A BIOGRAPHICAL DICTIONARY OF SCULPTORS IN BRITAIN 1660–1851

A BIOGRAPHICAL DICTIONARY OF SCULPTORS IN BRITAIN 1660–1851

Ingrid Roscoe

Emma Hardy & M G Sullivan

Published for the Paul Mellon Centre for Studies in British Art
and The Henry Moore Foundation
by Yale University Press
New Haven and London

Typesetting by Alliance Data Technology, Pondicherry, India
Printed by TJ International, Padstow

Library of Congress Cataloging-in-Publication Data

A biographical dictionary of sculptors in Britain, 1660–1851 /
edited by Ingrid Roscoe, Emma Hardy, and M.G. Sullivan.
p. cm.
Rupert Gunnis's Dictionary of British Sculptors, 1951 (revised 1968) provides the starting point for the new dictionary, which also makes use of his extensive unpublished archive.
Includes bibliographical references and index.
ISBN 978-0-300-14965-4 (alk. paper)
1. Sculptors--Great Britain--Biography--Dictionaries. I. Roscoe, Ingrid.
II. Hardy, Emma (Emma Elizabeth) III. Sullivan, M. G.
IV. Gunnis, Rupert. Dictionary of British sculptors, 1660–1851.
NB496.B56 2009
730.92'241--dc22
[B]

2009013999

A catalogue record for this book is available from The British Library

CONTENTS

INTRODUCTION

Rupert Gunnis's *Dictionary of British Sculptors* has been the standard work of reference on its subject ever since it was published in 1953. The author modestly described it as an 'attempted dictionary' and was most anxious that in due course it should be expanded and brought up to date. All he was able to arrange himself was a lightly amended reprint which appeared in the guise of a second edition in 1968 after his death. The present book, we hope, is the one he would truly have wished for. In places the text is still recognisably his but it has been vastly expanded to take account of more than fifty years of research and publication on British sculpture. Over a thousand of the entries are entirely new and all the major lives have been rewritten with the lists of works rigorously overhauled. Financial support has been generously provided by the Henry Moore Foundation and the Paul Mellon Centre for Studies in British Art to whom we are most grateful.

The project has been gently steered by a committee of management whose first, and most important task was to recruit a scholar of sufficient calibre to lead it. We were very fortunate to find that person in Ingrid Roscoe and she, in turn, quickly showed good judgement by engaging Greg Sullivan and Emma Hardy to assist her. This team of three has written the bulk of the text. Their list of acknowledgements reveals the great range of advice and help on which they have been able to draw and we are grateful to each and every one of the persons mentioned. The final stages of writing and editing have not been easy. Work began in earnest with the Millennium to a five-year plan. In the event, the plan has stretched out to eight years. That it has now been completed is almost entirely to Dr Roscoe's hard work and determination. Our thanks are due to Yale University Press for undertaking the production of the book and to Brian Allen, Director of Studies at the Paul Mellon Centre who has shown care, consideration, kindness and sympathy throughout.

Adam White
September 2007

ACKNOWLEDGEMENTS

The starting point for this volume was Rupert Gunnis's *Biographical Dictionary of British Sculptors* (1953), a work of scholarship awesome in its breadth and accuracy but now half a century out of date. In 1998 a pilot study to assess the value of commissioning a new dictionary was commissioned by the Henry Moore Institute in Leeds and following that report Adam White approached two funding bodies, the Paul Mellon Centre for Studies in British Art and the Henry Moore Foundation, who agreed to finance the compilation of a new dictionary. Their generous support has been constant throughout. Dr White provided the template and subsequently became chairman of the committee of management overseeing the new project. He has worked closely with me over the past eight years, giving invaluable direction on all aspects of the book. The other members of the managing committee, Brian Allen, Malcolm Baker, Penelope Curtis, John Physick and Benedict Read have all been unstinting in their help and support. I am particularly grateful to Brian Allen for his encouragement and accessibility throughout and to John Physick for putting at our disposal his extensive Gunnis revision typescript, lodged at the Henry Moore Institute. Thanks are due to Malcolm Baker and to Paul Greenhalgh, Head of the Research Department of the Victoria and Albert Museum, Penelope Curtis, Curator of the Henry Moore Institute and to the School of Fine Art, University of Leeds, for providing my co-authors with desks and full research facilities.

The resources of the Conway Library at the Courtauld Institute, which houses Gunnis's photographic archive and his unpublished material, have been essential in preparing the new dictionary and thanks are due to Geoffrey Fisher and Philip Ward-Jackson for their patient assistance and for direction and information in their particular fields.

It has been heart-warming to find that the good initial response of experts to the proposed dictionary was followed by much generous giving, both of unpublished material and practical assistance. Particular thanks are due to the late Howard Colvin, Alastair Laing and Nicholas Penny who provided access to their annotated Gunnis and Pevsner volumes and other help. David Alexander, Jon Bayliss, John Davis, Terry Friedman, the late Katharine Gibson, Douglas Merritt, Roy Morris, Denis Perriam, Fiona Pearson, Ann Saunders, Helen Smailes and Hilary Young have all proffered significant archival material, Jonathan Marsden provided information on the Royal Collections, John Kenworthy-Browne compiled the list of works for Joseph Nollekens and Gordon Balderston (GB) for Michael Rysbrack. Tim Knox and Todd Longstaffe-Gowan submitted detailed information on the sculpture in their collection. Caroline Jordan, Lucy Jessop, Loraine Long, Caroline Maddox, Opher Mansour and Pat Whatmore scoured record repositories in London. Kate Eustace made detailed searches through archives in Oxford and Bristol. Marjorie Trusted and Paul Williamson gave help and encouragement throughout.

Valuable assistance has come from archivists, librarians and curators of museum collections. These include GMD Booth, Senior Archivist, Warks CRO; Geoffrey Fisher (GF) of the Conway Library, Courtauld Institute; April Connett-Dance, AGBI Archives, Burlington House; Catherine Casley of the Ashmolean Museum; Steven Tomlinson of the Bodleian Library; Philip Gale of the Church of England Record Centre; Janet Seeley of the Council for the Care of Churches; Penelope Fussell of the Drapers' Company; the Clerk, Goldsmiths' Hall; Stephen Freeth of the Guildhall Library, MSS section; Pamela Hunter of Hoare's Bank; Francis Marshall of the Harris Art Gallery, Preston; Helen Burton of Keele University, Special Collections; Clare Brown of Lambeth Palace Library; the Clerk to the Mercers' Company; Charlotte Henwood of the Ministry of Defence Art Collection; Richard Elvin and Anthony Smith of the Historic MSS Commission; Mark Pomeroy and Helen Valentine of the Royal Academy; Christopher Lloyd, Jane Roberts and Pamela Clark of the Royal Collection; Pamela Forde and Bryony Kelly of the Royal College of Physicians; Christopher Denvir of the Royal Society of Arts; Katie George of the Salters' Company, Joseph Wisdom of St Paul's Cathedral Library; Helen Dorey, Susan Palmer of Sir John Soane's Museum; Andrea Cameron of the Stationers' Company; Bernard Nurse of the Society of Antiquaries; Frances Collard of the Wellington Museum, Apsley House; Richard Mortimer of the Muniment Room and Library, Westminster Abbey; William Tyan of the Warburg Institute; Philip McCaughley, Constance Clement and Jane Nowosadko of the Yale Center for British Art.

In addition there have been many valuable contributions from county record offices: we should particularly like to thank James Collett-White (Beds and Luton Archives), Rob Petre (Bristol RO); Mark Forrest (Dorset RO), Crispin Powell (Northants RO), Mrs SM Payne (Lincs RO), Sarah Bridges (Northants RO) and GMD Booth (Warks CRO).

Christopher Ridgway, curator at Castle Howard has been unsparing in his help. Charles Noble, Stuart Band and Andrew Peppitt at Chatsworth, Andrea Garahy and Jane Crease of Croome Court Estates, Bruce Bailey at Drayton House, Nicky Ingram at Petworth and Kate Harris at Longleat have all been most helpful. Assistance has also come from June Bonell of the Wedgwood Museum, Barlaston, Staffs, Helen Burton, archivist at Keele University and Ann Mitchell, archivist at Woburn Abbey. The NADFAS Church Recorders have submitted information on a wealth of previously unrecorded monuments.

Other valued contributors in specialized areas include Dorothy Abel Smith, Steven Allen, Francis Ames-Lewis, Paul Atterbury, Martin Barnes, Shelley Bennett, Diane Bilbey, Bruce Boucher, Roger Bowdler, Oliver Bradbury, Simon Bradbury, Sighle Breathnach-Lynch, Trevor Brighton, Hugh Brigstocke, Kerry Bristol, Anthony Burton, Helen Burne, David Carrington, Edward Chaney, Charlotte Chastel-Rousseau, Bridget Cherry, Viccy Coltman, David Connell, the late John Cornforth, Joan Coutu, Matthew Craske, Lucy Cullen, Lucy Cutler, Elisabeth Darby, Fiona Darling-Glinski, Jo Darke, Aileen Dawson, Ptolemy Dean, Angela Delaforce, Hilary Diaper, Larry Dohey, Dianne Duggan, Clive Easter, Richard Elvin, Mark Evans, Patrick Eyres, Peter Fairweather, Christine Faunch, James Fenton, Nicola Figgis, Jonathan Finch, Ros Fisher, Nigel Forbes Adam, Eric Forster, Joseph Friedman, Susan Fyler, Andrea Garahy, Andor Gomme, Gordon Grant, Ruth Gilding, Matthew Hargraves, John Harris, Andrew Heard, Richard Hewlings, Paul Hetherington, Gordon Higgott, Claude Hitching, Jane Hogan, Shannon Hunter Hurtado, Ralph Hyde, John Ingamells, Nicky Ingram, Alain Jacobs, Anna Jackson, Sally Jeffery, Janet Kennish, Milo Keynes, Susan Lambert, James Lawson, Ronald Lee, Ian Leith, Lesley Lewis, Julian Litten, Michael Liversedge, Nigel Llewellyn, Philip McEvansoneya, RJ Malden, Nicholas Merchant, Melody Mobus, Edward Morris, Tessa Murdoch, Paula Murphy, Pieter van der Merwe, John Newman, Maria Ranauro, Anthony Reeve, Emma Roberts, Frank Salmon, Cinzia Sicca, Jacob Simon, Andrew Skelton, Sarah

Skinner, Kim Sloan, Bobbie Smith, Richard Smith, Michael Snodin, Jane Southcott, Paul Spencer-Longhurst, Lindsay Stainton, Mary Ann Steggles, Alexander Stoddart, Simon Stock, David Sturdy, Steven Tomlinson, Paul Turnell, Helen Valentine, Wendy Walker, Mike Wall, Alicia Weisberg-Roberts, Pat Wengraf, David Whitehead, Christopher Whitehead, David Wickham, Stephen White, David Wilson, Philip Winterbottom, Richard Wood, Katherine Wyndham and Victoria Worsley, archivist at the Henry Moore Institute.

The task of second reading certain major entries has been willingly undertaken by Brian Allen, Bruce Bailey, Gordon Balderston, Geoffrey Beard, Julius Bryant, Marie Busco, Timothy Clifford, Joan Coutu, Elisabeth Darby, John Davis, Kate Eustace, Geoffrey Fisher, Eric Foster (EF), Margrethe Floryan, Peggy Fogelman, Cristiano Giometti, Martin Greenwood, Eileen Harris, Hugh Honour, David Irwin, Alison Kelly, James Lawson, Martin Levy, Derek Linstrum, John Lord, Katherine Macdonald, Mary Mauchline, John Martin Robinson, Douglas Merritt, Fiona Pearson, Nicholas Penny, John Physick, Ben Read, Christopher Ridgway, Alicia Salter, John Sankey, Ann Saunders, Tony Sharp, Helen Smailes, Timothy Stevens, Mark Stocker, Marjorie Trusted, John Turpin, Philip Ward-Jackson, James West, Adam White, Robin Woodward and Alison Yarrington. Guilland Sutherland has my unqualified admiration for meticulously reading the entire dictionary and Sally Salvesen has seen the book through Yale University Press with authority and patience.

Preparation of copy has been almost entirely an in-house exercise but a few external experts have provided biographies and these are acknowledged at the end of their respective articles. Special mention should however be made of the following: Sylvia Allen, who prepared no less than twelve substantial articles, Jon Bayliss, Donald Cameron, Fiona Darling-Glinsky, Moira Fulton, Caroline Jordan, Rocco Lieuallen, Melody Mobus, Gerardine Mulcahy, the late Corita Myerscough, Michael Paraskos and John Physick.

Barry Herbert devised the sophisticated database on which this dictionary was compiled and has shown great patience whilst making regular modifications as the parameters expanded.

My husband, Marshall Roscoe has been prepared to take a back seat in our household over nearly a decade, restoring my equilibrium with his dry humour when work on the dictionary became obsessive.

Finally, an enormous debt of thanks and much respect are due to Emma Hardy and to Greg Sullivan. Dr Sullivan's exhaustive bibliography formed the starting point for the book and he has subsequently steered me through various difficult areas with wisdom and enterprise. Emma Hardy has been particularly valuable for her quiet tenacity and her knowledge of Victorian sculpture. The two began work on the dictionary as editorial assistants, but their analytical skills, flair for language, dedication and enthusiasm have made them indispensable advisors and co-authors. Their active participation and support have made preparation of this dictionary a zestful, satisfying and engrossing experience.

Ingrid Roscoe
Editor
November 2008

USING THE DICTIONARY

The dictionary aims to include all known sculptors, modellers, wood and ivory carvers active in Britain and the British Empire in the period 1660–1851, as well as foreign sculptors working abroad who supplied sculpture for British patrons. In the last case the entries provide a general account of the sculptor's life but focus principally on works with British connections. The new dictionary has the same date span as Gunnis's dictionary.

Some of the sculptors in this dictionary were clearly little more than masons and almost nothing is known of their careers, but they have been given entries if they signed even a single work. They are also included if the only available information is a record of premiums and medals for sculpture awarded by the Royal Academy and other institutions, or if their name and trade as a carver or modeller appears in contemporary exhibition catalogues. Others are known only from advertisements in contemporary newspapers or listings in trade directories. A considerable number for whom there is also no biographical information appear in the accounts of private patrons, public buildings, livery companies and other institutions. All entries from Gunnis's dictionary have a place, often with supplementary information added, and his unpublished archives in the Conway Library at the Courtauld Institute of Art have been incorporated. In addition much information has been supplied by scholars and enthusiasts. The bibliography lists over 3,000 manuscript and published sources used in preparing the dictionary.

The dictionary includes more than 35,000 individual works. It has been difficult to know what precisely to include in the case of minor works by monumental masons and some of the lists of wall tablets by these sculptors are almost certainly incomplete.

Biographies

All entries except the very small ones are divided into two sections, a biography and a list of works. Emboldened names in the biographies cross-refer to other sculptors with entries in the dictionary and emboldened numbers relate to works listed below. At the end of the biographical section is a list of sources consulted, sub-divided into published and manuscript material. Additional manuscript sources which have not been consulted have been included under a separate heading since they may be of use to scholars. References are given to drawings which can not at present be related to the works listed. Brief information on auctions of sculptors' possessions is expanded in a separate appendix. Known portraits of the sculptor complete the biographical section.

Lists of works

Works have been listed in a hierarchy of categories with funerary monuments first, followed by statues, busts, chimneypieces, architectural sculpture, reliefs and finally miscellaneous subjects. This means that if a work of art falls into more than one category, it is listed under the category which comes first: a statue, for example, which was erected as a funerary monument is listed as a monument rather than a statue. An exception is made of reliefs on chimneypieces, which are listed under the latter category. The category of funerary monuments includes all sculpture which commemorates a burial, whether in a church or a mausoleum. Statues and statuettes are listed under statues with a note, if appropriate, that they are statuettes or 'figures'. Fixtures in churches such as fonts, screen figures and other miscellaneous sculpture that can sensibly be listed as architectural sculpture, appear as such.

Works are credited to the master of a workshop, with a note of assistants involved, if known. Information on each known work is arranged in six columns as follows:

(a) Date. Where the date of a piece of commemorative sculpture differs from that of the subject's death, the latter is given after the name. If the date of a monument is uncertain then the date of death (†) of the subject appears in the chronological listing. If there is a known date span between the year of a commission and its conclusion both years are given, but listing is by completion date. A question mark often precedes works taken from Gunnis's dictionary (1968 edition) if it is unclear whether his date refers to a monument's erection or the subject's demise.

(b) Subject. If a work was designed by someone other than the sculptor, the designer's name is given below the title of the work. Costs are also included in this column but caution should be used when analysing figures since it is often unclear whether materials, freight and installation are included in the sum.

(c) Materials. The material used for monuments is marble unless otherwise stated, marble being broadly defined as any stone which will take a polish. Materials are given in abbreviated form, as follows: alabaster (a); bronze (b); iron (i); lead (l); marble (m); plaster (pl); plaster, bronzed (pb); slate (sl); stone (s); terracotta (tc); wax (w); wood (wd). The term terracotta covers all types of clay regardless of chemical properties or firing methods. The term bronze is used loosely to encompass all objects of copper alloy, whether they are bronze in the strictest sense (copper and tin) or brass (copper and zinc). Works in mixed media, where marble is the dominant material, are listed under marble.

(d) Location. Where an object has been moved the original site is given in square brackets and is followed by current whereabouts, if known. The dedication of a church is given only when there is more than one in the area. Locations within religious foundations are given only in the case of Westminster Abbey and St Paul's Cathedral. All works appearing at Christie and Sotheby auctions were offered in London unless otherwise indicated.

(e) Details of signature and date are abbreviated 'S', 'D' or 'SD'.

(f) Bibliographical references to individual works. Inaccurate or out-of-date material has been omitted. Gunnis's manuscript references have been checked where possible, but a number have not been located, in which case a note is added that the source is Gunnis himself. Material in the National Archive is cited by the current abbreviation (TNA) rather than the old one (PRO). The abbreviation 'Conway Lib (repr)' indicates that a photograph exists in the Conway Library. It is only used when no published illustration has been found.

Attributions are confined to a few key works, clearly labelled to distinguish them from authenticated items. Signed drawings and drawings by a sculptor that relate to a monument in the characteristic style of the sculptor have been included in the lists of works under the sculpture to which they relate.

County names.

The county names used are those which preceded the boundary changes introduced by the Local Government Act of 1974.

IR

BIOGRAPHICAL DICTIONARY OF SCULPTORS

ABBOTT, Charles, of Aylsham fl 1802–29

Gunnis considers his work typical of the early 19th-century Norwich school. At some stage he worked in partnership, for the monument to Sir John Lubbock is signed 'Abbott and Thompson' (7). It seems likely that this co-sculptor was **J Thompson of Aylsham**. Abbott's premises in Aylsham were taken over in 1834 by his assistant **John Freeman**, who had worked for Abbott for 'many years' (*Norwich Mercury*, 20 Sept 1834).

Literary References: *Gunnis* 1968, 13

Funerary Monuments

1.	?1802	Charles Smith	Southrepps, Norfolk	S	*Gunnis* 1968, 13
2.	?1803	Anne Bond	Southrepps, Norfolk	S	*Gunnis* 1968, 13
3.	?1805	Edward Piggon	Aylsham, Norfolk	S	*Gunnis* 1968, 13
4.	?1811	Charles Hornor	Irstead, Norfolk	S	*Gunnis* 1968, 13
5.	†1814	Major James Harrison Baker	Cawston, Norfolk	S	
6.	?1817	Robert Doughty	Hanworth, Norfolk	S	*Gunnis* 1968, 13
7.	?1823	Sir John Lubbock (co-sculptor: Thompson)	North Walsham, Norfolk	S	*Gunnis* 1968, 13
8.	†1829	Thomas Elvin	Aylsham, Norfolk	S	

ABBOTT, George 1803–83

He showed regularly with the major exhibiting societies over a period of 30 years, though his entire corpus appears to have disappeared. Abbott was born in London on 18 July 1803 and showed at the Royal Academy in 1829 from 38 Frith Street, Soho. He joined the Academy Schools on the recommendation of the engraver Benjamin Wyon in 1839, giving his address as 61 Poland Street. He changed his London address frequently, dying at 27 Lupus Street, Pimlico, on 21 June 1883. His wife, Eliza Frances, is mentioned in the census records of 1881 and in his will. There appear to have been no children.

He carved a number of portrait busts of family members and private clients, but found commercial success with his representations of national figures. His bronze cabinet busts of the Duke of Wellington and Sir Robert Peel were replicated in large numbers (**15, 17**). In 1862 he was responsible for small seated models of the Duke of Wellington and Prince Albert, translated by Copeland to parianware (**2, 4**). The image of Prince Albert was judged 'good as a likeness, and graceful as a figure' (*AJ*, 1862, 211). His *Alexander the Great crossing the Granicus* was shown at the Great Exhibition of 1851 and again at the British Institution, where it was priced at £25 (**3**). He used the British Institution exhibitions to market groups or reliefs of children (**34, 35**).

His will, proved on 18 July 1883, valued his personal estate at £297 13s, but it was re-sworn in August 1892, when the value had risen to £7,162 4s 10d. A sculptor, John Adrian Raemakers, of whom nothing is currently known, of 22 Bloomfield Terrace, Pimlico, was one of the executors.

Literary References: 1881 census records; *Graves* 1875, 1; *Graves* I, 1905–6, 1; *Gunnis* 1968, 13

Archival References: RA Admissions, 1839

Will: PPR, fol 570

Statues

1.	1838	P Thomas, cabinet statue, 'sketch'	[Exhib Soc of BA, 606]; untraced	GPC
2.	1843	Arthur, 1st Duke of Wellington, model	[Exhib RA, London, 1378]; untraced	*Graves* I, 1905–6, 1
3.	1844	Alexander the Great crossing the Granicus	[Exhib RA, London, 1239]; untraced	*Graves* 1875, 1; *Graves* I, 1905–6, 1; *Gunnis* 1968, 13
4.	1862	Albert, the Prince Consort, model for Copeland Parian statuette	Untraced	*Darby and Smith* 1983, 97 (ceramic repr)

Busts

5.	1834	Mrs George Abbott	[Exhib RA, London, 1085]; untraced	*Graves* I, 1905–6, 1
6.	1834	One of Mrs George Abbott's children	[Exhib RA, London, 1089]; untraced	*Graves* I, 1905–6, 1
7.	1836	Master Browne	[Exhib RA, London, 1071]; untraced	*Graves* I, 1905–6, 1
8.	1837	John Clark	[Exhib Soc of BA, 586]; untraced	GPC
9.	1837	Rev Watts Wilkinson	[Exhib Soc of BA, 588]; untraced	GPC
10.	1838	Dr Solomon Herschell, High Priest	[Exhib RA, London, 1334]; untraced	*Graves* I, 1905–6, 1

11.	1838	Queen Victoria		[Exhib Soc of BA, 601]; untraced	GPC
12.	1838	W Amory		[Exhib Soc of BA, 600]; untraced	GPC
13.	1839	Captain Alsager MP		[Exhib RA, London, 1330]; untraced Other versions: exhib RA 1841, 1150	*Graves* I, 1905–6, 1
14.	1840	Thomas Blizzard FRS		[Exhib RA, London, 1120]; untraced	*Graves* I, 1905–6, 1
15.	1842	Arthur, 1st Duke of Wellington, cabinet bust	b	[Exhib RA, London, 1311]; untraced Other versions: Stratfield Saye, Hants, replica	*Graves* I, 1905–6, 1
16.	1846	Rev R Sanderson		[Exhib RA, London, 1373]; untraced	*Graves* I, 1905–6, 1
17.	1850	Sir Robert Peel, cabinet bust	b	untraced Other versions: replicated by Messrs Hetley of Soho Square	*Gunnis* 1968, 13
18.	1857	Field-Marshall Lord Raglan		[Exhib RA, London, 1267]; untraced	*Graves* I, 1905–6, 1
19.	1858	Miss Driggs		[Exhib RA, London, 1296]; untraced	*Graves* I, 1905–6, 1
20.	1858	Unidentified lady		[Exhib RA, London, 1228]; untraced	*Graves* I, 1905–6, 1
21.	1863	Maria Dickinson		[Exhib RA, London, 1176]; untraced	*Graves* I, 1905–6, 1
22.	1867	Unidentified lady		[Exhib RA, London, 1177]; untraced	*Graves* I, 1905–6, 1

Miscellaneous

23.	1829	' "The Rival Suitors". After Stephanoff'	[Exhib RA, London, 1110]; untraced	*Graves* I, 1905–6, 1
24.	1829	' "The Sisters". After Stephanoff'	[Exhib RA, London, 1105]; untraced	*Graves* I, 1905–6, 1
25.	1836	Group of Bacchanalians	[Exhib Soc of BA, 867]; untraced	GPC
26.	1843	William Rufus, model	[Exhib RA, London, 1374]; untraced	*Graves* I, 1905–6, 1
27.	1854	'And when our loved ones', from a poem by Sir Edwin Arnold	[Exhib RA, London, 1459]; untraced	*Graves* I, 1905–6, 1
28.	1854	Fidelity	[Exhib BI, 577]; untraced	*Graves* 1875, 1
29.	1854	The wandering thought	[Exhib BI, 582]; untraced	*Graves* 1875, 1
30.	1855	The pavement	[Exhib BI, 550]; untraced	*Graves* 1875, 1
31.	1855	The road	[Exhib BI, 552]; untraced	*Graves* 1875, 1
32.	1856	The first step Payment(s): 25 gns	[Exhib BI, 553]; untraced	*Graves* 1875, 1
33.	1856	The great plague of London Payment(s): 15 gns	[Exhib BI, 550]; untraced	*Graves* 1875, 1
34.	1857	'Leap frog. One of a series of English games'	[Exhib BI, 553]; untraced	*Graves* 1875, 1
35.	1860	'Childhood. "Dream'st thou of Heaven?" Mrs Hemens' Payment(s): marble: £70; casts: 3 gns	[Exhib BI, 643]; untraced	*Graves* 1875, 1
36.	1862	Miss Robinson	[Exhib RA, London, 1141]; untraced	*Graves* I, 1905–6, 1
37.	1863	Ophelia	[Exhib RA, London, 1155]; untraced	*Graves* I, 1905–6, 1
38.	1863	Signor Belli	[Exhib RA, London, 1189]; untraced	*Graves* I, 1905–6, 1
39.	1864	Benjamin C Jones	[Exhib RA, London, 1028]; untraced	*Graves* I, 1905–6, 1
40.	1864	Juliet. 'O Romeo, Romeo, wherefore art thou Romeo!'	[Exhib BI, 640]; untraced Other versions: exhib RA 1865, 1026	*Graves* 1875, 1; *Graves* I, 1905–6, 1
41.	1864	Ophelia 'And will he not come again'	[Exhib BI, 643]; untraced	*Graves* 1875, 1
42.	1866	C J Dodd	[Exhib RA, London, 1023]; untraced	*Graves* I, 1905–6, 1

ABINGTON, L J fl 1814

He married Jane, the daughter of John Sandys, a Baptist minister, and eventually became the owner of a pottery in Staffs. In 1814 he was responsible for all the decorative carving on the market cross at Devizes (1). Later he superintended the decorative carving at Soane's Bank of England.

Literary References: *Devizes* 1859, 479

Archival References: GPC

Architectural Sculpture

1.	1814	Decorative carving (designed by Benjamin Wyatt)	Market cross, Devizes, Wilts	GPC

ABLEWHITE, of Louth fl 1819

Funerary Monuments

1.	†1819	Rev John Emeris	Tetford, Lincs	S	Pevsner, *Lincs*, 1989, 752

ABRAHAM, Charles J 1816–85

The son of an architect, Robert Abraham, he attended the Royal Academy Schools in 1833, giving his age as 17 and his address as 27 Keppel Street, Russell Square. By his own account he was a pupil of **R W Sievier**, 'no mean artist,' and studied for three years in Paris and Rome (*Sydney Morning Herald*, 3 March 1845). In 1841 he carved 'an admirably executed statue' of the Duke of Wellington for a Mr J N Franklyn, who placed the figure on the lawn of his house near Bristol (**2**). With its pedestal it was 14 feet high, and could apparently be seen from the road (*GM*, 1841, 2, 407).

In 1842 he emigrated to Sydney, Australia, where one of his first subjects was the Surveyor-General (**10**). In 1845 he exhibited a number of busts of notable figures in Sydney, several of them draped *all'antica* (**4–10**). The *Sydney Morning Herald* advertised the exhibition, though the newspaper wrongly described Abraham as a self-taught artist, so occasioning the artist's publication of his educational credentials. Abraham exhibited at the Paris Exhibition in 1855. He returned to England, where he died in 1885.

Literary References: *Moore* 1934, 2, 71–2; *Gunnis* 1968, 13

Archival References: RA Admissions

Funerary Monuments

1.	nd	Robert Hancock, statue	Rockwood Cemetery, Australia	*Moore* 1934, 2, 72

Statues

2.	1841	Arthur, 1st Duke of Wellington	s	[Henbury Hill, Bristol]; untraced	*GM* 1841, 2, 407; *Gunnis* 1968, 13

Busts

3.	1845	Charles Windeyer		[Exhib Royal Hotel, Sydney]; untraced Other versions: Police Court, Liverpool Street, Sydney Family coll, Hunter River	*Moore* 1934, 2, 72
4.	1845	Daniel O'Connell		[Exhib Royal Hotel, Sydney]; untraced	GPC
5.	1845	Dr Bennett		[Exhib Royal Hotel, Sydney]; untraced	*Moore* 1934, 2, 72
6.	1845	Dr Nicholson		[Exhib Royal Hotel, Sydney]; untraced	*Moore* 1934, 2, 72; GPC
7.	1845	Hon and Mrs E Deas Thomson		[Exhib Royal Hotel, Sydney]; untraced	*Moore* 1934, 2, 72
8.	1845	Mr Justice à Becket		[Exhib Royal Hotel, Sydney]; untraced	*Moore* 1934, 2, 72
9.	1845	Robert Lowe		[Exhib Royal Hotel, Sydney]; untraced	*Moore* 1934, 2, 72; GPC
10.	1845	Sir Thomas Mitchell	m	[Exhib Royal Hotel, Sydney]; untraced Other versions: Pioneers Club, Sydney, plaster reproduction Mitchell Library, Sydney, plaster reproduction Royal Empire Society, London, plaster reproduction	*Moore* 1934, 1, 139; 2, 72; GPC
11.	1847	George Suttor		[Exhib Soc for the Promotion of the Fine Arts, Sydney]; untraced	*Moore* 1934, 2, 72
12.	1847	Sir George Gipps		[Exhib Society for the Promotion of the Fine Arts, Sydney]; untraced	*Moore* 1934, 2, 72
13.	1856	Richard Windeyer	p	Parliament House, Sydney	*Moore* 1934, 2, 72; GPC
14.	1866	Sir Henry Parkes		Royal Australian Historical Society, Sydney, Education Department	*Moore* 1934, 1, 141
15.	nd	Dr Bland		Mitchell Library, Sydney, Australia	*Moore* 1934, 1, 140
16.	nd	L Leichhardt		Hobart Gallery, Australia	*Moore* 1934, 139
17.	nd	Mrs Wentworth		Mitchell Library, Sydney, Australia	*Moore* 1934, 1, 140
18.	nd	W C Wentworth		Mitchell Library, Sydney, Australia	*Moore* 1934, 1, 139; 2, 72

ABRAHAM, Nicholas fl 1678–88

He signs the ambitious polychrome monument with kneeling life-size figures of Walter Langdon at St Martin by Looe. The figures are separated by a prayer desk and framed by columns and a broken pediment (1). On 29 April 1686 he and Peter Abraham 'gave a noat & was admitt' to the Masons' Company (*Court Book*, MS 5304/1, fols 89v & 90r). In 1688 he obeyed the summons of the London Masons' Company to appear before them as 'a foreigner of the Mason's trade' (not hailing from the City of London), 'to be sworn of the company.'

His son, Nicholas Abraham II (†1727), was apprenticed to Thomas Shadbolt in 1695 and made free of the Company on 30 June 1703. It was probably this son who built a house on the south side of Conduit Street, in 1719, which was insured with the Westminster Fire Office for £1,000. In 1723 it belonged to John Evelyn. Peter Abraham, who may have been a relative, was made free as a 'foreign member' on 29 April 1686 (Masons' Co Freemen List).

Literary References: *Gunnis* 1968, 13

Archival References: Masons' Co, *Apprentices*, 1695–1795; *Freemen*, fol 1; WFO, PR, no 307 (4 Sept 1719)

Funerary Monuments

1.	1678	Walter Langdon (†1667)	St Martin by Looe, Cornwall	SD	*Gunnis* 1968, 13; Pevsner, *Cornwall*, 1970, 188

ADAIR fl c1785

Chimneypieces

1.	c1785	Description unavailable	[Temple of Winds, Mount Stewart]; untraced	AL/RG

ADAIR, John fl 1763

He was listed in Mortimer's *Director* of 1763 as a 'Carver and Gilder' of Wardour Street, Soho (p 3).

ADAM, of Edinburgh fl 1734–48

Chimneypieces

1.	1734	Veined	m	Blair Castle, Perths	GPC
2.	1748	Description unavailable	m	Blair Castle, Perths	GPC

ADAM, William and Company fl 1781–2

Artificial stone manufacturers, they invented a terracotta substance known as 'Liardels Composition' (GPC). They were paid in February 1782 for work for the Earl of Coventry (1).

Architectural Sculpture

1.	1781	Various, including two low-relief figures Payment(s): £20 for reliefs	sa	[Croome Court, Worcs]; untraced	*Beard* 1993, 93; GPC

ADAMS, George Gammon 1821–98

A successful sculptor and medallist, he was born at Staines, Middx on 21 April 1821 and educated at Kepler House School. At 16 he went to work at the Royal Mint, where he was apprenticed to the chief engraver, **William Wyon RA**. He was admitted to the Royal Academy Schools in 1840, giving his address as 1 South Place, Pimlico, and that year won a silver medal for a head of *Melpomene* (**31**, RA Premium list). In 1841 he sent three relief medallions to the Royal Academy (**118–20**). He exhibited there regularly in the years that followed, showing medallions, busts and medals, as well as a few ideal works. After leaving the Royal Mint Adams received informal instruction in modelling and the cutting of medal and coin dies from **Benedetto Pistrucci**, who was then living in retirement near Windsor.

Adams sent two works to the Westminster Hall Exhibitions, held in 1844 and 1845 to select artists to provide sculpture for the new Palace of Westminster. He secured no commissions but his contributions were noticed by the press. One writer thought his statue of an *Ancient Briton* (**15**) 'a capital figure for an aspirant' displaying 'great decision in the muscular development, as well as in character and drawing' and declared, 'Mr. Adams has done this well, but he'll live to do better' (*Lit Gaz*, 1844, 483). Another critic praised the *Contest between the minstrel and the nightingale* for its 'grace and elegance' but noted that the effect was 'in some degree diminished by the lines formed by the arms of the figure' (*AU*, 1845, 258) (**16**).

In 1846 he travelled to Rome, where he studied briefly under **John Gibson**. In 1847 the RA awarded him a gold medal for a group of the *Massacre of the innocents* (RA Premium list; **17**) and a silver for a steel die engraved with a head of *Melpomene*. He was entitled to the RA's travelling studentship, but having recently returned from Rome, he did not use it. He sent several ideal works to the Great Exhibition of 1851 (**15**, **17**, **134**) and entered the international competition for the Great Exhibition Juror's medal. He won 100 guineas for his design, which, with a few modifications suggested by Prince Albert, was used for the verso of the medal and helped to establish the artist's reputation as a medallist. He went on to produce many medals, including those commemorating the Duke of Wellington's funeral, the official inauguration of Blackfriars Bridge and the Holborn Viaduct and Queen Victoria's Golden Jubilee.

Meanwhile, Adams's practice as a portrait sculptor also thrived. In 1852 he was commissioned to make the death mask of the Duke of Wellington (**137**). From this he executed a marble bust (**37**), which was apparently admired, for the Duke's heir wrote to the sculptor that it was 'considered by myself and those gentlemen who knew him best, as well as by his servants, as by far the best that has appeared, and we are obliged to you for thus making a likeness which hereafter will be considered as authentic' (*Wellesley* 1935, cited by *Gunnis* 1968, 13–14). It was much copied. Further commissions for busts, including several of army officers, followed. Palgrave ridiculed those of General Sir Edward Lugard and T H Franks (**57**, **58**), exhibited at the RA in 1863, saying that they 'grapple so ineffectually with the exigencies of the uniform, moustache, &c, that they look more like caricatures on the profession than monuments to the gallant originals' (*Palgrave* 1866, 41). These criticisms do not appear to have discouraged Adams's patrons.

He executed a number of public statues that elicited mixed responses (**18**, **19**, **24**, **26**, **28**). When his figure of General Sir Charles James Napier (**19**) was erected in Trafalgar Square in 1856 one commentator found much to praise, in spite of some reservations: 'The figure stands well, and the likeness is strongly marked. Simplicity and breadth characterise the treatment, and these are admirable qualities. We must, nevertheless, be permitted to say, rather with reference to works to follow than to this, that carried to extremes, especially in bronze, these qualities result in baldness and insipidity' (*Builder*, 1856, 446). In 1862 the *Art Journal* condemned it as 'dull and soulless' and 'perhaps the worst piece of sculpture in England', though it blamed the committee who oversaw the commission rather than the sculptor (*AJ*, 1862, 98). It has been suggested that another sculptor, John Adams-Acton, may have changed his name to avoid becoming associated with this particular work (*Read* 1982, 14).

By contrast, the statue of Hugh McNeile, Dean of Ripon, for St George's Hall, Liverpool, seems to have met with unanimous approval, though McNeile was a controversial figure because of his extreme anti-Catholic views (**28**). When the model for the statue was exhibited the *Art Journal* commented that it 'has quiet bearing, yet seems to speak' (*AJ*, 1871, 180), while the *Illustrated London News* praised the statue's naturalistically depicted drapery and dignified pose (*ILN*, 22 April 1871, 398). The *Daily Post* paid tribute to the sculptor who had produced 'the one good statue in St George's Hall' (*Daily Post*, 15 Dec 1870, cited by *Cavanagh* 1997, 282).

Through much of his career Adams lived and had his studio at 126 Sloane Street, in Chelsea, London. He was married and had a son who was studying architecture at the time of the 1881 census. His last works were a medal commemorating Queen Victoria's Diamond Jubilee in 1897 and a bust of W E Gladstone for Eton College (**115**). He died on 4 March 1898 at his home, Acton Green Lodge, Chiswick, and was buried in the family vault in the churchyard of St Mary, Staines. The sculptor's death seems to have passed unremarked by the periodical press. However, when the sculptor's widow sent a near-complete set of his medals to auction in 1900 they realized high prices. His works are represented in two national museum collections: the National Portrait Gallery acquired a number of plaster casts from his family soon after his death (**34**, **36**, **38**, **41**, **43**, **50**, **59**, **60**, **67**, **70**, **93**, **126**) and his daughter, Miss I D Adams, apparently presented a number of works to the Victoria and Albert Museum as late as 1980 (**22**, **29**, **30**, **37**, **38**, **67**, **84–91**, **93**, **126**).

EH

Literary References: *Graves* 1, 1905–6, 6–7; *Gunnis* 1968, 13–14; *Bilbey* 2002, 172–78

Archival References: RA Admissions; RA Premium list; 1881 census records

Additional MS Sources: Adams Papers 1; Adams Papers 2; Clyde Bust Papers

Wills and Administrations: PPR, administration, 18 July 1898, effects valued at £343

Auction Catalogues: Adams 1900

Portraits of the Sculptor: Self-portrait, bust (**84**); anon, oil on canvas, *c*1836, VAM P&D P.43-1982; John Bagnold Burgess, oil on canvas, VAM P&D P.44-1982; photograph, VAM AAD

Funerary Monuments

No.	Date	Subject	Location		References
1.	1854	Arthur, 1st Duke of Wellington, memorial (design only?)	[Exhib RA, London, 1379]; untraced		*Graves* I, 1905–6, 6
2.	†1855	William Brown	St Stephen, Rochester Row, Westminster, London		Pevsner, *London: Westminster*, 1997, 181, GPC
3.	1859	General Sir Charles James Napier (†1853)	St Paul's Cathedral, London, north transept		Pevsner, *London: City*, 1997, 174–5; *Morris* 2002, 26
4.	1860	Captain Henry Thompson (†1856)	St Paul's Cathedral, London		*Gunnis* 1968, 14
5.	1862	General Sir Harry Smith (†1860)	Whittlesey, Cambs		*Ormond* 1973, 421
6.	†1862	Sir Duncan MacDougall	St Paul's Cathedral, London, crypt		*Graves* I, 1905–6, 7; Pevsner, *London: City*, 1997, 180
7.	1863	General Sir William Napier (†1860)	St Paul's Cathedral, London, crypt	S	*Ormond* 1973, 335; Pevsner, *London: City*, 1997, 181
8.	1864	Augustus de Burgh	West Drayton, Middx	S	*Gunnis* 1968, 14
9.	1868	Admiral Sir Charles Napier (†1860)	St Paul's Cathedral, London		*Ormond* 1973, 332
10.	†1869	Rev Alexander Dallas	St Patrick's Cathedral, Dublin		GPC; C Lib (repr)

No.	Date	Subject	Medium	Location	Signed	Literature
11.	1873	Henry Sharpe		Hampstead, London		GPC
12.	†1875	Sir Edmund Saunderson Prideaux		Farway, Devon		Pevsner, *Devon*, 1989, 447
13.	†1882	Hon Rev Gerald Wellesley		Stratfield Saye, Hants		*ILN*, 20 Oct 1883, 381, 382 (repr); *Gunnis* 1968, 14
14.	nd	Mr Tuke, founder of The Retreat, York		Untraced		GPC
Statues						
15.	1844	Ancient Briton		[Exhib Westminster Hall, London, 162]; untraced Other versions: 'An ancient Briton as a scout' exhib RA, London, 1847, (1391); untraced		*AU*, 1844, 216; *ILN*, 6 Sept 1851, 289 (repr); *Graves* I, 1905–6, 6
16.	1845	Contest between the minstrel and the nightingale		[Exhib Westminster Hall, London, 125]; untraced Other versions: Exhib RA, 1877, 1451; untraced		*Westminster* 1845, 15; *AU*, 1845, 258; *Graves* I, 1905–6, 6, 7
17.	1847	Massacre of the Innocents Payment(s): £350		[Exhib RA, London, 1357 (gold medal)]; untraced		*ILN*, 8 Dec 1847, 400 (repr); *Graves* I, 1905–6, 6, 7
18.	1851	Arthur, 1st Duke of Wellington	b	[Marketplace, Norwich, until 1937]; The Close, Norwich, Norfolk		*Graves* I, 1905–6, 7; GPC; *Barnes* 2001, 29 (repr)
19.	1856	General Sir Charles James Napier Model(s): VAM A.126-1980, plaster	b	Trafalgar Square, London, south west corner		*Blackwood* 1989, 256–7 (repr); *Morris* 2002, 26, 28 (repr); *Bilbey* 2002, 173–4 (repr)
20.	1856	St John the Baptist		[Exhib RA, London, 1246]; untraced		*Graves* 187; GPC
21.	1858	The good shepherd (for St Stephen, Rochester Row, Westminster)		[Exhib RA, London, 1200]; untraced		*Graves* I, 1905–6, 7
22.	c1861	Major-General Sir Henry Havelock (model only)	pm	[coll sculptor's family]; VAM A.128-1980		*Bilbey* 2002, 174 (repr)
23.	1862	Night		[Int Exhib]; untraced		*Gunnis* 1968, 14
24.	1862	Richard Cobden	b	St Peter's Square, Stockport, Lancs		*ILN*, 4 Dec 1886, 599, 600 (repr); *Ormond* 1973, 108
25.	1863	Nymph after the bath	m	Sold Christie, Wrotham Park, 21 June 1994	S	*Graves* I, 1905–6, 7
26.	1866	Field Marshal John, 1st Baron Seaton (cast by Elkington & Co) Model(s): VAM A.127-1980, plaster	b	Devonport, Devon		*ILN*, 15 Dec 1866, 584 (repr); *Graves* I, 1905–6, 7; *Ormond* 1973, 413; *Bilbey* 2002, 174–5 (repr)
27.	1870	Aegle Model(s): VAM A.119-1980, plaster (in fragmentary condition)	m	[Exhib RA, London, 1166]; untraced		*Graves* I, 1905–6, 7; *Johnson* 1975, 2; *Bilbey* 2002, 176–7
28.	1870	Rev Dr Hugh McNeile, Dean of Ripon (†1879) Payment(s): approx £1,000	m	St George's Hall, Liverpool, Lancs		*Graves* I, 1905–6, 7; *Cavanagh* 1997, 280–2 (repr)
29.	1850–1898	Owl, statuette	m	[coll sculptor's family]; VAM A.131-1980		*Bilbey* 2002, 178 (repr)
30.	1850–1898	Standing figure (in fragmentary condition)	p	[coll sculptor's family]; VAM A.118-1980		*Bilbey* 2002, 176
Busts						
31.	1840	Melpomene		[RA, London, silver medal]; untraced		RA Premium list
32.	1849	Elizabeth, Marchioness of Londonderry		[Exhib RA, London, 1272]; untraced		*Graves* I, 1905–6, 6; GPC
33.	1849	Frederick, 4th Marquess of Londonderry		[Exhib RA, London, 1291]; untraced		*Graves* I, 1905–6, 6;
34.	c1849	General Sir Harry Smith	p	NPG 1255 Other versions: ex United Services Club, London, 1849, marble; untraced		*Graves* I, 1905–6, 6; *Gunnis* 1968, 14; *Ormond* 1973, 421 (repr 836)
35.	1849	Mrs Wood		[Exhib RA, London, 1266]; untraced		*Graves* I, 1905–6, 6
36.	1850	Hugh, Viscount Gough	p	NPG 1202	SD	*Graves* I, 1905–6, 6; *Ormond* 1973, 191 (repr 359)
37.	1852	Arthur, 1st Duke of Wellington	m	Stratfield Saye, Hants Other versions: Corsham Court, Wilts, marble, SD 1852 Burghley House, Lincs, marble, SD 1852 Walmer Castle, SD 1852 Badminton House, marble, SD 1852 VAM A.113-1980, marble VAM A.125-1980, bronze Wellington Museum, Apsley House, London, 1852, SD (1446–1948) Parke Bernet sale, NY, 2 March 1959, lot 104 (ex Stowe, Bucks) marble, SD 1852 Gov Art Coll, SD 1852 Royal Coll, Buckingham Palace, SD Gov Art Coll, 1853, SD, (acq 1952) Sold Christie, 11 Dec 1979, marble, SD 1855		*Graves* I, 1905–6, 6; *Gunnis* 1968, 14; *Bilbey* 2002, 172 (repr)
38.	1853	General Sir Charles James Napier	m	[coll sculptor's family]; VAM A.115-1980 Other versions: NPG 1198, plaster, SD 1853 SNPG, small bronze, 1853		*Ormond* 1973, 333–4 repr 660); *Bilbey* 2002, 173 (repr)
39.	1854	Henry, 7th Duke of Beaufort	m	Badminton, Glos	SD	*Graves* I, 1905–6, 7; *Gunnis* 1968, 14; *Ormond* 1973, 31
40.	1854	Sir Francis Burdett		Westminster School, London		*Graves* I, 1905–6, 7; GPC

No.	Date	Subject		Location		Literary references
41.	1855	Colin Campbell, 1st Baron Clyde	p	NPG 1201 Other versions: SNPG, Edinburgh, plaster, D 1861	SD	*Graves* I, 1905–6, 7; *Ormond* 1973, 104 (repr 185)
42.	1855	Frederick Le Gros Clark	m	St Thomas's Hospital, London, central hall	SD	*Cavanagh* forthcoming 2007 (Lambeth 2); C Lib (repr)
43.	1855	General Sir William Napier	m	NPG 1197 Other versions: SNPG, p	SD	*Graves* I, 1905–6, 7; *Ormond* 1973, 335 (repr 661)
44.	1855	Sir John Pennefather	m	Chelsea Hospital, London		*Gunnis* 1968, 14
45.	1855	Sir Samuel Bignold		[Exhib RA, London, 1532]; untraced		*ILN*, 24 Feb 1855, 181 (repr); *Graves* I, 1905–6, 7; GPC
46.	1855	William Brown	m	St George's Hospital, London		*Graves* I, 1905–6, 7; *Gunnis* 1968, 14
47.	1856	General Sir F Pennefather		[Exhib RA, London, 1344]; untraced		*Graves* I, 1905–6, 7; GPC
48.	1857	Hon Mrs F Walpole	m	Private coll	SD	*Graves* I, 1905–6, 7; C Lib (repr)
49.	1858	Lady Stafford		[Exhib RA, London, 1238]; untraced		*Graves* I, 1905–6, 7
50.	1858	Major L Thompson		[Exhib RA, London, 1274]; untraced		*Graves* I, 1905–6, 7; GPC
51.	1858	Major-General Sir Henry Havelock	p	NPG 1204	D	*Ormond* 1973, 217 (repr 409)
52.	1859	Arthur, 1st Duke of Wellington		[Exhib RA, London, 1356]; untraced		*Graves* I, 1905–6, 7
53.	1859	General Aichison		[Exhib RA, London, 1367]; untraced		*Graves* I, 1905–6, 7
54.	1859	Lord Charles Wellesley	m	Stratfield Saye, Hants		*Gunnis* 1968, 14
55.	1859	Mrs Hunter		[Exhib RA, London, 1324]; untraced		*Graves* I, 1905–6, 7
56.	1862	Mrs G G Adams		[Exhib RA, London, 1095]; untraced		*Graves* I, 1905–6, 7
57.	1863	General Sir Edward Lugard		[Exhib RA, London, 1197]; untraced		*Palgrave* 1866, 41; *Graves* I, 1905–6, 7
58.	1863	General Sir T H Franks		[Exhib RA, London, 1019]; untraced		*Graves* I, 1905–6, 7; GPC
59.	1863	John Bird Sumner, Archbishop of Canterbury	p	NPG 1207	SD	*Graves* I, 1905–6, 7; *Ormond* 1973, 439 (repr 876, 877)
60.	1863	John, 1st Baron Seaton	p	NPG 1205 Other versions: ex coll United Services Club, London, marble; untraced	SD	*Graves* I, 1905–6, 7; *Ormond* 1973, 413 (repr 818)
61.	1864	John Mason		Epworth Press, City Road, London, boardroom		RG/JP, I, 7
62.	1864	Unidentified lady		[Exhib RA, London, 1013]; untraced		*Graves* I, 1905–6, 7
63.	1866	Adolphus, 1st Duke of Cambridge		Royal Coll (Frogmore, Berks)		*Graves* I, 1905–6, 7; C Lib (repr)
64.	1866	Colonel Sir Edmund Prideaux Bt		[Exhib RA, London, 1013]; untraced		*Graves* I, 1905–6, 7; GPC
65.	1866	G A de Burgh		[Exhib RA, London, 994]; untraced		*Graves* I, 1905–6, 7
66.	1866	General Sir Joshua Jebb		[Exhib RA, London, 1014]; untraced		*Graves* I, 1905–6, 7
67.	1866	Henry, 3rd Viscount Palmerston	m	[coll sculptor's family]; VAM A.120-1980 Other versions: NPG 1206, p	SD	*Graves* I, 1905–6, 7; *Ormond* 1973, 358 (pl 710); *Bilbey* 2002, 174 (repr)
68.	1867	Francis, Duke of Teck		[Exhib RA, London, 991]; untraced		*Graves* I, 1905–6, 7; GPC
69.	1868	H Crabb Robinson		[Exhib RA, London, 979]; untraced		*Graves* I, 1905–6, 7; GPC
70.	1868	Sir James Brooke, Rajah of Sarawak	p	NPG 1200	SD	*Ormond* 1973, 64 (repr 108)
71.	1869	Angela, Baroness Burdett Coutts	m	[Exhib RA, London, 1291]; untraced		*Graves* I, 1905–6, 7; *Gunnis* 1968, 14; *Ormond* 1973, 81
72.	1869	Henry, 1st Baron Brougham and Vaux Payment(s): £300 17s 6d	m	[Guildhall, London]; destroyed Other versions: House of Lords, Palace of Westminster, London, nd, p		*Graves* I, 1905–6, 7; *Gunnis* 1968, 14
73.	1874	Unidentified gentleman		[Exhib RA, London, 1569]; untraced		*Graves* I, 1905–6, 7
74.	1874	Unidentified lady		[Exhib RA, London, 1567]; untraced		*Graves* I, 1905–6, 7
75.	1876	Thomas Proctor	m	Mansion House, Bristol		*Gunnis* 1968, 14
76.	1876	Unidentified lady		[Exhib RA, London, 1460]; untraced		*Graves* I, 1905–6, 7
77.	1878	Thomas, Baron Cottesloe		[Exhib RA, London, 1496]; untraced		*Graves* I, 1905–6, 7; *Ormond* 1973, 117
78.	1880	Edmund Charles Johnstone		[Exhib RA, London, 1641]; untraced		*Graves* I, 1905–6, 7
79.	1880–1881	Spring Payment(s): £63	m	[Exhib Soc of BA, London, 959]; untraced		*Johnson* 1975, 2
80.	1882	Arthur, 2nd Duke of Wellington	m	Stratfield Saye, Hants		*Gunnis* 1968, 14
81.	1884	Arthur, 1st Duke of Wellington (wearing formal jacket and bow tie)		Stratfield Saye, Hants	SD	C Lib (repr)
82.	1884	Arthur, 1st Duke of Wellington (wearing loose garment and garter star)	m	Stratfield Saye, Hants Other versions: Apsley House, London, marble, 1884 Stratfield Saye, marble, nd	SD SD S	C Lib (repr)
83.	1888	George, 2nd Duke of Cambridge	m	Windsor Castle, RCIN 31613,	SD	
84.	1850–1898	George Gammon Adams (self-portrait) Model(s): VAM A.130-1980	m	[coll sculptor's family]; VAM A.114-1980 Other versions: coll B Read		*Bilbey* 2002, 175 (repr)
85.	1850–1898	The sculptor's niece (?)	p	[coll sculptor's family]; VAM A.121-1980		*Bilbey* 2002, 177 (repr)
86.	1850–1898	Unidentified child (probably a boy)	p	[coll sculptor's family]; VAM A.123-1980		*Bilbey* 2002, 178 (repr)
87.	1850–1898	Unidentified man (in fragmentary condition)	p	[coll sculptor's family]; VAM A.117-1980		*Bilbey* 2002, 176
88.	1850–1898	Unidentified man in classical dress		[coll sculptor's family]; VAM A.124-1980		*Bilbey* 2002, 176 (repr)
89.	1850–1898	Unidentified woman	m	[coll sculptor's family]; VAM A.116-1980		*Bilbey* 2002, 177 (repr)
90.	1850–1898	Unidentified woman	p	[coll sculptor's family]; VAM A.122-1980		*Bilbey* 2002, 177 (repr)
91.	1850–1898	Unidentified woman	m	[coll sculptor's family]; VAM A.129-1980		*Bilbey* 2002, 178 (repr)
92.	nd	Admiral Briggs		Untraced		GPC

No.	Date	Subject	Medium	Location		Bibliography
93.	nd	Albert, the Prince Consort	p	NPG 1199	S	*Ormond* 1973, 9 (repr 20)
94.	nd	Bishop Wilberforce		Untraced		GPC
95.	nd	Earl of Beaconsfield		Untraced		GPC
96.	nd	Field Marshal, the Marquis of Anglesey		Untraced		GPC
97.	nd	General Sir H Atwell Lake		Untraced		GPC
98.	nd	General Thomas Wood		Untraced		GPC
99.	nd	General Wyndham		Untraced		GPC
100.	nd	J A Beaumont Esq		Untraced		GPC
101.	nd	Lord Derby		Untraced		GPC
102.	nd	Lord Mayo		Untraced		GPC
103.	nd	Lord Mayor William Hunter		Untraced		GPC
104.	nd	Lord Winmarleigh	m	Gawsworth Hall, Cheshire	S	*Gawsworth Guide*, 44
105.	nd	Rt Hon Spencer Walpole		Untraced		GPC
106.	nd	Samuel Graves	m	Walker, Liverpool		*Gunnis* 1968, 14
107.	nd	Sir Clarke Kennedy		Untraced		GPC
108.	nd	Sir Fenwick Williams		Untraced		GPC
109.	nd	Sir John Aitcheson		Untraced		GPC
110.	nd	Sir Robert Harvey		Untraced		GPC
111.	nd	Sir William Bunbury		Untraced		GPC
112.	nd	'The late Prince Imperial'		Untraced		GPC
113.	nd	The Shah of Persia		Untraced		GPC
114.	nd	William Bovill Esq, QC		Untraced		GPC
115.	nd	William Ewart Gladstone		Eton College, Windsor, Berks		*Forrer* I, 23
116.	nd	William Moore		Untraced		GPC
Architectural Sculpture						
117.	nd	Pedestals for busts with relief scenes	m	[coll Baroness Burdett Coutts]; untraced		*Gunnis* 1968, 14
Reliefs						
118.	1841	Melpomene, medallion		[Exhib RA, London, 1115]; untraced		*Graves* I, 1905–6, 6
119.	1841	Unidentified gentleman, medallion		[Exhib RA, London, 1116]; untraced		*Graves* I, 1905–6, 6
120.	1841	Unidentified lady, medallion		[Exhib RA, London, 1120]; untraced		*Graves* I, 1905–6, 6
121.	1842	Miss Wood, medallion		[Exhib RA, London, 1190]; untraced		*Graves* I, 1905–6, 6
122.	1843	Lady Littledale, medallion		[Exhib RA, London, 1352]; untraced		*Graves* I, 1905–6, 6
123.	1843	Unidentified lady, medallion		[Exhib RA, London, 1356]; untraced		*Graves* I, 1905–6, 6
124.	1844	Unidentified gentleman, medallion		[Exhib RA, London, 1260]; untraced		*Graves* I, 1905–6, 6
125.	1844	Unidentified lady, medallion		[Exhib RA, London, 1261]; untraced		*Graves* I, 1905–6, 6
126.	1845	Field Marshall Henry, Viscount Hardinge, medallion	p	NPG 1207a	SD	*Ormond* 1973, 212 (pl 401)
127.	1848	Adolphus, 1st Duke of Cambridge, medallion		[Exhib RA, London, 1300]; untraced		*Graves* I, 1905–6, 6
128.	1848	Albert, the Prince Consort, medallion		[Exhib RA, London, 1315]; untraced		*Graves* I, 1905–6, 6
129.	1866	William Dyce, medallion		[Exhib RA, London, 951]; untraced		*Graves* I, 1905–6, 7; *Ormond* 1973, 154
130.	1872	Mrs Charles Fowler, medallions		[Exhib RA, London, 1459]; untraced		*Graves* I, 1905–6, 7
131.	1878	Francis, Duke of Teck and Mary Adelaide, Duchess of Teck, medallion	w	[Exhib RA, London, 1538]; untraced		*Graves* I, 1905–6, 7
132.	1879	Arthur, 1st Duke of Wellington, medallion		Wellington Barracks, London, royal military chapel		GPC
133.	1850–1898	Spaniel in a kennel	p	[coll sculptor's family]; VAM A.313-1980		*Bilbey* 2002, 178 (repr)
134.	nd	John, Duke of Marlborough	m	Wellington Barracks, London, royal military chapel		GPC
Miscellaneous						
135.	1844	Combat of centaurs and lapithae		[Exhib RA, London, 1293]; untraced		*Graves* I, 1905–6, 6; GPC
136.	1848	Music's martyr		[Exhib RA, London, 1356]; untraced Other versions: coll Mr Greenall, Walton Hall, Lancs, 1875; untraced		*Graves* I, 1905–6, 6; *Gunnis* 1968, 14; GPC
137.	1852	Arthur, 1st Duke of Wellington, death mask	p	NPG 2155a		
138.	1856	The strife is o'er		[Exhib RA, London, 1236]; untraced		*Graves* I, 1905–6, 7
139.	1860	'Play' (Lena Bruce)		[Exhib RA, London, 959]; untraced		*Graves* I, 1905–6, 7
140.	1861	General O'Brien		[Exhib RA, London, 1085]; untraced		*Graves* I, 1905–6, 7; GPC
141.	1861	Sir Henry Bunbury		[Exhib RA, London, 1079]; untraced		*Graves* I, 1905–6, 7
142.	1862	Captain G T Gordon RN		[Exhib RA, London, 1134]; untraced		*Graves* I, 1905–6, 7
143.	1863	Mrs Adams		[Exhib RA, London, 863]; untraced		*Graves* I, 1905–6, 7
144.	1864	The captive kitten		[Exhib RA, London, 926]; untraced		*Graves* I, 1905–6, 7
145.	1865	General Sir Alexander Kennedy		[Exhib RA, London, 1039]; untraced		*Graves* I, 1905–6, 7
146.	1865	Mrs Smith		[Exhib RA, London, 950]; untraced		*Graves* I, 1905–6, 7
147.	1866	Captain Sir John Mildmay		[Exhib RA, London, 1033]; untraced		*Graves* I, 1905–6, 7
148.	1868	A youth diving		[Exhib RA, London, 992]; untraced		*Graves* I, 1905–6, 7
149.	1868	Thomas Joseph Pettigrew FRS		[Exhib RA, London, 1018]; untraced		*Graves* I, 1905–6, 7
150.	1870	Lady Lugard		[Exhib RA, London, 1196]; untraced		*Graves* I, 1905–6, 7
151.	1871	Charles, 2nd Viscount Canterbury		[Exhib RA, London, 1216]; untraced		*Graves* I, 1905–6, 7; GPC
152.	1872	Sir Christopher Charles Teesdale		[Exhib RA, London, 1396]; untraced		*Graves* I, 1905–6, 7
153.	1872	Sir Sills Gibbons, lord mayor of London		[Exhib RA, London, 1439]; untraced		*Graves* I, 1905–6, 7; GPC
154.	1873	Lady Prideaux		[Exhib RA, London, 1571]; untraced		*Graves* I, 1905–6, 7
155.	1874	Mrs James Scott		[Exhib RA, London, 1456]; untraced		*Graves* I, 1905–6, 7
156.	1874	R F Spicer		[Exhib RA, London, 1463]; untraced		*Graves* I, 1905–6, 7
157.	1876	The diver		[Exhib RA, London, 1426]; untraced		*Graves* I, 1905–6, 7; GPC
158.	1879	James Robinson Planché		[Exhib RA, London, 1555]; untraced		*Graves* I, 1905–6, 7
159.	nd	A gleaner		Untraced		GPC
160.	nd	A subdued Amazon		Untraced		GPC
161.	nd	Industry		Untraced		GPC
162.	nd	Strada		Untraced		GPC

ADAMS, W J fl 1830

Busts

1.	1830	Unidentified artist		[Exhib Soc of BA, London, 854]; untraced	Exhib Cat SBA, 33

ADAMS, William 1746–1805

Son of a stoneware manufacturer, Adams ran a pottery firm in Burslem from 1769 and opened a factory at Greengates, Tunstall in 1779. His jasperware rivalled that of Josiah Wedgwood, and the relief subjects that appeared on ceramics from his factory were sometimes taken from the same sources.

Literary References: *Pyke* 1973, 4; *Reilly* 1995, 12

Reliefs

1.	nd	Unidentified woman	w	Stanton Harcourt, Oxon	*Pyke* 1973, 4

ADDISON, Robert fl 1726–

He was described as a freemason of King's Meaburn when he made the font for Bampton church, Westmorland in 1726 (1). A mason of the same name was listed in Mortimer's *Director* of 1763 (p 49) as running a business from Hungerford Market. A Robert Addison, of St Martin in the Fields, was made free of the Masons' Company via service with George Lee on 30 March 1758.

Literary References: *Gunnis* 1968, 14; *Webb* 1999, 1

Architectural Sculpture

1.	1726	Font	m	Bampton, Westmorland	*Gunnis* 1968, 14

ADRON FAMILY

William Adron I –1809
Samuel Adron
William Adron II 1780–1867
Charles Adron *c*1787–1865

Masons of the name of Adron are known to have been active in London from 1748. By the turn of the 19th century the firm was based in the New Road, where it was still recorded in 1836. Identified monuments of the firm date from *c*1793. Gunnis considered their best work to be the monument by **William Adron II** to Henry Bewes, which has a relief of a woman mourning by a pillar carrying a portrait-medallion of the deceased (1). On the whole, Gunnis regarded the monuments as 'uninspired, though the details of the tablets are carefully carved' (*Gunnis* 1968, 15). One of the last known works of the firm was the temple in the Greek style to the memory of Dr Richard Valpy, headmaster of Reading School (8).

A William Adron, 'mason', was listed in the Westminster Poll-Book for 1748 in King Street, Golden Square. In 1809 the will was published of **William Adron I**, a mason living in the New Road, near Fitzroy Square, St Pancras. He may be the King Street mason. In his will, which was proved on 23 September 1809, he left sums amounting to about £100 to his brothers, sisters and nephews and the residue of his estate to his brother **Samuel Adron**. He appears to have been the uncle of William Adron II and **Charles Adron**.

Samuel Adron was the residual legatee of his brother William I's estate. There is an undated payment to a mason called Samuel Adron for a chimneypiece supplied to Shugborough Hall (13).

William Adron II was born on 20 September 1780 and christened at St Marylebone church, the son of Samuel Adron and Elizabeth, née Wheeler. His parents had married the previous year. In 1825–26 William II and his brother Charles were clearly running the firm, for their names appear on bills paid by John Nash for decorative ornaments at Buckingham Palace (15). They charged £6 14s 9d for 24 1/2 days' masonry work, which included dismantling the marble chimneypiece in the state apartments. William II is buried with his brother Charles in Kensal Green Cemetery. Works produced by the firm after 1809 are listed under William's name and works produced after 1825 are assumed to be joint productions of William and his brother Charles.

Literary References: *Gunnis* 1968, 14–15; *Robinson* 1989, 37; *Curl* 2001, 197–8, 213n

Archival References: TNA WORK 5/125 fol 332, fols 340–70; Longleat HA, 1800–1818 (accounts from 'Messrs Adron-statuary'); IGI

Will: William Adron I, PROB 11/1502/420

Funerary Monuments

1.	?1793	Henry Bewes		Duloe, Cornwall	S	*Gunnis* 1968, 15; Pevsner, *Cornwall*, 1970, 64
2.	?1800	William Golding		Southwark Cathedral, London	S	*Gunnis* 1968, 15
3.	?1805	Thomas Manning		Diss, Norfolk	S	*Gunnis* 1968, 15
4.	?1814	Sir James Musgrave		North Leigh, Oxon	S	*Gunnis* 1968, 15
5.	?1816	Aretas Akers		Yalding, Kent	S	*Gunnis* 1968, 15
6.	?1835	Thomas Easton		Ryton, Durham	S	*Gunnis* 1968, 15
7.	?1836	Clare Thornhill		Riddlesworth, Norfolk	S	*Gunnis* 1968, 15
8.	†1836	Dr Richard Valpy (by William Adron II and Charles Adron, designed by John Griffith)	s	Kensal Green Cemetery, London	S	*Curl* 2001, 197–8
9.	?1838	Major-General Adye		Woolwich parish church, London	S	*Gunnis* 1968, 15

Chimneypieces

10.	1792	Several Payment(s): £220	m	[Glevering Hall, Suffolk]; untraced	*Gunnis* 1968, 15
11.	1812	Two, of marble Payment(s): £314 18s 6d		Longleat, Wilts	Longleat HA, 1800–1818
12.	1810–1813	Several (by William Adron II) Payment(s): £318		[Ashridge Park, Berkhamstead, Herts]; untraced	*Gunnis* 1968, 15, citing archives, Lord Brownlow
13.	nd	(by Samuel Adron)		[Shugborough, Staffs]; untraced	Staffs RO D615/E(H)2/4 (receipted acct); *Robinson* 1989, 37

Architectural Sculpture

14.	1825–1826	Decorative work (by William Adron II and Charles Adron)		[Buckingham Palace, London]; untraced	TNA WORK 5/125 fols 332, 340–70; *Gunnis* 1968, 15

ADYE (or ADY), Thomas fl 1712–53

Adye was sculptor to the Society of Dilettanti from 1737 to 1744. In 1738 he carved an ornamental ballot box for the Society depicting the *Tomb of Bacchus* (**12**) and other work in ivory. When the Mansion House in London was being furnished in 1752 he submitted estimates for lamp-stands, 'six rich carved frames with looking glasses' and 'six brackets richly carved'. These do not appear to have been accepted, though he was paid later in the year for 'atlases and globes of glass for lights' (City Corp MSS Mansion House Box 2, 644 and 663, cited by *Gunnis* 1968, 15).

He signs a few funerary monuments, with portrait medallions, sometimes held by a seated female figure. They are adaptations of designs published by James Gibbs in *A Book of Architecture*, 1728. The monument to Charles Sergison has a draped personification of *Prudence* perched on a sarcophagus, reminiscent of Gibbs's and **Michael Rysbrack**'s monument to John Smith in Westminster Abbey. Adye adds a cherub (**2**). The William Mitchell monument is very similar, though here the boy holds an extinguished torch and the seated woman is identifiable as Mitchell's widow (**7**). The boy with a torch appears by himself holding the medallion on the monument to Lane Harrison at Perivale (**4**); two boys hold draped portrait medallions on the monuments to Sir John Cotton, Hugo Raymond and Humphrey Hall (**1, 3, 6**) and a lady alone supports Sir James Hallett's profile portrait (**8**). Whinney says that Adye modelled his style on Rysbrack's work in his treatment of the figures and draperies, but that his knowledge of anatomy was weak.

Adye's bust of the 7th Earl of Westmorland, 1742, was almost certainly ordered by Lord Cobham for the Temple of Friendship at Stowe (**9**), where it was sited with busts by **Peter Scheemakers** and Rysbrack. He is presented in classical armour and with cropped hair, looking authoritatively to his right. His expression carries conviction and the armour is finely realised. On stylistic grounds Adye is thought to have carved the bust of Paul Joddrell, *c*1740 (VAM), another classicising portrait with short curled hair, draperies and a severe demeanour. He apparently left his widow badly off, for in 1762 she had to apply for financial assistance from the Society of Artists.

Literary References: *Gunnis* 1968, 15; *Whinney* 1971, 71–5; *Whinney* 1988, 149, 247, 248; *Bilbey* 2002, 43–4

No.	Date	Work		Location		Reference
Funerary Monuments						
1.	†1712	Sir John Cotton		Landwade, Cambs	S	Pevsner, *Cambs*, 1970, 422
2.	1734	Charles Sergison (†1732)		Cuckfield, Sussex	S	*Gunnis* 1968, 15; *Whinney* 1988, 247–8 (repr)
3.	†1737	Hugo Raymond		Beckenham, Kent	S	*Gunnis* 1968, 15; Pevsner, *Kent: W & Weald*, 1976, 146
4.	†1740	Lane Harrison		St Mary, Perivale, Middx (West London arts centre)	S	*Whinney* 1988, 248; Pevsner, *London: N W*, 1991, 190
5.	†1742	Bishop Weston, his wife (†1741) and daughter (†1762)		Exeter Cathedral, Devon		Pevsner, *Devon*, 1989, 381
6.	?1742	Humphrey Hall		Bengeo, Herts	S	*Gunnis* 1968, 15
7.	†1745	William Mitchell and his wife Elizabeth (†1748)		Fowlmere, Cambs	S	*Gunnis* 1968, 15; *Whinney* 1988, 248
8.	†1753	Sir James Hallett		Little Dunmow, Essex		*Whinney* 1988, 248; Pevsner, *Essex*, 1965, 278
Busts						
9.	1742	John, 7th Earl of Westmorland Model(s): Socle with arms and trophies, all clay, ex coll Lord Fortescue; Ebrington Park, Glos	m	VAM A.65-1949 Other versions: Dashwood coll, West Wycombe Park	SD	*Whinney* 1971, 72–3 (repr); Pevsner, *Bucks*, 1994, 732; *Bilbey* 2002, 43 (repr)
Architectural Sculpture						
10.	1748	Carved work on the altar and other work including 'the Vase upon the Type of ye Pulpit' Payment(s): £29; £1 11s 6d outstanding		St John, Church Row, Hampstead, London		Hampstead parish church Trustees Minutes, 1744–96, 18 April 1748
11.	1753	Carved work for Augusta, Princess of Wales		[probably for Leicester House, London]; untraced		GPC
Miscellaneous						
12.	1737–1739	Ballot-box (designed by George Knapton) Payment(s): 15 gns plus 11 gns for the lid		[Soc of Dil, London]; untraced		*Cust* 1914, 31–2 (repr); *Gunnis* 1968, 15
13.	1755	Carved work		[Carlton House, London]; untraced		GPC

AFFLECK fl 1837

Assistant to **John Henning II**. He was sent to Manchester by his employer in April 1837 in order to carry out preliminary carving on the reliefs of Architecture, Painting, Sculpture, Wisdom, Astronomy and Mathematics on the Manchester City Art Gallery. He was paid £1 a week for his efforts.

Literary References: *Malden* 1977, unpag

AGAR, Samuel fl 1763

Listed as a 'Carver' in Church Street, St Anne's, Soho in the *Director* (*Mortimer* 1763, 3).

AGLIO, Augostino 1816–85

The son of Agostino Aglio of 36 Newman Street, a painter who exhibited at the Royal Academy, 1807–1834. In 1831, while living at 36 Newman Street, he received a medal from the Society of Arts for a bust (**1**). The following year he exhibited a 'bust of a gentleman' at the Manchester Academy (**2**). In 1836 he showed at the Society of British Artists from 2 Osnaburgh Street, Regent's Park. Like his father, Aglio subsequently specialised chiefly in watercolour painting.

Literary References: RSA *Transactions*, vol 48, 1831, 550; *Graves* I, 1905–6, 14; *Yockney* 1940, 129–30; *Yockney* 1943, 145–6; *Gunnis* 1968, 15; *Johnson* 1993, 3

No.	Date	Work	Location	Reference
Busts				
1.	1831	Unidentified subject, modelled from the life	[Soc of A, silver Isis medal]; untraced	*Gunnis* 1968, 15
2.	1832	Unidentified gentleman	[Exhib Manc A]; untraced	*Gunnis* 1968, 15
3.	1836	P Spagnoletti	[Exhib SBA, 892]; untraced	*Johnson* 1993, 3
4.	1838	Agostino Aglio, the sculptor's father	[Exhib SBA, 634]; untraced	*Johnson* 1993, 3

AIREY, of Kendal fl 1795–1851

He flourished in the first half of the 19th century. A William Airey, mason of Kendal, is referred to in the *Cumberland Pacquet* of 10 February 1795. The same mason, or possibly another with the same surname, signs a well-carved marble tablet to Anne Stewardson in Westmorland (1). Another tablet in Skipton, with a cross, descending dove, palm branches and bible, is signed 'T Airey' (2).

The *Carlisle Journal* of 20 March 1813 reported that Airey, a stone mason, had married Elizabeth Fawcett, also of Kendal. Thirty years later the same newspaper advertised the sale of marble chimneypieces at the house of Thomas Airey at Battle Borough, Appleby (26 April 1845). It stated that Airey was about to move to Kendal. In 1851 a Cumberland directory gave his profession and address as 'Stone Masons and Builders of Stricklandgate.' **Edward Bayliffe of Kendal** also worked from this street in 1845.

Literary References: *Gunnis* 1968, 15; *Hall* 1979, 1; RG/JP, 1, 14v-15 (Add inf. Denis Perriam)

Funerary Monuments

1.	?1815	Anne Stewardson		St Andrew Kendal, Westmorland	S	*Gunnis* 1968, 15; *Hall* 1979, 1
2.	†1817	Margaret Chippindale		Skipton, W R Yorks	S	

ALBACINI, Filippo 1777–1858

An Italian sculptor, born in Rome. In 1825 he carved a statue of *Wounded Achilles* for William, 6th Duke of Devonshire (1). A replica of this work, made in 1854, is in the Accademia di San Luca, Rome.

Literary References: *Panzetta* 1994, 17

Statues

1.	1825	Wounded Achilles Payment(s): 400 louis	m	Chatsworth, Derbys, sculpture gallery	*JKB* 1972 (3), 330, 331 (repr)

ALBERT, the Prince Consort 1819–61

Statues

1.	c1845	Eos (the Prince's favourite greyhound) (co-sculptor: John Francis)	b	Royal Coll, Osborne House, I of W	*Read* 1982, 137 (repr), 139

ALCOCK, J Rutherford fl 1820–26

A 'student in surgery' living at 11 New Burlington Street, he was awarded a medal from the Society of Arts in 1825 (2) and another in 1826 (3).

Reliefs

1.	1820	Unidentified man	w	VAM (L114 Bate)	*Pyke* 1973, 4 (repr)

Miscellaneous

2.	1825	Anatomical model in coloured wax		[Soc of A, gold Isis medal]; untraced	RSA *Transactions*, vol 43, 1825, xlviii
3.	1826	Coloured model in wax of a dissected arm	w	[Soc of A, gold medal]; untraced	RSA *Transactions*, vol 44, 1826, xliv

ALCOCK, Nicholas fl 1690–1702

He assisted **Grinling Gibbons** and **William Emmett** at Nottingham House (now Kensington Palace) in the years after William III's accession in 1688, laboriously working with Emmett on such items as '1405 feet of Ionicke modillion' and '942 feet of picture frame over ye Doores and Chimneyes'. Very little of this work survives. Green suggests that he may be the Alcock who carved a head of the King for the Tower of London Royal Armouries in 1702.

Literary References: *Green* 1964 (1), 67, 137

Busts

1.	by 1702	King William III		Royal Armouries, Tower of London	*Green* 1964 (1), 67, 137

Architectural Sculpture

2.	1690–1691	'the King's Armes with the Garter and Imperiall Crowne 2 boyes holding Trumpetts at Topp and a Lyon and Unicorne couching at Bottome' (co-sculptor: William Emmett) Payment(s): £10	wd	Kensington Palace, London	*Colvin* 1973–76, 5, 186–7
3.	1690–1692	Cornices, overdoors and chimney-frames (co-sculptor: William Emmett)	wd	Kensington Palace, London	*Colvin* 1973–76, 5, 186–7

ALCOTT, of Coventry fl 1803–1854?

The death of the wife of a 'Mr Alcott, mason of Coventry,' was reported in the *Monthly Magazine* in 1803 (2, 387). He is probably the mason who was employed 1796–1802 on the rebuilding of Arbury, Warks, where he carved a great number of gothic ornaments reminiscent of those at Strawberry Hill (7). In October 1809 a 'John Alcott of Coventry' entered into an agreement to take down and rebuild the four pinnacles of the steeple of Holy Trinity, Coventry, together with other masonry work, at a cost of £108 10s. A John Alcott, presumably from another generation of the same family, had yards at Coventry and Rugby, and signs a number of tablets from the 1830s to the 1850s. These are mostly Gothic in design.

Literary References: *Poole* 1870, 202; *Gunnis* 1968, 15

Funerary Monuments

1.	?1831	Rev Arthur Mill		Over Whitacre, Warks	S	*Gunnis* 1968, 15
2.	?1833	Andrew Gresley		Meriden, Warks		GPC
3.	?1833	Maria Powys		Thorpe Achurch, Northants	S	*Gunnis* 1968, 15
4.	?1840	Rev Henry Walpole		Winslow, Bucks	S	*Gunnis* 1968, 15
5.	?1847	Thomas Eagle		Alsley, Warks	S	*Gunnis* 1968, 15
6.	?1854	Henry Wise		Leek Wooton, Warks		GPC

Architectural Sculpture

7.	1796–1802	Gothic decoration, including pinnacles, panels and coats of arms	s	Arbury, Warks, interior and exterior	*Gunnis* 1968, 15; *Musgrave* 1966, 1–8

ALEFOUNDER, John fl 1784

Winner of a silver medal for sculpture at the Royal Academy (**1**). He was perhaps related to the John Alefounder, portrait painter of Bow Street, Covent Garden, whose will was proved on 10 October 1795 (PROB 11/1266).

Archival References: RA Premium list

Miscellaneous

1.	1784	An Academy figure or a bas-relief		[RA silver medal]; untraced	RA Premium list

ALKEN (or ALKIN), Oliver –1769

The brother of **Sefferin Alken**, he was one of the principal woodcarvers at Lansdowne House (**1**). By his will, which gives his address as Little Titchfield, Marylebone and his profession as 'Carver', he entrusted the care of his son (also called Sefferin) and daughter Ann to his brother's apprentice, **Richard Lawrence**, and to **James Thorne.**

Literary References: *Beard* 1981, 241; *Beard* 1985, 693

Will: PROB 11/947/119

Chimneypieces

1.	1767–1768	Description unavailable Drawing(s): Soane 22:118, dated 1768		[Lansdowne House, London, drawing room and other rooms]; untraced	*Harris* 2001, 347, n42; GPC

Architectural Sculpture

2.	1767–1768	Unspecified carving	wd	[Lansdowne House, London, interior]; untraced	GPC
3.	1766–1768	Unspecified carving		[German Lutheran chapel, the Savoy, London]; untraced	WCA 90/8

ALKEN (or ALKIN), Samuel 1756–1815

Born on 22 October 1756, the son of **Sefferin Alken**, he was involved in the family business by April 1771, when he presented his father's invoice for work at Audley End (Essex RO D/Dby/A30/11). He joined the Royal Academy Schools as a sculptor on 15 October 1772, giving his age as 16, and won a silver medal in 1773.

Alken assisted his father at Somerset House, providing work in wood and stone after his father's death in 1782 (**1, 2**). He is better known as an engraver: *A New Book of Ornaments Designed and Etched by Samuel Alken*, 1779, established him as accomplished in the new technique of aquatint. He died at St Pancras in 1815 and was buried on 9 November that year. His will was proved the following February.

Literary References: *Hutchison* 1960–62, 138; *Gunnis* 1968, 16; *Colvin* 1973–76, 5, 466; *Connor* 1979; *Beard and Gilbert* 1986, 8

Will: PROB 11/1576

Architectural Sculpture

1.	1781–1782	'Twenty-nine faces in Portland stone of composite capitals' and 9 'Goat's heads over windows to principal floor' (co-sculptor: Sefferin Alken (or Alkin)) Payment(s): £293 14s 9d	s	Somerset House, London	Chambers/Somerset Hse CHA/3 boxes 6–8; *Gunnis* 1968, 16; *Jenkins* 2000–1, 28
2.	nd	Unspecified interior carving	wd	[Somerset House, London]; untraced	*Gunnis* 1968, 16, citing building accts, Somerset House

ALKEN (or ALKIN), Sefferin 1717–82

Alken is best remembered as a carver of sophisticated neoclassical decoration for furniture, but he also worked in marble and stone. He appears to have been a member of the Alken family of sporting painters. He was a political refugee from Alken in North Jutland, Denmark and was in England by 1744, when he provided decorative carving for the saloon at Stourhead (**14**). His name continues to appear in the Hoare account books as a carver of wood and marble until the mid-1750s. Items provided included gilt picture frames charged at 8 guineas each, as well as a support in the shape of a unicorn for a German mannerist silver dish, still at Stourhead. Much of Alken's work at Stourhead was lost in a house fire early in the 20th century.

During the period when he worked for Henry Hoare he lived in the parish of St James, Westminster. In 1746 he took as an apprentice **Richard Lawrence**, who may subsequently have become his partner, for the business is referred to as 'Alken and Lawrence' in the Shardeloes accounts for 1763 (**21, 22**).

Alken worked extensively for Robert Adam, who employed Alken from *c*1761 as a wood and stone carver at some of his most important buildings. On many occasions from 1758 onwards Alken was entrusted with the carving of furniture supplied by William Vile and John Cobb, at Croome Court and elsewhere (**19, 23, 24, 41–45, 47–49, 51, 53, 55, 56**). Adam also employed him on a stone pediment for a greenhouse at Croome (**18**). Alken later subscribed to Adam's *Ruins of the Palace of the Emperor Diocletian at Spalatro* (1764).

In 1757 Alken provided a relief for St Margaret's, Westminster (**16**). A pamphlet of 1761 discussing repairs to the church notes that 'directly under the window is placed in a square moulding our Saviour at Emaus [*sic*], represented in basso-relievo and well executed by Mr. Alkin, of St. Anne's Westminster, from the famous painting by Titian' (quoted in *Gunnis* 1968, 16). In 1760 he took **Thomas Engleheart** as an apprentice.

Alken also had a long working relationship with Sir William Chambers and subscribed to the architect's *Designs for Chinese Buildings* (1757) and *Treatise of Civil Architecture* (1759). In 1764 he carved a bookcase to Chambers's design (**23**), and in 1767 he was employed by Chambers on work for Lord Charlemont's Casino at Marino (**26**). Chambers admired Alken's work, but also felt it was expensive and wrote to Lord Charlemont on 12 September 1767, 'Alken has carved one of the little heads for the corner of the doors of the medal-cases. It is very fine, but as he tells me that he cannot do them under three guineas and a half a head, I have stopped his further progress till I hear from your Lordship.' Later in the same letter Chambers writes: 'Alkin I have set about a head of Plato to match that of Homer and also about a pattera for to supply the places of the heads' (*HMC* 1891, 1, 284). One of his medal-cases, formerly at Elveden Hall, Suffolk, is now in the Courtauld Institute in London. In 1770 Chambers employed the carver again at Blenheim (**29**).

Mortimer's *Director* for 1763 lists Alken as a 'Carver in Wood and Stone' giving his address as 'Dufour's-court, Broad-Street, near Golden Square' (*Mortimer* 1763, 3). His only known monument, to Ann Littlejohn, was carved for export after 1771, to a design by the architect James Arrow (**1**). It is an assured and competent wall-monument, making use of the traditional motif of flying *putti* pulling back a tassled curtain to reveal an inscription. This baroque formula is combined with neoclassical details, such as paterae and a serpent-handled fluted vase.

In his last years Alken was much employed by Chambers on wood and stone carving for Somerset House (**28, 30–32, 54**). It is likely that Alken worked on this commission with one of his sons, **Samuel Alken**, who continued to receive payments after his father's death in 1782. In his will Sefferin Alken, 'Carver of St James Westminster', bequeathed his estate to his wife Ann. He also left a ring to 'his much esteemed good friend', the architect John Oldfield, of Scotland Yard (PROB 11/1090/143). Beard has described him as 'one of the most important neo-classical carvers'.

MGS

Literary References: *HMC* 1891, 1, 284; *Shaw Sparrow* 1931, 247–53; *Lewis* 1965–67, 11, 297; *Thornton* 1968, 419–20; *Gunnis* 1968, 15–16; *Beard* 1981, 242; *Beard* 1985, 693–4; *Beard and Gilbert* 1986, 8; *Murdoch* 1992, 44–7; *Grove* 1996, 1, 647 (Alexander); *Coleridge* 2000, 8–19; *Beard* 2004, 81–3

Archival References: Hoare private accounts, 1734–49, 1750–66; TNA AO 1/2495 (Somerset House)

Will: PROB 11/1090/143, proved 8 May 1782

Funerary Monuments					
1.	†1771	Ann DeLapierre Littlejohn (designed by James Arrow)		St Andrew, Halfway Tree, Jamaica	S *Lewis* 1965–67, 11, 297 (repr)
Busts					
2.	1767	Plato, head		[The Casino, Marino, near Dublin]; untraced	*HMC* 1891, 1, 284
Chimneypieces					
3.	c1742	Description unavailable Payment(s): £6 15s with other works over several years		Wimpole Hall, Cambs, gallery	Pevsner, *Cambs*, 1970, 491
4.	1753	Description unavailable Payment(s): £67 19s 8d		[Stourhead, Wilts]; destroyed	Hoare private accts, 1750–66; *Gunnis* 1968, 16
5.	1753	'for carving Sr Richds Chimney' Payment(s): £67 16s	m	[perhaps for Barn Elms, Surrey, Sir Richard Hoare's home]; untraced	Hoare private accts, 23 Nov 1753; *Gunnis* 1968, 16
6.	1754	Description unavailable Payment(s): £59 10s		[for Mrs Christopher Arnold, wife of a partner in Hoare's Bank]; untraced	Hoare private accts, 1750–66, 5 April 1754; *Gunnis* 1968, 16
7.	1763	Description unavailable	s	[Croome Court, Worcs]; untraced	GPC
8.	1765–1766	Description unavailable		[Normanton Park, Rutland]; untraced	*Beard and Gilbert* 1986, 8
9.	1769	Six, and miscellaneous carving Payment(s): £36 3s 8d		[for the Marquis of Tavistock]; untraced	*Beard and Gilbert* 1986, 8
10.	1770	Several Payment(s): £16 3s 2d		[Blenheim Palace, Oxon]; untraced	Chambers's letter-books, Ad MS 41133, fol 5; *Gunnis* 1968, 16
11.	1780	Four		Somerset House, London, east wing, basement storey and ground floor	Chambers/Somerset Hse CHA 3/1/8, fol 267
12.	1780	Three		Somerset House, London, Royal Society's Library and Museum, attic and mezzanine storeys; anteroom, principal floor	Chambers/Somerset Hse, CHA 3/1/8, box 6, fols 264–6
13.	1777–1783	Several	wd	[Somerset House, London, interior]; untraced	TNA AO 1/2495; *Gunnis* 1968, 16
Architectural Sculpture					
14.	1744	Decorative carving Payment(s): £187 10s 4d		[Stourhead, Wilts, saloon]; untraced	Hoare private accts, 1734–49; *Gunnis* 1968, 15–16
15.	1754	A 'richly carved pier glass' Payment(s): £60		[Marston House, Somerset (for Lady Boyle, Henry Hoare's daughter)]; untraced	Hoare private accts, 1750–66; *Gunnis* 1968, 16
16.	c1758	Christ at Emmaus, reredos relief, after Titian Payment(s): £93 17s 4d with other carving		St Margaret, Westminster, London	*Gunnis* 1968, 16; *Friedman* 2004, 90, pl 79
17.	1759	Capitals		[Longford Castle, Wilts]; untraced	Radnor archives; *Gunnis* 1968, 16
18.	1761	A large basket of flowers and festoons (designed by Robert Adam) Payment(s): £35 10s	s	Croome Court, Worcs, greenhouse, pediment	*Beard* 1981, 67; *Coleridge* 2000, 14
19.	1761	Alcove bed		[Croome Court, Worcs]; untraced	*Harris* 2001, 338 n17
20.	1761	Lord Coventry's arms Payment(s): £27 15s Model(s): in limewood, £1 18s; untraced		[Croome Court, Worcs]; untraced	*Beard* 1981, 66
21.	1763	Carved work (co-sculptor: Richard Lawrence) Payment(s): £543 12s		[Shardeloes, Bucks]; untraced	*Beard* 1985, 693
22.	1763	Carving on mahogany doors (designed by Robert Adam) (co-sculptor: Richard Lawrence) Payment(s): £15 17s 2d and £11 13s 6d	wd	[Shardeloes, Bucks]; untraced	*Beard* 1985, 693
23.	1763	Embellishments on bookcases Payment(s): £121 9s 8d	wd	[Croome Court, Worcs, library]; VAM	*Beard* 1993, 91, 94; *Harris* 2001, 45 (repr)
24.	1763	Font 'carv'd in oak, all ye mouldings to pedistal, body and cover enriched, also several ornaments' Payment(s): £11 14s	wd	[Croome Court, Worcs]; Evesham Town Museum	*Beard* 1993, 94; *Harris* 2001, 338 n21
25.	1764	Bookcase, with festoons of 'Musick, War, Painting and Sculpture' (designed by Sir William Chambers) Payment(s): £27 9s 6d		[coll Marquis of Tavistock]; untraced	*Beard and Hayward* 1988, 398

26.	1767	'a pattera'		[The casino, Marino, near Dublin]; untraced		*HMC* 1891, 1, 284
27.	1767	One 'little head' for the 'corner of the doors of the medal-cases' Payment(s): 3 1/2 gns		[The casino, Marino, near Dublin]; Courtauld Institute, London		*HMC* 1891, 1, 284; *Beard and Gilbert* 1985, 8
28.	1776–1777	Truss with rich foliage leaf and moulding in front and scrolls on profile Payment(s): £1 15s 0d	s	Somerset House, London		TNA AO3/1244; *Jenkins* 2000–1, 27
29.	1778	'4 pier glasses with carved frames gilt in burnish'd gold'		[Blenheim Palace, Oxon]; untraced		*Beard* 1985, 694
30.	1777–1778	Five 'fronts of Corinthian capitals to pillasters,' seven fronts to three column capitals, one Corinthian capital Payment(s): Plus repairs and joinery work £115 2s 6 1/2d Model(s): Listed in bill	s	Somerset House, London		Chambers/Somerset Hse, CHA 3/1/3, box 6, fol 82; *Gunnis* 1968, 16; *Jenkins* 2000–1, 28
31.	1780	'No 8 faces of Composite Capitals to pillasters'		Somerset House, London, great stairs		Chambers/Somerset Hse, CHA 3/1/8, box 6, fol 266
32.	1781–1782	'Twenty-nine faces in Portland stone of composite capitals' and nine 'Goat's heads over windows to principal floor' (co-sculptor: Samuel Alken (or Alkin) Payment(s): £293 14s 9d	s	Somerset House, London		Chambers/Somerset Hse, box 6, CHA 3/1/3 fol 82, box 7, CHA 3/2; *Gunnis* 1968, 16; *Jenkins* 2000–1, 28
33.	nd	Chair and lectern (designed by John Hobcraft) Payment(s): £13		Audley End, gothic chapel		*Beard and Gilbert* 1986, 8; *Harris* 2001, 344 n40
Miscellaneous						
34.	1747	Unspecified work Payment(s): £20 10s		[Stourhead, Wilts]; untraced		Hoare private accts, 1734–49
35.	1748	Unspecified work Payment(s): £32 14s paid 'in full' in August		[Stourhead, Wilts]; untraced		Hoare private accts, 1734–49
36.	1750	Unspecified work		[for Lord Fitzwilliam]; untraced		*Gunnis* 1968, 16, citing Fitzwilliam papers
37.	1746–1752	Carving		[Cleveland House, St James's, London]; destroyed		*Beard* 1985, 693
38.	1754	Unspecified work Payment(s): £67 19s 8d		[Henry Hoare's house, Clapham]; untraced		Hoare private accts, 1750–66; *Gunnis* 1968, 16
39.	1759	Five gilt picture frames (designed by Robert Adam)		[Kedleston Hall, Derbys, breakfast room]; untraced		*Beard* 1985, 693; *Harris* 2001, 23
40.	1759	Six term figures Payment(s): £50 8s	s	Longford Castle, Wilts, gardens		Radnor archives; *Gunnis* 1968, 16
41.	1761	Pulpit, sounding boards, desks and other fittings Payment(s): £33		Croome Court, Worcs	S	*Beard* 1981, 206 (repr 125); *Beard* 1985, 693; *Beard* 1993, 94
42.	1764	Two gilded picture frames and mouldings in the tapestry room Payment(s): Frames: £32 10s with gilding bills of £14 12s; mouldings: £13 9s		[Croome Court, Worcs]; untraced		*Beard* 1981, 66; *Beard* 1993, 95
43.	1765	Ornaments for chairs and sofas (designed by Robert Adam)	wd	Croome Court, Worcs		*Beard* 1993, 100; *Coleridge* 2000, 14, 16; *Harris* 2001, 53
44.	1765	Two table frames and two glass frames (designed by Robert Adam) Payment(s): £51 6s for the table frames, £67 12s for the glass frames		[Croome Court, Worcs]; Met NY and Philadelphia Museum of Art		*Beard* 1993, 95 (repr 4); *Harris* 2001, 52
45.	1768	Two carved gilt-wood table frames (designed by Robert Adam) Payment(s): £43 2s 9d, plus £34 19s for gilding and joinery	wd	[Coventry House, London]; private coll		*Beard* 1993, 102; *Harris* 2001, 57, 58 (repr)
46.	1750–1768	Unidentified work		[for the Duke of Northumberland]; untraced		*Beard and Gilbert* 1986, 8
47.	1769	'2 glass frames', ornamented with honeysuckle, two female figures, a basket of fruit, and foliage Payment(s): £68 16s 7d plus £60 12s 3d for gilding and joinery		[Coventry House, London]; untraced		*Beard* 1993, 103; *Harris* 2001, 57, 340 n17
48.	1769	A glass frame with a standing figure and rams' heads Payment(s): £23 8s 4d		[Croome Court, Worcs, anteroom]; untraced		*Beard* 1993, 102
49.	1770	'an oval dressing glass frame. . with coat of arms at top & supporters at bottom standing on rock work 2 women & foilige at sides & festoons of husks over glass'		[Coventry House, London, first floor dressing room]; untraced		*Murdoch* 1992, 46; *Beard* 1993, 95
50.	1771	Carving		[Woburn Abbey, Beds]; untraced		*Beard and Gilbert* 1986, 8
51.	1772	'two carved oval gilt glass frames' (designed by Robert Adam) Payment(s): £80 Drawing(s): Adam, Soane, vol 20, 68	wd	[Croome Court, Worcs]; untraced		*Murdoch* 1992, 44–7 (repr); *Harris* 2001, 63 (repr)

52.	1774	Unspecified work		[Milton Hall, Cambs]; untraced	*Gunnis* 1968, 16, citing Fitzwilliam papers
53.	1778	'4 Pier glasses with carved frames gilt in burnish'd gold' and 'A large picture frame for the present family picture'		[Blenheim Palace, Oxon]; untraced	*Beard and Gilbert* 1986, 8
54.	1780	Chimneypiece and carved cornice		Somerset House, Royal Antiquarian Library	Chambers/Somerset Hse CHA 3/1/8 fol 266
55.	1782	Frames		[Croome Court, Worcs]; untraced	*Beard* 1993, 95
56.	nd	Large mahogany clothes-press (designed by Robert Adam)	wd	[Croome Court, Worcs]; VAM	*Murdoch* 1992, 46; *Harris* 2001, 59 (repr)

ALLCOTT (or ALCOT), Joseph fl 1799–1811

An anecdotal account in the *Builder* relates that he began life as a carpenter and was sent to Stoke Park to prepare wooden pillars for the Italian artists to cover with scagliola, but being an ingenious man he watched the workmen and soon learnt the secret of the process. 'He then obtained a piece of marble and imitated it so well as to please the architect [Wyatt], more than what had been done by the Italians' (*Builder*, 1845, 50). Allcott's name as a supplier of scagliola appears in the accounts of numerous country houses and a letter from him to a patron, written in 1799, survives in the Newdigate archives. In it Allcot tells Sir Roger Newdigate that he has 'received an order from his Grace the Duke of Bridgewater for an imitation of a very fine porphyry table in his Grace's possession' (Newdigate Archives CR 136/B2635d). He was also involved in rebuilding work that included extensive carving for Newdigate at Arbury (1–4).

Literary References: *Gunnis* 1968, 16; *Baird* 1998, 84–7

Chimneypieces

1.	1799	with 'twenty small Doric flutes in each column'		[Arbury Hall, Warks]; untraced	*Gunnis* 1968, 16
2.	*c*1800	with ogee arch	m	Arbury Hall, Warks, school room	Pevsner, *Warks*, 1966, 70
3.	1800	with porphyry columns		[Arbury Hall, Warks]; untraced	*Gunnis* 1968, 16

Architectural Sculpture

4.	1796	Twenty scagliola columns of 'yellow antique marble' and four 'of jasper', pinnacles, panels, coats of arms etc, for the interior and exterior Payment(s): £84	p	[Arbury Hall, Warks]; untraced	Newdigate accts, 1796–1802, CR 136/V119; *Gunnis* 1968, 16
5.	1806	Columns with elaborate composite capitals		Goodwood, Sussex, entrance hall	Goodwood accounts in GPC; *Mason* 1839, 17; *Baird* 1998, 86
6.	1807	Scagliola work Payment(s): £36		[Grosvenor House, London]; untraced	Grosvenor archives in GPC
7.	1811	Scagliola columns Payment(s): £180		[Coventry House, Piccadilly, London]; untraced	Archives, Earl of Coventry quoted in *Gunnis* 1968, 16
8.	1807–1811	Scagliola work Payment(s): £215 17s 9d		[Dodington Park, Glos]; untraced	Codrington archives in GPC

ALLEN fl 1681

The wall monument to Sir Thomas Allen is a large and bold architectural structure 8 feet high, with Corinthian pillars, an open pediment and a flaming urn in the centre (1). The work was 'erected by Edward Allen' and signed 'Allen fecit', but it is not clear whether the two inscriptions refer to the craftsman only, or to the patron and craftsman respectively. Gunnis points out that the only craftsman with this surname who was a member of the Masons' Company at the time was Peter Allen, so the monument is possibly his work. Peter Allen became free by redemption in 1674, and was the father of **Theophilus Allen.**

Literary References: *Gunnis* 1968, 16–17; Pevsner, *London: N*, 1998, 120

Archival References: Masons' Co, Freedom Register, 1674

Funerary Monuments

1.	1681	Sir Thomas Allen (†1681) and wife (†1683)	St Mary-at-Finchley, Middx	S	Pevsner, *London: N*, 1998, 120

ALLEN, James I, of Bristol fl 1752–1810

A statuary and architect of Bristol, he was the son of John Allen, a joiner. In 1752 James was apprenticed to **James Paty II of Bristol** and on 18 September 1780 he received his freedom of the city as a carver. He was appointed one of three City Surveyors in 1788, but resigned in 1792. He became bankrupt in 1790.

His tablets are well executed but conventional in design, featuring in most cases an urn set against a pyramid. His architectural work included repairs to St Mary Redcliffe, Bristol, where one of his tablets was erected (1). He was still living in 1810.

Literary References: *Gunnis* 1968, 17; *Colvin* 1995, 74

Funerary Monuments

1.	?1765	Ann Taylor	St Mary Redcliffe, Bristol	S	*Gunnis* 1968, 17
2.	?1775	Priscilla Colley	Barnstaple, Devon	S	*Gunnis* 1968, 17
3.	?1775	Samuel Smith	Powick, Worcestershire	S	*Gunnis* 1968, 17
4.	?1780	John Bennet	Camerton, Somerset	S	*Gunnis* 1968, 17
5.	†1781	Susanna Matthew	St Mary, Thornbury, Glos	S	

ALLEN, James II, of Bristol fl 1756–before 1780

Described as a stonecutter when he was admitted a freeman of Bristol on 23 February 1756, by marriage with Ann, daughter of John Weaver, 'Gentl. dece'd'. He was dead by 16 December 1780, the date on which his son James became a freeman of Bristol.

Archival References: BRO, Burgess Books 04359, microfiche FC/BB/1(q)2 (fol Or p 42); microfiche FC/BB/1(u)4 (fol Or p 97)

ALLEN, Michael, of St Paul's, Birmingham fl 1830–1856

Funerary Monuments

1.	†1831	Michael Beasley	Stourbridge Unitarian chapel, Worcs	S	GPC
2.	†1834	William Scott	Stourbridge Unitarian chapel, Worcs	S	GPC
3.	†1835	Thomas Beasley	Stourbridge Unitarian chapel, Worcs	S	GPC
4.	†1839	Mr and Mrs Moseley	Stourbridge Congregational church, Worcs	S	GPC
5.	1847	Richard and Ann Silvey	Bilston, Staffs	S	

ALLEN, of Plymouth fl *c*1795–*c*1802

He signs a few tablets in Devon, the best of which commemorates James Luce (1).

Literary References: *Gunnis* 1968, 17

Funerary Monuments

1.	?1795	James Luce	St Budeaux, Devon	S	*Gunnis* 1968, 17
2.	?1798	Sir Thomas Byard	St Budeaux, Devon	S	*Gunnis* 1968, 17
3.	?1802	William Forbes	Plympton, Devon	S	*Gunnis* 1968, 17

ALLEN, Theophilus fl 1687–1727

He was the son of Peter Allen and was apprenticed to his father in 1687, but did not become free until 1694, when his name appears in the general search of the Masons' Company. Two more masons of that name are mentioned in the Company archives, one who was made free on 29 October 1679 by service to another mason of the same surname, and another who was made free by patrimony on 6 October 1726.

Literary References: *Knoop and Jones* 1935, 77; *Gunnis* 1968, 16–17

Archival References: Masons' Co, Freedom Register, 1674; Masons' Co, Freemen; Masons' Co, Court Book, 1677–94, fol 105v

Funerary Monuments

1.	†1727	Jonathan (†1704) Whiting and wife	St Bartholomew-the-Great, City of London	Pevsner, *London: City*, 1997, 202

ALLEN, William, of Norwich fl 1820–45

Notices of the erection of the monument to Charles Chapman (1) appeared in the *Norwich Mercury* on 21 April 1827.

Literary References: *Gunnis* 1968, 17

Funerary Monuments

1.	1826	Rev Charles Chapman (designed by Arthur Brown)	St Peter Mancroft, Norwich, Norfolk	*Gunnis* 1968, 17; Pevsner, *Norfolk: N-E and Norwich*, 1997, 250

ALLWOOD (or ALWOOD), Thomas fl 1769–72

He joined the Royal Academy Schools on 9 December 1769 and exhibited at the Society of Artists between 1770 and 1772. In 1771 he was elected a Fellow of the Society. In 1770 he gave his address as Great Russell Street, Bloomsbury.

Literary References: *Graves* 1907, 2; *Hutchison* 1960–62, 135; *Gunnis* 1968, 17

Busts

1.	1771	Unidentified gentleman		[Exhib Soc of Artists, London, 208]; untraced	*Graves* 1907, 2
2.	1771	Unidentified lady		[Exhib Soc of Artists, London, 209]; untraced	*Graves* 1907, 2
3.	1772	Unidentified gentleman	tc	[Exhib Soc of Artists, London, 3]; untraced	*Graves* 1907, 2

Miscellaneous

4.	1770	A vestal, model		[Exhib Soc of Artists, London, 162]; untraced	*Graves* 1907, 2

AMBROSE, Edward 1814–90

Born in Cork, by 1845 he was in London, where he enrolled as a student at the Royal Academy. He subsequently studied in Paris, Rome and Louvain and returned to England around 1851, when he exhibited at the Royal Academy (1). In 1864 he received a medal from the Liverpool Academy. His London address was 101 Stanhope Street, Mornington Crescent, Regent's Park. In the latter part of his life he returned to Cork, where he died on 29 April 1890.

Literary References: *Strickland* 1, 1913, 6; *Murray* 1991, 167

Statues

1.	1851	Psyche discovering Cupid	m	[Exhib RA, London, 1277 Manc Art Treas Exhib, 32]; untraced		*Manchester Art Treasures* 1857, 133; *Graves* I, 1905–6, 30; *Murray* 1991, 167; *Morris and Roberts* 1998, 43
2.	1852	Cupid and Psyche, statuette	m	Crawford MAG, Cork	SD	*Murray* 1991, 137, 262 (repr)
3.	by 1852	Spring, statuette	m	Crawford MAG, Cork (698-S)	S	*Murray* 1991, 137 (repr); *Morris and Roberts* 1998, 43
4.	1857	Cupid and Psyche	m	[Manc Art Treas Exhib, 28 ?Exhib RHA 1858 ?Exhib LSFA, Liverpool, 16]; untraced		*Manchester Art Treasures* 1857, 133; *Murray* 1991, 167; *Morris and Roberts* 1998, 43

Busts

5.	1876	Unidentified gentleman	m	Crawford Municipal Art Gallery, Cork (692-S)	SD	*Murray* 1991, 137 (repr)
6.	1878	Unidentified gentleman	m	Crawford Municipal Art Gallery, Cork (693-S)	SD	*Murray* 1991, 137 (repr)

ANDERSON fl 1760–70

A 'Mr Anderson' exhibited a copy of a tripod, after the design by James 'Athenian Stuart', at the Free Society of Artists in 1761 (2).

Literary References: *Graves* 1907, 3; *Gunnis* 1968, 17

Architectural Sculpture

1.	1760–1770	Extensive decorative carving	Penicuick House, Midlothian	*Gunnis* 1968, 17

Miscellaneous

2.	1761	Tripod (after design by James Stuart)	[Exhib Free Soc of A, 102]; untraced	*Graves* 1907, 3; *Gunnis* 1968, 17

ANDERSON, David, of Perth 1804–47

He was born in Perth in 1804 and from 1837 to 1845 worked as a marble and stone carver at County Place, Perth. He had considerable local success with a statue of *Tam O'Shanter* (2). In 1846, he moved to Liverpool, where in 1847 he exhibited several groups of stone (2–4). He died there of typhoid in the same year and was buried in Perth. The *Gentleman's Magazine*, described him as 'the celebrated Perthshire statuary, a man of great ability as an artist' (*GM*, 1847, ii, 668) while the *Liverpool Mercury* stated that 'like most men of genius he was modest, retiring, plain and unassuming' (October 1847). His only known surviving works are a series of sandstone statues depicting characters from Scottish literature in the grounds of Fingask Castle (2–7) and a monument commemorating David, Viscount Stormont at Scone Palace (1). He was survived by a son, **William Anderson**, who inherited his business.

Literary References: *Gunnis* 1968, 17; *Woodward* 1977, vol 1, pt 2, 7

Funerary Monuments

1.	nd	David, Viscount Stormont		Scone, Perths	RG/JP, 1, 21

Statues

2.	pre-1846	Tam O'Shanter	s	Fingask Castle, Perths, gardens	*Gunnis* 1968, 17; *Woodward* 1977, vol 1, pt 2, 8
3.	by 1847	Kirkton Jean	s	Fingask Castle, Perths, gardens	*Woodward* 1977, vol 1, pt 2, 8
4.	by 1847	Watty and Meg	s	Fingask Castle, Perths, gardens	*Woodward* 1977, vol 1, pt 2, 8
5.	nd	The highland drover	s	Fingask Castle, Perths, gardens	*Woodward* 1977, vol 1, pt 2, 8
6.	nd	The last minstrel	s	Fingask Castle, Perths, gardens	*Woodward* 1977, vol 1, pt 2, 8
7.	nd	Willie brew'd a peck o' maut	s	Fingask Castle, Perths, gardens	*Woodward* 1977, vol 1, pt 2, 8

ANDERSON, Edward 1696–1781

The son of Edward Anderson, a Chelsea farmer, he was apprenticed in 1720 to Benjamin Denny, 'citizen and mason of London.' He became free of the Masons' Company on 7 January 1730 and set up independently at the 'Horse-ferry near Chelsea' early in 1731. He was still described as 'Mason, Chelsea' when a search of the Company was carried out around 1740 (Masons' Co Assistants, fol 3). Between 1747 and 1749 he was employed on stonework at the theatre of Surgeons' Hall (Archives, Royal College of Surgeons) and a year later he became Master of the Masons' Company.

It was during Anderson's term of office that the Company began to experience financial difficulties. The court book for 1750 carries a note that there was to be 'a frugal dinner next election day and to have neither ladies or musick.' In 1751 Anderson was appointed churchwarden of Chelsea Old Church. Soon after he became master mason to Chelsea Hospital and he later held the same post at three royal palaces.

In 1778 he was paid £157 17s 10d for three stone obelisks for use at the observatory at Richmond (1), which he charged with unspecified mason's work and a block of Portland stone. He died on 17 June 1781 and was buried in Chelsea Old Church, where a slab of touch in the floor of the porch commemorates him and his father. The epitaph describes him as mason 'to His Majesty's Palaces at Hampton Court, Richmond and Kew.' The will of an Edward Anderson, mason, was proved on 2 July 1785 (PROB 11/1131).

Literary References: *Gunnis* 1968, 17

Archival References: Masons' Co, Freemen, fol 1; Court Book, 1695–1722, MS 5304/2, fols 176v-188r; Court Book, 1722–51, MS 5304/3 7 Jan 1731, 14 June 1749 & 4 May 1750

Architectural Sculpture

1.	1778	Three obelisks, time markers Payment(s): £157 17s 10d	Old Observatory, Richmond, Surrey	TNA WORK 5/66; Pevsner, *London: S*, 1983, 520

ANDERSON, Joshua fl 1825

David Dunbar I used Anderson's models for several of his own sculptured busts. An article on Dunbar in the *Carlisle Examiner* of 13 November 1858 (p 2) describes Anderson 'an amateur artist possessed much good taste and made several excellent models particularly of his friends, the late Mr Saul of Greenrow, Dr Blamire, Robert Anderson and Dean Milner [of Carlisle]' (1–4). (Inf. Denis Perriam)

Busts

1.	1825	Dr T Blamire	[Exhib Carlisle Acad of Fine Art, 165]; untraced	*Carlisle Examiner* 13 Nov 1858; *Carlisle Exhibs*, 1973
2.	nd	Dean Milner	Untraced	*Carlisle Examiner* 13 Nov 1858
3.	nd	Mr Saul of Greenow, model	Untraced	*Carlisle Examiner*, 13 Nov 1858
4.	nd	Robert Anderson (the poet)	Untraced	*Carlisle Examiner*, 13 Nov 1858

ANDERSON, Nicolaus fl 1763

Listed as a 'Modeller and chaser' of Gerrard Street, Soho in *Mortimer* 1763, 3.

ANDERSON, of Chester fl 1812

Architectural Sculpture

1.	1812	Coats of arms and unspecified carving	Eaton Hall, Chester	Grosvenor archives in GPC

ANDERSON, William, of Perth –1867

The son of **David Anderson**, he continued the family business at County Place, Perth after his father's death in 1847. He showed a figure of a *Highlander throwing the putting-stone* with reliefs illustrating highland games on the pedestal at the Great Exhibition of 1851 (3). In the same year he went into partnership with **Alexander Christie**. He received his first important commission, for a bust of Robert Peel for the Peel Memorial in Forfar, in 1852 (9). A review of the work in the *Illustrated London News* described Anderson as a young sculptor of promise and noted that he had executed the bust for a nominal fee (*ILN*, 21 May 1853, 397). The Forfar memorial is reputed to be the first permanent memorial to Peel erected in Scotland. In 1854 Anderson executed a heroic statue of Burns, which he presented to his native town (5). It was described by the *Builder* as 'of manly make' and 'enveloped in the homely folds of a Scottish plaid' (*Builder*, 1854, 295). The sculptor died at Perth in 1867.

Literary References: *Woodward* 1977, vol 1, pt 2, 8–9

Statues

1.	c1845	Flora MacDonald	s	Fingask Castle, Perths, grounds	*Woodward* 1977, vol 1, pt 2, 9
2.	c1845	Prince Charles Edward Stuart	s	Fingask Castle, Perths, grounds	*Woodward* 1977, vol 1, pt 2, 9
3.	1851	Highlander throwing the putting-stone		[Gt Exhib]; untraced	*Laperriere* 1, 1991, 49
4.	1851	William Wallace	s	Kinfauns Castle, Perths	*Woodward* 1977, vol 1, pt 2, 9
5.	1854	Robert Burns	s	County Place, Perth	*Woodward* 1977, vol 1, pt 2, 9
6.	1856	The curlers, statuette		[Exhib R Sc A, Edinburgh, 715]; untraced	*Laperriere* 1, 1991, 49
7.	1865	'Burns and Highland Mary, the vow', sketch for a larger group		[Exhib R Sc A, Edinburgh, 896]; untraced	*Laperriere* 1, 1991, 49
8.	nd	Unknown warrior	s	Kinfauns Castle, Perths	*Woodward* 1977, vol 1, pt 2, 9

Busts

9.	1853	Robert Peel	m	Peel Monument, Newmont Hill, Forfar, Angus	*Ormond* 1973, 373; *Woodward* 1977, vol 1, pt 2, 9
10.	1855	Master A Ogilvy		[Exhib R Sc A, Edinburgh, 765]; untraced	*Laperriere* 1, 1991, 49
11.	1866	Andrew Bannantyne		[Exhib R Sc A, Edinburgh, 897]; untraced	*Laperriere* 1, 1991, 49

Miscellaneous

12.	1858	Neil Gow		[Exhib R Sc A, Edinburgh, 774]; untraced	*Laperriere* 1, 1991, 49
13.	1858	Portrait of an unidentified child		[Exhib R Sc A, Edinburgh, 760]; untraced	*Laperriere* 1, 1991, 49
14.	1861	Master Walter Ogilvy		[Exhib R Sc A, Edinburgh, 815]; untraced	*Laperriere* 1, 1991, 49
15.	1861	Our little Jack		[Exhib R Sc A, Edinburgh, 811]; untraced	*Laperriere* 1, 1991, 49

ANDRAS, Catherine 1775–1860

She was born in Bristol. As an orphan, she grew up with her three sisters who ran a toy and perfumery business in the city. She is said to have modelled in wax a number of prominent people in Bristol, including John Wesley and the Polish General Kosciuszko (**41, 47**), before moving to London. There she lodged with Robert Bowyer, the painter and proprietor of the Historic Gallery, who subsequently adopted her. Her first work exhibited at the Royal Academy was a portrait of her adoptive father, shown in 1799 (**2**). In 1802 she submitted a portrait model of the young Princess Charlotte (**10**), for which she was awarded the silver palette by the Society of Arts. In 1805 she was asked to model a full-length effigy of Admiral Lord Nelson for Westminster Abbey. This was based on a likeness *ad vivum* which she had earlier modelled, possibly the one exhibited at the RA in 1801 (**6**). The effigy was dressed in Nelson's own clothes. In 1810 she gave her address as 52 Great Titchfield Street and the following year she was at 80 Pall Mall. She exhibited at the Royal Academy until 1824. She died in London. Gunnis owned more than 30 of her works, now in the VAM.

Literary References: *Graves* 1905–6, 1, 34; *Pyke* 1973, 5; *Pyke* 1981, 3; *Knox* 1998, 90, 95 n31

Busts

1.	nd	Rose Rainey	w	NGI 8080	*Pyke* 1973, 5; *Wynne and White* 1975, 5

Reliefs

2.	1799	Robert Bowyer	w	VAM	*Graves* I, 1905–6, 34; *Pyke* 1973, 5 (repr 6)
3.	1800	Admiral Sir A Mitchell	w	[Exhib RA, London, 864]; untraced	*Graves* 1905–6, 1, 34
4.	?1800	Mr and Mrs Plummer	w	Private coll	*Graves* I, 1905–6, 34; *Pyke* 1981, 3
5.	1801	A Davison	w	[Exhib RA, London, 1030]; untraced	*Graves* 1905–6, 1, 34
6.	1801	Admiral Lord Nelson	w	[Exhib RA, London, 1030]; untraced Other versions: Private coll, Canada, 1805 Westminster Abbey, lifesize effigy, 1806, £104 14s 9d (*Pyke* 1973, 5, repr) NMM Sotheby 21 Oct 1968, lot 101 VAM L55; L59 Bate Sotheby 25 July 1977, lot 5	*Graves* I, 1905–6, 34; *Pyke* 1973, 5; *Pyke* 1981, 3
7.	1801	Dr Webster	w	[Exhib RA, London, 1030]; untraced	*Graves* 1905–6, 1, 34
8.	1801	Unidentified male subjects	w	VAM A.117-1965; A.130-1965; A.137-1965; A.138-1965; A.139-1965	*Pyke* 1973, 5
9.	1802	Duke of Bedford	w	[Exhib RA, London, 1076]; untraced	*Graves* 1905–6, 1, 34
10.	1802	HRH Princess Charlotte	w	VAM A.113-1965 Other versions: VAM A.120-1965; A.121-1965; A.127-1965; A.134-1965	*Graves* 1905–6, 1, 34; *Pyke* 1973, 5
11.	1802	William Pitt the Younger	w	Christie 11 Oct 1977, lot 2 Other versions: NMM 1805 Private coll, Canada, 1806 Chevening, Kent, 1821 VAM A.131-1965 Stanton Harcourt, Oxon Private coll, USA, 1806 Exhib RA, London, 1807, 909	*Graves* 1905–6, 1, 34; *Pyke* 1973, 5; *Pyke* 1981, 3
12.	1803	Earl Moira	w	[Exhib RA, London, 789]; untraced	*Graves* 1905–6, 1, 34
13.	1803	Rev Mason of York	w	[Exhib RA, London, 823]; untraced	*Graves* 1905–6, 1, 34
14.	?1805	Charles James Fox	w	Stanton Harcourt, Oxon Other versions: NMM VAM L54 Bate	*Graves* 1905–6, 1, 34; *Pyke* 1973, 5
15.	?1805	Lord Thurlow	w	Private coll Other versions: VAM A.119-1965 VAM A.136-1965	*Graves* 1905–6, 1, 34; *Pyke* 1973, 5

16.	?1807	Kynaston Powell	w	Sotheby 13 April 1981, lot 10	*Graves* 1905–6, 1, 34; *Pyke* 1981, 3
17.	1807	Lady C Butler	w	[Exhib RA, London, 909]; untraced	*Graves* 1905–6, 1, 34
18.	1808	Mr Welles	w	Private coll	*Pyke* 1973, 5
19.	1809	G Sharp	w	[Exhib RA, London, 667]; untraced	*Graves* 1905–6, 1, 34
20.	1809	M Dechemant	w	[Exhib RA, London, 667]; untraced	*Graves* 1905–6, 1, 34
21.	1809	T Clarkson	w	[Exhib RA, London, 667]; untraced	*Graves* 1905–6, 1, 34
22.	?1810	Arthur, 1st Duke of Wellington	w	VAM L.56 Bate Other versions: Private coll	*Graves* 1905–6, 1, 34; *Pyke* 1973, 5
23.	1810	George Stephenson	w	Private coll, USA	*Pyke* 1973, 5
24.	1810	John Andras	w	Sotheby, 30 Nov 1964, lot 78; untraced	*Pyke* 1973, 5
25.	1810	Lady Charlemont	w	[Exhib RA, London, 610]; untraced	*Graves* 1905–6, 1, 34
26.	?1810	Marquess Wellesley	w	Stratfield Saye, Hants	*Graves* 1905–6, 1, 34; *Pyke* 1973, 6
27.	1810	Unidentified man	w	Phillips 31 Jan 1978, lot 31; untraced	*Pyke* 1981, 3
28.	?1811	Sir William Dolben	w	VAM	*Graves* 1905–6, 1, 34; *Pyke* 1973, 5
29.	1815	Marshal Prince Blucher	w	[Exhib RA, London, 843]; untraced	*Graves* 1905–6, 1, 34
30.	1817	Rev C Jerram	w	[Exhib RA, London, 949]; untraced	*Graves* 1905–6, 1, 34
31.	1820	King George III	w	BM Other versions: Met NY NMM VAM A.111-1965 VAM A.112-1965 private coll	*Pyke* 1973, 5
32.	1823	T Pagan	w	[Exhib RA, London, 1013]; untraced	*Graves* 1905–6, 1, 34
33.	1824	G Young, Esq, medallic portrait		[Exhib RA, London, 915]; untraced	*Graves* 1905–6, 1, 34
34.	1824	Unidentified lady, medallic portrait		[Exhib RA, London, 943]; untraced	*Graves* 1905–6, 1, 34
35.	nd	Broadly Wilson	w	Madame Tussaud's, London	*Pyke* 1973, 6
36.	nd	Charles, 1st Marquess Cornwallis	w	NMM	*Pyke* 1973, 5
37.	nd	Dr Robert Watts	w	sold Sotheby 1964; untraced	*Pyke* 1973, 5
38.	nd	Duke of Fife	w	sold Sotheby 1964; untraced	*Pyke* 1973, 5
39.	nd	Edward, Duke of Kent	w	VAM	*Pyke* 1973, 5
40.	nd	Elizabeth Fry	w	Private coll	*Pyke* 1973, 5
41.	nd	General Kosciuszko	w	[Bristol]; untraced	*Pyke* 1973, 6
42.	nd	George, 6th Duke of Argyll	w	VAM	*Pyke* 1973, 5
43.	nd	Granville Sharp	w	Sotheby 1964; untraced	*Pyke* 1973, 5
44.	nd	Granville, Marquess of Stafford	w	VAM	*Graves* 1905–6, 1, 34; *Pyke* 1973, 5
45.	nd	Hannah More	w	Private coll	*Pyke* 1973, 5
46.	nd	Henry Wilberforce	w	Madame Tussaud's, London	*Pyke* 1973, 6
47.	nd	John Wesley	w	[Bristol]; untraced	*Pyke* 1973, 6
48.	nd	King George II	w	Stanton Harcourt, Oxon	*Pyke* 1973, 5
49.	nd	King George IV	w	Minneapolis Institute of Arts	*Pyke* 1973, 5
50.	nd	King George IV	w	VAM A.116-1965 Other versions: VAM A.128-1965	*Pyke* 1973, 5
51.	nd	King George IV as Prince of Wales	w	VAM A.115-1965	*Pyke* 1973, 5
52.	nd	King William IV	w	Private coll	*Pyke* 1973, 6
53.	nd	Lord Holland	w	Sotheby 1964; untraced	*Pyke* 1973, 5
54.	nd	Lord Moira	w	VAM A.125-1965 Other versions: VAM A.126-1965	*Pyke* 1973, 5
55.	nd	Mr and Mrs Proctor	w	Sotheby 1964; untraced	*Pyke* 1973, 5
56.	nd	Mr Wyndham	w	Sotheby 1964, lot 80	*Pyke* 1973, 6
57.	nd	Mrs Searle	w	Sotheby 1964; untraced	*Pyke* 1973, 5
58.	nd	Princess Sophia	w	VAM	*Pyke* 1973, 5
59.	nd	Recumbent dog	w	VAM A.140-1965	*Pyke* 1973, 5
60.	nd	Rev Rowland Hill	w	Private coll	*Pyke* 1973, 5
61.	nd	Samuel Wilberforce	w	Private coll	*Pyke* 1973, 6
62.	nd	Sir Walter Scott	w	Private coll	*Pyke* 1973, 5
63.	nd	Thomas Clarkson	w	Madame Tussaud's, London	*Pyke* 1973, 5
64.	nd	Thomas Eyton	w	Private coll	*Pyke* 1973, 5
65.	nd	Thomas, 1st Baron Erskine	w	VAM	*Pyke* 1973, 5
66.	nd	Unidentified man	w	VAM	*Pyke* 1973, 5
67.	nd	Unidentified man	w	Private coll	*Pyke* 1973, 5
68.	nd	William Wilberforce	w	Madame Tussaud's, London	*Pyke* 1973, 6
Miscellaneous					
69.	1801	Admiral Lord Nelson		[Soc of A, greater silver palette]; untraced	RSA *Transactions*, vol 19, 1801, 376
70.	1801	HRH Princess Charlotte, from the life, model		[Soc of A, greater silver palette]; untraced	RSA *Transactions*, vol 19, 1801, 376

ANDREWS, James, of Olney 1735–1817

Andrews taught William Cowper to draw when Cowper lived at Olney. The poet called him 'my Michelangelo,' and in a letter to a Mr Newton said that 'James Andrews pays me many compliments on my success in the art of drawing, but I have not yet the vanity to think myself qualified to furnish your apartment (*Wright* 1886, 32). Andrews also drew Cowper's portrait.

He signs a number of local monuments and tablets, the best of which commemorates Alexander Small (1). Gunnis writes that the fine terra-cotta bust of Small is known from the parish records to have been executed by **Peter Scheemakers**. The work, however, is not typical of Scheemakers and it has not been possible to verify Gunnis's source. Pevsner notes a number of tombstones by Andrews in the churchyard at Olney. Wright described them as 'well-carved gravestones . . . embellished with representations of angels, skeletons, cherubs and books', the finest of which commemorates a pasture-keeper of Weston Underwood, William Lambry (**4**). It has a 'farmyard scene – a cut haystack, sheep, trough, crook, shears &c' (*Wright* 1886, 30–1). Pevsner notes a number of tablets by Andrews in Piddington, Northants.

Literary References: *Gunnis* 1968, 18; Pevsner, *Northants*, 1973, 344; Pevsner, *Bucks*, 1994, 588

Funerary Monuments

1.	†1752	Alexander Small (bust perhaps by Peter Scheemakers)	Clifton Reynes, Bucks	S	*Gunnis* 1968, 18; Pevsner, *Bucks*, 1994, 253
2.	?1776	Ann Buck	Weston-Underwood, Bucks	S	*Gunnis* 1968, 18
3.	?1778	Bartholomew Higgins	Weston-Underwood, Bucks	S	*Gunnis* 1968, 18
4.	†1779	William Lambry	Olney, Bucks	S	*Wright* 1886, 31; *Gunnis* 1968, 18
5.	?1787	Charles Small	Clifton Reynes, Bucks	S	*Gunnis* 1968, 18
6.	?1787	John Campion	Sherrington, Bucks	S	*Gunnis* 1968, 18
7.	?1793	Thomas Skevington	Newton Blossomville, Bucks	S	*Gunnis* 1968, 18
8.	†1795	Charles and Barbara Morgan	[Olney, Bucks]; untraced		*Wright* 1886, 32

ANDREWS, Samuel, of Wisbech fl 1768–1835

His tablets, the best of which are listed below, are nonetheless of provincial workmanship. At Yaxley there is a large wall tablet to Captain William Papp, 1797 (**2**). This has an urn and military trophies and is signed 'S. Andrews, of Yaxley' who can perhaps be identified with S Andrews of Wisbech. A 'Mr. Andrews' of Wisbech built the church, almshouses and school at Upwell, Norfolk in 1847 (*Builder*, 1848, 8).

Literary References: *Gunnis* 1968, 18

Funerary Monuments

1.	†1768	Thomas Sharpe	Tydd St Mary, Lincs		Pevsner, *Lincs*, 1989, 771
2.	†1797	Captain William Papp	Yaxley, Hunts	S	*Gunnis* 1968, 18
3.	?1801	M Smith	Yaxley, Hunts		*Gunnis* 1968, 18
4.	?1824	Robert Wing	Walsoken, Norfolk		*Gunnis* 1968, 18
5.	1826	Mr or Mrs Wallis	St Mary, Long Sutton, Lincs		Pevsner, *Lincs*, 1989, 536
6.	?1835	James Smith	Wisbech, Cambs		*Gunnis* 1968, 18

ANGELINI, Giuseppe 1742–1811

An Italian-born sculptor who worked in England in the 1770s. In his edition of J T Smith's *Nollekens and His Times* (II, 58) Whitten claims that Angelini was born in 1735, but when he joined the Royal Academy Schools on 14 December 1772 he gave his age as thirty.

He had studied in Rome under **Bartolomeo Cavaceppi** and is known to have carried out a considerable amount of restoration work with his master in the 1760s. He attended the Academy of Saint Luke before coming to England *c*1770. J T Smith writes that he lodged in Union Street at the back of the Middlesex Hospital until 1776, when the premises were taken by **G B Locatelli**. Angelini's address is, however, recorded in the list of exhibitors at the Society of Artists as 'at Mr Dufour's, Berwick Street' in 1775 (*Graves* 1907, 3). That year he exhibited a group entitled *Chastity rejecting profane love* (**14**).

He was employed by **Joseph Nollekens**, with whom he must have worked in Cavaceppi's studio in Rome. Angelini was often mistaken for his master from 'his dashing method of dressing in a fashionable coat and red morocco slippers.' One of the works executed by him in England was a life-size group of the *Virgin and Child* (**1**), which he was unable to sell. He was forced to dispose of it by means of a lottery (*Smith* 1828, II, 122). He was apparently in financial difficulties by 1777, for that year he applied for assistance to the Royal Academy, which granted him a 'charitable donation' of 25 guineas. Angelini was clearly well thought of by his colleagues, for the disbursement was recommended by Nollekens, **Edward Burch** and **Agostino Carlini**, as well as the engraver Francesco Bartolozzi and the history painter Benjamin West (RA Council Minutes, vol 1, June 1777, fol 240).

Angelini returned to Rome soon after. A letter of 1777 from **Thomas Banks** to Ozias Humphrey seems to suggest that 'Sigr. Angelini the Sculptor' was expected in Rome imminently (*Bell* 1938, 21). Angelini was certainly in his native city by 1779, for on 10 November the young **Antonio Canova** visited his studio and noted the over-life size statue of G B Piranesi, which Angelini was executing for the architect's tomb. The work bears some similarity to Nollekens's statue of Sir Thomas Salusbury at Great Zoffley. Angelini was one of the sculptors who was approached by **Henry Webber** to execute models for Josiah Wedgwood in 1787 (**2–11, 13**). He died in Rome in 1811. J T Smith described Angelini as 'an artist of superior talent'.

Literary References: *Smith* 1828, II, 122; *Honour* 1959, 242; *Hutchison* 1960–62, 135; *Gunnis* 1968, 18; *Pyke* 1973, 7; *Wilton Ely* 1976, 592–5; *Penny* 1977 (1), 11; *Haskell and Penny* 1981, 88; *Emmerson* 1995, 22–33; *Gennaccari* 1996, 153–285

Archival References: RA student register

Statues

1.	nd	Virgin and child	m	Untraced	*Gunnis* 1968, 18

Reliefs

2.	1787	Apollo with the muse Erato (for Wedgwood)		[Rome]; untraced	*Meteyard* 1866, 2, 591
3.	1787	Apotheosis of a young prince (for Wedgwood)		[Rome]; untraced	*Meteyard* 1866, 2, 591
4.	1787	Hercules (for Wedgwood)		[Rome]; untraced	*Meteyard* 1866, 2, 591
5.	1787	Mercury (for Wedgwood)		[Rome]; untraced	*Meteyard* 1866, 2, 591
6.	1787	Pluto carrying off Proserpine (for Wedgwood)		[Rome]; untraced	*Meteyard* 1866, 2, 591
7.	1787	Silenus (for Wedgwood)		[Rome]; untraced	*Meteyard* 1866, 2, 591
8.	1787	The pleasures of the Elysian fields (for Wedgwood)		[Rome]; untraced	*Meteyard* 1866, 2, 591
9.	1787	Two bacchantes (for Wedgwood)		[Rome]; untraced	*Meteyard* 1866, 2, 591
10.	1787	Two fauns (for Wedgwood)		[Rome]; untraced	*Meteyard* 1866, 2, 591
11.	1787	Victory (for Wedgwood)		[Rome]; untraced	*Meteyard* 1866, 2, 591
12.	nd	The rape of Proserpine	w	Lady Lever	*Pyke* 1973, 7

13.	nd	The whole fable of Meleager (for Wedgwood)	[Rome]; untraced	*Meteyard* 1866, 2, 591
Miscellaneous				
14.	1775	Chastity rejecting profane love	[Exhib Soc of Artists, London, 1]; untraced	*Graves* 1907, 3; *Gunnis* 1968, 18

ANNIS, James *c*1709–75

The son of John Annis, he was apprenticed to his brother, another **John Annis,** in 1723 and became free of the Masons' Company on 1 May 1730. He succeeded his brother as mason to the Ironmongers' Company in 1740 and worked there, 1743–46, possibly in partnership with his mother, for a payment of 1744 is made to them both. He also worked as a mason at St Bartholomew's Hospital, receiving £361 between 1754 and 1767. His yard was in Aldersgate Street and one of his long-term assistants was a Richard Finch.

Annis was a competent statuary and Gunnis considered his monument to Sir George Fettiplace, 1743, at Swinbrook, (**2**) to be 'of real importance, for the modelling and cutting of the portrait-bust is magnificent and not unworthy of a Rysbrack'. Whinney concurred with this judgement, though the bust is poorly articulated, revealing Annis's lesser abilities. He also signs the monument to Zachariah Foxall which has a cherub unveiling a medallion portrait (**4**). He, not his sibling, must have been responsible for the architectural monuments to Thomas Hawes (**1**) and John Styleman (**3**).

On 24 April 1756 Annis married Sarah Chapman at St Dionis Backchurch in London. He was renter warden of the Masons' Company in 1764, upper warden in 1765, and became master a year later. In 1748 he took as an apprentice his nephew William, son of John Annis. William Annis gained his freedom on 7 May 1756.

He died in Aldersgate on 14 June 1775. He asked to be buried with a 'handsome head and foot stone' in his late brother's vault. He left £300 to his wife and the dividends from shares valued at £500. Over £600 in named gifts was distributed to other members of the family.

Literary References: *Gunnis* 1968, 18; *Whinney* 1988, 245

Archival References: Masons' Co, Freemen, fol 1; Assistants, fols 3, 5; Court Book, 1722–51 (28 March 1723); 1751–96 (14 June 1765 & 14 June 1766, 14 June 1775); Ironmongers WA, vol 12; IGI

Additional MS Sources: Archives, Royal College of Physicians; St Bartholomew's Hospital Archives

Will: PROB 11/1008/218

Funerary Monuments					
1.	*c*1740	Thomas Hawes and family	Leyton, Essex	S	*Gunnis* 1968, 19
2.	†1743	Sir George Fettiplace	Swinbrook, Oxon	S	*Gunnis* 1968, 18; *Whinney* 1988, 245 (repr)
3.	post-1750	John Styleman (†1734)	St Mary, Bexley, Kent	S	Pevsner, *Kent: W & Weald*, 1976, 157
4.	†1758	Zachariah Foxall	St Botolph, Aldersgate, City of London	S	*Gunnis* 1968, 19; Pevsner, *London: City*, 1997, 207

ANNIS, John –1740

The son of John Annis of Beckenham, he was apprenticed to William Holland in 1714. On 5 May 1721 he was made free of the Masons' Company and set up on his own account in Aldersgate Street. He was employed as a mason at the College of Physicians in Warwick Lane in 1727. From 1730 until his death 10 years later he was mason to the Ironmongers' Company, responsible for work at their hall, barge-houses and almshouses on Old Street in 1732 and 1738–9. A payment was made in 1740 to his widow and executrix, Elizabeth.

In his will, proved on 7 November 1740, Annis, described as a 'Mason of Saint Botolph Aldersgate,' left £5 each to his mother, Anne Simmonds, his brother **James Annis** and his three sisters. The residue of his estate went to his wife. He was buried in the family vault at Beckenham, Kent. When his widow died in 1747 she left cash and property in trust for her son, John, and funds for the apprenticeship of another son, William. This son was apprenticed to his uncle, James Annis, in 1748.

The monument to William Strode, who died in 1732, signed 'Johannis Annis Londini fecit' is thought to be by this mason (**1**). It is a curious hybrid in style and execution. Two crudely carved and old-fashioned kneeling figures pray either side of a sarcophagus of a type associated with **Henry Cheere**. Above is a sophisticated relief carving of the four surviving children and a second relief decorates the sarcophagus. The monument to Henry Baldwyn, † 1737, is signed 'Annis Londini Fecit' and may date from the next generation of the family workshop (**2**).

Literary References: *Gunnis* 1968, 19; *Whinney* 1988, 245; *Baker* 2000, 78

Archival References: Masons' Co, *Freemen*, fol 1, 5 May 1721; Ironmongers, WA, vol 11 (several entries)

Wills: John Annis PROB 11/705; Elizabeth Annis PROB 11/755/168

Funerary Monuments					
1.	†1732	William Robinson Lytton Strode	Knebworth, Herts	S	*Whinney* 1988, 245; *Baker* 2000, 78 (repr)
2.	†1737	Rev Henry Baldwyn	Pontesbury, Salop	S	

ANSPACH, Elizabeth, Margravine of 1750–1828

The daughter of the 4th Earl of Berkeley, she married the 6th Earl of Craven in 1767. A fortnight after the latter's death in 1791 she became the wife of Christian, Margrave of Brandenburg-Anspach.

She is best remembered as a playwright and travel journalist but her talents extended to sculpture. In 1806 she received the silver medal from the Society of Arts for a bas-relief in clay of her second husband, who had died the previous year (**1**). An illustration of this work forms the frontispiece of the second volume of her autobiography, *Memoirs of the Margravine of Anspach. . . Written by Herself* (1826).

Literary References: *Farington, passim*; RSA *Register*, 1778, 32; RSA *Transactions*, vol 24, 1806, 18; *Gunnis* 1968, 19

Reliefs				
1.	1806	Christian, Margrave of Brandenburg-Anspach, clay bas-relief	[Soc of A, silver medal]; untraced	RSA, *Transactions*, vol 24, 1806, 18; RSA *Register*, 1778, 32

ARCHER, Frederick Scott 1813–57

Though a trained and practising sculptor, Archer is best remembered as the inventor of the wet collodion process, which greatly reduced the exposure time necessary to take a photograph. He was the second son of a butcher from Bishop's Stortford and was apprenticed to Mr Massey, a silversmith of Leadenhall Street, London. In 1836 he entered the Royal Academy Schools on the recommendation of Edward Hawkins, giving his address as Hamilton Place, King's Cross. He first exhibited at the Royal Academy that year (**23**).

By 1842 he had moved to 18 Tavistock Street and in January 1844 he married Frances Garratt Machin of Bexley, Kent. The same year he exhibited a statue of Alfred the Great at Westminster Hall (**2**). The work was ill-received by the *Literary Gazette* which considered that 'to fulfil our idea of Alfred the figure should be grand and powerful, but Mr Archer seems to think that a tame, spiritless specimen of vulgarity will do' (*Lit Gaz*, 1435, 20 July 1844, 466). In 1850 Archer carved the monument to Lady Henrietta Maria Conyngham, which was illustrated in the *Gentleman's Magazine*. It has an urn in low relief and is decorated with a band of 'XP' monograms, placed alternately in crowns of thorns and laurel wreaths (**1**). He also exhibited busts of distinguished sitters at the Royal Academy.

He died on 2 May 1857 and was buried in Kensal Green Cemetery. A subscription list was opened by the Photographic Society to help his indigent family and over £700 was raised. His widow died the following year, so the money supported his children. They were also granted a pension of £50 by the Crown, on the grounds that their father's photographic discoveries had been of no benefit to him, though they had been extremely profitable to others.

Literary References: *AJ* 1857, 230; *Graves* I, 1905–6, 57; *Gunnis* 1968, 19; *Heyert* 1979; *Bertram* 1985; *Dommasch* 1989, 334–6; *Ray* 1989, 28–9

Archival References: RA Admissions; IGI

Funerary Monuments

No.	Date	Subject		Location	References
1.	1850	Lady Henrietta Maria Conyngham (†1841)		Mickleham, Surrey	*GM* 1850, 1, 510 (repr); *Gunnis* 1968, 19

Statues

No.	Date	Subject		Location	References
2.	1844	Alfred the Great with the book of common law		[Exhib Westminster Hall, London]; untraced	*Builder* 1844, 367; *Lit Gaz* 1844, 466; *Gunnis* 1968, 19
3.	1845	A boy playing		[Exhib Westminster Hall, London, 132]; untraced	*Westminster* 1845, 16
4.	1851	Gertrude Hanson		[Exhib RA, London, 1272]; untraced	*Graves* I, 1905–6, 57

Busts

No.	Date	Subject		Location	References
5.	1838	Unidentified little boy		[Exhib RA, London, 1342]; untraced	*Graves* I, 1905–6, 57
6.	1839	Sir George Smart	m	[Exhib RA, London, 1363]; untraced	*Graves* I, 1905–6, 57
7.	1840	Unidentified boy		[Exhib RA, London, 1090]; untraced	*Graves* I, 1905–6, 57
8.	1841	Richard Hollier		[Exhib RA, London, 1281]; untraced	*Graves* I, 1905–6, 57
9.	1842	John Lee		[Exhib RA, London, 1371]; untraced	*Graves* I, 1905–6, 57
10.	1843	Charles Few		[Exhib RA, London, 1456]; untraced	*Graves* I, 1905–6, 57
11.	1843	Nicholas Carlisle		[Exhib RA, London, 1474]; untraced	*Graves* I, 1905–6, 57
12.	1844	Alexander Sim		[Exhib RA, London, 1381]; untraced	*Graves* I, 1905–6, 57
13.	1845	Unidentified lady, posthumous		[Exhib RA, London, 1443]; untraced	*Graves* I, 1905–6, 57
14.	1846	Thomas Weeding		[Exhib RA, London, 1485]; untraced	*Graves* I, 1905–6, 57
15.	1847	George Sim		[Exhib RA, London, 1373]; untraced	*Graves* I, 1905–6, 57
16.	1848	Francis Smedley		[Exhib RA, London, 1426]; untraced	*Graves* I, 1905–6, 57
17.	1848	The dean of Manchester	m	[Exhib RA, London, 1389]; untraced	*Graves* I, 1905–6, 57
18.	1849	John Hodgkin		[Exhib RA, London, 1298]; untraced	*Graves* I, 1905–6, 57
19.	1850	Spencer, 2nd Marquess of Northampton	m	[Exhib RA, London, 1451]; untraced	*Graves* I, 1905–6, 57
20.	1851	Benjamin Webster		[Exhib RA, London, 1372]; untraced	*Graves* I, 1905–6, 57

Reliefs

No.	Date	Subject		Location	References
21.	1841	Sir M I Brunel, portrait medallion		[Exhib RA, London, 1310; 1842, 1302]; untraced	*Graves* I, 1905–6, 57
22.	1849	Unidentified subject, bas-relief		[Exhib RA, London, 1236]; untraced	*Graves* I, 1905–6, 57

Miscellaneous

No.	Date	Subject		Location	References
23.	1836	Falling angels		[Exhib RA, London, 1154]; untraced	*Graves* I, 1905–6, 57
24.	1848	Young Britons receiving instruction		[Exhib RA, London, 1351]; untraced	*Graves* I, 1905–6, 57

ARMINGER, William 1752–93

Born on 22 November 1752, he joined the Royal Academy Schools on 21 March 1774. J T Smith describes Arminger as 'a raw-boned man, full six feet in height' and relates that he came to **Joseph Nollekens** one day saying that he was a 'cutter of funeral inscriptions come from the City of Norwich, and would be glad of a job.' Nollekens took him into his employment and allowed him to cut the inscription for the monument to the writer, Oliver Goldsmith, to be erected in Westminster Abbey. Arminger carried this out so well (from a shed in the yard) that Nollekens gave him regular work, and he afterwards cut many of his employer's best busts (*Smith* 1828, 1, 57–8, 116).

He died in 1793 and was buried in Paddington. Smith relates that he made 'what is called a very pretty fortune' (*ibid* 57). The sale catalogue of his works held by Greenwood on 6 March 1794 suggests a man of discernment, since it includes a selection of 'choice' French, Italian and English prints, a small 'but valuable' library of books (including subscription volumes) and some drawings. Several of the lots were purchased by Nollekens. A number of reliefs of ideal subjects were included in the sale.

Literary References: *Hutchison* 1960–62, 140; *Gunnis* 1968, 19

Auction Catalogues: Arminger 1794

Chimneypieces

No.	Date	Subject		Location	References
1.	nd	'The Aurora of Guido, stained upon marble for Tablet of a Chimney-Piece' Payment(s): sold in 1794 for £2 6s	m	Untraced	Arminger sale cat, 1794, lot 75 (£2 6s); *Gunnis* 1968, 19

Reliefs

2.	nd	'Adam and Eve Conducted by St Michael Out of Paradise, basso relievo' Payment(s): Sold in 1794 for £1 16s	Untraced	Arminger sale cat, 1794, lot 112; *Gunnis* 1968, 19
3.	nd	Slaughter of the innocents Payment(s): 9s	Untraced	Arminger sale cat, 1794, lot 113; *Gunnis* 1968, 19

ARMSTEAD, Henry Hugh 1828–1905

Henry Hugh Armstead was a talented and versatile sculptor who also worked as a metalworker and illustrator. He was born in Bloomsbury, London, on 18 June 1828, the fourth and youngest son of a heraldic chaser, John Armstead, and his wife Ann. He received little formal education but was a 'wide-reader from youth' (DNB). He started work in his father's workshop at the age of eleven and about two years later was sent to the Government School of Design at Somerset House. He also attended classes at two well-known private art schools in London, run by Francis Stephen Cary and James Matthews Leigh. He then found employment with the silversmiths Hunt and Roskell and studied under **Edward Hodges Baily**. In 1847 he entered the Royal Academy Schools, giving his address as 37 Liquorpond Street (a small thoroughfare running out of Gray's Inn Road which was later subsumed into Clerkenwell Road).

In 1849 Armstead was awarded a premium of £21 by the Art Union of London for a relief depicting the *Death of Boadicea* (**73**). This was cast by Elkington's and casts were distributed by the Art Union in 1850 and 1851 but none has been traced. In 1851 he won the first prize in the Art Union sculpture competition with a statuette of *Satan dismayed*, which was published as a small edition of five bronzes the following year (**23**). It depicts the scene in Milton's *Paradise Lost* when the fallen angels are turned into snakes and includes a writhing, half-serpentine figure coiled around the base. Armstead exhibited at the Royal Academy from 1851 onwards, from Percy Street, Grafton Street and St Paul's Road, Camden Town, showing several reliefs, portrait busts and statuettes. During the early part of his career, however, he concentrated mainly on metalwork, designing, modelling and chasing sculptural trophies and exhibition pieces for Hunt and Roskell and C F Hancock & Co. The most important of these, the *Outram Shield* (VAM), was presented in 1862 to Sir James Outram, the celebrated soldier who served in India. It is decorated with scenes from his life, modelled in very low relief. Disappointed by the critical response to this masterpiece, Armstead adopted sculpture as his principal profession soon after its completion.

In the early 1860s Armstead worked with the architectural partnership of John Pritchard and John Pollard Seddon designing an ambitious series of 20 reliefs illustrating the history of the Shirley family for Ettington Hall (**54**). He was subsequently employed at the new Palace of Westminster, where he designed a series of relief panels of Arthurian subjects, executed in wood for the queen's robing room (**78**). His 'original and very unTennysonian' interpretation of the subject was appreciated by contemporaries (*Spielmann* 1901, 13).

A long-lasting and fruitful association with the architect Sir George Gilbert Scott began during the same period when Armstead modelled the sculptural parts of Scott's model for the Albert Memorial (**53**). He also worked on the memorial itself, providing four bronze statues of *Rhetoric, Astronomy, Chemistry*, and *Medicine* and carving friezes representing *Poets and musicians* and *Painters* for the south and east sides of the podium (**64**). This work did not go smoothly. There was 'some little professional jealousy' between Armstead and **John Birnie Philip**, who was responsible for the *Architects* and *Sculptors* friezes on the other faces of the podium, which made them 'unwilling to consult one another and to work together' (BM Add MS 38992, fols 246–9, cited by *Brooks* 2000, 182). Armstead later fell out with John Kelk, the building contractor, and the reliefs were completed several years late and exceeded the budget. Scott nonetheless considered Armstead's work the most successful sculptural contribution to the memorial. He wrote in his memoirs 'I doubt whether either the central figure or a single group, as executed, is superior to the miniature models furnished by Mr Armstead. They remain to speak for themselves, while the two sides of the podium and the four bronzes which he designed, give a fair idea of what his models would have proved if carried out at the real size' (*Scott* 1879, 266). The architect employed Armstead again, together with John Birnie Philip, at his Italianate Foreign and Commonwealth Office in Whitehall, a building remarkable for the extent and quality of its sculptural decoration (**60–63, 65**). With so much large-scale architectural work in hand Armstead had moved by 1868 to a big studio in Bridge Place, Eccleston Bridge, at the back of Victoria Station.

Meanwhile he developed a thriving practice as a sculptor of funerary monuments. These range from modest examples, including a Renaissance-style wall tablet incorporating a portrait medallion (**18**) to full-size effigies, such as those erected in memory of Dean Howard, Bishop Wilberforce, Bishop Ollivant and Lord Winmarleigh (**3, 5, 16, 21**). These were admired for their naturalism. He secured several commissions for public statues, including a seated figure of the architect George Edmund Street for the Royal Courts of Justice. This has a relief on the pedestal depicting artists and craftsmen at work (**31**). He was also responsible for a lively portrait in Chatham of Lieutenant Thomas Waghorn, who had pioneered the overland route to India (**33**).

Armstead exhibited a few portrait busts and imaginative works at the RA such as *My dainty Ariel*, a nude statue of a young girl with a kitten called *Playmates* and a relief of *Hero with the dead body of Leander* (**29, 34, 79**). He also worked as an illustrator. He was elected an ARA on 16 January 1875 and became an RA on 18 December 1879, when he submitted a relief of Aphrodite drawn by dolphins entitled *The ever-reigning queen* as his diploma work (**80**). He taught in the Academy Schools from 1875 and Walter Armstrong noted that he 'gave proof of unusually fine taste as an arranger of works of art' when it was his turn to place the sculpture in the annual exhibitions (DNB). One of his last works, an expressive marble figure of Lady Macbeth entitled *Remorse*, was purchased for the nation by the Trustees of the Chantrey Bequest (**35**). Armstead died at his home, 52 Circus Road, St John's Wood, on 4 December 1905 and was buried in Highgate Cemetery.

His significance as a forerunner to the New Sculpture movement was recognised by contemporary critics, including Edmund Gosse and M L Spielmann. They argued that his training as a craftsman and the naturalism that is evident in many of his works distinguish him from the academic sculptors of his own generation and link him to the younger school.

EH

Literary References: *The Graphic*, XI, 20 Feb 1875, 171; *Scott* 1879, 265–7; *Gosse* 1883, 171–5; *Spielmann* 1901, 13–8; *The Times*, 6 Dec 1905, 6; 9 Dec 1905, 5; 11 Dec 1905, 6; *Haskell* 1975, 61–79, 104–10; *Houfe* 1978, 222; *Read* 1982, *passim; Beattie* 1983, *passim*; *Avery and Marsh* 1985, 332–3; *Grove* 2, 1996, 474 (Ward-Jackson); *Brooks* 2000, *passim*; *ODNB* (Hardy)

Archival References: RA Admissions

Additional MS Sources: Armstead albums; Armstead archive; Armstead/Craik; Armstead/Cusins; Armstead death duty accounts; Armstead/Dilke; Armstead/Fildes; Armstead/Gosse; Armstead/Layard; Armstead letter; Armstead/Scott; Armstead/VAM; Armstead/Pascal; Armstead/Philip; Armstead/Spielmann (1); Armstead/Spielmann (2); Pearson/Armstead

Miscellaneous Drawings: study after the Antique, standing *Discobolus*, HMI 53/1992

Wills: PPR, will, 27 December 1905, fol 1520 (effects valued at £14,602 17s 10d)

Portraits of the Sculptor: J E Hodgson, oil on canvas, 1884, Aberdeen Art Gallery, Macdonald Collection (repr ODNB); Lock & Whitfield, photograph, *Men of Mark* VII, 1883, 26; A J Melhuish, photograph, nd, VAM P&D PH.362-1888; engraving (after photograph by Messrs Fradelle and Marshall) *The Graphic*, 20 Feb 1875, 172; engraving, after photograph, *ILN*, 1875, 66; woodcut, after photograph, *Mag of Art*, vol 3, 1880, 420; H T Wells, painting, exhib RA 1878, ex coll H W Armstead (untraced); T Blake Wingman, canvas, exhib Society of Portrait Painters, 1892; H von Herkomer, canvas, exhib Society of Portrait Painters, 1898; W Robert Colton, bust, exhib RA, 1903 and 1904, ex coll H W Armstead (repr *RA Pictures*, 1903, 17)

Funerary Monuments

No.	Date	Subject		Location		References
1.	†1863	Henry Thomas (designed by John Pritchard)		Llandaff Cathedral, Glamorgan		Pevsner, *Glamorgan*, 1995, 254; C Lib (repr)
2.	1868	Lady John Thynne (designed by Sir George Gilbert Scott)		Haynes, Beds		Pevsner, *Beds, Hunts & Peterborough*, 1968, 96; C Lib (repr)
3.	1872	H E Howard, Dean of Lichfield (†1868) (designed by Sir George Gilbert Scott)		Lichfield Cathedral, Staffs		*Graves* I, 1905–6, 62; Pevsner, *Staffs*, 1974, 185; *Read* 1982, 128, 262 (repr)
4.	1873	James Henry Holis Atkinson (†1871)		Hartburn, Northumbs	SD	Pevsner, *Northumbs*, 1957, 165; C Lib (repr)
5.	†1873	Samuel Wilberforce, Bishop of Oxford and Winchester (designed by Sir George Gilbert Scott)		Winchester Cathedral, Hants		*Spielmann* 1901, 17; Pevsner, *Hants*, 1967, 682
6.	†1875	Blanche, Baroness Scarsdale		Kedleston, Derbys		C Lib (repr)
7.	1877	Frederick Walker ARA (†1875)		Cookham, Berks		*Gosse* 1883, 174–5; *Graves* I, 1905–6, 62; Pevsner, *Berks*, 1966, 122
8.	†1878	Edward Rice		Tilmanstone, Kent	S	Pevsner, *Kent: NE & E*, 1983, 479
9.	1879	Archdeacon Moore (†1876) (designed by Sir George Gilbert Scott)		Lichfield Cathedral, Staffs	D	*Graves* I, 1905–6, 62; Pevsner, *Staffs*, 1974, 185; *Read* 1982, 128
10.	†1881	Lord John Thynne, Dean of Westminster (designed by J L Pearson)		Westminster Abbey, London, nave		*Spielmann* 1901, 17; Pevsner, *London* 1, 1973, 452; C Lib (repr)
11.	1881	Theodore Mansel Talbot (†1876)		Margam Abbey, Glamorgan	SD	Pevsner, *Glamorgan*, 1995, 100, 426 (pl 95); C Lib (repr)
12.	†1882	Archibald Campbell Tait		Westminster Abbey, London, south transept		Pevsner, *London* 1, 1973, 443; C Lib (repr)
13.	†1882	William Gibbs		St Michael, Exeter, Devon		Pevsner, *Devon*, 1989, 101, 393; C Lib (repr)
14.	†1885	Charles Longuet-Higgins		Turvey, Beds	S	Pevsner, *Beds, Hunts & Peterborough*, 1968, 160n
15.	1885	Rev Francis Close (†1882)		Carlisle Cathedral, Cumberland	SD	*Builder*, 23 May 1885, 730 (repr); *Graves* I, 1905–6, 62; Pevsner, *Cumberland & Westmorland*, 1967, 93; *Read* 1982, 262
16.	1887	Alfred Ollivant, Bishop of Llandaff (†1882)		Llandaff Cathedral, Glamorgan	S	*Graves* I, 1905–6, 62; *Read* 1982, 262, 349; Pevsner, *Glamorgan*, 1995, 251; C Lib (repr)
17.	†1888	Lord Douglas Gordon		Orton Longueville, Hunts		Pevsner, *Beds, Hunts & Peterborough*, 1968, 301
18.	1889	Mrs Craik (†1887)		Tewkesbury Abbey, Glos		*Graves* I, 1905–6, 62; *Read* 1982, 262, 349 (repr)
19.	*c*1889	Rev Benjamin Webb (†1885)		St Paul's Cathedral, London		*Graves* I, 1905–6, 62; Pevsner, *London* 1, 1973, 139; C Lib (repr)
20.	1890	Unidentified only daughter (the guardian angel)		[Exhib RA, London, 1890, 2063]; untraced		*Spielmann* 1901, 17 (repr); *Graves* I, 1905–6, 62
21.	1894	John, Lord Winmarleigh		St Elphin, Warrington, Lancs		*Spielmann* 1901, 13, 18 (repr); *Graves* I, 1905–6, 62; *Read* 1982, 262, 349; *CIIA* 4/8/123–8 (repr)
22.	1896	Richard Walmesley, effigy	m	[Exhib RA, London, 1912]; untraced		*Graves* I, 1905–6, 62

Statues

No.	Date	Subject		Location		References
23.	1851	Satan dismayed, model		[Art Union sculpture competition, first prize]; untraced Other versions: five small bronzes issued by the Art Union of London, 1852 other bronze statuettes produced after 1852		*Manchester Art Treasures* 1857, 135; *Avery and Marsh* 1985, 332, 333 (repr)

No.	Date	Subject		Location		Literary references
24.	1857	Alfred the Great, statuette		[Exhib RA, London, 1234]; untraced		*Graves* I, 1905–6, 62; *Read* 1982, 262
25.	1857	William the Conqueror, statuette		[Exhib RA, London, 1245]; untraced		*ILN*, 18 July 1857, 53, 54 (repr); *Read* 1982, 262
26.	1874	Sir William Molesworth Bt		[Exhib RA, London, 1573]; untraced		*Graves* I, 1905–6, 62
27.	1878	William, Earl of Pembroke		[Exhib RA, London, 1481]; untraced		*Graves* I, 1905–6, 62
28.	1882	David and the lion		[Exhib RA, London, 1685]; untraced		*Graves* I, 1905–6, 62
29.	c1882	My dainty Ariel	m	[coll E Gotto]; Boughton Monchelsea Place sale, Christie, South Kensington, 21 Jan 1998		*Gosse* 1894, 202 (repr); *Graves* I, 1905–6, 62; *Daily Telegraph*, 22 Jan 1998, 13 (repr)
30.	1884	Dean Close, clay model		Untraced		*CJ*, 25 April 1884, 5
31.	1886	George Edmund Street		Royal Courts of Justice, London		*ILN*, 27 March 1886, 323 (repr); Pevsner, *London* 1, 1973, 322
32.	1887	Ladas dying at the goal		[Exhib RA, London, 1946]; untraced		*Graves* I, 1905–6, 62
33.	1888	Thomas Waghorn		Railway street, Chatham, Kent		*ILN*, 18 Aug 1888, 182 (repr); *Graves* I, 1905–6, 62; *Read* 1982, 262, 349
34.	1897	Playmates	m	[Exhib RA, London, 2100]; untraced		*Spielmann* 1901, 17; *Graves* I, 1905–6, 62
35.	1903	Remorse	m	Tate N01929		*Graves* I, 1905–6, 63; *Read* 1982, 349; C Lib (repr)
36.	nd	Aristotle		Oxford University Museum		Pevsner, *Oxford*, 1974, 282; C Lib (repr)
Busts						
37.	1853	D Grounds		[Exhib RA, London, 1391]; untraced		*Graves* I, 1905–6, 62
38.	1856	Mr Tevener		[Exhib RA, London, 1289]; untraced		*Graves* I, 1905–6, 62
39.	1876	Florence Boyce		[Exhib RA, London, 1476]; untraced		*Graves* I, 1905–6, 62
40.	1878	James Laycock		[Exhib RA, London, 1516]; untraced		*Graves* I, 1905–6, 62
41.	1878	Philip, 5th Earl Stanhope (after Lawrence Macdonald)	m	NPG 499		*Ormond* 1973, 428 (pl 849)
42.	1882	Dr John Deakin Heaton	m	LMG, W R Yorks inv 37.1/72		*Graves* I, 1905–6, 62; *Leeds* 1996, 13 (repr)
43.	1884	King Edward III		[Exhib RA, London, 1717]; untraced		*Graves* I, 1905–6, 62
44.	c1885	Maidenhood		Walker, Liverpool		*Graves* I, 1905–6, 62
45.	1887–1888	Queen Victoria		Guildhall, Exeter		Pevsner, *Devon*, 1989, 402
46.	1891	Master Philip Street		[Exhib RA, London, 1980]; untraced		*Graves* I, 1905–6, 62
47.	1895	Augustus Mordan	b	[Exhib RA, London, 1641]; untraced		*Graves* I, 1905–6, 62
48.	1897	Henry C Stephens	m	[Exhib RA, London, 2060]; untraced		*Graves* I, 1905–6, 62
49.	1898	Mrs Hugh Wells Armstead	m	[Exhib RA, London, 1940]; untraced		*Graves* I, 1905–6, 62
50.	1904	Sir Henry Cotton, for Cotton College, Assam	m	[Exhib RA, London, 1795]; untraced		*Graves* I, 1905–6, 63
51.	nd	George Edmund Street		RIBA		*ODNB*
Architectural Sculpture						
52.	c1850	Decorative sculpture (carved by Milo Griffith and Wiliam Clarke) Drawing(s): Armstead Albums, RA		[Llandaff Cathedral, Glamorgan, interior]; destroyed		*Read* 1982, 260–1; Pevsner, *Glamorgan*, 1995, 251
53.	c1863	Model for the Albert Memorial, sculptural parts (designed by Sir George Gilbert Scott)		VAM A.13-1973		*Bilbey* 2002, 355–6 (repr)
54.	1861–1863	The history of the Shirley family, twenty reliefs (carved by Edward Clarke)		Ettington Hall, Warks, above ground floor windows	S	*Read* 1982, 261–2; *Noszlopy* 2003, 37–9 (repr)
55.	1867	Frieze with scenes from the life of Christ, part of the reredos		Westminster Abbey, London		*ILN*, 7 Sept 1867, 272 (repr)
56.	1866–1869	Statues		New Palace Yard, Westminster, London, arcade		*Read* 1976, 235–6; *Read* 1982, 262
57.	c1869	Statues, designs only (carved by Milo Griffith and Wiliam Clarke) Drawing(s): Clarke workshop, Llandaff		Llandaff Cathedral, Glamorgan		*Read* 1982, 261; Pevsner, *Glamorgan*, 1995, 93, 250; C Lib (Oliphant repr)
58.	1871	Moses, David, St Peter and St Paul, reredos statues		Westminster Abbey, London		Pevsner, *London* 1, 1973, 421; *Read* 1982, 249; C Lib (repr)
59.	1873	Comus, design for a fountain		[Exhib RA, London, 1199]; untraced		*Gosse* 1883, 174; *Graves* I, 1905–6, 62
60.	1873–1874	Colonial secretaries, statues in niches on the upper storeys		Foreign and Commonwealth office, Whitehall, London		*AJ*, 1874, 374; *Read* 1982, 269, 271
61.	1873–1874	Education, Prudence, Valour, Government, Europe, Africa, America and Australasia, spandrel reliefs		Foreign and Commonwealth office, Whitehall, London		*Graves* I, 1905–6, 62; *Read* 1982, 269–71 (repr); *Beattie* 1983, 38–40 (repr)
62.	1873–1874	Justice, Fortitude, Truth and Obedience, reliefs over principal doorway		Foreign and Commonwealth office, Whitehall, London		*Read* 1982, 269, 271
63.	1873–1874	Navigation and Legislation, parapet statues		Foreign and Commonwealth office, Whitehall, London		*AJ*, 1874, 374
64.	1868–1874	Poets, Musicians and Painters friezes; figures of Rhetoric, Astronomy, Chemistry and Medicine Model(s): VAM 178-1906, 179-1906		Albert Memorial, Kensington Gardens, London		*Graves* I, 1905–6, 62; *Read* 1982, 100, 101 (repr); *Brooks* 2000, *passim* (repr); *Bilbey* 2002, 180–1 (repr)
65.	1873–1874	Queen Elizabeth, Drake, Livingstone, Wilberforce, Cooke and Franklin, medallion portraits above first floor windows		Foreign and Commonwealth office, Whitehall, London		*Read* 1982, 269, 271

66.	1876	Pulpit (designed by George Edmund Street)		Hythe, Kent	Pevsner, *Kent: NE & E*, 1983, 359
67.	1874–1879	Founder's fountain	b	King's College, Cambridge	*Spielmann* 1901, 14; *Graves* I, 1905–6, 62; Pevsner, *Cambs*, 1970, 95; C Lib (repr)
68.	1881	The entombment, reredos (designed by George Edmund Street)		Hythe, Kent	*Spielmann* 1901, 14; Pevsner, *Kent: NE & E*, 1983, 359
69.	*c*1885	Main entrance spandrels		Metropole buildings, Northumberland Avenue, London	Pevsner, *London* 1, 1973, 372
70.	1890	Roundels in the spandrels of the arcades and a lectern		Holy Trinity, Sloane Street, London	*Read* 1982, 335; Pevsner, *London 3*, 1991, 559; C Lib (lectern repr)
71.	1890	St Matthew, St Mark, the Good Shepherd, St Luke and St John, reredos statues	m	St Mary, Aberaven, Port Talbot, Glamorgan	*Spielmann* 1901, 16, 17 (repr); *Graves* I, 1905–6, 62; Pevsner, *Glamorgan*, 1995, 532; C Lib (repr)
72.	nd	Doorway	m	A Holborn restaurant, London	*Spielmann* 1901, 14
Reliefs					
73.	1849	Death of Boadicea		[Art Union premium]; untraced Other versions: Published as a small-scale bronze by the Art Union of London, 1850–1851, cast by Elkington & Co (no examples traced)	*Avery and Marsh* 1985, 332–3
74.	1853	Behold! he travaileth with iniquity		[Exhib RA, London, 1344]; untraced	*ILN*, 14 May 1853, 392; *Graves* I, 1905–6, 62
75.	1853	Introduction of music to the Arcadians		[Exhib RA, London, 1331]; untraced	*ILN*, 14 May 1853, 389, 392 (repr); *Graves* I, 1905–6, 62
76.	1863	Alice Wells, medallion		[Exhib RA, London, 1091]; untraced	*Graves* I, 1905–6, 62
77.	1863	Sidney Wells, medallion		[Exhib RA, London, 1093]; untraced	*Graves* I, 1905–6, 62
78.	1866–1870	Arthurian legends, 18 panels	wd	House of Lords, Palace of Westminster, London, queen's robing room	*Read* 1982, 262
79.	*c*1875	Hero and the dead body of Leander	m	Tate N02054	*Graves* I, 1905–6, 62
80.	1879	The ever-reigning queen (RA diploma work)		RA, London	*Spielmann* 1901, 17; *Graves* I, 1905–6, 62
81.	1880	The courage of David (David and the lion)	m	[Wellington Barracks, London, Guards' chapel]; destroyed	*Spielmann* 1901, 14, 17 (repr); *Graves* I, 1905–6, 62
82.	1881	The obedience of Joshua (Joshua and the angel)	m	[Wellington Barracks, London, Guards' chapel]; destroyed	*Spielmann* 1901, 17; *Graves* I, 1905–6, 62
83.	*c*1889	Lottie Armstead (the sculptor's daughter)	m	NMW A 2993	*Graves* I, 1905–6, 62
84.	1899	Frau Dr Fischer-Nissen, medallion	b	[Exhib RA, London, 2004]; untraced	*Graves* I, 1905–6, 62
85.	1899	G P Boyce, medallion		[Exhib RA, London, 2018]; untraced	*Graves* I, 1905–6, 62
Miscellaneous					
86.	1851	Satan beguiling Eve		[Exhib RA, London, 1283]; untraced	*Graves* I, 1905–6, 62
87.	1856	Adam and Eve, conscious of their fall		[Exhib RA, London, 1264]; untraced	*Graves* I, 1905–6, 62
88.	1872	Lord John Thynne, dean of Westminster		[Exhib RA, London, 1418]; untraced	*Graves* I, 1905–6, 62
89.	1880	G A Selwyn, Bishop of Lichfield		[Exhib RA, London, 1534]; untraced	*Graves* I, 1905–6, 62
90.	1880	In memoriam, B W K		[Exhib RA, London, 1524]; untraced	*Graves* I, 1905–6, 62
91.	1882	Anthony Gibbs		[Exhib RA, London, 1673]; untraced	*Graves* I, 1905–6, 62
92.	1883	John Mowlem		[Exhib RA, London, 1693]; untraced	*Graves* I, 1905–6, 62
93.	1891	Miss Hester Armstead		[Exhib RA, London, 2072]; untraced	*Graves* I, 1905–6, 62

ARMSTRONG, Michael fl 1771

In the *Hereford Journal* of 4 June 1771, Armstrong is noted as a 'Carver in wood and stone . . . from London, at the top of Wide Marsh Street, Hereford' (GPC).

ARMSTRONG, W fl 1832

Busts				
1.	1832	King Henry VIII	[Exhib Soc of BA, London, 862]; untraced	*Exhib Cat SBA*, 11

ARNALD, Sebastian Wyndham 1806–

A son of the landscape painter, George Arnald, ARA, he was christened on 4 January 1806 at Grasmere, Westmorland. He attended the Royal Academy Schools in 1824, winning the gold medal in 1831 for his group, *The massacre of the innocents* (**1**), the first of numerous works on biblical subjects. He exhibited this work, and also *War in heaven* (**12**) at Burlington House the following year. The former was considered 'not a subject for the public eye' as it could 'be viewed by the artist or amateur only as [an] academic exercise[s]' (*Lit Gaz*, no 805, 23 June 1832, 395). The latter, now lost, was described at some length by the *Library of Fine Arts* and was praised as 'a composition in no way discreditable to the English school.' The critic, however, felt that the falling figures showed such ability that one might wish that 'more majesty had been given to the archangel, whose position and form seem inadequate to the task he has accomplished of ejecting the rebel host' (*Library of Fine Arts* 1831, 1, 430). Arnald exhibited at the Royal Academy, 1823–1841, showing both ideal works and busts, including heads of his father (**2**) and of **George Garrard** (**5**). He also exhibited at the Birmingham Society of Artists.

He may later have abandoned sculpture for painting, since he did not exhibit at the Academy for some years after 1840. When finally he submitted a work in 1846 it was a canvas of *Christian and Pliable in the Slough of Despond.*

Literary References: *Gunnis* 1968, 66; *Pyke* 1973, 7

Archival References: RA Premium list; IGI

Statues					
1.	1831	The Massacre of the innocents, group		[RA gold medal 1831]; untraced	RA Premium list; *Graves* I, 1905–6, 66
Busts					
2.	1823	George Arnald ARA		[Exhib RA, London, 1062]; untraced	*Graves* I, 1905–6, 66
3.	1825	Deputy Whitby		[Exhib RA, London, 1072]; untraced	*Graves* I, 1905–6, 66
4.	1827	James Pearson		[Exhib RA, London, 1083]; untraced	*Graves* I, 1905–6, 66
5.	1828	George Garrard ARA	m	[Exhib RA, London, 1202]; untraced	*Graves* I, 1905–6, 66
6.	1829	A painter in seventeenth century costume		[Exhib RA, London, 1222]; untraced	*Graves* I, 1905–6, 66
7.	1829	Miss A M Arnald		[Exhib RA, London, 1152]; untraced	*Graves* I, 1905–6, 66
8.	1829	Miss Smith		[Exhib RA, London, 1155]; untraced	*Graves* I, 1905–6, 66
9.	1831	Rev Edward Irvine	m	[Exhib RA, London, 1204]; untraced	*Graves* I, 1905–6, 66
10.	1836	Samuel Taylor Coleridge	m	[Exhib RA, London, 1119]; untraced	*Graves* I, 1905–6, 66
Reliefs					
11.	1832	Rev Edward Irvine, portrait medallion		[Exhib RA, London, 1170]; untraced	*Graves* I, 1905–6, 66
12.	1830–1832	War in Heaven, alto-relief Model(s): 'Design' – Exhib RA, London, 1825, 553		[Exhib RA, London, 1138]; untraced	*Graves* I, 1905–6, 66; *Gunnis* 1968, 20
13.	1833	Unidentified subject, medallion	w	[Exhib RA, London, 1077]; untraced	*Graves* I, 1905–6, 66
14.	1838	'Isaiah XI', medallions		[Exhib RA, London, 1290, 1292]; untraced	*Graves* I, 1905–6, 66
Miscellaneous					
15.	1826	The death of Abel, sketch		[Exhib RA, London, 1051]; untraced	*Graves* I, 1905–6, 66
16.	1827	Perseus and Andromeda		[Exhib RA, London, 1072]; untraced	*Graves* I, 1905–6, 66
17.	1828	Satan and his angels cast out of Heaven		[Exhib, RA, London, 611]; untraced	*Graves* I, 1905–6, 66
18.	1830	The sounding of the seventh angel		[Exhib RA, London, 1264]; untraced	*Graves* I, 1905–6, 66
19.	1832	The golden age		[Exhib RA, London, 1191]; untraced	*Graves* I, 1905–6, 66
20.	1832	The iron age		[Exhib RA, London, 1195]; untraced	*Graves* I, 1905–6, 66; *Gunnis* 1968, 20
21.	1833	Bacchus		[Exhib RA, London, 1197]; untraced	*Graves* I, 1905–6, 66; *Gunnis* 1968, 20
22.	1833	Infant Moses on the Nile		[Exhib RA, London, 1067]; untraced	*Graves* I, 1905–6, 66
23.	1833	The millennium	w	[Exhib RA, London, 1194]; untraced	*Graves* I, 1905–6, 66
24.	1834	A group		[Exhib RA, London, 1034]; untraced	*Graves* I, 1905–6, 66
25.	1834	Design from Revelations		[Exhib Birmingham Soc of A]; untraced	*Gunnis* 1968, 20
26.	1834	Judaea capta		[Exhib RA, London, 1115]; untraced	*Graves* I, 1905–6, 66
27.	1837	Increase and decrease of the waters at the deluge		[Exhib RA, London, 558]; untraced	*Graves* I, 1905–6, 66
28.	1837	Righteousness and peace have kissed each other		[Exhib RA, London, 847]; untraced	*Graves* I, 1905–6, 66
29.	1841	A captive naiad	p	[Exhib RA, London, 1307]; untraced	*Graves* I, 1905–6, 66
30.	1841	A naiad	p	[Exhib RA, London, 1306]; untraced	*Graves* I, 1905–6, 66

ARNOLD, A fl 1815–19

A deaf and dumb amateur. His advertisement in the *Norwich Mercury* of 26 August 1815 stated that he would execute any orders on moderate terms, as 'his principal objective is amusement.'

Literary References: RG/JP, 1, 29v, (inf. David Cubitt).

Miscellaneous					
1.	1815	Sphinx	s	[Exhib for sale at Robert de Carle's premises in Norwich]; untraced	RG/JP, 1, 28v.
2.	1819	'a Vase and Candelabrio of statuary marble'		[Exhib Messrs Freeman's, carvers and gilders, 2 London Lane, Norwich]; untraced	*Norwich Mercury*, 28 Aug 1819

ARTHUR, John, of Cilycwm fl 1732

As a sculptor he is known only for one well-executed classical monument in a remote Carmarthenshire village (1). He also provided wall-paintings for the church.

Literary References: *Dale-Jones and Lloyd* 1989, 46

Funerary Monuments					
1.	†1732	Mary Lloyd		Cilycwm, Carmarthen	*Dale-Jones and Lloyd* 1989, 46

ASHBY, J fl 1835

He was paid £114 4s for 'carver's work', at Goldsmiths' Hall in 1835. This was largely for a clock case designed by Philip Hardwick, but it also included the carving of two shields with supporters (1).

Architectural Sculpture					
1.	1835	'a Unicorn & shield the Company's supporters' and another, larger one Payment(s): £5 10s and £3 10s	wd	[Goldsmiths' Company, London]; untraced	Goldsmiths CB, bk 18, 615; Goldsmiths Abstract E.1.2.a48f

ASHCROFT, Edmund, of Liverpool fl 1820–29

He may be related to 'Mr Henry Ashcroft, of Liverpool, stonemason', who died in 1810 at the age of 70 (*GM*, 1810, 2, 493). Ashcroft signed a large wall tablet to Thomas Hewitt at Rostherne, Cheshire (1). In 1825 his address was given as 66 Byrom St, Liverpool in *Baines' Gazeteer* (Inf. Nicholas Penny).

Literary References: *Gunnis* 1968, 20

Funerary Monuments

1.	?1820	Thomas Hewitt	Rostherne, Cheshire	S	*Gunnis* 1968, 20
2.	†1829	Thomas Davies	Llangynhafal, Denbighs		Pevsner, *Clwyd*, 1986, 226

ASHMORE, John fl 1662

He was paid £4 7s in 1662 for the font in Wirksworth Church, Derbys (1). This is described by Cox as being of 'octagon design and ornamented with patterns of unusual style, having more resemblance to Egyptian art, than anything that pertains to either Gothic or Renaissance'.

Architectural Sculpture

1.	1662	Octagonal font, carved with a set of florid initials Payment(s): £4 7s	Wirksworth, Derbys		*Cox* 1875–9, 2, 552; *Gunnis* 1968, 20; Pevsner, *Derbys*, 1978, 358

ASHTON, Henry, of London fl 1813–14

He was the son of **Robert Ashton I** and in 1813–14 was the mason responsible for building 18, Park Lane, London. On 22 August 1812 Lord Ashburnham recorded a payment of £5 11s for a quantity of 'Plimouth Marble slab' at 12/- a foot sent to Ashburnham Place. Attached to the account details is a receipt.

Literary References: *Gunnis* 1968, 20

Archival References: Ashburnham Accts, ASH 2804

ASHTON, Robert I –1805

He was first the pupil and later the assistant of **William Tyler RA** and together they signed a number of large and important monuments. That to the antiquarian Martin Folkes in Westminster Abbey was designed by Tyler and executed by Ashton. It has a full-size statue of Folkes, in loose-fitting robes, leaning on folio editions of his works (2).

Ashton also carved chimneypieces as part of a more wide-ranging masonry business (5, 6). In 1788 he tendered for building the Freemasons' Tavern, quoting a figure of £7,283. Since the lowest tender was under £5,000 he did not get the commission, though he was employed on decorative carving for the building from 1791 until 1792 (7).

The will of Robert Ashton, 'Stone Mason of Vine Street, Piccadilly', was proved on 17 December 1805. He left his business, utensils and stock in trade to his son **Robert Ashton II**, together with leasehold properties in Exeter Street, Chelsea and household items. Ashton was clearly a successful businessman, for he left £3,000 in shares to his daughter, and nearly 20 properties in Chelsea, Knightsbridge and Woolwich. One of his executors was **John Tombling.**

Literary References: *Gunnis* 1968, 20; *Whinney* 1988, 271

Will: PROB 11/1434

Funerary Monuments

1.	†1779	Elizabeth Yorke (co-sculptor: William Tyler RA)	Marchwiel, Flint	S	*Gunnis* 1968, 20; Pevsner, *Clwyd*, 1986, 251
2.	1788	Dr Martin Folkes (†1754) (co-sculptor: William Tyler RA)	Westminster Abbey, London, nave	S	Pevsner, *London: Westminster*, 1973, 459; *Whinney* 1988, 271–3 (repr)
3.	1788	William Pym (co-sculptor: William Tyler RA) Model(s):	Sandy, Beds	S	*Gunnis* 1968, 20
4.	1790	William Franks (co-sculptor: William Tyler RA)	Kentish Town, London	S	*Gunnis* 1968, 20, 404

Chimneypieces

5.	*c*1788	Several Payment(s): £94 (drawing room); £73 (dining room); £73 (duchess's dressing room); £40 (duke's dressing room); £36 (duke's bedroom)	[Chiswick House, London, drawing room, Duke of Devonshire's dining room, bedroom and dressing room]; untraced		*Gunnis* 1968, 20
6.	1790	Description unavailable	[for John Weyland, Woodeaton Hall, Staffs]; untraced		Soane bill book 4, fol 241; *Gunnis* 1968, 20

Architectural Sculpture

7.	1791–1792	Decorative carving	[Freemasons' Tavern, City of London?]; untraced		*Gunnis* 1968, 20

ASHTON, Robert II fl 1801–36

The son of **Robert Ashton I**, he inherited the profitable family business in December 1805, and had probably joined it by September 1801, when his father's partner **William Tyler RA** left him £100 in his will. The younger Ashton signs a number of monuments and tablets, the best being that commemorating Christian Gosselin, which has a finely cut relief (8). The tablet to Anne Norton at Little Gaddesden, Herts, has a relief of a mourning woman seated by a sarcophagus, a broken lily in her hand (3). It is signed 'ASHTON /Marylebone St /Piccadilly.' In 1813 he was employed by Lord Ashburnham at his house in Dover Street, where he may also have carved a chimneypiece.

Literary References: *Gunnis* 1968, 20

Wills: William Tyler RA, PROB 11/1363; Robert Ashton I, PROB 11/1434

Funerary Monuments

1.	†1768	William Edmunds	Wendover, Bucks	S	Pevsner, *Bucks*, 1994, 717
2.	?1795	Mrs Dinwiddie	Grosvenor Chapel, London	S	*Gunnis* 1968, 20
3.	†1796	Anne Norton	Little Gaddesden, Herts	S	Pevsner, *Herts*, 1977, 237
4.	?1813	John Bailey	Great Wenham, Suffolk	S	*Gunnis* 1968, 20
5.	†1816	William, 1st Earl Beauchamp	Madresfield, Worcs	S	*Gunnis* 1968, 20
6.	†1817	George Collings	St John, Hampstead, London		GPC

7.	1818	Houghton family	St Botolph's, Aldersgate, City of London	S	*Gunnis* 1968, 20
8.	1824	Christian Gosselin	Faversham, Kent	S	*Gunnis* 1968, 20
9.	†1830	Samuel Butler	Strensham, Worcs		Pevsner, *Worcs*, 1968, 273
10.	?1836	Mrs Zenogle	Farnham Royal, Bucks	S	*Gunnis* 1968, 20

ASHTON, Thomas fl 1815–35

He signed a number of tablets and was presumably a member of the family firm founded by **Robert Ashton I**. In 1819 he was paid small sums for sundry work at the Earl of Ashburnham's London house in Dover Street.

Archival References: Ashburnham abstract of bills 1819, no 7

Funerary Monuments

1.	†1815	James Bennett	North Cadbury, Somerset	S	*Gunnis* 1968, 20
2.	†1815	Rev B Barnard	Peakirk, Northants	S	*Gunnis* 1968, 20
3.	?1818	Hon Margaret Grenville	Chevening, Kent	S	GPC
4.	†1835	Eliza Jane Robson	Erbistock, Denbighs	S	Pevsner, *Clwyd*, 1994, 160

ASSITER, Thomas, of Maidstone –1826

Responsible for a number of tablets in Kent which Gunnis thought 'good for a provincial statuary' (*Gunnis* 1968, 21). He considered the tablet commemorating Sir John Twisden, with its relief reminiscent of the work of **John Bacon II**, to be his best work (**2**). Assiter was employed by the Earl of Romney on mason's work during the rebuilding of 'The Mote', near Maidstone (Building accounts, Maidstone Museum). He is buried in the graveyard of Maidstone Parish Church.

Literary References: *Gunnis* 1968, 21

Funerary Monuments

1.	?1778	William Jewell		Seal, Kent	S	*Gunnis* 1968, 21
2.	†1810	Sir John Twisden Bt		East Malling, Kent	S	*Gunnis* 1968, 21; Pevsner, *Kent: W & Weald*, 1976, 266
3.	?1814	William Bowles		Aylesford, Kent	S	*Gunnis* 1968, 21
4.	†1816	William Bryant	m	Maidstone, Kent	S	*Gunnis* 1968, 21
5.	?1818	Robert Foote		Boughton Monchelsea, Kent	S	*Gunnis* 1968, 21

ATHOW FAMILY, of Norwich fl 1787–1845

John Athow, who lived in the precincts of Norwich Cathedral, married the widow of a linen-draper, Elizabeth Waller, in December 1787, at St Luke's Chapel in Norwich. Athow carved several monuments in partnership with **Thomas Stafford**.

'**John Athow Jnr**' advertised in the *Norwich Mercury* on 6 July 1799. He announced that a move from St Andrews to a house at the 'Back of the Inns' where he 'Executes Monuments, Chimney Pieces, Black Marble Grave-Stones, Portland Head Stones, and every other branch of business in the neatest manner, on reasonable terms.' In the same newspaper on 7 August 1802 John Athow, marble and stone mason, advertised for an apprentice and a 'good mason.' A further advertisement appeared on 16 July 1803. John Athow's death was announced on 12 October 1822.

Another John Athow was listed in White's *Directory* in 1845 as a 'mason' and as a 'statuary and surveyor of city pavements, in Castle Street, Norwich.' Like his predecessors he executed monuments, chimneypieces, black marble gravestones and other items.

Literary References: *Gunnis* 1968, 21, 365

Archival References: IGI; GPC

Funerary Monuments

1.	1775	Thomas Wright	Kilverstone, Norwich, Norfolk	S	*Gunnis* 1968, 21
2.	†1780	Bartholomew Day (co-sculptor: Thomas Stafford, of Norwich)	Wicklewood, Norfolk	S	*Gunnis* 1968, 365; Pevsner, *Norfolk: N W & S*, 1999, 776
3.	†1786	Robert Tilyard	Hemsby, Norfolk	S	Pevsner, *Norfolk: N E & Norwich*, 1997, 546
4.	†1788	Robert Plumptre (co-sculptor: Thomas Stafford, of Norwich)	Norwich Cathedral, Norfolk	S	Pevsner, *Norfolk: N E & Norwich*, 1997, 210
5.	1792	Dr George Horne, Bishop of Norwich (co-sculptor: Thomas Stafford, of Norwich)	Norwich Cathedral, Norfolk		Pevsner, *Norfolk: N E & Norwich*, 1997, 210
6.	1792	William Bullock	Walsingham, Norfolk	S	*Gunnis* 1968, 21
7.	?1795	William Fell (co-sculptor: Thomas Stafford, of Norwich)	Horsham St Faith, Norfolk	S	*Gunnis* 1968, 365
8.	1797	Rev W Enfield	Octagon Chapel, Norwich	S	*Gunnis* 1968, 21
9.	†1803	Henry Partridge	Methwold, Norfolk		Pevsner, *Norfolk: N W & S*, 1999, 540

ATKINS, Robert fl 1800–15

His yard was in Charlotte Street, Brompton. He signed a very pretty little tablet at Buntingford, Herts to Edward Saunders, 1800 (**1**).

Funerary Monuments

1.	?1800	Edward Saunders	Buntingford, Herts	S	*Gunnis* 1968, 21
2.	?1815	Major Chambers	St Margaret, Lowestoft, Suffolk	S	*Gunnis* 1968, 21

ATKINS, William I fl 1703–20

He became free of the Masons' Company by service with **William Stanton** on 8 April 1703. In 1720 he made several chimneypieces for the Duke of Wharton's house, 'The Wilderness'.

Archival References: Masons' Co, *Freemen*, fol 1

Chimneypieces

1.	1720	Several	[Duke of Wharton's house]; untraced		*Gunnis* 1968, 21, citing Archives, Lord Braye

ATKINS, William II fl 1761

In 1761 he made a marble chimneypiece for the second Earl of Ashburnham which he sent down to Ashburnham Place, Sussex with his man, Joseph Gilliam (1). The latter was paid £2 10s in subsistance allowance during the time he spent erecting this (Ashburnham Archives).

Literary References: *Gunnis* 1968, 21

Chimneypieces

1.	1761	Description unavailable	m	[Ashburnham Place, Sussex, drawing room]; untraced		*Gunnis* 1968, 21

ATKINS, William, of Ludlow fl 1786–1817

Funerary Monuments

1.	†1786	William Toldervy		Barrow, Salop	S	GPC
2.	?1817	Richard Harper		Ashford Bowdler, Salop	S	*Gunnis* 1968, 21

ATKINS (or ADKINS), John fl 1761–77

On 3 April 1761 he received a premium of 30 guineas from the Society of Arts for a relief in stone of *Regulus returning to Carthage* in the under-25 class (2). He exhibited it the same year at the Society of Free Artists. Atkins was a pupil of **L F Roubiliac** and his name is noted on the list of those attending the latter's funeral in 1762. He then became assistant to **Joseph Wilton** and, according to J T Smith, it was Atkins and **Nathaniel Smith** who modelled and carved the statues on Somerset House for which Wilton received the payment and the credit.

Literary References: *Press Cuttings* 1723–1800, fol 107; RSA *Register*, 1778, 31; *Dossie* 1782, 439; *Smith* 1828, 2, 178; *Gunnis* 1968, 21; *Whinney* 1988, 267; *Bindman and Baker* 1995, 221

Funerary Monuments

1.	†1777	Unidentified subject, tablet		Southill, Beds		Pevsner, *Beds, Hunts & Peterborough*, 1968, 145

Reliefs

2.	1761	Regulus returning to Carthage	s	[Soc of A, premium, 30 gns]; untraced		RSA *Minutes*, 1760–61 seq 3 fols 48, 53; *Dossie* 1782, 439; *Graves* 1907, 16

ATKINSON, Charles, of London fl 1750–70

Atkinson was responsible for most of the chimneypieces at Holkham Hall, Norfolk. He signs the large monument, 20 feet high, of the Earl of Leicester, at Tittleshall (1). The busts of Lord and Lady Leicester which form part of it are the work of **L F Roubiliac**. The *London Directory* of 1768 notes that Atkinson's yard was in Leadenhall Street.

Literary References: *Gunnis* 1968, 21

Funerary Monuments

1.	1760	Thomas, Earl of Leicester (†1759) and Lady Leicester (†1775)		Tittleshall, Norfolk	S	*Bindman and Baker* 1995, 357

Chimneypieces

2.	nd	Several		[Holkham Hall, Norfolk]; untraced		*Gunnis* 1968, 21

ATKINSON, John, of London *c*1799–1856

A mason and paviour who was responsible for a number of funerary tablets. His son practised as an architect. Atkinson had a yard at 100, Goswell Road, London, where, as a very young man, he was joined in partnership by **Thomas Whitfield Browne**. As contracting masons Atkinson and Browne built Salters' Hall, the clerk's house and offices, 1823–27, to the designs of Henry Carr (**8**). Their tender of £17,362 was the lowest submitted in July 1823, though in the end, owing to various alterations and additions, they exceeded this figure by over £10,000. As early as August 1823, the clerk to the Salters' Company wrote to them to express the great dissatisfaction of the Building Committee 'at the extreme slowness and want of energy with which they had hitherto proceeded'. In addition to the buildings, they were responsible for most of the carved stonework and for a number of chimneypieces (**6**). They also tendered for eight carved wooden columns in the great hall which were to be done in scagliola to 'imitate Sienna and Statuary' for £670. The committee decided to pay them £440 instead and to choose a different finish. A summary of their payments to 25 October 1825 showed that they had been paid £27,544 to that date. The partners built the new hall of Christ's Hospital in 1824, where they executed all the carved stonework (**7**). A tradecard for a 'John Atkinson' is listed under 'Sculptors and Masons' in the Heal collection, BM, 106.1. Atkinson's death on 5 April 1856 at Frindsbury, Kent was noted in the *Gentleman's Magazine*. He was 57.

Literary References: *GM* 1856, i, 660; *Gunnis* 1968, 21; *Colvin* 1995, 81

Archival References: Salters, Ct Mins, 1821–27; Salters BCM 1821–27, 129, 226, 242, 263; Salters C1/23, 125–9, 149–53, 376, 408

Funerary Monuments

1.	†1812	John Besant		King's Chapel, Gibraltar	S	GPC
2.	1815	Joanna Howland (co-sculptor: Thomas Whitfield Browne)		Haverhill, Suffolk	S	*Gunnis* 1968, 21
3.	†1828	Ann Waller (co-sculptor: Thomas Whitfield Browne)		St Dunstan in the West, London	S	
4.	1830	John Kipling (co-sculptor: Thomas Whitfield Browne)		Overstone, Northants	S	*Gunnis* 1968, 21
5.	†1831	Lucy Hopkins (co-sculptor: Thomas Whitfield Browne)		St Dunstan in the West, London	S	

Chimneypieces

6.	1823–1827	For the court room (35 gns), election hall and waiting room, dining room (£40), breakfast and drawing room of the clerk's house (£20 each) (co-sculptor: Thomas Whitfield Browne)		Salters' Hall, City of London		*Gunnis* 1968, 21 citing Salters' Co archives

Architectural Sculpture

7.	1824	Carved stonework (co-sculptor: Thomas Whitfield Browne)	s	Christ's Hospital, new hall	*Gunnis* 1968, 21 citing Christ's Hospital archives
8.	1823–1827	Carved stonework (co-sculptor: Thomas Whitfield Browne)	s	Salters' Hall, City of London	*Gunnis* 1968, 21 citing Salters' Co archives

ATKINSON, Joseph, of York –1792

He was in partnership with **Thomas Atkinson of York** as 'stone and marble mason' until 1765 (*York Courant*, 21 May 1765). His death is noted in the *York Herald* of 19 May 1792, and his widow Elizabeth announced her intention of carrying on the business in the *York Herald* of 26 May 1792.

Archival References: GPC

ATKINSON, Richard b 1749/50

He was one of the first students of sculpture to enrol at the Royal Academy Schools, on 14 February 1769, when he gave his age as 19.

Literary References: *Hutchison* 1960–62, 133

ATKINSON, Thomas, of London fl 1790–1804

Between 1790 and 1804 he worked at Stourhead, where he built the wings of the house and provided the ornamental carving (**1**). These were saved when the rest of the building was destroyed by fire in the early part of the 20th century.

Literary References: *Gunnis* 1968, 22

Architectural Sculpture

1.	1790–1804	Decorative carving	s	Stourhead, Wilts, exterior wings	*Gunnis* 1968, 22

ATKINSON, Thomas, of York –1798

Atkinson was one of the leading architects in Yorkshire in the second half of the 18th century. He belonged to a long-standing family of York bricklayers and stonemasons and lived in the parish of St Saviour, York, with his first wife, Anne. Both husband and wife became Catholics during the 1760s and after Anne's death he married another Catholic, and raised a second family. He took his son James as an apprentice in 1761, a year after he had become a freeman of York. Another son, Joseph, had been apprenticed to Samson White, 'stonecutter of York', in 1767, rather than his father, probably because the latter was, at that time, classed as a 'foreigner' (York City Archives). In 1763 he embarked on his major architectural work, the Gothic front and the gate-house of Bishopthorpe Palace for Archbishop Drummond, completed in 1769. He also made chimneypieces for the house (**10**). He was also employed at the Bar Convent in York, 1791–3. His monuments are of good provincial workmanship and are executed in coloured marbles.

On 1 May 1765 he dissolved a partnership with **Joseph Atkinson of York**, who may perhaps have been his brother. Thomas stated in the local press that he had built a new shop adjoining the previous one, and that he was prepared to make estimates for 'Churches, Monuments and Chimney Pieces'. Joseph Atkinson countered on 21 May by announcing in the *York Courant* that he would carry on the 'marble and stone business at St. Andrew's Gate' in its various branches and that 'all future favours will ever be gratefully acknowledged and executed with great exactness'.

Thomas's sudden death was reported in the *York Herald* on 4 May 1798. **John Platt** wrote to Mr Iveson, the steward at Burton Constable 'May 5. 1798. Mr Thomas Atkinson dropt down dead between 12 and one o'clock yesterday near his own door' (Chichester-Constable Archives quoted in GPC). He left his business to his son, John. There is a tablet commemorating Thomas in St Saviour, York.

Literary References: *Gunnis* 1968, 22; *Aveling* 1970, 129, 150

Archival References: GPC

Funerary Monuments

1.	†1765	Marmaduke Prickett		Kilham, E R Yorks		Pevsner, *Yorks: E R & York*, 1995, 575
2.	1782	John Dixon (†1782)		St Peter, Leeds, W R Yorks		*Gunnis* 1968, 22; *Pullan* 2006, 67 (repr)
3.	†1789	Ann Prickett		Kilham, E R Yorks	S	Pevsner, *Yorks: E R & York*, 1995, 575
4.	1794	Sir Henry Vane		Long Newton, Durham		Pevsner, *Durham*, 1983, 355
5.	?1795	Lady Vane		Long Newton, Durham		*Gunnis* 1968, 22
6.	†1797	Elizabeth Scarisbrick		Holy Trinity, York		Pevsner, *Yorks: E R & York*, 1995, 163

Chimneypieces

7.	1756	Description unavailable Payment(s): £27		[Newby Hall, W R Yorks]; untraced	GPC
8.	1760	Doric (paid for 'setting up')		[Hovingham Hall, N R Yorks]; untraced	Archives of Sir William Worsley, Bt in GPC
9.	1767	with Roman Doric columns	s	Burton Constable Hall, E R Yorks, great hall	Pevsner, *Yorks: E R & York*, 1995, 375
10.	1763–1769	Several		[Bishopthorpe Palace, York, drawing and dining rooms]; untraced	*Gunnis* 1968, 22
11.	1769	With carved panel illustrating sacrifice to Aesculapius and Hygea	m	Burton Constable Hall, E R Yorks, dining room	Pevsner, *Yorks: E R & York*, 1995, 375
12.	1789	Description unavailable	m	[Farnley Hall, W R Yorks]; untraced	GPC
13.	nd	Three Payment(s): £21 12s 4d (dining room) £60 (others)	m	Newburgh Priory, N R Yorks, dining and other rooms	GPC

Miscellaneous

14.	1762	'Gothick stone press' Payment(s): £61 6s 6d		[Newby Hall, W R Yorks]; untraced	Compton of Newby archives in GPC

ATKINSON, William, of London –1766

Atkinson was the step-son of **Joseph Pickford**, who married Atkinson's widowed mother, Mary, in 1734. He appears to have entered into partnership with Pickford soon after, and they were working together as late as 1758 from premises between Brick Street and Down Street, Piccadilly. Atkinson was one of Pickford's executors and with his mother inherited Pickford's stock-in-trade and the yard by Hyde Park Corner, where he was still living in 1763. Like Pickford, Atkinson married when he was middle-aged, in 1762. Sarah Atkinson outlived her husband and continued to live at Hyde Park Corner until 1772.

From 1754 to 1758 the partners were building Stephen Wright's University Library at Cambridge, for which they received nearly £5,000. Atkinson himself seems to have provided most of the decorative stone carving and was paid £333 for his work (**8**). In 1759 he was responsible for the masonry work when wings were added to Copt Hall, Essex under the direction of the architects Sir Roger Newdigate and Thomas Prowse, for which he received £86.

He provided the wall monument to Sir John and Lady Bendyshe, which has a conventional double portrait medallion supported by a weeping cherub (**1**). The memorial to Walter Cary is described by Pevsner as 'boldly handled, with cartouche, wreath, and large lettering' (**2**) and another wall monument with a fine bust celebrates Lewis Dymoke (**5**). He was also involved in two monuments in Ireland. That to the Earl and Countess of Bessborough, †1758, is his most ambitious work (**3**). In an elaborate architectural setting, the Earl and Countess are represented half-length above a sarcophagus, wearing Roman togas. They hold hands in a classical pose emblematic of conjugal fidelity, deriving from a Roman tomb, engraved and published in the 17th century by P S Bartoli. The monument to Mrs Osborne, who did not die until 1798, is signed by Carew of Waterford (perhaps the father of **J E Carew**), but incorporates a medallion of a man mourning over an urn signed by Atkinson (**6**). It seems likely that the medallion originally came from another of Atkinson's memorials.

The will of William Atkinson, 'Architect and Builder', was proved on 7 July 1766. Two posthumous auctions catalogues of his stock-in-trade survive. The sale of 24–25 July 1766 conducted at his house and yard in Piccadilly, near Hyde Park Corner by a Mr Webster, comprised models, casts, moulds, figures, carved ornaments and utensils. Among the lots was a head of Apollo, 'two side frizes of statuary carved with Diana's trophies', '5 figures in Portland stone (the Stuart family) and one pedestal'; 'Figures of Peace, Plenty and Cleopatra', 'Two vases, one on a pedestal ornamented with vine leaves and a Janus's head, the other on a truss ornamented' and 'a fine cast of dolphin and boys by Rysbrack'. The second sale, conducted by Burnsall, on 2–3 April 1767, offered vases, alabaster statuary, plasters and moulds after the antique. The items included 'a large and magnificent vase in Bath stone, designed by Mr. Kent' and 'a most beautiful and magnificent table inlaid with horses' teeth and different rich marbles in fret and with a statuary marble border'. Also listed were 'Garden terms in Portland stone 7 ft. high of Alcibiden and a Grecian Venus' and a bust of Lord Westmorland. The unusually diverse range of sculpture and materials suggests a busy shop, which perhaps also dealt in work by outside craftsmen.

Literary References: *Mortimer* 1763, 49; *Gunnis* 1968, 22; *McCarthy* 1973, 26–36 (Copt Hall); *Potterton* 1975, 34; McCarthy 1979, 382 (Copt Hall); Pevsner, *London 3: NW*, 1991, 423; *Saunders* 1993, 11–16

Archival References: GPC

Will: PROB 11/920

Auction Catalogues: Atkinson 1766; Atkinson 1767

Funerary Monuments

1.	?c1740	Sir John Bendyshe Bt (†1707) and Lady Bendyshe (†1705) (co-sculptor: Joseph Pickford)	Steeple Bumpstead, Essex	S	C Lib (repr)
2.	†1757	Walter Cary	Heston, Middx	S	Pevsner, *London: N W*, 1991, 423
3.	†1758	Brabazon, Ist Earl of Bessborough and Sarah, his 1st wife (†1733)	Fiddown, Co Kilkenny	S	*Potterton* 1975, 34
4.	†1758	Brabazon, 1st Earl of Bessborough, and Elizabeth, his 2nd wife (†1738)	Fiddown, Co Kilkenny	S	*Potterton* 1975, 25, 34 (repr)
5.	†1760	Lewis Dymoke Model(s): terracotta model for bust of 'Champion Dymoke', Atkinson sale, 2 April 1767	Scrivelsby, Lincs	S	Pevsner, *Lincs*, 1995, 630
6.	†1798	Mrs Osborne, medallion only (monument by J E Carew)	Fiddown, Co Kilkenny	S	*Gunnis* 1968, 22

Chimneypieces

7.	1765	Description unavailable Payment(s): £84	Corsham Court, Wilts, alcove bedroom		Methuen Accounts, 11 Feb 1765; *Gunnis* 1968, 22

Architectural Sculpture

8.	1754–1758	'Four heads representing The Seasons' (£32), 'twenty two large festoons of fruits and flowers' (£159), two vases (£9) and other ornaments (designed by Stephen Wright)	s	University Library, Cambridge	*Gunnis* 1968, 22; *Saunders* 1993, 13 (repr)

AURIOL fl 1697

Statues

1.	1697	Several, including some for a fountain	[Chatsworth, Derbys]; untraced	Chatsworth Building Accts, 1697–98, 5

AUSTIN, Cornelius –1704

He carried out wood carving of the highest quality at Pembroke College, Cambridge (1). The wall ornaments incorporate swags, cartouches and naturalistic elements. He also provided carved work at St John's College, King's College Chapel, Emmanuel College Chapel and Trinity College, all in Cambridge. He employed a small workforce, lived in the parish of All Saints and owned a large inn, 'The Cardinal's Hat', in Trumpington Street. He appears to have been succeeded in business by a son of the same name around 1704.

Literary References: *Green* 1964 (1), 80–2); *Beard and Gilbert* 1986, 26; *Esterly* 1998, 74–6, 78, 161–2

Architectural Sculpture

1.	post-1660	Decorative carving	wd	Pembroke College, Cambridge, chapel	C Lib (repr)
2.	nd	Decorative carving, including the cedar bookcases, limewood coats of arms and the cypher of Robert Drake	wd	Trinity College, Cambridge	*Green* 1964 (1), 80–2 (repr 114)

AUSTIN, Felix fl 1817–72

Austin described himself in the trade directories as an architect, statuary mason and sculptor as well as an artificial stone manufacturer. An article in *The Builder* of 1868 notes that a Dutchman, **Van Spangen I**, set up in competition with the **Coade Factory** in about 1820, when he established an artificial stone manufactory at Bow. He later went into partnership with a Mr Powell, but the firm broke up about 1828 and the moulds were purchased by Austin, who was then experimenting with a compound of Portland cement, broken stone, pounded tile and coarse sand.

He lived at 1–3 Keppel Row, New Road, Fitzroy Square from 1830 and had premises further down the street. In 1834 he was paid for five garden vases to **Sir Francis Chantrey**'s design (or at least to be placed according to his design) at Holkham Hall, Norfolk (**11**). Austin was joined by **John Seeley** before 1841 and they later opened premises at 24 Church Street, Rotherhithe. The Specimen Book of Austin and Seeley's Artificial Stone Manufactury, published in 1841 in French and English, indicates that they imported or traded in artificial stone figures with France. The English title page reads 'Collections of ornaments at Austin and Seeley's Works, nearly opposite Trinity Church, New Road, London, for Gardens, Parks and Pleasure Grounds, consisting of fountains, tazzas, vases and pedestals, ornamental fish ponds, flower pots, sun-dials, sphinxes, eagles, lions &c, church fonts, tables, monuments, and screens, crosses, pinnacles and other Gothic decorations'. Special lines were the Medici and Borghese vases. The engravings were numbered, with measurements, but with prices suppled only in French currency (East Riding Archives Office, DDCC (2)/45A/22). In 1842 *The Ecclesiologist* mercilessly attacked Austin and Seeley's artificial stone fonts.

Austin signed a number of tablets alone. Those to Frances Samwell (**6**) and Sophia Pym (**7**) also carried Seeley's signature. Like his predecessor, Mrs Coade, Austin was shrewd enough to employ leading architects to work for him. He provided oriental vases designed by Sydney Smirke for the Pantheon Bazaar in 1833 and a pedestal for Ironmongers' Hall in 1834. J B Papworth and others designed a number of large fountains for him (**12, 13, 14**). The firm was still operating in 1872, when the Duke of Atholl paid £25 for a composition statue, *Diana and a deer* (Archives Duke of Atholl, quoted by RG/JP, 1, 41). His tradecard is listed under 'Sculptors and Masons' in the Heal Collection, BM, 106.2.

Literary References: 'Notice of Some Manufacturers in Artificial Stone', *The Conductor* 1834–5 (LMA 45.09 AUS 2.0); *Ecclesiologist*, 1842, 1, 127; *Builder*, 25 July 1868, 546; *Hadfield* 1960, 280; *Gunnis* 1960 (3); *Gunnis* 1968, 22–3; *Kelly* 1990, 51, 5 (inf. Gerardine Mulcahy)

Funerary Monuments

1.	†1817	Elizabeth Jocelyn		Stanstead Abbots, Herts	S	
2.	1826	William Ruddiman		St John's Wood Chapel, Marylebone, London	S	*Gunnis* 1968, 23
3.	1830	Catherine Petre		Selby, W R Yorks	S	*Gunnis* 1968, 23
4.	1830	Countess of Athlone		Sacombe, Herts	S	*Gunnis* 1968, 23
5.	1832	Lieutenant-Colonel Dashwood		Kirtlington, Oxon	S	*Gunnis* 1968, 23
6.	1841	Frances Samwell (designed by B Watson) (co-sculptor: John Seeley)		Upton, Northants	S	*Gunnis* 1968, 23
7.	†1841	Sophia Pym (co-sculptor: John Seeley)		William, Herts		Pevsner, *Herts*, 1977, 407

Statues

8.	post-1850	Diane de Gabies (co-sculptor: John Seeley)	sa	Sotheby, South Kensington 23–24 May 2000, lot 504; untraced	Sale cat (repr)
9.	1872	Diana and a deer (co-sculptor: John Seeley)	sa	[coll Duke of Atholl]; untraced	RG/JP, 1, 41, citing archives, Duke of Atholl

Chimneypieces

10.	1829	Several, gothic		Addington Palace, Surrey	RG/JP, 1, 40 citing Lambeth Palace Account Book

Architectural Sculpture

11.	1834	Five garden vases Payment(s): £23 1s 3d		Holkham Hall, Norfolk	NP/RG
12.	by 1834	Fountain (designed by J B Papworth)	sa	[Pantheon Bazaar, London]; untraced	*Archit Mag*, 1834, 295
13.	by 1834	Fountain (designed by J B Papworth)	sa	[Earl Amherst, Montreal House, Sevenoaks, Kent]; untraced	*Archit Mag*, 1834, 295
14.	by 1835	Fountain (designed by J B Papworth)	sa	[Alton Towers, Staffs]; untraced	*Archit Mag*, 1835, 123
15.	1859	A horse (co-sculptor: John Seeley) Payment(s): £10 10s	sa	[Blair Hotel, Perths, stable-yard archway]; untraced	RG/JP, 1, 40 citing archives, Duke of Atholl

Miscellaneous

16.	1845	Two pedestal tripods supporting brackets (co-sculptor: John Seeley) Payment(s): £14 14s	sa	[coll Lord Glenlyon]; Blair Castle, Perths	RG/JP, 1, 40 citing archives, Duke of Atholl

AUSTIN, T fl 1767

He is listed in the catalogue of exhibitors at the Society of Artists in 1767 as 'sculptor', although his only exhibited work appears to be a plaster cast (1).

Literary References: *Graves* 1907, 17

Reliefs

1.	1767	The Prince of Brunswick, in Roman character, introduced by Britannia to the Temple of Hymen, cast from a gold plate	p	[Exhib Soc of Artists, London, 198]; untraced		*Graves* 1907, 17

AVRAY, Robert fl 1754–56

He signs the monument at St Crux, York to Sir Tancred Robinson, twice Lord Mayor of York, who died in 1754 (1). This fine work, begun by **Harvey of London** and apparently designed by **Charles Mitley**, has a cherub holding a medallion portrait. Behind are naval trophies and below, the emblems of the Lord Mayor. In the account book of Sir William Robinson is a payment of £100, made on 29 May 1756 to 'Mr [William] Carr [of York] and Mr Avary for finishing and putting up Sir Tancred's monument' (Compton of Newby Archives, in GPC).

Literary References: *Gunnis* 1968, 23

Funerary Monuments

1.	†1754	Rear-Admiral Sir Tancred Robinson bt		St Crux parish room, York	S	Pevsner, *Yorks: E R & York*, 1995, 164; GPC

AWBREY, John fl c1727

Architectural Sculpture

1.	c1727	John Skutt, relief portrait		Poole, Dorset, harbour office front	S	Pevsner, *Dorset*, 1972, 321

AYLING, Thomas fl 1731

Ayling is described as a 'stone-mason' in the record of payment for a chimneypiece for Earl Fitzwalter (1) in 1731 (Mildmay Account Book 15 M 50/31, Hants RO).

Archival References: GPC

Chimneypieces

1.	1731	'Of Plimouth marble' Payment(s): £20	m	[Moulsham Hall, Essex]; untraced		*Edwards* 1977, 30

B, A fl 1764

All that is known of the sculptor is his initials carved on the Horne monument, a rococo wall tablet with naval trophies including a cannon and anchor.

Funerary Monuments

1.	†1764	Edmund Horne		Pentrich, Derby	S	C Lib (repr)

BABEL, Peter fl 1763

Listed in Mortimer's *Universal Director* of 1763 as 'Designer and Modeller, Long Acre, near James-Street – One of the first improvers of Papier Maché ornaments for ceilings, Chimney-pieces, picture-frames, &c an invention of modern date, imported by us from France, and now brought to great perfection'.

BACON, Charles 1821–c1885

A gem-engraver and sculptor in bronze and marble, his life remains obscure though he was responsible for some major civic sculpture. He exhibited for the first time at the Royal Academy in 1842 as an intaglio engraver of gemstones, giving his address as 15, White Conduit Grove, Pentonville. Works in this material were shown until 1849, including two after subjects by **E H Baily** (**26, 30**), and one after **John Flaxman** (**29**). In 1844 his address was 2, Strand and in 1845 he lived at 18 Greek Street. In 1846 he enrolled at the Academy Schools on the recommendation of the poet Alaric Watts (1797–1864), and in 1847, perhaps as a show of gratitude, he exhibited a bust of Watts, his first-known three-dimensional work of sculpture (**9**).

Bacon tried his hand at ideal subjects including a marble statue of *Helen veiled before Paris*, for which he asked a sum of 500 guineas (**2**). He also carved a number of busts, and his head of John Hullah won him a notice in the *Illustrated London News* (**12**). By 1849 Bacon had begun to work in bronze and in 1855, when he showed at the British Institution, he gave his address as 'The Statue Foundry, Lower Belgrave Place, Pimlico' (*Graves* 1875, 19). In 1857 he was living at 7, Loughborough Place, Brixton, from where he submitted for exhibition his bronze statue of Felix Mendelssohn (**4**). The statue, which shows the composer thoughtfully touching his chin, was the centrepiece of the Mendelssohn Festival at the Crystal Palace, Sydenham in May 1860.

In 1861 Bacon was commissioned to provide a bronze statue to be erected at Spilsby in memory of a famous Arctic explorer born in Spilsby, Sir John Franklin (**5**). Despite his earlier successes Bacon was still apparently little known, for on hearing of his selection as executant, a correspondent in the *Art Journal*, asked: 'Who is Mr. Bacon? We do not know of any living sculptor of that name' (*AJ* 1861, 29). Bacon produced an imposing full-length statue of the explorer with a telescope and other nautical attributes. A series of commissions followed, including a conventional bust of Warren Stormes Hale, the Lord Mayor of London (**15**), a frontal bust of G F W Mortimer which combined modern dress with draperies *all'antica* (**16**) and a colossal head of Shakespeare for the Agricultural Hall, Islington (**14**).

The apogee of Bacon's career came with the commission from Charles Oppenheim for a bronze equestrian statue of the Prince Consort, erected at Holborn Circus in 1874 (**7**). Bacon chose a pose that he had earlier used for his statue of the politician, John Erle-Drax, who was presented on a prancing horse, waving an enormous top hat at an imaginary crowd (**3**). Prince Albert also waves a cocked hat. The pedestal, financed by the City Corporation, is decorated with formal, static reliefs celebrating the Prince's achievements. The statue, which cost £2000 and was unveiled on 17 January 1874, was ill-received. The *Art Journal* remarked only that 'on the principle that one must not too narrowly examine a gift horse, we abjure criticism' (*AJ* 1874, 61). Lord Edward Gleichen, who did not abjure, considered it 'a poor thing' (*Gleichen* 1928, 134). Bacon's last major work was the figure of John Candlish, MP for Sunderland, which was erected by public subscription at a cost £1000, and was cast at the foundry of H. Young & Co in Pimlico (**8**). The sculptor continued to exhibit at the Royal Academy until 1884, and his name appeared in the directory of artists published in *The Year's Art* in 1885. Nothing is known of him after that date, which may have been the year of his death. He was then living at Bolton Studios in South Kensington, where he had been since 1873.

According to Graves, a '**G Bacon**' (of whom there is no other trace) showed heads of *Minerva, Antinous* and *Ariadne* at the Royal Academy between 1846 and 1848 (*Graves*, I, 1905–6, 87). Since this address is the same as that given for Charles Bacon, he may be a brother or some other relation (unless, of course, the 'G' in the catalogue is a misprint for 'C').

MGS

Literary References: *Graves* 1875, 19; *Graves* I, 1905–6, 87; *Gunnis* 1968, 24; *Usherwood* 2000, 181–2
Archival References: RA Admissions
Miscellaneous Drawings: Design for a monument to Princess Charlotte Augusta, Royal Coll RL 23461

No.	Date	Subject		Location		References
Funerary Monuments						
1.	1872	George Grote (†1871), bust		Westminster Abbey, London, south transept		*Graves*, I, 1905–6, 87; *Ormond* 1973, 205; Conway Lib (repr)
Statues						
2.	1853	Helen veiled before Paris Payment(s): asking price 500 gns	m	[Exhib BI, London, 570]; untraced		*Graves* 1875, 19; Conway Lib (repr)
3.	1853	John Erle-Drax		Olantigh, Wye, Kent		Conway Lib (repr)
4.	1857	Felix Mendelssohn	b	[Exhib RA, London, 1247]; untraced		ILN, 17 Dec 1859, 570 (repr); ILN, 12 May 1860, 461
5.	1861	Sir John Franklin	b	Spilsby, Lincs, marketplace	SD	*Gunnis* 1968, 24; *Ormond* 1973, 181; Conway Lib (repr)
6.	1864	Charles, Earl of Yarborough, equestrian sketch		[Exhib RA, London, 952]; untraced		*Graves* I, 1905–6, 87
7.	1869–1874	The Prince Consort, equestrian statue, with seated figures of Commerce and Peace and allegorical reliefs Payment(s): £2,000		Holborn Circus, City of London	SD	*Blackwood* 1989, 60–1 (repr); *Ward-Jackson* 2002, 442–53
8.	1875	John Candlish	b	Mowbray Park, Sunderland	SD	*Usherwood* 2000, 181–2 (repr)
Busts						
9.	1847	Alaric A Watts		[Exhib RA, London, 1421]; untraced		*Graves*, I, 1905–6, 87; *Ormond* 1973, 497
10.	1849	Edward, Baron Lytton	b	(coll H G Daniel)		*Ormond* 1973, 286
11.	1849	John Erle-Drax	m	Olantigh, Wye, Kent	SD	RG/JP, 1, 42
12.	1850	John Hullah		[Exhib RA, London, 1410]; untraced		*ILN*, 1850, 117 (repr); *Graves* I, 1905–6, 87
13.	1864	Henry Faudel		[Exhib RA, London, 1025]; untraced		*Graves* I, 1905–6, 87
14.	1864	William Shakespeare	m	Agricultural Hall, Islington		*ILN*, 30 April 1864, 417 (repr); *Gunnis* 1968, 24
15.	1865	Warren Stormes Hale	m	CL Coll, City of London School, acc 180		*Graves* I, 1905–6, 87; *Knight* 1986, 329 (repr)
16.	1866	Dr G F W Mortimer	m	CL Coll, City of London School, acc 267		*Graves* I, 1905–6, 87; *Knight* 1986, 329 (repr)
17.	1866	E F Flower		[Exhib RA, London, 991]; untraced		*Graves* I, 1905–6, 87
18.	1866	Henry Graves		[Exhib RA, London, 999]; Shakespeare Memorial Theatre, Stratford-upon-Avon, Warks		*Graves* I, 1905–6, 87
19.	1866	Innocence Payment(s): £31 10s	m	[Exhib Soc of BA, London, 1096]; untraced		*Johnson* 1975, 17
20.	1867	Alfred, Duke of Edinburgh		[Exhib RA, London, 989]; untraced		*Graves* I, 1905–6, 87
21.	1867	J M Levy	m	[Exhib RA, London, 1047]; untraced		*Graves* I, 1905–6, 87
22.	1884	Bishop of Chichester		[Exhib RA, London, 1822]; untraced		*Graves* I, 1905–6, 87
Reliefs						
23.	1861	T Brewer, medallion		[Exhib RA, London, 1030]; untraced		*Graves* I, 1905–6, 87
24.	1862	Mrs C Bacon, medallion		[Exhib RA, London, 1071]; untraced		*Graves* I, 1905–6, 87
Miscellaneous						
25.	1842	Edward VI, intaglio on cornelian		[Exhib RA, London, 1189]; untraced		*Graves* I, 1905–6, 87
26.	1842	Eve, intaglio on cornelian after E H Baily		[Exhib RA, London, 1187]; untraced		*Graves* I, 1905–6, 87
27.	1843	Demosthenes		[Exhib RA, London, 1371]; untraced		*Graves* I, 1905–6, 87
28.	1843	Queen Victoria		[Exhib RA, London, 1369]; untraced		*Graves* I, 1905–6, 87
29.	1844	Mercury and Pandora, intaglio after John Flaxman RA		[Exhib RA, London, 1254]; untraced		*Graves* I, 1905–6, 87
30.	1845	Paris, intaglio after E H Baily		[Exhib RA, London, 1302]; untraced		*Graves* I, 1905–6, 87
31.	1846	Arthur, 1st Duke of Wellington, equestrian, intaglio		[Exhib RA, London, 1379]; untraced		*Graves* I, 1905–6, 87
32.	1849	Albert Smith		[Exhib RA, London, 1322]; untraced		*Graves* I, 1905–6, 87
33.	1849	Eve and Neptune, onyx cameos		[Exhib BI, London, 510]; untraced		*Graves* 1875, 19
34.	1850	Infancy		[Exhib BI, London, 495]; untraced		*Graves* 1875, 19
35.	1855	Ariadne Payment(s): asking price 40 gns		[Exhib BI, London, 556]; untraced		*Graves* 1875, 19
36.	1861	Master Jeffreyes		[Exhib RA, London, 1047]; untraced		*Graves* I, 1905–6, 87
37.	1864	Jones Webb		[Exhib RA, London, 1023]; untraced		*Graves* I, 1905–6, 87
38.	1865	Sir George Barrow Bt		[Exhib RA, London, 1014]; untraced		*Graves* I, 1905–6, 87
39.	1866	Rt Hon B S Phillips, Lord Mayor		[Exhib RA, London, 988]; untraced		*Graves* I, 1905–6, 87
40.	1867	J Marr Johnson		[Exhib RA, London, 1192]; untraced		*Graves* I, 1905–6, 87
41.	1867	Robert Lowe MP		[Exhib RA, London, 1162]; untraced		*Graves* I, 1905–6, 87
42.	1867	W Leaf		[Exhib RA, London, 1150]; untraced		*Graves* I, 1905–6, 87
43.	1868	George Peabody		[Exhib RA, London, 1153]; untraced		*Graves* I, 1905–6, 87
44.	1868	H B Berthron		[Exhib RA, London, 1158]; untraced		*Graves* I, 1905–6, 87
45.	1868	Robert Alexander Gray		[Exhib RA, London, 982]; untraced		*Graves* I, 1905–6, 87
46.	1868	W MacArthur, Sheriff		[Exhib RA, London, 1151]; untraced		*Graves* I, 1905–6, 87
47.	1868	William Fernley Allen, Lord Mayor		[Exhib RA, London, 974]; untraced		*Graves* I, 1905–6, 87

48.	1871	C M Levy	[Exhib RA, London, 1221]; untraced	*Graves* I, 1905–6, 87
49.	1871	'Lister, Esq, FRS'	[Exhib RA, London, 1189]; untraced	*Graves* I, 1905–6, 87

BACON, G fl 1846–48

Graves records that 'G Bacon' of 18 Greek Street, Soho exhibited at the Royal Academy between 1846 and 1848. Since he exhibited from the same address as **Charles Bacon**, he may have been a relative. Alternatively the 'G' in the catalogue may be a misprint for 'C'.

Literary References: *Graves*, I, 1905–6, 87

Busts

1.	1846	Minerva	[Exhib RA, London, 1384]; untraced	*Graves* I, 1905–6, 87
2.	1847	Antinous	[Exhib RA, London, 1307]; untraced	*Graves* I, 1905–6, 87
3.	1848	Ariadne	[Exhib RA, London, 1309]; untraced	*Graves* I, 1905–6, 87

BACON, John I, RA 1740–99

Bacon was a designer, modeller and sculptor, a singularly successful and influential commercial artist and the first great British sculptor of the Industrial Revolution. He was born in Southwark, London on 24 November 1740, the son of Thomas Bacon (†1767), a cloth-worker, and Anne, née Greenwood, and was apprenticed to Nicholas Crisp of Bow churchyard, a jeweller and watchmaker, on 7 June 1755. Crisp owned a porcelain factory in Vauxhall, where Bacon apparently first saw the models that inspired him to become a sculptor (*Euro Mag* 1790, 83–4). By 1759 he had begun to make his own models and that year he was awarded a premium by the newly-formed Society for the Encouragement of Arts, Manufactures and Commerce for a figure of *Peace* (**122**).

Bacon's submission to the Society was no doubt encouraged by Crisp, who was one of its founders and a member of the award-giving committee. Bacon won premiums again in 1760, 1761 and 1764 (**209, 210, 214, 215, 216**). In July 1764 he left Crisp, who was now bankrupt, but he continued to enter works for Society of Arts prizes until 1778 (**127, 130, 134, 216**). He later wrote to the Society expressing gratitude for their encouragement, which had enabled him 'to pursue those studies which a disadvantageous situation had otherwise made difficult, if not impossible' (Bacon/RSA).

He married Elizabeth Wade at St Saviour, Southwark on 2 March 1767, and their first child, Ann, was born in 1768. That year Bacon exhibited with the Society of Artists, giving his address as 'Mr Tucker's, Cox's Square, Spital Fields' (*Graves* 1907, 18). By 1769 he had moved from the City to George Yard, Soho Square.

Bacon seems to have worked principally as a modeller from 1764 to 1769. The first known record of his work for Wedgwood is a letter dated 21 March 1769 from Peter Swift, Wedgwood's London agent: 'Mr. Bacon hath brought a model of Apollo and Daphne (**219**) which I have got a cast of – he asks for your futhur instructions since which I have found a paper with two drawings of vases and some references for modelling' (Wedgwood MSS E5/30858, Swift to Wedgwood, 21 March 1769). Between July 1769 and February 1771 he also received payments totalling £104 9s 7d for models prepared for the Chelsea-Derby factory (**228**).

From the evidence of Bacon's trade card, *c*1764–6 (BM Banks Coll, 106.2) he also worked for **Daniel Pincot**, the artificial stone manufacturer of Paternoster Row, Spitalfields, but it was with Pincot's remarkable successor, **Eleanor Coade**, that Bacon found extensive employment. Bacon appears to have begun working for Coade in Lambeth shortly after she opened her business in 1769. In September 1771 *The Daily Advertiser* announced that Coade's manufactory was now superintended by Bacon, a sculptor 'whose merit as an artist' was 'too well known to need any encomiums' (*Kelly* 1990, 40). His early models for the manufacturers were direct copies, executed with notable confidence. He used classical sources for *Antonia with urn* (**218**) and French rococo elements for *Apollo and Daphne*, both for Wedgwood, and was to work intermittently for manufacturers throughout his later career. Bacon clearly also had loftier ambitions for on 24 June 1769 he enrolled as a student at the Royal Academy Schools.

He won the first gold medal given by the RA for sculpture in 1769 with a relief, *Aeneas and his family escaping from Troy* (**217**). This was purchased by the architect, Sir William Chambers, but later copied by Bacon for other clients. In 1770 Bacon was elected an ARA, and in 1771 he exhibited a life-size statue of *Mars* with the Society of Arts (**127**), which he later presented to that Society. This figure apparently drew an exclamation from the painter, Benjamin West: 'If this is his first essay, what will this man be when he arrives at maturity?' (*Cunningham* 3, 203). The *Mars* also impressed William Markham, Archbishop of York, who commissioned a bust of George III from Bacon for Christ Church College, Oxford (**158**). It is not clear where Bacon learnt his skills as a sculptor, but this early work in marble is a remarkably fluent performance. The softness of the modelling, the fine carving of the chains and robes, and the harmony and accessibility of the portrait charmed the royal household, who ordered three replicas. Bacon's biographer, Richard Cecil, later recounted that the King sat for the bust and was impressed by Bacon's courtly manners. He appears to have won the King's favour and to have benefited from his support in many later public competitions.

In June 1774 Bacon took a long lease on a house at 17 Newman Street, rated at £60, which was to be the home and workshop of the Bacon family for two generations. Bacon's practice was becoming increasingly diverse; he was Coade's chief designer, he continued to work for Wedgwood (**133, 139, 221**) and he was employed by Matthew Boulton, who was producing a wide range of ornamental goods in Sheffield plate (**128**).

Bacon was meanwhile developing his practice as a sculptor, carving more busts for Christ Church, Oxford (**159–61**) and exhibiting a marble chimneypiece at the RA in 1775 (**184**). He was also beginning to establish himself as a monumental sculptor. His first Westminster Abbey monument, a bust of the Earl of Halifax, 1772 (**7**), was followed by a portrait-medallion with a muse commemorating the poet Thomas Gray (**8**). His monument to Thomas Guy (**9**), the founder of Guy's Hospital, is one of his outstanding achievements. A tableau recalling the parable of the *Good Samaritan*, with the founder in contemporary dress, raising up a sick, cadaverous man, is placed before a low relief of the hospital's courtyard. Bacon presented a bust of the sick man's head as his diploma work after his belated election as an academician in February 1778 (**167**). The institution had rejected three earlier applications.

The Academy's reservations about Bacon were not shared by the King, whose influence helped Bacon win the commission for the monument in Westminster Abbey to William Pitt, Earl of Chatham, in 1779 (**21**). Chatham was presented in contemporary dress. The work cost over £6,000 and was considered his masterpiece. An anonymous writer in the *European Magazine* felt that it would 'at all times remain a proof of the genius of the artist who produced it' (*Euro Mag*, August 1790, 84). William Cowper, extolled the sculptor's skills in his poem, *The Task*: 'Bacon there / Gives more than female beauty to a stone / And Chatham's eloquence to marble lips'. Horace Walpole noted that a 'numerous crowd of spectators' turned out for its opening in October 1782 (*Anecdotes* 1937, vol 5, 138–9). Whilst working on the Westminster Abbey monument, Bacon was busy on another memorial to Chatham for the Guildhall (**18**). The bustling asymmetry of the Guildhall monument, which depicts Chatham *all'antica*, appealed to contemporary sensibilities and earned Bacon a bonus from his patrons. A later generation of artists disapproved of its 'Baroque confusion' and one critic suggested that the compositional elements appeared to have been poured out of a wagon from the top of the pyramid (*Cunningham* 1829–33, 3, 212).

Bacon's wife died in February 1782 and he married Martha Holland at Marylebone church in October that year. By now he was a much respected sculptor and in 1784 **John Deare**, who occasionally worked for Bacon, called him 'the first man in the kingdom in sculpture' (*Smith* 1828, vol 2, 311). In 1784 the *Morning Chronicle* wrote of the 'beauteous shrine' to Captain Foulis in Woodford (**20**): 'Thus honour'd, who would murmur at their doom? / Who would not die to gain so fair a tomb?' (*Anecdotes* 1937, 139). Bacon's monumental practice was in a process of continual expansion. To increase his output he made modifications to the pointing machine, used to transfer dimensions from the model to the block. By the 1790s he employed about twenty assistants and the premises at Newman Street were expanded to incorporate more workshops linking them to the road and so improving accessibility for transport.

Robert Cecil, the Methodist minister at St John's chapel, Bedford Row and a personal friend of the sculptor, later claimed that Bacon saw sculpture as a means to encourage Christian morality. The pelican in her piety, an emblem for Christian charity, recurred so often in his work that it was said that Bacon routinely asked clients if the deceased had ever displayed even the slightest tendency to philanthropy, so that he could justify utilising 'our old friend the pelican' (*Cunningham* 1829–33, vol 3, 243). Nevertheless, he also made use of elements from a classical iconography, particularly the grieving woman by a cinerary urn.

In the 1780s Bacon became one of the few sculptors of his time to work in bronze. He installed a furnace in his premises and used new casting techniques, learnt from a founder who had worked under **John Nost III** (Bacon's assistant **Benjamin Grant** later attempted to take the credit for these innovations). Bacon's figures of *Hercules* and *Atlas* for the Radcliffe Library in Oxford (**143**) were followed by an ambitious composition for Somerset House, a statue of King George III with a personification of the River Thames, cast in 1789 (**148**). Bacon's *River god* was taken from a model he had made for Coade *c*1777 (**139**).

Bacon, whose patriotism had an intensity rare among Academicians, was horrified by events in France during the Revolution. He armed and drilled his apprentices in readiness for a French invasion, and chided a preacher at his church for referring to 'equality' in a sermon (*Farington*, 3, 765). This chauvinism helped cement his position as the King's favourite sculptor and other artists grumbled that Bacon made use of his access to the royal family. James Wyatt, the architect, told Farington in 1798 that, when Parliament voted funds for monuments to national heroes in St Paul's Cathedral and Westminster Abbey, Bacon suggested to the King that he might execute them all in a single cut-price contract (*Farington*, 3, 1119). The proposal, which was not implemented, prompted Henry Fuseli, the painter, to retort: 'If Bacon is to do all the stone-work for the Army and Navy, they ought also to give him the contract for hams and pork' (*Cunningham* 1829–33, vol 3, 223). Bacon's son, **John Bacon II**, called Fuseli's slur 'a gratuitous, unqualified falsehood' in *The Builder* (1863, 167–8), but Bacon did enter competition models for all the proposed monuments and his prices were always the lowest (St Paul's Monuments Costs).

His extraordinary success cannot be attributed solely to royal favour. He was willing to bid for any contract and had an unerring ability to find a pleasing and accessible design, a skill that had been developed during his years as a commercial modeller. The statue of Admiral Rodney (**150**) helped to open up an export market for Bacon, who subsequently received numerous commissions for monuments sent to Jamaica (**41, 49, 56, 72, 74, 82, 96, 105, 108, 110, 112**).

Bacon carved the first two monuments erected in St Paul's Cathedral, for the prison reformer, John Howard (**83**), and the great lexicographer, Samuel Johnson, the latter originally intended for Westminster Abbey (**89**). Both are presented in classical draperies, a decision that met a mixed reception. Bacon justified his decision to classicise Johnson's effigy in the *Gentleman's Magazine* in March 1796 (p180) and argued the propriety of classical dress in debates on the garb for **JCF Rossi RA**'s Lord Cornwallis at Academy committee meetings (*Farington*, 2, 369). The extent of work in preparation that year is clear from a letter to Francis Humberston Mackenzie: 'For myself I am buried in a marble Quarry besides two or three considerable works not yet begun Johnson's Howard for St Paul's Ld Heathfields for Buckley near Plymouth; Ld Effingham's for Jamaica belong to the first class Admiral Pocock's for Westm Abbey; Sir J Cust's; Ld Cornwallis for the East India Company. . .' (Bacon/Mackenzie, 12 April 1796).

At the time of his death he was working on further monuments for St Paul's, one to Sir William Jones, which has a fine oriental relief (**117**) and another to Thomas Dundas (**120**). He also designed the large and ambitious relief for the pediment of East India House, with a resolute King George III, garbed *all'antica*, commanding a pyramidal throng of figures representing the commerce of East and West (**206**). These works and numerous others were completed by the sculptor's sons, John Bacon II and **Thomas Bacon**, who gradually took over the workshop during their father's later years. Bacon's obituary in the *Gentleman's Magazine* related that the sons had 'almost entirely modelled and finished. . . every capital performance' since 1792 (*GM* 1799, vol 69, pt 2, 810).

Bacon died at Newman Street of an 'inflammation in the bowels' on 7 August 1799. Farington recorded his death, noting that Benjamin West 'expressed his sorrow for the loss of Mr Bacon' and adjourned an RA committee. West, Farington, **Joseph Wilton** and others 'sat together abt an hour & then separated' (*Farington*, 4, 1264).

He left £17,000 and considerable property to be divided among his wife and eight surviving children, but he gave his youngest son by his first marriage, John Bacon II, the opportunity to take over the house and workshops in Newman Street. He left a bequest to the Eclectic Society, a non-conformist group, and 12 guineas for the purchase of a teapot by which they could remember him. Bacon was a committed Methodist and numerous contemporaries testified to his piety. He was buried next to his first wife at Whitefield's Tabernacle, Tottenham Court, under a slab with an epitaph composed by himself: 'What I was as an artist seemed of some importance while I lived; what I really was as a believer in Jesus Christ is the only thing of importance to me now'. The church was destroyed in the Second World War, but a drawing of the monument survives (VAM E.1047-8).

Bacon's lengthy obituary in the *Gentleman's Magazine*, written by Robert Cecil, describes his attractive appearance and personality, but also indicates that he was dogmatic in articulating his Christian beliefs: 'In communicating his ideas he was sometimes forcible and happy, but frequently circuitous and obscure. Religion was with him, his grand concern' (*GM*, 1799, 810). Cecil expanded his account of the sculptor into a *Memoir*, which told the reader more about Bacon's activities as a pillar of the church than about his professional career.

A profile of the sculptor published in 1790 in the *European Magazine* described Bacon as a truly national artist, who had acquired his reputation without studying abroad, a stirring exemplar of home-matured talent. Later critics contrasted his work unfavourably with the international neoclassicism of Wilton, Banks and their heirs. Flaxman, in his *Address on the Death of Thomas Banks*, wrote that he showed 'much ingenuity' but was 'void of greatness and simplicity' (*Farington*, 5, 2511). In his life of Bacon, **Allan Cunningham** disparagingly contrasted the sculptor's background in the manufacturing industry, his appeal to the 'grosser faculties of the people at large' and his limited powers of invention, with the achievement of Banks, the progressive neoclassicist who attracted august patrons. Cunningham also tore the veil from Bacon's Christian stance, drawing attention to his grasping approach to business. Peter Cunningham later expressed remorse at the harsh judgment meted out by his father and declared that Bacon was 'one of the greatest sculptors England has produced' (*Builder* 1863, 168).

Bacon was one of the most influential British modellers and sculptors of his time. His works were among the effects of Robert Adam, **John Cheere** and **Joseph Rose Jnr**. He trained the celebrated sculptor **Anne Seymour Damer**, employed **Joseph Theakston** and John Deare, and exerted a formative influence on **E H Baily**. He also trained or employed a host of minor monumental sculptors including **George Napper, John Osborne** and **John Spiller**. Bacon's ability to turn out large numbers of well-carved but repetitive monuments made him a precursor of the mass-producing 'New Road' workshops of the 19th century. Among these was the practice set up by his son John with **Samuel Manning**, whose brother **Charles Manning** had been Bacon's pupil. Bacon's designs for the manufacturers provided an eclectic range of sophisticated styles and subjects for consumption by a mass-market. His work in this field was continued by his pupil **Henry Webber**.

MGS

Literary References: *GM*, Jan 1790, 3–4; *Euro Mag* 1790, 83–4; *Univ Mag.* 1800, pt 2, 184; *Farington, passim*; *GM* 69, 2, 1799, 808–10; *Cecil* 1801; *New Mont Mag*, 5, Jan-June 1816, 37; *Cunningham* 1829–33, vol 3, 200–46; *Builder* 1863, 167–8; *Graves* 1907, 18; *Anecdotes* 1937, 5, 138–9, 144; *Cox-Johnson* 1961, *passim*; *Cox-Johnson* 1962, 705–9; *Hutchison* 1960–62, 133; *Gunnis* 1968, 24–28; *Clifford* 1985, 288–304; *Goodison* 1985, 241–242; *Tattersall* 1985, 36–42; *Whinney* 1988, *passim*; *Kelly* 1990, *passim*; *Dawson* 1999, 30; *Ward-Jackson* 2003, *passim*, but esp 447–8

Archival References: Letters from Bacon to his wife and son, 1790s, private coll (*Cox-Johnson* 1961, 26–7); miscellaneous letters and family memoirs transcribed in *Cecil* 1801; RA Council Minutes, vol 1, 1770, fol 85; Bacon / Boulton; Bacon /RSA (*Cox-Johnson* 1962, 705–9); Bacon /Tracy; Bacon / Long; Bacon / Howard; Bacon / Mackenzie; Wedgwood-Bacon Receipt; *Press Cuttings* 1723–1800, c.fol 107; St Paul's Monuments Costs (transcribed in *Whinney* 1988, 470 n13); IGI

Will: PROB 11/1328 p171

Collections of Drawings: Sheet of designs for pedestals, pencil on paper, c1775, priv coll, reproduced in *Clifford* 1985, 296; 19 designs for monuments, VAM E1531-1931, E1539-1556-1931

Miscellaneous Drawings: Designs for unidentified funerary monuments, HMI 15/1991 (*Friedman* 1993, 91, cat no 15, repr); study for a wine-cooler, pencil and wash, RA; unsuccessful competition design for the monument to Captain James Montagu, St Paul's Cathedral (competition won by John Flaxman), BM PDL 1878, 0713.1248-50 and for the relief 1934, 0320.1; portrait of the artist's wife in profile, BM PDL 1943, 1102.3; design for an unidentified monument, BM PDL 1878, 0713.1777; design for an unidentified monument, Chicago AI; pencil drawing of son, John Bacon II, VAM E.410-1943, 'Uncle Thomas' E.403-1943, 'Aunt Raybould' E.404-1943, 'Aunt Nancy' E.408-1943 and an unidentified sitter E.407-1943

Portraits of the Sculptor: William Bate, after Mason Chamberlin, 1785, enamel on copper, NPG 6289; John Russell, c1792, crayon, VAM 94.D.35 (*Clifford* 1990, 231, repr and *Cox-Johnson* 1961, 18, 24 repr), engraving after this work NPG D12044; George Dance, drawing, RA, engravings after this work NPG D12044 and D12140; Henry Singleton, *The Royal Academicians under the Presidentship of Benjamin West*, oil on canvas, 1793–5, RA; John Bacon II, bust, 1798, exhib RA (*Smith* 1828, vol 2, 165; *Graves* 1905–6, 88); self-portrait (?), BM PDL 1943, 1102.2

Representation of the Sculptor's Premises: Plan of the house and workshops of 17 Newman Street, London County Council MS E/BN/44 (*Cox-Johnson* 1961, 24–5 pl 2)

Funerary Monuments

1.	†1756	Robert, Lord Hewytt, Lord Chancellor of Ireland		Sawbridgeworth, Herts	S	
2.	†1767	Mary Mason (designed by James Stuart)		Bristol Cathedral		*Mason* 1811, 1, 141; *Cox-Johnson* 1961, 42 fn12
3.	†1769	Thomas Langton Freke Drawing(s): private coll	p	Kings Sutton, Northants		Pevsner, *Northants*, 1973, 279; *CIIA* 4/3/92–5 (repr)
4.	c1770	Joseph Withers		St Swithun, Worcester, Worcs	S	Pevsner, *Worcs*, 1968, 3211 C Lib (repr)
5.	c1770	Mrs Withers		[St Mary, Worcester]; untraced		*New Mont Mag*, 5, 1816, 36
6.	post-1771	Robert, Lord Viscount Jocelyn (†1756)		Sawbridge, Herts	S	Pevsner, *Herts*, 1977, 335
7.	1772	George, 2nd Earl of Halifax (†1771)		Westminster Abbey, London, north transept	SD	*Cox-Johnson* 1961, 15; *MacMichael* 1977, 85–86; C Lib (repr)
8.	post-1777	Thomas Gray (†1771) Drawing(s): VAM E.1529-1931		Westminster Abbey, London, south transept	S	*Mason* 1811, 1, 137; *Cox-Johnson* 1961, 15; *MacMichael* 1977, 94; C Lib (repr)
9.	1779	Thomas Guy (†1724) Payment(s): £1,760 10s Model(s): RA, London		Guy's Hospital, Southwark, London	SD	*Cox-Johnson* 1961, 13 (repr 5); *Penny* 1977 (1), 141–2 (repr); *Whinney* 1988, 304–5 (repr); *Cavanagh* forthcoming 2007 (Southwark, Dulwich to Walworth)
10.	1780	Elizabeth Draper (†1778) Drawing(s): RA, London, Jupp coll		Bristol Cathedral	SD	*Graves* I, 1905–6, 88; *Cox-Johnson* 1961, 16 (repr IV); *Whinney* 1988, 308

11.	1780	James Harris (†1780) Drawing(s): VAM E.1530-1931		Salisbury Cathedral, Wilts	S	Pevsner, *Wilts*, 1975, 415
12.	†1780	John and Frances Johnson (†1776)		Leicester Cathedral	S	Pevsner, *Leics & Rutland*, 1984, 209
13.	1780	Robert, 4th Earl of Holdernesse (†1778)		Hornby, N R Yorks	S	Pevsner, *Yorks: N R*, 1966, 192; C Lib (repr)
14.	1780	Urn commemorating Lord Chatham		[Burton Pynsent, Somerset]; Chevening Park, Kent, the park		*GM* 1799, 809; *Cox-Johnson* 1961, 26; Pevsner, *Kent: W & Weald*, 1976, 213
15.	1781	James Marwood (†1767) Drawing(s): VAM E.1533-1931		Widworthy, Devon	S	*Penny* 1977 (1), 219 n3; C Lib (repr)
16.	†1781	John Leman		Warboys, Hunts		Pevsner, *Beds, Hunts & Peterborough*, 1968, 363
17.	†1781	Lady Miller		Bath Abbey, Somerset	S	*GM* 1799, 809; Pevsner, *Somerset: N & Bristol*, 1958, 103; C Lib (repr)
18.	1778–1782	William Pitt, Earl of Chatham Payment(s): £3,421 14s Drawing(s): BM PDL 1886, 0111.33-4		CL Coll, Guildhall, City of London, great hall, acc 42	SD	*Cox-Johnson* 1961, 26; *Knight* 1986, 329 (repr); *Ward-Jackson* 2002, 378–85
19.	†1782	William, Earl Talbot		Sutton, Surrey	S	C Lib (repr)
20.	1783	Captain Charles Foulis and his wife		St Mary the Virgin, Woodford, Essex		*Anecdotes* 1937, 139; Pevsner, *Essex*, 1965, 432
21.	1779–1783	William Pitt, Earl of Chatham (†1778) Payment(s): £6,085 8s 6d Model(s): Plaster model, Somerley, Hants, gallery; model for a figure of The Thames (statuette), t-c painted black, Sotheby, London, 4 July, 1996, lot 79		Westminster Abbey, London, north transept	S	*Euro Mag*, 1790, 84; *Cox-Johnson* 1961, 24–5; *Whinney* 1988, 306–7 (repr)
22.	1784	Charles Roe (†1781)		Christ Church, Macclesfield, Cheshire	S	*GM* 1796, 181–2; *Penny* 1977 (1), 174–5 (repr); *Carr* 1990, 32 (repr)
23.	1784	Figure for a monument	m	[Exhib RA, London, 506]; untraced		*Graves* I, 1905–6, 88
24.	†1784	John Broadley		Eastry, Kent	S	*Gunnis* 1968, 27
25.	†1784	John Dorrien Drawing(s): VAM E.1528-1931, pencil and wash		Berkhamstead, Herts		Pevsner, *Herts*, 1977, 97
26.	†1784	Jonas Langford Brooke		Rostherne, Cheshire	S	Pevsner, *Cheshire*, 1971, 324; C Lib (repr)
27.	1784	Major Francis Pierson (†1781) Payment(s): 300 gns Drawing(s): RA (*Cox-Johnson* 1961, repr 8)		Jersey, St Helier	SD	*Cox-Johnson* 1961, 33
28.	1785	John Bentley Ashley (†1761) and Jane Ashley (†1784)		Ashby St Ledgers, Northants	SD	Pevsner, *Northants*, 1973, 90; *CIIA* 4/3/3–7 (repr)
29.	1785	Liberality and Genius, figures for a monument	m	[Exhib RA, London, 510]; untraced		*Graves* I, 1905–6, 88
30.	1786	Dr Jeremiah (†1784) and Edith Milles (†1761)		St Edmund the King, Lombard St, City of London		*GM* 1786, vol 56, 1, 480; Pevsner, *London: City*, 1997, 218
31.	†1786	Joseph Hague		[Glossop, Derbys]; St Matthew, Hayfield, Derbys		Pevsner, *Derbys*, 1978, 241
32.	†1787	General Augustin Prevost		St Mary, East Barnet, Herts, churchyard		*GM* 1787, vol 57, 2, 660; *Cox-Johnson* 1961, 33; Pevsner, *London: N*, 1998, 114
33.	1787	Matthew Ridley (†1778)		Newcastle Cathedral	SD	Pevsner, *Northumbs* 1992, 422; C Lib (repr)
34.	†1787	Robert Dundas of Arnistoun		Borthwick, Midlothian		*Pearson* 1991, 14
35.	1788	'A Monument in Marble'		[Exhib RA, London, 494]; untraced		*Graves* I, 1905–6, 88
36.	1788	James Dennis, Baron Tracton (†1782)		St Nicholas, Cork	SD	*Cox-Johnson* 1961, 45; *Gunnis* 1963, 1175 (repr); *Potterton* 1975, 35
37.	†1788	Samuel Martin Drawing(s): VAM E.1532-1931		Canford Magna, Dorset	S	*Cox-Johnson* 1961, 40; Pevsner, *Dorset*, 1972, 126; C Lib (repr)
38.	†1788	Savile Finch		Thrybeurgh, W R Yorks	S	Pevsner, *Yorks: WR*, 1967, 517; C Lib (repr)
39.	1788	Viscountess Galway		Brewood, Worcs		*Jeavons* 1959, 72
40.	1789	Henry Sayer		St Paul, Deptford, London		RG/JP, I, 54
41.	1789	John Wolmer (†1729)		St Thomas, Kingston, Jamaica	SD	*Cox-Johnson* 1961, 31; *Lewis* 1965–7, June 1966, 196–8 (repr); *Coutu* 1998, 50, n.31
42.	1789	Sir Waldon Hanmer Bt		St Thomas & St Nicholas, Simpson, Bucks	S	Pevsner, *Bucks*, 1994, 549; C Lib (repr)
43.	†1790	Elizabeth Strode		Warboys, Hunts		*Penny* 1977 (1), 219 n3
44.	1790	William Jackson (†1789)		St Mildred, Canterbury, Kent	SD	Pevsner, *Kent: NE & E*, 1983, 243
45.	1791	Ann Allardyce (†1787)		West Church, Aberdeen	SD	*Pearson* 1991, 15; *Whinney* 1988, 308
46.	1791	Ann Whytell (†1788) Drawing(s): VAM E.1548-1931		Westminster Abbey, London, nave	SD	*Physick* 1969, 154–55 (repr); *Whinney* 1988, 311–2 (repr)
47.	?1791	Colonel Francis Robertson		Grosvenor Chapel, South Audley St, London		RG/JP, I, 55
48.	1791	Figure of Peace, for a monument		[Exhib RA, London, 524]; untraced		*Graves* I, 1905–6, 88

49.	1791	George McFarquhar (†1786)	St James, Montego Bay, Jamaica	SD	*Lewis* 1965–7, Nov 1966, 370 (repr); *Pearson* 1991, 14
50.	1791	Henrietta Wilkie (†1790)	Canford Magna, Dorset	SD	*Cox-Johnson* 1961, 40; Pevsner, *Dorset*, 1972, 126
51.	?1791	Jacob Forbes	Great Stanmore, Middx		*Gunnis* 1968, 27
52.	1791	John Dalton Drawing(s): RA, Jupp Catalogue	Great Stanmore, Middx	SD	*Cox-Johnson* 1961, 32, 39; Pevsner, *London: N W*, 1991, 291; C Lib (repr)
53.	1791	Thomas Wyld (†1789)	Speen, Berks	SD	*Whinney* 1988, 311; C Lib (repr)
54.	†1791	Walter Beatty	United Reformed Church, Newport Pagnell, Bucks		Pevsner, *Bucks*, 1994, 576
55.	1792	Admiral Samuel Graves (†1787)	Buckerell, Devon	SD	Pevsner, *Devon*, 1989, 221; C Lib (repr)
56.	1792	Dr Fortunatus Dwarris (†1790) and his niece, Anne Neufville (†1782) Drawing(s): VAM E.1570-1931	Kingston, Jamaica	SD	*Cox-Johnson* 1961, 31; *Lewis* 1965–7, July 1966, 234–5 (repr)
57.	1792	Mr Justice Willes (†1787)	Burnham, Bucks	SD	*Cox-Johnson* 1961, 31; Pevsner, *Bucks*, 1994, 205; C Lib (repr)
58.	1792	Samuel Egerton (†1780) and family	Rostherne, Cheshire	SD	*Whinney* 1988, 309–10 (repr)
59.	1792	Sir Richard Brooke, 4th Bt	Runcorn, Cheshire	S	Pevsner, *Cheshire*, 1971, 324
60.	1793	Brigadier-General Henry Hope (†1789)	Westminster Abbey, London, north transept	SD	*Cox-Johnson* 1961, 39; *Whinney* 1988, 311; *Headley* 1994, 255 (repr)
61.	1793	Ethelred Anne Cust (†1788)	Belton, near Grantham, Lincs	SD	Pevsner, *Lincs*, 1989, 135
62.	†1793	Fysh de Burgh	St Martin, West Drayton, Middx		Pevsner, *London: NW*, 1991, 367
63.	*c*1793	John Milton Drawing(s): private coll (C Lib repr)	St Giles, Cripplegate, City of London		Pevsner, *London I: City*, 1997, 220
64.	†1793	Lady Dynevor	Llandeilo, Carmarthen		*Dale-Jones and Lloyd* 1989, 42, 46
65.	1793	Lancelot Brown (†1783)	Fenstanton, Hunts		Pevsner, *Beds, Hunts & Peterborough*, 1968, 245
66.	†1793	Lucy Metcalfe	Hawstead, Suffolk	SD	Pevsner, *Suffolk*, 1974, 256; C Lib (repr)
67.	†1793	Sarah Winford	Astley, Worcs		Pevsner, *Worcs*, 1968, 73
68.	1793	Sir Thomas (†1791) and Anwaer (†1799) Rimbold	St Andrew & St Mary, Watton-at-Stone, Herts		Pevsner, *Herts*, 1977, 392
69.	†1794	Captain John Harvey	Eastry, Kent	S	WAM; Pevsner, *Kent: NE & E*, 1983, 308; C Lib (repr)
70.	1794	John Morton, Chief Justice of Chester (†1780)	Tackley, Oxon	S	Pevsner, *Oxon*, 1974, 803
71.	1794	Lieutenant-Colonel John Nugent (†1792)	Mumbai (Bombay) Cathedral, India	SD	
72.	1794	Malcolm (†1781) and Eleanor Laing (†1747)	St Thomas, Kingston, Jamaica	SD	*Cox-Johnson* 1961, 31; *Lewis* 1965–7, June 1966, 199–200 (repr)
73.	1794	Rev John Jones	Mullaghbrack, Co Armagh		*Potterton* 1975, 35; C Lib (repr)
74.	1794	Rosa Palmer (†1790)	St James, Montego Bay, Jamaica	SD	*Cox-Johnson* 1961, 31; *Lewis* 1965–7, Nov 1966, 372–3; *Coutu* 1997, 82–3 (repr)
75.	1794	Samuel Thorpe	St Katharine Cree, City of London		*Cox-Johnson* 1961, 39–40; Pevsner, *London: City*, 1997, 229
76.	†1794	Sarah Smith	Godstone, Surrey		Pevsner, *Surrey*, 1971, 260
77.	†1794	Sir Francis Henry Drake	Buckland Monachorum, Devon		Pevsner, *Devon*, 1989, 233
78.	1794	William (†1765) and Elizabeth Peere-Williams (†1792)	Ottery St Mary, Devon	SD	Pevsner, *Devon*, 1989, 621; C Lib (repr)
79.	1794	William Naper (†1791)	Sherborne, Glos	SD	*CIIA* 4/4/81–2 (repr); Pevsner, *Glos: Cotswolds*, 1999, 602
80.	†1795	Arthur Blayney	Tregynon, Montgomery	S	Pevsner, *Powys*, 1979, 200 (repr)
81.	1795	Catherine Vernon (†1794)	Bristol Cathedral	SD	C Lib (repr)
82.	1795	E Prince	Port Antonio, Jamaica, WI		C Lib (repr)
83.	1791–1795	John Howard (†1790), statue with a relief of Howard attending to a prisoner Payment(s): 1,800 gns earmarked for monument with two figures; 1,300 gns paid	St Paul's Cathedral, London, crossing	SD	*GM*, 1796, 178–80 (repr); *Penny* 1977 (1), 143–5 (repr); *Saunders* 2001, 128–31 (repr)
84.	1795	Mary Marow, Lady Eardley (†1794)	Berkswell, Warks	SD	Pevsner, *Warks*, 1966, 91 (repr); *Whinney* 1988, 308
85.	1795	Rev John Hickson (†1794)	North Mimms, Herts	SD	Pevsner, *Herts*, 1977, 263
86.	1795	Thomas Lane	St John the Baptist, Hillingdon, Middx	SD	Pevsner, *London: N W*, 1991, 335; C Lib (repr)
87.	1795–1796	Admiral Lord Heathfield	Buckland Monachorum, Devon		*GM* 1799, 809; Pevsner, *Devon*, 1989, 233
88.	1796	Admiral Sir George Pocock KB (†1792) Drawing(s): VAM E.1534-1931 (*Bilbey* 2002, 45) Model(s): poss F J B Watson (1969), SD	Westminster Abbey, London, Chapel of St John the Evangelist	S	*Cox-Johnson* 1961, 39; *Physick* 1969, 158–60 (repr)
89.	1791–1796	Dr Samuel Johnson (†1784) Payment(s): Price fixed at £600; Bacon was eventually paid £927 13s 6d	St Paul's Cathedral, London, crossing	SD	*GM*, Jan 1790, 304; *Saunders* 1985, 632–6 (repr); *Whinney* 1988, 308 (repr); *Saunders* 2001, 130–1 (repr)
90.	1796	Faith supporting Hope, figures for a monument	[Exhib RA, London, 784]; untraced		*Graves* I, 1905–6, 88
91.	1796	Frances Elizabeth Aust (†1794)	St Mary, Paddington Green, London	SD	Pevsner, *London: N W*, 1991, 676; C Lib (repr)
92.	1794–1796	George, Lord Waldegrave (†1794)	Eton College, Windsor, Berks, chapel	S	*Cox-Johnson* 1961, 29 (repr 3); *Whinney* 1988, 313

No.	Date	Subject		Location		Literature
93.	1796	Rev William Romaine		[St Andrew-by-the-Wardrobe, City of London]; destroyed		*Cox-Johnson* 1961, 40; Pevsner, *London I*, 1973, 146
94.	1796	Sir Richard Brooke, 5th Bt		Runcorn, Cheshire		Pevsner, *Cheshire*, 1971, 325
95.	1796	Soame Jenyns (†1787)		Bottisham, Cambs	SD	Pevsner, *Cambs*, 1970, 305
96.	1796	Thomas, 4th Earl and Catherine, Countess of Effingham (both †1791) Payment(s): £1,000 (setting up by John Welsh: £345)		Spanish Town Cathedral, Jamaica	SD	*Cox-Johnson* 1961, 32; *Lewis* 1965–67, April 1966, 129–31 (repr)
97.	1797	Captain Josias (†1795), Lieutenant James and Lieutenant Josias Rogers Drawing(s): VAM E.1547-1931		St Thomas, Lymington, Hants	SD	Pevsner, *Hants & Isle of Wight*, 1967, 325; *Physick* 1968, 156–7 (repr)
98.	†1797	Hon and Rev William Cadogan		St Giles, Reading, Berks		*Gunnis* 1968, 28
99.	?1797	Joseph Bushnan		Ridge, Herts		*Gunnis* 1968, 28
100.	†1797	Rev Joseph Milner [completed by John Bacon II]		Holy Trinity, Hull, E R Yorks		*GM* 1799, 810; Pevsner, *Yorks: E R & York*, 1995, 508
101.	1797	Rev William Romaine, AM (†1795) Drawing(s): VAM E.1535-1931		[St Ann, Blackfriars]; untraced		C Lib (repr)
102.	†1797	Robert Austen		Shalford, Surrey		Pevsner, *Surrey*, 1971, 452
103.	1796–1797	Sir John (†1734) and Lady Cust (†1779) Payment(s): £510 Drawing(s): VAM D.130-1890		St George, Stamford, Lincs	SD	*Ashmolean* 1967, 10, cat 57; Pevsner, *Lincs*, 1989, 101, 690 (repr)
104.	1795–1797	Sir John Fenn		[Exhib RA, London, 1795, 1095]; Finningham, Suffolk		*Graves* I, 1905–6, 88; Pevsner, *Suffolk*, 1974, 213
105.	1798	Anne Williamson (†1794)		Spanish Town Cathedral, Jamaica	SD	*Cox-Johnson* 1961, 32; *Lewis* 1965–7, May 1966, 158–9 (repr)
106.	1798	Joseph Yorke, Lord Dover (†1792), and Lady Dover (†1793)		Wimpole, Cambs	SD	Pevsner, *Cambs*, 1970, 493; C Lib (repr)
107.	†1798	Peter Downes		Pott Shrigley, Cheshire		Pevsner, *Cheshire*, 1971, 314
108.	1798	Richard Batty (†1796)		Spanish Town Cathedral, Jamaica	SD	*Lewis* 1965–7, March 1966, 77 (repr)
109.	1799	Catherine Willett (†1798) Drawing(s): VAM E.1538-1931		Canford Magna, Dorset	SD	*Cox-Johnson* 1961, 40; Pevsner, *Dorset*, 1972, 126; C Lib (repr)
110.	1799	Francis Rigby Brodbelt (†1795)		Spanish Town Cathedral, Jamaica	SD	*Lewis* 1965–67, May 1966, 164–5 (repr); *Cox-Johnson* 1961, 32
111.	†1799	Gregory Way		Great Yeldham, Essex		Pevsner, *Essex*, 1965, 214
112.	?1799	Mary Carr (†1798)		Kingston Cathedral, Jamaica	SD	*Gunnis* 1968, 28; C Lib (repr)
113.	1799	Rev Ralph Drake Brockman		Newington, Kent	S	Pevsner, *Kent: NE & E*, 1983, 400
114.	1799	Samuel Thomas (†1796)		St Clement, Cornwall	SD	Pevsner, *Cornwall*, 1970, 164; C Lib (repr)
115.	1799	Samuel Whitbread (†1796) [completed by John Bacon II] Payment(s): 1,300 gns		Cardington, Beds	SD	*Cox-Johnson* 1961, 41; *Whinney* 1988, 312–3 (repr)
116.	1799	Sir John Gardiner (†1797)		Tackley, Oxon		Pevsner, *Oxon*, 1974, 803
117.	1799	Sir William Jones (†1794) [completed by John Bacon II]		St Paul's Cathedral, London, crossing	SD	*GM* 1799, 810; *Penny* 1977 (1), 147 (repr)
118.	1799	William Mason (†1797) (co-sculptor: John Bacon II) Drawing(s): VAM E.1529-1931; pen and pencil NPG, London, 2690		Westminster Abbey, London, south transept	SD	*GM* 1799, 810; *Cox-Johnson* 1961, 39; *Physick*, 1969, 162–3 (repr)
119.	1798–1804	Captain John Harvey (†1794) and Captain John Hutt (†1794) (co-sculptor: John Bacon II) Payment(s): £3,150 Drawing(s): Pencil and wash, Sotheby, 25–26th April 1990, lot 445		Westminster Abbey, London, nave	SD	TNA MPD 78 (48), 1 July 1798; *GM* 1799, 810; *Whinney* 1988, 464 n13; C Lib (repr)
120.	1798–1806	Major-General Thomas Dundas (co-sculptor: John Bacon II) Drawing(s): PRO MPD 78,00 with agreement and bond; another for the pedestal, MPD 78,00		St Paul's Cathedral, London	SD	*GM* 1799, 810; *Whinney* 1988, 364, 366 (repr); *Yarrington* 1988, 64, 70–1 (repr 27)
Statues						
121.	1759	Peace, 'figure'		[Soc of A, premium, 10gns]; untraced		RSA *Minutes* 1758–60, seq 1 fol 78; *Dossie* 1782, 438; *Cox-Johnson* 1961, 4
122.	1762	Interview between Coriolanus and Volumnia, model in clay		[Exhib Free Soc, London, 172]; untraced		*Graves* 1907, 18
123.	1768	A Bacchanalian, model		[Exhib Soc of Artists, London, 197]; untraced		*Graves* 1907, 18
124.	post-1769	'Charity Assisting a Poor Boy', a group of two figures modelled 'under the direction of Jonas Hanway' (reproductions in Coadestone)	sa	Marine Society of London		*Coade* 1799, 320 (no 30); *Cox-Johnson* 1961, 8 (pl. 5); *Clifford* 1985, 303; *Kelly* 1990, 42 (repr)
125.	1772	A child, model	tc	[Exhib RA, London, 2]; untraced		*Graves* I, 1905–6, 88
126.	1772	'a Groupe of figures in Artificial Stone for Eleanor Coade' Payment(s): 16 gns		Audley End, Essex, chapel		Essex RO D/D By A 30/2

No.	Date	Work		Location		Literature
127.	1772	Mars, life-size cast Model(s): cast entered for a Soc of A premium, awarded 20 gns		[Soc of A, premium, 20 gns, presented by the sculptor, 1778, companion to 'Venus']; untraced Other versions: Usher Art Gall, Lincoln, made for Lord Yarborough [for Matthew Boulton]; untraced		*Dossie* 1782, 439; *Cox-Johnson* 1962, 706 (repr); *Clifford* 1985, 290; *Whinney* 1988, 304, 464–5 n6; *Lord* 1998, 916 (repr)
128.	1773	'Model and mould of a figure of Urania' Payment(s): £5 10s 6d				*Goodison* 1985, 241–2
129.	1774	The Seasons, four figures (reproductions in Coadestone and Wedgwood) Payment(s): £31 10s		Untraced		*Clifford* 1985, 292–4, 303–4 (repr); *Irwin* 1968, 216 (repr)
130.	1774	Venus, life-size cast	p	[Soc of A, premium, 50 gns, presented by the sculptor as a companion to the cast of Mars]; untraced		*Dossie* 1782, 439; *Cox-Johnson* 1962, 705–9 (repr)
131.	1775	King George III, model	tc	[Exhib RA, London, 6]; untraced		*Graves* I, 1905–6, 88
132.	1775	Minerva		[Exhib RA, London, 9]; untraced		*Graves* I, 1905–6, 88
133.	1775	Venus, model		[Exhib RA, London, 7]; untraced		*Graves* I, 1905–6, 88
134.	1776	Narcissus, life-size cast		[Soc of A, premium, 50 gns]; untraced		RSA, *Transactions*, vol 2, 1784, 127; *AJ* 1848 (repr); *Cox-Johnson* 1962, 70
135.	1777	Bacchus, Apollo, Andromache and Weeping Dacia (reproduced by Wedgwood)		Untraced Other versions: Fitzwilliam, Wedgwood ware Private coll, Wedgwood ware		*Clifford* 1985, 292–4,304 (repr)
136.	1777	'Figure of Thames, Colossal'		[Soc of A, premium, 50 gns]; untraced		*Dossie* 1782, 439; *Cox-Johnson* 1961, 13
137.	1777	Psyche and Hymen, statuettes for candlesticks (reproductions in Coadestone)		untraced		*Coade* 1799, 33 no 101–2; *Clifford* 1985, 291, 293 (repr)
138.	1778	'model of a human figure'		[Soc of A, premium, 50 gns]; untraced		RSA, *Transactions*, vol 2, 1784, 133; *Cox-Johnson* 1962, 707
139.	1777–1779	River god Payment(s): Coadestone figures offered at £105 in 1784 catalogue Drawing(s): 1777–1779, catalogue design (*Whinney* 1988, 303)		Untraced Other versions: Ham House, Surrey Terrace gardens, Richmond, Surrey		Pevsner, *Surrey*, 1971, 296, 440; *Clifford* 1985, 303
140.	pre-1784	A fountain nymph, reclining upon an urn		Untraced Other versions: reproduced in Coadestone		*Coade* 1799, 19, no 24; *Clifford* 1985, 303, 304; *Kelly* 1990, 127–9 (repr)
141.	pre-1784	Contemplation 'as executed for Dr Lettsom, at Grove-hill, Camberwell'		Untraced Other versions: reproduced in Coadestone		*Coade* 1799, 32 (no 34); *Clifford* 1985, 303
142.	pre-1784	'Flora. A study'		Untraced Other versions: reproduced in Coadestone		*Coade* 1799, 29 (no 73); *Clifford* 1985, 303
143.	c1784	Hercules and Atlas with globe	b	Radcliffe Observatory, Oxford		*Cox-Johnson* 1961, 28 (repr 7); Pevsner, *Oxon*, 1974, 272
144.	1784	Sir William Blackstone Payment(s): £539	m	All Souls College, Oxford, Codrington Library		*Cox-Johnson* 1961, 28 (repr 7); *Whinney* 1988, 308–9 (repr)
145.	pre-1784	Urania 'with a glass globe on her head, adapted for a lamp'		Untraced Other versions: reproduced in Coadestone		*Coade* 1799, 26 (no 56); *Clifford* 1985, 303
146.	pre-1784	Vesta 1	sa	Untraced Other versions: reproduced in Coadestone		*Coade* 1799, 27 (no 59); *Clifford* 1985, 303
147.	1786	King Henry VI Payment(s): £700	m	Eton College, Windsor, Berks, upper chapel	S	*Cox-Johnson* 1961, 29; Pevsner, *Bucks*, 1994, 305; C Lib (repr)
148.	1789	King George III and the River Thames Payment(s): £2,000 (PRO AO3/1244) Drawing(s): by GB Cipriani, Royal coll 13248 Model(s): Thames exhib RA, London, 1778, 4	b	Somerset House, London, courtyard		*Builder* 1862, vol 20, 692; *Graves* I, 1905–6, 88; *Esdaile* 1939, 168; *Cox-Johnson* 1961, 14; *Jenkins* 2000–1, 25, 28 (repr)
149.	1787'1789	Statuette figures of 'Vigilance' and 'Patience' for a clock produced by Benjamin Vulliamy	m	[Buckingham House, saloon]; Windsor Castle, Queen's presence chamber	S	*Clifford* 1990, 232, 234 (repr)
150.	1786–1790	Admiral Lord Rodney all'antica, on a pedestal with reliefs of Britannia protecting Jamaica, the Battle of the Saints and Britannia Triumphant Payment(s): approx £2,500	m	Spanish Town, Jamaica	SD	*Cox-Johnson* 1961, 29–30; *Lewis* 1965–7, Dec 1966, 365–71 (repr); *Coutu* 1998, 46–57 (repr)
151.	1791	Charity, with three children	sa	Fishmongers' Hall, City of London		*Kelly* 1990, 133; Pevsner, *London: City*, 1997, 387; C Lib (repr)

No.	Date	Subject	Material	Location		Literature
152.	pre-1795	Four Seasons		Untraced Other versions: reproductions in Derby porcelain		*Clifford* 1995, 296
153.	1793–1796	Marquess Cornwallis (pedestal completed by John Bacon II) Payment(s): £525 Drawing(s): VAM, design for pedestal	m	[East India House, Leadenhall Street, City of London, court room]; Foreign and Commonwealth Office, London		*Cox-Johnson* 1961, 42; *Archer* 1965, 406; Pevsner, *London: Westminster*, 1973, 548; C Lib (repr)
154.	1796–1797	Sir William Jones (co-sculptor: John Bacon II)	m	Kolkata (Calcutta)		Bacon/Mackenzie, 2 Sept 1797; *Gunnis* 1968, 26
155.	1794–1808	King William III, equestrian (cast by John Bacon II)	b	St James's Square, London	SD	*Cox-Johnson* 1961, 41; *Blackwood* 1989, 46–7 (repr)
156.	nd	Two tigers 'modelled. . . from nature, for Sir Francis Bassett at Tehidy-park in Cornwall' (reproductions in Coadestone)	sa	Untraced		*Coade* 1799, 20 (no 28); *Clifford* 1985, 303
Busts						
157.	1773	Unnamed sitter	m	[Exhib RA, London, 3]; untraced		*Graves* I, 1905–6, 88
158.	1774	King George III	m	[Exhib RA, London, 3]; Christ Church, Oxford, hall Other versions: for George III, c1774, marble; Soc Antiq University of Gottingen, Germany, c1774, marble for George, Prince of Wales, marble 1775: Royal Coll, Windsor Castle (RCIN 31610)		*Graves* I, 1905–6, 88; *Webb* 1953 (1), 242; *Whinney* 1988, 304, 465 n8 (repr)
159.	1776	General John Guise Payment(s): £259 7s 1d with busts of Trevor and Robinson	m	Christ Church, Oxford		*GM* 1799, 809; *Cox-Johnson* 1961, 13
160.	1776	Richard Robinson, Bishop of Armagh Payment(s): £259 7s 1d with busts of Trevor and	m	Christ Church, Oxford		*Cox-Johnson* 1961, 13; C Lib (repr)
161.	1776	Guise Richard Trevor, Bishop of Durham Payment(s): £259 7s 1d with busts of Robinson and Guise	m	Christ Church, Oxford		*British Portraits* 1956–7, 102; *Cox-Johnson* 1961, 13; Pevsner, *Oxon*, 1974, 127; C Lib (repr)
162.	1776	Unidentified sitter	m	[Exhib RA, London, 7]; untraced		*Graves* I, 1905–6, 88
163.	1777	Jupiter Tonans		[Exhib RA, London, 7]; untraced		*Graves* I, 1905–6, 88; *Cox-Johnson* 1961, 13
164.	1777	Unidentified gentleman	m	[Exhib RA, London, 8]; untraced		*Graves* I, 1905–6, 88
165.	1777	Unidentified sitter	m	[Exhib RA, London, 9]; untraced		*Graves* I, 1905–6, 88
166.	1778	Samuel Foote		[Exhib RA, London, 5]; untraced		*Graves* I, 1905–6, 88
167.	1778	Sickness (RA diploma work)	m	RA, London	SD	RA Council Minutes, vol 1, Nov 1778, f261; *Radcliffe* 1969, 46 (repr); *Whinney* 1988, 465 n9
168.	c1780	Inigo Jones	m	Carpenters' Hall, City of London		*Gunnis* 1968, 26
169.	c1780	Sir Francis Dashwood		West Wycombe Park, Bucks, mausoleum		*Gunnis* 1968, 26
170.	1785	Dr Jeremiah Milles	m	Soc Antiq, London	SD	*British Portraits* 1956–7, 93; *Whinney* 1988, 313
171.	1788	George III and Queen Charlotte	m	[coll Samuel Whitbread]; Southill, Beds		*Cox-Johnson* 1961, 32–3; C Lib (repr)
172.	1790	Professor Anthony Shepherd	m	Trinity College, Cambridge	SD	*Baker* 1995 (3), 135; C Lib (repr)
173.	1793	John Howard		Shrewsbury Prison, Salop, over archway of lower entrance wing		Pevsner, *Salop*, 1958, 269
174.	1793	Lord John Cavendish		Wentworth Woodhouse, W R Yorks, mausoleum	SD	*Penny* 1977 (1), 62; C Lib (repr)
175.	1793	William, 3rd Duke of Portland	m	[Exhib RA, London, 650]; Wentworth Woodhouse, W R Yorks, mausoleum	SD	*Graves* I, 1905–6, 88; *Penny* 1977 (1), 62
176.	1796	Sir Francis Bacon	m	Raveningham Hall, Norfolk	SD	
177.	1798	Dean Colet	m	St Paul's School, City of London		*Gunnis* 1968, 26
178.	1798	Marquis Cornwallis		[Exhib RA, London, 966]; untraced		*Graves* I, 1905–6, 88
179.	1812	Unidentified subject		Port Eliot, entrance hall	S	
180.	nd	Mr Justice Willis		Stoneleigh Abbey, Warks	S	
181.	nd	Ossian (colossal)	m	Untraced		*Gunnis* 1968, 24
182.	nd	Samuel Johnson (copy of a bust by Nollekens)		[coll of Samuel Whitbread]; Pembroke College, Oxford		*Saunders* 1985, 634; C Lib (repr)
Chimneypieces						
183.	1775	of marble	m	[Exhib RA, London, 8]; untraced		*Graves* I, 1905–6, 88
184.	1776	With figures carrying musical instruments in niches and relief of the 'Aldobrandini Marriage' (designed by James Wyatt) (co-sculptor: James Wyatt)		Burton Constable Hall, E R Yorks, great drawing room		Pevsner, *Yorks: E R & York*, 1995, 376; *Mulcahy* 2006, 26–7 (repr)
185.	1777	'Two muses for a chimneypiece'		[Exhib RA, London, 9]; untraced		*Graves* I, 1905–6, 88
186.	c1786	Two		Admiralty House, Portsmouth, Hants, reception and dining rooms		Pevsner, *Hants & Isle of Wight*, 1967, 413; C Lib (repr)
187.	1787	Description unavailable		[Governor Hornby's new mansion, Portman Square, London]; untraced		*The World*, 11 May 1787
188.	c1787	Description unavailable		[Fonthill Splendens, Wilts]; untraced		Soane, Journal I, 33; *Woodward* 1998, 32

189.	1789	Description unavailable		[Buckingham Palace, London]; Windsor Castle, state apartments	Pevsner, *Berks*, 1966, 290
190.	1793	Description unavailable Payment(s): £63 (£2 17s 6d to install)	m	For Warren Hastings, Daylesford House, Glos	BL Ad MS 29227-31; *Bell* 1938, 91; *Cox-Johnson* 1961, 39; Pevsner, *Glos: Cotswolds*, 1999, 312
191.	nd	'a handsome marble chimneypiece'	m	Pishobury, Herts, drawing room	*Neale* 1819, 2, 34, unpag; C Lib (repr)
192.	nd	Description unavailable	m	[War Office, London]; MOD, London	Pevsner, *London: Westminster*, 1973, 538

Architectural Sculpture

193.	1760	David and Abigail, clay		[Soc of A, premium, 15 gns]; untraced	RSA, *Minutes*, 1748–60, seq 4 f 49; *Dossie* 1782, 438; *Cox-Johnson* 1961, 5
194.	1770	Tympanum model	tc	Skinners' Hall, City of London, principal front (Coadestone)	*Wadmore* 1902, 133; Pevsner, *London: City*, 1997, 403; C Lib (repr)
195.	c1776	Caryatids, and relief of 'The Attempts of Time to Destroy Sculpture and Architecture defeated by the Vitrifying Aid of Fire'		[Eleanor Coade's manufactory, Lambeth, London, façade]; untraced	*Clifford* 1985, 303–4; *Whinney* 1988, 303–4
196.	1778	'Fame' and the 'Genius of England', with the British arms, a festoon of laurel and the insignia of the Order of the Garter Payment(s): £367 10s (Strand front), £307 10s (tritons)	s	Somerset House, Strand front, London	RIBA MS 335 A; *Jenkins* 2000–1, 28; *Cox-Johnson* 1961, 14
197.	1778	Keystone		[Great Arch, Somerset House, London, Embankment front]; untraced	RIBA MS 335A; *Cox-Johnson* 1961, 14
198.	1778	Two Tritons, supporting the British arms, adorned with coral and 'other marine productions' Payment(s): £367 10s	s	Somerset House, London, river front	RIBA MS 335a; *Cox-Johnson* 1961, 14; C Lib (repr)
199.	1777–1779	Allegorical tympanum group: three reliefs of blood-letting and two niche statues of Aesculapius and Hygeia Payment(s): £762	s	Guy's Hospital, Southwark, London, pediment	Pevsner, *London 2: S*, 1983, 581; *Cavanagh* forthcoming 2007 (Southwark, Dulwich to Walworth); C Lib (repr)
200.	1784	Models, designs for pediments Payment(s): £31 10s	tc	Royal Naval Hospital, Greenwich (ORNC)	TNA ADM 68/813, 11 May 1874; *Gunnis* 1968, 27
201.	1785	Two angels Payment(s): £630		Royal Naval Hospital, Greenwich (ORNC), east end of chapel	TNA ADM 68/816; *Gunnis* 1968, 27
202.	1789	Frieze for doorway into chapel Payment(s): £168		Royal Naval Hospital, Greenwich (ORNC)	TNA ADM 68/824; *Gunnis* 1968, 27; Pevsner, *London: City*, 1997, 117
203.	1790–1792	Plaques representing 'Justice and Boy', 'Mercy and Boy', 'Wisdom and Boy' Payment(s): £151 paid to Coade	sa	Shire Hall, Chelmsford, Essex	*Kelly* 1990, 81–2, 172 (repr); Pevsner, *Essex*, 1965, 117
204.	1792–1794	The winds (reliefs)	s	Radcliffe Observatory, Oxford	*Cox-Johnson* 1961, 28; Pevsner, *Oxon*, 1974, 272
205.	1793–1796	King George III and Queen Charlotte (medallions) and panel of the 'Genius of Navigation', and the Corporation arms		Trinity House, Tower Hill, City of London, façade	*Richardson* 1802–8, vol 1, 7 (repr XXIII); *Ward-Jackson* 2002, 890
206.	1797–1799	King George III defending the Commerce of the East (completed by John Bacon II) Payment(s): £2,342 Drawing(s): VAM D.1953-1889		[East India House, London]; Foreign and Commonwealth Office, London	*Physick* 1968, 161 (repr)
207.	nd	Oval medallions and tablets in terracotta and plaster		[Adam sale, 1818, lots 5, 7, 15]; untraced	Adam sale, 1818, 1–2
208.	nd	Reliefs, models (reproductions in Coadestone)		[for Hooton Hall, Cheshire]; untraced	*Gunnis* 1968, 24

Reliefs

209.	1760	David and Abigail, clay		[Soc of A, premium, 10 gns]; untraced	RSA *Minutes*, 1758–60, seq 4 fol 49; *Dossie* 1782, 438
210.	1761	Samson and Delilah, clay		[Soc of A, premium, 15 gns]; untraced	RSA *Minutes*, 1760–61, seq 3 fol 48; *Dossie* 1782, 438; *Cox-Johnson* 1962, 706
211.	1763	Cleopatra, model in alto-relievo		[Exhib Free Soc, London, 3]; untraced	*Graves* 1907, 18
212.	1763	Death of Virginia, clay		[Soc of A, premium, 10 gns]; untraced	RSA *Minutes*, 1762–63, seq 2 fol 64; RSA *Premiums*, 1762, 32
213.	1763	Mark Anthony, model in alto-relievo		[Exhib Free Soc, London, 2]; untraced	*Graves* 1907, 18
214.	1764	Death of Virginia, clay		[Soc of A, premium, 10 gns]; untraced	RSA, *Minutes*, 1762–63, seq fol 64, 69; RSA, *Premiums*, 1762, 32; *Dossie* 1782, 438; *Cox-Johnson* 1962, 706

215.	1764	Mucius Scaevola		[Soc of A, premium, 15 gns]; untraced		*RSA, Minutes*, 1763–64, seq 3 fol 83; RSA *Premiums*, 1763, 37; RSA *Register*, 1778, 31; *Cox-Johnson* 1961, 5
216.	1765	'Cincinnatus 2nd Dictatorship', clay		[Soc of A, premium, 20 gns]; untraced		RSA, *Minutes*, 1764–65, seq 3 fol 61; *Dossie* 1782, 439; RSA *Register* 1778, 31; *Cox-Johnson* 1961, 5
217.	1769	Aeneas and his family escaping from Troy (awarded first RA gold medal for sculpture)	p	[William Chambers's house, 53 Berners Street, London]; R Soc of Med, Marylebone, London Other versions: SJSM VAM W52A-1914) Foundling Hospital, London 5 Heriot Row, Edinburgh on the stairs at the Inchbold School of Design, 7 Eaton Gate, London, staircase		RA Premium list; *Cox-Johnson* 1961, 10–11 (repr 3); *Clifford* 1985, 301; *Sakula* 1988, 172–3; Pevsner, *London: N W*, 1991, 611
218.	1769	Antonia with urn, model	tc	Wedgwood Museum, Barlaston		*Clifford* 1985, 291, 294, 304 (repr)
219.	1769	Apollo and Daphne		Wedgwood Museum, Barlaston (mould) Other versions: reproduced by Wedgwood		Wedgwood/Bacon E5/30858; *Gunnis* 1968, 24–5; *Clifford* 1985, 292–3, 304 (repr)
220.	1769	King George III, medallion		[Exhib RA, London, 1]; untraced		*Graves*, I, 1905–6, 88
221.	c1769	The elements (four oval bas-reliefs)		[Crystal Palace, Sydenham, casts, 1854]; untraced		*Gunnis* 1968, 26
222.	1769	The god of day and the god of night (reproduced by Wedgwood)		Untraced		*Cox-Johnson* 1961, 7; *Clifford* 1985, 294
223.	1770	The good Samaritan		[Exhib RA, London, 1]; untraced		*Graves*, I, 1905–6, 88
224.	1777	'Small heads of the King and Queen' (reproduced by Wedgwood)		Untraced		*Clifford* 1985, 294, 304
225.	1785	Mason Chamberlin RA	m	NPG 2653	SD	NPG cat; C Lib (repr)
Miscellaneous						
226.	pre-1759	Models for Nicholas Crisp's manufactory		[Private coll (family descendants, 1961)]; untraced		*Cox-Johnson* 1961, 4
227.	1769	Bacchanalians, model		[Exhib RA, London, 2]; untraced		*Graves* I, 1905–6, 87; *Cox-Johnson* 1961, 11
228.	1769	Unidentified subjects for Derby porcelain factory Payment(s): £104 9s 7d		Untraced		*Cox-Johnson* 1961, 8; *Clifford* 1985, 295, 304
229.	1773	Design for his own doorplate		[Exhib RA, London, 4]; Bacon family coll		*Graves* I, 1905–6, 88; C Lib (repr)
230.	1779	Admiral Keppel's freedom box (design only) Drawing(s): six designs, pen, ink and wash, VAM, E.248-253-1946		Museum of London, 25142		*Murdoch and Snodin* 1993, 403–410 (reprs); *Cox-Johnson* 1961, 25
231.	1786	Two nymphs holding festoons	m	[Exhib RA, London, 615]; untraced		*Graves* I, 1905–6, 88
232.	1790	'The Woman touching the hem of Christ's garment' and Mr John Newton DD (models only, for engraved gems by Edward Burch)		Untraced		*Clifford* 1985, 300

BACON, John II 1777–1859

Bacon inherited one of the most celebrated sculpture businesses in London and was responsible for numerous commissions during his relatively brief active career. He was born at 17 Newman Street on 13 March 1777, the second son of **John Bacon RA** and Elizabeth, née Wade. He trained in his father's workshop and at the Royal Academy Schools, which he entered on 29 March 1790. In 1815 an article in the *European Magazine* claimed that he had been given a central role in his father's workshop at a young age, executing figures for monuments from the age of eleven (*Euro Mag*, vol 67, Jan-June 1815, 3). A family friend, Richard Cecil, reported that John and his brother, **Thomas Bacon**, modelled and finished almost every major work produced by the studio after 1792 (*GM* 1799, vol 69, pt 2, 810). Given this early practical experience, it is not surprising that young Bacon turned out to be an exceptional RA student, winning a silver medal in 1793 for his 'Model of an Academy figure' (**355**) and a gold medal in 1794, awarded by unanimous vote for his relief of *Adam contemplating Eve sleeping* (**353**; *Farington*, vol 1, 268).

Bacon was responsible for the workshop when his father was away in the late 1790s and, although he was a younger son, his father left him the premises, stock and business at his death in August 1799. That year the young Bacon completed three of his father's major commissions, statues of William Jones in St Paul's Cathedral and William Mason in Westminster Abbey, and a relief for East India House. Over the next nine years Bacon worked on numerous other contracts won by his father and considered many of them to be his own work. He signed the monuments to Thomas Dundas and to the Captains Harvey and Hutt, and was at pains to inform the press that he was responsible for casting the bronze statue to William III in St James's Square after his father's death (*Euro Mag*, vol 54, July 1808, 37).

Bacon well understood his father's business strategies and continued to run the workshop successfully, frequently adapting his father's designs and motifs for new clients. The deathbed scene on Samuel Whitbread's monument, begun by his father and completed by the younger Bacon, was re-utilised in barely modified form for the memorials to Thomas Starkey (**68**), Thomas Tyrwhitt Drake (**158**), Theodora de Fries (**174**) and Sir Egerton Leigh (**244**). Other motifs were also borrowed from his father's repertory, such as the bowed female grieving over an urn or a sarcophagus (**18, 56, 91**), and the 'pelican in its piety' (**17, 96, 132, 286**). Like his father, Bacon adapted designs by **Louis François Roubiliac**, notably the deceased visited by Death in the form of a skeleton (**55, 284**), or emerging from the coffin at the Last Trump (**137**). Following a family tradition, he also made use of delightful naturalistic elements, such as a fire engine in relief on the monument to the founder of the Phoenix Fire Insurance Company (**52**), or an exterior elevation of St Mary de Castro, Leicester, on the monument to a vicar (**185**).

By 1802 Bacon was considered by many to be at the forefront of his profession. Sir Roger Newdigate, writing to Bacon about his wife's monument (**36**), flattered the sculptor by adding that the work 'may be some little addition to the general reputation which your works have deservedly acquired' (*White* 1995, 302–3). In January 1803 Bacon exhibited his statue of Charles, Marquess Cornwallis, before it was shipped to India (**319**). Farington claimed that 400–500 people visited it daily (*Farington*, vol 5, 1967). Despite the popular interest in his work the Royal Academy declined to elect Bacon an Associate in 1802. It became apparent to the sculptor that the Academicians regarded him merely as an adjunct to his father, with no claim to originality. Farington suggested that his work might be reassessed if he showed a bust of a famous academician at the next Academy exhibition, a suggestion Bacon appears not to have pursued (*Farington* vol 5, 1928). Further failed election attempts followed in 1803, 1804, 1806 and 1811, when Bacon failed to attract a single vote.

In 1806 Bacon competed with the overbearing **J C F Rossi RA** for the commission to execute a statue of Marquess Wellesley, Governor-General of India, for Kolkata (Calcutta) (**321**). Rossi considered it demeaning to compete with Bacon, and the architect Robert Smirke felt that Bacon's model, exhibited together with Rossi's at 15 Portland Place, London, 'was in so bad a taste that were it to be executed & put up here it would disgrace the country' (*Farington*, vol 7, 2704). Nevertheless, Bacon won the commission, with the support of Charles Long, later Lord Farnborough, and others. Bacon went on to execute a second statue of Wellesley and of Cornwallis for Bombay (**322, 323**). These prestigious commissions formed part of the workshop's growing market for sculpture in the colonies. A large number of his monuments were shipped to India and the West Indies, most of them standard designs. Occasionally there were concessions to the work's intended context such as 'Indian' figures (**75, 322**), elephants (**142, 223, 322**) and orientalised putti (**162**).

In 1808 Bacon passed the daily running of his workshop to **Charles Manning**, who had worked for his father. An extensive agreement, dated 24 June 1808, allowed Manning to buy one quarter of Bacon's designs, marble and stock, valued at £1,068, and to manage the business full-time in Bacon's name from 17 Newman Street. Bacon himself would 'not be obliged to attend there further or otherwise than as he shall think fit and proper' (*Cox-Johnson* 1959, 239). Three-quarters of the profits were to be returned to Bacon. The partnership continued until Manning's death in 1812. Since Manning was a prize-winning Royal Academy student and a capable sculptor, many of the works signed 'John Bacon' in the years 1808–1812 may well have been Manning's work, perhaps carved without Bacon's supervision.

Bacon continued to compete successfully for major public commissions. In 1810 he won the commission for the monument in St Paul's Cathedral to the hero of Corunna, Sir John Moore (**204**), after which Rossi declared that he was never again going to apply for any competition judged by the Committee of Taste (*Farington* vol 10, 3669). The innovative work, completed after Manning's death, rates as one of the finest early nineteenth-century monuments in the cathedral. A muscular near-naked man and a winged angel lower the lifeless corpse of the hero into his simple sarcophagus, watched by a cherub holding the colours. The composition inverts the familiar conceit of the deceased rising from the tomb and so evokes pity not hope. Bacon later claimed that he had ignored all modifications to the design proposed by the Committee of Taste and, furthermore, that they had failed to notice. **Antonio Canova** praised the work on his visit to London in November 1816. Bacon, thrilled by the visit of the Italian sculptor, insisted on sketching his portrait.

Late in 1812 Bacon completed a statue of George III for the Bank of Ireland (**324**) and again exhibited the work for public scrutiny before it was shipped to its destination. He wrote to the Countess of Normanton in January 1813 that, although he had not been accorded a sitting, he had been flattered that it was a strong likeness. Farington, perhaps reflecting the antipathy of the Royal Academy, curtly refused to go to see the work (*Farington* vol 12, 4304).

In 1815 Bacon held an extensive exhibition of recently completed work and the *European Magazine* produced a flattering account of his career. The journal saluted his independence of patronage in favour of a 'general appeal to the taste and opinion of his country' (*Euro Mag*, vol 67, Jan-June 1815, 3). The article also alluded obliquely to the improper manner in which some of his rivals for public commissions had conducted themselves during competitions, and saluted Bacon for refusing to name his less-successful rivals as he had 'too high a respect for the character and talents of many of the artists who did not chance to succeed against him' (*ibid*, 4).

By 1818 Bacon had gone into business with his former partner's son, **Samuel Manning I**. Manning moved into Newman Street in 1819. No details survive of their partnership agreement but the monument to Christopher Metcalfe, 1820 (**259**), with its familiar relief of a woman mourning over a sarcophagus, was signed 'Bacon inv Manning fec', which suggests that Manning was now in charge of carving works from Bacon's designs. Bacon's well-used vocabulary of motifs continued to be used by the workshop, though modifications appeared occasionally for subjects from a military background, such as a woman grieving over a cannon (**169**), or a soldier over a sarcophagus (**196, 198**). Bacon's design for the monument to Roger Holland and family combined several of the well-tried motifs, including the weeping female, a broken column, a sarcophagus and wilting flowers, to which were added portrait medallions (**296**).

In 1823 Bacon left London with his wife Susannah and his large family of ten children and also moved out of his country house at Bromley in Kent. They went to live at Sidcliffe, near Sidmouth, and later in Winchester. In 1824 he exhibited at the Royal Academy for the last time. Bacon had always been comfortably off; he owned and developed 72 properties in London, had other business interests, and earned a steady income from the workshop. He continued to produce designs from his home in Sidcliffe, but virtually retired from active work, and in the 1830s the workshop ceased production. Samuel Manning remained at Newman Street until his death in 1836 and the premises were taken over for a short time by **E H Baily RA**.

In 1837 Bacon moved again, to Mount Radford, a suburb of Exeter, to be close to his daughter, Christina, who died in 1841. The diarist, Caroline Fox, recorded that Bacon 'after having given up his craft for twenty-five years, resuming it at the request of his dying daughter to make her monument,. . .found himself as much at home with his tools as ever' (*Fox* 1882, vol 2, 94–5). The monument is quite different from the rest of his oeuvre, depicting a recumbent effigy of his daughter, her hands clasped in prayer, within a gothic niche (**312**). The *Ecclesiologist* said of it that 'it is not too much to say that few of the best ages of Christian art surpass it. . . the face (which is said to be a striking likeness) has all the sweetness and composure distinctive of Catholick times.' (*Ecclesiologist* XIV, XV, Oct 1842, 58). It was probably also around this date that Bacon carved the altarpiece for St Lawrence, Exeter (**351**), which Beatrix Cresswell called 'very remarkable, not to say remarkably ugly' (*Cresswell* 1908, 76).

This brief return to his profession appears to have stirred Bacon to letters, and in 1843 he published two essays on sculpture. The first was a transcription of a speech he had given to the Exeter Diocesan Society, in which he expressed his despondency at the way in which modern monumental sculpture had disfigured English churches. For a man whose firm had produced over 300 monuments, this can only have been an expression of penitence. This was followed by *A letter to the Rt Hon Sir Robert Peel*, a reminiscence of Bacon's dealings with the Committee of Taste, which had in his opinion imposed a unifying banality on most of the monuments in St Paul's by its excessive interference. Bacon hoped that the current commission appointed to decorate the Houses of Parliament would avoid this error.

In the 1840s Bacon moved to lodgings at 5 Bath House, Worthing. By coincidence the residence was shared with Peter Cunningham, the son of the elder Bacon's venomous biographer. Cunningham recalled meeting 'a staid, demure, elderly gentleman' (*Builder* 7 March 1863, vol 21, 167), whose opinions he later used when revising his father's account of Bacon's father. In 1847 Bacon began his own *Reminiscences of the late John Bacon Esquire RA and other persons of his time. . .* (1847–50), in which he recalled a father he clearly held in great regard, but found irritable and severe. This is an important source for the life and character of both father and son.

Bacon subsequently moved with his daughter Elizabeth to Bathwick Hill, near Bath, where he died on 14 July 1859. In his will he left £13,000, numerous properties, a large art collection, and models and drawings, both by himself and his father. His death notice in *The Gentleman's Magazine* did not record his profession, but merely that he was 'son of the late John Bacon, R.A., sculptor' (*GM*, Sept 1859, 202, 314).

Bacon's family background was both a blessing and a hindrance. Although his early training rendered him a highly skilled and able sculptor and works such as the Moore and Medley monuments show him to have been capable of exceptional work, his reliance on his father's designs gave the impression that he could not establish a separate identity as a sculptor. His large inheritance allowed him to withdraw from the profession when he became disillusioned by a lack of artistic recognition, and his decision to do so appears to have given him a severe sense of failure, which he recorded in sorry detail in his diaries.

During his lifetime Bacon received public acclaim, the support of many connoisseurs, and had an inexhaustible stream of customers. Nevertheless his fellow sculptors, Rossi, **John Flaxman RA** and **Nathaniel Marchant** all held a low opinion of his work (*Farington, passim*). A century and a half later Rupert Gunnis showed a similar dismissive attitude: he considered Bacon inferior to his father as a sculptor and his monumental workshop productions to be a lamentable blot on the ecclesiastical landscape. The discovery of numerous family documents by Ann Saunders (née Cox-Johnson) in the 1950s has, however, helped to flesh out a career which is more interesting than most of the works it produced. As an illustration of early 19th-century workshop practice, as a vignette of the personal and aesthetic politics of the Royal Academy and as a case study of a privileged and sensitive child failing to cope with his paternal inheritance, John Bacon's story is surely worthy of more attention.

MGS

Literary References: *Farington, passim*; *Bacon II* 1843 (1), 117–26; *Bacon II* 1843 (2); *Cox-Johnson* 1959, 236–242; *Cox-Johnson* 1961; *Gunnis* 1968, 28–31; *Whinney* 1988, 313, 324, 370, 371, 442 n8; *Yarrington* 1988, 67, 119; *White* 1995, 302–3; *Groseclose* 1995, *passim*; *Clifford* 1995, 15–16

Archival References: Bacon/Normanton; Bacon/Hoare; Bacon/Anon; Bacon/MC Wyatt; Bacon family archives, including diaries running from August 1815–October 1824; Bacon reminiscences 1847–50; Bacon property papers (used extensively in *Cox-Johnson* 1959, 236–242, and *Cox-Johnson* 1961); IGI; Ann Saunders typescript (coll the author).

Wills: John Bacon RA, PROB 11/1328, p171; John Bacon II (details Ann Saunders MS).

Collections of Drawings: VAM, designs for unidentified monuments, 8818-1-120; two designs for an unidentified monument, marked 'Sidcliff', watercolour, E.1566-7-1931; design for unidentified monument, after 1828, E.1568-1931; 11 designs for unidentified monuments on 11 sheets, E.1571-1581-1931; designs for unidentified church monuments 8520-9, 8417-2, 8417-4, 8516-2; signed pencil drawings of 'Mr E. Thornton, E.393-1943, and E.400-1943, 'Mrs Blair' E.401-1943, 'Mr Blair' E.402-1943, and 'Patty Bacon' 1793, E.406-1943

Miscellaneous Drawings: portrait of Antonio Canova, pencil, 1815, private coll (*Clifford* 1995, 14, repr)

Portraits of the Sculptor: John Bacon RA, pencil portrait as a boy, VAM E.410-1943; T Blood engr, portrait of Bacon, after an original canvas by John Russell RA for *Euro Mag*, Jan 1815 (*Cox-Johnson* 1959, repr 40); self-portrait, bust (**347**); Charles Manning, bust, exhibited RA 1812, untraced

Funerary Monuments

1.	†1770	Rev George Whitfield (co-sculptor: Bacon workshop) Drawing(s): VAM E.1048-1966	[Whitfield's Tabernacle, Tottenham Court Road, London]; destroyed		
2.	†1780	Sir John Meredith Drawing(s): VAM E.1572-1931	Brecon Cathedral		Pevsner, *Powys*, 1979, 290; C Lib (repr)
3.	†1782	Elizabeth, wife of John Bacon RA (co-sculptor: Bacon workshop) Drawing(s): VAM E.1047, 1049-1966	[Whitfield's Tabernacle, Tottenham Court Road, London]; destroyed		
4.	†1794	Ann Frances Waring Drawing(s): VAM E.1051-1966	[Whitfield's Tabernacle, Tottenham Court Road, London]; destroyed		
5.	c1794	John Thomas, Bishop of Rochester (†1793)	Westminster Abbey, London, nave	S	*MacMichael* 1977, 16
6.	1795	Rachel Tyrwhitt Drake (†1784)	Amersham, Bucks	S	Pevsner, *Bucks*, 1994, 132
7.	†1797	Joseph Milner	Hull, E R Yorks	S	C Lib (repr)
8.	†1798	John and Charlotte (†1797) Mellish (co-sculptor: Samuel Manning I)	Braughing, Herts	S	
9.	1798	John Daintry	Leek, Staffs	S	*Gunnis* 1968, 29; C Lib (repr)
10.	?1799	Rev Ralph Brockman	Newington, Kent		*Gunnis* 1968, 29

11.	1800	Anna Rhodes (†1796) Drawing(s): VAM E.1556-1931	[St James, Hampstead Road, London]; VAM, on loan from London Diocesan Fund)	S	*Graves* I, 1905–6, 88; *Physick* 1969, 178–9; *Busco* 1994, 141 (repr); *Bilbey* 2002, 183 (repr)
12.	1800	Countess of Northampton	Abbots Langley, Herts		Pevsner, *Herts*, 1977, 62
13.	1800	Dr Duncan Anderson (†1796)	St James, Montego Bay, Jamaica	SD	*Graves* I, 1905–6, 88; *Lewis* 1965–7, Nov 1966, 372–4 (repr)
14.	†1800	Frances Andrew	Prestwold, Leics		Pevsner, *Leics and Rutland*, 1984, 349
15.	?1800	Francis Shephard	Ware, Herts		*Gunnis* 1968, 29
16.	†1800	Fysh de Burgh (born Coppinger)	West Drayton, Middx		Pevsner, *London: NW*, 1991, 367
17.	1800	George (†1782) and Anne Gostling (†1799)	St Mary, Twickenham, Middx	S	Pevsner, *London: S*, 1983, 539; C Lib (repr)
18.	†1800	Henry, 5th Lord Middleton and his wife, Dorothy (†1808)	Wollaton, Notts		*Gunnis* 1968, 30; Pevsner, *Notts*, 1979, 274
19.	?1800	Hon George Murray (†1797)	Ockham, Surrey		*Gunnis* 1968, 29
20.	?1800	Joseph Bland	Hatfield, Herts		*Gunnis* 1968, 29
21.	1800	Katherine Kirkpatrick (†1766)	Mumbai (Bombay) Cathedral, India	S	C Lib (repr)
22.	c1800	Lady Mary Archer (†1776)	Theydon Garnon, Essex		*Gunnis* 1968, 29
23.	1800	Nicholas Skottowe (†1798) Drawing(s): VAM E.1536, 1537-1931	Chesham, Bucks	S	Pevsner, *Bucks*, 1994, 238; C Lib (repr)
24.	?1801	Ann Clitherow	[St Laurence, Brentford, Middx]; untraced		*Gunnis* 1968, 29
25.	c1801	Anna Rhodes (†1796) Drawing(s): VAM E.1050-1966	[Whitfield's Tabernacle, Tottenham Court Road, London]; destroyed		*Physick* 1969, 179
26.	†1801	Christopher Barton Metcalfe (co-sculptor: Samuel Manning I)	Hawstead, Suffolk	S	Pevsner, *Suffolk*, 1974, 256
27.	†1801	Elizabeth Tyrwhitt Drake and two infant children Drawing(s): rejected designs, pencil and wash, E1558, 1559-1931	Amersham, Bucks	S	Pevsner, *Bucks*, 1994, 132
28.	†1801	George John Borlase Warren	Stapleford, Notts		Pevsner, *Notts*, 1979, 336
29.	?1801	William Heberden	St John the Baptist, Windsor, Berks		*Gunnis* 1968, 29
30.	†1802	Ann Dorrien	Berkhamsted, Herts	SD	C Lib (repr)
31.	?1802	Barbara Barron	Shepperton, Middx		*Gunnis* 1968, 29
32.	post-1802	Charles Parker (†1795) Drawing(s): VAM E.1563-1931	Harefield, Middx	S	*Graves* I, 1905–6, 88; Pevsner, *London: N W*, 1991, 317; C Lib (repr)
33.	1802	Harriet Winford (†1801)	Astley, Worcs	S	*Graves* I, 1905–6, 88; Pevsner, *Worcs*, 1968, 73; C Lib (repr)
34.	?1802	John Rice	Tooting, Surrey		*Gunnis* 1968, 29
35.	†1802	John Thomas Hughes	St James, Montego Bay, Jamaica	S	*Lewis* 1965–7, Nov 1966, 369 (repr)
36.	1802	Lady Hester Newdigate (†1800)	Harefield, Middx	S	Pevsner, *London: N W*, 1991, 318; *White* 1995, 302–3; C Lib (repr)
37.	†1802	Margaret Bearsley	St Mary Aldermary, City of London		Pevsner, *London* I, 1973, 169
38.	†1802	Mrs Warren	Stratton Audley, Oxon		Pevsner, *Oxon*, 1974, 795
39.	1802	Richard, Baron Rokeby (†1794)	Armagh Cathedral	SD	*Potterton* 1975, 35; C Lib (repr)
40.	?1802	Thomas Bayley	Eccles, Cheshire		*Gunnis* 1968, 29
41.	†1802	Thomas Cookes	St Peter, Carmarthen	S	*Dale-Jones and Lloyd* 1989, 46
42.	1802	William Tyrwhitt Drake (†1796)	Amersham, Bucks	SD	Pevsner, *Bucks*, 1994, 132; C Lib (repr)
43.	?1803	Captain John Garvey	Trinity, Palmetto, St Kitts, churchyard	SD	*Gunnis* 1968, 29
44.	†1803	Daniel Seton Model(s): relief of Britannia attended by Peace and Plenty, SJSM	Mumbai (Bombay) Cathedral, India		*Dorey* 2004, 61; C Lib (repr)
45.	?1803	John Archer	Welford, Berks		*Gunnis* 1968, 30
46.	?1803	John Harwood	Deane, Hants		*Gunnis* 1968, 30
47.	?1803	John Newman	Sudbury, Derbys		*Gunnis* 1968, 29
48.	1803	Laetitia Austin (†1801)	Barbados Cathedral, Bridgetown	SD	*Perowne* 1951, 1942 (repr); *Gunnis* 1968, 29; C Lib (repr)
49.	1803	Lieutenant John (†1791) and Lieutenant Richard (†1799) Forbes	Westminster Abbey, London, Chapel of St Andrew		*MacMichael* 1977, 53–4
50.	†1803	Richard Jolly	Worcester Cathedral		Pevsner, *Worcs*, 1968, 313
51.	†1803	Sir John and Lady Rose	Horsell, Surrey	S	Pevsner, *Surrey*, 1971, 320; C Lib (repr)
52.	1803	Thomas Stonestreet	St Stephen Walbrook, City of London		*Penny* 1977 (1), 175–7; Pevsner, *London: City*, 1997, 264
53.	†1803	William and Jane (†1783) Boys	St Clement, Sandwich, Kent	S	*Cox-Johnson* 1959, 240; *Gunnis* 1968, 29
54.	†1804	Elizabeth Creuzé	St John the Evangelist, Guildford, Surrey	S	Pevsner, *Surrey*, 1971, 272; C Lib (repr)
55.	†1804	John Berkeley Burland	Wells Cathedral, Somerset	S	Pevsner, *Somerset: N & Bristol*, 1958, 312; C Lib (repr)
56.	†1804	John Way	Acton, Middx, churchyard		*Cox-Johnson* 1959, 240; Pevsner, *London: N W*, 1991, 156
57.	1804	Richard Down's children	Friern Barnet, Middx	SD	Pevsner, *London: N*, 1998, 131
58.	1804	Richard Solly (†1803)	Worcester Cathedral		*Graves* I, 1905–6, 88; C Lib (repr)

59.	1804	Richard Solly's children	Friern Barnet, Middx		RG/JP, I, 63
60.	1804	William Northrop (†1800)	Bradford Cathedral, W R Yorks	SD	*Gunnis* 1968, 29
61.	†1805	Charles Polhill	Otford, Kent		*Cox-Johnson* 1959, 240; Pevsner, *Kent: W & Weald*, 1976, 446
62.	†1805	Godfrey Thornton	Blunham, Beds		Pevsner, *Beds, Hunts and Peterborough*, 1986, 58
63.	†1805	John Puget	Totteridge, Herts	S	Pevsner, *London: N*, 1998, 188; C Lib (repr)
64.	?1805	Lucy Burr	Banstead, Surrey		*Gunnis* 1968, 30
65.	†1805	Paul Fielde	Stanstead Abbots, Herts		Pevsner, *Herts*, 1977, 342
66.	1805	Peter de la Rive (†1803)	Kingston-upon-Thames, Surrey	SD	C Lib (repr)
67.	†1805	Peter Dobrée	St Peter Port, Guernsey	S	
68.	1805	Thomas Starkey (†1802) Drawing(s): VAM E.1543-1931	Wrenbury, Cheshire	S	Pevsner, *Cheshire*, 1971, 392; C Lib (repr)
69.	†1805	William Bridges	Beddington, Surrey	S	*Gunnis* 1968, 30; C Lib (repr)
70.	1806	Captain Edward Cooke (†1799) Drawing(s): VAM 8417.7	Westminster Abbey, London, north transept	SD	*Graves* I, 1905–6, 88; *Physick* 1969, 176–7 (repr)
71.	†1806	Charles Duncan	St John, Hampstead, London	S	Pevsner, *London: N*, 1998, 202
72.	?1806	Elizabeth Towry	St Mary, St Marylebone (new church), London		*Gunnis* 1968, 30
73.	†1806	Elizabeth Upcher	Ormesby St Michael, Norfolk	S	Pevsner, *Norfolk: NE & Norwich*, 1997, 630; C Lib (repr)
74.	1806	Frances Inglis, James and Ann Sutherland	St Thomas, Kingston, Jamaica	SD	*Lewis* 1965–7, June 1966, 198 (repr)
75.	1806	Frederick Christian Schwartz (†1798)	St Mary, Fort St George, Chennai (Madras), India	SD	*Graves* I, 1905–6, 88; *Archer* 1984, 50 (repr); *Groseclose* 1995, 91–3 (reprs)
76.	1806	John Castell (†1804)	Holy Trinity, Clapham, London		Pevsner, *London* 2, 1983, 380; C Lib (repr)
77.	†1806	John Monins	Ringwould, Kent	S	Pevsner, *Kent: NE & E*, 1983, 434
78.	1806	John, Lord Henniker	Rochester Cathedral, Kent	S	*Graves*, I, 1905–6, 88; Pevsner, *Kent: W & Weald*, 1976, 485; C Lib (repr)
79.	1806	Lloyd, Lord Kenyon (†1802)	Hanmer, Flint (damaged by fire, 1889)	SD	Pevsner, *Clwyd*, 1986, 361; C Lib (repr)
80.	1806	Margaret Taylor (†1806)	St Thomas, Kingston, Jamaica	SD	*Lewis* 1965–7, June 1966, 201 (repr)
81.	†1806	Rev James Moody	Warwick United Reformed Church, Brook St, London		RG/JP, I, 63
82.	1806	Richard Watt (†1796)	Standish, Lancs	S	*Penny* 1977 (1), 175, 223 n11 (repr)
83.	†1806	Robert Jocelyn	Stanstead Abbots, Herts	S	Pevsner, *Herts*, 1977, 342; C Lib (repr)
84.	?1806	Sir Richard Sullivan	Thames Ditton, Surrey		*Gunnis* 1968, 30
85.	†1806	William Egerton	St Wilfred, Wythenshawe, Lancs		Pevsner, *Lancs: S*, 1969, 342; *CIIA 4/8/59–62* (repr)
86.	†1807	Captain George Warden	Mumbai (Bombay) Cathedral, India	S	*Groseclose* 1995, 136 n32; C Lib (repr)
87.	1807	Charlotte Willes	Hungerford, Berks		*Cox-Johnson* 1959, 240; *Gunnis* 1968, 30
88.	†1807	General Charles Crosbie Drawing(s): VAM E.1573-1931	St Mary, Paddington Green, London	S	Pevsner, *London: N W*, 1991, 676; C Lib (repr)
89.	1807	John Harvey Yorke (†1805)	Speldhurst, Kent	SD	Pevsner, *Kent: W & Weald*, 1976, 542; C Lib (repr)
90.	1807	Lady Wilhelmina Maria Micklethwaite (†1805)	Sprowston, Norfolk		*Penny* 1975 (1), 324 (repr 47); Pevsner, *Norfolk: NE & Norwich*, 1997, 672 (repr 85)
91.	1807	Lieutenant-Colonel William Yorke (†1793) and Martin Yorke (†1798)	Speldhurst, Kent	SD	Pevsner, *Kent: W & Weald*, 1976, 542
92.	1807	Mrs William Mordaunt Milner (†1805)	Bolton Percy, W R Yorks	SD	Pevsner, *Yorks: W R*, 1967, 116; C Lib (repr)
93.	†1807	Pleasance Pratt	Ryston, Norfolk	S	Pevsner, *Norfolk: N-W & S*, 1999, 623; C Lib (repr)
94.	c1807	Rear-Admiral Thomas Totty (†1802)	Westminster Abbey, London, Chapel of St Andrew		*MacMichael* 1977, 54
95.	?1807	Sarah Freeman (†1806)	Astley, Worcs	SD	*Gunnis* 1968, 30; C Lib
96.	1807	Sir Thomas Parkyns (†1806)	Bunny, Notts	SD	Pevsner, *Notts*, 1979, 85; (repr) C Lib (repr)
97.	1807	V G Warren	Mumbai (Bombay) Cathedral, India		GPC
98.	1808	'Admiral Louis'	Untraced		*Cox-Johnson* 1959, 240
99.	†1808	Anthony Calvert	St Peter's-in-Thanet, Broadstairs, Kent	S	*Gunnis* 1968, 30
100.	1808	Captain George Duff (†1805) Payment(s): at least £1,050	St Paul's Cathedral, London, crypt	S	*Cox-Johnson* 1959, 240; *Yarrington* 1988, 87; *Saunders* 2001, 144 (repr)
101.	1808	Charlotte Smith	Stoke, near Guildford, Surrey		*Cox-Johnson* 1959, 240; *Gunnis* 1968, 30
102.	†1808	Colonel Charles James Morgan Drawing(s): VAM E.1562-1931	Winchester Cathedral, Hants		Pevsner, *Hants & Isle of Wight*, 1967, 684
103.	?1808	Colonel Charles Taylor	St Mary, Reading, Berks		*Gunnis* 1968, 30
104.	1808	Dr Robert Petrie (†1803)	Reigate, Surrey		*Cox-Johnson* 1959, 240; *Gunnis* 1968, 29
105.	1808	'Earl of Rosse'	untraced		*Cox-Johnson* 1959, 240
106.	1808	Frances Heneage (†1807)	Hainton, Lincs	S	Pevsner, *Lincs*, 1989, 356; C Lib (repr)

No.	Date	Subject	Location		Bibliography
107.	1808	Frances, Princess Bariatinsky (†1807)	Sherborne, Glos	S	*Cox-Johnson* 1959, 240; *CIIA* 4/4/88–90 (repr); Pevsner, *Glos: Cotswolds*, 1999, 602
108.	1808	Henrietta, Lady Langham (†1807)	Cottesbrooke, Northants	S	*Cox-Johnson* 1959, 240; Pevsner, *Northants*, 1973, 162; *CIIA* 4/3/39, 41–2 (repr)
109.	1808	Herman Katencamp (†1808)	Bath Abbey, Somerset	S	*Cox-Johnson* 1959, 240; Pevsner, *Somerset: N & Bristol*, 1958, 105; C Lib (repr)
110.	1808	Hon Frances Erskine (†1805)	Hampstead, London	S	*Cox-Johnson* 1959, 240; Pevsner, *London: N*, 1998, 202
111.	†1808	Jane Amelia Russell	St Mary, Fort St George, Chennai (Madras), India	S	*Archer* 1984, 50; *Groseclose* 1995, 97–8 (repr)
112.	1808	Lieutenant Thomas Alston (†1807), with a relief of the Battle of Montevideo	Odell, Beds	S	*Cox-Johnson* 1959, 240; Pevsner, *Beds, Hunts & Peterborough*, 1968, 130; C Lib (repr)
113.	1808	Lieutenant-Colonel James Achilles Kirkpatrick (†1805)	St John, Kolkata (Calcutta)	S	*Groseclose* 1995, 101–3 (reprs)
114.	1808	'Mr Crockett'	Untraced		*Cox-Johnson* 1959, 240
115.	1808	'Mr Sanderson'	Untraced		*Cox-Johnson* 1959, 240
116.	1808	'Mrs Arbuthnot'	Untraced		*Cox-Johnson* 1959, 240
117.	1808	'Mrs Arnold'	Untraced		*Cox-Johnson* 1959, 240
118.	1808	'Mrs Garrow', wife of Sir William Garrow (tomb)	s Untraced		*Cox-Johnson* 1959, 240
119.	1808	'Mrs Greathead'	Untraced		*Cox-Johnson* 1959, 240
120.	1808	'Mrs Nimage'	Untraced		*Cox-Johnson* 1959, 240
121.	1808	'Mrs Price'	Untraced		*Cox-Johnson* 1959, 240
122.	1808	'Mrs Sibley'	Untraced		*Cox-Johnson* 1959, 240
123.	?1808	Penelope Sheffield	Burton-upon-Stather, Lincs		*Gunnis* 1968, 30
124.	1808	Rear-Admiral Richard Kempenfelt (†1782)	Westminster Abbey, London, north transept	S	Pevsner, *London* I, 1973, 448; C Lib (repr)
125.	1808	Rev John Farrer	Witton-le-Wear, Durham		Pevsner, *Durham*, 1983, 509
126.	c1808	Rhoda (†1808) and Sylvia (†1807) Astley	Melton Constable, Norfolk		Pevsner, *Norfolk: NE & Norwich*, 1997, 611
127.	1808	Robert Andrew (†1807)	Harlestone, Northants		*Cox-Johnson* 1959, 240; *Gunnis* 1968, 30
128.	1808	Thomas Dawson (†1807)	Edwardstone, Suffolk		*Cox-Johnson* 1959, 240; Pevsner, *Suffolk*, 1974, 198
129.	†1808	William (†1808) and Catherine Hutchinson, their son and daughter (co-sculptor: Samuel Manning I)	St Mary, Beverley, ER Yorks	S	Pevsner, *Yorks: E R & York*, 1995, 299
130.	†1809	Ann Seward and three family members	Lichfield Cathedral, Staffs		Pevsner, *Staffs*, 1974, 187; C Lib (repr)
131.	†1809	Catharine de Burgh	West Drayton, Middx		Pevsner, *London: NW*, 1991, 367
132.	†1809	George, Earl of Coventry	Croome d'Abitot, Worcs	S	Pevsner, *Worcs*, 1968, 126; C Lib (repr)
133.	†1809	Henry and James Edward (†1796) Hanson	Great Bromley, Essex		*Gunnis* 1968, 30
134.	?1809	Henry Evelyn	[St James, Hampstead Road, London]; destroyed		*Gunnis* 1968, 30
135.	1809	John Jackson (†1794)	Crayford, Kent	SD	*Gunnis* 1968, 30; C Lib (repr)
136.	1809	John Jennings (†1808)	Wrenbury, Cheshire	SD	Pevsner, *Cheshire*, 1971, 392
137.	1809	Joseph Sykes (†1805)	Kirk Ella, Hull, E R Yorks	SD	*Cox-Johnson* 1959, 240; Pevsner, *Yorks: E R & York*, 1995, 585; C Lib (repr)
138.	†1809	Lieutenant-General Stibbert	South Stoneham, Southampton, Hants		Pevsner, *Hants*, 1967, 574
139.	1809	Lord Lavington	[Antigua, WI]; Destroyed		*Hoare* 1809, 42; *Cox-Johnson* 1959, 240; *Gunnis* 1968, 28–9
140.	†1809	Martha Bacon (the sculptor's sister)	Epsom, Surrey		*Cox-Johnson* 1961, 28
141.	1809	Sir Hugh Owen	Monkton, Pembrokes		*Gunnis* 1968, 30
142.	†1809	Sir William Bensley	Bletchingley, Surrey	S	Pevsner, *Surrey*, 1971, 115, C Lib (repr)
143.	1810	Captain Percy Burrell (†1807) Drawing(s): VAM E.1562-1931	Cuckfield, Sussex	SD	*Cox-Johnson* 1959, 241; *Physick* 1969, 177; C Lib (repr)
144.	1810	Charles Lawson (†1807)	Manchester Cathedral, Lancs		*Graves* I, 1905–6, 88; *Cox-Johnson* 1959, 240; *Penny* 1977 (1), 160 (repr); *CIIA* 4/8/52 (repr)
145.	†1810	Elizabeth Prowse	Wicken, Northants	S	C Lib (repr)
146.	†1810	Elizabeth Raynsford	[Faxton, Northants]; VAM A.12-1965	SD	
147.	†1810	Elizabeth Sharp	Wicken, Northants	S	Pevsner, *Northants*, 1973, 462
148.	†1810	Elizabeth Woollett	Rye, Sussex	S	C Lib (repr)
149.	†1810	Jane Rowe	Epsom, Surrey	S	Pevsner, *Surrey*, 1971, 215; C Lib (repr)
150.	†1810	John Herring	St George Colegate, Norwich, Norfolk	S	*Graves* I, 1905–6, 88; Pevsner, *Norfolk: NE & Norwich*, 1997, 235; C Lib (repr)
151.	†1810	Juliana, Lady Langham	Cottesbrooke, Northants	S	Pevsner, *Northants*, 1973, 162; *CIIA* 4/3/45–6 (repr)
152.	1810	Marianne Langham (†1809)	Cottesbrooke, Northants	SD	Pevsner, *Northants*, 1973, 162; *CIIA* 4/3/40 (repr)
153.	?1810	Mary Rice	Tooting, Surrey		*Gunnis* 1968, 30
154.	†1810	Mary, Viscountess Carleton	Hawstead, Suffolk	S	Pevsner, *Suffolk*, 1974, 256; C Lib (repr)

No.	Date	Subject	Location		Bibliography
155.	†1810	Osmond de Beauvoir	St Peter Port, Guernsey	S	
156.	?1810	Sir Henry Harvey	Walmer, Kent		*Gunnis* 1968, 30
157.	?1810	Thomas Godfrey (†1802)	Woodnesborough, Kent	S	*Gunnis* 1968, 30; C Lib (repr)
158.	†1810	Thomas Tyrwhitt Drake Drawing(s): VAM E.1543-1931	Amersham, Bucks		Pevsner, *Bucks*, 1994, 132; C Lib (repr)
159.	c1811	Captain George Bryan (†1809)	Westminster Abbey, London, nave		WAM (88); Pevsner, *London I*, 1973, 452
160.	†1811	Charlotte Elizabeth, Lady Gardner	St Peter, Nottingham (moved from chancel to north aisle above porch, 1961)	S	Pevsner, *Notts*, 1979, 224
161.	†1811	Elizabeth Oakes	Nowton, Suffolk	S	Pevsner, *Suffolk*, 1974, 381; C Lib (repr)
162.	†1811	George Keble Drawing(s): VAM E.1581-1931	St Mary, Fort St George, Chennai (Madras), India	S	*Archer* 1984, 50; *Groseclose* 1995, 87–8 (relief repr)
163.	1811	John Littlehales (†1810)	Winchester Cathedral, Hants	S	*Graves* I, 1905–6, 88; Pevsner, *Hants*, 1967, 684; C Lib (repr)
164.	†1811	Louisa Lownds	St John, Hampstead, London		*Cox-Johnson* 1959 (repr 41); Pevsner, *London: N*, 1998, 202
165.	†1811	Rev Francis Annesley	Eydon, Northants		Pevsner, *Northants*, 1973, 211
166.	c1812	Dr John Plenderleath (†1811)	Westminster Abbey, London, nave		WAM (85); *MacMichael* 1977, 29
167.	†1812	General Crauford and General Mackinnon	St Paul's Cathedral, London	S	Pevsner, *London: City*, 1997, 174; C Lib (repr)
168.	1812	Hannah Doorman (†1807)	Wanstead, Essex	D	*Gunnis* 1968, 30
169.	1812	Hon Edward Waldegrave (†1809)	Navestock, Essex	SD	*Graves* I, 1905–6, 88; Pevsner, *Essex*, 1965, 304; C Lib (repr)
170.	1812	John Buckeridge	St John the Baptist, Windsor, Berks		RG/JP, I, 63B
171.	†1812	Lieutenant-Colonel Charles Macleod	Westminster Abbey, London, Chapel of St John the Baptist		W A archives
172.	†1812	Lydia Bulkeley	Brockhampton-by-Bromyard, Herefs, new chapel	S	Pevsner, *Herefs*, 1963, 89
173.	1812	Mary Clayton	Marlow, Bucks		*Gunnis* 1968, 30
174.	†1812	Theodora de Fries	Luz RC Church, Chennai (Madras)	S	*Groseclose* 1995, 97–8 (repr)
175.	†1812	William (†1803), Sarah (†1812) and Harriet Dawson (†1771)	St George's Chapel, Windsor, Berks	S	*Bond* 1999, 87
176.	†1813	2nd Lord Heathfield	Buckland Monachorum, Devon		*Gunnis* 1968, 31
177.	?1813	Admiral Sir William Rowley	Stoke-by-Nayland, Suffolk		*Gunnis* 1968, 30
178.	?1813	Baron de Roll	Bidborough, Kent, churchyard		*Gunnis* 1968, 31
179.	†1813	Charles Johnson	St Mary the Virgin, Oxford		RG/JP, I, 63B
180.	?1813	George Fraser	Canterbury Cathedral, Kent	S	*Gunnis* 1968, 31
181.	†1813	Henry Skrine	St Mary, Walton-on-Thames, Surrey	S	Pevsner, *Surrey*, 1971, 496; C Lib (repr)
182.	†1813	John Bones (co-sculptor: Samuel Manning I)	Fen Ditton, Cambs	S	Pevsner, *Cambs*, 1970, 384
183.	1813	John Tharp (†1811)	St James, Montego Bay, Jamaica	SD	*Lewis* 1965–7, Dec 1966, 405–7 (repr)
184.	†1813	Rev John Venn	Holy Trinity, Clapham, London	S	Pevsner, *London 2: S*, 1983, 380
185.	†1813	Rev Thomas Robinson Drawing(s): VAM E.1564-1931, pencil	St Mary de Castro, Leicester	S	Pevsner, *Leics & Rutland*, 1984, 215; C Lib (repr)
186.	†1813	Sarah Mansfield	Birstall, Leics	S	Pevsner, *Leics & Rutland*, 1984, 103
187.	1813	Sophia Lambard	Ash, Kent		Pevsner, *Kent: W & Weald*, 1976, 132
188.	1813	Thomas Lambard	Ash, Kent		Pevsner, *Kent: W & Weald*, 1976, 132
189.	1814	Captain George Nicholas Hardinge (†1808)	Mumbai (Bombay) Cathedral, India	SD	*Graves* 1905–6, vol 1, 89; *Archer* 1984, 53–5; *Groseclose* 1995, 58–60 (reprs)
190.	1814	Captain Hodson	Jamestown, St Helena		RG/JP, I, 64
191.	?1814	Henry Jodrell	Letheringsett, Norfolk		*Gunnis* 1968, 31
192.	†1814	John Johnson (designed by the subject)	Leicester Cathedral		Pevsner, *Leics and Rutland*, 1984, 209
193.	†1814	Lieutenant-Colonel Sir Henry Sullivan Bt	Thames Ditton, Surrey	S	*Gunnis* 1968, 31
194.	?1814	Lutterell Wynne	Westminster Abbey, London, cloisters		*Gunnis* 1968, 31
195.	?1814	Mary Markham	Westminster Abbey, London, cloisters		*Gunnis* 1968, 31
196.	?1815	Captain William Hanson (†1813)	Great Bromley, Essex	SD	*Gunnis* 1968, 31; C Lib (repr)
197.	1815	Charles, Earl of Normanton, Archbishop of Dublin (†1809)	Westminster Abbey, London, nave	SD	*Graves* I, 1905–6, 89; WAM (61); *MacMichael* 1974, 26,28; C Lib (repr)
198.	†1815	Colonel Sir Henry Ellis	Worcester Cathedral	S	Pevsner, *Worcs*, 1968, 313; *Busco* 1994, 37 (repr)
199.	1815	Elinor Starkey (†1811)	Wrenbury, Cheshire	SD	Pevsner, *Cheshire*, 1971, 392; C lib (repr)
200.	c1815	General Sir Thomas Trigge (†1814)	Westminster Abbey, London, nave		*MacMichael* 1977, 34
201.	†1815	Josias Nottidge	Bocking, Essex	S	*Gunnis* 1968, 31; C Lib (repr)
202.	†1815	Lieutenant Peter Lawtie (co-sculptor: Samuel Manning I) Drawing(s): VAM E.1575-1931	Banff	S	C Lib (repr)
203.	†1815	Lieutenant Peter Lawtie Drawing(s): VAM E.1575-1931	St John, Kolkata (Calcutta)		*Groseclose* 1995, 68 (repr)

No.	Date	Subject		Location		References
204.	1815	Lieutenant-General Sir John Moore (†1809)		St Paul's Cathedral, London, south transept	SD	*Cox-Johnson* 1959, 241; *Whinney* 1988, 370–1 (repr); *Yarrington* 1988, 75 (repr 32)
205.	†1815	Major George Bean		St Mary Magdalene, Richmond, Surrey		Pevsner, *London: S*, 1983, 518
206.	c1815	Major-General Coote Manningham (†1809)		Westminster Abbey, London, north transept		*Graves* I, 1905–6, 89; *MacMichael* 1977, 86
207.	1815	Robert, 1st Earl of Belvidere (†1814)		Tyrrelspass, Co Westmeath	SD	*Potterton* 1975, 35; C Lib (repr)
208.	†1815	Sir John Sheffield		Burton-upon-Stather, Lincs	S	Pevsner, *Lincs*, 1989, 201; C Lib (repr)
209.	1815	Sir William Langham (†1812) and family	sa	Cottesbrooke, Northants	SD	Pevsner, *Northants*, 1973, 162; *CIIA* 4/3/47–51 (repr)
210.	†1815	Thomas Langford Brooke		Rostherne, Cheshire		Pevsner, *Cheshire*, 1971, 324
211.	?1815	William Shepherd		Edwardstone, Suffolk		*Gunnis* 1968, 31
212.	†1816	Charles Robert Ross		St Mary, Fort St George, Chennai (Madras), India		*Gunnis* 1968, 31; *Groseclose* 1995, 88–9 (relief repr)
213.	†1816	Elizabeth Fydell		St Botolph, Boston, Lincs	S	Pevsner, *Lincs*, 1989, 161
214.	†1816	Mary Foster-Pigot		Abington Pigotts, Cambs	S	Pevsner, *Cambs*, 1970, 291
215.	1816	Mrs Clarke		Ickenham, Middx		AL/RG
216.	†1816	Rev Charles Tyrwhitt Drake		Amersham, Bucks		*Gunnis* 1968, 31
217.	?1816	Rev William Goode Drawing(s): VAM E.1561-1931 (?)		St Andrew-by-the-Wardrobe, City of London		*Gunnis* 1968, 31
218.	†1816	Robert, Earl of Buckinghamshire		Nocton, Lincs		Pevsner, *Lincs*, 1989, 577
219.	?1816	Sir Henry Strachey		Chew Magna, Somerset		*Gunnis* 1968, 31
220.	?1816	Thomas and William Crowther		St Mary, Battersea, London		*Gunnis* 1968, 31
221.	1817	Edward Farnham (†1775) Drawing(s): VAM E.1557-1931		Quorndon, Leics	S	C Lib (repr)
222.	1817	Elizabeth, Duchess of Chandos		Worlingworth, Suffolk	S	*Graves* I, 1905–6, 89; Pevsner, *Suffolk*, 1974, 507; C Lib (repr)
223.	1817	Hon Jonathan Duncan (†1811)		Mumbai (Bombay) Cathedral, India	SD	*Archer* 1984, 53, 55 (repr); *Groseclose* 1990, 507–10 (repr)
224.	†1817	Lieutenant-Colonel Henry Powlett		Alderley, Glos		Pevsner, *Glos: Cotswolds*, 1999, 133
225.	†1817	Rev Philip Gurdon		Assington, Suffolk		Pevsner, *Suffolk*, 1974, 78
226.	†1817	Rev Richard Frank (†1810) and wife, Elizabeth (neé Drake)		Amersham, Bucks		AL/RG
227.	†1817	Sir John Lombe		Bylaugh, Norfolk	S	Pevsner, *Norfolk: NE & Norwich*, 1997, 423; C Lib (repr)
228.	†1817	William Clerk (co-sculptor: Samuel Manning I)		Stretton-on-Dunsmore, Warks		Pevsner, *Warks*, 1966, 421
229.	†1817	William Kennedy		Mumbai (Bombay) Cathedral, India	S	C Lib (repr)
230.	1818	Captain Bunn		Jamestown, St Helena		RG/JP, I, 64
231.	?1818	Elizabeth Swale		Mildenhall, Suffolk		*Gunnis* 1968, 31
232.	?1818	Francis Fortescue		Stoke-by-Nayland, Suffolk		*Gunnis* 1968, 31
233.	†1818	General Edmund Fanning		St Mary Abbots, Kensington, London		Pevsner, *London: N W*, 1991, 460; C Lib (repr)
234.	?1818	Hon George Berkeley		West Molesey, Surrey		*Gunnis* 1968, 31
235.	1818	Lieutenant Thomas Davies and Lieutenant John William Nattes, with a relief of the Siege of Mallegaon		St Mary, Fort St George, Chennai (Madras), India	S	*Groseclose* 1995, 133 n13
236.	†1818	Louisa Fullerton (co-sculptor: Samuel Manning I) Drawing(s): VAM E.1560-1931 (related)		Thrybergh, W R Yorks		RG/JP, I, 69
237.	†1818	Marianne Araminta Beresford		St John, Hampstead, London		*Cox-Johnson* 1959 (repr 39); Pevsner, *London: N*, 1998, 202
238.	†1818	Mary Brewer		Worcester Cathedral	S	AL
239.	1818	Mrs Abraham		Bagshot, Surrey		*Graves* I, 1905–6, 89; *Gunnis* 1968, 31
240.	†1818	Philip Booth and wife Elizabeth (†1798) (co-sculptor: Samuel Manning I)		Stanstead Abbots, Herts	S	Pevsner, *Herts*, 1977, 342; C Lib (repr)
241.	†1818	Philip Metcalfe (co-sculptor: Samuel Manning I)		Hawstead, Suffolk	S	Pevsner, *Suffolk*, 1974, 256
242.	†1818	Robert, Viscount Kilmorey (co-sculptor: Samuel Manning I)		Adderley, Salop	S	Pevsner, *Salop*, 1958, 53
243.	†1818	Rt Hon Warren Hastings		Westminster Abbey, London, north transept	S	*Cox-Johnson* 1959, 241; *MacMichael* 1974, 87; C Lib (repr)
244.	†1818	Sir Egerton Leigh Drawing(s): VAM E.1543-1931		Newbold-on-Avon, Warwick		C Lib (repr)
245.	1818	Sir Jacob Astley (†1817) (co-sculptor: Samuel Manning I)		Melton Constable, Norfolk	S	C Lib (repr)
246.	1818	Sir William and Lady Meredith		[Exhib RA, London, 1090]; untraced		*Graves* I, 1905–6, 89
247.	†1818	Sir William Fraser		St Mary, St Marylebone, London		Pevsner, *London: N W*, 1991, 603
248.	†1818	Thomas Ormerod		New College, Oxford, cloister		GPC
249.	†1819	Abbot Upcher (co-sculptor: Samuel Manning I)		Upper Sheringham, Norfolk	S	Pevsner, *Norfolk: NE & Norwich*, 1997, 661 (repr 86)
250.	†1819	Edward Madden		Chichester Cathedral, Sussex	S	*Gunnis* 1968, 31
251.	†1819	Elizabeth Delves		Peasmarsh, Sussex		Pevsner, *Sussex*, 1965, 578; *Gunnis* 1968, 31

No.	Date	Subject		Location		Reference
252.	†1819	John Parsons, Bishop of Peterborough		Balliol College Chapel, Oxford		Pevsner, *Oxon*, 1974, 102
253.	†1819	John Woollett (co-sculptor: Samuel Manning I)		Rye, Sussex	S	C Lib (repr)
254.	†1819	Joseph Howell		Markyate, Herts	S	*Gunnis* 1968, 31
255.	?1819	Louisa Lushington		Hanwell, Middx		*Gunnis* 1968, 31
256.	*c*1819	Sir William Augustus Pitt (†1809) and wife (†1819) (co-sculptor: Samuel Manning I) Drawing(s): VAM E.1572-1931		Heckfield, Hants		Pevsner, *Hants & Isle of Wight*, 1967, 287; C Lib (repr)
257.	†1820	Admiral S H Linzie		St Andrew, Plymouth		AL/RG
258.	1820	Captain Newton Chambers (†1815)		[Exhib RA, London, 1071]; untraced		*Graves* I, 1905–6, 89
259.	1820	Christopher Metcalfe (†1794) (co-sculptor: Samuel Manning I)		Hawstead, Suffolk	SD	Pevsner, *Suffolk*, 1974, 256; C Lib (repr)
260.	†1820	George Stainforth, wall-tablet with little sarcophagus (co-sculptor: Samuel Manning I)		Holy Trinity, Clapham, London	S	
261.	1820	Jervys family		Britford, Wilts	S	Pevsner, *Wilts*, 1975, 143
262.	†1820	Rev Browse Trist and family (co-sculptor: Samuel Manning I)		St Mary, Totnes, Devon		RG/JP, I, 69
263.	†1820	Richard Terveys (co-sculptor: Samuel Manning I)		Britford, Wilts		RG/JP, I, 69
264.	†1820	Walter, Marquess of Ormonde and his wife Anna Maria (co-sculptor: Samuel Manning I)		Ulcombe, Kent	S	Pevsner, *Kent: W & Weald*, 1976, 588
265.	†1821	Ann Callant		All Saints, Maidstone, Kent		RG/JP, I, 65
266.	1821	Archibald Seton, with a figure of Benevolence supported by Fortitude and Integrity		[Exhib RA, London, 1155]; untraced		*Graves* I, 1905–6, 89
267.	†1821	George Gunning		Frindsbury, Kent	S	Pevsner, *Kent: W & Weald*, 1976, 289
268.	?1821	John Swale		Mildenhall, Suffolk		*Gunnis* 1968, 31
269.	†1821	Patrick Campbell Baird		Mumbai (Bombay) Cathedral	S	*Groseclose* 1995, 90 (repr)
270.	†1821	Sir Peter de Haviland		St Peter Port, Guernsey	S	
271.	1822	Abel Ram		Ellastone, Staffs		GPC
272.	?1822	Admiral Sir John Borlase-Warren		Stratton Audley, Oxon		*Gunnis* 1968, 31
273.	?1822	Augusta Slade		Chester Cathedral		*Gunnis* 1968, 31
274.	†1822	Laetitia Mangles		Great Bromley, Essex	S	*Gunnis* 1968, 31
275.	†1822	William Godson (co-sculptor: Samuel Manning I)		Tenbury Wells, Worcs		Pevsner, *Worcs*, 1968, 278; *Gunnis* 1968, 32
276.	1823	Arthur Pott (co-sculptor: Samuel Manning I)		Eltham, Kent		*Gunnis* 1968, 32
277.	†1823	Dr Charles Grant (co-sculptor: Samuel Manning I)		St George, Bloomsbury, London	S	Pevsner, *London: N*, 1998, 258; C Lib (repr)
278.	†1823	James Antrobus Newton (co-sculptor: Samuel Manning I)		St Mary, Stockport, Cheshire		Pevsner, *Cheshire*, 1971, 340
279.	†1823	Oliver Hanson		Great Bromley, Essex	S	
280.	†1823	Sir Mark Masterman Sykes (co-sculptor: Samuel Manning I)		Sledmere, E R Yorks	S	Pevsner, *Yorks: E R & York*, 1995, 692; *Mulcahy* 2006, 75; C Lib (repr)
281.	†1823	Thomas, Mary and Elizabeth (†1823) Beckley	m	St Thomas, Lymington, Hants	S	
282.	†1824	Sarah Jenkins (co-sculptor: Samuel Manning I)		Stroud, Glos	S	Pevsner, *Glos: Cotswolds*, 1999, 650
283.	?1824	William Gurdon (co-sculptor: Samuel Manning I)		St Mary, St Marylebone, London		*Gunnis* 1968, 32
284.	†1825	Anne Smith (co-sculptor: Samuel Manning I)		St Thomas, Kingston, Jamaica	S	*Lewis* 1965–7, July 1966, 232–4; C Lib (repr)
285.	†1825	Caroline Curteis (co-sculptor: Samuel Manning I)		Wartling, Sussex	S	*Gunnis* 1968, 32; C Lib (repr)
286.	†1825	George Vansittart, his wife Sarah (†1819), their son George (†1824)		Bisham, Berks		C Lib (repr)
287.	?1825	Mary Blackett		Ovingham, Northumberland		*Gunnis* 1968, 31
288.	†1825	Samuel (†1805) and Ann Foyster (†1825)		St Pancras new parish church, London	S	*Gunnis* 1968, 31; C Lib (repr)
289.	†1825	Sir John B Walsh (co-sculptor: Samuel Manning I)		Warfield, Berks	S	Pevsner, *Berks*, 1966, 257; *Gunnis* 1968, 32
290.	†1826	Rev Charles Warburton, Bishop of Cloyne (co-sculptor: Samuel Manning I)		Cloyne Cathedral, Ireland	S	C Lib (repr)
291.	?1827	Ann Dollond (co-sculptor: Samuel Manning I)		Tuxford, Notts		*Gunnis* 1968, 32
292.	†1827	Francis Penoyre		Clifford, Herefs		Pevsner, *Herefs*, 1963, 102
293.	†1827	Rebekah Gillam Williams (co-sculptor: Samuel Manning I)		Berrington, Salop	S	Pevsner, *Salop*, 1958, 73
294.	?1828	Augustus Henry East (co-sculptor: Samuel Manning I)		Bisham, Berks	S	*Gunnis* 1968, 32; C Lib (repr)
295.	†1828	Edward (†1818) and Frances Maxwell (co-sculptor: Samuel Manning I)		Rumboldswyke, Chichester, Sussex	S	
296.	†1828	Roger Holland and his children Mary (†1823) and Roger (†1832) Drawing(s): VAM E.1579-1931		Bolton, Lancs		C Lib (repr)
297.	†1830	Frances Jane Metcalfe (co-sculptor: Samuel Manning I)		Hawstead, Suffolk	S	*Gunnis* 1968, 32; Pevsner, *Suffolk*, 1974, 256
298.	†1830	Sir Thomas Staines (co-sculptor: Samuel Manning I)		St John the Baptist, Margate, Kent	S	Pevsner, *Kent: N E & E*, 1983, 383
299.	†1830	William Dawson (co-sculptor: Samuel Manning I)		St George's Chapel, Windsor, Berks	S	*Bond* 1999, 89
300.	†1831	Arthur Tyrwhitt Drake		Amersham, Bucks		Pevsner, *Bucks*, 1994, 132

No.	Date	Subject		Location		Literary references
301.	†1831	Catherine Scott		Jesus Church, Southampton, Hants		Pevsner, *Hants & Isle of Wight*, 1967, 593
302.	†1831	Thomas, 6th Baron Despencer (co-sculptor: Samuel Manning I)		Rotherfield Greys, Oxon	S	*Gunnis* 1968, 32; Pevsner, *Oxon*, 1974, 735; C Lib (repr)
303.	†1832	Captain Richard Burton (co-sculptor: Samuel Manning I)	m	St Peter's-in-Thanet, Broadstairs, Kent	S	*Gunnis* 1968, 31; C Lib (repr)
304.	†1832	Francis, 1st Earl of Kilmorey (co-sculptor: Samuel Manning I)		Adderley, Salop		*Gunnis* 1968, 32
305.	†1833	George Heneage (co-sculptor: Samuel Manning I)		Hainton, Lincs	S	C Lib (repr)
306.	1833	Margaret Maude (co-sculptor: Samuel Manning I)		Langham, Essex	S	*Gunnis* 1968, 32; C Lib (repr)
307.	†1835	Susannah Sophia Bacon, the sculptor's wife (table tomb)	s	[West Hall Cemetery, Winchester]; untraced		Ann Saunders MS
308.	†1836	John Sargent and sons (co-sculptor: Samuel Manning I)		East Lavington, Sussex		RG/JP, I, 70
309.	†1836	Rev George Clarke (†1809) and his wife Elizabeth (†1836)	m	Meysey Hampton, Glos	S	CIIA 4/4/iv (repr); Pevsner, *Glos: Cotswolds*, 1999, 475
310.	†1838	Rev John Drake and his wife, Mary		Amersham, Bucks		AL/RG
311.	1841	Sir Astley Paston Cooper (co-sculptor: Samuel Manning I)		Hemel Hempstead, Herts		GPC
312.	1842	Christina Medley (†1841)	s	St Thomas, Exeter, Devon		*Ecclesiologist*, 14–15 Oct 1842, 58; *Cox-Johnson* 1959, 241–2 (repr pl 38); *Penny* 1977 (1), 128–31 (repr)
313.	1844	Tablet to the 44th Regiment, commemorating the dead of the Afghan War (co-sculptor: Samuel Manning I)		Alverstoke, nr Gosport, Hants		*ILN*, 11 April 1846, 245 (repr)
314.	†1845	William (†1829) and Sophia Dawson (†1845) (co-sculptor: Samuel Manning II)		St George's Chapel, Windsor, Berks	S	*Bond* 1999, 88
315.	?1846	Thomas Baskerville (co-sculptor: Samuel Manning II)		St Andrew, Redbourn, Herts		GPC

Statues

No.	Date	Subject		Location		Literary references
316.	1797	Cassandra		[RA, London, gold medal]; untraced		*Gunnis* 1968, 28
317.	1802	Angel, with emblems of Justice and Victory		[Exhib RA, London, 953]; untraced		*Graves* I, 1905–6, 88
318.	1802	Lion's head		[Exhib RA, London, 973]; untraced		*Graves* I, 1905–6, 88
319.	1803	Charles, Marquess Cornwallis (designed by John Bacon RA)		Victoria Memorial Hall, east quadrangle, Kolkata (Calcutta), (formerly Town Hall)	D	*Farington* V, 1967; *Archer* 1984, 53 (repr); *Groseclose* 1995, 105–109 (reprs); *Steggles* 2000, 60–61
320.	1806	William Pitt the Younger (competition model for Cambridge, commission won by Nollekens)		Somerley, Hants (poss Earl of Normanton)		*Gunnis* 1968, 28; *Liscombe* 1977, 701
321.	1806–1808	Richard, Marquess Wellesley, 2nd Earl of Mornington Payment(s): £6,000		Victoria Memorial Hall, Kolkata (Calcutta), (formerly town hall)		*Graves* I, 1905–6, 88; *Cox-Johnson* 1959, 240; *Archer* 1984, 53; *Steggles* 2000, 215
322.	1806–1808	Richard, Marquess Wellesley, 2nd Earl of Mornington Payment(s): £5,000		Dr Bhau Daji lad Museum, Mumbai (Bombay), India, gardens (formerly Churchgate until 1874)		*Graves* I, 1905–6, 88; *Cox-Johnson* 1959, 240; *Gunnis* 1968, 29; *Steggles* 2000, 216–8 (repr)
323.	1810	Charles, 1st Marquess Cornwallis Payment(s): at least £3,333 6s 8d	m	Dr Bhau Daji lad Museum, Mumbai (Bombay), India (formerly Bombay Green)		*Graves* I, 1905–6, 88; *Cox-Johnson* 1959, 240; *Steggles* 2000, 61–64
324.	1812	King George III (designed by T Kirk) Drawing(s): VAM E.938-1965 (design for pedestal)		Bank of Ireland, Dublin		*Farington* XII, 4304; C Lib (repr)

Busts

No.	Date	Subject		Location		Literary references
325.	1798	John Bacon RA, the artist's father Drawing(s): VAM E. 1048-1966		[Exhib RA, London, 1053]; untraced		*Graves* I, 1905–6, 88
326.	1804	Dr Garthshore		[Exhib RA, London, 938]; untraced		*Graves* I, 1905–6, 88
327.	1804	Lady Ribblesdale	m	YCAG		*Graves* I, 1905–6, 88; *Burl* 2003, 897 (repr)
328.	1804	Unidentified woman	m	Sotheby, 1 Nov 1991	SD	C Lib (repr)
329.	1804	William Markham, Archbishop of York	m	Christ Church, Oxford Other versions: Royal Coll, Windsor Castle, marble, SD 'J. BACON JUN^{R}. / 1813'		*Graves* I, 1905–6, 88; Pevsner, *Oxon*, 1974, 127; C Lib (repr)
330.	1808	Charles, 1st Marquess Cornwallis		Unidentified location, Mumbai (Bombay), India		*Cox-Johnson* 1959, 240
331.	1808	HRH Princess Charlotte	m	[Exhib RA, London, 986]; untraced		*Graves* I, 1905–6, 88
332.	c1808	Richard, Marquess Wellesley, 2nd Earl of Mornington	m	Indian Museum, Kolkata (Calcutta) Other versions: NPG, London, 992, marble		*Graves* I, 1905–6, 88, 89; *Cox-Johnson* 1959, 240; *Steggles* 2000, 215
333.	1810	George Canning		[Exhib RA, London, 728]; untraced		*Graves* I, 1905–6, 88
334.	1810	Hon Mrs R F A Lee		[Exhib RA, London, 869]; untraced		*Graves* I, 1905–6, 88
335.	1810	Lord le Despencer		[Exhib RA, London, 895]; untraced		*Graves* I, 1905–6, 88
336.	1811	The Persian Ambassador		[Exhib RA, London, 909]; untraced		*Graves* I, 1905–6, 88
337.	1812	George, 4th Earl of Aberdeen (†1860)		[Exhib RA, London, 928]; untraced		*Graves* I, 1905–6, 89
338.	1812	Richard Payne Knight	m	BM Other versions: NPG 4887, marble with bronze drapery, SD 1814	SD	*Graves* I, 1905–6, 88, 89; *Bullock* 1988, 144–5 (repr); *Dawson* 1999, 124–6 (repr)

339.	1812	William Pitt the Younger	m	BM		*Dawson* 1999, 164–5;
340.	1813	Edward Augustus, Duke of Kent and Strathearn	m	Windsor Castle RCIN 35404	SD	*Graves* I, 1905–6, 89; *Gunnis* 1968, 29; C Lib (repr)
341.	1816	Mrs Arbuthnot		[Exhib RA, London, 934]; untraced		*Graves* I, 1905–6, 89
342.	1816	'Portrait of a gentleman'		[Exhib RA, London, 1816, 714]; untraced		*Graves* I, 1905–6, 89
343.	1817	Sir Joshua Reynolds		[Exhib RA, London, 1045]; untraced		*Graves* I, 1905–6, 89
344.	1818	Two unidentified subjects Payment(s): £315 with another bust		[Carlton House, London]; untraced		*Gunnis* 1968, 29
345.	1820	Antonina, daughter of Lord Le Despencer	m	Sold Christie's, London, 29 Sept 1988 (formerly property of Duke of Northumberland)	S	*Graves* I, 1905–6, 89
346.	1820	Lavinia, Countess Spencer	m	Althorp, Northants	SD	*British Portraits* 1956–7, 127; C Lib (repr)
347.	nd	Self-portrait	m	Private coll		C Lib (repr)
Architectural Sculpture						
348.	1796	Figures of 'Providence' and 'Vigilance' 'for Trinity House'		[Exhib RA, London, 783, 790]; untraced		*Graves* I, 1905–6, 88
349.	c1803	Two seated sailors leaning on a globe, ships' rigging in relief behind	s	37–38 Threadneedle Street (formerly British Linen Bank), City of London		Pevsner, *London: City*, 1997, 605; *Ward-Jackson* 2003, 402–3 (repr)
350.	1814–1816	'Raving' and 'Melancholy Madness' (restoration only, original work by C G Cibber)		[Bethlem Hospital, Moorfields, London, above broken pediment on main gates]; Bethlem Hospital, Beckenham, Kent		*Allderidge* 1977, 5
351.	nd	Altarpiece, depicting an angel holding a cross rising towards a crown	m	St Lawrence, Exeter, Devon		*Cresswell* 1908, 76
Reliefs						
352.	1792	Moses striking the rock		[Exhib RA, London, 611]; untraced		*Graves* I, 1905–6, 88
353.	1794	'Adam contemplating Eve sleeping'		[RA gold medal winner]; untraced		RA Premium list; *Farington* I, 268; *Graves* 1875, 19
354.	1802	'Lord Howe's Victory, etc'		[Exhib RA, London, 947]; untraced		*Graves* I, 1905–6, 88
Miscellaneous						
355.	1793	'Model of an academy figure'		[RA silver medal winner]; untraced		RA Premium list; *Farington* I, 111
356.	1796	The Ascension		[Exhib RA, London, 874]; untraced		*Graves* I, 1905–6, 88
357.	1807	'A tribute of conjugal affection to a deceased parent'		[Exhib BI, 1807]; untraced		*Graves* 1875, 19
358.	1809	Mary at the feet of Christ, for an unidentified monument		[Exhib RA, London, 772]; untraced		*Graves* I, 1905–6, 88

BACON, Thomas 1771–

The eldest son of **John Bacon RA** and Elizabeth, née Wade, he was born in Wardour Street, London, on 21 March 1771. He worked in his father's studio and exhibited at the Royal Academy between 1793 and 1795. These early works were all from scripture, perhaps influenced by the strict religious upbringing imposed by his father (1–3).

During the 1790s Thomas and his brother, **John Bacon II,** appear gradually to have taken over the family workshop: Robert Cecil, a family friend who prepared the obituary for John Bacon RA, wrote that the two sons had for 'many years conducted the executive part of the business' (*GM* 1799, vol 69, pt 2, 810). They completed several works left unfinished at their father's death, including the monument to Samuel Whitbread, which was exhibited at the Royal Academy, described as being 'by John Bacon and Sons' (*Graves* I, 1905–6, 88).

Cecil predicted that the loss to British sculpture occasioned by their father's death 'will be compensated by the genius of his sons' (*GM* 1799, vol 69, pt 2, 810). He was optimistic: Thomas seems not to have taken any interest in the profession after and it was John Bacon II who continued the business alone.

Literary References: *Cox-Johnson* 1961, 7, 12 n1; *Graves* I, 1905–6, 90; *Grove* 3, 1996, 26 (Bryant)

Miscellaneous					
1.	1793	The prodigal son	tc	[Exhib RA, London, 828]; untraced	*Graves* I, 1905–6, 90
2.	1794	Christ and the woman of Samaria		[Exhib RA, London, 604]; untraced	*Graves* I, 1905–6, 90
3.	1795	Christ in the garden		[Exhib RA, London, 685]; untraced	*Graves* I, 1905–6, 90

BAILES, Henry fl 1823–32

He gave his address as 434 Oxford Street in 1823, the year he was awarded a silver Isis medal from the Society of Arts (1). Another silver Isis medal followed in 1827 (2) and, in 1828, a large silver medal (3).

Reliefs					
1.	1823	Carving of flowers	wd	[Soc of A, silver Isis medal]; untraced	RSA *Transactions*, vol 41, 1823, xxxix
Miscellaneous					
2.	1827	'copy of a figure carved in wood'		[Soc of A, silver Isis medal]; untraced	RSA *Transactions*, vol 45, 1827, xxxi
3.	1828	'an original group of figures carved in wood'		[Soc of A, large silver medal]; untraced	RSA *Transactions*, vol 46, 1828, xxvii
4.	1832	Unidentified lady	w	[Exhib Soc of BA, London, 892]; untraced	*Johnson* 1975, 18

BAILEY, George, of Kingston-upon-Hull fl 1847–48

White's *Directory* of 1846 lists Bailey & Furness, stone and marble masons of 10 St John Street, Hull. A bill dated 1848 for masonry work, materials and lodgings at Burton Constable Hall is made out to 'George Bailey Statuary and Mason, successor to the late Joseph Earle' (EYCRO DDCC/2/72). (Inf. Gerardine Mulcahy)

Funerary Monuments				
1.	†1847	Unidentified subject (co-sculptor: Furness)	Bridlington Priory, E R Yorks	S

2.	?1850	Margaret Nainby		Barnoldby le Beck, Lincs	S	GPC
3.	†1854	Tommy (†1837) and George (†1854) Hawdon and family		Selby Abbey, W R Yorks	S	
4.	†1855	William and Ann (†1855) Hawdon		Selby Abbey, W R Yorks	S	
5.	†1857	Jane Bannister		Paull, E R Yorks	S	Pevsner, *Yorks: E R & York*, 1995, 646
6.	†1862	William Harland		Burton Pidsea, E R Yorks	S	Pevsner, *Yorks: E R & York*, 1995, 379
7.	?1863	Richard Nainby		Barnoldby le Beck, Lincs	S	GPC

BAILEY, John fl 1851–61

Bailey, whose address was given as 8 Conduit Street, Paddington, exhibited portrait busts at the Royal Academy and at the Society of British Artists between 1851 and 1861. He signs a monument with two portrait medallions commemorating Colonel Warren Firth and his wife at Nursling (**1**).

Funerary Monuments

1.	†1854	Colonel Warren Firth		Nursling, Hants	S	

Busts

2.	1851	Charles Pemberton		[Exhib RA, London, 1346]; untraced		*Graves* I, 1905–6, 92
3.	1851	James Campbell		[Exhib RA, London, 1338]; untraced		*Graves* I, 1905–6, 92
4.	1851	Mrs Charles Pemberton		[Exhib RA, London, 1325]; untraced		*Graves* I, 1905–6, 92
5.	1852	Dr MacIntyre		[Exhib RA, London, 1432]; untraced		*Graves* I, 1905–6, 92
6.	1852	Henry Milford Bovelle		[Exhib RA, London, 1413]; untraced		*Graves* I, 1905–6, 92
7.	1852	John Bailey QC		[Exhib RA, London, 1444]; untraced		*Graves* I, 1905–6, 92
8.	1852	Regnier Winkley Moore		[Exhib RA, London, 1447]; untraced		*Graves* I, 1905–6, 92
9.	1852	Richard Bethell, Baron Westbury		Wadham College, Oxford		*Graves* I, 1905–6, 92; *Ormond* 1973, 501
10.	1853	Dr Laurie, model		[Exhib Soc of BA, London, 746]; untraced		*Johnson* 1975, 18
11.	1853	Edwin Canton, model		[Exhib Soc of BA, London, 745]; untraced		*Johnson* 1975, 18
12.	1853	Mrs Richard Bethell		[Exhib RA, London, 1453]; untraced		*Graves* I, 1905–6, 92
13.	1853	R Woolaston, model		[Exhib Soc of BA, London, 747]; untraced		*Johnson* 1975, 18
14.	1853	William Edward Kilburn		[Exhib RA, London, 1361]; untraced		*Graves* I, 1905–6, 92
15.	1854	Albert, the Prince Consort		[Exhib Soc of BA, London, 750]; untraced		*Johnson* 1975, 18
16.	1854	Arthur, 1st Duke of Wellington		[Exhib Soc of BA, London, 735]; untraced		*Johnson* 1975, 18
17.	1854	Dr Currie		[Exhib Soc of BA, London, 736]; untraced		*Johnson* 1975, 18
18.	1854	Emperor Napoleon III, model		[Exhib Soc of BA, London, 734]; untraced		*Johnson* 1975, 18
19.	1854	General Duncan MacLeod Model(s): Exhib RA, London, 1853, 1378		[Exhib RA, London, 1446]; untraced		*Graves* I, 1905–6, 92
20.	1854	James Blyth		[Exhib RA, London, 1443]; untraced		*Graves* I, 1905–6, 92
21.	1854	Rev F W Robertson		[Exhib Soc of BA, London, 738]; untraced		*Johnson* 1975, 18
22.	1854	W Morgan	m	[Exhib Soc of BA, London, 737]; untraced		*Johnson* 1975, 18
23.	1855	Mrs James Blyth		[Exhib RA, London, 1464]; untraced		*Graves* I, 1905–6, 92
24.	1855	Queen Victoria	m	Gov Art Coll	SD	Gov Art Coll archives; *Johnson* 1975, 18
25.	1860	General Sir Archdale Wilson		[Exhib RA, London, 1074]; untraced		*Graves* I, 1905–6, 92
26.	1860	John, Baron Lawrence		[Exhib RA, London, 1049]; untraced		*Graves* I, 1905–6, 92; *Ormond* 1973, 265
27.	1861	Mr Justice Maule		[Exhib RA, London, 1092]; untraced		*Graves* I, 1905–6, 92
28.	1861	Mrs David D Keane		[Exhib RA, London, 1107]; untraced		*Graves* I, 1905–6, 92

BAILY, Edward Hodges RA 1788–1867

Baily was admired by contemporaries principally for his 'ideal' works but is now best remembered for the iconic statue of Admiral Lord Nelson in Trafalgar Square. He was born in Bristol on 10 March 1788, the son of a talented ship's carver (*AJ*, 1867, 170). At school he apparently showed more interest in carving portraits of his classmates than in following the curriculum and his first position, in a merchant's counting-house, lasted only two years. He began his artistic career as a modeller of small busts in wax (*AJ*, 1867, 170), but was drawn to 'a higher aspiration' by **John Bacon RA**'s monument to Elizabeth Draper in Bristol Cathedral (*AU*, 1847, 260).

Early encouragement is said to have come from a young surgeon called Leigh, who lent him **John Flaxman RA**'s designs for Homer's *Iliad* and commissioned from him two small groups based on the drawings. The results were so successful that Leigh recommended Baily to Flaxman, who accepted him as a pupil in 1807 (*AJ*, 1867, 170). Baily remained in Flaxman's studio for seven and a half years and was apparently his favourite assistant.

In 1808, whilst living in Upper Cleveland Street, Baily was awarded a silver medal from the Society of Arts for a plaster cast of the *Laocoon* (**113**). The same year he joined the Royal Academy schools, where he won a silver medal in 1809, and the gold, with a prize of 50 guineas in 1811 for *Hercules rescuing Alcestis from Orcas* (**326**). His first exhibited work to attract attention was a figure of *Apollo discharging his arrows against the Greeks* (**116**), which led to his election as an associate member of the Royal Academy in 1817. His celebrated *Eve at the fountain* (**119**), said to have been designed as a handle for the lid of a soup tureen ordered by a City livery company (*Builder* 1867, 387), was exhibited in 1820 and the following year he was elected a Royal Academician, depositing a marble of *Eve* as his diploma work. He showed regularly at the Royal Academy between 1810 and 1862 and at the British Institution from 1812 to 1840. Through most of his career Baily lived in the area around Tottenham Court Road, London; his address was 8 Percy Street between 1824 and 1847 and 17 Newman Street from 1848 until 1855.

In 1815 he began work as a designer and modeller with the goldsmiths Rundell, Bridge and Rundell, where he seems to have been employed to make detailed drawings from outline designs by more famous artists such as Flaxman, Thomas Stothard and **William Theed I**. In 1833, shortly before the death of his employer, John Bridge, Baily moved to the firm of Hunt and Roskell, where he worked until 1857, designing a large number of works, including candelabra, presentation plate and racing trophies such as the Russian Imperial Ascot Trophy, 1846 (Al-Tajir Collection).

Several major patrons helped to establish his formidable reputation as a sculptor of 'ideal' works. Joseph Neeld, the great-nephew of Philip Rundell (of Rundell, Bridge and Rundell) commissioned statues from him over a period of forty years, including *Adam and Eve* (**158**) and *The tired hunter* (**153**) and displayed them in the vast central hall of his neo-Romanesque mansion, Grittleton House. Baily carved marble statues of the *Pastoral Apollo* (**120**) and *Maternal love* (**130**) for the 3rd Earl of Egremont's gallery at Petworth and the merchant Elkanah Bicknell ordered statues of *Paris, Psyche, Cupid and Paris*, and showed them with his collection of British painting at his house in Herne Hill, which was visited by many art lovers (**136–9**).

The sculptor was involved in several major contracts in London during the 1820s, commissioned by the Royal Family and Office of Works. His most lucrative contract, valued at more than £6,000, was for statues and architectural ornaments intended for the Marble Arch (**315–16**), some of which appear to have been used on other buildings including, perhaps, the National Gallery (TNA WORK 19/3). There were difficulties, however, in extracting a final payment for the Arch and in 1831 he and **Sir Richard Westmacott RA** were obliged to remind the Treasury that a third and final payment was three years overdue (TNA WORK T. 1/3489 box 1, labelled 1833/back to 1829). Baily provided architectural ornaments and interior friezes for the throne room at Buckingham Palace (**318**), but another royal commission, for eight statues on the gateway at Hyde Park Corner, collapsed because of the King's death in 1830.

Baily had a large practice in funerary monuments and these were admired and even celebrated in verse, though he was never as popular as his rival, **Sir Francis Chantrey RA**. Echoes of Flaxman's designs are apparent in many, for instance the Denys memorial at Easton Neston, which features a group of three linear angels floating above the family tomb (**62**). As with most sculptors, his quality varied: Viscount Brome's recumbent figure at Linton, Kent (**63**) was considered by Gunnis far to surpass Chantrey's admired effigy of Lady Frederica Stanhope in the same county, but the monument to Sir William Ponsonby in St Paul's Cathedral was condemned by him as 'utter bathos' (**8**).

His statues elicited a mixed response. *Eve at the fountain*, the figure which gave him a European reputation, was seen as 'a marble inspiration softened into life' (*Builder*, 1867, 387), but the figure of Lord Chief Justice Tindal (**146**), exhibited at the Royal Academy in 1847, aroused a venomous response in the *Art Journal*, which accused him of 'patching up' an old model of Sir William Blackstone by John Bacon RA. Baily's portrait busts were not highly regarded, except for the image of Douglas Jerrold, a journalist and playwright well known in his day for his contributions to *Punch* (**291**), which was admired by the *Builder* for its interpretative power (1867, 387).

The sculptor's enduring work is the statue of Horatio, Lord Nelson, in Trafalgar Square (**135**). In 1838 Baily was one of 150 artists competing for this prestigious commission and he suggested a figure of the Admiral standing on a rock at the foot of an obelisk, surrounded by a mythological group. This design came second to William Railton's suggestion for a simple Corinthian column. A new competition was held the following year, and eventually the committee compromised by choosing Railton's column supporting an 'unadorned' statue by Baily. Other major public works included statues of William Murray, 1st Earl of Mansfield (**156**) and Charles James Fox (**157**) for St Stephen's Hall, at the Palace of Westminster.

Baily had a succession of notable pupils and studio assistants including **Musgrave Lewthwaite Watson, William Theed II, William Calder Marshall RA, Joseph Durham, Edward Bowring Stevens** and **Alfred Gatley**.

The sculptor must have been affluent at times during his career, but he seems to have been extravagant and may have had financial problems as early as 1833, when he wrote to the council of the Royal Academy, asking them to adopt measures to improve the distressed state of sculpture. In 1857 he was one of the sculptors submitting a design for the Duke of Wellington's monument in St Paul's Cathedral, but was unsuccessful, and he applied to the Royal Academy that year for financial assistance. Finally, in 1863, he was made an Honorary Retired Academician with a pension of £200. He did not exhibit again and died at Holloway, London, on 22 May 1867. His daughter Amelia was given a pension of £25, rising to £35, in the years 1867–71.

Though Baily's achievement has been overshadowed both by Chantrey's and Flaxman's, his obituary in the *Art Journal* accorded him a distinctive place as one of the most successful sculptors of his century, an artist who upheld the dignity of his profession (*AJ*, 1867, 170). The many portraits of Baily suggest that he enjoyed celebrity thoroughout his mature career.

EH

Literary References: *Smith* 1931, *passim*; *K-Browne* 1966, 708–12; *Oman* 1966, 174–83; *Gunnis* 1968, 32–6; *Physick* 1969, 41–2, 181, 186; *Radcliffe* 1969, 44–51; *Ormond* 1973, 22–3; *Penny* 1975 (1), 314–32; *Potterton* 1975, 36; *Penny* 1977 (1), *passim*; *Ormond and Rogers* 2, 1979–81, 11; *Read* 1982, *passim*; *Whinney* 1988, *passim*; *Kelly* 1990, 221; *Sporting Glory* 1992, 62–3; *Groseclose* 1995, 74; *Kader* 1996, 177–82; *Grove* 1996, 3, 78–9 (Eustace); *Bennett* 1998, 130; *Dawson* 1999, 44–5, 96–9, 212; *Curl* 2001, 242

Archival References: Baily/RA Council (re submission of *Eve* as diploma work, 31 Nov 1821; Baily / RA Council (2) (deploring effect on British sculptors of unfair competition from Italy, 15 Nov 1833); Baily /RA Council (3) (requesting financial assistance 6 Dec 1837, £30 paid); Baily/RA Council (4) (defending himself against allegations that he had worked on models by students in Antique school who were candidates for prizes, Nov 1843); RA/GA, 1867–71

Additional MS Sources: *Baily Biog Coll; Baily Corresp; Baily/White;* coll for a biography including some original correspondence, BL Add MSS 38678

Wills and Administrations: PPR, 21 June 1867, fol 393, letters of administration with will annexed, effects under £50

Miscellaneous Drawings: Album of designs for plate for Rundell, Bridge and Rundell, including some perhaps by Baily, VAM, E.70-124-1964; several sketches of winged figures, HMI Archive

Portraits of the Sculptor: J Dinham, bust, exhib RA, 1826, 1092; J Lonsdale, canvas, exhib RA, 1828, 91; Sir William Beechey, canvas, exhib RA, 1829, 301; Miss Turner, lithograph, BM, NPG; T Mogford, canvas, exhib RA, 1843, 13; T Bridgford, drawing, exhib RA, 1843, 1059, engraved by J Smyth for the *Art Union*, 1847; drawing, Charles Hutton Lear, drawing, NPG, c1846, NPG 1456 (1); watercolour, artist unknown, c1850, NPG 6364; T Mogford, exhib RA 1854, 535; E G Papworth the younger, plaster statue, executed for Joseph Neeld, exhib RA, 1856, 1297; E G Papworth the younger, bust, exhib RA, 1856, 1331; G Tuson, canvas, exhib RA, 1858, 588; J E Williams, canvas, exhib RA, 1863, 693; self-portrait, canvas, nd, coll T C Bates; woodcut, published ILN, L (1867), 569; E G Papworth junior, bust, exhib RA 1868, 1127; A B Wyon, bronze medallion, nd, issued by the Art Union; photographs, NPG

Funerary Monuments

No.	Date	Subject	Location		Literature
1.	†1845	Caroline Savill-Onley	Stisted, Essex	S	Pevsner, *Essex*, 1965, 372; C Lib (repr)
2.	?1853	John Ogle	Whalton, Northumbs		*Gunnis* 1968, 36
3.	?1812	Archibald Randolph	Much Hadham, Herts		*Gunnis* 1968, 35
4.	c1819	Calverley Bewicke (†1815) (designed by William Theed)	Newcastle Cathedral, Northumbs		*Graves* I, 1905–6, 93; Pevsner, *Northumbs* 1992, 423; C Lib (repr)
5.	?1819	Elizabeth Hughes	Uffington, Berks		*Gunnis* 1968, 35
6.	†1819	Joseph Sheepshanks	Holy Trinity, Leeds, W R Yorks	S	
7.	†1820	George Gostling	Egham, Surrey		Pevsner, *Surrey*, 1971, 209
8.	1820	Major-General Sir William Ponsonby (†1815) (designed by William Theed)	St Paul's Cathedral, London, crypt	S	*Graves* I, 1905–6, 93; *Saunders* 2001, 144 (repr)
9.	†1821	Anne Sheepshanks	Holy Trinity, Leeds, W R Yorks	S	
10.	?1821	Elizabeth Russell	Moseley, Birmingham, Warks		*Gunnis* 1968, 35
11.	†1821	Sarah Fortescue	Little Torrington, Devon		Pevsner, *Devon*, 1989, 539
12.	†1822	Rebecca Dulaney	Patching, Sussex	S	C Lib (repr)
13.	†1823	Charles, 2nd Marquess Cornwallis	Culford, Suffolk	S	Pevsner, *Suffolk*, 1974, 181
14.	†1823	John, 1st Earl St Vincent	St Paul's Cathedral, London, crypt	SD	*Gunnis* 1968, 35; C Lib (repr)
15.	†1823	Joseph Bainbridge	Newcastle Cathedral, Northumbs		*Penny* 1977 (1), 6 (repr)
16.	†1823	Maria, 1st wife of James, 5th Earl Cornwallis	Linton, Kent	S	Pevsner, *Kent: W & Weald*, 1976, 381
17.	†1823	Robert Taylor	Thames Ditton, Surrey		*Gunnis* 1968, 35
18.	†1824	James, 4th Earl Cornwallis, Bishop of Lichfield and Coventry	Lichfield Cathedral, Staffs	S	
19.	†1824	Rev Thomas Roberts	All Hallows, Tottenham, Middx		*Gunnis* 1968, 35; C Lib (repr)
20.	†1824	Sir Francis Bayley	Christchurch Cathedral, Oxford		*Gunnis* 1968, 35
21.	†1824	Sir Francis Bayley	St John, Hackleton's Cliff, Barbados, WI	S	
22.	†1824	Thomas Parry	St George's Cathedral, Chennai (Madras), India	S	*Groseclose* 1995, 74 (repr)
23.	†1825	Professor Peter Paul Dobrée	Trinity College, Cambridge	S	*Graves* I, 1905–6, 94; Pevsner, *Cambs*, 1970, 168; C Lib (repr)
24.	?1825	Sir Richard Richards	Dolgelley, Merioneth		*Gunnis* 1968, 35
25.	†1826	Eliza Mortimer	St Martin, Exeter, Devon		*Penny* 1977 (1), 97 (repr)
26.	†1826	Harriet Middleton	Bristol Cathedral	S	*Penny* 1977 (1), 72–3 (repr)
27.	†1826	William Salmon	St John, Devizes, Wilts		Pevsner, *Wilts*, 1975, 207; C Lib (repr)
28.	?1827	Catherine Verney	Middle Claydon, Bucks		*Gunnis* 1968, 35
29.	†1827	Frederick-Augustus, Duke of York and Albany (after Nollekens) Model(s): RA, London, 1823, 1113	Freemasons' Hall, Holborn, London		*Graves* 1906, 1, 93; Pevsner, *London: N*, 1998, 267
30.	†1827	George Pelham, Bishop of Lincoln	Buckden, Hunts	S	*Penny* 1977 (1), 73 (repr)
31.	?1827	Lieutenant-General John Skinner	Heston, Middx		*Gunnis* 1968, 35
32.	1828	'A Monument'	[Exhib RA, London, 1193]; untraced		*Graves* I, 1905–6, 94
33.	†1828	Alan Walker Heneage	Compton Bassett, Wilts		Pevsner, *Wilts*, 1975, 189
34.	†1828	Captain Joseph Builderson	All Saints, Hessle, E R Yorks		Pevsner, *Yorks: E R & York*, 1995, 468
35.	†1828	Lydia Gostling	Egham, Surrey	S	Pevsner, *Surrey*, 1971, 209; C Lib (repr)
36.	1829	'A Monument'	[Exhib RA, London, 1171]; untraced		*Graves* I, 1905–6, 94
37.	?1829	Clare Colville	Hawstead, Suffolk		*Gunnis* 1968, 35
38.	†1829	Elizabeth Bell	St James, Grimsby, Lincs		Pevsner, *Lincs*, 1989, 338
39.	†1829	Thomas Turner	[St Mary Major, Exeter, Devon]; untraced	S	GPC; C Lib (repr)
40.	†1830	George, 3rd Earl of Pomfret	Easton Neston, Northants (2004)	S	*Graves* I, 1905–6, 94; *CIIA* 4/3/66–7 (repr)
41.	1830	John Smith (†1826)	Newcastle Cathedral, Northumbs	SD	C Lib (repr)
42.	c1830	Lieutenant-Colonel Sir Richard Fletcher (†1813)	Westminster Abbey, London, north west tower	S	WAM (7), 66271, 66267, 66270; *MacMichael*, 1974, 22; C Lib (repr)
43.	1830	Mrs Vernon	Ardington, Berks		*Penny* 1977 (1), 73–4; GPC
44.	1830	Resurrection, model for a monument executed in marble	[Exhib Soc of BA, London, 859]; untraced		*Johnson* 1975, 18
45.	?1830	Rev Thomas Whalley	Ecton, Northants		*Gunnis* 1968, 35
46.	†1831	John and Charles (†1821) Spearing	Potterne, Wilts	S	Pevsner, *Wilts*, 1975, 371
47.	†1831	John Ogle	Whalton, Northumbs		Pevsner, *Northumbs*, 1992, 623
48.	1832	'Monument at Millbrook'	[Exhib RA, London, 1213]; untraced		*Graves* I, 1905–6, 94
49.	†1832	Rev Daniel Durand	St Peter Port, Guernsey	S	
50.	†1832	Rev George Crabbe	St James, Trowbridge, Wilts		Pevsner, *Wilts*, 1975, 533
51.	†1833	David Taylor	Wotton-under-Edge, Glos	S	Pevsner, *Glos: Cotswolds*, 1999, 757
52.	†1833	Hannah More	Wrington, Somerset		Pevsner, *Somerset: N & Bristol*, 1958, 350
53.	†1833	John Jebb, Bishop of Limerick, with portrait medallion	Holy Trinity, Clapham Common, London	S	Pevsner, *London: S*, 1983, 380; GPC
54.	†1833	Matthew Davies Williams	Llanbadarn Fawr, Aberystwyth		*Penny* 1977 (1), 73
55.	†1834	Robert Gray, Bishop of Bristol	Bristol Cathedral	S	Pevsner, *Somerset: N & Bristol*, 1958, 383
56.	?1835	Gertrude Shuckburgh	Shuckburgh, Warks		*Gunnis* 1968, 36
57.	†1835	Lieutenant C J Mann	Linton, Kent		*Gunnis* 1968, 36; AL/RG
58.	1835	'Monument at Cwm, Aberystwyth'	[Exhib RA, London, 1079]; untraced		*Graves* I, 1905–6, 94
59.	†1835	Mr Horne	St Edmund the King,City of London		Pevsner, *London: I*, 1997, 218

No.	Date	Subject	Location		Bibliography
60.	†1835	Rev Lewis Evans	Llandre, Cardigan		GPC
61.	1836	John Jebb, Bishop of Limerick (†1833)	[Exhib RA, London, 1060]; Limerick Cathedral, Ireland	S	*Graves* I, 1905–6, 94; *Potterton* 1975, 36; GPC
62.	1818–36	Peter Denys (†1816), Lady Charlotte Denys (†1835) and Charlotte Denys (†1815) Payment(s): £430 15s	Easton Neston, Northants	SD	*Graves* I, 1905–6, 94; Chantrey Ledger, 103; *CIIA* 4/3/68, 71 (repr)
63.	†1836	Viscount Brome and Lady Jemima (†1836) Wykeham-Martin	Linton, Kent		Pevsner, *Kent: W & Weald*, 1976, 381
64.	1837	Charles, Viscount Brome (†1835)	[Exhib RA, London, 1837, 1167]; Linton, Kent	S	*Graves* I, 1905–6, 94; *Penny* 1977 (1), 122–3
65.	†1837	George, 3rd Earl of Egremont	Petworth, Sussex		*Graves* I, 1905–6, 94; Pevsner, *Sussex*, 1965, 296; *Penny* 1977 (1), 39
66.	†1837	Hannah Gostling	Egham, Surrey		Pevsner, *Surrey*, 1971, 209; C Lib (repr)
67.	1839	Hon Sir James Park (†1838)	St Mary the Virgin, Wimbledon, Surrey	SD	*Gunnis* 1968, 36
68.	1839	John Marshall (†1837)	Worfield, Salop	S	GPC
69.	1839	Thomas Telford (†1834)	[Exhib RA, London, 1296]; Westminster Abbey, London, north transept		*Graves* I, 1905–6, 94; Pevsner, *London: 1*, 1973, 449; C Lib (repr)
70.	1840	Francis Harington (†1836)	St James, Sydney, Australia	SD	
71.	†1840	Laura, Countess Cornwallis	Linton, Kent		Pevsner, *Kent: W & Weald*, 1976, 381
72.	†1840	Sir Henry Fane	Fulbeck, Lincs		Pevsner, *Lincs*, 1989, 291
73.	1840	Thomas Tregonna Biddulph (†1838)	St James, Bristol	SD	Pevsner, *Somerset: N & Bristol*, 1958, 390; GPC
74.	†1841	Dr William Brame Elwyn	Bristol Cathedral	S	Pevsner, *Somerset: N & Bristol*, 1958, 382; GPC
75.	†1841	Elizabeth Sparrow	Colwich, Staffs	S	Pevsner, *Staffs*, 1974, 107; GPC
76.	1842	Admiral Sir Pultney Malcolm (†1838)	St Paul's Cathedral, London, crypt	SD	*AU*, 1842, 128; *Graves* I, 1905–6, 94; Pevsner, *London: City*, 1997, 181; C Lib (repr)
77.	1842	Archibald Randolph (†1841)	Much Hadham, Herts		RG/JP, 1, 83
78.	†1842	Mrs Colby Loftus	Woolland, Dorset		Pevsner, *Dorset*, 1972, 498
79.	†1842	Sarah Russell	St Mary, Handsworth, Birmingham, Warks		*Penny* 1977 (1), 104, 105 (repr)
80.	1842	Sir Astley Cooper (†1842) Model(s): exhib RA, London, 1842, 1298	St Paul's Cathedral, London		*Graves* I, 1905–6, 94; Pevsner, *London: City*, 1997, 181; C Lib (repr)
81.	1843	Dean Henry Dawson (†1840)	St Patrick's Cathedral, Dublin	SD	*AU*, 1844, 170; *Graves* I, 1905–6, 94; *Potterton* 1975, 36
82.	1843	Dr James Wood	St John's College, Cambridge, chapel		*Graves* I, 1905–6, 94; Pevsner, *Cambs*, 1970, 154
83.	†1843	John Carey	St James-the-Less, Longton, Staffs	S	Pevsner, *Staffs*, 1974, 261; C Lib (repr)
84.	1843	Samuel Butler, Bishop of Lichfield	[St Mary, Shrewsbury, Salop]; destroyed		*Graves* I, 1905–6, 94; Pevsner, *Salop*, 1958, 269
85.	†1843	Thomas Botfield	Hopton Wafers, Salop	S	Pevsner, *Salop*, 1958, 154
86.	1843	Thomas Claughton (†1842)	Winwick, Lancs		AL/RG
87.	1843	Vice-Admiral Sir Thomas Hardy (†1839)	Royal Hospital, Greenwich (ORNC), chapel	S	
88.	†1844	Eliza Paynter	Stoke, Guildford, Surrey	S	C Lib (repr)
89.	1844	Model of a monumental statue	[Exhib RA, London, 1275]; untraced		*Graves* I, 1905–6, 94
90.	?1844	Samuel Paynter	Richmond, Surrey		*Gunnis* 1968, 36
91.	1845	General Sir Thomas Saumarez (†1845)	St Peter Port, Guernsey	SD	
92.	1845	Isaac Watts (†1748)	Abney Park Cemetery, Stoke Newington, London		Pevsner, *London: N*, 1998, 537
93.	†1845	John 'Gentleman' Jackson	Brompton Cemetery, Kensington, London		Pevsner, *London: N W*, 1991, 471
94.	†1845	Philip Miles	Abbotsleigh, Somerset	S	Pevsner, *Somerset: N & Bristol*, 1958, 77; C Lib (repr)
95.	1845	Robert Southey (†1843)	Bristol Cathedral		*ILN*, 27 June 1846, 413 (repr); *Read* 1982, 103
96.	†1846	Georgiana Caldecott	Baldock, Herts	S	Pevsner, *Herts*, 1977, 821; C Lib (repr)
97.	†1846	Henry, 4th Earl of Carrick	Lumley Chapel, Cheam, Surrey		*Gunnis* 1968, 36
98.	?1846	Sara Ogle	Whalton, Northumbs		*Gunnis* 1968, 36
99.	†1846	Sophia Dickson	Holy Trinity, Fareham, Hants	S	Pevsner, *Hants & Isle of Wight*, 1967, 222; GPC
100.	?1847	George Fullerton	South Stoneham, Hants		*Gunnis* 1968, 36
101.	*c*1847	Henry, 3rd Baron Holland (†1840)	Westminster Abbey, London, north transept		Pevsner, *London: 1*, 1973, 454
102.	†1847	Julia, Countess Cornwallis	Linton, Kent		Pevsner, *Kent: W & Weald*, 1976, 381
103.	1848	Afghan and Sikh memorial	Norwich Cathedral,	S	*Barnes* 2001, 30 (repr)
104.	1848	Elizabeth Williamson	Norfolk Grosvenor Chapel, South Audley Street, London		RG/JP, 1, 83
105.	†1849	Robert Vernon	Ardington, Berks		Pevsner, *Berks*, 1966, 67
106.	1850	Major Eldred Pottinger (†1843)	Mumbai (Bombay) Cathedral, India		*ILN*, 13 April 1850, 244 (repr)
107.	?1850	Mary Fullerton	South Stoneham, Hants		*Gunnis* 1968, 36
108.	?1850	Rev Edward Benbow	Aldenham, Herts		*Gunnis* 1968, 36
109.	†1851	John Thackery	St Mary, Lewisham, London	S	Pevsner, *London: S*, 1983, 415; C Lib (repr)
110.	1851	Thomas Fleming (†1848)	Manchester Cathedral, Lancs		*Graves* I, 1905–6, 95; *CIIA* 4/8/44–5 (repr)

111.	1853	Edward Pendarves		Camborne, Cornwall		Pevsner, *Cornwall*, 1970, 50
112.	† to 1854	Gostling children		Effingham, Surrey	S	
Statues						
113.	1808	Laocoon, plaster cast		[Soc of A, silver medal]; untraced		RSA *Transactions*, vol 36, 1808, 20
114.	1812	Neptune, figure		[Exhib BI, London, 216]; untraced		*Graves* 1875, 19
115.	1814	Hercules wrestling with Achelous, sketch		[Exhib BI, London, 229]; untraced		*Graves* 1875, 20; *Graves* I, 1905–6, 93
116.	1815	Apollo discharging his arrows against the Greeks		[Grittleton House, Wilts]; untraced		*Graves* 1875, 20; *Graves* I, 1905–6, 93; *Gunnis* 1968, 35; *Johnson* 1975, 18
117.	1817	'Flora (for the Earl of Darnley)'	m	[Exhib RA, London, 1062]; untraced		*Graves* I, 1905–6, 93
118.	1821	Eve, diploma work		RA, London		Baily/RA Council
119.	1822	Eve at the fountain Model(s): Bristol Museum and Art Gallery N6929; VAM A.3-2000	m	Bristol MAG Other versions: Ny Carlsberg Glyptotek, Copenhagen, replica	SD	*Manchester Art Treasures* 1857, 133; *Graves* I, 1905–6, 93; *Johnson* 1975, 18; *Grove* 3, 1996, 78; *Bilbey* 2002, 185–6 (repr)
120.	1824	Pastoral Apollo	m	Petworth House, Sussex		*Grove* 3, 1996, 79
121.	1825	Edward Jenner, sketch		[Exhib RA, London, 1046]; untraced		*Graves* I, 1905–6, 93
122.	1826	Painting deriving inspiration from Poetry, group		[Exhib RA, London, 1069]; untraced		*Graves* 1875, 20;*Graves* I, 1905–6, 94; *Johnson* 1975, 18
123.	1827	Edward Augustus, Duke of Kent and Strathearn		[Sketch exhib RA, London, 1822, 991]; Freemasons' Hall, London		*Graves* I, 1905–6, 93; Pevsner, *London: N*, 1998, 267
124.	c1827	Justice		Old Council House, Bristol		Pevsner, *Somerset: N & Bristol*, 1958, 414; C Lib (repr)
125.	c1830	Pallas Athene		Athenaeum Club, London, porch		Pevsner, *London: 1*, 1973, 668
126.	c1830	Rt Hon George Canning (†1827) statuette	p	Bristol MAG (on loan)		
127.	1833	Marius among the ruins of Carthage	p	VAM 8126-1862		*Graves* I, 1905–6, 94; *Bilbey* 2002, 186 (repr)
128.	c1835	A baby lying on a cushion	m	Foundling Hospital, London	SD	
129.	1835	Mother and child	m	[Cressbrook Hall, Derbys]; Manchester CAG 1886.2		*Graves* I, 1905–6, 94; *Gunnis* 1968, 35
130.	1837	Maternal love	m	[Grittleton House, Wilts]; VAM A.33-1964 Other versions: Petworth House, Sussex Fitzwilliam M.3-1974, SD 1841 Reproduced in Parian ware	SD	*Graves* 1875, 20; *Graves* I, 1905–6, 93–4; *JKB* 1966, 712; *Johnson* 1975, 18; *Atterbury* 1989, 12, repr 6 (Parian version repr); *Bilbey* 2002, 186–7 (repr)
131.	1838	Charles, 2nd Earl Grey (on a column by Benjamin Green)	s	Eldon Square, Newcastle, Northumbs		*Graves* I, 1905–6, 94; *Usherwood* 2000, 96–8 (repr)
132.	1839	The children of Sir F Shuckburgh Bt, group		[Exhib RA, London, 1300]; untraced		*Graves* I, 1905–6, 94
133.	1841	Eve listening to the voice	m	VAM 468-1875 Other versions: Ex coll Joseph Neeld, Grittleton Hall, SD 1849; untraced Ex coll Elkanah Bicknell, Herne Hill; untraced	SD	*Graves* I, 1905–6, 94; *Read* 1982, 203; *Bilbey* 2002, 188 (repr)
134.	1841	Sir Richard Bourke, model, for Sydney	m	Royal Botanical Garden, Sydney, NSW, Australia		*Graves* I, 1905–6, 94
135.	1839–1843	Admiral Lord Nelson (on a column designed by William Railton) Drawing(s): design BI, London, 1840, 447 Model(s): Admiralty House, London MOD 20179 (ID557)		Trafalgar Square, London		*Graves* I, 1905–6, 94; *Read* 1982, 61–2, 87–90 (repr); *Yarrington* 1988, 293–317 (repr 110); *Darke* 1991, 36–8 (repr)
136.	1843	Helen unveiling herself to Paris	m	[Elkanah Bicknell, of Herne Hill, London; sold 1863, £162]; untraced		Bicknell sale cat, 1863, 24; *Graves* I, 1905–6, 94; *Gunnis* 1968, 34, 35
137.	1843	Psyche	m	[Elkanah Bicknell, of Herne Hill, London; sold 1863, lot 144, £315]; untraced		Bicknell sale cat, 1863, 24; *Graves* I, 1905–6, 94; *Gunnis* 1968, 34, 35
138.	1844	Cupid Model(s): exhib RA, London, 1844, 1282		[Elkanah Bicknell, of Herne Hill, London; sold 1863, lot 145, bt Rhodes, £252]; untraced		Bicknell sale cat, 1863, 24; *Graves* I, 1905–6, 94; *Gunnis* 1968, 34
139.	1844	Paris Model(s): exhib RA, London, 1844, 1269	m	[Elkanah Bicknell, of Herne Hill, London; sold 1863, lot 142, £154]; untraced		*AU*, 1844, 170; Bicknell sale cat, 1863, 24; *Graves* I, 1905–6, 94; *Gunnis* 1968, 33–4
140.	1844	Sir Charles Metcalfe Model(s): exhib RA, London, 1845, 1326		Kingston, Jamaica		*AU*, 1845, 195; *Graves* I, 1905–6, 95; *Gunnis* 1968, 34
141.	1845	Flora		Grittleton House, Wilts (1955)		GPC
142.	1845	Nymph preparing for the bath	m	[Joseph Neeld MP, Grittleton House, Wilts]; Grittleton sale, lot 11, bt Old Clock House, 260 gns; untraced Other versions: cast shown Gt Exhib with The tired hunter (bronze medal)	SD	*AU*, 1844, 195; *Graves* I, 1905–6, 95; *JKB* 1966, 710; *Grittleton Marbles*, 1966
143.	1846	Augustus Frederick, Duke of Sussex		Freemasons' Hall, London		*AU*, 1846, 188; *Graves* I, 1905–6, 95; Pevsner, *London: N*, 1998, 267
144.	1846	David Hare		[Sanskritt College, Kolkata (Calcutta)]; Presidency college, Kolkata		*AU*, 1846, 188; *Graves* 1906, 1, 95; *Steggles* 2000, 133–4 (repr)

No.	Date	Title		Location		Literature
145.	1846	Mother and child	m	Glasgow Museums S.6		inf: Glasgow Museums
146.	1847	Lord Chief Justice Sir Nicholas Conyngham Tindal Model(s): exhib RA, London, 1847, 1328		Tindal Square, Chelmsford, Essex		*AU*, 1847, 200; *Graves* I, 1905–6, 95; *Read* 1982, 104; *Darke* 1991, 193–4 (repr)
147.	1849	Infant Bacchus	m	[coll A H Novelli]; untraced		*Manchester Art Treasures* 1857, 134; *Graves* I, 1905–6, 95
148.	1849	John Flaxman, seated		[Exhib RA, London, 1208]; University College, London		*Graves* I, 1905–6, 95; *Kader* 1996, 179
149.	1849	The three graces, group	m	[Grittleton House, Wilts]; Grittleton sale; bt Ferguson, 320 gns	SD	*Graves* 1906, 1, 95; *JKB* 1966, 710–2 (repr); *Grittleton Marbles* 1966, 10 (repr II)
150.	1850	Sleeping girl	m	Bristol MAG	SD	*Graves* I, 1905–6, 95; *Gunnis* 1968, 35
151.	1851	George Stephenson	m	[Euston Station, London]; NRM, York		*Usherwood* 2000, 149
152.	1851	Sir Robert Peel Model(s): Bury Art Gallery, Lancs, plaster	b	Bury, Lancs, marketplace		*Graves* I, 1905–6, 95; *Ormond* 1973, 372; *Read* 1982, 29–30, 107, 147, 148 (repr)
153.	1851	The tired hunter (youth returning from the chase; a youth and his dog)	m	[Joseph Neeld MP, Grittleton House, Wilts]; Grittleton sale, lot 12, bt Des Roches, 750 gns	SD	*Graves* I, 1905–6, 95; *Grittleton Marbles*, 1966, 12 (repr III); *Read* 1982, 141, 142 (repr)
154.	1853–1854	The morning star	m	CL Coll, Mansion House, City of London, 144	SD	*Knight* 1986, 14, 330 (repr); *Jeffery* 1993, 306; *Ward-Jackson* 2003, 245–6 (repr)
155.	1855	Sir Charles James Napier, 'sketch for a colossal statue'		[Exhib RA, London, 1555]; untraced		*Graves* I, 1905–6, 95; *Ormond* 1973, 334
156.	1855	William Murray, 1st Earl of Mansfield	m	Palace of Westminster, London, St Stephen's Hall	SD	*Walker* 1961, 45, 97–8, cat 49
157.	1856	Charles James Fox Model(s): exhib RA, London, 1857, 1210	m	Palace of Westminster, London, St Stephen's Hall	SD	*Graves* I, 1905–6, 95; *Walker* 1961, 28, cat 30; *Read* 1982, 83 (repr)
158.	1857	Adam and Eve (Adam consoling Eve after the evil dream)	m	[Grittleton House, Wilts]; Grittleton sale; bt Crowther, 320 gns	SD	*Graves* I, 1905–6, 93, 95; *JKB* 1966, 710–2 (repr); *Grittleton Marbles* 1966, 13
159.	1856–1857	The fate of genius (spirit of the woods)	m	[CL Coll, Mansion House, City of London, acc 135]; destroyed		*Graves* I, 1905–6, 95; *Knight* 1986, 14, 330 (repr); *Ward-Jackson* 2003, 249–50 (repr)
160.	1858	Joseph Mallord William Turner RA		[Exhib RA, London, 1184]; untraced		*Graves* I, 1905–6, 95
161.	1858	Valentine Knight		[Exhib RA, London, 1281]; untraced		*Graves* I, 1905–6, 95
162.	1860	Rev T J Judkins, statuette		[Exhib RA, London, 963]; untraced		*Graves* I, 1905–6, 95
163.	1862	A clergyman, statuette		[Exhib RA, London, 1047]; untraced		*Graves* I, 1905–6, 95
164.	1862	Late Archdeacon of Liverpool, statuette		[Exhib RA, London, 1043]; untraced		*Graves* I, 1905–6, 95
165.	nd	'Child standing by its mother'	m	[Cartwright sale, Christie, London, 28 Feb 1865]; untraced		
166.	nd	George Stephenson, statuette		[Christie, London, 22 June 1861]; untraced		GPC
167.	nd	John Flaxman		[Grittleton House, Wilts]; untraced		*Kader* 1996, 178 n6, 179 n15
168.	nd	King George IV on a rearing horse, statuette (cast by Rundell, Bridge & Rundell)	b	Royal Coll	S	JM
169.	nd	'Mother nursing a child'	m	[Cartwright sale, Christie, London, 28 Feb 1865]; untraced		GPC
170.	nd	Sir Robert Peel, statuette		[Christie, London, 22 June 1861]; untraced		GPC
171.	nd	Thomas Stothard		[Grittleton House, Wilts]; untraced		*Kader* 1996, 178, n6
172.	nd	Wrestlers	p	[Lawrence sale, 1830, lot 58, bt Hutchinson, £3]; untraced		Lawrence sale cat
173.	nd	Sir Henry Havelock, statuette		[Christie, London, 22 June 1861]; untraced		
Busts						
174.	1818	Benjamin Robert Haydon		[Exhib RA, London, 1085]; untraced		*Graves* I, 1905–6, 93
175.	1818	Mr Baily, the sculptor's father		[Exhib RA, London, 1087]; untraced		*Graves* I, 1905–6, 93
176.	1819	An artist		[Exhib RA, London, 1234]; untraced		*Graves* I, 1905–6, 93
177.	1820	Edward Hodges	m	[Exhib RA, London, 1116]; YCBA B 1977.14.1	SD	*Graves* I, 1905–6, 93
178.	1821	A clergyman		[Exhib RA, London, 1123]; untraced		*Graves* I, 1905–6, 93
179.	1821	C Muss		[Exhib RA, London, 1147]; untraced		*Graves* I, 1905–6, 93
180.	1821	John Bridge		Piddletrenthide school, Dorset Other versions: coll Derek Sherborn (*c*1985)		Pevsner, *Dorset*, 1972, 314; GPC
181.	1821	T Bigg		[Exhib RA, London, 1119]; untraced		*Graves* I, 1905–6, 93
182.	1821	W L Thomas		[Exhib RA, London, 1149]; untraced		*Graves* I, 1905–6, 93
183.	1823	J T Barker Beaumont		[Exhib RA, London, 1095]; untraced		*Graves* I, 1905–6, 93
184.	1823	John Flaxman	m	[65 Russell Square, London; Lawrence sale 1830 (2)]; RA, Burlington House, London, members' rooms		*Graves* I, 1905–6, 93; *Kader* 1996, 179, 181 (repr)
185.	1823	Michael Faraday		untraced		*Ormond* 1973, 169
186.	1823	P Norton		[Exhib RA, London, 1089]; untraced		*Graves* I, 1905–6, 93
187.	1823	R Hart-Davis		Sotheby, 5 Oct 2000, lot 142		*Graves* I, 1905–6, 93; AL/RG
188.	1823	Unidentified gentleman		[Exhib RA, London, 1105]; untraced		*Graves* I, 1905–6, 93
189.	1824	Henry Fuseli	m	[65 Russell Square, London]; Hazlitt, Gooden and Fox, London (2001); untraced	SD	*Graves* I, 1905–6, 93; *Kader* 1996, 178–80, 181, (repr)

190.	1824	Master Emilius Watson Taylor		[Erlestoke 1832, lot 180]; untraced		*Graves* I, 1905–6, 93; *Gunnis* 1968, 34
191.	1825	Joseph Munden		[Exhib RA, London, 1030]; untraced		*Graves* I, 1905–6, 93; *Johnson* 1975, 18
192.	1825	Samuel Dobrée	m	Merchant Taylors' Hall, City of London		*Graves* I, 1905–6, 93; *Gunnis* 1968, 34
193.	1825	Thomas Bewick	m	Lit and Phil Soc, Newcastle, Northumbs		*Dawson* 1999, 44
194.	1826	George, 6th Lord Byron	m	Harrow School, old schools Other versions: several recorded		*Graves* I, 1905–6, 94; *Johnson* 1975, 18; Pevsner, *London: NW*, 1991, 266
195.	1826	John Benwell Davis MD		[Exhib RA, London, 1044]; untraced		*Graves* I, 1905–6, 93
196.	1826	Mr Deviande, model		[Exhib RA, London, 1058]; untraced		*Graves* I, 1905–6, 93
197.	1826	Rev W Thorp, of Castle Green Chapel, Bristol		[Exhib RA, London, 1065]; untraced		*Graves* I, 1905–6, 94
198.	1826	Sir William Beechey RA (replicated)	m	Burlington House, London	SD	*Graves* I, 1905–6, 94; *Gunnis* 1968, 34
199.	1826	Thomas Campbell	m	Glasgow Museums S.26 Other versions: Hunterian GLAHA 44183, 1828		*Graves* I, 1905–6, 94; *Pearson* 1991, unpag
200.	1826	Thomas Stothard	m	[65 Russell Square, London; Lawrence sale, 1830 (2)]; RA, London	SD	*Graves* I, 1905–6, 93; *Kader* 1996, 180, 181 (repr)
201.	1827	Unidentified gentleman		[Exhib RA, London, 1112]; untraced		*Graves* I, 1905–6, 94
202.	1828	Francis Bacon	m	Magdalen College, Oxford, old library	S	Pevsner, *Oxon*, 1974, 154
203.	1828	J Norton		[Exhib RA, London, 1156]; untraced		*Graves* I, 1905–6, 94
204.	1828	John Locke	m	Magdalen College, Oxford, old library	S	Pevsner, *Oxon*, 1974, 154
205.	1828	Rev Mr Judkin		[Exhib RA, London, 1191]; untraced		*Graves* I, 1905–6, 94
206.	1828	Robert Medcalf		[Exhib RA, London, 1174]; untraced		*Graves* I, 1905–6, 94
207.	1828	Robert Smirke	m	[65 Russell Square, London; Lawrence sale, 1830 (2)]; untraced Other versions: NPG, London 4525 (plaster)		*Graves* I, 1905–6, 94; *Kader* 1996, 180, 181 (repr)
208.	1828	Samuel Johnson (after Joseph Nollekens)	m	[coll Robert Vernon]; NPG 996, Beningbrough, N R Yorks	SD	*Gunnis* 1968, 34; *Yung and Pettman* 1981, 309 (repr)
209.	1828	Sir Isaac Newton (after Louis François Roubiliac)	m	[coll Robert Vernon]; NPG 995, Beningborough, N R Yorks	SD	*Gunnis* 1968, 34; *Yung and Pettman* 1981, 415 (repr)
210.	1828	Sir William Rawlins		[Exhib RA, London, 1173]; untraced		*Graves* I, 1905–6, 94
211.	1828	Unidentified gentleman		[Exhib RA, London, 1172]; untraced		*Graves* I, 1905–6, 94
212.	1828	Unidentified young woman		Worcs County Museum, Hartlebury Other versions: Worcs county library, s		
213.	1829	Armour Donkin		[Exhib RA, London, 1194]; untraced		*Graves* I, 1905–6, 94
214.	1829	George Canning (after Joseph Nollekens)		[coll Robert Vernon]; Tate Britain N02247 Other versions: 10 Downing Street, London		*Gunnis* 1968, 34; www.tate.org.uk; GPC
215.	1829	Rev W Turner	m	Lit and Phil Soc, Newcastle, Northumbs		*Graves* I, 1905–6, 94; RG/JP, 1, 86
216.	1829	Sir Richard Carr Glyn		[Exhib RA, London, 1195]; untraced		*Graves* I, 1905–6, 94
217.	1829	Unidentified sitter		Cragside, Northumbs		AL/RG
218.	1828–1830	Arthur, 1st Duke of Wellington (after Joseph Nollekens)	m	[coll Robert Vernon]; Tate Britain N02236 Other versions: Palace of Westminster, London 10 Downing Street, London		*Walker* 1961, 76a, cat 91; *Gunnis* 1968, 34; www.tate.org.uk
219.	1830	John Waller	m	Bristol MAG		*Gunnis* 1968, 34
220.	1830	Michael Faraday (reproduced in plaster)	m	[Exhib RA, London, 1244]; untraced		*Graves* I, 1905–6, 94; *Ormond* 1973, 169
221.	1830	Sir Thomas Lawrence PRA (replicated)	m	Bristol MAG N6930		*Graves* I, 1905–6, 94; *Gunnis* 1968, 34; *Johnson* 1975, 18; *Kader* 1996, 177 (repr)
222.	1830	Unidentified gentleman		[Exhib RA, London, 1221]; untraced		*Graves* I, 1905–6, 94
223.	1830	William Wilkins RA	m	Trinity College, Cambridge		*Graves* I, 1905–6, 94
224.	1831	Henry, 1st Lord Brougham		[Exhib RA, London, 1213]; untraced		*Graves* I, 1905–6, 94; *Morris and Roberts* 1998, 55
225.	1831	J Lonsdale, model		[Exhib RA, London, 1198]; untraced		*Graves* I, 1905–6, 94; *Morris and Roberts* 1998, 55
226.	1831	John Northcote RA		[Exhib RA, London, 1212]; untraced		*Graves* I, 1905–6, 94
227.	1832	'A young lady'		[Exhib RA, London, 1179]; untraced		*Graves* I, 1905–6, 94
228.	1833	George Clint ARA		[Exhib RA, London, 1151]; untraced		*Graves* I, 1905–6, 94
229.	1833	J Lonsdale Jnr		[Exhib RA, London, 1187]; untraced		*Graves* I, 1905–6, 94
230.	1833	John Lawless		[Exhib RA, London, 1207]; untraced		*Graves* I, 1905–6, 94
231.	1834	'A Lady of Quality'		[Exhib RA, London, 1082]; untraced		*Graves* I, 1905–6, 94
232.	1834	'A Lady of Quality'		[Exhib RA, London, 1083]; untraced		*Graves* I, 1905–6, 94
233.	1834	Friend of the artist		[Exhib RA, London, 1081]; untraced		*Graves* I, 1905–6, 94
234.	1834	Lady Braybrooke		Audley End, Essex	SD	GPC
235.	1836	George Blackerton		[Exhib RA, London, 1136]; untraced		*Graves* I, 1905–6, 94
236.	1836	William Shakespeare		Shadwell Park, Norfolk		GPC
237.	1837	Admiral Sir Michael Seymour Bt		[Exhib RA, London, 1281]; untraced		*Graves* I, 1905–6, 94
238.	1837	Charles, 2nd Earl Grey		[Exhib RA, London, 1273]; Newcastle, Northumbs		*Graves* I, 1905–6, 94; *Ormond* 1973, 203
239.	1837	Eve	m	[coll Duke of Newcastle]; untraced		*Manchester Art Treasures* 1857, 136; *Graves* 1906, 1, 94; *Graves* I, 1905–6, 32; *Gunnis* 1968, 34
240.	1837	Sir William Knighton Bt		[Exhib RA, London, 1276]; untraced		*Graves* I, 1905–6, 94
241.	1837	Unidentified gentleman	m	[Exhib RA, London, 1280]; untraced		*Graves* I, 1905–6, 94

No.	Date	Subject		Location		Literary references
242.	1837	Unidentified man	m	Worcester City Art Gallery and Museum	SD	
243.	1838	Unidentified lady, model		[Exhib RA, London, 1289]; untraced		*Graves* I, 1905–6, 94
244.	1838	Unidentified man		Grittleton House, Wilts (1955)		GPC
245.	1838	W Seguier, model		[Exhib RA, London, 1370]; untraced		*Graves* I, 1905–6, 94
246.	c1840	Admiral Lord Nelson	p	NMM, Greenwich, SCU0087		
247.	1840	Edmund Burke, MP (after Hickey, J)	m	NGI		*le Harivel* 1988, 553 (repr)
248.	1840	Joseph Neeld		Grittleton House, Wilts (1955)		GPC
249.	1840	Philip Rundell	m	[Grittleton House, Wilts]; Grittleton sale, 1966; bt Sanders, 80 gns	SD	*Graves* I, 1905–6, 94; *Grittleton Marbles* 1966, 8 (repr 1)
250.	1840	Sir R Bourke		[Exhib RA, London, 1193]; untraced		*Graves* I, 1905–6, 94
251.	1840	Sir Robert O'Callaghan	p	Compton Place, Eastbourne, Sussex Other versions: Sotheby, 5 July 2000, lot 135, marble		*Gunnis* 1968, 34; AL/RG
252.	1841	Albert, the Prince Consort	m	[Grittleton House, Wilts]; VAM A.34-1964	SD	*Ormond* 1973, 11; *Read* 1982, 172; *Bilbey* 2002, 187 (repr)
253.	1841	Master J T D'Almain Mackinlay	m	[Exhib RA, London, 1323]; untraced		*Graves* I, 1905–6, 94
254.	1842	Joseph Neeld		Grittleton House, Wilts (1955)		GPC
255.	1842	Lord George Cavendish Bentinck	m	Russell-Cotes AG, Bournemouth, Dorset		*Ormond* 1973, 36
256.	1843	Kiallmark	m	[Exhib RA, London, 1524]; untraced		*Graves* I, 1905–6, 94
257.	1843	Thalberg	m	[Exhib RA, London, 1525]; untraced		*Graves* I, 1905–6, 94
258.	1844	James Lonsdale	m	NPG, London	SD	*Yung and Pettman* 1981, 353 (repr)
259.	1844	Master J Pintor		[Exhib RA, London, 1392]; untraced		*Graves* I, 1905–6, 95
260.	1844	Sir Charles Metcalf (or Metcalfe)	m	Metcalfe Hall, Kolkata (Calcutta)		*Graves* I, 1905–6, 95; *Gunnis* 1968, 35
261.	1844	Unidentified gentleman		[Exhib RA, London, 1393]; untraced		*Graves* I, 1905–6, 95
262.	1845	C Tawke		Vintners' Hall, City of London		Pevsner, *London: City*, 1997, 410
263.	1845	Lord Fitzgerald		[Exhib RA, London, 1450]; untraced		*Graves* I, 1905–6, 95
264.	1845	Rev T J Judkin		[Exhib RA, London, 1442]; untraced		*Graves* I, 1905–6, 95
265.	1845	Sir Henry de la Beche	b	[Crystal Palace, Sydenham, 1854]; untraced		*Ormond* 1973, 134
266.	1846	Prof Sir Richard Owen	m	[RCS, London]; destroyed		*Manchester Art Treasures* 1857, 136; *Graves* I, 1905–6, 95; *Graves* I, 1913–5, 32; *Ormond* 1973, 353
267.	1846	Sir John Jeremie		Freetown, Sierra Leone Cathedral		*Gunnis* 1968, 35
268.	1847	Charles Mackintosh		[Exhib RA, London, 1445]; untraced		*Graves* I, 1905–6, 95
269.	1847	Lord Chief Justice Sir Nicholas Conyngham Tindal		[Exhib RA, London, 1430]; untraced		*Graves* I, 1905–6, 95
270.	1848	Frederick Henry Paul, 2nd Baron Methuen	m	[Exhib RA, London, 1457]; Corsham Court, Wilts	SD	*Graves* I, 1905–6, 95
271.	1848	Hon J R Morrison, of China		[Exhib RA, London, 1459]; untraced		*Graves* I, 1905–6, 95
272.	1848	Philip Rundle		[Grittleton House, Wilts]; untraced		RG/JP, 1, 80
273.	1849	Francis Baily, presented to the Royal Astronomical Society		[Exhib RA, London, 1319]; untraced Other versions: NMM, Greenwich ZBA 1715, 1848		*Graves* I, 1905–6, 95
274.	1849	Unidentified lady	m	[Exhib RA, London, 1315]; untraced		*Graves* I, 1905–6, 95
275.	1850	Hugh, 1st Viscount Gough, model		[Exhib RA, London, 1441]; untraced		*Graves* I, 1905–6, 95; *Ormond* 1973, 191
276.	1850	Sir John Herschel Bt	m	St John's College, Cambridge		*Graves* I, 1905–6, 95; *Ormond* 1973, 224–5
277.	1850	Unidentified gentleman		[Exhib RA, London, 1437]; untraced		*Graves* I, 1905–6, 95
278.	1850	Unidentified gentleman	m	[Exhib RA, London, 1432]; untraced		*Graves* I, 1905–6, 95
279.	1850	Unidentified lady	m	[Exhib RA, London, 1433]; untraced		*Graves* I, 1905–6, 95
280.	1850	Unidentified man (possibly David Kent)	m	VAM A.71-1965	SD	*Bilbey* 2002, 188 (repr)
281.	?1850	William Whewell		[Crystal Palace portrait coll, Sydenham, 1854]; untraced		*Ormond* 1973, 503
282.	1851	Alderman Donkin	m	Public library, Newcastle, Northumbs		*Gunnis* 1968, 35
283.	1851	Joan Lever	m	Guy's Hospital, London		*Gunnis* 1968, 35
284.	1851	William Smyth	m	Fitzwilliam		*Gunnis* 1968, 35
285.	1851	William Whewell		[Exhib RA, London, 1852, 1440]; Trinity College, Cambridge, library		*Graves* I, 1905–6, 95; Pevsner, *Cambs*, 1970, 175
286.	1852	'A young lady'		[Exhib RA, London, 1438]; untraced		*Graves* I, 1905–6, 95
287.	1852	Arthur Blakestone	m	Foundling Hospital, London		*Gunnis* 1968, 35
288.	1852	Dr J C W Lever MD		[Exhib RA, London, 1479]; untraced		*Graves* I, 1905–6, 95
289.	1852	L C Humphrey		[Exhib RA, London, 1437]; untraced		*Graves* I, 1905–6, 95
290.	1852	Unidentified lady		[Exhib RA, London, 1439]; untraced		*Graves* I, 1905–6, 95
291.	1853	Douglas Jerrold	m	[coll Douglas Jerrold]; NPG, London Other versions: Duplicated in plaster	SD	*Manchester Art Treasures* 1857, 136; *Ormond* 1973, 243 (pl 469)
292.	1853	R Stephenson		[Exhib RA, London, 1443]; untraced		*Graves* I, 1905–6, 95
293.	1853	Wynn Ellis		[Exhib RA, London, 1439]; untraced		*Graves* I, 1905–6, 95
294.	pre-1854	Charles James Fox		Untraced		
295.	1854	Colonel Boldero		[Exhib RA, London, 1463]; untraced		*Graves* I, 1905–6, 95
296.	1856	Charles Geach MP		[Exhib RA, London, 1360]; untraced		*Graves* I, 1905–6, 95
297.	1856	John Estlin	m	Bristol MAG		*Gunnis* 1968, 35
298.	1856	Unidentified lady		[Exhib RA, London, 1363]; untraced		*Graves* I, 1905–6, 95
299.	1858	John Foster White, Treasurer of St Bartholomew's Hospital		[Exhib RA, London, 1237]; untraced		*Graves* I, 1905–6, 95
300.	1858	Sir John Neeld	m	[Grittleton House, Wilts]; sold Christie, 22 Sept 1966; bt Nugent, 28 gns	SD	*Grittleton Marbles* 1966, 7
301.	1860	Admiral Blake	m	Shire Hall, Taunton, Somerset		*Ret to Life*, 25
302.	1860	Mrs Valentine Knight		[Exhib RA, London, 1078]; untraced		*Graves* I, 1905–6, 95
303.	nd	Agnes Strickland		Untraced		*Ormond* 1973, 437
304.	nd	Edward Forbes		Untraced		*Ormond* 1973, 176

No.	Date	Subject		Location		Bibliography
305.	nd	John Milton		[Elkanah Bicknell, of Herne Hill, London; sold 1863, lot 127]; untraced		Bicknell sale cat, 1863, 22
306.	nd	Oliver Cromwell	s	Untraced		
307.	nd	Queen Victoria	m	Glasgow Museums S.85		inf: Glasgow Museums
308.	nd	William Shakespeare		[Elkanah Bicknell, of Herne Hill, London; sold 1863, lot 125, bt Graves, £33 12s]; untraced		Bicknell sale cat, 1863, 22
309.	nd	William, 2nd Viscount Melbourne, PM (after Joseph Nollekens)		10 Downing Street, London		GPC
Architectural Sculpture						
310.	1816	General Sir Thomas Picton, column with statue and relief (designed by John Nash)		[Carmarthen]; destroyed		*Whinney* 1988, 471 n36; *Yarrington* 1988, 262, 268–9; *Dale-Jones* 1989, 69–70
311.	c1823	Frieze		Masonic Hall, Bristol	S	Pevsner, *Somerset: N & Bristol*, 1958, 436
312.	c1828	Britannia acclaimed by Neptune and Tritons being drawn in her chariot (designed by John Flaxman) Payment(s): £2,500	s	Buckingham Palace, London, east front, pediment		TNA WORK 19/3, 5/119 fol 307 (exterior work); *Smith* 1931, 62, (repr 48); Pevsner, *London: 1*, 1973, 506; *Colvin* VI, 1976, 300
313.	c1828	Four statues of victories (originally intended for Marble Arch)		National Gallery, London, façade		*Colvin* VI, 1973, 295–297; *Yarrington* 1988, 229–45 (reprs 88, 89)
314.	c1828	Minerva (part of a group of Britannia supporting a medallion of Nelson flanked by a lion and a unicorn originally intended for the Marble Arch)		National Gallery, London, east façade		*Colvin* VI, 1973, 295–297; *Yarrington* 1988, 229–45 (pl 85)
315.	c1828	Nelson receiving the Spanish surrender after the Battle of St Vincent (intended for Marble Arch)		Shepperton Film Studios, 1985; Christie, 13 Dec 1985; untraced		*Daily Telegraph*, 11 Nov 1985 (repr); *Whinney* 1988, 471 n39; *Busco* 1994, 61–2 (repr)
316.	c1828	Relief panels of 'A Naval Warrior with a Figure of Justice' and 'Peace and Plenty', and other ornaments, Britannia, medallion of Nelson, lion and unicorn for attic pedestal, Trafalgar side		Marble Arch, London		TNA WORK, 19/3, 20, 1–40; *Colvin* VI, 1973, 295–297; *Yarrington* 1988, 229–45 (repr 81)
317.	post-1828	The Seasons		Buckingham Palace, London, east front		BM Ad MS 38, 687
318.	1828	Wars of the Roses, four friezes Payment(s): £1,300 Drawing(s): design by Thomas Stothard		Buckingham Palace, London, throne room		*Smith* 1931, 143, pl 142, 144
319.	c1846	Reredos figures (after Thorwaldsen)		Leigh Delamere, Wilts		Pevsner, *Wilts*, 1975, 295
Reliefs						
320.	1817	Kemble crowned by Melpomene (designed by John Flaxman RA)	p	SJSM		Soane Museum inventory
321.	1817	Kemble inspired by the genius of Shakespeare	p	SJSM		Soane Museum inventory
322.	1830	Thomas Lawrence PRA, medallion	b	[Exhib RA, London, 1234]; NPG, London, 1507 Other versions: Heim Gallery; San Marino (CA), Huntington art coll	S	*Graves* I, 1905–6, 94
323.	1831	Maternal affection		[Exhib RA, London, 1162]; untraced		*Graves* I, 1905–6, 94
Miscellaneous						
324.	post-1808	Adam outstretched on the cold ground, small model	p	SJSM		Soane Museum inventory
325.	1810	Study from nature		[Exhib RA, London, 729]; untraced		*Graves* I, 1905–6, 93
326.	1811	Hercules rescuing Alcestis from Orcas		[RA gold medal]; untraced		RA Premium list; *Graves* 1875, 19
327.	1811	'Model of a gentleman'		[Exhib RA, London, 698]; untraced		*Graves* I, 1905–6, 93
328.	1811	Neptune drives off the winds and calms the sea		[Exhib RA, London, 904]; untraced		*Graves* I, 1905–6, 93
329.	1813	Hercules restoring Alcestis to Admetus		Untraced		*Graves* 1875, 20; *Graves* I, 1905–6, 93; *Morris and Roberts* 1998, 55
330.	1814	Hercules throwing Lychas into the sea		[Grittleton House, Wilts]; untraced		*Graves* I, 1905–6, 93; *Gunnis* 1968, 35; *Johnson* 1975, 18
331.	1816	Achilles contending with Scamander		[Exhib RA, London, 928]; untraced		*Graves* 1875, 20; *Graves* I, 1905–6, 93
332.	1817	'Fame and Victory supporting the dying hero (sketch for a National Monument)'		[Exhib RA, London, 1069]; untraced		*Graves* I, 1905–6, 93
333.	1817	Fame embracing a dying hero		[Exhib RA, London, 1070]; untraced		*Graves* I, 1905–6, 93
334.	1817	Fame encouraging genius		[Exhib RA, London, 1068]; untraced		*Graves* I, 1905–6, 93
335.	1818	Cupid disarmed; an anacreontic		[Exhib RA, London, 1112]; untraced		*Graves* 1875, 20; *Graves* I, 1905–6, 93
336.	1820	Satan addressing the sun		[Exhib RA, London, 1038]; untraced		*Graves* I, 1905–6, 93
337.	1823	Adam comforting Eve after her dream		[Exhib RA, London, 1114]; untraced		*Graves* I, 1905–6, 93
338.	1827	Piety, for Bristol Cathedral		[Exhib RA, London, 1091]; untraced		*Graves* I, 1905–6, 94; *Morris and Roberts* 1998, 55
339.	1827	'small mother and child, etc'		[Exhib RA, London, 1104]; untraced		*Graves* I, 1905–6, 94
340.	1830	Mother and child	m	[Exhib RA, London, 1171]; untraced		*Graves* I, 1905–6, 94; *Johnson* 1975, 18

341.	1832	'Tis only nature lulled to sleep'		[Exhib RA, London, 1214]; untraced	*Graves* I, 1905–6, 94
342.	1836	Sleeping nymph	m	[Exhib RA, London, 1142]; untraced	*Graves* I, 1905–6, 94; *Gunnis* 1968, 35
343.	1854	Child on the sea-shore		[Exhib RA, London, 1368]; untraced	*Graves* I, 1905–6, 95
344.	1855	The Circassian slave		Royal Coll	*Gunnis* 1968, 35
345.	1856	Resignation: 'Thy will be done'		[Exhib RA, London, 1242]; untraced	*Graves* I, 1905–6, 95
346.	1856	The pet bird, or killed with kindness		[Exhib RA, London, 1223]; untraced	*Graves* I, 1905–6, 95

BAILY, R fl 1838

Funerary Monuments

1.	1838	William Owen of Glansevern (†1837)	Berriew, Montgomery	S	Pevsner, *Powys*, 1979, 77

BAKER, Andrew, of London fl 1717

Funerary Monuments

1.	1717	Colonel Robert Bridges (†1675)	Finglas, Dublin	S	*Potterton* 1975, 36

BAKER, Benjamin, of Liverpool fl 1817–44

Baker's wall-monuments to Thomas Brooks at Whalley, Lancs and to the Rev Samuel Sewell at Prescot are in the neo-Greek style (**2, 3**). He carved the tablet with military trophies to George Vernon, 1844, at North Mimms with a partner named Earle (**5**).

Literary References: *Gunnis* 1968, 36

Funerary Monuments

1.	†1817	Charlotte Potts	Chester Cathedral	S	
2.	†1831	Thomas Brooks	St Mary, Whalley, Lancs	S	Pevsner, *Lancs: N*, 1969, 258
3.	?1833	Rev Samuel Sewell	Prescot, Lancs	S	*Gunnis* 1968, 36
4.	†1837	Sarah Payne	St George, Bridgetown, Barbados	S	
5.	?1844	George Vernon (co-sculptor: Earle)	North Mimms, Herts		*Gunnis* 1968, 36

BAKER, Robert Charles, of Southampton fl 1836–51

Funerary Monuments

1.	†1836	Charles Baker		Upton, Bucks	S	*Gunnis* 1968, 36
2.	1851	Cemetery memorial	tc	[Gt Exhib, London]; untraced		*Gunnis* 1968, 36

BAKER, Thomas, of London fl 1755–63?

Perhaps identifiable with a mason named Baker who is listed in Little Arundel Street, Strand in 1763.

Literary References: *Mortimer* 1763, 49

Funerary Monuments

1.	†1755	Abraham Weekes	Ashley, Hants	Pevsner, *Hants & Isle of Wight*, 1967, 83

BALDWIN (or BALDWYN), Stephen fl 1661–62

The family worked as stonemasons in Gloucester for many years. Stephen may have been the son of Samuel Baldwin, a monumental mason who died on 27 August 1645 and was buried at St Nicholas, Gloucester. In 1661 Stephen was paid £20 'for cuttinge and settinge up' a statue of King Charles II in Worcester Guildhall and he later received a further £8 12s for his 'men's wages in settinge up the Pediston and the Arch' (Worcester Audit of Account Books, 3, 1640–1669, cited by *Gunnis* 1968, 36) (**2**). The statue must either have been damaged or become worn, for **Thomas White** was paid for repairing it in 1712. Baldwin also replaced the damaged statue of King Charles I on Worcester High Cross, and his personification of *Justice* originally stood at the upper end of the High Street (**1, 4**). In 1662 the city of Gloucester ordered a similar figure of King Charles II (**3**). This was removed in the mid-18th century and was lost for many years before being discovered in pieces in a garden at Chaxhill in 1945.

Literary References: *Gunnis* 1968, 36; *Gibson* 1997 (1), 165

Archival References: GPC

Statues

1.	1661	King Charles I	[Market cross, Worcester]; untraced	*Gibson* 1997 (1), 165
2.	1661	King Charles II Payment(s): £20	Guildhall, Worcester	*Gibson* 1997 (1), 165, 372
3.	1662	King Charles II	[Wheat Market, Southgate Street, Gloucester]; Three Cocks Lane, Gloucester	*Gibson* 1997 (1), 165
4.	nd	Justice	[High Street, Worcester]; untraced	*Gibson* 1997 (1), 165

BALL, Abraham, of Spilsby fl 1716–29

In September 1716 Ball entered into a contract with Joseph Banks of Revesby to supply Ketton stone paving and hearth stones for Revesby Hall, Lincs. In 1729 he was paid £1 1s for cutting an inscription for the almshouses which Banks built in the village of Revesby.

Literary References: *Hill* 1952, 26–7, 106

BALL, William fl 1763

Listed in Mortimer's *Universal Director* of 1763 as a mason of Carnaby Market (p 49).

BALLANT, Theodore fl 1767

On 1 May 1767 he received a premium of 25 guineas from the Society of Arts for a bas-relief (**1**). At that time his address was 3 Headin Street, near Swallow Street, Piccadilly, London. There is no further mention of him. He may have been related to the Theodore Balant who, according to J T Smith, taught **Michael Rysbrack**.

Literary References: RSA *Register*, 1778, 32; *Smith* 1828, II, 111; *Gunnis* 1968, 36; *Whinney* 1988, 449, n 3

Archival References: RSA Minutes, PR/GE/112/12/8 seq 3 f34, 36

Reliefs

1.	1767	The sacrifice of Iphigenia	[Soc of A, premium, 25 gns]; untraced	RSA *Minutes*, 1766–67, seq 3 fol 34, 36; *Dossie* 1782, 440

BALLANTINE, Alexander fl 1842–63

Ballantine had a yard at 126 Upper Dorset Street, Dublin. He was clearly more than an ordinary monumental mason, for some of his memorials have fine carved reliefs. The tablet commemorating Caroline Hamilton features two weeping figures and his memorial to John Fletcher at Killeskey has an unusual relief of a child and a female figure kneeling by a coffin (**2, 5**). The memorial to George O'Connor has a bust of the deceased but since the memorial is signed 'A. Ballantine & Kirwan fecit' it is possible that the bust was sculpted by Kirwan, who is otherwise unknown (**1**).

Literary References: *Potterton* 1975, 36

Funerary Monuments

1.	†1842	Rev George O'Connor (co-sculptor: Kirwan)	Castleknock, Dublin	S	*Potterton* 1975, 36
2.	†1845	Caroline Hamilton	Castleknock, Dublin		*Potterton* 1975, 36
3.	†1848	Rev and Mrs Hinson	New Ross, Co Wexford		*Potterton* 1975, 36
4.	†1850	John Newell	Cowran, Co Kilkenny	S	*Potterton* 1975, 36
5.	†1854	Rev John Fletcher	Killiskey, Co Wicklow		*Potterton* 1975, 36
6.	†1863	James Hamilton	Castleknock, Dublin		*Potterton* 1975, 36

BALLANTINE, R fl 1845–57

Probably related to **Alexander Ballantine**, he too had his yard in Dorset Street, Dublin, at number 11.

Literary References: *Potterton* 1975, 36

Funerary Monuments

1.	†1845	Henry Faulkner	Staplestown, Co Carlow	S	*Potterton* 1975, 36
2.	†1849	Isabella Longworth	Castleknock, Dublin	S	*Potterton* 1975, 36
3.	†1857	Rev Moore Morgan	Dunlavin, Co Wicklow	S	*Potterton* 1975, 36

BALLARD, Francis 1751–1811

Funerary Monuments

1.	†1804	Mary Gibbs (tombstone)	South Littleton, Worcs	S	*Gunnis* 1968, 36

BALLY, William 1829–56

William Bally was a phrenologist and sculptor. He was born in Switzerland but by the 1830s he was working in Birmingham, where he employed George Jacob Holyoake, who later came to prominence as a leading secularist and pioneer of the co-operative movement. He accompanied the influential phrenologist Johann Gaspar Spurzheim on lecture tours between 1829 and 1831, and under his direction produced sets of small plaster phrenological busts which seem to have been widely marketed with an explanatory text by Spurzheim (**1**). He ran the phrenological gallery on King Street, Manchester, in the 1830s and 1840s and served as curator of the Manchester Phrenological Society in 1838. Over 100,000 visitors attended the special phrenological exhibition he set up at the Manchester Mechanics Institute during the Christmas holidays in 1844. The display included a complete set of busts displaying the individual organs of the brain and another set of the most notorious murderers. Bally also taught wax modelling and plaster casting at the Manchester Mechanics Institute and lectured on phrenology at the Manchester Athenaeum. He retired to Switzerland in 1848, donating his collection of over 1,000 casts to the Manchester Mechanics Institute, but was apparently in England in June 1856. The base of a death mask of William Palmer, 'the Rugeley poisoner', in the Winchester Museums Service collection is inscribed 'The first cast of William Palmer taken by William Bally, Phrenologist of Manchester, the 14th June 1856 Stafford' (**7**).

Literary References: *Gunnis* 1968, 36; *Pyke*, 1973, 29; *Cooter* 1984, 150, 274, 350 n57; *Cooter* 1989, 18, 107, 171–2, 189, 313, 330

Busts						
1.	c1831	Set of 60 small phrenological busts	p	Science Museum A642804 Other versions: Institute of the History of Medicine, Johns Hopkins Univ, Baltimore		Science and Society Picture Library
2.	1832	Rev R Newton		[Manchester Exhib]; untraced		*Gunnis* 1968, 36
3.	1832	Samuel Hope, model		[Exhib Liverpool Ac, 375]; untraced		*Morris and Roberts* 1998, 57
4.	1837	Thomas Henry Ilidge		[Exhib Liverpool Ac, 687]; untraced		*Morris and Roberts* 1998, 57
5.	1844	John Burn		[Exhib Liverpool Ac, 1844, 560]; untraced		*Morris and Roberts* 1998, 57
6.	1846	Two unidentified clergymen		[Manchester Exhib]; untraced		*Gunnis* 1968, 36
7.	1856	William Palmer, death mask	p	Winchester Museums Service	S	
Reliefs						
8.	1837	John, 1st Earl of Eldon	w	VAM A.69-1970		*Gunnis* 1968, 36; *Pyke* 1971, 9 (repr 13); *Pyke* 1981, 5
9.	1851	Tom Sayers	w	Untraced		*Pyke* 1971, 9
Miscellaneous						
10.	1832	Colonel Wildman, of Newstead, model		[Exhib Liverpool Ac, 358]; untraced		*Morris and Roberts* 1998, 57
11.	1832	Mr Berend, model		[Exhib Liverpool Ac, 373]; untraced		*Morris and Roberts* 1998, 57
12.	1832	'The Lady of Colonel Wildman', model		[Exhib Liverpool Ac, 360]; untraced		*Morris and Roberts* 1998, 57

BALSHAW (or BELSHAW), John fl 1732–33

In 1732 **John Boson** executed much of the woodwork in Canterbury Cathedral, including carvings for the altar and reredos. This work appears to have been completed by Balshaw, who in 1733 received payments totalling £582 for work in the chancel (**1**). Among items mentioned are 'Six shafts of Corinthian columns £84' and 'Six capitals £30'. The cost of packing and freight from London came to £50, which the architect, John James, considered too much, though he passed the other charges (Canterbury Cathedral Fabric Account Book).

Archival References: GPC

Architectural Sculpture

1.	1733	Altarpiece and 'Wainscot work upon the North and South sides of the Altar' (co-sculptor: John Boson) Payment(s): £379, £203	wd	[Canterbury Cathedral, Kent]; untraced	GPC

BANCKES, Henry 1679–1716

He was the son of Matthew Bankes (†1706), who became His Majesty's Master-Carpenter under Charles II in 1663 and was reappointed by William and Mary in 1689. Young Banckes was apprenticed to **Edward Strong I** in 1695, and from 1705 onwards he was working at Blenheim Palace, where he built the colonnades of the Great Court. He also occasionally supplied small quantities of stone for Blenheim from the quarry he owned at Guiting, near Winchcomb. He was employed at Marlborough House between 1709 and 1712, and in 1713 received £41 for work at the Royal Mews, Charing Cross. In 1715 he went to Windsor Castle, where he was paid for stonework and flooring 'at the altar', seats 'with bear' and sideboards (TNA WORK AO 1/2448/149). He died in 1716 and was buried at Hampton, Middx, where a much-worn slab on the floor of the church tower commemorates him.

Literary References: *Malcolm* IV 1803–7, 317; *Wren Society*, VII, 228; XV, 122; XVI, 167, 177; XVIII, 164; *Green* 1951, *passim*; *Gunnis* 1968, 37

Chimneypieces

1.	1715	Description unavailable	s	Windsor Castle	*Gunnis* 1968, 37

BANKES (or BANCKES), John fl *c*1671

He may have been related to **Henry Banckes.**

Literary References: *Gunnis* 1968, 37

Architectural Sculpture

1.	*c*1671	'5 staggs heads for ye Hall' Payment(s): £25	[Sir Robert Clayton's banking house, Old Jewry, City of London]; untraced	Clayton & Morris, f241

BANKS, Charles *c*1745–92

He was the youngest son of William and Mary Banks and the brother of **Thomas Banks**. According to his niece, Lavinia Forster, Banks received most of his early instruction from Thomas. By 1764 he was a pupil of **L A Holm,** and a year later he was working for a Mr Powell of Oxford Road. In 1764 he was awarded a premium of 3 guineas from the Society of Arts (**10**) and in 1765 a 15 guinea premium (**11**). Three further prizes followed by 1768 (**2, 6, 7**). In October 1769 he entered the Royal Academy Schools. He must have been a promising student, since he was awarded a silver medal in 1771 (**12**) and a gold for a group in 1774 (**3**). On the latter occasion he also submitted a sketch (perhaps a drawing) of *Pyramus and Thisbe.*

Banks first exhibited at the Royal Academy in 1775 (**3**), giving his address as 'At Mr Taylor's, Shug Lane, near Haymarket' (*Graves* I, 1905–6, 104). He continued to exhibit intermittently over the following 17 years, on each occasion from a different address. In 1783 he resided at 89 Queen Anne Street East, in 1784 at 18 Little Castle Street, Oxford Market, in 1787 at 4 Upper Marylebone Street, and in the year of his death in Portland Place.

In a letter to Allan Cunningham, published in 1863, Mrs Forster gave details of her family history. Of her uncle she wrote that 'he died young, and was not, I believe, very industrious, therefore nothing remains of his talents in his profession' (*Builder* 1863, 4). Gunnis noted that the description of an early death was hardly accurate, for Banks must have been in his late forties when he died.

Literary References: *Graves* I, 1905–6, 104; *Bell* 1938, 94–5; *Hutchinson* 1960–2, 134; *Gunnis* 1968, 37; *Pyke* 1973, 9

Archival References: Archives, Soc of A; RA Premium list

Funerary Monuments						
1.	1783	Design for a monument		[Exhib RA, London, 404]; untraced		*Graves* I, 1905–6, 104
Statues						
2.	1767	Adonis erect, clay model		[Soc of A, premium, 20 gns]; untraced		RSA, *Minutes*, 1766–67, seq 3 f 23, 26; RSA, *Register*, 1778, 32
3.	1774	Pygmalion and his statue		[RA, London, gold medal]; untraced		RA Premium list; *Gunnis* 1968, 37
4.	1775	Adonis sleeping, clay model		[Soc of A, premium, 15 gns]; untraced Other versions: Exhib RA, London, 1775, 10		RSA *Minutes*, 1765–66, seq 3 fol 42; RSA, *Premiums*, 1763, 29; *Graves* I, 1905–6, 104
5.	1784	Lot and the Angels, model		[Exhib RA, London, 530]; untraced		*Graves* I, 1905–6, 104
Reliefs						
6.	1768	Death of Julius Caesar, clay model		[Soc of A, premium, 20 gns]; untraced		*Dossie* 1782, 439
7.	1768	Death of Lucretia		[Soc of A, premium, 20 gns]; untraced		*Dossie* 1782, 439
8.	1787	Unidentified subject, a sketch in bas-relief	w	[Exhib RA, London, 651]; untraced		*Graves* I, 1905–6, 104
Miscellaneous						
9.	1760	Victory and Peace	w	Untraced	SD	*Pyke* 1973, 9
10.	1764	Model of ornaments in clay		[Soc of A, premium, 3 gns]; untraced		RSA *Minutes*, 1763–64, seq 3 f84; RSA *Premiums*, 1763, 37
11.	1765	Model in clay		[Soc of A, premium, 15 gns]; untraced		RSA *Minutes*, 1764–65, seq 3 f 61
12.	1771	Unspecified subject, in the class of academy figure or bas-relief		[RA, London, silver medal]; untraced		RA Premium list
13.	1792	Diana and Endymion		[Exhib RA, London, 749]; untraced		*Graves* I, 1905–6, 104

BANKS, Matthew fl 1699–1708

He became free of the Masons' Company in 1699, by service with **Thomas Strong I**. In 1708 he was listed as living in Woodstock.

Archival References: Masons' Co, *Freemen*, 1677–1795 (1699); *Company Members*, 1708

BANKS, Thomas RA 1735–1805

Best remembered for his poetic subjects and influential monuments, Banks was hailed by his contemporaries as Britain's first truly neoclassical sculptor. He was born in a house on Kennington Common, South London on 22 December 1735, the son of William and Mary Banks. His brother **Charles Banks** was also a sculptor. Their father was a gardener to the Duke of Beaufort at Badminton, Glos (*Farington*, 2, 402) and Banks apparently went to school at Ross-on-Wye. At the age of 15 he was sent to London, where he was apprenticed to **William Barlow II**, an ornamental carver, with whom he served his full 7 years. According to Farington and **John Flaxman RA**, who presumably had the information from the sculptor himself, Banks also had some training with **Peter Scheemakers**. Farington clearly states that this was after his time with Barlow, but Flaxman's anecdotal account relates that the young sculptor drew and modelled in Scheemakers's studio late in the evenings during his apprenticeship years.

Banks showed early promise by winning five premiums from the Society of Arts between 1763 and 1769. One, reflecting his training, was for ornamental carving (**118**) and the others were for classical subjects and heralded his future sphere of interest (**40, 41, 103–5**). Around this time he was studying at the St Martin's Lane Academy and may also have been living or studying with **Richard Hayward**, for **Joseph Nollekens RA** addressed a letter to 'Mr. Thomas Banks, Sculptor, at Mr. Hayward's, Piccadilly, London' *c*1763–6 (*Whitley* 1930, 40). On 31 August 1766 Banks married Elizabeth Hooton, whose recent inheritance of a small property in Mayfair gave the couple some financial security. In 1767 the newlyweds moved to a house in New Bird Street, Oxford Road, from which address he first exhibited at the Free Society of Artists. Over the next few years he coped with the rising rateable value of the property, which changed from £10 in 1769 to £34 in 1772.

On 24 June 1769 Banks joined the Royal Academy Schools and the following year he won the gold medal for a relief, *The rape of Proserpine* (**106**). He was evidently ambitious, for he applied (unsuccessfully) to become an ARA the same year. Banks showed at the first two RA exhibitions (**1, 119**). In 1772 he won the Academy's scholarship to study in Rome.

Banks and his wife stayed in Rome for three years supported by the scholarship and another four at their own expense. His surviving letters, and references in Thomas Jones's *Memoirs*, indicate that he was part of the vibrant community of artists and collectors in the city, who included the sculptors **Michael Foy, Christopher Hewetson, Nathaniel Marchant**, the Swede Johan Tobias Sergel, and the Italian **G B Capizzoldi**. From Capizzoldi Banks received training in the cutting of marble ('in which the Italians beat us hollow') (*Smith* 2, 1828, 194), but it was Henry Fuseli, the Swiss painter, who particularly impressed him. Several of Banks's Rome reliefs were influenced by Fuseli's dramatic subject matter and echo his lithe, mannered figures. *The death of Germanicus* (**108**) and *Thetis and her nymphs rising from the sea to console Achilles for the death of Patroclus* (**110**) also show a new compositional inventiveness and a unity of subject and treatment. The *Germanicus* consists of a series of interacting, jarring, semi-circular shapes created by limbs and drapery, which stand out in high relief against a simple ground. A similar compositional formula is used for the *Thetis*, except that here the swirl of limbs and drapery harmoniously rims the contours of the oval frame. A sense of depth is created by the use of gradated relief carving.

Banks's daughter, Lavinia, was born in Rome, probably in 1775, and from 1777 to 1778 the family lived with the painter James Durno in the Stalla di Mignanelli, near the Piazza di Spagna. The Rome years ended unhappily, since Banks's patrons failed to give him proper support. The Earl-Bishop, Frederick Hervey, commissioned a group of *Cupid catching a butterfly on his wing* (**43**), and then decided not to take it. George Grenville (later Marquess of Buckingham) ordered a relief of *Caractacus before Claudius* (**109**) for 200 guineas and then refused to pay more than 100. Banks challenged Grenville's decision, which he said treated him 'with too much contempt both as an Artist & a man' (*Bindman* 2000, 772). By November 1778 Banks had become feverish and melancholic, a condition he blamed on his unreliable patrons. He submitted a late and unsuccessful design for Lord Chatham's memorial at Guildhall in the City of London (**2**). Meanwhile his wife sought to borrow money from friends in England. On 18 May 1779 Banks and his family left home for England, perhaps financing the journey by the raffle of his oval relief of *Alcyone* (**107**), won by Henry Swinburne and given to his friend, Sir Thomas Gascoigne.

In London Banks took a house at 5 Newman Street, rated at £60, where his neighbours included **John Bacon RA**, the miniaturist Ozias Humphrey and Benjamin West, the subject of a bust shown at the RA in 1780 (**58**). Banks also exhibited the sculpture rejected by his patrons in Rome (**47, 111**), together with a design for a monument to Captain Cook, perhaps intended to advertise his ability as a monumental sculptor (**4**). His first executed monument is a finely-characterised bust of the academic and poet, Isaac Watts (**3**), above an animated relief of Watts at his desk, receiving dictation from 'divine poetry'. Flaxman believed he could see the benefit of Banks's training in ornamental carving in the floral grotesques around the oval relief. The commission did not lead to further work and, in June 1781, Banks left for St Petersburg. Little is known of his time in Russia, except that he arrived there in August and, through the influence of Lord Malmesbury and Prince Potemkin, was able to sell his *Cupid* (**43**) for 4,000 roubles to the Empress Catherine II. He won only two commissions in St Petersburg (**44, 112**), perhaps because Malmsbury's influence at court was in decline, and in 1782 Banks returned to England.

He did not leave Britain again and lived in Newman Street until his death. Despite his earlier absences abroad, Banks had a reputation as a serious sculptor in England and he attracted the support of the writer George Cumberland, who recommended him to several potential patrons. In August 1783 Cumberland described Banks as a statuary who 'to a very refined judgement adds great learning and perfect mechanical skill, the result of many years' intense study and labour, the consequence is he has produced but few works but these of a quality to recommend and endear him to real judges' (*Bell* 1938, 56). One such judge was the historian and MP, Thomas Johnes of Hafod, a patron over a period of 20 years. Johnes commissioned a marble version of the model for a statue of *Achilles enraged*, shown at the RA in 1784 (**45**). The model received enthusiastic notices in the press that year, particularly from the *Morning Herald*, which described it as 'superior to most modern performances, and equal to many of the antique' (*Bell* 1938, 61). Although the marble version was never completed, Banks did carve a chimneypiece for Johnes at Hafod (**94**), as well as several busts (**71, 77**), a commemorative garden urn (**115**), and the innovative statue of Mrs Johnes as *Thetis dipping the infant Achilles in the river Styx* (**48**). Around the oval base are waves and sea-monsters.

In November 1784 Banks was elected an ARA and won his first public commissions, the statue and monument to Sir Eyre Coote (**46, 11**), commander-in-chief of the forces in India. These were both financed by the East India Company. The 26 foot high monument in Westminster Abbey has a central figure of *Victory* placing a medallion of Coote over quasi-eastern martial trophies commemorating the territorial benefits of Coote's military successes. It was the figure of a weeping Mahratta captive, exhibited at the RA, which excited particular admiration. Banks subsequently developed an iconography merging classical and Indian forms. He carved a chimneypiece for the former Governor-General of India, Warren Hastings, replacing the traditional caryatid figures of Dacian slaves with Indian women returning from the Ganges and adding a processional relief in the Roman manner, that bears debts to a painting of life in an Indian harem (**92**). Banks later executed several portrait busts of Hastings (**67, 68**).

Banks spent seven years from 1793 working on a statue of Marquess Cornwallis commissioned by the citizens of Madras to celebrate the end of the Mysore wars (**50**). The statue was the subject of a long and earnest debate amongst Academicians on the decorum of presenting Cornwallis in contemporary dress instead of the classical alternative. The work's emotional force comes from the relief on the base, illustrating the poignant moment when Tipu Sultan had been forced to surrender two sons to British protection until conditions for restitution were met. This metonym for the nurturing of an undeveloped nation by the paternal British empire is typical of Banks's major works of this period, for he focusses on moments of heightened emotion, often depicting the grief of a divided family.

His monuments of the 1780s and 1790s are amongst the most innovative and influential sculptural works of the eighteenth century. He executed considerably fewer monuments than either Bacon or Joseph Nollekens and never repeated designs, though he did develop certain themes, particularly the mourning widow grieving over a funerary urn (**7, 10, 13, 15, 17, 25**). The monument to Anne Martha Hand (**6**) focusses attention on the full-length figures of George Watson Hand and his dead wife, cradled in his arms, by reducing extraneous decoration to a minimum. Cornelia Milbanke's dead children are resurrected to welcome their mother to Heaven as mannerist cherubs in a swirling figure-of-eight composition (**26**). Major Delap Halliday, in his shroud, reaches out to his grieving widow across the mortal divide, suggested by a central obelisk (**30**). Banks's statue of Penelope Boothby of Ashbourne, a life-size child sleeping on a mattress (**22**), was said to have reduced Queen Charlotte and her daughters to tears when it was exhibited at the Royal Academy. The work is justly remembered as an early masterpiece of British sentimental romanticism and its site in Ashbourne church, facing the wall at the end of the Boothby Chapel, stresses the tragic curtailment of the family line. The sculptor's careful thoughts about the context of his monuments led Flaxman to proclaim that Banks could transform a church into 'a museum of sacred sculpture' (*Flaxman* 1838, 293).

In 1786 Banks became a full Academician. His diploma work, *The falling Titan*, crashes to earth amid falling rocks, as a tiny satyr and goats run for cover. This bravura performance was considered by J T Smith to be the finest work of sculpture ever produced by an Englishman (**47**). Banks played a major role at the Academy until his death, appeared regularly at general meetings and dinners, served on numerous committees (such as that to investigate **G B Locatelli**'s pay dispute with Lord Orford in July 1788) and featured frequently in Farington's diaries. But the sculptor was also prepared to sacrifice his chance of official honours by his commitment to radical politics. Banks was regarded as a blunt and serious man, whose uncompromising stance, (according to Flaxman), had hurt his interest 'both in Italy and in England' (*Farington*, 2, 636). In the 1790s Banks joined the Society for Constitutional Information (SCI), becoming a central figure in the group around the radical reformer, John Horne Tooke, and in January 1794 Farington described the sculptor as a 'violent democrat' (*Farington* vol 1, 144). That year Tooke and several other leading radicals were charged with treason, and in June 1794 Banks himself was arrested and questioned by the Privy Council. Although he was released almost immediately and Tooke was later acquitted, the event prejudiced the Council against him.

His political enthusiasm remained undiminished. In 1795 he cropped his hair (a signifier of political opposition) and his letters indicate an increasing association with Tooke and his circle in his later years. He modelled portraits of Tooke (**80**) and other active members of the SCI, Felix Vaughan, Dr John Warner and Lord Daer, sat for him (**78, 79, 113**). Among Banks's effects, and possibly by him, were busts of Tooke's co-defendant at his trial, Thomas Holcroft, the radical writer Mary Wollstonecroft (whose husband William Godwin recorded meeting Banks at a Wimbledon dinner in his diary), and Napoleon Bonaparte (**86**), for whom Banks expressed some support, before it became clear that the Emperor was no democrat ('he is chang'd & I have done with him') (*Bell* 1938, 148).

Given Banks's opposition to England's participation in the Napoleonic Wars, it is a tribute to the sculptor's reputation and ability that he was chosen to execute two of the monuments to war heroes in St Paul's Cathedral (**34, 36**). Banks felt the contradiction, describing the memorials phlegmatically as works to the memory of 'naval heroes who have been kill'd in attempting to kill others', but he also recognised that the business 'may be of some consequence to me' (*Bell* 1938, 118). It was: the contract for the Captain Westcott's monument earned him 4,000 guineas (*Farington*, vol 5, 1781).

Avarice was certainly not Banks's driving force. He was a gifted portraitist (Speaker Addington described the unidealised portrait of his father) (**69**) as the only bust he 'could ever talk to', (*Farington*, vol 3, 962), but did not exploit this lucrative genre, carving heads only for a limited circle of friends and patrons. He was suspicious of manufacturers like Matthew Boulton and, although courted by the Derby porcelain works (in 1787), he remained aloof from commercial modelling. He also disapproved of the practice among artists of acting as dealers ('a sign that the love of gain prevails more than the love of art'). His daughter later claimed that her father lived frugally, was 'very strict in his religious tenets', and expended 'considerable sums' on alleviating distress (*Bell* 1938, 6, 137).

In May 1803 Banks had a paralytic stroke, which impaired the use of his hands. After this date his work at St Paul's must largely have been the work of assistants. The names of his apprentices and workmen are largely unrecorded, although Joseph Panzetta later claimed to have worked on the relief of Shakespeare (**99**), and his bust of John Boydell was completed by F W Smith (**16**). The sculptor is known to have given tuition in drawing to the painter William Mulready.

In November 1803 Banks applied unsuccessfully for the post of Keeper of the Royal Academy, a post traditionally reserved for impecunious or inactive artists. His political history may have militated against him. Banks's last days do not, however, seem to have been inactive or penurious, for he continued to oversee his grandiose monument to Westcott, and to make visits to Wimbledon, Bath and Wells. By January 1805, however, he was very ill, and on 2 February he died.

He was buried in Paddington churchyard and a small tablet was erected in his memory in Westminster Abbey, with the lines 'Whose superior abilities in his profession added a lustre to the arts of his country, and whose character as a man reflected honour on human nature'. His wife and his daughter, Lavinia Forster, were his sole beneficiaries. There is no indication of the size of his estate, though Mrs Forster later claimed that he left 'a handsome provision' for them. On 22 May 1805 there was an auction of the contents of Banks's studio, which included many of the original terracottas for Banks's most famous works, sculpture by Joseph Wilton and Foy, as well as oddities such as 'four highly curious Gothic figures' rescued from the façade of the old Guildhall (**101**), and an antique fragment dredged from the Thames. It is impossible to be certain which of the plaster casts and busts listed are by Banks. Numerous other models were kept in the family (which moved to Paris ten years later), and then fell into the hands of **J C F Rossi** and ultimately **Sir Francis Chantrey**, who is said to have destroyed many of them (*Builder*, 3 Jan 1863, xxi, 5). *Achilles arming* (**42**) is a rare and celebrated survival.

Many notices in the press and comments in unpublished memoirs attest to Banks's status as one of England's greatest sculptors. Farington recalled Flaxman telling William Hamilton RA that Banks was the equal of **Antonio Canova** (*Farington* 2, 302). Banks was the subject of an extended biographical notice in the *European Magazine* in 1790, and in February 1805 Flaxman composed an address to the Royal Academy's Council *On The Death of Thomas Banks*, in which Banks was cast as Britain's first truly neoclassical sculptor, the artist who saved Britain from a cocktail of Puritan iconoclasm and the pernicious influence of Bernini. Flaxman's lecture was not delivered publicly, as many had hoped, since Farington and others fretted over whether their celebration of an artist who had been 'proclaimed to be democratical' might lead to the King's displeasure. Instead the eulogy was appended to the second edition of Flaxman's *Lectures* in 1838.

Banks's reputation remained high in the nineteenth century, aided by numerous hagiographic notices by his daughter (in *The Builder* and elsewhere) and a 'Life' by **Allan Cunningham** (1830). J T Smith felt that 'England had no sculptor of mind until the appearance of Thomas Banks' (*Smith* 1828, II, 185). His sculpture was shown at the International Exhibition in 1862, and seen by Palgrave as being the originator of the British school. But Banks's only modern full-length biographer has been an unsympathetic descendant. C.F. Bell's *Annals of Thomas Banks* (1938), a thorough piece of scholarship, posits the subject's works as quaint and outmoded and suggests that the character of the man is indelibly tainted by his 'heady democratic idealism' (*Bell* 1938, 170). Yet the influence of Banks's neoclassicism, combined with dramatic and sentimental subject-matter and innovatory composition and treatment, can be felt throughout the 19th century and deserves greater attention. The serious and high-principled nature of his approach to art and life marks him out as one of the more engaging characters in the history of British sculpture.

MGS

Literary References: *Farington, passim*; *Smith* II, 1828, 185–201; *Flaxman* 1838, 271–294; *Whitley* 1930, 40–1; *Anecdotes* 1937, 140, 146; *Bell* 1938; Jones, *Memoirs* 1951, 53, 73, 75, 89; *Hutchison* 1960–62, 134; *Stainton* 1974, 327–331; *Read* 1982, 19; *Bryant* 1983, 742–5; *Bryant* 1985, 49–64; *Whinney* 1988, 322–336; *Bryant* 1991, 409–11; *Bricknell* 1995, 16; *Groseclose* 1995, 57–8, 64; *Grove* 1996, 3, 183–5 (Bryant); *Ingamells* 1997, 48; *Bewley* 1998, 120, 153, 185; *Bindman* 2000, 769–772; *Bilbey* 2002, 46–53; *Bryant* 2005 (1), 51–8; *Bryant* 2005 (2)

Archival References: Poor Rate Books, St Marylebone, reel 19, 1780; RA Council Minutes, vol 1, 28 June 1770, fol 82; Banks/Upscott, Banks/Cumberland, Banks/Hastings; Banks/Humphry (most of Banks's surviving correspondence is published in *Bell* 1938 or *Bindman* 2000, 769–772)

Additional MS Sources: RA/GA, travelling scholarship, minutes of council, I, 137, 171, 191; minutes of general assembly I, 64

Will: Thomas Banks, 1 March 1805, PROB 11/1421, fol 324

Miscellaneous Drawings: double page from a sketchbook, unknown subject, SD 1803, HMI, 9/1990, *Leeds* 1999, 8; study of a male nude, signed in monogram 'TB', University of Glasgow; portrait of John Malin, 'a late model to the RA', exhib RA 1771, 6, RA (*Whitley* 1928, 2, 374)

Auction Catalogues: *Banks* 1805

Portraits of the Sculptor: Richard Cosway, graphite, before 1794, (BM, P&D 1965, 1211.34); James Northcote, canvas, 1792, RA; George Dance, chalk, 1793, chalk, RA; George Dance, 1794, graphite BM, P&D, 1898, 0712.12; anon, plaster mask cast from life, before 1791, RA; Henry Singleton, *The Royal Academicians under the Presidentship of Benjamin West, c*1793–5, RA; John Flaxman, graphite profile drawing, 1804, BM, P&D 1965, 1211.33; John Flaxman, pencil, 1804, pencil, Fitzwilliam. All these, and others of Banks's wife and child, are reproduced in *Bell* 1938, pls I, XXV, XXVI, XXVII, XLI

Funerary Monuments

1.	1771	Cherub decorating an urn, model, probably for a monument		[Exhib RA, London, 5]; untraced		*Bryant* 1985, 50
2.	1779	Design for a monument to the Earl of Chatham (commission won by John Bacon RA)	tc	[Models, 'sale of a nobleman', Christie, 17 May 1782, and Banks sale, 1805, lot 103]; untraced		*Bell* 1938, 39; *Gunnis* 1968, 39; *Bryant* 1985, 50
3.	1779	Dr Isaac Watts (†1748) Model(s): bas-relief sold Christie, 17 May 1782, lot 15; clay model, Banks sale, 1805, lot 82	m	Westminster Abbey, London, nave	S	*Bell* 1938, 42; *Bryant* 1985, 50–51, 52 (repr)
4.	1780	Design for a monument to Captain Cook (unexecuted) Drawing(s): aquatint of lost drawing, BM PDL		[Model exhib RA, London, 474; Banks sale, 1805, lot 104]; untraced		*Bell* 1938, 43, repr IV; *Bryant* 1985, 52
5.	†1782	Thomas Newton, Bishop of Bristol and Dean of St Paul's Payment(s): £200 (part-payment)		[St Mary-le-Bow, City of London]; destroyed		*Bell* 1938, 52, pl. VII; *Bryant* 1985, 53–54 (repr)
6.	1785	Anne Martha Hand (†1784) Model(s): exhib RA, London 1785 (500); 1787 (656); Banks sale, 1805, lot 90		[St Giles, Cripplegate, City of London]; destroyed		*GM*, Sept 1786, 808; *Bell* 1938, 66, 70 (repr VII and VIII); *Bryant* 1985, 55–56, 59 (repr)
7.	†1787	Dr William Smith, Dean of Chester Model(s): relief, Banks sale, 1805, lot 92		Chester Cathedral, Cheshire	S	*Bell* 1938, 70, 9 (repr XII); *Bryant* 1985, 55
8.	†1787	Edmund Law, Bishop of Carlisle Model(s): a female with a mitre, Banks sale, 1805, lot 97		Carlisle Cathedral, Cumberland	S	*Bell* 1938, 71 (repr XII); *Whinney* 1988, 328
9.	†1787	John Heaviside Drawing(s): model sold Banks sale, 1805, lot 96		St Etheldreda, Hatfield, Herts	S	*Bell* 1938, 70–1 (repr XIII); Pevsner, *Herts*, 1977, 164
10.	1788	Dr Robert Markham (†1786), Model(s): Banks sale, lots 92 and 94		['Piety weeping at the tomb of Benevolence', exhib RA, London, 1788, 504]; St. Mary, Whitechapel, London		*Bell* 1938, 72, (repr X); *Bryant* 1985, 55

11.	1784–9	General Sir Eyre Coote (†1783) Model(s): two, Banks's sale, 1805, lots 85 (unexecuted), 106 (plaster)		[Exhib RA, 1789, 611; Banks sale, 1805]; Westminster Abbey, London, north transept	S	*Bell* 1938, 58, 70; *Bryant* 1985, 51, 54–5 (repr)
12.	†1789	Giuseppe Baretti, mural monument (designed by Cipriani) Model(s): bust of Baretti and model, Banks sale, 1805, lots 37 and 95		St Mary-le-bone old church, London	S	*Bell* 1938, 75, pl. XIII
13.	†1790	Philip, 2nd Earl of Hardwicke Payment(s): £550 Model(s): Banks sale, 1805, lot 81		Wimpole, Cambs	S	*Bell* 1938, 82; *Penny* 1977, 68, 69 (repr)
14.	1790	Philip, 2nd Earl of Hardwicke (†1790)		Flitton, Beds, de Grey mausoleum	S	*Penny* 1977, 67–8 (repr); *Bryant* 2003, 79–80 (repr)
15.	1791	Hon Mary Pakenham (†1789) Model(s): Statue of 'Filial Piety', exhib RA, 1791, 634; sketch of two reliefs, Banks sale, 1805, lot 65 and 98; cast, SJSM M 278		[Summerhill, Co Meath, mausoleum]; destroyed		*Bell* 1938, 83–4 (repr XVII); *Bryant* 1985, 57–60 (repr)
16.	c1791	John Boydell, Lord Mayor of London, model (executed in marble by F W Smith, 1820) Model(s): VAM A.19-1931, painted plaster		[St Olave Jewry, City of London]; St Margaret Lothbury, City of London, 1888	S	*Bell* 1938, 85–6 (repr XX); *Whinney* 1988, 334; *Bilbey* 2002, 51–2
17.	†1792	Shukbrugh Ashby		Hungarton, Leics		Pevsner, *Leics & Rutland*, 1984, 182
18.	1791–1792	William Woollett (†1785) Model(s): bas-relief and model, Banks sale, 1805, lots 52, 65, 72, 89, 113		Westminster Abbey, London, cloisters	S	*Bell* 1938, 82–3, pl. XVIII; *Bryant* 1985, 57
19.	†1793	Anna Helena Matthews Model(s): Banks sale, 1805, lot 84		Chester Cathedral, south transept	S	*Bell* 1938, 97–8 (repr XXX); *Bryant* 1985, 58
20.	1793	Governor John Gideon Loten (†1789) Payment(s): £550 Model(s): plaster model of 'Generosity' and portrait, Banks sale 1805, lot 91		Westminster Abbey, London, nave	SD	WAM; *Bell* 1938, 96–7; *Bryant* 1985, 59
21.	†1793	Joseph Hurlock and his wife, Sarah		Stoke Newington, London	S	*Bryant* 1985, 58
22.	1793	Penelope Boothby (†1791) Model(s): Banks sale, 1805, lot 101; plaster, SJSM M 44		['Statue of a Sleeping Girl' exhib RA, London, 1793, 677]; Ashbourne, Derbys	D	*Bell* 1938, 95–6, pl. XXVIII–XXIX; *Penny* 1977, 115–7 (repr); *Thornton and Dorey* 1992, 61 (repr); *Dorey* 2004, 62–3
23.	†1794	Sir Clifton Wintringham Model(s): bas-relief and female figure, Banks sale, lot 87 and 97		Westminster Abbey, London, north transept	S	*Bell* 1938, 99, pl. XXX; *Bryant* 1985, 57–58
24.	1795	Margaret Petrie (†1791) Model(s): Banks sale, 1805, lot 105; Chelsea Hospital; destroyed World War II		St Mary, Lewisham, London	S	*Bell* 1938, 103, repr XXXII; *Bryant* 1985, 50, 58–60 (repr); *Dorey* 2004, 59
25.	†1795	Mrs Hallifax		Ewell, Surrey		Pevsner, *Surrey*, 1971, 224
26.	1796	Cornelia Milbanke (†1785) Model(s): exhib RA, 836; 'plaster on marble' model, Banks sale, 1805, lot 102		Croft, N R Yorks		*Bell* 1938, 108; *Penny* 1977, 59, 60, 91 (repr)
27.	†1796	Rev T Clarke		Ickenham, Middx		Pevsner, *London: NW*, 1991, 339
28.	†1796	Stephen Storace Model(s): 'Hand of death grasping a lyre', Banks sale, 1805, lot 81		St Mary, St Marylebone, London		*Bell* 1938, 111 (repr XXXV); *Bryant* 1985, 59
29.	1797	Colonel Robert Kyd Model(s): Banks sale, 1805, lot 71		[Exhib RA 1797, 1183]; Botanical gardens, Kolkata (Calcutta)		*Calcutta Gazette*, Jan 5, 1797; *Bell* 1938, 114–5, (repr XXXVI)
30.	1797	Major John Delap Halliday Model(s): Banks sale, 1805, lots 72, 89 and 100		[Exhib RA 1797, 1105]; Halesowen, Worcs		*Bryant* 1985, 56, 59, 61, 62 (repr)
31.	1797	Sarcophagus to contain the body of the daughter of Richard Cosway (†1796)	m	[Richard Cosway's house, 20 Stratford Place, London, drawing room]; untraced		*Farington*, II, 636; vol. 3, 913; *Wheatley* 1891, vol 3, 327
32.	1799	Weeping figure for a monument Model(s): 'A monumental figure weeping', Banks sale, lot 88		[Exhib RA, London, 1095]; untraced		*Bell* 1938, 128
33.	†1800	John G Clarke		Ickenham, Middx		*Bryant* 1985, 59
34.	1797–1802	Captain Richard Rundle Burgess (†1797) Drawing(s): PRO MPD 78,00 with agreement and bond Model(s): Bust and plaster model, Banks sale, 1805, lots 52 and 108		St Paul's Cathedral, London, chapel of St Michael and St George	D	*Bell* 1938, 149–50, (repr XXXIX); *Whinney* 1988, 330–33 (repr)
35.	1802	Model for a projected monument to Earl Howe in St Paul's Cathedral (commission won by John Flaxman)	p	[Banks sale, 1805, lot 86]; SJSM, Flaxman recess	SD	*Bell* 1938, 150–1, 158, (repr XXXVIII); SJSM inventory
36.	1802–1805	Captain George Blagdon Westcott (†1798) Payment(s): 4,000 gns Model(s): plaster, Banks sale, 1805, lot 107		St Paul's Cathedral, London, chapel of St Michael and St George	SD	*Bell* 1938, 150, 173, (repr XLII); *Whinney* 1988, 332, 365 (repr); *Yarrington* 1988, 64–5, 73–4 (repr 31a, 31b)

No.	Date	Subject	Material	Location	Literature
37.	nd	Lady Strange (perhaps unexecuted) Model(s): Banks sale, 1805, lot 83		Untraced	*Bell* 1938, 194
38.	nd	Mr Hawkins Model(s): Banks sale, 1805, lot 99		[St Mary, Whitechapel, Middx]; untraced	*Bell* 1938, 72; *Bryant* 1985, 54–5
Statues					
39.	1769	'a whole figure of Garrick'		[Soc of A, premium, 20 gns]; untraced	RSA, *Minutes*, 1768–69, seq 3 f 11
40.	1769	'original model in clay, of a naked human figure as large as the life' (Prometheus)		[Soc of A, premium, 30 gns]; untraced	RSA, *Minutes*, 1768–69, seq 3 f 30; *Bell* 1938, 12
41.	1769	Perseus, model		[Exhib Free Soc, London, 245]; untraced	*Bell* 1938, 15
42.	*c*1777	Achilles arming, statuette	tc	VAM A.22-1955 Other versions: Musée Girodet, Montargis (patinated tc)	*Whinney* 1971, 134–5 (repr); *Neoclassicism* 1972, 190; *Bilbey* 2002, 46–7 (repr)
43.	*c*1778	Cupid catching a butterfly on his wing Payment(s): 4,000 roubles Model(s): Banks sale, 1805, lot 74, with another Cupid companion piece	m	[Exhib RA, 534, 1781; Tsarksoe Selo, Russia, grotto]; untraced	*Bell* 1938, *passim*; *Grove*, 184
44.	1781	Empress Catherine of Russia, model	tc	[coll Prince Grigori Potemkin]; untraced	*Bell* 1938, 50
45.	1784	'Achilles, enraged for the loss of Briseis, retires to the seashore and complains to Thetis', model	p	[Exhib RA, London, 538]; British Institution, entrance hall; RA, Burlington House, vestibule; untraced	*Bell* 1938, 60–66; *Monthly Mag*, vol 23, pt 1, 1807, 486; *Bryant* 1983 (1), 742–5 (repr)
46.	1784	General Sir Eyre Coote	m	[East India House, City of London]; Foreign and Commonwealth Office, London	*Bell* 1938, 60, pl. X; *Archer* 1965, 406; Pevsner, *London: Westminster*, 1973, 548
47.	1786	The falling Titan, diploma work Model(s): plaster, Banks sale, 1805, lot 73	m	RA, London	SD *Manchester Art Treasures* 1857, 134; *Bell* 1938, 68–9 (repr X); *Whinney* 1988, 325, 466 n16
48.	1790	Thetis dipping the infant Achilles in the river Styx Model(s): plaster, Banks sale, 1805, lot 75	m	[Exhib RA, 658; Hafod, Radnor]; Clumber House sale, Christie, 19 Oct 1937, lot 337; VAM A.101-1937	*Bell* 1938, 75–79, repr XV; *Whinney* 1971, 130–1 (repr); *Bilbey* 2002, 49–50
49.	*c*1792	The Hindu deity Camadeva and his mistress on a crocodile, small model of a group	p	[Banks sale, 1805, lots 66–8]; SJSM A12	*Bell* 1938, pl. XXIII; SJSM Inventory
50.	1793–1800	Charles, 1st Marquess Cornwallis (with pedestal relief of the sons of Tipu Sultan, Abdul Khaliq and Muiz-ud-din, as hostages) Model(s): statue, bas-relief and two figures, mould and sketch, Banks sale, 1805, lots 14, 59 and 60	m	[Exhib RA, London, 1800, 1087 and 1096]; Fort St George Museum, Chennai (Madras), India	*Bell* 1938, 134–5; *Groseclose* 1995, 64 (repr); *Coutu* 1998, 50–1 (repr)
51.	1801	Two anatomical crucifixions (cast from the corpse of a murderous Chelsea pensioner), one lost	p	[Banks sale, 1805, lot 34]; RA, London	*Bell* 1938, 193; *Bryant* 1991, 409–411 (repr)
52.	nd	Benjamin West's dog	p	[Banks sale, 1805, lot 114]; untraced	*Bell* 1938, 42
53.	nd	Small copy of Mr Towneley's bronze Hercules	p	[Banks sale, 1805, lot 30]; untraced	*Bell* 1938, 193
54.	nd	The dying patriot, statuette, sketch model in clay		SJSM 1106	*Bell* 1983, 193, repr XL; Soane Museum inventory
Busts					
55.	1777	Maria Walpole, Duchess of Gloucester	tc	[Exhib RA, London, 514, 1782; Banks sale, 1805, lot 45]; untraced	*Bell* 1938, 53
56.	1778	Thomas Jones of Penkerrig, Radnor Model(s): Banks sale, 1805, lot 115		[Exhib RA, London, 1045 (sent from Rome)]; untraced	*Graves* I, 1905–6, 106; *Jones Memoirs* 1951, 75
57.	1778	Unidentified lady	m	[Exhib RA, London, 418]; untraced	*Bell* 1938, 42
58.	1780	Benjamin West RA Model(s): mould, nobleman's sale, Christie, 1782	tc	[Exhib RA, London, 424; Banks sale, 1805, lot 40]; Burlington House, London	*Bell* 1938, 42
59.	1781	Robert Home, the artist	tc	[Exhib RA, 437; Banks sale, 1805, lot 41]; untraced	*Bell* 1938, 48
60.	1783	'Head of a Majestic Beauty, composed on Mr [Alexander] Cozens principles'		[Exhib RA, London, 386]; untraced	*Bell* 1938, 55
61.	1784	Maria Cosway	m	[Exhib RA, London, 427]; untraced Other versions: Banks sale, 1805 (plaster)	*Bell* 1938, 56
62.	1785	Sir Joseph Bankes	m	[Erlestoke sale 1832, lot 165]; untraced	*Erlestoke* 1832, 167
63.	1785	Sir Joshua Reynolds		[Erlestoke sale 1832, lot 162]; untraced	*Erlestoke* 1832, 167
64.	†1787	Dr John Egerton, Bishop of Durham Model(s): two, clay, Banks sale, 1805, lots 46–7, sold with a mould	m	[Banks sale, 1805]; untraced	*The World*, 25 July 1787; *Bell* 1938, 69
65.	†1788	Johann Samuel Schroeter	tc	[Banks sale, 1805, lot 48; William Tassie sale, Christie, 12 July 1805, lot 208]; untraced	*Bell* 1938, 71; *Gunnis* 1968, 39

No.	Date	Subject	Material	Location	References
66.	c1789	Mrs John Taylor Model(s): (mould), Banks sale, 1805, lot 115		[Banks sale, 1805]; untraced	*Bell* 1938, 75–6
67.	1790	Warren Hastings (1st version) Payment(s): £73 10s Model(s): t-c, Victoria Memorial Hall, Calcutta; t-c, William Tassie sale, Christie, 12 July, 1805, lot 207; Banks sale, 1805, 5 lots relating to this or the 2nd version, lots 5, 53–56	m	[Daylesford House, Worcs]; Foreign and Commonwealth Office, London Other versions: five identified casts Another, identical to first marble version but with portion of drapery cut away from each shoulder, 1794, bronze, NPG, London, 209	*Bell* 1938, 79–80 (repr XXXI)
68.	c1790	Warren Hastings (2nd version, but draped all'antica)		[coll William Seward]; untraced Other versions: **1796, £73 10s, SD; Gov art coll (1954)**	*Bell* 1938, 79–80, (repr XXXI); *Whinney* 1988, 334 (repr); *British Portraits* 1956–7, 114
69.	1790–1791	Dr Anthony Addington Model(s): mask, Banks sale, lot 5; cast in artificial stone, painted, R C Physic	m	[Up-Ottery Manor, Devon]; private coll, USA Other versions: VAM A.2-1955	*Bell* 1938, 84 (repr XIX); (*Wolstenholme* 1964, 18–19, model repr); *Whinney* 1971, 132–3 (repr); *Bilbey* 2002, 50–51
70.	1792	'Master Cockerell in the character of Harpocrates' Model(s): mould of the back, Banks sale, 1805, lot 115		[Exhib RA, London, 739]; untraced	*Bell* 1938, 88
71.	1792	Mrs Jane Johnes and Mariamne Johnes (two) Model(s): casts and moulds of both, Banks sale, 1805, lot 38		[Hafod, Radnor]; (Jane Johnes only) Dolancothy, Llandeilo, South Wales	*Bell* 1938, 86–7, (repr XIX); *Whinney* 1988, 334
72.	1794	Unidentified lady		[Exhib RA, London, 391]; untraced	*Bell* 1938, 99
73.	1796	Anna Maria, Lady Lawley Model(s): moulds, Banks sale, 1805, lot 51		[Exhib RA, London, 463; Banks sale, 1805]; untraced	*Bell* 1938, 108
74.	1796	Charles, 1st Marquess Cornwallis Model(s): a mask, bust and mould, Banks sale, 1805, lots 5, 50, 60	m	[Exhib RA, London 1796, 872]; coll Major J Warde Other versions: cast, Banks sale, 1805; untraced	*Bell* 1938, 108–9, 135
75.	1796	Melpomene (Mrs Siddons)		[Exhib RA, London, 873]; untraced	The *True Briton*, 26 April, 1796; *Bell* 1938, 109
76.	1796	Sir Robert Lawley Model(s): moulds of Lord and Lady Lawley, Banks sale, 1805, lot 51	p	[Exhib RA, London, 877; Banks sale, 1805]; untraced	*Bell* 1938, 109
77.	1798	Thomas Johnes Model(s): Banks sale, 1805, lot 115		[Exhib RA, London, 1045]; untraced	*Bell* 1938, 119
78.	pre-1799	Felix Vaughan (†1799)	p	[Mould and bust, Banks sale, 1805, lot 128]; untraced	*Bell* 1938, 128
79.	pre-1800	Dr John Warner (†1800) Model(s): mask and clay bust, Banks sale, 1805, lots 5 and 46	tc	[Banks sale, 1805]; untraced	*Bell* 1938, 134
80.	1800	John Horne Tooke Model(s): a mask and two busts, Banks sale, 1805, lots 5, 35, 42	m	[Banks sale, 1805 (plaster cast)]; untraced	*Bell* 1938, 138–9
81.	1803	Miss Rose, daughter of George Rose Model(s): 'Bust of Miss Rose', Banks sale, 1805, lot 39	p	[Hafod, Radnor, music room; Banks sale, 1805]; untraced	*Bell* 1938, 163
82.	1803	Oliver Cromwell Model(s): masks of Cromwell, Banks sale, 1805, lots 5 and 43		[Exhib RA, 937; Hafod, Radnor]; private coll, London	*Bell* 1938, 161
83.	c1804	George Soane	p	SJSM SC 69	*Bell* 1938, 174
84.	nd	General Martin (and another 'when young'), Mrs Campbell, unidentified sitters, and Mr or Mrs 'Palmer'	p	[Banks sale, 1805, lots 37, 39, 42, 49]; untraced	*Bell* 1938, 193
85.	nd	Head of Agrippina		[Christie, 17 May 1782]; untraced	*Gunnis* 1968, 39
86.	nd	Prince of Wales, Governor Hollwell, Mary Wollstonecroft, [Thomas] Holcroft, Napoleon Bonaparte	p	[Banks sale, 1805, lots 5, 35]; untraced	*Bell* 1938, 193
87.	nd	Warren Hastings (3rd version, with drapery diagonal across the chest)	m	Private coll, London	S
Chimneypieces					
88.	1787	Description unavailable		[Governor Hornby's new mansion, Portman Square, London]; untraced	*The World*, 11 May 1787
89.	1790	'With a rich ornamented Tablet, festoon of Laurel leaves and ribbons on Friezes; Vitruvian scrool & flutes on Architrave' and 'Angular Columns with staff & ribbon and twisted flutes' Payment(s): £64	m	[Bank of England, City of London, Mr Newland's apartment]; untraced	Soane bank acct, vol 1, fol 91; *Gunnis* 1968, 38
90.	1787–1792	Description not available (designed by Sir John Soane) Payment(s): £93 3s 6d	m	[Egyptian Hall, Fonthill Splendens, Wilts, apartments to left of hall]; untraced	Soane Journal I, 34; *Britton* 1801–1815, vol 1, 214; *Gunnis* 1968, 38
91.	1787–1792	Several, including one with a female head representing the sun and two term figures	m	[Richard Cosway, 20, Stratford Place, London]; untraced	*Wheatley* 1891, vol 3, 327; *Bell* 1938, 90–1

92.	1792	With caryatids of Indian women returning from the Ganges and central frieze of a Harem Model(s): plaster and a cast, Banks sale, lots 69 and 70; in Ambrose Poynter's coll, 1863	m	Daylesford House, Glos, drawing room	*Bell* 1938, 88–9, (repr XXI–XXII); *Walch* 1965, 90; Pevsner, *Glos: Cotswolds*, 1999, 312 (repr 98)
93.	1792	With panel of Brahma between two elephants Model(s): Banks sale, lot 68	m	Daylesford House, Glos, central drawing room	*Bell* 1938, 90–1, (repr XXIII); *Watkin* 1968, 234
94.	pre-1803	With heads of Socrates, Plato, Alcibiades, Sappho and others		[Hafod, Radnor, dining room]; destroyed	*Bell* 1938, 90
95.	nd	Statuary marble with 'an enriched tablet'	m	[Fonthill House, Wilts, bedchamber]; untraced	*Bell* 1938, 90
Architectural Sculpture					
96.	1783	The four quarters of the globe Model(s): 4 small whole-lengths, 2 in clay, 2 in plaster, Banks sale, 1805, lot 63	s	Customs House, Dublin, north front, one damaged	*Bell* 1938, 54–5
97.	1784–1785	Trophies and military Ornaments Payment(s): £289 10s	s	Somerset House, Strand, London, north front in great square and centre of building next to river	*Colvin* 1973–76, vol 5, 466; *Jenkins* 2000–1, 27–8
98.	1788	The Graces and candelabrum		[Exhib RA, London, 622]; untraced	*Bell* 1938, 72
99.	1789	Shakespeare between the Dramatic Muse and the Genius of Painting Model(s): small models, Banks sale, 1805, lots 57, 64 (£153)	s	[Shakespeare Gallery, Pall Mall, London (until 1868)]; New Place, Stratford-upon-Avon, Warks, gardens	Boydell sale cat; *Bell* 1938, 73–77, repr XIV; Pevsner, *Warks*, 1966, 418; *Noszlopy* 2003, 50–1 (repr)
100.	*c*1795	Two angels holding a festoon, part of an altar		[St Paul's Church, Covent Garden]; untraced	*Bell* 1938, 107
101.	*c*1798	Three medieval statues, representing religion, temperance and fortitude, formerly on the façade of the Guildhall, London (restoration only)		[Guildhall; Banks sale, 1805, lot 110, bought by William Bankes, presumably for Corfe Castle, £100]; Guildhall, City of London	*Bell* 1938, 177–8; *Athenaeum* 1846, n996, 1223; *Farington*, III, 963
102.	1803	Term Model(s): Banks's Sale, 1805, lots 61 and 112? [Model for a term, Hercules and the lion skin]		[Exhib British School, Berners Street, 232]; untraced	*Bell* 1938, 160
Reliefs					
103.	1763	The death of Epaminondas, of Portland stone		[Soc of A, premium, 30 gns]; untraced	RSA, *Minutes*, 1762–63, seq 2 fol 64, 68; RSA *Premiums*, 1762, 32; *Bell* 1938, 12
104.	1765	The redemption of Hector's body	m	[Soc of A, premium, 25 gns]; untraced	RSA, *Minutes*, 1764–65, seq 3 f 63; *Dossie* 1782, 440; *Bell* 1938, 12
105.	1766	Judgement of Paris	m	[Soc of A, premium, 10 gns]; untraced	RSA, *Register*, 1778, 32; *Dossie* 1782, 440; *Bell* 1968, 15
106.	1770	The rape of Proserpine		[RA, London, gold medal]; untraced	RA Premium list; *Bell* 1983, 15
107.	*c*1774	Alcyone discovering the dead body of her husband Ceyx	m	[Exhib RA, London, 1775, 400]; LMG 7.660/68	*Stainton* 1974, 327–331 (repr); *Bryant* 1985, 52, 54 (repr)
108.	1774	The death of Germanicus Model(s): Banks sale, 1805, lot 77	m	Holkham Hall, Norfolk	*Bell* 1938, 35, 39, 40, 43, pl. II; *Whinney* 1988, 323 (repr)
109.	1774–1777	Caractacus before Claudius Payment(s): 200 gns estimate; patron prepared to pay only 100 gns Model(s): Banks sale, 1805, lot 78; SJSM, clay	m	[Exhib RA, London, 1780, 476]; Stowe House, Bucks	*Bell* 1938, *passim*, (repr II); *Bindman* 2000, 769–772; *Dorey* 2004, 65–6
110.	1777–1778	Thetis and her nymphs rising from the sea to console Achilles for the death of Patroclus Model(s): Banks sale, 1805, plaster, lot 76	m	VAM A.15-1984	*Whinney* 1971, 128–9 (repr); *Bryant* 1985, 49, 61, 62 (repr); *Bowron and Rishel* 2000, 228–9 (repr); *Bilbey* 2002, 47–9
111.	1772–1779	'Morning or the East', and 'Evening or the West' (roundels after the antique 'Sol' and 'Luna' from the Arch of Constantine)	p	[Pitzhanger Manor, Ealing, entrance hall]; SJSM Other versions: SJSM, ante-room, *c* 1803, tc	*Bell* 1938, 147, repr XXXVII; *Dorey* 2004, 58–9 (repr)
112.	1781–1782	Armed neutrality	m	[coll Empress Catherine II of Russia]; untraced	*Bell* 1938, 52
113.	pre-1794	Lord Daer (†1794), bas-relief and medallion	p	[Banks sale, 1805, lots 36, 115]; untraced	*Bell* 1938, 101
114.	1801	Morning, or the East (river Ganges) and Evening, or the West (the Thames)	m	Bank of England, City of London, Lothbury Court	*Ward-Jackson* 2002, 88–9
115.	1803	Mariamne Johnes grieving over the death of her pet robin redbreast, urn relief		[Hafod, Radnor, gardens]; Nat Lib of Wales, Aberystwyth	*Bell* 1938, 163–4, repr XL; *Bryant* 1985, 58
116.	nd	'Circular bas-relief allegorical of the Revolution of King William III', bust medallions of G B Cipriani, and an Italian poetess		[Banks sale, 1805, lots 37, 62]; untraced	*Bell* 1938, 194
117.	nd	Sketch of a battle between Jupiter and the Titans		Untraced	*Bell* 1938, 69

Miscellaneous

118.	1769	'A Design for Ornamental Furniture' Payment(s): £21		[Soc of A, premium]; untraced	*Bell* 1938, 12
119.	1770	Aeneas and Anchises escaping from Troy		[Exhib RA, London, 3, 4]; untraced	*Bell* 1938, 15
120.	1772	Mercury, Argus and Io, model		[Exhib RA, London, 3]; untraced	*Bell* 1983, 16
121.	1781	'Royal Personage as Psyche plucking the golden wool' (model, intended as a portrait of Princess Sophia of Gloucester)		[Exhib RA, London, 465]; untraced	*Bell* 1938, 49
122.	*c*1792	Angel in adoration, for the head of Lavinia Banks's harp	wd	VAM A.8-1965	*Bell* 1938, 93–4, pl.XXIV; *Bilbey* 2002, 52 (repr)
123.	1802	Portrait of a baby		[Exhib RA, London, 1088]; untraced	*Bell* 1938, 150
124.	nd	Seven sketches of Homeric and other classical subjects		[coll the sculptor]; destroyed	*Bell* 1938, 195–7

BANKS (or BANKES), Richard fl 1626

'Richard Banks, of St. Bartholomew the Great, mason' married Mary Miller at St Nicholas Cole Abbey, in the City of London, on 26 January 1626 (*Chester* II, 1887, 161). He may perhaps be identified with the Richard Bankes, who is described as *3 Bus Regibus Lapicidae* on the tablet commemorating his son-in-law and daughter, the Rev and Mrs Francis Clerke (†1715), in Shoreditch Parish Church. The monument bears both his arms and those of the Bankes family.

Literary References: *Gunnis* 1968, 37

Archival References: RG/JP, 1, 96; IGI

BANSON, Richard fl 1765

Perhaps identifiable with **Richard Benson**, who won a Society of Arts premium in 1764

Archival References: RSA, Minutes, 1764–65, seq 3 fol 61

Miscellaneous

1.	1765	Model in wax		[Soc of A, premium, 3 gns]; untraced	RSA, *Minutes*, 1764–65, seq 3 f 61

BAQUET fl 1773

A French artist, he exhibited at the Society of Artists giving his address as 3 Bartholomew Close, London.

Literary References: *Gunnis* 1968, 40; *Pyke* 1973, 9–10

Miscellaneous

1.	1773	Unidentified subjects, two portrait models	w	[Exhib Soc of Artists, London, 52, 53]; untraced	*Graves* 1907, 20

BARATTA, Giovanni di Isidoro 1670–1747

Born in Carrara on 13 May 1670, he was one of a large family of sculptors. He studied in Florence under **Giovanni Battista Foggini** and probably learned to sculpt in bronze under Massimiliano Soldani, before spending four years in Rome, where he studied in the studio of Camillo Rusconi. In 1697 he returned to Florence, where he created his earliest known work, a relief of *Tobias and the Angel* for the church of Santo Spirito, 1698. Among his ever-growing circle of international patrons was Frederick IV of Denmark, but his major commissions were for religious institutions in Italy and included a group, *The freeing of the slaves* for the high altar of San Ferdinando in Livorno, executed between about 1710 and 1717. He was employed by the royal court of Savoy from 1719 onwards and carved four colossal statues of doctors of the Church in the crossing of the chapel of Sant' Uberto at Venaria Reale, considered to be his masterpiece. Baratta was ennobled by the Duke of Massa in 1731.

The sculptor secured one significant British commission. On 28 April 1710 the architect Nicholas Hawksmoor wrote to the Duke of Marlborough about statues for Blenheim Palace. He informed the Duke that 'Baratta (whom Your Grace had directed last year to make two figures but could not being engaged by the King of Denmark) now offers to do something for Your Grace. He is in very great Esteem; and if Your Grace thinks fit to make a couple of figures for a trial, I believe it would be best to leave them to his own fancy' (*Whistler* 1954, 236). Marlborough was in accord and Baratta carved two over-life-size figures representing *Valour* and *Glory* which he completed in 1715 (**1, 2**). The Duchess of Marlborough then decided that she did not want them and they were left, only partly paid for, in the sculptor's studio for more than five years.

In 1721 James Brydges, Duke of Chandos, obtained the Duchess of Marlborough's permission to purchase the rejected figures for Canons. Shortly after they arrived in Britain the Duchess was informed, erroneously, that one of them represented her recently deceased husband and so Chandos offered to give her both figures on the condition that they would be returned to his family upon her death. The offer was declined and the statues were installed at Canons, where they remained until the contents of the house were sold after the death of Chandos in 1744. *Glory* is now in the Fitzwilliam Museum, Cambridge, but the location of the companion figure of *Valour* is unknown. It appears to have been at Ditton Park, Bucks in the 18th century and can probably be identified with a 'beautiful statue of the Great Duke of Marlborough in the character of Mars attributed to Joseph Baratta', which was sold at Christie's on 25 April, 1804 for 180 guineas.

Meanwhile, in 1714 Thomas, Earl of Strafford, wrote to Christopher Crowe, the British Consul at Livorno, enquiring about buying marble for columns, pilasters and pedestals for the gallery at Wentworth Castle. Crowe wrote to ask whether the columns were to be completely finished in Italy and recommended Baratta for the commission, adding that he 'did some very fine ones for the King of Denmark, and as he has a respect for the English, heele be very proud of being employed for your Lordshipp, not only in this but likewise for Statues if you had a need for any' (BM Add MS 22, 221, fols 259, 261, 263, 265). Lord Strafford declined. Baratta died on 21 May 1747 and was buried in the church of S Andrea at Carrara.

Literary References: *Honour* 1958 (2), 222–3, 226 n13; *Honour* 1958 (3), 170–77; *Gunnis* 1968, 40; *Grove* 3, 1996, 198–9; *Sicca and Yarrington* 2000, 6–7

Archival References: GPC

Statues

1.	1715	Glory	m	[Canons, Middx, 1721–44]; Fitzwilliam	SD	*Winter* 1958, 307–8 (repr); *Honour* 1958 (2), 226 n13; *Jenkins* 2005, 167, 192, n40
2.	1715	Valour	m	[Canons, Middx, 1721–44]; untraced		*Honour* 1958 (2), 222, 226 n13 (repr); *Jenkins* 2005, 167, 192, n40

BARBER fl 1835?

The Bennett monument takes the form of a sarcophagus with a scroll hanging from it.

Funerary Monuments

1.	?1835	Mary Bennett	Martock, Somerset	S	*Gunnis* 1968, 40

BARDELLE, W E fl c1850

He was a medallist and die-sinker, who worked principally for W J Taylor of London. He signs a small bust in the British Museum (1).

Literary References: *Dawson* 1999, 116; *Forrer* VII, 1904–30, 47

Busts

1.	nd	Unidentified man, possibly William Richard Hamilton FRS, FSA	p	BM	S	*Dawson* 1999, 116–7 (repr)

BARDI fl 1848

Signor Bardi carved the richly ornamented Quattrocento-style sarcophagus designed by Professor Ludwig Grüner which forms part of the monument to Princess Sophia in Kensal Green Cemetery (1). The rest of the monument was by a London mason, **Edward Pearce.**

Funerary Monuments

1.	†1848	Princess Sophia (designed by L Grüner) (co-sculptor: Edward Pearce)	Kensal Green Cemetery, London	Pevsner, *London: NW*, 1991, 469; *Curl* 2001, 200–1, 223 (repr)

BARKER, Jonathan fl 1733

Barker's only known work is a white marble tablet with cherubs at its top and cherubs' heads below, commemorating James Ashe, †1733 (1). It is possible that he was the John Barker, carver of Clerkenwell and Westminster, whose will was proved by the Archdeaconry Court of London in February 1735.

Funerary Monuments

1.	†1733	James Ashe	Halstead, Kent	S	Pevsner, *Kent: W & Weald*, 1976, 314

BARLOW, William I fl 1718

In 1718 he agreed with Lord Cowper to finish a house in Great George Street, Hanover Square. Writing to Cowper about chimneypieces for the house, Barlow added 'I will giet such as your Lordship shall like, as to sort and maner, both plain and Italen molded, tho. I think the molded ones are not so much used now' (GPC) (1). He can perhaps be identified with the William Barlow who in 1725 paid 7s 6d rates on a property in Oxford Street, next door to **Robert Hartshorne** and not far from **Michael Rysbrack** in Vere Street (St Marylebone Rate Books, reel 1, 1683–1731).

Archival References: St Marylebone rate books, reel 1, 1683–1731; GPC

Chimneypieces

1.	1718	Various, plain and moulded	[Lord Cowper, Great George St, Hanover Square, London]; untraced	GPC

BARLOW, William II fl 1740–52

Best remembered as the master of **Thomas Banks,** he became a director of the Westminster Fire Office in 1734. Between 1740 and 1754 he was employed on wood-carving at the house of the Rt Hon Henry Pelham in Arlington Street, where in 1750 he received £109 11s 1 1/2d for carving in the 'great room' (Pelham, box 1, 152) (6). He became free of the Masons' Company by redemption on 18 June 1751 and the following day agreed to supply twelve chimneypieces to 'Mr Dance's Drawings and Particulars', for the second floor and attic of the Mansion House by Michaelmas 1752. These were priced at £350 (MH Papers, Box 2, cited by *Jeffery* 1993, 299) (2). **Christopher Horsnaile II** also tendered for the work but quoted the much higher price of £690. Barlow received £50 on account on 20 December 1751 and the balance of £150 in 1752. He supplied more elaborate chimneypieces for the Lord Mayor's bed chamber and ante-chamber and received £16 for two lavatory basins for the same building (3, 4, 7). The sculptor also signs a large architectural monument with a triangular pediment and central sarcophagus commemorating Sir George Savile at Thornhill (1).

He can probably be identified with 'William Barlow Carver in Swallow Street St Thomas Westminster' whose will was proved on 8 May 1756. He may have been related to John Barlow who was granted the freedom of the Masons' Company by redemption on 3 August 1792 (Masons' Co Freemen List, fol 7) or to Thomas Barlow, a master carpenter and speculative builder who worked in London from about 1700 until his death in 1730 (see *Colvin* 1995, 100).

Literary References: *Farington*, vol II, 407; *Flaxman* 1838, 274; *Gunnis* 1968, 40; *Jeffery* 1993, 126–7, 273, 299

Archival References: Masons' Co, *Freemen*, fol 7, 18 June 1751, 3 August 1792; WFO, MN 343/5, 17 Oct 1734; GPC

Will: PROB 11/822

Funerary Monuments

1.	†1743	George Savile of Rufford	Thornhill, W R Yorks	Pevsner, *Yorks: W R*, 1967, 511

Chimneypieces

2.	1751–1752	Five of statuary marble for second floor rooms and seven of white and veined marble for the attic Payment(s): £350	Mansion House, City of London	*Gunnis* 1968, 40; *Jeffery* 1993, 126, 299, 273 (repr 250)

3.	1751–1752	With Apollo's head in tablet, ornaments and Ionic pilasters	m	Mansion House, City of London, Lord Mayor's bed chamber	*Jeffery* 1993, 127
4.	1751–1752	With Vitruvian scroll cross-member and carved pilasters	m	Mansion House, City of London, Lord Mayor's antechamber	*Jeffery* 1993, 127 (repr 93)
Architectural Sculpture					
5.	1747	Heads of cherubim	s	[Greenwich Hospital Chapel, keystone of chancel arch]; destroyed	TNA (Admiralty Papers) 68/743; *Bold* 2000 (2), 166
6.	1749–1750	Carving in the great room including friezes with foliage, festoons, shells & flowers and long carved panels on shutters Payment(s): £109	wd	[Rt Hon Penry Pelham's house, Great Arlington St, London]; untraced	Pelham Box I, fol 152
7.	1752	Two lavatory basins Payment(s): £16	m	Mansion House, City of London	*Jeffery* 1993, 93

BARLOW & MULLEY, of London fl 1830–40

Their small monument to John Miles at Cheshunt has a cherub mourning by an urn (2).

Literary References: *Gunnis* 1968, 40

Funerary Monuments					
1.	1829	Stephen Atkinson	Friern Barnet, Middx	S	
2.	†1834	John Miles	Cheshunt, Herts	S	Pevsner, *Herts*, 1977, 124

BARNARD, John c1740–

He was trained by his father and won premiums from the Society of Arts in 1760 and 1763, both in the 'sculptors under 22' category. He also exhibited with the Society of Free Artists.

Literary References: RSA *Minutes*, 1761–62, seq 3 f 64; *Gunnis* 1968, 40

Reliefs					
1.	1763	Tablet in clay		[Soc of A, premium, 15 gns]; untraced	*Dossie* 1782, 437
Miscellaneous					
2.	1760	Ornamental composition in clay (prize announced 1760, awarded 1762)		[Soc of A, premium, 3 gns]; untraced	RSA *Minutes*, 1761–2, seq 3 f 64
3.	1762	'model in clay, piece of flowers'	tc	[Exhib Soc of Free Artists, London]; untraced	*Gunnis* 1968, 40
4.	1762	'piece of ornament with two swans'	tc	[Exhib Soc of Free Artists, London]; untraced	*Gunnis* 1968, 40

BARNES, John, of Warwick fl 1716–41

He was employed as a marble mason in the Beauchamp Chapel at St Mary, Warwick, 1716–41. In 1716 he was paid £16 6s for a tabernacle (1) and on 14 July 1731 he received £95 9s for a black and white marble pavement. In 1735 he was given £1 15s 2d for 'taking down the old monument' plus £190 8s 10 1/2d for supplying and erecting the new altarpiece (Foxley (Lady Leveson's) Charity, Warks CRO, 1618/W15/15a). A payment of £93 for a white and veined marble pavement followed in 1737. In 1741 he was paid £38 2s 6d 'for worke done at ye Lady Chapell in Warwick to finish ye other part of ye altar piece which was left undone'. This included white and veined Italian marble for two great panels and the two 'cornishes', two large pieces of fine dove-coloured marble for the 'frizes' and capitals and black and yellow marble for the pilasters (2) (Dugdale MSS 1321 U, vouchers for repairs to the Beauchamp Chapel, 1735–42, archives Dugdale family of Merevale and Blythe Hall, family coll). The altarpiece was removed about 1760 and replaced with one by **William Collins**.

Literary References: *Churches of Warks* 1847, vol 1, 64

Archival References: GPC; RG/JP, 1, 108

Architectural Sculpture				
1.	1716	Tabernacle	[St Mary, Warwick, Beauchamp Chapel]; untraced	*Churches of Warks*, 1847, vol 1, 64
2.	1735–1741	Altarpiece	[St Mary, Warwick, Beauchamp Chapel]; dismantled c1760	GPC

BARNES, W fl c1800

He was responsible for a number of slate tablets and headstones, dating from c1800, at St Andrew, Timberland, Lincs.

Literary References: Pevsner, *Lincs*, 1989, 766

BARNETT, William 1786–1824

For further information the reader is referred to *Pyke* 1973, 10.

BARRATT, John fl 1676–84

An apprentice to **Abraham Storey**, he assisted Storey as mason for building St James, Piccadilly, 1676–84.

BARREL (or BARRELL), Henry I and II fl 1775–1805

At least two craftsmen of this name worked in London during the 18th century. A Henry Barrell, described as the son of Robert Barrell, was apprenticed to Antoine Jary, a carver of St James, Westminster, in 1737. It is not clear whether this man was related to Henry Barrel I, who worked as a mason and carver in the parish of St Martin-in-the-Fields. He was in business by 1775, when he received £85 from Lord Radnor in part payment for the 'capitals of the chapel columns' at Longford Castle (4) and he died in the spring of 1790. His son, Henry Barrel II, was apprenticed to a mason called Emmanuel Williams on 10 November 1781 and became free in 1788 (Masons' Co, Freemen List, fol 7).

The elder Barrel was employed at Guy's Hospital, where he was paid £72 10s for 'statuary work', 1777–78 (5). This included '12 faces' and '5 pattern's for ye frieze' costing £50 and £6 6s respectively. He worked for **Sir Robert Taylor** at General John Burgoyne's house, 3 Grafton Street, London, and at Gorhambury, Herts, in 1780 (6). From 1786 onwards he was employed at the 'new building next the Admiralty', receiving £139 for wood carving and chimneypieces (TNA ADM/17/1) (1, 7). The latter came from a demolished house at Blackheath belonging to Sir Gregory Page, so Barrel only had to reset most of them, though he did recut one. The last payments for this work were made in 1791, some time after Barrel's death, so it is possible that it was completed by his son. The Barrells, or perhaps only Henry Barrel II, were employed by Sir John Soane on mason's work, including a great deal of ornamental stone carving, at the Bank of

England between 1788 and 1805 (8). Payments included £4 for a mask-head in 1788 and £75 for four Corinthian capitals in 1789. The younger Barrel worked again for Soane in 1795 as the mason responsible for building 146 Piccadilly for a Mr Crauford. There he received £700, including payments for chimneypieces (2). He also made chimneypieces for the offices of the Commercial Commissioners in 1798, again for Soane (3).

Literary References: *Gunnis* 1968, 40–1; *Binney* 1984, 62

Archival References: Masons' Co, *Freemen*, fol 7; GPC

Will: PROB 11/1191

Chimneypieces

1.	1786–1791	Several installed and one recut Payment(s): £139 (with wood carving)		[for the 'new building next the Admiralty']; untraced	TNA ADM/17/1
2.	1795	Several		[Mr Crauford's House, 146 Piccadilly, London]; untraced	GPC
3.	1799	Several		[Offices of the Commercial Commissioners, 7 Austin Friars, City of London]; untraced	Soane bill book A, fols 288–9; *Gunnis* 1968, 40

Architectural Sculpture

4.	1775	'Capitals of the chapel columns' Payment(s): £85 (part payment)		Longford Castle, Wilts	*Gunnis* 1968, 40
5.	1777–1778	'Statuary work' Payment(s): £72 10s	s	[Guy's Hospital, London, central building]; untraced	*Gunnis* 1968, 40
6.	1780	Carving Payment(s): £138		[Gorhambury, Herts, library, dressing and drawing rooms]; untraced	*Gunnis* 1968, 40
7.	1786–1791	Wood carving Payment(s): £139 (with chimneypieces)	wd	[for the 'new building next the Admiralty']; untraced	TNA ADM/17/1
8.	1788–1805	Ornamental stone carving Payment(s): mask-head £4 (1788); capitals £58 (1788)	s	[Bank of England, City of London]; destroyed	Soane bank acct, vol 1, fol 20; *Gunnis* 1968, 40

BARRETT, B, of London fl 1838

Funerary Monuments

1.	†1838	Lady Boothby (designed by LN Cottingham)	Ashbourne, Derbys	Pevsner, *Derbys*, 1986, 62

BARRETT, G fl 1846–49

He exhibited at the Royal Academy, giving his address in 1846 as 6 Tufton Street, Westminster, and as 27 Clipstone Street, Fitzroy Square, in 1849.

Literary References: *Graves* I, 1905–6, 128

Miscellaneous

1.	1846	Mercury and Pandora	[Exhib RA, London, 1520]; untraced	*Graves* I, 1905–6, 128
2.	1849	Mercury and Argus	[Exhib RA, London, 1300]; untraced	*Graves* I, 1905–6, 128

BARRETT, James, of Norwich 1701/2–69

On 24 March 1733, Barrett, 'Mason and Carver', advertised in the *Norwich Gazette* that he had taken over the 'stock and shop of Mr **Augustine Curtis** deceased Carver, at the White-Swan in St Peter's Mancroft'. He stated that his work would be 'performed well and as cheap as any other stone-cutter on this Side London', and added that 'For some Years he has designed Drawings, and carved for most of the Masters in this City'. Barrett signs the monument to his predecessors, Augustine Curtis I and II, at St Peter Mancroft (2). This unusual work is about 8 feet high and takes the form of a central Corinthian pillar with a curtain behind it and curtains supported by cherub-heads hanging to left and right. Gunnis noted that it is similar in design to the monument to Mrs Hodgson (†1743) at Dersingham, Norfolk, which was carved by **Francis Stafford.** When Barrett died, aged 68, in December 1769, a local newspaper suggested that his works would provide 'lasting Evidence of his great Abilities in his Profession' (*Norwich Mercury*, 23 December 1769).

Literary References: *Gunnis* 1968, 41; RG/JP, 1, 109v, 110

Archival References: GPC

Funerary Monuments

1.	†1728	George Warren	Horstead, Norfolk	Pevsner, *Norfolk: NE & Norwich*, 1997, 568
2.	†1732	Augustine Curtis (†1731) and Augustine Curtis (†1732)	St Peter Mancroft, Norwich, Norfolk	Pevsner, *Norfolk: NE & Norwich*, 1997, 250

BARRY, John fl 1791–1842

Probably a Scarborough mason, he signs a number of local tablets.

Funerary Monuments

1.	†1791	Robert Wardrobe	St Mary, Scarborough, N R Yorks	S
2.	†1828	Richard Williamson	St Mary, Scarborough, N R Yorks	S
3.	†1828	Robert Tindall	St Mary, Scarborough, N R Yorks	S
4.	†1833	Elizabeth Borton	St Mary, Scarborough, N R Yorks	S
5.	†1842	Henry Leasley	St Mary, Scarborough, N R Yorks	S

BARTOLI, Domenico fl 1761–1805

He and his partner **John Augustus Richter** were the leading scagliola makers in London in the 1770s. Bartoli came from Leghorn. The earliest evidence of his presence in England is a court record of 1761, in which he is described as a carver, with an address in Newman Street, Westminster. He was probably the first inlayer of scagliola to work in England, although **Charles Clerici** was engaged in producing architectural work such as columns, pilasters and wall panels as early as 1737. Some indication of his materials is given by bills in the Burton Constable Accounts which itemise a silk sieve, a small quantity of 'Terra Sciena' and cuttle fish bone. These may have been fixatives.

In the years 1763–66 Bartoli was employed as a stuccoist by William Constable at Burton Constable, where he was paid a guinea a week and the cost of his materials (**1, 2, 16, 27–29**). A receipt in Bartoli's hand states that on 13 December 1764 he received 'Fifty Four pounds twelve shillings in full for a year's work' (**2**). The work he produced was remarkably accomplished and the chimneypiece he made for the state bed dressing room at Burton Constable appears to be the first time scagliola was inlaid into white statuary marble, as opposed to the coloured marbles used by the Florentine school.

In 1767 Bartoli went into business with Richter, working from premises in Great Newport Street, near Leicester Square. Although they are frequently spoken of as an enduring entity, the partnership appears to have been a relatively brief one, lasting only 10 years, from 1767 to 1777/8. Their work was almost exclusively for Robert Adam (**3, 4, 6, 10, 33**). After the partnership was dissolved both men continued working for the architects James Wyatt at 15 St James's Square (**25**), Thomas Leverton at Watton Wood (**12**) and George Steuart at Attingham (**15**) amongst others. In 1794–95 Bartoli went to Ireland to work for James Wyatt at Castle Coole in Co Fermanagh (**26**).

The last record of his work is a receipt dated 11 March 1805 for a pair of table tops for Carlton House, London (**36**). On 24 March 1807 a half-circular slab he supplied to Carlton House was returned to him, 'not being approved of' (*Jutsham*). (Add inf. Gerardine Mulcahy)

Donald Cameron

Literary References: *Gunnis* 1968, 41; *Wragg* 1957, 718–21; *Tite* 2001, 143; *Harris* 2001, 9; *Cameron* 2004, *passim*

Archival References: Middx sessions papers, London Met Archives SP 1761/02/011(1761); Royal Archives RA GEO/25189 (request for payment), 25190a (payment of £84)

Miscellaneous Drawings: Design for an inlaid table top, Burton Constable acc 1610 (1765)

Chimneypieces

No.	Date	Work	Location	Reference
1.	1763–1766	Inlaid with scagliola	Burton Constable Hall, E R Yorks, long gallery	Constable Accounts DDCC/2/52
2.	1763–1766	Scagliola inlaid in white statuary marble	Burton Constable Hall, E R Yorks, state dressing room	Constable Accounts DDCC/2/51
3.	1771	Inlaid with scagliola (co-sculptor: John Augustus Richter)	20 St James's Square, London	*Harris* 2001, 266
4.	1774	Inlaid with scagliola (co-sculptor: John Augustus Richter)	[Northumberland House, London, glass drawing room]; Syon House, London	*Harris* 2001, 101
5.	1774	Inlaid with scagliola (co-sculptor: John Augustus Richter)	20, St James's Square, London	Wynnstay MSS, box 115/7; *Harris* 2001, 360, n48
6.	1775	Inlaid with scagliola (co-sculptor: John Augustus Richter) Drawing(s): Osterley OPH 407/1949	Osterley Park, Middx	*Harris* 2001, 352, n92
7.	1775	Inlaid with scagliola	[Panton, Lincs]; Basildon Park, Berks	Basildon Park, NT Studies, 1991, 20
8.	1775	'Scagliola work done to the chimneypiece in my Lady's dressing room' (surround by John Hinchliff) Payment(s): £33 (part payment)	[for Sir William Watkins Wynn]; untraced	Wynnstay Accounts, box 115/7; *Harris* 2001, 360, n48
9.	1776	Two, inlaid with scagliola (co-sculptor: John Augustus Richter) Drawing(s): Soane Adam Drawings, vol 23, 67	Home House, London	
10.	1777	Inlaid with scagliola (co-sculptor: John Augustus Richter)	[Bolton House, London]; untraced	*Harris* 2001, 8
11.	?1777	Inlaid with scagliola (co-sculptor: John Augustus Richter) Drawing(s): Soane Adam Drawings, vol 17, 36	17 (formerly 31) Hill Street, London, hall	
12.	1779–1780	Two, inlaid with scagliola	Watton Wood, Herts, hall and dressing room	DC
13.	1784	Neoclassical design inlaid with scagliola Payment(s): £225 16s 16d	Burghley House, Northants, third George room	Lord Exeter's day book, 6 Nov 1784
14.	1785	Inlaid with scagliola Payment(s): £864	[Carlton House, London]; St James's Palace, London	King's Works RA/GEO 34975
15.	1785	Inlaid with scagliola	Attingham, Salop	DC

Architectural Sculpture

No.	Date	Work	Location	Reference
16.	1763–1766	Constable coat of arms (in an overmantel by Fisher of York) Drawing(s): Burton Constable LDS 1587, pencil and grey wash	Burton Constable Hall, E R Yorks, great hall, acc 961	Constable Accounts DDCC/2/55
17.	*c*1767	Scagliola columns in imitation of porphyry (co-sculptor: John Augustus Richter)	Holland House, Kingsgate, Kent, saloon	*Gunnis* 1968, 321
18.	*c*1770	Ionic pilasters of verd antique	Kedleston, Derbys, saloon	*Britton* IV, 1805, 414; *Harris* 2001, 39
19.	1772	Columns in imitation of giallo antiquo (co-sculptor: John Augustus Richter)	[Pantheon, London]; untraced	*Wragg* 1957, 719
20.	pre-1773	Scagliola columns in imitation of Sicilian jasper	Stowe, Bucks	*Seely* 1773, 31
21.	?1777	Scagliola columns in imitation of Siena marble, with gilt capitals, mouldings and ornaments	Stowe House, Bucks, music room	*Lipscomb* 3, 1847, 90; *Gunnis* 1968, 41
22.	1785	Pilasters	[Gorhambury, Herts]; untraced	Herts CRO MS XI.71
23.	1785–1786	Columns, panels and other work Payment(s): £424	Packington Hall, Warks	*Binney* 1970, 226–9
24.	1793	Pilasters Payment(s): £301	Cobham Hall, Kent, great hall	*Gunnis* 1968, 41
25.	1794	Columns	15, St James's Square, London	*Survey of London*, XXIX, 148
26.	1795	Scagliola pilasters and columns	Castle Coole, Co Fermanagh	*Rowan* 1979, 178

Miscellaneous

27.	1765	Britannia side-table, scagliola topped	Burton Constable Hall, E R Yorks, great hall, acc 970	Constable Accounts DDCC/2/53; *Hall* 1976, 1476 (repr), 1478
28.	1765	Two side tables with porphry veneered slab top on mahogany fluted Doric column supports	Burton Constable Hall, E R Yorks, great hall, acc 904, 905	Constable Accounts DDCC/2/56
29.	1763–1766	Scagliola-topped table with scene of a castellated town	Burton Constable Hall, E R Yorks, great hall, acc 971	Constable Accounts DDCC/2/54; *Hall* 1976, 1478
30.	1768	Tables inlaid with scagliola (co-sculptor: John Augustus Richter)	[Coventry House, London]; private coll	Croome Court archives 8/12/68
31.	1768	Two scagliola tables, each supplied with leather covers (co-sculptor: John Augustus Richter) Payment(s): £65 each Drawing(s): Soane Adam Drawings, vol 39:8	[Croome Court, Worcs]; untraced	Croome Court archives 8/12/68; *Beard* 1993, 41–3; *Harris* 2001, 101
32.	1774	Table top inlaid with scagliola (co-sculptor: John Augustus Richter) Drawing(s): Soane Adam Drawings vol 39, pl 8	[Northumberland House, London]; Syon House, Middx	DC
33.	1775	Table top inlaid with scagliola (co-sculptor: John Augustus Richter)	Osterley Park, Middx	*Harris* 2001, 171
34.	1777	Semi-circular inlaid scagliola table tops with eagle motifs (co-sculptor: John Augustus Richter)	Nostell Priory, W R Yorks	West Yorks R O, NP C3/1/5/4/5; *Harris* 2001, 206
35.	1797	Repairs to a mosaic table	Burghley House, Northants	Lord Exeter's Day Book, 17 Nov 1797
36.	1805	Table tops	[Carlton House, London]; untraced	King's Works, /Geo/25190, 21590A
37.	nd	Scagliola table top, 'ornamental'	Untraced	*CL*, 159, 3 June 1976, 1476
38.	nd	Table top inlaid with scagliola	Private coll, London	DC

BARTOLINI, Lorenzo 1777–1850

A Florentine sculptor, his studio attracted large numbers of British visitors between 1815 and 1824. His early works are neoclassical in style, but while in Paris at the turn of the century he developed an interest in the art of the *Quattrocento* and his later works combine neoclassical and neorenaissance elements with a strong taste for naturalism.

He was born near Prato, in Tuscany, on 7 January 1777, the son of a blacksmith. The family moved to Florence and he was there employed as a craftsman in various workshops before moving to Volterra in 1795, where he worked in the studio of the French sculptor Barthélemy Corneille (c1760–1812). In 1799 he went to Paris, where he studied under Pierre-Jean David. He won the Prix de Rome in 1802 with a relief of *Cleobis and Briton* (plaster fragment, priv coll, Italy) and undertook several commissions for the Napoleonic government, including a bronze relief of the *Battle of Austerlitz* for the Vendome Column (destroyed 1871). In 1807 Elisa Bonaparte appointed him professor of sculpture at the Accademia di Carrara and in 1810 he received an important commission for a colossal, semi-nude marble statue of Napoleon for Livorno. Completed in 1814, as the French empire crumbled, it was rejected and remained in the sculptor's studio for many years, before it was finally erected at Bastia, Corsica, in 1854. In 1814 Bartolini followed Napoleon into exile on the island of Elba, before settling in Florence some time after 1815.

As a Bonapartist Bartolini was excluded from public and grand ducal commissions for some years, but made a living with private commissions for portrait busts and statues, including a number of British travellers. After visiting his studio in 1817, Henry Matthews wrote, 'Bartolini is an excellent workman and takes admirable likenesses . . . It is now the fashion among the English to sit to him; – and you find all your acquaintances drawn up in fearful array, in hard marble; – some at full length!' (*Matthews* 1820, cited by *JKB* 1978, 1655). His subjects included Lord Byron, who agreed to sit for Bartolini on condition that he also modelled a bust of Byron's mistress, Countess Teresa Guiccioli (**23, 25**). The poet was unimpressed by his portrait, which he described as resembling a 'superannuated Jesuit' before adding 'though my mind misgives me it is hideously like. If it is I cannot be long for this world, for it overlooks seventy' (*Marchand* 1973–94, vol 9, 213).

Bartolini was also involved in the lucrative trade in copies of ancient and modern sculpture. In 1817 Matthews observed, 'Casts have been imported from London of busts of the King, Fox, Pitt, Nelson, Perceval, and many others. Bartolini reproduces in marble, and sends back to London, all expenses of carriage included, for twenty-two pounds each' (*Matthews* 1820, in GPC). In this area of his business Bartolini collaborated with other workshops, displaying their products for sale at his premises and taking a share of the profits in return. The 6th Duke of Devonshire purchased reproductions for Chatsworth (**7, 28, 36, 37**).

During this period Bartolini secured several commissions for ideal works which greatly enhanced his reputation in Italy and abroad. These included a *Reclining Venus* after Titian's famous painting in the Uffizi, executed around 1822 for the 3rd Marquis of Londonderry, and a *Reclining bacchante* commissioned by the Duke of Devonshire in 1822 (**8, 10**). He seems to have had little involvement with British patrons after the mid-1820s, perhaps because he was able to attract more prestigious commissions from such grandees as the Duke of Tuscany and Prince Anatole Demidov. His most famous work, a kneeling adolescent female nude entitled *Trust in God*, was commissioned by the Milanese Marchesa Poldi Pezzoli in memory of her husband (Museo Poldi Pezzoli, Milan, 1834–6). Towards the end of his career Bartolini executed a number of funerary monuments for the church of Santa Croce in Florence, including a tomb for the Polish Countess Sophia Zamoyska, erected in 1844.

By the time of his death, on 20 January 1850, he was recognised as a leading European sculptor. A large collection of plaster models from his studio, comprising around 300 models for portrait busts and almost all of the models for his most important funerary and ideal sculptures, is preserved in the gallery of the Accademia de Belle Arti in Florence. His work has attracted considerable scholarly attention in Italy and France but is less well-known in Britain.

EH

Literary References: *Gunnis* 1968, 41; *JKB* 1972 (3), 328, 331; *Penny* 1977, 73, 89, 206 n 30; *JKB* 1978, 1655–6; *Grove* 3, 1996, 294–7 (Spalletti); *Passeggia* 2000, 167–8; *Sicca and Yarrington* 2000, 12, 13; *Encyc Sc*, vol 1, 134–5 (Cinelli)

Archival References: GPC

Collections of Drawings: Museo Comunale, Prato, Italy; Uffizi, Florence, Italy

Portraits of the Sculptor: Jean Auguste Dominique Ingres, 1806, Musée Ingres, Mountauban, France; Jean Auguste Dominique Ingres, oil on canvas, 1820, Louvre, Paris, France; Pasquale Romanelli, posthumous marble bust, 1854, collezzione comunali, Prato (repr *Bartolini* 1978, 302)

No.	Date	Subject	Medium	Location		References
Funerary Monuments						
1.	†1818	Henrietta Stratford Canning		Lausanne Cathedral, Switzerland		*Bartolini* 1978, 287 (repr); *Grove* 3, 1996, 295
2.	†1820	Sir Vyell Vyvyan		Mawgan-in-Meneage, Cornwall	S	Pevsner, *Cornwall*, 1970, 114
Statues						
3.	c1818	'Mme Tay' or 'Milady Tait' Payment(s): 500 luigi Model(s): Galleria dell' Accademia, Florence, inv 1207, plaster	m	[Sent to Dublin]; untraced		*Bartolini* 1978, 24–5 (repr); *JKB* 1978, 1655–6 (repr)
4.	c1820	A nymph	m	[Garendon Hall, Leics]; untraced Other versions: Galleria dell' Accademia, Florence, inv 1214, plaster ex coll Jean-Gabriel Eynard, marble; untraced		*JKB* 1972 (2), 1102 (repr); *Bartolini* 1978, 26–7 (repr)
5.	c1820	Lady Emma and Lady Julia Campbell Model(s): Galleria dell' Accademia, Florence, inv 1183, plaster	m	[coll Mr Campbell]; Inverary Castle, Argyll		*Bartolini* 1978, 32–3 (repr); *JKB* 1978, 1656 (repr); *Grove* 3, 1996, 295
6.	1815–1820	Mary Tighe Model(s): Galleria dell' Accademia, Florence, plaster		Untraced		*Grove* 3, 1996, 295
7.	1822	Copy of the Venus de Medici Payment(s): £70	m	Chatsworth, Derbys, orangery		*JKB* 1972 (3), 328, 331
8.	c1822	Reclining Venus Payment(s): 600 luigi Model(s): Galleria dell' Accademia, Florence, inv 1313, plaster		[coll Charles, 3rd Marquis of Londonderry]; Musée Fabre, Montpelier, France Other versions: Lady Lever, Liverpool, m		*Grove* 3, 1996, 296
9.	1823	Frances, Marchioness of Londonderry with her son, George (later 4th Marquis of Londonderry) Model(s): Galleria dell' Accademia, Florence, inv 1205, plaster	m	Wynyard Park, Durham		*Bartolini* 1978, 40–1 (repr); *JKB* 1978, 1656 (repr); *Grove* 3, 1996, 295
10.	1822–1834	Reclining bacchante Payment(s): 600 luigi Model(s): Galleria dell' Accademia, Florence, inv 1204, small plaster	m	Chatsworth, Derbys, sculpture gallery Other versions: ex coll Comte de Poutalès-Gorgier, reduced marble; untraced		*JKB* 1972 (3) 328, 331 (repr); *Bartolini* 1978, 46–7 (repr)
11.	nd	Lady Louisa Russell (after Chantrey)		Kilruddery Castle, Co Wicklow	S	GPC
12.	nd	Venus coming from the bath		[The Deepdene, Dorking, Surrey]; untraced		*Gunnis* 1968, 41
Busts						
13.	1814	Emperor Alexander of Russia	a	[Exhib RA, London, 778]; untraced		*Graves* I, 1905–6, 136
14.	c1815	Lady Burghersh		Untraced		*JKB* 1978, 1655
15.	c1815	Lord Burghersh (later 11th Earl of Westmorland)		Untraced		*JKB* 1978, 1655
16.	By 1816	Mrs Foley		Untraced		*JKB* 1978, 1655
17.	By 1816	Mrs Middleton		Untraced		*JKB* 1978, 1655
18.	1816	Virgil	m	Bowood, Wilts		
19.	1815–1818	Elizabeth, Marchioness of Bristol Model(s): Galleria dell' Accademia, Florence, plaster	m	Ickworth, Suffolk (NT)		*Bartolini* 1978, 71 (repr); *JKB* 1978, 1655 (repr)
20.	c1818	Frederick, 1st Marquess of Bristol	m	Ickworth, Suffolk (NT)		*JKB* 1978, 1655 (repr); *Grove* 3, 1996, 295
21.	1819	Lady Morgan		Untraced		*JKB* 1978, 1655
22.	1819	Thomas Moore	p	[coll Thomas Moore]; untraced		*JKB* 1978, 1655
23.	1821	George Gordon, Lord Byron Model(s): Galleria dell' Accademia, Florence, plaster	m	NPG 1367 Other versions: South African Library, Cape Town, South Africa, marble Galleria d'Arte Moderna, Palazzo Pitti, Florence, marble coll Lord Malmesbury, 1882; untraced Istituto d'Arte, Parma, plaster	SD	*Notes and Queries*, Nov 1882, 422; *Bartolini* 1978, 74 (repr); *JKB* 1978, 1656 (repr); *Grove* 3, 1996, 295 (repr)
24.	c1821	Jonathan Hatfield Model(s): Galleria dell' Accademia, Florence, inv 159, plaster	m	[coll Jonathan Hatfield]; Manchester CAG 1957.410	S	*JKB* 1978, 1655; *Treuherz* 1983, 110–2 (repr)
25.	1821	Teresa Gamba Guiccioli Model(s): Galleria dell' Accademia, Florence, inv 1284, plaster	m	South African Library, Cape Town Other versions: Biblioteca Classense, Ravenna, marble Instituto d'Arte, Parma, plaster		*Bartolini* 1978, 75 (repr); *Grove* 3, 1996, 295
26.	1823	Charles, 3rd Marquis of Londonderry		Untraced		*JKB* 1978, 1656

27.	1824	Charles James Fox		Untraced Other versions: several replicas produced	GPC
28.	nd	Copy of an Egyptian double bust of Isis and Serapis	m	Chatsworth, Derbys, sculpture gallery	*Chatsworth Handlist*, 26
29.	nd	Count d'Orsay		[Countess of Blessington's sale, Phillips, Kensington, 7–26 May 1849]; untraced	GPC
30.	nd	Countess Maria Potocka	m	Chatsworth, Derbys, north corridor	*Chatsworth Handlist*, 5
31.	nd	Daniel Tighe		Ballyna House, Co Wicklow	GPC
32.	nd	Henry Hope		[The Deepdene, Dorking, Surrey]; untraced	*Gunnis* 1968, 41
33.	nd	Lord Frederick Montagu		Untraced	*JKB* 1978, 1655–6
34.	nd	Marguerite, Countess of Blessington		[Countess of Blessington's sale, Phillips, Kensington, 7–26 May 1849, lot 262]; untraced	*Ormond* 1973, 40
35.	nd	William Tighe		Ballyna House, Co Wicklow	GPC
Architectural Sculpture					
36.	1819	Copy of the Medici vase	m	Chatsworth, Derbys, orangery	*JKB* 1972 (3) 328, 331; *Haskell and Penny* 1981, 316
37.	1822	Marble bath à l'antique		Chatsworth, Derbys	*JKB* 1972 (3) 328

BARTON, William, of Derby fl 1839

Busts					
1.	1839	John Gibson		[Exhib Derby Mechanics Institute]; untraced	*Gunnis* 1968, 41
Reliefs					
2.	1839	Queen Victoria, medallion		[Exhib Derby Mechanics Institute]; untraced	*Gunnis* 1968, 41
3.	1839	Rev William Falkner, medallion portrait		[Exhib Derby Mechanics Institute]; untraced	*Gunnis* 1968, 41
4.	1839	Sir Richard Arkwright, medallion portrait		[Exhib Derby Mechanics Institute]; untraced	*Gunnis* 1968, 41
Miscellaneous					
5.	1839	A greyhound	a	[Exhib Derby Mechanics Institute]; untraced	*Gunnis* 1968, 41

BARUZZI, Cincinnato –1878

Baruzzi was a pupil of **Canova** and after his master's death in October 1822 he completed the unfinished reclining figure of *Dirce*, commissioned from Canova by George IV for Carlton House. The 6th Duke of Devonshire visited Baruzzi's studio in Rome on 19 December 1822 and noted in his diary that he was 'enchanted with Lord Kinnaird's Salmacis' (3). Two days later he returned and ordered 'an original group' from the sculptor. When the Duke saw the full-sized model of *Venus and Cupid* after work on the marble had already begun, he did not like it (1). Baruzzi offered to make something else and by November 1824 he had modelled an alternative figure of *Diana* but the Duke eventually agreed to accept the *Venus and Cupid*, perhaps because he felt committed or because he feared that the *Diana* would be even less successful. When the group arrived at Chatsworth it was erected in the central niche of the orangery instead of being placed in the Sculpture Gallery.

Literary References: *JKB* 1972 (3), 326, 328, 331; *Roberts* 2002, 143 (*Dirce*)

Statues					
1.	1825	Venus and Cupid Payment(s): 300 louis	m	Chatsworth, Derbys	*Chatsworth Handlist*, 28; *JKB* 1972 (3), 326, 329, 331 (repr)
2.	pre-1857	The nymph Salmacis gazing upon the son of Mercury and Venus	m	[coll Townley Parker]; untraced	*Manchester Art Treasures* 1857, 134
Miscellaneous					
3.	1822	Salmacis		[coll Lord Kinnaird]; untraced	*JKB* 1972 (3), 326

BASTARD FAMILY, of Blandford

Thomas Bastard I †1720
John Bastard I *c*1687–1770
William Bastard *c*1689–1764
Thomas Bastard II *c*1686–1731
Benjamin Bastard *c*1698–1772
John Bastard II 1722–1778

The Bastards were a family of builders and architects whose activities centred on the south coast counties of Hampshire and Dorset. Initially the family were masons, joiners and carpenters, though in this period such labels could be fluidly applied to fit particular commissions. In the early 18th century the dominant figure in the business was **Thomas Bastard I**, who worked from Blandford. It is unlikely that very much, if any, work that could be described as sculptural came from the family during this period, but this was to change in the next generation.

After his death his three eldest sons, **John Bastard I, William Bastard** and **Thomas Bastard II**, set up together in Blandford as **Bastard and Company**. This was primarily a means of continuing their father's business, but it also allowed the brothers to expand the architectural side of the firm, so opening the way for more sculpture-related activity. Little is recorded of the firm's work during the first ten years of its existence, and not all their work was executed in partnership. The monument to Henry Dirdoe and family members, *c*1724, is signed by John alone. It comprises a circular relief of carved angels' heads, which Gunnis thought delightful (1).

The lack of documentary evidence for this period may be due to a devastating fire that struck Blandford on 4 June 1731, destroying most of the town and its records. Those that do survive indicate that much of the partners' early activity was building work and sculptural elements were restricted to architectural ornaments and chimneypieces. Later in 1731 Thomas Bastard II died, but the two remaining brothers used the opportunity provided by the destruction of Blandford to expand their business activities and played a major role in rebuilding the town. The rebuilding of

Blandford was largely their work. This may not have been due simply to their abilities as builders, for they also had political power in the town. John and William owned the principal bank and between them held the position of town mayor nine times between 1729 and 1759. John became a director of the Westminster Fire Office in 1761.

The rebuilding of Blandford took only 30 years and so has a remarkable consistency of style. Austere Georgian forms predominate and the architectural decoration that formed the greater part of the Bastards' sculptural work is restricted to carved capitals and small-scale carved detailing on classical façades. An example of the latter is the lion on the front of the Red Lion Inn, *c*1750 (**7**). Their capitals can be seen on numerous buildings around the town, including the parish church, the interior of which has a series of Ionic capitals (**4**), and the façade of the Old Greyhound Hotel, which has four Corinthian capitals (**5**). The notable feature of many of their capitals is the use of a baroque motif taken from Borromini in which the volutes turn inwards, an early appearance of this form in England. Also in Blandford is the Bastards' monument to the fire, which takes the form of a water fountain and fire hydrant, erected in 1760 in the Market Square at the Bastards' own expense (**8**).

Outside Blandford, they were responsible in 1749 for building a town house for the merchant Sir Peter Thompson at 25 Market Close, Poole. Like the Red Lion in Blandford, this building has a sculpted lion rampant, and a florid rococo-style coat of arms on its façade (**6**).

Neither John nor William married and at their deaths their business interests were inherited by two nephews, both named Thomas, who also inherited considerable wealth and had little interest in continuing the business. One nephew only lived a year after inheriting, leaving the second 'to assume the status of a gentleman' until his death in 1791 (*Colvin* 1947, 190).

Another son of Thomas Bastard I, **Benjamin Bastard**, also became a mason. After an apprenticeship with **William Townesend, of Oxford**, he set himself up independently in Sherborne. He was responsible for the monument to Peter Davis in the cloisters of Wells Cathedral (**2**). Rising to 4.25 metres in height, it has a conventional neoclassical cherub with an inverted smoking torch, standing in front of a pyramid. Another monument, to Anna Maria Sharp (†1747) in St John the Evangelist, Wicken, Northants, has been confidently attributed to Benjamin Bastard since it is 'identical to the Davis monument' (Pevsner, *Northants*, 1973, 462).

Thomas Bastard II had a son, **John Bastard II**, who was apprenticed to Benjamin Bastard and worked as a mason and architect for Lord Winterton and at Stoneleigh Abbey in 1764, the Middlesex Hospital, London in 1766 and at Greenwich Palace in the early 1770s.

Michael Paraskos

Literary References: *Hutchins* 1870, IV, 205; *Webb* 1925, 144–50; *Colvin* 1947, 178–95; *Adams* 1968, 445–50; *Gunnis* 1968, 41; Pevsner, *Northants*, 1973, 462; *Stillman* 1978, 175–213; *Cornforth* 1984, 268–9; *Manco* 1991, 145–70; *Legg* 1994, 15–42; *Colvin* 1995, 108–10; *Smith and Hall* 2000, 38–41

Archival References: John Bastard, *A Book of Works to the South West Pavillion, King Charles's Building*, 1 Oct 1771–30 Sept 1773 (PRO 68/876); John Bastard's notebook, Dorset RO D6, MIC/R/37 and R/114; WFO, MB, 343/11 (15 Oct 1761)

Miscellaneous Drawings: vol by Bastard family members, VAM, P&D, E.1310-2001

Wills: John Bastard II, PROB 11/957; William Bastard, PROB 11/926; Thomas Bastard I, Dorset RO MK/T50

Portraits: Unidentified artist, portrait of John Bastard II, Blandford Town Hall (repr *Colvin* 1947, 193); unidentified artist, portrait of William Bastard, Blandford Town Hall (repr *Colvin* 1947, 193)

Funerary Monuments					
1.	?1724	Henry Dirdoe (by John Bastard I)	Gillingham, Dorset	S	*Gunnis* 1968, 41
2.	†1749	Peter Davis (by Benjamin Bastard)	Wells Cathedral, Somerset	S	*Colvin* 1995, 110
Chimneypieces					
3.	1760	Several (by Bastard and Company)	[Kingston Hall, Blandford, Dorset]; untraced		*Legg* 1994, 16
Architectural Sculpture					
4.	*c*1733	Capitals (by Bastard and Company)	Sts Peter and Paul, Blandford, Dorset		*Webb* 1925, 146 (repr)
5.	*c*1740	Capitals (by Bastard and Company)	Greyhound Inn, Blandford, Dorset		*Adams* 1968, 448 (repr)
6.	*c*1746	Lion and coat of arms (by Bastard and Company)	25 Market Close, Poole, Dorset		*Adams* 1968, 450 (repr)
7.	*c*1750	Lion rampant and capitals (by Bastard and Company)	Red Lion Inn, Blandford, Dorset		*Adams* 1968, 446, 448 (repr)
8.	1760	Blandford Forum fire monument, fountain and fire hydrant (by Bastard and Company)	Market Square, Blandford, Dorset		*Colvin* 1947, 189
9.	*c*1760	Capitals (by Bastard and Company)	26 Marketplace, Blandford, Dorset		*Adams* 1968, 446 (repr)

BATCHELOR, George, of Buckingham fl 1825–45

Possibly a descendent of **Richard Batchelor**, he signs small tablets in a number of Buckinghamshire village churches including Oakley, Padbury and Buckingham parish church.

Literary References: *Gunnis* 1968, 42

BATCHELOR, John, of Oxford 1734–1810

A labourer's son from Headington, he was apprenticed to Jacob Hayfield, a mason of Oxford, on 15 April 1751. £2 was paid 'by parent' and a further £10 came as charity from the University. He was admitted to the liberties of Oxford on 15 January 1762 and died, aged 74, in 1810. He may have been a member of the same family as **George** and **Richard Batchelor, of Buckingham.**

Literary References: *GM*, 1810, ii, 91; *Gunnis* 1968, 42

Archival References: Hanaster EB, L 5.5 (unpag)

BATCHELOR, Richard, of Buckingham fl 1750–60

On 3 March 1759 Mrs Purefoy of Shalstone, Bucks, signed an agreement with Richard Batchelor, of Buckingham, 'mason and statuary', for a marble monument to herself which was to be made in a 'good, sound substan[t]ial, firm, neat and workmanlike manner . . . according to the Pal or Draught . . . annexed' (*Records of Bucks*, XII, 261ff). This monument, which was erected in Shalstone church, is an architectural work with Corinthian capitals and a broken pediment enclosing a bust of Mrs Purefoy in the centre (**1**). There were originally two cherubs on the pediment, but a 19th-century vicar, who objected to their nakedness, had them removed. The work cost £93 13s 6d with a further 'ffive pounds . . on ffinishing the Inscription' (after Mrs Purefoy's death) and included £30 for the carving of the 'bosto' and the 'two boys' in marble (*op cit*). Batchelor was also employed as a mason on repairs at Buckingham church between 1754 and 1757.

Literary References: *Gunnis* 1968, 41–2

Funerary Monuments

1.	1759	Mrs Purefoy	Shalstone, Bucks	*Records of Bucks*, XII, *Eland* I, 1931, xv (repr 2); Pevsner, *Bucks*, 1994, 617

BATE, Richard, of Shrewsbury fl 1814–23

Bate became a burgess of Shrewsbury in 1814 (Shrewsbury Town Archives, cited by *Gunnis* 1968, 42). His only recorded work is a large wall-tablet to the Birch family. Gunnis noted that at first sight this appears to be a typical London product of the late 18th century and that it shows how slowly new designs reached the more distant counties.

Literary References: *Gunnis* 1968, 42

Funerary Monuments

1.	1823	Birch family	St. Martin, Salop	*Gunnis* 1968, 42

BATESON, William, of York fl 1725–before 1755

In 1729 he made a chimneypiece for York Guildhall (**1**). His name appears frequently in the York Minster Fabric Rolls between 1725 and 1755, when a payment was made to his widow. In 1731, he and his partner, William Ellis, became the master-masons at York Assembly Rooms after the dismissal of **Leonard Smith**. Bateson and Ellis took over the shell of the building and 'worked all the columns', which were finished before the year was out, though the hall was not roofed until 1736. These columns, forty in number, with very fine Corinthian capitals, are closely spaced and divide all the four sides of the main room, or Egyptian Hall, from its aisles (**2**). A year later, as well as executing a great deal of masonry-work, the partners carved 'the cornice stone of ye Corinthian order'. For some reason the partners were not allowed to finish the building, which was completed by the reinstated Leonard Smith. Bateson's widow, 'Elizabeth Bateson, mason', took a Richard Waddington as an apprentice in 1757.

Literary References: *Gunnis* 1968, 42

Archival References: Assembly Rooms Directors' Minutes, Ledgers & Receipt Books, 1730–1925, York City Archives M23/1–18; York Minster Fabric Rolls, Minster Library, Dean and Chapter Archives, E4a, fol 40v (1726), fol 58r (1755)

Chimneypieces				
1.	1729	Description unavailable	Guildhall, York	*Gunnis* 1968, 42
Architectural Sculpture				
2.	1731–32	Columns with Corinthian capitals and cornice	Assembly rooms, York	*Gunnis* 1968, 42

BATTERSBY, William fl 1760

In 1760 he was paid £124 for stone work including 'moulded work' and 'stone bannisters', at Serlby Hall, Notts, then being built by James Paine for the 2nd Viscount Galway.

Archival References: Archives, Viscount Galway in GPC

BATTLE fl 1779

Funerary Monuments

1.	†1779	Bargrave family	Eastry, Kent	S	

BAX, John, of Deal fl 1821–43

'J. Bax, Statuary and Mason, nearly opposite the Bank, Queen-Street, Deal' advertised in the *Kentish Gazette* on 1 September 1821 that he had 'taken the above business of Mr B. Eastes, that was conducted by the late Mr W. Bailey' and was able to provide 'Tombs, Monuments, Chimney Pieces, and every other kind of masonry, executed on the shortest notice, and most reasonable terms' (GPC). Gunnis considered his two wall-tablets in Walmer parish church 'unexciting' (**1, 2**).

Literary References: *Gunnis* 1968, 42

Funerary Monuments

1.	*c*1830	Henry and Richard Harvey	Walmer, Kent	S	*Gunnis* 1968, 42
2.	†1837	Sir Richard Lee	Walmer, Kent	S	*Gunnis* 1968, 42
3.	†1843	Charles (†1791) and Mary Matson	Worth, Deal, Kent	S	

BAYES, Robert and Joseph, of Kettering fl 1810–45

The firm comprised Robert Bayes and his son Joseph, who later succeeded him. Their wall-tablet to Robert Stanley at Weekley has a semi-urn (**1**), while that to the Rev James Hogg at Geddington takes the form of a hatchment (**2**).

Literary References: *Gunnis* 1968, 42

Funerary Monuments

1.	1821	Robert Stanley	Weekley, Northants	S	*Gunnis* 1968, 42
2.	1844	Rev James Hogg	Geddington, Northants	S	*Gunnis* 1968, 42

BAYES, William, of Great Yarmouth fl 1810

The *Norfolk Chronicle* of 14 April 1810 carried an advertisement for Bayes 'Marble & Stone-Mason, North Quay, Great Yarmouth', which stated that he had 'for sale, a variety of Marble, and Stone Chimney Pieces . . . Monuments, Tombs, and Grave-stones executed in the neatest manner'.

Archival References: RG/JP, 1, 115v

BAYLIFF, Edward, of Kendal fl 1834–51

In 1834 a Cumberland directory compiled by Pigot & Co listed his address as Stricklandgate, Kendal. **Thomas Airey** was working in the same street by 1851.

Literary References: *Gunnis* 1968, 42; RG/JP, 1, 116

Chimneypieces

1.	1832	Several, including one of black Italian marble for the drawingroom and another of black Kendal marble for the dining room	[Mr Dunslay's house, Micklegate Bar, York]; untraced	*Gunnis* 1968, 42

BAYLISS, Edward, of Helmdon fl 1738–39

On 19 December 1739 William Purefoy wrote to Bayliss asking him to 'set up a Turkey marble mantle piece & to lay 2 marble slobs [sic]', which had been supplied by **William Palmer** for Shalstone House, Bucks. Two months later he wrote again asking for the work to be redone as Bayliss's men had 'set the marble up in our best parlour so that the marble that goes over athwart the Chimney is exposed to the fire, it being six or eight inches below the stone mantelpiece within side' and so the fireplace could not be used (*Eland* 1931, 55). Gunnis describes the monument to Job Hanmer at Simpson as architectural, with a broken pediment and well-carved details (1).

Literary References: *Gunnis* 1968, 42

Funerary Monuments

1.	†1738	Job Hanmer	Simpson, Bucks	Pevsner, *Bucks*, 1994, 549

BAYLISS, Nathaniel –1768

On 30 June 1760 Bayliss advertised in the *Northampton Mercury* that he had purchased the stock of the late Mr Ward, stonemason, at Ampthill, Beds and that he proposed to carry on business in that town, as well as continuing his existing business at Woburn. He was employed at Woburn Abbey from 1762 until his death in 1768 and was buried at Woburn. He was probably responsible for the monument to George Hadley, at Flitton, which is signed 'Bayliss'.

Literary References: *Gunnis* 1968, 42

Archival References: Woburn Building Accts, R5/1092, pp 124, 210, £64 8s paid 21 July 1792, £2 14s 9d paid 9 Feb, 1762; GPC

Additional MS Sources: Bedford Papers

Funerary Monuments

1.	1768	George Hadley	Flitton, Beds	S	*Gunnis* 1968, 42

BAZZANTI, Pierre and Nicholas, of Florence fl 1823–45

The Bazzanti family owned a sculpture shop, Galleria Bazzanti, in the Lungarno Corsini, Florence, where, over many years, they sold copies of well-known works of sculpture as well as originals by various Italian sculptors. Their copies of works by English sculptors included busts of Wellington and Scott after **Sir Francis Chantrey**. In the first half of the 19th century they were responsible for a number of British funerary monuments. Those to Isabella Cave and Mary Jones are signed by Nicholas and both have reliefs in the classical tradition (2, 3). The monument to Lady Sophia Pierrepoint is the work of Pierre (1). Gunnis noted that the model for this work and the correspondence surrounding its dispatch to England survives in the collection of the Duke of Wellington. The letters are signed by Pierre Bazzanti and his partner, Joseph Moise, who gave their address as '*pres du Palais Corsini*'. In the grounds of Scarisbrick Hall, Lancs are a number of bronze copies of classical works signed by Pierre Bazzanti and his undated statue of *Aphrodite kneeling* is in the Wellcome Institute collection. Examples of their work in Italy include a marble statue of *Orcagna*, carved by Nicholas for the Uffizi in 1843, and several monuments in the Old Protestant Cemetery in Florence.

Literary References: *Gunnis* 1968, 43; *Rowan* 1973, 1158; *Sicca and Yarrington* 2000, 12

Archival References: GPC; NP/RG

Funerary Monuments

1.	1823	Lady Sophia Pierrepoint (by Pierre Bazzanti) Model(s): coll Duke of Wellington	Holme Pierrepoint, Notts	S	Pevsner, *Notts*, 1979, 147
2.	†1827	Isabella Cave (by Nicholas Bazzanti)	Henbury, Glos	S	Pevsner, *Somerset: N & Bristol*, 1958, 467
3.	†1828	Mary Jones (by Nicholas Bazzanti)	St Mary, Southampton, Hants	S	Pevsner, *Hants & Isle of Wight*, 1967, 573–4
4.	1835	Richard Jodrell (by Pierre Bazzanti)	Lewknor, Oxon	S	Pevsner, *Oxon*, 1974, 684
5.	1845	Captain Lewis Shedden (†1844) (by Nicholas Bazzanti)	Jesus Church, Southampton, Hants	S	Pevsner, *Hants and Isle of Wight*, 1967, 593

BEAL, F, of Barnstaple fl 1790–96

Gunnis considered Beal's tablet to John Palmer, which has an urn of coloured marble against a pyramid, the best of his works (3).

Literary References: *Gunnis* 1968, 43

Funerary Monuments

1.	1790	Colonel M . . . [illegible]	St Peter and St Paul, Barnstaple, Devon	S	*Gunnis* 1968, 43
2.	1796	Henry Tippitts	St Peter and St Paul, Barnstaple, Devon	S	*Gunnis* 1968, 43
3.	nd	John Palmer	St Michael, Great Torrington, Devon		*Gunnis* 1968, 43; Pevsner, *Devon*, 1989, 461

BEAL, J, of Exeter fl 1789–92

Gunnis notes that his tablets, like those by **F Beal**, of Barnstaple, are in marble and well executed.

Literary References: *Gunnis* 1968, 43

Funerary Monuments

1.	1789	Rev John Penneck	Gulval, Cornwall	S	*Gunnis* 1968, 43
2.	1792	William Harris	Gulval, Cornwall		*Gunnis* 1968, 43

BEAL, John, of Doncaster fl 1713–44

He became a freeman of Doncaster on 19 September 1713. In 1744 the town council decided that he should be employed for 'the inside masons' work at ye Mansion House', then being built to the designs of James Paine. His son, John Beal II, became a freeman on 28 December 1742, and William Beal, who was probably another relation, on 1 October 1750. They were both described as masons (Doncaster Corp Archives, cited by *Gunnis* 1968, 43).

Literary References: *Gunnis* 1968, 43

BEARD, Thomas 1727–1803

The son of Robert Beard, a barber of Navestock, Essex, he was apprenticed to William Heatley in 1740 and turned over to **William Spratt** in 1745, becoming free of the Masons' Company in 1747. He became renter warden in 1779, upper warden in 1780, and finally master of the Company in 1781. His son Robert was apprenticed to him in 1774 and made free on 1 April 1784. Thomas died in 1803 and was buried at Islington. His tombstone describes him as 'citizen and mason of London, 35 years an inhabitant of this parish' (*Nelson* 1811, 329).

Literary References: *Gunnis* 1968, 43

Archival References: Masons' Co, Court Book, 1722–51 (2 May 1740, 6 Sept 1745); 1751–96 (14 June 1779, 14 June 1780, 14 June 1781); Masons' Co Freemen, fol 7 (7 Jan 1747, 1 April 1784)

Will: PROB 11/1391

Funerary Monuments

1.	1748	Owen and Elinor Phillips	Haverfordwest, Pembrokes	*Gunnis* 1968, 43; GPC
2.	†1750	Katherine Masters	Meopham, Kent	Pevsner, *Kent: W & Weald*, 1976, 418

Chimneypieces

3.	1785	Description unavailable	[House designed by Robert Mylne, Bridge Street, London]; untraced	GPC

BEARD (or BARD), William fl 1674–80

In 1674 he was paid £2 for finishing the moulds and casting the plaster for the great model of St Paul's Cathedral. This must have been an exacting task, for Beard was paid on the basis of 12 days' work (*Bolton* 1939, 202).

Four years later 'Mr Beard the stone-cutter' travelled from London to repair 'the breaches and decays in the Earl of Leicester's and Ambrose Earl of Warwicks monuments' in the Beauchamp Chapel, St Mary, Warwick (**1**). That year Beard wrote to Sir William Dugdale, Garter King of Arms, that he had 'almost completed ye Lord Ambrose's monument which will be very handsome and commendable'. Later in the letter Beard says 'I must gett a crownet for his head and three more for ye Lord Lesters tombe is wanting, and one more for the Lord Ambrose at the end of his tombe. I will make a mould and fix them all on before I go hence' (Archives, Sir William Dugdale of Merevale in GPC).

Beard was also employed by **Joshua Marshall** to erect the monument to Lady Katherine Leveson in the same chapel. It is possible therefore that he and Marshall had a professional connection. It is clear however that Beard also worked independently, for in 1680 he contracted to carve the monument to Edward Bonham, younger son of William Bonham of Bocking Ash, Essex (**2**). The agreement, in which the sculptor is described as 'William Bard (sic) citizen and stone-cutter of London', was drawn up and witnessed by Sir William Dugdale and it survives in the archives of Sir William Dugdale of Merevale. Dugdale noted in his diary on 15 June 1680 that he had 'delivered to Mr. William Beard, stone cutter, the summe of ten pounds in pt of the summe of £20 for a monument of white marble for Mr. Edward Bonham, which summe of £20 Mrs. Eliz. Dilke is to pay to my son at Coventre' (*Hamper* ed 1827, 143).

While undertaking his various works at St Mary, Warwick, the sculptor seems to have fallen foul of the local mayor, who was also a trustee of the Beauchamp chapel. Beard wrote to Dugdale 'Mr Mayor hath ordered my landlord to trust me no further than Thursday night, which was last night. Now for my part I have and do work like a horse in a mill to finish it, but if I cannot have a little victuals I must desist and shall, except you be pleased upon sight of this to speak to Mr. Mayor to-day to continue me there at my lodgings and to satisfy them' (Archives, Sir William Dugdale of Merevale in GPC).

It was probably Beard's son, another William Beard, who was apprenticed to **Edward Pearce** in 1686. It seems likely that this was the 'William Beard, Carver of St Andrew Holborn' whose will was proved on 4 July 1734 (PROB 11/1766).

Literary References: *Hamper* ed, 1827, 140 *Gunnis* 1968, 43

Archival References: GPC

Funerary Monuments

1.	1678	Earl of Leicester, and Ambrose, Earl of Warwick (repairs only) Payment(s): £1 2s 6d	St Mary, Warwick	*Churches of Warks* 1847, 1, 63; *Gunnis* 1968, 43
2.	1680	Edward Bonham (†1679) Payment(s): £20	Ryton-on-Dunsmore, Warks	*Hamper* (ed) 1827, 143; *Gunnis* 1968, 43; GPC

BEATTIE, William fl 1829–68

William Beattie was a versatile sculptor and modeller who worked in several media, including silver. Between 1829 and 1867 he showed at the Royal Academy, the British Institution, the Society of British Artists, the Royal Scottish Academy, the Liverpool Academy and the Birmingham Society of Arts, from addresses in London, Stoke-on-Trent, Birmingham and Edinburgh. His first exhibit was an embossed silver plate illustrating *John Knox admonishing Mary Queen of Scots*, after a painting by Sir William Allan. This was followed by *Adam and Eve lamenting the death of Abel* in silver (BI, London, 1837, 450 and R Sc A, Edinburgh, 1846, 556), several portrait busts, a bronze medallion of Lord Elcho and a statue of *Lord Bacon as Chancellor to Queen Elizabeth I* (**33, 1**).

For Elkington & Co he designed a silver vase representing *The triumph of science and the industrial arts in the Great Exhibition*, which was prominently displayed by the firm at the exhibition. It was decorated with four statuettes of 'Newton, Bacon, Shakespeare, and Watt, commemorating Astronomy, Philosophy, Poetry, and Mechanics respectively' and with four bas-reliefs displaying 'the practical operations of Science and Art' between them. The figures on the base represented 'War, Rebellion, Hatred, and Revenge overthrown' and the whole was surmounted by a figure of Prince Albert 'who as patron of the Exhibition, is rewarding the successful contributors' (*AJ Cat* 1851, 195).

Other designs for testimonial plate included an épergne presented to Mr Ewing of Glasgow in 1860 and a vase presented to the family of John Strang, the City Chamberlain of Glasgow, in 1864. Beattie seems to have been particularly successful as a designer of groups for production in parian ware and he modelled for several Staffordshire manufacturers including Adams, Bates, Copeland, Minton, Wedgwood, Sir James Duke and Brown-Westhead and Moore. He died some time before 14 November 1868 when the *Illustrated London News* published a woodcut of his last work, an ornament for the mess table of the 92nd Highlanders. It took the form of a Peterhead granite obelisk with silver figures of soldiers at the base, 'most beautifully and carefully modelled by the late Mr W. Beattie' (*ILN*, 14 November 1868, 473, 478).

Literary References: *ILN*, 9 August 1851, 189; 25 February 1860, 180; 5 March 1864, 232–3; *Gunnis* 1968, 43; *Atterbury* 1989, 260

Statues

1.	1848	Lord Bacon as Chancellor to Queen Elizabeth Model(s): exhib RA, London, 1844, 1237	b	[Exhib BI, London, 467]; untraced		*Graves* 1875, 36; *Graves* I, 1905–6, 152
2.	c1850	The Queen of Sheba's visit to Solomon, model		Untraced Other versions: reproduced in Parian ware		*Atterbury* 1989, 255 (repr 885)
3.	1851	Love restraining wrath, model		Untraced Other versions: reproduced in Minton Parian ware (example shown Great Exhib 1851)		*Atterbury* 1989, 69 (repr 99)
4.	by 1853	The golden age, model		Untraced Other versions: reproduced in Copeland Parian ware (eg Royal Coll, Osborne House, I of W)		*Atterbury* 1989, 171 (repr 564)
5.	by 1853	William Burns and Highland Mary, model (after a painting by Thomas Faed)		Untraced Other versions: reproduced in Copeland Parian ware (eg Royal Coll, Osborne House, I of W)		*Atterbury* 1989, 169 (repr 559)
6.	1850–1855	The finding of Moses in the bullrushes, model		Untraced Other versions: reproduced in Wedgwood Parian ware		*Atterbury* 1989, 190 (repr 630)
7.	1856	David's triumph and reward, model		Untraced Other versions: reproduced in Minton Parian ware		*Atterbury* 1989, 78 (repr 119)
8.	1856	Robert the Bruce, statuette	b	[Exhib R Sc A, Edinburgh, 726, lent by the Art Union of Glasgow]; untraced Other versions: reproduced in Parian ware c1870		*Atterbury* 1989, 254 (repr 874); *Laperriere* 1, 1991, 105
9.	1856	The good race, model		Untraced Other versions: reproduced in Minton Parian ware		*Atterbury* 1989, 74 (repr 110)
10.	1856	William Wallace, statuette	b	[Exhib R Sc A, Edinburgh, 734, lent by the Art Union of Glasgow]; untraced Other versions: reproduced in Parian ware c1870		*Atterbury* 1989, 254 (repr 874); *Laperriere* 1, 1991, 105, 106
11.	1857	Coronation of Esther	m	Untraced Other versions: copies issued to Glasgow Art Union prizewinners		*ILN*, 8 Aug 1857, 141–2 (repr)
12.	1858	Daniel in the lions' den (Daniel saved)		[Exhib R Sc A, Edinburgh, 761]; untraced Other versions: reproduced in Minton Parian ware 1866 (eg at St Werburgh, Derby)		*Atterbury* 1989, 88 (repr 142); *Laperriere* 1, 1991, 106
13.	1859	England, Scotland, Ireland and America, models	tc	Untraced Other versions: reproduced in Wedgwood Parian ware		*Gunnis* 1968, 43; *Atterbury* 1989, 190–1 (repr 633, 636)
14.	c1860	Hannah, model		Untraced Other versions: reproduced in Parian ware		*Atterbury* 1989, 252 (repr 860)
15.	c1860	Innocence protected, model		Untraced Other versions: reproduced in Parian ware		*Atterbury* 1989, 255 (repr 884)
16.	c1860	Terpsichore, model		Untraced Other versions: Parian ware statuette issued by the Art Union of Glasgow		*Atterbury* 1989, 252 (repr 860)
17.	nd	Christ healing the blind man, model		Untraced Other versions: reproduced in Wedgwood Parian ware		*Atterbury* 1989, 194 (repr 641)
18.	nd	Interpretation, Joseph before Pharaoh, model		Untraced Other versions: reproduced in Wedgwood Parian ware		*Atterbury* 1989, 194 (repr 640)
19.	nd	Isaac and Rebekah, model		Untraced Other versions: reproduced in Wedgwood Parian ware		*Atterbury* 1989, 190 (repr 635)
20.	nd	Sir Isaac Newton, statuette	b	Royal Astronomical Soc Other versions: Windsor Castle, Berks	S	*Gunnis* 1968, 43; GPC
21.	nd	The flute player, model for Wedgwood	tc	Untraced		*Gunnis* 1968, 43
22.	nd	The sacrifice, model		Untraced Other versions: reproduced in Wedgwood Parian ware		*Atterbury* 1989, 190 (repr 629)

Busts

23.	1839	Unidentified gentleman		[Exhib RA, London, 1362]; untraced		*Graves* I, 1905–6, 152
24.	1845	Robert Burns		[Exhib Soc of BA, London, 836]; untraced		*Johnson* 1975, 34
25.	1845	Unidentified lady		[Exhib RA, London, 1432]; untraced		*Graves* I, 1905–6, 152
26.	1846	Rev C H Hassells		[Exhib Soc of BA, London, 780]; untraced		*Johnson* 1975, 34
27.	1847	Master Forrest		[Exhib RA, London, 1356]; untraced		*Graves* I, 1905–6, 152
28.	1849	Hon Cecilia Campbell		[Exhib RA, London, 1286]; untraced		*Graves* I, 1905–6, 152

29.	1850	Unidentified young lady		[Exhib RA, London, 1406]; untraced	*Graves* I, 1905–6, 152
30.	1859	Rev John Angell James		Untraced	*ILN*, 22 Oct 1859, 392, 400 (repr)
31.	1863	Princess Alexandra, model		Untraced Other versions: reproduced in Minton Parian ware	*Atterbury* 1989, 122 (repr 402)
32.	nd	Edward, Prince of Wales, model		Untraced Other versions: reproduced in Minton Parian ware	*Atterbury* 1989, 122 (repr 402)
Reliefs					
33.	1863	Lord Elcho, portrait medallion	b	[Exhib RA, London, 1187]; untraced	*Graves* I, 1905–6, 152
Miscellaneous					
34.	1851	William Shakespeare	b	[Exhib Liverpool Ac, 588]; untraced	*Morris and Roberts* 1998, 70
35.	1855	A Group of Boys		[Exhib Birmingham Soc of Arts]; untraced	*Gunnis* 1968, 43
36.	by 1862	Models for a Copeland Parian ware table service (from designs suggested by Madame Temple, who commissioned the work)		Untraced Other versions: example shown Int Exhib, London, 1862	*Atterbury* 1989, 173 (repr 567)
37.	1864	Jeannie Deans		[Exhib RA, London, 977]; untraced	*Graves* I, 1905–6, 152
38.	1864	Mental Culture		[Exhib RA, London, 940]; untraced	*Graves* I, 1905–6, 152

BEAUCHAMP, Ephraim –1728

Beauchamp is thought to have come from Burford, Oxon. He was the brother-in-law of **Edward Strong I** (who married Martha Beauchamp in 1675) and was probably the uncle of Edward Beauchamp who served his apprenticeship under **Edward Strong II** between 18 July 1705 and 14 June 1717. He may also have been related to Thomas Beauchamp who built Founders' Hall between 1669 and 1671 (Founders Company Archives, cited by *Gunnis* 1968, 44). He was made free of the Masons' Company by redemption on 16 October 1684, became a renter warden in 1697, upper warden in 1698, and master in 1701.

He was employed as a master mason at St Paul's Cathedral for many years. Working there on his own account in 1684 (St Paul's Aquittance Book, cited by *Knoop and Jones* 1935, 33), he supplied stone for the building from 1688 until 1698 and between 1691 and 1707 he carried out building and carved stonework in partnership with **Christopher Kempster**. In 1699 he was employed at Greenwich Palace, either as a partner or assistant of Edward Strong I and Edward Strong II. He worked independently at St Dunstan-in-the-East, 1696–7, receiving £30 from the vestry in June 1697 when he promised to 'hasten the fitting up of the church and finishing the steeple' (*Wren Soc*, XIX, 19). He was at Sir Edward de Bouverie's London house in 1698 (Longford Castle Archives, cited by *Gunnis* 1968, 44). In May 1716 he was called in to advise upon the condition of the cloisters at Christ's Hospital, Newgate Street, which had become 'not only ruinous but very dangerous' (*Wren Soc*, XI, 79).

Beauchamp appears to have retired from business and to have left London by 1708, for his address was recorded as 'Tottenham High Cross' in a list of members of the Masons' Company that year. He was buried at All Saints, Tottenham, where his tomb bore a long inscription stating that he died on 16 September 1728, that he was for many years one of the governors of the Christ Church, Bethlem and Bridewell Hospitals, and that his widow, Laetitia, daughter of John Coppin of Pullox Hill, Bedford, died in 1739, at the age of seventy-two (*Cansick* 1875, 53).

Literary References: *Knoop and Jones* 1935, 32–33; *Gunnis* 1968, 44; Wren Soc VI, 40; XIV, *passim*; XV, *passim*; XVI, 66

Archival References: Masons' Co, *Freemen*, fols 4, 5 (16 Oct 1684, 14 June 1717); Masons' Co, Masters and Wardens (1697, 1698, 1701); *Company Members* (1708)

Chimneypieces				
2.	by 1694	'a Portland chimneypiece. . .with an Italian moulding the jambs (co-sculptor: Christopher Kempster)	St Paul's Cathedral, London	TNA C106/145
Architectural Sculpture				
3.	by 1694	Decorative carving including capitals and 'great leaves and lace in the chaptring' (co-sculptor: Christopher Kempster)	St Paul's Cathedral, London	TNA C106/145

BEAUCLERC (or BEAUCLERK), G fl 1848–51

G Beauclerc, of 23 Grosvenor Street West, exhibited at the Royal Academy in 1848 and at the Great Exhibition. He was described as a 'Talented Amateur' when a number of his terracotta models, mostly of classical subjects, were sold by Philips, on 17 July 1850 (GPC).

Literary References: *Graves* I, 1905–6, 153; *Gunnis* 1968, 44

Archival References: GPC quoting archives Messrs Phillips, Son & Neale

Miscellaneous					
1.	1848	Cupid and Psyche		[Exhib RA, London, 1384]; untraced	*Graves* I, 1905–6, 153
2.	By 1850	Models, mainly classical subjects	tc	[Phillips, 17 July 1850]; untraced	GPC
3.	1851	Female figure on a couch		[Gt Exhib, London]; untraced	*Gunnis* 1968, 44
4.	1851	Sleeping nymph		[Gt Exhib, London]; untraced	*Gunnis* 1968, 44

BEAUCLERK, Lady Diana 1734–1808

Josiah Wedgwood's *Catalogue* of 1787 includes the statement 'I have lately been enabled to enrich it with some charming groups, which Lady Diana Beauclerk and Lady Templeton, whose taste is universally acknowledged, have honoured me with the liberty of copying from their designs' (Wedgwood/Templetown).

For further information the reader is referred to *Pyke* 1973, 11

BEAUPRE fl 1764–83

Beaupré was a French sculptor who 'came over to try his fortune in England' (*Angelo* I, 1904, 113). He exhibited at the Society of Artists between 1764 and 1767, giving his addresses as 'At Mr. Machau's, in the Piazza, Covent Garden', 'The Orange Coffee House' and 'At Mr. Burrel's, Charing Cross'. He showed a sketch for a monument at the Free Society in 1766 (1). J T Smith describes Beaupré as an excellent carver of flowers who was recommended to **Joseph Wilton RA** by the French sculptor Jean-Baptiste Pigalle (1714–1785). Under Wilton's direction he provided the model for the lead statue of George III, erected by the King's sister, Princess Amelia, in Berkeley Square (3). The statue was well received at the time, but by 1827 it was in a state of collapse and had to be supported with props. It was removed shortly afterwards and presumably melted down. In 1777 Beaupré moved to Dublin, where he remained for six years, living in Dame Street. He does not appear to have exhibited in Ireland and nothing is known of his work there.

Literary References: *Smith* II, 1828, 181; *Strickland* I, 1913, 53; *Gunnis* 1968, 44

Funerary Monuments					
1.	1766	'A sketch for a Monument for Mr. Churchill'		[Exhib Free Soc, London, 8]; untraced	*Graves* 1907, 27
Statues					
2.	1764	Paris	p	[Exhib Soc of Artists, London, 149]; untraced	*Graves* 1907, 27
3.	1766	King George III, equestrian, model (under the direction of Joseph Wilton)	l	[Berkeley Square, London]; removed 1827	*Blackwood* 1989, 346
Busts					
4.	1765	Unidentified subject	p	[Exhib Soc of Artists, London, 169]; untraced	*Graves* 1907, 27
Reliefs					
5.	1764	Bacchanals		[Exhib Soc of Artists, London, 150]; untraced	*Graves* 1907, 27
Miscellaneous					
6.	1767	Sketch of a sacrifice		[Exhib Soc of Artists, London, 201]; untraced	*Graves* 1907, 27

BECK, J, of Broad Street, Birmingham fl 1845

Funerary Monuments				
1.	†1845	Thomas English	Birmingham Cathedral	S

BECKHAM, Humphrey –1671

Beckham was chamberlain of the Joiners' Guild in 1621 and warden in 1635. He carved his own monument in St Thomas, Salisbury, which is of wood and has a 'primitively carved' relief of the Resurrection (1). It is inscribed 'Here under lyeth the Body of Humphry Beckham who died 2nd day of February Anno 1671 Aged 83 yrs. His own Worke'.

References: inf. Claude Blair

Funerary Monuments					
1.	†1672	Humphrey Beckham	wd	St Thomas, Salisbury, Wilts	Pevsner, *Wilts*, 1975, 441; R C, *Survey of Salisbury*, I, 1980, (repr 47); *Wells-Cole* 1987, 304, n19

BEDBOROUGH, James, of Windsor fl 1808–26

Much employed at Windsor Castle under Sir Jeffry Wyattville, following the death of **John Slingsby** in 1808, he became chief mason and thereafter described himself as 'statuary and stonemason to His Majesty'. He received £1,042 for building part of the terrace walk at Windsor in 1810 and two years later constructed the royal vaults beneath St George's Chapel, for which he was paid £3,626 (*Gunnis* 1968, 44 incorrectly cites PRO AO1/2501). He also signed a few tablets.

Literary References: *Gunnis* 1968, 44

Funerary Monuments				
1.	1823	Henry Neech	St John the Baptist, Windsor, Berks	*Gunnis* 1968, 44
2.	1818	John Mackie	Feltham, Middx	*Gunnis* 1968, 44
3.	1826	Maurice Swabey	Langley Marish, Bucks	*Gunnis* 1968, 44
4.	1826	Mrs Wagstaffe	Horton, Bucks	*Gunnis* 1968, 44

BEDBOROUGH, Robert fl 1743

Bedborough was employed on mason's work at Cliveden in 1743.

Archival References: Duchy of Cornwall Archives in GPC

Chimneypieces					
1.	1743	Two, of Portland stone	s	Cliveden, Bucks	GPC

BEDFORD, John and Sons, of London fl 1809–98

This popular monumental masonry firm had a yard in Oxford Street. Gunnis thought most of their work 'apt to be obvious and conventional in design' but on a few occasions, 'not too unfortunate' (*Gunnis* 1968, 44). Examples include the monument commemorating William Tallents, which has a profile relief portrait surrounded by a wreath half hidden by drapery (14). The firm was responsible for a number of naval and military memorials, including those commemorating Edward Long, Mrs Dawson, Captain Ellice, Barkly and Hugh Reid (**1, 22, 36, 58, 63**). The first two feature reliefs of the wreck of the *Isis* and a mourning naval officer, while the last depicts the captain in naval uniform, standing against the white ensign, his telescope tucked under his arm and his cap at his feet. The monument to Captain Henry Trelawney has a relief of a uniformed soldier mourning at the sarcophagus of his dead comrade (32).

Thomas Bedford of Mulgrave Road, Sutton, Surrey, who died on 9 February 1875 aged 78, was presumably a family member, since his will states that he was formerly of Oxford Street and his two sons, both executors, are described as of 256 Oxford Street. On his death certificate he is described as a 'Gentleman'. He evidently executed the monument in Bridgetown Cathedral, Barbados, which is signed 'T. Bedford, 256 Oxford Street' (15).

Literary References: *Gunnis* 1968, 44–5; *Potterton* 1975, 36

Archival References: GPC

Funerary Monuments					
1.	†1809	Edward Long	Seale, Surrey	S	Pevsner, *Surrey*, 1971, 448
2.	?1821	John Hope (†1813) and son	St Ewe, Cornwall	S	Pevsner, *Cornwall*, 1970, 174
3.	†1822	Sir Thomas Metcalfe	Winkfield, Berks	S	Pevsner, *Berks*, 1966, 306

4.	†1823	Fanny Lowe	Bramber, Sussex	S	
5.	†1830	Francis, 1st Earl of Bandon	Bandon, Co Cork		GPC
6.	1831	Henry (†1807) and Mary Vernon	Broadwater, Sussex	S	
7.	?1832	Sarah Metcalfe	St Mary, Penzance, Cornwall	S	Pevsner, *Cornwall*, 1970, 139
8.	†1834	John Pidcock	Wordsley, Staffs	S	
9.	†1835	Charles, 1st Earl of Charleville (designed by John Blore)	Tullamore, Co Offaly	S	GPC
10.	?1836	Sarah Bott	Bromfield, Salop	S	*Gunnis* 1968, 45
11.	?1837	Harriot Cotton	Birchington, Kent	S	*Gunnis* 1968, 45
12.	†1837	Rear Admiral John Richard Delap Tollemache	Helmingham, Suffolk	S	Pevsner, *Suffolk*, 1974, 259
13.	†1837	Rear Admiral John Richard Delap Tollemache	Tilstone Fearnall, Cheshire		Pevsner, *Cheshire*, 1971, 364
14.	†1837	William Tallents	St Mary Magdalene, Newark, Notts		Pevsner, *Notts*, 1979, 186
15.	†1839	Charlotte Crichlow	Barbados Cathedral, Bridgetown	S	
16.	?1841	Jane Bonnell	St Mary, Walthamstow, Essex	S	*Gunnis* 1968, 45
17.	†1841	John Nixon	Carlisle Cathedral	S	
18.	†1841	Sir Thomas Stanley	Eastham, Cheshire		Pevsner, *Cheshire*, 1971, 206
19.	†1842	Captain Davidson	Llanstephan, Carmarthen		*Dale-Jones and Lloyd* 1989, 46
20.	†1843	Elizabeth Farr	Christchurch Priory, Hants	S	
21.	†1843	George Errington	St John, Hampstead, London	S	
22.	?1843	Mrs Dawson	Barnes, Surrey (badly damaged by fire June 1978)		*Gunnis* 1968, 44
23.	1843	Samuel Boddington	St Andrew, Enfield, Middx	S	
24.	†1844	Captain Samuel Remington	Kensal Green Cemetery, London, catacombs	S	
25.	1844	Lieutenant-General Sir Richard Jones (†1835) and George Jones (†1844)	Broadwater, Sussex	S	*Gunnis* 1968, 45
26.	†1846	Lord Metcalfe	Winkfield, Berks		Pevsner, *Berks*, 1966, 306
27.	†1846	Reuben Mangin	Aston Rowant, Oxon	S	Pevsner, *Oxon*, 1974, 427
28.	?1846	Sir Edward Page-Turner	Bicester, Oxon	S	*Gunnis* 1968, 45
29.	†1849	Francis Wrightson Robinson	Rochester Cathedral, Kent	S	
30.	1850	Charles, 2nd Earl Grey (†1845) (designed by J Francis)	Howick, Northumbs	S	Pevsner, *Northumbs*, 1992, 351
31.	†1850	William McTaggatt	Chennai (Madras) Cathedral, India	S	
32.	†1851	Captain Henry Trelawney	Castledawson, Co Derry		*Potterton* 1975, 36; C Lib (repr)
33.	†1852	Georgiana Pidcock	St Mary, Watford, Herts	S	
34.	1852	Mr and Mrs Smythe	Worfield, Salop		GPC
35.	†1853	Ann and Thomas (†1858) Hawkes	Himley, Staffs	S	
36.	†1853	Captain Ellice	Hampton, Middx	S	Pevsner, *London: S*, 1983, 478
37.	†1853	George Pidcock	St Mary, Watford, Herts	S	
38.	1854	Devey family	Worfield, Salop		GPC
39.	1854	J R Phillips	Christ Church, Barbados	S	
40.	†1854	Mary Eliza Knight	Barbados Cathedral, Bridgetown	S	
41.	†1854	William Windham	Felbrigg, Norfolk	S	
42.	†1855	Colonel T G Egerton	Chester Cathedral, Cheshire	S	C Lib (repr)
43.	†1855	Rev Samuel Gamlen	Kirkby Mallory, Leics	S	AL
44.	1856	Sir Thomas Digby Aubrey	Boarstall, Bucks		Pevsner, *Bucks*, 1994, 184
45.	1857	Catherine Hildyard (†1855)	Catherston Leweston, Dorset	SD	
46.	†1857	Dorothea Methold	Tanfield, Durham		Pevsner, *Durham*, 1983, 474
47.	†1857	Harriot Prescott	Digswell, Herts	S	
48.	?1857	Sophia Greaves	St Nicholas, Tooting, London	S	*Gunnis* 1968, 45
49.	1857	William Patrick	Kensal Green Cemetery, catacombs	S	
50.	†1858	Francis Richard Price	Overton, Flint	S	Pevsner, *Clwyd*, 1986, 411
51.	†1858	Lieutenant Philip Phillips	Upton, Torquay, Devon	S	
52.	†1858	Lieutenant Robert Moorson	Rochester Cathedral, Kent	S	
53.	†1859	Lieutenant George Hallam	Furneux Pelham, Herts	S	
54.	†1860	Henry Pepys, Bishop of Worcester	Hartlebury, Worcs	S	
55.	†1860	Peter Wickens Fry	Axbridge, Somerset	S	
56.	†1861	Captain John Evans	Chagford, Devon	S	
57.	†1861	John Pidcock	Wordsley, Staffs	S	
58.	†1862	Barkly Reid	Codicote, Herts	S	
59.	†1862	Lieutenant General Sir Henry Somerset	Great Badminton, Glos	S	
60.	1862	Mary Burton	Dowles, Worcs		GPC
61.	1863	Officers and men of the 84th (York and Lancaster) Regiment (†1859–60 India)	York Minster, south choir aisle	S	*Aylmer* 1977, 470, 471 (repr); *Pattison and Murray* 2001, 126
62.	1864	Arthur Saltmarshe	Howden, E R Yorks		*Gunnis* 1968, 45
63.	†1865	Hugh Reid	Codicote, Herts	S	
64.	†1865	William Thomas	Heol Awst Congregational Chapel, Carmarthen		*Dale-Jones and Lloyd* 1989, 46
65.	†1866–1868	General Sir Adolphus (†1866) and Ann (†1868) Dalrymple	Aldenham, Herts	S	
66.	†1841–1868	John (†1841) and Mary (†1868) Buchanan Mansfield	Digswell, Herts	S	
67.	†1869	Philip Lovell Phillips	St Lucy, Barbados	S	
68.	†1872	Henry Lushington Comyn Robinson RN	Rochester Cathedral, Kent	S	
69.	†1898	Louise Hallam	Furneux Pelham, Herts	S	
70.	nd	Green family members	Wilby, Suffolk		Pevsner, *Suffolk*, 1974, 490
71.	nd	Mary, Countess Bandon	Bandon, Co Cork		GPC
72.	nd	Unidentified subject	Lostwithiel, Cornwall		Pevsner, *Cornwall*, 1970, 107

BEHNES, William *c*1795–1863

William Behnes was a major portrait sculptor and the master of a large studio, where many notable sculptors received their training. In spite of his considerable success, he was beset by severe financial problems throughout much of his career.

He was born in St Marylebone, London, the son of a piano-maker from Hanover and his English wife. His date of birth is uncertain but his obituary in the *Art Journal* suggests it was about 1794 (*AJ* 1864, 83). Behnes himself gave his age as eighteen when he joined the Royal Academy Schools in 1813. His father had come to London after completing his apprenticeship in Germany, perhaps because he already had a link with Britain through his elder brother, a surgeon in the British navy on board HMS *Cumberland*. When William was quite young he moved to Ireland with his parents and two younger brothers. His father continued to work as a piano-maker but with little apparent success. The sculptor, **Henry Weekes** who later worked for William, said that the child had been brought up in almost abject misery.

William was expected to follow his father's trade and began to help in the workshop as soon as he was old enough to handle the tools. It soon became clear, however, that his consuming interest was in drawing and he began to spend his spare time at the Dublin Society's Schools, where he is said to have distinguished himself by the accuracy and finish of his studies (*AJ* 1864, 83).

Piano-making in Ireland did not prove profitable, so the family returned to London and settled near the Tower of London, where they continued to manufacture musical instruments. They appear to have moved soon afterwards, for Behnes exhibited from Delahay Street, Westminster in 1815–16 and from Charles Street, near the Middlesex Hospital, in 1817. William and his brother Henry (the family's middle son, who later changed his name to **Henry Behnes Burlowe** because he was so ashamed of William) in the meantime continued to study art. William developed a thriving practice as a portrait painter, whose success enabled the family to move to better lodgings in Newman Street in 1818. A change of artistic direction came after informal lessons from the sculptor **Peter Francis Chenu**, who also lodged in the house in Charles Street. Behnes perhaps later regretted his decision to take up sculpture, saying wistfully near the end of his life 'I should like to paint a picture before I die' (*AJ* 1864, 83). The author of his obituary considered his portraits on vellum 'among the most beautiful we have ever seen' (*ibid*).

Weekes described him as an energetic sculptor, of limited intellect but considerable versatility. His positive qualities led to early success: he won silver medals from the Royal Academy in 1816, 1817 and 1819, a silver medal from the Society of Arts in 1816 and the Society's gold medal in 1819 for inventing 'an instrument for transferring points to marble' (Archives, Society of Arts, quoted by *Gunnis* 1968, 45). He exhibited at the Royal Academy from 1815 until 1863 and by 1818 he was an established and sought after artist.

Behnes was most active as a sculptor of portrait busts and his head of Thomas Clarkson (**235**) was particularly admired. He also depicted several members of the Royal family (**123, 124, 147, 148, 164, 166, 191, 331**) and his bust of Princess Victoria was particularly successful (**170**). On her succession to the throne, the Queen appointed Behnes Sculptor in Ordinary, though this distinction did not lead to further royal commissions.

Behnes was responsible for a number of important monuments. That to **Joseph Nollekens** (**7**) has a relief of the sculptor with his commemorative statue of Mrs Howard. Others, particularly to Esther North (**6**) and John Bourne (**21**), feature dramatic angels, in a style later widely imitated in Victorian cemeteries. Gunnis thought the monument to Charlotte Botfield (**9**), which has a relief of her son, Beriah, mourning by her coffin, well carved and very moving (*Gunnis* 1968, 46). His statue of Dr William Babington in St Paul's Cathedral (**37**) was considered particularly successful.

He had many commissions for public statues, including three of Sir Robert Peel, in Leeds, London and Bradford (**80, 83, 84**). However, one writer in the *Art Journal* considered these 'by no means comparable with his busts' and thought his last statue, of Sir Henry Havelock (**87**), executed for Trafalgar Square and replicated for Sunderland, 'the least worthy of all' (*AJ*, 1864, 84).

He exhibited at the major international exhibitions, showing a colossal statue of Sir William Follett (**56**) and a statuette of Lady Godiva (**74**) at the Great Exhibition in 1851 and *Cupid with two doves* (**70**) at the International Exhibition of 1862.

Behnes's financial problems appear to have begun in 1823 when he moved into premises in Dean Street, Soho, which were unsuited for a workshop. The expense incurred in trying to adapt the house and build on a modelling room high enough to take statues of heroic proportions crippled him financially. His problems were not helped by his extravagant habits and he fell into the hands of moneylenders. Weekes later recalled that he became neglectful of his pupils and the courtesies expected by clients. He became an alcoholic and his reputation for probity came into question. In 1861 he was declared insolvent.

Most of his works were executed in Osnaburg Street, where he lived from 1833 until his bankruptcy. He was still playing an active public role as late as 1856, when he was one of a group of sculptors who sent a letter to the *Daily News* protesting at the lack of opportunities for British sculptors to carry out major public commissions.

During his final years he lived alone in miserable lodgings in Charlotte Street, where his health deteriorated. He died of 'paralysis' in the Middlesex Hospital on 3 January, 1864 after being found 'literally in the gutter with threepence in his pocket' (*Hall* II, 1883, 238). He was buried in Kensal Green cemetery, and a committee was formed, with George Cruikshank as its secretary, to raise money for a monument and bust over his grave and for a bronze bust to be presented to the National Gallery. Insufficient funds were raised and instead a modest classical sarcophagus tomb in Portland stone was made by his last pupil, Morton Edwards.

Behnes's many significant pupils and assistants included **John Carew, John Graham Lough, Musgrave Lewthwaite Watson**, Henry Behnes Burlowe (his brother), **Henry Timbrell, Timothy Butler**, Henry Weekes, **Alfred Gatley, Edward** and **John Henry Foley, Neville Northey Burnard, Thomas Woolner** and **George Frederick Watts.** Woolner later claimed to have learnt more by working with Behnes than during his studies at the Royal Academy Schools and his mature style owes clear debts to the crisp, characterful drapery style of Behnes's Botfield monument (**9**) and his statue of Babington (**37**) in St Paul's.

Behnes was much admired by contemporary critics and younger sculptors. Palgrave praised the powerful modelling and grace of his work, although he thought that Behnes lacked 'poetic inventiveness' and was critical of the draperies on some of his statues (*Palgrave* 1866, 219–220). Weekes wrote that his busts showed 'greater freedom of handling, less mannerism, more variety, and greater difference of character' than those of **Sir Francis Chantrey**. Weekes and Palgrave particularly praised his portraits of children. Behnes was never elected to the Royal Academy despite his achievements, probably because of the irregularities that characterised his personal life.

EH

Literary References: *Farington*, XIV, 5119; *Passavant* 1836, v2, 284; *Hall* II, 1883, 238–9; *AJ* 1864, 83–4; *Palgrave* 1866, passim; *Redgrave* 1878, 35–6; *Weeks* 1880, 2–3, 294–317; *Graves* I, 1905–6, 166–9; *DNB*, II, 131–2; *Gunnis* 1968, 45–8; *Physick* 1969, 41; *Potterton* 1975, 36; *Penny* 1977 (1), 11, 106, 161, 178; *Read* 1982, passim; *Stafford* 1982, 4–11; *Whinney* 1988, 464, n.11; *Read and Barnes* 1991, 21; *Bennett* 1998, 130; *Grove* 3, 1996, 509–10 (Greenwood); *Dawson* 1999, 69, 79–81; *Curl* 2001, 226, 236–7, 242; *ODNB* (Stocker)

Archival References: RA Premium list

Additional MS Sources: *Behnes Papers; Peel Papers*, 1841, BM Add MSS 40493; *Behnes/Hone; Behnes/Panizzi*

Miscellaneous Drawings: Two portraits of Frederick Marryat, exhib Victorian Exhibition, New Gallery, London, 1892, 406 and 506, both subsequently engraved; portrait of Sydney, Lady Morgan, NPG 1177, engraved by H Meyer; portrait of Princess Anne Feodorowna of Leiningen, s&d 1828, VAM P&D E.438-1949; the seven ages, an allegorical composition attributed to Behnes, VAM P&D, E.51-1948; study for a large monumental sculpture, HMI/LMG 34.1/1988

Funerary Monuments

1.	†1848	Caroline Benfield	Bingley, W R Yorks		Pevsner, *Yorks, W R*, 1967, 102
2.	1811	3rd Duke of Grafton	Euston, Suffolk		GPC
3.	?1819	John Tunno	St John's Wood Chapel, Marylebone, London		*Gunnis* 1968, 47
4.	1821	Michael Bennet	Bodmin, Cornwall		Pevsner, *Cornwall*, 1970, 43
5.	?1822	James Strachan	St Leonard, Streatham, London		*Gunnis* 1968, 47
6.	†1823	Esther North	Old Alresford, Hants	S	*Penny* 1977 (1), 216 n 68; C Lib (repr)
7.	†1823	Joseph Nollekens RA	St Mary, Paddington Green, London	S	*Whinney* 1988, 464 n 11; Pevsner, *London: N W*, 1991, 676; C Lib (repr)
8.	1824	John Macalister	St George, Penang		*Gunnis* 1968, 47
9.	†1825	Charlotte Botfield	Norton, Northants		*CIIA* 4/3/107–8 (repr)
10.	†1825	John Russell	North Ockenden, Essex	S	Pevsner, *Essex*, 1965, 308; C Lib (repr)
11.	†1825	William, 1st Baron Radstock	Navestock, Essex	S	*Gunnis* 1968, 47; C Lib (repr)
12.	†1826	Sir Thomas Gooch (†1781) and his son, Sir Thomas	Benacre, Suffolk		Pevsner, *Suffolk*, 1974, 97
13.	†1827	John, 1st Earl of Stradbroke	Wangford, Suffolk	S	Pevsner, *Suffolk*, 1974, 475
14.	?1828	Isaac James	West Wickham, Kent		*Gunnis* 1968, 48
15.	?1828	Joseph Russell	North Ockenden, Essex		*Gunnis* 1968, 47
16.	†1829	John Alderson	Holy Trinity, Hull, E R Yorks		Pevsner, *Yorks: E R & York* 1995, 508
17.	†1829	Josiah Spode	St Peter, Stoke-on-Trent, Staffs	S	*Gunnis* 1968, 48; C Lib (repr)
18.	1831	Sir Charles Knowles	Holy Trinity, Guildford, Surrey		GPC
19.	†1832	Dr Andrew Bell	Westminster Abbey, London, nave Other versions: relief, plaster, Foundling Hospital, London		*Graves* I, 1905–6, 168; *Penny* 1977 (1), 161 (repr); *Stewart* 1, 1985, 47
20.	†1832	Vice-Admiral Sir Henry Blackwood	Westminster Abbey, London, north transept	S	*MacMichael*, 1977, 86
21.	†1833	John Bourne	St Peter, Stoke-on-Trent, Staffs	S	*Penny* 1977 (1), 216 n 68; C Lib (repr)
22.	†1833	John Chappel Woodhouse, Dean of Lichfield	St Peter, Stoke-on-Trent, Staffs	S	*Gunnis* 1968, 48; C Lib (repr)
23.	†1833	Maria Thomas	Holy Trinity, Tunbridge Wells, Kent		Pevsner, *Kent: W and Weald*, 1976, 580; C Lib (repr)
24.	1833	Rev John Watkins	Clifton Campville, Staffs	S	Pevsner, *Staffs*, 1974, 105; C Lib (repr)
25.	?1833	Rev S Pope	St Mary, Lambeth, London		*Gunnis* 1968, 48
26.	?1833	Richard Seyer	St Michael, Bristol		*Gunnis* 1968, 48
27.	†1833	William Praed	Tyringham, Bucks	S	*Penny* 1977 (1), 177–8, 223 n15 (repr)
28.	†1834	Lord James Henry Fitzroy	Grafton Regis, Northants		*CIIA* 4/3/77 (repr)
29.	1834	William Knox, Bishop of Londonderry Payment(s): £500 (raised by subscription)	Londonderry Cathedral		*Potterton* 1975, 37; C Lib (repr)
30.	1835	Captain Oakley	Bodmin, Cornwall		Pevsner, *Cornwall*, 1970 43
31.	†1835	Jane Lashley	St Mary, Scarborough, N R Yorks	S	
32.	†1835	John Orton Harrison	St James, Piccadilly, London	S	GPC
33.	†1835	Lieutenant Donald Campbell	Glasgow Cathedral, Lanarks	S	Pevsner, *Glasgow*, 1990, 134; C Lib (repr)
34.	†1835	Mary Wilson	Seamer, N R Yorks		Pevsner, *Yorks: N R*, 1966, 336
35.	?1835	Richard Harrison	S Warnborough, Hants		*Gunnis* 1968, 48
36.	†1836	Sir Henry Russell	Swallowfield, Berks		*Gunnis* 1968, 48
37.	1837	Dr William Babington (†1833) (co-sculptor: Musgrave Lewthwaite Watson)	St Paul's Cathedral, London, south transept		*Lonsdale* 1866, 85–6; *Graves* I, 1905–6, 168; *Read* 1982, 67
38.	1837	James Praed	Tyringham, Bucks		Pevsner, *Bucks*, 1994, 703
39.	†1837	Michael Barne	Dunwich, Suffolk	S	Pevsner, *Suffolk*, 1974, 193
40.	†1837	Richard Wilson	Seamer, N R Yorks		GPC
41.	†1838	John Tomlinson	St Peter ad Vincula, Stoke-on-Trent, Staffs	S	*Pevsner, Staffs*, 1974, 262; C Lib (repr)
42.	†1839	Sir John St Aubyn	Crowan, Cornwall		Pevsner, *Cornwall*, 1970, 60
43.	?1840	John Wordsworth	Trinity College, Cambridge, chapel		*Gunnis* 1968, 48
44.	?1840	Mr and Mrs Spaldin	Sculcoates, Hull, E R Yorks		*Gunnis* 1968, 48

No.	Date	Subject		Location		References
45.	?1840	Thomas Blankarne		Great St Helen's, Bishopsgate, City of London		*Gunnis* 1968, 48
46.	?1842	Alexander Trotter		St Nicholas, Warwick		*Gunnis* 1968, 48
47.	†1842	John Heddle		Mumbai (Bombay) Cathedral	S	C Lib (repr)
48.	1843	Admiral Sir Thomas Hardy (†1839)		Royal Hospital, Greenwich (ORNC), chapel Other versions: Royal Coll, RCIN 31669, SD 1836, bust only United Services Club, bust only		*Graves* 1905–6, 1, 168; *Gunnis* 1968, 47; C Lib (repr)
49.	†1843	General Sir John Jones		St Paul's Cathedral, London, south transept	S	Pevsner, *London: City*, 1997, 173; C Lib (repr)
50.	?1843	John Mousley		Clifton Campville, Staffs	S	*Gunnis* 1968, 48; C Lib (repr)
51.	†1843	Rev George Beckett		Corringham, Lincs		Pevsner, *Lincs*, 1989, 234; C Lib (repr)
52.	†1844	Anne Frewen		Northiam, Sussex		Pevsner, *Sussex*, 1965, 574
53.	c1846	Bishop Wilson, of Calcutta		St Paul's Cathedral, Kolkata (Calcutta)		*Graves* I, 1905–6, 168; *Gunnis* 1968, 47
54.	†1846	George, 7th Earl Waldegrave		Navestock, Essex	S	Pevsner, *Essex*, 1965, 304
55.	†1849	George, 5th Earl of Buckinghamshire		Great Hampden, Bucks		
56.	1850	Sir William Webb Follett (†1845)		Westminster Abbey, London, Chapel of St Michael		*Graves* I, 1905–6, 168; *Ormond* 1973, 176; *MacMichael* 1977, 52
57.	1855	George Cruikshank, bust	m	[Kensal Green Cemetery, London]; untraced Other versions: several, in marble and plaster		*Graves* I, 1905–6, 168; *Ormond* 1973, 124–5 (pl 228); *Dawson* 1999, 79–81 (repr); Curl 2001, 191–2
58.	1855	Oliver Walford		Charterhouse Chapel, City of London	S	*Gunnis* 1968, 48
59.	?1855	Samuel Rogers		Hornsey parish church, London		*Gunnis* 1968, 48
60.	1858	Mrs Elsworth		Highgate Cemetery, London		*Gunnis* 1968, 48
61.	1861	Martha Harrison		St James, Piccadilly, London		GPC
62.	†1873	5th Marchioness of Waterford		Clonegan, Co Waterford		*Potterton* 1975, 37 (repr)
63.	†1874	Countess of Portarlington		Emo, Co Laois		*Potterton* 1975, 37 (repr)
Statues						
64.	1823	Hon Charles Lambton		[Lambton Castle, Co Durham]; untraced		*Graves* I, 1905–6, 167; *Gunnis* 1968, 45, 46
65.	1824	Alexander Hope playing with a rabbit	m	[The Deepdene, Dorking, Surrey, new library; Hope sale, 1917, lot 1150]; untraced		*Graves* I, 1905–6, 1, 167; *Watkin* 1968, 43
66.	1826	An infant	m	[Exhib RA, London 1019]; untraced		*Graves* I, 1905–6, 167
67.	1826	Master Sutherland	m	[Exhib RA, London 1025]; untraced		*Graves* I, 1905–6, 167
68.	1826	Young girl playing on a lyre	m	Boyle's Auctioneers, Copenhagen (1996)	SD	GPC
69.	1830	Cupid	m	[Exhib RA, London, 1274]; untraced		*Graves* I, 1905–6, 167
70.	1830	Cupid with two doves		[coll E R Tunno, of Upper Brook Street, London]; untraced Other versions: Int Exhib, 1862		*Palgrave* 1866, 219; *Gunnis* 1968, 46
71.	1839	George, 3rd Earl of Egremont	m	Petworth House, Sussex		*Graves* I, 1905–6, 168; *Gunnis* 1968, 46
72.	1840	Baron Joy		[Dublin]; untraced		*Gunnis* 1968, 46
73.	1844	Lady Emily Somerset		Untraced		*Gunnis* 1968, 46; C Lib (repr)
74.	c1844	Lady Godiva, statuette (co-sculptor: Thomas Henry Nicholson)	p	Council House, Coventry, Warks		*Graves* I, 1905–6, 168; *Gunnis* 1968, 46; *Grove* 3, 1996, 509
75.	1844–1845	Sir Thomas Gresham Payment(s): £550	s	Royal Exchange, City of London, east front		*Leith* 1997, 340, 342 (repr); *Ward-Jackson* 2003, 322–3 (repr)
76.	1822–1846	King George IV (co-sculptor: Constantine Panormo)	m	RDS, Dublin		*Gunnis* 1968, 46; *White and Bright* 1998, 86–7
77.	1849	The startled nymph		[Exhib RA, London, 1205]; untraced		*Graves* I, 1905–6, 168
78.	1851	Sir Robert Peel, statuette		[Exhib RA, London, 1293]; untraced		*Graves* I, 1905–6, 168
79.	1852	Henry Hall		Leeds Infirmary, W R Yorks		*Gunnis* 1968, 46
80.	1852	Sir Robert Peel (cast by Frederick Robinson, of Pimlico) Payment(s): £1,800 raised by subscription Drawing(s): Study for head, Leeds City Art Gallery, c1852	b	[Court House exterior, Leeds, W R Yorks]; Woodhouse Moor, Leeds, W R Yorks	SD	*Stafford* 1982, 4–11 (repr)
81.	1853	Lord George Bentinck, statuette		[Exhib RA, London, 1339]; untraced		*Graves* I, 1905–6, 168; *Ormond* 1973, 36; *Bilbey* 2002, 193 (repr)
82.	1853	William Wordsworth, statuette		[Exhib RA, London, 1341]; untraced		*Graves* I, 1905–6, 168
83.	1855	Sir Robert Peel Payment(s): £7,000	b	[Cheapside, City of London]; Metropolitan Police College, Hendon, Middx		*Blackwood* 1989, 184 (repr); *Ward-Jackson* 2003, xii–xiv (repr)
84.	1855	Sir Robert Peel	b	[Peel Place, Bradford, W R Yorks]; Peel Park, Bradford, W R Yorks	S	*Gunnis* 1968, 46; *Ormond* 1973, 373
85.	1852–1855	Sir Robert Peel (?), statuette		VAM A.28-2000		*Bilbey* 2002, 193 (repr)
86.	1858	Edward Baines		Leeds Town Hall, W R Yorks		*Hall* 1995, 12
87.	1861	Sir Henry Havelock	b	Trafalgar Square, London Other versions: Another sent to Sunderland, 1861		*Blackwood* 1989, 258–9 (repr)
Busts						
88.	1815	Mr Badger		[Exhib RA, London, 476]; untraced		*Gunnis* 1968, 45; *Graves* I, 1905–6, 166
89.	1815	Rev Thomas Frognall Dibdin Drawing(s): BM PDL 10636		[Exhib RA, London, 678]; untraced		*Graves* I, 1905–6, 166
90.	1816	Portrait of a gentleman		[Exhib RA, London, 662]; untraced		*Graves* I, 1905–6, 166
91.	1816	Portrait of a gentleman		[Exhib RA, London, 407]; untraced		*Graves* I, 1905–6, 166
92.	1816	Portrait of a gentleman		[Exhib RA, London, 551]; untraced		*Graves* I, 1905–6, 166

93.	1816	Portrait of a gentleman		[Exhib RA, London, 757]; untraced		*Graves* I, 1905–6, 166
94.	1816	Portrait of a lady		[Exhib RA, London, 726]; untraced		*Graves* I, 1905–6, 166
95.	1817	Henry Earle	p	Foundling Hospital, London	S	*Gunnis* 1968, 46; C Lib (repr)
96.	1817	J North		[Exhib RA, London, 449]; untraced		*Graves* I, 1905–6, 166
97.	1817	Lord Elmley		[Exhib RA, London, 570]; untraced		*Graves* I, 1905–6, 166
98.	1817	Mr Evans		[Exhib RA, London, 534]; untraced		*Graves* I, 1905–6, 166
99.	1817	Mrs Cooper		[Exhib RA, London, 575]; untraced		*Graves* I, 1905–6, 166
100.	1817	Mrs W Brooks		[Exhib RA, London, 583]; untraced		*Graves* I, 1905–6, 166
101.	1817	Portrait of a gentleman		[Exhib RA, London, 446]; untraced		*Graves* I, 1905–6, 166
102.	1817	Portrait of a lady		[Exhib RA, London, 467]; untraced		*Graves* I, 1905–6, 166
103.	1817	William, Earl Beauchamp		[Exhib RA, London, 1047]; untraced		*Graves* I, 1905–6, 166
104.	1818	Lady Sophia Kent		[Exhib RA, London, 1070]; untraced		*Graves* I, 1905–6, 166
105.	1818	Portrait of a gentleman		[Exhib RA, London, 849]; untraced		*Graves* I, 1905–6, 166
106.	1818	Portrait of a gentleman		[Exhib RA, London, 882]; untraced		*Graves* I, 1905–6, 166
107.	1818	Portrait of a lady		[Exhib RA, London, 807]; untraced		*Graves* I, 1905–6, 166
108.	1818	Portrait of a lady		[Exhib RA, London, 817]; untraced		*Graves* I, 1905–6, 166
109.	1818	Portrait of a lady		[Exhib RA, London, 829]; untraced		*Graves* I, 1905–6, 166
110.	1818	Shute Barrington, Bishop of Durham	m	[Exhib RA, London, 1819, 1223]; untraced		*AJ*, 1864, 38; *Graves* I, 1905–6, 166
111.	1818	Sir Thomas Plumer, Master of the Rolls		[Exhib RA, London, 1100]; untraced		*Graves* I, 1905–6, 166
112.	1818	Unidentified gentleman and his son		[Exhib RA, London, 875]; untraced		*Graves* I, 1905–6, 166
113.	1818	William, 1st Baron Radstock	p	[Exhib RA, London, 1101]; NMM, Greenwich, SCU0060	S	*Graves* I, 1905–6, 166
114.	1819	Hon Miss Moreton		[Exhib RA, London, 1218]; untraced		*Graves* I, 1905–6, 166
115.	1819	J Bindley		[Exhib RA, London, 732]; untraced		*Graves* I, 1905–6, 166
116.	1819	John, 1st Earl of Eldon	m	[Exhib RA, London, 533]; Inner Temple, London		*Graves* I, 1905–6, 166; *Gunnis* 1968, 46
117.	1819	Master Boswell		[Exhib RA, London, 986]; untraced		*Graves* I, 1905–6, 166
118.	1819	Mr Marsden		[Exhib RA, London, 509]; untraced		*Graves* I, 1905–6, 166
119.	1819	Mr Murdoch		[Exhib RA, London, 901]; untraced		*Graves* I, 1905–6, 166
120.	1819	'Portrait of a gentleman'		[Exhib RA, London, 716]; untraced		*Graves* I, 1905–6, 166
121.	1819	'Portraits of two ladies'		[Exhib RA, London, 650]; untraced		*Graves* I, 1905–6, 166
122.	1819	Rev Dr Fisher		[Exhib RA, London, 526]; untraced		*Graves* I, 1905–6, 166
123.	1819	Victoria, Duchess of Kent and Strathearn	m	[Exhib RA, London, 1231]; Leighton House, London		*Graves* I, 1905–6, 1, 167
124.	1820	Augusta, Duchess of Cambridge	m	Royal Coll, Windsor Castle	SD	*Graves* I, 1905–6, 167; C Lib (repr)
125.	1820	Benjamin West PRA	m	[Exhib RA, London, 1820, 1061, coll Lord de Tabley]; untraced		*Graves* I, 1905–6, 167; *Gunnis* 1968, 46
126.	1820	Unidentified lady		[Exhib RA, London, 1051]; untraced		*Graves* I, 1905–6, 167
127.	1820	W S Clarke		[Exhib RA, London, 747]; untraced		*Graves* I, 1905–6, 167
128.	1821	Beriah Botfield	p	Longleat, Wilts		GPC
129.	1821	Charles Young	m	[Exhib RA, London, 1114]; untraced		*Graves* I, 1905–6, 167
130.	1821	Francis Cramer	m	[Exhib RA, London, 1060]; untraced		*Graves* I, 1905–6, 167
131.	1821	George, 5th Viscount Barrington	m	[Exhib RA, London, 1143]; untraced		*Graves* I, 1905–6, 167
132.	1821	Miss Barrington	m	untraced		*Graves* I, 1905–6, 167
133.	1821	Miss Wilson		[Exhib RA, London, 1158]; untraced		*Graves* I, 1905–6, 167
134.	1822	George Tierney	m	NPG, London, 173 Other versions: RDS, plaster	SD	*Graves* 1905–6, 1, 167; *Gunnis* 1968, 46; GPC
135.	1824	John, 1st Earl of Durham	m	[Exhib RA, London, 1005]; untraced		*Graves* I, 1905–6, 167; *Ormond* 1973, 152
136.	1824	Joseph Marriot	m	St George, Grenada		*Graves* I, 1905–6, 167; *Gunnis* 1968, 46
137.	1824	Walter Geough	m	[Exhib RA, London, 996]; untraced		*Graves* I, 1905–6, 167
138.	1824	William, Baron Stowell		[Exhib RA, London, 1013]; Inner Temple, London Other versions: NPG, London Middle Temple, London		*Graves* I, 1905–6, 167; *Gunnis* 1968, 46
139.	1825	Charles, 2nd Earl Grey		[Exhib RA, London, 1008]; untraced		*Graves* I, 1905–6, 167; *Ormond* 1973, 202
140.	1825	James Northcote RA	m	[Exhib RA, London, 1039]; untraced		*Graves* I, 1905–6, 167
141.	1825	Miss Fitzgerald	m	[Exhib RA, London, 1026]; untraced		*Graves* I, 1905–6, 167
142.	1825	Mrs Thomas Gent	m	[Exhib RA, London, 1036]; untraced		*Graves* I, 1905–6, 167
143.	1825	Rev J Townsend	m	[Exhib RA, London, 1010]; untraced		*Graves* I, 1905–6, 167
144.	1825	S Weston	m	[Exhib RA, London, 1002]; untraced		*Graves* I, 1905–6, 167
145.	1825	Unidentified lady	m	[Exhib RA, London, 1022]; untraced		*Graves* I, 1905–6, 167
146.	1826	Colonel Thomas Perkins	m	Athenaeum, Boston, USA		*Gunnis* 1968, 46
147.	1826	Edward Augustus, Duke of Kent and Strathearn (†1820)	m	Buckingham Palace, London, RCIN 2005	SD	JM
148.	1826	Frederick Augustus, Duke of York and Albany	m	[Exhib RA, London, 1826, 1076]; Buckingham Palace, London		*Graves* I, 1905–6, 167; GPC; C Lib (repr)
149.	1826	George, 3rd Earl of Egremont	m	Petworth House, Sussex	S	*Graves* I, 1905–6, 167; *Gunnis* 1968, 46; C Lib (repr)
150.	1826	James Christie	m	[Exhib RA, London, 1026]; untraced		*Graves* I, 1905–6, 167
151.	1826	Lady Beresford	m	[Exhib RA, London, 1045]; untraced Other versions: busts of Field Marshal Visc and Lady Beresford sold Sotheby, 27 April 2001, lot 161		*Graves* I, 1905–6, 167
152.	1826	Luke White		[Exhib RA, London, 1089]; untraced		*Graves* I, 1905–6, 167
153.	1826	M Baine	m	Sotterley, Suffolk	S	
154.	1826	Sir Thomas Coffin	m	Athenaeum, Boston, USA		*Gunnis* 1968, 46
155.	1826	Unidentified lady	m	[Exhib RA, London, 1087]; untraced		*Graves* I, 1905–6, 167
156.	1827	Charles, 3rd Baron Southampton and his wife, Harriet		[Exhib RA, London, 1103]; untraced		*Graves* I, 1905–6, 167

No.	Date	Subject		Location		Literature
157.	1827	Countess of Jersey	m	[Exhib RA, London, 1113]; untraced		*Graves* I, 1905–6, 167
158.	1827	Mr Young of Covent Garden	m	[Exhib ALRI, Liverpool, 285]; untraced		*Morris and Roberts* 1998, 72
159.	1827	Oliver Goldsmith Payment(s): £84 15s 5d	m	Trinity College, Dublin, Long Room Other versions: RDS, Dublin (two), plaster		*Crookshank* 1986, 24; *White and Bright* 1998, 26–7, 77
160.	1827	Rev Daniel Bogue		[Exhib RA, London, 1096]; untraced		*Graves* I, 1905–6, 167
161.	1827	Unidentified woman	m	VAM A.66-1949	SD	*Bilbey* 2002, 191 (repr)
162.	1828	Dr Helenus Scott	m	University of Sydney, New South Wales, Australia	SD	
163.	1828	Elizabeth, Marchioness of Cleveland	m	Raby Castle, Durham		*Graves* I, 1905–6, 167; *Gunnis* 1968, 47
164.	1828	Ernest Augustus, Duke of Cumberland and King of Hanover	m	Windsor Castle, RCIN 31625	SD	*Graves* I, 1905–6, 167; C Lib (repr)
165.	1828	George, 4th Duke of Grafton	m	[Exhib RA, London, 1161]; untraced		*Graves* I, 1905–6, 167
166.	1828	Prince George of Cumberland	m	Windsor Castle, RCIN 69/688	SD	*British Portraits* 1956–7, 132; *Gunnis* 1968, 47; C Lib (repr)
167.	1828	Unidentified gentleman	m	[Exhib RA, London, 1184]; untraced		*Graves* I, 1905–6, 167
168.	1829	Lady Elizabeth Gower	m	[Exhib RA, London, 1214]; untraced		*Graves* I, 1905–6, 167
169.	1829	Prince George of Hanover	m	[Exhib RA, London, 1182]; untraced		*Graves* I, 1905–6, 167; *Gunnis* 1968, 45
170.	1829	Queen Victoria as a child	m	Windsor Castle, RCIN 35417 Other versions: several	SD	*Grove* 1996, 3, 509; *Ormond* 1973, 479; C Lib (repr)
171.	1829	W Manning, MP	m	[Exhib RA, London, 1192]; untraced		*Graves* I, 1905–6, 167
172.	1830	'A young lady'	m	[Exhib RA, London, 1268]; untraced		*Graves* I, 1905–6, 167
173.	1830	Beriah Botfield	m	Longleat House, Wilts		*Gunnis* 1968, 47; C Lib (repr)
174.	1830	Charles, 1st Earl Camden (after a bust by Joseph Wilton)	m	Bayham Abbey, Sussex Other versions: Eton College, Windsor, Berks		*Gunnis* 1968, 47; *Ormond and Rogers* 2, 1979–81, 35
175.	1830	Henry, 1st Baron Brougham and Vaux	m	Lincoln's Inn, London Other versions: Peers' Library, Palace of Westminster	SD	*Walker* 1961, 8, cat no 11
176.	1830	Henry, 3rd Viscount Clifden, as a child	m	[Exhib RA, London, 1831, 1182]; Althorp, Northants		*Graves* I, 1905–6, 167; C Lib (repr)
177.	1830	Hugh, Lord Ebrington	m	Barnstaple Infirmary, Devon		*Graves* 1906, 1, 167; *Gunnis* 1968, 47
178.	1830	John, Earl of Stradbroke	m	[Exhib RA, London, 1232]; Henham Hall, Suffolk		*Graves* I, 1905–6, 167; C Lib (repr)
179.	1830	Rev Dr Richards	m	[Exhib RA, London, 1236]; untraced		*Graves* I, 1905–6, 167
180.	1830	Thomas Lucy MP	m	[Exhib RA, London, 1246]; untraced		*Graves* I, 1905–6, 167
181.	1830	Unidentified gentleman	m	[Exhib RA, London, 1219]; untraced		*Graves* I, 1905–6, 167
182.	1831	Colonel John Jones	m	[Exhib RA, London, 1211]; untraced		*Library of Fine Arts* 1831, vol 1, 432; *Graves* I, 1905–6, 167
183.	1831	Countess of Sheffield	m	[Exhib RA, London, 1183]; untraced		*Graves* I, 1905–6, 167
184.	1831	Dr William Babington	m	R C Physic, London	SD	*Graves* I, 1905–6, 167; *Wolstenholme* 1964, 38–9 (repr)
185.	1831	Henry, 1st Viscount Sidmouth	m	NPG, London, 3917	SD	*Graves* I, 1905–6, 167; *Ormond and Rogers* 2, 1979–81, 194; C Lib (repr)
186.	1831	John Nash	m	[Exhib RA, London, 1184, coll Sir James Pennethorne]; Corton Denham House, Dorset Other versions: RIBA, plaster All Souls', Langham Place, London, façade, copy by Cecil Thomas		*Library of Fine Arts* 1831, vol 1, 433; *Graves* I, 1905–6, 167; *Davis* 1966, 18–19; GPC
187.	1831	John, 1st Earl of Eldon	m	Middle Temple, London		*Graves* I, 1905–6, 167; *Gunnis* 1968, 47
188.	1831	Lady Ebrington	m	Castle Hill, Devon		*Gunnis* 1968, 47; C Lib (repr)
189.	1831	Master Robert Peel Dawson	m	[Exhib RA, London, 1214]; untraced		*Graves* I, 1905–6, 167
190.	1831	Mrs Lucy, of Charlecote	m	[Exhib RA, London, 1170]; untraced		*Graves* I, 1905–6, 167
191.	1831	Prince George of Cambridge	m	Windsor Castle, RCIN 35424	SD	*Graves* I, 1905–6, 167; C Lib (repr)
192.	1831	Sir Richard Keats, RN, KCB	m	Windsor Castle, RCIN 33442	SD	C Lib (repr)
193.	1832	Dudley, 1st Earl of Harrowby	m	Sandon Park, Staffs		*Graves* I, 1906, 167; *Gunnis* 1968, 47; C Lib (repr)
194.	1832	Edward, 1st Baron Skelmersdale	m	[Exhib RA, London, 1163]; untraced		*Graves* I, 1905–6, 167
195.	1832	Frederick, 1st Marquess of Bristol	m	Ickworth Park, Suffolk Other versions: Ickworth Park, Suffolk, 1833 Ickworth Park, Suffolk, 1838		*Graves* I, 1905–6, 167; *Gunnis* 1968, 47
196.	1832	Samuel Woodburn	m	Ashmolean WA 1865.1	SD	*Penny* 1992, 10 (repr)
197.	1832	Sir Francis Burdett (with plinth relief)	m	Coutts Bank, Strand, Westminster, London		
198.	1833	Alderman Atkins	m	[Exhib RA, London, 1130]; untraced		*Graves* I, 1905–6, 167
199.	†1833	Edward Hamlin Adams	m	[Middleton Hall, Carmarthen]; County Museum, Carmarthen		*Dale-Jones and Lloyd* 1989, 59
200.	1833	Michael Sadler		Leeds Lit and Phil Soc, W R Yorks		GPC
201.	1833	Richard Whately	m	Oriel College, Oxford		*Gunnis* 1968, 47
202.	1833	Samuel Woodington	m	[Exhib RA, London, 1201]; untraced		*Graves* I, 1905–6, 167
203.	1834	James Franck		Wellcome Museum	SD	C Lib (repr)
204.	1834	Sir Henry Hotham		Dalton Hall, E R Yorks		GPC
205.	1834	Vice-Admiral George Granville Waldegrave	p	NMM, Greenwich, SCU0061	SD	
206.	1834	W T Copeland	m	Spode Museum, Stoke-on-Trent, Staffs	SD	*Graves* I, 1905–6, 167
207.	1834	William, Baron Stowell	m	Gov Art Coll (1955)	SD	Gov Art Coll archives

208.	1835	Admiral Sir J Hawkins Whitched		Welbeck Abbey, Notts		*Graves* I, 1905–6, 168; GPC
209.	1832–1835	Admiral Sir Richard Keats	m	Royal Hospital, Greenwich (ORNC)		*Graves* I, 1905–6, 167
210.	1835	Admiral Sotheron		[Exhib RA, London, 1114]; untraced		*Graves* I, 1905–6, 168
211.	1835	Charles James Blomfield, Bishop of London		[Exhib RA, London, 1123]; untraced		*Graves* I, 1905–6, 168; *Ormond* 1973, 41
212.	1835	Dr Frank	m	[Exhib RA, London, 1102]; untraced		*Graves* I, 1905–6, 168
213.	1835	Lord Charles Fitzroy	m	[Exhib RA, London, 1111]; untraced		*Graves* I, 1905–6, 168
214.	1835	Martin Farquar Tupper	m	[Exhib RA, London, 1088]; Joanna Barnes Fine Art (1991)		*Graves* I, 1905–6, 168; *Ormond* 1973, 470; C Lib (repr)
215.	1835	Unidentified man	m	Cliveden, Bucks		C Lib (repr)
216.	1836	George, Lord Morpeth, later 6th Earl of Carlisle	m	Castle Howard, N R Yorks		*Gunnis* 1968, 47
217.	1836	James, 1st Baron de Saumarez		[Exhib RA, London, 1123]; untraced		*Graves* I, 1905–6, 168
218.	1836	John Knowles		[Exhib RA, London, 1093]; untraced		*Graves* I, 1905–6, 168
219.	1836	Nassau William Senior		[Exhib RA, London, 1134]; untraced		*Graves* I, 1905–6, 168
220.	1836	Sir Benjamin Brodie Bt		Wellcome Museum	SD	*Graves* 1905–6, 1, 168; C Lib (repr)
221.	1836	Sir William Brodie	p	RCS, London		*Gunnis* 1968, 47
222.	1836	William Hey	m	Leeds Infirmary, W R Yorks		*Gunnis* 1968, 47
223.	1837	Henry, 1st Baron Brougham and Vaux	m	[Lowther Castle, Westmorland]; untraced	SD	*Graves* I, 1905–6, 168; *Gawsworth Guide*, 47
224.	1837	John Paris	m	R C Physic, London		*Gunnis* 1968, 47
225.	1837	Miss Kirkpatrick	m	[Exhib RA, London, 1287]; untraced		*Graves* I, 1905–6, 168
226.	1837	Rev Dr Penfold	m	[Exhib RA, London, 1230]; untraced		*Graves* I, 1905–6, 168
227.	1837	Sir J Beckett	m	[Exhib RA, London, 1227]; untraced		*Graves* I, 1905–6, 168
228.	1837	Unidentified woman	m	Cliveden, Bucks	SD	C Lib (repr)
229.	1837	Young woman leaning on a ledge	m	Christie, London, 23 Nov 1990, lot 103; untraced		Sale cat, C Lib
230.	1838	Benjamin Travers	m	[Exhib RA, London, 1307]; untraced		*Graves* I, 1905–6, 168
231.	1838	C E Carrington	m	[Exhib RA, London, 1382]; untraced		*Graves* I, 1905–6, 168
232.	1838	Henry Earle	m	St Bartholomew's Hospital, City of London		*Graves* I, 1905–6, 168; *Gunnis* 1968, 47
233.	1838	Nicholas, 1st Baron Bexley	m	[Exhib RA, London, 1381]; untraced		*Graves* I, 1905–6, 168
234.	1839	H E Kendell	tc	RIBA		GPC
235.	1839	Thomas Clarkson	m	[Guildhall Lib, City of London]; destroyed		*AJ* 1864, 83; *Gunnis* 1968, 47
236.	1839	Unidentified man	m	[Ellicombe, Minehead, Somerset]; Grittleton sale, 1966, lot 28, bt Sykes, 18 gns; untraced	SD	*Grittleton Marbles* 1966, 22
237.	1840	Alderman Venables	m	[Exhib RA, London, 1148]; untraced		*Graves* I, 1905–6, 168
238.	1840	Colonel William Martin Leake	m	Fitzwilliam		*Graves* 1905–6, 1, 168; *Gunnis* 1968, 47; *Griefenhagen* 1985, 123–4 (repr)
239.	1840	Henry, 7th Duke of Beaufort	m	Badminton House, Glos	SD	*Graves* I, 1905–6, 168; *Ormond* 1973, 31; C Lib (repr)
240.	by 1840	King George III		[Christie, 19 April 1849]; untraced		RG/JP, 1, 128
241.	by 1840	Lord Munster's daughter		[Exhib for sale at the Colosseum, Regent's Park, London, 1849]; untraced		RG/JP, 1, 128
242.	1840	Miss Bland		Cliveden, Bucks	SD	*The British Face* 1986, 136–7 (repr)
243.	1840	Unidentified lady	m	[Exhib RA, London, 1173]; untraced		*Graves* I, 1905–6, 168
244.	1840	W Hobson	m	[Exhib RA, London, 1187]; untraced		*Graves* I, 1905–6, 168
245.	1841	John Beresford, Archbishop of Armagh	m	[Exhib RA, London, 1341]; untraced		*Graves* I, 1905–6, 168
246.	1841	John, 1st Baron Lyndhurst	p	VAM A.27-2000 Other versions: Lincoln's Inn, London Trinity College, Cambridge, library, 1844, marble	SD	*Graves* I, 1905–6, 168; Pevsner, *Cambs*, 1970, 175; *Ormond* 1973, 283; *Bilbey* 2002191–2 (repr)
247.	1841	King William IV	m	NMM, Greenwich, SCU0064		
248.	1841	Lady Emily, daughter of the 7th Duke of Beaufort	m	[Exhib RA, London, 1249]; untraced		*Graves* I, 1905–6, 168
249.	1841	Rev Hobart Caunter	m	[Exhib RA, London, 1252]; untraced		*Graves* I, 1905–6, 168
250.	1841	Unidentified lady	m	[Exhib RA, London, 1331]; untraced		*Graves* I, 1905–6, 168
251.	1842	A Dent	m	[Exhib RA, London, 1400]; untraced		*Graves* I, 1905–6, 168
252.	1842	Alderman Lucas	m	[Exhib RA, London, 1389]; untraced		*Graves* I, 1905–6, 168
253.	1842	Frederick, Lord North	m	Eton College, Windsor, Berks		*Gunnis* 1968, 47; C Lib (repr)
254.	1842	Sir B Malkin	m	[Exhib RA, London, 1368]; untraced		*Graves* I, 1905–6, 168
255.	1842	Sir Jonathan Frederick Pollock		Inner Temple, London	SD	*Graves* I, 1905–6, 168; *Ormond* 1973, 381; *Read* 1982, 174
256.	1842	Sir William Molesworth Bt	m	Reform Club, Pall Mall, London Other versions: Parliament Buildings, Ottawa		*AU*, 1842, 129; *Graves* I, 1905–6, 168; *Ormond* 1973, 323
257.	1842	Thomas Poynder	m	[Exhib RA, London, 1384]; untraced		*AU*, 1842, 129; *Graves* I, 1905–6, 168
258.	1843	Alfred Guillaume Gabriel, Count D'Orsay	p	[Exhib RA, London, 1519]; untraced Other versions: Royal Coll, 1846		*Graves* I, 1905–6, 168; *Ormond* 1973, 149
259.	1843	Edward Coplestone, Bishop of Llandaff	m	Oriel College, Oxford		*Graves* I, 1905–6, 168; *Gunnis* 1968, 47
260.	1843	George Grote	m	Untraced		*Ormond* 1973, 205
261.	1843	Henry, 4th Duke of Newcastle	m	Eton College, Windsor, Berks	S	*Ormond and Rogers* 2, 1979–81, 156
262.	1843	Sir William Webb Follett	m	[Exhib RA, London, 1520]; untraced		*Graves* I, 1905–6, 168; *Ormond* 1973, 176

No.	Date	Subject		Location		Literature
263.	1844	Edward Maltby, Bishop of Durham		Fitzwilliam		*Graves* I, 1905–6, 168; *Ormond and Rogers* 1, 1979–81, 142
264.	1844	Fitzroy Kelly		[Exhib RA, London, 1236]; untraced		*AU*, 1844, 171; *Graves* I, 1905–6, 168
265.	1844	Sir John Barrow Bt, MP		[Exhib RA, London, 1329]; untraced		*Graves* I, 1905–6, 168
266.	1844	Thomas Slingsby Duncombe		[Exhib RA, London, 1376]; untraced		*Graves* I, 1905–6, 168; *Ormond* 1973, 151
267.	1843–1844	William Charles Macready	m	NPG, London, 1504		*AU*, 1844, 171; *Ormond* 1973, 298 (repr 590)
268.	1845	Countess of Chesterfield	m	[Exhib RA, London, 1454]; untraced		*Graves* I, 1905–6, 168
269.	c1845	George Cruickshank	p	NPG, London 1300	S	
270.	1845	Richard Porson	m	Eton College, Windsor, Berks	SD	*British Portraits* 1956–7, 108; *Read* 1982, 174
271.	1845	Richard, 1st Earl Howe	m	Eton College, Windsor, Berks	S	*Gunnis* 1968, 46
272.	1846	Benjamin Bond Campbell		[Exhib RA, London, 1459]; untraced		*Graves* I, 1905–6, 168
273.	1846	Edward, 11th Duke of Somerset		[Exhib RA, London, 1502]; untraced		*Graves* I, 1905–6, 168
274.	1846	Francis, 3rd Marquess of Hertford		Ragley Hall, Warks		GPC
275.	1846	Joseph Hume MP		[Exhib RA, London, 1464]; untraced		*Graves* I, 1905–6, 168
276.	1846	Sir Henry Pottinger, 1st Bt		[Exhib RA, London, 1507]; untraced		*AU*, 1846, 189; *Graves* I, 1905–6, 168
277.	1846	Sir Jonathan Frederick Pollock		[Exhib RA, London, 1496]; untraced		*Graves* I, 1905–6, 168
278.	1846	'Thesiger, Attorney General'		[Exhib RA, London, 1465]; untraced		*Graves* I, 1905–6, 168
279.	1847	Benjamin Disraeli	m	Hughenden Manor, Bucks		*AU*, 1847, 200; *Graves* I, 1905–6, 168; *Gunnis* 1968, 47
280.	1847	Countess of Malmesbury		[Exhib RA, London, 1384]; untraced		*Graves* I, 1905–6, 168
281.	1847	Dr William Lister	m	St Thomas's Hospital, London	SD	*Cavanagh* forthcoming 2007 (Lambeth 2); C Lib (repr)
282.	1847	George, 6th Earl of Chesterfield		[Exhib RA, London, 1438]; untraced		*AU*, 1847, 200; *Graves* I, 1905–6, 168
283.	1847	John Moorhouse, Common Serjeant		[Exhib RA, London, 1398]; untraced		*Graves* I, 1905–6, 168
284.	1847	Joseph Carpue MD	m	St George's Hospital, London, medical school library	SD	*Graves* I, 1905–6, 168; *Gunnis* 1968, 47
285.	1847	Richard Jones	m	[Guildhall, London]; destroyed		*Gunnis* 1968, 47
286.	1847	Sir John Pirie Bt		[Exhib RA, London, 1402]; untraced		*Graves* I, 1905–6, 168
287.	1847	William Pitt, 1st Earl of Chatham	m	Eton College, Windsor, Berks, upper school	S	*Gunnis* 1968, 47; *Ormond and Rogers* 2, 1979–81, 42
288.	1848	Alderman Moon		[Exhib RA, London, 1440]; untraced		*Graves* I, 1905–6, 168
289.	1848	Colonel Peter Hawker		[Exhib RA, London, 1401]; untraced		*Graves* I, 1905–6, 168
290.	1848	J T Houlton		[Exhib RA, London, 1395]; untraced		*Graves* I, 1905–6, 168
291.	1848	Sir George Seymour		[Exhib RA, London, 1393]; untraced		*Graves* I, 1905–6, 168
292.	1848	Sir John Swinburne		[Exhib RA, London, 1448]; untraced		*Graves* I, 1905–6, 168
293.	1849	Colonel Forbes		[Exhib RA, London, 1305]; untraced		*Graves* I, 1905–6, 168
294.	1849	Edward Stanley, Bishop of Norwich	p	Linnean Soc, London		*Graves* I, 1905–6, 168; GPC
295.	1849	Henry, Lord Hammond	m	Eton College, Windsor, Berks, upper school	SD	*Gunnis* 1968, 47; C Lib (repr)
296.	by 1849	King Leopold		[Christie, 19 April 1849]; untraced		RG/JP, 1, 128
297.	by 1849	Princess Charlotte		[Messrs Town and Emanuel; Christie, 19 April 1849]; untraced		RG/JP, 1, 128
298.	1849	R R Pennington MD		[Exhib RA, London, 1268]; untraced		*Graves* I, 1905–6, 168
299.	1849	Robert Vernon	m	Tate Britain, London		*Read* 1982, 172
300.	1849	Sir Charles Barry	m	[Exhib RA, London, 1267]; untraced		*Graves* I, 1905–6, 168; *Ormond* 1973, 29
301.	1849	Sir Felix Booth Bt		[Exhib RA, London, 1240]; untraced		*Graves* I, 1905–6, 168
302.	1849	Thomas Arnold	m	[coll James Lee, Bishop of Manchester]; NPG, London, 168 Other versions: Rugby School, Warks, plaster	SD	*Ormond* 1973, 17 (repr 23)
303.	1850	Chevalier Bunsen		[Exhib RA, London, 1429]; untraced		*Graves* I, 1905–6, 168
304.	1851	Arthur, 1st Duke of Wellington	m	County Buildings, Winchester, Hants Other versions: coll, King of Prussia		*ILN*, 29 Nov 1851, 641; *Gunnis* 1968, 47
305.	1851	Mrs Moray	m	[Exhib RA, London, 1380]; untraced		*Graves* I, 1905–6, 168
306.	1852	Alderman Wire	m	[Exhib RA, London, 1480]; untraced		*Graves* I, 1905–6, 168
307.	1852	George Grote	m	University College, London, provost's room	S	*Ormond* 1973, 205; C Lib (repr)
308.	1853	Arthur, 1st Duke of Wellington		[Exhib RA, London, 1364]; untraced		*Graves* I, 1905–6, 168
309.	1853	Samuel Rogers		[Exhib RA, London, 1424]; untraced		*Graves* I, 1905–6, 168
310.	1855	Arthur, 1st Duke of Wellington		[Exhib RA, London, 1520]; untraced		*Graves* I, 1905–6, 168
311.	1855	Edmund Lawrence		[Exhib RA, London, 1546]; untraced		*Graves* I, 1905–6, 169
312.	1855	John Dupasquer		[Exhib RA, London, 1538]; untraced		*Graves* I, 1905–6, 169
313.	1855	Sir David Salomons	m	CL Coll, City of London School, acc 1861 Other versions: C L coll, acc 168		*Graves* I, 1905–6, 169; *Knight* 1986, 330 (repr)
314.	1856	Edward, 11th Duke of Somerset		[Exhib RA, London, 1317]; untraced		*Graves* I, 1905–6, 169
315.	1856	Rev Dr Croby		[Exhib RA, London, 1358]; untraced		*Graves* I, 1905–6, 169
316.	1856	Sir Charles Adam	m	[Exhib RA, London, 1354]; NMM SCU0001		*Graves* I, 1905–6, 169
317.	1857	George Norman	m	Guildhall, Bath		*Gunnis* 1968, 47
318.	1857	Isaac Hargreaves	m	Kent and Sussex Hospital, Tunbridge Wells, Kent	SD	*Gunnis* 1968, 47; C Lib (repr)
319.	1857	Rev Canon Dale		[Exhib RA, London, 1345]; untraced		*Graves* I, 1905–6, 169
320.	1858	Benjamin Travers	m	RCS, London	SD	*Read* 1982, 172; C Lib (repr)
321.	1858	'J Malcolmson's daughter'		[Exhib RA, London, 1309]; untraced		*Graves* I, 1905–6, 169

322.	1858	John Bowyer Nichols		[Exhib RA, London, 1308]; untraced		*Graves* I, 1905–6, 169
323.	†1858	Richard Bright	m	R C Physic, London		*Wolstenholme* 1964, 84–5 (repr)
324.	1858	Sir Charles Locock, 1st Bt		[Exhib RA, London, 1250]; untraced		*Graves* I, 1905–6, 169
325.	1858	Sir Henry Havelock	m	CL Coll, Guildhall Museum, City of London, acc 167 Other versions: several		*Ormond* 1973, 217, 218; *Knight* 1986, 331 (repr)
326.	1859	Richard Godfrey Bosanquet		[Exhib RA, London, 1343]; untraced		*Graves* I, 1905–6, 169
327.	1861	Archibald Campbell Tait, Archbishop of Canterbury		Lambeth Palace, London	S	*Graves* I, 1905–6, 169; C Lib (repr)
328.	1861	James, 8th Earl of Elgin	m	[Exhib RA, London, 1020]; Federal Government of Canada (on loan to Lord Elgin Hotel, Ottawa, Ontario)		*Graves* I, 1905–6, 169; *Ormond and Rogers* 3, 1979–81, 63
329.	1863	Hon Mountstuart Elphinstone	m	[Exhib RA, London, 1031]; private coll	SD	*Graves* I, 1905–6, 169
330.	1866	Duchess of Somerset (perhaps Lady Emily Somerset)	p	VAM A.26-2000	SD	*Bilbey* 2002, 192 (repr)
331.	nd	Augustus Frederick, Duke of Sussex	m	Leighton House, London		C Lib (repr)
332.	nd	Dr Bell		[Exhib for sale at the Colosseum, Regent's Park, London, 1849]; untraced		RG/JP, 1, 128
333.	nd	Edward Augustus, Duke of Kent and Strathearn	m	Royal Coll, RCIN 31619		JM
334.	nd	Hugh, Earl Fortescue	m	Powderham Castle, Devon	S	*Gunnis* 1968, 47
335.	nd	John Sleath		Private coll	S	
336.	nd	Mrs Thomas Hope	m	[The Deepdene, Dorking, Surrey, sculpture gallery]; untraced		*Watkin* 1968, 43, 171
337.	nd	Sir Joshua Reynolds		Plymouth Museum and Art Gallery		RG/JP, 1, 132
338.	nd	William Maltby	m	Fitzwilliam		*Gunnis* 1968, 47
339.	nd	William Manton	p	Linnean Soc, London		GPC
Architectural Sculpture						
340.	1829	'Group of figures' (designed by John Nash) Payment(s): £700	s	Buckingham Palace, London, clock tower		TNA WORK 19/3, f 363; *Gunnis* 1968, 45
341.	1847	Apollo, Morning and Night, statues		Buckingham Palace, London, east front		GPC
342.	post-1870	Stag and dragon		Curraghmore, County Laois, on tower and pediment		*Potterton* 1975, 37
Reliefs						
343.	*c*1830	Seven ages of man	tc	Untraced		*Graves* I, 1905–6, 167; *Gunnis* 1968, 46
344.	1839	A teacher and pupils at lessons	p	Foundling Hospital, London	S	
345.	1850	Robert Vernon, portrait medallion		[Exhib RA, London, 1393]; untraced		*Graves* I, 1905–6, 168
346.	1852	Jabez Bunting, medallion	b	NPG, London, inv no 4880	SD	
Miscellaneous						
347.	1814	'Outline of the Gladiator Repellens'		[Soc of A, silver medal]; untraced		*Bennett* 1998, 130
348.	1817	'A lady and child'		[Exhib RA, London, 470]; untraced		*Graves* I, 1905–6, 166
349.	1820	'Lady and family of distinction'		[Exhib RA, London, 604]; untraced		*Graves* I, 1905–6, 167
350.	1821	'A lady and child'		[Exhib RA, London, 922]; untraced		*Graves* I, 1905–6, 167
351.	1843	'Queen of Beauty' (Lord Seymour's horse, head)		Untraced		*ILN*, 30 Sept 1843, 221 (repr); *Gunnis* 1968, 45
352.	1848	'Europa, a sketch'		[Exhib RA, London, 1370]; untraced		*Graves* I, 1905–6, 168

BELL, Alexander, of Newcastle-upon-Tyne fl 1764–76

He was employed at Seaton Delaval between 1764 and 1768 and returned there in 1776 to build the mausoleum.

Literary References: *Gunnis* 1968, 48, citing Archives, Lord Hastings

Architectural Sculpture

1.	1764–1768	Capitals and other carving Payment(s): £211 for stonework; £7 4s each for capitals, £15 3s 8d for frieze around entrance door	s	Seaton Delaval Hall, Northumbs		*Gunnis* 1968, 48

BELL, Sir Charles

For information the reader is referred to *Pyke* 1973, 11

BELL, F B fl 1827

Funerary Monuments

1.	†1827	Thomas Salmon		Olveston, Glos	S	

BELL, John 1811–95

A prolific sculptor, particularly of romantic and literary subjects, many of them reproduced in bronze and iron and in ceramic materials, which brought them to a wider market. His technological and commercial versatility contrasts with his stylistic conservatism.

Bell came from a family of substance. He was born on 19 August 1811, the eldest son of Samuel Bell of Hopton Hall, Suffolk, a landowner, solicitor and the Collector of Customs in Great Yarmouth. He received a traditional classical education with a local vicar at Catfield Rectory, Norfolk and may have taken his first drawing lessons in Norwich. In 1827 Bell moved to London to study at Henry Sass's School of Drawing in Soho, living nearby at 3 Frith Street. In 1829 he was admitted to the Royal Academy Sculpture School, where **(Sir) Richard Westmacott RA** had recently become a professor. After completing his training Bell, whose parents actively supported their son's choice of career, was able to set up his own workshop, exhibiting his first work, a religious group, at the RA in 1832 (**106**). He showed regularly over the next forty-seven years, at the RA and British Institution and with the Society of

British Artists in Suffolk Street. His secure financial position enabled him to concentrate largely on ideal works, rather than busts and funerary monuments. In 1834 he moved to 43 Cambridge Street, Belgravia. He became a founder member of the Etching Club in 1838 and later produced etchings for editions of Oliver Goldsmith's *Deserted Village*, Thomas Gray's *Elegy Written in a Country Churchyard* and Shakespeare's *Songs and Ballads.*

Bell made his name as a sculptor with two imaginative works, *The Eagleslayer* (**19**) and *Dorothea* (**16**). *The Eagleslayer* was first shown at the RA in 1837 and then in 1844 at the exhibition held in Westminster Hall to select artists for the new Houses of Parliament. It was hailed as 'a performance so striking and masterly that it at once fixes the attention, not only by the novelty of the subject, but by the ability of the treatment' (*Lit Gaz*, 1435, 20 July 1844, 466). Large-scale versions were produced in marble, bronze and iron and the Art Union issued it as a small bronze statuette. Its success in the Westminster Hall exhibition eventually led to commissions for statues of two historic heroes for the Palace of Westminster, Viscount Falkland (**32**), and Sir Robert Walpole (**43**). *Dorothea*, a subject from Miguel de Cervantes' *Don Quixote*, was exhibited at the RA in 1839 and proved to be Bell's most popular work. The sculptor carved two marble versions, it was copied as a statuette in bronze and it was reproduced commercially in Parian ware.

He also worked as an industrial designer, collaborating with a number of metal-working and ceramics firms. He was closely associated with Felix Summerly's Art Manufactures, founded by Henry Cole in 1847 to promote higher standards in the decorative arts. Manufacturers, including Coalbrookdale, Minton and Doulton, executed works designed by Bell and examples were displayed at national and international exhibitions. Bell's novel designs for the Great Exhibition of 1851 included an 'Hours' clock, cast by Elkington; a matchbox in the form of a crusader's altar tomb reproduced in Parian by Minton and in ormolu by Dee and Fargues; a chess set for Minton; the 'Victoria Regia Cot' executed in papier-maché by Jennens and Bettridge; and a *Cerberus* doorstopper, manufactured by Stuart and Smith of Sheffield. His *Deerhound hall table* (**118**), cast in iron by the Coalbrookdale Company and exhibited at the Paris Exhibition of 1855, was an arresting and inventive composition featuring four large seated hounds supporting the table top. This was dismissed by Gunnis as a canine monstrosity when High Victorian ingenuity was at the nadir of its artistic reputation.

In 1842 Bell moved to Kensington, living first at 1 Marlborough Place and then in Douro Place, where he bought land in 1846 and built a house and studios. That year he married Eugenie, the only daughter of a wealthy artist, Robert Sullivan. They had one daughter. In 1846 Bell took on an apprentice, Charles Stoatt, who remained with him until the sculptor's death. In 1847 he was elected a member of the Society of Arts: he remained a member for 30 years and served on the Council on three separate occasions.

Bell's statues of enslaved female nudes enjoyed considerable success and can be linked to Hiram Powers's more famous works in this genre. *The Octoroon* (**39**), a mildly erotic standing figure, appropriate for private consumption, was purchased for Blackburn Town Hall and was also reproduced in bronze, iron and Parian. Another chained beauty, *Andromeda* (**31**), exhibited by Coalbrookdale at the Great Exhibition as an example of the firm's skill in bronze casting, was purchased by Queen Victoria for Prince Albert and mounted above a fountain at Osborne House.

Examples of many of Bell's most popular works were displayed at the Crystal Palace when it was re-erected at Sydenham in 1854. Bell also modelled four large statues for the building, *Australia*, *Birmingham*, *California* and *Sheffield* (**35**), cast in terracotta by **J M Blashfield**. *Australia* is said to have been the largest piece of sculpture fired in one piece at that time. Bell also designed several figures (**36, 37, 41**) and a fountain (**97**) for Blashfield.

Bell and the painter, Richard Redgrave, advised on the display of British sculpture at the Paris Exhibition of 1855. Several of Bell's statues, including a new work, *Omphale mocking Hercules* (**42**) were on show. This was the sculptor's first journey abroad and he visited the Louvre to see the classical sculpture.

He submitted two models for the Wellington Memorial competition in 1857 (**5**). Neither was chosen over the next two years and the sculptor wrote numerous articles on the subject of this notoriously badly managed commission. In 1859 he won his first public commission, the Crimean War Guards Memorial, Waterloo Place, London (**6**). It combines a group of three realistic guardsmen in bearskins and greatcoats and an allegorical figure of *Honour*, poised over them, clutching oak wreaths in her outstretched hands. The juxtaposition of ideal and naturalistic elements, which caused difficulties for many Victorian sculptors, was not successfully handled and the figure of *Honour* was ridiculed in the press as 'the quoits player'.

Bell proposed that a monument should be raised to commemorate Prince Albert and his role in the Great Exhibition and in 1858 he submitted a model in the form of an obelisk with symbolic figures at the corners of the base (**99**). The idea was not implemented until after the Prince Consort's death, when the Queen and her advisers chose a Gothic design by the architect George Gilbert Scott in preference to Bell's suggestion. He responded with a model for the central figure of the Prince, represented kneeling in the armour of a medieval knight (**58**). This too was rejected. The sculptor was responsible, however, for the group representing *America* (**64**), which won acclaim. *The Times* preferred it to the other groups of Continents carved by **John Henry Foley**, **William Theed II** and **Patrick MacDowell**, judging it 'the finest conception and composition of the four groups, and the boldest and most vigorous in every way' (*The Times*, 2 July 1872).

The late 1870s saw the emergence of 'The New Sculpture', developed by a generation of sculptors who sought to combine greater naturalism with a wide imaginative range and the use of new materials. In one respect Bell can be seen as a forerunner of the movement for, like the New Sculptors, he executed small-scale works for domestic interiors. But his generalised forms and bland style must have appeared outdated in the new context.

Bell retired in 1879, at the age of 68. He lived an increasingly secluded life at Douro Place, where he wrote poetry and carved a few statues, including a version of *Dorothea*, given as a wedding gift to his daughter Marguerita in 1881. A collection of 14 works from his studio was presented to Kensington Town Hall. Bell wrote a catalogue to this collection and was a regular contributor to *Building News* and other journals, for which he wrote articles that combined erudition and eccentricity, on such diverse topics as *The four primary sensations of the mind* (*JDM*, 1849) and *An Attempt towards the restoration of the Venus of Melos* (*Mag of Art*, 1894, 16–7). He died in his sleep on 14 March 1895 and was buried at Kensington cemetery, Hanwell, on the outskirts of London.

Many of his works were removed from their original site or destroyed during the next fifty years. At the time of his death two were on display at the South Kensington Museum, but within a few years *Babes in the wood* (**21**), one of his most popular works, loaned to the museum by the sculptor, was returned to the family and the iron version of *The Eagleslayer* was relegated to Bethnal Green Museum. When the Crystal Palace at Sydenham burned down in 1936 plaster versions of many of Bell's works were lost and during the Second World War the collection of sculpture at Kensington Town Hall and at Bell's former home and studio were destroyed by bombs. Gunnis was critical of much of Bell's work, writing of his groups exhibited at the Royal Academy 'They were much admired at the time and are typical of the work which has brought the sculpture of the late Victorian era [sic] so deservedly into disrepute' (*Gunnis* 1968, 49). As with his contemporaries, **Joseph Durham, William Theed** and **Henry Weekes**, Bell has not been rehabilitated as a sculptor, though he does enjoy some respect for his contribution to industrial design.

EH

Literary References: *AU*, 1842, 128; *AJ*, 1861, 30, 158; *Mag of Art*, 1894, 16–7; *The Times*, 28 March 1895, 10; *Athenaeum*, April 6 1895, 449; *DNB Suppl* I, 1901, 165–6; *Gunnis* 1968, 48–9; *Physick* 1970, 46 n5, 156–7; *Lawley* 1980, 18–21; *Bayley* 1982, *passim*; *Read* 1982, *passim*; *Avery and Marsh* 1985, 237–38; *Grove* 3, 1996, 629 (Stocker); *Barnes* 1999 (with comprehensive list of Bell's publications); *ODNB* (Dodgson rev. Edwards)

Additional MS Sources: *Bell/Gosse*; *Bell/Holland*; *Bell/Lubbock*; *Bell/Soden-Smith*; *Biography Handbook Papers*, 1860, Add MSS 28509 fol 131; *Layard Papers*, 1866–9, BM Add MSS 38992–7, 58166 fol 68, 58223 fols 8, 10; *Sherborn Autographs*, 1846, Add MSS 42575 fol 47

Will: PPR, probate, 26 April 1895, effects £220 14s 2d

Portraits of the Sculptor: Rachel Bird (née Glover), paper silhouette of John Bell and family on the beach, 1838 (*Barnes* 1999, repr1); photograph, 1867, family coll (*Barnes* 1999, repr 64); photograph, *c*1888, family coll (*Barnes* 1999, pl 91); engraving, from a photograph by W H Grove (*Mag of Art*, 1894, 16).

Funerary Monuments

No.	Date	Subject		Location		References
1.	1839	Admiral Lord Nelson, model		[Royal Naval College, Greenwich]; untraced		*Barnes*, 1999, 22–23
2.	1845	Thomas, 1st Earl of Leicester (†1842), design only (monument by John Henning II)		[Exhib BI, London, 511]; untraced		*Graves* 1875, 40; *Barnes* 1999, 28
3.	1847	Mrs Legard		[Exhib RA, London, 1341]; untraced		*Graves* I, 1905–6, 174
4.	1854–1857	Arthur, 1st Duke of Wellington Model(s): exhib RA, London, 1855, 1430 (small model of Wellington); RA, London, 1856, 1253 (War); RA, London, 1856, 1259 (Peace); Crystal Palace, Sydenham, London, 1856f (Peace and War)		Guildhall, City of London, great hall	SD	*Graves* I, 1905–6, 174; *Knight* 1986, 331 (repr); *Barnes* 1999, 47, 51, 53, 156–58 (repr); *Ward-Jackson* 2003, 177–81 (repr)
5.	1857	Arthur, 1st Duke of Wellington, for Westminster Abbey, two designs (monument by Alfred Stevens)		[Exhib Westminster Hall, London]; untraced		*Physick* 1970, 46 n5, 156–7
6.	1860	Crimean War Guards Memorial	b	Waterloo Place, London		*Graves* I, 1905–6, 174; *Read* 1982, 13 (repr); *Barnes* 1999, 54–5, 160–3 (repr)
7.	1861	James Montgomery Payment(s): £1,000 Model(s): formerly at Cutlers' Hall, Sheffield	b	[Sheffield Cemetery, W R Yorks]; Sheffield Cathedral precinct, W R Yorks		*Barnes* 1999, 63–4, 140 (repr)
8.	*c*1861	Sir William Reid, obelisk		Bermuda		*Barnes* 1999, 61
9.	1868	John Crome (†1821)		St George, Norwich, Norfolk	S	*Barnes* 1999, 185 (repr)
10.	†1871	Theodosia, Lady Waveney		Flixton, Suffolk		*Barnes* 1999, 74, 186–87 (repr)
11.	†1875	John Sinclair, Vicar of Kensington		St Mary Abbotts, Kensington, London	S	

Statues

No.	Date	Subject		Location		References
12.	1833	The quarterstaff player		[Exhib Soc of BA, London, 834]; untraced		*Johnson* 1975, 36
13.	1835	Ariel		[Exhib Soc of BA, London, 800]; untraced		*Johnson* 1975, 36
14.	1837	Infant Hercules strangling the snakes		[Exhib RA, London, 1197]; untraced		*Graves* I, 1905–6, 174
15.	1838	David	b	Ironbridge Gorge Museum, Coalbrookdale, Salop		*Graves* I, 1905–6, 174; *Johnson* 1975, 36; *Barnes* 1999, 6, 20, 43
16.	1839	Dorothea	m	Bowood, Wilts Other versions: several recorded, in marble, bronze, Parian ware and terracotta		*Graves* 1875, 40; *Graves* I, 1905–6, 174; *Johnson* 1975, 36, 37; *Barnes* 1999, *passim* (repr)
17.	1840	Child's play, 'model of a group'		[Exhib Soc of BA, London, 728]; untraced Other versions: copied in Parian ware		*Johnson* 1975, 36; *Barnes* 1999, 6, 24
18.	1841	Queen Victoria, statuette		[Exhib RA, London, 1242]; untraced		*Graves* I, 1905–6, 174; *Ormond* 1973, 483; *Johnson* 1975, 36; *Barnes* 1999, 6, 26
19.	1841	The Eagleslayer (The Eagle Shooter, The Archer)	m	[Wentworth Woodhouse, W R Yorks]; Tanenbaum coll, Christie NY, 26 May 1994; private coll Other versions: several recorded, including one in iron, VAM A.28-1959	S	*Graves* I, 1905–6, 174; *Johnson* 1975, 36; *Read* 1982, 27, 29, 83, 208, 289 (repr); *Grove* 3, 1996, 629; *Barnes* 1999, *passim* (repr); *Bilbey* 2002, 194–6 (repr)
20.	1841	The wounded Clorinda		[Exhib RA, London, 1240]; untraced Other versions: copied in Parian ware by Minton		*Graves* I, 1905–6, 174; *Barnes* 1999, 24, 135 (repr)
21.	1842	Babes in the wood	m	[VAM, London, *c*1881–1895]; Castle Museum, Norwich, Norfolk Other versions: copied in Parian ware by Minton, eg Osborne House, I of W		*Graves* I, 1905–6, 174; *Barnes* 1999, *passim* (repr)
22.	1842	Eve the bride, sketch		[Exhib RA, London, 1274]; untraced		*AU*, 1842, 127–8
23.	1843	A sleeping infant		[Exhib RA, London, 1407]; untraced		*Graves* I, 1905–6, 174

24.	1844	Jane Shore		[Exhib Westminster Hall, London, 134]; untraced		*Lit Gaz*, 1435, 20 July 1844, 466; *Read* 1982, 27; *Barnes* 1999, 6, 27, 47
25.	1845	The child's attitude	m	Royal Coll		*AU*, 1846, 189; *Graves* I, 1905–6, 174; *Barnes* 1999, 6, 29
26.	1845	William Shakespeare	p	[Exhib Westminster Hall, London, 127]; untraced Other versions: several recorded in bronze and Parian ware		*Westminster* 1845, 15; *AU*, 1845, 258; *Barnes* 1999, 6, 27, 28, 45, 47
27.	1847	Una and the lion	m	[Gt Exhib, London, 1851]; destroyed Other versions: copied in parian ware by Minton (eg at VAM and Osborne House, I of W)		*AJ Cat* 1851, 325 (repr); *Barnes* 1999, 32–3, 16, 45, 47, 117 (repr); *Victorian Nude* 2001, 72 (repr); *JKB* 2006, 197 (Crystal Palace cast)
28.	1850	Cupid indignant, statuette		Untraced Other versions: several recorded in Parian ware by Minton (including an example at Osborne), and in iron by Coalbrookdale		*Barnes* 1999, 43, 110 (repr)
29.	1850	Miranda	m	Private coll Other versions: copied in Parian ware by Minton		*Barnes* 1999, 43, 134 (repr)
30.	1850	Queen Victoria and Albert, the Prince Consort, statuettes (cast in bronze and ormolu by Dee and Fargues)	b	[Gt Exhib, London, 1851]; untraced		*Barnes* 1999, 6, 45
31.	1851	Andromeda (for a fountain designed by L Grüner) Payment(s): £300	b	Royal Coll, Osborne House, I of W, RCIN 41823 Other versions: Ironbridge Gorge Museum		*AJ Cat* 1851, 225 (repr); *Read* 1982, 29, 199–200 (repr); *Barnes* 1999, 6, 41–2, 46, 47, 122–25 (repr)
32.	1848–1852	Lucius, 2nd Viscount Falkland Model(s): Gt Exhib, 1851	m	Palace of Westminster, London, St Stephen's Hall	S	*Walker* 1961, 25, cat 27; *Read* 1982, 84, 164 (repr)
33.	1853	Eve	m	[coll Lord Truro]; untraced Other versions: VAM 4332-1854, *c*1853, bronze statuette		*Barnes* 1999, 44, 136 (repr); *Bilbey* 2002, 196–7 (repr)
34.	1853	The maid of Saragossa	p	[Exhib RA, London, 1307]; destroyed		*ILN*, 2 July 1853, 533; *Graves* I, 1905–6, 174; *Barnes* 1999, 47, 133 (repr)
35.	1854	California, Australia, Birmingham and Sheffield		[Crystal Palace, Sydenham, London, terrace]; destroyed		*Barnes* 1999, 47–8
36.	1854	Diana (cast by J M Blashfield)		Untraced		*Barnes* 1999, 6, 48
37.	1854	Erin (cast by Blashfield)		[Exhib RA, London, 1382]; untraced		*ILN*, 14 March 1857, 241; *Graves* I, 1905–6, 174; *Barnes* 1999, 48
38.	1854	Queen Margaret, statuette	b	sold Sworder & Co, Essex, 1998; private coll		*Barnes* 1999, 45, 132 (repr)
39.	1854	The Octoroon	m	Blackburn Town Hall, Lancs Other versions: copied in bronze and iron by Coalbrookdale and in Parian ware by Minton		*Graves* I, 1905–6, 174; *Barnes* 1999, 49, 153 (repr)
40.	1855	Armed Science Model(s): exhib RA, London, 1855, 1420	m	Artillery Officers' Mess, Woolwich, London Other versions: several recorded in terracotta bronze statuette cast by Coalbrookdale		*Graves* I, 1905–6, 174; *Barnes* 1999, *passim* (repr)
41.	1855	Hibernia (cast by Blashfield)	tc	Untraced		*Barnes* 1999, 48
42.	1855	Omphale mocking Hercules	m	[Paris Exhib]; destroyed		*Gunnis* 1968, 49; *Barnes* 1999, 6, 51
43.	1845–1855	Sir Robert Walpole, 1st Earl of Orford Payment(s): £5,000 Model(s): exhib RA, London, 1854, 1378	m	Palace of Westminster, London, St Stephen's Hall	S	*Walker* 1961, 48, cat 53; *Barnes* 1999, 27, 178 (repr)
44.	1856	Angelica, from Ariosto, model		[Exhib RA, London, 1232]; untraced		*Graves* I, 1905–6, 174; *Barnes* 1999, 53
45.	*c*1856	King Charles II	p	[Crystal Palace, Sydenham]; destroyed		*Barnes* 1999, 6, 45, 47
46.	1856	Lalage	m	Wentworth Woodhouse, W R Yorks Other versions: copied in Parian ware, eg National Gallery of Victoria, NSW (D313/1977)		*Graves* I, 1905–6, 174; *Edwards* 1978, 74–5; *Read* 1982, 129, 132; *Barnes* 1999, 6, 53, 64, 86
47.	*c*1858	'The Indian Mutiny Quelled 1858', a lion crushing a serpent under its claws, model only		Untraced		*Barnes* 1999, 55; C Lib (repr)
48.	1859	The star of Bethlehem		[Exhib RA, London, 1260]; untraced Other versions: others recorded in marble and Parian ware		*Graves* I, 1905–6, 174; *Johnson* 1975, 36; *Barnes* 1999, 7, 56, 68–9
49.	1859	Winged Leonine Andro Sphinx, model	p	Untraced		*Barnes* 1999, 7, 56, 60, 166 (repr)
50.	1860	9th statue, 'Arabian Nights', model		[Exhib RA, London, 1007]; untraced		*Graves* I, 1905–6, 174
51.	1861	Ceres (executed by Coalbrookdale)	ir	Untraced Other versions: copied in bronze		*Barnes* 1999, 63, 145 (repr)
52.	1861	Oliver Cromwell	ir	Bridge Street, Warrington, Lancs		*Barnes* 1999, 61–2, 65, 139, 141 (repr)

53.	1861	Temperance	ir	Untraced	*Barnes* 1999, 7, 63, 138 (repr)
54.	1861	Victory (Crimean War Artillery Memorial)	b	Woolwich Arsenal, London	*Barnes* 1999, 58, 159 (repr)
55.	1853–1862	A daughter of Eve (The American slave)	b	[coll Lord Hertford]; Cragside, Northumbs Other versions: several recorded in bronze and Parian, reduced size	*Graves* I, 1905–6, 174; *Barnes* 1999, 49, 64, 86, 137 (repr); *Wenley* 2004, 82 (repr)
56.	1862	Fame (four statues incorporated into Coalbrookdale gates)	ir	Warrington, Lancs, park gates	*Barnes* 1999, 62, 142–43 (repr)
57.	1862	Sir Francis Chantrey	p	[Int Exhib]; Norton, Sheffield, W R Yorks	*Barnes* 1999, 65–6, 184 (repr)
58.	1863	Albert the Good, for Albert Memorial, design only (statue by John Henry Foley)	p	Untraced	*Barnes* 1999, 66, 87, 177 (repr)
59.	1866	The Archfiend, statuette Payment(s): £157 10s	b	[Exhib Soc of BA, London, 1090]; untraced	*Johnson* 1975, 36; *Barnes* 1999, 70
60.	1868	The last kiss		[Exhib RA, London, 1042; Phillips 4 June 1883]; private coll Other versions: copied in Parian ware	*Graves* I, 1905–6, 174; *Barnes* 1999, 7, 69
61.	1869	Imogen	m	[coll Lord Coleridge]; untraced Other versions: copied in Parian ware by Minton	*Graves* I, 1905–6, 174; *Gunnis* 1968, 49; *Barnes* 1999, 69, 152 (repr)
62.	1871	The dove's refuge	m	[Exhib RA, London, 1304; Phillips, 4 June 1883]; private coll	*Graves* I, 1905–6, 174; *Barnes* 1999, 7, 69, 91, 180 (repr)
63.	1871	The five doves	m	Private coll	*Barnes* 1999, 7, 69, 180 (repr)
64.	1864–1872	America	m	Albert Memorial, Kensington Gardens, London	*Bayley* 1981, *passim* (repr); *Read* 1982, 99–100 (repr); *Barnes* 1999, 67–8, 70–1, 74–7, 168–76 (repr)
65.	1874	George, 4th Earl Clarendon	m	Foreign and Commonwealth Office, London	*Barnes* 1999, 77, 87, 179 (repr)
66.	1875	Cursetjee Manockjee, on a column with water fountain and iron naiads at base	b	Mumbai (Bombay), India (beside Byculla flyover)	*Gunnis* 1968, 49; *Barnes* 1999, 7, 78
67.	1875	Samson guarding Israel	tc	Untraced	*Barnes* 1999, 7, 77
68.	1876	Peace contemplating the map of the world, model (intended for Foreign Office, London, main hall)	tc	[Exhib RA, London, 1347]; destroyed	*Graves* I, 1905–6, 175; *Barnes* 1999, 77, 86
69.	1877	Peace and the soldier's return Payment(s): 300 gns	m	[Guildhall, City of London]; destroyed	*Barnes* 1999, 7, 78
70.	1878	Christ	tc	Untraced	*Barnes* 1999, 7
71.	1884	Unity of empire	tc	Untraced	*Barnes* 1999, 86, 188 (plaster repr)
72.	nd	The Abyssinian slave, statuette	b	Sotheby 9 Dec 2000; private coll Other versions: copied in Parian ware by Minton	*Barnes* 1999, 6, 44–5, 152 (repr)

Busts

73.	1833	Unidentified gentleman		[Exhib RA, London, 1119]; untraced		*Graves* I, 1905–6, 174
74.	1833	Unidentified sitter, model		[Soc of A, silver medal]; untraced		*Barnes* 1999, 14
75.	1837	Amoret (chastity in distress)		[Exhib BI, London, 446]; untraced		*Graves* 1875, 40; *Graves* I, 1905–6, 174
76.	1837	Psyche		[Exhib BI, London, 441]; untraced		*Graves* 1875, 40
77.	1837	Young Hercules		[Exhib BI, London, 444]; untraced		*Graves* 1875, 40
78.	1842	Two unidentified gentlemen		[Exhib Soc of BA, London 802, 303]; untraced		*Johnson* 1975, 36
79.	1848	Sir Thomas Fowell Buxton Bt	m	Freetown Cathedral, Sierra Leone		*Graves* 1, 1905–6, 174; *Ormond* 1973, 83
80.	1858	Sir Robert Walpole	m	[Exhib RA, London, 1301]; Eton College, Windsor, Berks		*Gunnis* 1968, 49
81.	1859	Raphael		Untraced		*Barnes* 1999, 6, 43
82.	1864	Angelica Payment(s): £31 10s	m	[Exhib Soc of BA, London, 1048]; untraced		*Johnson* 1975, 36
83.	1864	Dorothea Payment(s): £31 10s	m	[Exhib Soc of BA, London, 1049]; untraced Other versions: reproduced in Parian ware		*Johnson* 1975, 36; *Barnes* 1999, 43, 68–9
84.	1864	William Shakespeare		[Exhib Soc of BA, London, 1056]; untraced		*Johnson* 1975, 36
85.	1866	Dr William Clark	m	[Anatomical Museum, Cambridge]; untraced		*Gunnis* 1968, 49; *Barnes* 1999, 7, 70
86.	1867	Dr Hugh Falconer	m	Unidentified hospital, Chennai (Madras), India		*Barnes* 1999, 7, 70
87.	1867	Mr Cooper	m	Cambridge Town Hall		*Barnes* 1999, 7, 70 *Graves* I, 1905–6, 175; *Gunnis* 1968, 49
88.	1877	George, Lord Byron	tc	[Exhib RA, London, 1503]; untraced		
89.	by 1883	My Lady Fern		[Philips, 4 June 1883]; untraced		GPC
90.	by 1883	Spirit of sweet dreams		[Philips, 4 June 1883]; untraced		GPC
91.	nd	Earl Fitzwilliam (after Nollekens)		Wentworth Woodhouse, W R Yorks		GPC
92.	nd	Sir George Melleish		Untraced		*Barnes* 1999, 87
93.	nd	Unidentified man	i	Sotheby, 6 April 1995; untraced	S	GPC

Architectural Sculpture

94.	1842	Scientia and Industria, reliefs	s	Guild Hall, Derby, exterior	Pevsner, *Derbys*, 1978, 174; *Barnes* 1999, 26, 120 (repr)
95.	1843	Commerce and Agriculture	s	Corn Exchange, Newark, Notts, tower	*ILN*, 3 Feb 1849, 69; Pevsner, *Notts*, 1979, 191
96.	1851	Cupid and swan fountain	b	[Gt Exhib, London]; Ironbridge Gorge Museum, Coalbrookdale, Salop	*Barnes* 1999, 42, 45, 126–28 (repr)

97.	1854	Triton fountain	tc	Old Radcliffe Infirmary, Oxford	*Barnes* 1999, 48, 130 (repr)
98.	1858	Heads of animals	ir	[Metropolitan Cattle Market, Pentonville, London]; untraced	*Gunnis* 1968, 49; *Barnes* 1999, 63
99.	1858	Proposal for a memorial to Albert, the Prince Consort, obelisk, model		Untraced	*Barnes* 1999, 55–6, 167 (repr)
100.	1861	Samuel Gurney commemorative obelisk		Stratford Broadway, Newham, London	Pevsner, *Essex*, 1965, 374; *Barnes* 1999, 61
101.	1863	Your good health, fountain Payment(s): £105	m	[Kew Gardens, London, main entrance niche]; Castle Museum, Norwich	*Johnson* 1975, 36; *Barnes* 1999, 70, 181 (repr)
102.	1870	Cross, model		[Exhib RA, London, 1043]; untraced	*Graves* I, 1905–6, 174
Reliefs					
103.	c1850	Dorothea, medallion	m	Cecil Higgins Art Gallery, Bedford	*Graves* I, 1905–6, 174
104.	1864	The cross of prayer	tc	[Exhib RA, London, 983]; untraced	*Graves* I, 1905–6, 174; *Barnes* 1999, 68, 114 (repr)
105.	1864	William Shakespeare, tricentenary medallion	p	Untraced	*Barnes* 1999, 7, 68
Miscellaneous					
106.	1832	'When the wicked man . . .', a religious group		[Exhib RA, London, 1227]; untraced	*Graves* I, 1905–6, 174
107.	1833	A girl at a brook		[Exhib RA, London, 1114]; untraced	*Graves* I, 1905–6, 174
108.	1833	A young John the Baptist		[Exhib RA, London, 1225]; untraced	*Graves* I, 1905–6, 174
109.	1834	Psyche borne by the Zephrys		[Exhib RA, London, 1045]; untraced	*Graves* I, 1905–6, 174
110.	1835	Sketch	tc	[Exhib RA, London, 1098]; untraced	*Graves* I, 1905–6, 174
111.	1836	Psyche feeding a swan		[Exhib RA, London, 1085]; untraced	*Graves* I, 1905–6, 174
112.	1836	Youth, spring and infancy		[Exhib RA, London, 1153]; untraced	*Graves* I, 1905–6, 174
113.	1837	A praying boy		[Exhib Soc of BA, London, 599]; untraced	*Johnson* 1975, 36
114.	1837	Psyche and the dove		[Exhib RA, London, 1173]; untraced	*Graves* I, 1905–6, 174
115.	1838	The dreamer		[Exhib RA, London, 1285]; untraced	*Graves* I, 1905–6, 174
116.	1840	Madonna and child		[Exhib RA, London, 1082]; untraced	*Graves* I, 1905–6, 174
117.	1840	Mother and child		[Exhib RA, London, 1124]; untraced	*Graves* I, 1905–6, 174
118.	1855	Deerhound hall table, design (cast by Coalbrookdale)	ir	[Paris Exhibition, 1855]; Ironbridge Gorge Museum, Coalbrookdale, Salop	*Barnes* 1999, 50–1, 144, 146 (repr)
119.	1857	The descent of Pandora		[Exhib RA, London, 1224]; untraced	*Graves* I, 1905–6, 174
120.	1858	Sir Isaac Newton		[Exhib RA, London, 1223]; untraced	*Graves* I, 1905–6, 174; *Johnson* 1975, 36
121.	1858	The Farnesina		[Exhib RA, London, 1177]; untraced	*Graves* I, 1905–6, 174
122.	1862	Africa, America, Asia and Europe, lampstands (cast by Coalbrookdale)	ir	Ironbridge Gorge Museum, Coalbrookdale, Salop (Africa and Asia only)	*Barnes* 1999, 63, 148, 149, 183 (repr)
123.	1864	A partridge (The first of September) Payment(s): £10 10s	m	[Exhib Soc of BA, London, 1050]; untraced	*Graves* I, 1905–6, 174; *Johnson* 1975, 36; *Barnes* 1999, 7, 68–9
124.	1865	Cherub with primroses	m	[Exhib RA, London, 969]; untraced	*Graves* I, 1905–6, 174; *Barnes* 1999, 69
125.	1865	Dream of the wild waves Payment(s): 80 gns	m	[Exhib Soc of BA, London, 1030]; untraced	*Johnson* 1975, 36; *Barnes* 1999, 7, 70
126.	1866	The foot of the cross		[Exhib RA, London, 1006]; untraced	*Graves* I, 1905–6, 174; *Barnes* 1999, 70
127.	1874	Wellington and victories		[Exhib RA, London, 1588]; untraced	*Graves* I, 1905–6, 174
128.	1875	Hypnos	tc	[Exhib RA, London, 1364]; untraced	*Graves* I, 1905–6, 174; *Barnes* 1999, 77
129.	1875	The friend of the family		[Exhib RA, London, 1354]; untraced	*Graves* I, 1905–6, 174
130.	1875	The struggle of good and evil		[Exhib RA, London, 1240]; untraced	*Graves* I, 1905–6, 174
131.	1876	The heart that bled for all mankind	tc	[Exhib RA, London, 1478]; untraced	*Graves* I, 1905–6, 175
132.	1877	Herod stricken on his throne	tc	[Exhib RA, London, 1499]; untraced	*Graves* I, 1905–6, 175
133.	1877	On the sea shore		[Exhib RA, London, 1473]; untraced	*Graves* I, 1905–6, 175
134.	1879	Lost paradise, fragment	tc	[Exhib RA, London, 1544]; untraced	*Graves* I, 1905–6, 175
135.	1890	Pandora brought to Epimetheus	tc	Untraced	*Barnes* 1999, 7, 88

BELL, Lady Maria 1755–1825

Maria Hamilton was born in Chelsea on 26 December 1755 and baptized at St Martin-in-the-Fields, Westminster, the daughter of William Hamilton, an architect of Scottish descent, and his wife Sarah. She studied painting under her brother, William Hamilton RA, and Sir Joshua Reynolds, many of whose works she copied. These copies, which were principally portraits of celebrated ladies, were much admired by the *Gentleman's Magazine*, which considered them 'the more valuable because they retain their fine colouring of which time has deprived the originals' (*GM*, 1825, i, 570). She also copied the works of Rubens at Carlton House. She exhibited at the British Institution in 1807 and 1809 and at the Royal Academy between 1816 and 1820, showing mainly pictures. About 1808 she married Thomas Bell, sheriff of Middlesex, who was knighted in 1816. Her 1819 RA exhibits included a portrait bust of her husband and another of a Miss Bell, who may have been her daughter (1, 2). She died in London at her home, 47 Dean Street, Soho, on 9 March 1825.

Literary References: *Gunnis* 1968, 49–50; *ODNB* (Peach)

Portraits of the Sculptor: G Clint, mezzotint (after self-portrait by M Bell), BM; E Scriven, stipple, published 1821 (after miniature by W S Lethbridge), NPG; W S Lethbridge, miniature (untraced)

Busts

1.	1819	Miss Bell	[Exhib RA, London, 1213]; untraced	*Graves* I, 1905–6, 175
2.	1819	Sir Thomas Bell	[Exhib RA, London, 1213]; untraced	*Graves* I, 1905–6, 175

BELL, R fl 1746

His monument to Samuel Walford has a curved pediment, and a skull with bats' wings at the base.

Literary References: *Gunnis* 1968, 50

Funerary Monuments

1.	1746	Samuel Walford	Stratford-upon-Avon, Warks	S	*Gunnis* 1968, 50

BELLAMY, Thomas fl 1714–54

The son of Richard Bellamy, a tailor of St Botolph's, Aldgate, he was apprenticed to James Paget (or Padgett) on 12 March 1714 and became free of the Masons' Company on 30 June 1721. He signed two large architectural monuments (**1, 2**). He was employed at the house of James West in Lincoln's Inn Fields in 1753 (Archives, West of Alscot Park, cited by *Gunnis* 1968, 50). In March 1754 Bellamy, whose workshop was in Camberwell, wrote to the Masons' Company asking to be allowed to resign from the post of Assistant to the Court, as being 'oblig'd on account of my Health, to live in the country'. His request was granted.

Literary References: *Gunnis* 1968, 50

Archival References: Masons' Co, Court Book, 1751–96 (28 March 1754); Freemen, fol 5 (30 June 1721)

Funerary Monuments

1.	†1733	Sir Thomas Halton		Long Stanton, Cambs	S	*Gunnis* 1968, 50
2.	†1746	Sir Henry Fetherston Bt		Stanford-le-Hope, Essex	S	*Gunnis* 1968, 50

BENAGLIA, Francesco 1787–1846

William, 6th Duke of Devonshire went to Rome shortly after **Canova** died in 1822. He ordered copies of Canova's famous lions on the Rezzonico monument in St Peter's from **Rinaldo Rinaldi** and Benaglia. They were completed and set up at Chatsworth ten years later as a 'monument' to Canova, with a bust of Canova by **Thomas Campbell** and a copy of a self-portrait bust of Canova made by Rinaldi, in niches above them.

Literary References: *JKB* 1972 (3), 327

Statues

1.	1823	Sleeping lions, after Canova (co-sculptor: Rinaldo Rinaldi) Payment(s): 1,100 scudi	m	Chatsworth, Derbys, sculpture gallery		*Chatsworth Handlist*, 27; *JKB* 1972 (3), 327, 330, 331

BENET, Thomas c1800–

Benet, 'Of Christ Parish', was apprenticed to **John Fisher II** of York for a term of seven years on 22 January 1814, without premium.

Archival References: York App Rec D15, 283

BENNETT, James and Son, of Birmingham fl 1835–54

Funerary Monuments

1.	†1835	Ann Fereday		Sedgley, Staffs	S	
2.	†1838	Elizabeth Smith		Sedgley, Staffs	S	
3.	†1854	Hannah Swann		Stourbridge Presbyterian (Unitarian) Chapel, Worcs	S	

BENNETT, of Soho –1770

The stone and brass sundial bearing the Herbert coat of arms in the Fountain Garden at Powis Castle is signed 'Bennett of Crown Court, Soho, London' (**1**).

Miscellaneous

1.	nd	Sundial with Herbert coat of arms	s	Powis Castle, fountain garden	S	

BENNETT, T, of Frampton fl 1827–56

Funerary Monuments

1.	†1827	Daniel Palmer		Moreton Valence, Glos	S	Pevsner, *Glos: Vale & Forest of Dean*, 1976, 302
2.	†1856	Jasper Hawkins		Whitminster, Glos	S	Pevsner, *Glos: Vale & Forest of Dean*, 1976, 403

BENNETT, Thomas, of York –1831

Bennett worked in partnership with **John Flintoft** in the early-19th century. An advertisement for 'Bennett and Flintoft, Sculptors and Masons' appeared in the *York Courant* on 13 January 1812 and they signed two monuments together (**1, 2**). The sculptor may also have been responsible for a tablet to an unknown subject at Kirkby Moorside, N R Yorks, dated 1826 and signed 'Bennet' (Pevsner, *Yorks: N R*, 1966, 215). He married Hannah Watson of York in 1815 (*York Courant*, 20 November 1815) and her death was recorded in the *York Gazette* on 29 November 1828. Bennett's own death was announced in the same newspaper on 1 October 1831, where he was described as 'sculptor, of St. Andrewgate'.

Archival References: GPC

Funerary Monuments

1.	?1815	Mary Fothergill (co-sculptor: John Flintoft, of York)		Pickering, N R Yorks	S	
2.	†1820	John Dawker (†1816) and wife (co-sculptor: John Flintoft, of York)		Salton, N R Yorks	S	Pevsner, *Yorks: N R*, 1966, 317

BENNIER (or BESNIER), John fl 1681

On 23 December 1681 John Bennier agreed to cast 'in hard metle or hardened leads' (statues) at £40 each, of 'Diana, the Sabine Woman, Hercules, Commodus, and Antoninus, which shall be in full proportion of posture, dimensions, and full as large as those figures so called now standing and being in his Majesties privie garden, upon which figures hee . . . will make and take off his moulds for the more exact casting of the aforesaid figures'. The contract stated that he should 'cast upon the privie partes of the last mentioned figures . . . a piece of drapery or other ornament' and wait until these modifications had been approved by the Duke and Duchess before casting these last two statues. He also agreed to make sixteen smaller statues, measuring two and a half feet in height, in the same material, for which he would receive £5 each (**1**).

Literary References: *RCHM* 1879, pt II, 752; *Gunnis* 1968, 50

Statues

1.	1681	Four large, sixteen small		[coll Duke of Ormonde]; untraced		*Gunnis* 1968, 50

BENNIER (or BESNIER), Peter –1693

A French sculptor and the brother of Isaac Besnier, who had collaborated with Hubert le Sueur on the monument to George Villiers, 1st Duke of Buckingham, erected in Westminster Abbey in 1634. Peter Bennier may have been trained in France but was living in England before October 1643, when he was appointed sculptor to King Charles I. He was required to look after the 'Moulds, Statues and Modells' in the Royal collection, a duty previously performed by his brother, in return for the use of a house and £50 pa from the privy purse. The Civil War prevented him from taking up his duties and he was deprived of his office during the Commonwealth. At the Restoration he petitioned to be reinstated on the grounds that the late King had granted him the 'place of sculptor to His Majesty and the custody of his statues, etc, but by reason of the most unhappy distraction befallen since, hee injoyed not the same place, but was reduced into very great poverty and want through his faithfulness and constancy' (TNA SP 29/2, no 66-1, quotedby *Faber* 1926, 14). His request was granted on 15 March 1661 (TNA, LC3/25, 113, cited by *Gibson* 1997 (1), 163) and he held the post until his death, when he was succeeded by **Caius Gabriel Cibber**.

Bennier is listed as a ratepayer of Covent Garden, 1649–51, and among the Ashburnham Papers is a reference to a tenement occupied by Bennier near Common Street in 1664 (LMA, ACC/0524/045,046,047,048, cited by *Gibson* 1997 (1), 163). It has been tentatively suggested that he worked for Hubert le Sueur. He signed the monument with a 'noble' portrait-bust to Sir Richard Shuckburgh (1) (*Gunnis* 1968, 50). The monument to Sir Hatton Fermor at Easton Neston, Northants, has been attributed to him because the bust is similar to the Shuckburgh one and the two families intermarried. In 1655 Bennier was employed at Lamport Hall, Northants, carving shields and 'pictures', which were probably statues (Northants RO, IL 3956, cited by *White* 1999, 11, 12 n 10–11) (2). He also did unspecified work for the crown at Somerset House in 1661–2.

Literary References: *Gunnis* 1968, 50; *Colvin* V, 1973–6, 255; *Whinney* 1988, 90, 93, 439 n 16, n 21, 440 n 2–3; *McEvansoneya* 1993, 532–5; *Grove* 3, 1996, 875 (Physick); *White* 1999, 11–12

Funerary Monuments

1.	†1656	Sir Richard Shuckburgh	Upper Shuckburgh, Warks	S	*McEvansoneya* 1993, 533, 534 (repr); *White* 1999, 11

Architectural Sculpture

2.	1655	Shields and 'pictures'	Lamport Hall, Northants		*White* 1999, 11, 12, nn 10, 11

BENNIER (or BESNIER), Thomas c. 1663–1693

Vertue writes that Bennier reputedly cast the bronze statue of James II by **Grinling Gibbons** in Trafalgar Square. He describes Bennier as 'a curious ingenious Statuary. Born in England of French parents, his works in small in Marble from the Life, or modells are very fine. The anatomy figure commonly seen at apothecarys was from his Original model many other things are in the hands of the Curious of his doing. He was much imployed by Mr. Salmon for the wax work figures shown in Town. He us'd to cutt in Marble from the Life a Portrait for 2 guineas. Being industrious & young & very quick at his work. He *livd & died* near fleet ditch aged about 30 ano 1693' (*Vertue* I, 89). It seems likely that he was related to Isaac Besnier, who is known to have worked with Hubert Le Sueur. He was buried at St Ann's, Blackfriars, on 18 September 1693.

Literary References: *Vertue* I, 89; *Gunnis* 1968, 50; *Pyke* 1973, 13; *Whinney* 1988, 443 n.41; *Baker* 2000, 86

BENNISON, Appleton, of Kingston-upon-Hull *c*1750–1830

Bennison was a mason and architect with a yard in Mytongate, Hull. In 1801 he advertised in the *Hull Advertiser*, 'Plans and Elevations drawn at shortest notice; Marble Chimney Pieces and Monuments executed in the neatest manner'. He worked principally in the East Riding of Yorkshire. From 1792 to 1820 he was engaged on works in Bridlington Harbour and in 1804–5 he rebuilt the bridge over the River Hull at Tickton designed by William Chapman. In 1800 he contracted to build the Register Office at Beverley and in 1804–14 he erected the court house and gaol there to the designs of Charles Watson. He prepared designs himself for rebuilding Routh rectory in 1815 (Bothwick Institute, York, MGA 1815/4) and designed the Zion congregational chapel at Cottingham in 1819. He refitted the interior of St Augustine, Skirlaugh in the same year and rebuilt the nave of All Saints, Bishop Burton in 1820–1. He may also have carried out building work at All Saints, Northallerton in the North Riding. He died on 25 March 1830 aged 80 (*GM*, 1830, i, 381).

Literary References: *Gunnis* 1968, 50; *Colvin* 1995, 121

Funerary Monuments

1.	†1808	Sir James Pennyman Bt	Stainton, N R Yorks	S	Pevsner, *Yorks, N R* 1966, 354
2.	?1819	Henry Legard	Kirk Ella, E R Yorks	S	*Gunnis* 1968, 50
3.	1821	William Williamson	Kirk Ella, E R Yorks	S	*Gunnis* 1968, 50

BENOIST, Antoine 1632–1717

For information the reader is referred to *Pyke* 1973, 13.

BENSON, Richard fl 1763

In 1763 he won a 3 guinea premium from the Society of Arts. Perhaps identifiable with **Richard Banson**, who won a Society of Arts premium in 1765.

Literary References: *Dossie* 1782, 435

Miscellaneous

1.	1763	Ornamental group of wax flowers	[Soc of A, premium, 3 gns]; untraced	*Dossie* 1782, 436

BENZONI, Giovanni Maria 1809–73

An Italian sculptor who worked for a time as an assistant to **John Hogan** in Rome. He exhibited marble groups of *Fidelity* and *Gratitude* at the Great Exhibition of 1851 and in the same year, during a visit to London, worked on at least twenty-five commissions for British clients. He attracted considerable British and American patronage during the second half of the nineteenth century and examples of his sculpture were displayed at the London International Exhibition of 1862 and the Dublin Exhibition of 1872.

Literary References: *Bostrom* 2000, 151–5; *Bryant* 2002, 20

BERCHETT (or BURKETT) fl 1692–1706

He did a good deal of work at Chatsworth. In the third quarter of 1692 'Mr Borkett' and his partner 'Mr Carnall' were paid for setting up heads in the great hall. The following year Burkett and another partner, Finch, supplied terminals, receiving their first payment in September 1693 (2). In 1694 they supplied a grey marble basin, which stands beneath the window in the lower state landing and was probably designed for the dining room (3), and they were later paid for pedestals supporting two statues of sphinxes by **Caius Gabriel Cibber** on the west front (4). They also 'cleansed and set up' eight heads on the staircase and in the hall, working at a daily wage of 3s 9d (*Thompson* 1949, 114, 125, 212). Berchett later worked at the Inner Temple, receiving £21 10s for 'the eight figures at the end of the Robert Sawyer's building' in 1706 (*Inderwick* 1896–1936, vol III, 399).

Literary References: *Gunnis* 1968, 51–2

Statues

1.	1706	Eight figures Payment(s): £21 10s		Inner Temple, London, Robert Sawyer's building	*Inderwick* 1896–1936, vol III, 399

Architectural Sculpture

2.	1693	Stone terminals (co-sculptor: Finch)	s	Chatsworth, Derbys	*Thompson* 1949, 212
3.	1694	Grey marble basin (co-sculptor: Finch)	m	Chatsworth, Derbys, great stairs	*Thompson* 1949, 125
4.	post-1694	Pedestals (co-sculptor: Finch)		Chatsworth, Derbys, west terrace	*Thompson* 1949, 125

BERESFORD fl 1737

Funerary Monuments

1.	†1737	Ambrose Phillipps (designed by Robert Taylor)	Shepshed, Leics	S	Pevsner, *Leics and Rutland*, 1984, 376

BERNARD, John fl 1763

He was taught by his father and in 1763 won a premium of 15 guineas from the Society of Arts in the under 22 category (1).

Reliefs

1.	1763	Tablet in clay	[Soc of A premium, 15 gns]; untraced	*Dossie* 1782, 437

BERNASCONI, Francis 1762–1841

The most fashionable purveyor of Gothic stucco work in England during the Regency period, he worked under the architects Sir Jeffrey Wyatville, James Wyatt, Sir Robert Smirke and George Dance. He is thought to have been the son of Bernato Bernasconi, one of a family of stuccoists originating from Riva San Vitale, near Lugarno. Bernato was employed as a plasterer at Claydon House, Bucks, 1770–85, and apparently settled in the county, for it was as 'a poor man with a large fameley [*sic*] in the town of Buckingham' that he asked to be paid by Lord Verney, who was then on the verge of bankruptcy (Verney archives, quoted by *Gunnis* 1968, 51). Francis had a son, also Francis, who was made a freeman of the Plasterers' Company on 9 November 1805. John and Peter Bernasconi, who in 1805 repaired the exterior of Jesus College, Cambridge using Roman cement, were probably brothers.

Francis Bernasconi was employed extensively as a plasterer at country houses between 1800 and 1839. Among his many commissions he provided Gothic ornaments and other work at Cobham Hall, Kent, capitals for scagliola columns at Shugborough, Staffs and external and internal plasterwork at Compton Place, Sussex. He worked for the Grosvenor family at Grosvenor House, London and at Eaton Hall, Cheshire; refaced the exterior of Ashburnham Place, Sussex; and decorated a great hall in the gothic style at Blithfield Hall, Staffs, a house where he was employed for more than 20 years. For his work at Stafford House, London, he was paid £6,696, the largest of many four-figure sums. There were also commissions in Wales and Scotland.

The Prince Regent, later George IV, employed him at Carlton House in 1804 and at Windsor Castle, where he worked under Wyatville and was paid in 1805 for 'Gothic elliptical arches, elliptical soffits, Gothic compo mouldings, twelve enriched spandrels, the Royal Arms, thirteen angels with plain shields etc' (TNA WORK 5/93; 19/3 f 327). In about 1820 he modelled four groups designed by Thomas Stothard for the grand staircase at Buckingham Palace (3) and in 1833 Bernasconi & Son were paid for work at Kensington Palace.

Bernasconi restored medieval church fittings in several cathedrals. He was responsible for plasterwork in the lantern of Westminster Abbey for James Wyatt in 1803 and returned there in 1825 to execute an altarpiece (4) which 'consisted of a series of shrines, or rather ornamental niches, canopied with a profusion of delicate tabernacle work' (*GM* 1825, ii, 226–7). In 1803 he worked in the south transept of York Minster and made stucco birds and a new finial on the canopy of Archbishop de Grey's monument (York Minster Library, Fabric Rolls and Bills, E3, E4A). He returned to York in 1814 to repair the screen. At Southwell Minster, Notts, he made good the damaged sedilia and pulpitum and, at Christ Church Cathedral, Oxford, repaired the canopy over a statue of Cardinal Wolsey. He also modelled a plaque, with an ostrich and a wreath of oak leaves, which was cast in artificial stone by the **Coade Factory of Lambeth** for the pediment of a lodge designed by Samuel Wyatt at Holkham Hall, Norfolk (1).

Bernasconi lived at Alfred Place, Tottenham Court Road, London from 1806 until his death. He had experienced financial difficulties in the early years of the century but died a wealthy man on 1 January 1841, leaving an estate of £90,000.

Literary References: *Allen* II, 1828–31, 284; *Willis and Clark* II, 1886, 147, 497, 667; *Hiscock* 1946, 206; *Gunnis* 1968, 51; *Beard* 1975, *passim* (list of decorative plasterwork, 205–6); *Aylmer* 1977, 463; *Beard* 1981, 246; *Frew* 1984, 684; RG/JP, 1, 151; *Grove* 29, 1996, 834 (Beard)

Archival References: GPC

Will: PROB 11/1940, proved 10 February 1841 (Francis Bernasconi): PROB 11/1885 (Peter Bernasconi, plasterer of 178 Tottenham Court Road, proved 21 October 1837)

Architectural Sculpture

1.	1799	Coade stone plaque with ostrich and wreath of oak leaves (co-sculptor: Coade Factory, of Lambeth)	sa	Palmer's Lodge, Holkham Hall, Norfolk	*Kelly* 1990, 364; Pevsner, *Norfolk: NW & S*, 1999, 422
2.	1805	'eagles 83 long 38 high of very strong embossed and much relieved' (co-sculptor: his son)		Buckingham Palace, London	TNA WORK 5/93, f 352
3.	post-1820	Four groups of lunette figures	m	[Buckingham Palace, London, grand staircase]; untraced	Pevsner, *London: 1*, 1973, 508; *Beard* 1981, 246
4.	1825	Altarpiece (designed by B D Wyatt)		Westminster Abbey, London	*GM* 1825, ii, 226–7; *Cocke* 1995, 63

BERRISFORD, Anthony, of Bakewell fl c1750

Berrisford's mid-18th century tradecard, advertising chimneypieces, tables, monuments, statues, busts and all kinds of ornaments in marble '& Curious Chrystalline Substances, Done in the Best manner And at Reasonable Rates' is preserved in the Heal Collection (BM PDL Heal 106.3). He may have been employed on masonry work at Okeover, Staffs, for his estimate for a patio survives in their archives.

Literary References: *Oswald* 1964, 224; *Snodin* 1986, 103 (trade card repr)

BERRY, John, of Barnstaple fl 1753–90

He carved a number of sundials for churches in Devon. One of the most elaborate, which shows the time in the principal capitals of Europe and other locations including Cairo and Babylon, is above the south door at St Peter, Tawstock (**2**). Berry was later assisted by his son Thomas.

Literary References: *Gunnis* 1968, 51

Funerary Monuments						
1.	1763	John Thorn		Marwood, Devon	S	*Gunnis* 1968, 51
Architectural Sculpture						
2.	1753	Sundial		Tawstock, Devon, above door	SD	*Gunnis* 1968, 51; Pevsner, *Devon*, 1989, 791
3.	1762	Sundial	sl	St Thomas, Kentisbury, Devon, porch	SD	Pevsner, *Devon*, 1989, 516
4.	1762	Sundial		St Michael, Marwood, Devon	SD	Pevsner, *Devon*, 1989, 563
5.	1764	Sundial	sl	Bittadon, Devon	SD	Pevsner, *Devon*, 1989, 186
6.	1780	Sundial		Pilton, Devon	SD	Pevsner, *Devon*, 1989, 629
7.	nd	Sundial		East Buckland, Devon, porch	SD	Pevsner, *Devon*, 1989, 346

BERRY, William

For information the reader is referred to *Pyke* 1973, 15

BERTUCCINI, C fl 1730–31

Funerary Monuments						
1.	c1730	John Conyers		Great Staughton, Hunts	S	
2.	†1731	George Heneage and his two wives		Hainton, Lincs	S	*Lord* 1986 (1), 101

BERVILLE, Augustine fl 1754

Berville, who came from a French family, studied modelling at the Dublin Society Schools. He lived in Cope Street, Dublin and carved 'gentleman's likenesses modelled in the most beautiful and excellent manner' (*Universal Advertiser*, August 1754). These included a bust of Malone, in plaster, which he advertised in 1754 (**1**). He also introduced a pasteboard stucco for ornamenting houses, on which he modelled 'ornaments for ceilings, and history pieces in alto-relievo, beasts, birds, flowers, etc., all ready for immediate fixing' (*Universal Advertiser*, April 1757). In 1756, describing himself as a 'paper stucco worker', he petitioned the Dublin Society for assistance, but was refused.

Literary References: *Strickland* 1, 1913, 60–61

Busts						
1.	1754	[Anthony?] Malone	p	Untraced		*Strickland* I, 1913, 61

BETT, George, of Harlaxton –1795

A Kesteven slate headstone engraver from a well-established family of masons, there are 16 headstones in Kesteven signed by him between 1757 and 1792. His eldest son, William, followed him in the craft for some years before leasing a public house in Barkston.

Literary References: *Neave and Heron* 1969, 8

BEVAN, George, of Ffrwd fl c1740

Funerary Monuments						
1.	†1740	Lucy Mansel and forbears		Pembrey, Carmarthen		*Dale-Jones and Lloyd* 1989, 46

BEVAN, Silvanus 1691–1765

An apothecary and ivory carver, he was the son of Silvanus Bevan and Jane (née Phillips), both of Swansea. After moving to London he traded as an apothecary in Cheapside and from 1715 at 2 Plough Court, Lombard Street. On 10 September 1715 he married Elizabeth, the daughter of Daniel Quare, clockmaker to Queen Anne, at the Meeting House in White Hart Court, Gracechurch Street. The ceremony was attended by several eminent Quakers including William Penn, the founder of Pennsylvania, and persons of rank such as Sarah, Duchess of Marlborough. In 1736 Bevan was joined in partnership by his younger brother, Timothy, who inherited the business when Silvanus died without issue in 1765.

Thirty busts and reliefs carved by Bevan remained in the possession of the family until 1880, when the collection was dispersed, and only a handful of his works is known today. The most significant of these is the profile portrait of William Penn, thought to be the only reliable portrait of him in existence (**1**). Penn's presence at Bevan's wedding indicates that they knew each other well, so it is possible that it was carved from the life around 1715. However, in a letter to Lord Kames, dated 3 January 1760, Benjamin Franklin related an anecdote that Bevan 'an old Quaker apothecary, remarkable for the notice he takes of countenances, and a knack he has of cutting in ivory strong likenesses of persons he has once seen' carved the bust from memory some years after Penn's death for Lord Cobham who was then setting up the statues of famous men in the gardens at Stowe and could find no likeness of Penn. Josiah Wedgwood is thought to have used Bevan's carvings of Penn, Dr Mead, Dr Pemberton, Sir Hans Sloane and Sir Isaac Newton as models for jasperware medallions produced during the last quarter of the eighteenth century (**2, 3, 6, 7**).

Literary References: *Tait* 1959, 126–32; *Dawson* 1999, 142, 156

Reliefs						
1.	1715–1718	Sir William Penn	i	[coll Paul Bevan, 1857]; coll Michael Waterhouse Other versions: ex Loganian Library, Philadelphia, USA; untraced Christies, 10 July 1916, lot 143, plaster cast, bought by Huggins for £1 10s; untraced		*Watson* 1850, 1, 111; *Tait* 1959, 127–9 (repr 15B)

2.	post-1740	Dr Richard Mead	i	[coll Paul Bevan, 1857]; BM	*Tait* 1959, 127, 129–30 (repr 16A)
3.	nd	Dr Pemberton	i	[coll Paul Bevan, 1857]; untraced	*Tait* 1959, 127, 130
4.	nd	George Vertue (?)	i	coll Michael Waterhouse	*Tait* 1959, 131–2 (reprs 18B–C)
5.	nd	Silvanus Bevan, self-portrait		coll Michael Waterhouse	*Tait* 1959, 126 (repr 15A)
6.	nd	Sir Hans Sloane	i	[coll Paul Bevan, 1857]; untraced	*Tait* 1959, 127, 130–1
7.	nd	Sir Isaac Newton	i	[coll Paul Bevan, 1857]; untraced	*Tait* 1959, 127

BEYNON, D, of Cilycwm fl 1819–74

He signs some, at least, of his earlier monuments 'D. Benyon Cilycwm' (**1, 2, 4**). By 1868 he was living in the adjacent parish, for Slater's *Directory* for that year lists his address as Glanrhyderryd, Llandingat. His father may have been Rees Beynon, a mason of Llandovery, listed in Pigot's *Directory* of 1831. Dale-Jones and Lloyd note that Beynon was 'clearly a competent workman who enjoyed the patronage of the lesser local gentry' but describes his works as 'stiff and unadventurous' in execution. J Beynon, who signs a three-panelled gothic monument to the Rees family in the church of St Dingat, Llandovery, may have been his son.

Literary References: *Dale-Jones and Lloyd* 1989, 46

Funerary Monuments

1.	†1819	Rev John Price	Mydfai, Carmarthen	S	*Dale-Jones and Lloyd* 1989, 46
2.	†1843	Rev William Thomas	Llanfair-ar-y-bryn, Carmarthen	S	*Dale-Jones and Lloyd* 1989, 46
3.	†1843	William and Catherine Jones	Cilycwm, Carmarthen	S	*Dale-Jones and Lloyd* 1989, 46
4.	†1844	William and Anne Jones	Llandovery, Carmarthen	S	*Dale-Jones and Lloyd* 1989, 46
5.	†1848	Anne Jeffreys	Cilycwm, Carmarthen	S	*Dale-Jones and Lloyd* 1989, 46
6.	†1854	David Powell Price	Cilycwm, Carmarthen	S	*Dale-Jones and Lloyd* 1989, 46
7.	†1867	Mary Anne Jones	Cilycwm, Carmarthen	S	*Dale-Jones and Lloyd* 1989, 46
8.	†1874	Eliza Jenkins	Cilycwm, Carmarthen	S	*Dale-Jones and Lloyd* 1989, 46

BICKHAM, George 1684–1760

For information the reader is referred to *Pyke* 1981, 8

BIDFORD, W Manley fl 1818

Bidford's tablet to William Smith at Alcester takes the form of a curtain, bunched and corded at the corners.

Literary References: *Gunnis* 1968, 51

Funerary Monuments

1.	†1818	William Smith	Alcester, Warks	*Gunnis* 1968, 51

BIELFIELD, Charles F fl 1821–32

He received a silver Isis medal from the Society of Arts for an original portrait bust in 1821 (**1**) at which time he was living in St Martin's Lane. In 1832, when he exhibited at the Royal Academy, Bielfield's address was given as 11 Old Church Street, Paddington. He may perhaps be identified with Charles Frederick Bielefeld who manufactured papier-mâché architectural ornaments in London in the mid-19th century.

Literary References: RSA *Transactions*, vol 39, 1821, xxxviii; *Graves* I, 1905–6, 191; *Gunnis* 1968, 51; *DeVoe* 1975, 30–32

Archival References: GPC

Busts

1.	1821	Unidentified subject	[Soc of A, silver Isis medal]; untraced	RSA, *Transactions*, vol 39, 1821, xxxviii

Reliefs

2.	1832	J Thrupp, 'medallic portrait'	[Exhib RA, London, 1050]; untraced	*Graves* I, 1905–6, 191

BIENAIME, Angelo fl 1829–51

Bienaimé was born at Carrara and studied under **Thorvaldsen** before he came to London *c*1828. The following year he showed busts of Sir Astley and Lady Cooper at the Royal Academy (**6, 7**). His statue of *Innocence mourning the loss of her dove*, purchased second-hand by Joseph Neeld for his collection at Grittleton House, Wilts in 1847, was probably carved in Italy since it is dated 1826 (**1**). Gunnis notes that a statue of *Innocence* had been commissioned in Italy by the Marchesa Somareva, but was unfinished when she died and was accordingly sent over to London. He adds that it was exhibited at the Colosseum in Regent's Park in 1829 and later bought by Sir Matthew Ridley. A version of the same subject was shown at the Royal Academy in 1838. The sculptor's *Recumbent bacchante*, executed in 1836, is at Powerscourt (**2**). Bienaimé made a replica for the emperor of Russia the following year and later produced another for Sir Augustus Clifford. Clifford also commissioned statues of *Narcissus* and the four seasons (**3, 5**), as well as six marble vases for his house at Westfield, on the Isle of Wight. It seems likely that the small statue of *Spring* exhibited at the RA in 1846, and described as 'elegantly executed' by the *Art Union*, was one of those made for Clifford (*AU*, 1846, 189). Gunnis suggests that this sculptor was responsible for eight statues and two vases commissioned by the Duke of Devonshire for Chatsworth but these may rather have been made by **Francesco Bienaimé**, who was perhaps a relative.

Literary References: *Le Grice* 1844, I, 127–30; II, 96–105; *Gunnis* 1968, 51; *Read* 1982, 141

Archival References: GPC

Statues

1.	1826	Innocence mourning the loss of her dove	m	[coll Dr Nevinson]; Grittleton 1966, lot 22; untraced Other versions: ex coll Sir Matthew Ridley; untraced exhib RA, London, 1838, 1253	SD	*Graves* I, 1905–6, 191; *Grittleton Marbles* 1966, 19; *Gunnis* 1968, 51; *Read* 1982, 141
2.	1836	Recumbent bacchante		Powerscourt, Ireland Other versions: ex coll Emperor of Russia, 1837; untraced ex coll Sir Augustus Clifford; untraced		*Gunnis* 1968, 51
3.	?1846	The four seasons		[coll Sir Augustus Clifford]; untraced Other versions: small marble statue of Spring exhib RA, London, 1842, 1434		*AU*, 1846, 189; *Graves* I, 1905–6, 191; *Gunnis* 1968, 51

4.	1850	Love triumphant	m	[Exhib RA, London, 1344]; untraced		*Graves* I, 1905–6, 191; *Gunnis* 1968, 51
5.	nd	Narcissus		[coll Sir Augustus Clifford]; untraced		*Gunnis* 1968, 51
Busts						
6.	1829	Lady Cooper		[Exhib RA, London, 1165]; untraced		*Graves* I, 1905–6, 191
7.	1829	Sir Astley Cooper	m	[Exhib RA, London, 1159]; untraced		*Graves* I, 1905–6, 191
8.	*c*1840	Sir Robert Peel	m	Felbrigg Hall, Norfolk	S	*Gunnis* 1968, 51
9.	1848	Boy playing the mandolino	m	[Exhib RA, London, 1468]; untraced		*Graves* I, 1905–6, 191
10.	nd	Arthur, 1st Duke of Wellington	m	[Mr Joseph's sale, Phillips, 12 June 1854]; untraced		GPC
11.	nd	Sir Walter Scott	m	[Mr Joseph's sale, Phillips, 12 June 1854]; untraced		GPC
12.	nd	William Shakespeare	m	[Mr Joseph's sale, Phillips, 12 June 1854]; untraced		GPC
Architectural Sculpture						
13.	nd	Four vases		[Westfield, I of W, coll Sir Augustus Clifford]; untraced		*Gunnis* 1968, 51
Miscellaneous						
14.	1845	Sleeping boy		[Exhib RA, London, 1343]; untraced		*Graves* I, 1905–6, 191
15.	nd	Psyche with the lamp		[coll Lord Selsey]; untraced		GPC
16.	nd	The guardian angel		[coll Sir Matthew Ridley]; untraced		GPC

BIENAIME, Francesco fl 1844–57

Francesco Bienaimé's workshop in Carrara specialised in marble copies of classical statues. His patrons included the 6th Duke of Devonshire, who stated that he had purchased eight statues and two vases from Bienaimé for the gardens at Chatsworth in his 1844 *Handbook to Chatsworth and Hardwick* (**1, 3**). These probably included statues of *Apollo* and *Diana*, a vase and a bath that he bought in March 1841 for £375 with carriage (Devonshire MSS Accounts of the 6th Duke of Devonshire, 23, cited by *Sicca and Yarrington*, 200, 8). A similar set of statues and vases was purchased for the People's Park in Halifax, which opened in August 1857 (**2, 4**).

Literary References: *Haskell and Penny* 1981, *passim*; *Sicca and Yarrington* 2000, 8, 13

Statues						
1.	by 1844	Eight statues, including an Apollo Belvedere	m	Chatsworth, Derbys, south lawn		*Devonshire* 1999, 36–38 (repr)
2.	1857	Music girl, Sophocles, Telemachus, Diana, Apollo, Venus, Hercules and dancing girl, after the Antique	m	People's Park, Halifax, W R Yorks		inf: Calderdale Metropolitan Borough Council
Architectural Sculpture						
3.	by 1844	Two vases	m	Chatsworth, Derbys		*Devonshire* 1982, 209; *Sicca and Yarrington* 2000, 8
4.	1857	Borghese vase and Medici vase	m	People's Park, Halifax, W R Yorks		inf: Calderdale Metropolitan Borough Council

BIGEE, Nicholas fl 1700–12

Bigée's monument to General Cornelius Wood has a portrait bust set against a great baroque trophy of arms, in the centre of which is the club of Hercules, crowned with a plumed helm. To either side of the trophy are skulls with bats' wings, holding in their teeth heavy fringed curtains which fall in thick folds (**3**). An entry in the Register of St Peter-in-East, Oxford, records the baptism of 'Thomas son of Nicholas Bygee' on 18 September 1707.

Literary References: *Gunnis* 1968, 51–2

Archival References: RG/JP, 1, 153

Funerary Monuments						
1.	†1700	Sir John Busby		Addington, Bucks		Pevsner, *Bucks*, 1994, 127
2.	1707	Seth Wood and family members		St Leonards, Bucks	S	Pevsner, *Bucks*, 1994, 614
3.	†1712	General Cornelius Wood		St Leonards, Bucks	S	Pevsner, *Bucks*, 1994, 614
Miscellaneous						
4.	1712	Two eagles (co-sculptor: John Woodward)		St John's College, Cambridge, gate adjoining bridge		*Gunnis* 1968, 51–52

BIGGLESTONE, J fl 1837

Funerary Monuments						
1.	*c*1837	James family		Hampton Bishop, Herefs	S	Pevsner, *Herefs*, 1963, 141

BIGGS, Josiah, of Bath fl 1821–36

A minor local statuary, his tablet to Theodore Haultain is inscribed: 'This marble came from Pompeii' (**3**).

Literary References: *Gunnis* 1968, 52

Funerary Monuments						
1.	1821	Thomas Morgan		Hinton Charterhouse, Somerset	S	*Gunnis* 1968, 52
2.	1832	Rev Benjamin Richardson		Farleigh Hungerford, Somerset	S	*Gunnis* 1968, 52
3.	1832	Theodore Haultain		St Mary, Bath, Somerset	S	*Gunnis* 1968, 52
4.	1835	William Whipham		Calne, Wilts	S	*Gunnis* 1968, 52
5.	1836	Susanna Manifold		Brackley, Northants	S	*Gunnis* 1968, 52

BIGGS, Richard, of Bath fl 1735–58

He was apprenticed to his father, Richard Biggs, of Bath, in 1735 and became free in 1744. In 1749 he was working in London, as a mason at St Bartholomew's Hospital (Hospital Archives, cited by *Gunnis* 1968, 52).

Literary References: *Gunnis* 1968, 52

Archival References: Masons' Co, Freemen, fol 7 (4 December 1744)

Funerary Monuments						
1.	†1758	Sir Everard Fawkener		Bath Abbey, Somerset	S	*Gunnis* 1968, 52

BIGGS, William, of Bath fl 1730–44

William Biggs became free of the Masons' Company by redemption on 23 March 1730. He was employed on the new buildings of St Bartholomew's Hospital between 1731 and 1739, executing most of the carved stonework and three chimneypieces for the 'Great Room', for which he received £68 in 1734 (Hospital Archives, cited by *Gunnis* 1968, 52) (**3, 2**). On 26 March 1741 he was engaged by John Wood to build the Bristol Exchange. Biggs was then living at Monkton Combe, near Bath, and he gave Ralph Allen, the postal reformer and philanthropist, as security. His estimate for the freestone walls was almost £1,000 less than those submitted by the other masons, including **Thomas and James Paty**. He was employed on freestone work for the building almost continuously between May 1741 and September 1744. This included mouldings, columns, pilasters, capitals, balustrades, a pediment, windows and cornices. He did not give total satisfaction and on 4 September 1741 he was 'summon'd to attend the Committee' and 'Mr. Wood told him great Complaints were made of his work & admonished him to keep strictly to his Contract'. On 11 September he signed the minute ordering him to pull down the work 'not done according to the Contract' and rebuild it (BRO Exchange Minute Book, M/BCC/XCM/1, unpag).

Biggs described himself as 'citizen and mason of London' on the tomb he erected to two of his children in Monkton Combe churchyard (*Church Rambler*, vol I, 105, cited by *Gunnis* 1968, 52) (**1**). Benjamin Biggs, the mason responsible for building Bath Guildhall between 1760 and 1770, was another member of the family.

Literary References: *Gunnis* 1968, 52

Archival References: Masons' Co, Freemen, fol 6 (23 March 1730)

Funerary Monuments					
1.	nd	Two of the sculptor's children		Monkton Combe, Bath, churchyard	*Gunnis* 1968, 52
Chimneypieces					
2.	1734	Three Payment(s): £68		St Bartholomew's Hospital, London, great room	*Gunnis* 1968, 52
Architectural Sculpture					
3.	1731–1739	Carved stonework	s	St Bartholomew's Hospital, London	*Gunnis* 1968, 52
4.	1741–1744	Carved stonework	s	Bristol Exchange, Somerset	BRO Exchange Building Accounts, 04223 ff 16, 18, 19; 04221[1/c30] ff 29v, 53v, 55v, 88v; BRPO Exchange Minute Book, M/BCC/XCM/1, unpag (26 March, 4 Sept, 11 Sept, 1741)

BINFIELD, W

For information the reader is referred to *Pyke* 1973, 16

BINGHAM, E, of London fl 1831

The sculptor gave his address as '103 Fulham Road, Brompton, London' when signing the Despard monument, which has a weeping willow and draped sarcophagus.

Literary References: *Potterton* 1975, 37

Funerary Monuments					
1.	†1831	Francis Despard	St Mary, Kilkenny	S	*Potterton* 1975, 37

BINGHAM, Edward, of Peterborough –1796

The son of John Bingham, he was apprenticed to William Charlton of Wisbech 'mason' in 1730 (TNA IR 49/260 in GPC). In 1750 he carved chimneypieces for Lord Fitzwilliam at Milton Hall (**28**) and from 1773 was employed there under Sir William Chambers on marble carving (**31**). A letter from Fitzwilliam to Chambers, dated 17 August 1776, contains the following instructions: 'I enclose Mr Bingham's bill for your examination – upon no account to shew it to Lord Bessborough for there are two articles of the marble frieze & the cleaning of the Columns which I intend should not appear in his bill – as the whole estimate amounted but to 314 £ I am afraid His bill is larger than it should be. . .' (Chambers's Letters, RIBA, CHA/2.47).

Bingham specialised in architectural monuments and tablets in coloured marbles. Examples include the memorial to Ralph Lane, which features pretty rococo decoration and the tablet to William Gery, a classically inspired design which incorporates some subtle gothic detailing (**3, 20**). A contemporary described Bingham as 'a top workman for best mason work' (the estate book of Prebendary John Russell, *c*1760, quoted by *Lewis* 1953, 21) and Gunnis thought him an excellent provincial statuary. He died on 16 July 1796.

Literary References: *GM*, 1796, ii, 621; *Lewis* 1953, 19–38; *Gunnis* 1968, 52; *Penny* 1977 (1), 111

Archival References: GPC

Funerary Monuments					
1.	*c*1750	George (†1743) and Mary (†1741) Denshire	All Saints with St John, Stamford, Lincs	S	Pevsner, *Lincs*, 1989, 689
2.	†1751	Colonel John Creed	Titchmarsh, Northants	S	Pevsner, *Northants*, 1973, 433
3.	†1754	Ralph Lane (†1732) and wife	St Mary, Gamlingay, Cambs	S	Pevsner, *Cambs*, 1970, 391
4.	?1756	Jane Squire	Oundle, Northants		*Gunnis* 1968, 52
5.	?1758	John Digby	North Luffenham, Rutland		*Gunnis* 1968, 52
6.	†1760	John Simcoe	Cotterstock, Northants	S	Pevsner, *Northants*, 1973, 161
7.	?1764	Jane Forster	Elton, Northants		*Gunnis* 1968, 52
8.	?1767	James Edings	Clinton, Northants		*Gunnis* 1968, 52
9.	1767	Rev Bland (†1761) Payment(s): £15 8s 6d	Edenham, Lincs	S	*Lord* 1986, 100
10.	?1767	Richard Tryce	Peterborough Cathedral, Northants		*Gunnis* 1968, 52
11.	†1769	Edmund Turner	St Wulfram, Grantham, Lincs	S	Pevsner, *Lincs*, 1989, 320
12.	†1771	Richard Moore	Sleaford, Lincs	S	Pevsner, *Lincs*, 1989, 653
13.	†1782	George Denshire	All Saints with St John, Stamford, Lincs	S	Pevsner, *Lincs*, 1989, 689
14.	?1782	Rev Thomas Harrison	Ryhall, Rutland		GPC

15.	?1783	William Bowker	St John, Peterborough, Northants		*Gunnis* 1968, 52
16.	†1785	James Davie	St Martin, Stamford, Lincs	S	Pevsner, *Lincs*, 1989, 693
17.	†1786	Rev John Image	St John, Peterborough, Northants	S	Pevsner, *Beds, Hunts & Peterborough*, 1968, 326
18.	?1788	Francis Low	Paston, Northants		GPC
19.	†1788	John Truman	St Martin, Stamford, Lincs	S	Pevsner, *Lincs*, 1989, 693
20.	†1788	William Gery (†1787) and wife	Peterborough Cathedral, Northants		*Penny* 1977 (1), 111 (repr)
21.	?1790	Lord James Manners	Ufford, Northants		*Gunnis* 1968, 52
22.	?1792	Lucas family	Ancaster, Lincs		GPC
23.	?1792	Mary Griffiths	Whittlesey, Cambs		GPC
24.	?1792	Richard Arnold	Clinton, Northants		*Gunnis* 1968, 52
25.	?1793	Henry Fryer	St Martin, Stamford, Lincs		*Gunnis* 1968, 52
26.	?1795	Thomas Sambrook	St John, Peterborough, Northants		*Gunnis* 1968, 52
27.	nd	Curtis family	Wilsthorpe, Lincs	S	Pevsner, *Lincs*, 1989, 802
Chimneypieces					
28.	1750	Description unavailable	[Milton Hall, Northants]; untraced		*Gunnis* 1968, 52, citing Fitzwilliam (Milton) archives
29.	1767	Description unavailable Payment(s): £25 1s 6d (with Bland monument)	[for Peregrine, 3rd Duke of Ancaster]; untraced		GPC
30.	*c*1789	Several	Casewick Hall, Uffington, Lincs	S	Pevsner, *Lincs*, 1989, 214
Architectural Sculpture					
31.	1773	Marble carving	Milton Hall, Northants		*Gunnis* 1968, 52, citing Chambers Corr, RIBA Library

BINGHAM, James, of Peterborough fl 1800–20

He was probably the son or grandson of **Edward Bingham.**

Literary References: *Gunnis* 1968, 52–3

Funerary Monuments

1.	†1803	William Harper	St Martin, Stamford, Lincs	S	Pevsner, *Lincs*, 1989, 693
2.	1816	Eleanor Wing (ledger)	Sedgebrook, Lincs	S	*Gunnis* 1968, 53

BINGHAM, Margaret, Countess of Lucan 1740–1814

For further information the reader is referred to *Pyke* 1981, 9

BINGLEY, John, of London fl 1773–96

A mason of John Street, Tottenham Court Road, he went into partnership with **J C F Rossi** about 1790, principally producing works in terracotta or artificial stone. The partners modelled statues of *Music* and *Dancing* for the Assembly Rooms at Leicester in 1796 (**12**). Their employees included **James George Bubb** who, Bingley later stated, worked for them on Rossi's monument to Captain Robert Faulknor in St Paul's Cathedral (CLRO Misc MSS 207–8). The partnership does not seem to have been a success and was later dissolved. As an independent practitioner Bingley executed a number of chimneypieces and church monuments. He was also employed by Lord Radnor at 6 Grosvenor Street in 1802, and in 1807 received £655 from Earl Grosvenor for unidentified work at Grosvenor House, London.

Literary References: *Farington* 14, 4913; *Gunnis* 1968, 53, 326

Archival References: GPC

Funerary Monuments

1.	†1773	Mary Darker		St Bartholomew-the-Less, City of London	S	Pevsner, *London: City*, 1997, 204
2.	†1784	John Darker		St Bartholomew-the-Less, City of London	S	Pevsner, *London: City*, 1997, 204
3.	†1787	James Worsley of Stanbury		Godshill, I of W	S	Pevsner, *Hants & Isle of Wight*, 1967, 747
4.	1793	James Blicke		St Mary, Twickenham, Middx	S	*Gunnis* 1968, 53
5.	†1793	James Evelyn		Godstone, Surrey	S	Pevsner, *Surrey*, 1971, 260
6.	†1796	John Davenport		Teddington, Surrey	S	*Gunnis* 1968, 53
7.	†1798	Captain Willcox		St Bees, Cumberland	S	Pevsner, *Cumberland & Westmorland*, 1967, 184
Chimneypieces						
8.	1792	Description unavailable Payment(s): £78 18s 4d	m	[Calke Abbey, Derbys, drawing room]; untraced		GPC citing a payment in Jenney archives, Calke Abbey
9.	1796	Description unavailable Payment(s): £46 15s	m	[Cleveland House, London, drawing room]; untraced		*Gunnis* 1968, 53, citing Brownlow archives
10.	1796	Description unavailable Payment(s): £18	m	[Cleveland House, London, anteroom]; untraced		*Gunnis* 1968, 53, citing Brownlow archives
11.	1799	'an elegantly neat Statuary Marble Chimney piece with vein'd marble slab' Payment(s): £38	m	[Betchworth Castle, Surrey, drawing room]; untraced		Soane bill book B, fols 306r & v; *Gunnis* 1968, 53
Architectural Sculpture						
12.	1796	Music and Dancing, two statues (co-sculptor: J C F Rossi)		Assembly Rooms, Leicester		*Cavanagh* 2000, 124–6 (repr)

BIRCH, Robert fl 1726–37

Birch worked at Thoresby Hall, during the 1720s and 1730s. A first payment, for a Derbyshire marble chimneypiece 'which was delivered before His Grace's death and is now in the wardrobe at Thoresby', is recorded in the executors' accounts of the estate of Evelyn, 1st Duke of Kingston, †1726 (Archives, Lord Monson, in GPC) (**1**). Birch subsequently worked for the 2nd Duke, receiving a payment of £24 4s 4d in 1736 for 'paving the marble room at the stables with diamond paving and black marble squares'. He also supplied 'piers for the garden' and a marble chimneypiece in 1737 (Archives, Earl Manvers, Nottingham Univ 4544, in GPC) (**2**).

Gunnis notes that he made several chimneypieces for Welbeck Abbey, including those for the Duke of Portland's bedroom and dressing room and for the Duchess's bedroom, in 1746 to 1747 (Welbeck Abbey Archives, cited by

Gunnis 1968, 53). However, another source suggests that these were supplied by a firm called Thomas Birch and Co (*Turberville* 1938–9, vol 1, 394).

Literary References: *Turberville* 1938–9, vol 1, 394; *Gunnis* 1968, 53

Archival References: GPC

Chimneypieces

1.	1726	Derbyshire marble	m	Thoresby Hall, Notts, wardrobe	GPC
2.	1737	Description unavailable	m	[Thoresby Hall, Notts]; untraced	GPC

BIRCH, William fl 1749

In 1749 he received over £1,000 for mason's work at Welbeck Abbey, and two years later he was paid a further £944 for building the riding-house, stables and other buildings (Welbeck Abbey Archives cited by *Gunnis* 1968, 53).

BIRD, Edward Chapman –1792

He was one of six surviving children and probably the only son of **Francis Bird** and his wife Hester, the daughter of **Edward Chapman**, who were married in 1706. He had a considerable business as a marble merchant and is known to have supplied **Henry Cheere, Thomas Carter** and **Louis François Roubiliac**, for his name appears in their bank accounts. In 1770 he became bankrupt and a sale of his stock-in-trade was held at his yard at Millbank on 4 April, 1771. The lots included a 'Head of Venus', reliefs of 'The Crucifixion' and the 'Death of Lucretia', 'Sicilian Jasper marble tablets', a 'rare sized slab of lumatella [sic] antica', which fetched 2 guineas, chimneypieces and vases. He appears to have continued in the same line of business, in spite of this setback, for in 1777 a 'Mr Bird' bought uncarved blocks of marble, tables and carved chimneypieces from **Thomas Carter II.** Bird was insolvent again at his death on 22 February 1792. His sister, Hester Bird, and son, Christopher Chapman Bird, are named as executors in his will.

Literary References: *Gunnis* 1968, 53; *Rendel* 1972, 207; *Penny* 1977 (1), 204; *Bindman and Baker* 1995, 214, 382 n 12

Will: PROB 11/1217, 91, r-v; 11/633, 1144-115r

Auction Catalogues: Bird 1771

BIRD, Francis 1667–1731

The foremost sculptor in London during the first two decades of the 18th century, Bird was later described by George Vertue as 'the most famous statuary, that this Nation ever bred' (*Vertue* III, 49, 1730). Vertue, who was a fellow Catholic and a close friend, provides the fullest record of Bird's life. Both men became members of the circle of artists around Edward, Lord Harley, later 2nd Earl of Oxford (1689–1741) and his wife, Henrietta, the daughter and heiress of the 1st Duke of Newcastle.

Bird was born in London to recusant parents, probably in the parish of St Martin-in-the-Fields. Nothing further is known of his background. He was unique among British sculptors of his generation in having an extensive Continental training, first in Flanders, where he was apprenticed at about the age of 11 to an obscure sculptor named Cozins, and then in Rome, where he remained until about 1689. He returned to London and worked briefly under **Grinling Gibbons** and then **Caius Gabriel Cibber**, before going back to Rome for a further nine months, where he studied under Pierre Legros (1666–1719), who was carving sculptural ornaments for Rome's great baroque churches. Bird finally settled in London shortly after 1700. In 1706 he married Hester, the daughter of **Edward Chapman**, another recusant and a successful stonemason and contractor. The couple had several daughters, educated by the Blue Nuns, and a son, **Edward Chapman Bird**, who made his living principally as a marble merchant, one of his father's secondary activities. In 1708 he was obliged to take the Oath of Allegiance to the Crown. Bird travelled to Rome a third time in 1711, when John Talman, the antiquary, recorded meeting him.

His cosmopolitan training brought him to public attention soon after his second return from Italy. This coincided with the death of Cibber, who was working on architectural sculpture for St Paul's Cathedral shortly before 1700. Bird's knowledge of contemporary sculpture in Roman churches put him in a prime position to succeed Cibber at St Paul's and he enjoyed a virtual monopoly of the figurative work over the next two decades. His first contract, a relief panel of *St Paul preaching to the Bereans*, was set above the west door before March 1706 (**47**). This was followed immediately by the enviable but daunting order for a large tympanum relief representing the *Conversion of St Paul* for the west front (**46**). Two designs for the elevation had been prepared by Sir Christopher Wren's office in 1685, perhaps drafted by Gibbons or Cibber, and these formed the starting point for Bird's terracotta model, which incorporated all the features later realised in stone. Bird's relief has a sense of drama never before achieved in England on this scale: Saul of Tarsus is presented in the centre of a group of horsemen, surprised by the rays of light penetrating through a cloud in the apex of the pediment. He has fallen from his horse and looks up, blinded, while horses rear to either side of him. It is not known what assistance Bird received with the work, but a final payment of £650 was recorded in the building accounts in December 1706. Two further reliefs for the west front illustrating episodes in the life of St Paul were probably carved between 1706 and 1712 (**48, 49**) and another six panels on the same theme were added by about 1713 (**50–55**). The later panels appear to have been charged at £75 each.

Bird was also responsible for a statue of Queen Anne, which became the focal point of the paved enclosure outside the west front (**35**). Her standing image in coronation robes is mounted on a circular pedestal with personifications of her dominions grouped radially below her. The composition is indebted to baroque fountains in Rome and Paris, but also to Cibber's group of King Charles II surrounded by the four great rivers of England, carved for Soho Square in 1681. Bird's group was conceived as an integral part of the Cathedral complex and Wren was involved in its design and in the choice of sculptor. It is not known when Bird received the commission, but a warrant for the provision of three blocks of marble for the Queen's statue, given at her instruction from the royal store yard, is dated 14 April 1709. The building accounts for St Paul's include a large number of payments to Bird in connection with the statue. The figure of the Queen 'with all enrichments' cost £250, the four 'kingdoms' came at £220 each and the Queen's sceptre at £4. The work was erected in 1712 to celebrate the completion of St Paul's, but kept inside a hoarding for many years, probably because of work in the vicinity. At an appropriate moment, the thanksgiving service for the Peace of Utrecht on 7 July 1713, it was revealed for public scrutiny. Vertue merely called the work 'noble', a modest tribute in his vocabulary. The Opposition critic, James Ralph, considered 'the whole modell'd in a tolerable taste, and executed as well', but condemned the stolid effigy of the Queen as stiff and affected (*Ralph* 1734, 20). For a short while it seemed likely that many other statues of the Queen would be ordered from Bird's workshop, for in 1713 the Commission for Building Fifty New Churches in London resolved that a statue of Queen Anne by Gibbons or Bird should be set up in a focal point at each of the churches. The scheme came to nothing, partly because the Queen died the following year.

Bird's obituary made mention of 'many lofty tombs and magnificent monuments in Westminster Abbey and other churches' (*GM*, 1731, 83) and he was a subscriber to Dart's *Westmonasterium*, 1723, which included designs for monuments. Several works in the Abbey have been attributed to the sculptor solely on stylistic grounds and are not included in this account, but ten are signed and a score can be identified as Bird's work since he passed the inscriptions to John le Neve for publication in *Monumenta Anglicana*, 1717–19 (**1–6, 9, 11–22, 29**). Le Neve had applied to several London sculptors for transcripts of their epitaphs and he paid tribute to Bird's helpful response in his publication. The most remarkable of the sculptor's early monuments, that to Dr Richard Busby, a noted headmaster of Westminster School, was carved with the assistance of his father-in-law, Edward Chapman, and erected in 1703 (**10**). It was singled out as the finest monument of the period in Westminster Abbey by Whinney, who noted Bird's disciplined sense of design and particularly admired the relaxed pose of the effigy, leaning on one elbow with a book in the other hand. Other early monuments introduced European patterns to a nation hungry for Italian novelties: the wall-monument to Sir Orlando Gee at Isleworth (**12**), a virtuoso work with a garlanded architectural frame and an apron carved with a *gloria* of cherubs, is an early example in England of a memorial with an effigy truncated just below the waist. The monument to Admiral Priestman in Westminster Abbey (**21**) makes use of another novelty, a portrait medallion suspended from a ribbon. This motif became popular for monuments in Augustan England.

By 1711, Bird was a leading figure in the artistic Establishment and that year he became the only sculptor of note among the 60 founder members of Sir Godfrey Kneller's prestigious but short-lived Academy of Painting. Another member was the architect James Gibbs, who was also a Catholic and who worked with Bird a little later.

After the Jacobite rebellion of 1715, Bird and his father-in-law were obliged to register their estates as recusants. Bird's practice might have been in jeopardy, but for the continuing support of Tory patrons. In 1719 Alexander Pope, another fellow Catholic, whose means were relatively modest but whose literary reputation was second to none, gave Bird a prestigious order for a white marble tablet to commemorate his family at Twickenham (**26**). By this time Bird had also become a close associate of Lord Harley. In January 1720 Humfrey Wanley, Harley's librarian, noted Bird's offer to lend Harley, a noted bibliophile, any book Harley might want from his library. Bird also offered to 'assist my lord in buying . . . antique bustos' from a Mr Austin (*Wanley Diary* 1, 21, 20 Jan 1719/20).

The Harleys commissioned the monument in Westminster Abbey to Dr John Ernest Grabe (†1711), a Prussian-born theologian with High Church leanings (**29**). The finely carved, relaxed effigy perches on a sarcophagus in his Geneva robes, a book in one hand and a pen in the other. Grabe's epitaph was published by Le Neve in 1717, so work on the monument must have been well in hand by that date. There were to be long delays before its erection. On 27 August 1724, Wanley noted that 'Mr Bird came, desiring me to look over his copy of an inscription for Dr Grabe's monument; which I did & found to be faulty' (*Wanley Diary*, 2, 311). Wanley made minor changes and returned the inscription. Nearly two years later, on 25 May 1726, Wanley noted 'Mr Bird came, & having made Dr Grabe's monument, desired me to call at his house to see if the epitaph be rightly laid-down with black lead, before it be graven' (*Wanley Diary* 2, 424). The fee for its erection was paid early in 1727.

Bird's largest and least successful monument is the towering edifice commissioned by Lady Harley for her father, the Duke of Newcastle, in 1721 (**31**). Gibbs provided a design for a convex architectural structure inspired by a recent altarpiece in the Gesu church, Rome, to be carved in polychrome marbles. Bird's knowledge of Roman sculpture and his 'great dealings in Italy for Marbles' (*Vertue* III, 49), as well as his contacts with the Harley family, made him the obvious choice as sculptor, though **John Nost II** submitted an alternative design. Bird made the model, now lost, in pearwood and clay. Newcastle reclines on a sarcophagus in contemporary armour, flanked by personifications of *Wisdom* and *Charity*. He looks upwards to heaven and to his own armorial bearings, which are flanked by angels and cherubs on the attic storey. Ralph was merciless in his condemnation of the showy monument: 'it gives no pleasure to the elegant and knowing, and is only the admiration of the vulgar . . . the figure of the Duke himself is full of absurdities . . . the two statues on each side are equally tame and unmeaning' (*Ralph* 1734, 69). Lord Harley, however, was evidently satisfied, for he employed Bird and Gibbs again in 1728 on the monument to members of the Cavendish family at Bolsover (**32**).

In 1718 Bird was selected as sculptor for a statue of William III at Greenwich, but although a block of marble was purchased by the Hospital, the project came to nothing. Between 1717 and 1721 he provided a number of portraits of founders and other statues for collegiate buildings in Oxford (**37, 38, 41–43**) and in 1718 he returned to St Paul's Cathedral, where his team was active for the next six years. During this period **Peter Scheemakers** and **Laurent Delvaux** were employed briefly by him at St Paul's, but no other workshop members have been identified.

Bird's knowledge of Italian architectural sculpture again came into play at the Cathedral as he worked on an extensive series of parapet figures, a novel setting for statues in England (**56–59**). Negotiations for seven statues for the west front, each about 11 feet in height, began in 1716, when Bird and a Mr Carpenter, probably **Andrew Carpenter**, were asked to provide estimates for figures in marble or Portland stone, which was the material eventually chosen. In February 1718 a contract was drawn up with Bird by John James, the assistant surveyor of the Cathedral, for seated statues of the four Evangelists, all in the act of writing their gospels, with their symbolic companions, an angel, a lion, an ox and an eagle, beside them. These groups were sited at the feet of the west towers. Standing figures of St Peter looking upwards with a crowing cock on a stump at his feet and St James with a pilgrim flask and bottle were placed in the corners of the pediment and St Paul, holding a sword and the gospels, on the apex. All seven were painted in oil. Bird was paid the balance for these figures in 1721.

In 1720 his team began work on statues for the pediments on the north and south fronts. Each pediment had seated figures on the outer corners and three standing ones on the centre gables (**57–9**). The standing figures, which were between 11 and 12 feet in height, cost £140 each and the seated images, of the saints Simon, Matthias, Barnabas and John the Baptist, totalled £500. Several of these are lost or heavily restored and the untouched survivors are severely eroded.

Bird produced little in the last years of his life. He assisted **Giovanni-Battista Guelfi** with the monument to James Craggs, 1724–7 (**30**), very likely on the recommendation of Alexander Pope who supervised the work, but the partnership between the two sculptors was uneasy and on 30 October 1727 Guelfi wrote twice in one day to Alexander Pope, to complain about Bird. Guelfi then took to his bed, leaving Pope in a state of anxiety about the monument's completion. Bird must have carried on without Guelfi, for a month later the statue on the monument was in place and Bird had only to cut an inscription for the urn. His last known work is the monument in Westminster Abbey to William Congreve (**33**). Bird ignored the new taste for classicism, instead carving a medallion portrait of Congreve in modern dress after the Kit Kat portrait by Sir Godfrey Kneller. The playwright is shown surrounded by attributes of his art.

In 1729 Bird's father-in-law, Edward Chapman, died, leaving the greater part of his considerable estate, including a property in Windsor, to the sculptor and his wife. They did not have long to enjoy the windfall together. That Christmas Bird had a serious accident. He was coming out of a tavern near his home one frosty night when he slipped and broke his leg, which was badly set by the surgeon. In January 1731, 'he became swelled, his body and legs like a dropsy and this continued until he died on 27 February, 1731, aged sixty-five' (*Vertue* III, 49). He was buried in the vault at St Andrew, Holborn. It was 20 years before his collection was auctioned.

Bird's work varies in quality. His finest achievements are his architectural sculpture for St Paul's and some of the smaller monuments in Westminster Abbey (**10, 14, 21, 29**). In stylistic terms his major contribution was the introduction and popularisation of Italian baroque fashions into English sculpture.

IR

Literary References: *Le Neve, passim*; *Vertue* III, 18–19, 34, 49; *Farington* 7, 2494; *Esdaile* 1938, 164–9; *Esdaile* 1942, 176–97; *Wren Soc* VI, 71 (extract from the minute book for the building of Greenwich, 5 April 1718), XV, 146, 165, 207, 208; *Sherburn* 1956, II, 456–7; *Wanley Diary*, 1966 ed, vol 1, 21, vol 2, 311, 314, 414; *Physick* 1969, 69; *Rendel* 1972, 206–9; *Friedman* 1984, 40, 80; *Whinney* 1988, 150–6; *Grove* 4, 1996, 79 (Physick); *Ward-Jackson* 2003, *passim*; *ODNB* (Craske)

Archival References: GPC

Additional MS Sources: Talman Letter Book

Wills and Administrations: Francis Bird (admon) PROB 6/1–7 sig 55 (March 1731); Edward Chapman PROB 11/633, 114r–115r

Miscellaneous Drawings and Models: Design and model for the monument to Sir Godfrey Kneller in Westminster Abbey, executed by Michael Rysbrack, untraced (*Vertue* III, 43); model for Queen Anne's coronation medal, c1702, untraced (*Vertue* V, 47)

Auction Catalogue: Bird 1751

Bird's Collection of Sculpture: Vertue refers to several artefacts that suggest that Bird collected with discrimination. He owned a cast of Bernini's lost bust of Charles I which had been at Whitehall Palace (*Vertue* II, 50); a *Laocoon* and an *Apollo and Daphne* by Nicholas Stone the Younger, modelled in Rome (perhaps the *Daphne and Apollo* offered in Bird's sale on 30 April 1751, lot 4) (*Vertue* I, 90); a counterfeit gold medal of Oliver Cromwell (*Vertue* II, 50) and a *Faun* after the Antique, bought at the 1st Earl of Oxford's sale (*Vertue* V, 7). Three works 'by Bernini', a *Neptune* and two reliefs of angels, were sold at the 1751 auction (lots 44, 52); 'A large flying boy, by Algardi' formed lot 47 and there were several works by Duquesnoy ('Fiamingo'), including a head of Christ (lot 59) and a *Flora*, a *Farnese Hercules* and an *Antinous* (lots 59–61).

Funerary Monuments

No.	Date	Subject	Location		References
1.	†1661	John Michel	Old Windsor, Berks		*Le Neve* 1650–1679, 86
2.	†1668	Hugh Darrell (†1668), his wife and grandson	St Lawrence, West Wycombe, Bucks		*Le Neve* 1650–1679, 125–6; Pevsner, *Bucks*, 1994, 739
3.	†1669	Anne Duke (previously Michel)	Old Windsor, Berks		*Le Neve* 1650–1679, 141
4.	†1683	Benet Michel	Old Windsor, Berks		*Le Neve* 1680–1699, 45
5.	†1696	Humphrey Michel	Old Windsor, Berks		*Le Neve* 1680–1699, 176–7
6.	†1699	Martha Fitzherbert, ledger stone	Tissington, Derbys		*Le Neve* 1680–1699, 205; *Whinney* 1988, 152; C Lib (repr)
7.	post-1700	Thomas Shadwell (†1692)	Westminster Abbey, London, south transept	S	*Dart* 1, 1823, 76–7 (repr); *Whinney* 1988, 150
8.	†1702	Jane Wren	St Paul's Cathedral, London, crypt	S	*Whinney* 1988, 152; *Saunders* 2001, 80 (repr)
9.	†1702	Sir Arthur Ingram (†1681), his daughter (†1693) and his wife (†1702)	[St Dionis, City of London; moved to All Hallows, Lombard St, City of London]; untraced		*Le Neve* 1680–1699, 24–5
10.	1703	Dr Richard Busby (†1695) (co-sculptor: Edward Chapman) Payment(s): £130	Westminster Abbey, London, south transept		WAM; *Dart*, 1, 1723, 92–4 (repr); *Vertue* III, 18, 50; V, 72; *Whinney* 1988, 150; *Physick* 1995 (2), 7–8
11.	†1705	George, 8th Earl of Huntingdon	St James, Piccadilly, London		*Le Neve* 1700–1715, 75–6; *Vertue* III, 122; Pevsner, *London: Westminster*, 1973, 491; C Lib (repr)
12.	†1705	Sir Orlando Gee	All Saints, Isleworth, Middx		*Le Neve* 1700–1715, 96; *Whinney* 1988, 152–3 (repr)
13.	†1706	Elizabeth Eyre, perhaps a ledger stone	[Salisbury Cathedral, Wilts]; untraced		*Le Neve* 1700–1715, 100
14.	†1707	Brigadier-General Robert Killigrew	Westminster Abbey, London, nave		*Le Neve* 1700–1715, 133; *MacMichael* 1977, 25; C Lib (repr)
15.	†1707	John Alchorne, his wife and Richard Savage (†1707)	Untraced		*Le Neve* 1650–1718, 221–2
16.	†1709	Louis, 2nd Earl of Feversham	French Chapel of the Savoy, (Savoy Chapel), London		*Le Neve* 1700–1715, 165–6; *Physick* 1991, 42–6
17.	†1709	Rev John Cawley	St Mary, Henley-on-Thames, Oxon	S	*Le Neve* 1700–1715, 169; Pevsner, *Oxon*, 1974, 637
18.	†1710	Richard Stiles and his wife Judith (†1708), ledger stone	Untraced		*Le Neve* 1700–1715, 158
19.	†1710	Thomas Singleton, 'late of Molland in this parish'	Untraced		*Le Neve* 1700–1715, 200
20.	†1711	Henry Stiles	Untraced		*Le Neve* 1700–1715, 225–6
21.	†1712	Admiral Henry Priestman	Westminster Abbey, London, nave		*Dart* 2, 1723, 109–10 (repr); *Whinney* 1988, 153; C Lib (repr)
22.	†1714	Elizabeth Wilks	Untraced		*Le Neve* 1700–1715, 269
23.	1715	Rev Anthony Wingfield	Stonham Aspal, Suffolk, churchyard		Pevsner, *Suffolk*, 1974, 441; C Lib (repr)

No.	Date	Subject		Location		References
24.	†1716	Dr Robert South		Westminster Abbey, London, south transept		*Dart* 1, 1723, 94–7 (repr); *MacMichael* 1977, 91; *Whinney* 1988, 153
25.	†1716	Vice-Admiral John Baker		Westminster Abbey, London, nave	S	*Dart* 2, 1723, 108 (repr); *MacMichael* 1977, 26
26.	*c*1719	Alexander Pope and his parents		St Mary, Twickenham, Middx		Pevsner, *London 2: S*, 1983, 539
27.	†1720	Dr Thomas Sprat, Dean of Westminster and Bishop of Rochester (†1713) and Thomas Sprat		Westminster Abbey, London, nave; formerly in St Nicholas's Chapel	S	*Ashmolean* 1967, 3, cat 15; *MacMichael* 1977, 17
28.	pre-1723	Sidney, 1st Earl Godolphin (†1712) Drawing(s): VAM 8933.41 (attrib)		Westminster Abbey, London, nave	S	*Dart* 2, 1723, 92 (repr); *MacMichael* 1977, 17
29.	1717–1727	Dr John Ernest Grabe (†1711)		Westminster Abbey, London, south transept	S	*Le Neve* 1700–1715, 214 –5; *Wanley Diary*, 1966 ed, 2, 311, 314, 414; *Whinney* 1988, 153–5 (repr)
30.	1724–1727	James Craggs (†1721) (co-sculptor: Giovanni-Battista Guelfi)		Westminster Abbey, London, nave		*Physick* 1969, 69; *Sherburn* 1956, II, 456–7
31.	1721–1727	John, 1st Duke of Newcastle (†1711) (designed by James Gibbs) Payment(s): £50 paid 16 May 1721, and £81 on 22 April, 1727 (BL, Portland Papers loan 29/387) Drawing(s): Wren, fol II, no 59 (Soane); Welbeck Abbey Archives 010716, on loan RIBA (by Gibbs); Soc Antiq, Harley Coll VI, f18 (by Gibbs) Model(s): 'neatly done in pear tree and the figures done in beard earth £40'; untraced		Westminster Abbey, London, north transept	S	*Dart* 2 1723, 124 (repr); *Vertue* III, 19, 108–9; *Physick* 1969, 32, 60–61; *Friedman* 1984, 87–89, 314 (repr); *Whinney* 1988, 155–6, 448 n18
32.	1727–1728	Henry, 2nd Duke of Newcastle and other members of the Cavendish family (designed by James Gibbs) Drawing(s): By Gibbs, Ashm Gibbs III, 104		Bolsover, Derbys	SD	*Friedman* 1984, 88, 90, 298 (repr)
33.	†1729	William Congreve Model(s): 'a Cast of Congreve's monument, and several others', Bird's sale, 30 April 1751, lot 1		Westminster Abbey, London, nave	S	*MacMichael* 1977, 15

Statues

No.	Date	Subject		Location		References
34.	1702–1703	King Henry VIII	s	St Bartholomew's Hospital, City of London, gatehouse niche		*Vertue* III, 18; *Ward-Jackson* 2003, 349–50 (repr)
35.	1706	Queen Anne Payment(s): £47 18s 6d	l	Market House (former Town Hall), Kingston-upon-Thames, Surrey		*Gunnis* 1968, 541; C Lib (repr)
36.	1709–1712	Queen Anne on a pedestal above personifications of Britannia and France holding the Royal Arms, and Ireland and America Payment(s): £1,180 for the Queen; £220 for surrounding figures; £50 for shield Model(s): 'The original model of Q Anne, and 4 figures representing the four parts of the world', Bird's Sale, 1751, lot 35	m	[St Paul's Churchyard, City of London]; Holmhurst, Sussex Other versions: cast, Bird's sale, 1751, lot 17		*Vertue* III, 19, 50; *Whinney* 1988, 152, 448 n10; *Ward-Jackson* 2003, 374–81 (repr)
37.	1717	Dr John Radcliffe		University College, Oxford, Radcliffe Quadrangle, over entrance arch		*Gunnis* 1968, 54; Pevsner, *Oxon*, 1974, 212; C Lib (repr)
38.	1719	Cardinal Wolsey		Christ Church, Oxford, Tom Tower		*Vertue* III, 19; *Whinney* 1988, 448 n23
39.	1719	King Henry VI Payment(s): £443 17s 11d	b	Eton College, Windsor, Berks, school yard		*Vertue* III, 19; *Stukeley* 26 Dec 1748; Pevsner, *Bucks*, 1994, 308
40.	1719	Queen Anne		Minehead, Somerset		*Whinney* 1988, 152; C Lib (repr)
41.	1720	Queen Anne		University College, Oxford		RG/JP, II, 161
42.	1720	Queen Mary		University College, Oxford		*Gunnis* 1968, 55
43.	1721	Earl of Clarendon Payment(s): £55		Clarendon Building, Oxford, west side		*Gunnis* 1968, 55; Pevsner, *Oxon*, 1974, 257
44.	nd	'Nine figures, by Mr Bird &c', models	tc	Untraced		Bird's sale, 30 April 1751, lot 34

Busts

No.	Date	Subject		Location		References
45.	nd	Six models		Untraced		Bird's sale, 30 April 1751, lots 29–32

Architectural Sculpture

No.	Date	Subject		Location		References
46.	1706	Conversion of St Paul, tympanum relief Payment(s): £650 Drawing(s): All Souls, Oxford, Wren vol II, 37 and 39 (by Wren) Model(s): St Paul's Cathedral, Trophy Room, Jb-mod-6, clay, incorporated in a pinewood model of the west portico	s	St Paul's Cathedral, London, west front	S	*Vertue* III, 19; *Wren Soc* XV, 146 (repr 19); *Whinney* 1988, 151; *Saunders* 2001, 114 (repr); *Ward-Jackson* 2003, 365–6 (repr)

47.	1705–1706	St Paul preaching to the Bereans, relief panel Payment(s): £300	s	St Paul's Cathedral, London, over great west door	*Ward-Jackson* 2003, 368–9 (repr)
48.	1706–1712	Ananias putting his hands on Saul and restoring his sight, relief panel	s	St Paul's Cathedral, London, west front, over north door	*Ward-Jackson* 2003, 367 (repr)
49.	1706–1712	Saul receiving letters from the high priest, relief panel Payment(s): £620	s	St Paul's Cathedral, London, west front, north side of upper storey above portico	*Ward-Jackson* 2003, 366 –7 (repr)
50.	1712–1713	St Paul and the gaoler of Philippi, relief panel	s	St Paul's Cathedral, London, west front, inside portico on north side wall	*Ward-Jackson* 2003, 370 (repr)
51.	1712–1713	St Paul before Agrippa, relief panel Payment(s): £75	s	St Paul's Cathedral, London, within portico to right of great west door	*Ward-Jackson* 2003, 369–70 (repr)
52.	1712–1713	St Paul before Felix, relief panel Payment(s): £75	s	St Paul's Cathedral, London, within portico to left of great west door	*Ward-Jackson* 2003, 369 (repr)
53.	1712–1713	St Paul bitten by a viper on Malta, relief panel	s	St Paul's Cathedral, London, within west portico	*Ward-Jackson* 2003, 370 (repr)
54.	?1713	The baptism of Saul, relief panel	s	St Paul's Cathedral, London, over south door on west front	*Ward-Jackson* 2003, 368 (repr)
55.	?1713	The stoning of St Stephen, relief panel	s	St Paul's Cathedral, London, west front, over south door	*Ward-Jackson* 2003, 367 (repr)
56.	1718–1721	Four Evangelists (Matthew, Mark, Luke and John), and St Peter, St James and St Paul Payment(s): £950 Model(s): 'The figures of St Peter and St Paul', Bird's sale, 1751, lot 26	s	St Paul's Cathedral, London, at foot of side towers and on west pediment	*Vertue* III, 19; *Ward-Jackson* 2003, 363–5 (repr)
57.	1720–1724	St Barnabas, St Philip, St James the Less, St Jude, St John the Baptist, parapet figures	s	St Paul's Cathedral, London, north pediment	*Vertue* III, 19; *Ward-Jackson* 2003, 371–2
58.	1722–1724	St Simon and St Matthias, seated figures	s	St Paul's Cathedral, London, south pediment, outer corners (substantial additions by Henry Poole, 1923–5)	*Vertue* III, 19; *Ward-Jackson* 2003, 372 (St Simon repr)
59.	?1720–1724	St Thomas, St Andrew and St Bartholomew		[St Paul's Cathedral, south pediment, on central gable]; destroyed	*Ward-Jackson* 2003, 371–2
60.	1725	Altar (designed by John James)	m	St Paul's Cathedral, London	*Northampton Mercury*, 31 May, 1725; *Wren Soc* XVI, 137; *Colvin* 1995, 537
61.	1726–1727	Font	m	St Paul's Cathedral, London	Pevsner, *London I: City*, 1997, 164; C Lib (repr)

Miscellaneous

62.	nd	'Four figures, a group, and a busto, by Mr Bird, &c', models		Untraced	Bird's sale, 30 April 1751, lot 41
63.	nd	'Fourteen figures, 2 bustos, and 2 boys, by Mr Bird &c', models	tc	Untraced	Bird's sale, 30 April 1751, lot 36

BISHOP, Edward, of Tenterden 1757–1822

He is buried at Tenterden, where a gravestone in the churchyard commemorates him and his wife, Ann, née Cloake.

Literary References: *Gunnis* 1968, 56

Funerary Monuments

1.	1817	William Stringer	Goudhurst, Kent	S	*Gunnis* 1968, 56

BISHOP, of London fl 1848

The Lister monument, a simple tablet with shield, is signed 'Bishop of London'.

Funerary Monuments

1.	†1848	Matthew Lister	Burwell, Lincs	S	Pevsner, *Lincs*, 1989, 202

BISSET, T fl 1815–20

Several monuments in the Houff graveyard in Dundee are signed by T Bisset. Most of these incorporate relief carvings of sailing ships, anchors, sheaves of wheat or other emblems of a trade or profession. Among the more notable are those commemorating James Irons, Catherine Meldrum and David Ewing (1–3).

Literary References: *Woodward* 1977, vol 1, pt 2, 14

Funerary Monuments

1.	1815	James Irons	The Houff, Dundee	S	*Woodward* 1977, vol 1, pt 2, 14
2.	1818	Catherine Meldrum	The Houff, Dundee	S	*Woodward* 1977, vol 1, pt 2, 14
3.	†1820	David Ewing	The Houff, Dundee	S	*Woodward* 1977, vol 1, pt 2, 14

BISWICK fl 1743–45

Probably a Bristol mason, he was employed by Maynard Colchester as a stonecarver during the building of Westbury Court, Glos, between 1743 and 1745. In February–March, 1745 he was paid for carving 'Lions', probably heraldic beasts for a shield-of-arms, or for the gate piers (1) (Archives, Sir Francis Colchester-Wemyss, cited by *Gunnis* 1968, 56).

Literary References: *Gunnis* 1968, 56

Architectural Sculpture

1.	1743–1745	Stone carving, including lions	s	Westbury Court, Glos	*Gunnis* 1968, 56

BLACK, Robert fl 1838

Funerary Monuments

1.	1838	John Dick DD (†1833)	Glasgow Necropolis	Pevsner, *Glasgow*, 1990, 140

BLACKBURN, John I and II, of Norwich fl c1774–1813

They were stone and marble masons active in Norwich c1774–1813. In 1774 John Blackburn I advertised in the *Norwich Mercury* that he had taken over the business of **John Ivory** 'in all its branches' and was ready to take orders. In 1776 another notice in the same paper stated that Ivory had 'about two years since by Deed in Writing, in consideration of one Hundred Pounds then paid him, resigned the above yard all his business in the Stone mason way to the said John

Blackburn'. In 1788 Blackburn placed an advertisement in the *Bury Post* stating that 'the articles which existed between Mr. Ivory and him confining him from executing marble business has been for some time by mutual consent entirely dissolved. He now executes every article in the stone and marble branches. Monuments, ornamental and plain chimney-pieces in the most improved taste, best manner and on reasonable terms'.

In 1784 Blackburn's son, John Blackburn II advertised that he had 'taken Part of his Father's Yard in the Roselane, King Street, where he executed on his own Account every article in the Stone and Marble business' (*Norwich Mercury*, 14 Feb 1784). It is, therefore, unclear which of the Blackburns became a freeman of Norwich in 1788 and was employed by Sir Thomas Proctor Beauchamp on repairs to Langley Park, Norfolk, in 1796 (Beauchamp Archives, cited by *Gunnis* 1968, 56). It was probably the younger Blackburn who sold the stock in trade of his business at Castle Meadow, Norwich, in 1813 (*Norwich Mercury*, 14 Aug 1813) and died the following year 'aged about fifty years, after a lingering illness' (*Bury Post*, 18 May 1814).

Literary References: *Gunnis* 1968, 56; RG/JP, 2, 163

Archival References: GPC

Funerary Monuments

1.	1786	John Woodbine	East Dereham, Norfolk	S	*Gunnis* 1968, 56
2.	1793	Richard Pillans	East Dereham, Norfolk	S	*Gunnis* 1968, 56
3.	1810	William Powell	St Saviour, Norwich	S	*Gunnis* 1968, 56

BLACKWELL fl 1822–47

Blackwell signs two known monuments. Another sculptor with the same name, who may have been related to him, signs the monument to William Stinchcombe (†1870) at St Mary, Cheltenham.

Funerary Monuments

1.	†1822	Thomas Ducket	Quadring, Lincs	S	Pevsner, *Lincs*, 1989, 605
2.	†1847	John Cox	Swindon, Glos	S	Pevsner, *Glos: Vale & Forest of Dean*, 1976, 354

BLAGDEN, John, of Sheffield fl 1792–1805

Funerary Monuments

1.	†1792	Elizabeth Bapshaw	St Mary and All Saints, Chesterfield, Derbys	S	Pevsner, *Derbys*, 1978, 144
2.	1805	Elizabeth Jackson	Badsworth, W R Yorks	S	*Gunnis* 1968, 56

BLAIN, L, of Carlisle fl 1828

Funerary Monuments

1.	1828	Unidentified subject, tablet	Beltingham, Northumbs	S	Pevsner, *Northumbs*, 1992, 170

BLAKE, Francis fl 1679

He became free of Richard Hutchinson on 25 November 1679 (Masons' Co, *Freemen*, fol 4).

BLAKE, John fl 1704

John (or perhaps Robert, son of John) Blake became free of the Masons' Company by service with **Thomas Wise II** on 14 June 1704 (Masons' Co *Freemen*, fol 4). About 1740 he, or another mason with the same name, was recorded as a member of the London Masons' Company living in Winchester (Masons Co, *Assistants*).

Literary References: *Webb* 1999, 4

BLAKE, William, of Basingstoke fl 1753

In 1753 he agreed with Anthony Chute to lay a pavement of Portland stone and black and white marble in the gallery at the Vyne for £91 13s 4d (Archives, Sir Charles Chute Bt, cited by *Gunnis* 1968, 56).

BLANCHARD, Mark H 1816–

He was born on 9 November 1816 at Portsea, Hants and christened on 30 August 1817. After working at the **Coade Factory** during its declining years he set up on his own account as a manufacturer of terracotta architectural ornaments and sculpture in Blackfriars Road, south London. He probably bought some of the Coade moulds when they were finally sold off in 1843, and some of his earlier works are remarkably similar in both material and design to pieces made by the Coade Factory. He later produced more strongly coloured terracottas. On 29 December 1855 he advertised in *The Builder* that he was 'late of Coade's original works and successor to them in the manufacture of this invaluable material' (quoted by *Kelly* 1990, 51). **John Marriott Blashfield** established a rival ornamental terracotta firm after seeing Blanchard's prizewinning exhibits at the Great Exhibition of 1851 (**7–9**). At the sales of Blanchard's stock in trade held on 27 March 1860 and 5 April 1861 the lots included statues based on works by **John Bell, Sir Richard Westmacott** and **John Gibson** (**1–4**), as well as pieces designed for Mrs Coade by **John Bacon RA, Charles Felix Rossi** and **John Flaxman RA**.

His most important contract was for architectural ornaments at the Victoria and Albert Museum (**14**). During the 1870s he moved to Bishops Waltham, Hants, where his factory began to concentrate on producing utilitarian bricks and roofing and paving tiles. The 1881 census lists him in Bishop's Waltham with his wife and two adult children.

Literary References: *Gunnis* 1968, 56; *Penny* 1977 (1), 13; *Kelly* 1978, 25; *Kelly* 1990, 51, 313; *Stratton* 1993, *passim*

Archival References: 1881 census; GPC; IGI

Auction Catalogues: Blanchard 1860; Blanchard 1861

Statues

1.	by 1861	Gleaning girl (after John Bell)	tc	[Blanchard sale 1860/1861]; untraced	GPC
2.	by 1861	Pandora (after Sir Richard) Westmacott)	tc	[Blanchard sale 1860/1861]; untraced	GPC
3.	by 1861	Psyche (after Sir Richard Westmacott)	tc	[Blanchard sale 1860/1861]; untraced	GPC
4.	by 1861	Venus (after John Gibson)	tc	[Blanchard sale 1860/1861]; untraced	GPC

Architectural Sculpture

5.	c1850	Garden vase and pedestal	tc	Seago, Pimlico Road, London (1989)	*Burl*, 128, Sept 1988, 31 (repr); 131, Sept 1989, xxvii (repr)
6.	1850–1851	Balustrade, vases, finials and capitals (designed by Charles Barry)	tc	Cliveden, Bucks	*AJ Cat* 1851, 164 (repr); *Builder*, 1852, 34; *Stratton* 1993, 50, 222 (repr)

7.	1851	'pinnacles and tracery windows for the new chapel, Tottenham and for Kingston church'	tc	[Gt Exhib, London]; untraced		*AJ Cat* 1851, 164 (repr); *Builder* 1852, 34
8.	1851	Vase	tc	[Gt Exhib, London]; untraced		*AJ Cat* 1851, 157 (repr)
9.	1851	Vase and pillar, 'white terracotta'	tc	[Gt Exhib, London]; untraced		*AJ Cat* 1851, 157 (repr)
10.	1861–1862	Cornice of 'red terracotta'	tc	Messrs Hunt and Crombie's building, Eastcheap, London		*Stratton* 1993, 66, 68 (repr)
11.	1864	Decorative ornaments	tc	[Star and Garter Hotel, Richmond Hill, Surrey]; demol 1919		*Gunnis* 1968, 56
12.	1864	Moulded details	tc	Charing Cross Hotel, London		*Stratton* 1993, 67
13.	1864–1866	Decorative ornaments	tc	Canon Street Hotel, London		*Gunnis* 1968, 56; *Stratton* 1993, 67
14.	1862–1866	Decorative ornaments (designed by F Fowke, G Sykes and others)	tc	VAM, London		*Stratton* 1993, 58, 61 (repr)
15.	1869	Decorative ornaments	tc	Grand Hotel, Cairo, Egypt		*Builder*, 1869, 925, 927; *Gunnis* 1968, 56; *Stratton* 1993, 68
16.	1869–1872	Decorative ornaments	tc	Brighton Aquarium, Sussex		*Gunnis* 1968, 56
17.	1863–1873	Decorative mouldings	tc	Wedgwood Institute, Burslem, Staffs		*Stratton* 1993, 64, 65 (repr)
18.	1863–1873	The months of the year, relief panels (modelled by Rowland Morris)	tc	Wedgwood Institute, Burslem, Staffs		*Stratton* 1993, 64, 65 (repr)
19.	nd	Vase	tc	Sotheby, Billingshurst, Sussex, 26 Sept 1989, Lot 721	S	C Lib (repr)
20.	nd	Vase	tc	(coll Oliver Stocker)		C Lib (repr)

BLAND, Thomas ?1799–1865

Bland worked in rural Westmorland in the mid-19th century. The son of a yeoman farmer, he inherited land at Reagill in the Vale of Lyvvenet, where he laid out an Italianate garden filled with his own sculpture and oil paintings (2). The statues included figures of Joseph Addison, Robert Burns, the geologist Hugh Miller and Sir Walter Scott, who was presented on a pedestal with three reliefs depicting characters from his novels. A statue of *Music holding a lute* symbolised the River Lyvvenet. The last of the paintings, which included local scenes and subjects from Shakespeare, were removed before 1910, but much of the sculpture remains *in situ.*

Bland also made an obelisk with a medallion portrait of King Charles II on the pedestal, to commemorate his halt at Black Dub in 1650 (3) and he set up a stone to mark the place where Joseph Addison's forefathers had lived. In 1842 he carved the statue of *Britannia* and bas-reliefs on the octagonal column erected at Shap Wells Spa, Westmorland, to commemorate Queen Victoria's accession (1). The north panel has a palm and olive wreath, emblematic of peace and plenty, surmounted by the Lowther arms, while the east panel presents the British lion, with its paw resting on a globe. On the east side is a relief of the goddess *Hygeia*, pouring medicinal waters from a goblet into a shell held by an aged invalid. A local guide published soon after noted that Bland was a self-taught sculptor and that he had donated the statue and reliefs (*Westmorland* 1851, 223). The sculptor celebrated the anniversary of the Queen's accession each year by opening his garden to the public and engaging a band for the occasion.

Bland had at least one opportunity to further his artistic career: David Cox the Younger, impressed by some of his drawings, wished to introduce him to the London art world, but Bland was not interested in fame and the offer came to nothing. He died unmarried in September 1865.

Literary References: *Bates* 1855; *Gunnis* 1968, 56; *Read* 1982, 369

Statues

1.	1842	Britannia, and three reliefs	s	Queen Victoria Monument, Shap Wells, Westmorland	S	*Bates* 1955; Pevsner, *Cumberland & Westmorland*, 1967, 288; *Read* 1982, 369 (repr)
2.	nd	Garden figures and reliefs		Yew Tree Farm, Reagill, Westmorland		*Read* 1982, 369; C Lib (repr)

Architectural Sculpture

3.	nd	Obelisk commemorating King Charles II	s	Black Dub, Crosby Ravensworth, Westmorland		*Bates* 1955

BLASHFIELD, John Marriott –1882

An enterprising business man, he was involved in a number of ventures connected with ceramics, sculpture and architecture. He was Minton's representative in London and a partner in the firm of Wyatt, Parker & Co of Millwall, manufacturers of cement, scagliola and mosaic pavements, which he took over in 1846. As a property developer he built a number of grand houses in Kensington Palace Gardens, but was unable to sell most of them and was declared bankrupt in 1847. He is best known as a manufacturer of sculpture and architectural decorations in terracotta. He first became interested in the material around 1839 when he engaged **James Bubb** on experimental terracotta work for model cottages at Canford, Dorset, but only turned to terracotta production after seeing pieces by **M H Blanchard** at the Great Exhibition of 1851.

Blashfield soon won a prestigious contract, to cast a series of colossal terracotta statues representing *Australia, California, Birmingham* and *Sheffield* for the Crystal Palace (1). **John Bell** provided the models for these figures and for various other works produced by the firm (**2–4, 14, 29**). To publicise his works Blashfield published *An Account of the History and Manufacture of Ancient and Modern Terra Cotta* (1855) and several catalogues, including *A Catalogue of Five Hundred Articles* (1857). The items available included replicas of classical statuary and vases, such as the *Niobe* group in the Uffizi and the Borghese and Medici vases (**10, 15, 16**). Blashfield was proud of the fact that his products were hand-finished and taken from the best moulds. His version of the *Apollo Belvedere*, for example, was made from a cast taken from the original for the 'gallery of the late Mr Nash' (7). Other plaster figure makers sold inferior copies of broken casts.

In 1859 production was transferred from London to Stamford in order to exploit a bank of Jurassic clays. The opening of the new works attracted considerable public interest. The local aristocracy attended the drawing of the first kiln and one of the busts of the Queen that had been fired was presented to her the following day (**11**). In 1865 the firm made a statue of Prince Albert from a model by **William Theed II** for the infirmary at Bishops Waltham, Hants (**5**). It was of 'clays from the estate of Mr Arthur Helps, at Bishops Waltham, and clay from the Marquis of Exeter's celebrated pit at Wakerley, mixed with feldspar and Lynn sand' and was assembled inside the kiln and fired in one piece. It emerged from the kiln 'without flaw' and 'as hard as black marble' (*Builder* 1865, 709–10). This use of complex blends of ingredients and the highly wrought finish were typical of Blashfield's scientific approach to terracotta production. By contrast, other manufacturers, including Blanchard and Gibbs and Canning, favoured the use of a simple homogenous clay body and a notional approach to modelling, to produce a less refined but more spontaneous effect.

In 1870 Blashfield secured an important American contract, to supply architectural ornaments for the new Museum of Fine Arts in Boston (**26**). He seriously underestimated the logistical difficulties involved in shipping large consignments of fragile blocks across the Atlantic. He soon realised that he had accepted an uneconomic contract and his company began to incur serious debts when payments were delayed. Delivery of one consignment was held back when a ship had to turn back to England and other payments were delayed when the building contractors were unable to relate the pieces supplied to the intended spaces on the building. From the beginning of 1873 Blashfield was requesting money from his American clients with increasing desperation and by December 1874 the Stamford works, including models, moulds and machinery, was offered for sale. In the following month Blashfield announced that the firm was being wound up and he was declared bankrupt in 1878. After the collapse of the business a number of Blashfield's former employees emigrated to America, where they played an important role in the introduction of architectural terracotta. He died 'after a short illness of bronchitis followed by paralysis' on 15 December 1882 (*Builder*, Dec 1882, 826).

EH

Literary References: *Gunnis* 1968, 56; *Girouard* 1971, 1268–1270; *Penny* 1977 (1), 13; *Haskell and Penny* 1981, *passim*; *Kelly* 1990, 51, 54, 223, 227, 313; *Stratton* 1993, *passim*; *Barnes* 1999, 47–9, 92

Statues

No.	Date	Title	Material	Location		Reference
1.	1854	Australia, California, Birmingham and Sheffield (modelled by John Bell)	tc	[Crystal Palace, Sydenham, upper terrace]; untraced		*Barnes* 1999, 47–8
2.	1854	Diana (modelled by John Bell)	tc	Untraced		*Stratton* 1993, 49; *Barnes* 1999, 6, 48
3.	1854	Erin (modelled by John Bell)	tc	[Exhib RA, London, 1382]; untraced		*Graves* I, 1905–6, 174; *Barnes* 1999, 48
4.	1855	Hibernia (modelled by John Bell)	tc	Untraced		*Barnes* 1999, 48
5.	1865	Albert, the Prince Consort (modelled by William Theed II)	tc	[Bishops Waltham Infirmary]; destroyed		*Darby and Smith* 1983, 114 n85
6.	nd	Amazon	tc	Dodington House, Glos		NP/RG
7.	nd	Apollo Belvedere	tc	[coll Earl of Normanton]; untraced		*Gunnis* 1968, 56; *Haskell and Penny* 1981, 122–3
8.	nd	Diana and a stag	tc	Stoke Rochford Hall, Lincs	S	RG/JP, 2, 165
9.	nd	Diane de Gabies, after the Antique	tc	Untraced		*Haskell and Penny* 1981, 198
10.	nd	Statuettes based on the Antique Niobe group in the Uffizi	tc	Untraced		*Haskell and Penny* 1981, 278, 279 n 43

Busts

No.	Date	Title	Material	Location		Reference
11.	1859	Queen Victoria	tc	[Presented to Queen Victoria]; untraced		*Stratton* 1993, 49
12.	1862	Albert, the Prince Consort	tc	[Int Exhib, London]; untraced		*Builder* 1865, 709–10; *Darby and Smith* 1983, 114 n85

Architectural Sculpture

No.	Date	Title	Material	Location		Reference
13.	1854	Fountain	tc	[Crystal Palace, Sydenham, Renaissance court]; untraced		*Gunnis* 1968, 56
14.	1854	Triton fountain (modelled by John Bell)	tc	[Crystal Palace, Sydenham]; untraced Other versions: Radcliffe Infirmary, Oxford		*Barnes* 1999, 48, 130 (repr)
15.	1857	Borghese vase	tc	[Listed in Blashfield catalogue]; untraced		*Haskell and Penny* 1981, 315
16.	1857	Medici vase	tc	[Listed in Blashfield catalogue]; untraced		*Haskell and Penny* 1981, 316
17.	1863	Portico with Corinthian columns	tc	[Viscount Strangford's house, Cumberland Street, Hyde Park, London]; untraced		*Builder*, 1863, 899
18.	*c*1865	Entrance gateway and clock-tower	tc	Victoria Park, Mumbai (Bombay), India		*Stratton* 1993, 145–7 (repr)
19.	1866	Decorative ornaments	tc	Farnham Town Hall, Surrey		*Gunnis* 1968, 56
20.	1865–1867	Decorative detailing (designed by Charles Forster Haywood)	tc	Duke of Cornwall Hotel, Plymouth, Devon		*Stratton* 1993, 68
21.	1867–1868	Fountains, pedestals, balustrades and gate piers (designed by Matthew Digby Wyatt)	tc	Castle Ashby, Northants		*Builder*, 1868, 44; *Stratton* 1993, 66, 67 (repr)
22.	1868–1869	Parapets and decorative panels (designed by Charles Sturgis)	tc	Pinebank, Jamaica Plain, Boston, Mass		*Stratton* 1993, 144
23.	1866–1870	Decorative ornaments (designed by Charles Barry Jnr)	tc	Dulwich College, London		*Stratton* 1993, 66, 68–70 (repr)
24.	1870	Pair of classical vases	tc	Stokesay Court sale, Sotheby, 28 Sept 1994	SD	C Lib (repr)
25.	1863–1873	Processes of the pottery industry, relief panels (modelled by Matthew Eden)	tc	Wedgwood Institute, Burslem, Staffs		*Stratton* 1993, 64, 65 (repr)
26.	1870–1876	Architectural ornament (designed by J H Sturgis, Charles Brigham and J K Colling)	tc	[Museum of Fine Arts, Boston, USA]; demol 1906		*Stratton* 1993, 144–6 (repr)

27.	nd	Decorative ornaments	tc	Alford House, Somerset		*Gunnis* 1968, 56
28.	nd	Decorative ornaments	tc	Sun Fire office, Charing Cross, London		*Gunnis* 1968, 56
29.	nd	Large group supporting a tazza (modelled by John Bell)	tc	Untraced		*Stratton* 1993, 49
30.	nd	Pair of classical urns	tc	Ragley Hall, Warks		GPC
31.	nd	Pair of Warwick vases	tc	Stokesay Court sale, Sotheby, 28 Sept 1994, lot 432	S	Sotheby sale cat (GPC)
32.	nd	Pineapples, a pair	tc	Aldermaston, Berks, churchyard wall		RG/JP, 2, 165
33.	nd	Royal arms and frieze of roses, shamrocks and thistles	tc	English Church, Bagni di Lucca, Italy		GPC
34.	nd	Urns	tc	Royal Mausoleum, Windsor		*Gunnis* 1968, 56
35.	nd	Vases	tc	Buckingham Palace, London		*Gunnis* 1968, 56
36.	nd	Vases	tc	Kew Palace, Surrey		*Gunnis* 1968, 56
37.	nd	Vases	tc	Hampton Court Palace, Middx		*Gunnis* 1968, 56

BLAXLAND, H, of Milton-next-Sittingbourne, Kent fl 1802–28

He signs a few small tablets in churches around Faversham and Sittingbourne.

Literary References: *Gunnis* 1968, 57

BLAYNEY, John, of Chester fl 1822–41

Most of his tablets are Hellenistic in style.

Funerary Monuments

1.	?1822	John Corser	Moreton Say, Salop	S	*Gunnis* 1968, 57
2.	?1833	Elizabeth Panton	Chester Cathedral	S	*Gunnis* 1968, 57
3.	†1834	Edward Janes	Chester Cathedral	S	
4.	†1835	Mary (†1823) and Richard (†1835) Boydell	Gresford, Denbighs	S	Pevsner, *Denbighs*, 1994, 173
5.	†1836	Ellen Mathie	Worthenbury, Flint	S	Pevsner, *Clwyd*, 1986, 458
6.	?1837	Harriet Evans	Tarvin, Cheshire	S	*Gunnis* 1968, 57
7.	†1838	Roger Barnston	Chester Cathedral		Pevsner, *Cheshire*, 1971, 144
8.	†1841	Robert Bickerstaff	Chester Cathedral	S	Pevsner, *Cheshire*, 1971, 144
9.	by 1841	W Whitehall Davies	Worthenbury, Flint		Pevsner, *Clwyd*, 1986, 458
10.	nd	Mr Jones	Llangynhafal, Denbighs		Pevsner, *Clwyd*, 1986, 226

BLORE, Robert, of Derby 1810–68

He was the son of Joseph Blore, a monumental mason of Derby. Around 1837 he modelled a figure of the *Sleeping Endymion*, based on a work by **Canova**, later reproduced in biscuit porcelain by the Derby china works (**1**). In 1841 he moved to Middlesbrough, where he worked for Moss, Isaac Wilson and Co, who had opened a pottery there in 1838.

Literary References: *Gunnis* 1968, 57

Statues

1.	*c*1837	Sleeping Endymion, after Canova, model	Untraced Other versions: reproduced by Derby in biscuit porcelain	*Gunnis* 1968, 57

Busts

2.	1839	Rev Noah Jones	Untraced	*Gunnis* 1968, 57
3.	1851	Sir Joseph Paxton	Untraced	*Gunnis* 1968, 57

Architectural Sculpture

4.	*c*1840	Vases	Derby Arboretum	Pevsner, *Derbys*, 1978, 210

BLORE, Robert I and II, of Piccadilly fl 1759–1806

Monuments and tablets by the Blores can be found all over England and as far afield as Gibraltar and Barbados. It is difficult to distinguish between works by the father and son, since they seem to have worked together from about 1790. Gunnis comments that although the firm's works are always well carved, the designs are dull and uninteresting. The monument to William Ettrick was originally intended for Bishop-Wearmouth church but was too large and so was erected at High Barnes, the Ettrick family seat (**27**). It cost 'with the addition of a basement or pedestal by **Jopling of Gateshead**, upward of £500' (*Surtees* I, 1816–42, 239). The modest tablet to the Bishop of Ely, which has a dove marble ground and white marble inscription and vase, cost £85 4s with package and freight (**29**; Archives Lady Lucas and Dingwall, in GPC).

The elder Blore became bankrupt in 1818 and retired about two years later. In 1795 his son married Emma Earley, who was related to the **Carter** family of sculptors, at St Luke, Chelsea. He continued the business and some time after 1830 went into partnership with a former pupil, George Wilcox. The younger Blore became the subject of considerable public interest in 1825 when he brought an action for libel against John Stockdale, publisher of the *Memoirs* of the courtesan Harriette Wilson. He objected to Harriette's claim that, as a married man, he had proposed to Harriette's sister Fanny and that she described him as a ridiculous and uncouth figure. The court upheld his complaint and awarded him £300 in damages. He died in 1838 and is buried in Kensal Green cemetery (Add inf. Bob Moulder).

Literary References: *The Times*, 27 July 1818, 2; 24 August 1818, 2; 2 July 1825, 3–4; 14 November 1825, 3; *Gunnis* 1968, 57; *Wilson* 2004, 233–8

Funerary Monuments

1.	†1759	John White	Selborne, Hants	S	GPC
2.	†to 1759	Lockwood family	Gayton, Northants		Pevsner, *Northants*, 1973, 222
3.	†1780	Francis (†1777) and Frances Gwyn	Forde Abbey, Chard, Somerset, chapel	S	
4.	†1786	Hon William Murray	St Mary Abbots, Kensington, London	S	*Gunnis* 1968, 57
5.	?1786	John Simpson	Ryton, Durham		*Gunnis* 1968, 57
6.	?1791	Ann Read	Ramsbury, Wilts		*Gunnis* 1968, 57
7.	†1796	Edward Harvey	Holcot, Beds	S	Pevsner, *Beds, Huntingdon and Peterborough*, 1968, 101
8.	1796	Unidentified subject, tablet	Ely Cathedral, Cambs, north porch (formerly in north transept)	S	Pevsner, *Cambs*, 1970, 365
9.	?1799	Elizabeth Coghlan	St Mary, Paddington, London		*Gunnis* 1968, 57

10.	?1799	John Escott	Chertsey, Surrey		*Gunnis* 1968, 57
11.	1799	John Morrison	King's Chapel, Gibraltar		GPC
12.	?1802	Rev Edward Lockwood	St Peter, Northampton		*Gunnis* 1968, 57
13.	†1803	H Gwynne Browne	Evenley, Northants	S	Pevsner, *Northants*, 1973, 210
14.	?1803	Mayers family members	Barbados Cathedral, Bridgetown		*Gunnis* 1968, 57
15.	1804	J Wilkin	Chatton, Northumbs	S	Pevsner, *Northumbs*, 1992, 217
16.	1804	Lord Thomas Pelham Clinton	King's Chapel, Gibraltar		GPC
17.	†1805	Edward Foley (designed by C H Tatham)	Stoke Edith, Herefs		*GM*, vol LXXV, 1805, i, 278; Pevsner, *Herefs*, 1963, 292
18.	?1805	Lady Edwards	Hampton, Middx		*Gunnis* 1968, 57
19.	†1806	Anne Southby	Appleton, Berks	S	Pevsner, *Berks*, 1966, 65
20.	†1806	Lieutenant-General Sir William Myers	Barbados Cathedral, Bridgetown	S	*Gunnis* 1968, 57
21.	†1806	Mary Ann Webb	St Mary Abbots, Kensington, London	S	
22.	†1807	Dr John Wasdale	St Paul's Cathedral, London		Pevsner, *London: City*, 1997, 180
23.	†1807	Elizabeth Gwyn	Forde Abbey, Chard, Somerset, chapel	S	Pevsner, *Dorset*, 1972, 211
24.	?1807	Richard Lyster	Alberbury, Salop		*Gunnis* 1968, 57
25.	?1807	William Sherborn	East Bedfont, Middx		*Gunnis* 1968, 57
26.	†1808	Charles (†1774) and Anne Maysey	Mamble, Worcs	S	
27.	†1808	William Ettrick	High Barnes, Durham		*Surtees* I, 1816–40, 239 (repr)
28.	1790–1809	Forster family	Bolton Chapel, Northumbs	S	Pevsner, *Northumbs*, 1992, 197
29.	1809	James Yorke, Bishop of Ely (†1808) Payment(s): £85	Forthampton, Glos	S	Pevsner, *Glos: Vale & Forest of Dean*, 1976, 187
30.	†1809	John James Todd	Catherington, Hants	S	
31.	?1810	George Wyndham	Cromer, Norfolk		*Gunnis* 1968, 57
32.	†1811	Elizabeth Busby	St Mary Abbots, Kensington, London	S	
33.	?1812	Sir Thomas Fletcher	Betley, Staffs		*Gunnis* 1968, 57
34.	†1813	Charlotte Pigott	Exeter Cathedral, Devon		GPC
35.	†1813	Francis Gostling RN	St Mary Abbots, Kensington, London	S	
36.	†1815	Thomas Porter	Rockbeare, Devon		Pevsner, *Devon*, 1989, 702
37.	†1817	George Brooks (by Robert Blore II)	Stoke Poges, Bucks	S	Pevsner, *Bucks*, 1994, 652
38.	†1818	Robert John Atkyns	Burnham, Bucks	S	
39.	†1818	Thomas Curtis Chase	St Mary Abbots, Kensington, London	S	*Gunnis* 1968, 57
40.	†1818	W G Braddyll	Ulverston, Lancs		Pevsner, *Lancs: N*, 1969, 251
41.	†1819	Charles Stratton	St John's Wood Chapel, Marylebone, London		*Gunnis* 1968, 57
42.	?1819	Edward Downes	Pott, Cheshire		*Gunnis* 1968, 57
43.	?1819	Martha Cherry	St John's Wood Chapel, Marylebone, London		*Gunnis* 1968, 57
44.	†1821	Edward Ommaney Wrench, his daughter Catherine (†1802) and Lieutenant-Colonel William Handfield	Chester Cathedral, Cheshire	S	*Gunnis* 1968, 57
45.	†1821	Elizabeth, Countess of Mexborough	Methley, W R Yorks		*Gunnis* 1968, 57; Pevsner, *Yorks: W R*, 1967, 365
46.	†1821	Elizabeth, Countess of Mexborough	Westminster Abbey, London, Chapel of St John the Baptist		*MacMichael* 1977, 59
47.	?1822	Mrs Christian Mackenzie	Burwash, Sussex		*Gunnis* 1968, 57
48.	?1823	Thomas Winstanley	St Peter-in-the-East, Oxford		*Gunnis* 1968, 57
49.	?1824	Thomas Rennell	Winchester Cathedral, Hants		*Gunnis* 1968, 57
50.	?1828	Hon Henry Savile	Methley, Yorks		*Gunnis* 1968, 57
51.	?1828	Hon Henry Savile	Darfield, W R Yorks		GPC
52.	?1831	Martha Jadis	Iver, Bucks		*Gunnis* 1968, 57
53.	†1831	Montagu Cholmeley (by Robert Blore II) (co-sculptor: G Wilcox)	Stoke Rochford, Lincs	S	Pevsner, *Lincs*, 1989, 720

Chimneypieces

54.	1806	Several	[for W H Fellowes, Ramsey Abbey, Hunts]; untraced		Soane bill book D fol 553; *Gunnis* 1968, 57

BLUNDELL, William, of Daventry *c*1770–1865

Gunnis notes that his monuments to John Lucas, John King and David Rattray have well-cut details (**1, 2, 3**).

Literary References: *Gunnis* 1968, 57

Funerary Monuments

1.	?1810	John Lucas	Dunchurch, Northants	S	*Gunnis* 1968, 57
2.	†1816	John King	Long Buckley, Northants	S	*Gunnis* 1968, 57
3.	†1820	Colonel David Rattray	Daventry, Northants	S	*Gunnis* 1968, 57
4.	†1834	John Wildegose	Daventry, Northants	S	
5.	†1836	Rev Thomas Speidell	Crick, Northants	S	
6.	†1770–1848	Aholiab West Bradshaw and family	Priors Marston, Warks	S	

BOAG, Maitland and David, of London *c*1760–1817

Maitland Boag, or Bog, and his son David were the principal stone-carvers engaged on the restoration of Henry VII's Chapel in Westminster Abbey in 1809. The father was born *c*1760 and died in December 1817.

Literary References: *GM*, 1817, ii, 630; *Neale and Brayley* II, 1818–23, 26; *Gunnis* 1968, 58

BOGAERT, E fl 1829

'Bogaert, Em.' of 72 Wardour Street, Soho, exhibited one work at the Society of British Artists in 1829.

Literary References: *Johnson* 1975, 46

Busts

1.	1829	Paris, after Canova	[Exhib Soc of BA, London, 854]; untraced		*Johnson* 1975, 46

BOGLE fl 1738

A carver who worked for Henry Watson at Trentham Hall, Staffs in May 1738.

Literary References: *Brighton* 2001, 72

BOHSE fl 1773

He was an assistant of **John Francis Moore** and gave his address as 'At Mr Moore, Berners Street' when he exhibited at the Free Society of Artists in 1773.

Literary References: *Gunnis* 1968, 58

Chimneypieces

1.	1773	Vase with grapes and swags, tablet for a chimneypiece		[Exhib Free Soc, London, 23]; untraced		*Graves* 1907, 35

BOND, Henry, of Falmouth fl 1808–15

Funerary Monuments

1.	†1808	John Marshall	sl	King Charles the Martyr, Falmouth, Cornwall	S	
2.	†1815	Henry and Ann (†1804) Steel		King Charles the Martyr, Falmouth, Cornwall	S	

BONE, Charles 1791–

Bone entered the Royal Academy Schools in 1811, giving his age as 20. He exhibited at the RA in 1815 and 1826 and sent his 1815 RA exhibition work, *Ulysses throwing the rocky fragment*, to the British Institution in 1816 (**2**). His addresses are recorded as 15 Clarendon Street, 17 Upper Titchfield Street and 29 Winchester Row.

Literary References: *Hutchison* 1960–2, 166; *Gunnis* 1968, 58

Funerary Monuments

1.	1826	Monumental figure	[Exhib RA, London, 1063]; untraced	*Graves* I, 1905–6, 225

Miscellaneous

2.	1815	Ulysses throwing the rocky fragment	[Exhib RA, London, 896]; untraced	*Graves* 1875, 53; *Graves* I, 1905–6, 225

BONE, Edward –1816

Edward Bone was apprenticed to **Richard Westmacott I** in 1776 (PRO Apprenticeship Lists). His will was proved on 8 May 1816. It describes him as 'Sculptor, of Saint Marylebone, Middlesex' (PROB 11/1580).

BONOMI, Joseph 1796–1878

Bonomi began his career as a sculptor but later achieved prominence as an Egyptologist and draughtsman. He and his twin sister, Mary Ann, were born at 76 Great Titchfield Street, London, on 9 October 1796, the fourth and fifth surviving children of Joseph Bonomi ARA (1739–1808), an Italian-born architect, and his wife Rosa née Florini. He was baptised 4 days later in the Venetian chapel in London, when his sponsors (by proxy) were Giovanni Carlo Bonomi, his uncle, and Angelica Kauffman, the painter, who was his mother's cousin. Bonomi's parents died while he was young but he was left well provided for. He went to school at Carshalton, Surrey.

Bonomi had become interested in sculpture by 1815, when he was awarded a silver medal by the Society of Arts for an original bas-relief in plaster (**16**). He gave his address at that time as Charlotte Street. He joined the Royal Academy Schools the following year and won their silver medals in 1817 and 1818. He also studied anatomy under the eminent surgeon and anatomist Sir Charles Bell. **Joseph Nollekens** was a family friend and *c*1818 Bonomi entered his studio as a pupil. Nollekens seems to have been fond of the young man, whom he took on excursions to see the Parthenon marbles and on his regular Sunday evening walks. J T Smith records that 'it was generally supposed that he would have left a considerable part of his immense property' to his pupil in his will 'from his long continued attachment to him from his birth' (*Smith* 1828, I, 39). In fact Nollekens bequeathed him only £100 but he also left the same sum to each of Bonomi's five brothers and sisters. Joseph's brother Ignatius Bonomi (1787–1870) trained under his father and set up his own architectural practice in County Durham. He went on to design a number of funerary monuments, including two carved by **Charles Harriott Smith**.

One of Joseph Bonomi's earliest works is the monument to Captain Charles Showers, in Kolkata (Calcutta) Cathedral, which he signed '[Bonomi] / Nollekens / Discipulus / Fecit 1819' (**1**). It has a relief of the battle at Malown, during which Showers and his lieutenants, Bagot and Broughton, were killed in 1815. Rupert Gunnis considered it 'fine'. Bonomi exhibited *Jacob wrestling with the angel* at the British Institution in 1820 (**19**) and showed several portrait busts at the Royal Academy in 1820 and 1821 (**7–9**). The following year he travelled to Rome, intending to study under **Antonio Canova**, but the plan collapsed because Canova died before Bonomi arrived in the city. There he became acquainted with **John Gibson RA** and executed at least two works (**6, 17**). A critic who saw them wrote that 'this accomplished and intelligent artist is particularly distinguished by animation, freedom and simplicity in his works, very different from the usual manner of his countrymen' (*Lit Gaz*, 1824, 668).

In spite of this encouraging review, sculpture soon became a secondary occupation. In Rome he met Robert Hay, a naval officer who was to lead an expedition to Egypt, and was persuaded to join the explorers to help record their discoveries. This occupation must have been congenial, for between 1824 and 1834 Bonomi travelled extensively in Egypt and the Near East, with a number of leading Egyptologists, making drawings of hieroglyphics, monuments and ancient sites. He also took casts of antiquities, including one of the head of the colossal statue of Rameses II at Memphis, which was later displayed at the British Museum. After his return to England in 1834 he illustrated books on ancient Egypt and coloured plaster-casts of Egyptian sculpture for the British Museum. He even became involved in two architectural commissions, designing an Egyptian façade for John Marshall's Temple Mills in Leeds and an unrealised 'carved and painted tympanum' for James Wild's masterpiece, Christ Church, Streatham, in South London. In 1842 Bonomi and Wild joined a Prussian research team, led by Professor Karl Richard Lepsius, in Egypt. Between expeditions Bonomi continued to work as a sculptor and exhibited several works at the Royal Academy in 1837 and 1838 (**3, 4, 10, 13**).

Bonomi settled permanently in Britain in 1844 and married Jessie, a daughter of the painter John Martin, the following year. The couple's first four children all died of whooping cough in 1852. They went on to have four more, but Jessie died in 1859 and Joseph brought up his young family with the assistance of his sister-in-law, Isabella Mary Martin. He found that his combined expertise in art and Egyptology could be put to good use in a number of enterprises at home. In collaboration with two other artists, Henry Warren and Joseph Fahey, Bonomi produced and exhibited two moving panoramas depicting a trip along the Nile and a journey through the Holy Land. Highlights of the Nile panorama, which was put on display at the Egyptian Hall in London in July 1849, included a tableau of Abu Simbel seen by torchlight and a representation of a sandstorm overtaking a caravan in the Libyan desert. In 1852–53 Bonomi and Owen Jones designed the Egyptian Courts for the Crystal Palace at Sydenham. Bonomi oversaw the decorative sculpture and executed much of it himself (**14**). In 1857 he and James Wild jointly prepared a model for the national Wellington Memorial competition but were not successful (**5**) (*Bonomi Papers* Add 9389/2/W/60). In 1861 Bonomi was appointed Curator of the Sir John Soane Museum, in spite of objections from architects who pointed out that the post was officially reserved for a member of their profession. He also published a treatise, *The Proportions of the Human Body*, and invented a measuring device which he suggested might be used by artists and to identify individuals for legal purposes.

He died on 3 January 1878, after a short illness. His last known sculptural work was a pair of reliefs for the principal front of his family home, 'The Camels', in Prince's Road, Wimbledon, which was built by Ignatius Bonomi between 1865 and 1866 (**15**). They depicted the riddle famously posed by the sphinx in Sophocles's *Oedipus the King* and the camels that gave the house its name were prominently featured. They were presumably demolished with the rest of the building. He bequeathed his portrait bust of the painter and dramatist, Prince Hoare the Younger (**12**) and a portrait of his father by John Francis Rigaud to the Royal Academy.

Bonomi is remembered chiefly for his contribution to the study of the ancient monuments of Egypt and the Near East. One of his most popular publications, *Nineveh and its palaces. The discoveries of Botta and Layard, applied to the elucidation of Holy Writ*, was reprinted several times between 1852 and 1894. One obituary recalled that 'The kindness and urbanity of his disposition and his philanthropy endeared him to many friends, while his knowledge of the sites and monuments of ancient Egypt was freely imparted to all who sought his assistance or advice' (*Athenaeum*, 1878, i, 316).

EH

Literary References: RSA, *Transactions*, vol 33, 1815, 22; *Smith* 1828, *passim*; *Farington*, 14, 5119; *Builder*, 1861, 165; *The Times*, 5 March 1878, 10; 17 May 1878, 11; *DNB* V, 1886, 364 (Lane-Poole); *Simpson* 1895, 548–9; *Gunnis* 1968, 58; *Ormond* 1973, 43, pl 67; *Altick* 1978, 182, 206, 460; *Darby* 1983, *passim*; *Jenkins* 1992, 116, 127–8; *Colvin* 1995, 142; *Grove* 4, 1996, 333 (Meadows); *Curl* 2001, 57; *ODNB* (Meadows)

Additional Manuscript Sources: Bonomi Autograph 1; Bonomi Autograph 2; Bonomi Miscellania; Bonomi Papers; Bonomi/Catherwood; Bonomi/Douce; Bonomi/Eastlake; Bonomi/Hay 1; Bonomi/Hay 2; Bonomi/Hérékyan Bey; Bonomi/Lee 1; Bonomi/Lee 2; Bonomi/Lee 3; Bonomi/Panizzi; Bonomi/Smythe; Bonomi/Trevelyan; Bonomi/Wornum; Collectanea Ægyptiaca; Eclipse Scrapbook

Wills and Administrations: PPR, will, 1 May 1878, effects under £8,000

Collections of Drawings: Drawings, watercolours and sketches made in Egypt, Nubia, Palestine and elsewhere, Griffith Institute, Oxford University

Portraits of the Sculptor: Matilda Sharpe, canvas, 1868, NPG 1477 (Ormond 1973, pl 67); C Martin, painting, exhib RA, London, 1867, 493; J Pastorini, miniature, exhib RA, 1816, 732; woodcut published ILN, LXXII (1878), 245

No.	Date	Subject		Location		Reference
Funerary Monuments						
1.	1819	Captain Charles Showers, Lieutenant Humphrey Bagot and Lieutenant Edward Broughton (†1815)		St John's Cathedral, Kolkata (Calcutta)	SD	*Groseclose* 1995, 61
2.	†1819	Lieutenant-Colonel John Weston		Old Cathedral, Kolkata (Calcutta)	S	RG/JP, 2, 170
3.	1837	An infant child (model only)		[Exhib RA, London, 1195]; untraced		*Graves* I, 1905–6, 238
4.	1838	Unidentified subject (for Dorking, Surrey)		[Exhib RA, London, 1282]; untraced		*Graves* I, 1905–6, 239
5.	1857	Arthur, 1st Duke of Wellington (†1852), competition model (designed by J W Wild)		[Westminster Hall, London]; untraced		RG/JP, 2, 169v.
Statues						
6.	1823–1824	A Muse		[Rome]; untraced		*Lit Gaz*, 1824, 668; *Gunnis* 1968, 58
Busts						
7.	1820	'A young lady'		[Exhib RA, London, 1010]; untraced		*Graves* I, 1905–6, 238
8.	1821	James Northcote		[Exhib RA, London, 1109]; untraced		*Graves* I, 1905–6, 238; *Johnson* 1975, 48
9.	1821	Joseph Hume	p	New York Hist Soc, 1858–91	SD	*Graves* I, 1905–6, 238; *Ormond* 1973, 235; www.nyhist.org
10.	1838	Henry Parks		[Exhib RA, London, 1380]; untraced		*Graves* I, 1905–6, 239
11.	nd	Dr John Lee	p	Aylesbury Museum, Bucks		RG/JP, 2, 170
12.	nd	Prince Hoare	p	[Crystal Palace, Sydenham, 1854]; untraced		RG/JP, 2, 170
Architectural Sculpture						
13.	1837	Homer, one of a series of metopes for the decoration of a library		[Exhib RA, London, 1203]; untraced		*Graves* I, 1905–6, 238
14.	1852–1853	Decorative sculpture		[Crystal Palace, London, Egyptian court]; destroyed		*Gunnis* 1968, 58
15.	1865–1866	The riddle of Oedipus, a pair of reliefs		[The Camels, Prince's Road, Wimbledon Park, London]; destroyed		*Simpson* 1895, 549
Reliefs						
16.	1815	Unidentified subject	p	[Soc of A, silver medal]; untraced		*Gunnis* 1968, 58
17.	*c*1823	Dancing Bacchanal		[Rome]; untraced		*Lit Gaz*, 1824, 668; *Gunnis* 1968, 58

Miscellaneous

18.	c1820	Cast of the right hand of 'the French giant', perhaps Lois Franz	Untraced Other versions: Royal College of Surgeons		*Smith* II, 1828, 326–7
19.	1820	Jacob wrestling with the angel	[Exhib BI, London, 136]; untraced		*Graves* 1875, 56

BOOBYER, James, of Bath fl 1780–1821

James Boobyer I (fl 1780–90) was succeeded in the business by his son, James Boobyer II.

Literary References: *Gunnis* 1968, 58

Funerary Monuments

1.	?1785	James Moutray	Bath Abbey, Somerset	S	*Gunnis* 1968, 58
2.	†1821	John Owen Herbert	Kerry, Montgomery	S	Pevsner, *Powys*, 1979, 114

BOOL, George M 1812–

He entered the Royal Academy Schools in December 1833 on the recommendation of **John Francis**. The RA archives record that he was then 21 and his address was 56 Albany Street, Regent's Park. He won a silver medal in 1836, having shown various medallic portraits, busts and bas-reliefs over the previous four years. The *Literary Gazette* considered his colossal bust of William IV to be 'one of the most perfect resemblances of the King that has yet been executed; the effect of it is very grand' (4) (*Lit Gaz* 1834, 299). He appears to have exhibited his bust of *Democritus* (2), first shown at the Society of British Artists in 1833, for a second time at the RA in 1868.

Literary References: *Graves* I, 1905–6, 239; *Gunnis* 1968, 58

Archival References: RA Admissions, RA Premium list

Statues						
1.	1833	Ulysses, sketch		[Exhib RA, London, 1110]; untraced		*Graves* I, 1905–6, 239
Busts						
2.	1833	Democritus		[Exhib Soc of BA, London, 826]; untraced		*Graves* I, 1905–6, 239; *Johnson* 1975, 48
3.	1833	Unidentified artist		[Exhib Soc of BA, London, 845]; untraced		*Johnson* 1975, 48
4.	1834	King William IV	m	[Exhib Soc of BA, London, 868]; untraced		*Johnson* 1975, 48
5.	1834	Unidentified young lady		[Exhib RA, London, 1051]; untraced		*Graves* I, 1905–6, 239
6.	nd	Queen Adelaide		Royal Coll (Frogmore, Berks)	S	C Lib (repr)
Reliefs						
7.	1832	Adam		[Exhib RA, London, 1131]; untraced		*Graves* I, 1905–6, 239
8.	1833	Unidentified young lady, medallion		[Exhib RA, London, 1135]; untraced		*Graves* I, 1905–6, 239
9.	1833	Unidentified young lady, medallion		[Exhib RA, London, 1137]; untraced		*Graves* I, 1905–6, 239
10.	1835	Medallic study of heads	m	[Exhib RA, London, 1107]; untraced		*Graves* I, 1905–6, 239
11.	1835	Unidentified subject(s), medallions	m	[Exhib Soc of BA, London, 774]; untraced		*Johnson* 1975, 48
Miscellaneous						
12.	1834	Lion		[Exhib BI, London, 565]; untraced		*Graves* 1875, 56
13.	1834	The Saviour in the wilderness		[Exhib RA, London, 1037]; untraced		*Graves* I, 1905–6, 239
14.	1835	The millennium, a sketch		[Exhib RA, London, 1117]; untraced		*Graves* 1875, 56; *Graves* I, 1905–6, 239
15.	1836	Madonna		[Exhib RA, London, 1100]; untraced		*Graves* I, 1905–6, 239

BOOTH, of Nottingham fl ?1827–?1832

Funerary Monuments

1.	?1827	Phyllis and Elizabeth Booker	Dudley, Worcs	S	GPC
2.	†1830	Charles Beaumont	East Bridgford, Notts	S	Pevsner, *Notts*, 1979, 113
3.	?1832	Philip Palmer	East Bridgford, Notts	S	GPC

BOOTH & JOHNSON, of Nottingham fl c1770–1801

Funerary Monuments

1.	c1770	John Bulstrode	Keyworth, Notts	S	*Gunnis* 1968, 58
2.	?1778	Elizabeth Cripple	Ruddington, Notts	S	*Gunnis* 1968, 58
3.	?1780	Hawksley family	St Nicholas, Nottingham	S	*Gunnis* 1968, 59
4.	?1781	Clarkstone family, altar tomb	East Bridgford, Notts, churchyard	S	GPC
5.	†1789	Samuel Heywood	St Mary, Nottingham	S	
6.	†1797	Elizabeth Bainbrigge	Lockington, Leics	S	Pevsner, *Leics & Rutland*, 1984, 277
7.	?1799	Robert Wright	St Mary, Nottingham		*Gunnis* 1968, 59
8.	†1801	Rev Henry Swindell	Ockbrook, Derbys		

BOSON, John c1696–1743

A carver in wood and marble, he was probably the 'John Boson, son of Michael Boson of Witham, Suffolk,' who was apprenticed to Jarvis Smith, a joiner for eight years on 1 May 1711 (Joiners' Apprentices 1710–24, fol 5). In the 1720s and early 1730s he was employed on four of the new Queen Anne churches built by Nicholas Hawksmoor, St John, Westminster, St George, Bloomsbury, St Alphege, Greenwich and St Luke, Old Street (**8, 9, 17, 18, 21, 26**). In 1727 he petitioned the authorities for payment for his work at St George's, having received only £73 of the £221 owing to him and claiming to be 'a young man in Trade reduced to very great inconvenience' (Lambeth Palace Library MS/2690-2750/2728 f55). His yard was at Greenwich, where he produced altar, pulpit and screen carving in wood, as well as a font in marble (**8, 9**). Boson received further commissions for ecclesiastical furniture carving in Westminster Abbey and Canterbury Cathedral (**10, 12**). At the latter, where he worked under the architect John James, he carved the altar, on which he appears to have worked with **John Balshaw, or Belshaw**, who received payments for carving work on the same. He was also responsible for the ornaments on the façade of East India House, in partnership with **John How** (**15**), and also supplied chimneypieces (**7**). He was paid £189 19s 7d for unspecified 'carver's work' by the company in April 1730, which may be the bill for either of these commissions.

He continued his diverse practice in the 1730s. For the Prince of Wales alone he produced a marble chimneypiece, ornate picture frames, and carving on the Prince's state barge (**3, 24, 32, 34**). The connection was a lasting one: at the time of Boson's death he appears to have been working for the Prince, who paid his last bill to Boson's executors.

Boson's most notable work is the marble frame for the monument to Anne, Duchess of Richmond (**1**). The design, featuring caryatid figures and classical decoration, is taken from the frontispiece to the English edition of the *Fabbriche Antique disegnate da Andrea Palladio* (1730), published by Lord Burlington in 1730. William Kent was responsible for this frontispiece. The monument is signed '[Joan]nes Boson Anglus Sculpsit' and 'Andreas Pallad[io] Vincentinus Invent'. The bust of the deceased in the centre of the frame is by the Italian sculptor **Giovanni-Battista Guelfi.** It is possible that Boson's inclusion of 'Anglus' on his signature was intended to stress the native roots of the carver, in contradistinction to the bust's author. Boson carved furniture to designs by William Kent for Lord Burlington's villa at Chiswick. The pier tables with matching glass frames are a rare example of known surviving furniture carved by Boson (**29**). He was later a subscriber to Isaac Ware's edition of the *Four Books of Andrea Palladio* (1738). Boson clearly had a longstanding interest in architectural carving: in 1726 he subscribed to Giacomo Leoni's English edition of Alberti's *Della Architettura.*

In 1735 Boson leased a house from Lord Burlington, a handsome tripartite, pedimented building at 22/23 Savile Row. This may have been designed by William Kent. Boson lived there with his wife until his death, 'of an age not considerably above middle aged' in 1743 (*Vertue* III, 116). In his will, proved in April that year, the carver left his estate in the hands of three trustees, James Horne, the architect and surveyor John Thornhill, and George Lambert, the painter. He made bequests to his brothers Michael and Francis, his sisters Martha and Mary and his foreman, Thomas Nicholls the Elder, who received £10. To Mary Norman, the daughter of Barak Norman, a musical instrument maker of St Paul's Churchyard, he left the contents of his dwelling-house in St Ann's Hill, Chertsey. In a telling addition he also left her £15 yearly for each of her children yet unborn and that 'shall be born before the expiration of nine months after death.' He also mentions his father-in-law Francis Rayer. Vertue described Boson as 'a man of great ingenuity' who 'undertook great works in his way for the prime people of quality and made his fortune very well in the world' (*Vertue* III, 116). The lack of surviving work makes it difficult to assess his achievements, but his connections to the leading taste-makers of his day, Hawksmoor, Kent, Burlington and the Prince of Wales, suggest that Boson was a craftsman of some distinction.

MGS

Literary References: *Webb* 1955 (1), 143; *Gunnis* 1968, 59; *Beard and Gilbert* 1986, 88–9; *Whinney* 1988, 161
Archival References: GPC
Will: PROB 11/725/99 15 April 1743 'John Boson, Carver of St James's Westminster'

Funerary Monuments						
1.	1734	Anne, Duchess of Richmond (†1722), frame only: bust by G B Guelfi (designed by William Kent) (co-sculptor: Giovanni-Battista Guelfi) Payment(s): £211 'for carved work' (Account book, Boughton, Northants)		Deene, Northants	S	*Webb* 1955 (1), 141–143 (repr); GPC
Chimneypieces						
2.	1732	'chimney piece wch is gilt' Payment(s): £5 12s		[Earl Fitzwalter, Pall Mall, London, dining room]; untraced		Mildmay Accounts, Hants R O 15M50/31 cited in GPC
3.	1732–1734	Richly ornamented chimney piece and other work Payment(s): £177 (including £50 for the chimneypiece)	m	[Kew Palace, Surrey, for Frederick, Prince of Wales]; untraced		*Beard and Gilbert* 1986, 89; GPC
4.	1735	In the great room, and other carving Payment(s): £61		[Baylies, Stoke Poges, Bucks]; untraced		*Gunnis* 1968, 59; *Beard and Gilbert* 1986, 89
5.	1736	Description unavailable		Culverthorpe Hall, Lincs, great room		*Gunnis* 1968, 59; Pevsner, *Lincs,* 1989, 245; *Beard and Gilbert* 1986, 89
6.	1740	'Chimney piece with frame over it with scrolls, coronets etc' and other work Payment(s): £71 5s 7d for chimneypiece		[for Lord Noel Somerset]; untraced		GPC
7.	nd	Several (co-sculptor: John How)		[East India House, Leadenhall St, London]; untraced		*Gunnis* 1968, 59
Architectural Sculpture						
8.	1725–1726	Altar table with festoons and grapes, pulpit carved with cherub heads, reading desk, screens and front of gallery Payment(s): £220 (bill including marble font)	wd	[St John, Westminster, London]; untraced		*Beard and Gilbert* 1986, 89; *Friedman* 2004, 50–51; GPC
9.	1725–1726	Font Payment(s): £220 (bill including carving of altar table, pulpit, reading desk, screens and front of gallery)	m	[St John, Westminster, London]; untraced		*Friedman* 2004, 50–51
10.	1729	Carved woodwork for screen and organ gallery Payment(s): £33	wd	Westminster Abbey, London		*Gunnis* 1968, 59
11.	1730	Coat of arms above hall door Payment(s): £42		[Moulsham Hall, Essex]; untraced		*Edwards* 1977, 39; GPC

12.	1732	Carved work, including seven urns above the altar, Corinthian capitals and cherubs' heads (co-sculptor: John Balshaw or Belshaw) Payment(s): £279 4s 3d	wd	[Canterbury Cathedral, Kent]; untraced	*Gunnis* 1968, 59; GPC citing Fabric Acct Book, Cathedral library
13.	1732	Decorative ornaments Payment(s): £33 3s		[Cley (a house belonging to the Duke of Montrose), during room and stairs]; untraced	*Beard and Gilbert* 1986, 89 citing SRO GD 220/6/31/p640 Montrose Papers, cashbook, 1732
14.	1735	Heraldic shields		Westminster Abbey, London, in frieze below great west window	RG/JP, 2, 172–5
15.	nd	Carving (co-sculptor: John How)	wd	[East India House, Leadenhall St, London, façade]; untraced	E I Co archives in *Gunnis* 1968, 59; *Archer* 1965, 405
Miscellaneous					
16.	1727–1729	Unidentified work Payment(s): £140		[Home of Henry, 1st Duke of Kent at 4 St James's Square, London]; untraced	Hoare's Customer Ledger, 1725–1728, vol I, fol 460; Hoare's Customer Ledger, 1728–1731, vol K, f29; *Beard and Gilbert* 1986, 89; GPC
17.	1720–1730	Decorative ornaments Payment(s): £220, of which £73 still owing to him, 1727; paid after complaint to Bishop of London	wd	[St George, Bloomsbury, London]; untraced	*Gunnis* 1968, 59; *Beard and Gilbert* 1986, 89; GPC
18.	1732	Decorative ornaments		[St Alphege, Greenwich]; untraced	GPC
19.	post-1732	Unidentified work		[for Frederick, Prince of Wales, Cliveden, Bucks]; untraced	*Beard and Gilbert* 1986, 88
20.	1732	Unidentified work Payment(s): £19		[Holkham Hall, Norfolk]; untraced	*Beard and Gilbert* 1986, 89
21.	1727–1733	Decorative ornaments		[St Luke, Old Street, London]; untraced	*Gunnis* 1968, 59; GPC
22.	1733	Picture frame Payment(s): £20	wd	[All Souls' College, Oxford]; untraced	GPC
23.	1730–1733	Sundry carved work Payment(s): £58 8s (1730); £41 9s 6d (1732); £136 14s 2d (1733)		[Kelham, Notts, for Bridget, Duchess of Rutland]; untraced	GPC citing executors' accounts of Bridget, Duchess of Rutland (†1734), Belvoir Muniments
24.	1732–1733	Unidentified carved work Payment(s): £120 (1732); £30 (1733)		[Kew Palace, Surrey, for Frederick, Prince of Wales]; untraced	*Beard and Gilbert* 1986, 89; GPC
25.	1728–1733	Unidentified work		[St John, Horsleydown, London]; untraced	*Gunnis* 1968, 59
26.	1732–1734	Unidentified work (co-sculptor: John Darby)		[St Luke, Old Street, London]; untraced	GPC
27.	1734	Unidentified work Payment(s): £16		[for Frederick, Prince of Wales]; untraced	*Beard and Gilbert* 1986, 89; GPC
28.	1735	Carved work Payment(s): £233 19s 5d		[for Frederick, Prince of Wales, St James's Park, Westminster]; untraced	*Beard and Gilbert* 1986, 89
29.	1735	Two 'rich Glas frames,' two 'Mahogany Tables with Tearmes', decorated with owl crest (designed by William Kent) Payment(s): £43 4s (with stands)		[Chiswick House, Middx]; Chatsworth, Derbys	*Beard and Gilbert* 1986, 88, 89
30.	1735	Two 'stands with Boys heads' Payment(s): £43 4s (with frames and tables)		[Chiswick House, Middx]; untraced	*Beard and Gilbert* 1986, 88, 89
31.	1737	Unidentified work Payment(s): £8 2s 6d		[Ditton Park, Berks]; untraced	Andrew Marchant's Accounts, Boughton, Northants, 28 Jan 1737 (inf Geoffrey Beard)
32.	1738	Carved frames Payment(s): £24 5s		[for Frederick, Prince of Wales]; untraced	*Beard and Gilbert* 1986, 89
33.	1738	Mahogany carved bedstead Payment(s): £10 5s	wd	[for Sir Richard Hoare]; untraced	*Beard and Gilbert* 1986, 89 citing V&A lib, MS 86, NN 3, no 12
34.	1738	Ornaments for the state barge, including a carved taffrail or stern-board (designed by William Kent) Payment(s): £10 15s	wd	[for Frederick, Prince of Wales]; NMM, Greenwich	*Beard and Gilbert* 1986, 89; GPC citing Duchy of Cornwall, vol VIII, fol. 253
35.	1739	Unidentified work Payment(s): £50		[St Olave, Southwark, London]; untraced	GPC; *Beard and Gilbert* 1986, 89
36.	1740	Chimney mouldings, table frames and oval sconces Payment(s): £71 5s 7d		[for Lord Charles Somerset]; untraced	*Beard and Gilbert* 1986, 89 citing Badminton archives, Glos R O, D2700/QJ3/11
37.	1740	Unidentified work Payment(s): £94		[for the 1st Earl of Guilford]; untraced	*Beard and Gilbert* 1986, 89 citing Bodl MS North C58, F99
38.	1740	Various works, including 'peers to the Park Gate the two Pedestalls to the Vases' Payment(s): £1,440 8s 6d (£1,162 10s of which was for work on the Octagon Building in St James's Park)		[for Frederick, Prince of Wales]; untraced	GPC citing Duchy of Cornwall Accts

39.	1741	Ornaments Payment(s): £95 (for organ case?)	wd	Westminster Abbey, London	*Gunnis* 1968, 59
40.	1742	Mahogany stand, in the form of a Roman triumphal arch for 'Pope's Cabinet'	wd	[Stourhead, Wilts]; untraced	*Beard and Gilbert* 1986, 88, 89
41.	1743	'Frame and Figures &c' Payment(s): £53 13s		[Stourhead, Wilts]; untraced	Hoare Private Accounts 1734–49
42.	1740–1743	Unidentified work (under Henry Flitcroft)		[St Giles's House, Wimborne St Giles, Dorset]; untraced	MS Accounts 1743, St Giles's House, Wimborne, E/A/78
43.	1745	Carved work including two picture frames enriched mouldings, architraves, columns and capitals, and a chimneypiece Payment(s): £328		[Leicester House, London]; untraced	*Beard and Gilbert* 1986, 89; GPC citing Duchy of Cornwall Accts, vol VIII, fol 253

BOSSOM, Charles and Son, of Oxford fl 1822–37

Charles Bossom died on 14 June 1830 aged 42 and was buried in the churchyard of St Giles, Oxford. His tombstone describes him as a sculptor. He was succeeded in the business by his son, who signs tablets commemorating the Joy family and Lord Stavordale (5, 6). The *Gentleman's Magazine* for March 1828, which mentions the tablet to Dr Loveday (4), adds that Bossom 'has given other specimens of his art at New College'.

Literary References: *Gunnis* 1968, 59

Funerary Monuments

1.	1822	Mrs Deane	Kingston Bagpuize, Berks	S	*Gunnis* 1968, 59
2.	1822	Rev Henry Potter	Enfield, Middx	S	
3.	1825	John Oglander	Merton College Chapel, Oxford	S	*Gunnis* 1968, 59
4.	1828	Dr Arthur Loveday (†1824)	Magdalen College, Oxford	S	*GM*, vol XCVIII, March 1828, i, 209 (repr III)
5.	1833	Joy family	St Mary the Virgin, Oxford	S	GPC
6.	1837	Lord Stavordale	Farley, Wilts	S	*Gunnis* 1968, 59

BOSWOOD, J fl 1829–32

He exhibited a marble bust at the Royal Academy in 1832 from 57 Russell Square (1). Boswood posed for the artist George Richmond (1809–1896) on a number of occasions. A pen and ink portrait sketch by Richmond is dated 10 September 1829 (coll Prof Philip Rieff, Pennsylvania, USA, repr *Lister* 1981, 17). Several anatomical sketches of the sculptor by the same artist came onto the British art market in 2000 (C Lib repr).

Busts

1.	1832	Unidentified gentleman	m	[Exhib RA, London, 1182]; untraced	*Graves* I, 1905–6, 245

BOTTOMLEY FAMILY, of Norfolk and Cambridge fl 1729–1812

A number of sculptors called Bottomley who may have been inter-related were active in Norfolk and Cambs during the 18th and early 19th centuries.

George Bottomley went into partnership with **Robert Singleton** about 1729, and together they sign two monuments in Norwich (1, 2). The partnership was dissolved by 31 December 1737, when an advertisement in the *Norwich Mercury* announced that **Robert Page** had bought their stock-in-trade. William Cole, the antiquary, noted that the cartouche tablet to John Stevenson at Newton, near Cambridge, was the work of 'Bottomley, a mason in Cambridge, who was to have thirty guineas for it' (BL Add MS 5803, cited by *Palmer* 1932, 258) (4). This was probably **Charles Bottomley**, who married Susannah Flowerday at St James, Bury St Edmunds in 1849. He signs the obelisk commemorating Gregory Wale, erected on a hill between Shelford and Newton, and a ledger to Elizabeth Wenyade at Brettenham in Suffolk (7, 3). His widow appears to have carried on the business after his death for in 1757 she was paid for 'mason's work to the back of the Senate House' (Vice-Chancellor's Accounts, cited by *Gunnis* 1968, 59).

In 1778 another **Charles Bottomley**, of Wells-next-the-Sea, Norfolk, advertised that he could execute 'Chimney Pieces, Monuments, Tombs, Grave-stones, Coats of Arms in marble or any other stone' (*Norwich Mercury*, 13 Nov 1778). In 1787 he placed a notice in another local paper stating that although 'some malicious Persons have reported he means to decline that Branch of Business . . . he never had such intention; but that all Branches of Masonry will be executed at his Shop in Wells as usual' (*Norfolk Chronicle*, 5 May 1787).

Other masons likely to be from the same family are 'Mr. Bottomley of East Dereham' who died in 1827 and **Joseph Bottomley**, who lived at Wells-next-the-Sea in 1845. A tablet of 1791 is signed 'Bottomley' (5) and in 1812 a Bottomley was paid £13 8s 10d for the tablet to Edward Wright at Holkham (6).

Literary References: *Gunnis* 1968, 59

Archival References: GPC; RG/JP, 2, 175; NP/RG

Funerary Monuments

1.	†1729	Thomas Batchelor (by George Bottomley and Robert Singleton)	Norwich Cathedral, Norfolk	S	*Friedman* 1984, 267
2.	?1734	Daniel Fromanteel (by George Bottomley and Robert Singleton)	St Mary Coslany, Norwich, Norfolk	S	*Gunnis* 1968, 59
3.	?1747	Elizabeth Wenyade, ledger stone (by Charles Bottomley, of Bury and Cambridge)	Brettenham, Suffolk	S	*Gunnis* 1968, 59
4.	†1749	John Stevenson Payment(s): 30 gns	Newton, Cambs	S	*Palmer* 1932, 258
5.	?1791	Mr and Mrs Long	Gedney, Lincs	S	GPC
6.	by 1812	Edward Wright (†1809) Payment(s): £13 8s 10d	Holkham, Norfolk		NP/RG

Architectural Sculpture					
7.	c1739	Obelisk commemorating Gregory Wale (by Charles Bottomley, of Bury and Cambridge)		Magots Mount, Harston, Cambs	S	*Palmer* 1932, 147; Pevsner, *Cambs*, 1970, 403

BOUCHARDON, Edmé 1698–1762

A French sculptor, Bouchardon travelled to Rome in 1723 after winning the Prix de Rome with the subject *Gideon choosing his soldiers by watching them drinking* (untraced). He remained there for ten years and during that period executed a series of portrait busts, including several of British sitters. In 1727 he carved a severely classical bust of the German antiquary Baron Philipp von Stosch (Staatliche Museen, Skulpturensammlung, Berlin). This was followed by two portraits of English patrons, John Gordon of Invergordon and John, Lord Hervey (**1, 2**). Both men shared Stosch's antiquarian interests and are depicted in the same distinctive classicizing manner, with short hair and bare torsos truncated low on the chest. Lady Lechmere must have sat for her bust, later used on her memorial, when she and her husband, Sir Thomas Robinson, visited Rome in the early months of 1730 (**3**). Since Robinson's death in 1777 it has stood on his monument beside his bust, which was carved by Filippo della Valle, though Bouchardon may perhaps have provided the model (*Baker, Harrison and Laing* 2000, 755–6). Bouchardon also received a commission for a full-length statue of the Earl of Radnor but it is unclear whether it was ever executed.

Literary References: *Grove* 4, 1996, 508–11 (Harrison); *Baker, Harrison and Laing* 2000, 752–762

Busts						
1.	1728	John Gordon of Invergordon	m	coll Highland Council, Inverness	SD	*Baker, Harrison and Laing* 2000, 752–3, 754 (repr)
2.	1729	John, Lord Hervey	m	Melbury House, Dorset Other versions: Ickworth House (NT), tc, 1729	SD	*Treasure Houses* 1985, 312 (repr); *Bowron and Rishel* 2000, 230 (repr); *Baker, Harrison and Laing* 2000, 753, 754 (repr)
3.	1730	Elizabeth, Lady Lechmere	m	Robinson monument, Westminster Abbey, London		*Baker, Harrison and Laing* 2000, 753–5, 762 (repr)
4.	1731–1732	Catherine, Duchess of Buckingham	m	Private coll		*Baker, Harrison and Laing* 2000, 756, 757 (repr)

BOUCOCK, George fl 1787–90

William Miller and George Boucock, masons of 'St. Martin's, Ludgate', received £9,000 for building Wanstead church, Essex between 1787 and 1790. The contract for this work survives in the church archives.

Literary References: *Gunnis* 1968, 260

BOULTON fl 1783

Funerary Monuments					
1.	†1783	T Whinyates and family	Charleton, nr Kingsbridge, Devon	S	Pevsner, *Devon*, 1989, 254

BOUQUET, W V fl 1782–1827

Bouquet exhibited at the Royal Academy between 1782 and 1827 and at the Society of Arts in 1783, showing largely unidentified wax portraits. This peripatetic modeller was recorded 'At Mr. Richard's, Bear Street, Golden Square'; '112, Bunhill Row, Moorfields'; '2, Charles Street, Hatton Garden' and '18, Hoxton Square' (*Graves* I, 1905–6, 251). His only known surviving work is an undated wax portrait of a churchman (**1**).

Literary References: *Gunnis* 1968, 59; *Pyke* 1973, 18

Reliefs						
1.	nd	Unidentified divine	w	VAM A.103-1965	S	*Pyke* 1973, 18 (pl 33)
Miscellaneous						
2.	1782	Unidentified lady, model	w	[Exhib RA, London, 351]; untraced		*Graves* I, 1905–6, 251
3.	1783	Head of Ganymede, from a gem		[Exhib Soc of Artists, London, 40]; untraced		*Graves* 1907, 37
4.	1783	Hebe, model		[Exhib Soc of Artists, London, 39]; untraced		*Graves* 1907, 37
5.	1783	Trophy of friendship		[Exhib Soc of Artists, London, 41]; untraced		*Graves* 1907, 37
6.	1783	Trophy of friendship		[Exhib Soc of Artists, London, 42]; untraced		*Graves* 1907, 37
7.	1783	Unidentified gentleman		[Exhib RA, London, 278]; untraced		*Graves* I, 1905–6, 251
8.	1783	Unidentified lady, model	w	[Exhib Soc of Artists, London, 40]; untraced		*Graves* 1907, 37
9.	1783	Unidentified young gentleman	w	[Exhib RA, London, 284]; untraced		*Graves* I, 1905–6, 251
10.	1784	A philosopher	w	[Exhib RA, London, 244]; untraced		*Graves* I, 1905–6, 251
11.	1784	Hercules, model	w	[Exhib RA, London, 243]; untraced		*Graves* I, 1905–6, 251
12.	1784	Unidentified gentleman	w	[Exhib RA, London, 237]; untraced		*Graves* I, 1905–6, 251
13.	1784	Unidentified lady	w	[Exhib RA, London, 236]; untraced		*Graves* I, 1905–6, 251
14.	1785	Unidentified gentleman, model	w	[Exhib RA, London, 262]; untraced		*Graves* I, 1905–6, 251
15.	1785	Unidentified lady	w	[Exhib RA, London, 267]; untraced		*Graves* I, 1905–6, 251
16.	1785	Unidentified lady, model	w	[Exhib RA, London, 367]; untraced		*Graves* I, 1905–6, 251
17.	1786	Charlotte decorating the tomb of Werter		[Exhib RA, London, 265]; untraced		*Graves* I, 1905–6, 251
18.	1786	Unidentified young gentleman	w	[Exhib RA, London, 373]; untraced		*Graves* I, 1905–6, 251
19.	1787	Unidentified gentleman, model	w	[Exhib RA, London, 653]; untraced		*Graves* I, 1905–6, 251
20.	1787	Unidentified young lady, model		[Exhib RA, London, 639]; untraced		*Graves* I, 1905–6, 251
21.	1788	Unidentified lady, model	w	[Exhib RA, London, 613]; untraced		*Graves* I, 1905–6, 251
22.	1791	Unidentified gentleman, model		[Exhib RA, London, 655]; untraced		*Graves* I, 1905–6, 251
23.	1797	Unidentified minister, model		[Exhib RA, London, 847]; untraced		*Graves* I, 1905–6, 251
24.	1798	Unidentified young lady, model		[Exhib RA, London, 838]; untraced		*Graves* I, 1905–6, 251
25.	1827	Rev Mr Wilkinson		[Exhib RA, London, 1000]; untraced		*Graves* I, 1905–6, 251
26.	1827	Rev S Stennet		[Exhib RA, London, 994]; untraced		*Graves* I, 1905–6, 251

BOURNE, J, of Sleaford fl 1783

Funerary Monuments

1.	†1783	William Thacker		Dorrington, Lincs	S	Pevsner, *Lincs*, 1989, 258

BOWD, D, of Cheltenham fl 1809–60

Funerary Monuments

1.	†1809	Mary Ramus		Bishop's Cleeve, Glos	S	Pevsner, *Glos: Vale & Forest of Dean*, 1970, 107–8
2.	†1847	William (†1845) and Mary Proctor		Elkstone, Glos	S	Pevsner, *Glos: Cotswolds*, 1999, 358
3.	†1860	William Ansell		Burford, Oxon	S	

BOWENE (or BOURN), Herbert fl 1707–08

The 'Cities Mason', he received £200 in 1707 for repairs to the Guildhall and its chapel. He was paid a further £72 10s in 1708 and £80 in 1709, but during these later years he did not hold the post of City Mason, which was vacant.

Archival References: City Cash Accts, 01/25 fol 212r; fols 170r, 177v

BOWER, John fl 1844

In 1844 'Mr. John Bower ye carver and stone-cutter' was employed at Westbury Court, Glos, then being built by Maynard Colchester to the designs of **Michael Sidnell** (Archives, Sir Francis Colchester Wemyss, cited by *Gunnis* 1968, 59–60).

Literary References: *Gunnis* 1968, 59–60

BOWER, Joseph I and II fl 1714–59

The Bowers, father and son, were master-masons for the building of Wentworth Castle, Yorks, for Sir Thomas Wentworth, 1st Earl of Strafford, between 1714 and 1722. They were also responsible for carved stonework for the house and later erected a number of structures in the gardens. In 1725 the younger Bower was paid £92 2s for making 'the cascade in the menagerie' at Stainborough and two years later he built three miniature towers named after the Earl's daughters, Lucy, Anne and Harriett, each costing £4 15s. In 1734 his work included an obelisk erected in the park to the memory of Queen Anne and in 1739 he built a temple copied from one at Tivoli. In 1734–37 he received payments for an obelisk with incised lettering, and in 1742 for a column on a pedestal erected by William, 2nd Earl of Strafford in honour of his father-in-law, John, 2nd Duke of Argyll.

Literary References: *Gunnis* 1968, 59; *Baker* 1992, 793 n

Archival References: Strafford Papers, BM, Ad MS 22,241 fol 19, 34, 35, 63, 67, 82; Bower/Strafford Accts fol 75, 82, 89 (21 June 1739, Dec 1742, 30 Nov 1744)

BOWERS, George fl 1671–77

Bowers was one of three sculptors involved in work on the Monument, 1671–77, with **C G Cibber** and **Edward Pearce** (**1**). The bronze urn that tops the edifice was cast by Robert Bird and raised into position on 15 July 1676. Bowers had 'begun ye ornamentall work about the Urne' on 5 July (CLRO, Journal of the City Lands Committee, fol 58r, Minutes of 5 July 1676) and was ordered to affix his decorations on 6 August (*ibid*, fols 66r-67, 6 August 1676).

Literary References: *Ward-Jackson* 2003, 260, 264, 268 n22, n25

Architectural Sculpture

1.	1676	Ornaments for the urn	b	The Monument, City of London		*Ward-Jackson* 2003, 260, 264, 268

BOWIE, John fl 1844–after 1853

The red sandstone monuments in Fenwick churchyard erected to Mr Guthrie in 1844 and Captain Paton in 1853 are signed by J Bowie (**1, 2**). In his *History of Kilmarnock* (3rd ed, 1864, 5) Archibald Mackay states that Bowie was a Kilmarnock sculptor and mentions a work that has not been traced, a statue of Captain Paton carved by Bowie (**3**).

Literary References: *Woodward* 1977, vol 1, pt 2, 15–6

Funerary Monuments

1.	1844	Mr Guthrie	s	Fenwick, Ayrshire, churchyard	S	*Woodward* 1977, vol 1, pt 2, 15
2.	1853	Captain Paton	s	Fenwick, Ayrshire, churchyard	S	*Woodward* 1977, vol 1, pt 2, 15

Statues

3.	pre-1864	Captain Paton		[Kilmarnock, Ayrshire]; untraced		*Woodward* 1977, vol 1, pt 2, 16

BOWLES, Richard fl 1721–65

Richard Bowles was made free of the Masons' Company by service to William Holland in 1721. He was an assistant in the company by about 1740, when he lived in Shoreditch. In 1765 Trevor, Bishop of Durham, who was building a church at Glynde in Sussex, paid him £20 for a 'handsum veined marble font, properly ornemented' (Archives, Brand of Glynde, cited by *Gunnis* 1968, 60) (**2**).

Literary References: *Gunnis* 1968, 68

Archival References: Masons' Co, *Assistants*, c1740, fol 1; Masons' Co, *Freemen*, fol 5 (20 Oct 1721)

Funerary Monuments

1.	†1736	William Williams		Broxbourne, Herts	S	Pevsner, *Herts*, 1977, 114

Chimneypieces

2.	1765	Font Payment(s): £20	m	Glynde, Sussex		*Gunnis* 1968, 60

BOYD, Joseph 1822–99

A number of competently carved portrait medallions in both sandstone and marble are among the works signed by Joseph Boyd in Ayr cemetery. His own gravestone, which is in the cemetery, describes him as a sculptor who worked in Ayr until his death on 26 August, 1899. He was predeceased by his wife Mary, née Hollis.

Literary References: *Woodward* 1977, vol 1, pt 2, 16

BOYLE, James fl 1763

He is listed in Mortimer's *Universal Director* of 1763 as a 'Carver in wood and stone, Great Pulteney-Street, Golden Square' (p 3).

BOYLE, Richard Barrington 1811–91

Born in Dublin, he worked as a wood carver in his native city for many years. In 1835 he was in Swift's Row, moving in 1846 to 107 Middle Abbey, in 1850 to 19 Mary Street, and in 1857 to 82 Marlborough Street. He was employed on the restoration of St Patrick's Cathedral during the 1860s (1). He also worked in Westland Road church, and at St James, James Street, where he carved a reredos (2). He provided ornamental carving and furniture, including an elaborate sideboard for the brewer Sir Benjamin Guiness (7). After moving to Marlborough Street he was assisted by his sons Richard Barrington Boyle II (*c*1838–95) and James F Boyle (*c*1847–1911). The father and sons later worked as ornamental cabinet makers at 20 Upper Gloucester Street. Boyle died on 28 January 1891.

Literary References: *Strickland* 1, 1913, 74–75

Architectural Sculpture

1.	1860–1865	Woodwork, including stall of the knights of St Patrick and two chairs, carved in oak from the old roof of the cathedral	wd	St Patrick's Cathedral, Dublin	*Strickland* I, 1913, 74
2.	nd	Reredos (designed by Patrick Byrne)	wd	St James, James Street, Dublin	*Strickland* I, 1913, 74

Reliefs

3.	1853	The judgment of Solomon	wd	[Dublin Int Exhib]; untraced	*Strickland* I, 1913, 74
4.	nd	The Grecian chiefs in the tent of Achilles	wd	Untraced	*Strickland* I, 1913, 74

Miscellaneous

5.	1836	The arms of the lord lieutenant, Lord Mulgrave, carved in Irish oak	wd	[Exhib RHA, Dublin, 264]; untraced	*Stewart* I, 1985, 68
6.	1844	Infants		[Exhib RHA, Dublin, 444]; untraced	*Stewart* I, 1985, 68
7.	nd	Sideboard with arms and panels depicting and ancient boar hunt, harvesting and vine culture	wd	[coll Sir Benjamin Lee Guiness Bt]; untraced	*Strickland* I, 1913, 74

BOZZONI, Luigi, of Carrara fl 1838–47

Bozzoni was a native of Florence and studied in Rome under Bartolomeo Pinelli, a printmaker, painter, sculptor and draughtsman, before coming to England. In September 1838 he took as his studio part of the ground floor of the Imperial Hotel in Covent Garden, London. There he executed a series of 18 life-sized statues of apostles and martyrs and 18 reliefs for the Roman Catholic chapel at Everingham Hall, Yorks, recently built by a local landowner, William Constable Maxwell, later 10th Lord Herries (1, 2). A critic writing in the *Art Union* pronounced Bozzoni 'a man of genius', after viewing models for the first two statues, St Peter and St Paul (*AU*, 1839, 106). When the sculptor sent the figures of St Andrew and St John to the Westminster Hall Exhibition of 1844 the *Literary Gazette* noted that they displayed 'good modelling about the drapery' but added 'as much cannot be said for the figures' (*Lit Gaz*, 1435, 20 July 1844, 466). In 1847 Bozzoni exhibited a subject from Book XI of Virgil's *Æneid* at the Royal Academy (3). He probably died the same year.

Literary References: *AU*, 1839, 106; 1840, 114; *Gunnis* 1968, 60

Statues

1.	1839–1844	Twelve apostles and four martyrs	m	Chapel of the Virgin, Everingham Hall, E R Yorks	*AU*, 1839, 106; Pevsner, *Yorks: E R & York*, 1995, 412

Reliefs

2.	1839–1844	Religious subjects, 18 relief panels		Chapel of the Virgin, Everingham Hall, E R Yorks	*AU*, 1839, 106; Pevsner, *Yorks: E R & York*, 1995, 412

Miscellaneous

3.	1847	A subject from The Aeneid		[Exhib RA, London, 1318]; untraced	*Graves* I, 1905–6, 263

BRADBURY, R, of Ashford fl 1813

Funerary Monuments

1.	†1813	Elizabeth Howsley	Youlgreave, Derbys	S	

BRADDOCK, C, of Oundle fl 1757

Funerary Monuments

1.	1757	Rev Richard Cooke (†1752) and wife (†1767)	Ringstead, Norfolk	S	

BRADLEY, of Coleford fl 1793

Funerary Monuments

1.	†1793	Thomas Hopkins	Weston, Herefs		*Gunnis* 1968, 60

BRADLEY, Richard, of York fl *c*1840–58

About 1840 he opened a showroom and began to do business at 39 Gillygate, York, after having worked at the Minster as carver and mason. In 1858 he was working at St Helen's church. He carved heads of French and English generals and admirals who took part in the Crimean War for a house in Bootham Terrace, York (4). Other Bradleys worked in the city as statuaries and masons, including William, master mason at York Minster in 1705, John, a freemason, who became a freeman of York in 1739, and Robert, who described himself as 'sculptor' in the York directory of 1841.

Literary References: *Gunnis* 1968, 60

Archival References: GPC

Funerary Monuments

1.	†1842–1848	Cattle family members		Sheriff Hutton, N R Yorks	S

Architectural Sculpture

2.	nd	Carved heads and other ornaments		Scarborough College, N R Yorks	GPC
3.	nd	Heraldic shields	s	St Michael-le-Belfry, York	GPC
4.	nd	Keystone heads	s	10 Bootham Terrace, York	GPC

BRADLEY, Roger, of Hertford fl 1790–1817

Between 1790 and 1815 he provided masonry work for Lord Grimston at Gorhambury, Herts (General Accts, 3rd Viscount Grimston, Herts Archives & Local Studies, XI, 74). He was also employed by Lord Melbourne at Brocket Hall. He was one of the master masons at Ashridge Park, Herts, where he was paid over £2,000 between 1815 and 1817 (Archives, Lord Brownlow, cited by *Gunnis* 1968, 60).

Literary References: *Gunnis* 1968, 60

BRADLEY, William Frederick, of the Butts, Worcester fl 1807–49

Funerary Monuments

1.	†1807	Michael Harward	Hartlebury, Worcs	S	RG/JP, 2, 178v.
2.	†1849	John (†1832) and Elizabeth Nott (†1849)	Rock, Worcs	S	

BRADLEY, William, of Halifax and Selby fl 1806–37

Funerary Monuments

1.	?1806	Joseph Hulme	St John, Halifax, W R Yorks	S	*Gunnis* 1968, 60
2.	?1806	Rev Matthew Powbey	Dewsbury, W R Yorks	S	GPC
3.	?1807	William Norris	St John, Halifax, W R Yorks	S	*Gunnis* 1968, 60
4.	?1820	James Waddington	St John, Halifax, W R Yorks	S	*Gunnis* 1968, 60
5.	?1832	Joshua Jackson	St John, Halifax, W R Yorks	S	*Gunnis* 1968, 60
6.	?1835	Children of Edward Russell	Snaith, W R Yorks	S	*Gunnis* 1968, 60
7.	?1837	John Dobson	Selby Abbey, W R Yorks	S	*Gunnis* 1968, 60

BRADSHAW, of South Molton fl 1740–41

The town hall at South Molton, Devon, erected between 1740 and 1741 to the plans of a Mr Cullen, incorporates various fragments from the recently demolished Stowe at Kilkhampton, including four Corinthian capitals and pilasters, the 'ornaments of three windows', a 'carved architrave', a picture of *The Triumph of King Charles II* and a ton of lead (South Molton Town Archives, cited by *Gunnis* 1968, 60). Bradshaw was responsible for the rest of the carved stonework.

Literary References: *Gunnis* 1968, 60

Architectural Sculpture

1.	1740–1741	Shields, festoons, Corinthian capitals and other ornaments	s	Town Hall, South Molton, Devon	*Gunnis* 1968, 60

BRADSHAW, W, of Manchester fl 1735–72

He signs large wall-tablets to William Lawson, 1735, in Wakefield Cathedral, and to the Massey family, 1765, at Rostherne, Cheshire. (1, 3). Samuel Hibbert, in his *History of the Foundations in Manchester*, describes Bradshaw's monument to William Clowes in Manchester Cathedral as 'a mural monument which for elegance is not exceeded by any one within the church' (4).

Literary References: *Hibbert* vol II, 1828, 316; *Gunnis* 1968, 60

Funerary Monuments

1.	?1735	William Lawson	Wakefield Cathedral, W R Yorks	S	*Gunnis* 1968, 60
2.	?1746	Mary Dicconson	Eccleston, Lancs		GPC
3.	?1765	Massey family	Rostherne, Cheshire	S	*Gunnis* 1968, 60
4.	?1772	William Clowes	Manchester Cathedral, Lancs	S	*Gunnis* 1968, 60

BRAITHWAITE, William 1757–

He was born on 13 October 1757 and on 31 July 1771 was apprenticed to **John Walsh**. He joined the Royal Academy Schools on 25 March 1776 and in 1782 won a medal (1). Nothing more is known of him.

Literary References: *Hutchison* 1960–62, 142; *Gunnis* 1968, 60

Archival References: TNA Apprenticeship Lists, in GPC

Miscellaneous

1.	1782	Model of an Academy figure or bas-relief	[RA silver medal]; untraced	RA Premium list

BRANSON, Henry fl 1739

Branson carved the wood model for the London Mansion House, for which he was paid £192 3s 10d in June 1739. The model itself was made by John Cordwell (Mansion House Comm 01/1 pp 273–5).

BRANWHITE, Charles, of Bristol 1817–80

Born on 7 June 1817, he was the son of Nathan Cooper Branwhite, an engraver of Bristol. In 1836 he received a medal from the Society of Arts for a bas-relief (6) and during this period he executed a number of busts of Bristol worthies (1–4). In spite of these early successes his career as a sculptor was shortlived, for he abandoned sculpture for painting late in 1838. He died at his home, Bramford House, Westfield Park, Redland, on 15 February 1880.

Literary References: *AJ*, 1880, 208; *Gunnis* 1968, 60–1

Archival References: GPC

Will: Bristol Probate Registry, 15 March 1880, estate valued at under £6,000

Busts

1.	1837–1838	Dr Symonds	Untraced	GPC
2.	1837–1838	Rev Somers	Untraced	GPC
3.	1837–1838	Robert Hall	Untraced	GPC
4.	1837–1838	Sir John Haberfield	Untraced	GPC
5.	1845	W J Muller	Bristol Cathedral Other versions: Bristol Museum and Art Gallery, plaster	*Gunnis* 1968, 61

Reliefs

6.	1836	Unknown subject	[Soc of A, silver medal]; untraced	RSA *Transactions*, vol 52, 1838, xv

BRAYNE, T, of London fl c1797

Funerary Monuments

1.	†1797	Sir George Booth	Cotterstock, Northants	*GM*, 1812, ii, 220–1

BREAMER, Frederick Christian, of London fl 1793–1816

His address in 1793 was 8 New Road, opposite Fitzroy Square, London. In 1816 he supplied a number of chimneypieces for the Brighton Pavilion and also for the architect John Nash's London house (4, 5).

Literary References: *Graves* I, 1905–6, 271

Archival References: Nash MS, Oct 1816

Funerary Monuments						
1.	1804	Sir Richard Clode		Orpington, Kent	S	*Gunnis* 1968, 61
2.	1809	Mrs Oswald Smith		Bexley, Kent	S	*Gunnis* 1968, 61
Chimneypieces						
3.	1801	Several		[Henry Dundas's residence, Charles Street, Berkeley Square, London]; untraced		Soane bill book C, fols 127v-128r; *Gunnis* 1968, 61
4.	1816	Five of statuary and two of veined grey Payment(s): £143 1s with those for Brighton Pavilion	m	[John Nash's residence, Langham Place, London]; untraced		Nash MS, Oct 1816
5.	1816	Nine, including two of dove grey marble Payment(s): £143 1s with those for Nash's London house		Royal Pavilion, Brighton, Sussex		Nash MS, Oct 1816, p 22
Reliefs						
6.	1793	Tablet of flowers	m	[Exhib RA, London, 824]; untraced		*Graves* I, 1905–6, 271

BRETON, Luc-François 1731–1800

Born at Besançon in 1731, he was apprenticed to Julien Chambert, a local woodcarver, and then entered the studio of the sculptor Claude-François Attiret at Dôle. In 1754, he set out for Italy to complete his studies. In 1758 he won first prize for sculpture at the Accademia di San Luca with a terracotta relief of *Metellus rescuing Palladium from the temple of Vesta*. This work established his reputation and he decided to settle in Rome, where he stayed for several years, working mainly for French patrons. In 1771 he returned to Besançon, where he remained until his death.

Though he never came to England, Breton worked for Robert Adam, modelling the relief for his monument to Lieutenant-Colonel Townshend in Westminster Abbey (1). Adam's design for the Townshend monument consisted of two caryatid figures supporting a sarcophagus, with a relief depicting Townshend's death at the battle of Ticonderoga on the front and a trophy of arms above. In the spring of 1760 the architect sent Breton a drawing of the proposed relief, instructing him to make a full-scale model in terracotta and giving him the liberty to make changes to the design should he see fit. A few months later James Adam wrote to Robert from Venice to say that he had seen a drawing of Breton's finished relief: 'he has altered the whole design, has crowded it with horses and figures so that I was a good deal surprised to see your license so abused, as also to see at the foot of the drawing *Breton invt*' (13 August 1760, cited by *Fleming* 1962 (2), 166–8). The reasons for Breton's alterations and embellishments became clear when James went to Rome early in 1761. On 7 March he reported to Robert that he had been 'to see Breton's bas-relief. The first is really magnificent and I imagine might cost as much to execute as half the price of the whole monument. From the resemblance of the subject the English here explained it to Breton to be for General Wolfe and consequently he thought he could not make it too Magnificent'. His letter continued, 'He has since done a sketch of another, as much underacted as the other was overacted, and when I told him the corrections and asked him when he could finish it he told me he could not begin for some time, so that I must yet apply to another and am in hopes you will be perfectly happy with the execution of it' (*ibid*, 168). Unfortunately James did not specify what corrections he suggested for Breton's second sketch model, neither is it clear whether another modeller was brought in, but it seems probable that Breton completed the work in the next two months. It had been fired and dispatched from Leghorn by 3 July. The monument was erected in Westminster Abbey by **Benjamin** and **Thomas Carter II** in November 1761 and the marble version of the relief is prominently signed by **John Eckstein I**.

Literary References: *Fleming* 1962 (2), 163–171; *Stainton* 1983, 12, 18

Funerary Monuments					
1.	1760–1761	Lieutenant-Colonel the Hon Roger Townshend (†1759), model for relief only (monument executed by Benjamin and Thomas Carter II and John Eckstein I)	tc	Untraced	*Fleming* 1962 (2), 163–171; *Whinney* 1988, 251
Architectural Sculpture					
2.	nd	Keystone with a consular figure, from the Antique	tc	[Adam sale, 1818, lot 20]; untraced	*Adam Sale* 1818, 2

BREWER, Francis, of Petersfield fl 1820–23

Funerary Monuments					
1.	1820	John Clement	Steep, Hants	S	*Gunnis* 1968, 61
2.	1823	Baker family	Steep, Hants	S	*Gunnis* 1968, 61
3.	nd	Unidentified subject, wall-tablet	Hambledon, Hants	S	Pevsner, *Hants & Isle of Wight*, 1967, 271

BREWER, James fl 1778

Chimneypieces				
1.	1778	Two Payment(s): £24	[for Lord Archibald Hamilton, Rendlesham Hall, Suffolk]; untraced	Soane Priv Corr IV/9c/9, fols 36–7

BREWER, John, of Beccles fl 1778–89

In 1778 John Brewer announced that he had entered into partnership with **Edward Holl**, who had for several years conducted the business of the late **Robert Page of Norwich**. Brewer and Holl advertised that they executed monuments and tombs in the modern taste and gave their address as the Yard, Beccles, Suffolk. The partnership was dissolved in 1789, when it was announced that Holl would continue the business alone.

Literary References: *Norfolk Mercury*, 24 Oct 1778; *Norwich Mercury*, 10 Jan 1789

BREWER, William, of Box and Colerne fl 1761–c1836

Brewer was apprenticed to Henry Hill of Marlborough, 'Carver', in 1761 (Apprenticeship Books, 1760–63, TNA, IR 1/54 fol 116). He executed monuments and tablets in marble and stone, repeating a charming design with a bow at the top on several occasions. In 1799 he supplied stone and provided masonry work at Dodington Park, Glos, when James Wyatt rebuilt the house for Christopher Codrington (Codrington Archives, cited by RG/JP, 2, 181). The William Brewer who was paid £120 for lions for the gate piers at Bowood in 1853 was, presumably, a descendant of this sculptor (Archives, Marquess of Lansdowne, in GPC).

Literary References: *Gunnis* 1968, 61

Funerary Monuments

1.	?1778	Anne Cullurne	Malmesbury, Wilts	S	*Gunnis* 1968, 61
2.	?1778	Richard Legg	Market Lavington, Wilts	S	*Gunnis* 1968, 61
3.	?1779	Fanny Warner	St Peter and St Paul, Marlborough, Wilts	S	*Gunnis* 1968, 61
4.	?1783	Elizabeth Millington	Cliffe Pypard, Wilts	S	*Gunnis* 1968, 61
5.	c1785	William Merewether and family (†1783–1792)	Market Lavington, Wilts	S	*Gunnis* 1968, 61
6.	?1787	James White	St Peter and St Paul, Marlborough, Wilts	S	*Gunnis* 1968, 61
7.	?1787	Thomas Pinnell	Malmesbury, Wilts	S	*Gunnis* 1968, 61
8.	†1788	John Shergold	Market Lavington, Wilts	S	C Lib (repr)
9.	?1794	Rachel Neate	Aldbourne, Wilts	S	*Gunnis* 1968, 61
10.	?1799	William Fry	Malmesbury, Wilts	S	*Gunnis* 1968, 61
11.	†1809	John Painter	St John the Baptist, Hinton Charterhouse, Somerset		Pevsner, *Somerset: N & Bristol*, 1958, 206
12.	?1812	John Neate	Aldbourne, Wilts	S	*Gunnis* 1968, 61
13.	†1813	Daniel Gingell	Atworth, Wilts	S	
14.	?1813	Lucia Pyke	Great Somerford, Wilts	S	*Gunnis* 1968, 61
15.	c1836	Unidentified subject, tablet	Marksbury, Somerset	S	Pevsner, *Somerset: N & Bristol*, 1958, 224

BREWIN, Thomas, of Great Ponton 1733–82

A Kesteven slate headstone engraver, he came from a family of masons. There are five slate gravestones by him in Kesteven.

Literary References: *Neave and Heron* 1969, 8

BREWSTER, John, of Spittlegate, Grantham

There are 12 engraved slate headstones by him in Kesteven.

Literary References: *Neave and Heron* 1969, 9

BRIANT, S fl 1828

In 1828, while living at 34 Monmouth Street, London, he won a medal and £5 from the Society of Arts (1).

Reliefs

1.	1828	Model of St Clement's church	[Soc of A, silver Isis medal and £5]; untraced	RSA *Transactions*, vol 46, 1828, xxvii

BRICE, E, of London fl 1780

Reliefs

1.	1780	Innocence	[Exhib RA, London, 417]; untraced	*Graves* I, 1905–6, 277

BRIDGENS, Richard Hicks 1785–1846

Bridgens is best known as an architect and designer of furnishings, but he also exhibited at least one piece of sculpture early in his career. Little is known of his early life but an obituary described him as 'the fellow student and intimate friend, in early life of the celebrated **Chantrey**', which suggests that he may originally have come from Sheffield (cited by *Bullock* 1988, 17). As a young man he worked for **George Bullock**, from whose premises in Liverpool he exhibited at the Liverpool Academy in 1810, 1811 and 1812. His contributions included designs for a monument and for a chimneypiece at Speke Hall, Liverpool, together with a model of *A nymph attiring* (1). He moved to Bullock's London premises at 4 Tenterden Street, Hanover Square by 1814, when he sent two more drawings, of Joseph Ridgway's house at Ridgmont, Horwich, Lancs, to the Liverpool exhibition.

After Bullock's death in 1818 Bridgens attempted to set up an architectural practice in Birmingham, where James Watt of Aston Hall employed him to design oak furniture in a Jacobean style to match the house. In 1822 he published a volume of engravings of the medieval church at Sefton, Lancs. He may have visited Rome at about that time for in 1822 he exhibited at the Royal Academy 'an attempt to improve the Barberini candelabrum now erecting in bronze' and a 'View of the Forum in Rome – showing the excavation made at the charge of Her Grace the Duchess of Devonshire'. In about 1825 he closed the Birmingham practice, which had failed to attract sufficient clients, and moved to the West Indies, where his wife had inherited a sugar plantation. He was in England soon after April 1831 and two years later he published a volume entitled *Furniture with Candelabra and Interior Decoration Applicable to the Embellishment of Modern and Old English Mansions*, which included influential designs in the newly fashionable Elizabethan and Jacobean revival styles. A second revised edition appeared in 1838. Bridgens was again employed at Aston Hall between 1834 and 1837, where a porch was built to his designs in about 1836 (demol 1856).

Towards the end of his life Bridgens served as Superintendent of Public Works in Port of Spain, Trinidad, a post to which he was apparently unsuited, for he often committed 'faults which the humbler mechanic could have seen and avoided' (*Bullock* 1988, 17). He died in Trinidad in November 1846.

Literary References: *Graves* I, 1905–6, 278; *Gunnis* 1968, 61; *Joy* 1977, 114–7, 143, 175, 256; *Glenn* 1979, 54–67; *Bullock* 1988, 17–20; *Colvin* 1995, 160–1; *Grove* 4, 1996, 806–7 (Austen); *Morris and Roberts* 1998, 99

Statues

1.	1811	A nymph attiring	[Exhib Liverpool Ac, 159]; untraced	*Gunnis* 1968, 61; *Morris and Roberts* 1998, 99

BRIDGES fl 1796

Gunnis notes that his tablet commemorating H Bale at Bishops Waltham is 'of good workmanship'.

Funerary Monuments

1.	?1796	H Bale	Bishops Waltham, Hants	S	*Gunnis* 1968, 61

BRIDGES, Emanuel fl 1825–28

He described himself on the Tordiffe monument as Bridges of Chedworth.

Funerary Monuments

1.	†1825	Anne Pitt	Chedworth, Glos	S	Pevsner, *Glos: Cotswolds*, 1999, 222
2.	†1828	Harriett Tordiffe	Cranham, Glos	S	

BRIDGES, of Knightsbridge fl 1775

Bridges was an artificial stone manufacturer, whose workshop was in Knightsbridge, London. On 26 May 1775, his stock-in-trade, consisting of 'a great Variety of Statues, Vases, Bustos, and various kinds of Ornaments in Artificial Stone' was sold by Messrs Christie, on the occasion of his 'quitting that Branch of Business' (*Public Ad*, 24 May 1775, 4). Among the lots sold were medallions of the kings Alfred and Ethelred (**8, 9**); busts of Homer and Pitt (**6, 7**), statues of Ceres, Flora and Samson (**2, 3, 5**) and statuettes of Rubens and Van Dyck (**4**). A number of the lots, including a statue of a druid (**1**), were purchased by Eleanor Coade (see **Coade Factory, of Lambeth**). She also bought the Knightsbridge factory itself, for in December 1778 she announced that she intended to sell all the equipment of 'Mrs COADE's Manufactory at Knightsbridge . . . the Whole to be sold extremely cheap, on Account of clearing the Premises, the Business being carried on at King's Arms' Stairs, Lambeth' (*Daily Ad*, 24 December 1778). Some of Bridges's moulds appear to have remained in use at the Coade factory, including those for the statue of a druid, which Bridges himself had probably acquired indirectly from **George Davy**.

Literary References: *Gunnis* 1968, 61; *Valpy* 1986, 217–8, 222; *Kelly* 1990, 34, 44–5, 134

Auction Catalogues: Bridges 1775; Coade Factory 1779

Statues

1.	by 1775	A druid	sa	[Bridges sale, 1775]; untraced	*Gunnis* 1968, 61
2.	by 1775	Ceres	sa	[Bridges sale, 1775]; untraced	*Gunnis* 1968, 61
3.	by 1775	Flora	sa	[Bridges sale, 1775]; untraced	*Gunnis* 1968, 61
4.	by 1775	Rubens and Van Dyck, statuettes	sa	[Bridges sale, 1775]; untraced	*Gunnis* 1968, 61
5.	by 1775	Samson	sa	[Bridges sale, 1775]; untraced	*Gunnis* 1968, 61

Busts

6.	by 1775	Homer	sa	[Bridges sale, 1775]; untraced	*Gunnis* 1968, 61
7.	by 1775	William Pitt, 1st Earl of Chatham	sa	[Bridges sale, 1775]; untraced	*Walker* 1961, 13; *Gunnis* 1968, 61

Reliefs

8.	by 1775	King Alfred, medallion	sa	[Bridges sale, 1775]; untraced	*Gunnis* 1968, 61
9.	by 1775	King Ethelred, medallion	sa	[Bridges sale, 1775]; untraced	*Gunnis* 1968, 61

BRIDGEWATER, Thomas fl 1724

He was employed by James Gibbs at St Martin-in-the-Fields, receiving payments totalling £107 5s in 1724, and worked on the pulpit, designed by Gibbs and made by the joiner Charles Griffith (**1**).

Literary References: *Friedman* 1984, 71, 310

Architectural Sculpture

1.	*c*1724	Ornamental carving for the pulpit (designed by James Gibbs) Payment(s): £107 5s	St Martin-in-the-Fields, London	*Friedman* 1984, 71

BRIGHAM, Ada

For information the reader is referred to *Pyke* 1973, 19–20 and *Pyke* 1981, 9

BRINE, John and sons, of London fl 1774–1886

Brine, whose workshop was at 135 Euston Road, was assisted and later succeeded by his sons George and James. He is buried in Kensal Green Cemetery, where he is commemorated with a neo-Greek monument. The family flourished 1774–1866.

Literary References: *Gunnis* 1968, 61; *Curl* 2001, 213

Funerary Monuments

1.	?1829	John Elmslie	Windsor, Berks		*Gunnis* 1968, 61
2.	†1830	Elizabeth (†1818) and John Williamson	Letchworth, Herts	S	
3.	?1837	Dick family	St Mary, Chilham, Kent		Pevsner, *Kent: NE & E*, 1983, 273
4.	?1840	John Rogers	Streatham, London		*Gunnis* 1968, 61
5.	?1846	Lady Preston	Beeston St Lawrence, Norfolk		*Gunnis* 1968, 61
6.	†1848	Lieutenant-Colonel Francis Copland	Kensal Green Cemetery, catacombs	S	
7.	1861	Sir George Maclean	Kensal Green Cemetery, catacombs	S	

Statues

8.	1826	Several, unidentified subjects	[Wrest Park, Beds, gardens]; untraced	*Gunnis* 1968, 61, citing Archives, Lady Lucas and Dingwall

Chimneypieces

9.	1824	Several Payment(s): £155 16s 9d	[for the Royal Pavilion, Brighton, Sussex]; untraced	Nash MS, p 117
10.	1824	Several, of statuary marble Payment(s): £2,265 16s 1 1/2d	[for sundry houses in the Quadrant, Regent Street, London]; untraced	Nash MS, p 117
11.	1851	Several	[Gt Exhib]; untraced	*Gunnis* 1968, 61

BRISLEY, Thomas William, of Rochester 1800–

Brisley's name was given as 'Thomas' when he was apprenticed to his father in 1814, but a local directory of 1828 calls him 'William'. He was the son of Thomas Brisley, a mason who became a freeman of Rochester by purchase in 1795 (Rochester City Archives, cited by *Gunnis* 1968, 61). Gunnis notes that the medallion on his monument to James Forbes in Rochester Cathedral (2) is 'a charming and competent work, surprisingly good for a local statuary'.

Funerary Monuments					
1.	?1836	William Burke	Rochester Cathedral, Kent	S	*Gunnis* 1968, 62
2.	?1837	James Forbes	Rochester Cathedral, Kent	S	*Gunnis* 1968, 62
Chimneypieces					
3.	1834	Description unavailable	Cobham Hall, Kent		*Gunnis* 1968, 61–2

BRITTAN, Joseph and Son, of Tamworth fl *c*1759–*c*1813

Joseph Brittan started his business as a stone and marble mason in Eldergate Street, Tamworth about 1759 and was succeeded by his son Thomas *c*1790. Thomas was joined by H Y Mitchell some 15 years later and he took over the firm when Brittan died.

Literary References: *Jeavons* 1960, 54

Funerary Monuments					
1.	?1810	M Blakesley	Wigginton, Staffs		*Jeavons* 1960, 54
2.	?1813	W Allport	Tamworth, Staffs		*Jeavons* 1960, 54

BRITTON, T fl early 19th century

He is responsible for several early 19th-century headstones with 'very pretty inscriptions' at West Buckland (1).

Funerary Monuments					
1.	nd	Unidentified subjects, headstones	West Buckland, Devon, churchyard		Pevsner, *Devon*, 1989, 899

BROAD, C, of Cork fl 1793–1800

Potterton comments, 'one would suspect that he was merely a mason-plasterer' but for the fact that his monument to Rev Alexander Lamillière Snr has a 'competently executed female figure in high relief mourning at an urn' (2). A monument to Richard Musgrave (†1785) at Lismore may be Broad's work and there are unsigned memorials in Cloyne Cathedral that are in his style.

Literary References: *Potterton* 1975, 37

Funerary Monuments					
1.	†1793	Robert Pratt	Castlemartyr, Co Cork	S	*Potterton* 1975, 37
2.	†1800	Alexander Lamillière	St Nicholas, Cork	S	*Potterton* 1975, 37
3.	†1800	John Musgrave	Lismore, Co Cork	S	*Potterton* 1975, 37

BROAD, David fl 1787

He also worked as a surveyor.

Architectural Sculpture					
1.	1787	Font Payment(s): £10	Manchester collegiate church, Lancs		*Hibbert* II, 1828, 247

BROAD, John fl 1777

Funerary Monuments					
1.	†1777	Joseph Racster and family	Suckley, Worcs	S	

BROAD, Richard fl 1692–1720

Broad was working at Longleat before 30 April 1692 when he received £9 for unspecified work. Vouchers issued between 1705 and 1710 record that he supplied stone and carved pedestals for two figures by **Claude David** in the new plantation (3). He also provided 'great copeing' for 'ye pallasaids stands at ye opening nere ye middle of ye wilderness' and stone to be fashioned into dolphins and basins for the Hall Court.

Gunnis identifies the Longleat mason with Richard Broad of Box, who was responsible for two signed Wiltshire monuments. The Tipler memorial (1) is a large wall monument with an architectural frame flanked by standing cherubs, with two more in the elaborate cresting above. The other commemorates the wife and children of Thomas Smith (2). In his diary for 1720, Thomas Smith noted that he 'walked this morning, being frosty, to Broad, the stone-cutter near Bath, to see a monument he has just finished to be put up in memory of my dear spouse and children' (Diary of Thomas Smith, reprinted in J A Neale's *Charters and Records of Neale*, 207).

Literary References: *Gunnis* 1968, 62

Archival References: Longleat HA 200, 01/01/1705; Longleat HA 275, 30/04/1692; 275, 01/11/1709; 16/11/1709; 23/09/1710

Funerary Monuments					
1.	1719	Tipler family (†1651–1710)	Seend, Wilts	S	Pevsner, *Wilts*, 1975, 465
2.	1720	Wife and children of Thomas Smith	Melksham, Wilts	S	*Gunnis* 1968, 62
Architectural Sculpture					
3.	1705–1710	Pedestals and sundry work	Longleat, Wilts		Longleat HA, 1687–1712

BROAD, Richard, of Worcester fl 1752–68

He became a freeman of Worcester in February 1752. In 1766 he submitted designs for the new Worcester Infirmary, which were rejected in favour of others by Anthony Keck, and in 1768 he made a plan of the city. He signs two large tablets in coloured marbles at Stoke Edith, Herefs (1, 2).

Literary References: *Gunnis* 1968, 62; *Colvin* 1995, 162

Funerary Monuments					
1.	†1738	Henry Wolstenholme	Stoke Edith, Herefs	S	*Colvin* 1995, 162
2.	†1749	Mary Wolstenholme	Stoke Edith, Herefs	S	*Colvin* 1995, 162

BROADBENT, Messrs, of Leicester fl *c*1840–*c*1860

The firm carved the marble cenotaph commemorating the protestant martyr Hugh Latimer at Thurcaston (1). Pevsner writes that this is remarkable in being neither gothic nor classical, nor indeed Tudor, but a free treatment of early-18th century motifs. The *Gentleman's Magazine* of May 1847 notes its considerable cost and that Broadbent was responsible for the subsequent restoration work at Anstey church. The article adds 'Many persons of eminence have visited this church, and have awarded great praise to the builders, Messrs Broadbent and Hawley, of Leicester, whose ability and skill are thus manifest, both in the architectural and operative departments'. During the 1860s they were employed at two Northamptonshire country houses: they were the contractors responsible for building Overstone Hall to the designs of William Milford Teulon and they provided the ceilings in the South and Yellow Drawing Rooms at Althorp.

Literary References: *GM*, vol XXVII, May 1847, i, 539; *Builder*, 1862, 149; *Gunnis*, 1968, 62

Archival References: RG/JP, 2, 184

Funerary Monuments

1.	1843	Hugh Latimer, Bishop of Worcester (†1555)		Thurcaston, Leics	*GM*, vol XXVII, May 1847, ptI, 539, Pevsner, *Leics & Rutland*, 1984, 408

BROCKEDON, William 1787–1854

For information the reader is referred to *Pyke* 1973, 20

Busts

1.	nd	Richard Lander	p	Royal Geographical Society, London	*Ormond* 1973, 253

BRODIE, Alexander 1829–67

Brodie was born at 8 Virginia Street, Aberdeen in 1829, the son of a seaman, John Brodie, and his wife Mary, née Waker. He was 14 years younger than his more famous brother **William Brodie**. After leaving school he was apprenticed to a brass finisher for several years until he came to the attention of Sheriff Watson, one of his brother's early patrons. With Watson's assistance he moved to Edinburgh in the early 1850s, where he worked in his brother's studio and attended classes at the Trustees' School of Design. In 1856 he was awarded the School's highest prize for a model after the Antique. By this time he had already shown 'great promise of outstripping his brother in the race for fame' (*Daily Free Press*, 31 October 1881, cited in ODNB). In 1858 Brodie returned to Aberdeen, where he soon established a considerable practice in portrait busts and graveyard monuments. He lived at Catto Square, Footdee and had his studio in Bothwell's Court, Justice Street until 1863, when he moved to 56 Enoch Street.

His first significant commission was for a statue of the Reverend Charles Gordon (**17**). He had completed the model by August 1858, when it was exhibited at a special exhibition in the county buildings. This was followed by two further major commissions in the early 1860s for statues of the Duke of Richmond and Queen Victoria (**6, 9**). Brodie originally represented the Queen in court dress but later, reputedly at the Queen's request, added a tartan plaid fastened with a thistle brooch on the left shoulder. The Queen sat for Brodie in 1865, both for the statue and for a portrait bust (**15**). The statue was completed the following year and the sculptor then turned his attention to finishing the bust. His striving to perfect that work is generally regarded as a contributory factor in, if not the cause of, the mental breakdown which resulted in his suicide on 30 May 1867 at the age of 37. His unfinished bust of Queen Victoria was completed by William Brodie after the Queen sat for Brodie at Balmoral in October of the same year.

Literary References: *Gunnis* 1968, 62; *Woodward* 1977, vol 1, pt 2, 17–20; *ODNB* (Smailes)

Will: NAS SC1/36/61/3, Aberdeen Sheriff Court inventory, 2 July 1867

Portraits of the Sculptor: J Bissett, photo, after 1858, private coll (repr *Scottish Notes and Queries*, 3rd series, vol 1, 1923, 33)

Funerary Monuments					
1.	1859	Charles Adams Beattie		St Nicholas, Aberdeen, churchyard	*Woodward* 1977, vol 1, pt 2, 20
2.	1863	William Copland		St Nicholas, Aberdeen, churchyard	*Woodward* 1977, vol 1, pt 2, 20
3.	1865	John and Mary Brodie (the sculptor's parents)		St Clement, Aberdeen, churchyard	*Woodward* 1977, vol 1, pt 2, 20
Statues					
4.	1862	Mercury	m	Bowood House, Wilts	*Woodward* 1977, vol 1, pt 2, 20
5.	1862	Oenone		[Int Exhib, London]; untraced	*AJ Cat* 1862, 317 (repr); *Gunnis* 1968, 62
6.	1863	Charles, 5th Duke of Richmond	m	Huntley, Staffs, the Square	*Gunnis* 1968, 62; *Woodward* 1977, vol 1, pt 2, 20
7.	1863	Twelve apostles	p	St Mary's Cathedral, Aberdeen	*Woodward* 1977, vol 1, pt 2, 20
8.	1864	The mitherless lassie		[Exhib RA, London, 1008]; untraced	*Palgrave* 1866, 87; *Graves* I, 1905–6, 293
9.	1866	Queen Victoria	m	[Aberdeen, junction of Union St and St Nicholas St, until 1888]; Aberdeen City Chambers	*Ormond* 1973, 488; *Woodward* 1977, vol 1, pt 2, 20
10.	nd	Highland Mary	m	Aberdeen Art Gall	*Woodward* 1977, vol 1, pt 2, 20
Busts					
11.	1860	Colonel Sykes	m	Aberdeen Trinity Hall	*Woodward* 1977, vol 1, pt 2, 20
12.	1861	Colonel Leith Hay CB		[Exhib R Sc A, Edinburgh, 809]; untraced	*Laperriere* 1, 1991, 178
13.	1861	Lady Ann Duff, model		[Exhib R Sc A, Edinburgh, 806]; untraced	*Laperriere* 1, 1991, 178
14.	1861	Miss Gordon Cumming		[Exhib R Sc A, Edinburgh, 799]; untraced	*Laperriere* 1, 1991, 178
15.	1868	Queen Victoria (co-sculptor: William Brodie)	m	Royal Coll, Balmoral	*Woodward* 1977, vol 1, pt 2, 20
16.	nd	John Brodie (the sculptor's father)	p	[Exhib R Sc A, Edinburgh, 1916, 66]; untraced	*Laperriere* 1, 1991, 178
Architectural Sculpture					
17.	1858	Rev Charles Gordon, statue		Nelson Street School, Aberdeen, façade	*Woodward* 1977, vol 1, pt 2, 18, 20
Miscellaneous					
18.	1852	Frame of cameo portraits		[Exhib R Sc A, Edinburgh, 553]; untraced	*Laperriere* 1, 1991, 178
19.	1858	John Ballantyne		[Exhib R Sc A, Edinburgh, 759]; untraced	*Laperriere* 1, 1991, 178
20.	1864	Cupid and mask		[Exhib RA, London, 1033]; untraced	*Graves* I, 1905–6, 293

BRODIE, William 1815–81

Brodie was a successful portrait sculptor who worked in Edinburgh during the second half of the 19th century. He was born at Banff on 22 January 1815, the eldest son of a merchant seaman, John Brodie, and his wife Mary, née Waker. **Alexander Brodie**, who also practised as a sculptor, was his younger brother. The family settled in Aberdeen *c*1821 where, after serving an apprenticeship, William was employed as a plumber at the Broadford Works. In his leisure hours he studied science and art at the Aberdeen Mechanics Institute. He soon became proficient in modelling portrait medallions and miniature busts in wax and clay and by 1840 had begun to cast portraits of well-known figures in lead. During the same period he received additional instruction in drawing from George Washington Wilson, the pioneering photographer, and he developed a keen interest in phrenology, which was to inform his mature practice as a sculptor. He also studied oil painting and is reputed to have painted a number of portraits, particularly in the years after his marriage in 1841 to Helen Chisholm, herself an amateur painter.

In 1846 a number of Brodie's wax medallions were exhibited by a Mr Hay, of Market Street, Aberdeen. The exhibition attracted the attention of two of Brodie's earliest and most important patrons, Sheriff Watson of Aberdeen and the historian John Hall Burton. With their encouragement, Brodie moved to Edinburgh, where he attended the Trustees' School of Design between 1847 and 1851 and was taught to model on a larger scale and to carve portrait busts. In 1848 he gained the highest premiums for modelling from the life and from the Antique. He exhibited annually at the Royal Scottish Academy from 1847 onwards, showing principally portrait busts. He also sent works to the Royal Academy in London, the Royal Glasgow Institute of Fine Arts and the Great Exhibition of 1851, where his contribution was a group of *Little Nell and her grandfather* (**23**). He was becoming well-established in Edinburgh by 1852 when he was elected an associate member of the Royal Scottish Academy.

At about this time Hall Burton introduced Brodie to the Glasgow merchant and philanthropist James Buchanan. As well as commissioning an architectural monument incorporating an undated marble bust for Dean Cemetery, Edinburgh (**1**), Buchanan financed the sculptor's journey to Rome in 1853. There Brodie worked in the studio of **Lawrence MacDonald** and under his guidance executed a marble figure of *Corinna, the lyric muse* (**26**). It was exhibited to acclaim at the Royal Scottish Academy in 1855 and reproduced in Copeland parian ware in 1856. This commercial exploitation of Brodie's first major ideal work and the adoption of the porcelain statuette as a prize by the Royal Association for the Promotion of the Fine Arts in Scotland set a precedent and his representations of *Ruth* and *Penelephon, the beggar maid* were promoted in the same way (**45, 294**).

Following his return to Edinburgh in 1854 Brodie worked from 10 Randolph Cliff for three years before moving to 9 Coates Place, West Maitland Street, where he remained until 1865, when he established a studio, named St Helen's, in Cambridge Street. He attracted numerous commissions for portrait busts and his sitters included leading Scottish lawyers and politicians, such as Lord Rutherfurd, Henry Cockburn and Lord Moncrieff (**93, 89, 122**). After his death *The Times* credited him with having 'executed more busts in portraiture than any other in the same line' (*The Times*, 1 Nov 1881, 6). In addition he exhibited a number of large-scale portrait reliefs, a category later explored by his most distinguished pupil, James Pittendrich Macgillivray.

In 1862 Brodie carved a posthumous marble statue of Lord Cockburn for the Faculty of Advocates at Parliament House, Edinburgh (**36**). It was well received and prestigious public commissions in several Scottish cities followed, including the freestone monument to Prince Albert in Perth and a marble figure of Sir David Brewster for the University of Edinburgh (**38, 54**). The sculptor's most prominent public works are two bronze seated statues commemorating Thomas Graham in Glasgow and Sir James Young Simpson in Edinburgh (**44, 52**). Although his proposal for the Scottish national memorial to the Prince Consort was rejected in favour of a design by **Sir John Steell**, he provided one of the four subsidiary groups which flank Steell's statue of the Prince and represent different classes paying homage (**51**). He also competed unsuccessfully for the Glasgow statues of Dr David Livingstone and Thomas Campbell, both of which were executed by **John G Mossman**.

Brodie's best loved work is a small bronze statue of *Greyfriars' Bobby*, a Skye terrier famous for remaining faithfully beside his master's grave in Greyfriars' churchyard for fourteen years (**260**). The figure was commissioned by the philanthropist Baroness Burdett Coutts in 1871 and modelled from the life shortly before the dog's death. During the same period the sculptor started work on a number of freestone statues depicting characters from the *Waverley* novels which decorate the architectural canopy of the Sir Walter Scott monument on Princes Street, Edinburgh (**56**).

In November 1876 Brodie was appointed Secretary to the Royal Scottish Academy, a post which he held until 1880, when he resigned due to failing health. On 30 October 1881, after almost two years of illness, he died of heart disease and oedema of the lungs at his principal residence, Douglas Lodge, Merchiston Place, Edinburgh. The sculptor, who was survived by his wife, a son and three daughters, was buried in Dean cemetery. His estate was valued at more than £11,700 and a sale of his studio equipment and stock-in-trade was conducted by Dowell's of Edinburgh on 16, 17 and 19 December 1881.

EH

Literary References: *Gunnis* 1968, 62–3; *Woodward* 1977, vol 1, pt 2, 21–9; *Read* 1982, *passim*; *ODNB* (Smailes)

Additional MS Sources: *Brodie Correspondence*

Will: NAS SC70/4/192, 211 and 217, ESC will and inventory, 8 December 1881, with an additional inventory, 1 September 1882, property valued at £9,732 0s 8d and £2,508 4s 10d

Auction Catalogues: Brodie 1881

Portraits of the Sculptor: J G Tunny, photo, *c*1854, R Sc A, Edinburgh; J Phillip, canvas, exhib R Sc A, Edinburgh, 1859; A Rhind, canvas, 1875, formerly private coll, Scotland (untraced); Nesbitt & Lothian, *carte de visite* photo, NPG, London; J Phillip, canvas, nd, Aberdeen Art Gallery; photos, NLS, Edinburgh

Funerary Monuments

1.	†1848	Eliza Paton	s	Dean Cemetery, Edinburgh	*Woodward* 1977, vol 1, pt 2, 29
2.	†1856	Robert Cook	b	Rosebank Cemetery, Edinburgh	*Woodward* 1977, vol 1, pt 2, 29
3.	*c*1860	Duncan Macfarlan	b	Glasgow Necropolis	*McKenzie* 2002, 459
4.	1861	Alexander Cowan	b	Grange Cemetery, Edinburgh	*Woodward* 1977, vol 1, pt 2, 29; *Laperriere* 1, 1991, 181

No.	Date	Subject		Location		Literature
5.	1861	Rev Robert Story		Rosneath, Dunbarton		RG/JP, 2, 188
6.	1864	93rd Sutherland Highlanders (†1857–8)		St Giles, Edinburgh		*Gunnis* 1968, 63
7.	1866	Alexander and John Runciman	s	Canongate churchyard, Edinburgh		*Woodward* 1977, vol 1, pt 2, 29
8.	1866	Frances, Lady Kinnaird		Rossie Priory, Perths		*Gunnis* 1968, 62; *Laperriere* 1, 1991, 182; *ODNB*
9.	1867	71st Highland Light Infantry (†1863)		Glasgow Cathedral		*Woodward* 1977, vol 1, pt 2, 29
10.	1868	Alexander Smith		Warriston Cemetery, Edinburgh		*Gunnis* 1968, 63; *Woodward* 1977, vol 1, pt 2, 29
11.	1871	Olivia Barbara Kinnaird		Rossie Priory, Perths		*Woodward* 1977, vol 1, pt 2, 26
12.	†1873	Rev John Paul		St Cuthbert, New Town, Edinburgh		Pevsner, *Edinburgh*, 1991, 276
13.	1873	Robert Thomson		Dean Cemetery, Edinburgh		*Woodward* 1977, vol 1, pt 2, 29
14.	1873	Thomas Guthrie		St Columba, Edinburgh		Pevsner, *Edinburgh*, 1991, 168
15.	1873	Unidentified subject		St Clements churchyard, Aberdeen		*Woodward* 1977, vol 1, pt 2, 29
16.	1875	Thomas Guthrie		St John, Edinburgh		*Gunnis* 1968, 63
17.	1879	Sam Bough	b	Dean churchyard, Edinburgh		*CJ*, 18 July and 26 Aug 1879; Pevsner, *Edinburgh*, 1991, 390
18.	1879	Sir James Young Simpson Bt (†1870)		Westminster Abbey, Chapel of St Andrew	S	*Graves* I, 1905–6, 294; *MacMichael* 1977, 54; *Laperriere* 1, 1991, 183
19.	†1881	James and Jane (†1883) Buchanan with relief attrib to Sir John Steell (co-sculptor: Sir James Steell RA)		Dean Cemetery, Edinburgh Other versions: Merchants Hall, Glasgow, reduced bust, marble, nd		*Skinner* 1977, 259 (repr); *McKenzie* 2002, 195
20.	nd	John Graham Gilbert		Glasgow Necropolis		*McKenzie* 2002, 458
21.	nd	John Hill Burton (†1881)		Dean churchyard, Edinburgh		Pevsner, *Edinburgh*, 1991, 390
22.	nd	Mary Doig	s	Portobello Cemetery, Edinburgh		*Woodward* 1977, vol 1, pt 2, 29
Statues						
23.	1850	Little Nell and her grandfather		[Exhib R Sc A, Edinburgh, 459]; untraced		*Gunnis* 1968, 62; *Laperriere* 1, 1991, 180
24.	1851	Affection		[Exhib R Sc A, Edinburgh, 660]; untraced		*Laperriere* 1, 1991, 180
25.	1852	Bruce in defence of liberty, 'group in bronzed type metal'		[Exhib R Sc A, Edinburgh, 692]; untraced		*Laperriere* 1, 1991, 180
26.	c1853	Corinna, the lyric muse	p	Private coll Other versions: marble bust exhib R Sc A, Edinburgh, 1854, 709 marble statue exhib R Sc A, Edinburgh, 1855, 782 (lent by William Wilson Esq of Banknock) reproduced in Parian ware, 1857 marble statuette exhib R Sc A, Edinburgh, 1863, 830 (lent by James Hay of Leith)		*Gunnis* 1968, 62; *Pearson* 1991, unpag; *Laperriere* 1, 1991, 180
27.	1854	Arthur, 1st Duke of Wellington, model only		[Exhib R Sc A, Edinburgh, 705]; untraced		*Laperriere* 1, 1991, 180
28.	By 1856	Captive Chaldean, statuette	m	[coll Robert Roberts Jun]; untraced		*Laperriere* 1, 1991, 180, 181; *Morris and Roberts* 1998, 102
29.	1856	Hecamede	m	[coll Rt Hon Henry Labouchère]; untraced		*Gunnis* 1968, 62; *Laperriere* 1, 1991, 181
30.	1856	Little Mary, daughter of Edward James Jackson		[Exhib R Sc A, Edinburgh, 742]; untraced		*Laperriere* 1, 1991, 180
31.	1856	Nursery Music, statuette		[Exhib R Sc A, Edinburgh, 714]; untraced		*Laperriere* 1, 1991, 180
32.	1857	The thunderstorm		[Exhib R Sc A, Edinburgh, 246]; untraced		*Laperriere* 1, 1991, 181
33.	1858	Oenone Model(s): exhib R Sc A, Edinburgh, 1856, 748		Avington Park, Hants		*Gunnis* 1968, 62; *Laperriere* 1, 1991, 181, 182
34.	1862	Architecture crowning the theory and practice of her art	s	[James Gowan, Rockville, Napier Road, Edinburgh]; West Princes St Gardens, Edinburgh		*Woodward* 1977, vol 1, pt 2, 26 (repr 33); Pevsner, *Edinburgh*, 1991, 317
35.	1862	Dr Thomas Alexander	m	Prestonpans, East Lothian	D	*Woodward* 1977, vol 1, pt 2, 26; *Read* 1982, 104, 106 (repr)
36.	1862	Henry, Lord Cockburn	m	Faculty of Advocates, Edinburgh		*Gunnis* 1968, 62; *Woodward* 1977, vol 1, pt 2, 26; *Laperriere* 1, 1991, 181
37.	1863	Jeannie Deans		[coll Alexander Ross, Forfar]; untraced		*Laperriere* 1, 1991, 855
38.	1864	Albert, the Prince Consort Payment(s): £280	m	Perth		*Darby and Smith* 1983, 76, 78, 79 (repr)
39.	1867	Kilmeny		[coll Alexander Ross, Forfar]; untraced		*Laperriere* 1, 1991, 182
40.	1869	Sunshine	m	[Exhib R ScA, Edinburgh, 1004]; untraced		*Laperriere* 1, 1991, 182
41.	1870	John Graham Gilbert	m	Glasgow Museums S.40		*Gunnis* 1968, 62; *Laperriere* 1, 1991, 182
42.	1871	James Hay, statuette	m	[Exhib R Sc A, Edinburgh, 763]; untraced		*Laperriere* 1, 1991, 182
43.	1872	David Livingstone, statuette	m	David Livingstone Centre, Blantyre, South Lanarkshire		*Woodward* 1977, vol 1, pt 2, 29; *Billcliffe* 1, 1990–92, 172; *Laperriere* 1, 1991, 182, 183

44.	1871–1872	Dr Thomas Graham Model(s): exhib R Sc A, Edinburgh, 1871, 776 and RGIFA, Glasgow, 1871, 627 (head, lent by James Young of Kelly)	b	George Square, Glasgow	SD	*Billcliffe* 1, 1990–92, 171; *Laperriere* 1, 1991, 182; *McKenzie* 2002, 139–40 (repr)
45.	1872	Ruth	m	Art Gall, Aberdeen		*Pearson* 1991, unpag; *Laperriere* 1, 1991, 182
46.	1873	Blind girl reading, statuette	m	[coll James G Orchar, of Dundee]; McManus Galleries, Dundee		*Woodward* 1977, vol 1, pt 2, 29; *Laperriere* 1, 1991, 183
47.	1874	Charles Cowan, statuette	m	Beeslack Stables, Penicuik, Midlothian		*Woodward* 1977, vol 1, pt 2, 29 (pl 31); *Laperriere* 1, 1991, 183
48.	1874	Education	m	The Mary Erskine School, Edinburgh		Pearson 1991, unpag; *Laperriere* 1, 1991, 183
49.	1874	The mathematician, statuette		[coll James G Orchar, of Dundee]; McManus Galleries, Dundee		*Woodward* 1977, vol 1, pt 2, 29 (pl 32)
50.	1875	Rebecca at the well, statuette		[Exhib R Sc A, Edinburgh, 656]; untraced		*Laperriere* 1, 1991, 183
51.	1865–1876	Nobility (and bas-reliefs of heraldic emblems)		Albert Memorial, Charlotte Square, Edinburgh		*Gunnis* 1968, 62; *Darby and Smith* 1983, 70; Pevsner, *Edinburgh*, 1991, 294
52.	1876	Sir James Young Simpson Bt	b	West Princes St Gardens, Edinburgh		Pevsner, *Edinburgh*, 1991, 316
53.	1877	Michael Alexander Russel	m	[Exhib R Sc A, Edinburgh, 667]; untraced		*Laperriere* 1, 1991, 183
54.	1877	Sir David Brewster	m	University of Edinburgh, King's buildings		*Ormond* 1973, 52; *Woodward* 1977, vol 1, pt 2, 26
55.	1880	George Brown		Toronto, Canada		*Gunnis* 1968, 62
56.	1871–1881	Oliver Cromwell, Earl of Leicester, Helen MacGregor, Amy Robsart, Edith of Lorne, Jeannie Deans, Madge Wildfire, the Laird of Dumbiedykes	s	Scott Monument, Princes Street, Edinburgh Other versions: Peebles Public Library, Amy Robsart, marble exhib RGIFA, Glasgow, 1879, 693, Edith of Lorne, marble, £84; untraced		*Woodward* 1977, vol 1, pt 2, 26–7, 29; *Read* 1982, 117; *Billcliffe* 1, 1990–92, 172; *Laperriere* 1, 1991, 183, 184
57.	nd	Hercules supporting the heavens (cast by Elkington & Co)	b	Harbour steps, Portmeirion, Merionethshire		*Gunnis* 1960 (2), 1508; *Clough-Williams* 1960, 1, 394 (repr)
58.	nd	Lord Provost Thomas Marshall	b	Perth MAG		*Woodward* 1977, vol 1, pt 2, 26
Busts						
59.	1847	Sir Thomas Dick Lauder		[Exhib R Sc A, Edinburgh, 630]; untraced		*Laperriere* 1, 1991, 179
60.	1847	Unidentified gentleman		[Exhib R Sc A, Edinburgh, 632]; untraced		*Laperriere* 1, 1991, 179
61.	1848	Rt Hon Lord Advocate		[Exhib R Sc A, Edinburgh, 607]; untraced		*Laperriere* 1, 1991, 179
62.	1849	Dante		[Exhib R Sc A, Edinburgh, 602]; untraced		*Laperriere* 1, 1991, 180
63.	1849	Haidee	m	[Exhib R Sc A, Edinburgh, 347]; untraced		*Laperriere* 1, 1991, 179
64.	1849	William Watson		[Exhib R Sc A, Edinburgh, 609]; untraced		*Laperriere* 1, 1991, 180
65.	1850	Francis, Lord Jeffrey	p	[Exhib RA, London, 1398]; untraced Other versions: miniature bust exhib R Sc A, Edinburgh, 1852, 696		*Graves* I, 1905–6, 294; *Laperriere* 1, 1991, 180
66.	1850	Mrs J H Burton	m	[Exhib R Sc A, Edinburgh, 646]; untraced		*Laperriere* 1, 1991, 180
67.	1850	Sir James Young Simpson Bt	m	[Exhib R Sc A, Edinburgh, 481]; untraced Other versions: exhib R Sc A, Edinburgh, 1852, 699 miniature Manc Art Treas exhib, 1857, 143, m (lent by J Pender)		*Manchester Art Treasures* 1857, 136; *Laperriere* 1, 1991, 180
68.	1851	Child praying	m	[Exhib R Sc A, Edinburgh, 667]; untraced		*Laperriere* 1, 1991, 180
69.	1851	Mary Queen of Scots		[Exhib R Sc A, Edinburgh, 670]; untraced		*Laperriere* 1, 1991, 180
70.	1851	Rev David Welsh	m	New College, Edinburgh		*Woodward* 1977, vol 1, pt 2, 28; *Laperriere* 1, 1991, 180
71.	1851	William Shakespeare		[Exhib R Sc A, Edinburgh, 663]; untraced		*Laperriere* 1, 1991, 180
72.	1852	Dr John Scott		[Exhib R Sc A, Edinburgh, 700]; untraced		*Laperriere* 1, 1991, 180
73.	1852	Professor James Syme		[Exhib R Sc A, Edinburgh, 701]; untraced		*Laperriere* 1, 1991, 180
74.	1852	Thomas Faed		[Exhib R Sc A, Edinburgh, 682]; untraced		*Laperriere* 1, 1991, 180
75.	1852	Unidentified lady		[Exhib R Sc A, Edinburgh, 680]; untraced		*Laperriere* 1, 1991, 180
76.	1852	Unidentified lady		[Exhib R Sc A, Edinburgh, 697]; untraced		*Laperriere* 1, 1991, 180
77.	1852	Unidentified lady		[Exhib R Sc A, Edinburgh, 698]; untraced		*Laperriere* 1, 1991, 180
78.	1853	David Shaw		[Exhib R Sc A, Edinburgh, 683]; untraced		*Laperriere* 1, 1991, 180

No.	Date	Subject		Location		Literature
79.	1853	Hope	m	[Exhib R Sc A, Edinburgh, 693]; untraced		*Laperriere* 1, 1991, 180
80.	1853	Miss Grey		[Exhib R Sc A, Edinburgh, 686]; untraced		*Laperriere* 1, 1991, 180
81.	1854	Miss Rutherford	m	[Exhib R Sc A, Edinburgh, 699]; untraced		*Laperriere* 1, 1991, 180
82.	1854	Rev David Welsh	m	Free Church College, Edinburgh		*Woodward* 1977, vol 1, pt 2, 28
83.	1854	Thomas Constable		[Exhib R Sc A, Edinburgh, 707]; untraced		*Laperriere* 1, 1991, 180
84.	1854	Unidentified subject	m	[Exhib R Sc A, Edinburgh, 716]; untraced		*Laperriere* 1, 1991, 180
85.	1855	Charlotte, daughter of D O Hill		[Exhib R Sc A, Edinburgh, 750]; untraced		*Laperriere* 1, 1991, 180
86.	1855	Dr Richard J Mackenzie	m	RCS, Scotland, Edinburgh		*Woodward* 1977, vol 1, pt 2, 28 (pl 28)
87.	1855	George, 1st Duke of Argyll	m	Dunrobin Castle, Sutherland		*Walker* 1961, 2
88.	1855	Harry George, son of Deputy-Commissary General Weir		[Exhib R Sc A, Edinburgh, 770]; untraced		*Laperriere* 1, 1991, 180
89.	1855	Henry, Lord Cockburn	m	SNPG, Edinburgh Other versions: R Sc A, Edinburgh (diploma work), marble, 1856		*Gunnis* 1968, 63; *Woodward* 1977, vol 1, pt 2, 27; *Laperriere* 1, 1991, 180
90.	1855	Lord Handyside	m	Faculty of Advocates, Edinburgh		*Woodward* 1977, vol 1, pt 2, 27; *Laperriere* 1, 1991, 180
91.	1855	Unidentified lady		[Exhib R Sc A, Edinburgh, 760]; untraced		*Laperriere* 1, 1991, 180
92.	1856	Alexander Campbell	m	[Exhib R Sc A, Edinburgh, 736]; untraced		*Laperriere* 1, 1991, 180
93.	1856	Andrew, Lord Rutherfurd	m	Faculty of Advocates, Edinburgh		*Woodward* 1977, vol 1, pt 2, 28; *Ormond and Rogers* 2, 1979–81, 187; *Laperriere* 1, 1991, 180
94.	1856	Mrs Lenox Kennedy	m	[Exhib R Sc A, Edinburgh, 728]; untraced		*Laperriere* 1, 1991, 180
95.	1857	Alexander Cowan	m	[Exhib R Sc A, Edinburgh, 682]; untraced		*Laperriere* 1, 1991, 181
96.	1857	Alfred, Lord Tennyson Model(s): R Sc A, Edinburgh, 1856, 729; RA, London, 1857, 1354	m	Fine Art Soc, London, 1992	S	*Palgrave* 1866, 87; *Graves* I, 1905–6, 294; *Laperriere* 1, 1991, 180; *Read* 1992, 12, 52, cat 6 (repr)
97.	1857	La Penserosa	m	[Exhib R Sc A, Edinburgh, 683]; untraced		*Laperriere* 1, 1991, 181
98.	1857	Mrs Millar	m	[Exhib R Sc A, Edinburgh, 685]; untraced		*Laperriere* 1, 1991, 181
99.	1857	Mrs Sydney Dobell		[Exhib R Sc A, Edinburgh, 677]; untraced		*Graves* I, 1905–6, 294; *Laperriere* 1, 1991, 181
100.	1857	Rt Hon Lord Advocate	m	[Exhib R Sc A, Edinburgh, 693]; untraced		*Laperriere* 1, 1991, 181
101.	1858	A Scotch lassie (after Patric Park)	m	R Sc A, Edinburgh		*Woodward* 1977, vol 1, pt 2, 28; *Laperriere* 1, 1991, 181
102.	1858	Hugh Miller	m	SNPG, Edinburgh		*Gunnis* 1968, 63; *Woodward* 1977, vol 1, pt 2, 28; *Laperriere* 1, 1991, 181, 184
103.	1858	James, 1st Baron Dunfermline	m	SNPG, Edinburgh Other versions: New College, Edinburgh, m, 1859		*Graves* I, 1905–6, 294; *Gunnis* 1968, 63; *Woodward* 1977, vol 1, pt 2, 27; *Ormond and Rogers* 2, 1979–81, 68; *Laperriere* 1, 1991, 181
104.	1858	Laura		Bowood, Wilts		*Gunnis* 1968, 63
105.	1859	George, 9th Baron Kinnaird	m	[Corn Exchange, Dundee]; Dundee City Art Gallery		*Gunnis* 1968, 63; *Woodward* 1977, vol 1, pt 2, 27; *Ormond and Rogers* 3, 1979–81, 112; *Laperriere* 1, 1991, 181
106.	1859	John Hill Burton	m	Scotsman newspaper office, Edinburgh Other versions: SNPG, Edinburgh, m		*Woodward* 1977, vol 1, pt 2, 27 (pl 29); *Laperriere* 1, 1991, 182
107.	1859	Madeleine Smith	m	Fine Art Society, Edinburgh		*Woodward* 1977, vol 1, pt 2, 28
108.	1859	Storm	m	[Exhib R Sc A, Edinburgh, 731]; untraced		*Graves* I, 1905–6, 294; *Billcliffe* 1, 1990–92, 171; *Laperriere* 1, 1991, 181
109.	1859	Sunshine	m	[Exhib R Sc A, Edinburgh, 733]; untraced		*Graves* I, 1905–6, 294; *Laperriere* 1, 1991, 181
110.	1860	Charles Hay Forbes	m	Bank of Scotland, George Street, Edinburgh		*Woodward* 1977, vol 1, pt 2, 27
111.	1860	Earl of Rothes	m	[Exhib R Sc A, Edinburgh, 849]; untraced		*Laperriere* 1, 1991, 181
112.	1860	William P Allison	m	R C Physic, Edinburgh		*Woodward* 1977, vol 1, pt 2, 27
113.	1861	Amy, daughter of John Philip RA		[Exhib R Sc A, Edinburgh, 801]; untraced		*Laperriere* 1, 1991, 182
114.	?1861	Charles MacLaren	m	Royal Scottish Museum, Edinburgh Other versions: SNPG, Edinburgh, copy by J Hutchison, m, 1861		*Woodward* 1977, vol 1, pt 2, 28; *Laperriere* 1, 1991, 181
115.	1861	John Pender	m	[Exhib R Sc A, Edinburgh, 797]; untraced		*Laperriere* 1, 1991, 182
116.	1861	Mrs Pender	m	[Exhib R Sc A, Edinburgh, 790]; untraced		*Laperriere* 1, 1991, 181

No.	Date	Subject		Location	Literature
117.	1861	Rev Alexander Monteith	m	New College, Edinburgh Other versions: New College, Edinburgh, m, 1862	*Woodward* 1977, vol 1, pt 2, 28; *Laperriere* 1, 1991, 855
118.	1861	Thomas Guthrie		[Exhib R Sc A, Edinburgh, 804]; untraced	*Laperriere* 1, 1991, 182
119.	1862	Aunty Bella	m	[Exhib R Sc A, Edinburgh, 826]; untraced	*Graves* I, 1905–6, 294; *Laperriere* 1, 1991, 181
120.	1862	Henry, Lord Cockburn	m	Faculty of Advocates, Edinburgh	*Woodward* 1977, vol 1, pt 2, 27
121.	1863	Amy	m	[Exhib RA, London, 1083]; untraced	*Graves* I, 1905–6, 294
122.	1863	James, Lord Moncrieff	m	Faculty of Advocates, Edinburgh	*Woodward* 1977, vol 1, pt 2, 28; *Ormond and Rogers* 2, 1979–81, 149; *Laperriere* 1, 1991, 181
123.	1863	John A Rankin	m	[Exhib R Sc A, Edinburgh, 798]; untraced	*Laperriere* 1, 1991, 855
124.	1863	Maurice Lothian	m	[Exhib R Sc A, Edinburgh, 822]; untraced	*Laperriere* 1, 1991, 181
125.	1863	Professor John Blackie	p	R Sc A, Edinburgh Other versions: SNPG, Edinburgh, 1863 SNPG, Edinburgh, nd	*Gunnis* 1968, 63; *Woodward* 1977, vol 1, pt 2, 27
126.	1863	Rev William Cunningham	m	New College, Edinburgh	*Woodward* 1977, vol 1, pt 2, 27; *Laperriere* 1, 1991, 181
127.	1864	Charles Lawson		[Exhib R Sc A, Edinburgh, 736]; untraced	*Laperriere* 1, 1991, 182
128.	1864	John, Lord Glencorse	m	Faculty of Advocates, Edinburgh	*Graves* I, 1905–6, 294; *Woodward* 1977, vol 1, pt 2, 27; *Ormond and Rogers* 3, 1979–81, 78; *Laperriere* 1, 1991, 182
129.	1864	Juanita	m	[Exhib R Sc A, Edinburgh, 732]; untraced	*Graves* I, 1905–6, 294; *Laperriere* 1, 1991, 182
130.	1864	La Vignarola		[Exhib R Sc A, Edinburgh, 710]; untraced	*Billcliffe* 1, 1990–92, 171; *Laperriere* 1, 1991, 182
131.	1864	Provost William Lindsay	m	Leith Town Hall	*Woodward* 1977, vol 1, pt 2, 28; *Laperriere* 1, 1991, 182
132.	1864	Robert Burns	m	Lady Stair's House, Edinburgh	*Woodward* 1977, vol 1, pt 2, 27; *Billcliffe* 1, 1990–92, 171
133.	1864	Unidentified subject	m	[Exhib R Sc A, Edinburgh, 703]; untraced	*Laperriere* 1, 1991, 182
134.	1864	William Smith, for the Philosophical Institution, Edinburgh	m	[Exhib R Sc A, Edinburgh, 709]; untraced	*Laperriere* 1, 1991, 182
135.	1865	Frances, Lady Kinnaird	m	Rossie Priory, Perths	*Woodward* 1977, vol 1, pt 2, 27
136.	1865	Mrs Robert Hislop Jnr	m	[Exhib R Sc A, Edinburgh, 894]; untraced	*Laperriere* 1, 1991, 182
137.	1865	Mrs Rutherford Clark	m	[Exhib R Sc A, Edinburgh, 876]; untraced	*Laperriere* 1, 1991, 182
138.	1866	Dr Macleod	m	[Exhib R Sc A, Edinburgh, 907]; untraced	*Laperriere* 1, 1991, 182
139.	1866	John Ritchie	m	Scotsman newspaper office, Edinburgh	*Graves* I, 1905–6, 294; *Woodward* 1977, vol 1, pt 2, 28; *Laperriere* 1, 1991, 182
140.	1866	Lady Gibson Maitland		[Exhib RA, London, 860]; untraced	*Graves* I, 1905–6, 294
141.	1866	Miss Duncan	m	[Exhib R Sc A, Edinburgh, 912]; untraced	*Laperriere* 1, 1991, 182
142.	1866	Miss Home	m	[Exhib R Sc A, Edinburgh, 879]; untraced	*Laperriere* 1, 1991, 182
143.	1866	Unidentified lady	m	[Exhib R Sc A, Edinburgh, 871]; untraced	*Laperriere* 1, 1991, 182
144.	1866	William Thomas Thomson, for Colonial Life Assurance Co	m	[Exhib R Sc A, Edinburgh, 885]; untraced	*Laperriere* 1, 1991, 182
145.	1867	Miss Ballantyne	m	[Exhib R Sc A, Edinburgh, 909]; untraced	*Laperriere* 1, 1991, 182
146.	1867	Miss Imlach	m	[Exhib R Sc A, Edinburgh, 933]; untraced	*Laperriere* 1, 1991, 182
147.	1867	Professor James Syme	m	RCS, Scotland, Edinburgh Other versions: Edinburgh University, m, 1872	*Woodward* 1977, vol 1, pt 2, 28; *Laperriere* 1, 1991, 182
148.	1867	Sir William Hamilton	m	Edinburgh University	*Woodward* 1977, vol 1, pt 2, 27
149.	1867	Unidentified child	m	[Exhib R Sc A, Edinburgh, 896]; untraced	*Laperriere* 1, 1991, 182
150.	1867	Unidentified gentleman	m	[Exhib R Sc A, Edinburgh, 898]; untraced	*Laperriere* 1, 1991, 182
151.	1867	Unidentified lady	m	NGS, Edinburgh	*Woodward* 1977, vol 1, pt 2, 28
152.	1867	Unidentified lady	m	[Exhib RA, London, 1042]; untraced	*Graves* I, 1905–6, 294
153.	1867	Unidentified lady	m	[Exhib R Sc A, Edinburgh, 935]; untraced	*Laperriere* 1, 1991, 182
154.	?1868	Dr Francis Adams		Aberdeen University	*Gunnis* 1968, 63
155.	1868	James Young	m	[Exhib R Sc A, Edinburgh, 1032]; untraced	*Billcliffe* 1, 1990–92, 171; *Laperriere* 1, 1991, 182
156.	1868	John Phillip RA	m	Art Gall, Aberdeen	*Graves* I, 1905–6, 294; *Ormond* 1973, 377; *Woodward* 1977, vol 1, pt 2, 28; *Billcliffe* 1, 1990–92, 171; *Laperriere* 1, 1991, 182
157.	1868	Lady Seton Stewart of Touch		[Exhib RA, London, 965]; untraced	*Graves* I, 1905–6, 294

No.	Date	Subject	Medium	Location	Literary references
158.	1868	Our Dora	m	[Exhib R Sc A, Edinburgh, 1030]; untraced	*Laperriere* 1, 1991, 182
159.	1868	Queen Victoria (co-sculptor: Alexander Brodie)	m	Royal Coll, Balmoral Other versions: SNPG, Edinburgh, m, 1868 Merchant company, Edinburgh, m, 1869 St Conan, Lochawe, Argyll, m, nd	*Graves* I, 1905–6, 294; *Ormond* 1973, 489; *Woodward* 1977, vol 1, pt 2, 28; *Billcliffe* 1, 1990–92, 171; *Laperriere* 1, 1991, 182
160.	1868	Robert Cox		[Exhib R Sc A, Edinburgh, 1018]; untraced Other versions: Edinburgh university, copy by J S Rhind, 1897	*Woodward* 1977, vol 1, pt 2, 27; *Laperriere* 1, 1991, 182
161.	1868	William Burns	m	[Exhib RGIFA, Glasgow, 809]; untraced	*Billcliffe* 1, 1990–92, 171
162.	1869	A Scots girl	m	NGS, Edinburgh	*Woodward* 1977, vol 1, pt 2, 28
163.	1869	Ada Barclay		SNPG, Edinburgh	*Gunnis* 1968, 63; *Laperriere* 1, 1991, 182
164.	1869	Alexander MacDuff	m	Highland Tolbooth Church, Edinburgh	*Woodward* 1977, vol 1, pt 2, 28; *Laperriere* 1, 1991, 182
165.	1869	Alexander Smith		[Exhib R Sc A, Edinburgh, 977]; untraced	*Billcliffe* 1, 1990–92, 171; *Laperriere* 1, 1991, 182
166.	1869	James McClelland	m	[Exhib RA, London, 1167]; untraced	*Graves* I, 1905–6, 294
167.	1869	John Stewart	m	[Exhib RA, London, 1263]; untraced	*Graves* I, 1905–6, 294; *Laperriere* 1, 1991, 182
168.	1869	Rev Robert Lee	m	New College, Edinburgh	*Woodward* 1977, vol 1, pt 2, 28; *Laperriere* 1, 1991, 182
169.	1869	Thomas Carlyle	m	Dick Institute, Kilmarnock, Ayrshire Other versions: SNPG, Edinburgh, 1879 University College, Dundee, m, 1879	*Gunnis* 1968, 63; *Ormond* 1973, 94; *Woodward* 1977, vol 1, pt 2, 27; *Billcliffe* 1, 1990–92, 172; *Laperriere* 1, 1991, 184
170.	1869	Willie	m	[Exhib R Sc A, Edinburgh, 1000]; untraced	*Laperriere* 1, 1991, 182
171.	1870	Little Judy	m	[Exhib R Sc A, Edinburgh, 913]; untraced	*Laperriere* 1, 1991, 182
172.	1870	Mrs MacLellan	m	[coll Keith MacLellan Esq, Sri Lanka]; untraced	*Billcliffe* 1, 1990–92, 171; *Laperriere* 1, 1991, 182
173.	1870	Professor John Goodsir	m	Edinburgh University	*Graves* I, 1905–6, 294; *Woodward* 1977, vol 1, pt 2, 27
174.	1870	Thomas Constable	m	SNPG, Edinburgh	*Woodward* 1977, vol 1, pt 2, 27; *Ormond and Rogers* 3, 1979–81, 44; *Laperriere* 1, 1991, 182
175.	1870	Unidentified lady	m	[Exhib R Sc A, Edinburgh, 910]; untraced	*Laperriere* 1, 1991, 182
176.	1870	Unidentified lady	m	[Exhib R Sc A, Edinburgh, 941]; untraced	*Laperriere* 1, 1991, 182
177.	1871	Donald Horne	m	[Exhib R Sc A, Edinburgh, 779]; untraced	*Laperriere* 1, 1991, 182
178.	1871	J G Dymock	m	[Exhib R Sc A, Edinburgh, 790]; untraced	*Laperriere* 1, 1991, 182
179.	1871	John Graham Gilbert		Glasgow Corporation	*Gunnis* 1968, 63
180.	1871	Mrs Hallard	m	[Exhib R Sc A, Edinburgh, 764]; untraced	*Laperriere* 1, 1991, 182
181.	1871	Mrs Mungo Burton	m	[Exhib R Sc A, Edinburgh, 790]; untraced	*Laperriere* 1, 1991, 182
182.	1871	Professor Robert Christison MD	m	Edinburgh University	*Graves* I, 1905–6, 294; *Woodward* 1977, vol 1, pt 2, 27; *Billcliffe* 1, 1990–92, 171; *Laperriere* 1, 1991, 182
183.	1872	Edward, Lord Barcaple	m	Faculty of Advocates, Edinburgh	*Woodward* 1977, vol 1, pt 2, 27; *Ormond and Rogers* 3, 1979–81, 13; *Laperriere* 1, 1991, 182
184.	1872	Lord Provost William Law	m	New Council Chamber, Edinburgh	*Woodward* 1977, vol 1, pt 2, 27; *Laperriere* 1, 1991, 183
185.	1872	Mrs David Chalmers	m	[Exhib R Sc A, Edinburgh, 664]; untraced	*Laperriere* 1, 1991, 183
186.	1872	Mrs Farquharson, of Invercauld	m	Braemar, Invercauld, Aberdeenshire	*Gunnis* 1968, 63; *Woodward* 1977, vol 1, pt 2, 27; *Laperriere* 1, 1991, 183
187.	1872	Mrs Heugh	m	[Exhib R Sc A, Edinburgh, 666]; untraced	*Graves* I, 1905–6, 294; *Billcliffe* 1, 1990–92, 171; *Laperriere* 1, 1991, 183
188.	1872	Mrs John Boyd	m	[Exhib R Sc A, Edinburgh, 635]; untraced	*Laperriere* 1, 1991, 182
189.	1872	Robert Balfour, for Edinburgh Academy	m	[Exhib R Sc A, Edinburgh, 639]; untraced	*Laperriere* 1, 1991, 183
190.	1872	Sir James Young Simpson Bt	m	Edinburgh University Other versions: RC Surg, Edinburgh, marble, 1871 RC Physic, Edinburgh, m, 1871	*Woodward* 1977, vol 1, pt 2, 28; *Read* 1982, 126, 128 (repr); *Billcliffe* 1, 1990–92, 171; *Laperriere* 1, 1991, 183, 184
191.	1872	Unidentified subject		[Exhib RGIFA, Glasgow, 699]; untraced	*Billcliffe* 1, 1990–92, 171
192.	1872	Unidentified subject		[Exhib RGIFA, Glasgow, 703]; untraced	*Billcliffe* 1, 1990–92, 171
193.	1872	William Brand	m	Bank of Scotland, Edinburgh	*Woodward* 1977, vol 1, pt 2, 27; *Laperriere* 1, 1991, 183

No.	Date	Subject		Location		References
194.	1873	Janie	m	[Exhib RA, London, 1452]; untraced		*Graves* I, 1905–6, 294
195.	1873	Master Patrick Balfour	m	[Exhib R Sc A, Edinburgh, 640]; untraced		*Laperriere* 1, 1991, 183
196.	1873	Mrs J B Balfour	m	[Exhib R Sc A, Edinburgh, 645]; untraced		*Laperriere* 1, 1991, 183
197.	c1873	Mrs Law	m	Glasgow Museums S.138		*Laperriere* 1, 1991, 183
198.	1873	Provost Swan	m	[Exhib R Sc A, Edinburgh, 653]; untraced		*Laperriere* 1, 1991, 183
199.	1873	Rev Robert Candlish	m	St George's West Church, Edinburgh		*Woodward* 1977, vol 1, pt 2, 27; *Billcliffe* 1, 1990 –92, 171; *Laperriere* 1, 1991, 183
200.	1873	Thomas Jamieson Boyd	m	Merchant Company, Edinburgh		*Woodward* 1977, vol 1, pt 2, 27; *Laperriere* 1, 1991, 183
201.	1874	Adam Black Duncan	m	[Exhib R Sc A, Edinburgh, 571]; untraced		*Laperriere* 1, 1991, 183
202.	1874	Alexander Rhind	m	Glasgow University Other versions: coll Mrs Millard (the sculptor's granddaughter)		*Woodward* 1977, vol 1, pt 2, 28
203.	1874	Angela, Baroness Burdett-Coutts		Coutts Bank, London Other versions: ex coll Rupert Gunnis; untraced replica exhib R Sc A, Edinburgh, 1876, 728		*Graves* I, 1905–6, 294; *Gunnis* 1968, 63; *Ormond* 1973, 81; *Laperriere* 1, 1991, 183
204.	1874	David Jeffrey	m	[Exhib R Sc A, Edinburgh, 591]; untraced		*Laperriere* 1, 1991, 183
205.	1874	J S Fleming	m	[Exhib R Sc A, Edinburgh, 573]; untraced		*Laperriere* 1, 1991, 183
206.	pre-1874	James Beaumont Neilson	m	Glasgow Museums S.53		*Billcliffe* 1, 1990–92, 171
207.	1874	Mrs David Jeffrey	m	[Exhib R Sc A, Edinburgh, 589]; untraced		*Laperriere* 1, 1991, 183
208.	1874	Rev James Robertson DD	m	Highland Tolbooth Church, Edinburgh		*Woodward* 1977, vol 1, pt 2, 28; *Laperriere* 1, 1991, 183
209.	1874	Unidentified man		Royal College of Science and Technology, Glasgow	SD	
210.	1875	Professor John Bennett	m	Edinburgh University		*Woodward* 1977, vol 1, pt 2, 27
211.	1875	'The rising lily's snowy grace . . .'	m	[Exhib R Sc A, Edinburgh, 660]; untraced		*Laperriere* 1, 1991, 183
212.	1875	Thomas Guthrie	p	Greyfriars Church, Edinburgh Other versions: Inverary Manse, Argyll		*Gunnis* 1968, 63; *Woodward* 1977, vol 1, pt 2, 27
213.	1875	'With laurel leaves her folded robe, Was lightly wreathed round . . .'	m	[Exhib R Sc A, Edinburgh, 662]; untraced		*Laperriere* 1, 1991, 183
214.	1876	Eliza Lockhart	m	[coll James Young]; untraced		*Billcliffe* 1, 1990–92, 171
215.	1876	John Clapperton	m	George Watson's School, Edinburgh		*Woodward* 1977, vol 1, pt 2, 27; *Laperriere* 1, 1991, 183
216.	1876	Lady Coxe	m	[Exhib R Sc A, Edinburgh, 740]; untraced		*Laperriere* 1, 1991, 183
217.	1876	Miss Frances R MacGregor	m	[Exhib R Sc A, Edinburgh, 724]; untraced		*Laperriere* 1, 1991, 183
218.	1876	Mrs MacGregor	m	[Exhib R Sc A, Edinburgh, 725]; untraced		*Laperriere* 1, 1991, 183
219.	1877	Alexander Russel	m	SNPG, Edinburgh Other versions: Scotsman newspaper office, Edinburgh, m, 1877		*Woodward* 1977, vol 1, pt 2, 28 (pl 30); *Laperriere* 1, 1991, 184
220.	1877	Dr Robert Moffat	m	David Livingstone Centre, Blantyre, South Lanarkshire		*Woodward* 1977, vol 1, pt 2, 28; *Billcliffe* 1, 1990–92, 171; *Laperriere* 1, 1991, 183
221.	1877	Joseph Jefferson	m	[Exhib RA, London, 1437]; untraced		*Graves* I, 1905–6, 294; *Laperriere* 1, 1991, 184
222.	1877	Prof Thomas J Crawford	m	Edinburgh University		*Woodward* 1977, vol 1, pt 2, 27; *Laperriere* 1, 1991, 183
223.	1877	Sir John Melville	m	New Council Chamber, Edinburgh		*Woodward* 1977, vol 1, pt 2, 28
224.	1877	Unidentified boy	m	[Exhib R Sc A, Edinburgh, 677]; untraced		*Laperriere* 1, 1991, 183
225.	1878	Dr David Livingstone	p	Hunterian Museum, Glasgow University Other versions: ex coll Livingstone Bruce, marble; untraced		*Graves* I, 1905–6, 294; *Ormond* 1973, 273; *Woodward* 1977, vol 1, pt 2, 28; *Laperriere* 1, 1991, 184
226.	1878	Hugh Blair	m	[Exhib R Sc A, Edinburgh, 763]; untraced		*Laperriere* 1, 1991, 183
227.	1878	Mrs James Ogston	m	[Exhib R Sc A, Edinburgh, 672]; untraced		*Laperriere* 1, 1991, 183
228.	1878	Mrs Montgomery Neilson	m	[Exhib R Sc A, Edinburgh, 744]; untraced		*Laperriere* 1, 1991, 183
229.	1878	Robert Bryson	m	Merchant Company, Edinburgh		*Woodward* 1977, vol 1, pt 2, 27; *Laperriere* 1, 1991, 184
230.	1878	Rt Hon Lyon Playfair	m	[Exhib RA, London, 1455]; untraced		*Graves* I, 1905–6, 294
231.	1879	Dr Angus Smith	m	[coll James Young]; untraced		*Billcliffe* 1, 1990–92, 171
232.	1879	Helen Alice, daughter of Colin MacKenzie of Portmore	m	[Exhib R Sc A, Edinburgh, 749]; untraced		*Laperriere* 1, 1991, 184
233.	1879	Henry Irving	m	[Exhib RA, London, 1457]; untraced		*Graves* I, 1905–6, 294; *Billcliffe* 1, 1990–92, 172; *Laperriere* 1, 1991, 184
234.	1879	Mrs Bell	m	[Exhib R Sc A, Edinburgh, 801]; untraced		*Laperriere* 1, 1991, 184

235. 1879	Mrs James Auldjo Jamieson	m	[Exhib R Sc A, Edinburgh, 748]; untraced		*Laperriere* 1, 1991, 183
236. 1879	Rev William Smith	m	Highland Tollbooth Church, Edinburgh		*Woodward* 1977, vol 1, pt 2, 28
237. 1879	Robert Horn	m	[Exhib R Sc A, Edinburgh, 779]; untraced		*Laperriere* 1, 1991, 184
238. 1879	Unidentified lady		Coll F Brodie, Canterbury	SD	
239. 1879	Unidentified man	m	R Sc A, Edinburgh		*Woodward* 1977, vol 1, pt 2, 28
240. 1880	Ellen Terry	m	Shakespeare Memorial Theatre, Stratford, Warks		*Graves* I, 1905–6, 294; *Billcliffe* 1, 1990–92, 172; *Laperriere* 1, 1991, 184
241. 1880	G P Chalmers RSA	m	[Exhib RGIFA, Glasgow, 787]; untraced		*Billcliffe* 1, 1990–92, 172
242. 1880	Mr McKinley		Untraced		RG/JP, 2, 188
243. 1880	Mrs Connel Black	m	[Exhib R Sc A, Edinburgh, 783]; untraced		*Laperriere* 1, 1991, 184
244. 1880	Mrs H Brown	m	[Exhib RA, London, 1569]; untraced		*Graves* I, 1905–6, 294; *Billcliffe* 1, 1990–92, 172; *Laperriere* 1, 1991, 184
245. 1880	Rev Principal Harper	m	[Exhib R Sc A, Edinburgh, 782]; untraced		*Laperriere* 1, 1991, 184
246. 1880	William Nelson	m	SNPG, Edinburgh		*Woodward* 1977, vol 1, pt 2, 28; *Laperriere* 1, 1991, 184
247. 1881	Mrs Asher	m	[Exhib RA, London, 1457]; untraced		*Graves* I, 1905–6, 294
248. 1881	Professor W B Hodgson	m	Edinburgh University		*Woodward* 1977, vol 1, pt 2, 27
249. 1881	Unidentified lady	m	Huntly House Museum, Edinburgh		*Woodward* 1977, vol 1, pt 2, 28
250. 1881	Unidentified man	m	(coll Robin Woodward)		*Woodward* 1977, vol 1, pt 2, 28
251. 1881	Unidentified man	m	Nicolson's Antiques, High Street, Edinburgh		*Woodward* 1977, vol 1, pt 2, 28
252. 1882	James Young	m	[Exhib R Sc A, Edinburgh, 739]; untraced		*Laperriere* 1, 1991, 184
253. nd	Ekemhalmt(?)		Coll Mrs Millard		RG/JP, 2, 188
254. nd	Lady Gowans		Coll Mrs Millard		RG/JP, 2, 188
255. nd	Mrs Hutchison	m	[Exhib R Sc A, Edinburgh, 1916, 2]; untraced		*Laperriere* 1, 1991, 184
256. nd	Sir Rowland Hill	m	Untraced		*Ormond* 1973, 226
257. nd	Thomas Knox		Untraced		RG/JP, 2, 188
258. nd	Young Augustus		Untraced		RG/JP, 2, 186
Architectural Sculpture					
259. 1864	Portraits of the Cowan family	b	Royal Bank stationery warehouse, Edinburgh		Pevsner, *Edinburgh*, 1991, 331
260. 1872	Greyfriars Bobby, fountain figure	b	Victoria St, Edinburgh Other versions: Huntly House Museum, Edinburgh, small marble reproduction, nd		*Read* 1982, 177 (repr)
261. *c*1872	St Andrew, statue		[City of Glasgow Life Assurance Building, Renfield Street, Glasgow, Lanarks]; untraced		*McKenzie* 2002, 444
262. 1873–1874	Young scholar and reliefs		Greenview School, Greenhead Street, Glasgow Other versions: City Art Gallery, Dundee, version 'in small'		*McKenzie* 2002, 195 (repr); *Laperriere* 1, 1991, 183
263. 1875	The ram, fountain statue	b	Moffat, Dumfriesshire		*Woodward* 1977, vol 1, pt 2, 27
Reliefs					
264. 1847	Unidentified subject, portrait medallion		[Exhib R Sc A, Edinburgh, 636]; untraced		*Laperriere* 1, 1991, 179
265. 1847	Unidentified subject, portrait medallion		[Exhib R Sc A, Edinburgh, 637]; untraced		*Laperriere* 1, 1991, 179
266. 1847	Unidentified subject(s), portrait medallions		[Exhib R Sc A, Edinburgh, 651]; untraced		*Laperriere* 1, 1991, 179
267. 1851	Industry bringing peace, medallion		[Exhib R Sc A, Edinburgh, 653]; untraced		*Laperriere* 1, 1991, 180
268. 1851	Victory of peace, medallion		[Exhib R Sc A, Edinburgh, 654]; untraced		*Laperriere* 1, 1991, 180
269. 1853	Unidentified gentleman, medallion		[Exhib R Sc A, Edinburgh, 688]; untraced		*Laperriere* 1, 1991, 180
270. 1854	Fun		[Exhib R Sc A, Edinburgh, 704]; untraced		*Laperriere* 1, 1991, 180
271. 1855	Dante and Beatrice, medallion	m	[Exhib R Sc A, Edinburgh, 750]; untraced		*Laperriere* 1, 1991, 180, 184; *Morris and Roberts* 1998, 102
272. 1856	Hon Lady Mary Labouchère, medallion		[Exhib R Sc A, Edinburgh, 730]; untraced		*Laperriere* 1, 1991, 180
273. 1859	George Combe, medallion	p	SNPG, Edinburgh		*Woodward* 1977, vol 1, pt 2, 29; *Laperriere* 1, 1991, 181, 184
274. 1859	Unidentified subject, medallion	m	[Exhib R Sc A, Edinburgh, 742]; untraced		*Laperriere* 1, 1991, 181
275. 1860	Sir John Bowring, medallion		[Exhib R Sc A, Edinburgh, 873]; untraced		*Laperriere* 1, 1991, 181
276. 1861	Elizabeth, Lady Kinnaird, medallion	m	[Exhib R Sc A, Edinburgh, 784]; untraced		*Laperriere* 1, 1991, 181
277. 1861	James, Lord Moncrieff, medallion	b	[Exhib R Sc A, Edinburgh, 793]; untraced		*Laperriere* 1, 1991, 182
278. 1861	Lord Kinnaird, medallion	m	[Exhib R Sc A, Edinburgh, 787]; untraced		*Laperriere* 1, 1991, 181
279. 1861	Matty, head in high relief		[Exhib R Sc A, Edinburgh, 791]; untraced		*Laperriere* 1, 1991, 181
280. 1861	Willie, head in high relief		[Exhib R Sc A, Edinburgh, 796]; untraced		*Laperriere* 1, 1991, 182

281. 1865	Faith, part of a mural monument	m	[Exhib R Sc A, Edinburgh, 862]; untraced	*Laperriere* 1, 1991, 182
282. 1867	In memoriam		[Exhib R Sc A, Edinburgh, 922]; untraced	*Laperriere* 1, 1991, 182
283. 1876	The parting of Abradates and Panthea	m	[Exhib R Sc A, Edinburgh, 751]; untraced	*Laperriere* 1, 1991, 183
284. 1877	Hesiod	m	[Exhib R Sc A, Edinburgh, 680]; untraced	*Laperriere* 1, 1991, 183
285. 1877	Homer	m	[Exhib R Sc A, Edinburgh, 682]; untraced	*Laperriere* 1, 1991, 183
286. nd	Thomas Guthrie	s	Craig Dhu House, Inverary, Argyll	*Woodward* 1977, vol 1, pt 2, 29
Miscellaneous				
287. 1847	Unidentified officer		[Exhib R Sc A, Edinburgh, 642]; untraced	*Laperriere* 1, 1991, 179
288. 1847	Unidentified officer in Highland uniform		[Exhib R Sc A, Edinburgh, 641]; untraced	*Laperriere* 1, 1991, 179
289. 1848	Unidentified family group		[Exhib R Sc A, Edinburgh, 602]; untraced	*Laperriere* 1, 1991, 179
290. 1852	The pet		[Exhib R Sc A, Edinburgh, 686]; untraced	*Laperriere* 1, 1991, 180
291. 1860	Col Hugh Morrison		[Exhib R Sc A, Edinburgh, 863]; untraced	*Laperriere* 1, 1991, 181
292. 1864	Winter		[Exhib R Sc A, Edinburgh, 699]; untraced	*Laperriere* 1, 1991, 181
293. 1867	Light in darkness	m	[Exhib RA, London, 1042]; untraced	*Graves* I, 1905–6, 294; *Laperriere* 1, 1991, 182
294. 1867	Penelephon, the beggar maid	m	[Exhib R Sc A, Edinburgh, 918]; untraced	*Laperriere* 1, 1991, 182
295. 1868	Egeria Payment(s): £20	p	[Exhib RGIFA, Glasgow, 810]; untraced	*Billcliffe* 1, 1990–92, 171
296. 1881	A daughter of the artist		[Exhib R Sc A, Edinburgh, 723]; untraced	*Laperriere* 1, 1991, 184
297. 1881	James Mylne		[Exhib R Sc A, Edinburgh, 722]; untraced	*Laperriere* 1, 1991, 184
298. 1881	Miss Young		[Exhib R Sc A, Edinburgh, 725]; untraced	*Laperriere* 1, 1991, 182
299. nd	Adam and Eve		Untraced	RG/JP, 2, 186
300. nd	Martha and Mary		Untraced	RG/JP, 2, 186
301. nd	Robert Herdman		[Exhib R Sc A, Edinburgh, 1926, 27]; untraced	*Laperriere* 1, 1991, 184

BROMFIELD, Benjamin, of Liverpool fl 1757–88

Bromfield carved a number of chimneypieces and monuments in Wales and the northwest of England. He was christened on 2 August 1752 at Old Swinford, Worcs. His father, Robert, was a builder who held the post of clerk of works at Hagley Hall and in 1765 arbitrated in a dispute between the Newport estate and the architect **Thomas Farnolls Pritchard** over bills for work carried out at the Red Lion Inn and Deanery house in Wolverhampton. Benjamin was the youngest of four sons who were all employed in the sculpture and building trades. **Charles Bromfield** was, like Benjamin, a marble mason working from Liverpool and Robert, who was baptised at Whitchurch, Salop, on 8 July 1736, was a carver. The most successful member of the family was Joseph Bromfield (1744–1824), who worked as a plasterer, architect and surveyor in Shrewsbury and is thought to have executed plaster decoration for a number of houses associated with Pritchard.

A Liverpool trades directory for 1790 gives Benjamin's address as Marble Street, Islington, a district close to the city centre. In 1773 he carved the imposing white and red marble chimneypiece in the saloon at Chirk Castle (**17**) and in 1788 Sir Corbet Corbet paid him £400 for chimneypieces for Adderley Hall (**18**). Gunnis noted that all his monuments and tablets had 'good details' and were 'obviously influenced by those of **Sir Henry Cheere**'. The date of his death is uncertain but he was buried in a vault in Holy Trinity, Saint Anne Street, Liverpool.

Literary References: *Gunnis* 1968, 63; *Beard* 1975, 76, 207; *Beard* 1981, 248; *Colvin* 1995, 162–3; *Ionides* 1999, *passim*

Archival References: Bromfield Affidavit; IGI

Funerary Monuments					
1. ?1757	George Cotymore	Conway, Carnarvon		*Gunnis* 1968, 63
2. ?1764	Mary Eyton	St Mary-on-the-Hill, Chester		*Gunnis* 1968, 63
3. ?1769	Rev L Richmond	Stockport, Cheshire		*Gunnis* 1968, 63
4. ?1769	Robert Lloyd	Oswestry, Salop		*Gunnis* 1968, 63
5. †1770	George Warrington	Gresford, Denbighs	S	Pevsner, *Clwyd* 1994, 172
6. †1770	William Yates	Beetham, Westmorland		RG/JP, 2, 189
7. †1771	Robert Comberbach	St Michael, Chester, Cheshire		Pevsner, *Cheshire*, 1971, 152
8. †1771	Robert Wynne	Llanfair Talhaiarn, Denbighs		RG/JP, 2, 189
9. 1775	Richard Price Thelwall	St Asaph Cathedral, Flint		Pevsner, *Clwyd*, 1986, 439
10. ?1776	Nathaniel Wettenhall	Audlem, Cheshire		*Gunnis* 1968, 63
11. ?1776	Robert Howard	Conway, Carnarvon		*Gunnis* 1968, 63
12. †1776	Samuel Crook	Leyland, Lancs		RG/JP, 2, 189
13. pre-1781	John Stanley	Winwick, Lancs		*Gunnis* 1968, 63
14. †1781	Sir William Farmington	Leyland, Lancs		RG/JP, 2, 189
15. †1784	John Holland	Llanelian-yn-Rhos, Denbighs	S	Pevsner, *Clwyd*, 1986, 202
16. †1787	Francis Parry Price	Overton, Flint		Pevsner, *Clwyd*, 1986, 411
Chimneypieces				
17. 1773	White marble and red jasper	Chirk Castle, Denbighs, saloon		Pevsner, *Clwyd*, 1986, 125 (repr)
18. 1788	Several Payment(s): £400	[Sir Corbet Corbet, of Adderley Hall, Salop]; untraced		*Gunnis* 1968, 63

BROMFIELD, Charles 1739–

Charles Bromfield, an older brother of **Benjamin Bromfield**, worked as a marble mason in Liverpool. He was baptised on 6 October 1739 at Patshull, Staffs, where his father, Robert Bromfield, was probably employed in the rebuilding of Patshull Hall under **Francis** and **William Smith of Warwick**. He placed the following advertisement in an American newspaper: 'Liverpool, 1770. Charles Bromfield, Begs leave to acquaint his Friends and the Public, That he is establish'd in the Marble Trade, on a very extensive Plan, having a Large and curious Assortment of all the different Kind that is produced in Italy, and the valuable Sorts of other Countries: any Gentlemen who are pleased to apply to him, at his Yard in Williamson's Square, for any kind of manufactured Goods, may depend on having their Orders executed with the greatest Punctuality, in the neatest and cheapest Manner, having ready made a Variety of Chimney Pieces, Statues, Busts, Urns, Vases, Tables, Water Closet Cisterns, Mortars, &c. &c. He makes Monuments, Fonts and Tombs. N.B. He also will supply the Inland Manufacturers with Marble in the Block, on as good Terms as from any other Part of this Kingdom' (*The New-York Gazette and the Weekly Mercury*, 5 February 1770, cited by *Gottesman* 1970, 228). He signs two monuments in Denbighshire.

Literary References: *Gottesman* 1970, 228

Archival References: Bromfield Affidavit; IGI

Funerary Monuments

1.	†1767	Jane Hughes	St Grwst, Llanwrst, Denbighs	S	Pevsner, *Clwyd*, 1986, 234
2.	†1776	Philip Puleston	St Giles, Wrexham, Denbighs	S	Pevsner, *Clwyd*, 1986, 302

BROMHALL (or BROOMHALL), James and others fl 1679–1732

They were a large and confusing family embracing at least two generations. A James Broomhall was apprenticed to Jasper Latham in 1679 and another family member with the same name was the son of **Thomas Bromhall** and was apprenticed to his father in 1697, being made free of the Masons' Company on 12 October 1716. In 1726 Benjamin Hoare, who was then engaged in building Boreham House, near Chelmsford, paid 'John Broomhall' seven guineas for a model, though on 1 April 1732, James Broomhall received £26 in full for joiner's work. It is not clear whether two members of the family were employed by Hoare.

Literary References: *Webb* 1999, 5

Archival References: Masons' Co, Freemen, fol 5 (1716); Freedom Register, 1663–94 (1679); Court Book, 1722–51 (2 August 1723); Hoare Partnership Ledger, 1725–34, fol 141 (1726), f233 (1732)

BROMHALL (or BROOMHALL), Thomas and sons, of Fleet Ditch, London fl 1670–1723

From a flourishing family of masons, seven of whose apprenticeships are recorded in the registers of the Masons' Company. Thomas, the son of Richard Bromhall of Madeley, Salop, became a husbandman to James Smith (perhaps **James Smith I**) on 9 December 1670 and was made free of the Masons' Company in 1677. Bromhall's name is listed with John Walker, his apprentice, in the general search of 1678, under the heading 'Mr **Edward Strong**'s men at St Pauls Church' (*Knoop and Jones* 1935, 75). In 1705–7 he made several marble chimneypieces for Samuel Tufnell (**1**). Only two marble tablets have been identified (**2, 3**).

He had three sons, all of whom were formally apprenticed to their father. Samuel was apprenticed in 1693, Richard in 1703 and Joseph in 1705. In 1684 Bromhall took **Henry Gates** as an apprentice and in 1723 Michael, the son of **James Bromhall**, joined the workshop.

Literary References: *Gunnis* 1968, 63; *Webb* 1999, 5

Archival References: Masons' Co, *Freemen*, fol 4, 11 Dec 1677; *Freemen*, 1703; *Apprentices*, 1705; *Freemen*, 1716

Chimneypieces

1.	1705–1707	Several	m	Langley's, Chelmsford, Essex	*Gunnis* 1968, 63, citing Tufnell archives

Miscellaneous

2.	1717	Tablet recording the benefactions of Sir George Shiers		Fetcham, Surrey	*Gunnis* 1968, 63
3.	1717	Tablet recording the benefactions of Sir George Shiers		Great Bookham, Surrey	*Gunnis* 1968, 63

BROMLEY, A fl 1847–57

In 1847 his address was 46 Richmond Street Bank, Leeds.

Literary References: *Morris and Roberts* 1998, 103

Statues

1.	1847	Termosiris and Telemachus	p	[Exhib Liverpool Ac, 757]; untraced	*Morris and Roberts* 1998, 103

Busts

2.	1856	Thomas Nunneley		LGI, Leeds, W R Yorks	RG/JP, 2, 190
3.	1857	Richard Hobson		LGI, Leeds, W R Yorks	RG/JP, 2, 190

Miscellaneous

4.	1847	The young springer	m	[Exhib Liverpool Ac, 762]; untraced	*Morris and Roberts* 1998, 103

BROMLEY FAMILY, of Keswick

John Bromley I 1772–1841
William Bromley 1811–1861
John Bromley II 1833–1911
Joseph Bromley 1839–1906

A Cumbrian family of sculptors and stonecutters. **John Bromley I** was born in Beckermet, Cumberland, the son of a weaver, and chose to become a stone cutter and engraver. It is not certain where he served his apprenticeship but it may have been in Whitehaven, where several monumental masons were established and where he set up in business in 1792. In 1794 he married Elizabeth Ashburner, the daughter of a well-to-do farmer. Bromley specialised in slate headstones, a material that was ideal for fine engraving and had excellent weathering qualities. He rarely signed his work, but Hughes claims that his distinctive style is easily recognised and that he may well have earned a reputation as a carver of coats of arms. Several heraldic headstones testify to his skill (**3, 4, 6**). He died on 20 June 1841 and is buried at Crossthwaite. His obituary in the *Cumberland Pacquet* describes him as a celebrated stone cutter, with a remarkably retentive memory and a developed sense of humour (*CP*, 22 June 1841).

The business was taken over by his sixth son, **William Bromley**, who was apprenticed to his father and married a dressmaker, Mary Wilson. Two of the finest slate headstones ever produced in the county came from the Bromley workshops during his lifetime. Both incorporate panels of partially free-standing sculpture: Joseph Dover's headstone has a central panel depicting *Hope*, flanked by two side panels, one containing a dove with an olive leaf and the other a paschal lamb (**2**). The other, commemorating Joseph Cherry, has a central panel filled with a carving of *Time* with a *Tree of life* and a ruined building, and side panels with books on the themes of *Eternity* and *Transience* (**5**).

William's sons, **John Bromley II** and **Joseph Bromley**, continued the business, trading as J & J Bromley. During this period the firm was responsible for memorials over a wide area, including 50 in Cockermouth alone. By 1871 there was sufficient work to employ seven men and two boys. The last member of the family business died in 1957.

Literary References: Pevsner, *Cumberland & Westmorland*, 1967, 115; *Hughes* 1974, 186–97

Portraits of the Sculptor: Anon, John Bromley I, canvas (*Hughes* 1974, repr)

Funerary Monuments

1.	†1797	Elizabeth Hodgson, headstone (by John Bromley I)	Crossthwaite, Cumberland		*Hughes* 1974, 188
2.	†1810	Joseph Dover (by William Bromley)	Keswick, Cumberland		*Hughes* 1974, 192
3.	†1812	George Wood (by John Bromley I)	Crossthwaite, Cumberland		*Hughes* 1974, 190
4.	†1815	William Hartley (by John Bromley I)	Beckermet, Cumberland		*Hughes* 1974, 191
5.	†1818	Joseph Cherry (by William Bromley)	Keswick, Cumberland		*Hughes* 1974, 192–3 (repr)
6.	c1827	John Ashburner and wife (the sculptor's parents-in-law) (by John Bromley I)	Gosforth, Cumberland	S	*Hughes* 1974, 191

BROOKS, William fl 1782–88

His tradecard of 1788 describes him as a mason of Castle Street, Bloomsbury (Banks 106.4).

Funerary Monuments

1.	†1782	Melior Mary Weston	Holy Trinity, Guildford, Surrey	S

BROOKSHAW, George 1751–1823

Brookshaw exhibited six works, including 'A sacrifice to Cupid; a frieze for a chimneypiece', at the Free Society of Artists in 1780 and is described as 'Sculptor, etc' by Graves. He was not however a sculptor but a cabinet maker who specialised in furniture and chimneypieces, decorated with elaborately painted wood, marble and copper panels. He went out of business in the mid-1790s but re-emerged as an author and illustrator of painting manuals and horticultural works in the early years of the 19th century. He is thought to have spent the intervening decade working as a flower painter under the assumed name of George Brown, perhaps because his reputation was damaged by a financial or sexual scandal.

Literary References: *Graves* 1907, 41; *Gunnis* 1968, 63; *Wood* 1991 (1), 301–6; *Wood* 1991 (2), 383–97

BROTHERS, P, of London fl 1838

Funerary Monuments

1.	?1838	Robert Laurence	St Mary, St Marylebone, London	S	*Gunnis* 1968, 63

BROUGH, John, of London fl 1779–84

Brough was employed extensively at Greenwich Hospital between 1779 and 1784, working on the Queen Mary east building, the east colonnade, Augusta ward, the Royal Charles staircase, Queen Anne's Building, the infirmary and the north and south fronts of the hospital. In 1779 he made chimneypieces to replace those destroyed in a fire (**1**). In 1781 he rebuilt the north colonnade and, three years later, a school near the hospital. In 1781 he made pedestals for Coade stone figures in the vestibule outside the chapel (**2**) and erected the southwest staircase in the King William building.

Literary References: *Gunnis* 1968, 64

Archival References: TNA ADM 68/825–30, 68/813 and 68/880

Chimneypieces

1.	1779	Several	Royal Hospital, Greenwich (ORNC)	*Gunnis* 1968, 64

Architectural Sculpture

2.	1791	Pedestals	Royal Hospital, Greenwich (ORNC) vestibule outside the chapel	*Gunnis* 1968, 64

BROWN, Alfred fl 1844–56

Brown won a silver medal for a model at the Royal Academy Schools in 1844 (**10**) and a second silver medal the following year, together with the gold medal for a relief, *The hours leading forth the horses of the sun* (**7, 13**). He exhibited at the RA between 1845 and 1855 and sent a statuette of the Duke of Wellington to the British Institution in 1853 (**4**). His statue of *David before Saul* was displayed at the Great Exhibition of 1851 (**2**). M H Grant later commented 'His art was chiefly poetical and mythological, but he excelled in horses, whilst statues of C Napier [3] and David showed another side to his accomplishment' (*Grant* 1953, cited by *Bilbey* 2002, 224). Brown was also a designer of silver. His models for the trophy presented by the Emperor of Russia for Ascot races in 1845 and a large candelabrum presented to the 8th Marquess of Tweeddale by his friends in India in 1850 were exhibited at the RA (**11, 18**). He designed a magnificent jewelled and enamelled gold vase decorated with reliefs and surmounted by a group representing 'the United Kingdom as symbolised by Britannia, Scotia and Hibernia' (*AJ Cat* 1851, 281) and a testimonial centrepiece with figures of 'the sister muses who preside over dramatic and musical festivals' (**19, 20**) which were displayed at the Great Exhibition (*AJ Cat* 1851, 57–8). The latter was executed by the silversmiths Hunt and Roskell and in 1856 Brown designed and modelled a silver centrepiece for the 7th Earl of Stamford, realised by the same firm (**21**). This cost £2,500 and must have been a substantial piece, for it weighed 112 pounds.

Literary References: *Gunnis* 1968, 64; *Bilbey* 2002, 224

Archival References: RA Premium list

Statues

1.	1847	Satan falling from Heaven	p	[Loaned to South Kensington Museum by James Brown 1875]; untraced	*Graves* I, 1905–6, 304; *Bilbey* 2002, 224

2.	1850	David before Saul (David took a harp)	p	[Loaned to South Kensington Museum by James Brown 1875]; deteriorated beyond repair, 1932	*Graves* I, 1905–6, 304; *Gunnis* 1968, 64; *Bilbey* 2002, 224
3.	*c*1852	Sir Charles James Napier, equestrian figure	pb	VAM A.21-1936	*Graves* I, 1905–6, 305; *Ormond* 1973, 334; *Bilbey* 2002, 224 (repr)
4.	1853	Arthur, 1st Duke of Wellington, statuette Payment(s): 12 gns	p	[Exhib BI, London, 575]; untraced	*Graves* 1875, 69
5.	1853	The dying standard bearer	p	[RA, London, 1853, 1320; awarded gold medal]; loaned to South Kensington Museum by James Brown 1875; deteriorated beyond repair, 1932	*Graves* I, 1905–6, 305; *Bilbey* 2002, 224
Chimneypieces					
6.	1848	Several	m	Army and Navy Club, Pall Mall, London	*Gunnis* 1968, 64
Reliefs					
7.	1845	The hours leading forth the horses of the sun	p	[Loaned to South Kensington Museum by James Brown 1875]; deteriorated beyond repair, 1932	*Graves* I, 1905–6, 304; *Gunnis* 1968, 64; *Bilbey* 2002, 224
8.	1855	The fall of the wicked		[Exhib RA, London, 1492]; untraced	*Graves* I, 1905–6, 305
9.	1855	The resurrection of the just		[Exhib RA, London, 1491]; untraced	*Graves* I, 1905–6, 305
Miscellaneous					
10.	1844	Unidentified subject, model		[Awarded RA silver medal]; untraced	RA Premium list
11.	1845	Portraits of three horses for the Emperor of Russia's Ascot race cup		[Exhib RA, London, 1425]; untraced	*Graves* I, 1905–6, 304
12.	1845	The despair of Cain after the murder of Abel		[Exhib RA, London, 1344]; untraced	*Graves* I, 1905–6, 304
13.	1845	Unidentified subject, model		[RA, silver medal]; untraced	RA Premium list
14.	1846	Cupid watching his arrows		[Exhib RA, London, 1412]; untraced	*Graves* I, 1905–6, 304
15.	1848	Una and the lion		[Exhib RA, London, 1345]; untraced	*Graves* I, 1905–6, 304
16.	1849	Nymph and Cupid		[Exhib RA, London, 1230]; untraced	*Graves* I, 1905–6, 304
17.	1849	Phineas petrified by the Medusa's head		[Exhib RA, London, 1206]; untraced	*Graves* I, 1905–6, 304
18.	1850	Scots fighting Danes, group, part of a candelabrum executed in silver and presented to the Marquess of Tweeddale		[RA, London, 1850, 1359]; untraced	*AJ Cat* 1851, 58–9 (repr); *Graves* I, 1905–6, 305
19.	1851	Gold vase with group representing the United Kingdom, model		Untraced	*AJ Cat* 1851, 281
20.	1851	Lumley testimonial centrepiece, model for Hunt and Roskell		Untraced	*AJ Cat* 1851, 57–8 (repr)
21.	1856	Stags in Bradgate Park, model for silver centrepiece for Hunt and Roskell		Untraced	*Gunnis* 1968, 64

BROWN, C, of Kings Lynn fl 1822–25

He was the master-mason responsible for rebuilding Hillington Hall for Sir William Folkes, for a sum of £757 (inaccurately cited in GPC as Norwich Public Library Archives, 11672) (**1, 2**).

Archival References: GPC

Chimneypieces				
1.	1822–1825	Description unavailable Payment(s): £32	[Hillington Hall, Norfolk]; untraced	GPC
Architectural Sculpture				
2.	1822–1825	Ornamental carving	[Hillington Hall, Norfolk]; demol *c*1946	GPC

BROWN, Charles 1749–95

For information the reader is referred to *Pyke* 1973, 20

BROWN, F I, of Salisbury fl 1775–1811

He was appointed master-mason to Salisbury Cathedral in 1804 and was paid two years later for 'two Portlandstone columns and capitals' for that building. He signs several monuments of 'good workmanship' in Wiltshire.

Literary References: *Gunnis* 1968, 64

Funerary Monuments					
1.	?1775	William Batt	Nunton, Wilts	S	*Gunnis* 1968, 64
2.	1779	Mayne family	Teffont Evias, Wilts	SD	*Gunnis* 1968, 64
3.	?1799	William Brooker	West Dean, Wilts	S	*Gunnis* 1968, 64
4.	?1805	John Wyche	St Martin, Salisbury, Wilts	S	*Gunnis* 1968, 64
5.	*c*1811	Thomas King (†1787) and his son Thomas (†1811)	Alvediston, Wilts	S	Pevsner, *Wilts*, 1975, 89
Architectural Sculpture					
6.	1806	'two Portland-stone columns and capitals'	Salisbury Cathedral, Wilts		*Gunnis* 1968, 64

BROWN, F II, of Salisbury fl 1835–40

The son of F **Brown I of Salisbury**, he was responsible for a few minor tablets, but his chief work, executed about 1835, was an imposing marble chimneypiece at Somerley.

Literary References: *Gunnis* 1968, 64

Chimneypieces				
1.	?1835	With two white maidens Drawing(s): coll Lord Normanton	Somerley, nr Ringwood, Hants, new drawing room	*Gunnis* 1968, 64; Pevsner, *Hants & Isle of Wight*, 1967, 509

BROWN, George fl 1795–96

Chimneypieces

1.	1795	'veined marble'	m	[for Mrs Yorke, Sydney Lodge, Hamble, Southampton, Hants, drawing room]; untraced	Soane bill book 5, fols 105–6; *Gunnis* 1968, 64
2.	1796	Description unavailable	m	[for Thomas Lewis, Palmers Green, Middx]; untraced	Soane bill book 5, fol 258; *Gunnis* 1968, 64

BROWN, George, of Kidderminster 1803–77

He was born on 16 December 1803, the third child of George Brown, an Ayrshire mason who moved to Bewdley, Worcs, to work with Telford on the construction of the Severn Bridge and later lived at Bridgnorth, Salop. The elder George and his sons John (1799–1874) and George worked as masons at Bridgnorth until 1840, when the younger George set up for himself at Kidderminster. He died there on 2 December 1877.

Archival References: GPC

Funerary Monuments

1.	†1842	John Lavender	Wolverley, Worcs	S	GPC

BROWN, J, of London fl 1830?–57

A sculptor called J Brown (or Browne) exhibited a group of *Caractacus before Claudius* at the Westminster Hall Exhibition of 1844 (**17**). One critic considered it 'abominally bad' and advised the artist to 'break the whole thing up' (*Lit Gaz*, 1844, cited by *Gunnis* 1968, 64). He may have been responsible for a number of monuments and tablets signed either 'J Brown' or 'J Browne', including a large gothic monument with standing figures of *Hope* and *Charity* commemorating Philip Saltmarshe at Howden, Yorkshire (**12**). It is not clear whether he was connected with **Joseph Browne.**

Literary References: *Gunnis* 1968, 64

Funerary Monuments

1.	?1830	10th Lord Saye and Sele	Broughton, Oxon	S	*Gunnis* 1968, 64
2.	1836	Charles Shaw Lefevre (†1823)	Heckfield, Hants	S	Pevsner, *Hants & Isle of Wight*, 1967, 287; C Lib (repr)
3.	†1836	Charlotte Tremaine	Kensal Green Cemetery, London	S	*Gunnis* 1968, 64; *Curl* 2001, 251–2
4.	1837	Anne Fox (†1817) and Jane Smith (†1824)	St Mary, Finchley, Middx	SD	
5.	†1838	Deborah Barker	Kensal Green Cemetery, catacombs	S	
6.	?1839	Thomas Baldwin	Leyland, Lancs		GPC
7.	?1842	Emma Sparkes	Shalford, Surrey	S	*Gunnis* 1968, 64
8.	?1846	11th Lord Saye and Sele	Broughton, Oxon	S	*Gunnis* 1968, 64
9.	†1848	Ann Jones	St Giles-in-the-Fields, City of London	S	RG/JP, 2, 197v.
10.	?1848	Church family	Hatfield, Herts	S	*Gunnis* 1968, 64
11.	1847–1848	Elizabeth Saltmarshe (†1834)	Howden, E R Yorks	S	Pevsner, *Yorks: E R & York*, 1995, 489
12.	1847–1848	Philip Saltmarshe (†1846)	Howden, E R Yorks	S	Pevsner, *Yorks: E R & York*, 1995, 489
13.	1848	Sir Nicholas Tindal (†1846)	St Giles-in-the-Fields, City of London		RG/JP, 2, 197v.
14.	1849	Admiral Nicholas Tomlinson (†1847)	Berechurch, Essex	SD	C Lib (repr)
15.	1849	Colonel Courtney Chambers (†1848)	St James, Piccadilly, London		
16.	1857	Henrietta Maria Clarissa Hutchinson (†1857)	Hernhill, Kent	SD	

Statues

17.	1844	Caractacus before Claudius	[Exhib Westminster Hall, London]; untraced		*Gunnis* 1968, 64

BROWN, John, of Colchester fl 1823

Funerary Monuments

1.	?1823	Robert Torrin	Kelvedon, Essex	S	*Gunnis* 1968, 64

BROWN, L, of London fl 1846–48

He exhibited at the Royal Academy in 1846 and 1848 from 13 Clarendon Place.

Literary References: *Gunnis* 1968, 64; *Pyke* 1973, 20

Miscellaneous

1.	1846	Dogs setting a hare, model	w	Untraced	*Graves* I, 1905–6, 309
2.	1848	Caesar passing the Rubicon		[Exhib RA, London, 1372]; untraced	*Graves* I, 1905–6, 309

BROWN, Nathan fl 1817

He is listed in Johnstone's *Directory* of 1817 as 'Nathan Brown 197 Tottenham Ct Rd Modeller and Figure Caster' (Inf. Hilary Young)

BROWN, R, of Drury Lane, London fl 1827

Funerary Monuments

1.	†1827	Thomas Stringfield	St George, Bloomsbury, London	S	

BROWN, R, of Shrewsbury fl 1830

Busts

1.	1830	Mr Barton	[Exhib RA, London, 1256]; untraced	*Graves* I, 1905–6, 313

BROWN, Richard and Sons, of Derby

Richard Brown I fl 1735– †before 1785
Richard Brown II 1736–1816
Richard Brown III fl 1816–1829

The firm was founded in 1735 by **Richard Brown I,** whose advertisement that year in the *Derby Mercury* stated that he 'performed monuments, gravestones, chimney-pieces on reasonable terms.' In 1759, and again in 1782, he was paid for paving the floor at All Saints, Derby. In 1765 he made a pair of 'purple obelisks' for Kedleston, probably the magnificent pair made of blue-john that are still in the house (**10**).

He was succeeded by his son, **Richard Brown II**, who was in his turn followed by his son **Richard Brown III**, grandson of the founder. The firm leased a water-driven mill, the Derby Marble Works on the banks of the Derwent, from the corporation of the City of Derby. The lease on this building terminated in 1802 and they moved to premises on the site of the old monastery of St Helen, where they remained until 1829. The third Richard Brown sold this workshop to **Joseph Hall the Younger of Derby**.

On 7 November 1797 an auction of the property of 'a statuary and mason going abroad' was held by Mr Christie. One of the lots was a chimneypiece of Derbyshire Spar 'manufactured at considerable expense at Mr. Brown's of Derby for the late Mr. Harris of the Strand' (**3**) (see **Charles Harris**). The use of a range of local 'marbles' is a feature of the firm's work at this period and they also provided decorative carving. The altarpiece at Stapleford (**11**) was described by Nichols shortly after the turn of the century as 'just completed by Brown of Derby, and is beautifully formed of marble, with borders of black, statuary and dove colour. In the centre is a neat tablet, with the emblems of Hope and Eternity, an anchor suspended on an encircled serpent; and at the top a handsome urn' (*Nichols* 1795–1815, 2, 1, 340).

The firm also had a workshop in Matlock Bath until 1811, and by 1818 they were in possession of the extensive mill for sawing and polishing Derbyshire marbles at Ashford-in-the-Water, founded in 1748 by **Henry Watson**. Between 1828 and 1831 the Ashford works were recorded as being in the hands of John Brown, presumably another member of the family. The Browns quarried 'entrochial' marble in mines at Monyash owned by the Duke of Devonshire, for whose seat at Chatsworth the firm carried out work (**12**). They also quarried shiny 'Derbyshire black' marble (carboniferous limestone) at mines in Ashford. At the Ashford mill marble was carved 'into chimneypieces, vases, ornaments etc... equal in quality and beauty to any in the world; consequently, it is in great request in this kingdom, and finds a ready market in distant countries' (*Glover* 1831–3, 2, 266). Chimneypieces could be had at prices ranging from 30s to £60 and more, and they found an international clientele: in his *Picturesque Excursions in the High Peak* (1819) Henry Moore recorded that 'Mr Brown sold in 1818 in Ashford, an enriched black marble chimney piece to Archduke Michael, who was progressing through Derbyshire' (**6**, quoted in *Tomlinson* 1996, 42).

Literary References: *Glover* 1831–3, 1, 71; 2, 55, 266; *Gunnis* 1968, 64–5; *Tomlinson* 1996, 18, 19, 42, 43

Archival References: GPC

Funerary Monuments						
1.	?1761	Samson Bulkeley (by Richard Brown I)		Leek, Staffs	S	*Gunnis* 1968, 65
2.	1780	Sir John Every Bt, ledger stone (by Richard Brown I) Payment(s): £4 6s		Egginton, Derbys		GPC
Chimneypieces						
3.	pre-1797	Of Derbyshire Spar marble, 'manufactured at considerable expense' (by Richard Brown II)	m	[for Mr Harris, of the Strand]; untraced		Christie, 7 Nov 1797; *Gunnis* 1968, 64
4.	1805	One (by Richard Brown II)		[Meynell Langley Hall, Derbys, drawing room]; untraced		GPC citing Meynell of Meynell Langley archives
5.	1812	Description unavailable (by Richard Brown II)		[Alton Abbey (Towers), Staffs]; untraced		GPC citing archives, Earl of Shrewsbury
6.	1818	'Enriched black marble'	m	[for 'Archduke Michael']; untraced		*Tomlinson* 1996, 18
7.	1818	One Payment(s): £14 14s		[Meynell Langley Hall, Derbys, dining room]; untraced		GPC citing archives, Meynell of Meynell Langley
8.	1823	More than one Payment(s): £23 2s		[Derby Prison, near Uttoxeter Road]; untraced		*Glover* 1831–3, 2, 477, 479
Architectural Sculpture						
9.	1739	Font, in Derbyshire marble (by Richard Brown I) Payment(s): £17	m	Cottered, Herts		Church records
10.	1765	Pair of 'purple obelisks' (by Richard Brown I)		[Kedleston Hall, Derbys]; possibly the 'Blue John' obelisks still in situ, family corridor		*Gunnis* 1968, 64; *Kedleston* 1998, 21
11.	*c*1795	Altarpiece of marble and Derbshire blue john (by Richard Brown II)		Stapleford, Leics	S	*Nichols* 1795–1815, 2, 1, 340; *Gunnis* 1968, 65; Pevsner, *Leics & Rutland*, 1984, 386; C Lib (repr)
12.	*c*1831	Unidentified work	m	[Chatsworth, Derbys, north wing]; untraced		*Glover* 1831–3, 2, 266; *Gunnis* 1968, 65

BROWN, Richard I, of London 1674–1720

Brown was buried in Highgate churchyard, where his epitaph described him as 'Citizen and Mason of London' and stated that he was 'a very ingenious Artist in his way and a zealous Son of the Church of England' (*Mottley* II, 1734–5, 859, in GPC). He died on 21 March 1720, in his 47th year.

Archival References: GPC

BROWN, Richard II, of London fl 1817–22

Most of his tablets are Hellenistic in style.

Funerary Monuments					
1.	?1817	John Thornhill	Stanmore, Middx	S	*Gunnis* 1968, 65
2.	?1820	Robert, 2nd Earl of Roden	Sawbridgeworth, Herts	S	*Gunnis* 1968, 65
3.	?1822	William Dodd	Sutton Valence, Kent	S	*Gunnis* 1968, 65

BROWN, Richard Rushton, of Manchester –1851

He exhibited at the Liverpool Academy and the Academy of the Liverpool Royal Institution from several addresses in Liverpool and Manchester between 1812 and 1831 and showed five works at the Exhibition of Contemporary Art in Manchester in 1827. He was employed as a modeller by **Felix Austin** and **John Seeley** from 1841 until his death.

He can probably be identified with the 'Brown' who executed 'a relief descriptive of the argonauts expedition of 1,263BC . . . in a very hard plaster', which may have been a type of artificial stone. This was for the Great Hall of Francis Goodwin's Manchester Town Hall (2). This Greek Revival building was erected between 1822 and 1838 and demolished in 1912.

Literary References: *Manchester School of Architecture*, Sketch-book No. 1, 1915 (Univ of Liverpool Library, arch. 72.02. M26); *Gunnis* 1968, 65
Archival References: AGBI, vol 5, 137 (application by Mrs Ellen Brown, 1851); NP/RG

Busts

1.	1827	Unidentified gentleman	[Manchester Contemporary Art Exhib]; untraced	*Gunnis* 1968, 65

Architectural Sculpture

2.	?1822–1838	Expedition of the Argonauts, relief	[Old Town Hall, Manchester, Lancs]; demol 1912	

Reliefs

3.	1822	Unidentified artist, medallion portrait	[Exhib ALRI, Liverpool, 175]; untraced	*Morris and Roberts* 1998, 107

Miscellaneous

4.	1812	Cupid	[Exhib Liverpool Ac, 262]; untraced	*Morris and Roberts* 1998, 107
5.	1812	The woman accused of adultery	[Exhib Liverpool Ac, 306]; untraced	*Morris and Roberts* 1998, 107
6.	1812	Young bacchanals	[Exhib Liverpool Ac, 264]; untraced	*Morris and Roberts* 1998, 107
7.	1813	A bacchanalian lamenting over a dead panther	[Exhib Liverpool Ac, 315]; untraced	*Morris and Roberts* 1998, 107
8.	1814	Diana, a sketch	[Exhib Liverpool Ac, 294]; untraced	*Morris and Roberts* 1998, 107
9.	1822	Fear	[Exhib ALRI, Liverpool, 176]; untraced	*Morris and Roberts* 1998, 107
10.	1827	The infant Hercules strangling a serpent	[Manchester Contemporary Art Exhib]; untraced	*Gunnis* 1968, 65
11.	1827	Three unidentified works	[Manchester Contemporary Art Exhib]; untraced	*Gunnis* 1968, 65
12.	1830	Don Juan	[Exhib ALRI, Liverpool, 280]; untraced	*Morris and Roberts* 1998, 107
13.	1831	Love elevates the soul	[Exhib Liverpool Ac, 406]; untraced	*Morris and Roberts* 1998, 107
14.	1831	The dying crusader	[Exhib Liverpool Ac, 407]; untraced	*Morris and Roberts* 1998, 107

BROWN, Robert, of London fl 1823–57

Brown, whose premises were at 58 Great Russell Street, showed at the Great Exhibition of 1851 (**33**). Many of his monuments and tablets are Gothic in style but some are classical, including that to Archibald Little, 1844, at Chipstead, Surrey, which has a relief of a mourning woman described by Gunnis as being 'not unlike a minor work by **Chantrey**' (**22**).

Literary References: *Gunnis* 1968, 65

Funerary Monuments

1.	†1823	William Philpot	St Giles-in-the-Fields, City of London	S	
2.	†1831	Anne Browne Russell	Llanbrynmair, Montgomery	S	Pevsner, *Powys*, 1979, 120
3.	†1832	Jean Rougier	St Peter Port, Guernsey	S	
4.	?1833	James Foster	Streatham, London	S	*Gunnis* 1968, 65
5.	†1833	Lieutenant-Colonel Baillie of Leys Castle, MP	Inverness High Church	S	
6.	?1833	Lieutenant-Colonel Richard Boteler	Eastry, Kent	S	*Gunnis* 1968, 65
7.	†1837	Richard Buckner	Chichester Cathedral, Sussex	S	*Gunnis* 1968, 65
8.	†1838	Benjamin Freeman Coleman	St Catherine, Ventnor, I of W	S	Pevsner, *Hants & Isle of Wight*, 1967, 772
9.	†1840	Peter Carey	St Peter Port, Guernsey	S	
10.	†1840	Ralph Addison	St George, Bloomsbury, London	S	
11.	†1840	William Gentle	St John's Cathedral, Belize (formerly British Honduras)		*Hammond* 2000, 89–90
12.	†1841	Elizabeth and John Mearby	St George, Bloomsbury, London	S	
13.	†1841	Nathaniel Baron	North Cave, E R Yorks	S	Pevsner, *Yorks: E R & York*, 1995, 625
14.	†1841	Thomas Day	St George, Bloomsbury, London	S	
15.	?1842	Charles Williams	Gwennap, Cornwall	S	*Gunnis* 1968, 65
16.	†1843	Emily Larkin	St Giles-in-the-Fields, City of London	S	
17.	†1843	Francis Abbot	St George, Bloomsbury, London	S	
18.	†1843	J Parry Crooke	Boldre, Hants	S	
19.	†1843	John Jortin	North Nibley, Glos	S	Pevsner, *Glos: Cotswolds*, 1999, 521
20.	†1843	Sir Francis Sykes	Basildon, Berks		Pevsner, *Berks*, 1966, 76
21.	?1843	Sir Gregory Turner	Ambrosden, Oxon		GPC
22.	†1844	Archibald Little	Chipstead, Surrey		Pevsner, *Surrey*, 1971, 157
23.	†1844	Rev John Casberd	Penmark, Glamorgan	S	Pevsner, *Glamorgan*, 1995, 504
24.	†1844	Walter Rankin Johnson	West Wycombe, Bucks		Pevsner, *Bucks*, 1994, 739
25.	†1845	Elizabeth (†1806), John (†1821) and Susanna (†1845) Yenn	St George, Bloomsbury, London	S	
26.	?1845	Rev Edward Levett	Hampstead parish church, London		GPC
27.	†1846	Lady Shuckburgh	Upper Shuckburgh, Warks	S	Pevsner, *Warks*, 1966, 439
28.	†1847	Rev William Watts	St Giles-in-the-Fields, City of London	S	
29.	?1848	George Watlington	Aldenham, Herts	S	*Gunnis* 1968, 65
30.	†1848	Wynne Peyton	Sarratt, Herts	S	
31.	?1849	Benjamin Biddulph	Burghill, Herefs	S	*Gunnis* 1968, 65
32.	?1849	Caroline Williams	Gwennap, Cornwall	S	*Gunnis* 1968, 65
33.	1851	'A sepulchral monument of the Decorated period'	[Gt Exhib, London]; untraced		*Gunnis* 1968, 65
34.	†1851	Captain Francis Grantham	Scawby, Lincs		Pevsner, *Lincs*, 1989, 625
35.	†1852	Rev Henry Hughes	[All Saints, Gordon Square, St Pancras, London]; St Pancras new parish church, London	S	

36.	?1855	Rev William Peart	St John the Baptist, Windsor, Berks		GPC
37.	?1857	Henry Kemble	Bray, Berks	S	*Gunnis* 1968, 65

BROWN, Sarah –1840?

In 1809, when living in Hansworth, Staffs, she was awarded the smaller silver palette from the Society of Arts for wax modelling (RSA *Transactions*, vol 24, 1809, 20). For further information the reader is referred to *Pyke* 1973, 20.

Miscellaneous

1.	1809	'modelling in wax'	[Soc of A, smaller silver palette]; untraced	RSA, *Transactions*, vol 24, 1809, 20

BROWN, Thomas

In 1764 Thomas Brown 'from London' announced in the New York press that he had 'open'd a Marble Quarry, in this Government, little inferior to the Italian, out of which will be made Chimney Pieces, Marble Tables, Monuments, Tombs, Head Stones for Graves, &c. in the compleatest Manner, and on the most reasonable Terms'. He also offered lessons in 'the useful and necessary Arts of Drawing, and Architecture' at his premises in 'Water-street, on the upper Side of Peck-slip' (*The New-York Gazette or the Weekly Post-Boy*, 30 August 1764). In 1773 he advertised 'Italian, English, and Irish Marble for Chimney Pieces, &c. &c. To be sold as cheap as can be imported, By Thomas Brown, Marble Cutter, in Chapel-Street. Also Grave Stones and Jersey Stone Chimney Pieces, executed in the neatest manner' (*The New-York Gazette and the Weekly Mercury*, 26 July 1773)

Literary References: *Gottesman* 1938, 228–9

BROWN, W G, of Cheltenham fl c1840

Architectural Sculpture

1.	c1840	Caryatid figures between shop fascias	Cheltenham, Glos	S	Pevsner, *Glos: Vale & Forest of Dean*, 1976, 140

BROWN, W, of Stonehouse, Devon fl 1808–51

Most of his tablets are classical in design, though the monument to George Ogle Moore at Carlow, in Ireland, is in the gothic style (5).

Literary References: *Gunnis* 1968, 65; *Potterton* 1975, 37–8

Funerary Monuments

1.	?1808	Margaret Nesham	Anthony, Cornwall		*Gunnis* 1968, 65
2.	?1820	William Rowe	Liskeard, Cornwall		*Gunnis* 1968, 65
3.	?1835	Charles Matthews	St Andrew, Plymouth, Devon		*Gunnis* 1968, 65
4.	?1835	Sarah Body	Wonersh, Surrey		*Gunnis* 1968, 65
5.	†1849	George Ogle Moore	Carlow, Ireland	S	*Potterton* 1975, 38
6.	?1849	James Burnet	Stoke Damerel, Devon	S	GPC
7.	?1851	William Hodge	Stoke Damerel, Devon	S	GPC

BROWN, William, of Liverpool –1836

Brown (or Browne) exhibited works in 1812–13 from Slater Street, Liverpool (1. 3). He may have been related to **Richard Rushton Brown**, who exhibited from the same address in those years, and he can probably be identified with William Browne of Brownlow Hill, Liverpool, who exhibited a bust of Richard Rushton in 1814 (2). When his widow, Elizabeth, applied to the Artists General Benevolent Institution for financial assistance in 1837, she said that her husband had died of apoplexy on 31 December 1836.

Literary References: *Gunnis* 1968, 65; *Morris and Roberts* 1998, 106, 107

Archival References: AGBI, vol 3, 52, 89, 113, 149, 178, 215

Statues

1.	1812	Time, figure	[Exhib Liverpool Ac, 326]; untraced	*Morris and Roberts* 1998, 106

Busts

2.	1814	Richard Rushton	[Exhib Liverpool Ac, 298]; untraced	*Morris and Roberts* 1998, 107

Miscellaneous

3.	1813	Diana	[Exhib Liverpool Ac, 312]; untraced	*Morris and Roberts* 1998, 106

BROWN, William, of London 1799–

Brown joined the Royal Academy Schools on 1 September 1820, at the age of twenty-one. He married Elizabeth, the daughter of **John Francis** and his wife Mary. She was born 11 April 1807, died a widow on 29 July 1859 and was buried with her parents in Highgate Cemetery.

Literary References: *Cansick* II, 1869–72, 122; *Hutchison* 1960–62, 173; *Gunnis* 1968, 65

Archival References: GPC

Funerary Monuments

1.	1845	John, 2nd Viscount Sydney (†1831)	Chislehurst, Kent	*Gunnis* 1968, 65

BROWN, William, of Porter Street, London fl 1766–69

A sculptor of this name, who lodged with Mr Rush and then with Mr Frewin in Porter Street, London, exhibited at the Society of Artists in 1766 and 1769 (1, 2). In 1767 and 1768 he showed intaglios and an engraved portrait of the king.

Literary References: *Graves* 1907, 42

Archival References: RG/JP, 2, 197–8

Busts

1.	1766	Ganymede	[Soc of Artists, London, 200]; untraced	*Graves* 1907, 42

Miscellaneous

2.	1769	King George III	[Soc of Artists, London, 220]; untraced	*Graves* 1907, 42

BROWNE, Thomas Whitfield

See Atkinson, John

BROWNE, Joseph fl 1814–45

Browne was a supplier of marble, scagliola and artificial stone, who also occasionally worked as an architect. He was in business by 1814, for in that year he enlarged the dining room (now the library) at Raby Castle, County Durham, adding a screen of scagliola Ionic columns. The following year he provided scagliola columns and *verd antique* stands for Ashridge Park, Herts and ornaments for Ashburnham Place, Sussex, including scagliola columns and 4 composition capitals. A bill for carpenters' and joiners' work receipted by Ashburnham on 11 July 1815 amounted to £11,738 3s 2d. When **James George Bubb** became bankrupt in 1820, Browne took over his artificial stone business. He continued to oversee this enterprise until about 1827, employing Bubb as a designer and modeller. Between 1823 and 1829 Browne was employed at Buckingham Palace, supplying marble chimneypieces at a cost of £6,000 (**17**), as well as Corinthian columns, bases and pilasters for the Picture Gallery, pilasters with sunken panels at a cost of £1,278 for the Bow Drawing Room, and scagliola columns of lapis lazuli for the Blue Drawing Room (TNA WORK 5/119 fols 26–8). He also supplied marble to the value of £4,698 2s 9d, for which the Office of Works failed to pay him, so bringing him 'to the very verge of ruin' (*ibid*). He was the principal marble contractor for the Marble Arch (**20**) and in 1827 received a payment of £1,077 for work on the Arch, comprising 'six cornices, 64 modillions, 58 coffers and six very large laurel wreaths in solid ravaccione marble' (TNA WORK 19/3 fols 39, 56, 164–7).

In 1830, he held an exhibition of his collection of Antique marbles and other works of art, 'forming together nearly two thousand elegant specimens of ancient and modern art', at his premises in University Street, Bloomsbury (*Library of Fine Arts*, I, 178). He later added to this collection, buying a version of Johann Zoffany's famous painting, *Life class at the Royal Academy* (Royal Coll, Windsor Castle) for £37 16s from Bubb's sale in 1833.

Browne's monument to the Peninsular War veteran General Chowne, which has a scrolled top and Doric frieze, is a close copy of the 3rd-century BC Roman sarcophagus of Cornelius Lucius Scipio in the Vatican Museum, Rome (**5**). Gunnis considered Browne's monumental tablets dull but noted that one, commemorating William Kay at Tring, Herts, has a neo-Hellenic relief of a woman seated by an amphora (**13**). It is possible that some, or even all of the works listed under **J Brown (or Browne) of London** could be from his workshop.

Literary References: *GM*, 1833, I, 252; *Gunnis* 1968, 65–6, 67–8; RG/JP, 2, 199; *Penny* 1977 (1), 13; *Kelly* 1977 (2), 1432; *Colvin* 1995, 171; *Curl* 2001, 188, 216

Archival References: Ashburnham Accts ASH 2816 (1814–16); 2862

Miscellaneous Drawings: Design for a mausoleum, for Gordon Castle (?), SRO, Edinburgh, RHP 2378 no 42; design for a Grecian temple, for Gordon Castle (?), SRO, Edinburgh, RHP 2413

Tradecard: 'Joseph Brown' 1815, Heal Coll, BM 106.5

Funerary Monuments

1.	†1813	Caroline, Countess of Portarlington		Winterbourne Came, Dorset		*Gunnis* 1968, 66
2.	†1825	Hon Lionel Damer (†1807) and Williamsea Damer	s	Winterbourne Came, Dorset		*Gunnis* 1968, 66
3.	?1832	William Bray		Shere, Surrey		*Gunnis* 1968, 66
4.	?1833	Elizabeth Pughe		St Mary Aldermanbury, London		*Gunnis* 1968, 66
5.	†1834	General Christopher Chowne		Kensal Green Cemetery, London	S	*Curl* 2001, 216 (repr)
6.	†1835	Sarah Elizabeth Smith		Kensal Green Cemetery, London		*Curl* 2001, 188
7.	?1836	Hon Mrs Cox		Mistley, Essex		*Gunnis* 1968, 66
8.	?1837	Gurney family		North Runcton, Norfolk		GPC
9.	?1838	Rankin family		Royston, Cambs, churchyard		*Gunnis* 1968, 66
10.	†1839	Joseph Hockley		Holy Trinity, Guildford, Surrey	S	
11.	1844	Jane Mills		Barford, Warks		Pevsner, *Warks*, 1966, 85; *Gunnis* 1968, 66
12.	1845	Hon Cassandra Graves (†1843)		Burnham, Bucks	SD	*Gunnis* 1968, 66
13.	1845	William Kay (†1838)		Tring, Herts, vestry (previously in chancel)	SD	*Gunnis* 1968, 66; Pevsner, *Herts*, 1977, 368

Chimneypieces

14.	1823	Several		[Unknown house, Carlton House Terrace, London]; untraced		*Gunnis* 1968, 66
15.	1830	For 'Lord Sherborne's room' Payment(s): £37	m	[Sherborne Court, Glos]; untraced		*Gunnis* 1968, 66, citing archives, Lord Sherborne
16.	1830	Several		[Stafford House, London]; untraced		*Gunnis* 1968, 66
17.	1827–1830	Several, including one for the Drawing Room, five for the Picture Gallery (£250 each) and one with 'pilasters, profiles and frieze carved with Greek leaf and ogee' (£145) Payment(s): £6,000	m	[Buckingham Palace, London]; untraced		TNA WORK T 1/3489, f 329; *Gunnis* 1968, 66
18.	1837	Designed by C S Smith		[Stoneleigh Abbey, Warks]; untraced		GPC
19.	1848	For the music room		[Westfield, I of W]; untraced		*Gunnis* 1968, 66

Architectural Sculpture

20.	1827	Decorative marblework Payment(s): £1,077	m	Marble Arch, London		*Gunnis* 1968, 66; *Colvin* VI, 1976, 296
21.	1827–1830	Six cornices, 64 medallions, 58 coffers and 3 very large laurel wreaths of 'solid ravaccioni marble' Payment(s): £717		Buckingham Palace, London		TNA WORK 19/3 f 381
22.	1835	Marble work Payment(s): £373	m	Bowood, Wilts		GPC

BROWNE & YOUNG fl 1816–20

The firm flourished between 1816 and 1820. Gunnis notes that their tablets have delicately carved details, a good example being one commemorating Sir Felton Harvey-Bathurst, 1819, at Egham, Surrey, which has reliefs of the numerous medals and decorations awarded to him during the Napoleonic Wars (**4**). In 1819 the firm agreed to supply the scagliola columns for the east end of St Pancras Church for £742 (*Britton and Pugin* I, 1823–1828, 154). In 1818–1820 they were paid £363 for scagliola pillars and pilasters for Lansdowne House, London (Marquess of Lansdowne archives in GPC) and in 1820 they received £23 4s 6d from the 5th Earl of Carlisle for 'Two Scagliola Verd Antique Pedestals' (CH, 5th Earl of Carlisle, Private Accounts, J14/81, April–July 1820).

Literary References: *Gunnis* 1968, 65

Archival References: GPC

Funerary Monuments

1.	?1816	John Bovill	Streatham, Lambeth, London	S	*Gunnis* 1968, 65
2.	?1816	John Kirkpatrick	Windsor, Berks	S	*Gunnis* 1968, 65
3.	?1817	Ann Drury	Upton, Bucks	S	*Gunnis* 1968, 65
4.	?1819	Sir Felton Harvey-Bathurst	Egham, Surrey		*Gunnis* 1968, 65

BROXUP, John fl 1686–1704

The design for Sir John Knatchbull's monument at Mersham, Kent survives among the Knatchbull Papers (**1**). The tablet itself has a gadrooned base, flanked by pilasters and floral volutes. Above is a pyramid, in front of which is a tented canopy, opened to disclose two nude boys, kneeling and holding a cartouche. On either side are flaming torches, while at the summit are balanced a large shield, helmet and mantling. Below the gadrooning is an apron with a winged cherub's head, swags of fruit, drapery and trumpets. On either side is a winged skull and 2 cherubs heads are at the base. The design, dated 8 May 1700, is endorsed 'I Acknowledge I have agreed with Mr. John Broxup for fourscore guineas for ye erecting such a marble monument exactly as this draught [sic] expresses. . .' and is signed 'Edw: Knatchbull'. Broxup was responsible for a very similar monument to Lee Warner at Rochester Cathedral (**2**). A document, dated September 1702, in the Cathedral Archives, records 'Rec'd from Mr Warner Lee's exec. By hand of Mr Broxup, stonecutter, for setting in Merton Chapel a monument to Mr Warner Lee £10' (Rochester Cathedral Treasurer's Books, 1700–01, Medway Archives DRC/FTb 35, p 1). Yet another monument to the same design commemorates Christopher Milles (†1700) at Herne, also in Kent. It seems likely that it was executed by the same sculptor but is unsigned and no documentary evidence has surfaced to confirm authorship. A note in the Masons' Company *Court Book* for 1686 reads 'John Broxup to appeare next Cort' (Masons' Co, *Court Book*, 1677–94, f 98v). He does not appear to have complied with that request. **John Friend** was apprenticed to him in 1704.

Literary References: *Physick* 2004, 16–17

Archival References: RG/JP, 2, 200; RG/JP, suppl 2

Funerary Monuments

1.	1700	Sir John Knatchbull (†1696) Payment(s): 80 gns Drawing(s): Centre for Kentish Studies, Maidstone, U951 E227, dated 1700	Mersham, Kent		*Physick* 2004, 17
2.	1701	Archdeacon Lee Warner (†1698)	Rochester Cathedral, Kent		Pevsner, *Kent: W & Weald*, 1976, 483; *Physick* 2004, 16–17 (repr)

BRUTE FAMILY, of Llanbedr

John Brute I 1665–1730
Thomas Brute 1699–1767
Aaron Brute 1731–1801
John Brute II 1752–1834

At least 4 generations of a family of stonemasons from Llanbedr, near Crickhowell in Breconshire, who produced many ledger-stones, chest tombs, grave stones and naive rococo stone and painted wall monuments in Brecon, Radnor and Monmouths. **John Brute I** is described as a mason in family records, but does not appear to have signed his work. 76 signed monuments have been identified by his son, grandson and great-grandson, the most prominent of which are listed below.

Literary References: *Silvester and Pitman* 1998, 29–34

Funerary Monuments

1.	†1724	Thomas Brute senior (by Thomas Brute)	Llanbedr, Brecon	S	
2.	†1730	Thomas Williams (by Thomas Brute)	Llandefalle, Brecon		Pevsner, *Powys*, 1979, 332
3.	†1742	Benjamin Williams (by Thomas Brute)	Llandefalle, Brecon		Pevsner, *Powys*, 1979, 332
4.	†1757	William Sanders (by Thomas Brute)	Partrishow, Brecon	S	Pevsner, *Powys*, 1979, 364
5.	†1773	Anne Lewis (by John Brute II)	Llangattock, Brecon	S	Pevsner, *Powys*, 1979, 346
6.	†1774	William Vaughan (by Aaron Brute)	Talgarth, Brecon	S	Pevsner, *Powys*, 1979, 372
7.	†1775	Jennet Cunvin (by Aaron Brute)	Llangattock, Brecon	S	Pevsner, *Powys*, 1979, 346
8.	†1775	Price family member (by Aaron Brute)	Walterstone, Herefs	S	Pevsner, *Herefs*, 1963, 308
9.	†1777	Mary Moses (by Aaron Brute)	Llangattock, Brecon	S	Pevsner, *Powys*, 1979, 346
10.	†1785	Margaret Saunders (by Aaron Brute)	Llanfrynach, Brecon	S	Pevsner, *Powys*, 1979, 346
11.	†1788	John (†1788) and William (†1766) Powell (by Aaron Brute)	Partrishow, Brecon	S	Pevsner, *Powys*, 1979, 364
12.	†1800	Henry Watkins (by John Brute II)	Llanfrynach, Brecon	S	Pevsner, *Powys*, 1979, 346
13.	†1804	Anne Griffiths (by John Brute II)	Partrishow, Brecon	S	Pevsner, *Powys*, 1979, 364

BRYAN FAMILY, of Painswick and Gloucester

Joseph BryanI	1682–1730
John Bryan I	1716–1787
Joseph Bryan II	1718–1779
John Bryan II	fl *c*1795

A family of masons and carvers who had quarries at Painswick in the Cotswolds. The principal members were **John Bryan I** and **Joseph Bryan II**, sons of Joseph Bryan of Painswick. John I is described as 'late of this town, carver' on his large pyramidal monument at Painswick: he left bequests to his two daughters, Anne Bryan and Mrs Loveday. Joseph II established himself in Gloucester. His son, John II, married his first cousin Anne, the daughter of John I, and inherited the business. He went into partnership with **George Wood of Gloucester** *c*1795.

On 20 May 1760 Joseph II advertised in the *Gloucester Journal* that he 'wanted a sober Mason that can work mouldings etc. in Free-stone . . . . Apply Joseph Bryan in the City of Gloucestershire or to John Bryan in Painswick'. The same newspaper reported on 31 January 1785 'On Monday last died, in her 70th year of her age, Mrs Bryan, mother of Mr. Bryan, stone cutter, in this city'. The journal also noted, on 26 December 1808, that on 'Thursday died Mrs. Bryan, relict of Mr. John Bryan, statuary, of the Black Friars in this City'.

Masonry-work executed by the firm included the tower of Great Whitcombe church, 1749, the rebuilding of the spire of Painswick church after it was destroyed by lightning in 1763 and the spire of St Nicholas, Gloucester, 1784. Their tablets and churchyard memorials have charming and well-carved details, while a delightful and intelligent use is made of coloured marbles. The polychrome wall-monument to Mary Singleton, †1761, in Gloucester Cathedral has a sarcophagus-shaped inscription tablet below a pyramid carved with a *gloria*: under the sarcophagus is a circular armorial panel, set off by confidently executed consoles (4). John Webb's wall-monument (†1795) in Gloucester Cathedral has a large concave inscription tablet ornamented with Adamesque scrolls, paterae and crossed torches: above is a pyramid carrying knotted ribbons, a shield and a striated sarcophagus end, decorated with an oval relief of a rising phoenix (27).

Literary References: *Gunnis* 1968, 66; *Colvin* 1995, 176–7

Archival References: GPC

Funerary Monuments

1.	†1746	Elizabeth Charlett	Fladbury, Worcs	S	
2.	†1750	Elizabeth Whitehead	Barnwood, Glos	S	Pevsner, *Glos: Vale & Forest of Dean*, 1976, 97
3.	†1754	Muriel Oldisworth	Fairford, Glos	S	Pevsner, *Glos: Cotswolds*, 1999, 368
4.	†1761	Mary Singleton	Gloucester Cathedral	S	Pevsner, *Glos: Vale & Forest of Dean*, 1976, 218
5.	†1763	Samuel (†1759), Radulf (†1758) and John Selfe	St John the Baptist, Cirencester, Glos	S	
6.	†1770	Noble Pitts	Much Marcle, Herefs	S	*Gunnis* 1968, 66
7.	†1772	William and Collis Smart	St Peter, Winchcombe, Glos	S	Pevsner, *Glos: Cotswolds*, 1999, 729
8.	†1775	Alexander Colston	Fairford, Glos	S	Pevsner, *Glos: Cotswolds*, 1999, 368
9.	†1776	Abigail Carter	Eldersfield, Glos	S	*Gunnis* 1968, 66
10.	†1777	Benjamin Baylis and five family members	Gloucester Cathedral	S	Pevsner, *Glos: Vale & Forest of Dean*, 1976, 218
11.	†1778	John Stephens	Stroud, Glos	S	Pevsner, *Glos: Cotswolds*, 1999, 650
12.	†1779	Rev Thomas Coxe (signed by Joseph Bryan II)	Rodmarton, Glos	S	Pevsner, *Glos: Cotswolds*, 1999, 582
13.	†1779	Thomas Cope	Rodmarton, Glos	S	
14.	†1782	John Browne	Salperton, Glos	S	Pevsner, *Glos: Cotswolds*, 1999, 588
15.	†1782	Joseph Boughton	Westbury-on-Severn, Glos	S	Pevsner, *Glos: Vale & Forest of Dean*, 1976, 400
16.	†1784	James Pitt	Maisemore, Glos	S	Pevsner, *Glos: Vale & Forest of Dean*, 1976, 296
17.	1785	Guise family	[Rendcomb, Glos]; destroyed		Pevsner, *Glos: Cotswolds*, 1999, 574
18.	†1786	Mrs Hughes	Cheltenham, Glos	S	Pevsner, *Glos: Vale & Forest of Dean*, 1976, 126
19.	†1787	Mary Smith	Bishop's Cleeve, Glos	S	Pevsner, *Glos: Vale & Forest of Dean*, 1976, 107
20.	?1788	Mary Morse	Gloucester Cathedral		*Gunnis* 1968, 66
21.	†1789	Edward Sheppard	Minchinhampton, Glos	S	Pevsner, *Glos: Cotswolds*, 1970, 480
22.	†1790	Ann Coxe (by John Bryan II)	Kemble, Glos	S	Pevsner, *Glos: Cotswolds*, 1999, 422
23.	?1793	Frances Turner	Chadlington, Oxon		*Gunnis* 1968, 66
24.	?1793	Mary Milborne	Abergavenny, Monmouths		*Gunnis* 1968, 66
25.	†1794	John Buckle	Elmstone Hardwicke, Glos	S	Pevsner, *Glos: Vale & Forest of Dean*, 1976, 182
26.	†1794	Rev John Kipling	Staverton, Glos	S	Pevsner, *Glos: Vale & Forest of Dean*, 1976, 348
27.	†1795	John Webb (†1795) and family members	Gloucester Cathedral	S	Pevsner, *Glos: Vale & Forest of Dean*, 1976, 218
28.	†1799	Edward (†1771), Mary (†1753) and Sarah Wilbraham	St John the Baptist, Cirencester, Glos	S	
29.	†1800	John Selfe	St John the Baptist, Cirencester, Glos	S	
30.	†1800	Thomas Parker	Barnwood, Glos	S	Glos: *Vale & Forest of Dean*, 1976, 97
31.	†1801	Lucy Dolphin (signed by Joseph Bryan)	Upper Slaughter, Glos	S	Pevsner, *Glos: Cotswolds*, 1999, 708
32.	1801	Rev D Pritchett	St David's Cathedral, Lampeter, Cardigan		*Gunnis* 1968, 66
33.	†1801	Richard Brereton (co-sculptor: George Wood, of Gloucester)	Edgeworth, Glos	S	
34.	1802?	Mary Probyn (co-sculptor: George Wood, of Gloucester)	Pershore Abbey, Worcs		*Gunnis* 1968, 66

35.	†1804	Samuel Hayward (†1790) and his wife Catherine	Gloucester Cathedral	S	Pevsner, *Glos: Vale & Forest of Dean*, 1976, 219
36.	†1831	Richard (†1817) and Sarah Selfe	St John the Baptist, Cirencester, Glos		
Architectural Sculpture					
37.	*c*1743	Reredos with fluted Ionic columns and segmental pediment containing the Commandments and gilded sunrays (signed by John Bryan I) Payment(s): 10 gns	Painswick, Glos	S	*Colvin* 1995, 177; Pevsner, *Glos: Cotswolds*, 1999, 543
38.	1748	Carved stone gatepiers with vermiculated panels and ball finials (designed and made by John Bryan I)	Painswick churchyard, Glos		Pevsner, *Glos: Cotswolds*, 1970, 359

BRYSON, David fl 1800–06

Mistakenly called Daniel by Gunnis, Bryson did a good deal of wood and stone carving under Sir John Soane and is mentioned several times in Soane's account books.

Statues					
1.	1800	Model of a figure		[for Bentley Priory, Middx, seat of Marquess of Abercorn]; untraced	Soane Abstract of Bills, 3, fol 30; *Gunnis* 1968, 66
Architectural Sculpture					
2.	1801	Carved stonework Payment(s): £65	s	[Messrs Praed's offices, Fleet Street, London]; untraced	Soane Abstract of Bills, 3, fol 74; *Gunnis* 1968, 66
3.	1802	Ionic capital		[for Robert Knight's house, Charles St, Grosvenor Square, London]; untraced	Soane bill book D fol 156
4.	1804	Carving Payment(s): £53		Aynho, Northants	*Gunnis* 1968, 66
5.	1806	Decorative stone details	s	[Messrs Peters's offices, Fountain Court, London]; untraced	Soane bill book, D fol 468; *Gunnis* 1968, 66

BUBB, James George ?1781–1853

A sculptor in marble and artificial stone, Bubb was responsible for some notable architectural ornaments. It seems likely that he is the James George Bubb who was christened on 23 September 1781 at Saint Martin-in-the-Fields, London, the son of James and Fanny Bubb. James Bubb senior was a tobacconist with a shop in the Strand, and the sculptor exhibited from an address in that same thoroughfare as a young man. In 1806 **Lawrence Gahagan** referred pejoratively to the sculptor as 'Tobacconist Bubb', which appears to confirm the connection (CLRO Misc MSS 207–8). Bubb married Margaret Alice, second daughter of Henry Blakey of Scots Yard, Bush Lane, on 9 May 1812 (*The News*, 31 May, 1812).

Bubb entered the Royal Academy Schools in 1801 and won a silver medal in 1805. He also worked before 1806 for **J C F Rossi RA** and **John Bingley**, who were then in partnership. According to Bingley, Bubb 'did studiously attend to the duties of his profession and was employed in the several works carried on in that period, particularly in marble, viz. Captain Faulkener's monument in St Paul's' (CLRO Misc MSS 207–8).

Although young and relatively unknown, in 1806 Bubb was able to secure the commission for the monument to William Pitt, to be erected in the Guildhall (**1**). Bubb, whose estimate of £3,500 was the lowest tender, won the contract in competition with **Samuel Percy**, **William Fisher**, Lawrence Gahagan and Rossi, his former employer. Rossi was infuriated by the decision, which he felt to be a result of miserliness by the Corporation of London, and he queried whether Bubb was qualified to carry out the work. When asked to supply a reference, Rossi commented sourly that as Bubb had not 'been employed during his continuance with me upon anything by which he could acquire any practical skill in the execution of such works as the one proposed' he could not 'give any opinion as to the executive ability of Mr Bubb' (CLRO Misc MSS 207–8). Farington intimated that Bubb had been guilty of sharp practice, having 'canvassed the Members of the Common Council and gave cards on the back of which he put the mark which he put on his model that it might be known' (*Farington* vol 8, 2919).

Bubb intended the work as a pendant to **John Bacon RA**'s monument to the Earl of Chatham in Guildhall, but the statue has less variety and dynamism than Bacon's composition. Pitt stands in an oratorical pose, whilst before him *Britannia* on horse-back emerges from the waves brandishing a fish (originally she carried a thunderbolt). Whinney called Bubb's work 'a tedious echo of the St Paul's style of Rossi' (*Whinney* 1988, 374).

Between 1809 and 1814 Bubb was recorded at three different addresses, Grafton Street East, 'Mr Brooks' in the New Road, Paddington, and 22 Tenby Street, Fitzroy Square. He is known to have taken **Allan Cunningham** as an assistant around this time, and in November 1811 he applied to become an associate Royal Academician, in competition with the sculptors **Christopher Prospera**, **William Theed I**, **Sir Francis Chantrey RA**, **Peter Turnerelli** and **John Bacon II**. The antipathy of his colleagues does not appear to have abated in the wake of the 1806 Guildhall competition for Bubb polled no votes.

Bubb produced a few busts, one of which is known to have survived, namely the impressive portrait of Admiral Lord Nelson, 1810 (**15**). His most notable works were decorative ornaments for buildings: an early commission for statues and a delightful bas-relief for Bristol's Commercial Rooms, *c*1811, demonstrates real ability (**19**). In 1818 he and J C F Rossi went into partnership, despite their earlier dispute, to carry out extensive sculptural work for David Laing's London Customs House (**20**). Bubb and Rossi used their own composition material, a type of terracotta, for the work, but within six years the badly-constructed building had been pulled down. *The New Monthly Magazine*, commenting in 1818, said of the sculpture that its material was 'of a brick-like ferruginous colour and the general effect is very unpleasing' whilst the figures were feeble, vulgar and 'entirely devoid of all that is requisite in art; they possess no sentiment, they express nothing, they are seen and forgotten'. Lamenting Bubb's failure to learn from the Elgin marbles, the article continued 'It is a thousand pities that the performance of so great a national work should have been withheld from such men as **Flaxman**, Chantrey, and others, and its execution intrusted to a burner of artificial stone, whose style of design is as inferior to theirs, as is the tasteless material in which he deals to the purest marble of Italy' (*New Monthly Mag*, 1818, vol 10, 154).

The tasteless material, referred to as 'lithargolite', was used for another of Bubb's architectural works, the frieze for the Italian Opera House in the Haymarket (**21**). The work, according to Thomas Allen's near-contemporary description, had *Apollo and the Muses* at its centre, and a carved allegory of the *Progress of Music*. The fragments that survive suggest a diverse iconography, from ancient Egyptian dancers to figures in contemporary dress.

Around this time Bubb experienced financial difficulties and he borrowed heavily in order to be able to complete his commissions (*Farington*, vol 16, 5652). In August 1820 he became bankrupt and his premises and kiln were taken over by **Joseph Browne**, who employed Bubb as a modeller and designer. Despite this setback, Bubb continued to attract large-scale commissions for architectural decoration. When the architect Francis Goodwin proposed to employ Bubb for the statuary on Manchester Town Hall (**27**), he described the sculptor as 'pre-eminent in this country . . . in this particular branch of the Arts' (PMSA National Recording Project MR/MCR54). Bubb certainly attracted attention for the scope of his work if not for its quality: the *Literary Gazette* commented of his pediment with 40 figures for Cumberland Terrace (**28**) that it was 'on so large a scale that it is only exceeded in size by that on St Paul's Cathedral' (*Lit Gaz* 1827, 65).

Bubb provided much ornament for the front of the Royal Exchange (**24**). In 1827, when **Joseph Wilton**'s statue of George III was taken down from the quadrangle because of its ill state of repair, the work disappeared into Bubb's studio, from which it appears never to have re-emerged. Within a few months Bubb had applied to create a replacement and he was given the task without competition by the Gresham Committee. Bubb refused to copy Chantrey's statue in the Guildhall as suggested and instead made a sketch 'grateful to his own feelings for taste' which depicted the King in robes of state rather than 'any foreign costume' (**10**, Letter MC, GR, 1824–29, 29 October 1828, transcribed in *Roscoe* 1997, 182). The committee was more stringent in awarding the commission for a statue of George IV, and after a competition that work was awarded to **Sebastian Gahagan**.

Bubb exhibited ideal works at the Royal Academy in 1830 and 1831 (**11**, **12**), but his business appears to have declined gradually over the following years. In 1833 he held a sale at his premises in Grafton Street of his 'architectural sculpture, casts &c'. He must have been something of a collector, because among the lots was Johann Zoffany's *Life class at the Royal Academy*, which was sold to Joseph Browne for £37 16s (*GM*, 1833, pt 1, 252). In 1835 he applied to the AGBI for support, having had scarcely any employment over the previous two years. Bubb stated that he was living in impoverished circumstances, his landlord had taken and sold his stock in lieu of rent, and he had a wife and two children to support. A later note said that his wife had eloped with a young man who had been living with him as a pupil.

In 1839 Bubb was employed by **J M Blashfield** on experimental terracotta work at Canford, Dorset, where Sir John Guest was seeking to build inexpensive model cottages for agricultural workers. A small quantity of moulded bricks, tiles and ornaments were made from sketches by Sir Charles Barry. The same year he produced a statue of *Pomona* for Sir William Middleton (**13**), but these are his last known works. Bubb left a son, Francis, who was employed by **John Seeley** of New Road. A James George Bubb was given a gift of £12 by the Royal Academy in 1860. If Bubb died in 1853, as stated by Gunnis, this must have been a family member.

Bubb has not been remembered favourably, if at all. Most of his major works have been lost, destroyed or dismembered, and the low opinion of him expressed by his contemporaries and embittered rivals has given the impression that he was a sculptor of meagre talent with a reputation for opportunism. Mrs Esdaile was, however, so impressed by the remains of the Italian Opera House frieze, that in 1929 she described Bubb as an example of the 'Illustrious Obscure', with a 'genius for relief' (*Esdaile* 1929 (1), 33–8).

MGS

Literary References: *Farington passim*; *Euro Mag*, 1820, vol 78, 87; *Builder*, 1868, July 25, 547; *Graves*, I, 1905–6, 324; *Esdaile* 1929 (1), 33–43; *Gunnis* 1968, 66–8; *Whinney* 1988, 374; *Roscoe* 1997, 182–6; *Ward-Jackson* 2003, 174–7

Archival References: RA Premium list; TNA WORK 5/144 (Mason's work at Customs House, executants unidentified); AGBI, vol 2, 181 (1835), vol 5, 189 (1853); IGI

Will: James Bubb, tobacconist of the Strand, proved 26 November 1808, PROB 11/1487, 395–6

Funerary Monuments						
1.	1807–1813	William Pitt the Younger Payment(s): £4,078		CL Coll, Guildhall, City of London, great hall, acc 85 Other versions: 'bust of a statue of Mercury, executed in marble, and erected in Guildhall [for the monument]' exhib RA, 1814, 787; untraced	SD	*Knight* 1986, 332 (repr); *Ward-Jackson* 2003, 173–7, 452 (repr)
2.	1818	The George children		Tonbridge, Kent		*Gunnis* 1968, 68
3.	†1819	Henry Manley		Halberton, Devon		Pevsner, *Devon*, 1989, 466
4.	1820	Margaret Pounsett		St Mary, Battersea, London	S	*Gunnis* 1968, 68; C Lib (repr)
5.	†1821	Richard Rothwell		St Mary, Battersea, London	S	*Gunnis* 1968, 68; C Lib (repr)
Statues						
6.	1809	Unidentified subject Model(s): 'small model of a figure', exhib RA, 758	s	[Hope Insurance Office, Ludgate Hill, London]; untraced		*Graves* I, 1905–6, 324
7.	*c*1819	Britannia		[County Fire Office, Piccadilly, London]; destroyed (1929)		GPC
8.	*c*1825	Goddess Diana, in flowing dress	tc	Crowther of Syon Lodge (1990)	S	*Apollo*, 131, Jan 1990, 13 (repr)
9.	1826	British worthies		Chester Terrace, Regents Park, London		*Builder*, 1868, 25 July, 547; *Gunnis* 1968, 67
10.	1828–1830	King George III Payment(s): £330 15s	s	[Royal Exchange, City of London]; untraced		*Roscoe* 1997, 182–3
11.	1830	Poetry		[Exhib RA, London, 1176]; untraced		*Graves* I, 1905–6, 324
12.	1831	Vertumnus	m	[Exhib RA, London, 1159]; untraced		*Graves* I, 1905–6, 324
13.	1839	Pomona		[Shrubland Park, Suffolk]; untraced		*Gunnis* 1968, 67
Busts						
14.	1805	Mrs Furniss		[Exhib RA, London, 738]; untraced		*Graves* I, 1905–6, 324

15.	1810	Admiral Lord Nelson	m	NMM, Greenwich, SCU0089	S	*Graves* I, 1905–6, 324; *British Portraits* 1956–7, 102; *Knox* 1998, 90, 93 (repr)
16.	1811	W Shield		[Exhib RA, London, 921]; untraced		*Graves* I, 1905–6, 324
17.	1818	H Howorth		[Exhib RA, London, 1056]; untraced		*Graves* I, 1905–6, 324
18.	1818	Matthew Wood MP		[Exhib RA, London, 1056]; untraced		*Graves* I, 1905–6, 324
Architectural Sculpture						
19.	c1811	Statues of Bristol, Commerce and Navigation and a relief of Britannia, Neptune and Minerva		Commercial Rooms, Bristol		Pevsner, *Somerset, N & Bristol*, 1958, 424; *Gunnis* 1968, 67; C Lib (repr)
20.	1818	Reliefs of Commerce, Prosperity and Britannia, accompanied by Strength, Justice, and other allegorical figures, and a large marine shell to surmount the clock (co-sculptor: John Charles Felix Rossi RA) Payment(s): Over £5,000	tc	[Customs House, London, façade]; destroyed		*New Mont Mag*, vol 10, 1818, 152–5; *Gunnis* 1968, 67; *Kelly* 1977 (2), 1430–2; *Kelly* 1990, 225–6
21.	1818	'The progress of Music from the earliest attention to sound to the extraordinary accomplishments of the modern Ballet', frieze	tc	[Italian Opera house, Haymarket, London]; private colls (fragments)		*Allen* 1827–37, 296; *Esdaile* 1929 (1), 33–43 (repr)
22.	1820	Portico of termini, with capitals formed of female heads	tc	[Harmonic Institution, Regent Street, London]; untraced		*Elmes* 1827, 102–3 (repr)
23.	1823	Reliefs and statues	tc	Bristol Exchange		*Gunnis* 1968, 67
24.	1823	Statues representing the four quarters of the globe, four colossal busts of Queen Elizabeth, and two bas-reliefs	sa	[Royal Exchange, City of London, Cornhill front]; Hatfield House, Herts (reliefs)	SD	*Elmes* 1827, 158 (repr of building); *Roscoe* 1997, 183–4 (repr of surviving work)
25.	1824	Arms and composition ornaments		[Salters' Hall, City of London, principal front]; untraced		*Gunnis* 1968, 67 citing Salters' Co archives
26.	1825	Overdoor arms	s	Teffont Evias, Wilts	S	Pevsner, *Wilts*, 1975, 518
27.	1822–1827	A group symbolising Manchester and statues of Solon and Alfred the Great		[Old Manchester Town Hall, King Street (removed due to poor condition in 1836)]; untraced		PMSA National Recording Project MR/MCR54
28.	1827	With forty figures		Cumberland Terrace, London, pediment		*Lit Gaz*, 1827, 65; *Gunnis* 1968, 67; *Johnson* 1975, 64
29.	nd	Royal arms		Museum of London, City of London		RG/JP, 2 203v.

BUCHAN, Walter –1878

Little is known of Buchan's life and career other than that he trained under **William Mossman**, 1837, and worked under **John Mossman**. Work by him is rare but distinguished. He died, obscure and in poverty, in London. Medallions after the Antique in the spandrels of Strathclyde House, 94 Elmbank Street, Glasgow are attributed to him by McKenzie.

Literary References: *Gildard* 1892, 294, 298; *McKenzie* 1999, 106

Architectural Sculpture				
1.	1844	Friezes: International Commerce and Trial by Jury	Former Municipal Buildings, Ingram Street, Glasgow, Lanarks	*McKenzie* 2002, 427–9 (repr)

BUCHARD, C fl 1716

John Timbs, in his *Curiosities of London*, 1855, wrote of the 'equestrian metal statue' of George I, then in Leicester Square, that it was 'modelled by C Buchard for the Duke of Chandos, and brought from Canons in 1747, when it was purchased by the inhabitants of the square; it was finely gilt and within memory was regilt' (1) (*Timbs* 1855, 783).

The statue, which was cast and gilded by **John Nost II**, is now missing and is probably destroyed. Gunnis supposed that Buchard (whom he calls 'Burchard') was a pupil or assistant of Nost and dated the work to c1716. The Canons accounts suggest that it was installed c1723. No other works by Buchard are currently known.

A print of the Canons statue in the Guildhall Library (Pr W2/LE1) shows that the figure and the horse were very similar to equestrian figures produced by the Nost workshop for the Dublin Corporation and at Stowe and Hackwood Park. The horse is clearly a replica of Hubert Le Sueur's steed carrying Charles I at Charing Cross, which Nost II applied to the Lord Chamberlain for permission to cast in 1719 (TNA LC/5157, p241). Nost was commissioned to reproduce the Canons statue 'in all and every respect the same and like manner' (except in the dress and the carvings on the pedestal) for Sir Richard Grosvenor in 1725 (*Gatty* 1921, 2, 209).

Literary References: N&Q 5th ser, vol 2, Oct 10 1874, 292; *Baker* 1949, 141; *Gunnis* 1968, 70

Statues				
1.	1716	King George I, equestrian model (co-sculptor: John Nost II)	[Canons, Middx]; untraced	*Timbs* 1855, 783; *Gunnis* 1968, 70

BUCK, John fl 1817–21

Buck exhibited three works, which Gunnis identifies as reliefs, at the Royal Academy and the British Institution between 1817 and 1821. His address was Nottingham Street in 1817 and 1 Great Chesterfield Street from 1819 onwards. In his dictionary of British Institution contributors Graves describes the artist as a sculptor and painter and the two studies from nature he exhibited there in 1833 were probably pictures (*Graves* 1875, 75). It is possible that he was the same John Buck who, together with **John Ely Hinchliff**, witnessed the will of **John Flaxman** in March 1820, though he then gave his address as 24 Great Marylebone Street (PROB 11/1720, 129).

Literary References: *Gunnis* 1968, 68

Reliefs

1.	1817	Hector is dead and Ilium is no more		[Exhib RA, London, 1036]; untraced	*Graves* I, 1905–6, 327; *Gunnis* 1968, 68
2.	1819	David slaying the lion		[Exhib RA, London, 1226]; untraced	*Graves* 1875, 75; *Graves* I, 1905–6, 327; *Gunnis* 1968, 68
3.	1821	Telemachus and Hippias		[Exhib RA, London, 1092]; untraced	*Graves* I, 1905–6, 327; *Gunnis* 1968, 68

BUCK, Thomas fl 1694

Chimneypieces

1.	1694	Description unavailable Payment(s): £5 10s	m	[for James Sotheby]; untraced	GPC

BUCKHAM, George, of Westminster fl 1799

He signed the large monument to the Earl of Kerry in Westminster Abbey but nothing else by him has emerged (1). Buckham was the owner of a wharf at Westminster from which he dispatched Portland and other stone to the provinces.

Literary References: *Gunnis* 1968, 68

Archival References: GPC

Funerary Monuments

1.	†1799	Francis, 3rd Earl (†1818) and Anastasia, Countess of Kerry (†1799)		Westminster Abbey, London, Chapel of St Andrew	*Gunnis* 1968, 68

BUCKINGHAM, Edward fl 1672–1719

Buckingham was apprenticed to Nathaniel Turner in 1672 and became free of the Masons' Company in 1681. He lived in the parish of St Clement Danes. He was the chief mason for the Inner Temple between 1693 and 1711, receiving £115 in part payment 'for work done around' the Temple Church in 1696 (*Inderwick* 1896–1936, III, 337). His son Jeremiah was apprenticed to him in the same year and was made free on 17 January 1704.

In 1701 Buckingham was at Knole, Sevenoaks, where he was paid £100 for unspecified work (Sackville Archives, cited by *Gunnis* 1968, 68). He was living in 'Clements Lane by Clare Market' in 1708 according to a list of Masons' Company members. He became Master of the Company in 1716.

Buckingham erected a number of houses in London as a speculative builder, insuring them with the Westminster Fire Office. They included two of brick in Great George Street (insured for £550 and £850) and another in Prince's Street, Spitalfields, built in 1718 (insured for £100). In 1719 he built a corner house in Great George Street, 'Shepards' Fields', which belonged to the Hon George Carpenter in 1723. It must have been of considerable size since it was insured for £1,500. A second house in Prince's Street, 'Shepard's Fields' was insured for £200. Buckingham also contracted to build a house in Grosvenor Square in 1728 (Archives Glyn, Mills & Co, in GPC).

He may have been related to John Buckingham who built a house in London before 1730 for Richard Woolley, one of the directors of the South Sea Company (Inventory of Directors, South Sea Company).

Literary References: *Gunnis* 1968, 68

Archival References: Masons' Co, *Court Book*, 1695–1722, fol 147 r; *Freemen*, fol 5 (17 Jan 1704); *Company Members*, 1708; WFO, PR, no 323 (19 Feb 1718), no 324 (19 Feb 1718), no 837 (1 Oct 1718), no 324 (27 June 1719), no 837 (27 June 1719); GPC

Funerary Monuments

1.	†1704	John Locke		High Laver, Essex	*Cranston* 1957, 481

BUCKLE, V fl 1781

For information the reader is referred to *Pyke* 1973, 21

BUCKLEY, G H fl 1828–32

A Cork artist of some talent who died young. He exhibited a 'Model of a Gothic Chapel' at the Cork Mechanics Institute in 1828, then sent a 'Design for a Cathedral Church and College attached – Gothic style' and a 'Model of the Principal Front for a Palace' to the Royal Hibernian Academy in 1832. He is responsible for a number of monuments in the cemetery at Cork, where he is himself buried.

Literary References: *Strickland* 1, 1913, 124; *Stewart* I, 1985, 96

BUCKTON, William –1793

A statuary who worked in Cork and died in the autumn of 1793. He made chimneypieces and was described in his death notice as 'the celebrated statuary' (*Cork Gazette*, 4 September 1793).

Literary References: *Strickland* 1, 1913, 125

BUDDLE (or BUDLE)

Richard I, son of George Budle of Camberwell, yeoman to **Thomas Wise II**, 18 July 1705
Richard II, son of Richard Buddle, apprenticed to his father, 29 June 1727
George I, son of Richard Budle, apprenticed to his father, 27 June 1734
Benjamin, son of Richard Buddle, apprenticed to his father, 2 October 1740
George II, son of Richard Buddle, apprenticed to his father, 18 November 1765

Budle is probably an alternative form of Buddle, but, if this is not the case, the craftsmen were very likely inter-related. **Richard II** lived at 'Wood Street, nr St John's Church, Westmr', about 1740 when he was working for 'Mr [**Thomas**] **Dunn**' and Mortimer lists a mason of the same name, in 'the Strand, opposite Surry-Street', in 1763. **George I** was working for 'Mr Chair' (**Sir Henry Cheere**) about 1740 and **George II** was made free of the Masons' Company on 5 October 1775.

Literary References: *Mortimer* 1763, 49; *Webb* 1999, 5–6

Archival References: Masons' Co, *Assistants*, fol 5 (c1740); *Freemen*, fol 7 (2 Sept 1743, 5 Oct 1775); GPC

BULL, Thomas –1750/1

The son of Henry Bull, goldsmith and citizen of London, he was admitted to the Masons' Company by patrimony in 1712 and became master in 1746. His yard was in Plum Tree Court, Shoe Lane. He signed a number of monuments, including a fine architectural memorial with a portrait bust of Sir Roger Hill at Denham (3). His monument to Eignon Benyon and his wife at Redbourn (1) has a bust under a draped *baldacchino* and is closely similar in design to several monuments commemorating members of the Halsey family at Great Gaddesdon, which have been attributed to **Giovanni Battista Guelfi** and **Michael Rysbrack**. He is buried at St Helen, Bishopsgate.

Another mason called Thomas Bull was apprenticed to Thomas Crowther in 1725 and made free of the Masons' Company by 1731 when he took an apprentice called Lissman. He was living in Broad Street by about 1740. A third Thomas Bull was made free by patrimony on 6 October 1748. It is not clear which of these was the mason responsible in 1750 for the London Assurance Building in Birchin Lane (Company's Archives, in GPC).

Literary References: *Gunnis* 1968, 68

Archival References: Masons' Co, Assistants (c1740); Masons' Co, Court Book, 1722–51 (29 October 1725, 14 June 1731, 14 June 1746); Masons' Co, Freemen, fols 5, 7 (8 October 1712, 6 October 1748)

Funerary Monuments

1.	†1717	Eignon Benyon (†1717) and wife (†1732)	St Mary, Redbourn, Herts		Pevsner, *Herts*, 1977, 277
2.	?1728	D'Heer Denis Dutry	[Dutch Church, Austin Friars, City of London]; destroyed	S	GPC
3.	†1729	Sir Roger Hill	Denham, Bucks	S	Pevsner, *Bucks*, 1994, 269
4.	?1732	Mary Eccleston	Redbourn, Herts	S	*Gunnis* 1968, 68

BULL, William –1762

William Bull was apprenticed to his father, **Thomas Bull**, in 1726, and became free of the Masons' Company in 1735. In 1737 he received £231 for alterations to Skinners' Hall and in 1742 he repaired a house at Cripplegate for a Mr Pinch. About 1740 his name was included in a list of assistants of the Masons' Company and his address was given as Mark Lane. The same document indicates that he employed Richard Bassett in Mark Lane and Mark Hawkins at 'Mr Bull's in Broad Street', so he may have had more than one workshop. In 1755 he was paid for repairing a coat of arms at Trinity House and in 1757–9 he received a further £170 for masonry work at the Trinity Alms Houses in Stepney (Trinity House Archives, cited in GPC). Bull became bankrupt in 1752 and died 10 years later.

Literary References: *GM*, vol XXII, Nov 1752, 536

Archival References: Masons' Co, Assistants, *c*1740, fol 1; Masons' Co, Court Book, 1751–96 (15 Jun 1762); Masons' Co, Freemen, 1677–1795, f 6 (27 March 1735); Skinners' Co, Court Books, 1, p 69

Funerary Monuments

1.	?1740	John Lloyd	Aston Hall, Salop, chapel	S	*Gunnis* 1968, 68
2.	†1742	Sir Robert Godschall	Albury, Surrey	S	*Gunnis* 1968, 68

BULLOCK, Charles fl 1824–27

The brother of **William Bullock**, he put on an exhibition of wax figures in Regent Street before February 1827 advertised as 'Mr Bullock's Exhibition' in an attempt to take advantage of his brother's good name. It was apparently not a success.

Literary References: *Costeloe* 2006, 295, n68

Statues

1.	1824	Chief Rabbi Solomon Hirschel, statuette	p	Jewish Museum, London C1999.2.85	SD

BULLOCK, Elizabeth –*c*1828

Elizabeth Bullock (*née* Smallwood) was the proprietress of a wax museum and model shop and was the mother of **George** and **William Bullock**. She held exhibitions of waxworks in Birmingham from 1794 onwards. The first exhibition opened 'in a commodious Room, in Mr Mansell's late Tea Warehouse, nearly the opposite of New Street' on 27 May 1794 (*Aris's Birmingham Gazette* [*ABG*]). The *ABG* carried a notice of its reopening two years later at 87 Bull Street (16 May 1796) and, after a period in Lichfield, Mrs Bullock announced in November 1796 that it was 'again opened for the inspection of the public, at her House, No. 29 Bull Street Birmingham, near the Bank' (*ABG*, 14 November 1796). She continued to advertise her exhibition from this address until 1798, periodically taking it to other towns. The waxes on show included portraits of members of the British Royal Family; the French Royal Family based on original models by the French sculptor Jean-Antoine Houdon; Tippoo Sultan and his two sons; Catherine, Empress of Russia; the late Earl of Chatham; and Benjamin Franklin. Later additions to the display included 'LIKENESSES of the PRINCE and PRINCESS of WIRTEMBERG' and of 'the poet FREETE of this Town' (*ABG*, 29 May 1797).

In 1797 Mrs Bullock took one of her sons, probably George, briefly into partnership and began to diversify her activities, announcing on 27 March 1797 the opening of a modelling class at 'Bullock and Son's Modelling and statuary warehouse, no 29 Bull Street Birmingham' (*ABG*). In 1798 she offered a wide range of services that foreshadowed the activities of both George and William Bullock: 'Likenesses modelled from one to twenty Guineas each, Miniature[s] painted. All Kinds of Statue Figures for Halls, Stair-cases, and Pleasure Grounds; Figures with Lamps, Girandoles for Side-boards, &c in Plaister of Paris, Hard Metal, Lead &c. Modelling in all its Branches' (*ABG*, 28 May 1798). During the same period she acquired a representation of Napoleon modelled in rice paste, described as 'one of the first productions of its kind' and advertised portraits 'modelled in wax or rice paste' (*ABG*, 2 July 1798). A traveller who visited the shop in 1797 wrote, 'I was highly entertained by the great variety which surrounded me, such as miniature paintings, models in wax, rice paste and plaster of Paris, which for delicacy of finishing surpassed anything of the kind I had ever seen'. He gave a five-minute sitting for his own portrait and a few days later received 'that which is universally allowed to be a good likeness' (*ABG*, 27 November 1797).

She probably died in 1828, as her advertisements ceased to appear abruptly after 30 July that year. She gave no indication that she planned to retire other than announcing a sale of plaster figures four weeks earlier 'as she intends to decline that Part of her Business' (*ABG*, 2 July 1798).

Literary References: *Pyke* 1973, 21; *Bullock* 1988, 40–1, 47 n 27

BULLOCK, George 1783–1818

Sculptor, marble-mason and cabinet-maker, the notice of his death gives his age as 35 in 1818, pointing to a date of birth of 1782 or 1783. His place of birth is unknown. He was the son of the '**Mrs Bullock**' who exhibited wax models at 29 Bull Street, Birmingham between 1794 and 1798, and the brother of **William Bullock**. It seems likely that George was trained by his mother, and was taken into the business at a young age. In 1797 'Mrs Bullock and Son' offered modelling and drawing lessons at their premises. A press report of 1797 noted the presence at the Bull Street rooms of a young boy modelling in wax, rice-paste and plaster, who was almost certainly the sculptor. In 1798 Bullock advertised that he, a 'young artist who gained such great repute in Birmingham', was 'returning to London, the statue business not answering his expectation. He now intends giving his whole attention to the modelling and painting of likenesses... his age does not exceed twenty' (*Aris's Birmingham Gazette* 27 Aug 1798, 3, quoted in *Bullock* 1988, 41). Bullock was, however, still in Birmingham the following year where he set up independently as a 'Miniature-painter and portrait-modeller in rice-paste' at 12 Anne Street (*Aris's Birmingham Gazette* 16 Sept 1799 quoted in *Bullock* 1988, 41).

George's brother, William Bullock, who was to have a notable career as an entrepreneur and showman, opened his first 'museum' at Portugal House in Birmingham in 1800, where he exhibited a variety of curiosities. It seems likely that the likenesses and models in rice paste shown there were the work of George Bullock (**35, 36, 38**). William Bullock moved his museum to Liverpool in March 1801, and George followed his brother there, lodging at the premises at 24 Lord Street. In 1804 Bullock advertised himself as 'Modeller and Sculptor' and during his early years in Liverpool he seems to have attracted a number of important patrons for his sculptural work, which he exhibited at the Royal Academy in London. These included the lawyer, politician and patron of the arts, William Roscoe (**11**), who seems to have had an important role in developing the young sculptor's career, and Henry Blundell of Ince Blundell Hall (**6**), whose bust appears in Joseph Allen's portrait of George Bullock, presented open-shirted, young and Byronic.

By June 1804 George had left his brother's museum and entered into a partnership with William Stoakes, a looking-glass maker. The two advertised as 'Cabinet Makers, General Furnishers and Marble Workers' (*Gore's Liverpool Directory* 1805), and they supplied a large range of goods. Their showrooms, called the 'Grecian Rooms' in explicit competition with his brother's museum, now styled the 'Egyptian Rooms', were at 48 Church Street. On show were a large collection of bronze and bronzed figures, marble tables and chimneypieces, as well as a variety of other decorations in marble, bronze and artificial stone. Bullock also exhibited his own collection of ancient and modern busts. The firm won a large commission to supply Gothic furniture to Cholmondeley Castle (*in situ*).

In 1806 Bullock moved to 23 Bold Street, and in 1807 advertised that his partnership with Stoakes was dissolved. Sometime around 1806 he acquired the Mona marble quarries at Llanvechell on the island of Anglesey for a lease of £1000. These contained two beds of marble, one resembling 'in colour and effect oriental porphyry and the other verd antique' (*Repository of Arts*, 1815, 278). The marbles were brought to Liverpool, where they were manufactured into elegant chimneypieces and other decorations. Marble was to play a key part in Bullock's furnishing designs, for instance in the refurbishing of Thomas Johnes' house at Hafod, where Bullock incorporated Mona marble columns and paving. He also sold his marble to other sculptors, who were not always satisfied. **White Watson** noted in his ledger, when paying his bill of expenses after a law-suit with Bullock, 'A rascal as he is, so much for his friendship' (GPC).

In 1807 Bullock entered a design for a public monument to be raised in Liverpool to Lord Nelson (**4**). It is unclear whether, like **John Flaxman, J C F Rossi, Sir Richard Westmacott RA** and **John Bacon II**, he was actually invited to do so. Bullock's design, with Nelson in contemporary dress standing above four captive sailors, man o' war prows, four couchant lions and descriptions of Nelson's major victories, was accompanied by a published explanatory pamphlet that also appeared in the press. In it Bullock stressed that his aim was to produce a suitable iconography which was 'indebted to no foreign or adventitious ornament for its support' and contained 'no heathen mythology' or 'foreign attribute'. No doubt also seeking to build a showpiece for his own marbles, Bullock added that 'it has been my principal ambition to erect such a nautical monument with British materials' (*Monthly Mag* 1807, 1, 396). The project was far more complex than any other sculptural work produced by Bullock but, because of its anti-classical nationalist iconography, it attracted press support. *Le Beau Monde or Literary and Fashionable Magazine* (1, 1801, 388–9) declared it the most spirited, chaste and appropriate of the designs that had been submitted' and that it was 'what the model of a monument for a British admiral ought to be – British'. The judges, however, were unmoved by Bullock's ostentatious patriotism and gave the commission to **M C Wyatt**, who was assisted by Sir Richard Westmacott to produce a more classical monument.

Around 1809 Bullock made another partnership, this time with the architect Joseph Michael Gandy. Bullock's business had become so extensive that he feared he would not be able to supply all his commissions, and hoped that Gandy's abilities and professionalism would enable him to carry out all his plans. The two advertised as 'architects, modellers, sculptors, marble masons, cabinet-makers and upholsterers' (*Gore's Liverpool Directory* in *Bullock* 1988, 44) and probably worked together on Storrs Hall in Cumbria, Bolton Hall in North Yorkshire and Speke Hall, Liverpool. A chimneypiece for the last location was designed by **Richard Bridgens**, who appears to have worked for the partners at this time and exhibited from their address. Bridgens later moved to London with Bullock and seems to have been a significant designer for the firm. The partnership between Bullock and Gandy foundered in 1810 over the issue of whether the firm was to become associated with the nascent Liverpool Academy. Gandy, as an ARA, was not permitted to join such a body, but Bullock saw an opportunity, and became the founding President. In 1810 he exhibited nine busts at their exhibition, including that of Elizabeth Rose Jolliffe (**20**), a portrait *all'antica* with deeply cut ringlets falling over the forehead. He continued in the role until 1812, securing the Prince of Wales as patron. His regional status did not necessarily win him plaudits in the south, however. Referring to Bullock, Fuseli cited lines from the poet Addio in a letter to William Roscoe: 'The gods made that man neither a digger nor a ploughman, nor skilled in any other way; he has failed in every art' (quoted in *Bullock* 1988, 127).

Between 1812 and 1814 Bullock gradually transferred his business to London, holding sales of his stock, collections and premises. Once again he followed his brother, who had left Liverpool in 1810 to open his 'Egyptian Hall' in Piccadilly. George opened his own 'Grecian Rooms' on the premises in 1813, but the following year moved to a large house in Tenterden Street, Hanover Square with manufacturing premises at the end of the gardens, in Oxford Street. According to a later testimony Bullock kept an 'hospitable house' (*Annals of Fine Arts*, VIII, 1819, 321–2) and, indeed, an invitation to dine there was extended to **Antonio Canova** on his visit to England in 1815. The Italian was invited to meet 'a few of the select artists' at Tenterden Street (Bassano del Grappa E.68/5654 in *Eustace* 1997 (2), 22). A couple of years later the house was to act as an exhibition space for the history painter Benjamin Robert Haydon.

In 1814 he appears to have visited Paris, where he met Jacques-Louis David. In 1815 he secured a commission to provide furnishings, including a Mona marble table (**40**), for New Longwood, St Helena, which was then being furnished to house Napoleon Bonaparte. Other major furnishing commissions of his later career include work for Blair Castle, Tew Park in Oxfordshire (at a cost of £4000), Battle Abbey in East Sussex and Abbotsford for Sir Walter Scott.

At considerable expense, Bullock now transported his Mona marble from Anglesey to London, where it became a fashionable material. Ackermann's *Repository* illustrated a Mona chimneypiece in 1816 (**31**), adding that 'the importance of this invaluable marble to the purposes of interior decoration, renders the discovery of it highly interesting' as 'it vies in richness of colour with the precious marbles of antiquity'. Bullock stressed the native origins of the marble, implying that the use of Mona marble in his designs for anything from tables to monuments was a patriotic act. Bullock also pioneered the use of native materials in his furniture, using local larch wood at Blair Castle and Drumlanrig oak at Abbotsford. While principally classically-inspired, his work also incorporated Gothic, Elizabethan and Jacobean elements. Native materials and designs gained Bullock a reputation as a patriot: one commentator described him as 'in every respect, an Englishman, and ambitious of his country's reputation' (*Annals of Fine Arts*, VIII, 1819, 321–2 quoted in *Bullock* 1988, 20–1).

Bullock's sculptural output decreased in his later career, although he produced some busts. His subjects included his business partner Colonel Charles Fraser (**25**) and William Hey, the aged Senior Surgeon of Leeds General Infirmary (**28**). This was based on a life mask taken by Bullock for Benjamin Gott. In 1814 Bullock was commissioned by the antiquary John Britton to take a cast of the figure of Shakespeare from Gerard Jansen's monument in Stratford (**27**). Bullock declared to Britton that in the course of this work he could see evident signs that the monument had been originally taken from a cast, and was therefore a true and genuine likeness of the Bard. Once again sensing a lucrative vein of nationalism, Bullock reproduced the cast numerous times. The casts were of some fame as the *Annals of Fine Arts* later wrote that to Bullock 'was entirely owing, our possession of the casts from Shakespeare's bust at Stratford, which bears the internal marks of its being a portrait' (quoted in *Bullock* 1988, 20–1).

Only three monuments by Bullock have been identified, of which two, to Glover Moore and Anna Maria Bold, are simple but striking wall-slabs with the incorporation of green Mona marble and additional Greek decoration (**2, 3**).

In 1817 Bullock's premises, which he held with his financial partner Colonel Charles Fraser, were insured by the Sun Company for £3,800. According to Daniel Terry, who later reflected on the last days of the business in a letter to Sir Walter Scott, there was a 'rapid and enormous increase in business beyond capital', whilst at the same time the finances were mishandled by Fraser, who Terry described as 'an old crackbrained East Indian jackass' (quoted in *Beard and Gilbert* 1986, 127). On 1 May the following year Bullock died 'suddenly' at his home in Tenterden Street (*GM* 1818, 476), and he was buried on 8 May at St George, Hanover Square. According to Terry the fortunes of the business had hastened Bullock's death. Bullock's wife was made sole executrix of his will, which has not been located. Sales of Bullock's stock, art collections and assets were held in Liverpool and London in 1819.

An obituary in the *Annals of Fine Arts* (VIII, 1819, 321–2) described Bullock's death as 'sudden and lacerating'. The writer recalled the sculptor as 'a man of very remarkable powers; every thing that he thought, or did, or executed, was on a grand or extended scale'. The writer was in no doubt that Bullock had carried taste in furnishing to a higher level than Britain had seen before. Although sculpture was only one aspect of a large, varied and entrepreneurial furnishing business, the obituarist felt that it was central to Bullock's enterprise: 'He appeared to have entered into his late pursuit from one much higher, and much more elevated, bringing more powers to his task than was merely requisite. He was originally a sculptor and modeller, and carried the taste and feeling of an artist into what he latterly directed' (quoted in *Bullock* 1988, 20–1).

MGS

Literary References: *Stranger in Liverpool* 1812, 138; *Ackermann* VIII, 1819, 321–2; *Graves* I, 1905–6, 335; *Edwards* 1969, 172–3; *Beard and Gilbert* 1986, 126–8; *Bullock* 1988; *Levy* 1989, 145–213; *Clifford* 1992, 45, 50; *Grove* 5, 1996, 168–9 (Allwood); *Morris and Roberts* 1998, 111

Archival References: GPC

Miscellaneous Drawings: An album of tracings by Thomas Wilkinson of Bullock's designs, Birmingham MAG. These include eight unidentified drawings for monuments (*Bullock* 1988, 128).

Auction Catalogues: Bullock 1806; Bullock 1812 (1); Bullock 1812 (2); Bullock 1812 (3); Bullock 1814; Bullock 1819 (1); Bullock 1819 (2)

Portraits of the Sculptor: Bust, Samuel Joseph, exhib RA 1819, *Graves* II, 1905–6, 287; Joseph Allen, portrait of George Bullock with his bust of Henry Blundell, oil on canvas, Walker AG, Liverpool, *Bullock* 1988 (repr frontispiece and 129)

Representations of the Premises: Richard Bridgens, 'View of the Ware Rooms of Mr. Geo. Bullock's Egyptian Hall, Piccadilly, London,' Exhib Liverpool Ac 1812, 268, *Morris and Roberts* 1998, 99

No.	Date	Work	Material	Location		References
Funerary Monuments						
1.	1807	Robert Blundell (†1807) Payment(s): £28 10s		Sefton, Lancs		*Bullock* 1988, 136 (repr)
2.	†1809	Rev Glover Moore Drawing(s): Tracing, Birmingham CMAG M.3.74		Halsall, Lancs	S	GPC; *Bullock* 1988, 136–8 (repr)
3.	†1813	Anna Maria Bold		Farnworth, Lancs	S	*Bullock* 1988, 138–40 (repr)
Statues						
4.	1807	Admiral Lord Nelson, model for monument in Liverpool (commission won by M C Wyatt)		Untraced		*Gunnis* 1968, 69; *Bullock* 1988, 148–52 (design repr)
Busts						
5.	1804	Dr Smyth		[Exhib RA, London, 855]; untraced		*Graves* I, 1905–6, 335
6.	by 1804	Henry Blundell	m	[Ince Blundell Hall, Lancs]; Walker, Liverpool Other versions: plaster (with cravat frills), for Stephen Tempest 1807, £5 5s, private coll	S	*Graves* I, 1905–6, 335; *Edwards* 1969, 172 (repr); *Bullock* 1988, 130–1 (repr); *Grove* 5, 1996, 169; *Morris and Roberts* 1998, 111

7.	1804	Sir James Edward Smith Model(s): Formerly Allerton Hall	p	Walker, Liverpool		*Graves* I, 1905–6, 335; *Bullock* 1988, 132–3 (repr); *Grove* 5, 1996, 169; *Morris and Roberts* 1998, 111
8.	1804	Unidentified gentleman		[Exhib RA, London, 850]; untraced		*Graves* I, 1905–6, 335
9.	1804	Unidentified gentleman		[Exhib RA, London, 851]; untraced		*Graves* I, 1905–6, 335
10.	1804	W Stevenson		[Exhib RA, London, 838]; untraced		*Graves* I, 1905–6, 335; *Morris and Roberts* 1998, 111
11.	1804	William Roscoe	p	Walker, Liverpool Other versions: Plaster, Liverpool Boys' Institute School		*Graves* I, 1905–6, 335; *Beard and Gilbert* 1986, 126; *Bullock* 1988, 132–3 (repr); *Grove* 5, 1996, 169; *Morris and Roberts* 1998, 111
12.	1805	J Burch Esq		[Exhib RA, London, 781]; untraced		*Graves* I, 1905–6, 335; *Bullock* 1988, 147
13.	1805	John Blackburne MP		[Exhib RA, London, 813]; untraced		*Graves* I, 1905–6, 335; *Bullock* 1988, 147–8; *Morris and Roberts* 1998, 111
14.	1805	Master Betty, the 'Young Roscius'		[Exhib RA, London, 800]; untraced		*Graves* I, 1905–6, 335; *Bullock* 1988, 42, 147; *Morris and Roberts* 1998, 111
15.	1806	Dr Wilkinson		[Exhib RA, London, 335]; untraced		*Graves* I, 1905–6, 335; *Bullock* 1988, 148; *Morris and Roberts* 1998, 111
16.	1806	William Henry, 2nd Duke of Gloucester and Strathearn		[Exhib RA, London, 839]; untraced		*Graves* I, 1905–6, 335; *Bullock* 1988, 148; *Morris and Roberts* 1998, 111
17.	1807	Sir William Elford Bt		[Exhib RA, London, 1081]; untraced		*Graves* I, 1905–6, 335; *Bullock* 1988, 148
18.	1808	Sarah Siddons in the character of Melpomene		[Exhib RA, London, 916]; untraced		*Graves* I, 1905–6, 335
19.	1810	Colonel John Bolton		[Exhib Liverpool Ac, 195]; untraced		*Bullock* 1988, 152; *Morris and Roberts* 1998, 111
20.	by 1810	Elizabeth Rose Jolliffe	m	Amerdown Park, Somerset	S	*Bullock* 1988, 138–9 (repr); *Morris and Roberts* 1998, 111; GPC
21.	1810	Mr Cukit		[Exhib Liverpool Ac, 199]; untraced		*Bullock* 1988, 152; *Morris and Roberts* 1998, 111
22.	1810	Unidentified sitter		[Exhib RA, London, 767]; untraced		*Graves* I, 1905–6, 335
23.	1811	Robert Sewallis Shirley, Lord Tamworth		[Exhib Liverpool Ac, 165]; untraced		*Bullock* 1988, 152; *Morris and Roberts* 1998, 111
24.	1812	Mr James Sadler ('the celebrated aeronaut')		[Exhib Liverpool Ac, 263; Exhib RA, London, 1813, 944]; untraced		*Graves* I, 1905–6, 335; *Bullock* 1988, 152; *Morris and Roberts* 1998, 111
25.	1813	Colonel Charles Fraser		[Exhib RA, London, 784]; untraced		*Graves* I, 1905–6, 335; *Bullock* 1988, 152–3
26.	1814	George, 4th Earl of Aberdeen (drapery only, bust by Joseph Nollekens)	m	Private coll		*Bullock* 1988, 144 (repr)
27.	1814	William Shakespeare (cast from the monument by Gerard Jansen in Holy Trinity, Stratford-on-Avon)	p	SJSM SC 18 Other versions: 20 known copies	S	*Gunnis* 1968, 69; *Bullock* 1988, 20, 141; *Penny* 1992, 14; GPC
28.	1816	Dr William Hey FRS	m	[coll Benjamin Gott of Armley, Leeds]; University of Leeds, Brotherton Library, special colls Other versions: Plaster copies known	SD	*Graves* I, 1905–6, 335; *Friedman* 1972, 18–25; *Bullock* 1988, 69, 142–4 (repr)
29.	nd	Julia Pitches (Mrs William John Jolliffe)	m	Private coll	S	C Lib (repr)
Chimneypieces						
30.	1811	'Egyptian'		[Broughton Hall, W R Yorks]; untraced		*Bullock* 1988, 157
31.	1816	Of Mona marble, with ormolu decoration		Untraced		*Repository of Arts* 1, 1816, 19 (repr)
32.	nd	Of Mona marble, with ormolu mouldings		[Bullock sale 1819, lot 108]; Towneley, Burnley		*Bullock* 1988, 97
Reliefs						
33.	1801	Henry Blundell, seated figure in an interior	w	LMG	SD	*Beard and Gilbert* 1986, 126; Bullock 1988, 129–30 (repr)
Miscellaneous						
34.	1800	Sarah Siddons		[Exhib William Bullock's rooms, Portugal House, New Street, Birmingham]; untraced		*Bullock* 1988, 145–6
35.	?1800	William Kemble in the character of Cato (executed in rice paste)		[Exhib William Bullock's Museum, Liverpool Exhib Egyptian Hall, Piccadilly, London, 1812]; untraced		*Gunnis* 1968, 69; *Bullock* 1988, 146
36.	1802	Edward the Black Prince, equestrian model (executed in rice paste)		[William Bullock's Museum, Liverpool]; untraced		*Bullock* 1988, 146–7
37.	1804	Candlesticks with classical female figures	p	Birmingham CMAG	SD	*Bullock* 1988, 134–5 (repr)
38.	by 1808	Sarah Siddons (executed in rice paste)		[William Bullock's Museum, Liverpool]; untraced		*Bullock* 1988, 146
39.	1811	'4 heads'		[Broughton Hall, W R Yorks]; untraced		*Bullock* 1988, 157
40.	1815	Table of green marble		[New Longwood House, St Helena]; untraced		*Bullock* 1988, 33

BULLOCK, Matthew fl 1796–1809

Bullock was employed at Cleveland House, St James's, London between 1796 and 1799 when the south front and interior were remodelled by James Lewis for the 3rd Duke of Bridgewater (Ashridge MSS, AH 1749, in GPC). In 1809 he succeeded **Thomas Engleheart** as one of the carvers at Dodington Park, Glos, under the direction of the architect James Wyatt (1) (Codrington Archives in GPC).

Architectural Sculpture

1.	1809	Corinthian capitals	Dodington Park, Glos, principal front	GPC

BULLOCK, Sybella fl 1825

In 1825 Miss Sybella Bullock of 119 Sloane Square, was awarded a medal by the Society of Arts for a bust from the life (1).

Literary References: RSA *Transactions*, vol 43, 1825, xlvii

Busts

1.	1825	Unidentified subject 'from life'	[Soc of A, large silver medal]; untraced	RSA *Transactions*, vol 43, 1825, xlvii

BULLOCK, William early 1780s–after 1843

William Bullock the naturalist, antiquary, explorer and entrepreneur, who famously established the Egyptian Hall in Piccadilly, London, was also involved in the production of sculpture for a short period early in his career. He was the son of William and **Elizabeth Bullock** and the brother of **George Bullock**. In 1800 he opened a Cabinet of Curiosities at Portugal House, New Street, Birmingham, which included 'Likenesses of some of the most conspicuous Characters of the present Age modelled in Wax' and 'A Collection of capital Models in Rice Paste' (*Aris's Birmingham Gazette* [*ABG*], 11 August 1800). Some of these models were probably inherited from his mother's exhibition and others may have come from Mr Curtius's Cabinet of Curiosities, which was on show in Birmingham in 1796–97.

By March 1801 he had closed the Birmingham business and re-opened at 24 Lord Street, Liverpool, describing himself as 'Silversmith, Jeweller, Toyman and Statue Figure Manufacturer' and advertising 'Likenesses Modelled in Rice Paste from Ten to Fifteen Guineas' (*Billinge's Liverpool Advertiser* [*BLA*], 16 March 1801). It is likely that he was providing a Liverpool outlet for his brother George, who joined him some time between 1801 and 1804. George went into partnership with William Stoakes in June 1804 and six weeks later William moved to a museum and bronze figure manufactory in Church Street, where he sold 'every article in the Bronze figure and ornamental business' (*BLA* various refs). The two brothers were clearly operating in direct competition with one another, for in March 1805, when George Bullock's bust of the popular actor Master Betty was on display in Liverpool, William advertised that another 'taken since his late illness by **Mr. Gahagan**, Sculptor' could be seen at his museum in Church Street. Copies could be purchased by subscription (*Liverpool Chronicle*, 13 March 1805).

In 1809 Bullock moved to London, where his exhibition became extremely popular, especially after 1812 when it was installed in George Bullock's newly erected Egyptian Hall. After auctioning off his collection in 1819 Bullock let the Egyptian Hall for other exhibitions and in 1822 set off on an expedition to Mexico, where he acquired many important pre-Colombian artefacts and natural specimens, which he put on display in London in April 1824. Five years later, after disposing of his Mexican collection and selling the lease on the Egyptian Hall, Bullock again travelled to Mexico and the United States. There he attempted to found a model community near Cincinnati, which he named Hygeia. The venture failed and Bullock ended his days in London some time after 1843.

Literary References: *Altick* 1978, 235–52; *Bullock* 1988, 41–3; *Clifford* 1992, 45–6, 49–50; *ODNB* (Baigent)

BULLOCK, William, of Charing Cross fl 1710–c1740

Bullock was made free of the Masons' Company on 23 Oct 1710, by service to **Thomas Wise II**. About 30 years later he appeared in a list of assistants and livery of the Masons' Company, as 'Bullock, William Mason at Wharfe near Charing Cross'.

Archival References: Masons' Co, *Assistants*, fol 5 (c1740); *Freemen*, fol 5 (23 October 1710)

BULLOCK & THACKWAY, of Hull fl 1716–20

In 1716–17 William Bullock and Thomas Thackway, who were probably Hull masons, built a house in East Gate, Beverley, for Sir Charles Hotham to designs by Colen Campbell. They were also responsible for the architectural carving (1).

Architectural Sculpture

1.	1716–1720	Architectural carving	[Sir Charles Hotham's House, East Gate, Beverley, E R Yorks]; demol c1760	Hotham archives in GPC

BULMAN, of Newcastle fl 1849

Funerary Monuments

1.	1849	Thomas Clennell	Alwinton, Northumbs	Pevsner, *Northumbs*, 1992, 145

BULMER, William, of Stockton fl 1833–58

A minor statuary, he signs tablets in Yorkshire and County Durham.

Funerary Monuments

1.	?1833	Elizabeth Wedderburn	Middleton St George, Durham	*Gunnis* 1968, 69
2.	?1837	Rev William Fontaine	Middleton St George, Durham	*Gunnis* 1968, 69
3.	?1842	John Rockliffe	Topcliffe, N R Yorks	*Gunnis* 1968, 69
4.	†1858	Amelia, Viscountess Falkland	Rudby, N R Yorks	*Gunnis* 1968, 69

BUMPSTEAD (or BUMPSTEED), John –1683

'Jno Bumpstead Carver' was paid £47 by the Corporation of London, on 23 May 1673, for 'work about the public stairs at Queenhithe and Grig Lane' (Guildhall Library MS 184/4, 24v). He was employed on masonry work at the Guildhall in the same year and later worked at Christ's Hospital (3, 4). In his diary for 22 November 1677 Robert Hooke noted that he 'Shewd Garaway his daughters monument for Peters poor done by Bomstead' (*Robinson and Adams* 1935, 329) (1). Garaway was the proprietor of a well-known coffee house in Change Alley, Cornhill. His daughter's monument is likely to have disappeared, for the church of St Peter-le-Poer was rebuilt in 1792 and demolished in the early-20th century. In 1679 Bumpstead carved a pair of life-size wooden statues of King Charles I and King James I for Clothworkers' Hall (**2**). These were destroyed in an air raid in 1941.

Gunnis states that Bumpstead was upper warden of the Masons' Company in 1676 and master two years later. However, when he took **William Kidwell** as his apprentice in 1678 he was a member of the Joiners' Company. He died in 1683 and his probate inventory survives (TNA PROB 4/5493, 19 July 1683). He may have been related to Stephen Bumpsted who took an apprentice through the Masons' Company in 1673 and worked on the rebuilding of Trinity House in 1671, following the Great Fire of London (Trinity House Archives, in GPC). In 1683 William Bumpsted, who was perhaps John's son, was paid £7 for carving at the Mathematical School, Christ's Hospital.

Literary References: *Gunnis* 1968, 69

Archival References: Joiners' Apprentices, 1678, fol 143r or 8052, fol 56v; Christ's H, TAB 12819/10, 723; 12819/11, 274

Funerary Monuments

1.	1677	Garaway's daughter		[St Peter-le-Poer, City of London]; destroyed (?)	*Robinson and Adams* 1935, 329

Statues

2.	1679	King James I and King Charles I Payment(s): £40 plus £14 for gilding	wd	[Clothworkers' Hall, City of London, west side]; destroyed	*Smith* 1999, 17 (repr); *Wickham* 2000, 106

Architectural Sculpture

3.	1677	Two dragons 'on Leadenhall' Payment(s): £7		[Christ's Hospital, Newgate, City of London]; untraced	CH, TAB
4.	1683	Carving Payment(s): £17		[Royal Mathematical School, Christ's Hospital, Newgate, City of London]; untraced	*Gunnis* 1968, 69

BURCH, Edward I RA 1730–1814

One of a handful of London gem-engravers, Burch was also a wax modeller and medallist. He was baptised on 30 October 1730 at St Botolph-without-Aldgate, the son of Andrew and Hannah Burch. He worked initially as a Thames waterman, and his 'first effort in painting was exercised in the imitation of a gold band round his hat and the superior style of the interior of his wherry' (*New Monthly Mag* 1816, 417).

In 1760, when he showed at the first Society of Artists exhibition, he was working as a seal engraver in Bedford St, Bedford Row and his submission was an engraving on a semi-precious hardstone (**2**). This form of gem carving was classical in origin and the popularity of engraved gems with British grand tourists prompted the Society for the Encouragement of Arts, Manufactures and Commerce to attempt to found a native school. The society offered a series of premiums, several of which were awarded to Burch between 1763 and 1766, including one for a head of the *Apollo Belvedere* in 1764 (**6**).

Burch studied drawing and modelling at the St Martin's Lane Academy and in the Duke of Richmond's gallery of casts after the Antique. In Mortimer's *Director* of 1763, he described himself as 'Burch, Edward, engraver in stone. The upper end of Red-lion-court, Fleet Street' (*Mortimer* 1763, 4). By 1764 he had taken **Nathaniel Marchant** as an apprentice, and in 1765 he relocated to Warwick Street, Charing Cross. That year he was elected a fellow of the Society of Artists and in 1768 he and Marchant were made directors on the governing committee. Marchant wrote to the committee in October asking that he and his former master be described as 'sculptors', because the term was 'more applicable' to their profession than the word engraver (*Seidmann* 1987, 7–8). His skill won him important patrons, including the Duke of Marlborough, who commissioned some of Burch's most attractive surviving work (**8, 9, 23, 24, 27, 30**).

On 2 September 1769, aged 39, Burch enrolled as a student at the newly founded Royal Academy Schools. The following year he was elected an ARA, and in March 1771 he presented to the council 'a small model of a figure of Neptune, in wax as a specimen of his abilities'. The council asked him also to supply an intaglio or cameo, since it was for this work that he was renowned (**10**). In June he became the first Royal Academician to be elected by his fellow members (RA Council Minutes, vol 1, 1770, fols 82, 85; 1771, fol 109).

At the Academy exhibitions Burch exhibited portraits and carvings of models from the Academy life class in poses of biblical and classical figures (**53, 68**). An interest in anatomical precision influenced a good deal of his work and he was a close friend and admirer of the Professor of Anatomy, Dr William Hunter. He executed an *écorché* figure for Hunter (**1**) and also designed the Hunter medal, which has a portrait of the anatomist on one side and a scene of the doctor instructing an anatomy class on the reverse. In 1788 Burch described himself as 'Engraver to his majesty for medals and seals in stones and to HRH the Duke of York' and in 1790 as the medallist and gem-engraver to the King of Poland. He also worked for Wedgwood (**21, 82, 83**) and with the Scot, James Tassie.

In spite of these honours Burch struggled to make a living and in 1794 he was appointed librarian to the Royal Academy, a post traditionally given to indigent artists, which Burch filled with erratic application. In 1794 he alone voted for himself as future president of the Royal Academy after the death of Sir Joshua Reynolds. He seems not to have endeared himself to his fellow academicians by his coarseness of manner and expression. In 1795 he had privately printed his *Catalogue of One Hundred Proofs from Gems, Engraved in England by E Burch RA*, in an apparent move to drum up trade. The attempt must have failed, for in that year **John Bacon RA** told Joseph Farington that Burch (who on occasion engraved Bacon's designs on gems) had repeatedly and unsuccessfully asked Bacon for money. In 1796, when living at 2 Paynes Place, Kentish Town, he complained to Farington that he had only two commissions in hand, an oft-repeated carving of a head of Shakespeare (which he had taken from **Peter Scheemakers**'s portrait) and an image of Lady Mansfield's favourite cow (**34, 26**).

Burch became increasingly dependent on the Royal Academy's charity. In February 1800 he was described as 'in great distress' as a result of 'long illness and want of employment' and he was advanced a quarter of his salary, and granted £50. Between 1811 and 1814 he received a pension of £40 pa (RA *Council Minutes*, vol 3, fols 47, 51, 56, 85; vol 4, fol 377; vol 5, fol 59). He died on 11 February 1814. His obituary, probably written by his son Henry Jacob Burch, remarked that the gem-engraver's profession had become virtually obsolete, but that 'our artist's self-taught knowledge warrants the term genius' (*New Monthly Mag*, vol 1, 1814, 192, quoted in *Seidmann* 1997, 265).

Burch's works have subsequently occupied an historiographical no-man's land, between sculpture and engraving, and have received little serious consideration in the text books of either discipline. Gertrud Seidmann's work has recently done much to illuminate his life and career and to place his technically remarkable work in the visual culture of the day.

MGS

Literary References: *Farington, passim*; *Graves* I, 1905–6, 340; *Graves* 1907, 43; *Hutchison* 1960–62, 134; *Brown* 1980, 44; *Stainton* 1983, 18; *Seidmann* 1985, 150–153; *Seidmann* 1987, 5–8, 16, 19, 20, 21, 26; *Grove* 1996, 187 (Seidmann); *Seidmann* 1997, 263–279

Archival References: IGI

Representations of the Sculptor: J Zoffany *Life School at the Royal Academy* 1771–2, oil on canvas (Royal coll); Edward Burch Jr, exhib RA 1814, untraced

Statues

1.	pre-1769	Ecorché (anatomical statuette)	w	[coll Dr William Hunter]; Hunterian	*Grove* 1996, 187; *Bilbey* 2002, 56

Reliefs

2.	1760	St George and the dragon, onyx cameo		[Exhib Soc of Artists, 76]; untraced	*Graves* 1907, 43; *Seidmann* 1997, 265, 276 n32
3.	1762	'Apollo de Villa Medici', engraved in onyx		[Soc of A, premium, 20 gns]; untraced	*Dossie* 1782, 441
4.	1763	Head of Alexander, engraved in onyx		[Soc of A, premium, 20 gns]; untraced	*Dossie* 1782, 441
5.	1764	Head of Antinous	p	[Exhib Soc of Artists, 151]; untraced	*Graves* 1907, 43
6.	1764	Head of Apollo Belvedere, gem-engraving		[Exhib Soc of Artists, premium winner]; untraced	*Graves* 1907, 43; *Seidmann* 1997, 266
7.	1765	Head of the Apollo Python, engraved in cornelian		[Soc of A, premium, 20 gns]; untraced	*Dossie* 1782, 441
8.	1769	Head of Ganymede, in sardonyx		[coll George, 4th Duke of Marlborough]; untraced Other versions: Reproduced in sulphur	*Seidmann* 1997, 266 (cast repr)
9.	c1769	Hermes, in amethyst		[coll George, 4th Duke of Marlborough]; untraced Other versions: Reproduced in sulphur	*Seidmann* 1997, 266, 267 (cast repr)
10.	1771	Neptune, cornelian intaglio		RA, London (diploma work)	*Graves* I, 1905–6, 340; *Grove* 1996, 187
11.	1778	Two portrait medallions		[Exhib RA, London, 24]; untraced	*Graves* I, 1905–6, 340
12.	post-1779	David Garrick	w	BM	*Pyke* 1973, 22
13.	1780	Head of Bacchus, sardonyx		[Exhib RA, London, 246]; untraced	*Graves* I, 1905–6, 340
14.	1782	Hebe, model for a gem		[Exhib RA, London, 312]; untraced	*Graves* I, 1905–6, 340
15.	1782	Jupiter and Leda, a gem		[Exhib RA, London, 312]; untraced	*Graves* I, 1905–6, 340
16.	1782	Portrait of a lady, a gem		[Exhib RA, London, 312]; untraced	*Graves* I, 1905–6, 340
17.	1785	Alexander taming Bucephalus, model designed for gem engraving	w	[Exhib RA, London, 268; 1798, 763]; untraced	*Graves* I, 1905–6, 341
18.	1786	Ariadne and Hercules, two cameos		[Exhib RA, London, 314]; untraced	*Graves* I, 1905–6, 341
19.	1787	HRH Frederick, Duke of York, the Marquis of Rockingham, and a Vestal, three cameos		[Exhib RA, London, 263]; untraced	*Graves* I, 1905–6, 341
20.	c1789	19 horses	w	Untraced Other versions: Reproduced in Wedgwood jasperware	*Pyke* 1973, 22; *Grove* 1996, 187
21.	pre-1789	King George III	w	Wilton House, Wilts Other versions: Stanton Harcourt, Oxon, wax	*Pyke* 1973, 22 (rep pl 41)
22.	pre-1795	Anatomical figure, intaglio on sardonyx		Untraced Other versions: Reproduced in sulphur	*Seidmann* 1997, 270–1 (repr)
23.	pre-1795	Bacchus, in cornelian		[coll George, 4th Duke of Marlborough]; untraced Other versions: Reproduced in sulphur	*Seidmann* 1997, 268 (repr)
24.	pre-1795	Time (Chronos gnawing at the remains of the Torso Belvedere)		[coll George, 4th Duke of Marlborough]; untraced Other versions: Reproduced in sulphur	*Seidmann* 1997, 268, 271 (repr)
25.	pre-1795	Young Jupiter, in sardonyx		[coll Henry Constantine Jennings]; untraced Other versions: Reproduced in sulphur	*Seidmann* 1997, 266 (cast repr)
26.	1797	Portrait of a favourite cow, a lion and a bull, two cameos		[Exhib RA, London, 894]; untraced	*Graves* I, 1905–6, 341
27.	nd	Antinous, cornelian intaglio		[coll George, 4th Duke of Marlborough]; untraced Other versions: Private coll	*Seidmann* 1993, 175–8 (repr); *Seidmann* 1997, 266, 267 (repr)
28.	nd	Hercules, nicolo		[coll George, 4th Duke of Marlborough]; untraced	*Seidmann* 1997, 266
29.	nd	Hercules, citrine intaglio		BM	*Grove* 1996, 187
30.	nd	Sabina, yellow sardonyx		[coll George, 4th Duke of Marlborough]; Walters AG, Baltimore	*Grove* 1996, 187; *Seidmann* 1997, 266, 277 (repr)
31.	nd	'Sacrifice to Minerva', chalcedony intaglio		Hermitage, St Petersburg, Russia	*Grove* 1996, 187
32.	nd	Sir Isaac Newton, chalcedony intaglio		Christie, 4 Oct 1989, lot 435	*Grove* 1996, 187
33.	nd	Unidentified man	w	VAM (L.45 Bate loan)	*Pyke* 1973, 20 (repr pl 37)
34.	nd	William Shakespeare, cornelian intaglio		Fitzwilliam	*Grove* 1996, 187

Miscellaneous

35.	1764	'Figure of a Venus from the Bath'		[Exhib Soc of Artists, 152]; untraced Other versions: Reproduced in sulphur	*Graves* 1907, 43; *Seidmann* 1997, 270–1 (repr)
36.	1764	'Figure of Judith with the head of Holofernes'		[Exhib Soc of Artists, 152]; untraced	*Graves* 1907, 43
37.	1764	Head of Silence		[Exhib Soc of Artists, 152]; untraced	*Graves* 1907, 43
38.	1764	Portrait of a lady		[Exhib Soc of Artists, 152]; untraced	*Graves* 1907, 43
39.	1765	'Head of Faustina from a plaister bust'		[Exhib Soc of Artists, 170]; untraced	*Graves* 1907, 43
40.	1765	Head of Julia 'from the Roman coin'		[Exhib Soc of Artists, 170]; untraced	*Graves* 1907, 43
41.	1765	Head of Shakespeare 'from the plaister bust by Mr Scheemaker'		[Exhib Soc of Artists, 170]; untraced	*Graves* 1907, 43
42.	1765	Hercules reposing from his labours		[Exhib Soc of Artists, 170]; untraced	*Graves* 1907, 43
43.	1766	A model	w	[Exhib Soc of Artists, 202]; untraced	*Graves* 1907, 43
44.	1767	Head of Demosthenes 'from a bust'		[Exhib Soc of Artists, 204]; untraced	*Graves* 1907, 43
45.	1768	'A dancing figure from the painting of Herculaneum'		[Exhib Soc of Artists, 199]; untraced	*Graves* 1907, 43
46.	1768	A head of Inigo Jones 'from Vandyke'		[Exhib Soc of Artists, 200]; untraced	*Graves* 1907, 43
47.	1768	'Hercules reflecting on his misconduct in permitting Omphale to preside over him'		[Exhib Soc of Artists, 198]; untraced Other versions: Sulphur casts	*Graves* 1907, 43; *Seidmann* 1997, 270–1 (repr)
48.	1769	Diana after hunting, model	w	[Exhib Soc of Artists, 223]; untraced	*Graves* 1907, 43
49.	1769	Jupiter and Leda, model	w	[Exhib Soc of Artists, 221]; untraced	*Graves* 1907, 43
50.	1769	Narcissus, model	w	[Exhib Soc of Artists, 222]; untraced	*Graves* 1907, 43
51.	1769	Neptune resting on his trident, model	w	[Exhib Soc of Artists, 224]; untraced	*Graves* 1907, 43
52.	1771	'A portrait'	w	[Exhib RA, London, 20]; untraced	*Graves* I, 1905–6, 340
53.	1772	A deposition, 'Academy model'		[Exhib RA, London, 32]; untraced	*Graves* I, 1905–6, 340
54.	1772	A river god		[Exhib RA, London, 34]; untraced	*Graves* I, 1905–6, 340
55.	1772	'An Academy model, representing the River Tiber'		[Exhib RA, London, 33]; untraced	*Graves* I, 1905–6, 340
56.	1773	Neptune raising a storm, Academy model	w	[Exhib RA, London, 372]; untraced	*Graves* I, 1905–6, 340
57.	1775	Dr Robinson, Primate of Ireland, model	w	[Exhib RA, London, 46]; untraced	*Graves* I, 1905–6, 340
58.	1775	Unidentified lady	w	[Exhib RA, London, 47]; untraced	*Graves* I, 1905–6, 340
59.	1776	Empress Catherine of Russia	w	[Exhib RA, London, 37]; untraced	*Graves* I, 1905–6, 340
60.	1776	Unidentified gentleman, model	w	[Exhib RA, London, 38]; untraced	*Graves* I, 1905–6, 340
61.	1777	Unidentified gentleman	w	[Exhib RA, London, 27]; untraced	*Graves* I, 1905–6, 340
62.	1777	Unidentified lady	w	[Exhib RA, London, 26]; untraced	*Graves* I, 1905–6, 340
63.	1779	Unidentified gentleman	w	[Exhib RA, London, 35]; untraced	*Graves* I, 1905–6, 340
64.	1780	Hercules supporting Menalippe, model	w	[Exhib RA, London, 246]; untraced	*Graves* I, 1905–6, 340
65.	1780	Unidentified gentleman	w	[Exhib RA, London, 36]; untraced	*Graves* I, 1905–6, 340
66.	1782	Unidentified gentleman	w	[Exhib RA, London, 256]; untraced	*Graves* I, 1905–6, 340
67.	1784	Bacchus and Ceres	w	[Exhib RA, London, 278]; untraced	*Graves* I, 1905–6, 340
68.	1786	An Academy model representing a Roman slave, model for a cameo	w	[Exhib RA, London, 254]; untraced	*Graves* I, 1905–6, 341
69.	1787	Academy model of a sleeping Bacchante, designed for a gem	w	[Exhib RA, London, 643]; untraced	*Graves* I, 1905–6, 341
70.	1787	Academy model of the Birth of Venus, designed for a gem	w	[Exhib RA, London, 641]; untraced	*Graves* I, 1905–6, 341
71.	1788	The triumph of Venus, model	w	[Exhib RA, London, 626]; untraced	*Graves* I, 1905–6, 341
72.	1789	Head of Ariadne, model designed for a large cameo	w	[Exhib RA, London, 594]; untraced	*Graves* I, 1905–6, 341
73.	1790	Bacchus tantalising Cupid, Academy model	w	[Exhib RA, London, 695]; untraced	*Graves* I, 1905–6, 341
74.	1791	'A lady of quality'	w	[Exhib RA, London, 640]; untraced	*Graves* I, 1905–6, 341
75.	1791	General Pasquale Paoli	w	[Exhib RA, London, 639]; untraced	*Graves* I, 1905–6, 341
76.	1791	Neptune, model	w	[Exhib RA, London, 626]; untraced	*Graves* I, 1905–6, 341
77.	1792	Eve, from Milton's Paradise Lost, book IV, 460, model	w	[Exhib RA, London, 750]; untraced	*Graves* I, 1905–6, 341
78.	1793	Venus, model	w	[Exhib RA, London, 404]; untraced	*Graves* I, 1905–6, 341
79.	1794	The three Graces, design for a gem	w	[Exhib RA, London, 467]; untraced	*Graves* I, 1905–6, 341
80.	1796	Hymen's triumph in celebrating the nuptials of Cupid and Psyche, model for a cameo	w	[Exhib RA, London, 633; 1797, 894]; untraced	*Graves* I, 1905–6, 341
81.	1797	Discobolus, model designed for a gem	w	[Exhib RA, London, 893]; untraced	*Graves* I, 1905–6, 341
82.	nd	King George III, portrait (model for Wedgwood)		Untraced	*Pyke* 1973, 22
83.	nd	Queen Charlotte, portrait (model for Wedgwood)		Untraced	*Pyke* 1973, 22

BURCH, Edward II fl 1789–92

He exhibited at the Royal Academy between 1789 and 1792 from 24 Charlotte Street, Portland Place and then from 23 Denmark Place. For further information the reader is referred to *Pyke* 1973, 21.

Literary References: *Graves* I, 1905–6, 341

BURCH, Henry Jacob 1763–

The son of **Edward Burch I**, he was a gem-engraver, wax-modeller and painter. He entered the Royal Academy Schools in 1779 and exhibited at the RA between 1787 and 1831, as well as showing three works at the Society of Artists in 1790.

Literary References: *Graves* 1907, 43; *Graves* I, 1905–6, 341; *Pyke* 1973, 22

BURFORD, John fl 1763

In his *Universal Director* of 1763 Mortimer lists Burford as 'Carver and Gilder. On the Pavement, St Martin's Lane' (p 3).

BURGESS, Clement, of Petworth –1855

In the Sussex directory of 1828 Burgess describes himself as 'Statuary and Architect'.

Funerary Monuments						
1.	?1820	John Salter		Fittleworth, Sussex	S	*Gunnis* 1968, 70
2.	†1839	Vice-Admiral Sir Charles Paget and family members (†to 1843)		St Bartholomew, Reigate, Surrey	S	
Architectural Sculpture						
3.	1830	Pedestals of Portland stone		Petworth House, Sussex		*Gunnis* 1968, 70, quoting Archives, Lord Leconfield

BURGESS, D, of Sandbach fl c1740

Gunnis notes that the Wilkins tablet has well-cut lettering.

Funerary Monuments						
1.	?1740	John Wilkins		High Offley, Staffs	S	*Gunnis* 1968, 70

BURGESS, of Great Yarmouth fl 1826

Funerary Monuments						
1.	1826	Unidentified subject		Sloley, Norfolk		Pevsner, *Norfolk: NE & Norwich*, 1997, 665

BURGISS, E, of Uxbridge fl 1832–40

He was the son of **John Burgiss of Uxbridge** and succeeded him in the family business.

Literary References: *Gunnis* 1968, 70

Funerary Monuments						
1.	?1832	Charlotte Raine		Little Missenden, Bucks	S	*Gunnis* 1968, 70
2.	?1840	Thomas Clarke		Ickenham, Middx	S	*Gunnis* 1968, 70

BURGISS, John, of Uxbridge fl 1800?–29

In 1802 he was employed under Sir John Soane on masonry-work at the Treaty House, Uxbridge (Soane Bill Book D fol 70). He signs a number of tablets in Middx and Bucks.

Literary References: *Gunnis* 1968, 70

Funerary Monuments						
1.	?1800	John Bell		Harefield, Middx	S	*Gunnis* 1968, 70
2.	†1803	Thomas Markham		Fleet Marston, Bucks		Pevsner, *Bucks*, 1994, 331
3.	?1804	Peter Parker		Chalfont St Giles, Bucks	S	*Gunnis* 1968, 70
4.	?1820	Alexander Stewart		Wingrave, Bucks	S	*Gunnis* 1968, 70
5.	†1824	John Baptist and Elizabeth Shackle		Hayes, Middx	S	C Lib (repr)
6.	?1827	Mrs Tillyer		Harmondsworth, Middx	S	*Gunnis* 1968, 70
7.	1829	Thomas Allen		Chalfont St Giles, Bucks	S	*Gunnis* 1968, 70

BURGOYNE, R fl early 19th century

Funerary Monuments						
1.	nd	Several, unidentified subjects	sl	Huntington, Herefs	S	Pevsner, *Herefs*, 1963, 198

BURKE, W H & Co, of London fl 1820–79

The firm had premises at 17 Newman Street and 144 Regent Street, London.

Literary References: *Dale-Jones and Lloyd* 1989, 46

Funerary Monuments						
1.	†1820	Lady Frances Wade		Sarratt, Herts	S	
2.	†1847	John Edmonds		All Saints, Hastings, Sussex		Pevsner, *Sussex*, 1965, 520
3.	†1869	Stephen Showers	s	Holy Trinity, Cheltenham, Glos	S	
4.	†1870	Catherine Davies	s	Llangadog, Carmarthen		*Dale-Jones and Lloyd* 1989, 46
5.	†1871	Robert Henderson		Nuthurst, Sussex	S	
6.	†1879	Edward Bowen Jones	s	Heol Awst Congregational Chapel, Carmarthen		*Dale-Jones and Lloyd* 1989, 46

BURLOWE, Henry Behnes 1801/2?–37

A sculptor of portrait busts and the younger brother of **William Behnes**, Burlowe was the second of three sons of an impoverished German piano maker and his English wife and was probably born in London in 1801–1802, though one source suggests that the birth took place in Dublin in 1796 (*Thieme-Becker*, 3, 204). Burlowe was certainly brought up in Dublin, but by 1813 the family had returned to London, where the brothers assisted their father in his trade as well as studying art. The *Art Journal* noted that 'Henry Behnes first, then William, formed the resolution of settling definitively to sculpture as their profession' after receiving informal lessons from **Peter Francis Chenu**, a fellow lodger in the family home in Charles Street (*AJ*, 1864, 83). Henry entered the Royal Academy Schools in October 1821, aged 19, and was awarded a silver medal two years later. Around that time he adopted the name Burlowe so that his works would not be confused with those of his famous brother and perhaps because he was ashamed of William, whose dissolute life-style was well known.

In the 1820s Burlowe established a practice as a sculptor of portrait busts and he had some notable sitters, including the auctioneer James Christie II, the poet John Clare, the engraver John Pye and Henry Bathurst, Bishop of Norwich (**4, 6, 13, 17**). His bust of Samuel Carter Hall, editor of the *Art Journal*, suggests scientific pretensions for it is signed

'HB. BURLOWE / SCULPTOR / AND PHRENOLOGIST' (**26**). Burlowe exhibited at the Royal Academy in 1831 and 1833 and at the Society of British Artists, Suffolk Street, in 1831, giving his address as 10 Lower Southampton Street. During this period he also executed his two known monuments (**1, 2**).

He went to Rome *c*1834, where he received many commissions from English visitors to the city. E V Rippingille later recalled seeing a female head, thought to be the first work executed by Burlowe in Rome (**24**). He was surprised and delighted by its individuality and sophistication and commented that it was executed 'in a style directly opposed to that which was prevalent among the artists of Rome generally, being much broader and bolder' (*Rippingille* 1859, 202). Greenwood has noted that Burlowe's busts, with their 'lively naturalism, and a varied treatment of facial contours', differ markedly from the neoclassical works of established British sculptors in the city such as **John Gibson** and **Lawrence Macdonald** (ODNB).

In 1837 most of the English residents fled Rome to escape the cholera epidemic, but Burlowe chose to stay, against the advice of his friends, 'as he had so many busts in progress and he could not afford to leave them'. He was convinced that 'if a person took care to purify his stomach, there was little danger of being attacked by the malady' (*AU*, 1840, 193). He contracted cholera and by the time his plight was discovered by the artist Charles Lambert, he was already dying. He was buried in the Protestant cemetery at Monte Testaccio, Rome, shortly after his death on 4 September 1837 and a monument was later erected to his memory. His death was recorded in the *Norwich Mercury* on 30 September 1837.

The *Art Union* obituary noted that 'No person ever had more friends, or earned them, and merited them better. . . A more upright, manly or "straight-forward" person never lived; and it will not be too much to say that no one with means so limited ever did more good to those who required assistance' (*AU*, 1840, 193). One of his friends was Anna Jameson, the writer and art historian, who described Burlowe as 'my best friend, the dearest to me on earth' (cited by *Thomas* 1967, 144). The *Art Journal* observed that, although he was 'in every way superior to his brother as a man', Henry was William's 'inferior as an artist' (*AJ*, 1864, 84), but S C Hall believed that 'he would certainly have attained distinction' if he had lived longer (*Hall* II, 1883, 238).

EH

Literary References: *AU*, 1840, 193; *Rippingille* 1859, 201–2; *AJ*, 1864, 83–4; *Palgrave* 1866, 225; *MacPherson* 1878, 65, 177; *Hall* II, 1883, 238; *Thieme-Becker*, 3, 204; *DNB*; *Hutchison* 1960–62, 174; *Thomas* 1967, 144–5; *Gunnis* 1968, 70; *Read* 1982, 69; *Bilbey* 2002, 227; *ODNB* (Greenwood)

Additional MS Sources: *Behnes/Clare*; *Behnes Papers*

Funerary Monuments

1.	?1828	Robert Houston		Carshalton, Surrey		*Gunnis* 1968, 70
2.	†1832	Katherine Noel		Kirkby Mallory, Leics	S	*Gunnis* 1968, 70; C Lib (repr)

Busts

3.	1822	William Hey Junior		Leeds Lit and Phil Soc, W R Yorks		RG/JP, 2, 213
4.	*c*1827	James Christie II		Christie, London		*Gunnis* 1968, 70
5.	1828	Charles Seymour		Northants Central Library, Northampton		RG/JP, 2, 213
6.	1828	John Clare, the poet	pb	Northants Central Library, Northampton		*Bate* 2003, 539 (repr 19); GPC
7.	1829	Josephine Bache		[coll Miss C Clive]; untraced		*Gunnis* 1968, 70
8.	1831	Dr Leonard Stewart		[Exhib RA, London, 1228]; untraced		*Graves* I, 1905–6, 350
9.	1831	Emma		[Exhib RA, London, 1156]; untraced		*Graves* I, 1905–6, 350
10.	1831	G Clint ARA		[Exhib RA, London, 1135]; untraced		*Graves* I, 1905–6, 350
11.	1831	Henry Graves	m	[Exhib RA, London, 1174]; untraced		*Graves* I, 1905–6, 350
12.	1831	James Maude		[Exhib RA, London, 1146]; untraced		*Graves* I, 1905–6, 350
13.	1831	John Pye	p	NPG 2190	SD	*Gunnis* 1968, 70
14.	1831	Rev J Styles		[Exhib Soc of BA, London, 902]; untraced		*Johnson* 1975, 67
15.	1831	Richard Hart Davis MP		[Exhib Soc of BA, London, 898]; untraced		*Johnson* 1975, 67
16.	1831	Unidentified lady		[Exhib RA, London, 1127]; untraced		*Graves* I, 1905–6, 350
17.	1832–1833	Dr Bathurst, Bishop of Norwich		[Exhib RA, London, 1149]; untraced		*Norwich Mercury*, 2 June 1832; *Graves* I, 1905–6, 350
18.	1833	Infant son of R J Lane		[Exhib RA, London, 1215]; untraced		*Graves* I, 1905–6, 350
19.	1833	James Maule	m	[Exhib RA, London, 1128]; untraced		*Graves* I, 1905–6, 350
20.	1832–1833	Sir James Mackintosh	m	[Exhib RA, London, 1155]; untraced		*Lit Gaz*, 1832, 364; *Graves* I, 1905–6, 350
21.	1833	Stephen Lushington MP		[Exhib RA, London, 1124]; untraced		*Graves* I, 1905–6, 350
22.	1834	Charles Seymour	m	Althorp, Northants		C Lib (repr)
23.	1834	Dr Roberts		Untraced		*Gunnis* 1968, 70
24.	1834	Female head		[coll Lord de Clifford]; untraced		*AJ*, 1859, 202
25.	1834	Frederick Seymour, Lord Alcester	m	Althorp, Northants		C Lib (repr)
26.	1834	Samuel Carter Hall	m	VAM A.5-2000	SD	*Graves* I, 1905–6, 350; *Bilbey* 2002, 227 (repr)
27.	1837	George Clifford		Stonyhurst College, Lancs		*Gunnis* 1968, 70
28.	1837	Lady Ogle		Sotheby, 6 June 1997, lot 57	SD	
29.	1837	Sir Peter Hesketh-Fleetwood		Fleetwood, Lancs		*Gunnis* 1968, 70

BURMAN, Belthasar fl 1674–80

The son of **Thomas Burman** and his wife, Rebekah, he is likely to have trained with his father before becoming free by patrimony of the Masons' Company in July 1678. In 1674 he inherited his father's house and yard in Drury Lane, where his mother continued the business until he had completed his training. He carved the magnificent free-standing figure of Rachel, Countess of Bath (†1680), standing in coronation robes on a circular pedestal (**2**). This, except for the pedestal, is a replica of the elder Burman's statue of the Countess of Shrewsbury at St John's College, Cambridge. He also signed the monument to Brian Duppa in Westminster Abbey, an inscribed tablet with carved floral and foliate side scrolls and an apron carved with an angel's head and wings (**1**).

Literary References: *Gunnis* 1968, 70–71

Archival References: Masons' Co, Freemen, fol 4, 2 July 1676

Funerary Monuments

1.	†1662	Brian Duppa, Bishop of Winchester	Westminster Abbey, London, upper chantrey chapel	S	*Dart* 1723, 2, mt 73; *Gunnis* 1968, 70–71; *MacMichael* 1977, 56
2.	†1680	Rachel, Countess of Bath	Tawstock, Devon		*Gunnis* 1968, 71; Pevsner, *Devon*, 1989, 790; C Lib (repr)

BURMAN, Thomas 1617/18–74

Burman was a successful London sculptor who employed at least six apprentices and assistants in the 1660s. Something of his character can perhaps be gathered from George Vertue's story that one of his team, **John Bushnell**, was trapped by his master into marrying a servant Burman had himself seduced.

He was apprenticed to **Edward Marshall** in 1632–33 under the auspices of the Masons' Company, joined the livery in 1657–58 and became upper warden in 1673. He was said to have suffered poverty during the Commonwealth but appears to have become prosperous in later years and at his death owned a considerable amount of real estate. He lived in Drury Lane, Covent Garden from *c*1649 with his wife Rebekah, who carried on the business after his death, taking on two new apprentices in 1675 and a third in 1679.

His first known works were the effigy of the third Earl of Essex, 1646 (1) and an engraved plate for his coffin. The signed bill for the effigy survives (BM Add MS 46189, fol 113). He supplied two designs in 1651–52 for the family monument that Sir Ralph Verney intended to erect at Middle Claydon, Bucks, but the commission went to his former master, Marshall. One of Verney's agents described Burman as negligent. In 1652 John Stone noted in his memorandum book that one of five heads commissioned from him by Sir William Paston was roughed out by a Mr Ellis (probably **Anthony Ellis**) and finished by 'Mr Boreman' (*Vertue* I, 94).

A considerable number of monuments have been attributed to Burman on stylistic grounds, but only three surviving ones have been authenticated. In 1661 he signed the large wall-monument to Sir John Dutton at Sherborne, a standing figure with hooded eyes and hollow cheeks, clothed in a tightly-stretched shroud, set within an elaborate architectural frame (2). Vertue records that there was documentary evidence (now lost) for the wall-monument to Bartholomew and Katherine Beale at Walton, Bucks, *c*1672, which has two delicate high-relief portrait busts in oval niches (3). A third commission, the reclining figure of Frances, Lady Chandos, at Chenies (4) is documented: a bill submitted after Burman's death includes the item 'for the new tomb of black and white marble and alabaster £90-00-0'. The endorsement on the bill, which includes £12.10s for restoration work on other memorials in the Bedford chapel, reads '4 June 1675: £45 paid to Mistress Burman in part . . . 14th March 1675 [ie 1676] – £47 to Mistress Burman in full' (Russell box 262).

Soon after Charles II's restoration Burman received the prestigious commission for a black and white chimney-piece for the King's bedchamber at Whitehall (7), but there is no evidence of further royal employment. Gunnis considers Burman's most important work to have been the statue of Mary, Countess of Shrewsbury, 1671, erected over a gateway in St John's College, Cambridge (5). He may have provided the statue of Lady Margaret Beaufort, 1674, also at St John's College.

Burman's apprentices included, in addition to John Bushnell, Thomas Ashurst, who was listed in the Masons' Company Apprenticeship Records for 1666, John Dannett (1667), Matthew Pennyall (1667), William Robbins (1668), Oliver Fawcett (1669), Henry Prescott (1669), John Collins (1671) and John Cillinys. Nothing is known of their subsequent careers.

He died in March 1674 and was buried in the vault at St Paul, Covent Garden. His swagged table-tomb in the churchyard was sketched by Vertue (*Vertue* IV, 34). By his will he made bequests to his widow and three daughters; his son, **Belthasar Burman**, inherited his house and yard in Drury Lane and two of the apprentices, John Cillinys and William Carter (whose name does not appear in the Masons' Company records), received £3 each. His friends, **Joshua Marshall** and **Abraham Storey** were each given £5 for a mourning ring. In 1675 Rebekah Burman was paid £2 14s 3d as Thomas's widow for work on the gallery at the west end of St Paul's, Covent Garden.

It is not possible to evaluate Burman's status in the creative climate of Restoration London since so few of his works have been securely identified. A little earlier, during the Commonwealth period, he was described in a letter to Sir Ralph Verney as 'one of ye best stone cutters . . . in London' and one of Verney's agents commended him as having 'la reputation d-estre bon artisan' (*Stone* 1955–6, 2, 74). Writing nearly a century after his death, Vertue was ambivalent about his achievement, describing him both as 'A good mason & Carver of that time' (*Vertue* I, 128) and as 'No extraordinary Artist' (*ibid*). Gunnis considered him to have been a sculptor of considerable merit, though Whinney, judging him by the Dutton monument, felt he did not have much talent. Beyond enlarging the possible corpus of his work, no later writers have sought to rehabilitate him.

IR

Literary References: *Vertue* I, 86, 89, 90, 94, 128, IV, 34; *Willis and Clarke* 1886, II, 320; *Knoop and Jones* 1935, 24; *Stone* 1955–6, 2, 67–82; *Gunnis* 1968, 71; *Stone* 1955–6, 67–82; *Survey of London*, vol 36, St Paul, Covent Garden, 1970, 105n; *Whinney* 1988, 95, 437 n50; 440 n12; *Grove* 5, 263 (White); *White* 1999, 13–17; *Webb* 1999, *passim*

Will: PROB 11/344/33

Funerary Monuments

1.	†1646	Robert, 3rd Earl of Essex (funeral effigy)	Destroyed		*Stone* 1955–56, 74; *White* 1999, 13, 15 n11
2.	1661	John Dutton (†1656)	Sherborne, Glos	SD	*Grove* 5, 1996, 263; *White* 1999, 14; C Lib (repr)
3.	*c*1672	Rev Bartholomew Beale (†1660) and his wife, Katherine Payment(s): £45	Walton, Bucks		*Vertue* IV, 169; *Grove* 5, 1996, 263; *White* 1999, 14; C Lib (repr)
4.	*c*1674	Frances, Lady Chandos (†1623) Payment(s): £90	Bedford chapel, Chenies, Bucks		Russell, box 262

Statues

5.	1671	Mary, Countess of Shrewsbury Payment(s): £58 2s	St John's College, Cambridge, over gateway to second court		*Willis and Clarke* 1886, II, 320; *Whinney* 1988, 440 n12; *White* 1999, 13, 16 n16

Busts

6.	1652	Unidentified subject begun by 'Mr Ellis', for Sir William Paston		Untraced	*Vertue* I, 94; *Spiers* 1918–19, 27

Chimneypieces

7.	1661	Black and white marble Payment(s): £21 10s		[King's bedchamber, Whitehall Palace, London]; destroyed	*Colvin* 1973–76, V, 266; *White* 1999, 13, 16 n15
8.	1672	Description unavailable Payment(s): £38	m	[Robert Clayton's Banking House, Old Jewry, London]; untraced	Clayton & Morris f241v; *Gunnis* 1968, 71

BURN, Robert fl 1799

Burn sculpted a marble bust of James Gillespie for the Merchant Company, Edinburgh in 1799. It is a work of extraordinary quality and design for Scotland at that period. Virtually nothing is known about him except that he worked as a marble cutter at Leith Walk, Edinburgh from 1790 until 1816.

Literary References: *Woodward* 1977, vol 1, pt 2, 35–6; *Pearson* 1991, 14, 19

Busts

1.	1799	James Gillespie	m	Merchant Company, Edinburgh	*Pearson* 1991, unpag, 14, 19, 22 (repr)

BURNARD, Nevil Northey 1818–78

He was a Cornish sculptor of humble origins who achieved a national reputation as a portrait sculptor, but died in poverty not far from his birthplace. Burnard was born on 11 October 1818 at Penpont, a small village on Bodmin Moor, the son of George, a stonemason. He received a rudimentary education from his mother, Jane, who kept a dame school and supplemented the family income by making straw bonnets. Methodism was an important influence on Burnard's early life. His aunt and uncle, Elizabeth and Digory Isbell, had been among John Wesley's first Cornish followers and are remembered for building the region's first Methodist meeting place, the Wesley Cottage at Trewint. The Burnards and the Isbells were both well-established local families who specialised in stoneworking, and Burnard was related, through his uncle, to **Robert Isbell of Stonehouse** and **James Isbell of Truro**.

When he was 10 Burnard started work as his father's assistant or mortar-boy, and as they travelled between building jobs he must have become familiar with the region's architecture and monuments. In his spare time he amused himself by drawing or carving in wood and soon progressed to working in slate. His earliest known works are a shell cameo portrait of the hymn-writer James Montgomery and a slate tombstone commemorating his nine-year-old cousin Grace Burnard, both executed when he was 12 (**52, 1**). While still in his teens, Burnard carved several gravestones and tablets for local churches (**2–6**), a relief head of John Wesley on local polyphant stone for the façade of the Altarnun Methodist Chapel (**51**) and a small, delicate relief of Homer on slate (**53**). In 1832–3 he was employed at Place House, Fowey, a Tudor mansion then being extensively re-modelled by Joseph Treffry, a wealthy industrialist. Burnard probably carved medallions and other architectural ornaments (**49**). Treffry evidently took an interest in the young sculptor's progress, later commissioning an expensive porphyry pedestal for Burnard's bust of the Prince of Wales (**39**) and sitting for his own portrait (**46**).

In 1835, the recently established Royal Cornwall Polytechnic Society held its first exhibition at Falmouth and Burnard submitted a small relief of *Laocoön* based on an engraving in *The Penny Magazine*, for which he was awarded a silver medal (**54**). He continued to exhibit with the society, winning bronze medals for carvings of *Christ bearing the cross* and *Jupiter and Thetis* in 1836 and 1837 (**55, 56**). These works brought him to the attention of Sir Charles Lemon, the MP for Carclew and first President of the Royal Cornwall Polytechnic Society, who introduced him to **Sir Francis Chantrey RA**. Burnard carved a farmyard scene of a sow and her litter as a demonstration piece (**57**) and Chantrey was impressed enough to find him employment in the London studio of his former pupil, **Henry Weekes RA**. Soon after arriving in London Burnard struck up a friendship with the artist G F Watts, who showed him the city. He went on to work for **E H Baily RA, William Calder Marshall RA** and **J H Foley RA** and exhibited works independently at Falmouth in 1841 and 1843 (**58, 13**).

A turning point in his career came in 1847 when, through Sir Charles Lemon's influence, Queen Victoria granted him permission to model a bust of the young Prince of Wales (**16**). This was Burnard's first Royal Academy exhibit: it established his reputation and in due course brought him a number of important commissions. When it was exhibited at Falmouth, Burnard was entertained by the Fox family at their home, Penjerrick, where eminent writers, scientists and politicians were frequent visitors. This connection with the Foxes and their circle must have been useful for Burnard's future career. Caroline Fox described him as 'a great powerful pugilistic-looking fellow of twenty-nine; a great deal of face, with all the features massed in the centre; mouth open and all sorts of simplicities flowing out of it'. She considered his bust of the Prince of Wales 'a beautiful thing, very intellectual, with a strong likeness to the Queen' (*Fox* II, 1882, 89–90).

In 1849 Burnard started work on a statue commemorating the Cornish explorer Richard Lander, to be placed on a Doric column in Truro (**14**). It was described soon after its completion in 1852: 'The figure is clad in loose trowsers and paletot, or frock coat, and holds a palm branch in one hand, while pointing with a scroll in the other, to a map of the Niger. The countenance in place of staring into indefinite space or vacancy, is directed towards the spectators in front' (*Builder*, 1852, 205). This was followed by a second public statue honouring Ebenezer Elliott, 'the Corn-Law Rhymer', erected in Sheffield in 1854 (**15**). Burnard seems to have admired Elliott and to have been sympathetic to his radical political views. He published a poem lamenting Elliott's death (*The West Briton*, 30 Jan 1852, cited by *Martin* 1978, 49) and wrote to a member of the Elliott statue committee of his 'love for the poet of the poor' (*Burnard/Fowler*, cited by *Martin* 1978, 48–9). Between 1847 and 1873 Burnard was engaged chiefly in carving portrait busts and he portrayed many contemporary celebrities including Harriet Beecher Stowe, William Makepeace Thackeray, Richard Cobden, John Bright and W E Gladstone (**27, 33, 34, 35, 38**).

In his 50s Burnard seems to have lost the will to continue his career as a sculptor. He became discontented and unsettled, left his wife, drank heavily and neglected his work. His unhappiness was caused, or perhaps compounded, by the death of his youngest daughter, Lottie, of scarlet fever in March 1870. She was buried with her uncle, a little-known artist called Tom Nicholson, and Burnard carved an unusual headstone with profile portraits for their grave (11). Finally, Burnard left his London studio and returned to Cornwall. There he wandered the countryside, staying with old friends and neighbours, to whom he presented drawings and poems in return for hospitality, and writing political lampoons and verses for local newspapers. For some months in 1875–6 he lodged with the Dawes family at Crow's Nest, St Cleer, near Liskeard and an album of his drawings and poetry survives in family hands (*Dawes Album*). Burnard died at Redruth workhouse on 27 November 1878 of a heart and kidney complaint and was buried in Camborne churchyard. The only mourners are said to have been masons who were working at the church. His son, Thomas, was also a sculptor and exhibited at the RA from 1868 onwards, when he showed a bust of Sir Charles Lemon.

Although Burnard has been little studied nationally by sculpture historians, he is celebrated as a talented and colourful local figure in his native Cornwall. One early-20th-century local historian wrote of him, 'Burnard was cast in such an ample mould that he rarely failed to arrest attention: tall, broad-shouldered, well-knit, with limbs of a giant, and the flashing eye of a man who knows the heart of humanity. He was the ideal of physical perfection. Had he cared he could have carved for himself a niche in the temple of fame by the side of the country's greatest sculptors' (*Davey* 1910, cited by *Martin* 1978, 45). In 1954, Camborne Old Cornwall Society erected a headstone of local Delabole slate over his previously unmarked grave, and in 1968 the 150th anniversary of his birth was celebrated with a memorial service at Altarnun and a plaque was erected at his birthplace. Ten years later an account of his life, which stresses the importance of his Cornish roots, was published by Mary Martin.

EH

Literary References: *Palgrave* 1866, 225; *Fox* II, 1882, 89–90, 94–5, 109; *DNB* VII, 1886, 382–3; *Gunnis* 1968, 71; RG/JP, 2, 216–7; *Martin* 1978, *passim*; *Read* 1982, 50–2, 69; *ODNB* (Burnard and Peach)

Archival References: GPC

Additional Manuscript Sources: *Dawes Album* (including drawings and poetry, see *Martin* 1978 reprs 57–68)

Miscellaneous Drawings: 'Hieraspistes: A Defence of the Ministry of the Church of England' (1831) and pencil portraits of Betty Venning (1876), Emily Herring, John Vosper, Emma Bath, Edward Nicholls Vosper, William Bickford Smith, Henry Richards and Jane Richards, various private colls, Cornwall; portraits of Rev William Rowe and unidentified gentleman, Royal Cornwall Museum, Truro (*Martin* 1978, reprs 45–6).

Portraits of the sculptor: self-portraits, medallions (**59, 68**); self-portrait pencil drawing, *Dawes Album* (*Martin* 1978, frontispiece)

No.	Date	Subject		Location		Literature
Funerary Monuments						
1.	1830	Grace Burnard	sl	Royal Cornwall Museum, Truro		*Martin* 1978, 19, 58 (repr 7)
2.	1832	George and Elizabeth Burnard (the sculptor's grandparents)	sl	Altarnun, Cornwall, churchyard		*Martin* 1978, 19, 58 (repr 9)
3.	†1833	Alice and Elizabeth Webb	sl	Bodmin, Cornwall	S	*Martin* 1978, 19, 58 (repr 12)
4.	1833	Arthur Peter, tombstone		North Hill, Cornwall, churchyard		*Martin* 1978, 19, 58 (repr 30)
5.	1833	James Whitburn	sl	Gwennap, Cornwall		*Martin* 1978, 58 (repr 36)
6.	†1835	Elizabeth Willcocks		Fowey, Cornwall	S	*Martin* 1978, 26, 58 (repr 33)
7.	†1854	Rev Robert Newton		Wesley Chapel, City Road, London	S	*Gunnis* 1968, 71; *Martin* 1978, 59; C Lib (repr)
8.	†1858	Michael Williams		Gwennap, Cornwall		*Martin* 1978, 60 (repr 56)
9.	?1858	Rev Hugh Rogers		Camborne, Cornwall	S	*Gunnis* 1968, 71; *Martin* 1978, 44, 59 (repr 69)
10.	?1868	Dr George Smith		Wesley Chapel, Camborne, Cornwall		*Martin* 1978, 44, 59 (repr 47)
11.	1870	Lottie Burnard and Tom Nicholson		St Nicholas, Broadway, Weymouth, churchyard		*Martin* 1978, 57, 59 (repr)
12.	nd	Robert Nicholl, tombstone		Altarnun, Cornwall, churchyard		*Martin* 1978, 60
Statues						
13.	1843	Contentment, an unfinished group		[Exhib Royal Cornwall Polytechnic Soc, Falmouth, silver medal]; untraced		*Martin* 1978, 46–7, 58
14.	1849–1852	Richard Lander		Lemon Street, Truro, Cornwall (on Doric column)		*Builder* 1852, 205; Pevsner, *Cornwall*, 1970, 233; *Ormond* 1973, 254; *Martin* 1978, 27–8, 59 (repr 40–42)
15.	1854	Ebenezer Elliott		[Market Square, Sheffield]; Weston Park, Sheffield, W R Yorks		*Builder*, 1854, 467; *Martin* 1978, 28, 32, 48–9, 59 (repr 48–9)
Busts						
16.	1847	Albert Edward, Prince of Wales (later King Edward VII)	m	Royal Cornwall Polytechnic Soc, Falmouth		*AU*, 1848, 179–80; *Graves* I, 1905–6, 351; *Martin* 1978, 26–7, 43, 58 (repr 37)
17.	1847	Dr Carlyon	m	Council chamber, Truro, Cornwall		*Martin* 1978, 58
18.	1848	A child		[Exhib RA, London, 1431]; untraced		*Graves* I, 1905–6, 351
19.	1849	John Crouch Adams	b	Royal Astronomical Soc		*Graves* I, 1905–6, 351; *Martin* 1978, 58 (repr 50)
20.	1849	Sir Charles Lemon		[Exhib RA, London, 1296]; untraced		*Graves* I, 1905–6, 351
21.	1850	General Lord Gough		Untraced		*DNB*, VII, 1886, 382; *Martin* 1978, 58
22.	1850	George Greenough	m	Geological Museum, London		*Martin* 1978, 58 (repr 53)
23.	1851	Charles William Peach		[Exhib Royal Cornwall Polytechnic Soc, Falmouth]; untraced		*Graves* I, 1905–6, 351; *Martin* 1978, 58
24.	1851	Ludwig van Beethoven		[Exhib RA, London, 1352]; untraced		*Graves* I, 1905–6, 351; *Martin* 1978, 59
25.	1851	The Prince of Peace		[Gt Exhib]; untraced		*Gunnis* 1968, 71; *Martin* 1978, 58
26.	1852	Lajos Kossuth		[Exhib Royal Cornwall Polytechnic Soc, Falmouth]; untraced		*Martin* 1978, 59
27.	1853	Harriet Beecher Stowe		[Intended for the Crystal Palace, presented to Committee of the British and Foreign Anti-Slavery Soc by the Anti-Slavery cause]; untraced		*Martin* 1978, 32, 59
28.	1855	Gerald Massey		[Exhib RA, London, 1515]; untraced (Royal Cornwall Falmouth Soc, Falmouth)		*Graves* I, 1905–6, 351

29.	1855	Professor Edward Forbes	m	Douglas, Isle of Man Other versions: Geological Museum, London, copy by I C Lough (?)		*Graves* I, 1905–6, 351; *Martin* 1978, 59 (repr 52)
30.	1858	Ebenezer Elliott (two versions)	p	Rotherham Public Library, W R Yorks		*Graves* I, 1905–6, 351; *Martin* 1978, 32; GPC
31.	1858	James Montgomery		[Exhib RA, London, 1289]; untraced		*Graves* I, 1905–6, 351
32.	1866	Erwin Harvey Wadge Payment(s): £105		[Bought by the west country miners of Lewannick]; untraced		*Martin* 1978, 59
33.	1866	Richard Cobden, unfinished	m	[Exhib RA, London, 906]; untraced		*Graves* I, 1905–6, 351; *Laperriere* 1, 1991, 229
34.	1867	William Makepeace Thackeray	m	[Cottonian Museum, Plymouth Library, Devon]; untraced Other versions: NPG 738, Bodelwyddan		*DNB*, VII, 1886, 383; *Graves* I, 1905–6, 351; *Ormond*, 1973, 462 (pl 919); *Martin* 1978, 59 (repr 54)
35.	1869	John Bright	m	[Exhib RA, London, 1287]; untraced		*Graves* I, 1905–6, 351; www.chain.org.uk
36.	1871	C P Villiers MP		Manchester Town Hall, Lancs	SD	*Graves* I, 1905–6, 351; C Lib (repr)
37.	1871	John Benjamin Smith	m	[Exhib RA, London, 1314]; untraced		*Graves* I, 1905–6, 351
38.	1871	William Ewart Gladstone	m	[Exhib RA, London, 1310]; untraced		*Graves* I, 1905–6, 351
39.	1873	Albert Edward, Prince of Wales	m	Truro Town Hall, Cornwall		*Gunnis* 1968, 71
40.	1873	E A Leatham MP		[Exhib RA, London, 1550]; untraced		*Graves* I, 1905–6, 351
41.	nd	Admiral Boscawen (? after a plaster model by Roubiliac)	m	[coll Earl of Falmouth]; untraced		*Martin* 1978, 29, 60
42.	nd	Charles Buller		Untraced		*Martin* 1978, 47, 60
43.	nd	Charles Dickens		Untraced		*Martin* 1978, 60
44.	nd	Dr William Borlase	p	Royal Cornwall Museum, Truro		*Martin* 1978, 60 (repr 44)
45.	nd	Hon Mrs Tremayne		Untraced		*Martin* 1978, 60
46.	nd	Joseph Thomas Treffry		Place House, Fowey, Cornwall		*Martin* 1978, 60 (repr 35)
47.	nd	Michael Williams		Untraced		*Martin* 1978, 60
48.	nd	Richard Trevithick	m	Royal Cornwall Museum, Truro		*Martin* 1978, 60 (repr 39)
Architectural Sculpture						
49.	1832–1833	Decorative carving		Place House, Fowey, Cornwall		*Martin* 1978, 24–6 (repr 34)
50.	c1833	Three shields		National Schools, Tywardreath, Cornwall		*Martin* 1978, 60 (repr 31)
51.	1836	John Wesley, relief portrait	s	Old Methodist chapel, Penpont, Altarnun, Cornwall Other versions: copy, chapel of Lis Escop, Truro, Cornwall	D	*Martin* 1978, 15, 58, 60 (repr 4)
Reliefs						
52.	c1830	James Montgomery, cameo		Wesley Cottage, Trewint, Cornwall		*Martin* 1978, 15 (repr 6)
53.	1831	Homer, profile head	sl	Royal Cornwall Polytechnic Soc, Falmouth		*Martin* 1978, 19–20, 58 (repr 26)
54.	1834	Laocoon and his sons	sl	Royal Cornwall Polytechnic Soc, Falmouth		*Martin* 1978, 20, 21, 58 (repr 27)
55.	1836	Christ bearing the cross	sl	Royal Cornwall Polytechnic Soc, Falmouth		*Martin* 1978, 20, 58
56.	1837	Jupiter and Thetis	sl	Royal Cornwall Polytechnic Soc, Falmouth		*Martin* 1978, 20, 58
57.	c1840	A sow and her family	sl	Untraced		*Martin* 1978, 20, 58
58.	1841	Unidentified subjects, three portrait medallions	m	[Exhib Royal Cornwall Polytechnic Soc, Falmouth]; untraced		*DNB*, VII, 1886, 382; *Martin* 1978, 58
59.	c1850	Nevil Northey Burnard, self-portrait, medallion		Untraced (perhaps at Penpont House, Brecknock)		*Martin* 1978 (repr 51)
60.	1851	Mary Kelynack, portrait medallion		[Exhib Royal Cornwall Polytechnic Soc, Falmouth]; untraced		*Martin* 1978, 58
61.	1855	Father Gavazzi, portrait medallion		[Exhib Royal Cornwall Polytechnic Soc, Falmouth]; untraced		*Martin* 1978, 59
62.	1875	Olive Louise Burnard, portrait medallion		(coll Lady Sayer)		*Martin* 1978, 59 (repr 55)
63.	nd	Caricature profile of a man in medieval hat and hood	sl	Royal Cornwall Museum, Truro		*Martin* 1978, 23, 60 (repr 18)
64.	nd	Catherine Enys, portrait medallion	m	Royal Cornwall Museum, Truro		*Martin* 1978, 60 (repr 38)
65.	nd	Elizabeth Heard, portrait medallion		Private coll, Truro		*Martin* 1978, 60
66.	nd	J S Enys, portrait medallion	p	Untraced		*Martin* 1978, 60
67.	nd	Mr Benallack, portrait medallion		Untraced		*Martin* 1978, 60
68.	nd	Nevil Northey Burnard, self-portrait, medallion	p	Royal Cornwall Museum, Truro		*Martin* 1978, 60 (repr 11)
69.	nd	The sculptor's mother, portrait medallion	p	Royal Cornwall Museum, Truro		*Martin* 1978, 60 (repr 10)
Miscellaneous						
70.	nd	Hand of Richard Cobden	m	[Commissioned for the Fine Art Galleries Brighton, by John Bright]; untraced		*Martin* 1978, 32, 60
71.	nd	The schoolmistress	sl	[coll F R Todd, of Trebartha Hall]; untraced		*Martin* 1978, 60

BURNELL, Thomas and Sons, of London fl 1760–1821

The firm is thought to have comprised Thomas Burnell, his son Henry and the latter's son, Thomas. The elder Thomas was born about 1740, the son of John Burnell 'citizen and joiner' and was apprenticed to Edward Anderson in 1754. He was made free of the Masons' Company on 1 April 1762 and became Master in 1783. He was living in Wine Office Court, Fleet Street, London in 1774, when his name appeared in the apprenticeship binding book. His grandson, who was apprenticed to his father, Henry, gained his freedom by patrimony on 10 November 1795. In the late-18th century they were joined by a George Burnell, who had taken up his freedom in 1772.

The family may have been kinsmen of John Burnell, an alderman who served as Lord Mayor of London in 1788, since on his death in 1790 the *Gentleman's Magazine* announced 'His fortune, which is 60,000l. in the funds and Middlesex houses goes to his nephews, Mr. Tibbs and Mr. Burnell, the mason' (*GM* 1790, i, 89). Thomas later attracted press attention through his acquaintance with Mary Anne Clarke, the colourful mistress of Frederick, Duke of York. One account of her life, published many years later, claims that as a young woman she lived in a house belonging to Burnell and in 1791 eloped with one of his apprentices (*The News*, 5 February 1819, cited by RG/JP 2, 217–8).

On 9 May 1792 Thomas was appointed mason to the Inner Temple. His grandson Thomas succeeded him in the post and was employed under the architect James Savage on the restoration of the Temple Church. The project's soaring costs led to an inquiry and on 30 April 1841 the Committee of Members resolved that 'Mr. Burnell be discharged from his present employment as Mason at the Temple Church' (*Gunnis* 1968, 72).

Gunnis noted that monuments executed by the firm in the 18th century have 'finely cut and beautifully finished details' (*Gunnis* 1968, 72). The two most important examples are both in Northants. The D'Anvers family's monument at Culworth, which is 16 feet high, takes the form of a sarcophagus with a cherub standing on either side (4). That commemorating John Blencowe at Marston St Lawrence has a finely executed urn (2).

An architect called Thomas Burnell who trained under **Sir Robert Taylor** exhibited architectural drawings at the Royal Academy in 1802 and 1806 and was still practising as an architect in Chancery Lane in 1814. He was probably a kinsman.

Literary References: *Gunnis* 1968, 72; *Colvin* 1995, 192

Archival References: Masons' Co, Freemen, fols 7, 62; Court Book, 1751–96 (3 Oct 1754, 7 Aug 1772, 14 June 1783); Apprentice binding book (2)

Funerary Monuments

1.	†1760	Samuel Baldwin	St Leonards, Bucks	S	*Gunnis* 1968, 72
2.	†1777	John Blencowe	Marston St Lawrence, Northants	S	Pevsner, *Northants*, 1973, 302
3.	1783	Benjamin Wheeler	Ewelme, Oxon	S	*Gunnis* 1968, 72
4.	?1790	D'Anvers family	Culworth, Northants	S	Pevsner, *Northants*, 1973, 172
5.	†1794	Robert Gosling	Langley Marish, Bucks	S	Pevsner, *Bucks*, 1994, 639
6.	?1795	Major Richard Boorn	Romsey, Hants	S	*Gunnis* 1968, 72
7.	?1797	Stephen Wright	St Paul, Hammersmith, London	S	*Gunnis* 1968, 72
8.	?1807	Captain John Barfott	St Matthias, Poplar, London	S	*Gunnis* 1968, 72
9.	?1821	Joseph Peel	Burton-on-Trent, Staffs	S	*Gunnis* 1968, 72

BURNELL, Thomas, of London fl 1733–49

It has not been possible to discover whether this sculptor, who signs two monuments, was related to the family of the same name who were active in London between 1761 and 1841.

Literary References: *Gunnis* 1968, 62

Funerary Monuments

1.	?1733	Elinor Phillips	Haverfordwest, Pembrokes	S	*Gunnis* 1968, 72
2.	†1749	John Warden (†1730) and his wife, Hopestill	Cuckfield, Sussex	S	*Gunnis* 1968, 72

BURNETT, Benjamin, of Bungay fl 1806–11

In April 1806 'Benjamin Burnett, Marble and Stone Mason, Halesworth' advertised that he had 'taken the Stock in Trade of Mr B Gosling, Bungay' and intended to continue his business supplying 'Marble and Stone Chimneypieces, Monuments, Tombs, Grave-stones, Carn Floors &c &c' (*Norfolk Mercury*, 5 April 1806). In August 1809 he announced that he had purchased 'a large quantity of British Marbles from the Babicombe Quarry, in the possession of Mr J. P. Hubbard' and that he had it in his power to 'furnish Monuments, Chimney-Pieces, Slabs, Tables . . .' (*Norfolk Chronicle*, 26 August 1809). He must subsequently have become bankrupt for on 6 July 1811 the *Norwich Mercury* notified the public that he had 'assigned all his Estate and Effects to Philip L. Powell, Esq. and Charles Brightly, Gent. in trust for the benefit of his Creditors'. Shortly afterwards another advertisement announced that Burnett and **De Carle** 'had entered into Partnership'. It is not clear which De Carle this was.

Archival References: RG/JP, 2, 217v

BURNETT, Francis *c*1810–

Burnett was born in Dublin about 1810. He was employed by **Thomas Kirk** for some years but from about 1835 worked on his own in Paradise Row and then Phibsborough Road. He exhibited at the Royal Hibernian Academy, 1829–56, showing figures, reliefs and portrait busts, including two of his former master (7, 8) His statue of *The young musician*, first exhibited in 1850, was later shown at the Dublin International Exhibition of 1853 and another version of the subject was exhibited in 1856 (4). Burnett's younger brother, William Burnett, who was born about 1819, exhibited a bust of Archbishop Murray at the RHA in 1852.

Literary References: *Strickland* 1, 1913, 130

Statues

1.	1843	Child at play	m	[Exhib RHA, Dublin, 667]; untraced	*Stewart* I, 1985, 101
2.	1843	Child at play, small figure		[Awarded as a prize by the Royal Irish Art Union to Archdeacon Magee of Limerick]; untraced	*Strickland* I, 1913, 130
3.	1845	The expulsion	m	[Exhib RHA, Dublin, 435]; untraced	*Stewart* I, 1985, 101
4.	1850	The young musician	s	[Exhib RHA, Dublin, 341]; untraced Other versions: Exhib RHA, Dublin, 1856, 397	*Stewart* I, 1985, 101

Busts

5.	1829	Rev Mr Bardin	m	[Exhib RHA, Dublin, 285]; untraced	*Stewart* I, 1985, 101
6.	1836	Unidentified gentleman		[Exhib RHA, Dublin, 251]; untraced	*Stewart* I, 1985, 101

7.	1837	Thomas Kirk		[Exhib RHA, Dublin, 258]; untraced		*Stewart* I, 1985, 101
8.	1838	Thomas Kirk RHA, colossal		[Exhib RHA, Dublin, 227]; untraced		*Stewart* I, 1985, 101
9.	1840	Miss E Kirk		[Exhib RHA, Dublin, 350]; untraced		*Stewart* I, 1985, 101
Reliefs						
10.	1841	Arthur, 1st Duke of Wellington	m	[Exhib RHA, Dublin, 411]; untraced		*Stewart* I, 1985, 101
11.	1847	The mourner	m	[Exhib RHA, Dublin, 457]; untraced		*Stewart* I, 1985, 101
Miscellaneous						
12.	1842	Innocence, model		[Exhib RHA, Dublin, 477]; untraced		*Stewart* I, 1985, 101
13.	1846	The first lesson		[Exhib RHA, Dublin, 490]; untraced		*Stewart* I, 1985, 101

BURNS fl *c*1800?

Robert Adam's sale of 1818 included 'ten tablets and parts of friezes modelled by Burns', followed by 'thirteen ditto by Adam, Rose and Burn [sic]' (**1**).

Literary References: *Gunnis* 1968, 72

Auction References: Adam 1818, 1, lots 3–4

Architectural Sculpture

1.	nd	'Ten tablets and parts of friezes' and several other pieces	[Adam sale 1818, lot 3, 4]; untraced	Sale cat

BURT, John, of Callington fl 1753

The large ledger commemorating Ann Holiday has a relief of a woman kneeling by a prayer-desk.

Funerary Monuments

1.	?1753	Ann Holiday, ledger stone	sl	Callington, Cornwall	S	Pevsner, *Cornwall*, 1970, 49

BURTON fl 1786

Gunnis notes that he was probably a local craftsman and that his ledger to Ann Wigley has a fine coat of arms and mantling.

Funerary Monuments

1.	?1786	Ann Wigley, ledger stone	Scraptoft, Leics	S	*Gunnis* 1968, 72

BURTON, William

A 'modeller and sculptor', his premises were in St Alkmund's churchyard, Derby. (Inf. Maxwell Craven of Derby Museum and Art Gallery)

BUSHNELL, John 1636–1701

The first English sculptor to handle the Italian Baroque style with confidence, he was dismissed by Horace Walpole as 'an admired statuary in his own time, but only memorable to us by a capricious character' (*Anecdotes* III, 1782, 258). Many of the anecdotes noted below derive from Vertue's accounts.

He was the son of Richard Bushnell, a plumber, and his wife, Mary, and was baptised at St Andrew, Holborn on 22 April 1636. He was apprenticed to **Thomas Burman**, but before his seven-year term was completed, he was trapped by his master into marrying a servant Burman had himself seduced. When Burman sent him down to the country in 1656 or 1657 to supervise the erection of a monument Bushnell seized his chance to escape, taking with him £15 of his master's money. He fled to the Continent and, according to Bushnell's sons, remained there for at least ten years.

He apparently stayed two years in France and then posed as a labourer in Rome, Germany and several Flemish cities, thereby arousing astonishment by his skill in carving. He was certainly in Venice by the autumn of 1663, assisting with an ambitious project supervised by a Flemish master, Giusto de Corte, the monument to General Alvise Mocenigo, which fills the west end of S. Lazzaro dei Mendicanti (**1**). Bushnell was responsible for two elaborate reliefs depicting Mocenigo's victories over the Turks in 1650. Payments totalling 2,500 ducats, a considerable sum, were made to Giovanni Businelli 'inglese scultore' between October 1663 and May 1665.

A visiting English aristocrat is said to have persuaded Bushnell to return home, *c*1667, and he set up in Hatton Garden. Soon after, he was presented to King Charles II and, despite Bushnell's arrogance, which irritated courtiers from the outset, the King received him with courtesy and privately commissioned plaster statues of himself and his father, perhaps for the palace of Whitehall, but long missing (**14**). Among other untraced works Vertue records a marble statue of Mark Antony (**15**), his first work after returning to London, and a bust of William Talman with an exaggerated *contrapposto* pose, a long, feminine neck and hair arranged in an unusual manner (**24**).

Early in 1669, at a time when Bushnell was short of work, he was commissioned by Sir Robert Gayer, the Sheriff of Buckinghamshire, to carve three colossal works of Portland stone for his gardens at Stoke Poges (**20**). When the blocks arrived they were too large for the Hatton Garden workshop, so he found another studio in Whitehall and, when that proved inadequate, a third in Wandsworth. Practical problems and the lure of a prestigious public commission prevented Bushnell from completing within the stipulated two years and in due course led to a protracted and acrimonious court action, the first of several legal wrangles involving the sculptor.

The rival contract was for statues of three Stuart kings and Queen Elizabeth I for Temple Bar (**18**). He seized the opportunity to show his knowledge of recent developments in Roman sculpture and the figures, in modified classical garb, turn in an exaggerated manner, their cloaks falling into strong diagonal folds. In the same year he made the effigy for the Duke of Albemarle's state funeral in Westminster Abbey, executing the face and hands in wax and the rest in plaster (**26**).

In 1670–1 he carved statues of Charles I and Charles II for the Cornhill front of the Royal Exchange (**17**), and received £300 through **Thomas Cartwright**, who supervised the rebuilding project after the Great Fire of 1666, for 'Setting up the statues of the two kings' (MC, GR, 3, 1669–76, 25 January 1672/3). Both figures are dressed *all'antica*, but with long hair and moustache, and Charles I's attitude, hand on breast, is intended to draw attention to his sufferings. The statues have twisting poses and the influence of Bernini is apparent also in their finish: the faces, hands and feet bear chisel marks in imitation of the textural surface of Bernini's St Longinus, in St Peter's, Rome. Bushnell also supplied a statue of the Exchange's founder Sir Thomas Gresham for the south entrance, modelled on a figure by an unknown sculptor that had survived the Fire (**16**). Vertue noted that the model for the head was of terracotta and suggested that **Edward Pearce** carved the statue. Bushnell evidently thought that he had the contract also for the line of Royal statues to be sited in niches in the inner courtyard, for he began work on six or seven, including Edward VI, Queen Mary I, Queen Elizabeth I, King James I, King Charles I and II (**18**). He then discovered that another sculptor, **C G Cibber**, had been appointed to carve some of the kings and refused to proceed further.

The size of Bushnell's practice in commemorative monuments cannot be fully gauged since none is signed and documentation is scant, but Vertue says that he provided many and he lists six. One of the earliest, to Abraham Cowley, 1674, in Westminster Abbey (**3**), an urn on a pedestal, was paid for by the Duke of Buckingham. A more ambitious monument, to William and Lady Jane Ashburnham (**5**), is a tableau framed by a curtained *baldacchino*; the disconsolate husband kneels, his arm outstretched towards his dying wife, who is crowned by a cherub with the wreath of immortality. Flanking the tomb chest are four balusters carrying emblematic objects. Gunnis notes that there is a brief reference to Bushnell and the black marble background in the Ashburnham archives. The reclining figure of Jane Ashburnham provided a pattern for two wall monuments erected in 1676, to Dame Mary May (raised for herself) and to Elizabeth, Lady Myddelton (**6**, **7**). For the latter, a painted portrait was sent up to London 'for Bushnell the stone-cutter to draw a pattern'. Among his wall-memorials with portrait busts were one to Sir Thomas and Lady Myddelton, 1676 (**8**), and another to Mrs Grew, †1685 (**10**).

A more inventive composition is the monument to Viscount Mordaunt (**4**), a standing effigy with a swaggering pose, the head dramatically turned to the right and counterbalanced by a swirling, deeply undercut cloak draping the torso. As with the Ashburnham (**5**), Bushnell makes use of four short, flanking balusters here supporting inscription tablets, a coronet and gauntlets emphasising Mordaunt's illustrious ancestry. In 1688 the sculptor was paid for part-demolishing the monument so that Lady Mordaunt's body could be interred with her husband (Fulham Ch W Accts, 1668). Another unusual work was the monument to Sir Palmes Fairborne, Governor of Tangiers, in Westminster Abbey (**9**), an inscribed pedestal, originally flanked by obelisks supporting profile medallions of Turkish subjects and reliefs of the siege of Tangiers, where Fairborne was killed. Bushnell's last known tomb, raised to the Earl of Thomond at Great Billing by his widow in 1700, is an anachronistic composition (**11**). Kneeling effigies of the Thomonds and two children, memorable for their crude faces and stocky build, lean over a relief tablet carved with profile representations of five younger children. Below is a tomb chest of marked refinement.

Bushnell was an arrogant man, who regarded all English rivals as inferiors and responded to any slight on his reputation. When some fellow sculptors taunted him by declaring that he could not model a naked statue, Bushnell proceeded to make one of Alexander the Great (**13**), which Vertue saw many years later: he thought the body and limbs remarkably beautiful but the head, hands and feet ill-formed. On another occasion Bushnell heard courtiers discussing the wooden horse of Troy and declaring it would be impossible to construct such a thing. Again he could not resist proving his superiority and set about making a horse of wood covered in plaster, of such a size that the head alone was large enough to contain a table where twelve men might sit. When it was practically finished a sudden gale blew it over and smashed it. Two vintners, who had made an agreement with the sculptor to use the horse as a tavern, offered to pay for its re-creation after the gale, but Bushnell had not the heart to begin again, though the failed project lost him £500.

Bushnell had property interests which brought considerable anxiety and finally unbalanced him. In 1678 he leased a house at Goose Green, Wandsworth, which he extended at his own expense. Some years later a former owner emerged and claimed the building, precipitating a court action. In 1685 he took another lease on a large property at the junction of Tyburn Lane and Piccadilly, near Hyde Park, and again faced legal proceedings since he mortgaged the lease for a loan of £200 and failed to pay the interest. Bushnell's failure to maintain yet another dwelling at Thorndon, near Canterbury, led to a case at the Court of Chancery and finally, in 1690, he inherited a home at Stratfield Mortimer, near Reading, Berks, from a godfather, but under such complex terms that further litigation dogged his last years. Another venture, a scheme to import coal to London, failed, bringing near ruin.

He died in the Hyde Park house of 'gout of the stomach' in May 1701 and was buried at St Mary, Paddington, his occupation being recorded in the parish register as 'image-maker'. His two sons, John (who was made free of the Masons' Company by patrimony in 1719) and and a younger boy, Richard (b 1679), were still living in the house in the 1720s, refusing entry to visitors and even destroying their father's work since they felt it was insufficiently appreciated. Vertue managed to get in, however, and was surprised to see the staircase and floors still uninstalled. In Bushnell's studio he noted several marble statues and an equestrian figure of Charles II in plaster, intended for casting in bronze, which he considered spirited but not graceful (**21**). The statue of Alexander (**13**) and Talman's bust (**24**) were still intact and he saw also the abandoned Royal Exchange figures in various stages of completion (**17**). Apparently their poses were unconvincing and the legs ill-carved. Vertue also found evidence that Bushnell worked as a painter, for against one wall was a large triumphal scene painted on cloth, but in such a dilapidated state that its quality could not be assessed.

Bushnell's full-blown baroque style must have been a revelation to practitioners who had not travelled abroad. His dramatic use of torsion, diagonals and undercutting all had an impact on English sculpture. Whinney suggests that he may also have popularised a wider range of materials, drawing attention to the use of wax for the face and hands of Albemarle's effigy and plaster for the body. Critics from the 18th century onwards have agreed that his sculpture is often crude and pretentious by comparison with contemporary Continental work and his standing figures tend to be ill-balanced.

IR

Literary References: *Vertue* I, 29, 86–7, 90, 128–9; II, 8, 9; IV, 152; *Esdaile* 1926–7, 21–45; *Whinney* 1988, 95–102; *Grove* 5, 293–4 (Physick); *Gibson* 1997 (1), 168–71, 371–72, 376; *Gibson* 1997 (2), 138–173; *Gibson* 2001, 49–60; *Ward-Jackson* 2003, 415; *ODNB* (Gibson)

Archival References: PR, St Martin-in-the-Fields, 1685, WCA F 412; Hay Hill, St Martin-in-the-Fields, 1686, F 412; 1686, Hyde Park Road, 1686, F 413; Tyburn Lane, St Martin-in-the-Fields, 1691, F 419; Masons' Co, *Freemen*, 1719 (John Bushnell)

Wills: PROB 6/78, fol 93: PROB 6/87, fol 45; PROB 6/107, fol 52v

Miscellaneous Drawings: Design for a garlanded urn surrounded by the royal crown (Bodleian, Radcliffe) b.20, no 169 (f.171), inscribed in William Talman's hand 'Bushnell fect'

Funerary Monuments

1.	1663–1665	General Alvise Mocenigo, 'Siege of Martinengo' and 'Battle of Paros', reliefs		S Lazzaro dei Mendicanti, Venice	*Borean*, 1999 (repr)
2.	†1669	Elizabeth Pepys		St Olave, Hart St, City of London Other versions: plaster cast of the bust, NPG 4824, unsigned	*Whinney* 1988, 101
3.	1674	Abraham Cowley (†1667)		Westminster Abbey, London, south transept	*Dart* 1, 1723, 88–9 (repr)
4.	†1675	John, Viscount Mordaunt of Avalon Payment(s): £400		All Saints, Fulham, London	*Whinney*, 1988, 97–98 (repr)
5.	1675	William and Lady Jane (†*c*1669) Ashburnham		Ashburnham, Sussex	*Gibson* 2001, 55–6 (repr)
6.	1676	Dame Mary May (†1681) Drawing(s): BM Add MS 5676, f.33, author unknown		Mid-Lavant, Sussex	*Bayley* 1969, 1–11 (repr); *Whinney* 1988, 100 (repr)
7.	1676	Elizabeth, Lady Myddelton (†1675)		Chirk, Denbighs	*Myddelton* 1931, 119; *Whinney* 1988, 101; C Lib (repr)
8.	1676	Sir Thomas and Lady Myddelton		Chirk, Denbighs	*Whinney* 1988, 101
9.	†1680	Sir Palmes Fairborne		Westminster Abbey, London, nave	*Dart* 2, 1723, 87–9 (repr)
10.	†1685	Mrs Grew		[Christ Church, Newgate St, City of London]; untraced	*Whinney* 1988, 101
11.	1700	Henry, 6th Earl of Thomond (†1691) and family		Great Billing, Northants	*Whinney* 1988, 101 (repr)

Statues

12.	?*c*1667	St Peter and St Paul		[Somerset House, London, chapel]; untraced	*Gunnis* 1968, 74
13.	?*c*1670	Alexander the Great		[Bushnell's studio, *c* 1721]; untraced	*Vertue* I, 86; II, 8
14.	pre-1670	King Charles I, King Charles II	p	[Unknown royal palace]; untraced	*Vertue* II, 8
15.	pre-1670	Mark Antony	m	[Unknown merchant's house, *c*1721]; untraced	*Vertue* I, 90
16.	1670	Sir Thomas Gresham Payment(s): £75		[Second Royal Exchange, London, Cornhill front]; CL Coll, Central Criminal Court, Old Bailey, City of London, antechamber, acc no 965	*Vertue* I, 106; *Knight* 1986, 332; *Gibson* 1997 (2), 147–8 (repr); *Ward-Jackson* 2003, 67–8
17.	1670–1671	King Charles I and King Charles II Payment(s): £300	s	[Second Royal Exchange, London, Cornhill front]; Central Criminal Court (Old Bailey), City of London, antechamber	*Knight* 1986, 332; *Gibson* 1997, 147–8 (repr); *Ward-Jackson* 2003, 68–70 (repr)
18.	1670–1671	Queen Elizabeth I, King James I, King Charles I, King Charles II Payment(s): £440	s	Temple Bar, London	Guildhall restoration, *passim*; *Gibson* 2001, 57–8 (repr); *Ward-Jackson* 2003, xv
19.	*c*1671	Six or seven English sovereigns for the Royal Exchange	m	[Bushnell's studio, *c*1721]; untraced	*Vertue* II, 8
20.	1669–1675	Aeneas and Anchises, Samson with his lion, David, with pedestals Payment(s): £125	s	[Stoke Poges, Bucks, gardens]; untraced	*Gibson* 2001, 49–60; *Gibson* 2002, 49–60
21.	1685	King Charles II (or King James II)	s	[Southwark Town Hall, London, until 1793]; untraced	Corp of London Bridge House Estates Committee Accts, 12 June 1686, Guildhall MS, 60.4; *Gibson* 1997 (1), 161; *Cavavagh* 2007 (lost or removed works)
22.	pre-1685	King Charles II on horseback	p	[Bushnell's studio, *c*1721]; untraced	*Vertue* II, 8
23.	?1685–1688	King James II		Crawford Municipal Art Gallery, Cork	*Murray* 1991, 139

Busts

24.	nd	William Talman	m	[Bushnell's studio, *c*1721]; untraced	*Vertue* I, 129; II, 8; *Wren Soc* XVII, 8

Architectural Sculpture

25.	1701	Two marble frames, possibly for a marble buffet room Payment(s): £7 10s		[Drayton House, Northants]; untraced	Drayton Archive MM/A/442

Miscellaneous

26.	1670	General George Monck, 1st Duke of Albemarle (funeral effigy)	wp	Westminster Abbey, Chapter Library (mask only)	*Vertue* I, 86; *Whinney* 1988, 101

BUSHROD, William, of Weymouth fl *c*1791

The son of H Bushrod of Weymouth, mason, he signs a large marble tablet at Maiden Newton, Dorset.

Literary References: *Gunnis* 1968, 74

Funerary Monuments

1.	?1791	Charlotte Chaning	Maiden Newton, Dorset	S	*Gunnis* 1968, 74

BUSSELL, William, of Gloucester fl 1826–47

Funerary Monuments

1.	†1826	Samuel Commeline	Hempsted, Glos	S	Pevsner, *Glos: Vale & Forest of Dean*, 1976, 268
2.	*c*1830	Sophia Morris	Kidwelly, Carmarthen	S	*Dale-Jones and Lloyd* 1989, 46
3.	†1847	Charles Owen Cambridge	Whitminster, Glos	S	Pevsner, *Glos: Vale & Forest of Dean*, 1976, 403
4.	nd	Unidentified subject, tablet	Christ Church, Gloucester	S	Pevsner, *Glos: Vale & Forest of Dean*, 1976, 230

BUTLER, Abraham fl 1739

A 'carver', he worked for **Henry Watson** at Wentworth Woodhouse, W R Yorks, in March 1739. His arrival is recorded in Watson's account book (Bodleian MS Eng Misc f383, f163).

Literary References: *Brighton* 2001, 72

BUTLER, Timothy 1806–

He was christened on 24 October 1806 at Camersham, Oxon, the son of Timothy Butler and his wife Sarah. Nothing is known of his early life but he trained as a sculptor in the studio of **William Behnes** at 91 Dean Street, Soho. In 1824 he won a large silver medal from the Society of Arts for a plaster model after the antique (**15**) and in November 1825 entered the Royal Academy Schools, where he was awarded a silver medal in 1827. He exhibited at the RA between 1828 and 1879, showing about 100 portrait busts. He appears to have established his own studio by 1835, when his address was 30 Gower Place. He moved to 1 Middlesex Place in 1845 and then to 270 Marylebone Road in 1858.

Butler was a popular portrait-sculptor and his busts seem to have been excellent likenesses. In 1842 he executed one of Sir James Eyre (**40**) which the *Art Union* considered 'a work which would do honour to the greatest of our sculptors' (*AU*, 1842, 128). The outspoken art critic F T Palgrave was an admirer of the sculptor's work. He described the bust of Professor Narrien (**93**) as 'in the grand and thoroughly sculpturesque manner of Mr. Behnes' and noted that, like other works by the artist it was 'careful and conscientious in every detail' and appeared 'to convey a genuine likeness' (*Palgrave* 1866, 83). A number of Butler's busts were posthumous portraits including that of the infant Charles William O'Malley (**49**). He executed statues of the Earl of Leicester for Dereham town hall, and Richard Cobden for Bradford wool exchange (**16, 17**).

Butler also undertook decorative work, designing lamp standards which were set up on the Thames Embankment 'at the landing place between Waterloo and Hungerford Bridge' in 1870 and lions' heads for 'the pedestals both on the north and south side of the river'. The lamps featuring figures of boys climbing the shaft of the lamp to light the globe at the top, were intended to represent 'the energetic spirit which characterises the British nation' (*Builder*, 1870, 210).

The census records show that by 1881 Butler was a widower, living at 186 Euston Road with a daughter, who was a sculptress, and a son who was an artist. John Adams-Acton, a successful portrait sculptor of the later 19th century, trained in Butler's studio.

Literary References: *Palgrave* 1866, 42, 83, 206, 221, 225, 294; *Gunnis* 1968, 74–5; *Read* 1982, 21, 69, 123

Archival References: RA Admissions; RA Premium list; IGI

Funerary Monuments						
1.	†1830	James (†1829) and Mary (†1830) Piggott Ince		Hadley, Herts	S	*Gunnis* 1968, 74
2.	1831	Anne Marriott		Horsmonden, Kent		*Gunnis* 1968, 74
3.	†1832	Frances and Charlotte (†1831) Bellasis		Carisbrooke, I of W	S	GPC
4.	1836	William Prescott		Hendon, Middx		*Gunnis* 1968, 75
5.	1841	Lord Douglas Hallyburton		Kensal Green Cemetery, London		*Gunnis* 1968, 75
6.	?1841	Peter Burrowes MP (medallion only)		Burrowes monument, Kensal Green Cemetery, London	S	*Curl* 2001, 199, 225
7.	1845	James Ince		Hadley, Herts		*Gunnis* 1968, 75
8.	1846	Edward Miller		Goudhurst, Kent		*Gunnis* 1968, 75
9.	1849	Jackson, the pugilist (†1845)		West Brompton Cemetery, London		*Gunnis* 1968, 75
10.	†1850	Charles Ince		Hadley, Herts	S	*Gunnis* 1968, 75
11.	1850?	Thomas (†1836) and Mary (†1850) Palmer		Hendon, Middx	S	
12.	†1851	Robert Haynes		St John, Hackleton's Cliff, Barbados	S	
13.	1861	General Peter de la Motte		Kensal Green Cemetery, London		*Gunnis* 1968, 75
14.	c1868	Lady Jane (†1833) and Sir Henry Thompson (†1868)		Holy Trinity, Fareham, Hants	S	Flaxman Account Book 1794–1810, 73; Pevsner, *Hants & Isle of Wight*, 1967, 221–2; C Lib (repr)
Statues						
15.	1824	Model of a figure from the antique		[Soc of A, large silver medal]; untraced		RSA, *Transactions*, vol 42, 1824, xlvi
16.	1858	Thomas, 1st Earl of Leicester		[Corn Hall, Dereham, Norfolk, exterior]; destroyed by lightning 1950		*Gunnis* 1968, 74; Pevsner, *Norfolk: NW & S*, 1999, 286
17.	1876	Richard Cobden	m	Wool exchange, Bradford, W R Yorks	SD	*Gunnis* 1968, 74
Busts						
18.	1833	Unidentified gentleman	m	[Exhib RA, London, 1209]; untraced		*Graves* I, 1905–6, 365
19.	1835	Charles Lingen		[Exhib RA, London, 1110]; untraced		*Graves* I, 1905–6, 365
20.	1835	Mrs R M Jarvis	m	[Exhib RA, London, 1105]; untraced		*Graves* I, 1905–6, 365
21.	1836	Professor Samuel Cooper		[Exhib RA, London, 1076]; untraced		*Graves* I, 1905–6, 365
22.	1836	Rev R Vaughan, Professor of History, London University		[Exhib RA, London, 1086]; untraced		*Graves* I, 1905–6, 365
23.	1836	Unidentified gentleman	m	[Exhib RA, London, 1127]; untraced		*Graves* I, 1905–6, 365
24.	1837	A bencher of the Middle Temple		[Exhib RA, London, 1282]; untraced		*Graves* I, 1905–6, 365
25.	1837	Mrs Thomas Jarvis	m	[Exhib RA, London, 1206]; untraced		*Graves* I, 1905–6, 365
26.	1837	Thomas Wood	m	[Exhib RA, London, 1223]; untraced		*Graves* I, 1905–6, 365
27.	1838	Edward Turner, Professor of Chemistry, London University	m	[Exhib RA, London, 1364]; untraced		*Graves* I, 1905–6, 365
28.	1838	William Leatham		[Exhib RA, London, 1305]; untraced		*Graves* I, 1905–6, 365
29.	1839	Bishop Musgrave of Hereford		[Exhib RA, London, 1331]; untraced		*Graves* I, 1905–6, 365
30.	1839	Mrs Wilson		[Exhib RA, London, 1353]; untraced		*Graves* I, 1905–6, 365
31.	1839	Rev Eckersall		[Exhib RA, London, 1360]; untraced		*Graves* I, 1905–6, 365
32.	1839	William Wilson of Pion House, Herefs		[Exhib RA, London, 1355]; untraced		*Graves* I, 1905–6, 365
33.	1840	Dr Edwin Edlin of the East India Company		[Exhib RA, London, 1142]; untraced		*Graves* I, 1905–6, 365
34.	1840	Rev H Dudley Ryder	m	[Exhib RA, London, 1160]; untraced		*Graves* I, 1905–6, 365
35.	1840	Rev Lewis Bowerbank		[Exhib RA, London, 1111]; untraced		*Graves* I, 1905–6, 365
36.	1841	Dr Elliotson FRS	m	[Exhib RA, London, 1282]; untraced		*Graves* I, 1905–6, 365
37.	1841	George, 6th Earl of Granard		[Exhib RA, London, 1268]; untraced		*Graves* I, 1905–6, 365

38.	1841	John William Buckle		[Exhib RA, London, 1314]; untraced		*Graves* I, 1905–6, 365
39.	1842	Peter Burrowes, of Dublin	m	[Exhib RA, London, 1363]; untraced		*AU*, 1842, 129; *Graves* I, 1905–6, 365
40.	1842	Sir James Eyre	m	[coll Corporation of Hereford]; untraced		*AU*, 1842, 128; *Gunnis* 1968, 74
41.	1843	Mrs James Jay		[Exhib RA, London, 1518]; untraced		*Graves* I, 1905–6, 365
42.	1843	Mrs Lingen		[Exhib RA, London, 1527]; untraced		*Graves* I, 1905–6, 365
43.	1843	W Bullock		[Exhib RA, London, 1480]; untraced		*Graves* I, 1905–6, 365
44.	1844	Captain Colin MacKenzie		[Exhib RA, London, 1396]; untraced		*AU*, 1844, 171; *Graves* I, 1905–6, 365
45.	1844	Caroline, Lady Stirling-Maxwell (Mrs Norton)	m	[coll J B Sheridan Jnr]; untraced		*AU*, 1844, 171; *Graves* I, 1905–6, 365; *Gunnis* 1968, 74
46.	1844	Charles Kemble	p	Russell Cotes AG, Bournemouth, Dorset Other versions: marble exhib RA, London, 1846, 1426		*AU*, 1844, 171; *AU*, 1846, 189; *Graves* I, 1905–6, 365; *Gunnis* 1968, 74
47.	1844	Mrs James Whittle		[Exhib RA, London, 1390]; untraced		*Graves* I, 1905–6, 365
48.	1844	William Charles Chopple Norton	m	[Exhib RA, London, 1310]; untraced		*Graves* I, 1905–6, 365
49.	1845	Charles William O'Malley, aged 2 years ten months	m	[Exhib RA, London, 1404]; untraced		*Graves* I, 1905–6, 365
50.	1845	Dr Watson		[Exhib RA, London, 1453]		*Graves* I, 1905–6, 365
51.	1846	Captain Grover FRS		[Exhib RA, London, 1442]; untraced		*Graves* I, 1905–6, 365
52.	1846	Dr Sayer		[Exhib RA, London, 1491]; untraced		*Graves* I, 1905–6, 365
53.	1846	Dr Wolff		[Exhib RA, London, 1443]; untraced		*Graves* I, 1905–6, 365
54.	1846	Professor John Frederick Daniell, of King's College, London	m	[Exhib RA, London, 1454]; untraced		*AU*, 1846, 189; *Graves* I, 1905–6, 365
55.	1846	R C Kirby	m	[Exhib RA, London, 1506]; untraced		*AU*, 1846, 189; *Graves* I, 1905–6, 365
56.	1847	Edward R Daniell	p	Gov Art Coll RCJ 15414	SD	*Graves* I, 1905–6, 365
57.	1847	James Berkeley Ince	m	[Exhib RA, London, 1419]; untraced		*Graves* I, 1905–6, 365
58.	1847	Mrs W E Bell	m	[Exhib RA, London, 1359]; untraced		*AU*, 1847, 200; *Graves* I, 1905–6, 365
59.	1847	Unidentified gentleman (posthumous portrait)	m	[Exhib RA, London, 1346]; untraced		*Graves* I, 1905–6, 365
60.	1847	William Attree, surgeon to King George IV and King William IV	m	[Exhib RA, London, 1350]; untraced		*AU*, 1847, 200; *Graves* I, 1905–6, 365
61.	1848	Mrs Shearburn of Snaith, Yorks		[Exhib RA, London, 1378]; untraced		*Graves* I, 1905–6, 365
62.	1848	Mrs Thomas Longman	m	[Exhib RA, London, 1442]; untraced		*Graves* I, 1905–6, 365
63.	1848	William Shearburn	m	[Exhib RA, London, 1434]; untraced		*Graves* I, 1905–6, 365
64.	1849	Dr John Elliotson		[Exhib RA, London, 1288]; untraced		*Graves* I, 1905–6, 365
65.	1850	James Moncrieff Arnott, President, R C Surg	m	[Exhib RA, London, 1376]; untraced		*Graves* I, 1905–6, 366
66.	1850	Mrs Hurd	m	[Exhib RA, London, 1383]; untraced		*Graves* I, 1905–6, 366
67.	1850	Vincent George Dowling		[Exhib RA, London, 1387]; untraced		*ILN*, 13 Nov 1852, 408 (repr); *Graves* I, 1905–6, 366
68.	1851	Mrs Klein, unfinished		[Exhib RA, London, 375]; untraced		*Graves* I, 1905–6, 366
69.	1851	Professor Samuel Cooper		RCS, London		*Graves* I, 1905–6, 366; *Read* 1982, 123
70.	1852	Dr Robert C Edwards	m	[Exhib RA, London, 1421]; untraced		*Graves* I, 1905–6, 365, 366; *Read* 1982, 123
71.	1853	Colonel J B Gardiner, 1st Life Guards		[Exhib RA, London, 1451]; untraced		*Graves* I, 1905–6, 366
72.	1853	Dr Bariard van Oven		[Exhib RA, London, 1419]; untraced		*Graves* I, 1905–6, 366
73.	1853	Dr Guy of King's College, London		[Exhib RA, London, 1379]; untraced		*Graves* I, 1905–6, 366
74.	1853	Hananel de Castro		[Exhib RA, London, 1395]; untraced		*Graves* I, 1905–6, 366
75.	1854	Captain Paley	m	[Exhib RA, London, 1413]; untraced		*Graves* I, 1905–6, 366
76.	1854	James Jay of Litley Court, Hereford		[Exhib RA, London, 1435]; untraced		*Graves* I, 1905–6, 366
77.	1854	Mr Scobie		[Exhib RA, London, 1433]; untraced		*Graves* I, 1905–6, 366
78.	1854	'Third son of P.W. Cunningham, secretary of King's College'		[Exhib RA, London, 1508]; untraced		*Graves* I, 1905–6, 366
79.	1855	Robert Reece		[Exhib RA, London, 1523]; untraced		*Graves* I, 1905–6, 366
80.	1856	Alexander Shaw		[Exhib RA, London, 1325]; untraced		*Graves* I, 1905–6, 366
81.	1856	Fanny Watney	m	[Exhib RA, London, 1356]; untraced		*Graves* I, 1905–6, 366
82.	1857	Charles Kean		[Exhib RA, London, 1313]; untraced		*Graves* I, 1905–6, 366; *Ormond* 1973, 247
83.	1857	The late Mrs Mitchell	m	[Exhib RA, London, 1244]; untraced		*Graves* I, 1905–6, 366
84.	1858	Mrs Masdell Smith	m	[Exhib RA, London, 1252]; untraced		*Graves* I, 1905–6, 366
85.	1858	Spencer Smith, surgeon to St Mary's Medical School		[Exhib RA, London, 1211]; untraced		*Graves* I, 1905–6, 366
86.	1859	Annie Holland	m	[Exhib RA, London, 1341]; untraced		*Graves* I, 1905–6, 366
87.	1859	John Edmund Reade	m	[Exhib RA, London, 1320]; untraced		*Graves* I, 1905–6, 366
88.	1859	Thomas Mosdell Smith		[Exhib RA, London, 1345]; untraced		*Graves* I, 1905–6, 366
89.	1860	J W Bazalgette		[Exhib RA, London, 1061]; untraced		*Graves* I, 1905–6, 366; *Gunnis* 1968, 74
90.	1862	Miss Lingen		[Exhib RA, London, 1056]; untraced		*Graves* I, 1905–6, 366
91.	1862	Sir Richard Kirby CB		[Exhib RA, London, 1030]; untraced		*Graves* I, 1905–6, 366; *Gunnis* 1968, 74
92.	1863	Dr Jacob Bell	m	Pharmaceutical Soc, London	SD	*Palgrave* 1866, 42; *Graves* I, 1905–6, 366; GPC
93.	1864	Memorial to John Narrien FRS		Staff College, Sandhurst, Farnborough, Berks		*Graves* I, 1905–6, 366
94.	1865	Mr Thomas and Mr Eton		Bristol General Hospital		*Gunnis* 1968, 74
95.	1866	Amy Murchison	m	[Exhib RA, London, 920]; untraced		*Graves* I, 1905–6, 366
96.	1866	Hon Agnes Rollo		[Exhib RA, London, 917]; untraced		*Graves* I, 1905–6, 366
97.	1866	Hon William Wordsworth, Master of Rollo	m	[Exhib RA, London, 916]; untraced		*Graves* I, 1905–6, 366

98.	1866	Hugh Falconer FRS	m	Royal Society, London	*Graves* I, 1905–6, 366
99.	1867	Dr William Clark FRS		Trinity College, Cambridge	*Graves* I, 1905–6, 366; *Gunnis* 1968, 74
100.	1867	Lord Rollo		[Exhib RA, London, 1137]; untraced	*Graves* I, 1905–6, 366; *Gunnis* 1968, 74
101.	1868	Eric Rollo		[Exhib RA, London, 1111]; untraced	*Graves* I, 1905–6, 366
102.	1869	C H Cooper FSA		[Exhib RA, London, 1267]; Cambridge Town Hall	*Graves* I, 1905–6, 367; *Gunnis* 1968, 74
103.	1870	Arthur Purvis		Cocanada, Chennai (Madras) Presidency, India	*Graves* I, 1905–6, 367; *Gunnis* 1968, 74
104.	1870	Richard Burdon Sanderson, of Jesmond, Northumberland		[Exhib RA, London, 1211]; untraced	*Graves* I, 1905–6, 367
105.	1871	Constance Rollo		[Exhib RA, London, 1311]; untraced	*Graves* I, 1905–6, 366
106.	1871	Herbert Rollo		[Exhib RA, London, 1309]; untraced	*Graves* I, 1905–6, 366
107.	1872	Cuthbert Finch MD	m	[Exhib RA, London, 1429]; untraced	*Graves* I, 1905–6, 366
108.	1872	Miss Snow		[Exhib RA, London, 1554]; untraced	*Graves* I, 1905–6, 366
109.	1873	William Gilstrap of Fornham Park, Suffolk		[Exhib RA, London, 1536]; untraced	*Graves* I, 1905–6, 366
110.	1873	William Pulling, of Hereford, for that city		[Exhib RA, London, 1556]; untraced	*Graves* I, 1905–6, 366
111.	1874	Mrs Gilstrap	m	[Exhib RA, London, 1464]; untraced	*Graves* I, 1905–6, 366
112.	1875	Bernard Rollo		[Exhib RA, London, 1258]; untraced	*Graves* I, 1905–6, 366
113.	1875	W A Miller FRS		King's College, London	*Graves* I, 1905–6, 366
114.	1876	Daniel Sturdy		[Exhib RA, London, 1372]; untraced	*Graves* I, 1905–6, 367
115.	1877	Cicely Rollo		[Exhib RA, London, 1442]; untraced	*Graves* I, 1905–6, 367
116.	1877	William Joynson	m	[Exhib RA, London, 1418]; untraced	*Graves* I, 1905–6, 367
117.	1878	T Hughes	m	[Exhib RA, London, 1443]; untraced	*Graves* I, 1905–6, 367; *Gunnis* 1968, 74
118.	1879	Gilbert Rollo	m	[Exhib RA, London, 1470]; untraced	*Graves* I, 1905–6, 367
Architectural Sculpture					
119.	1870	Lamp standard with climbing boys, model (executed in bronze for Albert Bridge, Chelsea, London, 1874)		Untraced Other versions: Chelsea Old Church, London, 1874, bronze	*Ward-Jackson* 2003, 418–9
120.	1868–1870	Lion's head mooring ring, model (executed in bronze for Thames Embankment lamp pedestals)		Untraced	*Ward-Jackson* 2003, 418–9
Reliefs					
121.	1862	Albert, the Prince Consort, medallion	p	[Statistical Society, meeting room]; untraced	*Darby and Smith* 1983, 63, 112 n21
122.	1871	Christopher Thomas, of Bristol, medallion		[Exhib RA, London, 1326]; untraced	*Graves* I, 1905–6, 366
123.	nd	Prince Albert, the Prince Consort, medallion	p	R C Physic, London	*Ormond* 1973, 15
Miscellaneous					
124.	1828	Mars		[Exhib RA, London, 1134]; untraced	*Graves* I, 1905–6, 365
125.	1856	Memorials		[Exhib RA, London, 1109]; untraced	*Graves* I, 1905–6, 366
126.	1868	The hand of Mrs Grote	m	[Exhib RA, London, 1075]; untraced	*Graves* I, 1905–6, 366

BUTLIN, W 1794–1836

When Butlin's widow applied to the AGBI for help she stated that her husband 'had been sent to visit Rome by the assistance of Lord Spencer to perfect his art'. He exhibited various works at the Royal Academy and the Society of British Artists between 1828 and 1835, including a model for a statue of Lord Althorp to be executed in bronze, which 'wanted proportion' (*GM*, 1834, i, 631) (1). In 1836 he applied to the RA for assistance and was awarded 8 guineas. He died the same year and his widow, who was left with seven children, was granted a pension in 1837.

Literary References: *Gunnis* 1968, 75

Archival References: AGBI, vol 3, 36, 61, 109, 143; vol 4, 35, 105, 169, 201

Statues					
1.	1834	John Charles, Viscount Althorp and 3rd Earl Spencer, model (to be executed in bronze)		[Exhib RA, London, 1035]; untraced	*Graves* I, 1905–6, 367; *Gunnis* 1968, 75
Busts					
2.	1829	J Gawthorn		[Exhib Soc of BA, London, 838]; untraced	*Johnson* 1975, 69
3.	1830	Rev T B Bull		[Exhib Soc of BA, London, 842]; untraced	*Johnson* 1975, 69
4.	1830	Sir W Franklin		[Exhib RA, London, 1217]; untraced	*Graves* I, 1905–6, 367
5.	1830	Unidentified child		[Exhib Soc of BA, London, 836]; untraced	*Johnson* 1975, 69
6.	1830	Unidentified child		[Exhib Soc of BA, London, 840]; untraced	*Johnson* 1975, 69
7.	1831	Unidentified child, posthumous		[Exhib RA, London, 1190]; untraced	*Graves* I, 1905–6, 367
8.	1832	John Charles, Viscount Althorp and 3rd Earl Spencer	m	Althorp, Northants	*Graves* I, 1905–6, 367
Miscellaneous					
9.	1828	Psyche		[Exhib RA, London, 1195]; untraced	*Graves* I, 1905–6, 367
10.	1830	Orpheus		[Exhib RA, London, 1276]; untraced	*Graves* I, 1905–6, 367
11.	1831	Myrene's escape, sketch		[Exhib RA, London, 1209]; untraced	*Graves* I, 1905–6, 367
12.	1834	The grateful slave		[Exhib RA, London, 1116]; untraced	*Graves* I, 1905–6, 367

BUTTERFIELD, Daniel *c*1771–

The son of Thomas Butterfield of Pickhill, N R Yorks, he was apprenticed to **John Fisher I** of York for 7 years on 7 July 1785, at a premium of £2

Archival References: York App Reg D14, 7 July 1785, 275

BUTTON, Benjamin fl 1791–1802

Button was probably a Northamptonshire statuary. Gunnis notes that his tablet to George Ashby, at Hazelbeach, has 'excellent details' (3).

Literary References: *Gunnis* 1968, 75

Funerary Monuments

1.	?1791	Joseph Hearne, tombstone	Kelmarsh, Northants, churchyard	S	*Gunnis* 1968, 75
2.	1798	Mary Alcock	Hazelbeach, Northants	S	*Gunnis* 1968, 75
3.	†1802	George Ashby	Hazelbeach, Northants	S	Pevsner, *Northants*, 1973, 252

BUTTON, John fl 1769–78

John Button received £789 for masonry work at Bowood, Wilts, between 1769 and 1777 (Archives, Marquess of Lansdowne, cited by *Gunnis*, 1968). The following year he was paid for carving two groups of colossal figures on the Strand and Bank fronts of Somerset House (1).

Literary References: *Gunnis* 1968, 75

Architectural Sculpture

1.	1778	Two groups of colossal figures	s	Somerset House, London, Strand and Bank fronts	TNA AOI/2495/414

BUXTON, Joseph 1783–

Buxton entered the Royal Academy Schools on 20 January 1803. Four years later he was awarded a silver medal.

Literary References: *Hutchison* 1960–2, 161

Statues

1.	1807	An Academy figure, model	[Awarded RA silver medal]; untraced	RA Premium list

BYRD (or BIRD), William, of Oxford 1624–90?

A sculptor, mason and architect of Oxford, he was the son of Thomas Bird and was baptised at St Nicholas, Gloucester, on 1 June 1624. Byrd served an 8-year apprenticeship with William Nicholls, a Gloucester mason, and must have moved to Oxford around 1647, for in 1681, when giving evidence in a lawsuit, he stated that he had worked in that city for 34 years. In 1652 his name appeared for the first time in the overseer's ratebooks for the parish of St Peter-in-the East. By then he had a wife, Mary, and a daughter was baptised at St Mary Magdalene in November 1652.

In the difficult years after the Civil War when there was little work for masons, he experimented with stone pigmentation. In 1658 he 'invented a method of staining or painting marble by sinking a colour of considerable depth into the body of polished white marble, by application of it to the outside only, so that the same figure delineated without, shall be perfectly represented within' (*Plot* 1677, 277). The achievement made a considerable stir in local circles and encouraged him to present a specimen of his work to King Charles II.

By 1667 he was occupying a tenement near the racket court at the corner of Smith Street, Oxford, where he lived with his wife, two children, a boarder and two journeymen, Richard and **Thomas Wood**, to whom he paid £8 in wages. His yard was at Holywell in the Oxford suburbs. He remained at the Smith Street house until his death and in his last years paid rates for the whole house. In 1668 a payment of £24 0s 6d was made to Byrd 'for repairing and setting up the remainder of the Marbles given by my Lord Howard and Mr Selden and £10 in part for ye. two inscriptions intended for them' (Oxford, Vice-C's Accts, Archive WP/21/5, fol 12). This refers to the Arundel Marbles and the inscription tablets are now in the Ashmolean Museum.

Byrd claimed in the 1681 lawsuit that he had worked on 'several noble buildings' in different counties, though most of his work was in Oxford. He was mason at Wadham College by 1656 and was involved in work on Wren's Sheldonian Theatre, 1666–69. Wren commissioned Byrd to make a model of the theatre and Byrd supplied much carved work there (14). He was also responsible in 1660–69 for minor masonry work in the area, including 'worke done in securing the Vault of the Divinity Schole, making the new Doore, altering the Professors Seat and ye windowes' (Oxford, V-C's Accts, WP/21/5 1667–1697, fols 13v, 20v). In 1670 he made the ornamental centrepiece for the fountain in Tom Quad at Christ Church (15). This took the form of a large rock, gilded and studded with the celestial planets, and a fountain of water, conveyed through the centre of the rock by a pipe running through the mouth of a serpent. The whole structure cost more than £250. The serpent was replaced in 1695 by a statue of *Mercury*.

In 1671–77 Byrd worked intermittently at New College, where he provided carved panels for the senior common room (16). He stated that he also build the chapel of St Edmund Hall (1680–86) and he designed and partly built the garden quadrangle at New College (1682–85), using a plan that was probably influenced by Wren's recently prepared design for the palace of Charles II at Winchester. In November 1683, before the New College quadrangle was completed, Wren summoned Byrd to Winchester as building contractor for the south wing of the palace.

A large number of monuments in Oxford and Berkshire have been ascribed to Byrd, but only a handful are signed or documented. The Bishop Brideoake follows the convention for monuments to senior members of the Church, for it has a reclining figure in full vestments inside an architectural surround (2). The Fettiplace is much more elaborate than his other signed works (7). It has 3 life-sized, reclining figures in armour inside a composite frame, tiered one above the other on shelves, and was clearly designed to match an earlier monument in the church to members of the same family. The Dunch, Guise and Sandys monuments are all oval tablets set in elaborately carved frames, incorporating *putti* as well as foliate ornaments and heraldic shields (3, 4, 6).

Byrd signed his deposition in the lawsuit Wood v Frogley on 7 June 1681 as 'Gulielmus Bird de Oxon' and then as William Byrde. He stated that since becoming a master mason he 'hath in divers Counties work'd at sev'all noble buildings (too many to be here mentioned)'. Stephen Clement, mason, noted that Byrd had been responsible for work at the Bishop's palace and a chimneypiece at Hasely (10). (OU, Chancellor's Ct Papers, fol 17, fol 14).

His wife died in 1680 and Byrd married again quickly, for a union between William Byrd and Grace Keeble is registered in the parish records of St Peter-in-the-East. A son, John, was born in 1682. Byrd appears to have ceased work in the late 1680s and in the last quarter of 1690 the words 'not collected' are written against his name in the poor rate lists. His fullest biographer, Mrs Cole, described his work as 'daring, lavish. . .clumsy, showing an imagination greater than his powers'. Only one autograph monument in which he used his polychrome technique appears to have survived (3).

IR

Literary References: *Cole* 1947, 63–74; *Cole* 1952–3, 193–99; *Gunnis* 1968, 55; Pevsner, *Oxon*, 1974, 800, 808; *Colvin* 1995, 203–4; *Grove* 1996, 5, 336 (White); IGI

Archival References: GPC

No.	Date	Work		Location		Reference
Funerary Monuments						
1.	1664	William of Wykeham's tomb, repairs only		Winchester Cathedral, Hants		*Colvin* 1995, 204
2.	†1678	Ralph Brideoake, Bishop of Chichester		St George's Chapel, Windsor, Berks	S	Pevsner, *Berks*, 1966, 278; *Bond* 1999, 43
3.	†1679	M Dunch		Pusey, Berks	S	*Cole* 1949, 72; Pevsner, *Berks*, 1966, 195
4.	†1683	William Guise		St Michael, Oxford	S	*Gunnis* 1968, 55; C Lib (repr)
5.	†1684	William Wilmot		St Peter & St Paul, Wantage, Berks	S	*Cole* 1949, 72 n48; Pevsner, *Berks*, 1966, 253
6.	†1685	Samuel Sandys		Ombersley, Worcs	S	Pevsner, *Worcs*, 1968, 230; C Lib (repr)
7.	1686	Fettiplace family		Swinbrook, Oxon	S	Pevsner, *Oxon*, 1974, 800; *Kemp* 1985, 18 (repr)
8.	nd	Lord Williams of Thame, repairs including new unicorn and greyhound		Thame, Oxon		Pevsner, *Oxon*, 1974, 808
9.	nd	Smith family, ledger		Untraced		*Cole* 1949, 72 n48
Chimneypieces						
10.	pre-1681	of Burford stone Payment(s): £4 5s		[Mr Lentall's house at Hasely]; untraced		OU, Chancellor's Ct Papers, fol 14; *Gunnis* 1968, 55
Architectural Sculpture						
11.	1659	Sundial		All Souls College, Oxford, now on Codrington Library wall		*Cole* 1949, 66; *Gunnis* 1968, 55
12.	1662	Royal arms, repairs only		Physic garden gate, Oxford		*Cole* 1949, 67
13.	1665	Royal arms		Christ Church, Oxford, Canon's Lodgings		*Cole* 1949, 67; *Gunnis* 1968, 55
14.	1666–1669	Ornamental carving, including fourteen 'Emperors' heads' for the screen (now replaced) Payment(s): £307	s	Sheldonian Theatre, Oxford		*Cole* 1949, 67; *Colvin* 1995, 178
15.	1670	Ornamental centrepiece and fountain		[Great 'Tom' Quadrangle, Christ Church, Oxford]; destroyed		*Cole* 1949, 67–8
16.	1676–1677	Panel carving	wd	New College, Oxford, senior common room		*Cole* 1949, 68
17.	1679–1682	Extensive carved ornament, including founder's coat of arms, twelve terms, trophies, the king's arms and six cartouches		Ashmolean		Oxford, V-C's Accts, Archive WP/21/5; Pevsner, *Oxon*, 1974, 255
Miscellaneous						
18.	1668	Repairs and setting up of the Arundel Marbles with two related inscriptions Payment(s): £52 15s		Dispersed		*Gunnis* 1968, 55

C, W † 1767

There has been speculation about the identity of this sculptor. Penny draws attention to G N Wright's *Historic Guide to Bath*, 1864, 183, which described the monument to James Bosanquet, †1767, with its gradated relief of the *Good Samaritan*, as being 'from the design and chisel of W. Carter' (1). Penny suggests this may be **Thomas Carter II**. A photograph of the monument in the Conway Library is, however signed W C, who might concievably be **William Collins**, for it bears a resemblance to his work in Magdalene College, Cambridge.

CACCIATORI (or CACCIATORE), B, of Milan 1794–1871

No.	Date	Work	Location		Reference
Funerary Monuments					
1.	1840	Lady St J Mildmay	Dogmersfield, Hants	S	Pevsner, *Hants & Isle of Wight*, 1967, 192

CACKETT, W fl 1793

No.	Date	Work	Location		Reference
Funerary Monuments					
1.	1793	Isaac Wildash Payment(s): £225	Newington, Kent, churchyard		*Gunnis* 1968, 76

CADE, H, of Bristol fl 1851–57

He signed several funerary tablets in Devon and sent out one to the West Indies (2). He can presumably be identified with 'H Cade', who signed two works in Gloucestershire (3, 5).

No.	Date	Work	Location		Reference
Funerary Monuments					
1.	†1851	Mary Meek	Holy Trinity, Ilfracombe, Devon	S	
2.	†1852	Henry Husbands Haynes	St John, Hackleton's Cliff, Barbados	S	
3.	†1855	John Langham	Parkend, Glos	S	Pevsner, *Glos: Vale & Forest of Dean*, 1976, 319
4.	†1855	Rear-Admiral Edward Down	Holy Trinity, Ilfracombe, Devon	S	
5.	†1857	Rev Henry Poole	Parkend, Glos	S	Pevsner, *Glos: Vale & Forest of Dean*, 1976, 319

CADES, Alessandro 1734–1809

For further information the reader is referred to *Pyke* 1973, 22.

CAESAR, Anthony fl 1727–35

Architectural Sculpture

1.	1727	Coat of Arms, supplied with mirror frames		[Lord Bingley's house in Cavendish Square, London, over hall door]; untraced	*Gunnis* 1968, 76

Reliefs

2.	1735	For Frederick, Prince of Wales's bathing room Payment(s): £21	s	[Pavilion, St James's Park, London]; untraced	Accounts of Frederick Prince of Wales, Duchy of Cornwall, vol V, 1735

CAKEBREAD, George, of Bloxham fl 1806–48

Cakebread worked in marble and stone, producing tablets with careful and well-cut details. On 4 January 1817 he placed an advertisement in the *Northampton Mercury*, stating 'G.Cakebread, Statuary, Bloxham, Oxfordshire, Returns his most grateful Acknowledgement to the Nobility, Gentry and his numerous Friends, for the very liberal support with which they have favoured him, and most respectfully begs Leave to inform them, he has, at this Time, a large Stock of beautiful Sienna, Statuary, white and veined, dove and other Marble Chimney Pieces, worked to the most modern Taste, ready for Inspection and sale, at Prices unusually low, and pledges himself that every Attention shall be paid to the Execution of any Orders he may receive in the Chimney Piece, Monumental, Tomb or Gravestone Departments'.

Literary References: *Gunnis* 1968, 76

Funerary Monuments

1.	†1817	Fiennes Sanderson	Radway, Warks	S	
2.	c1810	Woolston Family	Adderbury, Oxon, churchyard		RG/HC
3.	?1814	Elizabeth Blencoe	Marston St Lawrence, Northants		*Gunnis* 1968, 76
4.	?1818	Mary Hitchcock	Dedington, Oxon, churchyard		*Gunnis* 1968, 76
5.	?1823	Richard Kirby	Bicester, Oxon		*Gunnis* 1968, 76
6.	?1830	John Jackson Blencowe	Marston St Lawrence, Northants		*CIIA* 4/3/101 (repr)
7.	?1836	Richard Austen	Bodicote, Oxon		*Gunnis* 1968, 76
8.	?1838	Rev Moses Bartholomew	Edgcote, Northants		*Gunnis* 1968, 76

CAKEBREAD, Samuel, of Warwick fl 1827–31

Funerary Monuments

1.	†1827	John Webb	Sherborne, Warks	S
2.	†1831	Thomas Biggs	Pedmore, Worcs	S

CALDWELL, George, of Chester fl 1824–36

Busts

1.	1824	Mr Harrison, the architect		[Exhib ALRI, Liverpool, 167]; untraced	*Gunnis* 1968, 76; *Morris and Roberts* 1998, 119
2.	1836	Robert, Earl Grosvenor	m	Eaton Hall, Chester	GPC

CALE, J, of Hempsted fl 1821

Funerary Monuments

1.	†1821	John Somerset	Hempsted, Glos	S	Pevsner, *Glos: Vale and Forest of Dean*, 1976, 268

CALEGARI

Architectural Sculpture

1.	nd	Angel	Oratory of St Philip Neri, Kensington, London, organ gallery	S	Pevsner, *London: N W*, 1991, 463

CALI, Ernesto fl 1857

A Neapolitan sculptor, he was responsible for the wall relief at Ingestre to Lady Victoria Talbot, who died in Naples in 1856 (1). Penny notes that 'every lace fringe of the peacefully dead woman [is] rendered with delicate care' (*Penny* 1977 (1), 132.)

Funerary Monuments

1.	1857	Lady Victoria Susan Talbot (†1856)	Ingestre, Staffs	S	Pevsner, *Staffs*, 1974, 156

CALVERT, James c1737–

In 1766 he was a pupil of **John Francis Moore** in Berners Street, Oxford Road. That year he received a premium of 15 guineas in the under 30 category from the Society of Arts, for a Portland stone relief of the *Death of Socrates* (5). In 1770 he deserted sculpture for the stage and appeared in Dublin in Otway's *Venice Preserved*, but though favourably received he did not remain an actor for long, but returned to his old profession and started to model wax portraits in Dublin.

Calvert later came back to England and worked with **Crashley** for a period, showing his waxes from Crashley's figure shop in Long Acre (1–4, 6–7). He was also apparently employed by **Joseph Wilton RA**, for in 1787 he went to Jamaica to erect his master's monument to Sir B Keith in the Cathedral. By 1783 he had returned to Britain. He exhibited wax portraits at the Free Society and the Society of Artists between 1765 and 1783.

Literary References: RSA *Premiums*, 1763, 29; *Strickland* 1, 1913, 149–50; *Graves* 1907, 47, 48; *Gunnis* 1968, 76; *Pyke* 1973, 23;

Archival References: GPC

Miscellaneous Drawings: head of Scipio Africanus exhib free Soc, 1767 (60); drawing of Democritus exhib Free Soc, 1767 (61)

Busts

1.	1783	Unidentified gentleman	w	[Exhib Soc of Artists, 49]; untraced	*Graves* 1907, 47
2.	1783	Unidentified gentleman	w	[Exhib Soc of Artists, 52]; untraced	*Graves* 1907, 47
3.	1783	Unidentified lady	w	[Exhib Soc of Artists, 50]; untraced	*Graves* 1907, 47
4.	1783	Unidentified officer	w	[Exhib Soc of Artists, 51]; untraced	*Graves* 1907, 47

Reliefs					
5.	1766	Death of Socrates, in Portland stone		[Soc of A, premium (15 gns)]; untraced	RSA, *Minutes*, 1765–66, seq 3 f 42; RSA *Premiums*, 1763, 29; *Graves* 1907, 48
6.	1783	Mr Hemet		[Exhib Soc of Artists, 48]; untraced	*Graves* 1907, 47
7.	1783	Mr Lewis, Theatre Royal, Covent Garden	w	[Exhib Soc of Artists, 49]; untraced	*Graves* 1907, 47

CALZA, Francesco

For further information the reader is referred to *Pyke* 1973, 23.

CAMINADA, C, of Hull fl 1842–64

A plaster-figure manufacturer and ornamental caster who had premises at 2 South Street, Kingston-on-Hull in 1846. In 1864 he was at 5 Paragon Street. He exhibited at the Mechanics' Institute in Hull in 1842. (Inf. Gerardine Mulcahy)

Literary References: *White*, 1846; Jones, *Mercantile Directory*, 1863–4

Statues					
1.	1842	Adonis ('for sale')	p	[Exhib Mechanics Institute, Hull, 26]; untraced	Exhib Cat, Mechanics' Inst

CAMPBELL, Thomas 1790–1858

An Edinburgh-born sculptor who practised in London and Rome, Campbell is chiefly known for portrait sculpture in the neo-classical style. He was the son of Douglas Campbell, described as a gentleman's servant and his wife, Helen, née Thorburn. A younger brother James (1810–1833) eventually became his pupil and studio assistant in Rome and latterly in London.

Campbell was born on 1 May 1791 and was apprenticed at an early age to a marble-cutter, John Marshall, who died during his apprenticeship. He completed his training with John Dalzell, who took over Marshall's business. Campbell received his first recorded independent commission as a figure sculptor *c*1813 when he executed two freestone heads for the portico of St Mary's Chapel (**112**). In 1816, after modelling a bust of Professor Robert Blair (**31**), probably carved subsequently in Rome, he attracted patronage from Gilbert Innes of Stow, the Depute Governor of the Bank of Scotland (**32**), who was impressed by the intellect of the young man when Campbell installed a chimneypiece in his home. Innes provided Campbell with the financial means to study at the Royal Academy Schools in London in 1818 and from 1819 in Rome.

During the winter of 1818, Campbell studied in Paris where the Dowager Duchess of Devonshire supplied him with a letter of introduction to **Antonio Canova** in Rome. The following year he met both Canova and **Bertel Thorvaldsen**, with whom he was to maintain amicable relations. Like many contemporaries he aspired towards the 'ideal', but was obliged to earn his living as a portrait and monumental sculptor. He maintained a good network of Scottish connections, acting as the accredited agent for the Board of the Trustees' Academy of Edinburgh, for whom he managed to secure first casts of works by Canova and Thorvaldsen, and probably also casts after the antique for the use of students. He attracted some prestigious Scottish patrons and in 1820 was in a position to open a studio at 12 Piazza Mignanelli. Among his clients was Baron Kinnaird, who commissioned his own bare-chested, staunchly classical bust (**40**) and also a statue of his son, depicted as a curly-haired Ascanius, distracted from the act of tying his sandal (**11**). In 1824 Campbell was selected in competition with **Samuel Joseph** to provide an equestrian statue for the Earl of Hopetoun in Edinburgh (**15**). Executed in Rome and shipped back in 1829, the monument suggests Hopetoun's patriotic virtue by showing him as a Roman citizen in a toga. The Earl is presented in a novel manner, leaning on the neck of his horse.

By 1823 Campbell had secured the patronage of the 6th Duke of Devonshire, who ordered a colossal portrait bust of himself (**38**). Devonshire went on to commission another of Princess Pauline Borghese (**48**), Napoleon's sister, whose legendary beauty and links to recent history captivated the attention of the Duke and many others in Rome. This was followed by an order for a seated statue of the Princess (**22**) to accompany **Antonio Canova's** statue of Napoleon's mother, Madame Mère, in the sculpture gallery at Chatsworth. The Princess sat several times for Campbell, who also took casts of her famously elegant hands and feet. He kept the exasperated Duke waiting for 16 years before finally delivering the statue, which depicts the Princess doting on a medallion of her brother. The base was inlaid with numerous iron medallions, left by Pauline to the Duke on her death in 1825. By 1826, when he executed marble busts for King George IV of Pope Pius VII and Cardinal Consalvi, both after originals by Thorvaldsen, Campbell was the doyen of Scottish expatriate sculptors in Rome (**47, 46**).

Campbell had returned permanently to London by February 1830 with commissions in hand said to be worth £30,000. He took a studio at 28 Leicester Square and then, in 1834, at 16 Great Marlborough Street, retaining a studio in Rome, where both marble and labour were cheaper. Henceforth the preliminary carving of his major works took place in Italy, after which they were shipped to England, where Campbell provided the finishing touches. In his close personal control over both conception and final appearance, his modus shares something with Canova, whose work Campbell sought to emulate.

One of Campbell's aristocratic patrons was the 5th Duke of Buccleuch, who commissioned the monument to Elizabeth Buccleuch at Warkton (**4**), which the *Art Journal* later described as Campbell's most important work. The effigy is seated stiff-backed on a classical throne rising nearly 10 feet in height and is attended, in Campbell's own words, by figures, one 'representing the Angel of Death the other a female figure recording the memory of her Grace's virtues' (Dalkeith Muniments, in GPC). Buccleuch also commissioned a statue of the Duke of Wellington (of whom Campbell produced numerous busts) in the pose of Donatello's St George at Orsan Michele, Florence (**10**). Another notable Buccleuch commission was the monument to the Countess of Courtown in Ireland, which has a recumbent effigy (**3**). In December 1836 Campbell submitted an estimate of £6,490 to Buccleuch for works in hand, and by the time these were completed in 1847 Campbell had been paid nearly £8,000.

In 1837 George Cleghorn, in his *Remarks on Ancient and Modern Art*, cited the work of Campbell with that of **Lawrence Macdonald** and others, as evidence of the rebirth of the sculptural arts in Scotland. Campbell was not however to become the favourite sculptor in his homeland. He had offended members of the Edinburgh establishment, especially Sir Thomas Gibson-Craig, by his late delivery of the Hopetoun monument, and so failed to be selected for such prestigious public commissions as the monument to Sir Walter Scott. He executed a number of other less glamorous works for Scottish patrons, including a *contrapposto* statue of the Duke of York (**21**) and a figure for Aberdeen of the Duke of Gordon, robed as a Roman General with his foot on a cannon (**25**).

Campbell produced only a few funerary monuments. They included a standing figure of Sir William Hoste (**2**), and the memorial to Lady Whichcote, a severely classical stele relief of a woman reading (**9**). His busts were almost exclusively classical in style. They included several versions of the head of Earl Grey (**51, 52, 60, 61**), a portrait of the Duchess of Bedford in ringlets (**87**) and another of the rustic-featured surgeon, Robert Liston (**79**). The *Art Journal* described his works in this genre as 'masterpieces of conception and invention' which forcefully embodied the character of the sitter (*AJ* 1858, 107).

He died of bronchitis and emphysema on 4 February 1858 at 1 Great Castle-street, Regent Street and was buried at Kensal Green Cemetery. He was accorded no monument. Despite the large sums earned at his zenith from members of the aristocracy, he left effects worth less than £600. His remaining stock-in-trade, including an alto-relievo of Sarah Siddons, intended for her monument (**5**) was said to have been dispersed at an unrecorded posthumous studio sale. His estate was administered by the artist John Grey.

Campbell's obituary states that he was 'of middle stature, and of a robust frame; lively in temperament, although occasionally subject to depression of spirits' (*AJ*, 1858, 107). As a sculptor he was obsessively painstaking, building up his ideas in close detail and refusing to deliver commissions until he was convinced of their perfection. He does not appear not to have won wide fame, but was clearly appreciated by a small circle of wealthy patrons and friends.

MGS

Literary References: *Haydon Autobiography* 1853, vol 1, 343; *AJ* 1858, 107–8; *Graves* I, 1905–6, 386; *Macready Diaries*, II, 1912, 117; *DNB*; *JKB* 1971, 208–212; *JKB* 1972 (3), 322–331; *Penny* 1977 (1), 10; *Smailes* 1987, 709–14; *Pearson* 1991, 64–69; *Dawson* 1999, 210–1; *Curl* 2001, 242; *Bilbey* 2002, 231; *ODNB* (Smailes)

Additional MSS References: Correspondence 1826–1851, Beinecke Library, Yale GEN MSS/226; Letter-book, National Library of Scotland, MS146; Campbell/Buccleuch Letters

Will: PPR 7 July 1851

Portraits of the Sculptor: Christian Albrecht Jensen, oil on canvas, 1838, untraced (ODNB)

Funerary Monuments

1.	†1827	Robert Leslie		Protestant Cemetery, Rome		GPC
2.	1833	Captain Sir William Hoste Bt		St Paul's Cathedral, London, south transept	SD	*AJ*, 1858, 107; Pevsner, *London: City*, 1997, 173; C Lib (repr)
3.	1836	Charlotte, Countess of Courtown (†1836) Model(s): part of the monument to Lady Charlotte Stopford, in Courtown church, Ireland, exhib RA, London, 1836, (1284)		Kiltennel, Co Wexford	SD	*AJ*, 1858, 107; *Graves* I, 1905–6, 387; *Potterton* 1975, 38; *Smailes* 1987, 711
4.	1830–1843	Elizabeth, Duchess of Buccleuch (†1827) Payment(s): £4,500		Warkton, Northants	S	Campbell / Buccleuch Letters, 1836, 1841; *AJ*, 1858, 107; *Webb* 1953 (2), 199; *CIIA* 4/3/139–145 (repr); *Smailes* 1987, 710; *Pearson* 1991, 155 (repr);
5.	1843	Sarah Siddons, relief designed for her monument	m	NPG, London		*Graves* I, 1905–6, 387; *Pearson* 1991, 66, 69 n11 (repr)
6.	by 1845	Admiral Sir Frederick Maitland		[Portsmouth, dockyard chapel]; destroyed		*ILN* 27 Sept 1845, 208 (repr); *AJ*, 1858, 107; GPC
7.	†1845	Charles, 2nd Earl Grey		Howick, Northumbs		*Gunnis* 1968, 77
8.	1845	Sarah Siddons (†1831)		Westminster Abbey, London, St Andrew's Chapel	SD	*Macready Diaries*, vol II, 117, 277, 298, 315 (1841–1846): *ILN* 6 Oct 1849, 229 (repr); *AJ*, 1858, 107; *MacMichael*, 1977, 54
9.	†1849	Marian, Lady Whichcote		Aswarby, Lincs	S	*AJ*, 1858, 107; Pevsner, *Lincs*, 1989, 109; C Lib (repr)

Statues

10.	1828–c1847	Arthur, 1st Duke of Wellington Payment(s): £1,890	m	Dalkeith Palace, Midlothian		Campbell/Buccleuch Letters, 1836, 1841; *AJ*, 1858, 107; *Gunnis* 1968, 77; *Smailes* 1987, 711–12 (repr); *Pearson* 1991, 66
11.	1822	Arthur Fitzgerald, 10th Baron Kinnaird as the Young Ascanius, statuette	m	Private coll	SD	*AJ*, 1858, 107; *Pearson* 1991, unpag, 66; C Lib (repr)
12.	1822	Psyche opening the vase	p	VAM A.4-2000 Other versions: for R Christopher Nisbett Hamilton, 1830; untraced Sotheby 7 July 1988, lot 292, marble	SD	*AJ*, 1858, 107; *Graves* I, 1905–6, 386; *Bilbey* 2002, 232 (plaster repr)
13.	1825	Lord Conyers Osborne (as a young Roman soldier)	m	Brocklesby Park, Lincs		GPC
14.	1829	Frederick Augustus, Duke of York and Albany	m	United Service Club, City of Westminster, staircase	SD	*AJ*, 1858, 107; Pevsner, *London: Westminster*, 1973, 612n

No.	Date	Subject		Location		Literature
15.	1824–1829	John, 4th Earl of Hopetoun, equestrian	b	St Andrew's Square, Edinburgh	S	*ArJ*, 1858, 107; *Read* 1982, 113, 116 (repr); *Smailes* 1987, 712; *Pearson* 1991, 66 (repr)
16.	1829	Viscountess Sandon (later Countess of Harrowby)	m	Sandon Park, Staffs	SD	*AJ*, 1858, 107; *Gunnis* 1968, 77; C Lib (repr)
17.	pre-1830	Cupid and Psyche, group Drawing(s): Woburn Abbey, signed 'Thos Campbell Sculp Rome'		[coll Christopher Nisbet Hamilton]; untraced		*ODNB*; C Lib (repr)
18.	1830	The daughter of Lady Julia Lockwood		[Exhib RA, London, 1177]; untraced		*Graves* I, 1905–6, 386
19.	1831	Portrait of a lady as a muse		[Exhib RA, London, 1227]; untraced		*Great Exhib* 1851 (1), vol 2, 844; *Graves* I, 1905–6, 386; *Gunnis* 1968, 77
20.	1838	Charles, 2nd Earl Grey, 'sketch', to be executed in marble		[Exhib RA, London, 1831, 1180]; coll Lady Mary Howick		*Graves* I, 1905–6, 386; *Ormond* 1973, 203
21.	1839	Frederick Augustus, Duke of York and Albany	b	Edinburgh Castle, esplanade		*AJ*, 1858, 107
22.	1824–1840	Princess Pauline Borghese (†1825) Payment(s): £500	m	[coll William, 6th Duke of Devonshire]; Chatsworth, Derbys		*AJ*, 1858, 107; *JKB* 1971, 208, 211, 212 (repr); *JKB* 1972 (3), 331; *Pearson* 1991, 64, 66 (repr); *Sicca and Yarrington* 2000, 150
23.	1821–1841	Ganymede with the Eagle Model(s): exhib RA, London, 1841		[Rossie Priory, Perths]; untraced Other versions: VAM 1859–4, plaster		*AJ*, 1858, 107; *Graves* I, 1905–6, 387; *Bilbey* 2002, 231 (plaster repr)
24.	1843	Earl of Dalkeith (as a hunter boy, with greyhound) Payment(s): £480	m	[Dalkeith Palace, Midlothian]; Bowhill, Roxburghs		Campbell/Buccleuch Letters, 1843, 1845; *AJ*, 1858, 107; *Graves* I, 1905–6, 387; *Gunnis* 1968, 77; *Smailes* 1987, 711; GPC
25.	1844	George, 5th Duke of Gordon (cut by MacDonald and Leslie)		Golden Square, Aberdeen		*ILN* 11 May 1844, 312 (repr); 30 Oct 1897, 611 (repr); *Aberdeen Journal*, 24 April, 1844; *AJ*, 1858, 107; *Meldrum* 1987, 80 (repr); *Smailes* 1987, 712
26.	1851	George, Lord Bentinck (†1848)	b	Cavendish Square, London		*ILN*, 29 Nov 1851, 640 (repr); *AJ*, 1858, 107; *Blackwood* 1989, 182 (repr)
27.	nd	Lady Mary Christopher (later Mary Nisbett Hamilton), seated		Untraced		*AJ*, 1858, 107
28.	nd	Queen Victoria		Windsor Castle		*DNB*; PMSA recording project
29.	nd	Seated woman all'antica	m	Untraced	S	GPC; C Lib (repr)
30.	nd	'Son of the present Lord Kinnaird'		Untraced		*AJ*, 1858, 107
Busts						
31.	1815	Robert Blair Model(s): University Library, Edinburgh, signed		University Library, Edinburgh	S	*ODNB*; C Lib (repr)
32.	1816–1821	Gilbert Innes		Untraced Other versions: Plaster, SNPG		*AJ*, 1858, 108
33.	1822	Sir Henry Raeburn	m	SNPG, Edinburgh	SD	*Smailes* 1987, 710; *Pearson* 1991, unpag, 66; C Lib (repr)
34.	1823	'A man and a woman'	m	Astley Cheetham Public Library and Art Gallery		RG/JP, 2, 237
35.	1823	Lady Charlotte Lane Fox	m	Brocklesby Park, Lincs	SD	C Lib (repr)
36.	1823	Richard Colley Wellesley, Marquess Wellesley	m	[coll Admiral Sir L. Keppel Hamilton]; BM	SD	*Dawson* 1999, 222–5 (repr)
37.	1823	Viscountess Sandon	m	Sandon Park, Staffs Other versions: Same location, bronze		C Lib (repr)
38.	1823	William, 6th Duke of Devonshire, colossal Payment(s): £40	m	Chatsworth, Derbys, sculpture gallery Other versions: Model Exhib RA, London, 1832, 1109 'to be executed in bronze', bronze; untraced		*AJ*, 1858, 107; *Gunnis* 1968, 77; *JKB* 1971, 211; *JKB* 1972 (3), 323, 327, 331 (repr); *Pearson* 1991, 66
39.	1823	Young woman	m	Gov Art Coll (16168) Other versions: 1824, sold Sotheby, 7 April 1975, lot 169		C Lib (repr)
40.	1824	Charles, 8th Baron Kinnaird	m	NGS (loan)		*Graves* I, 1905–6, 386; *Pearson* 1991, 66; C Lib (repr)
41.	1824	Lady Arethusa Susanna Cullum	m	Bury St Edmunds Town Hall, Suffolk	D	*British Portraits* 1956–7, 115; *Gunnis* 1968, 77; C Lib (repr)
42.	1824	William, 6th Duke of Devonshire	m	Althorp, Northants Other versions: Replica with rounded truncation, Castle Howard, E R Yorks, marble, SD 'Roma' 1824	SD	*Gunnis* 1968, 77
43.	c1825	Countess of Shrewsbury	m	[Alton Towers, Staffs]; untraced		*Gunnis* 1968, 77
44.	c1825	Earl of Shrewsbury	m	[Alton Towers, Staffs]; untraced		*Gunnis* 1968, 77
45.	1825	Frederick Augustus, Duke of York and Albany	m	Stratfield Saye, Hants Other versions: Hopetoun House, Lingithlow, marble	SD	*Gunnis* 1968, 77; C Lib (repr)

46.	1826	Cardinal Consalvi	m	Royal Coll Other versions: Alton Towers, Staffs		*Gunnis* 1968, 77; *ODNB*
47.	By 1826	Pope Pius VII (after Bertel Thorvaldsen)	m	Royal Coll		*ODNB*
48.	1824–1826	Princess Pauline Borghese	m	Chatsworth, Derbys	SD	*Gunnis* 1968, 77; *JKB* 1971, 208, 212 (repr); *JKB* 1972 (3), 328, 331 (repr)
49.	post-1827	Arthur, 1st Duke of Wellington	m	Thirlestane Castle Other versions: Christie 15 Dec 1982, SD 1827, marble		*Smailes* 1987, 709 (repr)
50.	1827	Arthur, 1st Duke of Wellington	m	Stratfield Saye, Hants Other versions: Marble, 1827, Sotheby, 15 Dec 1982, lot 341 (repr) ex coll Lord Westmorland, 1845; untraced Replica, Hopetoun House, Linlithgow, 1833, marble	S	*Gunnis* 1968, 77; *Smailes* 1987, 710
51.	1827	Charles, 2nd Earl Grey	m	Christie 28 Jan 1988, lot 173	SD	C Lib (repr)
52.	1827	Charles, 2nd Earl Grey	m	Palace of Westminster, London, Committee Corridor	SD	*Walker* 1961, 35, cat no 36; *Ormond* 1973, 202 (repr 380)
53.	1828	Arthur, 1st Duke of Wellington	b	Brynkinalt, Denbigh, Clwyd		*Graves* I, 1905–6, 386; *Gunnis* 1968, 77
54.	1828	Lady Caroline Sackville	m	Drayton House, Northants		*Gunnis* 1968, 77
55.	1828	Unidentified woman	p	Drayton House, Northants	SD	C Lib (repr)
56.	1830	Colin Mackenzie of Portmore	m	Signet Library, Edinburgh Other versions: Castle Fraser, Aberdeens, signed, marble, 1830	SD	C Lib (repr)
57.	1830	Earl of Belfast	m	[Exhib RA, London, 243]; untraced		*Graves* I, 1905–6, 386
58.	1830	George, 2nd Marquess of Donegal	m	[Lowther Castle, Westmorland]; Sold Christie, 20 March 1984, lot 21	SD	*Gawsworth Guide*, 45, 46 (repr)
59.	1830	Olivia, daughter of Charles, 8th Baron Kinnaird	m	Rossie Priory, Perths		C Lib (repr)
60.	1831	Charles, 2nd Earl Grey	m	Howick, Northumbs	SD	C Lib (repr)
61.	1831	Charles, 2nd Earl Grey	b	[Exhib RA, London, 1832, 1219]; (coll Lady Mary Howick) Other versions: Royal Coll, 1836 Doncaster Art Gall, W R Yorks, 1838, marble		*AJ*, 1858, 107; *Graves* I, 1905–6, 386; *Ormond* 1973, 202
62.	1832	Earl of Lonsdale	b	[Grand jury room, Carlisle Courts]; untraced Other versions: Whitehaven Library, Cumberland (1838)		*Hodgson/Lonsdale*, 20 Nov 1832, 13, 20 March, 1838
63.	1832	Lady Ashley	m	[Exhib RA, London, 1166]; untraced		*Graves* I, 1905–6, 386
64.	1833	John T Hope	b	[Exhib RA, London, 1108]; untraced		*AJ*, 1858, 108; *Graves* I, 1905–6, 386
65.	1835	Walter, 5th Duke of Buccleuch	m	Boughton, Northants		*Graves* I, 1905–6, 386; *Gunnis* 1968, 77
66.	1836	Charlotte, Duchess of Leeds	m	Brocklesby Park, Lincs	SD	C Lib (repr)
67.	1836	George, 5th Duke of Gordon	m	Windsor Castle		*Gunnis* 1968, 77
68.	1837	Sir John Cam Hobhouse Bt		[Exhib RA, London, 1263]; untraced		*AJ*, 1858, 108; *Graves* I, 1905–6, 386
69.	1838	Charles, 2nd Earl Grey	p	Eton College, Berks	SD	C Lib (repr)
70.	1838	Lady Arthur Lennox	m	[Exhib RA, London, 1366]; untraced		*Graves* I, 1905–6, 387
71.	1838	Mrs Henry Baring	m	[Exhib RA, London, 1313]; untraced		*Graves* I, 1905–6, 386
72.	1841	Marchioness of Douro	m	Stratfield Saye, Hants		*AU*, 1842, 129; *Gunnis* 1968, 77
73.	1841	Walter, 5th Duke of Buccleuch Payment(s): £106	m	Dalkeith Palace, Midlothian		Campbell/Buccleuch Letters, 1841
74.	1843	Mrs Henry Labouchère	m	[Exhib RA, London, 1439]; untraced		*Graves* I, 1905–6, 387
75.	1844	Lord Wallace	m	[coll Sir Charles Monck]; untraced		*Gunnis* 1968, 77
76.	1845	Sir Robert Smirke	m	[coll The sitter, presented by his pupils]; BM Other versions: RIBA	SD	*Graves* I, 1905–6, 387; *Dawson* 1999, 210–212 (repr)
77.	1848	George, Lord Bentinck (†1848)	m	NPG 134	SD	*Ormond* 1973, 36 (repr 58)
78.	1849	Sir Henry Lawrence	m	[coll Sir Henry Lawrence]; NPG, London 1989	SD	*AJ*, 1858, 108; *Graves* I, 1905–6, 387; *Ormond* 1973, 263 (repr 515)
79.	1850	Robert Liston	m	University College Hospital, London Other versions: Same location, marble, SD 1850	SD	*AJ*, 1858, 108; *Graves* I, 1905–6, 387; *Gunnis* 1968, 77; C Lib (repr)
80.	1850	Sir Edmund Antrobus		[Exhib RA, London, 1371]; untraced		*AJ*, 1858, 108; *Graves* I, 1905–6, 387
81.	1853	Henry Home Drummond	m	[Exhib RA, London, 1441]; untraced		*AJ*, 1858, 108; *Graves* I, 1905–6, 387; *Gunnis* 1968, 77
82.	1853	John Dalrymple FRS	m	RCS, London	SD	*AJ*, 1858, 108; *Graves* I, 1905–6, 387; *Gunnis* 1968, 77; C Lib (repr)
83.	1853	Lord Denman	m	Eton College, Windsor, Berks	SD	*Gunnis* 1968, 77; C Lib (repr)
84.	1856	Lord de Mauley	m	[Exhib RA, London, 1315]; untraced		*AJ*, 1858, 108; *Graves* I, 1905–6, 387
85.	1857	George, Lord Bentinck (†1848)	m	[Exhib RA, London, 1340]; untraced		*Graves* I, 1905–6, 387

No.	Date	Subject		Location		References
86.	nd	10th Duke of Hamilton		Untraced		*AJ*, 1858, 107; *ODNB*
87.	nd	Anna Maria Stanhope, Duchess of Bedford	m	Woburn Abbey, Beds		*Gunnis* 1968, 77; C Lib (repr)
88.	nd	Arthur, 1st Duke of Wellington	m	Sandon Park, Staffs		C Lib (repr)
89.	nd	Arthur, 1st Duke of Wellington and Earl Grey, 'speaking busts'		Royal Coll		*AJ*, 1858, 107
90.	nd	Charles, 2nd Earl Grey	b	Stratfield Saye, Hants		C Lib (repr)
91.	nd	Earl of Newburgh	b	Chatsworth, Derbys		*Gunnis* 1968, 77; C Lib (repr)
92.	nd	General Grey, 'brother of the late Earl'		untraced		*AJ*, 1858, 108
93.	nd	General Sir Alexander Hope of Lufness		untraced		*AJ*, 1858, 108
94.	nd	J P Potter		[University College London]; untraced		*AJ*, 1858, 108
95.	nd	John McVicar of Ardarrock		Untraced		*AJ*, 1858, 108
96.	nd	Lady Charlotte Stopford		Untraced		*AJ*, 1858, 108
97.	nd	Lady Kinnaird		Untraced		*AJ*, 1858, 108
98.	nd	Lord Balgonie (later Earl of Leven and Melville)		Untraced		*ODNB*
99.	nd	Lord Courtown's father		Untraced		*AJ*, 1858, 108
100.	nd	Lord Dudley Coutts Stuart	b	Sandon Park, Staffs	S	*AJ*, 1858, 108; C Lib (repr)
101.	nd	Marchioness of Tweedale		Untraced		*AJ*, 1858, 107
102.	nd	Miss Tytler, daughter of Peter Frazer Tytler		Untraced		*AJ*, 1858, 108
103.	nd	Napoleon Bonaparte	m	Sandon Park, Staffs		C Lib (repr)
104.	nd	Peter Frazer Tytler		Untraced		*AJ*, 1858, 108
105.	nd	R Christopher Nisbett Hamilton		Untraced		*AJ*, 1858, 108
106.	nd	Sir H Pottinger		Untraced		*AJ*, 1858, 108
107.	nd	Sir Thomas Gibson-Craig of Riccarton Bt	m	Signet Library, Edinburgh Other versions: Plaster NPG 351		*AJ*, 1858, 108; C Lib (repr)
108.	nd	The son of General Sir Alexander Hope of Lufness		Untraced		*AJ*, 1858, 108
109.	nd	Thomas Maitland, 11th Earl of Lauderdale	m	Apsley House, London		*AJ*, 1858, 107; C Lib (repr)
110.	nd	Wife of William Burn, architect		Untraced		*AJ*, 1858, 108
111.	nd	William Burn, architect		Untraced		*AJ*, 1858, 108

Architectural Sculpture

No.	Date	Subject		Location		References
112.	1813	Two heads		St Mary's Chapel Edinburgh, now St Mary's Metropolitan Cathedral		*ODNB*
113.	1846	Navigation, Commerce, Manufacture, Science, Art and Agriculture, parapet statues		Bank of Scotland, St Andrew Square, Edinburgh		Pevsner, *Edinburgh*, 1991, 326

Reliefs

No.	Date	Subject		Location		References
114.	nd	Duke and Duchess of Gordon, medallions		['put up at their seat']; untraced		*AJ*, 1858, 107

Miscellaneous

No.	Date	Subject		Location		References
115.	1832	Bacchus, 'sketch'		[Exhib RA, London, 1117]; untraced		*Graves* I, 1905–6, 386
116.	1836	Hon A Kinnaird	m	Rossie Priory, Perths		*Gunnis* 1968, 77
117.	1841	Oak carving Payment(s): £115	wd	[coll Walter, 5th Duke of Buccleuch]; untraced		GPC
118.	1841	Repairs to the 'groupe of Hercules & Stag, painting glass shade etc' Payment(s): £15		[coll Walter, 5th Duke of Buccleuch]; untraced		GPC
119.	1849	Frederick Robinson		[Exhib RA, London, 1264]; untraced		*Graves* I, 1905–6, 387
120.	1851	George, 4th Earl of Courtown		[Exhib RA, London, 1385]; untraced		*AJ*, 1858, 108; *Graves* I, 1905–6, 387

CAMPELLMAN, Robert and Ralph fl 1784

Probably York masons, in 1784 they built the stable block at Castle Howard.

Archival References: Castle Howard Building Accts, G 4/2

Architectural Sculpture

No.	Date	Subject		Location		References
1.	1784	Carved work		Castle Howard, NR Yorks, stable block		*Gunnis* 1968, 77

CAMPION, J L, of Carlow c1782–1868

Funerary Monuments

No.	Date	Subject		Location		References
1.	†1838	Rev Francis Armstrong and Rev Henry Garnett		Carlow, Co Carlow	S	*Potterton* 1975, 38

CANE, R b 1796 fl 1818

He attended the Royal Academy Schools in 1818 and showed a bust that year, giving his address as 9 Soll's Row, Hampstead (1).

Literary References: *Graves* I, 1905–6, 388; *Gunnis* 1968, 77

Busts

No.	Date	Subject		Location		References
1.	1818	Mr Brindle		[Exhib RA, London, 1055]; untraced		*Graves* I, 1905–6, 388

CANOVA, Antonio 1757–1822

A sculptor, painter, architect and diplomat, Canova was in his day the most celebrated artist in Europe. Although he was only in Britain briefly towards the end of his career, he was closely connected with a network of British patrons, sculptors, connoisseurs, and admirers from an early period, and he exercised a considerable influence on the development of British sculpture.

He was born at Possagno, near Treviso on 1 November 1757, the son of Pietro Canova, a stonecutter. In 1768 he was apprenticed to the sculptor Giuseppe Bernardi in Pagnano, near Asolo, and he followed his master to Venice, where he worked in the studio of the sculptor Giovanni Ferrari and studied at the Venice Academy. In 1775 he set up a studio in Venice and during the next four years executed a number of works for members of the leading Venetian families. In October 1779 Canova set off on his first journey from Venice to Rome, pausing for a few days in Florence where he visited the studio of **Francis Harwood.**

Canova appears to have cultivated close ties with the British and Irish communities in Rome. One of his early champions was the Scottish painter, archaeologist and connoisseur, Gavin Hamilton, whose studio Canova visited in January 1780. In June 1780, in company with the sculptor **Giuseppe Angelini**, Hamilton viewed the plaster cast of Canova's *Daedalus and Icarus* (Correr, Venice), a cast that Canova had sent to the Venetian ambassador in Rome, Girolamo Zulian, as a demonstration of his skill. Hamilton, who admired the work for its naturalism, was one of those who persuaded Zulian to invite Canova to Rome on a more permanent basis, so that the sculptor could study the 'true' (neoclassical) style. Zulian gave Canova a block of marble to carve as he wished and provided him with a studio in Palazzo di Venezia. Canova chose as his subject *Theseus and the Minotaur*, but after modelling a composition of the two figures in combat, he accepted Hamilton's advice and carved a static group of the hero calmly seated on the body of the dead monster. The work, which demonstrated sound neoclassical principles and established Canova's fame in Rome, was sold to an Austrian buyer through whose family it finally passed to England (7).

During the 1780s Canova drew on Hamilton's paintings for a series of reliefs of subjects from the *Iliad*, the *Odyssey* and the *Aeneid*. In 1783 Hamilton recommended Canova as executant for the monument to Pope Clement XIV Ganginelli in SS Apostoli, his first major commission. A commission for a second papal tomb, to Clement XIII, followed in the same year (St Peter's, Rome). Hamilton strongly advised Canova to turn from traditional formulae for papal monuments and instead to pursue a more independent aesthetic, based on the study of Nature and the masterpieces of antique Greek sculpture. A portrait bust of the pontiff by **Christopher Hewetson**, a friend of Canova since 1780, provided guidelines for Canova's representation and the tomb's completion was celebrated at a party given by Hewetson in 1787.

By the mid-1780s Canova was beginning to attract the attention of English visitors. In March 1784 the diarist Miss Berry visited his studio and reported that he was doing 'wonders in the way of sculpture' and that his *Theseus* rivalled the masterpieces of antiquity (*Honour* 1959, 227). His first and most loyal British patron was Colonel John Campbell, later Lord Cawdor (**8, 10, 11, 15, 17, 30**), who in 1787 commissioned a statue of *Amorino* (**8**), the first of Canova's works to arrive in England, and also ordered a delicate and erotic *Cupid Awakening Psyche*, much admired as an innovative interpretation (**10**). Another enthusiastic English collector, Henry Blundell, bought a *Psyche* from Canova, to be housed with his Antiquities in purpose-built galleries at Ince in Lancashire (**9**). In 1790 the sculptor was approached by Frederick Hervey, the Earl-Bishop of Derry, who offended the Italian by complaining, in the sculptor's company, that his prices were too high. Despite the Earl-Bishop's retractions and flattering correspondence Canova steadfastly refused to work for him after this slight. Nevertheless, Canova was always generous in his promotion of other sculptors, and it was he who recommended **John Flaxman RA** to the Earl-Bishop. In 1792 Canova was learning English: his notebook with copies from the correspondence of Alexander Pope and useful conversational phrases is preserved at Bassano (*Honour* (ed) 1994, 231–250).

Canova's reputation continued to grow during the French Revolutionary Wars when the British were unable to travel on the Continent, but after the short-lived Peace of Amiens, 1802, they returned briefly to Rome. Sir Simon Houghton Clarke, a Jamaican plantation owner, asked for versions of the Antique pugilists, *Creugas* and *Damoxenos* (Vatican), and Adam Ferguson, the Edinburgh philosopher and historian, offered a price of £2000 for a statue of the Scottish politician Henry Dundas, 1st Viscount Melville. The resumption of the French wars prevented the execution of both these commissions.

Canova's most illustrious patrons during the wars were the Emperor Napoleon and his family, but commissions from Britain's enemy did not prevent negotiations for a statue of William Pitt the Younger for the Senate House, Cambridge. The initiative came from the 4th Earl of Aberdeen, who was authorised by the Pitt Monument Committee to make enquiries as to whether Canova would be interested in undertaking the work. Despite an encouraging response from the sculptor the committee were lukewarm about the prospect of employing Canova without his coming to England, and an outcry against the possibility by British artists led to the approach being abandoned. The commission went to **Joseph Nollekens RA**. A second significant attempt to enlist Canova's services, for the monument to Admiral Nelson in St Paul's Cathedral, was championed in *The Director* by the MP and dilettante Charles Francis Greville. Canova provided a model for a severe, free-standing sarcophagus, decorated with allegories of Nelson's birth, death and apotheosis (**2**). Again there was an angry response to the suggestion that native sculptors were incapable of providing an appropriate work. The commission eventually went to John Flaxman.

After the Napoleonic wars, visits to Canova's studio in Vicolo delle Colonette di San Giocomo degli Incurabili once again became popular with British tourists, who regularly recorded their impressions of the great man's workplace in their journals and letters. Lord Cawdor visited in January 1815 with the Duke of Bedford, who ordered his own version of the *Three Graces*, a subject Canova was then carving for the son of Napoleon's first wife, the Empress Josephine (**19**). Canova took the opportunity to improve upon his first interpretation and this sensuous masterpiece has, as the Duke of Bedford hoped, become the cornerstone of Canova's reputation in Britain.

In August 1815 the Roman Senate sent Canova to Paris to negotiate for the return of works of art removed by Napoleon's armies during the Italian campaigns. Canova's success in his mission, as he later acknowledged, was due largely to the support of the Duke of Wellington, Viscount Castlereagh, the Foreign Secretary, and particularly Castlereagh's Under-Secretary of State William Richard Hamilton. Arguing the moral case and the principle of the inviolability of property, the British delegation succeeded in forcing the French to return the priceless antiquities, and gave Canova 250,000 franchi to cover the costs of packaging and transport. As a mark of his gratitude Canova later presented 'ideal heads' to Wellington, Castlereagh, Hamilton and Charles Long, the Paymaster General (**31–34**).

In late October 1815 Canova made his first and only visit to England with his half-brother, Giovanni Battista Sartori. The visit lasted a little over a month and was prompted, at least in part, by an invitation to give his opinion on the Elgin Marbles at a time when the British government were contemplating their purchase. Canova's report was appended to the report of the Select Committee of the House of Commons. Canova professed to admire their animation, expression and concealed skill so much that he would have been 'perfectly contented with having come to London on their account alone' (*Visconti* 1816, xxii). His visit also encompassed a number of glamorous social encounters, probably engineered by his friend WR Hamilton, including an official visit to Downing Street and a farewell ball in which he was presented to the Prince Regent. He also made an array of social visits to collections, patrons, artists and acquaintances made in Rome. Canova visited Westminster Abbey, the Townley marbles in the British Museum, the Shelburne marbles at Lansdowne House, Thomas Hope's collection in Duchess Street, Richard Payne Knight's collection, the Royal Society in Somerset House, Hampton Court and Windsor Castle. In St Paul's Cathedral he admired the work of **John Bacon RA** and of **John Bacon II**, on whom he subsequently paid a visit. He called on his patrons, Sir Simon Houghton Clarke at High Barnet and the Duke of Bedford at Woburn, in the company of his long-standing friend **Sir Richard Westmacott RA** and the architect Jeffrey Wyatt, who later built the Woburn temple for the *Three Graces*. Westmacott also accompanied Canova to Holland House, Ashridge Park and to Bromley Hill, Kent, the home of Sir Charles Long.

The Royal Academy was slow to issue an invitation to Canova, perhaps, as Benjamin Robert Haydon suggested, because the Academicians were suspicious that the Italian had come to London to attract national commissions. **JCF Rossi RA**, who knew Canova in Rome, propagated this rumour and it gained such currency that Canova's allies took pains to rebut it in the press. An RA dinner was eventually held in his honour on 1 December, a few days before his departure, when he charmed the company. Sir Thomas Lawrence told Farington that he considered 'the manners of Canova a pattern for an artist' and that 'he had modest but manly deportment' (*Farington*, vol 13, 4746). Canova's social graces won him many friends and his views on a range of topics, from the Raphael cartoons and the architecture of Waterloo Bridge to the view of London from Sydenham, were meticulously recorded by witnesses. Canova's own brief notes of his visit appear in his manuscript, *Appunti sul Viaggio in Inghilterra* (1815).

He left London on 5 December, returning to Rome, where, in recognition of his services, the Pope created him Marchese d'Ischia. He paid tribute to his English hosts in the following year, when, in his capacity as Perpetual President of the Academy of St Luke in Rome, he arranged for Lawrence, Flaxman, Henry Fuseli and Benjamin West to be elected members. He also supervised the preparation of twenty-nine casts of antiquities from the Vatican collections, which were given to the Prince Regent by the Pope. The Prince Regent proposed to house the casts in the British Institution, but Lawrence persuaded the Prince that the RA's special bond with Canova made the Academy their more fitting home. It was rumoured that the government had given £5,000 to Canova to found a British school of painting in Rome (*GM*, April 1816, vol 86, pt 1, 364).

Canova provided no national monuments in Britain, but his charm and known skills won him important patrons and encouraged a special affection between the British art world and the Italian sculptor. The Prince Regent himself gave a major sum towards the monument in St Peter's, Rome, commemorating the Stuart line (**4**), and he also commissioned a group of *Mars and Venus* as an allegory of the advent of European peace (**23**). In 1817, in a spirit of triumphalism, the nation bought Canova's statue of *Napoleon as Mars* and presented it to the Duke of Wellington (**14**).

The Royal Academy agreed to exhibit Canova's *Hebe* and *Terpsichore* (**15, 16**), both owned by British patrons, in 1817. The display of these lightly polychromed figures acted as a public showcase for Canova's work and he received commissions from Lord Lansdowne, the Duke of Hamilton, the Earl of Liverpool and notably, the 6th Duke of Devonshire, who by his own admission became 'famished' for Canova's work (*Watson* 1957, 406), and was not sated until he had bought six major pieces (**12, 15, 24, 28, 35, 42**).

Canova's activities were followed in the British press and a major new work, the colossal equestrian statue of Ferdinand IV (Naples), was one of those eagerly described in the *Gentleman's Magazine* (*GM*, September 1820, vol 90, pt 2, 255). Lord Byron, who had earlier celebrated in verse Canova's bust of *Helen* (1811, Albrizzi Palace, Venice), wrote a prefatory passage eulogising the sculptor before Canto IV of *Childe Harold's Pilgrimage* (1818). Casts of Canova's work reached a popular market through **Benjamin** and **Robert Shout** of Holborn. In Rome, Canova continued to pay special attention to British travellers, taking Thomas Lawrence and **Francis Chantrey RA** on one occasion for a private candlelit viewing of his statue of Pauline Borghese (Borghese Palace, Rome). Canova's insistence on personal control of the conception and finish of a work were recorded in Mrs Eaton's *Rome in the 18th Century. . .* (1820), and his aesthetic of eroticised mythology, high finish and subtly tinted marble had an important influence on a number of British sculptors, including Sir Richard Westmacott, **E H Baily RA, Lawrence Macdonald, Thomas Campbell, R J Wyatt** and **John Gibson RA**. Gibson spent five years using Canova's studio in Rome, and was subsequently recommended by the Italian to British patrons.

In the early 1820s a small group of British connoisseurs, including the Earl of Minto and Lord Dunstanville, began to decry Canova's work, choosing instead to champion the more austere compositions of **Bertel Thorvaldsen**. Thomas Lawrence probably spoke for the majority however, when he retorted that the Dane was 'much inferior' to Canova, 'the ablest sculptor that had appeared since the Greeks' (*Farington* vol 16, 5677).

The news of Canova's death in Venice on 13 October 1822 shook the Italian people, who mourned him as a liberal benefactor, patron, and an honour to his age and country. Canova's heart was preserved in a monument in the Frari church, Venice, his right hand in a vase at the Venice Academy, and the rest of his body in the mausoleum at Possagno, which the sculptor had designed and decorated with his own paintings and sculpture. Shortly after his death, Elizabeth, Duchess of Devonshire organised a subscription to build a monument in Rome. This latter project, which was to be overseen by Thorvaldsen and partly carved by **Pietro Tenerani**, aborted when the new Pope, Leo XII, withdrew his support for its construction.

John Flaxman's *Address on the Death of Canova*, delivered at the Royal Academy in 1822, stressed the extent to which Canova had begun to be thought of as an adoptive Briton: 'This sculptor. . . has a claim to the affectionate regard of Englishmen in particular, not only by his strong attachment to the institutions and manners of our country, but by his polite and careful attentions to our countrymen in Italy, of whom I believe it may be truly said, that no English traveller ever sought a reasonable service from Signor Canova in vain' (*Flaxman* 1838, 296–7).

He was the subject of numerous memoirs and biographies in Italian and the knowledge of his oeuvre was extended in England with the publication of an English edition of Countess Isabella Albrizzi's *Opere di scultore e di plastica di Antonio Canova*. This was published as *The Works of Antonio Canova*, with engravings after the original plates by Henry Moses (1822–4). The sculpture galleries of Woburn and Chatsworth were centred around his sculpture and casts of 19 of his works were placed for teaching purposes in the Crystal Palace at Sydenham. Victorian sensibilities led to anxieties about the carnality of Canova's statues. Mrs Fox of Penjerrick feared the works might arouse dangerous animalistic passions (*Fox* 1882, 67) and John Ruskin, in *The Stones of Venice*, famously argued that the glorification of sensuality in marble was a symptom of the degeneracy of the English upper classes. Lord Holland's account of the arrival of the semi-nude *Sleeping Endymion* at Devonshire House in July 1823 suggests a *frisson*, for it was 'exhibited much to the real or affected horror of some ladies' (*Fox* 1923, 172).

The interest in Canova, his role in the development of European neoclassicism and his relationship with the British, revived in the second half of the 20th century, particularly through the work of Hugh Honour. The Woburn *Three Graces* attracted a new audience for the sculptor's work between 1988 and 1994, when a series of government interventions prevented its sale to the Getty Museum in Los Angeles. Eventually a fund-raising campaign secured the work for the National Galleries of Scotland and the Victoria and Albert Museum. Canova's correspondence with British friends and patrons between 1816 and 1817 has recently been published in volume 18 of the *Edizione Nazionale* of the sculptor's writings.

The following list of works consists only of those commissioned or contributed to by British patrons, works presented by Canova to British friends, one design for a British state memorial, and pieces bought by British collectors during Canova's lifetime. Canova published his own *Catalogo cronologico delle sculture di Antonio Canova* in Rome in 1816, with an addendum in 1819, in order to avoid erroneous attributions of his work. This was updated at the time of Canova's death in 1823 by Leopoldo Cicognara and was subsequently used by Melchior Missirini and later writers. Serious doubt is therefore cast on works such as the monuments at Speen and Elvaston (**1, 5**), which are not included in these lists, even if inscribed and based on Canova's designs.

MGS

Literary References: *Farington, passim*; *Visconti* 1816, xxii; *GM* 1816, vol 86, pt 1, 555, 630; 1836, vol 159, 186; *Passavant* 1836, *passim*; *Hartmann* 1955, 205–35; *Watson* 1957, 403–6; *Honour* 1959, 241–5, 225–31; *Honour* 1962, 137–8; *Neoclassicism* 1972, 195–214; *JKB* 1974 (1), 982–4; *Pavanello* 1976; *Liscombe* 1977, 700–705; *Read* 1982, *passim*; *Licht* 1983; *Whinney* 1988, *passim*; *Clifford* 1995; *Honour* (ed) 1994; *Busco* 1994, 21, 175 n103; *Grove* 5, 1996, 625–33 (Pavanello); *Ingamells* 1997, 176–7; *Eustace* 1997 (2); *Baker* 2000, 159–168; *Yarrington* 2000, 132–155; *Yarrington* 2002, 30–43; *Honour and Mariuz* (eds) 2002

Archival References: Appunti sul Viaggio in Inghilterra (MS 6087, Bassano, Museo Civico), transcribed, annotated and reproduced in *Honour* (ed) 1994, 383–394; Canova/Castlereagh; Canova/Sir Richard Westmacott VAM; Canova/Sir Richard Westmacott NY Met; Canova/Lawrence (one of these letters, dated 20 March 1820, transcribed in *George* 1996, 30–1); Canova/Bedford; Canova/Cawdor; Canova/Hamilton; Canova/Wellington

Selected Portraits of the Sculptor: Hugh Douglas Hamilton *Antonio Canova in his Studio with Henry Tresham and a Plaster Model for the Cupid and Psyche*, 1788–9, pastel, VAM E.406-1998, *Clifford* 1995, 8 (repr); John Bacon II, 1815, pencil, private coll, *Clifford* 1995, 14 (repr); Thomas Phillips, drawing, 1815, etched by Mary Turner, 1815, *Eustace* 1997 (2), 25, 26 (repr); Richard Reinagle, drawing, 1815, untraced, *Eustace* 1997 (2), 26; John Flaxman, drawing, 1815, untraced, *Eustace* 1997 (2), 26; Sir Thomas Lawrence, 1815–18, oil on canvas, Gipsoteca, Possagno, *Clifford* 1995, frontispiece (approximately 20 versions and copies known, *Eustace* 1997 (2), 95–6); George Hayter, 1817, oil on canvas, Gov Art Coll (British Embassy, Paris), *Clifford* 1995, 18, 87 (repr); **Henry Rossi**, bust, 1817, untraced; **Raimondo Trentanove**, marble bust after Canova's self-portrait, several versions including Woburn Abbey, Beds; **W Ewing**, ivory portrait, 1820, untraced

Funerary Monuments

1.	†1806	Christian, Margrave of Anspach, Brandenburg and Bareith	Speen, Berks		*Gunnis* 1968, 78; *Whinney* 1988, 376–7 (repr)
2.	1806–1807	Models for a monument to Admiral Lord Nelson in wax, plaster and terracotta (commission won by John Flaxman) Drawing(s): Museo-Biblioteca-Archivio, Bassano del Grappa	Gipsoteca, Possagno		*Honour* 1962, 137–8 (reprs); *Neoclassicism* 1972, 206; *Pavanello* 1976, 116 (reprs)
3.	1815–1818	Sophia, Countess Brownlow (†1814) Payment(s): £1350 Model(s): plaster, Pontificio Seminario Romano Maggiore, Rome; plaster, Accademia di San Luca, Rome	Belton, Lincs		*Pavanello* 1976, 125, 126 (repr); *Penny* 1977 (1), 43, 100 (repr); *Clifford* 1995, 13 (repr)
4.	1817–1819	Cenotaph to the House of Stuart: James, the Old Pretender (†1766), Charles the Young Pretender (†1788) and Prince Henry Benedict, Cardinal York (†1807) Payment(s): Prince Regent contributed 50,000 franchi Drawing(s): first idea, Biblioteca Nazionale, Florence; Museo-Biblioteca-Archivio, Bassano del Grappa Model(s): plaster, Gipsoteca, Possagno (x4)	St Peter's, Rome		*GM* 1816, vol 86, pt1, 270; 1819, vol 89, pt2, 62; *Pavanello* 1976, 127–8 (repr); *Rudolph* 1980, 44–54 (repr); *Clifford* 1995, 15, 16 (repr)
5.	†1829	Charles, 3rd Earl of Harrington	Elvaston, Derbys	S	*Gunnis* 1968, 78; Pevsner, *Derbys*, 1978, 210

Statues

No.	Date	Title	Material	Details	Literature
6.	*c*1783	Model for a figure of Piety or Humility for the monument to Pope Clement XIV Ganganelli (Santi Apostoli, Rome)	tc	[Acquired by Henry Blundell of Ince]; private coll	*Pavanello* 1976, 92, 93 (repr); *Clifford* 1995, 11 (repr); *Bowron and Rishel* 2000, 234–5 (repr)
7.	1781–1783	Theseus and the minotaur Payment(s): 1000 zecchini	m	[Commissioned by Girolamo Zulian, Venetian Ambassador to Rome. Later bought by Robert, Viscount Castlereagh and transported to London 1814–22]; VAM A.5-1962	*Honour* 1959, 225; *Honour* 1969, 1–15; *Pavanello* 1976, 91–2 (repr)
8.	1787–1789	Amorino Payment(s): 600 zecchini Model(s): plaster, Gipsoteca, Possagno	m	[Commissioned by John, 1st Baron Cawdor]; Anglesey Abbey, Cambs Other versions: for Princess Lugumirsky, Lancut Castle, Poland 1786–8, marble for John La Touche, NGI, Dublin, 1790–1, marble with wings, for Nikolaj Jusupov, Hermitage, St Petersburg, 1794, bought by a Parisian, Ms Jullot, 1798; untraced	*Honour* 1959, 227; *Pavanello* 1976, 93 (reprs); *Honour* 1994, 129–40; *Clifford* 1995, 11, 90 (repr)
9.	1789–1791	Psyche and butterfly Payment(s): 600 zecchini, and 100 as a gift	m	[Bought by Henry Blundell of Ince]; private coll Other versions: Kunsthalle, Bremen, 1793–4, originally a gift for Girolamo Zulian	*Honour* 1959, 225; *Neoclassicism* 1972, 202–03; *Pavanello* 1976, 98 (repr); *Clifford* 1995, 12, 91 (repr)
10.	1787–1793	Cupid awakening Psyche Payment(s): 2000 zecchini Drawing(s): Museo-Biblioteca-Archivio, Bassano del Grappa EB 112.1123 Model(s): clay, Gipsoteca, Possagno; clay, Museo Correr, Venice	m	[Commissioned by John, 1st Baron Cawdor, passed on to Joachim Murat]; Louvre, Paris	*Honour* 1959, 227–8; *Pavanello* 1976, 98 (reprs); *Clifford* 1995, 8, 11, 89
11.	1796–1800	Cupid and Psyche standing Drawing(s): pencil, Museo-Biblioteca-Archivio, Bassano del Grappa, EB 112.1123	m	[Commissioned by John, 1st Baron Cawdor]; Louvre, Paris Other versions: St Petersburg, also commissioned by John, Lord Cawdor, 1800–3, marble	*Pavanello* 1976, 102–3 (repr); *Clifford* 1995, 11, 83 (drawing repr); *Bowron and Rishel* 2000, 238–9 (repr)
12.	1804–1808	Letizia Ramolino Bonaparte, Napoleon's Mother, seated (Madame Mère) Model(s): plaster, Gipsoteca, Possagno	m	[Louvre, Paris Bought by William, 6th Duke of Devonshire in 1818]; Chatsworth, Derbys	*Watson* 1957, 406 (repr); *JKB* 1972 (3), 322, 324, 330, 331 (repr); *Pavanello* 1976, 110 (repr)
13.	1809	Venus	m	[Bought by Lucien Bonaparte, then sold to Henry, 3rd Marquis Lansdowne by 1819]; Hearst San Simeon State Historical Monument, California Other versions: Residenzmuseum, Munich Named 'Venere Italica' Galleria Palatina, Florence	*Honour* 1972 (2), 666 n55; *Pavanello* 1976, 112 (repr); *Whinney* 1988, 376; *Palazzo Pitti* 2003, 193–209 (Hugh Honour)
14.	1802–10	Napoleon Bonaparte, as Mars Pacificator Payment(s): Bought by the British government for 66.000 francs Drawing(s): Museo-Biblioteca-Archivio, Bassano del Grappa; Biblioteca, Forlì	m	[Louvre, Paris Presented by the Prince Regent to the Duke of Wellington in 1817]; Wellington Museum, Apsley House, London, vestibule, 1442–1948 Other versions: Brera, Milan, 1809, bronze	*GM* 1817 Sept, vol 87, pt 2, 271; *Pavanello* 1976, 109–10 (repr); *Yarrington* 1988, 53, 223
15.	1808–1814	Hebe Drawing(s): Museo-Biblioteca-Archivio, Bassano del Grappa Model(s): plaster, Gipsoteca, Possagno	m	[Commissioned by John, 1st Baron Cawdor, bought by William, 6th Duke of Devonshire]; Chatsworth, Derbys Other versions: for G G Albrizzi, National Gallery, Berlin, marble, 1796 for Empress Josephine, Hermitage, St Petersburg, marble, 1800–05 for Veronica Guarini di Forlì, Pinacoteca Comunale, marble, 1816–17	*Graves* I, 1905–6, 388; *Pavanello* 1976, 119 (reprs); *JKB* 1972 (3), 323, 331; *Eustace* 1997 (2), 27, 51–2
16.	1814–1816	Terpsichore Model(s): plaster, Villa Carlotta, Tremezzo	m	[Commissioned by Sir Simon Houghton Clarke for Oak Hill, East Barnet, Herts]; Cleveland Museum of Art, Ohio Other versions: Fondazione Magnani Rocca, Mamiano, Parma, 1808–18, marble	SD *Graves* I, 1905–6, 388; *Hawley* 1969, 287–305 (repr); *Pavanello* 1976, 119 (repr); *Clifford* 1995, 13; *Eustace* 1997 (2), 23
17.	1815–1817	Reclining naiad or fountain nymph, roused by the music of Cupid Drawing(s): Museo-Biblioteca-Archivio, Bassano del Grappa; Biblioteca, Cagli; Uffizi, Florence Model(s): plaster, Gipsoteca, Possagno, two	m	[Commissioned by John, Lord Cawdor, passed on to George, Prince Regent]; Royal Coll, RCIN 2039 Other versions: without Cupid, bought by Charles Londonderry *c*1823, possibly that commissioned by Lord Darnley in *c*1821, NY Met, marble, 1819–22	*Watson* 1957, 405; *JKB* 1972 (1), 206–7 (repr); *Pavanello* 1976, 125, 126 (reprs); *Roberts* 2002, 141 –2 (repr); *Eustace* 1997 (2), 27

18.	1817	Seated young John the Baptist Model(s): Gipsoteca, Possagno	m	[Commissioned by Marquess of Douglas, later 10th Duke of Hamilton. Commission transferred to Duke de Blacas]; untraced Other versions: for Alexander Baring, 1821–22, marble, untraced		*Missirini* 1824, 512; *Pavanello* 1976, 129, 133 (plaster repr); *Clifford* 1995, 16
19.	1815–1817	Three Graces Payment(s): 6000 zecchini Drawing(s): Museo Correr, Venice, Biblioteca A74.CL.III, 1798 BIS Model(s): t-c, Giancarlo Gallino, Turin; Museo Correr, Venice; Musée des Beaux-Arts, Lyon; full size plaster, 1813, Gipsoteca, Possagno	m	[Commissioned by John Russell, 6th Duke of Bedford for Woburn Abbey, Beds, Sculpture Gallery]; VAM A.4–1994 and NGS Other versions: commissioned by Josephine de Beauharnais, Hermitage, St Petersburg, 1813–17, marble		*Clifford* 1995 (repr); *Baker* 2000, 159–68 (repr); *Yarrington* 2002, 30–43 (repr)
20.	1818–1820	Venus (The Hope Venus) Payment(s): 2000 zecchini Model(s): Gipsoteca, Possagno	m	[Bought from the sculptor by Thomas Hope in 1820]; LMG, W R Yorks 213/59 Other versions: plaster cast presented by the sculptor to Trustees Academy, Edinburgh, 1821; untraced		*Honour* 1972 (2), 658–70 (repr); *Pavanello* 1976, 129 (repr); *Clifford* 1995, 97 (repr); *Leeds* 1996, 5 (repr)
21.	1818–1822	Dancer with her hands on her hips	m	[Commissioned by Sir Simon Houghton Clarke]; NGC Other versions: for Josephine Beauharnais, Hermitage, St Petersburg, 1805–12, marble		*Missirini* 1824, 512; *Pavanello* 1976, 129 (repr); *Clifford* 1995, 13
22.	1819–1822	Fainting Magdalene Model(s): plaster, Gipsoteca, Possagno	m	[Commissioned by Robert, 2nd Earl of Liverpool]; untraced		*Watson* 1957, 405; *Pavanello* 1976, 130 (plaster repr); *Clifford* 1995, 79
23.	1815–1822	Mars and Venus Payment(s): 5,000 gns with Dirce Drawing(s): Museo-Biblioteca-Archivio, Bassano del Grappa Model(s): plaster, Gipsoteca, Possagno	m	[Commissioned by George, the Prince Regent]; Royal Coll		*Pavanello* 1976, 128, 129 (repr); *Carlton House* 1991–2, 225; *Clifford* 1995, 16, 79 (repr)
24.	1819–1822	Sleeping Endymion Payment(s): £1,500 Model(s): plaster, Gipsoteca, Possagno (x2)	m	[Commissioned by William, 6th Duke of Devonshire]; Chatsworth, Derbys		*Watson* 1957, 405; *JKB* 1972 (3), 323, 324, 326, 330, 331 (repr); *Pavanello* 1976, 130–1 (repr)
25.	1820–1822	Sleeping Nymph (unfinished at death) Payment(s): £500 Model(s): plaster, Gipsoteca, Possagno	m	[Commissioned by Lord Lansdowne]; VAM A.30-1930		*Canova/Lansdowne;* *Grove*, 630; *Watson* 1957, 406; *Pavanello* 1976, 130, 131 (repr)
26.	1819–1824	Dirce Payment(s): 5,000 gns with Mars and Venus Model(s): plaster, Gipsoteca, Possagno	m	[Proposed by the sculptor to George, the Prince Regent in 1820]; Royal Coll, RCIN 2042		*Missirini* 1824, 511; *Pavanello* 1976, 130, 131 (repr); *Carlton House* 1991–2, 225; *Roberts* 2002, 143 (repr)
27.	nd	Models (3) for Maria Louisa Habsburg as Concord (Galleria Nazionale, Parma); for the Romanzov Peace (National Museum, Kiev, Ukraine); and for a Dancer	tc	[Given to Miss Mary Berry, 1820 or 1821]; untraced		*Clifford* 1995, 17, 94–5 (reprs)
Busts						
28.	?1804–1805	Letizia Ramolino Bonaparte, Napoleon's Mother (Madame Mère)	m	[Bought by William, 6th Duke of Devonshire, in 1823]; Chatsworth, Derbys		*Pavanello* 1976, 110 (repr); *JKB* 1972 (3), 323, 330, 331; *Clifford* 1995, 93 (repr)
29.	1814	Napoleon Bonaparte	b	[Commissioned by Lady Holland for Holland House, London]; untraced		*Busco* 1994, 19
30.	1814	Peace		[Acquired by John, 1st Baron Cawdor]; untraced		*Missirini* 1824, 508; *Pavanello* 1976, 123; *Clifford* 1995, 11, 89
31.	1816	Ideal head	m	[Presented by the sculptor to William Richard Hamilton]; Ashmolean WA 1996.395	S	*Missirini* 1824, 509; *Pavanello* 1976, 127; *Eustace* 1997 (2), 68–9, 76–8 (repr)
32.	1816	Ideal head	m	[Presented by the sculptor to Sir Charles Long, later 1st Baron Farnborough]; Kimbell Art Museum, Fort Worth, Texas	S	*Missirini* 1824, 509; *Pavanello* 1976, 127; *Eustace* 1997 (2), 72–3, 81–3 (repr)
33.	1816	Ideal head (head of a dancer)	m	[Presented by the sculptor to Arthur, 1st Duke of Wellington]; Wellington Museum, Apsley House, London 1455–1948	S	*Missirini* 1824, 509; *Pavanello* 1976, 127 (repr); *Eustace* 1997 (2), 70–1, 79–80 (repr)
34.	1816	Ideal head (Helen)	m	[Presented by the sculptor to Robert, 1st Viscount Castlereagh]; private coll Other versions: for Contessa Isabella Teotechi Albrizzi, Palazzo Albrizzi, 1811, marble ex coll Marchesa Groslier, marble, 1817–18; untraced	S	*Missirini* 1824, 509; *Neoclassicism* 1972, 207; *Pavanello* 1976, 126, 127 (repr); *Eustace* 1997 (2), 74–5, 84–5 (repr)

35.	1817	Laura	m	[Bought from the sculptor by William, 6th Duke of Devonshire in 1819]; Chatsworth, Derbys	*JKB* 1972 (3), 323, 324, 330, 331 (repr); *Pavanello* 1976, 126, 127 (repr); *Clifford* 1995, 96 (repr)
36.	1819	Herm of Sappho Payment(s): 100 luigi Model(s): ?plaster, Gipsoteca, Possagno		[Commissioned by William John Bethel]; private coll	*Missirini* 1824, 511; *Pavanello* 1976, 132; *Honour* 1991, 193–200
37.	1819	Herm of Tuccia Vestal		[Commissioned by Frederick Webb, London]; untraced	*Missirini* 1824, 511; *Pavanello* 1976, 131
38.	1821–1822	A Muse	m	[Commissioned by Alexander Baring, London]; untraced	*Missirini* 1824, 513; *Pavanello* 1976, 132
39.	1822	Herm of Beatrice	m	[Commissioned by Alexander Baring, London]; untraced	*Missirini* 1824, 513; *Pavanello* 1976, 132
40.	1822	Herm of Peace	m	[Commissioned by Alexander Baring, London]; untraced	*Missirini* 1824, 132; *Pavanello* 1976, 132
41.	1822	Lucrezia d'Este	m	[Commissioned by Alexander Baring, London]; untraced	*Missirini* 1824, 513; *Pavanello* 1976, 133
42.	1803–1822	Napoleon Bonaparte	m	[Bought by Dowager Marchioness of Abercorn, given by her to William, 6th Duke of Devonshire]; Chatsworth, Derbys	*Missirini* 1824, 512; *Watson* 1957, 406; *JKB* 1972 (3), 323, 325, 330, 331 (repr); *Pavanello* 1976, 109 (repr)
43.	1823	Lansdowne Venus		[Exhib Carlisle Ac, 157]; untraced	*Carlisle Ac Exhibs*, 1823, 13
44.	nd	William Richard Hamilton	p	Gipsoteca, Possagno	*Eustace* 1997 (2), 29

CANSICK, H fl 1826

Funerary Monuments

1.	1826	James Redfern		Kentish Town, London	*Gunnis* 1968, 78

CAPIZZOLDI (or CAPITSOLDI) fl 1755–74

C F Bell suggests that he can perhaps be identified with Giovanni Battista Capezzuoli, who was working in Florence about 1760 and again in 1777 and who appears to have come to England. Gunnis states that Capizzoldi was born in Italy and worked in Florence, but yielded to the persuasion of **Joseph Wilton RA**, whom he met in Florence, and accompanied him to England in 1755. On his arrival in London Capizzoldi took the attic storey of a house in Warwick Street, Golden Square, where he proceeded to improve the appearance of his poorly furnished sitting-room by painting chairs, pictures and curtains on the bare walls. **Nathaniel Smith** was a frequent guest and J T Smith noted that he was served with breakfast, or an oyster and a pot of porter.

During his stay in England he worked with Wilton, and when the latter received the commission from Parliament to execute the Westminster Abbey monument to General Wolfe it was Capizzoldi who carved the relief depicting Wolfe's death (1). This was described as a 'spirited and interesting bronze bass-relievo, inlaid in the lower part of the monument, exhibiting the seige of Quebec' (*JT Smith* 2, 1828, 176). The work was unveiled in 1772, but it is not known whether the Italian was still in England at the time. He had certainly returned home by 1774, for in that year **Thomas Banks** met him in Rome and received instruction from him on marble-cutting. Banks wrote to Nathaniel Smith on 4 February 1774 'Your good friend Capitsoldi has been truly kind to me; he has improved me much by the instructions he has given me in cutting the marble, in which the Italians beat us hollow' (*Smith* 2, 1828, 194).

Literary References: *Smith* 2, 1828, 170; *Bell* 1938, 20–1; *Gunnis* 1968, 78; *Pyke* 1973, 24; *Baker* 2000, 85–6, 93

Funerary Monuments

1.	1772	General Wolfe's death, relief (monument by Joseph Wilton)	l	Westminster Abbey, London, north ambulatory	*Baker* 2000, 85 (repr)

Miscellaneous

2.	*c*1762	Model in wax of King George III's state coach (perhaps executed with Voyez)		Mansion House, City of London	*Pyke* 1973, 24

CARABELLI, Casimoro and Donato fl 1800–03

The brothers came from Milan and were sent over to England by the Earl-Bishop of Bristol to install terracotta friezes after **John Flaxman RA**'s Homeric designs round the dome at Ickworth. They appear to have worked in association with the **Coade Factory of Lambeth**. The Ickworth Papers list payments of £28 7s a month made between 1800 and 1803, plus free lodging, washing and ale. Their assistant received 10/6d a week.

Literary References: *Kelly* 1990, 175–6

Archival References: GPC

Architectural Sculpture

1.	1800–3	Frieze	tc	Ickworth Hall, Suffolk, rotunda	Pevsner, *Suffolk*, 1974, 286; *Irwin* 1979, 172–3 (repr)

CARDELLI, Dominico, of Rome fl 1786–1810

Responsible for classically inspired monuments in Continental Europe, his only known work in England is the memorial to John Smith, drowned off Staten Island, New York. **P Cardelli** may have been his son.

Literary References: *Gunnis* 1968, 78; *Hartmann* 1969, 9–38; *Licht* 1982, 1259

Funerary Monuments

1.	1789	Lieutenant John Smith		St Mary Aldermanbury, City of London	*Gunnis* 1968, 78

CARDELLI, P fl 1815–16

P Cardelli, who may be the son of **Domenico Cardelli**, exhibited at the Royal Academy in 1815–16 and at the British Institution in the latter year. His address in 1815 was 22 Gerrard Street and the following year he moved to 42 Greek Street. He may be Pietro Cardelli (1776–1822), who exhibited in the Paris salon of 1804 and met considerable success in the United States.

Literary References: *Graves* I, 1905–6, 392; *Worley* 1993, 41–50

Busts

1.	1816	Unidentified gentleman	[Exhib RA, London, 902]; untraced	*Graves* I, 1905–6, 392
2.	1816	Unidentified gentleman	[Exhib RA, London, 902]; untraced	*Graves* I, 1905–6, 392
3.	1816	Unidentified gentleman	[Exhib RA, London, 902]; untraced	*Graves* I, 1905–6, 392

Miscellaneous

4.	1815	Love reposing	[Exhib RA, London, 902]; untraced	*Graves* I, 1905–6, 392
5.	1816	Cupid sleeping (perhaps identifable with 'Love reposing')	[Exhib BI, London, 269]; untraced	*Graves* 1875, 86

CARDWELL, Holme 1815–

Born in Manchester, he attended the Royal Academy Schools in 1834 on the recommendation of **Sir Francis Chantrey RA**, giving his age as 19 and his address as 14 Percy Street. He won a silver medal for a model in 1839 (**24**) and in 1841 went to Paris, where he is thought to have studied for 3 years under the sculptor **David d'Angers** and to have distinguished himself at the Académie Royale. From Paris he moved to Rome and remained there for some considerable time. In 1844 a vistor to Cardwell's studio mentioned that he had just arrived in the city and was engaged on a group of *Greyhounds Playing* (**6**), which 'shows a keen observation of Nature, and great power' (*GM*, 1844, i, 71). The article added 'He has executed but few groups, one of which, Mrs Beaumont, of Yorkshire, ordered' (**5**, *ibid*). In 1852 Cardwell sent to England his colossal marble group of *The Good Samaritan*, which had taken him two years to complete (**7**). A correspondent for the *Art Journal* noted that the composition and its spirited execution were said to have been highly praised by **John Gibson RA** and other sculptors in Rome. The article went on to say: 'The *Manchester Courier* informs us that the sculptor went over to Paris some years since and studied for three years under David; he distinguished himself at the *Academie Royale.* He then returned to Manchester and carried off the first "Heywood Medal," afterwards he came to London and was much noticed by Chantrey, and gained the silver medal of the Royal Academy' (*AJ*, 1853, 297).

Cardwell exhibited at the Royal Academy between 1837 and 1856. In the years 1837–41 he gave his address as 38a Edward Street, Hampstead Road and then 48 Greek St, Soho. In 1856 he submitted *Sabrina* directly from Rome (**8**).

Literary References: *Graves* 1875, 86; *Graves* I, 1905–6, 393; *Gunnis* 1968, 78

Archival References: RA Premium list, 1839

Statues

1.	1836	Bathers, sketch for a large group		[Exhib Soc of BA, London, 875]; untraced		*Johnson* 1975, 75
2.	1837	Girl and lizard		[Exhib RA, London, 1177]; untraced		*Graves* I, 1905–6, 393
3.	1840	Group of Italian greyhounds		[Exhib BI, London, 454]; untraced		*Graves* 1875, 86
4.	1841	Group of boys with a bird's nest		[Exhib RA, London, 1221]; untraced Other versions: 'Two boys with a bird and nest' listed in inventory of 1st Lord Leverhulme, 1855, marble		*Graves* I, 1905–6, 393; *Lady Lever* 1999, 81
5.	1844	A group, subject unknown		[coll Mrs Beaumont of Yorkshire]; untraced		*GM* II, 1844, 71
6.	1844	Greyhounds playing		Untraced		*GM* 1844, 1, 71
7.	c1853	The Good Samaritan	m	[Cheltenham Hospital, Glos]; Birmingham MAG, inv P.95'77		Pevsner, *Glos: Vale & Forest of Dean*, 1976, 133; *Silber* 1987, 20, cat 47
8.	1856	Sabrina		[coll J Murray]; Hove Museum, Sussex		*Manchester Art Treasures* 1857, 133; *Graves* I, 1905–6, 393
9.	pre-1857	Huntsman and a stag	b	[coll R Openshaw]; untraced		*Manchester Art Treasures* 1857, 135; *Conn* vol 197, April 1978, 43 (cover repr)
10.	pre-1857	The shepherd Paris	m	[coll J Pender]; untraced		*Manchester Art Treasures* 1857, 134
11.	pre-1857	Venus Victrix	m	[coll R Openshaw]; Manchester CAG 1914.59		*Manchester Art Treasures* 1857, 134; *Gunnis* 1968, 78
12.	1862	Diana		[Exhib Manchester]; untraced		GPC
13.	1868	Lydia and the blind boy		Mrs Magson, of Bournemouth, Hants (c1960)	SD	GPC
14.	1870	Callisto		[Exhib Cardwell's studio, Rome]; untraced		GPC
15.	nd	Group of two greyhounds playing under a side-table		Ascot, Bucks (NT)	S	
16.	nd	Ione and Nydia	m	Birmingham MAG, inv no 61'99		*Silber* 1987, 43, cat 48
17.	nd	Nymph with a bow and quiver		[Christie, 21 May 1887, 100 gns]; untraced		*Gunnis* 1968, 78

Busts

18.	1837	John Kennedy		[Exhib RA, London, 1259]; untraced	*Graves* I, 1905–6, 393
19.	1837	Unidentified gentleman		[Exhib Soc of BA, London, 578]; untraced	*Johnson* 1975, 75
20.	1840	Dr Calvert, warden of the collegiate church, Manchester		[Exhib RA, London, 1161]; untraced	*Graves* I, 1905–6, 393
21.	1840	Dr Dalton	m	[Exhib RA, London, 1128]; untraced	*Graves* I, 1905–6, 393
22.	1840	Dr Marsh		[Exhib Birmingham Soc of A]; untraced	*Gunnis* 1968, 78
23.	1840	Thomas Henshaw		[Exhib RA, London, 1175]; untraced	*Graves* I, 1905–6, 393

Miscellaneous

24.	1839	A model, unidentified subject	[RA silver medal]; untraced	RA Premium list

CAREW, F, I fl 1834

He showed two busts at the Royal Academy, giving his address as Brighton.

Literary References: *Graves* I, 1905–6, 393

Busts

1.	1834	Dr Jenks	[Exhib RA, London, 1103]; untraced	*Graves* I, 1905–6, 393
2.	1834	Mr Wigan	[Exhib RA, London, 1055]; untraced	*Graves* I, 1905–6, 393

CAREW, F, II fl 1841–49

In 1849 his address was 40 Cambridge Street, Hyde Park, London.

Literary References: *Graves* I, 1905–6, 393

Statues					
1.	1849	Sketch in plaster for a statue in marble	[Exhib RA, London, 1243]; untraced		*Graves* I, 1905–6, 393
Busts					
2.	1841	William Shakespeare	Liverpool Playhouse, Foyer	S	
Miscellaneous					
3.	1849	Diana after the Chase	[Exhib BI, London, 514]; untraced		*Graves* 1875, 86

CAREW, John Edward *c*1782–1868

He worked initially as **Sir Richard Westmacott RA's** principal carver, but then spent 14 years carving portrait busts and mythological subjects for one patron, the 3rd Earl of Egremont, for Petworth. After Egremont's death, the sculptor was beset by financial problems, but he continued to exhibit and undertook a number of prominent public commissions.

Little is known of his early life. He was born about 1782, at Tramore, County Waterford, and is thought to have been the son of an Irish sculptor. The slender evidence for his father's occupation is the memorial to Rebecca Briscoe (†1798) once in Waterford Cathedral, signed 'Carew Fecit Waterford' (*Strickland* I, 1913, 152). By 1975 this had been removed, probably to Fiddown, County Kilkenny, where there is a Briscoe monument signed 'I. Carew fecit'. Potterton has plausibly suggested that this memorial may be an early work by Carew himself, not his father.

Carew may have had some training in Dublin, though there is no record of his attendance at the Dublin Society. He was perhaps apprenticed to a sculptor in the city or he could have attended another school. He left Ireland for London, where he assisted Sir Richard Westmacott from 1809 until 1826 or 1827 and again in 1828–9 (**75**). In 1812 Carew exhibited his first work, a bust, at the Royal Academy (**52**). That year he submitted a model in competition for a monument to be erected in Rio de Janeiro (**25**). Only three models were submitted and in 1815 Carew was awarded the 3rd prize of £50 (*Farington* XIII, 4667). In 1821 he set up his own studio with one of his brothers at 62 Edgware Road. He may also have worked as a mason for in 1822 'J. E. Carew' submitted a tender, which was not accepted, for building St Peter's, Regent Square, London (*New Churches Report Book*, 97).

Carew's practice was profitable. He later claimed that although at first Westmacott paid him only 5 or 6 pounds a week, by 1823 he was earning about £1,700 annually from Westmacott (Westmacott put the figure at £1,200 p a). In addition there was the income from his own commissions, which amounted to about £800 annually.

A turning point in Carew's career came when he was introduced to the 3rd Earl of Egremont, a generous supporter of British artists, whose country home, Petworth House, was famous as a centre for artistic society. In 1824 Egremont bought Carew's statue of *Arethusa* (**28**), so beginning a close association between sculptor and patron which lasted until the Earl's death in 1837. On 5 May 1829 the *Cumberland Pacquet* carried a report that Egremont had given £10,000 'for some very elegant groups' by Carew, a report contradicted by the Earl a fortnight later. Nonetheless in 1831 Carew moved to Brighton, at Egremont's request, in order to be nearer to Petworth and in 1835 moved again, to Grove House, Petworth, a property belonging to the Earl. There is a superb collection of Carew's works at Petworth, including 'ideal', neoclassical subjects, such as *Adonis and the Boar* (**29**), *Venus at Vulcan's Forge* (**31**) and *Prometheus and Pandora* (**41**) and a number of portrait busts (**59–63**). Most of these are displayed in the Promethean Hall, which was built in 1836–7, under Carew's supervision, specifically to house his works. It was exceptional for such a large collection of one sculptor's works to be displayed together in a purpose-built gallery. Carew undertook several further architectural projects on Egremont's behalf, including alterations to the chancels at Tillington and Petworth and the design of the Earl's Brighton lodge. He employed a number of workmen, including James Welch, Carew's foreman from 1822 onwards, James Lane, a marble mason and W Griggs, who worked as Carew's assistant for about three months in 1831.

After the Earl's death Carew claimed that his former patron owed him a considerable sum, successively escalating in his estimates from £5,326 11s 7d to £50,310 5s. In a statement delivered to the Earl's executors on 13th March 1838 Carew claimed a balance outstanding of £22,485 and argued that in 1823 Egremont had offered to pay him £1,700 a year to leave Westmacott's employment and work principally for him. He continued by describing the arrangement made between them, 'I was eight years in Town after that period, during which Lord Egremont occupied the greater portion of my time, and from that period to the present (upwards of seven years) having been induced to quit London on purpose, I devoted the whole of my time and services to his Lordship, sacrificing all the prospects which a residence in town and competition with other sculptors held out during the best period of my life. I built a House and large Studio and Gallery at Brighton at the desire of Lord Egremont and expended upon those, and also with my changes of residence, considerable sums' (*Carew v Burrell* 1840, 167).

Two legal disputes ensued, involving Carew and the Earl's executors. At the first hearing at Lewes Assizes in 1840 his counsel withdrew the suit, since the defence argued persuasively that the Earl had remunerated the sculptor amply, though irregularly, when he thought it appropriate. This was not the end of the matter. During the insolvency proceedings, Carew again argued that giving up an independent career and leaving London at a time when his reputation was growing, in order to work for the Earl, had left him badly out of pocket. This situation was particularly difficult for he was the head of a large family. Carew's fine statue of William Huskisson in Chichester Cathedral was discussed (**10**). Carew maintained that the statue had been executed on Egremont's behalf, whilst the Earl's executors refused to accept that he had commissioned it. Evidence that the Earl had frequently seen and commented upon the statue whilst the Huskisson Memorial Committee had almost no contact with the sculptor persuaded the court that this work could be claimed as a commission from the Earl. In his summing up, Carew's lawyer noted the difficulties of defending him against such powerful adversaries. He concluded that Carew was clearly much worse off than he had been before he had entered into his arrangement with the Earl and that it was impossible to make much sense of the figures as neither Carew nor the Earl had kept proper financial records. There was evidently some public sympathy for Carew's predicament as the *Times* (19 May 1842, 6) reports that this speech was greeted by a burst of applause by the spectators in the Court. The court ruled that Carew's total claim against the Egremont estate amounted to £19,207 18s 5d but he had already been paid £21,331 9s 1d and he was declared bankrupt.

Carew continued to exhibit until 1848 when his eye-sight started to fail, showing largely portraits and religious subjects. In 1842 several went on display at the British Institution, where a statue of a boy playing marbles, *The last stake* (**44**), received an enthusiastic response. It was described in the *Art Union* as 'a noble and beautiful statue, satisfactory to the anatomist and most valuable to the lover of Art'. A model of the *Adoration of the Magi* (**82**) was considered even more successful, and the *Madonna and Child* which formed the focal point of the group and was also exhibited in marble was described as 'a glorious conception executed with perfect skill' (*AU*, 1842, 77).

Carew undertook several prominent public commissions in the years after the court case. His best-known work, a statue of *Sir Richard Whittington listening to the London Bells* for the façade of the Royal Exchange, was executed in 1844 (**46**). In the same year he exhibited *A Sleeping Falconer* (**45**) at the Westminster Hall exhibition, having already shown it at the British Institution in 1843. Its success eventually led to a statue of Henry Grattan for St Stephen's Hall in the Palace of Westminster, completed in 1857 (**49**). On the advice of Sir Charles Eastlake, he was selected to make *The death of Nelson*, one of the four bronze reliefs at the base of Nelson's Column in Trafalgar Square (**83**). This was attached to the pedestal in December 1849, but there was an uncomfortable postscript to the commission; the founders, Christy, Adams and Hill, were later prosecuted for cheating the government by using metal of an inferior quality for the casting. The work is still in position.

He was responsible for several significant works for Roman Catholic churches. These included an altarpiece depicting the *Baptism of Christ* for the Chapel of St John the Baptist in Brighton (**76**). Carew later claimed that the Earl of Egremont had commissioned this work and owed him money for it, although the Earl had written to the local press specifically denying this claim and stating that he had never contributed to the building or decoration of any Catholic church. Carew executed a number of statues still *in situ* (**47, 48, 50**) for the magnificent Italianate cathedral at St John's, Newfoundland and an elaborate altarpiece, which was dismantled during the remodelling of the church in the 1950s (**79**).

He was awarded a donation of £20 by the Royal Academy shortly before his death in 1868, having lived in retirement for some years and was buried in an unmarked grave in Kensal Green Cemetery. The RA assisted the 'Misses Carew' with a sum of £30 in 1869 and a similar sum the following year. His death seems to have gone unnoticed by the press. Other members of his family appear to have become sculptors, for an 'F Carew' and 'F Carew Junr' exhibited sculpture at the RA in 1834 and 1849 respectively.

Carew has been described as a feckless but charming character. He was considered an exceptionally able carver, whose sculpture combined neo-classical dignity with emotion and realism, but his works were felt to lack intellectual content: his friend, Benjamin Robert Haydon, wrote, 'as rapid as lightening with his chisel but idle in thought, preferring the chat of a gossiping Coffee House to the glory of fame . . . cutting heads from memory & statues without Nature, the wonder is he does so well!' (*Haydon Diary* III, 1963, 172). (Add inf. Alastair Laing)

EH

Literary References: *CP*, 5 May 1829, 1, 19 May 1829, 3; *AU*, 1840, 50–1; 1842, 77; 1844, 216; *Carew v Burrell* 1840; *Carew Insolvency Proceedings* 1842; *The Times*, 1841–1845, *passim*; *Builder*, 1844, 419; 1853, 624; *Strickland* I, 1913, 152–4; *Palgrave* 1866, 125; *Finch* 1966, 84–96; *Gunnis* 1968, 78–80; *JKB* 1972 (3), 329, 331 n27; *JKB* 1973 (3), 1640–3; *Potterton* 1975, 38–9; *JKB* 1977 (2), 367–73; *Read* 1982, *passim*; *Busco* 1994, 42, 93, 175 n115; *Grove* 5, 1996, 740–1 (Turpin); *Egremont* 1985, 280–7; *Curl* 2001, 237–8, 242; *FitzGerald* 2002, 46–65; *Laing* 2003, *passim*; *ODNB* (Wroth/Rev Turpin)

Archival References: Orchard Wyndham MSS, 1838–41; RA/GA, 1868–70

Portraits of the Sculptor: George Clint, The sculptor with *Prometheus and Pandora* in the background, c1837, oil on canvas, Petworth House, Sussex; John Simpson, nd, painting, nd, untraced (repr *Finch* 1966, 84)

Funerary Monuments

1.	†1798	Mrs Osborne	Fiddown, Co Kilkenney		
2.	?1818	General Sir John Floyd	St James, Hampstead Road, London		*Gunnis* 1968, 80
3.	?1823	Rev Henry Williams	Marlesford, Surrey		*Gunnis* 1968, 80
4.	†1825	Charles, Earl Whitworth	Sevenoaks, Kent		Pevsner, *Kent: West & Weald*, 1976, 511
5.	?1825	Mary Field	St John, Hackney, London		*Gunnis* 1968, 80
6.	?1828	Henry Hoare	Morden, Surrey		*Gunnis* 1968, 80
7.	†1829	Rear-Admiral Richard Willis	Petworth, Sussex		Pevsner, *Sussex*, 1965, 296
8.	†1831	Dr John Johnson	Petworth, Sussex		Pevsner, *Sussex*, 1965, 296; *Finch* 1966, 93
9.	†1831	Rev Denis O'Donnell	Tallow, Co Wexford	S	*Potterton* 1975, 38
10.	1831	William Huskisson (†1830)	Chichester Cathedral	S	C v B, 1840, 8, 19, 67–71, 78, 151–54, 166, 171, 172; 1842, 19, 124–7, 148–9, 152–4, 248–9, 286, 290–7, 353–5, 497–9; Appdx, 34, 46, 50, 54–5; Pevsner, *Sussex*, 1965, 153
11.	†1833	Thomas Eyre	Hassop, Derbys		Pevsner, *Derbys*, 1978, 239
12.	†1834	Canon James Clarke	Tillington, Sussex		Pevsner, *Sussex*, 1965, 351
13.	1834	Edmund Woods (†1833) and his womenfolk	Chichester Cathedral, Sussex	SD	C v B, 1840, 9–10, 25–6, 71–2, 167, 171, 173; 1842, 20, 232; Appdx 34, 46, 50; Pevsner, *Sussex*, 1965, 154; *Finch* 1966, 95
14.	†1835	Ann Child	Petworth, Sussex		
15.	†1836	William French	Lyminster, Sussex	S	Pevsner, *Sussex*, 1965, 268
16.	†1837	Mrs Fitzherbert	St John the Baptist, Brighton, Sussex		Pevsner, *Sussex*, 1965, 432; *Finch* 1966, 93, 96 (repr)
17.	1837	Percy family (with a relief figure of Faith, originally intended for the monument to Rev Curran, Wexford)	Petworth, Sussex	S	Pevsner, *Sussex*, 1965, 296; *Finch* 1966, 95–6 (repr)

18.	c1838	Admiral, Lord Nelson, model only		Untraced		Orchard Wyndham MSS, 18 May 1838
19.	1837–1838	George, 3rd Earl of Egremont, colossal clay model, later broken up		Destroyed		Orchard Wyndham MSS, 18 May 1838; C v B, 1842, 35
20.	†1844	Robert Gibbings		St Nicholas, Brighton, Sussex	S	
21.	†1845	Sir Henry James Tichbourne		Tichborne, Hants		Pevsner, *Hants & Isle of Wight*, 1967, 621
22.	1846	Michael Nugent (†1845)		Kensal Green Cemetery, London		*Curl* 2001, 237–8
23.	†1847	Hugh, 3rd Duke of Northumberland		St Paul, Alnwick, Northumbs		Pevsner, *Northumbs*, 1992, 134
24.	†1850	Rev Edward Cullen		St John the Baptist, Brighton, Sussex		Pevsner, *Sussex*, 1965, 432; *Finch* 1966, 93
Statues						
25.	1812	Royal equestrian statue for Rio de Janeiro, model		[RA, London]; untraced		*Farington* XIII, 4667, 11 July 1815
26.	1817	J P Curran		[Exhib RA, London, 1018]; untraced		*Graves* I, 1905–6, 393
27.	c1822	Young Dick Whittington listening to Bow bells		[Whittington Almshouses, Islington; Phillips, 16 March 1860]; Felbridge, Surrey (1967)		*AJ Cat* 1851, 298 (repr); Pevsner, *London: N*, 1998, 703; *Ward-Jackson* 2003, 323
28.	1822–1824	Arethusa Payment(s): £700	m	Petworth House, Sussex Other versions: cast presented to the RHA (destr 1916)	SD	Orchard Wyndham MSS, 18 May 1838; C v B, 1840, 16–7, 51, 159, 172; 1842, 3, 123, 286; Appdx, 13–15, 50; *Graves* 1875, 86; *Finch* 1966, 85–7; *JKB* 1973 (3), 1643; *JKB* 1977 (2), 371, 373 (repr); *Stewart* 1, 1985, 119;
29.	1824–1825	Adonis and the boar Payment(s): £1,000	m	Petworth House, Sussex		Orchard Wyndham MSS, 18 May 1838; C v B, 1840, 17, 166, 171–2; 1842, 3–4, 19, 286; Appdx, 32, 46, 50; *Graves* 1875, 86; *Johnson* 1975, 75; *JKB* 1973 (3), 1643 (repr); *JKB* 1977 (2), 371, 373 (repr); *Stewart* 1, 1985, 119
30.	c1827	Diana	m	Royal Hib Ac		*Gunnis* 1968, 79; *Johnson* 1975, 75
31.	1825–1827	Venus at Vulcan's forge Payment(s): £4,000	m	Petworth House, Sussex, north gallery		C v B, 1840, 17, 166, 171, 172; 1842, 4, 19, 286; Appdx, 32, 156–60; *JKB* 1977 (2), 372, 373 (repr); *Rowell* 2000 (2), 45 (repr)
32.	1830	Gladiator and bear in the arena, model		[Exhib RA, London, 1227]; untraced Other versions: Colossal clay model made for Lord Egremont after 1831 and broken up at an uncertain date		C v B, 1842, 242; *Graves* I, 1905–6, 393
33.	1830	Group of boys	m	[coll Earl de Grey]; Wrest Park, Silsoe, Beds		*Grey Memoirs*, 1846, 82–85; *Gunnis* 1968, 79
34.	1829–1830	King William IV, colossal clay model for a fountain		[Commissioned by Mr D'Egville for Brighton]; destroyed		C v B, 1840, 21–2, 30, 167, 171, 172, 393; Appdx, 34, 46, 50; *JKB* 1977 (2), 373
35.	1829–1830	Satan, colossal model	p	Destroyed		C v B, 1840, 172; *JKB* 1977 (2), 373
36.	1829–1830	Theseus and the minotaur, colossal clay model		[Exhib RA, London, 1230]; destroyed		C v B 1840, 22, 23, 46, 82, 145, 167, 171; 1842, 5, 19, 109, 240–1; Appdx, 34, 46, 50; *Graves* I, 1905–6, 393; *Finch* 1966, 87–9
37.	1829–1831	The falconer Payment(s): £1,500	m	Petworth House, Sussex, north gallery Other versions: Portland stone version prepared for the exterior of Shingleton Park House, Bramley, bt by Egremont, 1838–9, but left with the sculptor		Orchard Wyndham MSS, 26 July 1838, 16 July 1839, 8 July 1840; C v B, 1840, 18, 78–9, 145, 166, 171, 172; 1842, 4, 19, 109, 286; Appdx, 32, 46, 56, 78–81; *Graves* 1875, 86; *Read* 1982, 201 (repr); *Rowell* 2000 (2), 45 (repr)
38.	1832–1835	Antique torso restored as Bacchus Payment(s): £500		Petworth House, Sussex		C v B, 1840, 18, 60, 145, 158, 166, 171, 172; 1842, 19, 109, 286, 324; *JKB* 1977 (2), 373
39.	1833–1835	Edmund Kean		Theatre Royal, Drury Lane, London		C v B, 1840, 29; *Finch* 1966, 86, 89 (repr); *Gunnis* 1968, 79
40.	1834–1835	Small putti 'for the outside of a house he was building in the country'		Wrest Park, Beds		C v B 1840, 31; 1842, 36
41.	1835–1837	Prometheus and Pandora Payment(s): £4,000	m	Petworth House, Sussex, north gallery		*Finch* 1966, 88–9 (repr); *JKB* 1977 (2), 373; *Rowell* 2000 (2), 45
42.	1838	George, 3rd Earl of Egremont, small seated figure with dog	m	Orchard Wyndham, Somerset, drawing room		Orchard Wyndham MSS, 26 July 1838; *Hearn, Upstone, Waterfield*, 1998, cat 79, 65 (repr)

No.	Date	Subject		Location		References
43.	1838–1839	Girl trapping a bird, unfinished figure	m	[for the 4th Earl of Egremont]; untraced		Orchard Wyndham MSS, 20 Nov, 12 Dec 1838, 23 March 1841; *Graves* I, 1905–6, 393
44.	1842	The last stake (boy shooting a marble) Drawing(s): two, Orchard Wyndham MSS	m	[for 4th Lord Egremont at Silverton House, Devon]; untraced		Carew/Egremont Corr, 16 July, 1 Dec, 10 Dec 1839, 18 July 1840, 27 Feb, 23 March 1841; *AU*, 1842, 77; *Graves* 1875, 86
45.	1843	A sleeping falconer	m	[Exhib RA, London, 1405]; untraced		*Graves* I, 1905–6, 393
46.	1844	Sir Richard Whittington Payment(s): £430	s	Royal Exchange, City of London, n front		*Graves* 1875, 86; *Leith* 1997, 340, 341 (repr); *Ward-Jackson* 2003, 323 (repr)
47.	c1850	St Joseph	m	Basilica of St John the Baptist, St John's, Newfoundland, Canada		www.stjohnsarchdiocese.nf.ca
48.	c1855	St Francis of Assisi; St Patrick	m	Basilica of St John the Baptist, St John's, Newfoundland, Canada, Piazza		www.stjohnsarchdiocese.nf.ca
49.	1856–1857	Henry Grattan	m	Palace of Westminster, London, St Stephen's Hall	S	*Walker* 1961, 34, cat no 35; *Finch* 1966, 88, 91 (repr)
50.	1858	The Immaculate Conception	m	Basilica of St John the Baptist, St John's, Newfoundland, Canada, Piazza		www.stjohnsarchdiocese.nf.ca
51.	nd	Meleager		Royal Hib Ac		*Gunnis* 1968, 79
Busts						
52.	1812	Dr Roche		[Exhib RA, London, 920]; untraced		*Graves* I, 1905–6, 393
53.	1813	Arthur, 1st Duke of Wellington		Stratfield Saye, Hants Other versions: coll. John Harris Esq		*Graves* I, 1905–6, 393; *Finch* 1966, 93–4 (repr)
54.	1813	Unidentified lady		[Exhib RA, London, 897]; untraced		*Graves* I, 1905–6, 393
55.	1818	George Ponsonby		[Exhib RA, London, 1061]; untraced		*Graves* I, 1905–6, 393
56.	1820	King George III		[Exhib RA, London, 1034]; untraced		*Graves* I, 1905–6, 393
57.	1830	Edmund, 3rd Baron Thurlow		Untraced		C v B, 1840, 33; *Gunnis* 1968, 80
58.	1830	General Sir George Brown		Untraced		C v B, 1840, 33; *Gunnis* 1968, 80
59.	1830–1832	Colonel (later General) Sir Henry Wyndham	m	Petworth House, Sussex, north gallery Other versions: For General Wyndham; untraced		C v B, 1840, 23, 85, 167, 171, 172; 1842, 20; Appdx, 34, 46, 50; *Graves* I, 1905–6, 393; *Barrett* 1971 (1), 79 (repr 25); *Rowell* 2000 (2), 44
60.	1832	John, 4th Marquess Townshend		Petworth House, Sussex Other versions: Raynham Hall, Norfolk Woburn Abbey, Beds		C v B, 1840, 23, 167, 171, 172; 1842, 20; Appdx, 34, 46; *Graves* I, 1905–6, 393; *Gunnis* 1968, 80; *Rowell* 2000 (2), 44
61.	c1832	Miss Harriet King		Petworth House, Sussex		C v B, 1840, 23–4, 167, 171, 172; 1842, Appdx, 34, 46, 50; *Finch* 1966, 93; *Gunnis* 1968, 80
62.	1831–1834	George, 3rd Earl of Egremont	m	Petworth House, Sussex, north gallery		Orchard Wyndham MSS, 8 July 1840; C v B, 1840, 23, 167, 171, 172; 1842, 20; Appdx, 34, 48, 50; *JKB* 1977 (2), 373 (repr); *Rowell* 2000 (2), 44
63.	1831–1834	Mrs John King	m	Petworth House, Sussex, north gallery		C v B, 1840, 25, 167, 171, 172; 1842, 20; Appdx, 34, 46, 50; *Finch* 1966, 93; *Gunnis* 1968, 80; *Rowell* 2000 (2), 44
64.	1835	Captain Frederick Marryat	m	[Exhib RA, London, 1112]; untraced		*Graves* I, 1905–6, 393
65.	1835	Rev Dr H M Wagner	m	National School, Church St, Brighton, Sussex		C v B, 1840, 34; *Graves* I, 1905–6, 393; RG/JP, 2, 245
66.	1843	Edward Cooke	m	[Exhib RA, London, 1428]; untraced		*Graves* I, 1905–6, 393
67.	1844	Theobald Mathew		[Exhib Adelaide Gallery]; untraced		*Gunnis* 1968, 80
68.	1845	Unidentified lady	m	[Exhib RA, London, 1382]; untraced		*Graves* I, 1905–6, 393
69.	1846	General Sir Robert Sale		[Exhib RA, London, 1504; Phillips, 16 March 1860]; untraced		*Graves* I, 1905–6, 393
70.	1846	Lady Georgiana Fane		[Exhib RA, London, 1453]; untraced		*Graves* I, 1905–6, 393
Chimneypieces						
71.	pre-1825	Five		[for Sir Robert Peel]; untraced		BL Ad MS 40605 f358
72.	1829	Two Payment(s): £500		Buckingham Palace, London		TNA WORK 19/3 f364; *Gunnis* 1968, 79
73.	c1838	Neo-rococo Payment(s): £150	m	Orchard Wyndham, Somerset, drawing room		Orchard Wyndham MSS, 26 July 1838
74.	c1838	Neo-rococo, identical to the Orchard Wyndham chimneypiece Payment(s): £150	m	[Silverton House, Devon]; Killerton, Devon		Orchard Wyndham MSS, 26 July 1838, 13 Aug 1839
Architectural Sculpture						
75.	1828–1829	The Progress of Navigation, frieze relief (designed by Sir Richard Westmacott RA)		Buckingham Palace, London, façade		*Busco* 1994, 25

76.	1837	Baptism of Christ, altarpiece		St John the Baptist, Brighton, Sussex	C v B, 1840, 9, 24, 146–51, 166, 171, 173; 1842, 19, 111–22, 147–8, 158–9, 250–6, 286; Appdx, 34, 46, 50, 54–9, 297–304, 355–63, 394–7 Pevsner, *Sussex*, 1965, 432 (repr); *Finch* 1966, 88–9 (repr)
77.	1844	Royal Arms Payment(s): £350		Royal Exchange, London	MC GR, 29 March 1844; *Leith* 1997, 336
78.	1853	The Assumption, altarpiece Payment(s): £1,000		Our Lady of the Assumption and St Gregory, Warwick St, London	*Builder* 1853, 624; *Finch* 1966, 90–3 (repr); Pevsner, *London: Westminster*, 1973, 498
79.	nd	Baptism of Christ, altarpiece	s	[Basilica of St John the Baptist, St John's, Newfoundland, Canada, High Altar]; untraced	www.stjohnsarchdiocese.nf.ca
Reliefs					
80.	1839	The Good Samaritan	m	[Exhib RA, London, 1281]; untraced	*Graves* I, 1905–6, 393
81.	1841	Descent from the Cross, model only (?)		[Sculptor's studio]; untraced	Orchard Wyndham MSS, 9 Jan, 23 March 1841; *Lit Gaz*, 1265, 17 April 1841, 252; *The Times*, 22 April 1841, 4; *Lit Gaz*, 1841, 252
82.	1842	Adoration of the Magi, small model; Madonna and Child, the centre of this composition executed in marble		[Exhib BI, London, 451 and 452]; untraced	*AU*, 1842, 77; *Graves* 1875, 86
83.	1849	Battle of Trafalgar (Death of Nelson)	b	Trafalgar Square, London, base of Nelson's Column	*CIIA* 4/2/31 (repr); *Read* 1982, 90; *Yarrington* 1988, 317–8 (pl 114)
84.	1851	'Alto-relievo for a Temple in Sussex'		[Great Exhib]; untraced	RG/JP, 2, 245
Miscellaneous					
85.	1813	Rape of Proserpine		[Exhib RA, London, 909]; untraced	*Graves* I, 1905–6, 393
86.	pre-1824	Unspecified work for Lord Whitworth		Untraced	C v B, 1842, Appdx, 5
87.	1828	Cupids and swans, sporting		[Exhib Soc of BA, London, 891]; untraced	*Johnson* 1975, 75

CARLINE FAMILY, of Shrewsbury

John Carline I 1761–1835
John Carline II 1792–1862
Thomas Carline 1799–1868

The Carline family had been stonemasons in Lincoln where they were evidently well-known, since a road is named after them. John I's father, another John (1730–98) moved to Shrewsbury where he oversaw the building of the English Bridge between 1769 and 1774. His mother, Anne, was related to **John Hayward II of Lincoln**.

John Carline I ran a flourishing business as an architect, builder and monumental mason in Shrewsbury. He built himself a house in the Abbey foregate and his stone-yard was in the area now occupied by the Abbey Gardens, where some salvaged fragments of architectural sculpture, which he probably collected, can still be seen. For a time he worked in partnership with a bricklayer, John Tilley. Together they were employed by Thomas Telford to erect Montford Bridge, Salop, 1790–92 and to rebuild the bridge over the Rea Brook at Coleham Head, Shrewsbury after the flood of 1795. They also built the Welsh Bridge at Shrewsbury to their own designs, 1793–95. In 1791 the partners announced that they had purchased the stock in trade of the carver and marble mason **Van der Hagan of Shrewsbury**, and that they intended to continue his business in monuments and chimneypieces (*Shrewsbury Chronicle* 1791, inf James Lawson). Tilley apparently died 5 years later and Carline formed a new partnership with Tilley's stepson Henry Linell in 1797.

John Carline II, who was in partnership with his father for some years, took over the business at his father's death and it survived until the mid-19th century. He was granted the freedom of Shrewsbury in 1817 and exhibited a monument at the Royal Academy in 1825 (**44**). He was a prominent local figure who served as a Conservative councillor and is said to have made copies of the Parthenon Marbles which were for a time in Shrewsbury Museum. He joined forces with a **Richard Dodson** in 1835 or soon after, but Dodson ended the partnership in 1845. At about that time Carline found himself in financial difficulties. He lost a considerable sum in connection with the restoration of Hereford Cathedral, where he had contracted to work under the architect L N Cottingham. He was also owed money by his brother Thomas Carline. Disheartened by these problems he went to live with another brother, Richard, who was a successful solicitor in Lincoln. The business was continued for a time by his clerk, James Hewitt, but was eventually disbanded. John II died at Lincoln in 1862. Several descendants of the Carline family became artists, including Hilda Carline who married the painter Stanley Spencer, but none took up sculpture.

The firm's building and architectural works included a portico at Adderley Hall, Salop for Sir Corbet Corbet (1787–8, demolished 1877), St Alkmund, Shrewsbury (1793–5), the dining room at Pradoe, Salop for Sir Thomas Kenyon (1810), Claremont Buildings, Shrewsbury (nd) and Pellwall House, Market Drayton Staffs, built for Purney Sillitoe to designs by Sir John Soane (1822–8). As marble masons they provided a chimney piece for the library at Eaton Hall (**69**) and in 1812 received a payment of £1,446 for a marble floor in the entrance hall (Grosvenor Archives, in GPC). John Carline II, who was interested in ecclesiology and archaeology, specialised in gothic and romanesque church buildings and designed neo-Norman churches at Grinshill and Albrighton, Salop.

John I and II were responsible for a large number of funeral monuments. They executed the Poore family monument in Salisbury Cathedral (**28**). This is in an archaeologically accurate gothic revival style and has a finely carved canopy over a tomb-chest. It was described at the time as 'perhaps one of the most perfect specimens of florid Gothic in the Kingdom' (*New Monthly Mag*, 1817, 563). Sir Corbet Corbet's wall monument at Adderley has a graceful seated woman, carved in the round, under a draped canopy suspended from stylised flowers (**39**). The 'noble and splendid' gothic memorial to the Rev J B Blakeway in St Mary, Shrewsbury (**48**), was designed by John II *c*1818 and carved with 'exquisite talent' by the Carline firm a decade later (*GM*, 1828, ii, 315–7). They also erected the monument commemorating Lieutenant-Colonel John Hill, carved by **Sir Francis Chantrey**, 1815, at Hodnet, Shropshire and provided elegantly carved Grecian surrounds for Chantrey's busts of John Simpson and William Hazeldine in St Chad, Shrewsbury (**33**, **57**). Their most prominent public work is the group of four lions, carved in local Grinshill stone, at the base the column celebrating the military achievements of Rowland, 1st Viscount Hill, which was designed by Edward Haycock and erected in Shrewsbury in 1817 (**70**).

Thomas Carline entered the Royal Academy Schools in 1821 and there met and formed a close friendship with Philip Corbet (1801–1877), who later married Carline's sister Jane and established himself as a portrait painter in Shropshire. The two men travelled to Holland together in 1830 and Corbet's portraits include depictions of several members of Carline's family. Carline won the Society of Arts' silver Isis medal for a single figure in 1821 (**67**) and exhibited at the RA between 1825 and 1828, first showing a model for part of a monument commemorating Sir John Hill of Hawkstone (**43**). On viewing the monument, with its 'admirably executed' relief of a funeral procession, one critic declared 'never did sculpture tell its tale more forcibly, or with more congeniality to the hearts and feelings of Englishmen than this' (*GM*, 1826, II, 589). In 1826 he exhibited 'a most interesting and expressive group of two orphan children (**74**) which was fortunate enough to obtain one of the best situations in the sculpture-room' at the RA (*GM*, 1826, II, 589). Thomas Kenyon of Pradoe, Salop commissioned the statue of his son, Henry Kenyon, exhibited in 1828 (**68**): the child, who died in 1827 at the age of 5, is shown sleeping. In spite of this period of initial success, Carline failed to maintain his reputation as a sculptor and ended his career as a surveyor of bridges in the North Riding of Yorkshire.

In the following list all monuments by 'John Carline', unless otherwise indicated, are listed as the work of John Carline I until 1835, the year of his death.

EH

Literary References: RSA *Transactions*, vol 39, 1821, xxxviii; *Carline* 1958, 13–5; *Corbet and Carline Families* 1958, *passim*; *Hobbs* 1960, 17–8; *Gunnis* 1968, 80–1; *Colvin* 1995, 215–6

Archival References: GPC

Additional Manuscript Sources: Carline Order Book; Carline/Downward

Collections of Drawings: books of plans and drawings, 1771–1802 and plan of Shadwell Hall, Mainstone, 1812, Salop CRO

Miscellaneous Drawings: plan for a proposed museum and library in Shrewsbury, by John Carline II, nd, coll S Morley Tonkin

Funerary Monuments

1.	†1770	Catharine Lacon Childe (by John Carline I)	Kinlet, Salop	S	
2.	†1780	William Edwards (by John Carline I) (co-sculptor: Henry Linell)	Guilsfield, Montgomery		Pevsner, *Powys*, 1979, 107
3.	?1789	Francis Cunliffe (by John Carline I)	Llanyblodwel, Salop		*Gunnis* 1968, 80
4.	*c*1790	Catherine Baldwyn (by John Carline I)	Kinlet, Salop		*Gunnis* 1968, 80
5.	†1790	Hester Bright (by John Carline I) (co-sculptor: Tilley)	North Lydbury, Salop	S	*Gunnis* 1968, 80
6.	?1794	R W Lloyd (by John Carline I)	Oswestry, Salop		*Gunnis* 1968, 80
7.	†1801	John (†1789) and Bold Oliver (by John Carline I) (co-sculptor: Henry Linell)	Pontesbury, Salop	S	
8.	†1802	Richard Maurice (by John Carline I)	Llangedwyn, Denbighs		Pevsner, *Clwyd*, 1986, 214
9.	†1805	Thomas Jelf Powys (by John Carline I)	Berwick Chapel, Salop	S	
10.	†1806	John Bright (by John Carline I)	North Lydbury, Salop	S	
11.	?1806	Robert Laurence (by John Carline I)	St Julian, Shrewsbury, Salop		*Gunnis* 1968, 80
12.	?1806	William Kinaston (by John Carline I)	Ruyton, Salop		*Gunnis* 1968, 80
13.	†1808	John Jones (by John Carline I)	Llanllwchaiarn, Montgomery		Pevsner, *Powys*, 1979, 147
14.	?1808	Lucy Minor (by John Carline I)	Shawbury, Salop		*Gunnis* 1968, 80
15.	†1808	Sir Richard Hill (by John Carline I)	Hodnet, Salop	S	*Gunnis* 1968, 80; C Lib (repr)
16.	?1810	Richard Phillips (by John Carline I)	St Martin's, Salop		*Gunnis* 1968, 80
17.	†1811	John Oakeley (by John Carline I)	Bishop's Castle, Salop	S	*Gunnis* 1968, 80
18.	†1811	Sir Thomas Tyrrwhitt Jones (by John Carline I)	St Alkmund, Shrewsbury, Salop	S	
19.	?1813	Francis Leighton (by John Carline I)	St Chad, Shrewsbury, Salop		*Gunnis* 1968, 80
20.	?1813	Mary Corbet (by John Carline I)	Moreton Corbet, Salop		*Gunnis* 1968, 80
21.	?1813	Maurice Lloyd (by John Carline I)	Llanfair, Denbighs		*Gunnis* 1968, 80
22.	?1814	Charles Groby (by John Carline I)	Market Drayton, Salop		*Gunnis* 1968, 80
23.	†1814	Maria Bucknall (by John Carline I)	St Nicholas with St Giles, Sidmouth, Devon	S	

No.	Date	Subject		Location		Bibliography
24.	†1814	Valentine Vickers (by John Carline I)		Worfield, Salop	S	
25.	†1815	Stephen Sayer (by John Carline Carline I)		Atcham, Salop	S	
26.	†1816	Margaret Owen (by John Carline I)		Penrhos, Montgomery		Pevsner, *Powys*, 1979, 183
27.	?1816	Sarah Mason (by John Carline I)		Worfield, Salop		GPC
28.	1817	Edward (†1780) and Rachel Poore (†1771) (designed by Archdeacon Hugh Owen; by John Carline I)		Salisbury Cathedral, Wilts	S	*Penny* 1977 (1), 114 (repr)
29.	†1817	John Corbet (by John Carline I; designed by Archdeacon Hugh Owen)		Battlefield, Salop	S	Pevsner, *Salop*, 1958, 70
30.	†1818	Margaret Smitherman (by John Carline I)		Buildwas, Salop	S	
31.	†1819	Stephen Leeke (by John Carline I)		Chester Cathedral	S	*Gunnis* 1968, 80
32.	†1820	Edward Jenkins (by John Carline I)		Shrewsbury Abbey, Salop	S	
33.	post-1820	John Simpson (†1815) (by John Carline II, with bust by Sir Francis Chantrey)		St Chad, Shrewsbury, Salop		Pevsner, *Salop*, 1958, 258; *Penny* 1977 (1), 182, 183, 223 n23 (repr)
34.	1820	Mr Conwy and Mr Shipley (by John Carline I)		Rhuddlan, Flint	S	Pevsner, *Clwyd*, 1986, 426
35.	†1821	Edward Gatacre (by John Carline I)		Claverley, Salop		GPC
36.	†1821	Richard Scott (by John Carline I)		St Chad, Shrewsbury, Salop	S	*Gunnis* 1968, 80
37.	?1822	Elizabeth Clive (by John Carline II)		Moreton Say, Salop		*Gunnis* 1968, 81
38.	?1822	Paul Panton (by John Carline I)		Pentreath, Anglesey		GPC
39.	†1823	Sir Corbet Corbet Bt (by John Carline I)		Adderley, Salop	S	Pevsner, *Salop*, 1958, 53
40.	†1824	Annabella Puleston (by John Carline I)		Nannerch, Flint		Pevsner, *Clwyd*, 1994, 402
41.	†1824	William Childe (by John Carline I)		Kinlet, Salop	S	*Gunnis* 1968, 81
42.	†1825	Mary Williams (by John Carline I)		Welshpool, Montgomery	S	
43.	c1825	Sir John Hill (†1824) (by Thomas Carline)		Prees, Salop	S	*Graves* I, 1905–6, 394; Pevsner, *Salop*, 1958, 231 (repr 38b)
44.	1825	Thomas Taylor (by John Carline II)		[Exhib RA, London, 730]; untraced		*Graves* I, 1905–6, 394
45.	†1826	T Evans (by John Carline I)		Llanfechain, Montgomery		Pevsner, *Powys*, 1979, 130
46.	?1827	Joseph South (by John Carline I)		Wellington, Herefs		*Gunnis* 1968, 81
47.	†1828	Cecil, 1st Lord Forester (by John Carline I)		Willey, Salop		*Gunnis* 1968, 81
48.	1828	Rev J B Blakeway (†1826) (designed by John Carline II)	s	St Mary, Shrewsbury, Salop	S	*Colvin* 1995, 216
49.	†1829	Catharine Edwardes (by John Carline I) (co-sculptor: Dodson)		Buildwas, Salop		
50.	?1829	Sir Thomas Tyrwhitt Jones (†1782) (by John Carline I)		St Alkmund, Shrewsbury, Salop	S	*Gunnis* 1968, 81
51.	†1832	Rev George Scott (by John Carline I)		St Chad, Shrewsbury, Salop	S	*Gunnis* 1968, 80
52.	†1832	Rev Maurice Anwyll (by John Carline I)		Pennal, Merioneth		GPC
53.	†1832	Thomas Pemberton (by John Carline I)		Munslow, Salop	S	Pevsner, *Salop*, 1958, 214
54.	†1833	Ann Collins (by John Carline I)		Much Wenlock, Salop	S	
55.	?1834	Mary Heber (by John Carline I)		Hodnet, Salop		*Gunnis* 1968, 81
56.	†1840	Sir Richard Puleston (by John Carline II)		Worthenbury, Flint		Pevsner, *Clwyd*, 1986, 457–8
57.	†1840	William Hazeldine (by John Carline II, with bust by Sir Francis Chantrey)		St Chad, Shrewsbury, Salop	S	*Chantrey Ledgers*, 1991–92, 259
58.	?1842	Mr Scott and Rev John Wall (†1817) (by John Carline II) (co-sculptor: Richard Dodson)		Aberdovey, Merioneth	S	GPC
59.	†1842	Rowland, 1st Viscount Hill of Almarez and Hawkstone (by Thomas Carline)		Hadnall, Salop	S	Pevsner, *Salop*, 1958, 136
60.	?1844	Rev John Basnett (by John Carline II)		Baschurch, Salop		*Gunnis* 1968, 81
61.	1844	Rev John Wall (†1817) (by John Carline I) (co-sculptor: Richard Dodson)		Quatt, Salop	S	GPC
62.	†1845	Rev R Powell (by John Carline II)		Munslow, Salop		Pevsner, *Salop*, 1958, 214
63.	†1846	Richard Powell (by John Carline II)		Munslow, Salop	S	
64.	†1848	Anne Ravenshaw (by John Carline II)		Atcham, Salop	S	

65.	†1848	Hinton family (by John Carline II)		Much Wenlock, Salop	S	
66.	†1858	Richard Collins (by John Carline II)		Much Wenlock, Salop	S	
Statues						
67.	1821	Unidentified figure (by Thomas Carline)		[Soc of Arts, silver Isis medal]; untraced		*Gunnis* 1986, 81
68.	1828	Henry Kenyon, exhibited 'in a sleeping attitude peculiar to the child' (by Thomas Carline)	m	Pradoe, Salop	S	*Graves* I, 1905–6, 395; *Carline* 1958, 14; *Corbet and Carline* 1958, 7; GPC; C Lib (repr)
Chimneypieces						
69.	1806	For the library (by John Carline I)		Eaton Hall, Cheshire		GPC
Architectural Sculpture						
70.	1817	Four lions couchant (by Thomas Carline)		Lord Hill Column, Abbey foregate, Shrewsbury, Salop		*Yarrington* 1988, 162, 164 (pl 58)
71.	1834	Screen (by John Carline I)	s	[St Mary, Shrewsbury, Salop]; destroyed		*Colvin* 1995, 216
72.	c1840	Pulpit, pews and other work (by John Carline II)		St Giles, Shrewsbury, Salop		*Colvin* 1995, 216
73.	nd	Saints Peter and Paul, statues		Shrewsbury Abbey, Salop, façade		*Carline* 1958, 15
Miscellaneous						
74.	1826	Orphans at the grave of their parents (by Thomas Carline)		[Exhib RA, London, 1070]; untraced		*Graves* I, 1905–6, 394
75.	1827	The good Samaritan (by Thomas Carline)		[Exhib RA, London, 1076]; untraced		*Graves* I, 1905–6, 394

CARLINI, Agostino RA *c*1718–90

Carlini was one of the leading sculptors in Britain in the 1770s, and his surviving works show considerable virtuosity and invention. Although details of his life and work are sparse, he was a founder member of the Royal Academy and was hailed by one later commentator as 'the finest sculptor of the day' (*Passavant* 1836, vol 2, 276).

18th-century sources give his place of birth as Genoa, and Farington recorded his death at the age of 72. Nothing is known of his training or career before 1748, when he received payments for himself and his workmen at Huis ten Bosch in the Hague from the architect Pieter de Swart. These payments, for decorative carving commissioned by the Dutch court, continued until 1751. Carlini made a model for the Dutch royal barge, which was rejected because the quotation of 5,000 guilders was considered excessive, and in 1751 he carried out 'carved work' for the 'bed of parade' in which William IV of Orange lay in state and was carried to his grave. Royal patronage in the Netherlands seems to have ended with the monarch's death, and the only further reference to his work there is an advertisement inserted by the Hague sculptor, Anthoni Wapperom in the *Gravenhaegse Courant* (18 Dec 1754) for a sumptuous horse-sleigh in the shape of a gilded centaur 'made by the famous sculptor A. Carlini'. The sledge was advertised again in 1756, and in 1765 it was auctioned; its subsequent fate is unknown. By this time however Carlini was established in London.

The date of Carlini's arrival in England is uncertain; he is first recorded as an exhibitor at the Society of Artists in 1760, showing a design for General Wolfe's monument intended for Westminster Abbey (**1**). His earliest surviving work for a British patron, a full-sized marble statue of the famous quack doctor Joshua Ward (**11**), indicates that Carlini had considerable experience of working in marble. Ward, the inventor of the medicinal 'Pill and Drop', which bore his name, made a fortune from his questionable concoctions, and had many celebrated patients, including George II. He was also a philanthropist who founded hospitals for the poor. Ward is said to have paid Carlini an annuity of 200 guineas until the doctor's death in December 1761 in order to keep the sculptor in England. The statue, which may have been intended for a projected monument to Ward, shows him in all his bulk, his flabby face, bursting waistcoat and billowing coat giving ample scope for Carlini to demonstrate his broad and exuberant carving.

In 1768 Carlini was living in Dean Street, Soho, 'next door to the tin-shop at the corner of Compton Street' (*Public Advertiser* 13 and 14 April 1768), where his property was rated at £36. In 1768 he was one of the 22 artists who successfully petitioned George III to found the Royal Academy, and he served as one of the original nine 'Visitors' appointed as visiting instructors and superintendents. At the first Academy exhibition in 1769 he showed a plaster model for an equestrian portrait of George III (**13**), copies of which could be bought for 6 guineas each. This was acclaimed by the press as the finest image of the monarch carved to date. It must have brought the sculptor to royal attention, for in 1773 he produced a marble bust of the king (**22**), described at the time as 'a strong expressive likeness' (*Trusted* 1992, 783). Both the model and bust were acquired by the Royal Academy, and were subsequently displayed at Somerset House. The architect William Chambers commissioned Carlini to make some decorative sculpture for the Strand front of the building (**25, 26**) and the sculptor may have brought in **Giuseppe Ceracchi**, who lodged with Carlini in Soho in 1776, and worked on the ornaments before 1778.

In 1783 Carlini became Keeper of the Academy Schools, a post he kept until his death. J T Smith commented that he filled it with little distinction, since he failed to 'control the students sufficiently, but allowed them to take liberties with their superiors which would later have met with expulsion' (*Smith* 1828, 1, 159). Carlini appears as 'Agostino Turnthekey' in Pasquin's *The Royal Academicians. A Farce* (London 1786). He was also a member of the National Academy of Design of America.

Smith described Carlini as 'an Italian who associated mostly with foreigners' (*Smith* 1828, 2, 202), and the sculptor certainly appears to have worked closely with other Italians in London. In January 1771 he submitted a model in competition for Alderman William Beckford's monument (**5**), producing a design incorporating a seven foot high statue with bronze ornaments and gold lettering, estimated at £1500. Although unsuccessful, the model was drawn by Biagio Rebecca, engraved by Francesco Bartolozzi and issued as a print in 1772. Bartolozzi also engraved Carlini's equestrian model for the statue of George III mentioned above (**13**), as well as his later design for a monument to the composer, Johann Christian Bach. In Carlini's posthumous sale engraved plates of these works fetched £37 5s 6d, £47 5s, and £12 12s respectively, fetching notably higher prices than most of the sculpture in the auction.

Carlini was also a close associate of his fellow academician, **Giovanni Battista Cipriani**, to whom, it was rumoured, he was often indebted for his designs (*Smith* 1828, 2, 203). At the 1787 Academy exhibition Carlini showed a model for Cipriani's monument (**9**), drawing a hostile reaction from the press, who commented 'the medallion of [Cipriani's] head possesses neither the least likeness nor character of the worthy original; but this Mr Carlini will no doubt correct in the marble; – as well as give more forcible expression to the weeping genius' (*Press Cuttings* 1686–1835, II, 337). Carlini, stout and elegant and holding his sculptor's hammer, appears with Bartolozzi and Cipriani in a portrait by John Francis Rigaud, 1777 (NPG 3186).

The most notable of Carlini's executed monuments, to Lord and Lady Milton at Milton Abbey, Dorset, was designed by Robert Adam. The composition is a revival of a seventeenth-century formula, featuring a grieving husband reclining by the recumbent figure of his deceased wife (**8**). Like his other known funerary monuments, the Milton memorial displays the grace and skilful handling of draperies which were highlighted in Carlini's obituary. He died at 14 Carlisle Street, London on 16 August 1790 (*GM* 1790, 2,769) unmarried and intestate, and the administration of his will was granted to his sole heiress, 'Elizabeth Watton, spinster', who was apparently his housekeeper. In January 1791 she held a sale of Carlini's prints, models, books, equipment and other possessions, including his Royal Academy diploma.

The scattered references to Carlini's life in 18th- and 19th-century sources give little insight into his personality, although JT Smith penned a characteristically colourful impression of the sculptor; 'When Carlini was Keeper of the Royal Academy, he used to walk from his house to Somerset-place, with a broken tobacco-pipe in his mouth, and dressed in a deplorable great coat; but when he has been going to the Academy-dinner, I have seen him getting into a chair, and full-dressed in a purple silk coat, scarlet gold-laced waistcoat, point-lace ruffles, and a sword and bag' (*Smith* 1828, 205).

Contemporary sculptors clearly held his work in high regard, for Nathaniel Smith and Joseph Nollekens were amongst those who purchased work at his posthumous sale. Farington noted that Nollekens was collecting information on Carlini 15 years after the Italian's death. Other commentators were less willing to accord undiluted respect to a foreign sculptor. A contemporary press report, for instance, commented that although 'Carlini had great abilities' and 'He might have been stiled a genius . . . the superior minds of our English sculptures left him in this respect – far – far behind' (*Trusted* 1993, 201). J T Smith was also prepared to grant that he was 'a man of talent', whilst criticising his work as displaying 'foreign affectation' (*Smith* 1828, 2, 203). Carlini was indeed one of the very few foreign sculptors working in England in the 1770s and 1780s, and arguably the most important. Following the acquisition in 1991 of the statue of Dr Ward by the Victoria and Albert Museum, scholarly interest has begun to revive in this important but still enigmatic artist.

MGS

Literary References: *Press Cuttings* 1686–1835, vol 2, 337; *Pasquin* 1786, *dramatis personae*; *GM*, 2, 1790, 769; *Farington*, 1794, 1, 132; 1805, VII. 2524; *New Mont Mag*, 1816, vol 418, 1 June, n29; *Smith* 1828, I, 159, 2, 202–5; *Passavant* 1836, 2, 276; *Colvin* V 1973–76, 372–3, 466; *Penny* 197 (1), 109, 128, 206, 210; *DBI* 1960–2000, vol 20; *Hutchison* 1986, 24–5, 27–8; *Whinney* 1988, *passim*; *RSA J* 1991, 433; *Trusted* 1992, 776–84; *Trusted* 1993, 190–201; *Bindman and Baker* 1995, 337; *Baarsen* 1998, 172–83

Archival References: WCA Poor Rate, St Anne, Soho 1770 (A239)

Will: PROB 6-166, fol 221

Miscellaneous Drawings: Design for an unidentified monument, signed, pen and ink, Witt coll, Courtauld Institute of Art, 1420; attributed drawings for unexecuted or untraced works, BM, Anderdon coll, 1869, fol 305); Soane (repr *Trusted* 1992, 777); VAM (repr *Bindman and Baker* 1995, 337); impressions of an engraving by Bartolozzi after a lost design for a monument to J C Bach, BM Add. MS 38072 f17, VAM 29 599B

Auction Catalogues: *Carlini* 1791

Portraits of the Sculptor: Charles Maucourt *Agostino Carlini* 1762, watercolour and bodycolour on ivory (NPG 5388); Johan Zoffany *Life Class at the Royal Academy* 1771–2, oil on canvas (Royal coll); Peter Rouw the Elder, *Agostino Carlini* RA, exhib RA 1788, no 639, wax (untraced)

Funerary Monuments						
1.	1760	'Design for General [James] Wolfe's monument, near Buckingham Gate'		[Exhib Soc of Artists, 77]; untraced		*Graves* 1907, 49; *Trusted* 1992, 777, 778; *Bindman and Baker* 1995, 337 (repr)
2.	1764	'A model of a monument to be erected in Westminster Abbey to the memory of Dr Ward'		[Exhib Soc of Artists, 153]; untraced		*Graves* 1907, 49; *Trusted* 1992, 781
3.	1765	John, Earl of Shelburne (†1761) (designed by Robert Adam)		Bowood, Wilts, mausoleum		*Trusted* 1993, 192 (repr)
4.	1768	'A design for General [James] Wolfe's monument; a model'		[Exhib Soc of Artists, 142]; untraced		*Graves* 1907, 49; *Trusted* 1992, 777
5.	1770	Alderman William Beckford (†1770), model for the Guildhall monument competition Payment(s): 30 gns		Untraced		*GM*, I, 1819, 43; *Trusted* 1992, 784; *Trusted* 1993, 190–1 (repr)
6.	†1771	Harriet Benson, Lady Bingley Payment(s): £150 (part-payment?)		Bramham Park, W R Yorks, chapel		*Trusted* 1993, 195 (repr)
7.	†1771	Lady Sophia Petty, Countess of Shelburne Drawing(s): Bowood, Wilts		High Wycombe, Bucks, south chapel	S	*Trusted* 1993, 193–4 (repr); Pevsner, *Bucks*, 1994, 386
8.	1775	Joseph Damer, Lord Milton (afterwards Earl of Dorchester) and Caroline, Lady Milton (†1775) (designed by Robert Adam) Drawing(s): Soane, 62, 63, and 64, v.19 Model(s): 'Model of a monument for the late Lady Milton' exhib RA, 1784, 507		Milton Abbey, Milton Abbas, Dorset	SD	*Graves* I, 1905–6, 395; *Penny* 1977 (1), 109–110 (repr); *Trusted* 1993, 196–8 (repr)
9.	1787	Giovanni Battista Cipriani (†1785), (model for a projected monument)		[Exhib RA, London, 588]; untraced		*Graves* I, 1905–6, 395; *Trusted* 1993, 198
10.	†1839	Ann Joyce		West Norwood Cemetery, Lambeth		Pevsner, *London: S*, 1983, 341
Statues						
11.	1761–1764	'Dr' Joshua Ward Drawing(s): BM PDL1920, 0420-4 (attrib)	m	[coll Ralph Ward]; VAM A.2-1991		*Trusted* 1992, 778–9 (repr); *Bilbey* 2002, 57 (repr)
12.	1765	A dog	m	[Exhib Soc of Artists, 171]; untraced		*Graves* 1907, 49

No.	Date	Work		Location		References
13.	1769	Model for an equestrian statue of King George III, statuette Model(s): exhib RA, London, 1769, no 9	p	RA, London (diploma work)	S	*Graves* I, 1905–6, 395; *Radcliffe* 1969, 44–51 (repr); *Trusted* 1992, 781, 782 (repr)
14.	1776	Ecorché cast (Smugglerius)		Copy cast, RA, London		*Trusted* 1992, 783
15.	nd	'A beautiful model of a dog'		[Carlini sale, 1791, lot 32]; untraced		*Trusted* 1992, 784
16.	nd	A model of [William Augustus] the old duke of Cumberland 'in a case, and pedestal', statuette		[Carlini sale, 1791, lot 52]; untraced		*Trusted* 1992, 784
17.	nd	'A model of [William Augustus] the old duke of Cumberland', statuette		[Carlini Sale, lot 51]; untraced		*Smith* 1828, v.1, 205; *Trusted* 1992, 784
18.	nd	'Mars and Venus, and 2 Jews', statuettes	tc	[Carlini Sale, lot 31]; untraced		*Trusted* 1992, 784
19.	nd	'Two [figures] of mercury and Neptune', statuette	tc	[Carlini Sale, lot 49]; untraced		*Trusted* 1992, 784; *Trusted* 1993, 200
20.	nd	'Two boys – a groupe – and 5 more in clay', statuette		[Carlini Sale, lot 47]; untraced		*Trusted* 1992, 784
21.	nd	'Two figures of Romans in plaster, and a pedestal', statuettes		[Carlini Sale, lot 50]; untraced		*Trusted* 1992, 784
Busts						
22.	1773	King George III	m	RA, London	SD	*Graves* I, 1905–6, 395; *Radcliffe* 1969, 44–51 (repr); *Trusted* 1992, 782–3 (repr)
23.	1776	'Portrait of a young nobleman'		[Exhib. RA, London, 44]; untraced		*Graves* I, 1905–6, 395
24.	nd	'A colossal head of his Majesty, and a cast from the life, when a youth'		[Carlini sale, 1791, lot 40]; untraced		*Trusted* 1992, 784
Architectural Sculpture						
25.	1776–1778	Keystones, masks representing the Rivers Dee, Tyne and Severn Payment(s): £21 each Drawing(s): Soc Antiq, Green portfolio no2, 20, 'by William Chambers'	s	Somerset House, London, Strand façade		Chambers/Somerset Hse CHA 3/1/2; *Harris* 1970, 101; *Colvin* 1973–76, V, 372; *Trusted* 1993, 199, 201 (repr)
26.	1776–1778	Statues of Justice and Prudence Payment(s): £120 each	s	Somerset House, London, Strand façade		*Colvin* 1973–76, V, 373; *Trusted* 1993, 198–200 (repr)
27.	c1783	Design model for the Irish arms on Dublin Customs House		Untraced		*Bell* 1938, 54; *Leask* 1945, 188–9
28.	1783–85	Neptune and Mercury		[Dublin Customs House, attic storey of s. front]; destroyed		*Pinkerton* 1906, 200 (repr); *Bell* 1938, 54; *Trusted* 1993, 200
Reliefs						
29.	1770	'An emblematical figure representing maritime power and riches; a sketch'	w	[Exhib RA, London, 28]; untraced		*Smith* 1828, v.1, 205; *Graves* I, 1905–6, 395
Miscellaneous						
30.	1764	Mars and Venus, model		[Exhib Soc of Artists, 154]; untraced		*Graves* 1907, 49
31.	1766	A general, model		[Exhib Soc of Artists, 203]; untraced		*Graves* 1907, 49
32.	1771	A model		[Exhib RA, London, 27]; untraced		*Graves* I, 1905–6, 395
33.	1771	Two candlesticks, carved with seated revellers holding sheets of music Payment(s): £21	wd	[coll Charles Rogers]; Plymouth Museum and Art Gallery		*Trusted* 1993, 191–2 (repr); GPC
34.	1772	A model		[Exhib RA, London, 37]; untraced		*Graves* I, 1905–6, 395
35.	1783	'A model of Plenty'		[Exhib RA, London, 426]; untraced		*Graves* I, 1905–6, 395
36.	1785	'Mercury; a model'		[Exhib RA, London, 613]; untraced		*Graves* I, 1905–6, 395; *Trusted* 1993, 200
37.	1785	'Neptune; a model'		[Exhib RA, London, 575]; untraced		*Graves* I, 1905–6, 395; *Trusted* 1993, 200
38.	nd	'A model of the death of [James] Wolfe'		[Carlini sale, 1791, lot 53]; untraced		*Trusted* 1992, 777
39.	nd	'Dr Ward, and several other heads, &c'		[Carlini Sale, lot 41]; untraced		*Trusted* 1992, 784
40.	nd	'Four figures and 2 heads in plaster'		[Carlini Sale, lot 48]; untraced		*Trusted* 1992, 784
41.	nd	'Four plaster basso relievo, and sundry legs, &c'		[Carlini Sale, lot 37]; untraced		*Trusted* 1992, 784
42.	nd	Model 'for a watch'	wd	[Carlini Sale, lot 33]; untraced		*Trusted* 1992, 784
43.	nd	'Venus, Mercury, Neptune and a head, in plaster'		[Carlini Sale, lot 39]; untraced		*Trusted* 1992, 784; *Trusted* 1993, 200

CARPENTER, Aaron, of London fl 1762–67

No.	Date	Work		Location		References
Statues						
1.	1762	Acteon	m	[Exhib Free Soc of Artists]; untraced		*Gunnis* 1968, 82 quoting the *London Magazine*, 1762, 173

CARPENTER, Edmund fl 1688

In the late 1680s he was employed by Sir John Brownlow, who was then building Belton Hall, Lincs, to provide wood overmantels of quality in several parade rooms.

Literary References: *Gunnis* 1968, 82; *Beard* 1989 (1), 44

No.	Date	Work		Location		References
Chimneypieces						
1.	1688	Carved with birds, fruit and flowers Payment(s): £25	wd	Belton Hall, Lincs, drawing room next to little parlour		*Gunnis* 1968, 82

2.	1688	Carved with fish, shells, birds, fruit and flowers Payment(s): £26	wd	Belton Hall, Lincs, drawing room next to great parlour	*Gunnis* 1968, 82
3.	1688	With fruit and flowers Payment(s): £18	wd	Belton Hall, Lincs, great parlour	*Beard* 1989 (1), 44

CARPENTER, John fl *c*1727

Chimneypieces

1.	*c*1727	Description unavailable	Newby Hall, N R Yorks, 'Petter Banks roome'	GPC

Architectural Sculpture

2.	*c*1727	Ionic Capitals for the Venetian Room and 82 cartouches	Newby Hall, N R Yorks	GPC

CARPENTER, Robert 1750/51–

Only one work by this sculptor, has been identified, a wood relief inscribed 'Executed by Robert Carpenter of Bath, 1808, aged 57 / Sarah Palmer and Anne Carpenter the gift of their Beloved Father, Seymour Street'. The *Bath Chronicle* of 11 December 1817 mentions a Mr R Carpenter as a sculptor of sacred and historical works.

Literary References: *Lady Lever* 1999, 6–7

Reliefs

1.	1808	Queen Margaret and the robbers	wd	Lady Lever (inv LL 148)	*Lady Lever* 1999, 6–7 (repr)

CARPENTER, Samuel, of London fl 1712–32

His only recorded employer was Earl Fitzwalter of Moulsham Hall, who made payments to him in 1730–32.

Literary References: *Gunnis* 1968, 82

Archival References: GPC

Statues

1.	1729	Several, including Diana and Mercury	m	[Moulsham Hall, Chelmsford, Essex, exterior]; Diana and Mercury at Wood Hill, Danbury, Essex (*c*1960)	Pevsner, *Essex*, 1965, 156; *Gunnis* 1968, 82; GPC; C Lib (repr)
2.	1730	Three Payment(s): £63	l	[Moulsham Hall, Chelmsford, Essex]; untraced	Mildmay Accts; GPC

Busts

3.	1732	'leaden Busto of Venus, Bronz'd Payment(s): £3 13s	l	[Moulsham Hall, Chelmsford, Essex]; untraced	Mildmay Accts; GPC

Architectural Sculpture

4.	1729	'Lyons over the great piers' Payment(s): £26 10s	l	[Moulsham Hall, Chelmsford, Essex]; untraced	Mildmay Accts; *Gunnis* 1968, 82; GPC

Reliefs

5.	1732	Head of Seneca (medal) Payment(s): £1 11s		[Moulsham Hall, Chelmsford, Essex]; untraced	Mildmay Accts; GPC

CARPENTER, Samuel, of York 1660–1713

A decorative carver in wood and stone, he was probably responsible for a number of modest sepulchral monuments in Yorkshire. He became free of the Masons' Company of York in 1684 and was made a freeman of the city the following year. He worked at Ripon in 1702 (5) and at Castle Howard in 1705–6, where he provided wood carving in several rooms and extensive architectural ornaments on the exterior elevations (**6, 8**). In November 1705 he was paid for carving the highly unusual satyr heads on the sides of the Satyr Gate into the kitchen garden, as well as baskets of ornamental stone flowers above (7). The bill includes work on the house (CH Archives G2/2/18).

Carpenter signed the monument with a portrait bust to Lady Elizabeth Stapleton, 1684, at Snaith (**1**). The bust is described as 'lovely' by Gunnis and 'large and imperious' by Pevsner. In 1710 he was commissioned by the antiquary, Ralph Thoresby, to provide a monument to Thoresby's friend, Mr Thomson, for St John's, Leeds (**2**), and a bust of his father for Leeds Parish Church (**3**). On 25 January 1710 Thoresby recorded in his diary that he was 'with Mr Carpenter about the monument for my dearest father; left his picture & a model with him.' He visited Carpenter at least thrice in York to watch progress and evidently the two liked one another for he, Carpenter and Thoresby's cousin, Lumley of York dined together 'after, at his [Carpenter's] request, sitting for my picture in crayons.' The monument was completed by 3 March 1712, when Thoresby 'was all day at church, with Mr Carpenter, setting up a monument for my honoured and dear father.' In 1714 it was engraved by Sturt in London, and the engraving appeared in Thoresby's *Ducatus Leodiensis* 1715 (*Thoresby Diary*, vol 2, 76, 77, 80, 90, 222).

He died on 27 June, 1713 and was buried at St Lawrence, York. His wife, Frances, died in 1731, aged 69, but for some reason was not buried with her husband but in the church of St Dennis, York.

Literary References: *Gunnis* 1968, 82; *Saumarez Smith* 1990, 62, 122

Archival References: Castle Howard masons/carvers, 1706 G2/2/28; Castle Howard building accts G1/1; G1/2

Funerary Monuments

1.	1684	Lady Elizabeth Stapleton	Snaith, W R Yorks	S	Pevsner, *Yorks, W R*, 1967, 490; *Gunnis* 1968, 82; *Whinney* 1988, 446 n6
2.	?1710	Mr Thomson	[St John, Leeds, W R Yorks]; untraced		*Gunnis* 1968, 82
3.	1710–1712	John Thoresby (†1679)	St Peter, Leeds, W R Yorks		*Thoresby Diary*, vol. 2, 64, 76, 77, 80, 90, 222; *Thoresby* 1715, 48 (repr); *Friedman* 1973 (1), 7, 12 n14; *Pullan* 2006, 21, 152 (repr)
4.	nd	Unidentified subject, cartouche tablet	St Mary, Bishophill Senior, York		*Gunnis* 1968, 82

Architectural Sculpture

5.	1702	Carving on the obelisk (designed by Nicholas Hawksmoor) Payment(s): £72 3s 3d	s	Ripon, W R Yorks, marketplace	*Hewlings* 1981, 47

6.	1705	Cartouches for the Drawing Room, cornice for a closet, Corinthian capitals for Lord Carlisle's Dressing Room and other ornaments	wd	Castle Howard, N R Yorks	*Gunnis* 1968, 82; *Saumarez Smith*, 1990, 62
7.	1705–1706	Satyr heads for Satyr Gate and baskets of ornamental flowers above		Castle Howard, N R Yorks, entrance to kitchen garden	*Saumarez Smith* 1990, 122 (repr)
8.	1705–1706	'thirty-six pilaster capitals of the Corinthian order and seventeen pilaster capitals for the West Wing', ornaments for north and south fronts including festoons and bust, a dragon (£10), a shield on the South front and cherubim over a window Payment(s): £206	s	Castle Howard, N R Yorks, n and w fronts	*Gunnis* 1968, 82

CARPENTER, Stephen, of Blandford fl 1749–74

The son of another Stephen Carpenter, he was apprenticed to **Francis Cartwright of Bryanston** in 1749. Between 1770 and 1775 he was the master-mason responsible for building Milton Abbey, Dorset, a house designed by Sir William Chambers. Lord Milton appears to have been dilatory in settling his accounts, for Gunnis writes that in 1774 Chambers was forced to inform him that 'Carpenter has been with me and is much distressed for money to pay debts contracted' (BM, Add MS 41,136, fol 165,169). This letter, dated 29 March 1774 describes problems over payments, but makes no mention of Carpenter.

Literary References: *Gunnis* 1968, 82

Archival References: Apprenticeship Books, TNA, IR 1/18 fol 176

CARPENTER (or CHARPENTIERE), Andrew *c*1677–1737

Carpenter, 'a Man in his time esteemed for his Skill' (*Vertue* III, 83) was responsible for a number of major statues and monuments in marble and was the most successful designer and modeller of lead garden figures in the generation between **John Nost I** and **John Cheere**.

His background is obscure, though the diarist, George Vertue, who knew him well, noted that 'Charpentiere' had been born between 1675 and 1677. He may have been a native of the French-speaking Netherlands. Carpenter told Vertue that he had been instructed in 'the rudiments of drawing' by the French academician, Peter Eude, who later settled in Scotland (*Vertue* IV, 35). No details are known of his early training, but he was John Nost I's principal assistant, engaged in modelling and carving over several years for Nost before he set up independently (*Vertue* III, 83). Carpenter's name first appears in the rate-books in 1703, when he acquired premises in Portugal Row, close to the Nost workshop. His neighbours were predominantly French and included the sculptor **Nadauld**, the decorative painter Louis Laguerre and, from 1707 to 1714, the ironsmith Jean Tijou. J T Smith recorded that the workshop stood on the site in Piccadilly later occupied by Egremont House.

Carpenter's first major commission and one of his finest works was the statue of Queen Anne for the Moot Hall in Leeds, commissioned by Alderman William Milner and erected in 1713 (**8**). The Leeds antiquary, Ralph Thoresby, paid numerous visits to the sculptor's London workshop to check the work's progress and persuaded Carpenter to make a drawing of the statue to be engraved for Thoresby's *Ducatus Leodiensis* (1715). In tones that suggest intense civic pride, Thoresby described the erection of this 'most noble magnificent statue of her Majesty . . . to the full proportion; in the best white marble.' The statue, in a niche on the principal front of the hall above the town's coat of arms, 'was viewed by many of the nobility and gentry who generally esteemed it the best that was ever made, not excepting the most celebrated one [by **Francis Bird**] in St Paul's Churchyard' (*Ducatus Leodiensis*, 250). The directors of the building scheme at St Paul's Cathedral were sufficiently impressed with Carpenter's work to approach him as well as Bird in 1716 when they contemplated commissioning statues for the west end of the cathedral, but they gave the contract to Bird.

On one visit to the workshop in May 1714 Thoresby recorded that as well as works in marble he also saw 'curious workmanship' by Carpenter in lead (*Diary* 2, 209) and leadwork appears to have been Carpenter's mainstay. In 1716 he supplied garden sculpture to the 1st Earl of Bristol (**9**) and in 1722, an 'abundance of works' to the Duke of Chandos for Canons (**10**). Drawing on Nost's work, as well as classical and renaissance prototypes and his own innovations, Carpenter built up a substantial repertoire of lead figures. His price list submitted to Lord Carlisle at Castle Howard who made purchases in 1723 gives some indication of the range as well as the dimensions and prices of his garden ornaments:

	Feet	Pounds
Cain and Abel	16	20
Do	6	20
Hercules & Wild Boar	6	20
Dianna & Stagg	6	20
Narcifsus	7 1/2	27
Venus de medici	6	15
Antonius	6	18
Saturnus	6 1/2	20
Triton	6	20
Bacchus sitting	6	18
Faunus	6	20
Meleager	6	20
Adonis	6	18

Apollo	6	18
Flora	6	16
A Gladiator	6	12
Duke of Marlborough	6	28
Roman Wrestlers		20
Narcissus	5 1/2	20?
Neptune	5 1/2	9
Mercury	5 1/2	10
Antinous	5	8
Venus	5	10
Do	5	7
a Bagpiper	5	10
An Indian	5	8
Apollo	5	9
Flora	5	9
Mercury	5	9
Cleopatra	5	7
Daphne	5	8
A french paisant & paisanne [two figures]	4	10
Jupiter	4 1/2	6
Apollo	4	5
Winter & Autumn [2 :fig]	4 1/2	8:08:0
4 Signs of ye Zodiac	4	16
A faunus & Nimph [two figures]	4	8:08:0
Mercury & fame [two figures]	3	6:06:0
Apollo	3 1/2	3:10:0
Love & disdain [two figures]	3 1/2	8
A large vase	6	20
3 do	5	24
1 do	4	6
Boys and Girls		18:18:0
4 Large Bustos		16
a pr of vase		7
6 vases		22
12 flower potts large & small		24

The list was not comprehensive, for it did not include Carlisle's chosen figures (**12**). The sculptor was also prepared to provide bespoke items: William Aikman visited Carpenter and several other Hyde Park Corner figure makers in November 1725 on behalf of Sir John Clerk of Mavisbank and reported that although he was not impressed by the goods in stock it was possible to 'get something done a-purpose after a good design' (*Fleming* 1962 (1), 38). Packing and freight for leads required as much care as for marbles: Carlisle paid £84 for his statues, packing cases cost £9 7s 9d, and it took a workman nine and a half days, twenty-one pounds of 'spike' and a thousand 'double-tenns' nails to prepare the works for the journey to Yorkshire.

Carpenter clearly prospered in his middle years, for in 1718 he took a second site in Portugal Row, described in the rate-books as 'workhouse and land.' He also invested in property at Edgware, building 'some houses and an Inn' on the outskirts of the Canons estate. Vertue relates that the sculptor advertised his presence in the area with one of his own works 'and in the middle of the road way put up a statue for a sign' (*Vertue* III, 83). Chandos was incensed at this vulgarity, but the sculptor refused to remove the figure.

There were other influential patrons. In 1719 he provided garden ornaments under the direction of the architect, James Gibbs, for Wimpole Hall (**23**) and in 1722 he transported marble figures from Chatsworth to Chiswick and bronzed busts for Lord Burlington (**25**). Gibbs and Carpenter collaborated again on allegorical figures at Ditchley Park in 1722 (**11**), and on the monument to Montague Garrard Drake, 1725 (**2**), which cost £180. Carpenter's monument to the 'restless malcontent' Henry Booth, 1st Earl of Warrington (**6**), erected by his son, George, in 1734, was inspired by Gibbs's dramatic design for the monument to Katharine Bovey, 1727–8, in Westminster Abbey, illustrated in *A Book of Architecture*, 1728. The focal point of the Bovey monument is a pair of allegorical Virtues representing *Learning* and *Truth*, who point towards Mrs Bovey's portrait, to emphasize her particular qualities. The same attendant figures appear again on the Warrington monument, but as fashionable trappings to an epitaph extolling Warrington's revolutionary principles and exonerating him from allegations of corruption.

Carpenter's monuments make use of ornaments familiar from John Nost I's work, including scrolls, flaming urns, cartouches and putti. He appears to have kept his prices competitive, charging only £389 for the Warrington, a monument comparable in its materials and carving to Nost's memorial to Viscount Irwin, 1697, at Whitkirk, which cost £600. Carpenter's work did not suffer as a result of his careful budgeting: the reclining figure of Sir John Thornycroft, bewigged, in his nightgown and in mid-speech, is intricately carved, particularly the gesturing fingers and fleshy undersides of the feet (**3**).

In his later years Carpenter had business anxieties. He was increasingly obliged to give 'time & study to Cast Leaden figures' and complained that prices paid for work at this less prestigious end of the market were diminishing and that 'he had much ado to hold up his head at last' (*Vertue* III, 83). In January 1736 he announced in the *Daily Journal* that he intended to 'leave off entirely the casting of lead figures' and intended to sell 'his entire stock of Statues of Figures in Hard Lead, Vases, Pots and Pedestals'. Perhaps encouraged by two recently completed commissions in Cheshire (**6, 7**), he advertised an intention to 'apply himself solely to his other business, viz the Statuary and Carving Part in Marble and Stone' (*ibid*).

The advertisement had little effect. Carpenter is not known to have won any further major commissions and 'age and cares brought him to his end' in July 1737, aged a little over 60. He was buried in his parish church, St George, Hanover Square (*Vertue* III, 83). In his will the sculptor left all his 'cottages, houses, lands, tenements and estate' in Edgware to his wife Ann, together with his chattels and shop contents. His son, John Carpenter, who 'had been an Idle fellow many years' (*Vertue* III, 83) received the proverbial shilling. Ann Carpenter continued to pay rates on the Hyde Park property and in May 1744, a sale was held there of her late husband's 'Metal Statues or Figures in Hard Metal . . . together with his Moulds, Models and casts in Plaister' (*Daily Advertiser*).

There is no known portrait of the sculptor, 'a gross heavy man allwayes' (*Vertue* III, 83). He was of particular value to Vertue while gathering information for his intended history of British painting and sculpture, since Carpenter provided accounts of several artists including **Arnold Quellin**, the elder Nost, **John Nost II** and Louis Laguerre.

Carpenter's monuments have been described by Margaret Whinney as transitional works, hovering stylistically between the ornamental baroque of Nost and the new Gibbsian designs, which drew on developments in Continental sculpture. His lead garden figures, particularly the ambitious groups supplied for Powis Castle (**19, 20**), are masterpieces of the genre.

MGS

Literary References: *Vertue* III, 83, IV, 35; *Daily Journal*, 26 Jan 1736 (Burney 319B); *Daily Ad*, 4 May 1744 (Burney 381B); *Thoresby Diary* (1830), vol 2, 98, 190, 209, 215, 221–2; *Smith* 1846, 15–16; *DNB*; *Bolton* 1939, 128, 132; *Friedman* 1973 (1); *Friedman* 1984 (1), *passim*; *Fleming* 1962 (1), 38–9; *O'Connell* 1987, 804–5; *Whinney* 1988, 244–251; *Davis* 1991 (1), *passim*

Archival References: WCA, Poor Rates, St Martin-in-the-Fields, 1703, (F1262), 1718 (F447); St George, Hanover Square 1727, (C97), 1737, (C127); Carpenter-Carlisle, list

Will: PROB 11/684 sig 155

Auction Catalogues: *Carpenter* 1736; *Carpenter* 1744

Funerary Monuments

1.	†1722	Sir John Fermor		Sevenoaks, Kent	S	Pevsner, *Kent: W & Weald*, 1976, 511; C Lib (repr)
2.	1725	Montague Garrard (†1698) and Jane (†1724) Drake (designed by James Gibbs) Payment(s): £180		Amersham, Bucks	S	*Friedman* 1984, 92, 291 (repr)
3.	†1725	Sir John Thornycroft		Bloxham, Oxon	S	*Gunnis* 1968, 33 (repr); Pevsner, *Oxon*, 1974, 479 –80; *Whinney* 1988, 245
4.	†1727	John Leng, Bishop of Norwich		St Margaret, Westminster, London	S	C Lib (repr)
5.	1730	Hon Charles (†1727) and Mrs Bertie (Mary), with portrait busts Payment(s): £150 Drawing(s): Lincs RO ANCX/A/10, p7		Theddlethorpe All Saints, Lincs	S	*Lord* 1986 (1), 100; *Lord* 2002, 107–13 (repr)
6.	1734	Henry, 1st Earl of Warrington (†1694) and his wife, Mary (†1691) Payment(s): £389		Bowdon, Cheshire	SD	*Whinney* 1988, 245 (repr)
7.	1735	Langham (†1724) and Henry (†1727) Booth		Bowdon, Cheshire	SD	Pevsner, *Cheshire*, 1971, 110; C Lib (repr)

Statues

8.	1712–13	Queen Anne	m	[Moot Hall, Leeds, niche in façade]; LMG, W R Yorks, 71/1887	SD	*Friedman* 1973, 5–13 (repr); *Leeds* 1996, 2 (repr)
9.	1716	The Seasons, four figures Payment(s): £20 'except for ye cases'		[coll John Hervey, 1st Earl of Bristol]; untraced		*Hervey* 1894, 150
10.	1722	An 'abundance of works' Payment(s): £60		[Canons, Middx]; untraced		*Vertue* III, 83; *Baker* 1949, 142
11.	1722–1723	Fame and Loyalty, two figures Payment(s): £55	l	Ditchley Park, Oxon, over the attic		Dillon DIL I/P/4X 2); *Friedman* 1984, 118–20, 318–9 (repr);
12.	1723	Farnese Hercules, Spartan Boys, Sitting Venus, Faunus Payment(s): £84	l	Castle Howard, N R Yorks, parterre, s front		*Gomme* 1989, 88 *Saumarez Smith* 1990, 139 (repr); *Davis* 1991 (1), 37, 43, 44 (repr)
13.	post-1730	A blackamoor and a gladiator	l	[Wrest Park, Beds, gardens]; untraced		*Gunnis* 1968, 83 citing archives, Lady Lucas and Dingwall
14.	1730	Several, including a 'little miller' with a pedestal and a blackamoor Payment(s): £28		Wrest Park, Beds		*Gunnis* 1968, 83; Wrest (Lucas) Archive (2), letters 130/8/39/7, L30/8/39/8 and 9; Hoare's Customer Ledger, 1728–1731, vol K, f263
15.	1731	Sabina, Faustina, Crispina and Giulia Mammea, four sibyls	l	Castle Howard, N R Yorks, outside Temple of the Four Winds		Castle Howard letters, 6 Dec 1731; *Saumarez Smith* 1990, 146 (repr)
16.	1730–2	Three unspecified, and lions Payment(s): £63 for three leaden figures, £25 for lions	l	[Moulsham Hall, Essex (lions for the 'Great Piers')]; untraced		*Edwards* 1977, 40–3; *Friedman* 1973 (1), 12–13 n16
17.	pre-1735	Hercules and Antaeus	l	[Stowe House, Bucks]; Trent Park, Middx		*Milles* 1735, 63; *Clarke* 1990, 63; *Davis* 1991 (1), 33
18.	By 1737	Unidentified figures Payment(s): £34 10s		[Stowe House, Bucks]; untraced		Stowe Accounts 1736–41, May 1737, Huntington ST 161
19.	nd	Hercules slaying the Nemean lion	l	Powis Castle, Montgomery, top terrace	S	*Powis* 1993, 47

20.	nd	Pegasus and Fame, equestrian group (probably taken from a model by John Nost I)	1	Powis Castle, Montgomery, courtyard	S	*Davis* 1991 (1), 32, 41–2; *Darke* 1991, 125–6 (repr)
Busts						
21.	1716	Cicero Payment(s): £2	1	[coll Lord Ashburnham]; untraced		Ashburnham Accts, 12 May 1716; *Gunnis* 1968, 83
22.	1732	Venus, bronzed Payment(s): £3 13s	1	[Moulsham Hall, Essex]; untraced		Mildmay Acct Book; GPC
Architectural Sculpture						
23.	1719–1720	12 vases and 24 baskets (designed by James Gibbs) Payment(s): £85 10s (vases: £7 each; baskets £1 10s each) Drawing(s): Bodleian, Gough, Maps, 46		Wimpole, Cambs, gardens		*Friedman* 1984, 166–7, 295 (designs repr)
24.	1720	Vases and other work Payment(s): £50 for 'vauzes', June 30th 1720; balance £23, October 31 1720		[Briggens, Herts]; untraced		*Chester Inventory* 1721, 49, 52
Miscellaneous						
25.	1721/2	Marble figures (transport only) and the bronzing of 'three heads' Payment(s): £7 10s		[Chatsworth House to Chiswick House, Middx]; untraced		*Davis* 1991 (1), 43
26.	1716	Two flowerpots Payment(s): £2 13s 9d	1	[coll John, 1st Earl of Bristol]; untraced		*Hervey* 1894, 150
27.	1720	'Figures and flower pots' Payment(s): £128	1	[Purley Hall, Berks]; untraced		S S Co Inventories, Hawes no 7 in 3, p 69
28.	1732	'A Medal of Seneca's head' Payment(s): £1 11s 6d		[Moulsham Hall, Essex]; untraced		*Mildmay Accts*, Hants RO, 15/M/50/31; *Edwards* 1977, 46

CARR, Joseph, of London –1768

In 1754–58 he built part of the Horse Guards in Whitehall, where he provided a marble frieze (**3**). He was responsible for two monuments in widely disparate areas, which suggests an extensive business in memorials. These were the polychrome architectural wall monument to Francis Fawkes (**1**) and the ledger with a coat of arms to Charles Monson (**2**). In 1753 he took an apprentice, John Hincks.

Carr was made bankrupt in 1768 and on 13 September a sale of his stock-in-trade was held at his yard at Mill Bank, Westminster. Among the lots were a number of marble chimneypieces. A note on the sale catalogue reads: 'The business will be continued as usual by Joseph Carr, Junior, who begs the favour of his father's friends and customers' (Carr Sale 1768).

One of his contemporaries was William Carr, son of Edward Carr, 'citizen of London and barber-surgeon,' who was apprenticed to Henry Daintry in 1741 and became free in 1748 (*Gunnis* 1968, 84).

Literary References: *Gunnis* 1968, 84; *Webb* 1999, 17

Auction Catalogues: Carr 1768

Funerary Monuments					
1.	1754	Francis Fawkes	Otley, W R Yorks	S	Pevsner, *Yorks: W R*, 1967, 386; *Gunnis* 1968, 84
2.	1765	Charles Monson Payment(s): £18, £3 6s for carving the coat of arms and £1 5s 6d for cutting 153 letters	Broxbourne, Herts		Monson archives, cited in *Gunnis* 1968, 84
Architectural Sculpture					
3.	1757–1758	Marble frieze carved and polished with cables, flutes and tongues Payment(s): £7 10s	Horse Guards, Whitehall, London		Board of Works/Horseguards, HOR/1/3 i; *Colvin* 1973–76, V, 438

CARRECK (or CARRICK), William, of Ashford fl 1815

He is only known to have signed one tablet. A 'Charles Carrick' of Canterbury, possibly a relation, showed 'a loo table, inlaid with various coloured woods' at the Great Exhibition of 1851.

Literary References: *Gunnis* 1968, 84

Funerary Monuments					
1.	†1815	Captain Thomas Smart	Ashford, Kent	S	*Gunnis* 1968, 84

CARTER, Benjamin 1719–66

He was the younger brother of **Thomas Carter I** and the uncle of **Thomas Carter II**, with whom he worked in partnership, 1756–66. He was christened in Datchet, Bucks, on 8 July 1719. Nothing is known of his training or early career, except that he supplied chimneypieces for Longford Castle, Wilts, in 1739 (**4**). He appears to have worked with Thomas I from 1751 until his brother's death in 1756 and was rated on a property next door in Piccadilly. Thomas I clearly considered Benjamin competent enough to take over the business, because under the terms of his will he left his brother all the 'working shops' and utensils, and the lease of his house, rated at £24. Benjamin was also given the option to buy 'all the drawings, models, marble and Portland stone'. Benjamin seems to have wasted little time in consolidating his position. By 28 September 1756, he had entered into co-partnership with Thomas Carter II, who began to pay annual rates of £10 on the property next to Benjamin in 1758.

One of their first collaborative commissions was on 3 chimneypieces for the London house of Thomas Bridges at 18 Cavendish Street (**6–8**). The partners both signed receipts for payments for this work, completed between May and September 1757 at a cost of £210. The architect Henry Keene supervised the contract, endorsed the designs and guaranteed that the entire commission, including the polishing, would be approved by him personally. Benjamin appears to have been one of the team of craftsmen employed by Keene, which included the carpenter John Phillips (who was Thomas Carter I's executor), the mason **Thomas Gayfere** and the carver **Thomas Dryhurst**. In 1760 Carter, Gayfere, Dryhurst and several other craftsmen were the subjects of a conversation-piece commissioned from the painter, Robert Pyle, as a gift for Keene. The central figure is Keene himself, pointing to a plan on the table for an unidentified building. Carter, in a wig and coat, appears to be challenging Gayfere, for the two craftsmen face each other, leaning awkwardly over the backs of their chairs.

In 1752 Carter provided the model for a lion which later became a local landmark above the central elevation of Northumberland House, London (**3**), then being refurbished by Keene. The Carters completed two fine chimneypieces for the house in 1757 (**5**). The cross-members had relief tablets, one carved with putti draping a lion with festoons and the other, putti draping an eagle. Each massive overmantel was supported by caryatid figures, variants of the *Farnese Captives*. The two sculptors received a handsome sum, £292, for their work.

The taste for classically-inspired ornaments was well served by the Carter workshop. In 1761 Benjamin modelled plaster reliefs for Henry Hoare's Pantheon at Stourhead at a cost of £268 (**24**). These reliefs, long thought to be by **Michael Rysbrack**, included a *Roman Marriage Ceremony* and a *Triumphal Procession of Bacchus*, both after engravings in Montfaucon's *L'Antiquité Expliquée*, 1721. A number of other payments to Carter appear in the Hoare Accounts including a pedestal of coloured marbles for the 'Florence box', and another, for an unknown site, of 'Sienna, Genoa green, and black marble' (**25**). They have not survived and were probably destroyed when the house was gutted by fire in 1902.

In 1763 the partners supplied slabs of marble to Horace Walpole and his architect, Richard Bentley, for a pair of commodes at Strawberry Hill (**28**). There is a curious reference among Walpole's letters which indicates that this was not his first contact with the sculptors. In July 1755 Bentley suggested that Walpole should 'traffic with Carter' personally and Walpole responded acidly 'do you think I can turn broker, and factor, and I don't know what?' (*Lewis* 1937–83, vol 35, 231).

Walpole was involved in the preliminary stages of Carter's most notable project, the monument to Lieutenant-Colonel Roger Townshend erected in 1761 in Westminster Abbey (**2**). Lady Townsend asked Walpole to recommend an artist to design a monument for her 'brave son' and Walpole, whose talents did not include draughtsmanship, provided a drawing himself (*Lewis* 1937–83, vol 40, 166–8). It was not used, but the monument as realised was an exemplary instance of collaborative practice. It was designed by Robert Adam, the low relief of the dying hero was modelled by **Luc-François Breton**, and the work's construction seems to have been directed by the two Carters, who also probably carved the handsome caryatid figures supporting the sarcophagus. These take the form of North American Indians and allude to Townsend's death at the battle of Ticonderoga in 1759. The monument was signed by both Carters and by the German sculptor, John Eckstein, who was employed by the workshop to carve the relief from Breton's model. The architect, Matthew Brettingham, felt that there was 'nothing equal to it in the Abbey' (*Fleming* 1962 (2), 169).

In the 1760s the Carters were employed extensively by Robert Adam to execute his designs for chimneypieces at Bowood (**15–19**), Lansdowne House (**13**) and Syon House (**23**). At Syon they collaborated with ormolu manufacturers to execute Adam's designs for opulent fireplaces, charging £144 6s 6d for designing and modelling ornaments, carving mouldings to encase the metalwork and 'fitting and working the ornaments together' (*Harris* 2001, 78). Their assistant, Robert Staveley, was responsible for setting up the Bowood chimneypieces, and also worked for them at Ashburnham Place, Sussex (**12**).

The precise nature of the Carter partnership is unclear but it seems likely that Benjamin was in control for in 1763 the workshop was advertised in Mortimer's *Universal Director* under 'Carter, Benjamin, Statuary, Hyde Park Corner' (p 6). He died late in 1766 and was buried in Datchet, leaving his share of the business, including all the 'stocks and effects' to his son John and wife Ann, who also inherited his household goods; he also made provision for three younger children. One of his executors was the marble merchant **Edward Chapman Bird**. Benjamin's son, John Carter (1748–1817), was the celebrated and eccentric antiquary, draughtsman and writer, noted for his championship of medieval sculpture and architecture. He later claimed that from the age of 12 he had prepared designs for assistants in his father's workshop.

MGS

Literary References: *GM*, April 1812, 82, pt 1, 341; *Smith* 1828, II, 307; *DNB*; *Smith* 1945, 556; *Fleming* 1962 (2), 169; *Gunnis* 1968, 84; *Lewis* 1973, vol 35, 231; vol 40, 166–8; *Haskell and Penny* 1981, 170; *Allen* 1983, 200; *Harris* 2001, 78

Archival References: *IGI*; Poor Rate, St George, Hanover Square, WCA, 1751 (C240), 1757 (C298), 1758 (C300); Carter/Keen Accounts; Archives, Marquess of Lansdowne; Ashburnham Archives; Hoare Private Accounts 1750–66, *passim*; 1752–78, I May 1759

Wills: Thomas Carter, 3 Sept 1756, PROB 11/824 fol 313–5; Benjamin Carter, 13 Nov 1766, PROB 11/923 fol 173–6

Miscellaneous Drawings: design for a chimney-piece, signed, sold as part of an album of chimneypiece drawings, Marlborough Rare Books, cat 81, 25 November 1977, lot 68 (repr)

Portraits of the Sculptor: Robert Pyle, *Henry Keene and his Craftsmen*, 1768, formerly at Buxted Place, Sussex (destroyed); *Smith* 1945, 556–7 (repr); John Carter, after Robert Pyle, nd, pen, ink, wash and watercolour, BM, PDB, 1908, 0714.48

Funerary Monuments

1.	†1759	Sarah Currer (co-sculptor: Thomas Carter II)		Bath Abbey, Somerset	S	*Gunnis* 1968, 84
2.	1761	Lieutenant-Colonel the Hon Roger Townshend (†1759), relief by John Eckstein (designed by Robert Adam and L-F Breton) (co-sculptor: Thomas Carter II) Drawing(s): Soane, Adam vol 14, no8; vol 18 no85; vol 19, no 9, 10, 66, 68, 72, 85; design for panels, Adam vol 19/69 & 70		Westminster Abbey, London, nave	S	*Fleming* 1962 (2), 163–171 (reprs); *Whinney* 1988, 251–2 (repr)

Statues

3.	1752	Lion	l	[Northumberland House, Strand, London]; Syon House, Isleworth, Middx		*GM*, April 1812, vol 82, pt1, 341

Chimneypieces

No.	Date	Description		Location	Source
4.	1739	Several Payment(s): £30		Longford Castle, Wilts	Pevsner, *Wilts*, 1975, 307
5.	1757	A pair, with caryatid figures of slaves (co-sculptor: Thomas Carter II) Payment(s): £292 the pair Drawing(s): VAM E.912-1921 (possibly by Henry Keene)	m	[Northumberland House, London]; VAM A.60-1951 and Syon House, Middx	*Allen* 1983, 200 (repr)
6.	1757	'French' with an astragal, mantle and jambs of statuary marble, and carved black marble covings; other parts of wood (co-sculptor: Thomas Carter II) Payment(s): £144	m	18 Cavendish Square, London	LMA, Cavendish Square Accounts fols 245, 250, 252, 262; Pevsner, *London N W*, 1991, 635
7.	1757	Of statuary marble and jasper, with Doric columns and a tablet depicting a lion and boys (co-sculptor: Thomas Carter II) Payment(s): £144, for this and another	m	18 Cavendish Square, London	LMA, Cavendish Square Accounts fols 245, 250, 252, 262; Pevsner, *London N W*, 1991, 635
8.	1757	With a tablet image of Cybele, black marble coving, Siena ground and statuary trusses (co-sculptor: Thomas Carter II) Payment(s): £52 10s	m	18 Cavendish Square, London, parlour	LMA, Cavendish Square Accounts f245, 250, 252, 262, 263
9.	1759	Description unavailable (co-sculptor: Thomas Carter II) Payment(s): £400		[Sir Matthew Featherstonhaugh, Dover House, Whitehall, London]; untraced	GPC
10.	1761	Description unavailable (co-sculptor: Thomas Carter II) Payment(s): £147		[Shardeloes, Bucks, library]; untraced	*Gunnis* 1968, 86
11.	1759–1761	Marble (co-sculptor: Thomas Carter II) Payment(s): £122 13s		Stourhead, Wilts	Hoare Private Accounts 1752–78, 1 May 1759; Hoare Partnership Ledger 1751–1764, fol 97; *Gunnis* 1968, 84
12.	1762	Marble (co-sculptor: Thomas Carter II)		Ashburnham Place, Sussex	*Gunnis* 1968, 84 citing Ashburnham archives
13.	1763	Designed by Robert Adam (co-sculptor: Thomas Carter II) Payment(s): £239 with one for the N E Room	m	[Lansdowne House, London, square room]; untraced	GPC citing Lansdowne House archives
14.	1763	More than one (co-sculptor: Thomas Carter II) Payment(s): £222		[Petworth House, West Sussex ?]; untraced	*Rowell* 2000 (2), 76
15.	1763	Of Portland stone (co-sculptor: Thomas Carter II)	s	[Bowood, Wilts, hall]; untraced	GPC
16.	1763	Three, two 'plain vein'd' with 'statuary Plynths' and another of 'Black and white and purple' (co-sculptor: Thomas Carter II)	m	[Bowood, Wilts, unidentified rooms]; untraced	GPC
17.	1763	Two (from designs by Robert Adam) (co-sculptor: Thomas Carter II) Payment(s): £239		[Bowood, Wilts, north-east room and square room]; untraced	GPC
18.	1764	Statuary marble with variegated brocatella and Corinthian columns (designed by Robert Adam) (co-sculptor: Thomas Carter II) Payment(s): £276 2s 6d Drawing(s): Soane 22:96	m	[Bowood House, Wilts, then Lansdowne House, London, drawing room]; untraced	*Harris* 2001, 110, 121, 346 (repr)
19.	1764	Statuary marble with variegated brocatella and Corinthian columns (designed by Robert Adam) (co-sculptor: Thomas Carter II) Payment(s): £276 2s 6d Drawing(s): Soane 22.96	m	[Bowood, Wilts, great room; sold 30 June 1955, lot 165]; untraced	*Cornforth* 1972, 1450; *Harris* 2001, 109–10, 346 n13 (repr)
20.	1764	Two (co-sculptor: Thomas Carter II) Payment(s): £46, £53		[Sir Richard Lyttleton's house, Piccadilly, London]; untraced	*Gunnis* 1968, 86
21.	1765	Two (co-sculptor: Thomas Carter II) Payment(s): £150		[Croome Court, Worcs, dressing room and ante room]; untraced	*Gunnis* 1968, 86
22.	1766	Several (co-sculptor: Thomas Carter II)	m	Mersham Hall, Kent	Pevsner, *Kent: W & Weald*, 1976, 426
23.	1766	With fluted Corinthian columns, embellished with ormulu (designed by Robert Adam) (co-sculptor: Thomas Carter II) Payment(s): £282 8s 4d	m	Syon House, Middx, drawing room	*Harris* 2001, 77, 78 (repr)

Architectural Sculpture

No.	Date	Description		Location	Source
24.	1761	Eight relief panels (co-sculptor: Thomas Carter II) Payment(s): £162 9s	p	Stourhead, Wilts, Pantheon	Hoare Private Accounts, 1750–66, 9 April, 3 Nov, 20 Dec 1761; Hoare Partnership Ledger 1751–1764, fl55; Pevsner, *Wilts*, 1975, 499
25.	nd	Sphinx above two Tuscan columns		Lacock Abbey, Wilts	Pevsner, *Wilts*, 1975, 289

Miscellaneous

26.	1760	Pedestal for the 'Florence box', charged with 'the great Glass frame' Payment(s): £50 6s 10d	m	[Stourhead, Wilts]; destroyed	Hoare Private Accounts 1750–66, 15 Aug 1760; *Gunnis* 1968, 84
27.	1762	Work including 'two granate tables' (co-sculptor: Thomas Carter II) Payment(s): £74 1s		[Croome Court, Worcs]; untraced	*Beard* 1993, 98
28.	1763–1764	Supply of materials for commodes (co-sculptor: Thomas Carter II)	m	[Strawberry Hill, Twickenham, Middx]; untraced	*Toynbee* 1927, 10, 111
29.	1764–5	Unspecified work (co-sculptor: Thomas Carter II) Payment(s): £350		[Northumberland House, London]; untraced	*Allen* 1983, 200
30.	nd	Pedestal of 'Sienna, Genoa green, and black marble'	m	[Stourhead, Wilts]; destroyed	*Gunnis* 1968, 84

CARTER, C J fl 1806

His tradecard, engraved by R Havell and dated 1806, has sketches of inlaid stone pavement, a unicorn's head, portcullis and crown. It gives his address as 1 Dean Street, Soho (Banks 106.6).

CARTER, Charles fl 1816

His yard was in Dean Street, Soho, London.

Miscellaneous

1.	1816	'Stone-carving' Payment(s): £237 3s 11d	s	[for the Duke of Bridgewater, probably for a London house]; untraced	Archives, Lord Brownlow, cited in *Gunnis* 1968, 84

CARTER, James fl 1812–17

He was employed at Ashburnham Place 1812–17, working under the direction of the architect, George Dance junior. His masonry work included turned and carved columns and ballusters for the gallery and grand staircase and 'carving branch Leaf Pattern' on the staircase. A letter to Lord Ashburnham of 26 April 1817 suggests that Carter managed the team, for it refers to payments made or due to other masons, particularly **Thomas Nuttall** and Joseph Dawes (Ashburnham Accts, ASH 2806, 8 Aug–12 Sept 1812, 5 Feb–2 July 1814, ASH 2812 19 April–21 Aug 1813).

CARTER, John *c*1744–by 1782

Dossie notes that he was 'apprentice to [**Henry**] **Cheere**' in 1762, when on 3 June he won a premium from the Society of Arts for an ornamental composition in clay, awarded to sculptors under 19 (3). That year he gained a second premium for a clay model (1). A third premium came his way on 24 May 1765 (2). Dossie noted in his *Memoirs* that Carter was dead by 1782.

Literary References: *Dossie* 1782, 438–9

Archival References: RSA Minutes, 1761–62, seq 3, f 64

Statues

1.	1762	'Slave taking the thorn from a Lion's foot', clay model	[RSA premium, 15 gns]; untraced	*Dossie* 1782, 438

Reliefs

2.	1765	'Cincinnatus' 2nd Dictatorship', clay model	[RSA premium, 5 gns]; untraced	RSA *Minutes*, 1764–65, seq 3 fol 61; *Dossie* 1782, 439; RSA *Register* 1778, 31

Miscellaneous

3.	1762	Ornamental composition	[RSA premium, 3 gns]; untraced	RSA *Minutes*, 1761–62, seq 3 f 64

CARTER, Thomas I 1702–56

He founded a major London workshop, one of the first to specialise in elaborate marble chimneypieces. Carter was born on 2 May 1702 in Datchet, Bucks, the son of Thomas and Anne Carter. The unsigned monument with a portrait medallion to Thomas Carter Senior (†1726) in Datchet seems likely to be a tribute carved by the Carter children for their father. The family was of well-established yeoman stock, but Thomas, his brother **Benjamin Carter**, and his nephew **Thomas Carter II**, all pursued successful careers as sculptors in London.

A colourful vignette published in the *European Magazine* (vol II, 178) a century after his birth, described Carter's first premises as 'a shed near the chapel in Mayfair' where he scratched a living for himself, his wife and his child, pursuing 'the *lower branches* of his profession, such as tomb-stones, grave-slabs, &c.' and labouring 'from the rising until the setting of the sun.' The author, Joseph Moser, who as a young man met Carter, wrote that the sculptor's luck had changed when a near-neighbour, Charles Jervas, Principal Painter to the King, noticed his work and lent Carter (depicted as an industrious but incredulous simpleton) £100 to buy materials and hire an assistant. However fanciful the anecdote, it is possible that Jervas, a keen collector of sculpture, provided early contacts, for one of Carter's major commissions was the monument to William Conolly, Speaker of the Irish Parliament, and his wife, both patrons of Jervas (**6**). This is a remarkably assured early work, with two full length reclining effigies in a towering architectural setting. Catherine Conolly, who holds a book, is on a slightly raised platform behind her husband and leans on her hand to look down at him. The *Dublin Gazette* recorded the work's completion on 17–19 August 1736 – 'On Friday last two curious fine monuments, lately finished by Mr Carter near Hyde Park Corner, was put on board a ship in the river in order to be carried to Ireland' (*Pottertor* 1975, 39).

In 1734 Carter moved into a yard rated at £12 annually on Portugal Row. The Carter workshop stood here for over fifty years. His immediate neighbour was **Thomas Manning**, the lead ornament manufacturer, and the lead workshops of **Andrew Carpenter** and **Catherine Nost** were nearby. In the 1730s it appears that Carter found employment as a carver on development projects. He worked under the architect John Wilkins on the building of 13–17 Queen Street, Soho in 1733, and under Isaac Ware and Charles Carne involved in the rebuilding of William Pulteney's houses on

Chandos Place in 1737 (**29**). Most of Carter's signed or documented monuments also date from the 1730s, and include wall-tablets with portrait medallions commemorating Mary Carew (**1**) and William Arnold (**3**), and the memorial with two busts to Sir Cecil Wray, Churchwarden of St George, Hanover Square, and his wife (**5**).

The full sized reclining figures of Colonel Thomas Moore, in Roman armour (**4**), and the muscular Sir Henry Every (**2**) both demonstrate Carter's skill and show a sensitivity to the work of foreign masters in London. Moore's effigy was modelled on a canvas portrait in his family's possession, lent 'to Mr. Carter, the stonemason, who is making a monument' (Bodl MS North Archives, b.14, fol 19). The effigy is reminiscent of **Michael Rysbrack**'s monument to Lord Stanhope in Westminster Abbey. The Every memorial was erected by his widow, Anne, Lady Guise, whose family was well-satisfied with the results. In a letter of 1734 written by Sir Simon Every to his sister-in-law, he expressed 'most humble thanks for ye beautiful monument you have given my brother' (Every/Guise). The full extent of the monument's beauty can no longer be appreciated, since the impressive effigy is all that has survived the Victorian restoration of the church.

In the 1740s the Carter workshop began to specialise increasingly in chimneypieces. These were often elaborate, incorporating polychrome marbles, reliefs of literary subjects, classically-derived telamonic figures and carving of the highest quality. They must have been marketed in keen competition with the rich, multi-coloured confections on offer from **Henry Cheere.** For the Great Apartments at Holkham Hall, Carter and another London neighbour, **Joseph Pickford**, provided architectural chimneypieces 'for the most part copied from Inigo Jones's works' (*Brettingham* 1773, ix). In other rooms Carter used colourful Sicilian and Sienese marbles as grounds for reliefs of subjects after the Antique, taken from engravings in Montfaucon's influential *L'Antiquité Expliquée*, 1719 (**19, 23**). Sir Matthew Featherstonehaugh of Uppark paid Carter nearly £1000 between 1747 and 1756 for fireplaces decorated with caryatid figures of classical philosophers and tablets representing *Androcles and the Lion* and *Romulus and Remus* (the former relief employed also at Saltram and perhaps elsewhere) (**22**). Carter used the novel 'gothic' style, a fashionable alternative to tired classical ornaments, for chimneypieces at Welbeck Abbey (**11**) and Bolsover Castle (**13**). The style had recently been explored by William Kent for interiors at Rousham, by the antiquarian James West at his London home and by the architect Sanderson Millar at Belhus. Carter supplied fireplaces for all these sites (**8, 12, 17**). A clue to the associations attached to the style comes from the Countess of Oxford's proud description of Carter's 'Gothic chimneypiece' for Welbeck (**11**). This was 'designed partly from a fine one at Bolsover, but composed of great variety of English, Scotch and Irish marbles and alabaster, and not one bit of foreign in it' (*Turberville* 1938, 394).

In 1741 Carter extended his premises in Portugal Row and was now liable for £16 in annual rates. By that date he clearly presided over an extensive business. In a letter to Lady Oxford's agent, Thompson, in 1746, Carter boasted that 'I have more than forty men under me and, thank God, without any disturbance in the least' (Portland Archives quoted by *Gunnis* 1968, 84–5).) and numerous names of assistants appear in the house accounts. **William Kay** and **[John?] Wildsmith**, whose mutual animosity at Welbeck prompted the letter to Lady Oxford, were two of his best masons and **Thomas Ker**, another mason, with John Baker, a polisher, stayed at Blair Castle for 4 months whilst 9 chimneypieces were installed (Atholl Accounts) (**16**). Kay travelled between Welbeck and Okeover to set up chimneypieces, supported by Leak Okeover, who paid both his travelling and living expenses (Carter/Okeover MS). The extravagant owner of Okeover Hall paid Carter £98 for a chimneypiece in 1743 (**10**), and a bill for an unidentified mason sent out by Carter made allowance for maintenance over 176 days, which amounted only to £28 12s. In 1746–9 a mason worked at Okeover for 679 days, charged at £113 5s. Whilst relying on a large number of employees, Carter continued to control workshop production and to provide designs. In 1746, he informed Kay that he had sent Lady Oxford 'a drawing of a Gothick chimney-piece' (Carter I/Kay), which may be the surviving drawing in the Welbeck Archives.

At Okeover Carter acted as a supplier of sculpture from another neighbour in Piccadilly, **John Cheere.** The accounts show that £8, with 18s for casing, was paid for 'work done by order of Mr Carter per John Cheere. To making a statue of a black' (*Oswald* 1964, 175). In addition to the Blackamoor, which arrived in 1741, it is possible that 'two spinx', supplied by Carter in 1740, also came from Cheere's workshop. The most prestigious name associated with the Carter workshop is **Louis Francois Roubiliac**, who, according to the painter James Northcote, was 'working as a journeyman for a person of the name of Carter' in or around 1752 (*Northcote* 1813, 29). Roubiliac had an independent workshop by this date, but may have assisted Carter or worked in sub-contract. Roubiliac later owned a bust of 'Mr Carter, Statuary,' although this could be by Benjamin rather than Thomas I.

From 1751 Carter's much younger brother Benjamin was rated on the property next door to the Piccadilly yard and it seems likely that Benjamin and Thomas had some kind of working relationship, though perhaps not of a formal nature. The rateable value of Thomas Carter's principal yard had risen to £24 in 1756, suggesting that the last few years of his professional life were the most prosperous. In the years 1751–6, for instance, Carter supplied nine chimneypieces to Blair Castle at a cost of £606 16s 7d (**16, 21**), as well as fulfilling the extensive contracts at Holkham and Uppark.

He died in 1756 and was buried at Datchet, Bucks, where a grave-slab commemorates him and two of his children. A notice in the *European Magazine* of 1803 stated that he was then a very rich man, with a handsome house in Halfmoon Street, Piccadilly. In his will, proved on 3 September, he divided his estate between his wife, Mary (who inherited all his household goods), his daughter Ann, a minor, and another daughter, Elizabeth, described as 'the wife of my nephew,' **Thomas Carter II**. He asked to be buried in the family vault at Datchet, with the remains of his deceased children. To his brother Joseph he left £50, and to his brother, Benjamin, the work-shops, lease of his house, working utensils and 'all the drawing, models, marble and Portland stone.' His executors were his neighbour John Cheere, and the master-builder and carpenter, John Phillips of Brook Street. Cheere and Phillips certified Carter's bank account at Drummonds from June 1756 (Carter I Bank Account). After his death outstanding payments from the Duke of Atholl for 8 chimneypieces were made to his widow.

Carter is chiefly remembered as the one time employer of Roubiliac, although Moser's anecdote suggests that Carter's own tale of success was considered noteworthy nearly fifty years after his death. Moser also suggested that Carter benefited from the new fashion for rich architectural decoration, 'previously very sparingly introduced'. He clearly ran a profitable business providing elegant focal points for the grand rooms of fashionable houses.

MGS

Literary References: *Brettingham* 1773, *passim*; *Moser* 1803, 178–9; *Northcote* 1813, 29; *Turberville* 1938, 394; *Gunnis* 1958, 334; *Gunnis* 1959 (1), 72; *Gunnis* 1963, 1174–6; *Oswald* 1964, 175; *S of.*, vol 33 (1966), 166; vol 36 (1970), 264; *Gunnis* 1968, 84–5; *Potterton* 1975, 39; *Guinness* 1981, 896–905; *Whinney* 1988, *passim*; *Bindman and Baker* 1995, 48, 214, 373; *Baker* 2000, *passim*

Archival References: Datchet parish registers; IGI; Poor Rates St George, Hanover Square, WCA C120–1 (1734), C240 (1751), C297 (1756); Carter/Okeover MS; Atholl Accounts; Carter I/Kay; Carter I Bank Account; GPC

Will: PROB 11/824 f313–5

Miscellaneous Drawings: Projections and design for a chimneypiece in the Pillar Parlour at Bolsover, pen, ink and wash, Welbeck Abbey 010720 (*Turberville* 1938, 397). On loan RIBA library

Portraits of the Sculptor: 'Mr Carter, Statuary,' bust, plaster, untraced. Roubiliac's sale, 12 May 1762, lot 12 (*Bindman and Baker* 1995, 364)

Funerary Monuments

No.	Date	Work		Location		Reference
1.	1731	Mary Carew		Antony, Cornwall	S	Pevsner, *Cornwall*, 1970, 37
2.	c1734	Sir Henry Every (†1709)		[Newton Solney, Derbys, chancel]; Newton Solney, tower		Pevsner, *Derbys*, 1978, 288; C Lib (repr)
3.	†1734	William Arnold		St Margaret, Westminster, London		Vestry Minutes, 2 Oct 1735 (E 2419)
4.	†1735	Colonel Thomas Moore		Great Bookham, Surrey		*Whinney* 1988, 250–1 (repr)
5.	pre-1735	Sir Cecil (†1735) and Dame Mary Wray (†1745)		Branston, Lincs	S	*Lord* 1986, 98; C Lib (repr)
6.	1736	Mr Speaker William Conolly (†1729) and his wife Catherine, figures only (frame possibly by William Kidwell)		Celbridge churchyard, Co Kildare	S	*Potterton* 1975, 39 (repr)

Statues

No.	Date	Work		Location		Reference
7.	nd	Two figures Payment(s): £52 10s for 2 figures		[Blair Castle, Perths]; untraced		Atholl archives in GPC

Chimneypieces

No.	Date	Work		Location		Reference
8.	1737	Description unavailable		Rousham Park, Oxon, probably 'Gothic', in saloon		*Gunnis* 1968, 85
9.	1739	Description unavailable Payment(s): £70		Longford Castle, Wilts		GPC
10.	1743	Large statuary Payment(s): £98	m	[Okeover Hall, Staffs]; untraced		*Oswald* 1964, 227
11.	1744	Three, one of them 'Gothic', in coloured marbles Payment(s): £1057 3s 9 1/2d Drawing(s): RIBA N35/9 for 'Gothick' chimneypiece with MS list of 'Marbles chosen. . . for this chimneypiece;' three more designs for chimneypieces N35/11		[Welbeck Abbey, Notts]; untraced		Welbeck archives, Notts R O, DD 6/1/1; *Turberville* I, 1938–9, 394
12.	1745	Of black and gold marble	m	[James West's house, Lincoln's Inn Fields, London]; untraced		*Gunnis* 1968, 85
13.	1746	Design only (pen, ink and wash)		[Bolsover Castle, Derbys, for pillar parlour]; Welbeck Abbey 010720, on loan RIBA		
14.	1746–7	Two statuary marble, one veined Payment(s): £201 for Great Room in 1747; £44 15 10s for the other two in 1746	m	[Moulsham Hall, Essex, great room, west dressing room, west bedchamber]; untraced		*Edwards* 1977, 64, 79
15.	1750	Description unavailable Payment(s): £23 19s		Milton Hall, near Peterborough, Northants		*Gunnis* 1968, 85, Fitzwilliam of Milton Accts, Northants RO F (M) misc vol 156
16.	1751	Veined, including 'the Apollo's head and two pieces of ornament to the friese in statuary marble' Payment(s): £62 11s	m	Blair Castle, Perths, dining room		*Oswald* 1949, 1436 (repr)
17.	1752	Description unavailable		Belhus, Essex		WCRO, Letter from J Barrett to Sanderson Miller, 24 March 1752, CR.125.B. 433
18.	c1752	Description unavailable	m	[Felbrigg Hall, Norfolk, cabinet]; replaced 1824		*Rococo* 1984, 202; *Jackson-Stops* 1987 (3), 13, 20
19.	1753	Two, in Sicilian marble, with bas-reliefs	m	Holkham Hall, Norfolk, saloon		*Brettingham* 1773, 2 (reprs 15, 48); Pevsner, *Norfolk: N W & S*, 1999, 418
20.	1753	With relief of Androcles and the Lion Payment(s): £144 10s		Saltram, Devon, entrance hall		Pevsner, *Devon*, 1989, 712; *Saltram* 1992, 11; C Lib (repr)
21.	1756	Eight, one with Ionic colums in jasper and brocatelle (described as 'the same as in Lord Townsend's library') and another ('the same as in Lord Townsend's drawing-room') Payment(s): £544 5s 7d		Blair Castle, Perths, small and great drawing room, Duchess Strange's room, and other rooms		*Oswald* 1949, 1435–6 (repr)
22.	1747–1756	Two, one with relief of 'Romulus and Remus', the other of 'Androcles and the Lion' Payment(s): nearly £1,000	m	Uppark, Sussex, saloon		*Uppark* 1999, 59 (reprs 7, 19, 59, 61)

23.	nd	Ornaments after the antique in Fior di Persica, with a bas-relief showing 'The Birth of the Poet Lucan' (after Montfaucon)	m	Holkham Hall, Norfolk, north state bedchamber	*Brettingham* 1773, 10 (repr 51); C Lib (repr)
24.	nd	'Thermes, with heads of the younger Empress Faustina'		Holkham Hall, Norfolk, state bedchamber	J Dawson, *The Stranger's Guide to Holkham*, 1817, in GPC
25.	nd	Two, one of Siena, one of Egyptian	m	[Heythrop, Oxon, little blue room, drawing room, great drawing room]; destroyed	*Oxford Guide* 1805, 140, 142; *Gunnis* 1963, 1175
26.	nd	With 'ornaments within the sunk pilasters (instruments from the Roman Sacrifice), copied from a very fine fragment of the same size, in the gardens of the Villa Medici'		Holkham Hall, Norfolk, north state bedchamber	J Dawson, *The Stranger's Guide to Holkham*, 1817, in GPC
27.	nd	With term figures and heads of the young Empress Faustina, on a ground of Siena	m	[Holkham Hall, Norfolk, state bedchamber]; untraced	*Brettingham* 1773, 8 (repr 50)
Architectural Sculpture					
28.	1733	Unspecified work (under John Wilkins)		[13–17 Queen Street, St Anne, Soho]; untraced	*S of L*, vol 33 (1966), 166
29.	1737	Unspecified work (under Isaac Ware and Charles Carne)		[Chandos Place, Long Alley, London]; untraced	*S of L*, vol 36 (1970), 264
30.	1740	'Festoons of oak leaves' Payment(s): £6		[Okeover Hall, Staffs]; untraced	*Oswald* 1964, 175
31.	1740	'Pedestal for a dial plate' Payment(s): £8		[Moulsham Hall, Essex]; untraced	*Edwards* 1977, 61
32.	1743	2 large vases in Portland stone Payment(s): £25	s	Okeover Hall, Staffs, gardens	GPC
33.	nd	Foliage scrolls in archway pilasters	wd	[Holkham Hall, Norfolk, 'archway leading to the sideboard']; untraced	*Brettingham* 1773, 5
Miscellaneous					
34.	1739	Two tables	m	[Okeover Hall, Staffs]; untraced	*Oswald* 1964, 175
35.	1742	Large black and white cistern for bottles Payment(s): £28		[Moulsham Hall, Essex]; untraced	*Edwards* 1977, 77
36.	1751	Wine cistern Payment(s): £35 15s	m	Blair Castle, Perths	*Rococo* 1984, 300 (repr); *Pearson* 1991, 142 (repr)

CARTER, Thomas II –1795

In the mid-19th century at least one scholar suggested that Carter had been 'reckoned among the first statuaries of the kingdom' in his day (*Hutchins* 1861, vol 1, 403). He was the nephew and son-in-law of **Thomas Carter I**, and the business partner of **Benjamin Carter**, 1756–66. Like his kinsmen, Thomas II was the master of a prosperous workshop, which sent out fine chimneypieces, and also two of the most distinctive monuments of late 18th-century England.

He married his cousin Elizabeth in February 1752 and was already established as a sculptor by 1756 when he was described as a 'statuary' in his father-in-law's will. Elizabeth inherited a third of her father's property, so that within a few weeks her husband was in a position to go into formal partnership with his uncle, Benjamin Carter, and began to pay annual rates of £10 on a property next to Benjamin on Hyde Park Road. The partnership ended when Benjamin died.

Benjamin's complex (and partly illegible) will directed that his half share in the business should pass to his wife and son at the formal expiration date of the partnership with Thomas, but that in the meantime an annual allowance should be made for the maintenance of Benjamin's family. This financial arrangement seems to have agitated Thomas. One of the last contracts completed in partnership with Benjamin was for chimneypieces at Sir Edward Knatchbull's house at Mersham, Kent (**25, 27, 28**). Thomas wrote to Knatchbull requesting payment for work undertaken at Mersham, since 'the Executors of my late partner have advised me to settle all my accounts.' The response was not encouraging, for Sir Edward declared himself 'a stranger as to what engagements you have entered upon concerning your partner' and added callously, 'you may have heard of buying a pig in a poke' (T Carter II/Knatchbull).

Carter's financial difficulties do not appear to have had any adverse effect on the range, output and quality of his independent workshop. By 1768 he had taken over Benjamin's former premises, rated at £24, and rates on the smaller adjacent property were paid by a 'Mr Cramphorn,' perhaps a relation of **William Cramphorn**, who was apprenticed to Thomas Carter on 9 June that year. Carter continued to offer ornate chimneypieces as his principal stock-in-trade. These were often designed by leading architects, including Robert Adam, who had worked with the Carter partnership for several years (**2, 4, 17, 18, 20, 22, 29, 31, 33, 39, 40, 41**). Thomas's new connections included **Robert Mylne the Younger** (**36**), Sir William Chambers (**45**), Henry Holland and Sir John Soane. He worked on a number of commissions in conjunction with Soane, earning £935 for chimneypieces at one residence (**58**). In or around 1783 Carter was employed by Henry Holland, who was altering Carlton House for the Prince Regent (**53**). Carter also worked to his own designs: Lady Louisa Connolly, who negotiated with Carter on behalf of her sister, Emily, Duchess of Leinster, sent the Duchess 'three drawings of Mr Carter's for chimney-pieces' on 28 March 1776 (**47**). An accompanying letter suggests that the sculptor was accustomed to penny-pinching clients; 'he [Carter] says that Corinthian capitals are much the most expensive part of the chimney-piece, so that in another order you may have as showy a chimney-piece for much less money' (*Fitzgerald* 1957, vol 3, 192).

Carter's numerous apprentices included **John Daintrey (or Daintee)**, **John Walsh**, and **Thomas Earley**, who was probably a relative. **Joseph Nollekens** apparently commented that 'Tom Carter always had a clever fellow with him to produce his work' (*Smith* 1828, II, 307), and it seems that Carter made a practice of choosing talented assistants, whether as full-time employees or for a single contract. **Peter Vangelder**, who joined the workshop *c*1769 was paid 2 guineas a week and specialised in floral decoration, although he is known to have carved an unnamed statue in around 1776. **John Deare**, who was articled to Carter around 1776, was initially paid as little as half a guinea a week, but 7 years later he provided Carter with a tablet for a chimneypiece at a cost of 24 guineas. Deare felt that Carter took advantage of his assistants: 'it is a custom with him to make large promises to young fellows, by which means he has gained grease to keep his carriage going' (*ibid*, 309). Though he accused Carter of cupidity, they ended their working relationship amicably and he judged Carter 'a blustering fellow, but a good man' (*ibid*, 304).

Around the time that Deare joined the workshop, Carter provided a monument to a noted 17th-century politician, Chaloner Chute, Speaker of the House of Commons in the Long Parliament (**7**). It was commissioned by a descendant, John Chute, an amateur architect and friend of Horace Walpole, and erected in a specially constructed chapel at The Vyne in Hampshire. The memorial has a full-size figure of the Speaker, reclining on a woven pallet, his head resting on his hand, a hat and book by his side. A near-contemporary, Samuel Egerton Brydges, recorded that the effigy was carved by **John Bacon RA** from a portrait by Van Dyck, a plausible suggestion since sub-contracting was a practice of the workshop. The terracotta model for the figure is finely detailed and possesses all the harmony and grace of the finished work (VAM). The Speaker is clad in the dress of his day but rests on a large, classically-inspired pedestal with fluted Ionic columns, interspersed with mannerist cartouches recording the family's history. Carter's detailed invoice makes it clear that he oversaw each aspect of the production and erection of the monument, and gives a breakdown of costs including marbles at £335 9s 11d, carving of the effigy and ornaments at £504, packaging, transport, and the travel costs of the mason and polisher sent down to Hampshire. The total cost was £940 17s 9d (*Chute* 1954, 1733).

In 1777 Carter moved from the large house on Hyde Park Road (now renamed Piccadilly) to another property in the same street, where he stayed until 1789. The move prompted two auctions of his superfluous stock, including marble 'wrought and unwrought,' second hand chimneypieces, tables, busts, casts, tablets, figures and 'four models of terra quota.' These were displayed beforehand in his yard, and in 'The Great Room upstairs' was an array of stones and marbles from sites throughout the British Isles, Italy, Egypt and Africa. 'Mr Bird', almost certainly the marble merchant, **Edward Chapman Bird**, was a major purchaser of the uncarved blocks. It seems that Carter was also involved in the marble trade, for in the same year the auctioneer, Willoughby, advertised a sale of newly imported marbles at 'Mr Carter's Wharf called Stangate Wharfe, on the Surry side of Westminster-Bridge.' The catalogue invited orders for Portland stone.

Carter continued to provide monuments from his new premises, the most notable of which commemorated Mary Benyon (**8**). This graphic work, commissioned by Richard Benyon of Gidea Hall, Essex, illustrates in high relief the moment of his mother's death. An attendant tries to support her dead mistress's head, whilst another gazes on in agonised disbelief. It is not clear whether Carter himself had a hand in this theatrical tour-de-force, though he certainly received a part-payment of £100. The sculptor largely responsible for another monument has been identified: **Peter Mathias Vangelder**, who worked regularly for Carter and carved the ornaments on the monument to Mrs Frampton (**9**), a tablet framed by cultivated and wild flowers. Vangelder was working under Carter's direction before June 1776, earning 2 guineas a week, and was 'one of the best hands in London at foliage' (*Smith* 1828, II, 306). The monument was 'esteemed by connoisseurs one of the completest pieces of sculpture in the kingdom' (*Hutchins* 1861, vol 1, 403).

The Carter workshop completed one notable monument in the 1780s, a draped pyramid with portrait medallions and rich ornaments to Carew Hervy Mildmay (**10**), and continued to supply chimneypieces, for instance at Woburn Abbey, until the early 1790s (**55**). In 1789 the sculptor ceased to pay rates on the property in Piccadilly, and at the time of his death in 1795 he was living in Sloane Street, in the village of Knightsbridge. He was a wealthy man, who left leasehold and freehold estates, farms, lands and tenements, as well as bequests totalling more than £4000. His will suggests that his personal life was complicated. He provided for his wife, his daughter Rebecca, and his granddaughter Emma Earley, but also left a substantial inheritance to his 'reputed son', Thomas, and gifts of £500 each to 7 other children mothered by a Mrs Sarah Moss.

During the earlier-20th century Thomas Carter was largely forgotten, but the discovery of his responsibility for the Chute monument led to a re-appraisal of his work. In 1954 the sculpture historian Margaret Webb, believing that Carter had personally carved Chute's effigy, suggested that 'he must now rank as one of England's greatest sculptors' (*Webb/Gunnis* 1954, 25). The claim is exaggerated, but Thomas Carter II and his two forebears deserve recognition as shrewd proprietors of a long-lived and thriving family business. The high quality of their chimneypieces and monuments is a testament both to their artistic standards and to their skill in recognising and utilising the talents of emerging sculptors.

MGS

Literary References: *Brydges* 1789–91, 59–60; *Smith* 1828, II, 304–7; *Hutchins*, 3rd ed. 1861, vol 1, 403, vol 4, 248–9; *Webb/Gunnis* 1954, 25; *Chute* 1954, 1733–4; *Fitzgerald* 1957, vol 3, 192; *Gunnis* 1958, 334; *Cummings* 1968, 659–67; *Gunnis* 1968, 85–6; *Whinney* 1988, *passim*

Archival References: Rate-Books, St George, Hanover Square, WCA, 1758 (C300), 1768 (C311), 1777 (C348), 1789 (C369); T Carter II/Knatchbull; GPC; IGI

Wills: Thomas Carter I, PROB 11/824 fol 313–5; Benjamin Carter, PROB 11/923 fol 173–6; Thomas Carter II, PROB 11/1257, f152

Auction Catalogues: Carter II, 1777 (1); Carter II, 1777 (2); Carter II 1777 (3)

Funerary Monuments

1.	†1759	Sarah Currer (co-sculptor: Benjamin Carter)	Bath Abbey, Somerset	S	*Gunnis* 1968, 84
2.	1761	Lieutenant-Colonel the Hon Roger Townshend (†1759) with relief by John Eckstein (designed by Robert Adam and L-F Breton) (co-sculptor: Benjamin Carter) Drawing(s): Soane, Adam vol 14, no 8; vol 18, no 85; vol 19, nos 9, 10, 66, 68, 72, 85; design for panels, Adam vol 19, 69 & 70	Westminster Abbey, London, nave	S	*Fleming* 1962 (2), 163–171 (reprs); *Whinney* 1988, 251–2 (repr)
3.	1768	Sir George (†1766) and Dame Anna Maria Amyand (†1767) Payment(s): £65	Carshalton, Surrey		Amyand Estate Accts, Herefs RO J/vi/6; *Skelton* 1996, 5
4.	†1769	Frances, Viscountess Palmerston (designed By Robert Adam)	Romsey Abbey, Hants	S	Pevsner, *Hants*, 1967, 486; *Colvin* 1995, 61

No.	Date	Work		Location		Reference
5.	†1774	Ann Rodney		Walton-on-Thames, Surrey	S	
6.	1774	Elizabeth Dayrell (†1768)		Shudy Camps, Cambs	S	*Palmer* 1932, 149; Pevsner, *Cambs*, 1970, 456
7.	1775–1776	Chaloner Chute (+†1659) Payment(s): £940 17s 9d Model(s): VAM (effigy) A8–1911		The Vyne, Hants		*Brydges* 1789–91, vol 1, 59–60; *Chute* 1954, 1733; *Whinney* 1988, 251, 253 (repr); *Howard* 1998, 28–9 (repr); *Bilbey* 2002, 59 (repr); *Bowdler* 2002, 46–50
8.	1778	Mary Benyon (†1777) Payment(s): £100 (part payment)		Englefield, Berks		Benyon Accts cited by *Gunnis* 1968, 84; Pevsner, *Berks*, 1966, 137; *Whinney* 1988, 25
9.	†1782	Mrs Frampton (co-sculptor: Peter Mathias Vangelder)		Moreton, Dorset		*Hutchins* 1861, vol 1, 403; *Whinney* 1988, 315
10.	†1784	Carew Hervy Mildmay and first wife, Dorothy (†1743)		Sherborne Abbey, Dorset		*Hutchins* 1861, vol 4, 248–9; Pevsner, *Dorset*, 1972, 375
Chimneypieces						
11.	1757	Of statuary marble and jasper, with Doric columns and a tablet with lion and boys (co-sculptor: Benjamin Carter)		[for Thomas Bridges]; 18 Cavendish Square, London		LMA, Cavendish Square Accounts f245, 250, 252, 262; Pevsner, *London NW*, 1991, 635
12.	1757	Two, with caryatid figures of slaves (co-sculptor: Benjamin Carter)		[Northumberland House, London]; Syon House, Middx and VAM A.60–1951		*Allen* 1983, 200 (repr)
13.	1757	With a tablet of Cybele, black marble covings and statuary trusses (co-sculptor: Benjamin Carter)		[for Thomas Bridges]; 18 Cavendish Square, London, parlour		LMA, Cavendish Square Accounts, 18 Cavendish Square, London f245, 250, 252, 262
14.	1761	Description unavailable (co-sculptor: Benjamin Carter)		[Shardeloes, Bucks, library]; untraced		*Gunnis* 1968, 86
15.	1759–1761	Marble (co-sculptor: Benjamin Carter)		Stourhead, Wilts		*Gunnis* 1968, 84
16.	1762	Marble (co-sculptor: Benjamin Carter)		Ashburnham Place, Sussex		*Gunnis* 1968, 84
17.	1762	Statuary marble with variegated brocatella and Corinthian columns (designed by Robert Adam) (co-sculptor: Benjamin Carter)		[Bowood House, Wilts, then Lansdowne House, London, drawing room]; untraced		*Harris* 2001, 110, 121, 346 n14
18.	1763	Designed by Robert Adam (co-sculptor: Benjamin Carter)		[Lansdowne House, London, square room]; untraced		RG/JP, 2, 260
19.	1763	Of Portland stone (co-sculptor: Benjamin Carter)		[Bowood, Wilts, hall]; untraced		GPC
20.	1763	Statuary marble with variegated brocatella and Corinthian columns (designed by Robert Adam) (co-sculptor: Benjamin Carter) Payment(s): £552 Drawing(s): Three by Adam, Soane vol 22, 94–96, with alternatives		[Bowood, Wilts, great room]; untraced		*Cornforth* 1972, 1450; *Harris* 2001, 109–10, 346 n 13 (repr)
21.	1763	Three, two 'plain vein'd' with 'statuary Plynths' and another of 'Black and white and purple' (co-sculptor: Benjamin Carter)		[Bowood, Wilts, unidentified rooms]; untraced		GPC
22.	1763	Two (from designs by Robert Adam) (co-sculptor: Benjamin Carter)		[Bowood, Wilts, north-east room and square room]; untraced		GPC
23.	1764	Two (co-sculptor: Benjamin Carter)		[Sir Richard Lyttleton's house, Piccadilly, London]; untraced		*Gunnis* 1968, 86
24.	1765	Two (co-sculptor: Benjamin Carter) Payment(s): £150		[Croome Court, Worcs, dressing room and ante-room]; untraced		*Gunnis* 1968, 86
25.	1766	Description unavailable (co-sculptor: Benjamin Carter)		Mersham Hatch, Kent, ante-room		*Gunnis* 1968, 86
26.	1766	Description unavailable		[Lansdowne House, Berkeley Square, London, ante-room]; untraced		*Gunnis* 1968, 86 citing Lansdowne archives
27.	1766	Marble (co-sculptor: Benjamin Carter) Payment(s): £155		Mersham Hatch, Kent, drawing room		*Gunnis* 1968, 86
28.	1766	Two, of Portland stone (co-sculptor: Benjamin Carter)	s	Mersham Hatch, Kent, hall		*Gunnis* 1968, 86
29.	1766	With fluted Corinthian columns embellished with ormolu (designed by Robert Adam) (co-sculptor: Benjamin Carter)		Syon House, Middx, drawing room		*Harris* 2001, 66, 78 (repr)
30.	1767	More than one Payment(s): £137 13s		[Sir George Amyand's house, 11 Great George Street, London]; untraced		Amyand Accts, Herefs RO J/vi/5
31.	1768	Designed by Robert Adam Drawing(s): by Robert Adam, Soane 22/240, 241		[5 Grosvenor Square, London, front and back first floor drawing rooms]; demol *c*1961		*S of L*, vol 40, 1980, 121
32.	1768	One with relief of the 'Labours of Hercules', possibly others		Saltram House, Devon, saloon, another attrib work in velvet drawing room		Pevsner, *Devon*, 1989, 712; *Saltram* 1992, 14–15 (reprs); *Harris* 2001, 233, 358; *S of L*, vol 40 (1980), 121
33.	1768	Two (designed by Robert Adam) Payment(s): £29, £38 Drawing(s): by Robert Adam, Soane 22/240, 241		[No 5, Grosvenor Square, London, front and back first floor drawing rooms]; demol *c*1961		

34.	1769	Description unavailable Payment(s): £260		[Croome Court, Worcs, drawing room]; untraced	*Gunnis* 1968, 86 citing Croome Estate Trustees; *Beard* 1993, 93
35.	1769	Description unavailable Payment(s): £260		[for Lansdowne House, London, drawing room]; untraced	Lansdowne archives in GPC
36.	1770	Description unavailable (under Robert Mylne) Payment(s): £128 16s		[Mr Berry's house, address unknown]; untraced	RG/JP, 2, 267 citing Robert Mylne's Journals, poss Miss Mylne
37.	c1770	With putti and caryatids	m	Claydon House, Bucks, saloon	Pevsner, *Bucks*, 1994, 479
38.	1774	Designed by James Stuart Payment(s): £59 19s	m	[Bowood, Wilts, library]; untraced	*Cornforth* 1972, 1450; *Gunnis* 1968, 86; GPC
39.	1774	Statuary marble, with clawed feet on the columns (designed by Robert Adam) Drawing(s): by Adam, dated Feby 28, 1774 and inscribed 'Mr Carter has this': Soane 23.47	m	[Derby House, Grosvenor Square, London, first drawing room]; demol 1862	*Harris* 2001, 284–5 (repr)
40.	1773–1774	Statuary, with a frieze carved with a wyvern and deer (designed by Robert Adam) Drawing(s): by Adam, dated 1773, inscribed 'Carter £59'; Soane 22.43	m	[Derby House, Grosvenor Square, London]; house demol 1862	*Harris* 2001, 282, 283, 284 (repr)
41.	1774	To a design by Robert Adam Drawing(s): Soane 23.46, inscribed 'Mr Car[ter] has th [is]'		[Derby House, Grosvenor Square, London, second drawing room]; demol 1862	*Harris* 2001, 286, 362 n32
42.	1773–1774	With inlaid scagliola ornments by Richter and Bartoli Drawing(s): by Adam, Soane 23.51, dated 1774, inscribed 'Mr Carter has not got this yet the drawing at large being not quite finished'	m	[Derby House, Grosvenor Square, London, Lady Derby's apartment]; untraced	*Harris* 2001, 292, 293, 363 n61 (repr)
43.	1773–1775	Description unavailable (under James Wyatt)		[William Drake's residence, 16 Grosvenor Square, London]; untraced	*S of L*, vol 40, 1980, 130
44.	c1775	One		Shardeloes, Amersham, Bucks, library	Pevsner, *Bucks*, 1994, 619
45.	1774–1775	Several projected, only one known to have been executed (designed by Sir William Chambers) Payment(s): 110 gns		[Milton Abbey, Dorset, unidentified rooms]; untraced	*Oswald* 1966, 209–10
46.	1775–1776	Statuary marble		[for John Chute at The Vyne, Hants. Not accepted since it 'was not executed according to time and agreement']; untraced	*Chute* 1954, 173–4
47.	1776	Three designs for chimneypieces with Corinthian capitals (probably executed)		[Lady Louisa Connolly, Black Rock House, Dublin]; untraced	*Fitzgerald* 1957, vol 3, 192
48.	1776	Two	m	[Bowood, Wilts, circular room and 'room next the circular room']; untraced	Lansdowne archives in GPC
49.	1777	Several and other masonry work Payment(s): £757		[for General Smith, Chilton, Hungerford, Berks]; untraced	Soane Bills to 1785, fols 136–9
50.	1777	Several, including one with tablet carved with 'Venus attended by the Graces', for the museum, part of a much larger contract Payment(s): £70 for the relief; whole contract £564		[for Sir Robert Barker, Busbridge, Surrey]; untraced	Soane Bills to 1785, fols 134–6
51.	1778	Several, and masonry work Payment(s): £251		[for John Crunden's development of 3 houses in Park St, London, named the North, South and Centre houses]; untraced	Soane Bills to 1785, fols 139–42
52.	1782	Description unavailable		[Lord Delaval's house, Hanover Square, London]; untraced	*Gunnis* 1968, 86
53.	1789	With three-quarter columns Payment(s): £47 10s	m	[Carlton House, London, ante-room]; untraced	*Carlton House* 1991–2, 211
54.	c1791	Description unavailable (co-sculptor: Benjamin Carter)		[Sir Matthew Featherstonhaugh, Dover House, Whitehall, London]; untraced	RG/JP, 2, 266
55.	1791	Of statuary marble, supplied with several others Payment(s): £119 3s 6d	m	Woburn Abbey, Beds	Woburn Building Accts, R5/1105, 24 Dec 1791; *Gunnis* 1968, 86
56.	1791	Several Payment(s): £444		[for Messrs Ransom, Morland and Hammersley of Pall Mall, London]; untraced	Soane Bills to 1785, ff 53–6
57.	nd	More than one (co-sculptor: Benjamin Carter)		[for Lord Egremont, probably at Petworth House, Sussex]; untraced	*Rowell* 2000 (2), 76
58.	nd	Several Payment(s): £935		[for Nicholas Kenny's house, St James's Street, London]; untraced	Soane Bills to 1785, ff 132–3
Architectural Sculpture					
59.	1761	Eight relief panels (co-sculptor: Benjamin Carter)	p	Stourhead, Wilts, Pantheon	Pevsner, *Wilts*, 1975, 499
60.	post-1777	Unspecified work (under John Crunden)		[11–19 Hertford Street, London]; untraced	*S of L.*, vol 40 (1980), 174

61.	1778	For two houses in Hertford Street, London, built for Thomas Pitt	Untraced	Soane Bills to 1778, fols 144–5
62.	nd	Scrolls in 'open pilasters'	[Holkham Hall, Norfolk, north dining room, archway]; untraced	*Gunnis* 1968, 86, citing archives, Earl of Leicester
Miscellaneous				
63.	1762	'Two granate tables' and sundry work (co-sculptor: Benjamin Carter)	[Croome Court, Worcs]; untraced	*Beard* 1993, 98
64.	1763–1764	Marble tables for commodes (co-sculptor: Benjamin Carter)	[Strawberry Hill, Twickenham, Middx]; untraced	*Toynbee* 1927, 10, 111
65.	1764–1765	Unspecified work (co-sculptor: Benjamin Carter)	[Northumberland House, London]; untraced	*Allen* 1983, 200

CARTWRIGHT, Francis, of Bryanston *c*1695–1758

A master-builder of Blandford, Dorset, he described himself as a 'carver' in his will. He was responsible for building Creech Grange, where he provided chimneypieces (**1**), and King's Nympton Park, Devon. In 1732 he was working for Henry Hoare II at Stourhead, Wilts, receiving payments totalling £510 between 1741 and 1747. This included the provision of a large carved frame, work in the saloon and other unspecified labour. In 1736 he took John Plimmer of Brinson, Dorset as an apprentice.

Cartwright is buried at Blandford St Mary, Dorset, where a wall tablet commemorates him. Below the inscription are carved dividers, a ruler, a T-square and a scroll of paper on which is incised the front of Came House, Dorset, which was probably also his work. This had fine composite capitals and pediment sculpture. He died on 24 April 1758, leaving a newly-built house in Blandford, and requested that his stone, marble, timber, boards and tools be sold for the benefit of his wife and daughter.

Literary References: *Oswald* 1953, 492; *Penny* 1977, 17; *Colvin* 1995, 231

Archival References: Hoare Private Accounts 1734–49; Hoare Partnership Ledger, 1725–34, f272, Jan 6 1732/3

Chimneypieces				
1.	1739	Three Payment(s): £5 19s 3d	[Creech Grange, near Corfe, Dorset]; untraced	GPC
Miscellaneous				
2.	1742–1743	Unidentified carving	[Blandford Forum Church, Dorset]; untraced	*Colvin* 1995, 231

CARTWRIGHT, Joseph fl 1673–84

The son of **Thomas Cartwright I** and father of **Thomas Cartwright III**. His father was closely involved with the Masons' Company and Joseph was made free of the Company by patrimony on 10 June 1673. He was admitted to the livery on 29 October 1674. He married Elizabeth Wigley of Camberwell on 23 August 1676, at which time he was living in the parish of St Olave, Southwark (Lic Vic Gen). Joseph probably assisted his father in the contracting business and succeeded him as Master Mason at London Bridge in July 1673, holding the post for 11 years until June 1684. In this capacity he was paid £753 *in toto* in 1682–3 and £110 in 1683–4, as well as a salary of £4 pa. During his tenure of office, he took 3 apprentices, Thomas Durham, bound in 1675, Walter Vincent in 1676 and Bartholomew Jackson in 1680. Durham and Jackson both worked at the Bridge. Joseph's name disappeared from the Bridge Accounts on 21 June 1684 and he may have died shortly afterwards.

Literary References: *Knoop and Jones* 1935, 37

Archival References: Bridge House Rentals 1673–86; GPC

CARTWRIGHT, Thomas I *c*1617–1702

Cartwright was one of the foremost London mason-contractors in the latter part of the 17th century and was responsible for several fine funerary monuments. Nothing is known of his family background, but he was apprenticed to Daniel Chaloner in 1631–32 under the auspices of the Masons' Company and was turned over to Christopher Kingsfield in 1637–38. Cartwright took an active part in the affairs of the Masons' Company throughout his mature years: he joined the livery by 1663, became an assistant in 1668, a warden in 1671 and was twice master, in 1673 and again in 1694. Two sons, **Thomas Cartwright II** and **Joseph Cartwright** both followed their father's profession and took a part in Masons' Company affairs.

Cartwright's professional activities in the first 40 years of his life are a mystery, but he was evidently considered a reliable contractor for in 1656–7 he was given £53 1s as a part-payment for paving the Temple church and in 1659 he was involved in masons' work at the Middle Temple. He was also working on a number of sculptural commissions. An account book covering the period from January 1657 to November 1659 details 3 monuments and 10 gravestones sent out of London, as well as a number of chimneypieces and architectural ornaments, all for clients not certainly identified (**1–4, 11, 12, 17, 18**).

His business expanded after the restoration of Charles II in 1660 and particularly after the Great Fire of 1666. In 1667 he provided chimneypieces for Whitehall Palace (**13–15**) and that year received the first of several contracts from the City's livery companies, for masonry work at the new Weavers' Hall and two houses nearby. In 1668 he was commissioned to rebuild Drapers' Hall in Throgmorton Street, where he also supplied a chimneypiece and a pair of carved gate-piers which so pleased the Company that they paid him £6 instead of the £4 he had requested (**16, 22**). The minute book for the Drapers' Hall rebuilding programme records sums totalling more than £1,100 paid to Cartwright between July 1668 and January 1672. He was also issued with a warrant for £250 on 11 November 1672 for work on Bridewell prison (City Lands Rough Minutes 03/001). Cartwright was also a developer: on 19 August 1670 he was granted the lease of a plot of the company's land with kitchen buildings that he was already converting for other use.

In the years 1667–71 he was the contracting mason for the new Royal Exchange, responsible to the surveyor Edward Jerman. In December 1667 he received a first payment of £200 for work to date. The keen pace slackened in 1668 for Jerman, who was losing control of the enterprise, appeared on site less regularly, and that autumn he died.

Cartwright took charge of the ailing scheme: he 'declared himself master of the wholle designe intended for that building; whereupon the Committee desired him to proceed vigoerously in the work' (MC, GR, II, 340). On 26 March 1670 his design for the frontispiece and cupola was accepted by the Joint Gresham Committee and the building was finished a year later. Cartwright negotiated with **John Bushnell** for statues of Charles I and Charles II for the Cornhill frontispiece and he paid Bushnell £300, later reimbursed by the Committee. Cartwright was given 'the City moiete' of his fee for Bushnell's statue of Gresham in November 1671. He was involved again in the sculptural programme in 1685, when he made the payment and perhaps subcontracted the commission to **Arnold Quellin** for a statue of Edward IV, ordered by the Ironmongers for the line of kings in the quadrangle.

Cartwright's proved managerial skills brought major contracts during the 1670s, for he was employed as mason for the rebuilding of Haberdashers' Hall, 1671, Tallow Chandlers' Hall, where he was paid £150 in 1672–3, and Mercers' Hall, completed in 1672. In 1673 he and **John Young** received £500 from the Mercers for 'stone and workmanship about the porch and columns' and other work. Payments for masonry work are recorded in the Guildhall restoration accounts for the years 1671–1675 at Poultry Compter, Fleet Ditch and Holborn Bridge (paid jointly with John Young) and he was also employed in rebuilding Moorgate (£1,400) and Ludgate (£1,160), where he may have provided the statue of Queen Elizabeth. In 1676, he supplied statues of the cardinal virtues for Newgate (**24**). He was Master Mason at London Bridge for the short period from August 1672 to July 1673, when he passed on the post to his son, Joseph. Cartwright was also the contractor administering large sums at three of Wren's churches, St Benet Fink, 1670–81 (£1,838), St Mary-le-Bow, 1670–81 (£3,488) and St Antholin, 1678–82 (£3,524). In all three he was responsible for carved stone work (**19–21**). Robert Hooke, who worked closely with Wren as co-surveyor under the Act for rebuilding London, records that he 'agreed with Cartwright for Bow tower for £2,500' (Hooke Diary, 1 March 1676, quoted by *Robinson and Adams*, 219). Cartwright also worked under Hooke at Bethlehem Hospital in Moorfields. Hooke's diary has the cryptic reference 'At Bedlam governors, Cartwright foold' on 19 October, 1674, and the architect laconically records on 28 September 1675 'To Cartwright saw his statues, for Bedlam Gates' (**23**; *Robinson and Adams*, 127, 183). On 7 December 1677 he submitted a bill of £31 5s 7d to the Corporation of London for masonry work at 'Lady Dacre's Hospital' in 'Tuttle Feilds' (the Emmanuel Hospital in Tothill Fields, Westminster). In 1675 he completed work on his only known domestic building, Sir William Turner's house in Warwick Lane.

In the mid-1670s he was responsible for two commissions of greater sophistication than his other known works of sculpture, the elegant monuments to Sir John Langham and to Sir John Lewys (**5, 6**). Payments for both were itemised in the ledgers at Clayton and Morris's bank. The Langham has two recumbent effigies in contemporary dress on a tomb chest carved with bold, fleshy cartouches. The sculptor received £290 for the monument in 1676. In the following year Cartwright completed the Lewys, which is now free-standing, and has a pair of semi-reclining figures one above another on a stepped base. It was originally against a wall, and the top part of the monument, a moderate-sized architecturally-framed inscription tablet, remains on the wall. He advertised the metropolitan origins of the work with the words '*Londini sculptore*' appended to his name and was paid £180 in two instalments.

Cartwright supervised the rebuilding of St Thomas's Hospital in Southwark, London from about 1680 to 1702. In 1681 he presented the governors with a design for a frontispiece on the Borough High Street 'containing pillars and the Kings Armes and the effigies of King Edward the Sixth and fower cripples to be carved in stone to be executed in Purbeck marble' (**25**; Court Minutes, 11 Nov 1681). His tender for the contract was £190 and he was eventually paid £206 'for the frontispiece of stone at the forecourt, graving and other work' (Cash Book, Nov 1681, June 1682). By the early 1720s the gateway had become too narrow and the structure was moved to the hospital's central quadrangle over a passage leading to the inner square. The statues have been relocated a number of times since. The timidly posed figure of the king is now on a pedestal on the hospital's river front and the cripples are inside the hospital. They are four lively figures of patients, a woman with her arm in a sling, another leaning on a stick, a poor man on crutches and a well-dressed man with a wooden leg.

He continued to accept contracts until shortly before his death, perhaps helped by his son, Thomas. In 1701 he was engaged on masons' work at Christ's Hospital School, Ware and in 1700 he was employed in building St Thomas, Southwark.

The names of several of Cartwright's apprentices are recorded in the Masons' Company apprentice bindings book, but little is known of them. Samuel Ward, the son of an Oxfordshire mason, joined him in 1668, Bostock Knight became his 'husbandman' in 1678 and John Porter his mason in 1687. His son, Thomas Cartwright II, was apprenticed to him in 1673 and **Thomas Davis**, who may be the sculptor employed at Chatsworth and Hampton Court in the 1690s, became his clerk of works in 1668. **Thomas Green of Camberwell** served with Cartwright as a journeyman.

Cartwright's work as a sculptor was integral to his career as a leading mason contractor in the City's rebuilding programme. His workshop had the skills to provide competent architectural ornaments and monuments, but the Lewys and Langham memorials are of another order. Gunnis pays tribute to the 'great artistic importance' of the 'magnificent' Langham monument, which 'proves conclusively that its creator was one of the foremost sculptors of the seventeenth century' (*Gunnis* 1968, 87).

IR

Literary References: *Inderwick* II, 1898, 325; *Weaver* 1915, 18, 19, 21, 27, 37; *Knoop and Jones* 1935, 38; *Robinson and Adams*, 1935, 127, 183; *Gunnis* 1968, 86–7; *Colvin* 1995, 232; *Grove* 13, 614 (Friedman); *Saunders* 1997, 129–33; *Gibson* 1997 (2), 148, 161; *White* 1999, 17–18; *Webb* 1999, 10, 20, 26, 34; *Smith* 1999, 14–25; *Ward-Jackson* 2002, 67, 68, 69, 129, 349

Archival References: Cartwright Accounts, 1657–1659; Whitehall O/E 1666–67; Weavers Subs, p 58; Turner Misc Accounts; Guildhall restoration, Poultry Compter, 29v, 29 June 1671, Holborn Bridge, 37r, 7 Feb 1675, Bridewell Prison, 46v, 30 Nov 1671, Moorgate, 52r, 31 Oct 1673; Tallowchandlers, WA, vol 3; St Thomas's Hospital, Cash Book, 26 August 1681; St Thomas's Hospital, Court Minutes, 11 Nov 1681; Masons' Company, Apprentice binding book (1); Corp of London, Emmanuel Hosp, CLA/071/AD/01/007; GPC

Funerary Monuments

1.	*c*1657	'a marble monument for ye lady St John', perhaps Christian, Lady St John and her infant son (†1653) Payment(s): £70	Staveley, Derbys	Cartwright Accounts, 1657–59; *White* 1999, 17, 18 nn11,12; C Lib (repr)

2.	c1657	A monument of black and white marble 'like to Mr Seldens in ye temple church', probably Sir Roland St John (†1645), his wife Sibyl (†1656) and son Oliver, Baron St John (†1662)		Woodford, Northants		Cartwright Accounts 1657–59; *White* 1999, 17, 18 nn13, 14; C Lib (repr)
3.	c1659	'one Allter Toombe sett up neare Malden in esex', almost certainly to John Strange (†1658)		Purleigh, Essex		Cartwright Accounts 1657–59; *White* 1999, 17, 18 nn10, 15, 16
4.	1657–1659	Ten gravestones, including three sent 'to Oxford to Mr Jackson'		Untraced		Cartwright Accounts 1657–59; *White* 1999, 17, 18 n9
5.	1676	Sir John Langham Bt (†1671) Payment(s): £290		Cottesbrooke, Northants		*Clayton & Morris* 6428/3, part 1, 85, 21 July 1676; *Gunnis* 1968, 87; C Lib (repr)
6.	1677	Sir John Lewys Bt (†1671) and wife Payment(s): £280		Ledsham, W R Yorks	SD	*Clayton and Morris* 6428/3, part 1, 84, 9 April and 18 Sept 1677; *Gunnis* 1968, 87; C Lib (repr)
7.	†1689	John Polhill		Burwash, Sussex	S	*Gunnis* 1968, 87; C Lib (repr)
8.	†1689	Sir John Witham Bt		Temple Church, London	S	*Esdaile* 1933 (2), 73; Pevsner, *London: City*, 1997, 270; C Lib (repr)
9.	†1691	Charles Thorold		St Andrew Undershaft, City of London	S	Pevsner, *London: City*, 1997, 193
10.	1692	Edward Sulyard		Runwell, Essex	S	*Gunnis* 1968, 88
Statues						
11.	1657–1659	Eight figures of unidentified subjects, seven of them alabaster		Untraced		Cartwright Accounts 1657–59; *White* 1999, 17, 18 n8
Chimneypieces						
12.	1657–1659	Twenty-one or twenty-three, for unidentified sites		Untraced		Cartwright Accounts 1657–59; *White* 1999, 17, 18 n5
13.	1667	Black marble	m	[Whitehall Palace, London, Duke of York's lodging]; untraced		Whitehall O/E; *Gunnis* 1968, 87 (PRO Works 5/9 incorrectly cited)
14.	1667	Black marble	m	[Whitehall Palace, London, Duke of Kendal's bed chamber]; untraced		Whitehall O/E; *Gunnis* 1968, 87
15.	1667	Black marble	m	[Whitehall Palace, London, Countess of Rochford's lodging]; untraced		Whitehall O/E; *Gunnis* 1968, 87
16.	1668	'in the Ladies Chamber'; the hearth 'laid with firestone' in 1669 Payment(s): £8		[Drapers' Hall, City of London]; untraced		Drapers' rebuilding, 18 Nov 1668; *Gunnis* 1968, 87
Architectural Sculpture						
17.	1657–1659	Coat of arms for an unidentified site		Untraced		Cartwright Accounts 1657–59; Bodl MS Rawlinson C 495; *White* 1999, 17, 18 n7
18.	1657–1659	Six sundials; in three cases 'rubinge and gravings and settinge' only		Untraced		Cartwright Accounts 1657–59; Bodl MS Rawlinson C 495; *White* 1999, 17, 18 n6
19.	post-1666	Eight capitals, two cherub-heads and eight flambeaux on the spire Payment(s): £46 for the capitals and cherub heads; £36 for the 'flambeaus'	s	St Antholin, City of London		*Gunnis* 1968, 87 citing Bodl, Rawlinson MS 495
20.	post-1666	'four draperies and two festoons, 4 ft. long' and six capitals Payment(s): £9 for the draperies and festoons; £27 for the capitals	s	St Benet Fink, City of London		*Gunnis* 1968, 87 citing Bodl, Rawlinson MS 495
21.	post-1666	Ten Corinthian capitals, four pinnacles and carving on the steeple, four flaming urns (co-sculptor: John Thompson) Payment(s): £8 for the capitals, £250 for 'pinacles and carving', £20 for urns		St Mary-le-Bow, City of London		*Gunnis* 1968, 87 citing Bodl, Rawlinson MS 495
22.	1669	Gate piers	s	[Drapers' Hall, City of London]; untraced		Drapers' rebuilding, 10 March 1669; *Gunnis* 1968, 87
23.	1675	Several statues		[Bedlam Gate, City of London]; untraced		*Robinson and Adams*, 1935, 183
24.	1676	Justice, Mercy, Truth,		[Newgate, City of London]; untraced		*Gunnis* 1968, 87
25.	1681	Liberty Frontispiece with statues of King Edward VI and 'two pairs of cripples' Payment(s): £190	s	[St Thomas's Hospital, Southwark]; St Thomas's Hospital, Lambeth (statues only)		*Stow* 1754–5, 278; *Gunnis* 1968, 87; *Blackwood* 1989, 36–7 (repr); *Cavanagh* forthcoming 2007 (Lambeth 2): C Lib (repr)
26.	1682	Two lions for the gate piers Payment(s): £30		[Ailesbury House, Clerkenwell, London]; untraced		*Gunnis* 1968, 87
27.	1696	Two large urns and 'a sun dyall with scroul's inriched with carving'		[St Thomas, Southwark, London, Chapel]; removed 1730		*Gunnis* 1968, 87

CARTWRIGHT, Thomas II 1655–1711

He was the son of **Thomas Cartwright I** and was apprenticed to his father on 21 January 1673. Like his father, he took an active interest in Masons' Company's affairs, becoming renter warden in 1704, upper warden in 1705, and master in 1710. He continued his father's work at St Thomas's Hospital, London, receiving a payment for mason's work on 26 April 1710 (£11). A second payment of £5 12s was made on 30 May 1711 principally for his work on the dome. His authenticated memorials are cartouches with scrollwork and feigned drapery.

Cartwright died on 15 November, 1711, and was buried at St Mary, Rickmansworth, Herts, where a stone once commemorated him and his wife, the daughter of Roger Touchet of Rickmansworth.

Literary References: *Cussans* 1870, III, part II, 157; *Gunnis* 1968, 87–8

Archival References: Masons' Co, Masters and Wardens, 1704, 1705, 1710; St Thomas's Hospital, Account Books, 26 April 1710, 30 May 1711

Funerary Monuments

1.	†1703	William Underwood and his wife (†1684)	Whittlesey, Cambs	S	C lib (repr)
2.	†1706	Benjamin Dodd (†1706) and Mary Craddock	St John, Hackney, London		*Stow* 1720, appendix, facing 128 (repr); *Gunnis* 1968, 88; C Lib (repr)
3.	†1706	Elizabeth Poole	Oaksey, Wilts	S	Pevsner, *Wilts*, 1975, 362

Architectural Sculpture

4.	1703	Cartouche with painted heraldry	St Mary, Whittlesey, Cambs	S	

CARTWRIGHT, Thomas III –1740

He was the son of **Joseph Cartwright** and the grandson of **Thomas Cartwright I**. His father, who had become free of the Masons' Company by patrimony in 1673, died in 1702, the year in which Thomas himself was admitted to the freedom of the Company, also by patrimony (26 March 1702). In 1733 Henry Hoare employed him at one of his houses, possibly Stourhead. The Hoare partnership ledgers have an entry for 20 December 1733, 'To Joh [or Jos] Cox's bill to Tho: Cartwright £50'.

Thomas's son, Newman Cartwright, was apprenticed to his father in 1723 and was working with him in 1731, the year in which he became free. Thomas died in 1740 and was survived by his widow Elizabeth, who received a pension from the Masons' Company until her death in 1770.

Literary References: *Knoop and Jones* 1935, 38 n4; *Gunnis* 1968, 88; *Webb* 1999, 6

Archival References: Hoare Partnership Ledger, 1725–34; Masons' Co, Court Book 1731 (freedom); Freemen, fols 9, 10

Funerary Monuments

1.	†1716	John Isham	All Souls College, Oxford	Isham Papers, Northants RO

Chimneypieces

2.	1739	One Payment(s): £53	Longford Castle, Wilts	*Gunnis* 1968, 88 citing Radnor archives

Miscellaneous

3.	1733	Unspecified work	[for Henry Hoare, perhaps at Stourhead, Wilts]; untraced	*Gunnis* 1968, 88 citing archives, Hoare's Bank (untraced)

CASONI, Castoro fl 1792–94

An Italian sculptor, he taught **Sir Richard Westmacott RA** in England, before accompanying his pupil to Paris in the winter of 1792 and then on to Rome. The two were given permission to sketch in the Uffizi in May 1794. Westmacott later said of Casoni that he was 'a native of Carrara, a man of considerable knowledge in the profession, under whom I studied sometime in England' (letter from Westmacott to James Elmes, 25 October 1822, RA Jupp Catalogue, 6/154–5 quoted in *Busco* 1994, 7, 172 n22).

Literary References: *Busco* 1994, 7–9

CASS, Christopher I 1678–1734

A conspicuously successful master mason whose team worked in London, Cambridge and at a number of large country houses, he was also apparently responsible for the remarkable monument to Jane and Edward Bray (1). Cass may have come from a family of masons since a Thomas Cass was master-mason at the Tower of London in 1668 (TNA, Works 5/145) and another Thomas Cass took an apprentice through the Masons' Company in 1711. He was apprenticed to Henry Parker in 1692 and made free of the Masons' Company on 8 July 1701. By 1704 he was one of the chief masons working under **Edward Strong I** and with **Edward Strong II** at Greenwich, where Cass was still employed on the west front of the Queen Anne building in 1725–6.

His work on London churches after the Fifty New Churches Act of 1711 included the completion of St John, Westminster, 1729–31, where he was responsible for 'pointing the Joints of the 4 Towers making good Fractures to keep out the Weather' (LPL MS 2701, fol 499, quoted by *Friedman* 2004, 43). He and **Andrews Jelfe** were responsible for the paving and other work at St Luke, Old Street, 1732–3. Cass built the tower of St Alphege, Greenwich, for which he received £3,043 and he worked as master mason at St Anne, Limehouse. Church commissions outside the Fifty Churches scheme included the building of St George's Chapel, Red Lion Fields, completed in 1719, and St George, Hanover Square, where he succeeded **Joshua Fletcher I** in 1725 and was responsible for most of the carved stone work (3). He was the mason at St Martin-in-the-Fields, 1722–6, working under the architect, James Gibbs, and received payment for his work in 1733, a full seven years after its completion (4).

On 16 December 1719, Cass wrote to the Bishop of Carlisle offering himself for the post of master mason at Westminster Abbey in place of **Edward Tufnell**, who had recently died. He felt well qualified 'having been bred in the buildings part of the Masons Trade in ye most considerable Publick Buildings lately advanced, which I have conducted where I have been concerned so farr as related to ye immediate executive part, and from that experience doubt not to do ye same work equally well at £20 pr. cent. cheaper than the Abbey have paid for ye same' (WA Muniments 65615). Cass added that he had been 'ye lowest Bidder among many competitors for ye Balistrades to St Paul's which I have just finished'.

Cass also worked on a large number of grand domestic buildings. He and **Joshua Fletcher I** were the principal masons at Blenheim from 1716, and in 1717 he was paid £159 for mason's work at Chevening. Around 1719 he built Briggens, near Hunsdon, Herts, for Robert Chester, one of the directors of the South Sea Company. In 1720, when the 'Bubble' burst and the directors were arrested and forced to give an account of their financial position, Chester wrote that he was 'indebted to Christopher Cass, mason, for stone and marble used, and work done, in building my house in Hertfordshire, £928 3s. 7d., as by his accompts, which not being according to agreement, I cannot adjust it at present' (Chester Inventory 1721, 51). Cass and Fletcher were responsible for the stonework front of Burlington House, London, 1719–22. Cass was also employed at Canons, near Edgware, 1724; at the London house of the architect, Nicholas Hawksmoor, 1727, and at Lord Bristol's house in St James's Square, London, 1732. He was master mason at Wolterton Hall, Norfolk (5). Cass, who was Master Mason to His Majesty's Ordnance, was employed at least twice on royal commissions: in 1727 he worked at the White Lodge in Richmond New Park and he was employed intermittently at Kew Palace in the years 1731–44, assisted by Andrew Jelfe (7).

Under Gibbs's direction Cass worked at Cambridge University from 1721. He built the south-east and north sides of the Senate House, where he was responsible for all the carved stonework (6) and in 1724 he was mason for the Fellows' Building, King's College. In 1727 he worked at Trinity Hall.

Cass provided much architectural ornament during his career but only one unsigned monument has been identified, to the children of Sir Edmund Bray (1). This is credited to Cass on the strength of a note on the back of the design which reads 'To Mr Chri Cass to be left att the George Inn; in Woodstock Oxfordshire'. The monument has a simple architectural ground above a large pedestal on which is presented a touching and dramatic scene. An angel holds the hands of two young children in contemporary dress, a girl in front who looks up trustingly and a boy who is reluctant to move forward, so causing the angel to twist round, encouraging him on. Clouds envelop the feet of all three. The two effigies, the angel and the inscription are London work, but the monument was clearly assembled by a local mason using a freestone instead of white marble.

Cass bound several apprentices through the Masons' Company: Jeremiah Bond joined him in 1714, Thomas Brooks and Henry Keble in 1717, James Prosser in 1718, his son **Christopher Cass II** in 1721 and Charles Pauling in 1732. His foreman at the time of his death was **Thomas Gayfere I**.

He died in London and was buried in the cemetery of St John, Westminster, under a heavy granite monument inscribed 'Chr. Cass, master-mason to his Maj. Ordnance. Dy'd Ap. 21, 1734'. In a report to the RIBA 'On the Mechanical Processes of Sculpture' **Charles Harriott Smith** suggested that this monument was one of the earliest works in England to be executed in granite, and that 'its mouldings, though such as would now be considered rude in form and execution, were highly esteemed in his (Mr. Smith's) boyhood' (*Builder*, 1851, 215). In his will Cass originally expressed a wish to be buried in a vault beneath the portico of St Martin-in-the-Fields, but he substituted St John's burial-ground in a codicil. To **Edward Strong II**, 'my friend and benefactor', he left £50, declaring that he owed him what 'I and my family, under the good providence of God, have'. He named Andrews Jelfe his executor, and bequeathed him 100 guineas. Thomas Gayfere received £20 and 'all his wearing apparel, linen and woollen of all kind'.

Cass's widow survived him and died in 1742. Andrews Jelfe, writing in that year to William Dixon, tells him that 'Mrs. Cass was buried last week. She had left all her part to Mr. Bright, a young lawyer, who married her daughter'.

IR

Literary References: *Webb* 1967, 115; *Gunnis* 1968, 88–9; *Physick* 1969, 27, 66–68; *Colvin* 1973–76, V, 232; *Friedman* 1984, 70, 234, 237, 293–5, 310–1; *Colvin* 1995, 542; *Skelton* 1994–1996, 111–128; *Webb* 1999, *passim*; *Bold* 2000 (2), 155; *Friedman* 2004, 43; BHO

Archival References: Masons' Co, Freemen, fol 8 (1701); Company Members, 1708, 6 (working in Woodstock); Greenwich Hosp bills, 82, 85–90; Graham/Collier Accts (Burlington House); GPC

Additional MS Sources: LPL, Papers of the Commission for Building Fifty New Churches, Lambeth Palace Library, MSS/2690–2750; BM, Ad MS 27587 (Hawksmoor's London house)

Will: PROB 11/667 (24 Oct 1734)

Funerary Monuments

1.	†1720	Jane (†1711) and Edward Bray Drawing(s): VAM 3436.424		Great Barrington, Glos	*Physick* 1957, 223; *Physick* 1969, 66–68; *Penny* 1977 (1), 98 (repr)

Architectural Sculpture

2.	by 1719	Eight Corinthian capitals (£112), 32 faces of Corinthian capitals (£120) and other work		[St George's Chapel, Red Lion Fields, London (St George, Queen Square)]; untraced	Lambeth Pal Lib, 'New Churches', box VII; GPC
3.	1725	Carved stonework		St George, Hanover Square, London	GPC
4.	1722–1726	Extensive carved ornaments Payment(s): £1,623 (portico and pediment sculpture)	s	St Martin-in-the-Fields, London	*Friedman* 1984, 70
5.	*c*1730	Walpole arms and other ornaments		Wolterton Hall, Norfolk, south front pediment	GPC
6.	1724–1731	Carved work in the tympana of the two pediments and stone posts before the theatre (designed by James Gibbs)		Senate House, University of Cambridge	*Gunnis* 1968, 88; *Friedman* 1984, 194–5

Miscellaneous

7.	*c*1731	Chimneypieces and other carving (co-sculptor: Andrews Jelfe) Payment(s): £450		[Kew Palace, Surrey]; untraced	Duchy of Cornwall Accts, vol II; GPC

CASS, Christopher II –1732

The son of **Christopher Cass I**, to whom he was apprenticed under the auspices of the Masons' Company on 23 August 1721. It seems likely that he worked in the successful family building concern until his premature death, but he also carved in marble, for his father's will mentions 'a marble pedestal done by my late son, Christopher Cass', bequeathed to young Christopher's sister, Sarah Gilbert.

Literary References: *Gunnis* 1968, 89; *Webb* 1999, 6

Will: PROB 11/667 (Christopher Cass I)

Chimneypieces

1.	nd	Pedestal	m	Untraced	*Gunnis* 1968, 89

CASSWELL, Richard, of Rippingale 1746–87

One of the most prolific and pleasing slate headstone engravers in the Kesteven area: the headstone to Edward Dawson is particularly fine and has lettering painted in gold.

Literary References: *Neave and Heron* 1969, 9

Funerary Monuments

1.	†1787	Edward Dawson	s	Threekingham, Lincs	S	*Neave and Heron* 1969, 9

CASTEL, J, of Oxford fl 1840–52

He exhibited an image of Abel at the Royal Academy in 1849, with a long quotation from Lord Byron (3). His address was given as Cowley Road, Oxford. He also exhibited at the Great Exhibition (2) and provided carved work in his home town (1).

Literary References: *Gunnis* 1968, 89

Statues						
1.	1851	Two		St Mary, Oxford, façade		*Gunnis* 1968, 89
Architectural Sculpture						
2.	1851	Font decorated with angels and foliage	s	[Gt Exhib, London]; untraced		*AJ Cat* 1851, 245 (repr)
Miscellaneous						
3.	1849	Abel		[Exhib RA, London, 1234]; untraced		*Graves* II, 1905–6, 13

CATHERWOOD, Thomas fl 1805–07

Brass worker or supplier, employed by the Marquess of Buckingham in 1807.

Literary References: *Gunnis* 1968, 89

Chimneypieces

1.	1805–1807	Of brass, supplied with a brass fender Payment(s): £100 (chimneypiece); £64 (fender)	b	Stowe, Bucks, gothic library		Soane bill book E fol 148; Pevsner, *Bucks*, 1994, 670

CATION, David fl 1737–42

A mason and carver, thought to have been responsible, with **Mungo Naismith**, for five keystone masks on Glasgow Town Hall, 1737–42. Four of these are now in St Nicholas Garden, Glasgow. He certainly worked on the Town Hall, for the Council minutes record that he was paid half a crown a day for over a year to carve ornaments, with one shilling a day for his apprentice.

Literary References: *McKenzie* 1999, 479

Chimneypieces

1.	1742	Jambs and hearthstones only Payment(s): £3 2s		[Town Hall, Trongate, Glasgow, Lanarks]; untraced		*McKenzie* 2002, 479

CATTERNS, Joseph fl 1678–84

The general search by the Masons' Company of 1678 listed 'Joseph Katernes' at the address of 'Mr Tompson' (**John Thompson**). Catterns was 'not free, bound att Joyners Hall' – that is, a member of the Joiners' Company (Masons' Co, Court Books 1677–94, fol 13r).

The only confirmed work by Catterns is the monument to Sir John Finch, an anatomist and diplomat, and Sir Thomas Baines, his friend and lifelong companion (1). It has high relief medallion portraits of the pair (based on paintings by Carlo Dolci, now in the Fitzwilliam), on separate pedestals but united by a single garland. Above and between the two is a flaming urn and hanging between their portraits is a knotted ribbon. The epitaph and the design, which recalls monuments associated with family and particularly marriage, encapsulate their exemplary Platonic friendship, the commingling of their lives and careers, and the unity in death of their souls and ashes. Gunnis described it as 'lovely', but Whinney felt that the design lacked unity and the *putti* showed the sculptor's limitations. Wilson has recently focussed on the relationship between Finch and Baines, who were founder members of the Royal Society, and analysed the iconography of the monument within the context of Cambridge Platonism and the celebration of exemplary friendship.

Literary References: *Gunnis* 1968, 89; Pevsner, *Northants*, 1973, 414; *Whinney* 1988, 138, 446 n7; Pevsner, *Bucks*, 1994, 613; *Wilson* 1995, 70–83

Funerary Monuments

1.	1684	Sir John Finch (†1682) and Sir Thomas Baines (†1681)		Christ's College, Cambridge, Chapel	S	Pevsner, *Cambs*, 1970, 52 (repr 46); *Whinney* 1988, 138, 446 n7; *Wilson* 1995, 71 (repr)

CAULFIELD, Mrs fl 1778

For further information the reader is referred to *Pyke* 1973, 25

CAVACEPPI, Bartolomeo 1716–99

He was a carver and restorer of antiquities, much employed in restoration work in the papal and aristocratic collections of Rome. His restored marbles found their way into the collections of Catherine the Great of Russia and Gustavus III of Sweden.

In the 1750s Cavaceppi requested permission from the Papal authorities to export antique statues to England, dealing directly with Thomas Anson of Shugborough and the antiquarian, Lyde Browne. His introduction to these British patrons was probably facilitated through contacts with the painter, Gavin Hamilton, and the dealer, Thomas Jenkins, both of whom conducted a flourishing trade in antiquities. Among the many British clients for whom he supplied restored statues and copies were the 2nd Marquess of Rockingham, who acquired a figure of *Antinous* in 1749–50 and Henry Blundell, for whom Cavaceppi carved a reduced version of *Trajan's Column* in the 1770s, supplied with the wooden model painted *en grisaille.* In 1768 Cavaceppi published a large illustrated volume of the antique statues that had been repaired at his studio. Of the sixty plates, thirty-four reproduced works owned by Englishmen.

Joseph Nollekens joined Cavaceppi's studio before 1764 and there learnt many dubious restoration techniques. In 1765 Nollekens acquired the earliest known casts of the *Furietti Centaurs* from Cavaceppi, which he sold to Anson.

Literary References: *Honour* 1959, 242; Pevsner, *Yorks: W R*, 1967, 650; *Haskell and Penny* 1981, 47, 68, 178; *Bowron and Rishel* 2000, 238; *Ingamells* 1997, 21, 141

Statues

1.	*c*1771	The Dog of Alcibiades	p	Burton Constable Hall, E R Yorks		*Mulcahy* 2006, 14

CAVALIER, Jean ?*c*1660–1699

Cavalier worked as an ivory-carver, medallist and wax-modeller, three related crafts, since the preliminary step for an ivory or metal relief was a model in wax. He is thought to have come from Dieppe, an established centre for the craft of ivory-carving and a port used by French Protestants fleeing to England to avoid Catholic persecution. He can probably be identified with John Cavalier, whose name is listed among the denizations of Huguenots in London on 16 May 1683.

His first known English ivories are signed and dated 1684. An uncomfortable head and shoulders portrait of Isabella, Duchess of Grafton, a daughter-in-law of Charles II, presents her face in profile and her upper torso from a three-quarters viewpoint, though there is no indication of torsion in the neck (1). The relief of Charles II on horseback, an image derived from the Great Seal, is entirely in profile, but for a slight turn of the horse's head (2). This is Cavalier's most ambitious known composition in an *oeuvre* otherwise devoted to small portrait medallions. The King is presented in finely-detailed classical armour and a cloak, holding a baton in his outstretched right hand in the manner of Antique equestrian statues. The horse is caparisoned in an elaborately embroidered saddle-cloth and walks among grassy hillocks past the trunk of a gnarled oak. On the verso is a delicately chiselled tree and a flower.

English subjects included aristocrats and luminaries such as the Principal Painter, Sir Godfrey Kneller (10) and the diarist, Samuel Pepys (4), as well as King William III and his wife Mary, both of whom were represented at least twice (3, 7). In the portrait of Queen Mary, his only surviving female portrait other than the Grafton, Cavalier again uses shifting perspective to display a strong profile and rounded, lightly covered breasts. The male portraits are treated in a dry, linear manner similar to contemporary medals, and Cavalier sometimes adds an upper case inscription round the border in the manner of a medal (4, 7).

He was appointed Medallist in Ordinary to Charles II in 1684, an appointment confirmed by William III in 1690, when a letter signed on the King's behalf gave 'le Sieur Jean Cavalier Notre Medalliste a Pais Estrangers' permission to travel abroad (PRO. S P Dom Warrant Book 35, 497, 11 December 1690, quoted in *Julius* 1926, Bil A). He spent a period in Germany and then Denmark, where in 1693 he carved another profile in ivory with an inscription round the rim, a portrait of Ulrich Frederick, Count Guldenlowe (VAM A.8-1928). In 1694 he joined the Swedish Court and it was on a diplomatic mission from Sweden to Russia and Persia that he died in Isfahan, Persia, in May 1699. Four of his portrait medallions in wax of European aristocrats are known to have survived.

Cavalier was the only well-known ivory-carver working in late Stuart England before the arrival, *c*1695, of **David le Marchand**, who injected new vitality and plasticity into the craft. The cost of the material and inevitable restrictions in size meant that ivories only ever appealed to a small market as cabinet-pieces. Several 18th-century sculptors, known principally for their work in marble, carved a few pieces, among them, **Peter Scheemakers** and **Peter Turnerelli. Gaspar van der Hagen** specialised in ivory carving in the middle decades of the century. In the 19th century **Benjamin Chesterton** and particularly **Richard Cockle Lucas** revived an interest in ivories, prompted perhaps by the renewed enthusiasm for medieval art. In the later-18th century the wax modeller **Isaac Gosset** discovered a composition that he claimed imitated ivory and reproduced inexpensive likenesses in the material.

IR

Literary References: *Julius* 1926; *Rasmussen* 1948, 159–63, 191; *Pyke* 1973, 25–6; *Friedman* 1981 (2), 4–13; *Theuerkauff* 1984, 29–33; *Murdoch and Hebditch* 1985, 205–7; *Avery* 1996, 15–15, 51; *Grove* 6, 101 (Friedman); *Gibson* 1998, 164

Reliefs

1.	1684	Isabella, Duchess of Grafton, oval medallion	i	VAM A.97-1980	SD	*Friedman* 1981 (2), 12–13 (repr)
2.	1684	King Charles II on horseback, oval medallion	i	LMG 27/80	SD	*Friedman* 1981 (2), 4–13; *Murdoch and Hebditch* 1985, 206–7 (repr); *Grove* 6, 101
3.	1686	Princess Mary, later Queen Mary II, oval medallion	i	VAM A.201-1929 Other versions: Staatliche Museen, Berlin, SD 1690 Kassel, West Germany	SD	*Friedman* 1981 (2), 4, 6 (repr); *Murdoch and Hebditch* 1985, 206
4.	1688	Samuel Pepys, circular medallion	i	Clothworkers' Company, City of London	SD	*Friedman* 1981 (2), 12 –13, n5; *Murdoch and Hebditch* 1985, 206–7 (repr); *Avery* 1996, 74 (repr)
5.	?*c*1690	A gentleman, probably Lord William Amphlett, circular medallion	i	Untraced	S	*Theuerkauff* 1984, 29–30 (repr)
6.	1690	Charles, 6th Earl of Dorset, circular medallion Payment(s): £21 10s with his wife's portrait	i	Untraced		*Friedman* 1981 (2), 4, 13, n7; *Murdoch and Hebditch* 1985, 206
7.	*c*1690	King William III, circular medallion	i	VAM A.18-1938 Other versions: Staatliche Museen, Berlin Kassel, Germany		*Friedman* 1981 (2), 4, 7 (repr); *Murdoch and Hebditch* 1985, 206–7 (repr)
8.	1690	Mary, Countess of Dorset, medallion Payment(s): £21 10s with her husband's portrait		Untraced		Sackville Papers Kent CRO A191/1; *Friedman* 1981 (2), 4, 13, n7; *Murdoch and Hebditch* 1985, 206
9.	1690	Master Wriothesley Russell, circular medallion	i	Sotheby, 19 March 1979, cat S 100, lot 211; private coll	SD	*Theuerkauff* 1984, 29–30, n5
10.	*c*1690	Sir Godfrey Kneller, circular medallion	i	NPG, London		*Piper* 1963, S 191, no 1740 (repr)

CAVANAGH, J, of Belfast fl 1843

Funerary Monuments

1.	†1843	Rev Charles Campbell	Newry, Co Down	S	*Potterton* 1975, 39

CAVE, J

For further information the reader is referred to *Pyke* 1973, 26 and *Pyke* 1981, 10–11

Reliefs

1.	nd	King George IV, seated on a sofa	wd	VAM A.76-1965	*Knox* 1996, 90, 92, 95 n31

CAWCY, Diacinto fl 1673–75

Cawcy (mistakenly called 'Jacinthe De Coucy' by Gunnis) was an Italian who was brought to Britain by Sir Thomas Cullum to decorate his seat, Hawstead Hall, Suffolk. In the local church is the patron's extraordinary monument (1). In consists of a sarcophagus standing between two square fluted columns, supporting a heraldic achievement with huge billowing mantling almost overpowering the monument. Parts of the background are of painted plaster imitating marble, but inset into the sarcophagus and surrounding the inscription plate, are panels of scagliola with scrolled foliage and floral designs. A step surrounding the monument has further scagliola panels, including at the corner a delightful floral bouquet. All the scagliola work is close in design to a window cill slab in the queen's closet at Ham House, where there is a fireplace surround of the same material. A receipt in the Tollemache archive records a payment to Baldassare Artima 'Roma' 1673. Gunnis states that the Hawstead monument bears 'De Coucy's signature'. Today there is no sign of a signature on this monument. Gunnis records his authority as Gage, *Hundred of Thingoe*, p 459. There is similar scgaliola furniture at Drayton House, Northants, acquired by Henry, 2nd Earl of Peterborough, who is known to have been on an embassy to Modena for James, Duke of York in 1673, and another table, formerly at Warwick Castle, is now in the Victoria and Albert Museum. The supposition is that several Italian craftsmen came to England *c*1670 and set up a manufactory for this material, and the Hawstead monument remains as one of the more bizarre examples of their work.

Literary References: *Gunnis* 1968, 125; *Blatchly and Fisher* 2004, 443–54

Funerary Monuments

1.	1675	Sir Thomas Cullum	p	Hawstead, Suffolk	*Gage* 1838, 458–9; Pevsner, *Suffolk*, 1974, 256

Architectural Sculpture

2.	pre-1675	Decorative work		[Hawstead Hall, Suffolk]; untraced	*Gunnis* 1968, 125

CENRATH, Giuseppe fl 1839

He signs a monument with a large-scale low relief of the deceased to Henry Bushe (1). Since no other work by him is known in the British Isles the inference is that this work was imported from Italy.

Funerary Monuments

1.	1839	Henry Bushe		Lismore Cathedral	SD *Potterton* 1975, 39

CERACCHI, Giuseppe 1751–1801

Ceracchi had one of the most peripatetic, turbulent and romantic careers of any 18th-century artist. He worked in Italy, Germany, Holland, Austria, France and the USA and produced images of several of the most powerful personalities of his day. His formative years, 1773–80, were spent in England, where he carved portraits in the neoclassical style, which he was to use throughout his career.

He was born in Rome on 4 July 1751, the son of Domenico Ceracchi, a goldsmith, and Lucia, née Balbi. He studied under Tommaso Righi and Andrea Bergondi and at the Accademia di San Luca and then worked in Milan and Florence between 1771 and 1773. In October 1773 **Richard Hayward** recorded in his list of British visitors to Rome that 'Giuseppe Carachi Italian sculptor' had come to England.

Ceracchi's reasons for embarking on a career in London are not recorded, but he had already cultivated connections with the British community in Italy. He was recommended to English patrons by Horace Mann, the British envoy to Florence, and arrived in England with letters of recommendation from Matthew Nulty (†1778), the British painter and antiquarian, who was a member for many years of the expatriate community in Rome. The first record of Ceracchi's activities in England is in 1776, when he exhibited a bas-relief at the Royal Academy of a subject from *The Iliad* (**19**). This was reportedly made for the Earl of Shelburne, for whom Ceracchi provided another work around this time (**30**).

It seems likely that the connection with Shelburne was made through Ceracchi's fellow-countryman **Agostino Carlini**, who had recently executed the monument to Lady Shelburne in High Wycombe. In 1777 Ceracchi was living at King's Square Court, Dean Street, Soho, where Carlini had his home and workshop. It is possible that Ceracchi began work as an assistant to Carlini soon after his arrival in England and it may well have been by Carlini's recommendation to Sir William Chambers, the architect of Somerset House, that Ceracchi won the commission for two of four statues for its façade, inspired by the antique Dacian slaves (PRO AO 1/2495). The others were Carlini's work. Ceracchi was paid £203 3s for his figures (**4**).

Perhaps encouraged by his early success, Ceracchi left Carlini's workshop in 1778 and moved to extensive premises in Margaret Street, Westminster, rented from a Mr George Watkins. J T Smith, who remembered Ceracchi visiting **Joseph Nollekens**'s studio, was taken to the Italian's premises, and described him as 'a short, thin man, with a piercing black eye, and a very blue beard' (*Smith* 1828, 2, 120).

Ceracchi carried out work for the architect Robert Adam. Among Adam's effects was 'a piece of foliage' executed by Ceracchi (**17**), as well as a relief modelled by Ceracchi after a design by the Venetian painter Antonio Zucchi (**23**). Ceracchi's only known use of artificial stone was for Adam (**18**). He also modelled at least one medallion for Wedgwood, the portrait of Joseph Priestley, which was reproduced in the series of *Illustrious Moderns* in 1779 (**25**).

Horace Walpole described Ceracchi as 'particularly successful in likenesses in busts. . . all which were to be known at the first glance' (*Anecdotes* 1937, 141–2), and his lively portraits are the most notable feature of his surviving English work. His head of Sir Joshua Reynolds (which was modelled in England but carved in Rome) is thought to be the only bust *ad vivum* of the Royal Academy's President (**9**). Ceracchi used as his source the antique bust of the Emperor Caracalla, presenting Reynolds in classical draperies, turning sharply to his left, his brow furrowed. J T Smith noted that this work was widely reproduced by plaster figure-makers. Ceracchi's masterful bust of the naval commander and Whig politician, Viscount Keppel, is reminiscent of the Reynolds, but the turn of the head is less extreme and the draperies more vital (**10**).

Walpole may have been responsible for introducing Ceracchi to his protégé, **Anne Seymour Damer**. Apparently smitten by her 'graceful nymph-like person' the Italian 'begged her to sit to him, and he made a most charming statue of her, whole length as large as life, in terracotta' (*Anecdotes* 1937, 142). This was later translated to marble and is one of Ceracchi's most inventive compositions. Damer is depicted as a personification of sculpture, standing with her tools at her feet and a statuette of a sea god in her hands (2). Damer, who had previously only sculpted portrait profiles in wax, subsequently received 'two or three lessons' in modelling from Ceracchi, after which she began to work in terracotta (*Anecdotes* 1937, 142).

The list of Ceracchi's exhibits at the Royal Academy in 1779 suggests that in addition to his market for busts of notable sitters, he hoped to execute great public works. He showed busts of Count Belgioioso, the Lombard minister at the Court of St James (11), and Pasquale Paoli, the Corsican patriot (13), but also a sketch for a proposed memorial to William Pitt, Earl of Chatham (1) to be erected in St Paul's Cathedral. The envisaged site was a novelty, for there were no contemporary monuments in St Paul's. Ceracchi made two allegorical designs in terracotta 'in one of which the character of Disinterestedness rejecting presents was fine and striking' (*Anecdotes* 1937, 142). If Ceracchi hoped his scheme would be realised he was to be disappointed: no monument was raised in St Paul's, and the monuments to Chatham that were erected in Westminster Abbey and the Guildhall were secured by **John Bacon RA**.

Walpole considered Ceracchi 'an excellent young Italian sculptor,' (*Anecdotes* 1937, 141–2) and William Chambers is said to have given the Italian work at Somerset House to encourage him to remain in England. Despite such powerful support, Ceracchi failed to find patrons and he won only four votes when his name was put forward for election as an Associate of the Royal Academy in 1779. It appears that his fortunes failed for he disposed of his premises in Margaret Street and left England in February 1780 to escape his creditors, whilst pretending that he had been summoned by the Emperor of Germany (*ibid*).

He left London for Vienna, where he carved a fine bust in the classical style of Prince von Kaunitz-Rietberg (Vienna, Kunsthistorisches Museum). The commission came through the recommendation of Count Belgioioso. He spent the 1780s working also in Berlin, Rome and Amsterdam, continuing chiefly to carve portraits, and among his sitters was Pope Pius VI (1790, Genoa, Galleria di Palazzo Bianco). His monument to Jan Van der Capellen de Pol (1785–89, Villa Borghese, Rome, gardens) was his most ambitious project, but had to be abandoned through political circumstances.

In 1791 Ceracchi left for the United States, where he hoped (in vain) to win the commission for George Washington's monument, then under debate in Congress. He did however carve several stern neo-classical busts of Washington and other American leaders, including John Jay (Supreme Court, Washington), George Clinton, Vice-President of New York (NY Hist Soc, X.42) and over 30 others. In 1792 Ceracchi returned to Italy with his wife, Therese Schlishan, and their 4 children, but he was driven out by the Papal authorities who were suspicious of his connections with Protestant Holland and the Republican USA.

After another short spell in Philadelphia in 1794, Ceracchi arrived in Paris, where his passion for sculpture was gradually relegated in favour of politics. He supported the French invasion of Italy in 1798 in the hope of seeing political reforms in his homeland. Then he changed loyalties. After giving allegiance to Napoleon, whose bust he modelled during the Italian campaign, Ceracchi gradually became disillusioned with Bonaparte. On 11 October 1800 he participated in a plot to assassinate the First Consul at the Paris Opera, and after a much-publicised trial, he was guillotined at the Place de Grève on 31 January 1801.

Ceracchi continued to have a reputation as a sculptor in England after his departure in 1780. In 1801 his 'celebrated' bust of Napoleon was brought to England under the ownership of a commercially alert dealer, Henry Richter of 26 Newman Street, who had the work engraved and offered casts after the original. Publishing twenty-seven years after the sculptor's death, J T Smith evaluated Ceracchi as 'highly gifted' but frustrated by the lack of encouragement he received in England, a judgment borne out by the high quality of his English work, and by its limited extent.

The legend of the sculptor's dramatic demise steadily began to eclipse any serious evaluation of his work as a sculptor. Smith enjoyed relating a fantastic story that Ceracchi had gone to the guillotine dressed as a Roman emperor in a bespoke chariot. In 1839 the playwright Samuel Naylor dramatised the sculptor's last days in *Ceracchi: A Drama*. Its vaunted purpose was to show 'the misdirected energies of a noble nature, erring in its departure from habitual contemplation of the exalted ideal of Art, into the vain pursuit after its semblance in Man' (*Naylor* 1839, vi–vii). In recent years Ceracchi's international career has begun to receive scholarly attention, though much still remains to be discovered about his formative years in London.

MGS

Literary References: Robert Adam's sale, 1818; *Smith* 1828, vol 2, 119–21; *Naylor* 1839; *Graves* 1905–6, vol 1, 19; *Whitley* 1928, vol 1, 338; *Pesci* 1934, 170–4; *Anecdotes* 1937, 141–2, 237; *Honour* 1963, 368–76; *Desportes* 1963, 140–79; *Hubert* 1964, 24–37; *DBI*; *Stainton* 1983, 15, 29–30; *Whinney* 1988, 319, 461 n.40; *Campitelli* 1993–1994, 121–41; *Reilly* 1995, 99; *Grove* 6, 323–4 (Bryant)

Archival References: WCA, St Anne Soho Poor Rate 1776 (A255); PRO AO 1/2495; St Marylebone Rate Books, 1778, reel 19, p25; RA/GA, 1 Nov 1779

Portraits of the Sculptor: John Trumbull, oil, Met NY (*Ceracchi Exhib Cat* 1989, 13, repr)

Funerary Monuments

1.	1779	'Sketch in clay of the Earl of Chatham's monument; designed for a niche in St. Paul's'	tc	[Exhib RA, London, 49]; untraced	*Anecdotes* 1937, 141–2; *Graves* II, 1905–6, 19

Statues

2.	c1777	Anne Seymour Damer as the muse of sculpture	tc	Untraced	*Anecdotes* 1937, 142; *Dawson* 1999, 85–9 (repr)
3.	c1778	Four colossal statues representing Music, Painting, Astronomy and History		Untraced	*Pesci* 1934, 170; *Ceracchi Exhib Cat* 1989, 8, 30
4.	1778	Temperance and Fortitude Payment(s): £200 3s, including costs of erection	s	Somerset House, London, Strand front	*Colvin* 1973–76, V, 373, 466; *Ceracchi Exhib Cat* 1989, 29–31 (repr); *Jenkins* 2000–1, 28
5.	1776–1779	Hebe		Untraced	*Ceracchi Exhib Cat* 1989, 30, 89
6.	1776–1779	River Xanto		Untraced	*Ceracchi Exhib Cat* 1989, 30, 89
7.	nd	Seated Britannia, holding a medallion of Queen Charlotte	p	[Stowe, Bucks, Queen's Temple]; untraced	*Rumsey Foster* 1848, lot 126; Stowe Sale 1921; Pevsner, *Bucks*, 1994, 683

Busts

8.	1777	Mercury		[Exhib RA, London, 52 and 1778, 43]; untraced		*Graves* II, 1905–6, 19; *Pesci* 1934, 170; *Ceracchi Exhib Cat* 1989, 90
9.	1778	Sir Joshua Reynolds Model(s): t-c, formerly Burlington House, London, destr	m	RA, London	S	*Radcliffe* 1969, 46 (repr); *Neoclassicism* 1972, 217; *Penny* 1986, cat 172; *Ceracchi Exhib Cat* 1989, 30, 49 (repr)
10.	1779	Augustus, Viscount Keppel of Elveden	m	[Exhib RA, London, 51]; Wentworth Woodhouse, W R Yorks, mausoleum Other versions: Belvoir Castle, Rutland, marble, 1779	SD SD	*Graves* II, 1905–6, 19; *British Portraits* 1956–7, 97; *Ceracchi Exhib Cat* 1989, 87; *Penny* 1977 (1), 62
11.	1779	Count Ludovico Barbiani di Belgioioso	m	[Exhib RA, London, 45]; untraced		*Graves* II, 1905–6, 19; *Ceracchi Exhib Cat* 1989, 45
12.	1776–1779	Dr Fardyce		Untraced		*Anecdotes* 1937, 142; *Pesci* 1934, 170; *Ceracchi Exhib Cat* 1989, 90
13.	1779	General Pasquale Paoli	m	[Exhib RA, London, 46]; untraced		*Graves* II, 1905–6, 19; *Ceracchi Exhib Cat* 1989, 45

Architectural Sculpture

14.	1777–1778	Several models for keystones (for Somerset House, London) Payment(s): £3 3s	w	Untraced		*Pesci* 1934, 173; *Ceracchi Exhib Cat* 1989, 30, 32, 89 (repr); *Jenkins* 2000–1, 28
15.	1776–1779	170 figures in bas-relief for several English architects		Untraced		*Ceracchi Exhib Cat* 1989, 30
16.	1774–1779	Ornamental urn	m	[for the Earl of Glasgow]; untraced		*Desportes Doctorat* nd; *Ceracchi Exhib Cat* 1989, 89
17.	nd	A 'piece of foliage' (designed by Robert Adam)		[Adam sale, 1818, lot 1]; untraced		Sale cat
18.	nd	'Sacrifice of Bacchus', relief model with 20 figures (for Robert Adam)	sa	[Desenfans's house, Portland Road, London, back front]; untraced		*Smith* 1828, vol. 2, 119–20; *Ceracchi Exhib Cat* 1989, 89

Reliefs

19.	1776	Thetis entreating Jupiter to revenge the wrongs her son Achilles had suffered from Agamemnon		[Exhib RA, London, 53]; untraced		*Graves* II, 1905–6, 19; *Ceracchi Exhib Cat* 1989, 89
20.	1777	Castor surprised in the chase by Pollux		[Exhib RA, London, 49]; untraced		*Graves* II, 1905–6, 19; *Ceracchi Exhib Cat* 1989, 89
21.	?1777	Profile medallion of a young boy	m	[Exhib RA, London, 1777, 50 (?)]; untraced	S	Christopher Gibbs sale, Christie 25–26 Sept 2000, lot 47 (repr)
22.	1777	Two medallions of young noblemen		[Exhib RA, London, 50]; untraced		*Graves* II, 1905–6, 19
23.	1779	'A basso-relievo in marble, the Rape of Europa; a model'	m	[Exhib RA, London, 48]; untraced		*Graves* II, 1905–6, 19
24.	1779	'A basso-relievo.. representing Love flying from Contention'	m	[Exhib RA, London, 47]; untraced		*Graves* II, 1905–6, 19
25.	1777–1779	Dr Joseph Priestley, medallion (for Josiah Wedgwood, reproduced in jasper and black basalt)	p	Wedgwood Museum, Barlaston, Stoke on Trent	S	*Ceracchi Exhib Cat* 1989, 50 (repr); *Reilly* 1995, 99
26.	nd	'figures sacrificing, a bass relief in three parts' (designed by Antonio Zucchi for Robert Adam)		[Adam sale, 1818, lot 13]; untraced		Sale cat
27.	nd	'one large circular medallion'		[Adam sale, 1818, lot 15]; untraced		Adam Sale 1818, 2

Miscellaneous

28.	1778	Lindzy		Untraced		*Ceracchi Exhib Cat* 1989, 90
29.	1778	'Lucretia; a sketch'		[Exhib RA, London, 42]; untraced		*Graves* II, 1905–6, 19
30.	1779	'a model in marble in a gilt frame' Payment(s): £25		[for Lord Shelburne]; untraced		GPC

CHADWICK, William, of Pentonville fl 1808–29

A monumental mason who signs a number of tablets. Chadwick was the master-mason employed in building the Board of Trade Office in Whitehall in 1825, and the hospital of St Katherine, Regent's Park, in the following year. For his work on the latter he was paid more than £435 in 1829. In the *Minute Books* of the Commissioners for building new churches (Lambeth Palace Library), he is recorded as master mason for the building of St Peter, Walworth, 1823–1825, and a church in Beckford Place, Newington.

Literary References: *Gunnis* 1968, 90

Archival References: TNA Work 5/119 fols 5, 20, 21, 162; 5/125 fol 172; GPC

Funerary Monuments

1.	c1808	Robert Hinde	Hitchin, Herts	S	*Gunnis* 1968, 90
2.	1819	Robert Hinde the Younger	Hitchin, Herts	S	*Gunnis* 1968, 90
3.	1821	John Smith	St Giles-in-the-Fields, London	S	*Gunnis* 1968, 90

CHALKLEY, Edward, of Portsea fl c1824

Funerary Monuments

1.	?1824	William Bowles	Boarhunt, Hants	S	*Gunnis* 1968, 90

CHALLIS, John, of Braintree fl 1805–20

In 1805 he was appointed by the vicar of Great Waltham to supply tombstones for the parish. His tablets have pleasant classical details.

Literary References: *Gunnis* 1968, 90 citing Great Waltham parish records.

Funerary Monuments

1.	1790	Sarah Jones	Braintree, Essex	S	Pevsner, *Essex*, 1965, 100; *Gunnis* 1968, 90
2.	?1797	Rev John Harrison	Falkbourn, Essex	S	*Gunnis* 1968, 90
3.	?1811	Rev Jeremy Pemberton	Belchamp St Paul, Essex	S	Pevsner, *Essex*, 1965, 82; *Gunnis* 1968, 90
4.	?1819	Bernard Seale	Braintree, Essex	S	*Gunnis* 1968, 90
5.	?1820	Joseph Lucas	Braintree, Essex	S	*Gunnis* 1968, 90

CHAMBERLAIN, Richard, of Newark fl 1809–25

He signs a 'charming' altar tomb with a well-carved urn to Sarah Thompson at Winthorpe (1). Her epitaph begins: 'This monitor of human instability' which Gunnis regarded as a charming, but unexpected, way to begin a valedictory inscription (*Gunnis* 1968, 90). The monument to the Maltby family also makes use of an urn on a table, but with tapering columns as legs and a sarcophagus beneath (2).

Funerary Monuments

1.	†1809	Sarah Thompson	Winthorpe, Notts, churchyard	S	*Gunnis* 1968, 90; Pevsner, *Notts*, 1979, 381
2.	*c*1825	Maltby family	Coates, Lincs	S	Pevsner, *Lincs*, 1989, 227

CHAMBERS, of Scarborough fl 1774–1815

His work 'is good for a local artist and he makes intelligent use of coloured marbles' (GPC). He signs numerous tablets in Yorkshire, including that to Richard Hudson, carved with an urn, drops, paterae and palm fronds (14).

Funerary Monuments

1.	†1774	Rev William Minithorpe	Folkton, E R Yorks	S	Pevsner, *Yorks: E R & York*, 1995, 423
2.	†1784	Elizabeth Wardrobe	St Mary, Scarborough, N R Yorks	S	GPC
3.	†1785	Fanny Sollittt	St Mary, Scarborough, N R Yorks	S	
4.	1787	Hannah Wright	Hutton Buscel, N R Yorks		*Yorks: N R*, 1966, 198; GPC
5.	†1788	Rev Thomas Bowness	Nafferton, E R Yorks	S	Pevsner, *Yorks: E R & York*, 1995, 619
6.	†1790	John Bell	Scalby, N R Yorks	S	Pevsner, *Yorks: N R*, 1966, 318
7.	?1791	John Smith	St Mary, Scarborough, N R Yorks	S	GPC
8.	†1792	Christopher Foster	Filey, E R Yorks		Pevsner, *Yorks: E R & York*, 1995, 416
9.	†1796	Unidentified subject	Hutton Buscel, N R Yorks	S	Pevsner, *Yorks: N R*, 1966, 198
10.	†1797	Richard Sollitt	St Mary, Scarborough, N R Yorks	S	GPC
11.	†1800	Martin Lowish	Thwing, E R Yorks	S	Pevsner, *Yorks: E R & York*, 1995, 724; GPC
12.	†1800	Mrs Wolley	Brompton, N R Yorks		Pevsner, *Yorks: N R*, 1966, 89
13.	†1801	Elizabeth Woodall	Seamer, N R Yorks		Pevsner, *Yorks: N R*, 1966, 336
14.	†1802	Richard Hudson	St Crux Parish Room, York		Pevsner, *Yorks: E R & York*, 1995, 164
15.	1807	Elizabeth Cayley	Brompton, N R Yorks		GPC
16.	†1807	Robert Lowish	Thwing, E R Yorks	S	*Yorks: E R & York*, 1995, 724; GPC
17.	†1737–1809	Paul family members	Nafferton, E R Yorks	S	Pevsner, *Yorks: E R & York*, 1995, 619
18.	?1812	Ann Webb	Thornton-le-Dale, N R Yorks		GPC
19.	?1814	Jane Smith	St Mary, Scarborough, N R Yorks	S	GPC
20.	†1815	James Tindall	St Mary, Scarborough, N R Yorks	S	GPC

CHAMBERS, Robert 1711–84

A mason, sculptor, architect and pioneer of marble staining, Chambers was christened at Minchinhampton, Glos on 19 December 1711, the son of Timothy and Hannah Chambers. He claimed descent from Francis Chambers, mason to King Henry VI, who had worked on the steeple of Minchinhampton church.

In 1759 Chambers won a premium of 10 guineas from the Society of Arts for 'staining marble' (Soc of A Archives, cited by *Gunnis* 1968, 90), and the following year Mendez da Costa, the librarian to the Royal Society, published an essay on 'Experiments on several pieces of marble stained by Mr. Robert Chambers' (*Philosophical Transactions*, vol 50, 30). Unfortunately the precise method was not disclosed. In 1761 Chambers began exhibiting specimens of his stained marble at the Free Society.

By 1763 he was living at Mr Kilby's in High Holborn, near Broad St Giles. Mortimer's *Director* for that year describes him as a 'Sculptor and Stainer in marble,' adding 'This ingenious artist stains various colours, Ornaments, and Emblematical Devices in marble; and copies there in Mosaic Work, or ancient Tescillation, in their proper colours.' Several examples were exhibited at the Free Society that year, including marble tables stained with a rose, a tulip, and a baron's coronet. The puff added '[he] performs Inscriptions on Monuments, Tombs, etc. in a manner which renders them more durable than the method now in use' (*Mortimer* 1763, 7). Examples of his lettering were exhibited intermittently at the Free Society between 1762 and 1782. These included 'The Hebrew alphabet', 1778, for which he appears to have had a passion, and 'the name of God in five characters' in 1782 (*Graves* 1907, 54–6).

Mortimer's *Director* also advertised that Chambers 'executes Ionic, Corinthian, and composite capitals' and 'draws designs in architecture' (*Mortimer* 1763, 7). There are no known examples of the former, but his designs for chimneypieces for a 'Bone-house' in St Mary's, Dover and for a canopy for a monument in Lee Churchyard, Kent, survive. A number of elaborate designs for fireplace surrounds are still at Claydon House, Bucks. Whilst none of these correspond exactly with chimneypieces at the house, there are similarities and they suggest an involvement at Claydon. Dated drawings fall between 1779 and 1782. Chambers exhibited architectural drawings at the Free Society in 1763, 1769, 1776, and 1782.

The memorial to the Earl of Stafford is signed 'invented and stained by Robert Chambers' (2). It is described by Brayley as a 'white marble tablet stained with the arms and ancient badges of the families connected with the Howards' (*Neale and Brayley* 1818–23, 2, 160, 161). The progress of the commission is recorded in correspondence of the widowed Countess. At the time of its completion in October 1764 she wrote 'I am told by all who have seen it, [it] has a very good effect, and that it is simple and noble; which is just what I wished it, and what my Lordship himself would have chose for any friend. Chambers has executed it in perfection. They say the colouring and badges are admirably well done, and that it has been much admired' (*Nichols* 1812–15, 708). A press notice in March that year informed readers that 'the whole was designed, executed, and the arms, &c stained in proper colours in the marble by a chemical process, by Mr Robert Chambers.' It also claimed that this 'is the first monument in England done in that manner' (*Anecdotes* 1937, 142–3).

Chambers lived at a number of addresses in Holborn, including 'Mr Franklyn's, in Bartlet's buildings' in 1765, 265 High Holborn in 1771, and 12 Brownlow Street in 1782. He was still active as a monumental sculptor in the latter year when he submitted a bill for the monument to Colonel Molyneux (**9**). The wall-monuments to Richard Savage and Peter Eaton both have inscriptions in Hebrew: the Savage is decorated with two fat palm branches (**4**) and the Eaton has baroque and rococo motifs suspended above a Grecian sarcophagus (**3**). The remarkably good condition and legibility of the monuments to Stafford and Sir John Evelyn (**2, 8**) suggest that his claim for the durability of his innovations in lettering technology were well founded. His will describes him as a 'sculptor' and a 'master-mason'. He was apparently a wealthy man, for he left property in Leics and Warks as well as Holborn and Clerkenwell.

Mendez da Costa later recalled that Chambers was 'a very curious person' who 'painted arms, flowers, fruit, Hebrew and other characters on marbles . . . he painted, or stained, on marble, several roses, exquisitely well for me, and the blazoned arms of the present Duke of Norfolk on a marble slab for his Grace' (*GM* 1812, I, 517).

MGS

Literary References: *Nichols* 1812–15, 3, 253; 8, 708; *Graves* 1907, 54–6; *Anecdotes* 1937, 142–3; *Gunnis* 1968, 90–1; *Bowdler* 1993, 91–93; *Colvin* 1995, 235–6

Archival References: Loseley MS LM/1087/21/Box I (1087/XXII/73); IGI

Will: PROB 11/1121/497

Miscellaneous Drawings: Designs for chimneypieces, Verney Papers, Claydon House, Bucks (*Colvin* 1995, 236); design for a canopy to be placed over the tomb of Sir Samuel and Sir Thomas Fludyer at Lee, Kent, s&d 21 Nov 1769, Lewisham Local History Centre, Manor House Library (*Bowdler* 1993, 91–3 (repr); 'A drawing for monumental tombs', exhib Free Soc 1783, untraced (*Graves* 1907, 56)

Funerary Monuments

1.	†1749	Joseph Iles, stained marble	Minchinhampton, Glos	S	*Gunnis* 1968, 90; Pevsner, *Glos: Cotswolds*, 1999, 480
2.	1764	John, 4th Earl of Stafford (†1762), stained marble	Westminster Abbey, London, St Edmund's Chapel	S	*Nichols* 1812–15, 8, 708–710; *Neale and Brayley* 1818–23, 2, 160; *Graves* 1907, 55; *Anecdotes* 1937, 142–3; Pevsner, *London: Westminster*, 1973, 432
3.	†1769	Peter Eaton, stained marble	St Mary, Dover, Kent	S	*Gunnis* 1968, 91; Pevsner, *Kent: N E & E*, 1983, 287
4.	†1772	Richard Savage, stained marble	Boughton Monchelsea, Kent	S	*Gunnis* 1968, 91; Pevsner, *Kent: W & Weald*, 1976, 176; C Lib (repr)
5.	†1774	Richard Wyatt (†1753) and Susannah Wyatt	Horsted Keynes, Sussex	S	Pevsner, *Sussex*, 1965, 540; C Lib (repr)
6.	†1774	Zachary Pearce, Bishop of Rochester	[Bromley, Kent]; destroyed World War II		*Gunnis* 1968, 91
7.	?1777	Sir Thomas Robinson	Merton, Surrey		GPC
8.	1778	Sir John Evelyn Bt (†1767), stained marble	Wotton, Surrey	S	*Gunnis* 1968, 91; Pevsner, *Surrey*, 1971, 542; C Lib (repr)
9.	1781	Colonel Thomas More Molyneux, stained marble	St Nicholas, Guildford, Surrey		Surrey History Centre, Loseley MSS/ 1087/21/Box1 (1087/XXII/73); *Gunnis* 1968, 91
10.	?1781	Peter Dore (designed by John Plaw)	Christ Church, Newgate, City of London	S	GPC

Chimneypieces

11.	1779–1782	More than one, including one with 'two marble cariatides already executed' one with lyre, one with a guitar	[Claydon House, Bucks, unidentified rooms]; untraced	*Claydon* 2002, 14–15

CHAMMOLL, Thomas fl 1667

He worked as a mason at the Palaces of Whitehall and Westminster. Chammoll made chimneypieces for the former building in 1667.

Literary References: *Gunnis* 1968, 91 (who incorrectly cites PRO Works 5/9)

Chimneypieces

1.	1667	Three in black marble	m	[Whitehall Palace, London, Duke of York's lodgings]; untraced	*Gunnis* 1968, 91

CHANCE, P F fl 1695–96

Funerary Monuments

1.	†1795	Lord Pigot	Patshull, Staffs	S	Pevsner, *Staffs*, 1974, 218
2.	†1796	Sir Robert Pigot	untraced		Pevsner, *Staffs*, 1974, 218

CHANDLER, Samuel –1769

A mason and monumental sculptor, his principal signed monument is the 'towering mass of marble' commemorating Edmund Humphrey (1). This has a reclining figure of the deceased with standing life-size figures of his parents and grandparents in niches above him. Humphrey approved the design before his death and directed that a sum of £1,000 and more if necessary should be spent on its erection. Gunnis regarded it as 'overpowering for a village church, but. . .nevertheless one of the most important early-eighteenth-century monuments in England' (*Gunnis* 1968, 91).

He also signs a monument with Corinthian pillars supporting a broken pediment in Worcestershire (2). In 1730 he was paid for the stone tablet over the doorway of Walthamstow Workhouse, a building now used as a museum (3; Workhouse Archives). From 1741 to 1758 Chandler was mason for the Trinity Almshouses, Stepney, London.

He was buried in Wanstead, Essex on January 30 1769. By his will, proved the following day, he left his business, stock in trade, books and all other belongings to Martha, his wife. His business was located in Mile End.

Literary References: *Rogers* 1957, 1371
Archival References: GPC
Will: PROB 11/945/62

Funerary Monuments

1.	†1727	Edmund Humphrey Payment(s): £1,000	Rettendon, Essex	S	*Rogers* 1957, 1371 (repr); Pevsner, *Essex*, 1965, 323; *Gunnis* 1968, 91; GPC
2.	†1741	William Taylor	Broadway, Worcs	S	Pevsner, *Worcs*, 1968, 102

Architectural Sculpture

3.	1730	Stone tablet	s	Walthamstow Museum (formerly workhouse), London, over door	*Gunnis* 1968, 91

CHANTREY, Sir Francis Legatt RA 1781–1841

The outstanding portrait sculptor of his generation, he was particularly admired for his penetrating studies of character and the uncluttered contours of his busts and statues. He was born in humble circumstances at Jordanthorpe, near Sheffield, on 7 April 1781, the son of a carpenter and tenant farmer who died when Chantrey was a child. The boy was apprenticed to Robert Ramsay, a local carver, gilder and dealer in plaster models. In his spare time Chantrey practised drawing and modelling. John Raphael Smith, the mezzotinter and draughtsman, saw his work at Ramsay's shop and encouraged him to develop his artistic skills. In 1802 Chantrey cancelled his indentures and set up in Sheffield as a portrait painter and miniaturist. He moved to London in May 1802, but then decided to tour the British Isles and in Dublin he fell seriously ill. By 1804 he had returned to England and he divided the next few years between London and Sheffield. In London he worked for a woodcarver, but studied informally in the Royal Academy Schools in the evenings. In 1804 he showed a competent canvas portrait of his uncle, Daniel Wale, at the Academy exhibition, giving his address as Chapel Street West, Mayfair. Chantrey made frequent visits to Sheffield, where he continued to paint portraits and modelled busts in plaster. In 1805 he won his first important commission, the monument to the Rev James Wilkinson, Rector of Sheffield (1). Wilkinson's bust, framed by a pyramid and looped marble curtain, is conservative in style and owes debts to the generation of sculptors active in the mid-18th century, particularly **Louis François Roubiliac**, whose naturalism Chantrey particularly admired. The monument showed no awareness of the neo-classical style fashionable in the metropolis.

In 1808 Chantrey took rooms in Curzon Street, London, and showed his first major work of sculpture at the Academy, a colossal head of *Satan* (**327**) with a 'gaze of dark malignant despair' (*Cunningham*, 1820, 50). This was a rare instance of Chantrey carving an ideal work. The following year he married Daniel Wale's daughter, Mary Anne, who brought a handsome dowry, so enabling him to set up a house and studio in Eccleston Street, Pimlico and to embark on his professional career as a sculptor.

In 1809 he won the contract for 4 large busts of admirals in plaster and wood for the exterior of the Naval Asylum, Greenwich (**328**). These helped to establish his reputation, but it was the Royal Academy exhibition of 1811, when he was already 30, that finally brought him to a wider public. He showed plaster busts of well-known personalities from both sides of the political spectrum. The Establishment was represented by busts of Benjamin West, PRA, and a posthumous portrait of William Pitt (†1806), the Tory Prime Minister (**332, 331**). More controversial were his heads of three radical politicians, his friends and mentors, John Raphael Smith, Sir Francis Burdett and particularly John Horne Tooke, who had a formative role in his education (**334–6**). Tooke's bust was a particular success, for it showed the sculptor's extraordinary flair in realising skin textures and in capturing a sitter's characteristic expression at a relaxed moment. **Joseph Nollekens RA** was so impressed with the bust that he conceded it a position at the exhibition intended for one of his own busts. Chantrey later estimated that the show brought in commissions for monuments and busts worth £20,000. Nollekens later allowed Chantrey to sculpt his portrait (**386**) and may have provided guidelines for workshop practice as Chantrey's studio expanded. After the exhibition Horne Tooke, who took an interest in Chantrey's progress, advised the sculptor that if he wished to succeed in London society, he must 'model at least half-a-dozen of the other [Tory] party' (Weekes, *Lectures*, 1880, 308, quoted by *Potts* 1981 (3), 73). In later years his clients came increasingly from the ruling classes.

Chantrey's first opportunity to carve a statue in marble presented itself in 1811 when he won the contract for a figure of George III for the London Guildhall, in competition with 15 other submitted designs (**291**). He had already had sittings from the king for a portrait bust in the previous year (**349**). There were suspicions among members of the Court of Common Council that Chantrey was insufficiently experienced for the task and its hesitant leader, Sir William Curtis, asked the sculptor whether he described himself as a painter or a sculptor. Chantrey responded neatly: 'I *live* by sculpture' (*Cunningham* 1820, 6). The completed work showed beyond doubt that Chantrey was able to translate the qualities evident in his busts into a major statue, for the king's fragile mental state was uncompromisingly captured in his portrait. It was completed in 1815, the year **Antonio Canova** visited London. Chantrey took the great Italian sculptor to see his work in Guildhall. The two sculptors became friends and Chantrey commissioned Canova's portrait from Jackson.

Commissions for statues of other prominent personalities came in while the king's image was in preparation and they allowed Chantrey to establish presentational formulae that he would use throughout his career. The image of a leading advocate, Robert Blair, 1812–17, for the Sessions House in Edinburgh, has a dignified and commanding head, but is seated with extreme informality and swathed in a voluminous cloak (**292**). The informally seated image was adopted for several later statues (**308, 302, 303**) and was particularly successful for the figure of Robert Dundas,

1820–24, also for the Sessions House (**299**). Whinney considered this the masterpiece of the series for its dignified and commanding head, relaxed pose and the simplified lines of the gown. A third statue for the Sessions House, the standing figure of Lord Melville, 1812–18 (**294**), provided a prototype for several statues of orators and statesmen, posed, speech in hand, with one foot determinedly forward (**118, 310, 260**). The statue of George Washington, sent overseas to Boston in 1826, is perhaps the most commanding of these standing men of action (**301**).

In several cases, the commission for a statue or monument followed a successful bust and led to Chantrey's selection as sculptor for the full-sized figure (**291, 52, 302, 311, 153, 306, 165**). An early example is the statue of George III (**291**), but several of the finest were of friends, whose physiognomy and character were familiar to the sculptor. The bust of James Watt, the engineer and inventor (**357**), which pre-dates the monuments (**52,130**), cranes forward with down-set mouth and an expression of focussed concentration in his mesmeric eyes. Chantrey and Watt had shared interests and corresponded on the subject of new pointing machines for sculpture. The bust of Sir Joseph Banks, President of the Royal Society (**368**), was presented by Chantrey to the Society the year after his election as a Fellow in 1818. Ten years separate the bust and monument, but the heads are similar, and they suggest close familiarity with the determined old scientist.

Chantrey was a sociable man and as he gained a reputation he was increasingly able to select his sitters for busts from among his many friends in artistic and professional circles. John Rennie was the civil engineer responsible for Waterloo Bridge: Chantrey's secretary, Allan Cunningham described his portrait (**385**), as a 'head of evident extended capacity and thought' (*Cunningham* 1820, 7–8). Dr James Scott's bust was a gift from the sculptor to a kindred spirit of humble origins, who had also made his name by the skill of his hands (**467**). It was one of 17 busts, statues and monuments celebrating medical men. A rare bust of a woman, the scientist, Mary Somerville, is a reflective image of an intellectual who was another of Chantrey's circle (**508**). The acclaimed portrait of Sir Walter Scott (**416**) was one of the few marbles produced entirely on Chantrey's own initiative and he kept it in the studio until 1828 when he presented it to the writer on condition that Scott agreed to sit for a new, more formal image, intended to convey his public achievement. Cunningham noted that the first bust appealed to contemporaries because it was felt to capture Scott's 'conversational look. . .when about to break into some sly funny old story' (*Potts*, 1981 (2), 53).

Chantrey was responsible for a large number of funerary monuments, many of them small and repetitive in composition. He paid lip-service to the classical taste with wall tablets of Greek stele shape, incorporating low-relief portrait medallions (**30, 51, 64**), or images of female mourners on sabre-leg stools (**68, 106**). More inventive were his kneeling women, carved both in relief and in the round (**37, 88, 92, 132, 148, 174**). The monuments which particularly appealed to contemporary sensibilities and brought him wide acclaim were large-scale deathbed dramas and disturbingly life-like images of dead children, carved in the second and third decades of the century. His first major achievement in funerary art was the monument to Mariamne Johnes, the daughter of Thomas Johnes of Hafod, a distinguished collector, remembered particularly as the patron of **Thomas Banks RA**. The commission followed a visit to Johnes in Cardiganshire, made with a friend, the painter and engraver, Thomas Stothard, who probably helped work out the composition (**8**). It is a striking tableau of triangular shape: the young woman lies on a couch while her father stands behind her, looking into her face, and her mother sits weeping at her feet. The model for the memorial was too large to exhibit at the Academy and so was shown at Spring Gardens, London, in 1812. Thomas Johnes was reportedly too overcome by emotion when he saw the finished work in the studio to take it back to Wales. It was destroyed by fire in 1932. Chantrey provided another magnificent death-bed scene in 1818, the monument to David Pike Watts at Ilam (**32**), the sculptor's most ambitious and costly funerary work. The old man is depicted raising himself from his pillows to bless his daughter and three little grandchildren. Tenderness between children and parents was again the theme in the group of Dorothy Jordan, the actress mistress of William IV, and two of her young children, 1834, which was designed for a secular context, but would have been as well-suited to a church (**313**).

The most popular of all Chantrey's monuments was to the daughters of William Robinson, Prebend of Lichfield Cathedral. Stothard again had a hand in the composition. The monument was known as *The sleeping children* because of the lifelike character of the entwined effigies, and it received rapturous acclaim when it was exhibited at the Academy in 1817 (**25**). Its success prompted Chantrey to consider carving a series of idealised portraits of young children, only three of which materialised (**295–7**). The 'sleeping' figure of Harriet Acland, 1819 (**297**), is clearly indebted to the Robinson Children, and was carved for her father's library. The standing figure of Louisa Russell, 1819, at Woburn Abbey (**295**) was commissioned as a pendant to her young sister Georgina's statue by the Danish neoclassicist, **Bertel Thorvaldsen**. This was an uncharacteristic work for Chantrey, since it formed part of an iconographic programme. The statues of the two small girls, placed in niches outside the Temple of the Graces, acted as attendants to Canova's *Three graces*, the focal point of the gallery.

The end of the long Napoleonic Wars gave Chantrey an opportunity to widen his horizons and cultivate his taste by foreign travel. In 1814 he visited Paris and admired the Italian treasures in the Louvre but apparently showed less enthusiasm for the French sculpture (*Cunningham* 1820, 6–7). The following year he returned to France with his wife and Stothard, and took the opportunity to sketch Gothic architecture in Rouen. Soon after his return to London, public honours began to come to him: in 1816 he was elected an Associate of the Royal Academy, becoming a full Academician in 1818. That year he was elected to the Royal Society and the Society of Antiquaries.

In 1819 he visited Italy to examine the ancient masterpieces, with the idea of launching himself on his return as a sculptor of 'ideal' gallery pieces, a prestigious but financially hazardous departure, since the return on the sculptor's time was often uncertain. Chantrey's ledgers for 1820 record orders for 'poetical' subjects received on his return from Italy from five great patrons, the Dukes of Devonshire and Bedford, the Earls of Egremont and Dartmouth and Lord Yarborough. Only a pair of indifferent reliefs for the Duke of Bedford were executed (**530, 531**). Among the many visitors to Chantrey's studio at this period was James Losh, who recorded on 13 June 1822 'Amongst other things

I saw today Mr Chantry, his workshop and rooms, with all of which I was much delighted. He is evidently a man of genious, plain and simple in his manners, but clear and vigorous in his opinions and expression – and his works do honour to his age and country' (*Losh* i, 159).

The 1820s were a turning point for Chantrey, for his reputation was at its zenith, and he now began to develop a grand, increasingly formal style, appropriate for portraits of leaders of the Establishment. The busts of Viscount Castlereagh, 1821, and the Duke of Wellington, 1823, both have partly bared chests, long, manly necks and a noble demeanour (**422, 431**). A glamorous bust of George IV, 1822 (**429**), modifies traces of the king's grossness, presenting him as a patrician with a haughty head, topped with intricately carved curls. The subjects of Chantrey's statues were presented in much the same manner whether in a church or public square. His figures of professional men and connoisseurs showed them in deep concentration (**304, 305, 322**), and the politicians and Empire builders were presented as aloof English gentlemen (**217, 260, 303, 311, 319, 310, 315**). Monuments to leading churchmen, kneeling in prayerful repose, gave an opportunity for the virtuoso carving of flowing robes (**201, 259**).

In 1831 Chantrey brought in Sir John Soane, whose bust he had carved as a present the previous year (**465**), to design a new ante-room for his studio at 20 Belgrave Place, Pimlico, round the corner from the sculptor's home in Belgrave Square. This studio became a sculpture gallery for his work, containing plaster casts of most of his busts and statues of eminent people, as well as casts of works by Canova and an important set of plasters from the Antique.

During the last decade of his life Chantrey became particularly interested in producing bronze sculpture, a notoriously difficult material to handle. In 1827 he established his own foundry in Eccleston Place, Pimlico, so that he might closely supervise the casting of two bronze figures, those of the Irish statesman Henry Grattan, for Dublin (**303**), and George IV for the Brighton Pavilion (**306**). The king's figure is an official image in garter robes, his arms arranged to suggest regal munificence. Orders for two equestrian figures in bronze followed in 1828–29: the statue of Sir Thomas Munro, Governor of Madras (**320**) is grand in scale and has an air of dignified control, reinforced by the motionless stance of his horse. The technically complex work took a decade to complete and was admired in the studio gallery by the Duke of Wellington, who particularly liked the horse. A second, equestrian statue of George IV, ordered at the king's personal request in 1829 (**309**), was intended to surmount the Marble Arch in London, but was incomplete at the king's death and eventually found a home in Trafalgar Square. Chantrey again avoided the conventional prancing steed in order to add to the sense of authority and lofty composure.

In 1830 he was appointed Sculptor-in-Ordinary to William IV and in 1835 he was knighted. By 1838 his health was deteriorating and he had to halt work temporarily on another official image, the bust of Queen Victoria (**509**). Nonetheless he wrestled again with the technical and compositional problems of bronze-casting in his last major work, the equestrian statue of the Duke of Wellington, 1839–44, sited outside the Mansion House in the City of London (**323**). Despite his eminence as a sculptor of the great, the contract was not a foregone conclusion. Supporters of a rival practitioner, **Matthew Cotes Wyatt**, argued that Chantrey had too much work in hand and that his bronze figures, particularly a statue of William Pitt in Hanover Square (**310**), were inferior in quality. In February 1839, after nearly two years of discussion and fund-raising, the Wellington Committee at the Mansion House approved his appointment and agreed to a fee of £7,000. The statue was completed under the direction of his assistant, **Henry Weekes**, after Chantrey's death, of a heart-attack, in November 1841.

Chantrey ran an efficient studio, sustaining high standards despite his vast output. He employed a large workforce, controlled by his secretary, **Allan Cunningham**, who came to him as a pointer, became his superintendent of works, and, as an accomplished writer, provided the best possible publicity for the studio. In 1814, when Chantrey started the account-books known as the Derby and Academy ledgers, he had a team of 7 assistants, all of whom were employed on the statue of George III for the Guildhall. They included **James Heffernan**, who worked for the practice until 1843 and is reputed to have carved many of Chantrey's busts. Henry Weekes was another long-serving assistant and eventually inherited the workshop and practice. **F A Legé** worked for him for a shorter time, but nonetheless carried out most of the cutting of the Robinson monument. **David Dunbar**, **Frederick William Smith** and three obscure assistants, William Elliott, Mr Purdy and Mr George were all in post in 1814. **Musgrave Lewthwaite Watson**, a pupil of Dunbar, worked as a modeller, employed on the reclining figure of Charlotte Digby, for Worcester Cathedral (**143**), but he resigned in 1833 when Chantrey refused his demands for a wage increase. Chantrey was apparently liberal in passing on commissions, for instance to Weekes, and this was a key to his practical success.

The sculptor's working procedure for portrait busts was described by an early biographer, John Holland, in 1851. Chantrey took pains to study the mannerisms of his sitters, sometimes inviting them to eat with him before work began and frequently introducing a third party into the studio so that the subject might relax in conversation. With the help of a *camera lucida* he made several drawings of the head in profile and full-face, which served as schematic indications of the sitter's features. Using these drawings, which were marked with small crosses to clarify the proportions, studio assistants built up the first rough bust in clay. The model was finished by Chantrey himself after as many as seven sittings. He took a cast of the mouth, but otherwise worked with considerable freedom, deciding the turn of the head only after he had finished modelling the face. The drapery, a secondary feature which served to set off the face, was modelled largely by assistants. Since the clay model was liable to crack in drying out, a permanent replica was cast in plaster and this plaster was kept in Chantrey's studio and used for making versions in marble. The roughing out of the marble block was done by assistants with a pointing machine. A more skilled carver then worked up the entire surface with a claw chisel at which point Chantrey again intervened, using a flat chisel to smooth over the surface and cut the finer details. His attention to the detailed working over of the marble was unique in England.

Detailed information on Chantrey's prices exists, thanks to the survival of three account ledgers and a daybook. The day-book is an important source for the sculptor's early years in London, providing lists of the busts, monuments and statues completed between 1809 and January 1813, and also details of payments to workers and sums paid for stone and marble. The three ledgers, all largely in Cunningham's hand but with annotations by Chantrey, cover transactions between 1809 and 1827 and give detailed information on the activities and wages of several assistants, particularly Legé, who spent nearly 176 days on the Robinson monument, for which he was paid £64 12s 7d. The success of Chantrey's practice depended on judging his market. His early plaster busts sold at £3–£5 each, but for his first marble heads Chantrey charged 100 guineas. This rose to 120 guineas by 1813 and to 150 guineas following his visit to Italy and his admission as a full Academician in 1819. In 1821, he introduced a charge of 200 guineas for a bust of George IV, which became his charge for prestigious commissions to a large format, such as royal portraits. A full-length statue would average around £3,000.

He was buried in Norton churchyard, Sheffield, close to members of his family. In his will he left a fortune of about £150,000, initially to his wife, reverting after her death to the Royal Academy. The Chantrey Bequest was to be used for the 'Encouragement of British Fine Art in Painting and Sculpture' and had parallels with his friend J M W Turner's bequest of his paintings to the nation. Many of his plaster models and casts were given by his wife to the Ashmolean Museum, Oxford, where some of them remain, though many were mutilated in 1939.

After his death, opinion was divided as to the merits of his work. A biographical notice in the *Evening Mail* for 10 November 1851 accused him of becoming 'greedy of commissions and money and anxious to secure everything' and the fear of possible insolvency perhaps accounts for his tendency to avoid ideal subjects, an area he could have afforded to explore. As a portrait sculptor he was without rival, but his readiness in the later years to provide the authoritative public images required by his august patrons, stifled the vitality and characterisation that were his great hallmarks.

IR

Literary References: *Cunningham* 1820, 3–10; *GM* 1842, 99–106; *Holland* 1851; C R Leslie, *Autobiographical Recollections*, ed T Taylor, 1860, 1, 74–7; *Graves* II, 1905–6, 40–42; *Denvir* 1956, 1416, 1418; *Gaunt* 1960, 626–7; *Shearstone* 1980; *Potts* 1981 (1), 17–27; Potts 1981 (2); *Potts* 1981 (3); *Lieberman* 1983; *Whinney* 1988, 398–425; *Chantrey Ledgers*, 1991–92; *Penny* 1991 (1), 255–64; *Dunkerley* 1995; *Grove* 6, 455–8 (Yarrington); *Bilbey* 2002, 234–371; *Ward-Jackson* 2002, 330–4; *ODNB* (Stevens)

Archival References: James Losh, *Diary*, Carlisle Library

Will: PROB 11/1954 sig 793

Miscellaneous Drawings: design for a monument, exhib RS, 1810 (730), untraced

Auction Catalogues: Chantrey 1842; Chantrey 1861

Portraits of the Sculptor: self-portrait, chalk, *c*1802, NPG, London; self-portrait, pencil, before 1809, NPG, London; self-portrait, canvas, *c*1810, Tate, London; F A Legé, bust, 1815, untraced; Thomas Phillips, canvas, *c*1817, NPG, London; George Crabbe, pencil drawing, s&d 1821, NPG, London; Paul Nixson of Carlisle, bust, 1823, Academy of Arts, Carlisle, pediment; F W Smith, bust, 1826, RA, London; James Heffernan, portrait medallion, 1842, SNPG, Edinburgh; another, 1843, NGI, Dublin; James Legrew, 'sketch', exhib RA, London, 1843, untraced; John Bell, statue, 1862, St James's, Norton, Sheffield; Thomas Earle, portrait medallion, wax, nd, formerly High Hazels Museum, Sheffield, W R Yorks, untraced

Funerary Monuments

No.	Date	Subject		Location		References
1.	†1805	Prebendary James Wilkinson		Sheffield Cathedral, W R Yorks		*Graves* II, 1905–6, 40; *Whinney* 1988, 399–400; *Chantrey Ledgers*, 1991–92, 332–3 (repr 5)
2.	1812	Lieutenant-Colonel George Henry Duckworth (†1811) Payment(s): £336 inclusive		Topsham, Devon		*Chantrey Ledgers*, 1991–92, 24–5 (repr 7)
3.	1813	Rev Stephen Sloane (†1812) Payment(s): £151 fully inclusive		North Stoneham, Hants		*Chantrey Ledgers*, 1991–92, 25 (repr 8)
4.	1814	Christopher D'Oyley (†1795) Payment(s): £500		St Mary, Walton-on-Thames, Surrey		*Chantrey Ledgers*, 1991–92, 46–7 (repr 29)
5.	1814	Thomas Kinnersly Payment(s): £250 10s fully inclusive		Untraced		*Chantrey Ledgers*, 1991–92, 37–8 (repr)
6.	1814–1815	John Mackenzie's two sons Payment(s): £110		Untraced		*Chantrey Ledgers*, 1991–92, 54–5
7.	1815	Lieutenant-Colonel John Hill (†1814)		Hodnet, Salop		*Chantrey Ledgers*, 1991–92, 47–8
8.	1811–1815	Mariamne Johnes (perhaps designed by Thomas Stothard) Payment(s): £3,265		[Hafod, Cardigan]; destroyed		*Whinney* 1988, 402; *Lieberman* 1990, 70–80 (repr); *Chantrey Ledgers*, 36 (repr 17)
9.	†1815	Sir Simon Richard Brissett Taylor Bt Payment(s): £367 10s		Lysson's Estate, Morant Bay, Jamaica	S	*Chantrey Ledgers*, 1991–92, 91–2
10.	1815	William Mason (†1814) Payment(s): £7 11s 9d		[Sledmere, E R Yorks]; untraced		*Chantrey Ledgers*, 1991–92, 52
11.	1816	Anne Bainbrigge Dobree (†1816) and family members Payment(s): £265		Walthamstow, Essex, churchyard		*Chantrey Ledgers*, 1991–92, 67
12.	1815–1816	Dr John Clarke MD (†1818) Payment(s): 100 gns		Tamworth, Staffs Other versions: another bust exhib RA 1817, 1043		*Chantrey Ledgers*, 1991–92, 63
13.	1814–1816	Granville Sharp (†1813) Payment(s): £60 1s 7 1/2d		Westminster Abbey, London, south transept		*Chantrey Ledgers*, 1991–92, 57
14.	1816	John Horne Tooke (†1812), tombstone Payment(s): £21		Ealing, Middx		*Chantrey Ledgers*, 1991–92, 41
15.	1815–1816	Lieutenant-Colonel Henry Cadogan (†1813) Payment(s): £315 Drawing(s): PRO MPF 78		St Luke, Chelsea, London Other versions: ex Downham, Wilts; untraced (£183 16s)		*Chantrey Ledgers*, 1991–92, 49 (repr 32)
16.	1812–1816	Major-General Daniel Hoghton (†1811) Payment(s): £1,575		St Paul's Cathedral, London		*Chantrey Ledgers*, 1991–92, 34 (repr 27)
17.	1814–1816	Mary Craven (†1811) Payment(s): £180	s	St John's churchyard, Hackney, London		*Chantrey Ledgers*, 1991–92, 39
18.	1814–1816	Matthew Craven (†1814) Payment(s): £110	s	St John's churchyard, Hackney, London		*Chantrey Ledgers*, 1991–92, 39
19.	†1816	Mr Bonsal		Aberystwyth, Dyfed	S	*Gunnis* 1968, 95
20.	1816	Richard Brinsley Sheridan (†1816), tombstone Payment(s): £19		Westminster Abbey, London, south transept	S	*Chantrey Ledgers*, 1991–92, 70

21.	1816	Sir Simon le Blanc (†1816) Payment(s): 100 gns	[Northaw, Herts]; destroyed		*Chantrey Ledgers*, 1991–92, 40
22.	1816	Vice-Admiral Sir Samuel Hood (†1814)	St Mary, Fort St George, Chennai (Madras)		*Chantrey Ledgers*, 1991–92, 50
23.	1817	Captain John Jervis Brenton (†1817) Payment(s): '10 or 15 gns'	Untraced		*Chantrey Ledgers*, 1991–92, 94
24.	1817	Elizabeth Dobrée (†1816) Payment(s): £70	[St Dionis Backchurch, City of London]; destroyed		*Chantrey Ledgers*, 1991–92, 68
25.	1815–1817	Ellen Jane and Mary Anne Robinson ('The sleeping children') Payment(s): £684 with their father's monument (29) Drawing(s): BL MS 35, 135, H.10, anon Model(s): ? sold Christie, 1930 (photo VAM archive); untraced	Lichfield Cathedral Other versions: reproduced in biscuitware	SD	*Graves* II, 1905–6, 41; *Penny* 1977 (1), 119; *Chantrey Ledgers*, 1991–92, 61–2 (repr 34); *Penny* 1992, 221 (plaster head of Ellen Jane repr)
26.	1817	Maria Wright Crockett (†1812) Payment(s): £183 3s	Church Eaton, Staffs		*Chantrey Ledgers*, 1991–92, 89
27.	1816–1817	Mr Lowndes Payment(s): £106 6s	[Glasgow Cathedral]; untraced		*Chantrey Ledgers*, 1991–92, 30
28.	1815–1817	Rev William Robinson (†1812) Payment(s): £650 with his daughters' monument (26)	Lichfield Cathedral (below his daughters)		*Chantrey Ledgers*, 1991–92, 61–2
29.	1817	Thomas D'Oyley (†1816)	Walton-on-Thames, Surrey	S	*Chantrey Ledgers*, 1991–92, 66
30.	1817	Thomas Tomkins (†1816) Payment(s): £107 inclusive	St Nicholas, Chiswick, Middx	S	*Chantrey Ledgers*, 1991–92, 58 (repr 40)
31.	1817–1818	Charles Moss, Bishop of Oxford (†1811) Payment(s): £40 7s 8d inclusive	Cuddesdon, Oxon		*Chantrey Ledgers*, 1991–92, 87
32.	1817–1818	David Pike Watts (†1816) Payment(s): £500	St John's Wood Chapel, Marylebone, London, churchyard		*Chantrey Ledgers*, 1991–92, 83 (repr 49)
33.	1818	Golding family (two tablets) Payment(s): 140 gns inclusive	untraced		*Chantrey Ledgers*, 1991–92, 99
34.	1818	Isabella Stewart Brenton (†1817) Payment(s): £49 11s 6d with a small tablet	Simonstown Cemetery, Capetown, South Africa		*Chantrey Ledgers*, 1991–92, 90
35.	1818	John Perceval (†1818) Payment(s): £17 19s	[for the West Indies]; untraced		*Chantrey Ledgers*, 1991–92, 95
36.	1817–1818	Lady Philippa Isham (†1786)	Orpington, Kent		*Chantrey Ledgers*, 1991–92, 68–9
37.	1818	Martha, Countess St Vincent (†1816) Payment(s): £600 exclusive of fixing etc Model(s): Ashm, plaster	Caverswall, Staffs	SD	*Chantrey Ledgers*, 1991–92, 64 (repr 50); *Penny* 1992, 222 (repr)
38.	1818	Rev Alexander Mackenzie (†1816) Payment(s): £300 Model(s): Ashm, plaster	Sheffield Cathedral, W R Yorks	S	*Chantrey Ledgers*, 1991–92, 55 (repr 30); *Penny* 1992, 237 (repr)
39.	1817–1818	Rev Hugh Cholmondeley, Dean of Chester (†1815) Payment(s): £52 10s	Brasenose Coll, Oxford, antechapel		*Chantrey Ledgers*, 1991–92, 60
40.	1817–1818	Richard Carew (†1791) Lady Philippa Isham (†1786)	Orpington, Kent	S	*Chantrey Ledgers*, 1991–92, 68–9
41.	†1818	Robert Carr Brackenbury	Raithby-by-Spilsby, Lincs	S	Pevsner, *Lincs*, 1989, 606
42.	1818	Sarah Rogers (†1816) Payment(s): £63 inclusive	Brampton Bryan, Herefs	SD	*Chantrey Ledgers*, 1991–92, 72 (repr 41)
43.	1816–1818	Six members of the Sharp family (design by 'Mr Bonomi', perhaps Ignatius Bonomi) Payment(s): £342 10s 6d	Durham Cathedral	S	*Chantrey Ledgers*, 1991–92, 70
44.	1817–1818	William Gee (†1815)	Orpington, Kent		*Chantrey Ledgers*, 1991–92, 68–9
45.	1818–1819	Amelia Ann Smyth (†1817) Payment(s): £114 18s	St Paul's, Halifax, Canada	S	*Chantrey Ledgers*, 1991–92, 75–76
46.	1819	Charles Fox Townshend (†1717) Payment(s): £157 10s	St John's Coll Chapel, Cambridge	S	*Chantrey Ledgers*, 1991–92, 78 (repr 39)
47.	1817–1819	Diana Warden (†1816) Payment(s): £219 5s	[Somerset Road Cemetery, Capetown]; National Museum, Capetown, South Africa	S	*Chantrey Ledgers*, 1991–92, 76
48.	1815–1819	Dr James Anderson MD (†1809) Payment(s): £1,000 Model(s): Ashm, plaster	Chennai (Madras) Cathedral, India	SD	*Graves* II, 1905–6, 41; *Steggles* 2000, 34–35 (repr); *Penny* 1992, 215 (repr)
49.	1818–1819	Elizabeth Acton (†1817) Payment(s): £111s 15s 3d fully inclusive	Shillingston, Dorset	S	*Chantrey Ledgers*, 1991–92, 98
50.	1819	George, Earl Pomfret (†1785) and his wife Anna Maria (†1787) Payment(s): £438 11s fully inclusive	Easton Neston, Northants		*Chantrey Ledgers*, 1991–92, 94–5 (repr 55)
51.	1819	Henry Kirke White (†1806) Payment(s): £91 fully inclusive Model(s): NPG, London, 93	[All Saints, Cambridge]; St John's College Chapel, Cambridge (1870)	S	*Chantrey Ledgers*, 1991–92, 80 (repr 42)

52.	1819	James Watt (†1819) Payment(s): £6,234	[Westminster Abbey, London, nave, north choir aisle]; St Paul's Cathedral, London, crypt		WAM (73); *Chantrey Ledgers*, 1991–92, 214–5 (repr 121); *MacMichael* 1977, 31
53.	1819	Lieutenant Rennie Payment(s): £46	[for the West Indies]; untraced		*Chantrey Ledgers*, 1991–92, 76–7
54.	1816–1819	Martha Davies (†1815) Payment(s): 150 gns	Aberystwth, Cardigan	S	*Chantrey Ledgers*, 1991–92, 70
55.	1818–1819	Mr Coltman Payment(s): £22 11s fully inclusive	Untraced		*Chantrey Ledgers*, 1991–92, 75
56.	1819	Professor Richard Porson (†1808) Payment(s): £178 10s fully inclusive Model(s): Ashm, plaster	Trinity College, Cambridge, chapel	S	*Chantrey Ledgers*, 1991–92, 77 (repr 37); *Penny* 1992, 242 (repr)
57.	1817–1819	Rev Edward Valentine Blomfield (†1816) Payment(s): £134	Bury St Edmunds, Suffolk		*Chantrey Ledgers*, 1991–92, 79
58.	1813–1819	Rt Hon Spencer Perceval MP (†1812) Payment(s): £140+£5 for 'fixing'	St Luke, Charlton, London	SD	*Chantrey Ledgers*, 1991–92, 40
59.	1819	Samuel (†1818) and Hannah (†1816) Tunnard Payment(s): £66 15s	Frampton, Lincs	S	*Chantrey Ledgers*, 1991–92, 126
60.	1818–1819	Sir Thomas Maynard Heselrige Bt (†1817) Payment(s): £31 14s inclusive	Hoxne, Suffolk	S	*Chantrey Ledgers*, 1991–92, 74
61.	1819	William Hanbury (†1807) Payment(s): £223 5s fully inclusive	Kelmarsh, Northants	S	*Chantrey Ledgers*, 1991–92, 114
62.	1817–1820	Admiral Sir John Duckworth Bt (†1817) Payment(s): £680 fully inclusive Model(s): Ashm, plaster, bust only	Topsham, Devon	S	*Chantrey Ledgers*, 1991–92, 96–7 (repr 58)
63.	1820	Assheton, Viscount Curzon (†1820) Payment(s): £326 4s fully inclusive	Penn, Bucks	SD	*Chantrey Ledgers*, 1991–92, 152
64.	1817–1820	Basil William, Lord Daer (†1794) Payment(s): £182 fully inclusive	Exeter Cathedral, Devon	S	*Chantrey Ledgers*, 1991–92, 84 (repr 43)
65.	1820	Colonel Charles Fox Canning (†1815) Payment(s): £49 9s 1d	The Waterloo Church, Belgium		*Chantrey Ledgers*, 1991–92, 130
66.	1818–1820	Francis Horner MP (†1817), portrait medallion, to be set into a sarcophagus	English Cemetery, Livorno, Italy. Medallion untraced but sarcophagus by local masons extant		*Chantrey Ledgers*, 1991–92, 108–9
67.	1817–1820	General Sir George Prevost (†1816) Payment(s): £525	Winchester Cathedral, Hants	S	*Chantrey Ledgers*, 1991–92, 95–6
68.	1817–1820	George Bowles (†1817) Payment(s): £525 plus extras	St Mary, Wanstead, Essex	SD	*Chantrey Ledgers*, 1991–92, 88 (repr 52)
69.	1820	George Canning II (†1820) Payment(s): £86 19s	St Mary Abbott, Kensington, London		*Chantrey Ledgers*, 1991–92, 129
70.	1818–1820	Henrietta Hartwell (†1818) Payment(s): £208 fully inclusive	Laleham, Surrey	S	*Chantrey Ledgers*, 1991–92, 100
71.	1819–1820	Hon Henry Annesley (†1818) Payment(s): £89 10s fully inclusive	Upper Arley, Worcs	S	*Chantrey Ledgers*, 1991–92, 114–5
72.	1818–1820	Jenney Mudge Rosdew (†1818) Payment(s): £163 fully inclusive	[St Andrew, Plymouth, Devon]; destroyed		*Chantrey Ledgers*, 1991–92, 110
73.	1819–1820	John Fuller MP (†1834) (co-sculptor: Henry Rouw) Payment(s): tablet £62 18s; bust £188 18s Drawing(s): Huntington Lib 72.54.38 Model(s): Ashm, plaster	Brightling, East Sussex Other versions: bust replicated for R I (*Walker* 1985, 626)	SD	*Walker* 1985, 626; *Chantrey Ledgers*, 1991–92, 120–1, 294 (repr 72); *Penny* 1992, 233
74.	post-1820	John Simpson (†1815) (bust only; monument by John Carline I and II) (co-sculptor: John Carline II and III, of Shrewsbury) Payment(s): £106 with packing	St Chad, Shrewsbury, Salop		*Pidgeon* 1851, 60; *Chantrey Ledgers*, 1991–92, 29–30 (repr 9)
75.	1819–1820	John Thomson MD (†1818)	Unitarian Chapel, Halifax, W R Yorks		*Chantrey Ledgers*, 1991–92, 118
76.	1818–1820	Lady Mary (†1814) and Lady Catherine (†1810) Feilding Payment(s): £217 9s inclusive	Berwick House, Salop, chapel	S	*Chantrey Ledgers*, 1991–92, 101
77.	1820	Lieutenant-Colonel William Eardley (†1805) Payment(s): £98 14s 3d fully inclusive	Berkswell, Warks	S	*Chantrey Ledgers*, 1991–92, 56
78.	1820	Mary Dutton Master (†1819), signed by Charles Rossi, perhaps in sub-contract	St John the Baptist, Cirencester, Glos		ATTRIB. *Chantrey Ledgers*, 1991–92, 153
79.	1819–1820	Rev Robert Mark Delfosse (†1819) Payment(s): £28 7s 10d	Petersham, Surrey		*Chantrey Ledgers*, 1991–92, 117
80.	1820	Samuel Parkes (†1811) Payment(s): £12 15s	Unitarian Chapel, Stourbridge, Worcs		*Chantrey Ledgers*, 1991–92, 125–6
81.	1819–1820	Sir Samuel (†1818) and Lady Ann Romilly (†1818) Payment(s): £67 18s	Knill, Powys		*Chantrey Ledgers*, 1991–92, 113
82.	1817–1820	Sir Simon Richard Brissett Taylor Bt (†1815)	Edington Priory, Wilts	S	*Chantrey Ledgers*, 1991–92, 91 (repr 54)
83.	1820	William Thoyts (†1817) Payment(s): £23 9s	Sulhamstead, Berks		*Chantrey Ledgers*, 1991–92, 150
84.	1821	Anna Maria Rooke Greaves (†1819) Payment(s): £550 plus extras	Waterperry, Oxon	SD	*Chantrey Ledgers*, 1991–92, 127 (repr 76)
85.	1817–1821	Anne Grant, Lady Cuyler (†1816) Payment(s): £63	Welwyn, Herts		*Chantrey Ledgers*, 1991–92, 84–5
86.	1819–1821	Isaac Hawkins Browne (†1818) Payment(s): £572 13s fully inclusive	Badger, Salop	S	*Chantrey Ledgers*, 1991–92, 110–1 (repr 66)

No.	Date	Subject	Location		Source
87.	1820–1821	Jesse Russell (†1820) Payment(s): £539 12s 8d	St Mary, Walthamstow, London, churchyard		*Chantrey Ledgers*, 1991–92, 137–8
88.	1821	Lady Octavia Ellenborough (†1819) Payment(s): £525 plus extras	North Cray, Kent	SD	*Chantrey Ledgers*, 1991–92, 139 (repr 74)
89.	1819–1821	Margaret Anne Johnstone (†1819) Payment(s): £549 2s fully inclusive	Hackness, N R Yorks	SD	*Chantrey Ledgers*, 1991–92, 128 (repr 78)
90.	1818–1821	Mrs Sconce Payment(s): £63 fully inclusive	Untraced		*Chantrey Ledgers*, 1991–92, 109
91.	1820–1821	Samuel Parkes (†1811) Payment(s): £12 15s	Stourbridge Unitarian Chapel, Worcs	S	*Chantrey Ledgers*, 1991–92, 125–6
92.	1820–1821	Susan Cornwall Warre (†1820) Payment(s): £331 4s 5 1/2d fully inclusive	Epsom, Surrey	SD	*Chantrey Ledgers*, 1991–92, 131–2 (repr 79)
93.	1820–1821	William Anthony Michell (†1819) Payment(s): £93 17s inclusive	Buckland, Herts		*Chantrey Ledgers*, 1991–92, 132
94.	1822	Admiral Sir George Campbell (†1821) Payment(s): £227 10s 4d	Untraced		*Chantrey Ledgers*, 1991–92, 156
95.	1822	Baroness Henrietta Maria Atherton (†1820) Payment(s): £213 4s with Thomas, 2nd Lord Lilford's monument	Thorp Achurch, Notts		*Chantrey Ledgers*, 1991–92, 173–4
96.	1820–1822	Carolette Bradshaw (†1820) Payment(s): £381 12s 5d	Whittlebury, Northants	S	*Chantrey Ledgers*, 1991–92, 144 (repr 75); *CIIA* 4/3/iv, 148 (repr)
97.	1819–1822	Colonel Charles Herries (†1819), bust only (plinth with relief of 'The Charge of Light Brigade', designed by Robert Smirke) Payment(s): £420 Drawing(s): WA, Muniment Room 66199 Model(s): Ashm, plaster	Westminster Abbey, London, nave	S	*Chantrey Ledgers*, 1991–92, 124 (repr 73)
98.	1819–1822	Dr Joseph Arnold MD (†1818) Payment(s): 120 gns	Beccles, Suffolk		*Chantrey Ledgers*, 1991–92, 117
99.	1819–1822	Edward, Lord Ellenborough (†1818) Payment(s): £664 fully inclusive	Charterhouse Chapel, London	S	*Whinney* 1988, 411; *Chantrey Ledgers*, 1991–92, 81–2 (repr 48)
100.	1820–1822	Hannah Roberts (†1819) Payment(s): £148 5s fully inclusive	Stoke Doyle, Northants	S	*Chantrey Ledgers*, 1991–92, 128–9 (repr 77)
101.	1819–1822	Lieutenant-Colonel Francis Wheler Hood (†1814) Payment(s): £108 0s 6d fully inclusive	[Coventry Cathedral, Warks]; destroyed	S	*Chantrey Ledgers*, 1991–92, 113
102.	1814–1822	Lieutenant-Colonel Henry Cadogan (†1813) Payment(s): £1548 17s Drawing(s): PRO, MPD 78, 00, with agreement and bond	St Paul's Cathedral, London	S	*Chantrey Ledgers*, 1991–92, 50 (repr 31)
103.	1814–1822	Major-General Bernard Foord Bowes (†1812) Payment(s): £1573 17s Drawing(s): PRO MPD 78,00 with agreement and bond	St Paul's Cathedral, London	S	*Liscombe* 1976, 35; *Chantrey Ledgers*, 1991–92, 51 (repr 33)
104.	1822	Martha Maria Arkwright (†1820) Payment(s): £220 4s	Cromford, Derbys		*Chantrey Ledgers*, 1991–92, 155–6
105.	1818–1822	Mary Brame Elwyn (†1818) Payment(s): £273	Bristol Cathedral	SD	*Chantrey Ledgers*, 1991–92, 108 (repr 65)
106.	1820–1822	Mary Gaulter (†1819) and her newborn son Henry Payment(s): £170 2s	Pear Tree Green, Itchen, Hants		*Chantrey Ledgers*, 1991–92, 143
107.	1821–1822	Matthew A'Deane (†1818) Payment(s): £174 14s 6d	Alderley, Glos	S	*Chantrey Ledgers*, 1991–92, 151
108.	1820–1822	Peter Patten Bold (†1819) Payment(s): £1,072 fully inclusive	Farnworth, Lancs	SD	*Chantrey Ledgers*, 1991–92, 149 (repr 103)
109.	1821–1822	Richard Bateman (†1821) Payment(s): £273 17s 2d	Derby Cathedral	SD	*Chantrey Ledgers*, 1991–92, 154 (repr 91)
110.	1821–1822	Richard Bayley Marsh (†1820) Payment(s): £329 15s 6d fully inclusive	Wombourn, Staffs	SD	*Chantrey Ledgers*, 1991–92, 151
111.	1819–1822	Robert Bernard Sparrow (†1805) and Robert Acheson Sparrow (†1818) Payment(s): £325 3s	Worlingham, Suffolk		*Chantrey Ledgers*, 1991–92, 116
112.	1822	Thomas, Lord Lilford (†1825) Payment(s): £213 4s with Baroness Atherton's monument	[Thorpe Achurch, Northants]; untraced		*Chantrey Ledgers*, 1991–92, 173–4
113.	1821–1822	Unidentified subject, ordered by Henry Porter of Mount Radford, near Exeter, and Mr Milman Payment(s): £218 4s 9d	Untraced		*Chantrey Ledgers*, 1991–92, 156
114.	1823	Dr Andrew Marshal MD (†1813) Payment(s): £52 with Dr Pitcairn's monument	Untraced		*Chantrey Ledgers*, 1991–92, 185
115.	1823	Dr David Pitcairn MD Payment(s): £52 with Dr Marshal's monument	Much Hadham, Herts		*Chantrey Ledgers*, 1991–92, 185
116.	1818–1823	Frances Puleston Cooke (†1818) Payment(s): £587 19s 6d	Owston, W R Yorks	SD	*Chantrey Ledgers*, 1991–92, 104 (repr 64)

No.	Date	Subject		Location		Reference
117.	1820–1823	Frances Thomasine, Lady Talbot (†1819) Payment(s): £325 9s		Ingestre, Staffs		*Chantrey Ledgers*, 1991–92, 132–3
118.	1817–1823	Francis Horner MP (†1817) Payment(s): £1,800 Model(s): Ashm, plaster		Westminster Abbey, London, north transept	SD	*Chantrey Ledgers*, 1991–92, 92–3 (repr 57); *Penny* 1992, 219 (repr)
119.	1820–1823	Frederica, Duchess of York (†1820) Payment(s): £664 16s fully inclusive		St James, Weybridge, Surrey	SD	*Chantrey Ledgers*, 1991–92, 157–8
120.	1823	Harriet Horton (†1814) Payment(s): £135 12s 4d fully inclusive		Croxall, Staffs		*Chantrey Ledgers*, 1991–92, 275
121.	1823	Henry Bengough (†1818) Payment(s): £700		St Mark, College Green, Bristol, Lord Mayor's Chapel	SD	*Chantrey Ledgers*, 1991–92, 125 (repr 83)
122.	1821–1823	Henry Peter (†1821) Payment(s): £171 12s or £171 2s		St Merryn, Cornwall	SD	*Chantrey Ledgers*, 1991–92, 155
123.	1817–1823	James Wildman (†1816) Payment(s): £2,545 fully inclusive Model(s): Ashm, plaster		Chilham, Kent	SD	*Chantrey Ledgers*, 1991–92, 89–90 (repr 53); *Penny* 1992, 223 (the mourners repr)
124.	1823	James, Earl of Malmesbury (†1820) Payment(s): £693 12s fully inclusive		Salisbury Cathedral, Wilts	SD	*Whinney* 1988, 412–4 (repr); *Chantrey Ledgers*, 1991–92, 160 (repr 104)
125.	1821–1823	John Hastell or Hatsell (†1820) Payment(s): £80 fully inclusive		[Temple Church, London]; destroyed		*Chantrey Ledgers*, 1991–92, 162
126.	1822–1823	John Rhodes (†1818) Payment(s): £318 13s 2d		Unitarian Chapel, Halifax, W R Yorks		*Chantrey Ledgers*, 1991–92, 170
127.	1821–1823	William Selwyn (†1817) Payment(s): £700		Chislehurst, Kent	SD	*Chantrey Ledgers*, 1991–92, 158
128.	1824	Dr Matthew Baillie MD (†1823) Payment(s): £52 10s		Duntisbourne Abbots, Glos		*Chantrey Ledgers*, 1991–92, 185–6
129.	1821–1824	Dr Walter Kennedy Craufuird MD (†1817) and his wife Emma Payment(s): £210 14s 1d fully inclusive		Bristol Cathedral	SD	*Chantrey Ledgers*, 1991–92, 163 (repr 94)
130.	1820–1824	James Watt (†1819) Payment(s): £2,000 plus extras Drawing(s): VAM E. 944-1965 Model(s): Ashm, plaster		St Mary, Handsworth, Warks	SD	*Graves* II, 1905–6, 41; *Penny* 1992, 222 (repr); *Potts* 1981 (3), 74–5; *Chantrey Ledgers*, 1991–92, 143–4 (repr 84); *Noszlopy* 1998, 68–9 (repr)
131.	1821–1824	John Winn (†1817) Payment(s): £755 6s 7d		Wragby, W R Yorks	SD	*Chantrey Ledgers*, 1991–92, 161 (repr 92)
132.	1817–1824	Lady Charlotte Finch (†1813) Payment(s): £563 7s 8d fully inclusive		Burley-on-the-Hill, Rutland	SD	*Chantrey Ledgers*, 1991–92, 85 (repr 51)
133.	1823–1824	Lieutenant-Colonel Thomas Hutchins (†1823) Payment(s): £111 5s fully inclusive		St Mary Abbots, Kensington, London		*Chantrey Ledgers*, 1991–92, 182
134.	1824	Louisa Meyer (†1822) Payment(s): £191 17s 5d		[Dutch Church, Austin Friars, London]; destroyed		*Chantrey Ledgers*, 1991–92, 177
135.	1824	'Molesworths Monument' Payment(s): £112 inclusive		[Cobham, Surrey]; untraced		*Chantrey Ledgers*, 1991–92, 182
136.	†1824	Rev Thomas Rennell		Salisbury Cathedral, Wilts		ATTRIB. *Chantrey Ledgers*, 1991–92, 331
137.	1821–1824	Rev William Hawkes of Manchester, ordered by Miss Duckworth of Guildford St, London Payment(s): £164 16s fully inclusive		Untraced		*Chantrey Ledgers*, 1991–92, 149
138.	1818–1824	Sir George Staunton (†1801) Payment(s): £399 17s Drawing(s): W A Muniments 66198		Westminster Abbey, London, nave	SD	WAM (68); *Chantrey Ledgers*, 1991–92, 102 (repr 59)
139.	1824	Thomas Coutts (†1822) Payment(s): £68 11s fully inclusive		Wroxton, Oxon		*Chantrey Ledgers*, 1991–92, 84
140.	1824	Thomas Fanshaw Middleton, Bishop of Calcutta (†1822) Payment(s): £70 with packing and cartage to the East India Wharf		Sibpur College Chapel, Chennai (Madras), (formerly Bishop's College)		*Chantrey Ledgers*, 1991–92, 184
141.	1824	William Townsend (†1823) Payment(s): £170 4s 6d inclusive		All Saints, Fulham, London		*Chantrey Ledgers*, 1991–92, 181–2
142.	1825	Brownlow North, Bishop of Winchester (†1820) Payment(s): £1036 19s		Winchester Cathedral, Hants	SD	*Chantrey Ledgers*, 1991–92, 171–2 (repr 101)
143.	1825	Charlotte Elizabeth Digby (†1820) Payment(s): £1,260 Model(s): Ashm, plaster		Worcester Cathedral	SD	*Lonsdale* 1866, 82–3; *Penny* 1992, 216 (repr); *Chantrey Ledgers*, 1991–92, 176–7 (repr 109)
144.	1820–1825	Cyril Jackson, Dean of Christ Church (†1819) Payment(s): £2,167 6s 11d inclusive Model(s): Ashm, plaster		Christ Church Cathedral, Oxford	SD	*Graves* II, 1905–6, 41; *Penny* 1992, 219 (repr); *Chantrey Ledgers*, 1991–92, 146–7
145.	*c*1825	James Watt (†1819), bust erected to replace the original monument	pb	Westminster Abbey, London, nave, window ledge		*MacMichael* 1977, 31
146.	1825	John Campbell, Baron Cawdor Payment(s): £71 14s		Bath Abbey, Somerset		*Chantrey Ledgers*, 1991–92, 175–6
147.	†1825	John Talbot		Ingestre, Staffs	S	*Gunnis* 1968, 96
148.	1825	Lady Georgiana Stanhope West (†1824) Payment(s): £222 17s 6d		Shelford, Notts	SD	*Chantrey Ledgers*, 1991–92, 188 (repr 111)
149.	1825	Sarah Capel (†1822) Payment(s): £431 15s 6d		St John's Wood Chapel, Marylebone, London	SD	*Chantrey Ledgers*, 1991–92, 187

No.	Date	Subject	Location		References
150.	1825	Thomas Master (†1823) Payment(s): £116 3s 6d	Cirencester, Glos		*Chantrey Ledgers*, 1991–92, 202–3
151.	1824–1825	William Brinton (†1823) Payment(s): £169 13s 9d inclusive	Speen, Berks	S	*Chantrey Ledgers*, 1991–92, 186
152.	1826	Archdeacon Francis Wollaston (†1823) Payment(s): £105	South Weald, Essex		*Chantrey Ledgers*, 1991–92, 200
153.	1817–1826	David Pike Watts (†1816) Payment(s): £6,090 inclusive Model(s): Ashm, plaster	Ilam, Staffs	SD	*Whinney* 1988, 362, 401, 402 (repr); *Penny* 1992, 223 (repr); *Chantrey Ledgers*, 1991–92, 82–3
154.	1826	Eusebius Horton (†1814) Payment(s): £522 11	Croxall, Staffs	SD	*Chantrey Ledgers*, 1991–92, 188–9
155.	1822–1826	Lady Louisa Theodosia, Countess of Liverpool (†1821) Payment(s): £1,500 Drawing(s): NPG, London Model(s): Ashm, plaster	All Saints, Kingston-upon-Thames, Surrey	SD	*Graves* II, 1905–6, 41; *Potts* 1981 (2), 32 (repr); *Chantrey Ledgers*, 1991–92, 169 (repr 108); *Penny* 1992, 220 (repr)
156.	1819–1826	Major-General Arthur Gore (†1814) and Major-General John Byrne Skerett (†1814) (designed by William Tollemache) Payment(s): 2,000 gns	St Paul's Cathedral, London		*Chantrey Ledgers*, 1991–92, 133–4
157.	1826	Major-General Sir Robert Rollo Gillespie (†1814) Payment(s): 1,500 gns Model(s): Ashm, plaster	St Paul's Cathedral, London	SD	*Chantrey Ledgers*, 1991–92, 73 (repr 56); *Penny* 1992, 218 (repr)
158.	1826	Sampson Gideon, Baron Eardley MP (†1824) Payment(s): £1063 10s	Erith, Kent	SD	*Chantrey Ledgers*, 1991–92, 198
159.	†1826	Sir Charles Oakeley, 1st Bt, Governor of Madras (†1826)	Lichfield Cathedral, Staffs	S	*Chantrey Ledgers*, 1991–92, 330–1
160.	1826	Sir Evan Nepean MP (†1822) Payment(s): £236 5s 2d	Loders, Dorset		*Chantrey Ledgers*, 1991–92, 205
161.	1822–1826	Thomas (†1819) and Mary (†1825) Kinnersly Payment(s): £2,047 18s 6d	Ashley, Staffs	SD	*Chantrey Ledgers*, 1991–92, 159 (repr 93)
162.	1826	Thomas Todd Payment(s): £210 inclusive	[Manchester, unidentified church]; untraced		*Chantrey Ledgers*, 1991–92, 205
163.	1826	William Baker (†1824) Payment(s): £73 10s	Bayford, Herts	S	*Chantrey Ledgers*, 1991–92, 204
164.	1824–1826	William Stuart, Archbishop of Armagh (†1822) Payment(s): £1,115 17s 9d inclusive	Armagh Cathedral, Northern Ireland	SD	*Chantrey Ledgers*, 1991–92, 191 (repr 102)
165.	1827	Dr Matthew Baillie MD (†1823) Payment(s): £636 fully inclusive	Westminster Abbey, London, north transept	SD	*Chantrey Ledgers*, 1991–92, 207 (repr 119)
166.	1825–1827	Dr Thomas James DD (†1804) Payment(s): £519 17s inclusive	Rugby School, Warks, Chapel	SD	*Chantrey Ledgers*, 1991–92, 55–6
167.	1827	Francis, 2nd Marquess of Hertford (†1822) Model(s): Ashm, plaster	Alcester, Warks		*Penny* 1992, 219 (repr); *Chantrey Ledgers*, 1991–92, 177–8 (repr 110)
168.	1827	Frederica, Lady Stanhope (†1823) Payment(s): £1,608 Model(s): Ashm, plaster	Chevening, Kent	SD	*Penny* 1992, 222 (repr); *Chantrey Ledgers*, 1991–92, 175 (repr 106)
169.	1827	General George Smyth (?), two tablets, one for America and another for England Payment(s): £211 16s	Untraced		*Chantrey Ledgers*, 1991–92, 211
170.	1819–1827	John Pinney (†1818) Payment(s): £329 7s 10d	Somerton, Somerset		*Chantrey Ledgers*, 1991–92, 121–2
171.	1827	Rev Frederick Iremonger, Prebendary of Winchester (†1820) Payment(s): £650 fully inclusive	Winchester Cathedral, Hants	s	*Chantrey Ledgers*, 1991–92, 180–1 (repr 105); *Yarrington* 1993, 38–42
172.	1827	Sophia, Lady Gomm (†1827) Payment(s): £134 13s	Untraced		*Chantrey Ledgers*, 1991–92, 226
173.	1824–1827	William Murdoch (†1839) Drawing(s): NPG, inscribed Will Murdock Model(s): Ashm, plaster	St Mary, Handsworth, Birmingham Other versions: plaster, after Chantrey, BMAG (*Silber* 1987, 24, cat 59)		*Penny* 1992, 239 (repr); *Chantrey Ledgers*, 1991–92, 93; *Noszlopy* 1998, 69 (repr)
174.	1819–1828	Caroline Leonora, Countess of Ilchester (†1819) Payment(s): £840	Melbury Sampford, Dorset	SD	*Chantrey Ledgers*, 1991–92, 111–2 (repr 67)
175.	1819–1828	Catherine Vansittart (†1810) Payment(s): 100 gns	Beckenham, Kent		*Chantrey Ledgers*, 1991–92, 123
176.	1828	General Sir Denis Pack (†1823) Payment(s): £593 15s Model(s): Ashm, plaster	Kilkenny Cathedral, Ireland	SD	*Penny* 1992, 241 (repr); *Chantrey Ledgers*, 1991–92, 213
177.	1828	General Sir Harry Calvert (†1826) Payment(s): £245 10s	Middle Claydon, Bucks	S	*Chantrey Ledgers*, 1991–92, 225
178.	1826–1828	Lady Mary Seymour (†1825) Payment(s): £657 3s	Orton Longueville, Cambs	SD	*Chantrey Ledgers*, 1991–92, 209
179.	1828	Rev Thomas Rennell DD (†1824) Payment(s): £200	St Mary Abbots, Kensington, London	S	*Chantrey Ledgers*, 1991–92, 220
180.	1824–1828	Rev Wadham Pigott (†1823) Payment(s): £335 9s 9d	Brockley, Somerset	S	*Chantrey Ledgers*, 1991–92, 194–5
181.	1828	Sir George Beaumont Bt (†1727) Payment(s): £57 15s	Coleorton, Leics		*Chantrey Ledgers*, 1991–92, 226
182.	1828	William Hoare (†1792) Payment(s): £522 16s	Bath Abbey, Somerset	SD	*Chantrey Ledgers*, 1991–92, 199–200 (repr 88)

183.	1828	William Lewis (†1811)	[Christ Church, Hunter St, Liverpool]; untraced	S	*Gunnis* 1968, 95
184.	1819–1828	William, 1st Baron Auckland (†1814) Payment(s): 100 gns	Beckenham, Kent		*Chantrey Ledgers*, 1991–92, 122–3
185.	†1828	Wilmot (†1815) and Martha Lambert	Banstead, Surrey		ATTRIB. *Chantrey Ledgers*, 1991–92, 330
186.	1829	Charlotte, Duchess of St Albans (†1797) Payment(s): £136 10s with the tablet for her husband, William, Duke of St Albans	St Andrew, Redbourne, Lincs		*Chantrey Ledgers*, 1991–92, 248
187.	1828–1829	Commodore Sir James Brisbane (†1826) Payment(s): £225 12s 6d fully inclusive	St James, Sydney, Australia	S	*Chantrey Ledgers*, 1991–92, 229–30
188.	1829	Edward Greaves, perhaps of Nettleworth, Lancs Payment(s): £150 inclusive	Untraced		*Chantrey Ledgers*, 1991–92, 215
189.	1827–1829	General Richard Vyse (†1825) Payment(s): £530 15s 6d with Mary Vyse Madan's monument (191)	Lichfield Cathedral, Staffs		*Chantrey Ledgers*, 1991–92, 224 (repr 124)
190.	1828–1829	George Macaulay (†1826) Payment(s): £156 2s including 'loading, Cartage and Mans wages shipping'	Presbyterian church, Charleston, South Carolina, USA		*Hershey* 1970, 803 (repr); *Chantrey Ledgers*, 1991–92, 228–9
191.	1829	John Taylor (†1824) Payment(s): £235 fully inclusive	Bolton, Lancs		*Chantrey Ledgers*, 1991–92, 220
192.	1827–1829	Mary Vyse Madan (†1827) Payment(s): £530 15s 6d with General Vyse's monument (188)	Lichfield Cathedral, Staffs		*Chantrey Ledgers*, 1991–92, 224 (repr 125)
193.	1829	Reginald Heber, Bishop of Calcutta (†1826) Payment(s): £300	Hodnet, Salop		*Chantrey Ledgers*, 1991–92, 222
194.	1829	Rev Zachariah Mudge (†1769) Payment(s): £525 with packing and freight Model(s): Ashm, plaster	St Andrew, Plymouth, Devon	SD	*Chantrey Ledgers*, 1991–92, 203 (repr 118); *Penny* 1992, 239 (repr)
195.	1827–1829	William Egerton (†1827) Payment(s): £316 17s 6d Model(s): Ashm, plaster	Gresford, Clwyd		*Chantrey Ledgers*, 1991–92, 242
196.	1829	William, 8th Duke of St Albans (†1825) Payment(s): £136 10 with the tablet for his first wife, Charlotte	St Andrew, Redbourne, Lincs		*Chantrey Ledgers*, 1991–92, 248
197.	1828–1830	Bryan Cooke MP (†1821) Payment(s): £763 2s inclusive	Owston, WR Yorks	SD	*Chantrey Ledgers*, 1991–92, 230 (repr 127)
198.	1830	Dr Clarke of Wiggenton Lodge, Brighton Payment(s): £9	Untraced		*Chantrey Ledgers*, 1991–92, 105
199.	1829–1830	Edward Hasell (†1825) Payment(s): £343 2s 1d	Dacre, Cumberland	SD	*Chantrey Ledgers*, 1991–92, 247
200.	1830	Mr Leyland of Liverpool Payment(s): 200 gns	Untraced		*Chantrey Ledgers*, 1991–92, 246
201.	1830	Reginald Heber, Bishop of Calcutta (†1826) Model(s): Ashm, plaster	St George's Cathedral, Chennai (Madras), India	SD	*Graves* II, 1905–6, 42; *Penny* 1992, 219 (repr); *Groseclose* 1990, 504; *Chantrey Ledgers*, 1991–92, 221–2 (repr 136, 137); *Steggles* 2002, 13 (repr)
202.	1829–1830	Rev Charles Pilkington (†1828) Payment(s): £213 17s inclusive	Chichester Cathedral, Sussex		*Chantrey Ledgers*, 1991–92, 246
203.	1831	Arabella, Duchess of Dorset (†1825) Payment(s): £829 2s 6d inclusive	Withyham, Sussex	S	*Chantrey Ledgers*, 1991–92, 233 (repr 130)
204.	1828–1831	Colonel John Noble (†1827) Payment(s): £650 inclusive	St Thomas, Chennai (Madras), India	SD	*Chantrey Ledgers*, 1991–92, 248
205.	†1831	Elizabeth, Lady Eldon	Corfe, Dorset		ATTRIB. *Chantrey Ledgers*, 1991–92, 328–9
206.	1831	John Webber Payment(s): £500	Untraced		Will of Henry Webber PROB 11/1717/79; *Tattersall* 1985, 42; *Chantrey Ledgers*, 1991–92, 249
207.	1831	Lady Henrietta Ann Barbara Sullivan (†1828) Payment(s): £130 inclusive	Iver, Bucks		*Chantrey Ledgers*, 1991–92, 255–6
208.	1831	Margaret, Countess Somers (†1831) Payment(s): £286 16s	Eastnor, Herefs		*Chantrey Ledgers*, 1991–92, 264
209.	1830–1831	Rev William Chamberlayne (†1829) Payment(s): £426 2s inclusive	Pear Tree Green, Itchen, Hants		*Chantrey Ledgers*, 1991–92, 260–1 (repr 157)
210.	1831	William Hazeldine (bust only; monument by John Carline I and II) Payment(s): £100 Drawing(s): NPG, London, several	**St Chad, Shrewsbury**		*Pidgeon* 1851, 60; *Chantrey Ledgers*, 1991–92, 259
211.	1830–1832	John Clarke of Liverpool Payment(s): £310 18s 8d fully inclusive	Untraced		*Chantrey Ledgers*, 1991–92, 256
212.	1831–1832	John Pringle (†1816) Payment(s): £175 inclusive of cartage etc and clergy and clerk's fees	Cowfold, Sussex		*Chantrey Ledgers*, 1991–92, 268–9
213.	1829–1832	Mary Kinnersly Attwood (†1823) Payment(s): £273 fully inclusive	Ashley, Staffs		*Chantrey Ledgers*, 1991–92, 252–3
214.	1832	Samuel Oldknow (†1828) Payment(s): £211	Marple, Cheshire		*Chantrey Ledgers*, 1991–92, 244

No.	Date	Subject	Location		Bibliography
215.	1832	Sarah Whinyates and her still-born child (†1828) Payment(s): £600 including freight	St Werburgh, Derby	SD	*Whinyates* 1894, correspondence, 1827–32; *Chantrey Ledgers*, 1991–92, 261 (repr 148)
216.	1832	Sir Hugh Inglis MP (†1820) Payment(s): £700 Model(s): Ashm, plaster	Milton Bryan, Beds	SD	*Chantrey Ledgers*, 1991–92, 201–2; *Penny* 1992, 219 (repr)
217.	1832	Sir Thomas Stamford Raffles (†1826) Payment(s): £1,500 Model(s): Ashm, plaster	Westminster Abbey, London, nave	SD	WAM (87); *Chantrey Ledgers*, 1991–92, 249 (repr 140); *Penny* 1992, 221 (repr)
218.	†1833	George, 1st Duke of Sutherland	[Dornoch Cathedral, Sutherland]; Dunrobin Castle, Sutherland, gardens		*Chantrey Ledgers*, 1991–92, 283–4
219.	1833	Hugh Owen Colby of Fynone Payment(s): £120	Untraced		*Chantrey Ledgers*, 1991–92, 273
220.	1833	Rev David (†1812/3) and Isabel (†1824) Wilkie	Cults, Fife	S	*Chantrey Ledgers*, 1991–92, 273–4
221.	1831–1833	Samuel Knight (†1829) Payment(s): £230	Milton, Cambs	S	*Chantrey Ledgers*, 1991–92, 267–8 (repr 149)
222.	1832–1833	Shute Barrington, Bishop of Durham (†1826) Payment(s): £1,260 Drawing(s): NPG, London Model(s): Ashm, plaster	Durham Cathedral	SD	*Penny* 1992, 215 (repr); *Chantrey Ledgers*, 1991–92, 276 (respr 156)
223.	1833	Sir Robert Cavendish Spencer	Great Brington, Northants		*Chantrey Ledgers*, 1991–92, 267
224.	1833	Sir Thomas Munro Bt, Governor of Madras (†1827) Payment(s): £52 10s	Fort St George, Chennai (Madras)		*Chantrey Ledgers*, 1991–92, 238
225.	1831–1833	Thomas Lett (†1815) Payment(s): £509 10s with expenses	St Mary, Lambeth (now Museum of Garden Hist)	SD	*Chantrey Ledgers*, 1991–92, 269
226.	1834	Admiral Sir Richard Bickerton (†1832) Payment(s): £521 16s fully inclusive	Bath Abbey, Somerset	SD	*Chantrey Ledgers*, 1991–92, 284–5 (repr 158)
227.	1832–1834	Charles, Viscount Camden (†1794) Payment(s): £200	Deal, Kent	SD	*Chantrey Ledgers*, 1991–92, 234–5
228.	1832–1834	John (†1797) and Thomas (†1805) Pratt Payment(s): £100	Deal, Kent		*Chantrey Ledgers*, 1991–92, 234–5
229.	1832–1834	Lady Caroline Stewart (née Pratt) Payment(s): £100	Deal, Kent		*Chantrey Ledgers*, 1991–92, 234–5
230.	1832–1834	Lady Frances Margaret Pratt (†1822) Payment(s): £100	Deal, Kent		*Chantrey Ledgers*, 1991–92, 234–5
231.	1834	Lady Mary Ann Bradford (†1830) Payment(s): £500 plus extras Model(s): Ashm, plaster	Hartburn, Northumbs	SD	*Chantrey Ledgers*, 1991–92, 268; *Penny* 1992, 216 (repr)
232.	1832–1834	Lord Chief Justice Sir John Pratt (†1724) Payment(s): £644 18s inclusive, charged with four others	Deal, Kent		*Chantrey Ledgers*, 1991–92, 234–5
233.	1834	Mary Ann Boulton (†1829) Payment(s): £1,500 exclusive of extras Model(s): Ashm, plaster	Great Tew, Oxon	SD	*Penny* 1977 (1), 87 (frontispiece repr); *Chantrey Ledgers*, 1991–92, 256–7; *Penny* 1992, 215 (repr)
234.	1834	Mrs Hall of Manchester Payment(s): £522 18s 6d	[for the Collegiate Church, Manchester]; untraced		*Chantrey Ledgers*, 1991–92, 280
235.	1834	Prebendary Thomas Baker (†1831) Payment(s): £225	Chichester Cathedral		*Chantrey Ledgers*, 1991–92, 273
236.	1832–1834	Rev Ralph (†1794) and Mrs Catherine (†1801) Nicholson Payment(s): £1024 10s 4d with the monument to William Nicholson	St James's Cemetery, Liverpool, Lancs, oratory		*Chantrey Ledgers*, 1991–92, 270–1
237.	1834	Rt Hon George Canning (†1827) Drawing(s): NPG, London Model(s): Ashm, plaster	Westminster Abbey, London, north transept	SD	*Potts* 1981 (3), 79–80; *Chantrey Ledgers*, 1991–92, 239 (repr 133)
238.	1834	William (†1768) and Martha (†1782) Le Marchant and their eight children Payment(s): £500 with packing and transfer to ship	St Peter Port, Guernsey	SD	*Chantrey Ledgers*, 1991–92, 279
239.	1834	William Nicholson (†1832) and six family members Payment(s): £1,024 10s fully inclusive	St James's Cemetery, Liverpool, Lancs, oratory	SD	*Chantrey Ledgers*, 1991–92, 270–1 (repr 150)
240.	1835	Admiral Sir Richard Keats Payment(s): £525	Royal Naval College, Greenwich (ORNC), chapel		*Chantrey Ledgers*, 1991–92, 289–90
241.	1835	Major Edmund Fortescue (†1821) Payment(s): £154 6s	East Allington, Devon		*Chantrey Ledgers*, 1991–92, 282
242.	1835	Other, 6th Earl of Plymouth (†1833) Payment(s): £547 fully inclusive	Tardebigge, Worcs	D	*Chantrey Ledgers*, 292 (repr 162)
243.	1835	Reginald Heber, Bishop of Calcutta (†1826) Payment(s): £2,035 14s Model(s): VAM A.29-1933	[St John's, Kolkata (Calcutta)]; St Paul's Cathedral, Kolkata		*Neoclassicism* 1972, 218; *Chantrey Ledgers*, 1991–92, 223 (repr 138, 139); *Bilbey* 2002, 236–7 (repr)
244.	1826–1835	Reginald Heber, Bishop of Calcutta (†1826) Payment(s): £3,000 Model(s): VAM A.29-1933, clay	St Paul's Cathedral, London, crypt	S	*Whinney* 1988, 414–5 (repr); *Chantrey Ledgers*, 1991–92, 242–3; *Bilbey* 2002, 236–7 (repr)

245.	c1835	Sir Humphrey Davy (†1829) Payment(s): £35	Westminster Abbey, London, St Andrew's Chapel		*Chantrey Ledgers*, 1991–92, 255
246.	†1835	Sophia, Baroness Howe	Penn, Bucks	S	ATTRIB. *Chantrey Ledgers*, 1991–92, 329–30
247.	1835	Thomas Wyatt (†1834) Payment(s): £150	St Mary, East Barnet, Herts		*Chantrey Ledgers*, 1991–92, 294
248.	1831–1836	Charlotte Chamberlayne (†1831) Payment(s): £626 fully inclusive	Pear Tree Green, Itchen, Herts	SD	*Chantrey Ledgers*, 1991–92, 280
249.	1836	Dr Thomas Young MD (†1829) Payment(s): £75 Drawing(s): WAM 66310	Westminster Abbey, London, St Andrew's Chapel		*Chantrey Ledgers*, 1991–92, 286–7
250.	1836	Frederica Mure (†1834) Payment(s): £218 6s fully inclusive	St Alban's Cathedral, Herts	S	*Chantrey Ledgers*, 1991–92, 295–6
251.	†1836	Harriet, Countess Howe	Penn, Bucks		ATTRIB. *Chantrey Ledgers*, 1991–92, 329–30
252.	1836	John (†1832), Harriot (†1832) and Nathaniel Hornby (†1835) Payment(s): £382 5s	St Peter, Titchfield, Hants	SD	*Chantrey Ledgers*, 1991–92, 296 (repr 164)
253.	1836	John Broadley Wilson (†1835) Payment(s): £509 15s fully inclusive	St Paul, Clapham, London	SD	*Chantrey Ledgers*, 1991–92, 297–8
254.	†1836	Samuel Northcote Payment(s): £200	St Andrew, Plymouth, Devon		*Chantrey Ledgers*, 1991–92, 266–7
255.	1836	Servants of Sir Hugh Inglis Payment(s): £21 14s 7d	Milton Bryan, Beds	S	*Chantrey Ledgers*, 1991–92, 281
256.	1837	Charles (†1837) and Dudley (†1837) Acland Payment(s): £200 Model(s): Ashm, clay sketch and plaster model	Selworthy, Somerset		*Chantrey Ledgers*, 1991–92, 262, 316–7
257.	1837	Charles Goring MP (†1829) Payment(s): £170 17s 6d	Wiston, Sussex	SD	*Chantrey Ledgers*, 1991–92, 306
258.	1837	Colonel John Bolton of Storrs, Westmorland Payment(s): £500	Untraced		*Chantrey Ledgers*, 1991–92, 313
259.	1837	Henry Ryder, Bishop of Lichfield (†1836) Model(s): Ashm, plaster	Lichfield Cathedral, Staffs	SD	*Graves* II, 1905–6, 42; *Penny* 1992, 222 (repr); *Chantrey Ledgers*, 1991–92, 312–3 (repr 172)
260.	1837	John Phelips (†1834) Payment(s): £612 11s 1d inclusive	Wells Cathedral, Somerset	SD	*Chantrey Ledgers*, 1991–2, 301 (repr 166)
261.	1837	John, 5th Viscount Downe (†1832) Payment(s): £1551 inclusive	Snaith, W R Yorks	SD	*Chantrey Ledgers*, 1991–92, 285 (repr 159)
262.	1837	Major-General Sir John Malcolm	Westminster Abbey, London, north transept		*Graves* II, 1905–6, 42; *MacMichael* 1977, 89
263.	1837	Maria Elizabeth, Countess de Gersdorff of Prussia (†1826) Payment(s): £215 11s 6d	Erith, Kent		*Chantrey Ledgers*, 1991–92, 216
264.	1837	Sir Charles Mill Bt (†1835) Payment(s): £277 10s	Eling, Hants		*Chantrey Ledgers*, 1991–92, 298
265.	1837	Sir Richard Johnstone Bt (†1807) Payment(s): £131 5s fully inclusive	Hackness, N R Yorks	S	*Chantrey Ledgers*, 1991–92, 300 (repr 165)
266.	1837	Thomas Harrison (†1818) Payment(s): £833 6s fully inclusive	Sheffield Cathedral, W R Yorks	S	*Chantrey Ledgers*, 1991–92, 226–7 (repr 126)
267.	1838	Harriet, Duchess of St Albans (†1837) Payment(s): £220	St Andrew, Redbourne, Lincs	S	*Chantrey Ledgers*, 1991–92, 314 (repr 173)
268.	1838	James Ramsbotham (†1835) Payment(s): £380	Stand, Lancs	SD	*Chantrey Ledgers*, 1991–92, 301–2
269.	†1838	Robert Gray	Holy Trinity, Sunderland	S	GPC
270.	1838	William Minshull (†1836) Payment(s): £163 18s	St John the Baptist, Kentish Town, London	S	*Chantrey Ledgers*, 1991–92, 306
271.	1839	Charles Thomas, Viscount Ingestre (†1826) and his wife, Frances Payment(s): £105	Ingestre, Staffs	SD	*Chantrey Ledgers*, 1991–92, 253, 299
272.	1839	Christopher Smith Payment(s): £189 11s	Untraced		*Chantrey Ledgers*, 1991–92, 312
273.	1839	Elizabeth Poyntz (†1830) Payment(s): £1069 4s 6d fully inclusive	Cowdray, Sussex	SD	*Chantrey Ledgers*, 1991–92, 272 (repr 151)
274.	1839	John, 1st Earl of Eldon (†1838)	Corfe, Dorset		ATTRIB. *Chantrey Ledgers*, 1991–92, 328–9
275.	c1839	Prebendary Evelyn Levett Sutton (†1835)	Westminster Abbey, London, nave	S	WAM (67); *Chantrey Ledgers*, 1991–92, 332
276.	1839	Sir Ralph Woodford Bt (†1828), Governor of Trinidad Payment(s): £1386 3s with another monument to Woodford, untraced Model(s): Ashm, plaster	Trinidad Cathedral Other versions: Another intended for the Roman Catholic Cathedral; untraced	SD	*Chantrey Ledgers*, 1991–92, 303; *Penny* 1992, 224 (repr)
277.	1839	Thomas Sharp (†1758) and three family members Payment(s): £747 7s 6d inclusive	Bamburgh, Northumberland	S	*Chantrey Ledgers*, 1991–92, 315–6
278.	1839	Thomas Taylor Vernon (†1835) Payment(s): £571 10s 3d inclusive Model(s): Ashm, plaster	Hanbury, Worcs	SD	*Chantrey Ledgers*, 1991–92, 308; *Penny* 1992, 222 (repr)
279.	post-1839	Thomas, 2nd Marquess of Bath (†1837)	Longbridge Deverill, Wilts		*Chantrey Ledgers*, 1991–92, 325
280.	1840	James Northcote RA (†1831) Payment(s): £1290 18s 8 1/2d Model(s): Ashm, plaster	Exeter Cathedral, Devon	SD	*Graves* II, 1905–6, 42; *Penny* 1992, 221 (repr); *Chantrey Ledgers*, 1991–92, 266 (repr 147)

No.	Date	Subject		Location		Literary references
281.	1840	Major-General Sir James Carmichael Smyth (†1838) Payment(s): £100		St George's Cathedral, Georgetown, Guyana Other versions: replica for Hall of Justice, Berbice, Guyana		*Chantrey Ledgers*, 1991–92, 324, 325
282.	1840	Mr Gawne of the Isle of Man Payment(s): £164		Untraced		*Chantrey Ledgers*, 1991–92, 317
283.	1840	Rev Edward Ward (†1835) Payment(s): £339 10s 1d inclusive		Iver, Bucks	SD	*Chantrey Ledgers*, 1991–92, 297
284.	1840	Sir James Carmichael Smyth Bt (†1838) Payment(s): £205 Model(s): Ashm, plaster		St George's Cathedral, Georgetown, Guyana Other versions: Bust replicated for the Hall of Justice, Berbice, Guyana	S	*Chantrey Ledgers*, 1991–92, 324, 325
285.	1841	Bishop Henry Bathurst (†1837) Model(s): Ashm, plaster		Norwich Cathedral, Norfolk	SD	*Graves* II, 1905–6, 42; *Chantrey Ledgers*, 1991–92, 311–2 (repr 171); *Penny* 1992, 215 (repr)
286.	1841	Isabella Read Lyon (†1836) Payment(s): £290 12s 6d		Goring-by-Sea, Sussex	SD	*Chantrey Ledgers*, 1991–92, 327 (repr 167)
287.	1841	Lady Elizabeth Smyth (†1840)		St John the Baptist, Weston-super-Mare, Somerset	SD	*Chantrey Ledgers*, 1991–92, 331–2
288.	1841	Richard Rosdew (†1837) Payment(s): £166 16s fully inclusive		Plympton St Mary, Devon	S	*Chantrey Ledgers*, 1991–92, 318–9
289.	1841	William Mason Smith (†1838) Payment(s): £250		St Philip, Charleston, USA	SD	*Hershey* 1970, 807 (repr); *Chantrey Ledgers*, 1991–92, 326
290.	nd	Elizabeth Nunn Agassiz		Bradfield, Essex	S	ATTRIB. *Chantrey Ledgers*, 1991–92, 328

Statues

No.	Date	Subject		Location		Literary references
291.	1811–1815	King George III Payment(s): £2,100; £310 18s 4d for the pedestal Drawing(s): Guildhall Record Office (*Chantrey Ledgers*, repr 12) Model(s): Ashm, plaster	m	[Guildhall, City of London, council chamber]; destroyed		*Penny* 1992, 217 (repr); *Chantrey Ledgers*, 1991–92, 31–2 (repr 11); *Ward-Jackson* 2002, xviii
292.	1812–1817	Robert Blair of Avontoun, President of the College of Justice, Edinburgh Payment(s): £4,000	m	Sessions House, Edinburgh, Faculty of Advocates Other versions: Thurso, Caithness, 1836 (RG/JP, 2, 297)	SD	*Whinney* 1988, 404; *Chantrey Ledgers*, 1991–92, 42–3 (repr 22)
293.	1817	Rt Hon Spencer Perceval Payment(s): £1,800		[All Saints, Northampton]; Northampton Town Hall	S	*Chantrey Ledgers*, 1991–92, 41–2 (repr 21)
294.	1812–1818	Henry, Viscount Melville (†1811) Payment(s): £3,500	m	Sessions House, Edinburgh, faculty of advocates	SD	*Graves* II, 1905–6, 41; *Whinney* 1988, 404 (repr); *Chantrey Ledgers*, 1991–92, 45–6 (repr 23)
295.	1818–1819	Lady Louisa Russell Payment(s): £367 10s Drawing(s): NPG, London Model(s): Ashm, plaster	m	Woburn Abbey, Beds		*Graves* II, 1905–6, 41; *Potts* 1981 (2), 31 (repr); *Chantrey Ledgers*, 1991–92, 87–8 (repr); *Penny* 1992, 221 (plaster repr); *Yarrington* 2002, 30–43 (repr)
296.	1818–1820	Alexander Boswell's daughter, Janet Theresa Eliot (†1836) Payment(s): £367 10s		Untraced		*Chantrey Ledgers*, 1991–92, 107
297.	1818–1820	Harriet Acland, an infant (†*c*1817) Payment(s): £367 10s Model(s): SJSM SC32, painted plaster		[Killerton Hall, Devon]; private coll, Westwood, New Jersey, USA (1943)	SD	*Chantrey Ledgers*, 1991–92, 105–6 (repr 35)
298.	1819–1820	Satan 'pursuant to a sketch' ('Lord Egremont's figure')		Abandoned		*Chantrey Ledgers*, 1991–92, 140–1
299.	1820–1824	Robert Dundas of Arniston, Lord Chief Baron of Scotland Drawing(s): NPG, London Model(s): Ashm, plaster	m	Sessions House, Edinburgh, faculty of advocates	SD	*Whinney* 1988, 404–5 (repr); *Chantrey Ledgers*, 1991–92, 135 (repr 24)
300.	1826	Dr William Hey MD Payment(s): £800 Model(s): Ashm, plaster	m	LGI, W R Yorks	SD	*Penny* 1992, 219 (repr); *Chantrey Ledgers*, 1991–92, 145 (repr 85)
301.	1819–1826	George Washington, President of the United States Payment(s): £2,250 fuly inclusive Model(s): Ashm, plaster	m	Boston State House, USA	SD	*Graves* II, 1905–6, 41; *Penny* 1992, 222 (repr); *Chantrey Ledgers*, 1991–92, 119–20 (repr 70)
302.	1826	Sir Joseph Banks FRS Payment(s): £2,100 Model(s): Ashm, plaster	m	[BM, London, entrance hall]; Natural History Museum, London	SD	*Graves* II, 1905–6, 41; *Potts* 1981 (3), 68–9 (repr 24); *Chantrey Ledgers*, 1991–92, 163–5 (repr 95, 96, 97); *Penny* 1992, 215 (repr)
303.	1827	Henry Grattan MP Payment(s): £2044 18s 3d fully inclusive Model(s): Ashm, plaster, exhib RA, London, 1826, 1067	b	City Hall, Dublin	SD	*Graves* II, 1905–6, 41; *Chantrey Ledgers*, 1991–92, 178–9 (repr 112); *Penny* 1992, 218 (repr)
304.	1824–1827	Thomas Coutts Payment(s): £2,120 8s 2d inclusive Model(s): Ashm, plaster	m	[coll Lady Harriet Coutts]; Coutts Bank, Strand, London Other versions: plaster, Coutts' Bank	SD	*Penny* 1992, 216 (repr); *Chantrey Ledgers*, 1991–92, 192 (repr 114)

305.	1828	Judge Stephen Babington Payment(s): £1,400 Model(s): Ashm, plaster	m	Asiatic Society, Mumbai (Bombay), India (formerly Town Hall)	SD	*Graves* II, 1905–6, 41; *Penny* 1992, 215 (repr); *Chantrey Ledgers*, 1991–92, 193 (repr 143)
306.	1822–1828	King George IV Payment(s): 3,000 gns Drawing(s): NPG, London Model(s): Ashm, plaster	b	Royal Pavilion Gardens, Brighton, Sussex Other versions: George St, Edinburgh, bronze, 1831 Windsor Castle, Berks, marble, 1836 Version for Jesse Watts Russel, marble George Street, Edinburgh, bronze, 1831 (£6,150)	SD	*Penny* 1992, 217 (repr); *Chantrey Ledgers*, 1991–92, 170–1, 218–9, 236 (repr 100, 122)
307.	1829	Sir Edward Hyde East Bt Payment(s): £1,338 1s 7d Drawing(s): NPG, London Model(s): Ashm, plaster	m	[RA, London, 1829, 1198]; High Court building, Kolkata (Calcutta)		*Graves* II, 1905–6, 41; *Chantrey Ledgers*, 1991–2, 218; *Penny* 1992, 217 (repr)
308.	1830	James Watt, after the monument formerly in Westminster Abbey, London Payment(s): £1,000	m	[Glasgow University]; Hunterian Museum, Glasgow Other versions: George Square, Glasgow, Lanarks, bronze, 1832 (£3,454) Watt Memorial Library, Greenock, SD 1838 (£2,000)	SD	*Chantrey Ledgers*, 1991–92, 213, 215, 217 (repr 120); *McKenzie* 1999, 50–1, no 6.22 (repr); *McKenzie* 2002, 393–4 (repr)
309.	1829–1830	King George IV, equestrian Payment(s): £3,150	b	[intended to surmount the Marble Arch, London]; Trafalgar Square, London		*Colvin* VI, 1973, 293–302; *Whinney* 1988, 409 (repr); *Yarrington* 1988, 236–241 (pl 84); *Chantrey Ledgers*, 1991–92, 244–5 (repr 135)
310.	1831	William Pitt the Younger Payment(s): £7,000 Model(s): Ashm, plaster	b	Hanover Square, London Other versions: George St and Frederick St intersection, Edinburgh, bronze, SD 1833 (£1,500)	S	*Walker* 1961, 56; *Potts* 1981 (3), 80; *Chantrey Ledgers*, 1991–92, 195–6, 275–6 (repr 115, 154, 155); *Penny* 1992, 221 (repr)
311.	1832	Rt Hon George Canning Payment(s): £3,150 Drawing(s): NPG, London Model(s): Ashm, plaster	m	Liverpool Town Hall, Lancs, main staircase Other versions: 1836, formerly at Trentham, Staffs; untraced (£1,130 14s 6d)	SD	*Graves* II, 1905–6, 42; *Chantrey Ledgers*, 1991–92, 241, 293–4 (repr 134); *Penny* 1992, 216 (repr); *Cavanagh* 1997, 75–9 (repr)
312.	1833	David with the head of Goliath		[Exhib BI]; untraced		*Gunnis* 1968, 96
313.	1831–1834	Dorothy Jordan and her two children Payment(s): 2,000 gns Model(s): Ashm, clay sketch and plaster model	m	Buckingham Palace, London RCIN 2177	SD	*Potts* 1981 (2), 32–3 (repr); *Chantrey Ledgers*, 1991–92, 262–3 (repr 144, 145); *Penny* 1992, 16 (repr)
314.	1834	Endymion (by Canova, finished by Chantrey) Payment(s): £420	b	Chatsworth, Derbys		*JKB* 1972 (3), 328–9; *Chantrey Ledgers*, 259–60
315.	1829–1834	Mountstuart Elphinstone, Governor of Bombay Payment(s): £2,571 2s 7d inclusive Model(s): plaster, Ashm	m	Asiatic Society, Mumbai (Bombay), India (formerly Town Hall)	SD	*Graves* II, 1905–6, 42; *Chantrey Ledgers*, 1991–92; 243; *Penny* 1992, 217 (repr); *Steggles* 2000, 91–2 (repr)
316.	1836	Sir John Sinclair		Thurso, Caithness		GPC
317.	1837	John Dalton Payment(s): £2,100 Drawing(s): NPG, London, dated May 1834 Model(s): Ashm, plaster, insc 'Chantrey 1834'	m	[R I, Manchester, Lancs]; Manchester Town Hall, Lancs, inv 1882.48	SD	*Graves* II, 1905–6, 42; *Chantrey Ledgers* 1991–92, 288, 335; *Penny* 1992, 216 (repr)
318.	1838	George, 1st Duke of Sutherland		Trentham Park, Staffs Other versions: Golspie, Sutherland, Ben Bragghie	S	*Chantrey Ledgers*, 1991–92, 299–300
319.	1838	Major-General Sir John Malcolm Payment(s): £2,500 Drawing(s): NPG, London Model(s): Ashm, plaster	m	Asiatic Society, Mumbai (Bombay), India, (formerly Town Hall), grand vestibule	SD	*Graves* II, 1905–6, 42; *Chantrey Ledgers*, 1991–92, 264–5, 282–3 (repr 146); *Penny* 1992, 220 (repr)
320.	1838	Sir Thomas Munro Bt, Governor of Madras, equestrian Payment(s): £8,012 9s 4d Model(s): Ashm, plaster	b	The Island, Chennai (Madras), India	SD	*Graves* II, 1905–6, 42; *Chantrey Ledgers*, 1991–92, 237; *Steggles* 2000, 141–2 (repr)
321.	1840	Sir Charles Forbes Bt, MP Payment(s): £1000 Model(s): Audley End, Essex; Ashm, plaster	m	Asiatic Society, Mumbai (Bombay), India (formerly Town Hall)		*Graves* II, 1905–6, 42; *Chantrey Ledgers*, 1991–92, 321; *Penny* 1992, 217 (repr)
322.	1841	William Roscoe Payment(s): £1,500 Model(s): Ashm, plaster		St George's Hall, Liverpool, Lancs	SD	*Graves* II, 1905–6, 42; *Chantrey Ledgers*, 1991–92, 295 (repr 168); *Penny* 1992, 221 (repr); *Cavanagh* 1997, 284–6 (repr)
323.	1839–1844	Arthur, 1st Duke of Wellington, equestrian (co-sculptor: Henry Weekes) Payment(s): £7,489 10s Drawing(s): NPG	b	City of London, outside the Mansion House	D	*Potts* 1981 (3), 80; *Chantrey Ledger*, 1991–92, 310–11 (repr 170); *Ward-Jackson* 2002, 330–4

Busts

324.	1805	Unidentified gentleman		[Exhib RA, London, 1805, 737]; untraced		*Graves*, II, 1905–6, 40; *Chantrey Ledgers*, 1991–92, 335
325.	1805	William Younge MD		[Exhib RA, London, 1805, 739]; untraced		*Chantrey Ledgers*, 1991–92, 334

No.	Date	Subject	Mat.	Location		Literature
326.	1806	J Bigland		[Exhib RA, London, 883]; untraced		*Graves* II, 1905–6, 40; *Chantrey Ledgers*, 1991–92, 334
327.	1808	Satan		[Exhib RA, London, 902]; untraced		*Graves* II, 1905–6, 40
328.	1809	Admirals Duncan, Howe, St Vincent and Nelson, of wood and plaster, colossal Payment(s): £42		[Royal Naval Asylum, Greenwich]; NMM, Greenwich: SCU0016 (Duncan), SCU0031 (Howe); SCU0032 (St Vincent), SCU0084 (Nelson) Other versions: Trinity House, London, 1810, plaster, destroyed		*Graves* II, 1905–6, 40; *Chantrey Ledgers*, 1991–92, 21 (repr 1–4)
329.	1810	Mr Cumfield		[Exhib RA, 721]; untraced		*Graves* II 1905–6, 40; *Chantrey Ledgers*, 1991–92, 334
330.	1810	Unidentified nobleman, 'Colossean'		[Exhib RA, London, 894]; untraced		*Graves* II, 1905–6, 40; *Chantrey Ledgers*, 1991–92, 335
331.	1810	William Pitt the Younger Payment(s): £94 10s	m	[Trinity House, London]; destroyed Other versions: Several plaster replicas	SD	*Graves* II, 1905–6, 40; *Chantrey Ledgers*, 1991–92, 22–3
332.	1811	Benjamin West PRA	p	[Exhib RA, London, 1811, 947]; untraced		*Graves* II, 1905–6, 40
333.	1811	Dr John Browne MD, 'with a Therme to support it' Payment(s): £125	m	Royal Infirmary, Sheffield, W R Yorks	S	*Chantrey Ledgers*, 1991–92, 23 (repr 6)
334.	1811	John Horne Tooke Payment(s): £105 (unpaid) Drawing(s): NPG, London	p	[Exhib RA, 1811, 945]; Ashmolean Other versions: Plaster 1811, YCBA, 1810–11 Marble, 1819, Fitz Marble, 1819, YCBA B 1977.14.2	S	*Graves* II, 1905–6, 40; *Potts* 1981 (2), 15–16 (repr); *Potts* 1981 (3), 70 (repr 26); *Whinney* 1988, 399–400, 473 n5 (repr); *Chantrey Ledgers*, 1991–92, 99–100 (repr 60); *Penny* 1992, 247 (repr)
335.	1811	John Raphael Smith Payment(s): £105	p	Ashmolean Other versions: VAM A.15-1920, 1825, marble	SD	*Graves* II, 1905–6, 40; *Whinney* 1971, 148–9 (repr); *Potts* 1981 (2), 18 (repr); *Potts* 1981 (3), 70; *Whinney* 1988, 419, 422 (repr); *Chantrey Ledgers*, 1991–92, 200 (repr 117); *Penny* 1992, 244 (repr); *Bilbey* 2002, 235–6 (repr)
336.	1811	Sir Francis Burdett	p	[Exhib RA 1811, 950]; Ashmolean	SD	*Graves* II, 1905–6, 40; *Potts* 1981 (3), 70; *Chantrey Ledgers*, 1991–92, 25, 29; *Penny* 1992, 228 (repr)
337.	1811	Thomas Johnes of Hafod MP Payment(s): £105 Model(s): Ashm, plaster	m	National Museum and Gallery of Wales, Cardiff Other versions: Mrs Turville Brown, nd Univ Col of Wales, Aberystwyth, 1817–19 (£161)	SD	*Graves* II, 1905–6, 40; *Chantrey Ledgers*, 1991–92, 36, 94; *Penny* 1992, 236 (repr)
338.	1811	William Vaughan Payment(s): £42	m	NPG, London, 4934 Other versions: formerly William Vaughan of Clapham Common, London, 1815, marble,	SD	*Chantrey Ledgers*, 1991–92, 22, 39 (repr 16)
339.	1810–1812	Admiral Sir John Duckworth Payment(s): £105		[Exhib RA, London, 1811(939); 1812 (897), coll William Baker]; untraced		*Graves* II, 1905–6, 40; *Chantrey Ledgers*, 1991–92, 24–5, 28; *Penny* 1992, 226 (repr)
340.	1812	Colonel Gordon, Quartermaster-General		[Exhib RA, London, 893]; untraced		*Graves* II, 1905–6, 40; *Chantrey Ledgers*, 1991–92, 334
341.	c1812	James Northcote RA	p	Ashmolean Other versions: Pynes, Devon, 1831 (RG/JP, 2, 300)		*Graves* II, 1905–6, 40; *Penny* 1992, 240 (repr)
342.	1812	John Philpott Curran, Master of the Rolls, Ireland Model(s): Ashm, plaster		[Exhib RA, London, 898]; untraced		*Graves* II, 1905–6, 40; *Chantrey Ledgers*, 1991–92, 334; *Penny* 1992, 230 (repr)
343.	1812	Mrs William Baker Payment(s): £105	m	[Exhib RA, London, 1813, 931]; untraced		*Graves* II, 1905–6, 40; *Chantrey Ledgers*, 1991–92, 28
344.	1812	Robert Ashby		[Exhib RA, London, 926]; untraced		*Graves* II, 1905–6, 40; *Chantrey Ledgers*, 1991–92, 334
345.	1812	Thomas Stothard RA Model(s): Ashm, plaster	p	[Exhib RA, London, 927]; untraced		*Graves* II, 1905–6, 40; *Chantrey Ledgers*, 1991–92, 334; *Penny* 1992, 245 (repr)
346.	c1813	Allan, 1st Lord Meadowbank	m	[Plaster versions sent to Sir George Mackenzie and George Joseph Bell, 1813]; untraced Other versions: Exhib RA, London 1816, 931 SD 1816, marble; untraced Maidstone Museum, Kent, ?1820, marble	S	*Chantrey Ledgers*, 1991–92, 44, 288, 341 (repr 28)
347.	1813	Dr Henry Cline MD Payment(s): 100 gns Drawing(s): NPG, London Model(s): Ashm, plaster	m	St Thomas's Hospital, London Other versions: R C Surg, London, SD 1826, marble ex coll J H Green, 1830; untraced	SD	*Manchester Art Treasures* 1857, 136; *Graves* II, 1905–6, 40; *Chantrey Ledgers*, 1991–92, 26–7, 190, 252; *Penny* 1992, 229 (repr)
348.	1813	G Robinson Payment(s): 10 gns	p	[coll Daniel Alexander?]; untraced		*Chantrey Ledgers*, 1991–92, 21–2

No.	Date	Subject	Material	Location	Signed/Dated	Literature
349.	1810–1813	King George III		Adelaide Art Gall, Australia Other versions: R C Surg, London, marble, SD, 1814 Goldsmiths Hall, City of London, 1814, presented by the sculptor London Hospital Medical School, Blizard Club, SD, 1825 Royal Coll	SD	*Graves* II, 1905–6, 40; *Harris, de Bellaigue, Millar* 1968, 184 (repr); *Potts* 1981 (2), 13 (repr); *Chantrey Ledgers*, 1991–92, 28, 35 (repr 13)
350.	1813	Lady Gertrude Sloane Stanley	p	[coll Sir Hans Sloane]; private coll Other versions: plaster, ex Cyril Humphreys, Walker, Liverpool	SD	*Graves* II, 1905–6, 40; *Chantrey Ledgers*, 1991–92, 27
351.	1813	Peter Denys Payment(s): 2 gns		[Exhib RA, London, 898]; untraced		*Graves* II, 1905–6, 40; *Chantrey Ledgers*, 1991–92, 334
352.	1813	Robert Blair of Avontoun		[Exhib RA, London, 899]; untraced Other versions: Copies provided for Mrs Maconochie (2), John Wauchope, Mrs Blair, John Clarke, James Breamer, Lord Robertson, James Wedderburn, Lord Meadowbank		*Graves* II, 1905–6, 40; *Chantrey Ledgers*, 1991–92, 335
353.	1813	Sir John Hatton Bt Payment(s): £48 6s inclusive		[Lincoln's Inn Fields, London]; untraced		*Chantrey Ledgers*, 1991–92, 24
354.	1813	Sir William Baker Payment(s): £105		Manchester CAG 1983.42	SD	*Graves* II, 1905–6, 40; *Chantrey Ledgers*, 1991–92, 28
355.	1813	William Sharp Model(s): Ashm, plaster		[Exhib RA, London, 928]; untraced		*Graves* II, 1905–6, 40; *Chantrey Ledgers*, 1991–92, 335; *Penny* 1992, 244 (repr)
356.	1814	T Brown (or J Brown) Payment(s): 80 gns	m	Whitbread and Co Other versions: Ashm, plaster	SD	*Graves* II, 1905–6, 40; *Chantrey Ledgers*, 1991–92, 26
357.	1815	James Watt Payment(s): 120 gns with six plaster copies	m	[coll Bolton family]; Soho House, Birmingham Other versions: SNPG, marble, nd Glasgow Museums S.286, 1816 James Watt Gall, Greenock, c1817 (Exhib Carlisle Ac, 1823, 161) Private coll, Radnor	SD	*Carlisle Ac Exhibs*, 1823, 13; *Graves* II, 1905–6, 40; *Potts* 1981 (2), 22 (repr); *Potts* 1981 (3), 73–4 (repr 27); *Pearson* 1991, unpag; *Chantrey Ledgers*, 1991–92, 52–3 (repr)
358.	1815–1816	Admiral John Jervis, 1st Earl St Vincent Payment(s): £126 Drawing(s): profile, inscribed 'To Capt. Parker with Chantrey's respects', Christie, 25 July 1972 Model(s): Ashm, plaster	m	[Exhib RA, London, 1817 (949)]; untraced		*Chantrey Ledgers*, 64; *Penny* 1992, 242 (repr)
359.	1816	Anne Maconochie		[Exhib RA, London, 1816, 931]; Christie, 20 June 1983; untraced		*Graves* II, 1905–6, 40; *Chantrey Ledgers*, 1991–92, 44 (repr 28)
360.	1816	Dr John Clarke MD Payment(s): £84	m	[Exhib RA, London, 1817, 1043]; untraced Other versions: another, for Charles Clarke, 1816 (£73 10s)		*Graves* II, 1905–6, 41; *Chantrey Ledgers*, 1991–92, 63
361.	1816	Edward Bird RA Model(s): Ashm, plaster	m	[Exhib RA, London, 1817, 1061]; NPG, London, 986 Other versions: 1816, Bristol MAG	SD	*Graves* II, 1905–6, 41; *Chantrey Ledgers*, 1991–92, 335; *Penny* 1992, 227 (repr)
362.	1815–1816	Henry, 1st Marquess of Anglesey Payment(s): £105 Drawing(s): VAM E.1137–1927 Model(s): Ashm, plaster	m	Plas Newydd, Anglesey	SD	*Graves* II, 1905–6, 40; *Chantrey Ledgers*, 1991–92, 59; *Penny* 1992, 226 (repr)
363.	1816	John Craven Payment(s): £105	m	Untraced		*Chantrey Ledgers*, 1991–92, 39
364.	1814–1816	John Wauchope		[coll Mrs Wauchope, gift of the sculptor]; untraced		*Chantrey Ledgers*, 1991–92, 52
365.	1816	Mr Crawford Payment(s): £21 for original model; £5 each for casts in plaster	p	Untraced		*Chantrey Ledgers*, 1991–92, 45
366.	1815–1816	Professor John Playfair, with an ornamental pedestal Payment(s): £105; £26 14s 6d for the pedestal Model(s): Ashm, plaster	m	Edinburgh, Old University Library	SD	*Graves* II, 1905–6, 40; *Chantrey Ledgers*, 1991–92, 38; *Penny* 1992, 242 (repr)
367.	1816	Sir Everard Home Drawing(s): NPG, London Model(s): Ashm, plaster	m	RCS, London	SD	*Graves* II, 1905–6, 40; *Chantrey Ledgers*, 1991–92, 35; *Penny* 1992, 236 (repr)
368.	1816	Sir Joseph Banks FRS Payment(s): £105 Model(s): Ashm, plaster	m	Petworth House, Sussex Other versions: Nat Gall of Victoria, Melbourne, Australia, SD 1818, marble Royal Soc, London, SD 1819, marble Linnean Soc, London, 1822, marble (120 gns)	S	*Graves* II, 1905–6, 41; *Whinney* 1988, 420, 422 (repr); *Potts* 1981 (2), 25 (repr); *Potts* 181 (3), 67–8; *Chantrey Ledgers*, 1991–92, 58–59, 161, 313 (repr 98); *Penny* 1992, 226 (repr)

No.	Date	Subject		Location		Literature
369.	1816	Sir Spiriton Foresti Payment(s): £21		[coll John Hawkins of Bignor Park, Sussex]; untraced	S	*Chantrey Ledgers*, 1991–92, 38
370.	1816	Sir William Blizard ARA Payment(s): £126	m	RCS, London Other versions: London Hospital Medical College	SD	*Graves* II, 1905–6, 41; *Potts* 1981 (2), 23 (repr); *Chantrey Ledgers*, 1991–92, 35–36, 139 (repr 14)
371.	1816	Susan, Lady Maconochie	m	Private coll (on loan to NGS)		*Pearson* 1991, unpag
372.	1816	Thomas Tomkins (†1816) Payment(s): £52 10s Drawing(s): Huntington 72.54.59 Model(s): Ashm, plaster	m	[Exhib RA, London, 1810, 873]; BM, London	SD	*Graves* II, 1905–6, 40; *Chantrey Ledgers*, 1991–92, 58; *Penny* 1992, 246 (repr); *Dawson* 1999, 215–7 (repr)
373.	?1817	Admiral Sir Pulteney Malcolm	p	NMM, Greenwich, SCU0038		
374.	1817	George Phillips MP Payment(s): £105	m	[Exhib RA, London 1820, 1019]; Park Bernet Chrysler, NY, 6 May 1960; untraced		*Graves* II, 1905–6, 41; *Chantrey Ledgers*, 1991–92, 29
375.	1817	Robert Dundas of Arniston Payment(s): £126	m	Arniston House, Midlothian	SD	*Chantrey Ledgers*, 1991–92, 62
376.	1817	Samuel Shore Payment(s): £84 Drawing(s): ?Huntington 72.54.48 (insc 'Mr Shore Esq')	m	[Exhib RA London, 1817, 1059]; VAM A.66-1965	SD	*Graves* II, 1905–6, 41; *Chantrey Ledgers*, 1991–92, 30; *Bilbey* 2002, 234 (repr)
377.	1817	Sir Thomas Stamford Raffles Payment(s): £126 Drawing(s): NPG, London	p	Foreign and Commonwealth Office, London		*Chantrey Ledgers*, 1991–92, 73–4 (repr 36)
378.	1818	Benjamin West PRA, diploma work Payment(s): £126 Model(s): Ashm, plaster	m	RA, London Other versions: NPG, London, SD 1818 several casts	SD	*Carlisle Ac Exhibs*, 1823, 13; *Manchester Art Treasures* 1857, 136; *Graves* II, 1905–6, 40, 41; *Potts* 1981 (2), 19 (repr); *Chantrey Ledgers*, 1991–92, 47, 101 (repr 25); *Penny* 1992, 248 (repr)
379.	c1818	Charles Fox Townshend Payment(s): £105	m	[Exhib RA, London, 1818, 1071]; untraced	S	*Chantrey Ledgers*, 1991–92, 78
380.	1817–1818	Francis Horner MP Payment(s): £147 Model(s): Ashm, plaster	m	SNPG, Edinburgh Other versions: 8 casts ordered with the marble Ackland Art Museum, Univ of North Carolina at Chapel Hill, marble, 1820	SD	*Graves* II, 1905–6, 41; *Chantrey Ledgers*, 1991–92, 79, 108, 109 (repr 46); *Penny* 1992, 236 (repr); *The British Face* 1986, 131–3 (repr)
381.	1818	Francis Humberstone Mackenzie, Baron Seaforth (?) Payment(s): £84 Model(s): Ashm, plaster	m	Institute of Arts, Detroit	SD	*Chantrey Ledgers*, 1991–92, 71
382.	1818	George, 2nd Earl Spencer Payment(s): £105 Drawing(s): NPG, London (1830) Model(s): Ashm, plaster	m	Althorp, Northants	SD	*Graves* II, 1905–6, 41; *Chantrey Ledgers*, 1991–92, 97, 168; *Penny* 1992, 244 (repr)
383.	1818	Henry Cowper Drawing(s): NPG, London Model(s): Ashm, plaster	m	VAM A.65-1965 (ex coll Rupert Gunnis)	SD	*Chantrey Ledgers*, 1991–92, 190; *Penny* 1992, 230 (repr); *Bilbey* 2002, 235 (repr)
384.	1817–1818	John Hookham Frere Payment(s): £105 Drawing(s): NPG, London, profile and full-face (repr *Ditner* 337)	m	NGC, Ottawa Other versions: Two replicas commissioned by Frere, the first in 1818	SD	*Graves* II, 1905–6, 41; *Ditner* 1988, 336–7 (repr); *Chantrey Ledgers*, 1991–92, 31, 69 (repr 10)
385.	1818	John Rennie Model(s): Ashm, plaster	m	NPG, London, 649	SD	*Manchester Art Treasures* 1857, 136; *Graves* II, 1905–6, 41; *Potts* 1981 (2), 24 (repr); *Chantrey Ledgers*, 1991–92, 86; *Ret to Life*, 2000, 50, 62 (repr)
386.	1818	Joseph Nollekens RA	m	BM Other versions: ex coll Watson Taylor MP, SD 1818, marble; untraced Woburn Abbey, Beds, SD 1819, marble		*Graves* II, 1905–6, 41; *Potts* 1981 (2), 19 (repr); *Chantrey Ledgers*, 1991–92, 65–6, 82, 88; *Penny* 1992, 240 (repr); *Dawson* 1999, 156 (repr) *Yarrington* 2002, 30–43 (repr)
387.	1818	Lady Louisa Russell	m	Woburn Abbey, Beds		
388.	1818	Sir Archibald Macdonald Payment(s): £105 Drawing(s): NPG, London		VAM A.64-1965	SD	*Graves* II, 1905–6, 41; *Chantrey Ledgers*, 1991–92, 78 (repr 44, 45); *Bilbey* 1992, 234–5 (repr)
389.	1818	Sir Harry Englefield Payment(s): £100 Drawing(s): VAM E. 1103-1927 Model(s): Ashm, plaster; another VAM, dated 1817	m	Cleveland Museum of Art, Ohio	SD	*Chantrey Ledgers*, 1991–92, 91; *Penny* 1992, 232 (repr)
390.	1818	William Fox Townshend		Raynham Hall, Norfolk		RG/JP, 2, 298; NP/RG
391.	1819	Edward Johnstone Payment(s): £126 Model(s): Ashm, plaster	m	Birmingham MAG, inv P.12'62	SD	*Potts* 1981 (2), 28–9 (repr); *Chantrey Ledgers*, 1991–92, 93 (repr 62); *Penny* 1992, 237 (repr); *Silber* 1987, 55, cat 55
392.	1819	Mrs Wilson Payment(s): £127 1s		[coll William Wilson, Dallem Tower, Westmorland]; untraced		*Chantrey Ledgers*, 1991–92, 113

No.	Date	Subject		Location		Literature
393.	1819	Rear-Admiral Sir Edward Codrington Payment(s): £105 Drawing(s): NPG, London; VAM E.1145-1927; Huntington, 1817 72.54.17 Model(s): Ashm, plaster	m	[Exhib RA 1819, 1221]; untraced		*Graves* II, 1905–6, 41; *Ormond* 1973, 110; *Chantrey Ledgers*, 1991–92, 74–5; *Penny* 1992, 229 (repr)
394.	1819	Rt Hon George Canning Payment(s): £127	m	National Museum and Gallery of Wales, Cardiff Other versions: House of Commons, Westminster, London, SD, 1819 NPG, London, 1821, marble Chatsworth, Derbys, 1826, marble National Gallery of Victoria, Melbourne	SD	*Graves* II, 1905–6, 41; *Walker* 1961, 11, cat 14; *Potts* 1981 (2), 16 (repr); *Potts* 1981, 30; *Chantrey Ledgers*, 1991–92, 106, 116 (repr 63)
395.	1818–1819	Sir Benjamin Hobhouse Bt Payment(s): £105 Drawing(s): NPG, London, several Model(s): Ashm, plaster		[Exhib RA, London, 1819, 1222]; Royal Bath, West and Southern Counties Soc, Shepton Mallett Other versions: Bath Art Galleries, plaster	SD	*Graves* II, 1905–6, 41; *Chantrey Ledgers*, 1991–92, 105; *Penny* 1992, 235 (repr)
396.	1818–1819	William Manning MP Payment(s): £105		[Exhib RA 1819, 1215]; untraced		*Graves* II, 1905–6, 41; *Chantrey Ledgers*, 1991–92, 96
397.	1820	Captain Sir W Bolton		[Exhib RA, London, 1041]; untraced		*Chantrey Ledgers*, 1991–92, 335
398.	1820	Charles Hatchett Payment(s): £105 Model(s): Ashm, plaster	m	Linnaean Soc, London	SD	*Chantrey Ledgers*, 1991–92, 120; *Penny* 1992, 234 (repr)
399.	1820	Charles Long MP		[Exhib RA, London, 1046]; untraced		*Graves* II, 1905–6, 41
400.	1819–1820	Charles, Lord Farnborough Payment(s): £126 Drawing(s): **NPG, London (*Eustace* 1997 (2), 93, repr)** Model(s): Ashm NBP 707	m	NPG, London, 2090 Other versions: copy for Lord Farnborough, 1820 Powis Castle, marble, h.73.5cm	SD	*Chantrey Ledgers*, 1991–92, 118–19, 288 (repr); *Eustace* 1997 (2), 91–4
401.	1818–1820	David Pike Watts Payment(s): £126	m	[Exhib RA, London, 1819, 1214]; untraced		*Graves* II, 1905–6, 41; *Chantrey Ledgers*, 1991–92, 81
402.	1819–1820	Dr James Anderson MD Payment(s): £105 Model(s): Ashm, plaster	m	Galleria d'Arte Moderna, Palazzo Pitti, Florence CG 703		*Penny* 1992, 226 (repr); *Chantrey Ledgers*, 1991–92, 61
403.	1820	Dr Samuel Kilderbee DD Payment(s): £126 with packing case	m	Ipswich Museum and Art Gallery, Suffolk	SD	*Chantrey Ledgers*, 1991–92, 111
404.	1817–1820	Francis Noel Charles Mundy Payment(s): £312 18s with pedestal	m	Derby County Hall, crown court	SD	*Chantrey Ledgers*, 1991–92, 64–5
405.	1818–1820	George Hume of Paxton, Berwickshire Payment(s): £143 6s Drawing(s): Huntington 72.54.69	m	Untraced		*Chantrey Ledgers*, 1991–92, 102
406.	1819–1820	George Watson Taylor MP Payment(s): £126 (unpaid) Drawing(s): NPG, London; Huntington(worked up version) Model(s): Ashm, plaster		[Exhib RA, London, 1820, 1044]; untraced		*Graves* II, 1905–6, 41; *Chantrey Ledgers*, 1991–92, 107; *Penny* 1992, 246 (repr)
407.	1817–1820	Henry Bone RA	m	RA, London	SD	*Manchester Art Treasures* 1857, 136; *Graves* II, 1905–6, 41; *Chantrey Ledgers*, 1991–92, 335
408.	1819–1820	Henry Colebrooke (†1837) Payment(s): £126 Drawing(s): NPG, London Model(s): Ashm, plaster	m	[East India House, Leadenhall Street, City of London]; Foreign and Commonwealth Office, London	SD	*Archer* 1965, 407 (repr); *Chantrey Ledgers*, 1991–92, 115 (repr 68); *Penny* 1992, 230 (repr)
409.	1818–1820	Hon Walter Charteris (or Hon Charteris Wemyss) Payment(s): Bust: £105; casts, £96 12s	m	[Exhib RA, London, 1821, 1126]; untraced Other versions: Several casts		*Graves* II, 1905–6, 41; *Chantrey Ledgers*, 1991–92, 103
410.	1820	John Hunter Payment(s): £126 Model(s): Ashm, plaster	m	RCS, London	SD	*Manchester Art Treasures* 1857, 136; *Chantrey Ledgers*, 1991–92, 36, 126 (repr 15); *Penny* 1992, 236 (repr)
411.	1820	Lady Nugent Payment(s): £126 Model(s): Ashm, plaster	m	[Exhib RA, London, 1047]; untraced		*Graves* II, 1905–6, 41; *Chantrey Ledgers*, 1991–92, 124–5; *Penny* 1992, 241 (repr)
412.	1820	Miss Riddell, model only Drawing(s): NPG (?); Huntington 72.54.65-6		Untraced		*Chantrey Ledgers*, 1991–92, 133
413.	1819–1820	Perkins (perhaps Henry Perkins †1855) Payment(s): £84 Model(s): Ashm, plaster		Untraced		*Chantrey Ledgers*, 1991–92, 127; *Penny* 1992, 241 (repr)
414.	1820	Sir Andrew Snape Hamond Bt Model(s): Ashm, plaster	m	[Exhib RA, London, 1821, 1139]; untraced		*Graves* II, 1905–6, 41; *Chantrey Ledgers*, 1991–92, 101; *Penny* 1992, 234 (repr)
415.	1820	Sir Hans Sloane Payment(s): £84 Drawing(s): NPG, London; VAM E.1195-1927; Huntington 72.54.50	m	Northampton Museum	SD	*Chantrey Ledgers*, 1991–92, 77 (repr 38)

No.	Date	Subject		Location		Literature
416.	1820	Sir Walter Scott Bt Drawing(s): Ashm Model(s): Ashm, plaster, death mask (2 versions), 1832, SNPG, Edinburgh	m	Abbotsford, Roxburgh Other versions: Stratfield Saye, marble, 1827 Gunnerside, 1828, marble Lady Lever, Liverpool, nd Gov. Art Coll, marble, nd Another, Lambeth House Bridge, nd Another Philadelphia Museum of Art, SD		*GM* 1842, 259; *Graves* II, 1905–6, 41; *Gunnis* 1968, 95; *Potts* 1981 (2), 21 (repr); *Potts* 1981 (3), 53–4, 59 (repr 17); *Chantrey Ledgers*, 1991–92, 136–7, 163, 173 (repr 80); *Penny* 1992, 243 (repr)
417.	1820	Thomas Main Payment(s): £126	m	Untraced		*Chantrey Ledgers*, 1991–92, 104
418.	1819–1820	Thomas, Baron Dundas (†1820) Payment(s): £126 Model(s): Ashm, plaster	m	Aske Hall, N R Yorks Other versions: ex coll Fitzwilliam family, Wentworth Woodhouse, SD 1820 (£126)	SD	*Chantrey Ledgers*, 1991–92, 131; *Penny* 1992, 231 (repr)
419.	1820	Viscount Villiers, later 6th Earl of Jersey, design only Drawing(s): NPG, London		Work abandoned		*Chantrey Ledgers*, 1991–92, 134
420.	1818–1821	Dr Benjamin Heath Malkin Payment(s): £84	m	St James's Middle School, Bury St Edmunds	SD	*Chantrey Ledgers*, 1991–92, 92
421.	1819–1821	P J Miles MP Payment(s): £126 Drawing(s): NPG, London	m	Untraced		*Chantrey Ledgers*, 1991–92, 122
422.	1821	Robert, Viscount Castlereagh, later Marquess of Londonderry Payment(s): 150 gns Drawing(s): NPG, London, several (*Eustace* 1997 (2), repr p 90) Model(s): Ashm, NPG 689, plaster	m	YCBA, New Haven, B 1977.13.3 Other versions: Haddo House, Aberdeen, 1827 RCIN 2136 Windsor Castle, 1826 Wellington Museum, Apsley House, London, nd (inv 1452–1948) Windsor Castle, Berks, 1828 (£157 10s) Ian Grant coll, Londonderry House sale, Sotheby, 16 Nov 1962 Earl of Aberdeen coll, 1828 (£157 10s) Sir Robert Peel coll, 1838 (£157 10s)	SD	*Graves* II, 1905–6, 41; *Chantrey Ledgers*, 1991–92, 145–6, 174, 232, 233; *Penny* 1992, 228 (repr); *Eustace* 1997 (2) 88–90 (repr)
423.	1821	Thomas Phillips RA Model(s): Ashm, plaster	m	Hovingham Hall, N R Yorks		*Graves* II, 1905–6, 41; *Chantrey Ledgers*, 1991–92, 335; *Penny* 1992, 242 (repr)
424.	1821	Unidentified gentleman		[Exhib RA, London, 1131]; untraced		*Graves* II, 1905–6, 41; *Chantrey Ledgers*, 1991–92, 335
425.	1821	Walter King, Bishop of Rochester Payment(s): £126 Drawing(s): Huntington 72.54.47 Model(s): Ashm, plaster	m	Corpus Christi College, Oxford Other versions: Los Angeles County Museum, M.76.77.2	SD	*Graves* II, 1905–6, 41; *Chantrey Ledgers*, 1991–92, 134, 135 (repr 71); *Penny* 1992, 237 (repr)
426.	1821	William Howley, Bishop of London, later Archbishop of Canterbury Payment(s): £157 10s Model(s): Plaster, Ashm	m	Symonton Court, Newbury, Berks Other versions: YCBA B 1977.14.4, 1821 Canterbury Cathedral Library Lambeth Palace, London	SD	*Chantrey Ledgers*, 1991–92, 150, 162 (repr 116); *Penny* 1992, 236 (repr)
427.	1822	Captain Joseph Cotton Payment(s): £105 Drawing(s): NPG	m	Untraced		*Chantrey Ledgers*, 1991–92, 148
428.	1822	Charles Hutton	m	Newcastle Lit and Phil Soc		*Gunnis* 1968, 94
429.	1822	King George IV Payment(s): £210 Model(s): Plaster, Ashm		Sotheby, 9 Dec 1976, lot 227; Chatsworth, Derbys Other versions: 17 known versions including Royal Coll RCIN 2136, 1826	SD	*Graves* II, 1905–6, 41; *Harris, de Bellaigue, Millar* 1968, 184 (repr); *Potts* 1981 (2), 13–14 (repr); *Potts* 1981 (3), 78 (repr 30): *Chantrey Ledgers, passim* (repr 99); *Carlton House*, 1991–2, 51; *Penny* 1992, 233 (repr); *Roberts* 2002, 144 (repr)
430.	1822	William Wordsworth Payment(s): £105 Drawing(s): NPG, London Model(s): Ashm, plaster	m	Indiana University, Bloomington, Indiana	SD	*Manchester Art Treasures* 1857, 136; *Graves* II, 1905–6, 41; *Potts* 1981 (2), 20–1 (repr); *Potts* 1981 (3), 56–8 (repr 18); *Chantrey Ledgers*, 1991–92, 138 (repr 81, 82); *Penny* 1992, 250 (repr)
431.	1823	Arthur, 1st Duke of Wellington Drawing(s): BM PDL 0528.87, 1859 (four) Model(s): Ashm NBP.778, plaster (1814)	m	Met, NY Other versions: 12 identified	SD	*Graves* II, 1905–6, 41; *Potts* 1981 (2), 17 (repr); *Potts* 1981 (3), 76, 78 (repr 28); *Crookshank* 1986, 25; *Chantrey Ledgers*, 141–2, 212, 238, 281, 308 (repr); *Penny* 1992, 248 (repr); *Eustace* 1997 (2), 86–7 (repr)
432.	1821–1823	Henry Russell Payment(s): £243 11s 9d Drawing(s): NPG, London (two) Model(s): Ashm, plaster		Untraced (Bolaram, India, 1905)		*Chantrey Ledgers*, 1991–92, 168; *Penny* 1992, 242 (repr)
433.	1823	John, 1st Marquess of Abercorn Payment(s): £157 10s Model(s): Ashm, plaster	m	Haddo House, Aberdeenshire	SD	*Chantrey Ledgers*, 1991–92, 140; *Penny* 1992, 226 (repr)

No.	Date	Subject		Location		Literature
434.	1823	William Baker		[Exhib Carlisle Ac, 169]; untraced		*Carlisle Ac Exhibs*, 1823, 13
435.	1823	William Hunter Baillie		RCS, London	SD	*Chantrey Ledgers*, 1991–92, 179
436.	1824	Dr Edward Daniel Clarke Payment(s): £210	m	[for the 'vestibule of the public library', Cambridge]; Fitzwilliam	SD	*Chantrey Ledgers*, 1991–92, 183
437.	1824	Dr Matthew Baillie MD (from a model by Joseph Nollekens)	m	R C Physic, London	SD	*Wolstenholme* 1964, 44–5 (repr); *Chantrey Ledgers*, 1991–92, 194 (repr 113)
438.	1824	Edward Troughton Payment(s): £73 10s Drawing(s): NPG, 1822 (2)		NMM, Greenwich, ZBA 1722	SD	*Chantrey Ledgers*, 1991–92, 209
439.	1824	Frederick Augustus Ellis Payment(s): £105 Drawing(s): NPG, London, several	m	Institute of Jamaica, Kingston, Jamaica	SD	*Chantrey Ledgers*, 1991–92, 157
440.	1825	Francis Burton (†1832) Payment(s): £126 Drawing(s): NPG, London Model(s): Ashm, plaster	m	Untraced		*Chantrey Ledgers*, 1991–92, 196; *Penny* 1992, 228 (repr)
441.	1825	Francis, 2nd Marquess of Hertford Payment(s): 200 gns Model(s): Ashm, plaster, damaged	m	Wallace Coll, London	SD	*Penny* 1992, 235 (repr); NACF *Review*, 1999, 133 (repr)
442.	1824–1825	Shute Barrington, Bishop of Durham Payment(s): £157 10s Drawing(s): NPG, London Model(s): Ashm, plaster	m	Manchester CAG 1981.83	SD	*Chantrey Ledgers*, 1991–92, 190; *Penny* 1992, 226 (repr)
443.	1825	Thomas, 5th Earl of Selkirk (†1820) Payment(s): £105	m	Destroyed		*Chantrey Ledgers*, 1991–92, 191
444.	1826	Dr James Lindsay DD Payment(s): £157 10s	m	Dr Williams Library, Gordon Square, London	S	*Chantrey Ledgers*, 1991–92, 192
445.	1826	Granville Sharp Payment(s): £210 Model(s): Ashm, plaster	m	[Guildhall, London]; destroyed		*Chantrey Ledgers*, 1991–92, 206–7; *Penny* 1992, 244 (repr)
446.	1826	Hastings Elvin Payment(s): £157 10s Drawing(s): NPG, London	m	Avon County Lib, Bath	SD	*Chantrey Ledgers*, 1991–92, 201
447.	1826	Miss Mundy Payment(s): £105 Model(s): plaster, Ashm, on loan to Belton House, Lincs	m	Untraced		*Chantrey Ledgers*, 1991–92, 206; *Penny* 1992, 239 (repr)
448.	1824–1826	Sir Henry Halford Payment(s): £157 10s Model(s): Ashm, plaster	m	R C Physic, London	SD	*Wolstenholme* 1964, 194–5 (repr) *Chantrey Ledgers*, 1991–92, 194; *Penny* 1992, 234 (repr)
449.	1826	Sir Sandford Graham Payment(s): £105 Drawing(s): NPG, London	m	Untraced		*Chantrey Ledgers*, 1991–92, 208
450.	1827	Charles Manners-Sutton, Archbishop of Canterbury (†1828) Payment(s): £157 10s Drawing(s): NPG, London Model(s): Ashm, plaster	m	Herrenhausen Museum, Hanover, Germany	SD	*Chantrey Ledgers*, 1991–92, 197
451.	1827	Mr Hyde Payment(s): £157 10s	m	Untraced		*Chantrey Ledgers*, 1991–92, 211
452.	1827	Sir James Edward Smith (†1828) Payment(s): £126 Drawing(s): NPG	m	Linnaean Soc, London	SD	*Chantrey Ledgers*, 1991–92, 210
453.	1827	Sir William Curtis Bt Payment(s): £200 Model(s): Ashm, plaster	m	[Exhib RA, London, 1828, 1170]; untraced		*Graves* II, 1905–6, 41; *Chantrey Ledgers*, 1991–92, 211–12; *Penny* 1992, 230 (repr)
454.	1828	Rt Hon Spencer Perceval (†1812) Payment(s): £105		Untraced		*Chantrey Ledgers*, 1991–92, 235
455.	1828	Sir Matthew Tierney Bt (†1845) Model(s): Ashm, plaster		Untraced		*Chantrey Ledgers*, 1991–92, 227; *Penny* 1992, 246 (repr)
456.	1828	William Stuart, Archbishop of Armagh Payment(s): £157 10 Model(s): Ashm, plaster	m	VAM A.137-1956	SD	*Chantrey Ledgers*, 1991–92, 219 (repr 123); *Penny* 1992, 245 (repr); *Whinney* 1971, 150–1 (repr); *Bilbey* 2002, 237 (repr)
457.	1828	William, Viscount Melbourne		Private coll		*Ormond* 1973, 314
458.	1829	George Granville Leveson-Gower, later 1st Duke of Sutherland Model(s): Ashm, plaster	m	[for BI, London]; Royal Horticultural Soc, London Other versions: Dunrobin, Sutherland, nd NPG, London 5597, 1830, marble	SD	*Potts* 1981 (2), 30 (repr); *Potts* 1981 (3), 52–3 (repr 16); *Chantrey Ledgers*, 1991–92, 232; *Penny* 1992, 246 (repr)
459.	1829	Lewis Bagot	m	Christ Church, Oxford, anteroom	SD	*Chantrey Ledgers*, 1991–92, 335
460.	1829	Marquess of Stafford		[Exhib RA, London, 1203]; untraced		*Graves* II, 1905–6, 41
461.	1828–1829	Thomas Coke of Norfolk, 1st Earl of Leicester Payment(s): A gift from the sculptor Drawing(s): NPG, London	m	Holkham Hall, Norfolk Other versions: Another, after a model by Roubiliac, Holkham Hall, 1830	SD	*Potts* 1981 (2), 29 (repr); *Potts* 1981 (3), 54; *Chantrey Ledgers*, 1991–92, 230–231 (repr 128)
462.	1829	W Granville Payment(s): £157 10s	m	Untraced		*Chantrey Ledgers*, 1991–92, 232

No.	Date	Subject	Material	Location		Literature
463.	1830	Augustus Frederick, Duke of Sussex Payment(s): £210 Drawing(s): NPG, London, several Model(s): Ashm, plaster	m	[Exhib RA, London, 1831, 1218]; Freemasons' Hall, London	SD	*Graves* II, 1905–6, 42; *Chantrey Ledgers*, 1991–92, 252; *Penny* 1992, 245 (repr)
464.	1830	George, 3rd Earl of Egremont Payment(s): £210 Drawing(s): NPG, London Model(s): Ashm, plaster		Royal Sussex County Hospital, Brighton	SD	*Chantrey Ledgers*, 1991–92, 251 (repr 142); *Penny* 1992, 232 (repr)
465.	1830	Sir John Soane (†1837) Payment(s): Presented to Soane by the sculptor Drawing(s): NPG, London Model(s): Ashm, plaster	m	SJSM M 931	SD	*Graves* II, 1905–6, 41; *Chantrey Ledgers*, 1991–92, 250–1 (repr 141); *Penny* 1992, 244 (repr); *Thornton and Dorey*, 1992, 77 (repr); *Dorey* 2004, 62–4 (repr)
466.	1830	William Hyde Wollaston Drawing(s): NPG, London Model(s): Ashm, plaster		RI London (1879)	SD	*Chantrey Ledgers*, 1991–92, 249–50; *Penny* 1992, 249 (repr)
467.	1831	Dr James Scott MD Drawing(s): NPG, London (*Potts* 1981 (2), 25) Model(s): Ashm, plaster	m	RCS, London	SD	*Potts* 1981 (2), 25 (repr); *Potts* 1981 (3), 62–4; *Chantrey Ledgers*, 1991–92, 269–70 (repr 152); *Penny* 1992, 243 (repr)
468.	1831	George Saunders Payment(s): £210 Drawing(s): NPG, London, several	m	Untraced		*Chantrey Ledgers*, 1991–92, 257
469.	1831	James, 8th Earl of Lauderdale (?)		Apsley House, London		*Gunnis* 1968, 94
470.	1831	William, 1st Earl of Lonsdale (?)		Apsley House, London		*Gunnis* 1968, 94
471.	1832	David Hume, Baron of the Scottish Exchequer	m	Edinburgh, Parliament House, faculty of advocates	SD	*Whinney* 1988, 422–3 (repr); *Chantrey Ledgers*, 1991–92, 228; *Penny* 1992, 236 (repr)
472.	1832	Henry, Viscount Melville Payment(s): £300 Model(s): Ashm, plaster	m	Royal Naval Hospital, Gosport, Hants		*Chantrey Ledgers*, 1991–2, 258; *Penny* 1992, 238 (repr)
473.	1832	John Ireland, Dean of Westminster Payment(s): £169 13s 4d Drawing(s): NPG, London Model(s): Ashm, plaster	m	Examination Schools, Oxford, lobby		*Chantrey Ledgers*, 1991–92, 238; *Penny* 1992, 236 (repr)
474.	1832	Major Thomas Otway Cave Payment(s): £210 Model(s): Ashm, plaster; NPG, London	m	Stanford Hall, Leics		*Chantrey Ledgers*, 1991–92, 264; *Penny* 1992, 228 (repr)
475.	1832	Robert Southey Payment(s): £157 10 Model(s): Ashm, plaster	m	NPG, London, 3956 Other versions: Private coll (RG/JP)	SD	*Potts* 1981 (2), 22 (repr); *Potts* 1981 (3), 60–62, (repr 19); *Chantrey Ledgers*, 1991–92, 239–30 (repr 131); *Penny* 1992, 244 (repr)
476.	1832	Sir Robert Cavendish Spencer, with a pedestal Payment(s): £315	m	Althorp, Northants		*Chantrey Ledgers*, 1991–92, 271
477.	1832	William Howley, Archbishop of Canterbury	m	Huntington	SD	*Chantrey Ledgers*, 1991–92, 150
478.	1833	Elizabeth, Lady Eldon Payment(s): £157 10s		Untraced		*Chantrey Ledgers*, 1991–92, 275
479.	1833	John Abernethy Payment(s): £126 Model(s): Ashm, plaster	m	RCS, London	SD	*Chantrey Ledgers*, 1991–92, 263; *Penny* 1992, 226 (repr)
480.	1833	Princess Louisa of Saxe Weimar (two, ordered by Queen Victoria) Model(s): Ashm, plaster		[Exhib RA, London, 1833, 1176]; untraced		*Graves* II, 1905–6, 42; *Chantrey Ledgers*, 1991–92, 277–8, 283; *Penny* 1992, 242 (repr)
481.	1833	Rev Vernon Harcourt Payment(s): £210 Model(s): Ashm, plaster	m	City Art Gallery, York Other versions: Miniature version, private coll (C Lib repr)	SD	*Chantrey Ledgers*, 1991–2, 272; *Penny* 1992, 234 (repr)
482.	1833	Sir Robert Peel	m	Gunnerside Lodge, Lancs (*c*1991) Other versions: Royal Coll, Windsor Castle, SD 1835, RCIN 35432 (drawing: NPG 316a 99)	SD	*Ormond* 1973, 369–70, 371 (pl 726); *Potts* 1981 (2), 17 (repr); *Chantrey Ledgers*, 1991–92, 258–9, 295 (repr)
483.	1833	William Pitt the Younger Payment(s): £105 Model(s): Ashm, plaster	m	Pembroke College, Cambridge, library Other versions: Cirencester Park,	SD	*Chantrey Ledgers*, 1991–92, 282; *Penny* 1992, 242 (repr)
484.	?1834	Allan, 2nd Lord Meadowbank Model(s): Ashm, plaster	m	Glos Maidstone Museum, Kent Other versions: marble, retained by the sculptor, 1820, presented to the sitter in 1834	S	*Chantrey Ledgers*, 1991–92, 44, 288
485.	1834	John Dalton DCL	p	Ashmolean		*Penny* 1992, 231 (repr)
486.	1834	Sir John Woolmore Payment(s): £105 Drawing(s): NPG, London, several	m	Private coll, Jersey (1933)		*Chantrey Ledgers*, 1991–92, 277
487.	1834	Sir Thomas Munro Bt, Governor of Madras Model(s): Ashm, plaster	m	Untraced		*Graves* II, 1905–6, 42; *Chantrey Ledgers*, 1991–92, 289; *Penny* 1992, 239 (repr)

No.	Date	Subject	Material	Location	Signed/Dated	Literary References
488.	1834	Thomas Harrison Payment(s): £157 10s	m	RI, London Other versions: another ordered by Mrs Harrison in marble, 1827 (£126)	SD	*Chantrey Ledgers*, 1991–92, 208, 223
489.	1834	William Sherbrooke Payment(s): £300 with pedestal	m	Shire Hall, Nottingham, grand jury room	SD	*Chantrey Ledgers*, 1991–92, 274 (repr 153)
490.	1835	Admiral Lord Nelson, colossal, paired with a bust of Wellington, the latter untraced Model(s): Ashm, plaster	m	Royal Coll, RCIN 69609 (on loan NPG) Other versions: NMM, Greenwich, SCU0084l834, bronze, colossal, NPG 4309, 1835, SD	SD	*Potts* 1981 (2), 18 (repr); *Chantrey Ledgers*, 1991–92, 286; *Penny* 1992, 240 (repr)
491.	1835	James Watt Payment(s): £80	m	Institut de France, Paris Other versions: Lord Brougham, 1839 BMAG (inv P.80'83), marble, SD 1841		*Chantrey Ledgers*, 1991–92, 53, 159, 301, 324 (repr 26); *Silber* 1987, 24, cat 56
492.	1835	John, 1st Marquess of Camden Payment(s): £157 10s; pedestal £25 Drawing(s): NPG, London Model(s): Ashm, plaster	m	NPG, London, 5241	SD	*Chantrey Ledgers*, 1991–92, 254, 281; *Penny* 1992, 228 (repr)
493.	1835	King William IV Drawing(s): NPG, London	m	Goldsmiths' Hall, City of London Other versions: 11 identified	SD	*Graves* II, 1905–6, 42; *Harris, de Bellaigue, Millar* 1968, 184–5 (repr); *Ormond* 1973, 512; *Potts* 1981 (2), 14 (repr); *Chantrey Ledgers*, *passim; Penny* 1992, 249 (repr)
494.	1835	Sir John Nicholl Payment(s): £162 15s Drawing(s): NPG, London, several Model(s): Ashm, plaster	m	Merthyr Mawr, Glamorgan		*Chantrey Ledgers*, 1991–92, 277; *Penny* 1992, 240 (repr)
495.	1836	Arthur Henry Hallam Payment(s): £84	m	Trinity College, Cambridge, chapel	S	*Chantrey Ledgers*, 1991–92, 289
496.	1836	Colonel Seymour Bathurst Payment(s): £210 Model(s): Ashm, plaster	m	Cirencester Park, Glos	SD	*Chantrey Ledgers*, 1991–92, 289; *Penny* 1992, 227 (repr)
497.	1836	Dr William Henry MD Payment(s): £157 10s Model(s): Ashm, plaster	m	[Manchester Lit and Phil Soc]; destroyed		*Chantrey Ledgers*, 1991–92, 309; *Penny* 1992, 234–5 (repr)
498.	1837	Frederick-Augustus, Duke of York and Albany (from an original by Nollekens)	m	[Temple of Military Fame, Kew]; Buckingham Palace, London, RCIN 2061 2034 Other versions: Gov Art Coll (1954), nd, marble Herrenhausen Museum, Hanover, formerly Royal Palace	SD	*Harris, de Bellaigue, Millar* 1968, 185 (repr); *Chantrey Ledgers*, 1991–92, 298, 307; *Roberts* 2002, 139
499.	1837	Professor Horace Wilson Drawing(s): NPG, London 316a (143) Model(s): Ashm, plaster	m	[Exhib RA, London, 1286]; Asiatic Society of Bengal, Kolkata (Calcutta)		*Graves* II, 1905–6, 42; *Ormond* 1973, 517; *Chantrey Ledgers*, 1991–92, 303; *Penny* 1992, 249 (repr)
500.	1837	Sir Jeffrey Wyatville RA Payment(s): £157 10s Model(s): Ashm, plaster	m	Windsor Castle, private apartments	SD	*Graves* II, 1905–6, 42; *Potts* 1981 (3), 62 (repr 20); *Chantrey Ledgers*, 1991–92, 305 (repr 169); *Penny* 1992, 250 (repr)
501.	1838	Samuel Whitbread Payment(s): £200	m	Bedford General Hospital, south wing	SD	*Chantrey Ledgers*, 1991–92, 302
502.	1839	Dr William Mill DD Payment(s): £210 Drawing(s): NPG, London Model(s): Ashm, plaster	m	Asiatic Society of Bengal, Kolkata (Calcutta)		*Graves* II, 1905–6, 42; *Chantrey Ledgers*, 1991–92, 319; *Penny* 1992, 239 (repr)
503.	1839	John, 6th Duke of Bedford, after a bust by Nollekens and from life Payment(s): £200 exclusive of extras	m	Bedford General Hospital	SD	*Chantrey Ledgers*, 991–92, 320–1 (repr 174)
504.	1839	Robert, 1st Marquess of Westminster (†1845) Payment(s): £210 Drawing(s): NPG, London, several Model(s): Ashm, plaster	m	Eaton Hall, Cheshire		*Chantrey Ledgers*, 1991–92, 265–6; *Penny* 1992, 248 (repr)
505.	1839	Sir Benjamin Brodie FRS Drawing(s): NPG, London	m	Untraced		*Chantrey Ledgers*, 1991–92, 323
506.	1840	James Dunlop Payment(s): £157 10s Drawing(s): NPG, London, dated 26 July 1836 Model(s): Ashm, plaster	m	[Exhib RA, London 1841, 1327]; untraced		*Graves* II, 1905–6, 42; *Chantrey Ledgers*, 1991–92, 309–10; *Penny* 1992, 231 (repr)
507.	1840	Major-General Sir John Malcolm, model Drawing(s): NPG, London Model(s): Ashm, plaster		Not completed		*Chantrey Ledgers*, 1991–92, 325; *Penny* 1992, 238 (repr)
508.	1840	Mary Somerville Payment(s): £210 Drawing(s): NPG, London 316a (114–5) Model(s): Ashm, plaster	m	Royal Society, London	SD	*Graves* II, 1905–6, 42; *Potts* 1981 (2), 26–7 (repr); *Chantrey Ledgers*, 1991–92, 290–2 (repr 161); *Penny* 1992, 244 (repr); *Grove* 6, 457

509.	1839–1840	Queen Victoria Drawing(s): NPG, London, several Model(s): Ashm, plaster	m	Royal Coll, RCIN 31618, 1839 Other versions: Schloss Callenberg, Coburg, Germany, 1840 NPG, London (1716), 1841 Dunrobin Castle, Sutherland	SD	*Graves* II, 1905–6, 42; *Chantrey Ledgers*, 1991–92, 320, 324 (repr 176); *Ormond* 1973, 476, 478 (drawings repr 945, 946); *Potts* 1982 (2), 15 (repr); *Roberts* 2002, 145 (repr)
510.	1839–1840	Sir Charles Forbes Bt, MP Payment(s): £210 Drawing(s): NPG, London, several	m	[Exhib RA, London, 1840, 1200]; untraced		*Graves* II, 1905–6, 42; *Chantrey Ledgers*, 1991–92, 322
511.	1840	Sir Charles Mansfield Clarke Bt, MD Drawing(s): NPG, London, several Model(s): Ashm, plaster	m	[Exhib RA London, 1199]; Sotheby 12 Dec 1985, lot 320; untraced		*Graves* II, 1905–6, 42; *Chantrey Ledgers*, 1991–92, 292–3; *Penny* 1992, 229 (repr)
512.	1841	James Morrison MP Payment(s): 200 gns Model(s): Ashm, plaster		[coll Ian Grant]; untraced	SD	*Graves* II, 1905–6, 42; *Ormond* 1973, 326; *Chantrey Ledgers* 1991–92, 317; *Penny* 1992, 239 (repr)
513.	1837–1841	John Palmer Payment(s): £409 10s	m	Town Hall, Kolkata (Calcutta)		*Chantrey Ledgers*, 1991–92, 315
514.	1841	Joseph Neeld MP Payment(s): £210 Drawing(s): NPG, London (several) Model(s): Ashm, plaster	m	[Grittleton House, Wilts]; untraced Other versions: Neeld Hall, Chippenham, Wilts, unsigned Chippenham Town Hall, Wilts, SD 1839	SD	*Graves* II, 1905–6, 42; *Chantrey Ledgers*, 1991–92, 316, 323; *Penny* 1992, 239 (repr); *Grittleton Marbles* 1966, 7
515.	1841	William Strutt (co-sculptor: Henry Weekes) Model(s): Ashm, plaster	m	Derby Art Gall (1977)	SD	*Potts* 1981 (2), 27 (repr); *Chantrey Ledgers*, 1991–92, 304; *Penny* 1992, 245 (repr)
516.	1841	William, Viscount Melbourne Drawing(s): NPG, London, several, 313–316a (87), 1838 Model(s): Ashm, plaster	m	Windsor Castle RCIN 35433	SD	*Ormond* 1973, 313; *Chantrey Ledgers*, 1991–92, 323–4 (repr 175); *Penny* 1992, 238 (repr)
517.	nd	Allan (or Francis) Cunningham	p	SNPG, Edinburgh		*Gunnis* 1968, 95; *Ormond* 1973, 127
518.	nd	Charles Manners Sutton, Archbishop of Canterbury	p	Ashmolean		*Penny* 1992, 246 (repr)
519.	nd	J W Croker (†1857)	m	Athenaeum, London		*Chantrey Ledgers*, 1991–92, 336
520.	nd	Mountstuart Elphinstone, Governor of Bombay	p	Ashmolean		*Penny* 1992, 232 (repr)
521.	nd	'Mr Warp' Model(s): Ashm, plaster	m	Christie, 24 Sept 1987, lot 149; untraced	S	*Penny* 1992, 248 (repr)
522.	nd	Reginald Heber, Bishop of Calcutta	p	Ashmolean		*Penny* 1992, 234 (repr)
523.	nd	Richard, Marquess Wellesley	b	NGI 8151		*le Harivel* 1988, 556
524.	nd	Sir James Rivett Carnac	m	Asiatic Society, Mumbai (Bombay), (formerly Town Hall)		GPC

Chimneypieces

525.	*c*1830	With female figures in the jambs and shells in the frieze	m	Matfen Hall, Matfen, Northumbs		Pevsner, *Northumbs*, 1992, 386

Architectural Sculpture

526.	1815	4 dolphins for a fountain Payment(s): 10 gns	l	[for Mr Simson, engineer]; untraced		*Chantrey Ledgers*, 1991–92, 65
527.	1818	Altar dedicated to Peace (ordered by Charles Sutton, Archbishop of Canterbury) Payment(s): £131 17s	m	Untraced		*Chantrey Ledgers*, 1991–92, 98

Reliefs

528.	1816	Plenty, mezzo-relievo	s	[coll D Brammall, Sheffield, W R Yorks]; untraced		*Gunnis* 1968, 95
529.	1821	Sarah Brooke (?), portrait medallion in an elm frame	m	[coll Brooke family]; Sotheby, 11 Dec 1986, lot 186	SD	
530.	1820–1828	Hector and Andromache (companion to Penelope with the Bow of Ulysses) Payment(s): £2,100 with Penelope relief Model(s): Ashm, plaster	m	Woburn Abbey, Beds, sculpture gall	SD	*Graves* II, 1905–6, 41; *Chantrey Ledgers*, 1991–92, 148 (repr 90); *Penny* 1992, 225 (repr); *Yarrington* 2002, 30–43 (repr)
531.	1820–1828	Penelope with the Bow of Ulysses (companion to Hector and Andromache) Payment(s): £2,100 with Hector relief Model(s): Ashm, plaster	m	Woburn Abbey, Beds, sculpture gall	SD	*Graves* II, 1905–6, 41; *Chantrey Ledgers*, 1991–92, 148 (repr 89); *Penny* 1992, 225 (repr); *Yarrington* 2002, 30–43 (repr)
532.	1832	'Signing the Reform Bill'		Holkham Hall, Norfolk		*Gunnis* 1968, 95
533.	1834	The Holkham Woodcocks Model(s): Ashm, plaster	m	Holkham Hall, Norfolk	SD	*Potts* 1982 (2), 33 (repr); *Chantrey Ledgers*, 1991–92, 287 (repr 160); *Penny* 1992, 225 (repr)
534.	*c*1835	'Noli me tangere'		Magdalen College, Oxford, chapel, above the reredos		Pevsner, *Oxon*, 1974, 152
535.	1840	John, 1st Earl of Eldon, medallion (after the bronze medallion on his monument)		Law Soc, London Other versions: Bonham, London, 1 July 2003, lot 99		*Gunnis* 1968, 95
536.	1840	The signing of Magna Carta Payment(s): £300	m	Holkham Hall, Norfolk	S	*Chantrey Ledgers*, 1991–92, 304–5 (repr 177)
537.	1841	Lord Stowell, medallion		Law Soc, London		*Gunnis* 1968, 95
538.	nd	Queen Adelaide, medallion	s	Ashmolean		*Ormond* 1973, 7

CHAPLIN, Samuel fl 1768

He is mentioned in the will of **Michael Rysbrack**, dated 5 March 1768, as a 'carver in Oxford Chapel Court' (PROB 11/954/28). Rysbrack left £10 to Chaplin, and £10 to Chaplin's son, John, who was Rysbrack's godson. The Chaplins may have been related to William Chaplin, who was apprenticed as a mason to William Trymmer in October 1717.

Literary References: *Balderston* 2001, n19

Archival References: Masons' Co Freemen, fol 9

CHAPLING, James fl 1746

A Norwich carver, he signs a tablet with cherubs' heads and urns at Rackheath.

Literary References: *Gunnis* 1968, 96

Funerary Monuments

1.	†1746	Sir Horatio (†1730) and Lady Pettus	Rackheath, Norwich	S	Pevsner, *Norfolk: N-E & Norwich*, 1997, 642

CHAPMAN, Edward –1729

The son of Edward Chapman, stonemason and contractor, he married Margaret Wilcocks (or Wilcox). They both appear to have been of Warwickshire stock, though the family had settled in London. The Masons' Company 'search' records for 1696 state that he was then working with his father. Chapman's yard was in Red Lion Square and in 1706 he was employing **William Palmer** as an assistant.

He made chimneypieces for Burley-on-the-Hill, Rutland, the home of Lord Nottingham, between 1699 and 1705 (**4**). He also provided other mason's work, including a marble basin to the design of a 'Mr Lumley', perhaps **John Lumley of Northampton**. In his correspondence with Lord Nottingham, Chapman protested 'I was sober all times', presumably in response to an accusation of intemperance (*Finch* 1901, 1, 75). This was not Chapman's only dispute with a patron. On 11 May 1699 Lord Ashburnham wrote to his banker, Henry Hoare, asking him to 'chuse five marble chimney-pieces of different colour'd marble and the newest fashion of the dimensions mentioned in the drawings.' A second letter followed in August 1699, when Ashburnham requested of Hoare 'I trust you will be so kind to take the trouble of going . . . to one Chapman of whom I have bought fine marble chymney pieces with slabbs, coves, Hearth Stones etc. all ready to come down & be sett up here in the new built lodgings. Chapman is to have 42-02= on his delivery of the goods which I desire you to pay to him accordingly . . . I desire you see they be well packed as they ought to be & that the word Marble be written in great letters upon every box or parcel' (Ashburnham Letterbook ASH 842, p 269). Hoare followed his instructions and Lord Ashburnham wrote again 'In my passage by London to Sussex, I hope to have time to view the marble chimney pieces . . . they ought to be extremely fyne being valued soe excessively deare.' Ashburnham may not have found time to see them, but trustingly he wrote to Hoare: 'Mr Chapman shall be paid the forty pounds for the five marble chimney-pieces . . . as for the cases to pack them upp, I will be at that charge and for the workmen to sett them upp alsoe.' They were sent down to Great Park, Ampthill, but when they arrived it was discovered that they were not the ones Ashburnham had seen in London. A letter to a Mr Abraham Smythe, dated 3 November, expressed the patron's displeasure that Chapman had failed to send the specified chimneypieces, two large ones of dove for the library and chamber, a white-veined and a small one, and 'one large mixed marble'. Instead Chapman had sent 'three mixed pieces'. Justifiably, Ashburnham, having paid the craftsman, felt 'very unjustly & ill-used' and proposed to 'proceed against him' if things were not immediately made right (ASH 842, 317–8). Ashburnham also wrote to Hoare: 'I take myself to have been very unjustly and ill used in this matter, and if Chapman will not fairly change those that I bargained for, bought and paid for, I will immediately proceed against him at lawe and right myselfe that way if it be possible'. After this angry letter, Chapman sent the chimneypieces originally selected (**2**).

Edward Chapman was the father-in-law of **Francis Bird**. After the Jacobite rising of 1715 they were both obliged to register their estates as recusants. In his will, signed in 1727, Chapman described himself as a mason of St-Giles-in-the-Fields. He left his wife, Margaret, an annuity of £100 from the income on his leaseholds and tenements in the parish of St Andrew. A number of bequests were made to other family members including his daughter, Catherine. The residue of his considerable estate went to his daughter Hester Bird and her sculptor husband. This included a substantial property near Windsor.

Literary References: *Vertue* III, 49; *Rendel* 1972, 206; *Gunnis* 1968, 96; *Lord* 1986, 99; *Whinney* 1988, 448 n21

Archival References: Masons' Co, Court Books, MS 5304/2, fol 13v; GPC

Will: PROB 11/633 114r–115r

Statues

1.	1705	'Italian figures' Payment(s): £60		Chatsworth, Derbys	*Gunnis* 1968, 96

Chimneypieces

2.	1699	Five, coloured marble Payment(s): £40	m	[Ampthill House, Beds]; untraced	*Gunnis* 1968, 96; GPC
3.	1699–1705	Description unavailable Payment(s): £39 15s (with cost of Reigate stone)		[Winslow Hall, Bucks]; untraced	*Bolton and Hendry* 1940, 55
4.	1699–1705	Several, in dove and statuary marble Payment(s): £300 11s 6d	m	[Burley-on-the-Hill, Rutland]; untraced	*Finch* 1901, 72

CHAPMAN, John fl 1833

In 1833 he exhibited at the British Institution, giving his address as 18 Margaret Street, Spa Fields, London.

Miscellaneous

1.	1833	David with the head of Goliath	[Exhib BI, London, 550]; untraced	*Graves* 1875, 96

CHAPMAN, Joseph and Son, of Frome fl 1805–63

The firm was established about 1805 by Joseph Chapman I. He was succeeded in about 1840 by his son who considerably increased the family business. An advertisement in Cuzner's *Handbook* to Frome, 1866–7, described the younger Chapman, who had a 'marble and stone works' in Portway, as 'architect, architectural and monumental sculptor.' It added that Chapman had 'a collection of designs for monumental erections, from the simplest to the most elaborate, such as can scarcely be surpassed in any provincial town.'

Cuzner extolled the sculptor in the text and listed some of his 'exquisite' works (**11–14**). He described how Chapman had visited cemeteries in Europe and America in order to keep pace 'with the improved and improving taste of the age'. Monuments from his yard were sent to the Cape of Good Hope, India, the West Indies and New Zealand. Cuzner mentions a mural monument of Purbeck marble and mosaic design in Westminster Abbey, which has not been identified, and an altar monument in Ambleside, which is probably to be the one to Captain Lutwige (**9**).

Gunnis recorded several other tablets by the firm, which he described as 'not very exciting'. These included the monument to John Smith, which features a small obese putto sitting on an urn (**4**). In his entry for the firm Gunnis also took the opportunity to deliver a scathing judgement on Joseph Chapman III, an architect who 'utterly destroyed' in 1863 the 'magnificent and untouched example of a fifteenth-century manor-house' known as 'King Ina's Palace' at South Petherton, Somerset. Built by Sir Giles Daubeny in the reign of Henry VI, Chapman rebuilt it in 'Cockney Gothic' (*Gunnis* 1968, 97).

Literary References: *Cuzner* 1866–7, 137–8; *Gunnis* 1968, 97

Funerary Monuments

1.	?1806	John Parsons	Midsomer Norton, Somerset	S	*Gunnis* 1968, 97
2.	?1809	Thomas Taylor	Devizes, Wilts	S	*Gunnis* 1968, 97
3.	?1824	James Carpenter	Beckington, Wilts	S	*Gunnis* 1968, 97
4.	†1829	John Smith	Midsomer Norton, Somerset	S	Pevsner, *Somerset: N & Bristol*, 1958, 229; *Gunnis* 1968, 97
5.	1830	William Crumbleholme	Horningsham, Wilts	S	*Gunnis* 1968, 97
6.	?1832	Thomas Latimer	Mere, Wilts	S	*Gunnis* 1968, 97
7.	† to 1840	Edward Lawrence and family	St Denys, Warminster, Wilts	S	
8.	†1848	Thomas Hancock	St James, Poole, Dorset		Pevsner, *Dorset*, 1972, 319
9.	†1861	Captain Lutwidge	St Mary, Ambleside, Westmorland	S	
10.	nd	Captain Marrish, cross	[Great Elm, Somerset, churchyard (1866)]; untraced		*Cuzner* 1866–7, 138
11.	nd	Pooll family member	[Rode, Somerset (1866)]; untraced		*Cuzner* 1866–7, 138
12.	nd	Stancombe family members, wall-tablet 'of Early English design'	[Trowbridge, Somerset, cemetery (1866)]; untraced		*Cuzner* 1866–7, 138
13.	nd	The 'Nonconformist memorial'	[Rook Lane Chapel, Frome, Somerset (1866)]; untraced		*Cuzner* 1866–7, 138

Architectural Sculpture

14.	nd	Memorial cross	[Dissenters' Cemetery, Frome, Somerset (1866)]; untraced	*Cuzner* 1866–7, 138

CHARDINI, P J fl 1842–43

In 1842 and 1843 he showed statues, a medallion and busts at the Royal Academy, including a bust, *ad vivum*, of the King of Holland. His address was given as 8 Percy Street in 1842 and 14 Cleveland Street in 1843.

Statues

1.	1843	Albert, the Prince Consort (†1861), equestrian		[Exhib RA, London, 1495]; untraced	*Graves* II, 1905–6, 45
2.	1843	Queen Victoria, equestrian		[Exhib RA, London, 1486]; untraced	*Graves* II, 1905–6, 45; *Ormond* 1973, 484

Busts

3.	1842	King of Holland		[Exhib RA, London, 1343]; untraced	*Graves* II, 1905–6, 45
4.	1843	Arthur, 1st Duke of Wellington		[Exhib RA, London, 1506]; untraced	*Graves* II, 1905–6, 45
5.	1843	Innocence	m	[Exhib RA, London, 1479]; untraced	*Graves* II, 1905–6, 45
6.	1843	Juno	m	[Exhib RA, London, 1437]; untraced	*Graves* II, 1905–6, 45

Reliefs

7.	1842	'Lablanche', medallion		[Exhib RA, London, 1391]; untraced	*Graves* II, 1905–6, 45

CHARLES, William, of Nottingham fl 1720–63

His tablets are usually executed in the local slate and have well-carved armorial bearings. There are several examples in Nottinghamshire, including that to Henry Fawks which incorporates the winged hourglass motif (**1**).

Literary References: *Gunnis* 1968, 97; Pevsner, *Notts*, 1979, 143, 290, 364

Funerary Monuments

1.	†1730	Henry Fawks	sl	Stanford-on-Soar, Notts, churchyard	Pevsner, *Notts*, 1979, 335
2.	?1752	Rev John Wood	sl	Wilford, Notts	*Gunnis* 1968, 97
3.	?1755	Rev Henry Wood	sl	Wilford, Notts	*Gunnis* 1968, 97
4.	?1757	James Bryans	sl	Willoughby-on-the-Wolds, Notts, churchyard	*Gunnis* 1968, 97
5.	?1763	Ann Bonner, gravestone	sl	St Nicholas, Deptford, London, churchyard	*Gunnis* 1968, 97

CHARLTON, William, of Cambridge and King's Lynn fl 1760–62

In the *Ipswich Journal* of 17 May 1760, he advertised that he had taken a wharf and shop near Lady Bridge at Lynn Regis [King's Lynn] and that he could execute orders 'both in the ancient and modern taste, viz statuary, monuments, chimney-pieces, sconces, chandeliers, girandoles, etc.' Over two years later, on 27 December 1762, Charlton advertised in the *Cambridge Chronicle*. He described himself as a 'Carver & Mason' and gave his address as the 'Stone-yard in Trumpington St, Cambridge.' He added that he could perform 'all sorts of statuary monuments, chimney pieces and other ornaments in stone or wood, all in the ancient or modern taste' as well as supplying 'Busts & figures in Plaster of Paris, the late stock of the Italian in Cambridge.' His one known monument (**1**) is a large wall tablet in coloured marbles.

Literary References: *Gunnis* 1968, 97

Archival References: GPC

Funerary Monuments

1.	?1759	Mrs and Miss Meader	Littleport, Cambs	S	GPC

CHASE, John, of Titchfield fl 1795–1825

Presumably related to N Chase.

Funerary Monuments

1.	†1795	Edward Otto	Titchfield, Hants	S	
2.	†1825	Rev Alexander Radcliffe	Titchfield, Hants	S	

CHASE, N, of Titchfield

Funerary Monuments

1.	nd	Bratby family member	Hamble, Hants	S	Pevsner, *Hants & Isle of Wight*, 1967, 265

CHEERE, Sir Henry Bt 1703–81

Cheere ran a major business in monuments, statues and chimneypieces, many of them carved by assistants and sub-contractors working under his direction. His public life is perhaps the most unexpected aspect of his career, for he was the first sculptor fellow of the Society of Antiquaries, was knighted and later became a baronet.

He was born in Clapham, Surrey, in 1703, the son of a prosperous merchant, John Cheere, who was probably of Huguenot origins and took an active role in the local community, regularly attending vestry meetings in the parish church. His younger brother was the lead figure maker, **John Cheere**. Henry appears to have been educated at Westminster School. He married Helen Randall, a woman of limited education, who pre-deceased him, and they had two sons, the Rev William, who inherited his baronetcy, and died without issue in 1808, and Charles (†1799) whose surviving daughter married Charles Madryll, of Papworth Hall, Cambs and took the name and arms of Cheere after William's death. There were no direct descendants.

Henry was apprenticed to a member of the **Hartshorne** family, probably Robert I, in December 1718. By 1726 he had acquired two premises in St Margaret's Lane, Westminster, one of them a 'shop'. The location was convenient for the transport of stone and finished work by river and also for commissions destined for Westminster Abbey. Within a year he was collaborating on monuments with the Flemish sculptor, **Henry Scheemakers**, who introduced him to Continental modelling and carving techniques. Their most ambitious work, signed conspicuously by both sculptors, is the memorial to the Duke of Ancaster, which has an elegant life-sized effigy of a Roman general with cropped hair, set in a grand architectural frame (**6**). The partnership lasted 7 years, ceasing when Scheemakers left England in 1733.

By 1732, Cheere's business was expanding. He had three premises, two of them workshops or yards in St Margaret's Lane, and he was beginning to compete for commissions with the most sought-after sculptor in the metropolis, **Michael Rysbrack**. Rysbrack was in favour with Queen Caroline, and perhaps expected to win the contract for her statue sited at the entrance of the Queen's College, Oxford, together with figures emblematic of *Law*, *Physic* and *Poetry*. The commission went to Cheere (**98**), who also won several other orders for statues of patrons and founders of the University (**94, 96, 99**). Another coup was the statue of William III for the Bank of England (**95**), which could also have gone to Rysbrack on the strength of his much-publicised image of King William for Bristol. By the late 1730s Cheere had made connections with the Westminster Abbey authorities, he had carved details for the south-west tower (**140**) and provided the first of a series of major monuments (**20**). By 1740 he was sufficiently well-established to move into larger premises in Old Palace Yard and in 1743 he was appointed Carver to the Abbey. He was one of several sculptors who in 1744 provided a design and a model for the pediment of the London Mansion House, which he estimated would cost £450. The contract went to [Sir] **Robert Taylor**.

During the 1740s Cheere became increasingly involved in public affairs, the ladder to gentrification. He became principal vestryman at St Margaret, Westminster, and in 1742 was sworn a juryman for the parish. He served two terms as a director of the Westminster Fire Office in 1745 and 1746 and in 1749 became Controller of Duties for the Free Fish Market of Westminster. Other distinctions followed, including his appointment as a Justice of the Peace and his election to the Antiquaries in 1750.

These appointments gave Cheere valuable contacts and he spent much time in cultivating men of fashion, among them George Bubb Dodington. His larger memorials began to incorporate rococo elements: the Hardy (**25**) and John Conduitt (**26**) make use of small, asymmetrical drapery folds. The ambitious monument to the Earl of Kildare (**31**), sent to Dublin in 1746, was the most dramatic tableau to come out of the workshop. Cheere's attention was now beginning to focus on the middle-class market and he sent out increasing numbers of formulaic works, carved with delicate garlands, shells and cherubs' heads, clad in the polychrome marbles which became his trademark. These could be produced at a relatively modest cost by assistants, but they were nonetheless stylistically recognisable and formed an alternative to the mass-produced classicising monuments available from the workshops of Rysbrack and **Peter Scheemakers**. Despite increased delegation, their quality remained high and though different hands are evident in the carving of surface textures and draperies, a consistency in composition indicates that it was Cheere who usually provided the drawings and that he retained overall control.

He found a market too for pretty chimneypieces carved with bucolic scenes, often taken from Aesop's *Fables* and counted Lord Baltimore, an acolyte of Frederick, Prince of Wales, among his clients for these focal points in rococo interiors (**127**). He was paid on a number of occasions between 1738 and 1742 for chimneypieces at Ditchley Park, Oxon (**112–4, 118, 120–2**). The payments described him initially as a mason but by 1739 he was identified as a statuary on notes of hand from the 2nd Earl of Lichfield to Frances and Samuel Child. Among the large surviving number of chimneypiece designs are a number of restrained classical compositions, which were appropriated by the architect George Dance the Elder for five rooms on the principal floor of London's Mansion House, as well as the pretty colour-washed confections favoured by the Leicester House set.

Cheere was not a member of the St Martin's Lane Academy, but he had associations with leading members of the set who met at Slaughter's Coffee House, and in 1748, after the peace of Aix-la-Chapelle, he travelled to Calais with William Hogarth and the painters Thomas Hudson and Francis Hayman. After 4 or 5 weeks spent on the Continent he returned to London. The style of his work was not much affected by his first-hand exposure to

French art: the monument to Admiral Medley combines the familiar English formula of a portrait bust on a sarcophagus with rococo garlands of naturalistic shells and irregularly placed trophies (**50**). The de Sausmarez has a traditional portrait medallion and sarcophagus; the medallion is supported by asymmetrical *putti* and the inscribed pedestal is bordered by vigorous s-scrolls (**36**).

Cheere became one of the first artists to join the Society for the Encouragement of Arts, Manufacture and Commerce, founded in 1754. In 1755 he gave a paper arguing for a national academy of arts, intended to stimulate a demand for work by English artists and so increase national self-esteem. He recommended associates from several eminent City families, who were also his patrons, for membership of the Society, and took an active part in judging competitions.

In 1760, in his role as a vestryman, Cheere organised the team of craftsmen who assembled a temporary fountain at Westminster in celebration of George III's coronation. These included **William Jelfe** and John Cheere. He was knighted by the King that year after presenting the loyal address from the county of Middlesex. Six years later he received a baronetcy, perhaps as a reward for his loyalty to the Westminster political establishment. By then he had virtually retired from the business and in 1770, after completing an equestrian statue of the Duke of Cumberland which drew censure from Sir Joshua Reynolds for its use of modern dress (**100**), he sold the Westminster yards. Later that year his former apprentice, **Richard Hayward,** noted the arrival in Rome of Cheere and his two sons.

The names of 7 of his apprentices are recorded in the London Apprenticeship Records, two of whom gained independent reputations. **[Sir] Robert Taylor** began his indentures in 1732, later became a major country house architect, and like Cheere received a baronetcy in recognition of his contribution in the public sphere. Richard Hayward, who joined the workshop in 1742, clearly took a major role in the workshop, for £1,901 was paid to him from Cheere's bank account in 1746. The size of these sums suggests that Hayward was purchasing marbles as well as paying assistants and sub-contractors. He was a major purchaser at Cheere's posthumous auction. **William Collins,** who was either an apprentice or an assistant, was described by J T Smith as 'the greatest modeller of chimney-tablets of his day' and is likely to have been responsible for many of the distinctive chimney-surrounds sent out by the workshop. He was a beneficiary in Cheere's will. **William Powell** and **William Woodman II** were both employed as sub-contractors (**11, 16**). Cheere is also thought to have employed **Louis François Roubiliac** during the 1730s and 1740s as an assistant principally engaged in modelling. J T Smith believed it was Cheere who introduced Roubiliac to Jonathan Tyers, the proprietor of Vauxhall Pleasure Gardens, and who suggested that, since Tyers wanted a statue emblematic of music, he could not do better than have a statue of Handel in the guise of Apollo.

The sculptor amassed a fortune of over £100,000, partly by taking advantage of the expanding London market for funerary monuments, but also by making large investments in the property market. He left his elder son a number of houses in Parliament Street, Canon Row, Charing Cross, the Strand and Church Court. He died in Clapham on 21 July 1787 and was buried in the family vault at St Paul's, Clapham, where his brother John and his two sons in due course joined him.

In 1745 George Vertue (whose patriotism matched Cheere's) named Cheere with **Francis Bird,** Rysbrack and Roubiliac as practitioners whose output compared with anything being created on the Continent. Cheere's inclusion in this galaxy confirms that work of a consistently high standard was sent out under his name and endorses his talent for business organisation and quality control.

A considerable number of works have been attributed to Cheere, several of them illustrated in the Conway Library files (C Lib). Only convincingly-argued attributions have been included in the list below.

IR

Literary References: Reynolds, *Discourse* X, 1780, line 386; *Smith* 1828, II, 94, 313; Esdaile typescript, nd, 1; *Webb* 1957 (3), 115–70; *Webb* 1958 (2), 232–40, 274–8; *Carswell and Dralle* 1965, *passim*; *Girouard* 1966, 188–90, 227; *Gunnis* 1968, 97–99, 310; *Physick* 1969, 34; *Whinney* 1971, 63; *Colvin* V, 1973–76, 428–30; *Friedman and Clifford* 1974; *Stainton* 1983, 13, 20; *Rococo* 1984, F 10, 278–87; *Allan* 1984, 204–7; *Baker* 1986 (2), 143–60; *Whinney* 1988, 191–7; *Craske* 1992, 40–81; *Jeffery* 1993, 159; *Baker* 1995 (1), 90–108; *Bindman and Baker* 1995, *passim*; *Craske* 2000, 94–113; *Baker* 2000, *passim* (with attributions); *ODNB* (Baker and Craske); *Friedman* 2004, 96–7

Archival References: Bank acct, Hoare, 1736–1737, 1744–1747; Watch Rates, Old Palace Yard, WCA, E.362-368 (1740–46), E 369–377 (1746–52) E 481 (1777); lease of a tenement in St Margaret, Westminster to Cheere, 18 February 1736, WAM 65639; Ch W, St Margaret, Westminster, 1762, E 136, E 3293/5, 5–10; Dillon DIL I/p/4ai-o (Lichfield to Samuel Child); WFO, GCB, 343/75 (17 Oct 1745, 17 Oct 1746)

Will: PROB 11/1073 fol 95, proved 31 January 1781

Miscellaneous Drawings: Studies and designs for monuments, VAM 8933; chimneypieces and decorative details including chimneypiece designs for the Mansion House, VAM 8934 E28; 28 designs for chimneypieces, colour washed, VAM D.715 (1-28)-1887; misc designs by Cheere and others, VAM 4910; design for a wall-monument, VAM E.640-1949; designs for monuments by Cheere and others, VAM 93.H.32. Among these drawings are sketches, highly finished coloured designs and copy or trace drawings.

Auction Catalogues: Cheere 1770

Funerary Monuments

1.	†1725	Anna Borrett	Shoreham, Kent	S	C Lib (repr)
2.	†1727	Hammond (†1727) and Anthony Twyman (†1722) (co-sculptor: Henry Scheemakers)	Westbere, Kent	S	*Webb* 1957 (3), 119, 121 (repr)
3.	c1727	Mathew Humberston (†1709)	Humberston, Lincs		*Rococo* 1984, 299
4.	†1728	James Walsingham	Little Chesterford, Essex	S	
5.	1728	Robert Davies (†1728)	Mold, Flints	SD	*Whinney* 1988, 193
6.	1728	Robert, 1st Duke of Ancaster (†1723) (co-sculptor: Henry Scheemakers)	Edenham, Lincs	S	*Webb* 1957 (3), 119, 121 (repr); *Lord* 1986, 96–8 (repr); *Lord* 2002, 107–13
7.	1729	Anne Nanney	Llanfachreth, Merioneth		*CL*, 2 Jan 1964 (repr)
8.	†1731	Atheluston Owen	Towyn, Merioneth		*Gunnis* 1968, 98
9.	1732	Dean Henry Aldrich (†1710)	Christ Church Cathedral, Oxford		*Baker* 1986 (2), 145
10.	1733	Chambers family	St Paul, Clapham, London, churchyard		*Craske* 2000, 74

No.	Date	Subject	Location		References
11.	c1733	Lady Susannah Thomas (†1731) and her mother, Dame Dorothy (†1726) (designed by Thomas Archer) (co-sculptor: William Powell)	Hampton, Middx	S	*Craske* 1992, 96, 150–1 (repr)
12.	†1734	Dr Richard Willis, Bishop of Winchester Payment(s): £600 Drawing(s): VAM 8933.144	Winchester Cathedral, Hants	S	*Webb* 1958 (2), 274 (repr); *Whinney* 1988, 194
13.	1735	Lady Denton (†1733)	Hillesden, Bucks	S	*Craske* 1992, 320; Pevsner, *Bucks*, 1994, 399
14.	1733–1735	Lord Chief Justice Robert, 1st Lord Raymond (†1732) (designed by Westby Gill) Payment(s): £1,000 Drawing(s): VAM 8933.19	Abbots Langley, Herts	S	*London Evening Post*, 25 Oct. 1735; *Whinney* 1988, 195–7 (repr)
15.	post-1735	Peter Nepueu (†1658) Drawing(s): VAM 8933.10	Hougham, Kent		*Physick* 1974, 1068 (design repr)
16.	1732–1735	William, 2nd Viscount (†1728) and Gertrude, Viscountess Newhaven (†1732) (co-sculptor: William Woodman I)	Drayton Beauchamp, Bucks	S	*London Evening Post*, 7 March 1732; *Whinney* 1988, 251, 253–4 (repr)
17.	†1738	Mary, Marchioness of Carnarvon	Chandos Mausoleum, St Lawrence, Whitchurch, Middx		Pevsner, *London: N W*, 1991, 296
18.	†1738	Sir Thomas Crosse	St Margaret, Westminster, London		St Margaret Vestry Minutes, 23 June 1738; C Lib (repr)
19.	1738	Thomas Archer (†1743) (designed by Archer, drawing on Marcantonio Raimondo's engraving of two sibylls) Model(s): VAM A.11-1934, for left Virtue, clay	Hale, Hants		ATTRIB *Baker* 2000, 97 (repr); *Bilbey* 2002, 63; *ODNB*
20.	pre-1739	Dr Samuel Bradford, Bishop of Rochester and Dean of Westminster (†1731)	Westminster Abbey, London, north transept	S	WAM 1731; *Baker* 1986 (2), 159
21.	†1739	General Joseph Sabine	Tewin, Herts		Sabine Papers, Herts CRO, AHH/4/2
22.	†1739	John and Elizabeth (†1725) Borrett	Shoreham, Kent	S	*Webb* 1958 (2), 234, 240 (repr)
23.	post-1740	Bowater Vernon (†1735)	Hanbury, Worcs		ATTRIB *Baker* 1986 (2), 147–8 (repr); *ODNB*
24.	†1741	Dame Mary Fowler	St George, Esher, Surrey	S	Pevsner, *Surrey*, 1971, 221
25.	1738–1742	Admiral Sir Thomas Hardy (†1732)	Westminster Abbey, London, nave, west end		*FFB* 1738; *Rococo* 1984, 284 (repr)
26.	c1742	John Conduitt (†1737) Drawing(s): VAM 8933-1882, cartouche only	Westminster Abbey, London, nave, west end		FFB 1738; *Rococo* 1984, 284
27.	†1742	Thomas Churchman	St Giles, Norwich, Norfolk		Pevsner, *Norfolk: N-E & Norwich*, 1997, 236
28.	1740–1745	Edward Vernon	Hanbury, Worcs		*Baker* 2000, 79–82 (repr)
29.	1745	Sir William Pole Bt (†1741) Payment(s): £319 10s Drawing(s): VAM 8933.172, perhaps by R Hayward	Shute, Devon		*Gunnis* 1968, 97; *Webb* 1958 (2), 274–8 (repr)
30.	1740–1745	William Wither (†1733)	Wootton St Lawrence, Hants		*Baker* 2000, 80, 81, 103 (repr)
31.	1743–1746	Robert, 19th Earl of Kildare (†1743)	Christchurch Cathedral, Dublin	S	*Pool and Cash* 1780, 100 (repr); *Gunnis* 1961, 5–6 (repr); *Baker* 1986 (2), 151–2 (repr)
32.	†1746	Sir Abraham Shand and Ruth Shand (†1744)	Shoreham, Kent	S	
33.	By 1746	Sir John (†1741) and Lady Harpur Payment(s): £200	Calke, Derbys		*Baker* 2000, 75, 76 (repr)
34.	1746	Sir John Chardin (†1713) Drawing(s): VAM 8933.20, 21	Westminster Abbey, London, nave		*MacMichael* 1977, 17; *Craske* 1992, 72
35.	1746	Theobald, 1st Viscount Mayo (†1741) Drawing(s): VAM	[? Ballintobber, County Mayo]; untraced		*Potterton* 1975, 40
36.	†1747	Captain Philip de Sausmarez	[St Andrew, Plymouth, Hants]; Destroyed		*Craske* 1992, 71
37.	1747	Dame Magdalene de Carteret Drawing(s): VAM 4910.17	Town Church, St Helier, Jersey		ATTRIB *Rococo* 1984, 299 (design repr)
38.	†1748	Benet Swayne	St Martin, Salisbury, Wilts		*Craske* 1992, 120 (repr)
39.	1745–1748	Dr Hugh Boulter, Archbishop of Armagh (†1742) Drawing(s): by H Cheere, compiled by J Schnebellie, Soc Antiq MS 263; alternatives (?) by Sir Robert Taylor, TI, fols 36r, 53r, 122r, 136r and 137r	Westminster Abbey, London, north transept		FFB, 1745; *GM*, April 1748; *Rococo* 1984, 285 (design & monument repr); *ODNB*
40.	1748	Peregrine, 2nd Duke of Ancaster (†1742)	Edenham, Lincs		*London Evening Post*, 2 Aug 1748; *Bindman and Baker* 1995, 358–9
41.	c1748	Robert Butts, Bishop of Ely (†1747) Drawing(s): VAM 8933 14, 15	Ely Cathedral, Cambs		*Penny Evening Post*, 2 Aug 1748; *Baker* 2000, 75, 76 (repr)

42.	1748	Roger Owen (†1718) and his wife Catherine	Condover, Salop		VCH *Salop*, VIII, 1968, 55; *Baker* 1986 (2), 151–3 (repr); *ODNB*
43.	1749	Captain William Cust (†1747)	St Wulfram, Grantham, Lincs		*Craske* 1992, 23
44.	†1749	George, 2nd Baron Carpenter Drawing(s): VAM 4910.2	Owlesbury, Hants		ATTRIB *Craske* 1992, 47 (repr)
45.	pre-1749	Henry, 1st Earl of Uxbridge (†1743)	Hillingdon, Middx		ATTRIB *Baker* 1986 (2), 149–50 (repr)
46.	†1749	Lord Thomas Bertie Drawing(s): VAM 4910.10	St Nicholas, Chislehurst, Kent		*Physick* 1974, 1068 (design repr); *Baker* 1986 (2), 148; C Lib (repr)
47.	c1749	Samuel Tufnell (†1748) Drawing(s): VAM 4910.29	Pleshey, Essex		*Webb* 1958 (2), 274–8 (repr); *Physick* 1969, 40 (repr)
48.	1744–1749	Sir George Cooke	[Hayes, Middx?]; Sotheby, 12 Dec 2003		Sotheby cat, 12 Dec 2003, lot 223 (repr)
49.	†1749	Sir William Joliff MP	Pleshey, Essex		ATTRIB *Webb* 1958 (2), 274–8 (repr)
50.	1749	Vice-Admiral Henry Medley (†1747) Payment(s): £262.10; iron railings £6.14	York Minster, north choir aisle		*Friedman and Clifford*, 1974, no 8; *Aylmer* 1977, 453–5 (repr)
51.	post-1750	John Merick (†1749)	Norwood, Middx		*Craske* 2000 (2), 99
52.	c1750	Sir John Molesworth Bt (†1723) and his wife Jane (†1714)	Egloshayle, Cornwall		*Baker* 2000, 75, 76 (repr)
53.	1752	'3 monuments att Bradford', probably including William Swann, †1737, in Bradford Cathedral	Bradford, W R Yorks		*Ingram* 1955, 4
54.	c1752	Edward Atkyns (†1755)	Ketteringham, Norfolk		*Baker* (2), 1986, 158; *Craske* 1992, 125–6
55.	†1752	Henrietta Vernon	Hodnet, Salop		Heber Percy/Hodnet, Box 1/bdl. 16/1; *Craske* 1992, 106
56.	1752	Jeremiah and Mary (†1744) Hollins Drawing(s): VAM 4910.37	St John, Halifax, W R Yorks		*Friedman and Clifford* 1974, no 9
57.	†1752	John Scrope	Lewknor, Oxon		ATTRIB *Whinney* 1988, 240
58.	1752	Thomas Grimston (†1751)	Kilnwick in Beswick, E R Yorks		*Ingram* 1955, 2–3; Pevsner, *Yorks: E R & York*, 1995, 578
59.	1753	Amy (†1750) and Margaret (†1752) Gwyn and their married sister	Great Baddow, Essex		Pevsner, *Essex*, 1965, 192
60.	†1754	George, John (†1725) and Elizabeth (†1724) Durell	Town Church, St Helier, Jersey		*Craske* 1992, 71
61.	1754	John Hampden (†1643)	Great Hampden, Bucks		*Craske* 1992, 320; Pevsner, *Bucks*, 1994, 346; C Lib (repr)
62.	†1754	John, 1st Viscount Tyrconnel	Belton, Lincs	S	*Webb* 1958 (2), 278 (repr 24)
63.	1754	Lady Mary Wrey	Tawstock, Devon		*Baker* 1986 (2), 158
64.	c1755	Captain Philip de Sausmarez (†1747) Drawing(s): VAM 4910.25; two others, Sausmarez family poss	Westminster Abbey, London, nave		WAM (64); *Webb* 1958 (2), 239–40; *Physick* 1969, 122–3 (repr); *Baker* 1986 (2), 153–4 (repr)
65.	c1755	Sir Edmund Prideaux Bt (†1729) and his wife Anne (†1741) Drawing(s): VAM 8933.2	Westminster Abbey, London, nave		WAM (64); *Physick* 1969, 124–5 (repr); *Rococo* 1984, 285
66.	1756	Sir Edward Atkyns (†1755) and family members Drawing(s): two by Cheere sold Christie, 14 Dec. 1982, lot 104, repr.cat.	Westminster Abbey, London, south transept		FFB, 1756; *Rococo* 1984, 285; C Lib (repr)
67.	1755–1757	David Polhill (†1754) Payment(s): £600 Drawing(s): VAM 4910.41	Oxford, Kent		*Physick* 1969, 19, 126–7 (repr)
68.	†1757	Elizabeth Drake	Amersham, Bucks		*Penny* 1977 (1), 67 (repr)
69.	†1757	Jane Rodney	Old Alresford, Hants		*Robinson* 1978, 18–21 (repr); *Rococo* 1984, 278–9 (repr)
70.	1757–1758	Charles (†1755) and Martha (†1742) Polhill	Oxford, Kent	S	*Physick* 1969, 19
71.	†1758	Charles Apthorp	King's Chapel, Boston, USA	S	*Gunnis* 1968, 99 (repr IV)
72.	1758	Charles Hosier (†1750) and wife	Wicken, Northants		Pevsner, *Northants*, 1973, 462
73.	1759	Arthur, 1st Viscount Doneraile (†1727) Payment(s): £325	Doneraile, Co Cork		*Potterton* 1975, 40
74.	†1759	Captain Nicholas le Messurier	St Peter Port, Guernsey		C Lib (repr)
75.	1759	Lord Chief Justice Sir Dudley Ryder (†1756) Payment(s): £420 9s (Sandon Hall Accts)	St Wulfram, Grantham, Lincs		*Webb* 1958 (2), 278–9 (repr 23)
76.	1759	Lord Chief Justice Sir John Comyns (†1739)	Writtle, Essex	S	*Webb* 1958 (2), 277–8; *Baker* 1986 (2), 158
77.	1760	Admiral Sir Charles Molloy	Shadoxhurst, Kent		Pevsner, *W Kent and the Weald*, 1969, 519 (repr 72); *Craske* 1992, 71 (repr)
78.	†1760	Dr Thomas Cheyney	Winchester Cathedral, Hants		ATTRIB *Craske* 1992, 41 (repr)

No.	Date	Subject		Location		Bibliography
79.	c1760	General James Wolfe, model only (monument by Joseph Wilton)		[Cheere sale, 26 March 1770, lot 75]; untraced		*Bindman and Baker* 1995, 336
80.	post-1760	Rev John Maryon		White Rothing, Essex		*Craske* 1992, 71
81.	1757–1761	Cholmley Turner (†1757) Payment(s): £262		Kirkleatham, N R Yorks, Mausoleum		*Friedman and Clifford* 1974, no 51; *Whinney* 1988, 457
82.	†1761	Jeremiah Lewis		Westminster Abbey, London, west walk of cloisters		FFB, 1766
83.	1761	Joseph Wilcocks, Bishop of Rochester and Dean of Westminster (†1756) Model(s): Cheere's sale, March 1770		Westminster Abbey, London, nave		*Whinney* 1988, 239, 457 n23; *Craske* 1992, 41 (repr)
84.	†1761	Lady Jane Coke		Sunbury, Middx		*Craske* 1992, 47
85.	†1761	Sir Crisp Gascoyne		Barking, Essex		*Baker* 1986 (2), 154
86.	1762	John Musgrave (†1762) and daughter (†1762)		St Margaret, Westminster, London		*Craske* 2000 (2), 98
87.	1747–1763	Barbara, Frances and another married sister of Sir Samuel Newman		Fifehead Magdalene, Dorset		*Craske* 2000 (2), 106
88.	†1763	Lucy Skipwith		Metheringham, Glos		*Craske* 1992, 47
89.	1763	Sir Griffith Boynton (†1761) Payment(s): £134 1s 8d		Burton Agnes, E R Yorks		NAL MSL/1969/4075; Pevsner, *Yorks: E R & York*, 1995, 366; *Mulcahy* 2006, 57–8 (repr)
90.	1766	Rev W Sandford (?design only) Drawing(s): VAM 4910.21		Monument untraced		
91.	nd	Cornet St Ledger		[Intended for Westminster Abbey, London]; untraced		*Craske* 2000, 98
92.	nd	Philip Durell		[St Andrew, Plymouth, Hants]; destroyed		*Craske* 1992, 71
93.	nd	Rev William Wynne Drawing(s): VAM 8933.28		Mold, Flintshire		
Statues						
94.	1732–1734	Christopher Codrington Payment(s): £148 9s 6d for statue and pedestal	m	All Souls College, Oxford		*Webb* 1958 (2), 236; *Baker* 1986 (2), 145–6; *Whinney* 1988, 194, 197 (repr)
95.	1733–1734	King William III Payment(s): £284	m	Bank of England, City of London, previously pay hall, now by Bartholomew Lane vestibule	S	*Ward-Jackson* 2003, 25–6 (repr)
96.	1735	King Charles II Payment(s): £120	s	Sheldonian Theatre, Oxford, previously above north door, now basement store		*Webb* 1958, (2) 236; *Gibson* 1997 (1), 374
97.	1735	King William III, on a Doric column Payment(s): £42	s	[Hartwell House, Bucks, column in central allée]; destroyed		*Friedman* 1984, 184, 292
98.	1734–1735	Queen Caroline, with figures of Law, Physic and Poetry Payment(s): £139 5s		The Queen's College, Oxford, main entrance		QCA, Building Accts, fol 34 (24 July 1734); *Northampton Mercury*, 27 Oct 1735; *Baker* 1986 (2), 145–6; *Whinney* 1988, 197
99.	1737–1738	Archbishop Sheldon and the Duke of Ormonde Payment(s): £223 7s 10d for two		Sheldonian Theatre, Oxford		*Gunnis* 1968, 97; *Whinney* 1988, 197
100.	1770	William Augustus, Duke of Cumberland	l	[Cavendish Square, London]; destroyed		*Gunnis* 1968, 97; *Yarrington* 1988, 42; *Blackwood* 1989, 346 (repr)
101.	nd	Vulcan and Venus, seated figures, statuettes	m	[Sir Robert Ainslie sale, Christie, 10 March 1809, 40 gns]; sold Cheffin's, Cambridge, 12 Feb 2004, lot 474; untraced		*Gunnis* 1968, 98
Busts						
102.	1736	Giles Bennet	p	All Souls College, Oxford, Codrington Library (above cornice)		ATTRIB *Webb* 1958 (2), 236; *Friedman and Clifford* 1974, Appendix B
103.	1736	Nicholas Hawksmoor	p	All Souls College, Oxford, buttery Other versions: several plaster copies, including one at Castle Howard, NR Yorks		*Baker* 2000, 80, 81, 102, 103 (repr)
104.	c1738	Archbishop William Laud (†1641)		Clarendon Building, Oxford		Pevsner, *Oxon*, 1974, 257
105.	c1738	Edward Hyde, Ist Earl of Clarendon (†1674)	tc	Clarendon Building, Oxford		*Walker* 1961, 16
106.	c1738	George Streatfeild	tc	Chiddingstone, Kent, Mausoleum		*Baker* 2000, 82 (repr)
107.	1738–1741	George Pitt MP	m	[Coll W Moreton Pitt; Stowe House sale, 1848, lot 751]; VAM A.7-1981		ATTRIB *Rococo* 1984, 288 (repr); *Bilbey* 2002, 61–2 (repr); *ODNB*
108.	1742	Three, unidentified subjects		[coll Lord Folkestone]; untraced		*Gunnis* 1968, 98
109.	1747	William Augustus, Duke of Cumberland	l	Belton House, Lincs, Bel / M /44 Other versions: Windsor Castle (attrib) VAM A.12-1947		*Gunnis* 1968, 98; *Penny* 1992, vol III, 158; *Bilbey* 2002, 64 (repr); *ODNB*
Chimneypieces						
110.	1731	Stone, carved, and two marble slabs		[Moulsham Hall, Essex]; untraced		Mildmay Account-book, Hants RO 15m 50/31; *Edwards* 1977, 42
111.	1734	With caryatids	m	Goldsmiths' Hall, City of London, court room		*Baker* 1986 (2), 157 n 42
112.	1739	Description unavailable Payment(s): £100		Ditchley Park, Oxon, 'the little room within the great room'		*Webb* 1958 (1), 278; *Gunnis* 1968, 97

No.	Date	Description		Location	Reference
113.	1739	With Bacchic mask flanked by foliate ornament on cross member and richly carved consoles with masks Payment(s): £96		Ditchley Park, Oxon, great room (white drawing room)	*Webb* 1958 (1), 278; *Cornforth* 1988 (2) 82, 84 (repr)
114.	1739	'with Bacchus Head in the Larger Dineing Room' Payment(s): £105 10s 6d plus casing at £2 11s 4d		Ditchley Park, Oxon	Dillon DIL I/P/3bd
115.	*c*1740	Description unavailable		Wallington, Northumbs	*Gunnis* 1968, 97
116.	*c*1740	With carved panel of two children as a shepherd and shepherdess Drawing(s): VAM D.715 (23)–1887	m	[Lambton Castle, Co Durham]; Biddick Hall, Durham	*Physick* 1969, 128–9 (repr)
117.	*c*1740	With carved panel of two children as shepherd and shepherdess	m	[43/44 Parliament St, Westminster, London]; untraced	*Physick* 1969, 128–9 (repr)
118.	1740	With garlanded cross member and caryatid supports	m	Ditchley Park, Oxon, blue drawing room	*Webb* 1958 (1), 278; *Cornforth* 1988 (2), 83 (repr)
119.	1741–1742	Several Payment(s): £800		Longford Castle, Wilts	*Gunnis* 1968, 97
120.	1743	Description unavailable Payment(s): £84		Ditchley Park, Oxon, tapestry room	*Webb* 1958 (1), 278; *Cornforth* 1988 (2), 84
121.	pre-1743	With head of Mercury, flanked by garlands Payment(s): £100	m	Ditchley Park, Oxon, velvet room (state bedroom)	*Webb* 1958 (1), 278; *Cornforth* 1988 (2), 84 (repr)
122.	1743	'with People Terms' Payment(s): £100		Ditchley Park, Oxon	Dillon DIL I/p/sbf
123.	*c*1745	Description unavailable		Wallington Hall, Northumbs	Pevsner, *Northumbs*, 1992, 602
124.	1747	Description unavailable Payment(s): £54		Kimbolton Castle, Huntingdon, drawing room	*Gunnis* 1968, 97
125.	1746, 1748	Two Payment(s): £189; £91		Kirtlington Park, Oxon	GPC
126.	1749	Description unavailable Payment(s): £26 16s 6d		[Worcester Lodge, Badminton]; Badminton House, Glos	Beaufort Accounts, 1749
127.	1740–1750	Rococo, with cartouche relief of a dog and foliage	m	[Woodcote Park, Surrey]; untraced	*Girouard* 1966, 61 (repr)
128.	pre-1750	With carving imitating a cave of icicles		[La Trappe, Prince Frederick's house at twickenham, Middx]; untraced	*Jones* 1961, 8, 20 n 15
129.	?*c*1750	With central tablet of boys and to either side, reliefs of goats on a grassy tussock Drawing(s): VAM D.715-1887, 27	m	Langley Park, Norfolk	*Jevons* 1960, 3288 (repr); *Baker* 1986 (2), 157
130.	1752	Five or more		[Kilnwick Hall, E R Yorks]; Hall Gareth, Goodmanham, E R Yorks and Reighton Hall, E R Yorks	*Craske* 2000 (2), 106 (repr)
131.	1752	Of Siena and statuary marble		[Kilnwick Hall, E R Yorks]; untraced	*Ingram* 1955, 2–6
132.	1749–1752	With central relief of children skating, flanked by carvings of a bear and a beaver; two others Drawing(s): VAM D. 715 (13)-1887		Picton Castle, Pembrokes, dining room, boudoir and hall	*Girouard* 1966, 188 (repr); *Physick* 1969, 128–9 (repr)
133.	*c*1753	Of coloured marbles		Saltram, Devon, morning room	Pevsner, *Devon*, 1989, 712
134.	1755	Three Payment(s): £96 13s		Grimsthorpe Castle, Lincs	*Baker* 1986 (2), 148, n 17
135.	1764	Description unavailable		Grimsthorpe Castle, Lincs	*Baker* 1986 (2), 148, n 17
136.	nd	Description unavailable		[John Trotter, Soho, London]; untraced	*Gunnis* 1968, 98
137.	nd	Description unavailable		30 Grosvenor Square, ground floor	LMA 57/1/MB/4SF/0372
138.	nd	Several Drawing(s): VAM D 715-1887, Music Room		West Wycombe Park, Bucks, dining room, music room and perhaps others	
139.	nd	Two, one with term supports with a garland of delicate floral ornamen		New Hailes, Midlothian, dining room, drawing room	*Pearson* 1991, 47

Architectural Sculpture

No.	Date	Description		Location	Reference
140.	1734–1744	Decorative details for south-west tower (designed by Nicholas Hawksmoor) Payment(s): £448 19s 4d		Westminster Abbey, London	WAM 35351, 18 Dec 1734; *ODNB*; *Friedman* 2004, 20
141.	1744	Mansion House pediment, London (design only, pediment by Sir Robert Taylor) Payment(s): estimate £400		Untraced	*Vertue* III, 122; *Jeffery* 1993, 45, 81
142.	*c*1745	Britannia	s	Bank of England, City of London, Lothbury Court	ATTRIB *Ward-Jackson* 2003, 239–42 (repr)
143.	1750	'Carving done to Two Gothic Doors etc'		Westminster Abbey, London, Islip Chapel	WAM 46770
144.	1766	Vestal Virgin, Urania		[Temple of Apollo, Stourhead, Wilts, façade]; untraced	*Fulton* 2001, repr 47 a,b

Miscellaneous

No.	Date	Description		Location	Reference
145.	1728	Unspecified work Payment(s): £23 19s		[For the Duke of Kent]; untraced	Hoare's Customer Ledger, 1725–1728, vol I, fols 318, 460
146.	1735	Unspecified work, possibly a pedestal for a statue of Marcus Aurelius Payment(s): 'Mr Cheere Stonemason on account £50; Mr Henry Cheere Stonemason in full £37.0.6'		[Wilton House, Wilts]; untraced	Household Accounts; *Webb* 1958 (1), 278

CHEERE, John 1709–87

John Cheere ran a thriving business for 50 years at Hyde Park Corner and dominated the market for high quality lead figures during the 1740s and 1750s. He supplied plaster statues, statuettes and busts as integral parts of parade room schemes and grand interiors and was one of the first to experiment with bronzing techniques for plaster busts.

He was the younger son of John and Mary Cheere of Clapham who were probably of French Huguenot origin, and was baptised in Clapham on 12 January 1709. His elder brother was the sculptor **Sir Henry Cheere.** John's first wife, Theodosia Maria, died in 1767 'of a broken heart for the death of her father and only son' (*GM* 1767, 280) and in 1768 he married Mary Wilmot of Clapham, who outlived him. They apparently had no children, for his nephews Charles Cheere and the Rev Sir William Cheere were the principal beneficiaries in his will.

At least one of his kinsmen was a haberdasher and John's name appeared in the Apprenticeship Books in August 1711, when he was indented to another haberdasher, Henry Crofts. He must have had training as a sculptor, perhaps in Henry's workshop and evidently acquired a sound knowledge of casting and mould-making techniques.

In 1737, Henry and John seem to have leased a property together from Anthony 'Noast' in Portugal Row, Piccadilly. Other sculptors in this growing centre for the trade included **Thomas Carter I, William Collins, Richard Dickinson** and **Thomas Manning. Andrew Carpenter** had ceased producing lead figures the previous year and it seems likely that Cheere acquired some of his early stock from Carpenter's sale, for, like Carpenter, he later marketed figures of a *Blackamoor with a Sundial* (**9**), the *Borghese Gladiator* (**6**) and *Diana with her Stag* (**78**). After Manning's death in 1747 John Cheere took over two of his yards.

His stock of lead subjects included figures after the antique, versions of 17th-century classical subjects at Versailles and some adaptations from the work of leading English contemporaries, particularly **Peter Scheemakers** (**17, 72, 89**) and **Michael Rysbrack** (**17, 50**). Since the leads were piece-moulded, Cheere could assemble parts in new configurations, for instance the figure of *Time* with a dial for Blair Castle (**126**), adapted from **John Nost I**'s *Indian* at Melbourne Hall, Derbys.

Cheere's first recorded commission came to a disappointing conclusion. A lead equestrian figure of William III on a 'curious' Portland stone pedestal (4) was commissioned by the householders for St James's Square, London, at a reported cost of 300 guineas. On 7 March 1739 *Read's Weekly Journal* stated that the figure was 'standing at his Yard', but it was never installed. Meanwhile Cheere caught the attention of powerful patrons creating extensive landscape gardens. In the late 1730s two colossal statues were dispatched to Lord Carlisle at Castle Howard, a *Borghese Gladiator* (**6**) and one of Cheere's bespoke items, a *Dancing Faun* (7), 'cast 'from a moddle made on purpose' (Castle Howard J14/28/21). At a similar period, Henry, Duke of Kent (†1739), who had planted an avenue celebrating the Glorious Revolution of 1688 at Wrest Park, obtained a statue of its instigator, King William III, derived from Henry Cheere's statue of the King at the Bank of England (4).

Cheere came to the attention of his most loyal early patron, the 2nd Duke of Atholl, before 1740, when lead figures forming the first of eight major orders were shipped north to Blair Castle (**125**). The client was evidently confident of Cheere's ability to work in another medium for the next shipment, billed in 1742, comprised seventeen plaster busts, largely of classical and modern Men of Letters, Cheere's first known series of library heads (**83**). The sculptor also sent up ten plaster statues and groups (**11**) with advice on their maintenance: 'they should be painted over carefully with Flake White and Turpentine Oile when they are set up . . . and a little Drying Oile'. Any parts broken during unpacking might be repaired with 'Comon Glew' (Cheere bills, bundle 55).

The business expanded considerably from the mid-1740s: in 1746, the year of the Battle of Culloden, Cheere sent to Ireland a statue of the hated victor, William Augustus, Duke of Cumberland (**14**). This was intended for St Stephen's Green, Dublin, but discretion led to its erection in a less conspicuous site, at Parsonstown, King's County (*General Advertiser*, 17 October 1746). In 1749 he opened an account with Drummond's Bank and in 1750 he completed the commission that established his pre-eminence as a supplier of library busts, a series of twenty-four distinguished Fellows of All Souls' College for the Codrington Library, Oxford (**90**). That year he also provided the celebrated *River God* for Stourhead (**21**), one of his most costly garden figures, a bespoke commission, never duplicated, for which he charged £98. In 1752 he was paid £38 for a statue of *Mars* for Hampton Court Palace (**26**).

Like any successful practioner in the luxury trades, Cheere kept abreast of stylistic trends and he responded to the rococo taste for naturalism by extending his range of garden figures to include *commedia dell'arte* and other rustic figures. The Duke of Atholl was a client once more. In 1753 his purchases included a gamekeeper 'painted in proper coulers' (**27**), sent with instructions that it should be washed carefully every two years and oiled with linseed. Two years later, ten bucolic subjects and six *commedia* figures (**40**) were sent up to Scotland to create a festive atmosphere in gardens evoking in miniature the public pleasure grounds of London.

Cheere's business in garden figures was at its height in the late 1750s when an order of daunting size came in from Portugal, probably through the recommendation of Dean Joseph Wilcocks, former Chaplain to the British Factory in Lisbon and an associate of of Henry Cheere. This was for over 90 separate statues and figure groups for the gardens of the Royal Palace at Queluz (**45**), which were being landscaped by King Pedro III. The execution of such an order was beyond the capabilities of any of his rivals, but seems to have posed no difficulty for Cheere; the order was dispatched in three shipments of 233 in 1755 and 1757. He received a prompt payment of £871 17s 1d for part of the order.

His yards, peopled with an increasingly eclectic range of near-life-size figures in white, gilt or polychrome paint was constituting something of a tourist attraction. An Irish clergyman visiting in 1761 was 'introduced to an Assembly of gods and Goddesses, Juno, Minerva, Venus de Medici, Jupiter, Mars, Neptune and many Rural Deities Pan & Frisking Satyrs with an Infinite Multitude of Meer Dancers, Haymakers, Gladiators, Wrestlers, Huntsman & Fowlers, also Eagles, Vulturs, Hawks, Kites, Ostrich, peacocks, Lions, Leopards, tygers' (*Journals of Visits to England in 1761 and 1762*, BL Add MSS 27951, 16 inset).

The demand for Cheere's rococo garden figures dwindled in the early 1760s with changing tastes in garden design and the sculptor seems to have been anxious about declining profits. His postscripts to bills for statues submitted to

Atholl in 1761 (**54**) and to Lord Coventry at Croome Court in 1763 (**63**) emphasize that he charged 'your Lordship . . . not a shilling more than if a merchant had them' (Croome F60/13). The tone sounds defensive.

Cheere then changed orientation and faced a new demand, for less familiar classically inspired sculpture to decorate façades and parade rooms, taken from lead casts after unfamiliar Antique statues and busts. These were probably from moulds commissioned in Rome during the early 1750s by the architect Matthew Brettingham the Younger and acquired by Cheere soon after 1760. These figures appeared on the exterior both of the Temple of Apollo (**118**) and the Pantheon at Stourhead (**119**), as well as on Robert Adam's exteriors at Kedleston (**120, 121**) and very likely at Saltram (**123**), whilst suites of plaster figures, notable for their fine detail, were introduced into the entrance hall at Bowood (**61**) and the Gallery at Croome Court (**70**). Cheere was also prepared to provide a maintenance service for his plaster figures: in 1756 Nathaniel Curzon was charged £1.16s for having two statues cleaned and polished in the workshop, and in 1779 the Earl of Coventry paid 8s to have 12 busts and a statue in his Piccadilly house cleaned, an annual event. On one occasion Cheere's men went down to Croome Court to clean and repair sculpture (**63**).

Despite his prolific output, Cheere did not need a large or highly paid workforce and probably took on casual assistants like **John Deare**, who provided several models for him, when the need arose. Casting techniques were easily learnt and wages in this trade were low by comparison with stone carving. Of his five known apprentices and assistants, two later started independent businesses. **James Hoskins**, who was taken apprentice by Cheere in 1747, became 'moulder and caster in plaster' at the newly founded Royal Academy in 1769 and in 1774 formed a partnership with another former apprentice, **Benjamin Grant**. They supplied plaster casts to the firm of Wedgwood and Bentley. The others, of whom nothing is known, were John Fulford, Richard Breach and John Candy, all listed as Cheere's apprentices in the *London Evening Post* on 10–12 December 1751 when they testified to the efficacy of a cure for William Collins's ulcerous leg.

Cheere died a wealthy man and was buried in his brother's vault in Clapham. His profits had been converted into leases and freeholds of 15 properties in the City and Westminster and he left cash bequests of over £5,000 of which £900 was earmarked for charitable causes. Charles Cheere inherited the entire contents of the yards, shop and showrooms in Piccadilly and offered the Royal Academy the choice of his uncle's casts. They selected a St Susanna. The residue went to auction in 1788 and were bought by 'a man from the Borough [of Southwark]'. At a second sale in 1812, the brewer, Samuel Whitbread, bought 20 statues for £975, 15 of which went to his gardens at Southill, Beds (**77**). A copy of Cheere's statue of Shakespeare, commissioned by David Garrick for the Jubilee of 1769, was presented by Whitbread to the Theatre Royal, Drury Lane (**72**).

Cheere's works were largely derivative, depending on models by other sculptors, but he in turn gave an impetus to the ceramics trade, who reproduced his more popular figures as statuettes (**50, 56**). His response to market trends and his attention to quality made him the most successful of the lead-figure men and brought a new refinement to the genre.

Only convincingly-argued attributions have been included in the list below. See also **William Cheere.**

Moira Fulton/IR

Literary References: *GM* 1768, 349; *Smith* II, 1828, 285; *Webb* 1951 (3), 54–56; *Webb* 1957 (3), 115–9; *Webb* 1958 (2), 232–40; *Phillips* 1964, 76–7, 271; *Gunnis* 1968, 99–100, 123; *Clifford and Friedman* 1974; *Avery* 1974, 551–3; *Kenworthy-Browne* 1983, 44; *Rococo* 1984, E6; *Cruft* 1984, 285–301; *Afonso and Delaforce* 1986, 16, 17, 36; *Davis* 1991, 31–2, 52–61, 370 n156; *Clifford* 1992, 40, 58–9, 65; *Kenworthy-Browne* 1993 248–52; *Craske* 1992, 32; *Fulton* 2001; *Fulton* 2003, 21–39

Archival References: Blair Castle, misc tradesmen's accounts, bundle 55, Cheere bills (*Fulton* 2001, appendix A 7–14); Croome, F60/13 (*Fulton* 2001, appendix A, 15–19); WCA PR, St George, Hanover Square, November 1737, WCA, C 127; Hoare Private Accounts 1734–49, 1750–66; Walton/Dunn Accts Burton C, 1764; GPC

Wills: PROB 11/1155 fol 314 (*Fulton* 2001, appendix F); Henry Cheere's will, PROB 11, 1073

Miscellaneous Drawings: *Hercules*, sketch, Burton Constable 1609

Auction Catalogue: Cheere 1788

Artist's impression of Cheere's yard (?): William Hogarth, *An Analysis of Beauty*, 1753, pl 1 (with illustrations of Venus de' Medici, Belvedere Antinous, Farnese Hercules, Apollo Belvedere, Sphinx)

Funerary Monuments					
1.	†1711	Deborah Gibbons	S	St Peter Vere, Jamaica	
2.	†1733	James Lawes	S	St Andrew, Halfway Tree, Jamaica	*Coutu* 1997, 77–9 (repr)
Statues					
3.	?1762	St Susanna, after François Duquesnoy	p	Stourhead, Wilts, Pantheon Other versions: Easton Neston, Northants, lead RA, London, plaster	*Fulton* 2001, 36 (repr 65a)
4.	by 1739	King William III (after Sir H Cheere's statue, Bank of England)	l	Wrest Park, Beds Other versions: for St James's Square, London; untraced	ATTRIB *Fulton* 2001, 32 (repr 55 a, c)
5.	c1740	Bacchus	l	[Kinmount, Dumfries]; Waddeson Manor, Bucks	
6.	c1740	Borghese Gladiator Payment(s): 14 gns	l	Castle Howard, N R Yorks Other versions: Hopetoun House, West Lothian, 1752, destroyed Burton Agnes Hall, E R Yorks	Castle Howard archives, J14/28/21; *Hopetoun Papers*, Hopetoun House, Box 3, bundle 5; *Fulton* 2001, 8, 12, 52 (repr 27b); *Fulton* 2003, 33 (repr); *Mulcahy* 2006, 51
7.	pre-1740	Dancing Faun, on a Portland stone base (bespoke figure) Payment(s): 17 gns	l	Castle Howard, N R Yorks	Castle Howard archives, J14/28/21; *Davis* 1991, 43; *Fulton* 2001, 8, 12, 52, Appendix 1, 52 (repr 27a)
8.	1740	Two Sphinxes and two gladiators Payment(s): £45 3s	l	[Newhailes, East Lothian]; untraced	*Davis* 1991, 55, 371n, 111, citing Newhailes archives

9.	1741	Blackamoor with a sundial (after John Nost I) Payment(s): £8 18s	l	Okeover Hall, Staffs, principal front		*Davis* 1991, 49 (repr); GPC
10.	1742	Two dogs, gilded and painted Payment(s): 7 gns plus 15s for painting	l	Blair Castle, Perths		*Fulton* 2001, Appendix A 8
11.	1742	Vestal virgin with an urn, Saturn with child, Leda with the swan, Amphitrite with dolphin and lobster, Hercules and Hydra, Faun with the tigerskin, Venus de' Medici, Callipygian Venus; four seasons (in marble), statuettes Payment(s): 12s each	p	Blair Castle, Perths		*Fulton* 2001, Appendix A 9
12.	1743	Farnese Hercules Payment(s): 25 gns	l	Blair Castle, Perths		*Fulton* 2001, Appendix A 10; *Fulton* 2003, 24 (repr)
13.	1745	Apollo and Diana Payment(s): £51 5s (with packing cases)		Stourhead, Wilts		Hoare Private Accounts 1734–49, 1 May 1745
14.	1746	William Augustus, Duke of Cumberland, crowned with laurels, on a Doric column	l	[Parsonstown, King's County, now Birr, Co Offaly]; Birr Museum, Co Offaly (head only)		*Cambridge Journal & Weekly Flying Post*, 18 Oct 1746; *Hill* 1998, 72 (repr); *Fulton* 2003, 24, 38 n 27
15.	1748	Sphinxes	l	Chiswick House, London Other versions: Castle Hill, Devon Syon House, Middx Compton Verney, Oxon Anglesey Abbey, Cambs Newhailes, East Lothian West Wycombe, Bucks Saltram, Devon Goodwood, Sussex Hopetoun House, West Lothian, two (£32 2s)		*Davis* 1991, 55–57, 95, 100 (repr); *Penny* 1992, vol III, 97' *Fulton* 2001, 8, 31; *Fulton* 2003, 29
16.	1748	Unidentified figure Payment(s): £37		[for Henry Hoare]; untraced		Hoare Private Accounts, 1734–49, 24 June 1748
17.	1749	10 statuettes, Shakespeare (after P Scheemakers), Homer, Spenser, Pope, Milton, Inigo Jones, Newton, Locke, Rubens and Van Dyck (after M Rysbrack) (all later reproduced in ceramic bodies or lead)	pb	[Kirkleatham Hall, N R Yorks]; Castle Museum, York, on loan YCAG	SD	*Friedman and Clifford* 1974, nos 36, 45, 52, 54, 55, 65, 67, 68, 72, 74 (8 repr); *Rococo* 1984, S28
18.	c1749	Alexander Pope, statuette	l	VAM A.4-1955 Other versions: York City Art Galls		ATTRIB *Bilbey* 2002, 67
19.	c1749	Edmund Spenser, statuette		VAM A.3-1955		ATTRIB *Bilbey* 2002, 66 (repr)
20.	1750	Britannia Payment(s): £18 9s		[London Assurance Office]; untraced		GPC
21.	1750	River God (bespoke) Payment(s): £98	l	Stourhead, Wilts, grotto		*Friedman and Clifford* 1974, 9; *Davis* 1991, 50, 52 (repr, colour repr 15); *Fulton* 2003, 29–30, 35 (repr)
22.	1751	'A head cast and finished for a figure of King George I in hard metal'		[Horse Armoury, Tower of London]; untraced		Ordnance Declared Accounts, TNA, A.o.1 and 160/164
23.	1751	Hercules, statuette Payment(s): £51 5s	p	Stourhead, Wilts	SD	*Friedman and Clifford* 1974, no 30 (repr 1); Hoare Partnership Ledger, 1742–51 f 195
24.	1751	King George II, 'in Armour richly gilt'	l	St Helier, Jersey, Channel Islands, marketplace (now Royal Square)		*General Advertiser*, 8 April 1751; *Legouix* 1975, 278–851 *Fulton* 2001, 33, 44 n 104, Appendix E, (repr 25a, 57a and b; *Fulton* 2003, 25 (repr)
25.	post-1751	King William III (adapted from the sculptor's George II, Jersey)	l	[Hoghton Hall, Lancs]; private coll, USA		ATTRIB *Weaver* 1909, 149–50; *Fulton* 2001, 44 (repr 25b)
26.	1752	Mars, large statue on a Portland stone plinth Payment(s): **£38 with carriage**, charged with the model and painted surface	l	Hampton Court Palace, Middx		TNA AOI/2461/187; *Fulton* 2001, 30, Appendix A 25 (repr 44)
27.	1753	'Gamekeeper made in the best manner and painted in proper Coulers', 'Mercury made in ye best and strongest Manner'	l	[Blair Castle, Perths]; untraced		*Fulton* 2001, Appendix A 11
28.	1753	Robert Gordon Payment(s): £73 18s 6d Model(s): Robert Gordon's College, Aberdeen, clay	m	Robert Gordon's College, Aberdeen (niche over south entrance)		ATTRIB *Caledonian Mercury*, 14 Aug 1753; *Pearson* 1991, 47, 48 (repr); *Fulton* 2001, 33–4 (59 a–c)
29.	by 1754	Archbishop John Tillotson, statuette (stock item)		No example traced		*Friedman and Clifford* 1974, no 105

No.	Date	Subject	Material	Location		Sources
30.	1754	Ceres	p	Maister House, Hull, E R Yorks, staircase hall niche		*Friedman and Clifford* 1974, no 20; *Fulton* 2001, 36 (repr 64)
31.	by 1754	Geoffrey Chaucer (stock item)		No example traced		*Friedman and Clifford* 1974, no 80
32.	by 1754	Horace, statuette (stock item)		No example traced		*Friedman and Clifford* 1974, no 89
33.	by 1754	John Dryden, statuette (stock item)		No example traced		*Friedman and Clifford* 1974, no 85
34.	by 1754	Robert Boyle, statuette (stock item)		No example traced		*Friedman and Clifford* 1974, no 77
35.	by 1754	Socrates, statuette (stock item)		No example traced		*Friedman and Clifford* 1974, no 103
36.	1754	Two, unidentified subjects, one from an original model		[Kilnwick Hall, Kilnwick-on-the-Wolds, E R Yorks]; untraced		ERAO, DDGR/42/4/71; *Fulton* 2001, 8, Appendix A 2
37.	1754	Unidentified figure Payment(s): £185		Stourhead, Wilts		Hoare Private Accounts 1750–66, 25 Jan 1754
38.	1754	Unidentified figure Payment(s): £18 5s		Untraced		Hoare Private Accounts, 1752–78, 26 Jan 1764
39.	by 1754	Virgil, statuette (stock item)		No example traced		*Friedman and Clifford* 1974, no 110
40.	1755	Male and female haymakers, sailor and his girl, Dutch skaters (male and female), gardener and girl with bird's nest, fiddler and bagpiper, Harlequin, Columbine, Pierrot, highland girl, Pantaloon and 'Herliquin woman', Bacchus, Pomona, Mercury	l	Blair Castle, Perths		*Fulton* 2001, Appendix A 12
41.	?c1756	Harlequin and Columbine	l	[Wrest Park, Beds, orangery]; destroyed		*Weaver* 1909, 27; *Fulton* 2001, 29–30
42.	post-1756	Nymph of the Grotto	l	Stourhead, Wilts, Grotto Other versions: ex Southill, perhaps the figure now at West Wycombe, Bucks		ATTRIB *Fulton* 2001, 27–8 (repr 31b)
43.	1756	Several, unidentified	p	[Boreham Hall, Essex]; untraced		Essex CRO D/DDc.118; *Gunnis* 1968, 99
44.	?c1756	Venus and Adonis, Diana and Endymion, abduction of Helen, Aeneas and Anchises, on lead plinths Payment(s): *Helen* **£100**		[coll Mr Brooke (?) of Southwark]; Wrest Park, Beds		ATTRIB *Webb* 1951 (3), 54–5; *Davis* 1991, 53–4 (repr); *Grey Memoirs*, 1846, 82–5; *Fulton* 2001, 26, 29, 47n19 (repr); *Fulton* 2003, 25 (Diana repr), 37 (Venus and Adonis repr)
45.	1755–1757	Approximately 90 figures and groups including Neptune and nymphs fountain, Nereid fountain, Adonis, Diana, Mars and Minerva, Meleager and Atalanta, Aeneas and Anchises, Vertumnus and Pomona, Samson slaying the Philistine, Ariadne and Bacchus, Venus and Adonis, four seasons, the rape of Proserpine, Farnese Hercules	l	Royal Palace, Queluz, Portugal (some lost)		*Afonso and Delaforce* 1986, *passim*; *Fulton* 2001, 15, 18 (repr); WMF appeal pamphlet, Oct 2003; *Delaforce* 2002, *passim*; *Fulton* 2003, 24 (Samson repr), 25 (Meleager repr), 36 (Venus and Adonis repr); *Fulton* 2004, 102–3 (Diana repr)
46.	1757	King George II, on a column (replacing a statue of King William III by Sir Henry Cheere) Payment(s): 150 gns	l	Hartwell House, Bucks		Pevsner, *Bucks*, 1994, 374; GPC
47.	1753–1757	King William III, equestrian, gilt (perhaps designed by Sir Henry Cheere)	l	[Petersfield House, Hants, coll Sir William Jolliffe]; Petersfield, Hants, Square		*Cambridge Journal and Flying Post Weekly*, 2 June 1753; *Webb* 1958 (2), 278; *Fulton* 2001, 14, 33 (repr 58c); GPC
48.	1755–1757	The Olympian courtship (or Meleager offering Atalanta the head of the Calydonian Boar) (identical to the group at Queluz)	l	[Copped Hall, Essex]; Anglesey Abbey, Cambs, NT.AA/M.204	SD	Pevsner, *Cambs*, 1970, 293
49.	1759	Augusta and Flora (after Farnese Flora) Payment(s): Flora: 8 gns	l	Longford Castle, Wilts (Flora only) Other versions: Southill, Beds		*Whinney* 1988, 241; *Davis* 1991, 110; *Fulton* 2001, 38 (Southill version repr)
50.	post-1759	Farnese Flora, statuette, after M Rysbrack (reproduced in porcelain by Bow factory)	pb	Stourhead, Wilts	S	*Friedman and Clifford* 1974, no 33 (repr 2)
51.	1757–1759	Frederick, Prince of Wales, equestrian Payment(s): £173 9s	l	[Hartwell House, gardens to south west of house]; Hartwell House, Bucks, principal front (1989)		VAM (NAL) 11.RC.G10; Bucks RO D/Le/D2/37; *Fulton* 2001, 10, 34, Appendix A 3
52.	1760	Triton boy, for the refreshment stand fountain celebrating George III's accession (temporary structure)		[Parish of St Margaret, Westminster]; destroyed		*Craske* 1992, 68–9; *Friedman* 2004, 96–7 (repr 81)
53.	c1760	Youthful satyr (after the Antique figure supplied to Holkham Hall)	l	Seago Antiques (1991)		*Davis* 1991, 57–8, 64 (repr)

54.	1761	Apollo, Diana, Bacchus, Flora Payment(s): £37 16s	l	[Blair Castle, Perths]; untraced		*Fulton* 2001, Appendix A 14; *Fulton* 2003, 32
55.	1762	Demosthenes (bespoke)	p	Burton Constable Hall, E R Yorks, great hall niche, acc 962		*Friedman and Clifford* 1974, 39; *Fulton* 2001, 38 (repr 71a-c); *Fulton* 2003, 28; *Mulcahy* 2006, 12 (repr)
56.	c1762	Demosthenes, statuette Drawing(s): Sketch, Burton Constable 1595 (1762), pencil and ink	pb	Burton Constable Hall, E R Yorks, acc 966 Other versions: reproduced in Staffs earthenware	S	*Friedman and Clifford* 1974, nos 38, 40; *Fulton* 2003, 27, 28 (design repr); *Mulcahy* 2006, 12 (repr)
57.	1762	Farnese Hercules, statuette Payment(s): £1 11s 6d	pb	Burton Constable Hall, E R Yorks, staircase hall	SD	*Friedman and Clifford* 1974, no 30; *Mulcahy* 2006, 18–19 (repr)
58.	1762	Hercules with Cerberus (bespoke)	p	Burton Constable Hall, E R Yorks, great hall niche, acc 963		*Friedman and Clifford* 1974, 39; *Fulton* 2001, 38 (repr 70a-c); *Fulton* 2003, 28; *Mulcahy* 2006, 13 (repr)
59.	1762	Meleager and others Payment(s): £23 15s with cases	p	Stourhead, Wilts, Pantheon Other versions: Easton Neston, Northants, lead		Hoare Private Accounts, 1750–66, 12 Nov 1762; *Friedman and Clifford* 1974, nos 90, 95; *Fulton* 2001, 10, 36 (repr 65b), Appendix A 5
60.	1762	Mercury Payment(s): £4 14s 6d		[Burton Constable Hall, E R Yorks]; untraced		ERAO, tin trunk DDCC 145/2, Chichester Constable papers; *Fulton* 2001, Appendix A 20
61.	1762–1763	Apollo, Callipygian Venus, Mercury, Venus de' Medici, Livia Augusta, Capitoline Flora, Ceres (largely stock figures) Payment(s): Livia, Flora, Ceres 10gns; two Venuses and Mercury, 8 gns	p	[Bowood, Wilts, entrance hall]; untraced		*Bolton* I, 1922, 214; *Friedman and Clifford* 1974, Appendix E
62.	1763	Farnese Flora, statuette Payment(s): £1 13s 6d	pb	Burton Constable Hall, E R Yorks, staircase hall		*Mulcahy* 2006, 18–19 (repr)
63.	1763	Flora and Ceres Payment(s): £53 1s 1d	l	[Croome Court, Worcs, 'Leasose Greenhouse']; untraced Other versions: Flora, ex Audley End, 1783, destroyed		Croome Court archives F60/13; *Fulton* 2001, 13, Appendix A 15 (repr 6, 8b, 8c)
64.	1764	A fox and goose 'painted like life'	l	Untraced		SRO, CS 181/11/19; *Pearson* 1991, 46
65.	c1765	Lion and lioness, statuettes	pb	Burton Constable Hall, E R Yorks, staircase hall Other versions: Heaton Hall, Manchester, Lancs, large lead Castle Hill, Devon, large lead Anglesey Abbey, Cambs, large lead Quenby Hall, Leics, large lead		*Friedman and Clifford* 1974, 92; *Davis* 1991, 35, 71, 91, 94 (repr)
66.	c1765	Livia Augusta Payment(s): 10 gns	p	Burton Constable Hall, E R Yorks, staircase hall, acc 1102		ERAO, tin trunk DDCC /2/51, Chichester Constable papers; *Fulton* 2001, 8, 38, Appendix A 22 (repr 69)
67.	1765	Several, unidentified Payment(s): £153 2s		Stourhead, Wilts		Hoare Private Accounts, 1750–66, 1765
68.	1765	Unidentified work Payment(s): £80		Stourhead, Wilts		Hoare Private Accounts, 1750–66, 12 June 1765
69.	1765–1766	Flora 'after the Antique Drapery Flora neat finished & polish'd' Payment(s): £14 9s 5d with a bust of Sappho Model(s): plaster, Burton Constable, acc 1099	m	Burton Constable Hall, E R Yorks, staircase hall, acc 1101	S	Walton/Dunn Accts, Burton C, ERAO DDCC/20A/6 and 2/52; Audley End Papers, Essex RO, D/DY A41/6; *Friedman and Clifford* 1974, no 33; *Fulton* 2001, 38, Appendix A 21, A 22 (repr 68)
70.	1767	Draped figures of Capitoline Flora, Isis, Camillus, Ganymede, Vesta and Urania and perhaps others Payment(s): £80 17s 5d with cases, iron cramps and a bill for repairing Flora	p	[Croome Court, Worcs, Gallery niches]; dispersed: Flora and Isis at LA County Museum, Mercury at Kenwood House, London Other versions: Isis, c 1765, Stourhead, Wilts		Croome Court archives F60/33; *Nornan-Wilcox* 1965, 14–31; *Fulton* 2001, 13, Appendix A 16 (repr 66); Fulton 2003, 32 (Isis at Stourhead repr)
71.	1768	Seven mythological subjects	l	Longford Castle, Wilts		*Gunnis* 1968, 99
72.	1769	William Shakespeare, after P Scheemakers, commissioned and donated by David Garrick	l	Town Hall, Stratford-upon-Avon, Warks, external niche Other versions: Theatre Royal, Drury Lane, London, over entrance reproduced in porcelain at Derby factory		*Webb* 1951 (3), 55; *Fulton* 2001, 26, 34 (repr 61); *Noszlopy* 2003, 71–2 (repr)
73.	1773	Sphinxes	l	Blenheim Palace, Oxon, the bridge		William Chambers's Letters-Book, BL Ad MS 41133, fols 98, 106, 108
74.	1778	4 sphinxes (bespoke; charged with the mould) Payment(s): £31 each	l	Somerset House, London, parapet		TNA AOI/2495/414; *Colvin* V 1973–6, 467; *Fulton* 2001, Appendix A 25

No.	Date	Subject		Location		References
75.	nd	Apollo	l	[Copped Hall, Essex]; Anglesey Abbey, Cambs		C Lib (repr)
76.	nd	Augusta	p	[Probably 29 Piccadilly, London]; untraced		Croome Court archives F60/33B; *Fulton* 2001, appendix A 18
77.	nd	Ceres, Minerva, Farnese Flora, Samson slaying the Philistine (after Giambologna), two of priests, Winter (after Girardon) Isis, Apollino, Rape of Proserpine, Diana and four others	l	[Cheere's estate, bt Samuel Whitbread 1812 (£975)]; private coll		*Webb* 1951 (3), 55 (repr 78–80); *Whinney* 1988, 241 (repr); *Fulton* 2001, 30 (repr 48a,b)
78.	nd	Diana with her stag		Hillam Hall, Pontefract, W R Yorks Other versions: Easton Neston, Northants Anglesey Abbey, Cambs		Pevsner, *Yorks: W R*, 1967, 632; C Lib (repr)
79.	nd	Mercury (from Lord Bateman's version), Sleeping Nymph, Sleeping Cleopatra/Ariadne, Faun/Satyr and others		[Cheere's estate, bt Samuel Whitbread 1812]; untraced		*Webb* 1951 (3), 54
80.	nd	Shepherd and shepherdess	l	North Mymms, Herts Other versions: Anglesey Abbey, Cambs		*Fulton* 2001 (repr 17a, d; 18 a-c, 19)
81.	nd	Vesta and ?Urania (Vesta identical to Croome Court Vesta)		[Bostock Hall, Middlewich, Cheshire]; LACM		*Norman-Wilcox* 1965, 14–32
82.	nd	William Augustus, Duke of Cumberland, statuette		Royal Coll, RCIN 35324	S	
Busts						
83.	1742	Cicero, Homer, Seneca, Horace, Aristotle, Plato, Newton, Milton, Swift, Dryden, Pope, Shakespeare, Vestal Virgin, Pomona, Madonna, Bacchus, two boys	p	Blair Castle, Perths		*Fulton* 2001, Appendix A 9
84.	1742	Eight, including Brutus and Seneca		[Wotton House, Surrey]; untraced		*Gunnis* 1968, 99, citing Evelyn archives
85.	1743	Eight	p	[Moulsham Hall, Essex]; untraced		*Gunnis* 1968, 99; *Edwards* 1977, 64
86.	1743	James, 2nd Duke of Atholl, 'hard metal on a marble neck', bronzed Payment(s): 7 gns plus 2 gns for gold bronzing	l	Blair Castle, Perths		*Pearson* 1991, 52 (repr)
87.	?c1745	Ben Jonson, William Shakespeare, John Milton	p	Malmesbury House, Salisbury, Wilts, staircase Other versions: Gilmore House, Clapham Common, London (Shakespeare and Milton)		*Friedman and Clifford* 1974, nos 18, 91; *Cavanagh* forthcoming 2007 (Wandsworth)
88.	1749	Five, unidentified subjects Payment(s): £9 6s		[Kilnwick Hall, Kilnwick-on-the-Wolds, E R Yorks]; untraced		*Friedman and Clifford* 1974, no 24
89.	1749	Matthew Prior (after A Coysevox), John Dryden (after P Scheemakers), William Congreve, Joseph Addison, Sir Francis Bacon (after L-F Roubiliac), Dr Samuel Clarke, Dean Swift, Cicero, Horace (Prior, Congreve and Bacon later reproduced in ceramic bodies)	pb	[Kirkleatham Hall, N R Yorks; presented by the Kirkleatham Museum]; York Castle Museum, on loan to YCAG		*Friedman and Clifford* 1974, nos 56, 57, 60, 61, 62, 71 (all repr); *Rococo* 1984, 300
90.	1749–1750	24 fellows of All Souls, with 25 companion vases Payment(s): £195 15s	pb	All Souls College, Oxford, Codrington Library, cornice		*Webb* 1958 (2), 236; *Friedman and Clifford* 1974, no 22, Appendix B; *Friedman* 1984, 240, 319
91.	c1750	Dr William Henry Salmon (probably after a model by Sir Henry Cheere)	l	VAM A.19-1921		ATTRIB *Bilbey* 2002, 64–5 (repr)
92.	c1750	Mary Salmon (probably after a model by Sir Henry Cheere)	l	VAM A.20-1921		ATTRIB *Bilbey* 2002, 65 (repr)
93.	1752	Homer and Sappho and perhaps seven others	pb	Felbrigg Hall, Norfolk, dining room		*Rococo* 1984, M11; *Maddison* 2001, 51
94.	1753	Unidentified subjects	p	[Henry Hoare's houses, Clapham and Barnes]; untraced		*Gunnis* 1968, 99 citing archives, Hoare's Bank
95.	c1754	Cicero, Horace, Seneca (stock items)	p	Temple Newsam House (LMG), library		*Friedman and Clifford* 1974, 41, 43, 44, Appendix I; *Leeds* 1966, 3 (repr)
96.	1754	Several Payment(s): £18 5s		[Henry Hoare's home at Barnes]; untraced		Hoare Private Accounts 1750–66, 25 Jan 1754
97.	pre-1756	Cornelia, Geta, Plautilla, Zingara, Cicero, Augustus, Livia, Seneca	p	[Red Hall, Winestead, E R Yorks]; (coll Nicholas Hildyard)		*Friedman and Clifford* 1974, nos 16, 82, 88, 99, 111
98.	1757	Venus, Zingara		[Sir Nathaniel Curzon's London house]; untraced		*Fulton* 2001, Appendix A 24
99.	1759	Several, unidentified subjects, on brackets Payment(s): £7 12s		[Uppark, West Sussex, staircase hall]; destroyed		*Uppark* 1999, 74
100.	1762	Faustina, Antinous (stock items) Payment(s): 4 gns		[Bowood, Wilts]; untraced		*Bolton* I, 1922, 214; *Friedman and Clifford* 1974, Appendix E; GPC

101.	1762	Mercury Payment(s): £4 14s		[Burton Constable Hall, E R Yorks]; untraced	Constable Accts, ERAO Tin Trunk DDCC145/2
102.	1762	Sir Isaac Newton (after L-F Roubiliac) and William Shakespeare Payment(s): 2 gns each	p	[Fairfax House, Castlegate, York, on brackets in staircase hall]; untraced Other versions: Newton: YCBA B 1977.14.5	Fairfax Papers, North Yorks CRO, ZDV (F) mic 1132/9519; *Stratton*, 1920, xxviii, 43 (pls XCVIII, XCIX, fig 37); *Friedman and Clifford* 1974, nos 21, 97, 102
103.	1763	Seneca Payment(s): £1 13s 6d	p	[Burton Constable Hall, E R Yorks]; untraced	Constable Accounts, ERAO, Tin Trunk DDCC145/2
104.	1765	Antoninus Pius Payment(s): 2 gns	p	Burton Constable Hall, E R Yorks, great hall mantelpiece, acc 965 Other versions: Bowood, Wilts	Constable Papers ERAO, DDCC/2/51; *Friedman and Clifford* 1974, no 26; *Fulton* 2001, 8, Appendix A 22; Mulcahy 2006, 13 (repr)
105.	1765	Sappho Payment(s): £14 9s 5d with a statue of Flora	p	Burton Constable Hall, E R Yorks, acc 964 Other versions: formerly at Red Hall, Winestead, E R Yorks; untraced	Walton/Dunn Accts, Burton C, 1764, ERAO DDCC20A/6; *Friedman and Clifford* 1974, no 101; *Mulcahy* 2006, 12–13 (repr)
106.	1765	Seneca Payment(s): 4s 6d	p	[Burton Constable Hall, E R Yorks]; untraced	ERAO, tin trunk, Chichester Constable papers; *Fulton* 2001, 8, 38, Appendix A 21
107.	pre-1768	Cicero, Socrates, Virgil, Homer, Horace, Seneca, Sappho, Marcus Aurelius, Vestal Virgin, Apollo, Antinous, Caracalla	p	[Probably 29 Piccadilly, London, coll Earl of Coventry]; untraced	Croome Court archives F60/33C; *Fulton* 2001, appendix A17, A 18
108.	1774	Aristotle, Shakespeare, Plato, Homer Payment(s): 10s 6d each	p	[for Josiah Wedgwood and Richard Bentley]; Wedgwood Museum, Barlaston, Staffs, acc 4615	Wedgwood/J Cheere L1/33, Cheere acct, 24 Feb 1774; *Friedman and Clifford* 1974, no 76, Appendix G
109.	1775	Five	p	[Wotton House, Surrey]; untraced	*Gunnis* 1968, 99 citing Evelyn archives
110.	pre-1780	Sir Isaac Newton, John Locke, John Milton and John Dryden (Newton after Rysbrack's Conduitt bust) Payment(s): £104	pb	West Wycombe Park, Bucks, music room	*Keynes* nd, 30
111.	pre-1780	Sir Isaac Newton, John Milton, Joseph Addison, Alexander Pope and Socrates	p	West Wycombe Park, Bucks, library	*Keynes* nd, 31
112.	nd	Portrait of a man, perhaps William Hogarth	l	VAM A 62-1926	ATTRIB *Bilbey* 2002, 67
113.	nd	Several, unidentified subjects	p	Arniston House, Midlothian, library	*Pearson* 1991, 48
Chimneypieces					
114.	1748	Several, including one with sunburst		Kirtlington Park, Oxon, saloon and unidentified rooms	*Gunnis* 1968, 100
Architectural Sculpture					
115.	1742	Obelisk carved with the Atholl crest, coronet, star and three Manx legs Drawing(s): Blair Castle Charter Room, bundle 55	s	Blair Castle, Perths on an eminence	*Fulton* 2001, Appendix A 9
116.	1758	Two pineapples, plus the expense of buying the fruit and making the pattern and moulds, set on Portland stone plinths ('work done by order of' Michael Henry Spang) Payment(s): £10 16s including cases	l	Kedleston Hall, Derbys	*Fulton* 2001, 8, Appendix A 24
117.	1759	Two wyverns Payment(s): £48 5s	l	[coll Trevor, Bishop of Durham]; Glynde Place, Sussex, gatepiers	Pevsner, *Sussex*, 1965, 510
118.	1766	Ceres, Pomona, Minerva, Vestal, Mercury, Apollino, Urania, Bacchus, Callipygian Venus Payment(s): £233 2s 11d	l	[Stourhead, Wilts, Temple of Apollo]; Stourhead, Wilts, formerly Temple of Apollo, now portico and terrace	Hoare Private Accounts, 1752–78; *Fulton* 2001, 30, Appendix A 5; *Fulton* 2003, 34 (Bacchus repr)
119.	1766	Vestal Virgin, Urania, Uffizi Mercury	l	[Pantheon, Stourhead, Wilts, façade]; untraced	*Fulton* 2001 (repr 47 a,b)
120.	?1767	Flora with a garland, Bacchus with vines and perhaps others	l	Kedleston, Derbys, south front niches	*Fulton* 2001, Appendix A 23
121.	1773	Bacchante, two Muses and a Vestal	l	Kedleston, Derbys, north front	*Kedleston* 1998, 5, 10 (repr); *Fulton* 2001, 9, 30, Appendix A 23
122.	1774	Large, 'neatly finish'd' relief Payment(s): 10 gns	p	[Stourhead, Wilts]; untraced	Wilts RO 383.4; *Fulton* 2001, Appendix A 5
123.	nd	Antinous, Vestal Virgin, Isis, Mercury	l	Saltram House, Devon, façade	ATTRIB *Fulton* 2001, 30 (repr 49a, b)
Reliefs					
124.	nd	Sir Robert Hildyard	p	[Red Hall, Winestead, E R Yorks]; Flintham Hall, Newark, Lincs	*Friedman and Clifford* 1974, no 16

Miscellaneous

125.	1740	Coat of arms (from a model made by Cheere), large Diana the Huntress on a Portland stone pedestal, group of boys and statues of Apollo, Flora and Ceres Payment(s): £94 18s 6d	l	[Blair Castle, Perths]; Flora and Ceres still in situ; Diana destroyed	*Fulton* 2001, Appendix A 7 (repr 9 a-d)
126.	1743	Statue of Time for a dial, statue of Fame gilt, 80 cut letters, and two flower pots Payment(s): £68 8s 4d		Blair Castle, Perths	*Davis* 1991, 50; *Fulton* 2001, Appendix A 9, A 10; *Fulton* 2003, 24 (Time repr)
127.	1747	Two sphinxes, busts &c Payment(s): £55 1s		Stourhead, Wilts	Hoare Private Accounts, 1734–49, 11 July 1747
128.	1747–1748	Busts of John Milton and John Dryden and small statues of Hercules, Milton and Dryden; bust of a Vestal Virgin, a statue of Shakespeare 'from the original'; five brackets		[Alscot Park, Warks]; untraced	West Papers, Alscot Park, box 42; *Whinney* 1988, 458 n35
129.	*c*1750	Brackets for Cheere's statuettes and busts	p	[Kirkleatham Hall, E R Yorks]; YCAG	ATTRIB *Friedman and Clifford* 1974, corrigendum to p 14; *Rococo* 1984, S 30, 31
130.	1753	Bust of Swift, low relief of Bacchus, Ceres and Venus bronzed and a frame gilt, a fine bracket with Fame and other ornaments Payment(s): 14 gns		Blair Castle, Perths	*Davis* 1991, 53; *Fulton* 2001, Appendix A 11
131.	1753	Mercury, (after Giambologna) 'gilding ye Wings Ball and Cadduce', two flower pots gilded and painted with Prussian blue Payment(s): Mercury £3 13s 6d; gilding 3s; pots 16s each	l	[Blair Castle, Perths]; untraced	*Fulton* 2001, Appendix A 11
132.	1758	4 statues of two boys and two girls, eight 'ornamented' vases Payment(s): 16 gns, £18		Blair Castle, Perths	*Fulton* 2001, Appendix A 13
133.	1766	Atlas, a figure, and glass globes (presumably lamps)		[coll Sir Robert Burdett]; untraced	Berks CAO, D/EBU. A.9/1
134.	nd	6 seats after those formerly in the exedra, Chiswick	l	Castle Hill, Devon	ATTRIB *Gunnis* 1968, 99; *Davis* 1991, 93, 95–6 (repr)

CHEERE, William –*c*1767

William appears to have been the son of **John Cheere**'s first wife, Theodosia Maria, who died in 1767 'of a broken heart for the death of her father and only son' (*GM* 1767, 280). He supplied sculpture to George Washington for Mount Vernon in response to Washington's order, which gave directions not only for the subject matter but also as to size, which was determined by his indented placement for these objects. Washington wrote: 'Directions for the Busts / 4-one of Alexr the Great-another of Julius Caesar-anr of Chs 12 Sweeden & a 4th of the King of Prussia. / N.B.–these are not to exceed 15 Inchs in highth nor 10 in width for brokn Pedimt. / 2 other Busts of Prince Eugene & the Duke of Marlborh-somewhat smallr. 2 Wild Beast-not to exceed 12 Inch in highth nor 18 in lenght. Sundry Small Ornaments for Chimy piece'.

In 1760 he received a shipment costing £12 11s 4d which contained 'A Groupe of Aeneas carrying his Father out of Troy with 4 Statues viz – his Father Anchises, his wife, Creusa, himself and his son Ascanius, [neatly] finished and bronzed with Copper. /Two Groupes, with two Statues each of Bachus & Flora finisht neat, & bronzd w' Coper £2.2 each / Two Ornamented Vases with Faces & festoons of Grape & Vine Leaves &c finished Neat & bronzd w' Coppr The above for ye Chimney Piece-/ Two Lyons after the Antique Lyon's in Italy finished neat & bronzd with Copper £1.5 each. An invoice of William Cheere, dated March 1760 relates to these works.

The tradesman from whom the pieces were purchased sent directions as to how they were to be placed, adding to the above invoice the note: 'this is ye best Ornaments I could possibly make for the Chimney Piece', adding 'of all the wild Beasts as could be made there is none thought better than the Lyons.' His instructions for displaying the other figures stated that 'the manner of placing them on ye Chimney piece shd be thus. A Group of Flora – Vase – Aeneas – Vase – Group of Bacchus'. He went on to add that: There is no Busts of Alexander ye Great [none at all of Charles 12th of Sweden] Jullius Caesar, King of Prussia, Prince Eugene nor Duke of Marlborough of the Size desired; and to make models would be very Expensive – at least 4 Guineas each. But I can make Busts exactly to the Size wrote for [15 Inches] also very good ones at the rate of 16s. Each of Homer, Virgil, Horace, Cicero, Plato, Aristottle, Seneca, Galens, Vestall, Virgin Faustina, Chaucer, Spencer, Johnson, Shakespear, Beaumont, Fletcher, Milton, Prior, Pope, Congreve, Swift, Addison, Dryden, Locke, Newton'.

The figural groupings and vases were intended to ornament a mantepiece, but the busts may have been for broken segmental overdoors or for mounting on brackets.

John Davis

Literary References: *Abbot* 1988, 355; *Vincent* 1988, 169

CHELI, C fl 1839

He exhibited at the Royal Academy in 1839, giving as his address the Imperial Hotel, Covent Garden.

Statues

1.	1839	Ganymede	m	[Exhib RA, London, 1295]; untraced	*Graves* II, 1905–6, 52

CHENEY, Bartholomew fl 1742

He acted as assistant to **Sir Robert Taylor** and carved the figures of *Fame* and *Britannia* on his master's monument to Captain Cornewall, 1742, in Westminster Abbey. According to J T Smith Taylor paid him £4 15s a week.

Literary References: *Smith* 1828, 1, 151

CHENU, D fl 1794

He attended the Royal Academy Schools in December 1794 and exhibited two busts in the same year. His address was given as 122 Wardour Road, the same as **Peter Francis Chenu**, who must have been kindred.

Literary References: *Hutchison* 1960–62, 155; *Gunnis* 1968, 100

Busts

1.	1794	Unidentified girl	[Exhib RA, London, 587]; untraced	*Graves* II, 1905–6, 52
2.	1794	Unidentified girl	[Exhib RA, London, 605]; untraced	*Graves* II, 1905–6, 52

CHENU, Peter Francis 1760–1834

Born on 8 October 1760, he attended the Royal Academy Schools in October 1784. In the Academy records he is listed as 'Pierre François Chenu' (*Hutchison* 1960–62, 148). He won a silver medal in 1785 (**24**) and in the following year was awarded the gold medal for a 'restoration' of the *Belvedere Torso* (**25**). In 1786 he submitted a sketch (perhaps a drawing) of *Daedalus and Icarus.* He first exhibited at the Royal Academy in 1788, giving his address as 28 Great Castle Street, Cavendish Square. Over the years he showed works in a variety of genres, including candelabra supports and wax models, as well as a bust, a bas-relief and a design for a monument. His monuments were judged by Gunnis to be 'of unequal merit, some have extremely well-cut reliefs, while others are not nearly so successful.' The relief on his tablet to Thomas Gorsuch (**16**), for instance 'is almost comic. It shows Time, who is knocking down an obelisk, while he holds in one hand what appears to be a wine-jar bearing the words "All sink to re-ascend" ' (*Gunnis* 1968, 100).

In the 1790s Chenu lived in Wardour Street, where in 1796 he was visited by Joseph Lygo, who was there to assess **Peter Turnerelli**'s skills for William Duesbury of the Derby manufactory. Turnerelli was at that time Chenu's pupil. Chenu bought a large number of pieces at various London auctions, which suggests that a key part of his output was in reproduction. He purchased several lots at the sales of **Joseph Rose the Younger** on 10 April 1799 and of **Thomas Scheemakers** and **Thomas Banks** in 1805.

In 1800 his address was 115 Great Portland Street and by 1811 he was at 23 Charles Street, Middlesex Hospital. He died in 1834 at 1 Union Street, Lambeth, a relatively wealthy man. In his will he left nearly £4,000 in shares. His premises and business went to his residuary legatee, Michael Nicholas Chenu. He asked to be buried in the parish of St Mary Lambeth.

Literary References: *Graves* II, 1905–6, 52; *Hutchison* 1960–62, 148; *Gunnis* 1968, 100; *Clifford* 1992, 51; *Bricknell* 1995, 95

Archival References: RA Premium list

Will: PROB 11/1836 (proved 10 Sept 1834)

Funerary Monuments

1.	?1796	Peter Smith	Ely Cathedral	S	*Gunnis* 1968, 100
2.	?1796	Sir Robert Pigot	Patshull, Staffs	S	*Gunnis* 1968, 100
3.	†1788	Walter (†1780), William (†1788) and Walter Strickland	Beverley Minster, E R Yorks	S	Pevsner, *Yorks: E R & York*, 1995, 292
4.	*c*1795	Lord Pigot	Patshull, Staffs	S	*Gunnis* 1968, 100
5.	†1796	James Andrew	Barkway, Herts	S	Pevsner, *Herts*, 1977, 87
6.	?1797	Charles Nairn	Cranbrook, Kent	S	*Gunnis* 1968, 100
7.	†1797	Henry Rice	St Mary, Dover, Kent	S	*Gunnis* 1968, 100; Pevsner, *Kent, NE and E*, 1983, 288
8.	†1797	Sir Francis Lumm	St James, Piccadilly, London		GPC
9.	†1802	Cox family member	Piddletrenthide, Dorset		Pevsner, *Dorset*, 1972, 314
10.	†1806	William Gyll	Wraysbury, Bucks	S	Pevsner, *Bucks*, 1994, 767
11.	?1807	Elizabeth, Lady Smith	Sydling St Nicholas, Dorset		GPC
12.	?1809	John Beaufoy	Upton Grey, Hants	S	*Gunnis* 1968, 100
13.	?1809	Mary Golding	Ditton, Kent	S	*Gunnis* 1968, 100
14.	?1813	Sir Thomas Style Bt	Wateringbury, Kent	S	*Gunnis* 1968, 100
15.	†1817	Mary Wathen	St Mary, Woodchester, Glos	S	*Gunnis* 1968, 100; Pevsner, *Glos: Cotswolds*, 1999, 744
16.	†1820	Thomas Talbot Gorsuch	Barkway, Herts	S	*Graves* II, 1905–6, 52; *Gunnis* 1968, 100; Pevsner, *Herts*, 1977, 87

Statues

17.	1819	Seated Hercules, statuette	b	[Sotheby, 12 Dec 2003]; untraced	SD	Sotheby Cat, 71 (repr)
18.	1833	Aurora, design for a time piece, statuette	b	[Exhib Soc of BA, London, 826]; untraced		*Johnson* 1975, 84

Busts

19.	1788	Dr Herschell	[Exhib RA, London, 654]; untraced	*Graves* II, 1905–6, 52

Architectural Sculpture

20.	1789	A Vestal for a candelabrum	[Exhib RA, London, 479]; untraced	*Graves* II, 1905–6, 52
21.	1810	Ornaments for a temporary structure	[for Grand National Jubilee, St James's Park, London]; untraced	TNA Work 5/112; *Gunnis* 1968, 100
22.	1811	A figure for a candelabrum	[Exhib RA, London, 918]; untraced	*Graves* II, 1905–6, 52

Reliefs

23.	1816	Bas-relief of 'Bacchus and Ariadne', for holding lights	[Exhib RA, London, 912]; untraced	*Graves* II, 1905–6, 52

Miscellaneous

24.	1785	Model of an Academy figure or a bas-relief	[RA, London, silver medal]; untraced	RA Premium list
25.	1786	Restoration of the Belvedere torso	[RA, London, gold medal]; untraced	RA Premium list; *Graves* II, 1905–6, 52; *Gunnis* 1968, 100

26.	1788	Mercury instructing Cupid in the Art of Commerce, model		[Exhib RA, London, 623]; untraced	*Graves* II, 1905–6, 52
27.	1790	Figure of genius, weeping		[Exhib RA, London, 519]; untraced	*Graves* II, 1905–6, 52
28.	1792	Model of Faith, Hope and Charity	w	[Exhib RA, London, 724]; untraced	*Graves* II, 1905–6, 52
29.	1794	Two figures for a chandelier or lamp		[Exhib RA, London, 590, 603]; untraced	*Graves* II, 1905–6, 52
30.	1796	A vestal designed to hold a lamp		[Exhib RA, London, 879]; untraced	*Graves* II, 1905–6, 52
31.	1796	Genius		[Exhib RA, London, 865]; untraced	*Graves* II, 1905–6, 52
32.	1800	The Good Samaritan, model		[Exhib RA, London, 1081]; untraced	*Graves* II, 1905–6, 52
33.	1811	Cupid and Psyche, for supporting lights		[Exhib RA, London, 920]; untraced	*Graves* II, 1905–6, 52

CHEVERTON, Benjamin 1796–1876

Cheverton invented a device for producing small-scale replicas of larger works of sculpture. His reducing machine was developed with the assistance of John Isaac Hawkins and was based on an earlier design by the steam pioneer James Watt. It was perfected for commercial use in 1836. A version of it, patented in 1844, is in the Science Museum, London. He used the mechanism for producing exquisitely detailed ivory reproductions of works by **Sir Francis Chantrey, Joseph Nollekens, L F Roubiliac, Joseph Durham** and others. He is also known to have used the machine for reproductions in ceramic materials. He exhibited numerous examples at exhibitions in London and Liverpool and in 1851 he exhibited a reduced copy of the Antique *Theseus* at the Great Exhibition to some acclaim. Cheverton is thought to have produced several hundred miniature busts with his machine, of which only a selection is listed. His address in 1835 was 72 Pratt Street, Camden Town.

Literary References: *Johnson* 1975, 84; *Silber* 1987, 24, 72; *Shedd* 1992, 39

Archival References: GPC

Portraits of the Sculptor: Parianware bust, Science Museum inv 1924-0293

Statues					
1.	1839	'An ivory statue – after Sir F Chantrey's Lady Russell'	i	[Exhib Liverpool Ac, 682]; untraced	*Morris and Roberts* 1998, 135
2.	1839	'Ivory statue – after the Companion to Lady Russell, modelled by Lege'	i	[Exhib Liverpool Ac, 684]; untraced	*Morris and Roberts* 1998, 135
3.	1851	Theseus, reduced copy		[Gt Exhib]; untraced	*Shedd* 1992, 39
Busts					
4.	1835	Basil Montague, 'after a model by Mr Clark'	i	[Exhib Soc of BA, London, 791]; untraced	*Johnson* 1975, 84
5.	1835	Charles James Fox, after Joseph Nollekens	i	[Exhib Soc of BA, London, 794]; untraced	*Johnson* 1975, 84; *Morris and Roberts* 1998, 135
6.	1836	Sir Robert Peel, after Sir Francis Chantrey	i	[Exhib Liverpool Ac, 211]; untraced	*Morris and Roberts* 1998, 135
7.	1836	Sir Walter Scott, after Sir Francis Chantrey	i	[Exhib Liverpool Ac, 212]; untraced	*Morris and Roberts* 1998, 135
8.	1837	Isaac Newton, after Louis-François Roubiliac		[Exhib Liverpool Ac, 703]; untraced	*Morris and Roberts* 1998, 135
9.	1837	John Milton, after Louis-François Roubiliac		[Exhib Liverpool Ac, 700]; untraced	*Morris and Roberts* 1998, 135
10.	1839	Dr Dalton	i	[Exhib Liverpool Ac, 683]; untraced	*Morris and Roberts* 1998, 135
11.	1842	Queen Victoria	i	[Phillips, 14 June 1931]; VAM A.28–1931	SD VAM SCP colls list, ivories
12.	1849	Jenny Lind, after Joseph Durham	i	[Exhib Soc of BA, London, 637]; untraced	*Johnson* 1975, 84; GPC
13.	nd	Chaucer	i	Untraced	GPC
14.	nd	Homer	i	Untraced	GPC
15.	nd	Lord Brougham	i	Untraced	GPC
16.	nd	Thomas Slingsby Duncombe	i	VAM A.32-1926	VAM SCP colls list, ivories
Miscellaneous					
17.	1837	Ajax, 'after an Antique in the Vatican'		[Exhib Liverpool Ac, 701]; untraced	*Morris and Roberts* 1998, 135
18.	1837	Isis, or Clytie, 'from an Antique in the British Museum'		[Exhib Liverpool Ac, 699]; untraced	*Morris and Roberts* 1998, 135
19.	1837	William Shakespeare, 'from the Chandos Gallery'		[Exhib Liverpool Ac, 702]; untraced	*Morris and Roberts* 1998, 135
20.	1838	A Danaid, 'from the original of Professor Rauch, of Berlin'		[Exhib Liverpool Ac, 661]; untraced	*Morris and Roberts* 1998, 135

CHICHELEY, Richard fl 1713–30

Between 1726 and 1730 Chicheley (or Chichley) and his partner, **Joseph Wade**, were responsible for a considerable amount of carving at Greenwich Palace (**3–6**). A carver called 'Richard Chichley of Rochester,' took Edward Batten of Chatham as an apprentice on 12 January 1744. It is possible that this may be a relative.

Literary References: *Webb* 1957 (3), 116; *Gunnis* 1968, 100; *Bold* 2000 (2), 155; *Penny* 1992, 20

Architectural Sculpture					
1.	1713	Repairs to the carved work over the Bone House Door and carved work to the organ Payment(s): £2 10s 6d		St Nicholas, Deptford	*Drake* 1886, 35
2.	1719–1720	Carved woodwork	wd	[St Paul, Deptford, London]; untraced	Accounts for building the New Churches, Lambeth Palace Library
3.	1726–1728	'Carving in the Great Pediment of the West middle front' (co-sculptor: J Wade)		[Greenwich Palace]; untraced	TNA ADM 68/706; *Gunnis* 1968, 100
4.	c1730	'12 faces of capitals Corinthian pillars' (£98 13s 4d), '40 modillions' (£20) and 2 scrolls (£2 each)	s	[Greenwich Palace, South Pavilion]; untraced	TNA ADM 68/710; *Gunnis* 1968, 100

5.	1730	'2 Mask heads over the chimney in the kitchen with a compartiment of leather work and scrolls' Payment(s): £4 for each head		[Greenwich Palace, South East Pavilion]; untraced		TNA ADM 68/707/8; *Gunnis* 1968, 100
6.	1730	'carved moldings in fir' and '14 faces of Corinthian capitals'		[Greenwich Palace, North East Pavilion]; untraced		TNA ADM 68/710
Miscellaneous						
7.	?1720–1730	Clock case crowned by a crowing cock and a figure of Time and flanked by boy angels	wd	Ashmolean		*Penny* 1992, III, 20–1 (repr)

CHINQUA, Amoy fl 1716

A Cantonese face-modeller, he signs a large figure, in painted plaster, of Joseph Collet, a merchant and administrator in Sumatra and Madras (1). Another statuette of an unidentified westerner is inscribed 'Amoy Chinquafe 1717' and is in the collection of the Peabody Museum of Salem.

Literary References: *Crossman* 1991, 307

Statues						
1.	1716	Joseph Collet	p	NPG 4005	S	

CHISLET, John, of Beaminster fl 1823–30

The *Gentleman's Magazine* states that he carved the 'chaste and elegant' monument to Admiral Sir William Domett (2) at Hawkchurch, Dorset (*GM* 1829, 2, 478). In Pigot's *Directory* for 1830 he describes himself as a 'Sculptor and Professor of Music' living in Hogshill Street (*Pigot* 1830, 275).

Literary References: *Gunnis* 1968, 100–1

Funerary Monuments						
1.	?1823	Joseph Bishop		Corscombe, Dorset	S	*Gunnis* 1968, 100
2.	1829	Sir William Domett		Hawkchurch, Dorset	S	*GM* 1829, 2, 478; *Gunnis* 1968, 101; Pevsner, *Devon*, 1989, 476

CHITQUA (or SHYKINGQUA) –1796

Chitqua was a Cantonese modeller. He appears to have been one of a number of sculptors who modelled faces or statuettes of western merchants visiting the port. Thomas Bentley wrote to Josiah Wedgwood that Chitqua was 'one of those artists who make the mandarin figures that are brought to England, a pair of which you may remember to have seen at Mr Walley's shop' (*Whitley* 1928, 1, 270). Unlike his contemporaries he actually visited England and because of his skills and exotic appearance became a celebrated guest of artists and aristocrats. He arrived from Canton in August 1769 on the *Hoisendon* East Indiaman under Captain Jameson. Apparently he had gained permission from the Chinese government to go to Bavaria but the *Gentleman's Magazine* states that 'curiosity and respect for the British, induced him to visit this island' (*GM* 1771, 41, 237–238). Others suggested that he was escaping debtors.

He took lodgings at a hatter's premises in Norfolk Street and on 22 April 1770 was a guest with the Earl of Carlisle, Horace Walpole, Edmund Burke and Charles Jennens, at the Royal Academy's grand dinner in Pall Mall (*Press Cuttings 1723–1800*, f 108). This was held to celebrate the opening of the Royal Academy exhibition, in which Chitqua exhibited a specimen of his work (3), giving his address as Arundell Street. An observer, Richard Gough, described him as 'a middle sized man, about or above forty, thin and lank . . . his upper lip covered with thin hair an inch long . . . on his head no hair except the long lock braided into a tail almost a yard long . . . his lips prominent, nose long, eyes not very lively, nails as long as one sees of our sedentary mechanics. He wears the dress of his own country, a pointed stiff cap, with a border turned up of quilted silk, an undervest like a banian of green silk, with a lining; his upper vest a kind of mantelet; his drawers much the same as his undervest, and his slippers yellow. He complained much of cold, but had no fire; and preferred the country to London only for quietness from noise, for he meets with no insults in the streets. He likes his own climate best, and returns with the next shipping' (quoted in *Sunderland* 1988, 142).

Chitqua's intention of returning home was frustrated. In 1771 he embarked on the *Grenville* at Gravesend, where the sailors considered him a Jonah, sure to bring bad luck to the ship because of his strange dress. After sustained abuse from the men and an unfortunate incident in which he fell overboard and nearly drowned, he begged to be put ashore at Deal. The Captain obliged and sent the pilot to accompany Chitqua to London, but on arriving in the city the sculptor could not recollect or express intelligibly where he lived and 'a mob gathered round the hackney coach and began to abuse and beat the pilot, for having, as they supposed, kidnapped a foreigner.' Chitqua was eventually rescued by a friendly gentleman who recognised him and conveyed him to lodgings in the Strand. The volume of the *Gentleman's Magazine* which carried the news of this scandalous event also gave a full description of his appearance, noting that he 'speaks the Lingua Franca mixt with broken English; is very sensible and a great observer. He is remarkably ingenious in forming small busts with a sort of China earth, many of which carry a striking likeness of the person they are designed to represent. He steals a likeness, and forms the busts from memory' (*GM* 1771, 41, 237–238).

He appears to have had numerous English patrons, including William Hickey, who was evidently appreciative of his detailed modelling and polychrome finish, for Hickey wore his most elaborate clothes for the occasion (2). Bentley noted that the modeller had also 'been with the King and Queen, who were much pleased with him, and he is to take the portraits of the Royal Infantry. He has ten guineas a piece for his little portraits, which are very small' (*Whitley* 1928, 1, 270). The only certain surviving work which Chitqua produced in England is the painted clay statuette of Dr Anthony Askew (1), seated on a rocky base and holding his customary gold-headed cane. Chitqua apparently wrote accounts on oriental gardening for a letter from Archdeacon Clive to 'SWC' of Berkeley Square, London refers to 'the explanatory discourse by Chitqua [on the subject] . . . which I have read with the highest satisfaction' (BM MS 41,136 fol 14, 28 March 1774).

The Chinaman returned to Canton in 1772 and died there in 1796. The *Gentleman's Magazine* reminded readers of the identity of 'Chitqua or Shykinqua (as some write the name), the ingenious artist.' They reported 'the news of his death, and of its having been occasioned by his taking poison' (*GM* 1797, 47, 1072).

There are numerous surviving examples of Cantonese statuettes modelled in painted clay depicting western figures of this period. These are frequently attributed to Chitqua and include a portrait of a Dutch merchant in painted and unfired clay in the Rijksmuseum, and a statuette with real hair in a private collection, thought to represent the actor David Garrick.

MGS

Literary References: *Graves* II, 1905–6, 60; *Piper* 1952, 198; *Charleston* 1958, 459–461; *Crossman* 1991, 314; *Rijksmuseum Portraits* 1995, 86; *Portraits of Garrick*, 2003, 69–70 (repr).

Representations of the Sculptor: John Hamilton Mortimer, portrait of Chit Qua, the Chinese Modeller, oil on canvas, private coll (*Sunderland* 1988, 142, repr); Charles Grignion, drawing, 1771, Asmolean (*Piper* 1952, 198, repr); J Zoffany *Life School at the Royal Academy*, 1771, RA

Statues

1.	c1770	Dr Anthony Askew, statuette (clay, polychromed)	tc	R C Physic, London	*Wolstenholme* 1964, 34–5 (repr); *Crossman* 1991, 311, 314 (repr)
2.	nd	William Hickey, statuette		Untraced	*Crossman* 1991, 314; *Portraits of Garrick* 2003, 69–70

Miscellaneous

3.	1770	'Portrait of a gentleman', model	[Exhib RA, London, 245]; untraced	*Graves* II, 1905–6, 60

CHOVET, Abraham 1704–90

For further information the reader is referred to *Pyke* 1973, 29

CHRISTIE, Alexander fl 1851–69

In Glenorchy Church, Dalmally Village, is an undated marble relief tablet commemorating the Campbells of Glenorchy. The artist signs it 'A. Christie sculpt. Perth'. He was probably a partner in the firm of Anderson and Christie, marble cutters of County Place, Perth. Alexander Christie joined the firm in 1851 and continued the business for two years after his partner, **William Anderson**, died in 1867.

Literary References: *Woodward* 1977, vol 1, pt 2, 45

Funerary Monuments

1.	nd	The Campbells of Glenorchy	Glenorchy Church, Dalmally, Argyll	S	*Woodward* 1977, vol 1, pt 2, 45

CHUKE, Michael, of Kilkhampton, Cornwall 1679–1742

He was the son of Stephen Chuke who was probably a London carver employed on decorative work at Grenville, Lord Bath's mansion at Stowe, near Kilkhampton in Cornwall, where he married and settled in the village. His son, Michael, was baptised there in 1769. As a boy Michael Chuke was sent to London and apprenticed to **Grinling Gibbons** 'who found him an apt pupil' (*Dew* 1933, 11). He later returned home where he married Elizabeth Braginton in 1713. Like his father, he worked at Stowe in Cornwall, apparently under Gibbons, where he carved and signed a pulpit in the chapel (**11**). When the house was pulled down in 1739, Lord Cobham bought the woodwork and moved it to the private chapel of Stowe House, Bucks.

Chuke carried out some decorative carving (**7–10**) and provided a handful of monuments in his Cornish neighbourhood. The latter included a headstone with a reclining figure commemorating his father (**6**). Its ornaments are very similar to the monument in the church to a member of the Cottell family (**5**).

He died in 1742 and was buried on the south side of Kilkhampton churchyard on 24 September. His headstone describes him as a carver. His widow survived him by 20 years, dying at the age of 78 on 1 November 1762. Roderick Dew, who wrote a history of Kilkhampton Church, stated that Chuke's work was 'in contemporary opinion considered little inferior to that of Gibbons himself,' but the author gives no supporting evidence for this claim (*Dew* 1933, 11).

Literary References: *Dew* 1933, 10–14; *Gunnis* 1968, 101

Funerary Monuments

1.	1700	John Warminster (†1700)		Kilkhampton, Cornwall		Pevsner, *Cornwall*, 1970, 85
2.	1704	Richard Westlake		Kilkhampton, Cornwall		*Dew* 1933, 13; Pevsner, *Cornwall*, 1970, 85
3.	1705	John Courtis		Kilkhampton, Cornwall		*Dew* 1933, 14; Pevsner, *Cornwall*, 1970, 85
4.	1714	Sir Bevil Grenville (†1643)		Kilkhampton, Cornwall		*Dew* 1933, 12; *Gunnis* 1968, 101
5.	nd	Cottell family member	sl	Kilkhampton, Cornwall		*Dew* 1933, 14
6.	nd	Stephen Chuke		Kilkhampton, Cornwall, churchyard		*Dew* 1933, 11; *Gunnis* 1968, 101

Architectural Sculpture

7.	nd	Royal arms	Marhamchurch, Cornwall	*Gunnis* 1968, 101; Pevsner, *Cornwall*, 1970, 114
8.	nd	Royal arms	Kilkhampton, Cornwall	*Gunnis* 1968, 101; Pevsner, *Cornwall*, 1970, 85
9.	nd	Royal arms	Launcells, Cornwall	*Dew* 1933, 10; *Gunnis* 1968, 101; Pevsner, *Cornwall*, 1970, 95
10.	nd	Royal arms	Stratton, Cornwall	*Gunnis* 1968, 101; Pevsner, *Cornwall*, 1970, 217

Miscellaneous

11.	nd	Pulpit and wainscoting in cedarwood	wd	[Grenville House, Stowe near Kilkhampton, Cornwall, Chapel]; Stowe, Bucks, chapel	S	*Dew* 1933, 11; *Gunnis* 1968, 101

CHURCHILL, Robert, of London fl 1690–1721

As 'Master Mason to His Majesty's Office of Ordnance' and 'of St. Margaret's Westminster', Churchill appears to have built a number of houses in London, which he insured with the Westminster Fire Office. They include three in Great Distaff Lane, 1717, and one in Old Change. Others were in Millbank (insured for £500), Vine Street (two, insured together for £150) and East Greenwich. He was a subscriber to John Dart, *Westmonasterium*, 1723, and his coat of arms is published in the preface with other subscribers. His daughter was the third wife of **Edward Stanton**.

Archival References: WFO, PR, no 1997 (23 March 1719), no 1348 (4 June 1719); GPC

CIBBER, Caius Gabriel 1630–1700

The son of a Danish royal cabinet-maker, Cibber was a sculptor to two English kings, Charles II and William III. He was born in Flensburg, Schleswig-Holstein and travelled to Italy around 1647 with a grant from Frederik III of Denmark and there studied classical art. Returning home through the Netherlands he may have come into contact with the sculptor Peter de Keyser, for when he arrived in London *c*1655, he joined the workshop of **John Stone**, de Keyser's kinsman, in Long Acre. Cibber worked as a journeyman and then foreman to Stone and when Stone suffered paralysis in Breda in 1660 while petitioning for a royal appointment from Charles II, Cibber brought him back to England. He ran Stone's workshop until his master's death in 1667 and then set up on his own.

Cibber married twice. Nothing is known of his first wife, but in 1670, while living in Southampton Street, Bloomsbury, he married Jane Colley, an heiress from Rutland, who 'had 6000 pounds fortune' (*Vertue* I, 99). Some of this was set aside for their three children, Veronica, Colley, who later became an actor, dramatist and poet laureate and Lewis, who went to Winchester College, where his father presented a statue of the founder on his son's behalf (**12**). Cibber gambled away the balance of his wife's fortune and insolvency dogged his mature years: he was periodically imprisoned for debt and twice, in 1680 and 1689, had to re-assert his standing with the Crown in order to continue work.

His independent career began with a flourish, when on 20 June 1667, he was appointed a member of the Royal Household and a sculptor to the King. This provided status but no guarantee of employment and he realised that his best opportunities lay in the City of London, where rebuilding was under way following the Great Fire of 1666. In 1668 Cibber joined the Leathersellers' Company, which gave him the right to work within the City Liberties, but characteristically, he was unable to find the fee of £25 and eventually paid in kind, presenting the Company with a fountain (**20**). In 1668 also, he was appointed Surveyor to the Steelyard and carved the arms of the Hanseatic League for the entrance to their headquarters in Thames Street (**21**). He was willing to make ephemeral structures for the City fathers, including decorations for the hustings at the lord mayor's banquets in the 1670s and the figures of *Gog* and *Magog* for the Guildhall, which he twice showed in 1672 to his frequent dining companion, Robert Hooke, one of the commissioners for rebuilding the City (**6**).

Meanwhile Cibber had already turned his attention to one of the most prestigious new building projects, the Royal Exchange. In December 1667 the Lord Chamberlain recommended him as sculptor for a sequence of 27 statues of English monarchs for niches in the inner courtyard and he submitted models which apparently pleased the King (**4, 5**). The Gresham Committee, who controlled the building project, evidently considered his submission premature, for they refused to consider commissioning statues when the foundations were barely laid and told him to apply again in due course. The statues were carved many years later by other sculptors while he was working in the Midlands. In 1668 Cibber was among those seeking the post of Surveyor of the New Exchange but was again unsuccessful.

The sculptor was an active member of the German Lutheran community. In 1672 these 'strangers and foreigners residing in London' obtained a charter from the King allowing them to build their own church in the City by private subscription (Guildhall MS 8358). Cibber, who offered his services as architect without fee, probably designed the severe, rectangular building in Little Trinity Lane, London.

In 1673 he won his first important public contract, for a large relief for the Monument, the memorial column commemorating the Great Fire (**23**). This brought him into contact with Sir Christopher Wren, Surveyor of the King's Works. The sculptor was given day release from the Marshalsea debtors' prison in Southwark to carve the ambitious allegorical tableau presenting the King as the benign force controlling the rebuilding programme. He earned £600 between 28 June 1673 and 8 September 1675, paid 'out of the cole money' for his 'hieroglifick ffigures' in relief (Guildhall MSS 184/4, fol 31) and also prepared estimates for several ideas for the finial above the column (Guildhall MS 5761). **Edward Pearce**, who carved the City griffins, emblematic swags and armorials, is not named in the accounts, which suggests that he worked in sub-contract to Cibber. The first English edition of Cesare Ripa's *Iconologia*, 1709, edited by Isaac Fuller the Younger, has a frontispiece showing the arrival of the Romans on British shores and pointing at Cibber's relief on the Monument. Several of the engravings are signed 'C.G.C. *Deli.*'

Soon after the Monument's completion Cibber won a second pivotal London contract for statues to flank the entrance to Bethlem Hospital for the Insane at Moorfields. He carved a pair of writhing near-naked figures of *Raving and Melancholy Madness* (**7**), whose bold and disturbing naturalism, which transcended all the sculptural conventions of the time, gives credence to the tradition articulated by George Vertue, the diarist and engraver, that they were modelled from life.

Cibber's monument to the 13-year old Thomas Sackville is another dramatic tableau (**2**). The twisting effigy reclining on a tomb-chest looks heavenwards, his hand on a skull, and is attended by life-sized figures of his grieving parents kneeling either side of the chest. The contract drawn up with Sackville's mother, the Dowager Countess of Dorset, made the unusual stipulation that the completed work must be approved by Sir Peter Lely, Principal Painter to the King, before a final payment would be authorized.

Cibber experimented with lead sculpture and helped to popularise this material for garden statuary and other works, including the statue of William of Wykeham (**12**). His stone figures found favour with aristocratic patrons, perhaps because he was prepared to travel to their country estates and to economise by using local materials. In 1680 the 9th Earl of Rutland ordered seven pastoral figures in Ketton stone for Belvoir Castle, at a cost of £35 each (**8**). Cibber evidently also thought that he also had the prestigious contract for monuments to the 7th and 8th Earls in Bottesford church, for he wrote to inform his patron's secretary that he had arranged freight of the necessary marble by river from Lyme Regis to Windsor and then by land to Stamford. In a postscript he sought to tempt the Earl with two colossal figures of gladiators, in preparation at Ketton. The monuments were carved two years later by **Grinling Gibbons** and the gladiators were not mentioned again.

From 1685–87 Cibber worked under the architect William Talman on a major commission for Lord Kingston at Thoresby Hall, Notts (**43**). His willingness to work in local materials is indicated by a memorandum inserted in the 1st Duke of Devonshire's Building Accounts at Chatsworth, which ends 'at this rate I will doe my endeavour to serva any Nobleman, in freestone' (Devonshire Building Accounts, vol VIII, f.5A). Cibber and Talman then moved on to Chatsworth where Cibber began to receive modest but regular payments in December 1687, eventually earning £450. He supplied figures in local stone for the gardens including a magnificent *Triton and sea-horses* for a fountain (**28**), provided marble statues for the great staircase and others in alabaster, carved in the round, for the chapel altarpiece (**9, 32**). He may also have have been responsible for the design of the altarpiece, though the decorative elements were probably carved by **Samuel Watson**.

Cibber's association with Wren was renewed in 1678, when the architect appears to have considered employing him as sculptor for a projected mausoleum for King Charles I in St George's Chapel, Windsor Castle (*Stewart*, 1977, 1–56). Wren gave him the contract in 1681 for allegorical figures for the parapet of his library at Trinity College, Cambridge (**25**) and in 1682 tried unsuccessfully to get him the contract for a statue for Tom Tower, Christ Church, Oxford. From 1690–94 they were both working at Hampton Court Palace (**30, 31, 34, 35**). Cibber's relief for the east front pediment of the palace was another patriotic tableau, *Hercules triumphing over Envy* (**37**), an allusion to King William III's victories over Louis XIV of France. He was paid £400 for 'the Great Frontispiece with Iconologicall figure, and for sevll. Journeys of himself witmen to look after the performance' (PRO E 351/3464).

In 1693 he was appointed Sculptor-in-Ordinary to William III in succession to **Peter Besnier**. This office carried an annual retainer of £50, but involved routine duties including custody of the royal collection of moulds, statues and models. Minor payments were made to him in 1693 for repairs to statues in the Queen's Garden.

Cibber returned to architectural design in 1694, when he was appointed surveyor, without fee, to the Danish Church for Scandinavian merchants in Wellclose Square, Poplar, after the Danish Elders rejected their appointed architect's plans. He also provided statues of Biblical figures in oak for the reredos (**38**) and probably the lead statues of Christian Virtues on the principal front (**36**).

During the last two years of his life Cibber worked under Wren once more, at St Paul's Cathedral. He must have had a considerable workforce to carve the keystones for the arches supporting the dome (**39**) and the pediment relief of a rising phoenix for the south transept front (**40**). He died in 1700 and was buried beside his wife in the Danish Church.

Little is known of Cibber's assistants. In April 1678 the Masons' Company conducted one of their periodic searches and listed five men, all foreigners of whom nothing is known, working for the sculptor. In 1691, two other assistants, one of them named Pearson, were left at Chatsworth to complete Cibber's contract. The only other clue to workshop members is George Vertue's brief statement that **Francis Bird** worked for Cibber after leaving Gibbons's employment.

Vertue described Cibber as 'a Gentleman-like man & a man of Good sense but died poor' (*Vertue* I, 39). His royal commissions attest to his contemporary reputation, but recent scholars, perhaps comparing his work with the virtuoso wood-carving of his rival, Gibbons, have dismissed him as no more than reasonably competent, a harsh judgment to pass on the author of the Sackville monument and the great *Hercules* relief at Hampton Court. Cibber's work testifies to the extraordinary versatility of a leading late-17th century workshop.

IR

Literary References: *Vertue* 1, 39, 91, 99; II, 36, III, 34, IV, 64, 178, 165; *Faber* 1926; *Robinson and Adams* 1935, *passim*; *Knoop and Jones* 1935, 25; *Thompson* 1949, *passim*; *Gunnis* 1968, 101–3; *Physick* 1969, 24–7, 54–5; *Colvin* 1973–6, 29, 162, 171, 190, 297; *Gold* 1984, 93–113; *Whinney* 1988, 110–15; *Davis* 1991, *passim*; *Colvin* 1995, 248, 929; *Grove* 7, 1996, 297–9 (Physick); *Stewart* 1977, 1–56; *Gibson* 1997 (2), *passim*; *Ward-Jackson* 2003, *passim*, but esp 266–9, 455; *Sackville* 2003; *ODNB* (Gibson)

Archival References: Sackville 1677, U269 E 611; DLW/550 (agreement and receipt, Sackville monument); GPC

Additional MS Sources: London Met Archives, Tyrwhitt-Drake E/TD/943, assignment to Cibber of leasehold, 1673

Miscellaneous Drawings: Design for a plain mural tablet, 1670, Isham Papers, Northants RO IL.3079/A46; design for a statue of Neptune, perhaps for Chatsworth, nd, VAM E 668-1949, signed, (*Physick* 1969, 25); attrib design for a memorial to King Charles I, All Souls, Oxford, 2.95 (*Stewart* 28); 44 drawings by Cibber for sepulchral monuments sold Sotheby and Wilkinson 27 Nov 1861, £1 3s (*Builder* 1868, 656)

Portraits of the Sculptor: Christian Richter, watercolour, nd, untraced, engraved J Bannerman (*Faber* 1926, frontispiece); Marcellus Laroon the Elder, canvas, formerly coll. Horace Walpole, untraced (*Vertue* VI, 85, 161); Oliver de Critz, miniature entitled Cibber the Carver, oil on copper, nd, Rosenbach Museum, Philadelphia; woodcut, nd, unsigned, (*Anecdotes* 1876, II, 167)

Funerary Monuments

1.	1677–1678	James Fox (†1677) Payment(s): £60		[Westminster Abbey, London, cloisters]; untraced	Fox Strangway Papers, 9 March and 4 May 1678
2.	1677–1680	Thomas Sackville (†1676) and Richard, 5th Earl of Dorset Payment(s): £350		Withyham, Sussex	*Faber* 1926, 41–2 (repr facing 41); *Joekes* 1982, 535–8 (repr)
3.	1681	William Fox (†1680) Payment(s): £20		Untraced	Fox Strangway Papers, 21 Dec 1681 and 10 Nov 1682

Statues

4.	1667	King Edward III, model only (statue by E Pearce)	tc	[for the Royal Exchange, London]; Skinners' Hall, City of London	*Gunnis* 1997 (1), 102; *Gibson* 1997, 160–1, 172 (colour repr IVb)
5.	1667	King Edward IV, model only (statue by A Quellin)	tc	[for the Royal Exchange, London]; Ironmongers' Hall, City of London	*Gibson* 1997 (2), 161, 172 (colour repr IVc)
6.	*c*1672	Gog and Magog		[Guildhall, City of London]; replaced 1708	*Robinson and Adams*, 1935, 10, 11
7.	*c*1676	Raving and Melancholy Madness Model(s): Raving Madness, Staatliche Museen, Berlin, acc 376, clay	s	[Bethlem Hospital, Moorfields, London, above broken pediment on main gates]; Bethlem Hospital, Beckenham, Kent	*Faber* 1926, 42–6 (reprs between 42–3); *Whinney* 1988, 112–3 (repr); *Allderidge* 1977
8.	1680–1684	Spring, Summer, Autumn, Winter, Juno, the senses taste and smell, with pedestals Payment(s): £35 each plus freight and cost of stone	s	Belvoir Castle, Rutland, gardens	*Manners* 1930, 382–3; *Davis* 1991, 103, 123–5 (repr)

No.	Date	Work		Location		Bibliography
9.	1688	Pallas, Apollo and Lucrece Payment(s): £50 with a triton Drawing(s): VAM E.946-1965 (Apollo and Lucrece)		Chatsworth, Derbys, great staircase		*Faber* 1926, 49–56 (repr facing 52); *Wren Soc* 17 (repr VI); *Physick* 1969, 54, 55 (repr)
10.	1680–1690	Boy playing the bagpipes	s	[Whitton Park, Middx]; VAM A.3–1930		*Faber* 1926, 36–9 (repr facing 36); *Whinney* 1988, 114; *Bilbey* 2002, 2–3 (repr)
11.	1687–1690	Two sphinxes, Flora, Diana, Venus and other classical subjects	s	Chatsworth, Derbys, gardens		*Faber* 1926, 49–56; *Davis* 1991, 125
12.	1697	William of Wykeham	l	Winchester College, Hants, School entrance	S	*Vertue* I, 91; *Faber* 1926, 72–3 (repr facing 72); *Wren Soc* VII, 20
13.	nd	'Extreordinary' model of 'An Adonis cast by Mr. Cibbert'		[coll Richard Osgood]; untraced		*Davis* 1991, 34, 370, n29
Busts						
14.	?1659	Oliver Cromwell, small head	p	[coll Dr Richard Mead]; untraced		Mead sale (2), p 252; *Faber* 1926, 24
15.	*c*1675	Mark Antony		[The sculptor's studio]; untraced		*Robinson and Adams* 1935, 177
16.	pre-1676	Robert Devereux, 3rd Earl of Essex (†1646)	wd	[Grecian Coffee House, Devereux Court, City of London]; Devereux Court		*Faber* 1926, 24 (pl facing 24)
Chimneypieces						
17.	1669	Marble Payment(s): £25	m	[Sessions House, Westminster, London]; untraced		Guildhall restoration, 18v; *Gunnis* 1968, 103; City Cash Accts 01/13 fol 137v
18.	1670	High Room mantelpiece (design by John Webb) Drawing(s): Northants RO IL 3079/A46		Lamport Hall, Northants		*Blatchly and Fisher* 2000, 460–9 (repr)
Architectural Sculpture						
19.	1660	Capitals and other decorative carving (co-sculptor: John Stone) Payment(s): to both sculptors		[Chesterton, Warks]; destroyed		*Grove* 7, 297
20.	*c*1668	'a stone mirmayd over the pumpe', fountain		Leathersellers' Hall, City of London, courtyard (head only)		*Faber* 1926, 21–3 (repr facing 20); *Whinney* 1988, 112
21.	1668–1670	Arms of the Hanseatic League	s	[The Steelyard, Thames St, City of London]; Museum of London		*Faber* 1926, 24–5 (repr); *Colvin* 1995, 248
22.	1674	City and Royal arms		[Newgate, City of London]; destroyed		Guildhall restoration, 15r; *Gunnis* 1968, 103
23.	1673–1675	King Charles II directing the rebuilding of the City of London, relief Payment(s): £600	s	The Monument, City of London, west side		Guildhall restoration, *passim*; *Whinney* 1988, 111–2 (repr); *Gibson* 1997 (1), 172–3, 380; *Ward-Jackson* 2003, 260–9 (repr)
24.	1675–1676	Liberty, Severity, Peace, Plenty, statues Payment(s): £100		[Newgate, London, west side]; Billingshurst sale, Sotheby, 30 May 2001, lots 402–3; dispersed		Guildhall restoration 16v; *Gunnis* 1968, 102
25.	1681	Divinity, Law, Physics and Mathematics, parapet figures Payment(s): £80, Grumbold Accounts	s	Trinity College, Cambridge, library		*Wren Soc* XVII, 79 (repr III), V, 40 (repr XXII); *Whinney* 1988, 113–4; *Baker* 1995 (3), 113
26.	1681	King Charles II surrounded by the four great rivers of England, the Thames, Humber, Tyne and Severn, fountain	s	[King's Square (Soho Square) until 1876]; Soho Square, London, 1938 (statue only; personifications of rivers at Grimsdyke, Harrow Weald)		*Vertue* I, 99; *Faber* 1926, 47–8; *Blackwood* 1989, 24–5 (repr); *ODNB*
27.	1683	Unspecified work Payment(s): £10		Sessions House, Northampton		*Colvin* 1995, 248
28.	1688–1690	Fountain with four seahorses, water nymphs and tritons with conch shells	s	Chatsworth, Derbys, gardens		*Faber* 1926, 49–56; *Davis* 1991, 106, 125 (f'piece, colour repr 36)
29.	post-1690	Unidentified work		[Kensington Palace, London]; untraced		*Beard* 1989 (1), 28
30.	*c*1690	Urn on pedestal supported by three baby satyrs, with relief of 'Meleager hunting the Calydonian Boar' (companion to an urn by Edward Pierce) Payment(s): £521 12s	s	[Hampton Court Palace, Middx, fountain garden]; Kensington Palace, London, orangery		*Faber* 1926, 58–60 (repr facing 60); Wren Soc VII, 132, XVII, 79 (repr VII); *Colvin* 1973–76, V, 171
31.	*c*1690	Vase with relief of Bacchus in a chariot drawn by leopards (companion to a vase by Edward Pearce) Payment(s): £234	m	[Hampton Court Palace, Middx, gardens, east front]; Windsor Castle		*Faber* 1926, 58–9 (repr facing 59); *Wren Soc* XVII, 79 (repr VII), IV, 25
32.	1688–1691	Faith and Justice, altarpiece figures Drawing(s): Chatsworth Library (Wren Soc 17, repr XXXIV attrib William Talman)	a	Chatsworth, Derbys, chapel		*Faber* 1926, 49–56 (repr facing 50); Wren Soc XVIII (repr XXXIV); *Whinney* 1988, 115 (repr)
33.	1691	Four great flowerpots, richly carved Payment(s): £187 10s	s	King's gallery, Kensington Palace, London, parapet		*Colvin* V, 1976, 190
34.	1691–1694	Royal coats of arms supported by cupids with garlands	s	Hampton Court Palace, Middx, clock court		*Faber* 1926, 58 (repr facing p57); *Wren Soc* 17 (repr V); *Colvin* V, 1973–76, V, 162

35.	1694	'several Statues and ffigures in Mettall' Payment(s): £530 (for these and 36 coats of arms)		[Hampton Court Palace, Middx, east front]; untraced	*Colvin* V, 1976, 162 n4; *Whinney* 1988, 115, 442 n18
36.	1695	Faith, Hope and Charity	l	[Danish Church, Wellclose Square, Poplar, London, west front]; Ny Carlsberg Glyptotek, Copenhagen, Sweden, 1908	*Faber* 1926, 65–6 (repr facing 64); *Grove* 7, 298–9
37.	1694–1696	Hercules triumphing over Envy, tympanum relief Payment(s): £400	s	Hampton Court Palace, Middx, east front	*Faber* 1926, 57–8 (repr facing 57); *Wren Soc* 17 (repr XVIII); *Colvin* 1973–76, V, 162
38.	1694–1696	Moses and Aaron, St Paul and St John the Baptist	wd	[Danish Church, City of London, niches flanking reredos]; Danish Church, Regent's Park, London, and Danish Church, Ming St, Poplar, London	*Faber* 1926, 66 (repr facing 66); *Gold* 1984, 93–113; *Colvin* 1995, 248
39.	1698	Keystones for eight arches supporting central dome with festoons and angels with crossed swords of St Paul and other emblems Payment(s): £298		St Paul's Cathedral, London	*Faber* 1926, 75; *Grove* 7, 298; *Wren Soc* III (repr 12), XV, 38 (repr 62); *Saunders* 2001, 112 (repr)
40.	1699	Phoenix, lunette relief Payment(s): £100	s	St Paul's Cathedral, London, south pediment	*Faber* 1926, 74–5; *Wren Soc* XV, 50 (repr 28); *Ward-Jackson* 2003, 372–3 (repr)
41.	1700	Four double festoons with 8 cherubim heads 'upon the pedestalls'		St Paul's Cathedral, London	*Faber* 1926, 75
42.	1700	'Four Insense Potts' on piers		St Paul's Cathedral, London, south front	*Faber* 1926, 75 (repr facing 72)
Miscellaneous					
43.	1685–1687	Pediment reliefs, a figure in the round with a boy on its shoulders, six statues, two dogs twelve heads of Caesars and a pair of sphinxes Payment(s): £536	s	[Thoresby House, Notts]; destroyed	Manvers archives, Nottingham Univ library, 4205, 4206; *Faber* 1926, 48–9; *Davis* 1991, 125; *ODNB*

CINGANELLI, Pietro 1760–1827

For further information the reader is referred to *Pyke* 1973, 30

CLARK, Edward fl mid 19th century

He was the carver responsible for the execution in stone of reliefs modelled by **Thomas Woolner** before 1858 at Llandaff Cathedral. His son, William Clarke, carried out a good deal of wood-carving with **James Milo ap Griffith**, also at Llandaff.

Literary References: *Read* 1982, 258

CLARK, J, of Hereford fl 1805–30

Little is known of him except that he signed a pair of tablets in Herefordshire (1, 2). George Clark, his son and assistant, became a Freeman of Hereford in 1832 (City Archives quoted in *Gunnis* 1968, 103).

Funerary Monuments					
1.	?1805	Benjamin Holland	Wellington, Herefs	S	*Gunnis* 1968, 103
2.	?1830	Susannah Davies	Pembridge, Herefs	S	*Gunnis* 1968, 103

CLARK, J, of Paris Street, Exeter fl 1833–34

Funerary Monuments					
1.	†1833	Dr Peter Hennis	Exeter Cathedral, Devon	S	
2.	†1834	Anne Salt	Exeter Cathedral, Devon		RG/JP, 3, 340v.

CLARK, Thomas, of Bristol 1764–1829

Clark of Lime Kilne Lane, Bristol, was an assistant to **Sir Richard Westmacott RA** and the principal stone-carver employed in building Eaton Hall, Cheshire. He also did a good deal of work in his native city. In 1821 he executed a 'very elegant canopy in the Perpendicular style' over the effigy of John Whitson, Mayor of Bristol, itself a copy of the original of 1629 in St Nicholas's church (2). In the following year he carved the tracery for the west window in the Lord Mayor's chapel (5) and in 1823 received £40 for decorating the stone gallery (6). The window-tracery was removed from the chapel by the architect, Pearson in 1890 and now stands in the grounds of a private house at Henbury, near Bristol. In 1825 he worked on the Bristol Council House (7, 4). He died in 1829 and was buried in the Lord Mayor's Chapel in Bristol, where there is a monument to his memory.

Literary References: *Roper* 1931, 134, n3, 135; Gunnis 1968, 103

Archival References: Bristol City Archives, cited by *Gunnis*, untraced

Funerary Monuments					
1.	c1810	Mark Howell	Long Ashton, Somerset	S	Pevsner, *Somerset: N & Bristol*, 1958, 220; *Gunnis* 1968, 103
2.	1821	Canopy for the tomb of John Whitson, Mayor of Bristol	St Nicholas, Bristol		*Roper* 1931, 135; *Gunnis* 1968, 103
3.	†1826	Mary Brydges	Winterbourne, Glos		Pevsner, *Glos: Vale & Forest of Dean*, 1976, 409
Chimneypieces					
4.	1825	Four Payment(s): £106 6s 4d with coat of arms for pediment	m	[Old Council House, Bristol]; untraced	*Gunnis* 1968, 103

Architectural Sculpture

5.	1822	Tracery		[St Nicholas, Bristol, Lord Mayor's Chapel, west window]; Private house, Henbury, near Bristol, garden	*Gunnis* 1968, 103
6.	1823	Decorative ornaments Payment(s): £40	s	St Nicholas, Bristol, Stone Gallery	*Gunnis* 1968, 103
7.	1825	Coat of arms Payment(s): £106 6s 4d with 4 chimneypieces		[Old Council House, Bristol]; untraced	*Gunnis* 1968, 103

CLARK, W fl 1806

Busts

1.	1806	Rev Isaac Saunders		St Andrew-by-the-Wardrobe, London	SD GPC

CLARKE, Elizabeth fl 1791

In 1791 she was paid for masonry work at Trinity House, Water Lane, London, receiving £16 (Trinity House Archives).

Literary References: GPC

CLARKE, George, of Birmingham 1796–1842

A pupil of **Sir Francis Chantrey**, he set up in Birmingham after leaving his master's studio. In 1821, whilst living at 24 Ann Street, Birmingham, he sent his first bust to the Royal Academy exhibition (**4**). By 1825 he had moved to London, where he lived in Drury Lane and then Museum Street.

In 1826 he was responsible for a statue commemorating the naval officer and political reformer John Cartwright (**2**). This commission reveals his opportunism: **Patrick Macdowell** had won the contract but the subscription fund failed to realise the desired sum. Clarke offered to execute the work for the money already collected. Macdowell recorded in his autobiography that Clarke could afford to carry out the work because of 'connexions' (in Birmingham) that Macdowell lacked (*AJ* 1850, 8). Macdowell also claimed that Clarke failed to impress the committee with the likeness of Cartwright and, with Macdowell's consent, used his original model.

In 1829 Clarke was renting premises in Charles Street, Covent Garden, where he executed a colossal head of the Duke of Wellington (**10**), 'the first sight of which', as the *Literary Gazette* rhapsodised that year, irresistibly drew from them the exclamation 'prodigious' (*Lit Gaz* 1829, 586). A representative from the journal, who visited the sculptor's studio, felt that Clarke's many busts evinced talents 'which, under auspicious circumstances, will no doubt raise their possessor to a distinguished rank in his profession' (*Lit Gaz* 1829, 586). Unfortunately for Clarke his circumstances were insufficiently auspicious and in 1832 he became bankrupt (a fact recorded by Macdowell with satisfaction).

In January 1835 Clarke advertised plaster casts after his busts of Col Harvey and Lord Wodehouse (**29, 30**) in the *Norfolk Chronicle*, adding that 'early application is solicited as Mr Clarke's stay is limited on account of his professional engagements in London'. In 1839 he exhibited from 34 Gower Place, London. On 12 March 1842, he died very suddenly in the shop of a Birmingham surgeon in New Hall-Street. He left a family of 9 children with no means of support. At the time of his death he was engaged in the arduous task of casting the leaves for the capital of Nelson's Column in Trafalgar Square, but had only completed two of them.

Literary References: *Lit Gaz* 1829, 586; *GM* 1842, 1, 453; *AJ* 1850, 8; *Graves* II, 1905–6, 68; *Gunnis* 1968, 103

Funerary Monuments

1.	1829	Lieutenant-Colonel Hercules Pepper (†1826)		St Mary, Fort St George, Chennai (Madras), India	S	*Lit Gaz* 1829, 586; *Steggles* 2000, 157–8 (repr)

Statues

2.	1831	Major John Cartwright (designed by Patrick MacDowell)	b	Cartwright Gardens, London		*AJ*, 1850, 8–9; *Blackwood* 1989, 176–7 (repr)
3.	nd	Children of E G Barnard, MP, of Gosfield Hall		[Christie, 7 July 1877]; untraced		*Gunnis* 1968, 104

Busts

4.	1821	Rev Samuel Parr	m	[Exhib RA, London, 1104 (?model); 1826, 1046]; untraced		*Lit Gaz* 1829, 586; *Graves* II, 1905–6, 68; *Gunnis* 1968, 104
5.	1822	Will Hamper FSA	m	Birmingham Reference Library		*Graves* II, 1905–6, 68; *Gunnis* 1968, 104
6.	1825	W Macready		[Exhib RA, London, 987 Sculptor's studio, London (1829)]; untraced		*Lit Gaz* 1829, 586; *Graves* II, 1905–6, 68; *Gunnis* 1968, 104
7.	1827	John Johnstone		[Exhib Birmingham Soc of A]; untraced		*Gunnis* 1968, 104
8.	1827	Mr Rolfe		[Exhib Birmingham Soc of A]; untraced		*Gunnis* 1968, 104
9.	1828	Rev Dr Maltby ('to be executed in marble')		[Exhib RA, London, 1187]; untraced		*Graves* II, 1905–6, 68
10.	1829	Arthur, 1st Duke of Wellington		[Sculptor's studio, London (1829)]; untraced		*Lit Gaz* 1829, 586; *Gunnis* 1968, 103
11.	1829	Clarkson Stanfield		[Sculptor's studio, London]; untraced		*Lit Gaz* 1829, 586; *Gunnis* 1968, 103
12.	1829	Colonel Shorte		[Exhib Birmingham Soc of A]; untraced		*Gunnis* 1968, 104
13.	1829	Dr Milner		[Sculptor's studio, London]; untraced		*Lit Gaz* 1829, 586; *Gunnis* 1968, 103
14.	1829	Mr Braham (a singer)		[Sculptor's studio, London]; untraced		*Lit Gaz* 1829, 586; *Gunnis* 1968, 103
15.	1829	Rev Dr Blomberg		[Exhib Birmingham Soc of A]; untraced		*Gunnis* 1968, 104
16.	1830	Basil Montague	m	[Exhib RA, London, 1206]; untraced		*Graves* II, 1905–6, 68
17.	1830	Dr Heath	m	[Exhib RA, London, 1238]; untraced		*Graves* II, 1905–6, 68

18.	1830	Rev Dr Samuel Buller, Head Master of Shrewsbury School	m	[Exhib RA, London, 1247]; untraced	*Graves* II, 1905–6, 68
19.	1832	Lady Sutherland		[Exhib Birmingham Soc of A]; untraced	*Gunnis* 1968, 104
20.	1832	Rajah Rammohun Roy	m	Kolkata (Calcutta)	*Graves* II, 1905–6, 68; *Gunnis* 1968, 104
21.	1833	Charles Silvestre, 'for the Philosophical room at Derby'		[Exhib RA, London, 1190]; Derby Art Gallery	*Graves* II, 1905–6, 68; *Gunnis* 1968, 104
22.	1833	John Mathewman	m	[Exhib RA, London, 1145]; untraced	*Graves* II, 1905–6, 68
23.	1833	Rev R Brandling	m	[Exhib RA, London, 1174]; untraced	*Graves* II, 1905–6, 68
24.	1833	Sir Charles Cockerell	m	[Exhib RA, London, 1154]; untraced	*Graves* II, 1905–6, 68; *Gunnis* 1968, 104
25.	1834	Francis, 6th Earl of Guilford	m	[Exhib RA, London, 1070]; untraced	*Graves* II, 1905–6, 68; *Gunnis* 1968, 104
26.	1834	John Spottiswoode		[Exhib RA, London, 1087]; untraced	*Graves* II, 1905–6, 68
27.	1834	Lady Burrell		[Exhib RA, London, 1099]; untraced	*Graves* II, 1905–6, 68; *Gunnis* 1968, 104
28.	1834	Lord Encombe		[Exhib Birmingham Soc of A]; untraced	*Gunnis* 1968, 104
29.	1835	Colonel Harvey		Untraced Other versions: Casts offered for sale	*Norfolk Chronicle*, 31 Jan 1835
30.	1835	Rt Hon Lord Wodehouse		Untraced Other versions: Casts offered for sale	*Norfolk Chronicle*, 31 Jan 1835
31.	1839	Colonel Thompson, late MP for Hull	m	[Exhib RA, London, 1357]; untraced	*Graves* II, 1905–6, 69
32.	1839	T P Thompson		Hull Guildhall	GPC
33.	1841	George Muntz		[Exhib RA, London]; untraced	*Gunnis* 1968, 104

CLARKE, I fl 1722

Funerary Monuments

1.	1722	William Settle (†1650)	Finglas, Co Dublin	GPC

CLARKE, II fl 1808

He was described as a carver and as such was paid £210 for work at Eaton Hall, Chester, in 1808.

Literary References: GPC citing Grosvenor Archives

CLARKE, John –1708

Clarke was apprenticed to Timothy Townsend and became free in 1669. He became a warden of the Masons' Company in 1693 and master four years later. In 1667 he was employed on mason's work including 'a sink of stone' and paving at Greenwich Palace and he worked with **George Pile** at Windsor Castle in 1686. The two were paid for masonry work, including a doorway into the pastry office, a chimney for 'the Queen's closett', sawing and laying several feet of white and black marble 'at the altar of his Majesty's Castle' and laying several feet more of white marble in the Queen's birdcage. They also provided a marble pedestal and several chimneypieces (1). In 1687 Clarke built Windsor Guildhall (Town Archives, cited in *Gunnis* 1968, 104).

During the period 1689–96, when extensive additions were made to Hampton Court, he acted with **Thomas Hill** as one of the principal masons and was paid over £7,000 for his work. Between 1688 and 1691 he built the New School at Eton, receiving £1,050 11s 8d. In 1694 he was there again rebuilding the stairs to the upper chapel. In 1703–4 he built the tower of St Mary, Aldermanbury. He was noted as living at Windsor in the list of members of the Masons' Company for the year 1708. His death later that year is recorded in the same document.

Literary References: *Willis and Clarke* 1886, 446; *Hope* 1913, 328; *Bolton and Hendry* 1942, 109; *Gunnis* 1968, 104

Archival References: Masons' Co, Freedom Register; Masons' Co, Masters and Wardens; Masons' Co, List of Company Members, p 4; BM Harleian 1658 fols 165, 169 (Greenwich); TNA E.351/3463; St Paul's Cathedral library, MS. WE.35; RG/JP, 3, 344

Chimneypieces

1.	1686	Several, of white, yellow and black marble (co-sculptor: George Pile)	m	[Windsor Castle, Berks, Queen's closets, bedchamber, bathing and dressing rooms]; untraced	*Gunnis* 1968, 104; *Hope* 1913, 328

CLARKE, of Wigmore Street fl 1829–*c*1845

Between 1829 and 1830 he was the master-mason responsible for additions to Lambeth Palace, where the total sum paid to him was £8,315. Part of this sum was for carving (5). His tablets to Lord Western and William Way are Gothic in style (2–4). Gunnis described them as large and very ugly. That to Adolphus Meetkerke is simpler (1).

Literary References: *Gunnis* 1968, 103

Funerary Monuments

1.	?1841	Adolphus Meetkerke	Rushden, Herts	S	*Gunnis* 1968, 103
2.	†1844	Baron Western of Rivenhall	Rivenhall, Essex		Pevsner, *Essex*, 1965, 325
3.	†1844	Robert Prickett	All Saints, Thwing, E R Yorks		Pevsner, *Yorks: E R & York*, 1995, 724
4.	?1845	Rev William Way	Denham, Bucks Other versions: ?Glympton, Bucks (GPC)	S	*Gunnis* 1968, 103

Architectural Sculpture

5.	1829–1830	Stone carving Payment(s): £355	s	Lambeth Palace, London	*Gunnis* 1968, 103

CLARKE, William fl 1829

In 1829 he was the master-mason responsible for repairs and additions to Lambeth Palace, carried out under the architect Edward Blore. Clarke received over £7,000 (Account Book, Lambeth Palace).

Literary References: GPC

CLARKE (or CLARK), Richard, of Reading fl 1811–36

A popular provincial statuary who also had yards at Wallingford and Watlington. His work, chiefly consisting of wall tablets, is 'in no way distinguished' (*Gunnis* 1968, 104). He had taken more than one of his offspring into the business by the time he produced the monument to Grace Norris, signed '& Sons' (**8**).

Funerary Monuments

1.	?1811	Richard Jervoise	Shalstone, Bucks	S	*Gunnis* 1968, 104
2.	?1812	Elizabeth Parker	St Leonard, Wallingford, Berks	S	*Gunnis* 1968, 104
3.	?1816	John Bushnell	Blewberry, Berks	S	*Gunnis* 1968, 104
4.	?1817	Henry Fludyer	St Leonard, Wallingford, Berks	S	*Gunnis* 1968, 104
5.	?1817	Samuel Rudge	Wheatfield, Oxon	S	*Gunnis* 1968, 104
6.	?1828	Henry Hopkins	Basildon, Berks	S	*Gunnis* 1968, 104
7.	?1829	Lady Caroline Kerr	Arundel, Sussex	S	*Gunnis* 1968, 104
8.	†1830	Grace Norris	Warblington, Hants	S	
9.	?1836	John Beaufoy	Upton Grey, Hants	S	*Gunnis* 1968, 104

CLAYTON, John Richard 1816–96

He was responsible for the image of *St George and the dragon* which surmounts the monument to the scholars of Westminster School killed in the Crimean War (**1**). He originally trained as a sculptor, but later became a stained glass artist.

Funerary Monuments

1.	nd	St George and the Dragon	Westminster School, Broad Sanctuary, London	*CIIA* 4/7/102 (repr)

CLAYTON, of Roche Abbey fl 1835

The Harvey is a large Gothic monument.

Funerary Monuments

1.	?1835	Rev John Harvey	Finningley, Notts	S	GPC

CLEARE, Richard fl 1680

He was paid £21 1s in 1680 for 'carving worke done upon the Hall Staircase' of the Mercers' Company (Mercers S & R W Accts).

CLEERE, Richard fl 1669–79

Cleere was paid £35 in 1669 for carving at Christ's Hospital and £5 in 1679 (Christ's H. TAB, 12819/10, 211, 862). He carried out carving work at the Guildhall, City of London, including its chapel, for which he was paid £81 19s in October 1671 (City Lands Comm Papers 04/1). He can perhaps be identified with **Richard Cleare**.

CLELANDS & Co fl 1810–32

The Clelands family first established a marble works in Glasgow in 1810. William Clelands and his son John worked from Bath Street until 1829 when the business moved to 5 Cathcart Street. In 1831 James and Alexander Clelands, who were either brothers or sons of John, joined the firm, as did **William Mossman**. The following year the business was taken over by **David Hamilton and Sons**.

Literary References: *Woodward* 1977, vol 1, pt 2, 46

Funerary Monuments

1.	1829	Lieutenant John Stirling (†1828)	Glasgow Cathedral	S	*Woodwward* 1977, 46; Pevsner, *Glasgow*, 1990, 134

CLEMENTS, John fl 1845

He exhibited two works in Liverpool in 1845 giving his address as 'London'.

Reliefs

1.	1845	Europa	[Exhib Liverpool Ac, 801]; untraced	*Morris and Roberts* 1998, 142

Miscellaneous

2.	1845	Mucius Scaevola	[Exhib Liverpool Ac, 805]; untraced	*Morris and Roberts* 1998, 142

CLEMSON, H fl 1838

Funerary Monuments

1.	†1838	William Stokes	sl	Willersey, Glos	S	Pevsner, *Glos: Cotswolds*, 1999, 724

CLERKE, John fl c1625

Edward Marshall was apprenticed to him and became free in January 1627.

Archival References: Masons' Co Quarterage Book (1), f 47v

CLERUCI, Charles fl 1769–82

Cleruci was a scagliola worker. Between 1769 and 1771 he was employed at Thoresby Park, Notts, by the architect, John Carr of York. In December 1769 there were payments to 'Carlo Clerici and Company for work at the Dome' and in the two following years he received nearly £600 for decorating the Marble Hall. There is also a note of a payment to 'Loftus Clifford for Mr Clericy's marble work' (Earl Manvers' Archives, 4420/21, Nottingham Univ Library). He was assisted by Ely Crabtree, who later set up as a plasterer in Lendal, York. In 1769 Cleruci was working and living at the town house of the Marquis of Rockingham in Grosvenor Square. In 1774 he was at Rockingham's seat at Wentworth Woodhouse, Yorks, where he again worked under Carr. He was paid a guinea a week plus board and lodging, and made casts, pedestals, scagliola tables and vine leaf insets for marble chimneypieces. His principal and most spectacular work was in the Grand Saloon where he constructed niches, columns and pedestals. During his stay Clerici impregnated a family maidservant, who subsequently died (to the evident relief of the household). At the conclusion of his work in August 1782 he was paid £475 10s 10d, the whole of his salary for 8 years 259 days.

Literary References: *Wragg* 1959, 356–7; *Gunnis* 1968, 104; GPC

CLEVELY, of Gloucester 1686–1743

He signs the large tablet in memory of Lucy Stokes in his home town (1). Clevely died on 17th February 1743, and was buried in St Mary de Lode, Gloucester.

Literary References: *Fosbrooke* 4, 1819, 349

Funerary Monuments

1.	†1732	Lucy Stokes	Gloucester Cathedral	S	*Gunnis* 1968, 104

CLIFFORD, Richard William, of Stow-on-the-Wold fl 1828–34

There were several Cliffords who were masons in the neighbourhood of Stow, including Richard Clifford (1734–1797) and William Clifford of Bourton-on-the-Water (1747–1833). The latter was employed by Warren Hastings to build Daylesford church in 1816. Gunnis was uncertain which of these was the father of Richard William Clifford, who signs three monuments in Stow Church. The earliest, to Leonard Hayward, 1828, takes the form of a classical urn and is a copy in marble of a Coade Factory terra-cotta erected in 1780 on the same wall (1). The other two are tablets.

Literary References: *Gunnis* 1968, 104–5

Funerary Monuments

1.	†1828	Leonard Hayward	Stow-on-the-Wold, Glos	S	Pevsner, *Glos: Cotswolds*, 1999, 640
2.	†1829	Ann Knight	Stow-on-the-Wold, Glos	S	Pevsner, *Glos: Cotswolds*, 1999, 640
3.	†1834	Elizabeth Cornbill	Stow-on-the-Wold, Glos	S	Pevsner, *Glos: Cotswolds*, 1999, 640

CLIFFORD, Theophilus, of Marlow fl 1823–42

Both identified works are tablets.

Literary References: *Gunnis* 1968, 105

Funerary Monuments

1.	†1823	Lieutenant-Commander Hippolyte da Costa	Hurley, Berks	S	Pevsner, *Berks*, 1966, 158; *Gunnis* 1968, 105
2.	?1826	Mary Waghorne	Bray, Bucks	S	*Gunnis* 1968, 105

CLIFTON PARIS, T fl 1831

In 1831, while living in Dover Street, Piccadilly, he was awarded a large silver medal by the Society of Arts.

Miscellaneous

1.	1831	Models of horses in sealing wax	[Soc of A, large silver medal]; untraced	RSA, *Transactions*, vol 48, 1831, 550

CLINT, Scipio 1805–39

The second son of George Clint, ARA, he worked chiefly as a medallist and gem-engraver but also carved several busts. In 1825, when living at 5 Rolls Buildings, Fetter Lane, he first exhibited at the Royal Academy, showing an impression from a steel seal after a bust of Thomas Lawrence by **E H Baily**. He produced other medallic portraits of great men of the age after busts by **William Behnes, Samuel Joseph** and **John Gibson**. He was appointed medallist to King William IV in 1831 and seal-engraver to Queen Victoria in 1838. At this time Clint lived at 19 Dean Street. In the 1830s he modelled and exhibited numerous busts, some of marble. Clint also acted as secretary to a Roman Catholic Society established to forward a Government plan of education. He died suddenly on 8 August 1839 in his home in 48 Greek Street, Soho, leaving four children. He had married Ann Randall Anderson at St Clement Danes on 20 August 1828. The *Art Union* described him as 'largely esteemed as an able artist' (*AU* 1839, 122). Clint had providently joined the Artists' Annuity Fund at the age of 22. His widow and 4 children were given financial aid from 12 December 1839, receiving £20 annually and £5 for each child from the orphans' fund.

Literary References: *AU* 1839, 122; *Graves* II, 1905–6, 86; *Gunnis* 1968, 105; *Morris and Roberts* 1998, 144

Archival References: AAF, CM, 23667/1, 84; 23667/4, pp 89, 98; AAF Proposals, 137; AAF, MGM

Statues

1.	1838	Rev Mr Blick, rector of Tamworth, cabinet statue		[Exhib RA, London, 1344]; untraced	*Graves* II, 1905–6, 87
2.	1838	Unidentified artist, miniature figure		[Exhib Soc of BA, London, 608]; untraced	*Johnson* 1975, 94

Busts

3.	1834	Margaret Watson		[Exhib RA, London, 1094]; untraced	*Graves* II, 1905–6, 87; *Gunnis* 1968, 105
4.	1834	Thomas Roscoe		[Exhib Soc of BA, London, 837]; untraced	*Johnson* 1975, 94
5.	1835	Olinthus Gregory FRS		[Royal Military Acad, Woolwich, London]; untraced	*Graves* II, 1905–6, 87; *Gunnis* 1968, 105; *Johnson* 1975, 94
6.	1835	Peter Barlow FRS		[Royal Military Acad, Woolwich, London]; untraced	*Graves* II, 1905–6, 87; *Gunnis* 1968, 105; *Johnson* 1975, 94
7.	1835	Unidentified gentleman		[Exhib RA, London, 1086]; untraced	*Graves* II, 1905–6, 87
8.	1836	George Ringer		[Exhib Soc of BA, London, 863]; untraced	*Johnson* 1975, 94
9.	1836	James Morison	m	[Exhib RA, London, 1133]; untraced	*Graves* II, 1905–6, 87
10.	1836	Rev Reginald Rabett		[Exhib Soc of BA, London, 880]; untraced	*Johnson* 1975, 94
11.	1836	W B Cooke		[Exhib Soc of BA, London, 894]; untraced	*Johnson* 1975, 94
12.	1836	William Lews		[Exhib Soc of BA, London, 887]; untraced	*Johnson* 1975, 94
13.	1837	Captain Macauly		[Exhib Soc of BA, London, 609]; untraced	*Johnson* 1975, 94

14.	1837	Cardinal Nicholas Wiseman	m	[Exhib Soc of BA, London, 581]; untraced		*Ormond* 1973, 518; *Johnson* 1975, 94; *Morris and Roberts* 1998, 144
15.	1837	G Lance		[Exhib Soc of BA, London, 601]; untraced		*Johnson* 1975, 94
16.	1837	Mr Robinson		[Exhib Soc of BA, London, 610]; untraced		*Johnson* 1975, 94
17.	1837	Mr Wagstaff		[Exhib Soc of BA, London, 607]; untraced		*Johnson* 1975, 94
18.	1837	Mrs Robert Graves	m	[Exhib RA, London, 1145]; untraced		*Graves* II, 1905–6, 87; *Gunnis* 1968, 105
19.	1837	Rev George Thomas Palmer		[Exhib Soc of BA, London, 604]; untraced		*Johnson* 1975, 94
20.	1837	The Venerable Archdeacon of Ferns		[Exhib Soc of BA, London, 608]; untraced		*Johnson* 1975, 94
21.	1837	Unidentified gentleman		[Exhib Soc of BA, London, 612]; untraced		*Johnson* 1975, 94
22.	1837	Unidentified lady		[Exhib Soc of BA, London, 611]; untraced		*Johnson* 1975, 94
23.	1837	W J Cooke		[Exhib Soc of BA, London, 602]; untraced		*Johnson* 1975, 94
24.	1838	Unidentified gentleman	m	[Exhib RA, London, 1314]; untraced		*Graves* II, 1905–6, 87
Reliefs						
25.	nd	William Roscoe, medallion	b	Manchester CAG 1981.12		

CLOTHIER, of the New Road, London fl 1841–42

He signs two known works, one of them the wall-tablet with a sarcophagus to William Hildyard (2).

Funerary Monuments

1.	†1841	Lieutenant-Colonel John Snodgrass	Halifax Cathedral, Nova Scotia		GPC
2.	†1842	William Hildyard	Winestead, E R Yorks		Pevsner, *Yorks: E R & York*, 1995, 757

CLOTHIERS, of New Road, London fl 1845

Funerary Monuments

1.	†1845	George White	Whippingham, I of W	S	

CLOUD, R fl 1801

Funerary Monuments

1.	?1801	John Knight	Axminster, Devon	S	*Gunnis* 1968, 105

CLOWES, Robert fl 1812

In 1812 he was paid £100 for building a temple at Alton Abbey (later Alton Towers), Staffs.

Archival References: GPC citing Archives, Earl of Shrewsbury

CLUTTEN, Henry, of Framlingham fl c1830–39

His monument to John Sheppard (1) is an exact copy of one by **Sir Richard Westmacott RA** in the same church.

Literary References: *Gunnis* 1968, 105

Funerary Monuments

1.	?1830	John Sheppard	Campsey Ash, Suffolk	S	*Gunnis* 1968, 105
2.	?1839	George Edwards	Framlingham, Suffolk	S	*Gunnis* 1968, 105

COADE, Eleanor 1733–1821

See **Coade Factory, of Lambeth**

COADE FACTORY, of Lambeth fl 1769–1840

Eleanor Coade's artificial stone manufactory produced a vast range of architectural and garden ornaments, decorative details and furnishings for interiors and also a number of funerary monuments and commemorative statues. The factory maintained high standards of design and production throughout its 70-year history and was employed by London's leading architects, Robert Adam, James Wyatt, John Nash and Sir John Soane. Coade, **John Sealy**, **William Croggon** and his son, **Thomas John Croggon** were all in turn directors of the business.

She was born in Exeter on 14 June 1833, the daughter of George Coade, a woollen cloth finisher from Lyme Regis, Dorset, and his wife Eleanor, née Enchmarch. The family's prosperity was adversely affected by a decline in the Exeter wool trade during the 1750s and in 1759 George Coade was declared bankrupt. The Coades moved to London soon after, living first at Charterhouse Square in the City and then at Charles Square, Hoxton. By 1766 Eleanor was in business on her own account as a linen draper. She never married but was referred to as Mrs Coade, the courteous form of address for a mature single woman in employment in the 18th century.

It is not clear how Mrs Coade became involved in the production of artificial stone, but she dated the foundation of her manufactory at Narrow Wall, by King's Arms Stairs in Lambeth (later known as Belvedere Road and now a part of the area occupied by the South Bank Centre) to 1769. There was already an artificial stone business run by **Daniel Pincot** on the site by 1767. Coade appears to have taken over Pincot's business and retained his services for some years, but the arrangement was unsatisfactory. In September 1771 she announced that Pincot was not a partner in the firm and 3 days later she declared that he was no longer employed by her (*Daily Ad*, 11 and 14 September 1771 cited by *Valpy* 1986, 215–6). **John Bacon RA** was appointed superintendent soon after. This proved to be an astute decision, for Bacon was a rising young sculptor and he provided the firm with some of its most popular designs over the next 3 decades.

The artificial stone produced by the factory was a ceramic material containing a large of proportion of ground pre-fired stoneware, or grog, with an additive of glass, which stabilised the body during firing. In its raw state the material lacked plasticity and could not easily be modelled, so it was rolled out in sheets and pressed into moulds. An enormous range of products, from simple architectural details like paterae and stringcourses to complex sculptural pieces such as the large statue of a river god at Ham House (**94**), were made by this method. Moulds could be reused and some of the most popular designs, such as the *Borghese* and *Medici Vases* (**196, 200**), were much repeated and remained in production over many years. Most stock items were reasonably priced: a lifesize statue of a charity school child could be bought for 16 guineas (**87**) and a bust of King Edward IV or Queen Elizabeth cost only three. Most works were cast in sections and then assembled before firing, which meant that they could easily be adapted to suit different purposes and tastes without the need for preparing a new model. A statue of *Urania* (**92**), for instance, could be transformed into a *Flora* (**95**) by the addition of some flowers.

Pincot, **Richard Holt, Batty Langley** and **George Davy** all preceded Coade as manufacturers of artificial stone and **Bridges of Knightsbridge** was a competitor during the 1770s, but her volume and scope of business greatly surpassed theirs. Her factory developed considerable expertise in controlling the firing process to produce a remarkably resilient material. The product marketed by her predecessors lacked the durability to withstand hard weather: the ornaments on Robert Adam's Brentford Gateway at Syon House, for instance, which were executed in an early artificial stone (perhaps supplied by Davy or Bridges), crumbled due to frost damage. They were later replaced by 'Coade stone' panels, which are still in pristine condition (**204**).

Adam's neoclassical architectural style was at the height of its popularity when Mrs Coade established her factory and Coade stone was the ideal material for the delicate, applied external ornaments he required, since the detail remained clear and sharp even in exposed situations. Coade also catered for the market requiring gothic architectural motifs and executed, notably, gate piers for Strawberry Hill (**201**), the screen at St George's Chapel, Windsor (**269**) and 10 candelabra decorated with dragons and tracery for the conservatory at Carlton House (**222**). The popularity of Coade's material was enhanced by the sustainedly high standard of design at the factory, where a number of prominent sculptors, particularly **John De Vaere, JCF Rossi RA, Joseph Panzetta** and Bacon provided the models.

Coade energetically promoted the factory's products. In 1773 she advertised that the firm was 'employed by many of the Nobility and first Architects in the Kingdom'. She published a catalogue listing 778 available items in 1784 and commissioned a series of engravings of products made by the company. In 1798 she built a row of houses in Pedlar's Acre, at the south end of Westminster Bridge, one of which became 'Coade's Gallery', the firm's showroom. The façade was decorated with a relief, *The attempts of Time to destroy Sculpture and Architecture, defeated by the vitrifying aid of fire* (**267**), a design that was adapted from the firm's tradecard designed by Bacon. A pamphlet describing the items on display and listing sites for which coade stone had already been supplied was published in 1799. The most impressive object was a colossal group of *Polyphemus, standing on a cave, hurling rocks down at Acis and Galatea* (**116**).

By 21 May 1789 John Sealy, a cousin of Eleanor Coade who had been employed at the factory for some years, had become a partner and the firm's name changed to Coade and Sealy. A son or nephew of John Sealy, Thomas Sealy, was also employed at the factory until he died prematurely after crashing drunkenly into a post when passing through Pedlar's Acre one night in January 1804. The factory reached the height of its success in the early-19th century when it received a number of prestigious commissions for public statues, including several commemorating the jubilee of George III in 1810 (**128–30**). The previous year a memorial column crowned with a statue of Admiral Nelson, was sent out to Montreal (**127**). The most ambitious commission was a spectacular tympanum relief celebrating Nelson for the Royal Naval Hospital at Greenwich, which was designed by the President of the Royal Academy, Benjamin West and modelled by Joseph Panzetta (**290**). The firm's ability to cast a ceramic relief over forty feet long and reaching ten feet in height demonstrates the factory's remarkable technical capabilities.

John Sealy died on 22 October 1813 and was buried in Lambeth churchyard, where a large coade stone monument marks the family vault (**35**). Mrs Coade then appointed as her manager a distant relation from Cornwall, William Croggon. He remained in the post until her death on 18 November 1821 and purchased the firm soon after. The terms of the transfer were disputed in the Chancery Court and Croggon's order, day and letter books for the period 1813–1821 were presented as evidence. These records are now in the PRO (C111/106) and they indicate a diminution in demand for the firm's architectural elements. Garden ornaments, vases and statues remained popular, but sales of relief plaques, medallions and friezes suffered as an austere, Greek-inspired classicism became the dominant architectural style. It was perhaps in response to these problems that the Coade factory turned to the production of scagliola, an imitation marble used for interior ornaments. The first order for scagliola came in 1817 and records show that production increased rapidly over the next few years. Croggon sought to expand the business by opening a showroom in Euston Road, close to the newly fashionable residential area of Regent's Park. It was managed by his eldest son, William Richard Croggon.

The firm's most prestigious later work was at Buckingham Palace, which was rebuilt from 1825 by John Nash. In addition to much ornamental work in scagliola and artificial stone (**335**), the factory supplied nine statues modelled by **Edward Hodges Baily RA** to designs by **John Flaxman RA** (**331**) and a further six modelled by JCF Rossi (**332**). These were all moved and some were lost during later alterations. William Croggon received payments of more than £10,000 for his work at the palace between 1825 and 1828.

Despite the size of the Buckingham Palace contract, Croggon was declared bankrupt in 1833. The reasons for his failure are not known, but he undertook much work for the Duke of York, for which he is unlikely to have been fully paid since the Duke died in 1827, owing large sums to tradesmen. The expense of setting up the Euston Road showroom may been another contributory factor. On 28 February 1834 Croggon wrote to Sir John Soane, stating that 'having formed a partnership with a gentleman who has purchased all the stock, plant, machinery and effects, the business in all its branches is resumed under the firm of William Croggon and Company . . . at Lambeth' (Croggon/Soane). A further sale of surplus stock took place on 30 July 1834. Croggon died soon after, in July 1835. His son, Thomas John Croggon, took over the lease on the factory but concentrated on business activities outside the production of artificial stone and he finally left Lambeth in 1837, when the factory was let to Thomas Routledge and John Danforth Greenwood. They ran a terracotta and scagliola works for a number of years and appear to have produced small numbers of coade stone ornaments until as late as 1840. A colossal lion made for the

Lion Brewery on Belvedere Road in 1837 (**157**) is stamped 'COADES' on its paw, but a bottle containing the trade card of Routledge & Greenwood was found in a cavity in its back during conservation work, and the charity boy at Vintners' Hall is marked 'COADE'S 1840' (**87**). The factory's moulds were finally sold by Rushworth and Jarvis in 1843. Some may have been purchased by **M H Blanchard** who manufactured a similar product for a period.

The firm's achievements were underestimated for many years, partly because coade stone imitates the natural substance and so has often failed to be properly identified. The excavation of the factory's site prior to construction of the Royal Festival Hall generated interest in the manufactury, and this was reinforced by the discovery of the Coade records in the Public Record Office during the 1960s. Recent studies, principally by Kelly, have revealed the scope and volume of the factory's output.

EH

Literary References: *Coade* 1784, *passim*; *Coade* 1799, *passim*; *Coade* c1808, *passim*; *The Times*, 9 Oct 1833, 2; 23 Oct 1833, 6; 30 Nov 1833, 3; *Builder*, 25 July 1868, 546; *S of L*, XXIII, 1951, 58–61; *Hamilton* 1954, 295–301; *Kessels* 1955, 141–6; *Gunnis* 1968, 105–9, 116–7,304, 346; *Ruch* 1968, 34–56; *Colvin* VI, 1973–76, 270–1, 283, 298–301; *Kelly* 1978, 14–25; *Valpy* 1986, 215–223; *Valpy* 1990, 112–3; *Kelly* 1990, *passim* (with a gazetteer of works including minor architectural ornaments); *Penny* 1990, 879–880; *Yorke* 1993, 54–55; *Grove* 7, 1996, 480 (Kelly); *ODNB* (Kelly)

Archival References: Voucher, dated 21 May 1789, for £83 18s 7d from William Constable to Mrs Coade and John Sealy, Artificial Stone Manufacturers, ERAO, Chichester Constable Papers DDCC/2/59

Additional MS Sources: Coade Papers

Collections of Designs: volumes of etchings BL 1802.b.24; NAL 37.E.218; GL A 3.5 no. 1; GL SL 68:5; Soane PC 115/14/2; RA

Will: PRO PROB 11/1651 (Eleanor Coade)

Auction References: Coade Factory 1779, 1834, 1843

Views of the Factory: interior of Coade kiln, engraving (*Euro Mag*, 1787, f 112); watercolour, c1800, GL Print Room q 9516811; George Shepherd, watercolour, c1800, GL Print Room q 9516828; Charles Tomkins, watercolour, 1801, GL Print Room q 9516834; Samuel Rawle, *The entrance to Coade's Gallery*, engraving, 1802, GL Print Room q 9516840

Funerary Monuments

1.	c1775	Frederick Frankland	sa	Stanmer House, Brighton, Sussex Other versions: George Holgate †1785, Brocklesby Park, Lincs Timothy Brett †1791, Mount Edgcumbe, Cornwall Patrick Sarsfield, Lucan House, Co Kildare		*Kelly* 1990, 229, 339, 362, 383 (repr)
2.	†1777	Edward Wortley Montagu	sa	Westminster Abbey, London, west side of cloisters		*Kelly* 1990, 245, 424
3.	†1779	Mary Pulton Payment(s): 30 gns	sa	Desborough, Northants Other versions: Elizabeth Minto (+1783), St James, Montego Bay, Jamaica, 1790		*Kelly* 1990, 366
4.	†1780	Leonard Hayward	sa	Stow-on-the-Wold, Glos		*Kelly* 1990, 350
5.	†1782	Edward Keepe (designed by Samuel Robinson)	sa	St Mary the Virgin, Woodford, Essex, churchyard Other versions: Martha Chivers, West Tarring churchyard, Sussex, 1807		*Kelly* 1988 (2), 192 (repr); *Kelly* 1990, 349
6.	1782	George Illington	sa	Winterborne Stickland, Dorset, churchyard		*Kelly* 1990, 253, 345
7.	†1784	Lettice Adderley	sa	Lea Marston, Warks		Pevsner, *Warks*, 1966, 332; *Kelly* 1990, 384
8.	†1786	Eleanor Lovett	sa	Soulbury, Bucks Other versions: Richard Coffin (†1796), Lawhitton, Cornwall Sarah Goring, Wiston, Sussex, 1798 Sir Charles Morgan, Bassalleg, Mon, 1806 Anne, Lady Stanhope (†1812), Melton Constable, Norfolk, 1814		*Kelly* 1990, 249, 336, 339, 365, 383 (repr)
9.	†1788	David Harvey	sa	Langley Marish, Bucks Other versions: John Camden (†1780) and Elizabeth Neild (†1791), St Mary, Battersea, London, 1791 Frances Brown, Fenstanton, Huntingdon, 1793 Sir William Hillman, VAM, 1800 Joseph Johnson, St Mary, Paddington, London, 1802 George Mitchell, Henstead, Suffolk, 1806 Mary Rockfort (†1819), Wootton, Isle of Wight		*Kelly* 1990, 248, 374, 392, 412, 417 (repr); *Bilbey* 2002, 238 (repr)
10.	1788	T S Jolliffe	sa	[Ammerdown, Radstock Somerset]; church demol; figures in gardens of Ammerdown House		*Kelly* 1990, 371
11.	1789	Rev Thomas and Mrs Ann Green	sa	Bramber, Sussex		*Kelly* 1990, 379
12.	1790	Bermingham family mausoleum (plaques, statuettes, urn)	sa	Athenry Friary, Galway	SD	*Kelly* 1990, 433; *Feely* 1996, 93 (repr)
13.	1790	Bernard Birch (†1780)	sa	St James, Montego Bay, Jamaica		*Kelly* 1990, 445
14.	1790	Finlater family member	sa	[St James, Montego Bay, Jamaica]; untraced		*Kelly* 1990, 445
15.	1790	Lawrence family member	sa	[St James, Montego Bay, Jamaica, W I]; untraced		*Kelly* 1990, 445

16.	1791	John Camden (†1780) and daughter (†1791)		St Mary, Battersea, London	SD	
17.	1789–1791	King Edward IV and Queen Elizabeth Woodville	sa	St George's Chapel, Windsor Castle		*Bond* 1999, 110
18.	1791	Mrs Simpson (designed by Humphrey Repton)	sa	[All Saints, Babworth, Notts]; untraced	S	*Kelly* 1990, 245–7, 368
19.	1792	Charles Hill	sa	Dewlish, Dorset, churchyard	SD	*Kelly* 1990, 344
20.	1792	Margaret Simpson	sa	Keynsham, Somerset		*Gunnis* 1968, 108
21.	†1793	Dorothy Cooper	sa	Kirkby Overblow, W R Yorks		Pevsner, *Yorks: W R*, 1967, 288
22.	1793	Lady Ann Henniker (†1792)	sa	Worlingworth, Suffolk		Pevsner, *Suffolk*, 1974, 507; *Kelly* 1990, 250
23.	1793	Lady Ann Henniker (†1792) (designed by 'Mr Banks,' probably Henry Bankes)	sa	Rochester Cathedral, Kent	SD	*Kelly* 1990, 250, 359 (repr)
24.	†1794	John Simmonds	sa	Congregational and Unionist Church, Faversham, Kent		*Kelly* 1990, 358
25.	†1794	Joseph Edmonds	sa	St Mary, Swanage, Dorset		*Kelly* 1990, 344
26.	†1794	Richard Newton Ogle	sa	Ponteland, Northumbs	S	*Kelly* 1990, 367
27.	†1795	Thomas Payler and family	sa	St Helen, York		Pevsner, *Yorks: E R & York*, 1995, 167
28.	1796	Lieutenant Philip Bromfield (†1795)	sa	Boldre, Hants	SD	
29.	1796	Stratford family	sa	Battinglass, Co Wicklow		*Kelly* 1990, 433
30.	1797	Emma Saunders	sa	St Andrew, Montserrat		*Gunnis* 1968, 108
31.	†1799	John Booth	sa	Stamford, Lincs		*Kelly* 1990, 363
32.	1799	Robert Wilmot	sa	St Mary, Lambeth, London, churchyard		*Gunnis* 1968, 108
33.	1800	Charles Carsane	sa	St Mary, Lambeth, London		*Kelly* 1990, 408
34.	1800	Rev Henry Harpur	sa	Tonbridge, Kent	SD	*Kelly* 1990, 359
35.	c1800	William (†1800) and John Sealy and family	sa	St Mary, Lambeth, London, churchyard	S	*Kelly* 1990, 408
36.	1801	Bulteel family	sa	Holbeton, Devon Other versions: W Seymour, Plympton, Devon, 1801 Elizabeth Perfect (+1802) Buckland, Berks William (+1805) and Charles Templer (+1806), Teigngrace, Devon Elizabeth Coppin (+1812) St Stephen, Norwich, Norfolk		*Kelly* 1990, 247, 332, 342, 343, 365 (repr)
37.	†1801	Dr Edward Boys	sa	Eastry, Kent	S	CMN, Summer 1992, 11
38.	1801	George Hutchinson	sa	Ifield, Crawley, Sussex		*Kelly* 1990, 381
39.	1801	Sir John Gale	sa	Lee, Lewisham, London, churchyard		*Kelly* 1990, 409
40.	†1802	Elizabeth Howard	sa	Coulsdon, Surrey		*Kelly* 1990, 376
41.	1802	Major-General Charles O'Hara	sa	King's Chapel, Gibraltar		*Kelly* 1990, 442
42.	1802	Mark Stuart Pleydell	sa	Coleshill, Berks	S	*Kelly* 1990, 118, 333
43.	†1802	Thomas Williams	sa	Cadoxton-juxta-Neath, Glamorgan		Pevsner, *Glamorgan*, 1995, 165
44.	†1803	Lord Henniker	sa	Great Dunmow, Essex		*Kelly* 1990, 250, 347
45.	1804	Henry Hunter	sa	Bunhill Fields Cemetery, London	S	*Kelly* 1990, 395
46.	1804	James Bryan	sa	St Mary, Lambeth, London		*Kelly* 1990, 408
47.	1804	William Mason (†1797)	sa	Aston, W R Yorks	SD	*Kelly* 1990, 141
48.	1805	Admiral Lord Nelson, cenotaph	sa	Teigngrace, Devon		*Kelly* 1990, 239, 343
49.	†1805	Anna Maria Crouch	sa	St Nicholas, Brighton, Sussex, churchyard	S	*Kelly* 1990, 379–80
50.	†1805	Lord Henry Murray (obelisk)	sa	Kirk Braddon, Isle of Man, churchyard		*Kelly* 1990, 360
51.	†1806	Mrs Asperne	sa	St Michael, Cornhill, City of London		Pevsner, *London: City*, 1997, 251
52.	1806	William Clarke	sa	Henstead, Suffolk		*Kelly* 1990, 374
53.	†1807	William Chivers	sa	Lee, Lewisham, London		*Gunnis* 1968, 109
54.	†1807	William Nesbit	sa	Speldhurst, Kent, churchyard	SD	*Kelly* 1990, 253
55.	1808	Joseph Hay	sa	St Leonard, Streatham, London, churchyard		*Kelly* 1990, 421
56.	1809	Lancelot 'Capability' Brown	sa	Croome Court, Worcs		*Kelly* 1990, 387
57.	1809	William Press	sa	Capel St Mary, Suffolk	SD	*Kelly* 1990, 373
58.	1810	Charlotte Trevanion	sa	Caerhays, Cornwall		*Kelly* 1990, 338
59.	1810	Elizabeth Meadows Martineau	sa	Thorpe, Norfolk	S	*Kelly* 1990, 365
60.	1810	Rev William Cooke	sa	St Lawrence, Brentford, Middx		*Kelly* 1990, 418
61.	1813	Isabella Jackson Hernon	sa	St Pancras old church, London		*Kelly* 1990, 418; Pevsner, *N London*, 1998, 348
62.	†1813	James Templer Payment(s): 80 gns	sa	Teigngrace, Devon		*Kelly* 1990, 343
63.	1813	Major-General Bernard Bowes Foord Bowes (†1812) (designed by Joseph Panzetta)	sa	Beverley Minster, E R Yorks	SD	*Kelly* 1990, 251, 388 (repr)
64.	1814	2nd Earl Harcourt (†1809) Payment(s): £262 10s	sa	Stanton Harcourt, Oxon		*Kelly* 1977 (1), 1516 (repr); *Kelly* 1990, 369–70 (repr)
65.	1814	Lieutenant Jones Payment(s): 25 gns	sa	[The Temple, Fleet St, London]; untraced		*Kelly* 1990, 422
66.	1814	Rev Dixon Payment(s): 12 gns	sa	[Sullington, Sussex]; untraced		*Kelly* 1990, 383
67.	1815	Monumental pedestal and vase commemorating Henry Thornton	sa	[Mrs Thornton, Battersea Rise, London]; Mottisfont Abbey, Hants		*Kelly* 1990, 392
68.	1815	Sir William Langham (†1812)	sa	Cottesbrooke, Northants		Pevsner, *Northants*, 1973, 162
69.	1815	Spong family Payment(s): 40 gns	sa	[Aylesford, Kent]; untraced		*Kelly* 1990, 356

No.	Date	Subject	Medium	Location		Bibliography
70.	*c*1817	Admiral (†1817) and Mrs William Bligh	sa	St Mary, Lambeth, London, churchyard		*Kelly* 1990, 195, 253–4
71.	†1817	Esther Jane Sheridan Payment(s): £63 1s	sa	St Peter, Old Windsor, Berks Other versions: ex Paddington churchyard, London; Charles Fryer, 1819; untraced George Todd, Hampstead churchyard, London, 1821		*Kelly* 1990, 253, 333
72.	1818	George Elliott	sa	[Laugharne, Carmarthen]; untraced		*Kelly* 1990, 427
73.	1818	Mrs Josiah John Guest	sa	[Billed to Dowlais House, Cardiff]; untraced		*Kelly* 1990, 426
74.	1818	Warren Hastings Payment(s): £55 8s 4d	sa	Daylesford, Glos, churchyard	D	*Kelly* 1990, 252
75.	1819	James Barry (bust)	sa	St Paul's Cathedral, London, crypt Other versions: One for Soc of Arts and two for Dr Fryer. One survives, private coll		*Kelly* 1990, 138–9, 418–9, (repr)
76.	1819	Mrs P Brayley	sa	[St Mark, Clapham Road, London]; untraced		*Kelly* 1990, 418
77.	1819	Solly family member	sa	Walthamstow, London, churchyard		*Kelly* 1990, 423
78.	1821	James Broadwood's son	sa	[Lyne Caple, Dorking, Surrey]; untraced		*Kelly* 1990, 376–7
79.	1821	Rev Henry Swann Payment(s): 60 gns	sa	[St James, Bury St, Dublin]; untraced		*Kelly* 1990, 435
80.	1828	Unidentified subject	sa	Old Shoreham, Sussex, churchyard, east end	SD	*Kelly* 1990, 253, 382
81.	nd	E S Cooper	sa	[Markree Castle, Co Sligo]; untraced		*Kelly* 1990, 438
82.	nd	Edward Wortley Montagu	sa	[Finedon Hall, Northants]; private coll		*Kelly* 1990, 195, 366
83.	nd	Harriet Thomson	sa	Putney burial ground, London	S	*Kelly* 1990, 415–6
84.	nd	Major Norman Ramsay	sa	Inveresk, churchyard		*Kelly* 1990, 251, 431 (repr)
85.	nd	Monkhouse Davison and Adrian Newman	sa	St Olave, Hart St, City of London		*Kelly* 1990, 418
86.	nd	Unidentified subject	sa	St Anne, Limehouse, London, churchyard	S	*Kelly* 1990, 195, 253, 416
Statues						
87.	1760	Charity boy, Charity girl	sa	St John's Old School, Wapping, London Other versions: St John's Primary School, Leicester, 1785 Archbishop Michael Ramsay School, Camberwell, London (boy only), 1785 Wyggeston's Hospital, Leicester, 1787 Fanmakers' Hall, City of London, 1821 ex 2 Queen's Row, Pentonville, London, 1821; untraced Vintners' Hall, City of London, 1840		Pevsner, *London: South*, 1983, 623; *Kelly* 1990, 133, 361, 393 (repr); *Cavanagh* 2000, 95–7, 122–4 (repr); *Field* 1995, 22 (repr)
88.	1772	Peacock	sa	[Bloxholm Hall, Lincs]; destroyed		*Kelly* 1990, 265, 362
89.	1772	Sibyl (or Contemplation)	sa	Audley End, Essex Other versions: several, including ten at Burghley House, Northants, *c*1777		*Kelly* 1990, *passim* (repr)
90.	1772	Vestal (designed by John Bacon RA) Payment(s): 15 gns	sa	Audley End, Essex Other versions: 12 identified		*Kelly* 1990, *passim* (repr)
91.	1773	Small lion couchant Payment(s): 4 gns each	sa	Stratford Place, London, porter's lodge Other versions: Audley End, Essex (pair) 1786 (4 gns each) Paxton House, Berwicks, 1789 Cullen House, Banff, 1816 ex Mr Boardman's house, Bolton, 1817; untraced ex Maresfield Park, Uckfield, Sussex, 1819 (pair, 8gns); destr		*Kelly* 1990, 257–9, 346, 382, 420, 429 (repr)
92.	1773	Urania, statue (designed by John Bacon RA)	sa	[Stourhead, Wilts]; untraced Other versions: Downton Castle, Herefs, 'Pantheon' room, *c*1778 Bowden Park, Wilts, oval hall, 1796 Private coll (ex Wentworth Woodhouse, Yorks) 1780–1799 Pitzhanger Manor, Ealing Grove, London, interior, 1802		*Graves* 1907, 60; *Kelly* 1990, 130–1, 386 (repr)
93.	1777	Four lions Payment(s): £113 12s	sa	Burghley House, Northants, bridge		*Kelly* 1990, 365
94.	*c*1777	River god (the Thames) (designed by John Bacon RA)	sa	Ham House, Surrey Other versions: ex Llewenny Hall, Denbighs, before 1789; untraced Terrace Gardens, Richmond, dmgd		*Kelly* 1990, frontisp, 127–8, 427 (repr); *Kelly* 1993, 915 (repr)

No.	Date	Subject		Location		Reference
95.	c1780	Flora	sa	Heveningham Hall, Suffolk, orangery Other versions: ex Callender House, Falkirk, 1787–88; untraced Burton Constable, E R Yorks, orangery, 1788–1789 ex Harewood House, Hanover Square, London, 1814; untraced ex coll Hon Frederick North, St James's Place, London, 1815; untraced ex Bellevue House, Walthamstow, Essex, 1816; untraced ex The Grange, Beckett Park, Leeds, W R Yorks, adapted for lamps, 1817; untraced ex Langham House, Portland Place, London, 1817; untraced ex Royal Palace, Rio de Janeiro, Brazil, lamp stand with dolphin pedestal, 1820; untraced		*Kelly* 1990, *passim* (repr)
96.	c1780	Pomona	sa	Heveningham Hall, Suffolk, orangery Other versions: Burton Constable, E R Yorks, Orangery, 1788–1789 ex Bellevue House, Walthamstow, Essex, 1816; untraced Ex Langham House, Portland Place, London, 1817; destr ex Royal Palace, Rio de Janeiro, Brazil, lamp stand with dolphin pedestal, 1820; untraced		*Kelly* 1985, 86; *Kelly* 1990, *passim* (repr)
97.	c1785	Boy with basket on goat	sa	[Belfield, Weymouth, Dorset]; private coll		*Kelly* 1990, 344–5
98.	1786	Northumberland lion with cap of dignity	sa	Audley End, Essex		*Kelly* 1990, 261, 347
99.	1786	Several, unidentified subjects	sa	[Dalkeith Palace]; untraced		*Kelly* 1990, 429
100.	1787–1788	Ceres	sa	[Callender House, Falkirk]; untraced Other versions: Burton Constable, E R Yorks, Orangery, 1788–1789		*Kelly* 1990, 210, 388, 428 (repr)
101.	1788	Fortitude and five other Virtues, six figures	sa	[Royal Pavilion, Brighton]; untraced Other versions: Fortitude, ex coll Hon Frederick North, 1815; untraced		*Kelly* 1990, 215–6, 379 (repr)
102.	1787–1788	Grecian sphinxes	sa	[Callender House, Falkirk]; untraced Other versions: Trent Park, Herts, with medallions of the seasons on their bases, 1785 Lisreaghan House, Bellevue, Galway, ?1792 Croome Court, Worcs, 1795 Castle Park Barracks, Dunbar, by 1799 Tullynally House, Ireland, by 1799 Gosford House, Lothian, c1800 Caledon, C Tyrone, 1813 Glos Regiment Depot, Gloucester, nd		*Kelly* 990, *passim*
103.	c1788	Major-General Stringer Lawrence (after Peter Scheemakers)	sa	Lawrence Castle, Dunchideock, Devon		*Kelly* 1990, 230, 342
104.	c1789	Faith, Hope, Charity and Humility, four figures (designed by Benjamin West PRA)	sa	Royal Hospital, Greenwich (ORNC), ante-chapel Other versions: Nuckel's Almshouses, Broadstairs, Kent, pediment (Charity) 1838		Pevsner, *London: S*, 1983, 264; *Kelly* 1985, 76; *Kelly* 1990, 133
105.	1789	Hygeia	sa	[St Bernard's Well, Edinburgh]; destroyed		*Kelly* 1990, 430
106.	1790	Charity, standing figure with three children (designed by John Bacon RA)	sa	Fishmongers' Hall, City of London		*Kelly* 1990, 133, 402
107.	pre-1791	Large lions couchant, pair	sa	[Stowe, Bucks, north portico]; untraced Other versions: ex St Lucy's Athboy, Co Meath, 1816; untraced ex Castlewellan, Co Down, 1821; private coll		*Kelly* 1990, 336
108.	1792	Four	sa	5 St James's Square, London	SD	*Kelly* 1990, 417
109.	1792	St George and the dragon	sa	[Mercers' Hall, Cheapside, City of London]; Museum of London	SD	*Kelly* 1990, 410
110.	c1794	Florentine lions (Medici or Michelangelo's)		Preston Hall, Lothian, gateway Other versions: ex Stowe, Bucks, s portico; untraced		*Kelly* 1990, 97, 208, 261, 432
111.	1798	Liberty and Hospitality	sa	[Arundel Castle, Sussex; sold April 1891, lot 281]; untraced		*Kelly* 1988 (2), 182; *Kelly* 1990, 123, 378–9
112.	by 1799	Charity, a group of two figures (modelled by John Bacon RA)	sa	Marine Soc, City of London		*Kelly* 1990, 42, 410 (repr)

No.	Date	Subject		Location		Bibliography
113.	1799	Justice	sa	Thetford Guildhall, Norfolk Other versions: Court of Request, Tower Hamlets, London, by 1799; untraced ex Hothfield Place, Kent, c1800; untraced Sessions House, Beverley, E R Yorks, 1807 ex Court House, Canterbury, Kent, 1808; untraced ex Kilkenny Court House, 1817; untraced		*Kelly* 1990, 365
114.	by 1799	Minerva	sa	[Fire Insurance Office, Charing Cross, London]; untraced Other versions: Huntingdon Literary Institute ex coll Hon Frederick North, 1815; untraced		*Kelly* 1990, 131, 356
115.	1799	Nymph with a shell ('Brito Martis')	sa	[Exhib Coade's Gallery]; untraced		*Kelly* 1990, 101
116.	1799	Polyphemous hurling rocks at Acis and Galatea	sa	[Exhib Coade's Gallery]; untraced		*Kelly* 1990, 68
117.	1799	Salmacis and Hermaphroditus	sa	[Exhib Coade's Gallery]; untraced		*Kelly* 1990, 97
118.	by 1799	Shakespeare with the comic and tragic muses	sa	[Edinburgh Theatre]; Bonaly Tower, Edinburgh, gardens (Shakespeare only)		*Kelly* 1990, 135, 430
119.	1800	Egyptian figures, a pair	sa	[perhaps coll Thomas Hope]; Buscot Park, Berks Other versions: Crowthers, Isleworth, 1968; untraced for Bullocks Museum, Piccadilly, London, 1812; untraced	SD	*Kelly* 1990, 94, 95, 332 (repr); *Kelly* 1993, 915, 917 (repr)
120.	1800	Sir Edward Coke, for a column designed by James Wyatt (modelled by J C F Rossi)	sa	Stoke Poges, Bucks		*Kelly* 1990, 230, 336; *Colvin* 1995, 1121
121.	c1800	Temperance	sa	[Hothfield Place, Kent]; untraced		*Kelly* 1990, 358
122.	1802	Clio	sa	Pitzhanger Manor, Ealing Grove, London, interior Other versions: Downton Castle, Herefs, Pantheon room, c1778 Bowden Park, Wilts, oval hall, 1796 ex Wentworth Woodhouse, Yorks, private coll 1780–1799 Powderham Castle, Devon, 1808 Essex Institute, Salem, Mass, before 1820		*Kelly* 1989 (1), 251–2, 253 (repr); *Kelly* 1990, *passim* (repr)
123.	1802	Norman archer	sa	[Clytha Park, Abergavenny, Monmouths]; Christie, 10 July 2003; untraced	SD	
124.	1803	Venus, with dolphins about her feet	sa	Destroyed		*Kelly* 1990, 131, 132, 143 n 33 (repr)
125.	1803–1805	King George III (designed by James Hamilton of Weymouth)	sa	The Esplanade, Weymouth, Dorset		*Kelly* 1990, 230–2, 345 (repr)
126.	1808	Urania (adapted to represent Flora)	sa	Powderham Castle, Devon Other versions: Essex Institute, Salem, Mass, before 1820	D	*Kelly* 1990, 342 (repr)
127.	1809	Admiral, Lord Nelson, on a column with reliefs on plinth (designed by Robert Mitchell)	sa	Place Jacques Cartier, Montreal, Canada (parts replaced with fibre-glass copies)		*Collard* 1969, 210–11 (repr); *Kelly* 1990, 234–5
128.	1809	King George III in Roman armour	sa	Southampton, Hants, Bargate Other versions: Taplow Court, Bucks, SD 1804	SD	*Kelly* 1990, 101, 233, 353
129.	1810	King George III	sa	[Portland Square, Bristol, Somerset]; destroyed		*Kelly* 1990, 233, 372
130.	1810	King George III (modelled by Joseph Panzetta)	sa	[Dunston Pillar, Nocton, Lincs]; Lincoln Castle (bust only)		*Kelly* 1990, 233–4, 362; *Darke* 1991, 205 (repr)
131.	†1812	Captain George Bettesworth	sa	Caerhays, Cornwall		*Kelly* 1990, 137, 338
132.	1813	Farnese Flora, statue	sa	[Illogan, Cornwall]; Tehidy Park, Truro, Cornwall Other versions: St John's College, Oxford		*Kelly* 1990, 339
133.	1814	Piping boy Payment(s): 26 gns (with pedestal)	sa	[Sunninghill Park, Berks]; untraced		*Kelly* 1990, 92, 334
134.	1814	Sculpture, Architecture, Geometry, Painting, Music and Poetry Payment(s): 150 gns	sa	[for John Nash, 29 Dover St, London]; destroyed		*Kelly* 1985, 86; *Kelly* 1990, 399
135.	1813–1814	Suraya (Indian sun god) and two Brahmin bulls	sa	Sezincote, Glos, Temple pool		*Kelly* 1990, 134, 206, 263, 264, 350 (repr)
136.	1810–1815	Lady Gardner and two children Payment(s): 200 gns	sa	[Court Garden, Marlow, Bucks]; untraced		*Kelly* 1990, 137, 251–2, 335
137.	1815	Lord Gardner and Lord Nelson Payment(s): 150 gns each	sa	[Little Marlow Manor, Bucks]; untraced		*Kelly* 1990, 137, 239, 335
138.	1815	Sleeping nymph Payment(s): £21	sa	Chicksands Priory, Biggleswade, Beds		*Kelly* 1990, 331
139.	1816	Laocoon, statuette Payment(s): 10 gns	sa	[90 Pall Mall, London, coll William Dennison]; untraced		*Kelly* 1990, 413

No.	Date	Work		Location		Sources
140.	1816	Livia (Pudicitia) Payment(s): 40 gns	sa	[Chicksands Priory, Biggleswade, Beds]; largely destroyed		*Kelly* 1990, 96, 331
141.	1816	Rowland, Baron Hill, of Almarez and Hawkstone (designed by Edward Haycock; modelled by Joseph Panzetta) Payment(s): £315	sa	Lord Hill column, Shrewsbury, Salop		*Kelly* 1990, 239, 371 (repr)
142.	1817	'an Eagle from one at the British Museum' Payment(s): £11 2s 8d	sa	[Chicksands Priory, Biggleswade, Beds]; untraced Other versions: Hexton House, Hitchen, Herts, 1820		*Kelly* 1990, 101, 331, 355
143.	1817	Small elephant Payment(s): 5 gns	sa	[Coleorton Hall, Ashby-de-la-Zouche, Leics]; untraced		*Kelly* 1990, 361
144.	1818	Ancient Briton, Norman Payment(s): 136 gns	sa	[Malvern Hall, Solihill, Warks]; untraced		*Kelly* 1990, 385
145.	1818	Gothic statue, two lions couchant and two eagles	sa	[Bletchington House, Oxon]; untraced		*Kelly* 1990, 369
146.	1818	Hope, with an anchor Payment(s): 55 gns	sa	[Holborn Fire Office, Oxford St]; destroyed		*Kelly* 1990, 406
147.	1818	Lions, a pair (designed by John Flaxman) Payment(s): £42	sa	St John's Lodge, Regents's Park, London		*Kelly* 1990, 260 (repr)
148.	1816–1818	William Shakespeare	sa	[Opera House, Haymarket, London]; Public library, Romford Road, Newham, London		*Kelly* 1990, 135, 136, 411 (repr)
149.	1819	Apollo Belvedere (and a pedestal with the nine muses) Payment(s): £119 4 0	sa	[Dryburgh Abbey, Kelso, Temple of the Muses]; untraced Other versions: Somerley, Hants, 1840		*Kelly* 1990, 134, 429
150.	1819	Piping Faun	sa	[Dryburgh Abbey, Kelso, coll Earl of Buchan]; untraced		*Kelly* 1990, 429
151.	1821	Bryce Smyth in Augustinian habit, representing St Mola n'Faidh Payment(s): £42	sa	Ballinatray House, Waterford, grounds		*Kelly* 1990, 117–8, 433
152.	1821	Faith	sa	Dover gaol, Kent		*Kelly* 1990, 358
153.	1828	Sculpture and architecture (designed by John Flaxman RA and modelled by Edward Hodges Baily RA) Payment(s): 150 gns each	sa	[Buckingham Palace, London, north wing pediment]; Lancaster House, London, garden	SD	TNA WORK 19/3. 252–90, f285; *Colvin* VI, 1976, 301; *Kelly* 1990, 221–2, 409
154.	*c*1830	Mercury (after Thorvaldsen)	sa	Private coll, New South Wales, Australia		*Kelly* 1990, 440
155.	1835	Sir John Crosby	sa	[Crosby Hall, Bishopsgate, London]; untraced		*Kelly* 1990, 136, 399
156.	1836	Lions, two small	sa	[Lion Brewery, Belvedere Road, Lambeth]; destroyed		*Kelly* 1990, 393, 408
157.	1837	Large standing lion (modelled by William Woodington)	sa	[Lion Brewery, Belvedere Road, Lambeth]; Westminster Bridge, London		*Kelly* 1990, 393, 408 (repr)
158.	nd	Diana the huntress	sa	[Heslington Hall, York]; destroyed		*Kelly* 1990, 131, 390
159.	nd	Father Time	sa	Anglesey Abbey, Cambs, gardens Other versions: Tyringham, Bucks, nd Henniker monument, Rochester, Kent, 1793 ex coll James Baxter, Turnham Green, 1818; untraced		*Kelly* 1990, 134, 144 n 57, 337; *Kelly* 1993, 915
160.	nd	Seated tiger	sa	[Alton Towers, Staffs]; Acton Round Hall, Bridgnorth, Salop		*Kelly* 1990, 370; *Kelly* 1993, 917
161.	nd	St George and the dragon	sa	Anglesey Abbey, Cambs		*Kelly* 1980, 106, 107 (repr); *Kelly* 1990, 337
162.	nd	Standing lion	sa	Millichope Park, Salop		*Kelly* 1990, 261
163.	nd	Venus, statuette	sa	Private coll		*Kelly* 1990, 69, 70 (repr)
164.	nd	Venus, statuette	sa	Private coll Other versions: Clothed version, D 1804, Sotheby Billingshurst, 1 June 1988, lot no 770		*Kelly* 1990, 69, 70 (repr)
Busts						
165.	1772	William Shakespeare and David Garrick, roundels with portrait busts	sa	Assembly rooms and theatre, Truro, Cornwall Other versions: Birmingham Central Reference Library, Warwicks, 1774 New Theatre, Newcastle under Lyme, Staffs (Shakespeare only) 1787–1788		*Kelly* 1990, 141, 339, 384; *Noszlopy* 1998, 38 (repr)
166.	1792	Gerard de Visme, bronzed	sa	Christie, April 1986; private coll		*Kelly* 1990, 139 (repr)
167.	1799	Isis Aphroditis, George III, Duke of Clarence and Dr Mead	sa	[Exhib Coade's Gallery]; untraced		*Kelly* 1990, 101
168.	by 1802	Warren Hastings (modelled by John Charles Felix Rossi)	sa	Melchet Park, Romsey, Hants		*Kelly* 1990, 352
169.	1806	Admiral Lord Nelson	sa	Bicton Gardens, Devon, orangery Other versions: NMM, Greenwich, SCU0101, 1808 and two others	SD	*Kelly* 1990, 140, 340, 411, 445 (repr)
170.	1806	Arthur, 1st Duke of Wellington (?) and Sir Walter Raleigh	sa	Bicton Gardens, Devon, orangery	SD	*Kelly* 1990, 340 (repr)

No.	Date	Subject		Location		References
171.	pre-1809	Venus and Caracalla	sa	[Christie, 24 Feb 1809]; untraced		*Kelly* 1990, 413
172.	1813	William Shakespeare, Joseph Addison, John Dryden, Matthew Prior and Ben Jonson	sa	[Uffington House, Stamford, Lincs]; untraced		*Kelly* 1990, 138, 363
173.	1815	Emperor of Russia, colossal Payment(s): 40 gns	sa	[Pulteney Hotel, Piccadilly, London]; untraced		*Kelly* 1990, 138, 414
174.	1817	John Milton and William Shakespeare, terms Payment(s): 7 gns each	sa	Coleorton Hall, Leics		*Kelly* 1990, 137, 361; *Kelly* 1993, 915
175.	post-1817	Michelangelo and Raphael, terms	sa	Coleorton Hall, Leics Other versions: Buckingham Palace, London		*Kelly* 1990, 137–8 (repr); *Kelly* 1993, 915
176.	1820	John Wesley Payment(s): 5 gns	sa	[Phoenix foundry, Sheffield, W R Yorks]; untraced Other versions: given to C H Tatham, 1820; untraced		*Kelly* 1990, 138
177.	nd	Homer, Marcus Aurelius, Vestinia (or Faustina), Horace, Cicero, Commodus	sa	Untraced		*Kelly* 1990, 102

Chimneypieces

No.	Date	Subject		Location		References
178.	1771	Two	sa	[Boreham House, Chelmsford, Essex]; untraced		*Kelly* 1990, 191, 346
179.	By 1771	With a tablet depicting a Roman Procession	sa	Seaton Delaval, Northumbs Other versions: Chicksands Priory, Biggleswade, Beds (tablet only)		*Kelly* 1990, 98, 331, 367
180.	1774	'from a design of Mr [John] Johnson'	sa	[Galloway House, Charles St, London]; untraced		*Graves* 1907, 60; *Kelly* 1990, 397
181.	1783	One Payment(s): 6 1/2 gns	sa	[Argyll House, Twickenham, Middx]; untraced		*Gunnis* 1968, 107; *Kelly* 1990, 392
182.	1783	With perpendicular tracery and a relief of Abraham and Isaac	sa	Lord Harborough's pew, Stapleford, Leics		*Kelly* 1990, 118, 361–2
183.	1789	With relief figures of dancing girls from Herculaneum	sa	[Belgrave Square, London]; Capesthorne, Cheshire Other versions: Wollaton Hall, Notts, ?1790s The Octagon, Washington DC, USA, 1801		*Kelly* 1990, 191–2, 368, 444 (repr)
184.	1790	Four Payment(s): £205	sa	[Fishmongers' Hall, City of London]; destroyed		*Kelly* 1990, 191, 402
185.	1790	With Faith, Hope and Charity	sa	[Belgrave Square, London]; Chelminski, King's Road, London (2001)	SD	*Kelly* 1990, 191–2, 337–8 (repr); *Apollo*, Dec 2001, 7 (repr)
186.	by 1799	Several	sa	[Erddig, Denbighs]; untraced		*Kelly* 1990, 428
187.	1801	With anchors, dolphins and seaweed	sa	The Octagon, Washington DC, USA		*Kelly* 1990, 282, 444 (repr)
188.	1813	Gothic Payment(s): £200	sa	[Taymouth Castle, Tayside]; untraced		*Kelly* 1990, 432
189.	1814	Gothic Payment(s): 140 gns	sa	[Ravensworth Castle, Co Durham]; untraced Other versions: ex Clay Hill, Enfield, Middx, 1820; untraced		*Kelly* 1990, 118, 345, 401
190.	1815	Gothic Payment(s): 42 gns	sa	[Battle Abbey, Sussex]; untraced Other versions: ex Clay Hill, Enfield, Middx, 1816; untraced		*Kelly* 1988, 183; *Kelly* 1990, 118, 379, 401 (repr)
191.	1816–1817	'A Rich Gothic Chimneypiece with a centre' Payment(s): £189	sa	[Michel Grove, Sussex]; destroyed		*Kelly* 1988 (2), 188; *Kelly* 1990, 382
192.	1817	Gothic, based upon one at Windsor Castle Payment(s): 60 gns	sa	Ettington Park, Stratford, Warks, Library Other versions: Lough Cutra Castle, Galway, 1818		*Kelly* 1990, 119, 384, 438
193.	nd	Bacchanalian procession (chimneypiece tablet)	sa	[Summerset, Lymington, Hants]; untraced Other versions: Chicksands Priory, Biggleswade, Beds		*Kelly* 1990, 331, 352
194.	nd	With faun and bacchante	sa	[Bretton Hall, W R Yorks]; removed 1946 Other versions: Caledon, Co Tyrone		*Kelly* 1990, 189, 190, 388 (repr)

Architectural Sculpture

No.	Date	Subject		Location		References
195.	*c*1769	Arms, statues, vases, capitals	sa	[St George's Fields, London]; destroyed		*Kelly* 1990, 416–7
196.	1770	Borghese Vase Payment(s): £12 14s 6d	sa	Stourhead, Wilts, Temple of Flora Other versions: seventeen identified		*Kelly* 1990, *passim* (repr); *Kelly* 1993, 915–6
197.	1770	Frieze of animal skin swags, pediment, capitals, coat of arms	sa	Skinners' Hall, City of London		*Kelly* 1990, 278 (repr)
198.	*c*1770	Lions	sa	[Tixall, Staffs, screen walls]; destroyed		*Kelly* 1990, 373
199.	*c*1770	Lions, roundels with classical heads, rams' heads and swags of oak leaves	sa	Thorndon Hall, Brentwood, Essex, gateway		*Kelly* 1990, 348

200.	c1771	Medici Vase	sa	Kedleston, Derbys, south front Other versions: Castle Howard, N R Yorks, Ray Wood, 1778 Cobham Hall, Kent, gardens, 1801 Hewell Grange, Tardebigge, Worcs, 1815 Chiswick House, London, c1814–17 Barlby Manor, Notts (ex Elvaston Castle, Derbys) 1817–18 Kew Gardens, London (two, one ex Royal Coll!) 1825, 1826 Coleorton Hall, Leics, 1827 Royal Coll, Buckingham Palace, grounds	*Kelly* 1990, passim (repr); *Kelly* 1993, 915–6, 920 (repr)
201.	1772	Gothic gate piers (designed by James Essex) Payment(s): £150	sa	[Strawberry Hill, Twickenham, Middx]; destroyed	*Kelly* 1985, 72–3; *Kelly* 1990, 107–8, 420 (repr)
202.	c1772	Ionic capitals, string course, paterae	sa	Heaton Park, Manchester, Lancs	*Kelly* 1985, 77; *Kelly* 1990, 150, 164, 360 (repr)
203.	1771–1773	Figures and medallion	sa	Redgrave Hall, Suffolk, orangery	*Kelly* 1990, 375
204.	1773	Ornaments (designed by Robert Adam)	sa	Syon House, Middx, Brentford gateway and screen Other versions: Zoological gardens, Rio de Janeiro, Brazil, c1812	*Kelly* 1984, 548–53 (repr); *Kelly* 1990, 207, 295, 296 (repr)
205.	c1775	Plaques, Ceres and America	sa	Whiteford, Callington, Cornwall, garden pavillion	*Kelly* 1990, 167, 339
206.	1776	Large medallion of Diana the huntress, capitals, frieze, vases and other ornaments	sa	Woolverstone Hall, Suffolk	*Kelly* 1985, 82; *Kelly* 1990, 167, 375 (repr)
207.	1777	Druid (originally a conduit)	sa	[South St, Chichester, Sussex]; Priory Park, Chichester, Sussex Other versions: Shugborough, Staffs, 1794 Croome Court, Worcs, 1795, 25 gns Erddig, Denbighs The Vyne, Hants *Kelly* 1988 (2), 185 notes that there is said to be another at Caigwell House, near Bognor.	*Kelly* 1990, 34, 134, 380, 373, 387, 428 (repr); *Kelly* 1997, 22, 23 (repr)
208.	1775–1777	Panels with swags and paterae, medallions of girls riding on mythical creatures, capitals and other decoration	sa	20 and 21, Portman Square, London	*Kelly* 1985, 74; *Kelly* 1990, 73, 156, 164, 415 (repr)
209.	c1777	Plaques, urns, swags and paterae	sa	Herstmonceux Place, Sussex	*Kelly* 1985, 79; *Kelly* 1990, 381
210.	1778	Corinthian capitals, frieze and plaques (including Aldobrandi Marriage and Phrygian shepherd and shepherdess)	sa	Croome Court, Worcs, Island Temple	*Kelly* 1990, 74, 98, 99, 162, 386 (repr); *Kelly* 1997, 22, 23 (repr)
211.	1775–1778	Plaques, niches with urns, capitals	sa	Market Hall and Theatre, Bury St Edmunds, Suffolk	*Kelly* 1985, 74
212.	1775–1779	Plaques between first and second floors, paterae and urns on gate piers, paterae on bridge	sa	Cottesbrooke Hall, Northants	*Kelly* 1990, 169, 365–6
213.	1779	Urns, reclining figures supporting escutcheon, plaques with swags and relief profiles, caryatids, recumbent lions, Corinthian capitals	sa	Heveningham Hall, Suffolk	*Kelly* 1990, 77, 132, 163, 374 (repr)
214.	c1780	Plaques (Borghese Dancers) and capitals	sa	Heveningham Hall, Suffolk, orangery	*Kelly* 1990, 96, 270, 374 (repr); *Kelly* 1993, 916
215.	1780	Plaques of tritons, badge and oars, pilaster capitals, swags	sa	Watermen's Hall, City of London, facade	*Kelly* 1990, 152, 424, 270 (repr)
216.	pre-1781	Lamp stands with three caryatid figures	sa	West Wycombe Park, Bucks, dining room Other versions: ex Queen's Lodge, Frogmore, Berks and Godmersham Park, Kent; both untraced	*Kelly* 1985, 77; *Kelly* 1990, 183, 337, 358 (repr)
217.	1783	Lions and vases for gateway known as the 'Kale Cross'	sa	[Newcastle, Northumbs]; Blagdon, Morpeth, Northumbs	*Kelly* 1985, 78; *Kelly* 1990, 367
218.	pre-1783	Panels, capitals and other ornaments	sa	[James Wyatt's house, Queen Anne St East, London]; Syon Lodge, Isleworth, Middx (elements only)	*Kelly* 1990, 402
219.	1783	Pedestal (triangular with three figures)	sa	Audley End, Essex, gardens Other versions: Syon House, Isleworth, Middx Wardour Castle, Wilts Weston Park, Salop (used as a sundial) ex coll Mr Gibbons, The Oaks, Wolverhampton, 1815; untraced	*Kelly* 1990, 205 (repr)
220.	1783	Tripod with lion monopodia	sa	Audley End, Essex, gardens	*Kelly* 1990, 205, 346 (repr)
221.	c1784	External ornaments including keystones, string course, urns and interior details	sa	Belmont, Lyme Regis, Dorset (Coade family home)	*Kelly* 1990, 24, 344 (repr)

No.	Date	Work		Location		References
222.	1783–1785	Fountain with dragons; statues of two ancient kings, two bishops and a pilgrim; ten Gothic candelabra Payment(s): £86; £96 12s; £500	sa	[Carlton House, London, conservatory]; dispersed		*Kelly* 1990, 219–20, 396 (repr); *Bilbey* 2002, 307 (repr)
223.	1785	Medallions of mourners and other ornaments	sa	Castle Upton, Co Antrim, Mausoleum		*Kelly* 1985, 74; *Kelly* 1990, 434
224.	c1785	Mermaids	sa	[Hurstbourne Priors, Hants]; Farleigh House, Farleigh Wallop, Hants, gate piers		*Kelly* 1985, 78; *Kelly* 1990, 269, 352 (repr)
225.	1785	The good Samaritan, plaque	sa	[Royal Infirmary, Lancaster]; untraced		*Kelly* 1990, 359
226.	1783–1785	Trophies of war, naval and military trophies Payment(s): £450	sa	[Carlton House, London, colonnade]; untraced		*Kelly* 1990, 215, 396
227.	1786	29 vases for parapets (designed by William Chambers RA) Payment(s): £193	sa	Somerset House, Strand, London Other versions: Alameda, Ampthill, Beds (pair)		*Kelly* 1990, 419
228.	1786	Frieze of bucrania and drapery, panels with swags, urns and pedestals	sa	Rotunda Hospital, Dublin		*Kelly* 1990, 161, 436; *Feely* 1996, 93
229.	1786	Gothic font (designed by Richard Holland)	sa	Debden, Essex Other versions: ex St George's Chapel, Windsor, 1787, destr (ex Milton Abbey, Dorset) c1789–1791, untraced Oaklands Park Museum, Chelmsford, Essex (simplified), 1803 Chignal St James, Essex, 1838		*Kelly* 1990, 110, 111, 116, 218–9, 344, 347 (repr)
230.	1787	Copies of six vases from the collection of Sir William Hamilton Payment(s): £45	sa	[Carlton House, London]; untraced		*Gunnis* 1968, 107; *Kelly* 1990, 219, 396
231.	c1788	Plaques on three fronts, coat of arms on west front	sa	Sledmere House, E R Yorks		*Kelly* 1973, 1798 (repr); *Kelly* 1990, 170–1, 390
232.	1780–1789	Reclining naiad (Sabrina) fountain (designed by John Bacon RA) Payment(s): 30 gns	sa	Croome Court, Worcs, by artificial grotto Other versions: ex Llewenny Hall, Denbighs, before 1789; untraced ex Gunnersbury Park, London; untraced		*Kelly* 1990, 128, 387, 427 (repr); *Kelly* 1997, 22 (repr)
233.	1788–1789	Statues, plaques (the seasons) and urns	sa	Burton Constable Hall, E R Yorks, orangery		*Kelly* 1990, 210, 388 (repr)
234.	1789	Statues, vases, fountains and other ornaments	sa	[Lord Aldborough's house, Dublin]; untraced		*Gunnis* 1968, 107; *Kelly* 1990, 205, 436
235.	1780–1789	Thirty-two capitals and bases, thirty-two cherubs' heads, the hospital arms, four oval medallions of the prophets Daniel, Micah, Zechariah and Malachi, six circular medallions from the Acts of the Apostles for the pulpit and reader's desk, six angels supporting the altar	sa	Royal Hospital, Greenwich (ORNC), chapel		*Kelly* 1990, 180, 223, 224, 403 (repr); *Bold* 2000 (2), 176
236.	c1790	Gothic ogee overdoors with Hope and Faith in tympana	sa	[Almshouses, Bordesley, Warks]; destroyed		*Kelly* 1990, 384
237.	c1790	Plaque, Britannia, with a barge, the Radcliffe Observatory and St Mary's in the background	sa	[Oxford Canal Company Offices]; Master's House, St Peter's College, Oxford		*Kelly* 1990, 20, 369 (repr)
238.	by 1790	Plaques of the Seasons, Music, Painting, Architecture, Commerce, Peace, Plenty, Law, Truth and Prudence	sa	[Dr Lettsom's house, Camberwell Grove, London]; destroyed		*Kelly* 1990, 395
239.	c1790	Three panels (Bacchus, satyr and Ceres), coat of arms, string course, pilaster capitals and balusters (plaques designed by J Biagio Rebecca)	sa	Castle Goring, Worthing, Sussex		*Kelly* 1990, 172–3, 380 (repr)
240.	1791	Caryatids and plaque symbolising Painting	sa	Schomberg House, 80–82 Pall Mall, London	D	*Kelly* 1990, 67, 170 (repr)
241.	1791	Duke of Richmond's fountain	sa	Merrion Square, Dublin		*Kelly* 1990, 205, 436 (repr)
242.	c1791	Four figures, lampholders	sa	Preston Hall, Lothian, hall Other versions: ex Selwood Park, Sunninghill, Berks, 1796, destr		*Kelly* 1990, 185, 261, 334, 432 (repr)
243.	c1792	Britannia (designed by J C F Rossi RA)	sa	Town Hall, Liverpool, Lancs, dome		*Kelly* 1985, 77; *Kelly* 1990, 102, 360
244.	1792	Font	sa	Hafod, Cardigan		*Gunnis* 1968, 108
245.	1792	Guilloche string course and plaques	sa	Iver Lodge, Bucks		*Kelly* 1990, 163, 335 (repr)
246.	c1792	Panels after the Borghese dancers, capitals, paterae and other decorative details	sa	City rooms, Leicester		*Kelly* 1990, 361; *Cavanagh* 2000, 126–7 (repr)
247.	1792	Plaque with a figure and view of house, medallions of the Seasons, capitals, urns and other decorations	sa	Belmont, Throwley, Kent		*Kelly* 1990, 79, 168, 171, 356 (repr)

248.	1792	Plaques based on the reliefs on the Borghese vase and capitals	sa	Hammerwood Park, East Grinstead, Sussex		*Kelly* 1990, 148–9, 381 (repr)
249.	1792	Screen and vaulting	sa	Langley Marish, Bucks, Harvey Chapel		*Gunnis* 1968, 108; *Kelly* 1990, 115–6
250.	1793	Caryatids, loosely based on the Erechtheion (six)	sa	[Buckingham House, London]; Anglesey Abbey, Cambs (NT) Other versions: West Dean Park, Sussex, 1793 (two) Bank of England, City of London, Rotunda, 1795 (twelve) Bank of England, London, Transfer Office 1799 (twelve) Pitzhanger Manor, Ealing, c1800 (four) SJSM, façade, 1812 (two) ex Hewell Grange, Tardebigge, Worcs, 1821; untraced	SD	*Kelly* 1989 (1), 249–51 (repr); *Kelly* 1990, 86, 102, 134–5, 141, 145 n 68, 383, 387, 394–5 (repr)
251.	1793	Decorative details	sa	[Mr WB Simond's house, Reading]; untraced		*Gunnis* 1968, 108
252.	1793	Plaques (Justice and boy, Mercy and boy, Wisdom and boy) and other decorative details (plaques designed by John Bacon RA)	sa	Shire Hall, Chelmsford, Essex Other versions: similar at County Hall, Lewes, Sussex, 1808–1812		*Kelly* 1990, 82, 171–2 (repr)
253.	1793	Standing naiad (originally a conduit) (designed by John Johnson) Payment(s): £108 12s	sa	[Chelmsford, near Shire Hall]; Chelmsford, Essex, inside Shire Hall		*Kelly* 1985, 81; *Kelly* 1990, 133
254.	1793	Swag and paterae plaques, Ionic capitals (designed by Charles Bulfinch)	sa	[Senator Bingham's house, Philadelphia, USA]; destroyed		*Kelly* 1990, 288, 290 (repr)
255.	1794	Ionic portico capitals, plaque on the cat monument, roundels on Lichfield lodges Payment(s): £141 5s	sa	Shugborough, Staffs		*Kelly* 1990, 80, 162, 373 (repr)
256.	c1794	Plaques of Morning, Noon and Evening, signs of the Zodiac and other ornaments (modelled by J C F Rossi RA)	sa	Radcliffe Observatory, Oxford		*Kelly* 1990, 173–4, 369 (repr)
257.	1794	Two oval vases and plaques	sa	Croome Park, Worcs, Punch-bowl Gateway	D	*Kelly* 1997, 21 (repr)
258.	1794–1795	Seven plaques, including representations of Ceres, Hibernia, an oak garland and a harp	sa	[Cuffnells, Hants]; Stratfield Saye, Hants (four)		*Kelly* 1989 (1), 249; *Kelly* 1990, 167
259.	post-1796	Coat of arms with palms, plaques, vases and capitals	sa	Great Saxham Hall, Suffolk		*Kelly* 1990, 169
260.	c1796	Font	sa	[All Saints, Newcastle, Northumberland]; untraced		*Kelly* 1990, 367
261.	†1797	Armorial above the oculus containing the coffin of Richard Muilman Trench Chiswell	sa	Debden, Essex, Chiswell burial vault	S	
262.	1797	King Alfred instituting trial by jury (modelled by J C F Rossi)	sa	Arundel Castle, Sussex (fragment)		*Kelly* 1990, 122–3
263.	1797	Rusticated blocks and keystones with bearded heads	sa	Croome Court, Worcs, Dry Arch bridge	D	*Kelly* 1997, 22, 23 (repr)
264.	1797	Two statues, adapted to hold lights	sa	Leith Hill Place, Surrey		*Kelly* 1990, 376
265.	1798	Howard lion and Fitzalan horse	sa	[Norfolk suspension bridge, Shoreham, Sussex]; Arundel Castle, Sussex		*Kelly* 1988 (2), 182; *Kelly* 1990, 265, 378, 382
266.	1777–1798	Plaques (including Florentine lion) and medallions	sa	Doddington Hall, Cheshire		*Kelly* 1990, 169, 338
267.	1798	Relief from the firm's trade card ('The Attempts of Time to Destroy Sculpture' and 'Architecture defeated by the Vitrifying Aid of Fire') and caryatids (designed by John Bacon RA)	sa	[Coade's Gallery, Lambeth, London, overdoor]; destroyed		*Kelly* 1990, 408
268.	by 1799	Bas relief figures and other ornaments	sa	[Freemantle, Southampton, Hants]; untraced		*Kelly* 1990, 351
269.	1790–1799	Gothic screen and statues of the Virgin, Edward the Confessor and St George (designed by Henry Emlyn) Payment(s): £1,685 8s od for screen and organ loft	sa	St George's Chapel, Windsor Castle, west front		*Darlington* 1955, 13–8, pl I; *Kelly* 1990, 216–8, 227, 335 (repr)
270.	1799	Pediment group	sa	[Pelican Life Insurance Office, Cornhill, City of London, pediment]; Horniman Museum, London		*Kelly* 1990 47, 406 (repr)
271.	c1799	Psyche and Hymen, statuettes incorporating candleholders (modelled by John Bacon RA)	sa	[Norbury Park, Dorking, Surrey]; Heaton Park, Lancs		*Kelly* 1990, 187, 360, 377 (repr)
272.	by 1799	Tiger and 'its companion' (modelled from life by John Bacon RA)	sa	[Tehidy Park, Truro, Cornwall]; untraced		*Kelly* 1990, 257, 263, 339
273.	1790–1800	Coat of arms and gothic details	sa	[Arundel Castle, Sussex]; untraced		*Kelly* 1988 (2), 182; *Kelly* 1990, 378–9

274.	c1800	Coat of arms, heraldic lions and swans, plaques (Judgment of Paris, Warriors at the altar of Diana, etc), roundels with profile heads (Bacchus, Ceres, Architecture, Health, Scotia, etc) (designed by Robert Adam)	sa	Gosford House, Lothian		*Kelly* 1990, 75, 146, 258, 268, 431 (repr)
275.	1800	Commemorative urn, pedestal and globe with inscription	sa	Myddleton memorial, Great Amwell, Herts		*Kelly* 1990, 230, 355
276.	1800	Hindu temple (executed by John Charles Felix Rossi)	sa	[Melchet Park, Wilts]; untraced		*GM* 1841, 2, 243 (repr); *Kelly* 1990, 209, 211
277.	c1800	Phoenix	sa	[Phoenix Fire Engine House, Chelmsford]; Brewery House, Chelmsford, Essex, gardens		*Kelly* 1990, 109, 346
278.	1800	Urn and plaque with a mourning woman	sa	Mylne Mausoleum, Great Amwell, Herts		*Kelly* 1990, 355
279.	1800–1801	Pair of swans Payment(s): £13 10s	sa	Vintners' Hall, City of London		*Kelly* 1990, 265
280.	c1801	Plaques (Griffins and ornament and the Seasons) and other decorations	sa	Stationers' Hall, City of London		*Kelly* 1990, 420
281.	1801	Statues of the four continents and vases Payment(s): £514 19s 6d	sa	[Bank of England, London, Lothbury Court]; P Dem		*Kelly* 1989 (1), 250–1 (repr); *Kelly* 1990, 225, 392 (repr); *Ward-Jackson* 2002, 887
282.	1801	Unicorn, recumbent	sa	[Hazelwood Castle, Tadcaster, W R Yorks]; Hazelwood Castle sale, 15 June 1972, lot 760, untraced	SD	*Kelly* 1990, 389
283.	1802	Egyptian lionesses	sa	Culzean, Ayrshire, Cat Gates Other versions: ex coll Thomas Hope, Deepdene, Surrey, 1820; private coll, Suffolk ex Castlewellan, Co Down; 1818, untraced	SD	*Kelly* 1990, 262–3, 373, 376, 429 (repr); *Kelly* 1993, 917
284.	1802	Four standing female figures in high relief	sa	Pitzhanger Manor, Ealing Grove, London, interior		*Kelly* 1989 (1), 251–2, 253 (repr); *Kelly* 1990, 86, 318, 415 (repr)
285.	1801–1803	Piers, ceiling and window tracery, figures of angels between the upper windows, corbels	sa	Chelmsford Cathedral, Essex		*Kelly* 1985, 81–2; *Kelly* 1990, 109, 346 (repr)
286.	1804	Portable font	sa	[Foundling Hospital, London, chapel]; Coram Foundation, London, court room	SD	*Gunnis* 1968, 108; *Kelly* 1990, 116
287.	1805	Two pairs of terms Payment(s): £63	sa	[Croome Court, Worcs]; untraced		*Kelly* 1997, 23
288.	1806	Label stops and tracery	sa	St Peter, Chertsey, Surrey, aisle windows		Pevsner, *Surrey*, 1971, 148; *Kelly* 1990, 114 (repr)
289.	1809	Triton fountain	sa	Petworth House, Sussex Other versions: ex Taymouth Castle, Tayside, 1813; untraced ex Norbiton Place, Surrey, 1819; untraced ex Flambards, Harrow, Middx, 1820; untraced ex Wilton Castle, Wexford; untraced		*Kelly* 1990, 202–3, 377, 382, 406, 432 (repr); *Kelly* 1993, 914, 917 (repr)
290.	1810–1812	Neptune handing over Nelson to Britannia, tympanum relief (designed by Benjamin West PRA; modelled by Joseph Panzetta) Payment(s): £2,584	sa	Royal Hospital, Greenwich (ORNC), quadrangle, King William block		*Kelly* 1985, 76; *Kelly* 1990, 235–7, 403–4 (repr)
291.	1813	Capitals and plaques (laurel wreaths, fasces and other ornaments)	sa	[Leeds Court House, W R Yorks]; destroyed		*Kelly* 1990, 155, 389 (repr)
292.	1799–1813	Gothic garden building	sa	Great Saxham Hall, Suffolk		*Kelly* 1990, 209, 374
293.	1799–1813	Shop sign with a relief of a cocoa tree	sa	[The Cocoa Tree, a chocolate house in the London area]; private coll	SD	*Kelly* 1990, unpag (repr)
294.	1814	Arms of the hospital with palms and laurels Payment(s): 150 gns	sa	Royal Hospital, Greenwich (ORNC), Trafalgar Block		*Kelly* 1985, 76; *Kelly* 1990, 404
295.	1814	Arms, festoons, lion's heads and other ornaments	sa	[St Thomas's Hospital, Southwark, London]; destroyed		*Kelly* 1990, 419
296.	1813–1814	Elephants and figures of Apollo	sa	[Sezincote, Glos]; untraced		*Kelly* 1990, 134, 206, 263 (repr)
297.	1814	'Peace and Victory with wings, a caduceus, olive branch, cornucopia etc' Payment(s): £103 1s 4d	sa	[Swansfield House, Alnwick, Northumberland, column]; untraced		*Kelly* 1990, 367
298.	1815	Candelabrum	sa	Tatton Park, Cheshire		*Kelly* 1990, 96, 338
299.	1815	Grecian capitals and paterae	sa	[Deepdene, Surrey]; destroyed		*Kelly* 1990, 152, 376
300.	1814–1815	Large gothic archway, 30 corbels, coat of arms Payment(s): £147 (archway) £78 15s (corbels)	sa	Battle Abbey, Sussex		*Kelly* 1988, 183; *Kelly* 1990, 119–20, 379 (repr)
301.	1816	'2 rich Gothic candelabras' Payment(s): £81 16s 4d	sa	[Michel Grove, Sussex]; untraced		*Kelly* 1988 (2), 188
302.	1816	Caryatid, copy of one from the Erechtheion	sa	[Ordered by Hon Frederick North for Athens]; untraced		*Kelly* 1990, 135, 417
303.	1816	Font Payment(s): 14 gns	sa	[Shiplake, Oxon]; untraced		*Kelly* 1990, 369
304.	1816	Four lions, supporters (designed by David Stephenson) Payment(s): £55 each	sa	Percy tenantry column, Alnwick, Northumbs		*Usherwood* 2000, 1–2 (repr)

305.	1816	'The French Eagle conquered by the British Lion' Payment(s): 45 gns	sa	[for George Palmer, St James's St, London]; The Grosvenor Arms, Pulford, Cheshire		*Kelly* 1990, 259, 260, 418 (repr)
306.	1817	'A rich Gothic candlestick' Payment(s): £35 16s 1d	sa	[Coleorton Hall, Ashby de la Zouche, Leics]; private coll		*Kelly* 1990, 361
307.	1817	Font, 'highly wrought, with cherubs' Payment(s): £36 15s	sa	[E I Co]; untraced		*Kelly* 1990, 116
308.	1817	Four vases, eagle with wings extended, two panels representing 'The Marriage of Cupid' Payment(s): 75 gns	sa	[William Chamberlayne MP, Weston Grove, Southampton, Hants]; untraced		*Kelly* 1990, 198, 265, 353
309.	1814–1817	Plaques, coats of arms and many other ornaments Payment(s): nearly £5,000	sa	Dalmeny House, Linlithgow		*Kelly* 1990, 120–3, 429 (repr)
310.	1817	Rampant lion, swags and bows, armorial shield	sa	Cullen House, Banff, gateway		*Kelly* 1985, 75; *Kelly* 1990, 428
311.	1817	Royal arms, Neptune on seahorse, Britannia, lion and shield	sa	[Custom House, City of London]; destroyed		*Kelly* 1990, 399
312.	1814–1817	Terms with girls' heads	sa	Chiswick House, London		*Kelly* 1990, 397
313.	1818	Eagles	sa	Castlewellan, Co Down, gate piers		*Kelly* 1990, 266, 434
314.	1818	Fountain, urns, two portrait plaques	sa	Syon House, Isleworth, Middx		*Kelly* 1990, 421
315.	1815–1818	Medallions of earth, water and Diana, lions	sa	Corby Castle, Carlisle, Cumberland		*Kelly* 1990, 339
316.	1818	Tablets with reclining figures emblematic of Commerce, Agriculture, Navigation, Arts and Manufactures	sa	Bank of Montreal, Canada, Head Office		*Kelly* 1990, 171, 441
317.	1818	Two hawks	sa	Farnley Hall, Otley, W R Yorks, gate piers		*Kelly* 1990, 389
318.	1819	Britannia, victories, dolphins and scrolls (designed by William Wilkins; modelled by Joseph Panzetta and Griffiths) Payment(s): £1368 2s 6d	sa	Nelson column, Great Yarmouth, Norfolk		*Kelly* 1990, 237–8, 364 (repr)
319.	1819	Decorative details	sa	[Union Assurance Office, Cornhill, London]; destroyed		*Gunnis* 1968, 108
320.	1819	Font Payment(s): 12 gns	sa	[St Mary, Welwyn, Herts]; removed		*Kelly* 1990, 116, 355–6
321.	1819	Inn sign, 'a swan on a ground'	sa	[The Swan Inn, Chichester, Sussex]; untraced Other versions: for John Lyall, of Chelsea, 1817; untraced ex Rickmansworth, Herts; untraced		*Kelly* 1988 (2), 184; *Kelly* 1990, 265
322.	1819	Pinnacles, window tracery, screen and other ornaments Payment(s): £823 10s 4d	sa	All Saints, Deane, Hants		*Kelly* 1977 (1), 1514–6 (repr); *Kelly* 1990, 111–3, 351 (repr)
323.	1820	'A Rich Gothic Font' Payment(s): about 25 gns	sa	[St Dunstan-in-the-East, London]; untraced		*Kelly* 1990, 116
324.	1820	Child and dolphin fountain	sa	Knole, Kent		*Kelly* 1990, 359; *Kelly* 1993, 917
325.	1820	'Royal Arms surrounded by wreaths of laurel . . . supported by 2 colossal statues of Justice and Truth' and 'statue St George with St John with eagle'	sa	[Royal Palace, Rio de Janeiro, Brazil]; untraced		*Kelly* 1990, 134, 144 n 59, 441
326.	1821	Neptune and sea horse Payment(s): £44	sa	[Mr Goldworthy, Exeter]; untraced		*Kelly* 1990, 341
327.	1821	Parts of frieze, plaques, columns and other ornaments	sa	Ickworth Park, Suffolk (NT)		*Kelly* 1990, 176, 374 (repr)
328.	1822	Coat of arms, heraldic animals, capitals and urns	sa	Easton Neston, Northants, entrance (now the entrance to Towcester Racecourse)		*Kelly* 1990, 207, 366 (repr); *Kelly* 1993, 916
329.	1824	Decorative details		[New Courts of Judicature, London]; untraced		*Gunnis* 1968, 117; *Kelly* 1990, 226
330.	1827	Decorative details		[Board of Trade, Whitehall, London]; untraced		*Gunnis* 1968, 117; *Kelly* 1990, 226
331.	1828	Astronomy, Geography, History, Painting, Commerce, Neptune, Navigation, statues (designed by John Flaxman and modelled by Edward Hodges Baily) Payment(s): 150 gns each	sa	[Buckingham Palace, London, pediments]; untraced		TNA WORK 19/3.252–90, f285; *Colvin* VI, 1976, 301; *Kelly* 1990, 221–2, 409
332.	1827–1828	Six Virtues, statues (modelled by J C F Rossi) Payment(s): £1,386	sa	[Buckingham Palace, London, west front around bow]; Buckingham Palace, London, behind royal mews		*Colvin* VI, 1976, 301; *Kelly* 1990, 221
333.	1828–1830	Three figures, including Agriculture and plaques	sa	Covent Garden Market, London		*Kelly* 1990, 399
334.	1835	Britannia (modelled by Joseph Panzetta)	sa	Town Hall, Plymouth, Devon, pediment		Pevsner, *Devon*, 1989, 675
335.	1826–1837	Frieze, four military trophes, four naval trophies, royal arms, 6 vases, capitals, consoles supporting balconies (frieze designed by John Flaxman)	sa	Buckingham Palace, London	SD	*Colvin* VI, 1976, 301; *Kelly* 1990, 85, 222–3, 395 (repr)
336.	1840	Townley vase	sa	Sotheby, Billingshurst, Sussex, May 1988		*Kelly* 1990, 101
337.	1840	Warwick vase	sa	Somerley, Hants	SD	*Kelly* 1990, 353
338.	nd	Ceres with lion and cornucopia (designed by James Giles)	sa	Clydesdale Bank, Aberdeen		*Kelly* 1990, 428

339. nd	Colonnade and gateway with crest, capitals and statues in niches	sa	[Glananea, Co Westmeath]; Rosemead (statues now in private coll)		*Kelly* 1990, 208, 437
340. nd	Dog kennel with relief decoration and cross over entrance	sa	[Hillam Hall, Yorks]; private coll	S	*Kelly* 1990, 389
341. nd	Font with gothic enrichment on clustered columns	sa	Swine, E R Yorks		*Kelly* 1990, 390
342. nd	Garden seats in the form of winged sphinxes	sa	Parham House, Sussex		*Kelly* 1998 (2), 188, 189 (repr); *Kelly* 1990, 93–4, 182–3, 382 (repr)
343. nd	Group of three boys, group of two boys and four vases, garden ornaments	sa	[Methley Hall, W R Yorks]; destroyed		*Kelly* 1990, 390
344. nd	Large plaque of a female profile and other ornaments	sa	Grove House, Roehampton, Surrey		*Kelly* 1990, 377
345. nd	Lion and unicorn	sa	Kensington Palace, London, gate piers		*Kelly* 1990, 226, 407 (repr)
346. nd	Plaque of Phoebus, statues, lions, royal arms, trophy and other ornaments	sa	[Coade Factory, Lambeth, London, exterior]; destroyed		*Kelly* 1990, 408
347. nd	Reliefs of Arts and Commerce	sa	Weglegen, Haarlem, Holland, behind portico		*Kelly* 1990, 442
348. nd	Spaniel	sa	Southill, Beds		*Kelly* 1990, 332
349. nd	Spring, summer, autumn and winter, lampholding figures (designed by John Bacon RA)	sa	City Rooms, Leicester, ballroom Other versions: East Park, Hull, E R Yorks (Spring and Summer), 1799 ex Wentworth Woodhouse, Yorks, 1814; private coll ex The Retreat, Reigate, Surrey, 1818; untraced		*Kelly* 1990, 129, 377; *Cavanagh* 2000, 127–9 (repr)
Reliefs					
350. *c*1777	Plaques with crossed arrows, cornucopiae, consoles	sa	Woodhall Park, Hertford, Herts		*Kelly* 1990, 356
351. 1787	Medallion with a pyramid, Isis-Hygeia, a Sphinx and ruins	sa	[Medical Society, Bolt Court, Fleet Street]; Medical Society of London, Marylebone, London Other versions: ex coll Dr Lettsom, Camberwell Grove, London; untraced	SD	*Kelly* 1990, 169, 396
352. 1788	Four panels of tritons	sa	[Admiralty, London]; untraced		*Gunnis* 1968, 107; *Kelly* 1990, 169
353. 1788	Medallions with putti on dolphins Payment(s): 4 gns each	sa	[Hooton Hall, Cheshire]; untraced Other versions: Chiswick House, London, bridge		*Kelly* 1990, 168, 338, 397
354. 1790	Panels of King George III and Queen Charlotte surrounded by graces and virtues and capitals (designed by R F Brettingham)	sa	Temple of Concord, Audley End, Essex		*Kelly* 1990, 153–4, 230, 231 (repr); *Kelly* 1993, 916
355. 1790	Plaques with nereids and dolphins Payment(s): £205 (with statue of Charity)	sa	[Fishmongers' Hall, City of London]; destroyed		*Kelly* 1990, 168–9, 402
356. 1791	7 plaques (reclining ladies and swags with paterae)	sa	Runnymede House, Egham, Surrey	SD	*Kelly* 1990, 377
357. 1796	Panels of putti engaged in agriculture, architecture, painting	sa	[20–21 Wellclose Square, Stepney]; 25 Belgrave Square, London Other versions: similar at Emo, Co Laois, 1790–1799		*Kelly* 1990, 437 (repr)
358. by 1799	Apollo, relief	sa	Corby Castle, Carlisle, Cumberland Other versions: ex East India House, Leadenhall St, London, 1814–1815, destr		*Kelly* 1990, 339
359. 1799	Prince of Wales and Duchess of Rutland, portrait medallions	sa	[Exhib Coade's Gallery]; untraced		*Kelly* 1990, 141
360. *c*1800	Nine muses, panel	sa	[Charles Fowler's office, Gordon Square, London]; Warburg Institute, London, hall		*Kelly* 1990, 177; Pevsner, *London: N*, 1998, 278
361. 1804	West Indiaman	sa	[West India Dock, London, above entrance]; untraced		*Kelly* 1990, 424
362. 1816	Alexander Pope, portrait medallion	sa	Saltram, Devon		*Kelly* 1990, 141, 343
363. 1816	Thomas Gray, portrait medallion	sa	Saltram, Devon Other versions: Strawberry Hill, Twickenham, Middx, nd		*Kelly* 1990, 107, 141, 343
364. 1817–1823	Eagle medallion (several examples recorded)	sa	[Eagle Fire Insurance Company, City of London]; untraced		*Kelly* 1990, 266, 400–1
365. 1832	Lion	sa	[Northwick Park, Glos, south front]; Parham House, Sussex, gardens	SD	*Kelly* 1988 (2), 188; *Kelly* 1990, 382 (repr)
366. nd	Duke and Duchess of Northumberland, portrait medallions (several)	sa	Alnwick Castle, Northumbs Other versions: Brizlee Tower, Hulne Priory, Alnwick, Northumbs	S	*Kelly* 1990, 74, 367
367. nd	John Milton (?) portrait medallion	sa	Private coll		*Kelly* 1990, 141
368. nd	Phoenix medallion (issued by the Phoenix Fire Insurance Company)	sa	National Westminster Bank, Weedon, Northants		*Kelly* 1990, 366 (repr)
Miscellaneous					
369. 1784	Dr Johnson's death mask	sa	Untraced		*Gunnis* 1968, 107

COATES, Enos, of Falsgrave fl 1798–1833

A Yorkshire restorer and monumental mason. His oval tablet to Mary Lamprey is of coloured marbles and features an urn in high relief (2). The Woodall monument, which has cornucopiae and an urn, was described as 'weird' by Pevsner and 'amusing' by Gunnis (1).

Literary References: Pevsner, *Yorks: N R*, 1966, 456;

Archival References: GPC

Funerary Monuments

1.	†1798	John Woodall	Seamer, N R Yorks		Pevsner, *Yorks: N R*, 1966, 456
2.	†1827	Mary Lamprey	Boynton, E R Yorks	S	Pevsner, *Yorks: E R & York*, 1995, 334
3.	†1829	Thomas Wharram	Burton Fleming, E R Yorks		Pevsner, *Yorks: E R & York*, 1995, 378
4.	?1833	John Taylor	Hackness, N R Yorks		GPC
5.	nd	Sir William St Quintin (†1649), restoration only	Harpham, E R Yorks	S	Pevsner, *Yorks: E R & York*, 1995, 450

COATES, F L, of Lambeth fl 1841

Architectural Sculpture

1.	*c*1841	Reapers, a group	Corn Exchange, Sudbury, Suffolk, above façade	Pevsner, *Suffolk*, 1974, 454

COCHRANE, J fl 1810

The plaster cast of **Thomas Banks**'s relief of *Thetis and her Nymphs rising from the Sea to console Achilles for the Death of Patroclus* in the Soane Museum is signed 'Published by J Cochrane . . . 1810' (inf. Helen Dorey). He must have been a plaster modeller or the owner of a plaster workshop.

COCHRANE, John fl 1837–49

In 1837 John Cochrane showed a model of a gentleman in Highland costume at the Royal Scottish Academy (1). In the exhibition catalogue his address was given as the National Monument, Edinburgh, which suggests that he was working with **Robert Forrest**, the custodian of the National Monument, Calton Hill, Edinburgh. Four years later Cochrane exhibited a figure of Sir Walter Scott from an address in Atholl Street, Perth (2). This was presumably the freestone statue of Scott which a Perth firm of mason sculptors, Cochrane Brothers, sold to the city of Perth on their departure for America in the 1840s.

Literary References: *Woodward* 1977, vol 1, pt 2, 46–7

Statues

1.	1837	Gentleman in Highland regimental dress, model	[Exhib R Sc A, Edinburgh, 367]; untraced	*Woodward* 1977, vol 1, pt 2, 46–7; *Laperriere* 1, 1991, 322
2.	1841	Sir Walter Scott	South Inch, Perth	*Woodward* 1977, vol 1, pt 2, 47; *Laperriere* 1, 1991, 322

COCKAINE, J fl 1817–18

He exhibited busts at the Royal Academy from 85 Newman Street and 5 New Road, London.

Busts

1.	1817	Rev J Disney DD	[Exhib RA, London, 1041]; untraced	*Graves* II, 1905–6, 90
2.	1818	Captain Rutherford RN	[Exhib RA, London, 1058]; untraced	*Graves* II, 1905–6, 90
3.	1818	Rev W Beloe	[Exhib RA, London, 90]; untraced	*Graves* II, 1905–6, 90

COCKBURN, P, of Dublin fl 1817–24

Funerary Monuments

1.	†1817	Rev Richard Bourne	St Werburgh, Dublin	S	*Potterton* 1975, 41
2.	†1820	John Rickaby	Collon, Co Louth	S	*Potterton* 1975, 41
3.	†1820	Matthew West	St Werburgh, Dublin	S	*Potterton* 1975, 41
4.	†1824	Sir Frederick Flood	St Anne's, Dublin	S	*Potterton* 1975, 41

COCKER, D fl *c*1840

His address is given on a wax bust as 8 Chenies Street, London.

Archival References: GPC

Busts

1.	*c*1840	Unidentified English admiral	w	coll Rupert Gunnis, untraced	GPC

COCKER, George Potts, of Derby fl 1839

A modeller at the Derby China Factory, he exhibited a number of works in that city.

Archival References: GPC

Busts

1.	1839	Admiral Lord Nelson, cabinet bust	[Derby Mechanics Exhib]; untraced	GPC
2.	1839	Arthur, 1st Duke of Wellington	[Derby Mechanics Exhib]; untraced	GPC
3.	1839	Daniel O'Connell, cabinet bust	[Derby Mechanics Exhib]; untraced	GPC
4.	1839	Dr Douglas Fox	[Derby Mechanics Exhib]; untraced	GPC
5.	1839	Sir Robert Peel, cabinet bust	[Derby Mechanics Exhib]; untraced	GPC

Miscellaneous

6.	nd	Three figures representing the three stages of drinking, intended as a warning against intoxication	[for Dr Douglas Fox, of Derby]; Brighton Museum, Sussex	GPC

COFFEE, H, of Derby and London 1795–

He was born in Lambeth on 14 May 1795 and was probably a son of **William Coffee**. A sculptor, modeller and designer of this name exhibited at the Royal Academy from 1819 to 1845 from a number of addresses in Westminster, changing location every few years until 1842 when he was at 6 Oxford Market, Oxford Street. In 1839 his *Boy and Foliage*, perhaps a tablet for a chimneypiece (7) was praised by the *Literary Gazette* who considered the sculptor had shown 'judgment and taste in his combinations; for it may be observed that nothing can be more suitable to the modulating lines of foliage than the easy flow of infantile forms' (*Lit Gaz* 1839, 379). His last exhibited work, *Death of a Boar*, was later executed in silver (**18**). Coffee applied to join the Artists' Annuity Fund in 1839. He was elected in the following year. He was still alive in 1863.

Literary References: *Gunnis* 1968, 109

Archival References: AAF, Proposals, 287

Funerary Monuments					
1.	1826	Devotion, design for a monument		[Exhib Soc of BA, London, 733]; untraced	*Johnson* 1975, 96
Statues					
2.	1822	Group of cattle		[Exhib RA, London, 1030; exhib Soc of BA, London, 1832, 882]; untraced	*Graves* II, 1905–6, 95; *Johnson* 1975, 96
3.	1832	A horse, model		[Exhib Soc of BA, London, 875]; untraced	*Johnson* 1975, 96
Busts					
4.	1821	Unidentified sitter, model ('to be executed in marble')		[Exhib RA, London, 1138]; untraced	*Graves* II, 1905–6, 95
5.	1825	Master F Pulley		[Exhib RA, London, 1053]; untraced	*Graves* II, 1905–6, 95; *Johnson* 1975, 96
6.	1826	Unidentified gentleman		[Exhib Soc of BA, London, 747]; untraced	*Johnson* 1975, 96
Chimneypieces					
7.	1839	'Boy and foliage, part of a chimneypiece executed for his late Majesty George IV'		[Exhib RA, London, 1278]; untraced	*Lit Gaz*, 1169, 15 June 1839, 1 379; *Graves* II, 1905–6, 95; *Gunnis* 1968, 109
Architectural Sculpture					
8.	1839	A young Triton; 'part of a fountain'		[Exhib RA, London, 1283]; untraced	*Graves* II, 1905–6, 95
Reliefs					
9.	1826	George III, medallic bust		[Exhib RA, London, 977]; untraced	*Graves* II, 1905–6, 95
Miscellaneous					
10.	1819	Cupid		[Exhib RA, London, 1225]; untraced	*Graves* II, 1905–6, 95
11.	1824	A group of boys		[Exhib RA, London, 999]; untraced	*Graves* II, 1905–6, 95
12.	1825	F Goodwin		[Exhib RA, London, 1066]; untraced	*Graves* II, 1905–6, 95
13.	1825	Unidentified lady	w	[Exhib RA, London, 956]; untraced	*Graves* II, 1905–6, 95
14.	1826	'Groupe of Bacchantes'		[Exhib RA, London, 1055]; untraced	*Graves* II, 1905–6, 95
15.	1827	Death of a bear, model of a hunt	w	[Exhib Soc of BA, London, 837]; untraced	*Graves* 1875, 109; *Johnson* 1975, 96
16.	1832	Group of two sleeping children		[Exhib Soc of BA, London, 865; exhib RA, London, 865]; untraced	*Graves* II, 1905–6, 95; *Johnson* 1975, 96
17.	1842	Unidentified lady, cabinet portrait		[Exhib RA, London, 1195]; untraced	*Graves* II, 1905–6, 95
18.	1845	Death of a boar		[Exhib RA, London, 1468]; untraced	*Graves* II, 1905–6, 95; *Gunnis* 1968, 109

COFFEE, John Thomas –1869

Coffee worked for Coade and Sealy (see **Coade Factory of Lambeth**) and exhibited at the Royal Academy in 1816 from 11 Brook Street, West Square, Lambeth. In the same year he emigrated to Charleston, South Carolina, and later went to New York, where he died after 1869.

One of his busts, of General Scott (2), was reproduced in 1877 on the United States 24 cent stamp. The Fort Beauséjour Museum, New Brunswick has a bust of John Watts by 'Thomas Coffee', probably the same artist.

Literary References: *Gunnis* 1968, 109

Busts					
1.	nd	Edward Ratchford Williamson, MD		Fort Beauséjour Museum, New Brunswick, Canada	*Gunnis* 1968, 109
2.	nd	General Scott		untraced	*Gunnis* 1968, 109
3.	nd	John Watts, copy after Robert Ball Hughes		Fort Beausejour Museum, New Brunswick, Canada	*Chamberlain* 1957, 384; *Gunnis* 1968, 109
Architectural Sculpture					
4.	1816	Gothic candelabrum	tc	[Exhib RA, London, 969]; untraced	*Graves* II, 1905–6, 95; *Gunnis* 1968, 109

COFFEE, William 1746–1840

A London modeller, he was the father of **William John Coffee**. He married Catherine Lee on 25 February 1772 at St Martin-in-the-Fields. Coffee appears to have been employed by a manufactory in Chelsea and also had connections with the Derby works, where his son subsequently worked. He is mentioned on a handful of occasions in Joseph Lygo's correspondence with William Duesbury. In January 1795 **J C F Rossi** told Lygo that the manufactory for which Coffee worked was 'intirely standing still' and that Coffee was now 'in some gentleman's service' (Lygo/Duesbury corr, quoted in *Bricknell* 1998, 19). In September 1795 Coffee wrote to Duesbury asking for his son to be re-employed at the Derby works, which he had left some months earlier (*Jewitt* 1876, 2, 98). Coffee also worked as an ornamental plasterer.

In 1829 he applied for financial help from the Artist's General Benevolent Association. He stated that he had 'carved several coats of arms and figures about different parts of England' and listed some of his commissions. They included work at Greenwich College Chapel (1), where Coffee must have been employed by **Eleanor Coade**. In 1831 he again applied for assistance, pleading that 'having lost his hearing he is now so feeble that he cannot earn one penny'. From 1830–1840 he received an annual pension from the Royal Academy, which totalled £118 16s over the period. In 1841 a 'Miss Coffee' was awarded £10 from the same source.

Literary References: *Gunnis* 1968, 109; *Kelly* 1990, 64; *Bricknell* 1995, 68–9, 77, 85, 89, 92–3; *Bricknell* 1998, 19

Archival References: RA/GA, 1830–41; AGBI, vol 2, 28, 55, 78, 112, 149, 162; vol 3, 33, 53, 83, 112, 143, 187; vol 4, 173, 210 (the latter applications made by his daughter)

Architectural Sculpture

1.	pre-1829	Decorative ornaments ('the apostles and prophets around the pulpit and reading desk' and 'the angels under the communion table')	[Greenwich College, Chapel]; untraced	*Gunnis* 1968, 109
2.	pre-1829	Figures and coats of arms	[for Lord Abergavenny]; untraced	*Gunnis* 1968, 109
3.	pre-1829	Figures and coats of arms	[for Lord Darnley]; untraced	*Gunnis* 1968, 109
4.	pre-1829	Figures and coats of arms	[for Lord Essex]; untraced	*Gunnis* 1968, 109
5.	pre-1829	Figures and coats of arms	[for Duke of Buckingham]; untraced	*Gunnis* 1968, 109
6.	pre-1829	Figures and coats of arms	[for Hon Mr Villiers]; untraced	*Gunnis* 1968, 109
7.	pre-1829	Figures and coats of arms	[for Squire Bedford]; untraced	*Gunnis* 1968, 109
8.	pre-1829	Royal arms	[Windsor Castle, Berks]; untraced	*Gunnis* 1968, 109
9.	pre-1829	Royal arms	['Outside Hatchett's, Long Acre, London']; untraced	*Gunnis* 1968, 109

COFFEE, William John 1773–after 1846

Coffee was a modeller, sculptor, painter and one of the first British sculptors to establish a career in America. He was the son of **William Coffee**, a modeller for **Eleanor Coade**, and Catherine, née Lee, and was baptised at St Clement Danes, London, on 12 September 1773. Coffee, like his father, was employed as a modeller by Coade, but he left Lambeth in mid-1792 when a dispute with another employee, a Mr Pritchard, brought him into conflict with Coade's manager and junior partner, **John Sealy**.

He married Martha Dudley on 21 May 1792 and their son, Henry, was born at the Lying-in Hospital for the Distressed Poor on 23 May 1793. The couple lived at Tottenham Street, London. On 3 November 1792 he registered for admission to the Royal Academy schools, but his admission was not completed. In April 1793 he considered an offer of employment from the Derby China Manufactory and on 28 May signed an agreement with William Duesbury II to become resident modeller at the Derby Works in succession to **John James Spängler**. Coffee received 3s 6d for each ten and a half hour day and was expected to work 63 hours a week. In 1794 changes in Duesbury's methods of payment (offering piece work in place of a flat rate) caused trouble with several of the staff including Coffee, who objected in writing. Joseph Lygo, Duesbury's assistant, did not 'much admire Mr Coffee's modeling' anyhow (quoted in *Bricknell* 1998, 25) and Spängler was re-employed at Derby where he worked with Coffee for about two months, before Coffee left the manufactory. A list of the designs thought to have been modelled by Coffee for the Derby works is given in Bricknell's monograph of 1998.

On 4 June 1795 Coffee was employed by another local firm, the Church Gresley China Factory, near Burton-upon-Trent. This business was short-lived and in September 1795 Coffee was in London looking for work. At his father's request, he was re-employed at Derby when Duesbury's attempt to appoint **Henry Webber** as chief modeller failed. In the autumn of 1796 he joined another short-lived ceramics manufacturing enterprise, this time a small white china factory in Friar Gate, Derby, which closed in 1798. On 3 November 1798 he became a travelling salesman for the Pinxton China works at 4s 2d a day, their highest paid employee. He travelled to London and took the opportunity to show specimens of his animal pieces at the Royal Academy (**59, 60**).

In 1803 he left Pinxton to establish his own business as a modeller and sculptor in Derby. His output expanded to embrace all kinds of sculptural work, including busts, monuments and reliefs, not only in terracotta and plaster but also in marble, alabaster, composition and artificial stone. His busts included local celebrities, such as a fiddler (**15**) and a women from Tutbury famed for feats of fasting (**46**). His bust of the Derby scientist Erasmus Darwin in artificial stone, was lauded by the national press (**9**): 'the materials of which it is composed not being liable to be injured by the properties of atmospheric air, it is admirably calculated to convey to posterity the image of one of the greatest physicians and philosophers of the age' (*Monthly Mag*, 1804, 557). In 1808 he exhibited at the Royal Academy from a London address, 32 Stanhope Street, though he continued to live and work in Derby. In 1810 he executed in marble a copy of the *Calydonian Boar* for Joseph Strutt (**3**), and also a full-size figure of *Aesculapius* for the Derby Infirmary (**2**). Coffee advertised his decision to 'carry [on] the business of sculptor in marble, alabaster etc' at his premises in Bridge Street, Derby in the *Derby Mercury* of 26 September 1810. He flattered himself that because of 'his knowledge of the antique (beyond which he has not the vanity to aspire) . . . he is capable of producing such designs as will meet with the approbation of the amateur' (*Bricknell* 1998, 38).

John Haslem relates that in 1812 Coffee moved to London where he opened an establishment in Oxford Market. He was certainly in London in 1814, where he witnessed the myriad celebrations marking the end of the Napoleonic Wars. That year he was back in Derby, where he painted a large number of transparencies for Derby's own festive illuminations. In May he advertised for two apprentices, indicating that 'boys from the country will be preferred, with whom a small premium will be expected' (*Derby Mercury*, quoted in *Bricknell* 1998, 39).

Coffee's diverse activities probably reflect a lack of patrons, and in late 1816 or early 1817 he emigrated with his daughter Catherine to America. Other sculptors, such as Coffee's acquaintance **J C F Rossi**, spoke of emigration in the difficult economic conditions of post-war England, but Coffee appears to be the first notable British sculptor to have done so. He set up in New York as a sculptor, modeller and painter. In 1817 he exhibited at the American Academy of the Fine Arts (**70**), and in 1818 he attracted the patronage of the former President, Thomas Jefferson (**31**). Through Jefferson's influence he modelled busts *ad vivum* of President James Monroe (**25**) and ex-President James Madison (**24**). In 1818, he wrote from 501 Greenwich Street, New York, to another former President, John Adams, outlining his working method: he needed sittings of one hour each day for 4 or 5 days, and his subject could sit, stand or move around freely. He charged $35 for a clay model and $10 for each copy.

Coffee was invited to Monticello, Jefferson's home in Virginia, on three occasions between 1818 and 1822. He advised Jefferson on engineering repairs using concrete for his country house and executed extensive decorative work on classical themes for the new buildings of the University of Virginia (**53**). By 1820 he was a naturalised American citizen. Despite his distinguished patrons, Coffee found it difficult to make a living. He worked as a portrait-painter and restorer and wrote to Jefferson about numerous unexecuted schemes that he hoped might bring in enough money to pay for a passage back to England. In 1824 he entered the competition for the commission, worth $500, to execute the tympanum relief for the portico of the Capitol in Washington. His design was for *Justice on a pedestal with figures of Wisdom and Truth.* The judges felt Coffee's design to be the best of the numerous works submitted, but decided, to Coffee's ire, not to choose any of the entries. In 1826 Coffee made ornaments in Roman cement for the Gothic church of Notre Dame in Montreal, Canada (**54**). That year his great patron, Thomas Jefferson, died.

In 1827, despite his hankering for England and his loathing of the cold climate of the East Coast, Coffee settled in Albany, New York State, where he appears to have remained for the rest of his life. Living at 13 Washington, he advertised in the *Albany Argus* on 3 December 1829 offering 'superior enrichments either in plaster or Roman cement, for external decoration' (*Bricknell* 1998, 51). He planned a subscription bust of President Andrew Jackson, and continued to canvas leading politicians such as Governor William Henry Seward for patronage (**43**). In 1839 he offered Seward a life-size plaster bust with drapery for $100 with $30 for each copy. The directories and census records list Coffee living in Albany in the 1840s with four of his relatives. There is no mention of him after 1847. Until the last decade of his life Coffee complained of hardship: in a letter penned in January 1841 he moaned that a lack of patronage and competition from Henry Kirke Brown (1814–1886) had left him uncertain 'how to obtain either wood or bread' for his family (*Bicknell* 1998, 53). Even then he still hoped to return to England.

The relatively small number of surviving works makes it difficult to assess Coffee's merits as a sculptor. The importance of his early work as a modeller is manifest in the detailed and expressive modelling of the busts of Darwin (**9**) and the portrait of an unidentified man, whose fat lips, sagging eyes and bursting waistcoat convey a real sense of character (**14**). His extant American work is also naturalistic, though the nobility of some of his subjects is indicated by the herm form (**16**), or by the use of pinned drapery *all'antica* (**17**). The detailed documentation of his life and career by Brian Bicknell has given an important case study of the economic difficulties faced by a professional modeller and sculptor in England and America in the late-18th and early-19th centuries.

At least one of Coffee's offspring followed him into the profession. Notes on a lawsuit of 1818 relating to the Derby China Works in the British Museum, mention 'Coffee's son who lives in Tottenham Court Road & is a modeller' (*Bricknell* 1998, 71).

MGS

Literary References: *Haslem* 1876, 156; *Jewitt* 1878, 1, 1878; *Graves* II, 1905–6, 95; *Rutledge* 1945, 297–312; *Groce* 1946, 14; *Gunnis* 1968, 109–110; *Bricknell* 1995, *passim*; Bricknell 1998

Archival References: GPC

Portraits of the Sculptor: Edward Foster, silhouette, private coll (*Bricknell* 1998, frontispiece)

Statues

1.	1808	A figure for a candelabrum		[Exhib RA, London, 870]; untraced		*Graves* II, 1905–6, 95
2.	1810	Aesculapius	tc	[Royal Derby Infirmary]; destroyed (1891)		Pevsner, *Derbys*, 1978, 188; *Bricknell* 1998, 38
3.	c1810	Boar	m	[for garden of Joseph Strutt, Derby]; destroyed		Derby Local Studies Library 29130
4.	1810	Models of a ram		[Sold Uttoxeter 1883]; untraced		*Bricknell* 1998, 36 n25; GPC
5.	1811	A lioness, model	tc	[Exhib RA, London, 919]; untraced		*Graves* II, 1905–6, 95
6.	1814	Unidentified old man and woman, painted statuettes	tc	Derby Museum 1937-721	SD	*Bricknell* 1998, 35 (repr 19)
7.	nd	An unidentified tinker	tc	Royal Crown Derby Museum		*Bricknell* 1998, 36
8.	nd	Setter lying down, small biscuit figure		Private coll	S	*Bricknell* 1998, 36

Busts

9.	1804	Dr Erasmus Darwin	sa	Untraced Other versions: plaster, Derby Art Gallery, SD 1804		*Monthly Mag* 1804, 557; *Bricknell* 1998, 33 (plaster, repr 11)
10.	1806	Admiral Lord Nelson	p	NMM, Greenwich, SCU0095	SD	*Bricknell* 1998, 34 (reprs 12 and 13)
11.	c1807	D'Ewes Coke, Deputy Recorder for Grantham (1774–1856)	sa	Private coll Other versions: Plaster, private coll, stamped 'W Coffee Efecit'	S	Bricknell 1995, 34 (reprs 16, 17)
12.	?1810	Daniel Parker		Royal Derby Infirmary		*Gunnis* 1968, 109
13.	?1810	Mr Robertshaw		Royal Derby Infirmary		*Gunnis* 1968, 109
14.	1811	Unidentified man	tc	Private coll	SD	*Bricknell* 1998, 35 (repr 18)
15.	1814	Unidentified man ('Finney the Fiddler')	tc	Private coll	SD	*Bricknell* 1998, 35
16.	1816	Hugh Williamson MD	p	NYHS, X.58	S	*Gunnis* 1968, 110; *Bricknell* 1998, 41
17.	1817	De Witt Clinton, Governor of New York	p	NYHS, 1818.2 Other versions: Medallion presented to Albany Female Seminary, 1829		*Bricknell* 1998, 41, 50, 83
18.	1818	Anne Cary Randolph Bankhead	tc	Thomas Jefferson Memorial Foundation, USA		*Bricknell* 1998, 83
19.	1818	Chief Justice John Marshall		Untraced Other versions: 10 t-c copies recorded		*Bricknell* 1998, 42, 50
20.	1818	Cornelia Jefferson Randolph	tc	Thomas Jefferson Memorial Foundation, USA		*Gunnis* 1968, 110; *Bricknell* 1998, 41, 83 (repr 22)
21.	1818	Dolley Madison Payment(s): $105 with busts of James Madison and John Payne Todd	tc	National Trust for Historical Preservation, Montpelier, USA		*Bricknell* 1998, 42, 83
22.	1818	Ellen Wayles Randolph	tc	Untraced		*Bricknell* 1998, 41, 84
23.	1818	Isaac A Coles	tc	Private coll, USA		*Bricknell* 1998, 42, 83

24.	1818	James Madison Payment(s): $105 with busts of Dolley Madison and John Payne Todd	tc	Untraced		*Bricknell* 1998, 42, 85
25.	1818	James Monroe		Untraced		*Bricknell* 1998, 85
26.	1818	John Coles III		Private coll, USA		*Bricknell* 1998, 42
27.	1818	John Payne Todd Payment(s): $105 with busts of James Madison and Dolley Madison	tc	Untraced		*Bricknell* 1998, 42, 85
28.	1818	Martha Randolph	tc	Untraced		*Bricknell* 1998, 41, 84
29.	1818	Mrs Margaret Nicholas	tc	Thomas Jefferson Memorial Foundation, USA		*Bricknell* 1998, 41 (fig 24)
30.	1818	Rebecca Elizabeth Tucker Coles	p	Private coll, USA		*Bricknell* 1998, 42, 83
31.	1818	Thomas Jefferson	tc	Untraced Other versions: Copy presented to Albany Female Seminary, 1829		*Gunnis* 1968, 110; *Bricknell* 1998, 41, 50
32.	1818	Thomas Jefferson Randolph		Untraced		*Bricknell* 1998, 43, 85
33.	1818	Walter Coles	p	Private coll, USA		*Bricknell* 1998, 42, 83 (repr 25)
34.	1821	General Charles Cotesworth Pinckney	p	[Presented to the South Carolina Acad of Fine Arts]; untraced		*Gunnis* 1968, 110; *Bricknell* 1998, 44, 85
35.	1821	General Thomas Pinckney		[Presented to South Carolina Acad of Fine Arts]; South Carolina Historical Society		*Rutledge* 1945, 304 (repr); *Bricknell* 1998, 44, 83
36.	c1822	Dr Samuel Latham Mitchell		Untraced		*Bricknell* 1998, 86
37.	1826	Stephen Van Rensselaer, President of the Albany Institute		Untraced		*Bricknell* 1998, 86
38.	1827	Pierre van Cortlandt Payment(s): $100 and copies offered at $25	p	Museum of the City of New York, USA		*Gunnis* 1968, 110; *Bricknell* 1998, 50
39.	1829	John Milton	p	Untraced		*Bricknell* 1998, 86
40.	1831	Simeon De Witt, Surveyor-General	p	[Albany Institute of History and Art, USA]; untraced		*Bricknell* 1998, 87
41.	1835	William James	p	Untraced		*Bricknell* 1998, 85
42.	1836	Erastus Corning		Untraced Other versions: Plaster copy donated to Albany Institute, USA		*Bricknell* 1998, 52–3, 87
43.	?1839	William Henry Seward, Governor of New York		Untraced		*Bricknell* 1998, 87
44.	1840	William Harrison, half-size		Untraced		*Bricknell* 1998, 87
45.	nd	Admiral Lord Nelson, hard-paste porcelain	tc	Private coll Other versions: terra-cotta, Detroit Institute of Arts, SD 1824	S	*Bricknell* 1998, 34, 84 (reprs 14, 26)
46.	nd	Ann Moore, the 'Tutbury fasting woman'		Untraced		*Bricknell* 1998, 35
47.	nd	Charles James Fox		Untraced		*Gunnis* 1968, 109; *Bricknell* 1998, 35
48.	nd	Daniel Parker Coke MP		[Sold Uttoxeter 1883]; untraced		*Bricknell* 1998, 35; GPC
49.	nd	Hannah More	tc	Untraced		*Bricknell* 1998, 35
50.	nd	Sir Richard Arkwright		Untraced		*Gunnis* 1968, 109; *Bricknell* 1998, 35
51.	nd	William Strutt		Derby Museum		*Gunnis* 1968, 109; *Bricknell* 1998, 35

Architectural Sculpture

52.	1821	Friezes, with masks and ox skulls		[Poplar Forest, Bedford, USA, dining room and parlour]; destroyed		*Bricknell* 1998, 44, 85
53.	1822–1825	Ornaments in lead and composition	l	University of Virginia, USA, pavilions (work for rotunda damaged 1895)		*Bricknell* 1998, 46, 83, 86
54.	1826	'Large [gothic] ornaments'	sa	[Notre-Dame, Montreal, Canada]; untraced		*Bricknell* 1998, 86
55.	nd	Urn		Radbourne Hall, Derbys	S	*Bricknell* 1998, 36

Reliefs

56.	1821	Joel Poinsett, medallion		[Presented to South Carolina Acad of Fine Arts]; untraced		*Bricknell* 1998, 44, 85
57.	1829	Martin van Buren, medallion		[Presented to Albany Female Seminary, USA]; untraced		*Bricknell* 1998, 50, 86
58.	c1829	Reliefs commemorating De Witt Clinton and Sir Walter Scott	p	[Albany City Hall, USA]; destroyed (1880)		*Bricknell* 1998, 51, 87

Miscellaneous

59.	1801	A brood horse, model		[Exhib RA, London, 898]; untraced		*Graves* II, 1905–6, 95
60.	1801	A brood mare, model		[Exhib RA, London, 895]; untraced		*Graves* II, 1905–6, 95
61.	1808	A greyhound, study from nature		[Exhib RA, London, 879]; untraced		*Graves* II, 1905–6, 95
62.	1808	A group of cattle		[Exhib RA, London, 876]; untraced		*Graves* II, 1905–6, 95
63.	1808	Welsh pony, study from nature		[Exhib RA, London, 871]; untraced		*Graves* II, 1905–6, 95
64.	1811	Cow		[Sold Uttoxeter 1883]; untraced		*Bricknell* 1998, 36 n25; GPC
65.	1811	Greyhound		[Sold Uttoxeter 1883]; untraced		*Bricknell* 1998, 36 n25; GPC
66.	1811	Old Time	tc	[Sold Uttoxeter 1883]; untraced		*Bricknell* 1998, 36 n25; GPC
67.	1816	A setter ('the property of M Allam of Derby')	tc	[Exhib RA, London, 958]; untraced		*Graves* II, 1905–6, 95
68.	post-1816	Canterbury pilgrims	p	[Albany Institute of History and Art, USA]; untraced		*Bricknell* 1998, 87

69.	post-1816	Cavalcade proceeding to the tournament		[Albany Institute of History and Art, USA]; untraced	*Bricknell* 1998, 87
70.	1817	The infant morpheus	tc	[Exhib American Acad of Fine Arts]; untraced	*Bricknell* 1998, 84
71.	nd	A dog		[Sold Uttoxeter 1883]; untraced	*Bricknell* 1998, 36 n25; GPC
72.	nd	Brace of partridges	tc	[Exhib Midland Counties Exhibition 1870]; untraced	*Bricknell* 1998, 36 n25
73.	nd	Floating swan		[Sold Uttoxeter 1883]; untraced	*Bricknell* 1998, 36 n25; GPC

COFFIN, Edmond, of Exeter fl 1759–70

Coffin, who may have been a brother of Thomas Coffin of Exeter, alderman and goldsmith, became a freeman of his native city in 1769. In 1759 he received £116 for work at the Mayoralty House and he was working at the Guildhall in 1767 (Exeter City Archives). He signs the large wall monument to Thomas Bolithoe, which depicts a mourning woman at an urn before a landscape in low relief, all set against a grey marble obelisk (1).

A 'William Coffin', son of Thomas the goldsmith, was apprenticed to **William Barlow** in 1755.

Literary References: *Gunnis* 1968, 110

Funerary Monuments

1.	†1753	Thomas Bolithoe	St Stephen, Exeter, Devon	S	Pevsner, *Devon*, 1989, 396
2.	†1770	Margaret Moe	Exeter Cathedral, Devon	S	GPC

COFFIN, Edmund, of London 1761–1826

He attended the Royal Academy Schools to study sculpture in October 1785, winning a medal ten years later (**20**) and was an honorary exhibitor at the Royal Academy in 1787. In 1788 he was living at 13 Poland Street, the same address as the wax modeller **John Charles Locheé** who was no doubt influential on Coffin's technique. Gunnis, who owned Coffin's 'beautifully modelled' wax portrait of Louis XVI (5), appreciated Coffin's 'great delicacy of treatment' (*Gunnis* 1968, 110).

By 1793 Coffin was living in a large house at 4 Mary Street, Tottenham Court Road, where he remained for the rest of his life. He exhibited works, mainly wax models, at the Royal Academy until 1803. His name appears in the *Workmens Ledger 1793–99* of the silversmiths John Wakelin and Robert Garrard, and he exhibited models for silver candelabra that may be connected with them (**22, 23**). He also produced at least one monument, a large wall-tablet to John Cole (**1**).

He died in 1826. He is described in his will, proved on 15 August 1826, as a 'Sculptor of St Pancras.' He left a wife, Sarah, and five children, to whom he bequeathed numerous properties, over £600 in cash, and annuities. Given that most of these properties were in Exeter it seems likely that Coffin was a native of the town and a relative of **Edmond Coffin of Exeter.**

Literary References: *Graves* II, 1905–6, 95; *Hutchison* 1960–62, 148; *Gunnis* 1968, 110; RG/JP, 3, 367; *Pyke* 1973, 31

Will: PROB 11/1715

Funerary Monuments						
1.	?1790	John Cole		Milborne St Andrew's, Dorset	S	*Gunnis* 1968, 110
Busts						
2.	1798	Unidentified boy		[Exhib RA, London, 1052]; untraced		*Graves* II, 1905–6, 95
Architectural Sculpture						
3.	c1807	Decorative ornaments		[Dodington Park, Glos]; untraced		Codrington archives in GPC
Reliefs						
4.	1792	Titan, model in bas-relief		[Exhib RA, London, 617]; untraced		*Graves* II, 1905–6, 95
5.	1793	King Louis XVI	w	VAM A.108-1965 (Gunnis bequest)	SD	*Graves* II, 1905–6, 95; *Gunnis* 1968, 110; *Pyke* 1973, 31
6.	1802	Model for a medal, showing Britannia crowning a figure of Minerva, inscribed 'Arts and Commerce Promoted/Britannia 1802'	w	VAM A.3-1924		*Gunnis* 1968, 110
7.	1803	Corinthian frieze, model		[Exhib RA, London, 1002]; untraced		*Graves* II, 1905–6, 95
Miscellaneous						
8.	1787	Portrait of an unidentified artist		[Exhib RA, London, 606]; untraced		*Graves* II, 1905–6, 95
9.	1788	Dr Herschell		[Exhib RA, London, 630]; untraced		*Graves* II, 1905–6, 95
10.	1788	Portraits of two unidentified gentlemen		[Exhib RA, London, 600, 629]; untraced		*Graves* II, 1905–6, 95
11.	1790	Anthony Pasquin, model		[Exhib RA, London, 298]; untraced		*Graves* II, 1905–6, 95
12.	1790	Student at law, model		[Exhib RA, London, 690]; untraced		*Graves* II, 1905–6, 95
13.	1790	Unidentified lady, model	w	[Exhib RA, London, 702]; untraced		*Graves* II, 1905–6, 95
14.	1792	Unidentified lady, deceased	w	[Exhib RA, London, 767]; untraced		*Graves* II, 1905–6, 95
15.	1792	Unidentified young lady	w	[Exhib RA, London, 770]; untraced		*Graves* II, 1905–6, 95
16.	1793	A senator, model	w	[Exhib RA, London, 414]; untraced		*Graves* II, 1905–6, 95
17.	1793	Unidentified 'celebrated actress'	w	[Exhib RA, London, 405]; untraced		*Graves* II, 1905–6, 95
18.	1793	Unidentified lady, model	w	[Exhib RA, London, 397]; untraced		*Graves* II, 1905–6, 95
19.	1794	Sisyphus		[Exhib RA, London, 589]; untraced		*Graves* II, 1905–6, 95
20.	1795	Model of an academy figure or a bas-relief		[RA, London, silver medal]; untraced		RA Premium list
21.	1796	Timon of Athens, model		[Exhib RA, London, 878]; untraced		*Graves* II, 1905–6, 95
22.	1800	Ceres and Bacchus, models for candelabra		[Exhib RA, London, 1025, 1027]; untraced		*Graves* II, 1905–6, 95
23.	1801	A group, model for a silver candelabrum		[Exhib RA, London, 1028]; untraced		*Graves* II, 1905–6, 95

COLBOURNE, William, of Lymington fl 1826–51

He signs monuments in Lymington, Hants. His father, also William Colbourne, who was a local statuary and mason, died in Bath in 1804, aged 97 (*Euro Mag 1804*, 79).

Funerary Monuments

1.	†1826	Charles (†1826) and Anne St Barbe	Lymington, Hants	S	*Gunnis* 1968, 110
2.	†1827	John Nike	Lymington, Hants	S	*Gunnis* 1968, 110
3.	†1851	Rev Henry Michell	Lymington, Hants	S	

COLE, John, of Stamford 1735–1797

Cole ran a general mason's business in Stamford, building houses for the Earl of Exeter. He became a freeman of Stamford in 1766. His death was noted in the *Gentleman's Magazine* of 1797 and that year his widow advertised that she would continue his business making tombs, wall-pieces and graves.

Literary References: *GM*, 1797, 534; *Stamford Mercury*, 18 Aug 1797; RG/JP, 3,366–8

Funerary Monuments

No.	Date	Subject		Location		Reference
2.	1796	Rev Richard Knowles		Tinworth, Rutland		*Gunnis* 1968, 110

COLEBOURNE, William, of Edinburgh fl 1735?–44

A marble mason of Edinburgh, he supplied chimneypieces to James Loch in 1744 (2). He was presumably the 'Coleburne of Edinburgh' who signs a monument in Lanarkshire (1).

Literary References: *Loch* 1934, 140

Archival References: GPC

Funerary Monuments

No.	Date	Subject		Location		Reference
1.	†1735	Walter Campbell		Bothwell, Lanarks	S	GPC

Chimneypieces

No.	Date	Subject		Location		Reference
2.	1744	More than one Payment(s): £83	m	[for James Loch of Drylaw, Edinburgh]; untraced		*Loch* 1934, 140

COLEBOURNE (or COLBOURNE), William, of London fl 1694–*c*1726

The Masons' Company's general search of 1694 states 'William Colbourne works att Mr Nest's [**John Nost I**], in the Haymarket, bound to Mr. Bumstead [**John Bumpstead**], not yet free' (Masons Co, *Court Book*, 1677–94, fol 165r). Colebourne, who also worked for **William Kidwell**, signs a fine and important monument to Jacob Holte, taking the form of a great urn in an architectural setting (1). He may have been related to the 'W. Coleburne Londinensi Architecto' who signs the monument in Armagh to Dean Drelincourt. The reclining figure of the dean is by **Michael Rysbrack.**

Literary References: *Gunnis* 1968, 110

Archival References: GPC

Funerary Monuments

No.	Date	Subject		Location		Reference
1.	*c*1722	Jacob Holte		Rochdale, Lancs	S	*Gunnis* 1968, 110
2.	?1726	Jefferay Gilbert		[Temple Church, London]; destroyed	S	*Gunnis* 1968, 110

COLEBURN, Edward fl 1737

The son of Richard Coleburn, late mason of London, he was apprenticed to James Mack, mason of Edinburgh, on 13 July 1737.

Archival References: Register of Edinburgh Apprentices, in GPC

COLECOM, James, of Merstham and Reigate fl 1825

Presumably related to **Samuel Colecom, of Merstham**. He was responsible for the ten-foot high obelisk with Grecian scenes commemorating the Masseres family and executed a series of tombs in Banstead churchyard, Surrey.

Literary References: Pevsner, *Surrey*, 1971, 103

Funerary Monuments

No.	Date	Subject		Location		Reference
1.	1825	Masseres family		St Mary, Reigate, Surrey, churchyard	S	Pevsner, *Surrey*, 1971, 426

COLECOM, Samuel, of Merstham fl 1812–43?

His tablets and monuments 'are above the usual standard of the provincial mason' (*Gunnis* 1968, 110).

Funerary Monuments

No.	Date	Subject		Location		Reference
1.	?1812	Mrs Bury		Nutfield, Surrey	S	*Gunnis* 1968, 110
2.	?1817	James Eldridge		Bletchingley, Surrey, churchyard	S	*Gunnis* 1968, 110
3.	?1824	General Robert Morse		St Mary, St Marylebone, London	S	*Gunnis* 1968, 110
4.	?1831	Harriet Clements		Reigate, Surrey	S	*Gunnis* 1968, 110
5.	?1831	Richard Dendy		Leigh, Surrey	S	*Gunnis* 1968, 110
6.	?1838	Sir E Banks		Chipstead, Surrey, churchyard	S	*Gunnis* 1968, 110
7.	?1843	Hilton Joliffe		Petersfield, Hants	S	*Gunnis* 1968, 110

COLES, John, of London fl 1790–1833

He was the son of John Coles, who had a yard at 21 Fleet Street in 1768 and was responsible for a number of tablets. In his later works he was assisted by his son Thomas.

Literary References: *Gunnis* 1968, 110

Funerary Monuments

No.	Date	Subject		Location		Reference
1.	?1795	Maria le Geyt		Canterbury Cathedral, Kent	S	*Gunnis* 1968, 110
2.	?1800	Thomas Marston		Hatfield, Herts	S	*Gunnis* 1968, 110
3.	?1817	Rev Thomas Marsham		Kew, Surrey	S	*Gunnis* 1968, 110
4.	†1823	Mrs Maitland		Hartfield, Sussex	S	Pevsner, *Sussex*, 1965, 517; *Gunnis* 1968, 110

Chimneypieces

No.	Date	Subject		Location		Reference
5.	1796–1797	Description unavailable Payment(s): £216	m	[Henham Hall, Suffolk]; untraced		Stradbrooke archives in *Gunnis* 1968, 110

COLES FAMILY, of Thrapston and Huntingdon

John Coles 1763–1816
James Coles 1791–1834

The father and son sign a number of tablets. They were buried at Islip, Northants, a village a mile from Thrapston, where their tombstone is still to be seen in the churchyard.

Literary References: *Gunnis* 1968, 110

COLLETT fl 1760–1804

Nicholas Collett †1804
Mr Collett
William Collett

Nicholas Collett was a specialist wood-carver, employed by **Joseph Wilton RA** on carving the state coach designed by Sir William Chambers (4). J T Smith described him as 'a little man, who from his superior ability was honoured by Mr Waldron, the actor, with the characteristic epithet of *A Garrick of a Carver*'.

Other woodcarvers of the same name and presumably from the same family were 'Mr Collett' who was employed to carve a horse for 'the late Mr Hackett, of Long-acre as large as the life, for the purpose of showing the harness upon (2)'. This was modelled from the measurements of a stud horse belonging to the King of Hanover. Part of the statue of Queen Elizabeth and 'some other woodwork' were carved by the same artist for her effigy in the Royal Armoury (1).

William Collett was a close friend of Thomas Gainsborough. His subjects 'were chiefly selected from the domestic animal fables of Aesop, and now and then to be met with in the tablets of chimneypieces.' One such was often repeated: 'a shepherd's boy, eating his dinner amidst his flock, under the shade of a tree, with his dog begging by his side' (*Builder* 1854, 72).

Literary References: *Marsden and Hardy* 2001, 6, 12 fn 31, 33

Statues

1.	nd	Face and hands of Queen Elizabeth		[Royal Armoury, Tower of London]; untraced		*Builder* 1854, 72
2.	nd	Horse	wd	[for Mr Hackett, Long Acre, London]; untraced		*Builder* 1854, 72
3.	nd	Horse	wd	[Royal Armoury, Tower of London]; untraced		*Builder* 1854, 72

Architectural Sculpture

4.	1760	Carving for the Royal State Coach (with Joseph Wilton, designed by Sir William Chambers and G B Cipriani)	wd	Royal Coll		*Marsden and Hardy* 2001, 5 (repr)

COLLEY, E fl 1858

Funerary Monuments

1.	†1858	Archdeacon Cowper		St Philip, Sydney, New South Wales, Australia		GPC

COLLEY, William

He signs a handsome marble table tomb in Virginia to John Custis (1). The epitaph states that Custis died 'Aged 71 years and yet liv'd but seven years which was the space of time he kept a bachelor's house at Arlington.' Colley signs the work 'Wm COLLEY mason in Fenn Church Street, London, Fecit'. Colley added of the curious epitaph 'this inscription on the tomb was by his own positive order'.

Funerary Monuments

1.	nd	John Custis IV		Custis family graveyard, Arlington, Northampton County, Virginia, USA	S	GPC

COLLIER, William fl 1717–after 1725

The son of a wheelwright, Maurice Collier of Bishop's Sutton, Hants, he was apprenticed to William Collier (perhaps his uncle) in 1717. He became free in September 1725. His yard was in Camomile Street. A George Collier was made free via service to Joshua Fletcher in July of the same year.

Archival References: Masons' Co, Freemen, fol 10; GPC

COLLINGWOOD, Henry 1797–1825

He attended the Royal Academy Schools as a sculptor in September 1820 and gained the silver medal two years later (5). He exhibited at the Academy in 1824 from 69 Berwick Street (1, 2). His relief of Henry Pelham (3) was formerly in the collection of Rupert Gunnis.

Literary References: *Hutchison* 1960–62, 173; *Gunnis* 1968, 111; *Pyke* 1981, 12

Archival References: RA Premium list

Busts

1.	1824	Unidentified man		[Exhib RA, London, 980]; untraced		*Graves* II, 1905–6, 109
2.	1824	Unidentified man		[Exhib RA, London, 978]; untraced		*Graves* II, 1905–6, 109

Reliefs

3.	1825	Henry Pelham, later 5th Duke of Newcastle	l	Knox/Longstaffe-Gowan coll (acq 1991)	SD	
4.	nd	4th Duke of Newcastle		Phillips, 8 July 1975, lot 38		*Pyke* 1981, 12

Miscellaneous

5.	1822	Model in the life academy		[RA, London, silver medal]; untraced		RA Premium list

COLLINGWOOD & SONS, of Grantham fl 1806–37

They sign tablets in Lincs, mostly of Hellenistic design. William Collingwood (1741–1805) was responsible for 30 identified headstones in Kesteven and was also responsible for several slate headstones at St Peter, Foston, and St Wulfram, Grantham.

Literary References: *Gunnis* 1968, 111; *Neave and Heron* 1969, 10; Pevsner, *Lincs*, 1989, 284, 320

Funerary Monuments

1.	?1806	Margaret Brudenell		Hougham, Lincs	S	*Gunnis* 1968, 111
2.	?1823	John Turney		Sedgebrook, Lincs	S	*Gunnis* 1968, 111
3.	?1826	Maria Kelly		Grantham, Lincs	S	*Gunnis* 1968, 111
4.	†1835	Sir John Thorold		Marston, Lincs	S	*Gunnis* 1968, 111; Pevsner, *Lincs*, 1989, 558
5.	†1837	Francis Musson		Hough-on-the-Hill, Lincs		Pevsner, *Lincs*, 1989, 400

COLLINS, Job, of Warwick fl 1750

The son of Thomas Collins of Warwick, he was apprenticed to John Dunckley of Warwick in 1726 (TNA I.R.49/79). Around 1750 he carved a stone vase for Lady Luxborough (1) and he carried out similar work for William Shenstone at the Leasowes (Letters of Lady Luxborough to William Shenstone in *Gunnis* 1968, 111) (2). He was for many years mason to St Nicholas, Warwick (Ch W Accts).

Literary References: *Gunnis* 1968, 111

Archival References: GPC

Architectural Sculpture

1.	1750	Vase	s	[Barrells, Warks, gardens]; untraced	*Gunnis* 1968, 111
2.	1750	Vases		[for William Shenstone of the Leasowes]; untraced	Letters of Lady Luxborough to William Shenstone cited in *Gunnis* 1968, 111

COLLINS, John, of London fl 1779–86

He was the master-mason for building the Middlesex Sessions House, 1779–1782. Gunnis identifies him with the 'J Collins' who exhibited a bust at the Royal Academy in 1806, from an address in Southampton Row.

Literary References: *Graves* II, 1905–6, 111; *Gunnis* 1968, 111

Busts

1.	1806	Mr Barrymore	[Exhib RA, London, 938]; untraced	*Gunnis* 1968, 111; *Graves* II, 1905–6, 111

COLLINS, of Driffield fl c1731

About 1731 he made the dramatic life-size lead statues of King Athelstan and St John of Beverley at the entrance to the choir of Beverley Minster (1). Oliver said of him that 'Mr Collins was a clever man. His models of animals were well managed, and his rural subjects, which he was fond of introducing, were generally executed with much taste and feeling. He was a native, either of Driffield or some village in its immediate neighbourhood, but for want of patronage he passed his working days in obscurity and wretchedness and was frequently reduced to absolute indigence.' The same author recounted that the figure of Athelstan was the artist's own composition, though that of St John 'is supposed to have been taken from a graceful and admirably expressed mould, representing Pope Gregory at the moment of regarding an angelic messenger.' Oliver regarded the former as 'formed without taste, judgement or consistent effort,' and bemoaned the 'false taste of the artist, under whose superintendence so much absurdity has been accomplished' (*Oliver* 1829, 326–7 n46).

Literary References: *Gunnis* 1968, 111

Statues

1.	c1731	King Athelstan and St John of Beverley (from a Choir screen)	l	Beverley Minster, E R Yorks	*Oliver* 1829, 326–7; Pevsner, *Yorks: E R & York*, 1995, 293

COLLINS, Thomas fl 1771

The nephew of **William Wilton**, he was 'bred to the plaistering business by his uncle' (*Farington* 3, 703). He worked with his uncle and his cousin **Joseph Wilton** at Parkstead and Styche in Shropshire, under the direction of Sir William Chambers. Collins was to have a lifelong association with the architect. He first appears in the list of payments made by Chambers in the account books of Drummond's Bank in 1762. He was paid small amounts until 1768, but in 1769 he received £530. In 1770 over £1,000 was made over to him and in 1771 he and Chambers had a joint account, suggesting a shared building project. That year the Royal Academy accepted a gift from Collins of works, presumably in plaster, made from designs by Chambers (1). Collins was the architect's principal executor. Farington relates that 'Chambers sent for Collins just before he died and asked him to take care of his wife' (*Farington* 3, 703). In 1796 he lived in Berners Street.

Literary References: *Farington* vol. 3, 703, 27 Nov 1796; *Harris* 1970, 53, 175; *Alcock* 1980, 209

Miscellaneous

1.	1771	'Two tripods and a figure in bas-relief' (designs by Sir William Chambers)	[RA, London (gift)]; untraced	RA Council Minutes, vol 1, 23 March 1771, f128

COLLINS, William 1721–93

Renowned in his day for his whimsical reliefs of pastoral scenes, Collins was a notable sculptor in marble and a highly competent modeller in plaster of religious and mythological scenes. He was born in 1721 but nothing is currently known of his family background. He became a pupil of **Sir Henry Cheere** and subsequent payments to Collins in his master's bank account suggest that he carved work in sub-contract for Cheere's thriving workshop.

In December 1751 Collins was described in the *London Evening Post* as 'a figure maker at Hyde Park Corner'. The article was a puff for 'Iron Pear-Tree Water,' a quack medicine which was claimed to have cured, in a mere 24 hours, a sore on Collins's leg, that had troubled him for two years. The miraculous recovery was confirmed by **John Cheere** and his assistants, and it is possible that Collins was at this time working for the branch of the Cheere business which produced multiples in plaster and lead in the Shepherd's Market area.

In December 1759 he was one of the pioneering group which included Francis Hayman, Sir Joshua Reynolds and **Joseph Wilton**, who founded the Society of Artists, Britain's first exhibiting society. At its early exhibitions Collins showed numerous bas-reliefs, including a distinguished scene for Magdalen College, Cambridge, designed by the architect Thomas Lightoler (32). This depicts the moment when Christ's tomb is found empty by his mourners and the guarding soldiers. The composition has several gradations of relief and the tumult of the drama is conveyed by thick swirling clouds weaving round the figural elements. Soon after its installation a local guide book singled out the work as being 'reckoned well worth the observation of the curious' (*Cambridge Depicta* 1763, 77). Lightoler also designed an *Annunciation* altarpiece executed by Collins for the Beauchamp chapel at St Mary, Warwick (25), which

John Hands described in his guide to the church as 'a fine bas-relievo of the Salutation, under a Gothic canopy, the whole exceedingly well executed' (*Hands* c1770, 36).

The bulk of Collins's exhibited reliefs appear to have been intended for chimneypieces, and J T Smith was later to describe him as 'the most famous modeller of chimney-tablets of his day' (*Smith* 1828, 2, 313). Smith, however, considered Collins's work to be lacking in nobility: 'his figures were mostly clothed, and exhibited pastoral scenes, which were understood by the most common observer such as, for instance, a shepherd-boy eating his dinner under an old stump of a tree, with his dog begging before him; shepherds and shepherdesses seated upon a bank surrounded by their flocks; anglers, reapers, etc' (*ibid*). Several tablets with pastoral motifs have been attributed to Collins (**7, 8, 19, 20**) and the similarity of Smith's description to a known design by Sir Henry Cheere in the Victoria and Albert Museum also suggests that Collins may have been the executant of many of Cheere's chimneypiece tablets. When Henry Cheere died in 1781 he left Collins £100 in his will.

By 1763 Collins had set up his own workshop in Channel-Row, Westminster, producing work in stone, plaster and marble, usually for decorative schemes in country houses. He executed an elaborate pediment relief at Worksop Manor under the architect James Paine, with an image of the old manor house, destroyed by fire in 1761 and a plan of the new, as well as symbols of the family's virtue (**26**). Another pediment relief, for Sandbeck Park (**18**), was described in Paine's book of plans as 'a very fine alto relievo, executed by the ingenious Mr William Collins' (*Paine* 1783, 12a).

Working under Robert Adam, he provided decorative roundels on the theme of country life for the external elevations at Kedleston Hall (**27**) and extensive plaster work for the interiors of Harewood House (**23, 29, 30, 38**). A number of Collins's works were offered in Adam's sale of 1818 (**9, 18, 42–45**). Adam's relationship with Collins was not always harmonious: on 18 August 1767 Adam wrote to Sir Rowland Winn of Nostell Priory, for whom he was designing a chimneypiece, telling him that 'Mr. Collins promised me to have the tablet for the library chimney sent to my house, end of last week, but has likewise disappointed me'. Collins eventually produced a tablet in a material so flimsy that Adam could not find anyone 'to undertake to fire it for fear of its breaking'. When it was fired the architect's worst fears were realised, for the piece warped and cracked. The design was finally realised in wood, apparently by another carver (*Brockwell* 1915, 16–18).

Collins's most notable works were perhaps for Burton Constable, where he was responsible for three full-size statues including a youthful *Mercury and Cupid*, competitively rolling dice on a rock (**1–3**). A design for the plaster oval of *Pan and the Graces* survives at Burton Constable, marked 'Collins' by the owner, William Constable (**37**). If this work is by Collins it demonstrates not only his developed skills in draughtsmanship, but also his ability to compose original designs.

He died on 24 May 1793 at his house in Tothill Fields, Westminster, and was buried in the old cemetery in King's Road, Chelsea. His entire estate, including properties in Bath and Weston-super-Mare, was left to his only daughter, Elizabeth. The *Gentleman's Magazine* carried a notice of his death in June, adding that his 'works as an artist have been long known and admired in this country' (*GM*, June 1793, 577). Collins appears to have been a highly regarded sculptor, as well as a friend to leading painters such as Thomas Gainsborough, whose bucolic aesthetic echoes Collins's own. The sculptor's gracious rococo works have since elicited charmed responses from commentators such as Timothy Clifford and Mark Girouard, though there has been no full account of his life and work. In Girouard's words 'William Collins is an artist who could do with further research' (*Girouard* 1966 (2), 189).

A number of convincingly-argued attributions have been included in the list below.

MGS

Literary References: *Mortimer* 1763, 8; *Smith* 1828, II, 313; *Graves* II, 1905–6, 62; *Soc of Artists Papers, 1759–61*, 116; *Girouard* 1965, 968; *Gunnis* 1968, 111–2; *Friedman and Clifford* 1974, Appendix C; *Clifford* 1992, 41–2; *ODNB* (MB); *Craske* 2000 (2), 100, 112 n16; *Baker* 2000, 77; *Bilbey* 2002, 68–9

Archival References: Walton and Dunn Accounts, Burton Constable, 1764; Collins/ Constable 1769

Will: Henry Cheere, PROB 11/1073/95; William Collins PROB 11/1233/303

Statues

1.	1768	Bacchus Payment(s): 16 gns	p	Burton Constable, E R Yorks, dining room	Collins/Constable 1768; *Mulcahy* 2006, 16–17; C Lib (repr)
2.	1768	Mercury and Cupid playing dice Payment(s): 15 gns	p	Burton Constable, E R Yorks, dining room	Collins/Constable 1768; *Mulcahy* 2006, 17 (repr)
3.	1768	Satyr and dog Payment(s): 12 gns	p	Burton Constable, E R Yorks, dining room	Collins/Constable 1768; *Mulcahy* 2006, 17; C Lib (repr)

Chimneypieces

4.	1760	Romulus and Remus, frieze model, for Brandenburg House, Hammersmith	tc	[Exhib Soc of Artists, London, 78]; Christie, London, 15 May 1798; untraced	*Graves* 1907, 62; *Gunnis* 1968, 112; AL/RG
5.	1760	Satyr and traveller, model of a tablet		[Exhib Soc of Artists, London, 79]; untraced	*Graves* 1907, 62
6.	1761	A clown and a country girl, bas-relief		[Exhib Soc of Artists, London, 144]; untraced	*Graves* 1907, 62
7.	c1761	Putti with a ram, relief tablet	m	VAM 1176-1882	ATTRIB *Bilbey* 2002, 69 (repr)
8.	c1761	Shepherd and shepherdess, relief tablet	m	VAM 1152-1882 Other versions: Bretton Hall, Wakefield, W R Yorks Lever, LL 131, LL 132, LL 133	ATTRIB *Snodin* 1984, 307–8 (repr); *Bilbey* 2002, 68–9 (repr)
9.	1764	Bacchus and Ariadne, tablet Model(s): Exhib Soc of A, London, 155		[Adam sale, 1818 (lot 11)]; untraced	Adam Sale, 22 May 1818, lot 11; *Gunnis* 1968, 111
10.	1765	Bacchanalian boys, a model for a tablet		[Exhib Soc of Artists, London, 173]; untraced	*Graves* 1907, 62
11.	1765	Oedipus interpreting the riddle of the Sphinx, model for a tablet		[Exhib Soc of Artists, London, 172]; untraced	*Graves* 1907, 62
12.	1766	The fable of the fox that had lost his tail, two tablets		[Exhib Soc of Artists, London, 204]; untraced	*Graves* 1907, 62

No.	Date	Work		Location	References
13.	1767	Overmantel relief of putti, representing the arts (designed by Robert Adam)	p	[for Nostell Priory, W R Yorks]; destroyed	*Brockwell* 1915, 16; Pevsner, *Yorks: W R*, 1967, 381; *Harris* 2001, 200
14.	1767	Zephyrus and Flora, model of a tablet		[Exhib Soc of Artists, London, 205]; untraced	*Graves* 1907, 62
15.	1768	Anacreon and Cupid, model of a tablet		[Exhib Soc of Artists, London, 144]; untraced	*Graves* 1907, 62
16.	1769	With tablet of 'Sacrifice to Aesculapius and Hygeia' Payment(s): 16 gns		Burton Constable, E R Yorks, dining room	Walton and Dunn Accts, Burton Constable 1769; *Mulcahy* 2006, 15–16; C Lib (repr)
17.	nd	A shepherd, tablet		Great Hasely Manor, Oxon	RG/JP, 3, 373 citing a letter from 'Mrs Bachmann'
18.	nd	Cupid, tablet		[Adam sale, 1818, lot 20]; untraced	Adam Sale, Christie, 22 May 1818, 20; *Gunnis* 1968, 111
19.	nd	Fox and pig, relief		Langley Park, Norfolk	ATTRIB *Gunnis* 1960 (1), 818, 821
20.	nd	Shepherd and begging dog		Sandbeck Park, W R Yorks, ballroom	ATTRIB *Girouard* 1965, 968 (repr)
21.	nd	Tame and Isis, tablet		[for the Margrave of Anspach]; Christie, 15 March 1798; untraced	*Gunnis* 1968, 112
22.	nd	With a tablet depicting 'the bear and the beehives'		Ancaster House, Lincoln's Inn Fields, London	*Gunnis* 1968, 111; C Lib (repr)
Architectural Sculpture					
23.	1760	Medallions of Liberty, Agriculture, Commerce and Britannia (designed by Antonio Zucchi)		Harewood House, W R Yorks, east and west wings	*Hargrove* 1789, 151; *Jewell* 1822, 22; *Gunnis* 1968, 111
24.	c1760	Pediment sculpture of Ceres and Cupid, alto-relievo	s	Sandbeck Park, W R Yorks	*Paine* 1783, 12a (repr 52); *Girouard* 1965, 966–8 (repr); *Girouard* 1966, 190; *Gunnis* 1968, 111
25.	c1760	The Annunciation, altarpiece (designed by Thomas Lightoler)		St Mary, Warwick, Lady chapel	*Gunnis* 1968, 111; *Hands* c1770, 36; C Lib (repr)
26.	1765	Pediment sculpture, with a view of the old manor house, and statues of Divine Virtue, Peace and Plenty (designed by James Paine)		Worksop Manor, Notts, garden (damaged)	*Paine* 1767 (repr 102); *Girouard* 1965, 969; Pevsner, *Notts*, 1979, 392
27.	1769	Vintage, harvest, pasturage, ploughing and boar hunting, medallions	s	Kedleston Hall, Derbys, north front	*Kedleston* 1998, 10, opp 72 (repr)
28.	1772	The origin and progress of civilization		[Merly, Dorset, library ceiling]; destroyed	*Willett* 1785; *Girouard* 1965, 969
Reliefs					
29.	1760	Antique marriage		[Harewood House, W R Yorks, little library overmantel]; untraced	*Jewell* 1822, 26
30.	1760	Oblong overmantel reliefs of 'Mars tamed by peace' and 'triumph of Neptune', and six large medallic trophies	p	Harewood House, W R Yorks, great hall	*Jewell* 1822, 25; *Gunnis* 1968, 111; *Harris* 2001, 139
31.	1761	A boy keeping sheep, large bas-relief		[Exhib Soc of Artists, London, 145]; untraced	*Graves* 1907, 62
32.	1761	The Marys at the sepulchre (designed by Thomas Lightoler)	p	Magdalen College Library, Cambridge (formerly chapel)	*Cantabrigia Depicta* 1763, 77; *Graves* 1907, 62; *Girouard* 1966 (2), 189 (repr); *Gunnis* 1968, 111
33.	1762	A lion hunting, bas-relief		[Exhib Soc of Artists, London, 139]; untraced	*Graves* 1907, 62
34.	1762	Boys sliding, bas-relief		[Exhib Soc of Artists, London, 140]; untraced	*Graves* 1907, 62
35.	1762	The fable of the fox and the cat, bas-relief		[Exhib Soc of Artists, London, 141]; untraced	*Graves* 1907, 62
36.	1763	Belisarius, bas-relief		[Exhib Soc of Artists, London, 141]; untraced	*Graves* 1907, 62
37.	1765–1769	Pan and the Graces, Bacchus and Ariadne (oval reliefs), medallions Payment(s): £27 6s plus travel costs of £3 3s; £6 for medallions and relief vases and packaging Drawing(s): Burton Constable, E R Yorks, pencil, pen and wash	p	Burton Constable, E R Yorks, dining room	Collins/Constable 1768; Collins/Constable 1769; *Girouard* 1966, 189; *Hall* 1970, no 46; *Clifford* 1992, 42, 52; Pevsner, *Yorks: E R & York*, 1995, 375; *Mulcahy* 2006, 14–15 (repr)
38.	c1769	Sacrifice of Venus and Sacrifice of Bacchus	p	Harewood House, W R Yorks, saloon overmantel	*Jewell* 1822, 30; *Harris* 2001, 140
39.	1769	The four seasons	p	Burton Constable, E R Yorks, dining room	Collins/Constable 1768; *Mulcahy* 2006, 16 (repr)
40.	post-1771	Roundels of 'harvest' and 'the vintage'	p	Kedleston, Derbys, dining room	*Kedleston* 1998, 46–7 (repr)
41.	c1773	Female sacrificial figure, after a gem by Picart		Heaton Park, Lancs Other versions: Westport House, Co Mayo, 1781 Wardour Castle, Wilts Private Coll	*Clifford* 1992, 52

42.	nd	Forty-one 'tablets and medallions in terracotta and plaster' (sold with works by John Bacon RA)		Untraced	Adam Sale, Christie, 22 May 1818, lots 7 and 8
43.	nd	Four medallions		Untraced	Adam Sale, Christie, 22 May 1818, lot 15
44.	nd	Pair of oval medallions		Untraced	Adam Sale, Christie, 22 May 1818, lot 15 1818,
45.	nd	'Two semicircular, four oval medallions' (sold with works by John Bacon RA)		Untraced	2 Adam Sale, Christie, 22 May 1818, lot 5
Miscellaneous					
46.	1760	Gypsies, model		[Exhib Soc of Artists, London, 81]; untraced	*Graves* 1907, 62
47.	1760	Representation of Spring; boys with a bird's nest		[Exhib Soc of Artists, London, 80]; untraced	*Graves* 1907, 62
48.	1769	Bacchic Vases, four	p	Burton Constable, E R Yorks, dining room	Collins/Constable 1768; *Mulcahy* 2006, 16 (repr)

COLQUHOUN, James fl 1641–83

Colquhoun was responsible for the statues of the Hutcheson brothers, two lawyers whose bequest led to the building of a hospital and school in Glasgow between 1641 and 1660 which bears their name (**1**). He was a mason and builder who also repaired and gilded the bell of the original building in 1683. The statues now stand on the new building, which dates from 1802–5. Colquhoun is credited with inventing Glasgow's first fire engine, and was a bailie on the town council.

Literary References: *McKenzie* 1999, 106

Statues					
1.	*c*1649	George and Thomas Hutcheson	s	[Hutchesons' Hospital, Trongate, Glasgow, Lanarks, garden front]; Hutchesons' Hall, Ingram Street, Glasgow, Lanarks	*McKenzie* 2002, 205–8 (repr)

COLSON, Francis, of Lichfield fl 1700

Funerary Monuments				
1.	†1700	R Schollar	Bakewell, Derbys	S

COMOLLI, Giovanni Battista 1775–1830

An Italian sculptor, he spent four years working in England. He was born in Valenza, Piedmont, on 19 February 1775, and studied at the Brera Academy in Milan under Giuseppe Franchi, and in Rome (possibly under **Antonio Canova**) between 1795 and 1798. In May 1795 he won a prize for a relief of *Joseph Confiding Benjamin to Juda* from the Accademia di San Luca. That year **Sir Richard Westmacott RA** won the first prize for the same subject.

In 1800 Comolli was in Grenoble, where he executed a series of portrait busts for the town's library. In January 1802 he paid his first visit to London during the Peace of Amiens. Later that year he was in Paris, where he executed a bust and a model for a colossal statue of Napoleon. He also made the acquaintance of **Giuseppe Ceracchi**. In February 1803 he departed for Turin, where he became Professor of Sculpture at the Imperial Academy. Between 1808 and 1812 he was chiefly in Carrara.

Following the collapse of the Napoleonic Empire and the loss of an important patron, Comolli, like his countryman Canova, attempted to develop a market in England. In 1816 he moved with his family to London where he remained until 1820. He rented a studio at 1 Seymour Terrace and enjoyed the patronage of the Grenville family and the Duke of Gloucester (**3, 5, 1**). The bust of Thomas Grenville (**5**) is presented *all'antica*, with the sitter depicted with furrowed, beetle-brows and an inscrutable expression. Comolli's most significant work was the altar (costing £1,000) and other architectural sculpture for the Roman Catholic Chapel in Moorfields (**6**). The altar was carved with foliage and two figures of angels with expanded wings. The church was pulled down in 1900 but Comolli's columns, inspired by the Choragic Monument of Lysicrates, were reused by the architect George Sherrin in the new church, built in 1900. In August 1820 he departed for Paris. He subsequently returned to Milan where he died on 26 December 1830.

Literary References: *Britton and Pugin* 1823–1828, 2, 9; *Gunnis* 1968, 112; *DBI* 1982, 619–626; *Grano and Grossi Grano* 1990; *Panzetta* 1994, 95; *Busco* 1994, 172 n30; *Grove* 1996, 7, 662 (Balderston); *Saur* 1998, 460–462; *Dawson* 1999, 109–11

Busts					
1.	*c*1820	William Frederick, 2nd Duke of Gloucester (†1834)		[Stowe sale, 15 Aug 1848, lot 76]; untraced Other versions: Knox/Longstaffe coll (2006), marble	Stowe Sale 1848; *Bilbey* 2002, 240
2.	nd	Charles James Fox		Untraced	*DBI* 1982, 27, 624
3.	nd	Lord William Wyndham Grenville (†1834)		[Stowe sale, 15 Aug 1848, lot 760]; untraced	*Dawson* 1999, 111 n9
4.	nd	Napoleon Bonaparte		Junior United Service Club, London	*Gunnis* 1968, 112
5.	nd	Thomas Grenville (†1846)	m	BM, London, MLA Dept Other versions: Stowe Sale 15 Aug 1848, lot 762	*Read* 1982 (repr), 129; *Dawson* 1999, 13, 14, 17, 109–111 (repr); *Bilbey* 2002, 240
Architectural Sculpture					
6.	1818–1821	Capitals and altarpiece Payment(s): £1,000 (altarpiece)	m	Roman Catholic Chapel, Moorfields, London (capitals only)	*Britton and Pugin* 1823–1828, 2, 9; *Gunnis* 1968, 112; *DBI* 1982, 27, 624

CONDE, Jean 1766–

Condé entered the Royal Academy schools in September 1787 as a painter, but in 1792 he won a prize for modelling (**1**).

Literary References: *Hutchison* 1960–62, 149

Miscellaneous				
1.	1792	Academy figure, model	[RA silver medal]; untraced	RA Premium list

CONNY (or CONEY), Christopher fl 1665–1708

He was apparently a Shrewsbury artist. According to a local historian, Thomas Phillips, 'the neat altar piece of the Corinthian Order' erected at St Mary's in 1708, was signed 'Christopher Coney, Projector and Carver' (3) (*Phillips* 1779, 95). One of his monuments to Richard Prynce is carved with a similarly grandiose signature: 'Cony arc. et projr.' (1).

Literary References: *Gunnis* 1968, 112

Archival References: GPC

Funerary Monuments						
1.	†1665	Richard Prynce		Holy Cross, Shrewsbury, Salop	S	*Gunnis* 1968, 112
2.	†1690	Richard Prince		Holy Cross, Shrewsbury, Salop	S	
Architectural Sculpture						
3.	1708	Altarpiece		St Mary, Shrewsbury, Salop	S	*Gunnis* 1968, 112; GPC

CONSTANCE fl 1726

He is described as 'Mr Constance, figure-maker' in a payment for two heads (1) in the account-book of the first Duke of Kent.

Literary References: *Gunnis* 1968, 112

Miscellaneous						
1.	1726	Two heads		[for Wrest Park, Beds]; untraced		*Gunnis* 1968, 112, citing archives, Lady Lucas and Dingwall

CONSTANT, Christopher fl 1763

Chimneypieces						
1.	1763	Description unavailable Payment(s): £28 7s	m	Bowood, Wilts		Lansdowne archives in GPC

CONTE fl 1848–51

An Italian sculptor living in London in 1848 when he carved a marble statue of the young Marquess of Stafford in highland dress (1). This was commissioned by the Duchess of Sutherland after an original work in bronze by a French artist. The *Art Union* recorded that the figure was 'executed in the purest marble by machinery, yet it is so delicately carved and so exquisitely finished in all its details, as to convey the idea of having been sculptured entirely by hand' (*AU* 1848, 343). He exhibited at the Great Exhibition (2): the catalogue noted 'M. Conté is an Italian artist, who has long resided in London, where, in his atelier, we have seen many most elegant works in marble, especially some statuettes' (*AJ Cat* 1851, 302).

Literary References: *Gunnis* 1968, 112

Statues						
1.	1848	George, 2nd Duke of Sutherland, in highland dress, copy after a bronze by a French sculptor	m	[for Stafford House]; untraced		*AU* 1848, 343; *Gunnis* 1968, 112
Chimneypieces						
2.	1851	Carved with a coat of arms, eagles and foliage		[Gt Exhib, London]; untraced		*AJ Cat* 1851, 302 (repr)

COOK, J fl 1800

He exhibited a bust at the Royal Academy in 1800 from Upper Norton Street, Marylebone, London (1).

Literary References: *Graves* II, 1905–6, 127

Busts						
1.	1800	Unidentified gentleman		[Exhib RA, London, 1010]; untraced		*Graves* II, 1905–6, 127

COOK, W, of Birmingham fl ?1838

Funerary Monuments						
1.	?1838	Gitton family		St Leonard, Bridgnorth, Salop	S	GPC

COOKE, G H, of Gloucester fl c1842–48

Presumably related to **James Cooke of Gloucester.**

Funerary Monuments						
1.	c1842	Unidentified subject		St John Northgate, Glos	S	RG/JP, 3, 375
2.	†1848	Ann Lane		Westbury-on-Severn, Glos	S	Pevsner, *Glos: Vale & Forest of Dean*, 1976, 400

COOKE, James, of Gloucester fl 1798–1844

The son of John Cooke of Gloucester, a pargeter who had become a freeman of that city in 1770, Cooke signed a number of tablets in Glos and Worcs. He spent a period in partnership with **James Millard of Gloucester** and together they signed a number of tablets (listed under the entry for Millard). Cooke's solo monumental works include a tablet in coloured marble to James Bennett (5), reliefs of grieving women for the Gardner family and Simon Adams (24, 39), and a neo-Greek slab for Thomas Blunt (11). Cooke was also a mason. He rebuilt the nave of St Mary de Lode in Gloucester and in 1838 remodelled Cowley rectory in the same county.

Literary References: *Gunnis* 1968, 112; *Colvin* 1995, 268

Funerary Monuments						
1.	†1798	William and Elizabeth (†1797) Hill (of copper)		Edgeworth, Glos	S	
2.	†1793	Ralph Grove		Thornbury, Glos	S	
3.	c1800	Lady Lyttleton		Malvern, Worcs		*Gunnis* 1968, 112
4.	†1803	Noah Buckle		Chaceley, Glos	S	Pevsner, *Glos: Vale & Forest of Dean*, 1976, 119
5.	†1804	James Bennett		Elkstone, Glos	S	Pevsner, *Glos: Cotswolds*, 1999, 358
6.	†1807	John Caruthers		Pitchcombe, Glos		Pevsner, *Glos: Cotswolds*, 1999, 561

7.	†1809	Sarah Yarnton		Sapperton, Glos	S	Pevsner, *Glos: Cotswolds*, 1999, 591
8.	?1810	Anne Skipp		Ledbury, Herefs		*Gunnis* 1968, 112
9.	†1811	Mary Mansell		St Peter, Carmarthen		*Dale-Jones and Lloyd* 1989, 47
10.	†1811	Susanna Colchester		Brockworth, Glos	S	Pevsner, *Glos: Vale & Forest of Dean*, 1976, 115
11.	†1811	Thomas Blunt		Mitcheldean, Glos	S	Pevsner, *Glos: Vale & Forest of Dean*, 1976, 300
12.	†1813	Catherine Canning		Hartpury, Glos	S	Pevsner, *Glos: Vale & Forest of Dean*, 1976, 265
13.	†1813	Joshua North		Gloucester Cathedral	S	*Gunnis* 1968, 259
14.	†1813	Sarah Donovan		Tibberton, Glos	S	Pevsner, *Glos: Vale & Forest of Dean*, 1976, 383
15.	†1814	Isaac Dickes and family members		Cherington, Glos	S	
16.	†1816	Richard Donovan		Tibberton, Glos	S	Pevsner, *Glos: Vale & Forest of Dean*, 1976, 383
17.	†1817	Henry Wyatt		Edgeworth, Glos	S	
18.	†1817	William Ricketts		St Andrew, Droitwich, Worcs	S	
19.	†1818	John Arkell		Boddington, Glos	S	Pevsner, *Glos: Vale & Forest of Dean*, 1976, 113
20.	1819	Unidentified subjects, two tablets		St Mary de Lode, Gloucester, Glos	S	Pevsner, *Glos: Vale & Forest of Dean*, 1976, 235
21.	†1820	Crawley-Boevey family		Flaxley, Glos	S	Pevsner, *Glos: Vale & Forest of Dean*, 1976, 185
22.	†1821	Thomas Turner		Down Hatherley, Glos	S	Pevsner, *Glos: Vale and Forest of Dean*, 1976, 172
23.	†1821	William Yarnton Mills and family members	m	Miserden, Glos	S	Pevsner, *Glos: Cotswolds*, 1999, 486
24.	†1822	Hester and James (†1801) Gardner		Gloucester Cathedral	S	Pevsner, *Glos: Vale & Forest of Dean*, 1976, 219; *CIIA* 4/4/48 (repr)
25.	†1822	Rev John Astley		Quenington, Glos	S	Pevsner, *Glos: Cotswolds*, 1999, 571
26.	†1823	Elizabeth Williams		Dursley, Glos	S	Pevsner, *Glos: Cotswolds*, 1999, 335
27.	†1823	Richard Raikes		Maisemore, Glos	S	Pevsner, *Glos: Vale & Forest of Dean*, 1976, 296
28.	?1824	Agge family		Overbury, Worcs		*Gunnis* 1968, 112
29.	†1825	Catherine Hodges		Pauntley, Glos	S	Pevsner, *Glos: Vale & Forest of Dean*, 1976, 320
30.	†1825	John Baylis		Winchcombe, Glos	S	Pevsner, *Glos: Cotswolds*, 1999, 729
31.	†1825	John Plumptre		Gloucester Cathedral		
32.	?1826	George Little		Goodrich, Hereford		*Gunnis* 1968, 112
33.	1824–1828	Unidentified subjects, two tablets		Hempsted, Glos	S	Pevsner, *Glos: Vale & Forest of Dean*, 1976, 268
34.	†1829	Anthony (†1819) and Ann Freston		Edgeworth, Glos	S	
35.	†1829	Edward Wallington		St James, Dursley, Glos	S	Pevsner, *Glos: Cotswolds*, 1999, 335
36.	†1831	Joseph Cooper		Redmarley d'Abitot, Glos	S	Pevsner, *Glos: Vale & Forest of Dean*, 1976, 328
37.	†1831	Richard Huntley		Boxwell, Glos	S	Pevsner, *Glos: Cotswolds*, 1999, 194
38.	†1833	Nathaniel Dyer		St George, Nailsworth, Glos	S	Pevsner, *Glos: Cotswolds*, 1999, 494
39.	†1833	Simon (†1801) and Sarah Adams		Anstey, Warks	S	
40.	†1834	Rev Daniel Lysons		Rodmarton, Glos	S	Pevsner, *Glos: Cotswolds*, 1999, 582
41.	†1836	Richard Selloway		Chipping Norton, Oxon	S	RG/JP, 3, 373 v.
42.	?1836	William Wakeman		Beckford, Glos	S	*Gunnis* 1968, 112
43.	†1837	Rev W C Holder		St George, Upper Cam, Glos	S	Pevsner, *Glos: Cotswolds*, 1999, 210
44.	†1838	Lieutenant-Colonal William Percy Cunningham		Gloucester Cathedral	S	
45.	†1840	Rev John (†1828) and Mary Michell (†1840)		Gloucester Cathedral	S	
46.	†1843	Lady Elizabeth Somerset		Tormarton, Glos	S	Pevsner, *Glos: Cotswolds*, 1999, 699
47.	1828–1844	Unidentified subjects, numerous tablets		Christ Church, Gloucester, Glos	S	Pevsner, *Glos: Vale & Forest of Dean*, 1976, 230
48.	*c*1846	Unidentified subject, tablet		Blaisdon, Glos	S	Pevsner, *Glos: Vale & Forest of Dean*, 1976, 112
49.	nd	Unidentified subject, tablet		Horsley, Glos	S	Pevsner, *Glos: Cotswolds*, 1999, 416
Busts						
50.	1800	Unidentified subject		[Exhib RA, London, 1010]; untraced		*Graves* II, 1905–6, 127

COOKE, Josiah

A 'Statuary and Mason' of New Road, Portland Road, London, he became bankrupt in December 1805 (*Euro Mag* 1805, 48, unpag).

COOKE, Richard, of London –1850

Between 1803 and 1809 he received £205 for 'marble work' at Cobham Hall, Kent. This almost certainly included the two large alcoves at each end of the dining-room (Archives, Earl of Darnley). He married Hannah Fox Cheeke, the daughter of a builder, on 22 August 1795. Cooke was at this time employed by Mr Cheeke, who was building part of Grove Terrace, Kentish Town. The marriage was against Cheeke's wishes and proved a failure. Mrs Cooke died in 1833 and Cooke in 1850 (*Survey of London*, 19, II, 1938, 36).

Literary References: *Gunnis* 1968, 112

Archival References: GPC

Chimneypieces

1.	1791	Two Payment(s): £91	[Mr C Hilton's house, Finsbury Square, London]; untraced	Mrs Barchard of Henfield archives in GPC

COOKE, Robert, of London fl 1780–1817

Cooke was a successful monumental sculptor. Gunnis considered the memorial to the Earl of Darlington his finest work (6). This has a high relief of Lord Darlington on his death-bed and in the background is a 'charming' vignette of Raby Castle. The monument to John Smeaton (8) has a model of the Eddystone Lighthouse, while that to Mary Styleman takes the form of an urn on a wreathed pillar (21). The Lovedon (2) portrays the deceased on a couch comforted by an angel, a design re-used for the monuments to Margaret, Countess of Darlington (15) and Jane Caygill (18).

Literary References: *Gunnis* 1968, 112

Funerary Monuments

1.	†1783	Edward Ives	Titchfield, Hants	S	Pevsner, *Hants & Isle of Wight*, 1967, 625
2.	†1784	Margaret Loveden	Buscot, Oxon	S	Pevsner, *Berks*, 1966, 108
3.	1786	Elizabeth Loveden (†1788)	Buscot, Berks	SD	*Gunnis* 1968, 112
4.	†1791	Bastard family member	Charlton Marshall, Dorset		Pevsner, *Dorset*, 1972, 142
5.	†1791	Rev Robert Ready	Buscot, Berks	S	*Gunnis* 1968, 112
6.	†1792	Henry, 2nd Earl of Darlington	Staindrop, Durham	S	*Gunnis* 1968, 112; Pevsner, *Durham*, 1983, 428
7.	1793	John Pybus (†1789)	Cheam, Surrey, Lumley chapel	SD	
8.	1793	John Smeaton	St Mary, Whitkirk, W R Yorks	SD	Pevsner, *Yorks: W R*, 1967, 350; *Gunnis* 1968, 112
9.	1793	Mary Meade	St Botolph Aldersgate, City of London	S	*Gunnis* 1968, 112; Pevsner, *London: City*, 1997, 207
10.	?1795	Elizabeth Richmond	Thorpe, Surrey	S	*Gunnis* 1968, 112
11.	†1795	Thomas Beale Browne	Salperton, Glos	S	Pevsner, *Glos: Cotswolds*, 1999, 588
12.	†1796	Jeremiah Millington	Coln Rogers, Glos	S	Pevsner, *Glos: Cotswolds*, 1999, 297
13.	?1796	Robert Mead	Christ Church, Philadelphia, USA	S	*Gunnis* 1968, 112
14.	†1797	John, 2nd Earl of Portsmouth	Farleigh Wallop, Hants	S	Pevsner, *Hants & Isle of Wight*, 1967, 228
15.	†1800	Margaret, Countess of Darlington	Staindrop, Durham	S	Pevsner, *Durham*, 1983, 428
16.	?1802	John White	Newington, Oxon	S	*Gunnis* 1968, 113
17.	†1806	Jane Selwyn	St John, Halifax, W R Yorks	S	Pevsner, *Yorks: W R*, 1967, 230
18.	?1807	Jane Caygill	Halifax, W R Yorks	S	*Gunnis* 1968, 113
19.	†1807	John Frank Nicholls	Barbados Cathedral, Bridgetown	S	
20.	†1807	Katharine Margaret, Countess of Darlington	Staindrop, Durham	S	Pevsner, *Durham*, 1983, 428
21.	†1807	Mary Styleman	Snettisham, Norfolk	S	*Gunnis* 1968, 112; Pevsner, *Norfolk: N W & S*, 1999, 655
22.	?1817	Elizabeth Baily	Gamston, Notts	S	*Gunnis* 1968, 113

Chimneypieces

23.	1793	Description unavailable Payment(s): £39 17s 6d	[Salisbury Guildhall, Wilts]; untraced	Salisbury city archives, cited in *Gunnis* 1968, 112
24.	1799	Description unavailable	[for Lord Radnor]; untraced	Longford Castle archives in *Gunnis* 1968, 112
25.	1807	Statuary marble Payment(s): £52 12s	Longleat, Wilts	Longleat HA, 1806–1818, 3 Dec 1807, fol 14r
26.	1807	Statuary marble Payment(s): £52 12s	Longleat, Wilts	Longleat HA, 1806–1818, 3 Dec 1807, fol 14r
27.	1808	Three Payment(s): £32 15s 6d	Longleat, Wilts	Longleat HA, 1806–1818, July 1808, fol 25r
28.	1808	Three Payment(s): £32 15s 6d	Longleat, Wilts	Longleat HA, 1806–1818, July 1808, fol 25r

COOKE, Thomas, of London fl 1776–?1820

Cooke, whose yard was in Fitzroy Square and later in the New Road, signs a monument with a portrait-bust in Southwark Cathedral (5). An earlier one in Somerset (1) has a relief of two praying Charity children and their school, which was endowed by the dead man.

Literary References: *Gunnis* 1968, 113

Funerary Monuments

1.	†1776	Richard Stephens	Frome, Somerset	*Penny* 1977 (1), 152
2.	?1800	William Selwin	Hatfield Broad Oak, Essex	*Gunnis* 1968, 113

3.	†1813	Walwyn Graves	Mickleton, Glos	S	Pevsner, *Glos: Cotswolds*, 1999, 476
4.	†1817	Samuel Weston	Wyke Regis, Dorset		*Gunnis* 1968, 113; Pevsner, *Dorset*, 1972, 502
5.	?1818	Aaron Morgan	Southwark Cathedral, London	S	*Gunnis* 1968, 113
6.	†1820	John Twemloe	St Mary, Finchley, Middx	S	*Gunnis* 1968, 113
7.	?1820	Viscountess Ranelagh	Fulham, London		*Gunnis* 1968, 113

COOLEY, William fl 1730–44

The son of Benjamin Cooley, a mason of Chelmsford. Both men helped in the building of Boreham Hall for Benjamin Hoare in the 1730s. Between 1744 and 1746 William Cooley was employed by Earl Fitzwalter at Moulsham Hall. A 'William Cooley,' possibly the same man, was made free of the Masons' Company via service to **Christopher Mason** on 19 November 1735. A mason named 'Cooley' was paid £34 when St Catherine's Cree was repaired in 1752 (GL MS 7767).

Literary References: *Gunnis* 1968, 113; *Edwards* 1977, 63, 134

Archival References: Hoare Partnership Ledger, 1725–34, fol 239; Hoare Partnership Ledger, 1734–42, fol 171; Masons' Co, Freemen, fol 10; GPC

Chimneypieces

1.	1744–1746	Description unavailable	m	[Moulsham Hall, Essex]; untraced	Fitzwalter archives in *Gunnis* 1968, 113

Miscellaneous

2.	1744	Unspecified work Payment(s): £30		[Moulsham Hall, Essex]; untraced	*Edwards* 1977, 63

COOPER, George, of Canterbury fl 1820–51

His father was John Cooper, a builder of Canterbury, who added the aisles to Ashford Church in 1827. George Cooper signs a number of tablets in Kent. According to the *Builder* the Gothic tablet in Caen stone to John Neame in 1851 (9) was from 'the atelier of Mr George Cooper of Canterbury and executed by **H[enry] J[ohn] Day**, a student in the Royal Academy' (*Builder* 1851, 23).

Literary References: *Gunnis* 1968, 113

Funerary Monuments

1.	†1820	Mary Deane		Holy Cross, Canterbury, Kent	S	Pevsner, *Kent: N E & E*, 1983, 240
2.	?1830	Rev Thomas de Lannay		East Langdon, Kent	S	*Gunnis* 1968, 113
3.	?1832	Mary Davies		Cranbrook, Kent	S	*Gunnis* 1968, 113
4.	†1835	Sir William Cosway MP, obelisk on a podium		Bilsington, Kent		Pevsner, *Kent: W & Weald*, 1976, 171
5.	?1836	John Sutton		Chartham, Kent	S	*Gunnis* 1968, 113
6.	†1844	John and Eleanor (†1831) Cooper		St Mildred, Canterbury, Kent	S	
7.	†1845	Edward Plummer		Staple, Sandwich, Kent	S	
8.	†1846	Richard Frend		Canterbury Cathedral, Kent, cloister	S	
9.	1851	John Neame (co-sculptor: Henry John Day)	s	Sellinge, Kent		*Builder* 1851, 23; *Gunnis* 1968, 113

COOPER, John, of London fl 1763

In 1763 he was listed as a 'Carver and Gilder' of Noble Street, Foster-lane, Cheapside.

Literary References: *Mortimer* 1763, 8

COOPER, John, of Maidenhead fl 1777

Cooper, who married a Miss Emlyn in 1757, was possibly a son of Thomas Cooper of Henley. He was the master-mason in charge of building the Town Hall at Maidenhead in 1777, and was also employed on repairs to Marlow Church (Ch W Accts).

Literary References: *Gunnis* 1968, 113

COOPER, of Stratford-le-Bow fl 1781

He signs a work in white and grey marbles.

Funerary Monuments

1.	†1781	John Major	Worlingworth, Suffolk	Pevsner, *Suffolk*, 1974, 507

COOPER, R, of Edinburgh fl 1737

He signs a monument to Alexander Banus with an inscription relating that he died 'on his way to the baths of Somerset' (1). The work appears to be of stained or painted marble, with a brass medallion portrait of Banus in the centre. Gunnis regarded the work as 'charming and unusual' (GPC).

Funerary Monuments

1.	†1737	Alexander Banus	Alnwick, Northumbs	GPC

COOPER, Thomas, of Henley fl 1740–54

Cooper, who was employed on repairs to Stonor Park, Oxon in 1754, signs a large monument to a Sidney family member at Turville (2).

Literary References: *Gunnis* 1968, 113

Funerary Monuments

1.	1740	Perry family	Turville, Bucks	S	Pevsner, *Bucks*, 1994, 698
2.	?1740	William Sidney	Turville, Bucks	S	*Gunnis* 1968, 113 citing de L'Isle and Dudley archives

COOPER, Thomas, of London fl 1838

Busts

1.	1838	Queen Elizabeth	Burghley, Northants	SD	*Gunnis* 1968, 113

COOPER, William 1700–54

He was the son of John Cooper (†1724), a mason of the parish of St James, Clerkenwell. William was apprenticed to his father in January 1716 and became free of the Masons' Company in 1722. In 1720 Sir Harcourt Masters paid £150 to 'Mr. William Cooper, the mason, in part for a monument to Mrs. Mary Masters in St. Paul's Church at Canterbury' (1) (S S Co, Harcourt Masters no 1 in 2, p 79). Mary Masters was Sir Harcourt's recently deceased cousin. It is possible that the payment was received by William Cooper, who was then still an apprentice, on behalf of his father. The monument has not survived, but it must have been of some importance judging by the size of the part payment.

John Cooper, another London mason, is noted *c*1740 as working for 'Mr Horsnail' (Masons' Co Assistants). This was presumably **Christopher Horsnaile II.**

Literary References: *Gunnis* 1968, 113

Archival References: Masons' Co, Apprentice binding book (1); Lists of Livery; Court Book, fol 145v; Freemen fols 8, 9; Court Book, 1751–96; GPC

Funerary Monuments

1.	1720	Mrs Mary Masters Payment(s): £150 part payment		[St Paul, Canterbury, Kent]; untraced	*Gunnis* 1968, 113

COPE, William

Cope's tradecard describes him as a 'Mason / Opposite the Hercules, Threadneedle Street / behind the Royal Exchange'. He offered 'all sorts of Monuments, Tombs, Chimney Pieces, Marble Tables. Bath Stones, Mortars' and that he bought and sold 'old marble chimneypieces, Tables' (Heal 106.10).

COPELAND, Robert fl 1722

He is known only for one small, old fashioned, tablet.

Funerary Monuments

1.	†1722	William Greene	Osbournby, Lincs	S	Pevsner, *Lincs*, 1989, 596

COPPING (or COPPIN), Nicholas and John fl 1712–30

Nicholas Copping, of the Queen's Arms near the Red Well, advertised in the *Norwich Gazette* on 26 January 1712, that he made grave-stones of all types and also carved in wood. On 24 March 1724 he advertised in the same paper, from 'the King's Arms in the Castel-Ditches', that he could supply chimneypieces and building stones and that he was also working from the 'White-Lyon-Yard' in Beccles. An advertisement in the *Norwich Gazette* on 22 August 1730, announced that following the death of Nicholas Coppin, stone-cutter, of the King's Arms Lane, Norwich, the business was being carried on by his son, John, of the same address.

CORBETT, Joseph fl 1792

He was under 14 when he won a premium from the Dublin Society in 1792 (1). He appears to have been a pupil of **Edward Smyth**, whom he assisted in carving statues on the Custom House, Dublin. He is said to have caught a cold whilst applying the finishing touches to this work and to have died as a result.

Literary References: *Strickland* 1, 1913, 209–210

Miscellaneous

1.	1792	Unidentified subject	m	[Dublin Society, premium]; untraced	*Strickland* 1, 1913, 209–210

CORBETT & MARSHALL, of Bromley fl ?1797

They sign a large tablet in Lewisham.

Funerary Monuments

1.	?1797	Susannah Hunter	St Mary, Lewisham, London	S	*Gunnis* 1968, 113

CORNEY, Robert, of Kirkleatham –?1774

He was the master builder responsible for Kirkleatham church in the North Riding of Yorkshire, *c*1761. In 1741/2 Corney built the very handsome chapel in the centre of Kirkleatham Hospital, receiving £198 6s for his work. The interior was not finished until 1748, when he was paid £108 8s 4d for 'Joiner's work at ye chapel'. He must therefore have been responsible for the magnificent mahogany pews and also the unusual capitals which support the roof.

A payment of £23 was made to Corney in 1748 for 'mason's work'. This may well be for the inscription recording the building of the chapel, the shield and coat-of-arms on the front, and the figures of two charity children which stand on the roof. In 1747 he was paid £60 for mason's work at the Master's house (these are the two brick buildings which stand either side of the chapel). In 1770 he was paid £121 for building the 'dining room', presumably the large room which adjoins the matron's house. There are further payments of £576 to Corney in 1773/4, the last of which was paid to 'Mr Smith, the balance due to the late Mr Corney' (Kirkleatham Archives).

Archival References: GPC

CORNMAN, H fl 1782

He exhibited at the Free Society of Artists in 1782 from 7 Little Street, Martin's Lane and was presumably a relative of **Philip Cornman**, though unlikely to have been his son, **Henry Cornman**, since Philip Cornman married in 1776.

Literary References: *Graves* 1907, 64; *Young* 1996, 481

Miscellaneous

1.	1782	A horse, model		[Exhib Free Soc of A, London, 257]; untraced	*Graves* 1907, 64; *Young* 1996, 481
2.	1782	The Ville de Paris, model	i	[Exhib Free Soc of A, London, 218]; untraced	*Graves* 1907, 64; *Young* 1996, 481

CORNMAN, Henry –1830

The son of **Philip Cornman**, he exhibited a large number of wax portraits and busts at the Royal Academy between 1799 and 1821. In 1799 his address was 5 Great Newport Street, where he lived with his father. By 1804 he was in partnership with the elder Cornman and together they worked as gold and silversmiths. In 1813 he entered his first mark as a plateworker.

In 1815 he showed a portrait of Mr Henderson, probably **John Henderson**, the dentist and amateur sculptor in ivory, who exhibited from the Cornmans' address at the Society of Artists in 1783 (**16**). By 1816 Cornman appears to have had his own premises at 29 Newman Street. He retired to Hampstead Road in 1825/6, where he died in 1830.

Literary References: *Graves* II, 1905–6, 170; *Gunnis* 1968, 113; *Pyke* 1973, 31; *Young* 1996, 481–486

Busts

1.	1803	Lord Carlisle		[Exhib RA, London, 865]; untraced	*Graves* II, 1905–6, 170; *Young* 1996, 482
2.	1805	Unidentified gentleman		[Exhib RA, London, 712]; untraced	*Graves* II, 1905–6, 170
3.	1806	Mr Downs		[Exhib RA, London, 863]; untraced	*Graves* II, 1905–6, 170
4.	1821	T Valentine	w	[Exhib RA, London, 1056]; untraced	*Graves* II, 1905–6, 170

Miscellaneous

5.	1799	'Portrait of a gentleman'		[Exhib RA, London, 1080]; untraced	*Graves* II, 1905–6, 170
6.	1800	Mr Downs		[Exhib RA, London, 668]; untraced	*Graves* II, 1905–6, 170
7.	1802	Mr Wilkinson, model		[Exhib RA, London, 1086]; untraced	*Graves* II, 1905–6, 170
8.	1805	Unidentified gentleman	w	[Exhib RA, London, 793]; untraced	*Graves* II, 1905–6, 170
9.	1805	Unidentified young lady	w	[Exhib RA, London, 798]; untraced	*Graves* II, 1905–6, 170
10.	1806	Captain Weltden, miniature		[Exhib RA, London, 634]; untraced	*Graves* II, 1905–6, 170
11.	1810	Unidentified gentleman		[Exhib RA, London, 623]; untraced	*Graves* II, 1905–6, 170
12.	1811	Unidentified lady		[Exhib RA, London, 696]; untraced	*Graves* II, 1905–6, 170
13.	1812	Two unidentified ladies	w	[Exhib RA, London, 622]; untraced	*Graves* II, 1905–6, 170
14.	1813	B West, model		[Exhib RA, London, 573]; untraced	*Graves* II, 1905–6, 170
15.	1813	Unidentified lady, model		[Exhib RA, London, 538]; untraced	*Graves* II, 1905–6, 170
16.	1815	Mr Henderson		[Exhib RA, London, 831]; untraced	*Graves* II, 1905–6, 170
17.	1816	Mr Stone		[Exhib RA, London, 867]; untraced	*Graves* II, 1905–6, 170
18.	1817	Lord Dudley and Ward		[Exhib RA, London, 971]; untraced	*Graves* II, 1905–6, 170
19.	1817	Princess Charlotte, model	w	[Exhib RA, London, 943]; untraced	*Graves* II, 1905–6, 170
20.	1817	Unidentified gentleman, model		[Exhib RA, London, 1017]; untraced	*Graves* II, 1905–6, 170
21.	1818	Captain Maxwell, model		[Exhib RA, London, 1004]; untraced	*Graves* II, 1905–6, 170
22.	1819	Unidentified lady		[Exhib RA, London, 1112]; untraced	*Graves* II, 1905–6, 170
23.	1820	Unidentified gentleman		[Exhib RA, London, 954]; untraced	*Graves* II, 1905–6, 170

CORNMAN, Philip *c*1754–1822

A silversmith, modeller, engraver and print-seller, he exhibited portraits in wax at the Royal Academy between 1788 and 1792. He was apprenticed to Christopher Binger I of St Pancras, a small-worker in gold, but was subsequently passed on to Herman Jacobi Walther, whose service he left without consent in 1772. In 1776 he married Elizabeth Hodgson at St-Martin-in-the-Fields, London, and towards the end of 1781 was running his business from premises in Cock Lane. In March 1786 he moved to a property in Great Newport Street, rated at £52 in 1791. By 1804 he was in partnership with his son, **Henry Cornman**, and they advertised as gold and silver workers. His mark appears on a number of major pieces in silver for patrons such as the Earl of Carlisle and the Earl of Selkirk. In 1800 he worked with **Lucius Gahagan** on a 'grand silver light' for the Earl of Carlisle. Charles Heathcote Tatham provided the design, Gahagan modelled the work in wax for £10 and Cornman was paid £38 for the silverwork. He died in 1822. He is best remembered for his massive centrepieces and other work for Rundell, Bridge and Rundell, the royal silversmiths.

Literary References: *Graves* II, 1905–6, 170; *Gunnis* 1968, 113; *Pyke* 1973, 31; *Young* 1996, 481–486

Miscellaneous

1.	1788	Two unidentified models	w	[Exhib RA, London, 634, 681]; untraced	*Graves* II, 1905–6, 170
2.	1791	Unidentified gentleman, model		[Exhib RA, London, 653]; untraced	*Graves* II, 1905–6, 170
3.	1791	Unidentified lady, model		[Exhib RA, London, 638]; untraced	*Graves* II, 1905–6, 170
4.	1792	Unidentified lady	w	[Exhib RA, London, 764]; untraced	*Graves* II, 1905–6, 170

COSTA, Pietro fl 1840–80

Principally known as a carver of monumental statues for cemeteries. He was born in Genoa, but moved to Rome in 1848. He signs a monument in Bedford.

Literary References: *Gunnis* 1968, 114

Funerary Monuments

1.	1847	Thomas Waller	St Mary, Luton, Beds	S	Pevsner, *Beds, Hunts & Peterborough*, 1968, 115

COSTOLI, Aristodeme, of Florence 1803–71

A painter and sculptor, he was born in Florence and carried out a number of commissions for English patrons, particularly the Sandfords of Corsham Court. He studied sculpture under Stefano Ricci, and by 1839 had become assistant master of sculpture under **Lorenzo Bartolini** at the Accademia in Florence. His first works for the Sandford family date from the mid-1830s and appear to have been commissioned and executed in that city. Costoli carved busts of several members of the family, including Anna Horatia Sandford (**7**), portrayed *all'antica*, with her hair drawn up on her head and showing her regular teeth. The monument to Henrietta Sandford (**2**) features a statue of a mourning winged youth with ringlets, his hands crossed over his chest. Among other works for the family was a terracotta model of the family dog, Duchess (**13**).

The monument to Eliza, Lady Rendlesham shows a creative engagement with the English neoclassical tradition (**3**). The wall-tablet has a graceful, simplified relief of the deceased ascending to heaven, set against a plain ground. This appears to be a response to **John Flaxman RA**'s monument to Mary Rendlesham in the same church, which has a similar relief, but with a sea of ice-cream clouds. Costoli's treatment of the theme is yet more linear and simplified.

Costoli exhibited his *Gladiator* at the Royal Academy in 1845 (**6**). *The Art Union* considered his 'masterly modelling' to be 'worthy of the antique' (*AU*, 1845, 195). His reputation in England did not however endure: Clement and Hutton remarked that he was 'skilful in design and in all the technique of his art, but before his work the heart remains placid and the pulse is not quickened' (*Clement and Hutton* 1879, 1, 162). Gunnis dismissed his monuments as 'in the florid Italian style of the period'.

Literary References: *Gunnis* 1968, 114; *Sborgi* 1983–1985, 329–347; *Grove* 1996, 8, 19; *Mutucci* 2003

Funerary Monuments						
1.	?1835	Richard Jodrell		Lewknor, Oxon		*Gunnis* 1968, 114
2.	1840	Henrietta Sanford (†1837)		Nynehead, Somerset	SD	*Gunnis* 1968, 114; *Matucci* 2003, 40–1 (reprs 32–34)
3.	1842	Eliza, Lady Rendlesham (†1840)		Rendlesham, Suffolk	SD	Pevsner, *Suffolk*, 1974, 402; *Matucci* 2003, 42, 43–4 (repr 35)
4.	†1855	Rev John Sanford		Nynehead, Somerset		*Matucci* 2003, 36–7 (repr 23)
Statues						
5.	1837	A Wounded Warrior		Corsham Court, Wilts	SD	*Gunnis* 1968, 114
6.	1845	Gladiator	m	[Exhib RA, London, 1328]; untraced		*AU*, 1845, 195; *Graves* II, 1905–6, 173; *Gunnis* 1968, 114
Busts						
7.	1835	Anna Horatia Caroline Sanford	m	Corsham Court, Wilts		*Matucci* 2003, 38 (repr 24)
8.	1836	Adelaide, Countess Spencer		Althorp, Northants		*Matucci* 2003, 39 (repr 30)
9.	1838	Young English lady	m	English art market, 1992; untraced		*Matucci* 2003, 3 (repr 29)
10.	nd	Elisabeth Georgina Sanford	m	Corsham Court, Wilts		*Matucci* 2003, 38 (repr 28)
11.	nd	Lorenzo the Magnificent		Corsham Court, Wilts		*Matucci* 2003, 39 (repr 31)
Miscellaneous						
12.	1836	The hand of Orazia Sanford	m	Corsham Court, Wilts		NP/RG
13.	1851	Duchess, a dog, model	tc	[Gt Exhib]; untraced		*Gunnis* 1968, 114; *Matucci* 2003, 39

COTTERILL, Edmund 1795–

He joined the Royal Academy Schools in January 1820, aged 25, and exhibited at Academy exhibitions from 1822. His early works are chiefly sketches of classical, literary and religious subjects. In 1822 he lived at 67 John Street, Fitzroy Square, but by 1829 he had moved to 31 Panton Street, just off the Haymarket, and from 1832 onwards he exhibited from 25 Haymarket. From 1833 he was the head of the design studio which produced models for Robert Garrard, the royal goldsmiths. It was presumably through this work that he gained access to the foundries, which allowed him to produce a number of works in bronze. He modelled numerous animal studies, including horses for the 'Alhambra' Table Fountain in the royal collection. The *Art Journal* noted these equine models, commenting that Cotterill's 'reputation in this class of work is universal' (*AJ* 1849, 159).

Literary References: *Graves* 1875, 126; *Graves* II, 1905–6, 177; *Hutchison* 1960–62, 172; *Bury* 1962, 353; *Gunnis* 1968, 114; *Johnson* 1975, 108

Statues					
1.	1839	Equestrian figure of the 1st Duke of Wellington on 'Copenhagen'	b	[exhib RA, London, 1839, 1311]; Glasgow Museums S.1 Other versions: small bronze, Powis Castle, h.63.5 (1837)	*Graves* II, 1905–6, 177; *Gunnis* 1968, 114
2.	1839	Small equestrian figure of Queen Victoria at the review of the Household troops at Windsor in 1837	b	[Exhib RA, London, 1308]; untraced	*Graves* II, 1905–6, 177
3.	1842	St George, group	b	[Exhib RA, London, 1307]; untraced	*Graves* II, 1905–6, 177
4.	1846	Equestrian statue of John, 1st Duke of Marlborough, half size model		[Exhib RA, London, 1409]; untraced	*Graves* II, 1905–6, 177
5.	1847	Equestrian figure of Henry, 1st Marquess of Anglesey as Colonel of the 7th Hussars	b	[Exhib RA, London, 1390]; untraced	*Graves* II, 1905–6, 177
6.	1848	The contest, group	b	[Exhib RA, London, 1349]; untraced	*Graves* II, 1905–6, 177
7.	1858	Horses playing, group	b	[Exhib RA, London, 1242]; untraced	*Graves* II, 1905–6, 177
Busts					
8.	1832	Sir Edward Banks		[Exhib Soc of BA, London, 851]; untraced	*Johnson* 1975, 108
9.	1836	R S Kirkby		[Soc of BA, London, 1836, 870]; untraced	*Johnson* 1975, 108
10.	1838	King William IV	b	[Exhib Soc of BA, London, 614]; untraced	*Johnson* 1975, 108
Reliefs					
11.	1834	'Description of the name of Buccleuch,' alto-relievo		[Exhib RA, London, 1041]; untraced	*Lit Gaz* 1834, 361; *Graves* II, 1905–6, 177; *Gunnis* 1968, 114
Miscellaneous					
12.	1822	A faun		[Exhib RA, London, 996]; untraced	*Graves* II, 1905–6, 177
13.	1823	The angel overcoming Satan, clay sketch	tc	[Exhib RA, London, 1093]; untraced	*Graves* II, 1905–6, 177
14.	1823	Theseus rescuing Hippodamia from the Centaur, clay sketch	tc	[Exhib RA, London, 1091; 1827, 1073 (?completed work) Exhib Soc of BA, London, 1829, 855]; untraced	*Graves* II, 1905–6, 177; *Johnson* 1975, 108
15.	1824	Hercules delivering Theseus from the infernal regions leaves Pirithous to his fate, sketch in clay	tc	[Exhib RA, London, 1000]; untraced	*Graves* II, 1905–6, 177
16.	1824	Titania, Bottom and the Sprites (from A Midsummer Night's Deam), sketch in clay	tc	[Exhib RA, London, 1016]; untraced	*Graves* II, 1905–6, 177
17.	1825	Hercules rescuing Hesione from the sea monster, clay sketch	tc	[Exhib RA, London, 1047]; untraced	*Graves* II, 1905–6, 177
18.	1825	Venus		[Exhib RA, London, 1060]; untraced	*Graves* II, 1905–6, 177
19.	1826	Castor and Pollux carrying off the daughters of King Leucippus		[Exhib RA, London, 1037]; untraced	*Graves* II, 1905–6, 177
20.	1826	Hero and Leander, a sketch		[Exhib RA, London, 1082]; untraced	*Graves* II, 1905–6, 177

21.	1827	Death of the stag, clay sketch	tc	[Exhib RA, London, 1100]; untraced	*Graves* 1875, 126; *Graves* II, 1905–6, 177
22.	1827	Ganymede, clay sketch	tc	[Exhib RA, London, 1099]; untraced	*Graves* II, 1905–6, 177
23.	1828	Poor Vulcan, a sketch		[Exhib RA, London, 1162]; untraced	*Graves* II, 1905–6, 177
24.	1828	The wolf and vulture contending over the body of the fallen warrior, sketch		[Exhib RA, London, 1166]; untraced	*Graves* II, 1905–6, 177
25.	1831	The gallant		[Exhib Soc of BA, London, 909]; untraced	*Graves* 1875, 126; *Johnson* 1975, 108
26.	1831	The sportsman		[Exhib Soc of BA, London, 906]; untraced	*Graves* 1875, 126; *Johnson* 1975, 108
27.	1831	Two characters from 'Waverley'		[Exhib Soc of BA, London, 907, 910]; untraced	*Johnson* 1975, 108
28.	1832	Dumbiedikes, from 'The Heart of Midlothian'		[Exhib BI, London, 594]; untraced	*Graves* 1875, 126
29.	1832	'Old Mortality'		[Exhib BI, London, 589]; untraced	*Graves* 1875, 126; *Johnson* 1975, 108
30.	1832	Study from nature		[Exhib Soc of BA, London, 881]; untraced	*Johnson* 1975, 108
31.	1833	Davie Gellatly with Ban and Buscar from 'Waverley'		[Exhib BI, London, 546]; untraced	*Graves* 1875, 126; *Johnson* 1975, 108
32.	1833	Edie Ochiltree		[Exhib BI, London, 549]; untraced	*Graves* 1875, 126; *Johnson* 1975, 108
33.	1833	Hawking, in silver, from a model by Cotterill		[Exhib Soc of BA, London, 873]; untraced	*Johnson* 1975, 108
34.	1833	The sand-boy		[Exhib Soc of BA, London, 852]; untraced	*Johnson* 1975, 108
35.	1834	A bacchanal		[Exhib BI, London, 560]; untraced	*Graves* 1875, 126
36.	1835	The foray		[Exhib Soc of BA, London, 799]; untraced	*Johnson* 1975, 108
37.	1836	Study from nature		[Exhib RA, London, 1110]; untraced	*Graves* II, 1905–6, 177
38.	1837	The invalid		[Exhib Soc of BA, London, 593]; untraced	*Johnson* 1975, 108
39.	1850	Spanish bull-fight		[Exhib RA, London, 1351]; untraced	*Graves* II, 1905–6, 177
40.	1851	Saphadin, the brother of Saladin, receiving knighthood from Richard Coeur de Lion		[Exhib RA, London, 306]; untraced	*Graves* II, 1905–6, 177
41.	1852	Encounter between Robert Bruce and Sir Henry de Bohun at Bannockburn		[Exhib RA, London, 1356]; untraced	*Graves* II, 1905–6, 177
42.	1855	A Turk taking his 'kef'		[Exhib BI, London, 557]; untraced	*Graves* 1875, 126
43.	1855	The stirrup-cup		[Exhib RA, London, 1514]; untraced	*Graves* II, 1905–6, 177
44.	1855	The Suffolk punch-cart horse		[Exhib RA, London, 1501]; untraced	*Graves* II, 1905–6, 177

COTTON & HUMPHREYS fl 1773

In 1773 the Syndics agreed to pay them £64 for the Doric columns at the Divinity Schools at Cambridge University (Vice-Chancellor's Accounts).

Literary References: *Gunnis* 1968, 114

COTTRELL (or COTTERELL), T, of Bristol fl 1830–34

'T Cotterell of Bristol' signs a plain rectangular slab monument in Carmarthan (1). He is assumed to be the 'T Cottrell' who exhibited in Birmingham around the same time. He exhibited at the Birmingham Society of Artists in 1830 and 1832 (2–4).

Literary References: *Gunnis* 1968, 114

Funerary Monuments				
1.	†1834	Anne Llewellyn	Carm, Carmarthen, Tabernacle	*Dale-Jones and Lloyd* 1989, 47
Statues				
2.	1830	Samuel Cottrell, miniature model	[Exhib Birmingham Soc of A]; untraced	*Gunnis* 1968, 114
Busts				
3.	1832	Charles, 2nd Earl Grey	[Exhib Birmingham Soc of A]; untraced	*Gunnis* 1968, 114
4.	1832	Lord Brougham	[Exhib Birmingham Soc of A]; untraced	*Gunnis* 1968, 114

COULMAN, of London fl 1800–18

Coulman's yard was in Portland Road. He signs a number of 'dull' tablets in the south and south-west of England (*Gunnis* 1968, 114).

Funerary Monuments					
1.	†1800	Lady Wheler	Leamington Hastings, Warwick		GPC
2.	†1809	Bishop Porteus	All Saints, Fulham, London	S	*Gunnis* 1968, 114
3.	?1812	Frances Hoskins	Appleton, Berks	S	*Gunnis* 1968, 114
4.	?1812	James Hatsell	Godstone, Surrey	S	*Gunnis* 1968, 114
5.	?1813	John and Elizabeth Ball	Berry Pomeroy, Devon	S	*Gunnis* 1968, 114
6.	?1818	George Lovibond	Hatfield Peverel, Essex	S	*Gunnis* 1968, 114
7.	nd	Edward Bovey	Staverton, Devon	S	Pevsner, *Devon*, 1989, 758

COULTON, J, of Braithwell fl 1792

He signs a large marble tablet in Yorkshire.

Funerary Monuments					
1.	?1792	Joseph Tomlinson	Tickhill, W R Yorks	S	*Gunnis* 1968, 114

COURBOULD, Edward Henry fl 1767?–1835

In 1835, while living at 5 Crescent Place, Burton Crescent, he was awarded a gold Isis medal from the Society of Arts.

Funerary Monuments

1.	†1767	James Bosanquet	Bath Abbey, Somerset	S	Pevsner, *Somerset: N & Bristol*, 1958, 104; *Penny* 1977 (1), 137, 219 n8 (repr)

Miscellaneous

2.	1835	St George and the Dragon	[Soc of A, gold Isis medal]; untraced		RSA *Transactions*, vol 51, 1838, xiv

COVELL, S E

For further information the reader is referred to *Pyke* 1973, 32 and *Pyke* 1981, 12

COWEY, Diocinto fl 1671

Chimneypieces

1.	1671	Two of 'counterfitt marble'	[Volary Building, Whitehall Palace, London, King's bedchamber and withdrawing room]; untraced		*Colvin* 1973–76, V, 274

COWGILL, Francis, of York –1807

For many years he was foreman to **Joseph Atkinson of York.** On 15 June 1799 he announced in the *York Herald* that he had opened a stoneyard within the 'gateway to Mr Nurbrown's garden in Mickelgate'. In 1806 he took **Henry Plows of York** into the business (*York Courant*, 6 October 1806). After Cowgill's death, his widow Catherine announced that Plows would continue it (*York Courant*, 18 May 1807).

Archival References: GPC

COWLE, of Gloucester fl 1792

Funerary Monuments

1.	†1792	William Hunter	Cranham, Glos	S	Pevsner, *Glos: Cotswolds*, 1999, 306

COWLEY, William fl 1770–71

William Cowley, a stone mason, received regular payments for work on the new bridge in Woburn Park, 1770–71 under the architect Samuel Miller.

Archival References: Woburn Building Accts, 1770–1773, R5/1093

COWLING TAYLOR, R fl 1830

All that is known of him is that he was living in Carlton Chambers, Regent Street when, in 1830, he received an award from the Society of Arts.

Miscellaneous

1.	1830	South Wales Coalfield, models	[Soc of A, gold Isis medal]; untraced		RSA, *Transactions*, vol 48, 1831, xxiv

COX, Henry, of Northampton 1725–1810

He was born on 14 August 1725, the son of **Samuel Cox I of Northampton** and Ann, née Brabrook. Between 1745 and 1750 he lived in his own house in Northampton, but after his father's death he returned to the family home in Derngate. A month later Cox inserted advertisements in the *Northampton Mercury* (25 Dec. 1749 and 1 Jan. 1750), stating that he intended to carry on his father's business and was prepared to execute 'all sorts of monumental structures, chimneypieces etc.' In addition he could provide 'Figures human or animal, alto and basso Relievos, compartments of drapery, leatherwork shields and mantling, arms and supporters, trophies, festoons, foliage and all other ornaments, enrichments and decorations of sculpture for churches, houses, gardens . . . in marble, other stone or wood, according to the most strict and approved rules of beauty and proportion, either antique or modern and after more compleat and elegant manner and taste than hath been hitherto practis'd in this country' (quoted in *Lewis* 1953, 22).

He was admitted a freeman by patrimony of his native town on 26 September 1752. On 16 Sept 1754 he advertised in the *Northampton Mercury* for an apprentice, preferably a 'strong, active willing lad, of a mild and quiet disposition, descended from sober, honest parents' (quoted in *Lewis* 1953, 23). In the same newspaper, on 29 March 1762, he offered drawing lessons at a property in Vigo-Lane, Northampton. He was people's churchwarden at St Giles in 1755 and sat on a church charities committee in 1786.

Gunnis describes his numerous monuments and tablets, as having 'well-carved details and he makes an ingenious use of coloured marbles.' His 'most delightful' commemorates Dr John Shipton (**5**) and shows a number of books lying on a ledge with a pot of ink and a realistic quill. His most lavish work is the architectural monument to Elizabeth Langham with its flaming lamps and urns (**19**), but of particular note was his collaboration with **Michael Rysbrack** on the monument to John Palmer. It is signed by both sculptors (**16**). In 1751 a drawing of the monument by Cox was engraved by T Jefferys.

Literary References: *Gunnis* 1968, 114; *Lewis* 1953, 19–38

Funerary Monuments

1.	†1717	Thomas Mercer	Piddington, Northants	S	*Lewis* 1953, 35
2.	†1726	Henry Chester	East Haddon, Northants	S	*Lewis* 1953, 33, 35; *Gunnis* 1968, 114
3.	?1731	John Ward	Guilsborough, Northants		GPC
4.	1732	Edward Bateman (†1731)	St Giles, Northampton	S	*Lewis* 1953, 35; *Gunnis* 1968, 114
5.	†1748	Dr John Shipton	Wollaston, Northants	S	*Lewis* 1953, 35; *Gunnis* 1968, 114; GPC
6.	†1751	Sarah Mansel	St Giles, Northampton	S	*Lewis* 1953, 32, 35; *Gunnis* 1968, 114
7.	†1753	Samuel Keynton	Bugbrooke, Northants	S	*Lewis* 1953, 32, 34, 35; *Gunnis* 1968, 114

8.	†1754	Charles Pinfold	Walton, Bucks	S	*Lewis* 1953, 35
9.	†1756	Robert Atkinson	Ware, Herts		*Gunnis* 1968, 114; Pevsner, *Herts*, 1977, 378
10.	†1756	Thomas Lucas	Guilsborough, Northants	S	*Lewis* 1953, 35; *Gunnis* 1968, 114; Pevsner, *Northants*, 1973, 243
11.	1757	John Barrow (†1744)	Potterspury, Northants	S	*Lewis* 1953, 35
12.	?1757	Sir Thomas Samwell	Upton, Northants		*Gunnis* 1968, 114
13.	1758	George Palmer (†1723)	St Giles, Northampton	S	*Lewis* 1953, 35; *Gunnis* 1968, 114
14.	†1759	Hannah Payne	Warkton, Northants	S	*Lewis* 1953, 35
15.	†1761	Henry Locock	All Saints, Northampton	S	*Lewis* 1953, 33, 35; *Gunnis* 1968, 114
16.	†1761	John Palmer (co-sculptor: Michael Rysbrack)	Ecton, Northants	S	*Webb* 1954, 222; Pevsner, *Northants*, 1973, 207
17.	†1762	Sarah Rudsdell	Doddridge Chapel, Northampton	S	*Lewis* 1953, 35
18.	1772	George Evans (†1757)	St Peter, Northampton	S	*Lewis* 1953, 35; *Gunnis* 1968, 114
19.	1773	Elizabeth Langham (†1756)	Preston Deanery, Northants	S	*Lewis* 1953, 31, 33, 35; Pevsner, *Northants*, 1973, 379
20.	1785	Colonel James Money (†1785)	Pitsford, Northants	S	*Lewis* 1953, 35; *Gunnis* 1968, 114
21.	1787	John Newcombe (†1765)	All Saints, Northampton	S	*Lewis* 1953, 35; *Gunnis* 1968, 114
22.	†1798	John Harvey Thursby II and wife	Abington, Northants	S	*Lewis* 1953, 26, 32, 35
23.	nd	Rev Francis Paris	Ringstead, Northants	S	GPC

COX, J R, of Deptford fl 1838–43

The son of John Cox, a mason who was apprenticed to George Drewett in 1765, became free of the Masons' Company in 1774 and then set up in Deptford. The younger Cox was master-mason to Woolwich Dockyard.

Literary References: *Gunnis* 1968, 115

Funerary Monuments

1.	?1838	Elizabeth Dobson	St Paul, Deptford, churchyard	S	*Gunnis* 1968, 115

Architectural Sculpture

2.	1843	Font	St Giles, Camberwell, London		Report of the Committee on the Rebuilding of St Giles, in GPC

COX, Samuel, of Daventry and Northampton III 1767–1851

He was born on 8 May 1767, the son of **Samuel Cox II of Daventry** and Martha, née Cole. He became a freeman of the town in October 1788. In 1793 he succeeded his grandfather **William Cox I of Northampton** in the family business in Northampton, though he continued to live in Daventry and to serve clients there. On 23 November 1793 he advertised his succession to the business in the *Northampton Mercury* and promised to execute his patrons' commissions with 'all the taste, accuracy and Dispatch which distinguished his predecessor.' At the same time he acquainted his patrons in Daventry that 'having engaged some able assistants he will endeavour so to conduct business there as to merit a continuance of those favours already conferred' (quoted in *Lewis* 1953, 24).

Cox became a justice of the peace in Daventry in 1824 and a bailiff in 1825. He acted as agent for the Sun Fire Office from 1819 to 1833. He married first Frances Cole of Daventry, by whom he had five children, and then Elizabeth Cooper of Daventry. His tablets are of standard 18th-century design, well out of date by the time he supplied them.

Literary References: *Gunnis* 1968, 115; *Lewis* 1953, 19–38

Funerary Monuments

1.	†1797	William Steer	St Sepulchre, Northampton	S	*Lewis* 1953, 37
2.	1801	James Fremeaux (†1799)	Kingsthorpe, Northants	S	*Lewis* 1953, 37
3.	†1801	William Mayo	Great Brington, Northants	S	*Lewis* 1953, 32, 37; *Gunnis* 1968, 115
4.	?1802	Edward Swinfen	Long Buckby, Northants	S	*Gunnis* 1968, 115
5.	†1802	Margaret Fremeaux	Kingsthorpe, Northants	S	*Lewis* 1953, 37; *Gunnis* 1968, 115
6.	†1803	Gertrude Joanna Portington	Kingsthorpe, Northants	S	*Lewis* 1953, 37
7.	1803	Samuel Clay (†1800)	Daventry, Northants	S	*Lewis* 1953, 37
8.	1816	John Clarke (†1805)	Welton, Northants	S	*Lewis* 1953, 32, 37; *Gunnis* 1968, 115; Pevsner, *Northants*, 1973, 457
9.	1820	Henry Bagshaw Harrison (†1801)	Daventry, Northants	S	*Lewis* 1953, 37
10.	1827	John Portington (†1789)	All Saints, Northampton	S	*Lewis* 1953, 37; *Gunnis* 1968, 115

COX, Samuel, of Daventry II –1772

Thought to be a son of **William Cox I of Northampton**, he moved to Daventry in 1766 presumably to set up a new branch of the Northampton business. The same year he married Martha Cole of Northampton. On 30 April 1767 he became freeman of Daventry. He was the father of **Samuel Cox III of Daventry and Northampton** and was succeeded in his stone-carving business by **William Cox II of Daventry**.

Literary References: *Lewis* 1953, 19–38

COX, Samuel, of Northampton I 1690–1749

The son of Joseph and Elizabeth Cox, he appears to have been the first stone carver in the family. His father was a carpenter and the monument to his memory in Hanslope churchyard, which was probably by one of his descendants, is carved with a relief showing the tools of his trade. In November 1704 he Cox left Hanslope for Northampton, where he served an 8-year apprenticeship with **John Lumley of Northampton**. Cox married Ann Brabrook of Olney on 11 November 1713 and they had 8 children. On 25 May 1715 he became a freeman of the town 'by birth' (Northampton

Borough Records 6/1, Freeman's Register, p 150). The family lived on the north side of Derngate, in the Parish of St Giles where he died on 19 November 1749. He was buried in St. Giles, Northampton and is commemorated by a tablet in the sanctuary. He was succeeded in the family business by his son **Henry Cox of Northampton**.

Samuel was known principally for his monuments though he was paid £10 17s in 1731–2 by Sir Justinian Isham for unidentified work, probably at Lamport Hall. Gunnis considered his monuments 'greatly superior to that turned out by other contemporary provincial statuaries. Most are architectural wall monuments of late-17th century style, with pillars and broken pediments. The Thursby has a life-size figure and is the most ambitious work by any member of the family (**9**). Thursby is depicted in barrister's robes beneath a *baldacchino*, the curtains of which appear to be tucked behind the flanking pilasters, only to reappear at the sides of the monument. The strongly-carved, vertical folds of his robe are echoed in the fluting of the pilasters. The monument to Downhall Thursby has a portrait-bust (**5**), considered 'very indifferent' by the antiquarian George Baker (*Baker* 1822–30, 1, 15).

Literary References: *Gunnis* 1968, 114; *Lewis* 1953, 19–38

Funerary Monuments

1.	†1722	William Ashton	Kimbolton, Hunts	S	*Lewis* 1953, 34; *Gunnis* 1968, 115
2.	†1726	Ann Woolston	St Giles, Northampton	S	*Lewis* 1953, 34; *Gunnis* 1968, 115
3.	1727	William Price (†1727)	St Giles, Northampton	S	*Lewis* 1953, 32, 34; *Gunnis* 1968, 115
4.	†1729	Dorcas Sargeant	All Saints, Northampton	S	*Lewis* 1953, 34; *Gunnis* 1968, 115
5.	1733	Downhall Thursby (†1706)	Abington, Northants	S	*Lewis* 1953, 26, 34; *Gunnis* 1968, 115
6.	?1733	Mrs Robb	Milton Ernets, Beds	S	*Gunnis* 1968, 115
7.	†1733	Roger Mercer	Piddington, Northants	S	*Lewis* 1953, 34
8.	†1736	Richard Thursby	Abington, Northants	S	*Lewis* 1953, 26, 34; *Gunnis* 1968, 115
9.	pre-1736	William Thursby (†1701)	Abington, Northants	S	*Lewis* 1953, 26, 27, 34 (repr); *Gunnis* 1968, 115; Pevsner, *Northants*, 1973, 344
10.	1737	George Tompson	St Peter, Northampton	S	*Lewis* 1953, 34; *Gunnis* 1968, 115
11.	†1737	Henry Lowth	Abington, Northants	S	*Lewis* 1953, 26, 34; *Gunnis* 1968, 115
12.	†1739	Thomas Mercer	Piddington, Northants	S	*Lewis* 1953, 34
13.	1740	Nicholas Jeffcut (†1739)	St Peter, Northampton	S	*Lewis* 1953, 34; *Gunnis* 1968, 115
14.	1741	Thomas Lucas (†1741)	Guilsborough, Northants	S	*Lewis* 1953, 32, 34
15.	†1745	Thomas Forster	Hanslope, Bucks	S	*Lewis* 1953, 34
16.	†1747	Mary Stanyan	St Giles, Northampton	S	*Lewis* 1953, 34
17.	1748	Dorothy Beckett (†1748)	All Saints, Northampton	S	*Lewis* 1953, 34; Pevsner, *Northants*, 1973, 319

COX, William fl 1725–?1752

Cox, who may have worked at Deptford, signs two 'very fine' portrait-busts of Thomas Bacon and William Horsmonden Turner (**1, 2**). The latter is 'an admirable work by a skilled hand' (*Gunnis* 1968, 115).

Busts

1.	1752	Josiah Bacon	m	[Bacon's School, Grange Rd, Bermondsey, over door]; Bacon's Comprehensive School, Camberwell	SD	*Gunnis* 1968, 115; *Cavanagh* forthcoming 2007 (Southwark, Dulwich to Walworth)
2.	nd	William Horsmonden Turner (1678–1753)	s	Maidstone Museum, Kent	S	*Gunnis* 1968, 115

COX, William I, of Northampton 1717–93

The son of **Samuel Cox I of Northampton** and Ann Brabrook, he was born on 29 June 1717 and married Sarah Brafield of Northampton. He must spent a period in the capital for on 29 March 1762 he placed an advertisement in the *Northampton Mercury* describing himself as 'William Cox, carver, from London.' At this date he was established in Northampton at 'The Urn in Cock Lane,' where he performed 'all sorts of statuary, monuments, tombs and gravestones, chimney pieces.' In addition he could provide ornaments in stone or wood and 'figures human or animal, alto and basso relievos for houses and gardens completed in the neatest manner according to the antient or modern taste' (quoted in *Lewis* 1953, 23).

Cox was also a poet, and received praise from no less an authority than William Cowper. In 1787 the clerk of All Saints applied to Cowper for some verses for his 'Bill of Mortality' and was referred by the poet to Cox, 'a statuary and a first-rate maker of verses.' The clerk replied that he had already had help from that source, but that Cox was 'a gentleman of so much reading that the people of our town cannot understand him' (letter from Cowper to Lady Hesketh, 27 Nov 1787, quoted in *Lewis* 1953, 24). His many tablets frequently comprise a pyramid with rococo flaming lamps on either side, and Lewis considered them 'somewhat stereotyped in design'. Gunnis notes that they have 'delightful details'.

His death is noted in the *Northampton Mercury* of 16 November 1793: 'Died Sunday, Mr William Cox of this town, carver; he was a man of great integrity and universally esteemed for his professional merit' (*Lewis* 1953, 24). He was buried in St Giles's on 14 November 1793 and was succeeded in business by his grandson, **Samuel Cox III of Daventry and Northampton**.

Literary References: *Lewis* 1953, 19–38; *Gunnis* 1968, 115

Funerary Monuments

1.	†1728	Frances Clark	Guilsborough, Northants	S	*Lewis* 1953, 36
2.	1745	Charles Sturges (†1745)	Orlingbury, Northants	S	*Lewis* 1953, 36
3.	†1753	Richard Kent	Gayton, Northants	S	*Lewis* 1953, 36
4.	†1754	Thomas Malcher	Spratton, Northants	S	*Lewis* 1953, 37

5.	†1755	Thomas and Mary White		Flitton, Beds	S	GPC
6.	1761	Mary Young (†1761)		Orlingbury, Northants	S	*Lewis* 1953, 36
7.	†1763	Hester Raynsford (née Isham)		[Faxton, Northants]; Lamport, Northants (1958)	S	*Lewis* 1953, 36; *Isham* 1965, 5
8.	†1763	Sir Arthur Hesilridge		Noseley, Leics		Pevsner, *Leics & Rutland*, 1984, 337
9.	†1765	Thomas Holmes		Doddridge Chapel, Northampton	S	*Lewis* 1953, 32, 36
10.	1766	Benjamin Okell (†1743)		Spratton, Northants	S	*Lewis* 1953, 37; *Gunnis* 1968, 115
11.	†1767	Edward Lye		Yardley Hastings, Northants	S	*Lewis* 1953, 37
12.	†1767	Harriet Knatchbull		Cosgrove, Northants	S	*Lewis* 1953, 35
13.	†1767	Mary Malcher		Spratton, Northants	S	*Lewis* 1953, 37
14.	†1769	Elizabeth Halford		Weston Favell, Northants	S	*Lewis* 1953, 37
15.	1769	Sir Charles Wake-Jones (†1755)		Courteenhall, Northants	S	*Lewis* 1953, 33, 36; Pevsner, *Northants*, 1973, 166
16.	?1769	Thomas Maydwell		Geddington, Northants		*Gunnis* 1968, 115
17.	†1770	Elizabeth Beynon		Spratton, Northants	S	*Lewis* 1953, 37; Pevsner, *Northants*, 1973, 407
18.	1770	Thomas Plampin (†1770)		Yelvertoft, Northants	S	*Lewis* 1953, 32, 37; Pevsner, *Northants*, 1973, 473
19.	1771	Richard Backwell (†1765)		All Saints, Northampton	S	*Lewis* 1953, 36; Pevsner, *Northants*, 1973, 319
20.	†1774	Edward Whitton		All Saints, Northampton	S	*Lewis* 1953, 36
21.	1774	Thomas Wills (†1774)		Yelvertoft, Northants	S	*Lewis* 1953, 37
22.	1775	William Ward (†1737)		Little Houghton, Northants	S	*Lewis* 1953, 32, 36; Pevsner, *Northants*, 1973, 294
23.	†1776	Clarke Adams		East Haddon, Northants	S	*Lewis* 1953, 36; Pevsner, *Northants*, 1973, 198
24.	?1777	Rev John Nixon		Cold Higham, Northants		GPC
25.	†1778	Francis Beynon		Spratton, Northants	S	*Lewis* 1953, 37; Pevsner, *Northants*, 1973, 407
26.	†1778	Francis Brownsmith		Great Houghton, Northants	S	*Lewis* 1953, 36
27.	†1778	Harriet Treslove		St Peter, Northampton	S	*Lewis* 1953, 36
28.	†1778	Pulter Forester		Cosgrove, Northants	S	*Lewis* 1953, 32, 36; Pevsner, *Northants*, 1973, 159
29.	1779	Isaac Ashley (†1757)		Welton, Northants	S	*Lewis* 1953, 37; Pevsner, *Northants*, 1973, 456
30.	?1779	John Wainwright		Welton, Northants		*Gunnis* 1968, 115
31.	†1780	Richard Kent		Gayton, Northants	S	*Lewis* 1953, 36
32.	?1780	Sanderson Miller		Radway, Warks		GPC
33.	†1781	George Tymms		Dallington, Northants	S	*Lewis* 1953, 33, 36
34.	1781	John Harvey Thursby (†1764) and Honor Harvey Thursby		Abington, Northants	S	*Lewis* 1953, 26, 28, 35 (repr)
35.	†1781	Richard Wadsworth		Cosgrove, Northants	S	*Lewis* 1953, 33, 36
36.	†1782	Elizabeth Mercer		Piddington, Northants	S	*Lewis* 1953, 37
37.	†1782	George Tymms		Dallington, Northants	S	*Lewis* 1953, 36
38.	†1782	Theophilus Goodfellow		Great Houghton, Northants	S	*Lewis* 1953, 36
39.	1785	Catherine-Maria Raynsford (†1777)		Bugbrooke, Northants	S	*Lewis* 1953, 35
40.	†1786	Bridget Wodnoth		St Giles, Northampton	S	*Lewis* 1953, 36
41.	†1786	Mary Lacy		All Saints, Northampton	S	*Lewis* 1953, 36
42.	1788	Edward Wodnoth (†1755)		St Giles, Northampton	S	*Lewis* 1953, 36
43.	1788	Matthew Maddock		Catworth, Hunts		RG/JP, 3, 388
44.	1790	Thomas Treslove (†1749)		St Peter, Northampton	S	*Lewis* 1953, 36
45.	1791	Thomas Thornton (†1783)		Brockhall, Northants	S	*Lewis* 1953, 35; Pevsner, *Northants*, 1973, 127
46.	†1792	John Revell (†1741)		All Saints, Northampton	S	*Lewis* 1953, 36
47.	?1792	Robert Lowndes		Soulbury, Bucks		*Gunnis* 1968, 115

Chimneypieces

48.	1775	Three		[Lamport Hall, Northants]; untraced		Isham archives cited in GPC
49.	1775	Three Payment(s): £36 16s 9d including travel and fixing	m	[Lamport Hall, Northants, great parlour, drawing room and 'sprig'd room']; untraced		*Lewis* 1953, 23

COX, William II, of Northampton –1784

He was almost certainly the son of **William Cox I of Northampton** and Sarah Brafield, and the brother of **Samuel Cox II of Daventry**. He succeeded Samuel in the branch of the family firm in Daventry in 1772 and was made a freeman of the town on 25 June 1772 that year. Cox died in 1784 and was buried in Northampton on 14 May. By his will, proved 19 June 1784, he left his entire estate to his wife Eleanor.

Funerary Monuments

1.	†1777	John Nixon	Cold Higham, Northants	S	*Lewis* 1953, 37
2.	†1778	John Wainwright	Welton, Northants	S	*Lewis* 1953, 37; *Gunnis* 1968, 115

COX & SON, of London fl 1844

Funerary Monuments

1.	†1844	John Le Cornu	Hathersage, Derbys	S

COYSEVOX, Antoine 1640–1720

The renowned French sculptor was responsible for the famous bust of the poet Matthew Prior, which was placed upon Prior's monument, designed by James Gibbs and carved by **Michael Rysbrack**, in Westminster Abbey (1). A note in the inventory of Prior's pictures states that the bust was completed in Paris in 1714. It was highly regarded by its British audience: **John Cheere** reproduced the bust in bronzed plaster and **Richard Dickenson** carved a version in marble.

Literary References: *Grove* 1996, 8, 93–4 (Souchal)

Archival References: BL, Ad MS 70362, f17

Busts

1.	1714	Matthew Prior (monument designed by James Gibbs and executed by Michael Rysbrack)	Westminster Abbey, London, south transept	*Dart*, 1723, II, repr p 61 (*sic*); *Friedman* 1984, 99–102, 314 (repr); *Physick* 1989, 54; *Whinney* 1988, 165 (repr); *Balderston* 2001, 20–1, n 4, 16; *Balderston* 2002, 29, n 2

CRABTREE & RUSHWORTH fl 1797

Architectural Sculpture

1.	1797	Vases	Market Cross, Beverley, E R Yorks	Pevsner, *Yorks: E R & York*, 1995, 305

CRAKE, Matthias John, of London 1805–

He joined the Royal Academy Schools in November 1825 on the recommendation of H Sass, giving his address as 64 Norton Street, Fitzroy Square. He won the silver Isis medal from the Society of Arts in the following year (**8**). In 1837 he carried out repairs to the Royal College of Physicians in Cockspur Street, for which he received £70.

He exhibited with the Society of British Artists in 1832 from 1 King's Road, Chelsea. He is probably, therefore, to be identified with the 'Crake of Chelsea' who signs a number of tablets in St Luke's, Chelsea, including the two listed here (**1, 4**), and one in Billingborough, Lincs (**3**). 'Crake of Chelsea' received a separate entry in Gunnis's *Dictionary*.

Literary References: *Gunnis* 1968, 116; *Johnson* 1975, 111

Archival References: RA Admissions

Funerary Monuments

1.	?1826	William Terwin	St Luke, Chelsea, London	S	*Gunnis* 1968, 116
2.	†1827	Elizabeth Noyes	Great Gaddesden, Herts	S	
3.	†1831	Mary Wayet	Billingborough, Lincs	S	Pevsner, *Lincs*, 1989, 145
4.	?1833	Richard Lee	St Luke, Chelsea, London	S	*Gunnis* 1968, 116
5.	?1837	Lady Harriet Capel	Watford, Herts	S	*Gunnis* 1968, 116
6.	?1840	John Payne	St Margaret, Lothbury	S	*Gunnis* 1968, 116
7.	?1852	Captain George Browne	Gibraltar Cathedral		GPC

Statues

8.	1826	'a figure in the round, a copy'	[Soc of A, silver Isis medal]; untraced		RSA, *Transactions*, vol 44, 1826, xliii

Busts

9.	1832	M M G Dowling	[Exhib Soc of BA, London, 859]; untraced		*Johnson* 1975, 111

CRAKE, Michael, of London fl 1801–29

Gunnis, who refers to bills in the Soane archives, notes that Crake worked under Richard Nash at the Brighton Pavilion, where he received £643 for statuary work and in 1822 he was paid £244 for chimneypieces executed for 7 Langham Place (**34**). These bills cannot be traced. His yard was in Portland Road and there he produced a large number of monuments and tablets, none of them, in Gunnis's view, 'particularly outstanding'. One of the monuments has a relief depicting the death of Eliza Musgrave, killed in a riding accident (**15**). At least three other monuments also make use of reliefs (**12, 14, 17**).

Literary References: *Gunnis* 1968, 116; *Potterton* 1975, 41

Funerary Monuments

1.	?1801	Mrs Schreiber	Laxton, Northants	S	*Gunnis* 1968, 116
2.	?1809	John Bye	St Giles-in-the-Fields, London		*Gunnis* 1968, 116
3.	†1810	Martha (†1802) and Charles Pybus	Cheam, Surrey, Lumley Chapel	S	*Gunnis* 1968, 116
4.	†1810	Walter Booth	Goostrey, Cheshire	S	*Gunnis* 1968, 116; Pevsner, *Cheshire*, 1971, 225
5.	†1811	John Hallam	St George's Chapel, Windsor, Berks	S	*Bond* 1999, 146
6.	†1811	Sarah Conant	St Mary-at-Finchley, Middx	S	
7.	c1811	Sir William Green	Plumstead, Kent	S	*Gunnis* 1968, 116
8.	?1812	Captain Charles Rand	St Michael, Lewes, Sussex	S	*Gunnis* 1968, 116
9.	†1812	Thomas and Elizabeth Fydell	St Botolph, Boston, Lincs	S	Pevsner, *Lincs*, 1989, 161
10.	?1813	Captain Peake	George Town, British Guiana		GPC
11.	?1813	General Carmichael	George Town, British Guiana		GPC
12.	?1813	Harriet Sweetland	Exeter Cathedral, Devon	S	*Gunnis* 1968, 116
13.	?1813	Mr and Mrs Fydell	Boston, Lincs		GPC
14.	†1814	William Acton	Stoulton, Worcs	S	*Gunnis* 1968, 116; Pevsner, *Worcs*, 1968, 268
15.	†1815	Eliza Musgrave	Antigua Cathedral, WI	S	*Coutu* 1997, 83–4 (repr)
16.	?1816	Anne Butt	Buntingford, Herts	S	*Gunnis* 1968, 116
17.	†1816	Grice Smith	Youghal, Co Cork	S	*Potterton* 1975, 41
18.	†1816	Rev Thomas Blundell	Halsall, Lancs		Pevsner, *Lancs: N*, 1969, 136
19.	?1816	Sir William Essington	All Saints, Wandsworth, Surrey	S	*Gunnis* 1968, 116
20.	?1818	Rev John Hargreaves	Burnley, Lancs	S	*Gunnis* 1968, 116
21.	†1818	Sir Charles Price	Richmond, Surrey	S	*Gunnis* 1968, 116
22.	1818	Unidentified subject, tablet	St Mary & St Nicholas, Spalding, Lincs		Pevsner, *Lincs*, 1989, 673
23.	?1819	Helen Holloway	Gibraltar Cathedral		GPC
24.	†1819	Joshua Cooper	Minster-in-Thanet, Kent	S	
25.	†1820	Francis and Elizabeth Horne	Holy Trinity, Clapham Common, London	S	
26.	†1822	Sarah and James Alexander	Finchley, Middx		RG/JP, 3, 390
27.	?1823	Countess of Cardigan	Navestock, Essex	S	*Gunnis* 1968, 116
28.	?1823	Hon Mary Denny	Aldenham, Herts	S	*Gunnis* 1968, 116
29.	?1823	James Alexander	Axminster, Devon		GPC
30.	1823	Lieutenant George Johnson	St Mary and St Nicholas, Spalding, Lincs		GPC
31.	†1826	Vere Fane	Fulbeck, Lincs		Pevsner, *Lincs*, 1989, 291
32.	1829	Unidentified subject, tablet	St Mary and St Nicholas, Spalding, Lincs		Pevsner, *Lincs*, 1989, 673

Chimneypieces

33.	1812	Description unavailable		[Alton Abbey, Staffs]; untraced		Earl of Shrewsbury archives in GPC
34.	1822	More than one Payment(s): £244		[7 Langham Place, London]; untraced		*Gunnis* 1968, 116

Architectural Sculpture

35.	1815–1819	'Statuary work' Payment(s): £643		[Royal Pavilion, Brighton]; untraced		*Gunnis* 1968, 116

CRAMPHORN, William I fl 1768–1809?

He was apprenticed to **Thomas Carter II** on 9 June 1768. A 'Mr Cramphorn' appears in the rates from 1768 to 1774 in a house formerly occupied by Carter on Hyde Park Road. Carter had moved next door to larger premises formerly occupied by his partner **Benjamin Carter**. It seems possible that Cramphorn or a relative was therefore running a branch of the Carter enterprise. Cramphorn exhibited a wax model at the Free Society of Artists in 1772 (**2**), and a chalk drawing of an urn which was perhaps a design for a monument. In 1807 and 1809 a sculptor of this name, presumably the same man, exhibited wax models at the Royal Academy from 31 Hart Street, Bloomsbury (**1, 3**). In 1809 he exhibited alongside **William Cramphorn II**.

Literary References: *Graves* 1907, 66; *Gunnis* 1968, 116

Archival References: Poor Rate, WCA C311, C318; GPC

Busts

1.	1809	Unidentified gentleman		[Exhib RA, London, 802]; untraced		*Graves* II, 1905–6, 193

Miscellaneous

2.	1772	Flowers, model	w	[Exhib Soc of Artists, London, 58]; untraced		*Graves* 1907, 66
3.	1807	Justice, model	w	[Exhib RA, London, 1017]; untraced		*Graves* II, 1905–6, 193

CRAMPHORN, William II 1788–1829

Probably the son of **William Cramphorn I**, he attended the Royal Academy Schools in January 1806, giving his age as 18. He won a silver medal in 1808 and exhibited wax portraits at the Academy in 1807 and 1809. At this time he was living in the family home at 31 Hart Street, Bloomsbury. A note in the Academy Council Minute-book dated 1807 records that a model by Cramphorn, which he valued at 17 guineas, had been stolen from the Exhibition Room. Four years later it was decided to pay him this sum, as there was no chance that the model would be recovered. His monument to Mrs Cumberbatch has a fine, and unusually corporeal relief of the deceased and her child rising from a shattered tomb (**1**).

The will of William Cramphorn, sculptor, of the parish of St Anne, Soho, was proved in February 1829. He left his son, James Cramphorn, all his stock-in-trade and his daughter, Mary Freeman, inherited all his household furniture and shares. In his will his former addresses were given as Warren Street near Fitzroy Square, Greek Street, Soho and Vernon Place, Bloomsbury Square. It was therefore he, rather than William Cramphorn I, who in 1819 exhibited at the Royal Academy from 13 Greek Street, Soho (**2**).

Literary References: *Graves* II, 1905–6, 193; *Hutchison* 1960–62, 162; *Gunnis* 1968, 116; *Penny* 1977 (1), 97

Will: PROB 11/1751/153

Funerary Monuments

1.	†1818	Charlotte Cumberbatch and son		St Mary, Paddington, London	S	Pevsner, *London: N W*, 1991, 676

Busts

2.	1819	Unidentified gentleman		[Exhib RA, London, 1186]; untraced		*Graves* II, 1905–6, 193

Miscellaneous

3.	1809	An officer defending his colours, model	w	[Exhib RA, London, 791]; untraced		*Graves* II, 1905–6, 193
4.	1812	King George III	w	[Exhib RA, London, 912]; untraced		*Graves* II, 1905–6, 193

CRANFIELD, John Smith 1758–1802

The son of **Richard Cranfield**, he first exhibited at the Society of Artists at the age of 11, describing the work as 'his first attempt.' He joined the Royal Academy Schools in London on 8 October 1779, aged 21. Strickland records that Cranfield lived for some time at 109 Capel Street, before taking on some lime-kilns near Ballybough Bridge. Sometime around 1782 he moved to the North Strand and from 1783 he was in business with his father. He died from 'the effects of a wetting while attending to his kiln' in April 1802 (*Strickland* 1, 1913, 220).

Literary References: *Hutchison* 1960–62, 144

Reliefs

1.	1773	Charity, bas-relief	m	[Soc of A, Dublin, premium, £9 2s]; untraced		*Strickland* 1, 1913, 220

Miscellaneous

2.	1769	'Model of a foot'		[Exhib Soc of Artists, Dublin]; untraced		*Strickland* 1, 1913, 220
3.	1772	Unidentified carving	wd	[Soc of Arts, Dublin, premium, 16 gns]; untraced		*Strickland* 1, 1913, 220

CRANFIELD, Richard 1731–1809

He was the son or nephew of Richard Cranfield of Abbey Street, a joiner and gilder who died in October 1750. In 1756 he was awarded a premium of £6 by the Dublin Society for a work of sculpture. He lived at this time on Hog Hill, but by 1765, when he exhibited at the Society's exhibition, he had moved to Church Lane. He later became treasurer of the Society of Artists and when the Society became bankrupt, their exhibition house in William Street fell into his hands. From 1783 he was in business with his son, **John Smith Cranfield**. He appears to have prospered for he owned properties in Irishtown and Sandymount. On retiring in 1797 he took up residence at Tritonville Lodge, Sandymount and founded 'Cranfield's Baths' at Merrion. He died on 21 January 1809 and was buried at St Andrews.

Literary References: *Strickland* 1, 1913, 218–20

Architectural Sculpture

1.	1765	'Emblematical group of Hibernia'	wd	[Exhib Soc of Artists, Dublin, for the Hibernian Silk Warehouse]; untraced	*Strickland* 1, 1913, 219
2.	1767	'the new chair for the Society's presiding member'		[Dublin Society premises, Grafton Street]; untraced	*Strickland* 1, 1913, 219
3.	1771	Unidentified carving and gilding		[Provost's House, Dublin]; untraced	*Strickland* 1, 1913, 219
4.	nd	Unidentified carving		[Dublin Society premises, Grafton Street]; untraced	*Strickland* 1, 1913, 219
5.	nd	Unidentified carving		[Bluecoat school, Dublin]; untraced	*Strickland* 1, 1913, 219

Reliefs

6.	1765	Elijah taken up into Heaven, bas-relief	wd	[Exhib Soc of Artists, Dublin]; untraced	*Strickland* 1, 1913, 219

Miscellaneous

7.	1766	Group of boys representing Painting, Sculpture and Architecture		[Exhib Soc of Artists, Dublin]; untraced	*Strickland* 1, 1913, 219

CRASHLEY (or CHRASHLEY), David fl 1775–77

Crashley was the proprietor of a 'figure-shop' at Sir Isaac Newton's Head in Long Acre. His tradecard in the British Museum describes him as a 'Carver and Gilder' and also the maker and vendor of 'All Sorts of Figures and Ornaments in Plaster of Paris' (BM Heal 32.13). He employed both **John Durant** and **James Calvert** as modellers. Crashley exhibited a number of reliefs designed by the former at the Society of Artists between 1775 and 1777.

Literary References: *Graves* 1907, 66; *Gunnis* 1968, 116; *Rococo* 1984, 63

Statues

1.	1775	Ceres, a figure	[Exhib Soc of Artists, London, 70]; untraced	*Graves* 1907, 66

Reliefs

2.	1775	Boys, four bas-reliefs (from a model by John Durant)	[Exhib Soc of Artists, London, 69]; untraced	*Graves* 1907, 66
3.	1775	The triumph of Neptune, alto-relievo (from a model by John Durant)	[Exhib Soc of Artists, London, 67]; untraced	*Graves* 1907, 66
4.	1775	Wisdom, Beauty and Power, alto-relievo (from a model by John Durant)	[Exhib Soc of Artists, London, 68]; untraced	*Graves* 1907, 66
5.	1776	Hero and Leander, alto-relievo (from a model by John Durant)	[Exhib Soc of Artists, London, 199]; untraced	*Graves* 1907, 66
6.	1776	Ino, with the infant Melicertes, received by Neptune, alto-relievo (from a model by John Durant)	[Exhib Soc of Artists, London, 198]; untraced	*Graves* 1907, 66
7.	1776	Jupiter and Asteria, alto-relievo (from a model by John Durant)	[Exhib Soc of Artists, London, 201]; untraced	*Graves* 1907, 66
8.	1776	Jupiter and Europa (from a model by John Durant	[Exhib Soc of Artists, London, 200]; untraced	*Graves* 1907, 66
9.	1777	The Elopement of Helen with Paris, alto-relievo (from a model by John Durant)	[Exhib Soc of Artists, London, 189]; untraced	*Graves* 1907, 66

CRAWFORD, Joseph

A 'carver', he owned a tenement on Great Carrington Street (Lease papers, BL MS 3542, fols 301–6).

Archival References: GPC

CRAWLEY, John –c1767

Crawley was placed with **John Nost III** by the Dublin Society in 1750 so that he might be instructed 'in the statuary art' (*Strickland* 1, 1913, 221). He won a premium of £5 from the Society in 1754 and a further sum in 1755. In 1757 he was sent to Italy at the expense of the Society and his arrival in Rome was noted in **Richard Hayward**'s list of visitors to the city in 1758. Like many artists, Crawley took lodgings on the Strada Felice. He appears not to have been popular with all his fellow travellers: the architect Robert Mylne described him as both impudent and foolish in a letter of June 1758.

Richard Pocock, Bishop of Ossory reported on Crawley's progress to the Dublin Society on 2 October 1758. He wrote 'I am sure it is Crawley's intention to return to Ireland and exercise his art of statuary, and to settle here, and if he does not I will repay the Society the eighty pounds they allowed. . . I find he goes on very well at Rome' (quoted in *Strickland* 1, 1913, 221). In January 1759 Crawley was still in Rome, where he was among the artists who settled the affairs of the deceased watercolourist Jonathan Skelton.

The sculptor seems never to have returned to Ireland but to have died in Italy. The history painter James Barry recollected after the death of the Scots painter John Runciman in Naples in 1768 that he had seen another artist 'helped out of this world,. . . one Crawley, a sculptor' (quoted in *Ingamells* 1997, 253). Barry arrived in Italy in October 1766, which suggests that Crawley died soon after.

Literary References: *Strickland* 1, 1913, 221; *Potterton* 1975, 85; *Stainton* 1983, 11, 20; *Ingamells* 1997, 253

CREED, Elizabeth fl 1710–14

The sister of John Dryden, she appears to have had a career as a painter and is noted by Pevsner as responsible for three painted monuments in Northants, all to family members.

Funerary Monuments

1.	†1710	Rev Theophilus Pickering	Titchmarsh, Northants	Pevsner, *Northants*, 1973 432–3
2.	†1714	Dorothy Creed	Barnwell, Northants	Pevsner, *Northants*, 1973, 102
3.	nd	John Dryden and parents	Titchmarsh, Northants	Pevsner, *Northants*, 1973, 433

CRESANT, Jacob fl 1738

Architectural Sculpture

1.	1738	Two vases	Elvaston Castle, Derbys, gardens	SD	Pevsner, *Derbys*, 1978, 210

CRIPPS, Charles fl 1821

He carved the monument to his wife in Speldhurst, Kent, a work which has echoes of the memorial to General Hargreave by **L F Roubiliac**.

Funerary Monuments

1.	†1821	Sophia Cripps	Speldhurst, Kent		Pevsner, *Kent: W & Weald*, 1976, 543

CROAD, John, of Plymouth fl 1756–61?

He signs two large architectural marble tablets in Cornwall. Croad was Master-Mason of the Ordnance at Plymouth. In the Carew-Pole archives, 1759–1769 (Ordnance Debentures), are references to dealings between Croad and Reginald Pole of Antony House, Cornwall.

Literary References: *Gunnis* 1968, 116

Archival References: GPC

Funerary Monuments

1.	?1756	Sir John Trelawney	Pelynt, Cornwall	S	*Gunnis* 1968, 116
2.	?1761	Rev Samuel Deeble	Sheviocke, Cornwall	S	*Gunnis* 1968, 116

CROCKER, of Plymouth

Funerary Monuments

1.	nd	Unidentified subject	Liskeard, Cornwall		Pevsner, *Cornwall*, 1970, 104

CROFT, Samuel fl 1763

In 1763 he was paid £25 for 'making and putting up the frontispiece over the door in front of the house' at Ashburnham Place, Sussex (1). A William Croft, who was possibly a relative, was engaged from 1760–1763 as Master Mason in charge of alterations then being carried out to the house.

Archival References: GPC citing Ashburnham Archives

Architectural Sculpture

1.	1763	'Frontispiece' or coat of arms	Ashburnham Place, Sussex		GPC

CROGGON, William fl 1818–34

From 1821 onwards he was manager of the **Coade Factory of Lambeth**. He also produced a small number of marble tablets.

Funerary Monuments

1.	†1818	Thomas Estcourt		Shipton Moyne, Glos	S	Pevsner, *Glos: Cotswolds*, 1999, 606
2.	1821	Lovell Badcock		Little Missenden, Bucks		*Gunnis* 1968, 117
3.	1822	Lord Henry Fitzgerald		St Mary, Paddington, London		*Gunnis* 1968, 117
4.	1823	Nicholas Parry		Little Hadham, Herts		*Gunnis* 1968, 117
5.	†1829	Jane Estcourt		Shipton Moyne, Glos	S	Pevsner, *Glos: Cotswolds*, 1999, 606
6.	1831	Rev Charles Hawtrey		Christ Church, Spitalfields, London		*Gunnis* 1968, 117
7.	†1833	Francis Browne		Frampton, Dorset		Pevsner, *Dorset*, 1972, 213
8.	†1833	Thomas Conway and family		St James Garlickhythe, London		RG/JP, 3, 393
9.	1834	Wither Bramston (†1832)		Deane, Hants	SD	Pevsner, *Hants & Isle of Wight*, 1967, 190

Statues

10.	*c*1826	Robert Aske	sa	[Haberdashers Aske's School, Hoxton]; Haberdashers Aske's School, New Cross, London	SD	*Blackwood* 1989, 87 (repr); *Cavanagh* forthcoming 2007 (Lewisham)

Architectural Sculpture

11.	1822	Royal arms		Christ Church, Spitalfields, above chancel beam	SD	*Columns*, autumn 2003, 1 (repr)
12.	1831	A rich, inlaid and polychrome scagliola floor Payment(s): £900		Syon House, Middx, vestibule		*Harris* 2001, 73, 341 n33

CROOK, James 1759–

He entered the Royal Academy as a student of painting in October 1776, but in 1779 won a silver medal for sculpture (1).

Literary References: *Hutchison* 1960–62, 142

Miscellaneous

1.	1779	An academy figure or a bas-relief	[RA, silver medal]; untraced		RA Premium list

CROOKE, John fl 1681–1700

The son of **Richard Crooke**, he was made free of the Masons' Company by patrimony on 4 October 1681. He became a renter warden in 1694 and upper warden in 1697. He succeeded his father as mason to the Grocers' Company, a post he held until 1700. In 1684 he worked at Christ's Hospital, and in 1692 John and his partner, **Samuel Fulkes,** built the Writing School there which was finished three years later at a total cost of £1,159. Between 1686 and 1699, minor payments for work at the Hospital were made to him alone.

Literary References: *Gunnis* 1968, 117

Archival References: Grocers WA, 1699–1700, 19

CROOKE (or COOKE), Richard –1686

Crooke was warden of the Masons' Company in 1667 and 1672 and master in 1674. Between 1670 and 1673 he and his partner **John Shorthose** received £1,300 for work at Ludgate. He worked as a mason at Christ's Hospital from 1667 to 1686, when his widow received a payment: in 1683 he built part of the Mathematical School, earning £396.

He was one of the masons responsible for rebuilding Grocers' Hall in 1680–82 but was not the sole mason: the principal carving was done by **Edward Pearce**, who was paid £105, whilst Crooke, described as a stone-cutter, was paid £15. Gunnis says that he worked on the library of the Royal College of Physicians in Warwick Lane in 1688.

It seems likely that his widow was responsible for this contract. A payment to 'Sarah Crooke, executrix to Richard Crooke' appears in the Grocers' Company accounts for 1697. His son **John Crooke** succeeded him as a mason at Grocers' Hall and continued his father's work at Christ's Hospital.

The register of marriage licences for London records the union of Richard Crooke, 'Cit and Mason' and Sarah Phillips of St Andrew, Holborn on 22 July 1667. Since the groom is described as a widower aged 'abt 59' it seems likely that the entry refers to an earlier generation of this family of masons, unless Richard Crooke became a very active octogenarian (*Armytage* 1892, vol 33, 1660–1668, 214). References to several other family members are recorded in the Masons' Company archives. Another John Crooke was made free via service to Richard Crooke in January 1683; Peter Cooke became free by service to Richard Crooke on 8 October 1678 and Charles Cooke by service to John Crooke in June 1702.

Literary References: *Gunnis* 1968, 117

Archival References: Guildhall MSS 184/4 'Payments for Restoration of Guildhall etc 1666', p31r; Masons' Co, Masters and Wardens; Freemen, fols 8, 9; Grocers' WA 11571/16 and 17; GPC; CH, TAB 12819/10, p 57; 12819/11, 421

CROOME, John, of Salisbury fl 1771–73

In 1771 and again in 1773 he worked at Longford Castle (Longford Castle Archives). Between 1789 and 1796 he was the master-mason responsible for building Salisbury Guildhall, where he also executed the carved stonework.

Literary References: *Gunnis* 1968, 117, citing City Archives

CROSKILL, Henry, of Great Yarmouth –1820

His father, Henry, was a ship's carpenter. Croskill was apprenticed to **John Ivory** of Norwich in or before 1769. He gained the freedom of Norwich by patrimony on 21 March 1778 and the freedom of Yarmouth by patrimony in 1779, by which time he had a workshop at Southtown, near Yarmouth bridge. On 9 and 16 May 1778, the *Norfolk Chronicle* carried the advertisement: 'HENRY CROSKILL, jun. Stone-Mason, at his Yard in South Town, near Yarmouth-Bridge, begs Leave to inform the Public and Friends, that he has imported a Quantity of fine Portland Stone, proper for Grave Stones of all Sorts, Chimney Pieces, and all Kinds of Work used in Building; likewise handsome Dove-coloured and veined Marble for Chimney Pices, Monuments &c. and black Marble Grave Stones. . .N.B. Sells Dutch Terras and Mortars for Apothecaries use'. In 1796 he took 'the Old Yard upon the Quay near the Custom House' and the stock of **Matthew Cufaude**, deceased (*Norwich Mercury*, 30 July 1796). Croskill's apprentices included Eldredge Smith (3 June 1782) and William Bays (1796) (Yarmouth Apprenticeship Rolls). (Add inf. Jon Bayliss).

Funerary Monuments

1.	†1817	Mary Custen (co-sculptor: Logdon of Great Yarmouth)	Gorleston-on-Sea, Norfolk	S	

CROSS, William fl 1763

He signs a rococo monument in Lincs.

Funerary Monuments

1.	†1763	Katherine Bowker	Long Sutton, Lincs, churchyard	Pevsner, *Lincs*, 1989, 536

CROUCHLEY, John Barber fl 1839

The Walker Art Gallery possesses a wax relief inscribed '**John Gibson RA** / modelled by his / fellow pupil / JB Crouchley' (2). Despite his pretensions as a sculptor, Crouchley appears have realised few, if any, of the sculptural projects he hoped to carry out. Among his letters in the Harris Art Gallery, Preston, is one in which he states that he had wished to study in Rome but had been forced to stay in Liverpool by his father. His designs include a self-portrait and a study of Lord Lyndhurst. He exhibited a model at the Liverpool Academy in 1839 (1). (Add inf. Francis Marshall, Harris Museum and Art Gall)

Additional MS Sources: 43 draft letters to John Gibson and **Benjamin Spence** at Rome (Harris M & AG)

Collections of Drawings: Portfolio of 128 sketches, drawings and designs for sculptural subjects; 57 sheets of sketches and designs for sculpture, one sketch book and four separate sheets (Harris M & AG)

Reliefs

2.	1839	Musidora, study in alto relievo for a group		[Exhib Liverpool Ac, 701]; untraced		*Morris and Roberts* 1998, 173
3.	nd	John Gibson RA	w	Walker, Liverpool	S	

CROWE, M, of Norwich fl 1779

Funerary Monuments

1.	†1779	William Crowe	Lakenham, Norfolk	S	Pevsner, *Norfolk: N E & Norwich*, 1997, 347

CROWLEY, Peter Lawrence 1818/24–60

Crowley was born in Ireland. There is confusion about his date of birth: when he joined the Royal Academy Schools he gave his birth date as 1818, but in 1859, when he applied for help to the AGBI, he said he was 35. He was a pupil in the Dublin Society schools, winning a prize for modelling in 1837. The following year he exhibited at the Royal Hibernian Academy from Bushfield, Donnybrook Road, Dublin.

In 1839 he attended the Royal Academy Schools in London on the recommendation of James Loft. He lived first at 73 Newman Street, but by 1844 he had set up at Upper Fitzroy Street, Fitzroy Square. That year he exhibited *Edward I Presenting His Son to the Welsh* at Westminster Hall, a portrait of the king in chain mail, holding the child with his left hand (1). The *Art Union* thought the King was 'a fine chivalrous figure, but rather easy than dignified in movement' (*AU* 1844, 217). The *Literary Gazette* sarcastically remarked that 'the standing leg is several inches too short and we must confess until now our ignorance of His Majesty's physical defect' (*Lit Gaz* 1844, 483). In 1851 Crowley was living both at his former address in Dublin and in London at 6 Cardington Street. He is recorded in University Street and Leverton Street, London in 1853 and 1859 respectively. He died of dropsy at Ingatestone, Essex, on 25 April 1860.

Literary References: *Graves* II, 1905–6, 216; *Strickland* 1, 1913, 239–240; *Stewart* 1985, 1, 184

Archival References: RA Admissions; AGBI, vol 6, 238

Statues

1.	1844	King Edward I presenting his son to the Welsh		[Exhib Westminster Hall, London, 181]; untraced	*AU*, 1844, 217; *Lit Gaz*, 1844, 483; *Gunnis* 1968, 117
2.	1844	Paolo and Francesca di Rimini, group		[Exhib RHA, 415]; untraced	*Strickland* 1, 1913, 240; *Stewart* 1985, 1, 184
3.	1845	Drowned Leander		[Exhib Westminster Hall, London, 143]; untraced	*Westminster* 1845, 17; *Graves* II, 1905–6, 216; *Gunnis* 1968, 117; *Stewart* 1985, 1, 184

Busts

4.	1838	Nicholas J Crowley		[Exhib RHA, 212]; untraced	*Strickland* 1, 1913, 240; *Stewart* 1985, 1, 184
5.	1850	T H Illidge		[Exhib RA, London, 1388]; untraced	*Graves* II, 1905–6, 216; *Gunnis* 1968, 117
6.	1850	Unidentified lady		[Exhib RA, London, 1443]; untraced	*Graves* II, 1905–6, 216
7.	1851	A little child	m	[Exhib RA, London, 1342]; untraced	*Graves* II, 1905–6, 216
8.	1851	A little child		[Exhib RHA, 365]; untraced	*Strickland* 1, 1913, 240; *Stewart* 1985, 1, 184
9.	1853	Cupid, model ('to be executed in marble')		[Exhib RA, London, 1345]; untraced	*Graves* II, 1905–6, 216
10.	1854	Unidentified child	m	[Exhib RA, London, 1509]; untraced	*Graves* II, 1905–6, 216
11.	1859	Sheridan Knowles	m	[Exhib RA, London, 1363]; untraced	*Graves* II, 1905–6, 216; *Gunnis* 1968, 117

CRUTCHER, Richard I 1659–1725

Crutcher's reputation rests on a single signed monument, to the City magnate and Lord Mayor, Sir Robert Clayton, commissioned by Clayton before his death. Crutcher was baptised on 24 April 1659 and was the son of Michael Crutcher, yeoman of Morden, Surrey, and his wife, Sarah. He was apprenticed to William King, citizen and mason, on 27 May 1674 and turned over to **Edward Pearce** by consent of both parties on 6 July 1680. He became free of the Masons' Company in 1681, steward in 1691, renter warden in 1707 and master in 1713. His son, Michael, who became free of the Company in 1712 by service to his father, not by patrimony, worked as his assistant and died during his father's lifetime.

Crutcher appears to have been reasonably successful as a mason in his mature years, but almost nothing is known about his early career. He was responsible for rebuilding Bakers' Hall, 1716–19 and in 1710 agreed to attend to all the masonry work for a house that Elias Rich was building at the Old Bailey (Guildhall Archives, 8790). In 1722 he and Michael Crutcher put in a tender, which was not accepted, for the building of Christ Church, Spitalfields, giving their address as 'Billiters Lane, Fan-Church Street' (Lambeth Palace Library, New Churches, box II).

It is not known how Crutcher came to the attention of Sir Robert Clayton, but it seems unlikely that Clayton would have commissioned Crutcher to provide his monument unless the mason had already proved his competence as a figure carver. In a codicil to Clayton's will, dated 22 May 1707, he directed that the 'hereditaments and premises in Bletchingley' should be charged with keeping in order the monument which he was 'then erecting for himself and his late wife in the South Chancel of the church in Bletchingley.' The work was singled out by Sacheverell Sitwell as having 'the most spendid of all the architectural frontispieces' and he considered it 'the finest monument of the Baroque in England' (*Esdaile* 1946, 28–9). Clayton stands in his mayoral robes holding a scroll which probably denotes his gifts to St Thomas's Hospital. His wife wears elegant contemporary dress and at their feet is their only child, a touchingly sensitive portrait of a baby who died 40 years before the monument's erection. The frontispiece has four Corinthian columns and pilasters and within is a canopy tied up with cords to reveal a glory of cherubim and the inscription. The two upper storeys have segmental pediments of diminishing size and support a pair of life-sized seated angels, a heraldic shield and four urns.

The names of several of Crutcher's apprentices, none of whom achieved an independent reputation, are recorded in the Masons' Company lists. Henry Mills was bound in 1689, Francis Dickens in 1696, Richard Wickham in 1718 and Isaac Andrews in 1723.

Crutcher was living in the parish of All Hallows Staining at the time of his death. He bequeathed most of his modest estate to his two daughters, Mrs Wilmot and Mrs Saunders. His grandson, **Richard Crutcher II**, who was probably Michael's son, was left £20, half of it to enable him to be placed in an apprenticeship. (He was made free of the Masons' Company by patrimony in March 1747). Gunnis suggests that the business was inherited by Richard's widow, Mary, though the evidence he offers, an entry in the court minutes of the Masons' Company, dated 4 October 1722, does not tally with Crutcher's death, which was in 1725. The entry reads 'William Crutcher (son of Peter Crutcher, late of Morston [sic], Surry [sic], Yeoman dec[eas]ed late apprentice to Michael Crutcher, late Citizen and Mason de[ceas]ed. By Ind[entu]res dated the 23rd Feb[ruary] 1713 for Seven Years (his Mistress Mary Crutcher, the Widow Testifying for his service), was admitted into the freedom of this Company by service . . .' (Guildhall Lib MS 5304/3). Several members of the family practised as masons and their kinship is hard to establish. In Morden churchyard is the tombstone of 'Mr William Crutcher, Citizen and Mason of London, who departed this life on 22 day of February 1728/9 in the 33 Year of his Age'. It has the coat-of-arms of the Masons' Company, carved in relief.

Literary References: *Gunnis* 1968, 117-8; RG/JP, 3, 396; *Whinney* 1988, 106–8; *Webb* 1999, 1, 9, 10, 22, 36; IGI

Archival References: Masons' Co, Freemen, fol 8 (1681), fol 9 (1712); Masons' Co, Masters and Wardens; Masons' Co, Court Book 1695–1722 (1713); memorandum, Crutcher and Rich, Guildhall Ms 8790

Wills: Sir Robert Clayton, Alderman of the City of London, proved 1 Aug 1707, PROB 11/495; Richard Crutcher, Mason of All Hallows Staining, City of London, proved 21 May 1725, PROB 11/603

Funerary Monuments

1.	†1707	Sir Robert and Lady Clayton	Bletchingley, Surrey	*Whinney* 1988, 106–108 (repr)

CRUTCHER, Richard II fl 1747

A grandson of **Richard Crutcher**, he was left the sum of £20 in his grandfather's will, half of which was earmarked to pay his apprenticeship fee. His father is likely to have been Michael Crutcher, who was made free of the Masons' Company in 1712 and died young. Richard Crutcher II became free of the Company by patrimony in March 1747.

Will: Richard Crutcher, FRC PROB 11/603, proved 21 May 1725

CUENOT, Jean-Antoine –1763

A French-born carver from Franche-Comté, there are several references to him in Robert Dossie's *Memoirs of Agriculture, and other Oeconomical Arts*, 1782, the primary source of reference on premiums awarded by the Society for the Encouragement of Arts. He appears in the rate books of St James, Piccadilly, between 1744 and 1762, where his name is variously misspelled and his Christian name is anglicised to John. His workshop was in Warwick Street, Golden Square, an area frequented by members of the furniture-making and allied trades.

Cuenot's major patron was the 9th Duke of Norfolk, who employed him principally at Norfolk House, St James's Square. There he was responsible for much elaborate rococo wood carving in parade rooms between 1753 and 1755, working to designs by the Piedmontese architect, Giovanni Battista Borra. He carved elaborate panels and pier-glasses in the music room, for which he charged a total sum of £647 7s 3d, making it his most expensive scheme at Norfolk House. He supplied two spendid doorcases for the great drawing room, charging £104 15s 1d for the carving, including £19 12s for the monkeys over the lintels (1). Cuenot also provided a triptych for the Duke of Norfolk for the private chapel at Arundel Castle (2). In 1759 he worked for George Brudenell, 4th Earl of Cardigan.

He died on 22 January 1763. His will, written in French on 10 August 1762, makes reference to a 'natural son', **John Cuenot**, who was also a carver, 'taught by his father'. Cuenot's executors were both carvers who worked in London, Robert Ansell and Joseph Duffour.

Literary References: *Mortimer's Universal Directory*, 1763, 8; *Gunnis* 1968, 90; *Rococo* 1984, 40, B16; *Beard* 2004, 80–1 (repr); *Murdoch* 2006, 54–63

Will: PROB 11/863, proved London 22 January 1763

Architectural Sculpture

1.	1753–1756	Carved decorations, overmantels and furniture Payment(s): £2,643 3s 81/2d	[Norfolk House, London (demol 1930s), great drawing room, green damask room, flowered velvet room, state dressing room]; VAM (music room and great drawing room doorcases), Arundel Castle (pier & sideboard tables)	*Murdoch* 2006, 54–63 (repr)
2.	nd	Triptych	Arundel Castle, Sussex	*Beard* 1984, 80–81

CUENOT (CEUNOT), John c1743–before 1782

The illegitimate son of **Jean-Antoine Cuenot**, he was mentioned in his father's will of 1762, when he was still under 22. In June 1762 he won a 7 guinea premium from the Society of Arts for a clay model of a festoon in the under 19 class (1) and won another in 1763 (2), at which time he was away in Paris, but generally resided in London with his guardian, Mr Emon of Soho. Dossie notes that he was taught by his father, a carver 'since dead' in 1763 (*Dossie* 1782, 437).

Literary References: *Dossie* 1782, 17 *Gunnis* 1968, 90; *Murdoch* 2006, 63

Archival References: RSA, Minutes, 1761–62, seq 3 fol 64

Reliefs

1.	1762	Model of a festoon	tc	[Soc of A premium, 7 gns]; untraced	RSA, *Minutes*, 1761–62, seq 3 f 64; *Dossie* 1782, 437
2.	1763	Clay festoon		[Soc of A, premium]; untraced	RSA, *Minutes*, 1762–63, seq 2 f 70

Miscellaneous

3.	1762	'piece of flowers'		[Exhib Free Soc, London]; untraced	RG/JP, 2, 279

CUFAUDE, Matthew 1731–96

He was in partnership with **Robert Page** from c1754 until Page's death in 1778, at which time his workshop address was the old yard on the quay near the custom house, Great Yarmouth. In the *Norfolk Chronicle* of 7 November 1778 Cafaude noted his 24-year association with Page, and informed 'the Public that he continues the Business of a STONE-MASON and CARVER, at the OLD YARD. where he has lately laid in a fresh Stock of Marble of various sorts, good Portland and other Stone fit for Building. . . He executes mural Monuments, cuts Coats of Arms on Marble Grave-Stones, Tombs, Head-Stones. . . Marble Chimney-Pieces &c. in the most modern Taste and neatest Manner'. He died in July 1796 aged 65, after a 'tedious illness' (*Norwich Mercury*, 6 August 1796), and a neatly-carved stone tablet commemorated him in St Nicholas, Yarmouth. His widow, Susanna, died in 1816, aged 93. Cufaude's yard and stock were taken over by **Henry Croskill** (*Norwich Gazette*, 30 July 1796). (Inf. Jon Bayliss)

Literary References: J Preston, *The Picture of Yarmouth*, 48 (tablet insc)

Will: PROB 11/1044

CUMBERWORTH, M –1852

Born in America, the son of an English officer and a Frenchwoman, he was taken to Paris as an infant and later studied sculpture there under the Swiss sculptor James Pradier (1790–1852). He appears to have lived in Paris throughout his life. In 1842 or 1843 he won from the Paris Academy the prize which would have enabled him to study in Rome, but on the eve of his departure it was discovered that he was not a Frenchman, and therefore not eligible for the award.

As the son of an Englishman, Cumberworth decided to send work to the Royal Academy in London in 1846, but unfortunately his group, *Paul and Virginia* (1), arrived two days after the official receiving date and could not be accepted. It was, however, later reproduced in parianware by Copeland and a large number of copies were sold. The *Art Union* reproduced the work to demonstrate the potential of the material to express the emotions and the educational benefits of reproducing art in affordable multiples. The *Art Journal* announced Cumberworth's death in Paris in 1852. They described him as 'a young and promising sculptor', known in England for his models for Copeland. His works, they added 'indicate pure taste and true talent combined with originality' (*AJ* 1852, 316).

Literary References: *AU* 1846, 299; *Gunnis* 1968, 118

Statues

1.	1846	Paul and Virginia		Untraced Other versions: reproduced in Copeland Parian ware		*Art U*, 1846, 299 (repr); *Gunnis* 1968, 118
2.	1851	The Indian fruit girl and the water-bearer, models for Copeland Parian ware statuettes		[Gt Exhib, London (parian statuettes)]; untraced		*AJ Cat* 1851, 167 (repr); *Art J* 1852, 316
3.	nd	Male and female slaves, group	b	[Phillips, 14 June 1856]; untraced		GPC

CUMMING, Sir William 1769–1852

For further information the reader is referred to *Pyke* 1973, 32.

CUMMINS, Robert fl 1793–1803

His works appear to date from the early-19th century and he can probably be identified with the carver and gilder of that name who worked at 23 South Bridge, Edinburgh from 1793 to 1803.

Literary References: *Woodward* 1977, vol 1, pt 2, 49

Busts

1.	nd	Rev Robertson DD	p	Aberdeen University Other versions: St Andrews University, plaster, signed	S	*Woodward* 1977, vol 1, pt 2, 49
2.	nd	William Smellie	p	SNPG		*Woodward* 1977, vol 1, pt 2, 49

CUNDY, James 1793–1826

The second son of Thomas Cundy, the architect, builder and surveyor of the Grosvenor estates in Belgravia and Pimlico, he enrolled at the Royal Academy Schools to study sculpture in January 1812. He appears to have exhibited at the Royal Academy in 1817 for his name appears in the index for the catalogue of that year, but unfortunately no details of the work were recorded. He showed literary subjects at the British Institution from 1817, giving his address as 7 Grosvenor Street West, and after 1823, simply as Pimlico.

He carved a number of memorial tablets, including one to Dr Benjamin Tate, illustrated in the *Gentleman's Magazine* of 1823 (4). His sepulchral works indicate an interest in Gothic architecture. He was employed as a designer and modeller by the silversmiths Rundell, Bridge and Rundell, and 'at the time of his death he was engaged in the design of one of the largest and most sumptuous vases ever made in England' (*GM* 1826, I, 569).

On 24 April 1826, while riding down Regent's Street, he was struck by the shaft of a butcher's cart, being 'driven at a furious rate from Piccadilly'. Cundy suffered a compound fracture of the leg that proved fatal. He died on 2 May 1826. The driver was later convicted of manslaughter and imprisoned. Cundy's obituary in the *Gentleman's Magazine* paid tribute to his intelligence, kindness and good humour. It recalled also his knowledge of the antique and of anatomy and the affection felt by his distinguished patrons. As a sculptor and modeller he apparently possessed 'an uncommon share of correct taste' (*ibid*, 569).

Literary References: *GM* 1826, I, 569; *Graves* 1875, 136; *Graves* II, 1905–6, 224; *Hutchison* 1960–62, 166; *Gunnis* 1968, 118; *Colvin* 1995, 284

Funerary Monuments

1.	†1813	Lady Heathcote	Edenham, Lincs	Pevsner, *Lincs*, 1989, 269
2.	?1815	Lemuel Shuldham	Marlesford, Suffolk	*Gunnis* 1968, 118
3.	?1822	George Tate	Mitcham, Surrey	*Gunnis* 1968, 118
4.	?1823	Dr Benjamin Tate (designed by Buckler)	Magdalen College, Oxford	*GM* 1823, 1, 133 (repr); *Gunnis* 1968, 118

Statues

5.	1825	Musidora	[Exhib Soc of BA, London, 351]; untraced	*Gunnis* 1968, 118; *Johnson* 1975, 115

Miscellaneous

6.	1817	Eve supplicating Adam, from Milton's 'Paradise Lost'	[Exhib BI, London, 239]; untraced	*Graves* 1875, 136
7.	1818	Comus, from Milton	[Exhib BI, London, 307]; untraced	*Graves* 1875, 136
8.	1818	The Judgement of Paris	[Exhib BI, London, 301]; untraced	*Graves* 1875, 136
9.	1823	Andromeda	[Exhib BI, London, 332]; untraced	*Graves* 1875, 136

CUNDY, Samuel 1816–67

The son of **James Cundy**, he was the mason responsible for repairs to Fulham Church in 1845 and built the staircase of Northumberland House, Charing Cross in 1851.

He worked under Sir George Gilbert Scott on repairs to churches in St Albans, including the Abbey Church and St Stephen's, and under the same architect he restored the monument to Philippa of Hainault in Westminster Abbey. Large fragments of this, including an entire alabaster canopy, had been purchased from **Thomas Gayfere III**, the Abbey mason, 35 years earlier and were located by Cundy at the museum of the noted Gothic revivalist architect L N Cottingham. The model, which was exhibited at the Great Exhibition, included figures by **John Birnie Philip** (7). Cundy used the Gothic style for the large tomb he executed to Lord Bateman (2).

Like other members of the family his practice was in Pimlico, where he also ran a marble works. His obituary commented that he was known for 'his portly person, always smiling lips, and rosy cheeks' (*Builder* 1867, 25, 464).

Literary References: *Builder*, 1852, 33; *Victorian Church Art*, 56; *Colvin* 1995, 284

Funerary Monuments

1.	?1838	William Gell	Westminster Abbey, London	*Gunnis* 1968, 118
2.	†1845	1st Lord Bateman	Kelmarsh, Northants, churchyard	*Gunnis* 1968, 118; Pevsner, *Northants*, 1973, 270

3.	?1846	General Sir William Clinton	Barkway, Herts		*Gunnis* 1968, 118
4.	†1847	Martha Sherborn	Bedfont, Middx		GPC
5.	?1848	Frederick Anson	St Luke, Chelsea, London		*Gunnis* 1968, 118
6.	?1849	Mr and Mrs Harris	Mitcham, Surrey		GPC
7.	1851	Model, reconstruction of the monument to Queen Philippa of Hainault (designed by Sir George Gilbert Scott)	VAM A.15-1973		*Victorian Church Art*, 56; *Bilbey* 2002, 354–5 (repr)
8.	1855	Sir Michael Hicks-Beach (†1854) (designed by G R Clarke)	Coln St Aldwyns, Glos, churchyard	S	*Gunnis* 1968, 118; Pevsner, *Glos: Cotswolds*, 1999, 299
Architectural Sculpture					
9.	1853	Font	St Gabriel, Pimlico		GPC
10.	1855	Reredos	North Marston, Bucks		*Gunnis* 1968, 118

CUNDY, Samuel Tansley fl before 1857

The name 'Samuel Tansley Cundy, Belgrave Wharf, Lower Belgrave Place, Pimlico, Statuary and mason' is listed under 'Bankrupts' in the *London Gazette* of 8 May 1857.

Archival References: GPC

CUNNINGHAM, Allan 1784–1842

Cunningham was a stonemason and long-term assistant to **Sir Francis Chantrey**. He was also a notable poet and one of the most influential early historians of British art. He was born in Keir, Dumfriesshire, on 7 December 1784, the 4th son of John Cunningham and Elizabeth Harley, was educated briefly in Quarrelwood and then apprenticed at the age of 11 to his brother, James, a stonemason of Dalswinton. By 1806 it was clear that Cunningham had literary ambitions and some of his works were published in *Literary Recreations* (1807). In 1809 he sent a series of ballads, penned by himself but presented as specimens of ancient Scottish songs, to the publisher R H Cromek. They were published in *Remains of Nithsdale and Galloway Song* (1809).

Cunningham left Scotland for London with Cromek's encouragement, arriving on 9 April 1810 and first found employment in the workshop of **J G Bubb**, at a wage of 26s a week, increased to 32s because of his superior abilities. He also wrote poetry for a journal, *The Day*, and published a volume of *Songs* in 1813. He married Jean Walker at Saint Saviour, Southwark on 1 July 1811.

In 1814 Chantrey, who had met Cunningham through Cromek, employed the Scotsman as a pointing assistant. Cunningham became Chantrey's superintendent of works at 27 Lower Belgrave Place, Pimlico, managed the workforce, conducted Chantrey's correspondence and proved an able publicist for the workshop. In April 1820 he published an account of Chantrey in *Blackwood's Edinburgh Magazine*. Cunningham combined his pivotal role within the business with a flourishing literary career: in 1822 he published two volumes of *Traditional Tales of the English and Scottish Peasantry*, and in 1825 4 volumes of *The Songs of Scotland, Ancient and Modern*.

In 1829 he published the first volume of *Lives Of The Most Eminent British Painters, Sculptors and Architects*, and five more followed during the next four years. The third volume, dedicated to Chantrey, comprised 9 biographies of sculptors from **Grinling Gibbons** to **John Flaxman**. Cunningham's intimate knowledge of sculpture and his penmanship make them the best informed and most readable histories of British sculptors of the 18th and early-19th centuries. The influence of his biographies, particularly that of **Anne Seymour Damer**, persisted into the 20th century, and their impact on sculptural historiography is matched only by the contemporary account of *Nollekens and his Times* by **J T Smith**. By Cunningham's own admission these were candid and opinionated sketches, in which all subjects received some level of adverse criticism. The essay on **John Bacon RA**, for instance, is so harsh in its critique of the sculptor's work and his pious personality that the author's son, Peter Cunningham, later publicly expressed his remorse to Bacon's son, **John Bacon II**. Further editions of the *Lives* were published in 1879, 1893 and 1908.

Cunningham's literary output in the 1830s included a number of romances and a biography of Robert Burns, as well as a series of articles on literary subjects in the *Athenaeum*. In 1841 the death of Chantrey ended their association, which had lasted for a quarter of a century. Some indication of Cunningham's pivotal role in the workshop is manifest in Chantrey's will, which directed that Cunningham ('my assistant and friend') was to continue to be employed after his death and to direct the completion of his remaining studio works by **Henry Weekes**. After these were finished and Cunningham had wound up Chantrey's affairs, he was to receive a legacy of £2,000 and an annuity of £100 for the rest of his natural life (PROB 11/1953/343). Unfortunately Cunningham soon died, on 29 October 1842, at 27 Lower Belgrave Place. He was buried in Kensal Green Cemetery on 4 November, where there is a monument to his memory carved by **M L Watson**. Another tablet by the same sculptor is in the church in Dumfries. His wife Jean survived him and received an annuity under the terms of Chantrey's will. The Reverend David Hogg published a *Life* of Cunningham in 1875.

MGS

Literary References: *Cunningham* 1820, 3–10; *Cunningham* 1829–33; *Hogg* 1875; *Esdaile* 1929 (1), 34, 37; *K-Browne* 1972 (3), 329; *ODNB* [Leslie Stephen, rev Hamish Whyte]

Additional MS Sources: Correspondence relating to the *Lives*, 1815–1841, Woodson Research Center, Fondren Library, Rice University, Houston, Texas, USA.

Portraits of the Sculptor: Henry Weekes, marble bust, 1842, SNPG (described in *AU* 1842, 129); Sir Francis Chantrey, plaster bust, SNPG; **F W Smith**, bust, 1823, untraced; **James Fillans**, marble bust, 1837, untraced

CUNNINGHAM, Francis fl 1729–c1740

He was made free of the Masons' Company via service to **Robert Taylor I** on 29 October 1729. A list of members of the Company dating from *c*1740 states that he was living in Piccadilly. William Cunningham, who may be a relation, was made free via service to **Walter Lee** in October 1734 and lived in Wardour Street *c*1740.

Archival References: Masons' Co, *Assistants* fol 5; Masons' Co, *Freemen*, fol 10; GPC

CUNNINGHAM, Patrick –1774

Strickland writes that Cunningham was the son of a wine-cooper from Dublin who won the lottery but squandered his winnings in a failed venture as a wine-merchant. He attended Robert West's drawing school in St George's Lane and was a prize-winner in 1748. The Dublin Society, who took a close interest in Cunningham's career, arranged his apprenticeship to **John Nost III** in May 1750. They provided other occasional support for the young sculptor including a bed and bed-clothes in 1750, and £5 to replenish his wardrobe in 1756, the last year of his apprenticeship. He was awarded a premium of £5 by the society in 1754, and under their patronage founded his own workshop. In August 1758 he advertised in *Faulkner's Journal* that he had 'opened a yard and shop in William Street, where he undertakes all manner of statuary work in clay, marble, brass, lead or plaster of Paris. As he is the first native that has been bred to that business he humbly hopes for the favour of the public' (*Strickland* 1913, 1, 247).

A number of busts are known from the early part of Cunningham's career. These include the celebrated portrait of Jonathan Swift, which Lord Macaulay described as 'much the best likeness of the Dean, striking and full of character' (**10**). Sir William Wilde noted that it 'exhibited the Dean's peculiar sloping forehead' (*Potterton* 1975, 42). Cunningham also worked in lead, and, like his master, John Nost III, appears to have run an extensive casting business. In March 1766, when based in College Green, he sold his collection of figures, including the *Farnese Hercules, Venus de Medici* and *The Sportsman*, as well as busts of modern and antique subjects, vases and moulds.

In 1766 Cunningham exhibited a number of wax portraits (**14**). The material, usually coloured, became a key part of his output in the following years. In 1767 he received the commission for a conversation piece of Richard Chappell Whaley, his wife and 7 children, apparently to be executed as a marble chimneypiece tablet. The tablet has not been located and may never have been executed, but a model thought to be for this work survives (**13**). It is a curious piece of genre sculpture depicting a vibrant, gesticulating family in a perspectival interior with black and white flagstones, modelled in gradated relief.

In 1772 he married a Miss Austin of Abbey Street and left Dublin to settle in London. His exhibited several works in wax at the Society of Artists exhibition, and in 1773 gave his address as Chidley Court, Pall Mall. He died in Paddington in December 1774. The *Hibernian Journal* of 14–16 December 1774 relates that he was 'a man of great fancy and imagination in architecture, statuary and waxwork, in the latter of which he excelled any in Europe, as may be seen by many of his performances' (*Strickland* 1913, 1, 249). He seems to have had only one pupil, the unnamed artist who advertised in *Faulkner's Dublin Journal* of 11–13 February 1777 that he was 'The only pupil the late ingenious and much regretted Mr Cunningham ever had, takes likenesses in wax at no 64, Dame Street' (*Pyke* 1973, 32).

Literary References: *Graves* 1907, 68; *Strickland* 1, 1913, 247–249; *Crookshank* 1966, 307; *Gunnis* 1968, 118–119; *Pyke* 1973, 32; *Potterton* 1975, 42; *Casey* 1995, 117–8

No.	Date	Work	Material	Location		References
Statues						
1.	1758	Dolphin, a 'figure'		[RDS]; untraced		*Strickland* 1913, 1, 247
2.	1758	Roman slave, a 'figure'		[RDS]; untraced		*Strickland* 1913, 1, 247
3.	1758	Venus, a 'figure'		[RDS]; untraced		*Strickland* 1913, 1, 247
4.	1760	King George II, equestrian		[RDS 10 guinea premium]; untraced		*Strickland* 1913, 1, 247–8
5.	1765	'The Farnesian Hercules'		[Exhib Soc of Artists, Dublin]; untraced		*Strickland* 1913, 1, 248
Busts						
6.	1759	John Lawson, librarian Payment(s): £34 2s		Trinity College, Dublin, Long Room		*Strickland* 1913, 1, 249; *Crookshank* 1986, 23
7.	1760	Frederick, King of Prussia	l	[Unidentified house in Prussia Street, exterior niche]; untraced		*Strickland* 1913, 1, 249
8.	1763	William Maple	m	RDS, Dublin	SD	*Crookshank* 1966, 307; *Harbison, Potterton and Sheehy* 1978, 173 (repr); *White and Bright* 1998, 55
9.	1765	Dean Delany	m	[Exhib Soc of Artists, Dublin]; untraced		*Strickland* 1913, 1, 248
10.	1766	Dean Jonathan Swift		[Exhib Soc of Artists, Dublin, coll George Faulkner, Parliament Square, Dublin]; Dublin Cathedral (since 1776) Other versions: NGI, marble		*Strickland* 1913, 1, 248; *Potterton* 1975, 42; *le Harivel* 1988, 558 (repr)
11.	1766	Several, of unidentified sitters	tc	[Exhib Soc of Artists, Dublin]; untraced		*Strickland* 1913, 1, 248
12.	1773	Unidentified gentleman, clay	tc	[Exhib Soc of Artists, London, 60]; untraced		*Graves* 1907, 68
Reliefs						
13.	1767	The family of Richard Chappell Whaley, model	w	Newman House, 86 St Stephen's Green, Dublin		*Casey* 1995, 117–8 (repr)
Miscellaneous						
14.	1766	'Portraits modelled in coloured wax'		[Exhib Soc of Artists, Dublin]; untraced		*Strickland* 1913, 1, 248
15.	1773	A group of children, coloured wax	w	[Exhib Soc of Artists, London, 61]; untraced		*Graves* 1907, 68
16.	1773	A madonna, in coloured wax	w	[Exhib Soc of Artists, London, 62]; untraced		*Graves* 1907, 68
17.	1773	A magdalen, in coloured wax	w	[Exhib Soc of Artists, London, 63]; untraced		*Graves* 1907, 68
18.	1773	Unidentified portraits in coloured wax, six	w	[Exhib Soc of Artists, London, 64–9]; untraced		*Graves* 1907, 68

CURRIE, Andrew fl 1855–81

Currie who worked at Darnick near Melrose between 1855 and 1881. He was responsible for statues of Mungo Park, in Selkirk, and James Hogg, 'the Ettrick Shepherd', on the banks of Loch St Mary in the Ettrick Valley. He also executed statues of *Edie Ochiltree* and *Old Mortality* for the Scott Monument in Edinburgh.

Literary References: *Woodward* 1977, vol 1, pt 2, 49–53; *Pearson* 1991, unpag.

CURRIE (or CORRIE), John *c*1820–79

Currie was born at Loch Foot near Dumfries and trained initially as a whinstone mason. He began to work in red and grey sandstone when he moved to Dumfries in the 1830s and in 1839 he exhibited a group, *Old Mortality and his pony* in Bond Street, Liverpool (3). The *Art Union* considered it 'very admirably executed in freestone – the size of life' (*AU*, 1, 1839, 116). Greatly encouraged by the success of this exhibition, he moved to Liverpool, where he began work on a group representing another two of Scott's characters, *Edie Ochiltree and Douster Swivel* (2). This was shown with *Old Mortality* in London in 1840. Another two statues inspired by Scottish literature, *Dominie Sampson* and *Meg Merrilies*, soon followed, but were not as well received as the earlier groups (4, 5).

Currie's stay in Liverpool did not bring the success he had hoped for and in the early 1840s he returned to Dumfries. There he raised funds by raffling the group of *Old Mortality*. It was won by an army surgeon, Dr Sinclair, who died in a gig accident near Chatham on the day the raffle was drawn. His executors presented the work to the Dumfries Museum and Observatory where an octagonal, open-sided temple was built to house it. Currie remained in Dumfries working as a portraitist and sculptor of architectural decorations from a studio at 130 High Street until his death on 31 December 1879. He was buried in St Michael's churchyard, Dumfries. Although his works are signed J Currie the sculptor's descendants, Richard and Alistair Corrie of Balmaclellan, claim the correct rendering of their grand-uncle's name to be Corrie.

Literary References: *Gunnis* 1968, 119; *Woodward* 1977, vol 1, pt 2, 49–53

Funerary Monuments					
1.	1870	Robert Paterson ('Old Mortality')	s	Caerlaverock Churchyard	*Woodward* 1977, vol 1, pt 2, 53
Statues					
2.	1839	Edie Ochiltree and Douster Swivel		Untraced	*AU*, Aug 1839, 116
3.	*c*1839	Old Mortality and his pony	s	Dumfries Museum and Observatory Other versions: Balmaclellan, Kircudbright coll Lord Templeton	*Gunnis* 1968, 119; *Woodward* 1977, vol 1, pt 2, 51–3
4.	*c*1841	Dominie Sampson	s	Carlton House, Kirkcudbright, gardens	*Gunnis* 1968, 119; *Woodward* 1977, vol 1, pt 2, 52
5.	*c*1841	Meg Merrilees	s	Carlton House, Kirkcudbright, gardens	*Gunnis* 1968, 119; *Woodward* 1977, vol 1, pt 2, 52
6.	nd	Cameron highlander	s	Private coll, Balmaclellan, Kircudbright	*Woodward* 1977, vol 1, pt 2, 53
7.	nd	Henry Duncan DD	m	Church Crescent, Dumfries Kircudbright	*Woodward* 1977, vol 1, pt 2, 53
8.	nd	The covenanter	s	Untraced	RG/JP, 3, 400
9.	nd	Unidentified recumbent male figure	s	Private coll, Balmaclellan, Kircudbrightshire	*Woodward* 1977, vol 1, pt 2, 53
Busts					
10.	1841	Mr Mackay, of the Theatre Royal Edinburgh		[Exhib R Sc A, Edinburgh, 550]; untraced	*Laperriere* 1, 1991, 381
11.	1842	Wellwood Maxwell	m	Dumfries Museum and Observatory	*Woodward* 1977, vol 1, pt 2, 53
12.	1848	Robert Thomson	m	Dumfries Museum and Observatory	*Woodward* 1977, vol 1, pt 2, 53
13.	*c*1850	Alexander Maxwell	m	Dumfries Museum and Observatory	*Woodward* 1977, vol 1, pt 2, 53
14.	nd	Richard Corrie	p	Private coll, Balmaclellan, Kircudbrightshire	*Woodward* 1977, vol 1, pt 2, 53
Architectural Sculpture					
15.	nd	Carved rope	s	St George's Hall, Buccleuch St, Dumfries	*Woodward* 1977, vol 1, pt 2, 53
16.	nd	Four lions and decorative carving	s	Dumfries Academy	*Woodward* 1977, vol 1, pt 2, 53
17.	nd	Hippocrates and Hygeia, two allegorial figures	s	Old Infirmary, Dumfries	*Woodward* 1977, vol 1, pt 2, 53
18.	nd	Sundial, gateposts, decorative fountain, vases and four lions	s	Holm House, Balmaclellan, Kircudbright	*Woodward* 1977, vol 1, pt 2, 53
19.	nd	Two lions	s	Gracefield Art Centre, Academy St, Dumfries	*Woodward* 1977, vol 1, pt 2, 53

CURTIS, F, of Bristol fl 1737–43

Gunnis described Curtis's monuments as 'large and important' and compared them stylistically to the works of the contemporary London sculptor **William Palmer**. The monuments produced by both workshops include a large acanthus leaf with out-turned leaves at their base. The monument to Thomas Rous (2) has fluted pilasters and an open pediment with an urn.

Literary References: *Gunnis* 1968, 119; Pevsner, *Glos: Cotswolds*, 1999, 757

Funerary Monuments					
1.	†1737	Henry Walter	Lord Mayor's Chapel, Bristol	S	*Gunnis* 1968, 119; *Eustace* 1982, 78 (repr)
2.	†1737	Thomas Rous	Wotton-under-Edge, Glos	S	*Gunnis* 1968, 119; Pevsner, *Glos: Cotswolds*, 1999, 757
3.	?1743	Thomas and Catherine George	Croscombe, Somerset	S	*Gunnis* 1968, 119

CURTIS, Laurentio fl 1671

Chimneypieces				
1.	1671	Description unavailable Payment(s): £12	[for Sir Robert Clayton's bank, Old Jewry, London]; untraced	Clayton & Morris, f 241 v; *Gunnis* 1968, 119

CURTIS FAMILY, of Norwich

Augustine Curtis I 1661–1731

Augustine Curtis II 1701–1732

The father and son together sign a monument in Norwich. On 20 October 1711 'Augustin Certis' (*sic*) advertised in the *Norwich Gazette* that he had moved to the White Swan in the market. The two men died within a year of one another and were buried at St Peter Mancroft, Norwich. Blomefield describes their monument as 'an unusual, but a well-looking composure, at the top is a shield, on which are the arms of Curtis. . supported by a neat pillar, surmounting a piece of marble, cut in the form of a pyramid.' The epitaph refers to them as 'carvers' and as 'son and grandson of John and Frances Curtis, late of this city'. They died on May 26 1731 and 26 October 1732 respectively (*Blomefield* 1745, 631).

An advertisement in the *Norwich Gazette* for 23 December 1732 noted that Mrs Deborah Curtis was the widow and executrix of the elder Augustine Curtis, and Mrs Deborah Curtis the Younger was the sister and executrix of **Augustine Curtis II**. On 24 March 1733, James Barrett advertised that he had taken over 'the stock and shop of Mr Augustine Curtis, deceased Carver, at the White Swan in St Peter's Mancroft.'

On 12 July 1698 Timothy Curtis was made free of the London Masons' Company via service to Deborah Curtis. She was perhaps the wife of Augustine I.

Literary References: *Gunnis* 1968, 119; RG/JP, 3, 400–1

Archival References: Masons' Co, Freemen, fol 8

Funerary Monuments

1.	?1728	Abigail Jenny		St John Maddermarket, Norwich	S	*Gunnis* 1968, 119

CUSHING, Joshua, of Norwich b 1775 † 1824

The son of Samuel Cushing, a church-carver of Norwich, he became a freeman of his native town in 1797. An advertisement in the *Norfolk Chronicle* of 6 June 1801 gave his address as 'opposite the Corn Exchange, Back Gate, St Andrew's, Norwich' and informed the public that he executed monuments, chimneypieces and gravestones. A few signed tablets by him are recorded in Norfolk. Another advertisement in *The Norwich Mercury* of 13 March 1802 gives his address as Bridge St Andrews and the *Norfolk Chronicle* of 16 June 1804 records a new domicile, Black Friar's Bridge. His first wife was Lydia, daughter of Mr Howard, a farmer of Flixton, whom he married in November 1803 (*Norwich Mercury* 12 Nov 1803).

In 1807 he exhibited in Norwich a 'beautiful' and 'neatly executed' model in stone for a proposed monument to Lord Nelson (3). This was from a design by Arthur Browne of Norwich. It took the form of an hexagonal temple with three triumphal entrance arches 'dedicated to the three grand victories'. Inside was a statue of the Admiral on a pedestal and there were rusticated pilasters, niches and tablets for inscriptions. It 'terminated with a hexagonal obelisk' (*GM* 1807, 126).

Cushing was declared bankrupt in 1813 (*Norwich Mercury*, 3 April 1813) and on 12 June it was announced that James Palmer had taken over his premises. Cushing, then 'late of Black Friars Bridge,' was again made bankrupt in 1816 (*Norwich Mercury*, 20 July, 3 August). He died at Norwich in 1824 and was survived by his second wife, Elizabeth, who died at the age of 69 in Norwich in 1850.

The death of a 'Samuel Cushing Jnr', presumably a relation, 'of the Parish of St Giles, Carver and Gilder' was announced in the *Norfolk Chronicle* on 13 January 1821. The advertisement solicited support for his widow and six children who were deprived of any immediate support. (Add inf. David Cubitt)

Literary References: *Gunnis* 1968, 119

Archival References: GPC; RG/JP, 3, 400

Funerary Monuments

1.	?1804	John Kerrison		Ranworth, Norfolk	S	*Gunnis* 1968, 119
2.	?1806	John Basely		St Saviour, Norwich	S	*Gunnis* 1968, 119
3.	1807	Admiral Lord Nelson, model in the form of an hexagonal temple (designed by Arthur Browne)	s	[Exhib Norwich]; untraced		*GM* 1807, 126; *Gunnis* 1968, 119
4.	?1808	Charles Garneys		Much Haddenham, Norfolk	S	*Gunnis* 1968, 119; Pevsner, *Cambs*, 1970, 400
5.	?1810	Rev Samuel Newton		Old Meeting House, Norwich		GPC
6.	?1817	Harriet Stracey		Rackheath, Norfolk	S	*Gunnis* 1968, 119

CUSWORTH, John, of Stoke Newington 1795–1856

A monumental mason whose address in 1830 was given as 'Near the bridge,' Stoke Newington. His monument, or rather mausoleum, to Andrew Ducrow, the equestrian circus performer and proprieter of Astley's Ampitheatre, was erected in 1837 (1). It is a fantastic work in the Graeco-Egyptian style, combining brick, marble and artificial stone, and decorated with reliefs of horses, angels, sphinxes, genii and bee-hives. Ducrow had it built in his lifetime to contain the body of his first wife at a cost of £3,000. He himself was buried in it in 1842, leaving in his will the further sum of £800 to 'decorate' the tomb. It is immodestly inscribed 'Erected by Genius for the reception of its own remains.' Gunnis was perplexed by the work, saying that 'among the many strange and curious monuments which throng Kensal Green Cemetery this is by far the most bizarre'.

Literary References: *Gunnis* 1968, 119; *Curl* 2001, 189, 218

Funerary Monuments

1.	1837	Andrew Ducrow, mausoleum (designed by George Danson) Payment(s): £3000		Kensal Green Cemetery, London		*Gunnis* 1968, 119; *Curl* 2001, 189–90, 218, 239 (repr)

CUSWORTH, of Stamford Hill fl 1864–70?

Presumably the heir of **John Cusworth of Stoke Newington**, he signs the inscription tablet surmounted by a pediment with a five-pointed star to John Mason (1). A Cusworth of Pentonville Road, London signs the monument to the Rev Joseph Pemberton (†1870) at Gingerland, Nevis, West Indies.

Funerary Monuments

1.	†1864	Rev John Mason		Wesley's Chapel, City Road, London	S	

DACRE, Lady Barbarina Brand 1768–1854

A poet, dramatist and amateur wax modeller. For further information the reader is referred to *Pyke* 1973, 35 and *Pyke* 1981, 12.

DAINTRY (or DAINTREE), John *c*1739–

In 1760, when 'under 22' and an apprentice of **Thomas Carter II**, he won a premium from the Society of Arts, followed by two others in 1761 and 1764 (1–3). Carter later employed him to carve tablets for chimneypieces. Dossie described him as 'ornamental carver, London'. A Henry Daintry, who could conceivably be a relative of this sculptor, became free of the Masons' Company through service to Mary Easton, on 6 October 1737. He later had premises in Aldersgate Street.

Literary References: *Dossie* 1782, 437; *Gunnis* 1968, 120

Archival References: Masons' Co, Assistants, fol 5; Masons' Co, Freemen, fol 13; RSA Minutes, 1758–60 seq 4, 50 53; 1760–61, seq 3 fol 48

Reliefs

1.	1764	Mucius Scaevola before Porsenna, clay model	[Soc of A, premium, 5 gns]; untraced	RSA, *Minutes*, 1763–64, seq 3 f 83; RSA, *Premiums*, 1763, 37

Miscellaneous

2.	1760	Clay model	[Soc of A, premium]; untraced	RSA *Minutes*, 1758–60, seq 1 f 50, seq 4 f 53
3.	1761	Clay model	[Soc of A, premium, 9 gns]; untraced	RSA *Minutes*, 1760–61, seq 3 f 48

DALE, Thur fl 1703

This cryptic signature appears on a monument to D Dale. The executant or designer was presumably a relative of the deceased.

Funerary Monuments

1.	†1703	D Dale	Bakewell, Derbys	S	

DALY, John fl 1720–50

Little is known of this sculptor, who may have received some training from **William Kidwell**. Both his known monuments are strongly architectural. His advertisement in the *Munster Journal* of February 1749–50 announced that 'John Daly, Marble Mason' had newly imported from London 'a large quantity of Ornaments of Stone and Lead such as Statues, Urns, Flower-potts, Vases, Pines, Lions, eagles, Foxes, hares, Rabetts and Sun Dial Pedestals, which goods he will sell cheaper than any gentleman can import; he likewise has imported a great sortment of British Window Glass' (*Potterton* 1975, 42).

Literary References: *Strickland* 1, 1913, 252

Funerary Monuments

1.	†1720	David Fleming	Doneraile, Co Cork	S	*Potterton* 1975, 42; *Strickland* 1, 1913, 252
2.	†1745	John Lysaght	Ballyclough, Co Cork		*Potterton* 1975, 42

DALZIEL, James *c*1779–1836

In 1820 James Dalziel succeeded to the Leith Walk marble cutting business previously owned by John Marshall and in the next two decades developed it into one of the more important workshops in Edinburgh. The firm acquired an international reputation and received several orders for decorative work from abroad, in particular from Brazil. Dalziel died on 13 August 1836, aged 57, and was buried in Calton Hill Burial Ground, Edinburgh.

Literary References: *Woodward* 1977 (vol 1, pt 2), 54

Funerary Monuments

1.	†1824	Colonel J Walker	St Andrew's Kirk, Chennai (Madras), India	S	GPC

DAMER, Anne Seymour 1748–1828

The only child of Field-Marshal Henry Conway, a distinguished soldier and Whig politician, and Lady Caroline, née Campbell, daughter of the 4th Duke of Argyll, Damer was born at Coomb Bank, Sundridge, Kent. Her father's cousin, Horace Walpole, acted as Damer's guardian when her parents were abroad, and took a close interest in the child from an early age: 'you know how courteous a Knight I am to distressed virgins of five years old' he wrote in a letter to Henry Conway (quoted in *Noble* 1908, 5). Accounts of 'Missy's' intellectual development recurred in Walpole's correspondence from her early childhood. He later recalled that she first displayed her talent for sculpture at 10 years old, when she modelled a Spenserian subject in period costume from pieces of candle wax. She later modelled dogs in bas-relief and heads 'in the manner of **Isaac Gosset**' (*HWC*, vol 12, 273). Walpole was quick to hail the arrival of an important artist: 'Goodnight. . . to the Infanta, whose progress in waxen statuary advances so fast that by next winter she may rival Rackstrow's olde man [presumably **Benjamin Rackstrow**]' (*Noble* 1908, 5). An anecdote, related much later by Allan Cunningham, reveals that it was her father's secretary, the philosopher and historian, David Hume, who first sparked Damer's talent. Apparently the child mocked the work of an itinerant plaster-modeller and Hume challenged her to produce something better.

On 14 June 1767 she married John Damer, the eldest son of Lord Milton (afterwards Earl of Dorchester) at Park Place. Her husband, who was heir to a great fortune, was a hopeless spend-thrift, and Damer too appears to have indulged in the trappings of high rank and fortune: her ear-rings alone were reputedly worth £4,000. The marriage was not a happy one and the couple separated. On 15 August 1776 he committed suicide in a tavern, the Bedford Arms in Covent Garden. Something of the scale of his spending is reflected in the extent of his wardrobe, which was sold after his death for £15,000.

Cunningham suggests that sculpture provided a consolation for Damer after the breakdown of her marriage. Another, anonymous account, in French and possibly autobiographical, says that the event led to a decision to engage less with the fashionable world and to pursue her desire to be an *artist* rather than a *dilettante* (quoted in *Yarrington* 1997, 33). Damer took 'two or three lessons' in modelling from **Giuseppe Ceracchi**, who was probably introduced to her by Walpole (*Anecdotes* 1937, 142). The Italian arrived in England in 1773 and subsequently immortalised Damer in a marble statue as *The Muse of Sculpture*. She received 6 lessons in carving from **John Bacon RA** and lessons in anatomy were provided by the surgeon William Cumberland Cruickshank. According to Walpole her 'first effort in marble' dated from 1780 and was the head of a *Niobed* (**19**, *HWC*, vol 12, 272); this conflicts with the account of John Gould who claims that a self-portrait in marble executed in 1778 was her first work (**18**). In 1784 she exhibited at the Royal Academy as an amateur or 'Honorary Exhibitor' (*Graves* II, 1905–6, 235), showing a bust of Lady Melbourne, a group of dogs and an ideal subject (**21, 5, 65**). In 1786 she received an important commission for two colossal keystones for the new bridge at Henley (**53**). These, like the *Niobed*, are carved in a broad manner, imitative of Greek sculpture. In the 1780s she was responsible for several works in which Society figures were glorified as antique characters, including Peniston Lamb as *Mercury* (**26**) and Prince Henry Lubomirski as *Bacchus* (**29**), both of which carry inscriptions in Greek. In addition to her other talents, Damer was apparently a classical scholar.

Her efforts were eulogised by her friends. Horace Walpole compared her favourably to Bernini and the sculptors of antiquity. He had the words 'Non me Praxiteles finxit at Anna Damer' cut on the terra-cotta model of a fishing-eagle which she presented to him in 1787 (**7**). On two of her early portraits Erasmus Darwin penned the lines: 'long with soft touch shall Damer's chisel charm/ with grace delight us and with beauty warm/ Forster's (**32**) fine form shall hearts unborn engage/ and Melbourne's smile enchant another age (**21**).' Sir William Hamilton, who was visited by Damer in Naples in 1782, felt that her *Ceres* excelled the work of any living Italian (**20**). She was in Italy again between October 1785 and July 1786 when she executed a profile portrait of a British visitor, Lady Elizabeth Foster (**58**).

In November 1790 Damer left England for Portugal for her health's sake. There she appears to have modelled a statue of King Joseph I, which was cast in Lisbon (**10**). She proceeded to Spain, where she visited the Alhambra, and then to France. After her return to London in May 1791 she completed the statue of George III for the Register House at Edinburgh (**12**). This commission came in 1787 through the good offices of her uncle, Lord Frederick Campbell, the Lord Clerk Register of Scotland. It was exhibited at the Rotunda, Blackfriars Road, London, in 1793. Its finishing touches were a bronze crown and sceptre, cast by the clockmaker Benjamin Vulliamy. A portrait of her close friend Mary Berry, also in bronze, dates from around this time and may have been cast by the same firm (**34**).

Damer was a high-profile public figure, and was praised and noticed for a variety of personal attributes and pursuits. A *Sapphick Epistle*, portraying her as a lesbian, appeared in 1771. As an 'inveterate Whig' she sympathised with the American Revolution and canvassed for Charles James Fox in the Westminster Election of 1784, with other notable aristocratic women, particularly Georgiana, Duchess of Devonshire (*Cunningham* 1829–33, 3, 255). Her sculptural pretensions, and perhaps the impropriety of a woman nurturing them, were satirised in a print entitled *The Damerian Apollo*, 1789, which portrayed Damer in a billowing dress, her hammer and chisel poised to emasculate a statue of the god.

She had an equivocal reputation with professional artists. Farington, for instance, balanced his interest in her as a celebrity (focussing particularly on her physical attributes) with a mistrust of her qualifications as a sculptor. After he accompanied Damer and Miss Berry to the Royal Academy exhibition of 1796 he commented 'the observations of Mrs Damer did not seem to me to prove that she has any exact knowledge of painting, whatever she may have of sculpture; and she did not make intelligent remarks on the latter. I think her manner and particularly her voice very affected and unpleasing' (*Farington* 2, 571). Although it was never doubted that Damer carried out her own modelling and it was common sculptural practice to employ assistants to carry out most of the heavy cutting work, Damer was criticised for using other hands in the course of her work. **James Smith II** was one of those assisting her and he helped undermine her reputation by claiming that 'she could carve little or none: I carved most of her busts for her' (*Cunningham* 1829–33, 3, 272).

Horace Walpole died early in 1797. He left Damer £4,000 and his beloved Gothic home, Strawberry Hill, with £2,000 per annum for its upkeep. Farington writes that Mrs Damer's behaviour became increasingly erratic and she took to wearing 'a man's hat, and shoes, and a jacket also like a man's – thus she walks abt the fields with a hooking stick'. He also ridiculed the ostentatious fondness she demonstrated for her friends, the Miss Berrys, from whom she took leave with such ecstasy that the servants compared the ritual to a parting before death (*Farington* 3, 1048). She remained at Strawberry Hill until 1811 and there organised a number of theatrical events, written and performed by herself and her circle. William Lamb's play *The Fashionable Friends. . .spoken by Hon Anne S Damer* was published in 1801. Around the same time she penned a novel, *Belmour*, which was republished in 1827. Damer's theatricality was central to Cunningham's critique of her character, for he presented her as impersonating the role of a deluded artist in a melodrama.

In November 1799, shortly after the Battle of the Nile, Damer modelled a portrait of Lord Nelson *ad vivum*. In the following years she presented busts of the Admiral to Napoleon Bonaparte (**36**) and the Corporation of London (**38**). The former was given to the First Consul in 1802 when Damer, his admirer and a friend of his wife, visited France during the Peace of Amiens. She also gave him her bust of Charles James Fox (**37**). The bust of Nelson for the Corporation was praised in a piece by Thomas Hope in the *Morning Post* on 5 May 1804, in which he admired the 'breadth of style. . . discarding every incidental minutiae' and the 'simplicity of attitude inseparable from real dignity' (*Yarrington* 1997, 37). Damer personally distributed 50 copies of the article. Here, as on numerous other occasions, the eulogies of her literary friends and admirers were at odds with the opinions of professional artists and art historians. Cunningham considered the bust crude and Farington regarded Hope's article as 'most extravagant & false & ridiculous' (*Farington* 9, 3223–4). **Lawrence Gahagan** cast a slur on Damer's status when he advertised his own bust of Nelson in *The Times* of 16 December 1805 as 'the only professional sculpted bust of the hero' (*Yarrington* 1997, 41). Damer's own confidence as a sculptor can be seen in her decision to compete against her professional counterparts for the commission to provide Nelson's monument after his death in 1805. The decision indicates that Damer had the workshop facilities, either at home or through subcontractors, to carry out such a large commission. In the event the job went to James Smith II, who narrowly defeated **J C F Rossi** in the final ballot.

Later that decade Damer executed two monuments for members of her family, both with busts. Her mother's is frontal, *all'antica*, and is now badly damaged (**2**). That to her grandmother is slightly turned, has arms and a naturalistic double chin. Some busts of the 1810s are innovative: the head of Caroline, Princess of Wales, has a slip of carved drapery round the head, which crosses over the breastbone (**44**). The bust of Sir Humphrey Davy is signed in Greek but is more naturalistic than classicising, conveying a good deal of character through the upturned corners of the scientist's mouth and the wisp of hair across his forehead (**42**). When she was advanced in years she had casts of her bust of Nelson made for the Duke of Clarence and the Rajah of Tanjore (**46**). Cunningham's satirical account suggests that the latter was presented in the belief that her art could civilise the Rajah's country. The Rajah thanked Alexander Johnston, Damer's relative who presented the bust, for 'a very beautiful specimen of an elegant art' (*Lit Gaz*, 1829, 427).

Damer died at her home in Upper Brook Street on 28 May 1828, and was buried at Sundridge. Her grave is marked with a plain slab carved with coats of arms and an epitaph requested in her will: 'HIC PROPE JACET, UNO CHARACUM MATRE IN LOCO, ANN SEYMOUR DAMER SCULPTRIX ET STATUARIA, ILLUSTRIS FEMINA'. She desired that her mallet, chisel, apron and the ashes of a favourite dog ('Fidèle') should be placed in her coffin. Damer also requested that when she was assumed to be dead her body should be 'thrown into quick lime. . . so as to prevent the possibility of my being buried alive, an idea which has always presented itself to my imagination with peculiar dread and horror'. She left her properties, York House, and Upper Brook Street, to relatives and large sums of money to servants and family. A snuff-box given to her by Napoleon was bequeathed to the British Museum. A sale of her extensive library was held in 1828, part of which is now at the Yale Center for British Art in New Haven.

Damer's biographers have been ambivalent about the importance of sculpture in her life's achievements. The obituarist writing for the *Gentleman's Magazine* accorded her the status of 'celebrated. . . amateur sculptor' and presented her art as one remarkable part of a generally notable and active aristocratic life. He referred to her works as 'gifts', indicators of friendship divorced from economic pressures (*Noble* 1908, 224). A similar approach can be seen in Percy Noble's biography, *Mrs Damer A Woman of Art and Fashion*, 1908, which, as its title suggests, deals as much with Damer's thespian and other social activities as with her sculptural work. For the professional artistic community, however, Damer presented a number of challenges. She could not be dismissed as a bumbling amateur since her commitment to her craft was tangible and her abilities were admitted to be of a very high standard. Cunningham's influential and nuanced *Life* presents her as a woman of deluded faith in her own genius who hoped to discard her aristocratic lineage and replace it with an immortal reputation as an artist. Cunningham expressed admiration for this ambition. The tragedy, however, as he presented it, was that Damer had no genius, her works were uneven in quality, and she would have received little or no notice had it not been for her rank and her rejection of the mental and physical expectations of a lady of quality. Of her works he was scathing, writing: 'She exhibits few symptoms of poetic feeling. . .she aspires only to the gentle and the agreeable; there is little of dignity in her Thalia (**30**) – of heroism in her Nelson – or of intellectual capacity in her Fox' (*Cunningham* 1829–33, 3, 273).

Latter-day accounts have addressed Damer's work largely within the same evaluative frameworks. Gunnis based his entry on *Cunningham* and on the very similar biography by John Gould. Noble offered little defence of his subject's artistic efforts, which he felt were 'rather rough and unfinished' (*Noble* 1908, viii). Whinney praised Damer's naturalistic treatment of animals, but presented her merely as an agreeable eccentric, and remarked that her Henley keystones were only 'an unusual achievement for a young lady of quality' (*Whinney* 1988, 319). Damer's practice and reputation have recently been reassessed in a thesis by Benforado and an article by Yarrington. The latter focusses closely on all aspects of the making of Damer's reputation and on the ways in which her gender, privileged background and semi-professional sculptural practice were negotiated in contemporary and near-contemporary biographies.

MGS

Literary References: *HWC*, vol 12, *passim*; *Farington*, vols 1–9, *passim*; *Cunningham* 1829–33, 3, 247–273; *Gould* 1834, 132; *Noble* 1908; *Anecdotes* 1937, 46, 49, 142, 172, 236–38; *Gunnis* 1968, 120–121; *Neoclassicism* 1972, 229–230; *Pyke* 1973, 36; *Benforado* 1986; *Yarrington* 1988, 92–4; *Whinney* 1988, 319; *Yarrington* 1997, 32–44; *Dawson* 1999, 30–2; *Pettit and Spedding* 2002, 2, 5

Archival References: GPC

Additional Archival References: Lewis Walpole Library, Farmington; Brynmor Jones Library, Hull University; BL MS 37727 ff143–275; Nat Library of Scotland, MS Coll, MS 629 ff1–52

Will: PROB 11/1741

Auction Catalogues: Damer 1828

Representations of the Sculptor: Angelica Kauffman, 1766, private coll (frontispiece to *Noble* 1908); Sir Joshua Reynolds, 1773, canvas, NPG (594) and YCBA (repr *Yarrington* 1997, 36); Giuseppe Ceracchi, *Anne Seymour Damer as the Muse of Sculpture*, c1777, marble, BM; Richard Cosway, 1785, watercolour on ivory, NPG (5236), engraved by W C Edwards for *Cunningham* 1829–33, 3, 247; H. Carr watercolour, 1788 SNPG; William Holland, *The Damerian Apollo* (satirical print), 1789, BM; anon, Came House (repr *Noble* 1908, opp 48); Richard Cosway, canvas, nd (repr *Noble* 1908, opp 98)

Funerary Monuments

1.	1807	Admiral Lord Nelson, 'sketch'		[Exhib RA, London, 1000]; untraced		*Graves* II, 1905–6, 236
2.	1808	Lady Caroline Conway (†1808)		Sundridge, Kent	SD	*Gould* 1834, 133; *Noble* 1908, 79; Pevsner, *Kent: W & Weald*, 1976, 554
3.	1808	Maria Bellenden, wife of the 4th Duke of Argyll (†1780)		Sundridge, Kent		Pevsner, *Kent: W & Weald*, 1976, 554

Statues

4.	c1784	A dog	tc	Chillington Hall, Staffs		*Whinney* 1988, 319
5.	c1784	Two sleeping dogs Model(s): t-c untraced, formerly Strawberry Hill	m	Goodwood, Sussex, tapestry room	S	*HWC*, vol 12, 272; *Gould* 1834, 133; *Noble* 1908, 81; *Gunnis* 1968, 120 (repr 7); *Treasure Houses* 1985, 301 (repr)
6.	1785	Two kittens, small	tc	['At Lady Melbourne's' ?Exhib RA, London, 641]; untraced		*HWC*, vol 12, 272
7.	1787	An osprey or fishing eagle	tc	[Exhib RA, London, 617 Presented to Horace Walpole]; untraced		*HWC*, vol 12, 272; *Gould* 1834, 133; *Graves* II, 1905–6, 235; *Noble* 1908, 79; *Gunnis* 1968, 120

No.	Date	Title	Material	Location	Signed	Literary References
8.	1788	Her own terrier (very like a greyhound), size of life, lying down, but as if listening eagerly, and ready to rise Model(s): t-c, 1787, untraced	m	Untraced		*HWC*, vol 12, 273
9.	1789	Two kittens, group	m	[for Horace Walpole, Strawberry Hill, Twickenham, Middx]; untraced		*HWC*, vol 12, 274; *Gould* 1834, 133; *Graves* II, 1905–6, 235; *Noble* 1908, 81
10.	*c*1791	King Joseph I of Portugal	b	[Lisbon, Portugal]; untraced		*Noble* 1908, 127; *Yarrington* 1997, 39, n59
11.	1792	Apollo		[Drury Lane Theatre, London]; destroyed		*Gunnis* 1968, 120; *Yarrington* 1997, 39
12.	1790–1794	King George III Model(s): t-c, 1787, 7ft high, untraced	m	Register House, Edinburgh		*HWC*, vol 12, 273–4; *Noble* 1908, opp p 75, 79 (repr); *Yarrington* 1997, 32
13.	nd	A greyhound, whole figure, smaller than life	tc	Untraced		*HWC*, vol 12, 272
14.	nd	A shock dog, whole figure	tc	['At General Conway's']; untraced		*HWC*, vol 12, 272
15.	nd	Dog	m	[Presented to Queen Charlotte]; untraced		*Gould* 1834, 133
16.	nd	Seated woman, statuette	tc	Chillington Hall, Wolverhampton		C Lib (repr)
17.	nd	Two kittens		Came House, Dorset		*Manchester Art Treasures* 1857, 135; *Gunnis* 1968, 120
Busts						
18.	1778	Self-portrait	m	Uffizi, Florence Other versions: several recorded		*Gould* 1834, 133; *Yarrington* 1997, 38; *Dawson* 1999, 90; C Lib (repr)
19.	1780	Niobed	m	Private coll	SD	*HWC*, vol 12, 272; *Yarrington* 1997, 37 n51; C Lib (repr)
20.	1782	Ceres, over life-size		[Executed in Naples]; untraced		*Yarrington* 1997, 37
21.	1784	Lady Melbourne	m	[Exhib RA, London, 499]; private coll		*HWC*, vol 12, 272; *Gould* 1834, 133; *Graves* II, 1905–6, 235; *Yarrington* 1997, 37, 38 (repr)
22.	1785	General Conway, the sculptor's father, in a helmet	tc	Untraced		*HWC*, vol 12, 272; *Gould* 1834, 133
23.	1785	Lady Melbourne's son, Frederick James Lamb, as infant Mercury	m	Untraced		*HWC*, vol 12, 272
24.	1785	Self-portrait, large as life	tc	Untraced		*HWC*, vol 12, 272
25.	1786	Self-portrait		Accademia di San Luca		*Neoclassicism* 1972, 230
26.	1787	Hon Peniston Lamb as Mercury	m	[Exhib RA, London, 625]; Sotheby, 10 Dec 2002	S	*HWC*, vol 12, 272; *Gould* 1834, 133; *Graves* II, 1905–6, 235; *Penny* 1992, III, 33; C Lib (repr)
27.	1787	Jupiter Serapis, repairs only		[coll Horace Walpole]; untraced		*HWC*, vol 12, 272–3
28.	1787	Miss Farren, the actress	tc	Untraced		*HWC*, vol 12, 273
29.	1788	Portrait of Prince Henry Lubomirski in the character of Bacchus	m	Ashmolean WA 1908.208	S	*HWC*, vol 12, 273; *Gould* 1834, 133; *Graves* II, 1905–6, 235; *Penny* 1992, III, 32–3 (repr)
30.	1789	Elizabeth Farren, Countess of Derby, as the muse Thalia	m	[Exhib RA, London, 585]; NPG, London 4469	S	*HWC*, vol 12, 274; *Gould* 1834, 133; *Graves* II, 1905–6, 235
31.	post-1789	Lady Ailesbury, veiled	m	Untraced		*HWC*, vol 12, 272, 273, 274
32.	*c*1789	Lady Elizabeth Foster, afterwards Duchess of Devonshire	m	untraced		*Gould* 1834, 133; *Gunnis* 1968, 120
33.	*c*1789	Miss Freeman as Isis Model(s): t-c	m	[Exhib RA, London, 613 Coll Thomas Hope]; VAM A.31-1931	S	*HWC*, vol 12, 274; *Gould* 1834, 133; *Graves* II, 1905–6, 235; *Watkin* 1968, 49; *Yarrington* 1997, 38 (repr); *Bilbey* 2002, 70 (repr)
34.	*c*1790	Mary Berry	b	NPG, London Other versions: Chillington Hall, Wolverhampton, bronze, SD 1793 (C Lib repr) Christie, London 10 Dec 1991, bronze, signed		*HWC*, vol 12, 274; *ILN* 11 Dec 1852, 517 (repr); *Berry Journals* 1865, 1, 160; *Clifford* 2000, 463 (repr)
35.	1795	Mrs Siddons as Melpomene, cast		[Exhib RA, London, 733]; untraced		*HWC*, vol 12, 274; *Graves* II, 1905–6, 235
36.	1802	Admiral Lord Nelson		[Coll Napoleon Bonaparte, Tuileries, Paris]; untraced		*Farington* V, 1848; *Gunnis* 1968, 120
37.	1802	Charles James Fox		[Presented to Napoleon Bonaparte]; Musée de Versailles, France		*Farington* V, 1848 (repr); *Gould* 1834, 133; *Graves* II, 1905–6, 235; *Gunnis* 1968, 120
38.	1803	Admiral Lord Nelson	m	CL Coll, Guildhall, City of London, acc 81 Other versions: Plaster casts offered for sale in *The Times*, 23 Nov 1805		*Gould* 1834, 133; *Graves* II, 1905–6, 235; *Knight* 1986, 334 (repr); *Yarrington* 1997, 37, 41
39.	1805	Master W H Betty		[Exhib RA, London, 784]; untraced		*Graves* II, 1905–6, 235

40.	1806	Sir Joseph Banks Bt		[Exhib RA, London, 838]; untraced		*Graves* II, 1905–6, 235
41.	1810	A muse	b	[Exhib RA, London, 884]; untraced		*Gould* 1834, 133; *Graves* II, 1905–6, 236
42.	1813	Professor Sir Humphrey Davy Model(s): Exhib RA, London, 1814, 768, terracotta	p	R I, London	SD	*Gould* 1834, 133; *Graves* II, 1905–6, 236; C Lib (repr)
43.	1813	Sir Joseph Banks Model(s): t-c, untraced	b	[Exhib RA, London, 912]; BM	S	*Gould* 1834, 133; *Graves* II, 1905–6, 236; *Dawson* 1999, 29–32
44.	1814	Caroline, Princess of Wales	tc	Ranger's House, Blackheath, London	SD	*Berry Journals* 1865, 3, 1; *Yarrington* 1997, 40
45.	1823	Self-portrait	m	[coll Richard Payne Knight]; BM	SD	*Gould* 1834, 133; *Dawson* 1999, 90
46.	1827	Admiral Lord Nelson (†1805)	b	[coll Duke of Clarence, presented by the sculptress]; Windsor Castle, RCIN 20743 (1829) Other versions: several known plaster replicas	SD	*Noble* 1908, 83; C Lib (repr)
47.	nd	Dawson Damer (the sculptor's husband)		Drayton, Northants		*Gunnis* 1968, 120; C Lib (repr)
48.	nd	Duke of Richmond	p	Goodwood, Sussex		*Gunnis* 1968, 120
49.	nd	Mercury ('Her own design')	p	[?Exhib RA, London, 1784, 521]; untraced		*HWC*, vol 12, 272; *Graves* II, 1905–6, 235
50.	nd	Miss Campbell, 'large as life'	tc	Untraced		*HWC*, vol 12, 272
51.	nd	Queen Caroline ('the late')	tc	Untraced		*Gould* 1834, 133
52.	nd	Self-portrait	m	Drayton, Northants		*Gunnis* 1968, 120; C Lib (repr)

Architectural Sculpture

53.	1786	Heads of the rivers Thame and Isis Model(s): coll Mrs Airey Neave, t-c	s	Henley Bridge, Oxon		*Gould* 1834, 133; *Graves* II, 1905–6, 235; *Noble* 1908, 79–80 (repr); *Neoclassicism* 1972, 230; *Whinney* 1988, 319
54.	nd	Nymph and urn, bas-relief for fountain at Buxton		[Plaster model exhib RA, London, 624 ('Hygeia, design for a fountain at Buxton, a cast')]; untraced		*HWC*, vol 12, 272; *Graves* II, 1905–6, 235

Reliefs

55.	1783	Princess Daskiou's daughter, medallion	m	['sent to Russia']; untraced		*HWC*, vol 12, 272
56.	1785–6	Lady Elizabeth Foster	w	[Executed in Italy]; untraced Other versions: Marble copy, for Duchess of Devonshire, untraced clay, 1789; untraced		*HWC*, vol 12, 272, 274
57.	nd	A shock dog, small bas-relief	w	[Park Place]; untraced		*HWC*, vol 12, 271
58.	nd	Anthony and Cleopatra Payment(s): 4 gns at Boydell's sale	tc	[Boydell's Shakespeare Gallery]; untraced		Boydell sale, 17 May 1805, lot 14; *HWC*, vol 12, 274; *Noble* 1908, 82 (repr)
59.	nd	Bas-relief of a scene from Coriolanus	tc	[for Boydell's Shakespeare Gallery]; untraced		*HWC*, vol 12, 274; *Noble* 1908, 82 (repr)
60.	nd	Coriolanus's triumphal return Payment(s): 3 gns at Boydell's sale	tc	[for Boydell's Shakespeare Gallery]; untraced		Boydell Sale, May 17 1805, lot 16; *HWC*, vol 12, 274
61.	nd	Lady Ailesbury, profile	w	[Park Place]; untraced		*HWC*, vol 12, 271
62.	nd	Miss Caroline Campbell, profile 'in the manner of Gosset'	w	['Park Place']; untraced		*HWC*, vol 12, 271
63.	nd	Sir Joseph Banks	w	Art Inst Chicago		*Pyke* 1973, 36 (repr 68)
64.	nd	Voltaire 'in the manner of Gosset' (HWC)	w	[Strawberry Hill, Twickenham, Middx]; sold 13 May 1842, lot 381; untraced		*HWC*, vol 12, 271; *Pyke* 1973, 36

Miscellaneous

65.	1784	Cupid catching a butterfly		[Exhib RA, London, 537]; untraced		*Graves* II, 1905–6, 235; *HWC*, vol 12, 272
66.	1787	'The Rossi's boy . . . as a young Paris'	m	Untraced		*Gould* 1834, 133; *Graves* II, 1905–6, 235; *HWC*, vol 12, 272, 273; *Penny* 1992, III, 33; *Yarrington* 1997, 37
67.	1800	A lap-dog		[Exhib RA, London, 1009]; untraced		*Graves* II, 1905–6, 235
68.	nd	Emperor Augustus (from a work in the collection of Sir William Hamilton)	w	[Strawberry Hill sale, 1842]; untraced		*HWC*, vol 12, 271; *Gunnis* 1968, 120–121
69.	nd	Lady Ailesbury (†1803)	w	[Strawberry Hill sale, 1842]; untraced		*Gunnis* 1968, 120–121
70.	nd	The fall of Phaeton		Untraced		Lawrence sale, 6 July 1830, lot 64 (bt Lewis, 4 gns)

DANCE, Giles –1751

Giles Dance appears as a 'Stone Cutter' in the accounts for work done at Tadworth Court, Banstead, Surrey for Leonard Wessell in 1705–7 (TNA C11/965/22). As a master-builder he was responsible in 1720 for Carshalton House, the home of Sir John Fellowes, a Director of the South Sea Company. He received £100 in December 1720, a further £200 in January 1721 and £102 and £54 in March that year. This work was perhaps carried out under **Henry Joynes**, for a payment to him as surveyor was made in March 1721. Dance was a member of Merchant Taylors' Company. He signed a large architectural monument to Richard Dawes (1), with a gadrooned base and fluted Doric pilasters, surmounted by cherubs and heraldic emblems. In his will he is described as being in partnership with his son, George Dance the Elder, the Mansion House architect (1695–1768). In the 1720s 'Messrs Dance and Co' worked on masonry at South Sea House, billed at over £700. George Dance the Younger (1741–1825), the grandson of Giles Dance, is known to have designed two monuments.

Richard Rawlinson, who recorded epitaphs, copied the inscription on the tomb-stone of the Rev John Dane (2) 'from the stone itself at the graver's Mr. Dance in Lothbury' (Bodleian Library, B.420, b. f50 in GPC). Dance was buried in Copford church, Essex. His will, which describes him as being of St Leonard, Shoreditch, was proved on 5 July 1751 (PROB 11/789).

Literary References: *Gunnis* 1968, 121; *Colvin* 1995, 287

Archival References: S S Co Inventories, Sir John Fellowes no 9 in 1, pp 10–11, 14; GPC

Funerary Monuments

1.	†1712	Richard Dawes		Wotton-under-Edge, Glos	S	*Gunnis* 1968, 121; *Colvin* 1995, 287; Pevsner, *Glos: Cotswolds*, 1999, 757
2.	†1713	Rev John Dane		untraced		GPC

DANDERS, of Shrewsbury fl 1765–69

A carver employed by **TF Pritchard**, who provided the designs for his 4 known chimneypieces and a pediment at Hatton Grange.

Chimneypieces

1.	1765–1769	Two Drawing(s): Pritchard D B (AIA 16, 32)		[for Mr Lloyd, Raven Street, Shrewsbury]; untraced	*Ionides* 1999, 328, 331, 366, 382 (repr)
2.	1765–1769	Two, with rococo ornament, for Miss Leighton's Bed Chamber and Dressing Room (co-sculptor: Nelson and Van der Hagen) Drawing(s): Pritchard D B (AIA 13)		[Condover Hall, Salop]; untraced	*Ionides* 1999, 328, 363 (repr)
3.	1765–1769	With frieze of oak leaves and acorns Drawing(s): Pritchard D B (AIA 15)		[for Richard Corbet Esq]; untraced	*Ionides* 1999, 329, 365 (repr)
4.	1765–1769	With gothic details (co-sculptor: Van der Hagen) Drawing(s): Pritchard D B (AIA 45)		[Condover Hall, Salop]; untraced	*Ionides* 1999, 333, 396 (repr)

Architectural Sculpture

5.	1765–1769	Pediment (co-sculptor: Nelson) Drawing(s): Pritchard D B (AIA 31)	s	Hatton Grange, Salop	*Ionides* 1999, 128–9, 331, 381 (repr)

DANTAN, Jean-Pierre 1800–69

He was born in Paris, one of a French family of sculptors and trained with his father, a wood-carver, before entering the Ecole des Beaux-Arts in 1823. He visited London on several occasions between 1833 and 1841 and carved caricature images of English subjects. He dates his bust of Talleyrand 'July 1833, London' (5).

Literary References: *Ormond* 1973, *passim*; *Grove* 1996, 8, 510 (Ward-Jackson).

Statues

1.	1833	Count Alfred D'Orsay, statuette	p	(coll Marquess of Londonderry)		*Ormond* 1973, 148
2.	1834	Daniel O'Connell, statuette (two)	b	Musée Carnavalet, Paris		*Ormond* 1973, 148
3.	1834	William IV, statuette	p	Musée Carnavalet, Paris		*Ormond* 1973, 514
4.	1851	Queen Victoria, seated, cast in zinc		[Gt Exhib]; untraced		*Grove* 1996, 8, 510

Busts

5.	1833	Charles Maurice de Talleyrand-Périgord	p	Wimpole Hall, Cambs	SD	
6.	1833	Samuel Rogers, cast	p	NPG 3888		*Grove* 1996, 8, 510

DARBEY, Joseph, of Dudley fl 1821–40

He signs a large tablet to Joseph Amphlett (1) and another to Alfred Howell (2). He is probably identical with the 'Darbey Jph. Mason' listed in a directory of Sedgley, near Dudley, published in 1834 (*White* 1834, 282).

Funerary Monuments

1.	?1821	Joseph Amphlett	Enville, Staffs	S	*Gunnis* 1968, 121
2.	1840	Rev Alfred Howell	Sedgley, Staffs	S	

DARBY, John fl 1759

A carver, he was paid £80 for making 'eight Girandoles for the Dancing Gallery' of the Mansion House in 1759 (MHCM 01/01/2, 805)

DARBY, Thomas fl 1712–46

A carver in wood and stone, employed on several Queen Anne churches. He appears to have been in partnership with **Gravas Smith.**

Literary References: *Gunnis* 1968, 121; *S of L*, 27, 161

Archival References: GPC

Architectural Sculpture

1.	1712–1724	Unspecified carved work		[St Anne, Limehouse, London]; untraced	*Gunnis* 1968, 121
2.	1723–1729	Unspecified carved work (co-sculptor: Gravas Smith) Payment(s): £243 for the wood carving, 1727	wd	[Christ Church, Spitalfields, London]; untraced	GPC, citing Accts for building the New Churches, Lambeth Palace Library
3.	1716–1729	Wood carving and other work (co-sculptor: Gravas Smith) Payment(s): £306 for wood-carving	wd	[St Mary Woolnoth, London]; untraced	*Gunnis* 1968, 121; GPC, citing Accts for building the New Churches, Lambeth Palace Library
4.	1728–1733	Unspecified carved work		[St John Horsleydown, London]; untraced	*Gunnis* 1968, 121

5.	1727–1733	Unspecified carved work		[St Luke's, Old Street, London]; untraced	GPC
6.	1746	Stone and wood-carving, including six stone Corinthian capitals Payment(s): £161, including £39 for the capitals		[Welbeck Abbey, Notts]; untraced	*Gunnis* 1968, 121 citing Welbeck Abbey archives

DARLEY, George fl 1787

A member of the building and quarrying family, active in speculative building on the north side of Dublin in the second half of the 18th century. He signs one monument.

Literary References: *Potterton* 1975, 42

Funerary Monuments

1.	†1787	John Baillie	Kilkenny Cathedral	S	*Potterton* 1975, 42

DARLEY, Henry fl 1775–after 1780

He was employed as a stone mason by the architect James Gandon on the Custom House in Dublin in the 1780s. The *Hibernian Magazine* for April 1775 gives his address as Abbey Street, Dublin and reports that he completed **John Nost III**'s memorial to Archbishop Smyth, 1775, in St Patrick's Cathedral (1). One of his assistants was **Edward Smyth.**

Literary References: *Crookshank* 1966, 308, 310; *Potterton* 1975, 42

Funerary Monuments

1.	1775	Archbishop Arthur Smyth (†1771) (co-sculptor: John Nost (or Van Ost) III)	St Patrick's Cathedral, Dublin	*Hibernian Magazine*, April 1775, 5, 193 (repr); *Potterton* 1975, 42

DARLEY, Moses fl 1723

Chimneypieces

1.	1723	Two of Kilkenny marble	m	[Trinity College, Dublin, library]; untraced	*Crookshank* 1986, 20

DARLEY, of Dublin fl 1787

The *Cumberland Paquet* of 2 May 1787 announced the erection of a monument by this sculptor (1), who may be identical with **Henry Darley**. (Add inf. Dennis Perriam).

Literary References: RG/JP, 3, 406v

Funerary Monuments

1.	1787	Rev Thomas Spalding (†1783)	St James, Whitehaven, Cumberland	*Cumberland Paquet*, 2 May 1787

DARNOI fl 1848

Busts

1.	1848	Unidentified man	p	Glasgow University	SD	*Woodward* 1977, vol 1, pt 2, 54

DAVID, Claude fl 1678–1721

A Burgundian sculptor, perhaps of aristocratic birth since he described himself as 'Chevalier David', he probably trained in France and certainly worked in Italy before coming to England. The first record of his activities is in 1678, when he was in Rome carving ivory crucifixes and by 1695 he was in Genoa working on the ambitious sculptural programme in S Maria in Carignano, where he was a successor to the noted French sculptor Pierre Puget (1620–94). In 1695 David is recorded as receiving 760 lire for a large figure of St Bartholomew for a niche in the church and in the same year he was commissioned to produce a stucco model for the high altar.

David was in England by 1700, at Windsor Castle, where he was paid £100 for unspecified work (Halifax MSS Ad.MS.10,119, in GPC). A second royal commission followed in 1702, for 2 marble figures ordered by Queen Anne for the gardens of St James's Palace (3). One of these may be the *Neptune*, now in the Victoria and Albert Museum. They were described as 'of a curious performance, and mightily commended by such who have any gust of things of this nature' (*Whinney* 1988, 449, n 15, quoting JP Malcolm, *Londinium Redivivium* IV, 1807, 242).

Royal patronage led to interest from the aristocracy. David received commissions from Lord Weymouth at Longleat, where he carved a number of garden figures (5). On 17 September 1708 the mason William Self was paid for 'one days work about ye figures by Caviler's order and Direction' (1st Visc Weymouth, 275 17/09/1708) and further bills from another artisan, **Richard Broad**, record the supplying of stone and carving of pedestals for two figures by David in the 'New plantation' (1st Visc, 275 01/11/1709 and 16/11/1709). David's garden sculpture was noted by George Harbin, the non-juring chaplain and librarian to the 1st Viscount: 'four marble statues in the garden the work of Cavalier David, amounted to £600' (Thynne Family Colls, *c*1718, Thynne Papers 185 fol 33r). He appears also to have been responsible for architectural designs and ornaments for the house. There are two designs thought to be by him in the Longleat archives, both for the main entrance: one has a pair of columns and a square-headed doorway with a segmental pediment, and the other a rounded arch surmounted by a swan neck pediment. The joiner's bill for 26 January 1705 refers to the making of a model of the door by Cavalier David's order (7). This may refer to the present front entrance of Longleat, which is surmounted by the Thynne arms and a viscount's coronet, both confidently executed. David is known to have been at Longleat in 1706 since a collection of poetry, ending with a list of borrowers of books from the Longleat library, 1700–1718, includes an entry penned shortly before 6 April 1706 'To Cavalier David the Life of K. Henry the 5th' (MS 259, f 56v). He was also responsible for the monument to James Thynne †1709, an uncle of the 1st Viscount, at Buckland (1). The Thynne papers carry the entry '[James Thynne's] Nephew and Heir Thomas Thynne Esquire, Father of the Present Lord Viscount Weymouth. . .erected a Marble Monument to his Memory against the Wall of the Chancell, which was the workmanship of the famous statuary Claude David (who made the fine Marble statues at Longleate) & cost 80£' (Thynne family colls, *c*1718, Thynne Papers 185 fol 33r).

In 1706 'le Chevalier Davy' and the decorative painter Louis Laguerre visited Ampthill, Beds where they discussed 'matters relating to their severall professions in knowledge' with Lord Ashburnham (Ashburnham Letterbook, 16 Nov 1706, ASH 846). David's work also interested the Norfolk connoisseur, Sir Andrew Fountaine, who obtained a statue of *Vulcan chained to a rock* for Narford Hall (**6**). This was sited on the landing halfway up the principal staircase. It was intended to be accompanied by a companion figure of King William III which appears not to have been executed. The two figures were to have formed an allegorical representation of the avoidance of war as a result of William's arrival and the Glorious Revolution. Vulcan is therefore fettered rather than fashioning the instruments of war.

The sculptor's best-known work is the monument to Philip Cartaret (†1710) in Westminster Abbey, which is signed 'Gidius David eques sculpsit'. It has a twisting figure of *Time* on a pedestal, closely reminiscent of the *Vulcan* at Narford, and though both are smaller-scale works, they recall the sculptor's statue of St Bartholomew in Genoa. The Cartaret monument is surmounted by a haughty portrait bust in contemporary dress (**2**).

David was less successful in his attempts to provide public works. In 1721 he tried to raise £2,500 by subscription for an equestrian statue of King George I to be erected in the centre of St James's Square, but only £100 was collected and the plan had to be abandoned. A second aborted plan was for an ambitious fountain over the Cheapside Conduit: Vertue saw a large print of the design and described it as having figures of river gods, an equestrian statue of the Duke of Marlborough, and a statue of Queen Anne surmounting the structure. The print was signed 'opus equitis Claudii David. Comitatis Burgundiae' and was apparently prepared from a model.

Given the status of his known patrons and a number of attributed monuments, it seems possible that David's commissions substantially exceeded the known works. It was his good fortune to be a sculptor from a prestigious European background active in England a generation before the arrival of such formidable potential competitors as **G B Guelfi**, **Michael Rysbrack** and **Peter Scheemakers**.

IR

Literary References: *Vertue* II, 87; *Lankheit* 1962, 149, 306; *Gunnis* 1968, 121; *Whinney* 1988, 449 n15; *Grove* 8, 550; *Baker* 2000, 28–31; *Bilbey* 2002, 71–2

Archival References: Misc Thynne Papers; GPC

Funerary Monuments

1.	†1709	James Thynne Payment(s): £80		Buckland, Glos		Thynne Papers Book 185 f.33r
2.	†1710	Hon Philip Cartaret		Westminster Abbey, London, nave	S	*Dart* 2, 1723, 111–2 (repr); *Gunnis* 1968, 121 (repr VIII); *Whinney* 1988, 449 n15; *Baker* 2000, 29–31 (repr)

Statues

3.	1702	'two excellent figures of marble'		[St James's Park, London]; untraced		*Whinney* 1988, 449, n 151; *Bilbey* 2002, 72
4.	1704	Neptune		Dyrham Park, Glos, deer park		Pevsner, *Glos: Cotswolds*, 1999, 345
5.	by 1708	The seasons (perhaps supplied with other figures)		Longleat, Wilts, formerly gardens, now stables parapet		Pevsner, *Wilts*, 1975, 311; *Baker* 2000, 29
6.	c1710	Vulcan (Prometheus)	m	[Narford Hall, Norfolk, staircase]; VAM A.3-1981		*Baker* 2000, 29–31; *Bilbey* 2002, 71 (repr)

Architectural Sculpture

7.	1705	Principal entrance doorway Drawing(s): Longleat HA, two		Longleat, Wilts		Longleat HA, 200, 01/01/1705
8.	nd	Design and model for a fountain with a statue of Queen Anne, the Duke of Marlborough on horseback and several river gods		[for Cheapside Conduit, City of London]; unexecuted		*Vertue* II, 87; *Ward-Jackson* 2003, 378
9.	nd	Truth, Liberty, Equity, Secrecy, Apollo and Mercury		[Buckingham House, London, parapet figures]; untraced		GPC

DAVID, Pierre Jean, of Angers 1788–1856

David d'Angers was one of the most celebrated European sculptors of his day. He visited England on two occasions and produced a number of busts and medallions of British sitters. He was born in Angers, and was taught by his father, a sculptor and decorator, entering the atelier of Philippe Roland in Paris, under whom he worked on decorative ornaments at the Louvre. In 1812 his native town granted him a scholarship to study in Italy, where he was greatly influenced by the work of **Antonio Canova**. After completing his studies he paid a brief visit to England in 1815 to admire the Parthenon marbles on Canova's recommendation. He attempted to meet **John Flaxman RA**, but was turned away. The Englishman apparently confused him with the Republican painter Jacques-Louis David, whose role in the execution of Louis XVI had disgusted Flaxman.

After returning to Paris he carried out a number of prestigious commissions and in 1826 became a Professor of the Academy. One of his most famous works, the relief on the Panthéon, was commissioned in 1830. Notable British sitters who visited his studio included the utilitarian philosopher Jeremy Bentham (**1, 20**) and Lady Morgan, an Irish woman with literary pretensions (**9**). The bust of Bentham was exhibited at the Royal Academy in 1829 and in 1844 belonged to John Bowring, another of David's sitters (**11**).

In 1828–29 he paid a second visit to London. He visited the British Museum, where he saw **L F Roubiliac**'s statue of Shakespeare. In his notebooks he recorded his reservations about the image, which he considered insufficiently austere in conveying the genius of Shakespeare, with a finger to his lips as if he had just had 'une idée malicieuse'. He concluded 'cette figure est horrible' (quoted in *Dawson* 1999, 203). Nonetheless in 1833 he made a gift of a plaster bust of George Cuvier by Amedeo Lavy to the British Museum.

David d'Angers carved busts and medallions of a number of British 'grand hommes' in the following years, including Flaxman, Lord Byron and the explorer, Sir John Franklin (**6, 21, 8**). He also produced models for James Tassie. A list of his pupils published by Henry Jouin included two otherwise unknown sculptors, Hawkins and

Jennings, who may have been British (*Jouin* 1878, 1, 581). Curiously, the list does not include **Holme Cardwell**, who is thought to have studied with him for 3 years in Paris.

David was a republican and an ardent patriot linked to the Romantic literary movement. He produced a vast corpus of work, including more than 150 busts and 500 medallions of public figures. In 1848 he became Mayor of a Parisian district, but was forced to seek exile following the coup d'état of Louis Napoleon. He returned to France in 1852 and died in Paris in January 1856.

Literary References: *Jouin* 1878; *Neoclassicism* 1972, 187–8; *Pyke* 1973, 37; *Grove* 1996, 8, 564–7 (Ward-Jackson); *Dawson* 1999, *passim*

Busts

1.	1825–1828	Jeremy Bentham		[Exhib RA, London, 1829, 1180]; untraced Other versions: several, in bronze	D	*Graves* II, 1905–6, 255; *Illustrated Times* 1844, 377; *Gunnis* 1968, 121; *Dawson* 1999, 40
2.	1830	Sydney, Lady Morgan	m	VAM A.1839-1971 Other versions: Musée des Beaux Arts, Angers, plaster		*Avery* 1972, 232 (repr); *Ormond* 1973, 325
3.	1833	Arthur O'Connor		Untraced		*Gunnis* 1968, 121
4.	1836	Amelia Opie		Untraced		*Gunnis* 1968, 121

Reliefs

5.	1827	George Canning, portrait medallion		Untraced		*Gunnis* 1968, 121
6.	1828	John Flaxman, portrait medallion		Untraced		*Gunnis* 1968, 121
7.	1829	Amelia Opie, portrait medallion		Untraced		*Gunnis* 1968, 121
8.	1829	Sir John Franklin, portrait medallion		Numerous versions		*Gunnis* 1968, 121; *Ormond* 1973, 181
9.	1829	Sydney, Lady Morgan, portrait medallion	b	Musée des Beaux Arts, Angers		*Ormond* 1973, 325
10.	1830	Sir Sidney Smith, portrait medallion		Untraced		*Gunnis* 1968, 121
11.	1832	Dr John Bowring, portrait medallion	b	[coll L Richard]; NPG, London 1082	SD	*Ormond* 1973, 47, pl 72
12.	1832	Joseph Pentland, portrait medallion		Untraced		*Gunnis* 1968, 121
13.	1834	George Pitt-Rivers, portrait medallion		Untraced		*Gunnis* 1968, 121
14.	1834	John Wilkes, portrait medallion		Untraced		*Gunnis* 1968, 121
15.	1836	Sir John Ross, portrait medallion	b	Musée des Beaux Arts, Angers		*Ormond* 1973, 402
16.	?1837	Dominique Jean Larrey	p	NGI	SD	*le Harivel* 1988, 559 (repr)
17.	1838	William Temple, portrait medallion		Untraced		*Gunnis* 1968, 121
18.	nd	Daniel O'Connor, portrait medallion		Untraced		*Gunnis* 1968, 121
19.	nd	James Watt, portrait medallion		Untraced		*Gunnis* 1968, 121
20.	nd	Jeremy Bentham, portrait medallion	b	[Christie, 17 July 1984, lot 31]; untraced		*Dawson* 1999, 40
21.	nd	Lord Byron, portrait medallion		Untraced		*Gunnis* 1968, 121
22.	nd	Mrs Somerville, portrait medallion		Untraced		*Gunnis* 1968, 121

DAVIES, John, of Wrexham fl 1834

He signs a large and elaborate monument in Denbighshire, with Gothic details and a tripartite canopy.

Funerary Monuments

1.	†1834	Sir Foster and Lady Harriet (†1830) Cunliffe	St Giles, Wrexham, Denbighs	S	Pevsner, *Clwyd*, 1986, 301

DAVIES, of Builth fl 1733–1806

Possibly a family firm.

Funerary Monuments

1.	†1733	Rev James Jones	Llanbadarn Fawr, Radnor	S	Pevsner, *Powys*, 1979, 241
2.	†1793	T Butts	Llanfinangel Rhydithon, Radnor	S	Pevsner, *Powys*, 1979, 253
3.	†1806	Rev Thomas Jones	Cefullys, Radnor	S	Pevsner, *Powys*, 1979, 225

DAVIES, of Chelsea fl 1841

Funerary Monuments

1.	1841	Countess Winterton	[St James, Hampstead Road, London]; church demol	S	*Gunnis* 1968, 121

DAVIES, of Clun fl 1790–1867

There are a number of monuments in Radnorshire carrying this signature, three of them signed 'B Davies' (**1, 4, 6**). Since 77 years separate the date of death of the first and last persons commemorated, more than one generation may have been involved in the business.

Funerary Monuments

1.	†1790	Evan Williams	Llanbedr Paincastle, Radnor	S	Pevsner, *Powys*, 1979, 244
2.	†1833	Edward Meredith	Llanbedr Paincastle, Radnor	S	Pevsner, *Powys*, 1979, 244
3.	†1834	Benjamin Bore	Llanfinangel Rhydithon, Radnor	S	Pevsner, *Powys*, 1979, 253
4.	†1834	Mary Evans	Llangynllo, Radnor	S	Pevsner, *Powys*, 1979, 254
5.	†1838	Rev David Lloyd	Llanbedr Paincastle, Radnor	S	Pevsner, *Powys*, 1979, 244
6.	†1867	Elizabeth (†1830) and Richard Bywater	Llanbedr Paincastle, Radnor	S	Pevsner, *Powys*, 1979, 244

DAVIES, of Hereford fl 1799

One work is listed by Pevsner, who notes several slate tablets in Huntington church by 'R Davies'.

Literary References: Pevsner *Herefs*, 198

Funerary Monuments

1.	†1799	Brickenden family member	St Andrew, Dinedor, Herefs		Pevsner, *Herefs*, 1963, 113

DAVIES, R G, of Newcastle-upon-Tyne fl 1820–57

Davies was responsible for a considerable number of wall tablets in Northumbrian churches, for instance in Woodhorn, Gosforth, Warkworth and Alston. He exhibited *Actaeon Devoured by His Hounds* at Westminster Hall in 1844 (**30**), apparently with limited success for the *Literary Gazette* remarked: 'We wish the unfortunate hunter had been entirely devoured, so that we might have been spared the sight of so disgusting a group' (*Lit Gaz*, 1436, 27 July 1844, 482). The *Illustrated London News* however published a woodcut of his newly erected monument to the artist Luke Clennell at Newcastle (**22**). This journal described him as 'a young sculptor of talent and rising reputation' but felt the work was ill served by an inscription of 'four lines of miserable verse which contain neither meaning nor truth' (*ILN* 1844, 326). The monument is carved with a palette, brush and laurels. His other wall monuments include an obelisk in low relief to Edward Moses (**1**), and a low relief portrait of Marcus Allen, set in a pillar (**20**).

Davies, who married at St Andrew's, Newcastle, in 1812, later took **Christopher Tate** into his studio. The latter died in 1841, leaving unfinished a statue of the Duke of Northumberland which was completed by his former master and erected at Tynemouth (**26**). On 8 August 1846 the *Carlisle Journal* carried a note on the Carlisle Exhibition with the information that 'Mr Davies introduced two clay models at a promenade on Thursday evening'. Davies was staying temporarily in Carlisle and his presence attracted considerable attention. It is not known when he finally left Newcastle, but by 1857 he had moved to Chester-le-Street in Durham.

Literary References: *Gunnis* 1968, 122; Pevsner, *Northumbs*, 1992, *passim*

Funerary Monuments

1.	†1813	Edward Moses		All Saints, Newcastle, Northumbs		Pevsner, *Northumbs* 1992, 426
2.	†1813	Phillis Craster		Ellingham, Northumbs		Pevsner, *Northumbs*, 1992, 266
3.	†1815	Winefrid Haggerston		Ellingham, Northumbs		Pevsner, *Northumbs* 1992, 266
4.	†1816	James Graham		Holy Trinity, Berwick-upon-Tweed, Northumbs	S	Pevsner, *Northumbs*, 1992, 172
5.	1817	Ralph Waters		St Andrew, Newcastle		GPC
6.	?1817	Sarah Dand		Warkworth, Northumbs		GPC
7.	†1819	David Stephenson		All Saints, Newcastle, Northumbs	S	Pevsner, *Northumbs*, 1992, 426; *Friedman* 2004, 140
8.	?1820	Robert Jopling		Bywell, Northumbs	S	*Gunnis* 1968, 122
9.	?1821	Jane Gowland		Bedale, N R Yorks	S	*Gunnis* 1968, 122
10.	1821	Margaret Clavering		Newcastle Cathedral	S	*Gunnis* 1968, 122
11.	?1821	Robert Dand		Warkworth, Northumbs		GPC
12.	?1822	Francis Johnstone		Newcastle Cathedral	S	*Gunnis* 1968, 122
13.	?1829	John Carr		Ford, Northumberland		GPC
14.	†1830	Anthony Compton		Carham, Northumbs		Pevsner, *Northumbs*, 1992, 212
15.	?1830	Joseph Fenwick		Warkworth, Northumbs		GPC
16.	1831	Elizabeth Woodifield		Durham Cathedral	S	*Gunnis* 1968, 122
17.	1836	Unidentified subject, tablet		Wooler, Northumbs		Pevsner, *Northumbs*, 1992, 634
18.	†1837	Unidentified subject, tablet		St Stephen, York		Pevsner, *Yorks: E R & York*, 1995, 177
19.	?1840	Widrington family		Warkworth, Northumbs		GPC
20.	†1843	Marcus Allen		St Paul, Newcastle upon Tyne, Northumbs		Pevsner, *Northumbs*, 1992, 429
21.	1844	Grace Darling		St Cuthbert's Chapel, Farne Islands		*Gunnis* 1968, 122
22.	1844	Luke Clennell (†1840)		St Andrew, Newcastle		*ILN* 1844, 325–6 (repr); *Gunnis* 1968, 122; GPC
23.	1846	'Monumental sketch'		[Exhib Carlisle Acad of Fine Art, 282]; untraced		*Carlisle Exhibs*, 1973
24.	†1849	Matthew Culley		Chatton, Northumbs		Pevsner, *Northumbs*, 1992, 217
25.	†1850	Unidentified subject, tablet		Alston, Cumberland		Pevsner, *Cumberland & Westmorland*, 1967, 60
26.	?1853	Joseph Crawhall		St Anne, Newcastle		GPC
27.	nd	Unidentified subjects, tablets		Warkworth, Northumbs		Pevsner, *Northumbs*, 1992, 613
28.	nd	Unidentified subjects, tablets		St Nicholas, Gosforth, Northumbs		Pevsner, *Northumbs*, 1992, 501

Statues

29.	post-1841	Hugh, 3rd Duke of Northumberland (co-sculptor: Christopher Tate)		Master Mariners' Homes, Tynemouth, Northumbs		*Gunnis* 1968, 122; Pevsner, *Northumbs*, 1992, 595
30.	1844	Actaeon devoured by his hounds		[Exhib Westminster Hall, London]; untraced		*Lit Gaz*, 1844, 482

Busts

31.	1828	Voltaire		[Exhib Suffolk Street Galleries]; untraced		GPC
32.	1844	Fanny Ternan		[Unidentified address, Newcastle-upon-Tyne]; untraced		*C J*, 28 Dec 1844
33.	1846	Archdeacon Reed		[Exhib Carlisle Acad of Fine Art, 279]; untraced		*Carlisle Ac Exhibs*, 1973
34.	1846	Female head, study from nature		[Exhib Carlisle Acad of Fine Art, 276]; untraced		*Carlisle Ac Exhibs*, 1973
35.	1846	J Buddle		[Exhib Carlisle Acad of Fine Art, 273]; untraced		*Carlisle Ac Exhibs*, 1973
36.	1846	William Bell Scott	tc	[Exhib Carlisle Acad of Fine Art, 272]; untraced		*Carlisle Ac Exhibs*, 1973

Architectural Sculpture

37.	1846	Monumental cross for Hexham Abbey, model		[Exhib Carlisle Acad of Fine Art, 281]; untraced		*Carlisle Ac Exhibs*, 1973

Miscellaneous

38.	1846	Old Man and Death	tc	[Exhib Carlisle Acad of Fine Art, 266]; untraced		*Carlisle Ac Exhibs*, 1973
39.	1846	Pair of whelps		[Exhib Carlisle Acad of Fine Art, 280]; untraced		*Carlisle Ac Exhibs*, 1973
40.	1846	Prodigal Son	tc	[Exhib Carlisle Acad of Fine Art, 268]; untraced		*Carlisle Ac Exhibs*, 1973

DAVIES, R, of Newcastle-upon-Tyne fl 1777–1800

Possibly the father of **R G Davies of Newcastle-upon-Tyne**, he is known only for three tablets.

Literary References: *Gunnis* 1968, 122

Funerary Monuments

1.	†1762	Thomas Peacock	Grindon, Durham	S	*Gunnis* 1968, 121–122
2.	1797	William Christopher	Norton, Durham	S	*Gunnis* 1968, 122
3.	†1828	Thomas Peacock (†1710) and later family members	Grinton, N R Yorks	S	Pevsner, *Yorks: N R*, 1966, 176

DAVIES, Richard

His tradecard is in the Banks collection at the British Museum (106.10).

DAVIES, Samuel fl 1759–74

Presumably the 'Samuel Davies, mason, of Adam and Eve Court, Oxford Street', whose wife Ann had a son, William, born at the Middlesex Hospital and baptised in the hospital on 30 October 1774 (Hospital Archives in GPC).

Literary References: *Gunnis* 1968, 122

Chimneypieces

1.	1759	Description unavailable Payment(s): £13 6s 6d	[Hoare's Bank, Fleet Street, London]; untraced	Hoare Partnership Ledger 1751–1764, fol 99; *Gunnis* 1968, 122

DAVIES (or DAVIS), David, of Carmarthen 1789–1861

A builder and monumental mason, he was born in 1789, the son of a clockmaker of the same name, in Llandyfaelog. He was the founder of a family firm, whose other members included William, Henry Francis and Wynford. Davies's uncle, a shoemaker, was the grandfather of **Edward Davis**.

Literary References: *Dale-Jones and Lloyd* 1989, 47, 48

Funerary Monuments

1.	†1802	Elizabeth Lewis	Llanglydwen, Carmarthen		*Dale-Jones and Lloyd* 1989, 47, 48
2.	†1813	Evan and Elizabeth Protheroe	Llanglydwen, Carmarthen		*Dale-Jones and Lloyd* 1989, 47, 48
3.	1833	John Evans, table tomb	Laugherne, Carmarthen, churchyard	S	*Dale-Jones and Lloyd* 1989, 47
4.	nd	The Charles family	Llangunnor, Carmarthen, churchyard	S	*Dale-Jones and Lloyd* 1989, 47

DAVIES (or DAVIS), Thomas fl 1681–1705

A mason-sculptor who in 1687 erected a cross for the bathing cistern at Bath (7), then an attraction for 'people of fashion' who 'bathe for pleasure.' This was erected at the expense of John, Earl of Melfort, Secretary of State to King James II, and commemorates the occasion in 1687 when the Queen bathed in the cistern (as a cure for infertility). It consisted of a large pedestal, decorated with putti, shells and festoons and was crowned by a dome with the cross of Christ, the Holy Ghost and a dove descending (*Wood* 1765, 259–61).

Davies also carried out work for the Duke of Devonshire and had some royal contracts. When he received payment in 1705 for one of his later chimneypieces at Hampton Court (**6**), he was also imbursed for 'working the marble bason' (TNA E351/3464). In 1690 the Earl of Dorset paid 'Mr. Davis, ye stone-cutter' £34 for unidentified work (Knole Archives in GPC). In 1712 he was the master-mason employed in building Lord Ashburnham's house in St James's Square. Both his recorded monuments were destroyed in the Second World War (**1, 2**).

Davies may concievably be the Thomas Davis, son of another Thomas, of Lechlade, who became clerk of works to **Thomas Cartwright I** on 23 October, 1668. On 29 April 1700 Davies took his son Edward as an apprentice.

Literary References: *Gunnis* 1968, 122; *Webb* 1999, 10

Funerary Monuments						
1.	1681	Humphrey Levins		[St Mary-le-Bow, London]; destroyed	S	*Gunnis* 1968, 122
2.	1689	Sir Thomas Hanmer		[Temple Church, London]; destroyed	S	*Gunnis* 1968, 122
Statues						
3.	1695	Faunus Payment(s): £23		[Chatsworth, Derbys]; untraced		Chatsworth Building Accts, 1695–6, 8
4.	1696	Mark Anthony Payment(s): £24		[Chatsworth, Derbys]; untraced		Chatsworth Building Accts, 1695–96, 57
Chimneypieces						
5.	1696	Seven	m	[Hampton Court Palace, Middx]; untraced		TNA AO 1/2482/297; *Gunnis* 1968, 122
6.	1705	Description unavailable		[Hampton Court Palace, Middx]; untraced		PRO E351/3464; GPC
Architectural Sculpture						
7.	1687	Cross	m	[The Cross Bath, Bath]; untraced		*Wood* 1765, 2, 259; *Gunnis* 1968, 122

DAVIS, Charles, of Bidford-on-Avon fl 1813

Pevsner notes several headstones by Davis in the churchyard of St Nicholas, Saintbury, Glos.

Literary References: Pevsner, *Glos: Cotswolds*, 1999, 587

Funerary Monuments

1.	†1813	Rev William Scott	Willersey, Glos	S	Pevsner, *Glos: Cotswolds*, 1999, 724

DAVIS, Edward 1813–78

Davis, whose family came from Carmarthen, was born in London, the son of Dr David Daniel Davis of Llandyfaelog, the physician who delivered Queen Victoria. He attended the Royal Academy Schools in 1833 on the recommendation of **E H Baily**, in whose workshop he also trained. He first exhibited at the Royal Academy in 1834, giving his address as 4 Fitzroy Street. Most of his known works of the following decade are portrait busts, and it is to be assumed that it was with this genre that he initially made his living. The *Art Union* commented on the bust of Francis Grant (**45**) that 'The free and flowing manner of the hair of this head seems to be precisely "as the winds have left it"; and in the whole there is as much of poetic sentiment as may be risked in portraiture' (*AU*, 1842, 128). The same journal was more equivocal in 1844, when Davis exhibited *The Power of the Law* (**7**) at Westminster Hall, a female figure with a chain. This was described as 'heavy in character, coarse in execution. . .nothing beyond a sketch' (*AU*, 1844, 217). The *Literary Gazette* was succinctly acid, when it remarked 'Would that this gentleman had the power of doing something better' (*Lit Gaz* 1844, 483).

Further adverse criticism greeted a major public work, the statue of the Duke of Rutland, 1850, for the City of Leicester. It was cast in bronze by a French firm and exhibited at the Great Exhibition (**10**). It was intended for a high pedestal and carved to be seen from below, but unfortunately it was shown at a low level and the exaggerated features elicited a jaundiced response. The *Builder* thought that the 'strange, loose figure of the Duke' was 'unfortunately a failure. . . His Grace is made to appear positively intoxicated; and as we may expect, if it be put up without alteration, to find the old proverb of "as drunk as a lord" giving place in Leicester to "as drunk as a Duke" ' (*Builder* 1851, 715). Once erected, however, the *Leicester Journal* encouraged all those who had only seen the work a yard above the ground to look at it *in situ*, where the effect of the 'noble statue' was 'absolutely electrifying' (*Cavanagh* 2000, 144).

Other important works included a statue of Sir William Nott for Davis's home town of Carmarthen (**9**), where Davis had retained connections. In July 1846 *The Welshman* carried a report that Davies 'a rising sculptor in the metropolis', had offered a bust of the Bishop of St David's to the City Corporation, who had accepted it (**54**) (*Dale-Jones and Lloyd* 1989, 48). Thirlwall went on to commission a monument to Bishop Richard Davies, a wall-tablet with a fine, angular relief of the seated cleric in his academic hat and robes (**2**).

He was also responsible for a statue of Josiah Wedgwood, erected by public subscription in Stoke. Wedgwood was depicted standing, bare-headed, holding the Portland vase in his left hand (**14**). Towards the end of his life he was commissioned by the Royal Academy to execute busts of the painters Daniel Maclise and John Constable (**95, 99**). He exhibited at the Academy until 1877, giving his address as 15 Fitzroy Street. He died on 14 August 1878.

Literary References: *AJ* 1864, 289–90; *Graves* 1905–6, 2, 259; *Gunnis* 1968, 122; *Dale-Jones and Lloyd* 1989, 48–9

Archival References: RA Admissions

No.	Date	Subject		Location		References
Funerary Monuments						
1.	†1842	David Saunders		Llangyndeyrn, Carmarthen		*Dale-Jones & Lloyd* 1989, 49
2.	†1849	Richard Davies, Bishop of St David's		Abergwili, Carmarthen		*Graves* II, 1905–6, 260; *Dale-Jones and Lloyd*, 1989, 39, 49 (repr)
3.	1851	Joseph Whalley		St Luke, Lancaster, Lancs		Pevsner, *Lancs: N*, 1969, 161
4.	1853	Colonel J Bugle Delap Model(s): part model exhib RA, London, 1853, 1336		Lillingstone Lovell, Bucks		*Graves* II, 1905–6, 260; Pevsner, *Bucks*, 1994, 433
5.	1857	Lieutenant Benyon		[Exhib RA, London, 1235, a part]; untraced		*Graves* II, 1905–6, 260
6.	1866	'The widow – a monumental sketch'		[Exhib RA, London, 931]; untraced		*Graves* II, 1905–6, 260
Statues						
7.	1844	'The Power of the Law', chained female figure Model(s): Exhib RA, London, 1844, 1290		[Exhib Westminster Hall, London, 182]; Cambridge Assize Courts		*Graves* II, 1905–6, 260; *Lit Gaz* 1844, 483; *AU*, 1844, 170, 217; *Gunnis* 1968, 122
8.	1849	Venus and Cupid	m	[Salford AG, Lancs]; untraced		*AJ Cat*, 1851, 151 (repr); *Graves* II, 1905–6, 260; *Gunnis* 1968, 122; *Wells* 1999, 42
9.	1851	Sir William Nott Model(s): Exhib RA, London, 1849, 1224	b	Nott Square, Carmarthen	S	*Graves* II, 1905–6, 260; *Gunnis* 1968, 122; *Dale-Jones and Lloyd* 1989, 48; *Darke* 1991, 129 (repr)
10.	1850–1852	John, 5th Duke of Rutland (cast by Simonet et fils, Paris)	b	[Cheapside, Leicester]; Marketplace (in front of Corn Exchange), Leicester Other versions: statuette, exhib RA, London, 1365	SD	*Graves* II, 1905–6, 260; *Builder* 1851, 715; *Cavanagh* 2000, xiv, 141–5 (repr)
11.	1856	George Lance		[Exhib RA, London, 1349]; untraced		*Graves* II, 1905–6, 260; *Ormond* 1973, 252
12.	1856	Rebecca		[Exhib RA, London, 1256 Int Exhib, London, 1862]; untraced		*Graves* II, 1905–6, 260; *AJ Cat* 1862, 318 (repr); *Gunnis* 1968, 122
13.	1858	Cupid caught flying, group		[Exhib RA, London, 1224]; untraced		*Graves* II, 1905–6, 260; *Morris and Roberts* 1998, 181
14.	1862	Josiah Wedgwood (†1795)	b	Wilton Square, Stoke-on-Trent, Staffs		*AJ*, 1864, 289–90; *Darke* 1991, 168–9 (repr)
15.	1864	'Lily-bud', Lilian Wyndham Barnard	m	[Exhib RA, London, 919]; untraced		*Graves* II, 1905–6, 260
16.	1864	St John, model ('to be executed in marble')		[Exhib RA, London, 1003]; untraced		*Graves* II, 1905–6, 260
17.	1866	Mr Watson		[Exhib RA, London, 1020]; untraced		*Graves* II, 1905–6, 260
Busts						
18.	1834	Professor Davis MD		[Exhib RA, London, 1097]; untraced		*Graves* II, 1905–6, 259
19.	1834	'The late' Mr Thelwall		[Exhib RA, London, 1031]; untraced		*Graves* II, 1905–6, 259
20.	1835	Dr Elliottson		[Exhib Soc of BA, London, 768]; untraced		*Johnson* 1975, 120
21.	1835	Dr Fellowes	m	[Exhib RA, London, 1076]; University College Hospital, London		*Graves* II, 1905–6, 259; GPC
22.	1835	Dr J B Davis	m	[Exhib RA, London, 1103]; University College Hospital, London		*Graves* II, 1905–6, 259; *Morris and Roberts* 1998, 181; GPC
23.	1835	E W Scadding		[Exhib RA, London, 1069]; untraced		*Graves* II, 1905–6, 259
24.	1835	Miss Bingham		[Exhib RA, London, 1083]; untraced		*Graves* II, 1905–6, 259

25.	1835	Rev Dr Moore		[Exhib RA, London, 1054]; untraced		*Graves* II, 1905–6, 259
26.	1836	Charles Kemble		[Exhib RA, London, 1073]; untraced		*Graves* II, 1905–6, 259
27.	post-1836	Charles Thomas Longley, Archbishop of Canterbury	m	Lambeth Palace, London	S	*Graves* II, 1905–6, 260; GPC
28.	1836	Mrs Farquhar Fraser	m	[Exhib RA, London, 1113]; untraced		*Graves* II, 1905–6, 259
29.	1836	William Tooke MP	m	[Exhib RA, London, 1103]; untraced		*Graves* II, 1905–6, 259; *Gunnis* 1968, 122; *Morris and Roberts* 1998, 181
30.	1837	Frederick Say		[Exhib RA, London, 1229]; untraced		*Graves* II, 1905–6, 259
31.	1837	Henry Blagrove		[Exhib RA, London, 1232]; untraced		*Graves* II, 1905–6, 259
32.	1837	John Wichelo		[Exhib RA, London, 1228; exhib Liverpool Ac, 676]; untraced		*Graves* II, 1905–6, 259; *Morris and Roberts* 1998, 181
33.	1838	Benjamin Aislabie		Marylebone Cricket Club, London		*Gunnis* 1968, 122
34.	1838	David Salomons	m	[Exhib RA, London, 1310]; untraced		*Graves* II, 1905–6, 259
35.	1838	F Raincock		[Exhib Liverpool Ac, 677]; untraced		*Morris and Roberts* 1998, 181
36.	1838	Hon Mrs Leicester Stanhope	m	[Exhib RA, London, 1308]; untraced		*Graves* II, 1905–6, 259
37.	1838	J G Middleton		[Exhib RA, London, 1312]; untraced		*Graves* II, 1905–6, 259
38.	1839	Joshua Mayhew	m	[Exhib RA, London, 1361]; untraced		*Graves* II, 1905–6, 259
39.	1839	Lord Ossulton MP	m	[Exhib RA, London, 1365]; untraced		*Graves* II, 1905–6, 259
40.	1839	'Terminal bust of Benjamin Nislake'		[Exhib RA, London, 1343 'for the pavillion of the Marylebone Cricket Club']; untraced		*Graves* II, 1905–6, 259
41.	1840	Daniel Maclise RA		[Exhib RA, London, 1077]; untraced		*Graves* II, 1905–6, 259; *Ormond* 1973, 295
42.	1840	Master Robert Kindersley	m	[Exhib RA, London, 1141]; untraced		*Graves* II, 1905–6, 259; *Morris and Roberts* 1998, 181
43.	1841	Mrs Parnell		[Exhib RA, London, 1339]; untraced		*Graves* II, 1905–6, 259
44.	1841	Rev John Giffard Ward, of St James's, Piccadilly	m	[Exhib RA, London, 1334; 1847, 1363; 1860, 1023]; untraced		*Graves* II, 1905–6, 259, 260
45.	1842	Sir Francis Grant		[Exhib RA, London, 1330]; untraced		*Graves* II, 1905–6, 259; *AU*, 1842, 128; *Ormond* 1973, 194
46.	1842	William R Collett, MP		[Exhib RA, London, 1378]; untraced		*Graves* II, 1905–6, 259
47.	1843	Duchess of Kent	m	[Exhib RA, London, 1386]; Royal Coll, RCIN 2012	SD	*Graves* II, 1905–6, 259; *Dale-Jones and Lloyd* 1989, 48
48.	1843	John, 14th Earl of Tyrconnel	m	[Exhib RA, London, 1516]; untraced		*Graves* II, 1905–6, 259
49.	1843	Sir Francis Doyle, Bt		[Exhib RA, London, 1453]; untraced		*Graves* II, 1905–6, 259
50.	1844	Charles Thomas Longley, Bishop of Ripon		Lambeth Palace, London		*Ormond* 1973, 275
51.	1844	Thomas Hood		[Exhib RA, London, 1845, 1410]; untraced		*Graves* II, 1905–6, 260; *Ormond* 1973, 230
52.	1846	Baron Alderson		[Exhib RA, London, 1449]; untraced		*Graves* II, 1905–6, 260
53.	1846	Colonel Rice Trevor	m	[Guildhall, Carmarthen]; untraced		*Graves* II, 1905–6, 260; *Dale-Jones and Lloyd* 1989, 48
54.	1846	Connop Thirlwall, Bishop of St David's		[Carmarthen Town Hall]; untraced Other versions: Westminster Abbey, 1876, marble		*Graves* II, 1905–6, 260, 261; *Gunnis* 1968, 122; *Dale-Jones and Lloyd* 1989, 48
55.	1846	W Sharman Crawford, MP		[Exhib RA, London, 1452]; untraced		*Graves* II, 1905–6, 260
56.	1847	Barclay F Watson		[Exhib RA, London, 1348]; untraced		*Graves* II, 1905–6, 260
57.	1848	Mr Huxley	m	[Exhib RA, London, 1430]; untraced		*Graves* II, 1905–6, 260
58.	1849	Mrs Pemberton Heywood	m	[Exhib RA, London, 1258]; untraced		*Graves* II, 1905–6, 260; *Morris and Roberts* 1998, 181
59.	1849	Sir John Jervis, Attorney-General	m	[Exhib RA, London, 1290]; Middle Temple, London		*Graves* II, 1905–6, 260; *Gunnis* 1968, 122
60.	1850	F C Skey, FRS		[Exhib RA, London, 1449]; untraced		*Graves* II, 1905–6, 260
61.	1850	John, Duke of Rutland	m	[Exhib RA, London, 1380]; Belvoir Castle, Rutland		*Graves* II, 1905–6, 260; *Gunnis* 1968, 122
62.	1851	Dr Blair		[Exhib RA, London, 1340]; untraced		*Graves* II, 1905–6, 260
63.	1851	Miss Juliet Smith		[Exhib RA, London, 1314]; untraced		*Graves* II, 1905–6, 260
64.	1853	John Hardy		[Exhib RA, London, 1383]; untraced		*Graves* II, 1905–6, 260
65.	1853	Mrs J Sant		[Exhib RA, London, 1380]; untraced		*Graves* II, 1905–6, 260
66.	1854	Benjamin Heywood Jones, model		[Exhib Liverpool Ac, 763]; untraced		*Morris and Roberts* 1998, 181
67.	1854	Robert Maken, model		[Exhib Liverpool Ac, 764]; untraced		*Graves* II, 1905–6, 260; *Morris and Roberts* 1998, 181
68.	1854	William Sant		[Exhib RA, London, 1431]; untraced		*Graves* II, 1905–6, 260
69.	1855	William Rathbone Model(s): exhib Liverpool Ac, 1854, 760		Walker, Liverpool Other versions: St George's Hall, Liverpool, 1857, marble		*Graves* II, 1905–6, 260; *Gunnis* 1968, 122; *Morris and Roberts* 1998, 181
70.	1855	William Stuart Model(s): exhib RA, London, 1856, 1302	b	[Railway bridge, Great Howard Street, Liverpool, Lancs]; NRM, York	SD	*Graves* II, 1905–6, 260; *Cavanagh* 1997, 69–70 (repr)
71.	1856	William Roscoe		Unitarian Chapel, Renshaw Street, Liverpool		GPC
72.	1857	George Guthrie		[Exhib RA, London, 1337]; RCS, London		*Graves* II, 1905–6, 260; *Ormond* 1973, 206
73.	1857	Mary Sant		[Exhib RA, London, 1315]; untraced		*Graves* II, 1905–6, 260
74.	1858	Major Levison		[Exhib RA, London, 1291]; untraced		*Graves* II, 1905–6, 260
75.	1859	Marion Hall Davis		[Exhib RA, London, 1351]; untraced		*Graves* II, 1905–6, 260
76.	1859	Miss Hamilton, posthumous bust		[Exhib RA, London, 1368]; untraced		*Graves* II, 1905–6, 260
77.	1860	Mr Edgar	m	[Exhib RA, London, 987]; untraced		*Graves* II, 1905–6, 260
78.	1860	Mrs Magniac, posthumous bust		[Exhib RA, London, 971]; untraced		*Graves* II, 1905–6, 260
79.	1860	William Peek	m	[Exhib RA, London, 1065]; untraced		*Graves* II, 1905–6, 260
80.	1862	Dr E A Parkes	m	[Exhib RA, London, 1075]; University College, London		*Graves* II, 1905–6, 260; *Gunnis* 1968, 122

81.	1862	Unidentified lady, posthumous		[Exhib RA, London, 1091]; untraced	*Graves* II, 1905–6, 260
82.	1863	Captain Francis Fowke, R E		[Exhib RA, London, 1152]; untraced	*Graves* II, 1905–6, 260
83.	1864	Mrs Frederick Mocatta		[Exhib RA, London, 906]; untraced	*Graves* II, 1905–6, 260
84.	1865	Mrs Mocatta	m	[Exhib RA, London, 1034]; untraced	*Graves* II, 1905–6, 260
85.	1865	Mrs Sant		[Exhib RA, London, 974]; untraced	*Graves* II, 1905–6, 260
86.	1866	'An old gentleman'		[Exhib RA, London, 983]; untraced	*Graves* II, 1905–6, 260
87.	1866	Colonel Leveson		[Exhib RA, London, 1004]; untraced	*Graves* II, 1905–6, 260
88.	1867	Sir Samuel Canning		[Exhib RA, London, 1154]; untraced	*Graves* II, 1905–6, 261
89.	1867	Thomas Hood	p	[Royal Society, London]; untraced	*Ormond* 1973, 230
90.	1868	Master Jemmy Sant		[Exhib RA, London, 1023]; untraced	*Graves* II, 1905–6, 261
91.	1868	Mr Newbon, posthumous		[Exhib RA, London, 1133]; untraced	*Graves* II, 1905–6, 261
92.	1868	Unidentified lady		[Exhib RA, London, 1197]; untraced	*Graves* II, 1905–6, 261
93.	1869	Dr Forbes Winslow	m	[Exhib RA, London, 1179]; untraced	*Graves* II, 1905–6, 261
94.	1870	Dr Quain	m	[Exhib RA, London, 1187]; untraced	*Graves* II, 1905–6, 261
95.	1871	Daniel Maclise	m	[Exhib RA, London, 1305]; RA, London	*Graves* II, 1905–6, 261; *Gunnis* 1968, 122; *Ormond* 1973, 295
96.	1871	Sir Francis Ronalds	m	[Exhib RA, London, 1259]; Royal Soc, London	*Graves* II, 1905–6, 261; *Ormond* 1973, 400
97.	1873	Dr Williams, FRS		[Exhib RA, London, 1424]; untraced	*Graves* II, 1905–6, 261
98.	1873	J Norman Lockyer F R S		[Exhib RA, London, 1425]; untraced	*Graves* II, 1905–6, 261
99.	1874	John Constable RA	m	[Exhib RA, London, 1549]; RA, London	*Graves* II, 1905–6, 261; *Gunnis* 1968, 122; *Dale-Jones and Lloyd* 1989, 48
100.	1874	Miss Hayes	m	[Exhib RA, London, 1547]; untraced	*Graves* II, 1905–6, 261
101.	1876	Miss Collmann	m	[Exhib RA, London, 1383]; untraced	*Graves* II, 1905–6, 261
102.	1876	Sir Francis Ronalds	m	Institute of Electrical Engineers, London	*Ormond* 1973, 400
103.	1877	Unidentified lady		[Exhib RA, London, 1510]; untraced	*Graves* II, 1905–6, 261
Reliefs					
104.	1840	The affrighted mother		[Exhib RA, London, 1094]; untraced	*Graves* II, 1905–6, 259
105.	1846	The Madonna	m	[Exhib RA, London, 1518]; untraced	*Graves* II, 1905–6, 260
106.	1850	Madonna and Child, alto relievo		[Exhib RA, London, 1455]; untraced	*Graves* II, 1905–6, 260
107.	1852	Diana and Endymion		[Exhib RA, London, 1358]; untraced	*Graves* II, 1905–6, 260; *Morris and Roberts* 1998, 181
108.	1854	Instruction		[Exhib RA, London, 1393]; untraced	*Graves* II, 1905–6, 260
109.	1855	Virgin and Saviour, alto-relievo		[Exhib RA, London, 1431]; untraced	*Graves* II, 1905–6, 260
110.	1858	Madonna and Child	m	[Exhib RA, London, 1330]; untraced	*Graves* II, 1905–6, 260
111.	1865	Madonna and Child, alto-relievo		[Exhib RA, London, 963]; untraced	*Graves* II, 1905–6, 260
112.	1875	The Swing, alto-relievo		[Exhib RA, London, 1239]; untraced	*Graves* II, 1905–6, 261
Miscellaneous					
113.	1840	William Charles Macready		[Exhib RA, London, 1097]; untraced	*Graves* II, 1905–6, 259; *Ormond* 1973, 299
114.	1855	A cottage scene		[Exhib RA, London, 1328]; untraced	*Graves* II, 1905–6, 260
115.	1858	Indian figure		[Exhib RA, London, 1214]; untraced	*Graves* II, 1905–6, 260
116.	1862	Sir James Dalrymple Hay Bt		[Exhib RA, London, 1099]; untraced	*Graves* II, 1905–6, 260
117.	1866	Andromeda		[Exhib RA, London, 856]; untraced	*Graves* II, 1905–6, 260
118.	1867	Love Triumphant		[Exhib RA, London, 1012]; untraced	*Graves* II, 1905–6, 260
119.	1868	Field Marshall Sir John Burgoyne Bt		[Exhib RA, London, 1139]; untraced	*Graves* II, 1905–6, 261
120.	1868	Sir W Jenner Bt, FRS		[Exhib RA, London, 1146]; untraced	*Graves* II, 1905–6, 261
121.	1869	R D Hampden, Bishop of Hereford	m	[Exhib RA, London, 1156]; untraced	*Graves* II, 1905–6, 261
122.	1870	Nymph and Cupid	m	[Exhib RA, London, 1132]; untraced	*Graves* II, 1905–6, 261
123.	1875	Cupid and Psyche	m	[Exhib RA, London, 1317]; untraced	*Graves* II, 1905–6, 261

DAVIS, George fl after 1770

An artificial stone manufacturer.

Miscellaneous					
1.	post-1770	Statues, medallions and other work	sa	[for Lord Rockingham]; untraced	Wentworth Woodhouse muniments, quoted in NP/RG

DAVIS, of Bath fl 1795–1858

Presumably a family firm, known to have been active between 1795 and 1858.

Funerary Monuments					
1.	1795	Henry Littledale and his daughter	St Nicholas, Whitehaven, churchyard		*CP*, 14 April 1795
2.	†1837	Elizabeth Harper	Drybrook, Glos	S	Pevsner, *Glos: Vale & Forest of Dean*, 1976, 174
3.	†1850	Rev John Allen	Upper Arley, Worcs	S	
4.	†1858	Elizabeth Law (signed R Davis)	Standon, Herts	S	

DAVIS, Roger fl 1682–*c*1700

The master-joiner at Chelsea Hospital with Charles Hopson and John Smallwell, where he worked under the wood-carvers **William Emmett** and **William Morgan**. He was also employed under **Grinling Gibbons** on the Choir at St Paul's Cathedral, again with Smallwell and Hopson. Under **John Oliver** he provided carved work at Mercers' Hall, completed by August 1682.

Literary References: *Green* 1964 (1), 58, 91, 139

DAVIS, William fl 1692

He worked at Chatsworth in 1692 under **Thomas Young**, the London woodcarver, and with **Joel Lobb** and **Samuel Watson**, carving ornaments in limewood for the Great Chamber.

Literary References: *Green* 1964 (1), 58, 91, 120, 139

Archival References: James Whildon's Accts, Chatsworth, 1685–99, 76

DAVY, George fl 1767–73

George Davy, an artificial stone manufacturer, took over the premises in Goulston Square, Whitechapel, London, formerly occupied by **Daniel Pincot**, some time between February and October 1767, when he advertised 'a large Quantity of Goods of near 100 different Subjects, such as Figures, Busts, Tablets, Friezes, Medalions, Vases, Capitals of Different Orders of various Sizes' for sale at his warehouse at 18 Long Acre, near Covent Garden. He claimed that these goods were 'more durable and higher finished than natural stone' and, furthermore, undertook to sell them at the same price or cheaper than any equivalent work available in plaster or wood (*Daily Ad*, 23 October 1767). At the end of December 1767 there was a sale of artificial stone produced at Goulston Square over the last year, at Christie's, perhaps including work by both Davy and Pincot. The catalogue survives in the Christie archive and shows that prices were considerably lower than those of comparable items listed in the catalogue of the **Coade Factory of Lambeth**, published in 1783.

In March 1768 Davy announced that a large quantity of his artificial stone had been sold by John Moreing at the Great Sale Room in Maiden Lane, Covent Garden, adding 'if due Encouragement is given to this Undertaking, the Proprietor intends to continue the Manufactory' (*Daily Ad*, 23/24 March 1768). Further sales at Moreing's auction house and then at Blyth's sale room in Dean Street, Soho were advertised throughout 1768 and in 1770. The public response appears to have been less than enthusiastic for Davy commented, 'the Proprietor has reason to think that many Gentlemen entertain a less opinion of Artificial Stone by the Reports of some whose Interest it may be to deprecate it' (*Daily Ad*, 27 May 1768).

Davy's last known advertisements appeared in April 1771 (*Daily Ad*, 29 April 1771) and by July 1773 he was financially ruined. He wrote to his patron, the 2nd Marquess of Rockingham requesting payment for four medallions of Alexander and Hercules (**6**), explaining that they 'were made by your particular Order and at the Sale I bought them for your Lordship but am now so poor that I cannot clare [*sic*] the lots therefore let me intreat your Lordship to be so kind as to advance me the money or else the goods will be resold and all the charges attending it will fall on me'. He also informed him that if he had any further orders he should approach a 'Mr Smith at Nightsbridge' who had bought all his moulds (*Rockingham Vouchers, Sheffield City Library*, No 1, microfilm A314). In October 1773 Davy wrote a yet more desperate letter to the Duke of Northumberland asking him to settle a bill for £14 8s for various pieces of artificial stone (**5**), 'for I must Actually go to Prison in a City Action if I can't raise fifteen pounds by the 15th or 16th of this month' (*Davy/Northumberland*).

Rockingham bought reliefs, busts and statues after the antique from Davy, as well as a statue of a druid (**2**) and charity children (**7**), both subjects later produced by the Coade Factory. Some of Davy's moulds may still have been in use at Lambeth more than 50 years later, for it seems likely that 'Mr Smith at Nightsbridge' was a predecessor or partner of **Bridges of Knightsbridge** whose factory was bought by Mrs Coade in 1775. This suggestion of a direct connection between Davy, Bridges and Coade is supported by the production of large-scale statues of druids by all three businesses (see **Bridges, of Knightsbridge**, 1 and **Coade Factory, of Lambeth**, 207).

EH

Literary References: *Valpy* 1986, 210–5, 220–1; *Coade* 1990, 33; *Penny* 1990, 879
Archival References: Rockingham Vouchers; Davy/Northumberland
Auction References: Pincot and Davy 1767; Davy 1768 (1); Davy 1768 (2); Davy 1768 (3); Davy 1768 (4); Davy 1770

Statues					
1.	1771	The dying gladiator Payment(s): 30 gns	sa	[coll Charles, 2nd Marquess of Rockingham]; untraced	*Penny* 1991 (2), 14, noting vouchers 1, 36, 54, 66, 77, 93, Wentworth Woodhouse Muniments, Sheffield City Libraries
2.	1768–1773	Druid	sa	[coll Charles, 2nd Marquess of Rockingham]; untraced	*Penny* 1990, 879
3.	1768–1773	Grecian Venus	sa	[coll Charles, 2nd Marquess of Rockingham]; untraced	*Penny* 1991 (2), 14, noting vouchers 1, 36, 54, 66, 77, 93, Wentworth Woodhouse Muniments, Sheffield City Libraries
Busts					
4.	1768–1773	Several busts from the antique, including Antoninus Pius	sa	[coll Charles, 2nd Marquess of Rockingham]; untraced	*Penny* 1991 (2), 14, noting vouchers 1, 36, 54, 66, 77, 93, Wentworth Woodhouse Muniments, Sheffield City Libraries
Architectural Sculpture					
5.	1773	'4 pieces of Cornis', patterae with lions heads, medallions with the head of the Duke of Northumberland Payment(s): £14 8s	sa	[for the Duke of Northumberland]; untraced	*Kelly* 1990, 33
6.	1773	Alexander and Hercules, four medallions	sa	[coll Charles, 2nd Marquess of Rockingham]; untraced	*Penny* 1990, 879
7.	1768–1773	Charity children	sa	[coll Charles, 2nd Marquess of Rockingham]; untraced	*Penny* 1990, 879
8.	1768–1773	Tablets and medallions, some with reliefs of dancing nymphs	sa	[coll Charles, 2nd Marquess of Rockingham]; untraced	*Penny* 1991 (2), 14, noting vouchers 1, 36, 54, 66, 77, 93, Wentworth Woodhouse Muniments, Sheffield City Libraries

DAVY, W fl 1816

He advertised in the *Norwich Mercury*, 17 February 1816, that he had recently taken the long-established yard of Blackburn Castle Meadows, near the 'new opening' King Street, Norwich. He was previously at 'St. George's Colegate.' He boasted that he could provide chimneypieces, gravestones and monuments. (Inf. David Cubitt)

DAW, James, of Berkeley fl 1807–45

He provided a number of tablets in Gloucestershire including one of coloured marbles to Elizabeth Dyer (1). Daw clearly had pretensions as an artist for he signed the Royal Arms of George III in Upper Cam 'James Daw, sculptor.' Since he added 'pinxit' to this work he may only have been responsible for painting the arms (10).

Funerary Monuments

1.	†1807	Elizabeth Dyer	Cromhall, Glos	S	Pevsner, *Glos: Vale & Forest of Dean*, 1976, 166
2.	†1826	Mary Tratman	Berkeley, Glos		Pevsner, *Glos: Vale & Forest of Dean*, 1976, 101
3.	†1786	Hopton Hadley	St George, Upper Cam, Glos	S	Pevsner, *Glos: Cotswolds*, 1999, 209
4.	†1810	William Turner	Upper Cam, Glos	S	Pevsner, *Glos: Cotswolds*, 1999, 209
5.	†1836	Clarissa Peach	Olveston, Glos	S	Pevsner, *Glos: Vale & Forest of Dean*, 1976, 316
6.	†1836	Samuel Cruger Peach	Olveston, Glos		
7.	†1845	Sir John Colt	St Michael, Hill, Glos	S	Pevsner, *Glos: Vale & Forest of Dean*, 1976, 272
8.	nd	Unidentified subject, tablet	St Martin, Horsley, Glos	S	Pevsner, *Glos: Cotswolds*, 1999, 416
9.	nd	Unidentified subject, tablet	Congregational Church, Upper Cam, Glos	S	Pevsner, *Glos: Cotswolds*, 1999, 210

Architectural Sculpture

10.	1816	Royal arms of King George III	Upper Cam, Glos	S	Pevsner, *Glos: Cotswolds*, 1999, 209

DAWSON, Francis fl 1793–95

It was noted in the *Cumberland Pacquet* of 8 January 1793 that Francis Dawson, a marble-cutter, had opened a marble yard at Brackenthwaite, Whitehaven. He had lately acted as foreman in one of the principal marble yards in London after some years in Dublin. He could provide chimneypieces, gravestones and monuments. The same paper reported on 14 April 1795 that Dawson's monument to Henry Littledale had been erected in Whitehaven (1). The paper feared that the Italian and Kilkenny marbles would suffer from exposure to the elements. (Inf: Denis Perriam)

Literary References: *Potterton* 1975, 42–3

Funerary Monuments

1.	1795	Henry Littledale	Whitehaven, Cumbria	*Potterton* 1975, 42

DAY, Charles, of Cambridge fl 1781

He was the master-mason responsible for building Cambridge Town Hall in 1781.

Literary References: Town Archives, cited in *Gunnis* 1968, 123

DAY, F S fl 1839

She was the sister of **Joseph Charles Day**. In 1839, while living with her brother at 41 Camden Street, Camden Town, she was awarded a medal from the Society of Arts (1).

Busts

1.	1839	Unidentified subject	[Soc of A, silver Isis medal]; untraced	RSA, *Transactions*, vol 53, 1841, xv

DAY, Henry John 1825–

Possibly a relative of **Joseph C Day** and **F S Day**, he attended the Royal Academy School of Sculpture in 1844. He gave his address as Dartford and was admitted on the recommendation of **William Behnes**. In 1851 was working as an assistant to **George Cooper of Canterbury**.

Literary References: *Gunnis* 1968, 123

Archival References: RA Admissions

DAY, J, of Westminster fl *c*1785–1825?

A statuary and marble mason of Brewers Row, Westminster, he may have been be related to **R Day of Camberwell** and possibly also to **John Day**. Holden's *Triennial Directory* for 1808 lists 'Day, J, mason, Brewers Row, Westminster'. He was the main supplier of finely worked marble for the elaborate neoclassical clocks made by Vulliamy & Son in the late-18th and 19th centuries. His association with Vulliamy perhaps started as early as 1785. The surviving records in the PRO confirm that Day was working for Vulliamy by 1797 and that he (or his successor) was still supplying them with marble in 1825. (Inf. Roger Smith)

DAY, John fl 1818

In 1818 he built the mausoleum for Sir Francis Bourgeois attached to the Dulwich Picture Gallery, from designs by Sir John Soane.

Literary References: *Gunnis* 1968, 123

Archival References: Soane Bill Book G fol 425; Soane Bill Book H, fols 238–9

DAY, Joseph Charles fl 1835–42

In 1835 and 1836 he exhibited at the Royal Academy, giving his address as 61 Poland Street (4, 5). In 1837 he won a medal from the Society of Arts for a 'medallic portrait' (3) and in 1839, while living at 41 Camden Street, Camden Town, was awarded another medal (1). He won a third in 1841, while living at 50 Frith Street, Soho (2). His sister was **F S Day**.

Literary References: *Graves* II, 1905–6, 276; *Gunnis* 1968, 123

Statues

1.	1839	Original figure modelled in clay		Untraced	RSA *Transactions*, vol 53, 1841, xiv
2.	1841	Moses upbraiding the Israelites	p	[Soc of A, silver medal]; untraced	RSA *Transactions*, vol 54, 1843, xiv

Busts

3.	1837	Medallic portrait	[Soc of A, silver Isis medal]; untraced	RSA *Transactions*, vol 52, 1838, xiv

Reliefs

4.	1835	The fall of Satan, from Paradise Lost, alto-relievo	[Exhib RA, London, 1118]; untraced	*Graves* II, 1905–6, 276; *Gunnis* 1968, 123

Miscellaneous

5.	1836	St John	[Exhib RA, London, 1130]; untraced	*Graves* II, 1905–6, 276; *Gunnis* 1968, 123

DAY, of Birmingham fl 1811

Chimneypieces

1.	1811	Green marble, supplied with a marble table top and shelves	Tatton Park, Cheshire	NP/RG

DAY, R, of Camberwell fl 1816–c1841

As a young man Day worked in partnership with his father, J Day, a mason who became bankrupt in September 1822. The insolvency notice gave their address as Camberwell Green (*Euro Mag* 1822, 277). He then worked on his own and was responsible for a good deal of stone-carving at Buckingham Palace in 1827–8. Nash referred to him in a letter as an 'extraordinarily excellent workman' and praised him for the speed with which he carved stone of every description. He added that 'rapid and cheep as he is he is nevertheless a poor man and. . .I was under the necessity of agreeing with him for prompt payment' (TNA Work 19/3, fols 327–8).

He designed and executed the richly decorated Graeco-Egyptian mausoleum commemorating Richard Budd (2). In his *History of Lambeth* Allen describes it as 'without doubt the finest sepulchral monument in the open air in the metropolis and perhaps not equalled by any one in the kingdom' (*Allen* 1826, 414).

Gunnis identifies Day with the 'R Day, architect' who exhibited at the Royal Academy between 1827 and 1841, showing models and designs of buildings and giving addresses in Lambeth, Walworth, Southwark and Newington Causeway. This architect exhibited models of Salisbury Cathedral and the Temple of Minerva from the Parthenon. His son Robert exhibited similar works. The failing fortunes of one of the two was reported in the *Builder* in 1848: 'There are few architects who are not acquainted with the admirable models made by Mr Day', it began, but 'after struggling for some years to make a living by the practice of art he finds his efforts fruitless, and he must either seek some other employment or starve. Some of our readers may, perhaps, be disposed to help him' (*Builder*, 1848, 490).

Literary References: *Graves* II, 1905–6, 276; *Gunnis* 1968, 123

Funerary Monuments

1.	†1816	Richard Shawe	Old Dulwich churchyard, London	S	GPC
2.	1825	Richard Budd (†1824)	St Matthew, Lambeth, London, churchyard		Pevsner, *London: S*, 1983, 338

Architectural Sculpture

3.	1827–1828	Various, including: capitals, 'rockwork bases, cornices and balustrades' for the terraces and 'wreaths for the four pediments of the conservatory'. Payment(s): £20 each for the wreaths	Buckingham Palace, London	TNA Work 19/3, fols 327–8; *Gunnis* 1968, 123

DAY, W fl 1840

In 1840, while living at 41 Camden Street, Camden Town, with his sister, **F S Day**, he won the Society of Arts silver medal. There is no further trace of him.

Statues

1.	1840	'Clay model of a group'	[Soc of A, silver medal]; untraced	RSA *Transactions*, vol 53, 1840, xvi

DAYMOND, J fl 1851–c1870

The son of **William Daymond**, he showed at the Great Exhibition (1).

Literary References: *Gunnis* 1968, 123

Chimneypieces

1.	c1870	Description unavailable		Thoresby, Notts, great hall	GPC

Architectural Sculpture

2.	1851	Vase of flowers	m	[Gt Exhib]; untraced	*Gunnis* 1968, 123

DAYMOND, William

A London statuary.

Literary References: *Gunnis* 1968, 123

DEAN, H fl 1794

In 1794 he exhibited at the Royal Academy, giving his address as 8 Great Newport Street.

Literary References: *Graves* II, 1905–6, 280

Reliefs

1.	1794	The good Samaritan, allegorical bas-relief	[Exhib RA, London, 602]; untraced	*Graves* II, 1905–6, 280

DEANE, John –1705

He was apprenticed to Thomas Shadbolt and turned over to **William Stanton** on 20 April 1686, becoming free of the Masons' Company on 14 June 1687. Deane served as City Mason from 1696 to 1705, and was responsible in 1701 for masonry work at the Emmanuel Hospital in Tothill Fields (2) (City Cash Accts 01/22–25). In 1702 he was due to be paid £57 12s for unspecified masonry work (City Cash Accts 01/110, 116–7). Shortly before his death he was working at the Guildhall, and at a meeting of the Building Committee it was reported that he had offered to 'do the whole front of the porch and chapel both as to imagery and masonry work for £60'. In 1703 he received £26 from Mr Tufnell of Langley's, Chelmsford, 'for a marble monument and gravestone', a work which Gunnis was unable to trace (1).

Deane's widow, Mary, who continued the business, received £33 in 1707 for work done at the Guildhall in 1705 (City Cash Accts 01/25 ff 129r) and a further £400 in 1708, part of which was owing to her husband at the time of his death (City Cash Accts 1/25). She was also paid £130 in 1712 for work done in 1708 but must have died by 1712, for a further payment of £90 appears that year to her administrator, Nathaniel Rawlins (City Cash Accts 01/27 fol 153v).

In the Panshanger Archives is John Deane's agreement with William Cowper of the Middle Temple to build a house at Colesgreen, Herts. It states that the 'four pilasters shall be built according to the Corinthian order with Capitals, Architrave, Frieze, and Cornish according to the same order, with modillions carved with flowers and carved in the Pannells and a Parapit in front of the same building over the said Cornish'. The house, which appears from the sketch accompanying the agreement to have been of great charm, was finished in 1706 and pulled down in 1801 (GPC).

Another John Deane, perhaps a relative, was made free of the Masons' Company on 29 June 1693 by service to **Ephraim Beauchamp.** A 'John Dean mason in Angell Abbey', who features in a list of assistants and livery of the Masons' Company *c*1740, may perhaps be a member of the same family (Masons' Co Assistants, fol 5).

Literary References: *Gunnis* 1968, 123; *Webb* 1999, 10

Archival References: Masons' Co, *Freemen*, fol 12

Funerary Monuments

1.	1703	Tufnell family member (?) Payment(s): £26		[for Samuel Tufnell]; untraced	*Gunnis* 1968, 123 quoting account book of Samuel Tufnell

Architectural Sculpture

2.	1701	Various, including cartouches and coats of arms	s	Emmanuel Hospital, Tothill Fields, London	*Gunnis* 1968, 123

DEARE, John 1759–98

John Deare spent most of his short career in Rome producing decorative reliefs for the mansions of wealthy British patrons. He was born in Liverpool on 26 October 1759, the son of a jeweller. Deare showed an interest in art from childhood and his earliest recorded work, carved when he was about 10, was a finely detailed wood skeleton (**3**).

By May 1776 Deare had moved to London, where he was apprenticed to **Thomas Carter II**. He was employed principally in carving tablets for chimneypieces but also worked on a monument 'for General Burgoyne's Lady, to be put up in the Abbey' (**1**) (*Smith* 1828, II, 308). On 31 December 1777 he enrolled at the Royal Academy Schools, giving his age as 18. Deare and two of his contemporaries, **John Flaxman RA** and **Thomas Proctor**, soon became known among the students for their fine draughtsmanship. Their efforts are said to have prompted **Joseph Nollekens RA**, who was then a visitor, to give up sketching altogether (*Smith* 1828, II, 12). In 1780 Deare became the youngest artist to win the Academy's gold medal. The competition was in two stages and Deare submitted a terracotta relief of *Adam and Eve* from Milton's *Paradise Lost* and a sketch of *The soldiers going to kill Marius in prison* (**25, 26**). The second work could have been a drawing or a terracotta relief.

He was employed by Carter until the summer of 1783 and went on to work for **John Cheere** and later for **John Bacon RA**, for whom he modelled figures for a monument. He also provided models for Derby biscuit porcelain figures to ornament several of Benjamin Vulliamy's elaborate clocks (**41**). Meanwhile, he executed a number of independent works in plaster and terracotta, including four reliefs of the seasons (**18**) and a pediment relief depicting *The war of Jupiter and the Titans* (**24**), commissioned by George Gosling of Whitton Park. In 1784 he exhibited several works at the Liverpool Society for the Promotion of Painting and Design (**4, 5, 40, 42**).

Deare was industrious and often worked late into the night, rarely sleeping before 3am. He studied anatomy, attended dissections and examining life casts at the RA and was particularly fascinated by the physiognomy of criminals. On one occasion J T Smith says he borrowed the head of a hanged criminal and crept into Cheere's yard late at night to make a cast of it (**10**). His enthusiasm and self-confidence are apparent from his letters home. In 1783 he wrote to his father, 'The Sculptors allow me to be the first young fellow in the kingdom, and sometimes come with a model, for me to do them the very great honour of giving it a touch' (*Smith* 1828, II, 310).

In 1785 Deare was narrowly beaten by **JCF Rossi** in the competition to win the Academy's travelling student scholarship to Rome. The Council however took the unusual step of awarding prizes to both students. Deare set out in May, visiting Bologna and Florence *en route* and arrived in Rome in the summer of 1785. He remained in Rome for the rest of his life.

He soon started work on a large relief, *The judgment of Jupiter* (**31**) which he intended to exhibit at the Academy. Deare was bitterly disappointed when it was rejected because of its size. It was an ambitious work, drawing upon a wide range of sources. The composition of 23 figures was lively and varied and high and low relief carving were combined to great effect. The plaster was later installed at Northwick Park, Worcs and a version in marble was commissioned by Sir Richard Worsley of Appuldurcomb. The marble was confiscated by the French during their occupation of Rome and was lost for many years.

Deare's first and only RA exhibition entry was a plaster of *Edward and Eleanor* (**30**), commissioned by Henry Blundell and shown in 1788. This relief depicts the legend of Queen Eleanor of Castile, risking her life to suck the poison from a wound sustained during the Crusades by her husband, King Edward I. Deare interpreted this British medieval subject in an heroic, neoclassical style. The subject matter and elements of the composition may have been suggested by Angelica Kauffman's painting of the same subject, exhibited at the RA in 1776, during Deare's time as a student.

In Rome Deare filled many notebooks with his studies of ancient sculpture and became a leader of the city's artistic community. The critic and collector George Cumberland described the sculptor's apartment in the Corso as an informal academy where students gathered to compare their studies and plan expeditions to ancient sites. Deare's circle included the painters Charles Grignion, Robert Fagan and Hugh Robinson. A close associate was John Penn, who had inherited a fortune from the sale of land in Pennsylvania. Penn commissioned a bust (**13**) and an overmantle relief of *Caesar invading Britain* (**20**).

Deare's scholarship from the Academy terminated in June 1788, but he had several commissions in hand and so was able to remain in Rome without financial support. By 1791 he was well established and he wrote to tell his brother, **Joseph Deare**, who also became a sculptor, 'I have several men who work for me, and a boy who acts as my servant. I have the best study in Rome and live like a gentleman' (*Smith* 1828, II, 324).

Most of Deare's patrons were English visitors to the city. They included Henry Blundell, the Earl-Bishop of Bristol, Prince Augustus Frederick, Edward Poore, Thomas Hope and Sir Andrew Corbet Corbet, who commissioned a marble version of *Edward and Eleanor* (**30**) and a chimneypiece with a frieze of the *Nine Muses* (**19**) for Adderley Hall, Salop. In 1787 Sir Cecil Bisshop ordered a relief, *Venus reclining on a sea monster with Cupid and a putto* (also known as the *Marine Venus*) for Parham Park (**29**). Deare's *Venus* relief drew on classical Roman depictions of nymphs riding on sea monsters, but he introduced a languid, sensuous quality derived from Florentine sculpture of the 16th century. The subject gave him an opportunity to demonstrate his virtuosity in rendering in marble such diverse textures as flesh, hair, animal fur and sea foam. Another version of the subject was commissioned by Sir Richard Worsley, who evidently boasted of his acquisition, for Nollekens is said to have commented 'I don't see the wonderful merit in [Deare's] Marine Venus that Sir Richard Worsley talks so much about' (*Smith* 1828, II, 49).

Deare was involved only marginally in the trade in antiquities. He collected excavated works himself, occasionally assisted British patrons who wished to make purchases and made several copies of ancient sculpture, including a bust of *Ariadne*, after a work in the Capitoline Museum (**11**). He carved copies of the *Apollo Belvedere* and the *Medici Venus* for Lord Berwick (**6, 7**). This lucrative commission evidently caused friction between Deare and a rival sculptor, **Christopher Hewetson**, for Deare accused Hewetson of trying to influence Lord Berwick against him. Deare was in general critical of sculptors who made their living restoring, faking and selling antiquities. His attitude did not endear him to Nollekens, who would comment on hearing of Deare's death 'he was a very upstart fellow, or he ought to have made money by sending over some antiques from Rome' (*Smith* 1828, I, 231–2).

Deare's career continued to flourish through the 1790s. In 1795 he wrote to Joseph that he had sold chimneypieces to the Prince of Wales (**22**) and the Earl-Bishop (**21**) and was working on busts of Prince Augustus Frederick (**15**) and Lady Webster (**16**). In 1797 it was thought that the Committee of Taste might commission him to carve a monument for St Paul's Cathedral (*Farington* III, 947), but the following year, on 17 August 1798, he died at the age of 38. Deare was buried in the Protestant Cemetery in Rome.

There are several accounts of his cause of death. Charles Grignion told Deare's family that he had died after suffering from 'bilious fever' for eight days. Another possibility, recorded by J T Smith, was that he had slept on a block of marble in the hope that this would inspire his next work and caught a chill which killed him in just a few days. Yet another colourful account claimed that he was murdered or died of a broken heart having been thrown into prison by the commander of the French troops, who had fallen in love with his wife. Deare left a young widow, who was six months pregnant, and a three year old daughter. The sculptor Vincenzo Pacetti was appointed his executor and ordered an inventory of the contents of his studio. This lists many pieces of unworked marble, some antiquities, casts and several reliefs, most of which are untraced.

Deare's work was admired by most contemporaries and it was generally felt that if only he had lived longer he would have been recognised as a very great sculptor. Since much of his work was either installed in private houses or dispersed during the French occupation of Rome, it is only in recent that years that it has come into the public domain and so received the attention it deserves. It is now again recognised for its originality and technical virtuosity.

EH

Literary References: *Farington, passim*: *Smith* 1828, I, 183, 231–2; II, 12, 49, 303–333; *Hutchison* 1960–62, 143; *Gunnis* 1968, 123–4; *Ford* 1974, 431; *Penny* 1977 (1), 10, 15; *Laing* 1983, 187; *Clifford* 1990, 227–30, 235; *Knox* 1996, 95 n35; *Grove* 8, 1996, 587–8 (Bryant); *ODNB* (Stevens); *Ingamells* 1997, 87–8; 287–9; *Fogelman* 2000, 85–126; *Avery* 2002, 50–7

Archival References: RA Council Minutes, vol 2, 1785, fol 1

Additional MS Sources: *Deare Inventory*

Collections of Drawings: two volumes of drawings (236) mainly of antiquities and statues in Rome, many SD, VAM P&D E.57-291-1966; volume of drawings (138) by Deare and James Paine, Roman subjects, some s, VAM P&D E.238-376-1968; 7 drawings, *Harris M & AG*, pl 23–9; sketchbook (79 drawings), Walker 6415–6494

Miscellaneous Drawings: study of two nude youths, BM PDB 1973, 9414.10; pensive male figure seated on a chair, BM, PDB 1973, 0414.9; *Venus and Cupid*, dated 9 September, 1786, pen and ink, VAM P&D E.575-1931; small triangular altar, Villa Albani, sgd John Deare 1788, pen, ink and wash, VAM P&D E.576-1931; a Roman Wedding, pen and ink, VAM P&D E.577-1931; scene from *Coriolanus*, VAM P&D E.578-1931; two male figures in attitudes of flight, VAM P&D E.579-1931; pine tree in Villa Pamphili, VAM P&D E.580-1931; Cypress on Monte Mario, VAM P&D E.581-1931; nude male figure with rearing horse, Walker, 10820; design for a tomb monument, private coll (*Fogelman* 2000, 120, repr)

Portraits of the Sculptor: Charles Grignion, pen and ink drawing, Harris M & AG, P130

No.	Date	Work		Location	Reference
Funerary Monuments					
1.	1778	Lady Charlotte Burgoyne (co-sculptor: Thomas Carter)		Untraced	*Smith* II, 1828, 308
2.	†1792	William Wilson		Ganton, E R Yorks	*Fogelman* 2000, 101–2
Statues					
3.	c1770	Human skeleton, statuette		[coll Deare family]; untraced	*Fogelman* 2000, 88
4.	1784	Bellerophon, model		[Exhib SPPDL, 21]; untraced	*Morris and Roberts* 1998, 186; *Fogelman* 2000, 89
5.	1792	Adam and Eve, group Payment(s): £250	m	[coll Mr Boehm of London]; untraced	*Fogelman* 2000, 102
6.	1792–1795	Apollo Belvedere Payment(s): £450	m	[Attingham Hall, Salop; sold 1827, lot 78]; untraced	Attingham Hall sale, 1827, lot 78; *Fogelman* 2000, 103
7.	1792–1795	Venus de' Medici		[for Lord Berwick but impounded by the French, 1797]; untraced	*Fogelman* 2000, 96–7
8.	nd	Faun with a kid (Faunus), small statue		[Lyons House, Co Kildare]; coll Cloncurry family	*Fogelman* 2000, 105
Busts					
9.	1781	The devil		[coll Deare family]; untraced	*Fogelman* 2000, 89
10.	c1783	A criminal	p	Untraced	*Fogelman* 2000, 89
11.	1789–1790	Ariadne, after an antique bust in the Capitoline Museum	m	Untraced	*Fogelman* 2000, 96

No.	Date	Work	Medium	Location	Signed	Reference
12.	1789–1790	Madame Martinville		[coll Mr Lattin]; untraced		*Fogelman* 2000, 96
13.	1791–1793	John Penn of Stoke Poges	m	[coll John Penn]; Eton College, Windsor, Berks, library Other versions: Stoke Poges church, Bucks, plaster	SD	*Fogelman* 2000, 101 (repr 33)
14.	1793	Marshal Stanislaus Malachowski	m	National Museum, Warsaw, Poland	SD	*Fogelman* 2000, 102 (repr 34)
15.	c1795	Augustus Frederick, Duke of Sussex		Untraced		*Fogelman* 2000, 103–4
16.	c1795	Lady Elizabeth Webster		Untraced		*Fogelman* 2000, 104
Chimneypieces						
17.	1783	Description unavailable		[for 'a Manchester gentleman']; Untraced		*Fogelman* 2000, 90
18.	c1783	The seasons, four reliefs for chimneypieces		Untraced		*Fogelman* 2000, 89–90
19.	1792	with frieze of the nine muses	m	[Adderley Hall, Salop]; private coll		*Avery* 2002, 50–7 (repr)
20.	1791–1794	Caesar invading Britain, overmantle relief	m	Stoke Manor, Stoke Poges, Bucks, originally in great marble hall, now in drawing room		*Fogelman* 2000, 100–1 (repr 32)
21.	c1795	Description unavailable		[for the Earl-Bishop of Bristol, but impounded by the French and sold Rome, 1804]; untraced		*Fogelman* 2000, 104
22.	c1795	Two, one with frieze depicting a racehorse, the other 'mosaic' Payment(s): £150 and £350		[for George, Prince of Wales but confiscated by the French, 1797]; untraced		*Fogelman* 2000, 104
23.	c1795	with festoons and masks (co-sculptor: Vincenzo Pacetti) Payment(s): £150		[Intended for George, Prince of Wales but must have remained unfinished in Deare's studio and was completed by Vincenzo Pacetti in 1800]; Royal Coll (Frogmore, Berks)		*Fogelman* 2000, 104 (repr 36)
Architectural Sculpture						
24.	1784	War of Jupiter and the Titans Drawing(s): Liverpool Public Library, Mayer Papers inv 920 May		[Whitton Park, Hounslow, Middx, destroyed 1847]; destroyed		*Fogelman* 2000, 89, 90, 106
Reliefs						
25.	c1780	Adam and Eve (The Angels surprising Satan at the ear of Eve)	tc	[RA, gold medal]; untraced		*Morris and Roberts* 1998, 186; *Fogelman* 2000, 85, 88–9
26.	c1780	The soldiers going to kill Marius in prison, probably a clay sketch		[for RA gold medal competition]; untraced		*Fogelman* 2000, 88–9
27.	post-1782	The good Samaritan		[Liverpool Dispensary, Lancs, destroyed c1829]; untraced		*Fogelman* 2000, 89
28.	c1783	Cupid and Psyche		Untraced		*Fogelman* 2000, 97
29.	1787	Venus reclining on a sea monster with Cupid and a putto (Marine Venus) Drawing(s): Pen and ink, 1786, Arthur M Sackler Coll, New York	m	[coll Sir Cecil Bisshop]; Parham Park, Pulborough, Sussex Other versions: JPGM 98.SA.4, c1788, m (?ex coll Sir Richard Worsley) Several contemporary versions, bronze	S	*Fusco* 1998, 104–5 (repr); *Fogelman* 2000, 94–6 (repr VII, 16–21)
30.	1790	Edward and Eleanor Drawing(s): VAM E.260-1968	m	[Adderley Hall, Salop]; private coll Other versions: Ince Blundell Hall, Lancs, 1786, plaster Walker 4418, 1786, plaster Lyons House, Co Kildare, plaster Wimpole Hall, Cheshire, plaster private coll, S 'ROBILLIAC. Sc.', marble	SD	*Graves* II, 1905–6, 283; *Avery* 2002, 50–7 (repr)
31.	1788–1790	The judgement of Jupiter	m	Los Angeles County Museum of Art, Cal M.79.37 Other versions: ex Northwick Park, Worcs (destr), 1786–7, plaster		*Bull. LACM*, 1980, 34–5 (repr); *Fogelman* 2000, 90–2 (repr 2–5)
32.	c1791	Cupid and Psyche Drawing(s): private coll, SD 1787	p	[coll Lord Cloncurry]; Lyons Demesne, Co Kildare Other versions: ex coll Thomas Hope, 1791, marble; untraced ex coll Robert Fagan; untraced		*Fogelman* 2000, 97–8 (repr 24)
33.	1791	Liberality, supported by justice and fortitude	m	[Exhib Soc of Artists, London, 64]; untraced		*Graves* 1907, 73; *Fogelman* 2000, 100
34.	1790–1792	Bacchus feeding a panther	m	[coll Edward Poore]; Art Institute of Chicago	SD	*Fogelman* 2000, 98–9 (repr 26, 27)
35.	1790–1792	Hebe feeding the bird of Jupiter Drawing(s): VAM E.64–1966	m	[coll Edward Poore; sold 1805]; untraced		*Fogelman* 2000, 99 (repr 30)
36.	1790–1795	Apollo with the muse Euterpe (?)		[Executed in competition with Canova]; untraced		*Fogelman* 2000, 99
37.	nd	A seated figure; portrait of the Pope; Time ravishing Youth		[coll Robert Fagan]; untraced		*Fogelman* 2000, 105
38.	nd	Boys		Untraced		*Fogelman* 2000, 92
Miscellaneous						
39.	1783	Spanish coat of arms, design only (?)		[for a Spanish nobleman]; untraced		*Fogelman* 2000, 89
40.	1784	Crucifix	tc	[Exhib SPPDL, 20]; untraced		*Morris and Roberts* 1998, 186; *Fogelman* 2000, 89
41.	c1784	Figures for clocks by Benjamin Vulliamy, models		Untraced		*Clifford* 1990, 226–236
42.	1784	Virginius and his daughter, cast		[Exhib SPPDL, 22]; untraced		*Morris and Roberts* 1998, 186; *Fogelman* 2000, 89

43.	1790–1791	Venus and Cupid	m	[for Lord Bristol]; untraced	*Fogelman* 2000, 96–7
44.	c1793	The three graces with the thread of life		Untraced	*Fogelman* 2000, 102
45.	1794	Centaur		[coll George Cumberland]; untraced	*Fogelman* 2000, 103
46.	nd	Antinous		[coll Thomas Hope]; untraced	*Fogelman* 2000, 105

DEARE, Joseph 1803–35

The nephew of **John Deare**, he was baptised on 27 May 1803 at St Nicholas, Liverpool, the son of Edward Deare, an attorney, and Margaret, née Wattle. He joined the Royal Academy Schools in April 1822, winning silver medals in 1823 and 1825, and a gold in the latter year for his group, *David and Goliath* (**3**). J T Smith reported a couple of years later that casts of this work could be bought at Deare's father's house at 12, Great St Helens, Bishopsgate 'where several other of his productions may be seen' (*Smith* 1828, 2, 331–2). The Society of Arts three times awarded him the silver Isis medal (**1, 2, 22**). By 1829 he had left the family home and set up at 58 Great Russell Street, moving again the following year to 38 Essex Street, Strand and then to 18 Hart Street, Bloomsbury.

From around 1832 he worked and exhibited in Liverpool. That year he showed eight busts at the Liverpool Academy from the house of William Clements, a printseller in Bond Street (**11–14, 17–20**). By 1834 he had moved to 4 Colquitt Street and he later had a studio in the old Excise Office in Hanover Street where he worked as a sculptor and portrait-painter. Late one night in 1835 he fell while trying to reach his studio by climbing a wall. He died of his injuries soon after, on 5 August 1835.

Literary References: *Gunnis* 1968, 124; *Graves* II, 1905–6, 283; *Hutchison* 1960–62, 174; *Morris and Roberts* 1998, 186; *ODNB* (Stevens)

Collections of Drawings: sketchbook, Liverpool Central Library, H741.91 DEA D 10617; album, Liverpool Central Library, riq 920 DEA, Eq 801

Statues				
1.	1823	Bacchus, 'plaster copy'	[Soc of A, silver Isis medal]; untraced	RSA, *Transactions*, vol 41, 1823, xxxix
2.	1824	Model of a group from the antique	[Soc of A, silver Isis medal]; untraced	RSA, *Transactions*, vol 42, 1824, xlvi
3.	1825	David and Goliath, model	[RA, gold medal]; destroyed	RA Premium list; *Graves* II, 1905–6, 283; *ODNB*
Busts				
4.	1828	Unidentified gentleman	[Exhib RA, London, 1206]; untraced	*Graves* II, 1905–6, 283
5.	1829	John Aston Key	[Exhib RA, London, 1154]; untraced	*Graves* II, 1905–6, 283
6.	1829	Unidentified gentleman	[Exhib RA, London, 1157]; untraced	*Graves* II, 1905–6, 283
7.	1830	Thomas Kearsey	[Exhib RA, London, 1180]; untraced	*Graves* II, 1905–6, 283
8.	1831	Francis B Thomas	[Exhib RA, London, 1221]; untraced	*Graves* II, 1905–6, 284
9.	1831	'The late' Thomas Lowten	[Exhib RA, London, 1231]; untraced	*Graves* II, 1905–6, 284
10.	1831	Unidentified gentleman	[Exhib RA, London, 1136]; untraced	*Graves* II, 1905–6, 284
11.	1832	Charles Nicholson, professor of the flute	[Exhib Liverpool Ac, 377]; untraced	*Morris and Roberts* 1998, 186
12.	1832	Dr Gall	[Exhib Liverpool Ac, 382]; untraced	*Morris and Roberts* 1998, 186
13.	1832	Dr Raffles	[Exhib Liverpool Ac, 376]; untraced	*Morris and Roberts* 1998, 186
14.	1832	Master W Patton	[Exhib Liverpool Ac, 193]; untraced	*Morris and Roberts* 1998, 186
15.	1832	Rev H S Cotton	[Exhib RA, London, 1110]; untraced	*Graves* II, 1905–6, 284
16.	1832	Unidentified gentleman	[Exhib RA, London, 1123]; untraced	*Graves* II, 1905–6, 284
17.	1834	Dr Stewart Traill	[Exhib Liverpool Ac, 441]; untraced	*Morris and Roberts* 1998, 186
18.	1834	John North	[Exhib Liverpool Ac, 435]; untraced	*Morris and Roberts* 1998, 186
19.	1834	Thomas Rodick	[Exhib Liverpool Ac, 436]; untraced	*Morris and Roberts* 1998, 186
20.	1836	Unidentified gentleman	[Exhib Liverpool Ac, 650]; untraced	*Morris and Roberts* 1998, 186
21.	nd	Lord Brougham	Untraced	*Gunnis* 1968, 124
Reliefs				
22.	1824	Original bas relief from the life of an unidentified subject	[Soc of A, silver Isis medal]; untraced	RSA, *Transactions*, vol 42, 1824, xlvi
23.	1828	Eleanor sucking poison	[Exhib Carlisle Ac of Fine Art, 209]; untraced	*Carlisle Ac Exhibs*, 1973
Miscellaneous				
24.	1823	Unidentified subject	[RA, silver medal]; untraced	RA Premium list
25.	1825	Academy figure, model	[RA, London, silver medal]; untraced	RA Premium list; *Hutchison* 1960–62, 174
26.	1831	Virginius and Virginia	[Exhib RA, London, 1131]; untraced	*Graves* II, 1905–6, 283
27.	1832	Specimen of casting from nature	[Exhib Liverpool Ac, 397]; untraced	*Morris and Roberts* 1998, 186

DEARLE, W, of London fl 1842

Funerary Monuments				
1.	†1842	Jane Pakre	Garrison Church, Colombo, Sri Lanka	GPC

DECAIX, Alexis fl 1794–1821

A Frenchman who may have fled to England during the French Revolution, he was in London from 1794. He worked for Garrard's, the silversmiths, from 1799 to 1804 and from 1800 to 1803 supplied 'bronze manufactures' to the Prince of Wales. He appears to have been responsible for a pair of recumbent bronze greyhounds supplied to the connoisseur and collector, Thomas Hope, for his mansion in Duchess Street, London. An engraving of Hope's picture gallery, published in *Magazine of Fine Arts*, 1821, has a sofa in the foreground with bronze dogs forming arm rests. These may be the dogs, 70cm in length, which were purchased by the Leeds industrialist, Sir Edward (later Lord) Brotherton at the great sale of Hope heirlooms conducted by Christie in July 1917 (lot 237) (**1**).

Literary References: *White* 1986, 23–25

Statues					
1.	pre-1821	Two greyhounds	b	LMG	*White* 1986, 23–5

DE CARLE FAMILY

Robert Brettingham de Carle	1748–1791
John de Carle	1750–1828
Benjamin de Carle	1788–1864

Robert de Carle II	1761–1837
Robert de Carle III	1785–1829
Mary de Carle	1792–1866
Robert de Carle IV fl	1795–1842

The de Carle family worked principally in Norwich though they, or perhaps another branch of the family, also ran workshops elsewhere in East Anglia. Robert Brettingham, John and Robert II were brothers; John was the father of Benjamin, Robert II was the father of Robert III and the latter married Mary de Carle, née Lock. Robert IV's kinship to the other family members is not clear, but he practiced in Bury St Edmunds and was at some stage in partnership with Benjamin.

Robert Brettingham de Carle worked as a modeller for the **Coade Factory**. He was the son of a bricklayer Robert de Carle I, and was baptised in Norwich on 17 July 1748. It is thought that he was named after his paternal grandmother, who was probably a sister of the architect Matthew Brettingham. He appears to have moved to London as a young man and he married Ann Davy at St George, Hanover Square on 18 February 1774. In 1785 he exhibited three works, including a wax portrait of a lady, at the Royal Academy, giving his address as Stangate Street, Lambeth (**33–35**). He was working for the Coade factory by the mid-1780s and in 1786 signed a gothic Coadestone font in Debden, Essex, together with the architect Richard Holland (**30**). Another signed work, also in Coadestone, is a lunette depicting three putti grouped around an urn which is fixed to a headstone at Yoxford, Suffolk (**4**). It commemorates Ann Davy, who may have been the sculptor's mother-in-law. After his death in London on 7 February 1791, he was described in the Press as 'the first artist of the Artificial Stone manufactory' and 'an eminent modeller, whose skill was unrivalled' (*Norfolk Chronicle*, 12 Feb 1791; *Bury Post*, 16 Feb 1791). His last work, a coat of arms in coade stone, was erected above the entrance to a shawl manufactory in St George, Colegate, Norwich, in September 1792 (**31**).

John de Carle worked as a marble mason and builder in Norwich, Bury St Edmunds and Cambridge. He was born on 17 September 1750, the son of a bricklayer, Robert de Carle I, and christened on 23 September at St Giles, Norwich. He served his apprenticeship under **John Ivory** in Norwich. On 6 April 1773 he married Alice Parkerson and the following year he became a freeman of Norwich. De Carle and Ivory became business partners in April 1776. De Carle paid Ivory £50, together with £171 7s for a half share of his stock, and they agreed to share all expenses and profits for the duration of the partnership, which was set at 11 years (Ivory/de Carle Indentures). A few months later they advertised that, as co-partners in the marble trade, they could provide marble chimneypieces and monuments executed 'in the neatest manner' (*Linnell and Wearing* 1952, 26). Together they signed a number of wall monuments in Norfolk churches which depict mourning putti in various attitudes, with funerary symbols such as broken columns and extinguished torches (**1–3, 5**).

In 1792 John de Carle and his brother, Robert de Carle II, jointly purchased the stock and premises of **Thomas Singleton of Bury St Edmunds** and advertised 'Chimney Pieces, Monuments, Gravestones, etc' executed with 'neatness, accuracy and dispatch' at both Norwich and Bury (*Bury and Norwich Post*, 20 Feb 1799). It seems that John ran the Bury workshop alone and Robert, who remained in Norwich, was merely a sleeping partner. He must have been successful for in 1799 he established a second branch of the business in Cambridge, while continuing to operate in Bury. He announced that he had 'taken Premises for the reception of his materials in Mr. Wedd's Corn Yard, near the Great Bridge' and that he could execute masonry, chimneypieces and monuments 'on terms equal to the prices charged in London, which he understands are much lower than those hitherto charged in Cambridge' (*ibid*).

John's practice as a builder was extensive and he was frequently employed to erect buildings designed by Sir John Soane. He built and carved the city's arms for Soane's Blackfriars bridge, Norwich, in 1783 (**29**). Between 1783 and 1788 he worked at several houses in Norfolk which were built or rebuilt to Soane's designs, including Burnham Hall, Earsham Hall, Saxlingham Rectory, Letton Hall and Shottesham Hall (Soane Bill Abstracts, 9–10, 78–9, 80; Soane Accounts 2, 4). In 1790–91 he and Robert de Carle II carried out alterations to Norwich Castle at a cost of £3,905, again under Soane's direction (*Soane Journal* I, 20). Later in his career he was much employed at Ickworth House, Suffolk. In 1817 he built the obelisk in memory of the 4th Earl of Bristol and Bishop of Derry (**32**) (De Carle Obelisk Bill; *Norwich Mercury*, 31 Jan 1818). Between 1822 and 1824 he and his son, Benjamin de Carle carried out work on the south and east fronts and prepared an estimate for a parapet outside the dining room (Ickworth Building Accounts 941/30/7, 11, 13). They had difficulty in obtaining sufficient good quality Portland stone for the portico at Ickworth, where they were working in 1826–27. John died on 7 July 1828 and was buried in the Abbey graveyard at Bury St Edmunds. He had several sons who followed his trade: James de Carle (1775–1825) acted as his assistant for a time, became free in 1797 and then established himself as a stonemason in Ipswich, Charles William de Carle (1783–1822) was apprenticed to John Ivory, like his father, became free in 1804, and Benjamin seems to have taken over the business in Bury after his father's death.

Robert de Carle II, his son, **Robert de Carle III** and **Mary de Carle** all worked as stonemasons in Norwich. They had premises at Duke's Palace, close to St John Maddermarket and were responsible for a number of monuments in Norfolk, Suffolk and Essex, including one commemorating the Robinson family at Denstone, Suffolk, which takes the form of a large altar-tomb in stone, marble and touch and is based on 16th-century work (**15**). Robert de Carle II was baptised on 24 August 1761, he married Mary Smith in February 1784 and their son, Robert III, was born on 15 May 1785. In 1792 Robert II and John de Carle jointly purchased the stock and premises of **Thomas Singleton of Bury St Edmunds** but it appears that Robert remained in Norwich, while John ran the Bury workshop alone (*Bury and Norwich Post*, 20 Feb 1799).

Robert III and Mary Lock married on 23 February 1813. Two years later the firm exhibited a Portland stone sphinx by **A Arnold**, a deaf and dumb sculptor, at their premises and informed the public that Arnold would 'execute any orders . . . on moderate terms, as his principal objective is amusement' (*Norwich Mercury*, 26 August 1815). In May 1829, shortly after her husband's death, Mary advertised that she intended to continue his statuary and masonry business for the benefit of herself and her seven children (*Norwich Mercury*, 27 June 1829). A few months later notice was given of the forthcoming auction of a 'dwelling house, stoneyard and masonry rooms' at St John Maddermarket, which may have been the de Carle business (*Norwich Mercury*, 1 Oct 1829). If so there must have been some change in Mary de Carle's circumstances as early the following year she placed another advertisement stating that she was carrying on the business under the superintendence of 'Mr De Carle Senior' (*Norwich Mercury*, 9 Jan 1830). This was presumably her father-in-law who died, aged 76, on Sunday 8th January 1837.

Three of Robert III and Mary de Carle's sons, Edward (1815–1848), Charles Gills (1823–1856) and Henry Lock (1826–1891) became stonemasons. Edward and Henry both worked from premises in Chapel Field Road, Norwich. Mary de Carle's business continued to thrive until the mid-19th century and was listed in a local directory for 1845 (*White* 1845, 206). She seems to have retired from business four years later since in 1849 she informed the public that the marble and stone works in Duke's Palace were to continue under the superintendence of one of her sons (*Norwich Mercury*, 7 April 1849). In the same advertisement she noted that the firm had been 'established upwards of a century', suggesting that Robert de Carle II had taken over an established business. Mary de Carle died at the age of 74 on 27 December 1866.

Robert de Carle IV was the master mason when additions were made to Culford Hall, Suffolk in 1796 and received £2,020 for his work. He was also responsible for building work at Haileybury College, 1806–9, the terrace at Ickworth, 1827 and gothic ornaments at Great Barton Hall, Suffolk. (Add inf. David Cubitt of Norwich).

EH

Literary References: *Burgess* 1960, 639; *Burgess* 1963, *passim*; *Gunnis* 1968, 125; *Pyke* 1973, 38; RG/JP, 3, 421–4; *Colvin* 1995, 155

Additional MS Sources: *De Carle Cash Book; De Carle Day Books: De Carle Letter Book; Ivory Stock Valuation*

Funerary Monuments

1.	†1762	Sir Randall Ward Bt (by John de Carle) (co-sculptor: John Ivory)		Bixley, Norfolk	S	RG/JP, 5, 740; Pevsner, *Norfolk: N W & S*, 1999, 208
2.	†1779	Thomas Moore (by John de Carle) (co-sculptor: John Ivory)		Norwich Cathedral, Norfolk	S	Pevsner, *Norfolk: NE & Norwich*, 1997, 210
3.	†1780	Cyril Wyche (by John de Carle) (co-sculptor: John Ivory)		Hockwold, Norfolk	S	Pevsner, *Norfolk: N W & S*, 1999, 410
4.	1786	Ann Davy (Coadestone lunette fixed to headstone) (by Robert Brettingham de Carle)	sa	Yoxford, Suffolk, churchyard	S	*Burgess* 1960, 639
5.	†1787	Sarah Norris (by John de Carle) (co-sculptor: John Ivory)		Barton Turf, Norfolk	S	Pevsner, *Norfolk: NE & Norwich*, 1997, 380
6.	1791	Margaret, Duchess of Norfolk (†1563) (by John de Carle)		St John Maddermarket, Norwich, Norfolk	S	*Gunnis* 1968, 125
7.	1797	William Wollaston (by John de Carle)		Great Finborough, Suffolk	S	*Gunnis* 1968, 125
8.	1799	Edmund Tyrell (by John de Carle)		Stowmarket, Suffolk	S	*Gunnis* 1968, 125
9.	†1806	William, 1st Earl of Clermont (by John de Carle)		Little Cressingham, Norfolk	S	*Gunnis* 1968, 125
10.	?1808	George Stone (signed R de Carle and Son)		Woodton, Suffolk		*Gunnis* 1968, 125
11.	?1808	George Stone (signed R de Carle and Son)		Bedlingham, Norfolk		*Gunnis* 1968, 125
12.	1814	Lieutenant-Colonel Collier (by Robert de Carle IV)		St Mary, Bury St Edmunds, Suffolk	S	*Gunnis* 1968, 125
13.	1820	Gertrude Dawson (by Robert de Carle IV)		Bardwell, Suffolk	S	*Gunnis* 1968, 125
14.	†1821	William Stevenson (designed by Arthur Browne; by John de Carle)		St Stephen, Norwich, Norfolk	S	Pevsner, *Norfolk: N E & Norwich*, 1997, 253
15.	1822	Robinson family, altar-tomb (by Robert de Carle IV)		Denstone, Suffolk		*Gunnis* 1968, 125
16.	1831	William Scott (by Benjamin de Carle)		Mildenhall, Suffolk		*Gunnis* 1968, 124
17.	1833	Sir James Affleck (by Robert de Carle IV)		Dalham, Suffolk	S	*Gunnis* 1968, 125
18.	†1834	Charles Earle		Cromer, Norfolk		RG/JP, 3, 423
19.	1834	Rev Ligonier Treadway (by Benjamin de Carle)		Gayton, Norfolk		*Gunnis* 1968, 124
20.	1839	Mary Gataker (by Benjamin de Carle)		Worlington, Suffolk		*Gunnis* 1968, 124
21.	1840	Emma Colvile (by Robert de Carle IV)		Hawstead, Suffolk	S	*Gunnis* 1968, 125
22.	1840	George Weller-Poley (by Robert de Carle IV)		Boxted, Suffolk	S	*Gunnis* 1968, 125
23.	1841	Henry Wright (by Benjamin de Carle)		St Lawrence, Norwich, Norfolk		GPC
24.	†1841	Lady Pilkington (by Robert de Carle IV)		Dedham, Essex	S	*Gunnis* 1968, 125
25.	†1842	Mary Turner		St Peter Mancroft, Norwich		RG/JP, 3, 423
26.	1846	William Killett (by Benjamin de Carle)		Kenninghall, Norfolk		*Gunnis* 1968, 124

Chimneypieces

27.	1787–1788	Several, of marble (by John de Carle)		[Letton Hall, Norfolk]; untraced		Soane bill book, 1, 64–8, 106–8
28.	1829	by Benjamin de Carle	m	Bank of England, Norwich		*Gunnis* 1968, 124

Architectural Sculpture

29.	1783	Norwich city arms (by John de Carle)	s	Blackfriars Bridge, Norwich, Norfolk		*Gunnis* 1968, 125
30.	1786	Font (designed by Richard Holland; by Robert Brettingham de Carle)	sa	Debden, Essex	SD	*Burgess* 1960, 639
31.	1792	Royal arms (by Robert Brettingham de Carle)	sa	[Shawl manufactory, St George's Colegate, Norwich, Norfolk]; untraced		*Norwich Mercury*, 8 Sept 1792; *Norfolk Chronicle*, 8 Sept 1792
32.	1817	Obelisk in memory of Frederick, 4th Earl of Bristol and Bishop of Derry (by John de Carle)		Ickworth Park, Suffolk		De Carle Obelisk Bill; *Norwich Mercury*, 31 Jan 1818

Miscellaneous

33.	1785	Portrait of a child (by Robert Brettingham de Carle)		[Exhib RA, London, 368]; untraced	*Graves* II, 1905–6, 289
34.	1785	Portrait of a lady (by Robert Brettingham de Carle)	w	[Exhib RA, London, 482]; untraced	*Graves* II, 1905–6, 289
35.	1785	Portrait of a lady (by Robert Brettingham de Carle)		[Exhib RA, London, 573]; untraced	*Graves* II, 1905–6, 289

DEEBLE, William fl 1823

Of 1 Seymour Place, Islington, he was awarded a silver Isis medal in 1823 'for his method of taking casts from leaves and foliage' (RSA *Transactions* vol 41, 1823, xxxix). Deeble's letter on the subject reveals that he was a landscape engraver and his aim in devising his casting technique was 'to supply myself with fac-similes of the form and texture of those plants, which . . . I might have to introduce in the foreground of landscapes' (RSA *Transactions*, vol 41, 1823, 95). Details of the process of wax-moulding were appended.

DEERING, Samuel fl 1766

In January 1766 Samuel Deering, a sculptor, took as his apprentice Martin Jean Parquot, a pupil at the Westminster French Protestant Charity School.

Literary References: *le May* 2001, 565

DEEVE, Thomas, of Bury St Edmunds fl 1705–15

Funerary Monuments

1.	1705	Unidentified subject, box tomb	St Gregory, Sudbury, Suffolk, churchyard	S	*Gunnis* 1968, 125
2.	1715	Unidentified subject, box tomb	St Gregory, Sudbury, Suffolk, churchyard	S	*Gunnis* 1968, 125

DEITERICH (or DIETTERECH), George fl 1758

Described in the RSA *Minutes* as an apprentice to Mr [**Henry**] **Cheere**, on 15 February 1758 he submitted a drawing for the modelling prize in clay (1). The subject was approved and he was awarded half the premium.

Literary References: *Dossie* 1782, 437

Archival References: RSA Minutes, 1757–58, fol 150

Miscellaneous

1.	1758	'drawing for the modelling prize in clay'	[RSA premium]; untraced	*Dossie* 1782, 437
2.	1758	Model in clay	[Soc of A, premium]; untraced	*Gunnis* 1968, 125

DE KEYSER, Hendrick 1613–65

In May 1663 Bishop John Cosin contracted with Hendrick de Keyser a 'sculptor' of Bishop Auckland in Durham, to pave the chapel floor in the palace at Bishop Auckland. This was to be completed in polished black marble and local stone, following a design by Roger Coates (*Cosin Letters* 1870, 362–3). The sculptor was presumably Hendrick de Keyser II, who was born in Amsterdam, the son of the renowned sculptor and architect of the same name (1565–1621). Hendrick II worked in England from 1633 to 1647 in the studio of Nicholas Stone, who was subsequently to become his brother-in-law.

Literary References: *Grove* 1996, 18, 8 (Rem)

DE KEYSER, William 1603–

A son of the distinguished Dutch sculptor, Hendrick de Keyser I (1565–1621), he came to England in the 1620s, where he probably worked for his brother-in-law, the English sculptor Nicholas Stone. He married Walburga Parker whilst in this country. In 1640 he returned to Amsterdam. Though he became City Mason and worked on the grand baroque tomb for Admiral Tromp in the Oude Kerk in Delft, he was unable to revive the flagging fortunes of the family dynasty. In 1658 he became bankrupt and made a second visit to England, where he provided decorative carving at Whitehall in the 1660s (2). He also supplied designs for Charles II's intended palace at Greenwich in July 1661 at a cost of £2.

He was living in London in 1674, and in 1678 was admitted to the Masons' Company as a foreign member. His date and place of death have not been ascertained.

According to Strickland, in 1683 William de Keyser 'carver in stone', contracted to carve two royal statues for Dublin (1). Henry Parris, a brazier, was paid £6 18s for a sceptre and spear of mixed metal for the statues. This seems a remarkably late work and may be the product of a second generation of the family. The poor state of repair of the statues occasioned their removal to another church in 1805, and later to the Cathedral.

Literary References: *Strickland* 1, 1913, 271–272; *Colvin* 1995, 299; *Grove* 1996, 18, 10 (Rem); *Scholten* 2003, 111

Statues						
1.	1680–1683	King Charles I and King Charles II Payment(s): £100 the pair	s	[Tholsel Gate, Skinners' Row, Dublin]; Christ Church Cathedral, Dublin, crypt (since 1806)		*Strickland* 1, 1913, 271; *Loeber* 1970, 19–21, (repr); *Gibson* 1997 (1), 167, 370
Architectural Sculpture						
2.	1661	'Draperyes' with two flying boys in them holding the curtains before the bedchamber alcove, and for two great eagles and a shield with a head on it Payment(s): £40		[Whitehall Palace, London]; destroyed		*Colvin* 1973–76, V, 266
Miscellaneous						
3.	1661–2	Unspecified work Payment(s): £140		[Somerset House, London]; untraced		*Colvin* 1973–76, V, 255

DELAISTRE, François Nicholas, of Paris 1746–1832

A French sculptor, born in Paris on 9 March 1746, he was responsible for the monument to Lord Boringdon, who died aged 11 in Paris in 1817 (1). The boy's father, the Earl of Morley, had wished to employ an English sculptor and had asked four London artists to submit designs, but only **Sir Richard Westmacott RA** agreed to the proposal, the other three refusing to engage in what they regarded as a competition. Morley accordingly decided to look elsewhere and engaged Delaistre 'a sculptor of some eminence' (*Boringdon* 1818, 16–17). The medallion which forms part of the monument was executed by the sculptor from a wax model of the child made by his mother. Delaistre died in Paris on 23 April 1832.

Literary References: *Boringdon* 1818, 16–17; *Gunnis* 1968, 123; *Grove* 1996, 8, 650 (Durey)

Funerary Monuments						
1.	1819	Henry, Viscount Boringdon (†1817)		St Mary, Plympton, Devon		*Boringdon* 1818, 16–17 (engr repr); *Gunnis* 1968, 125–6; Pevsner, *Devon*, 1989, 685

DELL, Isaac fl 1788

In the National Art Library are two copies of an indenture dated 26 April 1788 witnessing the apprenticeship of Isaac Dell, of Berkhamstead St Peters, Hertford, to **John Flaxman I**. Dell's mother, Harriot, paid Flaxman £31 10s to instruct Dell in the 'Moulding and Casting of Plaister Figures'. It was stipulated in an addendum that Dell's mother would fund her son in 'Washing, Mending and Apparel of all sorts' (NAL QQ. Box I (ii).)

Literary References: *Bilbey* 2002, 80

DELL, J fl 1793–97

Between 1793 and 1797, he showed works as an 'honorary exhibitor' at the Royal Academy. One of these was a portrait in ivory of an unidentified 'English sculptor in Rome' (1). In 1794 he gave his address as 420 Strand, and in 1794 as 4 Great May's Buildings, St Martin's Lane. Dell's signed wax portrait of Robert Burns is on loan from Mrs Bate at the Victoria and Albert Museum (2).

Literary References: *Gunnis* 1968, 126; *Pyke* 1973, 38

Reliefs						
1.	1793	Portrait of an English sculptor in Rome	i	[Exhib RA, London, 459]; untraced		*Graves* II, 1905–6, 298; *Gunnis* 1968, 126
2.	nd	Robert Burns	w	VAM (Bate)	S	*Gunnis* 1968, 126; *Pyke* 1973, 38 (pl 72)
Miscellaneous						
3.	1793	Atalanta		[Exhib RA, London, 403]; untraced		*Graves* II, 1905–6, 298
4.	1794	A physionomist, model	w	[Exhib RA, London, 588]; untraced		*Graves* II, 1905–6, 298
5.	1795	Bacchus and Ariadne		[Exhib RA, London, 674]; untraced		*Graves* II, 1905–6, 298
6.	1795	Portrait of an artist		[Exhib RA, London, 404]; untraced		*Graves* II, 1905–6, 298
7.	1797	Cupid		[Exhib RA, London, 1046]; untraced		*Graves* II, 1905–6, 298

DELVAUX, Laurent 1696–1778

Laurent Delvaux spent seven active years in England working principally with **Peter Scheemakers**, before embarking on a distinguished career in his homeland, the Southern Netherlands (now Belgium).

He was born in Ghent on 17 January 1696, the son of Godefroid Delvaux, a cornet in the Austrian cavalry and Françoise, née Chasselat, a supplier of provisions and a laundress working for her husband's regiment. There were no sculptors in his immediate family. Delvaux trained in Ghent under an obscure master, Gery Helderenberg (1651–1739), and around 1713–14, joined the Brussels studio of **Pierre-Denis Plumier**. While Delvaux was with him, Plumier was involved in a wide range of commissions including monuments, statues, liturgical furnishings and a fountain with river gods for the Hotel de Ville.

Plumier took his workshop to London in or before 1720 and Delvaux joined him by 1721. There he met Scheemakers, who had recently joined Plumier's team. Plumier died in 1721, shortly after winning the contract for the monument to John Sheffield, Duke of Buckingham in Westminster Abbey (1), leaving Delvaux and Scheemakers to execute the commission from his design and models. Delvaux carved a dramatic personification of *Time*, poised on a bracket above effigies of the duke in Roman armour, and his kneeling duchess. The status of the client, Buckingham's widow and the novel triangular composition guaranteed lively attention for the monument in the *Post-Boy* for 17–19 July 1722, and in several provincial newspapers.

George Vertue notes that Delvaux and Scheemakers both worked briefly for **Francis Bird**, but around 1723 they entered into an informal partnership together and from 1725 seem to have shared premises in Church Street, Millbank, Westminster, rated in 'Mr Delmore's' name. Its nominal value, £30 10s in 1725, was high for the district and suggests a need for extensive work space. On 27 May 1726 Delvaux left London briefly to marry Plumier's widow, Madeleine (née Pauwels), at Sint Jacobskerk in Antwerp. She died soon after in childbirth and Delvaux informally adopted her two children by Plumier, one of whom, Pierre Plumier, later joined his workshop in Nivelles.

Delvaux and Scheemakers together received a number of commissions for garden sculpture, particularly for pairs of classical subjects, which gave them an opportunity to pit their relative skills. Delvaux's colossal *Hercules*, 1722 (**7**), for Lord Castlemaine's pleasure-grounds at Wanstead (teamed with an *Omphale* by Scheemakers) is a powerful, muscular figure. By contrast, the tender group of *Vertumnus and Pomona* (**25**) for the 1st Duke of Chandos at Canons (a pendant to Scheemakers's *Apollo and Venus*) provided Delvaux with an early opportunity to explore a theme to which he would return in England, and later in Belgium, the subtle interaction between pairs of figures. The partners also turned out a number of seductive, recumbent Venus statuettes, including one for the distinguished collector, Sir Andrew Fountaine (**11, 13, 27**).

Three commissions for monuments were executed in tandem during the 1720s. The wall-monument to Sir Thomas Grantham at Bicester (**3**), which was probably carved soon after the two sculptors joined forces, is a conservative work with a heavy, scrolled frame, a wigged medallion portrait and an apron carved with a winged skull. Two large standing monuments (**2, 4**) reflect an awareness of the growing enthusiasm amongst Whig patrons and grand tourists for a classical vocabulary. Each has an architectural frame enclosing effigies in classical dress. Payments for the Rockingham (**2**), which was designed by Scheemakers, were made to Delvaux and suggest that he acted as the controlling partner. Delvaux was responsible for both extant designs for the Ongley (**4**).

Delvaux is known to have worked alone on two commissions in the 1720s. Around 1724 he carved a formal, stolid figure of George I in the guise of a Roman Emperor, for a niche above the judicial bench in the Rolls House in Chancery Lane (**8**). A commission for four figures of the Seasons now at West Wycombe was evidently more congenial to the sculptor, for these are sensuous, confidently executed groups of seated nudes attended by rotund babies (**21**).

Throughout their partnership years, Delvaux and Scheemakers fought without success to break **Michael Rysbrack**'s market dominance. Rysbrack had not visited Rome, but the classical veneer on his sculpture had a wide appeal. In 1728 Delvaux and Scheemakers made a striking bid to attract attention by selling their entire stock, announcing on the title page of their sale catalogue their intention of 'going to Italy'. Their decision was sufficiently noteworthy for Vertue to record that they were travelling south with an intention 'to form & improve their studies' (*Vertue* III, 36). Among the models sold at auction by Delvaux were several ideas for garden figures, which may have been executed, but of which there is no trace (**6, 9, 10, 12, 14, 16, 16–20, 22, 24, 35, 36**).

The partners travelled south in August 1728, taking with them an introduction from Sir Andrew Fountaine to Cardinal Lorenzo Corsini. In Rome they took lodgings in the Palazzo Zuccari, near the Spanish Steps, and began their studies of antique and baroque sculpture. Corsini's influence helped Delvaux to forge contacts with the Papal Court and he was commissioned to carve two colossal angels for the basilica of the Royal Palace at Mafra, Portugal, as well as portrait busts of Pope Benedict XIII and of Corsini, after his election as Pope Clement XII. Delvaux also made several fine copies in marble of antiquities and of Bernini's *David* (**26, 29–33**).

Scheemakers returned to London in 1730 leaving Delvaux, who was 'well imployed', in Rome (*Vertue* III, 44), though the partners had an outstanding commission in London which needed his attention. Before leaving for Italy they appear to have agreed to carve a monument in Westminster Abbey for the Duchess of Buckingham's obstetrician, Dr Hugh Chamberlen (**5**). Scheemakers provided the design for a reclining effigy on a sarcophagus flanked by two standing Virtues, *Hygeia* and *Longevity*. Vertue records 'one of the standing figures of Delvo. The others & ye statue of ye Dr. by Scheemaker' (*Vertue* III, 53). Delvaux's figure is probably *Longevity*, a statue notable for its airy draperies and gentle torsion. It is not known whether the figure was carved in London or sent over from Rome, but the monument was completed in 1731.

In 1732 Delvaux went to Brussels, taking with him a letter of recommendation from Pope Clement to the Habsburg regent of the Southern Netherlands, the Arch-Duchess Marie-Elisabeth. Shortly afterwards, on 28 January 1733, he was appointed her court sculptor, but in 1733 he also visited London for two months, taking with him a marble bust of *Caracalla* (**40**), 'A fine and Just imitation. . . done by him at Rome' (*Vertue* III, 66). Delvaux recorded in his *Répertoire des Ventes*, a notebook of business activities, a number of works left with Scheemakers to sell on commission. These were the copies of antiquities and five terracotta models (**34**). Through the good offices of John Sanderson, the Duke of Bedford's architect and a friend of Delvaux, Bedford bought the marbles in 1734. Sanderson bought the terracotta models and commissioned Delvaux's portrait by Isaac Whood.

There is no evidence that Delvaux returned to England again but he retained links with London over the next decade. Notes in the *Répertoire* indicate that in 1738 he organised the passage of marbles ordered by Scheemakers and sent to London via the burgermaster of Ostend. In 1741 he was involved in a curious piece of business with the retired sea-captain, Thomas Coram, later founder of the London Foundling Hospital, to whom he sent 'powder mill bluestones' costing 54,000 florins. In 1744, the entrepreneurial plasterer William Wilton sent his son, **Joseph Wilton**, to be trained under Delvaux in Nivelles, where Wilton spent 53.5 days assisting with the oak pulpit for the Carmelite church. Wilton's mature style combines naturalistic and classical elements in a manner similar to Delvaux's.

Delvaux's later career was highly successful. The Arch-Duchess was succeeded as Governor in 1750 by Duke Charles-Alexander, an active patron with a passionate desire to improve his palaces and gardens. Delvaux, hitherto known principally as a carver of devotional works, was re-appointed Court-sculptor and had a major hand in ornaments for the palaces. He died in Nivelles on 24 February 1778 and was seen posthumously as the reviver of a national school.

Despite the brevity of his London career, Delvaux's name was woven into the history of British sculpture. In 1749 Vertue named the four foreigners who had recently transformed the quality of the native product, Rysbrack,

Scheemakers, **Louis François Roubiliac** and Delvaux, who 'staid not long' (*Vertue* III, 145–6). He was given a short entry in the first edition of Horace Walpole's *Anecdotes of Painting*, with a portrait engraved by Hibbart after Whood. His craftsmanship was apparently still appreciated in the early-19th century, for when his vases for Wanstead (**44**) were auctioned in 1822, they fetched impressive sums, £80.17s and £78. 15s. Later critics have discussed his work principally in tandem with Scheemakers, drawing a distinction between Scheemakers's stiff classicism and Delvaux's animated and naturalistic carving.

IR

Literary References: *Vertue* III, 36, 44, 66, 146; *Anecdotes* 1762–1771, IV, 100; *Gunnis* 1968, 126; *Avery* 1980, 150–70; *Avery* 1983, 253–64; *Roscoe* 1987, 1–10; *Roscoe* 1990, *passim*; *Jacobs* 1996, 71–90; *Jacobs* 1997, 58–66; *Jacobs* 1999 (1); *Roscoe* 1999, 163–5, 173; *Roscoe* 2001, 106–8; *ODNB* (Roscoe)

Archival References: PR, St Margaret, Westminster, WCA E.344-348, E.352; L Delvaux, *Repertoire des Ventes*, 1734–42, coll Raymond Delvaux, Brussels

Auction Catalogues: Delvaux and Scheemakers 1728

Portraits of the Sculptor: Isaac Whood, *Laurent Delvaux with his bust of Caracalla*, canvas commissioned by John Sanderson, 1734, untraced; Alexander Vanhaecken, mezzotint after Whood's portrait (*Jacobs* 1999, frontispiece); I Wright, woodcut after Whood's portrait, (*Anecdotes* 1876, III, 41); G L Godecharle, bust, 1824, Musées royaux des Beaux-Arts, Brussels (*Jacobs* 1999, 14, repr)

Funerary Monuments

No.	Date	Subject		Location		References
1.	1721–1722	John, 1st Duke of Buckingham (†1721/2) and family (co-sculptor: Peter Scheemakers) Payment(s): £500 Drawing(s): Soane, vol 37/46 Model(s): Reclining figure for a monument sold 16 April 1728, lot 19; Time, lot 31; Time with a dial, lot 68; weeping figure for a monument, lot 69; model of the Buckingham monument by Delvaux and Scheemakers, lot 72		Westminster Abbey, London, Henry VII's Chapel	S	*Dart* 1, 1723, 162–3 (repr); *Vertue* I, 101; *Avery* 1980, 152–3, 156; *Whinney* 1988, 157–9 (repr); *Roscoe* 1999, 178–80
2.	1724–1725	Lewis, 1st Earl of Rockingham (†1723) and his wife Katherine (†1695) (co-sculptor: Peter Scheemakers) Payment(s): £400 Drawing(s): VAM 8408-1		Rockingham, Northants	S	*Whinney* 1988, 182–4 (repr); *Roscoe* 1999, 180–1 (repr 34, 35); *Jacobs* 1999, 226–8 (repr)
3.	c1725	Sir Thomas Grantham (†1718) (co-sculptor: Peter Scheemakers)		Bicester, Oxon	SD	*Roscoe* 1999, 182–3; *Jacobs* 1999, 225–6 (repr)
4.	1727–1728	Sir Samuel Ongley (†1725) (co-sculptor: Peter Scheemakers) Drawing(s): VAM 8949; Musées royaux des Beaux-Arts de Belgique 10.252		Old Warden, Beds	S	*Physick* 1969, 112–3 (repr); *Whinney* 1988, 184; *Roscoe* 1999, 181–2 (repr 36–38); *Jacobs* 1999 240–2 (repr)
5.	?1728–1731	Dr Hugh Chamberlen (†1728) (co-sculptor: Peter Scheemakers) Model(s): VAM, A.6-1927, effigy		Westminster Abbey, London, north choir aisle	S	WAM (92); *Vertue* III, 53; *Whinney* 1988, 183–5 (repr): *Roscoe* 1999, 184–5 (repr 40, 42)

Statues

No.	Date	Subject		Location		References
6.	pre-1721	'A Satyr and Venus, by Plimier and Delvo', model	tc	[Delvaux's and Scheemakers's sale, 16 April 1728, lot 60]; untraced		
7.	1722	Hercules Drawing(s): VAM D.1062-1887 Model(s): Hercules and Omphale, Delvaux's and Scheemakers's Sale, 16 April 1728, lot 64	m	[Wanstead House, Essex; sold 1822, lot 267]; Waddesdon Manor, Bucks		*Vertue* I, 102; *Hodgkinson* 1970, 208–11 (repr); *Avery* 1980, 155–6 (repr)
8.	c1724	King George I Model(s): 'A Figure of the late King' sold 16 April 1728, lot 71	m	[Rolls Chapel, London]; PRO, London	S	*Avery* 1980, 154, 156 (repr); *Jacobs* 1999, 224–5 (repr)
9.	pre-1728	A Venus washing, model	tc	[Delvaux's and Scheemakers's sale, 16 April 1728, lot 85]; untraced		
10.	pre-1728	Apollo and Venus, model	tc	[Delvaux's and Scheemakers's sale, 16 April 1728, lot 28]; untraced Other versions: Apollo, model, sold 16 April 1728, lot 64		
11.	pre-1728	Ariadne, statuette Model(s): 'A sleeping Figure, by Mr Delvo', Delvaux's and Scheemakers's Sale, 16 April 1728, lot 53; untraced	m	YCBA B 1977.14.31 Other versions: attrib, Huntington, before 1728, marble	S	*Avery* 1980, 162–3 (repr); *Jacobs* 1999, 237 (repr)
12.	pre-1728	Bacchus, model	tc	[Delvaux's and Scheemakers's sale, 16 April 1729, lot 17]; untraced		
13.	pre-1728	Cleopatra, statuette Model(s): Delvaux's and Scheemakers's Sale, 16 April 1728, lot 6	m	Huntington	S	*Avery* 1980, 162–3 (repr); *Jacobs* 1999, 236–7 (repr)
14.	pre-1728	Diana, model	tc	[Delvaux's and Scheemakers's sale, 16 April 1728, lot 9]; untraced		
15.	pre-1728	Farnese Flora (companion to Scheemakers's Ceres) Model(s): Namur, Musée Groesbeeck de Croix, Sc 38	m	Englefield House, Berks	S	*Jacobs* 1999, 246–7 (repr)
16.	pre-1728	Fawn and goat, model	tc	[Scheemakers's sale, 10 March 1756, lot 24]; untraced		
17.	pre-1728	Jupiter, model	tc	[Delvaux's and Scheemakers's sale, 16 April 1728, lot 38]; untraced		

18.	pre-1728	Leda, model	tc	[Delvaux's and Scheemakers's sale, 16 April 1728, lot 14]; untraced		
19.	pre-1728	Papyrius and his mother, model	tc	[Scheemakers's sale, 10 March 1756, lot 32]; untraced		*Gunnis* 1968, 126
20.	pre-1728	The rape of Proserpine, model	tc	[Delvaux's and Scheemakers's sale, 16 April 1728, lot 75]; untraced		
21.	pre-1728	The Seasons	m	[Nocton, Lincs]; West Wycombe Park, Bucks (c1770)	S	*Avery* 1980, 164–5 (repr); *Jacobs* 1999, 234–7 (repr)
22.	pre-1728	Three figures after the antique, models	tc	[Delvaux's and Scheemakers's sale, 16 April 1728, lots 81, 82, 83]; untraced		
23.	pre-1728	Two figures, models	tc	[Delvaux's and Scheemakers's sale, 16 April 1728, lot 39]; untraced		
24.	pre-1728	Venus and Cupid, model	tc	[Delvaux's and Scheemakers's sale, 16 April 1728, lot 28]; untraced		
25.	1725–1728	Vertumnus and Pomona Model(s): Pomona by Delvaux sold 16 April 1728, lot 66; Vertumnus by Scheemakers, lot 67; Vertumnus and Pomona, a group, by Delvaux, lot 70	m	[Canons, Middx]; VAM A.1-1949	S	*Avery* 1980, 160–2 (repr); *Jacobs* 1999, 231–4 (repr); *Bilbey* 2002, 73–4 (repr)
26.	1730	Hermaphrodite, after the Borghese hermaphrodite, statuette	m	Woburn Abbey, Beds Other versions: Jean Delvaux, Brussels	SD	*Avery* 1983, 253–64 (repr); *Jacobs* 1999, 240–50 (repr)
27.	c1730	Reclining Venus (conceivably by Scheemakers)	m	Narford Hall, Norfolk		*Moore* 1985, 109–11 (repr)
28.	1730–1732	Two kneeling cupids on scrolled brackets	tc	VAM 910-1855, 911-1855	S	*Bilbey* 2002, 74 (repr)
29.	pre-1733	Biblis and Caunus (or Hermaphroditus and Salmacis)	m	Woburn Abbey, Beds Other versions: ex coll marquis de Spontin, c1730, marble; private coll (*Avery* 1983, 257, repr 10)	S	*Avery* 1983, 253–64 (repr); *Avery* 1987, 454 (repr); *Jacobs* 1999, 253–9 (repr)
30.	pre-1733	Crouching Venus Model(s): Musées royaux des Beaux-Arts, Brussels, c1730	m	Woburn Abbey, Beds	S	*Avery* 1983, 253–64 (repr); *Jacobs* 1999, 252 (repr)
31.	pre-1733	David (after G-L Bernini)	m	Woburn Abbey, sculpture gallery Other versions: Black-Nadeau Gall, Monte Carlo, c1730, tc on carved oak stand	S	*Avery* 1983, 259–64 (repr); *Jacobs* 1999, 261–2 (repr)
32.	pre-1733	Lion	m	Woburn Abbey, Beds		*Avery* 1983, 253–64 (repr 21); *Jacobs* 1999, 259–60 (repr)
33.	pre-1733	Venus with the cockleshell Model(s): Musées royaux des Beaux-Arts, Brussels, clay	m	Woburn Abbey, Beds	S	*Avery* 1983, 253–64 (repr); *Jacobs* 1999, 251–2 (repr)
34.	pre-1734	Five models, including Crouching Venus and Roman Charity	tc	[coll John Sanderson, 1734]; untraced		*Avery* 1983, 255
35.	pre-1756	Faun and goat, model	tc	[Scheemakers's sale, 1756, lot 24]; untraced		*Gunnis* 1968, 126
36.	nd	'Chalcedonian Boar'	m	[Scheemakers's sale, 10 March 1756, lot 22]; untraced		
37.	nd	Dying Gaul, model		Woburn Abbey, Beds	S	
38.	nd	Sleeping putto with a sheaf of corn and a sickle, from a set of the four seasons, statuette	m	[Unidentified English coll]; untraced	S	*Avery* 1980, 163–5 (repr)
Busts						
39.	pre-1728	Four, models	tc	[Delvaux's and Scheemakers's sale, 16 April 1728, lots 62, 90]; untraced		
40.	pre-1733	Emperor Caracalla	m	Woburn Abbey, Beds	SD	*Vertue* III, 66; *Avery* 1980, 166–7 (repr); *Avery* 1983, 253–64; *Jacobs* 1999, 260–1 (repr)
41.	pre-1733	Emperor Hadrian	m	Sotheby, 6 June 1995, lot 166; private coll, London		*Jacobs* 1999, 262 (repr)
42.	pre-1733	Lucius Verus	m	Woburn Abbey, Beds	S	*Avery* 1983, 253–64 (repr); *Jacobs* 1999, 261 (repr)
43.	nd	Infant Nero	m	Private coll	S	*Jacobs* 1999, 262–3 (repr)
Architectural Sculpture						
44.	pre-1728	Two vases, carved with reliefs of a Sacrifice of Iphigenia and a Sacrifice to Bacchus, after the Borghese and Medici vases (companions to two by P Scheemakers)	m	[Wanstead House, Essex; sold 1822, lots 371, 372]; Anglesey Abbey, Cambs	S	*Roscoe* 1999, 292 (repr 95); *Jacobs* 1999, 228–30; *Laing* 2001, 34 (repr)
Reliefs						
45.	nd	Lion, after Flaminio Vacca	m	Jean Delvaux, Brussels		*Avery* 1983, 253–64 (repr)
46.	nd	Sacrifice to Diana	p	Hatfield Priory, Essex	S	*Jacobs* 1999, 230–1 (repr)
47.	nd	Sir Isaac Newton, medallion portrait	tc	Spalding Gentlemen's Society, Lincs Other versions: Nivelles, Musée communal d'Archéologie, nd, s, bronzed plaster Namur, musée de Groesbeeck de Croix, nd, s, marble Ixelles, coll Paul Saintenoy, nd, s, marble Brussels, Musées royaux d'art et histoire, nd, tc Brussels, coll Georges Fiévet	S	*Jacobs* 1999, 238–40 (repr)

Miscellaneous

No.	Date	Subject		Location	Reference
48.	1727	Unspecified work for the Duke of Kent Payment(s): £31 10s		Untraced	Hoare's Customer Ledger, 1725–1728, vol I, 251
49.	pre-1728	Pallas, model		[Delvaux's and Scheemakers's sale, 16 April 1728, lot 78]; untraced	
50.	pre-1728	'Two Boys lying', 'a boy', 'Three Boys, by Plimier and Mr. Delvo', 'Two sitting boys', 'Two Vases, with boys in plaster', models	tc	[Delvaux's and Scheemakers's sale, 16 April 1728, lots 23, 24, 48, 76, 91]; untraced	

DENHAM, Joseph
See **Joseph Dinham**

DENMAN, Maria 1776–1861

Born on 2 February 1776, she was baptized at St Mary, Whitechapel, the daughter of Ann and William Denman of Mansell Street. She was the sister of **Thomas Denman** and the sister-in-law and adopted daughter of **John Flaxman RA**. In 1807 she received a silver medal from the Society of Arts for a plaster model of a cupid's head, which may be the plaster of *Cupid and Bacchus* now in Sir John Soane's Museum (1). She exhibited this at the British Institution from 'Mr Flaxman's, Buckingham Street' in 1812 (*Graves* 1875, 153). She was also given a silver medal for drawings of the Society's new medal, used to make the engraving for the frontispiece of *Transactions of the Royal Society*, 1807. Her address that year was Buckingham Place, London.

Flaxman left her and **Mary Ann Flaxman** all his possessions. In his will he commended their 'exemplary conduct' and affectionate sisterly relationship (PROB 11/1720, 129). After the death of Mary Ann, Maria assumed control of Flaxman's estate, writing that she was 'the only one who had any claim on him'. When the National Gallery was founded she offered Flaxman's plaster models to the nation, expressing horror when the government offered to buy only a small selection for £500. In another letter she wrote that this financial offer constituted 'an ungrateful insult to the memory of the great artist'. She added: 'Moreover I should lose the right of imposing the only condition I had ever thought of exacting, that these casts should be suitably placed in some public edifice as national property' (Flaxman Papers Ad MS 39783, fols 17, 35).

In 1848, through the agency of Henry Crabb Robinson, who was a friend of Flaxman, Denman gave the 120 models to University College London. The process of housing them adequately was protracted, but finally they were installed in the 'Flaxman Gallery' in 1857. Denman also published Flaxman's *Compositions from the Tragedies of Aeschylus* (1831) and *Compositions of the "Acts of Mercy"* (1831). She died in 1861.

Literary References: RSA, *Transactions*, vol 25, 1807, a 2, 18, 20; *Gunnis and Whinney* 1967; *Gunnis* 1968, 127; *Read* 1982, 32

Archival References: Flaxman Papers Ad MS 39791; GPC

Reliefs

No.	Date	Subject		Location	Reference
1.	1807	Cupid and Bacchus, portrait medallion	p	[Soc of A, silver medal]; SJSM SC38	RSA *Transactions*, vol 25, 1807, 20

DENMAN, Thomas 1787–

The son of William and Ann Denman of Mansell Street, London and the brother of **Maria Denman**, he was born in 1787 and christened at St Mary Whitechapel in January 1788. He attended the Royal Academy Schools in January 1807 and in the same year won the lesser silver palette from the Society of Arts for a plaster model of Antinous (**66**). His address in 1807 was given as High Holborn. In 1813 he gained a silver medal from the Royal Academy for a drawing in the life academy. He first exhibited at the Royal Academy in 1815, showing a classical subject (**76**) and giving his address as 39 Frederick Place, Hampstead Road. By 1818 he had moved to 42 London Street.

He worked for many years in the studio of his brother-in-law, **John Flaxman**, and after the latter's death in 1826, completed his unfinished works. These included a statue of the Marquess of Hastings for Calcutta (**67**), for which Denman contributed some original elements: he exhibited his own design for a figure representing *Power, Peace and Justice* for the pedestal at the Royal Academy (*Graves* II, 1905–6, 305). He seems also to have completed other studio work such as the ideal relief of *Satan and the angel Gabriel* (**75**). In 1828 he was living with **Mary Ann Flaxman** and Maria Denman at Flaxman's premises at 7 Buckingham Street, where he remained until 1837. That year he moved to 56 Albany Street. Numerous works signed by Denman are reworkings of Flaxman's designs, such as the monuments to William Reymond Morris (**22**), Elizabeth Stephens (**25**) and Elizabeth Kelsall (**24**), which owe much to the angels on Flaxman's monument to Agnes Cromwell in Chichester.

Denman subsequently set up his own workshop at 83 The Quadrant, Regent Street. He produced a number of simple and harmonious tablet designs in a Flaxmanesque style, including some for Ireland (**19, 20, 33**) and others that went further afield (**28, 33, 34, 40, 43, 46, 61**). Gunnis remarked on his prolific output, but felt that much of the work was 'uninspired and dull' (*Gunnis* 1968, 127). Denman became bankrupt in 1847. His date of death has not been ascertained. A John Flaxman Denman (born 1808), who attended the RA schools as a painter in March 1825, was presumably a member of the same family.

Literary References: RSA, *Transactions*, vol 24, 1806, 20; *Graves* 1875, 153; *Graves* II, 1905–6, 305; *Gunnis* 1968, 127; *Hutchison* 1960–62, 162, 178

Archival References: IGI; RA Premium list; GPC

Funerary Monuments

No.	Date	Subject	Location		Reference
1.	†1814	Unidentified subject, tablet	Wigmore, Herefs		Pevsner, *Herefs*, 1963, 321
2.	c1817	George Lloyd	Snitterfield, Warks		*Gunnis* 1968, 127
3.	?1817	Sir Joseph Mawbey	Chertsey, Surrey		*Gunnis* 1968, 127
4.	†1818	William Dyke	Fighledean, Wilts		Pevsner, *Wilts*, 1975, 245
5.	†1820	William (†1802), Mary Ann (†1808) and Mary Adams	South Mimms, Herts	S	*Gunnis* 1968, 127
6.	1825	John Trevener	Helston, Cornwall	S	Pevsner, *Cornwall*, 1970, 81
7.	†1827	Henrietta Strickland	Boynton, E R Yorks		Pevsner, *Yorks: E R & York*, 1995, 334

8.	†1827	John Hudeeston Watson	Heston, Middx	S	Pevsner, *London: N W*, 1991, 424
9.	†1828	General Arabin	West Drayton, Middx	S	Pevsner, *London: N W*, 1991, 367
10.	?1828	Paul Benfield	St Mary, Leicester		*Gunnis* 1968, 127
11.	1829	A monumental figure, to be executed in marble	[Exhib RA, London, 1162]; untraced		*Graves* II, 1905–6, 305
12.	?1829	Henry Farmer (obelisk)	Cheam, Surrey, churchyard		*Gunnis* 1968, 127
13.	?1830	George Ellison	Marlow, Bucks		*Gunnis* 1968, 127
14.	1830	Hope, for a monument	[Exhib RA, London, 1197]; untraced		*Graves* II, 1905–6, 305; *Johnson* 1975, 129
15.	1830	Monumental figure	[Exhib Soc of BA, London, 848]; untraced		*Johnson* 1975, 129
16.	?1833	Francis Pym	Sandy, Beds		*Gunnis* 1968, 127
17.	?1834	Lieutenant-Colonel Booth	Writtle, Essex		*Gunnis* 1968, 127
18.	?1834	Rt Hon Charles Philip Yorke	Wimpole, Cambs		*Gunnis* 1968, 127
19.	†1835	James, 3rd Earl of Courtown	Kiltennel, Co Wexford		*Potterton* 1975, 42
20.	†1835	Rev James McCreight	Caledon, Co Tyrone		*Potterton* 1975, 42
21.	†1836	Anna Cust	Cockayne Hatley, Beds		AL/RG
22.	†1836	William Douglas Reymond Morris	Speldhurst, Kent	S	*Gunnis* 1968, 127; Pevsner, *Kent: W & Weald*, 1976, 542
23.	?1837	Admiral Tower	South Weald, Essex		*Gunnis* 1968, 127
24.	†1837	Elizabeth Kelsall	Holy Trinity, Fareham, Hants	S	Flaxman Account Book 1794–1810, 61; *Gunnis* 1968, 127
25.	†1837	Elizabeth Stephens	Holy Trinity, Fareham, Hants		*Gunnis* 1968, 127; Pevsner, *Hants & Isle of Wight*, 1967, 222
26.	?1837	Helen Anstey	Trumpington, Cambs		*Gunnis* 1968, 127
27.	1837	Peter Hill	Helston, Cornwall		Pevsner, *Cornwall*, 1970, 81
28.	?1838	Charles McMurdo	Jamestown, St Helena		GPC
29.	?1838	Charlotte Curteis	Wartling, Sussex		*Gunnis* 1968, 127
30.	†1838	Edward Brown	All Saints, Stamford, Lincs	S	
31.	†1838	John Crosdell	St Giles in the Fields, London		RG/JP, 3, 430
32.	?1838	John Longley	Roseau, Dominica		GPC
33.	†1838	John, 1st Marquess of Ormonde (of the second creation)	Kilkenny Cathedral		*Potterton* 1975, 42
34.	1838	Sir William Rough	Garrison Church, Colombo		GPC
35.	†1839	Captain Robert Honywood Monypenny	Rolvenden, Kent	S	
36.	†1839	George Milward	Lechlade, Glos	S	Pevsner, *Glos: Cotswolds*, 1999, 438
37.	†1839	Magdalen Wienholt	St Giles, Reading		*Gunnis and Whinney* 1967, 45
38.	†1839	Major John Johnson	Canterbury Cathedral, Kent	S	
39.	†1839	Robert and Susanna (†1833) Vincent	South Mimms, Herts		
40.	†1840	Charles Walker	Mumbai (Bombay) Cathedral	S	
41.	†1840	Henry and Elizabeth (†1837) Usbourne	Cowlinge, Suffolk	S	
42.	†1840	Hon Russell Barrington	Shrivenham, Berks		Pevsner, *Berks*, 1966, 218
43.	†1840	Lieutenant-Colonel Thomas MacLean	Chennai (Madras) Cathedral, India		*Gunnis* 1968, 127
44.	†1840	Peter Nichols	Yelverton, Norfolk		Pevsner, *Norfolk: N W & S*, 1999, 810
45.	?1841	Henry Jackson	Hartfield, Sussex		*Gunnis* 1968, 127
46.	?1841	James Laidlaw	Roseau, Dominica		GPC
47.	†1841	Rev Peter Payne	Irchester, Northants		RG/JP, 3, 429
48.	?1841	Sir Philip Broke	Nacton, Suffolk		*Gunnis* 1968, 127
49.	†1842	Charles Hayne	St Clement, Dartmouth, Devon	S	Pevsner, *Devon*, 1989, 322
50.	†1842	Harriet Mainwaring Ellerker	Rowley, E R Yorks		Pevsner, *Yorks: E R & York*, 1995, 662
51.	†1842	Lady Charlotte Heathcote	[Normanton, Rutland]; Edenham, Lincs	S	Pevsner, *Lincs*, 1989, 269
52.	?1842	Sir John Lawford	St John's Wood Chapel, Marylebone, London		*Gunnis* 1968, 127
53.	†1843	Horton family member	Croxall, Staffs		Pevsner, *Staffs*, 1974, 111
54.	?1843	Lieutenant James Fuller	Holy Trinity, Marylebone, London		*Gunnis* 1968, 127
55.	?1843	Mary Morphew	Terrington St Clement, Norfolk		*Gunnis* 1968, 127
56.	1843	Officers and Men of the 13th Light Infantry	Canterbury Cathedral, Kent	S	*Gunnis* 1968, 127
57.	†1844	Captain John Guyon	Richmond, Surrey		RG/JP, 3, 429
58.	†1844	Lucy Cust	Cockayne Hatley, Beds		AL/RG
59.	?1844	Sir Gore Ouseley	Hertingfordbury, Herts		*Gunnis* 1968, 127
60.	†1845	John Barkworth	Hessle, E R Yorks		Pevsner, *Yorks: E R & York*, 1995, 468
61.	?1846	Major-General John Hare	Jamestown, St Helena		GPC
62.	1846	Officers of the 47th Bengal Native Infantry	Woodmancote, Sussex	S	
63.	†1846	Rev Daniel Tremlett	Rodney Stoke, Somerset	S	
64.	?1847	Sir John Eardley-Wilmot	Berkswell, Warks		*Gunnis* 1968, 127
65.	nd	Unidentified subject, tablet	Stradsett, Norfolk	S	
Statues					
66.	1807	Antinous	[Soc of A, lesser silver palette]; untraced	p	RSA, *Transactions*, vol 24, 1806, 20
67.	1826–1830	Francis, 1st Marquess of Hastings (co-sculptor: John Flaxman RA) Model(s): Exhib RA, London, 1828, 1150 and 1158 models for figures of 'Power,' 'Peace' and 'Justice' for the pedestal	Victoria Memorial Hall, Kolkata (Calcutta), (formerly Town Hall)		*Graves* II, 1905–6, 305; *Gunnis* 1968, 127

68.	1833	Colossal group, sketch		[Exhib RA, London, 1833, 1132 'for General [Andrew] Anderson's institution in Elgin']; untraced	*Graves* II, 1905–6, 305
69.	1834	Dr Babington, sketch		[Exhib RA, London, 1120]; untraced	*Graves* II, 1905–6, 305
70.	1836	Thomas Telford, model	pm	[for George and Richard Tangye]; Lady Lever (inv no LL 301)	*Graves* II, 1905–6, 305; *Lady Lever* 1999, 9 (repr)
Busts					
71.	1830	John Flaxman		[Exhib RA, London, 1231]; untraced	*Graves* II, 1905–6, 305; *Johnson* 1975, 129
72.	1835	1st or 2nd Marquess of Hastings		[Exhib RA, London, 1090]; untraced	*Graves* II, 1905–6, 305
Architectural Sculpture					
73.	1829	Decorative work Payment(s): £600		Buckingham Palace, London	*Gunnis* 1968, 127
Reliefs					
74.	1831	Charity, group in alto-relievo		[Exhib RA, London, 1132]; untraced	*Graves* II, 1905–6, 305; *Library of Fine Arts*, vol I, 1831, 430
75.	nd	Satan and the angel Gabriel, bas-relief (co-sculptor: John Flaxman RA)	m	untraced	GPC
Miscellaneous					
76.	1815	Menelaus defending the body of Patroclus		[Exhib RA, London, 869]; untraced	*Graves* II, 1905–6, 305; *Gunnis* 1968, 127; *Graves* 1875, 153; *Johnson* 1975, 129
77.	1818	Adam and Eve lamenting over the dead body of Abel		[Exhib RA, London, 1045]; untraced	*Graves* II, 1905–6, 305
78.	1832	Endymion, alto-relievo		[Exhib RA, London, 1118]; untraced	*Graves* II, 1905–6, 305

DENNIS, LEE & WELSH, of Leeds fl 1816–48

They sign tablets in Yorkshire and Northumberland. The Howey monument has a garlanded urn (1) and the Bridlington work is a gothic wall tablet (2).

There are references in the Leeds Town Hall Committee Minutes to work by **Lee & Welsh, Lee and Walsh** and Dennis, Lee & Welsh, who are clearly interconnected. They read as follows: 26 Nov 1858. Lee and Welsh paid £33 4s for marble pedestals; 18 June 1865 Lee and Walsh paid £4 10s for a marble mantle piece; 27 Feb 1865. Dennis Lee and Welsh paid £7 15s 6d for cleaning statues; 1 Feb 1867. Dennis Lee and Welsh paid £29 9s for cleaning statues and marrble (HMI, misc file).

Funerary Monuments				
1.	†1816	Henry Howey	Beadnell, Northumbs	Pevsner, *Northumbs*, 1992, 160
2.	†1848	Unidentified subject, tablet	Bridlington Priory, E R Yorks	Pevsner, *Yorks: E R & York*, 1995, 346

DENT, Isaac fl 1744–71?

The large architectural monument surmounted by an obelisk to William Byrd is signed 'Isaac Dent, Crutched Fryers, London' (1). He may be the Isaac Dent who acted as master-mason at the Travellers' House at Rochester in 1771, and carved the large urn on the apex of the roof (Account-book, Travellers' House, cited by *Gunnis* 1968, 127).

Literary References: *Gunnis* 1968, 127

Archival References: GPC

Funerary Monuments					
1.	†1744	William Byrd	Westover, Charles City County, Virginia, USA, garden	S	GPC
Architectural Sculpture					
2.	1771	Urn	[Travellers' House, Rochester]; untraced		*Gunnis* 1968, 127

DERMOTT, T M fl 1818

A local statuary, he signs the large wall-tablet to John Postlethwaite at Ashton-under-Lyne (1). This is decorated with masonic emblems including the number of Postlethwaite's Lodge, and is one of the earliest monuments to embody such details that Gunnis encountered.

Literary References: *Gunnis* 1968, 127–8

Funerary Monuments				
1.	†1818	John Postlethwaite	Ashton-under-Lyne, Lancs	Pevsner, *Lancs: S.*, 1969, 68; *CIIA* 4/8/1 (repr)

DE VAERE, John 1755–1830

John De Vaere (De Vacre, De Vaare, Davaere) worked in England as a modeller and carver for more than 20 years. He appears to have been born in France and attended the Royal Academy Schools in 1786, giving the date of his birth as 10 March 1755.

In 1787 he was sent to Rome by Josiah Wedgwood to make models from the Antique under the supervision of **John Flaxman RA**. On 16 June 1787, shortly before their departure, Wedgwood wrote to Sir William Hamilton telling him that Flaxman 'has promised to employ for me all the time he can spare at Rome, and to superintend a modeller [De Vaere], who I have engaged to accompany him and to employ the whole of his time for me at Rome' (*Finer and Savage*, 1967, 307). De Vaere was set to work making a model of the Borghese vase relief and on 15 November 1788, Flaxman duly reported back to Wedgwood's partner, Byerly: 'Mr. De-veare has been at work with the utmost diligence ever since he has been here on the bas relief of the Borghese Vase in which he has succeeded very well, but it will still take him some weeks to finish and after he has done, I also shall have something to do to it, Mr. Wedgwood will easily conceive as this is new work to Mr. D. he must needs be slow at first especially as he takes so much pains. As a proof he follows his studies well he has already gained the Pope's first silver medal for a figure modelled at night in the Roman Academy' (Flaxman/Byerly quoted by *Constable* 1927, 110–11, n 4). De Vaere copied other reliefs in the Roman collections and designed plaques with Homeric and other classical themes, and he modelled the entire Borghese vase in miniature, apparently on his own initiative (**16**).

After his return to England in 1790, De Vaere worked for Wedgwood at Etruria, where in 1794 he succeeded **Henry Webber** as a senior modeller. His prefered method was to work in red or white wax on a slate ground in low or medium relief. He left the firm after Wedgwood's death in 1795 and moved to the **Coade workshop** where in 1797 he modelled a large overdoor group of emblematical figures, cast for the Pelican Life Insurance Office in Lombard Street (**10**). It features a standing representative of the company in the guise of a near-naked Roman centurion, who holds laurel wreaths above three distraught women, presumably widows being told their claims will be met. The tableau was illustrated in the *European Magazine* above an article on the Pelican Insurance Company, which described the sculpture as 'very striking and beautiful . . . the recumbent figure at the east end has been particularly admired for its graceful attitude and anatomical correctness' (*Euro Mag*, vol 39, 1801, 262–4). The design was used as the frontispiece of the Coade Gallery Handbook in 1799. His independent work was also on occasion translated to Coadestone: a tall candelabrum for a John Jarrett of Freemantle, described by Mrs Coade as 'a most exquisite piece of workmanship from the marble designed and executed by Mr. De Vaere', was described as being on offer in the Coade Gallery within a year of its execution in marble.

De Vaere exhibited for the first time at the Royal Academy in 1798 (**17**), giving his address as 14 Cleveland Street. By 1800, the year he seems to have set up by himself, he had moved to 4 Pedlar's Acre, Lambeth, at or near the Coade workshop During the next decade he signed a number of memorial tablets. Perhaps he failed to prosper for in 1810, shortly after joining a lodge of freemasons in London, he left England for Flanders, where he was appointed Professor of Sculpture to the Royal Academy of Ghent. He died at Tronchinnet-les-Grand in 1830.

Literary References: *Graves* I, 1905–6, 314; *Gunnis* 1968, 128; *Pyke* 1973, 34; *Irwin* 1979, 27–8; *Hendricks* 1984, 621–22; *Kelly* 1990, 47; RG/JP, 3, 432; *Tattersall* 1985, 36

Archival References: GPC

Portraits of the Sculptor: P J Farmer, bust, exhib RA, 1826, untraced

Funerary Monuments						
1.	†1795	William Drake		St Mary, Amersham, Bucks	S	Pevsner, *Bucks*, 1994, 132
2.	1806	Countess of Kenmare		St Giles-in-the-Fields, London	S	*Gunnis* 1968, 128
3.	†1806	General John McPherson ('The Wreck of the Rose in Bloom') Model(s): exhib RA, London, 1809, 763		[Intended for First Presbyterian Church, Charleston]; Gibbes Art Museum, Charleston, South Carolina		*Graves* I, 1905–6, 763; *Gunnis* 1968, 128; *Hershey* 1970, 806 (repr)
4.	1806	William Drake		Amersham, Bucks	S	*Gunnis* 1968, 128
5.	1808	Hannah Shirley		Bristol Cathedral	S	*Gunnis* 1968, 128
6.	†1809	Hon Edward Methuen Irby		Whiston, Northants	S	*CIIA* 4/3/149 (repr)
Statues						
7.	1800	Apollo	m	[Exhib RA, London, 1006]; Christie NY, 10 Jan 1990, lot 1006; untraced	SD	*Graves* I, 1905–6, 314
8.	nd	Mercury Belvedere		[The Deepdene, Dorking, Surrey; Hope sale 1917, lot 1167]; untraced		*Gunnis* 1968, 128
Chimneypieces						
9.	c1805	With Apollo, Minerva and a frieze of the Nine Muses	m	[Stratton Park, Hants, drawing room]; Sotheby, 10 July 1998, lot 7; untraced		*Avery* 2002, 56, 57 (repr)
Architectural Sculpture						
10.	1797	Allegorical group, model (designer: Lady Diana Beauclerk)		[Pelican Life Insurance Office, Lombard Street, London, cornice]; Geffrye Museum, London, grounds		*Whinney* 1988, 464 n4; *Kelly* 1990, 47, 60 (repr); *Cavanagh* forthcoming 2007 ('lost or removed works')
11.	1798	Candelabrum	m	Untraced Other versions: Reproduced in Coadestone		*Euro Mag*, vol 39, 262; *Graves* I, 1905–6, 1037; *Kelly* 1990, 185
12.	pre-1800	Large pair of eagles with outstretched wings, model for the Coade workshop, probably replicated for use on gate-piers		Untraced		GPC
13.	c1807	Decorative ornaments		Dodington Park, Glos		GPC
Reliefs						
14.	1788–1789	From the Borghese vase, model for Josiah Wedgwood		Untraced		*Irwin* 1979, 27–8
15.	1798	Admirals Nelson, St Vincent and Duncan, models for medallions Payment(s): £2 15s	w	Untraced		*Gunnis* 1968, 128; *Pyke* 1981, 13
Miscellaneous						
16.	1788–1789	Borghese Vase, model, probably small scale, for Josiah Wedgwood		Untraced		*Hendriks* 1984, 621–2
17.	1797	'Vesper, or the Morning Star'		[Exhib RA, London (1109)]; untraced		*Graves* I, 1905–6, 314
18.	1809	A father and his children deploring the loss of his wife		[Exhib RA, London, 827]; untraced		*Graves* I, 1905–6, 314

DEVALL, John I 1701–74

He was the son of a yeoman, 'George Devall, late of Ensham, Oxon' and was bound apprentice to **Joshua Fletcher II** on 2 August 1718 (Masons' Co, Court Book, 1695–1722 fol 170r, & 1722–51). Deval was admitted to the freedom of the Masons' Company on 20 February 1727. He worked for **Andrews Jelfe**, but afterwards set up independently.

Deval was employed as a mason at St Olave's, Southwark in 1737 and at Kimbolton Castle in 1738. In May 1738 he and **Thomas Dunn** tendered for the contract to build the Mansion House in London under the architect George Dance the Elder. Another estimate by a group comprising **John Townesend of London, Christopher Horsnaile II** and **Robert Taylor I** came in at exactly the same figure, £18,000. In July 1739 the Mansion House committee resolved to give the contract to all five masons at a cost of no more than £17,000. Deval also worked at Guy's Hospital in 1739 and Cornbury House, London in 1744.

A list of Masons' Company assistants compiled around 1740 gives Devall's address as Margaret Street, Oxford Square. In 1742 he became a Director of the Westminster Fire Office. Between 1742 and 1752 he was the mason responsible for building the Foundling Hospital and its chapel. In 1747 he informed the Committee that, on the demolition of Canons, he had purchased for £24 10s 'two Venetian windows which would be fit for the chappell of this hospital' and that he was prepared to part with them at the price he had paid for them. His offer was regretfully refused on the grounds that the windows were too large (Foundling Hospital Archives).

He was employed by the partners of Hoare's Bank in the 1750s (**6**) and was also at Woburn, the seat of the 4th Duke of Bedford. At Woburn he worked with **Michael Rysbrack** and carved a number of ornate marble chimneypieces with caryatid terms and foliage decoration (**13**). He also worked for the architect Henry Flitcroft, who paid him for work in 1751/2, and the sum of £352 in 1764.

In 1760 he became master of the Masons' Company. His son, **John Deval II**, was certainly involved in the business by 1768, for he received a payment for a chimneypiece at Coventry House that year. Another employee was Henry Gill, whose name appears in the Harewood House accounts and who set up Devall's chimneypieces. Devall was paid £863 for work at the Excise Office in the late 1760s, and Gunnis notes that the father and son were chief masons for the royal palaces, the Tower of London and the royal mews. In 1769 Devall became the chief mason at Newgate prison. The firm seems also to have had a connection with the architect Sir William Chambers, since there is a letter to 'Mr Devall' amongst the architect's letters, dated 26 May 1770 (Chambers's Letter-Books, Ad MS 41133, fol 15).

Devall's death is recorded in the *Hereford Journal* of 17 February 1774. He was buried at Isleworth. He left annuities of £10 and £20 to his servants, Ann Whitwell and John Stalker, and the residue of his personal estate to his son.

Literary References: *Gunnis* 1968, 128–9; *Colvin* V, 1973–76, 349; *Jeffery* 1993, 49–50, 67, 300; *Webb* 1999, 3, 14, 18, 20, 22, 31, 37; *Harris* 2001, 141

Archival References: Masons' Co, Freemen, fol 13; Assistants, fol 3; Westminster Fire Office, MB, 343/7, 21 Oct 1742; Woburn Building Accts, 1748–62, BLARS R5/1092, 24 Aug 1756 (£192), 1 May 1760 (£36 4s), 26 July 1762 (£19 8s); R5/1105, 24 Dec 1790 (£589 15s); GPC

Will: PROB 11/1002/392

Chimneypieces

1.	1734	Description unavailable Payment(s): £90 15s		[Kew Palace, Surrey]; untraced	GPC, citing Accts Frederick Prince of Wales, Duchy of Cornwall
2.	1737–1738	Four, for the 2nd Earl of Rockingham		18 Grosvenor Square, London	All Souls College, Oxford, Bodl MS North c. 21, fol 71
3.	1739	Description unavailable Payment(s): £85		[Barn Elms House, Surrey]; untraced	*Gunnis* 1968, 128 citing Hoare's bank archives
4.	1739	Perhaps several, description unavailable Payment(s): £85		[Mr Arnold's house at Clapham, London]; untraced	*Gunnis* 1968, 128 citing Hoare's bank archives
5.	1739	Perhaps several, description unavailable		[for Charles Lowndes, of Chesham Bury, Bucks]; untraced	*Gunnis* 1968, 128 citing Hoare's bank archives
6.	1745	Marble Payment(s): £94 14s		[Stourhead, Wilts, saloon]; untraced	Hoare Private Accounts, 1734–49, 20 June 1745
7.	1746	Description unavailable, supplied with grate, fender and hearth		[Okeover Hall, Staffs]; untraced	GPC citing Okeover Archives
8.	1749	Description unavailable	m	Foundling Hospital, London, office	*Gunnis* 1968, 128
9.	1753	Description unavailable Payment(s): £85 12s 8d	m	[Barn Elms, Surrey]; untraced	Hoare Private Accounts 1752–78, 27 Sept 1753; Hoare Partnership Ledger 1751–1764, 27 Sept 1753, fol 70
10.	1753	'Mrs Arnolds Chimneypiece' Payment(s): £25		Untraced	Hoare Private Accounts, 1750–66, 23 March 1753
11.	1755	Description unavailable		[Weald Hall, Essex]; untraced	*Gunnis* 1968, 128, citing Christopher Tower archives
12.	1756	Description unavailable Payment(s): £289	m	[Milton Hall, Northants]; untraced	*Gunnis* 1968, 129
13.	1756–1765	Several, including one in statuary and Siena (with a tablet carved by Michael Rysbrack), and one with 'profile terms carved with Diana's head' Payment(s): £125 (statuary and Siena) and £142 (profile terms); £35 4s for Marble Slabs & Chimney Pieces, 1 May 1760	m	Woburn Abbey, Beds, gallery and state rooms	Woburn Abbey Building Accts; 1 May 1760, p 122; *Gunnis* 1968, 129; *Beard and Hayward* 1988, 393, 398 (repr)
14.	1766	Tablet of half-boys flanking an orrery (designed by Robert Adam)		Harewood House, W R Yorks, library	*Harris* 2001, 153, 349 n64
15.	1766	With relief of Venus and Cupid (designed by Robert Adam) Drawing(s): Soane 22:181		[Harewood House, W R Yorks, dining room]; destroyed	*Harris* 2001, 149
16.	1767	decorated with Cupid and Psyche in bas-relief (designed by Robert Adam) Payment(s): £240 Drawing(s): Soane 20:67, 68		[Coventry House, Piccadilly, London]; untraced	*Harris* 2001, 58, 340 n21; GPC
17.	1767	Description unavailable Payment(s): £73 12s 2d	m	[Teddesley Park, Staffs, 'best parlour']; untraced	Stafford RO, Littleton D/260/M / E116, 117; GPC
18.	1767	Description unavailable Payment(s): £110 3s 8d		[Kings Weston, Glos]; untraced	GPC citing *Journals of Robert Mylne*, coll Miss Mylne.
19.	1767	Oval medallion of Cupid and Psyche, panels of arabesque ornament and winged sphinxes (designed by Robert Adam) Payment(s): £41	m	Nostell Priory, W R Yorks, tapestry drawing room	*Gunnis* 1968, 128; *Harris* 2001, 203 (repr); GPC
20.	1768	'carving a chimneypiece'		[Croome Court, Worcs]; untraced	*Beard* 1993, 93

No.	Date	Description		Location	Source
21.	1768	Description unavailable Payment(s): £19 10s 6d		[2 Grosvenor Square, London for Sir Watkin Williams-Wynn]; untraced	*Harris* 2001, 359 n6
22.	1768	Description unavailable Payment(s): £180		[Lansdowne House, London, dining room]; untraced	*Harris* 2001, 128; GPC
23.	1768	'Two chamber chimney pieces and architraves'		[Teddesley Park, Staffs]; untraced	Stafford RO, Littleton D/260/ M / E116, 117
24.	1769	Description unavailable (designed by Robert Mylne)		[Mr Hill's house, Hanwell, Middx]; untraced	GPC, citing *Journals of Robert Mylne*, coll Miss Mylne
25.	1769	With Corinthian pilasters and tablet showing a sphere flanked by two half-boys and foliage	m	Kenwood House, London	*Harris* 2001, 188
26.	1769	With Griffon tablets, urn and palmette friezes (designed by Robert Adam)	m	Harewood House, W R Yorks, saloon	*Harris* 2001, 140 (repr)
27.	1770	Description unavailable Payment(s): £92		[Teddesley Park, Staffs]; untraced	Stafford CRO, Littleton D/260/ M / E116, 117
28.	1767–1770	Several		[Government House, New Barn, North Carolina, USA]; untraced	GPC
29.	1771	Description unavailable Payment(s): £57 17s		[Hovingham Hall, N R Yorks]; untraced	GPC, citing Worsley archives
Architectural Sculpture					
30.	1738	Two large terms, carving the frieze with flowers, leaves and berries in the 'Front Room' and decorating others with shells, fruit and flowers Payment(s): £300 3s 7 1/2d claimed; reduced to £241 2s 6d		18 Grosvenor Square, London	All Souls College, Oxford, Bodl MS North c. 21, f71
Reliefs					
31.	*c*1751	Two bas-reliefs	m	[Woburn Abbey, Beds, hall]; untraced	Walpole, *Country Seats*, 17; *Gunnis* 1968, 128
Miscellaneous					
32.	1732–1733	Unidentified work Payment(s): £60		[Kew Palace, London]; untraced	GPC citing Accts, Frederick, Prince of Wales, Duchy of Cornwall
33.	1738	'stone & Marble' Payment(s): £94 10s		[Wolterton Hall, Aylsham, Norfolk]; untraced	Walpole at Wolterton, Sept 1738
34.	1738	Tables	m	[Longford Castle, Wilts, for Lord Folkestone]; untraced	*Gunnis* 1968, 129 citing Archives, Earl of Radnor
35.	*c*1753	Surround for relief of charity children engaged in husbandry and navigation (relief by Michael Rysbrack)		Foundling Hospital, London, court room	*Gunnis* 1968, 128; Pevsner, *London: N*, 1998, 269
36.	1767	Surround for wood carving Payment(s): £41 14s 6d	m	Nostell Priory, W R Yorks, library	*Harris* 2001, 354 n25

DEVALL, John II 1728–94

The son of **John Devall I**, he was admitted to the Masons' Company by patrimony on 9 January 1777. He was already involved in the family business by 1768, for in May that year he received payment for a finely decorated chimneypiece with foliage decoration for Coventry House (**2**). Devall II was much employed by the Crown and succeeded his father as master-mason to the royal palaces on the latter's death in 1774. In 1784 he became master of the Masons' Company. Before 1790 he had taken his son, **John Devall III**, into partnership.

Devall II was the mason-contractor responsible for the north and south fronts of Somerset House, 1777–1786; Coutts' bank, Strand, 1780–1789; the King's Bench prison, 1780–1784 (£4,590); the house for the marshal of the prison, 1781–1782 (£546); Argyll House, 1783; the government building next to the Admiralty, 1786–1791 (£1,875); the temple at Audley End, 1791 (£300) and the new guardroom at St James's Palace, 1793. He was also paid £1,536 for building the Chancellor of the Exchequer's house in Downing Street.

He was employed on additions or repairs to Cobham Hall, Kent, 1776–78; at Audley End, 1785, where he was paid £790, and at 4 St James's Square, London where he was paid a considerable sum by Sir Watkin Williams Wynn for unspecified mason's work. His firm carried out rich and extensive carving featuring foliage and angels for the Royal Chapel at Greenwich in 1788 (**17**). In the records of Carlton House, where he also worked, he was recorded as 'Mr Duval, of Mortimer Street, Cavendish-square' (**9**) (*Pyne* 1819, v3, n 12).

Between 1784 and 1789 he and **Richard Lawrence** rebuilt the Queen Mary block of Greenwich Palace following its destruction by fire. His bill, which included 3,366 feet of Portland Stone and '10 waggon loads of marble bases and capitals' came to £2,347 5s 8d (TNA ADM 68/813). In 1791–92 he carried out work at Woburn Abbey for a total sum of £1,653. Devall and his son also worked at Somerset House after 1790, receiving payments totalling £1,756 11s 2d.

Devall executed his own designs and those of others. In 1772 John Carr, the architect, wrote to the Duke of Portland 'The dining room at Burlington House [in York?] will be pretty near finished by Xmas. Did Your Grace speak to Deval about a chimneypiece for it? . . . There should also be one for the drawing room of about £60 value. If your Grace have not given the order for them it would be well to give Deval a line and refer him to my drawing for the model for the dining room chimney and leave the design of the drawing room to himself' (Portland Archives in GPC). Devall is also known to have sold the work of other sculptors through his shop: in a letter to Jacob Houblon of Hallingbury of 1775, **Henry Watson** referred to a mosaic table of his making, which could be seen at Devall's shop in Little Portland Street.

He must have had a number of assistants: two of his employees were **John Gilliam** and a mason, Henry Young. The latter had worked for the practice for 15 years when, working on a royal palace on 8 October 1785, he fell 33 feet from a ladder sustaining acute injuries and leaving his wife and children without support.

Devall produced a large number of high quality chimneypieces in competition with a neighbour, **R Maile**. In 1786 John Carr wrote (again) to the Duke of Portland about a house he was designing: 'I do not attempt to mark out the chimneypieces for the rooms because Your Grace may see a variety of patterns at Mr. Devall's or at Mr. Mails at the end of Great Portland Street' (Portland Archives in GPC).

The workshop was also responsible for at least one monument, to Thomas Spackman (1). Gunnis described the 18 foot high edifice with its life-size statue of Spackman, as 'exciting and arresting' and declared that Devall 'was undoubtedly a fine artist in the best English tradition' (*Gunnis* 1968, 129). It is possible, given the absence of any comparable production by the workshop, that Devall, like **Thomas Carter II**, sub-contracted figurative work on this scale to one of the more able sculptors of the day. This does not however diminish his achievement. The work depicts the energetic and heroic figure of Spackman, his arm outstretched in a gesture of blessing. At his feet lies a straw basket of carpenter's tools, while to left and right stand a boy and a girl, pupils of the charity school he endowed out of the fortune he made as a carpenter. More emblems of his trade are shown in relief at the base of the monument.

Devall was a figure of some note in his time and appears to have made a considerable fortune. In 1788 when Horace Walpole sought among his contemporaries for a craftsman comparable to **Robert Taylor I** (†1742), he alighted on Devall: Taylor, he wrote, was 'the greatest stone-mason of his time: like Devall in the present day, he got a vast deal of money; but again, unlike him altogether, he could not keep what he got' (*GM*, 1788, 930). Devall was evidently a shrewd money manager.

He died in 1794 and his will, a document of some length and complexity, was proved on 12 April that year. He left his recently furnished house at Upper Clapton to his wife, Ann, and the premises in Little Portland Street to his elder son, John. The workshops were clearly extensive for Devall refers to the 'shops, sheds, yards, gardens, backsides and tenements' in the grounds. In addition Devall left a property with lands and gardens at Heyford, Northants, to the same two beneficiaries. The will also mentions his younger children, Robert, Elizabeth, Susannah, Jane and Henrietta.

MGS

Literary References: *Pyne* 1819, v3, 12n; *Gunnis* 1968, 129; *Colvin* V, 1973–76, 466; VI, 39; *Harris* 2001, 61

Archival References: Masons' Co, Freemen, fol 13; Court Book 1751–96 (14 June 1784); Chambers/Somerset Hse, 25 Dec 1776–25 Dec 1777, fol 52, 53; Essex RO D/DBY.A.222; GP

Will: PROB 11/1244

Funerary Monuments

1.	†1786	Thomas Spackman Payment(s): £1,000 allocated in his will		Cliffe Pypard, Wilts	S *Gunnis* 1968, 129 (repr); *Penny* 1977 (1), 17–19 (repr)

Chimneypieces

2.	by 1768	Decorated with a relief of a lion and cupids (designed by Robert Adam) Payment(s): £136 6s 9d Drawing(s): Soane 22:70	m	Coventry House, Piccadilly, London, back parlour	*Harris* 2001, 61 (repr); GPC
3.	c1771	Description unavailable Payment(s): approx £60 for that in Drawing Room		[Burlington House, dining and drawing rooms]; untraced	GPC, citing Portland archives
4.	1780	Description unavailable Payment(s): £66		[Longford Castle, Wilts, long parlour]; untraced	*Gunnis* 1968, 129
5.	1783	Several		Earsham Hall, Norfolk	*Gunnis* 1968, 129; Pevsner, *Norfolk: N W & S*, 1999, 316
6.	1785	Description unavailable		Attingham Park, Salop, drawing and dining rooms	*Gunnis* 1968, 129; NP/RG
7.	1786	More than one, in Portland stone	s	Somerset House, London	*Gunnis* 1968, 129
8.	1787	Description unavailable		[Bedford House, London]; untraced	*Gunnis* 1968, 129
9.	1788	Chimneypieces and 'statuary work' Payment(s): £931		[Carlton House, London]; destroyed	TNA H.O. 73/18; *Pyne* 1819, v3, 12 n; *Gunnis* 1968, 129
10.	1788	Chimneypieces and statuary work Payment(s): £931		Untraced	*Gunnis* 1968, 129, citing PRO H.O. 73/18
11.	1790	Description unavailable		[Althorp, Northants, long library]; untraced	GPC; NP/RG
12.	1790	Description unavailable		[Althorp, Northants, yellow drawing room]; untraced	GPC (inf. Earl Spencer)
13.	1790	Description unavailable		[Althorp, Northants, blue sitting room]; untraced	GPC (inf. Earl Spencer)
14.	1786–1791	Veined marble Payment(s): £50	m	[Building adjoining the Admiralty Office, London]; untraced	TNA ADM 17/1
15.	1793	Description unavailable		[St James's Palace, London, waiting-room]; untraced	*Gunnis* 1968, 129

Architectural Sculpture

16.	1788	Marble work Payment(s): £73	m	[St James's Palace, Prince Edward's apartments]; untraced	*Gunnis* 1968, 129
17.	1788	Marble work including '591 feet of antique galoches of statuary in black marble' for 'four circular flowers of statuary and black marble and two large flowers' Payment(s): £1,897	m	Royal Hospital, Greenwich (ORNC), chapel	*Gunnis* 1968, 129; C Lib (repr)
18.	1791	Great Portland stone capital for column Payment(s): £163		Colne Park, near Colchester, Essex	*Gunnis* 1968, 129
19.	nd	'twenty-five faces of rich Corinthian capitals of columns' Payment(s): £213		Somerset House, London	*Gunnis* 1968, 129

Miscellaneous

20.	1776	Unidentified work		[for Sir William Watkins Wynn, 4 St James' Square, London]; untraced	GPC

DEVALL, John III –1830

He was the elder son of **John Devall II** and his wife Ann and was taken into the partnership c1786, after which the name of the firm is recorded in accounts at the Admiralty, Somerset House and elsewhere as 'John Devall and Son' (TNA ADM 17/1). He inherited the business premises in Little Portland Street on the death of his father in 1794. Whether he continued the masonry practice is unclear. He died in 1830, in possession of a large estate.

Literary References: *Gunnis* 1968, 129; *Colvin* V, 1973–76, 466

Wills: John Devall II, PROB 11/1244; John Devall III, PROB 11/1765/123–6

DE VEAUX (or DE VAUX), S J fl *c*1830–34

An 'S J De Vaux' exhibited intaglio portraits at the Royal Academy between 1832 and 1834, giving his address as 21 Bond Street in 1833 and 166 Regent Street in 1834 (*Graves* II, 1905–6, 314). Gunnis, who calls him 'John' owned his wax portrait of Sir Charles Colville (**10**). In 1831 De Veaux was living in Dublin, and advertised himself as 'Seal Engraver to His Majesty' in Wilson's *Dublin Directory* of 1831 (GPC). He later identified himself as gem and seal-engraver to the Duke of Sussex, and gave his address as 204 Oxford Street, London.

Literary References: *Gunnis* 1968, 129; *Pyke* 1973, 39

Reliefs

1.	c1830	Unidentified sitter	w	National Museum of Ireland		*Pyke* 1973, 39
2.	1832	Duke of York, intaglio gem		[Exhib RA, London, 1084]; untraced		*Graves* II, 1905–6, 314
3.	1832	King William IV, intaglio gem		[Exhib RA, London, 1084, coll Duke of Sussex]; untraced		*Graves* II, 1905–6, 314; *Ormond* 1973, 509
4.	1832	Marquess of Anglesey, intaglio gem		[Exhib RA, London, 1084]; untraced		*Graves* II, 1905–6, 314
5.	1833	HRH, The Duke of Sussex, gem portrait		[Exhib RA, London, 1046]; untraced		*Graves* II, 1905–6, 314
6.	nd	Duke of York, portrait medallion	w	NPG, London		*Gunnis* 1968, 129
7.	nd	King William IV, portrait medallion	w	NPG, London	S	*Ormond* 1973, 509 (pl 999); *Pyke* 1973, 39 (pl 73)
8.	nd	Unidentified man	w	[Sotheby 15 Feb 1966, lot 166]; untraced		*Pyke* 1973, 39

Miscellaneous

9.	1836	Arthur, 1st Duke of Wellington	w	Stratfield Saye, Hants	D	GPC
10.	nd	Sir Charles Colville	w	Untraced		GPC

DEVIGNE (or DEVISNE) fl 1706

He was employed by Thomas Coke of Melbourne Hall in 1706 to carve pedestals for lead work by **John Nost I.** Mr Sergeant, Coke's Derbyshire agent, writes to his master: 'Mr. Devigne will come about them [the pedestals] by next week. They are to be made from stone from the new quarry. Mr. Devigne and all the workmen think it will work as fine or finer than Donington.'

Coke refers to Devigne as 'ye French carver' and the sculptor seems to have returned subsequently to France. Late in 1706 Sergeant wrote to Coke: 'Mr. Devigne desires to know if you have any more occasion for him, for he thinks to leave this country in a little time' (Archives, Marquess of Lothian, quoted by *Gunnis* 1968, 129–30).

Literary References: *Gunnis* 1968, 129–130

Architectural Sculpture

1.	1706	Two baskets of fruit and flowers, pedestals for four seasons vase and groups of amorini Payment(s): £27	s	Melbourne Hall, Derbys		*Gunnis* 1968, 129–130; *Davis* 1991 (1), 37, 370 n33 (repr)

DE VILLE, James S 1777–1846

A plaster-cast manufacturer and phrenologist, he was born at Hammersmith on 12 March 1777 and raised by his maternal uncle, who ran a brick-making business. De Ville was apprenticed to **Charles Harris**, until the latter's death in 1796. In 1797 he married Jane Smith, who conducted a retail business from their home while De Ville worked as a journeyman moulder in plaster. As a young man he was employed by **Joseph Nollekens** to make casts from moulds and he later seems to have set up on his own account. In 1803 he opened a plaster works in Soho, before moving to a larger location at Leicester Square where he had eight employees. In 1809 the Rev James Hall wrote to **John Flaxman** on behalf of Lord Buchan who 'desired a cast from the face of Newton'. Flaxman replied that he could not supply one himself 'but the original mould from it belongs to Mr. de Ville figure maker in Newport Street, who sells them at two shillings or half a crown each' (Wedgwood/de Ville L1/215, John Flaxman to Rev James Hall, 19 May 1809). The *European Magazine* (1823, 84, 344) states that de Ville purchased 'the original moulds of busts from the models made by the late Mr Nollekens of all the distinguished characters who honoured that artist with sittings for the same' and that he also prepared casts from 'the original busts by Roubiliac of Hampden, Sidney and Cromwell and other eminent men.'

De Ville subsequently expanded into lamp-making and moved to larger premises at 367 Strand in 1814. His membership of the Institute of Civil Engineers brought him into contact with Bryan Donkin, a disciple of the Viennese phrenologist, J G Spurzheim. Donkin encouraged and employed De Ville to produce casts for phrenological investigation. De Ville developed a strong interest in the field and took a number of life casts which were marked with the phrenological regions and characteristics of the relevant portions of the brain. In pursuit of this interest he developed a method of taking life-casts with the aid of straws to prevent suffocation. In 1824 he published a standardised plaster bust demonstrating the layout of the phrenological regions, with an accompanying booklet. He was a co-founder of the London Phrenological Society in 1823 and gave a series of lectures on the subject at his shop. De Ville's zeal for his subject was renowned, although his speaking and writing skills were regarded by his more educated colleagues as little more than basic. From 1840–2 he was a member of the Phrenological Association. At his death the phrenological collection at his 'museum' consisted of 5,450 specimens, 3,000 of which were of non-human skulls.

He died on 6 May 1846 and his obituary described him as being 70 years of age and 'a plaster figure-maker, lamp manufacturer and phrenologist in the Strand (*GM* 1846, 2, 104).' He exhibited at the Royal Academy between 1823 and 1826, showing busts, which were probably original works carved with the help of life-masks. His bust of William Thackeray, made after a mould, was illustrated in the *Magazine of Art* in 1891 and depicted the writer aged 11 (**2**). 'The gentle expression in the youthful physiognomy is suggestive of the general aspect of the features in later years' (*Mag of Art* 1891, 289). His death mask of Rowland Hill, inventor of the Penny Post, was described by Edward Sidney as 'one of the most beautiful casts of Hill's features I ever saw' (**18**). Taken 'by the well-known Phrenologist Deville', it indicated 'a balmy rest in slumber, than the painful fixedness of a corpse in death. It indicated all his characteristics' (*Sidney* 1834, 407).

Literary References: *Smith* 1828, I, 400; *Graves* II, 1905–6, 315; *Gunnis* 1968, 130; *Ormond* 1973, 462; *Whye* 2002

Busts						
1.	1822	Casts, etc Payment(s): £30		[for Sir William Folkes, Hillingdon Hall, Norfolk]; untraced		Norwich Public Library Archives, II672, in GPC
2.	1822	William Makepeace Thackeray		[coll Lady Ritchie]; untraced Other versions: Electrotype, NPG		*Mag of Art* 1891, 289 (repr); *Ormond* 1973, 460–2 (pl 910)
3.	1823	General Maitland		[Exhib RA, London, 1079]; untraced		*Graves* II, 1905–6, 315
4.	1823	J Scarlett MP		[Exhib RA, London, 1087]; untraced		*Graves* II, 1905–6, 315
5.	1823	J Smith, Esq		[Exhib RA, London, 1127]; untraced		*Graves* II, 1905–6, 315
6.	1824	Captain Lyon RN		[Exhib RA, London, 1020]; untraced		*Graves* II, 1905–6, 315
7.	1825	David Pollock		[Exhib RA, London, 1005]; untraced		*Graves* II, 1905–6, 315
8.	1825	G Rose		[Exhib Soc of BA, London, 346]; untraced		*Johnson* 1975, 131
9.	1825	John Shute Duncan (†1844)	p	Ashmolean	SD	*Graves* II, 1905–6, 315; *Penny* 1992, III, 34
10.	1825	T Chevalier		[Exhib Soc of BA, London, 347]; untraced		*Johnson* 1975, 131
11.	1825	W Mudford		[Exhib Soc of BA, London, 345]; untraced		*Johnson* 1975, 131
12.	1826	Bernardino Rivadavin		[Exhib Soc of BA, London, 718]; untraced		*Johnson* 1975, 131
13.	1826	F Pollock		[Exhib Soc of BA, London, 749]; untraced		*Johnson* 1975, 131
14.	1826	James Buxton		[Exhib Soc of BA, London, 738]; untraced		*Johnson* 1975, 131
15.	1826	Sir Harford Jones		[Exhib RA, London, 1103]; untraced		*Graves* II, 1905–6, 315
16.	1826	The late Ambassador to Mexico		[Exhib Soc of BA, London, 739]; untraced		*Johnson* 1975, 131
17.	nd	Charles James Fox, miniature		Shugborough Hall, Staffs		GPC
18.	nd	Rev Rowland Hill		Untraced		*Gunnis* 1968, 130
Miscellaneous						
19.	1823	Plaster cast of the life mask of William Blake	p	NPG London		*Gunnis* 1968, 130

DEWER fl 1849

Statues						
1.	1849	Two griffins		Temple Gardens, City of London		Pevsner, *London: City*, 1997, 619

DEWICK, William Graham 1828–98

A sculptor and wax modeller, he attended the Royal Academy Schools and won a silver medal for a model in 1846. He may be identical with the William Graham Dewick who was christened in East Retford, Notts on 31 March 1828, a son of Francis and Lucy Dewick.

Literary References: *Pyke* 1973, 39

Archival References: RA Premium list; IGI

Busts						
1.	1862	Unidentified subject, perhaps an Ingleby family member	m	Ripley Castle, W R Yorks	SD	
Reliefs						
2.	nd	Unidentified man	w	Private coll		*Pyke* 1973, 39 (pl 74)
Miscellaneous						
3.	1846	Unidentified subject, model		[RA, London, premium]; untraced		RA Premium list

DICKENSON (or DICCONSON), Richard –1736

A statuary of Hyde Park Corner, he produced works in lead and plaster. The earliest recorded reference to him comes in 1719, in the account-book of the first Duke of Kent, where he is described as a 'figure-maker' (**1**). In 1721 James Gibbs commissioned a bust of Matthew Prior from Dickenson (**4**). It was apparently a version of the celebrated head by **Antoine Coysevox**, but modified by Gibbs 'after his own fancy.' According to Prior's secretary, Adrian Draft, 'the head is the same, but the other part is less, and in lieu of the cap, Mr Dickenson has put short hair a la romaine, which has this effect as to show a greater likeness of Mr Prior's face, and is more in the manner of the Ancient Bustos' (BL Ad MS 70362, f 164 in *Balderston* 2001, 1). Later the same year Dickenson was paid for three copies of a bust of *Flora* by **François Girardon** that had been in Prior's collection (**3**). The list of 'Disbursements Since Mr Prior's Decease. September the 18th 1721' noted that the poet had commissioned these as presents for James Gibbs, Charles Bridgeman and Michael Dahl (BL Ad MS 70362, f 80v in *Balderston* 2001, 20 n5).

He apparently retired in 1726, for an advertisement for *the Catalogue of the Curious Stock of R Dickenson, Figure Maker* appeared that year (Anderdon Cuttings, 1–303, fol 13). He was subsequently involved in property development. In 1732 he agreed with a Mr George Hamilton to build the first of several houses on Hyde Park Corner 'abutting west on Hamilton Street and North on Hyde Park,' one of which was the sculptor's own dwelling. A lease on one of these houses was given to Henry Fairfax, gentleman, in October 1733 for £270 (Middlesex Land Register 1733/3/355 in GPC). Dickenson's own house was rated at £15 in 1736, and was close to properties owned by **Thomas Manning, Joseph Pickford** and **Thomas Carter I**.

The *London Daily Post and Advertiser* of 6 September 1736 noted the sudden death of Mr Dickenson, 'an Eminent Statuary' of Hyde Park Corner (*Fulton* 2001, 38, n 20). A posthumous sale of his goods included 'a great variety of statues, bustos, bass relievos etc in hard metal and finely finished and in particular a very fine gladiator in hard metal' as well as plasters (*Baker* 2000, 120).

He left a widow, Mary Dickenson, who continued to pay rates on his property on Hyde Park Road. According to J T Smith, Dickenson's yard was on the site of Gloucester House, Piccadilly.

Literary References: *Smith* 1846, 15–16; *Gunnis* 1968, 130; *Baker* 1995 (3), 118; *Balderston* 2001, 1, 20

Archival References: GPC

Auction Catalogues: Dickenson 1726; Dickenson 1736

Statues

1.	1719	Several	p	[Wrest Park, Beds]; untraced		Lucas and Dingwallarchives in *Gunnis* 1968, 130
2.	1719	Several Payment(s): £32 8s		[for Lord Derby, Knowsley]; untraced		Lord Derby archives, 2005/5 cited in *Gunnis* 1968, 130

Busts

3.	*c*1721	Flora, three copies (after François Girardon) Payment(s): £15	l	[for Matthew Prior, cast as presents to 'Mr Gibbs, Mr Bridgeman and Mr Dhael']; untraced		*Wright and Montgomery* 1945, 200
4.	*c*1721	Matthew Prior		[The sculptor's studio, Piccadilly, London]; untraced		*Friedman* 1984, 101

DICKINSON, G, of Newark fl *c*1776

He signs a tablet with 'delightful decorative details' and a relief of *Hope* (1).

Funerary Monuments

1.	?1776	Elizabeth Dickinson	sl	Scrooby, Notts	S	*Gunnis* 1968, 130

DICKINSON, William fl 1673

He was clerk to **John Oliver**, deputy surveyor at St Paul's Cathedral. Like Oliver and several others he provided sketches for the Choir. He also worked at Windsor (1).

Literary References: *Green* 1964 (1), 91

Architectural Sculpture

1.	1673	Carved work Payment(s): £5 10s	wd	[Windsor Castle, Chapel, organ loft]; untraced		*Colvin* V, 1973–76, 315

DICKSON, Joseph

See **Joseph Dixon**

DIEMAR, Emmanuel Matthias 1720–95

He was born in 1720, the son of a Berlin gunmaker, Matthias Diemar and had two brothers, Nathaniel and Benjamin, who became well-known painters. Around 1760 Emanuel and Benjamin left Berlin, and by 1761 both were exhibiting at the Free Society in London. Over the two following decades Emanuel exhibited wax portraits, landscapes, still-life and literary subjects with the Society of Artists. In 1769 he gave his address as 'opposite the Lying-in Hospital, Westminster Bridge' (*Graves* 1907, 77). In 1771 Eleanor Coade lodged with 'Mr Demar' at 'Bridge Head, Lambeth', which may have been Diemar's address (*Kelly* 1990, 38, 43). In 1770 he was elected a fellow of the Society of Artists and in 1772 a director. By 1777 he had taken a shop at 377 Strand, on the north side between Carle Court and Maygold Court.

In addition to his work as a wax modeller, Diemar was a gunmaker and an engraver. A pair of signed flintlock pistols, which are chiselled and engraved, survive in the Royal Collection. In 1780 he published *The History and Amours of Rhodope*, which had engraved drawings by Angelica Kaufmann. In 1783, he took out a Sun Insurance policy on his household goods and stock valued at £800, giving his profession as gunsmith and printseller. In 1785 he moved to 114 Strand, London and issued an elaborate tradecard describing himself as 'Printseller and publisher' (Guildhall Library, reproduced in *Blackmore* 1989, 108).

Diemar clearly ran a prosperous concern for when his insurance was renewed in 1791 the value of his stock and goods was £2,000. In his will, prepared in 1790, he left his estate to his widow Ann, who carried on the business. His death on 24 April 1795 was announced in the *Gentleman's Magazine*. He was buried in the Lutheran church, Savoy, at a cost of £6. The will directed that 'three days after my decease before I am buried my coffin be filled up with hot rossin and immersed in plaister and afterwards interred in a plain decent manner' (PROB 11/1268 fol 678 in *Blackmore* 1989, 109).

Gunnis identified a second wax-modeller, John Emmanuel Diemar. It seems likely that this was Emmanuel Matthias and that the confusion is caused by inconsistent spelling in the exhibition catalogues of the Society of Artists.

Literary References: *Gunnis* 1968, 130; *Pyke* 1973, 39; *Blackmore* 1989, 105–142

Reliefs

1.	1777	Three bas-reliefs, impressions from a steel engraving	w	[Exhib Soc of Artists, London, 195]; untraced		*Graves* 1907, 77
2.	nd	David Garrick	w	Private coll		*Pyke* 1973, 39
3.	nd	Flower piece	w	VAM A.29-1939	S	*Blackmore* 1989, 107 (repr)

Miscellaneous

4.	1761	Two portraits	w	[Exhib Soc of Artists, London, 146]; untraced		*Graves* 1907, 77
5.	1768	Two frames of flowers, 'in their natural colours'	w	[Exhib Soc of Artists, London, 146]; untraced		*Graves* 1907, 77

6.	1769	Hunting group Payment(s): £5 5s		[coll Duke of Atholl]; untraced		Atholl archives in GPC
7.	1770	A fable, model	w	[Exhib Soc of Artists, London, 164]; untraced		*Graves* 1907, 77
8.	1770	A landscape, model	w	[Exhib Soc of Artists, London, 163]; untraced		*Graves* 1907, 77
9.	1772	Bear in an apiary, from Aesop's Fables	w	[Exhib Soc of Artists, London, 86]; untraced		*Graves* 1907, 77
10.	1772	Festoons of flowers	w	[Exhib Soc of Artists, London, 84, 85]; untraced		*Graves* 1907, 77
11.	1774	'A case with rich arms'	w	[Exhib Soc of Artists, London, 82]; untraced		*Graves* 1907, 77
12.	1774	A chandelier, three models	w	[Exhib Soc of Artists, London, 78, 79, 80]; untraced		*Graves* 1907, 77
13.	1775	Flowers	w	[Exhib Soc of Artists, London, 75]; untraced		*Graves* 1907, 77
14.	1778	A landscape, model	w	[Exhib Soc of Artists, London, 290]; untraced		*Graves* 1907, 77
15.	1780	Three portraits of unidentified ladies	w	[Exhib Soc of Artists, London, 291, 292, 293]; untraced		*Graves* 1907, 77
16.	1783	Four portraits of unidentified ladies	w	[Exhib Soc of Artists, London, 73, 74, 75, 76]; untraced		*Graves* 1907, 77
17.	1783	Two portraits of unidentified gentlemen	w	[Exhib Soc of Artists, London, 78]; untraced		*Graves* 1907, 77
18.	1790	Two portraits of unidentified ladies	w	[Exhib Soc of Artists, London, 62, 63]; untraced		*Graves* 1907, 77

DIEMAR, John Emmanuel

See Diemar, Emmanuel Matthias

DINHAM (or DENHAM), Joseph 1803–54

In 1820, while living in Pimlico, London, he won a large silver medal for a restored model of the *Ilissus* from the Elgin collection (**19**). That year he joined the Royal Academy Schools where he twice won the silver medal, in 1821 and 1824 (**20, 23**). When he exhibited at the RA in 1823 he was working in the studio of **Sir Francis Chantrey** in Belgrave Place. The following year he had moved to 25 Norfolk Street and during the 1820s he exhibited 1 Poland Street and 7 Cleveland Street. He showed at the RA until 1852 and his works included a bust of **E H Baily** (**8**). His last recorded address was 36 Wyndham Street. He died in December 1854, leaving a widow and five children.

Literary References: *Graves* II, 1905–6, 333; *Graves* 1875, 160; *Gunnis* 1968, 131

Funerary Monuments						
1.	†1840	Elizabeth Mackenzie		St James, Bermondsey, London	S	*Gunnis* 1968, 131
2.	?1853	Bishop Broughton		Sydney Cathedral, Australia		GPC
Statues						
3.	1826	Sleeping nymph, model		[Exhib RA, London, 1826, 1029 'for Sir M W Ridley Bt']; ? Blagdon, Northumbs		*Graves* II, 1905–6, 333; *Gunnis* 1968, 131
Busts						
4.	1824	Unidentified lady		[Exhib Soc of BA, London, 326]; untraced		*Johnson* 1975, 132
5.	1825	Francis Const		[Exhib RA, London, 1070]; untraced		*Graves* II, 1905–6, 333
6.	1825	Harriet Gouldsmith		[Exhib RA, London, 1070]; untraced	S	*Graves* II, 1905–6, 333
7.	1826	A child		[Exhib RA, London, 1094]; untraced		*Graves* II, 1905–6, 333
8.	1826	E H Baily RA		[Exhib RA, London, 1092]; untraced		*Graves* II, 1905–6, 333; *Gunnis* 1968, 131; *Johnson* 1975, 132
9.	1827	Sir Richard Birnie		[Exhib RA, London, 1078]; untraced		*Graves* II, 1905–6, 333
10.	1830	F Tatham		[Exhib Soc of BA, London, 132]; untraced		*Johnson* 1975, 132
11.	1830	John Flaxman		[Exhib Birmingham Soc of A]; untraced		GPC
12.	*c*1834	George Richmond	p	[coll George Richmond]; NPG, London 2157		*Ormond* 1973, 395 (pl 785)
13.	1844	Mrs Richmond	m	[Exhib RA, London, 1306]; untraced		*Graves* II, 1905–6, 333
14.	1847	'The late' George Gibbs, of Exeter College, Oxford		[Exhib RA, London, 1366]; untraced		*Graves* II, 1905–6, 333
15.	1849	Rt Hon Sir James Wigram, Vice-Chancellor		[Exhib RA, London, 1274]; untraced		*Graves* II, 1905–6, 333
16.	1850	Dr Ashburner		[Exhib RA, London, 1362]; untraced		*Graves* II, 1905–6, 333
17.	1851	'The late' Marquis of Hastings		[Exhib RA, London, 1351]; untraced		*Graves* II, 1905–6, 333
18.	1852	Unidentified lady		[Exhib RA, London, 1448]; untraced		*Graves* II, 1905–6, 333
Miscellaneous						
19.	1820	Restored model of the Illissus		[Soc of A, large silver medal]; untraced		RSA, *Transactions*, vol 38, 1820, xxxiv
20.	1821	Model in the antique academy		[RA silver medal]; untraced		RA Premium list
21.	1823	W Salter		[Exhib RA, London, 1078]; untraced		*Graves* II, 1905–6, 333
22.	1824	G Isaacson		[Exhib RA, London, 997]; untraced		*Graves* II, 1905–6, 333
23.	1824	Model in the life academy		[RA silver medal]; untraced		RA Premium list
24.	1825	Study from nature		[Exhib Soc of BA, London, 132]; untraced		*Johnson* 1975, 132
25.	1826	A child listening to a shell, model		[Exhib BI, London, 407]; untraced		*Graves* 1875, 160
26.	1826	Unidentified child		[Exhib RA, London, 1094]; untraced		*Graves* II, 1905–6, 333
27.	1827	A sleeping woman		[Exhib BI, London, 473]; untraced		*Graves* II, 1905–6, 333
28.	1828	Musidora		[Exhib BI, London, 518]; untraced		*Graves* 1875, 160
29.	1828	Walter Drew		[Exhib RA, London, 1183]; untraced		*Graves* II, 1905–6, 333
30.	1830	A daughter of C H Tatham		[Exhib RA, London, 1275]; untraced		*Graves* II, 1905–6, 333
31.	1830	Juno attiring		[Exhib RA, London, 1195]; untraced		*Graves* II, 1905–6, 333

32.	1830	The forsaken	[Exhib RA, London, 1186]; untraced	*Graves* II, 1905–6, 333; *Johnson* 1975, 858
33.	1832	Venus and Cupid	[Exhib RA, London, 1187]; untraced	*Graves* II, 1905–6, 333
34.	1839	Holy Family	[Exhib RA, London, 1387]; untraced	*Graves* II, 1905–6, 333
35.	1840	An infant's head, study	[Exhib BI, London, 449]; untraced	*Graves* 1875, 160
36.	1848	Young love meditating his first shot	[Exhib RA, London, 1341]; untraced	*Graves* II, 1905–6, 333
37.	1850	After the bath	[Exhib RA, London, 1358]; untraced	*Graves* II, 1905–6, 333

DIPPLE, Henry, of Richmond fl *c*1791–1808

He signs the Theobald monument alone (**1**), though he may have been one of the partners 'Dipple and Hudson' who in 1791 repaired Lord Willoughby de Broke's house at Richmond (Compton Verney Archives). In 1808 the firm was known as 'Dipple, Hudson and Dipple,' of Red Lion Street, Richmond, but by 1827 was owned alone by Henry Dipple of the same address.

Literary References: *Gunnis* 1968, 131

Archival References: GPC

Funerary Monuments

1.	?1796	Elizabeth Theobald	Kew, Surrey	S	*Gunnis* 1968, 131

DIXEY, John –1820

Dixey was born in Dublin. According to Strickland he went to London at an early age to become a student at the Royal Academy. The only student of that name recorded in the students' admission book was enrolled as a painter in October 1784 and gave his date of birth as 19 August 1763. Strickland records that Dixey was selected, as one of the most promising students, to be sent to Italy for further study, although he preferred instead to pursue opportunities in America. By 1801 he was established in New York, where he was employed on architectural decoration and executed some sculptural groups. He exhibited at the American Academy and became vice-president of the Academy of Fine Arts in Pennsylvania. His son, George Dixey, was also a sculptor.

Literary References: *Strickland* 1, 1913, 279–280; *Hutchison* 1960–62, 148

DIXON, John fl 1754–66

He was born in St Botolph-without-Aldgate, and was apprenticed in 1754 to **Henry Gregory**, becoming free of the Masons' Company in 1761. Dixon's monument to Bishop Sherlock is a sarcophagus on an altar tomb with scroll decoration (**1**).

Literary References: *Gunnis* 1968, 131

Funerary Monuments

1.	†1761	Bishop Sherlock (designed by John Vardy)	All Saints, Fulham, London, churchyard	S	*Gunnis* 1968, 131, 408; *Colvin* 1995, 1010
2.	1765	James, 1st Earl and James, 2nd Earl Waldegrave	Navestock, Essex	S	*Gunnis* 1968, 131
3.	†1766	Rev Henry Trotter	Graveley, Cambs	S	*Gunnis* 1968, 131; Pevsner, *Cambs*, 1970, 394

DIXON, Joseph –1787

Dixon (spelt Dickson in the Masons' Company list of freemen) appears to have been a son of Joseph Dixon, a Stamford carpenter. He was made free of the Masons' Company of London in 1760 'by virtue of an order of the Lord Mayor and Court of Aldermen.' In the same year he began to build Blackfriars bridge, working under the architect, Robert Mylne. This was completed in 1768. Dixon's work included the finely carved pillars, one of which survived the bridge's demolition in 1867 (**3**). He worked again under Mylne on Almack's Rooms in King Street, St James's.

In the 1760s he built a number of houses in Pall Mall together with his carpenter brother, Richard. In 1761 one of several payments was made to him for mason's work Woburn Abbey, and in 1766 he enlarged Coker Court, Somerset, for William Helyar.

His first London address was Air Street, Piccadilly, but by 1766 he had premises in St Alban's Street. In 1767 he became a director of the Westminster Fire Office. Around this time he took as a pupil John Carter, later to find fame as an architectural draughtsman and writer. Carter's father, **Benjamin Carter**, died in 1766 and Dixon appears to have taken the young man under his wing. The *Gentleman's Magazine* noted that Dixon allowed Carter 'to study under his instruction, till he came of age, at a liberal salary'. Carter remained with him 'for some years' (*GM* 1817, 2, 363).

Working as a mason-contractor under the architect Henry Holland, Dixon built, or altered, houses for Baron Atkinson at Putney in 1767; for Sir Thomas Robinson at Chelsea in 1769; for Philip Stephens at Fulham in 1770; for Mr Crawford in Hertford Street and for Sir Samson Gideon in St James's Square. He also carved chimneypieces for other buildings under Holland's supervision (**1, 2**). John Carter also worked for Holland for whom he made drawings in 1768.

Dixon was employed as a mason by two other notable architects, Matthew Brettingham, who used his services on the Earl of March's house in Piccadilly and Robert Adam, who queried his charges. In 1768 Dixon was paid £28 for work at Lansdowne House, but a note by Adam against his bill reads 'Wether or not an extravagant bill?' (Archives, Marquess of Lansdowne in GPC). Dixon and his brother nonetheless built the new south wing at Hitchin Priory, Herts, in 1770–2, to designs by Adam.

In 1773 Dixon offered his services to the Marine Society, who were commissioning a bust of their founder Jonas Hanway, to be carved after a wax model by **Patience Wright**. A note in the minute book of the Marine Society dated 26 May 1773 reads 'Mr Hanway's bust in wax made by Mrs Wright, intended for a model, is ready for the statuary. Mr Joseph Dickson, Statuary of Lambeth, asked to send for the model and submit an estimate' (GPC).

In December 1775 Dixon sold his stock in trade, auctioned by Hathwell on the premises, known as Dixon's Wharf at Pedlar's Acre, Lambeth. Among the lots were models for tablets and monuments, various busts and figures, terracottas of *Briseis and Agamemnon*, and a large statue of *Mercury*. Marble busts of Inigo Jones, Seneca, Dr Stukeley and Palladio, by 'Steff. Domine-Ceti' were also in the sale as well as 'two vases in statuary marble inlaid with sienna.' Other lots included 'An equestrian statue of the King of Prussia in plaster; a very capital wax model for a monument cloath'd and colour'd; two obelisks in statuary marble inlaid with Sienna' and two marble sphinxes.

In 1778 the *London Magazine* carried a notice of Dixon's bankruptcy. He was described as 'late of Pedlar's Acre, of St Mary, at Lambeth, Surry, stone merchant and mason' (*London Mag* 1778, 47, 190). His brother also became bankrupt that year. Dixon's last known commission was as architect of the new Battersea church, built between 1775 and 1777. He died in 1787 and was buried in that church 'without a fee' (*Taylor* 1925, 276). In his will Dixon was described as a 'senior bridge master,' although (apart from Blackfriars bridge) his most notable structure in this field was Exeter bridge, which collapsed in a flood in 1775. In 1789, Robert Mylne noted in his journal that Dixon's estate had paid a dividend of 10s in the pound (Mylne Archives in GPC).

MGS

Literary References: *GM* 1817, 2, 363; *Builder* 1850, 303; *Taylor* 1925, 99–113; *Gunnis* 1968, 131; *Colvin* 1995, 306–7
Archival References: Masons'Co, *Freemen*, 1677–1795 (1760); *Court Book*, 1751–96 (12 June 1760); Woburn Building Accts, 1748–62, BLARS R5/1092, 30 Nov 1761, p 123 (18s 6d); Soane Case 127, fol 130 (Baron Atkinson), fol 110 (Sir Thomas Robinson), fols 140–1 (Philip Stephens), fol 111 (Mr Crawford), fols 112–3 (Sir Samson Gideon); WFO DM 343/12, (22 Oct 1767); GPC
Auction Catalogues: Dixon 1775
Will: PROB 11/1152/171

Chimneypieces

1.	1769	Several Payment(s): £48	[Lord Warwick's house, St James Square, London, dining-room and others]; untraced	Soane Case 127, fols 127–9; *Gunnis* 1968, 131
2.	1769	Several Payment(s): £74	[for Colonel Scott of Charlton, Kent]; untraced	Soane Case 127, f 124; *Gunnis* 1968, 131

Architectural Sculpture

3.	1764	Pillars and pilasters (designed by Robert Mylne)	[Blackfriars Bridge, London]; one surviving pillar, Great Amwell, Herts	GPC

DOBSON, John fl 1783–93

His marriage to Miss S Sothren, daughter of G Sothren, of Norwich, was noted in the *Norfolk Chronicle* of 1783, and he placed an advertisement in the same paper on 31 May 1783. On 28 September 1793 it was announced that **Samuel Lincoln**, stone-mason, of St Andrew's, Bridge Street, Norwich, had taken over the stock and premises of John Dobson, for 'gravestones of every denomination'.

DOBSON, Richard

See **Richard Dodson**

DODSON, Richard fl *c*1835–81

One or more masons called Richard Dodson was active in the Shrewsbury area during the 19th century. A number of tablets in Shropshire and Wales are signed with this name, some of them perhaps dating from as early as the 1820s. **John Carline II of Shrewsbury** worked in partnership with a Richard Dodson *c*1835–1845, with whom he signed two tablets (**5, 6**). It seems that Dodson later set up on his own account, or perhaps took over Carline's yard, for *Slater's Directory of Shrewsbury* for 1850 lists a Richard Dodson at the 'Abbey Marble and Stone Works', Abbey Foregate. By 1877 a Richard Dodson was working from Swan Hill, Shrewsbury when an advertisement in the *Ludlow Advertiser* stated that he had been commissioned to execute the memorial to R B Bellyse in the market square at Audlem, Cheshire. The Bellyse memorial currently in the square is a cast-iron lamp-stand on a plain square plinth, perhaps erected by Dodson who might have carved the lettering of the inscription. The 1881 census records that Richard Dodson, a statuary mason who employed 5 men and one boy, was resident at 21 Swan Hill. It also states that he was born in 1819, at Ironbridge, Salop. He was, therefore, a mere 16 years old in 1835, which suggests that Carline's business partner was probably another, older man with the same name.

Literary References: RG/JP, 2, 248–9; 3, 444–5; *Colvin* 1995, 216

Funerary Monuments

1.	†1731	John Hill (re-cut by Dodson)	[Old St Chad, Shrewsbury]; St Chad, Shrewsbury, Salop	S	
2.	†1822	John Oliver	Much Wenlock, Salop		RG/JP, 3, 444
3.	†1823	Joseph Honeyborne	Kinver, Staffs	S	
4.	†1841	Rev Edward Tellett	Much Wenlock, Salop		RG/JP, 3, 444
5.	?1842	Mr Scott (co-sculptor: John Carline III, of Shrewsbury)	Aberdovey, Wales	S	RG/JP, 2, 248
6.	1844	Rev John Wall (†1817) (co-sculptor: John Carline III, of Shrewsbury)	Quatt, Salop	S	RG/JP, 2, 248
7.	†1845	Thomasine Dickin	Loppington, Salop	S	
8.	†1848	Rev Richard Scott (designed by Carline of Shrewsbury) (co-sculptor: Dodson)	Holy Cross, Shrewsbury, Salop	S	
9.	†1855	Rev Lewis Hughes	Pennal, near Aberdovey, Merioneth		RG/JP, 3, 444
10.	?1862	Humphrey Evans	Machynlleth, Powys		RG/JP, 3, 444
11.	?1864	Mary Lewis	Aberdovey, Merioneth		RG/JP, 3, 445
12.	?1866	Mary Breese	Machynlleth, Powys		RG/JP, 3, 445
13.	?1876	Rev John Williams	Aberdovey, Merioneth		RG/JP, 3, 445

DOE, John, of London fl 1723–72

The chief assistant to **Anthony Hart**, he carved a number of marble chimneypieces for Dudley North, of Glenham Hall, Suffolk. His contract, dated March 1723, stated that 'Mr. Doe shall do all the chimneys in the house at Glenham as Mr. North shall order at 5 shs. a foot, and the marble paving in ye middle of ye chapell at 2 shs. a foot' (1). In 1727 Doe also carved the capitals of the gate piers (3).

A John Doe 'of St Anne's Westminster stucco plaisterer' was buried at Islip, Oxon on 6 May 1772. The long date span suggests that there were at least two craftsmen of that name at work.

Literary References: *Gunnis* 1968, 131
Archival References: GPC

Chimneypieces

1.	1723	Several, including those in 'The Great Roome', the 'Roome next ye Chapell' and the 'Roome next ye Great stairs' Payment(s): 5s per foot	m	[Glenham Hall, Suffolk]; untraced	*Gunnis* 1968, 131, citing North archives

Architectural Sculpture

2.	1718	'Coping'		[Glenham Hall, Suffolk]; untraced	GPC

Miscellaneous

3.	1727	Capitals for gate piers		[Glenham Hall, Suffolk]; untraced	*Gunnis* 1968, 131 citing Dudley North archives

DOE, Robert fl 1717–40

The son of Thomas Doe of Reading, a yeoman, he was apprenticed to Richard King in 1717; two years later he was turned over to **James Paget**, and became free of the Masons' Company on 3 September 1725. In 1740 he supervised the erection of the Long Gallery chimneypieces at Temple Newsam House, Leeds.

Archival References: Masons' Co, Freemen, fol 13; GPC

DOLBIN fl 1698–1703

Dolbin was paid £2 19s on 4 January 1703 by Sir Francis Child, possibly for sculptural work (Child's Posting Book).

Archival References: GPC

Chimneypieces

1.	1698	Description unavailable Payment(s): £9 14s	m	[for Sir Edward Ernle]; untraced	Childs Bank, Ledger 1684–1698, fol 141

DORMAN, Joseph, of Chelmsford fl 1813–39

In 1801–13 he acted as foreman to G Wray, a mason of Chelmsford, but in the latter year set up for himself in acrimonious circumstances. On 9 and 16 April 1813 Dorman took out advertisements in the *Chelmsford Chronicle* publicising his treatment at the hands of his former master. He felt it 'necessary to inform his friends and the public, that having faithfully discharged the duties of Foreman to Mr G. Wray of Spitalfield, nearly twelve years, and having seven children', he had been encouraged by relatives to ask Wray either for a share in the business or an additional £6 per year. Wray would have none of it, since he had paid Denman 'and his boy of 16 years of age' (who was trained) £177 12s 4d during the past year. Dorman advertised on 9 June in the same paper that he was 'determined to execute all orders at most reduced prices, not withstanding that he has been undermined, by one of the trade, with several persons, who otherwise meant to employ him, and even came into the yard for that purpose.'

Literary References: RG/JP, 3, 445v

Funerary Monuments

1.	1823	Rev William Harty	Great Leighs, Essex	S	*Gunnis* 1968, 131
2.	†1838	William Rust	Good Easter, Essex	S	
3.	1839	John Poole	Bovinger, Essex	S	*Gunnis* 1968, 131
4.	1839	Unidentified subject, tablet	Bobbingworth, Essex	S	Pevsner, *Essex*, 1965, 90

D'ORSAY, Alfred, Count 1801–52

It is open to debate whether d'Orsay was a sculptor at all, since he may not have been the author of the artistic works that appeared under his name. Both **Thomas Henry Nicholson** and **William Behnes** are identified by contemporary sources as d'Orsay's 'ghost' sculptors. Though sub-contraction to other artists was not in itself an unusual practice in sculpture production, the way in which writers on d'Orsay have emphasised this point suggests that he was subject to a particular degree of animosity, which may have stemmed from his reputation in 19th-century England as a socialite rather than an artist.

He was born on 4 September 1801 in Paris. His father, Albert, Count d'Orsay, was one of Napoleon's generals, and his mother, Eleanor, née de Franquemont, the illegitimate daughter of the Duke of Würtemburg. D'Orsay himself joined the French army in 1821, but later that year journeyed to England to attend the coronation of King George IV. During this visit he rapidly gained a reputation as a dandy, wit and socialite. Returning to France in 1822, he met Lord and Lady Blessington at Valence, and was rapidly integrated into their social circle, remaining with them in Italy for much of the next seven years. Whilst there, d'Orsay married Lady Harriet Gardiner (1812–1869), a daughter from Lord Blessington's first marriage, which gave him the security provided by Lord Blessington's Irish property. The marriage appears to have been purely a financial arrangement, and the couple were distant and uncivil towards each other in public. D'Orsay was to conduct a barely concealed affair with Lady Blessington.

Returning to London in 1830, his wife left him and returned to Ireland, while d'Orsay helped Lady Blessington to establish one of London's most celebrated bohemian salons of the time, first at Seamore Place in Mayfair and later at Gore House, Piccadilly. This attracted many of the best-known artists, writers, politicians and other distinguished people, including Dickens, Tennyson, Disraeli and Wellington. As a well-known socialite, d'Orsay frequently sat to other artists and he also undertook many portraits of people who frequented Lady Blessington's salon. They included a relatively small number of figures such as Jenny Lind, the Emperors of Russia and Austria and Louis Napoleon, who was at the time living in exile in Britain, but would later to return to France as Napoleon III (**9, 2, 19, 10**). The most celebrated of these works of sculpture was d'Orsay's statuette, *Wellington on horseback*, 1845, which delighted the Duke so much that he claimed it was the portrait he would like posterity to remember him by (**5**). Writing to Henry Bulmer, the British ambassador in Madrid, d'Orsay claimed that the piece 'is almost causing a revolution here', and that the Duke 'comes here continually to admire himself' (*Sadleir* 1933, 334).

It seems unlikely that d'Orsay had any formal artistic training, but his work was clearly considered of high enough quality to be exhibited at the Royal Academy, 1843–48. Whether these exhibits were actually by him is difficult to ascertain. The *Art Journal* suggested that Nicholson was in fact the author of the Wellington statuette and other works, and he is said to have 'complained bitterly' at d'Orsay's attempts at carving in his absence, which caused Nicholson 'many an extra week's work' (*AJ*, 1870, 204). Henry Vizetelly also claimed that a series of miniature portrait busts, allegedly by d'Orsay, were modelled by **William Behnes** 'before he became celebrated as a sculptor' (*Sadleir* 1933, 325). While reporting these claims, Sadleir was sceptical of their veracity.

In keeping with his reputation as a playboy, d'Orsay was financially reckless and was forced in 1849 to flee to France to avoid his creditors. His profligacy ruined Lady Blessington, who was forced to sell her properties and possessions to settle his debts. In France he made repeated attempts to gain a government appointment from his friend, the newly returned Louis Napoleon, and was finally rewarded in 1852 with the post of director of the Ecole des Beaux Arts. Before he was able to take up this post, however, he contracted a spinal infection. He died on 4 August 1852.

Michael Paraskos

Literary References: *AJ*, 1870, 204; *Sadleir* 1933, *passim*; *Gunnis* 1968, 131–2; *ODNB* (Burton) *Breward* 2004, *passim*;

Selected Portraits of the Sculptor: E Landseer, drawing, 1832–35, NPG 4922; W Behnes, bust, 1843–47, royal coll; J Doyle, drawing, BM; R J Lane, drawing (repr *Sadleir* 1933, 296)

Statues					
1.	1844	Daniel O'Connell, MP, statuette	b	NGI	SD *le Harivel* 1988, 559 (repr)
2.	c1846	Emperor of Russia, statuette	b	[Countess of Blessington sale, Phillips, Gore House, Kensington, 7–26 May 1849]; untraced	*AU*, 1846, 189; *Gunnis* 1968, 132
3.	1846	Marquis of Anglesey, equestrian statuette, model		[Exhib RA, London, 1479]; untraced	*AU*, 1846, 189
4.	c1847	Sir Francis Grant, statuette	p	Coll Hon Mrs G Walsh	*Ormond* 1973, 194
5.	1852	Wellington on horseback, statuette	b	[Hatfield House, Herts]; Gov Art Coll	Gov Art Coll archives
6.	nd	Count Alfred D'Orsay, self-portrait statuette		[Blessington sale, Gore House, Kensington, 1849, lot 196]; untraced	*Ormond* 1973, 149; *Morris and Roberts* 1998, 201
7.	nd	Daniel O'Connell, statuette	b	[Blessington sale, Gore House, Kensington, 1849, lot 1475]; untraced	*Ormond* 1973, 349
8.	nd	Equestrian figure of Napoleon Bonaparte, statuette		[Blessington sale, Gore House, 1849]; untraced	*Gunnis* 1968, 132
9.	nd	Jenny Lind, statuette	m	[Blessington sale, Gore House, 1849]; untraced	*Gunnis* 1968, 132
10.	nd	Louis Napoleon (later Emperor Napoleon III), statuette (co-sculptor: Thomas Henry Nicholson)	b	[Blessington sale, Gore House, 1849]; untraced	*Gunnis* 1968, 132, 272
11.	nd	Sir James Grant, two statuettes		[Blessington sale, Gore House, Kensington, 1849, lots 264, 267]; untraced	*Ormond* 1973, 196
Busts					
12.	1847	Sir Francis Grant	m	[Exhib RA, London, 1434]; untraced	*Ormond* 1973, 194
13.	1847	William Behnes	m	[Exhib RA, London, 1397]; untraced	*AU*, 1847, 200
14.	1849	Viscountess Canterbury		[Exhib Colosseum, Regent's Park, London]; untraced	GPC
15.	nd	Alfred, Count d'Orsay, self-portrait	m	NPG, London, 3548	*Ormond* 1977, 149, repr 277
16.	nd	Alfred, Count d'Orsay, self-portrait	b	[Blessington sale, Gore House, Kensington, 1849, lot 194]; untraced	*Ormond* 1973, 149
17.	nd	Arthur, 1st Duke of Wellington	m	[Blessington sale, Gore House, 1949]; untraced	*Gunnis* 1968, 132
18.	nd	Edward, 14th Earl of Derby		Untraced Other versions: Parian ware bust after D'Orsay, ex coll Roger Fulford (†1869); untraced	*Ormond* 1973, 136
19.	nd	Emperor of Austria	b	[Blessington sale, Gore House, 1849]; untraced	*Gunnis* 1968, 132
20.	nd	Lord Brougham	b	[Blessington sale, Gore House, 1849]; untraced	*Gunnis* 1968, 132
21.	nd	Lord Lyndhurst	b	[Blessington sale, Gore House, 1849]; untraced	*Gunnis* 1968, 132
22.	nd	Marguerite, Countess of Blessington	m	[Blessington sale, Gore House, Kensington, 1849, lot 281]; untraced	*Ormond* 1973, 40
23.	nd	Albert, Count d'Orsay	b	[Blessington sale, Gore House, Kensington, 1849]; untraced	*Gunnis* 1968, 132
Reliefs					
24.	nd	Marguerite, Countess of Blessington		[Blessington sale, Gore House, Kensington, 1849, lot 220]; untraced	*Ormond* 1973, 40
Miscellaneous					
25.	1844	Napoleon		[Exhib Liverpool Ac, 557]; untraced	*Morris and Roberts* 1998, 201

DOUBLEDAY, William fl 1829–34

In 1829 he contracted to build Brighton Town Hall for £12,491 1s 7d, and he is therefore presumably responsible for the charming and unusual Corinthian capitals of the pillars of the interior, especially those in the top storey. The final payment to Doubleday was not made until 1834.

Archival References: GPC

DOUGHTY, Jean fl 1784

A carver of Charles Street, Westminster, in May 1784 he took as an apprentice Richard Rousset, a pupil at the French Protestant Charity School.

Literary References: *le May* 2001, 568

DOUGLAS, John fl 1769–83?

He was a London sculptor and is perhaps synonymous with Douglas, a mason, who sold his supply of stone in 1783.

Chimneypieces

1.	1785	White marble Payment(s): £99 6s	m	Leuchie House, near North Berwick, drawing room	Leuchie House archives in GPC

Architectural Sculpture

2.	1769	Pedestal for a statue of Diana Payment(s): £30	m	[Lansdowne House, London, staircase]; untraced	Archives, Marquess of Lansdowne in GPC

DOVELL, N, of Barnstaple fl 1813?

Funerary Monuments

1.	?1813	Augustus Willett	Westleigh, Devon	S	*Gunnis* 1968, 132

DOWER, John, of Marston 1646–

Dower (or Dener) was 35 when he was called to give evidence in 1681 in the suit between **Thomas Wood** and Richard Frogley, a carpenter. He told the court that he had served a 9-year apprenticeship to his father George Dower, late of Marston, and during that time worked at Brazenose College library and chapel, on the vestry and vault of St John's College and also at the theatre, all in Oxford. He had been employed under **William Byrd of Oxford** on 'the dorecases of the Divinity Schole in Oxon' and stonework at New College. He was now employed in the building 'of the Elaboratory within the University of Oxon' (OU, Chancellor's Ct Papers, Wood v Frogley, fol 16).

Literary References: *Gunnis* 1968, 126–7

Chimneypieces

1.	pre-1681	'in the Hall of Esqr. Lentall's house [at Hasley, Oxon], curiously wrought and carv'd'	Untraced	OU, Chancellor's Ct Papers, Wood v Frogley, fol 16

Architectural Sculpture

2.	pre-1681	Six 'dore cases of freestone' and other work	[Bishop of Oxford's Palace, Cuddesdon]; destroyed, 1960s	OU, Chancellor's Ct Papers, Wood v Frogley, fol 16

DOWYER, James and John fl 1726–31

An entry of 1726 in the private account book of the 1st Duke of Kent reads: 'Paid Dowyer the carver, third payment, on account of Lord Harold's monument, £40'; a fourth payment of £20 is noted later in the same volume (Archives, Lady Lucas and Dingwall, cited by *Gunnis* 1968, 132). The monument referred to is at Flitton, and has a life-sized reclining figure on a sarcophagus (1). Gunnis was not impressed: he considered the work 'generally clumsy, the attitude of the figure is awkward and the head is too big for the body; in fact, the only features of the monument worth noting are the curious feet of the sarcophagus, which are in the form of eagle's claws'. It seems strange, he added 'that the Duke should have engaged so obscure and second-rate a sculptor to execute the monument to his deeply loved, only surviving son'.

There were two Dowyer carvers, John and James. In 1729 both were working for Earl Fitzwalter, probably at Moulsham Hall, Essex. In 1729 Charles Beard, Earl Fitzwalter's steward, entered in his account book 'July 24 pd. John Dowyer and James Dowyer stone carver £6'. This was the first of 12 payments, all for sums between £4 and £6, made over the period until August 1730. Further payments were made to James alone between August and December 1731 (Hants RO, 15 M 50/31, 125–6). Another account book records a payment £101 9s 4d 'in full' made to a Mr Dowyer by Beard. The carvers are referred to as 'Mr Dowyer the Elder' and 'The lame one;' (Essex RO D/DM.A5).

Literary References: *Gunnis* 1968, 132; *Edwards* 1977, 40

Archival References: GPC

Funerary Monuments

1.	1726	Anthony, Earl of Harrold (†1721) Payment(s): £60 (part payment?)	Flitton, Beds, Grey Mausoleum	S	*Gunnis* 1968, 132; Pevsner, *Beds, Hunts & Peterborough*, 1968, 92; *Bryant* 2003, 78 (repr)

DRAKE, John fl 1735–40

In Westminster Public Library is a rough account-book of John Drake, itemising, among other matters, payments to his partner John Skinner. From this it appears that the partners built Weald Hall, Essex, between 1735 and 1740. ('The Temple', a building in the grounds, is also mentioned.) There are references to payments for work at 'Mr. Jelfe's house in New Palace Yard' (**Andrews Jelfe**), and also at the homes of Lord Nassau Paulet; Mrs Warner, Albemarle Street; Mr Page, Salisbury Street, and Mr Catwood, Clare Market.

Archival References: WPL MS.3127; GPC

DRAPER, John fl 1718–46

The son of John Draper, of St Andrew's, Holborn, he was apprenticed in 1718 to G Grosvenor 'Citizen and Joiner' (Apprenticeship Books, TNA IR 1/6 fol 134). In 1746 he was working at Welbeck Abbey with his partner, **William Wilson.**

Literary References: *Gunnis* 1968, 132

Architectural Sculpture

1.	1746	'Keystone with a lion's head' (co-sculptor: William Wilson)	[Welbeck Abbey, Notts]; untraced	Duke of Portland archives in *Gunnis* 1968, 132
2.	1746	'Large ornament with festoons of fruit and flowers' (co-sculptor: William Wilson)	[Welbeck Abbey, Notts]; untraced	Duke of Portland archives in *Gunnis* 1968, 132

DRAWATER, James fl 1768–75?

Drawater, who was described as 'of St. Mary le Bonne, Middlesex, mason,' became bankrupt in 1770 (*London Mag* 1770, 112), but apparently continued in business, for he was the mason employed six years later on repairs to Sir John Griffin's London house (Braybrooke Estate Accts, Essex RO, D./DBY A.34; D/DBY A 197). As a contractor he built two houses in Harrow Road in 1768 (Middlesex Building Affidavits). He signs the tablet to Richard Canning (1).

His father may have been the 'Barnwall Drawater, mason' employed in 1747 by the Hon George Fox at his house in Cavendish Square (Archives, Bramham Park in *Gunnis* 1968, 132).

Literary References: *Gunnis* 1968, 132

Funerary Monuments

1.	?1775	Richard Canning	St Helen, Ipswich, Suffolk	S	*Gunnis* 1968, 132

DREW, C, of Eaton Socon fl 1788

He signs a small mural tablet at Great Gadson and may well be synonymous with **Charles Drew of Bedford**.

Funerary Monuments

1.	1788	Charles Kettle	Great Gansdon, Huntingdon	S	

DREW, Charles, of Bedford –1826

Between 1808 and 1812 he assisted **Thomas Grundy** in building Moggerhanger House, Beds, for Stephen Thornton, to designs by Sir John Soane. A payment of £222 is recorded in Soane's accounts. He also worked as a statuary and his tablets usually have carefully carved details.

Literary References: *Gunnis* 1968, 132

Archival References: Soane, Abstract of Bills 4, fol 30

Funerary Monuments

1.	?1791	Henry Sharp	Flitton, Beds	S	*Gunnis* 1968, 132
2.	?1800	William Edwards	Arlesey, Beds	S	*Gunnis* 1968, 132
3.	?1805	Carter Shavington	Kempton, Beds	S	*Gunnis* 1968, 132
4.	?1814	John Osborn	Campton, Beds	S	*Gunnis* 1968, 132
5.	?1816	Alexander Small	Clifton Reynes, Bucks	S	*Gunnis* 1968, 132
6.	?1819	John Higgins	Weston Underwood, Bucks	S	*Gunnis* 1968, 132

DREW, of London fl 1767?

He signs one known tablet 'with charming details'.

Funerary Monuments

1.	?1767	Mrs Lloyd	Marylebone Chapel, London	S	*Gunnis* 1968, 132

DREW, Thomas, of Bury St Edmunds –1713

In 1706 he provided the black-marble ledger tomb commemorating Isabella, Countess of Bristol, at Ickworth (**1**). Drew married Ann Warren on 23 April 1685 at St James, Bury St Edmunds and was buried at St Mary, Bury St Edmunds, on 17 November 1713 (parish register). In his will, proved on 31 December 1713, probate was granted to his widow (Archdeaconry of Sudbury Administration).

Archival References: IGI; GPC

Funerary Monuments

1.	1706	Isabella, Countess of Bristol	Ickworth, Suff		*Gunnis* 1968, 132

DREWETT, William, of Bristol fl 1784–1803

He was foreman to **Thomas Paty** and set up for himself after Paty's death in 1789. In 1794 he agreed with John Colby to build, for a sum of £84 a Painswick-stone cantilevered staircase for Ffynone House, Pembroke and to supply a marble chimneypiece (**20**) (Colby Archives cited in *Gunnis* 1968, 132–3). Drewett alone signed the monument to Mary Teast, which is about 14 feet high and has a figure of *Hope*, and to Sir Robert Mackworth, which has a large draped sarcophagus (**4, 5**).

He carved a number of monuments in partnership with **Henry Jones** and **John Dunn**, several of them signed 'Jones, Dunn and Drewett' or 'Dunn and Drewett'. In 1800, in Bristol, the partners advertised their competence in 'monuments, chimney pieces and every description of ornamental work executed with elegance and dispatch on the most reasonable terms' (*Dale-Jones and Lloyd* 1989, 49). Their most notable monument is to Daniel and Margaret Prytherch (**12**), a polychrome work decorated with fluting and surmounted by a roundel enclosing a weeping lady. All identified works by the firm are listed below.

Literary References: *Gunnis* 1968, 132–3; *Dale-Jones and Lloyd* 1989, 49

Funerary Monuments

1.	†1784	John Arundell (by Jones, Dunn & Drewett of Bristol)	Ruishton, Somerset		Pevsner, *Somerset: S & W*, 1958, 283
2.	1785	Elizabeth Bailey	Olveston, Glos	S	Pevsner, *Glos: Vale & Forest of Dean*, 1976, 316
3.	?1789	Morgan Evans (by Jones, Dunn and Drewett, of Bristol)	Lydney, Glos	S	*Gunnis* 1968, 133
4.	1790	Mary Teast (†1766)	Henbury, Glos		Pevsner, *Somerset: N & Bristol*, 1958, 467; *Gunnis* 1968, 132
5.	1794	Sir Robert Mackworth	Neath, Glamorgan		*Gunnis* 1968, 132
6.	†1795	Christopher Nicholls (by Jones, Dunn & Drewett, of Bristol)	Old Sodbury, Glos	S	Pevsner, *Glos: Cotswolds*, 1999, 535
7.	†1798	Edward Hathway (by Jones, Dunn & Drewett, of Bristol)	Pucklechurch, Glos	S	Pevsner, *Glos: Vale & Forest of Dean*, 1976, 325
8.	†1798	Sexa James (†1798), William Ogbourn and William Robert James (by Jones, Dunn & Drewett, of Bristol)	Axbridge, Somerset	S	
9.	?1799	Hannah Hughes (by Jones, Dunn and Drewett, of Bristol)	St Mary Redcliffe, Bristol	S	*Gunnis* 1968, 133
10.	†1799	John Campion	Olveston, Glos	S	Pevsner, *Glos: Vale & Forest of Dean*, 1976, 316
11.	?1799	Samuel Webb (by Jones, Dunn and Drewett, of Bristol)	Widford, Somerset	S	*Gunnis* 1968, 133
12.	†1800	Daniel and Margaret Prytherch (by Jones, Dunn & Drewett, of Bristol)	Brechfa, Carmarthen		*Dale-Jones and Lloyd* 1989, 49

13.	†1802	Anna Underwood		Coaley, Glos	S	Pevsner, *Glos: Vale & Forest of Dean*, 1976, 162
14.	†1802	Esther Williams (by Jones, Dunn & Drewett, of Bristol)		St Peter, Carmarthen		*Dale-Jones and Lloyd* 1989, 49
15.	†1802	John and Elizabeth Lloyd (by Jones, Dunn & Drewett, of Bristol)		St Peter, Carmarthen	S	*Gunnis* 1968, 133; *Dale-Jones and Lloyd* 1989, 49
16.	†1802	Richard Howell (by Jones, Dunn & Drewett, of Bristol)		Llanstephan, Carmarthen		*Dale-Jones and Lloyd* 1989, 49
17.	†1802	Sarah Lowder		Tidenham, Glos	S	Pevsner, *Glos: Vale & Forest of Dean*, 1976, 384
18.	?1803	Eleanor Kemeys (by Jones, Dunn and Drewett, of Bristol)		Newport, Monmouths	S	*Gunnis* 1968, 133
19.	?1803	William Wheeler (by Jones, Dunn and Drewett, of Bristol)		St Augustine, Bristol	S	*Gunnis* 1968, 133
Chimneypieces						
20.	1794	Description unavailable	m	[Ffynone House, Pembroke]; untraced		*Gunnis* 1968, 132–3

DREWIT, Henry after 1744–

He was the son of Henry Drewit (or Druit), a carver who was apprenticed to John Cooper in 1721, and the grandson of Henry Druit, 'stone-carver' of Goodman's Fields. Dossie says that Drewit was 'taught by his father, a carver'. In 1763 he received a premium in the under 19 class from the Society of Arts (1).

Literary References: *Dossie* 1782, 437; *Gunnis* 1968, 133

Reliefs

1.	1763	Festoon in clay	[Soc of A, premium]; untraced	*Dossie* 1782, 437; *Gunnis* 1968, 133

DRUIT, Joseph, of London fl 1826–27

Druit is listed as a 'statuary' of Whitehorse Lane, Stepney in the London *Directory* of 1827 (*Pigot* 1826–7, 259).

Funerary Monuments

1.	?1826	Townsend family	Godmanchester, Hunts	S	*Gunnis* 1968, 133

DRYHURST, James fl 1729–31

A carver, he was probably related to **Thomas Dryhurst**.

Archival References: Hoare Partnership Ledger, 1725–34, fol 213

Architectural Sculpture

1.	1729–1731	Unspecified carved work Payment(s): £181	[for the partners of Hoare's Bank]; untraced	Hoare Partnership Ledger, 1725–34, fols 211–27

DRYHURST, Thomas fl 1757–63

Presumably a relative of **James Dryhurst**, he was employed by the architect Henry Keene, together with **Benjamin Carter** and **Thomas Gayfere**, on the building of Thomas Bridges's house at 18 Cavendish Square, London (2). He appears in Henry Pyle's painting of Keene and his craftsmen, formerly at Buxted Place, Sussex (destroyed but reproduced in *Smith* 1945, 556). He is in the centre of the composition, leaning over the back of a chair.

Archival References: LMA, Cavendish Square Accounts fols 223–264

Architectural Sculpture				
1.	1763	Unspecified carved work Payment(s): £15	[Sir Roger Newdigate's house, Spring Gardens, London]; untraced	Newdigate archives in GPC
Miscellaneous				
2.	1757–1759	Unidentified 'carving' Payment(s): £150	[18 Cavendish Square, London]; untraced	LMA, Cavendish Square Accounts fols 223–64

DU CHAIME (or DUCHESNE), Gideon fl 1706

He was employed, with **Nadauld**, as a stone-carver of interiors at Castle Howard in 1706, and submitted his bills in French.

Archival References: Castle Howard Building Accts, G/2/26, nd; G2/2/27, 22 Oct 1706; G2/2/28, 22 Oct 1706

Architectural Sculpture

1.	1706	Composite columns and other interior carving (co-sculptor: Nadauld) Payment(s): £52 13s 4d	s	Castle Howard, N R Yorks, great hall	Castle Howard Building Accts, G2/1/1, fol 94v; *Saumarez-Smith*, 1990, 66

DUBOURG fl 1769

The Royal Academy gave a donation of 5 guineas to 'Mr Dubourg, carver' in June 1769.

Archival Reference: RA Council Minutes, vol 1, 24 June 1769, fol 29

DUCKETT, of Margate fl 1863

He signs a stone and slate monument in Kent.

Funerary Monuments

1.	†1863	John Gaskell	St Nicholas-at-Wade, Kent	S

DUCKETT, Thomas, of Preston 1804–78

Duckett was a portrait sculptor who worked in Preston, Lancs during the mid-19th century, hailing from the Preston area, where his forebears were respectable farmers. He had no formal artistic training and was initially apprenticed to a local plasterer, but he became increasingly dissatisfied with that occupation and his indentures were eventually cancelled. He then found employment as a wood-carver with the cabinet-makers Gillow and Co in Lancaster but soon left them to work for **Franceys and Spence** in Liverpool. His first recorded sculptural work, a bust of the Rev J Dunn, was exhibited at the Liverpool Academy in 1828 (13). He later worked for **Francis Webster and Sons of Kendal** and was manager of their sculpture department for several years. Whilst employed by the Websters he carved a limestone group of *St George and the dragon* for the pediment of the Roman Catholic church in New Road, Kendal (28). Soon after it was completed he returned to Preston, where he set up home in Cannon Street and established a studio in Avenham Road.

Duckett executed a number of works for his native town. The most important of these is the statue of Sir Robert Peel, in Westmorland limestone, erected in Winckley Square in 1852 (7). A contemporary noted that the statue was considered a good likeness but criticised the incongruous character of the drapery covering the lower limbs. He felt that the sculptor had hesitated between yielding to the convention which invested all sculpture with Antique drapery, and boldly representing him in full modern dress: 'The clothing appears to cling to the lower limbs as though it had been soaked in water. Neither one nor the other object has been truly effected; but the vacillation has considerably injured the general effect of the statue' (*Hardwick* 1857, 434–5). Other local works include carved stone decoration for the Literary and Philosophical Institute (**24**), a marble altar for St Augustine's Church, Preston (**25**) and several funerary monuments (**1–5**). Duckett had little success in attracting commissions for public statues and was not well-known outside Preston. His plaster model for a colossal seated figure of Sir Richard Arkwright was admired by his friends, but was eventually demolished since it was not commissioned in marble or bronze (**12**). He competed for the Peel statue in Bury and the Wellington statue in Leeds, but was unsuccessful though his designs were highly commended (**7, 9**).

Duckett was twice married and had 5 children. His second son, also named Thomas, was a sculptor of some promise who died aged 29 in Australia, in 1868. The younger Duckett, who had studied under **Thomas Thornycroft** and in Rome, exhibited at the Royal Academy between 1861 and 1867 and at the British Institution in 1866. The father died on 13 February 1878, after a long illness.

Literary References: *AJ*, 1868, 158; 1878, 169, 207; *Preston Guardian*, 16 Feb 1878, 6; *Graves* 1875, 167; *Graves* II, 1905–6, 380–1; *Gunnis* 1968, 133

Funerary Monuments

1.	1841	Richard Gell		Walton-le-Dale, Lancs	S	*Gunnis* 1968, 133
2.	1854	T Lowndes		St George, Preston, Lancs		*Gunnis* 1968, 133
3.	1860	Giles Thornton		Poulton-le-Fylde, Lancs	S	*Gunnis* 1968, 133
4.	1861	Thomas Hart		St John, Preston, Lancs		*Gunnis* 1968, 133
5.	nd	Katherine Wyrley-Birch		East Wretham, Norfolk		GPC

Statues

6.	1838	John Horrocks, prize-winning design		Untraced		*Gunnis* 1968, 133
7.	c1851	Sir Robert Peel, for Bury (or Bolton), model only (commission awarded to Edward Hodges Baily)		Untraced		*AJ*, 1878, 169; NRP database
8.	1852	Sir Robert Peel	s	Winckley Square, Preston, Lancs		*ILN*, XX, 1852, 448 (repr); *Read* 1982, 107, 147 (repr)
9.	c1855	Arthur, 1st Duke of Wellington, for Leeds, model only (commission awarded to Carlo, Baron Marochetti)		Untraced		*Preston Guardian*, 16 Feb 1878, 6; *AJ*, 1878, 169
10.	1863	Unidentified subject		Harris S 78	SD	
11.	nd	Nymph disturbed at her bath	m	Towneley, Burnley		inf. Towneley Hall Art Gall
12.	nd	Sir Richard Arkwright, model only	p	Destroyed because no funds available to carve the statue in marble		*Preston Guardian*, 16 Feb 1878, 6

Busts

13.	1828	Rev J Dunn		[Exhib ALRI, Liverpool, 228]; untraced		*Morris and Roberts* 1998, 203
14.	1844	Thomas Batty Addison	m	Harris S 10	S	*Gunnis* 1968, 133
15.	1845	Rev Robert Harris	m	Harris S 6		*Gunnis* 1968, 133
16.	1847	Thomas German	m	Harris S 7	S	*Gunnis* 1968, 133
17.	1847	Thomas Miller		Harris S 7		
18.	1852	William Taylor	m	Harris S 8		*Gunnis* 1968, 133
19.	1861	John Addison	m	Harris S 11	SD	*Gunnis* 1968, 133
20.	1862	William, 11th Earl of Meath (from a model by the Earl's wife)	m	Kilkuddery House, Co Wicklow	SD	GPC
21.	1863	Unidentified subject		Harris S 79	SD	
22.	1870	Thomas Miller	m	Harris S 5	S	*Gunnis* 1968, 133
23.	1874	Miles Myres	m	Harris S 9	S	*Gunnis* 1968, 133

Architectural Sculpture

24.	1846	Carved stonework	s	Literary and Philosophical Institute, Preston, Lancs		*Gunnis* 1968, 133
25.	nd	Altar	m	St Augustine, Preston, Lancs		*Preston Guardian*, 16 Feb 1878, 6
26.	nd	Brockholes family coat of arms	m	Poulton-le-Fylde church, Lancs		*Gunnis* 1968, 133
27.	nd	Group of two children		Infants' school, Lancaster (gift of Mr Newsham)		*Preston Guardian*, 16 Feb 1878, 6
28.	nd	St George and the dragon	s	Holy Trinity and St George, Kendal, Cumbria, pediment		*Preston Guardian*, 16 Feb 1878, 6

DUDLEY, Cornelius, of Bristol fl 1738

Gunnis claims that he signs the monument to Anna Maria, daughter of Morgan Lloyd, though a recent search by Dale-Jones and Lloyd failed to locate this signature.

Funerary Monuments

1.	†1738	Anna Maria Lloyd	m	Llangadog, Carnarvon		*Gunnis* 1968, 133; *Dale-Jones and Lloyd* 1989, 49

DUDLEY, J J

Listed as a statuary and mason of Bermondsey New Road in Kent's *Directory* of 1827, he is perhaps to be identified with **J Dudley of London**.

Literary References: *Kent's Directory* 1827, 109

DUDLEY, J, of London fl c1850

Architectural Sculpture

1.	c1850	British monarchs, divines and evangelists, carvings on dripstones		Bicton, Devon		Pevsner, *Devon*, 1989, 174

DUGDALE, Thomas fl 1677–

In 1678 he executed the 'magnificent' panelling of the long gallery at Chirk Castle. The capitals were removed during a Georgian restoration. Gunnis speculated that he might be the 'Thomas Dugdale, of Liverpool, carver,' whose will was proved in 1714.

Literary References: *Gunnis* 1968, 133

Statues

1.	1678	Four figures	s	[for Sir Kenrick Eyton's house at Wrexham]; untraced	*Gunnis* 1968, 133

Architectural Sculpture

2.	1677	Fifteen capitals		[Chirk Castle, Denbighs, drawing-room]; removed	Myddleton archives cited in *Gunnis* 1968, 133
3.	1678	Panelling, overdoor and other ornaments	wd	Chirk Castle, Denbighs, long gallery	Pevsner, *Clwyd*, 1995, 125–126 (repr)

DUNAGE, Samuel fl 1724–

The son of Samuel Dunage, 'Cit & Weaver' of London, he was apprenticed for £4 10s on 20 May 1724 to **Adam Nost**, 'Cit & Mason'. Another Samuel Dunage, presumably a relative, was made free via service to Adam Morse on 2 October 1755.

Literary References: *Webb* (3), 1957, 115

Archival References: Masons' Co, Freemen, fol 13

DUNBAR, David I 1793–1866

A peripatetic sculptor of Scottish origin, he was christened in Dumfries on 29 April 1793, the son of Thomas Dunbar, a builder, mason and Deacon of the Squaremen, and Janet, née Johnston. The death of his father, with whom he was training as a mason, in 1805, changed his life. Through generous funding by friends, who had 'long watched the genius of the embryo sculptor', he studied in Rome and elsewhere (*Builder* 1866, 638). On his return to Britain he found employment in the studio of **Sir Francis Chantrey**, where in 1814 he was paid for work on the statue of George III for the Guildhall. In November 1815 he was given the task of cleaning other Guildhall monuments. He exhibited at the Royal Academy in 1815 from an address in Ebury Street, Pimlico (**1**) and must have married *c*1813 since the obituary of his wife Ann, née Stokes, states that they had been married 50 years and she died in 1863 (*C J* 13 Nov 1863, 5). His son David was baptised at Fisher Street Presbyterian church on 7 October 1825.

By 1822 he was living in Abbey Street, Carlisle, working for the mason and sculptor, **Paul Nixson**. Together they were the driving force behind the Carlisle Academy of Fine Art, founded in October 1822. Nixson provided the rooms, which Dunbar decorated with an allegorical statue and busts of three eminent artists, his former master, Chantrey, Sir Christopher Wren and Benjamin West PRA (**62**). Between October 1824 and December 1825, Dunbar was secretary of the Carlisle Mechanics' Institute (*The Citizen*, 23 April 1824, 81; 23 Oct 1824, 185; 16 Dec 1825). When presented a silver snuff box by the Institute for his services in establishing it, he was described as 'very pleasant, amiable, kind-hearted and good-natured' (*The Citizen*, 6 Jan 1826, 54). Dunbar was in Italy again in 1826–27 and on his return boasted at a Carlisle Academy dinner that he had been presented with a cast of **Bertel Thorvaldsen**'s *Venus* and that the professor of the Academy at Carrara (of which Dunbar was a member) had sent him a collection of drawings for use by the Carlisle students.

Dunbar taught modelling at the Carlisle Academy, numbering **M L Watson** among his pupils. He also showed more than 40 works of sculpture at the Academy's exhibitions between 1822 and 1833. He was sufficiently dynamic to persuade other sculptors to donate their work to the schools, including **Joseph Gott** who made a gift in 1827.

Dunbar appears to have been a driving force behind several regional exhibitions. In 1826 he showed in Leeds (**23**) and in 1828 and 1830 acted as a secretary for exhibitions held in Dumfries (*C J*, 9 Feb 1828). In the 1828 exhibition there were 234 modern paintings and 23 works of sculpture, including some of his own (*C J*, 24 May 1828). In 1829 he exhibited with the Birmingham Society of Artists (**39**), and in 1831 and 1832 held displays of his own work in Newcastle (where he had had a studio for some years) and Durham. In 1833 he advertised listed casts from his busts in his studio in the Royal Arcade, Newcastle (*C J*, 28 Sept 1833). He began corresponding with the Royal Manchester Institution in the mid-1830s and before 1838 he had presented them with a marble bust of **Antonio Canova** by an unidentified sculptor. In 1837 he exhibited at the Institution and may have moved to Manchester, for Pigot's *Directory* of 1838 lists a sculptor of that name at 30, Pool Street.

During the 1820s and 1830s Dunbar was responsible for several monuments. These included a bust on a high pedestal above a base carved with reliefs of the Christian Virtues for the merchant James Clegg (**10**), and a full-size, seated and cross-legged statue of the Chancellor of the County Palatine of Durham (**14**). Among his more affecting works was a depiction of a sleeping child for the tomb of his infant daughter in Carlisle (**20**). According to the historian William McDowall, the original of this work was carved in Italy during the sculptor's first visit as a reception piece for the Carrara Academy (**27**). Dunbar later used a version of the subject for another monument to his daughter in Dumfries (**19**). When the American writer Nathaniel Hawthorne visited Dumfries church in 1857 he was told that the naked statue which had stood on the monument for over 26 years had been sold to 'a gentleman from London' for 100 guineas, and that Dunbar had supplied a replacement, this time with a slip of drapery over the lower limbs (*Hawthorne Notebooks* 1941, 502).

During his lifetime Dunbar was particularly noted for his busts of famous sitters, particularly the author, Mrs Gaskell, the Earls of Lonsdale and Durham and the heroic Grace Darling (**39, 45, 52, 47**). Grace's father, William, manned a lighthouse on the Farne Islands and made headlines in September 1838 for rowing out with his daughter in treacherous seas to rescue survivors from a shipwreck. Dunbar, who must have had an entrepreneurial streak, arrived at the Darling home a little over a week after the rescue. His bust of Grace helped to make the comely face of this regional heroine into a national icon and copies of the head were in considerable demand. By the end of October he was exhibiting busts of both Darlings at his rooms in Oxford Street, Newcastle and Villiers Street, Sunderland, and offering casts at a guinea each. The bust was reproduced six times in marble.

In March 1843 the *Carlisle Journal* reported that Dunbar had given a series of lectures on sculpture in the city, illustrated with works by Thorvaldsen, Canova, **John Flaxman RA, Thomas Banks**, Chantrey, **E H Baily, Samuel Joseph** and M L Watson. Dunbar also carried out commissions during this time in Newcastle and Manchester. An estimate survives offering two versions of a memorial to Mr and Mrs Whelpdale of Penrith (†1844 and †1848) dated 17 June 1859, was sent from Dunbar at the Marble Works, Finkle Street (CRO D/Hud/15/22 and D/Hud/17/75).

The 1861 census states that Dunbar and his wife were then living at 23 Senhouse Street, Whitehaven, Cumberland. By 1864 he had returned to his native Dumfries and was living at 112, St Michael Street, from where he sold plaster casts of his most admired works (*Dumfries Standard* 10 Sept 1864). He died there on 12 August 1866, and was buried in a family vault at St Michael, Dumfries. His death was noted in the *Builder* (1866, 638), who commended his copies from the Antique (**37, 38**) and in the *Art Journal*, which described Dunbar as 'a portrait sculptor in good repute in Scotland' (*AJ*, 1866, 320). McDowall later saluted him as a sculptor who had done much to foster the visual arts in his homeland.

There has been considerable confusion about aspects of Dunbar's life and work since his career overlapped that of **David Dunbar II**, who was probably his son. Gunnis assumed that obituaries for the elder Dunbar, published in 1866, referred to the younger sculptor, thus misrepresenting both careers. (Inf. Denis Perriam)

MGS

Literary References: Catalogue 'of Mr Dunbar's First Exhibition of the Works of Foreign & British Sculptors', 1831, (Newcastle City Library): *Newcastle Exhib* 1831; *Mr Dunbar's Exhibition of Foreign and British Sculptors, Durham*, 1832 (Newcastle Central Library); *Newcastle Exhib* 1832; *RMI Exhib* 1838, 4; *Dumfries Standard* 10/9/1864; *AJ*, 1866, 320 (obit); *CJ*, 17 Aug 1866 (obit); *Builder* 1866, 638; *Graves* 1875, 169; *McDowall* 1876; *Graves* 1905–6, 385; *Gunnis* 1968, 133–4; *Carlisle Exhibitions* 1973, 9; *Ormond* 1973, 131–2; *Perriam* 1975, 300, 305n; *Friedman* 1980 (1), 27; *Chantrey Ledgers* 1991–92, 9, 34; *McEwan* 1994, 182

Archival References: Carlisle Lib notes D/CAR 730

Additional References: Dunbar/RMI

Portraits of the Sculptor: Photo, nd, Carlisle Library

Exhibition Catalogues: Catalogue of Mr Dunbar's First Exhibition of Foreign & British Sculptors, Oxford Street, Newcastle, 1831 (Newcastle Library); A Catalogue of Mr Dunbar's Exhibition. . .Foreign and British Sculptors, Palace Green, Durham, 1832 (Newcastle Library)

Funerary Monuments

No.	Date	Subject		Location		References
1.	1815	Robert Burns, model		[Exhib RA, London, 907]; untraced		*Graves* II, 1905–6, 385
2.	†1825	Elizabeth Connell		St Cuthbert, Carlisle, Cumberland	S	Pevsner, *Cumberland & Westmorland*, 1967, 96; *Gunnis* 1968, 134
3.	†1830	Rev Alexander Scott, with portrait bust		St Michael, Dumfries Other versions: plaster casts offered for sale, 1864	S	*Dumfries Standard* 10/9/1864; *Gunnis* 1968, 134; Pevsner *Dumfries and Galloway* 1996, 247
4.	1834	Rev Edward Stanley		Workington, Cumberland	S	*CJ*, 1 March 1834; *CP*, 19 Aug 1834, 2; *Gunnis* 1968, 134
5.	1834	Robert Anderson (†1833)		Carlisle Cathedral, Cumberland, south transept	S	*CJ*, 22 Feb 1834; Pevsner, *Cumberland & Westmorland*, 1967, 94; *Gunnis* 1968, 134; C Lib (repr)
6.	†1834	Sir J D A Gilpin		Carlisle Cathedral	S	*Carlisle Pat*, 22 Nov 1834
7.	†1835	George Gibson		Crosby Ravensworth, Westmorland		Pevsner, *Cumberland & Westmorland*, 1967, 244
8.	†1835	John Richardson		Christ Church, North Shields, Northumbs		Pevsner, *Northumbs* 1992, 526
9.	†1835	Rev James Taylor		St John the Baptist, Newcastle, Northumbs		Pevsner, *Northumbs*, 1992, 428
10.	+1836	James Clegg		Stand, Lancs	S	*CIIA* 4/9/143-6 (repr)
11.	†1837	John Hutchinson		Christ Church, North Shields, Northumbs		Pevsner, *Northumbs*, 1992, 526
12.	†1837	Rev Henry Griffith		St Andrew, Newcastle, Northumbs		Pevsner, *Northumbs*, 1992, 427
13.	†1838	Rev Robert Gray		Holy Trinity, Sunderland, Durham		*Gunnis* 1968, 134; Pevsner, *Durham*, 1983, 451
14.	1838	Robert Hopper Williamson (†1835) (designed by William Dobson)		Newcastle Cathedral	S	Pevsner, *Northumbs* 1992, 423; *Colvin* 1995, 315
15.	1843	Joseph Saul of Greenrow		[Exhib Mr Kirkbride's marble works on Finkle St, Carlisle; for Abbeytown]; Holme Cultram Abbey, Abbeytown, Cumberland		*CJ*, 9 Sept 1843
16.	*c*1843	Mary Benn Steward of Whitehaven		Moresby, Cumberland		*C J*, 4 Jan 1845
17.	1845	Miss Losh		Wreay, Cumberland		*C J*, 25 Jan 1845
18.	1850	Katherine Losh, with medallions of the girl's parents and an uncle		Wreay, Cumberland, Mausoleum		Pevsner, *Cumberland & Westmorland*, 1967, 212; *Gunnis* 1968, 134; *Wood* 1971, 1231 (repr)
19.	1860	Elizabeth Dunbar (†1821), (the sculptor's infant daughter)	s	Carlisle Cathedral, Cumberland, south transept	SD	*C J*, 6 Jan 1860; *Gunnis* 1968, 134
20.	*c*1860	Elizabeth Dunbar sleeping (the sculptor's infant daughter)		St Michael, Dumfries Other versions: plaster casts offered for sale, 1864		*Hawthorne Notebooks*, 502; *Dumfries Standard* 10/9/1864; *Gunnis* 1968, 134; Pevsner *Dumfries and Galloway* 1996, 247
21.	†1860	Joseph Benn		Corney, Cumberland		RG/JP, 3, 454

Statues

No.	Date	Subject	Location	References
22.	1823	Design for a statue for the music-room at Gilgarron	[Exhib Carlisle Ac, 156]; untraced	*Carlisle Ac Exhibs*, 1823, 14
23.	1826	Dr William Hey	[Exhib Royal Northern Soc, Leeds]; untraced	*Gunnis* 1968, 134

No.	Date	Subject		Location		Reference
24.	1830	Sir Joshua Reynolds, model		Untraced Other versions: model for Northern Ac of Fine Arts, Carlisle, 1835		*Carlisle Journal*, 20 Feb 1830, 3; *Carlisle Pat*, 25 July 1835
25.	1842	Admiral Sir Pulteney Malcolm (†1838)	s	Langholm, Dumfries, behind library (formerly Marketplace, moved 1878)		Pevsner *Dumfries and Galloway* 1996, 56, 401
26.	1858	'John Anderson, my Jo', group, model		['modelled expressly for the forthcoming gathering of the admirers of Burns' in Carlisle']; untraced		*Carlisle Examiner*, 11 Dec 1858, 3
27.	nd	Sleeping Child		[Exhib Royal Northern Soc, Leeds, 1828]; untraced		*Gunnis* 1968, 134; *MacDowall* 1876
Busts						
28.	1823	Captain Huddart, FRS		[Exhib Carlisle Ac, 158]; untraced		*Carlisle Ac Exhibs*, 1823, 13
29.	1823	Col Johns		[Exhib Carlisle Ac, 168]; untraced		*Carlisle Ac Exhibs*, 1823, 13
30.	1823	'F. Chantrey, R.A.'		[Exhib Carlisle Ac, 34]; untraced		*Carlisle Ac Exhibs*, 1823, 13
31.	1823	Hebe		[Exhib Carlisle Ac, 159]; untraced		*Carlisle Ac Exhibs*, 1823, 13
32.	1823	Master Thomas Dunbar		[Exhib Carlisle Ac, 179]; untraced		*Carlisle Ac Exhibs*, 1823, 14
33.	1823	'Mr Joseph Saul, Greenrow, from a model by an amateur'	m	[Exhib Carlisle Ac, 71]; untraced		*Carlisle Ac Exhibs*, 1823, 14
34.	1823	Rev William Dunbar of Applegarth, Dumfriesshire		[Exhib Carlisle Ac, 167]; untraced		*Carlisle Ac Exhibs*, 1823, 13
35.	1823	Robert Anderson, the Cumberland bard		[Exhib Carlisle Ac, 94]; untraced		*Carlisle Ac Exhibs*, 1823, 14
36.	1823	S B Denton		[Exhib RA, London, 1068]; untraced		*Graves* II, 1905–6, 385
37.	1824	Laocoon's son (after the antique)	m	Christie, London, 15 Dec 1982; untraced	SD	C Lib (repr)
38.	1826	Isis		[Exhib Royal Northern Soc, Leeds]; untraced		*Gunnis* 1968, 134
39.	1829	Elizabeth Stephenson (later Mrs Gaskell)		[Exhib 'Works by Foreign and British Sculptors,' Newcastle, 1831, 47]; Manchester City Library Other versions: ex coll Manchester City Art Gall, Lancs, plaster, 1831; untraced Gaskell memorial tower, Knutsford, plaster		*Newcastle Exhib* 1831; *Ormond* 1973, 185
40.	c1830	Duke of Buccleuch		Untraced		*Perriam* 1975, 304
41.	1831	Peter Dixon	m	[Exhib Newcastle 1831]; Carlisle MAG		*Cumberland Artists* 1971, 15; *Carlisle Ac Exhibs* 973, 9
42.	1832	Dr J R Fenwick	m	Durham Castle	S	RG/JP, 3, 453; C Lib (repr)
43.	1832	Earl Grey	m	untraced Other versions: plaster casts offered for sale, 1864		*CP*, 11 Sept 1832, 3; *Dumfries Standard* 10/9/1864; *AJ*, 1866, 320; *Builder* 1866, 638; *Perriam* 1975, 304
44.	1832	James Losh		Literary and Philosophical Institute, Newcastle	D	*Losh* ii, 106 (12 Feb 1831); Losh 29 April 1832, ii, 141; *Read* 1982, 123
45.	1833	William, 1st Earl of Lonsdale	m	[Lowther Castle, Westmorland]; untraced Other versions: plaster casts offered for sale, 1864		*C P*, 15 Oct 1833, 2; *Dumfries Standard* 10/9/1864; *Gunnis* 1968, 134; *Perriam* 1975, 304
46.	c1834	Robert Burns (from a portrait by Naysmith)	p	SNPG 183		*CJ*, 19 April 1834; *Smailes* 1990, 50
47.	1838	Grace Darling	m	[coll Edward Maltby, Bishop of Durham]; NPG 998 Other versions: Grace Darling Museum, Bamburgh, marble Royal National Life Boat Institution coll, marble 4 other known marble versions plaster casts offered for sale, 1838 and 1864	S	*Dumfries Standard* 10/9/1864; *C J*, 29 June 1860; *AJ*, 1866, 320; *Builder* 1866, 638; *Ormond* 1973, 131–2 (pl 243)
48.	1838	William Darling		Untraced Other versions: copies in plaster offered for sale, 1838		*Ormond* 1973, 132
49.	1841	Robert Cowen	m	Carlisle MAG	S	*Cumberland Artists* 1971, 15
50.	1850	Sir Robert Peel	m	[Exhib at the marble rooms of Messrs T & J Nelson, Carlisle]; untraced		*C J*, 18 Oct 1850
51.	nd	Alderman Wilson		Gateshead, Northumbs		*Gunnis* 1968, 134
52.	nd	Earl of Durham		Untraced		*AJ*, 1866, 320; *Builder* 1866, 638; *Perriam* 1975, 304
53.	nd	Hon and Rev Robert Liddell	m	Untraced Other versions: plaster casts offered for sale, 1864		*Dumfries Standard* 10 Sept 1864
54.	nd	Hon Lady Ravensworth	m	Untraced Other versions: plaster casts offered for sale, 1864		*Dumfries Standard* 10 Sept 1864
55.	nd	J Fergusson MP	m	Untraced Other versions: plaster casts offered for sale, 1864		*Dumfries Standard* 10 Sept 1864
56.	nd	Lady Bloomfield	m	untraced Other versions: plaster casts offered for sale, 1864		*Dumfries Standard* 10 Sept 1864
57.	nd	Lord Brougham		untraced		*AJ*, 1866, 320; *Builder* 1866, 638

58.	nd	Peter Johnston	m	[coll 'the late' Sir Alexander Johnston]; untraced Other versions: plaster casts offered for sale, 1864	*Dumfries Standard* 10 Sept 1864
59.	nd	Queen Victoria and Albert, the Prince Consort	m	[coll Ivie Mackie, Auchencairn House]; untraced Other versions: plaster casts offered for sale, 1864	*Dumfries Standard* 10/9/1864
60.	nd	Sir Joseph Gilpin	m	Untraced Other versions: plaster casts offered for sale, 1864	*Dumfries Standard* 10/9/1864
Architectural Sculpture					
61.	c1808	Capitals and other decorative parts		Lowther Castle, Westmorland	*CJ*, 17 Aug 1866
62.	1823	Statue of a sculptor with a head representing the Genius of Carlisle, and busts of Sir Christopher Wren, Benjamin West and Sir Francis Chantrey		[Carlisle Acad (also Nixson's Marble Works, Finkle Street)]; untraced	*Perriam* 1975, 300–2 (repr)
63.	1841	Royal arms		[Royal Arcade, Newcastle, Northumbs]; untraced	*Ross* 1841, 64
Reliefs					
64.	1823	Alto Relievo		[Exhib Carlisle Ac, 36]; untraced	*Carlisle Ac Exhibs*, 1823, 14
Miscellaneous					
65.	1817	The soldier's return ('She sunk within my arms and cried, Art thou my ain dear Willie' – Robert Burns)		[Exhib RA, London, 1028]; untraced	*Graves* II, 1905–6, 385
66.	1823	A lowland laird		[Exhib Carlisle Ac, 160]; untraced	*Carlisle Ac Exhibs*, 1823, 13
67.	1823	An odd fellow		[Exhib Carlisle Ac, 35]; untraced	*Carlisle Ac Exhibs*, 1823, 14
68.	1823	'The Ark, modelled from the seal of the Grand Lodge of England for the masonic procession at laying the foundation stone of the new prisons, Carlisle'		[Exhib Carlisle Ac, 164]; untraced	*Carlisle Ac Exhibs*, 1823, 13
69.	1828	Love		[Exhib Royal Northern Soc, Leeds]; untraced	*Gunnis* 1968, 134
70.	1829	A nymph		[Exhib Birmingham Soc of A]; untraced	*Gunnis* 1968, 134
71.	1840	A greyhound		[Exhib RA, London, 1116]; untraced	*Graves* II, 1905–6, 385

DUNBAR, David II 1828–73

He was the eldest son of George Dunbar, **David Dunbar I**'s brother and was born on 3 April 1828. David Dunbar I kept in close touch with his nephew: the younger man showed with his uncle at exhibitions of the works of 'Foreign and British Sculptors' held in Newcastle-upon-Tyne in 1833 and 1834, and when advertising his studio in Carlisle, Dunbar I also advertised his nephew's book of poems in the *Carlisle Journal* (12 June 1857). Dunbar II's marriage to Mary Anne Rawes at St Andrew, Newcastle, was reported in the *Carlisle Journal* on 18 February 1837. In 1837 he exhibited at the Royal Manchester Institution and may have moved to Manchester, for Pigot's *Directory* of 1838 lists a sculptor of that name at 30, Pool Street.

He appears subsequently to have moved to London, for the Royal Academy exhibition catalogues note that 'David Dunbar Junr' exhibited at the Royal Academy in 1841 from 11 Elizabeth Street, Pimlico (**2**). He gave no address in 1845 (**5**). In 1844 the *Literary Gazette* drily commented on his statue of Robert Burns depicted as a young man (**1**), that it would have been very pleasing 'had the execution been equal to the intention' (*Lit Gaz*, 27 July, 1844, 482). The *Art Union* was more generous, noting that it was 'executed with infinite nicety' and though the resemblance was not marked, the figure was 'distinguished by a simple grace' (*AU* 1844, 215).

Graves assumed that all works exhibited by 'David Dunbar' at the Royal Academy between 1840 and 1859 were by Dunbar II, although only those discussed above are distinctly marked in the original catalogues as his work. It is possible that some of the other works exhibited by 'David Dunbar' were by Dunbar I, and in the case of the medallions of Grace and William Darling (**6, 7**), it appears highly probable. (Add inf. Denis Perriam)

Literary References: *Pigot* 1838, 38, 86, 111; *Graves* II, 1905–6, 385; *Gunnis* 1968, 133–4; *Perriam* 1975, 305

Archival References: IGI

Statues					
1.	1842	Robert Burns, half-size		[Exhib RA, London, 1340]; untraced	*AU* 1844, 215; *Lit Gaz* 1844, 482; *RA Exhib Cat* 1842; *Graves* II, 1905–6, 385; *Gunnis* 1968, 134
Busts					
2.	1841	Unidentified gentleman		[Exhib RA, London, 1302]; untraced	*RA Exhib Cat* 1841; *Graves* II, 1905–6, 385
3.	1843	Dunbar (posthumous portrait of the artist's son)	m	[Exhib RA, London, 1484]; untraced	*RA Exhib Cat* 1843; *Graves* II, 1905–6, 385
4.	1844	Sir Martin B Folkes, Bt		[Exhib RA, London, 1361]; untraced	*RA Exhib Cat* 1844; *Graves* II, 1905–6, 385 *Gunnis* 1968, 134
Reliefs					
5.	1845	Unidentified lady, medallion		[Exhib RA, London, 1373]; untraced	*RA Exhib Cat* 1845; *Graves* II, 1905–6, 385
6.	1848	Grace Darling, portrait medallion		[Exhib RA, London, 1416]; untraced	*RA Exhib Cat* 1848; *Ormond* 1973, 132
7.	1848	William Darling, portrait medallion		[Exhib RA, London, 1415]; untraced	*RA Exhib Cat* 1848; *Graves* II, 1905–6, 385; *Ormond* 1973, 132

Miscellaneous

8.	1844	Study from nature	[Exhib BI, London, 433]; untraced	*Graves* 1875, 169
9.	1859	Miss Sarah Warner	[Exhib RA, London, 1281]; untraced	*RA Exhib Cat* 1859; *Graves* II, 1905–6, 385

DUNCALFE, Isaac, of Hitchen fl 1766

Funerary Monuments

1.	1766	Rev Edward (†1765) and Elizabeth (†1741) Young	St Mary, Welwyn, Herts	SD Pevsner, *Herts*, 1977, 393

DUNCKLEY, Samuel, of Warwick fl 1678–1708

Responsible for much masonry work at St Mary's collegiate church in Warwick, in 1678 he was paid for paving the Beauchamp Chapel. That year the Mayor of Warwick wrote to Sir William Dugdale, a fellow trustee of the Chapel: 'I have sent the worke man over to you that has paved over part of the Chapell to Durham Tume with new stone, the other part loocke very scandlius and I desire you to consider of it that it may be mayd all a like' (Archives, Sir William Dugdale of Merevale in GPC). By 1697/8 Dunckley was in partnership with **Francis Smith of Warwick**. After a fire damaged the church an agreement was made between the church administrators and 'Mr Smith and Mr Dunckley yt. they should take down the Chancell wall and build all ye Church Tower and Pinacles with all other Pinacles and Cornish mouldings. . . . Buttresses Pillars etc, and face ye staircase with Wimcote stone they to find all Lyme scaffolding and materialls for finishing ye works the workmen to have all ye old stone but pay for ye new stone yt was then getting so much as ye sd stone has cost in getting and carriage, for all which they are to have £2300 and £50 more if ye Comrs please' (*Churches of Warwicks*, 1847, 1, 34).

Dunckley also rebuilt the entrance to the Beauchamp chapel, completing the work in 1704. John Sabin, the parish clerk, recorded that Dunckley, 'a poor mason of Warwick', had 'designed, carved, built and finished that August Frontispiece in the Gothic Taste' (*Sabin* c1760, 23). He was a member of the Baptist community in the town and was for a time minister at the chapel on Castle Hill. In 1725/6 John Dunckley, presumably a son, was paid for repairs to the Beauchamp chapel. At about this time he took **Job Collins of Warwick** as an apprentice.

Literary References: *Churches of Warwicks* 1847, 1, 64; *Chatwin* 1949, 8, 9, 11, 37; *Gunnis* 1968, 134
Archival References: GPC

DUNN, Charles, of Greenwich –1762

He worked with his father, **Thomas Dunn**, and, after the latter's death in 1746, carried on the family business. He was the master-mason for building St Leonard, Shoreditch under the elder Dance. The inscription on the foundation stone, laid on 17 November 1736, relates 'Carolo Dunn et Gulielmo Goswell Artificibus' (*GM* 1736, 682). In 1743 he was the mason employed on the French Church, now the Great Synagogue. In 1749 the Corporation of Trinity House paid him £6 13s for a 'Boundary Stone at Newington' (Trinity House Archives).

Gunnis (who incorrectly cites the *London Magazine* 1757, 44) notes that Dunn became bankrupt that year. In 1758 however, he was working with his partner, John Townesend, the son of his father's old partner, **John Townesend of London**, on repairs at Greenwich Palace, including the laying of paving and taking down a chimneypiece. The death of Dunn, 'formerly an eminent marble and stone merchant of Newington, Surrey', was published in the *Court Magazine* (June 1762, 490).

Literary References: *Gunnis* 1968, 134
Archival References: TNA ADM/68/767; GPC

DUNN, John, of Bristol fl 1774

He was the partner of **William Drewett** and **Henry Jones**, and became a freeman of Bristol in 1774. His father was William Dunn, who had become a freeman of the city in 1744. The works of the firm are listed under the entry for William Drewett.

Literary References: GPC; *Dale-Jones and Lloyd* 1989, 49

DUNN, of Alnwick fl 1839

Funerary Monuments

1.	†1839	Henry Collingwood Selby	Alnwick, Northumbs	Pevsner, *Northumbs*, 1992, 133

DUNN, Thomas c1676–1746

Dunn was apprenticed to David Farmer of Southwark in 1690 and became free of the Masons' Company on 12 July 1698. He was the mason for Clapham Church in 1710. As a mason-contractor he was much employed by Nicholas Hawksmoor, for whom he built Christ Church, Spitalfields, 1714–1729, receiving payments totalling nearly £22,500, and St Mary Woolnoth, 1716–1727, which brought him nearly £12,000, including sums for carved work (**6, 7**). He was assisted at both churches by his partner, Thomas Bray. He also built the minister's house at Spitalfields and Stratford-le-Bow.

In 1720 he was appointed mason to the Grocers' Company and in 1722 he became renter-warden of the Masons' Company. In 1729 he was paid £37 by Mr and Mrs Hays for building a wall and balustrade for a house at Wimbledon (Surrey RO K172/4/3 a-d). The iron railings and gate alone cost £65. In 1729 also, he built the church at Stratford-le-Bow. Dunn was responsible for a considerable amount of work at Greenwich Palace, where he and his partner, **John Townesend II**, built the south, north, north-east, north-west and east pavilions of Queen Anne's Court between 1729 and 1731 (TNA AD 68/708710, ADM 68/708–10). In January 1732, Dunn and Townesend entered into a contract with the directors of the Bank of England to complete the building of the bank in Threadneedle Street by Michaelmas 1733.

Gunnis considered Dunn a statuary of considerable importance. His monument to Edward Peck has a portrait-bust, a *baldacchino* and two mourning boys (1). The work was cleaned in 1797 by **John Flaxman RA**, who erected the nearby monument to Sir Robert Ladbrooke. Another notable work is the monument to Edward Colman (2), which has a life-sized reclining figure in an elaborate architectural setting, with a *gloria* crowning the scene. Gunnis called it a dramatic and important work.

In 1739 Dunn became one of the mason-contractors for the London Mansion House. He tendered for the contract in partnership with **John Deval I** on 16 May 1738, competing with another group of masons comprising **John Townesend of London, Christopher Horsnaile II** and **Robert Taylor I**. Both teams quoted a figure of £18,000. Second, sealed proposals were requested, and Dunn's partnership came up with a price of £16,975, compared with the rival consortium's £17,200. After much delay a compromise was reached: all five were chosen by the Court of Common Council on 24 July 1739 to execute the work at a price not exceeding £17,200. Further work by the team followed in the dancing gallery in 1741–2 (£325), and in 1744 they were paid £134 for obelisks, plinths and paving at the front of the Mansion House. Dunn, like Deval and Horsnaile, was a freemason.

At the time of the Mansion House contract Dunn was based in Blackman Street, in the parish of St George the Martyr. By the time he died he owned a network of properties and land around these premises, known as Swan Yard. He had houses in Robin Hood's Court, Little Lamb Alley, Griffin Alley, Mint Street and Horsemonger Lane and a stone yard on the north side of Kent Street. Dunn owned buildings also at Lambeth Marsh and in Princes Street, Rotherhithe.

He died on 30 April 1746 and was buried close to his late wife at St George the Martyr, Southwark. In his will, proved 2 May 1746, he divided the bulk of his estate between his sons, Edward and **Charles Dunn** and his daughter Sarah, who was married to Towneshend Wottonhall, a merchant resident in Portugal. A codicil offered Charles Dunn the stock in trade of the family business, an option he appears to have accepted, for the business continued under Charles for several more years. Dunn also left £5 to **Richard Spangen**, an executor, and sums to purchase mourning rings to George Dance, the architect, **Christopher Horsnaile II** and **William Atkinson**.

MGS

Literary References: *GM* 1746, 272; *Malcolm* 1803–7, 2, 455; *Gunnis* 1968, 134; *Jeffery* 1993, 49–50, 67, 300

Archival References: Masons' Co, Freemen, fol 12; Court Book, 1677–94, fol 126v; Court Book, 1722–51 (14 June 1722); Grocers WA, 1720–21, 12; Ch W Accts, Clapham parish church; Grocers' Company archives, 1720; Accounts for building the New Churches, Lambeth Palace Library, MSS/2690-2750/2703 p32a; 2705 fols 69v, 79; 2706, fols 43, 98, 336; 2714, fols 21v-22; 2716 fols 186, 220; 2728 fol 118r-v; GPC

Will: PROB 11/747/12–15

Funerary Monuments

1.	†1736	Edward Peck	Christ Church, Spitalfields, London	S	Flaxman Account Book 1794–1810, 56; *Gunnis* 1968, 134
2.	1743	Edward Colman (†1739)	Brent Eleigh, Suffolk	S	*Gunnis* 1968, 134; Pevsner, *Suffolk*, 1974, 114

Chimneypieces

3.	1733	Description unavailable	[R C Physic, London, Dr Mead's apartments]; untraced	R C Physic, Cash Book 1726–1778, (1732/3 p14); *Gunnis* 1968, 135
4.	1733	Description unavailable Payment(s): £53	[for Benjamin Hoare of Boreham Hall, Essex]; untraced	Hoare Partnership Ledger, 1725–34, ff297, 299; *Gunnis* 1968, 135
5.	nd	14 for the North West Pavilion	Royal Hospital, Greenwich (ORNC)	*Gunnis* 1968, 135 citing PRO AD 68/709

Architectural Sculpture

6.	1716–1727	12 Corinthian capitals Payment(s): £192	[St Mary Woolnoth, London]; untraced	GPC
7.	1716–1727	Font Payment(s): £20	[St Mary Woolnoth, London]; untraced	GPC

DURANCE, of Lincoln fl 1830–38

Several Lincolnshire monuments are signed by this firm including one to William Wilkinson, which has reliefs of two Christ's Hospital boys in attitudes of mourning (**4**). The monument to William Featherby (**3**) is signed 'Durance and Son.'

Funerary Monuments

1.	†1830	Cecilia Young	Kingerby, Lincs	S	Pevsner, *Lincs*, 1989, 415
2.	†1780	Lady Sophia Nevile	Old Church, Aubourn, Lincs	S	Pevsner, *Lincs*, 1989, 110
3.	†1829	William Featherby	Cherry Willingham, Lincs	S	Pevsner, *Lincs*, 1989, 219
4.	†1838	William Wilkinson (†1837) and wife (†1838)	St Michael, Lincoln	S	Pevsner, *Lincs*, 1989, 499

DURANT, John fl 1757–74

He was apprenticed to **Joseph Wilton** in October 1757, when his wax model of *Marsyas* was approved by the Society of Arts (**2**). In 1774 he was employed at **Crashley**'s 'Figure shop' in Long Acre.

Literary References: *Graves* 1907, 83

Archival References: RSA Minutes 1757–58, 93

Reliefs

1.	1774	Minerva judging the Arts, alto-relievo		[Exhib Soc of Artists, London, 73]; untraced	*Graves* 1907, 83

Miscellaneous

2.	1757	Marsyas, model	w	[Soc of A approval, 5 Oct 1757]; untraced	RSA Minutes 1757–1758, f93

DURANT, Susan 1827–73

Susan Durant was a woman of strong character who made her mark as a sculptor at a time when it was rare for women from a privileged background to pursue a career. As her success grew, her circle of friends came to include other professional women who were experts in their own fields as artists, writers, doctors and social reformers. She had a lively intellect, was extremely well-read and keenly supported the enfranchisement and education of women.

She was born in Stamford Hill, London, the daughter of George Durant, a silk broker, and his wife Mary. As a young girl she travelled with her parents to Italy, spending at least one winter in Rome, and this was where, according to her obituary in *The Queen*, she became interested in sculpture. At first she experimented as an amateur, but eventually she decided to work professionally and became the pupil and later the assistant of the French sculptor, **Henri Triqueti**, working at his studio in the Rue Pigalle in Paris. In later years she divided her time between Paris and London where, after the death of her mother, she took responsibility for the household of her ailing father. She kept a small studio in Radnor Place, Paddington, close to her father's house, where she was able to work whilst in London.

In 1847 Prince Albert, as President of the Society of Arts, awarded Durant its silver Isis medal for an original bust in plaster (**6**). She showed two statues at the Great Exhibition of 1851, 'a study from nature' (**2**), and a figure of Belisarius, the legendary Byzantine general (**3**). In 1857 she lent a statue of Robin Hood to the Manchester Art Treasures Exhibition (**4**). The *Athenaeum* described this work as showing promise when it was first exhibited at the Royal Academy in 1856. Another 'ideal' work, *The negligent watchboy*, a subject from Theocritus, was shown at the Academy in 1858 and again at the British Institution in 1860, priced at 250 guineas in marble (**52**). It was described by the *Art Journal* as an 'elaborate and very admirable composition' (*AJ* 1858, 171). Whilst working in Paris in 1857, she met the American author, Harriet Beecher Stowe, who agreed to sit for her (**15**). *The Art Journal* considered the resulting bust a great success and an excellent likeness (*AJ* 1857, 176).

Durant was the only woman commissioned by the Corporation of London to execute one of the 17 statues for the Egyptian Hall at the Mansion House in 1861. These were to represent mythical or historical figures from English literature and she chose to depict *The faithful shepherdess*, the eponymous heroine of John Fletcher's early-17th century play (**5**). In 1864, Queen Victoria instructed Triqueti to provide plans for the decoration of a chapel at Windsor Castle, to be known as the Albert chapel, which would commemorate the Prince Consort. This was an ambitious project which included medallion portraits of 12 members of the Royal family. Triqueti gave Durant the contract for these reliefs, nine of which were exhibited at the Royal Academy (**30–32, 34, 36, 40, 41, 45, 46**) and they took her to Windsor, Osborne, Potsdam and Darmstadt to model the subjects from life. The commission led to close and enduring links with several members of the Royal family. The Queen allowed Durant to give lessons in sculpture to Princess Louise and she formed a lifelong friendship with the Crown Princess of Prussia, who was herself a talented artist. Whilst Durant was working at Osborne in 1865, the Queen's uncle, Leopold of Saxe-Coburg, King of the Belgians, died. The Queen asked Durant to carve his monument (**1**), to be placed in a prominent position in St George's chapel, Windsor, close to the monument to his first wife, Princess Charlotte Augusta. It depicts a recumbent effigy accompanied by two angels and the lion of Belgium. The Queen noted in her journal on 12 July 1867 that she had visited the chapel to see her beloved uncle's memorial and thought 'The likeness is remarkably good'. After Durant's death, it was moved to a side aisle and was then relocated in Christ Church, Esher Green, Surrey, *c*1879. In 1871 she received her last important commission when Queen Victoria chose Durant to execute a marble bust of herself, 'of heroic size', for the newly opened hall of the Inner Temple (**26**) (*Graves* II, 1905–6, 391). The hall was badly damaged during the Second World War and the bust has not survived.

Durant gave birth in secret to a son by Triqueti in 1869, whom she named Henry Paul Harvey. He had a distinguished career in the Foreign Office and in his retirement compiled the Oxford Companions to English, French and Classical Literature. On 1 January 1873, at the height of her career, Susan Durant died at 15 Rue Scribe in Paris, after an unsuccessful operation. She was buried at the cemetery of Père Lachaise. Her tombstone has a bronze relief, *A concert of angels*, by Triqueti. He died the following year.

Arthur Munby, a contemporary diarist, poet and philanthropist, described Susan Durant as 'a tall and very comely young woman' with a 'flashing face and massive rippling chestnut hair', who was 'dignified and self-reliant'. Her obituary paid tribute to her intellect, knowledge of literature and a personality that would make her loss 'well nigh irreparable' to a large circle of distinguished friends. The ornaments for the Albert chapel and the Queen's bust in the hall of the Inner Temple 'opened last year by Princess Louise', were mentioned in passing, but without critical judgment (*The Queen*, 17 January 1873).

Sylvia Allen

Literary References: *Great Exhib* 1851 (1), Fine Arts Section, 846, no 78; *Manchester Art Treasures* 1857, 134, cat 39; C E Stowe, *The Life of HBS*, 1889, 228; *Gunnis* 1968, 135; Derek Hudson, *Munby, Man of Two Worlds*, 1972, 218; *Jeffery* 1993, 239, 305–8; *Hurtado* 1994; *Cram and Allen* 1998/9, 418–24

Archival References: Census returns, 1861, 1871; Paul Harvey's marriage certificate, naming Henri de Triqueti as his father, Portswood parish church, County of Southampton, no 89, MXA 546125; Durant Papers, Royal A, Windsor Castle, RA VIC/, Add MSS, X/2; X 2/212; Queen Victoria's Journal, Royal A VIC/QVJ

Will: proved 30 Jan 1873

Auction announcement: 'Excellent furniture, china, glass effects', including marble statuary and medallions, the property of the late Susan Durant, to be sold 5 June, at 3 Bryanston Place, Bryanston Square (*The Times*, 7 May 1873)

Portraits of the Sculptor: self-portrait, 1853, formerly coll Emma Wallis, Barford, Warks, untraced; author unknown, photograph with her *carte de visite*, nd, Royal A VIC/Add X 2/1; Margaret Sarah Carpenter, 1860, canvas, exhib RA; author unknown, engraving, published with her obituary, 1873

Funerary Monuments

1.	1866–1867	Leopold, King of the Belgians (†1865) Payment(s): £500 plus cost of canopy		[St George's Chapel, Windsor Castle, Berks]; Christchurch, Esher Green, Surrey	SD	Royal archives RA/Vic/Add.X/212, RA/R40/48; *Bond* 1958, 128

Statues

2.	1850	A study from nature		[Exhib RA, London, 1346]; untraced		*Great Exhib* 1851 (1), vol 2, Fine Arts Section, 846, no 78; *Graves* II, 1905–6, 391; *Gunnis* 1968, 135
3.	1851	Belisarius, a group	p	[Gt Exhib]; untraced		*Great Exhib* 1851 (1), vol 2, Fine Arts Section, 843, no 5
4.	1856	Robin Hood ('the deere unfinished')	m	[Exhib RA, London, 1271]; untraced		*Manchester Art Treasures* 1857, 134; *Graves* II, 1905–6, 391; *Gunnis* 1968, 135; *Laperriere* 1996, I, 367
5.	1861–1863	The faithful shepherdess Payment(s): £700	m	Egyptian Hall, Mansion House, City of London	SD	*Graves* II, 1905–6, 391; *Knight* 1986, 334 (repr); *Jeffery* 1993, 239, 305–8

Busts

No.	Date	Subject	Material	Location	Signed	Literature
6.	1847	'An original bust in Plaster being a Portrait'	p	[RSA, London, silver Isis medal]; untraced		RSA MSS, Premiums offered and bestowed 1812–1850, 1847
7.	1847	Don Adolfo Bayo		[Exhib RA, London, 1418]; untraced		*Graves* II, 1905–6, 391
8.	1847	Miss Allwood		[Exhib RA, London, 1377]; untraced		*Graves* II, 1905–6, 391; *Gunnis* 1968, 135
9.	1848	Lidwell Heathom		[Exhib RA, London, 1423]; untraced		*Graves* II, 1905–6, 391
10.	1849	Unidentified lady		[Exhib RA, London, 1260]; untraced		*Graves* II, 1905–6, 391
11.	1850	Cavaliere Sebastiano Fuezi		[Exhib RA, London, 1364]; untraced		*Graves* II, 1905–6, 391
12.	1851	Daniel Whittle Harvey MP		[Exhib RA, London, 1337]; untraced		*Graves* II, 1905–6, 391; *Gunnis* 1968, 135
13.	1853	Self-portrait	m	[Exhib RA, London, 1449, coll Emma Beaufoy Wallis]; untraced		Royal A Vic Add Mss. X/2; *Graves* II, 1905–6, 391
14.	1856	John Joseph Mechi	m	[Exhib RA, London, 1311]; untraced		*Graves* II, 1905–6, 391
15.	1857	Harriet Beecher Stowe Model(s): Castle Howard, N R Yorks, plaster	m	[Exhib RA, London, 1353]; Harriet Beecher Stowe Center, Hartford, Conn	S	*Graves* II, 1905–6, 391; *Gunnis* 1968, 135
16.	1858	HH Toussoun Pasha, son of the Viceroy of Egypt, as a child, cast from a marble bust	p	[Exhib SFA, London, 206]; untraced		Royal A VIV/Add X 2/212; Englishwoman's Journal, 1 May 1858; *Hurtado* 1994, 225; *Laperriere* 1996, I, 367
17.	1858	Lady Killeen	m	[Exhib RA, London, 1315]; untraced		*Graves* II, 1905–6, 391; *Gunnis* 1968, 135
18.	1859	Harvey Brabazon Combe	m	[Exhib RA, London, 1350]; untraced		*Graves* II, 1905–6, 391
19.	1860	John Percy MD, FRS		[Exhib RA, London, 981]; untraced		*Graves* II, 1905–6, 391
20.	1860	Matthew Combe	m	[Exhib RA, London, 1055]; untraced		*Graves* II, 1905–6, 391
21.	1864	Baron Henri de Triqueti	m	[Exhib RA, London, 890]; Musée Girodet, Montargis, France	SD	*Graves* II, 1905–6, 391; *Gunnis* 1968, 135
22.	1866	Sir Arthur Helps		Untraced		*Hurtado* 1994, 227; Royal A VIC/Add X 2/212
23.	1866	Sir Charles Phipps 'upon his death'		Untraced		Royal A VIC/Add X 2/212
24.	1867	Woronzow Greig, clerk of the peace for Surrey	m	[Exhib RA, London, 1028]; R Soc Library, London, on loan from Surrey County Council	S	*Graves* II, 1905–6, 391
25.	1869	Ruth		Private coll, France	SD	*Graves* II, 1905–6, 391
26.	1872	Queen Victoria Payment(s): 200 gns	m	[Inner Temple, London, hall]; destroyed WW II		*Graves* II, 1905–6, 391; *ITC*, 1915, 88

Reliefs

No.	Date	Subject	Material	Location	Signed	Literature
27.	1852	Judge Matthew Begbie, portrait medallion		[Exhib RA, London, 1395]; untraced		*Graves* II, 1905–6, 391
28.	1862	George Grote, portrait medallion	m	[Exhib RA, London, 1135]; UCL, London, cloisters	SD	*Ormond* 1973, 201; *Hurtado* 1994, 226
29.	1863	Three, Thetis dipping Achilles in the Styx, Thetis receiving from Vulcan the arms of Achilles, Thetis mourning over the dead body of Achilles	m	[Exhib SFA, London]; untraced		*Hurtado* 1994, 228; *Laperriere* 1996, I, 367
30.	1865	Prince Leopold, later Duke of Albany, portrait medallion Payment(s): £60 Model(s): Osborne House, I of W, plaster	m	Albert chapel, Windsor Castle	SD	*Graves* II, 1905–6, 391; *Darby and Smith* 1983, 34 (repr)
31.	1865	Princess Helena, portrait medallion Payment(s): £60 Model(s): Osborne House, I of W, plaster	m	Albert chapel, Windsor Castle Other versions: two known copies in metal, NPG	SD	Royal archives RA PP/ Windsor/656; RA VIC /Add X 2/212; Osborne papers AML 79700255; *Graves* II, 1905–6, 391
32.	1865	Princess Louise, portrait medallion Payment(s): £60 Model(s): Osborne House, I of W, plaster	m	Albert chapel, Windsor Castle	SD	Royal archives RA PP/ Windsor/656; RA VIC /Add X 2/212; Osborne papers AML 79700256; *Graves* II, 1905–6, 391
33.	1866	Albert, the Prince Consort, (†1861), portrait medallion, executed for the Albert Chapel Model(s): Osborne House, I of W, SD 1866, plaster	m	Windsor Castle Other versions: two copies NPG		*Ormond* 1973, 13
34.	1866	Alfred, Duke of Edinburgh, portrait medallion Payment(s): £60 Model(s): Osborne House, I of W, plaster	m	Albert chapel, Windsor Castle		Royal archives RA PP/ Windsor/656; RA VIC /Add X 2/212; Osborne papers AML 79700254; *Graves* II, 1905–6, 391
35.	1866	Howard Blackwell, portrait medallion		Untraced		*Hurtado* 1994, 227
36.	1866	Princess Beatrice, portrait medallion Payment(s): £60 Model(s): Osborne House, I of W, plaster	m	Albert chapel, Windsor Castle		Royal archives RA PP/ Windsor/656; RA VIC /Add X 2/212; Osborne papers AML 79700259; *Graves* II, 1905–6, 391
37.	1866	Princess Feodora, portrait medallion	p	Royal Coll, Osborne House, I of W	SD	
38.	1866	Queen Victoria, portrait medallion Model(s): Osborne House, I of W, plaster	m	Windsor Castle	SD	*Graves* II, 1905–6, 391; *Ormond* 1973, 489
39.	1866	The five grandchildren of Queen Victoria, medallions		Untraced		*Hurtado* 1994, 226

40.	1866	The Princess Royal, Crown Princess of Germany, eldest daughter of Queen Victoria, portrait medallion Payment(s): £60 Model(s): Osborne House, I of W, plaster	m	Albert chapel, Windsor Castle	SD	Royal archives RA PP/Windsor/656 and RA VIC/Add X 2/212; Osborne papers AML 79700251; *Graves* II, 1905–6, 391
41.	1867	Alexandra, Princess of Wales, portrait medallion Payment(s): £60 Model(s): Osborne House, I of W, plaster	m	Albert chapel, Windsor Castle	SD	Royal archives RA PP/Windsor 656; RA VIC/Add X 2/212; Osborne papers AML 79700260; *Graves* II, 1905–6, 391
42.	*c*1867	Arthur, later Duke of Connaught, portrait medallion Payment(s): £60 Model(s): Osborne House, I of W, plaster	m	Albert chapel, Windsor Castle		Royal A PP/Windsor/656
43.	1867	Blanche, Madame Delessert, portrait medallion (daughter of Henri de Triqueti)		Untraced		*Hurtado* 1994, 227
44.	1867	Prince Louis and Princess Alice of Hesse, portrait medallions (cast by Barbedienne)		NPG 2023a (10), 2023a (10a)		Royal A VIC Add X 2/212
45.	1868	Albert Edward, Prince of Wales (later King Edward VII), portrait medallion Payment(s): £60 Model(s): Osborne House, I of W, plaster	m	Albert chapel, Windsor Castle	SD	Royal archives RA PP/Windsor/656; RA VIC/Add X 2/212; Osborne papers AML 79700252; *Graves* II, 1905–6, 391
46.	1868	Princess Alice, portrait medallion Payment(s): £60 Model(s): Osborne House, I of W, plaster	m	Albert chapel, Windsor Castle Other versions: four, NPG, London	SD	Royal archives RA PP/Windsor/656; RA VIC /Add X 2/212; Osborne papers AML 79700253; *Graves* II, 1905–6, 391
47.	1868	Princess Louise of Hesse 'Part of the decoration of Wolsey's Chapel'	m	[Exhib RA, London, 927]; untraced		*Graves* II, 1905–6, 391
48.	*c*1871	Nina Lehmann, as a child	m	[coll Campbell family]; private coll		*Agnew*, Misc Drawings and Sculpture, Nov / Dec 1989, cat 81 (repr)
49.	nd	Homer, portrait medallion	sl	The Ridgeway, Shere, Guildford, Surrey, over entrance door		*Hurtado* 1994, 228
50.	nd	Queen Victoria, two medals		[coll Sir Henry Paul Harvey]; NPG 2023a (1, 2), 1924		
Miscellaneous						
51.	1858	'How Sleep the Brave who sink to rest'		[Exhib SFA, London, 523]; untraced		*Laperriere* 1996, I, 367
52.	1858	'Negligent Watch-boy of the Vineyards Catching Locusts', unfinished	m	[Exhib RA, London, 1858, 1169]; untraced		*Graves* 1875, 170; *Graves* II, 1905–6, 391
53.	1858	Warwick the Kingmaker, model		[Exhib SFA 555]; untraced		*Hurtado* 1994, 228; *Laperriere* 1996, I, 367
54.	1866	Constance, 'her litil child lay weping on her arme etc'		[Exhib RA, London, 855]; untraced		*Graves* II, 1905–6, 391; *Hurtado* 1994, 228
55.	1867	Arthur Wellesley, small son of the Dean of Windsor, model		Untraced		Royal A VIC Add X 2/212
56.	1867	Miss Richie		[Exhib RA, London, 997]; untraced		*Graves* II, 1905–6, 391
57.	1867	Prince Sigismund, infant son of the Crown Prince and Princess of Prussia		[Exhib RA 1867, 1111]; untraced		*Graves* II, 1905–6, 391
58.	1869	Lily and Arthur Brooking, the children of Marmaduke Brooking		[Exhib RA, London, 1185]; untraced		*Graves* II, 1905–6, 391
59.	1873	Elizabeth Garrett Anderson MD		[Exhib RA, London, 1873]; untraced		*Graves* II, 1905–6, 391

DURHAM, Joseph FSA, ARA 1814–77

Durham was a talented, naturalistic sculptor. He received much praise for the work of his early years, but his reputation and fortunes declined sharply in later life, a fact openly attributed to the influence of alcohol.

He was born in London and apprenticed to **John Francis** before moving on to the studio of **E H Baily**. In 1835 he began to exhibit regularly at the Royal Academy, showing 128 pieces during his lifetime. His early works were principally busts and portrait medallions, many of now-forgotten sitters. It was one of his busts, a portrait of the Swedish opera singer Jenny Lind, that helped make his name in royal circles and with the public (**71**). In 1846 Lind gave a performance in Dresden, Germany, attended by Queen Victoria and Prince Albert, which resulted in an invitation to perform in London the following year. Whilst in England the singer sat for Durham, who produced a marble bust that was praised by the *Art Journal* as 'universally regarded as the most successful portrait [of Lind] brought out'. It was applauded as an 'admirable likeness' possessing 'the beauty of intelligence, amiability and modest deportment' characteristic of Lind herself (*AJ*, 1846, 340). The bust was reproduced in parian ware by the Copeland factory and became one of Copeland's most popular lines. It also started a professional relationship between Durham and Copeland that was to last many years. Among Durham's models reproduced by Copeland were popular figures of the time, such as Isambard Kingdom Brunel and Queen Victoria, 1863, and genre subjects like the *May Queen* and *The hop queen*, 1873 (**11, 15, 104, 111**).

One of Durham's first major commissions came in 1858 when he won the competition for the memorial to be erected in London's Hyde Park to commemorate the Great Exhibition of 1851 (**13**). This comprised a central statue of

Britannia, allegedly modelled on Queen Victoria, overlooking figures representing the continents of Europe, Africa, America and Asia, each of them modelled on appropriate racial sterotypes, holding objects representing the four continents. Following the death of Prince Albert in 1861, the monument was re-designed by Durham to become a memorial to the Prince, with Britannia replaced by a copper electrotype statue of Albert, designed by Durham and made by Elkington of Birmingham. This was unveiled in 1863 in the newly opened gardens of the Royal Horticultural Society in Kensington, and was described by the *Art Journal* as 'the best of the national monuments as yet erected in England' (*AJ*, 1863, 137). Praise came in from the Queen amongst others, but F T Palgrave was critical of the figure of the Prince Consort who was, he claimed, buried under incongruous courtly robes. Nonetheless, additional copies of the memorial were produced for St Peter Port, Guernsey, and Framlingham College.

Other statues by Durham commemorated both historic and contemporary figures including Francis Crossley, the MP for Halifax, George Stephenson and a group of British Worthies (**10, 30, 130**). These were straightforward representations, but for some of his memorials to public figures he moved beyond portraiture into the realm of association. In 1864, for example, he commemorated Florence Nightingale with a figure entitled *Santa Filomen* (*filomena* is the Latin for nightingale) (**20**). His public works also included designs for several Gothic Revival drinking fountains (**127, 129, 131**).

Much of Durham's output was not for public display. He was responsible for genre pieces for domestic consumption, including a series of gently nationalistic works celebrating British sporting prowess (**14, 21, 22, 27**). There were also homely representations of children, such as *Go to sleep*, 1861, and *The picturebook*, 1867, which depict Victorian children reflecting the contemporary ideal of middle class childhood (**12, 34**). In the first, a child cradles a lap dog as if it is a doll, while in the second two seated children look at a picturebook. Both are in keeping with the Victorian vogue for images of childhood innocence, but as the *Art Journal* noted in 1864, such subject matter was more familiar in contemporary painting than in sculpture. A similar adoption of painters' subject matter is perhaps also evident in Durham's representation of *Paul and Virginia*, the innocent lovers from Bernardin de Saint-Pierre's novel (**7**). These works shows that while Durham was an artist who reflected a mainstream Victorian cultural outlook that was realistic, sentimental and often tinged with nationalistic feeling, he could also stretch the conventional boundaries for sculpture in his choice of subject matter.

Durham was elected a fellow of the Society of Antiquaries in 1853 and an associate of the Royal Academy in 1866. After his death the *Builder* stated that 'Mr. Durham was of a genial and kindly disposition, and very popular with a large circle of friends in the earlier part of his career'. It noted, however, that commissions became less frequent in the latter part of his life and hinted that this had something to do with with his drinking. The *Builder* commented 'Probably with a little more power of self-restraint he might have attained a higher position on the ladder of fame' (*Builder*, 1877, 1110). This was confirmed by Durham's friend, Samuel Carter Hall, who wrote that Durham was a 'victim of the curse that has consigned so many men of genius to graves' (*ODNB*, 243). He died of consumption at his home at 21 Devonshire Street, Marylebone, London, after a long illness and was buried in Kensal Green Cemetery, where he is commemorated by an altar tomb decorated with reliefs of a sculptor's tools, which may have been his own work.

Michael Paraskos

Literary References: *Builder*, 1863, 336, 406–7, 422; 1877, 1110; *AJ*, 1864, 374; *Palgrave*, 1866, 37–8, 82, 86, 121–2, 123, 250; *Hall* II, 1883, 242–3; *Read* 1982, *passim*; *Darby and Smith* 1983, 1–2, 72, 82, 106 n11, 113 n39; *Curl* 2001, 188, 201–2, 226, 237, 242, 358n; *ODNB*

Will: PPR, 10 November 1877, fol 862

Auction References: Durham 1878

Portraits of the Sculptor: J Robson, oil painting(?), exhib RA, 1844, untraced; E Landseer, marble bust (?), exhib RA, 1868; Lock and Whitfield, Woodburytype photograph, NPG; cartes-de-visite, NPG; print, repr J Maas, *The Victorian Art World in Photographs*, 1984; wood engraving, NPG (repr *ILN*, 9 June 1866)

Funerary Monuments						
1.	1861	Thomas Dealtry, Bishop of Madras		Chennai (Madras) Cathedral, India	S	*Gunnis* 1968, 136
2.	1874	William Jerdan		Bushey, Herts, churchyard		*Gunnis* 1968, 136
Statues						
3.	1855	A sleeping child, Alice Evelyn Tupper Model(s): exhib RA, London, 1854, 1388; untraced	m	[Exhib RA, London, 1424]; untraced		*ILN*, 2 Sept 1854, 217 (repr); *Graves* II, 1905–6, 394
4.	1855	The fate of genius, model	p	[Exhib RA, London, 1419]; untraced	SD	*Graves* II, 1905–6, 394; *Jeffery* 1993, 306
5.	1856	Sunshine Model(s): Durham sale, Christie, 18 March 1878, lot 69, plaster	m	[Manc Art Treas Exhib, 1857, 85]; untraced Other versions: Sotheby, Belgravia, 6 July 1973, lot 47, marble, SD 1865		*AJ*, 1856, 352 (repr); *Manchester Art Treasures* 1857, 135; *Durham* 1878, 8
6.	1858	Hermione Model(s): C of L Coll acc 138, plaster	m	CL Coll, Mansion House, City of London, Egyptian Hall, acc 137 Other versions: Int Exhib, London, 1862, coll Francis Bennoch; untraced Durham sale, 18 March 1878, lot 116, bronze statuette; untraced	SD	*AJ Cat* 1862, 320 (repr); *Durham* 1878, 10; *Graves* II, 1905–6, 394; *Knight* 1986, 334 (repr); *Ward-Jackson* 2003, 252 (repr)
7.	1859	Paul and Virginia Model(s): Durham sale, Christie, 18 March 1878, lot 57, small plaster; untraced		[Exhib RA, London, 1270]; untraced		*AJ*, 1864, 374; *ILN*, 26 Sept 1868, 304 (repr); *Durham* 1878, 7; *Graves* II, 1905–6, 394, 395
8.	1859	William Caxton Model(s): exhib RA, London, 1859, 1239; Durham sale, Christie, 18 March 1878, lot 82, plaster, seated statuette; untraced		[Westminster Palace Hotel, Victoria St, London]; untraced		*Durham* 1878, 8; *Graves* II, 1905–6, 394; *Gunnis* 1968, 135

9.	1860	Chastity, statuette Model(s): Durham sale, Christie, 18 March 1878, lot 70, plaster; untraced	m	[Durham sale, Christie, 18 March 1878, lot 100]; untraced Other versions: Reproduced in Parian ware (eg Durham sale, Christie, 18 March 1878, lot 107A)		*ILN*, 4 Aug 1860, 98 (repr); *Durham* 1878, 8, 9; *Graves* II, 1905–6, 394; *Atterbury* 1989, 16 (repr)
10.	1860	Frank Crossley MP		People's Park, Halifax, W R Yorks		*Graves* II, 1905–6, 394; *Gunnis* 1968, 135
11.	1860	Isambard Kingdom Brunel		Untraced Other versions: reproduced in Parian ware		*Atterbury* 1989, 213 (repr)
12.	1861	Go to sleep Model(s): Durham sale, Christie, 18 March 1878, lot 61, plaster; untraced	m	[Joseph Arden sale, Christie, 26 April 1879]; untraced Other versions: Parian ware copies issued as prizes by the Art Union, 1863, 1864 and 1865		*AJ Cat* 1862, 324; *Durham* 1878, 7; *Graves* II, 1905–6, 394; *Atterbury* 1989, 34, 142 (repr)
13.	1863	Albert, the Prince Consort (Great Exhibition Memorial) Payment(s): £7,500 Drawing(s): competition design, Britannia presiding over the four corners of the globe, 1858, untraced Model(s): exhib RA, London, 1862, 998 (Europe); 1863, 1014, 1073 (Africa and America); 1864, 1043 (part of a design for a memorial to HRH the Prince Consort); Durham sale, Christie, 18 March 1878, lot 44 (Continents)		[Royal Horticultural Soc Gardens]; Kensington, London, in front of the Albert Hall Other versions: St Peter Port, Guernsey, 1863 Framlingham College, Suffolk, 1865 Four Continents and four heads in Portland stone, Durham sale, Christie, 18 March 1878, lot 106; untraced	S	*Graves* II, 1905–6, 394, 395; *Darby and Smith* 1983, 2, 78, 79 (repr); *Blackwood* 1989, 58–9 (repr); *Atterbury* 1989, 158 (repr); *Ward-Jackson* 2003, 199
14.	1863	Preparing to throw, statuette	b	[Exhib RA, London, 1864, 964]; untraced Other versions: Durham sale, Christie, 18 March 1878, lots 113, 114, two, bronze; untraced Christie, London, 15 May 1986, lot 31, bronze, SD 1863; untraced		*Durham* 1878, 10; *Graves* II, 1905–6, 395
15.	1863	Queen Victoria with the attributes of peace Model(s): Int Exhib, London, 1862; 'reduced model' exhib RA, London, 1863, 1034; untraced; Durham sale, Christie, 18 March 1878, lot 48, plaster; untraced	b	[coll Prince of Wales]; untraced		*AJ Cat* 1862, 316 (repr); *Durham* 1878, 7; *Graves* II, 1905–6, 394
16.	1863	Waiting his innings, statuette	b	[Exhib RA, London, 1864, 963]; untraced Other versions: Durham sale, Christie, 18 March 1878, lots 110, 115, two, bronze; untraced Christie, London, 15 May 1986, lot 28, bronze, SD 1863; untraced		*Durham* 1878, 10; *Graves* II, 1905–6, 394
17.	1864	Alastor Model(s): 'reduced model' exhib RA, London, 1865, 910; untraced	m	CL Coll, Mansion House, City of London, Egyptian Hall, acc 125	SD	*Graves* II, 1905–6, 395; *Knight* 1986, 335 (repr); *Jeffery* 1993, 307; *Ward-Jackson* 2003, 255 (repr)
18.	1864	Boating boys, statuette	b	[Exhib RA, London, 954]; untraced Other versions: Durham sale, Christie, 18 March 1878, lots 111–112, two, bronze; untraced Sotheby, London, 13–15 March 2002, lot 1146, bronze, signed; untraced		*Durham* 1878, 10; *Graves* II, 1905–6, 394
19.	1864	Preparing to catch, statuette	b	[Exhib RA, London, 961]; untraced Other versions: Durham sale, Christie, 18 March 1878, lots 113, 114, two, bronze (untraced) Christie, London, 15 May 1986, lot 32, bronze, signed; untraced		*Durham* 1878, 10; *Graves* II, 1905–6, 394
20.	1864	Santa Filomena Model(s): Durham sale, Christie, 18 March 1878, lot 76, plaster, life-size; untraced		Untraced Other versions: reproduced in Copeland Parian ware (egs Paris Int Exhib, 1867; Durham sale, Christie, 18 March 1878, lot 107A)		*Durham* 1878, 8, 9; *Gunnis* 1968, 135; *Atterbury* 1989, 154 (repr)
21.	1864	The batsman, statuette	b	[Exhib RA, London, 953]; untraced Other versions: Durham sale, Christie, 18 March 1878, lots 110, 115, two, bronze; untraced Christie, London, 15 May 1986, lot 29, bronze, signed; untraced		*Durham* 1878, 10; *Graves* II, 1905–6, 394
22.	1864	The bowler, statuette	b	[Exhib RA, London, 955]; untraced Other versions: Durham sale, Christie, 18 March 1878, lots 110, 115, two, bronze; untraced Christie, London, 15 May 1986, lot 30, bronze, signed; untraced		*Durham* 1878, 10; *Graves* II, 1905–6, 394

No.	Date	Title		Location		Literature
23.	1865	On the sea shore, a portrait of Savile Brinton Crossley (later 1st Lord Somerleyton) as a boy	m	Somerleyton Hall, Suffolk	SD	*Graves* II, 1905–6, 395; *Read* 1982, 212; *Atterbury* 1989, 142 (repr)
24.	1865	The Lady of the Lake, model	p	[Durham sale, Christie, 18 March 1878, lot 59]; untraced		*Durham* 1878, 7; *Graves* II, 1905–6, 395
25.	1865	Trying the lesson: Edith and G C Ashton Jonson	m	[Exhib RA, London, 904]; untraced		*Graves* II, 1905–6, 395
26.	1866	A perilous plaything, a portrait of George Herbert Guadet	p	[Durham sale, Christie, 18 March 1878, lot 60]; untraced		*Durham* 1878, 7; *Graves* II, 1905–6, 395
27.	1866	Waiting his innings, a portrait of Basil Edward Lawrence Model(s): Durham sale, Christie, 18 March 1878, lot 89A, plaster	m	[84, Holland Park, London]; CL Coll, Guildhall Art Gall, London, acc 585	SD	*Durham* 1878, 8; *Graves* II, 1905–6, 395; *Holland Park* 1957, unpag (repr); *Knight* 1986, 335 (repr)
28.	1867	A sleeping child, the infant son of W H Smith	m	[Exhib RA, London, 1004]; untraced		*Graves* II, 1905–6, 394
29.	1867	Euclid		Oxford University Museum	S	*Read* 1982, 235, 236 (repr)
30.	1867	George Stephenson Model(s): Durham sale, Christie, 18 March 1878, lot 84, small seated statuette, plaster; untraced		Oxford University Museum	S	*Durham* 1878, 7; *Gunnis* 1968, 136; *Read* 1982, 235
31.	1867	Girl at the spring Model(s): Durham sale, Christie, 18 March 1878, lot 78, plaster, life-size; untraced	m	[Samlesbury Hall, Lancs, fernery]; Blackburn Town Hall, Lancs Other versions: Somerleyton Hall, Suffolk, 1868 Gloucester Gate, Regents Park, London (part of fountain)	SD	*Graves* II, 1905–6, 395; *Durham* 1878, 8; *Gunnis* 1968, 135; *Read* 1982, 41–3 (repr)
32.	1867	Good night, a portrait of Maria Lilian Redhead Model(s): Durham sale, Christie, 18 March 1878, lot 50, plaster; untraced		[Exhib RA, London, 999]; untraced		*ILN*, 10 Aug 1867, 161 (repr); *Durham* 1878, 7; *Graves* II, 1905–6, 395
33.	1867	Lord John Douglas Scott		Dunchurch, Warks	S	*Graves* 1905–6, 2, 395; *Gunnis* 1968, 136; *Noszlopy* 2003, 19–20 (repr)
34.	1867	The picturebook, Mary and Richard Redhead Model(s): Durham sale, Christie, 18 March 1878, lot 81; untraced	m	Macclesfield Town Hall, Cheshire	S	*Durham* 1878, 8; *Graves* II, 1905–6, 395; *Read* 1982, 210, 212 (repr)
35.	1868	Going in for a paddle, a portrait of William Rawson Shaw		[Exhib RA, London, 957]; untraced		*Graves* II, 1905–6, 395
36.	1868	Peace Model(s): Durham sale, Christie, 18 March 1878, lot 53, 'Peace on Earth', plaster; untraced		[coll G Fox, of Harefield, Cheshire]; untraced		*Durham* 1878, 7; *Gunnis* 1968, 136
37.	1868	Ready for my bath, a portrait of Frederic Ougley Francis Model(s): Durham sale, Christie, 18 March 1878, lot 62, plaster; untraced		[Exhib RA, London, 936]; untraced		*Durham* 1878, 7; *Graves* II, 1905–6, 395
38.	1868	Sitting for our portraits, four daughters of Mr and Mrs W H Smith Model(s): Durham sale, Christie, 18 March 1878, lot 87, plaster; untraced		[Exhib RA, London, 946]; untraced		*Durham* 1878, 8; *Graves* II, 1905–6, 395
39.	1869	Only once a year Model(s): Durham sale, Christie, 18 March 1878, lot 67, plaster; untraced		[Exhib RA, London, 1225]; untraced Other versions: exhib RA, London, 1877, 1464, bronze 'grotto boy'; untraced Durham sale, Christie, 18 March 1878, lot 108, bronze, 48 in high; untraced		*Durham* 1878, 8, 10; *Graves* II, 1905–6, 395
40.	1870	Perdita and Florizel Model(s): Durham sale, Christie, 18 March 1878, lot 56, plaster; untraced		Walker, Liverpool		*AJ*, 1870, 152 (repr); *Durham* 1878, 7; *Gunnis* 1968, 136; *ODNB*
41.	1870	Unidentified young boy by a mile post	m	[Sotheby, London, 25/6 Nov 1982, lot 298]; untraced	SD	C Lib (repr & sale press cutting)
42.	1871	Hero Model(s): Durham sale, Christie, 18 March, 1878, lot 72, small plaster sketch; untraced	m	[coll G Fox, of Harefield, Cheshire]; untraced		*AJ*, 1871, 44 (repr); *Durham* 1878, 8; *Graves* II, 1905–6, 395; *Gunnis* 1968, 136
43.	1871	Leander Model(s): Durham sale, Christie, 18 March, 1878, lot 72, small plaster sketch; untraced	m	[Exhib RA, London, 1269]; untraced		*Durham* 1878, 8; *Graves* II, 1905–6, 395
44.	1872	A dip in the sea ('the first dip') Model(s): RA, London, 1871, 1224; Durham sale, Christie, 18 March 1878, lot 68, plaster; untraced	m	[coll Edward Brooke]; Christie, 4 March 1882 (200 gns); untraced		*AJ*, 1872, 264 (repr); *Durham* 1878, 8; *Graves* II, 1905–6, 395; *Gunnis* 1968, 135
45.	1873	Humility Model(s): Durham sale, Christie, 18 March 1878, lot 47, plaster; untraced	m	[Durham sale, Christie, 18 March 1878, lot 99]; untraced		*Durham* 1878, 7, 9; *Graves* II, 1905–6, 396

No.	Date	Title	Medium	Location	Signed	Literature
46.	1873	Master Tom Model(s): Durham sale, Christie, 18 March 1878, 45, 46, two, plaster; untraced	m	[Durham sale, Christie, 18 March 1878, lot 97]; untraced		*ILN*, 11 Oct 1873, 341 (repr); *Durham* 1878, 7, 9; *Graves* II, 1905–6, 396
47.	1873	Miss Ellie Model(s): Durham sale, Christie, 18 March 1878, 45, 46, two, plaster; untraced	m	[Durham sale, Christie, 18 March 1878, lot 96]; untraced		*ILN*, 11 Oct 1873, 341 (repr); *Durham* 1878, 7, 9; *Graves* II, 1905–6, 396
48.	1873	Pride Model(s): Durham sale, Christie, 18 March 1878, lot 46, plaster; untraced	m	[Durham sale, Christie, 18 March 1878, lot 98]; untraced		*Durham* 1878, 7, 9; *Graves* II, 1905–6, 396
49.	1875	The siren and the drowned Leander	m	[Deanery Gardens, Sonning, Berks]; Sotheby, Billingshurst, 26 Sept 1989, lot 550; untraced Other versions: Durham sale, Christie, 18 March 1878, lots 54, 103, 104 (a plaster, life-size marble and smaller marble) Private coll (Glos), p, SD, 1871	SD	*Durham* 1878, 7, 9; *Graves* II, 1906–6, 395, 396; *Gunnis* 1968, 135
50.	nd	Albert, the Prince Consort, statuette Model(s): Durham sale, Christie, 18 March 1878, lot 49, plaster; untraced	b	[Durham sale, Christie, 18 March 1878, lot 109]; untraced		*Durham* 1878, 7, 10
51.	nd	Boy with a basket, model	p	[Durham sale, Christie, 18 March 1878, lot 86]; untraced		*Durham* 1878, 8
52.	nd	Erin, statuette	p	[Durham sale, Christie, 18 March 1878, lot 66]; untraced		*Durham* 1878, 8
53.	nd	Flora, statuette	p	[Durham sale, Christie, 18 March 1878, lot 83]; untraced		*Durham* 1878, 8
54.	nd	Pandora, statuette	p	[Durham sale, Christie, 18 March 1878, lot 83]; untraced		*Durham* 1878, 8
55.	nd	Pitt, statuette	p	[Durham sale, Christie, London, 18 March 1878, lot 63]; untraced		*Durham* 1878, 7
56.	nd	Reading girl, model	p	[Durham sale, Christie, 18 March 1878, lot 80]; untraced		*Durham* 1878, 8
57.	nd	Swift, statuette	p	[Durham sale, Christie, London, 18 March 1878, lot 63]; untraced		*Durham* 1878, 7
58.	nd	The first step, model	p	[Durham sale, Christie, 18 March 1878, lot 55]; untraced		*Durham* 1878, 7
59.	nd	The plighted troth, model	p	[Durham sale, Christie, 18 March 1878, lot 58]; untraced		*Durham* 1878, 7
60.	nd	The sense of touch, a blind girl reading, model (one of a set of five illustrating the senses)	p	[Durham sale, Christie, 18 March 1878, lot 52]; untraced		*Durham* 1878, 7
61.	nd	The sleeping child, model	p	[Durham sale, Christie, 18 March 1878, lot 79]; untraced		*Durham* 1878, 8
62.	nd	Venus at the bath, model	p	[Durham sale, Christie, 18 March 1878, lot 77]; untraced		*Durham* 1878, 8
63.	nd	William Makepeace Thackeray, statuette	p	[Durham sale, Christie, 18 March 1878, lot 75]; untraced		*Durham* 1878, 8
Busts						
64.	1835	Unidentified gentleman	m	[Exhib RA, London, 1120]; untraced		*Graves* II, 1905–6, 393
65.	1836	The sculptor's mother		[Exhib RA, London, 1122]; untraced		*Graves* II, 1905–6, 393
66.	1841	Unidentified gentleman		[Exhib RA, London, 1270]; untraced		*Graves* II, 1905–6, 393
67.	1842	Unidentified youth		[Exhib RA, London, 1324]; untraced		*Graves* II, 1905–6, 393
68.	1844	Lady of Malohn Rymer		[Exhib RA, London, 1382]; untraced		*AU*, 1844, 171; *Graves* II, 1905–6, 393
69.	1846	Mirth, a study Model(s): exhib RA, London, 1845, 1389; untraced	m	[Exhib RA, London, 1439]; untraced		*AU*, 1846, 189; *Graves* II, 1905–6, 393
70.	1847	Unidentified subject		[Exhib RA, London, 1370]; untraced		*Graves* II, 1905–6, 393
71.	1848	Jenny Lind	m	Royal College of Music, London Other versions: over 100 Parian ware reproductions		*AJ*, 1850, 344 (repr); *Manchester Art Treasures* 1857, 136; *Graves* II, 1905–6, 393; *Atterbury* 1989, 185 (repr); *ODNB*
72.	1848	Sir David Pollock		[Exhib RA, London, 1375]; untraced		*Graves* II, 1905–6, 393
73.	1848	Sir Jonathan Frederick Pollock		[Exhib RA, London, 1399]; untraced		*Graves* II, 1905–6, 393
74.	1849	La Penserosa Model(s): Durham sale, Christie, 18 March 1878, lot 71, plaster; untraced	m	[coll W E Gladstone]; Christie, London, 23 June 1875; private coll Other versions: Durham sale, Christie, 18 March 1878, lot 91, marble, life-size; untraced		*Manchester Art Treasures* 1857, 136; *Durham* 1878, 8, 9; *Graves* II, 1905–6, 393; GPC
75.	1849	Thomas Hunt	m	[Exhib RA, London, 1336]; untraced		*Graves* II, 1905–6, 393
76.	1850	Captain R J Elliott RN	m	[Exhib RA, London, 1396]; untraced		*Graves* II, 1905–6, 393–4
77.	1850	F W L Ross	m	Exeter Art Gallery, Devon		*Graves* II, 1905–6, 394; *Gunnis* 1968, 136
78.	1850	Queen Victoria	m	Exeter Art Gallery, Devon		GPC
79.	1850	Thomas Wright		Soc Antiq, London		*Graves* II, 1905–6, 394
80.	1853	Dr T R Grahamsley, model	m	[Exhib RA, London, 1434]; untraced		*Graves* II, 1905–6, 394
81.	1854	Unidentified lady	m	[Exhib RA, London, 1502]; untraced		*Graves* II, 1905–6, 394

No.	Date	Subject		Location		Literature
82.	1855	Lady with flowers in her hair	m	[Phillips, Tatton Park, 14 May 1990, lot 43]; untraced	SD	C Lib (repr & sale press cutting)
83.	1856	Queen Victoria	m	[Guildhall, City of London, Council Chamber]; destroyed Other versions: Royal College of Music, marble Durham sale, Christie, 18 March 1878, lot 101, marble, 1856, lot 105, lot 107, Parian ware; all untraced Foundling Hospital, London, plaster, SD 1855 ex Royal Albert Memorial Museum, Exeter, plaster, 1855; untraced Christie, London, 15 June 1961, lot 20, biscuit porcelain, 1855 Maidstone Museum, Kent, Parian ware copy; untraced		*Manchester Art Treasures* 1857, 136; *Durham* 1878, 9; *Graves* II, 1905–6, 394; *Gunnis* 1968, 136; *Ormond* 1973, 487
84.	1856	W H Smith	m	Russell-Cotes AG, Bournemouth, Dorset	SD	*Graves* II, 1905–6, 394
85.	pre-1857	L'Allegra Model(s): Durham sale, Christie, 18 March 1878, lot 71, plaster; untraced	m	[Manc Art Treas Exhib, 154]; untraced		*Manchester Art Treasures* 1857, 136; *Durham* 1878, 8
86.	1857	Martin Farquhar Tupper		[Crystal Palace, Sydenham]; untraced		*Graves* II, 1905–6, 394
87.	1857	Thomas Hall		[Guildhall, City of London]; destroyed 1940		*Gunnis* 1968, 136
88.	1859	Sir Edward Sabine	m	Royal Soc, London		*Graves* II, 1905–6, 394; *Ormond* 1973, 409; C Lib (repr)
89.	1860	Head of an unidentified boy	m	[Exhib RA, London, 989]; untraced		*Graves* II, 1905–6, 394
90.	1861	Peace, an ideal head	m	[Durham sale, Christie, 18 March 1878, lot 95]; untraced		*Durham* 1878, 9; *Graves* II, 1905–6, 394
91.	1862	Albert, the Prince Consort Payment(s): £143 10s	m	[Council Chamber, Guildhall, City of London]; destroyed 1940		*Ormond* 1973, 14; *Darby and Smith* 1983, 63
92.	1862	William Hazlitt	p	Maidstone Museum, Kent	SD	C Lib (repr)
93.	1863	James Bunning		[Guildhall, City of London]; destroyed		*ILN*, 28 Oct 1865, 428 (repr); *Gunnis* 1968, 136
94.	1864	Lady Beatrice Clinton	m	[Exhib RA, London, 873]; untraced		*Graves* II, 1905–6, 394
95.	1864	William Makepeace Thackeray Model(s): Durham sale, Christie, 18 March 1878, lot 74, plaster; untraced	m	Garrick Club, London, inv 178 Other versions: NPG 495, plaster, SD 1864 NPG 495a, copy by Sir Joseph Edgar Boehm, clay, 1878	S	*Durham* 1878, 8; *Ormond* 1973, 460 (pl 918); *Ashton* 1997, 524 (colour repr 46r)
96.	1865	Head of an unidentified child	m	[Exhib RA, London, 957]; untraced		*Graves* II, 1905–6, 395
97.	1865	Sir Daniel Cooper		Parliament House, Sydney, NSW		*Graves* II, 1905–6, 395; GPC
98.	1866	Charles Knight		[coll Knight family]; untraced Other versions: NPG 393, marble, SD 1874		*Graves* II, 1905–6, 395; *Ormond* 1973, 250 (repr 490)
99.	1866	Henry, 5th Duke of Newcastle		[Exhib RA, London, 867]; untraced		*Graves* II, 1905–6, 395; *Ormond* 1973, 338
100.	1867	Henry, 3rd Viscount Palmerston		[Guildhall, City of London]; destroyed 1940		*Graves* II, 1905–6, 395; *Ormond* 1973, 361
101.	1867	John Blaxland		Parliament House, Sydney, NSW		GPC
102.	1867	John, Lord Romilly	m	PRO, London		*Graves* II, 1905–6, 395; *Gunnis* 1968, 136
103.	1867	Martha, Lady Crossley	m	Somerleyton Hall, Suffolk		*Graves* II, 1905–6, 395
104.	1868	The may queen, model		untraced Other versions: reproduced in Copeland Parian ware for the Crystal Palace Art Union (example sold Christie, London, 15 July 1993, lot 107)		*ILN*, 18 July 1868, 61 (repr); *Atterbury* 1989, 180 (repr)
105.	1869	John Crossley		[Exhib RA, London, 1243]; untraced		*Graves* II, 1905–6, 395
106.	1869	Leigh Hunt		Chelsea Town Hall, London Other versions: replica ex Kensal Green Cemetery, London; untraced		*ILN*, 23 Oct 1869, 413 (repr); *Gunnis* 1968, 136; *Curl* 2001, 201
107.	1870	Sir George Pollock	m	NPG 364	SD	*Graves* II, 1905–6, 395; *Ormond* 1973, 380 (pls 746, 747)
108.	1871	Mr Havers		[Freemasons' Hall, London]; untraced		*Gunnis* 1968, 136
109.	1873	'Julius Bru. . .'		Maidstone Museum, Kent	SD	C Lib (repr)
110.	1873	Sir Sidney Hedley Waterlow Bt Model(s): exhib RA, London, 1873, 1520; untraced		St Bartholomew's Hospital, London	SD	*Graves* II, 1905–6, 396; C Lib (repr)
111.	1873	The hop queen, model		Untraced Other versions: Parian ware version issued by the Ceramic and Crystal Palace Art Union		*Atterbury* 1989, 181 (repr)
112.	1875	George Bertram, son of R Milne Redhead		[Exhib RA, London, 1274]; untraced		*Graves* II, 1905–6, 396
113.	1875	John Brinton		[Exhib RA, London, 1256]; untraced		*Graves* II, 1905–6, 396

No.	Date	Subject	Medium	Location		Literary references
114.	1875	Rev John Barlow	m	R I, London		*Graves* II, 1905–6, 396; C Lib (repr)
115.	1875	William Hogarth Model(s): Durham sale, Christie, 18 March 1878, lot 73, plaster; untraced	s	Leicester Square, London		*Durham* 1878, 8; *Graves* II, 1905–6, 396; *Read* 1982, 170–1 (repr)
116.	1876	Edward Gibbon Wakefield		Foreign and Commonwealth Office, London		*Graves* II, 1905–6, 396; *Ormond* 1973, 494
117.	1876	Sir William R Grove	m	R I, London		*Graves* II, 1905–6, 396; C Lib (repr)
118.	1878	Mrs Peel	m	[Exhib RA, London, 1425]; untraced		*Graves* II, 1905–6, 396
119.	1878	Thomas Webster RA	m	[Exhib RA, London, 1456]; untraced		*Graves* II, 1905–6, 396
120.	nd	Geoffrey Chaucer	m	[Durham sale, Christie, 18 March 1878, lot 94]; untraced		*Durham* 1878, 9
121.	nd	John Milton	m	[Durham sale, Christie, 18 March 1878, lot 92]; untraced		*Durham* 1878, 9
122.	nd	Silence, a figure of an angel	p	[Durham sale, Christie, 18 March 1878, lot 51]; untraced		*Durham* 1878, 7
123.	nd	Sir Francis Crossley	m	Somerleyton Hall, Suffolk		www.somerleyton.co.uk
124.	nd	Thomas Knight	m	[Durham sale, Christie, 18 March 1878, lot 90]; untraced		*Durham* 1878, 9
125.	nd	Unidentified female sitter	m	Christie NY, 13 June 1981, lot 55; untraced	S	Christies Cat., 21
126.	nd	William Shakespeare	m	[Durham sale, Christie, 18 March 1878, lot 93]; untraced		*Durham* 1878, 9
Architectural Sculpture						
127.	1866	Moses striking the rock, relief, part of drinking fountain Model(s): Durham sale, Christie, 18 March 1878, lot 88, plaster; untraced	b	[Guildhall Yard, City of London]; St Lawrence Jewry, London		*ILN*, 18 Aug 1866, 161 (repr); *AJ*, 1869, 60 (repr); *Durham* 1878, 8; *Ward- Jackson* 2003, xxiv (repr)
128.	1866–1867	Queen Victoria, Queen Elizabeth I, Empress Matilda, Queen Anne	s	Former PRO, Chancery Lane, City of London, parapet of central tower		*Ward-Jackson* 2003, 304 (repr)
129.	1868	Fountain		Somerleyton Hall, Suffolk		*Gunnis* 1968, 135
130.	1869	Statues of British worthies: Sir Isaac Newton, William Harvey, Jeremy Bentham and John Milton Model(s): exhib RA, London, 1869, 1198, 1200, Harvey and Newton; Durham sale, Christie, 18 March 1878, lot 63, Milton and Bentham; all untraced		Royal Academy schools (former University of London headquarters), Burlington Gardens, London, façade		*Durham* 1878, 7; *Graves* II, 1905–6, 395; *Read* 1982, 226
131.	1876	Double drinking fountain Model(s): exhib RA, London, 1875, 1300; untraced	b	[On site of old town hall, Leek, Staffs]; Moorlands House, Stockwell St, Leek, Staffs (1988)		*ILN*, 6 May 1876, 452 (repr); *Graves* II, 1905–6, 396
132.	1872–1876	Phidias, William of Wykeham, figure		Burlington House, London, courtyard façade		Pevsner, *London: Westminster*, 1973, 624
133.	nd	Boy seated on a dolphin, design for a drinking fountain		[Durham sale, Christie, 18 March 1878, lot 65]; untraced Other versions: Durham sale, Christie, 18 March 1878, lot 64		*Durham* 1878, 7
134.	nd	Design for a pedestal with three female figures	p	[Durham sale, Christie, 18 March 1878, lot 85]; untraced		*Durham* 1878, 8
Reliefs						
135.	1836	Cupid		[Exhib RA, London, 1105]; untraced		*Graves* II, 1905–6, 393
136.	1840	Unidentified gentleman, medallion		[Exhib RA, London, 1106]; untraced		*Graves* II, 1905–6, 393
137.	1843	Unidentified gentleman, medallion		[Exhib RA, London, 1464]; untraced		*Graves* II, 1905–6, 393
138.	1848	Joshua Cristall, medallion		[Exhib RA, London, 1471]; untraced		*Graves* II, 1905–6, 393
139.	1851	Three bas reliefs in frame, intended for the panels of a pedestal		[Exhib RA, London, 1388]; untraced		*Graves* II, 1905–6, 394
Miscellaneous						
140.	1838	Grief, a study		[Exhib RA, London, 1326]; untraced		*Graves* II, 1905–6, 393
141.	1849	Guizot		[Exhib RA, London, 1297]; untraced		*Graves* II, 1905–6, 393–4
142.	1854	Joseph Arden		[Exhib RA, London, 1500]; untraced		*Graves* II, 1905–6, 394
143.	1854	The eldest son of Alexander Johnston		[Exhib RA, London, 1471]; untraced		*Graves* II, 1905–6, 394
144.	1857	Captain F R Pollock		[Exhib RA, London, 1323]; untraced		*Graves* II, 1905–6, 394
145.	1859	J P Gassiott		[Exhib RA, London, 1361]; untraced		*Graves* II, 1905–6, 394
146.	1861	Frank Crossley MP		[Exhib RA, London, 1042]; untraced		*Graves* II, 1905–6, 394
147.	1862	Emma Burrows	m	[Exhib RA, London, 1037]; untraced		*Graves* II, 1905–6, 394
148.	1862	Henry White FSA		[Exhib RA, London, 1027]; untraced		*Graves* II, 1905–6, 394
149.	1865	Miss Bateman	m	[Exhib RA, London, 940]; untraced		*Graves* II, 1905–6, 395
150.	1866	Miss Evelyn Hankey		[Exhib RA, London, 915]; untraced		*Graves* II, 1905–6, 395
151.	1869	Octavius Cohen		[Exhib RA, London, 1215]; untraced		*Graves* II, 1905–6, 395
152.	1870	Arthur Cecil Milne Redhead		[Exhib RA, London, 1200]; untraced		*Graves* II, 1905–6, 395
153.	1870	Joseph Crossley	m	[Exhib RA, London, 1165]; untraced		*Graves* II, 1905–6, 395
154.	1870	Miniature reproduction of the tomb of John Evelyn		[coll Mr Evelyn, of Wotton]; untraced		*AJ* 1870, 159; GPC
155.	1870	Mrs Birks	m	[Exhib RA, London, 1154]; untraced		*Graves* II, 1905–6, 395
156.	1871	Andreas Holtz	m	[Exhib RA, London, 1298]; untraced		*Graves* II, 1905–6, 395
157.	1871	Mrs Andreas Holtz	m	[Exhib RA, London, 1302]; untraced		*Graves* II, 1905–6, 395
158.	1874	Sir Sydney H Waterlow Bt MP		[Exhib RA, London, 1514]; untraced		*Graves* II, 1905–6, 396
159.	1874	Wilfred Milne Redhead		[Exhib RA, London, 1466]; untraced		*Graves* II, 1905–6, 396
160.	1877	A J Waterlow	m	[Exhib RA, London, 1427]; untraced		*Graves* II, 1905–6, 396

DURRANT, Eustace fl 1735

He was apprenticed to G Hart of London and set up for himself in Ipswich in 1735, announcing in the *Ipswich Gazette* that he made 'monuments, gravestones, coats of arms and chimney-pieces of the newest fashion', and that he was also prepared to make 'designs for any manner of building at reasonable rates'.

Literary References: *Gunnis* 1968, 136

DYCE, William 1806–64

The Scottish painter and designer was also responsible for some sculpture. A bust is recorded in the museum of his home town of Aberdeen.

Literary References: *Grove* 1996, 9, 473 (Pointon); *Read* 1982, 273

Busts

1.	nd	Unidentified sitter	m	City Art Gallery, Aberdeen		*Read* 1982, 273

EADS, J fl 1786

Funerary Monuments

1.	1786	Unidentified sailor, murdered at Hindhead (designed by R M Payne)		Thursley, Surrey, churchyard	S	Pevsner, *Surrey*, 1971, 485

EAMES (or EMES), M, of Exeter fl 1762–1808

Gunnis comments that though 'his tablets feature rather too often the draped urn against a pyramid' Eames was a 'careful, if uninspired, craftsman'. Towards the end of his career he went into partnership with **William Stephens of Exeter.** He was succeeded in the business by his son, **W Eames.**

Literary References: *Gunnis* 1968, 137

Funerary Monuments

1.	†1762	Rev Nathaniel Wells	East Allington, Devon	S	Pevsner, *Devon*, 1989, 346
2.	?1788	Richard Blake	Farway, Devon	S	*Gunnis* 1968, 137
3.	†1791	Vincent (†1764) and Elizabeth Darley	North Hill, Cornwall	S	Pevsner, *Cornwall*, 1970, 128
4.	?1792	Rebecca Burrows	Tawstock, Devon	S	*Gunnis* 1968, 137
5.	?1794	Margaret Graham	Littleham, Devon	S	*Gunnis* 1968, 137
6.	†1797	Samuel Needham	St Gregory, Dawlish, Devon	S	Pevsner, *Devon*, 1989, 331
7.	?1799	Egerton Filmore	Lympsone, Devon	S	*Gunnis* 1968, 137
8.	1801	Lady Charlotte Carr	Menheniot, Cornwall		Pevsner, *Cornwall*, 1970, 117
9.	†1803	Major-General Elliot	Littleham, Devon	S	Pevsner, *Devon*, 1989, 538
10.	†1808	John Kingdon (co-sculptor: William Stephens, of Exeter)	Bridgerule, Devon		Pevsner, *Devon*, 1989, 213
11.	?1812	William Holmes	Shobrooke, Devon	S	*Gunnis* 1968, 137

EAMES (or EMES), W, of Exeter fl 1829?

The son of M Eames, he took over the family business.

Literary References: *Gunnis* 1968, 137

Funerary Monuments

1.	?1829	Elizabeth Penton	Bampton, Devon	S	*Gunnis* 1968, 137

EARLE FAMILY, of Kingston-upon-Hull

George Earle I 1748–1827
John Earle I c1779–1863
John Earle II b 1816
George Earle II c1810–1835
Joseph Earle 1821–1844
Thomas Earle 1810–1876

The Earles were a family of accomplished sculptors and masons who ran a thriving practice for three generations. **George Earle I**, the son of a York bricklayer, migrated to Hull *c*1776 and established himself as a stonemason, architect and speculative builder. From the outset he cultivated sound business and social connections. In 1781 he married Mary, the daughter of a stone mason and carver-gilder, **Jeremiah Hargrave**, whose son Joseph was architect and surveyor to the town. One of the witnesses at their wedding was Charles Mountain, a bricklayer, plasterer and stuccoist who subsequently became one of Hull's most notable architects and builders. The Earles were involved with Mountain on a number of projects including Hesslewood, the country house built for the Hull merchant and banker J R Pease. They had three sons, George, Thomas and John. George and Thomas established a business as Hull merchants who were, for a time, the town's leading importers of slate, stone and Italian marble.

John Earle I joined his father's masonry business and was responsible for numerous competent but conventional funerary monuments in the East Riding and North Lincolnshire. His most unusual, to George Lambert, has a fine relief of a church organ, alluding to Lambert's 40 years as organist at Holy Trinity, Hull (**42**). By 1814 John was managing the Earle yard on Osborne Street, Hull. He continued to work as a mason and architect but by the 1820s styled himself 'sculptor'. The business flourished throughout the 1820s and Earle received a number of major commissions for architectural projects whilst continuing to provide a wide range of monuments. By October 1832, however, Earle's business had collapsed and he was declared bankrupt, though he managed to stay in business. Competition stiffened as an increasing number of architects and stone and marble masons became established in the town, including **George Bailey** 'statuary and mason', **John Waudby & Son**, sculptors 'of Hull and York', and particularly **William Day Keyworth.** As late as 1863, the year of his death, Earle and Keyworth were the only two sculptors listed in the local trades' directory.

Little is known of **John Earle II.** He undoubtedly received his initial training with his father before founding his own yard in Chapel Street, Hull. His only known work is a charming wall tablet with a mourning female figure (**29**). He appears to have left Hull sometime between 1841 and 1851.

George Earle II served his apprenticeship with his father and after working for a time at the Earle yard in Whitefriargate, he set up as a marble mason at 28 Junction Dock Street, Hull. He provided church monuments in Hull, the East Riding and North Lincolnshire and one further afield, at Barsham in Suffolk (**33**). He exhibited two portrait busts at the Exhibition of Fine Arts held in July 1827 at the Hull Assembly Rooms (**115, 116**). His finest monuments commemorate Simon Horner (**24**) and Horner Reynard (**36**). Both have delicate gothic detailing and are supported by figurative marble brackets.

George Earle II died prematurely. His father was in no position to take charge of his son's yard at Junction Dock and the business was controlled by trustees over the next eight years. George's younger brother **Joseph Earle** took over in 1843 and shortly afterwards he advertised his new 'spacious marble works' in the local press (*Hull Advertiser*, 21 April 1843). He had one yard at St John Street and another on Osbourne Street, the latter perhaps shared with his father, who was also working from Osborne Street. Joseph Earle died in February 1844, barely one year after taking charge. Only four signed works by him are known, all simple wall tablets (**11, 35, 45, 47**). His workshop at St John Street was taken over by George Bailey 'Statuary and Mason, successor to the late Joseph Earle' (E R Yorks Archives office, DDCC/2/72).

The most talented and successful family member was **Thomas Earle**. He was born in Hull and began his career as a sculptor at the age of 12, when it was already evident that he had a talent for modelling. He was undoubtedly apprenticed to his father, but supplemented his early education at the Mechanics' Institute where his father was among the founder members. Since there was no school of art in Hull until 1861, the Mechanics' Institute, established in 1825, was invaluable to aspiring artists, since it had a drawing class and a model room containing a 'good collection of casts and models' (*Sheahan*, 1868, 646). The Mechanics' Institute commissioned Thomas Earle's first public work in 1832, a statue of Dr John Alderson (**66**). When the statue was unveiled the Mechanics' Institute was congratulated for encouraging an enterprising young artist, who 'would at a future day, if blessed with life and health, deservedly rank with the most distinguished statuaries of Britain, or Europe' (*Hull Advertiser*, 16 September 1831).

Thomas Earle left Hull *c*1830–31 and became a designer and modeller for **Sir Francis Chantrey RA**, remaining with him for between eight and twelve years. In January 1832, on Chantrey's recommendation, he was admitted as a probationer at the Royal Academy and the following December became a student at the Academy schools. In 1839 he was awarded the Academy's gold medal for the best historic group, *Hercules deliverung Hesione from the sea monster* (**69**), which was exhibited at the Academy in 1840.

By 1851 Earle had his own London studio at Vincent Street, Ovington Square. He competed for national commissions, including the monuments to Nelson and the Duke of Wellington (**111, 94**), but it was his continued association with Hull that brought prosperity. Like his father and grandfather before him, Thomas Earle was a member of the Minerva lodge of freemasons in Hull. This fraternity played a significant role, for it brought sound professional associations with architects and builders and also led to patronage from fellow members including the Earls of Zetland and Yarborough (**128, 133, 154**). In 1846 Thomas married Mary, the daughter of a local builder, Frank Appleyard. The Appleyards had worked with the Earles on a number of building projects in Hull and were also freemasons. Earle's friendship with another freemason, C S Todd, the town clerk of Hull, appears to have been instrumental in securing him the commission for Hull's statues of Queen Victoria and Prince Albert (**102, 103**). Freemasonry may also have played a part in Thomas Earle's introduction to Sir Francis Chantrey, a member of the Royal Somerset & Inverness Lodge.

In February 1860 Todd wrote to Thomas Earle informing him that the Mayor, Z C Pearson, was to present Hull with a public park and that the authorities intended to commission a statue of the Queen, similar to **Matthew Noble**'s figure in Peel Park, Manchester (Hull City Archives, BHH 115/716). Since both Todd and Pearson were freemasons, Earle must have been confident of securing the commission. Having agreed terms, Earle prepared a small model (Hull City Archives, BHH 97/369) which found favour with the Mayor who then announced his intention of presenting the townspeople of Hull with a statue of the Queen executed by 'their townsman' Thomas Earle (Hull City Archives, BHH 116/462).

Pearson was declared bankrupt in 1862, but his successor, Mayor W H Moss, agreed to pay for the statue, which was unveiled on 29 October 1863. On 7 November the *Illustrated London News* reported: 'an intellectual expression has been produced, and the drapery and accessories, are elegant and graceful . . . The statue of the Queen has received the approval of several members of the Royal family'. Having secured the commission for Queen Victoria's statue, Todd wrote to Earle in April 1863 to suggest that 'with a little management' a commission for a statue of Prince Albert might be forthcoming 'as a companion' (Hull City Archives BHH 118/8). Earle's initial proposal, for placing a figure of Prince Albert on the same pedestal as the statue of the Queen, was rejected. He won approval for a replica of his statue of Prince Albert executed for the Licensed Victuallers' Asylum in Kennington (**102**). The Hull commission was again plagued by financial difficulties from the outset, but the statue of Albert was eventually unveiled on 14 October 1868.

Although Thomas Earle executed many portrait busts, few survive. His most ambitious and successful monument, to Thomas Ferres, has a life-sized figure of an angel supporting an exhausted seaman (**60**). A regular exhibitor at the Royal Academy and the British Institute, Earle had a passion for 'ideal' sculpture and his first work in the prestigious but often unremunerative genre was shown at the Academy in 1834, while he was still employed by Chantrey (**67**). In 1842 he exhibited the life-size relief, *Abel and Thirza* (**168**), which the *Art Union* considered 'a fine conception wrought out with much ability' (*AU*, 1842, 128). In 1844 he showed *An ancient Briton protecting his family* at Westminster Hall (**74**). The *Literary Gazette* maintained that 'nothing could surpass the arrangement and composition of the female and children, and the modelling of the young ones [is] most exquisite and masterly' (*Lit Gaz*, 1844, 483). When the work was exhibited the following year at the Leeds Polytechnic Exhibition it was described as 'a master-piece, worthy of any age or nation' a work that would 'ensure the artist a fame that will endure for ever' (*Leeds Polytechnic exhib cat*, 9 June, 1845, n p). Few of his ideal works were realised in marble, though the Earl of Yarborough commissioned two, *Happy as a queen* (**91**) and *Fisher boy* (**83**).

Thomas Earle was the last sculptor member of the Earle family and he died without issue in May 1876. He was interred at Spring Bank cemetery in Hull and since he was still considered a local celebrity, a large funeral procession paid tribute to the memory of the town's talented citizen. He is commemorated by a fine monument of his own workmanship at Holy Trinity, Hull (**65**).

His widow, Mary, sold some of the studio contents including a model of the Ferres monument (**60**), which went to Hull's Trinity House Seaman's Guild for £20. Several other works were donated to institutions including the South Kensington Museum (**93, 105**). Mary Earle was still in possession of numerous pieces (now lost) in 1881, which she loaned to the exhibition of works of local arts held at the Hull Temperance Club.

Gerardine Mulcahy

Literary References: *Jones's Mercantile Directory of the Shipping Port of Hull*, 1863–64; *Gunnis* 1968, 137–8; *Colvin* 1995, 327–8; *Mulcahy* 2000

Miscellaneous Drawings: *Original Sketches by Thos. Earle, Sculptor, of Hull*, Earle file, Hull Maritime Museum; these include a sketch of a foot 'from the Antique', (two versions, one signed); sketch of *The Wrestlers*; design for a medallion of a mother and two children; design for a church monument depicting a female mourning figure with a funerary urn; design for a church monument with a female mourning figure with flowing hair, and a draped funerary urn; design 'No. 4' for a church monument with a seated female mourning figure; design 'No. 5' for a church monument with a female mourning figure prostrate over a tomb chest (signed); design for a church monument featuring a semi-recumbent female figure with discarded book; design 'No. 81' for a church monument with two female mourning figures and a sarcophagus incorporating a portrait; design 'No. 38' for a church monument with two female mourning figures and a sarcophagus incorporating a portrait; *Faith supporting a rustic Cross*, design 'No 6' for a church monument (with dimensions and recommended materials) (*Mulcahy* 2000 (1), *passim*)

Portraits of the Sculptors: Anon, portrait of Thomas Earle, oil on canvas, nd., Wilberforce House Museum, Kingston-upon-Hull

Funerary Monuments

1.	†1740	Robert Pattinson (by John Earle I)	Easington, E R Yorks	S	*Mulcahy* 2000 (1), cat 6
2.	†1778	John Pease (by John Earle I)	St Mary Lowgate, Kingston-on-Hull, ER Yorks		*Mulcahy* 2000 (1), cat 5 (repr 4)
3.	†1803	John Helmsley (by George Earle I)	Bridlington Priory, E R Yorks	SD	*Mulcahy* 2000 (1), cat 2 (repr 1)
4.	†1808	Robert Pattinson (by John Earle I)	Easington, E R Yorks		*Mulcahy* 2000 (1), cat 7
5.	†1809	George Gibson (by John Earle I)	Sigglesthorne, E R Yorks	S	*Mulcahy* 2000 (1), cat 9 (repr 6)
6.	†1809	John Bell (by John Earle I)	Elstronwick, E R Yorks	S	*Mulcahy* 2000 (1), cat 8 (repr 5)
7.	†1810	Harriet Atty (by John Earle I)	Aswarby, Lincs	S	*Mulcahy* 2000 (1), cat 10 (repr 7)
8.	†1812	Henry Maister (by John Earle I)	Holy Trinity, Kingston-on-Hull, E R Yorks		*Mulcahy* 2000 (1), cat 11 (repr 8)
9.	†1812	William Corlass (by John Earle I)	Sculcoates, E R Yorks	S	*Mulcahy* 2000 (1), cat 12 (repr 9)
10.	†1813	John Rickaby (by John Earle I)	Bridlington, E R Yorks	S	*Mulcahy* 2000 (1), cat 13
11.	†1813	Thomas Harland (by Joseph Earle)	Bridlington Priory, E R Yorks	S	*Mulcahy* 2000 (1), cat 43 (repr 24)
12.	†1814	Rev Thomas Orme (by John Earle I)	St James, Louth, Lincs		*Mulcahy* 2000 (1), cat 14
13.	†1816	John Barker (by John Earle I)	St Mary, Kingston-on-Hull, E R Yorks		*Mulcahy* 2000 (1), cat 16 (repr 10)
14.	†1816	John Foster (by John Earle I)	North Cave, E R Yorks		*Mulcahy* 2000 (1), cat 17
15.	†1816	Thomas Owst (by John Earle I)	Halsham, E R Yorks	S	*Mulcahy* 2000 (1), cat 15
16.	†1819	John Emeris (by John Earle I)	St James, Louth, Lincs	S	*Mulcahy* 2000 (1), cat 18 (repr 11)
17.	†1819	Sir Henry Etherington and family (by John Earle I)	North Ferriby, E R Yorks	S	*Gunnis* 1968, 137; *Mulcahy* 2000 (1), 19 (repr 12)
18.	†1821	Thomas Grimston (by John Earle I)	Kilnwick-on-the-Wolds, E R Yorks		*Mulcahy* 2000 (1), cat 20
19.	†1822	Robert Holgate (by John Earle I)	Roxby, Lincs		*Mulcahy* 2000 (1), cat 21
20.	†1823	Richard Collinson (by John Earle I)	Sculcoates, E R Yorks		*Mulcahy* 2000 (1), cat 22
21.	†1824	William Haddesley (by John Earle I)	Hemingbrough, E R Yorks	S	Pevsner, *Yorks: E R & York*, 1995, 460; *Mulcahy* 2000 (1), cat 23 (repr 14)
22.	†1825	Richard Roadley (by George Earle II)	Searby, Lincs	S	*Mulcahy* 2000 (1), cat 49 (repr 26)
23.	†1828	Richard Dixon Roadley (by George Earle II)	Searby, Lincs	S	*Mulcahy* 2000 (1), cat 50 (repr 27)
24.	†1829	Simon Horner (by George Earle II)	Hutton Cranswick, E R Yorks	S	*Mulcahy* 2000 (1), cat 51 (repr 28, 29, 30)
25.	†1830	Rev Robert Todd (by John Earle I)	North Cave, E R Yorks	S	*Mulcahy* 2000 (1), cat 24
26.	†1830	Sir Henry Nelthorpe (by George Earle II)	Scawby, Lincs	S	*Mulcahy* 2000 (1), cat 52 (repr 31)
27.	†1831	George Green (by John Earle I)	Skipsea, E R Yorks	S	*Mulcahy* 2000 (1), cat 26
28.	†1831	Hugh Wright (by John Earle I)	Ottringham, E R Yorks	S	*Mulcahy* 2000 (1), cat 25 (repr 15)
29.	†1831	Jemima Dennis (by John Earle II)	Marfleet, E R Yorks	S	*Mulcahy* 2000 cat 42 (repr 23)
30.	†1832	John Storm (†1832) and 5 family members (by George Earle II)	Beverley Minster, E R Yorks	S	*Mulcahy* 2000 (1), cat 54
31.	†1832	Mr Sutcliffe (by Thomas Earle)	[Bolton Brow Methodist church, Sowerby, W R Yorks]; private coll	S	*Mulcahy* 2000 (1), cat 69 (repr 40)
32.	†1832	Nicholas Sykes and others (by George Earle II)	Kirk Ella, E R Yorks	S	*Mulcahy* 2000 (1), cat 53 (repr 32)
33.	†1833	Elizabeth Flavell (by George Earle II)	Barsham, Suffolk	S	*Mulcahy* 2000 (1), cat 55 (repr 33)
34.	†1833	Pearson Fox (by John Earle I)	Sculcoates, E R Yorks	S	*Mulcahy* 2000 (1), cat 27 (repr 16)
35.	†1834	Anthony Floyer and others (†1841) (by Joseph Earle)	South Ormsby, Lincs	S	*Mulcahy* 2000 (1), cat 44
36.	†1834	Horner Reynard (by George Earle II)	Hutton Cranswick, E R Yorks	S	*Mulcahy* 2000 (1), cat 56 (repr 34, 35)

No.	Date	Subject	Material	Location	Signed	Source
37.	†1835	Alice Whyte (by George Earle II)		Hotham, E R Yorks	S	*Mulcahy* 2000 (1), cat 57
38.	†1835	Mary Burland (by George Earle II)		South Cave, E R Yorks	S	*Mulcahy* 2000 (1), cat 58
39.	†1836	Henry Hutton (by George Earle II)		Cherry Willingham, Lincs	S	*Mulcahy* 2000 (1), cat 59
40.	†1836	William Dennis (by John Earle I)		Marfleet, Hull, E R Yorks	S	*Mulcahy* 2000 (1), cat 28
41.	†1837	Richard Parnell (by George Earle II)		Kelstern, Lincs	S	*Mulcahy* 2000 (1), cat 60
42.	†1838	George Lambert (by John Earle I)		Holy Trinity, Kingston-on-Hull, E R Yorks	S	*Mulcahy* 2000 (1), cat 29 (repr 17)
43.	†1838	Mary Howard Bell (by George Earle II)		Sutton, E R Yorks	S	*Mulcahy* 2000 (1), cat 61
44.	†1840	Bryan Taylor (by John Earle I)		Bridlington Priory, E R Yorks	S	*Mulcahy* 2000 (1), cat 30
45.	†1840	Sarah Parker (by Joseph Earle)		Rippingale, Lincs	S	*Mulcahy* 2000 (1), cat 45
46.	†1842	Ann Brankley (by John Earle I)		Humbleton, E R Yorks, churchyard	S	*Mulcahy* 2000 (1), cat 31 (repr 18)
47.	†1842	William Grantham (by Joseph Earle)		Scawby, Lincs	S	*Mulcahy* 2000 (1), cat 46 (repr 25)
48.	†1843	Isabella Owst (by John Earle I)		Halsham, E R Yorks	S	*Mulcahy* 2000 (1), cat 32
49.	†1843	Mary Bamford (by Thomas Earle)		Sculcoates, E R Yorks	S	*Mulcahy* 2000 (1), cat 70 (repr 41)
50.	†1844	John Belt (by John Earle I)		Humbleton, E R Yorks, churchyard	S	*Mulcahy* 2000 (1), cat 33
51.	*c*1845	Sir Robert Dundas (†1844) (by Thomas Earle) Drawing(s): Original sketches by Thos Earle, Sculptor, of Hull', SD 1845, (*Mulcahy* 2000, 214, repr 86)		Loftus, Cleveland	S	*Leeds Mercury*, 16 May 1846; *Mulcahy* 2000 (1), cat 71 (repr 42)
52.	†1846	Charles Wells (by John Earle I)		Marfleet, Hull, E R Yorks	S	*Mulcahy* 2000 (1), cat 35
53.	†1846	Elizabeth Pearson (by John Earle I)		[St Peter, Hull, E R Yorks, churchyard]; Drypool, E R Yorks	S	*Mulcahy* 2000 (1), cat 34 (repr 19)
54.	†1846	Sir Charles Anderson and his wife, Dame Francis Mary (†1836) (by George Earle II)		Lea, Lincs	S	*Mulcahy* 2000 (1), cat 63 (repr 36)
55.	†1848	Henry Carr (by John Earle I)		Elstronwick, E R Yorks	S	*Mulcahy* 2000 (1), cat 36
56.	†1849	James Brankley (by John Earle I)		Humbleton, E R Yorks, churchyard	S	*Mulcahy* 2000 (1), cat 37 (repr 20)
57.	†1850	Ann (†1834) and Thomas Earle (by George Earle II)		Holy Trinity, Hull, E R Yorks	S	*Mulcahy* 2000 (1), cat 48
58.	†1854	John Dennis (by John Earle I)		Marfleet, E R Yorks	S	*Mulcahy* 2000 (1), cat 38 (repr 21)
59.	†1858	John William Gray (by Thomas Earle) Drawing(s): 'Original sketches by Thos. Earle, Sculptor, of Hull' (*Mulcahy* 2000, 215, repr 87, 216, repr 88, 217) Model(s): 'part of a monument' exhib RA, London, 1865, 922		Holy Trinity, Kingston-on-Hull, E R Yorks	SD	*AJ*, 1865, 172; *Graves* II, 1905–6, 5; *Mulcahy* 2000 (1), cat 77 (repr 48)
60.	1859	Thomas Ferres (by Thomas Earle) Model(s): Trinity House Chapel, Kingston-upon-Hull, ER Yorks (*Mulcahy* 2000, 202)		Holy Trinity, Kingston-on-Hull, E R Yorks	SD	*Hull News*, 2 July 1859; *Mulcahy* 2000 (1), cat 72, 73, 202 (repr 44, 45)
61.	1860	Frank (†1850) and John (†1828) Appleyard (by Thomas Earle) Drawing(s): 'Original sketches by Thos Earle, Sculptor, of Hull (*Mulcahy* 2000, 218, repr 89)		Holy Trinity, Kingston-upon-Hull, E R Yorks	SD	Pevsner, *Yorks: E R & York*, 1995, 507; *Mulcahy* 2000 (1), 76 (repr 47)
62.	†1860	John Holmes (by Thomas Earle)		Sculcoates, E R Yorks	S	*Mulcahy* 2000 (1), cat 75
63.	1861	Charles Bamford (†1860) (by Thomas Earle) Drawing(s): Original sketches by Thos Earle, Sculptor, of Hull (*Mulcahy* 2000, cat 226 repr 97)		Sculcoates, E R Yorks	SD	*Mulcahy* 2000 (1), cat 74 (repr 46)
64.	†*c*1865	John Todd (by Thomas Earle)		Untraced		*Hull Advertiser*, 14 Oct, 1865; *Mulcahy* 2000 (1), cat 78
65.	†1876	Thomas Earle (the sculptor's own monument)		Holy Trinity, Kingston-on-Hull, E R Yorks	S	*Mulcahy* 2000 (1), cat 79 (repr 79)
Statues						
66.	1831	Dr John Alderson MD (by Thomas Earle)	s	City Hall, Kingston-on-Hull, E R Yorks		*GM*, May 1831, 456; *Mulcahy* 2000 (1), cat 188 (repr 64)
67.	1834	The age of innocence, group (by Thomas Earle)	p	[Exhib RA, London, 1114]; untraced		*Graves* II, 1905–6, 4; *Mulcahy* 2000 (1), cat 136
68.	1836	The minstrel boy, model (by Thomas Earle)		[Exhib RA, London, 1065]; untraced		*Graves* II, 1905–6, 4; *Mulcahy* 2000 (1), cat 137
69.	1839	Hercules delivering Hesione from the sea monster, group (by Thomas Earle)	p	[RA Schools, gold medal]; untraced		*Gunnis* 1968, 137; *Mulcahy* 2000 (1), cat 135
70.	1841	Child saying grace (by Thomas Earle)		[Exhib RA, London, 1291]; untraced		*Graves* II, 1905–6, 5; *Mulcahy* 2000 (1), cat 140
71.	1841	Pyramus and Thisbe, model (by Thomas Earle)		[Exhib RA, London, 1292]; untraced		*Graves* II, 1905–6, 5; *Mulcahy* 2000 (1), cat 141
72.	1843	'A sketch in clay' (by Thomas Earle)		[Exhib BI, 440]; untraced		*Graves* 1875, 173; *Mulcahy* 2000 (1), cat 143
73.	1843	Miss Todd (by Thomas Earle)	m	[Tranby Park, E R Yorks; sold 25 April 1949, lot 253]; untraced		*Graves* II, 1905–6, 5; *Mulcahy* 2000 (1), cat 87
74.	1844	An ancient Briton protecting his family (by Thomas Earle)		[Cottingham House, E R Yorks]; untraced		*AU*, 1844, 216; *Mulcahy* 2000 (1), cat 144

75.	1844	Edward I presenting the first Prince of Wales (by Thomas Earle)		[Cottingham House, E R Yorks]; untraced		*Gunnis* 1968, 137; *Mulcahy* 2000 (1), cat 145
76.	1844	The morning ablution, group, model (by Thomas Earle)	p	[Exhib RA, London, 1304]; untraced		*Graves* 1875, 173; *Graves* II, 1905–6, 5; *Gunnis* 1968, 137; *Mulcahy* 2000, cat 151
77.	1845	Sin triumphant, group (by Thomas Earle)	p	[Exhib Westminster Hall, London, 138]; untraced Other versions: Manchester Institute, 1857; untraced		*Westminster* 1845, 16; *AU*, 1845, 258; *Graves* 1875, 173; *Gunnis* 1968, 137; *Mulcahy* 2000, cat 150
78.	1845	The infant Christ bruising the head of the serpent (by Thomas Earle)		[Exhib BI, London, 517]; untraced		*Graves* 1875, 5
79.	1847	Cupid rejected, model (by Thomas Earle)		[Exhib BI, 554]; untraced		*Graves* 1875, 173; *Mulcahy* 2000 (1), cat 155
80.	1847	Genius receiving the award of merit (by Thomas Earle)		[Hull Central Museum, E R Yorks]; destroyed		*Graves* II, 1905–6, 5; *Gunnis* 1968, 137
81.	1847	Pastorella (by Thomas Earle)	m	[Exhib RA, London, 1333]; untraced Other versions: marble, under life-size, exhib BI 1848 (496)		*Graves* 1875, 468; *Graves* II, 1905–6, 5; *Gunnis* 1968, 138
82.	1847	Zephyr and Aurora, group (by Thomas Earle)	p	[Exhib RA, London, 1325]; untraced		*Graves* II, 1905–6, 5; *Mulcahy* 2000 (1), cat 154
83.	post-1848	Fisher boy (by Thomas Earle) Drawing(s): 'Original Sketches by Thos Earle, Sculptor, of Hull', nd, (*Mulcahy* 2000, 209, repr 78)	m	Brocklesby Park, Lincs Other versions: another, model, exhib RA 1848 (1368)		*Mulcahy* 2000 (1), cat 157, 158 (repr 58)
84.	1848	Ophelia, model (by Thomas Earle)		[Exhib RA, London, 1848, 1343]; untraced		*Graves* II, 1905–6, 5; *Gunnis* 1968, 138; *Mulcahy* 2000 (1), cat 156
85.	1849	Musidora (by Thomas Earle)	m	[Exhib BI, 518]; untraced		*Graves* 1875, 173; *Mulcahy* 2000 (1), cat 160
86.	1849	Sylvia and the wounded fawn, model (by Thomas Earle)		[Exhib RA, London, 1212]; untraced		*Graves* II, 1905–6, 5; *Mulcahy* 2000 (1), cat 159
87.	1850	Hindoo girl testing the fate of her lover, model (by Thomas Earle)		[Exhib BI, London, 491]; untraced		*Graves* 1875, 173
88.	1850	L'Allegro, model (by Thomas Earle) Model(s): exhib RA, London, 1852 (1318); untraced		[Exhib BI, London, 496]; untraced		*Graves* 1875, 173; *Graves* II, 1905–6, 5; *Mulcahy* 2000 (1), cat 164
89.	1850	Nature's mirror, model (by Thomas Earle)		[Exhib RA, London, 1850, 1339]; untraced Other versions: Exhib BI, London, 1852, 532		*Graves* 1875, 173; *Graves* II, 1905–6, 5
90.	1851	Jacob and Rachel, model (by Thomas Earle) Drawing(s): Two, 'Original sketches of Thos Earle, Sculptor, of Hull' (*Mulcahy* 2000, cat 212, 213, repr 81, 82)		[Gt Exhib, 1851, main hall]; untraced		*AJ Cat* 1851, 248 (repr); *Mulcahy* 2000 (1), cat 163
91.	1853	Happy as a queen (by Thomas Earle)	m	Brocklesby Park, Lincs Other versions: Exhib RA, London, 1858, 1188		*Graves* II, 1905–6, 5; *Gunnis* 1968, 138; *Mulcahy* 2000 (1), repr 61
92.	1853	Il Penseroso, model (by Thomas Earle)		[Exhib BI, London, 585]; untraced		*Graves* 1875, 173; *Mulcahy* 2000 (1), cat 165
93.	1854	Hyacinthus (by Thomas Earle)	p	VAM 383-1876	SD	*Graves* II, 1905–6, 5; *Mulcahy* 2000 (1), cat 167 (repr 60); *Bilbey* 2002, 255–6 (repr)
94.	1854	'small models for monuments to the late Duke of Wellington. . . Ditto ditto Equestrian' (by Thomas Earle)		[Exhib BI 1854, 585]; untraced		*Graves* 1875, 173; *Mulcahy* 2000 (1), cat 192, 193
95.	1856	Cinderella, model (by Thomas Earle) Drawing(s): Two, 'Original Sketches by Thos Earle, Sculptor, of Hull' (*Mulcahy* 2000, 210, 211, repr 79, 80)		[Exhib RA, London, 1262]; untraced		*Graves* II, 1905–6, 5; *Mulcahy* 2000 (1), cat 168
96.	1857	Titania (by Thomas Earle)		[Exhib RA, London, 1219]; untraced Other versions: Replicated in plaster		*Graves* 1875, 173; *Graves* II, 1905–6, 5; *Mulcahy* 2000 (1), cat 170
97.	1859	The first lesson (by Thomas Earle)		[Exhib RA, London, 1267]; untraced		*Graves* II, 1905–6, 5; *Mulcahy* 2000 (1), cat 172
98.	1860	A first dip (by Thomas Earle) Payment(s): £150	m	[Exhib BI, 638]; untraced Other versions: Duplicated in plaster at £10		*Graves* 1875, 173; *Graves* II, 1905–6, 5; *Mulcahy* 2000 (1), cat 173
99.	c1860	King Harold, model, for the Mansion House, City of London (by Thomas Earle)		Untraced		*Mulcahy* 2000 (1), cat 199
100.	1861	The novice (by Thomas Earle) Payment(s): £200	m	[Exhib BI, 638]; untraced Other versions: Duplicates in plaster (£20)		*Graves* 1875, 375; *Mulcahy* 2000 (1), cat 174
101.	1862	Hope (by Thomas Earle) Payment(s): £35		[Exhib BI, 644]; untraced		*Graves* 1875, 173; *Mulcahy* 2000 (1), cat 175

No.	Date	Subject		Location		Literature
102.	1863	Albert, the Prince Consort (by Thomas Earle)	m	[Licensed Victuallers' Asylum, Kennington]; Licensed Victuallers' Asylum, Denham, Bucks Other versions: Pearson Park, Kingston-on-Hull, E R Yorks, 1868		*ILN*, 28 March 1863, 358; 13 Aug 1864, 102; 20 Aug 1864, 119, 121 (repr); *Ormond* 1973, 14; *Blackwood* 1989, 60 (repr); *Mulcahy* 2000 (1), cat 196 (repr 67), 197
103.	1863	Queen Victoria (by Thomas Earle)	m	Pearson Park, Kingston-on-Hull, E R Yorks		*ILN*, 28 March 1863, 259, 358; 7 Nov 1863, 335; *Ormond* 1973, 489; *Mulcahy* 2000 (1), cat 194 (repr 65), 195
104.	1866	King Edward I (by Thomas Earle)	m	Guildhall, Kingston-on-Hull, E R Yorks		*Graves* II, 1905–6, 5; *Mulcahy* 2000 (1), 200 (repr 71), 201
105.	1866	Miranda (by Thomas Earle)	p	[Exhib RA, London, 900]; VAM 332-1876		*Graves* II, 1905–6, 5; *Mulcahy* 2000 (1), cat 176 (repr 63); *Bilbey* 2002, 256 (repr)
106.	1873	Flower-girl of Capri (by Thomas Earle)		[Exhib RA, London, 1518]; untraced		*Graves* II, 1905–6, 5; *Mulcahy* 2000 (1), cat 182
107.	1873–1876	Alexander the Great (by Thomas Earle)	m	Untraced		*Gunnis* 1968, 137
108.	nd	A girl at prayer (by Thomas Earle)		Untraced		*Mulcahy* 2000 (1), cat 179
109.	nd	Alexander before mounting Bucephalus (by Thomas Earle)		[Hull Central Museum, E R Yorks]; Destroyed		*Gunnis* 1968, 137
110.	nd	Andrew Marvell, with a pedestal, small model 'intended to be erected in Hull, much larger than life' (by Thomas Earle)		[Exhib Hull Temperance Club of the Works of Local Arts, 1881, 110a]; untraced		*Mulcahy* 2000 (1), cat 203
111.	nd	Design for a monument to Horatio, Lord Nelson and three allegorical figures, small models (by Thomas Earle)		Untraced		*Mulcahy* 2000 (1), cat 189
112.	nd	Eve, model (by Thomas Earle)		Untraced		*Mulcahy* 2000 (1), cat 178
113.	nd	The late Sir Robert Peel, with a pedestal, statuette (by Thomas Earle)		Untraced		*Mulcahy* 2000 (1), cat 190, 191
114.	nd	Titania and the bullrush (by Thomas Earle)		[Exhib Hull Temperance Club Exhib of the Works of Local Arts, 109a]; untraced		*Mulcahy* 2000 (1), cat 184
Busts						
115.	*c*1827	Daniel Sykes MP (by George Earle II)		[Exhib Hull and E R Institution for the Promotion of the Fine Arts, 251]; untraced		*Mulcahy* 2000 (1), cat 65
116.	*c*1827	Dr John Alderson M D (by George Earle II)	p	[Exhib Hull and E R Institution for the Promotion of the Fine Arts, 251]; untraced		*Mulcahy* 2000 (1), cat 64
117.	1829	John Earle, architect, 'taken from life' (by Thomas Earle)		[Second exhib of the Hull and E R Institution for the Promotion of Fine Arts, 226]; untraced		*Graves* II, 1905–6, 5; *Mulcahy* 2000 (1), cat 80
118.	1835	'a Boy's head from Nature' (by Thomas Earle)		[Exhib RA, London, 1129]; untraced		*Graves* II, 1905–6, 4; *Mulcahy* 2000 (1), cat 85
119.	1837	James Brothers (by Thomas Earle)		[Exhib RA, London, 1265]; untraced		*Graves* II, 1905–6, 4; *Mulcahy* 2000 (1), cat 85
120.	1839	Charles Roberts (by Thomas Earle)		[Exhib RA, London, 1373]; untraced		*Graves* II, 1905–6, 4; *Mulcahy* 2000 (1), cat 83
121.	1842	Thomas Watson (by Thomas Earle)	m	[Exhib RA, London, 1372]; untraced		*Graves* II, 1905–6, 5; *Mulcahy* 2000 (1), cat 84
122.	1843	John Todd (by Thomas Earle)	m	[Exhib RA, London, 1477; Wilson Todd, Anderson, Garland sale, 25 April 1949, lot 251]; untraced		*Graves* II, 1905–6, 5; *Gunnis* 1968, 138
123.	1843	Mrs Todd (by Thomas Earle)	m	[Exhib RA, 1843, 1503; Wilson Todd, Anderson, Garland sale, 25 April 1949, lot 252]; untraced		*Graves* II, 1905–6, 5; *Mulcahy* 2000 (1), cat 86
124.	1844	A gentleman (by Thomas Earle)		[Exhib RA, London, 1356]; untraced		*Graves* II, 1905–6, 5; *Mulcahy* 2000 (1), cat 88
125.	1845	George Haines of Kensington, model (by Thomas Earle)		[Exhib RA, London, 1399]; untraced		*Graves* II, 1905–6, 5; *Mulcahy* 2000 (1), cat 92
126.	1845	Richard, Baron Westbury (by Thomas Earle)	m	[Rise Hall, E R Yorks]; untraced		*Graves* II, 1905–6, 5; *Ormond* 1973, 501
127.	1845	Unidentified gentleman (by Thomas Earle)		[Leeds Third Polytechnic exhib, no 105]; untraced		*Mulcahy* 2000, cat 91
128.	1846	Lawrence, 1st Earl of Thomas, 2nd Earl of Zetland (by Thomas Earle)	p	Minerva lodge, Kingston-on-Hull, E R Yorks		*Graves* II, 1905–6, 5; *Gunnis* 1968, 138
129.	*c*1847	Alderman Thomas Thompson (by Thomas Earle)	m	[Plaster exhib RA, London, 1847, 1441]; Guildhall, Kingston-on-Hull, E R Yorks	S	*Hull Advertiser*, 21 Nov 1845; *Graves* II, 1905–6, 5; *Mulcahy* 2000 (1), cat 98 (repr); cat 99
130.	1847	Joseph Bates of Leeds (by Thomas Earle)	p	[Exhib RA, London, 1433]; untraced		*Graves* II, 1905–6, 5; *Mulcahy* 2000 (1), cat 95
131.	1847	Mrs J Bates of Leeds (by Thomas Earle)	p	[Exhib RA, London, 1351]; untraced		*Graves* II, 1905–6, 5; *Mulcahy* 2000 (1), cat 96
132.	1847	Thomas English (by Thomas Earle)	m	[Exhib RA, London, 1412]; untraced		*AU*, 1847, 200; *Sheahan*, 1868, 740; *Graves* II, 1905–6, 5; *Mulcahy* 2000 (1), cat 97

No.	Date	Subject	Medium	Location		Literature
133.	1848	Charles, 1st Earl of Yarborough (by Thomas Earle)	p	[Exhib RA, London, 1390]; Minerva lodge, Kingston-on-Hull, E R Yorks Other versions: ex Humber Minerva Masonic Lodge; destroyed		*Graves* II, 1905–6, 5; *Mulcahy* 2000 (1), cat 100 (repr); 101
134.	1849	Head of a girl, probably Ophelia (by Thomas Earle)	m	Ferens Art Gall, Kingston-on-Hull, E R Yorks, acc S110	SD	*Graves* 1875, 173; *Mulcahy* 2000 (1), 130 (repr 57)
135.	1850	George Walker of Killingbeck Hall, Leeds (by Thomas Earle)		[Exhib RA, London, 1374]; untraced		*Graves* II, 1905–6, 5; *Mulcahy* 2000 (1), cat 105
136.	1850	J B Pyne (by Thomas Earle)	m	[Exhib RA, London, 1370]; untraced		*Graves* II, 1905–6, 5; *Mulcahy* 2000 (1), cat 104
137.	1851	Frank Appleyard, two (by Thomas Earle)	p	[Exhib RA, London, 1355]; Minerva lodge, Kingston-on-Hull, E R Yorks Other versions: marble exhib RA, London, 1860, 983		*Graves* II, 1905–6, 5; *Mulcahy* 2000 (1), cat 106 (repr 54); 107 (repr 55); 108
138.	1853	W J Fox MP (by Thomas Earle)		[Exhib RA, London, 1392]; untraced		*Graves* II, 1905–6, 5; *Mulcahy* 2000 (1), cat 109
139.	1854	Andrew Marvell (by Thomas Earle)	p	[Exhib RA, London, 1487]; Wilberforce House, Kingston-on-Hull, E R Yorks		*Graves* II, 1905–6, 5; *Mulcahy* 2000 (1), cat 133
140.	1854	Rt Hon Thomas Sidney, Lord Mayor (by Thomas Earle)	m	[coll Mrs Sidney]; untraced		*Graves* II, 1905–6, 5; *Mulcahy* 2000 (1), cat 110
141.	1856	Mrs Wilson (by Thomas Earle)	m	[Exhib RA, London, 1333]; untraced		*Graves* II, 1905–6, 5; *Mulcahy* 2000 (1), cat 112
142.	1856	Samuel Warren MP (by Thomas Earle)		[Exhib RA, London, 1322]; untraced		*Graves* II, 1905–6, 5; *Mulcahy* 2000 (1), cat 111
143.	1859	Desire (by Thomas Earle) Payment(s): 30 gns	m	[Exhib BI, 590]; untraced		*Graves* 1875, 173; *Mulcahy* 2000 (1), cat 134
144.	1860	T S Neall (by Thomas Earle)	m	[Exhib RA, London, 1014]; untraced		*Graves* II, 1905–6, 5; *Mulcahy* 2000 (1), cat 113
145.	c1860	Z C Pearson, model (by Thomas Earle)	tc	Untraced		*Hull Advertiser*, 6 Oct 1860; *Mulcahy* 2000 (1), cat 121
146.	1861	Queen Victoria (by Thomas Earle)	m	Buckingham Palace RCIN 2069 Other versions: Sculptor's studio, 1876; untraced	SD	*AJ*, 6 May 1876, 236; *Graves* II, 1905–6, 5; *Ormond* 1973, 488
147.	c1862	Henry Blundell JP (by Thomas Earle)	m	[Brunswick House, Hull]; untraced		*Graves* II, 1905–6, 5; *Mulcahy* 2000 (1), cat 116
148.	1862	William Crosskill (by Thomas Earle)	m	County Hall, Beverley, E R Yorks		*Graves* II, 1905–6, 5; *Mulcahy* 2000 (1), cat 117
149.	c1865	Richard Thornton (by Thomas Earle)		Untraced		*Hull and Lincs Times*, 14 Oct 1865; *Mulcahy* 2000 (1), cat 120
150.	1867	Thomas Pridgin Teale FRS (by Thomas Earle)	m	[Leeds General Infirmary, W R Yorks]; LMG, W R Yorks Other versions: exhib RA, London, 1849, 1310	SD	*Graves* II, 1905–6, 5; *Mulcahy* 2000 (1), cat 103 (repr 53)
151.	1869	James Fullam (by Thomas Earle)		[Exhib RA, London, 1158]; untraced		*Graves* II, 1905–6, 5; *Mulcahy* 2000 (1), cat 118
152.	nd	Albert, the Prince Consort (by Thomas Earle)		[Hull Temperance Club Exhib of Local Arts, 112]; untraced		*Mulcahy* 2000 (1), cat 123
153.	nd	C S Todd (by Thomas Earle)		[Hull Temperance Club Exhib of Works of Local Arts, 113]; untraced		*Mulcahy* 2000 (1), cat 124
154.	nd	Charles, 2nd or 3rd Earl of Yarborough (by Thomas Earle)		[Hull Temperance Club Exhib of Works of Local Arts, 118]; untraced		*Mulcahy* 2000 (1), cat 127
155.	nd	J V Thompson (by Thomas Earle)		[Mechanics Institute, Hull]; untraced		*Mulcahy* 2000 (1), cat 119
156.	nd	'Portrait bust of a child' (by Thomas Earle)		[Hull Temperance Club Exhib of Works of Local Arts, 114]; untraced		*Mulcahy* 2000 (1), cat 125
157.	nd	'Portrait of a child' (by Thomas Earle)		[Hull Temperance Club Exhib of Local Arts, 115]; untraced		*Mulcahy* 2000 (1), cat 126
158.	nd	Unidentified female (by Thomas Earle)	m	[Halnaby Hall, Croft, N R Yorks; sold Wilson Todd, Anderson, Garland, 25 April 1949, lot 254]; untraced		*Mulcahy* 2000 (1), cat 129
159.	nd	Unidentified male (by Thomas Earle)	m	[Halnaby Hall, Croft, N R Yorks; Wilson Todd, Anderson, Garland sale, 25 April 1949, lot 254]; untraced		*Mulcahy* 2000 (1), cat 128

Chimneypieces

No.	Date	Subject	Medium	Location		Literature
160.	1827	Several		[Redbourne Hall, Lincs]; destroyed		Lincs City Archive 2 RED 4/4/14; *Mulcahy* 2000, cat 4
161.	1827	Several (by John Earle I)		[Redbourne Hall, Lincs]; destroyed		*Mulcahy* 2000 (1) cat 4
162.	1834	Surround (by George Earle II)	m	Burton Constable Hall, E R Yorks, blue drawing room		E R archives Office DDCC2/66; *Mulcahy* 2000 (1), cat 47

Architectural Sculpture

No.	Date	Subject	Medium	Location		Literature
163.	1822	Trophy of arms (by John Earle I)		Roland House (previously Ferrens Hospital), Kingston-on-Hull, E R Yorks		*Mulcahy* 2000, cat 3 (repr 2)
164.	1829	Sea and river gods with emblems of commerce (by Thomas Earle)		[Smith Bank, Whitefriargate, Hull, pediment]; Over 'Poundstretcher' shop, Whitefriargate, Kingston-on-Hull, E R Yorks, pediment		*Mulcahy* 2000 (1), cat 66 (repr 38)
165.	1831	Oceanus reclining (by Thomas Earle)		[Trinity Almshouse, Hull, E R Yorks, postern gate]; Trinity House Courtyard, Kingston-on-Hull, E R Yorks, Posterngate		*Mulcahy* 2000 (1), cat 67 (repr 39)
166.	nd	Justice and Mercy (by Thomas Earle)		[Mansion House, Hull]; destroyed		*Mulcahy* 2000 (1), cat 68

Reliefs

167.	1838	Maternal instruction (by Thomas Earle)		[Exhib RA, London, 1268]; untraced		*Graves* II, 1905–6, 4; *Mulcahy* 2000 (1), cat 138
168.	1840	Abel and Thirza, group, model (by Thomas Earle)		[Exhib RA, London, 1192]; untraced Other versions: Exhib RA, London, 1842 (1283)		*Westminster* 1845, 16; *Graves* II, 1905–6, 4; *Mulcahy* 2000 (1), cat 139
169.	1845	A gentleman, portrait in a gold frame (by Thomas Earle)		[Leeds Third Polytechnic Exhib, 45, coll Thomas Eagland]; untraced		*Mulcahy* 2000 (1), cat 89
170.	nd	Britannia rewarding Industry, model for a medal (by Thomas Earle)		Untraced		*Mulcahy* 2000 (1), cat 186
171.	nd	Grace before meat (by Thomas Earle)		Untraced		*Mulcahy* 2000 (1), cat 177
172.	nd	Morning, 'after Thorwaldsen' (by Thomas Earle)		[Humber Masonic Lodge, Hull, E R Yorks]; destroyed		*Shaw* 1935, 174; *Mulcahy* 2000 (1), cat 181
173.	nd	Night and day, 'after Thorwaldsen' (by Thomas Earle)		[Humber Masonic Lodge, Hull, E R Yorks]; destroyed		*Shaw* 1935, 174; *Mulcahy* 2000 (1), cat 180
174.	nd	Peace descending, model for a medal (by Thomas Earle)		Untraced		*Mulcahy* 2000 (1), cat 185
175.	nd	Poetry inciting Sculpture, model for a medal (by Thomas Earle)		Untraced		*Mulcahy* 2000 (1), cat 187
176.	nd	Sir Francis Chantrey, 'miniature medallion portrait' (by Thomas Earle)	w	[High Hazels Museum, Sheffield, W R Yorks]; untraced		*Hoole*, 1925, 45; *Mulcahy* 2000 (1), cat 122

EARLEY, John *c*1743–

In 1762 he won a premium from the Society of Arts in the under-19 class (1). He was then living in Datchet, Herts. Gunnis says that he modelled a number of tablets for chimneypieces.

Literary References: *Dossie* 1782, 437; *Gunnis* 1968, 138

Archival References: RSA Minutes, seq 3, f 64

Miscellaneous

1.	1762	Ornamental festoon in clay		[Soc of A premium, 7 gns]; untraced		RSA *Minutes*, seq 3, f 64

EARLEY (or EARLY), Thomas fl 1764

He was presumably a brother of **John Earley**. Gunnis states that he was awarded a prize by the Society of Artists for a model of *Neptune* when he was under 19, and on 18 May 1764 he won a premium from the Society of Arts in the under-25 class (**2**, **1**). At that time he resided 'at Mr Carter, Statuary, Hyde Park Corner' (RSA *Premiums*, 1763, 37).

Literary References: *Gunnis* 1968, 138

Miscellaneous

1.	1764	Model in clay		[Soc of A premium, 15 gns]; untraced		RSA *Minutes*, 1763–64, seq 3 f 83; RSA *Premiums*, 1763, 37
2.	nd	Neptune, model		[Soc of Artists, premium]; untraced		*Gunnis* 1968, 138

EARLSMAN, Edward fl 1713

Architectural Sculpture

1.	1713	Urns and a mitre		Salisbury Cathedral, Wilts		Salisbury Cathedral archives, cited by *Gunnis* 1968, 138

EARLSMAN, Richard I, of Salisbury fl 1737–50

He was the son of **Edward Earlsman** and the father of **Richard Earlsman II**. He was employed at Longford Castle between 1737 and 1750, receiving £8 for 'ye carving over ye green damask door', in 1742 and £16 for 'several ornaments' in 1750 (1).

Literary References: *Gunnis* 1968, 138

Architectural Sculpture

1.	1737–1750	Wood and stone carving		Longford Castle, Wilts		*Gunnis* 1968, 138

EARLSMAN, Richard II, of Salisbury 1745–1831

The son of **Richard Earlsman I**, he was apprenticed to Martin Moatyard, of Bryanston, Dorset, a carver, in 1762 (TNA IR 23/49, cited by RG/JP, 3, 464). Like his father he was employed as a mason at Longford Castle between 1776 and 1792, and in 1796 he was working as a stone-carver at Salisbury Cathedral. He died in 1831 and is buried in St Martin, Salisbury.

Literary References: *Gunnis* 1968, 138

Funerary Monuments

1.	?1786	Sir Alexander and Lady Powell		St Thomas, Salisbury, Wilts	S	*Gunnis* 1968, 138
2.	?1792	Samuel Foot		Berwick St John, Wilts	S	*Gunnis* 1968, 138
3.	?1795	Edward Doyle		All Saints, Colchester, Essex	S	*Gunnis* 1968, 138
4.	?1807	Philip Pinchnay		Berwick St John, Wilts	S	*Gunnis* 1968, 138

Architectural Sculpture

5.	1796	Stone carving		Salisbury Cathedral, Wilts		*Gunnis* 1968, 138

EARNELL, of Wisbech fl 1758–59

He was listed as 'Farnell' in the first edition of Gunnis's *Dictionary of British Sculptors*, but the monument to Nicholas Wildman at Long Sutton is signed 'Earnell (1) (Inf. Edmund Esdaile).

Literary References: *Gunnis* 1953, 143

Archival References: GPC

Funerary Monuments

1.	?1758	Nicholas Wildman		Long Sutton, Lincs	S	GPC
2.	†1759	Thomas Whitwell		Peterborough Cathedral, Northants		*Gunnis* 1953, 143

EARP, Thomas 1828–93

A stone carver who specialised in gothic architectural decoration and church fittings. He was born and brought up in Nottingham and moved to London to work for George Myers, a building contractor, in 1848. In 1850, while still employed by Myers, he carved an effigy of Father Charles Pratt (†1849) for the Roman Catholic church of Saint Marie in Sheffield, Yorkshire. The vast majority of Earp's work was produced during the second half of the nineteenth-century, after he established his own business in Lambeth, and falls outside the scope of this book.

Literary References: *Read* 1982, 246, 248, 250; *Mitchell* 1990, *passim*

Archival References: RG/JP, suppl 3

EASTON, Charles –1786

The son of **Robert Easton I**, he became free of the Masons' Company by redemption in 1728, upper warden in 1753 and master the following year. By about 1740 he had premises in Eastcheap, an address which he shared with another Easton family member (Masons' Co, *Assistants*, fol 3, *c*1740). He was apparently still there in 1763 when 'Easton', a mason at Eastcheap, was listed in Mortimer's *Universal Director*. Easton was mason to the Fishmongers' Company in 1740–2 and 1745–6, in succession to his father. He was responsible for building the original hospital of St Luke, Old Street, in 1751 (Hospital Archives, in GPC) and in 1752 carried out repairs to St Mary Woolnoth (Guildhall MS 7653, in GPC). Between 1762 and 1780 he served as City mason and in this capacity was employed on repairs to the Mansion House between 1762 and 1777. His death on 14 June 1786 is noted in the Court Book of the Masons' Company.

Literary References: *Mortimer* 1763, 49; *Gunnis* 1968, 138; *Metcalfe* 1977, 100–2

Archival References: Masons' Co, Court Book, 1751–96 (14 June 1786); Freemen, fol 16 (6 December 1728); Fishmongers P W Accts, 6, pp 45–6, 55–58, 90, 124, 160, 190, 228, 260, 298

Funerary Monuments

1.	?1722	Rev G Morton	St Margaret, Lothbury, London	S	*Gunnis* 1968, 138
2.	†1722	Thomas (†1714) and George Lewis	[All Hallows, Lombard St, London]; All Hallows, Twickenham, Middx	S	*Gunnis* 1968, 138
3.	†1726	Richard Ansell	Ickleford, Herts	S	*Gunnis* 1968, 138
4.	1736	Richard Watts (†1579) Payment(s): £50	Rochester Cathedral, Kent		*Friedman* 1984, 266–7, 348 n 43 (repr)
5.	†1771	Ennis and Margaret Read (†1745)	St Peter of the Alley, Vere, Jamaica	S	

EASTON, Robert I –*c*1725

Gunnis states that Easton was apprenticed to Charles Cotton, citizen and farrier, in 1692 and was turned over to James Paget, citizen and mason, becoming free in 1704 (GPC). The Masons' Company records indicate that he was in fact granted the freedom of the Company on 18 April 1705 (Masons' Co, Freemen, fol 16). By 1708 he had a yard in Bow Street, Covent Garden.

Easton was mason to the Fishmongers' Company, for whom he carved a marble statue of James Hulbert, erected at the Company's almshouses in Southwark in 1724 (**2**). Hulbert was prime warden of the Company when he died in 1719, leaving a considerable sum to fund an extension to the almshouses and provide for the needs of the 20 poor persons dwelling there. Two payments relating to the statue appear in the prime warden's account books under the general heading 'Payment for Repairation and Building at this Company's Hall & at St Peter's Almshouses at Newington'. The first, made between 1722 and 1724, details: 'Paid Robert Easton Mason in parte of the Effigie of Mr. Hulbert to be set upp in the New Square the Sum of £80' (Fishmongers P W Accts, 4, 233). The second, dating between 1724 and 1726 states: 'Paid the widow Easton in full of the Company's agreemt with her late Husband for the Marble Effigies of the late Mr. Hulbert – Set up in the Square there the Summ £102 – 10s.' In 1723 Skeat & Company were paid £41 for 'ironwork set round Mr Hulberts Effigies'. Easton was also paid for general mason's work at Newington (Fishmongers PW, pp 233–4; 5, p 16).

The almshouses were 'altogether a neat and imposing pile' consisting of three courts with gardens behind, a dining hall and a chapel surrounded by a low parapet wall (*Herbert* 1837, cited by *Ward-Jackson* 2003, 111). Hulbert's statue, which Gunnis describes as 'a fine work showing Hulbert . . . in contemporary costume', was erected in the courtyard which he had endowed. The almshouses were pulled down in 1851 but the statue remained at Newington Butts until 1923, when it was taken to another of the Company's almshouses, the Jesus Hospital at Bray, Berks. The lettering on the pedestal, including the sculptor's signature, was probably recut at that time since the signature now appears as 'Daston'. The statue was brought from Bray to London and erected behind the Company's Hall in 1978.

Easton's widow, Mary, continued the business after her husband's death taking on a number of apprentices in the years that followed. Gunnis notes that Robert Green was apprenticed to her in 1727 and the Masons' Company records show that Henry Daintry and Thomas Evans, who both became free in October 1737, and Thomas Morris, who was freed in December 1741, were also apprenticed to her (Masons' Co, Freemen, fols 13, 16, 45). Robert's sons, **Charles** and **Thomas Easton**, also worked as masons.

Literary References: *Gunnis* 1968, 138–9; *Ward-Jackson* 2003, 111–2

Funerary Monuments

1.	?1721	James Marriott		Hampton, Middx	GPC

Statues

2.	1724	James Hulbert Payment(s): £80; £102 10s	m	[St Peter's Hospital, Newington]; Fishmongers' Hall, City of London, courtyard	*Blackwood* 1989, 86 (repr); *Ward-Jackson* 2003, 111–2 (repr)

EASTON, Robert II fl 1756–63

The son of **Thomas Easton**, he was apprenticed to his uncle, **Charles Easton** in 1756. He became free of the Masons' Company in 1763.

Archival References: Masons' Co, Apprentices, 1756; Freemen, 1763

EASTON, Thomas 1704–

The son of **Robert Easton** and brother of **Charles Easton**, he was apprenticed to **Bartholomew Wolfe** in 1718 and turned over to his father in 1722. He was made free in March 1725/6, 'Mary Easton the widow Testifying for his Service', and he set up for himself 'against the Weig House in Little East Cheap' (Masons' Co, Freemen, fol 16, 4 March 1725; Court Book, 1722–51, 14 March 1725/6). In 1756 Thomas's son, Robert Easton II, was apprenticed to his uncle Charles Easton, which suggests that Thomas was dead before that date (Masons' Co, Apprentices, 1756).

Literary References: *Gunnis* 1968, 139

Funerary Monuments

1.	†1733	Sir Edward Bettenson	Chislehurst, Kent	S	Pevsner, *London: S*, 1983, 177

ECKFORD, C J fl 1835

He was paid £391 12s 6d for his work as a carver and gilder at the new Goldsmiths' Hall in 1835. This sum was largely for repairing and regilding frames for doors, mirrors and pictures.

Archival References: Goldsmiths CB, bk 18, 611; Goldsmiths, Abstract, E.1.2.a 48 ff

ECKSTEIN, George Paul 1739–1828

Born at Poppenreuth in Germany, the seventh son of Conrad Eckstein, a woodcarver and cabinet-maker, he was the younger brother of **John Eckstein**. He left for the Hague in 1760 and five years later went to London, where he settled in Marylebone. In 1770 he married Ann Mitchell in Faversham church. The two elder children of their family of 12 were born at Ospringe, Kent, and the others in London.

Eckstein exhibited at the Royal Academy from 1777 to 1801, showing several reliefs in marble and wax and also models of animals. In 1777 he gave his address as 'Green Man, Berwick Street' (*Graves* 1905–6, 3, 13) and in November 1783 the couple christened their son, George Frederick Eckstein, at St Andrew, Holborn. The RA exhibition catalogue records that in 1798 the Ecksteins were living at 41 Tash Street, near Gray's Inn Lane, where, according to J T Smith, Eckstein kept a public house at 'the sign of the Goat and Star' (*Smith* 1828, 1, 179). Eckstein's nephew, John Eckstein the Younger, exhibited his paintings from this address in 1787, so it can be assumed that the family lived at the public house from that date and perhaps earlier.

In about 1775 he carved two greyhounds in Portland stone for Ashburnham House in Dover Street (1). A terracotta statuette of Conrad Eckstein, the sculptor's father, is now at Yale (2). A note attached to the work records that the statue was mounted by George Frederick Eckstein, the sculptor's son.

By 1822 Eckstein was living in a house in Holloway, Islington. Gunnis believed he died in 1828, but his will was not proved until July 1829. Eckstein, who described himself as a victualler, left all his assets, including his business, house, pewter and shares in a brewery, to his daughter Jane Eckstein, in recognition of her years of labour and service.

Literary References: *Gunnis* 1968, 139

Archival References: IGI

Will: PROB 11/1758/112

Statues						
1.	1775	Two greyhounds	s	[Ashburnham House, Dover Street, London]; Ashburnham Place, Sussex		*Gunnis* 1968, 139
2.	nd	The sculptor's father, 'statuette'	tc	YCBA B 1977.14.7	S	
Reliefs						
3.	1777	Unidentified subject	m	[Exhib RA, London, 106]; untraced		*Graves* 1905–6, 3, 13
Miscellaneous						
4.	1777	A model	w	[Exhib RA, London, 107]; untraced		*Graves* 1905–6, 3, 13
5.	1798	A model	w	[Exhib RA, London, 1043]; untraced		*Graves* 1905–6, 3, 13
6.	1799	Bull, model		[Exhib RA, London, 1090]; untraced		*Graves* 1905–6, 3, 13
7.	1799	Dog, model		[Exhib RA, London, 1094; 1802, 957]; untraced		*Graves* 1905–6, 3, 13
8.	1801	Poetry		[Exhib RA, London, 83]; untraced		*Graves* 1905–6, 3, 13

ECKSTEIN, John I 1735–1818

A German-born sculptor, engraver and painter who worked briefly in London before establishing himself in his homeland and then in America. He was born at Poppenreuth near Nuremberg on 25 November 1735, the son of Conrad Eckstein, a woodcarver and cabinet-maker, and was the elder brother of **George Paul Eckstein**. He studied under Prieffler, the head of the Academy of Arts at Nuremberg, and travelled to England as a young man.

Eckstein evidently formed a professional connection with the workshop of **Benjamin** and **Thomas Carter II** before 1761, since in that year the Carters set up the monument to Roger Townshend in Westminster Abbey, which has Eckstein's signature prominently sited beneath the relief (1). The monument, which was designed by Robert Adam, has a relief of the General, depicted *all'antica*, expiring at the Battle of Ticonderoga. Adam is known to have sent his design to Rome, where it was modelled in terracotta by **Luc-François Breton**. It therefore seems likely that Eckstein was responsible only for translating the model to marble. Flaxman described the monument as 'one of the finest specimens of Art in the Abbey' (*Smith* 1828, 2, 307) and although mutilated, it demonstrates that Eckstein already possessed considerable carving ability.

On 23 April 1762 he was awarded a premium for a Portland stone relief in the under-26 class from the Society of Arts (2), which he exhibited the following year at the Society of Artists. Another premium followed in 1764 (3).

Eckstein must have established a reputation during his years in England for in 1765 he accepted an invitation from Frederick the Great to go to Prussia, where he became the King's principal sculptor and executed numerous works at Potsdam and Sans Souci. He remained there until 1769. He was next employed by the Duke of Mecklenburg, who in 1770 sent him to England on a special mission. Here he met with a flattering reception and exhibited wax portraits at the Royal Academy (4–6). During his stay his address was John Street, Oxford Street. On concluding his mission he appears to have left England for the last time, returning to the Grand Ducal Court at Ludwigslust. J T Smith's assertion that Eckstein was the unnamed 'German' who worked with **John Deare** in the Carter workshop in 1780, and entered the Royal Academy modelling competition, appears to be inaccurate (*Smith* 1828, 2, 307).

At Ludwigslust Eckstein is known to have produced wax reliefs, including a surviving portrait of Prince Friedrich Franz I, and also to have worked on the sculpture of the Hofkirche. He remained there until 1774. In 1775–76 he modelled for the porcelain manufactory in Berlin, where he lived and worked, exhibiting at the Berlin Academy. In 1786 he took the death mask of Frederick the Great at Potsdam, from which he made wax busts. He seems also to have been employed in carving metopes after Johann Gottfried Schadow's models for the Brandenburg Gate in Berlin in 1792.

Soon after this last commission Eckstein emigrated to America. On 10 November 1793 he and his son advertised an exhibition of their paintings, sculpture and wax models at their house at 323 Market Street, Philadelphia. Eckstein became one of the founders of the Philadelphia Academy and showed with the Society of Artists between 1810 and 1814. One of his exhibits was an equestrian figure of George Washington, *all'antica*, apparently intended for a monument to be erected in the city. He had earlier engraved a plate of a standing statue of Washington, *ad locutio*. One of his last works was a marble bust of the theologian Emanuel Swedenborg. In 1817 he set out for Cuba, but died on 27 June 1817, soon after reaching Havana. His energetic wax reliefs of the *Raising of Lazarus* and the *Raising of the daughter of Jairus* are in the Cincinatti Art Museum, USA.

Eckstein was the father of John Eckstein, a painter who exhibited at the Royal Academy between 1787 and 1802, and lived with George Paul Eckstein in Tash Street. He accompanied Samuel Hood in 1803 to the 'Diamond Rock' near Martinique, and sent back to England 15 pictures of the settlement there. He next went to Barbados and painted portraits of the officers stationed on the island. He apparently died in the West Indies about 1838. His portrait of Sir Sydney Smith is in the National Portrait Gallery. Another son, Frederick Eckstein, emigrated with his father to America and pursued a career in sculpture.

Much confusion surrounded the life and family of John Eckstein until Rupert Gunnis published information in his *Dictionary* from a privately printed history of the Eckstein family by Louisa V Alderstein, daughter of G P Eckstein.

MGS

Literary References: *Smith* 1828, 1, 179; 2, 307, *Graves* 1905–6, 3, 13; *Gunnis* 1958, 334; *Gunnis* 1968, 139–40; *Fleming* 1962 (2), 163–71; *Pyke* 1973, 44; *Anderson* 1980, 37; *Pyke* 1981, 16; *Whinney* 1988, 251, 459 n20; *Bott* 1995–7, 417–28; *Saur* 1998, 32, 112

Archival References: GPC

Funerary Monuments

1.	1761	Lieutenant-Colonel the Hon Roger Townshend (†1759), relief only (monument erected by Benjamin and Thomas Carter II; designed by Robert Adam and the relief modelled by L-F Breton Drawing(s): Soane, Adam v.14, no 8; v.18 no 85; v.19, no 9, 10, 66, 68, 72, 85; design for panels, Adam Vol 19/69 & 70		Westminster Abbey, London, nave	S	*Fleming* 1962 (2), 163–171 (reprs); *Whinney* 1988, 251–2 (repr)

Reliefs

2.	1762	The death of Epaminondas	s	[Soc of A, premium, 15 gns]; untraced	RSA, *Minutes*, 1761–62, seq 3 f 63; RSA, *Register*, 1778, 31; *London Mag*, 1762, 31, 174; *Smith* 1828, 1, 179
3.	1764	The rape of Cassandra	m	[Soc of A premium, 50 gns]; untraced	RSA, *Minutes*, 1763–64, seq 3 f 76; *Dossie* 1782, 439; *Smith* 1828, 1, 179

Miscellaneous

4.	1770	A family piece in coloured wax	w	[Exhib RA, London, 77]; untraced	*Graves* 1905–6, 3, 13
5.	1770	A landscape with figures in coloured wax	w	[Exhib RA, London, 79]; untraced	*Graves* 1905–6, 3, 13
6.	1770	Three portraits in coloured wax	w	[Exhib RA, London, 78]; untraced	*Graves* 1905–6, 3, 13

ECKSTEIN, John II –1838

For further information the reader is referred to *Pyke* 1973, 44.

EDEY

Martha Edey, a sculptor's widow, was awarded 3 guineas by the Royal Academy's council in 1768.

Archival References: RA/GA, 1769

EDMONDSON, J fl 1790–92

He exhibited at the Royal Academy, 1790–92, from 14 Warwick Street, Golden Square.

Reliefs

1.	1790	Unidentified subject	[Exhib RA, London, 508]; untraced	*Graves* III, 1905–6, 18
2.	1791	'An imitation of a bas relief'	[Exhib RA, London, 265]; untraced	*Graves* III, 1905–6, 18
3.	1792	'An imitation of a bas relief'	[Exhib RA, London, 605]; untraced	*Graves* III, 1905–6, 18

EDNEY, Thomas fl 1673

In March, April, June and November 1673 Thomas Edney 'stone-cutter' signed agreements with Sir Harbottle Grimstone to carry out stone and marble work in the chapel and shell house at Gorhambury, Herts (*HMC* 1906, 77, 79–80).

EDWARD, W fl 1796

Miscellaneous

1.	1796	Academy figure, model	[RA silver medal]; untraced	RA Premium list

EDWARDES & CO, of London fl 1836–60?

A tablet commemorating Mary, Baroness Sandys in Ombersley church is signed by Edwardes & Co of 17 Newman St, London (1). Three others in the same church, to Charles Hill and family (*c*1831), Arthur Hill (†1860) and Charlotte Hill (†1854), probably came from the same workshop.

Funerary Monuments

1.	†1836	Mary, Baroness Sandys	Ombersley, Worcs	S

EDWARDS, Alexander Wilson, of Wrexham fl 1806–13

Gunnis describes his three signed coloured marble wall tablets as 'charming'.

Literary References: *Gunnis* 1968, 140

Funerary Monuments

1.	†1806	William Travers and Mr Johnson	Gresford, Denbighs	S	Pevsner, *Denbighs*, 1994, 173
2.	?1811	Christiana Smith	Holt, Denbighs	S	*Gunnis* 1968, 139
3.	†1813	Susan Price	Overton, Flint	S	Pevsner, *Clwyd*, 1986, 411

EDWARDS, Edward 1803–27?

He attended the Royal Academy Schools in 1820 and gained a silver medal a year later. In 1823 the Society of Arts awarded him their gold Isis medal and a large silver medal (**1, 4**). His address at the time was 2 Newcastle Street, Clerkenwell. In 1824 he won two more medals (**5, 2**). He exhibited at the Royal Academy in 1825 and 1826, but after this date there is no further trace of him.

Literary References: *RSA Transactions*, vol 41, 1823, xxxix, vol 42, 1824, xlvi; *Gunnis* 1968, 140

Statues					
1.	1823	Ulysses and Calypso	p	[Soc of A, gold Isis medal]; untraced	RSA *Transactions*, vol 41, 1823, xxxix
Busts					
2.	1824	Unidentified subject	p	[Soc of A, silver Isis medal]; untraced	RSA, *Transactions*, vol 2, 1784, xlvi
3.	1825	Unidentified lady		[Exhib RA, London, 1071]; untraced	*Graves* III, 1905–6, 22
Reliefs					
4.	1823	Plaster model in the round after an unspecified original		[Soc of A, large silver medal]; untraced	RSA *Transactions*, vol 41, 1823, xxxix
5.	1824	Bas-relief from life	p	[Soc of A, large silver medal]; untraced	
6.	1824	Original bas-relief from life	p	[Soc of A, large silver medal]; untraced	RSA, *Transactions*, vol 42, 1824, xlvi
7.	1826	David and Goliath		[Exhib RA, London, 1093]; untraced	*Graves* III, 1905–6, 22
Miscellaneous					
8.	1826	Psyche		[Exhib RA, London, 1083]; untraced	*Graves* III, 1905–6, 22

EDWARDS, John fl 1719–22

Edwards, who was probably a native of Wrexham, was employed at Chirk Castle in 1719 and 1722. In the latter year he supplied pedestals for two lead figures by **John Nost** (**2, 3**).

Literary References: *Gunnis* 1968, 140, citing Chirk Castle Archives

Architectural Sculpture

1.	1719	'capitals and urns upon ye pillars by ye iron gates' Payment(s): £25	[Chirk Castle, Denbighs]; untraced	*Gunnis* 1968, 140
2.	1721	Pedestal for statue of Atlas	[Chirk Castle, Denbighs, North Court]; untraced	*Gunnis* 1968, 140
3.	1721	Pedestal for statue of Hercules	[Chirk Castle, Denbighs, North Court]; Chirk Castle, Denbighs, park	*Gunnis* 1968, 140

EDWARDS, Joseph 1814–82

Edwards was born on 5 March 1814 in Merthyr Tydfil, South Wales. His father was a stonecutter who carved inscriptions for gravestones and when the young boy showed a talent for carving, his father began to pass any stonework needing ornamentation to his son. Joseph's first work, a stone tablet inscribed with his name, age and the date 1821, is in Cyfarthfa Castle Museum, Merthyr Tydfil (**95**).

His mother came from a more privileged background and she ensured that her son was sent to a local school and encouraged him in artistic pursuits. Inspired by the sculpture collection at Margam Castle, he left home at about 17 to work for a statuary mason in Swansea where he soon became the foreman, earning 3s a day. After two years he returned home and joined his father, where he stayed until his 21st birthday, leaving for London in late March 1835. He took with him a note of introduction to **William Behnes**, who had no need for help but felt sorry for the young man and allowed him to stay at his studio and watch his assistants working. Behnes soon realised that Edwards had talent and took him on at a guinea a week.

In December 1837, after submitting a plaster relief of the *Farnese Hercules* to the Royal Academy from an address in Diana Place, Regent's Park (**75**), Edwards was admitted as a student. He co-ordinated his studies with work at the studio and in December 1838 was awarded the Royal Academy's silver medal for the best model from the antique. His friends in Merthyr were proud of his achievements and persuaded the architect Thomas Henry Wyatt (whose uncle was agent to the Duke of Beaufort at Troy House near Monmouth), to take an interest in the young sculptor. In 1839 he won the commission for a monument to the 6th Duke of Beaufort to Wyatt's design (**5**). The Beaufort family thought well of him and over the next few years he provided a bust of the 7th Duke (**58**) and memorials to the 7th Duke and his mother at Great Badminton (**13, 16**).

In 1838 Edwards left Behnes's studio to work for **Patrick MacDowell**. The following year he was awarded another silver medal by the Academy but did not continue with his studies because of workshop pressure. In 1840 he provided two Merthyr patrons, the Member of Parliament and the schoolmaster, with busts of their sons (**39, 41**). He also assisted MacDowell with works including *The triumph of Love* and *Virginius*. In 1843 he carved *The last dream*, a relief considered to be one of his finest works, which became the focal point of the monument to Margaret Hutton (**8**). It depicts a young girl asleep with a bible clasped in her hand, dreaming of the angels who float above her. It was exhibited at the Royal Academy in 1844. The composition was used again for the monument to Charlotte White (**9**) and he showed a version of the relief at the Great Exhibition of 1851. In 1853 he carved another poetic relief, *Religion consoling Justice* for the monument to Sir John Bosanquet (**14**) and was described as a young sculptor who 'possesses talents of no common order' by the *Art Journal* (*AJ* 1856, 188).

Edwards took infinite pains with his sculpture, often re-modelling a work several times before he was satisfied. He always made the finishing touches himself. In consequence, his commissions often took much longer than expected. In 1854 his high relief of *Hope* for the memorial to William Hawkins of Colchester which took six years to complete, was described by a critic as 'a monument of great beauty and refinement' (**24**) (*Davies* 2000, 33). The Hawkins family originally agreed to pay £258 (including carriage and installation) but became impatient with the delay, complaining that they had been overcharged. Edwards asked **John Henry Foley** for his opinion on the value of the work and was told that 500 guineas would be a moderate price and that he knew of another sculptor who would charge 800 guineas. In 1861 Edwards's statue of *Religion* was erected over the grave of Eliza Vaughan in Highgate Cemetery (**27**). Eleven years later he was asked to reproduce the statue for the Harries family memorial in Cefn-coed-y-cymmer Cemetery on the banks of the River Taff in Merthyr, where it is known locally as the 'White Lady'.

Edwards always received favourable reviews from the *Art Journal* and executed the memorials for both George Virtue, the proprietor, and Samuel Carter Hall, the editor (**28, 32**). Mrs S C Hall encouraged Edwards to design and execute an overmantel relief for their home in Surrey. The result was a charming panel entitled *The angel of Love and Truth*, which was exhibited at the Royal Academy in 1866 (**91**) and later became widely known when the design was used as the headpiece on the title page of the popular periodical, *The Girls' Own Paper*.

Edwards was deeply interested in religion and philosophy and was a member of the Cymmrodorion Society, established in 1751 for the encouragement of the Welsh Arts, Science and Literature. In 1880 he was asked to design a medal for the Society, a commission he considered particularly important. He did not marry because he felt he could never provide a wife with comfort and security.

From about 1860 he assisted **Matthew Noble**. Apparently he often worked on Sundays and at night, so earning the sobriquet 'sculptor's ghost'. When Noble was dying in 1876 he asked Edwards, who was by then 62, to supervise the completion of all his works. This was a daunting task for there were a number in hand. He had to deal with copious amounts of paperwork, and also dispose of as many original models as possible for the benefit of Mrs Noble and her two sons.

When all was settled, Edwards found himself in straitened circumstances and his friends including **Thomas Woolner** and G F Watts helped him apply to the Royal Academy to become a Turner annuitant, which entitled him to £50 a year. He died on 8 January 1882 and bequeathed all his models and books to the Cymmrodorion Society. He was buried at Highgate Cemetery and a committee collected £70 for a monument: 2 of his pupils executed a cameo portrait in high relief for his tombstone.

Sylvia Allen

Literary References: *Gunnis* 1968, 140–1; *Wilkins* 1994, 127–8; *Davies* 2000

Funerary Monuments

1.	†1800	Edward Harris of Gurno and his wife Jane (†1787)	Merthyr Tydfil, Glamorgan, Zoar chapel	S	
2.	†1816	Rees Davies	Merthyr Tydfil, Glamorgan		Pevsner, *Glamorgan*, 1995, 437
3.	†1829	Eleanor Estcourt (designed by T H Wyatt)	Shipton Moyne, Glos		Pevsner, *Glos: Cotswolds*, 1999, 606
4.	†1831	John Bishop	Myddfai, Carmarthen		*Dale-Jones and Lloyd*, 1989, 49
5.	c1837	Henry, 6th Duke of Beaufort (†1835) (designed by T H Wyatt)	Great Badminton, Glos	S	Pevsner, *Glos: Cotswolds*, 1999, 386
6.	c1840	Rees (†1816) and William Davis (†1820)	Merthyr Tydfil, Glamorgan, churchyard	S	*Cardiff & Merthyr Guardian*, 11 Jan 1840
7.	?1841	Lieutenant-Colonel Henry Booth	Northallerton, N R Yorks	S	*Gunnis* 1968, 141; Pevsner, *Yorks: N R*, 1966, 271
8.	1844	Margaret Hutton (†1833)	North Otterington, N R Yorks	S	*AJ*, 1858, 24 (repr); *Graves* III, 1905–6, 26; Pevsner, *Yorks: N R*, 1966, 273
9.	1848	Charlotte White (†1845)	Berechurch, Essex, Audley chapel Other versions: 'The Last Dream', relief, exhib RA, London, 1851	S	*Graves* III, 1905–6, 26; *AJ Cat* 1851, 204 (repr); *Penny* 1977 (1), 92–3 (repr)
10.	†1849	Thomas Morgan	Cyfarthfa Castle Museum, Merthyr Tydfil	S	*Wilkins* 1994, 30
11.	†1850	Charles Bosanquet	Rock, Northumbs	S	*Graves* III, 1905–6, 26; Pevsner, *Northumbs*, 1992, 551; C Lib (repr)
12.	1852	Lady Margaret Millbank	Well, N R Yorks		GPC
13.	†1853	Henry, 7th Duke of Beaufort (designed by T H Wyatt)	Great Badminton, Glos	S	*Davis* 2000, 18–19 (repr)
14.	1853	Sir John Bernard Bosanquet (†1847)	Dingestow, Monmouths	S	*AJ*, 1865, 188 (repr); *AJ Cat* 1862, f 88 (repr); *Graves* III, 1905–6, 26
15.	1857	A vision, monumental bas-relief, model	[Exhib RA, London, 1236]; untraced Other versions: three of marble; untraced		*AJ*, 1864, 28 (repr); *Graves* III, 1905–6, 26
16.	1857	Charlotte Sophia, Duchess of Beaufort (†1854) Model(s): exhib RA, London, 1859, 1279	Great Badminton, Glos	S	*Graves* III, 1905–6, 27; *CIIA* 4/4/59–60 (repr); Pevsner, *Glos: Cotswolds*, 1999, 386
17.	1857	'Suspiria', part of a monument	[Exhib RA, London, 1238]; untraced		*Graves* III, 1905–6, 27
18.	†1857	Thomas Evans	Kidwelly, Carmarthen		*Dale-Jones and Lloyd*, 1989, 49
19.	c1858	B J A Angell	St Mary, Calne, Wilts	S	*Graves* III, 1905–6, 27; *Cardiff & Merthyr Guardian*, 11 Sept 1858

20.	†1858	Mrs Morley		St David, Newtown, Montgomery	S	Pevsner, *Powys*, 1979, 174
21.	by 1859	Edward Squire (†1853)		[Portrait medallion, part of a monument, exhib RA, London, 1856, 1275]; Ainderby Steeple, N R Yorks		*ILN*, 5 Nov 1859, 454; *Graves* III, 1905–6, 26
22.	1860	Lewis Morgan (†1856)		[Craig Chapel, Abercanaid, Glamorgan]; Cyfarthfa Castle Museum, Merthyr Tydfil, Glamorgan	S	*Graves* III, 1905–6, 27; *Davies* 2000, 44
23.	1860	Mrs R P Davis Payment(s): £125		Tredegar, Monmouths	S	*Graves* III, 1905–6, 25; *Davies* 2000, 45
24.	1854–1860	William (†1843) and Mary Ann Hawkins		St Boltoph, Colchester, Essex	S	*Graves* III, 1905–6, 26; Pevsner, *Essex*, 1965, 132; *Davies* 2000, 33
25.	†1863	Arthur Bishop		Myddfai, Carmarthen		*Dale-Jones and Lloyd*, 1989, 49
26.	†1863	Thomas Evans		Myddfai, Carmarthen		*Dale-Jones and Lloyd*, 1989, 49
27.	1866	Eliza Vaughan Payment(s): £373		Highgate Cemetery, London Other versions: Cefn Cemetery, Merthyr, 1877	S	*Davies* 2000, 45
28.	1870	George and Helen Virtue		Walton-on-Thames Cemetery, Surrey	S	*Graves* III, 1905–6, 27; *Gunnis* 1968, 141
29.	?1870	Rev Evan Owen Payment(s): £300		Bryncoedifor, Merioneth	S	*Davies* 2000, 45
30.	c1872	Harries family		Cefncoedcymmer cemetery, Merthyr Tydfil	S	*Davies* 2000, 68–9
31.	1874	William Williams		Vaynor, Glamorgan		Pevsner, *Glamorgan*, 1995, 643
32.	†1889	Sarah Elizabeth Fielding (†1856), Anna Maria Hall (†1881) and Samuel Carter Hall		Addlestone, Surrey		
Statues						
33.	1846	William Williams		[for Aberystwyth]; untraced		*Gunnis* 1968, 140
Busts						
34.	1838	Sir John Josiah Guest MP		Cyfarthfa Castle Museum, Merthyr Tydfil	SD	
35.	1838	Thomas Evans		[Exhib RA, London, 1311]; untraced		*Graves* III, 1905–6, 26
36.	1839	E L Richards		[Exhib RA, London, 1385]; untraced		*Graves* III, 1905–6, 26
37.	1839	Unidentified lady		[Exhib RA, London, 1375]; untraced		*Graves* III, 1905–6, 26
38.	1839	Unidentified man	p	National Museum and Gallery, Cardiff		
39.	1841	Ab Iolo (Taliesin Williams)		[Exhib RA, London, 1328]; untraced		*Graves* III, 1905–6, 26
40.	1841	Lady Charlotte Guest		Cyfarthfa Castle Museum, Merthyr Tydvil	SD	
41.	1841	Master Ivor Bertie Guest	m	[Exhib RA, London, 1290]; untraced		*Graves* III, 1905–6, 26
42.	1842	Mrs E L Richards		[Exhib RA, London, 1394]; untraced		*Graves* III, 1905–6, 26
43.	1842	S R Bosanquet		[Exhib RA, London, 1329]; untraced		*Graves* III, 1905–6, 26
44.	1843	Edward Ormond Lyne		[Exhib RA, London, 1522]; untraced		*Graves* III, 1905–6, 26
45.	1845	B J Angell Angell		[Exhib RA, London, 1367]; untraced		*Graves* III, 1905–6, 26
46.	1845	Mr Thorburn		[Exhib RA, London, 1439]; untraced		*Graves* III, 1905–6, 26
47.	1845	Rev John Guthrie		[Exhib RA, London, 1397]; untraced		*Graves* III, 1905–6, 26; *Gunnis* 1968, 140
48.	1846	W Williams		[Exhib RA, London, 1455]; untraced		*Graves* III, 1905–6, 26; *Davies* 2000, 25
49.	1847	Mrs Angell		[Exhib RA, London, 1347]; untraced		*Graves* III, 1905–6, 26
50.	1848	Miss L A Cooper		[Exhib RA, London, 1466]; untraced		*Graves* III, 1905–6, 26
51.	1850	Sir Harry Smith Bt		[Exhib RA, London, 1446]; untraced		*Graves* III, 1905–6, 26
52.	1853	J Snow Beck MD		[Exhib RA, London, 1427]; untraced		*Graves* III, 1905–6, 26
53.	1853	Son of William Hunter		[Exhib RA, London, 1435]; untraced		*Graves* III, 1905–6, 26
54.	1855	Master Thomas Williams Angell Evans		[Exhib RA, London, 1524]; untraced		*Graves* III, 1905–6, 26
55.	1855	Samuel Bosanquet	m	[Exhib RA, London, 1478]; untraced		*Graves* III, 1905–6, 26
56.	1856	Mrs James Bosanquet		[Exhib RA, London, 1329]; untraced		*Graves* III, 1905–6, 26
57.	1857	Field Marshall Lord Raglan		[Exhib RA, London, 1355]; untraced		*Graves* III, 1905–6, 27; *Gunnis* 1968, 140
58.	1857	Henry, 7th Duke of Beaufort		[Exhib RA, London, 1326]; Badminton, Glos		*Graves* III, 1905–6, 27; *Gunnis* 1968, 140
59.	1858	Stephen Pearce		[Exhib RA, London, 1229]; untraced		*Graves* III, 1905–6, 27
60.	1859	Unidentified gentleman		[Exhib RA, London, 1331]; untraced		*Graves* III, 1905–6, 27
61.	1860	Archdeacon Williams		[Exhib RA, London, 970]; untraced		*Graves* III, 1905–6, 27; *Gunnis* 1968, 140
62.	1861	George Virtue		[Exhib RA, London, 1022]; untraced		*Graves* III, 1905–6, 27
63.	1864	Sir John Guest		Town Hall, Merthyr Tydfil, Glamorgan Other versions: Cyfarthfa Castle Museum, Merthyr Tydfil		*Gunnis* 1968, 140; *Davies* 2000, 50
64.	1867	Henry, 3rd Viscount Palmerston		Tiverton Town Hall, Devon		*Ormond* 1973, 361
65.	1869	Unidentified gentleman		[Exhib RA, London, 1177]; untraced		*Graves* III, 1905–6, 27
66.	1870	Unidentified lady		[Exhib RA, London, 1189]; untraced		*Graves* III, 1905–6, 27
67.	1873	G T Clark, ironmaster	m	[Exhib RA, London, 1564]; Cyfartha Castle Museum, Merthyr Tydfil, Glamorgan, 1033.995		*Graves* III, 1905–6, 27; *Gunnis* 1968, 140
68.	1874	Major Nanney		[Exhib RA, London, 1568]; untraced		*Graves* III, 1905–6, 27
69.	1874	Miss Edith Wynn		[Exhib RA, London, 1559]; untraced Other versions: exhib RA, London, 1875, 1257, marble; untraced		*Graves* III, 1905–6, 27

70.	1875	George Virtue	m	[Exhib RA, London, 1352]; untraced		*Graves* III, 1905–6, 27
71.	1878	James Walter		[Exhib RA, London, 1421]; untraced		*Graves* III, 1905–6, 27
72.	1878	Thomas Stephens	m	[Exhib RA, London, 1439]; untraced		*Graves* III, 1905–6, 27
73.	nd	S R Bosanquet		coll Robert Courthope (1956)	S	GPC
Reliefs						
74.	pre-1830	Copy of a medallion of Lord Byron		[Coll Lady Charlotte Guest]; untraced		*Davies* 2000, 11
75.	1837	Farnese Hercules	p	[RA, London]; untraced		*Davies* 2000, 17
76.	1839	H S Smith, portrait medallion		[Exhib RA, London, 1315]; untraced		*Graves* III, 1905–6, 26
77.	1845	E Ormond Lyne, portrait medallion		[Exhib RA, London, 1350]; untraced		*Graves* III, 1905–6, 26
78.	1845	James de Carle Sowerby, portrait medallion		[Exhib RA, London, 1381]; untraced		*Graves* III, 1905–6, 26
79.	*c*1846	Daughter of the Dawn, life size		Untraced		*AJ*, 1856, 188; *Davies* 2000, 25
80.	1846	J Petherick, portrait medallion		[Exhib RA, London, 1521]; untraced		*Graves* III, 1905–6, 26
81.	1846	The spirit ascending		[Exhib RA, London, 1519]; untraced		*Graves* III, 1905–6, 26
82.	1847	Unidentified young lady, medallion		[Exhib RA, London, 1344]; untraced		*Graves* III, 1905–6, 26
83.	1848	B J A Angell and wife, medallic portraits		[Exhib RA, London, 1473]; untraced		*Graves* III, 1905–6, 26
84.	1850	Miss Cross, portrait medallion		[Exhib RA, London, 1368]; untraced		*Graves* III, 1905–6, 26
85.	1851	A Philosopher, directing the attention of a youth to the celebrated Delphic precept, 'Know Thyself', inscribed over a niche containing the bust of Thales, sketch, part of a larger composition in bas-relief		[Exhib RA, London, 1289]; untraced		*Graves* III, 1905–6, 26; *Davies* 2000, 31–2 (repr)
86.	1851	Three bas-reliefs		[Gt Exhib, London]; untraced		*Gunnis* 1968, 140
87.	1852	J Ewing Ritchie, portrait medallion		[Exhib RA, London, 1342]; untraced		*Graves* III, 1905–6, 26
88.	by 1856	The weary reassured		Untraced		*AJ* 1856, 188
89.	1858	B J A Angell, monumental medallion		[Exhib RA, London, 1327]; untraced		*Graves* III, 1905–6, 27
90.	1858	W B Angell, medallion		[Exhib RA, London, 1263]; untraced		*Graves* III, 1905–6, 27
91.	1866	Angel of Love and Truth	p	National Museum & Gallery, Cardiff, acc A388 Other versions: Electrotype, NM &G, Cardiff, A 389; A 390 ex coll Mrs SC Hall, marble; untraced		*Graves* III, 1905–6, 27
92.	1866	Mrs Kennedy Erskine, medallion portrait		[Exhib RA, London, 966]; untraced		*Graves* III, 1905–6, 27
93.	1880	Hon Soc of Cymmrodorion medal, design		National Museum & Gallery, Cardiff, A13117		
94.	nd	G G Ferrari		Castle Howard, N R Yorks		*Gunnis* 1968, 140
Miscellaneous						
95.	1821	Oval tablet 'The First Stone engraved by Joseph Edwards of Ynysgau Aged 7: 1821'		Cyfarthfa Castle Museum, Merthyr Tydfil, Glamorgan		
96.	pre-1830	A child sleeping	s	[Coll Lady Charlotte Guest]; untraced		*Davies* 2000, 11
97.	1841	Infant daughter of J P Grant, model		[Exhib RA, London, 1237]; untraced		*Graves* III, 1905–6, 26
98.	1841	Lavinia		[Exhib RA, London, 1283]; untraced		*Graves* III, 1905–6, 26
99.	1848	The dying Christian's dream		[Exhib RA, London, 1412]; untraced		*Graves* III, 1905–6, 26
100.	1851	'Britannia in the presence of Minerva, rewarding the Genius and Industry of the World, while the Spirit of Peace attends the Crown, sketch'; design for a commemorative medal made for the Great Exhibition		[Exhib RA, London, 1273]; untraced		*Graves* III, 1905–6, 26; *Davies* 2000, 26
101.	1853	The high poet-priest of Science advocating the modern precept, 'Study Nature', inscribed on a tablet held in his hand		[Exhib RA, London, 1372]; untraced		*Graves* III, 1905–6, 26
102.	1858	Prof John Erichson		[Exhib RA, London, 1230]; untraced		*Graves* III, 1905–6, 27
103.	1859	Archdeacon John Williams, of Cardigan		[Exhib RA, London, 1301]; untraced		*Graves* III, 1905–6, 27
104.	1860	John Hutton		[Exhib RA, London, 995]; untraced		*Graves* III, 1905–6, 27; *Gunnis* 1968, 140
105.	1866	Star-crowned spirit of love and truth floating in light		[coll Mrs S C Hall]; untraced		*AJ*, 1867, 28 (repr); *Graves* III, 1905–6, 27
106.	1870	Laura Instone		[Exhib RA, London, 1142]; untraced		*Graves* III, 1905–6, 27
107.	nd	Dawn	p	National Museum & Gallery, Cardiff, acc A2894		

EDWARDS, William, of Didbrook fl 1833–50

Funerary Monuments						
1.	†1833	John Walker		St Michael, Guiting Power, Glos	S	Pevsner, *Glos: Cotswolds*, 1999, 395
2.	1850	Margaret Witts		Upper Slaughter, Glos, churchyard	S	Pevsner, *Glos: Cotswolds*, 1999, 708

EDWARDS & CO, of Wrexham fl 1820

Funerary Monuments						
1.	†1820	Lieutenant-Colonel Henry Tarleton		Malpas, Cheshire	S	Pevsner, *Cheshire*, 1971, 274

EGART, Daniel fl 1762

On 28 May 1762 he received a premium of 25 guineas for a basso relievo of *Iphigenia released* in the under-25 class, a work he had exhibited at the Society of Free Artists in the previous year.

Literary References: *Dossie* 1782, 439; *Gunnis* 1968, 141

Archival References: RSA, Minutes, 1761–62, seq 3 f 61

Reliefs

1.	1762	Iphigenia released	m	[Exhib Free Soc, London, 1762, 170]; untraced Other versions: replicated in Portland stone, 1863	RSA *Minutes*, 1761–62, seq 3 f 61; *Graves* 1907, 87

EGLINGTON FAMILY

Benjamin Eglington II, of Derby	*c*1730–1768
John Eglington, of Birmingham	1733–1787
Samuel Eglington I, of Ashbourne	1742–1788
Joseph Eglington, of Coventry	1746–1810
Samuel Eglington II, of Kineton	†1816
'Eglington Snr, Birmingham'	fl *c*1731
James Eglington, of Walsall	†1809

The Eglingtons were a family of masons and stone carvers working in the Midlands in the 18th century, most of whom were descended from Benjamin Eglington of Badby, Northants. He had several sons who became masons. The eldest, **Benjamin II**, was foreman-mason for the Derby Assembly Rooms, built to the designs by Joseph Pickford in 1763–64. **John** established himself in Birmingham and **Samuel I** worked as a stone-carver in Ashbourne, Derbys. **Joseph** moved to Coventry where he established a successful business as a builder-architect. He undertook building work at Holy Trinity church, 1775–87, and designed County Hall, 1783–84. In 1792 All Saints, Leek Wooton, Warks, was rebuilt to his designs. His payments there included £5 7s for 'taking down the Monument [unidentified] . . . Pollishing engraving and fixing' made on 10 December 1791. A further 17 guineas was paid to him on 5 April 1793 for a font (**4**) (Shakespeare Birthplace Trust, Leigh Papers DR18/3/32/25). In 1794 he supplied a chimneypiece for Arbury Hall (Newdigate Archives in GPC) (**3**). In 1805, he was paid £39 by Mr Bracebridge for repairs to Atherstone Hall, Warks, which was let to Lord Grey (Bracebridge Archives, in GPC). In the next generation **Samuel II** (the son of Benjamin II) worked as a mason at Kineton, Warks, where he died in 1816. He can perhaps be identified with 'Samuel Eglington, mason' who was paid £37 18s for work at Aston parish church, Birmingham, in 1789–90 (Ch W, cited by *Gunnis* 1968, 141).

The '**Eglington Snr, Birmingham**' who signed a large wall-tablet, with a pyramid and well-carved details, to Edward Brandwood at Aston, has not been identified (**1**). He may have been related to **James Eglington of Walsall**, who signed a tablet to Joanna Goodall (**2**). Samuel and John Eglington, masons, worked in Edmund Street, Birmingham, during the 1790s. In 1818 John Eglington, stonemason, was in Bridge Street, Walsall, and in 1828 John and James Eglington had a yard in Can Lane, Wolverhampton. In 1835 John Eglington was listed in Newport Street, Walsall. All trace of the family vanishes in the 1850s. (Add inf. Terry Friedman)

Literary References: *Jeavons*, 1960, 55; *Gunnis* 1968, 141; *Colvin* 1995, 337–8

Archival References: GPC

Funerary Monuments

1.	†1731	Edward Brandwood (signed 'Eglington Snr, Birmingham')	Aston, Warks	S	*Gunnis* 1968, 141; *Colvin* 1995, 338
2.	?1790	Joanna Goodall (signed by James Eglington, of Walsall)	Walsall Parish Church, Staffs	S	*Gunnis* 1968, 141

Chimneypieces

3.	1794	Italian marble (by Joseph Eglington, of Coventry)	Arbury, Warks		Newdigate archives, CR 136/B2635c (bill); *Gunnis* 1968, 141

Architectural Sculpture

4.	1793	'a Derbyshire Font compleat' (by Joseph Eglington, of Coventry)	Leek Wootton, Warks		Leigh Papers in GPC

EIZAT, Alexander fl 1677

Architectural Sculpture

1.	1677	Fluted Corinthian pilasters, overmantel with big festoons of foliage, acanthus leaf friezes, panelling and other ornaments	wd	Holyrood Palace, privy chamber, ante chamber, King's bed chamber and closet	Pevsner, *Edinburgh*, 1991, 144–5

EKINS, George, of Ware fl 1803–60

Funerary Monuments

1.	†1803	Adams family	Walkern, Herts	S
2.	†1829	Ensign George René Cathrow	Great Amwell, Herts	S
3.	†1843	Robert (†1837) and Mary Sworder	Little Hadham, Herts	S
4.	†1860	Rev John Montague Chumley	Standon, Herts	S

ELDERTON, James, of Southampton fl 1807–26

Elderton signs two Hampshire tablets. He was succeeded by his son, Charles Harben Elderton.

Funerary Monuments

1.	1807	Anna Lintott	Woolston, Hants	S	*Gunnis* 1968, 141
2.	1826	Rev Charles Philipson	Eling, Hants	S	*Gunnis* 1968, 141

ELDERTON, of Northampton

For further information the reader is referred to *Pyke* 193, 45.

ELDREDGE (or ELDRIDGE), William, of Kings Lynn 1749–1819

He was the son of Joseph Eldredge, a mason who had been apprenticed to **John Fellowes** in 1725. He signs several tablets in Norfolk.

Literary References: *Gunnis* 1968, 141

Funerary Monuments

1.	?1796	Francis Dalton	West Bilney, Norfolk	S	*Gunnis* 1968, 141
2.	?1805	Ann Lancaster	Pentney, Norfolk	S	*Gunnis* 1968, 141
3.	?1814	William Benezet	Swaffham, Norfolk	S	*Gunnis* 1968, 141
4.	?1815	Rev Horace Hammond	South Wooton, Norfolk	S	*Gunnis* 1968, 141

ELGER, John, of London fl 1835?

His yard was at South Street, Park Lane.

Archival References: GPC

Funerary Monuments

1.	?1835	Richard Turton	Beaumaris, Anglesey	S	GPC

ELLIOT, Richard

He practiced as a carver in 'Newgate-Street, opposite Warwick-lane' (*Mortimer* 1763, 10).

ELLIOT, Thomas, of Hull fl 1814

Funerary Monuments

1.	†1814	Edward Green	Lawford, Essex	S	*Gunnis* 1968, 141

ELLIS, Anthony 1620?–71

Ellis was apprenticed to Nicholas Stone in 1634–5. Stone described him as his 'servant' in his will of January 1641 and left him a small bequest. He is probably the 'Mr. Ellis' who in 1652 was paid by **John Stone** for carving 4 heads supplied to Sir William Paston at Oxnead Hall, Norfolk, and for roughing out a fifth. In the Restoration period he emerged from this humble background to become a builder and an architectural designer of consequence, responsible for remodelling Althorp House, Northants (1665/6–1668), where he is described in the building accounts as a surveyor. He joined the Yeomanry of the Masons' Company of London by 1663 and is known to have taken 2 apprentices under the Company's auspices. In 1666 he appears in the parish ratebooks for Pall Mall where he was again listed in the year of his death.

Literary References: *Knoop and Jones* 1935, 23; *White* 1999, 48–9

Will: PROB 11/337/121

Funerary Monuments

1.	†1651	Sir John Wentworth and his wife	Somerleyton, Suffolk	S	*White* 1999, 48–9

ELLIS, John, of Portsea fl 1803?–35?

Funerary Monuments

1.	?1803	Solomon Ferris	Southwick, Hants	S	*Gunnis* 1968, 141
2.	?1835	Sir Thomas McMahon	Portsmouth Cathedral	S	*Gunnis* 1968, 141

ELLIS, William I fl 1770

A mason called William Ellis received payments for 'making a new Gate Way on Woodcock Bank' on 31 August 1770 and again on 28 September 1770. See also **Matthew Freer**.

Archival References: Castle Howard Cash Book F4/11/4, pp 206, 210, 213

ELLIS, William II 1824–82

He was born in Sheffield and studied under **Edward Law** but went to London *c*1850, where he was associated with **Alfred Stevens**. He later returned to his native city and set up on his own account as a sculptor, but 'failed to reap the fruits of his persevering labours' and died suddenly on 19 July 1882 of 'exhaustion, disappointed and in poverty' (*Odom* 1926, 211).

Literary References: *Gunnis* 1968, 141

Busts

1.	post-1843	James Montgomery Model(s): Literary and Philosophical Society, Sheffield, W R Yorks, 1843, plaster	m	Cutlers' Hall, Sheffield, W R Yorks Other versions: Royal Infirmary, Sheffield, W R Yorks	*ILN*, 13 Oct 1855, 436 (repr); *Odom* 1926, 211
2.	1874	Thomas Sale	m	Sheffield Cathedral, W R Yorks	*Odom* 1926, 211; *Gunnis* 1968, 141
3.	1875	William Overend	m	Mappin Art Gallery, Sheffield, W R Yorks Other versions: Royal Infirmary, Sheffield, W R Yorks, plaster cast, nd	*Odom* 1926, 211; *Gunnis* 1968, 141
4.	1876	Alfred Stevens	m	Mappin Art Gallery, Sheffield, W R Yorks	*Odom* 1926, 211; *Gunnis* 1968, 141
5.	1881	John Arthur Roebuck MP	m	Cutlers' Hall, Sheffield, W R Yorks	*Odom* 1926, 211; *Gunnis* 1968, 141
6.	nd	Dr H C Sorby	m	Sheffield University, W R Yorks	*Odom* 1926, 211
7.	nd	Dr Henry Jackson	m	Royal Infirmary, Sheffield, W R Yorks	*Odom* 1926, 211
8.	nd	Ebeneezer Elliot	p	Central Public Libraries, Sheffield, W R Yorks	*Odom* 1926, 211
9.	nd	Rev Samuel Earnshaw	m	Sheffield University, W R Yorks	*Odom* 1926, 211
10.	nd	Sir Arnold J Knight MD	p	Literary and Philosophical Society, Sheffield, W R Yorks	*Odom* 1926, 211

Reliefs

11.	1852	James Montgomery, medallion (design for a Montgomery prize medal)	b	Mappin Art Gallery, Sheffield, W R Yorks Other versions: Literary and Philosophical Society, Sheffield, W R Yorks Central Public Libraries, Sheffield, W R Yorks, marble	*Odom* 1926, 211; *Gunnis* 1968, 141

ELSWORTH, John, of York fl 1703–15

He and his partner, **William Smith of York**, were the chief masons at Castle Howard between 1703 and 1714. They built the bridge in the park and the obelisk, receiving £80 and £168 respectively for these. They also provided carving in the house (**2**).

Literary References: *Gunnis* 1968, 141; *Saumarez-Smith*, 1990, 60

Archival References: Castle Howard Archives, G2/2 selected bills; Castle Howard Building Account Books G2/1/1-2

Chimneypieces

1.	1703–1714	Several, for lesser rooms (co-sculptor: William Smith)		Castle Howard, N R Yorks	*Gunnis* 1968, 141

Architectural Sculpture

2.	1703–1714	Cornice and capitals of the cupola, 'the south modillion cornish', vases on the north wing and other decorative work (co-sculptor: William Smith) Payment(s): £137 for 'the south modillion cornish'; £8 each for the vases	s	Castle Howard, N R Yorks	*Gunnis* 1968, 141
3.	1715	Vases for the mulberry garden, the Back Court gateway and the 'circular corridor' (co-sculptor: William Smith)	s	Castle Howard, N R Yorks	*Gunnis* 1968, 360

EMERSON, David fl 1722–25

He placed an advertisement in the *Norwich Gazette* on 28 April 1722 stating that 'all Gentlemen and others, that have Deceas'd, or shall have Occassion for any Marble Grave-Stones, or for other Grave-Stones, or Head-Stones for Graves . . . may have them of David Emerson, in the Gate right against the Rampant-Horse in St Stephen's in Norwich . . . and Coats of Arms or Inscriptions cut . . .'. The advertisement appeared again in the same paper on 13 March 1725.

EMERY, J fl 1849–53

His address was 14 North Street, Westminster until 1853 when he moved to 24 Harrington Street.

Literary References: *Graves* III, 1905–6, 53

Statues

1.	1849	The flower girl, model for a garden figure		[Exhib RA, London, 1245]; untraced	*Graves* III, 1905–6, 53
2.	1865	Edward, Baron Hatherton, statuette		[Exhib RA, London, 988]; untraced	*Graves* III, 1905–6, 53

Miscellaneous

3.	1852	The three chief virtues		[Exhib RA, London, 1339]; untraced	*Graves* III, 1905–6, 53
4.	1853	The convalescent	pm	[Exhib RA, London, 1315]; untraced	*Graves* III, 1905–6, 53

EMERY, of Haywood fl 1814?

He is known only for one large Hellenic tablet with an urn and coat of arms.

Funerary Monuments

1.	?1814	Edward Drakeford	St Mary, Stafford	S	GPC

EMETT, of Downend fl 1797

Funerary Monuments

1.	†1797	Thomas Mountjoy	St Michael, Winterbourne, Glos	S	Pevsner, *Glos: Vale & Forest of Dean*, 1976, 409

EMETT, S T fl 1769

Funerary Monuments

1.	†1769	Richard Oseland	Wapley, Glos	S	Pevsner, *Glos: Vale & Forest of Dean*, 1976, 398

EMETT, W, of Frenchay fl 1829–after 1850

Funerary Monuments

1.	†1829	William Cullimore	Tytherington, Glos	S	Pevsner, *Glos: Vale & Forest of Dean*, 1976, 394
2.	post-1850	Several unidentified subjects, tablets	Mangotsfield, Glos	S	Pevsner, *Glos: Vale & Forest of Dean*, 1976, 297

EMMETT, William *c*1641–

A carver in stone and wood who was in considerable demand at the royal palaces, he was the son of Maurice Emmett, who briefly held the post of Master Bricklayer in the Office of Works at the Restoration in 1660. He was probably born in 1641, for he was aged about 30 when as a 'Citizen & Joiner' he married Jane Brown at St Margaret, Westminster in 1671 (*Wren Society*, XIV, xxiii). He was the cousin of **Henry Phillips**, who was appointed master sculptor and carver in wood to the Crown in 1661. In 1688 Phillips retired from active work, though he continued to draw his salary until 1692, whilst Emmett carried out his duties. Phillips died in 1693 and was succeeded in his post by **Grinling Gibbons**. William's younger brother, Maurice Emmett, served as master bricklayer from 1677 until he died, aged 48, in 1694.

Emmett's surviving works include a 'spectacular martial overmantel' in the manner of Grinling Gibbons at the Royal Hospital, Chelsea, and a series of 'very fine' round windows carved with 'an ornament of Lyons Skins & Lawrell leaves & Berrys bound about with a fillet' at Hampton Court (*Green* 1964, 70; *Esterley* 1998, 130–2) (**22, 17**).

Literary References: *Green* 1964 (1), *passim*; *Gunnis* 1968, 141–2; *Beard* 1989 (1), 21, 24, 27, 28, 34; *Esterly* 1998, 22, 130–2; *Colvin* 1995, 346–7

Architectural Sculpture

No.	Date	Work		Location	References
1.	1670–1675	Unspecified carving Payment(s): £24		[St Christopher, Threadneedle Street, City of London]; untraced	*Wren Soc*, X, 46
2.	1680	A 'rich picktur frame wrought with flowers' and 'a cherubin's head with a compartment about for two festoones of leaves'		[St James's Palace, London, oratory beside Duchess of York's bedroom]; untraced	*Colvin* 1973–76, V, 234
3.	c1680	Extensive carved work Payment(s): £219		[St James's Palace, London, Duchess of York's bedroom]; untraced	*Colvin* 1973–76, V, 234
4.	1682	Carved work Payment(s): £3		[St Bartholomew, Exchange, City of London]; untraced	*Wren Soc*, XIX, 10
5.	1682	'carving work about the Altarpiece, pillars, pillasters, shields, festoons, &c' Payment(s): £45	wd	Temple Church, London	*Wren Soc*, X, pls 58–60; *Colvin* 1995, 346
6.	1679–1683	Heads of cherubim and festoons, rails and balusters		[St James's Palace, London, Queen's chapel]; untraced	*Colvin* 1973–76, V, 248, 252
7.	1685	'Carveing about the Altar and Pulpitt'		[Somerset House, London]; untraced	*Colvin* 1973–76, V, 257
8.	1685–1686	Carving in the Queen's apartments, the privy gallery, the council chamber and the vane room		[Whitehall Palace, London]; destroyed	*Wren Soc*, VII, 98, 99, 104, 114–5; *Green* 1964, 62; *Colvin* 1973–76, V, 289
9.	1687	Altarpiece and altar rails (co-sculptor: William Morgan)		Royal Hospital, Chelsea, chapel	*Wren Soc*, XIX, 73–4; *Green* 1964, 58; Pevsner, *London: N W*, 1991, 564
10.	1677–1687	Unspecified carving Payment(s): £6		[St Martin, Ludgate, City of London]; untraced	*Wren Soc*, X, 48, 124
11.	1686–1687	Unspecified carving		[Whitehall Palace, London, chapel, vestry, organ loft and staircase]; destroyed	*Wren Soc*, VII, 121, 124, 126; *Green* 1964, 60 n4; *Colvin* 1973–76, V, 291
12.	1685–1690	Carving, including font cover, two coats of arms, eight cherubim heads (co-sculptor: Newman) Payment(s): £10 (1687–8); £10 (1688–9); £15 (1689–90)	wd	St Mary Abchurch, City of London	*Wren Soc*, X, 124, (repr 19, 27, 41, 43, 51); XIX, 31; Pevsner, *London: City & Westminster*, 1957, 155; *Beard* 1989 (1), 34
13.	1689–1690	Cornices, overdoors and chimney-frames and brackets (co-sculptor: Nicholas Alcock) Payment(s): £206 11s 2 1/2d		[Kensington Palace, London, royal apartments]; untraced	*Colvin* 1973–76, V, 186
14.	1690	Enriched cornices, overmantel ornaments and ten brackets		[Hampton Court Palace, Middx, Thames gallery]; demol 1700	*Wren Soc*, IV, 22, 25, 44; *Green* 1964, 69; *Colvin* 1973–76, V, 158
15.	1690	Four keystones in the arches of the portico Payment(s): £6	s	[Hampton Court Palace, Middx, fountain (or quadrangle) court]; untraced	*Wren Soc*, IV, 52; *Green* 1964, 70
16.	1690	The King's 'Badges & Crownes'; '4 foliage flowers & husks'; '20 Roses 9 inch diameter'		[Kensington Palace, London, gates]; untraced	*Wren Soc*, VII, 171
17.	1691	17 round windows carved with 'a compartment of Lyon's skins and Lorril leaves on a round' Payment(s): £20 each	s	Hampton Court Palace, Middx, fountain (or quadrangle) court	*Wren Soc*, IV, 52; *Green* 1964, 70; *Colvin* 1973–76, V, 159–60
18.	1690–1691	Carved cornices (co-sculptor: Nicholas Alcock) Payment(s): £185 3s 5d	wd	Kensington Palace, Queen's apartments	*Colvin* 1973–76, V, 187
19.	c1691	Enriched cornices and overdoor picture frames Payment(s): £9 18s; £6 14s; £4 7s 6d		Royal Hospital, Chelsea, Council Chamber	*Wren Soc*, XIX, 77
20.	c1691	'Enrichments' for the presence chamber, privy chamber, great bedchamber, drawing room, eating room, little bedchamber, dressing room, closet and lobby		[Whitehall Palace, London]; destroyed	*Colvin* 1973–76, V, 295
21.	1690–1691	Keystones for three round-headed windows Payment(s): £4 10s		[Hampton Court Palace, Middx, king's stairs]; untraced	*Colvin* 1973–76, V, 160
22.	c1691	Overmantel carved with martial trophies Payment(s): £30	wd	Royal Hospital, Chelsea, council chamber	*Wren Soc*, XIX, 77; *Green* 1964, 58, 60 (repr); Pevsner, *London: N W*, 1991, 564–5; *Esterly* 1998, 130–2
23.	1690–1691	'ye King's Armes & Supporters with ye Garter & Imperial Crown' Payment(s): £10	wd	[Kensington Palace, London, Queen's bedchamber]; untraced	*Wren Soc*, VII, 157; *Colvin* 1973–76, V, 187
24.	1678–1692	Unidentified carving Payment(s): £12, £12 10s		St Bride, Fleet Street, City of London	*Wren Soc*, X, 124, (repr 16); XIX, 14; *Green* 1964, 178, n2
25.	c1692	Unidentified carving		[House of Commons, Palace of Westminster, London]; destroyed	*Colvin* 1973–76, V, 402
26.	1692–1693	'46 Ballisters in ye Raile before ye Altar in the Chapel'		[Kensington Palace, London]; untraced	*Wren Soc*, VII, 164, 181
27.	1693	Cornice with 'three enrichments' Payment(s): £18		[Whitehall Palace, London, Private Oratory]; destroyed	TNA WORK 5/46, f316
28.	1693	Keystone for the new portico to the waterstairs	s	[Whitehall Palace, London]; destroyed	PRO Works 4/46, cited by *Gunnis* 1968, 142

29.	1693	Picture frames for the great withdrawing room and the queen's new bedchamber		[Whitehall Palace, London]; destroyed	*Colvin* 1972–76, V, 296
30.	1691–1694	Unidentified carving Payment(s): £918 3s 5d		[Hampton Court Palace, Middx, state rooms]; untraced	*Wren Soc*, IV, 22, 25; *Colvin* 1973–76, V, 163; *Beard* 1989, 27
31.	nd	'excellent woodwork'		College of Arms, London, library	Pevsner, *London: City & Westminster*, 1957, 173
Miscellaneous					
32.	1688	Carved gnomon for the great sundial		[Whitehall Palace, London, Privy Garden]; destroyed	*Colvin* 1973–76, V, 294
33.	c1691	Mould for a lead cistern (for withdrawing room off the council chamber, Royal Hospital, Chelsea)		Untraced	*Wren Soc*, XIX, 78

ENGEL, Jozsef 1815–1901

A Hungarian sculptor, he began his artistic training in Vienna, where he was apprenticed to a wood carver and attended the Academy of Art, 1832–38. He then travelled to England, where he studied under **William Behnes** and entered the Royal Academy Schools in 1839 on the recommendation of **Sir Francis Chantrey** (RA Admissions). He exhibited at the RA between 1840 and 1847, from 25 Castle Street, Leicester Square, and won a medal in 1843 (**13**). His first important work was a group, *The Amazons and the Argonaut* which was bought by Prince Albert for £600 (**3**). It was displayed at the Great Exhibition of 1851 and is now at Osborne House. In 1847 Engel went to Rome, where he worked for nearly 20 years, returning to Hungary in 1866. He apparently visited London in 1888 for that year he exhibited three works at the Royal Academy, giving his address as 17 Burton Crescent (**5–7**).

Literary References: *Singer* V, 1901–7, 161; *Thieme Becker*, X, 530–1; *Gunnis* 1968, 142

Statues					
1.	1845	Cupid, statuette	i	[Exhib RA, London, 1320]; untraced	*Graves* III, 1905–6, 56
2.	1845	Hymen, statuette	i	[Exhib RA, London, 1318]; untraced	*Graves* III, 1905–6, 56
3.	1846	The Amazons and the Argonaut		[coll Prince Albert, the Prince Consort]; Royal Coll, Osborne House, I of W	*Gunnis* 1968, 142; *Read* 1982, 132, 134 (repr)
4.	pre-1857	Faith		[coll Sir David Saloman]; untraced	*Manchester Art Treasures*, 1857, 133
5.	1888	Innocence (the chase)	m	[Exhib RA, London, 1927]; untraced	*Graves* III, 1905–6, 57
6.	1888	Innocence lost (after the chase)	m	[Exhib RA, London, 1931]; untraced	*Graves* III, 1905–6, 57
7.	1888	The birth of Eve	m	[Exhib RA, London, 2066]; untraced	*Graves* III, 1905–6, 57
Busts					
8.	1838–1839	Queen Victoria and Albert, the Prince Consort		Untraced	*Singer* V, 1901–7, 161
9.	1840	Unidentified gentleman		[Exhib RA, London, 1152]; untraced	*Graves* III, 1905–6, 56
10.	1844	Mr Colnaghi		[Exhib RA, London, 1383]; untraced	*Graves* III, 1905–6, 56
11.	1845	W G Rogers, the woodcarver		[Exhib RA, London, 1411]; untraced	*Graves* III, 1905–6, 56
Reliefs					
12.	1846	The Hours bringing the horses to the chariot of Apollo, part of a frieze		[Exhib RA, London, 1429]; untraced Other versions: exhib RA, London, 1847, 1385	*Graves* III, 1905–6, 56–7
Miscellaneous					
13.	1843	Unidentified model		[Awarded RA silver medal]; untraced	RA Premium list
14.	1844	Crucifix	i	[Exhib RA, London, 1236]; untraced	*Graves* III, 1905–6, 56

ENGLEHEART, J –1809?

Miscellaneous					
1.	1783	Unidentified subject, portrait in wax		[Exhib RA, London, 277]; untraced	*Graves* III, 1905–6, 58

ENGLEHEART, Thomas 1745–1809

The sculptor and wax-modeller was one of a family of artists originating in Germany. His father, Francis, a modeller of decorative plasterwork, was born in Silesia but settled in England in 1721. Two of his brothers, John Dillman and Paul, carried on their father's business, while a third, George, became a successful miniature painter. Thomas's son, Francis, was a book illustrator.

Thomas may have been a pupil of **Sefferin Alken**, for Alken took an 'Engleheart' as his apprentice in 1760. He joined the Royal Academy Schools on 3 November 1769, giving his age as 23, and gained a silver medal in 1771 (*Hutchison* 1960–62, 134). A year later he won the gold medal, beating **John Flaxman RA** with a relief of *Ulysses and Nausicaa* (**7**). The sculptor's nephew, Nathaniel Engleheart, later wrote 'Flaxman assured me that, when fellow-students at the Royal Academy, he had no rival whom he envied so much as as Thomas Engleheart, and that such feelings assumed actual jealousy when the latter gained the Academy gold medal in a competition which lay only in point of fact between those two' (*Williamson and Engleheart* 1902, 4). In 1777 Engleheart was awarded a premium by the Society of Arts for a model, 6 feet high, of *John the Baptist in the desert* (**1**). He exhibited at the RA between 1773 and 1786 from several addresses, 4 Old Bond Street, 28 St James's Street, Little Carrington Street, Mayfair and Richmond, Surrey.

Pyke notes that Engleheart modelled for Josiah Wedgwood and his trade label, which is found on reliefs of George III and Queen Charlotte in the royal collection, indicates that he worked as a carver in wood and stone as well as making 'wax portraits at 2 guineas each' (*Pyke* 1973, 45) (**12, 14**). As a stone carver he worked on capitals for the principal front of Dodington Park, built for Christopher Codrington by James Wyatt, 1800–9 (**6**). After his death in 1809 a payment was made to 'Francis Engleheart on account of his father's carving' (Codrington Archives, in GPC).

Literary References: *Williamson and Engleheart* 1902, 4–5; *Williamson* 1936; 27–33; *Pyke* 1973, 45; *Beard and Gilbert* 1986, 8; *Grove* 10, 1996, 378 (Hunnisett)

Will: PROB 11/1506

Statues					
1.	1777	John the Baptist in the desert, model		[Soc of A premium, 25 gns]; untraced	RSA, *Transactions*, vol 2, 1784, 132; *Dossie* 1782, 439
Busts					
2.	1773	Thomas Fluelling		[Exhib RA, London, 96]; untraced	*Graves* III, 1905–6, 59
3.	1774	Unidentified subject, model		[Exhib RA, London, 84]; untraced	*Graves* III, 1905–6, 59
4.	1777	Unidentified subject	w	[Exhib RA, London, 119]; untraced	*Graves* III, 1905–6, 59
5.	1778	Unidentified subject	w	[Exhib RA, London, 102]; untraced	*Graves* III, 1905–6, 60
Architectural Sculpture					
6.	1800–1809	Corinthian capitals (co-sculptor: Lancashire)		Dodington Park, Glos, façade	Codrington archives in GPC; Pevsner, *Glos: Cotswolds*, 1999, 317
Reliefs					
7.	1772	Ulysses and Nausicaa		[RA gold medal]; untraced	*Public Advertiser*, 10 Dec 1772; *Williamson and Engleheart* 1902, 4
8.	1778	3 medallions	w	[Exhib RA, London, 103]; untraced	*Graves* III, 1905–6, 60
9.	1786	Edward, Duke of Kent	w	NPG 207	*Williamson and Engleheart* 1902, 4; *Gunnis* 1968, 142
10.	nd	Elizabeth Brown	w	[coll George Mackay, 1902]; destroyed before 1936	*Williamson and Engleheart* 1902, 4–5 (repr); *Williamson* 1936, 30, 33 (repr)
11.	nd	Hester Woolley	w	[coll George Mackay, 1902]; destroyed before 1936	*Williamson and Engleheart* 1902, 4–5 (repr); *Williamson* 1936, 30
12.	nd	King George III	w	Royal Coll	*Gunnis* 1968, 142; *Pyke* 1973, 45
13.	nd	Mary Woolley	w	[coll George Mackay, 1902]; destroyed before 1936	*Williamson and Engleheart* 1902, 4–5 (repr); *Williamson* 1936, 30, 33 (repr)
14.	nd	Queen Charlotte	w	Royal Coll	*Gunnis* 1968, 142; *Pyke* 1973, 45
Miscellaneous					
15.	1774	Three models	w	[Exhib RA, London, 85]; untraced	*Graves* III, 1905–6, 59
16.	1775	Three portrait models	w	[Exhib RA, London, 115]; untraced	*Graves* III, 1905–6, 59
17.	1776	Two portraits	w	[Exhib RA, London, 115]; untraced	*Graves* III, 1905–6, 59
18.	1777	A medal	w	[Exhib RA, London, 119]; untraced	*Graves* III, 1905–6, 59
19.	1779	A model	w	[Exhib RA, London, 89]; untraced	*Graves* III, 1905–6, 60
20.	1780	Unidentified gentleman	w	[Exhib RA, London, 295]; untraced	*Graves* III, 1905–6, 60
21.	1780	Unidentified lady	w	[Exhib RA, London, 294]; untraced	*Graves* III, 1905–6, 60
22.	1786	Unidentified subject, a portrait	w	[Exhib RA, London, 370]; untraced	*Graves* III, 1905–6, 60

ESSEX, Charles fl 1847–53

Essex exhibited busts and medallions at the Royal Academy, 1847–53. His gave his address as 22 Crawford Street, Portman Square (1847–1852) and 2 Percy Street (1853).

Literary References: *Graves* III, 1905–6, 61

Busts				
1.	1847	Alfred Essex	[Exhib RA, London, 1369]; untraced	*Graves* III, 1905–6, 61
2.	1849	Captain Maconochie	[Exhib RA, London, 1259]; untraced	*Graves* III, 1905–6, 61
3.	1850	Mr Williams	[Exhib RA, London, 1415]; untraced	*Graves* III, 1905–6, 61
4.	1850	Rev William Bruce	[Exhib RA, London, 1403]; untraced	*Graves* III, 1905–6, 61
5.	1850	Unidentified lady	[Exhib RA, London, 1372]; untraced	*Graves* III, 1905–6, 61
6.	1852	William Essex	[Exhib RA, London, 1324]; untraced	*Graves* III, 1905–6, 61
Reliefs				
7.	1851	Mrs Bird, medallion	[Exhib RA, London, 1281]; untraced	*Graves* III, 1905–6, 61
8.	1852	'L H', medallion	[Exhib RA, London, 1336]; untraced	*Graves* III, 1905–6, 61
9.	1853	'C E', medallion	[Exhib RA, London, 1457]; untraced	*Graves* III, 1905–6, 61

EUSTACE, Thomas fl *c*1715

Statues					
1.	*c*1715	2 charity school children	s	St Mary Abbots School, Kensington, London, exterior	*Holyoake* 1980, 1787

EVANS, E F, of Derby fl 1797–1800

Gunnis notes that he was probably a son of **Joseph Evans** and that 'his monuments in design and execution are better than those of the average provincial statuary of the time'.

Literary References: *Gunnis* 1968, 142

Funerary Monuments					
1.	†1797	George Bonsall	Alfreton, Derbys	S	Pevsner, *Derbys*, 1978, 56
2.	†1800	William Stevens	Repton, Derbys	S	Pevsner, *Derbys*, 1978, 305

EVANS, Eneas, of Derby fl 1761–65

Evans, who may have been the father of **Joseph Evans**, worked as assistant to **Joseph Hall I of Derby**, at Kedleston in 1761. Four years later he made chimneypieces for some of the bedrooms.

Literary References: *Gunnis* 1968, 142, citing Curzon Archives, 1761, 1765

Chimneypieces					
1.	1765	Several, black and yellow marble	m	Kedleston, Derbys, Bedrooms	*Gunnis* 1968, 142

EVANS, Joseph, of Derby fl c1770–89

The monument to Sir Brooke Boothby takes the form of an antique block *stele* decorated with ivy and tear vases (**1**). It is an early example of neoclassical sepulchral sculpture and of the use of ivy to symbolise clinging memory. It is unlikely that a provincial statuary like Evans could have conceived of such an original monument and the writer Sir Brooke Boothby (1744–1824), who commissioned the monument in memory of his parents, was probably responsible for the design. As a founder member of the Lichfield Botanical Society, Boothby had a particular interest in plants, and his friends included several of the leading artists of the day. He subsequently commissioned an important monument commemorating his daughter, Penelope, from **Thomas Banks.**

Literary References: *Gunnis* 1968, 142; *Penny* 1977 (1), 21, 24, 207

Funerary Monuments

1.	†1789	Sir Brooke Boothby and his wife, Dame Phebe (†1788)	a	Ashbourne, Derbys	S	*Penny* 1977 (1), 20–21 (repr)
2.	1797	Thomas Peach (†1790)		Dingley, Northants	S	*Gunnis* 1968, 142

EVEN

His tradecard, engraved by J Pye, has a picturesque scene with a tree trunk supporting a stone slab inscribed 'EVEN's/Sculptor/to/HRH'. A statue on a plinth is in the distance and in the foreground are callipers, an artist's palette and an open sketch book (Heal Coll BM 106.11).

EWINGS, W fl 1820–36

In 1820–21 Ewings was in Rome, where he carved ivory portraits of Canova and Pope Pius VII (**10, 11**). Two years later he exhibited these with other examples of his work in ivory at the Royal Academy, from 9 Percy Street, Bedford Square. He must have returned to Rome soon after, since his busts of Robert Finch and J Waldie were both executed in that city (**2, 5**). His monument to Owen Lewis (**1**) has a 'fine relief of a mourning woman in the manner of **Chantrey**' (*Gunnis* 1968, 142).

Literary References: *Gunnis* 1968, 142

Archival References: GPC

Funerary Monuments						
1.	?1824	Owen Lewis		Laugharne, Carmarthen	S	*Gunnis* 1968, 142
Busts						
2.	1826	Robert Finch	m	Taylorian Institute, Oxford	SD	
3.	1827	1st Lord Wenlock		Escrick Park, E R Yorks	D	GPC
4.	1831	Henry Crabb Robinson		Dr Williams's Library, Gordon Square, London	D	GPC
5.	1836	J Waldie		[Hendersyde Park, Roxburghs]; untraced		*Hendersyde* 1859 in GPC
6.	nd	Apollo Belvedere		[Hendersyde Park, Roxburghs]; untraced		*Hendersyde* 1859 in GPC
7.	nd	Emperor Augustus		[Hendersyde Park, Roxburghs] untraced		Hendersyde 1859 in GPC
Reliefs						
8.	1818	Major J C Sirr	i	VAM A.60-1940	SD	VAM SCP colls list, ivories
9.	nd	Unidentified man	i	Private coll	S	inf VAM SCP
Miscellaneous						
10.	1820	Antonio Canova	i	[Exhib RA, London, 1822, 922]; untraced		*Graves* III, 1905–6, 74
11.	1821	Pope Pius VII	i	[Exhib RA, London, 1822, 925]; untraced		*Graves* III, 1905–6, 74
12.	1822	Study from the head of an antique statue of Antinous	i	[Exhib RA, London, 929]; untraced		*Graves* III, 1905–6, 74
13.	1822	Unidentified young lady	i	[Exhib RA, London, 920]; untraced		*Graves* III, 1905–6, 74

EXLEY, Robert, of Malton fl 1837

Funerary Monuments

1.	1837	Jacob Stubbs		Crambe, N R Yorks	S	GPC

EYKYN, Roger, of Wolverhampton c1725–95

An architect and builder, he was born at Worfield, Staffs in 1724 or 1725 and established himself in Wolverhampton, where he is first noted in 1760 as a master joiner and subsequently as a nurseryman, architect and surveyor. He appears also to have worked as a mason for he signed three monuments, and provided carved ornaments at Stone, Staffs (**1, 2, 3, 7**). He is mentioned frequently in the account book of William Baker (1705–1771), an architect and surveyor of Audlem, Cheshire, who paid him for two vases in 1756 and £24 for a monument at Leighton in 1759 (**6, 3**). Baker employed Eykyn at a number of houses, including Oakely Hall, Salop, Dorfield Hall, Cheshire and Etwell Hall, Derbys. He also noted Ekyn's marriage in 1754. As an architect Eykyn supplied designs and a model for St Paul's, Birmingham, in 1777–9. His obituary notice in the *Birmingham Gazette* describes him as an 'eminent architect and surveyor'.

Literary References: *Oswald* 1954, *passim*; *Gunnis* 1968, 142; *Colvin* 1995, 359

Funerary Monuments

1.	†1747	Elizabeth Crompton		Broseley, Salop	S	*Gunnis* 1968, 142; *Colvin* 1995, 359
2.	†1748	George Weld		Willey, Salop	S	Pevsner, *Salop*, 1958, 320
3.	1756, 1759	Elizabeth (†1743) and Anthony (†1760) Leighton, tablet, and two vases Payment(s): Vases (1756) £1 16s; tablet (1759) £24		Leighton, Salop	S	*Colvin* 1995, 359
4.	1756–1759	Hayns family (?) Payment(s): £24		[For Leighton, Salop]; untraced		*Oswald* 1954, 134; *Colvin* 1995, 359

Chimneypieces

5.	1756	Description unavailable	Brand Hall, Norton-in-Hales, Salop, parlour	*Oswald* 1954, 125

Architectural Sculpture

6.	1756	Two vases Payment(s): £1 16s	[coll William Baker of Audlam]; untraced	*Colvin* 1995, 359
7.	*c*1785	Carving Payment(s): £4 10s	Stone church, Staffs	*Colvin* 1995, 359

FACONET, Martha –before 1790

Martha Faconet, the widow of a sculptor, was given a donation of 5 guineas by the Council of the Royal Academy in 1790.

Archival References: RA/GA 1790

FAGAN fl later 18th century

He flourished during the second half of the 18th century, when he was a pupil and assistant of **Simon Vierpyl** and probably worked on stone carving for the various public buildings where his master was employed.

Literary References: *Strickland* I, 1913, 329

FANELLI, Giovanni Battista 1605–72

The 'John Baptista Fenella' who is listed in *Gunnis* 1968 is probably Giovanni Battista Fanelli. The son of Francesco Fanelli, sculptor to King Charles I, he was baptised on 5 August 1605 in S Agnese, Genoa and trained in his father's workshop. He is not recorded in Italy after Francesco's departure for England *c*1628, so it is likely that he accompanied his father across Europe to London. Giovanni Battista appears to have resided in the Spanish Netherlands between about 1630/1 and 1633/4, was in London, and perhaps later in Oxford, from *c*1633/4 until about 1644, when he left England. He returned before April 1663, when Charles II issued a Royal Warrant granting him 'ye sum of £40 pr. ann. for and towards ye charge, and of providing a fit and necessary working-place, & other accommodations for ye performance of our service in his profession' (TNA, Calendar of State papers, Domestic, Charles II (1663–4), 9, 334). He remained in London until his death in 1672, which probably took place soon after he signed his will on 15 March 1672 in a hand that suggests extreme frailty (City of Westminster Archives, Act Book 70, 509).

Simon Stock/EH

Literary References: *Gunnis* 1968, 144

FARKSON, Benjamin

See **Fattson, Benjamin**

FARLEY, James Samuel 1811–66

J S Farley lived at Kensal Green where he established his business in 1833. It was carried on after his death by his son, another J S Farley, passing after the son's death to T Kemp. It currently trades as Jordan Farley Ltd, from the original premises opposite the entrance to Kensal Green Cemetery. The elder Farley was appointed chapel clerk and sexton of the cemetery in 1843, and was buried there. His monument to Mary Gibson (4) gives striking proof of the high level of craftsmanship achieved by commercial firms of Victorian monumental masons. It is an open-canopied tomb with a peristyle of 12 Corinthian columns and a frieze of lilies around the entablature. This supports 4 angels whose outstretched arms once held a crown of thorns.

The younger Farley was responsible for the monument to William Henry, 6th Earl Poulett, †1899, at Hinton St George, Somerset. The full size plaster model survives on the premises and the monument appeared as the frontispiece to Farley's catalogue of 1910.

Literary References: *Curl* 2001, *passim*

Funerary Monuments

1.	†1851	Colonel Edward Story		Kensal Green Cemetery, London, catacombs	S	
2.	†1857	Henry Mount	m	Nackington, Kent	S	
3.	†1863	Emma Hankey		Kensal Green Cemetery, catacombs	S	
4.	†1872	Mary Gibson		Kensal Green Cemetery, London		*Curl* 2001, 112, 184–5, 214, 237, 238 (repr)
5.	†1877	Margaret Anderson		Kensal Green Cemetery, catacombs	S	
6.	†1887	Mary Ramsey		Kensal Green Cemetery, catacombs	S	

FARMER, P J fl 1826–27

His address was 35 William Street in 1826, when exhibited a bust of the sculptor **John de Vaere** at the Royal Academy (1).

Literary References: *Graves* III, 1905–6, 88

Busts

1.	1826	John de Vaere, to be executed in marble		[Exhib RA, London, 1014]; untraced	*Graves* III, 1905–6, 88

Miscellaneous

2.	1827	Flowers, sketch	tc	[Exhib Soc of BA, London, 863]; untraced	*Johnson* 1975, 155

FARMER, Richard, of Swindon fl 1719–33?

Probably the son of James Farmer of Chippenham, he was apprenticed to Richard Smith, mason, of the same town in 1719 (TNA IR 1/6). Gunnis describes his memorial to Jane Scholes as 'a very pretty cartouche-tablet'.

Literary References: *Gunnis* 1968, 143

Funerary Monuments

1.	?1733	Jane Scholes	m	St Mary, Marlborough, Wilts	S	*Gunnis* 1968, 143

FARRELL, James RHA 1821–91

The eldest son of **Terence Farrell**, he studied in his father's studio in Dublin and exhibited at the Royal Hibernian Academy from 1836. Most of his life was spent in Ireland, but he sent over works to the Royal Academy in London between 1843 and 1869. He sometimes worked in collaboration with his father. A bust of the Dean of St Patrick's

Cathedral (17) exhibited at the RHA in 1842 was entered under the names of both James and Terence, and in 1843 James exhibited at the RA models of two groups of children and animals which Earl de Grey had commissioned from his father (3). His first important independent work was *The pet dove's return*, which was awarded the first prize of £15 by the Royal Irish Art Union in 1845 (4). It was subsequently executed in marble and exhibited at the RA in 1847 and the RHA in 1848. In 1853 he sent statues of the *Hunter Reposing* and *Our Lady of Refuge* to the Dublin International Exhibition (5, 6). Farrell was much employed in work on religious statues for both public and private patrons. He was elected an Associate of the RHA in 1880, and a full member 2 years later. He died at his home, 30 Mountjoy Square, Dublin, on 20 November 1891 and was buried in the vaults of Westland Row church.

Literary References: *Strickland* I, 1913, 331–2; *Gunnis* 1968, 143; *Potterton* 1975, 43

No.	Date	Work		Location	References
Funerary Monuments					
1.	1853	Archbishop Murray, sketch model		[Exhib RHA, Dublin, 472]; untraced	*Stewart* 1, 1985, 250
2.	†1854	Lieutenant Worthington		St George, Dublin	*Potterton* 1975, 43
Statues					
3.	1843	'Children and dogs' and 'children and goats' (co-sculptor: Terence Farrell RHA) Model(s): exhib RA, London, 1843, 1427, 1436; awarded Royal Irish Art Union first premium, 1844		[Wrest Park, Beds, gardens]; untraced	*Graves* III, 1905–6, 90; *Gunnis* 1968, 143; *Murphy* 1991–2, 75, 79 n9
4.	1845	The pet dove's return, model		[Awarded Royal Irish Art Union premium]; untraced	*Graves* III, 1905–6, 90; *Strickland* I, 1913, 331; *Stewart* 1, 1985, 250
5.	1852	Hunter reposing (the tired hunter)		[Exhib RHA, Dublin, 378]; untraced	*Strickland* I, 1913, 331; *Stewart* 1, 1985, 250
6.	1853	Our lady of refuge		[Int Exhib, Dublin]; Rathmines church, Dublin, portico	*Strickland* I, 1913, 331
7.	1858	The soft sleep of happy boyhood	m	[Exhib RA, London, 1193]; untraced	*Graves* III, 1905–6, 90; *Morris and Roberts* 1998, 227
8.	1859	Christ in the temple (the youthful saviour disputing with the elders) Payment(s): £50	m	Rathmines church, Dublin	*Strickland* I, 1913, 331; *Stewart* 1, 1985, 250
9.	1860	Oliver Goldsmith, statuette Payment(s): £2 2s		[Exhib RHA, Dublin, 513]; untraced	*Stewart* 1, 1985, 250
10.	1862	Erin, 'statue in Parian' Payment(s): £30		[Exhib RHA, Dublin, 464]; untraced	*Stewart* 1, 1985, 250
11.	1882	Calypso Payment(s): £25		National Museum, Kildare Street, Dublin	*Strickland* I, 1913, 331; *Stewart* 1, 1985, 250
12.	1888	William Ewart Gladstone, statuette Payment(s): £25		[Exhib RHA, Dublin, 492]; untraced	*Stewart* 1, 1985, 250
13.	1889	St Agnes and Fabiola Payment(s): £25		[Exhib RHA, Dublin, 504]; untraced	*Stewart* 1, 1985, 250
Busts					
14.	1836	Mrs Law		[Exhib RHA, Dublin, 254]; untraced	*Stewart* 1, 1985, 250
15.	1836	Unidentified child		[Exhib RHA, Dublin, 259]; untraced	*Stewart* 1, 1985, 250
16.	1841	Right Rev Dr Dickinson, Bishop of Meath		[Exhib RHA, Dublin, 397]; untraced	*Stewart* 1, 1985, 250
17.	1842	Henry Dawson, Dean of St Patrick's (co-sculptor: Terence Farrell RHA)		[Exhib RHA, Dublin, 467]; untraced	*Stewart* 1, 1985, 250
18.	1853	Unidentified gentleman		[Exhib RHA, Dublin, 458]; untraced	*Stewart* 1, 1985, 250
19.	1862	Mrs Stuart, model		[Exhib RHA, Dublin, 468]; untraced	*Stewart* 1, 1985, 250
Reliefs					
20.	1886	Unidentified lady, medallion		[Exhib RHA, Dublin, 600]; untraced	*Stewart* 1, 1985, 250
Miscellaneous					
21.	1856	Annunciation		St Francis Xavier, Gardiner Street, Dublin	*Strickland* I, 1913, 331; *Stewart* 1, 1985, 250
22.	1868	St Agnes Payment(s): £30		[Exhib RHA, Dublin, 438]; untraced	*Stewart* 1, 1985, 250
23.	1869	Boys and duck		[Exhib RA, London, 1304]; untraced	*Graves* III, 1905–6, 90
24.	1879	The Dauphin Payment(s): £30		[Exhib RHA, London, 552]; untraced	*Stewart* 1, 1985, 250
25.	1880	A bather Payment(s): £30		[Exhib RHA, London, 592]; untraced	*Stewart* 1, 1985, 250
26.	1880	Joy		[Exhib RHA, Dublin, 593]; untraced	*Stewart* 1, 1985, 250
27.	1880	Sorrow		[Exhib RHA, Dublin, 594]; untraced	*Stewart* 1, 1985, 250
28.	1881	The genius of the wood	p	[Exhib RHA, Dublin, 704]; untraced	*Stewart* 1, 1985, 250
29.	1883	'Has sorrow thy young days shaded . . .' Payment(s): £25		[Exhib RHA, Dublin, 644]; untraced	*Stewart* 1, 1985, 250
30.	1883	The bride Payment(s): £5		[Exhib RHA, London, 645]; untraced	*Stewart* 1, 1985, 250
31.	1884	Cimabue Payment(s): £25		[Exhib RHA, Dublin, 631]; untraced	*Stewart* 1, 1985, 250
32.	1884	The morning star Payment(s): £5		[Exhib RHA, Dublin, 633]; untraced	*Stewart* 1, 1985, 250
33.	1884	Twilight Payment(s): £5		[Exhib RHA, Dublin, 632]; untraced	*Stewart* 1, 1985, 250
34.	1885	The emigrant Payment(s): £35		[Exhib RHA, Dublin, 563]; untraced	*Stewart* 1, 1985, 250
35.	1885	The favourite doll Payment(s): £5		[Exhib RHA, Dublin, 564]; untraced	*Stewart* 1, 1985, 250

36.	1886	Genevieve Payment(s): £5		[Exhib RHA, Dublin, 609]; untraced	*Stewart* 1, 1985, 250
37.	1886	The message of love (love's messenger) Payment(s): £25		[Exhib RHA, Dublin, 599]; untraced	*Stewart* 1, 1985, 250
38.	1887	Cannera Payment(s): £50		[Exhib RHA, Dublin, 500]; untraced	*Stewart* 1, 1985, 250
39.	1889	A poetess Payment(s): £20		[Exhib RHA, Dublin, 506]; untraced	*Stewart* 1, 1985, 250
40.	1889	Beppo Payment(s): £10		[Exhib RHA, Dublin, 508]; untraced	*Stewart* 1, 1985, 250
41.	1889	Graziella Payment(s): £35		[Exhib RHA, Dublin, 507]; untraced	*Stewart* 1, 1985, 250
42.	1890	Lear and Cordelia		[Exhib RHA, Dublin, 516]; untraced	*Stewart* 1, 1985, 250
43.	1890	Solitude		[Exhib RHA, Dublin, 515]; untraced	*Stewart* 1, 1985, 250
44.	1891	Jealousy Payment(s): £20		[Exhib RHA, Dublin, 509]; untraced	*Stewart* 1, 1985, 250
45.	1891	Little Lord Fauntleroy Payment(s): £30		[Exhib RHA, Dublin, 508]; untraced	*Stewart* 1, 1985, 250
46.	nd	The sacred heart		Sion Hill Convent, Blackrock, Co Dublin	*Strickland* I, 1913, 331

FARRELL, John 1829–1901

The fourth son of **Terence Farrell**, he was a pupil at the modelling school of the Royal Dublin Society and won a prize in 1846 (**9**). He also studied drawing at the Royal Hibernian Academy. He worked principally in collaboration with his brothers on religious statues for churches. He exhibited at the RHA between 1849 and 1895 and sent works, including *The wanderer* and *Judith*, to the Dublin International Exhibitions of 1853 and 1872 (**1, 17**).

Literary References: *Strickland* I, 1913, 332

Statues					
1.	1853	The wanderer		[Dublin Int Exhib]; untraced	*Strickland* I, 1913, 332
2.	1872	Lord Gough, statuette		[Exhib RHA, Dublin, 430]; untraced	*Stewart* 1, 1985, 251
Busts					
3.	1862	Henry Pakenham, Dean of St Patrick's		[Exhib RHA, Dublin, 465]; untraced	*Stewart* 1, 1985, 251
4.	1862	Terence Farrell RHA		[Exhib RHA, Dublin, 466]; untraced	*Stewart* 1, 1985, 251
5.	1864	Alderman Roe		[Exhib RHA, Dublin, 443]; untraced	*Stewart* 1, 1985, 251
6.	1864	John Hatch Power		[Exhib RHA, Dublin, 446]; untraced	*Stewart* 1, 1985, 251
7.	1868	Unidentified subject	p	[Exhib RHA, Dublin, 448]; untraced	*Stewart* 1, 1985, 251
8.	nd	Rev Dr Yore		Convent of the Sisters of Charity, Merrion, Dublin	*Strickland* I, 1913, 332
Miscellaneous					
9.	1846	Unidentified subject, large model		[RHA prize]; untraced	*Strickland* I, 1913, 332
10.	1849	Devotion		[Exhib RHA, Dublin, 440]; untraced	*Stewart* 1, 1985, 250
11.	1856	La siesta		[Exhib RHA, Dublin, 402]; untraced	*Stewart* 1, 1985, 250
12.	1859	The hunter reposing		[Exhib RHA, Dublin, 330]; untraced	*Stewart* 1, 1985, 250
13.	1860	Sleeping youth Payment(s): £52 10s	m	[Exhib RHA, Dublin, 514]; untraced	*Stewart* 1, 1985, 250
14.	1860	The swimmer Payment(s): £5 5s		[Exhib RHA, Dublin, 516]; untraced Other versions: exhib RHA, 1862, 473, £10; untraced	*Stewart* 1, 1985, 250, 251
15.	1862	Nora Creina Payment(s): £20		[Exhib RHA, Dublin, 484]; untraced	*Stewart* 1, 1985, 251
16.	1868	A poetess reposing after her triumph		[Exhib RHA, Dublin, 426]; untraced	*Stewart* 1, 1985, 251
17.	1871	Judith	m	[RHA, Dublin, 1871, 402; Dublin Int Exhib, 1872]; untraced	*Strickland* I, 1913, 332; *Stewart* 1, 1985, 251
18.	1873	Design for a memorial, model		[Exhib RHA, Dublin, 373]; untraced	*Stewart* 1, 1985, 251
19.	1876	The Peri		[Exhib RHA, Dublin, 433]; untraced	*Stewart* 1, 1985, 251
20.	1879	Erin		[Exhib RHA, Dublin, 553]; untraced	*Stewart* 1, 1985, 251
21.	1880	Pandora		[Exhib RHA, Dublin, 591]; untraced	*Stewart* 1, 1985, 251
22.	1883	Mary Magdalen at the feet of our Lord		[Exhib RHA, Dublin, 647]; untraced	*Stewart* 1, 1985, 251
23.	1884	Hermione		[Exhib RHA, Dublin, 634]; untraced	*Stewart* 1, 1985, 251
24.	1886	St Michael		[Exhib RHA, Dublin, 601]; untraced	*Stewart* 1, 1985, 251
25.	1886	Susannah		[Exhib RHA, Dublin, 602]; untraced	*Stewart* 1, 1985, 251
26.	1887	Listening to the echoes		[Exhib RHA, Dublin, 495]; untraced	*Stewart* 1, 1985, 251
27.	1888	Zenobia		[Exhib RHA, Dublin, 491]; untraced	*Stewart* 1, 1985, 251
28.	1889	Jeptha's daughter		[Exhib RHA, Dublin, 509]; untraced	*Stewart* 1, 1985, 251
29.	1890	On she went with her maiden smile		[Exhib RHA, Dublin, 522]; untraced	*Stewart* 1, 1985, 251
30.	1894	'Improvisatrice' Payment(s): £10		[Exhib RHA, Dublin, 464]; untraced	*Stewart* 1, 1985, 251
31.	1894	Pastoral life Payment(s): £31 10s		[Exhib RHA, Dublin, 463]; untraced	*Stewart* 1, 1985, 251
32.	1895	Spring		[Exhib RHA, Dublin, 502]; untraced	*Stewart* 1, 1985, 251

FARRELL, Joseph 1823–1904

The second son of the Dublin sculptor **Terence Farrell**, he was born in 1823. He collaborated with his brothers, chiefly on work for churches. His small marble statue of *The blessed Virgin* (**1**) brought him to the attention of the Catholic clergy and 'until it was pirated by the Italian moulders in Dublin, the sale of copies in plaster brought him a considerable income' (*Strickland* I, 1913, 332–3). He exhibited at the Royal Hibernian Academy between 1850 and 1896 and sent *A bard, Looking at the sea* and *Saved from the wreck* to the Dublin International Exhibitions of 1853 and 1872 (**3, 14, 15**). He died in 1904 and was buried in Glasnevin Cemetery.

Literary References: *Strickland* I, 1913, 332–3

Statues					
1.	1850	The blessed Virgin	m	[Executed for William Nugent Skelly]; untraced Other versions: reproduced in plaster by Farrell and others	*Strickland* I, 1913, 332–3; *Stewart* 1, 1985, 251
2.	1851	A deaf and dumb child, statuette	m	[Executed for William Nugent Skelly]; untraced	*Stewart* 1, 1985, 251
3.	1853	A bard		[Dublin Int Exhib]; untraced	*Strickland* I, 1913, 333
4.	1887	Portion of a group of a Pieta		[Exhib RHA, Dublin, 497]; untraced	*Stewart* 1, 1985, 252
5.	nd	St Joseph		Convent of the Redemptorists, Drumcondra, Dublin	*Strickland* I, 1913, 333
Busts					
6.	1883	John Philpot Curran		[Exhib RHA, Dublin, 648]; untraced Other versions: exhib RHA, Dublin, 1884, 635; untraced	*Stewart* 1, 1985, 252
7.	1885	The Virgin Payment(s): £52 10s	m	[Exhib RHA, Dublin, 561]; untraced	*Stewart* 1, 1985, 252
Architectural Sculpture					
8.	nd	Altar		Waterford Cathedral	*Strickland* I, 1913, 333
9.	nd	Altar		Dundalk, Co Louth	*Strickland* I, 1913, 333
10.	nd	Altar		Convent of the Redemptorists, Drumcondra, Dublin	*Strickland* I, 1913, 333
Miscellaneous					
11.	1859	St Michael		[Exhib RHA, Dublin, 332]; untraced	*Stewart* 1, 1985, 251
12.	1862	Rebecca		[Exhib RHA, Dublin, 469]; untraced	*Stewart* 1, 1985, 251
13.	1863	Pieta (unfinished model)		[Exhib RHA, Dublin, 486]; untraced	*Stewart* 1, 1985, 251
14.	1871	Looking at the sea Payment(s): £100	m	[Exhib RHA, Dublin, 400]; untraced	*Strickland* I, 1913, 333; *Stewart* 1, 1985, 251
15.	1871	Saved from the wreck Payment(s): £100		[Exhib RHA, Dublin, 406]; untraced	*Strickland* I, 1913, 333; *Stewart* 1, 1985, 251
16.	1873	Sancta Maria		[Exhib RHA, Dublin, 366]; untraced	*Stewart* 1, 1985, 251
17.	1873	St Joseph		[Exhib RHA, Dublin, 367]; untraced	*Stewart* 1, 1985, 251
18.	1876	Godiva		[Exhib RHA, Dublin, 430]; untraced	*Stewart* 1, 1985, 251
19.	1881	Learn of me Payment(s): £95	m	[Exhib RHA, Dublin, 707]; untraced Other versions: exhib RHA, Dublin, 1882, 662; untraced	*Stewart* 1, 1985, 251
20.	1881	Mater salvatoris Payment(s): £60		[Exhib RHA, Dublin, 709]; untraced	*Stewart* 1, 1985, 251
21.	1881	Virgo fideles Payment(s): £95		[Exhib RHA, Dublin, 708]; untraced	*Stewart* 1, 1985, 251
22.	1882	Dulcis Virgo Maria		[Exhib RHA, Dublin, 663]; untraced	*Stewart* 1, 1985, 251
23.	1882	Nora		[Exhib RHA, Dublin, 649]; untraced	*Stewart* 1, 1985, 252
24.	1882	St Agnes		[Exhib RHA, Dublin, 664]; untraced	*Stewart* 1, 1985, 251
25.	1885	The Virgin, model		[Exhib RHA, Dublin, 561]; untraced	*Stewart* 1, 1985, 252
26.	1887	A racer Payment(s): £6		[Exhib RHA, Dublin, 496]; untraced	*Stewart* 1, 1985, 252
27.	1887	King and priest Payment(s): £2		[Exhib RHA, Dublin, 498]; untraced	*Stewart* 1, 1985, 252
28.	1887	Last look of St Agnes to heaven Payment(s): £35		[Exhib RHA, Dublin, 499]; untraced	*Stewart* 1, 1985, 252
29.	1895	Design for a memorial		[Exhib RHA, Dublin, 507]; untraced	*Stewart* 1, 1985, 252
30.	1895	Draped relievo, preparatory sketch		[Exhib RHA, Dublin, 506]; untraced	*Stewart* 1, 1985, 252
31.	1895	Pieta Model(s): sketch model exhib RHA, Dublin, 1895, 504		[Exhib RHA, Dublin, 503]; untraced	*Stewart* 1, 1985, 252
32.	1895	Saved		[Exhib RHA, Dublin, 505]; untraced	*Stewart* 1, 1985, 252
33.	1896	The bather		[Exhib RHA, Dublin, 441]; untraced	*Stewart* 1, 1985, 252

FARRELL, Terence RHA 1798–1876

He enjoyed some success as a sculptor of portraits and church monuments in Ireland in the mid-19th century and was the head of a large family workshop, with all six of his sons following his profession. He was born at Creve, County Longford, where his grandfather owned stone quarries. In 1810 his mother brought him to Dublin, where his elder brother was employed as a stone cutter, and he was placed in the modelling school of the Dublin Society, receiving instruction from **Edward** and **John Smyth**. On leaving the school he entered the studio of **Thomas Kirk**, as a pupil for nearly seven years and then as an assistant. He was still employed by Kirk when he first exhibited at the Royal Hibernian Academy in 1826, showing a miniature bust of George IV (**25**). Kirk worked on two commissioned portraits of the King during the same period.

After he married Maria Ruxton, at the age of 21, the couple lived on the south bank of the River Liffey in the parish of St Bride, a market area and poor residential quarter, where it seems likely that home and studio were one. As Farrell became established he moved to the north side of the city near most of the sculpture yards, opening premises in Lower Mecklenberg Street in 1841. The Farrell family workshop remained in this area, at Mecklenberg Street and North Gloucester Street, until the early 20th century.

During the 1830s Terence established a reputation as a portrait sculptor, exhibiting a number of commissioned busts at the RHA each year. He particularly specialised in miniature heads, such as the tiny herm-like classical portrait of Bartholomew Lloyd, Provost of Trinity College, which he carved from life in 1836 (**40**). Some of these were incorporated into church monuments, including one of Henry Dawson, Dean of St Patrick's Cathedral, which is mounted above a sarcophagus-shaped tablet at Castlecomer (**4**). In 1840 he applied for the post of master of the modelling school at the Royal Dublin Society but was unsuccessful, and the job went to **Constantine Panormo**. During the same period Farrell competed for the commission for a monumental statue of the late Dean of St Patrick's to be placed in the Cathedral, exhibiting his design at the RHA in 1842 (**15**). It was difficult for a sculptor of miniature busts to convince the committee that he could also work on a monumental scale and the commission was awarded to **E H Baily**. By this time his eldest sons, **James** and **Joseph Farrell**, were working in the sculpture-yard and they were soon joined by their younger brothers, **Thomas, John**, Michael (1834–1855) and William (1839-after 1913).

Farrell's most important patron was Thomas, Earl de Grey, who first came into contact with the sculptor when, in his capacity as lord lieutenant of Ireland, he commissioned a bust from Farrell in the early 1840s (**54**). De Grey found Farrell 'a modest, unassuming, diffident man' and was greatly impressed by his work (*Proceedings of the RDS*, 26 January 1843, Appendix III, xlix, quoted by *Murphy* 1991–2, 75). He commissioned a series of statues for the gardens at Wrest Park, including two groups of animals and children which were awarded the first premium in the category 'Modelling in Clay or Plaster' at the Royal Irish Art Union in 1844 (**16–18**). When de Grey resigned his position as Lord Lieutenant in 1844 the RDS commissioned a marble bust of the Earl, a former chairman of the Society, from Farrell (**66**). The bust, which was based on an earlier clay model made at the request of the Countess de Grey, was well received both by the RDS and later, when it was exhibited at the Dublin Exhibition of 1853.

Farrell's connection with Earl de Grey helped him secure a number of significant monumental commissions during the 1840s and 1850s. These included the large wall monument commemorating his countess for the de Grey mausoleum at Flitton (**9**). It is a conventional composition, depicting in relief the mourning family, with the earl standing behind a draped coffin and two daughters weep helplessly over it, whilst above them the countess is guided heavenwards by an angel. He also executed three memorials for St Patrick's Cathedral, Dublin: the tribute to members of the 18th Royal Irish Regiment who fell in the China War of 1840–42 has a relief illustrating the death of Colonel Tomlinson at Chappoo in 1842 (**5**), and the Burmah War Memorial relief represents the storming of the Shoe Dragon Pagoda in April 1832 (**12**). Both are supported by crouching Irish wolf-hounds, with the dragon of China and the sphinx of Egypt on either side. The monument to Charles Wolfe has a portrait medallion (**13**). The designs for the Countess de Grey and China War memorials were both displayed at the Dublin International Exhibition in 1853 and Farrell sent an ideal work, *Early affliction*, to the Great Exhibition in London, in 1851 (**19**).

During the 1850s Farrell received commissions for portrait statues of General Sir Galbraith Lowry Cole, commander of the 27th Regiment in the Peninsular War, and John Willoughby, 2nd Earl of Enniskillen, for Enniskillen (**22, 10**). Both men were brothers of the late Countess de Grey. General Cole's statue was placed on top of a column in Forthill Park, while that of the Earl of Enniskillen was erected as a funerary monument in the Anglican Cathedral of St McCarten. Farrell was, presumably, also responsible for a second, virtually identical statue of General Cole erected in the Cathedral (**6**). De Grey's influence also ensured that Farrell was involved in discussions on the completion of the Wellington testimonial in Phoenix Park, Dublin which had stood in an unfinished state since 1820, though he did not execute any of its sculpture.

Farrell, who had been an associate since 1851, was elected a full member of the RHA in 1859. He was by then already in his sixties and beginning to take a lesser role while his third son, Thomas Farrell, became the most prominent member of the family. The death of Earl de Grey in the same year lost him his most significant patron. He continued to exhibit at the RHA until 1866 showing principally portrait busts and in the early 1860s received an unusual commission from another lord lieutenant, Lord Carlisle. This was a memorial to his sister, Lady St Germans, which commemorates her with the image of a tree she had planted, which died in the year of her death. It takes the form of a simple cropped column, encircled by a garland of flowers, on a base with an inscription tablet, and is placed in a secluded spot amongst trees in the grounds of the vice-regal Lodge (**81**).

Farrell died on 19 March 1876, aged 78, and was buried in the crypt of St Andrew, Westland Row, Dublin. His death attracted little comment. The *Irish Builder* described him as 'a gentleman highly respected and esteemed' in a very short notice of his death, while The *Irish Times* carried a death notice and no obituary (*Irish Builder*, 15 April 1876 and *Irish Times*, 19 March 1876, cited by *Murphy* 1991–2, 78). Murphy comments that, 'while Farrell's carving shows diligent craftsmanship and sculptural talent, there is little creative expression manifest in the work' and suggests that this was perhaps because the opportunities provided by Earl de Grey's patronage came too late in his career (*Murphy* 1991–2, 78–9).

EH

Literary References: *Strickland* 1, 1913, 333–34; *Gunnis* 1968, 143; *Potterton* 1975, 43–4; *Murphy* 1991–2, 73–79

Funerary Monuments

1.	†1827	Father Kenrick	St Nicholas of Myra, Francis Street, Dublin		*Murphy* 1991–2, 74 (repr)
2.	†1827	Robert Kane (signed 'Farrell Sc.')	Castlecomer, Co Dublin	S	*Potterton* 1975, 43
3.	†1830	Anne, Countess of Ossory (signed 'Farrell Sc.')	Castlecomer, Co Dublin	S	*Potterton* 1975, 43
4.	1841	Henry Dawson, Dean of St Patrick's	Castlecomer, Co Dublin		*Potterton* 1975, 43; *Stewart* 1, 1985, 252; *Murphy* 1991–2, 74 (repr)
5.	†1840–1842	18th Royal Irish Regiment, China War memorial Model(s): Dublin Int Exhib, 1853	St Patrick's Cathedral, Dublin	S	*Strickland* I, 1913, 335; *Potterton* 1975, 43; *Murphy* 1991–2, 76, 77 (repr)
6.	†1842	Sir Galbraith Lowry Cole	Enniskillen, Co Fermanagh		*Potterton* 1975, 43; *Murphy* 1991–2, 77, 78 (repr)
7.	†1842	Sir Hussey Vivian	[St Mary, Truro, Cornwall]; Truro Cathedral	S	*Strickland* I, 1913, 335; *Murphy* 1991–2, 75, 79 n14
8.	†1843	John Crawford Smith	Christ Church Cathedral, Dublin, crypt		C Lib (repr)

No.	Date	Subject	Material	Location	Signed	References
9.	†1848	Henrietta, Countess de Grey Model(s): Dublin Int Exhib, 1853; untraced		Flitton, Beds	S	*Strickland* I, 1913, 335; *Penny* 1977 (1), 101–03 (repr); *Murphy* 1991–2, 76–7 (repr); *Bryant* 2003, 80 (repr)
10.	†1848	John, 2nd Earl of Enniskillen		Enniskillen, Co Fermanagh		*Potterton* 1975, 43; *Murphy* 1991–2, 78
11.	1849	John McDonagh		[for the Westland Row RC church]; untraced		*Stewart* 1, 1985, 252
12.	†1852	18th Royal Irish Regiment, Burmah War (1852) memorial		St Patrick's Cathedral, Dublin	S	*Potterton* 1975, 43; *Murphy* 1991–2, 77
13.	1853	Rev Charles Wolfe		St Patrick's Cathedral, Dublin		*Potterton* 1975, 43; *Stewart* 1, 1985, 253
14.	nd	Father O'Reilly		Navan RC church, Co Meath		*Potterton* 1975, 44
Statues						
15.	1842	Henry Dawson, Dean of St Patrick's, design for a marble statue		[Exhib RHA, Dublin, 464]; untraced		*Stewart* 1, 1985, 252; *Murphy* 1991–2, 73–4
16.	1843	'Children and dogs' and 'children and goats' (co-sculptor: James Farrell RHA) Model(s): exhib RA, London, 1843, 1427, 1436; awarded Royal Irish Art Union first premium, 1844		[Wrest Park, Beds, gardens]; untraced		*Graves* III, 1905–6, 90; *Gunnis* 1968, 143; *Murphy* 1991–2, 75, 79 n9
17.	*c*1843	The elements, four male figures		[Wrest Park, Beds, gardens]; untraced		*Murphy* 1991–2, 75
18.	*c*1843	The seasons, four male figures		[Wrest Park, Beds, the terrace]; untraced		*Strickland* I, 1913, 335; *Murphy* 1991–2, 75
19.	1848	Early affliction (or early sorrow)	m	[Exhib RHA, Dublin, 329]; untraced		*Stewart* 1, 1985, 252
20.	1851	'Faith, to be executed in Portland stone, 8 feet high, for the Church of St Nicholas, Francis Street'		[Exhib RHA, Dublin, 342]; untraced		*Stewart* 1, 1985, 253
21.	1860	Madonna Payment(s): £36 15s	m	[Exhib RHA, Dublin, 524]; untraced		*Stewart* 1, 1985, 253
22.	1850–1860	Sir Galbraith Lowry Cole Model(s): sketch model exhib RHA, Dublin, 1860, 510	s	Cole Monument, Forthill Park, Enniskillen, Co Fermanagh		*Strickland* I, 1913, 334; *Potterton* 1975, 43–4; *Stewart* 1, 1985, 253; *Murphy* 1991–2, 77, 78 (repr)
23.	nd	Four statues		Thorndon Park, Essex, Chapel		*Gunnis* 1968, 143
Busts						
24.	1829	Duke of York	m	[Exhib RHA, Dublin, 281]; untraced		*Stewart* 1, 1985, 252
25.	1829	King George IV	m	[Exhib RHA, Dublin, 283]; untraced		*Stewart* 1, 1985, 252
26.	1830	Mrs Henry		[Exhib RHA, Dublin, 294]; untraced		*Stewart* 1, 1985, 252
27.	1830	Unidentified lady		[Exhib RHA, Dublin, 296]; untraced		*Stewart* 1, 1985, 252
28.	1831	Lord Bishop of Down and Connor		[Exhib RHA, Dublin, 276]; untraced		*Stewart* 1, 1985, 252
29.	1831	Unidentified late Fellow of Trinity College, Dublin		[Exhib RHA, Dublin, 282]; untraced		*Stewart* 1, 1985, 252
30.	1832	Henry, Marquis of Anglesey		[Exhib RHA, Dublin, 276]; untraced		*Strickland* I, 1913, 334; *Stewart* 1, 1985, 252
31.	1832	Hon John Parsons		[Exhib RHA, Dublin, 274]; untraced		*Stewart* 1, 1985, 252
32.	1832	Lady Emily Paget		[Exhib RHA, Dublin, 275]; untraced		*Stewart* 1, 1985, 252
33.	1834	Mr Beresford	m	Coll Lord Reigate		C Lib (repr)
34.	1835	Archbishop of Dublin		[Exhib RHA, Dublin, 299]; untraced		*Stewart* 1, 1985, 252
35.	1835	General Sir Barry Close		[Exhib RHA, Dublin, 307]; untraced		*Stewart* 1, 1985, 252
36.	1835	Lord Bishop of Cork		[Exhib RHA, Dublin, 300]; untraced		*Stewart* 1, 1985, 252
37.	1835	Lord Bishop of Ferns		[Exhib RHA, Dublin, 301]; untraced		*Stewart* 1, 1985, 252
38.	1835	Mrs Mullins (designed for a monument)		[Exhib RHA, Dublin, 305]; untraced		*Stewart* 1, 1985, 252
39.	1835	Very Rev Dean Vignoles		[Exhib RHA, Dublin, 302]; untraced		*Stewart* 1, 1985, 252
40.	1836	Bartholomew Lloyd	m	coll John Gilmartin		*Strickland* I, 1913, 335; *Barrett* 1971 (1), 81; *Stewart* 1, 1985, 252; *Murphy* 1991–2, 73 (repr)
41.	1836	Lord Bishop of Meath		[Exhib RHA, Dublin, 261]; untraced		*Stewart* 1, 1985, 252
42.	1836	Mrs Batty		[Exhib RHA, Dublin, 250]; untraced		*Stewart* 1, 1985, 252
43.	1836	Rev Joseph Blanco White		[Exhib RHA, Dublin, 245]; untraced		*Stewart* 1, 1985, 252
44.	post-1840	Unidentified subject		[Commissioned by Earl de Grey, as Lord Lieutenant of Ireland]; untraced		*Murphy* 1991–2, 74
45.	1841	John, 3rd Earl of Donoghmore	m	[Exhib RHA, Dublin, 400]; untraced		*Strickland* I, 1913, 335; *Stewart* 1, 1985, 252
46.	1841	Richard Willes		[Exhib RHA, Dublin, 398]; untraced		*Stewart* 1, 1985, 252
47.	1841	Unidentified artist	m	[Exhib RHA, Dublin, 391]; untraced		*Stewart* 1, 1985, 252
48.	1841	Unidentified clergyman		[Exhib RHA, Dublin, 399]; untraced		*Stewart* 1, 1985, 252
49.	1841	Unidentified lady	m	[Exhib RHA, Dublin, 394]; untraced		*Stewart* 1, 1985, 252
50.	1841	William Morrison		[Exhib RHA, Dublin, 393]; untraced		*Stewart* 1, 1985, 252
51.	1842	Henry Dawson, Dean of St Patrick's (co-sculptor: James Farrell RHA)		[Exhib RHA, Dublin, 467]; untraced		*Stewart* 1, 1985, 252; *Murphy* 1991–2, 73
52.	1842	John Molloy	m	[Exhib RHA, Dublin, 475]; untraced		*Stewart* 1, 1985, 252
53.	1842	Rev Caesar Otway	m	[Exhib RHA, Dublin, 476]; untraced		*Stewart* 1, 1985, 252
54.	1844	Thomas, 2nd Earl de Grey Model(s): for Henrietta, Countess de Grey, clay; untraced		RDS, Dublin Other versions: Wrest Park, Beds, replica		*Strickland* I, 1913, 334–5; *Stewart* 1, 1985, 253; *Murphy* 1991–2, 75
55.	1849	Lady Alice Villiers		[Executed for the Countess of Clarendon]; untraced		*Stewart* 1, 1985, 252
56.	1849	Lady Constance Villiers		[Executed for the Countess of Clarendon]; untraced		*Stewart* 1, 1985, 252

No.	Date	Subject		Location	Bibliography
57.	1849	Lady Emily Villiers		[Executed for the Countess of Clarendon]; untraced	*Stewart* 1, 1985, 252, 253
58.	1849	Lord Hyde		[Exhib RHA, Dublin, 429]; untraced	*Stewart* 1, 1985, 252
59.	1851	Captain Webb		[Exhib RHA, Dublin, 375]; untraced	*Stewart* 1, 1985, 253
60.	1851	Lord Monck		[Exhib RHA, Dublin, 376]; untraced	*Stewart* 1, 1985, 253
61.	1853	Edward, 3rd Earl of St Germans	m	[Exhib RHA, Dublin, 473]; untraced	*Strickland* I, 1913, 335; *Stewart* 1, 1985, 253
62.	1853	James Hans Hamilton MP		[Exhib RHA, Dublin, 471]; untraced	*Stewart* 1, 1985, 253
63.	1853	John William, 4th Earl of Bessborough		[Exhib RHA, Dublin, 481]; untraced	*Strickland* I, 1913, 334; *Stewart* 1, 1985, 253
64.	1853	Lady Agnes Villiers		[Exhib RHA, Dublin, 469]; untraced	*Stewart* 1, 1985, 253
65.	1853	Theobald Wolfe Tone		[Exhib RHA, Dublin, 466]; untraced	*Stewart* 1, 1985, 253
66.	1853	Thomas, 2nd Earl de Grey	m	[Exhib RHA, Dublin, 470]; untraced	*Strickland* I, 1913, 335; *Stewart* 1, 1985, 253
67.	1853	Unidentified lady		[Exhib RHA, Dublin, 484]; untraced	*Stewart* 1, 1985, 253
68.	1853	William Nugent Skelly		[Exhib RHA, Dublin, 482]; untraced	*Stewart* 1, 1985, 253
69.	1853	William, 3rd Earl of Enniskillen		[Exhib RHA, Dublin, 474]; untraced	*Strickland* I, 1913, 335; *Stewart* 1, 1985, 253
70.	1861	Admiral Trench		[Exhib RHA, Dublin, 585]; untraced	*Stewart* 1, 1985, 253
71.	1861	Unidentified gentleman		[Exhib RHA, Dublin, 597]; untraced	*Stewart* 1, 1985, 253
72.	1861	Unidentified lady		[Exhib RHA, Dublin, 592]; untraced	*Stewart* 1, 1985, 253
73.	1862	W H Byrne		[Exhib RHA, Dublin, 463]; untraced	*Stewart* 1, 1985, 253
74.	1862	Wolfe Tone, from the marble to be executed for Mr Maxwell of New York		[Exhib RHA, Dublin, 457]; untraced	*Stewart* 1, 1985, 253
75.	1863	John Browne		[Exhib RHA, Dublin, 475]; untraced	*Stewart* 1, 1985, 253
76.	1863	Unidentified child		[Exhib RHA, Dublin, 475]; untraced	*Stewart* 1, 1985, 253
77.	nd	Sir Hussey Vivian		Untraced	*Strickland* I, 1913, 335
Reliefs					
78.	nd	John Finlay, medallion bust		[Exhib RHA, Dublin, 409]; untraced	*Stewart* 1, 1985, 252
Miscellaneous					
79.	1858	Colonel Blacker		[Exhib RHA, Dublin, 332]; untraced	*Stewart* 1, 1985, 253
80.	1859	'Pastime, models from which Marbles have been recently executed for Earl de Grey'		[Exhib RHA, Dublin, 323 and 328]; untraced	*Stewart* 1, 1985, 253
81.	1860–1865	Memorial to Lady St Germans (†1862)		Áras an Uachtaráin (former Vice-Regal Lodge), Phoenix Park, Dublin, grounds	*Strickland* I, 1913, 335; *Murphy* 1991–2, 78 (repr)

FARRELL, Sir Thomas PRHA 1827?–1900

Thomas Farrell, the third son of **Terence Farrell**, was the most successful sculptor working in Ireland in the second half of the 19th century. The first son of the family to be given a formal training outside his father's studio, he was admitted as a student at the modelling school of the Royal Dublin Society in 1842. The following year he was awarded a prize in the category 'Original Design in Clay' and he won premiums from the Royal Irish Art Union in 1844 and 1846 (**89, 90**). He exhibited at the Royal Hibernian Academy in 1849, and continued as a frequent exhibitor there until his death.

His first major work was the monument to Archbishop Daniel Murray (**3**). This prestigious commission was won in competition with **John Hogan**, an experienced and well-known sculptor, with a strictly neoclassical design comprising a kneeling figure of the Archbishop, flanked by two allegorical figures, *Meekness* and *Prudence*. After securing the commission Farrell visited Italy. Strickland states that he travelled there to choose the marble for the Murray monument and whilst in the country took the opportunity to visit Rome and Florence. Murphy suggests that the visit was primarily a study trip. By the summer of 1854 he was back in Dublin and starting work on the portrait statue of the Archbishop, erected in the Pro-Cathedral the following year. He was assisted by his younger brother, Michael, who carved the figure of *Prudence* shortly before he contracted a fever of which he died in 1855.

This early success brought Farrell prosperity and a degree of artistic and domestic independence. In 1856 he moved to Warrington Place on the south side of the city, near the canal, though he apparently continued to work at the family studio in Gloucester Street in north Dublin. A second significant commission was offered to him later in the 1850s when he was invited to model one of the bronze reliefs for the Wellington Testimonial in Phoenix Park (**88**). Other reliefs were commissioned from **Joseph Robinson Kirk** and John Hogan. Farrell's model, depicting the fall of the Earl of Uxbridge at the Battle of Waterloo, an incident which inspired the English cavalry to attack the French soldiers with renewed energy, was completed by March 1860 and sent to be cast at Thomas Potter's foundry in South Molton Street, London. The casting was completed the following spring but Farrell was appalled by the quality of Potter's work. He wrote: 'so battered and butchered is every part of it, that I had considerable difficulty in recognising any of my own work at all . . . Thank Heaven, it is gone up to such a height, for I would not for any consideration that it was seen on the ground as my work' (Letter to General Sir Thomas Larcom, 1 April 1861, quoted by *Murphy* 1993, 198–9).

As the most prominent sculptor in Dublin from the 1860s, Farrell was employed on a succession of public statues, most of them for sites in the city. He found patrons both in the Catholic and Protestant communities, and Murphy suggests that his commissions for portrait statues of Protestants, 'were frequently of a particular type and seem related to his being an Irish Catholic' (*Murphy* 1993, 200). Many of these were of individuals who took a particularly active interest in Irish culture and politics. Examples include the statues of Sir John Gray, a Protestant nationalist, the proprietor of *The Freeman's Journal* and an active member of the Dublin Corporation, who was commemorated in recognition of his work in improving the city's water supply (**32**); Sir Robert Stewart, a renowned organist and professor of music with a deep interest in ancient Irish music (**41**); and William Smith O'Brien, a Protestant revolutionary nationalist (**26**). In 1864 Farrell competed for the national monument to Daniel O'Connell, submitting a design for a three-tiered edifice consisting of a seated statue of O'Connell, with figures of *Erin, Law, Patriotism* and *Eloquence* seated around the pedestal and semi-reclining personifications of different aspects of *Liberty* at the base (**25**). He was unsuccessful and the commission, the most significant of its time in Ireland, was awarded to **John Henry Foley**.

The O'Connell monument was not completed until 1883 but a model of Foley's work was put on display in Dublin's City Hall in 1867 and this may have had an impact on Farrell's monument to Cardinal Paul Cullen, unveiled in 1882 (**11**). Like Foley's O'Connell, Farrell's statue of Cullen stands on a drum-pedestal with a frieze of figures in high-relief. Here the figures represent the various religious institutions, social, medical and educational, founded by the Cardinal. Other church monuments by Farrell include a relief of a soldier dying on the battlefield at Sebastopol, erected in memory of Lieutenant Thomas Kidd in Armagh Cathedral; a bust of Cardinal Newman in the University Church, Dublin and a reclining effigy of Archbishop Whately in St Patrick's Cathedral, Dublin (**4, 15, 6**). He also executed a number of monuments in Glasnevin Cemetery, including one to members of the Irish Republican Brotherhood, which features three symbolic figures *Erin, Fidelity* and *Patriotism* (**12**).

Farrell was a diffident and shy man who seems to have been uncomfortable at public occasions such as unveiling ceremonies and the banquets which sometimes accompanied them. He was nonetheless actively involved in the Royal Hibernian Academy for many years. In 1860 he was elected a full member, by-passing the associate stage under new rules introduced that year. He was appointed professor of sculpture in 1862, but the appointment was not renewed and passed to J R Kirk at the end of the year. He was subsequently a Council member on three occasions, auditor for one year and treasurer for twenty-two, until finally he was elected president in 1893. Two years later he was again appointed professor of sculpture at the Academy, which at that stage of his life was effectively an honorary position. He also served on the board of the National Gallery of Ireland from 1876, and in May 1894 he was knighted.

The Farrell sculpture yard remained in Gloucester Street, though Thomas moved from his house in Warrington Place to Mountjoy Square in 1881 and in 1895 to Redesdale House, a large property in Stillorgan, a suburb south of Dublin. When he died there on 2 July 1900 his 3 surviving brothers were living with him. His obituary in *The Irish Times* paid tribute to a 'great genius', the successor of Foley and Hogan, whose death left a gap which it would be hard to fill (*The Irish Times*, 5 July 1900, quoted by *Murphy* 1993, 206). This view was not shared by Potterton, who later wrote that Farrell was 'by no means a sculptor of genius, or even of any great imaginative powers; so that the majority, if not all, of his statues are extremely boring' (*Potterton* 1975, 44).

EH

Literary References: *Strickland* 1, 1913, 335–40; *Crookshank* 1966, 311; *Potterton* 1975, 44; *Murphy* 1992–3, 196–206; *Grove* 10, 1996, 815 (Murphy)

Funerary Monuments

No.	Date	Subject		Location		References
1.	1853	Design for a monument to an unidentified subject		[Exhib RHA, Dublin, 478]; untraced		*Stewart* 1, 1985, 253
2.	†1854	Henry Baldwin		Pro-Cathedral, Dublin		*Potterton* 1975, 44
3.	*c*1855	Daniel Murray, Archbishop of Dublin (†1852) (co-sculptor: Michael Farrell) Model(s): exhib RHA, Dublin, 1858, 337 and 338		Pro-Cathedral, Dublin	S	*Potterton* 1975, 44, 68 (repr); *Stewart* 1, 1985, 253; *Murphy* 1993, 196, 197–8 (repr)
4.	†1855	Thomas Kidd		Armagh Cathedral	S	*Potterton* 1975, 30, 44 (repr)
5.	†1861	Captain John McNeill Boyd RN		Derry Cathedral		*Potterton* 1975, 44
6.	†1863	Richard Whately, Protestant Archbishop of Dublin		St Patrick's Cathedral, Dublin		*Potterton* 1975, 44; *Murphy* 1993, 202, 203 (repr)
7.	1864	Captain John McNeill Boyd RN (†1861) Model(s): exhib RHA, Dublin, 1862, 470; 1863, 505		St Patrick's Cathedral, Dublin	S	*Strickland* I, 1913, 338; *Potterton* 1975, 44; *Stewart* 1, 1985, 253; *Murphy* 1993, 196, 197 (repr)
8.	*c*1864	Lieutenant Clifford		[for Thomastown, Co Kilkenny]; untraced		*Potterton* 1975, 44
9.	†1869	Rev Dr Edward Marks		St Patrick's Cathedral, Dublin		*Strickland* I, 1913, 339; *Potterton* 1975, 44
10.	†1881	Michael Canon Doyle		St Andrew, Westland Row, Dublin		*Potterton* 1975, 44
11.	1882	Cardinal Paul Cullen (†1878) Model(s): sketch model of bust of the cardinal exhib RHA, Dublin, 1881, 699		Pro-Cathedral, Dublin	SD	*Potterton* 1975, 44, 71 (repr); *Read* 1982, 194, 198 (repr); *Stewart* 1, 1985, 254; *Murphy* 1993, 201–2 (repr)
12.	1886	Members of the Irish Republican Brotherhood Model(s): exhib RHA, Dublin, 1892, 497, 498 & 499		Glasnevin Cemetery, Dublin (erected 1933)		*Stewart* 1, 1985, 255; *Murphy* 1993, 202–3 (repr)
13.	1887	Cardinal Edward McCabe		Glasnevin Cemetery, Dublin		*Murphy* 1993, 202
14.	*c*1888	Ellen Palles (†1885)		Glasnevin Cemetery, Dublin	S	*Stewart* 1, 1985, 254; *Murphy* 1993, 203
15.	*c*1891	Cardinal John Henry Newman (†1890)		University Church, St Stephen's Green, Dublin		*Strickland* I, 1913, 339; *Potterton* 1975, 44; *Stewart* 1, 1985, 255; *Murphy* 1993, 206 (repr)
16.	1894	Barry Sullivan Model(s): exhib RHA, Dublin, 1894, 452		Glasnevin Cemetery, Dublin	S	*Strickland* I, 1913, 337, 339; *Stewart* 1, 1985, 255
17.	nd	Dean O'Connell		[Our Lady Star of the Sea, Sandymount, Dublin]; untraced		*Strickland* I, 1913, 338; *Potterton* 1975, 44
18.	nd	Rev Thomas Leahy		[Our Lady Star of the Sea, Sandymount, Dublin]; untraced		*Strickland* I, 1913, 338; *Potterton* 1975, 44

Statues

No.	Date	Subject		Location		References
19.	1843	Unidentified figure, an 'Original Design in Clay'		[RDS prize]; untraced		*Murphy* 1993, 196
20.	1853	Master Barton		[Dublin Int Exhib]; untraced		*Strickland* I, 1913, 338
21.	1856	The infant Saviour and St John the Baptist	m	[Exhib RHA, Dublin, 386]; untraced		*Stewart* 1, 1985, 253, 254
22.	1858	The angelic mission	p	[Exhib RHA, Dublin, 325]; untraced		*Graves* III, 1905–6, 90; *Stewart* 1, 1985, 253; *Morris and Roberts* 1998, 227

23.	1861	Patrick, Earl of Lucan, sketch model design for a statue in bronze		[Exhib RHA, Dublin, 593]; untraced		*Stewart* 1, 1985, 253
24.	1863	William Dargan Model(s): exhib RHA, Dublin, 1862, 472	b	NGI, Dublin, front lawn	SD	*Potterton* 1974 (2), 145; *le Harivel* 1988, 561 (repr); *Stewart* 1, 1985, 253; *Murphy* 1991, 199 (repr)
25.	1864	Daniel O'Connell, national monument, sketch model only (commission awarded to John Henry Foley)		Untraced		*Murphy* 1993, 201
26.	1867	William Smith O'Brien	m	[Carlisle Bridge, Dublin, until 1929]; O'Connell Street, Dublin		*Stewart* 1, 1985, 254; *Murphy* 1993, 200–1 (repr)
27.	1868	The little pet	m	[Exhib RHA, Dublin, 435]; untraced		*Graves* III, 1905–6, 90; *Strickland* I, 1913, 340; *Stewart* 1, 1985, 254
28.	*c*1874	William Burke Drawing(s): design exhib RHA, Dublin, 1874, 328	s	Tuam Cathedral, Co Galway, forecourt		*Strickland* I, 1913, 338; *Stewart* 1, 1985, 254; *Murphy* 1993, 204–5
29.	1878	Daniel O'Connell, memorial for St Louis, Massachussets, USA, sketch model		[Exhib RHA, Dublin, 440]; untraced		*Stewart* 1, 1985, 254
30.	1878	Sir Alexander MacDonnell Bt Model(s): exhib RHA, Dublin, 1877, 498		[Tyrone House, Dublin, forecourt, until 1950]; NMI Store, Daingean, Co Offaly		*Read* 1982, 120; *Stewart* 1, 1985, 254; *Murphy* 1993, 200 (repr)
31.	1870–1879	John MacHale, Archbishop of Tuam		Cathedral of the Assumption, Tuam, Co Galway, forecourt		*Murphy* 1993, 204–5
32.	1879	Sir John Gray Model(s): exhib RHA, Dublin, 1877, 497	m	O'Connell Street, Dublin		*Stewart* 1, 1985, 254; *Murphy* 1993, 200 (repr)
33.	1884	Richard Lalor Shiel Model(s): exhib RHA, Dublin, 1884, 630; 1885, 555		[Four Courts, Dublin, main hall]; destroyed by fire (1922) Other versions: NGI 8183, plaster statuette		*le Harivel* 1988, 561 (repr); *Stewart* 1, 1985, 254; *Murphy* 1993, 199, 207 n13
34.	1885	Robert Emmett 'executed for the Emmett Memorial Committee'		[Exhib RHA, Dublin, 556]; untraced		*Stewart* 1, 1985, 254
35.	1886	Thomas, Lord O'Hagan Model(s): exhib RHA, Dublin, 1886, 598; 1887, 494		[Four Courts, Dublin, main hall]; destroyed by fire (1922)		*Graves* III, 1905–6, 90; *Stewart* 1, 1985, 254; *Murphy* 1993, 199, 207 n13
36.	1886	William Dease (†1798) Payment(s): £600	m	RCS, Dublin	S	*Strickland* I, 1913, 338; *Stewart* 1, 1985, 254; *Murphy* 1993, 204
37.	1891	Arthur, Lord Ardilaun Model(s): exhib RHA, Dublin, 1892, 494	b	St Stephen's Green, Dublin	SD	*Strickland* I, 1913, 337; *Stewart* 1, 1985, 254; *Murphy* 1993, 199 (repr)
38.	1893	The blessed Virgin, 'for the Church of the Apparition, Knock'		[Exhib RHA, Dublin, 461]; untraced		*Stewart* 1, 1985, 255
39.	1894	Queen Victoria, design 'in connection with the Museum of Science and Art, Dublin'		[Exhib RHA, Dublin, 451]; untraced		*Stewart* 1, 1985, 255
40.	1895	Bishop Butler, 'executed in marble for Limerick Cathedral'		[Exhib RHA, Dublin, 499]; untraced		*Stewart* 1, 1985, 255
41.	1898	Sir Robert Stewart	m	Leinster Lawn, Dublin		*Read* 1982, 119, 120 (repr); *Murphy* 1993, 200 (repr)
42.	nd	Queen Victoria		Guildhall, Derry		*Strickland* I, 1913, 339
Busts						
43.	1851	Unidentified gentleman	m	[Exhib RHA, Dublin, 373]; untraced		*Stewart* 1, 1985, 253
44.	1852	Wolfe Tone		Trinity College, Dublin, Long Room		*Crookshank* 1986, 25
45.	1856	'The late Thomas Farrell'		[Exhib RHA, Dublin, 398]; untraced		*Stewart* 1, 1985, 253
46.	1862	Mother Theresa Ball	m	Loreto Abbey, Rathfarnham, Dublin		*Murphy* 1993, 203, 205 (repr)
47.	1862	'The late Mrs Ball, from the marble in the Ursuline Convent, Rathfarnham'		[Exhib RHA, Dublin, 462]; untraced		*Stewart* 1, 1985, 253
48.	1863	Unidentified gentleman, posthumous portrait		[Exhib RHA, Dublin, 483]; untraced		*Stewart* 1, 1985, 253
49.	1864	'The late Archbishop of Dublin'		[Exhib RHA, Dublin, 426]; untraced		*Stewart* 1, 1985, 253
50.	1864	Unidentified lady		[Exhib RHA, Dublin, 425]; untraced		*Stewart* 1, 1985, 253
51.	1865	Unidentified gentleman		[Exhib RHA, Dublin, 468]; untraced		*Stewart* 1, 1985, 254
52.	1866	Judge Nicholas Ball		[Exhib RHA, Dublin, 504]; untraced		*Stewart* 1, 1985, 254; *Murphy* 1993, 199–200, 203
53.	1868	Unidentified gentleman		[Exhib RHA, Dublin, 446]; untraced		*Stewart* 1, 1985, 254
54.	1872	Mrs Anna Maria O'Brien		[Exhib RHA, Dublin, 452]; untraced		*Stewart* 1, 1985, 254; *Murphy* 1993, 203
55.	1872	Unidentified lady	m	[Exhib RHA, Dublin, 432]; untraced		*Stewart* 1, 1985, 254
56.	1878	Michael William Balfe	m	NGI 8044	S	*Wynne and White* 1975, 14; *le Harivel* 1988, 560 (repr)
57.	1880	Sir Richard Griffith Bt	m	RDS, Dublin	S	*Stewart* 1, 1985, 254; *White and Bright* 1998, 54
58.	1881	John Gunn		Gaiety Theatre, Dublin		*Strickland* I, 1913, 338; *Stewart* 1, 1985, 254
59.	1883	Denis Florence McCarthy		Blackrock College, Dublin		*Strickland* I, 1913, 338; *Stewart* 1, 1985, 254
60.	1884	Alexander Martin, cast of death mask	p	NGI		*le Harivel* 1988, 561 (repr)
61.	1885	A M Sullivan		[Exhib RHA, Dublin, 558]; untraced		*Stewart* 1, 1985, 254
62.	1885	Sir George Hodson Bt, 'erected in marble in Rathdown Union'		[Exhib RHA, Dublin, 557]; untraced		*Stewart* 1, 1985, 254
63.	1888	Canon James Roche		Cathedral Square, Wexford	S	*Strickland* I, 1913, 339; *Stewart* 1, 1985, 254

64.	1889	Edmund Dwyer Gray		[Exhib RHA, Dublin, 502]; untraced	*Strickland* I, 1913, 338; *Stewart* 1, 1985, 254
65.	1889	Sir John Gray		Roundwood Reservoir, Co Wicklow Other versions: Glasnevin Cemetery, Dublin, replica	*Strickland* I, 1913, 338
66.	1889	Unidentified lady		[Exhib RHA, Dublin, 500]; untraced	*Stewart* 1, 1985, 254
67.	1889	Unidentified lady		[Exhib RHA, Dublin, 501]; untraced	*Stewart* 1, 1985, 254
68.	1890	Lord O'Hagan		[Exhib RHA, Dublin, 521]; untraced	*Stewart* 1, 1985, 254
69.	1892	Arthur, Lord Ardilaun	m	[Exhib RHA, Dublin, 495]; untraced	*Stewart* 1, 1985, 254
70.	1893	Sir Charles Cameron	m	RCS, Dublin	*Strickland* I, 1913, 338; *Stewart* 1, 1985, 255; *Murphy* 1993, 206
71.	1893	T Sexton MP		City Hall, Dublin	*Strickland* I, 1913, 339; *Stewart* 1, 1985, 255
72.	1894	Alderman Joseph Meade	m	[Exhib RHA, Dublin, 455]; untraced	*Stewart* 1, 1985, 255
73.	1894	Joseph P Culverwell		[Exhib RHA, Dublin, 470]; untraced	*Stewart* 1, 1985, 255
74.	1898	Captain Alex Henry		[Exhib RHA, Dublin, 452]; untraced	*Stewart* 1, 1985, 255
75.	1899	Father Reiffe	m	Blackrock College, Dublin	*Strickland* I, 1913, 339; *Stewart* 1, 1985, 255
76.	1899	Sir Patrick Keenan	m	Department of Education (formerly Tyrone House), Marlborough Street, Dublin	*Stewart* 1, 1985, 255; *Murphy* 1993, 200 (repr)
77.	nd	Alderman Moore		Untraced	*Strickland* I, 1913, 339
78.	nd	John Hatch Power		RCS, Dublin	*Strickland* I, 1913, 339
79.	nd	John Mitchel (1815–1875), cast of a death mask	p	NGI	*le Harivel* 1988, 561
80.	nd	Major Singleton		Untraced	*Strickland* I, 1913, 339
81.	nd	Miss Duguid		Untraced	*Strickland* I, 1913, 339
82.	nd	Mrs Goodbody		Untraced	*Strickland* I, 1913, 339
83.	nd	Mrs Reid		Untraced	*Strickland* I, 1913, 339
84.	nd	Mrs Speedy		Untraced	*Strickland* I, 1913, 339
85.	nd	Thomas Pim		Untraced	*Strickland* I, 1913, 339
86.	nd	William Murphy		Untraced	*Strickland* I, 1913, 339
Architectural Sculpture					
87.	by 1890	Groups representing Painting, Sculpture, Architecture and Poetry Model(s): exhib RHA, Dublin, 1889, 503; 1890, 517, 518 & 519		[National Museum and Library, Kildare Street, Dublin]; removed	*Stewart* 1, 1985, 254; *Murphy* 1993, 205–6
Reliefs					
88.	1859–1861	Waterloo (cast by Thomas Potter, London) Model(s): exhib RHA, Dublin, 1860, 511	b	Wellington testimonial, Phoenix Park, Dublin	*Murphy* 1993, 198–9 (repr); *Stewart* 1, 1985, 253
Miscellaneous					
89.	1844	Nisus and Euryalus		[Royal Irish Art Union £10 prize; purchased by the RDS]; untraced	*Strickland* I, 1913, 336, 339
90.	1846	Young bather surprised (or 'boy and swans') Payment(s): £50		[Royal Irish Art Union £5 prize; purchased by the Art Union and awarded as a prize to Miss Hall of Lugan]; untraced	*Strickland* I, 1913, 336, 339
91.	1849	Innocent amusement		[Exhib RHA, Dublin, 422]; untraced	*Stewart* 1, 1985, 253
92.	1851	St Joseph, to be executed in marble		[Exhib RHA, Dublin, 360]; untraced	*Stewart* 1, 1985, 253
93.	1852	The lost one		[Exhib RHA, Dublin, 371]; untraced	*Strickland* I, 1913, 340; *Stewart* 1, 1985, 253
94.	1861	The nymph Eucharis and love		[Exhib RHA, Dublin, 404]; untraced	*Stewart* 1, 1985, 254
95.	1866	'The late Miss Murphy, of Baymount Castle'		[Exhib RHA, Dublin, 504]; untraced	*Stewart* 1, 1985, 254
96.	1868	HRH the Prince of Wales		[Exhib RHA, Dublin, 429]; untraced	*Stewart* 1, 1985, 254
97.	1870	A little dunce		[Exhib RHA, Dublin, 403]; untraced	*Strickland* I, 1913, 340; *Stewart* 1, 1985, 254
98.	1873	Miss Alicia Fitzpatrick		[Exhib RHA, Dublin, 361]; untraced	*Stewart* 1, 1985, 254
99.	1873	'The late Countess of Granard'		[Exhib RHA, Dublin, 360]; untraced	*Stewart* 1, 1985, 254
100.	1873	The Tarpeian rock Payment(s): £350	m	[Exhib RHA, Dublin, 359]; untraced	*Stewart* 1, 1985, 254
101.	1881	Playfellows		[Exhib RHA, Dublin, 701]; untraced	*Stewart* 1, 1985, 254, 255
102.	1882	The expulsion Payment(s): £25		[Exhib RHA, Dublin, 659]; untraced	*Stewart* 1, 1985, 254
103.	1883	St Agnes		[Exhib RHA, Dublin, 642]; untraced	*Stewart* 1, 1985, 254
104.	1884	Good night, beloved		[Exhib RHA, Dublin, 629]; untraced	*Stewart* 1, 1985, 254
105.	1884	Narcissus		[Exhib RHA, Dublin, 628]; untraced	*Stewart* 1, 1985, 254
106.	1885	Telemachus and love Payment(s): £20		[Exhib RHA, Dublin, 560]; untraced	*Stewart* 1, 1985, 254
107.	1888	Innocence, 'executed in marble for John Duguid, Esq. of Dover'		[Exhib RHA, Dublin, 490]; untraced	*Stewart* 1, 1985, 254
108.	1890	Caught		[Exhib RHA, Dublin, 520]; untraced	*Stewart* 1, 1985, 254
109.	1893	On the sands		[Exhib RHA, Dublin, 459]; untraced	*Stewart* 1, 1985, 255
110.	1895	In rosy cordage		[Exhib RHA, Dublin, 498]; untraced	*Stewart* 1, 1985, 255
111.	1896	A captive		[Exhib RHA, Dublin, 440]; untraced	*Stewart* 1, 1985, 255
112.	1898	Angelic succour		[Exhib RHA, Dublin, 451]; untraced	*Stewart* 1, 1985, 255
113.	nd	Girl with a dog		[coll Viscount Powerscourt]; untraced Other versions: replica in RA purchased by Mr Gerstenberg	*Strickland* I, 1913, 339

FARRELL & SON (GLASNEVIN MARBLE WORKS) fl 1834–59

A firm of monumental sculptors, they opened at the gates of the new Glasnevin Cemetery just outside Dublin in 1834. It has wrongly been assumed that **Terence Farrell** established the sculpture yard for the proprietors' names are recorded as Peter and John Farrell. John was probably Terence's brother, who had worked in Dublin as a stone-cutter. The firm of Farrell & Son still survives, but is no longer run by the family.

Literary References: *Murphy* 1991–2, 73, 79 n6

Funerary Monuments

1.	†1859	Father Byrne	Our Lady Star of the Sea, Sandymount, Dublin	S	*Potterton* 1975, 44

FARRINGTON, William fl 1715

Only one tablet is recorded, signed 'William Farrington, Jnr'.

Literary References: *Gunnis* 1968, 143

Funerary Monuments

1.	1715	Mary Farrington	Bereton, Staffs	S	*Gunnis* 1968, 143

FARROW, Thomas, of Diss fl 1824?–42

Gunnis notes that in 1842 he married a 'Mrs Maskett' of Palgrave Place in Norfolk.

Literary References: *Gunnis* 1968, 143

Funerary Monuments

1.	?1824	Lady Sophia Macdonald	Quidenham, Norfolk	S	*Gunnis* 1968, 143
2.	nd	Susanna Frere	Roydon, Norfolk	S	*Gunnis* 1968, 143

FATTSON (or FARKSON), Benjamin fl 1722?

Funerary Monuments

1.	?1722	Rev George Morton	St Margaret, Lothbury, London	S	

FAULKNER, Jonathan, of Chelsea fl 1833

In 1833 Faulkner repaired the monument to Sir Thomas More in Chelsea Old Church (1). He 'accomplished this difficult task with much skill, in imitating and preserving the antique style of the various mouldings, frieze, foliage, &c' (*GM*, 1833, ii, 485).

Funerary Monuments

1.	1833	Sir Thomas More (restoration only)	Chelsea Old Church (All Saints), London		*GM*, 1833, ii, 485

FAULKNER, Matthew, of Twickenham fl 1725–27

Between 1725 and 1727 he carved chimneypieces and decorative details for Little Deene, a house built in the grounds of Deene Park, Northants (**1, 2**). It was a building of some pretensions with enriched ceilings and other decorations. Apparently Faulkner had financial difficulties for in the Brudenell accounts is a note about 'poor Matt Faulkner's bill and letter from Prison' (Brudenell MSS ASR 118/209, cited by *Gunnis* 1968, 143).

Literary References: *Gunnis* 1968, 143

Chimneypieces

1.	1725–1727	Several	[Little Deene, Deene Park, Northants]; untraced		*Gunnis* 1968, 143

Architectural Sculpture

2.	1725–1727	Decorative details	[Little Deene, Deene Park, Northants]; untraced		*Gunnis* 1968, 143

FAULKNER, of Exeter fl early 19th century

Funerary Monuments

1.	nd	Nine Graeme family members	Stokeinteignhead, Devon	S	Pevsner, *Devon*, 1989, 766

FAWCET, of Liverpool and Lancaster fl 1838–70

Funerary Monuments

1.	†1838	Richard Clark	Lancaster Priory	S	
2.	†1834–1843	James Newby and family	Cartmel Priory, Lancs	S	Pevsner, *Lancs: N*, 1969, 90
3.	†1856	John Pritt	Lancaster Priory	S	
4.	†1862	James Hansbrow (?)	Lancaster Priory	S	
5.	†1783–1870	John Higgin	Lancaster Priory	S	

FAYROM (or FAREHAM), Thomas, of London fl 1717–48

Fayrom built a considerable number of houses in London between 1717 and 1719 and insured them with the Westminster Fire Office (Westminster Fire Office Archives, in GPC). In 1720 he built one for Sir Theodore Janssen in Hanover Square (Declared Accounts, Directors South Sea Company, Janssen, 44). Four years later he agreed to build another for the architect Edward Shepherd on the north side of Brook Street, undertaking to provide all the moulded work, white and veined marble chimneypieces and a black and white marble pavement (PRO C 105/32, in GPC) (**1**). In 1737 he acquired a building site from the 4th Lord Berkeley of Stratton, now the location of Berkeley Square (Westminster Public Library, Deeds 10/16).

Fayrom moved house several times: in 1717 he lived in the parish of St Anne, Westminster in 1724 in St Martin-in-the-Fields. In 1748 the Westminster Poll Book gave his address as Mount Street. He was described as 'Mason, of Hanover Square' when he became bankrupt in 1741 (*London Mag*, 1741, 258).

Archival References: GPC

Chimneypieces

1.	1724	Several, white and veined marble	[Edward Shepherd's house, Brook Street, London]; untraced		PRO C 105/32 in GPC

FEARN, George *c*1820–77

He was a monumental mason 'of limited talent'. On 12 May 1843, when he set up in High Street, Stamford, Lincs, he advertised that he had come from Derbyshire (*Stamford Mercury*, 12 May 1843. In 1859 he rebuilt his workshops in Scotgate, Stamford and in 1861 sold his stock (*ibid*, 20 May 1859, 6 December 1861). He died in Halifax, W R Yorks (*ibid*, 6 April 1877).

Archival References: JP Misc Corr

FELLOWS, William, of Kings Lynn fl 1721–65?

He was the son of **John Fellows** and was apprenticed to his father in 1721, becoming a freeman of his native town in 1758.

Literary References: *Gunnis* 1968, 144

Funerary Monuments

1.	†1735	William Browne	Westacre, Norfolk	S	*Gunnis* 1968, 144
2.	?1765	Christopher Adamson	Wereham, Norfolk	S	*Gunnis* 1968, 144

FELLOWS (or FELLOWES), John, of Kings Lynn fl 1714–65

As a 'free stone-mason' he became a freeman of his native town in 1714, and between 1714 and 1717 built the library at the west end of the south aisle of St Margaret's church, which was destroyed in 1874 (Town Archives, cited by *Gunnis* 1968, 143). In 1742, with John Parsons, of Wells, Norfolk, he rebuilt the nave of the same church, to the designs of Matthew Brettingham (Ch W, cited by *Gunnis* 1968, 143).

Literary References: *Gunnis* 1968, 143

Funerary Monuments

1.	?1714	Vokes Walsham	Woodstone, Hunts	S	*Gunnis* 1968, 143
2.	?1730	John Dickinson	Woodstone, Hunts	S	*Gunnis* 1968, 143
3.	†1738	Richard Dashwood	[Cockley Cley, Norfolk]; untraced	S	Pevsner, *Norfolk: N W & S*, 1999, 265
4.	†1742	Forster family member	Clenchwarton, Norfolk	S	Pevsner, *Norfolk: N W & S*, 1999, 264
5.	†1765	Adamson family member	Wereham, Norfolk	S	Pevsner, *Norfolk: N W & S*, 1999, 759

Chimneypieces

6.	1723	Black and grey marble	Raynham Hall, Norfolk, smoking room		*Gunnis* 1968, 143

FENTIMAN, John, of Stoke Newington fl 1789

In 1789 he received £4,116 for building Lewes Prison (Town Records, cited by *Gunnis* 1968, 144) and in the same year he contracted to build the county gaol at Dorchester for £12,000 (Dorset County Archives, in GPC).

FEODOROWNA, Maria, Empress of Russia 1759–1828

For further information the reader is referred to *Pyke* 1973, 88

FERGUSON, Hugh, of Belfast fl 1836

Funerary Monuments

1.	†1836	Major Robert Fulton	Lisburn Cathedral, Co Antrim	S	*Potterton* 1975, 45

FETCH (or FITCH), John fl 1663–86

The son of Habakkuk Fetch of Higham Ferrers, he was apprenticed to William Joyne on 11 September 1663 and was described as a 'citizen and mason of London' in the Masons' Company freeman list of 1673 (f 24). His apprentices included **Thomas Green of Camberwell** (apprenticed 1673), Peter West (1678) and James Tylee (1686). Fetch had a brother, Thomas, who was also apprenticed under the auspices of the Masons' Company, to **John Martin**, on 29 January 1666.

Literary References: *Webb* 1999, 12, 14, 34, 35

FEUCHERE, Jean Jacques 1807–52

Feuchère was a French sculptor, painter, decorative artist and collector. After seeing examples of his work at the Paris residence of James de Rothschild, George, 2nd Duke of Sutherland commissioned a bronze statue of his son, the young Marquis of Stafford, in Highland dress (1). The Duke had misgivings about the commission and expressed the hope that it would not look 'like one of those before tobacconists' shops taking a pinch of snuff' (*Gower* 1891, 216). Feuchère rose to the occasion however, producing an example of 'virtuoso modelling in celebration of childhood and exotic costume' (*Ward-Jackson* 1985, 148).

Literary References: *Grove* 11, 1996, 42 (Ward-Jackson)

Statues

1.	1837	George, Marquis of Stafford (later 3rd Duke of Sutherland) (cast by the Vittoz foundry)	b	[Stafford House, London, coll George, 2nd Duke of Sutherland]; Dunrobin Castle, Sutherland	*Ward-Jackson* 1985, 146, 148 (repr); *Pearson* 1991, 6 (repr)

FICKER, of Piccadilly fl 1765

He gave his address as Vine Street, Piccadilly, when he exhibited a tablet for a chimneypiece at the Free Society of Artists in 1765.

Chimneypieces

1.	1765	The four seasons, tablet	[Exhib Free Soc, London, 1765]; untraced	*Graves* 1907, 91

FIELD, H C fl 1826–36

He exhibited sculpture and paintings at the Society of British Artists between 1826 and 1836 from an address in Strand, London.

Busts

1.	1826	B Field	[Exhib Soc of BA, London, 746]; untraced	*Johnson* 1975, 158

Reliefs

2.	1829	Unidentified lady, medallic portrait	[Exhib Soc of BA, London, 887]; untraced		*Johnson* 1975, 158
3.	1833	Major G, medallic portrait	[Exhib Soc of BA, London, 870]; untraced		*Johnson* 1975, 158

FIELD, John, of Hampstead fl 1825?–51

Funerary Monuments

1.	?1825	C Cartwright	St John, Hampstead, London	S	
2.	?1833	Unidentified subject	St John, Hampstead, London	S	
3.	†1851	Harriott Mary More	More, Salop	S	Pevsner, *Salop*, 1958, 203

FILLANS, James 1808–52

Although Fillans spent many years in London, his success as a portrait sculptor depended almost entirely on Scottish patronage. He was born on 27 March 1808 at Wilsontown, near Lanark, the third-born but eldest surviving son of John Thomson Fillans and his wife Jean, née White. He was educated at the local parish school until about 1816 when his family moved to Busby, where Fillans worked with his father on the land. He was employed as a print assistant at the Busby calico printing works for about five years but when the family moved to Paisley he was apprenticed, apparently against his will, to a hand-loom weaver. During this period he spent much of his leisure time sketching and making models in wood, metal and clay.

His career as a sculptor began at the age of 17, when he was apprenticed to a Paisley stonemason, Hall McLatchie. After his master's death Fillans spent several years working as journeyman stonemason in Paisley, Greenock and Glasgow, where he carved capitals for the Royal Exchange (**64**). In about 1830 he opened his own studio in Paisley and began to model profile portraits, reliefs and statuettes for David Dick, a local bookseller who marketed copies of them in wax and plaster. His groups of *Watty and Meg* and of a well-known local character *Jamie Gemmell borne along by two policemen* were especially popular (**9, 7**). These were followed by a bust of Sheriff Campbell (**22**) which 'added vastly to the growing reputation of the artist, and brought him encouraging supplies of cash, as well as orders' (*Paterson* 1854, 24). He secured commissions from Glasgow patrons and in the early 1830s moved to Glasgow. There he set up a studio in Miller Street, employing his brothers, Robert and **John Fillans**, as assistants, and he attended Mr Warren's drawing classes. On 16 April 1833 he married Grace, the daughter of John Gemmell, a Paisley manufacturer.

Two years later, with financial assistance from his friend and patron James Walkinshaw, Fillans travelled to Paris, where he made a number of drawings from paintings in the Louvre. On his return he settled in London, establishing a studio at 5 High Holborn in 1836. He moved to 12 South Bank, Regent's Park, in 1838 and then to 82 Baker Street in 1840. He soon made the acquaintance of **Allan Cunningham**, whose bust he exhibited in 1837 (**25**). It was probably Cunningham who introduced Fillans to **Sir Francis Chantrey**, whose recommendation helped secure him the commission for a bust of Richard Oswald, the owner of the Auchincruive estate in Ayrshire (**40**). Since the sitter was in Italy, Fillans travelled to Florence to model the work. He remained there for several months in 1841 and again visited Paris before returning to London. Fillans exhibited at the Royal Academy throughout this period, showing 25 works between 1837 and 1850.

Although his principal studio was in London Fillans maintained strong links with Scotland. Many of his commissions came from patrons on the west coast and he spent much of his time in Glasgow and Paisley, modelling portrait busts. His most important work was a statue commemorating Sir James Shaw, Provost of Kilmarnock, erected in Kilmarnock in 1848 (**16**). After the ceremony Fillans was the guest of honour at a public banquet at which 'homage was rendered to him by all the leading persons of the town and neighbourhood' (*AJ* 1848, 314). The sculptor was elected an Academician of the West of Scotland Academy in 1841 and he exhibited there in 1842, 1847, 1849 and 1852. Since Fillans spent an increasing amount of time in Scotland his London residence became an unnecessary financial burden and in 1850 he finally moved back to Glasgow, where he worked from a studio in St Vincent Street. There he started work on a series of reliefs entitled *Taming the wild horse*, which were apparently inspired by a book about Texas (**78**), and he modelled a statuette of *The flying Dutchman*, a celebrated race horse belonging to the Earl of Eglinton (**18**). He also carved a monument commemorating William Motherwell, which included reliefs illustrating some of the poet's works a well as a portrait bust (**6**).

Two years later, on 27 September 1852, Fillans died of rheumatic fever and was buried in the family plot at Woodside Cemetery, Paisley. A crouching figure *Grief*, or *Rachel weeping for her children*, which he had designed as a monument to his father, was carved by **John Mossman** and placed over his own grave (**17**). A sale of the sculptor's remaining works and studio equipment, held in St Vincent Street on 16 March 1852, 'did not realise as much as might have been expected' (*Paterson* 1854, 108). One of the sculptor's daughters, Wilhelmina Fillans, exhibited sculpture at the Royal Scottish Academy in 1869 and 1871.

EH

Literary References: *AJ*, 1852, 350; *Paterson* 1854; *Athenaeum*, 1854, 1371–2; *Gunnis* 1968, 144; *Pyke* 1973, 47; *Woodward* 1977, vol 1, pt 2, 65–8; *Pearson* 1991, 91–2

Archival References: IGI

Portraits of the Sculptor: David Octavius Hill and Robert Adamson, James Fillans with his two daughters, calotype, 1843–8, NPG P6(120); *Paterson* 1854, frontispiece

Funerary Monuments

1.	1825–1830	Unidentified apprentice, headstone	[Johnstone, Renfrewshire, churchyard]; untraced	*Paterson* 1854, 22
2.	1840	James Dick	Old Kirkyard, Ayr	*Woodward* 1977, vol 1, pt 2, 68
3.	1841	Dugald Moore	Glasgow Necropolis	*McKenzie* 1999, 12, no 2.12; *McKenzie* 2002, 459
4.	1844	Captain Alexander Wilson (†1842)	Beith, Ayrshire	*Paterson* 1854, 52

5.	1846	Jacobus Brown		Glasgow Necropolis		*Woodward* 1977, vol 1, pt 2, 68
6.	1851	William Motherwell (†1835)	s	Glasgow Necropolis	S	*Paterson* 1854, 94–7 (repr XXV–XXVII); *McKenzie* 2002, 301–2 (repr)
Statues						
7.	*c*1830	Jamie Gemmell borne along by two policemen, model		Untraced Other versions: published in wax or plaster by David Dick		*Paterson* 1854, 23–4
8.	*c*1830	Man was made to mourn, statuette		[coll Grace Gemmell]; untraced		*Paterson* 1854, 24
9.	*c*1830	Wattie and Meg, model		Untraced Other versions: published in wax or plaster by David Dick		*Paterson* 1854, 23–4
10.	*c*1836	McGregor and the Bailie, group		[Commissioned by James Dick, for presentation to Mr Forest]; untraced		*Paterson* 1854, 32
11.	1838	Abelard and Heloise, unfinished group		Untraced		*Paterson* 1854, 35
12.	1840	Elizabeth Jane Walkinshaw, model for a marble figure		[Exhib RA, London, 1162]; untraced		*Graves* III, 1905–6, 109
13.	*c*1845	Boy and faun		Untraced		*Paterson* 1854, 46–7 (repr XVI)
14.	1845	The blind teaching the blind to read the Bible by means of raised letters		[Exhib RA, London, 1340]; untraced		*AJ*, 1852, 350; *Paterson* 1854, 43–5 (repr XV); *Graves* III, 1905–6, 109
15.	1847	Madonna and child	m	[Exhib RA, London, 1326]; untraced		*AU*, 1847, 200; *Paterson* 1854, 93 (repr XXIV); *Graves* III, 1905–6, 109
16.	1848	Sir James Shaw	m	Kilmarnock, Ayrshire		*AU*, 1848, 314; *Paterson* 1854, 64–70 (repr XVII); *Graves* III, 1905–6, 109; *Woodward* 1977, vol 1, pt 2, 68
17.	1849	Grief (Rachel weeping for her children), design only	p	[Glasgow Museums S.51]; destroyed Other versions: Woodside Cemetery, Paisley, Renfrewshire, carved by John Mossman as a monument to James Fillans		*Paterson* 1854, 98 (repr XXVIII); *Gildard* 1892, 294; *Graves* III, 1905–6, 109; *Woodward* 1977, vol 1, pt 2, 68; *Laperriere* 2, 1991, 52
18.	1850	The Flying Dutchman, statuette		Untraced Other versions: reproduced in bronze and composition		*Paterson* 1854, 85–90
19.	by 1851	Athena before Paris, statuette		[Fillans sale, 16 March 1852, lot 20]; untraced		*Paterson* 1854, 99, 107
20.	nd	Richard Oswald, statuette	m	[coll Lady Lillias Oswald]; untraced Other versions: Fillans sale, 16 March 1852, lot 14		*Paterson* 1854, 40, 107 (repr XIII)
21.	nd	The young ornithologist, 'a Fancy Figure'		[Fillans sale, 16 March 1852, lot 16]; untraced		*Paterson* 1854, 107
Busts						
22.	*c*1830	Sheriff Campbell		Untraced		*Paterson* 1854, 24
23.	*c*1830	William Motherwell		Untraced		*Paterson* 1854, 23
24.	1836	Charles Tennant		Untraced		*Paterson* 1854, 32
25.	1837	Allan Cunningham	m	[Exhib RA, London, 1255]; untraced		*Paterson* 1854, 38, 107; *Graves* III, 1905–6, 109
26.	1837	James Walkinshaw	m	[Exhib RA, London, 1251]; untraced		*Graves* III, 1905–6, 109
27.	1837	John Thomson		[Exhib Soc of BA, London, 585]; untraced		*Johnson* 1975, 158
28.	1837	Mrs Charles Tennant	m	[Exhib RA, London, 1235]; untraced		*Paterson* 1854, 32; *Graves* III, 1905–6, 109
29.	1837	William Walkinshaw	m	[Exhib RA, London, 1234]; untraced		*Graves* III, 1905–6, 109
30.	1838	Archibald Hastie MP	m	[Exhib RA, London, 1304]; untraced		*Paterson* 1854, 34–5; *Graves* III, 1905–6, 109
31.	*c*1838	Dr Kerr		Untraced		*Paterson* 1854, 36
32.	1838	Mr McArthur		Untraced		*Paterson* 1854, 35
33.	1839	Archibald, 1st Baron Blythswood, for County Hall, Paisley	m	[Exhib RA, London, 1313]; untraced Other versions: Glasgow Museums S.150, m, nd		*Paterson* 1854, 48; *Graves* III, 1905–6, 109
34.	1839	Sir Walter Scott	m	[Exhib RA, London, 1322]; untraced		*Paterson* 1854, 38, 107; *Graves* III, 1905–6, 109
35.	1840	Andrew Johnstone	m	[Exhib RA, London, 1131]; untraced		*Graves* III, 1905–6, 109
36.	1840	John Burnet FRS, model for a marble bust		[Exhib RA, London, 1171]; untraced		*Paterson* 1854, 107; *Graves* III, 1905–6, 109
37.	1840	Robert Napier		Institution of Mechanical Engineers		*Graves* III, 1905–6, 109
38.	1841	James Davidson		[Exhib RA, London, 1278]; untraced		*Graves* III, 1905–6, 109
39.	*c*1841	John Alston	m	[Glasgow Blind Asylum]; untraced		*Paterson* 1854, 43–4
40.	1841–1842	Richard Oswald of Auchincruive		[Presented to Richard Oswald by his tenantry]; untraced		*Paterson* 1854, 38–42; *Woodward* 1977, vol 1, pt 2, 66
41.	1842	Unidentified child Model(s): RA, London, 1842, 1374; untraced	m	Glasgow Museums S.105		*Graves* III, 1905–6, 109; *Laperriere* 2, 1991, 52
42.	1845	James Ewing	m	[Exhib RA, London, 1416]; untraced		*Graves* III, 1905–6, 109

No.	Date	Subject	Medium	Location		Bibliography
43.	1845	Mrs James Ewing		[Exhib RA, London, 1451]; untraced		*Graves* III, 1905–6, 109
44.	1845	Professor John Wilson	p	National Library of Scotland, Edinburgh Other versions: for County Hall, Paisley, 1848 Blackwood's, Edinburgh, miniature, reproduced by the Royal Porcelain Works, Worcester		*Paterson* 1854, 39, 53, 70–2 (repr XVIII); *Graves* III, 1905–6, 109; *Gunnis* 1968, 144; *Woodward* 1977, vol 1, pt 2, 68; *Laperriere* 2, 1991, 52
45.	1847	Poetic head		[Exhib BI, London, 558]; untraced		*Graves* 1875, 188
46.	1848	Colonel Mure MP	m	[Exhib RA, London, 1460]; untraced		*Graves* III, 1905–6, 109
47.	1849	Unidentified man	m	Paisley MAG, Renfrewshire		*Woodward* 1977, vol 1, pt 2, 68
48.	1850	Charles McIver	m	[Exhib RA, London, 1421]; untraced		*Graves* III, 1905–6, 109
49.	nd	James Coats	m	Paisley MAG, Renfrewshire		*Laperriere* 2, 1991, 52
50.	nd	James Ewing	w	Glasgow Museums S.259		inf: Glasgow Museums
51.	nd	James Hogg (the Ettrick Shepherd)		[Fillans sale, 16 March 1852, lot 3]; untraced		*Paterson* 1854, 107
52.	nd	Kirkman Finlay		[Fillans sale, 16 March 1852, 107]; untraced		*Paterson* 1854, 107
53.	nd	'Morning, Childhood, a Fancy Bust'		[Fillans sale, 16 March 1852, lot 13]; untraced		*Paterson* 1854, 107
54.	nd	'Morning, Head in Clay'	tc	[Fillans sale, 16 March 1852, lot 14]; untraced		*Paterson* 1854, 107
55.	nd	Mrs James Ewing	w	Glasgow Museums S.260		
56.	nd	'Name child' of Archibald McLellan		untraced		*Paterson* 1854, 81 (repr XIX)
57.	nd	Napoleon		Blackwoods, Edinburgh Other versions: reproduced by the Royal Porcelain Works, Worcester		*Woodward* 1977, vol 1, pt 2, 68 (repr 70)
58.	nd	Robert Burns		[Fillans sale, 16 March 1852, lot 4]; untraced		*Paterson* 1854, 107
59.	nd	Sir John Maxwell, 7th Bt	m	Stirling Maxwell coll, Pollok House, Glasgow PS.2		inf: Glasgow Museums
60.	nd	Unidentified man	p	Paisley MAG, Renfrewshire		*Woodward* 1977, vol 1, pt 2, 68
61.	nd	Unidentified man	m	Paisley MAG, Renfrewshire		*Woodward* 1977, vol 1, pt 2, 68
62.	nd	William Kennedy		[Fillans sale, 16 March 1852, lot 7]; untraced		*Paterson* 1854, 107
63.	nd	William Motherwell	p	Paisley MAG, Renfrewshire Other versions: Paisley MAG, plaster, nd		*McKenzie* 2002, 302
Architectural Sculpture						
64.	1828	Capitals		Gallery of Modern Art (former Royal Exchange), Exchange Square, Glasgow		*AJ*, 1852, 350; *Paterson* 1854, 23; *McKenzie* 2002, 455
65.	1825–1830	Four carvings of heads		[An ashlar fronted tenement, The Cross, Paisley, Renfrewshire]; untraced		*Paterson* 1854, 22
66.	1825–1830	'Time-dial . . . elaborately wrought with figures and other appropriate ornaments'	s	Untraced		*Paterson* 1854, 22
Reliefs						
67.	1831	Unidentified family group	w	Sold Christie, 5 Oct 1976 lot 11; coll J Glanz, London		*Pyke* 1981, 17
68.	1835	William Motherwell	w	SNPG, Edinburgh		*Woodward* 1977, vol 1, pt 2, 68
69.	1836	The birth of Burns		Untraced		*AJ*, 1852, 350; *Paterson* 1854, 33–4 (repr VII)
70.	1837	Unidentified subject		[Exhib RA, London, 1189]; untraced		*Graves* III, 1905–6, 109
71.	*c*1838	Coila crowning Burns		[Fillans sale, 16 March 1852, lot 10]; untraced		*Paterson* 1854, 35, 107 (repr IX)
72.	1840–1841	Kerr testimonial	m	[Presented to Dr Kerr by Paisley Water Company]; untraced		*Paterson* 1854, 36–7 (repr X)
73.	1842	Bacchus and Silenus		[Exhib RA, London, 1289]; untraced		*AU*, 1842, 128; *Graves* III, 1905–6, 109
74.	1842	Unidentified mother	w	Sold Christie, 5 Oct 1976 lot 11; coll Laurel G Blair, Toledo, Ohio		*Pyke* 1981, 17
75.	1843	Sir James Wylie	w	Paisley MAG D 97/8, Renfrewshire	SD	*Pyke* 1973, 47 (pl 96)
76.	1843	Unidentified daughter	w	Sold Christie, 5 Oct 1976, lot 12; coll Laurel G Blair, Toledo, Ohio		*Pyke* 1981, 17
77.	1849	Love pilots the soul		[Exhib Soc of BA, London, 638]; untraced		*Paterson* 1854, 99; *Johnson* 1975, 158
78.	*c*1850	Taming the wild horse, a series of reliefs		[Fillans sale, 16 March 1852, lot 1, purchased by Peter Coats for his mansion at Woodside, Paisley]; untraced		*Paterson* 1854, 85, 107 (repr XX–XXIII)
79.	by 1851	Head of Michel Angelo Buonarotti (two versions?)	m	[Fillans sale, 16 March 1852, lots 11 and 12]; untraced		*Paterson* 1854, 99, 107
80.	nd	An original design from Burns's 'The Twa Dogs'		[Fillans sale, 16 March 1852, lot 17]; untraced		*Paterson* 1854, 107
81.	nd	Mother and child, monumental relief		[Fillans sale, 16 March 1852, lot 19]; untraced		*Paterson* 1854, 107
82.	nd	William Motherwell	w	Mitchell Library, Glasgow		*Woodward* 1977, vol 1, pt 2, 68
Miscellaneous						
83.	1825–1830	Bacchus seated on a barrel, model	tc	[Presented to Captain Maxwell of the Brediland Pottery]; untraced		*Paterson* 1854, 21–2
84.	1825–1830	Figure of a horse, shop sign		[Blacksmith's shop, Lonend, Paisley, Renfrewshire]; untraced		*Paterson* 1854, 22

85.	1836–1838	Model for a jug with reliefs illustrating Tam o'Shanter (cast in silver for Archibald Hastie)		[Fillans sale, 16 March 1852, lot 23]; untraced		*Paterson* 1854, 108 (repr VIII)
86.	1850	William Chandler	m	[Exhib RA, London, 1379]; untraced		*Graves* III, 1905–6, 109
87.	nd	Morning, a fragment		[Fillans sale, 16 March 1852, lot 18]; untraced		*Paterson* 1854, 107

FILLANS, John *c*1817–67

For further information the reader is referred to *Pyke* 1973, 47 and *Pyke* 1981, 17

FINCH, T, of Islington fl 1801?

Funerary Monuments

1.	?1801	William White		High Barnet, Herts	S	

FINELLI, Carlo 1786–1853

In 1822, during a visit to Rome, the 6th Duke of Devonshire, saw and ordered a statue of *Cupid with a butterfly* from Finelli (2). He noted in his diary for 19 December 1822 that 'Poor **Canova**', who had recently died, 'used to wish me to employ this man' (quoted by *JKB* 1972, 326). The figure was admired by Count Hawks Le Grice, who wrote 'The simplicity, purity, gracefulness and repose, that characterise this statue of Cupid, together with its truth of expression, are truly, admirable, and bespeak a genius of the first order, who has thus stamped on a stone a divine type, the creation of his own mind' (*Le Grice*, II, 1844, 126). Le Grice states that a statue of *Cupid and Psyche* by the same artist was in the Devonshire collection. He appears to have been mistaken.

Literary References: *Le Grice* 1844, I, 125–6; II, 125–6; *JKB* 1972 (3), 326–7, 331

Statues

1.	1819–1822	Unidentified subject		[coll Lord Ashburton]; untraced		*JKB* 1972 (3), 327
2.	1822–1826	Cupid with a butterfly Payment(s): 150 louis	m	Chatsworth, Derbys, orangery		*JKB* 1972 (3), 326, 327, 331 (repr)

FINES, C fl 1833–46

He exhibited wax portraits at the Royal Academy, 1833–1846, giving his address as 14 Guildford Street, London.

Literary References: *Gunnis* 1968, 144; *Pyke* 1973, 47

Reliefs

1.	1833	Edward Jesse, model		[Exhib RA, London, 1083]; untraced		*Graves* III, 1905–6, 110
2.	1833	Rev Mr Levett, model		[Exhib RA, London, 1076]; untraced		*Graves* III, 1905–6, 110
3.	1842	Mr Chabot	w	[Exhib RA, London, 1083]; untraced		*Graves* III, 1905–6, 110
4.	1843	Miss Edith Chabot	w	[Exhib RA, London, 1351]; untraced		*Graves* III, 1905–6, 110
5.	1843	Mr G Jorden, medallic portrait		[Exhib RA, London, 1357]; untraced		*Graves* III, 1905–6, 110
6.	1844	Mr Craib	w	[Exhib RA, London, 1256]; untraced		*Graves* III, 1905–6, 110
7.	1846	Unidentified subject, posthumous portrait	w	[Exhib RA, London, 1378]; untraced		*Graves* III, 1905–6, 110

FIRBANK, Christopher –*c*1765

In 1759 he worked at Castle Howard (1). Considerable sums were paid to him for carving when Newburgh Priory was enlarged by Lord Fauconberg in 1763–5 (2). No details are given, but it seems likely that he may have been responsible for the four pretty stone urns on the roof of the new building. He must have died *c*1765 for a payment was made to 'Widow Firbank' early in 1766. He was succeeded as carver at Newburgh by Matthew Frear, who appears to have been his assistant (Wombwell Archives, in GPC).

Archival References: Castle Howard Building Accts, G3/3/68–74, July 1759–Jan 1760

Architectural Sculpture

1.	1759–1760	Stone carving	s	Castle Howard, N R Yorks, west wing		Castle Howard, selected bills, G3/1/1
2.	1763–1765	Stone carving		Newburgh Priory, N R Yorks		Wombwell archives in GPC

FIRMADGE, William, of Leicester 1755–1836

Born on 14 November 1755, he was the son of William Firmadge, slater and plasterer of Scraptoft, Leics, and his wife Ann. He became a freeman of Leicester in 1778 and is variously described in the directories and other sources as builder, slater, stone-mason, plasterer, architect and surveyor. He did a good deal of work as a monumental mason: Gunnis comments that his tablets 'have well-cut designs and he makes intelligent use of coloured marbles'. Slate headstones by him can be seen in several churchyards in Leicestershire and are all 'equally good' (*Gunnis* 1968, 144). He was employed extensively as a builder, constructing gaols in Leicester, Worcester, Oakham and other towns before 1812, when he began to concentrate on his architectural practice. In the latter capacity his only recorded works of any consequence are extensions to Leicester Lunatic Asylum (1794), the construction of the New Market, Leicester (1824) and Lutterworth House, Leics (1821–2).

He was a prominent member of the Corporation of Leicester, holding office as Mayor in 1809–10. His pupils included the Leicester architect, William Parsons. He died at Leicester on 27 March 1836 and was buried at Scraptoft. His second wife, Susanna Needham died in 1841.

Literary References: *Gunnis* 1968, 144; *Colvin* 1995, 363

Archival References: GPC

Additional MS Sources: Firmadge/King

Funerary Monuments

1.	?1778	Rev Richard Wynne		Gumley, Leics	S	*Gunnis* 1968, 144
2.	?1779	Henry Coleman		Burton Overy, Leics	S	*Gunnis* 1968, 144
3.	?1787	William Kemp		Belton, Rutland	S	*Gunnis* 1968, 144
4.	?1790	John Rowland		Enderby, Leics	S	*Gunnis* 1968, 144
5.	?1792	Miss Lee		Burton Overy, Leics	S	*Gunnis* 1968, 144
6.	?1792	Rev Barton Shuttleworth		Laughton, Leics	S	*Gunnis* 1968, 144
7.	?1792	Samuel Soames, ledger stone		Rolleston, Staffs	S	*Gunnis* 1968, 144
8.	?1793	Anne Firmadge		Scrapton, Leics	S	*Gunnis* 1968, 144

FISHER, James, of Camberwell 1682–1722

Fisher signed the magnificent monument with life-size standing figures of William, 1st Earl Fitzwilliam and his wife at Marholm (**2**). It was originally much larger, incorporating standing figures of *Piety* and *Grief* in arches flanking the effigies. The Virtues were probably removed when the church was restored in the late 1860s. A 'superb' drawing of the monument in the British Library is thought to be the sculptor's original design (BM Add MS 32467, fol 157, repr *Bailey* 1996, 116). The contract for the monument also survives. It is dated 28 August 1828 and endorses: 'Mr Fisher the stone-cutter of Camberwell his bill and acquittance for making and setting up the monument at Marham Church and for the little monument at North Runcton Church in Norfolk' (**1**). It gives a full specification for the Fitzwilliam monument and stipulates that when finished it was to be conveyed by Fisher to some 'wharf or stairs below London Bridge and shipped and put on board some vessel at his own cost and charges'. Fisher's witnesses were Richard Dixon and Robert Harper (Fitzwilliam Papers, Northants RO, cited by *Gunnis* 1968, 145).

The sculptor died on 30 March 1722, leaving his property to his wife Anne. He was buried in Camberwell churchyard, but the tombstone commemorating him is destroyed (*Mottley* 1734–5, II, 833, cited by *Gunnis* 1968, 145).

Literary References: *Gunnis* 1968, 144–5; *Bailey* 1996, x, 116

Archival References: GPC

Will: PROB 11/584

Funerary Monuments

1.	1718–1721	Sir John Cremor (†1668) Payment(s): £24 10s	North Runcton, Norfolk		Pevsner, *Norfolk: N W & S*, 1999, 574
2.	1718–1721	William, 1st Earl Fitzwilliam (†1719) and his wife Anne Payment(s): £900 Drawing(s): BM Add MS 32467, f 157	Marholm, Northants	S	Bridger, *History of Northants*, 1791, 2, 520; *Bailey* 1996, 116 (design repr)

FISHER FAMILY, of York

Richard Fisher I	*c*1705–*c*1770
John Fisher I	1735–1804
Samuel Fisher I	b 1738
John Fisher II	1771–1839
William Fisher	1776–1815
George Fisher	1788–1815
Samuel Fisher II	1780–1812
Richard Fisher II	1784–1819
Charles Fisher	1789–1861
John Fisher III	1823–1884
Richard Fisher III	active *c*1830 (?)

Richard Fisher appears to have arrived in Ripon around 1716, perhaps from Scotland, though apparently he spoke fluent French. He assumed the name of Fisher, learnt to carve in the Ripon area and married a local girl, Alice Bradley of Sharow. The couple had 2 sons who became sculptors, **John Fisher I** and **Samuel Fisher**. The workshop was active over 4 generations.

Richard's first recorded patron was Sir Henry Slingsby of Scriven Hall, Knaresborough, who made payments totalling £54 12s to 'Fisher, the Carver' between June 1729 and April 1731 (**223**). He worked on chimneypieces and decorative carving for Sir John Aislabie and his son William at Studley Royal, near Ripon, between 1732 and 1753 (**214, 224, 225, 227**) and in 1737 won his first known contract outside Yorkshire, for eight chimneypieces ordered by Sir Horatio Walpole at Wolterton Hall, Norfolk (**212**). At this time he had one unnamed apprentice and perhaps also employed **Robert Doe** as his assistant. Fisher was dismissed by Walpole after a year for breach of contract, since apparently he had been making moulds that were outside his brief. In a letter to the architect Thomas Ripley seeking payment for his work, Richard disputed the cause of his dismissal, which may have been engineered by jealous Norfolk craftsmen.

Fisher and 'his man' worked on chimneypieces for the 7th Viscount Irwin at Temple Newsam House, near Leeds, between 1740 and 1742 (**213**). Commissions in York may already have been coming his way, for on 15 July 1746 he placed an advertisement in the *York Journal* informing potential clients that he was 'now fix'd in the Minster Yard, York, where all sorts of Carved and Statuary work, both in wood, Marble and stone, either for Household Furniture, or Monumental and Sepulchral Ornaments, are performed in the Neatest Manner and at moderate Prices'.

In 1752 Sir Rowland Winn paid Fisher for carved work at Nostell Priory (**234**). By this time his sons John I and Samuel must have been working for Richard. Since the workshop was within the Minster precinct their apprenticeship did not need to be registered, just as Richard did not have to be a freeman of the City to engage in employment. By the early 1750s the Fisher name began to appear on funeral monuments.

A letter in the Studley Royal archives relates that between 1755 and 1761 the Fisher family 'left the country', perhaps for London (Aislabie Papers, letter from Doe to Aislabie, 3–4 April 1755). In 1761 Richard Fisher showed two marble statuettes at the Society of Artists' exhibition, *Christ carrying the cross* and *Jupiter with an eagle* (**194**). These works attracted the attention of the Marquess of Rockingham, who perhaps encouraged him to return to Yorkshire.

During the 1760s the Fishers supplied at least two chimneypieces for Rockingham at Wentworth Woodhouse, for which they charged £164 and £88 (**218**). This sum suggests they were of marble. The workshop also provided an elaborate overmantel at Burton Constable, for which they were paid £42, including £4 for packing (**215**). Various architects were content to use the Fishers to provide chimneypieces. Their work at Studley Royal and Temple Newsam, under the architects Colen Campbell and Daniel Garrett, has already been noticed. They may also have been involved in commissions at houses designed by the architect John Carr, who was employed by the Chomleys of Whitby and Howsham Hall, and Sir Charles Sheffield of Normanby Hall. The Fishers made monuments for these families (**4, 5, 16, 64, 25**). It is thought that the Fishers carved the parapet figures for John Carr's York Assize Courts between 1773 and 1777, but documentation is lacking since Carr's name is attached to all payments for the building.

It is not certain when Richard Fisher died and his sons inherited the workshop, but his wife was a widow in 1773 when her death was recorded in the registers of St Michael-le-Belfry, York. For a decade after their father's death John and Samuel worked from their shop in North Street, York, collaborating on chimneypieces, architectural ornaments and particularly church monuments: the relief tablet to Sybil Wilson, 1773, in Lancaster, which depicts the child's parents in classical costume, mourning by her death-bed, was particularly admired by Gunnis (**24**). He also praised the figure of *Hygeia* on the memorial to John Dealtry in York Minster and the personification of *Religion* on the memorial to Sir Charles Sheffield at Burton-on-Stather (**27, 25**).

In 1780 Samuel and his wife Ann (née Sanderson) left York for London, perhaps because Ann's brother James had established himself in the City, where he took an active role in civic affairs, earning a knighthood and eventually becoming lord mayor in 1792–3. Samuel and Ann were beneficiaries in her brother's will.

After Samuel's departure John Fisher led the workshop alone. He returned to Wentworth Woodhouse, where he supplied more chimneypieces (**219**) and also pedestals in the Rockingham mausoleum, for which Fisher charged £203 10s, with an additional £8 for 'horse hire and expenses'. The pedestal for **Joseph Nollekens RA**'s statue of the Duke was inscribed with 281 upper case letters. John's other patrons included Walter Fawkes of Farnley Hall (**220**), Lord Carlisle at Castle Howard (**238**) and Viscount Lonsdale, for whom he made two elaborately framed memorial tablets, topped with sarcophagi and resting on lions' paws (**1, 90**). A number of payments to him are also recorded in the Swinton Castle account books for 1793–94; he received £203 3s 10d for chimneypieces in the drawing room, library and perhaps other 'new rooms'.

John's most memorable achievement came in response to an advertisement in the *York Courant* on 6 January 1784, announcing the proposal to erect a statue in honour of the politician Sir George Savile by public subscription. This was originally intended to be sited in the courtyard of York Castle (**62**). Savile died three days later, but John, having sent 'an accurate Drawing or design, together with an Estimate of the Expence thereof' (*York Courant*, 9 March 1784) won the contract, and in 1789 the statue was erected in York Minster. The draped figure of Savile stands on a pedestal, holding in his right hand a scroll inscribed with the words 'The Petition of the Freeholders of York'. John advertised his skills by commissioning Francesco Bartolozzi, engraver to the King, to provide prints of the statue, which sold at a guinea each. The subscribers included the Prince of Wales and a number of Dukes.

Only one of John Fisher's workmen has been identified: the death of Abraham Swords as the result of 'a melancholy accident in 1777' happened in the yard in North street while watching the launch of a new brigantine. A gun was fired and a stray piece of wadding hit him in the throat (*York Courant*, 2 September 1777). In the 1770s the workshop was clearly prospering for he bought his and Samuel's freedom of the City of York, and by the 1780s John had enough work to keep five apprentices, his two sons, **John Fisher II** and **William Fisher**, as well as Daniel Butterfield, Thomas Benet and **Joseph Theakston**.

Around 1790 the business floundered and in 1792 Fisher was declared bankrupt. A letter of 1795 from John Carr to Benjamin Hall, Lord Fitzwilliam's steward, on the subject of a monument to Edmund Burke, gives a hindsight to the problems besetting the firm: 'All Fisher's best men have left him. They cannot get their wages of him' (Fitzwilliam archives, Sheffield, WWM Stw P (IV), (V), 6) His obituary, published in the *York Courant* on 2 July 1804, nonetheless saluted his achievement: 'On Saturday last died, after a tedious illness, Mr. John Fisher, statuary of this City, whose abilities ranked him amongst the most eminent of his profession'. The *Monthly Magazine* praised 'the purity and classic originality of his design, as well as the spirit and elegant chastity of its execution' (*Monthly Mag*, XVIII, 1804, 173).

It is not known where John's other sons, **George Fisher** and **Richard Fisher II** served their apprenticeships, but notices in the *York Courant* indicate that both were trained in London. **Samuel Fisher II** spent five years 'studying sculpture under an eminent and most distinguished artist in London' (*York Courant*, 10 Nov 1806), and **Charles Fisher** trained under 'that eminent artist, Mr [John] Bacon [II]' (*York Courant*, 11 Dec 1815). Of all John's sons, William Fisher was the most ambitious: he exhibited at the Royal Academy on several occasions and also at the Northern Society exhibitions, held in Leeds. He also entered the City of London's competition for a monument to commemorate William Pitt in the Guildhall, and in 1806 wrote that he 'was engaged with Mr. [Joseph] Nollekens, Mortimer Street' (Fisher Letters).

John II and Charles were the only two sons to live beyond their thirties. Charles ran the workshop until his death in 1861, after which his wife, Mary Anne (†1772), and son, **John Fisher III**, assumed control. The most important work carved by Charles is perhaps the memorial in Sowerby, executed in 1856 to honour men of the parish who had died in the Crimea (**183**). By the second quarter of the 19th century the business had changed: monuments had become less grand, but with the opening of York cemetery in 1837 came an increasing demand for gravestones and 143 signed by the Fisher workshop have been recorded.

The Fisher workshop was the most prominent sculpture business in 18th-century Yorkshire, at a time when craftsmen had the opportunity to capitalise on the extensive building work taking place in the county. The firm's monuments attained a high standard of craftsmanship: Gunnis particularly admired their 'intelligent and sympathetic' use of coloured marbles and the qualitative carving of neoclassical ornaments. Julius Bryant has suggested that John Fisher I's finest works, particularly the statue of George Savile and the *Hygeia* on the Dealtry monument, can be ranked alongside the best monuments by Joseph Nollekens and **John Bacon RA**.

Corita Myerscough

Literary References: *Gunnis* 1968, 145–6; *Aylmer* 1977, 454, 456–60, 463; *Fothergill* 1984, 238; *Beard* 1986, 219; *Whinney* 1988, 256, 319; *Grove* 11, 138 (Bryant); *Myerscough* 1996, vol I, thesis; vol II, houses; vol III, monuments to 1799; vol IV, monuments 1800–1884 (unpag); *Myerscough* 2000, 24–33

Archival References: York App Reg, D14, 25 Sept 1784, 262 (John Fisher I), D14, 10 Aug 1786, 287 (John Fisher II), D15, 25 Oct 1793, 71 (William Fisher cleared of apprenticeship); letter from Doe to Aislabie, Aislabie Papers, parcel 301, roll 29/f/10; Fisher letters, 1806

Funerary Monuments

1.	†1713	Richard, 2nd Viscount Lonsdale	Lowther, Westmorland	S	*Myerscough* 1996, III (repr)
2.	†1741	Alathea Jordan	St Olave, York	S	*Myerscough* 1996, III (repr)
3.	†1744	John Dunn	Howden, E R Yorks		*Gunnis* 1968, 146; *Myerscough* 1996, III
4.	†1755	Hugh and Katherine (†1748) Cholmley (by John Fisher I)	St Mary, Whitby, N R Yorks		*Myerscough* 1996, III (repr)
5.	†1755	Katherine Cholmley (by John Fisher I)	St Mary, Whitby, N R Yorks	S	*Myerscough* 1996, III (repr)
6.	†1756	Robertson and Thomas Morley	Brayton, W R Yorks	S	*Myerscough* 1996, III (repr)
7.	†1762	Andrew Perrott M D	St Saviour, York	S	*Myerscough* 1996, III (repr)
8.	†1766	Charles Floyer	Ripon Cathedral, W R Yorks	S	*Myerscough* 1996, III (repr)
9.	†1767	Henry Rousby	Sledmere, E R Yorks	S	*Myerscough* 1996, III (repr)
10.	†1767	Lady Graham	Wath, N R Yorks	S	*Myerscough* 1996, III (repr)
11.	†1769	Ann Cayley	Burton Agnes, E R Yorks	S	*Myerscough* 1996, III (repr)
12.	†1769	Henry Masterman	Settrington, E R Yorks	S	*Myerscough* 1996, III (repr)
13.	†1770	Richard Osbaldeston, Bishop of Carlisle, and family	Hunmanby, E R Yorks	S	*Myerscough* 1996, III (repr)
14.	†1771	Grace Staines (by John Fisher I)	Ripon Cathedral, W R Yorks		*Myerscough* 1996, III
15.	†1771	Thomas Bosvile	Ravenfield, W R Yorks		*Myerscough* 1996, IV (repr)
16.	†1772	Henrietta Catherine Cholmley (by John Fisher I)	St Mary, Whitby, N R Yorks	S	*Myerscough* 1996, III (repr)
17.	†1772	James Buller (by John Fisher I)	St Thomas, Exeter, Devon		*Myerscough* 1996, III
18.	†1772	Robert Stansfield (by John Fisher I)	Guiseley, W R Yorks	S	
19.	†1772	Thomas Outybridge (by William and Richard Fisher II)	[Clarborough, Notts]; untraced	S	*Myerscough* 1996, III (repr); Pevsner, *Notts*, 1979, 97
20.	1772	William Hutchinson	St Michael, Spurriergate, York Other versions: St Thomas, Osbaldwick, N R Yorks	S	*Myerscough* 1996, III (repr)
21.	†1773	Godfrey Heathcote (by John Fisher I)	Chesterfield parish church, Derbys		*Gunnis* 1968, 146; *Myerscough* 1996, III (repr)
22.	†1773	John Hill (by John Fisher I)	Thornton-le-Dale, N R Yorks	S	*Myerscough* 1996, III (repr)
23.	†1773	Mary Darby (by John Fisher I)	Harpham, E R Yorks	S	
24.	†1773	Sybilla Wilson (by John Fisher I)	St Mary, Lancaster, Lancs	S	*Gunnis* 1968, 145
25.	†1774	Sir Charles Sheffield	Burton-upon-Stather, Lincs	S	*Gunnis* 1968, 145
26.	†1774	Thomas Scrivener (by John Fisher I)	Barton-on-Humber, Lincs	S	
27.	1776	Dr John Dealtry MD (†1773) (by John Fisher I) (designed by William Mason)	York Minster, Lady Chapel	S	*Gunnis* 1968, 145; *Aylmer* 1977, 460–1 (repr); *Penny* 1977 (1), 112
28.	†1776	Francis White	Ripon Cathedral, W R Yorks	S	*Myerscough* 1996, III (repr)
29.	†1776	Mary Preston	Scalby, N R Yorks	S	*Myerscough* 1996, III (repr)
30.	†1776	Richard Bagshaw	Norton, E R Yorks	S	*Myerscough* 1996, III (repr)
31.	†1777	Dame Frances Legard	Ganton, E R Yorks	S	*Myerscough* 1996, III (repr)
32.	†1777	Thomas Bowes	St Crux Parish Hall, York	S	*Myerscough* 1996, III (repr)
33.	†1778	Hon Amelia Sparre	St Mary, Thirsk, N R Yorks	S	*Myerscough* 1996, III (repr)
34.	†1779	Elizabeth Young	Great Ouseburn, W R Yorks	S	*Myerscough* 1996, III (repr)
35.	†1779	Henry Stapylton (by John Fisher I)	Wighill, W R Yorks	S	*Myerscough* 1996, III (repr)
36.	†1779	John Etty and family	All Saints, Pavement, York	S	*Myerscough* 1996, III (repr)
37.	†1780	Henry Waite, by John Fisher I	St Crux Parish Hall, York	S	*Myerscough* 1996, III (repr)
38.	†1780	John Grimston	Kilnwick-on-the-Wolds, E R Yorks	S	*Aylmer*, 1977, 454; *Myerscough* 1996, III (repr)
39.	†1780	Thomas Fountayne	High Melton, W R Yorks	S	
40.	†1781	Edward Forster	Thorne, W R Yorks	S	*Myerscough* 1996, III (repr)
41.	†1781	John Royds (by John Fisher I)	St John, Halifax, W R Yorks	S	*Myerscough* 1996, III (repr)
42.	†1781	William Danby	Masham, N R Yorks	S	*Myerscough* 1996, III (repr)
43.	†1782	John Bell	St Peter and St Paul, Pickering, N R Yorks		
44.	†1783	John Rickaby (by John Fisher I)	Priory Church, Bridlington, E R Yorks	S	*Myerscough* 1996, III (repr)
45.	†1783	Ursula Blomberg (by John Fisher I)	Kirby Misperton, N R Yorks	S	*Myerscough* 1996, III (repr)
46.	†1784	Dr Stephen Simpson (by John Fisher I)	Lichfield Cathedral, Staffs	S	*Penny* 1977 (1), 6 [(repr); *Myerscough* 1996, III (repr)
47.	†1784	Hannah Mosley (by John Fisher I)	St Nicholas's Cathedral, Newcastle, Northumbs	S	Pevsner, *Northumbs* 1992, 423
48.	†1784	Rev John Varey (by John Fisher I)	Stillington, N R Yorks	S	*Myerscough* 1996, III (repr)
49.	†1785	Elizabeth Whalley (by John Fisher I)	Whalley, Lancs	S	*Myerscough* 1996, III (repr)
50.	†1785	Mary Cooke (by John Fisher I)	Owston, W R Yorks		*Gunnis* 1968, 146
51.	†1785	Rev George William and Lucy (†1830) Anderson (by John Fisher I)	York Minster, south choir aisle	S	*Pattison and Murray* 2001, 114
52.	†1785	Thomas Nelson (by John Fisher I)	Holtby, N R Yorks	S	*Myerscough* 1996, III (repr)
53.	†1786	Francis Fawkes (by John Fisher I)	Otley, W R Yorks		*Myerscough* 1996, III (repr)
54.	†1786	John Birtwhistle	Holy Trinity, Skipton, W R Yorks		*Gunnis* 1968, 146
55.	†1786	Katherine Johnson (by John Fisher I)	Belton-in-Axholme, Lincs	S	*Myerscough* 1996, III (repr)
56.	†1786	Mary Pulleyn (by John Fisher I)	York Minster, St Stephen's Chapel	S	*Aylmer* 1977, 460; *Pattison and Murray* 2001, 95
57.	†1786	Sir Thomas Davenport MP (by John Fisher I)	York Minster, north choir aisle	S	*Aylmer* 1977, 460; *Pattison and Murray* 2001, 94–5
58.	†1787	Eleanor Swinburne	York Minster	S	*Aylmer* 1977, 461 (repr); *Pattison and Murray* 2001, 95–6
59.	†1787	Thomas Rodwell (by John Fisher I)	[St Mary, Bishophill Senior]; St Clement, York	S	*Myerscough* 1996, III (repr)

60.	†1788	Edward Nelthorpe (†1788)	Scawby, Lincs	S	*Myerscough* 1996, III (repr)
61.	†1788	Rev Sir William Lowther (by John Fisher I)	Swillington, W R Yorks	S	*Myerscough* 1996, III (repr)
62.	1789	Sir George Savile Bt, MP (†1784) (by John Fisher I)	York Minster, north choir aisle	S	*Aylmer* 1977, 461–2 (repr); *Whinney* 1988, 319; *Pattison and Murray* 2001, 92–3
63.	†1791	Fairfax Fearnley (by J Fisher)	Harewood, W R Yorks	S	*Myerscough* 1996, III (repr)
64.	†1791	Nathaniel Cholmley (by John Fisher I)	St Mary, Whitby, N R Yorks	S	*Myerscough* 1996, III (repr)
65.	†1792	Constantine, 1st Lord Mulgrave	Lythe, N R Yorks	S	*Myerscough* 1996, III (repr)
66.	†1792	George Morewood (by John Fisher I)	Alfreton, Derbys	S	*Myerscough* 1996, III (repr)
67.	1778–1792	Roger Talbot	Thornton-le-Street, N R Yorks	S	*Myerscough* 1996, III (repr)
68.	†1792	Walter Fawkes	Otley, W R Yorks	S	*Myerscough* 1996, III (repr)
69.	†1792	William Mushet M D	St Mary, Castlegate, York	S	*Myerscough* 1996, III (repr)
70.	†1793	Captain Pelsant Reeves (by John Fisher I)	York Minster, north choir aisle	S	*Aylmer* 1977, 462; *Pattison and Murray* 2001, 98
71.	†1793	John Singleton	Great Givendale, E R Yorks	S	*Myerscough* 1996, III (repr)
72.	†1794	Deborah Read (by John Fisher I)	Sand Hutton, N R Yorks	S	*Myerscough* 1996, III (repr)
73.	†1794	Fowler Hickes	Richmond, N R Yorks		*Gunnis* 1968, 146; *Myerscough* 1996, III
74.	†1794	Richard Wharton	York Minster, north choir aisle	S	*Aylmer* 1977, 462; *Pattison and Murray* 2001, 99
75.	†1795	Matthew Boynton (born Langley) (by John Fisher I)	Snaith, W R Yorks	S	*Myerscough* 1996, III (repr)
76.	†1795	Thomas Brook	St Michael-le-Belfrey, York	S	*Myerscough* 1996, III (repr)
77.	†1796	Lieutenant-Colonel George Legard	Ganton, E R Yorks	S	*Myerscough* 1996, III (repr)
78.	†1797	James Muncaster	Felton, Northumbs	S	Pevsner, *Northumbs*, 1992, 280
79.	†1797	Thomas Marris and family members	Barton-on-Humber, Lincs		
80.	†1798	Amaziah Empson	Scawby, Lincs	S	*Myerscough* 1996, III (repr)
81.	†1798	John Greame	Priory Church, Bridlington, E R Yorks	S	*Myerscough* 1996, III (repr)
82.	†1798	Sir James Sanderson	St Magnus the Martyr, London Bridge, London	S	*Myerscough* 1996, III (repr)
83.	†1799	Beilby Thompson (by John Fisher I)	Escrick, N R Yorks		*Gunnis* 1968, 146
84.	†1799	David Lambert	Rillington, E R Yorks	S	*Myerscough* 1996, III (repr)
85.	†1799	George (†1792) and Isabella Cary	Rudby-in-Cleveland, N R Yorks		Pevsner, *Yorks: N R*, 1966, 314
86.	†1799	Sir John Nelthorpe	Barton-on-Humber, Lincs	S	*Myerscough* 1996, III (repr)
87.	†1801	Peter Drinkwater	St Peter, Bolton, Lancs	S	*Myerscough* 1996, IV (repr)
88.	† to 1801	William Roxby (†1744), Mary Carnham (née Roxby, †1795) and her family	Beverley, E R Yorks	S	Pevsner, *Yorks: E R and York*, 1995, 292; *Myerscough* 1996, IV (repr)
89.	†1802	Barnard Foord	Cowlam, E R Yorks	S	*Myerscough* 1996, III (repr)
90.	†1802	James, 4th Viscount Lonsdale	Lowther, Westmorland	S	*Myerscough* 2000, 32
91.	†1803	Dorothy Barstow	Acomb, York	S	*Myerscough* 1996, IV (repr)
92.	†1803	John Wilkinson	Millington, E R Yorks	S	*Myerscough* 1996, IV (repr)
93.	†1803	Thomas Sanderson	St Michael, Spurriergate, York	S	*Myerscough* 1996, IV (repr)
94.	†1804	Henry Hewgill	Great Smeaton, N R Yorks	S	*Myerscough* 1996, IV (repr)
95.	†1806	Robert Hotham (by William and Charles Fisher)	St Denys, York	S	*Myerscough* 1996, IV (repr)
96.	†1808	Alexander Strachan	Christ Church, Harrogate, W R Yorks	S	*Myerscough* 1996, IV (repr)
97.	†1808	John Atkinson	St Martin-cum-Gregory, York	S	*Myerscough* 1996, IV (repr)
98.	†1808	Rev Robert Mitton	Christ Church, Harrogate, W R Yorks	S	*Myerscough* 1996, IV (repr)
99.	†1809	Alexander Hunter MD	St Michael-le-Belfrey, York	S	*Myerscough* 1996, IV (repr)
100.	†1809	Joseph Thompson	Brayton, W R Yorks	S	*Myerscough* 1996, IV (repr)
101.	†1809	Mary Lister (by William and Richard Fisher II)	Bradford Cathedral, W R Yorks	S	*Myerscough* 1996, IV (repr)
102.	†1809	Richard Samuel Prosser	Durham Cathedral	S	*Myerscough* 1996, IV (repr)
103.	†1809	Thomas Outybridge	Clarborough, Notts	S	*Myerscough* 1996, IV (repr)
104.	†1809	William Richardson	Kendal St Andrew, Westmorland	S	*Myerscough* 1996, IV (repr)
105.	1810	Ensign Henry Whittam (†1809)	York Minster, south choir aisle	S	*Aylmer* 1977, 463, n 67; *Myerscough* 1996, IV (repr); *Pattison and Murray* 2001, 105–6
106.	†1810	John Hedges	Thrybergh, W R Yorks	S	*Myerscough* 1996, IV (repr)
107.	†1811	Julia Cooke	Owston, W R Yorks	S	*Myerscough* 1996, IV (repr)
108.	† to 1811	Saltmarshe family	Howden, E R Yorks	S	*Myerscough* 1996, IV (repr)
109.	†1811	Sir William Mordant Milner (by George Fisher)	Bolton Percy, W R Yorks	S	*Myerscough* 1996, IV (repr)
110.	†1811	Thomas Haskoll	Christ Church, Harrogate, W R Yorks	S	*Myerscough* 1996, IV (repr)
111.	†1811	Thomas Pilkington	Wakefield Cathedral, W R Yorks	S	*Myerscough* 1996, IV (repr)
112.	†1812	Anne Brooke	Sowerby, N R Yorks	S	*Myerscough* 1996, IV (repr)
113.	†1812	Lax family	Kirby Hill, N R Yorks	S	*Myerscough* 1996, IV (repr)
114.	†1813	George Dawson	[St Mary, Bishophill Senior]; St Clement, York	S	*Myerscough* 1996, IV (repr)
115.	†1813	John Hopwood	Rochdale parish church, Lancs	S	*Myerscough* 1996, IV (repr)
116.	†1813	Lieutenant John Crossland	St Michael-le-Belfrey, York	S	*Myerscough* 1996, IV (repr)
117.	†1813	Maria Fawkes	Otley, W R Yorks	S	*Myerscough* 1996, IV (repr)
118.	†1813	Roger Darvall	St Michael-le-Belfrey, York	S	*Myerscough* 1996, IV (repr)
119.	†1813	Sarah Rhodes	St Crux Parish Hall, York	S	*Myerscough* 1996, IV (repr)

120.	†1813	William, Lord Hotham	South Dalton, E R Yorks	S	*Myerscough* 1996, IV (repr)
121.	†1814	Caroline Lacon Wood	Otley, W R Yorks	S	*Myerscough* 1996, IV (repr)
122.	†1814	Charles Thyots	Hawnby, N R Yorks	S	Pevsner, *Yorks: N R*, 1966, 185
123.	†1814	John Tripp	Spofforth, W R Yorks	S	*Myerscough* 1996, IV (repr)
124.	†1814	Mary Fortescue (by Charles Fisher)	Ketton, Northants	S	*Myerscough* 1996, IV (repr)
125.	†1814	Rev Henry Wray	Newton Kyme, W R Yorks	S	*Myerscough* 1996, IV (repr)
126.	†1814	Robert Jefferson	Howden Minster, E R Yorks	S	*Myerscough* 1996, IV (repr)
127.	†1814	Thomas Robinson	St Michael, Malton, N R Yorks	S	*Myerscough* 1996, IV (repr)
128.	†1816	Elizabeth Hamilton	Christ Church, Harrogate, W R Yorks	S	*Myerscough* 1996, IV (repr)
129.	†1816	Richard Simpson	St Peter and St Paul, Pickering, N R Yorks	S	*Myerscough* 1996, IV (repr)
130.	†1816	Robert Driffield (by Charles Fisher)	Unitarian Chapel, York	S	*Myerscough* 1996, III (repr)
131.	†1817	Mary Ann Wilks (by Charles Fisher)	Sowerby, W R Yorks	S	*Myerscough* 1996, IV (repr)
132.	†1819	John Mathewman (by Charles Fisher)	Christ Church, Harrogate, W R Yorks	S	*Myerscough* 1996, IV (repr)
133.	†1820	Edward Topham	Cowlam, E R Yorks	S	*Myerscough* 1996, IV (repr)
134.	†1820	Hall Plume (by Charles Fisher)	Sheriff Hutton, N R Yorks	S	
135.	†1820	Richard Sawdon (by Charles Fisher)	Brompton, N R Yorks	S	*Myerscough* 1996, IV (repr)
136.	†1821	George Coates (by Charles Fisher)	Ripon Cathedral, W R Yorks	S	*Myerscough* 1996, IV (repr)
137.	†1821	Marion Lloyd	St Michael-le-Belfrey, York	S	*Myerscough* 1996, IV (repr)
138.	†1821	Nicholas Piper (by Charles Fisher)	St Peter and St Paul, Pickering, N R Yorks	S	*Myerscough* 1996, IV (repr)
139.	†1822	Digby Legard	Ganton, E R Yorks	S	*Myerscough* 1996, IV (repr)
140.	†1822	Rev Richard Davies	St Michael, Malton, N R Yorks	S	*Myerscough* 1996, IV (repr)
141.	†1822	Robert Harrison	St Michael-le-Belfrey, York	S	*Myerscough* 1996, IV (repr)
142.	†1823	Jane Marcella Brooke	Sowerby, N R Yorks	S	*Myerscough* 1996, IV (repr)
143.	†1823	John Hunter (co-sculptor: William Abbot of York Plows)	Christ Church, Harrogate, W R Yorks	S	*Myerscough* 1996, IV (repr)
144.	†1823	Simon Kettlewell	Kirklington, N R Yorks	S	*Myerscough* 1996, IV (repr)
145.	†1824	Eliza Outram	Christ Church, Harrogate, W R Yorks	S	*Myerscough* 1996, IV (repr)
146.	†1824	Sophia Bolton (by Charles Fisher)	St Michael-le-Belfrey, York	S	*Myerscough* 1996, IV (repr)
147.	†1826	Thomas Wilkinson	St Saviour, York		*Myerscough* 1996, IV (repr)
148.	†1827	Rev James Rudd	Full Sutton, E R Yorks		Pevsner, *Yorks: E R & York*, 1995, 429
149.	†1829	Rev William Rhodes	St Mary, Tadcaster, W R Yorks	S	*Myerscough* 1996, IV (repr)
150.	†1829	William Gage (by Charles Fisher)	St Martin-cum-Gregory, York	S	*Myerscough* 1996, IV (repr)
151.	†1830	Anne Lloyd	St Mary, Castlegate, York	S	*Myerscough* 1996, IV (repr)
152.	†1830	Ellen Jones, tombstone	St Stephen, Acomb, York	S	*Myerscough* 1996, IV (repr)
153.	†1830	James, 2nd Earl of Mexborough	Methley, W R Yorks	S	*Myerscough* 1996, IV (repr)
154.	†1830	Susanna Wray	St Martin-cum-Gregory, York	S	*Myerscough* 1996, IV (repr)
155.	†1831	Caroline Strangeways	Sowerby, N R Yorks	S	*Myerscough* 1996, IV (repr)
156.	†1831	Henry, 1st Earl of Mulgrave and Viscount Normanby (by Charles Fisher)	Lythe, N R Yorks	S	*Myerscough* 1996, IV (repr)
157.	†1831	Phebe Mallatratt	St Saviour, York	S	*Myerscough* 1996, IV (repr)
158.	†1831	Thomas Maude	Christ Church, Harrogate, W R Yorks	S	*Myerscough* 1996, IV (repr)
159.	†1832	Ann Bingley	Christ Church, Harrogate, W R Yorks	S	*Myerscough* 1996, IV (repr)
160.	†1832	Eliza Meek	Kirby Whiske, N R Yorks	S	*Myerscough* 1996, IV (repr)
161.	†1832	Elizabeth Bridgewater, tombstone	Cholera burial ground, York	S	*Myerscough* 1996, IV (repr)
162.	†1832	Rev John Tyson	Goodmanham, E R Yorks	S	*Myerscough* 1996, IV (repr)
163.	†1835	Rev Arthur Guinness	Christ Church, Harrogate, W R Yorks	S	*Myerscough* 1996, IV (repr)
164.	†1837	William Camac	Christ Church, Harrogate, W R Yorks	S	*Myerscough* 1996, IV (repr)
165.	†1838	Eliza Geldart	Kirk Deighton, W R Yorks	S	*Myerscough* 1996, IV (repr)
166.	†1838	Rev James Dallin	Holy Trinity, Goodramgate, York	S	*Myerscough* 1996, IV (repr)
167.	†1839	Rev James Geldart	Kirk Deighton, W R Yorks	S	*Myerscough* 1996, IV (repr)
168.	†1840	Albert Legard	Settrington, E R Yorks	S	*Myerscough* 1996, IV (repr)
169.	†1840	Hannah Hunter	Christ Church, Harrogate, W R Yorks	S	*Myerscough* 1996, IV (repr)
170.	†1840	James Robert Fryer	Holy Trinity, Goodramgate, York	S	*Myerscough* 1996, IV (repr)
171.	†1840	Maria Stevens	St John, Knaresborough, W R Yorks	S	*Myerscough* 1996, IV (repr)
172.	†1842	Christopher Wilson	Wighill, W R Yorks	S	*Myerscough* 1996, IV (repr)
173.	†1842	Mary Rivis	Sherburn, E R Yorks	S	Pevsner, *Yorks: E R & York*, 1995, 680
174.	†1843	Charlotte Bingley	Christ Church, Harrogate, W R Yorks	S	*Myerscough* 1996, IV (repr)
175.	†1844	Rev John Graham	[St Mary, Bishophill Senior]; St Clement, York	S	*Myerscough* 1996, IV (repr)
176.	†1846	Elizabeth Nicholson	Cawood, W R Yorks	S	*Myerscough* 1996, IV (repr)
177.	†1847	John Nelson	St Michael, Spurriergate, York	S	*Myerscough* 1996, IV (repr)
178.	†1847	Susanna Bingley	Christ Church, Harrogate, W R Yorks	S	*Myerscough* 1996, IV (repr)
179.	†1848	James Gladwell Ogilvie	Christ Church, Harrogate, W R Yorks	S	*Myerscough* 1996, IV (repr)
180.	†1851	Thomas and Margaret Lax	Kirby Hill, N R Yorks	S	*Myerscough* 1996, IV (repr)
181.	†1852	John Wright	Walton, W R Yorks	S	*Myerscough* 1996, IV (repr)
182.	†1855	Robert Stansfield	Sowerby, W R Yorks	S	*Myerscough* 1996, IV (repr)
183.	1856	Crimean War memorial (by Charles Fisher)	Sowerby, W R Yorks	S	*Myerscough* 1996, IV (repr)
184.	†1857	Hon Edmund Phipps	Lythe, N R Yorks	S	*Myerscough* 1996, IV (repr)
185.	†1858	Richard Bland	Dalby, N R Yorks	S	*Myerscough* 1996, IV (repr)
186.	†1861	Rev Timothy Fysh Foord-Bowes	Cowlam, E R Yorks	S	Pevsner, *Yorks: E R & York*, 1995, 392
187.	†1861	William Catton	St Crux Parish Hall, York	S	*Myerscough* 1996, IV (repr)
188.	†1865	William Whitelocke	Foston, N R Yorks	S	*Myerscough* 1996, IV (repr)

No.	Date	Subject	Material	Location		Bibliography
189.	†1868	Rev Joseph Crosby		St Crux Parish Hall, York	S	*Myerscough* 1996, IV (repr)
190.	†1870	Elizabeth Cowling		Unitarian Chapel, York	S	*Myerscough* 1996, IV (repr)
191.	†1873	Rev Metcalfe Thompson		St Crux Parish Hall, York	S	*Myerscough* 1996, IV (repr)
192.	†1874	Eliza Cowling		Unitarian Chapel, York	S	*Myerscough* 1996, IV (repr)
193.	†1877	David Cowling		Unitarian Chapel, York	S	*Myerscough* 1996, IV (repr)
Statues						
194.	1761	Jupiter with an eagle, and Christ carrying the cross (by Richard Fisher I)	m	[coll John Fisher, St Saviourgate, York]; Yorkshire Museum, York	S	*Graves* 1907, 92; *Myerscough* 1996, II; *Myerscough* 2000, 28
195.	1761	Our Saviour with the cross (by Richard Fisher I)	m	[coll Samuel Fisher]; York Minster (1907)	S	*Graves* 1907, 92; *Aylmer* 1977, 456–7 (repr); *Myerscough* 1996, II
Busts						
196.	1802	Napoleon Bonaparte (by William Fisher)		Untraced		*York Courant*, 4 Jan 1802 (advert); *Myerscough* 1996, II
197.	1807	Head of Christ (by William Fisher)		[Exhib RA, London, 1002]; untraced		*Graves* III, 1905–6, 118; *Myerscough* 1996, II
198.	c1808	An elderly nobleman (by William Fisher)		Private coll	S	*Myerscough* 1996, II (repr)
199.	1808	'Dr F' (by William Fisher)		[Exhib RA, London, 892]; untraced		*Graves* III, 1905–6, 118; *Myerscough* 1996, II
200.	1808	J Wheatley (by William Fisher)		[Exhib RA, London, 885]; untraced		*Graves* III, 1905–6, 118; *Myerscough* 1996, II
201.	1808	Miss Smith of Covent Garden Theatre (by William Fisher)		[Exhib RA, London, 993]; untraced		*Graves* III, 1905–6, 118; *Myerscough* 1996, II
202.	1808	The late Mr Fothergill (by William Fisher)		[Exhib RA, London, 866]; untraced		*Graves* III, 1905–6, 118; *Myerscough* 1996, II
203.	1808	William Pitt the Younger, after Joseph Nollekens (by Richard Fisher II) Payment(s): £21	m	Harewood House, W R Yorks, Spanish library Other versions: University of Leeds, Special Colls, Brotherton Library, 1810		WR CRO HAR/ACC/244; *Mauchline* 1992, 119
204.	1810	'The late Peregrine Wentworth'		[Exhib RA, London, 896]; untraced		*York Courant*, 13 Aug 1809; *Graves* III, 1905–6, 118
205.	1810	William Pitt the Younger (by Richard Fisher II)		Untraced		*York Courant*, 6 April 1812 (advert)
206.	1811	The late Sir C Turner (by William Fisher)		[Exhib RA, London, 916]; untraced		*Graves* III, 1905–6, 118; *Myerscough* 1996, II (repr)
207.	1812	The late Sir William Milner (by George Fisher)		Untraced		*York Courant*, 6 April 1812 (advert); *Myerscough* 1996, II (repr)
208.	post-1816	Arthur, 1st Duke of Wellington		[Exhib York Fine Art & Industrial Exhib, July 1866, cat 671]; untraced		*Myerscough* 1996, II (repr)
209.	nd	Sir Isaac Newton (by John Fisher)	m	Fisher family coll	S	*Myerscough* 1996, II
210.	nd	William Pitt the Younger (by William Fisher)		[Lowther Castle, Westmorland]; Gawsworth Hall, Cheshire	S	*Gawsworth Guide*, 44, 46 (repr)
211.	nd	William Shakespeare (by John Fisher)	m	York Minster Library	S	*Myerscough* 1996, II
Chimneypieces						
212.	1737	Eight (by Richard Fisher I)		Wolterton Hall, Norfolk, marble hall, state dining room, Venetian room, saloon, blue damask room, boudoir, state dressing room, east state bedroom		Wolterton/Fisher, 8/21; *Myerscough* 1996, II
213.	1740–1742	Several (by Richard Fisher I)		LMG, Temple Newsam House, W R Yorks, blue striped dressing room, boudoir, blue damask room, ante-room		*Myerscough* 1996, II
214.	1732–1753	Description unavailable		[Studley Royal, W R Yorks, library]; destroyed		*Myerscough* 1996, II
215.	1766	Overmantel (by John I and Samuel Fisher) Payment(s): £42	wd	Burton Constable Hall, E R Yorks, great hall		Pevsner, *Yorks: E R & York*, 1995, 375; *Myerscough* 2000, 28
216.	1766	Overmantel with ropes, garlands and crossed oak branches by John Fisher I and Samuel Fisher, supporting a scagliola shield by Domenico Bartoli Payment(s): £38 for carving the ornaments	wd	Burton Constable Hall, E R Yorks, great hall, acc 961		Constable Accts ERAO, DDCC 140/5, 21 April 1766; *Myerscough* 1996, II (repr)
217.	1766	Two		Swinton Castle, N R Yorks, drawing room and first library (by John Fisher I)		Danby ZS 2290; *Myerscough* 1996, 28 (repr)
218.	1768	Two Payment(s): £88, £164		Wentworth Woodhouse, W R Yorks, state dressing room, state bedroom		WW/Steward's Papers, 1768; *Myerscough* 1996, II (repr)
219.	1781–1782	Several Payment(s): £300 Drawing(s): Private coll, signed by John Fisher as receipt for payment	m	Wentworth Woodhouse, W R Yorks, grand drawing room and other rooms		*Myerscough* 1996, II (repr)
220.	1786–1789	Several (by John Fisher I)	m	Farnley Hall, W R Yorks, dining and other rooms		Letter, Farnley archives, uncat; *Gunnis* 1967, 145; *Myerscough* 1996, II (repr)

221.	1793	by John Fisher I		Swinton Castle, N R Yorks	Danby Papers ZS 2290
222.	1805	Two by William Fisher		Thornville Royal (Allerton Park), W R Yorks, breakfast and billiard rooms	*Fothergill* CXLII (1984)
Architectural Sculpture					
223.	1729	Unidentified work (by Richard Fisher I)		[Scriven Hall, Knaresborough, W R Yorks]; destroyed	Slingsby Papers, DD56 and 148, 12; *Myerscough* 1996, II
224.	1732	Exterior ornaments (by Richard Fisher I) Payment(s): £28 5s 4d	s	Studley Royal, W R Yorks, banqueting hall	Vyner MSS, 37, V.5619a, V.5508; *Myerscough* 1996, II (repr)
225.	1732	Interior ornaments (by Richard Fisher I)		Studley Royal, W R Yorks, banqueting hall	Vyner MSS, VR286, bundle A, [1], 25; bundle B [2], 12
226.	1741	Carved work (by Richard Fisher I)		Castle Howard, N R Yorks	Castle Howard archives
227.	1750	Doorcases and other works	wd	[Studley Royal, W R Yorks]; destroyed	*Myerscough* 1996, II
228.	1740–1750	Unidentified work		Nostell Priory, Wakefield, W R Yorks	*Myerscough* 1996, II
229.	1751–1752	Decorative carving (by Richard Fisher I and sons)		Nostell Priory, W R Yorks	West Yorks CRO NP/A4/1530/4
Reliefs					
230.	1794	Charles, Marquis of Rockingham, medallion portrait (by John Fisher I)		Untraced	*York Herald*, 2 Aug 1794
231.	1801	A greyhound course (by William Fisher)	m	[Exhib RA, London, 969]; untraced Other versions: Exhib RA, London, 969	*Graves* III, 1905–6, 117–8; *Myerscough* 1996, II (repr)
232.	c1830	Putti with goat (by Richard Fisher III (?)	s	Fairfax House, York	*Myerscough* 1996, II (repr)
Miscellaneous					
233.	1740–1742	Doorcase 'in the saloon'		LMG, Temple Newsam House, W R Yorks	TN/EA/13/28, f 40, 40F; Pawson / Accounts, p 15, parcel 7, box 4; *Myerscough* 2000, 26–27
234.	1751–1752	Unidentified carving (by Richard Fisher I)		Nostell Priory, Wakefield, W R Yorks	Winn Accounts, NP/A4/1530/4; *Myerscough* 2000, 27
235.	1732–1753	Apollo sunburst (formerly south tower: now in Fountains Hall), chimneypiece (east room), chimneypiece (red room), chimneypiece and ornaments (library)		Studley Royal, W R Yorks	Vyner MSS VR286, bundle B [2], 12, 33, 44; bundle C, 38; *Myerscough* 1996, II
236.	1732–1753	Unidentified work, probably bedroom chimneypieces, doorcases etc (by Richard Fisher I and sons)		Studley Royal, W R Yorks	Vyner MSS VR286, bundle B [2], 12, 33, 44; bundle C, 38
237.	1784–1793	Lettering and pedestals (by John Fisher I)		Rockingham Mausoleum, Wentworth Castle, W R Yorks	WW Muniments, Sheffield D1550B; *Myerscough* 1996, II (repr)
238.	1780–1794	Various works (by John Fisher I)		Castle Howard, N R Yorks	Castle Howard Cash Books, 1761–1815; CH Accounts, 1770–1816
239.	1797	Marble tables (by John Fisher I)		Harewood House, W R Yorks	*Mauchline* 1992, 119
240.	1806	A stag chase (by William Fisher)		[Exhib RA, London, 861]; untraced	*Graves* III, 1905–6, 118; *Myerscough* 1996, II
241.	1806	Fox's head (by William Fisher)		[Exhib RA, London, 846]; untraced	*Graves* III, 1905–6, 118; *Myerscough* 1996, II (repr)
242.	1807	Head of Christ		[Exhib RA, London, 1002]; untraced	*Graves* III, 1905–6, 00
243.	post-1816	Time cutting Cupid's wings		[Exhib York Fine Art & Industrial Exhib, July 1866, cat 671]; untraced	

FITZGERALD, J E fl 1845

A bust of the antiquary William Vaux signed 'J. E. Fitzgerald/Xmas 1845' was formerly at the British Museum. No information on Fitzgerald, who was presumably Irish, has come to light. He may have been in the circle of the artist Joseph Severn, who was a friend of Vaux.

Literary References: *Gunnis* 1968, 146; *Dawson* 1999, 222–3

Busts						
1.	1845	William Sandys Wright Vaux	p	[BM, London, Old Medal room]; destroyed 1941	SD	*Dawson* 1999, 18, 222–3

FITZGERALD, of Cork fl 1823

Funerary Monuments				
1.	†1823	Rev William Hoare (designed by James and G R Paine)	Limerick Cathedral	*Potterton* 1975, 73

FITZGERALD, Thomas fl 1798

Fitzgerald described himself as 'under indentures of apprenticeship to Mr Westmacott [**Richard Westmacott I**], statuary, in Mount-street, Grosvenor-square' on 12 September 1798, when giving evidence at a trial (Proceedings of the Old Bailey, t 17980912-54). He had been robbed of a silver watch, valued at 42 shillings and a silk handkerchief at the corner of Vere Street. Fitzgerald was lodging in Brown Street, Grosvenor Square, at the house of a Mrs Haycock. He was unmarried. The prisoner was sentenced to death.

FITZPATRICK, Thomas and W, of Belfast fl 1830–68

W Fitzpatrick signs the memorial with a kneeling figure of grief by an urn to Rev George Birch (**1**). Another monument, probably provided nearly 20 years later, to Colonel John Eliot Cairnes is signed by T and W Fitzpatrick (**2**). Thomas Fitzpatrick later established himself as an architectural carver and worked on many public buildings in Belfast, including the Custom House (1857), the Ulster Bank, Waring Street (1860), and 34 and 36 Victoria Street (1868). Potterton suggests that W Fitzpatrick may have been his father.

Literary References: *Potterton* 1975, 45; *Darby and Smith* 1983, 91

Funerary Monuments

1.	†1830	George Birch	Comber, Co Down	S	*Potterton* 1975, 45
2.	†1847	Colonel John Eliot Cairnes	Agherton, Co Londonderry	S	*Potterton* 1975, 45

FLATTERS, Johann Jakob 1786–1845

Flatters was born in Germany but trained and worked as a sculptor in Paris. He was in England in 1842–3 when he exhibited at the Royal Academy, giving his address as 2 Ranelagh Grove, Pimlico. He executed a bust of Queen Victoria (**3**).

Literary References: *Thieme-Becker*, XII, 76

Statues

1.	1842	Girl awakening	b	[Exhib RA, London, 1350]; untraced	*Graves* III, 1905–6, 123

Busts

2.	1842	J G Lockhart		[Exhib RA, London, 1339]; untraced	*Graves* III, 1905–6, 123
3.	1843	Queen Victoria	m	VAM	*Ormond* 1973, 485

FLAXMAN, John I 1726–1803

A modeller and caster of plaster figures, he is best remembered as the father of **John Flaxman RA**. The elder Flaxman was born at Aston Clinton, Bucks and christened there on 5 June 1726. He was a younger son of Robert Flaxman and Elizabeth, née Nunly. Nothing is known of his training. According to Allan Cunningham, Flaxman married a Miss Lee, and had a peripatetic early career. **William Flaxman** was their first child. In July 1755 Flaxman was in York, where his second son, John Flaxman RA, was born. A close friend during this period was William Lindley, the draughtsman who was chief assistant to the architect John Carr of York, and it is possible that Flaxman also found employment with Carr. He is said to have returned to London early in 1756.

In February 1763, following the death of his first wife, he married Elizabeth Gordon at St Anne's Soho, Westminster. Their daughter, the sculptress **Maria Ann Flaxman**, was born in 1768, and two other daughters followed. Flaxman had taken premises in New Street, Covent Garden by 1766 and one of his earliest known commissions was to repair Torrigiano's famous busts from the Holbein Gate, recently acquired by a coachmaker, Wright of Long Acre (**15**). Flaxman appears to have specialised in modelling plaster figures. In 1770 he was producing models of graceful classical statuettes for Matthew Boulton, the Birmingham ormolu manufacturer (**2**), and probably began to work for Wedgwood and Bentley. He supplied a great many designs for Wedgwood in 1775 (**5, 26–32, 37, 38**). He continued to work for Wedgwood until the 1780s, but the firm sought to attract the services of members of the newly-founded Royal Academy and undervalued Flaxman's models. Wedgwood wrote to Bentley in February 1771 'I wrote to you in my last concerning Busts, I suppose those at the Academy are less hackneyed and better in General than the plaister shops can furnish us with: besides it will sound better to say this is from the Academy, taken from an original in the Gallery of etc etc than to say we had it from Flaxman' (Wedgwood Archives, quoted in *Bindman* 1979, 47).

Flaxman lived at King Street, Covent Garden between 1773 and 1776 and a surviving trade card describes him as a 'figure maker' (BM Heal 103.12). His business must have flourished. In 1776 he took a lease on larger premises at 420 Strand, 'opposite Durham Yard' (BM Heal 103.13). Flaxman became known chiefly as a moulder, caster and purveyor of plaster figures, although he took on other work too. In 1781–82 he and his two sons worked for Edward Knight at Wolverley Hall, providing chimneypieces and miscellaneous decorative ornaments (**25, 39**).

Between 1785 and April 1787 Flaxman employed his son, John on miscellaneous work for his firm. Surviving bills give some indication of the more pedestrian aspects of the business and include references to the oiling of a mould, 'casting a small monument' for 1s 6d, supplying and fixing a pedestal for 'Mr Longe' and painting a bas-relief for 'Mr Montague.' Young Flaxman received 5/- a day as well as extra payments for specific works (Flaxman Papers BL, Ad MS 39791, ff124–8). Young John went to Italy late in 1787, which perhaps prompted Flaxman Senior to take an apprentice, Isaac Dell of Berkhamstead, in April 1788, at fee of £31 10s. Dell was to be instructed in the 'Moulding and Casting of Plaister Figures' (VAM NAL QQ. Box I (ii)).

Flaxman may have benefited from his son's period in Rome, for in 1791 young John recommended him as a suitable man to produce moulds of plaster casts from the antique for the portraitist George Romney, who was attempting to found an academy. It is not known whether anything came of the suggestion, but young John certainly saw an opportunity for his father to corner a potentially lucrative market. He wrote home 'I find from what I see of the English nobility and gentry here that the taste increases in England for plaster casts as well as other articles of sculpture' (BL MS 39780, fol 57, 3rd March 1792). The elder Flaxman responded by expressing a wish to expand his repertoire of cast subjects and in the same year he bought several moulds that had formerly belonged to **John Cheere**.

In March 1796 Flaxman signed a further 21-year lease on his premises on Strand at an annual rent of £60. Little is known of his later output, but many of his plasters were acquired by the 3rd Earl of Egremont for Petworth between 1798 and 1801 and they comprise a wide range of subjects, from classical mythology to animal anatomy (**10, 12, 23**). Flaxman died in 1803 and his will was proved in April. He left his wearing apparel to his son, William, and an ornamental ring to his son John. His daughter Maria Ann was the residuary legatee. His fortune was probable modest, for when Mary Ann died in 1833 her estate amounted to only £43 15s 4d. A sale of his work was held in June 1803.

Little is known of Flaxman as a person except his political leanings (Farington records that he voted for Charles James Fox in the Westminster election of 1796), and his personal appearance, which was recorded by his son in a pencil portrait of the old man, seated and holding his spectacles. His work, too, remains elusive because the documented pieces have largely perished. Contemporary sources and biographies of his son John however suggest that the shop was popular with many distinguished patrons, including the politician Frederick Montagu, the Reverend AS Matthews, Mr Crutchley of Sunninghill Park, and Lord Boringdon. Flaxman was said also to have been employed as a modeller by both **Louis François Roubiliac** and **Peter Scheemakers**. Nearly twenty-five years after his death, the *Gentleman's Magazine* described him as one of the last respectable plaster model makers 'which was not then so hackneyed a trade, as it has now become, by the large importation of Italians' (*GM*, 1827, vol 98, part 1, 273–6).

MGS

Literary References: *Farington*, vol 2, 581; *Cunningham* 1829–33, vol 3, 274; *Graves* 1905–6, II, 123; *Graves* 1907, 93; *Goodison* 1974, 98–103; *Irwin* 1979, 46, 223 n35; *Bindman* 1979, 26, 39, 47, 50; *Haskell and Penny* 1981, 80; *Galvin and Lindley* 1988, 894–5; *Reilly* 1995, 184

Archival References: IGI; Flaxman Leases; Grantham Correspondence; Flaxman Papers BL, Add MS 39791, fols 3, 120, 124–8, 196

Will: PROB 11/1390, 225–6

Auctions Catalogues: Flaxman 1803

Statues

1.	1767	Flora and Zingara, 'figures' Payment(s): £1 16s		[for James West, Alscot Park, Warks]; untraced	West Papers, Alscot Park, box 42; *Gunnis* 1968, 147
2.	1770	'Group of Hercules and Atlas,' statuettes for Matthew Boulton Payment(s): £3 1s, including cost of package, for these and the 'figure of Michelangelo's Anatomy'		Untraced	*Goodison* 1974 (1), 57–8; *Goodison* 1974 (2), 102–3
3.	c1772	Figures representing Architecture and Painting	m	Raby Castle, Durham	*Gunnis* 1968, 149; *Irwin* 1979, 6 (Architecture repr)
4.	1772	Hickes memorial: Charity protecting a poor boy	b	[Royal Exchange, London]; Marine Society, London	RG/JP, 4, 504
5.	1775	Two, unspecified subjects Payment(s): £2 2s		Untraced Other versions: reproduced by Wedgwood	*Clifford* 1992, 54
6.	1781	Alexander the Great Payment(s): £100		[coll Edward Knight, Wolverly House, Worcs]; untraced	*Hendricks* 1984, 618
7.	1785	'Figures' for lamps	p	[for Lord Boringdon]; untraced	Grantham Corr, Beds RO 130/15/54/295; L30/14/333/337
8.	1786	Unspecified figure (for the Derby Porcelain Manufactory) Payment(s): 9s, bill including repairs to '3 Large Vauses'	p	Untraced	*Bricknell* 1995, 12, citing Day-Book, Derby Local Studies Library, parcel 17x
9.	1787	'a cast of a female body' (executed for John Flaxman I by John Flaxman RA) Payment(s): £9 4s		Untraced	Flaxman Papers BL Add MS, fols 124–8
10.	1788–1789	Several, including 'An anatomical figure . . . The Anatomy of a Horse . . . Ditto of a Leg . . . Gainsborough's Horse' Payment(s): £3 18s 6d	p	[Petworth House, Sussex]; untraced	Petworth House archives, PHA 7556
11.	1792	Unspecified subjects	pb	[for Mr and Mrs Mathew Montagu]; untraced	*Blunt* 1923, vol 2, 284
12.	1801	'The Crouching Venus' and 'Venus with the Shell' Payment(s): £1 5s each		[Petworth House, Sussex]; untraced	Petworth House archives, PHA 7558

Busts

13.	1767	Alexander Pope Payment(s): £31 12s		[for James West, Alscot Park, Warks]; untraced	West Papers, Alscot Park, box 42; *Gunnis* 1968, 147
14.	1767	John Milton		[for James West, Alscot Park, Warks]; untraced	West Papers, Alscot Park, box 42; *Gunnis* 1968, 147
15.	c1769	Repairs to Pietro Torrigiano's busts of Henry VII, Henry VIII and Bishop John Fisher (possibly executed by John Flaxman RA)	tc	[Holbein Gate, Whitehall, London]; VAM A4-1935; Met NY	*Smith* 1807, 23; *Galvin and Lindley* 1988, 894–5
16.	1781	Dr Fothergale Payment(s): £1 4s		Untraced Other versions: reproduced by Wedgwood	*Gunnis* 1968, 147
17.	1781	Jean-Jacques Rousseau		Untraced Other versions: reproduced by Wedgwood	*Gunnis* 1968, 146
18.	1781	Laurence Sterne		Untraced Other versions: reproduced by Wedgwood	*Gunnis* 1968, 147
19.	1782	Several (possibly by John Flaxman RA) Payment(s): £20		[Wolverley House, Worcs]; untraced	*Hendricks* 1984, 625
20.	1784	Hercules		Untraced Other versions: reproduced by Wedgwood	*Gunnis* 1968, 147
21.	1786	Marshal Turenne (executed for John Flaxman I by John Flaxman RA) Payment(s): £2 8s for two, with two busts of 'Mr Lawrence'		Untraced	Flaxman Papers BL Ad MS, fols 124–8

No.	Date	Work		Location	Reference
22.	1786–1787	'Mr Lawrence' (executed for John Flaxman I by John Flaxman (RA) Payment(s): £2 8s for two, with two busts of 'Turenne' in 1786		Untraced Other versions: one, in form of a mask, 1787, 12s; untraced	Flaxman Papers BL Ad MS, fols 124–8
23.	1801	'Sappho and Zingara'		[Petworth House, Sussex]; untraced	Petworth House archives, PHA 7558
24.	nd	George Frederick Handel	p	Windsor Castle	*Gunnis* 1968, 147
Chimneypieces					
25.	1781–1782	Several (possibly in collaboration with John Flaxman RA)		[Wolverley Hall, Worcs]; untraced	*Hendricks* 1984, 625
Architectural Sculpture					
26.	1775	'An Antique Vase sculptured with figures' Payment(s): £1 15s		Untraced Other versions: reproduced by Wedgwood	*Clifford* 1992, 54
27.	1775	'Sacred to Bacchus' and 'Sacred to Neptune,' pair of ewers Payment(s): £3 3s		Untraced Other versions: reproduced by Wedgwood	*Bindman* 1979, 50 (copies repr)
Reliefs					
28.	1775	Bacchus, Ariadne, bas-reliefs Payment(s): 7s each		Untraced Other versions: reproduced by Wedgwood	*Clifford* 1992, 54
29.	1775	Jupiter, Juno, Minerva, Justice, Hope, bas-reliefs Payment(s): 10s 6d each		Untraced Other versions: reproduced by Wedgwood	*Bindman* 1979, 52; *Clifford* 1992, 54
30.	1775	Melpomene, Thalia, Terpsichore, Euterpe, Sappho, Apollo, Hercules with the lion, Hercules with the boar, Hercules and Cerberus, bas-reliefs (reproductions by Wedgwood) Payment(s): 10s 6d each		Untraced Other versions: reproduced by Wedgwood	*Clifford* 1992, 54
31.	1775	'Moulding & making a cast from a Medall of Lennaeus' (Carolus Linnaeus)		Untraced Other versions: reproduced by Wedgwood	*Clifford* 1992, 54; *Reilly* 1995, 184
32.	1775	The four seasons Payment(s): £2 2s		Untraced Other versions: reproduced by Wedgwood	*Bindman* 1979, 51 (Wedgwood repr)
33.	1786	Unspecified bas-relief (executed for John Flaxman I by John Flaxman RA) Payment(s): £4 4s		['for Mr Proctor']; untraced	Flaxman Papers BL Ad MS, fols 124–8
34.	nd	Inigo Jones	w	(coll John Harris)	
Miscellaneous					
35.	1770	'A sleeping Bacchus, 11 boys. ., 2 groups of ditto' for Matthew Boulton Payment(s): £3 7s, including cost of package		Untraced	*Goodison* 1974 (1), 57–8
36.	1770	'figure of Michelangelo's Anatomy' for Matthew Boulton Payment(s): £3 1s, including cost of package, with the 'Group of Hercules and Atlas'		Untraced	*Goodison* 1974 (1), 57–8
37.	1775	'Mending a Wax Medall & making a Mould from It' for Wedgwood Payment(s): 2s		Untraced	*Clifford* 1992, 54
38.	1775	Six cups and saucers Payment(s): 8s 6d		Untraced Other versions: reproduced by Wedgwood	*Clifford* 1992, 54
39.	1781	Moulding and taking 13 casts of a 'Lion Frieze' Payment(s): £2 3s for the moulding, £12 14s for the casts		[for Edward Knight, Wolverley House, Worcs]; untraced	*Hendricks* 1984, 621
40.	1786	Marius and Agrippina (executed for John Flaxman I by John Flaxman RA) Payment(s): £1 1s		Untraced	Flaxman Papers BL Ad MS, fols 124–8
41.	1787	'eight moulds' and 'a child's arm' (executed for John Flaxman I by John Flaxman RA) Payment(s): 16s and 1s		Untraced	Flaxman Papers BL Ad MS, fols 124–8
42.	1794	Unspecified work (for Derby Porcelain Manufactory) Payment(s): £1 18s 6d		Untraced	*Bricknell* 1995, 79
43.	1794	Venus and Cupid	p	Audley End, Essex	Essex RO, D/DBY A225; *Gunnis* 1968, 147
44.	1801	Unspecified work		[for Matthew Boulton]; untraced	*Irwin* 1979, 219, n28
45.	nd	'1 lion . . . base relief of ditto . . . ram's head . . . deer's head', of 'fine plaster', for Matthew Boulton Payment(s): £2 16s, including cost of package		Untraced	*Goodison* 1974 (1), 57–8
46.	nd	'masks of Garrick, Henderson and Mrs Robinson', 'a cast of Mrs Jordan's leg' and a 'bust of Lord Bathurst'		[Flaxman's studio, 420 Strand, London]; untraced	Flaxman sale, 1803

FLAXMAN, John II RA 1755–1826

A sculptor, illustrator, designer and lecturer, Flaxman was the most widely-known British sculptor in the decades around 1800 and had a profound influence on British 19th-century sculpture. He was born in York on 6 July 1755, the second son of **John Flaxman I** and the younger brother of **William Flaxman**. His mother's maiden name was Lee. Flaxman was born during one of his father's working trips into the country, though the family settled in London soon afterwards. He learnt to draw and model in his father's plaster shop, and, if his earliest biographers are to be believed, was a youthful prodigy, having learnt to read Latin whilst still a young boy. He is said to have received early encouragement from patrons of his father, such as the Reverend Anthony Stephen Matthews and his blue-stocking wife, Harriet, who held a salon in Rathbone Place, London and a Mr Crutchley of Sunninghill Park, who commissioned six chalk drawings from the young boy. The politician Frederick Montagu ordered one of Flaxman's earliest recorded works of sculpture, *The Death of Julius Caesar* (**313**). In 1767, 1768 and 1769 Flaxman exhibited with the Free Society (**237, 238, 266, 267**), and in 1766 and 1768 with its more prestigious rival, the Society of Artists (**312, 313**), where he won a premium in 1770 for his bust of David Garrick (**239**). The *Gentleman's Magazine* later paid tribute to the young man's erudition and skill, commenting 'our societies bestowed rewards upon him at an age when other children are still in the nursery' (*GM*, 1781, vol 51, 1781, 65).

In 1769 Flaxman entered the Royal Academy schools to study sculpture, won a silver medal for a *Neptune* (**379**) and exhibited at the academy exhibition of 1770. In 1771 he came to the attention of Josiah Wedgwood, who reported the opinion of an acquaintance, Mr Freeman, that 'young Flaxman is a coxcomb but does not think him a bit the worse for it, or less likely to be a great Artist' (Wedgwood Archives, quoted in *Bindman* 1979, 47). Flaxman later concurred with this judgement of his youthful character, owning that his conceit was only tempered by his failure to win the Royal Academy's gold medal in 1772, when he lost to **Thomas Engleheart**. By 1775 Flaxman, like his father, had begun to model for Wedgwood, supplying wax models, initially portraits of modern worthies, for which he received modest single payments and, as was standard commercial practice, received no recognition as the designer (**317, 318**). Wedgwood chose Flaxman because his prices were cheaper than those of his principal rival **Joachim Smith**, and Flaxman was to prove a valuable employee. His later reliefs for Wedgwood, such as the *Apotheosis of Homer* (**323**), were taken from antique vases in Sir William Hamilton's collection, published in D'Hancarville's *Collection of Etruscan. . . Antiquities* (1766–7). Hamilton said of Flaxman's work that he 'never saw a bas-relief executed in the true simple antique style half so well' (Wedgwood Archives, quoted in *Bindman* 1979, 47).

On 3 June 1781 Flaxman married Ann Denman, the daughter of a Whitechapel gunstock maker, at St Anne, Soho (parish registers, vol 17, 143), and about this time he left his father's workshop in the Strand to set up home at 27 Wardour Street. Ann was 'of a respectable family in London, not only an amiable, but a highly accomplished female' (*GM*, 1827, 1, 273), and their marriage, although childless, was apparently very happy. Her enthusiastic letters, many of which survive, have proved an important source for historians of Flaxman's career. His friends at this time included the painters William Blake and Thomas Stothard, with whom he shared a passion for medieval art and history, reflected in Flaxman's early sketchbooks and also, on rare occasions, in his commissions for Wedgwood. The bishop in the set of chess pieces modelled in 1783 was apparently based on a figure on the exterior of Wells Cathedral (**392**). In addition to his many designs for Wedgwood, Flaxman also carved chimneypieces for Wedgwood's home, Etruria Hall (**296**), and, together with his father and brother, works for Edward Knight, who was to prove a longstanding patron (**296, 297, 309, 354, 359**).

In 1780 Flaxman advertised his interest in executing funerary sculpture by providing a sketch for a monument to the poet Thomas Chatterton (**1**) and by the mid-1780s he had started to receive commissions in this field. A noteworthy early monument was ordered by the poet William Hayley, who had met Flaxman in 1783, for his father-in-law, Thomas Ball (**12**). Flaxman's early monuments reflect several influences: the Ball is a graceful, oval-framed mourning scene reminiscent of **Thomas Banks**, whilst the monuments to Ann Russell (**2**) and Sarah Morley (**10**) are elaborate ascension scenes which have the theatricality of monuments by **Louis François Roubiliac** and **Joseph Wilton.** The presence in all these scenes of guiding angels (possibly modelled on those on the Temple of the Winds in Athens) also suggests he was influenced by Emanuel Swedenborg's theological writings. Flaxman had joined the Theosophical Society founded to promote the theologian's writings in 1784 and he later became a member of the Council of the Swedenborg Society, but he seems never to have left the established church.

In the autumn of 1787, with financial assistance from his parents-in-law, Flaxman and his wife left for Italy. They saw much of France and visited a number of northern Italian cities before arriving in Rome in December. Their surviving letters and the sculptor's journals and sketchbooks provide a detailed record of the couple's period abroad. In January 1788 Flaxman visited Naples, Herculaneum, Pompeii, Portici and Paestum. In March he was back in Rome where he rented the rooms in the Stalla Mignanelli, near the Piazza di Spagna, occupied by Thomas Banks a decade earlier.

Much of Flaxman's time during his early years in Rome was spent in the study of old master paintings and sculpture and he received few commissions (**273, 275, 359**). Before leaving England he had made an informal arrangement with Wedgwood to supervise the work of **John De Vaere** in Rome, and when De Vaere completed his work for Wedgwood and returned to England in 1790, Flaxman also contemplated returning home. He extended his stay however when he received a commission for a marble group, *The Fury of Athamas*, from Frederick Hervey, Earl of Bristol, on the recommendation of **Antonio Canova** (**246**). The commission proved a mixed blessing. Flaxman was so delighted at the prospect of producing an ideal group that he accepted the derisory sum of £600, of which £550 was expended on marbles and workmen. Bristol was delighted with his bargain and declared that Flaxman 'will probably rise to be the first sculptor in Europe' (*Childe-Pemberton* 1925, vol 2, 438).

In 1791 the Flaxmans moved into rooms in the Strada Felice, where they existed on an income of about £120 a year. They had little social life but the sculptor was industrious, taking a course in anatomy in April 1792 and travelling to Orvieto to study the great renaissance cathedral in September. Late in 1792 he worked on a commission from Georgina Hare-Naylor, the scholarly daughter of the Bishop of Asaph, for a series of outline drawings illustrating Homer's *Iliad* and *Odyssey* for which she paid 15/- a sheet. Flaxman intended these minimal, linear drawings to be studies for future bas-reliefs, in imitation of the antique sarcophagi which he admired. The reliefs never materialised.

The drawings, which were engraved in 1793, received such widespread acclaim that they formed the basis for his European reputation. Thomas Hope, who ordered two groups from the sculptor (**244, 247**), also commissioned more than 100 drawings from Dante's *Divine Comedy* (first published in a private edition for Thomas Hope in 1795). Another admirer of Flaxman's graphic work, Countess Spencer, commissioned a series of drawings from the works of Aeschylus for which she paid a guinea a sheet (published in 1795). The illustrations were disseminated throughout Europe, attracting interest from the German writers Johann Wolfgang Goethe and August William von Schlegel. They were copied by art students in Denmark and France and subsequently influenced such artists as Francisco Goya, Jean-Auguste-Dominique Ingres, Theodore Géricault and Gustave Moreau.

The proximity of French invading forces in 1794 persuaded Flaxman and other British artists and connoisseurs to return to England. The Flaxmans left Rome in June and stayed 5 weeks in Florence before journeying back via Carrara, Venice and Innsbruck. Farington noted Flaxman's return, in the company of the painter Maria Cosway and 'young Bartolozzi' (presumably Gaetano) in November, adding that 'Flaxman's drawings and sculpture are highly spoken of' (*Farington*, vol 1, 260). In London Flaxman was so appalled by the import taxes imposed on his own works that he lobbied for a relaxation of customs duties for artists. His success in this campaign led to a signed letter of thanks from artists in Rome, including **Sir Richard Westmacott RA, Christopher Hewetson, John Deare** and **William Theed I**.

Flaxman set up his home and studio at 7 Buckingham Street, off Fitzroy Square, and employed 6 men. An early assistant was **James Smith**, and an early apprentice, **Thomas Hayley**, whose father, William, continued to be an influential champion of Flaxman's work. William Hayley was chiefly responsible for Flaxman's selection as executant of monuments to the poet William Collins, a *cavo-rilievo* portrait (**16**), and to the scholar George Steevens in the form of a stele (**59**). Hayley also eulogised his friend in verse. Flaxman's most notable commission of this period was the monument to the former Lord Chief Justice, William Mansfield, in Westminster Abbey (**68**). The design, apparently prepared by Flaxman and Sir William Hamilton, was for the first free-standing monument in the Abbey, and in its bold composition and limited ornament reflected the influence of Canova's papal monuments.

Flaxman was responsible for two celebrated busts in the mid-1790s, of a Mr Udney (**280**), considered by Nathaniel Marchant to be 'worthy of a place among the works of the Greeks' (*Farington*, vol 2, 425) and of the Corsican patriot Pasquale di Paoli, who sat for his bust (**281**). Thenceforth the bulk of Flaxman's practice was in church monuments, a choice made as much from conviction as necessity, since he believed that the purpose of art was the furtherance of Christian devotion. Flaxman's post-Italian monuments tend to be uncluttered classicising works, making use of the stele form and key-fret or strigil decoration, often above pious dicta in bronzed lettering, such as 'Go and do thou likewise' (**37**) and 'Blessed are they that mourn' (**44**). The monument to Agnes Cromwell (**49**), a linear composition in gradated relief, is an apotheosis scene: the deceased is raised to heaven by three guiding angels. Below is the inscription 'Come thou blessed'.

On 6 November 1797 Flaxman was elected an associate of the Royal Academy, defeating **J C F Rossi** in the second ballot. Initially his relationship with the Academy was not close. Thomas Banks commented that Flaxman had shown nothing at the exhibitions which 'corresponded with the reputation he bore' (*Farington*, vol 4, 1369) and Flaxman refused to attempt to ingratiate himself with the academicians. When he was elected a full academician in February 1800 Farington commented that this was because the sculptor was 'too able to be objected to' (*Farington*, vol 4, 1380). Flaxman took on the role of public commentator on sculptural issues, writing articles in the *Morning Chronicle* in 1796 and 1797. In 1799 he published a pamphlet, proposing the erection of a 230-foot high statue of *Britannia* in Greenwich Park to commemorate naval victories of the Napoleonic Wars, which would take ten years to erect and would cost around £70,000 (**248**). He wrote an essay on sculpture for Longman's *Encyclopaedia* in 1803, and in 1805 offered to deliver a public address on the death of Thomas Banks, the sculptor whom he considered to have established a new standard in sculpture.

After the Peace of Amiens in 1802 Flaxman travelled to Paris to examine sculpture in the Louvre looted by the French in the recent wars. The renewal of hostilities in due course brought Flaxman new opportunities in the form of prestigious commissions for monuments in St Paul's Cathedral to Admiral Nelson (**202**), Nelson's flag-captain, Ralph Miller (**105**), and Admiral Howe (**154**). Flaxman's skills were not best exhibited in these triumphalist works, which have none of the grace of his contemporaneous relief monuments to the scholars Joseph Warton (**97**), which depicts him teaching pupils at Westminster School, or to Abraham Balme, who is also shown instructing the ignorant (**162**).

Despite his celebrity, Flaxman does not seem to have amassed a great fortune. He inherited nothing but a ring from his father, who died in 1803 and he had no instinct for business. Although he regularly reinterpreted old designs for new monuments, for instance the inscription tablet flanked by a Christian Virtue, probably first used on the monument to Sir Simon Clarke (**52**), and adapted on at least 7 occasions, he never developed the profitable recycling techniques of **John Bacon RA** or his son. Throughout his life he produced designs for manufacturers, including the Royal Goldsmiths, Rundell, Bridge and Rundell, for whom he designed the Trafalgar Vase, the National Cup, and the *Shield of Achilles* (**403**), together with designs for cups and candelabra.

Flaxman was always busy: in 1808 he told Farington that he had 'work in hand that would employ him near seven years' (*Farington*, vol 9, 3328–9). In 1809 he was commissioned to design a series of reliefs for Covent Garden Theatre and provided rhythmic processions of draped figures representing *Ancient and Modern Drama* (**311**). These were executed in stone by **JCF Rossi**, who commented with some truth that Flaxman had little power 'in working upon marble and stone. His power is confined to designing and modelling' (*Farington*, vol 10, 3513–4, 3529). Apart from his attention to important details, Flaxman appears to have played little part in the carving of his works, which were transposed from half-size models and carved by his assistants. This accounts in part for the contemporary perception, hinted at by Canova, that Flaxman's execution was 'not equal to his imagination and taste' (*Farington*, vol 12, 4746).

In 1810 Flaxman was appointed the first professor of sculpture at the Royal Academy, with a stipend of £60 a year. His duties entailed the delivery of six annual lectures, the first series of public lectures on sculpture delivered by a British artist. Sir Joshua Reynolds, whose monument in St Paul's Cathedral was provided by Flaxman (**174**), had delivered only one discourse on sculpture, which Flaxman regarded in part as 'nonsense' (*ibid*, vol 5, 1980). Flaxman took his lectures seriously, placing the practice of sculpture within an expansive historical framework and in August 1812 he embarked on a study trip from Waltham to York to gather material and make drawings for his lectures. In 1813 he was also asked to give two at the Royal Institution. Flaxman's gravity of manner, though admired by some, was felt by others to be stultifying: Fuseli described the RA lectures as the 'sermons' of 'Reverend Flaxman' (*Cunningham* 1829–33, vol 3, 339).

At the close of the wars in 1815 Flaxman was once again in Paris, and in 1816 he gave the most extensive evidence of any artist to the Elgin Marbles Committee. In September 1816, through the intervention of Canova, he was elected a member of the Accademia di San Luca in Rome. He continued to receive a steady stream of commissions, not only for privately commissioned British funerary monuments, which sometimes included Gothic decoration, but also for public statues in marble and bronze for the city of Glasgow (**251, 252**), statues and monuments for export to India and a large monument for the East India Company (**187**). Flaxman also received commissions for two ideal works, the *Pastoral Apollo* and *Satan overcome by St Michael* (**255, 259**), from an enlightened patron, the 3rd Earl of Egremont. These appear to have been the first commissions for poetic works received by Flaxman since the 1790s, and he altered his working practice for the *St Michael*, producing a full-size model and as a result, a far more vivid and well-proportioned composition. Cunningham described it as 'a work of the highest merit – the conception is epic – the grouping grand, and the action godlike' (*Cunningham* 1829–33, vol 3, 355).

In 1820, the year Flaxman failed in his candidacy for presidency of the Royal Academy, his wife died, and was noted as an 'excellent Greek scholar' in her obituary (*GM*, vol 80, part 1, 281). Flaxman was subsequently cared for by his half sister, Mary Ann Flaxman, and his sister-in-law, Maria Denman, who moved into Buckingham Street. In 1822 he delivered an address on the death of Antonio Canova, with whom he was frequently compared, although the press recorded the general opinion that the two belonged in separate spheres: 'Canova excelling more in the exquisite delicacies of the human figure, and Flaxman in general and extensive composition of figures' (*GM*, 1827, vol 98, part 1, 275). Although Flaxman's studio continued to produce monuments in the 1820s, the sculptor's powers were diminishing. The architect C R Cockerell called on Flaxman in March 1825 and found him 'very feeble & slow. his lamp is expiring – little fruit can be expected from so old a stock however golden in his former productions – his religious learned & contemplative mind is too little of this world to feel powerfully the attractions of art & this will still diminish as he draws higher to the object of his thought' (*Diaries*, RIBA Library, quoted in *Bindman* 1979, 33). His last commission, to design decoration for the new Buckingham Palace, came from John Nash in 1826 and Flaxman did not live to complete the work. He contracted a severe cold and died on 7 December. He was buried by his wish after a private service on 15 December, next to his wife in St Giles-in-the-Fields burial ground, with an inscription honouring his 'angelic spirit.'

Flaxman left all his possessions including his collection of art, his books and his furniture, to **Mary Ann Flaxman** and Maria Denman with his 'living and dying benediction on their exemplary conduct and affectionate sisterly and disinterested tone and attention on all occasions'. He also arranged for money to be given to his female servants from the sale of his stocks of marble and utensils. The *Gentleman's Magazine* noted in a lengthy obituary that Flaxman 'was a man of warm benevolence and rigid integrity. In all pecuniary matters, he was so severely scrupulous against his own interest, that his profession was far less productive to him than most artists enjoying equal rank' (*GM*, vol 98, part 1, 276). His estate was valued at only £3,314 4s 8d. Remaining works in his studio, including the memorials to Kemble and Robert Burns (**232, 258**), were completed by his brother-in-law, **Thomas Denman**, and Flaxman's favourite assistant, **John Ely Hinchliff**. Another pupil, **E H Baily**, who was probably Flaxman's most notable protégé, may have completed other works.

Flaxman was remembered by his contemporaries as a small, thin, hunched man, possibly the result of an illness that forced him to walk on crutches as a boy. His features were irregular, although softened by a sweet smile and animated by large and intelligent eyes. He was profoundly pious and serious, although possessed of a great deal of humility. He dressed plainly, had no coach or livery, took his meals at unsociable hours, and never attended parties. Although all attested to his mildness of manner and generosity of spirit, his aloofness caused one unnamed Academician to conclude that Flaxman 'lived as if he did not belong to this world; his ways were not our ways' (*Builder*, 1863, 37).

Commentators, including Sir Richard Westmacott, who delivered an address to the Royal Academy on Flaxman's death, were in no doubt that Britain had lost its finest modern sculptor. Cunningham's highly influential account of Flaxman's life and work appeared in his *Lives* (1829–33). Flaxman's lectures were published in 1829, bringing his scholarship to a wider audience, and a second, extended edition of the lectures appeared in 1838. In 1848 Maria Denman gave University College, London a collection of 120 original models by the sculptor, which were housed in 1857 in their 'Flaxman Gallery.' In view of the importance which the sculptor placed on the modelling process, this collection probably represents the finest surviving testament to Flaxman's creative powers. The Royal Academy honoured him with a plaque in St Pancras church and also with a statue on the façade of Burlington House by **Henry Weekes**.

Although the celebrated Victorian image of Flaxman as the pious Fra Angelico of sculpture has fallen out of favour, his reputation as a sculptor has been sustained as a result of the growing post-war interest in neoclassicism and through the rigorous scholarship of Croft-Murray, Gunnis and Whinney. Attention has chiefly been focussed on his monumental sculpture, still admired for its combination of classicism and clarity of religious expression, but modern scholarship has begun to take account of his importance as an industrial designer for ceramics and silverwork. His reputation as an illustrator with an international reputation has remained constant. The full range of Flaxman's talents was displayed in an exhibition held in Hamburg and London in 1979, and in a monograph by David Irwin in the same year.

MGS

Literary References: *Farington, passim*; *Monthly Mag*, 1802, 362; *Cunningham* 1829–33, vol 3, 274–367; *AU*, Jan 1842, 13; *Constable* 1927; Flaxman Account Book, 1794–1810; *Irwin* 1959 (1), 212–17; *Hutchison* 1960–62, 134; *Oman* 1966, 174–82; *Gunnis and Whinney* 1967; *Gunnis* 1968, 147–151; *JKB* 1973 (3), 1640–1; *Pyke* 1973, 48–9; *K-Browne* 1977 (2), 367–73; *Penny* 1977 (1), *passim*; *Bindman* 1979; *Irwin* 1979; *Read* 1982, *passim*; *Whinney* 1988, *passim*; *Groseclose* 1995, *passim*; *Ingamells* 1997, 361–4; *Grove* 1996, 162–4 (Bindman); *Bold* 2000, 33, 251 n121; *Bindman* 2003; *Bilbey* 2002, 76–84

Archival References: Parish register of St Anne, Soho, vol 17, 143; Flaxman Papers, BM Ad MS 39791, fol 28, fol 48, fols 103–4, f167; John Flaxman papers, Univ of California, Bancroft Library, BANC MSS 76/94z, including letters to Prince Hoare and others; see also list of MS sources in *Irwin* 1979, 233–4; *Dorey* 2004, 57–70

Wills: John Flaxman I, 9 April 1803 (PROB 11/1390, 225–6); John Flaxman RA, 17 January 1827 (PROB 11/1720, 129)

Collections of Drawings: Album of designs for tombs and monuments, Tate T10823-90, T11724-5, T11732-3, designs for monuments T10178-241, T11663-9, design for a monument to Alderman Beckford T08461; two Roman sketchbooks, VAM, one of 71pp exhaustively analyzed in *Whinney* 1956, 269–82, the other of 170pp, with studies of figures and monuments, *Bindman* 1979, 78, 80–3 (repr); copies of Flaxman's drawings for Rundell, Bridge and Rundell, marked *Designs for Plate by John Flaxman etc*, VAM, *Oman* 1966, 174–82; Italian sketchbook, YCBA (*Ingamells* 1997, 362)

Miscellaneous drawings (sculpture only): several, including unrealised designs for Buckingham Palace, HMI/Leeds City Art Gallery (*Friedman* 1993, 91, cat 27, repr, and *Leeds* 1999, 16–18); several, including four for pediment sculpture at Buckingham Palace, Royal coll, RL 23228-31291; portrait of Flaxman's polisher, John Burge, pencil, Mus Fine Arts, Boston; portrait of Sarti, pencil, Mus Fine Arts, Boston; study for a monument, c1813, BM; study for a triumphal arch surmounted by a figure of Britannia, 1799, pen, ink and pencil, Art Museum, Princeton (*Irwin* 1979, 165, repr); study for a monument to John Howard, pen and wash, c1800, Hamburg, Kunsthalle (*Bindman* 1979, 117, repr); reconstruction of the west pediment of the Parthenon, c1802, pen, ink and wash, BM (*Irwin* 1979, 174, repr); design for *The modern Drama*, untraced, payment of 10 gns received in September 1809 (Flaxman Account Book 1809–26, 8, *Gunnis and Whinney* 1967, 60–1); design for unidentified monument, VAM 8970K; design for a chimneypiece (inscribed 'Sky light room'), pen and wash, VAM (*Bindman* 1979, 46, repr); designs for chimneypieces, sold Christie 24 March 1982, lots 106 and 107; drawings of sculpture to illustrate lectures, pen and wash, Hamburg, Kunsthalle (*Bindman* 1979, 133–4, repr); design for a Victory medal, 1802 or 1815, pen and wash, UCL (*Bindman* 1979, 136, repr); design for a prize medal of the Lyceum Medicum, London, 1785, VAM (*Bindman* 1979, 136, repr); designs for both sides of a Royal Academy medal, 1819, pencil and wash, RA; design for a naval medal of George III, pen and wash, VAM; design for roundel of Hypnos, pen, ink, pencil and wash, BM (*Bindman* 1979, 138, repr); study for a candelabrum with a hussar on top, c1805–15, pen and wash, VAM (*Bindman* 1979, 149, repr); sketch for a centrepiece presented to Sir Arthur Wellesley, c1810, pencil, pen and ink, VAM (*Bindman* 1979, 149, repr); design for a candelabrum, c1809, pen and wash, BM (*Bindman* 1979, 149, repr); studies for silverware, pen and wash, BM (*Bindman* 1979, 151, repr); sketchbooks from the sculpture tour of 1812 (*Irwin* 1979, 204); mythological designs for Rundell, Bridge and Rundell, 1824, BM, VAM, Huntington, Met Mus NY (*Bindman* 1979, 151, repr); designs for Buckingham Palace, London, 1826, pencil, BM, Huntington (*Irwin* 1979, 176–7, repr); *Mercury presenting Bacchus to the Nymphs*, design for a candelabrum, pen, wash and pencil, Huntington (*Irwin* 1979, 193, repr); design for the National Cup, pencil and wash, 1824, Royal Coll (*Physick* 1969, 170–1, repr)

Auction Catalogues: Flaxman 1828 (1); Flaxman 1828 (2)

Portraits of the Sculptor: Self-portrait 1778–9, pen and wash, Earls High School, Halesowen (*Bindman* 1979, 38, repr); self-portrait 1779, pen with flesh tinting, UCL 616 (*Bindman* 1979, 38, repr); self-portrait, 1790, NPG 2487; Guy Head, 1792, oil on canvas, NPG 823 (*Irwin* 1979, 51, repr); Archibald Skirving, 1791, pastel, YCAG (*Burl* 1993, 897, repr); George Romney, *Flaxman modelling the bust of William Hayley*, 1795, oil on canvas, YCBA (version or possibly a study for the final work, NPG, 101); Henry Howard, c1797, oil on panel, NPG 674; Thomas Cooley, 1810, pencil, NPG 4913b; George Cruikshank *The Antiquarian Society*, 1812, etching with caricature of Flaxman holding a bible (*Irwin* 1979, 123, repr); James Atkinson, 1826, pencil, ink and wash, NPG 823; E H Baily, marble bust, 1826, RA, London; David d'Angers, medallion portrait for a medal, Galerie David et Museé d'Angers (*Bindman* 1979, 139, repr); E H Baily, medallion portrait for a bronze coin, BM (*Bindman* 1979, 139, repr); Henry Weigall, medallion-portrait for a bronze coin, Fitz (*Bindman* 1979, 140, repr); Henry Weekes, *Flaxman leaning on Homer's Head*, statue, 1873–4, Royal Academy, façade; John Thomas Smith, watercolour, nd, BM, P&D, 1885,0509.1574; William Young Ottley, sketch, nd, BM, P&D, 1885, 0509.1575

Funerary Monuments

1.	1780	Thomas Chatterton (+1770), sketch		[Exhib RA, London, 453]; untraced		*Graves* III, 1905–6, 123; *Bindman* 1979, 22
2.	†1781	Ann Russell (†1780) and her infant son		Lydd, Kent		Pevsner, *Kent: W & Weald*, 1976, 392; *Irwin* 1979, 11–12 (repr)
3.	†1781	James Morris		St Mary, Lambeth, London (now Museum of Garden History)	S	Flaxman Account Book 1794–1810, 73–4
4.	†1782	Agatha Halsey		Great Gaddesden, Herts		Pevsner, *Herts*, 1977, 151; *Bindman* 1979, 45; C Lib (repr)
5.	1782	Sir Edward Sebright Bt and family Drawing(s): John Mallet		Flamstead, Herts	S	*GM*, vol 98, pt 1, 1827, 274; Pevsner, *Herts*, 1977, 143
6.	†1783	John Wickins (†1783) and wife, Philadelphia		Petworth, West Sussex	S	Pevsner, *Sussex*, 1965, 296; C Lib (repr)
7.	1784	'a tomb to the memory of Rousseau' Payment(s): £105	s	[Mr Fierville's estate near Stanmore]; untraced		*Irwin* 1979, 11, 220 n61
8.	†1784	Barbara Bourchier		St Mary, Newent, Glos		*CIIA* 4/4/79 (repr); *Bindman* 1979, 45 (repr); *Irwin* 1979, 11–12 (repr)
9.	†1784	Richard Spencer		Hornchurch, Essex		Pevsner, *Essex*, 1965, 245; C Lib (repr)
10.	†1784	Sarah Morley		Gloucester Cathedral	S	*Bindman* 1979, 27 (repr); *Irwin* 1979, 13 (repr); *Whinney* 1988, 339–40 (repr)
11.	†1785	William Lawrence		Kirby Fleetham, N R Yorks		Pevsner, *Yorks: N R*, 1966, 214; C Lib (repr)
12.	1784–1786	Rev Thomas Ball (†1770) Model(s): UCL, plaster, 1061		Chichester Cathedral, Sussex	S	*Gunnis and Whinney* 1967, 18 (model repr 2a); *Bindman* 1979, 27, 100 (repr); *Irwin* 1979, 10, 13–14 (repr)
13.	†1787	Zacchary Hubbersty		Holy Trinity, Kendal, Westmorland		Pevsner, *Cumberland & Westmorland*, 1967, 254

14.	1795	Captain Walter Serocold RN (†1794) Payment(s): £60 Drawing(s): VAM 8970.F	Cherry Hinton, Cambs	S	Flaxman Account Book 1794–1810, 55; Pevsner, *Cambs*, 1970, 317
15.	1795	John Bellamy (†1794) Payment(s): £110 Model(s): UCL, plaster, 1029	St Paul, Covent Garden, London	S	Flaxman Account Book 1794–1810, 55; *Gunnis and Whinney* 1967, 31–2 (model pl 14a)
16.	1795	William Collins (†1759) Payment(s): £96 16s Drawing(s): BM 1885-5-9 -1606a, 1606b and 1607 and 1926-11-15-25 (42 and 45); Whitworth Model(s): UCL, plaster, 1047	Chichester Cathedral, Sussex	S	Flaxman Account Book 1794–1810, 54; *Gunnis and Whinney* 1967, 29 (model repr 13); *Irwin* 1979, 60–1, 63 (drawing repr); *Bindman* 1979, 100, 113–15 (repr)
17.	1796	Catherine Susannah Bull (†1795) Payment(s): £74 8s 8d inc package and carriage	Shorwell, I of W		Flaxman Account Book 1794–1810, 58
18.	1796	Jane Smith (†1780) Payment(s): £123 6s 6d	Chichester Cathedral, Sussex	S	Flaxman Account Book 1794–1810, 59; *Irwin* 1979, 128
19.	1796	John Petrie	St Mary, Lewisham, London		*Gunnis* 1968, 150
20.	1795–1796	Philip (†1781) and Lady Frances Medows (†1795) Payment(s): £107 12s 5d Drawing(s): BM 1900-8-24-207	Kingston-upon-Thames, Surrey	S	Flaxman Account Book 1794–1810, 56 (repr XIVa); Pevsner, *London: S*, 1983, 312
21.	1795–1796	Rear-Admiral George Elliot (†1795) Payment(s): £20	[Commissioned by Miss Elliot, Copford near Colchester, Essex]; untraced		Flaxman Account Book 1794–1810, 56
22.	1796	Sarah Mapletoft (†1792) Payment(s): £30	St James, St Helena		Flaxman Account Book 1794–1810, 57
23.	1796	Timothy Earle (†1787), Dorothy Earle (†1781), and family members Payment(s): £89 5s	Rickmansworth, Herts		Flaxman Account Book 1794–1810, 57; Pevsner, *Herts*, 1977, 279
24.	1797	Rev John Parkhurst (†1797) Payment(s): £65 4s Drawing(s): VAM CAI 1090 (?) Model(s): UCL	Epsom, Surrey	S	Flaxman Account Book 1794–1810, 60
25.	1796–1797	Richard Neville Neville (†1793) Payment(s): £50 excluding erection	Ruscombe, Berks	S	Flaxman Account Book 1794–1810, 58; Pevsner, *Berks*, 1966, 209
26.	1795–1797	Sir Robert Ladbroke (†1773) Payment(s): £480 Model(s): UCL	Christ Church, Spitalfields, London	S	Flaxman Account Book 1794–1810, 55–6; C Lib (repr)
27.	1796–1797	Sir William Burrell Bt (†1796) Payment(s): £305 with monument in West Grinstead (28)	Cuckfield, Sussex	S	Flaxman Account Book 1794–1810, 57; Pevsner, *Sussex*, 1965, 478
28.	1796–1797	Sir William Burrell Bt (†1796) Payment(s): £305 with monument in Cuckfield (27) Drawing(s): VAM	West Grinstead, Sussex	S	Flaxman Account Book 1794–1810, 57–8 (pl XVIIIb); Pevsner, *Sussex*, 1965, 371
29.	1797	Thomas Owens (†1769), Elizabeth Weller (†1781) and Catherine Owens (†1797) Payment(s): £60 excluding cost of erection	Rye, Sussex	S	Flaxman Account Book 1794–1810, 59 (repr XVIIIc); Pevsner, *Sussex*, 1965, 595
30.	1798	James Dodsley (†1797) Payment(s): £19 4s 10d	St James, Piccadilly, London		Flaxman Account Book 1794–1810, 61; Pevsner, *London: Westminster*, 1973, 491
31.	1798	John Lewis (†1797) Payment(s): £50 excluding cost of erection	Old Radnor, Radnors	S	Flaxman Account Book 1794–1810, 62–3; Pevsner, *Powys*, 1979, 264
32.	1798	John Wilkes (†1797) Payment(s): £22 19s	Grovesnor Chapel, South Audley Street, London	S	Flaxman Account Book 1794–1810, 63
33.	1798	Julia, Lady Shuckburgh-Evelyn (†1797) Payment(s): 200 gns Model(s): UCL, plaster, 1032 (sketch model of whole monument) and 1066 (panel relief)	Upper Shuckburgh, Warks	S	Flaxman Account Book 1794–1810, 61 (pl XVId); *Gunnis and Whinney* 1967, 20–1, 36–7 (model repr 3b); *Irwin* 1979, 148 (repr)
34.	1798	Sir Edmund Head, 6th Bt (†1796) Payment(s): 50 gns excluding erection	Rochester Cathedral, Kent	S	Flaxman Account Book 1794–1810, 62; Pevsner, *Kent: W & Weald*, 1976, 484
35.	1796–1798	Sir William Jones (†1794) Payment(s): £500 Drawing(s): BM 1888-5-3-41 and 1900-8-24-210 and 211; VAM CAI 1093; MFAB, pencil Model(s): UCL, plaster, 1050	St Mary the Virgin, Oxford	S	Flaxman Account Book 1794–1810, 57 (repr XVIIb); *Gunnis and Whinney* 1967, 22 (model repr 6b, marble pl 7); *Penny* 1977 (1), 148–9 (repr); *Irwin* 1979, 122, 139, 141, 142, 168 (repr)

36.	1796–1798	Thomas Sainsbury (†1795) Payment(s): 150 gns excluding erection Model(s): UCL, plaster, 1005	Market Lavington, Wilts	S	Flaxman Account Book 1794–1810, 59; *Gunnis and Whinney* 1967, 41; C Lib (repr)
37.	1798	William Benson Earle (†1796) Payment(s): 200 gns Model(s): UCL	Salisbury Cathedral, Wilts	S	Flaxman Account Book 1794–1810, 60; Pevsner, *Wilts*, 1975, 415; C Lib (repr)
38.	1799	Countess of Guilford Payment(s): £35	Untraced		Flaxman Account Book 1794–1810, 63
39.	1799	Dr John Sibthorp (†1796) Payment(s): 50 gns excluding erection Model(s): UCL, plaster, 1028	Bath Abbey, Somerset		Flaxman Account Book 1794–1810, 64; *Gunnis and Whinney* 1967, 35; *Penny* 1977 (1), 26–8 (repr); *Bindman* 1979, 106 (repr)
40.	1799	Edward Hall MD (†1798) Payment(s): £115 10s Model(s): UCL, plaster, 1015	St Paul, Covent Garden, London	S	Flaxman Account Book 1794–1810, 64; *Gunnis and Whinney* 1967, 44 (model repr 14b)
41.	1799	Elizabeth Woodward (†1797) Payment(s): £37 16 excluding cost of erection	West Grinstead, W Sussex		Flaxman Account Book 1794–1810, 64; *Irwin* 1979, 166
42.	1799	John Smyth (†1771) Payment(s): £164 with the monuments to Lady Georgina Smyth and Sarah Caroline Smyth Drawing(s): VAM 8967 D and 8970 C (rejected design)	Kirkthorpe, W R Yorks	S	Flaxman Account Book 1794–1810, 64
43.	1799	Lady Georgina Smyth (†1799) and children Payment(s): £164 19s 2d with the monuments to Sarah Caroline Smyth and John Smyth (42, 46) Drawing(s): VAM 8967 D and 8970 C (rejected design)	Kirkthorpe, W R Yorks	S	Flaxman Account Book 1794–1810, 64; Pevsner, *Yorks: W R*, 1967, 294
44.	1798–1799	Mary Blackshaw (†1797) Payment(s): £200 excluding erection Model(s): UCL, plaster, 1078, 1096 (sketch-model for whole monument)	St Mary, Lewisham, London	S	Flaxman Account Book 1794–1810, 62; *Gunnis and Whinney* 1967, 25–6, 55 (model repr 10); *Bindman* 1979, 102 (repr); *Irwin* 1979, 125–6 (repr)
45.	1799	Mr Pinder	[St John, Hackleton's Cliff, Barbados]; untraced		*Gunnis* 1968, 150
46.	1799	Sarah Caroline Smyth (†1811) Payment(s): £164 with the monuments to Lady Georgina Smyth and John Smyth Drawing(s): VAM 8967 D and 8970 C (rejected design)	Kirkthorpe, W R Yorks	S	Flaxman Account Book 1794–1810, 64
47.	1799	Sarah Wilson (†1798) Payment(s): £50 excluding cost of erection	Ashurst, W Sussex		Flaxman Account Book 1794–1810, 65; C Lib (repr)
48.	1798–1799	Sir Charles Philip Jennings-Clerke Bt (†1788) Payment(s): 175 gns excluding erection Drawing(s): VAM 8970N	Lyndhurst, Hants		Flaxman Account Book 1794–1810, 60 (repr XVb); Pevsner, *Hants & Isle of Wight*, 1967, 327
49.	1798–1800	Agnes Cromwell (†1797) Payment(s): £50 excluding erection Drawing(s): BM PDL; Soane; UCL, sheet Q, 2 Model(s): UCL, plaster, 1082, 1101 and 1102 (the two latter on loan to VAM (*Bilbey* 2002, 77–8)	Chichester Cathedral, Sussex	S	Flaxman Account Book 1794–1810, 61; *Gunnis and Whinney* 1967, 15–16, 55–6 (models repr 22a and b); *Bindman* 1979, 103 (repr); *Irwin* 1979, 127–8 (repr
50.	1800	General Thomas Dundas, sketch	[Exhib RA, London, 1005]; untraced		*Graves* III, 1905–6, 124
51.	1800	Rev Christopher Dodson (†1784), and wife Mary (†1748) Payment(s): £30 excluding cost of erection	Hurstpierpoint, Sussex		Flaxman Account Book 1794–1810, 66; Pevsner, *Sussex*, 1965, 541; C Lib (repr)
52.	1799–1800	Sir Simon Clarke, 7th Bt (†1777) Payment(s): 100 gns excluding erection Drawing(s): VAM CAI 1065 Model(s): UCL, plaster, 1000; SJSM MR 71	Lucea, Jamaica	SD	Flaxman Account Book 1794–1810, 65; *Gunnis and Whinney* 1967, 32–4 (model repr 1 12a)
53.	†1800	Thomas Hayley	Eartham, Sussex	S	*Horsfield* 1835, 61–2; Pevsner, *Sussex*, 1965, 211; *Gunnis* 1968, 150; C Lib (repr)
54.	1800	Unidentified subject Payment(s): £100	[Erected for Lord Newark 'against Kensington Church']; untraced		Flaxman Account Book 1794–1810, 68
55.	1801	Captain James Robert Mosse and Captain Edward Riou (both †1801) (competition model for St Paul's, commission won by JCF Rossi)	p SJSM, M1103		Soane Museum Inventory

No.	Date	Subject	Location		Bibliography
56.	1800–1801	Charlotte Nicholas (†1800) Payment(s): 110 gns, excluding erection, packing and 'a Portland step' Drawing(s): BM 1862-3-8-28 Model(s): UCL	Ashton Keynes, Wilts		Flaxman Account Book 1794–1810, 67; *Irwin* 1979, 150
57.	1801	Elizabeth, Lady Pennyman (†1801) Payment(s): 80 gns excluding erection Model(s): UCL, plaster, 1007 (for whole monument), 1083 (for figures only)	Dawlish, Devon	S	Flaxman Account Book 1794–1810, 72; *Gunnis and Whinney* 1967, 16, 42
58.	1801	Frances, Lady Hoare (†1800) Payment(s): 120 gns excluding erection Model(s): UCL, plaster, 1088	Beckenham, Kent	S	Flaxman Account Book 1794–1810, 72 (repr XVIa); *Gunnis and Whinney* 1967, 56
59.	1800–1801	George Steevens (†1800) Payment(s): £100 excluding cost of erection Model(s): UCL	St Matthias, Poplar, London	S	Flaxman Account Book 1794–1810, 69; *Bindman* 1979, 13, 104 (repr)
60.	1800–1801	John Brathwaite Payment(s): 180 gns excluding erection Drawing(s): Sir Robert Will Model(s): UCL 1910, plaster	Epsom, Surrey	S	Flaxman Account Book 1794–1810, 69; *Gunnis and Whinney* 1967, 46
61.	1801	John Sainsbury (†1792) and wife Elizabeth (†1800) Payment(s): 100 gns, excluding erection	Petersfield, Hants	S	Flaxman Account Book 1794–1810, 71; Pevsner, *Hants & Isle of Wight*, 1967, 372
62.	1801	Lieutenant-Colonel Roger Morris (†1799) Payment(s): £27 13s 3d	St Mary, Lambeth, London (now Museum of Garden History)		Flaxman Account Book 1794–1810, 73–4
63.	1801	Marie-Josephe Godefrey de Tonnancour (†1799) Payment(s): £100	St Michael, Vaudreuil, Quebec, Canada		Flaxman Account Book 1794–1810, 68
64.	1801	Mary Harford (†1798) Payment(s): £60 excluding dove marble background	Stapleton, Somerset	S	Flaxman Account Book 1794–1810, 68; Pevsner, *Somerset: N & Bristol*, 1958, 472; C Lib (repr)
65.	1800–1801	Matilda Lockwood Maydwell and her infant daughter (†1800) Payment(s): 66 1/2 gns, excluding erection Drawing(s): VAM CAI 1001	Lambourne, Essex	S	Flaxman Account Book 1794–1810, 67; *Bindman* 1979, 29 (repr)
66.	1801	Sir William Jones (†1794) Payment(s): £245 Drawing(s): Sold Sotheby, 25th June 1981 Model(s): UCL, plaster, 1051, 1052	St Mary, Oxford	S	Flaxman Account Book 1794–1810, 71; *Gunnis and Whinney* 1967, 21–2; C Lib (repr)
67.	1801	William Aldersey (†1800) Payment(s): 140 gns, excluding erection Model(s): UCL, plaster, 1086	St John the Evangelist, Guildford, Surrey	S	Flaxman Account Book 1794–1810, 69; *Gunnis and Whinney* 1967, 54; Pevsner, *Surrey*, 1971, 272
68.	1793–1801	William, Earl of Mansfield (†1793) Payment(s): £2,500 Drawing(s): UCL, sheet Ω, Nos 4, 5 and 6; Scone Palace (*Pearson* 1991, unpag); Hamburg, Kunsthalle (unexecuted design); VAM Model(s): SJSM	Westminster Abbey, London, north transept	SD	Flaxman Account Book 1794–1810, 54–5; *Graves* II, 1905–6, 123; *Irwin* 1979, 62–6 (repr); *Bindman* 1979, 30, 31, 116 (repr)
69.	1800–1802	Admiral Samuel Barrington (†1800) Payment(s): 150 gns Drawing(s): VAM E.9870	Shrivenham, Berks	S	Flaxman Account Book 1794–1810, 70; Pevsner, *Berks*, 1966, 218
70.	1801–1802	Admiral Sir Charles Thompson (†1799) Payment(s): £210 excluding erection Model(s): UCL, plaster, 1002; Flint House, Great Amwell, Herts	Holy Trinity, Fareham, Hants		Flaxman Account Book 1794–1810, 73 (repr XIVd); *Gunnis and Whinney* 1967, 36; *Irwin* 1979, 162, 164 (drawing repr)
71.	1800–1802	Ann, Lady Clarke (†1800) Payment(s): 105 gns excluding erection and lettering Model(s): UCL, plaster, 1023 (sketch-model), 1091 (Faith); SJSM MR 78	Tewkesbury Abbey, Glos	S	Flaxman Account Book 1794–1810, 65 (repr XIVb); *Gunnis and Whinney* 1967, 31; *Irwin* 1979, 141, 143 (repr)
72.	1801–1802	Anthony Champion Payment(s): 100 gns, excluding erection Model(s): SJSM	[Temple Church, London]; destroyed		Flaxman Account Book 1794–1810, 71; *Gunnis and Whinney* 1967, 31
73.	1802	Eleanor Belfield Payment(s): 30 gns excluding erection	Epsom, Surrey	S	Flaxman Account Book 1794–1810, 76

No.	Date	Subject	Location	S	Bibliography
74.	1802	Hon Evelyn Pierrepont (†1801) Payment(s): 100 gns excluding erection Drawing(s): BM 1900-8-24-207	Holme Pierrepont, Notts		Flaxman Account Book 1794–1810, 75; Pevsner, *Notts*, 1979, 147; C Lib (repr)
75.	1802	John (†1795), Esther (†1797) and John Marsh (†1779) Payment(s): £252 excluding erection Model(s): UCL, plaster, 1030, 1115	Penn, nr Wolverhampton, Staffs	S	Flaxman Account Book 1794–1810, 77; *Gunnis and Whinney* 1967, 43–4, 60 (repr 16b); Pevsner, *Staffs*, 1974, 323
76.	1802	John Brathwaite (†1800) Payment(s): £200 Model(s): UCL, plaster, 1041	Bridgetown Cathedral, Barbados		Flaxman Account Book 1794–1810, 76; *Gunnis and Whinney* 1967, 26 (repr 11a)
77.	1801–1802	John Henry Warre (†1801) Payment(s): 100 gns excluding erection Model(s): UCL	Epsom, Surrey	S	Flaxman Account Book 1794–1810, 72–3; Pevsner, *Surrey*, 1971, 215; C Lib (repr)
78.	1802	Lieutenant-Colonel Arthur Brice Payment(s): £105	[Commissioned by Mrs Brice, 21 Welbeck Street]; untraced		Flaxman Account Book 1794–1810, 75
79.	1802–1803	Francis and Bridget Dear (†1802) Payment(s): £105 excluding erection Drawing(s): VAM CAI 1065 Model(s): UCL	Chichester Cathedral, Sussex	S	Flaxman Account Book 1794–1810, 76; Pevsner, *Sussex*, 1965, 160
80.	1801–1803	Helen Charlotte Knight (†1801) Payment(s): 100 gns excluding erection Model(s): Plaster, SJSM M 217	Wolverley, Worcs	S	Flaxman Account Book 1794–1810, 74; *Hendricks* 1984, 622–3; *Thornton and Dorey*, 1992, 61 (plaster repr)
81.	1802–1803	Isaac Hawkins Browne (†1760) Payment(s): 180 gns with the monument to Jane and Henrietta Browne excluding cost of erection	Untraced		Flaxman Account Book 1794–1810, 75
82.	1802–1803	Jane (†1783) and Henrietta Browne (†1802) Payment(s): 180 gns with the untraced monument to Isaac Hawkins Browne 1802–3	Badger, Salop	S	Flaxman Account Book 1794–1810, 75; Pevsner, *Salop*, 1958, 67; C Lib (repr)
83.	1803	Josiah Wedgwood (†1795) Payment(s): £86 12s 2d	Stoke-on-Trent parish church, Staffs		Flaxman Account Book 1794–1810, 79; *Penny* 1977 (1), 177, 223 n13; *Bindman* 1979, 48; *Irwin* 1979, 187; C Lib (repr)
84.	1803	Mrs Miller Payment(s): 100 gns	Untraced		Flaxman Account Book 1794–1810, 79
85.	1803	Rev Edmund Nelson (†1802) Payment(s): £49 13s 6d	Burnham Thorpe, Norfolk		Flaxman Account Book 1794–1810, 79 (repr XVIIId); Pevsner, *Norfolk: N W & S*, 1999, 235
86.	1800–1803	Sarah (†1782), Amelia (†1800), Marianne (†1795) and Henry (†1801), four children of Sir Thomas Frankland Payment(s): 100 gns Model(s): UCL, plaster, 1006	Thirkleby, N R Yorks	S	Flaxman Account Book 1794–1810, 66–7; *Gunnis and Whinney* 1967, 41–2 (repr 15a)
87.	1802–1803	William Cowper (†1800) Payment(s): 45 gns excluding erection	East Dereham, Norfolk		Flaxman Account Book 1794–1810, 74 (repr XVd); *Irwin* 1979, 167–8; Pevsner, *Norfolk: N W & S*, 1999, 285–6
88.	1803	William Miles (†1803) Payment(s): 400 gns excluding erection Model(s): UCL	Ledbury, Herefs	S	Flaxman Account Book 1794–1810, 80; *Irwin* 1979, 131, 133 (repr)
89.	1802–1803	William, 3rd Viscount Ashbrook (†1802) Payment(s): 100 gns excluding erection	Shellingford, Berks	S	Flaxman Account Book 1794–1810, 74 (repr XVIIIa); Pevsner, *Berks*, 1966, 215
90.	1798–1804	Captain James Montagu (†1794) Payment(s): Price of 3,500 gns agreed in 1798 Drawing(s): HMI, 16/1991 (dated 9 October 1798); another PRO Work 36/52, MPD 78 (T.62/78) Model(s): UCL	Westminster Abbey, London, north west tower	S	Flaxman Account Book 1794–1810, 63; WAM (20); *Graves* II, 1905–6, 124; *Irwin* 1979, 161–2 (repr)
91.	1804	Elizabeth Godfrey (†1803) Payment(s): £15 15s	St Mary Abbots, Kensington, London		Flaxman Account Book 1794–1810, 84
92.	1804	George, 1st Lord Rivers (†1803) Payment(s): £500 excluding erection Drawing(s): VAM CAI 1059 Model(s): UCL, plaster, 1065 (figures only)	Stratfield Saye, Hants	S	*Gunnis and Whinney* 1967, 18 (model repr 8); Flaxman Account Book 1794–1810, 81
93.	1801–1804	Henrietta Maria North (†1796) Payment(s): 200 gns excluding erection Model(s): UCL, plaster, 1037	Winchester Cathedral, Hants	S	Flaxman Account Book 1794–1810, 73; *Gunnis and Whinney* 1967, 38–9

No.	Date	Subject	Location		Literature
94.	1804	Henry, 2nd Viscount Palmerston (†1802) Payment(s): £200 excluding erection Model(s): UCL, plaster, 1018; 1107 (sketch-model for the whole monument)	Romsey Abbey, Hants	S	Flaxman Account Book 1794–1810, 81; *Gunnis and Whinney* 1967, 49, 58; C Lib (repr)
95.	1804	John (†1795) and Susannah Phillimore (†1762) Payment(s): 150 gns Drawing(s): BM 1888-5-3-63 and 1926-11-15-25 (43) Model(s): UCL, plaster, 1009 (sketch-model of whole monument), 1068	[St Stephen's, Coleman Street, London]; destroyed	S	Flaxman Account Book 1794–1810, 83; *Gunnis and Whinney* 1967, 11, 43; *Bindman* 1979, 107 (model repr)
96.	1804	John Blake (†1803) Payment(s): £42 15s including a case Model(s): UCL	St Martin, Salisbury, Wilts		Flaxman Account Book 1794–1810, 70; *Gunnis* 1968, 151
97.	1801–1804	Joseph Warton DD (†1800) Payment(s): £500 (from the Society of Wykehamists) Drawing(s): VAM 7345; BM PDL 1888-5-3-45	Winchester Cathedral, Hants	S	Flaxman Account Book 1794–1810, 70; *Physick* 1969, 172–3 (drawing repr); *Bindman* 1979, 118 (repr); *Irwin* 1979, 137, 139 (repr)
98.	1804	Mr Hubbersty Payment(s): 100 gns excluding erection	['to be in London Wall Church']; untraced		Flaxman Account Book 1794–1810, 82
99.	1803–1804	The three infant children of Francis Redfearn Payment(s): £105 Model(s): UCL, plaster, 1067, 1105 (sketch-model for whole monument)	St Cuthbert, New Town, Edinburgh		Flaxman Account Book 1794–1810, 77; *Gunnis and Whinney* 1967, 20; *Irwin* 1979, 132–4 (repr)
100.	1804	Unidentified subject Payment(s): 60 gns	[Commissioned by 'Mrs Holland']; untraced		Flaxman Account Book 1794–1810, 83
101.	1804	William Hamilton RA (†1801) Payment(s): £18 18s	St Anne, Soho, London		Flaxman Account Book 1794–1810, 82
102.	1805	Amelia Sloper (†1800) Payment(s): £70 with the monuments to Anna Maria Shipley (+1796) and Anna Maria Shipley (+1803)	[Twyford, Hants]; perhaps not executed		Flaxman Account Book 1794–1810, 85
103.	1805	Anna Maria Shipley (†1803) Payment(s): £70 with the monuments to Anna Maria Shipley (+1796) and Amelia Sloper	Twyford, Hants		Flaxman Account Book 1794–1810, 85
104.	1805	Anna Sophia Lawrence (†1802) Payment(s): £28 18s 10d	Kirby Fleetham, N R Yorks		Flaxman Account Book 1794–1810, 85
105.	1801–1805	Captain Ralph Willett Miller RN (†1799) Payment(s): £500 Drawing(s): VAM; poss Sir Robert Witt CBE Model(s): UCL, plaster, 1077	St Paul's Cathedral, London	S	Flaxman Account Book 1794–1810, 71; *Gunnis and Whinney* 1967, 21 (model pl 20b); *Irwin* 1979, 162, 164 (repr)
106.	1805	Frances Timson Payment(s): 100 gns excluding erection Drawing(s): BM 1862-3-8-27 Model(s): UCL	Farnham, Surrey	S	Flaxman Account Book 1794–1810, 86
107.	1799–1805	Frederick, 2nd Earl of Guilford (†1792) Payment(s): 250 gns excluding erection Model(s): UCL, plaster, 1055	Wroxton, Oxon	S	Flaxman Account Book 1794–1810, 65; *Gunnis and Whinney* 1967, 23
108.	1805	Friedrich Christian Schwartz Payment(s): £500 Drawing(s): BM 1888-5-3-50; VAM CAI 1095 and 1096 (? rejected designs)	Tanjore, India	S	Flaxman Account Book 1794–1810, 78 (pl XVIc); *Irwin* 1979, 150 (repr); *Archer* 1984, 52 (repr); *Groseclose* 1995, 91–2 (repr)
109.	1802–1805	George Speke (†1753) Payment(s): 50 gns	White Lackington, Somerset	S	Flaxman Account Book 1794–1810, 66
110.	1804–1805	Hon Anne Brudenell (†1803) Payment(s): 100 gns excluding cost of erection	St George's Chapel, Windsor, Berks		Flaxman Account Book 1794–1810, 83; *Bond* 1999, 51
111.	1805	Hon James Stuart-Wortley	Wortley, W R Yorks		*Gunnis* 1968, 151
112.	1805	Isaac Hawkins Browne Payment(s): 50 gns	['for Burton']; untraced		Flaxman Account Book 1794–1810, 81
113.	1804–1805	Isaac Hawkins Browne (†1760) Payment(s): £160 excluding erection Drawing(s): BM 1926-11-15-25; VAM CAI 1032; VAM E.951-1965 Model(s): UCL, plaster, 1100	Trinity College, Cambridge, chapel	S	Flaxman Account Book 1794–1810, 81; *Gunnis and Whinney* 1967, 58–9 (model repr 23b); *Bindman* 1979, 107 (repr); *Irwin* 1979, 127 (repr)
114.	1803–1805	John Stuart Wortley (†1797) Payment(s): 150 gns excluding erection Drawing(s): BM 1900-8-24-207	Wortley, W R Yorks		Flaxman Account Book 1794–1810, 79; *Bindman* 1979, 45 (drawing repr)

115.	1805	Mrs Troth Blisset (†1804) Payment(s): £100 excluding erection Drawing(s): BM 1862-3-8-27 Model(s): UCL, plaster, 1020	All Saints, Corn Street, Bristol	S	Flaxman Account Book 1794–1810, 84; *Gunnis and Whinney* 1967, 47; Pevsner, *Somerset: N & Bristol*, 1958, 387
116.	1805	Paul Panton (†1797) Payment(s): 100 gns excluding erection	Holywell, Flint	S	Flaxman Account Book 1794–1810, 85; Pevsner, *Clwyd*, 1986, 373
117.	1805	Rev Charles Robinson (†1805) Payment(s): 35 gns	Dawlish, Devon		Flaxman Account Book 1794–1810, 85; Pevsner, *Devon*, 1989, 331
118.	1804–1805	Sir Francis Sykes (†1804) Payment(s): 150 gns excluding erection Model(s): UCL, plaster, 1004	Lower Basildon, Berks	S	Flaxman Account Book 1794–1810, 82; *Gunnis and Whinney* 1967, 40–1; Pevsner, *Berks*, 1966, 76; C Lib (repr)
119.	1805	William Buchan MD (†1805) Payment(s): 30 gns	Westminster Abbey, London, cloisters		Flaxman Account Book 1794–1810, 86; *MacMichael* 1977, 101
120.	1805	William Ewin (†1804) Payment(s): 150 gns excluding erection Drawing(s): VAM CAI 1090 Model(s): UCL	St Lawrence, Brentford, Middx	S	Flaxman Account Book 1794–1810, 84; Pevsner, *London: N W*, 1991, 378; C Lib (repr)
121.	1804–1806	Agnes Squire (†1780) and daughter, Agnes (†1793) Payment(s): 150 gns excluding erection Model(s): UCL, plaster, 1003	St John, Peterborough	S	Flaxman Account Book 1794–1810, 83; *Gunnis and Whinney* 1967, 40
122.	1806	Dr Thomas Lawrence (†1783) Payment(s): 80 gns excluding erection Drawing(s): VAM CAI 1086	Canterbury Cathedral, Kent	S	Flaxman Account Book 1794–1810, 86; Pevsner, *Kent: NE & E*, 1983, 211; C Lib (repr)
123.	1804–1806	Elizabeth Catherine Ellis (†1803) Payment(s): 250 gns	St George, Esher, Surrey	S	Flaxman Account Book 1794–1810, 82
124.	1806	Francis Page (†1803) Payment(s): £33 19s 2d	Steeple Aston, Oxon		Flaxman Account Book 1794–1810, 88
125.	1806	Rev Richard Leslie (†1804) Payment(s): £100 Model(s): UCL	St Mary, Fort St George, Chennai (Madras), India		Flaxman Account Book 1794–1810, 87; *Groseclose* 1995, 93–4; C Lib (repr)
126.	1806	Rt Hon William Bingham (†1804) Payment(s): 250 gns excluding erection Drawing(s): BM 1926-11-15-25 (31)	Bath Abbey, Somerset	S	Flaxman Account Book 1794–1810, 88; Pevsner, *Somerset: N. & Bristol*, 1958, 104; C Lib (repr)
127.	1805–1806	Sir George Shuckburgh-Evelyn Payment(s): £100 excluding erection Drawing(s): VAM 8969 I (related)	Shuckburgh, Warks		Flaxman Account Book 1794–1810, 84
128.	1803–1806	Thomas Yarborough (†1772), his wife Johanna (†1762) and daughters Payment(s): £500 Drawing(s): BM 1888-5-3-51; Huntington Model(s): UCL, plaster, 1045, 1093 (sketch-model for the whole monument)	Campsall, W R Yorks	S	Flaxman Account Book 1794–1810, 80; *Gunnis and Whinney* 1967, 28, 53 (model repr 4); *Bindman* 1979, 77 (repr); *Irwin* 1979, 136–7 (repr)
129.	1806–1807	Charles (†1795), Marianna (†1785) and Maria (†1798) Colmore Payment(s): £105 excluding erection Model(s): UCL	Hendon, Middx	S	Flaxman Account Book 1794–1810, 87 (repr XIVc); Pevsner, *London: N*, 1998, 159
130.	1806–1807	Frances Hunter (†1805) Payment(s): 100 gns excluding cost of erection Model(s): UCL	Dawlish, Devon	S	Flaxman Account Book 1794–1810, 89; Pevsner, *Devon*, 1989, 330; C Lib (repr)
131.	1805–1807	Hon Barbara Lowther (†1806) Payment(s): 220 gns Model(s): UCL, plaster, 1092, 1103	St Mary Magdalene, Richmond, Surrey	S	Flaxman Account Book 1794–1810, 86 (repr XVa); *Gunnis and Whinney* 1967, 59 (model repr 19a and b); *Bilbey* 2002, 78–9 (model repr)
132.	1807	John (†1807), Edward (†1742), William (†1744) and Charlotte (†1781), children of William Hillersdon Payment(s): £105 Model(s): UCL	Leyton, Essex	S	Flaxman Account Book 1794–1810, 90; Pevsner, *Essex*, 1965, 268; C Lib (repr)
133.	1807	Josiah Webbe (†1804) Payment(s): £800 Model(s): UCL, plaster, 1019 (sketch-model of whole monument), 1053 (left-hand side of monument only)	St Mary, Fort St George, Chennai (Madras), India	S	Flaxman Account Book 1794–1810, 78 (repr XVIb); *Gunnis and Whinney* 1967, 23, 48 (model repr 9a); *Archer* 1984, 50–1 (repr); *Groseclose* 1995, 112–4 (repr)
134.	1807	Pasquale di Paoli (†1807) Payment(s): 150 gns Drawing(s): VAM	Westminster Abbey, London, nave	S	Flaxman Account Book 1794–1810, 90; *Irwin* 1979, 187; C Lib (repr)
135.	1806–1807	Rev John Courtail (†1806) Payment(s): £150 excluding erection Model(s): UCL	Burwash, Sussex	S	Flaxman Account Book 1794–1810, 88; Pevsner, *Sussex*, 1965, 463; C Lib (repr)

No.	Date	Subject	Location		References
136.	1807	Rev Pearce Mealy (†1801) and Lieutenant-Colonel Ridgeway Mealy (†1805) Payment(s): £38 excluding erection	Bangor Castle, Gwynedd		Flaxman Account Book 1794–1810, 90
137.	1807	Samuel Buck (†1806) Payment(s): £210 excluding erection Model(s): UCL, plaster, 1013 (for whole monument), 1059 (figures only)	All Saints, Rotherham, W R Yorks	S	Flaxman Account Book 1794–1810, 90; *Gunnis and Whinney* 1967, 18, 45; C Lib (repr)
138.	1806–1808	Admiral Mark Milbanke (†1805) Payment(s): 60 gns excluding erection	Untraced		Flaxman Account Book 1794–1810, 87
139.	†1808	Charlotte, Countess of Euston Payment(s): 150 gns Drawing(s): VAM	Grafton Regis, Northants	S	Flaxman Account Book 1809–26, 83; *CIIA* 4/3/78–81 (repr)
140.	1808	John Rowley (†1805) Payment(s): £500 agreed, but no record of payment Drawing(s): VAM CAI 1071 and 1097 (the latter inscribed 'J. Rowley')	Untraced		Flaxman Account Book 1794–1810, 92
141.	1808	Rev Hugh Moises (†1806)	Salisbury Cathedral, Wilts		RG/JP, 4, 520
142.	1808	Rev Nathan Wetherell (†1807) Payment(s): £200 excluding erection Drawing(s): BM 1888-5-3-37 Model(s): UCL, plaster, 1085	St Mary the Virgin, Oxford (damaged)	S	Flaxman Account Book 1794–1810, 92; *Gunnis and Whinney* 1967, 52; C Lib (repr)
143.	1807–1809	Anne Hill (†1804) Payment(s): 100 gns excluding erection	Broome, Worcs	S	Flaxman Account Book 1794–1810, 90; Pevsner, *Worcs*, 1968, 113
144.	1806–1809	Elizabeth Knight (†1800) Payment(s): £150 excluding cost of erection Drawing(s): BM 1888-5-3-87 Model(s): UCL, plaster, 1104 (sketch-model of whole monument) and 1054	Milton, Cambs		Flaxman Account Book 1794–1810, 87; *Gunnis and Whinney* 1967, 23–4, 60; *Irwin* 1979, 128–9, 130 (repr)
145.	†1809	John Monck Payment(s): 300 gns Model(s): UCL, plaster, 1070	St Mary, Reading, Berks		Flaxman Account Book 1809–26, 22; Pevsner, *Berks*, 1966, 202; *Gunnis and Whinney* 1967, 12; *Irwin* 1979, 150–1; C Lib (repr)
146.	1806–1809	Sir Rowland Winn Bt (†1765), and his wife Susannah (†1741) Payment(s): £200 excluding erection Drawing(s): BM 1926-11-15-25 (46)	Wragby, W R Yorks	S	Flaxman Account Book 1794–1810, 89; Pevsner, *Yorks: W R*, 1967, 560; C Lib (repr)
147.	1810	Colonel Thomas Vassal (†1807) (executed by John Charles Felix Rossi RA)	St Paul, Bristol		Pevsner, *Somerset: N & Bristol*, 1958, 406; C Lib (repr)
148.	1810	Dr Sydenham Payment(s): 60 gns	['St James's Church']; untraced		Flaxman Account Book 1809–26, 16
149.	1810	Georgiana Hare-Naylor (†1806) Payment(s): 50 gns	Twyford, Hants		Flaxman Account Book 1809–26, 14; Pevsner, *Hants & Isle of Wight*, 1967, 630; *Irwin* 1979, 131; C Lib (repr)
150.	1806–1810	Harriet, Lady Baring (†1804), Sir Francis Baring (†1810), 1st Bt and other members of the family Payment(s): £1,387 Drawing(s): VAM CAI 977 (from the life); BM 1888-5-3-39; UCL no703; Fitz Model(s): UCL, plaster, 1064 (finished model), 1072, 1076, 1087, 1098	Micheldever, Hants	S	Flaxman Account Book 1794–1810, 93; Flaxman Account Book 1809–26, 24; *Gunnis and Whinney* 1967, 12–13, 15, 19, 51–2, 61 (models repr 1, 11b); *Bindman* 1979, 109 (drawing repr); *Irwin* 1979, 129, 131, 133 (repr)
151.	1808–1810	Rev Hugh Moises (†1806) Payment(s): £450	St Nicholas's Cathedral, Newcastle, Northumbs	S	Flaxman Account Book 1794–1810, 91; Pevsner, *Northumbs*, 1992, 423
152.	1810	Sir Matthew White Ridley (†1813) Payment(s): £900 paid in February 1814	St Nicholas's Cathedral, Newcastle, Northumbs		Flaxman Account Book 1809–26, 64; Pevsner, *Northumbs*, 1992, 423
153.	1808–1810	Walter Long (†1807) Payment(s): £645 excluding erection Drawing(s): VAM CAI 1062; BM 1888-5-3-43 and ?1926-11-15-25 (32) Model(s): UCL	Salisbury Cathedral, Wilts	S	Flaxman Account Book 1794–1810, 91 (repr XVc); Pevsner, *Wilts*, 1975, 415; *Irwin* 1979, 167
154.	1803–1811	Admiral, 1st Earl Howe (†1799) Payment(s): £6300 Drawing(s): BM 1888-5-3-126; VAM CAI 1060, 8520.6 and 8968 D (?); YCAG, pen, ink and wash	St Paul's Cathedral, London	S	Flaxman Account Book 1794–1810, 78; *Irwin* 1979, 155–7 (repr); *Yarrington* 1988, 64–5, 71, 72–3 (repr 30)
155.	1809–1811	Ann Bowling (†1808) Payment(s): £120 excluding erection	[Croydon, Surrey]; destroyed		Flaxman Account Book 1794–1810, 93

No.	Date	Subject	Location		Bibliography
156.	1811	Deborah, Viscountess Ashbrook (†1810) Payment(s): £200	Hurley, Berks		Flaxman Account Book 1809–26, 26; Pevsner, *Berks*, 1966, 158; C Lib (repr)
157.	1811	Hon Henrietta Dillon (†1811) Payment(s): 150 gns Model(s): ?UCL, plaster, 1036	[All Saints, Southampton, Hants]; destroyed		Flaxman Account Book 1809–26, 30; *Gunnis and Whinney* 1967, 38
158.	1811	Lieutenant-General John Simcoe (†1806) Payment(s): £950 Drawing(s): VAM 8967A; Ionides Bequest 766	Exeter Cathedral, Devon	S	Flaxman Account Book 1809–26, 32; *Physick* 1969, 174–5 (repr); *Groseclose* 1995, 112–3
159.	1811	Margaret Wortley-Mackenzie (†1808) Payment(s): £500	Wortley, W R Yorks		Flaxman Account Book 1809–26, 18; Pevsner, *Yorks: W R*, 1967, 559
160.	1811	Rev Matthew Raine (†1811) Payment(s): 350 gns Model(s): UCL, plaster, 1089, 1116 (sketch-models for left and right-hand models respectively)	Charterhouse Chapel, City of London	S	Flaxman Account Book 1809–26, 36; *Gunnis and Whinney* 1967, 65; Pevsner, *London: N*, 1998, 620; C Lib (repr)
161.	1811	Sir Stewkley Shuckburgh Bt Payment(s): £150 paid in 1809	Shuckburgh, Warks		Flaxman Account Book 1809–26, 2; *Gunnis and Whinney* 1967, 41; C Lib (repr)
162.	1809–1812	Abraham Balme (†1796) Payment(s): £315 Model(s): UCL, plaster, 1056	Bradford Cathedral, W R Yorks	S	*Flaxman Account Book* 1809–26, 6; *Gunnis and Whinney* 1967, 24 (repr 6a); *Irwin* 1979, 137, 138 (repr)
163.	1810–1812	Captains James Walker and Richard Beckett (†1809) Payment(s): £700 Drawing(s): VAM; MFAB 63.203 Model(s): UCL, plaster, 1106	St Peter, Leeds, W R Yorks		Flaxman Account Book 1809–26, 10; *Gunnis and Whinney* 1967, 62 (model repr 20a); *Friedman* 1972, 23; *Irwin* 1979, 161–3 (repr); *Pullan* 2006, 19–23, 139 (repr)
164.	1812	Dr Nicholas Wanostrocht Payment(s): £150	[St Giles, Camberwell, London]; destroyed		Flaxman Account Book 1809–26, 50; *Gunnis* 1968, 151
165.	1809–1812	Rev Christian William Gericke (†1809) Payment(s): £189 Drawing(s): Huntington, pen, ink, pencil and wash Model(s): UCL, plaster, 1040 (sketch-model for whole monument), 1060	St Mary, Fort St George, Madras, India (damaged)	S	Flaxman Account Book 1809–26, 4; *Gunnis and Whinney* 1967, 17, 40; *Groseclose* 1995, 94 (repr); *Irwin* 1979, 138–9, 140 (drawing repr)
166.	1812	Sarah Udny (†1811) Payment(s): 150 gns	Chichester Cathedral, Sussex	S	Flaxman Account Book 1809–26, 46; *Gunnis and Whinney* 1967, 47; *Irwin* 1979, 152–3 (repr)
167.	1812	Thomas Greene, and another tablet to family Payment(s): £52 10s, and £47 5s	Untraced		Flaxman Account Book 1809–26, 42
168.	1813	Admiral Sir Charles Cotton (†1812) Payment(s): £200 Drawing(s): VAM E.8970	Madingley, Cambs		Flaxman Account Book 1809–26, 58; *Irwin* 1979, 166–7 (repr)
169.	1807–1813	Charles, 1st Marquess Cornwallis (†1805) Payment(s): £630 Model(s): UCL, plaster, 1021	[St George's, Penang (formerly Prince of Wales Island)]; destroyed		Flaxman Account Book 1794–1810, 89 (repr XVIIa); *Gunnis and Whinney* 1967, 48; *Groseclose* 1995, 63–6 (repr); *Irwin* 1979, 162
170.	1810–1813	Henry, 6th Duke of Bolton (†1794) Payment(s): £500 paid 1810 Model(s): UCL, plaster, 1014	Basing, Hants		Flaxman Account Book 1809–26, 20; *Gunnis and Whinney* 1967, 45–6; C Lib (repr)
171.	1810–1813	Matthew Boulton (†1809), bust Payment(s): 300 gns paid 1810	Handsworth, Warks Other versions: Tew Park, replica		Flaxman Account Book 1809–26, 12; *Irwin* 1979, 187 (repr); *Whinney* 1988, 355, 357 (repr); *Noszlopy* 1998, 67–8 (repr)
172.	1813	Matthew Quantock (†1812) Payment(s): £300 Drawing(s): BM, pen, ink and wash Model(s): UCL, plaster, 1033	Chichester Cathedral, Sussex	S	*Gunnis and Whinney* 1967, 37; *Irwin* 1979, 151–2 (repr)
173.	1813	Rev William Saltren (†1811) Payment(s): £300	Holme Pierrepont, Notts	S	Flaxman Account Book 1809–26, 52; *Gunnis and Whinney* 1967, 27; C Lib (repr)
174.	1808–1813	Sir Joshua Reynolds PRA (†1792), statue Payment(s): £1,150 Model(s): UCL; SJSM, plaster; Grittleton House, Wilts	St Paul's Cathedral, London, crossing	S	Flaxman Account Book 1794–1810, 92; *Graves* II, 1905–6, 124; *Irwin* 1979, 183–5 (repr)

No.	Date	Subject	Location		Bibliography
175.	1813	William Bromley (†1737) and other members of the family, the last William (†1810) Payment(s): £500 Drawing(s): UCL, 713 (inscribed 'Resignation'); BM Model(s): UCL, plaster, 1011	Baginton, Warks	S	Pevsner, *Warks*, 1966, 84; *Gunnis and Whinney* 1967, 44–5; *Bindman* 1979, 109, 117 (repr)
176.	1813	William Mills Payment(s): £100	Petersham, Surrey		Flaxman Account Book 1809–26, 56; C Lib (repr)
177.	1814	Caroline Elwes (†1812) Payment(s): 150 gns	Great Billing, Northants		Flaxman Account Book 1809–26, 71; *Irwin* 1979, 155 (repr); *CIIA* 4/3/91 (repr)
178.	†1814	Hon Charles Harris	Throwley, Kent		Flaxman Account Book 1809–26, 84; *Gunnis* 1968, 151; Pevsner, *Kent: NE & E*, 1983, 477
179.	1814	Mary, Lady Rendlesham Payment(s): £505 Model(s): UCL, prelim and final models; SJSM MRR 14, plaster	Rendlesham, Suffolk		Flaxman Account Book 1809–26, 77; *Irwin* 1979, 130 (repr); Soane Museum Inventory
180.	†1814	Mrs Ferguson	King's Caple, Herefs		Pevsner, *Herefs*, 1963, 204
181.	1814	Sir Isaac Pocock (†1810) Payment(s): £420 Model(s): UCL, plaster, 1024 (sketch-model of whole monument), 1079 (finished model of relief)	Cookham, Berks		Flaxman Account Book 1809–26, 67; *Gunnis and Whinney* 1967, 30, 34; C Lib (repr)
182.	1814	Sir Robert Chambers (†1803) Payment(s): £300	St Mary the Virgin, Oxford		Flaxman Account Book 1809–26, 76; C Lib (repr)
183.	†1814	Vice-Admiral Henry Frankland and Mary Frankland (†1823) Payment(s): 300 gns Model(s): part of monument exhib RA London 1814, 779	Chichester Cathedral, Sussex	S	Flaxman Account Book 1809–26, 75; *Graves* II, 1905–6, 124; *Gunnis and Whinney* 1967, 45; Pevsner, *Sussex*, 1965, 153; C Lib (repr)
184.	1812–1814	William Morgan James (†1798) and Rev Thomas James (†1812) Payment(s): 300 gns Drawing(s): UCL, pen, ink and pencil Model(s): UCL, plaster, 1008	Brecon Cathedral, Powys		Flaxman Account Book 1809–26, 44; *Gunnis and Whinney* 1967, 43; *Irwin* 1979, 134–5 (drawing repr)
185.	1815	George Lindsay Johnstone Payment(s): 360 gns	Westminster Abbey, London, gallery	S	Flaxman Account Book 1809–26, 65; Pevsner, *London: Westminster*, 1973, 461; C Lib (repr)
186.	†1815	John Lyon (†1592) Payment(s): £300 Drawing(s): UCL	Harrow-on-the-Hill, Middx		Flaxman Account Book 1809–26, 91; *Penny* 1977 (1), 160, 221 n56; Pevsner, *London: N W*, 1991, 262; C Lib (repr)
187.	1815	Major-General Sir Barry Close (†1813) Payment(s): £433 on account and £700 in India bonds, paid Jan 1815 Model(s): UCL, plaster, 1022 (sketch-model for the whole monument), 1058 (Muslim and Hindu figures)	St Mary, Fort St George, Chennai (Madras), India Other versions: bust only, marble, 1823, for Maxwell Close, Elm Park, Armagh, £105, Flaxman Account Book 1809–26, 23; untraced	S	Flaxman Account Book 1809–26, 78; *Gunnis and Whinney* 1967, 24, 30–1; *Archer* 1984, 51 (repr); *Groseclose* 1995, 13, 114–5 (repr)
188.	1814–1815	Mary Tighe Payment(s): £100 Model(s): UCL, plaster, 2810; Rothe House, Kilkenny	Inistioge, Kilkenny, mausoleum in churchyard		*Flaxman Account Book* 1809–26, 74; *Gunnis and Whinney* 1967, 49 (modelrepr 23a); *Potterton* 1975, 45 (repr); *Bindman* 1979, 110 (repr); *Irwin* 1979, 152, 154 (repr)
189.	†1815	William Antonie	Sharnbrook, Beds		Flaxman Account Book 1809–26, 109; Pevsner, *Beds, Hunts & Peterborough*, 1968, 141
190.	1813–1815	William Bosanquet (†1813) Payment(s): 200 gns Model(s): UCL, plaster, 1071 (figure composition only)	Leyton, Essex		Flaxman Account Book 1809–26, 54; *Gunnis and Whinney* 1967, 12; *Penny* 1977 (1), 140, 219 n7 (repr); *Irwin* 1979, 134–5 (model repr)
191.	1815	William Moore Payment(s): £105	[Temple Church, London]; untraced		Flaxman Account Book 1809–26, 79
192.	1816	Bishop John Skinner (†1816) Payment(s): £300	St Andrew, Aberdeen		Flaxman Account Book 1809–26, 94; *Irwin* 1979, 185
193.	1816	Elizabeth Caswall (†1815) Payment(s): £300 paid in February 1816 Drawing(s): UCL no 706, 'Religion comforting the Mourner' Model(s): UCL, plaster, 1069	Sacombe, Herts		Flaxman Account Book 1809–26, 85; *Gunnis and Whinney* 1967, 11; *Irwin* 1979, 134; C Lib (repr)

194.	1815–1816	John Miles (†1812) Payment(s): 150 gns	Ledbury, Herefs		Flaxman Account Book 1809–26, 69; *Gunnis and Whinney* 1967, 33 (repr 12a)
195.	1816	Miss Thompson Payment(s): 100 gns	Untraced		Flaxman Account Book 1809–26, 88
196.	1816	Monumental figure of Resignation Payment(s): 100 gns	[for John N Fazakerley MP, Lincoln]; untraced		Flaxman Account Book 1809–26, 87; *Gunnis and Whinney* 1967, 45
197.	1815–1816	Rev Thomas Brand (†1815) Payment(s): £125 Model(s): UCL, plaster, 1097	Wath, N R Yorks	S	Flaxman Account Book 1809–26, 80; *Gunnis and Whinney* 1967, 62; *Bindman* 1979, 110–1 (repr)
198.	†1817	Frances Schutz Drury	Kingsbridge, Devon		*Gunnis* 1968, 151; Pevsner, *Devon*, 1989, 520
199.	1816–1817	Harriet Susan, Viscountess Fitzharris (†1815) Payment(s): 200 gns Drawing(s): John Murray, London, pencil Model(s): UCL, plaster, 1038 (sketch-model of whole monument), 1043; SJSM MRR 11 (plaster)	Christchurch Priory, Hants		*Whinney* 1988, 356–8 (repr); *Penny* 1977 (1), 158 (repr); *Gunnis and Whinney* 1967, 26–7, 39 (repr 17a and b); *Irwin* 1979, 141–5 (repr)
200.	1817	Lady Ibbetson (†1816) Payment(s): £200	Hatfield Broad Oak, Essex	S	Flaxman Account Book 1809–26, 99; *Gunnis and Whinney* 1967, 49; Pevsner, *Essex*, 1965, 235
201.	1817	Mrs Carr Payment(s): 80 gns	Untraced		Flaxman Account Book 1809–26, 98
202.	1807–1818	Admiral Lord Nelson (†1805) Payment(s): £6300 Drawing(s): BM, pen, ink and wash; YCAG; Private coll	St Paul's Cathedral, London		Flaxman Account Book 1794–1810, 78; *Bindman* 1979, 30 (repr); *Irwin* 1979, 158–60 (repr); *Whinney* 1988, 346–8 (repr); *Yarrington* 1988, 63, 65, 79–92 (repr 41); *Irwin* 1979, 158 (repr)
203.	1817–1818	Admiral Thomas Western (†1814) Payment(s): 150 gns	Tattingstone, Suffolk		Flaxman Account Book 1809–26, 95; *Gunnis and Whinney* 1967, 45; C Lib (repr)
204.	1818	Rev Matthew Rolleston (†1817) Payment(s): £105 Model(s): UCL, plaster, 1117	University College, Oxford		*Flaxman Account Book* 1809–26, 102; *Gunnis and Whinney* 1967, 64–5; C Lib (repr)
205.	1818	Sophia, Lady Hesketh (†1817) Payment(s): £210 Model(s): UCL, plaster, 1016	Rufford, Lancs		Flaxman Account Book 1809–26, 101; *Gunnis and Whinney* 1967, 46–7; C Lib (repr)
206.	1818	William Long (†1818) Payment(s): £755	Salisbury Cathedral, Wilts		Flaxman Account Book 1809–26, 103
207.	1817–1819	Ann Fortescue (†1815) Payment(s): £168 Model(s): UCL, plaster, 1039 (sketch-model for whole monument), 1063	Buckland Fillegh, Devon		Flaxman Account Book 1809–26, 96; *Gunnis and Whinney* 1967, 19, 39
208.	1815–1819	George, 4th Duke of Dorset (†1815) Payment(s): 500 gns Model(s): UCL, plaster, 1012 (sketch-model for whole monument), 1081	Withyham, Sussex		Flaxman Account Book 1809–26, 81; *Gunnis and Whinney* 1967, 16, 42 (model repr 15b)
209.	1814–1819	Georgiana, Countess Spencer (†1814), conceived as a pendant to Nollekens's monument to her husband Payment(s): 450 gns, paid June 1816 Drawing(s): Huntington, pen, ink and wash; Althorp, Northants, pencil Model(s): UCL, plaster, 1044, 1090, 1099 (all for figure of Charity) and 1113 (figure of Faith); SJSM	Great Brington, Northants	S	Flaxman Account Book 1809–26, 89; *Gunnis and Whinney* 1967, 27, 62–3 (model repr 18a and b); *Irwin* 1979, 141, 143 (repr)
210.	1819	Rev John Clowes Payment(s): £150 Drawing(s): pen and ink, YCBA Model(s): UCL, plaster, 1034 (sketch-model for relief and frame), 1048	[St John, Manchester]; destroyed		Flaxman Account Book 1809–26, 106; *Gunnis and Whinney* 1967, 30, 37 (model repr 9b); *Penny* 1977 (1), 156–7 (repr); *Irwin* 1979, 116–7 (drawing repr)
211.	†1819	Rev Robert Delafosse Payment(s): £170 paid in 1821 Drawing(s): VAM E.949-1965	Petersham, Surrey		Flaxman Account Book 1809–26, 111
212.	1819	Richard Watson, Bishop of Llandaff (†1816) Payment(s): £105	Bowness-on-Windermere, Westmorland		Flaxman Account Book 1809–26, 105; Pevsner, *Cumberland & Westmorland*, 1967, 228

No.	Date	Subject		Location		Bibliography
213.	1820	Mary Ann Bosanquet (†1819) and child, Lewis (†1806) Payment(s): £210 Model(s): UCL, plaster, 1049, 1094 (sketch-model)		Llantilio Crosseney, Monmouths	S	*Gunnis and Whinney* 1967, 29, 54 (repr 3a); *Irwin* 1979, 150
214.	1819–1821	Chichester, 4th Earl of Masserene (†1816) Payment(s): 450 gns Drawing(s): Huntington Model(s): UCL, plaster, 1025		Antrim Church, Ireland		*Flaxman Account Book* 1809–26, 104; *Gunnis and Whinney* 1967, 34 (model repr 12); *Potterton* 1975, 45 (repr)
215.	1821	George Gostling (†1820) Payment(s): £450		Egham, Surrey		Flaxman Account Book 1809–26, 5; Pevsner, *Surrey*, 1971, 209; C Lib (repr)
216.	1821	Lord or Lady Dunalley		[Silvermines church, Co Tipperary (?)]; untraced		*Potterton* 1975, 45
217.	1822	Elizabeth Georgiana Ellis (†1820)		St George, Esher, Surrey	S	Flaxman Account Book 1809–26, 100; *Penny* 1977 (1), 25 (repr)
218.	1822	Nathaniel Marchant (†1816) Payment(s): 100 gns		Stoke Poges, Bucks		Flaxman Account Book 1809–26, 3; *Lipscomb* 1847, 565; Pevsner, *Bucks*, 1994, 652
219.	1823	Benjamin family Payment(s): £120		[Egham, Surrey]; untraced		Flaxman Account Book 1809–26, 17
220.	1822–1823	Emily Mawbey (†1819) Payment(s): £105 Model(s): UCL, plaster, 1073		Chertsey, Surrey	S	*Gunnis and Whinney* 1967, 13–14 (model repr 2b); *Irwin* 1979, 134, 136 (repr)
221.	1823	Hon Mrs Agneta Yorke (†1820) Payment(s): £200 Model(s): UCL, plaster, 1118, 1119 (sketch-models for right and left-hand side respectively)		Wimpole, Cambs		Flaxman Account Book 1809–26, 25; *Gunnis and Whinney* 1967, 63–4; Pevsner, *Cambs*, 1970, 493; C Lib (repr)
222.	1822–1823	Mary Arbuthnot Payment(s): £200		St John, New Town, Edinburgh		Flaxman Account Book 1809–26, 114; *Gunnis and Whinney* 1967, 28; *Irwin* 1979, 142 (repr)
223.	1824	Charles, 1st Marquess Cornwallis (†1805) Payment(s): £525		Ghazipur, India		*Archer* 1984, 53–4 (repr); *Steggles* 2000, 64–6
224.	1824	Edward Christian (†1823) Payment(s): £150 Model(s): UCL, plaster, 1027		Broxbourne, Herts	S	*Gunnis and Whinney* 1967, 35; Pevsner, *Herts*, 1977, 114; C Lib (repr)
225.	1824	Frances Hawkins (†1817) and infant daughter Payment(s): £200		Kingsbridge, Devon		Flaxman Account Book 1809–26, 29; *Gunnis and Whinney* 1967, 24; *Whinney* 1988, 352
226.	1824	Harriet Prevost Payment(s): £35		[Southrop, Glos]; untraced		Flaxman Account Book 1809–26, 39
227.	1824	Rev Kelsall Prescott (†1823) Payment(s): £100		All Saints (Old), Marple, Cheshire		Flaxman Account Book 1809–26, 31; Pevsner, *Cheshire*, 1971, 276; C Lib (repr)
228.	1825	Archdeacon John Mousley (†1819) Payment(s): £380		St George's Cathedral, Chennai (Madras), India	S	Flaxman Account Book 1809–26, 21; *Archer* 1984, 51; *Groseclose* 1995, 136 n33
229.	†1825	Edward Clarke Payment(s): £50, paid May 1825		Jesus College Chapel, Cambridge		Flaxman Account Book 1809–26, 49; Pevsner, *Cambs*, 1970, 87
230.	1825	Sophia Hoare (†1824) Payment(s): 200 gns Model(s): UCL, plaster, 1062		St Leonard, Streatham, London		Flaxman Account Book 1809–26, 45; *Gunnis and Whinney* 1967, 19–20; Pevsner, *London: S*, 1983, 391; C Lib (repr)
231.	1826	Harriot Peach (†1825) Payment(s): £100		Ketteringham, Norfolk		Flaxman Account Book 1809–26, 60; Pevsner, *Norfolk: N W & S*, 1999, 455; C Lib (repr)
232.	1826	John Philip Kemble (†1823) (completed by John Hinchliffe and Thomas Denman) Payment(s): £850 Model(s): SJSM SDR 11		Westminster Abbey, London, St Andrew's Chapel		Flaxman Account Book 1809–26, 37; Pevsner, *London: Westminster*, 1973, 460; C Lib (repr)
233.	1813–1827	Hon Harriet Pryse Payment(s): 150 gns		Llanbadarn Fawr, Cardiganshire		Flaxman Account Book 1809–26, 60; *Gunnis* 1968, 151
234.	1827	Rev John Davies (†1817) Payment(s): payment of £150 in 1823		Trinity College, Cambridge, ante-chapel		Flaxman Account Book 1809–26, 19; *Penny* 1977 (1), 24–6 (repr)
235.	†1832	James Lushington		St George's Cathedral, Chennai (Madras), India		*Gunnis* 1968, 151
236.	nd	Models for unidentified monuments	p	UCL 1017, 1026, 1031, 1035, 1046, 1095, 1111, 2811		*Gunnis and Whinney* 1967, 28–9, 34, 36, 38, 44, 50, 58
Statues						
237.	1767	Hercules, large model	p	[Exhib Free Soc, London, 115]; untraced		*Graves* 1907, 93; *Irwin* 1979, 10
238.	1767	Omphale, large model	p	[Exhib Free Soc, London, 116]; untraced		*Graves* 1907, 93; *Irwin* 1979, 10
239.	1770	David Garrick		[Soc of A, gold palette]; untraced		*Dossie* 1782, 439

240.	1772	History, figure		[Exhib RA, London, 85]; untraced		*Graves* III, 1905–6, 123
241.	1773	Grecian Comedy		[Exhib RA, London, 104]; untraced		*Graves* III, 1905–6, 123
242.	1787	Venus and Cupid		[coll Mr Knight, of Portland Place, London]; untraced		*Cunningham* 1829–33, vol 3, 293; *Graves* III, 1905–6, 123; *Hendricks* 1984, 621
243.	1790	Apollo and Marpessa Drawing(s): Fitz, pen, ink and wash	m	RA, London (presented as his diploma work in 1800)		*Radcliffe* 1969, 46–7 (repr); *Bindman* 1979, 101 (repr); *Irwin* 1979, 169–71 (repr)
244.	1790	Aurora visiting Cephalus on Mount Ida	m	[Thomas Hope's house, Duchess Street, London]; Lady Lever LL 713	S	*Irwin* 1979, 54–5 (repr); *Bindman* 1979, 28 (repr); *Lady Lever* 1999, 9–11 (repr)
245.	1787–1794	Apollo Belvedere, small model	p	SJSM, M1147		Soane Museum Inventory
246.	1790–1794	Fury of Athamas, group Payment(s): £600	m	Ickworth House, Suffolk		*Irwin* 1979, 55–8 (repr); *Bindman* 1979, 28, 33; *Whinney* 1988, 342–4 (repr); *Ingamells* 1997, 363
247.	1792–1795	Hercules and Hebe Payment(s): £341 of total 700 gns paid Model(s): UCL, painted plaster, 1084	m	[for Thomas Hope, 'to be executed in marble in Rome']; untraced		Flaxman Account Book 1794–1810, 56; *Gunnis and Whinney* 1967, 53 (model repr 24a); *Irwin* 1979, 58–9, 60 (repr); *Bindman* 1979, 28 (model repr)
248.	1799	Britannia by divine providence triumphant, competition model for colossal statue for Greenwich Park (unexecuted) Drawing(s): VAM, E.950-1965, inscribed 'Colossal statue 230 feet high proposed to be erected on Greenwich' Model(s): UCL	p	SJSM, M1079		*Flaxman* 1799; Soane Museum Inventory; *Bindman* 1979, 119 (drawing repr); *Irwin* 1979, 163, 166 (drawing repr)
249.	1803–1807	Sarfogi, Rajah of Tanjore Payment(s): £1200	m	Tanjore Palace, India		Flaxman Account Book 1794–1810, 78; *Irwin* 1979, 181 (repr)
250.	1809	Comedy Payment(s): £210		Covent Garden Theatre, London, façade		Flaxman Account Book 1809–26, 8; C Lib (repr)
251.	1808–1812	William Pitt the Younger (†1806) Payment(s): £1,300 Model(s): plaster, SJSM SC 41	m	[Town Hall, Glasgow]; Glasgow Museums S.30	SD	Flaxman Account Book 1794–1810, 91; *Irwin* 1979, 181–2 (repr); *Whinney* 1988, 348–9 (repr); *McKenzie* 2002, 264–6 (repr)
252.	1810–1818	Sir John Moore (†1809) (assisted by Sir Richard Westmacott) Payment(s): £3,200	b	Glasgow, George Square		Flaxman Account Book 1809–26, 38; *Irwin* 1979, 182–3 (repr); *Busco* 1994, 24, 176 n125; *McKenzie* 1999, 49, no 6.20
253.	1820	Warren Hastings (†1818) Payment(s): £1,000	m	[East India House, Leadenhall Street, City of London]; Foreign and Commonwealth Office, London		Flaxman Account Book 1809–26, 113; *Archer* 1965, 407; *Irwin* 1979, 183
254.	1824	Two small statues, Cupid and Psyche Payment(s): £105 Model(s): Cupid, plaster, SJSM SC 33		[for Samuel Rogers, St James's Place, London Sold in Roger's Sale, 1856, lot 835]; untraced		Flaxman Account Book 1809–26, 33; *Gunnis and Whinney* 1967, 49, 50
255.	1813–1825	Pastoral Apollo Payment(s): 900 gns	m	Petworth, Sussex		Flaxman Account Book 1809–26, 62; *JKB* 1977 (2), 368, 369 (repr); *Irwin* 1979, 178–80 (repr)
256.	1826	Michelangelo, small model (companion to Raphael)	p	SJSM, M1484 Other versions: Other plasters: BM; RA; UCL (destroyed)		*Bindman* 1979, 30, 111 (repr); Soane Museum Inventory
257.	1826	Raphael, small model (companion to Michelangelo) Drawing(s): UCL	p	SJSM, M1485 Other versions: Other plasters: BM; RA; UCL (destroyed)		*Graves* III, 1905–6, 125; *Bindman* 1979, 30, 111 (repr); Soane Museum Inventory
258.	1822–1826	Robert Burns Payment(s): £1,400 Model(s): plaster, City of Edinburgh Museums and Art Galleries	m	SNPG, Edinburgh		Flaxman Account Book 1809–26, 107, 109; *Irwin* 1979, 185–6 (repr); *Whinney* 1988, 348–50 (repr)
259.	1817–1826	Satan overcome by St Michael Payment(s): £3,500 Model(s): VAM, plaster, 312–1898; UCL, plaster, 999; SJSM SC7	m	Petworth, Sussex	SD	*Gunnis and Whinney* 1967, 51 (UCL model repr 24b); *JKB* 1977 (2), 367–373 (repr); *Irwin* 1979, 178–80 (UCL model repr); *McEvansoneya* 2001, 351–9 (repr); *Bilbey* 2002, 81 (VAM model repr)
260.	1826–1830	Francis, 1st Marquess of Hastings (completed by Thomas Denman) Model(s): SJSM, plaster, SDR 1	m	Victoria Memorial Hall, Kolkata (Calcutta), (formerly Town Hall)		*Irwin* 1979, 183; *Archer* 1984, 53
261.	nd	A Philosopher, statuette	tc	SJSM, BR 17		Soane Museum Inventory

262.	nd	Apollo		[Deepdene, Surrey]; untraced		*Gunnis* 1968, 149
263.	nd	Faith and Hope, statuettes (the latter with a bracket in the form of a head with curling hair)	p	Untraced		*Gunnis and Whinney* 1967, 56, 57
264.	nd	Hercules in the Garden of the Hesperides Model(s): SJSM, DR 14, wax on wood base	b	BM		Soane Museum Inventory
265.	nd	The rape of Ganymede	m	RA, London		*Manchester Art Treasures* 1857, 134
Busts						
266.	1768	'Rev Mr Whitfield'		[Exhib Free Soc, London, 96]; untraced		*Graves* 1907, 93
267.	1768	Unidentified gentleman		[Exhib Free Soc, London, 97]; untraced		*Graves* 1907, 93
268.	1772	Unidentified man	tc	[Exhib RA, London, 87]; untraced		*Graves* III, 1905–6, 123
269.	1782	Mercury		Untraced Other versions: cast offered to Wedgwood, 1782; untraced		*Graves* III, 1905–6, 123; *Bindman* 1979, 56
270.	1782	Several (possibly by John Flaxman I) Payment(s): £20		[Wolverley House, Worcs]; untraced		*Hendricks* 1984, 625
271.	1784	Unidentified gentleman		[Exhib RA, London, 519]; untraced		*Graves* III, 1905–6, 123
272.	1785	Venus Payment(s): £25		[for Edward Knight]; untraced		*Hendricks* 1984, 625
273.	1788	Harriet Hamilton		Untraced		*Irwin* 1979, 54; *Ingamells* 1997, 362, 363
274.	1788	King Louis XVI		Untraced	SD	RG/JP, 4, 10
275.	1790–1791	Homer Payment(s): £35	m	[for Edward Knight]; untraced		*Irwin* 1979, 224 nl; *Hendricks* 1984, 622, 625; *Ingamells* 1997, 363
276.	c1794	Henry Howard	p	SJSM, BR21		Soane Museum Inventory; *Irwin* 1979, 186
277.	c1794	John Flaxman, the sculptor's father	p	SJSM		Soane Museum Inventory; *Irwin* 1979, 186
278.	c1794	William Hayley	p	SJSM, BR 23		Soane Museum Inventory; *Bindman* 1979, 36, 100; *Irwin* 1979, 186
279.	1795	Jupiter Payment(s): £90		[for Anne, Lady Camelford]; untraced		Flaxman Account Book 1794–1810, 54
280.	1795	Mr Udney Payment(s): £52 10	m	Untraced		*Farington* II, 425; Flaxman Account Book 1794–1810, 54
281.	1796	Pasquale di Paoli Payment(s): £36 14s 6d	m	Untraced		*Farington* II, 509; Flaxman Account Book 1794–1810, 54
282.	1797	'Mr Wortley' Payment(s): £31 10s		Untraced		Flaxman Account Book 1794–1810, 59
283.	1798	Sir George Yonge Payment(s): £26 5s including a plaster cast of the same	tc	Untraced		Flaxman Account Book 1794–1810, 60
284.	1800	Mary Blackshaw Payment(s): £42 and a cast for 12s	m	[for Mrs Lushington, Shooter's Hill near Greenwich]; untraced		Flaxman Account Book 1794–1810, 68
285.	1803	Henry Philip Hope (†1839) Payment(s): £84	m	[Duchess Street, London, dining room; Hope sale, 1917, lot 1130]; Thorvaldsen Museum, Copenhagen G271	S	Flaxman Account Book 1794–1810, 80; *Bindman* 1979, 105 (repr); *Irwin* 1979, 186 (repr)
286.	1805	Admiral Lord Nelson	m	United Services Club, London Other versions: NMM, Greenwich, SCU0090, marble for Lord Orford; untraced		Pevsner, *London: Westminster*, 1973, 612; *Irwin* 1979, 161, 229 n57; C Lib (repr)
287.	1800–1805	John Hunter Payment(s): £60	m	RCS, London	S	Flaxman Account Book 1794–1810, 85; *Le Fanu* 1960, 42; *Irwin* 1979, 186; C Lib (repr)
288.	1806	Frederick, 2nd Earl of Guilford Payment(s): £170 for bust and marble term		Examination Schools, Oxford, lobby		Flaxman Account Book 1794–1810, 87; Pevsner, *Oxon*, 1974, 266
289.	?1807	Busts of Princepi and Principessa Plantamone di San Antonio, statue of child and an arrow		Untraced		NP/RG
290.	1809	John Forbes Payment(s): £63	m	Untraced		Flaxman Account Book 1809–26, 7
291.	1808–1809	William Pitt the Younger (†1806) Drawing(s): BM PDL	p	SJSM, M 1087		*Walker* 1961, 57; Soane Museum Inventory
292.	1810	Matthew Boulton Payment(s): £105		[for 'Mr Dumourge']; untraced		Flaxman Account Book 1809–26, 12
293.	1812	Alexander Munro Payment(s): 120 gns	m	Edinburgh University		Flaxman Account Book 1809–26, 40; C Lib (repr)
294.	1823	John Forbes	m	[Exhib RA, London, 1088]; untraced		*Graves* III, 1905–6, 124
295.	1826	Sir Matthew White Ridley Payment(s): £105	m	Untraced		Flaxman Account Book 1809–26, 66

Chimneypieces

No.	Date	Description		Location	Bibliography
296.	1780–1781	Marble, part of a decorative scheme designed by the sculptor Payment(s): £129 5s		[Etruria Hall, Staffs, saloon]; destroyed	*Bindman* 1979, 7
297.	1781–1782	Several, including one with lions and foliage (possibly in collaboration with John Flaxman I) Payment(s): £779 16s	m	[Wolverley House, Worcs]; untraced	*Hendricks* 1984, 621, 623
298.	1783–1784	With two small medallion busts in the corners, and with two classical nymphs or muses in the centre	m	Eartham, Surrey	*Bindman* 1979, 46, 100 (repr)
299.	1786	Marble Payment(s): £66 6s	m	Kingston Lacy, Dorset, saloon	*Kingston Lacy*, NT guidebook, 1998, 58; C Lib (repr)
300.	c1787	Description unavailable		[Fonthill Abbey, Wilts]; untraced	*Gunnis* 1968, 149
301.	1787	Two Payment(s): £25 4s and £31 3s 6d		[for Josiah Wedgwood]; untraced	*Gunnis* 1968, 149
302.	1800	Small Payment(s): £20 3s	m	[for Josiah Wedgwood the younger, probably for Tarrant Gunville Manor House, Dorset]; untraced	Flaxman Account Book 1794–1810, 69
303.	1800	Two Payment(s): £157 and £200	m	[for Thomas Hope, Hanover Square]; untraced	Flaxman Account Book 1794–1810, 68
304.	1802	With caryatids	m	Albury Park, Surrey, drawing room	*Gunnis* 1968, 149; Pevsner, *Surrey*, 1971, 93
305.	1803	With reliefs of a lyre-playing youth and a bowing maiden Model(s): UCL	m	[coll Charles Hoare]; Luscombe Castle, Devon, octagonal drawing room	Flaxman Account Book 1794–1810, 77; Pevsner, *Devon*, 1989, 544
306.	1804	Description unavailable Payment(s): £100, with £20 for two slabs of statuary marble for commodes		[for Sir Thomas Frankland, Thirkleby Park, N R Yorks]; untraced	Flaxman Account Book 1794–1810, 67
307.	1804	With reliefs of a muse holding a lyre, and Mnemosyne Payment(s): £105	m	[for Samuel Rogers, 22 St James's Place, London]; untraced	Flaxman Account Book 1794–1810, 77
308.	1823–1824	Grecian feast, relief Payment(s): £150 Drawing(s): Huntington Model(s): SJSM SC 28, plaster (dates from Italian period)	m	Northington Grange, Hants	Flaxman Account Book 1809–26, 51; *Irwin* 1979, 176–7 (repr); Soane Museum Inventory; *Bryant* 2003, 85 (repr)

Architectural Sculpture

No.	Date	Description		Location	Bibliography
309.	1785	Vase Payment(s): £19 19s		[Wolverley House, Worcs]; untraced	*Hendricks* 1984, 625
310.	1802–1803	Liberty, Peace, Agriculture and Commerce, tympanum figures for the Temple of Liberty, model (later carved in marble by Sir Richard Westmacott) Payment(s): 80 gns Drawing(s): BM 1888-5-3-53 (rejected design); private coll	p	UCL 1114 (marble at Woburn Abbey, Beds)	Flaxman Account Book 1794–1810, 76; *Gunnis and Whinney* 1967, 57; *Irwin* 1979, 172; *JKB* 1989, 29, 30 (repr marble)
311.	1809	The Ancient and Modern Drama, reliefs (executed in stone by JCF Rossi) Payment(s): £31 10s 6d for model	p	UCL 1109, 1110 Other versions: Covent Garden Theatre, London, façade, stone VAM A.8-1968, A.9-1968, casts	Flaxman Account Book 1809–26, 8; *Lady's Mag*, vol 40, Sept. 1809, 385–6 (repr); *Gunnis and Whinney* 1967, 60–1 (repr 21); *Irwin* 1979, 172–4 (repr); *Bilbey* 2002, 83–4 (repr)

Reliefs

No.	Date	Description		Location	Bibliography
312.	1766	Minerva, clay bas-relief		[Soc of A, premium, 10 gns]; untraced	*Dossie* 1782, 439; *Graves* 1907, 93
313.	1768	Death of Julius Caesar, clay bas-relief Drawing(s): Coll Christopher Powney (?)		[Soc of A, premium, 10 gns]; untraced	RSA, *Minutes* 1767–68 seq 3 f25; *Graves* III, 1905–6, 123; *Graves* 1907, 93; *GM*, vol 51, 1781, 65; *Bindman* 1979, 40; *Irwin* 1979, 10
314.	1769	Death of Cleopatra, clay		[Soc of A, premium, 10 gns]; untraced	*Dossie* 1782, 439
315.	1772	Mary Ann Flaxman, holding a doll	w	VAM 295-1864	*Irwin* 1979, 10–11 (repr); *Whinney* 1988, 338; *Bilbey* 2002, 76
316.	1773	A vestal, bas-relief		[Exhib RA, London, 105]; untraced	*Graves* III, 1905–6, 123
317.	1775	Dr Daniel Charles Solander, portrait-medallion		untraced Other versions: reproduced by Wedgwood	*Bindman* 1979, 47, 51 (Wedgwood repr)
318.	1775	Sir Joseph and Lady Banks, portrait-medallions		untraced Other versions: Second version c1779 reproduced by Wedgwood	*Bindman* 1979, 47, 50, 51 (Wedgwood repr); *Irwin* 1979, 19 (repr)
319.	1777	Six muses		Untraced Other versions: reproduced by Wedgwood	*Gunnis* 1968, 147; *Irwin* 1979, 20 (repr)
320.	1778	Dr Richard Mead, portrait-medallion		Untraced Other versions: reproduced by Wedgwood	*Irwin* 1979, 20

321.	1778	John Flaxman, the sculptor's father, medallion Model(s): SJSM S 43; A 19	tc	VAM		Soane Museum Inventory
322.	1778	Self-portrait Drawing(s): UCL; Earls High School, Halesowen, Worcs	tc	VAM 294-1864	SD	*Bindman* 1979, 39 (repr); *Bilbey* 2002, 76–7 (repr)
323.	1778	The apotheosis of Homer		Untraced Other versions: reproduced by Wedgwood		*Bindman* 1979, 9, 47, 56 (Wedgwood repr); *Irwin* 1979, 22 (Wedgwood chimneypiece repr)
324.	1778	The dancing hours		Untraced Other versions: reproduced by Wedgwood (reproductions in Wedgwood Museum, Barlaston, Staffs)		*Bindman* 1979, 47, 54 (Wedgwood repr)
325.	1778	'The marriage of Cupid and Psyche', and companion 'Cupids with goat'		Untraced Other versions: reproduced by Wedgwood (reproductions in Wedgwood Museum, Barlaston, Staffs)		*Bindman* 1979, 53 (Wedgwood repr)
326.	1778	William Pitt, 1st Earl of Chatham		Untraced Other versions: reproduced by Wedgwood (reproduction in Wedgwood Museum, Barlaston, Staffs)		*Bindman* 1979, 53 (Wedgwood repr)
327.	*c*1779	Self-portrait	p	BM		*Bindman* 1979, 39 (repr)
328.	1779	Self-portrait, aged 14		Wedgwood Factory (plaster mould) Other versions: reproduced by Wedgwood		*Bindman* 1979, 50 (modern replica repr)
329.	1779	The sacrifice to Ceres		Untraced Other versions: reproduced by Wedgwood		*Gunnis* 1968, 147
330.	1780	Unidentified subject		Papplewick Hall, Notts, morning room		Pevsner, *Notts*, 1979, 287
331.	1781	Acis and Galatea, bas-relief		[Exhib RA, London, 475]; untraced		*Graves* III, 1905–6, 123; *Irwin* 1979, 10
332.	1781	Ferdinand I, King of the Two Sicilies, portrait-medallion		Untraced Other versions: reproduced by Wedgwood		*Irwin* 1979, 20
333.	1782	Blind man's buff Payment(s): £11 0s 6d (?)	w	Wedgwood Museum, Barlaston, Staffs Other versions: reproduced by Wedgwood		*Bindman* 1979, 48, 55 (repr)
334.	*c*1782	George, Prince of Wales, portrait-medallion		Untraced Other versions: reproduced by Wedgwood		*Irwin* 1979, 20
335.	1782	Hermann Boerhaave, portrait-medallion		Untraced Other versions: reproduced by Wedgwood		*Bindman* 1979, 58 (Wedgwood repr)
336.	1782	Paul I of Russia, portrait-medallion		Untraced Other versions: reproduced by Wedgwood		*Irwin* 1979, 20
337.	1782	Psyche bound and attacked by Cupid		Untraced Other versions: reproduced by Wedgwood		*Gunnis* 1968, 147
338.	1782	Sacrifice to Cupid		Untraced Other versions: reproduced by Wedgwood		*Gunnis* 1968, 147
339.	1783	Charles James Fox, portrait-medallion		Untraced Other versions: reproduced by Wedgwood (reproduction in Wedgwood Museum, Barlaston, Staffs)		*Bindman* 1979, 65 (Wedgwood repr); *Gunnis* 1968, 147
340.	1783	Dr William Buchan, portrait-medallion Payment(s): £2 2s		Untraced Other versions: reproduced by Wedgwood (reproductions in Wedgwood Museum, Barlaston, Staffs)		*Bindman* 1979, 57, 58 (Wedgwood repr)
341.	1783	Sir William Herschel, portrait-medallion		Bath Art Gallery, Somerset		*Gunnis* 1968, 149
342.	1784	Bas-relief of Veturia and Volumnia entreating Coriolanus Payment(s): £9 9s	w	Untraced		*Bindman* 1979, 57, 59 (bronze repr)
343.	1784	Charles, 1st Earl Liverpool, portrait-medallion Payment(s): £2 2s		Untraced Other versions: reproduced by Wedgwood (reproduction in Wedgwood Museum, Barlaston, Staffs)		*Bindman* 1979, 57, 59 (Wedgwood repr)
344.	1784	Dr Samuel Johnson Payment(s): £2 2s	w	Untraced Other versions: reproduced by Wedgwood (reproduction in Wedgwood Museum, Barlaston, Staffs)		*Bindman* 1979, 57, 58 (Wedgwood repr)
345.	1784	Sarah Siddons, portrait-medallion Payment(s): £1 11s 6d		Untraced Other versions: Reproductions by Wedgwood		*Bindman* 1979, 57 (Wedgwood repr)
346.	1785	Gustavus III, King of Sweden, portrait-medallion Payment(s): £2 2s		Untraced Other versions: reproduced by Wedgwood		*Bindman* 1979, 60

No.	Date	Subject		Location	Bibliography
347.	1785	Hercules in the garden of the Hesperides Payment(s): £23		Untraced Other versions: reproduced by Wedgwood	*Bindman* 1979, 61 (Wedgwood repr)
348.	c1785	The apotheosis of Virgil		Untraced Other versions: reproduced by Wedgwood (reproduction VAM)	*Bindman* 1979, 62 (Wedgwood repr)
349.	1785	Warren Hastings, portrait-medallion Payment(s): £3 3s		Untraced Other versions: reproduced by Wedgwood (reproduction VAM)	*Bindman* 1979, 57, 58 (Wedgwood repr)
350.	1785	William Franklin, portrait-medallion		Untraced Other versions: reproduced by Wedgwood (reproduction in BM)	*Gunnis* 1968, 147; *Bindman* 1979, 59 (Wedgwood repr)
351.	1787	Maria I of Portugal, portrait-medallion Payment(s): 3 gns	w	Untraced Other versions: reproduced by Wedgwood	*Bindman* 1979, 63 (Wedgwood repr)
352.	1787	Mercury uniting the hands of Britain and France Payment(s): 13 gns Drawing(s): pen and wash, coll Christopher Lennox-Boyd	w	Wedgwood Museum, Barlaston, Staffs Other versions: reproduced by Wedgwood	*Bindman* 1979, 48, 64 (repr)
353.	1787	Peace preventing Mars from opening the gates of the Temple of Janus Payment(s): 15 gns	w	Wedgwood Museum, Barlaston, Staffs Other versions: reproduced by Wedgwood	*Bindman* 1979, 48, 63 (repr)
354.	1790	Hercules delivering Alcestis from Orcus		[for Edward Knight?]; untraced	*Hendricks* 1984, 622; *Ingamells* 1997, 363
355.	1787–1794	Self-portrait with Mrs Flaxman Model(s): plaster, SJSM		Untraced Other versions: reproduced by Wedgwood	*Bindman* 1979, 64 (Wedgwood repr)
356.	1795	'Two Tygers,' bas relief, model Payment(s): 3 gns		[for 'Mr Mott, Plaisterer. Little Titchfield Street']; untraced	Flaxman Account Book 1794–1810, 54
357.	1797	Sketches from the New Testament, bas-reliefs		[Exhib RA, London, 1106–8]; untraced	*Graves* III, 1905–6, 123
358.	1800	Design and model for a medal commemorating Lord St Vincent's approbation of the officers' and men's conduct on board the Ville de Paris		Untraced	Flaxman Account Book 1794–1810, 70; *Bindman* 1979, 136, 138 (medal repr)
359.	1802	Bacchanalian subject from the Borghese vase, bas-relief Payment(s): £157 10s Model(s): t-c, 1788, £35, untraced; plaster, SJSM	m	[for Edward Knight Wolverley House, Worcs (sold 1945, appendix 2, lot 512)]; untraced	Flaxman Account Book 1794–1810, 74; *Irwin* 1979, 54, 224 n1; *Hendricks* 1984, 620–2, 625 (plaster repr)
360.	1803	Models for face and reverse of a coin commemorating Francis, 5th Duke of Bedford		Untraced	Flaxman Account Book 1794–1810, 80
361.	1805	Mercury and Minerva, models for a Society of Arts prize medal Drawing(s): ?Christie's, 10 April 1862	w	Untraced	*Bindman* 1979, 136, 138 (repr medal)
362.	1805	Mercury conveying Pandora to Epimethus	p	Glyptotek, Copenhagen Other versions: Royal Coll, RCIN 41874, plaster oval UCL, plaster, 1057 SJSM SC46, sketch model	*Gunnis* 1968, 149; *Gunnis and Whinney* 1967, 25 (repr 5a); *Bindman* 1979, 108 (repr); *Irwin* 1979, 170–1 (plaster repr)
363.	1807	Medal depicting busts of Athena and Mercury		[Soc of A, first gold medal for the design of the Society's new medal]; Soc of A	RSA *Transactions*, vol 25, 1807, p a2, 19 (frontispiece repr)
364.	pre-1809	The cup of Theocritus Drawing(s): VAM	p	SJSM, BR26	Soane Museum Inventory; *Bindman* 1979, 150 (drawing repr); *Irwin* 1979, 192–4
365.	c1826	Adam and Eve in paradise	p	SJSM, M 959	Soane Museum Inventory
366.	c1826	Adoration of the Magi Drawing(s): BM, pen and wash Model(s): Plaster, SJSM MRR 10; Formerly UCL, University of Virginia	m	Private coll	*Bindman* 1979, 123 (drawing repr); Soane Museum Inventory
367.	c1826	'The Flight of Satan from Paradise,' from Milton, *Paradise Lost*, IV, 977-1015 (apparently unexecuted commission for Francis, 5th Duke of Bedford) Payment(s): Projected cost of the marble version £500	p	UCL, 1074, 1108 (sketch model); SJSM M 965 Other versions: Private Coll, Sweden, marble, perhaps completed by workshop after Flaxman's death	Flaxman Account Book 1809–26, 68; *Gunnis and Whinney* 1967, 14, 54 (repr 5b); *Irwin* 1979, 106, 172, 230 n5 (repr); Soane Museum Inventory; *Sandstrom* 1989, 631–3
368.	c1826	The golden age (for a vase for Rundell, Bridge and Rundell)	p	SJSM, SC45	Soane Museum Inventory
369.	nd	Count and Countess Meerman		Untraced Other versions: reproduced by Wedgwood	*Bindman* 1979, 48
370.	nd	Cupid and Psyche	p	UCL, 1001	*Gunnis and Whinney* 1967, 50
371.	nd	J C Smith		Untraced Other versions: reproduced by Wedgwood	*Bindman* 1979, 48

372.	nd	Joseph's Dream	p	SJSM, MRR 13	Soane Museum Inventory
373.	nd	Mrs Flaxman, the sculptor's mother, medallion	p	SJSM, SC 26	Soane Museum Inventory
374.	nd	Mrs Matthews, medallion	w	Untraced	RG/JP, 4, 510
375.	nd	The silver age	p	SJSM, SC47	Soane Museum Inventory
Miscellaneous					
376.	1767	Model in clay		[Soc of A, silver palette gilt]; untraced	RSA, *Minutes*, 1766–67, seq 3 fols 23, 26
377.	1768	Marquis of Granby, model	w	[Exhib Soc of Artists, London, 148]; untraced	*Graves* 1907, 93
378.	1769	Figure(s) modelled in clay		[Soc of A, silver palette gilt]; untraced	RSA, *Minutes*, 1767–68, seq 3 fol 27–8; RA Premium list 1768, 14
379.	1769	Neptune, model	w	[RA silver medal]; untraced	RA Premium list; *Graves* III, 1905–6, 123; *Bindman* 1979, 22
380.	1770	'Portrait of a gentleman', a model		[Exhib RA, London, 80]; untraced	*Graves* III, 1905–6, 123
381.	1770	'Portrait of a gentleman', model	w	[Exhib RA, London, 81]; untraced	*Graves* III, 1905–6, 123
382.	1771	Four portraits, models	w	[Exhib RA, London, 70]; untraced	*Graves* III, 1905–6, 123
383.	1775	Portrait	w	[Exhib RA, London, 119]; untraced	*Graves* III, 1905–6, 123
384.	1777	Agrippina after the death of Germanicus, model	tc	[Exhib RA, London, 123]; untraced	*Graves* III, 1905–6, 123
385.	1777	Pompey after his defeat at Pharsalia, model	tc	[Exhib RA, London, 122]; untraced	*Graves* III, 1905–6, 123; *Irwin* 1979, 10
386.	1777	'Portrait of a lady'	w	[Exhib RA, London, 124]; untraced	*Graves* III, 1905–6, 123
387.	1778	Hercules tearing his hair, after having put off the poisoned shirt given him by Deianeira, model	tc	[Exhib RA, London, 108]; untraced	*Graves* III, 1905–6, 123
388.	1778	Portrait	w	[Exhib RA, London, 109]; untraced	*Graves* III, 1905–6, 123
389.	1779	Portrait	tc	[Exhib RA, London, 91]; untraced	*Graves* III, 1905–6, 123
390.	1780	Unidentified work		[for Sir John Dick, Mount Clare, Roehampton]; untraced	*Riches* 1984, 259
391.	1781	Portrait	w	[Exhib RA, London, 272]; untraced	*Graves* III, 1905–6, 123
392.	1783	Chess pieces, models Payment(s): £1 5s for the Fool Drawing(s): Pen and wash, signed, Wedgwood Museum, Barlaston, Staffs, paid £6 6s	w	Wedgwood Museum, Barlaston, Staffs (King, Queen) Other versions: reproduced by Wedgwood and cast in silver by Rundell, Bridge and Rundell	*Bindman* 1979, 31, 48, 60–1 (model, Wedgwood copy and drawing repr); *Irwin* 1979, 26–7 (model repr)
393.	1783	Duchess of Devonshire		Untraced Other versions: reproduced by Wedgwood	*Gunnis* 1968, 147
394.	1783	Sir William Herschel Payment(s): £2 2s		Untraced Other versions: reproduced by Wedgwood	*Gunnis* 1968, 147; *Bindman* 1979, 57
395.	1784	Captain James Cook, portrait-medallion Payment(s): £2 2s	w	Untraced Other versions: reproduced by Wedgwood	*Bindman* 1979, 54, 57 (Wedgwood repr)
396.	1783–1784	Flora Payment(s): £70		[for Edward Knight]; untraced	*Hendricks* 1984, 625
397.	1784	Sir Joshua Reynolds		Untraced Other versions: reproduced by Wedgwood	*Gunnis* 1968, 147
398.	1784–1785	Piping Faun Payment(s): £70		[for Edward Knight]; untraced	*Hendricks* 1984, 625
399.	1800	St George and the Dragon Payment(s): £21	w	[for John, 1st Marquess Camden]; untraced	Flaxman Account Book 1794–1810, 66
400.	1803	'A tablet of marble & inscription to Mr Franklin' Payment(s): £12 7s 4d, packing case 13s 2d		['delivered to Mr Duff, 15 Finsbury Square']; untraced	Flaxman Account Book 1794–1810, 66
401.	1806	Victory Payment(s): £72 including model and installation		[for Thomas Hope, 2 Hanover Square, London]; untraced	Flaxman Account Book 1794–1810, 89
402.	1815	Restorations to a female figure in alto-relievo, a bust of Euripides, two medallions of Demosthenes and Homer Payment(s): £20 and £8 8s		[for Hon Frederick North, St James's Place]; untraced	Flaxman Account Book 1809–26, 82
403.	1818	The Shield of Achilles, model (for Rundell, Bridges and Rundell and cast in bronze) Payment(s): £600 Drawing(s): BM PDL; Christopher Powney Esq	p	SJSM (finished bronze in Ashmolean)	Flaxman Account Book 1809–26, 93; *Bindman* 1979, 30–1, 141, 145–7, 150 (shield and drawing repr); *Irwin* 1979, 194–202; *Dorey* 2004, 65
404.	1822	Sleeping child	m	[Exhib RA, London, 1024]; untraced	*Graves* III, 1905–6, 124; *Bindman* 1979, 24
405.	nd	Ganymede feeding the eagle	w	Untraced	RG/JP, 4, 510
406.	nd	'model of Dr Harriet Matthew'		Untraced	RG/JP, 4, 510
407.	nd	Sir John Soane's crest		Untraced	RG/JP, 4, 510

FLAXMAN, Mary Ann 1768–1833

A painter and wax modeller, she was born on 6 July 1768, the daughter of **John Flaxman I** and his second wife, Elizabeth Gordon and was christened at St Martin-in-the-Fields, London on 31 July. Her half-brothers were **John Flaxman RA** and **William Flaxman**.

She first exhibited at the Royal Academy in 1786, showing a work entitled *Turkish ladies* that is unlikely to have been three-dimensional, and in 1790 she exhibited a portrait in wax, the same year as her brother William (1). At this time she was living with her father at 420 Strand, where she had probably learnt to draw and model. She became governess to the children of Georgina Hare-Naylor, who had commissioned John Flaxman RA's designs for Homer's *Odyssey* and *Illiad* in the 1790s. Mary Ann shared her employer's passion for book illustration: many of the drawings which she exhibited at the Royal Academy between 1787 and 1819 are scenes from literature. She also exhibited drawings and portraits at the Society of Artists in 1790 and at the British Institution in 1811.

Mary Ann was the principal beneficiary in her father's will of 1803. In 1807 she was living with her half-brother John in Buckingham Street, London, but by 1817 she had moved to 19 Castle Street, Falcon Square. After 1820 she again lived with her half-brother, and she and her kinswoman, **Maria Denman**, cared for him after the death of his wife. There are regular payments to 'sister Mary' in John's accounts. When he died in 1826 his estate, valued at £3,314 4s 8d, was left jointly to Mary Ann and Maria Denman. Mary Ann played an important role in ensuring that her half-brother's *Lectures* were published after his death. She died at Norton Street, Fitzroy Square, on 17 April 1833, leaving an estate valued at only £43 15s 4d.

Literary References: *Graves* 1875, 191; *DNB*; *Graves* II, 1905–6, 125; *Graves* 1907, 93; *Pyke* 1973, 49; *Irwin* 1979, 4, 204, 232 n3

Archival References: IGI; Flaxman Papers, BL Add MS 39791, f121, 167, 196

Wills: John Flaxman I, 9 April 1803, PROB 11/1390, 225–6; John Flaxman RA, 17 January 1827, PROB 11/1720, 129

Miscellaneous

1.	1789	Portrait of unknown subject	w	[Exhib RA, London, 580]; untraced		*Graves* III, 1905–6, 125

FLAXMAN, William before 1755–after 1803

A wax modeller and wood carver, he was the son of **John Flaxman I** and the elder brother of **John Flaxman RA.** His date and place of birth are unknown. Flaxman exhibited at the Free Society of Artists in 1768 from his father's address in New Street, Covent Garden (6). In 1781, when he began exhibiting at the Royal Academy (7), he was living and possibly working at the premises of a Mr Harris of New Bolton Street in Long Acre, a district with many plaster shops. Flaxman went on to exhibit a cast work at the Royal Academy (8), but he appears also to have learnt how to carve. In 1781 he was paid for a carving in an unspecified medium for Wolverley House, Worcs, where he worked with his father and brother (5). **Allan Cunningham**, who garnered his information on the family principally from **Maria Denman** and **Mary Ann Flaxman** described William as a carver in wood, although none of his works in this medium has been identified. His only surviving piece, a wax bust of the actor Joseph George Holman, is a competent exercise (3). Flaxman changed address several times in London. In 1785 he lived at 9 Duke's Court, St Martin's Lane, in 1788 at 22 New Street, Covent Garden and in 1793 at 30 Grafton Street, Soho. The *DNB* suggests that he died in 1795, but he was still alive in 1803, when he inherited his father's rings and 'wearing apparel.' He had two daughters.

Literary References: *Cunningham* 1829–33, vol 3, 274; *DNB*; *Graves* II, 1905–6, 125; *Graves* 1907, 93; *Gunnis* 1968, 151–2; *Pyke* 1973, 49

Will: John Flaxman I, April 1803, PROB 11/1390, 225–6

Busts						
1.	1786	'Portrait of a gentleman'	w	[Exhib RA, London, 374]; untraced		*Graves* III, 1905–6, 125
2.	1787	'Portrait of a gentleman', model	w	[Exhib RA, London, 635]; untraced		*Graves* III, 1905–6, 125
3.	1793	Joseph George Holman	w	[Exhib RA, London, 410]; VAM 1118-1869	S	*Graves* III, 1905–6, 125; *Pyke* 1973, 49 (repr 99)
4.	1793	'Portrait of a gentleman', model	w	[Exhib RA, London, 125]; untraced		*Graves* III, 1905–6, 125
Architectural Sculpture						
5.	1781	'Carving' Payment(s): £84 9s		[Wolverley House, Worcs]; untraced		*Hendricks* 1984, 625
Reliefs						
6.	1768	Venus, a bas-relief		[Exhib Free Soc, London, 98]; untraced		*Graves* 1907, 93
Miscellaneous						
7.	1781	John Flaxman RA	w	[Exhib RA, London, 275]; untraced		*Graves* III, 1905–6, 125
8.	1793	'A cast from a model'		[Exhib RA, London, 802]; untraced		*Graves* III, 1905–6, 125

FLETCHER, Angus 1799–1862

Fletcher was born in Edinburgh, where he began to study law, later abandoned in favour of sculpture. In 1825 he entered the Royal Academy Schools on the recommendation of **Sir Francis Chantrey**. His address at this time was 32 Great Queen Street, Lincoln's Inn Fields (RA Admissions). He exhibited at the Carlisle Academy (1830), the Academy of the Liverpool Royal Institution (1830 and 1832) and the RA (1831–1839) from addresses in Edinburgh and London. Gunnis notes that Fletcher was a great friend of Charles Dickens, who used to call him 'Mr Kindheart'.

Literary References: *Gunnis* 1968, 152

Funerary Monuments						
1.	1832	Dr Chrystal		Glasgow Necropolis		*Woodward* 1977, vol 1, pt 2, 70
Busts						
2.	c1829	Felicia Hemans	m	NPG, London 5198	S	*Gunnis* 1968, 152; *Woodward* 1977, vol 1, pt 2, 70; *Morris and Roberts* 1998, 236
3.	1830	A child	m	[Exhib ALRI, Liverpool, 275]; untraced		*Morris and Roberts* 1998, 236
4.	1830	Daughter of Captain Basil Hall RN		[Exhib ALRI, Liverpool, 1830]; untraced		*Morris and Roberts* 1998, 236
5.	1830	George William, 6th Duke of Argyll		[Exhib Carlisle Acad of Fine Art, 252]; untraced		*Graves* III, 1905–6, 126; RG/JP, 4, 523; *Morris and Roberts* 1998, 236
6.	1834	J S B Morritt	m	[Exhib RA, London, 1086]; untraced		*Graves* III, 1905–6, 126
7.	1834	Miss Stewart McKenzie		[Exhib RA, London, 1052]; untraced		*Graves* III, 1905–6, 126
8.	1834	Mrs Lawrence of Studley	m	Ripon Town Hall, W R Yorks		*Graves* III, 1905–6, 126; *Gunnis* 1968, 152; *Woodward* 1977, vol 1, pt 2, 70

9.	1834	Son of Sir James Riddell Bt	m	[Exhib RA, London, 1053]; untraced		*Graves* III, 1905–6, 126
10.	1839	Charles Dickens	m	Dickens' House, London		*Graves* III, 1905–6, 126; *Ormond* 1973, 143
Reliefs						
11.	1839	Edmund Kean	m	St Mary Magdalene, Richmond, Surrey		*Woodward* 1977, vol 1, pt 2, 70

FLETCHER, Joshua I –1725

The son of William Fletcher, a brewer of St Margaret, Westminster, Fletcher was apprenticed to Robert Bushnell on 16 July 1691 and became free of the Masons' Company on 20 April 1699. The Masons' Company records reveal that he was living at Woodstock by 1708 and was still there in 1714. He was elected upper warden of the Company in June 1724. With **Christopher Cass I**, he was one of the principal masons at Blenheim Palace from 1716. He also worked with Cass at Burlington House, London, 1719–22 (Chatsworth, Burl Misc Box 3, Earl of Burlington's payments, 1719–22, 2, 22). In 1721–25 he was master mason at St George's, Hanover Square. After his death in 1725 the payments for 1725/6 were made to his administrators (Accounts for Building the New Churches, Lambeth Palace Library).

Literary References: *Gunnis* 1968, 152; *Webb* 1999, 13

Archival References: Masons' Co, Freemen, fol 20; List of Company Members, 1708, p 9; Quarterage Book (3), 1714, p 9; Court Book, 1722–51, 15 June 1724; GPC

Will: PROB 11/602

Chimneypieces						
1.	1725	Description unavailable Payment(s): £55 5s		[for Sir John Chester, Chicheley Hall, Bucks]; untraced		GPC

FLETCHER, Joshua II –1749

The son of **Joshua Fletcher I**, he was apprenticed to his father on 2 August 1723 and admitted to the Masons' Company in August 1730. He leased a site in Grosvenor Square for development around 1728 (Glyn, Mills & Co Archives, in GPC), acquired another site, in Berkeley Square in 1736 (Westminster Public Library, Deeds 10/16) and became a director of the Westminster Fire Office in 1740. At this time his address was Audley Street, Grosvenor Square (Masons' Co, *Assistants*, c1840, fol 1). The Westminster Poll Book for 1748 shows that he had moved to Mount Street and described him as a 'statuary' (*Gunnis* 1968, 152). Entries in the Masons' Company Court Book indicate that he died some time between October 1749 and June 1750. He may have been related to a Mr Fletcher, 'mason', who was paid £700 by Sir Matthew Featherstonehaugh in 1759 for work on his London house in Whitehall, later known as Melbourne House (Uppark Archives, in GPC).

Literary References: *Gunnis* 1968, 152; *Webb* 1999, 13

Archival References: Masons' Co, Freemen, fol 20, 7 August 1730; Court Book 1722–51, 30 October 1749, 14 June 1750; WFO, MB, 343/6, 16 Oct 1740; GPC

Chimneypieces						
1.	1748	Four, of dove, Egyptian, purple and veined marbles		[Blair Castle, Perths]; untraced		Archives, Duke of Atholl in GPC

FLETCHER, Z, of Stockton fl 1818–19?

Gunnis notes that his tablets have 'nicely carved details'.

Literary References: *Gunnis* 1968, 152

Funerary Monuments						
1.	?1818	Frances Brewster		Greatham, Durham	S	*Gunnis* 1968, 152
2.	?1819	Alice Barras		Norton, Durham	S	*Gunnis* 1968, 152

FLETCHERBY fl *c*1724

Chimneypieces						
1.	*c*1724	Description unavailable	m	Chicheley Hall, Bucks, entrance hall		Pevsner, *Bucks*, 1994, 247

FLIN, John fl 1763

Funerary Monuments						
1.	1763	Timothy Lucas		Killone Convent, Co Galway	S	*Strickland* I, 1913, 355

FLINTOFT, John, of York fl 1815–42

Flintoft worked in partnership with **Thomas Bennett** until about 1820. He is described as 'sculptor' in the York Directory for 1841.

Literary References: *Gunnis* 1968, 152

Archival References: GPC

Funerary Monuments						
1.	?1815	Mary Fothergill (co-sculptor: Bennett)		Pickering, N R Yorks	S	
2.	†1820	John Dawker (†1816) and wife (co-sculptor: Bennett)		Salton, N R Yorks	S	Pevsner, *Yorks: N R*, 1966, 317
3.	†1821	Unidentified subject		Kirby Hill, N R Yorks		Pevsner, *Yorks: N R*, 1966, 209
4.	†1825	Unidentified subject		Lastingham, N R Yorks	S	Pevsner, *Yorks: N R*, 1966, 226
5.	†1826	Unidentified subject		Middleton, N R Yorks		Pevsner, *Yorks: N R*, 1966, 254
6.	?1828	John Eadon		Snaith, W R Yorks	S	*Gunnis* 1968, 152
7.	?1829	Mr Richardson		St Michael-le-Belfrey, York	S	*Gunnis* 1968, 152
8.	†1842	Baldwin Wake		St Michael-le-Belfrey, York	S	Pevsner, *Yorks: E R & York*, 1995, 173

FLORY, James fl 1663–80

Flory received payments for work on the restoration of Guildhall in 1666 and 1673, when a warrant for £296 was issued for 'all worke at Guildhall hall' and other locations (City Lands Rough Minutes 03/001). He was paid for mason's work at Billingsgate Dock in November 1669 (Guildhall MSS 184/4, p23r). He was employed as a mason at

St Dunstan-in-the-East in 1671 and was paid £12 'in full of all accounts for his putting up St Dunstan in the East End of the Church' in 1671 (*Wren Soc* XIX, 18). He was described as of 'St Catherine Creechurch, Lond Mason, Widr. abt. 36' when he married 'Alice Williams of Wanstead. Essex, Wid. abt. 30' in February 1667/8 (*Armytage* 1892, vol 33, 1660–1668, 231). Flory served as mason to the Bakers' Company from 1672 until his death and in 1676 he was paid £50 for paving in marble the chapel of Emmanuel College, Cambridge (*Willis and Clark* 1886, cited by *Gunnis* 1968, 152). In 1680 he carved decorative details at St Michael Bassishaw (1). The payment for this work was made to his widow, so he must have died in 1680 or shortly afterwards. Mrs Flory also received payment for her husband's work at St Michael, Greenhithe (2) (Bodleian, Rawlinson MSS 387, cited by *Gunnis* 1968, 152).

Literary References: *Gunnis* 1968, 152

Architectural Sculpture

1.	1680	Decorative details, including cherubim-heads at the east end	St Michael Bassishaw, London	*Gunnis* 1968, 152; *Wren Soc* XIX, 42
2.	nd	'ten windows with ornaments' Payment(s): £110	St Michael, Greenhithe, London	*Gunnis* 1968, 152

FLOWER fl 1838?

Probably a local mason, he signs a monument at Long Sutton, Lincs.

Literary References: GPC

Funerary Monuments

1.	?1838	Mary Delamore	Long Sutton, Lincs	S	GPC

FLOWER (or FOWER), Henry fl 1809–12

He built a bridge over the river Churnet for Earl Talbot in 1809 and was paid £1,376 in 1812 as the master mason responsible for building part of Alton Abbey, Staffs (Archives, Earl of Shrewsbury in GPC).

Architectural Sculpture

1.	1812	Gothic columns, capitals and other carving	[Alton Abbey, Staffs (Alton Towers)]; destroyed	GPC

FLOWERS, of York fl 1826–27

Funerary Monuments

1.	1826–1827	Benjamin (†1792) and Mary (†1826) Dodsworth	Bossall, N R Yorks	S

FOGGINI, Giovanni Battista 1652–1725

Foggini was the leading Florentine sculptor of the late baroque period. He received a significant British commission in 1714 when the Commissioners for Building 50 New Churches entrusted him with making a bronze statue of Queen Anne for £340 (1). After discussing a number of possible sites the Commissioners decided that the statue should be placed at the top of a 200-foot column to be erected, from designs by James Gibbs, to the west of the new church of St Mary-le-Strand. This scheme was abandoned when the Queen died on 1 August 1714. In spite of this setback, Foggini continued to work on the statue while a number of alternative locations were investigated. Between them, John Talman, who was acting as the commissioners' representative in Italy, and Foggini came up with several designs for a monument with supporting allegorical figures for Lincoln's Inn Fields and on 4 May 1715 Talman wrote to inform the Commissioners that anticipating the adoption of this scheme, he had asked the sculptor to increase the size of the statue from 7 feet to 10 feet in height and introduce 'many rare ornaments' (Lambeth Palace Library MS 2716, cited by *Friedman* 1976 (2), 48–9). The commissioners decided not to commission the proposed allegorical figures and architectural surround but agreed to pay the increased price of £800 for the larger, more elaborate statue. By 24 May the statue was nearly, if not completely, finished and Talman was able to view it in its entirety in Foggini's studio. He enthusiastically reported that it will be 'y finest figure in Europe' (*ibid*, 49). However, due to political changes in Britain, the idea of erecting the statue was dropped, it was left on the sculptor's hands and has been lost.

Foggini's son, Vincenzo Foggini, carved a statue of *Samson and the Philistines*, which was acquired by the Marquess of Rockingham for Wentworth Woodhouse (VAM). The statue is signed and dated 1749, the same year that Rockingham sent his son to Italy to acquire sculpture. It may not have been made specifically for him since there is no record of its commission, and it is suggested that the roughed out block was in Giambologna's studio when it was taken over by Pietro Tacca in 1608, and that it was subsequently worked on by both G B and Vincenzo Foggini.

Literary References: *Friedman* 1976 (2), 39–56; *Treasure Houses* 1985, 291–2

Statues

1.	1715	Queen Anne	b	[for the Commissioners for Building Fifty New Churches]; untraced	*Friedman* 1976 (2), 39–56

Busts

2.	1718	Duke Cosimo III	m	[Commissioned by the Duke of Gordon]; VAM	*Pearson* 1991, 45, 46 (repr)

FOLEY, Edward Arlington 1814–74

The elder brother of **John Henry Foley**, he was born in Montgomery Street, Dublin. As a boy he showed a talent for modelling and received some instruction from his step-grandfather, **Benjamin Schrowder**. His formal training began in 1826, when he joined the Royal Dublin Society's schools and the following year he was apprenticed to **John Smyth**, a neighbour in Montgomery Street. His master was unable to provide him with work and before completing his indentures Foley went to London in search of employment. He had little success at first, but his fortunes improved after he carved a coat of arms (41) which so impressed **William Behnes** that he was immediately engaged as a studio assistant on a wage of £4 a week.

As 'an expert carver and an artist of some talent' Foley soon established himself as a sculptor specialising in portrait busts (*Strickland* I, 1913, 356). He exhibited at the Royal Academy between 1834 and 1873 and at the Liverpool Society of Fine Arts in 1859. In 1844 he showed *Canute reproving his courtiers* at the Westminster Hall Exhibition (1). This work won the approval of the *Literary Gazette* which praised the 'sarcastic dignity and appropriate action' of the seated figure (*Lit Gaz* 1844, 482). Another commentator thought it promising, but hastily executed (*AU*, 1844, 216). In 1860 half-size copies of Foley's bust of Rev David Laing (**23**), which the *Art Journal* felt suitable 'for a boudoir or drawing-room ornament' and perhaps of interest to 'friends and parishioners of the deceased clergymen', were produced by Overhead of Haverstock Hill (*AJ*, 1860, 319).

Foley drowned himself on 10 May, 1874 in the Regent's Canal. Although he called out for help he could not be reached in time to be saved. At the inquest into his death the coroner heard that the sculptor, who had been ill for a year, believed that he would never recover his health and he also had financial problems.

Literary References: *The Times*, 12 May 1874, 12; *Strickland* I, 1913, 356–7; *Gunnis* 1968, 152–3

No.	Date	Subject	Medium	Location		References
Statues						
1.	1844	Canute reproving his courtiers (perhaps by John Henry Foley)		[Exhib Westminster Hall, London, 145]; untraced		*AU*, 1844, 216; *Gunnis* 1968, 152
Busts						
2.	1834	Unidentified young lady		[Exhib RA, London, 1112]; untraced		*Graves* III, 1905–6, 130
3.	1835	Daughter of Professor Davis		[Exhib Soc of BA, London, 780]; untraced		*Johnson* 1975, 162
4.	1835	Samuel Lover's eldest daughter		[Exhib RA, London, 1104]; untraced		*Graves* III, 1905–6, 130; *Ormond* 1973, 275
5.	1836	Unidentified young man		[Exhib RA, London, 1077]; untraced		*Graves* III, 1905–6, 130
6.	1839	Samuel Lover	m	[coll Samuel Lover]; NPG, London	SD	*Graves* III, 1905–6, 130; *Ormond* 1973, 275 (pl 545)
7.	1840	Henry Morton Dyer's daughter		[Exhib RA, London, 1085]; untraced		*Graves* III, 1905–6, 130
8.	1842	Mrs Edward Tyrrell	m	[Exhib RA, London, 1385]; untraced		*AU*, 1842, 129; *Graves* III, 1905–6, 130
9.	1845	Edward Tyrrell	m	[Exhib RA, London, 1412]; untraced		*Graves* III, 1905–6, 130
10.	1845	Frank, eldest son of Richard Harris		[Exhib RA, London, 1377]; untraced		*Graves* III, 1905–6, 130
11.	1845	Mrs Warner		[Exhib RA, London, 1369]; untraced		*Graves* III, 1905–6, 130
12.	1849	Avery, son of Edward Tyrrell	m	[Exhib RA, London, 1316]; untraced		*Graves* III, 1905–6, 130
13.	1850	Robert William Warren		[Exhib RA, London, 1373]; untraced		*Graves* III, 1905–6, 130
14.	1851	Eldest son of William Hampton		[Exhib RA, London, 1336]; untraced		*Graves* III, 1905–6, 131
15.	1851	John Wilson		[Exhib RA, London, 1319]; untraced		*Graves* III, 1905–6, 131
16.	1851	Professor Murphy		[Exhib RA, London, 1320]; untraced		*Graves* III, 1905–6, 131
17.	1853	Mrs Harriet L Irwin		[Exhib RA, London, 1425]; untraced		*Graves* III, 1905–6, 131
18.	1855	Helen of Troy		[Exhib RA, London, 1012]; untraced		*Graves* III, 1905–6, 131; *Strickland* I, 1913, 356
19.	1855	Miss Catherine Hayes		[Exhib RA, London, 1507]; untraced		*Graves* III, 1905–6, 131; *Strickland* I, 1913, 356
20.	1857	Unidentified gentleman		[Exhib RA, London, 1262]; untraced		*Graves* III, 1905–6, 131
21.	1859	Head of a child		[Exhib LSFA, Liverpool, 778]; untraced		*Morris and Roberts* 1998, 237
22.	1859	Unidentified sitter		[Exhib LSFA, Liverpool, 764]; untraced		*Morris and Roberts* 1998, 237
23.	1860	Rev David Laing		[Exhib RA, London, 990]; untraced Other versions: Numerous small copies produced by Overhead of Haverstock Hill		*AJ*, 1860, 319; *Graves* III, 1905–6, 131; *Gunnis* 1968, 152
24.	1861	Madame Catherine Hayes		[Exhib RA, London, 1021]; untraced		*Graves* III, 1905–6, 131; *Strickland* I, 1913, 356
25.	1862	Douglas Jerrold	m	[Exhib RA, London, 1125]; untraced		*Graves* III, 1905–6, 131
26.	1864	Unidentified gentleman		[Exhib RA, London, 1040]; untraced		*Graves* III, 1905–6, 131
27.	1869	The nymph Œnone		[Exhib RA, London, 1170]; untraced		*Graves* III, 1905–6, 131; *Strickland* I, 1913, 356
28.	1870	Penelope		[Exhib RA, London, 1105]; untraced		*Graves* III, 1905–6, 131; *Strickland* I, 1913, 356
29.	1873	Portrait of an unidentified girl	m	NGI	SD	*le Harivel* 1988, 562 (repr)
30.	1873	The Morning Star		[Exhib RA, London, 1470]; untraced		*Graves* III, 1905–6, 131; *Strickland* I, 1913, 356
Reliefs						
31.	1852	Mrs N W Chapman, medallion portrait		[Exhib RA, London, 1338]; untraced		*Graves* III, 1905–6, 131
Miscellaneous						
32.	1850	Laura Sophia Foley		[Exhib RA, London, 1401]; untraced		*Graves* III, 1905–6, 130
33.	1858	Stephen S Alford		[Exhib RA, London, 1292]; untraced		*Graves* III, 1905–6, 131
34.	1859	George Samuel		[Exhib RA, London, 1322]; untraced		*Graves* III, 1905–6, 131
35.	1859	Miss Mary Warburton Waters		[Exhib RA, London, 1339]; untraced		*Graves* III, 1905–6, 131
36.	1862	Miss Edith Crossley		[Exhib RA, London, 1040]; untraced		*Graves* III, 1905–6, 131
37.	1866	Thomas Davies		[Exhib RA, London, 984]; untraced		*Graves* III, 1905–6, 131
38.	1867	Mrs Arthur Otto Robertson		[Exhib RA, London, 1176]; untraced		*Graves* III, 1905–6, 131
39.	1871	Scene from 'Twelfth Night'		[Exhib RA, London, 1200]; untraced		*Graves* III, 1905–6, 131
40.	1872	Master Arthur Lennox		[Exhib RA, London, 1416]; untraced		*Graves* III, 1905–6, 131
41.	nd	Coat of Arms		Untraced		*Strickland* I, 1913, 356

FOLEY, John Henry RA 1818–1874

John Henry Foley has been called the most important sculptor in mid-Victorian Britain (*Grove* 11, 1996, 237). His sculpture was admired for its realism and technical excellence. It showed greater vigour and originality than that of contemporaries such as **John Bell**, **Matthew Noble** and **William Theed II** who favoured a blander, more conventional neoclassical style.

He was born in Dublin on 24 May 1818, the son of Jesse Foley, a grocer. The boy had little formal education, but there were sculptors in the family: his step-grandfather was **Benjamin Schrowder**, and his elder brother **Edward Arlington Foley**. John Henry began his studies at the art schools of the Royal Dublin Society in 1831, under **John Smyth**, and won several prizes in 1833.

He moved to London at his brother's suggestion in 1834 and began to attend the Royal Academy Schools in 1835. He also found employment in the studio of **William Behnes**. Foley first exhibited at the RA in 1839, showing two ideal works *Innocence* and *The death of Abel* (**24, 117**). The following year he submitted a full-size plaster group of *Ino and the infant Bacchus*, which attracted considerable attention (**25**). Samuel Carter Hall, the editor of the *Art Journal*, later recalled first meeting Foley at that time and described him as a serious, thoughtful and hardworking but physically delicate young man (*AJ*, 1874, 306).

In 1844 Foley exhibited several works including *Youth at a stream* at Westminster Hall (**28**). An unidentified critic writing for the *Art Union* considered it the most beautiful work on show, comparable in quality to the sculpture of antiquity. He particularly admired the finely modelled head and concluded 'had such a figure been dug up in Rome, or near Naples, somewhat mutilated, it would have been pronounced a valuable specimen of classic Art' (*AU*, 1844, 216). Success in this competition led to commissions for statues of two 17th-century Parliamentarians, John Hampden and John Selden, for the Palace of Westminster (**30, 35**) and these set the seal on Foley's reputation as a sculptor.

Meanwhile, Foley executed *Ino and the infant Bacchus* in marble for Francis, 1st Earl of Ellesmere, for the substantial sum of 750 guineas. Lord Charles Townshend had first expressed an interest in the work, but changed his mind and asked Foley to return his part-payment. A legal dispute ensued, but a compromise was reached whereby Foley agreed to execute a single figure for Townshend without charge. The marble group was completed by 1849, when it was engraved for the *Art Journal* (*AJ*, 1849, 30). Some puritanical subscribers objected to the engraving, fearing that this depiction of a semi-nude woman might endanger 'the minds of those who found there such perilous stimulants' (*AJ*, 1874, 306).

Foley's practice expanded healthily from the mid-1840s and by 1848 he had set up his own studio at 19 Osnaburgh Street, Euston. In 1849 he was elected an ARA and in 1858 a full Academician. During the early 1860s he also became a member of the Royal Hibernian Academy and the Belgian Academy of Arts. He was one of only 4 sculptors asked to submit designs for the initial, ill-fated competition for the Wellington Memorial in St Paul's Cathedral, London, and was interviewed by the RA commissioners for their report of 1863. Despite this recognition, Foley could be critical of official institutions. He signed an open letter with 21 other sculptors, objecting to the unfair way in which the Wellington competition was organised, he voiced concerns about the teaching and display of sculpture at the RA, and after 1861 he ceased to show there because he objected to the arrangement of his works in exhibition.

As an established sculptor, Foley concentrated on portrait statues, busts and monuments, for which there was always a ready market. His sensitive rendering of naturalistic detail in portrait sculpture, far superior to the bland, conventional style of many sculptors of the period, is particularly evident in Hampden's statue and in the bust of Catherine Prendergast (**77**). Contemporaries held his equestrian statues in high regard, especially the portraits of Henry, Viscount Hardinge and Sir James Outram, both cast in bronze and erected in Calcutta (**37, 64**). The Hardinge, which is arguably Foley's finest work, was displayed briefly in London before being shipped to India to rapturous acclaim. It was hailed as a masterpiece almost without parallel 'for grandeur of design, for truth of action and for power and beauty of execution' (*AJ*, 1859, 36). A group of fellow artists formed a committee in a vain attempt to raise enough money for a replica to be kept in Britain.

Foley continued to execute occasional 'ideal' works when the opportunity arose; his *Egeria* (**34**) and *Caractacus* (**38**), both English literary subjects, were commissioned for the Egyptian Hall at the Mansion House during the 1850s and *The elder brother from Comus* (**39**) was presented by the sculptor to the RA in 1860 as his diploma work. He also provided several designs for metalwork including a centrepiece, the Samuel Courtauld Testimonial, which had figures representing *Civil and religious liberty triumphant* and was illustrated in the *Art Journal* in 1856 (p 28). Another commission was the seal of the Confederate States of America, 1862 (*AJ*, 1865, 29; Museum of the Confederacy, Richmond, Virginia, USA). Several of his designs were reproduced commercially; *Youth at a stream*, 1844 (**28**) and *Caractacus*, 1859 (**39**) were published as bronze statuettes by the Art Union of London in 1846 and 1861 respectively, and *Innocence*, 1839 (**24**) was realised in parian ware by Copeland in 1847.

Foley won a number of significant commissions for statues of national heroes in his native Ireland during the 1860s, including the figures of Oliver Goldsmith, the man of letters (**42**) and his contemporary, Edmund Burke, the political writer (**53**), both erected at their university, Trinity College, Dublin. His most ambitious and enduringly famous work in Dublin is the national monument to Daniel O'Connell (**70**). It is a tripartite structure, with a statue 4 metres high, above a drum carved with images of 50 Irish patriots, who hasten towards Erin to hear the proclamation of their liberty. The pedestal has allegorical winged Victories at each corner representing *Patriotism*, *Courage*, *Eloquence* and *Fidelity*. The work took 17 years to complete and was finally erected in 1883, nearly a decade after Foley's death.

Foley's reputation remained high throughout his later years and was endorsed again towards the end of his life when he was invited to contribute to the most prestigious commission of the 1870s, the Albert Memorial in Kensington Gardens, London. He sculpted both the marble group representing *Asia* (**61**) and also the iconic, gilt bronze, central figure of the seated Prince Consort (**68**), a commission passed to him after **Carlo, Baron Marochetti**'s death. Foley was said to have contracted the pleurisy which eventually killed him, either by sitting on the wet clay limbs of the central figure of the *Asia* group whilst modelling her bust (*Atkinson* 1882, 34), or while arranging the full-scale model of Prince Albert on the podium on a cold, windy day (*AJ*, 1874, 306).

The sculptor might have been knighted if he had lived to see the unveiling of the Albert Memorial in 1876. He died 2 years too soon, at his comfortable London house, The Priory, Hampstead, on 27 August 1874, and was accorded the significant honour of burial in the crypt of St Paul's Cathedral. He left most of his property to the Artists' Benevolent Fund and his models to the Royal Dublin Society. It is not known how many models were originally in the RDS collection but in 1931 14 statues were recorded and now only 6 full-size statues, two busts and one statuette, survive. Several commissions were unfinished at his death, including the Prince Consort's statue for the Albert Memorial (**68**), the O'Connell Monument (**70**) and the equestrian figure of Viscount Gough (**63**). These were completed by Foley's principal assistant and most successful pupil, Thomas Brock. He had many other pupils, including **Charles Bell Birch**, **Francis John Williamson**, Albert Bruce-Joy, **Mary Grant**, **George Mossman** and **Samuel Ferris Lynn**.

Foley was a central figure in the mid-Victorian artistic establishment, but his naturalistic style also influenced a younger generation of sculptors. Edmund Gosse, in his essay, 'The New Sculpture', argues that Foley thought nothing of surface and was therefore especially antagonistic to the New Sculptors (*Gosse* 1894, 138). There is evidence however that in practice, some of them were indebted to Foley's work. Alfred Gilbert, the most famous of the school, saluted Foley's importance in a professorial lecture delivered in 1901, when he called Foley 'a great man whose work . . . he had never ceased to admire for his prowess and for its fixed steadfast purpose' (*Dorment* 1985, 211). After Foley's death, Brock assisted Frederic Leighton in the execution of his *Athlete wrestling with a python*, 1877, a defining work of the movement. The pensive pose of William Hamo Thornycroft's statue of General Gordon, 1888, on the Thames Embankment in London, another key work of the New Sculpture, was influenced by Foley's Sidney, Lord Herbert of Lea (51). During his lifetime and in the immediate aftermath, Foley's work drew wide admiration but like most Victorian sculptors, his reputation went into eclipse during the 20th century. After a period of neglect, his achievement and that of his contemporaries has attracted long overdue scholarly interest.

EH

Literary References: *AJ*, 1849, 30, 49; *AJ*, 1859, 36; *AJ*, 1874, 305–6; *Palgrave* 1866, *passim*; *Monkhouse* 1875; *Atkinson* 1882, 1–34; *Hall* 1883, 239–41; *DNB* XIX, 1889, 353–4; *Gosse* 1894, 138–42; *Strickland* 1913, 357–65; *Crookshank* 1966, 312; *Gunnis* 1968, 153–5; *Physick* 1969, 41–2, 191, 193; *Physick* 1970, 28–31; *Ormond* 1973, 175; *Potterton* 1973, 1–11; *Read* 1974, 262–71; *Potterton* 1975, 46; *Harbison, Potterton and Sheehy* 1978, *passim*; *Turpin* 1979 (1), 42–53; *Turpin* 1979 (2), 108–116; *Bayley* 1981, *passim*; *Read* 1982, *passim*; *Beattie* 1983, 1–2, 12, 13, 182; *Dorment* 1985, 211; *Avery and Marsh* 1985, 331–2; *Read* 1985, 64; *Blackwood* 1989, 187–7 (repr); *Murphy* 1995, 155–6; *Grove* 11, 1996, 237–9 (Stocker); *Murphy* 1996, 22–6; *Hill* 1998, *passim*; *Murphy* 1999, 64–73; *Sankey* 1999, 87–92; *ODNB* (Stocker)

Archival References: RA/GA 1835, 1849, 1858

Additional MS sources: *Biography Handbook Papers*, 1860, Add MSS 28510 fols 47, 48; *Layard Papers*, 1866–9, Add MSS 38993–6; *Sherborn Autographs*, 1866, Add MSS 42575 f.270; *Reading Room Papers*, 1850, Add. 48340 ff. 125, 126; *Layard Papers*, 1866–1869, Add MSS 38993 fols. 170, 261, 38994 fols 103, 116, 38995 fols 80, 156, 163, 198, 199, 258, 373, 377, 396, 38996 fols 303, 356

Wills and Administrations: PPR, will, 23 November 1875, folio no 870, effects under £14,000

Portraits of the Sculptor: woodcut after a painting by E Walker, *AJ*, 1849, 49 (repr); C J Birch, wax relief, NGI 8157; woodcut, after a photograph by J Watkins, NPG, ILN, XXX, 1857, 419 (repr); E Edwards, photograph, (L Reeve, *Men of Eminence*, I, 1863, fol 13, repr); W Egley, miniature, exhib RA, 1868, 778, untraced; Thomas Brock, bust, exhib RA, 1873, 1432, *AJ*, 1877, 360 (repr), untraced; woodcut, after a photograph by the London Stereoscopic Co, *ILN*, LXV, 1874, 249; Charles Bell Birch, medallion, plaster, *c*1876, NPG 1541, (*Ormond* 1973, 175, repr); canvas after a photograph, coll Miss Herrick (1891), sketched by G Scharf, 'TSB' (NPC Archives, XXXVI, 30); T Mogford, canvas, INPG, (*Mag of A*, 1901, 515, repr); James Gamble, statue, 1905, VAM façade

Funerary Monuments

1.	?1839	Catherine Prendergast	St Mary, Fort St George, Chennai (Madras), India		*Gunnis* 1968, 154
2.	†1848	Joseph Ablett	Ruthin, Denbighs	S	Pevsner, *Clwyd*, 1986, 275
3.	†1848	Lieutenant-General John Williams Morris	Kensal Green Cemetery, London		*Curl* 2001, 236
4.	†1851	Sir Francis Lawley	Hints, Staffs		Pevsner, *Staffs*, 1974, 148
5.	1852	Admiral Sir William Cornwallis (†1819), Captain John Whitby (†1806), Mary Anne Whitby (†1850) Model(s): exhib RA, London, 1849, 1202	Milford-on-Sea, Hants		*Monkhouse* 1875, 53–6 (repr); *Graves* III, 1905–6, 131; *Strickland* I, 1913, 361
6.	1854	Arthur, 1st Duke of Wellington (†1852), design only (monument by Alfred Stevens)	[Exhib RA, London, 1396]; untraced		*Graves* III, 1905–6, 131; *Physick* 1969, 41–2; *Physick* 1970, 28–31, 37; *Read* 1974, 266
7.	*c*1854	Hon James Stuart Model(s): exhib RA, London, 1854, 1397	Colombo, Sri Lanka		*ILN*, 13 May 1854, 437; *Graves* III, 1905–6, 131; *Strickland* I, 1913, 363
8.	1856	Helen Faucit (†1898) (co-sculptor: Hughes)	Llantysilio, Denbighs Other versions: Royal Shakespeare Company, Stratford-on-Avon		*Monkhouse* 1875, 45–8 (repr); *Graves* III, 1905–6, 132; *Carlisle* 2000, 269–71 (repr)
9.	1857	John Jones (†1854) Model(s): exhib RA, London, 1859, 1298	Guilsfied, Montgomery	S	*Monkhouse* 1875, 57–60 (repr); *Graves* III, 1905–6, 132; Pevsner, *Powys*, 1979, 107
10.	*c*1857	Richard Sheepshanks (†1855)	Trinity College, Cambridge, chapel		*Graves* III, 1905–6, 132; Pevsner, *Cambs*, 1970, 168
11.	†1857	Sir Henry Lawrence, medallion	St Paul's Cathedral, Kolkata (Calcutta)		*Ormond* 1973, 263
12.	†1861	Captain John McNeill Boyd RN	St Patrick's Cathedral, Dublin		www.nmm.ac.uk/memorials
13.	1861	John Whittaker (†1840)	[Queen's Road Chapel, Hurst, Lancs]; Tameside Council, Manchester (2002)		Pevsner, *Lancs: S.*, 1969, 126; *Read* 1982, 186; www.tameside.gov.uk/citizenjune/septoo/news8.htm
14.	1862	Brigadier-General John Nicholson (†1857)	Lisburn Cathedral, County Antrim, Ireland	S	*ILN*, 10 May 1862, 475; *Monkhouse* 1875, 49–52 (relief repr); *Graves* III, 1905–6, 132; *Ormond* 1973, 343; *Potterton* 1975, 46
15.	†1862	Charles John, 1st Earl Canning Model(s): plaster, 28 in high, RDS	Westminster Abbey, London, north transept		*MacMichael* 1977, 89; *Turpin* 1979 (2), 112; *Ormond and Rogers* 3, 1979–81, 34
16.	?1862	William Richie	St Paul's Cathedral, Kolkata (Calcutta)		RG/JP, 4, 533
17.	?1865	Godfrey Wentworth Bayard Bosville	Rudstone, E R Yorks		RG/JP, 4, 533

No.	Date	Subject		Location		Bibliography
18.	1866	General the Hon Robert Bruce		Dunfermline Abbey, Fife		*ILN*, 17 June 1865, 593; *AJ*, 1866, 156 (repr); *Monkhouse* 1875, 61–2 (repr)
19.	1866	James Ward (†1859)		Kensal Green Cemetery, London		*Read* 1974, 266–7 (repr); Pevsner, *London: N W*, 1991, 470; *Curl* 2001, 66, 196, 225, 236
20.	1872	Dr Cooke (portrait medallion for a monument by John Boyd)		May Street Presbyterian Church, Belfast		*Potterton* 1975, 46
21.	?1872	William Cobbett		Farnham, Surrey		RG/JP, 4, 533
22.	1874	William Rathbone (†1868)		Ullet Road Unitarian Church, Liverpool, Lancs	SD	Pevsner, *Lancs: S*, 1969, 238
23.	nd	Bryan Proctor (Barry Cornwall)		Untraced Other versions: NPG (bust)		*Strickland* I, 1913, 363
Statues						
24.	1839	Innocence		[Exhib RA, London, 1316]; untraced Other versions: Copeland Parian ware, 1847, Royal Coll, Osborne House, I of W, reduced size		*Graves* III, 1905–6, 131; *Read* 1982, 65, 133 (repr); *Stewart* 1, 1985, 268; *Morris and Roberts* 1998, 237
25.	1840	Ino and the infant Bacchus	pm	RDS, Dublin, Ireland Other versions: Lord Ellesmere, 1840, current loc unknown reductions in Copeland Parian ware		*Graves* 1975, 192; *Graves* III, 1905–6, 131; *Read* 1982, 58–9, 83, 129 (repr); *Stewart* 1, 1985, 268
26.	1842	Venus rescuing Aeneas from Diomed		[Exhib RA, London, 1275]; untraced		*AU*, 1842, 128; *Graves* III, 1905–6, 131
27.	1843	The wanderer (The houseless)		[Exhib BI, London, 433]; untraced		*Graves* 1875, 192; *Turpin* 1979 (2), 108; *Stewart* 1, 1985, 268; *Morris and Roberts* 1998, 237
28.	1844	Youth at a stream	pm	RDS, Dublin, Ireland Other versions: Bancroft Gardens, Stratford-on-Avon, Warks, bronze, cast by J A Hatfield, 1851 Royal Albert Hall, marble ex RHS gardens, marble, 1869; untraced reproduced as a small bronze for the Art Union of London (one at Nat Gall of Ireland)		*Read* 1982, 28–9 (repr); *Stewart* 1, 1985, 268; *Noszlopy* 2003, 48 (repr)
29.	1845	Contemplation		[Exhib RA, London, 1341]; untraced		*Graves* III, 1905–6, 131; *Stewart* 1, 1985, 268
30.	1847	John Hampden Model(s): plaster, RDS, Dublin; model exhib Westm Hall, London, 1847; another, Gt Exhib, London, 1851	m	Palace of Westminster, London, St Stephen's Hall	SD	*Walker* 1961, 36, cat 37; *Read* 1982, 82, 84, 164, 177–9 (repr)
31.	1848	Innocence		[Exhib RA, London, 1848, 1330]; untraced Other versions: Private coll, small bronze		*Graves* 1875, 192; *Graves* III, 1905–6, 131; *Turpin* 1979 (1), 43, 51, n7; *Turpin* 1979 (2), 108–9
32.	1851	The homeless wanderer	m	[Gt Exhib, London]; untraced		*ILN*, 14 June 1851, 571; *Turpin* 1979 (2), 109
33.	1851	The mother, group	pm	RDS, Dublin, Ireland		*AJ*, 1852, 194 (repr); *Graves* III, 1905–6, 131; *Read* 1982, 35 169, 209 (repr); *Murphy* 1999, 68
34.	1853–1855	Egeria	m	CL Coll, Mansion House, City of London, 131 Other versions: Bury Art Gallery, Lancs, small marble ex coll A J Bostead, small marble; untraced	SD	*Graves* III, 1905–6, 132; *Read* 1982, 207, 208 (repr); *Knight* 1986, 336 (repr); *Morris and Roberts* 1998, 237; *Ward-Jackson* 2003, 246 (repr)
35.	1853–1855	John Selden Model(s): plaster, RDS, Dublin	m	Palace of Westminster, London, St Stephen's Hall	SD	*ILN*, 9 Dec 54, p 621; *Walker* 1961, 66, cat 69; *Read* 1974, 264, 268
36.	1855	Mrs James Stuart Wortley, model		[Exhib RA, London, 1425]; untraced		*Graves* III, 1905–6, 132
37.	1858	Henry, 1st Viscount Hardinge of Lahore, equestrian Model(s): exhib Int Exhib, London, 1862	b	[Government House, Kolkata (Calcutta)]; Penshurst Place, Kent, gardens		*Steggles* 2000, 110–2 (repr)
38.	1856–1859	Caractacus Model(s): C of L Coll 134, plaster	m	CL Coll, Mansion House, City of London, 37 Other versions: bronze statuette published by the Art Union of London (one in Nat Gall of Ireland)	SD	*Beattie* 1983, 1–2, 13 (repr); *Avery and Marsh* 1985, 333, 334 (repr); *Knight* 1986, 336 (repr); *Ward-Jackson* 2003, 250–1 (repr)
39.	1860	The elder brother from *Comus*	m	[Exhib RA, London, 960, Diploma Work]; RA, Burlington House, London		*Graves* III, 1905–6, 132; *Holland Park* 1957, unpag (repr); *Read* 1974, 268 (repr)
40.	1863	John Fielden (modelled by Foley: cast by Elkington & Co)	b	[Fielden Square, Todmorden, W R Yorks]; Centre Vale Park, Todmorden, W R Yorks	SD	*Read* 1982, 86, 87, 147 (repr)

No.	Date	Subject	Medium	Location		Bibliography
41.	1863	Manockjee Nesserwanjee (a Parsee merchant) Model(s): plaster, RDS, Dublin	b	Oriental Spinning and Weaving Company, Mumbai (Bombay), India		*Read* 1982, 168 (plaster model repr); *White and Bright* 1998, 68; *Murphy* 1999, 69; C Lib (repr)
42.	1863	Oliver Goldsmith Model(s): plaster, RDS, Pallas, Co Longford	b	College Green, Dublin, Ireland Other versions: Royal Coll 36124, small bronze, signed Coll Alderman G V Goldberg, small bronze Christie, London, 27 Sept 1990, small bronze YCBA B1997.24.2, small bronze		*Graves* III, 1905–6, 132; *Read* 1982, 128, 164, 166 (repr); *Stewart* 1, 1985, 268; *Hill* 1998, 98–100; *Morris and Roberts* 1998, 237
43.	1864	Father Theobald Mathew	b	Patrick Street, Cork, Ireland		*Hill* 1998, 109–11 (repr)
44.	1864	John, Lord Elphinstone (†1860)	m	Asiatic Society, Mumbai (Bombay), India (formerly Town Hall)	SD	*Steggles* 2000, 89–90 (repr)
45.	1865	Sir Charles Barry Payment(s): £908 15s	m	Palace of Westminster, London, Committee stairs	SD	Pevsner, *London: Westminster*, 1973, 527; *Read* 1982, 58–9 (repr)
46.	1866	Albert, the Prince Consort		[Cambridge University]; Madingley, Cambs		*Graves* III, 1905–6, 132; *Bayley* 1981, 60–6, 140, 142 (repr); *Read* 1982, 1, 3, 153 (repr); *Noszlopy* 1998, 143
47.	1866	Albert, the Prince Consort Payment(s): £2,000 raised by subscription	m	[Corporation Art Gallery, Birmingham, Warks]; Council House, Birmingham, Warks	SD	*Noszlopy* 1998, 142–3 (repr)
48.	1866	Queen Victoria, equestrian statuette, cast by Elkington & Co	b	NGI	SD	*le Harivel* 1988, 562 (repr)
49.	1866	Sir Henry Marsh		R C Physic, Dublin, Ireland	SD	*Turpin* 1979 (2), 112; *Read* 1982, 76
50.	1867	John McHale, Archbishop of Tuam	b	Mayo, Co Galway		*Strickland* I, 1913, 362; RG/JP, 4, 532
51.	1867	Sidney, 1st Baron Herbert of Lea Model(s): plaster, RDS, Dublin		[Pall Mall (outside old War Office), London]; Waterloo Place, London		*Read* 1974, 268–9 (repr); *Turpin* 1979 (2), 113; *Read* 1982, 149, 150, 174–7 (repr); *Beattie* 1983, 203, 205
52.	1868	Colin Campbell, Field Marshal Lord Clyde Payment(s): £1,200 Model(s): plaster, RDS, Dublin	b	George Square, Glasgow, Lanarks		*McKenzie* 2002, 136–9 (repr)
53.	1868	Edmund Burke Model(s): plaster, RDS, Dublin	b	College Green, Dublin, Ireland Other versions: Royal Coll 36131, small bronze Coll Alderman G V Goldberg, small bronze YCBA B1997.24.1, bronze		*ILN*, 7 March 1868, 233; *Hill* 1998, 98–100 (repr)
54.	1869	Sir Dominic Corrigan Model(s): plaster, NGI, SD 1863	m	R C Physic, Dublin, Ireland	SD	*Turpin* 1979 (2), 114; *Read* 1982, 76; *le Harivel* 1988, 562 (repr model); C Lib (repr)
55.	1870	George, 7th Earl of Carlisle	b	[Phoenix Park, Dublin]; Works Depot, Dublin, Ireland Other versions: Brampton Motte, nr Carlisle, Cumberland, 1870, bronze		*CJ*, 6 Oct 1871, 7; *Gunnis* 1968, 154; *Read* 1982, 40–1 (repr); *Hill* 1998 101–2
56.	1871	Albert, the Prince Consort	b	Leinster Lawn, Dublin, Ireland		*ILN*, 15.6.1872, 577; *Read* 1982, 119, 120, 153, 155 (repr); *Hill* 1998, 100–1 (repr); *Murphy* 2001, 39, 40, 42 (repr)
57.	1873	General Thomas J 'Stonewall' Jackson	b	Capitol Square, Richmond, Virginia, USA	SD	*Graves* III, 1905–6, 132; SIRIS
58.	1873	Henry Grattan	b	College Green, Dublin, Ireland		*Read* 1982, 117; *Hill* 1998, 104–6 (repr)
59.	1873	Sir Benjamin Lee Guinness	b	St Patrick's Cathedral, Dublin, Ireland, exterior		*Graves* III, 1905–6, 132; *Read* 1982, 72 (repr); *Hill* 1998, 109
60.	1873	Ulick Canning de Burgh, Lord Dunkellin		[Galway, Ireland]; destroyed		*Cunningham* 1990, 115–23 (repr); *Hill* 1998, 113–4
61.	1874	Asia	m	Albert Memorial, Kensington Gardens, London		*Bayley* 1981, 55, 100–9 (repr); *Read* 1982, 50, 51, 177, 179 (repr)
62.	1874	Charles John, 1st Earl Canning, equestrian (co-sculptor: Thomas Brock)	b	[Eden Gardens, Kolkata (Calcutta)]; Police hospital, Barrackpore, gardens		*Steggles* 2000, 52–3 (repr)
63.	1874	Hugh, 1st Viscount Gough, equestrian (co-sculptor: Thomas Brock)	b	[Phoenix Park, Dublin]; Chillingham Castle, Northumbs, park		*Hill* 1998, 107–8 (repr); *Usherwood* 2000, 22–4 (repr); *Murphy* 2001, 41–2 (repr)
64.	1874	Lieutenant-General Sir James Outram, equestrian	b	[Kolkata (Calcutta), near junction of Chowringhee Road and Park Street]; Victoria Memorial, Kolkata, gardens Other versions: several		*AJ*, 1874, 306; *Groseclose* 1995, 17–8 (repr); *Steggles* 2000, 154–5 (repr)
65.	1874	William Rathbone (co-sculptor: Thomas Brock)	m	Sefton Park, Liverpool, Lancs	SD	*Read* 1982, 72; *Cavanagh* 2000, 186–190 (repr)
66.	1874	William Stokes	m	R C Physic, Dublin	SD	*Turpin* 1979 (2), 115; *Read* 1982, 76

67.	1875	William, 3rd Earl of Rosse (co-sculptor: Thomas Brock)		St John's Mall, Birr, Co Offaly, Ireland	SD	*Harbison, Potterton and Sheehy* 1978, 224 (repr); *Read* 1982, 104, 106, 169, 179 (repr); *Hill* 1998, 114, 115 (repr)
68.	1876	Albert, the Prince Consort (co-sculptor: Thomas Brock)	b	Albert Memorial, Kensington Gardens, London		*Read* 1982, *passim* (repr); *Sankey* 1999, 87–92 (repr)
69.	1877	Michael Faraday (co-sculptor: Thomas Brock)	m	RI, London		*ILN*, LXX, 1877, 233 (repr); *Ormond* 1973, 169
70.	1866–1883	Daniel O'Connell MP (co-sculptor: Thomas Brock) Model(s): NGI, SD, plaster; RDS, Dublin, plaster	b	O'Connell Street, Dublin		*Potterton* 1973, 1–12 (repr); *Murphy* 1996, 22–6 (repr); *Hill* 1998, 93–7 (repr)
71.	nd	Leith Ritchie		Untraced		*Strickland* I, 1913, 363
72.	nd	Mrs Boustead, statuette		Untraced		*Strickland* I, 1913, 361
73.	nd	Winter, Summer Model(s): Winter, plaster, RDS, Dublin	pm	[Dunster House, Rochdale, Lancs; Nield 1879, lots 94, 95]; untraced Other versions: Winter, plaster, coll H Potterton Winter, plaster, RDS, Dublin		*Strickland* I, 1913, 364; *Gunnis* 1968, 154; *Turpin* 1979 (2), 109; *Read* 1982, 35 (repr)
Busts						
74.	1841	William Robert Dickinson		[Exhib RA, London, 1338]; untraced		*Graves* III, 1905–6, 131
75.	1842	William Farren		[Exhib RA, London, 1395]; untraced		*Graves* III, 1905–6, 131
76.	1843	Helen Faucit	m	NPG, London 1554 Other versions: plaster, NGI	SD	*Graves* III, 1905–6, 131; *le Harivel* 1988, 562
77.	1845	Catherine Prendergast	m	NGI 8045	SD	*Graves* III, 1905–6, 131; *Crookshank* 1966, 309 (repr); *le Harivel* 1988, 562 (repr)
78.	1845	James Oliver Annesley		[Exhib RA, London, 1378]; untraced		*Graves* III, 1905–6, 131; *Turpin* 1979 (2), 115
79.	1848	Sir James Annesley		[Exhib RA, London, 1449]; untraced		*Graves* III, 1905–6, 131
80.	1852	Rev Andrew Reed	m	[Exhib RA, London, 1477]; untraced		*ILN*, 28 July 1855, 125; *Graves* III, 1905–6, 131
81.	by 1853	Catherine Hayes		[Int Exhib, Dublin 1853]; untraced		*Murphy* 1999, 69
82.	1854	A youth's head	m	[Exhib BI, London, 587]; untraced		*Graves* 1875, 192
83.	1854	Field Marshall Henry, 1st Viscount Hardinge of Lahore	m	South Park, Penshurst, Kent Other versions: Maidstone Museum and Art Gallery, 668/28 (18) Royal Coll, 20745, 1860, replica	SD	*ILN*, 4.8.1860, 99; *Graves* III, 1905–6, 131–2; *Ormond* 1973, 213; *Read* 1974, 266, 267 (repr); Turpin 1979(2), 115–6; *Read* 1982, 133
84.	1854	Mrs Warner		[Exhib RA, London, 1480]; untraced		*Graves* III, 1905–6, 132
85.	1855	Thomas Mason		[Exhib RA, London, 1508]; untraced		*Graves* III, 1905–6, 132
86.	1856	Lady Hulse	m	[Exhib RA, London, 1326]; untraced		*Graves* III, 1905–6, 132
87.	1856	Richard Sheepshanks	m	[Royal Greenwich Observatory, Cambridge]; NMM, Greenwich, ZBA 1713	SD	
88.	1856	Sir Charles Hulse		[Exhib RA, London, 1321]; untraced		*Graves* III, 1905–6, 132
89.	1858	Major-General William Nairn Forbes	m	[The Mint, Kolkata (Calcutta), India]; untraced Other versions: cast, coll Asiatic Soc, Calcutta, plaster		*Graves* III, 1905–6, 132; *Strickland* I, 1913, 362
90.	1858	Sir George Biddell Airy		[Royal Greenwich Observatory, Cambridge]; NMM, Greenwich, ZBA 1714	SD	
91.	1860	John Purcell Fitzgerald	m	[Exhib RA, London, 1059]; untraced		*Graves* III, 1905–6, 132
92.	1860	Mrs Samuel R Healey	m	[Exhib RA, London, 1067]; untraced		*Graves* III, 1905–6, 132
93.	1860	R S Bertram James Vaughan	m	[Exhib RA, London, 1035]; untraced		*Graves* III, 1905–6, 132
94.	1861	Sir James Outram	m	Victoria Memorial Hall, Kolkata (Calcutta)		*Graves* III, 1905–6, 132; *Ormond* 1973, 351
95.	1862	John Julius Angerstein	m	[Angerstein family; sold Sotheby, 21–22 July 2003]; untraced	SD	
96.	1864	Lord Ashburton		Christie, 5 Dec 1950; untraced		*Turpin* 1979 (2), 116
97.	1865	Sidney, 1st Baron Herbert of Lea		Harrow School Other versions: Wilton House, Wilts		*Ormond* 1973, 223
98.	1866	John Sheepshanks		VAM 1-1881	SD	*Strickland* I, 1913, 363; *Barrett* 1971 (1), 84; *Bilbey* 2002, 260 (repr)
99.	1867	Sir William Rowan Hamilton		Trinity College, Dublin		*Turpin* 1979 (2), 113; *Crookshank* 1986, 24
100.	1868	Unidentified subject	p	RDS, Dublin	SD	*White and Bright* 1998, 69
101.	1869	Unidentified little girl	m	Private coll	SD	
102.	1870	Sir Herbert Edwardes		India Office Library, Westminster, London		*Ormond* 1973, 157
103.	1871	Albert, the Prince Consort	p	RDS, Dublin		*Turpin* 1979 (2), 116
104.	1871	Brigadier-General John Nicholson Model(s): RDS (plaster)	p	RDS, Dublin		*Strickland* I, 1913, 363; *Turpin* 1979 (2), 116
105.	1871	George, 7th Earl of Carlisle Model(s): plaster, RDS, Dublin	m	Morpeth Town Hall, Northumbs Other versions: two at Castle Howard, Yorks, one SD 1870		*Carlisle Express*, 8 Jan 1869, 5; *Turpin* 1979 (2), 116; *Ormond and Rogers* 3, 1979–81, 35
106.	1871	Michael Faraday		Royal Society, London		*Ormond* 1973, 169
107.	nd	Aidrian Hope		Untraced		*Strickland* I, 1913, 362;
108.	nd	Bryan Waller Procter (Barry Cornwall)	m	NPG, London	S	*Ormond* 1973, 385 (pl 758); *Murphy* 1999, 69

109.	nd	Charles, 5th Duke of Richmond		[Council Chamber, Chichester, Sussex]; untraced		*Strickland* I, 1913, 363
110.	nd	Mr Littledale		Untraced		*Strickland* I, 1913, 362
111.	nd	Sir Benjamin Lee Guinness		[coll Lord Iveagh]; untraced		*Strickland* I, 1913, 362
112.	nd	Sir Charles Barry		Untraced		*Strickland* I, 1913, 361
Reliefs						
113.	*c*1859	'The Tomb Revisited', relief for an unidentified monument		Untraced		*AJ*, 1859 (repr)
114.	1869	Augusta Jane Percival Fitzgerald with her children	m	[Boulge Hall, Woodbridge, Suffolk]; London Fertility Clinic, Harley St		
115.	nd	Charles Graves, Bishop of Limerick and Mrs Selina Graves, pendants	m	NGI	S	*le Harivel* 1988, 563 (repr)
116.	nd	William Hookham Carpenter	m	BM, London	S	*Dawson* 1999, 57–8 (repr)
Miscellaneous						
117.	1836	The death of Abel		[Exhib RA, London, 1839, 1290]; untraced		*Graves* III, 1905–6, 131; *Turpin* 1979 (2), 108
118.	1840	The death of Lear		[Exhib BI, London, 450]; untraced		*Graves* 1875, 192; *Graves* III, 1905–6, 131
119.	1841	Lear and Cordelia		[Exhib RA, London, 1260]; untraced		*Graves* III, 1905–6, 131
120.	1842	The dead warrior		[Exhib BI, London, 449]; untraced		*Graves* 1875, 192
121.	1843	Prospero relating his adventures to Miranda		[Exhib RA, London, 1485]; untraced		*Graves* 1875, 192; *Graves* III, 1905–6, 131; *Stewart* 1, 1985, 268
122.	1845	A study from nature		[Exhib BI, London, 519]; untraced		*Graves* 1875, 192; *Stewart* 1, 1985, 268
123.	1846	Pandarus overthrown by Diomed		[Exhib RHA, Dublin, 460]; untraced		*Strickland* I, 1913, 364; *Stewart* 1, 1985, 268
124.	1858	Dr G B Airey, Astronomer Royal		[Exhib RA, London, 1302]; untraced		*Graves* III, 1905–6, 132
125.	1863	A young girl		[Exhib RHA, Dublin, 479]; untraced		*Strickland* I, 1913, 364; *Stewart* 1, 1985, 268
126.	nd	Adversity; Prosperity; Imogen		Untraced		*Strickland* I, 1913, 364

FOOTE, David fl 1825–27

At the exhibition organised by the Royal Institution for the Encouragement of the Fine Arts in Scotland in 1827 he exhibited the bust of a younger son of Lord Campbell (**2**). It was well received by one reviewer who wrote that it was 'nature, without ostentation – without effort, – but so true – simple – and grateful, as to be, if we may so speak, intensely effective' (*Scotsman* no 472, 17 Feb 1827, 110). He also exhibited at the Royal Academy in London (**1**, **3**).

Literary References: *Woodward* 1977, vol 1, pt 2, 71

Busts				
1.	1825	Unidentified gentleman	[Exhib RA, London, 1069]; untraced	*Graves* III, 1905–6, 134
2.	1827	A younger son of Lord Campbell	[Exhib RIEFAS]; untraced	*Woodward* 1977, vol 1, pt 2, 71
Reliefs				
3.	1825	Unidentified subject	[Exhib RA, London, 991]; untraced	*Graves* III, 1905–6, 134

FORD, John I, of Bath 1711–67

He was the master-mason responsible for building Bath Grammar School in 1752 and almost certainly executed some of the earlier monuments listed under his son, **John Ford II**. He died on 6 September 1767 and was buried at Colerne, Wilts, where his epitaph declares that 'his abilities and enterprise in business in a great measure contributed to the erection of the handsome buildings and streets' of Bath.

Literary References: *Gunnis* 1968, 154–5

Archival References: GPC

FORD, John II, of Bath 1736–1803

The son of **John Ford I**, he exhibited a marble bust at the Free Society in 1764 (**27**). Three years later he was working as a statuary at the Royal Crescent, Bath. He died on 23 February 1803 and, like his father, was buried at Colerne, where a monument was erected to his memory. Henry Bromley notes a print of 'John Ford, statuary at Bath', by T Woolridge, in his *Catalogue of Engraved British Portraits*, 1793 (p 402).

Most of his monuments are of coloured marbles with large reliefs and he makes much use of a female figure mourning by an urn, with an obelisk in the background. Gunnis suggests just such a monument may have inspired an anonymous correspondent to send a sonnet to the *Gentleman's Magazine* in 1787, with the lines, 'Then, Sculptor, sparing of thy marble graces,/ Let thy taught chisel from my tomb-stone speak/ All dove-winged cherubs with fat baby faces,/ And Christian faith squat by a Roman urn!' (*GM*, 1787, ii, 352).

In the list of works given below some of the earlier ones are almost certainly by the elder Ford.

Literary References: *Gunnis* 1968, 155; *Potterton* 1975, 46; *Colvin* 1999, 244, n 27

Funerary Monuments					
1.	?1750	George Husey	Seend, Wilts		*Gunnis* 1968, 155
2.	†1755	Robert Smith	Combe Hay, Somerset	S	Pevsner, *Somerset: N & Bristol*, 1958, 173
3.	1756	Henry Long	North Bradley, Wilts	S	Pevsner, *Wilts*, 1975, 359
4.	†1758	John Russ	Castle Cary, Somerset	S	Pevsner, *Somerset: S & W*, 1958, 116
5.	†1759	Elizabeth Phillips	Bathford, Somerset	S	Pevsner, *Somerset: N & Bristol*, 1958, 140
6.	?1761	Sir Samuel Garrard Bt	Wheathampstead, Herts	S	*Gunnis* 1968, 155
7.	†1762	John Andrews	Bromham, Wilts	S	*Gunnis* 1968, 155
8.	?1763	Charles Holder	Bathampton, Somerset		*Gunnis* 1968, 155
9.	†1765	Lady Barbara Montagu	Charlcombe, Somerset	S	Pevsner, *Somerset: N & Bristol*, 1958, 152
10.	†1766	John St Albyn	Stringston, Somerset	S	Pevsner, *Somerset: S & W*, 1958, 307

11.	†1768	Jane Talbot		Keevil, Wilts	S	Pevsner, *Wilts*, 1975, 278
12.	†1770	Francis Turner Blythe		[Jackfield, Salop]; untraced		BL Ad MS 21237 fol 376
13.	†1770	Morgan Graves		Mickleton, Glos	S	Pevsner, *Glos: Cotswolds*, 1999, 476
14.	1770	Ward family		North Stoke, Somerset	S	Pevsner, *Somerset: N & Bristol*, 1958, 235
15.	?1771	Anne Wainhouse		Steeple Ashton, Wilts		*Gunnis* 1968, 155
16.	†1771	John Browne		Frampton, Dorset		Pevsner, *Dorset*, 1972, 213
17.	?1772	Charles Inman and Ralph Preston		Spanish Town Cathedral, Jamaica		*Gunnis* 1968, 155
18.	1772	Rev Samuel Woodforde Payment(s): £14 14s		Ansford, Somerset		*Beresford* I, 1924–31, 113
19.	†1772	Robert Browne		Frampton, Dorset		*Gunnis* 1968, 155
20.	?1773	Elizabeth and Robert Clavering		St Peter and St Paul, Marlborough, Wilts		*Gunnis* 1968, 155
21.	†1773	Thomas Coward		Batcombe, Somerset	S	Pevsner, *Somerset: N & Bristol*, 1958, 89
22.	†1779	Sir John Fust		Hill, Glos		C Lib (repr)
23.	†1790	Robert and George Cox (†1777)		Piddletrenthide, Dorset	S	Pevsner, *Dorset*, 1972, 314
24.	†1790	William Cox		Piddletrenthide, Dorset		C Lib (repr)
25.	nd	Day (or Dawe) family member		Ditcheat, Somerset	S	Pevsner, *Somerset: S & W*, 1958, 150
26.	nd	Unidentified subject		St Nicholas, Cork	S	*Potterton* 1975, 46
Busts						
27.	1764	Young Mr Worlidge	m	[Exhib Free Soc, London, 50]; untraced		*Graves* 1907, 94
Architectural Sculpture						
28.	1763	Twenty vases	s	[for Sir William Lee, of Hartwell]; untraced		GPC

FORD, Peter fl 1812

In 1812 he was working at Alton Abbey, Staffs (later Alton Towers) chiefly in the gardens.

Architectural Sculpture				
1.	1812	Basin and columns Payment(s): £46, £55	[Alton Abbey, Staffs, Bath House]; untraced	Archives, Earl of Shrewsbury in GPC

FORREST, Andrew Hume 1813–

He was 26 when he entered the Royal Academy Schools in 1839 on the recommendation of **William Behnes** (RA Admissions).

Miscellaneous				
1.	1851	The forsaken	[Gt Exhib]; untraced	*Gunnis* 1968, 155

FORREST, Robert, of Lanark 1790–1852

A Scottish mason-sculptor, he came to prominence in the 1830s after holding an exhibition of his works in Edinburgh. He was born on 28 June 1790 at Braidwood, Carluke, Lanarkshire, the son of Robert Forrest and Helen, née Hamilton, and trained as a stonemason in the quarries of Clydesdale where he began carving figurines and animals around 1810, after visiting the collections of several local noblemen. His career as a sculptor began in 1817 when he was apparently discovered carving animals in an old quarry by a Colonel Gordon, who had lost his way when out shooting. Gordon was sufficiently impressed by Forrest's work to commission a figure of *Bacchus* and to recommend him to his friends, including Mr Robertson of Hall Craig who commissioned a life-sized statue of a *Highland chieftain* (**3, 4**). Further orders followed and Forrest adopted sculpture as a profession, establishing a workshop in a quarry near Lanark, where he executed statues of *Old Norval, Falstaff* and *Rob Roy* (**5–7**). In 1820 he presented a statue of Sir William Wallace to the town of Lanark (**8**). His depiction of the Scottish national hero, dressed in a 'Roman costume with sword and buckler', was well received by the local population who, on the day of the unveiling, carried the sculptor 'in triumph through the streets, preceded by musk and the banners of the different trades' (*Georgian Era* 1834, cited by *Gunnis* 1968, 155).

Forrest was largely self-taught though he received some formal artistic training after he moved to Edinburgh in 1823 (*DNB*). There he studied at the Trustees School of Design, attended evening classes at the School of Arts and received private tuition in modelling. Two years later he was living in Glasgow, where he studied anatomy, drawing and modelling at Mr Warren's Academy. During the same period he found employment carving 2 prominent public monuments. In 1825 he executed a statue of John Knox from a model by **William Warren**, which was placed on a column designed by Thomas Hamilton in Glasgow Necropolis (**12**). This was followed by a figure of Lord Melville, designed by **Sir Francis Chantrey** and modelled by **Luke O'Neil** (**13**). It was erected on a column designed by William Burn, in St Andrew's Square, Edinburgh, in August 1827.

Forrest opened his own sculpture exhibition in the summer of 1832 next to the National Monument on Calton Hill, Edinburgh. Initially it consisted of four colossal equestrian groups representing Robert the Bruce, Mary Queen of Scots, the Duke of Marlborough and the Duke of Wellington, each carved from a single block of sandstone weighing approximately 20 tons (**14–17**). The exhibition grew steadily and by 1835, when the first of 3 descriptive catalogues was published, there were more than 16 pieces on display in a series of wooden huts behind the National Monument. The statues depicted popular characters from Scottish history, literature and folk lore in a lively, informal style. Examples included figures of *Symon* and *Bauldy* inspired by Allan Ramsay's pastoral poem, *The gentle shepherd*, and a group of King James V attacked by brigands in Cramond Wood (**18, 20, 21**). Forrest used his considerable skill as a showman to attract public attention to his spectacle and his activities were enthusiastically reported by the *Scotsman*. The exhibition became one of the city's most popular attractions and it greatly enhanced the sculptor's reputation.

In spite of the attention accorded to his exhibition, Forrest's attempts to attract patronage met with only limited success. In 1835 he competed for the prestigious Glasgow monument to Sir Walter Scott but the commission was awarded to his former assistant **John Greenshields**. He had a notable success however with a pair of figures of Nelson and Wellington, commissioned by Alexander Falconer for the façade of Falcon Hall in Edinburgh (**22**). Falconer may have financed the sculptor's journey to France and Italy in 1837. Forrest's most ambitious project, for an 80-foot-high seated statue of the Duke of Wellington for Arthur's Seat, Edinburgh, fell through when Lord Elgin, who had commissioned the work, died in 1841. However he successfully completed a public monument to Robert Ferguson of Raith which has a statue of Ferguson atop a Doric column, with 4 mourning figures at the base. It was erected at Haddington, East Lothian, in 1843 (**25**).

Forrest struggled to find a market for his work and faced increasingly serious financial difficulties during the 1840s. In 1849, when he refused to pay an increased rental for the ground occupied by his exhibition, Edinburgh Town Council asked the sculptor to leave, but he was unable to finance the removal of his statues. He attempted to raise the necessary funds through an exhibition of some of his works in Cheshire but the venture was a complete failure and only added to his debts. The authorities were unable to find a solution and the works were still standing on Calton Hill when Forrest died on 29 December 1852. There they remained for a further 14 years during which time the Town Council repeatedly demanded that Forrest's widow should remove the sculpture, which she could not afford to do. Eventually in 1865 the Council sought a warrant for the ejection of the statues and in 1866 paid for their removal and storage in Royal Crescent Park. They were finally sold by auction in November 1876.

Although Forrest's exhibition was a marked success as a popular entertainment his works have not generally been admired by art experts. In 1876, when Edinburgh Town Council briefly considered purchasing Forrest's works, 'Municeps Edinburgensis' wrote to the *Scotsman*, 'While no one can deny that for a self-taught mason these figures testify to great industry, enterprise, and perseverance, no one who knows anything of art can fail to see that they are of a very crude and commonplace description and void of artistic refinement' (*Scotsman*, 14 March 1876, 7). In a recent article Joe Rock has attempted to rehabilitate the sculptor, arguing that he did much to encourage public interest in sculpture in Scotland and produced works that were vigorous and immediate.

EH

Literary References: *Anderson* IX, 1882, 710; *Gunnis* 1968, 155; *Woodward* 1977, vol 1, pt 2, 71–5; *Forbes* 2000, 92–3; *Rock* 2003, 62–71; *ODNB* (Fagan, Rev McKenzie)

Archival References: IGI

Additional MS Sources: *Forrest Papers*

Auction Catalogues: Forrest 1876

Will: NAS SC70/1/79 and SC70/4/27, ESC will and inventory, 2 May 1852

Funerary Monuments

1.	1834	William McGavin	s	Glasgow Necropolis	*McKenzie* 2002, 297–8 (repr)
2.	1836	David Ritchie, 'the black dwarf', gravestone	s	Hallyards (Peebles?)	*Woodward* 1977, vol 1, pt 2, 75

Statues

3.	c1817	Bacchus		[coll Colonel Gordon]; untraced	*Gunnis* 1968, 155; *Woodward* 1977, vol 1, pt 2, 72
4.	c1817	Highland chieftain		[coll Mr Robertson]; untraced	*Gunnis* 1968, 155; *Woodward* 1977, vol 1, pt 2, 72
5.	c1820	Falstaff		Untraced	*Gunnis* 1968, 155; *Woodward* 1977, vol 1, pt 2, 72
6.	c1820	Old Norval		Untraced	*Gunnis* 1968, 155; *Woodward* 1977, vol 1, pt 2, 72
7.	c1820	Rob Roy		Untraced	*Gunnis* 1968, 155; *Woodward* 1977, vol 1, pt 2, 72
8.	?1820	Sir William Wallace	s	Lanark Tolbooth	*Woodward* 1977, vol 1, pt 2, 75; *Pearson* 1991, 73; *Rock* 2003, 63, 65–6 (repr)
9.	1823	Sir John Moore		[Douglas Park, Hamilton, Lanarks]; untraced	*McKenzie* 2002, 122
10.	1823	Souter Johnnie	s	[Calton Hill, Edinburgh, c1835–1866]; private coll	Forrest sale 1876; *Rock* 2003, 67, 68–9 (repr)
11.	1823	Tam o' Shanter	s	[Calton Hill, Edinburgh, c1835–1866]; private coll	Forrest sale, 1876; *Rock* 2003, 67, 68–9 (repr)
12.	1825	John Knox (†1572) (designed by Thomas Hamilton) (co-sculptor: William Warren)	s	Glasgow Necropolis	*McKenzie* 2002, 293–7 (repr)
13.	1827	Henry, 1st Viscount Melville (designed by Sir Francis Chantrey RA) Model(s): by Luke O'Neil; untraced	s	St Andrew Square, Edinburgh	Pevsner, *Edinburgh*, 1991, 322
14.	by 1832	Arthur, 1st Duke of Wellington, equestrian group		[Calton Hill, Edinburgh, 1832–1866]; untraced	*Gunnis* 1968, 155; *Woodward* 1977, vol 1, pt 2, 73
15.	by 1832	John, 1st Duke of Marlborough, equestrian group		[Calton Hill, Edinburgh, 1832–1866]; untraced	*Gunnis* 1968, 155; *Woodward* 1977, vol 1, pt 2, 73
16.	by 1832	King Robert the Bruce, equestrian group	s	[Calton Hill, Edinburgh, 1832–1866]; private coll	*Gunnis* 1968, 155; *Rock* 2003, 66, 68 (repr)
17.	by 1832	Queen Mary and Lord Herries, equestrian group		[Calton Hill, Edinburgh, 1832–1866]; untraced	*Gunnis* 1968, 155; *Woodward* 1977, vol 1, pt 2, 73
18.	1834	King James V attacked in Cramond Wood, equestrian group	s	[Calton Hill, Edinburgh]; private coll	*Read* 1982, 209; *Rock* 2003, 64, 67 (repr)
19.	1834	Mazeppa, fallen horse and rider	s	[Calton Hill, Edinburgh]; Hamilton Park, near Glasgow	Forrest sale, 1876; *Rock* 2003, 69, 70 (repr)
20.	by 1835	Bauldy	s	[Calton Hill, Edinburgh, c1835–1866]; private coll	*Rock* 2003, 68 (repr)
21.	by 1835	Symon	s	[Calton Hill, Edinburgh, c1835–1866]; private coll	*Rock* 2003, 68 (repr)
22.	1837	Arthur, 1st Duke of Wellington and Horatio, Admiral Lord Nelson, pair of figures		[Falcon Hall, Edinburgh]; untraced	*Daily Telegraph* 12 Oct 1992; *Rock* 2003, 69
23.	1841	Arthur, 1st Duke of Wellington, design for an equestrian group		[Exhib R Sc A, Edinburgh, 565]; untraced	*Laperriere* 2, 1991, 75

24.	1841	Napoleon, design for an equestrian statue		[Exhib R Sc A, Edinburgh, 564]; untraced	*Laperriere* 2, 1991, 75
25.	1843	Robert Ferguson	s	Haddington, Lothian	*Woodward* 1977, vol 1, pt 2, 75
26.	1851	Arthur, 1st Duke of Wellington	s	Falkirk, Stirlingshire, from 1854	*Gunnis* 1968, 155; *Woodward* 1977, vol 1, pt 2, 75 (pl 67)
27.	nd	Prodigal son	s	Falkirk, Stirlingshire	*Woodward* 1977, vol 1, pt 2, 72
Busts					
28.	1842	Unidentified lady		[Exhib R Sc A, Edinburgh, 521]; untraced	*Laperriere* 2, 1991, 75
29.	1842	Unidentified lady		[Exhib R Sc A, Edinburgh, 523]; untraced	*Laperriere* 2, 1991, 75
30.	1843	Unidentified gentleman		[Exhib R Sc A, Edinburgh, 587]; untraced	*Laperriere* 2, 1991, 75
31.	1844	Unidentified gentleman		[Exhib R Sc A, Edinburgh, 574]; untraced	*Laperriere* 2, 1991, 75
32.	1844	Unidentified lady		[Exhib R Sc A, Edinburgh, 575]; untraced	*Laperriere* 2, 1991, 75
Miscellaneous					
33.	1841	Death of Sir John Moore		[Exhib R Sc A, Edinburgh, 566]; untraced	*Laperriere* 2, 1991, 75
34.	nd	The careless shepherd		Untraced	*Pearson* 1991, unpag

FORSYTH, W, of Worcester fl 1828

Funerary Monuments

1.	†1828	Rev Alfred Worthington	Stourbridge Unitarian Chapel, Worcs	RG/JP, 4, 535v

FORTUNE, William fl 1677

The son of Humphrey Fortune, 'wharfinger', he hailed from Henley, Oxon. He was described as 'of St. Dunstan's in the West, Mason, Bachr. abt. 24', when he married Rebeccah Collier, of 'St. Dunstan's in the East, Spr. abt 25' in April 1677. Later the same year he became free of the Masons' Company by service to John Clarke.

Literary References: *Armytage* 1892, vol 34, 1669–1679, 193; *Webb* 1995, 13

Archival References: Masons' Co, Freemen, fol 20, 9 October 1677

FOSS, William, of Richmond, Yorkshire fl 1811–22

He was the son of John Foss, an architect and mason who held the office of Mayor of Richmond between 1811 and 1822. Foss signs several 'pretty tablets in coloured marbles' (*Gunnis* 1968, 155).

Literary References: *Colvin* 1995, 371–2

Funerary Monuments

1.	?1818	Sophia Milbanke	Well, N R Yorks	S	*Gunnis* 1968, 156
2.	?1819	Eleanor Milbanke	Croft, N R Yorks	S	*Gunnis* 1968, 156
3.	?1819	Thomas Colpitts	Barnard Castle, Durham	S	*Gunnis* 1968, 156
4.	?1821	William Milbanke	Well, N R Yorks	S	*Gunnis* 1968, 156
5.	nd	Henry Blegborough	Richmond, N R Yorks	S	*Gunnis* 1968, 156

FOSTER, Edward (or Edmund), of Hull fl 1774–99

Pevsner claims that Foster was responsible for the best Hull-produced monuments of the Georgian period. One example is the Sykes at Roos which features a double portrait medallion mounted on an obelisk (**2**). In a long letter to Sir Christopher Sykes of Sledmere, who commissioned the monument, Foster wrote, 'I have just now seen the Boy who rides the North Post from hence, he would gladly take the parcel (the Drawg. at large) but He cannot answer for its' being delivered at Malton. He goes no farther than Wieghton, from whence it must be committed to the next for York, so to a third for Malton, the doubt therefore of it coming safe to hand makes me unwilling to venture it that Way, by water it would be a most tedious conveyance' (Sykes Archives, 5 Jan 1784, in GPC).

Literary References: *Gunnis* 1968, 156; Pevsner, *Yorks: E R & York*, 1995, 69

Funerary Monuments						
1.	†1774	Ralph (†1768) and Bridget Pennyman		St Mary, Beverley, E R Yorks	S	Pevsner, *Yorks: E R & York*, 1995, 299
2.	†1783	Rev Sir Mark (†1783) and Lady Decima Sykes (†1793)		Roos, E R Yorks		Pevsner, *Yorks: E R & York*, 1995, 661
3.	†1790	John Huntington		Holy Trinity, Hull, E R Yorks		Pevsner, *Yorks: E R & York*, 1995, 507
4.	†1799	William Bethell		Rise, E R Yorks		Pevsner, *Yorks: E R & York*, 1995, 658
Architectural Sculpture						
5.	*c*1762	Richly carved rococo surround to the Mayor's seat	wd	Guildhall, Beverley, E R Yorks, court room		Pevsner, *Yorks: E R & York*, 1995, 302
6.	1765	Organ-case (designed by Timothy Lightowler)	wd	Beverley Minster, E R Yorks (parts incorporated into vestry screen)		Pevsner, *Yorks: E R & York*, 1995, 292
7.	1780	Ogee moulding, astragals and paterae	wd	Thorpe Hall, Rudston, E R Yorks		Pevsner, *Yorks: E R & York*, 1995, 665

FOSTER, James, of Bristol *c*1748–1823

He was the pupil and apprentice of **Thomas Paty**. Like Paty he combined architectural practice with the business of a statuary mason, executing, according to his own advertisement, 'monuments and chimneypieces in marble with peculiar grace and elegance' (cited by *Gunnis* 1968, 156). In Carmarthenshire Foster remodelled the Bishop's Palace at Abergwili, *c*1803, and signed a monument to George Oakley (**2**). Dale-Jones and Lloyd suggest that 4 identical unsigned tablets in the same county may be Foster's work. They commemorate Maria Lloyd (1806), Anne Blome (1807) and Thomas Blome (1810) at Abbergwili and Mary Warlow (1809) in St Peter's, Carmarthen.

Early in the 19th century Foster was joined in the business by his son James Foster II (†1836) and the firm's practice became exclusively architectural. It survived until 2001 and was responsible for many notable buildings in Bristol including Colston Hall, Foster's Almshouses in Colston Street and the City Museum in Queen's Road.

Literary References: *Gunnis* 1968, 156; *Colvin* 1995, 372–3; *Priest* 2003, 7

Funerary Monuments

1.	?1798	John Maxse	Brislington, Somerset	S	*Gunnis* 1968, 156
2.	†1801	George Oakely	St Peter, Carmarthen	S	*Dale-Jones and Lloyd* 1989, 49
3.	?1804	John Kernan	Stanton Drew, Somerset	S	*Gunnis* 1968, 156
4.	nd	Amelia Burges (co-sculptor: Walker)	St Augustine, Bristol	S	*Gunnis* 1968, 156

FOULIS, Robert fl 1755

In 1755 Foulis issued *A Catalogue of Pictures, Drawings, Prints, Statues and Busts in Plaster of Paris done at the Academy in the University of Glasgow.* He stated that he had 'lately employed some hands in moulding busts and figures from casts of the best statues', and listed two pages of casts in lead and plaster available both in Glasgow and Edinburgh. They included copies after the antique, 'Modern Busts', statuettes of poets and Cupids after Duquesnoy described as 'proper for putting over architraves and cornices'.

Literary References: *Pearson* 1991, 45–6

FOWLER, of Gloucester fl 1717

Funerary Monuments

1.	1717	Rowland (†1697) and Margaret Scudamore (†1716)	Llangarren, Herefs	SD	

FOX, Charles –1854

In 1847 he received a medal from the Society of Arts for a model of a group of children (4). At the Great Exhibition of 1851 he showed a model of a pediment with a relief representing *The Arts, Commerce and Manufactures promoted by the Great Exhibition* (1). His address was given as 3 Brighton Place, Brighton, when he exhibited with the Society of British Artists in 1850 and 1852.

Literary References: *Dossie* 1782, 439; *Gunnis* 1968, 156; *Johnson* 1975, 166

Architectural Sculpture				
1.	1851	The Arts, Commerce, and Manufactures promoted by the Great Exhibition, model for a pediment	[Gt Exhib, London]; untraced	*AJ Cat* 1851, 56 (repr)
2.	1853	Decorative panels	[Unidentified house, North Street, Brighton, East Sussex]; untraced	*Gunnis* 1968, 156
Reliefs				
3.	1850	Fairies floating through the air on a feather	[Exhib Soc of BA, London, 735]; untraced	*Johnson* 1975, 166
Miscellaneous				
4.	1847	Model of a group of children	[Soc of A, silver Isis medal]; untraced	*Gunnis* 1968, 156
5.	1852	St Bernard's dog finding a traveller	[Exhib Soc of BA, London, 166]; untraced	*Johnson* 1975, 166

FOX, Douglas fl 1826

A surgeon from Derby, he was awarded a large silver medal by the Society of Arts for an 'elastics mould for casts in wax or plaster of paris', designed to take casts of irregularly shaped objects such as 'a deer's horn or deformed foetus', for which moulds made from hard metals were inadequate. His moulds were of glue.

Literary References: RSA, *Transactions*, vol 44, 1826, 38–43

FOX, Edward fl 1851

The brother of **Charles Fox**.

Literary References: *Gunnis* 1968, 156

Statues

1.	1851	Edmund Spenser, statuette	[Gt Exhib, London]; untraced	*Gunnis* 1968, 156
2.	1851	Geoffrey Chaucer, statuette	[Gt Exhib, London]; untraced	*Gunnis* 1968, 156

FOX, of Green Street, Grosvenor Square fl *c*1737

'Mr Fox, Carver of Green Street, Grosvenor Square' is mentioned in the account book of **Henry Watson** *c*1737 (Bodleian MS Eng Misc f383, cited by *Brighton* 2001, 71).

FOXHALL, Edward –1815

The son of Martin Foxhall, he was responsible for decorative carving at various houses designed and built by his father's friend, Sir John Soane. In 1783 he received £1,069 11s 1d for all the carved woodwork in Philip Yorke's London house (3). Ten years later he was again employed by Yorke (now the Earl of Hardwicke) at Wimpole, Cambs (Soane, Wimpole Acct Bk 1791–94, fols 104, 105, 133). He worked at Malvern Hall under Soane for Sir Henry Lewis, 1785, in Grosvenor Square for the Marquess of Abercorn, 1787 (Soane, Abstract of Bills, I, fol 134), and in Pall Mall for Lady Louisa Manners, 1788 (Soane Abstract of Bills, 1, fol 152). He carved four Ionic capitals for the Marquess of Abercorn at Bentley Priory (7).

Foxhall provided two chimneypieces and the state bed for William Beckford at Fonthill (2). He was paid £580 5s, *c*1807, for 'Church Furniture' at Dodington, Glos, then under construction by James Wyatt for Christopher Codrington (Codrington Archives in GPC).

At the time of his death on 29 October 1815 he lived in Orchard Street (*GM*, 1815, ii, 636). He is described in his will as an 'Upholsterer of Saint Marylebone'. His son Edward Martin Foxhall (1793–1862) was an architect and surveyor (see *Colvin* 1995, 380).

Literary References: *Gunnis* 1968, 156

Archival References: GPC

Will: PROB 11/1575

Chimneypieces

1.	1783	For Thomas Pitt, Lord Camelford Payment(s): £10	[Burnham Hall, Norfolk]; untraced	Soane Abstract of Bills, I, fol 10
2.	1787	Two, and the state bed	[Fonthill Abbey, Wilts]; destroyed	Edward Boyd Alexander, *Life at Fonthill 1807–1822* in GPC

Architectural Sculpture

3.	1783	Carving, including 'six very rich girandoles carv'd and gilt in Burnished Gold' Payment(s): £1069	[for Hon Philip Yorke's house, New Cavendish Street, London]; untraced	Soane, New Cavendish St Acct Bk, 1781–4
4.	1785	16 Ionic capitals, and a 'run of frieze' with 'oxe's heads and festoons of fruits and flowers' Payment(s): £137	[Malvern Hall, Warks]; untraced	Soane Bills to 1785, fols 149–51
5.	1786	Snake carved at base of the column erected to the memory of Edward and Julia Evelyn Payment(s): £4 15s	[Felbridge, East Grinstead, Sussex]; Lemmington, Northumbs	Soane Acct Bk 1781–86, fol 76
6.	1791	Tablet with 'carvings of hops and hop leaves for the entrance hall'	[for Mr Simmonds, Reading, Berks]; untraced	GPC
7.	1799	Four Ionic capitals	[for Bentley Priory, Middx, seat of Marquess of Abercorn]; untraced	Soane bill book, fol 67; *Gunnis* 1968, 156

FOYE, Michael fl 1765–77

Foye entered the Dublin Society's Schools in 1765 and in 1767 exhibited two works with the Society of Artists in William Street, Dublin (**8, 9**). These were followed by bas reliefs of *Mercury instructing Cupid* and *Hercules resting from his labours*, for which he was awarded premiums by the Dublin Society (**5, 6**). By 1770 he was working in the studio of **John Nost III** and about 2 years later he travelled to Italy, arriving in Florence by 28 April 1772. He studied the ducal collections in Florence, making a cast of Michelangelo's *Bacchus* and a copy of Titian's *Venus of Urbino*, before proceeding to Rome before Easter, 1773, when he took lodgings in the Strada dei Greci. The following year he was living in the Via Babuino. Foye soon came into contact with **Thomas Banks**, who described him as 'a sculptor, a very ingenious, worthy young man; he is doing a copy of the Apollo Belvidere in marble, about five feet and a half high' (*Bell* 1938, 17) (**1**). In November 1776 the English painter Thomas Jones met Foye with Banks, **Christopher Hewetson, Nathaniel Marchant** and numerous other artists, at the Cafe degli Inglesi (*Jones Memoirs* 1951, 53). In 1777 'Mr Foy, at Rome' sent a 'Busto of an artist' to the exhibition of the Society of Artists in London (**3**). It is possible that this was the bust of Allan Ramsay now in the Scottish National Portrait Gallery (**4**). The last digit of the date on the Ramsay is missing but it was certainly executed during the 1770s. Another bust, in a private collection, was thought to be a representation of Sir William Hamilton but has recently been identified as Sir John Lindsay, a famous naval officer and Allan Ramsay's brother-in-law (**2**). Foy also carved a head in relief of the history painter James Durno which appeared in Thomas Banks's posthumous sale of 1805 (**7**). He is thought to have died in Rome soon after 1777. (Add inf. Nicola Figgis)

Literary References: *Strickland* I, 1913, 381; *Esdaile* 1924 (4), 237; *Gunnis* 1968, 156; *Stainton* 1983, 15, 23–4; *Ingamells* 1997, 379; *Wilson* 2005, 31–9

Statues

1.	1773	Apollo Belvedere, after the Antique		Untraced		*Bell* 1938, 17

Busts

2.	1776	Sir John Lindsay KB	m	Edward D Cohen coll (Salop)	SD	*Wilson* 2005, 31–9 (repr)
3.	1777	Unidentified artist		[Exhib Soc of Artists, London, 201]; untraced		*Graves* 1907, 95
4.	1770–1779	Allan Ramsay	m	SNPG	SD	*Potterton* 1975, 85; *Wilson* 2005, 32, 36–7 (repr)

Reliefs

5.	1768	Mercury instructing Cupid		[Exhib Soc of Artists, William Street, Dublin]; untraced		*Strickland* I, 1913, 381
6.	1770	Hercules resting from his labours		[Exhib Society of Artists, William Street, Dublin]; untraced		*Strickland* I, 1913, 381
7.	nd	James Durno		[Banks sale, 22 May 1805]; untraced		Christie's archives, cited by *Gunnis* 1968, 156; *Stainton* 1985, 24–5

Miscellaneous

8.	1767	Group of boys	p	[Society of Artists, William Street, Dublin]; untraced		*Strickland* I, 1913, 381
9.	1767	Venus and Cupid	m	[Exhib Society of Artists, William Street, Dublin]; untraced		*Strickland* I, 1913, 381

FRANCEYS, Samuel and Thomas, of Liverpool fl *c*1802–19

The brothers ran the leading firm of monumental masons in Liverpool between *c*1802 and 1819. Little is known of their background but they may have been related to the Samuel Franceys who was employed on decorative stucco-work at Melbourne Hall, Derbys, in 1760 (Archives, Marquis of Lothian, in *Gunnis* 1968, 156). According to one account they established themselves as builders and plasterers in Pleasant Street, Liverpool *c*1802 and 'having a taste for art, they entered into the manufacture of a sort of composition of oil stucco, then much in vogue for chimney pieces and ceilings' which 'led to the execution of works in marble' (*Picton* II, 1875, 214–5). By 1812 a wide range of products could be viewed at the firm's premises in Brownlow Hill. These included 'a great variety of marble chimneypieces . . . in the Egyptian, Grecian, Gothic and modern taste, and in various species of the most beautiful Italian, Egyptian, and British marbles. Marble tables for halls, sideboards, &c monuments, plain, or sculptured after elegant designs . . . various figures in marble, bronze and artificial stone to support dials and lamps; statues, busts &c., of excellent execution', (*Stranger in Liverpool* 1812, 139).

Their monuments could be quite elaborate. That to Joseph Brandreth, physician to the Duke of Gloucester and Lord Derby and founder of the Liverpool Dispensary, has a relief of the *Good Samaritan* caring for the unfortunate traveller, while the Cumming dramatically depicts a tomb, riven apart on the Day of Judgement and the mother and daughter ascending from it (**27, 26**). The figure of *Faith* embracing a cross on the memorial to Ursula Lloyd at Llanbedr was first used on the memorial to John Ford in Chester Cathedral (**15, 7**).

The German sculptor **F A Legé** was employed by the firm and **John Gibson, William Spence** and **Thomas Duckett** all began their careers in the Franceys workshops. When Samuel Franceys left the business and the partnership was dissolved in 1819 (*Euro Mag*, 1819, 282) Spence took his place. The reconstructed firm of **Franceys and Spence** continued in operation until about 1844, though Samuel Franceys died much earlier, on 20 May 1829. He was buried in the graveyard of the Wesleyan Chapel in Brunswick Street, Liverpool. Another family member was Mary Franceys, 'Sculptor' who is listed at 25 Pleasant Street in the *Liverpool Directory* for 1823–24.

Literary References: *Gunnis* 1968, 156–7; *Physick* 1969, 41–2, 180; *Yarrington* 1988, 119; *Curtis* 1989, *passim*

Funerary Monuments

1.	†1783	William Pate	Gresford, Denbighs	S	Pevsner, *Clwyd*, 1994, 173
2.	†1788	Jinnet Price	Llanfachreth, Merioneths	S	NP/RG
3.	†1792	John Parnell	Bebington, Cheshire		GPC
4.	†1800	Rev Thomas Edwards	Selattyn, Salop	S	*Gunnis* 1968, 157
5.	†1801	Thomas Lovett	Chirk, Denbighs	S	Pevsner, *Clwyd*, 1994, 129
6.	†1806	Thomas Smith	St Chad, Rochdale, Lancs	S	*Gunnis* 1968, 157; C Lib (repr)
7.	†1807	John Ford	Chester Cathedral	S	*Gunnis* 1968, 157; C Lib (repr)
8.	†1808	Watkin and Elizabeth (†1825) Williams	Nannerch, Flint	S	Pevsner, *Clwyd*, 1994, 402
9.	?1809	Benjamin Smith	St Chad, Rochdale, Lancs	S	*Gunnis* 1968, 157
10.	?1809	Rev William Loxham	Penwortham, Lancs		*Gunnis* 1968, 157
11.	†1810	Henry Blundell (designed and executed by John Gibson)	Sefton, Lancs	S	Pevsner, *Lancs: S*, 1969, 401
12.	†1810	John Henshall	Newchapel, Staffs		*Jeavons* 1960, 65
13.	?1810	Rev Joseph Venables	Oswestry, Salop	S	
14.	†1810	Thomas Davies	Llansilin, Denbighs	S	Pevsner, *Clwyd*, 1986, 242
15.	†1810	Ursula (†1795), John (†1806) and Margaret Lloyd	Llanbedr Dyffryn Clwyd, Denbighs	S	Pevsner, *Clwyd*, 1994, 188
16.	†1811	Rev Edward Jones and wife Mary (†1823)	Ruthin, Denbighs	S	Pevsner, *Clwyd*, 1986, 275
17.	?1811	Rev Robert Morgan	Llanbedr Dyffryn Clwyd, Denbighs	S	*Gunnis* 1968, 157
18.	?1813	Frances Bower	Stockport, Cheshire	S	*Gunnis* 1968, 157
19.	1813	George (†1786), Dulcibella (†1810) and William (†1813) Brownbill (designed by John Gibson)	Rainford, Lancs	S	*CIIA* 4/8/75–6 (repr)
20.	?1813	Rev John Hargreaves	Burnley, Lancs	S	*Gunnis* 1968, 157
21.	†1813	Rev Samuel Hall	St Ann, Manchester, Lancs	S	*Gunnis* 1968, 157; C Lib (repr)
22.	†1813	Sir Thomas Broughton	Broughton, Staffs	S	*Gunnis* 1968, 157
23.	†1814	Elizabeth France	Davenham, Cheshire	S	Pevsner, *Cheshire*, 1971, 196
24.	†1814	William Wright	St George, Bolton, Lancs	S	Pevsner, *Lancs: S.*, 1969, 80
25.	†1815	Anne and Edward Rowland	Ruabon, Denbighs	S	Pevsner, *Clwyd*, 1986, 270
26.	1815	Charlotte (†1813) and Sarah Cumming	Kirkheaton, W R Yorks		GPC
27.	†1815	Joseph Brandreth	Ormskirk, Lancs	S	C Lib (repr)
28.	†1816	Elizabeth Wynne	St Mary, Llanfair Talhaearn, Denbighs	S	Pevsner, *Clwyd*, 1986, 210
29.	1816	Robert Knowles (†1813)	St Peter, Bolton, Lancs	S	
30.	†1816	Thomas Ridgway	Horwich, Lancs		C Lib (repr)
31.	†1817	George Wood	St John, Longton, Staffs		*Jeavons* 1960, 65
32.	?1817	Hannah Hale	Audlem, Cheshire	S	*Gunnis* 1968, 157
33.	1818	George Johnson (†1816)	St Peter, Chester, Cheshire	S	Pevsner, *Cheshire*, 1971 152
34.	*c*1820	Isherwood family members	St Mary, Stockport, Lancs		NP/RG
35.	*c*1820	Owen Owen	Bangor Cathedral, Carnarvons		GPC

FRANCEYS AND SPENCE, of Liverpool fl 1801–*c*1844

Marble masons, they continued the business of Samuel and Thomas Franceys until *c*1844. The firm was controlled by Thomas Franceys and William Spence and then, after Franceys died in 1829, by Spence alone. They sign a number of monuments, and a terracotta bust of King George III is inscribed 'Pub by/T Franceys & Spence/Sculptors Liverpool/1820' (8). It seems likely that this work was modelled by Spence, whose bust of William Roscoe was also published at that time in the form of a small bronze.

Funerary Monuments

1.	†1801	Rice Jones		Llanfachreth, Merioneths	S	NP/RG
2.	*c*1820	John Lownes		Congleton, Cheshire	S	*Gunnis* 1968, 157
3.	†1823	Elizabeth Longton		St Luke, Farnworth, Lancs		*CIIA* 4/8/35 (repr)
4.	?1823	Rev Thomas Blackburne		Holt, Denbigh	S	*Gunnis* 1968, 157
5.	†1827	Meyrick Bankes		Billinge, Lancs	S	*CIIA* 4/8/23 (repr)
6.	?1833	Robert Reynolds		Colne, Lancs	S	*Gunnis* 1968, 157
7.	1844	Rev Richard Rothwell		Sefton, Lancs	S	Pevsner, *Lancs: S*, 1969, 401
Busts						
8.	1820	King George III, in old age	tc	Knox/Longstaffe-Gowan coll	SD	C Lib (repr)

FRANCHESCHI, B fl 1842–44

His address when exhibiting at the Royal Academy was given as 20 London Street in 1842 and 14 Carburton Street in 1844.

Literary References: *Gunnis* 1968, 157; *Graves* III, 1905–6, 156

Busts

1.	1842	Queen Victoria	[Exhib RA, London, 1337]; untraced	*Graves* III, 1905–6, 156
2.	1844	Albert, the Prince Consort	[Exhib RA, London, 1375]; untraced	*Graves* III, 1905–6, 156

FRANCIS, James, of Clapham *c*1751–1833

He was probably born in 1751, for an inscription tablet in St Paul's, Clapham records his death in 1833 at the age of 82. In 1795 he was paid £32 for the balcony of Sir John Crawford's house, 146 Piccadilly (Soane Archives, cited by GPC). He was also employed as a mason at Clapham parish church in 1802 and rebuilt the tower of St Anne, Soho, in the same year (Ch W, cited by *Gunnis* 1968, 157). His first wife, Susannah, died at Newington, Surrey, in October 1777, a few days after the birth of her only child, Charles. Charles was later apprenticed to the architect Francis Hurlbatt and established a cement works at Nine Elms, Vauxhall, *c*1810 (inf Major A J Francis, 1960, in GPC). James's second wife, Jane, née Hewson, died at Clapham in 1808, aged 49 (*Genealogists' Magazine*, II, 336, cited by GPC).

Literary References: *Gunnis* 1968, 157

Archival References: GPC

Funerary Monuments

1.	1798	B Carpenter (†1782) and family	St Eustace, Tavistock, Devon	S	Pevsner, *Devon*, 1989, 781
2.	1798	Elizabeth Davidson	St George the Martyr, Southwark, London	S	*Gunnis* 1968, 157

FRANCIS, John 1780–1861

Francis was born in Lincoln in 1780 and began his working life as a farmer in Thornham, Norfolk, marrying the local miller's daughter, Mary Evetts of Burnham Thorpe, a relation of Lord Nelson. In 1806 he travelled to London to attend Nelson's funeral and on his return carved a model of the funeral carriage from pieces of jet he had collected at the seashore. A member of the influential Vernon family saw the model and encouraged him to take up sculpture, promising future patronage. Thomas William Coke, the renowned agriculturist of nearby Holkham Hall, also took an interest in Francis and advised him to go to London and study with an established sculptor. Francis took this advice and worked first under **Samuel Joseph** and then with **Frances Chantrey**. He found it hard to make a living as a sculptor and was forced to return three times to the Norfolk farm.

He exhibited at the Royal Academy for the first time in 1820, showing busts of his patron Thomas William Coke (**26**) and Sir William Bolton, who had served at Trafalgar (**25**). Two years later he exhibited a bust of Horatia Nelson (**27**) and subsequently decided to settle permanently in London with his wife and four children. His wife was evidently not happy with this arrangement for she threw one of his first commissioned busts out of a window. Over the next few years he received a number of prestigious orders for busts, including heads of George IV and Queen Caroline, and of the late Princess Charlotte (**29, 33**).

In 1830 Francis rescued a woman who had jumped from a bridge into the Serpentine and so was awarded a testimonial on vellum by the Royal Humane Society. This brought him to the attention of the Duke of Sussex, who took a keen interest in the Society and, being much impressed by his character, became one of his most important patrons. It was no doubt through the Duke's influence that he became a favourite sculptor of the Whig party, carving portraits, amongst others, of Earl Grey (**47**), Earl Russell (**49**) Lord Brougham (**57**) and Earl Spencer (**63**), all prominent supporters of the 1832 Reform Bill. Francis also provided busts of the Duke's brothers and fellow freemasons, King William IV and the late Duke of Kent (**52, 54**).

In 1835, **Thomas Thornycroft**, an immature young man from Cheshire with an aptitude for sculpture, was introduced to the Duke of Sussex. The Duke suggested that Thornycroft should go to London and become one of Francis's pupils, where he would gain useful instruction whilst being kept away from the temptations of city life. Thornycroft arrived at Albany Street, Regents Park and joined the Francis household, which included two other pupils, **Joseph Durham** and **Matthew Noble** He found contentment and purpose with the homely Francis family and in 1840 married the eldest daughter, **Mary Francis (Thornycroft)**.

Francis continued his association with the royal family, executing a bust of Queen Victoria in 1837, the year of her accession (**64**). When she married in 1840 he was asked to carve a bust of Prince Albert (**74**). The prince took a keen interest in sculpture and early in 1844 he commissioned Francis to assist him with a bust of his father, the Duke of Saxe Coburg, who had recently died (**80**). The prince himself was actively involved in modelling the head when it was dropped and, as the Queen noted in her diary on 3 March, 'was broken into atoms or rather squashed to a lump' (*Roberts* 1987, 116, n 105). Francis re-worked the bust, the prince made the finishing touches and a few days later the royal couple watched the casting process. Prince Albert's much-loved greyhound died in 1844 and Francis was called to Windsor to work on a model of the dog under the Prince's direction. The bronze statue was placed over the dog's grave in the Home Park at Windsor and a cast was made for the terrace at Osborne House, Isle of Wight (**20**). The model was exhibited at the RA in 1848.

Francis continued to be a regular exhibitor at the Royal Academy until 1857, principally showing largely portrait busts. He had the satisfaction of seeing his daughter Mary Thornycroft follow in his footsteps to become one of the royal family's favourite sculptors. He died on 30 August 1861, aged 81, at his home in Albany Street and was buried at Highgate Cemetery.

Sylvia Allen

Literary References: *Graves* 1905–6, III, pp 159–160; *Thornycroft* 1932, 6–13; *Manning* 1982, 21–24, 39; *Roberts* 1987, 116–17; *Wake* 1988, 89

Archival References: Royal Humane Society Records, Annual Report, 1831, 42–44

Funerary Monuments

1.	?1823	Hon Frances Warren	Stockport, Cheshire		*Gunnis* 1968, 158
2.	?1827	William Walcot	Oundle, Northants		*Gunnis* 1968, 158
3.	†1829	Sir Richard Brooke	Great Oakley, Northants		Pevsner, *Northants*, 1973, 236
4.	†1835	George Charles, Lord Vernon and wife	Sudbury, Derbys	S	Pevsner, *Derbys*, 1978, 331
5.	†1842	Thomas, 1st Earl of Leicester, bust only (canopy by Joseph Hall II of Derby)	Longford, Derbys		Pevsner, *Derbys*, 1978, 268
6.	?1843	Anne, Viscountess Anson	Colwich, Staffs		*Gunnis* 1968, 158
7.	1844	Elizabeth Johnson (†1843)	St Mary and St Nicholas, Spalding, Lincs		Pevsner, *Lincs*, 1989, 673

Statues

No.	Date	Subject		Location		Reference
8.	1830	Arthur, 1st Duke of Wellington		[Exhib Soc of BA, London, 852]; untraced		*Johnson* 1975, 168
9.	1831	John, 1st Earl Russell	m	[NPG, London, 1883]; Westminster Abbey, London, Norman porch	D	*Graves* III, 1905–6, 160; *Walker* 1965, 21, cat 82
10.	1832	Charles, 2nd Earl Grey, cabinet statue	m	[Exhib RA, London, 1226]; untraced		*Graves* III, 1905–6, 160
11.	1832	King George IV		Freemasons' Hall (New), Holborn, London		Pevsner, *London: N*, 1998, 267
12.	1834	George, 1st Duke of Sutherland	m	[Exhib RA, London, 1107]; untraced		*Graves* III, 1905–6, 160
13.	1834	Lord Brougham	m	[Exhib RA, London, 1109]; untraced		*Graves* III, 1905–6, 160
14.	1835	Lady Adeliza Howard	m	[Exhib RA, London, 1131]; untraced		*Graves* III, 1905–6, 160
15.	1837	Augustus Frederick, Duke of Sussex, statuette	m	[Exhib RA, London, 1288]; untraced		*Graves* III, 1905–6, 160
16.	1837	Il Penseroso Payment(s): £85		[Francis studio sale, 6 March 1862]; untraced		*Graves* III, 1905–6, 160; Phillips archives in GPC
17.	1837	William, Viscount Melbourne, statuette	m	[Exhib RA, London, 1254]; untraced		*Graves* III, 1905–6, 160
18.	1843	Duke of Sutherland	m	[for Dornoch Cathedral, Sutherland]; untraced		*Graves* III, 1905–6, 160
19.	1844	Albert, the Prince Consort		[Exhib Westminster Hall, London, 144]; untraced		*AU*, 1844, 215
20.	1848	Eos, Prince Albert's greyhound (modelled by Prince Albert) Model(s): exhib RA, London, 1848, 1470	b	Royal Coll, Windsor, RCIN 41483 Other versions: Osborne House, terrace, cast		*Graves* III, 1905–6, 160; *Read* 1982, 137, 139 (repr)
21.	nd	Queen Victoria Payment(s): £165		[Francis studio sale, 6 March 1862]; untraced		Phillips archives in GPC

Busts

No.	Date	Subject		Location		Reference
22.	1818	Richard, 2nd Earl of Mornington (after Nollekens)		Wellington Museum, Apsley House, London 1456–1948	SD	*Gunnis* 1968, 158
23.	1820	E R Pratt		[Exhib Norwich Soc of Artists]; untraced		inf: Norma Watt, Norwich Castle Museum
24.	1820	J Bloom		[Exhib Norwich Soc of Artists, 158]; untraced		inf: Norma Watt, Norwich Castle Museum
25.	1820	Sir W Bolton RN		[Exhib RA, London, 1041]; untraced		*Graves* III, 1905–6, 159
26.	1820	Thomas William Coke, subsequently 1st Earl of Leicester		[Exhib RA, London, 1016]; untraced		*Graves* III, 1905–6, 159
27.	1822	Horatia Nelson		[Exhib RA, London, 994]; untraced		*Graves* III, 1905–6, 159
28.	1822	Mr Scott		[Exhib RA, London, 1005]; untraced		*Graves* III, 1905–6, 159
29.	1823	George IV and Queen Caroline, a pair	m	[Charles and Barbara Robertson coll]; sold Sotheby, Bond St, 16 Dec 2002, lot 68		GB
30.	1823	T Devitt MP		[Exhib RA, London, 1128]; untraced		*Graves* III, 1905–6, 159
31.	1824	Thomas Coke, later 1st Earl of Leicester		Woburn Abbey, Beds		*Gunnis* 1968, 158
32.	c1825	Cicero		Woburn Abbey, Beds		*Gunnis* 1968, 158
33.	1825	Princess Charlotte	m	[Exhib RA, London, 1015]; untraced		*Graves* III, 1905–6, 159
34.	1825	T Devitt		[Exhib RA, London, 1034]; untraced		*Graves* III, 1905–6, 159
35.	1827	Mr Vernon		[Exhib RA, London, 1069]; untraced		*Graves* III, 1905–6, 159
36.	1827	Mrs Vernon		[Exhib RA, London, 1092]; untraced		*Graves* III, 1905–6, 159
37.	1828	Captain Francis Vernon		[Exhib RA, London, 1200]; untraced		*Graves* III, 1905–6, 159
38.	1828	Unidentified gentleman		[Exhib RA, London, 1186]; untraced		*Graves* III, 1905–6, 159
39.	1828	Unidentified gentleman		[Exhib RA, London, 1197]; untraced		*Graves* III, 1905–6, 159
40.	1828	Unidentified lady		[Exhib RA, London, 1149]; untraced		*Graves* III, 1905–6, 159
41.	1828	Unidentified lady		[Exhib RA, London, 1198]; untraced		*Graves* III, 1905–6, 159
42.	1829	Lord Holland	m	[Holland House, London]; untraced		*Graves* III, 1905–6, 159
43.	1830	Arthur, 1st Duke of Wellington, miniature marble		Woburn Abbey, Beds		*Graves* III, 1905–6, 159; *Gunnis* 1968, 158
44.	1830	Leopold of Saxe-Coburg, later first King of the Belgians		Windsor Castle		*Gunnis* 1968, 157
45.	1832	Arthur, 1st Duke of Wellington (after Nollekens)		Stratfield Saye, Hants		*Graves* III, 1905–6, 159
46.	1832	Bernard, 6th Duke of Bedford		Woburn Abbey, Beds		*Graves* III, 1905–6, 160; *Gunnis* 1968, 158
47.	1832	Charles, 2nd Earl Grey	m	[Exhib RA, London, 1148]; untraced Other versions: Francis studio sale, 6 March 1862, marble; untraced ex coll Rupert Gunnis; untraced		Phillips archives in GPC; *Graves* III, 1905–6, 159; *Read* 1982, 137, 139 (repr); *Knox* 1996, 92, 95 n 41
48.	1832	Duke of Kent		[Mansion House, City of London]; destroyed 1940		GPC
49.	1832	John, 1st Earl Russell	m	NPG, London, 678 Other versions: Windsor Castle, Berks, 1838 exhib RA, London, 1848, 1405, marble; untraced Francis studio sale, 6 March 1862, marble; untraced	SD	*Graves* III, 1905–6, 160; *Gunnis* 1968, 157; *Ormond* 1973, 407 (pl 803); Phillips archives in GPC
50.	1832	John, 5th Earl of Essex		[Exhib RA, London, 1185]; untraced Other versions: Francis studio sale, 6 March 1862, plaster copy; untraced		*Graves* III, 1905–6, 159; Phillips archives in GPC
51.	1832	King William IV		[Mansion House, City of London]; destroyed 1940 Other versions: Freemasons' Hall, London, 1832		*Graves* III, 1905–6, 159; GPC
52.	1832	King William IV (former Grand Master)	m	Freemasons' Hall, Great Queen Street, London	SD	*Gunnis* 1968, 158

53.	1832	King William IV, small	m	Royal Coll RCIN 11919	SD	JM
54.	1833	Edward, Duke of Kent, KG (Grand Master of the Ancients)	m	Freemasons' Hall, Great Queen Street, London	SD	*Gunnis* 1968, 158
55.	1833	G J Vernon MP, later 5th Baron Vernon, model		[Exhib RA, London, 1153]; untraced		*Graves* III, 1905–6, 160
56.	1833	Hon Mrs Vernon, model		[Exhib RA, London, 1148]; untraced		*Graves* III, 1905–6, 160
57.	1833	Lord Brougham	m	[Exhib RA, London, 1175]; untraced Other versions: exhib Soc of BA, London, 1835, 764 Madame Tussaud's, London, nd Studio sale, 6 March 1862, marble; untraced		*Graves* III, 1905–6, 160; *Johnson* 1975, 168; GPC
58.	1834	George, 1st Duke of Sutherland		Dunrobin Castle, Sutherland		*Graves* III, 1905–6, 160; *Gunnis* 1968, 158
59.	1834	George, 2nd Duke of Sutherland		Dunrobin Castle, Sutherland		*Graves* III, 1905–6, 160
60.	1836	Henry Bathurst, Bishop of Norwich		[Exhib RA, London, 1107]; untraced		*Graves* III, 1905–6, 160
61.	1836	William, Viscount Melbourne		[Exhib RA, London, 1117]; untraced		*Graves* III, 1905–6, 160
62.	1837	Harcourt Johnson		Eridge Castle, East Sussex		GPC
63.	1837	John, 3rd Earl Spencer		Althorp, Northants		*Graves* III, 1905–6, 160
64.	1837	Queen Victoria	m	CL Coll, Guildhall, London, acc no 100 Other versions: seven identified		*AU*, 1842, 127; *Graves* III, 1905–6, 160; *Ormond* 1973, 483, 484, 487; *Johnson* 1975, 168; *Knight* 1986, 338 (repr)
65.	1837	William, Viscount Melbourne	m	[Exhib RA, London, 1289]; untraced		*Graves* III, 1905–6, 160
66.	1838	Admiral Edward Vernon (after Rysbrack's bust at Sudbury Hall, Derbys)	m	NMM, Greenwich, SCU0056	S	
67.	1838	Arthur, 1st Duke of Wellington	m	[Exhib RA, London, 1258]; untraced		*Graves* III, 1905–6, 160
68.	1838	George, 1st Duke of Sutherland		Buckingham Palace, London		*Gunnis* 1968, 157
69.	1838	Lord Holland		Buckingham Palace, London Other versions: Windsor Castle, Berks		*Gunnis* 1968, 157
70.	1838	William, Viscount Melbourne	m	[Royal Coll (presented by the sitter)]; Gov Art coll (1920)		Gov Art Coll archives
71.	1839	Colonel C R Fox	m	[Exhib RA, London, 1341]; untraced		*Graves* III, 1905–6, 160
72.	c1839	John, 6th Duke of Bedford		Tavistock Library (formerly Abbey Gatehouse), Devon		Pevsner, *Devon*, 1989, 783
73.	1839	Lady Fox	m	[Exhib RA, London, 1345]; untraced		*Graves* III, 1905–6, 160
74.	1840	Albert, the Prince Consort	m	[Mansion House, City of London]; CL Coll, Guildhall, London, acc 105 Other versions: five identified		*AU*, 1844, 170; *Graves* III, 1905–6, 160; *Ormond* 1973, 9, 12, 13 (repr 16); *Knight* 1986, 338 (repr); Pevsner, *London: City*, 1997, 384
75.	1840	Harriet, Countess of Sutherland		[Exhib RA, London, 1172]; untraced		*Graves* III, 1905–6, 160
76.	1840	James Locke MP	m	Stoke College, Suffolk		*Graves* III, 1905–6, 160
77.	1840	Queen Louise of Belgium		Windsor Castle		*Gunnis* 1968, 157
78.	1841	Princess Augusta		[for the Duke of Sussex]; untraced		*Graves* III, 1905–6, 160
79.	1843	Bernard, 12th Duke of Norfolk	m	[Exhib RA, London, 1430]; untraced		*Graves* III, 1905–6, 160
80.	1844	Ernst, Duke of Saxe-Coburg and Gotha (Ernst I) Payment(s): £105, with four casts for £20	m	Royal Coll RCIN 31323 Other versions: Royal Coll RCIN 2037; RCIN 34363	SD	JM
81.	1845	Charlotte, Duchess of Norfolk	m	[Exhib RA, London, 1458]; untraced		*Graves* III, 1905–6, 160
82.	1845	Henry, 13th Duke of Norfolk	m	[Exhib RA, London, 1366]; untraced		*Graves* III, 1905–6, 160
83.	1846	Duke of Saxe-Coburg and Gotha (probably Ernst II)		Buckingham Palace, London		*Gunnis* 1968, 157
84.	1847	Augustus Frederick, Duke of Sussex	b	[Exhib RA, London, 1355]; untraced		*Graves* III, 1905–6, 160
85.	by 1847	Ernst, Duke of Saxe-Coburg and Gotha, small (?Ernst II), probably a pair with 109		[coll Queen Victoria 1847]; Windsor Castle, RCIN 34114		
86.	1849	Hon Edward Petre	m	[Exhib RA, London, 1329]; untraced Other versions: studio sale, 6 March 1862, plaster copy; untraced		*Graves* III, 1905–6, 160; Phillips archives in GPC
87.	1851	H W Eaton	m	[Exhib RA, London, 1327]; untraced		*Graves* III, 1905–6, 160
88.	1851	Master Eaton	m	[Exhib RA, London, 1384]; untraced		*Graves* III, 1905–6, 160
89.	1851	Master Herbert Eaton	m	[Exhib RA, London, 1347]; untraced		*Graves* III, 1905–6, 160
90.	1851	Master William Eaton	m	[Exhib RA, London, 1344]; untraced		*Graves* III, 1905–6, 160
91.	1851	Miss Eaton	m	[Exhib RA, London, 1361]; untraced		*Graves* III, 1905–6, 160
92.	1851	William Lascelles MP	p	Castle Howard, N R Yorks	SD	*Gunnis* 1968, 158
93.	1852	Arthur, 1st Duke of Wellington	m	NPG, London 218	SD	*Gunnis* 1968, 158
94.	1852	Hon W S Lascelles		[Exhib RA, London, 1378]; untraced		*Graves* III, 1905–6, 160
95.	1853	Arthur, 1st Duke of Wellington	m	[Exhib RA, London, 1406]; untraced		*Graves* III, 1905–6, 160
96.	1853	George, 7th Earl of Carlisle	m	Castle Howard, N R Yorks Other versions: exhib RA, London, 1852, 1375		*Graves* III, 1905–6, 160
97.	1854	Hon and Rev James Norton	m	[Exhib RA, London, 1445]; untraced Other versions: Francis studio sale, 6 March 1862, plaster copy		*Graves* III, 1905–6, 160; Phillips archives in GPC
98.	1855	Admiral Sir Charles Napier		[RA, London, 1855, 1443]; untraced Other versions: Francis studio sale, 6 March 1862, marble; untraced		Phillips archives in GPC; *Graves* III, 1905–6, 160

99.	1859	George, 4th Earl of Aberdeen		[Exhib RA, London, 1348]; untraced	*Graves* III, 1905–6, 160
100.	nd	Cherub with a goose, after the antique	b	Royal Coll RCIN 41484	JM
101.	nd	Duke and Duchess of Saxe-Coburg		Royal Coll, Osborne House, I of W	*Gunnis* 1968, 157
102.	nd	Ernst, Duke of Saxe-Coburg and Gotha	b	Windsor Castle, RCIN 2159	JM
103.	nd	General Harcourt	p	[Francis studio sale, 6 March 1862]; untraced	Phillips archives in GPC
104.	nd	George, Duke of Sutherland		Sutton Place, Guildford	*Gunnis* 1968, 157
105.	nd	Lady Vernon	m	[Francis studio sale, 6 March 1862]; untraced	Phillips archives in GPC
106.	nd	Lord Vernon	p	Untraced	Phillips archives in GPC
107.	nd	Mrs Johnston	p	[Francis studio sale, 6 March 1862]; untraced	Phillips archives in GPC
108.	nd	Mrs Norris	p	[Francis studio sale, 6 March 1862]; untraced	Phillips archives in GPC
109.	nd	Princess Alexandrine, wife of Ernst, Duke of Saxe-Coburg and Gotha, small	m	Royal Coll RCIN 3411	JM
110.	nd	Sir Robert Peel	m	[Francis studio sale, 6 March 1862]; untraced	Phillips archives in GPC; *Ormond* 1973, 373
111.	nd	Sir Walter Scott		Madame Tussaud's, London	GPC
Chimneypieces					
112.	1805	Several Payment(s): £55 14s		[for the London house of Mr Bracebridge, of Atherstone, Warks]; untraced	Bracebridge archives in GPC
Miscellaneous					
113.	1808	Nelson's funeral carriage, carved from jet, model		Untraced	*Manning* 1982, 22 (repr)
114.	1837	Sleeping child		[Exhib RA, London, 1186]; untraced	*Graves* 1879, 197; *Graves* III, 1905–6, 160

FRANCIS, Mary

See **Thornycroft, Mary**

FRANKHAM, Jeremiah and Sons fl 1797–1821

The builders of Doddington Park, Glos between 1797 and 1821, they were responsible for all the masonry work, which is very fine. James Wyatt was the architect until his death in 1813, and the patron was Christopher Codrington (Codrington Archives, in GPC).

FRANKLIN, Joseph, of Cirencester, Purton and Stroud fl 1766–1850

Gunnis describes his monuments and tablets as 'uninteresting' (*Gunnis* 1968, 158).

Funerary Monuments					
1.	†1766	Ann Bond	Pitchcombe, Glos	S	Pevsner, *Glos: Cotswolds*, 1999, 561
2.	†1768	Thomas Jones	South Cerney, Glos	S	Pevsner, *Glos: Cotswolds*, 1999, 619
3.	†1773	Edmund Hinton and his wife, Ann (†1758)	Daglingworth, Glos	S	Pevsner, *Glos: Cotswolds*, 1999, 309
4.	†1776	Richard Aldridge	St Laurence, Stroud, Glos	S	Pevsner, *Glos: Cotswolds*, 1999, 650
5.	†1789	John Ballinger	Chedworth, Glos	S	Pevsner, *Glos: Cotswolds*, 1999, 222
6.	†1789	John Eycott	Withington, Glos	S	Pevsner, *Glos: Cotswolds*, 1999, 741
7.	†1790	Mary Nayler	St John the Baptist, Gloucester	S	Pevsner, *Glos: Vale & Forest of Dean*, 1976, 232
8.	†1790	Samuel Spencer	Stonehouse, Glos	S	Pevsner, *Glos: Vale & Forest of Dean*, 1976, 352
9.	†1790	William Carruthers	Painswick, Glos	S	Pevsner, *Glos: Cotswolds*, 1999, 544
10.	†1791	Esther Jones	South Cerney, Glos	S	Pevsner, *Glos: Cotswolds*, 1999, 619
11.	†1791	Jonathan Skinn	St John the Baptist, Cirencester, Glos	S	Pevsner, *Glos: Cotswolds*, 1999, 254
12.	?1791	Thomas Pearce	Ashbury, Berks	S	*Gunnis* 1968, 158
13.	†1792	William Hewer	St John the Baptist, Cirencester, Glos	S	Pevsner, *Glos: Cotswolds*, 1999, 254
14.	†1793	Ann Price and family members	Duntisbourne Abbots, Glos	S	Pevsner, *Glos: Cotswolds*, 1999, 329
15.	†1793	John Cripps	St John the Baptist, Cirencester, Glos	S	Pevsner, *Glos: Cotswolds*, 1999, 254
16.	†1799	John (†1789) and Ann Adams (†1799)	South Cerney, Glos	S	Pevsner, *Glos: Cotswolds*, 1999, 619
17.	†1801	John Jones	South Cerney, Glos	S	Pevsner, *Glos: Cotswolds*, 1999, 619
18.	?1802	John Bryant	Purton, Wilts		*Gunnis* 1968, 158
19.	†1802	John Phelps	Chiselden, Wilts	S	
20.	?1803	Richard Broome	Cliffe Pyppard, Wilts		*Gunnis* 1968, 158
21.	†1804	Rev Richard Bowles	St Lawrence, Lechlade, Glos	S	Pevsner, *Glos: Cotswolds*, 1999, 438
22.	?1807	Catherine Tarrant	Ashbury, Berks	S	*Gunnis* 1968, 158
23.	†1808	Crowdys family member	Chiselden, Wilts	S	
24.	?1811	John Sadler	Purton, Wilts		*Gunnis* 1968, 158
25.	?1812	Henry Wilson	Wootton Bassett, Wilts		*Gunnis* 1968, 158
26.	†1814	Catherine Bowles	St Lawrence, Lechlade, Glos		Pevsner, *Glos: Cotswolds*, 1999, 438

27.	?1822	William Stratton	Brinkworth, Wilts		*Gunnis* 1968, 158
28.	†1836	Thomas Colley	Chiselden, Wilts	S	
29.	†1838	William Crowdy	Highworth, Wilts		Pevsner, *Wilts*, 1975, 269
30.	†1839	Matthew Vivash	Purton, Wilts		Pevsner, *Wilts*, 1975, 375

FRANKS, of Brentford fl *c*1679–1711

He can probably be identified with 'Thomas Francks' who was granted the freedom of the Masons' Company by service to Robert Waters, on 25 November 1679 (Masons' Co, *Freemen*, fol 20). In 1687 Franks received £12 10s from the 1st Earl Fauconberg for work at Sutton Court, Chiswick, and there are payments to him noted in most years until 1704, some of them considerable sums (Wombwell Archives, in GPC). He was described as a 'stone cutter' when William Lowndes paid him £18 15s in 1700 for carved work and stone hearth-paving at Winslow Hall, Bucks, designed by Sir Christopher Wren (1). Lord Raby (afterwards Earl of Stafford) paid him £74 in 1708, and a further £59 in 1711 for work at his house near London (BM, Add MS. 22, 234, in GPC).

Literary References: *Gunnis* 1968, 158

Architectural Sculpture

1.	1700	A 'pair of Plints, a pair of Necks carved and Acorns to Sett up betweene the two gardens' Payment(s): £14	[Winslow Hall, Bucks]; untraced	*Wren Society*, XVII, 62

FRATODDI, Angelino

For further information the reader is referred to *Pyke* 1973, 50

FREEBAIRN, Richard G 1797–1825

Freebairn attended the Royal Academy Schools in 1814 and later studied in Rome, returning to England in 1821. He exhibited at the Royal Academy between 1818 and 1835 and at the British Institution in 1819. In 1822 he showed a bust of King George III 'under his afflicting malady' at the RA (*Lit Gaz*, 1822, 346) (**2**). His most important work, carved just before his death in 1825, was a marble statue of Psyche (**1**). *The Literary Gazette* considered that he had 'wrought it with sufficient variation to entitle him to credit for a very successful work' (*Lit Gaz*, 1825, 428).

Literary References: *Gunnis* 1968, 158

Statues

1.	1824	Psyche Model(s): exhib RA, London, 1824, 987; untraced	m	[Exhib RA, London, 1825, 1051]; untraced	*Graves* III, 1905–6, 167

Busts

2.	1821	King George III, model	[Exhib RA, London, 1164]; untraced	*Lit Gaz*, no 228, 2 June 1821, 346; *Graves* III, 1905–6, 167

Miscellaneous

3.	1818	A nymph	[Exhib RA, London, 1097]; untraced	*Graves* III, 1905–6, 167
4.	1819	Love and innocence	[Exhib BI, London, 9]; untraced	*Graves* 1875, 201
5.	1820	The deluge	[Exhib RA, London, 1072]; untraced	*Graves* III, 1905–6, 167
6.	1823	La ballerina	[Exhib RA, London, 1117]; untraced	*Graves* III, 1905–6, 167
7.	1823	Spring	[Exhib RA, London, 1123]; untraced	*Graves* III, 1905–6, 167
8.	1824	Cupid and Psyche, a sketch	[Exhib RA, London, 1018]; untraced	*Graves* III, 1905–6, 167

FREELOVE, John fl 1744

Described in *The Daily Advertiser*, 24 May 1744 as a carver (Burney 381b). (Inf. Terry Friedman)

FREEMAN, John, of Norwich fl 1806–34

Admiral Nelson presented the sword surrendered to him by the Spanish Admiral at the Battle of Cape St Vincent to the city of Norwich. It is displayed on a wall-monument in the Council Chamber of the Guildhall and was executed by 'Mr J Freeman of Norwich' (*Norfolk Chronicle* of 17 May 1806) (**1**).

The *Norwich Mercury* for 20 September 1834 stated that Freeman, 'Stone and Marble Mason of Aylsham' had taken over the premises of Mr **Charles Abbott**, to whom he had for many years been an assistant, and that he executed 'monuments, tombs, gravestones and chimney-pieces'.

Archival References: RG/JP, 4, 548v (inf. David Cubitt, 1991)

Miscellaneous

1.	1806	Monument displaying sword surrendered to Nelson at the battle of Cape St Vincent	Guildhall, Norwich, council chamber	*Norfolk Chronicle*, 17 May 1806

FREEMAN, William fl 1824–38

Between 1824 and 1828 he was employed in building the east wing of the British Museum, where he was paid sums totalling nearly £10,000 for stone and mason's work, some of it in collaboration with the mason Samuel Baker.

Literary References: *Gunnis* 1968, 158

Architectural Sculpture

1.	1824–1828	Four Ionic capitals Payment(s): £100	BM, London, East Wing	TNA WORK 5/119-5/125

FREER, Matthew fl 1770

The accounts at Castle Howard include a payment to 'Matthew Freer Jnr', made on 31 October 1770 for 'Carving the gate-way on Woodcock bank' (**1**), now known as the Exclamation Gate, which was designed by William Chambers and became the principal entrance to the estate for travellers journeying from York. Work on this structure is recorded in Castle Howard cash books of the period, but under the name of **William Ellis**, not Freer. Gunnis suggests that Freer may have carved the pair of stone dogs which were on the Woodcock Bank gate and were later removed to go above the front of the stables, where they still are. (inf. Christopher Ridgway)

Archival References: GPC

Architectural Sculpture

1.	1770	'Carving the gate-way on Woodcock bank'	[Castle Howard, N R Yorks]; untraced	Castle Howard Accounts in GPC

FRIEND (or FREND), John, of Canterbury fl 1704–47

He was apprenticed to **John Broxup** in 1704 and appointed chief mason to Canterbury Cathedral in 1731, a post he retained until 1747. His work there included repairs to the tracery of the windows, for which he received £500 between 1734 and 1735 (Canterbury Cathedral Archives, cited in *Gunnis* 1968, 158). He signs two architectural monuments in St Margaret's, Canterbury, which Gunnis describes as 'well executed and typical of their period, with weeping cherubs on either side' (**1, 2**). In 1702 he also supplied a sideboard with a marble slab for Lord Folkestone's house at Bifrons, Kent (Longford Castle Archives, cited in *Gunnis* 1968, 159). Gunnis suggests that Friend may have been responsible for the monument to Thomas Chafin (†1691) at Chettle. John Hutchins, in his *History of Dorset*, says that it is 'curiously sculptured and was made at Canterbury and erected in 1708' (*Hutchins* III, 1861–70, 570).

Literary References: *Gunnis* 1968, 158–9

Funerary Monuments

1.	†1709	John Barrett	St Margaret, Canterbury, Kent	S	Pevsner, *Kent: N E & E*, 1983, 240
2.	†1709	Paul Lukin	St Margaret, Canterbury, Kent	S	Pevsner, *Kent: N E & E*, 1983, 240

FULKES, Samuel –1714

Fulkes had a 'long and honourable career as a mason' (*Knoop and Jones* 1935, 33). He is first recorded working at 2s 6d per day on the Duke of York's Lodgings at Whitehall in 1664 (BM Harl MS 1618, cited by *Knoop and Jones* 1935, 33). He was the principal mason for the Haberdashers' Company at Aske's Hospital (1). On 1 September 1671 he was admitted to the freedom of the Haberdashers' Company by redemption and in the 1670s he had small contracts connected with the rebuilding of St Bride's, St Mary Aldermanbury, St Swithin's, and St Michael Queenhithe. In 1683, in partnership with **William Wise**, he accepted a contract at Winchester Palace calling for the employment of 28 masons and setters and 14 sawyers and labourers. During the 1680s he was also the contractor for significant amounts of masonry work at All Hallows, Bread Street, St Alban's, Wood Street, St Margaret Pattens and St Margaret's, Lothbury.

Fulkes may have worked for **Thomas Strong** and **Edward Strong I** as an overseer or foreman at St Paul's Cathedral. In the Masons' Company general search of 1678 the first name to appear under the heading 'At St Paul's' is 'Mr ffulkes, Haberdasher' and the fact that no other mason in the group was described as 'Mr' suggests that he held the most responsible post under the contractor (*Knoop and Jones* 1935, 33). He was later described in an Ely Cathedral building contract of 1699 as 'Overseer of the Masons' work on the Cathedral Church of St Paul's, London' (Ely Chapter Order Book, 25 November 1699, 229, cited by *Knoop and Jones* 1935, 33). If at times Fulkes served as an overseer he was also a contractor on quite a big scale for he received a large number of payments for work at St Paul's between about 1688 and 1700. There his work included carved shields and festoons, keystones and cherub-heads, Corinthian capitals, the great tribune at the west end, four scrolls in the library, the capitals on the north-west tower, the decorative work of the west portico and part of the great upper portico (**6**). The general search of 1694 shows that he was employing 16 men at St Paul's, as well as another 3 at his house in Fetter Lane. The sum he finally received for masonry and carved work for the building amounted to no less than £23,115.

In 1695 Fulkes was the master-mason at Aske's Hospital, Hoxton, and on 28 May that year the Minute-book of the Haberdashers' Company notes that Mr Fulkes was ordered 'to go on with the figures for the Great Gate' (*Gunnis* 1968, 159). These apparently stood on the piers of one of the entrance gates to the building and were described as 'two stone statues representing two of Aske's hospital men in full proportion' (*Stow* 1720, 212). In the same year the sculptor was paid for 'bassos, capitals and pineapples according to the modell' (Haberdashers' Company Archives, cited by *Gunnis* 1968, 159). During the 1690s he also worked in partnership with John Crooke, the son of **Richard Crooke** at Christ's Hospital, Newgate Street.

In 1707 Fulkes was elected warden of the Haberdashers' Company and on 1 December 1708 he was sworn on to the Court of Assistants (Haberdashers' Company Archives, Minutes of the Court of Assistants, 31 December 1707, 1 December 1708, cited by *Knoop and Jones* 1935, 34). One of Fulkes's daughters married **Edward Stanton**. She died in 1712 at the age of 38 and the epitaph on her tomb in the churchyard of St Andrew, Holborn, was recorded by Le Neve in his *Monumenta Anglicana* (*Le Neve* IV, 104, cited by *Gunnis* 1968, 159). Fulkes himself died 2 years later.

Literary References: *Weaver* 1915, 16, 18, 20–2; *Knoop and Jones* 1935, 33–4, 41, 42, 44, 46–9, 51–2, 57; *Gunnis* 1968, 159; *Wren Soc*, VII, X, XIV, XV, XIX, *passim* (see index XX, 75)

Will: PROB 11/542, 22 Sept 1714

Statues

1.	1695	'ye ffigures for ye..Gate [piers]' on Pitfield Street, and 'bassos, capitals and pineapples according to the modell'		[Aske's Hospital, Hoxton, London]; untraced	Haberdashers Minutes, 35, 40, 44; *Gunnis* 1968, 159

Chimneypieces

2.	1683	'Two surcular whitt marble chimny pieces' for the 'Belton Room' and the 'Duchess Closet'		[Northumberland House, Charing Cross, London]; untraced	Archives, Duke of Northumberland in GPC

Architectural Sculpture

3.	1685	Font Payment(s): £15		St Swithin, Cannon Street, London	*Wren Soc*, X, 36 (repr)
4.	1686	Pillars and capitals	s	[Winchester Palace, Hants]; untraced	PRO E 351/3460 in GPC
5.	1695	'bassos, capitals and pineapples'		[Aske's Hospital, Hoxton, London]; untraced	Haberdashers' Co archives, cited by *Gunnis* 1968, 159
6.	1688–1700	Decorative carving		St Paul's Cathedral, London	*Wren Soc*, XIV and XV, *passim*
7.	nd	'eight freestone pillar-capitals and five pillaster capitals'		[St Margaret, Lothbury, London]; untraced	Bodleian, Rawlinson MSS 387, cited by *Gunnis* 1968, 159
8.	nd	Three Corinthian capitals Payment(s): £39		[St Margaret Pattens, London]; untraced	Bodleian, Rawlinson MSS 387, cited by *Gunnis* 1968, 159

FURNESS, of Kingston-upon-Hull

See **Bailey, George.** Furness is not known to have executed any works alone.

FURNISS, B C fl 1829–33

He exhibited at the Royal Academy in 1829 from Doctors Commons and in 1833, from 45 Kirby Street, Hatton Garden.

Literary References: *Graves* III, 1905–6, 182; *Gunnis* 1968, 159

Busts

1.	1829	Lord Cosmo Russell	[Exhib RA, London, 1067]; untraced	*Graves* III, 1905–6, 182

Reliefs

2.	1833	W Martin Coates, medallion	[Exhib RA, London, 1084]; untraced	*Graves* III, 1905–6, 182

Miscellaneous

3.	1829	Michael the archangel casting the angels out of Heaven	[Exhib RA, London, 1082]; untraced	*Graves* III, 1905–6, 182

G, II (or JJ) fl 1848

A small bust of Mark Kennaway in Exeter is signed with the initials 'IIG', or possibly 'JJG' (**1**). The sculptor has not been identified.

Archival References: GPC

Busts

1.	1848	Mark Kennaway	m	Rougemont House, Exeter, Devon	SD

GAFFIN, Thomas and Edward

Thomas Gaffin 1780–1855
Edward Gaffin 1819–1869

The Gaffin firm flourished between 1800 and the early 1900s and comprised at least 3 generations. Their showroom was at 63 Regent Street and they were responsible for large numbers of simple mural tablets in black and white marble. Gunnis describes them as the most prolific statuaries of the first half of the 19th century noting that from their workshop 'poured forth an apparently unceasing flood of tame, dull and uninteresting monuments and memorial tablets. The number they produced must have run into thousands, the majority of which have a strong family likeness; unfortunately it was such a very plain family'. He adds that their best works, including a monument with a 'lovely relief' commemorating John Willis at Greatford, Worcs (**38**), date from the 1830s but 'the memorials become duller and plainer as the years go on'.

From 1827 they had a workshop at Kensington Place, Millbank, though they clearly changed premises more than once for Edward Gaffin's undated tradecard describes him as a statuary and mason, supplying monuments, marble chimneypieces etc, from 37 Warwick Street and 1 Green's Court, Little Pulteney Street, Golden Square. Edward Gaffin died on 28 July 1855 and is described on his death certificate as 'Retired Sculptor Master'. The 1851 census states that his son, Thomas, was born in County Mayo. Edward died at his home in Bessborough Gardens, Pimlico, on 24 October 1869. Thomas and Edward are both buried at All Souls, Kensal Green.

Literary References: *Gunnis* 1968, 160; *Potterton* 1975, 47; *Curl* 2001, 197, 237

Archival References: GPC

Tradecard: for 'M. Gay and E. Gaffin', Heal Collection, BM 106.14f

Wills and Administrations: PPR, will of Thomas Gaffin, 18 November 1869, effects valued at under £1,600. The following list is arbitrary, but seeks to provide some idea of geographical distribution of the firm's works:

Funerary Monuments

1.	†1789	Arthur Raymond		St Michael, Lyme Regis, Dorset		Pevsner, *Dorset*, 1972, 259
2.	†1790	William Joseph Lockwood (by Thomas Gaffin)		Lambourne, Essex	S	
3.	†1797	Ann Carvile (by Edward Gaffin)		Paull, E R Yorks	S	Pevsner, *Yorks: E R & York*, 1995, 646
4.	†1797	Jane Stovin (by Edward Gaffin)		Paull, E R Yorks	S	Pevsner, *Yorks: E R & York*, 1995, 646
5.	†1801	Robinson and Ann Groome (by Edward Gaffin)		Aldeburgh, Suffolk	S	
6.	1806	Thomas Quintin (by Edward Gaffin)		Hatley St George, Cambs	S	Pevsner, *Cambs*, 1970, 405
7.	†1810	Edmund Filmer (by Edward Gaffin)	a	East Sutton, Kent	S	
8.	†1811	Sir John Stepney		St Elli, Llanelli, Carmarthen		*Dale-Jones and Lloyd* 1989, 49
9.	?1814	Sir Richard Neave		South Weald, Essex		*Gunnis* 1968, 160
10.	†1816	Unidentified subject, tablet (by Thomas Gaffin)		Beckington, Somerset		Pevsner, *Somerset: N & Bristol*, 1958, 142
11.	†1819	Charles, 4th Duke of Richmond (by Thomas Gaffin)		Chichester Cathedral, Sussex	S	
12.	†1821	Andrew Cowell		St Elli, Llanelli, Carmarthen		*Dale-Jones and Lloyd* 1989, 49
13.	†1821	Mary Stepney Cowell		St Elli, Llanelli, Carmarthen		*Dale-Jones and Lloyd* 1989, 49
14.	†1826	Louisa Garrard (by Thomas Gaffin)		Wheathampstead, Herts	S	
15.	?1827	Jemima Harvey		Langley Marish, Bucks		*Gunnis* 1968, 160
16.	†1827	Rhoda Pearce (by Edward Gaffin)		Staverton, Glos	S	Pevsner, *Glos: Vale & Forest of Dean*, 1976, 348
17.	?1827	Sophia St John		Coltishall, Norfolk		*Gunnis* 1968, 160
18.	†1828	Frances and Rev Henry (†1826) Alington (by Edward Gaffin)		Swinhope, Lincs	S	Pevsner, *Lincs*, 1989, 738
19.	†1828	William Torriano (by Edward Gaffin)		Stansted Mountfitchet, Essex		Pevsner, *Essex*, 1965, 366
20.	†1829	Dr Samuel Slade DD (by Edward Gaffin)		Chichester Cathedral, Sussex	S	

21.	†1829	Mary Atkyns (by Edward Gaffin)	Ketteringham, Norfolk	S	Pevsner, *Norfolk: N W & S*, 1999, 455
22.	†1830	Dr Mary Mudden (by Edward Gaffin)	St George, Bloomsbury, London	S	
23.	†1831	James Fawcett (by Edward Gaffin)	Mumbai (Bombay) Cathedral, India	S	GPC
24.	†1831	Susannah Gordon	All Saints, St John's Wood, London		RG/JP, 4, 552
25.	†1831	William Cookes (by Edward Gaffin)	Burgh-le-Marsh, Lincs	S	Pevsner, *Lincs*, 1989, 196
26.	†1832	Henry Augustus, Viscount Dillon (by Thomas Gaffin)	Spelsbury, Oxon	S	Pevsner, *Oxon*, 1974, 775
27.	†1833	Mary Vizard (by Edward Gaffin)	Little Faringdon, Oxon	S	Pevsner, *Oxon*, 1974, 685
28.	†1833	Mrs Hearle Rodd (by Edward Gaffin)	North Hill, Cornwall	S	Pevsner, *Cornwall*, 1970, 1282
29.	†1833	Mungo Dick	Richmond, Surrey	S	
30.	†1833	Two, to Pellew, Viscount Exmouth (by Edward Gaffin)	Christow, Devon	S	Pevsner, *Devon*, 1989, 261
31.	?1834	John Monck	St Mary, Reading, Berks		*Gunnis* 1968, 160
32.	†1834	Major Thomas Scott (by Edward Gaffin)	Fordwich, Kent	S	
33.	†1834	Richard (†1828) and Mary Lea (by Thomas Gaffin) (co-sculptor: Lovelock, of Beckenham)	Beckenham, Kent	S	
34.	†1834	Sarah and John (†1831) William	St Leonard, Bilston, Staffs		RG/JP, 4, 552
35.	?1834	Sarah Winfield	Tyringham, Bucks		*Gunnis* 1968, 160
36.	†1834	Sophia Hennis (by Edward Gaffin)	Exeter Cathedral, Devon	S	Pevsner, *Devon*, 1989, 383
37.	†1835	Anne Langton (by Edward Gaffin)	Warham, Norfolk	S	Pevsner, *Norfolk: N E & Norwich*, 1997, 707
38.	†1835	John Willis MD (by Thomas Gaffin)	Greatford, Lincs	S	Pevsner, *Lincs*, 1989, 328
39.	†1835	Mary Patten Bold (by Edward Gaffin)	St Luke, Farnworth, Lancs	S	*CIIA* 4/8/32–4 (repr)
40.	†1836	F Hearle Rodd (by Edward Gaffin)	North Hill, Cornwall	S	Pevsner, *Cornwall*, 1970, 128
41.	†1836	James Digby	Bourne, Lincs	S	Pevsner, *Lincs*, 1989, 173
42.	†1836	Robert Bradshaw (by Edward Gaffin)	King's Langley, Herts	S	
43.	1836	William Coryton	St Mellion, Cornwall	S	Pevsner, *Cornwall*, 1970, 190
44.	†1837	Hon Emily Wingfield (by Edward Gaffin)	Adlestrop, Glos	S	Pevsner, *Glos: Cotswolds*, 1999, 132
45.	1837	Mary Owen	Conway, Carnarvon		RG/JP, 4, 552
46.	T1838	Lady Sarah Wandesforde	Ulcombe, Kent	S	Pevsner, *Kent: W & Weald*, 1976, 589
47.	†1838	Rev Charles Neat (by Edward Gaffin)	Bishops Hatfield, Herts	S	
48.	†1838	W H Ord	St John, Whitfield, Northumbs		Pevsner, *Northumbs* 1992, 624
49.	†1839	Anne Howkins (by Edward Gaffin)	Orpington, Kent	S	
50.	†1840	Caroline Dashwood	St John the Baptist, Stanford-on-Soar, Notts		Pevsner, *Notts*, 1979, 335
51.	†1840	Deborah Hindes	Earl Soham, Suffolk		Pevsner, *Suffolk*, 1974, 194
52.	†1840	Elizabeth White	Stradbroke, Suffolk	S	Pevsner, *Suffolk*, 1974, 447
53.	†1841	Abraham Pole (by Edward Gaffin)	Todenham, Glos	S	Pevsner, *Glos: Cotswolds*, 1999, 697
54.	†1842	Edward Hamlin Adams	Llanarthey, Carmarthen		*Dale-Jones and Lloyd* 1989, 49
55.	†1842	Elizabeth (†1829) and George (†1842) Cathrow (by Edward Gaffin)	Great Amwell, Herts	S	
56.	†1842	General Lord Robert Edward Somerset (by Thomas Gaffin)	Great Badminton, Glos	S	
57.	†1842	John Jones MP	St Peter, Carmarthen		*Dale-Jones and Lloyd* 1989, 42, 49 (repr)
58.	†1842	Maria Sarah Moore (by Edward Gaffin)	St Mary the Virgin, Monken Hadley, Herts	S	
59.	†1842	Mary Jane Phillips (by Edward Gaffin)	Stoke D'Abernon, Surrey	S	
60.	?1843	Admiral the Hon Jacob Henniker	Hartfield, Sussex		*Gunnis* 1968, 160
61.	†1843	Charles Savill-Onley (by Edward Gaffin)	Stisted, Essex	S	Pevsner, *Essex*, 1965, 372
62.	†1843	Rev Edward John Cathrow (by Edward Gaffin)	Great Amwell, Herts	S	
63.	†1843	Robert Pauncefoote (by Edward Gaffin)	Preston, Glos	S	Pevsner, *Glos: Vale & Forest of Dean*, 1976, 324
64.	†1844	William Cookes	Burgh-le-Marsh, Lincs	S	Pevsner, *Lincs*, 1989, 196
65.	1845	William, 4th Earl of Mornington	Grosvenor Chapel, London	S	RG/JP, 4, 552
66.	†1846	Charles Clayton (†1846) and Charles Hill (†1845)	Irchester, Northants	S	
67.	†1846	Christiana and Emanuel (†1853) Goodhart (by Thomas Gaffin)	Beckenham, Kent	S	
68.	†1846	Helen Fellowes	Warblington, Hants	S	
69.	†1847	Charlotte Pye (by Thomas Gaffin)	Swinhope, Lincs	S	Pevsner, *Lincs*, 1989, 738

70.	?1847	Herbert Curteis and family	Wartling, Sussex		*Gunnis* 1968, 160
71.	†1847	Susannah Briggs	Oxcombe, Lincs	S	Pevsner, *Lincs*, 1989, 599
72.	†1847	Thomas Spencer Frost (by Thomas Gaffin)	Braydeston, Norfolk		Pevsner, *Norfolk: N E & Norwich*, 1997, 412
73.	†1848	Alexander Cumine Peat (by Thomas Gaffin)	Mumbai (Bombay) Cathedral, India	S	
74.	†1848	Joseph (†1844) and Maria Peyton (by Edward Gaffin)	Ardingly, Sussex	S	
75.	†1848	Mrs Wallis	Great Barrow, Cheshire	S	Pevsner, *Cheshire*, 1971, 226
76.	†1848	Robert Sutton (by Thomas Gaffin)	St Leonards, Bucks	S	
77.	†1849	Charles Booker	Holy Trinity, Guildford, Surrey	S	
78.	†1849	Robert Shedden	Hardmead, Bucks	S	Pevsner, *Bucks*, 1994, 371
79.	†1849	Sir Thomas Reade	Congleton, Cheshire	S	Pevsner, *Cheshire*, 1971, 182
80.	†1850	Hon Paul Horsford (by Thomas Gaffin)	Antigua Cathedral, WI	S	
81.	†1850	Thomas Thistlethwayte (by Thomas Gaffin)	Southwick, Hants	S	
82.	†1851	Henry Davis (by Thomas Gaffin)	Compton Greenfield, Glos	S	Pevsner, *Glos: Vale & Forest of Dean*, 1976, 164
83.	†1851	Lady Jane Sherard	Leadenham, Lincs	S	Pevsner, *Lincs*, 1989, 430
84.	†1851	Walter de Winton (by Thomas Gaffin)	Sandhurst, Glos	S	Pevsner, *Glos: Vale & Forest of Dean*, 1976, 334
85.	†1852	Captain Henry James Matson RN, and six shipmates (by Thomas Gaffin)	Emsworth, Hants	S	
86.	†1852	Frances Hutchinson (by Thomas Gaffin)	Hemhill, Kent	S	
87.	†1852	Henry Alleyne (by Thomas Gaffin)	St James, Holetown, Barbados	S	
88.	†1852	John Smalman	Quatfrod, Salop	S	
89.	†1852	Lieutenant-Colonel George (†1818) and Maria Clara Robertson	Carisbrooke, I of W	S	
90.	†1852	Mr Paxton	Barbados Cathedral, Bridgetown	S	
91.	†1852	Patty Crawfurd (by Thomas Gaffin)	St Swithun, East Grinstead, Sussex	S	
92.	†1852	Payne brothers	St Elli, Llanelli, Carmarthen		*Dale-Jones and Lloyd* 1989, 49
93.	†1853	Sarah Catherine Ramsay	St James (C of E), King Street, Sydney, New South Wales,	S	
94.	†1854	George Abercromby (by Thomas Gaffin)	Carisbrooke, I of W	S	
95.	†1854	John Thomas Hope (by Thomas Gaffin)	Dorrington, Salop	S	
96.	†1854	Thomas Shute	Christchurch Priory, Hants	S	RG/JP, 4, 551 rev.
97.	†1854	Valentine Gould	Kensal Green Cemetery, London	S	
98.	†1855	Charles Dorrington (by Thomas Gaffin)	Bisley, Glos	S	Pevsner, *Glos: Cotswolds*, 1999, 175
99.	†1855	Field-Marshall James, 1st Baron Raglan (by Thomas Gaffin)	Great Badminton, Glos	S	
100.	†1855	George Norman (by Thomas Gaffin)	Holy Trinity, Bromley, Kent	S	Pevsner, *Kent: W & Weald*, 1976, 185
101.	†1855	Henry Cobbe (by Thomas Gaffin)	Donabate, Co Dublin	S	*Potterton* 1975, 47
102.	†1856	John Cutting Packer	Barbados Cathedral, Bridgetown	S	
103.	†1856	Lucy Lord (by Thomas Gaffin)	Tythegston, Glamorgan	S	Pevsner, *Glamorgan*, 1995, 641
104.	†1857	Captain Henry King	Rochester Cathedral, Kent		RG/JP, 4, 551v
105.	†1857	Captain Samuel Read	Rochester Cathedral, Kent	S	RG/JP, 4, 552
106.	†1857	William Moore (by Thomas Gaffin)	All Souls, Langham Place, London	S	Pevsner, *London: N W*, 1991, 599
107.	†1858	Frances Reeve (by Thomas Gaffin)	Leadenham, Lincs	S	Pevsner, *Lincs*, 1989, 430
108.	†1858	Lady Sheffield (by Thomas Gaffin)	Burton-on-Stather, Lincs	S	Pevsner, *Lincs*, 1989, 201
109.	†1858	Matilda Shute	Wootton, I of W	S	
110.	†1859	Ann Isabella Sealy (by Thomas Gaffin)	St John, Hackleton's Cliff, Barbados	S	
111.	c1859	Legge family, tablets (by Thomas Gaffin)	Brimscombe, Glos	S	Pevsner, *Glos: Cotswolds*, 1999, 197
112.	†1859	Thomas Price	Richmond, Surrey	S	RG/JP, 4, 552
113.	1860	Charles and Ann Lascelles	Grosvenor Chapel, London	S	RG/JP, 4, 552
114.	†1860	Colonel A Pack (by Thomas Gaffin)	Kilkenny Cathedral	S	*Potterton* 1975, 47
115.	†1860	Edward (†1840) and Philip Frederick Honeywood (by Thomas Gaffin)	Elmsted, Kent	S	
116.	†1860	George Browne	Barbados Cathedral, Bridgetown	S	
117.	†1860	Joseph Liggins (by Thomas Gaffin)	Antigua Cathedral	S	
118.	†1861	George Lawrence	Salisbury Cathedral, Wilts	S	RG/JP, 4, 552
119.	†1861	Major-General Matthew Griffith (†1828) and his wife Louisa (†1861)	Padworth, Berks	S	
120.	†1862	Francis Head	St Elli, Llanelli, Carmarthen		*Dale-Jones and Lloyd* 1989, 49
121.	1862	Joseph Locke (†1860) (co-sculptor: A MacDonald, of Aberdeen)	Kensal Green Cemetery, London	S	*Curl* 2001, 197 (repr)
122.	?1863	Colin Campbell, Baron Clyde (†1863)	Westminster Abbey, London, nave		*Gunnis* 1968, 160

123.	†1863	Dr Benjamin Golding (by Thomas Gaffin)	St Osyth, Essex	S	
124.	†1863	Henrietta Vere	Kensal Green Cemetery, catacombs	S	
125.	†1863	Hon Charlotte Angerstein (by Thomas Gaffin)	Castleblaney, Co Monaghan	S	*Potterton* 1975, 47
126.	†1863	Rev John Netherton Harward (by Thomas Gaffin)	St Swithun, East Grinstead, Sussex	S	
127.	†1864	H L Wickham	East Worldham, Hants		RG/JP, 4, 551 rev.
128.	†1864	Lord Arthur Lennox	Chichester Cathedral, Sussex	S	
129.	†1865	Captains Robert (†1864) and Frederick Glover (†1865)	Hartley Wintney, Hants		RG/JP, 4, 551 rev.
130.	†1865	Jemima Wilson (co-sculptor: of Beckenham Lovelock)	Beckenham, Kent	S	
131.	†1865	Rev Frederick Vane	Great Canfield, Essex		RG/JP, 4, 551 rev.
132.	†1865	William Cameron	Christchurch Priory, Hants		RG/JP, 4, 551 rev.
133.	†1866	Emily, Lady Davis (by Thomas Gaffin)	Compton Greenfield, Glos	S	Pevsner, *Glos: Vale & Forest of Dean*, 1976, 164
134.	†1866	Hon James Watson Sheriff	Antigua Cathedral, WI	S	
135.	1868	John Hay Hill	Gressenhall, Norfolk	S	
136.	†1868	Major Richard Wellington (by Thomas Gaffin)	Templemore, Co Waterford	S	*Potterton* 1975, 47
137.	†1869	Dr Philip Phillips	St Mary, Upton, Torquay, Devon		RG/JP, 4, 551 rev.
138.	†1869	Ennis and Albert (†1868) Twyford (by Edward Gaffin)	Trotton, Sussex	S	
139.	†1869	Lieutenant Frank, Admiral William and Louisa Dashwood (by Thomas Gaffin)	Lyndhurst, Hants	S	
140.	†1871	Matthew Thompson	Cosby Garrett, Cumberland	S	
141.	†1872	Captain E H Gage Lambert (by Gaffin & Co)	Whitsbury, Hants		Pevsner, *Hants*, 1967, 651
142.	†1872	Simon Frase Campbell	Goathurst, Somerset	S	
143.	†1874	Anna Maria Spenser Phillips (by Thomas Gaffin)	Boreham, Essex	S	
144.	1874	Men of the 23rd Royal Welch Fusiliers († 4th Ashanti campaign 1873)	St Giles, Wrexham, Denbighs		Pevsner, *Clwyd*, 1986, 301
145.	†1875	William Vere	Kensal Green Cemetery, London, catacombs	S	
146.	†1876	Lieutenant Thomas Boydell	Gresford, Denbighs	S	
147.	†1876	William Wilkinson Whittaker	Ripon Cathedral, NR Yorks	S	
148.	†1879	William Augustus St Clair	Lingfield, Surrey	S	
149.	†1880	Captain Francis Bourne	Weston-sub-Edge, Glos		Pevsner, *Glos: Cotswolds*, 1979, 470
150.	†1880	Elizabeth Coulson and her parents	Père Lachaise Cemetery, Paris	S	
151.	†1881	George (†1854) and Rose Buxton	Mildenhall, Wilts	S	
152.	† to 1883	Petten family (by Edward Gaffin)	Bradford-on-Tone, Somerset	S	
153.	†1885	Miss L Wickham	East Worldham, Hants		RG/JP, 4, 552
154.	†1887	Lord Northwick	Blockley, Glos		Pevsner, *Glos: Cotswolds*, 1979, 122
155.	†1889	Charlotte Eva Edward	Ruthin, Denbighs	S	Pevsner, *Clwyd*, 1986, 270
156.	†1895	Colonel William Honeywood	Elmsted, Kent	S	
157.	†1898	E Brewster	St Mary, Leyton, Essex		Pevsner, *Essex*, 1965, 268
158.	†1908	Rev James Fleming	Kensal Green Cemetery, London		*Curl* 2001, 237
159.	nd	Lady Northwick	Blockley, Glos		Pevsner, *Glos: Cotswolds*, 1979, 122
160.	nd	Unidentified subject, tablet	Bunny, Notts	S	Pevsner, *Notts*, 1979, 85

GAHAGAN, C fl 1824–44

In 1828 he was employed as an assistant by **John Flaxman RA**, who paid him 3 guineas a week. He exhibited at the Society of British Artists in 1824 and 1828, and at the Royal Academy between 1831 and 1836, from a number of London addresses. His submission to the Westminster Hall Exhibition of 1844 drew a derisory comment from the art critic of the *Literary Gazette*: 'If the union conferred as little benefit upon the kingdoms as this gentleman upon the arts, the dissolution were most devoutly to be wished' (*Lit Gaz*, 1844, 483).

He can perhaps be identified with Charles Gahagan II (b *c*1801), a marble carver who was the grandson of **Lawrence Gahagan** and the son of Charles Gahagan I (b *c*1765) who was apprenticed to Charles Schofield, a liveryman of the Painters' Company. Charles Gahagan II was still alive in 1871 when he was listed in the census returns with his wife Mary Ann and three children.

Literary References: *Gunnis* 1968, 160

Archival References: City of London Apprenticeships 1442-1858; Flaxman Papers BM, Ad MS 39784, AA, fol 22

Busts					
1.	1831	Unidentified child		[Exhib RA, London, 1157]; untraced	*Graves* III, 1905–6, 189
2.	1832	Pierce Mahony		[Exhib RA, London, 1224]; untraced	*Graves* III, 1905–6, 189
3.	1836	Lewis Stevens		[Exhib RA, London, 1126]; untraced	*Graves* III, 1905–6, 189
Miscellaneous					
4.	1844	An allegorical representation of the union of the three kingdoms		[Exhib Westminster Hall, London]; untraced	*Gunnis* 1968, 160
5.	1824	Head of a dog		[Exhib Soc of BA, London, 358]; untraced	*Johnson* 1975, 172
6.	1828	Unidentified lady, model	w	[Exhib Soc of BA, London, 889]; untraced	*Johnson* 1975, 172
7.	1828	Unidentified lady, model	w	[Exhib Soc of BA, London, 892]; untraced	*Johnson* 1975, 172

GAHAGAN, Edwin *c*1806–58

The son of **Vincent Gahagan,** he exhibited at the Royal Academy and between 1831 and 1837 and showed a statue of Newton at Westminster Hall in 1844 (**4**). The *Art Journal* reported that it possessed 'marked merit' and gave 'promise of future excellence' (*AJ*, 1844, 215), while the *Literary Gazette* commented, 'Among so much that is worthless, it is a pleasure when we come to speak of that which can be admired. There is a charming softness in the finish of this piece, though the lower extremities appear to be exaggerated in length for the sake of importing elegance' (*Lit Gaz*, 27 July 1844, 482). He also exhibited at the British Institution in 1831 and perhaps in 1832, though the works shown in the latter year may have been by his father. He died on 5 July 1858. His son **Stephen Gahagan** was also a sculptor.

Literary References: *Gunnis* 1968, 160; SDA

Statues				
1.	1831	Infant Hercules, figure	[Exhib Soc of BA, London, 835]; untraced	*Graves* 1875, 205; *Johnson* 1975, 172
2.	1832	Frederick-Augustus, Duke of York and Albany, equestrian (possibly by Vincent Gahagan)	[Exhib BI, London, 593]; untraced	*Graves* 1875, 205
3.	1832	King William IV, cabinet statue	[Exhib Soc of BA, London, 855]; untraced	*Johnson* 1975, 172
4.	1844	Sir Isaac Newton	[Exhib Westminster Hall, London, 132]; untraced	*AU*, 1844, 215
Reliefs				
5.	1857	Medallion portrait	[Exhib RA, London, 1300]; untraced	*Graves* III, 1905–6, 190
Miscellaneous				
6.	1831	A falconing party in the costume of the seventeenth century	[Exhib RA, London, 1208]; untraced	*Graves* III, 1905–6, 190
7.	1831	Apollo repelling the attack of Diomed on Aeneas	[Exhib RA, London, 1139]; untraced	*Graves* III, 1905–6, 189
8.	1831	Infant Bacchus	[Exhib BI, London, 560]; untraced	*Graves* 1875, 205
9.	1831	Infant Jupiter	[Exhib BI, London, 559]; untraced	*Graves* 1875, 205
10.	1832	Achilles dragging the body of Hector round the walls of Troy	[Exhib Soc of BA, London, 857]; untraced	*Johnson* 1975, 172
11.	1832	The prodigal son	[Exhib Soc of BA, London, 856]; untraced	*Johnson* 1975, 172
12.	1837	Model of a boy	[Exhib RA, London, 1184]; untraced	*Graves* III, 1905–6, 190

GAHAGAN, Lawrence *c*1735–1820

The first known member of the Gahagan dynasty of sculptors, Lawrence was born in Ireland, where he won a premium from the Royal Dublin Society in 1756 (**3**). Shortly afterwards he moved to London and changed his name from Geoghegan to Gahagan. In 1762 he married Phoebe Hunter, with whom he had 4 sons, Charles (born *c*1765) and **Lucius, Vincent** and **Sebastian Gahagan.** It is not known whether Lawrence remained in London throughout his mature years or, like his son Lucius, moved to Bath, but he exhibited sculpture at the Royal Academy from 22 Dean Street in 1798, Pershore Place, New Road in 1800, 5 Little Tichfield Street in 1801 and 12 Cleveland Street, Fitzroy Square from 1809 until 1817.

The full extent of Gahagan's output cannot be gauged, since most of the works credited to him are undated and are identified only as being by 'L Gahagan'. Some of these may be by his son, Lucius. Graves lists 19 works, mostly portrait busts, by 'L Gahagan', exhibited at the RA in the years 1798–1817. The title page of a second major source for Lawrence's work, the sale catalogue of a Miss Fenton of Chandos House, Westgate Buildings, Bath, also fails to give a full first name. It reads 'Catalogue of Works of Art. . .by the *late* L. Gahagan, sculptor'. There is a pencilled notation '1840', and if the date is accurate, this opens up the possibility that some of the many busts, a few figures and a number of reliefs may be the work of Lucius. Indeed one of the subjects, a group of Maria Bagnell and her murderer, Gilham (described as Gillingham in the sale catalogue) illustrates a notorious murder that took place in 1828 and so must be by Lucius, for Lawrence had by then been dead eight years. Another subject, a bust of Mayor Goldney of Chippenham, depicts a worthy who did not come into office until 1853. It seems likely that Miss Fenton's sale was principally of Lawrence's work, but that Lucius, who, like Miss Fenton, had lodgings in his later years at Chandos House, included some of his own sculpture in the sale, including the Bagnell tableau and Goldney bust. It is possible that sculpture by outsiders was included in the auction and wrongly credited to L Gahagan.

In 1777 Lawrence was awarded a premium by the Society of Arts for a relief 6 feet high, depicting *Alexander exhorting his troops* (**85**). In 1801 he was employed on decorative work at Castle Howard (**84**) and in 1806 he submitted a model for the proposed monument to Pitt at Guildhall (**6**). His design was rejected and he later wrote to the Committee that he had 'made four applications at your office for my model, but could not obtain it until last Saturday and then in a very mutilated state' (Guildhall Committee/Lawrence Gahagan). Gahagan's two colossal statues of Isis and Osiris, commissioned in 1811, formed part of the façade of William Bullock's Egyptian Hall in Piccadilly (**8**). Though the subjects are Egyptian, their elegantly turned poses and vulnerable faces have affinities to the 18th-century tradition of blackamoor figures.

Gahagan was known for his portrait busts of celebrities, many of them produced as multiples available in a variety of materials and sizes. His subjects included members of the Royal family (**75, 76**), statesmen (**42, 44, 68**), national heroes (**43, 63, 66, 73**) and the poet Byron (**56**). Mary Anne Clarke (**53**), the Duke of York's mistress, who was depicted like the Antique *Clytie*, rising 'roguishly feminine from a sunflower' (*Kerslake* 1966, 162), had used her influence with the Duke to obtain army appointments, a transgression which led to a heated parliamentary enquiry. Madame Catalani was a noted opera singer (**69**) and Sir Edward Parry, a famous explorer (**81**). Other subjects had a particular appeal for West Country clients: George Whitfield, the preacher and missionary, came from Gloucester (**82**), William Jay was a popular Bath preacher (**62**) and Sir William Struth was Mayor of Bristol (**59**). Gahagan's subjects evidently respected his work, for the Chandos House catalogue relates that in 1798 Lord Nelson honoured the sculptor with seven sittings for his bust (**43**), which was later engraved by Barnard. A trade card issued in 1815 by 'L Gahagan' informed the public that 'the only Bust to which His Imperial Majesty, the Emperor of all the Russias, ever condescended to sit is on view at the sculptor's study, 12 Cleveland Street, Fitzroy Square' (**65**) (Heal Coll, BM D.2.1324).

The provision of popular images extended to statuettes, some of which formed an obvious postscript to a well-received bust. Hannah More is best known as a leader of the Sunday School movement (**11**) and Princess Caribou was a Devonian who famously tricked people into believing she was a Javanese princess (**30**). Subjects from the Bath Establishment included Ralph Allen of Prior Park (**32**), the Francis Taylors and the Harding family (**14, 28, 29, 34, 35, 37**).

Sylvia Allen/IR

Literary References: *Graves* III, 1905–6, 190, 191; *Strickland* 1, 1913, 391–392; *Kerslake* 1966 (1), 159; *Gunnis* 1968, 160–1; *Ward-Jackson* 2003, 231–2; SDA

Additional MS sources: Tradecard for 'L. Gahagan', undated, BM, Banks Coll, 106.12

Miscellaneous Drawings: *Giving the Flitch of Bacon at Dunmow*, large drawing, Chandos House sale, untraced

Auction Catalogues: Chandos House, Bath (?1840)

Portraits of the Sculptor: Vincent Gahagan, 'portrait of his father', exhib RA, London, 1804 (898), untraced

Funerary Monuments

1.	1810	Joseph Baldwin		Cholebury, Bucks	S	*Gunnis* 1968, 161
2.	†1816	Rev Nathaniel Thornbury		Avening, Glos	S	Pevsner, *Glos: Cotswolds*, 1999, 150

Statues

3.	1756	'a piece of sculpture', probably a statuette of Rubens		[Royal Dublin Society]; untraced		*Gunnis* 1968, 160
4.	1800	A bull, statuette		[Exhib RA, London, 969]; untraced		*Graves* III, 1905–6, 190
5.	1803	Two Egyptian winged female figures, statuettes	p	Corsham Court, Wilts, dining room	SD	
6.	1806	Rt Hon William Pitt, model		[for Guildhall, City of London]; untraced		*Gunnis* 1968, 160
7.	1809	Venus directing the arrow of Cupid, model		[Exhib BI, London, 339]; untraced		*Graves* 1875, 205
8.	1811	Isis and Osiris		[Egyptian Hall, Piccadilly]; Museum of London	SD	*Ward-Jackson* 2003, 231–2
9.	1811	King George III, statuette (perhaps by Lucius Gahagan)	b	Untraced Other versions: Multiples in plaster, 1820 (jubilee souvenirs)		GPC
10.	1818	King George III, polychrome statuette	p	Melbourne Art Gallery, Australia Other versions: Royal Coll, SD 1818 YCBA B 1977.14.11, *c*1820, signed, Christie, London 20 April 1988, 1818, SD; untraced	SD	
11.	1822	Hannah More, seated with a standing child, statuette, patinated black (perhaps by Lucius Gahagan)	p	[Chandos House, Bath]; Knox/Longstaffe-Gowan coll (acq 1994) Other versions: ex coll Derek Sherborn, Brighton, 1835, SD Killerton, Devon (NT), biscuit	SD	Chandos House sale
12.	nd	'A young sailor and several other large figures' (perhaps by Lucius Gahagan)		[Chandos House, Bath]; untraced		Chandos House sale
13.	nd	Admiral Lord Nelson, two statuettes (perhaps by Lucius Gahagan)		[Chandos House, Bath]; untraced		Chandos House sale
14.	nd	'Col Harding in Hussar dress, with his horse', statuette (perhaps by Lucius Gahagan)		[Chandos House, Bath]; untraced		Chandos House sale
15.	nd	Cupid with his bow, statuette (perhaps by Lucius Gahagan)		[Chandos House, Bath]; untraced		Chandos House sale
16.	nd	Esculapius, Hippocrates, Hygeia, Pitt, Fox and others, models (perhaps by Lucius Gahagan)		[Chandos House, Bath]; untraced		Chandos House sale
17.	nd	'figure of an Indian runner' (perhaps by Lucius Gahagan)		[Chandos House, Bath]; untraced		Chandos House sale
18.	nd	'figure of Britannia', statuette (perhaps by Lucius Gahagan)		[Chandos House, Bath]; untraced		Chandos House sale
19.	nd	'Gentleman and 2 children, group', small figures (perhaps by Lucius Gahagan)		[Chandos House, Bath]; untraced		Chandos House sale
20.	nd	Innocence with the dove, statuette (perhaps by Lucius Gahagan)		[Chandos House, Bath]; untraced		Chandos House sale
21.	nd	King George III, leaning on a cane and holding a telescope in his left hand, statuette	b	Christie, 20 April 1988; untraced	S	Christie, London, 20 April 1988
22.	nd	'King George IV, figure' (perhaps by Lucius Gahagan)		[Chandos House, Bath]; untraced Other versions: 'another very handsome figure of George IV', Chandos House sale; untraced		Chandos House sale
23.	nd	King William IV seated in a chair, model (perhaps by Lucius Gahagan)	tc	[Chandos House, Bath]; untraced		Chandos House sale

24.	nd	'Large and handsome group of the Holy Family' (perhaps by Lucius Gahagan)		[Chandos House, Bath]; untraced		Chandos House sale
25.	nd	Lord Brougham, statuette (perhaps by Lucius Gahagan)		[Chandos House, Bath]; untraced		Chandos House sale
26.	nd	'Lord Shield at study', small figure (perhaps by Lucius Gahagan)		[Chandos House, Bath]; untraced		Chandos House sale
27.	nd	Miss Bowles, statuette (perhaps by Lucius Gahagan)		[Chandos House, Bath]; untraced		Chandos House sale
28.	nd	Mr Francis Taylor, small group (perhaps by Lucius Gahagan)		[Chandos House, Bath]; untraced		Chandos House sale
29.	nd	Mrs Francis Taylor, small group (perhaps by Lucius Gahagan)		[Chandos House, Bath]; untraced		Chandos House sale
30.	nd	Princess Caribou, statuette (perhaps by Lucius Gahagan)		[Chandos House, Bath]; untraced		Chandos House sale
31.	nd	'Queen in her coronation robes', statuette (perhaps by Lucius Gahagan)		[Chandos House, Bath]; untraced		Chandos House sale
32.	nd	Ralph Allen of Prior Park, statuette (perhaps by Lucius Gahagan)		[Chandos House, Bath]; untraced		Chandos House sale
33.	nd	'Sitting figure of a child, with a bird's nest, suitable for holding a light' (perhaps by Lucius Gahagan)		[Chandos House, Bath]; untraced		Chandos House sale
34.	nd	'standing figure of Miss H Harding', statuette (perhaps by Lucius Gahagan)		[Chandos House, Bath]; untraced		Chandos House sale
35.	nd	'the late Col Harding', statuette (perhaps by Lucius Gahagan)		[Chandos House, Bath]; untraced		Chandos House sale
36.	nd	'The late Lady Hood of the Circus', statuette (perhaps by Lucius Gahagan)		[Chandos House, Bath]; untraced		Chandos House sale
37.	nd	'the late Miss Harding with piano', statuette (perhaps by Lucius Gahagan)		[Chandos House, Bath]; untraced		Chandos House sale
38.	nd	'the late Mrs Ford (mother of the present Captain Ford)', statuette (perhaps by Lucius Gahagan)		[Chandos House, Bath]; untraced		Chandos House sale
39.	nd	'the Queen, George III, Coke, Nelson, Cranmer and Latimer', small figures (perhaps by Lucius Gahagan)		[Chandos House, Bath]; untraced		Chandos House sale
40.	nd	'very pretty sitting statuette of Pitt' (perhaps by Lucius Gahagan)		[Chandos House, Bath]; untraced		Chandos House sale
Busts						
41.	1798	Admiral Sir Thomas Paisley		[Exhib RA, London, 1046]; untraced		*Graves* III, 1905–6, 190
42.	1798	Charles James Fox	tc	Gov Art Coll (1938)	SD	*Graves* III, 1905–6, 190
43.	1798	'Sir Horatio Nelson' (perhaps by Lucius Gahagan)		[Exhib RA, London, 1050]; Lord Cottesloe Other versions: Bath Art Gallery, Avon, 1804 NMM, Greenwich, 1804, plaster NMM, Greenwich, SCU0096, bronze, nd NMM, Greenwich, SCU0097, tc, nd NMM, Greenwich, SCU0098, plaster, 1839		Chandos House sale; *Graves* III, 1905–6, 190; *Yarrington* 1997, 41, GPC
44.	1800	Rt Hon William Pitt		[Exhib RA, London, 1092]; untraced		*Graves* III, 1905–6, 190
45.	1801	Unidentified gentleman, 'bust'		[Exhib RA, London, 994]; untraced		*Graves* III, 1905–6, 190
46.	1801	Unidentified gentleman, 'head'		[Exhib RA, London, 993]; untraced		*Graves* III, 1905–6, 190
47.	1807	Unidentified man wearing a medallion inscribed 'The Triumph of Truth'	m	NGI 8058	SD	*Harbison, Potterton and Sheehy* 1978, 178 (repr); *le Harivel* 1988, 565 (repr)
48.	1809	Bishop of St Pol de Leon		[Exhib RA, London, 757]; untraced		*Graves* III, 1905–6, 190
49.	1809	The late Dr Hawes, treasurer of the Humane Society		[Exhib RA, London, 861]; untraced		*Graves* III, 1905–6, 190
50.	1809	Unidentified child		[Exhib RA, London, 781]; untraced		*Graves* III, 1905–6, 190
51.	1809	Unidentified gentleman		[Exhib RA, London, 860]; untraced		*Graves* III, 1905–6, 190
52.	1811	Arthur, 1st Duke of Wellington	b	Stratfield Saye, Hants		*Gunnis* 1968, 160
53.	1811	Mary Anne Clarke	m	NPG, London 4436	SD	*Crookshank* 1966, 308
54.	1812	Sir Thomas Lawrence	b	NGI 8068	SD	*le Harivel* 1988, 565; *Wynne and White* 1975, 18
55.	1812	Unidentified subject	b	ex coll Rupert Gunnis, untraced		*Gunnis* 1968, 160
56.	?c1814	Lord Byron (perhaps by Lucius Gahagan)	tc	[Chandos House, Bath]; untraced Other versions: ex coll David Verey (1953); untraced		Chandos House sale; GPC
57.	1816	Rev Dr Parr of Bristol		[Exhib RA, London, 944]; untraced Other versions: Exhib RA, 1816 (944)		*Graves* III, 1905–6, 190
58.	1816	Sir Samuel Romilly		[Exhib RA, London, 940]; untraced		*Graves* III, 1905–6, 190
59.	1816	Sir William Struth, Mayor of Bristol		[Exhib RA, London, 938]; untraced		*Graves* III, 1905–6, 190
60.	1817	Unidentified gentleman		[Exhib RA, London, 1063]; untraced		*Graves* III, 1905–6, 190
61.	1817	Unidentified gentleman		[Exhib RA, London, 1066]; untraced		*Graves* III, 1905–6, 190
62.	1839	Rev William Jay (perhaps by Lucius Gahagan)	p	[Chandos House, Bath]; Knox/Longstaffe-Gowan coll (acq 1994)	SD	Chandos House sale
63.	nd	Arthur, 1st Duke of Wellington (perhaps by Lucius Gahagan)		[Chandos House, Bath]; untraced Other versions: ex coll Miss Fenton, Chandos House, Bath; untraced		Chandos House sale

64.	nd	Captain Berry (perhaps by Lucius Gahagan)	[Chandos House, Bath]; untraced	Chandos House sale
65.	nd	Emperor Alexander I, bronze or terracotta model (perhaps by Lucius Gahagan)	[Chandos House, Bath]; untraced	Chandos House sale
66.	nd	General Blücher (perhaps by Lucius Gahagan)	[Chandos House, Bath]; untraced	Chandos House sale
67.	nd	Head of a boy (perhaps by Lucius Gahagan)	[Chandos House, Bath]; untraced	Chandos House sale
68.	nd	Lord Brougham (perhaps by Lucius Gahagan)	[Chandos House, Bath]; untraced Other versions: small versions in the Chandos House sale; untraced	Chandos House sale
69.	nd	Madame Catalani (perhaps by Lucius Gahagan)	[Chandos House, Bath]; untraced	Chandos House sale
70.	nd	Marquess of Albuquerque (perhaps by Lucius Gahagan)	[Chandos House, Bath]; untraced	Chandos House sale
71.	nd	'Mormon leaders' (perhaps by Lucius Gahagan)	[Chandos House, Bath]; untraced	Chandos House sale
72.	nd	Mr Trevor (perhaps by Lucius Gahagan)	[Chandos House, Bath]; untraced	Chandos House sale
73.	nd	Napoleon Bonaparte (perhaps by Lucius Gahagan)	[Chandos House, Bath]; untraced	Chandos House sale
74.	nd	'Perceval' (probably Spencer Perceval); (perhaps by Lucius Gahagan)	[Chandos House, Bath]; untraced	Chandos House sale
75.	nd	Queen Adelaide (perhaps by Lucius Gahagan)	[Chandos House, Bath]; untraced	Chandos House sale
76.	nd	Queen Victoria 'when young' (perhaps by Lucius Gahagan)	[Chandos House, Bath]; untraced Other versions: 'another of the Queen when very young', Chandos House sale; untraced	Chandos House sale
77.	nd	Rev East (perhaps by Lucius Gahagan)	[Chandos House, Bath]; untraced	Chandos House sale
78.	nd	Rev Owen (perhaps by Lucius Gahagan)	[Chandos House, Bath]; untraced	Chandos House sale
79.	nd	Rev Romain (perhaps by Lucius Gahagan)	[Chandos House, Bath]; untraced	Chandos House sale
80.	nd	Rev Totenham (perhaps by Lucius Gahagan)	[Chandos House, Bath]; untraced Other versions: 'Tottenham', Chandos House sale	Chandos House sale
81.	nd	Sir Edward Parry (perhaps by Lucius Gahagan)	[Chandos House, Bath]; untraced	Chandos House sale
82.	nd	'Whitfield and numerous others in different sizes' (perhaps by Lucius Gahagan)	[Chandos House, Bath]; untraced	Chandos House sale
Architectural Sculpture				
83.	1800	Candelabrum, for Earl Spencer, model	[Exhib RA, London, 1026]; untraced	*Graves* III, 1905–6, 190
84.	1801	Decorative ornaments	Castle Howard, N R Yorks	*Gunnis* 1968, 160 citing Castle Howard archives
Reliefs				
85.	1777	Alexander exhorting his troops	[Soc of A, premium, 30 gns]; untraced	RSA, *Transactions*, vol 2, 1784, 132; *Dossie* 1782, 439
86.	nd	A Missionary preaching to to the South Sea Islanders (perhaps by Lucius Gahagan)	[Chandos House, Bath]; untraced	Chandos House sale, ? 1840
87.	nd	Death of Nelson (perhaps by Lucius Gahagan)	[Chandos House, Bath]; untraced	Chandos House sale
88.	nd	'George IV presenting Peace to the Goddess of the Earth, in background equestrian figure of Wellington' (perhaps by Lucius Gahagan)	[Chandos House, Bath]; untraced	Chandos House sale, ? 1840
89.	nd	The Death of Spencer Perceval	[Chandos House, Bath]; untraced	Chandos House sale
Miscellaneous				
90.	1801	A figure of Spring designed to support a pot of flowers	[Exhib RA, London, 963]; untraced	*Graves* III, 1905–6, 190
91.	1801	A spaniel	[Exhib RA, London, 992]; untraced	*Graves* III, 1905–6, 160
92.	1801	Portrait of an unidentified child	[Exhib RA, London, 1027]; untraced	*Graves* III, 1905–6, 190
93.	nd	anatomical busts, and fine models of wild and domesticated animals (perhaps by Lucius Gahagan)	[Chandos House, Bath]; untraced	Chandos House sale
94.	nd	'many children's busts and figures' (perhaps by Lucius Gahagan)	[Chandos House, Bath]; untraced	Chandos House sale
95.	nd	'models of Charlcombe & Bathampton Churches' (perhaps by Lucius Gahagan)	[Chandos House, Bath]; untraced	Chandos House sale
96.	nd	'numerous fancy brackets' (perhaps by Lucius Gahagan)	[Chandos House, Bath]; untraced	Chandos House sale

GAHAGAN, Lucius 1773–1855

Lucius was the second son of **Lawrence Gahagan** and the brother of **Vincent** and **Sebastian Gahagan.** He married Sarah Proudman in 1794 and they had four children, two of whom appear to have had minor careers as sculptors. It is likely that 'Gahagan L, junr', who exhibited at the Royal Academy in 1817, was Lucius (**12**). On this occasion he gave his address as 9 Swallow Street, London and he is thought to have moved to Bath around 1820, where he lived in a house called 'Lo Studio'. He later took rooms at Chandos House, Westgate Buildings, a large dwelling in the centre of Bath, designed as lodgings by John Wood the Elder in 1828–30. Here Gahagan must have come to know a fellow lodger, Miss Fenton. The auction of Miss Fenton's 'Works of Art . . . by the late L. Gahagan, sculptor', which appears to have taken place in 1840, was principally of sculpture by Lawrence Gahagan, but probably also included works by Lucius. Among these was a statuette commemorating the notorious murder in 1828 of Maria Bagnell (**9**).

Gahagan was responsible for some satisfying architectural sculpture (**18–20**) and for works in bronze and plaster as well as marble. He appears also to have worked in wax, for in an undated letter, a correspondent writing to **Joseph Nollekens** said that 'Lady Holland wants a good modeller in wax'. On the bottom of this letter Nollekens noted that he had recommended Lucius Gahagan (*Nollekens Sketchbook*, Ashm, in GPC). His few known monuments, which have 'of Bath' appended to the signature, are well-carved, but conventional classicising exercises. A characteristic example, to Archdeacon Thomas in Bath Abbey, has a figure of *Faith* standing by a column (**3**).

Gahagan appears to have produced relatively little work during his long life and his obituary in the *Bath and Cheltenham Gazette*, published on 19 December 1855, relates that he lived in penury during his later years: 'Dec 14 at Chandos House aged 82, Mr Lucius Gahagan, sculptor of this city. His reward will be hereafter. In this world he has passed a long and strictly virtuous life exemplifying abilities which only the very few appreciated and which the many failed to reward. More than half his life has been, as to worldly means, that of mere subsistence and in poverty he has resigned his temporal difficulties. His son, who inherits his father's talents and who will, we understand, continue the profession in this city, will, we trust, live to see a change for the better'. Gahagan's effects amounted to less than £200.

Little is known of the two children who practised as sculptors. No work has been identified by Lucius Gahagan II (1798–1866), the son mentioned in his father's obituary. The sculptress daughter, Sarah or **Sally Gahagan** (1801–1866), who administered her father's modest estate, was perhaps responsible for a bust of a child exhibited at the Royal Academy in 1817, in which case she was an extraordinarily youthful exhibitor.

Sylvia Allen/IR

Literary References: *Graves* III, 190; *Gunnis* 1968, 161; SDA

Will: FRC microfiche, 1858–1930, 1855

Miscellaneous Drawings: Dancing Jerry, lithograph, BM 1906-8-20-3; John Parrish Esq, lithograph, BM 1906-8-20-4; seven silhouettes, BM 1906-8-20-2; two drawings of unidentified subjects, pencil, BM 1906-8-20-1; Queen Charlotte, pencil drawing, *c*1818, inscribed 'the original drawing taken at Bath whilst taking the Baths', Museum of London C2397

Auction Catalogue: Chandos House, Bath (?1840)

Funerary Monuments

1.	†1804	Hon George Napier		Redland Chapel, Bristol	S	*Gunnis* 1968, 161
2.	†1814	Arthur (†1795), Alexander (†1798) and Samuel Hood		Butleigh, Somerset	S	Pevsner, *Somerset: S & West*, 1958, 112; C Lib (repr)
3.	†1820	Archdeacon Josiah Thomas		Bath Abbey, Somerset	S	Pevsner, *Somerset: N & Bristol*, 1958, 104
4.	†1831	Mary Sophia, Viscountess Bridport		Cricket St Thomas, Somerset	S	Pevsner, *Somerset: S & West*, 1958, 141; C Lib (repr)

Statues

5.	1811	King George III, statuette	b	Mr G Rose Other versions: Another, plaster, 1820, coll Mr Rose Two, Royal Coll RCIN 36983, unsigned, bronze and plaster	SD	RG/JP, 4, 555
6.	1823	Richard Beadon, Bishop of Bath and Wells, statuette	p	NPG, London 4901	SD	
7.	1834	Lady Filmer and her two small daughters, statuette Payment(s): £17 17s		[coll Stuart Beazley]; untraced		GPC
8.	1834	Unidentified man, seated with a dog at his feet, statuette	tc	Joanna Barnes (1995)	SD	
9.	nd	'A large Model of the Murdered Figure of Maria Bagnell and Gillingham [*sic*] the Murderer', statuette		[Chandos House, Bath]; untraced		Chandos House sale

Busts

10.	1809	King George III		[Chandos House, Bath]; untraced	SD	St Giles's House, Dorset sale, Christie, 26 June 1980, lot 4
11.	1810	Sir Thomas Best	p	Museum of London A21083	SD	
12.	1817	Rev J Hyatt		[Exhib RA, London, 1077]; untraced		*Graves* III, 1905–6, 190
13.	1831	David Garrick		Garrick Head Hotel, Bath, principal front		*Gunnis* 1968, 161; Pevsner, *Somerset: N & Bristol*, 1958, 120
14.	1834	Miss Munro Payment(s): 3 gns		Untraced		GPC; C Lib (repr)
15.	1836	Five miniature female portraits	p	Victoria Art Gallery, Bath	SD	
16.	nd	Caleb Parry		[Victoria Art Gall, Bath]; destroyed		*Gunnis* 1968, 161
17.	nd	Gabriel Goldney, Mayor of Chippenham		[Chandos House, Bath]; untraced		Chandos House sale

Architectural Sculpture

18.	1824	Mercury, Commerce and Genius		Royal Bank of Scotland, 9 Quiet Street, Bath, Avon, façade, built as the Auction House and Bazaar		*Gunnis* 1968, 161
19.	nd	Hygeia, Hippocrates and Aesculapius		[Pittville Pumproom, Cheltenham, Glos]; Corporation depot, Cheltenham, Glos		GPC
20.	nd	Two, in roundels		Old Bazaar, Oriel Street, Bath, Somerset, exterior		Pevsner, *Somerset: N & Bristol*, 1958, 127

Reliefs

21.	1832	Arthur, 1st Duke of Wellington, portrait medallion		Stratfield Saye, Hants	SD	RG/JP, 4, 555

GAHAGAN, Mr fl 1805

It is unclear which member of the Gahagan family was responsible for this bust of the child actor William Henry West Betty in one of his most famous roles, marketed by **William Bullock** in 1805.

Busts

1.	1805	Master Betty in 'Achmet'	[William Bullock's Showroom, Church Street, Liverpool]; untraced	*Bullock* 1988, 42, 147

GAHAGAN, Sally 1801–66

Busts

1.	1817	Unidentified child	[Exhib RA, London, 1055]; untraced	*Graves* III, 1905–6, 190

GAHAGAN, Sebastian 1779–1838

The fourth son of **Lawrence Gahagan** and the younger brother of **Lucius** and **Vincent**, he married Ann Parker in 1799 and they had six children, none of whom appear to have been sculptors. A second wife, Catherine, received an RA pension after his death. Strickland states that he was born in Dublin, though his father settled in London about two decades before his birth. Gahagan's active years were spent in London: he gave his address as 58 Titchfield Street, London in 1802, the first time he exhibited at the Royal Academy and moved several times during his career, first to King Street, Edgware Road, Westminster (by 1817), then to 57 Ernest Street, Regent's Park (by 1833) and finally to Little Clarendon Street, Somers Town in 1835.

Gahagan showed regularly at the RA throughout his career. He also exhibited several times at the British Institution, winning the premium in the class 'modelling in heroic or poetic composition' in 1808 for *Samson breaking the bonds* (**33**). By this date he had become an assistant to **Joseph Nollekens** and he was responsible for carving the statue of William Pitt for the Senate House, Cambridge (**9**). Nollekens exploited Gahagan, passing on only £300 of the £4,000 charged for Pitt's statue and pedestal. J T Smith later commentated 'Mr Nollekens paid him, I am sorry to say, a miserly small sum' (*Smith* 1828, I, 368). For versions of the bust of Pitt, which were presumably turned out with virtually no finishing by Nollekens, Gahagan and other assistants were paid about £25 each, while Nollekens received 120 guineas (**17**). Nonetheless Gahagan retained links with his former master: he was one of the 11 mourners at Mrs Nollekens's funeral in 1817, but was left only a modest £100 when Nollekens died in 1823. Unfortunately, in the face of the financial constraints then plaguing him, Gahagan did not receive the bequest 'till several years had elapsed, during which time he had undergone many serious vicissitudes of ill fortune' (*Smith* 1828, 1,368).

It is not known how long Gahagan remained with Nollekens but by 1816 he must have had an independent reputation for that year he won his most prestigious commission, the monument in St Paul's Cathedral to the flamboyant General, Sir Thomas Picton, who had died at the battle of Waterloo (**4**). The Committee of Taste controlling the erection of national memorials in the Cathedral approved his proposal for a pyramidal structure with an authoritative portrait bust at its apex and, in a line below, life-sized figures of *Genius* and *Valour* with a lion, facing a statue of *Victory* with a laurel wreath. The frieze-like composition has clear debts to the Elgin Marbles. Gahagan capitalised on the work involved in preparing the monument by issuing a number of busts of Picton, one of which was exhibited at the RA in 1818 (**18**).

In the wake of the Picton monument, Gahagan met a considerable demand for busts, though he suffered from a problem common to many sculptors, pirating by Italian scultors who reproduced the heads cheaply. The memorial to Sir Charles Burney in Westminster Abbey features a portrait head (**6**) and among the busts for a secular context, the head of Dr Charles Hutton was singled out by the *Gentleman's Magazine* as 'admirably created' (**24**) (*GM*, 93, pt I, 232). This was commissioned by his many friends in the world of science and was bequeathed by Hutton to the Literary and Philosophical Society of Newcastle to be placed in their new institution. A number of casts were provided by Gahagan for Hutton's friends.

He was also responsible for a number of statues. Edward Augustus, Duke of Kent, the father of Queen Victoria, was considerably involved in charitable activities in his later years and soon after his death in 1820 a group of noblemen and gentlemen met at Freemasons' Hall to consider erecting his statue somewhere in London. They chose Gahagan as executant, no doubt on the strength of the Picton monument. The imposing bronze statue, completed in 1825, presents the Duke in magnificently-realised garter robes, with an expression of aristocratic benevolence on his face and the charter granting him freedom of the City of London in his hand (**10**). It was paid for by supporters of the many charities in which he had involved himself.

The commission for another royal statue came in March 1831, several months after the death of King George IV, when the Gresham Committee, the controlling body of the Royal Exchange, resolved to add his statue to the line of kings in the quadrangle. The work was put to competition and seven sculptors responded by providing models and estimates, including Gahagan, whose quotation of £420 was second in cost only to **Benedetto Pistrucci** (£525). The other competitors were 'J Manning' (perhaps **Samuel Manning I**), **William Croggan**, whose model would have been executed by **Joseph Kendrick, R W Sievier, J G Bubb** and **Richard Westmacott III**, who failed to submit a model. Gahagan's proposal was chosen as 'much superior to any of the others', though adaptations were considered necessary for the proposed location and the budget was reduced to £350. On 3 June 1832, when Gahagan attended the Committee with a new model and drawing, the Committee informed him that no payment would be made until the work was completed, so creating a considerable difficulty at the initial stage when the sculptor needed to make outlays on materials. However, having nominated a guarantor, the sum of £115 was released to Gahagan, with further payments forthcoming at the half way stage and on completion. It was ready for viewing in December 1831, when Gahagan raised an important issue: there were no empty niches on the east side of the quadrangle, where the statue chronologically belonged. Several of the royal statues were therefore resited so that Gahagan's figure could take its proper place next to JG Bubb's statue of King George III.

Like many contemporary sculptors working with intense competition in a very limited market, he was frequently in financial difficulties. J T Smith noted that Gahagan had appealed to him for help, but that Smith felt unable to assist. Gahagan also applied to the AGBI for relief. In 1835 he received a donation of eight guineas from the Council of the Royal Academy. The Academy awarded his widow an annual pension of £10, rising to £15 in 1875.

The last notable sculptor member of the Gahagan family, Sebastian was perhaps the ablest.

IR

Literary References: *Smith* 1828, I, 344, II, 44, 438–9; *GM* 1823, vol I, 232; Graves 1875, 205; *Strickland* 1, 1913, 392–393; *Crookshank* 1966, 308; *Penny* 1977 (1), 11, 13, 205 n16, 206 n30; *Whinney* 1988, 369, 470 n.28; *Roscoe* 1997, 184–5; GGW (Gahagan website)

Archival References: RA/GA *passim*; MC/GR, 1830–36, 10 May 1831; AGBI, vol 2, 178

Funerary Monuments

1.	1804	'Affliction and Consolation, a monumental sketch'		[Exhib RA, London, 899]; untraced		*Graves* III, 1905–6, 190
2.	1807	'A monumental sketch'		[Exhib RA, London, 1007]; untraced		*Graves* III, 1905–6, 190
3.	1814	Sketch for a monument to the Rt Hon Spencer Perceval		[Exhib RA, London, 771]; untraced		*Graves* III, 1905–6, 190
4.	1816	Sir Thomas Picton Model(s): exhib RA, London, 1818, 1098		St Paul's Cathedral, London		*Graves* III, 1905–6, 190; *Whinney* 1988, 369, 470 n28 (repr); *Yarrington* 1988, 76 (repr 34)
5.	post-1817	William Wyndham (†1814) Model(s): exhib RA, London, 1817 (1021)		St Brides Major, Glam, St Bridget		*Graves* III, 1905–6, 190; Pevsner, *Glamorgan*, 1995, 550
6.	1819	Dr Charles Burney (†1814)		Westminster Abbey, London, nave		*Gunnis* 1968, 161; *MacMichael* 1977, 30
7.	1821	'The Grave; a monumental subject'		[Exhib RA, London, 1148]; untraced		*Graves* III, 1905–6, 190
8.	1825	A monumental figure, 'Let my Prayer be directed, etc'		[Exhib RA, London, 990]; untraced		*Graves* III, 1905–6, 190

Statues

9.	1812	William Pitt (working as an assistant to Joseph Nollekens)		Senate House, Cambridge		*Penny* 1977 (2), 1336–7 (repr)
10.	1825	Edward Augustus, Duke of Kent	b	Portland Place, London		*Crookshank* 1966, 308; *Blackwood* 1989, 88–9 (repr)
11.	1825	King George IV, model		[Exhib RA, London, 1062]; untraced		*Graves* III, 1905–6, 190
12.	1830–1831	King George IV Payment(s): £350		[Royal Exchange, City of London]; untraced		*Roscoe* 1997, 173, 184–85
13.	1833	Monsieur Louel as a troubadour in a performance before George IV at the Egyptian Hall in 1829, model		[Exhib RA, London, 1133]; untraced		*Graves* III, 1905–6, 190
14.	1835	Charles, 2nd Earl Grey, model		[Exhib RA, London, 1094]; untraced		*Graves* III, 1905–6, 191; *Ormond* 1973, 203

Busts

15.	1803	'A portrait; a study'		[Exhib RA, London, 907]; untraced		*Graves* III, 1905–6, 190
16.	1805	Unidentified lady		[Exhib RA, London, 722]; untraced		*Graves* III, 1905–6, 190
17.	by 1805	William Pitt (working under Joseph Nollekens)		Untraced		*Strickland* I, 1913, 391–3
18.	1816	Lieutenant-General Sir Thomas Picton	m	[Iscoed, Carmarthen]; untraced Other versions: ex coll John Colby, of Ffynone, Pembroke; untraced exhib RA, 1818 (1115); untraced		*Graves* III, 1905–6, 190; *Gunnis* 1968, 162; *Dale-Jones and Lloyd* 1989, 59
19.	1816	Rev E Picton		[Exhib RA, London, 963]; untraced		*Graves* III, 1905–6, 190
20.	1819	Henry, 1st Earl of Mulgrave		Mulgrave Castle, N R Yorks		GPC
21.	1821	C Beloe Esq		[Exhib RA, London, 1146]; untraced		*Graves* III, 1905–6, 190
22.	1821	Unidentified portrait		[Exhib RA, London, 1821]; untraced		*Graves* III, 1905–6, 190
23.	1821	William Windham (†1810) (after Joseph Nollekens)	m	Felbrigg Hall, Norfolk	SD	*Gunnis* 1968, 161
24.	1822	Charles Hutton		[Exhib RA, London, 1034]; untraced Other versions: Newcastle Literary Soc, 1832		*Graves* III, 1905–6, 190; *Gunnis* 1968, 161
25.	1822	George Cholmondeley		[Exhib RA, London, 1032]; untraced		*Graves* III, 1905–6, 190
26.	1823	Dr Patrick Kelly		[Exhib RA, London, 1084]; untraced		*Graves* III, 1905–6, 190
27.	1824	Sir Peter Laurie, Sheriff of London		[Exhib RA, London, 986]; untraced		*Graves* III, 1905–6, 190
28.	1834	E Sampays		[Exhib RA, London, 1084]; untraced		*Graves* III, 1905–6, 190
29.	nd	William Pitt (copy of a bust by Nollekens)	m	Palace of Westminster, London	S	Walker 1961, 57, cat 62

Reliefs

30.	1819	The cradle hymn; portraits, 'Hush, my babe, lie still, etc'		[Exhib RA, London, 1247]; untraced		*Graves* III, 1905–6, 190

Miscellaneous

31.	1802	'Prudence, a sketch for a time piece'		[Exhib RA, London, 955]; untraced		*Graves* III, 1905–6, 190
32.	1808	Cradle hymn		[Exhib BI, London, 140]; untraced		*Graves* 1875, 205
33.	1809	Samson breaking the bonds, model		[Exhib BI, London, 340]; untraced		*Graves* 1875, 205
34.	1811	A Nymph tantalising Cupid		[Exhib BI, London, 310]; untraced		*Graves* 1875, 205
35.	1815	Judith and Holofernes		[Exhib BI, London, 238]; untraced		*Graves* 1875, 205
36.	1818	Crescent and pillar in commemoration of the Battle of Trafalgar		[Exhib RA, London, 1039]; untraced		*Graves* III, 1905–6, 190
37.	1818	Innocence – a portrait		[Exhib RA, London, 1108]; untraced		*Graves* 1875, 205; *Graves* III, 1905–6, 190
38.	1821	Priam imploring Achilles for the body of Hector		[Exhib RA, London, 1165]; untraced		*Graves* III, 1905–6, 190
39.	1823	Design for the Shakespeare commemoration		[Exhib RA, London, 1094]; untraced		*Graves* III, 1905–6, 190
40.	1832	Let my prayer be directed as incense in thy sight, and the elevation of my hands as an evening sacrifice		[Exhib Soc of BA, London, 899]; untraced		*Johnson* 1975, 172

GAHAGAN, Stephen 1832–

The son of **Edwin Gahagan**, he attended the Royal Academy Schools in 1850 and Gunnis states that he showed a medallion portrait at Burlington House in 1857, though there is no record of this work in Graves's dictionary of RA exhibitors (1). He was dead by the time of the 1881 national census and his children were in the care of their maternal aunt.

Literary References: *Gunnis* 1968, 160; GGW

Reliefs

1.	1857	Unidentified subject, medallion portrait	[Exhib Burlington House, London]; untraced	*Gunnis* 1968, 160

GAHAGAN, Vincent 1776–1832

He was the third son of **Lawrence Gahagan** and the brother of **Lucius** and **Sebastian**. In 1803 he married Elizabeth Kay, who died in childbirth shortly afterwards, and the following year he took a new wife, Mary Ann Lewis. They had six children including perhaps three who were connected with their father's profession, **Edwin**, Basil Augustine (1815–1884) who was listed in the 1871 and 1881 census records as 'marble carver (mason)' and Vincent (1817–40), of whom little is known. Gahagan was married for the third time in 1827 to Maria Dupais. His premises appear to have remained in the area west of Bloomsbury throughout his career: in 1804, when he first exhibited at the Royal Academy, he gave his address at 106 Titchfield Street, by 1814 he was at 269 Oxford Street, and from 1817 at 11 Molyneux Street, Edgware Road.

In 1811 the Portuguese Ambassador asked the Royal Academy to arrange a competition for a royal equestrian statue to be erected in Rio de Janeiro, offering a prize of £200 for each of the 2 best models and £50 for the 3rd (RA Council Minutes, vol 4, April 1812, f364–6). Farington relates that models by **JCF Rossi**, **John Edward Carew** and Gahagan were deposited at the RA in 1812, but that the decision on their merit was postponed until other sculptors could also submit. The Academy took pains to find more competitors, but some of the best known did not respond. Long before the works were ready to be judged in 1815 the Ambassador began to regret his offer, but the Academy refused to allow him to go back on his word. The first 2 prizes were awarded to Gahagan (1) and Rossi, and Carew came 3rd. It is not certain that the successful sculptors were paid for their work. Gahagan exhibited at the Royal Academy sporadically 1804–23, showing animal studies (**5, 6**), classical and biblical subjects (**2, 7, 8, 9, 10**). It is not clear whether these were models. According to the *Literary Gazette* he showed a *Hawking party* and an equestrian statue of the Duke of York at the 'British Gallery' in 1832 (**3, 11**). The writer considered the latter 'both in feature and in figure an admirable resemblance of His Royal Highness', but could not 'praise the nag' (*Lit Gaz* 1832, 170). It is possible that both these works were in fact exhibited by Edwin Gahagan for they are listed under his name in Graves's dictionary of British Institution exhibitors (p 205).

In 1832 Gahagan was employed as an assistant to **Sir Richard Westmacott RA** and was working on a statue of the Prime Minister, George Canning, which collapsed on him, causing his death. The inquests column of *The Times* briefly noted 'Vincent Gahagan Killed by a statue of Mr Canning' (*The Times* 31 December 1832, 4). His widow, who was left with six step-children (most of them fully grown) and little means of support, applied for assistance to the Artists' General Benevolent Institution, graphically drawing attention to her husband's dramatic death, 'Frightfully destroyed at Pimlico by the falling of the statue of George Canning while working on the statue'. None of Gahagan's works appears to have survived.

Sylvia Allen/IR

Literary References: *Farington* XIII, 4667, 11 July 1815; *Graves* III, 1905–6, 191; *Crookshank* 1966, 308; *Gunnis* 1968, 162; SDA

Archival References: AGBI, vol 3, 170, 209; vol 4, 39, 71, 104

Statues

1.	1811	Royal equestrian statue for Rio de Janeiro, model	[RA, London]; untraced	*Farington* XIII, 4667, 11 July 1815; *Gunnis* 1968, 162
2.	1814	Design for a statue of Apollo	[Exhib RA, London, 755]; untraced	*Graves* III, 1905–6, 191
3.	1832	Frederick-Augustus, Duke of York and Albany, equestrian (possibly by Edwin Gahagan)	[Exhib British Gallery]; untraced	*Lit Gaz*, 17 March 1832, 170

Busts

4.	1804	Portrait of the artist's father	[Exhib RA, London, 898]; untraced	*Graves* III, 1905–6, 191

Miscellaneous

5.	1804	Study of a lion	[Exhib RA, London, 967]; untraced	*Graves* III, 1905–6, 191
6.	1804	Study of a lion and kid	[Exhib RA, London, 965]; untraced	*Graves* III, 1905–6, 191
7.	1817	Satan in council, design for the end of a garden walk	[Exhib RA, London, 1025]; untraced	*Graves* III, 1905–6, 191
8.	1821	The triumph of Achilles over the body of Hector	[Exhib RA, London, 1090]; untraced	*Graves* III, 1905–6, 191
9.	1822	'Dido. And this, shall kindly speed me to the realms below' (from Virgil)	[Exhib RA, London, 999]; untraced	*Graves* III, 1905–6, 189
10.	1823	The prodigal son	[Exhib RA, London, 1065]; untraced	*Graves* III, 1905–6, 191
11.	1832	Hawking party	[Exhib British Gallery]; untraced	*Lit Gaz*, 17 March 1832, 170
12.	1832	Hawking party (possibly by Edwin Gahagan)	[Exhib BI, London, 590]; untraced	*Lit Gaz*, 791, 17 March 1832, 170; *Graves* 1875, 205

GALL, James fl 1850–64

He exhibited annually at the Royal Scottish Academy in the years 1850–54 and again in 1857–64, showing principally portrait busts. His address was 20 Gayfield Square, Edinburgh from 1850 until 1854 when he moved to 26 Gayfield Square. In 1863 he moved again, to 10 St John Street.

Literary References: *Woodward* 1977, vol 1, pt 2, 75–6

Busts

1.	1850	Rt Hon William Johnston	[Exhib R Sc A, Edinburgh, 472]; untraced	*Laperriere* 2, 1991, 108
2.	1851	Hugh Miller	[Exhib R Sc A, Edinburgh, 669]; untraced	*Laperriere* 2, 1991, 108

3.	1851	Professor Simson		[Exhib R Sc A, Edinburgh, 671]; untraced	*Laperriere* 2, 1991, 108
4.	1851	Unidentified boy		[Exhib R Sc A, Edinburgh, 661]; untraced	*Laperriere* 2, 1991, 108
5.	1851	Unidentified lady		[Exhib R Sc A, Edinburgh, 675]; untraced	*Laperriere* 2, 1991, 108
6.	1852	Miss Wakefield		[Exhib R Sc A, Edinburgh, 687]; untraced	*Laperriere* 2, 1991, 108
7.	1852	Rev G R Davidson		[Exhib R Sc A, Edinburgh, 693]; untraced	*Laperriere* 2, 1991, 108
8.	1852	Unidentified officer		[Exhib R Sc A, Edinburgh, 694]; untraced	*Laperriere* 2, 1991, 108
9.	1853	Unidentified boy	m	[Exhib R Sc A, Edinburgh, 696]; untraced	*Laperriere* 2, 1991, 108
10.	1853	Unidentified child	m	[Exhib R Sc A, Edinburgh, 698]; untraced	*Laperriere* 2, 1991, 108
11.	1854	Sir Thomas Brisbane	m	[Exhib R Sc A, Edinburgh, 719]; untraced	*Laperriere* 2, 1991, 108
12.	1854	Unidentified gentleman		[Exhib R Sc A, Edinburgh, 722]; untraced	*Laperriere* 2, 1991, 108
13.	1854	Unidentified lady		[Exhib R Sc A, Edinburgh, 727]; untraced	*Laperriere* 2, 1991, 108
14.	1854	William Marshall	m	[Exhib R Sc A, Edinburgh, 721]; untraced	*Laperriere* 2, 1991, 108
15.	1857	Son of M T Martin	m	[Exhib R Sc A, Edinburgh, 692]; untraced	*Laperriere* 2, 1991, 108
16.	1857	Unidentified child	m	[Exhib R Sc A, Edinburgh, 691]; untraced	*Laperriere* 2, 1991, 108
17.	1858	Unidentified gentleman	m	[Exhib R Sc A, Edinburgh, 751]; untraced	*Laperriere* 2, 1991, 108
18.	1858	Unidentified gentleman	m	[Exhib R Sc A, Edinburgh, 771]; untraced	*Laperriere* 2, 1991, 108
19.	1858	Unidentified lady	m	[Exhib R Sc A, Edinburgh, 757]; untraced	*Laperriere* 2, 1991, 108
20.	1859	J S Cunningham	m	[Exhib R Sc A, Edinburgh, 719]; untraced	*Laperriere* 2, 1991, 108
21.	1859	John Gibson		[Exhib R Sc A, Edinburgh, 714]; untraced	*Laperriere* 2, 1991, 108
22.	1859	Unidentified lady	m	[Exhib R Sc A, Edinburgh, 718]; untraced	*Laperriere* 2, 1991, 108
23.	1860	James Russell	m	[Exhib R Sc A, Edinburgh, 843]; untraced	*Laperriere* 2, 1991, 108
24.	1860	Mrs Hope Scott	m	[Exhib R Sc A, Edinburgh, 866]; untraced	*Laperriere* 2, 1991, 108
25.	1862	Hon Mrs Johnstone	m	[Exhib R Sc A, Edinburgh, 831]; untraced	*Laperriere* 2, 1991, 108
26.	1862	Mrs Hunter	m	[Exhib R Sc A, Edinburgh, 856]; untraced	*Laperriere* 2, 1991, 108
27.	1862	Robert Graham Esq	m	[Exhib R Sc A, Edinburgh, 834]; untraced	*Laperriere* 2, 1991, 108
28.	1862	Unidentified lady	m	[Exhib R Sc A, Edinburgh, 833]; untraced	*Laperriere* 2, 1991, 108
29.	1863	Professor Nichol	m	[Exhib R Sc A, Edinburgh, 806]; untraced	*Laperriere* 2, 1991, 108
30.	1864	Unidentified boy		[Exhib R Sc A, Edinburgh, 739]; untraced	*Laperriere* 2, 1991, 108
Reliefs					
31.	1851	Rt Hon the Lord Provost, medallion		[Exhib R Sc A, Edinburgh, 668]; untraced	*Laperriere* 2, 1991, 108
32.	1861	Rev Dr Duff, 'medallion in Parian from a bust'		[Exhib R Sc A, Edinburgh, 798]; untraced	*Laperriere* 2, 1991, 108
Miscellaneous					
33.	1853	An only child – a restoration in marble	m	[Exhib R Sc A, Edinburgh, 691]; untraced	*Laperriere* 2, 1991, 108
34.	1853	The infant Samuel		[Exhib R Sc A, Edinburgh, 681]; untraced	*Laperriere* 2, 1991, 108

GALLAGHER, John 1805–

Gallagher was born in Ireland and studied sculpture at the Royal Dublin Society Schools, where he won several prizes. When **William Behnes** offered to take two boys into his studio for instruction, Gallagher and **Constantine Panormo** were selected by the Society as their most promising pupils and sent to London. In 1824, before joining Behnes, Gallagher attended the Royal Academy Schools, gaining a silver medal in 1825 (7). He was with Behnes the following year. He later went to Rome at the expense of the Dublin Society, but the promise of his early years does not seem to have been fulfilled, for little more is heard of him. In 1840 he was an unsuccessful candidate for the mastership of the Royal Dublin Society's Modelling School. He exhibited at the Royal Academy from 1834 to 1844, giving several addresses around Marylebone and showed a design for a fountain at the Great Exhibition of 1851 (5).

Literary References: *Strickland* I, 1913, 393–394; *Gunnis* 1968, 162

Statues					
1.	nd	Prometheus chained to the rock		RDS, Dublin	*Strickland* I, 1913, 395
Busts					
2.	1834	Colonel Hodges		[Exhib RA, London, 1032]; untraced	*Graves* III, 1905–6, 195
3.	1837	Baron de Lagos	m	[Exhib RA, London, 1208]; untraced	*Graves* III, 1905–6, 195
4.	1844	Unidentified gentleman		[Exhib RA, London, 1364]; untraced	*Graves* III, 1905–6, 195
Architectural Sculpture					
5.	1851	Design for a fountain		[Gt Exhib]; untraced	*Gunnis* 1968, 162

Reliefs

6.	1835	Count Ugolino and his sons in prison		[Exhib RA, London, 1078]; untraced		*Graves* III, 1905–6, 195

Miscellaneous

7.	1825	Model in the Antique Academy		[Awarded RA silver medal]; untraced		RA Premium list

GAMES, of Talgarth fl 1765

Funerary Monuments

1.	†1765	William James		Llanfaredd, Radnor	S	Pevsner, *Powys*, 1979, 252

GARDENER fl mid 18th century

His 'fine contemporary wax portrait of David Garrick' is in the Royal Collection (*Gunnis* 1968, 162).

Miscellaneous

1.	nd	David Garrick	w	Royal Coll Other versions: Christie, London, 11 Dec 1978, lot 134; untraced		*Gunnis* 1968, 162; *Pyke* 1973, 52

GARDENER (or GARDNER), George, of Tewkesbury fl 1793–1847

Funerary Monuments

1.	?1793	John Hancock		Chastleton, Oxon	S	*Gunnis* 1968, 162
2.	?1813	John Jones		Chastleton, Oxon	S	*Gunnis* 1968, 162
3.	†1818	William Pearce		Staverton, Glos	S	Pevsner, *Glos: Vale & Forest of Dean*, 1976, 348
4.	†1826	James Olive		Twyning, Glos	S	Pevsner, *Glos: Vale & Forest of Dean*, 1976, 393
5.	†1833	A P Mainwaring		Longdon, Worcs	S	
6.	1833	Kenelm Chandler (†1809)		Tewkesbury Abbey, Glos	S	Pevsner, *Glos: Vale & Forest of Dean*, 1976, 368
7.	†1837	John Roughton		St Thomas, Dudley, Worcs	S	
8.	?1838	Rev Joseph Baugh		Ripple, Worcs	S	*Gunnis* 1968, 162
9.	?1839	Lady Wheler		Leamington Hasting, Warks	S	
10.	1844	Catherine Price		Tewkesbury Abbey, Glos	S	Pevsner, *Glos: Vale & Forest of Dean*, 1976, 368
11.	†1847	Mary Roughton (perhaps by W M Gardener of Cheltenham, Pimlico and Tewkesbury)		St Thomas, Dudley, Worcs	S	

GARDENER (or GARDNER), W M, of Cheltenham, Pimlico and Leamington fl 1812–43

Funerary Monuments

1.	1780	Unidentified subject, tablet		St John the Baptist, Gloucester	S	Pevsner, *Glos: Vale & Forest of Dean*, 1976, 232
2.	†1781	James Clarke		Bishampton, Worcs	S	
3.	†1803	Rev Thomas Stock		St John Northgate, Gloucester	S	
4.	†1810	Colonel John Callow		Bishampton, Worcs	S	
5.	†1812	Edward Parsons		Presteigne, Radnor	S	Pevsner, *Powys*, 1979, 269
6.	†1812	William Hill		Leigh, Glos	S	Pevsner, *Glos: Vale and Forest of Dean*, 1976, 287
7.	†1820	John Barnes		Hasfield, Glos		Pevsner, *Glos: Vale & Forest of Dean*, 1976, 266
8.	†1829	Edward Southose		Prestbury, Glos		Pevsner, *Glos: Vale & Forest of Dean*, 1976, 266
9.	†1830	R L Townsend		Bishop's Cleeve, Glos	S	Pevsner, *Glos: Vale & Forest of Dean*, 1976, 107
10.	†1832	Timothy Jones		Leonard Stanley, Glos	S	
11.	†1834	Captain Edward Stopford RN		St Lawrence, Swindon, Glos	S	Pevsner, *Glos: Vale & Forest of Dean*, 1976, 354
12.	†1836	John Bevry (?)		Holy Trinity, Cheltenham, Glos	S	
13.	†1838	Charlotte Edwardes		Laugharne, Carmarthen	S	*Dale-Jones and Lloyd* 1989, 49
14.	†1840	John Gibbs		Holy Trinity, Cheltenham, Glos	S	
15.	†1841	Rev James Beebee		Presteigne, Radnor	S	Pevsner, *Powys*, 1979, 269
16.	?1843	Lieutenant-Colonel Cyprian Bridge		Harwich, Essex	S	*Gunnis* 1968, 162
17.	†1845	Anna Maria George		Laugharne, Carmarthen	S	*Dale-Jones and Lloyd* 1989, 49
18.	†1847	Mary Roughton (perhaps by George Gardener of Tewkesbury)		St Thomas, Dudley, Worcs	S	
19.	†1848	Mary Annesley		Holy Trinity, Cheltenham, Glos	S	
20.	†1854	Courtland Skinner Shaw		Laugharne, Carmarthen		*Dale-Jones and Lloyd* 1989, 49
21.	†1854	Mary (†1850) and Elizabeth Bilbie		Old Milverton, Warks	S	
22.	†1859	Ann Lockett		Old Milverton, Warks	S	

Statues

23.	1831	King William IV		Cheltenham, Glos		*Ormond* 1973, 512

GARDIE, Louis fl 1850–64

Busts

1.	1850	H Wilde	m	[Exhib RA, London, 1424]; untraced		*Graves* III, 1905–6, 201
2.	1850	Victoria Mary Louisa, Duchess of Kent		[coll Alderman Joseph Fletcher; donated to Salford AG, 1876]; untraced	SD	*Gawsworth Guide*, 46, 47 (repr); *Wells* 1999, 41, 45, 46; Sotheby, 23–24 May 2000, lot 576 (repr)
3.	1851	Henry, 3rd Viscount Palmerston		Broadlands, Hants		RG/JP, 4, 560
4.	1851	Marquis de la Roche Jacquelin		untraced		*Gunnis* 1968, 162
5.	1851	Sir Robert Peel	b	[Gt Exhib, London]; untraced		*Gunnis* 1968, 162
6.	1851	Unidentified gentleman	m	[Exhib RA, London, 1343]; untraced		*Graves* III, 1905–6, 201
7.	1852	W Danter	m	[Exhib RA, London, 1441]; untraced		*Graves* III, 1905–6, 201

8.	1853	Charles Wilkins		[Exhib RA, London, 1355]; untraced		*Graves* III, 1905–6, 201
9.	1854	Arthur, 1st Duke of Wellington	m	[Exhib RA, London, 1414]; untraced		*Graves* III, 1905–6, 201
10.	1864	John Hanning Speke	p	[coll Mr King, solicitor of Bath]; NPG, London 1739 Other versions: Royal Geographical Society, London, 1865	SD	*Ormond* 1973, 426 (repr 844)
Miscellaneous						
11.	1850	G Marciller		[Exhib RA, London, 1409]; untraced		*Graves* III, 1905–6, 201

GARDNER (or GARDINER), Richard, of Stow fl 1812–32

Funerary Monuments						
1.	†1812	William Hill		Leigh, Glos	S	Pevsner, *Glos: Vale & Forest of Dean*, 1976, 287
2.	†1814	Rev Richard Harvey	sl	Upper Swell, Glos	S	Pevsner, *Glos: Cotswolds*, 1999, 711
3.	†1814	Unidentified subject, tablet	sl	Broadwell, Glos	S	Pevsner, *Glos: Cotswolds*, 1999, 201
4.	†1820	John Barnes		Hasfield, Glos	S	Pevsner, *Glos: Vale & Forest of Dean*, 1976, 266
5.	†1829	Edward Southouse		Prestbury, Glos	S	Pevsner, *Glos: Vale & Forest of Dean*, 1976, 322
6.	†1832	Rev Timothy Jones		Leonard Stanley, Glos	S	Pevsner, *Glos: Cotswolds*, 1999, 445

GARLAND fl 1843

Busts						
1.	1843	John Dollond		Royal Society, London	SD	*Gunnis* 1968, 163
2.	nd	George Dollond		Royal Society, London	S	*Gunnis* 1968, 163

GARLAND, Thomas P fl 1840–after 1850

An architectural modeller, he worked under **John Thomas** on ornaments for the Houses of Parliament during the 1840s and 1850s. He was principally employed in making full-size models of heraldic devices for carvers to work from.

Literary References: *Read* 1976, 242

GARLAND & FIELDWICK, of Camberwell fl 1807–47

In 1816 the firm built the portico of Camberwell church. Gunnis considered their tablets 'dull', with the exception of one in Brixton parish church which has 'a fine relief of a mourning woman' (**10**). Groseclose notes that their monument to Admiral Maitland in Bombay, which features a profile cameo mounted underneath a draped urn and a military trophy, 'boasts exquisite detail, skillful carving, and refined composition' (*Groseclose* 1995, 62) (**8**).

Literary References: *Gunnis* 1968, 163

Archival References: GPC

Funerary Monuments						
1.	?1807	Mary Walter		Crayford, Kent		*Gunnis* 1968, 163
2.	1815	Hitchens family		St Ia, St Ives, Cornwall	S	Pevsner, *Cornwall*, 1970, 181
3.	?1820	Ann Hedges		Whitchurch, Bucks		*Gunnis* 1968, 163
4.	†1824	Louisa Schroder		Old Burial Ground, Dulwich Village, London		*Gunnis* 1968, 163
5.	?1828	Ellen Caldecott		Shimpling, Suffolk		*Gunnis* 1968, 163
6.	?1833	William Old		St Mary-at-Hill, City of London		*Gunnis* 1968, 163
7.	?1836	Captain Borlase		Fareham, Hants		*Gunnis* 1968, 163
8.	†1839	Admiral Sir F L Maitland		Mumbai (Bombay) Cathedral, India	S	*Gunnis* 1968, 163; *Groseclose* 1995, 62
9.	†1839	Arthur Teagle		Antigua Cathedral	S	*Gunnis* 1968, 163
10.	?1841	Joseph Newcomb		Brixton, London		*Gunnis* 1968, 163
11.	?1847	William Morris		Woodford, Essex, churchyard	S	*Gunnis* 1968, 163
Architectural Sculpture						
12.	1839	Font		St Peter, Southwark, London		Pevsner, *London: South*, 1983, 577

GARNETT, Martha fl 1825

Baines's Lancashire directory of 1825 lists her as a 'statuary' of Booth Street, Manchester (NP/RG).

GARRARD, Charles 1798–

The son of **George Garrard**, he attended the Royal Academy Schools in 1816, winning a silver medal the following year (**20**). He exhibited at the RA, the British Institution and the Society of British Artists between 1816 and 1829, giving his address as 4 Queen's Buildings, Brompton.

Literary References: *Graves* III, 1906–6, 206–7; *Gunnis* 1968, 163

Statues						
1.	1827	A charger belonging to the King	b	[Exhib Soc of BA, London, 855]; untraced		*Johnson* 1975, 174
2.	1827	A horse, property of Mrs Wills, model		[Exhib Soc of BA, London, 857]; untraced		*Johnson* 1975, 174
3.	1829	Frederick-Augustus, Duke of York and Albany, equestrian, model for a bronze		[Exhib RA, London, 1140]; untraced		*Graves* III, 1905–6, 206
Busts						
4.	1816	Unidentified youth		[Exhib RA, London, 921]; untraced		*Graves* III, 1905–6, 206
5.	1817	Unidentified young lady		[Exhib RA, London, 1026]; untraced		*Graves* III, 1905–6, 206
6.	1817	Unidentified young lady		[Exhib RA, London, 1017]; untraced		*Graves* III, 1905–6, 206
7.	1818	Mr Raymond, of Drury Lane Theatre		[Exhib RA, London, 1051]; untraced		*Graves* III, 1905–6, 206

8.	1818	Unidentified gentleman		[Exhib RA, London, 1067]; untraced	*Graves* III, 1905–6, 206
9.	1818	Unidentified young lady		[Exhib RA, London, 1064]; untraced	*Graves* III, 1905–6, 206
10.	1819	Mr Clift, model		[Exhib RA, London, 1244]; untraced	*Graves* III, 1905–6, 206
11.	1820	Unidentified young lady		[Exhib RA, London, 1068]; untraced	*Graves* III, 1905–6, 206
12.	1821	Alexander Mitchell		[Exhib RA, London, 1145]; untraced	*Graves* III, 1905–6, 206; *Johnson* 1975, 174
13.	1821	Unidentified young lady		[Exhib RA, London, 1098]; untraced	*Graves* III, 1905–6, 206
14.	1822	Miss Cooke		[Exhib RA, London, 1015]; untraced	*Graves* III, 1905–6, 206
15.	1823	Unidentified lady		[Exhib RA, London, 1074]; untraced	*Graves* III, 1905–6, 206
16.	1824	Unidentified gentleman		[Exhib Soc of BA, London, 325]; untraced	*Johnson* 1975, 174
17.	1826	J Watts		[Exhib RA, London, 1105]; untraced	*Graves* III, 1905–6, 206
18.	1827	Unidentified young lady		[Exhib Soc of BA, London, 867]; untraced	*Johnson* 1975, 174
19.	nd	A girl		Powderham Castle, Devon	*Gunnis* 1968, 163
Miscellaneous					
20.	1817	Model 'in the Antique Academy'		[RA silver medal]; untraced	RA Premium list
21.	1818	Ecce Homo, study		[Exhib RA, London, 1113]; untraced	*Graves* III, 1905–6, 206
22.	1822	The infant St John, model from a painting by Reynolds		[Exhib RA, London, 995]; untraced	*Graves* 1875, 207; *Graves* III, 1905–6, 206
23.	1823	Peter Coxe		[Exhib RA, London, 1129]; untraced	*Graves* III, 1905–6, 206
24.	1824	'Sketch in clay in memory of a lady in the costume of Minerva'	tc	[Exhib RA, London, 984]; untraced	*Graves* III, 1905–6, 206
25.	1826	Emma Whitbread Battye		[Exhib RA, London, 1027]; untraced	*Graves* III, 1905–6, 206
26.	1826	Model of a charger	b	[Exhib BI, London, 412]; untraced	*Graves* 1875, 207

GARRARD, George 1760–1826

George Garrard was born in London on 3 May 1760, the second son of Robert and Miriam Garrard. As a boy he studied under Sawrey Gilpin RA, the animal painter, whose daughter Matilda he later married. In 1778 he was accepted as a student at the Royal Academy and in 1781 exhibited for the first time at Burlington House, emulating his master's subject-matter by showing a painting entitled *Two Horses*. In 1784 Garrard's canvas, *View of a Brewhouse Yard*, was bought by Sir Joshua Reynolds PRA. In 1795 Garrard began to make models of cattle, which he felt might be useful to landscape painters. His new interest in sculpture led him to petition Parliament, backed by two patrons, Samuel Whitbread II and Sir Harry Mildmay, in support of a bill to secure copyright for works of plastic art. The petition was successful and in 1798 when 'An Act for encouraging the art of making new models and casts of busts and other things therein mentioned' was passed (38 George III. C. 71).

Gilpin introduced Garrard to the Whitbread brewing family. Samuel Whitbread I bought a house at Southill, Beds in 1795, but died the following year. His son, Samuel II, engaged the architect Henry Holland to rebuild the house and over the next six years Garrard and Sawrey Gilpin worked almost exclusively for Whitbread, providing paintings and in Garrard's case, models of animals and overdoors in low-relief (**9, 13, 14, 128**).

By 1799 he was working under the patronage of the Board of Agriculture on a series of scale models of breeds of cattle of Great Britain and Ireland (**8**) and in 1800 published *Garrard's Prize Cattle*, which contained descriptions of the different breeds, accompanied by engravings. That year that he was elected an ARA. He never became a full Academician. He started to exhibit portrait sculpture at the Royal Academy in 1797 (**39**). Many of the busts depicted men closely connected with his life and work: they included Samuel Whitbread, his great patron (**51**), Benjamin West, PRA (**42**), Arthur Young, Secretary to the Board of Agriculture (**47**), Sawrey Gilpin (**45**) and Rev William Gilpin (**58**), his wife's uncle.

Garrard's association with Whitbread paved the way for an introduction to the Duke of Bedford, a near neighbour. In 1804 Garrard produced a detailed painting of *Woburn Sheep Shearers* in which he depicted himself, seated at a small table, selling plaster models. He later worked on architectural features for Woburn Abbey including low-relief plaster overdoor panels (**133**), an eagle in high relief for the *Temple of Graces* (**130**), tympanum reliefs for the sculpture gallery (**131**) and lions for gate piers on the west front (**130**). He continued to work for Whitbread and in 1806 made a model for a memorial to Mrs Whitbread's favourite spaniel (**2**), realised in Coade Stone and placed on a pedestal designed by Henry Holland for use as a drinking trough in the gardens of Southill.

In 1807 Garrard was invited, with **Richard Westmacott I, John Flaxman RA, John Bacon II** and **Joseph Nollekens** to submit a model for a commemorative statue to William Pitt the Younger for the Senate House, Cambridge. Nollekens's design was selected. Garrard unsuccessfully entered two further competitions, both for equestrian statues, to Sir John Moore, 1812 (**23**), and the Duke of Wellington, 1814 (**28**).

The Drury Lane Theatre in London burnt down in 1809 and Whitbread was instrumental in raising money for its restoration. Garrard made a copy of **Louis Francois Roubiliac**'s statue of Shakespeare in Garrick's *Temple of Shakespeare* at Hampton for the new theatre (**25**). A second copy for Garrick's temple was provided by Garrard in 1823 when Roubiliac's original went to the British Museum under the terms of Garrick's will.

Garrard received no great acclaim for his work and suffered many disappointments, despite his gifts as a painter, engraver and sculptor (**Nollekens** described him as a 'jack of all trades'). He lost his principal patron in 1815 when Whitbread committed suicide. Garrard continued to exhibit at the Royal Academy until shortly before his death on 8 October 1826, at his home at Queen's Building, Brompton, London. He collapsed suddenly whilst at prayer with his family, and his wife, who had given birth to 12 children during their marriage, was left in straitened circumstances, and with an invalid daughter. The Royal Academy awarded her an annuity of £45 and a donation of £50. Garrard's son **Charles Garrard** became a sculptor but the Garrard name was to achieve more lasting fame through his nephews, who became crown jewellers to Queen Victoria in 1843.

Sylvia Allen

Literary References: Redgrave 1878, 168; *Graves* III, 1905–6, 208–9; *Smith* 1905, 289–290; *Webb* 1951 (3), ch 4; *Whitbread and Croft-Murray* 1960, *passim*; *Robinson* 1976, 276–279; *Penny* 1976 (1), 302–3; *Liscombe* 1977, 700–4; *Penny* 1977 (2), 1,336–7; *Whinney* 1988, 320–32; *Dawson* 1999, 202, 204; *ODNB* (Asleson)

Funerary Monuments

No.	Date	Subject	Material	Location	Signed/Dated	Literature
1.	†1799	Anne Nottidge		Bocking, Essex	S	*Gunnis* 1968, 164
2.	1806	Jock, a favourite spaniel (plinth designed by Henry Holland)	sa	Southill Park, Beds, garden		*Webb* 1951 (3) 58 (repr 81); *Penny* 1976 (1), 302–3 (repr)
3.	†1809	Paul Burrard		Lymington, Hants	S	*Gunnis* 1968, 164
4.	1816	Countess Conyngham		Hughenden, Bucks		*Gunnis* 1968, 164
5.	1816	John Weech		Wiveliscombe, Somerset		*Gunnis* 1968, 164
6.	†1816	Thomas Nottidge		Bocking, Essex	S	*Gunnis* 1968, 164
7.	†1818	Lady Campbell		Latton, Essex		Pevsner, *Essex*, 1965, 222

Statues

No.	Date	Subject	Material	Location	Signed/Dated	Literature
8.	1796	Cattle, sheep, draft-horse, statuettes (set of 20 commissioned by the Board of Agriculture)	p	Southill Park, Beds		*Graves* III, 1905–6, 207; *Webb* 1951 (3), 58 (repr 86)
9.	1796	Reindeer from Lapland, group, statuette	p	Southill Park, Beds		*Graves* III, 1905–6, 207
10.	1797	Cow and calf, model		[Exhib RA, London, 1112]; untraced		*Graves* III, 1905–6, 207
11.	1797	Equestrian model		[Exhib RA, London, 1176]; untraced		*Graves* III, 1905–6, 207
12.	1798	A pointer, owned by Sir Charles Turner, model		[Exhib RA, London, 975]; untraced		*Graves* III, 1905–6, 207
13.	1799	Pointer, statuette	p	Southill Park, Beds	SD	*Webb* 1951 (3), 58
14.	1799	Two pointers	b	Southill Park, Beds		*Gunnis* 1968, 164
15.	post-1800	Thoroughbred stallion rearing, statuette	b	Ashmolean WA 1988.338		*Penny* 1992, III, 70 (repr)
16.	1806	Two dogs	m	Southill Park, Beds		*Gunnis* 1968, 164
17.	1808	Death of Adonis, sketch	tc	[Exhib RA, London, 877]; untraced		*Graves* III, 1905–6, 208
18.	1809	William Pitt in an MA gown, model (made at the request of the Cambridge committee)		[Exhib RA, London, 760]; untraced		*Graves* III, 1905–6, 208
19.	1811	King George III, model		[Exhib RA, London, 942]; untraced		*Graves* III, 1905–6, 209
20.	1811	King George III, study for an equestrian statue		[Exhib RA, London, 922]; untraced		*Graves* III, 1905–6, 209
21.	1812	A terrier, a bulldog and a greyhound, three statuettes	b	[Exhib RA, London, 907]; untraced		*Graves* III, 1905–6, 209
22.	1812	Bull-bitch owned by R P D Burrell		[Exhib RA, London, 918]; untraced		*Graves* III, 1905–6, 209
23.	1812	Sir John Moore, bronze mounted figure, model for a statue	b	Southill Park, Beds		*Graves* 1875, 207; *Graves* III, 1905–6, 209, 210; *Whinney* 1988, 321; *Gunnis* 1968, 164
24.	1812	The boxers, group, statuette	p	Southill Park, Beds	SD	*Graves* 1875, 207; *Graves* III, 1905–6, 209; *Gunnis* 1968, 164
25.	*c*1812	William Shakespeare (after Roubiliac's statue for Garrick's Villa)	p	[coll Samuel Whitbread]; Theatre Royal, Drury Lane, London Other versions: coll David Garrick, Hampton, *c*1823; untraced		*Smith* 1905, 289–90; *Webb* 1951 (3), 56; *Dawson* 1999, 202
26.	1816	Unidentified subject, model		[Exhib RA, London, 933]; untraced		*Graves* III, 1905–6, 209
27.	1817	Bull-calf, model		[Exhib RA, London, 1076]; untraced		*Graves* III, 1905–6, 210
28.	1818	Arthur, 1st Duke of Wellington, equestrian statuette, model for a statue (unexecuted)	b	Birmingham MAG, inv P.35'57	SD	*Graves* 1875, 207; *Graves* III, 1905–6, 210; *Whinney* 1988, 321; *Silber* 1987, 42, cat 120 (repr)
29.	1820	'The Downfall of Usurpation', equestrian model		[Exhib RA, London, 1011]; untraced		*Graves* III, 1905–6, 210
30.	1822	A 7-year old elephant, statuette	b	[Exhib BI, London, 327]; untraced		*Graves* 1875, 207
31.	1822	King George IV, equestrian model		[Exhib BI, London, 324]; untraced		*Graves* 1875, 207
32.	1822	Pegasus, modelled from Copenhagen	b	[Exhib BI, London, 325]; untraced		*Graves* 1875, 207
33.	1826	A group of pigs		[Exhib Soc of BA, London, 719]; untraced		*Johnson* 1975, 174
34.	1826	A group of pointers		[Exhib Soc of BA, London, 753]; untraced		*Johnson* 1975, 174
35.	1826	A horse trotting		[Exhib Soc of BA, London, 720]; untraced		*Johnson* 1975, 174
36.	1826	Cow, bull and calf		[Exhib Soc of BA, London, 754]; untraced		*Johnson* 1975, 174
37.	1826	Unidentified equestrian statue		[Exhib Soc of BA, London, 760]; untraced		*Johnson* 1975, 174

Busts

No.	Date	Subject	Material	Location	Signed/Dated	Literature
38.	1796	Samuel Whitbread III as a child	pb	Christie, 10 May 2006, lot 83 (repr)	SD	
39.	1797	An infant		[Exhib RA, London, 1192]; untraced		*Graves* III, 1905–6, 207
40.	1801	Unidentified young lady		[Exhib RA, London, 896]; untraced		*Graves* III, 1905–6, 208
41.	1802	Emperor Napoleon	pb	Uppark, Sussex	D	*Uppark* 1999, 51
42.	1803	Benjamin West		[Exhib RA, London, 1022]; untraced		*Graves* III, 1905–6, 208
43.	1803	Earl Fauconberg		[Exhib RA, London, 1026]; untraced		*Graves* III, 1905–6, 208
44.	1803	P Cox		[Exhib RA, London, 1019]; untraced		*Graves* III, 1905–6, 208
45.	1803	Sawrey Gilpin RA	p	Burghley House, Northants		*Whinney* 1988, 321
46.	1803	Thomas Adkin	m	Southill Park, Beds	SD	*Webb* 1951 (3), 59
47.	1804	Arthur Young		Petworth House, W Sussex	SD	*Graves* III, 1905–6, 208; *Gunnis* 1968, 164
48.	1804	J Heaviside		[Exhib RA, London, 935]; untraced		*Graves* III, 1905–6, 208
49.	1804	Lord Somerville		[Exhib RA, London, 856]; untraced		*Graves* III, 1905–6, 208
50.	1804	Rev Dr Willis	p	Burghley House, Northants	SD	*Graves* III, 1905–6, 208
51.	1804	Samuel Whitbread		[Exhib RA, London, 933]; untraced		*Graves* III, 1905–6, 208
52.	1804	Sir Joseph Banks	tc	Burghley House, Northants Other versions: Glasgow University, p		*Graves* III, 1905–6, 208
53.	1805	A Newland		[Exhib RA, London, 787]; untraced		*Graves* III, 1905–6, 208

54.	1805	Charles James Fox	pb	[Uppark, Sussex]; destroyed by fire, 1989		*Graves* III, 1905–6, 208; *Uppark* 1999, 51
55.	1805	Francis, 5th Duke of Bedford	pb	[Uppark, Sussex]; destroyed by fire, 1989		*Uppark* 1999, 51
56.	1805	Major Batten		[Exhib RA, London, 810]; untraced		*Graves* III, 1905–6, 208
57.	1805	Mr Fullar		[Exhib RA, London, 803]; untraced		*Graves* III, 1905–6, 208
58.	1805	Rev Mr Gilpin		[Exhib RA, London, 780]; untraced		*Graves* III, 1905–6, 208
59.	1805	William Battine, FRS	pb	Uppark, Sussex	D	*Uppark* 1999, 51
60.	1806	Henry Holland	m	Southill Park, Beds	SD	*Graves* III, 1905–6, 208; *Webb* 1951 (3), 59 (repr 90)
61.	1806	T W Coke	m	Ingestre Hall, Staffs (coll Lord Shrewsbury)	SD	*Graves* III, 1905–6, 208; C Lib (repr)
62.	1806	Thomas Coke	m	Shugborough, Staffs	SD	C Lib (repr)
63.	1806	Unidentified lady		[Exhib RA, London, 851]; untraced		*Graves* III, 1905–6, 208
64.	1807	George, 3rd Earl of Egremont	m	Petworth House, W Sussex, inv 135		*Gunnis* 1968, 164
65.	1807	J C Curran		[Exhib RA, London, 1104]; untraced		*Graves* III, 1905–6, 208
66.	1807	John, Earl St Vincent		[Exhib RA, London, 1097]; untraced		*Graves* III, 1905–6, 208
67.	1807	Rt Hon J Foster		[Exhib RA, London, 1100]; untraced		*Graves* III, 1905–6, 208
68.	1807	Unidentified young lady		[Exhib RA, London, 1084]; untraced		*Graves* III, 1905–6, 208
69.	1807	William Pitt		[Exhib RA, London, 1082]; untraced		*Graves* III, 1905–6, 208
70.	1808	J C Curwen		[Exhib RA, London, 989]; untraced		*Graves* III, 1905–6, 208
71.	1808	Mr Pugett, model		[Exhib RA, London, 994]; untraced		*Graves* III, 1905–6, 208
72.	1808	Sawrey Gilpin RA	m	Southill Park, Beds	SD	*Graves* III, 1905–6, 208; *Webb* 1951 (3) 59 (repr 85)
73.	1808	Unidentified lady, model		[Exhib RA, London, 869]; untraced		*Graves* III, 1905–6, 208
74.	1808	Valentine Green ARA		[Exhib RA, London, 884]; untraced		*Graves* III, 1905–6, 208
75.	1808	William Pitt	tc	Fitzwilliam		*Graves* III, 1905–6, 208; *Gunnis* 1968, 164
76.	1809	Captain Thompson, Coldstream Guards, model		[Exhib RA, London, 876]; untraced		*Graves* III, 1905–6, 208
77.	1809	H Ashby, model		[Exhib RA, London, 880]; untraced		*Graves* III, 1905–6, 208
78.	1809	Rev T Fry, model		[Exhib RA, London, 882]; untraced		*Graves* III, 1905–6, 208
79.	1809	Unidentified lady		[Exhib RA, London, 768]; untraced		*Graves* III, 1905–6, 208
80.	1809	William Pitt in the robes of the Chancellor of the Exchequer, model		[Exhib RA, London, 862]; untraced		*Graves* III, 1905–6, 208
81.	1810	Dr S H Jackson, model		[Exhib RA, London, 727]; untraced		*Graves* III, 1905–6, 208
82.	1810	Humphrey Repton, model		[Exhib RA, London, 720]; untraced		*Graves* III, 1905–6, 208
83.	1810	Samuel Whitbread, model		[Exhib RA, London, 898]; untraced		*Graves* III, 1905–6, 208
84.	1810	T Tompkins, model		[Exhib RA, London, 873]; untraced		*Graves* III, 1905–6, 208
85.	1810	William Wilberforce, model		[Exhib RA, London, 897]; untraced		*Graves* III, 1905–6, 208
86.	1811	Sir J Sinclair Bt, model		[Exhib RA, London, 933]; untraced		*Graves* III, 1905–6, 209
87.	1811	Unidentified lady, model		[Exhib RA, London, 903]; untraced		*Graves* III, 1905–6, 208
88.	1811	Unidentified youth, model		[Exhib RA, London, 935]; untraced		*Graves* III, 1905–6, 209
89.	1811	W Adam, model		[Exhib RA, London, 901]; untraced		*Graves* III, 1905–6, 208
90.	1812	General Tarleton, model		[Exhib RA, London, 925]; untraced		*Graves* III, 1905–6, 209
91.	1812	Unidentified man, model		[Exhib RA, London, 895]; untraced		*Graves* III, 1905–6, 209
92.	1813	R B Sheridan	p	SJSM		*Graves* III, 1905–6, 209; *Johnson* 1975, 174; Soane Museum Inventory
93.	1813	Unidentified young lady, model		[Exhib RA, London, 922]; untraced		*Graves* III, 1905–6, 209
94.	1814	Arthur, 1st Duke of Wellington		Althorp House, Northants	SD	*Webb* 1951 (3), 60n
95.	1814	Time, study		[Exhib BI, London, 226]; untraced		*Graves* 1875, 207
96.	1814	Unidentified infant		[Exhib RA, London, 765]; untraced		*Graves* III, 1905–6, 209
97.	1814	Unidentified young lady		[Exhib RA, London, 756]; untraced		*Graves* III, 1905–6, 209
98.	1815	Arthur, 1st Duke of Wellington, for the Queen's apartments at Windsor		[Exhib RA, London, 897]; untraced		*Graves* III, 1905–6, 209
99.	1815	Lord Lascelles, model		[Exhib RA, London, 874]; untraced		*Graves* III, 1905–6, 209
100.	1815	Miss Lascelles, model		[Exhib RA, London, 887]; untraced		*Graves* III, 1905–6, 209
101.	1815	Prince Hoare, model		[Exhib RA, London, 879]; untraced		*Graves* III, 1905–6, 209
102.	1815	Sir J Gilpin		[Exhib RA, London, 893]; untraced		*Graves* III, 1905–6, 209
103.	1815	T Frankland, model		[Exhib RA, London, 885]; untraced		*Graves* III, 1905–6, 209
104.	1815	Unidentified gentleman, model		[Exhib RA, London, 898]; untraced		*Graves* III, 1905–6, 209
105.	1816	Arthur, 1st Duke of Wellington	m	Southill Park, Beds	SD	*Graves* III, 1905–6, 209; *Webb* 1951 (3), 61
106.	1816	Samuel Whitbread, model for a monumental bust		[Exhib RA, London, 936]; untraced		*Graves* III, 1905–6, 209
107.	1816	Unidentified gentleman, model		[Exhib RA, London, 922]; untraced		*Graves* III, 1905–6, 209
108.	1816	W Wiltshire, model		[Exhib RA, London, 936]; untraced		*Graves* III, 1905–6, 209
109.	1817	Unidentified artist, model		[Exhib RA, London, 1035]; untraced		*Graves* III, 1905–6, 210
110.	1817	Unidentified lady, study for a monumental bust		[Exhib RA, London, 1054]; untraced		*Graves* III, 1905–6, 210
111.	1818	Henry Holland	m	Woburn Abbey, Beds	SD	*Webb* 1951 (3) 59; *British Portraits* 1956–7, 108
112.	1818	Princess Charlotte, model		[Exhib RA, London, 1091]; untraced		*Graves* III, 1905–6, 210
113.	1819	Rev W Coxe, Archdeacon of Wiltshire, model		[Exhib RA, London, 1230]; untraced		*Graves* III, 1905–6, 210
114.	1820	Arthur, 1st Duke of Wellington	b	[Exhib RA, London, 1056]; untraced		*Graves* III, 1905–6, 210
115.	1820	Samuel Whitbread	b	[Exhib RA, London, 1058]; untraced		*Graves* III, 1905–6, 210
116.	1824	General Mina, model		[Exhib RA, London, 1036]; untraced		*Graves* III, 1905–6, 210
117.	1824	Joseph Barrett	tc	[Exhib RA, London, 994]; untraced		*Graves* III, 1905–6, 210
118.	1825	Master Lane Fox, model		[Exhib RA, London, 1006]; untraced		*Graves* III, 1905–6, 210
119.	1825	Miss Lane Fox, model		[Exhib RA, London, 1018]; untraced		*Graves* III, 1905–6, 210
120.	1825	Unidentified gentleman	b	[Exhib RA, London, 1045]; untraced		*Graves* III, 1905–6, 210
121.	1826	Mrs Lane Fox, model		[Exhib RA, London, 1077]; untraced		*Graves* III, 1905–6, 210
122.	1826	Unidentified gentleman	b	[Exhib RA, London, 1081]; untraced		*Graves* III, 1905–6, 210
123.	1826	Unidentified lady	b	[Exhib RA, London, 1084]; untraced		*Graves* III, 1905–6, 210

No.	Date	Subject	Medium	Location	Signed	Literary references
124.	1826	Unidentified lady, model		[Exhib RA, London, 1073]; untraced		*Graves* III, 1905–6, 210
125.	1826	Unidentified man, perhaps 3rd Earl of Egremont	b	Knox/Longstaffe-Gowan coll (acq 2000)	SD	*Graves* III, 1905–6, 211
126.	nd	Thomas Girtin		[Garrard's studio; sold 1827, lot 68]; untraced		*Gunnis* 1968, 164

Chimneypieces

No.	Date	Subject	Medium	Location	Signed	Literary references
127.	1796	Tablet for a chimneypiece		[Exhib RA, London, 884]; untraced		*Graves* III, 1905–6, 207

Architectural Sculpture

No.	Date	Subject	Medium	Location	Signed	Literary references
128.	1797	Duncan's maddened horses; lion, lioness and cubs; fighting bulls; Norway elk pursued by wolves; camels	p	Southill Park, Beds, entrance hall overdoors		*Graves* III, 1905–6, 207, 208; *Webb* 1951 (3), 32, 58 (repr 87a and b); *Whinney* 1988, 320–1 (repr)
129.	1811	Eagle of Jove, bearing laurel and thunderbolts		Woburn Abbey, Beds, above entrance to Temple of the Graces		*Clifford* 1995, 64, 65 (repr)
130.	1811	Lions on gate piers Model(s): exhib RA, London, 1811, 934		Woburn Abbey, Beds, w front		*Graves* III, 1905–6, 209; *Webb* 1951 (3), 58
131.	1812	Bacchic bull, tympanum relief		Woburn Abbey, Beds, sculpture gallery, s façade		*Clifford* 1995, 64
132.	1825	Gothic truss, with busts of a lady and her seven daughter		[Exhib RA, London, 994]; untraced		*Graves* III, 1905–6, 210
133.	nd	Four overdoor reliefs depicting scenes from Gay and Aesop's fables	pb	Woburn Abbey, Beds, first state room		*Webb* 1951, 60

Reliefs

No.	Date	Subject	Medium	Location	Signed	Literary references
134.	1804	Stag at bay	pb	Uppark, Sussex, dining room		*Uppark* 1999, 51
135.	1804	'The wanton courser thus with reins unbound, Breaks from his stall'	pb	Uppark, Sussex, dining room		*Graves* III, 1905–6, 208; *Uppark* 1999, 51
136.	1805	'As when some huntsman with a flying spear'		[Exhib RA, London, 703]; untraced		*Graves* III, 1905–6, 208
137.	1806	Plaques of animals		Burghley House, Northants, corridor etc		*Gunnis* 1968, 164
138.	1812	(?) John, 6th Duke and Georgiana, Duchess of Bedford, medallion		[Exhib RA, London, 905]; untraced		*Graves* III, 1905–6, 209
139.	1812	Mr Cribb, medallion		[Exhib RA, London, 940]; untraced		*Graves* III, 1905–6, 209
140.	1813	A boa-serpent crushing a tiger, study for a bas-relief for James Wheeler		[Exhib RA, London, 915]; untraced		*Graves* III, 1905–6, 209
141.	1817	Unidentified lady, medallion		[Exhib RA, London, 1020]; untraced		*Graves* III, 1905–6, 209
142.	1819	A bull, from an antique gem		[Exhib RA, London, 1239]; untraced		*Graves* III, 1905–6, 210; *Johnson* 1975, 174

Miscellaneous

No.	Date	Subject	Medium	Location	Signed	Literary references
143.	1796	The Nil Gaw antelope, model		[Exhib RA, London, 795]; untraced		*Graves* III, 1905–6, 207
144.	1797	A stag from the banks of the Ganges, model		[Exhib RA, London, 1184]; untraced		*Graves* III, 1905–6, 207
145.	1797	Group of lambs		[Exhib RA, London, 1177]; untraced		*Graves* III, 1905–6, 207
146.	1797	Pugilists, group		[Exhib RA, London, 1125]; untraced		*Graves* III, 1905–6, 207
147.	1799	Alexander and Bucephalus		[Exhib RA, London, 1109]; untraced		*Graves* III, 1905–6, 207
148.	1799	Bison and Jebu		[Exhib RA, London, 982]; untraced		*Graves* III, 1905–6, 207
149.	1799	Irish pig, Berkshire hog		[Exhib RA, London, 1002]; untraced		*Graves* III, 1905–6, 207
150.	1799	Nessus and Deianeira		[Exhib RA, London, 1101]; untraced		*Graves* III, 1905–6, 207
151.	1801	Holderness cattle, from the King's stock at Windsor		[Exhib RA, London, 904]; untraced		*Graves* III, 1905–6, 208
152.	1801	The infant son of Sir J Mildmay, reclining on a mattress		[Exhib RA, London, 911]; untraced		*Graves* III, 1905–6, 208
153.	1802	Peasant attacked by wolves		[Exhib RA, London, 765]; untraced		*Graves* III, 1905–6, 208
154.	1813	Three models of dogs and a horse		[Exhib RA, London, 914]; untraced		*Graves* III, 1905–6, 209
155.	1815	The fall of Phaeton, for a salver		[Exhib RA, London, 877]; untraced		*Graves* III, 1905–6, 209
156.	1817	Comet, an improved short-horn bull		[Exhib RA, London, 1042]; untraced		*Graves* III, 1905–6, 210
157.	1819	Model for a public monument	tc	[Exhib RA, London, 1241]; untraced		*Graves* III, 1905–6, 210
158.	1819	Victory and fame, model for a monument	tc	[Exhib RA, London, 1242]; untraced		*Graves* III, 1905–6, 210
159.	1826	A case containing ten subjects		[Exhib Soc of BA, London, 755]; untraced		*Johnson* 1975, 174
160.	1826	The Marquis of Exeter's mare, Augusta, four studies for a piece of sculpture		[Exhib RA, London, 327]; untraced		*Graves* III, 1905–6, 210

GARRATT fl 1711–

He worked under William Townesend at Queen's College, Oxford with a Mr Smith. The entry in Townesend's accounts reads, '1711. Paid Mr. Garratt 16 days for carving the pediment towards the College. £3 4s (1). Paid Mr. Smith for 17 days work on the same pediment'. Later there is a payment of £7 16s to Garratt for 39 days work 'carving ye pediment towards ye street'. Smith again assisted and was paid £6 for 36 days' work (2).

Literary References: *Hiscock* 1946, 43; *Gunnis* 1968, 164

Archival References: QC, Wm Townesend Accts, 22 December 1711

Architectural Sculpture

No.	Date	Subject	Location	Literary references
1.	1711	Pediment (co-sculptor: Smith)	The Queen's College, Oxford, west wing of the front quadrangle	*Gunnis* 1968, 164; GPC
2.	post-1711	Pediment (co-sculptor: Smith)	The Queen's College, Oxford, street façade	GPC

GARRATT, J, of Portsea fl 1822–30?

Funerary Monuments

1.	?1822	William Veasey	Holy Trinity, Gosport, Hants	S	GPC
2.	?1830	John Battershell	Alverstoke, Hants	S	GPC

GARRETT, George and Jonathan, of Southampton fl 1832?

Funerary Monuments

1.	?1832	Anne Northage	Itchen (Pear Tree Green), Hants		*Gunnis* 1968, 164

GARRETT, Joseph fl c1740

Joseph Garrett, 'Mason in Gravel Lane, Southwark', was a Liveryman of the Masons' Company c1740 (Masons' Co Assistants, c1740, f3).

GATES, Henry fl 1684–1722

He was the son of William Gates of Kingston-on-Thames and was apprenticed in 1684 to **Thomas Broomhall**. In 1692 he became free of the Masons' Company (Masons' Co, *Freemen*, fol 24, 3 Jan) and the list of members for 1708 gives his address as Vauxhall. He made a marble chimneypiece for Stourhead in 1722 for which he charged £5 10s (Hoare Private Accounts, 1714–31, 11 Oct 1722).

Archival References: Masons' Co, *Apprentice binding book* (1), 1684

Chimneypieces

1.	1722	Description unavailable	m	Stourhead, Wilts	*Gunnis* 1968, 164

GATES, William I fl 1731–61

The son of **Henry Gates**, he was apprenticed to his father on 15 June 1713 and became free in 1722. He was admitted to the livery of the Masons' Company on 26 June 1760, and in the following year lived near Fishmongers' Hall.

Literary References: *Gunnis* 1968, 164; *Webb* 1999, 13

Archival References: Masons' Co, Court Book, 1751–96 (26 June 1760); Freemen, fol 24 (14th June 1722)

Funerary Monuments

1.	?1746	John Wise	Totnes, Devon	S	*Gunnis* 1968, 164

GATES, William II fl 1740–85?

The son of **William Gates I**, he was apprenticed to Samuel Stretton on 27 March 1740, becoming free of the Masons' Company in 1747. Mortimer's directory of 1763 lists a William Gates, mason, near Dyers-wharf, Thames-street but it is not clear whether this was the father or the son (p 49). It was presumably the younger Gates who was employed as the mason in charge of building St Luke's Hospital, Old Street, in 1785. Since **Daniel Pinder** and **William Norris** took over from him the following year it is possible that Gates had died (Hospital Archives, in GPC). Alternatively, he could be the 'William Gates, Mason of All Hallows the Less, City of London', who died on 17 March 1802 (TNA PROB 11/1371).

Literary References: *Gunnis* 1968, 164

Archival References: Masons' Co, *Freemen*, fol 25 (1 May 1747); GPC

GATLEY, Alfred 1816–63

Gatley received considerable critical acclaim for his work but nonetheless struggled to make a living as a sculptor. His father, William, owned and worked two stone-quarries in the Kerridge Hills near Macclesfield. His mother Betty (or possibly Hannah, née Henshaw) died when Gatley was only 7. He was given space in his father's yard and taught how to use a stonemason's tools from an early age. At 17 he produced a finely carved bust in Kerridge stone of the poet John Milton, proudly signed and dated 'Alfred Gatley, A.D. 1833' (**23**). In the same year he carved a pair of Kerridge stone statuettes, copies of **James Thom**'s celebrated figures, *Tam O'Shanter* and *Souter Johnnie* (**13, 14**). **Sir Francis Chantrey** is said to have admired the skilful execution of these early works, particularly given the basic tools and materials then available to Gatley.

His talent was recognised and encouraged by a local clergyman, James Sumner of Pott Shrigley. Sumner arranged for Gatley to be sent to London to receive formal training and an introduction was arranged to **Edward Hodges Baily**. Baily was apparently impressed by Gatley's ability but only offered him a salary of 10/- a week since he had no experience of working with marble. Gatley diligently applied himself to his studies: he drew and modelled in Baily's workshop in the evenings, studied books on anatomy and the antique and gained permission to draw at the British Museum. Within 2 years he was accepted at the Royal Academy Schools where he obtained silver medals in the antique and life academy in 1841, 1842, and 1844. His bust of *Hebe* (**24**) was his first work to attract public notice: this was selected by one of the prize-winners of the Art Union of London. Gatley was paid £20 and the bust was cast in bronze by the firm of J A Hatfield. Editions were distributed to lottery winners. Gatley was the first sculptor to benefit from the Union's patronage; his bust was was included on the frontispiece to the *London Art Union Prize Annual* in 1845 together with figures by more established sculptors. In 1843 Gatley moved to the studio of **Musgrave Lewthwaite Watson** and in 1847 he established himself as an independent sculptor. He continued to receive much-needed encouragement from his friends in Cheshire; a subscription was raised for a bust of the Bishop of Chester, John Sumner (**36**). Other important commissions for busts include one of General Espartero, ex-regent of Spain (**33**) and another of the theologian Richard Hooker (**43**).

Having worked in London for some years with only limited success Gatley moved to Rome in 1852, where he hoped his talent would receive greater encouragement. He took a studio near the Porta Pinciana and became a friend of **John Gibson RA**, with whom he shared an admiration for Greek art. He produced his first full-size classical figures at this time, *Echo* and *Night* (**17, 18**). *Echo* was one of Gatley's favourite subjects and at least 3 versions in marble are known. Another important work from this period is *A Greek hero leading a bull to sacrifice* (**19**). Gatley was also recognised for his animal studies, particularly his lions and tigers (**20–22**), which earned him the title 'the Landseer of sculpture' (*Athenaeum*, 1863, 748). In 1851 he was consulted by Samuel Christie-Miller MP on the decoration for a mausoleum to commemorate the bibliophile William Henry Miller (**12**). W H Miller had left his fortune and estates at Craigentinny and Britwell to his cousin, Samuel Christie (subsequently Christie-Miller) on the stipulation that a sizeable mausoleum should be erected to his memory. Gatley suggested the subject of *Pharaoh and his army in the Red Sea* and, to his delight, he was given the commission, with another for a companion relief, *Song of Moses and Miriam.* These two epic scenes were inspired by ancient Greek and Egyptian relief sculpture and share dynamic compositions, angularity of style and deep, incisive cutting. For a period Gatley's prospects looked good, his reputation grew and he moved to larger studios behind the Piazza del Popolo. In 1862 his *Pharaoh* relief was given a place at the International Exhibition in London. It was widely admired: *The Queen* magazine described it as 'among the noblest productions of modern art' (July 1863) while the *Art Journal* declared that 'there is not a sculptor in Europe who would not consider it an honour to have been its author' (1863, 181). Gatley also submitted *Echo* and *Night* along with some animal studies. Although his work was well received, nothing was sold and no new pieces were commissioned. Bitterly disappointed, Gatley returned to Rome where he continued to work on the *Miriam* relief. He was however plagued by financial worries and deeply concerned about his future prospects to such an extent that he considered emigrating to Australia to make a fresh start. In June 1863 he caught a severe chill, which developed into acute dysentery and on 28 June 1863 he died.

Gatley was buried in the Protestant Cemetery in Rome. The inscription over his grave described him as: 'great in his works, a loyal citizen, beloved by many and respected by all. He had a kindness of heart, and a hatred of all that was false. He lived a Christian's life, and died at the age of 47'. Gatley never married. He was described as deeply religious, honourable and conscientious but also shy, sensitive and prone to melancholy. He was apparently 'pale and careworn' in appearance, but possessed a 'fine face' and 'luminous eyes' through which his 'intellectual and imaginative power shone' (*Sumner* 1885, 731). In its obituary, the *Art Journal* attempted to account for Gatley's lack of commercial success: 'The style he chose admitted of no facile compromise of the classical with the pictorial. It descended not to seek an easily-purchased popularity by softly-blended forms, after the manner of the romantic. The school to which he belonged was stern and strict. The English public failed to comprehend the largeness of his manner.' (*AJ*, 1863, 322).

Caroline Jordan

Literary References: *Palgrave* 1862, 145, 269; *Athenaeum*, 25 July 1863 (obit); *Sumner* 1885, 722–36; *Alfred Gatley: Kerridge boy who became famous sculptor*, Bollington Festival Prog, 1964; *Reaney* 1968, 34–5; *Avery and Marsh*, 1985, 328–37; *Wells* 1999, *passim*

Archival References: Gatley corr transcribing copies of letters sent by him to friends & family, started in Rome 1853 and including account of visit to Florence, priv coll; Gatley/Atkinson; Gatley/Cope; Gatley/Rathbone

Portraits of the Sculptor: J Adams-Acton, exhib RA 1860; another, Marcianno da Tuna, Roma, 1862 (private coll)

Funerary Monuments

1.	1840	Bridget Downes		Pott Shrigley, Cheshire	S	*Gunnis* 1968, 165
2.	†1846	John Lowe		Mottram, Lancs	S	*Gunnis* 1968, 165; C Lib (repr)
3.	1846	Mary Legh		Newton-in-Markerfield, Lancs	S	*Gunnis* 1968, 165
4.	1850	Mural tablet, design only		[Exhib RA, London, 1454]; untraced		*Graves* III, 1905–6, 215–6
5.	†1851	Elizabeth Clayton		Hazel Grove, Cheshire	S	Pevsner, *Cheshire*, 1971, 236
6.	1851	George Lockwood		Lambourne, Essex	S	C Lib (repr)
7.	1851	John Clayton (†1848)		Marple, Cheshire	SD	C Lib (repr)
8.	1851	Mural tablet, design only		[Exhib RA, London, 1269]; untraced		*Graves* III, 1905–6, 215–6
9.	1851	Mural tablet, design only		[Exhib RA, London, 1389]; untraced		*Graves* III, 1905–6, 215–6
10.	1853	Mural monument, design only		[Exhib RA, London, 1414]; untraced		*Graves* III, 1905–6, 215–6
11.	†1857	Thomas Legh		St Mary, Disley, Cheshire		*Gunnis* 1968, 165; Pevsner, *Cheshire*, 1971, 198
12.	1855–1863	W H Miller, mausoleum with reliefs of 'Pharoah and his Army in the Red Sea' and 'The Song of Miriam'		Craigentinny, Edinburgh		LIE, 1862; *Gunnis* 1968, 165; *Reaney* 1968, 34–5; *ODNB*

Statues

13.	1833	Tam O'Shanter, statuette	s	Untraced		*Sumner* 1885, 724; *Reaney* 1968, 54; C Lib (repr)
14.	1844	Souter Johnnie, statuette	s	Untraced		*Sumner* 1885, 724; *Reaney* 1968, 54; C Lib (repr)
15.	1851	Unidentified subject, design only		[Exhib RA, London, 1291]; untraced		*Graves* III, 1905–6, 215–6
16.	1851	Unidentified subject, design only		[Exhib RA, London, 1348]; untraced		*Graves* III, 1905–6, 215–6
17.	1853	Echo	m	[Salford AG, Lancs, 1871]; Gawsworth Hall, Cheshire (1999) Other versions: Another, SD 1859, sold Christie, 15 July 1993, lot 258 Another, stone, nd, Gawsworth Hall, Cheshire (ex Lyme Park), marble, SD	SD	*Gawsworth Guide*, 44, 45; *Gunnis* 1968, 165; *Wells* 1999, 44, 46, 56 (repr)
18.	*c*1853	Night	m	[Gallery of C W Wass, of Crystal Palace (for auction)]; untraced		*ODNB*
19.	1861	Greek hero leading the bull to sacrifice		Salford Art Gallery, Greater Manchester		SAG catalogue, 1883; *Gunnis* 1968, 165; *Wells* 1999, 48, 46 (repr)
20.	1862	A tiger in the act of springing	m	Untraced		*LIE* 1862; *Sumner* 1885, 734; *DNB*; *Reaney* 1968, 55
21.	1862	Sleeping lioness	m	Untraced		*Sumner* 1885, 734; *DNB*; *Reaney* 1968, 55
22.	1862	Three lions and a lioness, four statuettes		Untraced		*LIE* 1862; *Sumner* 1885, 734; *DNB*; *Reaney* 1968, 54

Busts

23.	1833	John Milton	s	[formerly Gawsworth Hall, Cheshire]; private coll	SD	*Gawsworth Guide*, 44; *Reaney* 1968, 54
24.	1834	Hebe	m	[Exhib RA, London, 1444]; untraced		*Graves* III, 1905–6, 215–6; *Avery and Marsh*, 329–30 (repr 329, 337)
25.	1841	Unidentified gentleman		[Exhib RA, London, 1295]; untraced		*Graves* III, 1905–6, 215–6
26.	1842	Richard Willis		[Exhib RA, London, 1405]; untraced		*Graves* III, 1905–6, 215–6
27.	1843	Miss Rylance		[Exhib RA, London, 1475]; untraced		*Graves* III, 1905–6, 215–6
28.	1843	Unidentified gentleman		[Exhib RA, London, 1511]; untraced		*Graves* III, 1905–6, 215–6
29.	1844	Cupid	m	[Exhib RA, London, 1389]; untraced		*Sumner* 1885, 726
30.	1844	Psyche	m	[Exhib RA, London, 1403]; untraced		*Graves* III, 1905–6, 215–6; *Sumner* 1885, 726

No.	Date	Subject		Location		References
31.	1845	Mrs Maude Legh, unfinished		Newton Coll, Lyme Park		*Graves* III, 1905–6, 215–6
32.	1845	Thomas Legh of Lyme	m	Newton Coll, Lyme Park		*Graves* III, 1905–6, 215–6; *Gunnis* 1968, 165
33.	1846	General Espartero, Duke of Vittoria and Morella, ex-regent of Spain		[Exhib RA, London, 1488]; untraced		*Graves* III, 1905–6, 215–6; *Gunnis* 1968, 165
34.	1847	J H Smith Barry		[Exhib RA, London, 1364]; untraced		*Graves* III, 1905–6, 215–6
35.	1847	Mrs Smith Barry		[Exhib RA, London, 1364]; untraced		*Graves* III, 1905–6, 215–6; *Gunnis* 1968, 165
36.	1848	John Sumner, Archbishop of Canterbury		[Exhib RA, London, 1397]; untraced		*Graves* III, 1905–6, 215–6; *Ormond* 1973, 439
37.	1848	Mrs Hulton	m	Bolton Art Gallery		*Graves* III, 1905–6, 215–6
38.	1848	William Hulton		Bolton Art Gallery		*Graves* III, 1905–6, 215–6; *Gunnis* 1968, 165; C Lib (repr)
39.	1849	Unidentified lady		[Exhib RA, London, 1312]; untraced		*Graves* III, 1905–6, 215–6
40.	1850	S Christie MP		[Exhib RA, London, 1381]; untraced		*Graves* III, 1905–6, 215–6
41.	1851	Captain the Hon Augustus Vernon		[Exhib RA, London, 1328]; untraced		*Graves* III, 1905–6, 215–6
42.	1851	Mrs Forster	m	[Exhib RA, London, 1359]; untraced		*Graves* III, 1905–6, 215–6
43.	1851	Richard Hooker		[Temple Church, London]; destroyed		*ILN*, 6.9.1851, 285; *Graves* III, 1905–6, 215–6; *Gunnis* 1968, 165
44.	1852	A J Coffin		[Exhib RA, London, 1419]; untraced		*Graves* III, 1905–6, 215–6; *Gunnis* 1968, 165
45.	*c*1853	Alastor, or the spirit of solitude		Untraced		*Sumner* 1885, 728; *DNB*
46.	1853	Angel of Mercy	m	[Exhib RA, London, 1374]; untraced		*Graves* III, 1905–6, 215–6
47.	1857	Unidentified man		Private coll, London	S	
48.	1873–1874	Euripides, after the antique		Salford AG, Lancs (in store 2005)		Salford Museum cat, 1883; *Wells* 1999, 55
49.	1871–1875	Paris (or Alexander), after the antique		[Salford AG, Lancs]; untraced		*Wells* 1999, 55
50.	nd	Elizabeth Swindells		Waterhouse Medical Centre, Bollington, Cheshire	S	
51.	nd	George Swindells		Waterhouse Medical Centre, Bollington, Cheshire	S	
52.	nd	Homer, after the Antique		[Salford AG, Lancs]; untraced		*Wells* 1999, 55

Reliefs

No.	Date	Subject		Location		References
53.	nd	Triumph of Britannia	s	[Gawsworth Hall, Cheshire]; untraced		*Gawsworth Guide*, 45

Miscellaneous

No.	Date	Subject		Location		References
54.	*c*1835	Reliquary	s	[Gawsworth Hall, Cheshire]; private coll		*Gawsworth Guide*, 45
55.	1846	The hours leading out the horses of the sun		[Britwell Court (home of the Miller family)]; untraced		*Graves* III, 1905–6, 215–6
56.	1848	Religious instruction		[Exhib RA, London, 1346]; untraced		*Graves* III, 1905–6, 215–6

GAWEN, Joseph 1825–

Gawen was 22 and living at 20 Great James St, Bedford Row, when he joined the Royal Academy Schools in 1847, on the recommendation of **William Behnes**. He occasionally exhibited at the RA from various London addresses between 1850 and 1882, and was awarded a medal for a model in 1852 (7).

Literary References: *Gunnis* 1968, 165

Archival References: RA Admissions

Statues

No.	Date	Subject		Location		References
1.	1855	Arthur, 1st Duke of Wellington, equestrian statuette		[Exhib RA, London, 1495]; untraced		*Graves* III, 1905–6, 217
2.	1857	Field-Marshal Lord Raglan, statuete		[Exhib RA, London, 1240]; untraced		*Graves* III, 1905–6, 217

Busts

No.	Date	Subject		Location		References
3.	1850	W Blanchard Jerrold		[Exhib RA, London, 1412]; untraced		*Graves* III, 1905–6, 217
4.	1854	Master Little		[Exhib RA, London, 1476]; untraced		*Graves* III, 1905–6, 217
5.	1868	George Cruikshank	m	[Exhib RA, London, 1032]; untraced		*Graves* III, 1905–6, 218
6.	1882	Rev Samuel Smith	m	[Exhib RA, London, 1640]; untraced		*Graves* III, 1905–6, 218

Miscellaneous

No.	Date	Subject		Location		References
7.	1852	Unidentified subject, model		[RA medal]; untraced		RA Premium list
8.	1861	Achilles and Lycaon		[Exhib RA, London, 1075]; untraced		*Graves* III, 1905–6, 218

GAY, M L, of London fl 1818–21?

Gay's flamboyant tradecard, which combines architectural and sculptural trophies describes him as a 'Bath Stone Mason' of 20 Buckingham Place, Fitzroy Square, London (BM Heal 106.14). He was declared bankrupt in 1818.

Literary References: *Gunnis* 1968, 165

Funerary Monuments

No.	Date	Subject		Location		References
1.	?1821	Mrs Knipe		Bath Abbey, Somerset	S	*Gunnis* 1968, 165

GAYFER, James

See **John Gilbert**.

GAYFERE, Thomas I 1685–

He was born on 28 January 1685 at Bury St Edmunds and married Mary Townshend of Burford, who was probably a member of the family of Oxford masons. He became foreman to **Christopher Cass I** and by 1730 had his own mason's yard in St Ann's Lane, Westminster. About a decade later his name appeared at this address in a list of assistants and livery of the Masons' Company. He had at least three sons: James was apprenticed in 1736 to a joiner, Thomas Adey, and in 1748 he was described as 'of Westminster, mason' when another son, Richard was apprenticed to **George Mercer** (TNA IR 15/21). The third was **Thomas Gayfere II**. Thomas I was probably the Thomas Gayfere who was the mason for Westminster Bridge, opened in 1750. He died on 26 June 1756.

Literary References: *Chester* 1876, 483; *Toynbee* 1927, 157; *Gunnis* 1968, 165

Archival References: Masons' Co Assistants, f6; GPC

GAYFERE, Thomas II 1720–1812

The eldest son of **Thomas Gayfere I** and Mary, née Townsend, he was born on 31 August 1720 at Ratcliffe Street, St Dunstan's, Stepney. In 1734 he was apprenticed to **Andrews Jelfe**. He became free on 30 June 1743, and on 3 March 1752 married Frances, the daughter of Edmund Le Neve. It was probably he, rather than his father, who in 1756 built 18, Cavendish Square for Thomas Bridges as one of a team of craftsmen including **Benjamin Carter**, who were working under the architect Henry Keene. In 1760 Gayfere, Carter and several other craftsmen appeared in a conversation-piece commissioned from the painter Robert Pyle as a gift for Keene. The central figure is Keene himself, pointing to a plan on the table for an unidentified building. Gayfere is in the central foreground leaning over his chair, apparently engaged in a dispute with Carter.

Gayfere was appointed master-mason to Westminster Abbey by October 1762 when his name and position were mentioned in the Abbey records. He remained the sole holder of this post until 7 December 1802, when the patent was confered again jointly to him and his son, **Thomas Gayfere III**. In 1773 he built (and helped design) the Portland stone front of Horace Walpole's chapel at Strawberry Hill at a cost of £230 6s. Gayfere's close knowledge of the gothic architecture of Westminster Abbey enabled him to produce one of the most authentic approximations of the true medieval style at Walpole's mock-gothic mansion. Gayfere was also responsible for the chimneypiece in the great north bedroom (1) and for masons' work, for which he was paid £50 in June 1774. In 1773 he became Master of the Masons' Company. During the same period Gayfere worked for Sir Roger Newdigate. In 1768–69 he carried out repairs to Harefield Church, Middx, for which he received £53, and in 1779 he was paid £259 for work on Newdigate's house in Spring Gardens, London (Newdigate Archives). Gayfere also acted as a stone merchant and in 1773 supplied materials for the building of Osterley Park by Robert Child.

His wife Frances died on 22 March 1770 and was buried in Westminster Abbey. Gayfere himself died on 4 April 1812, and was buried on 10 April in the west cloisters of the Abbey. His estate was sworn at under £10,000, and was administered by his only surviving child, Thomas Gayfere III.

Literary References: *London Marriage Licences*; *Chester* 1876, 483; *Toynbee* 1927, 156–7; *Smith* 1945, 556–7, 868; *Gunnis* 1968, 165–6; *Crook* 1973, 1726–30

Archival References: Masons' Co, Freemen, fol 25; Court Book, 1751–96 (14 June 1773); LMA Acc 85/f223; GPC

Portraits of the Sculptor: Robert Pyle, conversation piece, 1760, formerly Buxted Place, Sussex, destroyed

Chimneypieces

1.	1773	Description unavailable		Strawberry Hill, Twickenham, London, great north bedroom	*Gunnis* 1968, 165; Pevsner, *London: S*, 1983, 548

Reliefs

2.	c1766	King Alfred, medallion, part of a chimneypiece	m	University College, Oxford, hall	Pevsner, *Oxon*, 1974, 210; C Lib (repr)

GAYFERE, Thomas III 1755–1827

He was born on 9 January 1755 in Church Street, Millbank, the son of **Thomas Gayfere II**. He exhibited drawings at the Society of Artists in 1774 and 1777 and at the Royal Academy in 1778, 1779 and 1780. Gayfere married Ann, daughter of Evan Jones, of Oakham, Rutland.

On 7 December 1802 he succeeded to the position of Master-Mason to Westminster Abbey, a post he initially held jointly with his father. Gayfere superintended the repairs to Henry VII's chapel, 1809–22, an exercise he performed with scrupulous attention to detail. He visited quarries in St Albans, Woburn and Bath before finding the appropriate stone at Coombe Down, Somerset, and took measurements and casts of all the surviving ornaments of the chapel before making full working drawings. His carvers included **Maitland** and **David Boag**, **John Teasdale I** and **John Teasdale II**. Brayley felt that 'the spirit and correctness,' with which the decoration was executed showed 'skill, judgment, and ingenuity'. Furthermore it was 'no eulogium to say that the execution of this task could not have been entrusted to a more capable artizan than Mr Gayfere' (*Neale and Brayley* 1818–23, 23).

Gayfere's work initially aroused controversy but he was quick to deflect criticism. In 1810 the *Gentleman's Magazine* indignantly reported that he proposed 'to knock up a sky light' in the ceiling of Henry VII's chapel, an act which would have mutilated and disfigured the building (*GM* 1810, 539). Gayfere responded by attempting to take John Carter, the architectural writer and source of the article, to law. Gayfere himself signed a letter to the magazine from his home in Abingdon Street in 1811 with a sworn statement that the allegation was untrue.

In 1814, two years after his father's death Gayfere undertook repairs to the great rose window. He also signs the monument in the Abbey to Mrs Vincent (1). In 1819–22 he restored the north front of Westminster Hall with Bath stone under the direction of JW Hiort of the Office of Works. In 1810 he was employed at Somerset House (PRO, AO 1/2499). Gayfere retired as mason to the Abbey in 1823.

He died in Burton-on-Trent on 20 October 1827 and was buried at Newton Solney, Derbys. His tombstone reads: 'His qualities as a man will find their best memorial in the affection of his survivors; while the restoration of Henry VII's Chapel and the Hall at Westminster will prove a lasting monument of his abilities as an architect.' A street in Westminster was named after him in recognition of his work for the Abbey. His obituary in the *Monthly Magazine* declared that 'the faithfulness of his workmanship will be a lasting testimony to his abilities and it is by no means too great praise to aver that to no other individual could the interests of that edifice [Westminster Abbey] have been better entrusted. At its completion the antiquary rejoiced and the fears which had been long entertained gave way to feelings of gratification' (*Monthly Mag* 1828, 224).

Literary References: *GM* 1811, 341; *Chester* 1876, 483; *Toynbee* 1927, 157; *Gunnis* 1968, 165; *Colvin* 1995, 395

Archival References: GPC

Auction Catalogues: Gayfere's Library, BL SCS 138/7

Funerary Monuments

1.	†1807	Hannah Vincent	Westminster Abbey, London, south transept	S	*Gunnis* 1968, 166

GAZLEY, Martha

For further information the reader is referred to *Pyke* 1973, 52.

GEEFS, Guillaume 1805–83

This Belgian sculptor was the eldest and most famous member of a sculpting family of seven brothers. In 1838 he married Fanny Corr, a Belgian girl of Irish parentage, and it was no doubt through his wife that Geefs moved to Ireland. He is reputed to have executed statues of *Ireland* and *Art and Industry* for the 'Industriepalast' in Dublin (7). These were probably made for the Dublin international exhibition of 1853 or 1865 but are not mentioned in the exhibition catalogues. At the 1853 exhibition one of the family (the catalogue gives only 'Geefs') exhibited *Cupid in the attitude of supplication*. Potterton suggests that it is 'just possible' that this could be the figure of an angel on the unsigned memorial to the 6th Baron Carbery (†1845) in Rosscarbery, Co Cork (*Potterton* 1975, 47). In the same church is a full length statue of Baron Carbery, signed 'Gme. Geefs, statuaire de S. M. le Roi des Belges, Bruxelles 20 July 1848' (1). His memorial to Sir Maziere Brady, Lord Chancellor of Ireland and a patron of the arts, features an angel holding a portrait medallion (2).

In 1851 Geefs sent several works to the Great Exhibition and one of these, a group of 2 sleeping children entitled *Paul et Virginie*, was bought by Prince Albert, who gave it to Queen Victoria as a Christmas present (4). Ten of the sculptor's works were later displayed in the Crystal Palace at Sydenham.

Literary References: *Potterton* 1975, 47; *Read* 1982, 37, 132, 139; *Grove* 12, 1996, 230 (van Lennep)

Funerary Monuments						
1.	1848	6th Baron Carbery (†1845)		Rosscarbery, Co Cork	S	*Potterton* 1975, 47
2.	†1871	Sir Maziere Brady, lord chancellor of Ireland		St Patrick's Cathedral, Dublin		*Potterton* 1975, 47
Statues						
3.	1851	Genevieve of Brabante		[Gt Exhib, London]; untraced		*AJ Cat* 1851, 288 (repr)
4.	1851	Paul et Virginie		[Gt Exhib, London]; Royal Coll, Osborne House, I of W		*Read* 1982, 132, 135 (repr)
5.	1851	The faithful messenger		[Gt Exhib, London]; untraced		*AJ Cat* 1851, 234 (repr)
6.	1858	Le lion amoureux	m	[Exhib LSFA, Liverpool, 317]; untraced		*Morris and Roberts* 1998, 252
7.	nd	'Ireland' and 'Art and Industry'		[for the 'Industriepalast', Dublin]; untraced		*Potterton* 1975, 47

GEERTS, Charles, of Louvain 1807–55

A Belgian sculptor, in 1856 a collection of about 150 of his models, largely religious statues and groups, was put on display at the Crystal Palace in Sydenham in the hope of securing 'a provision' for his widow (*AJ*, 1856, 376–7).

Literary References: *Gunnis* 1968, 166

Funerary Monuments				
1.	?1852	Harriot Rushout	Burford, Salop	S	*Gunnis* 1968, 166

GELL, Robert fl 1814

His address was recorded as Marble Works, Lime Street, Liverpool, when he exhibited a bust at the Liverpool Academy in 1814.

Busts				
1.	1814	William Byrom	[Exhib Liverpool Ac, 293]; untraced	*Morris and Roberts* 1998, 252

GEORGE, George *c*1741–

He was apprenticed to **John Wildsmith** in 1762 but was free by 1764 and working on his own account as an ornamental carver, probably of tablets for chimneypieces. On 23 April 1762 he was awarded 4 guineas in compensation from the Society of Arts for the breakage of his model. He won a premium on 3 June 1762 for an ornamental composition in clay awarded to sculptors under the age of 22 (2) and in 1763 gained another for a tablet (1). A final award came from the Society on 18 May 1764 for an ornamental composition in clay by a youth under 22 (3). At this time he was living at 'Mr Sams, Down Street, Hyde Park Corner'.

Literary References: RSA *Premiums*, 1763, 37; *Dossie* 1782, 437; *Gunnis* 1968, 166

Archival References: RSA Minutes 1761–62, seq 3 fol 64; 1763–64 seq 3 fol 83

Reliefs				
1.	1763	Tablet	[RSA premium, 15 gns]; untraced	*Dossie* 1782, 437
Miscellaneous				
2.	1762	Ornamental composition in clay	[RSA premium, 4 gns]; untraced	RSA *Minutes*, 1761–62, seq 3 f 64
3.	1764	Ornamental composition in clay	[RSA premium, 6 gns]; untraced	RSA *Minutes* 1763–64, seq 3 f 83

GERAERSTEN (or GEERAERSLIUS), Jan fl 1688–92

He worked at Chatsworth as an assistant to **Cibber** from 1688 to 1691 and then on his own account in 1691–2, making statues for the fountains.

Literary References: *Thompson* 1949, 86; *Gunnis* 1968, 166

Archival References: Chatsworth Building Accounts, 1687–94, 8, 9; GPC

Miscellaneous				
1.	1688–1692	Statues for fountains	Chatsworth, Derbys	*Thompson* 1949, 86

GERMAIN fl 1695–96

In 1695 the 1st Earl Fauconberg purchased 'Two Great Potts' for his orangery at Sutton Court, Chiswick, from Germain for £14. The following year two more were bought for £12 and Fauconberg paid him a further £4 for 'bronzing two other Potts'.

Archival References: GPC

GERMAIN, François-Thomas 1726–91

The French silversmith François-Thomas Germain spent some time in England after he became bankrupt in Paris. On 17 October 1769 the 'sieur Germain, sculptor, gold and silversmith' gave 'notice to artists in these branches' that he was to open a 'manufactory at Pimlico, near the queen's palace' in about a month's time. He intended to produce, 'sculpture, bronzes, gold and silversmiths' works; and in general all articles that relate to the decoration or ornamenting of apartments, in bronzes, &c., the designs of which are all in the genuine antique taste and style'. He required '15 chasers, 10 gold and silversmiths, two modellers of figures, and three of ornaments' and stated that he would employ 'English artists and workmen in preference to those of any other country' (*Anecdotes* 1937, 145).

GHEYS, James I –1752

The son of James Gheys of Bromley, Kent, he was apprenticed to Samuel Roussett of St Martin-in-the-Fields, 'carver' in 1730 (PRO, IR 12/31, in GPC). In 1750 he asked the Barber Surgeons' Company for the skeleton 'that used to hang up in the theatre', offering an 'ornamental figure in plaster-of-Paris in exchange'. A bargain was struck, and the Barber Surgeons received a head of Inigo Jones in return for their skeleton. Two years later an advertisement appeared which stated 'This day are published, 1752 PROPOSALS for casting in plaister of Paris by subscription, two curious figures from the antique, which were never before published in England. Subscriptions are taken, and specimens to be seen at the proprieters James Gheys, Carver, in May-fair; at Mr Pickford's, a mason, Hyde-Park-Corner . . .' (Anderdon Cuttings, fol 140).

Literary References: *Gunnis* 1968, 166

Archival References: GPC

Busts

1.	c1750	Inigo Jones	[Barber Surgeons' Company]; untraced		*Gunnis* 1968, 166 citing Barber-Surgeons' Company archives

GHEYS, James II 1749–

Gheys was born on 6 August 1749, the son of **James Gheys I** and joined the Royal Academy Schools on 16 March 1773, giving his age as 24 and his date of birth as 6 August (*Hutchison* 1960–62, 139). In 1776 he received a premium from the Society of Arts for a model of *Lucretia*, five feet or more in height (**3**). He exhibited at the Academy, 1774–1778. The monument to the Lort family at Tenby, is signed 'Gheys, Marylebone'.

Literary References: *Hutchison* 1960–62, 139; *Gunnis* 1968, 166

Funerary Monuments					
1.	1778	Lort family	Tenby, Pembrokes	S	*Gunnis* 1968, 166
Miscellaneous					
2.	1774	A vestal Virgin, model	[Exhib RA, London, 101]; untraced		*Graves* III, 1905–6, 227
3.	1776	Lucretia, model	[Soc of A premium, 15 gns]; untraced		*Dossie* 1782, 439; RSA, *Transactions*, vol 2, 1784, 126
4.	1778	Apollo, model	[Exhib RA, London, 127]; untraced		*Graves* III, 1905–6, 227
5.	1778	Poetry, model	[Exhib RA, London, 128]; untraced		*Graves* III, 1905–6, 227

GIANNELLI (or GIANELLI), Family fl 1777–1841

There appear to have been several craftsmen of this name working in London in the later 18th and early 19th centuries, well known for their plaster busts, casts and the like, both bronzed and unbronzed. Considerable confusion surrounds their identities. **Giovanni Battista Giannelli I** (fl 1777–1809) was chiefly employed in making plaster busts, vases, statues and architectural ornaments. He exhibited a number of subjects at the Great Rooms by Exeter Exchange in 1777 (**1, 6, 7**) and his wife showed 'a dish of fruit in coloured wax' at the same exhibition. There are references to Giannelli in the archives of the Marquess of Lansdowne: in 1777 he was paid for plaster-work at Bowood, and there is also an item for 'Carrying model to exhibition £1 3.' This was probably the exhibition at Exeter Exchange. Some of the figures shown may have been for Bowood (GPC). In 1785 he was employed by Robert Mylne, the architect, on decorative work at his house in Bridge Street (destroyed when Blackfriars railway was built) and in 1790 he was working at the house Mylne was building for himself at Great Amwell, Herts (*Journals of Robert Mylne*, poss Miss J Mylne, in GPC). In the early years of the 19th century he was apparently employed as a modeller at the 'Old Hall' pottery works at Hanley. A figure modelled by him is inscribed 'Statue and Figure Maker to His Royal Highness the Prince of Wales at the Royal Academy. Figures and Animals as large as life. No. 33 Cock Lane, Snow Hill' (GPC).

In his article on plaster shops of the rococo and neoclassical era, Clifford lists a **Giovanni Battista Giannelli** (1787–1825) and a **Giovanni Domenico Giannelli** (1775–1841). The latter had been a student in the Copenhagen Academy, winning its gold and silver medals in 1797 and 1799. In 1801 he applied for permission to go to England. His daughter Rosa applied for assistance to the AGBI after her father's death on 14 December 1841. Pyke notes that he had a brother, Pietro Leonardo, who was a wax modeller, probably in Copenhagen. Giovanni Domenico exhibited at the Royal Academy 1809–20, also from 33 Cock Lane, Snow Hill, and provided a 'fine bronze bust of Professor Porson' (**12**), and 'a very faithful bust' of John Nichols (**16**) (*Gunnis* 1968, 167).

Literary References: *Gunnis* 1968, 166–7; Pyke 1973, 53; *Clifford* 1992, 39–65; *Bricknell* 1995, 40

Archival References: AGBI, vol 3, 169; GPC

Statues

1.	1777	Flora, Hebe, Mercury, Venus (by Giovanni Battista I)		[Exhib Great Rooms by Exeter Exchange, London]; untraced		*Gunnis* 1968, 166
2.	1789	Isis, Flora, Antinous and the Discobolus, with pedestals painted in imitation of porphyry and verde antico marble (by Giovanni Battista I) Payment(s): £63	p	[Carlton House, London, great hall]; untraced		*Carlton House* 1991–2, 208
3.	1805	Egyptian figure, probably made to hold a hanging lamp (by Giovanni Domenico)		VAM	SD	*Fitzgerald* 1968, pp 11, 12 (repr)

No.	Date	Subject	Medium	Location		Source
4.	1807	Chinoiserie figures, statuettes (by Giovanni Domenico)	p	A pair sold Christie, Wateringbury Place, Maidstone, 31 May–2 June 1978, lot 204	SD	NP/RG
5.	1809	A pair of classical allegories, statuettes, painted and gilt (by Giovanni Domenico)	p	Untraced	SD	NP/RG
Busts						
6.	1777	King Alfred (by Giovanni Battista I)		[Exhib Great Rooms by Exeter Exchange, London]; untraced		*Gunnis* 1968, 166
7.	1777	Socrates (by Giovanni Battista I)		[Exhib Great Rooms by Exeter Exchange, London]; untraced		*Gunnis* 1968, 166
8.	1794	Unidentified subject (by Giovanni Battista I)		[for Lord Abercorn, Bentley Priory]; untraced		*Gunnis* 1968, 166
9.	1806	Unidentified subject (by Giovanni Battista I)		[coll Lord Bridport]; untraced		*Gunnis* 1968, 166
10.	1808	Mounted on a Regency bookcase (by Giovanni Domenico)	pb	VAM W.2-1967	SD	
11.	1808	Pitt the Younger and Charles James Fox, of bronzed plaster, supporting the entablature of a mahogany book case designed by Sheraton (by Giovanni Domenico)		[Clifton Castle, N R Yorks]; VAM		*Fitzgerald* 1968, 9–12 (repr)
12.	1809	Professor Richard Porson (by Giovanni Domenico)	b	Eton College, Windsor, Berks, library Other versions: NPG 673, plaster cast, 1808 NPG 673a, Elkington & Co electrotype, 1883		*Gunnis* 1968, 167; *Graves* III, 1905–6, 227
13.	1810	J C Saunders (by Giovanni Domenico)		[Exhib RA, London, 860]; untraced		*Graves* III, 1905–6, 227
14.	1812	Mr Baldwin (by Giovanni Domenico)		[Exhib RA, London, 904]; untraced		*Graves* III, 1905–6, 227
15.	1812	Mr Bell (by Giovanni Domenico)		[Exhib RA, London, 889]; untraced		*Graves* III, 1905–6, 227
16.	1814	John Nichols FSA (by Giovanni Domenico)		[Exhib RA, London, 785]; untraced		*Gents Mag*, 1826, Pt 2, 502; *Graves* III, 1905–6, 227
17.	1814	Unidentified lady (by Giovanni Domenico)		[Exhib RA, London, 807]; untraced		*Graves* III, 1905–6, 227
18.	1820	Dr Wachul (by Giovanni Domenico)		[Exhib RA, London, 1013]; untraced		*Graves* III, 1905–6, 227
19.	1829	Unidentified man, sketch model (by Giovanni Domenico)	w	VAM A.25-1947	SD	*Gunnis* 1968, 167; *Pyke* 1973, 52 (repr 107)
20.	nd	Samuel Pett (by Giovanni Domenico)	pb	Dr Williams Library, Gordon Square, London		GPC
Architectural Sculpture						
21.	1783	Vases (by Giovanni Battista I)		[Wimpole, Cambs]; untraced		*Gunnis* 1968, 166
22.	1783	Vases (by Giovanni Battista I)		[Cavendish House, New Cavendish Street, London]; untraced		*Gunnis* 1968, 166
23.	1785	Decorative work (by Giovanni Battista I)		[Robert Mylne's house, Bridge Street, London]; destroyed		RG/JP, 4, 576
24.	1807	A pair of figural candelabra, ebonised tc and gilt metal (by Giovanni Domenico)		Sotheby Parke Bernet, NY, 26 Oct 1990, lot 264	SD	NP/RG
Miscellaneous						
25.	1777	Cast of a dog's head (by Giovanni Battista I)	p	[coll Lord Shelburne]; untraced		*Gunnis* 1968, 166
26.	1804	'Lion & Dog' (by Giovanni Domenico) Payment(s): £65 12s		Woburn Abbey, Beds		Woburn Accts, BLARS R3/2114/521

GIBBONS, Grinling 1648–1721

Grinling Gibbons is the acknowledged master of English limewood carving, the material he introduced to this country as a versatile alternative to native oak. Horace Walpole wrote 'There is no instance of a man before Gibbons who gave to wood the loose and airy lightness of flowers' (*Anecdotes* III, 1782, 148–9). His marble and stone carving, a new departure in the later 1670s, only occasionally achieved a comparable distinction. Gibbons's immense output obliged him to keep a team that at times numbered as many as fifty assistants and to bring in specialists for work which was beyond his normal range (**43, 47, 51**).

Gibbons was born in Rotterdam on 14 April 1648, the son of James Gibbons, a draper and freeman of the Drapers' Company of London and Elizabeth (née Grinling), from whom he acquired his unusual Christian name. Her father had established himself as a tobacco merchant in Rotterdam. It is not known where Gibbons received his training, but his early work has affinities with the limewood sculptural tradition of Southern Germany. There were however two great workshops closer to home and Gibbons may have been apprenticed either to Artus Quellin I (1609–68), the sculptor responsible for much of the carving at Amsterdam Town Hall, or to his cousin, Artus Quellin II (1625–1700), who worked principally in Antwerp. These two produced work in both classical and naturalistic idioms, as Gibbons was to do in England. Artus II's sons, **Arnold** and **Thomas Quellin**, were later employed by Gibbons.

Gibbons came to England *c*1667 and first settled in York, perhaps through connections in the wool trade, where he was employed by John Etty (c1634–1707), the pre-eminent York architect and carver of his day. Two independent works are known from this period (**111, 112**). Etty and Gibbons remained in touch and in July 1684 Gibbons wrote to Etty about a visit by one of his assistants to York, in connection with a monument to be erected in York Minster (**9**).

Shortly before 18 January 1671, Gibbons moved to Deptford, where there was plentiful employment for ships' carvers, though Gibbons had aspirations of a higher order. An apochryphal meeting with the diarist John Evelyn, who discovered him carving a relief copy of a *Crucifixion* by Tintoretto (**113**) in 'a poore solitary thatched house in a field in our Parish' (*Evelyn* 1959, 549, 18 January 1671), apparently led to an introduction at the Court, where King Charles II considered acquiring the relief panel, for which Gibbons asked £100. The King was apparently dissuaded from the purchase by the Queen. Immediate hopes of royal patronage were dashed, but the relief found a purchaser, Sir George Viner, who paid a respectable £80 for this work by a virtually unknown carver. Evelyn found Gibbons engaging, describing him as 'Musical, & very Civil, sober & discreete in his discourse' (*Evelyn* 1959, 549) and his enthusiasm for the sculptor's skills as a wood-carver perhaps led to Gibbons's first commission in London, for capitals and other ornaments in wood for the proscenium arch in the fashionable Dorset Garden Theatre (**70**). Sir Peter Lely, Principal Painter to the King, who also came from a Dutch background, admired the ornaments, met the sculptor and probably proposed him for election to St Luke's Club, a convivial society for artists and lovers of art. Gibbons was to serve twice as its steward, in 1691 and 1709. It may have been Lely who first encouraged Gibbons to work in marble, for he and the architect, Hugh May, negotiated the price of Gibbons's first work in that medium, a monument (**1**), and after Lely died in 1680, the commission for his own monument, which had a portrait bust, went to Gibbons (**3**).

Little is known of the sculptor's professional life in the early 1670s, but he became a liveryman of the Drapers' Company by patrimony in 1672 and registered his first apprentice in the Drapers' Company books that year. Eight more were recorded in the years 1675–96, but only 1 of them, John Hunt, went on to have an independent career as a sculptor. Gibbons must have married around 1671; his wife, Elizabeth, appears as a plump beauty in a double portrait with her husband by Closterman. She bore their first child in 1672 and at least 11 more followed, most of whom died in childhood. Gibbons's address in 1672 was given as La Belle Sauvage, a coaching-inn on Ludgate Hill in the City of London. He had premises on the hill at least until the 1680s, though by 1678 he had moved to an elegant house known as The King's Arms in Bow Street, Covent Garden, an area particularly popular with artists. Entries in the Hand-in-Hand fire insurance company records for 1705 and again for 1712 describe a structure of substantial size, valued at £700, with a summerhouse behind. It had a picture gallery for his growing collection, where he displayed his own early limewood relief of The stoning of St Stephen (114). Evelyn's kindness to Gibbons was at some stage rewarded with the gift of a rich walnut and lime table carved by the sculptor (Evelyn Inventory 1702). The diarist visited him with the Duchess of Grafton and the Earl and Countess of Arlington in 1679, where they found the house 'furnish'd like a Cabinet, not onely with his owne work, but divers excellent Paintings of the best hands' (Evelyn 1959, 671, 8 August 1679). The house collapsed in 1702, but was rebuilt and Gibbons lived there until his death; the posthumous auction of his collection of paintings was held in the picture gallery in 1722.

The sculptor's first known carvings for interiors using the vocabulary of naturalistic elements that became closely associated with his name were limewood overmantels and picture frames, provided for two country houses in the mid-1670s (**55, 56**). By 1677 he had begun a major contract for the King at Windsor Castle (**57, 58, 72–76**) working in collaboration with **Henry Phillips**, master sculptor and carver in wood to the Crown, under the direction of Hugh May, the Comptroller of the Works. Bills totalling over £1,200 for work in the royal apartments were submitted by Phillips and Gibbons in 1677 and 1678, but by 1679 Gibbons was in sole charge of the contract. He employed a team of assistants from the Low Countries, including **John Nost I**, **Laurens Vandermeulen**, **Anthony Verhuke** and **Arnold Quellin**, these last three described as his servants in a residence permit issued in 1679. The richest ornaments at Windsor were concentrated in the King's Chapel (**78**), where the woodwork acted as a foil for decorative paintings by Antonio Verrio. Evelyn saw the chapel and described the carvings as 'stupendious, & beyond all description'. He continued 'nor doubt I at all, but he will prove as greate a Master in the statuary Art' (*Evelyn* 1959, 743, 16 June 1683). In 1682, after completing his contract at Windsor, Gibbons was retained as Surveyor and Repairer of the Carved Work at Windsor, with a salary of £100 a year. This continued to be paid at least until 1713.

In 1682 Gibbons completed the 'Cosimo' panel, regarded as his finest work in limewood, a gift ordered by the King for the Grand Duke of Tuscany (**115**). It is an extraordinary *tour de force* of refined and precise carving. At its centre are emblems of Painting, Architecture and Music, a quiver of arrows and a pair of coronets, the whole being set in a wreath of leaves, flowers and fruits, surmounted by a pair of billing doves. Immediately below the doves is an array of cravats, a speciality of Gibbons, which gave particular scope to his skill in cutting intricate pierced detail. Among the musical trophies is a score of such accuracy that it has been suggested that Gibbons was a practising musician. Sheets of contemporary music appear elsewhere in his work with accurate carvings of violins, citterns and shawms (**83, 91, 116**).

Gibbons worked in formal partnership with Quellin from 1681 until May 1683, when a quarrel temporarily ended their association. Their contract stipulated that Quellin was to do 'all sort of carvers worke in Stone, joyntly to be undertaken between them . . .' (PRO C9/415.2503). A wide array of commissions was in progress at this time, including several ambitious monuments (**5–9**). The Ferrers (**4**), *c*1681, one of the most remarkable works in marble to come out of the Gibbons workshop, has two life-sized crouching figures in full-bottomed wigs and Roman dress, dramatically posed on either side of the inscription panel. These are thought to be Quellin's work (*Beard* 1989 (1) 56) and Quellin may also have been responsible for the imposing reclining figure of Archbishop Richard Sterne in York Minster (**9**). The two sculptors may have collaborated on a model in wood for a statue of King Charles II cast by **Josias Ibach** at Windsor (**38**). Its pedestal, which has four elaborate marble reliefs, combines martial trophies with swagged flora and fauna. The statue, invoiced with a sundial pedestal for Windsor (**76**), was paid for by Tobias Rustat, Master of the Robes.

Charles II's popularity led to several commissions for royal statues by Gibbons alone or in partnership with Quellin. In 1682 the Company of Merchant Adventurers offered to give a statue of the King to the new Royal Exchange, to be sited in the centre of the courtyard. This was designed and executed by Gibbons (**39**), charged at £500 and celebrated by Samuel Phillips in 1684 in a poem addressed to 'Mr Grinsted Gibbons, his carving the matchless statue of the King' (BL 806 k16, 131). The uniformly classical image in Portland stone showed the monarch with short hair, in the garb of a Roman general, on a pedestal carved with cupids and the arms of France, Ireland and Scotland.

On 25 October 1683, Gibbons's partnership with Quellin, which had terminated in May that year, was formally dissolved by a proceeding in Chancery. The document indicates why. Quellin was failing to advance his agreed share towards the cost of raw materials, a major outlay at the start of a commission. Gibbons appears to have worked without Quellin on two bronze statues, which were commissioned by Rustat shortly after the King's death in 1685: one of the late king, for the new Chelsea Hospital (**43**) and a second of his brother, now James II, for the Pebble Court in the Palace of Whitehall (**47**). Gibbons brought in experts in both cases: Vandermeulen apparently modelled the Charles II, which was cast by him and another Low Countries craftsman, **Dievot of Malines** (*Vertue* V, 59). James II's statue was cast by **Thomas Bennier** (*Vertue* I, 89). Rustat's own monument, c1686, a work 'of consummate mastery' (*Beard* 1989 (1), 65) is attributed to Gibbons and was ordered nearly eight years before Rustat's death and set up in the courtier's house.

Gibbons and Quellin came together again for a short period in 1685–6. Quellin may therefore have collaborated on the two less inventive monuments to the 7th and 8th Earls of Rutland, which have standing effigies. Both were completed in 1686, the year of Quellin's death (**11–12**). At a similar period, work was in progress on an ambitious monument to the 3rd Viscount Campden, his 4 wives and many children, at Exton, Rutland (**10**). This grand familial statement has a backdrop 20 feet in height and heavy obelisks and urns flanking dumpy, life-sized effigies of the Viscount and his last wife, but the relief vignettes commemorating the earlier wives and many offspring, and the garlands have a delicacy comparable to Gibbons's best work in wood.

In May 1685, the new king, James II commissioned a splendid Roman Catholic chapel at the palace of Whitehall, and all the leading craftsmen of the Office of Works were engaged to work on it under the control of the Surveyor-General, Sir Christopher Wren. Wren designed the high altar, using Gibbons and Quellin as executants (**84**). This had to be completed in a short period. The sculptors undertook to 'employ constantly . . . fifty workmen or soe many Marblers, Sculptors, Sawyers, Pollishers & Labourers' to ensure that the work would be ready within 5 months (PRO 5/145, fol 184.5). Vertue noted that **Francis Bird** worked for Gibbons in the mid or late 1680s, so he may have been associated with the project (*Vertue* III, 18, 34). The altarpiece had 4 large statues, numerous cherubs' heads, several relief panels and two graceful, life-sized angels, which are thought to be Quellin's work. The chapel fell into disuse after the succession of the Protestant William and Mary in 1688, and in 1695, after a fire which destroyed much of the palace, Gibbons dismantled the altarpiece. It was eventually installed by Gibbons and Wren in Westminster Abbey in 1706, where it remained until 1821, when the elements were dispersed. Gibbons also worked on overmantels in the royal apartments at Whitehall (**60**).

Work at Whitehall continued under the new monarchs (**61–62**) and by 1690 Gibbons was also heading a team working on decorative schemes, largely in pine and pearwood, for the King's and Queen's Apartments at Kensington Palace (**97**) and also at Hampton Court, where his charges came to the substantial sum of £1,265 (**99–101**). He took over the position of Master Sculptor and Carver in Wood to the Crown in 1693 and the following year, when Queen Mary died, he provided the embellishments for her catafalque, to designs by Wren (**22**). Work in the royal palaces ceased with the Queen's death and was only resumed several years later (**97, 99–101**).

The sculptor's most important collaboration with Wren was at St Paul's Cathedral, where his workforce was responsible for extensive work, mainly in the years 1694–7. They carved ornaments in stone, oak and lime for the choir and also the case and screen for the great west organ (**96**). The astonishing oak ornaments for the choir included canopies of foliage, doves and pelicans above two banks of stalls, cut in remarkably low relief for such a complex composition. By September 1696, Gibbons's mounting charges were giving concern and Wren was obliged to adjust certain prices with the sculptor, particularly for the organ-cases. A force of stonecarvers worked on the pendentives of the dome and externally, on pedimental reliefs for the north front and festoons under the windows (**93, 94, 96, 98**). Gibbons was paid nearly £3000 for his wood carving and another £586 for his work in stone.

In the years after 1702, when Queen Anne ascended the throne and limewood carving went out of fashion, Gibbons's workshop concentrated principally on sculpture in stone. This work is of varied quality. Gibbons had carved a clumsy marble statue of the 6th Duke of Somerset for Wren's library at Trinity College, Cambridge, in 1691 (**48**). On the other hand, his monument to a child, Robert Cotton (†1697) has superbly carved flowers and palms surrounding a sensitive medallion portrait (**27**). Some of the later monuments are ambitious compositions with reclining, standing and kneeling effigies below cloud-wrapped putti, framed by architectural surrounds (**30, 33**). The finest is the memorial to the 1st Duke of Beaufort, 1699–1701, at Badminton, Somerset (**30**), which cost over £1,000 and has an imposing, reclining figure of the Duke in a full-bottomed wig and pierced cravat. He is flanked by graceful, standing Virtues. Less successful is the effigy of Admiral Sir Cloudesly Shovell in Westminster Abbey (**34**), a flaccid representation that drew censure from Joseph Addison because Shovell, 'a brave rough English admiral', was depicted as a beau 'dressed in a long periwig, and reposing himself on velvet cushions under a canopy of state' (*The Spectator*, no 26, March 1710). Gibbons's last monument, commemorating the 1st Duke of Chandos, *c*1717 (**37**), was executed 30 years before the subject's death and depicts him looking imperious in a wig and Roman armour, with 2 of his 3 wives kneeling at either side. Though Chandos was famous for his extravagance, he quibbled about the final instalment of Gibbons's bill, a sum of £350.

Gibbons died on 3 August 1721 and was buried in London at St Paul's, Covent Garden a week later, next to his wife, who predeceased him by two years. The sculptor's baroque carving, which had earned him such acclaim, went out of fashion during the Hanoverian period, when Whig politics found its visual expression in an austere classical style. It was only in March 1969, at the insistence of Gibbons's modern biographer, David Green, that a memorial was placed in the church where he was buried, a limewood wreath of flowers which had been carved by the sculptor for St Paul's Cathedral.

IR

Literary References: *Vertue* I–V, *passim*; *Evelyn* 1959, *passim*; *Croft-Murray and Hulton* 1960, 332–6; *Douglas Stewart* 1963, 125–7; *Green* 1964 (1); *Gunnis* 1968, 167–70; *Colvin* V 1976, *passim*; *Beard* 1989 (1); *Davis* 1997, (2), 150; *Gibson* 1997 (2); RG/JP 4, 581–91; *Esterly* 1998; *Gibson* 1999; *Esterly* 1999, 355–6; *Sayce and Esterly* 2000, 11–21; *Moore* 2002, 433–4; *ODNB* (Esterly)

Archival References: Charges connected with the funeral of Queen Mary II including two lions and unicorns, £16, eight great candlesticks, £16, TNA WORK fol 292; Drapers' Declarations MS, 1704; Drapers' Dinner Book, MS, 9 August 1705; Hand-in-Hand, 1705, 1712; letter from Gibbons to John Evelyn, 23 March 1683, asking for Evelyn's help in obtaining a 'verij consedrebell' commission for carving from Lord Kildare, Evelyn MSS, BL uncat; GPC

Additional MS Sources: Evelyn Inventory, 1702, Evelyn MSS, BL, uncat

Will: FRC PROB 6/97

Miscellaneous Drawings: Collaborative drawings are included only if they are essentially by Gibbons. Designs for several interiors in the King's and Queen's apartments, Hampton Court Palace, *c*1690 (perhaps by Hawksmoor), Hampton Court Album, Soane 110:30 (*Esterly* 1998, repr p170); designs for a monument for King Charles I supported by emblematic figures, *c*1678, All Souls Coll, Oxford, 2.94 (*Douglas Stewart* 1997, 21–64, repr); design for a monument for Queen Mary II, 1695, All Souls Coll, Oxford, 2.5 (*Green* 1964, 1, 160, repr 92); studies for a statue, probably either of Charles II or James II, BM, PDL 1889-6-3-254 (1–5); design for a monument to King William III and Queen Mary II, attrib, *c*1703, BM 1881-6-11-164 (*Green* 1964, 163, repr 93); design for an iron gate at Kilkenny Castle, presented in competition with William Robinson, nd (*Barnard and Fenlon* 2000, 151)

Sales of the Sculptor's Collection of Paintings: Gibbons had a secondary career as a picture dealer. On 2 June 1684, together with Parry Walton, Supervisor and Repairer of the King's Pictures, he was allowed to hold an auction of paintings at the Banqueting House, Whitehall, 2 years later a similar event took place, again at the Banqueting House, when Gibbons and Walton sold *A Collection of the best Italian Masters, both Ancient & Modern* (*London Gazette*, 2136, 6–10 May 1686; 2139, May–June 1686, quoted in *Moore* 2002, 433–4). His own collection of paintings, drawings, books and models, were sold from his home in Bow Street from 15 November 1722. This sale attracted the attention of the leading collectors of the day including Sir Robert Walpole (BL MSS, HARL.5947 120; Mic: BL Rare Books B915/10 quoted in *Moore* 2002, 433–4).

Portraits of the Sculptor: Self-portrait, medallion, Modena panel, c1685, limewood (121); Sir John Baptist Medina c1686, drawing, BM 1852/0214/375 (*Beard* 1989 (I), frontispiece repr); Sir Godfrey Kneller, *Gibbons measuring a cast of the head of Proserpine from Bernini's Pluto and Proserpine*, by 1690, oil on canvas, Hermitage Museum, St Petersburg (*Moore* 2002, 297–8 repr); another version of Kneller's painting, NPG 2925; John Smith, *The sculptor with his wife, Elizabeth*, mezzotint after a lost painting by John Closterman, *c*1691, NPG (*Esterly* 1998 repr p 58)

Funerary Monuments

1.	*c*1679	Sir Roger Burgoyne Bt (†1677)	Sutton, Beds	*Beard* 1989, (1), 53–4, 56, 194–5 (repr 67); *Esterly* 1998, 56
2.	1680	Frances, Lady North (†1678) Payment(s): £72 16s	Wroxton, Oxon	*Beard* 1989 (1), 213–4 (repr 75); GPC
3.	†1680	Sir Peter Lely	[St Paul's, Covent Garden]; destroyed	*Whinney* 1988, 129, 444 n59
4.	*c*1681	John (†1680) and Sir Humphrey (†1678) Ferrers (co-sculptor: Arnold Quellin)	Tamworth, Staffs	*Beard* 1989 (1), 56–7, 195, 198 (repr 68–70)
5.	1681	Robert Southwell (†1677) and his wife Helena (†1679) (co-sculptor: Arnold Quellin)	St Multose, Kinsale, County Cork	*Loeber* 1983, 84–101 (repr 7); *Beard* 1989 (1), 55 (repr 75)
6.	1680–1682	Dame Catherine Perceval (née Southwell) (†1679) (co-sculptor: Arnold Quellin)	St Multose, Kinsale, County Cork	*Loeber* 1983, 85, 86 (repr 4); *Beard* 1989 (1), 54–5
7.	1683	Sir Richard Browne, father-in-law of John Evelyn (co-sculptor: Arnold Quellin)	[St Nicholas, Deptford, London]; destroyed	*Gunnis* 1968, 168; *Green* 1964 (1), 151; *Beard* 1989 (1), 57, 209
8.	1683–1684	German and Anne Pole (co-sculptor: Arnold Quellin) Payment(s): £300	Radbourne, Derbys	*Beard* 1989 (1), 57–9, 69, 106 (repr 76–8); GPC
9.	1683–1684	Richard Sterne, Archbishop of York (†1683) (co-sculptor: Arnold Quellin)	York Minster, resited in choir aisle, 1949	*Douglas Stewart* 1976, 508–9; *Beard* 1989 (1), 11, 59, 68, 196, 199 (repr 79–80)
10.	1684–1686	Baptist, 3rd Viscount Campden (†1683) and family Payment(s): £1,000	Exton, Rutland	*Vertue* V, 25; *Whinney* 1988, 122–4 (repr); *Beard* 1989 (1), 64–5, 75, 82, 198, 201 (repr 89–93)
11.	1684–1686	George, 7th Earl of Rutland (†1641)	Bottesford, Leics	*Beard* 1989 (1), 62–4, 197 (repr 85–6)
12.	1685–1686	John, 8th Earl of Rutland (†1679) and his wife, Frances	Bottesford, Leics	*Beard* 1989 (1), 62–4, 197 (repr 87–8)
13.	1687–1688	Archbishop John Dolben (†1686) Payment(s): £300	York Minster, south choir aisle	*Harris* 1998, 829–32 (repr)
14.	1689	Elizabeth Jefferys (†1688) Drawing(s): Soc Antiq, Prattinton Colls, parishes vol VII, Cha-Cli, fol 123r, with contract on verso	Clifton-on-Teme, Worcs	*Green* 1964 (1), 158; *Beard* 1989 (1), 67, 199 (repr 100–1)
15.	†1689	Sir Richard Head	Rochester Cathedral, Kent	*Whinney* 1988, 127, 129; *Beard* 1989 (1), 199 (repr 99); *Physick* 1995, 31
16.	*c*1690	John, 4th Lord Coventry (†1687) Payment(s): £322 10s+ £26 17s 6d for iron gate	Croome d'Abitot, Worcs	Agreement, Croome Court archives; 1690; *Douglas Stewart* 1976, 508–9; *Beard* 1989 (1), 65–6 (repr 97)
17.	1691	Archbishop Thomas Lamplugh (†1691) Payment(s): £100	York Minster, south choir aisle	*Beard* 1989 (1), 68–9, 199 (repr 103)

No.	Date	Subject		Location		Literature
18.	1691	William Windham (†1689), his wife Katherine (†1729), and his daughter, Mary (†1747) Payment(s): £51 19s with carriage		Felbrigg, Norfolk		*Beard* 1989 (1), 67–8
19.	†1692	Sarah, Duchess of Somerset, wife of the 4th Duke Payment(s): £500 left in will		Westminster Abbey, London, St Michael's Chapel		*Douglas Stewart* 1963, 125–7 (repr); *Beard* 1989 (1), 69, 199 (repr 104)
20.	1693	Henry Newdigate (†1629) Payment(s): £10		Ashtead, Surrey		Newdigate archives (contract, 22 July 1693), CR 136/B2445-8; *Gunnis* 1968, 168; *Beard* 1989 (1), 69
21.	†1694	Charlotte Mostyn		Nannerch, Flint		*Beard* 1989 (1), 70 (repr 105)
22.	1694	Embellishments for Queen Mary's catafalque (designed by Sir Christopher Wren) Payment(s): £99 8s 7d		Destroyed		*Green* 1964 (1), 73 (repr 91); *Colvin* 1973–76, V, 455
23.	1693–1694	Mary, Lady Newdigate (†1692) Drawing(s): BCH, LDS 5279, SD 'GK 1699' (probably Godfrey Kneller)		Harefield, Middx		*Gunnis* 1968, 168; *Beard* 1989 (1), 70; *Esterly* 1998, 36–7
24.	†1695	Dorothy, Lady Clarke (†1695) and Samuel Barrow (†1682) Payment(s): £300		All Saints, Fulham, London		*Green* 1964 (1), 161 (repr 233); *Whinney* 1988, 444 n63
25.	†1695	Sarah, Lady Newdigate Drawing(s): BCH LDS 5279, SD 'GK 1699'		Harefield, Middlesex		*Green* 1964 (1), 160 (repr 228)
26.	1697	Dr William Holder FRS (†1697) Drawing(s): Fitz (1)		St Paul's Cathedral, London, crypt		*Green* 1964 (1), 161–2 (repr 230, 231); *Beard* 1989 (1), 72–3, 200 (repr 110)
27.	†1697	Robert Cotton		Conington, Cambs	S	*Whinney* 1988, 126–7 (repr); *Beard* 1989 (1), 71, 200 (repr 107)
28.	1698–1699	Theophilus, 7th Earl of Huntingdon (†1701) and family		Ashby-de-la-Zouch, Leics		BM Harley MS 4712, f 366; Bodleian MS Smith 50, fol. 181; *Douglas Stewart* 1963, 125–7 (repr); *Beard* 1989 (1), 73
29.	1700	Elizabeth, Lady Fox (†1696) (co-sculptor: John Goodfellow of Salisbury)		Farley, Wilts		*Millar* 1995, 518–28
30.	1701	Henry, 1st Duke of Beaufort (†1700) Payment(s): £1,000		[Beaufort Chapel, St George's Chapel, Windsor Castle, until 1854]; Great Badminton, Glos (re-erected 1875)		*Beard* 1989 (1), 74–5, 200 (repr 111–116); *Lees-Milne* 1998, 115, 151; *Esterley* 1998, 206, 209–10 (repr)
31.	†1702	Sir Robert Southwell (designed by Sir Henry Sheers)		Henbury, Glos		*Archit Hist* X, 1967, 25 (repr 49); *Beard* 1989 (1), 55–6 (repr 75)
32.	†1702	William Courten Payment(s): £130 (estimate)		[St Mary Abbots, old church, London, churchyard]; St Mary Abbots, new church, fragment only, porch		*Green* 1964 (1), 164
33.	†1705	Mary Beaufoy		Westminster Abbey, London, nave		*Dart* 2, 1723, 103–4 (repr); *Potterton* 1974 (3), 1784–5; *Beard* 1989 (1), 77–8, 213 (repr 119)
34.	1708	Admiral Sir Cloudesly Shovell (†1707)		Westminster Abbey, London, nave		*Dart* 2, 1723, 79–80 (repr); *Beard* 1989 (1), 78–9, 201 (repr 120–1)
35.	1710	Admiral George Churchill Drawing(s): London, Westminster Reference Library (1)		Westminster Abbey, London, nave		*Beard* 1989 (1), 80–81 (repr 123–4)
36.	†1713	Archbishop Narcissus Marsh		St Patrick's Cathedral, Dublin		*McParland* 1994, 108–9 (repr)
37.	*c*1717	James, Duke of Chandos (†1744) with his wives Mary (†1719) and Cassandra (†1735) (valued at £1,000 in 1725)		Whitchurch, Middx		*Beard* 1989 (1), 81–2, 201–2 (repr 125); *Jenkins* 2005, 165
Statues						
38.	1678–1679	King Charles II, equestrian (bronze; cast by Josias Iback), with pedestal reliefs (marble) Payment(s): £1,300 (£400 for reliefs)		Windsor Castle, brick court Other versions: Parliament Square, Edinburgh, 1684–5, lead	S	*Vertue* 1, 126; *Evelyn* 1959, 686, 24 July 1680; *Beard* 1989 (1), 59–62 (repr 17–18); *Gibson* 1997 (1), 179–83, 368–9; *Gibson* 1999, 21–9
39.	1683–1684	King Charles II, on a pedestal Payment(s): £500	s	[Royal Exchange, London, centre of courtyard]; destroyed		*Vertue* IV, 35; *Gunnis* 1968, 168; *Gibson* 1997 (1), *passim*; *Gibson* 1997 (2) 151–6 (repr); *Ward-Jackson* 2003, 70, 317, 324–5
40.	1684	King James I Payment(s): £50	s	[Royal Exchange, London, line of kings on the façade of the piazza]; unraced		*Gibson* 1997 (2), 156, 166, 172 (repr)
41.	1684–1685	King Edward VI Payment(s): £50	s	[Royal Exchange, London, line of kings on the façade of the piazza]; untraced		*Gibson* 1997 (2), 156, 166, 172 (repr)
42.	1685	Queen Mary I Payment(s): £50	s	[Royal Exchange, London, line of kings on the façade of the piazza]; untraced		*Gibson* 1997 (2), 156, 162, 170, 172 (repr); *Gibson* 1999, 24–5

No.	Date	Subject	Medium	Location		Sources
43.	1685–1686	King Charles II	b	Royal Hospital, Chelsea, London, Figure Court	S	*Vertue* V, 58; *Evelyn* 1959, 938, 12 May 1691; *Gibson* 1997 (1), 370–1; *Gibson* 1997 (2), 153–4 (repr 50); *Gibson* 1999, 26–7
44.	1686	King James II		[Royal Exchange, London, line of kings on the façade of the piazza]; untraced		*Gibson* 1997 (2), 165, 172
45.	1688	Horse (co-sculptor: Thomas Quellin)	wd	Tower of London Armoury		*Beard* 1989 (1), 198–9 (repr 98)
46.	1685–1688	King Charles I, equestrian figure Payment(s): £40	wd	Tower of London Armoury		Exchequer, Declared Accounts, Treasurers, Paymasters of the Ordnance, E.351/2673, June 1688; *Blakiston* 1957, 57; *Green* 1964 (1), 136 (repr 192); *Borg* 1975, 320 (repr LXXIIIa)
47.	1687–1688	King James II Payment(s): £300; (£40 'for erecting and gilding')	b	[Whitehall Palace, London, Pebble Court]; Trafalgar Square, London		*Vertue* V, 58–9; *Whinney* 1988, 119–121 (repr); *Beard* 1989 (1), 61 (repr 83–4); *Gibson* 1999, 27–8
48.	1691	Charles, 6th Duke of Somerset Payment(s): £245	m	Wren Library, Trinity College, Cambridge		*Whinney* 1988, 124; *Beard* 1989 (1), 35–6, 189 (repr 28); *Esterly* 1998, 210 (repr)
49.	1692	Several figures	l	[Petworth House, West Sussex, probably on the west front]; untraced		*Rowell* 2000 (2), 7
50.	1696–1698	Sir John Moore, President of Christ's Hospital Payment(s): £90	m	[Christ's Hospital, Newgate Street, City of London, new writing school]; Christ's Hospital, Horsham, Sussex		Christ's H, TAB 12819/11, 979; 12819/12, 101; *Green* 1964 (1), 134, 135; *Beard* 1989 (1), 72, 76–7, 200 (repr 109)
51.	1700–1701	King William III, equestrian figure in Roman armour, on a pedestal with low-relief trophies Payment(s): £800	b	[College Green, Dublin]; destroyed		Dublin Assembly Roll, 20 June 1700; *Beard* 1989 (1), 77; *Hill* 1988, 42–3 (repr); *Murphy* 2001, 40, 41 (repr)
52.	1701–1702	Sir Robert Clayton, on a pedestal Payment(s): £200	m	[St Thomas's Hospital, Southwark, Clayton quadrangle]; St Thomas's Hospital, Lambeth, London, principal front		*Green* 1964 (1), 135–6 (repr 190); *Beard* 1989 (1), 76–77, 201 (repr 118)
Busts						
53.	1688	King Charles II, bust only, to be placed in a suit or armour Payment(s): £40	wd	Tower of London Armoury		*Ffoukes* 1916, 2, 442; *Green* 1964 (1), 136 (repr 194); *Gibson* 1997 (1), 379
54.	nd	Self-portrait	m	untraced		*Vertue* III, 10; IV, 35
Chimneypieces						
55.	1675–1677	Overmantel frame with birds, shells and foliate side-drops; picture surround; limewood	wd	[Holme Lacy, Herefs, inner library]; untraced		*Esterly* 1998, 62, 63–4, 73, 81, 183–4 (repr)
56.	1678	Overmantel frame with festoons of fruit and game, limewood Payment(s): £40	wd	Sudbury Hall, Derbys, drawing room		*Beard* 1989 (1), 37–38, 191 (repr 43–4); *Esterly* 1998, 68, 177–8 (repr)
57.	1676–1679	Overmantel frames	wd	Windsor Castle, Queen's presence chamber and King's dining room		*Esterly* 1998, 84–6, 90, 184 (repr)
58.	1678–1679	Two overmantel frames 'carved with flowers and fruites' Payment(s): £63 5s	wd	[Windsor Castle, Berks, privy chamber and King's drawing room]; untraced		*Colvin* 1973–76, V, 325
59.	1683	Overmantel frame with cresting of swags of fruit, fish and game, overdoor drops, limewood	wd	Badminton House, Glos, great parlour (cresting lost)		*Beard* 1989 (1), 41–2, 200 (repr 45–46); *Esterly* 1998, 90–2, 101–3 (repr)
60.	1685–1688	Four overmantel frames Payment(s): £100	wd	[Whitehall Palace, London, little bedchamber, dressing room, closet, lobby]; destroyed		*Beard* 1989 (1), 24–5
61.	1688	Marble chimneypiece with limewood overmantel carved with crowns, coat of arms and drapery Payment(s): £180		[Whitehall Palace, London, great bedchamber]; destroyed		TNA WORK 5/42; *Beard* 1989 (1), 24; Esterly 1998, 105
62.	c1689	Chimneypiece with two figures 'as big as the life a Crowne and Cushion and a pedistall over the chimney'; marble and wood Payment(s): £180		[Whitehall Palace, London, drawing room]; destroyed		*Colvin* 1973–76, V, 295; *Beard* 1989 (1), 24; *Esterly* 1998, 105
63.	c1690	Overmantel with wheat, fruit, flowers, draped folds, two doves and a bright and sorrowing cherub's head	wd	Kensington Palace, London, King's presence chamber		*Beard* 1989 (1) 29, 188 (repr 20); *Esterly* 1998, 106–7 (repr)
64.	c1690	Two gilt overmantels with volutes, drapes and festoons of flowers	wd	Kensington Palace, London, Queen Mary's Gallery		*Beard* 1989 (1), 28–9, 188 (repr 21)
65.	1692	Marble Payment(s): £18	m	[John Evelyn's house at Wotton, Surrey]; untraced		*Gunnis* 1968, 168
66.	1689–1694	Overmantel frames, cornices and other ornaments	wd	[Kensington Palace, London, Queen Mary's bedchamber and other staterooms]; largely dispersed: cornice in Queen Mary's bedchamber still *in situ*; pine and pearwood carvings in orangery		*Beard* 1989 (1), 28–9 (repr 20, 21)

No.	Date	Work	Medium	Location	Literary references
67.	1680–1700	Overmantel	wd	Drumlanrig Castle, Dumfriesshire	*Esterly* 1998, 177 (repr)
68.	1701	Neptune and Galatea, overmantel relief Payment(s): £80	m	[Moor Park, Herts]; Dalkeith Palace, Midlothian, great closet, 1703	*Beard* 1989 (1), 45–6, 193 (repr 57–9); *Esterly* 1998, 105, 210–1 (repr)
69.	1699–1701	Three overmantels with chains of leaves and flowers Payment(s): £30, £28, £25 Drawing(s): Wren Papers, Codrington Library, All Souls, Oxford (Esterly 1998, repr 90, p. 120)		Hampton Court Palace, Middx, King's apartments, withdrawing room, privy chamber, eating room	*Esterly* 1994, 32–8 (repr); *Esterly* 1998, 120–9 (repr); *Sayce and Esterly* 2000, 11–21 (repr)
Architectural Sculpture					
70.	1671	Ornaments for the proscenium arch	wd	[Dorset Garden Theatre, London]; untraced	*Vertue* I, 125; *Esterly* 1998, 52, 54–6 (repr)
71.	1678	Carved ornaments for chimney-pieces, doorcases, pedestals and pictures (co-sculptor: Henry Phillips) Payment(s): £614 17s 8d	wd	[Windsor Castle, Berks, several rooms]; some survivals	*Colvin* 1973–76, V, 321
72.	1676–1678	Picture frame surrounds, decorative overdoors, overmantels and other carving	wd	[Windsor Castle, Berks, King's eating room, Queen's audience chamber, chapel]; destroyed	*Colvin* 1973–6, V, 321; *Beard* 1989 (1), 20–23, 187–8 (repr 13–16)
73.	1676–1678	Surrounds for three alcove panels with rabbits, swagged gamebirds and fruit	wd	Windsor Castle, King's dining room	*Esterly* 1998, 88, 90 (repr)
74.	1676–1679	Overdoor surrounds	wd	Windsor Castle, Queen's audience chamber, Queen's presence chamber	*Esterly* 1998, 86–7 (repr)
75.	1678–1679	'sixty pannells Carved with fflowers, ffruites, shells, and severall other Ornaments' Payment(s): £60	wd	[Windsor Castle, Berks, King's great and little bedchambers and closet, over corner fireplaces]; untraced	*Colvin* 1973–76, V, 325
76.	1678–1680	'Mouldings & ornaments for ye pedistall of ye large dial'	m	Windsor Castle, north terrace	*Beard* 1989 (1), 59 (repr 19)
77.	c1680	Overmantels and picture surrounds, limewood	wd	[Cassiobury Park, Herts, inner library]; Art Institute of Chicago and Cleveland Museum of Art (overmantels)	*Evelyn* 1959, 682, 17 April 1680; *Esterly* 1998, 26, 64, 77, 177, 183 (repr)
78.	1680–1682	28 round-headed niches and above each, a pelican with her young; between these, bunches of flowers and fruit, ribbons and palm leaves; ornaments over the King's seat	wd	[Windsor Castle, King's chapel]; removed 1827; some re-used in Waterloo Chamber	*Evelyn* 1959, 742, 16 June 1683; *Colvin* 1973–76, V, 326; *Beard* 1989 (1), 23; *Esterly* 1998, 154–5; *Esterly* 1999, 355
79.	c1682	Altar, screen, pedestals and 'a carved panell under the organ'		[St James's Palace, London, Chapel]; untraced	*Colvin* 1973–76, V, 250–2
80.	1682–1683	Arms of Queen Catherine of Braganza	wd	St James's Palace, the Queen's Chapel, over east window	*Colvin* 1973–76, V, 244–54 (repr 29A)
81.	1684	Adam and Eve font, with cameo reliefs of Noah's Ark, the Baptism of Christ and the Baptism of the Eunuch of Candace by St. Philip	m	St James, Piccadilly, London	*Beard* 1989 (1), 33–4, 191 (repr 39)
82.	1684	Reredos with pelican in her piety in the cresting and acanthus scroll, floral and foliate drops; limewood	wd	St James, Piccadilly, London	*Evelyn* 1959, 786, 7 Dec 1684; *Esterly* 1998, 100–3, 168 (repr)
83.	1683–1685	Decorative ornaments, perhaps including overmantel in black and yellow bedroom, trophies over three overdoors in the 1st George room, and a point-cravat	wd	Burghley House, Northants	*Vertue* IV, 34; *Beard* 1989 (1), 42–4; *Esterly* 1998, 93–6 (repr); *Sayle and Esterly* 2000, 11–21
84.	1686	Reredos relief panels with putti holding the arms of Ireland and Scotland	wd	[Whitehall Palace, London, Roman Catholic Chapel]; untraced	*Beard* 1989 (1), 26
85.	1681–1686	Reredos with pelican in her piety, urns, cherubs and royal arms	wd	St Mary Abchurch, City of London	*Beard* 1989 (1), 33, 34, 54, 190 (repr 37)
86.	1686	Stoup	m	[Whitehall Palace, London, Roman Catholic Chapel]; untraced	TNA, WORK, 5/54 f230; *Gunnis* 1968, 169
87.	1686–1687	High altarpiece with four statues of saints, cherubs, angels and relief panels (designed by Sir Christopher Wren) (co-sculptor: Arnold Quellin)	m	[Whitehall Palace, London, Roman Catholic Chapel, dismantled 1695]; Canons' Gardens, Westminster (statues); Burnham, Somerset (angels and relief panels); Dean's Yard, Westminster and VAM (reliefs)	*Vivian-Neal* 1935, 127–32; *Evelyn* 1959, 857–8, 29 Dec 1686; *Green* 1962, 164–6; *Colvin* 1973–76, V, 290–3 (plan repr); *Whinney* 1988, 121–3 (repr), 443–4 n45; *Beard* 1989 (1), 25–6 (repr 73–4)
88.	1686–1687	Pulpit with relief figures of the Evangelists, cherubs and vegetation Payment(s): £90	wd	[Whitehall Palace, London, Roman Catholic Chapel]; untraced	*Colvin* 1973–76, V, 293; *Beard* 1989 (1), 26
89.	c1688	Low relief of Goliath with a marble base '2 marble Boyes and cornucopes . . . over the chimney' and other carving Payment(s): £100		[Whitehall Palace, London, great bedchamber]; destroyed	TNA WORK 5/42; *Colvin* 1973–76, V, 295; *Beard* 1989 (1), 24–5
90.	1690–1691	Ornaments for the queen's apartments, state rooms and privy suite Payment(s): £1,265 3s 4d		Hampton Court Palace, Middx	*Colvin*, 1973–76, V, 162–5

No.	Date	Description	Material	Location		Literature
91.	1692	Two elaborate double portrait surrounds surmounted by ducal coronets, limewood Payment(s): £150	wd	Petworth House, Sussex, carved room		*Vertue* II, 8; IV, 149; *Beard* 1989 (1), 38–41, 192–3 (repr 51–6); *Esterly* 1998, 108–17, 170, 172 (repr); *Rowell* 2000; (1), 19–26 (repr); *Sayce and Esterly* 2000, 11–21; *Rowell* 2002, 40–7
92.	1693	Reredos frame with putti heads, arabesques and flowers		Trinity College, Oxford, chapel		*Esterly* 1998, 118–20, 168, 170 (repr)
93.	1694	Ornaments in pendentives of the dome	s	St Paul's Cathedral, London		*Beard* 1989 (1), 30
94.	1695	26 festoons on the exterior under the windows Payment(s): £13 each	s	St Paul's Cathedral, London, nave		*Beard* 1989 (1), 30
95.	1690–1695	Limewood swags and drops, overdoor ornaments, 24 benefactors' panels and 4 plaster busts over the book-cases		Wren Library, Trinity College, Cambridge		*Beard* 1989 (1), 35–6, 189–90 (repr 26–7); *Baker* 1995 (3), 112; *Esterly* 1998, 154–62, 171
96.	post-1696	Great west organ case in oak; richly decorated limewood choir stalls, bishop's throne and stall, lord mayor's and dean's stall, in oak and limewood (designed by Sir Christopher Wren) Drawing(s): 2 for the organ case and door surround, Guildhall Lib, London, St Paul's deposit	wd	St Paul's Cathedral, London, organ-case relocated in the Cathedral, 1872		*Beard* 1989 (1), 30–31 (repr 31–36); *Esterly* 1998, 162–5, 167 (repr)
97.	c1696	'Worke done in the New Gallery Building in the King's Great and little Closset in three Rooms under the King's Apartment in the King's Gallery' Payment(s): £839 4s 5d		[Kensington Palace, London]; destroyed		*Colvin* 1973–76, V, 190
98.	1698	Angels with the royal arms, lunette relief Payment(s): £120	s	St Paul's Cathedral, London, north pediment		*Ward-Jackson* 2003, 372–3 (repr)
99.	1699–1700	Overdoor festoons, limewood	wd	Hampton Court Palace, Middx, King's apartments, presence chamber		*Colvin* 1973–76, V, 164; *Esterly* 1994, 32–8 (repr)
100.	1701	Lion and unicorn, for gate piers	s	Hampton Court Palace, Middx		TNA WORK, 5/52; *Gunnis* 1968, 170
101.	1701–1702	Ornaments and carving over doors and windows, oak Payment(s): £572 including £150 for 25 Corinthian capitals		Hampton Court Palace, Middx, King's apartments, guard chamber, privy chamber, ante-room, drawing room, cartoon gallery, painted room, staircase and passage		*Colvin*, 1973–76, V, 168–70; *Esterly* 1994, 37
102.	1704	Archbishop Tenison's throne	wd	[Canterbury Cathedral, Chancel]; Canterbury Cathedral, Kent, store		*Vertue* V, 38; *Green* 1964 (1), 147 (repr 217)
103.	1706	Eight capitals		[House of Commons, London]; untraced		TNA E 351/3312; *Gunnis* 1968, 170
104.	c1707	Overmantel, mirror frame, 'a Cock's Head for the Duchess of Marlborough's Side Board', and a 'Snake's head for the Basin at the Queen's Back Stairs' Payment(s): £39 19s 10d	wd	[Windsor Castle, Berks, various rooms]; untraced		*Colvin* 1973–76, V, 334
105.	1709	Piers enriched with vermiculated carving and topped with baskets of flowers Payment(s): £8 each for baskets	s	[Blenheim Palace, Oxon, gate on west front]; Blenheim Palace, Hensington Gate, Woodstock Rd		*Beard* 1989 (1), 49 (repr 63)
106.	1711	Carving in the queen's drawing room	wd	Hampton Court Palace, Middx		*Colvin* 1973–76, V, 175
107.	c1711	Reredos surround Payment(s): £941 14s 9d		Hampton Court Palace, Middx, Chapel Royal		*Esterly* 1998, 129
108.	1708–1712	Ducal arms for tympanum on north front, coronetted finials for four great towers, trophies for the roofline, 18 statues for north front quadrants, two lions and capitals for the north front, and interior ornaments Payment(s): £20 each Drawing(s): One, for the Saloon, by Hawksmoor with sculptural elements filled in by Gibbons, Bodl MS. Top. Oxon, a.37* fol 32	s	Blenheim Palace, Oxon (two surviving statues)		RG/JP 4, 589; *Beard* 1989 (1), 14, 47–50, 193–4 (trophies repr 62); *Esterly* 1998 130, 206
109.	1715	'for carving a new picture over a new door'		Hampton Court Palace, Middx, princess's dressing room		TNA WORK AO1/2448/149
110.	c1718	Gallery columns and other ornaments Payment(s): £156	wd	[St Alfege, Greenwich]; destroyed		Pevsner, *London: S*, 1983, 246
Reliefs						
111.	c1670	King David playing a harp and Saint Cecilia playing an organ (after an engraving by Johannes Sadeler), boxwood	wd	[Probably for Sir Robert Barwick of Toulston, Recorder of York]; coll Alfred Taubman	S	*Esterly* 1998, 41–5 (repr); *Sayce and Esterly* 2000, 11–21 (repr)

112.	c1670	'The History of Elijah under the Juniper Tree' (probably a relief)	wd	[coll Ralph Thoresby, Leeds]; untraced		*Esterly* 1998, 44
113.	1671	The Crucifixion (after Tintoretto's painting, Scuola San Rocco, Venice), limewood	wd	[coll Sir George Viner]; tentatively identified with the relief over the library chimneypiece, at Dunham Massey Hall, Cheshire, in place by by 1758 (NT)		*Evelyn* 1959, 549, 552; *Beard* 1989 (1), 15–16, 17, 185–6 (repr 4); *Esterly* 1998, 19–25, 31–33 (repr)
114.	c1671	The stoning of St Stephen, limewood panel	wd	[coll 1st Duke of Chandos]; VAM 446–1898		*Vertue* II, 3, 48; V, 34; *Beard* 1989 (1), 16, 186 (repr 5); *Esterly* 1998, 34–5, 48–51 (repr); *Bilbey* 2002, 4–5 (repr); *ODNB* (Esterly)
115.	1680–1682	Panel presented to Duke Cosimo III of Tuscany (the 'Cosimo' panel), limewood Payment(s): £150	wd	[Bargello, Florence]; Pitti Palace, Florence	S	*Colvin* 1973–76, V, 328; *Beard* 1989 (1), 17–18, 186–7 (repr 6–11); *Esterly* 1999, 355–6; ODNc (Esterly)
116.	c1685	The 'Modena' panel, limewood	wd	[coll Alfonso IV, Duke of Modena]; Galleria Estense, Modena	S	*Beard* 1989 (1), 18–19, 187 (repr 12); *Esterly* 1998, 145–9 (repr); *Sayce and Esterly* 2000, 11–21
117.	1686	Organ case	wd	[Whitehall Palace, London, Roman Catholic Chapel]; St James, Piccadilly, London, since 1691		*Beard* 1989 (1), 26, 33
118.	1690–1700	The 'Kirtlington' panel, with fish, fowl and crustaceans, limewood	wd	[Kirtlington Park, Oxon]; private coll		*Esterly* 1998, 97–9, 152–3, 188–9 (repr)
119.	nd	Charles II, medallion portrait, set in an oval frame, with two angels holding a wreath above, oak	wd	Christie, 13 April 1983, lot 23; untraced		Wolterton sale, Christie's 13 April 1983 (repr)
120.	nd	The 'Cullen' panel		[Cullen House, Banffshire]; untraced		*Esterly* 1998, 150, 152 (repr), 215n17, 216, n18; *Sayce and Esterly* 2000, 11–21 (repr)
Miscellaneous						
121.	c1679	'carvings of Mr. Gibbons' and 'an excellent Pendule-Clock inclosed in the curious flower-work of Mr Gibbons'	wd	[Mr Bohune's house, near Sayes-Court, Deptford, Kent]; untraced		*Evelyn* 1959, 672, 25 Aug 1679; 728, 30 July 1682
122.	?1679	Ornaments, a 'fret', a clockcase and a chimneypiece		[Christopher Boone's house, Lee Place, near Greenwich]; untraced		*Esterly* 1998, 136–7 (repr)
123.	post-1682	Point cravat	wd	[coll Sir Robert Gayer]; VAM W 181-1928		*Vertue* I, 85, 160; II, 10–11; *Esterly* 1998, 136–7 (repr)
124.	1684–1686	Two altarpieces, overmantels, picture frames and two foliate panels for the 'Confession Chair' Payment(s): £96 19s 9d		[Windsor Castle, King's and Queen's chapel, Queen's apartments]; untraced		*Colvin* 1973–76, V, 330
125.	1686–1687	Model for a marble bathing cistern with a wainscot border, with copper water pipes		[Windsor Castle, Berks, bathing room]; untraced		*Colvin* 1973–76, V, 331
126.	?c1699	Two overmantels with drops but without cresting and a frieze of acanthus, songbirds, fruit and wheat ears	wd	Hampton Court Palace, Middx, King's apartments, great bedchamber		*Esterly* 1994, 36–7

GIBBONS, John, of Bristol fl 1741–52

A freestone cutter who was working regularly on the Exchange and Market at Bristol 1741–52. In 1747 he was paid for '4 Plain Archve Windows', '2 Venetian windows pedestals' and '25 Feet extraordinary in ye 2 Coats of Arms'.

Archival References: BRO, Exchange Building-Accts, 04221 [l/c30], fols 1–3, 28, 33, 37, 47; 04223 fols 45, 48, 50, 52–4, 66; 04224

GIBBS, Samuel, of Axminster fl 1773–1821

Gunnis comments that his firm's work 'is well above the average of the contemporary small-town statuary of the period' (*Gunnis* 1968, 170).

Funerary Monuments

1.	?1773	Robert Coade	Lyme Regis, Dorset	S	*Gunnis* 1968, 170
2.	?1775	Benjamin Studley	Broadwindsor, Dorset	S	*Gunnis* 1968, 170
3.	?1775	William Drake	Axminster, Dorset	S	*Gunnis* 1968, 170
4.	?1779	Jane Steer	Axminster, Dorset	S	*Gunnis* 1968, 170
5.	?1799	Christopher Joliffe	Kingsdon, Somerset	S	*Gunnis* 1968, 170
6.	?1813	Samuel Sparks	Crewkerne, Somerset	S	*Gunnis* 1968, 170
7.	?1816	John Ellard	Axminster, Dorset	S	*Gunnis* 1968, 170
8.	?1819	Rev Maurice Hopkins	Stoke Abbott, Dorset	S	*Gunnis* 1968, 170
9.	?1821	Elizabeth Cozens	St Peter, Dorchester, Dorset	S	*Gunnis* 1968, 170

GIBBS, W, of Basingstoke fl 1803–42

Gunnis notes that his best work is the monument to Sarah Debary (4) which has 'a well-carved relief' (*Gunnis* 1968, 170).

Funerary Monuments

1.	?1803	Peter Waldo	Worting, Hants	S	*Gunnis* 1968, 170
2.	†1806	Rev Isaac Lefroy	Ashe, Hants	S	Pevsner, *Hants & Isle of Wight*, 1967, 83
3.	?1814	Thomas Matthew	Upton Grey, Hants	S	*Gunnis* 1968, 170
4.	†1823	Sarah Debary	Hurstbourne Tarrant, Hants	S	Pevsner, *Hants & Isle of Wight*, 1967, 302

5.	?1824	Lady Ashley	Evesley, Wilts	S	*Gunnis* 1968, 170
6.	†1841	Catherine (†1835) and James Edwards	King's Somborne, Hants	S	
7.	?1842	John Ker	Weyhill, Hants	S	*Gunnis* 1968, 170

GIBSON, Benjamin 1811?–51

The youngest brother of **John Gibson**, Benjamin was born near Conway and moved to Liverpool as a child. He exhibited at the Academy of the Liverpool Royal Institution between 1822 and 1830 from addresses in Lime Street, Haymarket and Duncan Street East, showing ideal works and portrait busts, including one of his mother (**16**). He also produced a number of monuments for churches in Liverpool and the surrounding area, including one commemorating Matthew Gregson, erected in St John's, Liverpool, in 1829, which consisted of a draped urn above a tablet ornamented with four branches of honeysuckle (**4**).

In 1836 Benjamin joined John Gibson in Rome. There he lived with his elder brother and worked in his studio, 'assisting him in his professional engagements and contributing to his domestic circle an unvarying amiability of disposition and cheerful and pleasing manners' (*GM*, 1851, ii, 552). In 1840 the *Gentleman's Magazine* reported that Benjamin had recently sent a copy of his brother's group of *Psyche borne by Zephyrs* to Liverpool and was working on an original composition entitled *Shepherd boy and dog* (*GM*, 1840, i, 404) (**8, 9**). Thomas Byrth, the Rector of Wallasey, visited Gibson's studio in the later 1840s and wrote 'Gibson's studio was open. The Gibson is in England, but his brother [Benjamin] was at his post, finishing a statue. He is a very unaffected manly kind of person. Several of the sculptures in the studio are intended for England' (*Byrth* 1851, 228).

In 1848 the *Art Union* noted that he had just completed a *Bacchante Listening to Pan*, 'an ingenious and pleasing composition, half life-size, for Mr. Lousanda' (*AU*, 1848, 50) (**11**). Other works in progress in his studio at that date included a small plaster group of *Minerva chasing Cupid, who runs to Venus*, which was to be executed for Richard Vaughan Yates, the Liverpool ironmaster, and a bas-relief of a *Wounded Amazon*, another copy of a work by his brother, for Eliza Huskisson, widow of the politician William Huskisson (**13, 20**). Benjamin was an authority on Greek and Latin literature and translated classical texts for John Gibson, who called him 'my classical dictionary' (*Eastlake* 1870, 194). He also wrote a number of papers on Italian antiquities for the *Gentleman's Magazine* and for the Society of Antiquaries and his remarks on the monuments of ancient Lycia were published by the archaeologist Sir Charles Fellows. His art and 170 antiquarian books collected in Rome were given to the Royal Liverpool Institution on his death and became the nucleus of Liverpool University Library.

Benjamin Gibson died at the Baths of Lucca on 13 August 1851, after a long, painful illness, and was buried in the Protestant cemetery there. He was, according to his obituary, 40 years old (*GM*, 1851, ii, 552). John Gibson executed the simple monument marking his grave, which describes him as a member of the British Archaeological Association, adding 'He resided 14 years at Rome, where his learning, amiability and virtue made him beloved and esteemed' (*Eastlake* 1870, 198). John justified not describing Benjamin as a sculptor on his headstone as 'His health did not permit him to exercise himself in sculpture: He has not done enough to be considered a sculptor. His real hobby were his books' (Gibson/Sandbach, Leghorn, 17 Oct 1851).

Eric Foster/EH

Literary References: *GM*, 1840, i, 404; *AU*, 1848, 50; *GM*, 1851, ii, 552; *Eastlake* 1870, 194–9; *Sampson* ed, 1895 (catalogue of Gibson's library); *Gunnis* 1968, 170; *Grove* 12, 1996, 597–9 (Greenwood-'Gibson, John (i)')); *Morris and Roberts* 1998, 253–4

Archival References: Gibson/Sandbach Papers NLWMS 20567E-127

Portraits of the Sculptor: Self-portrait, stone bust, private coll, USA

Funerary Monuments

1.	?1826	Margaret Clough		[Mold, Flint]; untraced	S	*Gunnis* 1968, 170
2.	?1827	John Hodson		Standish, Lancs	S	*Gunnis* 1968, 170
3.	?1829	Major Hilton		Chester Cathedral, Cheshire	S	*Gunnis* 1968, 170
4.	1829	Matthew Gregson (†1824)		[St John, Liverpool, Lancs]; destroyed		*GM*, 1829, ii, 652
5.	1834	Richard Uniacke (†1834) Payment(s): £400		Halifax Cathedral, Nova Scotia, Canada		C Lib, listed under John Gibson (repr)
6.	1842	Egerton Smith		[for Richard Vaughan Yates of Liverpool]; untraced		inf: Eric Foster

Statues

7.	1840	Proserpine, statuette (reduced copy of a statue by John Gibson)		[coll William Lassells, of Liverpool]; untraced		inf: Eric Foster
8.	1840	Psyche borne off by Zephyrs (after John Gibson)		Walker, Liverpool Other versions: Wolverhampton AG, Staffs, 1840,		*GM*, 1840, i, 404
9.	1840	Shepherd boy and dog		S Wolverhampton AG, Staffs (broken remains only) Other versions: sold to 'a lady passing thro' to Naples' 1849		*GM*, 1840, i, 404
10.	1840	William Huskisson, statuette (reduced copy of a statue by John Gibson)		[coll Mrs Huskisson]; untraced		inf: EF
11.	1848	Bacchante listening to Pan	m	[coll Mr Lousanda]; untraced		*AU*, 1848, 50
12.	1848	Cupid disguised as a shepherd boy (after John Gibson)		[Claughton Manor House, Birkenhead, Cheshire]; untraced Other versions: several reduced copies: ex coll daughters of John Ashton Yates, of Liverpool, 1839–40; untraced ex coll Dr Cot, 1849; untraced ex coll Mr Griffiths of Shropshire, 1849; untraced coll Eric Forster		*AU*, 1848, 50; inf: EF

13.	1848	Minerva chasing Cupid, who runs to to Venus for protection	p	Untraced		*AU*, 1848, 40
14.	nd	Hylas and the nymphs		[coll Dwarkenarth Tagore, of India]; untraced		inf: EF
Busts						
15.	1824	A matron		[Exhib ALRI, Liverpool, 175]; untraced		*Morris and Roberts* 1998, 253
16.	1828	The artist's mother		[Exhib ALRI, Liverpool, 232]; untraced		*Morris and Roberts* 1998, 253
17.	1829	Unidentified gentleman		[Exhib ALRI, Liverpool, 343]; untraced		*Morris and Roberts* 1998, 254
18.	1847	Queen Victoria (after John Gibson)	m	[Prince Anatole Demidoff]; Gov Art Coll	S	Gov Art Coll archives
Reliefs						
19.	1840	Minerva driving away Cupid		[coll Richard Vaughan Yates of Liverpool]; untraced		inf: EF
20.	1848	Wounded Amazon (after John Gibson)		[coll Mrs Huskisson]; untraced		*AU*, 1848, 50
Miscellaneous						
21.	1822	Infant Hercules		[Exhib ALRI, Liverpool, 179]; untraced		*Morris and Roberts* 1998, 253
22.	1822	Nymph and river god		[Exhib ALRI, Liverpool, 170]; untraced		*Morris and Roberts* 1998, 253
23.	1824	Cain and Abel		[Exhib ALRI, Liverpool, 183]; untraced		*Morris and Roberts* 1998, 253
24.	1824	Centaur and bacchante		[Exhib ALRI, Liverpool, 185]; untraced		*Morris and Roberts* 1998, 253
25.	1824	Venus disarming Cupid		[Exhib ALRI, Liverpool, 180]; untraced		*Morris and Roberts* 1998, 253
26.	1828	Cupid		[Exhib ALRI, Liverpool, 238]; untraced		*Morris and Roberts* 1998, 253
27.	1830	Penelope following Ulysses		[Exhib ALRI, Liverpool, 270]; untraced		*Morris and Roberts* 1998, 254
28.	1835	Dying gladiator		[coll H Jones, of Liverpool]; untraced		inf: EF
29.	1840	Arm of a beautiful child		[coll unidentified English peer]; untraced		inf: EF
30.	1846	Innocence		[Claughton Manor House, Birkenhead, Cheshire, coll W Jackson]; untraced		*Gunnis* 1968, 170
31.	1846–1847	'Hand of Miss York' Payment(s): £5		Untraced		inf: EF

GIBSON, John RA 1790–1866

John Gibson trained under **Antonio Canova** and **Bertel Thorvaldsen** in Rome, where he spent most of his life and became a central figure in the international artistic community. He was the most important British neoclassical sculptor of the mid-19th century but is now chiefly remembered for his controversial polychrome sculpture.

He was born near Conway in North Wales, the son of a market gardener, William Gibson, who moved with his family to Liverpool in 1799. Two of his brothers, **Solomon Gibson** and **Benjamin Gibson** also became sculptors. John showed an interest in art from an early age and later recalled how he had made copies of the images displayed in print shop windows and was beaten at school for drawing during lessons. He received early encouragement from his mother and from John Turmeau, a miniature painter and dealer in prints and artists' materials, who lent him drawings and casts to copy.

In 1804 Gibson began his apprenticeship as a cabinet-maker in the Liverpool business of Southwell and Wilson but he found this occupation uncongenial and the terms of his apprenticeship were changed so that he could instead work as a wood-carver, making decorative mouldings for furniture. He was later introduced to the sculptor, **F A Legé**, who was working for **Samuel** and **Thomas Franceys**, the Liverpool carvers, and Gibson made copies of some of Legé's models, including a small head of *Bacchus* (**76**). The Franceys partners were sufficiently impressed by these early efforts to pay Gibson's employers £70 to cancel his indentures so that he could work for them. The monument to Henry Blundell (**1**), signed by Franceys, is an example of Gibson's early work, executed whilst he was employed by the firm.

Gibson's first patron was William Roscoe, the Liverpool banker and connoisseur. Roscoe commissioned a narrative relief of *Alexander the Great* for his library at Allerton Hall (**130**). The source was an engraving by Marcantonio Raimondi, after a fresco by Raphael in the Vatican. Gibson frequently visited Allerton to study Roscoe's fine collection of old master drawings and particularly admired Michelangelo, whose influence is evident in a drawing, *The fall of Satan and the rebel angels*, executed *c*1811 (Walker, Liverpool). Roscoe advised him however that as a sculptor he should emulate the purity and simplicity seen to be the essence of ancient Greek art and Gibson turned his attention to casts and prints from classical sources. He studied designs for sculpture after the antique by **John Flaxman RA** and began to think of travelling to Rome. During this period Gibson also attended anatomy classes, given by Dr Vose, the surgeon, where he watched the dissection of human bodies. In order to continue these studies more informally after the doctor's lecture season, Gibson and his fellow students stole corpses from a city graveyard.

He exhibited drawings and models at the Liverpool Academy from 1810 and in 1816 showed a relief of *Psyche carried by zephyrs* at the Royal Academy (**133**). In 1817 he completed his apprenticeship, and as opportunities for talented artists in Liverpool were limited, went to London, where he met a number of influential artists including Henri Fuseli, William Blake, Benjamin West, **Joseph Nollekens RA** and also James Christie the Younger, the auctioneer. He was introduced to Flaxman, who praised his work and encouraged him to pursue his plans to go to Rome. In 1816 George Watson Taylor, of Erlestoke Park, a friend of the Prince Regent, commissioned busts of himself, his wife and children (**80**), together with one of William Roscoe (**82**).

Gibson arrived in Rome on 20 October 1817. He may have worked briefly under Nollekens, since a *Theseus and centaur* modelled by 'Gibson in Mr Nollikens's study' appeared in the sale of Nollekens's effects held at Christie's in 1823 (**166**). Gibson was certainly introduced to Canova, who received him kindly and offered to support him. He studied modelling and life drawing in Canova's studio, at Canova's Academy and at the Academy of St Luke. He also received instruction from Thorvaldsen and studied Greek and Graeco-Roman sculpture. By 1821 Gibson had established his own studio in the Via Fontanella, off the Via Babuino. His first original work modelled in Rome was *The Sleeping shepherd boy* (**40**), a subject he re-interpreted several times in marble. In 1819 the 6th Duke of Devonshire commissioned a group of *Mars restrained by Cupid* (**41**). Gibson was so inexperienced that he agreed to a price of £500 for the work, which cost him £520 to execute. Another important early work was the group of *Psyche borne by Zephyrs* for the connoisseur Sir George Beaumont (**44**).

By the 1830s Gibson was a well-established sculptor and the leader of a group of English sculptors working in Rome which included **Richard James Wyatt, Lawrence Macdonald** and **Joseph Gott**. Some of his friends suggested that he should return to London, where they felt that he could earn larger sums for his work. He prefered however to remain in Rome, making only occasional summer visits to England and wrote euphorically 'I thank God for every morning that opens my eyes in Rome' (*Gunnis* 1968, 171). Gibson particularly valued the easy, informal communication between artists working in the city and thought that in England he would be less able to concentrate on 'ideal' works. On 3 November 1833 he was elected an associate and on 10 February 1836 a full member of the Royal Academy, submitting a version of *Narcissus* as his diploma work (**47**). He won numerous commissions from English collectors visiting Rome, including several wealthy industrialists and merchants from Liverpool. Henry Sandbach, a shipping heir, and his wife Margaret, a grand-daughter of William Roscoe, bought many of his works, including *Hunter and dog* (**57**) and *Aurora* (**62**) for Hafodunos Hall, the gothic revival mansion they had built in North Wales. He also provided Tommaso and Luigi Saulini, the Italian cameo carvers, with designs.

Throughout his career Gibson worked in a neo-classical style strongly influenced by Canova and Thorvaldsen and by the writings of Johann Joachim Winckelmann. He aimed to achieve 'the sublime and the purest beauty' in his sculpture through study of the human form perfected to the standards of classical sculpture. Gibson felt the sculptor's role was to select and combine the most beautiful parts of nature to create a harmonious whole, which would delight and elevate the viewer. He later described his use of a number of male and female models for a figure of *Bacchus* (**67**). Gibson believed that deviation from the principles of classical art for the sake of novelty could only produce inferior sculpture. He specifically condemned the use of contemporary dress, writing 'The human figure concealed under a frock-coat and trousers is not a fit subject for sculpture' (*Matthews* 1911, 100). Certain critics mocked him for depicting men of his day in classical draperies: the statue of Sir Robert Peel in Westminster Abbey (**27**) was dismissed by Palgrave as 'Gibson's tasteless and unresembling Peel in a toga' (*Palgrave* 1866, 333). *Narcissus* is typical of Gibson's mature work, for it combines a classical allegory with an observed genre scene. Gibson later revealed that the statue was inspired by the sight of a boy sitting on the edge of a fountain during his morning walk along the Monte Pinciano.

Gibson's most controversial work was the *Tinted Venus* (**66**), commissioned by a Liverpool manufacturer, Robert Preston, and his wife in 1851. Gibson's use of colour was prompted by classical Greek antecedents, discussed in the influential writings of Quatremère de Quincy and other scholars. He also admired contemporary polychrome architectural decoration by Leo von Klenze in Munich. Gibson applied colour to several works, including *Love cherishing the soul, while preparing to torment it* (**55**), his first statue of Queen Victoria (**65**) and *Pandora* (**64**) but he developed the idea to its fullest extent with the *Tinted Venus*, which he considered his finest work. He described it as 'the most carefully executed work I ever executed' adding 'I tinted the flesh like warm ivory – scarcely red – the eyes blue, the hair blonde, and the net which contains the hair golden' (*Eastlake* 1870, 211). He became so attached to the finished statue that he kept it in his studio for 4 years in spite of Mrs Preston's repeated protests. The work caused consternation when it was displayed in a temple designed by Owen Jones, at the 1862 International Exhibition. Many found it too life-like and thought that the use of colour compromised the icy purity that was deemed necessary for a nude statue to avoid indecency.

Gibson executed a number of royal portraits, including the standing figure of Queen Victoria for Buckingham Palace (**60**), later replicated for Osborne, and another seated one, with supporting figures of *Justice* and *Clemency*, for the Palace of Westminster (**65**). He carved only a few public statues, including the William Huskisson (**61**) and George Stephenson for Liverpool (**63**), generally preferring to avoid commissions which would take him away from Rome for lengthy periods. Gibson was invited to compete against **EH Baily, JH Foley** and **Carlo, Baron Marochetti** in the first, ill-fated, competition for the Wellington Monument for St Paul's Cathedral, but declined to do so. He did, however, submit a model for the second competition (**33**) which was unsuccessful. After Prince Albert's death in 1861 the Queen sought Gibson's advice on the form her husband's memorial should take and later asked him to carve one of the groups. He demurred on the grounds that after so many years in Rome, returning to the cold climate of England might be harmful to his health.

Gibson assisted a number of younger sculptors in Rome including **William Theed II, Richard Westmacott III, Alfred Gatley, Henry Timbrell, William Calder Marshall, Mary Thornycroft, George Gamon Adams, John Hogan** and **Benjamin Edward Spence**, and Benjamin Gibson worked in his studio from 1837 until his death in 1851. Lady Eastlake nonetheless maintained that his only real pupil was the American sculptor, Harriet Hosmer. Gibson received many honours in recognition of his achievement, including the *légion d'honneur*, awarded by the French government in 1864. A statue of Gibson (now destroyed) was erected at the Glyptothek in Munich probably in 1859.

Gibson's biographers represent him as an unworldly and impractical man who led a happy and peaceful life devoted to his art. Harriet Hosmer remarked, 'He is a god in his studio, but God help him when he is out of it' (*Eastlake* 1870, 231). However, he clearly had some business acumen as he ran a busy workshop, amassed a large fortune and gave financial support to his brother Solomon. Gibson never married, but he formed deep and lasting friendships with a number of women, including Margaret Sandbach, his correspondent over many years. He died in Rome on 27 January 1866 and was buried in the Protestant Cemetery. He bequeathed most of the models and unfinished works in his studio and his fortune of £32,000 to the RA, with the intention that this should finance a regular display of his work as an aid to young artists. A room dedicated to the display of his work was created in Burlington House (now the library). He also left an account of his life, in the form of notes and letters, which was edited and published by Lady Eastlake in 1870 and, in a new edition, by Thomas Matthews in 1911.

EH

Literary References: *AU*, 1839, 106; *Builder*, 1847, 223, 540; 1866, 76, 104, 132, 925; *AJ*, 1853, 63–4; 1857, 273–5; 1866, 90–1, 113–5; *ILN* 48, 1866, 137, 159–61; *Palgrave* 1866, 39, 80–1, 222, 249, 294; *Eastlake* 1870, *passim*; *Hall* II, 1883, 237; *DNB* XXI, 1890, 278–281; *Matthews* 1911, *passim*; *Gunnis* 1968, 171–3; *Physick* 1969, 41–2, 180; *Physick* 1970, 21–3, 25, 28, 36n, 41n, 166–7; *Cooper* 1971, 84–92; *Morris* 1971, 397–9; *Neoclassicism* 1972, 239–40; *Fletcher* 1972, 336–40; *JKB* 1972 (3), 325–7, 329, 330, 331; *Brumbaugh* 1973, 122–7; *Ormond* 1973, 185–8; *Wilton* 1973, 118–19; *Fletcher* 1974, 2–5; *Carr* 1975, 170–81; *Penny* 1977 (1), *passim*; *Fletcher* 1977, 60–2; *Darby* 1981, 37–53; *Read* 1982, *passim*; *Read* 1985, 59–60, 64; *Whinney* 1988, 422; *Curtis* 1989, *passim*; RG/JP, 4, 589–98; *Blühm* 1996, *passim*; *Grove* 12, 1996, 597–9 (Greenwood); *Morris and Roberts* 1998, 254; *Bilbey* 2002, 271–74; *ODNB* (Greenwood)

Archival References: RA/GA, 1833, 1836, 1866

Additional MS sources: Gibson Albums; Gibson Letters; Gibson Papers (1); Gibson Papers (2); Gibson/Blair; Gibson/Hall; Gibson/Hall; Gibson/Horner; Gibson/Lawrence; Gibson/Lyttleton; Gibson/Mozley; Gibson/Rogers; Gibson/Sandbach; Gibson/Shaw; Gibson/Thomas; Gibson/Thrupp; Menai Francis Essay; Penry Williams Letters; Tinted Venus Papers

Will: PPR, with three codicils, 3 May 1866, fol 309, effects under £40,000

Miscellaneous drawings: *The fall of Satan and the rebel angels*, c1811, pen and wash and pencil, Walker; *study of a rebel angel*, c1811, pen and ink and pencil, BM, PDB, 1872-10-12-3266; *Christ blessing the little children*, BM, PDB, 1885,0509.1641; *Psyche borne by zephyrs*, BM, PDB, 1858,1009.361; *a bacchanal*, after an antique relief, BM, PDB 1875,0814.1172; *Woman and child*, BM, PDB, 1885,0711.265; about 60 life drawings, studies after the antique and designs for monuments, 1810–1817, VAM, P&D. PD 156 and PD 156A, inv D.1333-1898, D.1335-1889, E.645-1948

Selected portraits of the sculptor: John Partridge, 1825, pencil on paper, NPG 3944(32); A Geddes, 1830, painting, Walker; William Brockedon, 1844, chalk on paper, NPG 2515(96); J Graham-Gilbert, 1847, painting, NGS (smaller replica NMW); Sir Edwin Landseer, c1850, painting, RA 03/1235 (replica, Walker); William Theed the Younger, 1852, bust, Conway parish church, another c1852 RA 03/3725, another, marble, c1868, NPG 1795; R Lehmann, 1853, drawing, BM, PDB, 1906, 0419.14; Margaret Sarah Carpenter, 1857, oil on canvas, NPG 232; Field Talfourd, 1859, coloured chalks on buff paper, BM, PDB, 1909, 0723.3; Sir George Scharf, 1860, drawing, NPG 6050; unknown artist, c1860, pencil on paper, NPG 1370 (another identical drawing BM); Nadar (Gaspard Félix Tournachon), c1862, salt print, NPG P227; John Adams Acton, marble bust, 1862, Walker, Liverpool, another, 1862, RA, 03/1669; Sir W Boxall, 1864, painting, RA 03/443; Isabel Cholmeley, painted plaster bust, 1863, RA 03/1692; J S Wyon, 1875, bronze medal, issued by the Art Union of London, NPG D2918; Harriet Hosmer, nd, marble medallion, NPG 5342 (other versions at Watertown Free Public Library, Mass, USA and on Gibson's tomb, Protestant cemetery, Rome); anon, nd, silhouette, SNPG; Henry Meyer, nd, pencil touched with watercolour, BM, PDB, 1871, 0812.1807; Penry Williams, oil on canvas, version at NMW, Cardiff (14102); marble bust, nd, Stanford Hall, Northants

Funerary Monuments

1.	1813	Henry Blundell (†1810) Drawing(s): VAM D.1321-98; VAM D.1322-98	p	St Helen, Sefton, Lancs		*Penny* 1977 (1), 163 (repr); *Grove* 12, 1996, 597; *Morris and Roberts* 1998, 254
2.	†1819	Ann Earle		[St James the Less, Liverpool, Lancs]; untraced		C Lib (repr)
3.	†1822	Le Gendre Starkie		Padiham, Lancs		Pevsner, *Lancs: N*, 1969, 187; C Lib (repr)
4.	†1822	Thomas Earle		[Our Lady and St Nicholas, Liverpool, Lancs]; untraced	S	C Lib (repr)
5.	†1823	Anna Maria Allott		[Cemetière du Calvaire, Lausanne, France]; untraced		
6.	†1823	Frances Bovell		Barbados Cathedral, Bridgetown	S	*Perowne* 1951, 1942 (repr); *Gunnis* 1968, 173
7.	1825	Dr Dixon		[St Nicholas, Whitehaven, Cumberland]; destroyed		*CP*, 4 Oct 1825
8.	1830	Emily Robinson (†1829) Model(s): relief, RA colls, plaster		St James's mortuary chapel, Liverpool		*Matthews* 1911, 72; *Curtis* 1989, 48–9; *Sharples* 1991, 12; C Lib (repr)
9.	†1832	Henry Holinshead		[St George, Liverpool, Lancs]; untraced	S	C Lib (repr)
10.	†1832	William Hammerton		St James's the Less, Liverpool, Lancs, cemetery chapel Other versions: Relief, RA colls, labelled 'Charity', plaster	S	*Penny* 1977 (1), 162–4 (repr); *Curtis* 1989, 48–9 (repr); *Sharples* 1991, 10–11 (repr)
11.	1833	Dudley North (†1829)		Little Glemham, Suffolk		*Matthews* 1911, 74–5, 245; Pevsner, *Suffolk*, 1974, 336; C Lib (repr)
12.	†1833	John Westcar		Whitchurch, Bucks	S	*Penny* 1977 (1), 185–6 (repr); Pevsner, *Bucks*, 1994, 748
13.	†1833	Sarah Byrom		Daresbury, Cheshire Other versions: Relief, RA colls, plaster	S	*Holland Park* 1957, unpag (repr); Pevsner, *Cheshire*, 1971, 195; *Penny* 1977 (1), 80, 81 (repr)
14.	1831–1833	William Huskisson MP (†1830)		[Huskisson Mausoleum, St James's Cemetery, Liverpool, Lancs]; NMG Merseyside, Conservation Centre (2003)		*Matthews* 1911, 79–80, 245 (repr); *Cavanagh* 1997, 151
15.	†1834	Eyre Coote Model(s): Relief, RA colls, labelled 'Consolation', plaster		Rockbourne, Hants	S	Pevsner, *Hants & Isle of Wight*, 1967, 476
16.	1837	'Monumental statue'		[Exhib RA, London, 1164]; untraced		*Graves* III, 1905–6, 230
17.	†1839	William Earle Model(s): Relief, RA colls, plaster		The Oratory, St James's Cemetery, Liverpool, Lancs	S	*Curtis* 1989, 48–9; *Sharples* 1991, 6–7 (repr)
18.	†1840	Edward (†1834) and Margaret Roscoe (†1840) Model(s): Relief of 'Hope', RA colls, plaster		Unitarian Church, Ullet Road, Liverpool, Lancs	S	*Gunnis* 1968, 173; Pevsner, *S Lancs*, 1969, 238; C Lib (repr)

No.	Date	Subject	Medium	Location	Signed	Bibliography
19.	1841	Bishop William van Mildert (†1836)		Durham Cathedral		*Penny* 1977 (1), 76 (repr)
20.	†1844	Anne Amelia, Countess of Leicester Model(s): relief of 'Angel carrying an infant and leading the mother to heaven', RA colls, plaster		Longford, Derbys		Pevsner, *Derbys*, 1978, 268; C Lib (repr)
21.	†1848	Harriet Cheney		Badger, Salop Other versions: relief, RA colls, plaster	S	Pevsner, *Salop*, 1958, 67; C Lib (repr)
22.	1851	Richard James Wyatt (†1850)		Protestant Cemetery, Rome		*Matthews* 1911, 136, 245; *Gunnis* 1968, 173
23.	†1852	'Angel plucking flowers for the four Bonomi Children'		Untraced		Gugliemi, *Engravings from Original Compositions* (VAM Gen Coll, ref 106.A.41)
24.	1852	Benjamin Gibson (†1851)		Anglican Cemetery, Bagni di Lucca, Italy		
25.	†1852	Harriet Pigott Model(s): 'angel leading the spirit to heaven': plaster relief for the monument RA colls (Gibson bequest)		Badger, Salop	S	Pevsner, *Salop*, 1958, 68; *Penny* 1977 (1), 215 n52; C Lib (repr)
26.	†1852	Margaret Sandbach		[Hafodunos Hall, Denbighs]; Walker, Liverpool Other versions: relief, Walker, Liverpool 7505, marble relief, RA colls, plaster	S	*Eastlake* 1870, 254; *Matthews* 1911, 244; Walker, Liverpool, *Annual Reports*, vols II–IV, 1971–4, 30–1
27.	1852	Sir Robert Peel Bt (†1850)		Westminster Abbey, London, north transept	S	CSC, *Journal*, 101–2; Pevsner, *London: Westminster*, 1973, 449; *Read* 1982, 166 (repr)
28.	†1856	Eliza Huskisson Model(s): relief, RA colls, plaster		Chichester Cathedral, Sussex		*Matthews* 1911, 223–4, 245; Pevsner, *Sussex*, 1965, 155; C Lib (repr)
29.	†1856	Selina Knightley Model(s): relief, RA colls, labelled 'Angel receiving the spirit', plaster		Fawsley, Northants	S	Pevsner, *Northants*, 1973, 214; C Lib (repr)
30.	1863	Edward Lloyd		Llanbedr Dyffryn, Denbighs	S	Pevsner, *Clwyd*, 1986, 188
31.	1865	Emily Lutley (co-sculptor: John Adams Acton)		[Brockhampton, Herefs]; untraced	SD	
32.	1865	Three angels, relief, part of the monument to Sarah, Baroness Braye (†1862) (monument by Mary Thornycroft)		Stanford, Northants		*CIIA* 4/3/116, 118 (repr)
33.	nd	Arthur, 1st Duke of Wellington (model only, monument in St Paul's Cathedral executed by Alfred Stevens)		Untraced		*Matthews* 1911, 218–221; *Physick* 1970, 36, 41, 166–7
34.	nd	Blundell Holinshead Model(s): the guardian angel, relief, RA, London (Gibson bequest)	p	Liverpool Cemetery Chapel, Lancs		
35.	nd	Robert Preston of Abercromby Square		[St Katherine's, Abercromby Square, Liverpool]; untraced		NLW photo
36.	nd	William Hammond (erected 1895)		Pulborough, Sussex	S	*Gunnis* 1968, 173
Statues						
37.	1823	Augusta Pierrepont		Stratfield Saye, Hants	S	*Gunnis* 1968, 172; C Lib (repr)
38.	1824	Nymph reposing		[coll Count Schonberg of Bavaria]; untraced		*Eastlake* 1870, 250; *Matthews* 1911, 242
39.	1819–1824	Paris	m	[Erlestoke Park, Wilts; Erlestoke sale, 25 July 1832, lot 166]; untraced		*Graves* III, 1905–6, 230; *Matthews* 1911, 55, 63–4, 69–71; AL/RG
40.	1824	Sleeping shepherd boy	m	[coll Lord George Cavendish]; Exhib Chelminski, London, Sept–Oct 2002 Other versions: Walker, Liverpool, marble coll James Lennox, 1881, New York Public Library RA colls, 1818, plaster Alnwick Castle, Northumbs, called 'Repose' (AL/RG)		*Graves* III, 1905–6, 230; *Matthews* 1911, 49–51, 62, 241; *Curtis* 1989, 57–9; *Grove* 12, 1996, 597, 598
41.	1825	Mars restrained by Cupid Payment(s): £500	m	Chatsworth, Derbys	S	*JKB* 1972 (3), 325, 327, 331 (repr)
42.	1826	Cupid drawing his bow	m	[coll Sir Watkin Williams Wynn, 5th Bt]; Glasgow Museums TEMP.15367		*Graves* III, 1905–6, 230; *Matthews* 1911, 66–7, 242; *Gunnis* 1968, 172; *Grove* 12, 1996, 598
43.	1826	Hylas surprised by the Naiads (Hylas and the water nymphs)	m	[coll Robert Vernon]; Tate Britain, London		*Graves* III, 1905–6, 230; *Matthews* 1911, 66, 242 (repr); *Holland Park* 1957, unpag (repr)
44.	1822–1827	Psyche borne by zephyrs		[coll Sir George Beaumont]; untraced Other versions: Galleria Corsini, Rome Hermitage Museum, St Petersburg, 1820s Prince Torlonia, 1839 for the Palazzo Torlonia, Rome.		*Graves* III, 1905–6, 230; *Matthews* 1911, 54–5, 67–8, 73, 110, 241, 242 (repr); *Dukelskaya* 1979, 328–9 (repr)

45.	c1830	Cupid disguised as a shepherd boy (Love disguised as a shepherd)	m	[coll Sir John Johnstone]; Peel Heirlooms sale, 1900: untraced Other versions: Sir Robert Peel, for Drayton Manor, Staffs, 1834 ex coll Hereditary Grand Duke of Russia; Hermitage, St Petersburg, 1830s Walker, c1840 Museum of Fine Arts, Boston, USA, c1840; untraced	S	*Graves* III, 1905–6, 230; *Matthews* 1911, 75–8; *Dukelskaya* 1979, 329 (repr); *Sc J*, 1998, 155 (repr)
46.	1830	Flora		[coll Lord Durham]; untraced Other versions: Walker, 1874 RA colls, plaster		*Matthews* 1911, 75, 242; *Gunnis* 1968, 172; RG/JP, 4, 593
47.	1830	Narcissus Payment(s); £300	m	[coll Lord Barrington]; untraced Other versions: Art Gallery of New South Wales, Sydney Royal Coll, Osborne House, I of W Richard Fort of Manchester, ?1833–1839 RA, London (diploma work) 03/1918, 1838, marble RA, London 04/730 Mr Errington, c1842; untraced	S	*Graves* III, 1905–6, 230; *Holland Park* 1957, unpag (repr); *Fletcher* 1977, 60–2 (repr)
48.	1824–1831	Nymph untying her sandal (Nymph preparing for the bath)	m	[coll Charles, 1st Earl of Yarborough]; Usher Art Gall, Lincoln Other versions: RA colls, plaster	S	*AJ Cat* 1862, f.208 (repr); *Graves* III, 1905–6, 230; *Matthews* 1911, 73–4, 242; *Grove* 12, 1996, 598
49.	c1831	Sappho		[Allerton Hall, Lancs]; untraced Other versions: RA colls, plaster		*AJ*, 1857, 275; *AJ*, 1866, 115; *Matthews* 1911, 80–1, 242
50.	1831	Venus kissing Cupid	m	[coll Charles, 1st Earl of Yarborough]; Usher Art Gallery, Lincoln Other versions: RA colls, plaster	S	*Graves* III, 1905–6, 230; *Matthews* 1911, 78, 242 (repr)
51.	1832	Proserpine in the fields of Enna		[coll Joseph Ablett of Llanbedr Hall, North Wales]; untraced Other versions: For Dwarkanath Tagore of Calcutta; untraced RA colls, plaster		*Matthews* 1911, 106–7, 242
52.	1833	Nymph kissing Cupid (Venus kissing Cupid)	m	NMW, Cardiff Other versions: For John Malcolm of Poltalloch For W R Sandbach For the Prince of Wales, Marlborough House, tinted RA colls, plaster	S	Sale cat, Sotheby, 9 Dec 1993
53.	1833	Venus Verticordia (untinted)		[coll Joseph Neeld of Grittleton]; Fitzwilliam	S	*Graves* III, 1905–6, 230; *Matthews* 1911, 179–85
54.	1836	William Huskisson MP	m	[Royal Exchange, London]; Pimlico Gardens, Grosvenor Rd, London		*Graves* III, 1905–6, 230; RG/JP, 4, 594; *Read* 1982, 173, 174 (repr); *Cavanagh* 1997, 151
55.	1839	Love cherishing the soul, while preparing to torment it (Cupid tormenting the soul, Cupid and a butterfly)	m	[coll Lord Selsey]; untraced Other versions: For Richard Yates Esq, Liverpool For R S Holford Esq, Dorchester House, tinted Walker, Liverpool RA, London, 04/278, marble Harewood House, WR Yorks, marble		*Graves* III, 1905–6, 230; *Matthews* 1911, 106, 230, 242; *Gunnis* 1968, 172; C Lib (repr)
56.	1840	Wounded Amazon	m	[coll Mrs Preston]; NMW, Cardiff Other versions: coll Duke of Westminster, Eaton Hall, Cheshire, marble coll Mrs Preston, Chesterfield House, Richmond		*Graves* III, 1905–6, 230; *Eastlake* 1911, 85–7; *Matthews* 1911, 85–7, 242; *Gunnis* 1968, 172; C Lib (repr)
57.	c1842	Hunter and dog (Meleager)	m	[Hafodunos Hall, Denbighs]; private coll Other versions: Earl of Yarborough J L Clare, Liverpool Norwich Castle Museum, c1847 Usher Art Gallery, Lincoln, 1847 George Moore sale, Christie, London, 29 May 1880 small bronze version, Sotheby, London, 20 Nov 1997, lot 130 ex coll Judge Josephson, Art Gall of New South Wales, Sydney, small bronze version, Italian or English, cast from a model by Gibson, Frick Art Museum, Pittsburgh RA colls, plaster		*Manchester Art Treasures* 1857, 133; *Matthews* 1911, 96–7, f98 (repr); *Gunnis* 1968, 173; *Grove* 12, 1996, 598
58.	1842–1844	Kirkman Finlay	m	Merchants' House, Glasgow, Lanarks	S	*Matthews* 1911, 109, 245; *McKenzie* 2002, 415–6 (repr)

No.	Date	Subject	Medium	Location		Literary references
59.	1845	Catherine, Countess Beauchamp (Hon Mrs Murray)	m	[coll Baroness Bray]; Stanford Hall, Northants	S	*GM* ii, 1844, 71; *Graves* III, 1905–6, 230; *Matthews* 1911, 197–8, 245; RG/JP, 4, 596
60.	1844–1846	Queen Victoria	m	Buckingham Palace, London RCIN 2071 Other versions: Royal Coll, Osborne House, I of W, 1849	S	*Harris, de Bellaigue, Millar* 1968, 187 (repr); *Fletcher* 1974, 2 (repr); *Darby* 1981, 37–9 (repr); *Read* 1982, 131, 132 (repr)
61.	1847	William Huskisson MP	b	[Canning Place, Liverpool, Lancs, outside Customs House]; The Oratory, St James's Mount Gardens, Liverpool, Lancs	SD	*Cavanagh* 1997, 150–3 (repr)
62.	1848	Aurora (Eos)	m	[Hafodunos Hall, Denbighs]; NMW, Cardiff Other versions: RA colls (two) Dr Henry 1843–5, replica	S	*GM*, ii, 1844, 71; *Graves* III, 1905–6, 230; *Matthews* 1911, f96, 97–8, 242 (repr); *Gunnis* 1968, 173; *Grove* 12, 1996, 598; *Morris and Roberts* 1998, 254
63.	1851–1854	George Stephenson	m	St George's Hall, Liverpool, Lancs	S	*Graves* III, 1905–6, 230; *Cavanagh* 1997, 269–70 (repr)
64.	1856	Pandora		[coll Lady Marian Alford]; Lady Lever, inv LL718 Other versions: VAM A.3-1922, marble Sotheby, Belgravia, 13 Nov 1974, lot 23, marble; untraced		*Gunnis* 1968, 173; *Fletcher* 1974, 2–3 (repr); *Lady Lever* 1999, 35–40 (repr); *Bilbey* 2002, 273–4 (repr)
65.	1850–1856	Queen Victoria, flanked by Justice and Clemency Payment(s): £3,835	m	Palace of Westminster, London, Prince's Chamber	S	*Matthews* 1911, 175–8, 242 (repr); *Walker* 1961, 74, cat 77; *Darby* 1981, 42–4 (repr); *Read* 1982, 120–1; *Read* 2000, 260–2 (repr)
66.	1851–1856	'Tinted Venus' (Venus verticordia)	m	[coll Mr and Mrs Robert Preston of Liverpool]; Walker, Liverpool Other versions: RA, London, two, 03/6185 and 03/1922, marble and plaster Royal Coll, reduced version, marble AGNSW, Sydney, ex coll Judge Josephson Sotheby, 21 June 1988; untraced Sotheby, 19 April 2000; untraced	S	*Read* 1982, 25–6, 60, 141, 200, 201, 203 (col repr 2); *Blühm* 1996, 122–3 (repr)
67.	*c*1860	Bacchus (Dionysus)	m	RA, London, 04/725	S	*Matthews* 1911, 214–8; *Fletcher* 1974, 3–5 (repr)
68.	1860	Hebe	m	[coll Howard Galton]; untraced Other versions: Astley Cheetham Art Gallery, Stalybridge, Lancs University College, London RA, London 04/727 (tinted)	S	*Matthews* 1911, 227, 243 (repr); RG/JP, 4, 596; *Radcliffe* 1969, 48, 49 (repr)
69.	*c*1860	The wounded warrior	m	RA, London 04/724		*Matthews* 1911, 228, 243; *Read* 1982, 35 (repr)
70.	1863	Psyche carrying a cake to Cerberus		Untraced Other versions: RA colls, labelled Psyche, plaster		*Eastlake* 1870, 251; *Matthews* 1911, 234, 243
71.	1865	Theseus and the robber	p	[Hafodunos Hall, Denbighs]; untraced Other versions: smaller model, ex coll Harriet Hosmer, then at Hafodunos Hall; untraced		*Matthews* 1911, 238, 243; *Read* 1982, 34
72.	nd	Dancing nymph		Wolverhampton AG Other versions: ex Stirling coll, Glasgow; untraced	S	*Eastlake* 1870, 251; *Matthews* 1911, 243
73.	nd	Hunter and wounded fawn		[Lord Herbert of Lea; Christie, 27 March 1863]; untraced Other versions: Academy of St Luke, Rome, plaster		*Gunnis* 1968, 172, 173
74.	nd	Pugilist (after Canova)		[coll Penry Williams]; untraced		*Eastlake* 1870, 48
75.	nd	The three graces		Walker, Liverpool		*Gunnis* 1968, 173; C Lib (repr)
Busts						
76.	?1805	Bacchus, copied from a work by F A Legé	tc	Untraced		*Matthews* 1911, 9, 241, 246; *Gunnis* 1968, 171
77.	?1805	Mercury	m	[coll Mrs Vose]; untraced		*Matthews* 1911, 9; *Gunnis* 1968, 171
78.	1814	John Philip Kemble Drawing(s): four studies, BM, PDL, 1894, 0516.11 and 10	b	NPG, London, 149 Other versions: SJSM M303, plaster	SD	*Eastlake* 1870, 37–8; *Matthews* 1911, 26, 246; *Gunnis* 1968, 173; *Walker* 1985, 292–3 (repr); *Morris and Roberts* 1998, 254
79.	1816	'A young lady'		[Exhib RA, London, 914]; untraced		*Graves* III, 1905–6, 230
80.	*c*1816	George Watson Taylor, his wife and four of their children	m	[Erlestoke Park, Wilts; Erlestoke sale, 1832]; untraced		*Graves* III, 1905–6, 230; *Matthews* 1911, 34–5, 41, 246; *Bilbey* 2002, 271–2 (repr)
81.	1816	Henry Park		[Exhib RA, London, 924]; untraced		*Graves* III, 1905–6, 230
82.	1819	William Roscoe	m	[coll George Watson Taylor]; YCBA B 1983.13 Other versions: Liverpool University Ullet Road Unitarian Church, Liverpool	SD	*Matthews* 1911, 37–8, 72, 246; *Gunnis* 1968, 171, 173; Pevsner, *Lancs: S*, 1969, 238

83.	1820	George James		Untraced		*Gunnis* 1968, 173;
84.	1822	C Ellison		[Exhib RA, London, 1026]; untraced		*Graves* III, 1905–6, 230
85.	1822	Charles, 1st Baron Colchester	m	Westminster School, London		RG/JP, 4, 596
86.	1823	A nobleman		[Exhib RA, London, 1115]; untraced		*Graves* III, 1905–6, 230
87.	c1828	Walter Savage Landor	m	NPG, London, 2127 Other versions: Plaster NPG, inv 1950, SD 1828		*Walker* 1985, 307–8 (repr)
88.	1829	Lord Monson		[Gatton Park, Surrey]; untraced		Gibson Letters, 2 May 1829
89.	1825–1829	Unidentified young woman	m	YCBA B 1980.35	S	
90.	?1830	A Greek girl		[Ilam Hall, Staffs]; untraced		*Gunnis* 1968, 173
91.	1825–1830	Helen of Troy	m	VAM A.25-1950 Other versions: Derby City Art Gallery Art Gallery of New South Wales Walker, Liverpool, ex Phillips coll	S	*Read* 1992, 21, 53, cat 22 (repr); *Bilbey* 2002, 272 (repr)
92.	c1835	Ideal female head	m	Cecil Higgins Art Gallery, Bedford		www.cecilghigginsartgallery.org
93.	c1840	A woman	m	Sotheby, 2–3 Nov 1989, lot 104	S	C Lib (sale cat cuttings)
94.	c1840	Sir Charles Eastlake, PRA	m	[coll Sir Charles Eastlake]; NPG, Bodelwyddan	S	*Ormond* 1973, 155 (repr 296)
95.	1842	Grazia	m	Manchester CAG 1979.538 Other versions: VAM 1149-1882, SD 1843, marble Royal Coll RCIN 31171, SD 1843, marble Royal Coll RCIN 2019, SD 1843, plaster RA Coll, plaster	SD	*Eastlake* 1870, 95–7, 252; *Matthews* 1911, 205–10, f212, 246 (repr); *Bilbey* 2002, 273 (repr)
96.	1848	Queen Victoria	m	[Liverpool Town Hall, Lancs]; Walker, Liverpool Other versions: plaster cast, VAM	S	*British Portraits* 1956–7, 163; *Ormond* 1973, 486; C Lib (repr)
97.	1848–1850	Queen Victoria	m	Russell-Cotes AG, Bournemouth, Dorset	S	*Bills* 2001, cat 1 (repr)
98.	1851	Countess Fitzwilliam		[Wentworth Woodhouse, W R Yorks]; private coll		RG/JP, 4, 596
99.	by 1851	Queen Victoria	m	Royal Coll, RCIN 69064		JM
100.	1853	Luisa – A Woman of the Sabines	p	RA colls	S	*Eastlake* 1870, 252; *Matthews* 1911, f212, 246 (repr)
101.	1857	Elizabeth, Duchess of Wellington	m	[Apsley House, London]; Stratfield Saye, Hants (?)	SD	*Matthews* 1911, 192–4, 246; *British Portraits* 1956–7, 141; *Gunnis* 1968, 173; C Lib (repr)
102.	1861	Sir Charles Lyell		Private coll, Scotland		*Eastlake* 1870, 252; *Matthews* 1911, 228, 246; C Lib (repr)
103.	1862	Anna Brownell Jameson	m	NPG, Bodelwyddan	S	*Cooper* 1971, 85 (repr); *Ormond* 1973, 240 (repr)
104.	1863	Alexandra, Princess of Wales	m	Buckingham Palace, London RCIN 2078 Other versions: RA colls, plaster RCIN 2023 s	SD	*Graves* III, 1905–6, 230; *Matthews* 1911, 230–2, 146 (repr); *British Portraits* 1956–7, 163
105.	1864	Edith Margaret Mozley	m	[coll Edith Mozley]; VAM A.15-1968 Other versions: RA colls, small plaster, painted to imitate terracotta	S	*Bilbey* 2002, 274 (repr)
106.	nd	Aurora	m	YCBA B 1978.5	S	C Lib (repr)
107.	nd	Catherine, Countess Beauchamp (Hon Mrs Murray)		Stanford Hall, Northants		C Lib (repr)
108.	nd	Edward, 1st Viscount Cardwell	m	Colnaghi, London (1986)	S	*Eastlake* 1870, 252; *Matthews* 1911, 246; *The British Face* 1986, 138–9 (repr)
109.	nd	Flora		[Mr Rogers; sold Christie, 2 May 1871]; untraced		*Gunnis* 1968, 173
110.	nd	General Burnaby	m	Leicester Museum		RG/JP, 4, 597
111.	nd	Girl, after statue of 'Nymph untying her sandal'		Walker, Liverpool Other versions: ex coll Elhanan Bicknell, of Herne Hill, sold 25/4/1863, lot 137 (bt Agnew) Walker, Liverpool 7508 Sotheby, London, 20 May 1994, lot 92 (repr) Huntingdon, LA		Walker, Annual Report, vols II–IV, 1971–4, 31
112.	nd	James Dundas of Ochtertyre	m	Signet Library, Edinburgh		RG/JP, 4, 597
113.	nd	John Howard Galton	m	Birmingham MAG, inv 147'38	S	*Silber* 1987, 46–7, cat 131 (repr)
114.	nd	John Lloyd Wynne		[Corwen, Merioneth]; untraced		*Eastlake* 1870, 252; *Matthews* 1911, 246
115.	nd	Joseph Strutt		Untraced		*Silber* 1987, 92, cat no 288
116.	nd	Lilah Clifden	p	RA colls (Gibson bequest)		
117.	nd	Mr and Mrs Henry Sandbach		[Hafodunos Hall, Denbighs]; private coll		*Eastlake* 1870, 252; *Matthews* 1911, f106, 246 (repr)
118.	nd	Mrs Mainwaring		Untraced		*Eastlake* 1870, 252; *Matthews* 1911, 246
119.	nd	Naiad		Christie, London, 11 Dec 1978	S	C Lib (repr)
120.	nd	Prince Duleep Singh	m	Kyburg Ltd, London (1988)	S	*Eastlake* 1870, 252; *Matthews* 1911, 225, 246

No.	Date	Subject	Medium	Location		Literary references
121.	nd	The young Augustus	m	Walker, Liverpool		*Matthews* 1911, 246; *Gunnis* 1968, 173
122.	nd	Unidentified man		Michael Hall Fine Arts Inc (1985)	S	C Lib (repr)
123.	nd	Venus	m	Exhib Fine Art Soc, London (1992)		*Read* 1992, 20, 53, cat 21 (repr)
124.	nd	Victoria of Albano		Untraced		*Eastlake* 1870, 252; *Matthews* 1911, 246
125.	nd	Viscountess Clifden		Untraced Other versions: plaster, RA colls, inscribed 'Lilah Clifden'		*Eastlake* 1870, 252; *Matthews* 1911, 229, 246
126.	nd	William Bewick	m	Tate Britain, London, inv TO 6866	S	C Lib (repr)
Chimneypieces						
127.	c1816	With 'two female figures in alto-rilievo' (perhaps identical to 135)		[for Sir John Gladstone]; probably at Fasque House, Kincardine		*Eastlake* 1870, 39–40
128.	c1821	Overmantel reliefs		Wentworth Woodhouse, W R Yorks, marble saloon		Pevsner, *Yorks: W R*, 1967, 542
129.	1852	With a flat slab representing 'The Fall of Phaeton'		[for Lord Fitzwilliam]; untraced		CSC, *Journal*, Nov 1852, 101–2
Reliefs						
130.	1810	'Alexander the Great ordering the works of Homer to be placed in the sarcophagus of Achilles'	tc	Hornby Library, William Brown Street, Liverpool, Lancs	SD	*Cavanagh* 1997, 251–2 (repr); *Morris and Roberts* 1998, 254
131.	1811	Psyche	m	[Exhib Liverpool Ac, 161]; untraced		*Morris and Roberts* 1998, 254
132.	1813	William Roscoe, portrait medallion	tc	BM, London Other versions: replicated	SD	*Dawson* 1999, 176–9 (repr); *Morris and Roberts* 1998, 254
133.	1816	Psyche carried by zephyrs		[Exhib RA, London, 937]; untraced		*Graves* III, 1905–6, 230; *Matthews* 1911, 31, 35, 243; *JKB* 2006, 181
134.	?1822–1823	Hero and Leander Payment(s): £200	m	Chatsworth, Derbys, sculpture gallery Other versions: RA colls, plaster		*Graves* III, 1905–6, 230; *JKB* 1972 (3), 329, 331
135.	1826	The hours and the horses of the sun; Phaeton driving the chariot of the sun Model(s): RA colls, plaster (both subjects)		Wentworth Woodhouse, W R Yorks Other versions: NMW, Cardiff, S, marble (Phaeton)		*Graves* III, 1905–6, 230; *Matthews* 1911, 139–42, 243; *Gunnis* 1968, 173
136.	†1833	Sarah Byron Model(s): relief of the husband mourning his dying wife with his child in his arms, RA, London, plaster (Gibson bequest)	p	Darnsbury, Warrington, Cheshire	S	
137.	1833	Unidentified subject		[Exhib Carlisle Acad, 256]; untraced		*Carlisle Ac Exhibs*, 1973
138.	1839	Venus and Cupid	m	VAM A.22-1963 Other versions: RA colls, marble, S RA colls, plaster, S Hafodunos Hall, Denbighs	S	*Graves* III, 1905–6, 230; *Cooper* 1971, 88, 90 (repr); *Bilbey* 2002, 272 (repr)
139.	1840	Amalthea nursing the infant Jupiter	m	[Castle Howard, NR Yorks]; untraced Other versions: RA colls, plaster		*Eastlake* 1870, 253; *Matthews* 1911, 243; *Gunnis* 1968, 173
140.	1840	Eteocles and Polynices, Jocasta intervening Model(s): RA colls, plaster	p	[Exhib RA, London, 1084]; untraced		*Matthews* 1911, 201–3, 243; *Graves* III, 1905–6, 230; *Morris and Roberts* 1998, 254
141.	1841	Eros and Anteros struggling for the soul Model(s): plaster relief, RA colls		[coll Lady Davy]; untraced		*Eastlake* 1870, 101–3, 253; *Matthews* 1911, 244; AL/RG
142.	1841	Oenone deserted by Paris		[Wentworth Hall (Surrey?)]; untraced		*Eastlake* 1870, 110–1; *Matthews* 1911, 244
143.	1841	Unidentified subject, described in *The Athenaeum* as 'a mother holding a drinking cup to the lips of her child'	m	[Exhib RA, London, 1231]; untraced		*The Athenaeum* 1841, p 406; *Graves* III, 1905–6, 230
144.	c1854	Cupid pursuing Psyche Drawing(s): HMI 18/1992	m	[Hafodunos Hall, Denbighs]; Walker, Liverpool, acc 7272 Other versions: Duke of Northumberland Miss Webb RA colls, marble	S	*Eastlake* 1870, 253; *Matthews* 1911, 243; *Friedman* 1993, 13, 91, cat no 19 (repr); *Taylor* 1999, 22; Walker, Liverpool, *Annual Report*, vol I, 1970, 15–16
145.	1861	Lady Mary C Stanhope, portrait medallion		Untraced		*Matthews* 1911, 228
146.	1862–1864	Christ blessing little children		[Hafodunos Hall, Denbighs]; Walker, Liverpool, acc 7273 Other versions: RA colls, plaster	S	*Eastlake* 1870, 238–9, 253; *Matthews* 1911, 228–9, 237, 244 (repr); *Gunnis* 1968, 173; Walker, Liverpool, *Annual Report*, vol I, 1970–1, 16

147.	nd	'Birth of Venus – received by persuasion'; Cupid wounding Sappho (?); Love between beauty and fortune; Hippolytus (?); Venus and Cupid appearing to Sappho to console her; love and idleness (?) Model(s): Venus and Cupid / Sappho, RA colls, plaster; Birth of Venus, RA colls, plaster	p	RA colls		*Eastlake*, 1870, 255;
148.	nd	Cupid and Psyche (Cupid and Psyche embracing)	m	[coll Mrs Huskisson]; untraced Other versions: RA colls, marble, s	S	*Eastlake* 1870, 253; *Matthews* 1911, f48, 243 (repr)
149.	nd	Cupid and Psyche (Cupid and Psyche seated on a couch)	m	Royal Coll (1845), RCIN 41062	S	C Lib (repr)
150.	nd	Juno conducting Hypnos to Jupiter		[Windsor Castle]; Royal Coll (?)		*Eastlake* 1870, 253; *Matthews* 1911, 243
151.	nd	Marriage of Psyche and celestial love Drawing(s): RA, London		Windsor Castle		*Eastlake* 1870, 253; *Matthews* 1911, 243
152.	nd	Minerva bringing Pegasus to Bellerophon		[coll C S Dickens Esq]; Private coll, London Other versions: RA colls, plaster		*Eastlake* 1870, 253; *Matthews* 1911, 244
153.	nd	Psyche receiving nectar from Hebe in the presence of celestial love Model(s): RA colls, plaster		[Wentworth Hall (Surrey ?)]; untraced		*Matthews* 1911, f94, 244 (repr)
154.	nd	Several	p	Hafodunos, Denbys		Pevsner, *Clwyd*, 1986, 218
155.	nd	Wounded amazon and horse		[coll Mrs Huskisson]; untraced Other versions: RA colls, plaster		*Eastlake* 1870, 253; *Matthews* 1911, 243
156.	nd	Zephyrus and Psyche		Untraced Other versions: RA colls, plaster		*Eastlake* 1870, 253
Miscellaneous						
157.	1801	'Model of a chimaera' Payment(s): £5 5s		[for Thomas Hope]; untraced		Flaxman Account Book 1794–1810, 74
158.	1810	Psyche (perhaps a drawing)		[Exhib Liverpool Ac, 189]; untraced		*Morris and Roberts* 1998, 254
159.	1811	Holy family (perhaps a drawing)		[Exhib Liverpool Ac, 228]; untraced		*Morris and Roberts* 1998, 254
160.	1811	Pomona (perhaps a drawing)		[Exhib Liverpool Ac, 158]; untraced		*Morris and Roberts* 1998, 254
161.	1812	Design from the story of Bestia (perhaps a drawing)		[Exhib Liverpool Ac, 200]; untraced		*Morris and Roberts* 1998, 254
162.	1812	Portrait of a young lady (perhaps a drawing)		[Exhib Liverpool Ac, 282]; untraced		*Morris and Roberts* 1998, 254
163.	1813	A bacchante diverting the attention of a tiger with her cymbals (perhaps a drawing)		[Exhib Liverpool Ac, 309]; untraced		*Morris and Roberts* 1998, 254
164.	1813	'Come, seize your prey, ye ministers of pain!' (perhaps a drawing)		[Exhib Liverpool Ac, 278]; untraced		*Morris and Roberts* 1998, 254
165.	1814	Mercules mad (perhaps a drawing)		[Exhib Liverpool Ac, 291]; untraced		*Morris and Roberts* 1998, 254
166.	pre-1817	'Theseus combating a centaur by the elder Gibson, (now at Rome), modelled in Mr. Nollikens's study'	tc	Untraced		Nollekens sale (2), lot 53
167.	1833	Cupid blindfolded		[Exhib Carlisle Acad, 271]; untraced		*Carlisle Ac Exhibs*, 1973
168.	nd	Head of a horse	m	Birmingham MAG, inv 146'38		*Silber* 1987, 46, cat no 130

GIBSON, Solomon, of Liverpool 1796–1866

A younger brother of **John Gibson**, Solomon was born near Conway, North Wales, a few years before his family moved to Liverpool. Few details have emerged of his early life but it is possible that he began his career working for **Samuel and Thomas Franceys of Liverpool** with his brother John. He exhibited for the first time in 1812, showing four works at the Liverpool Academy, including a terracotta statuette of *Venus lamenting the death of Adonis*, the only one of the four known to have survived (**22, 27, 28, 29**). In 1813 he showed a seated figure of *Mercury* (**21**). This was admired by the portrait painter Sir Thomas Lawrence who, when he was presented with a copy of the figure, sent the sculptor a £10 note 'as an encouragement'. Lord Colborn later bought a bronze cast of the statuette as the 'the work of an unknown genius' and was much surprised when John Gibson told him that it was, in fact, by his brother (DNB).

Gibson was working independently by 1816, the year the Liverpool street directories listed him as an artist for the first time, residing at 69 Islington. In 1818 he lived at 1 Green Lane, Pleasant Street and he changed address several times before settling in 1826 at 1 Hanley Street, where for the first time the directories described him as a sculptor rather than an artist. In 1817 he carved a marble relief depicting *Charity leading blind children to the tomb of their patron* for the Royal School for the Blind in Liverpool to commemorate Pudsey Dawson, a philanthropist and former mayor (**4**). Another locally important commission was the monument to Dr Barrow, who had died heroically during a typhoid outbreak (**5**). He also executed a few portrait busts, including one of Dr Thomas Trail, a physician well known as a promoter of the arts in Liverpool (**26**). However, Gibson never really fulfilled his early promise. Much of his career was spent in designing and executing modest neoclassical funeral monuments for churches in Liverpool and the surrounding counties and he exhibited only sporadically, showing works at the Liverpool Academy and the

Academy of the Liverpool Royal Institution in 1812–14, 1822, 1824 and 1830 and at the Royal Academy in 1816 and 1822. *The kaleidoscope* reviewed the Liverpool Exhibition of 1830–1 and noted 'Mr Solomon Gibson has favoured the Exhibition with only two specimens since his return from Italy' (vol 11, 110).

For many years he was financially dependent on John Gibson, whose work he defended at least twice in the Press. In 1834 he sent an anonymous letter to *The Times* headed 'Statue of the Late Huskisson', in which he complained of the inadequacy of the mausoleum designed by John Forster, the Liverpool architect, to house John's statue of Huskisson, which he described as 'a roundhouse for the temporary confinement of trespassers' (3 Dec 1834, 3). Solomon had himself submitted a design 'founded on the tomb of Lysicrates at Athens' (*ibid*). He took to the Press in his own name in 1853 in a dispute with Sir Archibald Alison over a claim that John had originally been commissioned to provide a statue of the Duke of Wellington for Glasgow, a work executed by **Carlo Marochetti** (*North British Mail*, 25 Jan 1853).

He was also a classical scholar and had a good knowledge of ancient Welsh literature. He visited his brother in Rome between 1826 and 1830. There he produced a plan for the restoration of Trajan's Forum, which 'showed great research and knowledge' but was 'very defective in drawing and perspective' (*Lit Gaz*, 1819, 649, cited by *Gunnis* 1968 174). In 1835 he was elected a member of the Liverpool Literary and Philosophical Society, where he delivered papers on a remarkably diverse range of subjects. He also belonged to the Liverpool Polytechnic Society. In 1848 he designed a silver cradle for Joseph Mayer, the Liverpool silversmith and antiquary, which was presented to Mrs Horsfall, the mayor's wife, on the birth of her daughter and exhibited at the Great Exhibition in 1851.

Solomon died at 117, Rue de Lafayette, Paris on 24 January 1866 on his way to Rome to see John Gibson, who was also going through his final illness. The Royal Academy claimed and won Solomon's estate on 22 January on the grounds that he had died before his brother John and that they were entitled to the money. He seems to have been a rudderless character: in a lost manuscript memoir of the sculptor, Joseph Mayer wrote, 'There was an absence of purpose in the direction of his studies, and he passed through life a strange and useless though not commonplace man' (DNB). John Gibson apparently thought him quite mad.

Eric Foster/EH

Literary References: *Liverpool Directories* 1816, 1818, 1826; *Eastlake* 1870, *passim*; *DNB*; *Gunnis* 1968, 173–4; *ODNB* (Stevens)

Additional MS Sources: *Gibson/Ellis*

Wills and Administrations: PPR admin, 22 March 1866, effects under £600

Miscellaneous Drawings: study of a head, after Raphael, VAM P&D (pressmark K.5.b)

Portraits of the Sculptor: T Griffiths (*ODNB*)

Funerary Monuments

No.	Date	Subject		Location		References
1.	1814	Monumental design		[Exhib Liverpool Ac, 299]; untraced		*Morris and Roberts* 1998, 254
2.	†1814	Rev Archibald McDonald		St Peter RC, Seel St, Liverpool, Lancs	S	Pevsner, *Lancs: S*, 1969, 154
3.	†1816	Rev William Tarleton		St Peter RC, Seel St, Liverpool, Lancs	S	Pevsner, *Lancs: S*, 1969, 154
4.	1817	Pudsey Dawson (†1816) Payment(s): £126		[Royal School for the Blind, Liverpool, Lancs]; destroyed		*Morris and Roberts* 1998, 254; *ODNB*
5.	?1819	Dr Barrow		[St Nicholas, Liverpool, Lancs]; destroyed		*Morris and Roberts* 1998, 254; *ODNB*
6.	†1820	Mary Ann Congreve		St Nicholas, Burton, Cheshire	S	Pevsner, *Cheshire*, 1971, 122
7.	?1822	Charles Morrall		Dudleston, Salop	S	*Gunnis* 1968, 174
8.	1822	Design for a monument		[Exhib ALRI, Liverpool, 173]; untraced		*Morris and Roberts* 1998, 254
9.	?1824	Rev Hope Eyton		Mold, Flint	S	*Gunnis* 1968, 174
10.	†1824	Thomas Aldersey		St Boniface, Bunbury, Cheshire	S	inf. Eric Foster
11.	†1825	General Charles Cotesworth Pinckney		St Michael, Charleston, South Carolina, USA	S	*Gunnis* 1968, 174; *Hershey* 1970, 805 (repr)
12.	?1825	Mrs Ann Edwardes		Dudleston, Salop	S	*Gunnis* 1968, 174
13.	†1825	Scrope Colquitt		Childwall, Lancs	S	*Gunnis* 1968, 174
14.	?1825	William Challnor		Dudleston, Salop	S	*Gunnis* 1968, 174
15.	?1826	Mary Hilton		Dudleston, Salop	S	*Gunnis* 1968, 174
16.	1830	Design for a monument		[Exhib ALRI, Liverpool, 278]; untraced		*Morris and Roberts* 1998, 255
17.	†1830	John Hughes		Llanfair Dyffryn, Denbighs	S	Pevsner, *Clwyd*, 1986, 207
18.	1830	Monumental figure		[Exhib ALRI, Liverpool, 240];		*Morris and Roberts* 1998, 255
19.	?1844	Dr John Davies		Mallwyd, Montgomery	S	*Gunnis* 1968, 174
20.	nd	Jacob Aemelius Irving		St James, St James's Place, Liverpool, Lancs	S	inf. Eric Foster

Statues

No.	Date	Subject		Location		References
21.	c1812	Mercury, statuette		[Exhib Liverpool Ac, 1813, 311]; untraced Other versions: several copies, including one presented to Sir Thomas Lawrence; untraced Merseyside Maritime Museum, Liverpool, acc 11.3.1.L, Herculaneum Pottery earthenware Birmingham MAG, inv 416'35, pl, 1815 tc model sent to Henry Ellis at the BM, 1826; untraced		BL Ad MS 4132 fol 47; *Graves* III, 1905–6, 232; *Gunnis* 1968, 173; *Silber* 1987, 44, cat 129; *Morris and Roberts* 1998, 254
22.	1812	Venus lamenting the death of Adonis, statuette	tc	Walker, Liverpool		*Grove* 12, 1996, 599; *Morris and Roberts* 1998, 254

Busts

No.	Date	Subject		Location		References
23.	1822	J Rosson	m	[Exhib RA, London, 1037]; untraced		*Graves* III, 1905–6, 232; *Gunnis* 1968, 174
24.	1822	Miss Traill		[Exhib ALRI, Liverpool, 187]; untraced		*Morris and Roberts* 1998, 254
25.	1824	A druid		[Exhib ALRI, Liverpool, 182]; untraced		*Morris and Roberts* 1998, 254
26.	1824	Dr T S Traill		[Exhib ALRI, Liverpool, 171]; untraced		*Morris and Roberts* 1998, 254

Miscellaneous

27.	1812	Cupid and Psyche	[Exhib Liverpool Ac, 260]; untraced	*Morris and Roberts* 1998, 254
28.	1812	Venus consoling Sappho	[Exhib Liverpool Ac, 330]; untraced	*Morris and Roberts* 1998, 254
29.	1813	The disconsolate widow, model	[Exhib Liverpool Ac]; untraced	inf. Eric Foster
30.	1822	Resignation – 'Thy will be done'	[Exhib ALRI, Liverpool, 174]; untraced	*Morris and Roberts* 1998, 254
31.	1824	Design for a national monument in memory of Princess Charlotte	[Exhib ALRI, Liverpool, 195]; untraced	*Morris and Roberts* 1998, 254

GIBSON, William fl 1763

A carver of 'Warner-Street, Coldbath-fields' (*Mortimer* 1763, 11).

GIFFORD, Lord fl *c*1822–62

He may be George Hay, Earl of Gifford (1822–1862), who married Caroline Norton's sister in 1862.

Busts

1.	nd	Caroline, Lady Stirling-Maxwell (Caroline Norton) as a young woman	m	Stirling Maxwell Coll, Pollok House, Glasgow, Lanarks E.80.1977.7	*Ormond* 1973, 433

GILBERT, Daniel, of Stamford 1795/1800–1862

He married at St John, Stamford in 1818 and in 1841 was living in Tinwell Road, where he also had a workshop. His stock in trade was sold after his death in 1862.

Literary References: *Stamford Mercury*, 26 September 1862

Archival References: RG/JP, 4, 598v.

Funerary Monuments

1.	†1823	Joseph Percy		St Mary, Stamford, Lincs	S	
2.	†1826	William Kilner Scott		All Saints, Stamford, Lincs	S	Pevsner, *Lincs*, 1989, 691
3.	†1828	John Lawson		St Martin, Stamford, Lincs	S	Pevsner, *Lincs*, 1989, 693
4.	†1829	James McGuffog		St Mary, Stamford, Lincs	S	
5.	†1829	William Allen		St Mary, Stamford, Lincs	S	
6.	†1840	Mary McGuffog		St Mary, Stamford, Lincs	S	
7.	†1845	Mary (†1842) and Thomas John Davis		St Mary, Stamford, Lincs	S	
8.	†1847	Chamberlin White		St John, Stamford, Lincs	S	
9.	†1847	Irving family member	sl	St John, Stamford, Lincs	S	

GILBERT, Henry, of Stamford fl 1827–48

He was the son of John Gilbert. In 1827 he advertised as sculptor and marble mason in Haymarket, Broad Street, Stamford, at which time he exhibited his copy of **L F Roubiliac**'s bust of Sir Isaac Newton (2). He provided a polished marble slab for Apethorpe Hall, Northants in 1848.

Archival References: RG/JP, 4, 598v.

Statues

1.	1845	Lions for the bridge	s	Burghley House, Leics	Burghley Estate Office Account Book, Northants RO, W (A) X 2898; Pevsner, *Beds, Hunts & Peterborough*, 1968, 225

Busts

2.	1827	Sir Isaac Newton, after Roubiliac		Untraced	RG/JP, 4, 598v.

GILBERT, John fl 1732–67

The son of William Gilbert of Shadwell, Middx, he was apprenticed to John Sutton, citizen and joiner, for 7 years on 4 January 1732, becoming free of the Joiners' Company on 6 February 1738. He executed a great deal of carving for the Mansion House (1). On 6 July 1749 he submitted his first estimate of £1,844 16s against **James Gayfer**'s estimate of £1,900, for carved decoration on the principal floor. These both exceeded the architect George Dance's estimate and so were dismissed. Fresh proposals were submitted by Gilbert, Thomas Darby, Henry Branson and John Preston on 19 July 1749 and Gilbert secured the contract with his estimate of £1,665. The contracts for the decoration of the second and third storeys were also awarded to Gilbert, on 19 June 1751, priced at £1,500. He undertook to finish the work by the following summer, with a penalty of £300 for late completion. Work was virtually complete by the autumn of 1752 and the final account was settled in October 1754. Examples of his work include the fine carved profile heads with festoons, acanthus foliage and drops in the passage room.

He may be identified with 'John Gilbert, carver' who, in 1756, received payments of £67 3s and £86 1s for work at East India House, Leadenhall Street, London and with 'J Gilbert' who carried out carving at Croome Court in 1767 (**2, 3**). A John Gilbert is described by Dossie in 1764 as a 'carver and gilder, of Mount street', the year he won a premium from the Society of Arts (4). He was also listed in Mortimer's *Universal Director* of 1763 (p 11).

Literary References: *Dossie* 1782, 438; *Archer* 1965, 405; *Jeffrey* 1993, 113–5, 140, 301 (repr 103)

Architectural Sculpture

1.	1732–1754	Decorative carving	Mansion House, City of London	*Jeffrey* 1993, 113–5, 140, 301 (repr 103)
2.	1756	Unidentified work	[East India House, Leadenhall Street, London]; untraced	*Archer* 1965, 405
3.	1767	Unidentified carving	[Croome Court, Worcs]; untraced	*Beard* 1993, 93

Miscellaneous

4.	1764	Model of ornaments in clay	[Soc of A premium, 3 gns]; untraced	RSA *Minutes*, 1763–64, seq 3 f 84; RSA *Premiums*, 1762, 37

GILBERT, John and Henry, of Stamford and Cambridge fl 1802–49?

The Gilbert family were masons in Lincolnshire in the 18th century. **John Gilbert** (1774–1839) was at Stamford by 1802, when his daughter was christened at St Martin's. In 1807 he advertised that he had moved from Deeping

St James and had worked for **George Sparrow**. He set up his own establishment in Beast Market [Broad Street] as a marble mason, making monuments and chimneypieces. By 1825 he was in Cambridge, where he died in Brunswick Place. He was succeeded in the business by his son, **Henry Gilbert**, who carved the later tablets, but Gunnis notes that 'neither of them produced any outstanding work'.

Literary References: *Stamford Mercury*, 9 Oct 1807, 16 Aug 1822, 1 March 1839; *Cambridge Chronicle*, 1 July 1825; *Gunnis* 1968, 174

Archival References: Stamford Hall Books; RG/JP, 4, 598v; JP, Misc Corr

Funerary Monuments

1.	?1811	Rev Humphrey and Miss Hyde	Dowsby, Lincs		RG/JP, 4, 599
2.	?1812	Sally Mounsay	Greystock, Cumberland		*Gunnis* 1968, 174
3.	?1816	Mary Graham	Belton, Rutland		*Gunnis* 1968, 174
4.	?1822	John Bailey	Thorney, Cambs		*Gunnis* 1968, 174
5.	†1822	Susanna Paillet	Yaxley, Hunts	S	*Gunnis* 1968, 174
6.	?1824	John and Hannah Robinson	Surfleet, Lincs		RG/JP, 4, 600
7.	?1824	Mary Hurrell	Newton, Cambs	S	*Gunnis* 1968, 174
8.	?1824	Mrs Bonney	Kingscliffe, Northants		*Gunnis* 1968, 174
9.	?1824	Rev Stephen Wright	Castor, Northants		*Gunnis* 1968, 174
10.	?1824	William Belgrave	Preston, Rutland		*Gunnis* 1968, 174
11.	?1825	Charles Harrison	Holbeach, Lincs		RG/JP, 4, 600
12.	?1826	Josiah Neale	St Clement, Cambridge	S	*Gunnis* 1968, 174
13.	?1827	Rev Richard Lucas	Great Casterton, Rutland		*Gunnis* 1968, 174
14.	?1828	Rev Thomas Kerrich	Dersingham, Norfolk	S	*Gunnis* 1968, 174
15.	?1837	Joseph Phillips	St Martin, Stamford, Lincs		*Gunnis* 1968, 174
16.	?1849	Charles Harrison	Surfleet, Lincs		RG/JP, 4, 600

GILES, of Wakefield fl 1834?

Funerary Monuments

1.	?1834	Samuel Haxley	Brotherton, W R Yorks	S	*Gunnis* 1968, 174

GILL, John, of London fl 1808

In 1808 he provided a chimneypiece for the Marquess of Bute's villa at Petersham, then being built under the direction of Robert Mylne (**1**). In the same year he received £113 for marble chimney-pieces for the Bank of England (**2**). Three years later he was one of the principal masons building Mr Coutts's house in Stratton Street, Piccadilly (Coutts Bank Archives, cited by *Gunnis* 1968, 174).

Chimneypieces

1.	1808	Description unavailable Payment(s): £41		[Marquess of Bute's villa, Petersham, Surrey]; untraced	GPC citing Journals of Robert Mylne, poss Miss J Mylne
2.	1808	Several Payment(s): £49 18s and £77 10s	m	[Bank of England, London]; destroyed	Soane bank acct, vol 8, fols 10 & 64–5; *Gunnis* 1968, 174

GILLIAM, John fl 1776–98

Gilliam supplied a number of chimneypieces for Clumber Park (**1, 2**). As the junior partner of **John Deval II** he was employed on building work at Somerset House between 1776 and 1794, and after Devall's death in 1794, with **Thomas Wood**. Gilliam also worked extensively on his own account at Somerset House (**3–8**). In 1782 he was the master-mason building the Fleet Prison, where he received a total sum of £2,211 (PRO, AO 1/2495, cited by *Gunnis* 1968, 174).

There were a number of other masons called Gilliam, including some in Lincolnshire. A William Gilliam, of Welburn, was apprenticed to his father, Thomas Gilliam, mason, in 1718. Joseph Gilliam, an assistant to **William Atkins**, was sent down to Ashburnham Place, Sussex, in 1761 to set up a chimney-piece made by his master (Ashburnham Archives, cited by *Gunnis* 1968, 174).

Literary References: *Gunnis* 1968, 174

Archival References: Clumber Archives, Nottingham Univ, bundle 274, in GPC; Shide Ledger, Somerset House, RIBA CHA/3/1/2 box 6 (1777); 3/1/8 (1780); box 6, 3/3, box 8 (1790)

Chimneypieces

1.	1775	'marble chimneypiece in the Great Dining Room' Payment(s): £208 Drawing(s): VAM P&D	m	[Clumber Park, Notts]; Buxted Park, Uckfield, Sussex, dining room	*Gunnis* 1968, 174
2.	1775–1777	Several		[Clumber Park, Notts]; untraced	Clumber archives, bundles 272–80
3.	1780	Several, supplied with paving sink stones &c		Somerset House, London, Strand side building	Chambers/Somerset House, box 6, CHA 3/1/8 fo 176
4.	1786	Several		Somerset House, London	Shide Ledgers
5.	1790	Portland stone		Somerset House, Strand, houses of 2nd, 3rd and 4th Commissioners of the Navy	Chambers/Somerset Hse, box 8, CHA 3/3, fo 179
6.	1790	Portland stone, supplied with paving		Somerset House, London	Shide Ledgers

Architectural Sculpture

7.	1777	3 ox skulls and drapery to back of keystones Payment(s): £4 12s		Somerset House, London, vestibule	Chambers/Somerset Hse, box 6, CHA 3/1/2, fo 54
8.	1777	38 moulded trusses to windows, with rich shells enriched into bean pods & roses in centre of scrolls Payment(s): £8 10s		Somerset House, London, principal floor	Chambers/Somerset Hse, box 6, CHA 3/1/2, fo 75

GILLINGHAM, James, of Winchester fl 1814–38

Funerary Monuments

1.	?1814	Chaloner Ogle	Winchester Cathedral, Hants	S	*Gunnis* 1968, 174–5
2.	?1835	John Terry	Dummer, Hants	S	*Gunnis* 1968, 175
3.	?1838	Sarah Wickham	Wonston, Hants	S	*Gunnis* 1968, 175

GINN, John 1813–

He was 17 in 1830 and living at Holywell Street, Millbank, when he entered the Royal Academy Schools on the recommendation of John Constable RA. In the same year he won a medal from the Society of Arts for a model of a bust from life (**2**). He exhibited at the Academy in 1832 and 1833, and showed a bust of Lord Brougham at the Suffolk Street Galleries in 1833 (**3**).

Literary References: RA Admissions; RSA, *Transactions*, vol 48, 1831, xxiii; *Gunnis* 1968, 175

No.	Date	Subject	Material	Location	Signed	References
Statues						
1.	1833	Adam and Eve		[Exhib RA, London, 1217]; untraced		*Graves* III, 1905–6, 244
Busts						
2.	1830	Unidentified subject, model		[Soc of A, large silver medal]; untraced		RSA *Transactions*, vol 48, 1831, xxiii
3.	1833	Lord Brougham		[Exhib Soc of BA, London, 824]; untraced		*Johnson* 1975, 180
4.	1833	Unidentified gentleman		[Exhib RA, London, 1118]; untraced		*Graves* III, 1905–6, 244
Miscellaneous						
5.	1832	Psyche borne by Zephyrs		[Exhib RA, London, 1203]; untraced		*Graves* III, 1905–6, 244

GLAZELEY, Joseph fl 1775

No.	Date	Subject	Material	Location	Signed	References
Architectural Sculpture						
1.	1775	Pelican in her piety, altarpiece	wd	S Michael Cornhill, City of London		Pevsner, *London: City*, 1997, 250

GLOCK fl 1800

No.	Date	Subject	Material	Location	Signed	References
Funerary Monuments						
1.	†1800	Elizabeth Skrine (†1800) and Elizabeth, her daughter (†1800)	m	St Thomas the Apostle, Lymington, Hants	S	

GOBLET, Lewis Alexander 1764–

He attended the Royal Academy Schools in 1792, won a medal in 1794 (**8**), and then became an assistant to **Joseph Nollekens.** He remained with Nollekens as his principal carver until his master's death in 1823, and perhaps did not long outlive him. J T Smith states that Goblet carved 'the whole of the figures' for the monument to Mrs Coke at Tittleshall, Norfolk (**3**). This has a full-length effigy in relief, leaning on a column with an elegant twisted pose, while an angel, borne aloft by clouds, gestures heavenwards. A *putto* seated at Mrs Coke's feet holds up a flaming heart symbolising her husband's enduring love. Goblet also executed the figure of *Religion* from Nollekens's design for the monument to Mrs Howard at Wetheral, Cumberland (**1**) and he cut busts from Nollekens's models. J T Smith later commented that although Nollekens received 120 guineas for each version of his bust of William Pitt the Younger he paid Goblet, **Sebastian Gahagan** and another assistant as little as £24 for carving them (**11**). During the last months of Nollekens's life Goblet slept in his house so that he could be 'at all times ready, night and day, to render him every assistance in his power' and he was present at the sculptor's deathbed (*Smith* 1920, II, 16). In his will Nollekens left Goblet all the working tools and marbles in his yard, and Goblet's children Henry and Louisa were bequeathed £100 and £30 respectively. Several of Goblet's works were auctioned in the sale of Nollekens's effects which took place on 3 July 1823 (**19, 44, 45**).

Goblet also carved busts and monuments in his own right and exhibited at the RA between 1799 and 1822, from various London addresses. Gunnis suggests that he may have had a studio of his own at one time, since his address was given as 20, Upper Marylebone Street in a London directory of 1809.

Literary References: *Smith* 1920, *passim*; *Gunnis* 1968, 175; *Whinney* 1971, 155–157; *Penny* 1977 (1), 11, 54; *Dawson* 1999, 50, 55

No.	Date	Subject	Material	Location	Signed	References
Funerary Monuments						
1.	1803	Religion, part of the monument to Hon Maria Howard of Corby (†1789), working as assistant to Joseph Nollekens		Wetheral, Cumberland		*Smith* 1920, II, 15 n2; *Whinney* 1971, 155 (repr); *Bilbey* 2002, 104
2.	?1804	Rev J Boucher		Epsom, Surrey	S	*Gunnis* 1968, 175
3.	1805	Jane Coke (†1800), working as an assistant to Joseph Nollekens Drawing(s): VAM E.4358-1900		Tittleshall, Norfolk		*Smith* 1920, II, 15 nl; *Physick* 1969, 150–1 (repr); *Penny* 1977 (1), 54, 56 (repr)
4.	1816	'Affection decorating a tomb with the emblems of grief, a monumental figure'		[Exhib RA, London, 968]; untraced		*Graves* III, 1905–6, 252
5.	?1818	Dr Charles Burney		St Paul, Deptford, London	S	*Graves* III, 1905–6, 252; *Gunnis* 1968, 175
6.	1818	Rev Charles Burney		Westminster Abbey, London, nave Other versions: St Paul, Deptford, London, plaster, S, 1818		*Gunnis* 1968, 175; *Dawson* 1999, 55
7.	1819	Monumental tablet to the memory of Princess Charlotte (designed by Miss Byam)		[Exhib RA, London, 1062]; untraced		*Graves* 1875, 217; *Graves* III, 1905–6, 252
Statues						
8.	1794	Academy figure, model		[RA silver medal]; untraced		RA Premium list
Busts						
9.	1802	Unidentified artist		[Exhib RA, London, 1057]; untraced		*Graves* III, 1905–6, 252
10.	1802	Unidentified child		[Exhib RA, London, 1055]; untraced		*Graves* III, 1905–6, 252
11.	c1806	William Pitt the Younger, working as assistant to Joseph Nollekens		Untraced		*Smith* 1920, I, 370–1
12.	1807	'The gentleman who first obtained the sixpences for the debtors in Ipswich gaol'		[Exhib RA, London, 1018]; untraced		*Graves* III, 1905–6, 252
13.	1808	Madame Catalini		[Exhib RA, London, 996]; untraced		*Graves* III, 1905–6, 252
14.	1808	Mr Violet		[Exhib RA, London, 891]; untraced		*Graves* III, 1905–6, 252

15.	1811	Henry Goblet		[Exhib RA, London, 907]; untraced		*Graves* III, 1905–6, 252
16.	1811	The sculptor's daughter		[Exhib RA, London, 910]; untraced		*Graves* III, 1905–6, 252
17.	1812	Mr Giani		[Exhib RA, London, 919]; untraced		*Graves* III, 1905–6, 252
18.	1814	Unidentified child		[Exhib RA, London, 754]; untraced		*Graves* III, 1905–6, 252
19.	1814	Unidentified gentleman		[Exhib RA, London, 759]; untraced		*Graves* III, 1905–6, 252
20.	1816	Joseph Nollekens		[Exhib RA, London, 945]; untraced		*Graves* III, 1905–6, 252
21.	1817	Charles, 11th Duke of Norfolk (?)		[Exhib RA, London, 1039]; untraced		*Graves* III, 1905–6, 252
22.	1818	J L Blackmore		[Exhib RA, London, 1040]; untraced		*Graves* III, 1905–6, 252
23.	1818	Mr Lonsdale RA		[Exhib RA, London, 1083]; untraced		*Graves* III, 1905–6, 252
24.	1818	Rt Hon Mr Ponsonby		[Exhib RA, London, 1041]; untraced		*Graves* III, 1905–6, 252
25.	1818	Unidentified male sitter	m	Untraced	SD	*The British Face* 1986, 130–1 (repr)
26.	1818	W C Chambers		[Exhib RA, London, 1059]; untraced		*Graves* III, 1905–6, 252
27.	1820	Angelica Catalani	m	NPG 5039	SD	
28.	1820	Jas Pulham		[Exhib RA, London, 1014]; untraced		*Graves* III, 1905–6, 252
29.	1820	P Violet		[Exhib RA, London, 1037]; untraced		*Graves* III, 1905–6, 252
30.	1821	Joseph Nollekens Model(s): plaster, SD 1821, loaned to Ashm 1971	m	VAM A.70-1965 Other versions: exhib RA, London, 1822, 1041; untraced exhib Soc of BA, London, 1826, 740; untraced		*Whinney* 1971, 156–7 (repr); *Johnson* 1975, 183
31.	nd	Joseph Nollekens		[Nollekens sale, Christie, 4 July 1823, lot 112]; untraced		*Gunnis* 1968, 175
32.	nd	Unidentified woman		[Sotheby, 17 April 1980, lot 279]; untraced		RG/JP, suppl 2
Miscellaneous						
33.	1799	Flora		[Exhib RA, London, 1062]; untraced		*Graves* III, 1905–6, 252
34.	1800	A Bacchus		[Exhib RA, London, 1008]; untraced		*Graves* III, 1905–6, 252
35.	1801	Eloisa receiving the news of Abelard's misfortune		[Exhib RA, London, 1029]; untraced		*Graves* III, 1905–6, 252
36.	1804	Cupid trying his dart	p	[Exhib RA, London, 930]; untraced		*Graves* 1875, 217; *Graves* III, 1905–6, 252
37.	1805	Miss Hume		[Exhib RA, London, 707]; untraced		*Graves* III, 1905–6, 252
38.	1805	Unidentified gentleman		[Exhib RA, London, 708]; untraced		*Graves* III, 1905–6, 252
39.	1806	Unidentified subject, a sketch		[Exhib RA, London, 878]; untraced		*Graves* III, 1905–6, 252
40.	1808	Admiral Lord Nelson, model	tc	[Exhib BI, London, 144]; untraced		*Graves* 1875, 217
41.	1809	Bacchus pressing a bunch of grapes, model		[Exhib BI, London, 342]; untraced		*Graves* 1875, 217
42.	1821	Mrs Connelly		[Exhib RA, London, 1161]; untraced		*Graves* III, 1905–6, 252
43.	1821	Temptation		[Exhib RA, London, 1089]; untraced		*Graves* III, 1905–6, 252
44.	nd	A fawn		[Nollekens sale, Christie, 4 July 1823]; untraced		*Gunnis* 1968, 175
45.	nd	Joseph and Potiphar's wife		[Nollekens sale, Christie, 4 July 1823]; untraced		*Gunnis* 1968, 175

GODDARD, F fl 1840

The Rev F Goddard carved the 'very fine' font at Clyffe Pypard.

Literary References: Pevsner, *Wilts*, 1975, 182

Architectural Sculpture

1.	1840	Font	Clyffe Pypard, Wilts	Pevsner, *Wilts*, 1975, 182

GODDARD, James, of Kings Lynn fl 1801–23

On 17 June 1801 he advertised for workmen and apprentices in the *Bury Post*. In the same newspaper he announced in 1802 that he had opened another yard at Watton. His wife, Frances, died in 1823, aged 30.

Literary References: *Gunnis* 1968, 175

Archival References: GPC

Funerary Monuments

1.	?1794	Elizabeth Postlethwaite	Dersingham, Norfolk	S	*Gunnis* 1968, 175
2.	?1822	Rev William Atkinson	Hillington, Norfolk	S	*Gunnis* 1968, 175

GODFREY, William I, of Abingdon fl 1756–59

He was apprenticed to Gilbert Burgess of Oxford and became a freeman of that city in 1756. In 1759 he was paid £22 by University College for the monument to their benefactor, Sir Simon Benet (1).

Literary References: GPC, citing Oxford City Archives and University College Archives

Funerary Monuments

1.	1759	Sir Simon Bennet Payment(s): £22	Beachampton, Bucks	GPC

GODFREY, William II, of Abingdon fl 1800–42?

Probably the son or grandson of **William Godfrey I**. He signs a number of tablets in Berkshire.

Literary References: *Gunnis* 1968, 175

Funerary Monuments

1.	?1800	Mary Anthony	Appleton, Berks	S	*Gunnis* 1968, 175
2.	?1801	Robert Sellwood	Appleton, Berks	S	*Gunnis* 1968, 175
3.	?1811	Bernard Bedwell	St Helen, Abingdon, Berks	S	*Gunnis* 1968, 175
4.	?1820	Thomas Lintall	St Helen, Abingdon, Berks	S	*Gunnis* 1968, 175
5.	?1836	Thomas Humfrey	Blewberry, Berks	S	*Gunnis* 1968, 175
6.	?1842	Charles King	St Helen, Abingdon, Berks	S	*Gunnis* 1968, 175

GOLDEN, John, of Holborn fl 1760–1805

Golden was apprenticed to William Halfpenny, of St George the Martyr, mason in 1760 (PRO, IR 22/151, in GPC). In 1781 he carried out repairs to Mr Wood's house in Red Lion Square (Archives, Lord Brownlow, cited by *Gunnis* 1968, 175). Gunnis notes that his monuments are executed in coloured marbles and frequently have charming

Adamesque details. His yard was in Upper North Place, Gray's Inn Road. A tradecard of 1781, with a draped female figure pointing at a scroll, gives the information 'IN GOLDEN/MASON/and/STATUARY/no 97 High Holborn' (Banks 106.3).

Literary References: *Gunnis* 1968, 175

Funerary Monuments

1.	?1778	Joseph Fitch		St Thomas, Kingston, Jamaica	S	RG/JP, 4, 603
2.	†1780	Thomas Allen		St Mary-at-Finchley, London	S	GPC
3.	?1781	Henry Doughty		Mapledurham, Oxon	S	*Gunnis* 1968, 175
4.	†1781	John Williamson Drawing(s): Norwich RO, bound volume presented by Walter Rye		Finningham, Suffolk	S	Pevsner, *Suffolk*, 1974, 213; GPC
5.	†1784	John Badcock		Paul, Cornwall	S	Pevsner, *Cornwall*, 1970, 131
6.	?1785	John Bates		Beaconsfield, Bucks	S	*Gunnis* 1968, 175
7.	†1790	John and Anne Denne		St Mary, Watford, Herts	S	Pevsner, *Herts*, 1977, 386
8.	?1790	John Carpenter		Watford, Herts	S	*Gunnis* 1968, 175
9.	†1796	Joseph Brooke		Southfleet, Kent	S	Pevsner, *Kent: W & Weald*, 1976, 540
10.	†1805	Dorothea (†1793) and Sir Beversham Filmer	a	East Sutton, Kent	S	Pevsner, *Kent: W & Weald*, 1976, 270

GOLDSMITH, Mrs

For further information the reader is referred to *Pyke* 1973, 55–6 and *Pyke* 1981, 18.

GOODFELLOW, William fl 1705

He was paid £30 for carving the monument to Mrs Charles Fox in 1705 (1). He may have been related to 'Mr John Goodfellow Stone Cutter or Mason at Sarum' who appears to have assisted **Grinling Gibbons** with the monument to Lady Fox in the same church, receiving a payment in 1699 of £20 from Sir Stephen Fox 'on acctt of makeing a Monument for my Lady Fox Deceased'. A mason called Goodfellow was also employed in building Kingston Lacy, Dorset, during the 1660s.

Literary References: Pevsner, *Dorset*, 1972, 245; *Millar* 1995, 523, 528

Funerary Monuments

1.	1705	Mrs Charles Fox (†1704) Payment(s): £30	Farley, Wilts	*Millar* 1995, 523

GOODLIFF fl 1806?

Funerary Monuments

1.	?1806	Frances Pochin	Morcott, Rutland	S	*Gunnis* 1968, 175

GOODWILLIE, Thomas fl 1841

Funerary Monuments

1.	1841	Henry Geutzener	South Leith, Edinburgh, churchyard	Pevsner, *Edinburgh*, 1991, 458

GOODWIN, Robert I, of Stamford *c*1771–before 1844

Goodwin was one of a family of masons, several generations of whom were christened Robert. He was apprenticed to **John Haines** of Stamford. Later in life he became the landlord of the Masons' Arms, Scotgate, Stamford. His building works included Snowden's Hospital, 1822–1823. His son **Robert Goodwin II** was also a general mason. Another family member was James Goodwin, who died in 1803, aged 45.

Archival References: JP Misc Corr

Funerary Monuments

1.	?1796	Samuel Allen	St John, Stamford, Lincs	S	*Gunnis* 1968, 175

GOODWIN, Robert II, of Stamford 1799–1871

He was the son of **Robert Goodwin I** and was a general mason, like his father.

Archival References: JP Misc Corr

Funerary Monuments

1.	†1824	William Pears	s	Barnack, Northants	S	*Gunnis* 1968, 175
2.	†1845	Mary Harrison, headstone		St Martin, Stamford, Lincs	S	

GOOLD, of Swindon fl 1816?

Funerary Monuments

1.	?1816	Walter Brind	Liddington, Wilts	S	*Gunnis* 1968, 175

GORDON, John fl 1781

His tradecard for 1781 is listed under 'Sculptors and Masons', in the Banks Collection, BM 106.13.

GOSLING, B, of Bungay fl 1806

The *Norwich Mercury* of 5 April 1806 carried an advertisement stating that Benjamin Barnett had taken over the stock in trade of Mr B Gosling of Bungay and intended to continue his business providing 'Marble and Stone Chimney-pieces, Monuments, Tombes, Grave-stones, Barn Floors, &c. &c.'

GOSSET, Gideon 1707–85

For further information the reader is referred to *Pyke* 1973, 56

GOSSET, Isaac 1713–99

One of the most successful wax-modellers of the 18th century, Gosset was born on 3 May 1713, the son of Jean Gosset and Susanne D'Allain. He was descended from a family of Normandy Huguenots who had fled to Jersey at the time of the revocation of the Edict of Nantes and later settled in London. Vertue says that Gosset was brought up by his uncle, **Matthew Gosset**, in a house in Berwick Street, and he is thought to have trained the young man in carving and modelling. Isaac married Françoise Buisset on 17 December 1737. The first of their five children was born in 1743.

Gosset worked initially with his brother Gideon as a frame-carver, a business he continued to practice intermittently throughout his career. In 1774, presumably in this capacity, he was appointed 'Joyner of his Majesty's Privy Chamber'. He worked for many of the most notable painters of the day, including William Hogarth, Thomas Gainsborough and Allan Ramsay.

By the 1740s Gosset had begun to gain a reputation as a wax modeller and was producing profiles *ad vivum* of notable sitters including members of the Stanhope and Murray families (**1, 2**). In 1752 Vertue commented that the 'Ingenious' Gosset (a complimentary term repeated in his obituary) had popularised the art, as his skill 'has been so universally approvd on for likeness' (*Vertue* III, 160). By this date Gosset had already modelled the profiles of several members of the Royal Family (**10–13**) and other 'people of quality, learned men etc' (*Vertue* III, 160).

Gosset's working practice was to carve the portrait and then produce moulds from which he cast copies in a white or honey-coloured wax composition. The composition was thought by the *Gentleman's Magazine* to have been invented by Gosset himself and an advertisement for the sculptor's commemorative wax of General James Wolfe (**32**) suggests that the colour and texture were intended to be 'in imitation of ivory' (*Whitley* 1928, 2, 246–7). In 1752 Vertue recorded that the original models were offered at 4 guineas each and the copies at 1 guinea, and that they were 'sold all over the town and country' (*Vertue*, III, 160). By the 1760s, Gosset was sufficiently in demand to increase the price of the copies to £1 10s 6d.

His work was valued and utilised by his artistic peers. **Anne Seymour Damer** worked initially in wax, in imitation of Gosset. **Louis François Roubiliac** was sent Gosset's wax portrait of Thomas Winnington by relatives of the deceased who wanted a good likeness for a bust monument (**9**). In 1772 Gosset, who had modelled the subject, gave **Richard Hayward** advice on the physiognomy of Baron de Botetourt, for a statue at the House of Burgesses in Williamsburg, Virginia (**38**). A merchant from Virginia, John Norton, who was acting for the House in London, sent 4 copies of the wax portrait to notables of the House in 1772. Since they were small and relatively cheap, Gosset's works were used as gifts on other occasions, for instance by Thomas Hollis, who donated 13 portraits to the University of Leiden (**16–25**). These works show Gosset's skill in historical portraiture: Hollis, who was a noted Whig, chose to commission a series of British worthies who embodied his own commitment to civil and religious liberties.

Gosset showed at the Society of Artists, 1760–78. He was awarded a special exhibition by that Society in 1768, and became a director in 1772. He also exhibited at the Free Society in 1761, but appears not to have exhibited at the Royal Academy. Several of his models were adapted for reproduction by Wedgwood, including Princess Augusta (**121**), Frederick, Prince of Wales (**10**), William, Duke of Cumberland (**13**), George III, and Queen Charlotte (**126**). James Tassie reproduced Gosset's portrait of Professor Francis Hutcheson (**124**) in enamel paste.

He died in December 1799 at his home in Edward Street, Portman Square, where he had lived since 1774. He bequeathed £4,000 to his son, the Reverend Isaac Gosset, who was also made his sole executor and residuary legatee. His daughter, Elizabeth Ann, was granted an annuity and gifts of money were made to three French charities in London, including the French Hospital in Old Street, where Gosset had once been a director.

In its obituary, the *Gentleman's Magazine* commented that Gosset modelled portraits 'in the most exquisite manner' and was 'one of those ingenious men, so rarely met with, who are at the same time equally amiable and inoffensive' (*GM* vol 69, 1799, 1088). During his lifetime his work was admired by royalty and the nobility, and was noted and recommended by Vertue, Mrs Delany, Horace Walpole and the philosopher and historian David Hume.

Gosset's reputation remained high throughout the 19th century, and his works were bought, amongst others, by the writer and collector, Peter Cunningham. More recently, Gunnis, who was a keen collector of waxes, described Gosset as 'one of the best of the eighteenth-century wax-modellers'. Yet, apart from a family memoir, there is still no full-length notice of this very successful sculptor, whose skilful work in a cheap material forms an interesting case study in 18th-century aesthetics and commercial innovation.

MGS

Literary References: *HWC*, vol 12, 271; N&Q, vol 11, Jan 27 1855, 66; vol 6, 3rd series, Dec 24 1864, 516; *Gosset* 1888–91, 540–68; *DNB*; *Graves* 1907, 103–4; *Norton* 1937, 225–6, 245, 264–7; *Gunnis* 1968, 175–6; *Pyke* 1973, 56–58; *Pyke* 1981, 18–9; *Murdoch and Hebditch* 1985, 313–17; *Simon* 1994, 444–55; *Strien* 2000, 4–34

Portraits of the Sculptor: anon (?Jean Etienne Liotard), c1772, pastel, private coll, *Murdoch and Hebditch* 1985, 215, repr

Will: PROB 11/1334/46-7

Reliefs

1.	1745	Grisel, Countess Stanhope	w	Chevening, Kent		*Pyke* 1973, 57; *Murdoch and Hebditch* 1985, 216 (repr)
2.	1745	Grisel, Lady Murray	w	Chevening, Kent	D	*Pyke* 1973, 57; *Murdoch and Hebditch* 1985, 216 (repr)
3.	1745	Hon George Baillie	w	Chevening, Kent	D	*Murdoch and Hebditch* 1985, 216 (repr); *Pyke* 1973, 56
4.	1745	Hon Rachel Hamilton	w	Chevening, Kent	D	*Pyke* 1973, 57; *Murdoch and Hebditch* 1985, 216 (repr)
5.	1745	Lady Grizel Baillie	w	Chevening, Kent	D	*Pyke* 1973, 56; *Murdoch and Hebditch* 1985, 216 (repr)
6.	1745	Philip, 4th Earl of Chesterfield	w	Chevening, Kent	D	*Graves* 1907, 104; *Pyke* 1973, 57; *Murdoch and Hebditch* 1985, 216 (repr)
7.	1745	Rachel, Lady Binning	w	Chevening, Kent	D	*Pyke* 1973, 56; *Murdoch and Hebditch* 1985, 216 (repr)
8.	1745	Thomas, 7th Earl of Haddington	w	Chevening, Kent	D	*Pyke* 1973, 57; *Murdoch and Hebditch* 1985, 216 (repr)

No.	Date	Subject	Medium	Location	Literary references
9.	pre-1750	Thomas Winnington	w	[coll Henry Fox]; untraced	*Baker* 2000, 84
10.	?by 1752	Frederick, Prince of Wales (three)	w	Windsor Castle, library Other versions: ex-coll Horace Walpole, Strawberry Hill (sold Robins 14 May 1847, lot 81) VAM A.55-1970; A.30-1970 Northampton, Northants (Mrs IH Gosset) Sotheby, 2 June 1975, lot 136 and 15 Dec 1975, lot 1 reproduced by Wedgwood	*Vertue* III, 160; *Walpole* 1798–1825, vol 2, 432–3; *N&Q*, vol 6, 3rd series, 24 Dec, 1864, 516; *Gunnis* 1968, 176; *Pyke* 1973, 56, 58; *Pyke* 1981, 19; *Reilly* 1995, 206
11.	?by 1752	George, Prince of Wales (later King George III)	w	Windsor Castle, library	*Vertue* III, 160; *Gunnis* 1968, 176; *Pyke* 1973, 56;
12.	?by 1752	King George II (two)	w	Windsor Castle Other versions: VAM Cheltenham Art Gallery and Museum, Glos coll E J Pyke, London (1981) Sotheby, 2nd June 1975, lot 137; untraced	*Pyke* 1981, 19 *Vertue* III, 160; *Pyke* 1973, 56; *Pyke* 1981, 19
13.	?by 1752	William, Duke of Cumberland	w	Windsor Castle Other versions: VAM 414:1358-1885 coll R E Santo, Lisbon, Portugal Walters Art Gallery, Baltimore ex coll E J Pyke, London; untraced Cheltenham Art Gallery and Museum, Glos Toledo Museum of Lithophanes and Wax Miniatures	*Vertue* III, 160; *Gunnis* 1968, 176; *Pyke* 1973, 57
14.	1756	Thomas Hoadley, Bishop of Winchester	w	[Strawberry Hill, Twickenham, Middx]; untraced Other versions: ex coll Peter Cunningham (1864); untraced VAM A.105-1965 Sotheby, 15 Dec 1980	*Walpole* 1798–1825, vol 2, 432–3; *N&Q*, vol 6, 3rd series, 24 Dec 1864, 516; *DNB*; *Gunnis* 1968, 176; *Pyke* 1981, 19
15.	1757	Richard Trevor, Bishop of Durham	w	[coll George Montagu]; untraced	*DNB; HWC*, vol 9, 213
16.	1758	Algernon Sydney	w	[Presented to the University of Leiden by Thomas Hollis]; untraced	*Pyke* 1973, 57; *Strien* 2000, 16
17.	1758	Andrew Marvell	w	Academisch Historisch Museum der Rijksuniversiteit, Leiden	*Pyke* 1973, 57; *Strien* 2000, 12, 15 (repr)
18.	1758	Edmund Ludlow	w	Academisch Historisch Museum der Rijksuniversiteit, Leiden	*Pyke* 1973, 57; *Strien* 2000, 12, 14 (repr)
19.	1758	Francis Bacon, Lord Verulam	w	Academisch Historisch Museum der Rijksuniversiteit, Leiden	*Pyke* 1973, 57; *Strien* 2000, 12, 13 (repr)
20.	1758	George Buchanan	w	[Presented to the University of Leiden by Thomas Hollis]; untraced	*Pyke* 1973, 57; *Strien* 2000, 13, 16
21.	1758	Isaac Newton	w	Academisch Historisch Museum der Rijksuniversiteit, Leiden	*Pyke* 1973, 57; *Strien* 2000, 12, 14 (repr)
22.	1758	James Harrington	w	[Presented to the University of Leiden by Thomas Hollis]; untraced	*Pyke* 1973, 57; *Strien* 2000, 14, 16
23.	1758	John Locke	w	Academisch Historisch Museum der Rijksuniversiteit, Leiden	*Pyke* 1973, 57; *Strien* 2000, 12, 15 (repr)
24.	1758	John Milton	w	Academisch Historisch Museum der Rijksuniversiteit, Leiden Other versions: coll Mrs B Pratt, Frogmore, near Kingsbridge, Devon	*Pyke* 1973, 57; *Strien* 2000, 12 (repr)
25.	1758	John Wycliffe	w	Academisch Historisch Museum der Rijksuniversiteit, Leiden	*Pyke* 1973, 57; *Strien* 2000, 11, 12, 13 (repr)
26.	1758	Robert Boyle	w	[Presented to the University of Leiden by Thomas Hollis]; untraced	*Pyke* 1973, 57; *Strien* 2000, 13–14, 16
27.	1760	Field-Marshall Henry Seymour Conway	w	NPG 1757, London	*Gunnis* 1968, 176; *Pyke* 1973, 56
28.	1761	King George III, model	w	[Exhib Soc of Artists, London, 147]; untraced	*Graves* 1907, 103, 104
29.	1763	Miss Conyers and Miss Palmer Payment(s): 10 gns	w	Untraced	Newdigate archives, CR 136/B2645a&b (bill); *Gunnis* 1968, 176
30.	1764	Duchess of Atholl	w	Blair Castle, Perths	*Pearson* 1991, unpag
31.	c1765	Henry Pelham	w	[Uppark, Sussex]; destroyed	*Uppark* 1999, 23
32.	c1765	Major-General James Wolfe	w	[Uppark, Sussex]; destroyed Other versions: VAM Royal Ontario Museum, Toronto, Canada	*Pyke* 1973, 57, 58; *Uppark* 1999, 23
33.	1765	Portrait of a nobleman	w	[Exhib Soc of Artists, London, 174]; untraced	*Graves* 1907, 103
34.	c1765	Sophia, Lady Shelburne (1745–71)	w	Bowood, Wilts	*Gunnis* 1968, 176; *Pyke* 1973, 57; *Trusted* 1993, 193
35.	c1765	Thomas, 1st Duke of Newcastle Model(s): model in wax, exhib Soc of A, 1768, 149	w	[Uppark, Sussex]; destroyed Other versions: ex coll Trevor, Bishop of Durham, 1767, £1 11s 6d' untraced	*Gunnis* 1968, 176; *Uppark* 1999, 23

36.	1766	Lord Camden, model	w	[Exhib Soc of Artists, London, 205]; untraced		*Graves* 1907, 103
37.	1768	Sir Jeffery Amherst, model	w	[Exhib Soc of Artists, London, 150]; untraced		*Graves* 1907, 103
38.	pre-1770	Norborne, Baron de Botetourt (+1770)	w	Untraced Other versions: 4 copies made for members of the Williamsburg House of Burgesses, Virginia, USA, 1772; untraced		*Norton* 1937, 225–6, 245, 264–7
39.	1776	Jean-Jacques Rousseau	w	Untraced		*Pyke* 1973, 58
40.	c1776	Mrs Delany	w	Untraced		*Llanover* 1861, vol 2, 225; *DNB*; *Gunnis* 1968, 176
41.	1778	Bishop Hurd	w	Hartlebury Castle, Kidderminster, Worcs	D	*Gunnis* 1968, 176; *Pyke* 1973, 57
42.	1778	Portrait of a Prelate	w	[Exhib Soc of Artists, London, 301]; untraced		*Graves* 1907, 104
43.	1779	General Maclean	w	Buxted Park, Sussex		*Gunnis* 1968, 176
44.	nd	Anne, Princess of Orange	w	Colonial Williamsburg Foundation, Virginia		*Pyke* 1981, 18
45.	nd	Anne, Princess Royal	w	Stanton Harcourt, Oxon		*Pyke* 1973, 56
46.	nd	Apuleius	w	Dr H Gosset, Christchurch, New Zealand		*Pyke* 1973, 56
47.	nd	Aristophanes	w	Dr H Gosset, Christchurch, New Zealand		*Pyke* 1973, 56
48.	nd	Augustus, 3rd Duke of Grafton	w	Walters Art Gallery, Baltimore Other versions: Caroline Rogers, London		*Pyke* 1973, 56
49.	nd	Benjamin Franklin	w	American Philosophical Society, Philadelphia, USA		*Pyke* 1973, 56
50.	nd	Charles Townshend	w	[Strawberry Hill, Twickenham, Middx]; untraced Other versions: Cracow, Poland NPG 1756, London		*Walpole* 1798–1825, vol 2, 432–3; *N&Q*, vol 6, 3rd series, 24 Dec 1864, 516; *Gunnis* 1968, 176; *Pyke* 1973, 57; C Lib (repr)
51.	nd	Charles Yorke	w	Hartlebury Castle, Kidderminster, Worcs		*Gunnis* 1968, 176; *Pyke* 1973, 57
52.	nd	Col Frederick Clinton	w	Warnford Cottage, Thoralby, NR Yorks		*Pyke* 1981, 18
53.	nd	David Garrick	w	Untraced		*Gunnis* 1968, 176
54.	nd	Democritus	w	Dr H Gosset, Christchurch, New Zealand		*Pyke* 1973, 56
55.	nd	Diogenes	w	Dr H Gosset, Christchurch, New Zealand		*Pyke* 1973, 56
56.	nd	Dr Harris	w	Mrs I H Gosset, Northampton		*Pyke* 1973, 56
57.	nd	Dr Linné (two)	w	Mrs A E Hamill, Lake Forest, Illinois, USA		*Pyke* 1973, 56
58.	nd	Dr Walker	w	Mrs I H Gosset, Northampton		*Pyke* 1973, 56
59.	nd	Edward, Duke of York	w	Windsor Castle, library Other versions: coll R E Santo, Lisbon, Portugal		*Gunnis* 1968, 176; *Pyke* 1973, 56
60.	nd	Elizabeth Serecold	w	Mrs A E Hamill, Lake Forest, Illinois, USA		*Pyke* 1973, 56
61.	nd	Emperors Augustus, Claudius, Caligula, Tiberius, Domitian, Vitellius, Galba, Otho, Vespasian and Titus		New Zeland, dispersed Other versions: Christie, 5 Oct 1976, lot 28		*Gunnis* 1968, 176; *Pyke* 1973, 56, 57; *Pyke* 1981, 19
62.	nd	Epicurus	w	Dr H Gosset, Christchurch, New Zealand		*Pyke* 1973, 56
63.	nd	Farnese Hercules	w	[Strawberry Hill, Twickenham, Middx]; sold Robins 14th May 1847, lot 82; untraced		*Pyke* 1973, 58
64.	nd	Ferdinand, Duke of Brunswick	w	Windsor Castle, library		*Gunnis* 1968, 176; *Pyke* 1973, 56
65.	nd	Fisher Littleton	w	Hartlebury Castle, Kidderminster, Worcs		*Gunnis* 1968, 176; *Pyke* 1973, 57
66.	nd	Frederick Augustus, Bishop of Derry and 4th Earl of Bristol	w	Ickworth Park, Suffolk		*Gunnis* 1968, 176
67.	nd	Frederick-Augustus, Duke of York and Albany	w	Windsor Castle		*Pyke* 1973, 56
68.	nd	Frederick, Earl of Guilford	w	Dr H Gosset, Christchurch, New Zealand Other versions: coll R Margolis, Tolado, New Jersey Sotheby, 24 July 1976, lot 56		*Pyke* 1973, 56; *Pyke* 1981, 19
69.	nd	General Aratus	w	Christchurch, New Zealand (Dr H Gosset)		*Pyke* 1973, 56
70.	nd	General Pasquale Paoli	w	London (E J Pyke) Other versions: ex coll Miss D Gosset, Horsham, West Sussex		*Pyke* 1973, 57
71.	nd	General Sir John Ligonier	w	D Nicholas, Goring-on-Thames, Oxon		*Pyke* 1973, 57
72.	nd	George Edwards (reproduced by Wedgwood)	w	Untraced		*Reilly* 1995, 206
73.	nd	George Grenville	w	Untraced		*Gunnis* 1968, 176
74.	nd	George Selwyn	w	Untraced		*Gunnis* 1968, 176
75.	nd	George Townsend	w	Met NY		*Pyke* 1973, 57
76.	nd	Gideon Gosset	w	Mrs I H Gosset, Northampton		*Pyke* 1973, 56
77.	nd	'Greek philosopher and writer'	w	Christie, 5 Oct 1976, lot 26; untraced		*Pyke* 1981, 19
78.	nd	Henry Hoare	w	Walters Art Gallery, Baltimore, USA		*Pyke* 1973, 57
79.	nd	?Henry Swinburne	w	Calne, Somerset (J R Hickish)		*Pyke* 1973, 57

80.	nd	Henry, 1st Baron Holland	w	VAM 414:1363-1885	*Pyke* 1973, 56
81.	nd	Heraclitus	w	Christchurch, New Zealand (Dr H Gosset)	*Pyke* 1973, 56
82.	nd	Hon Henry Cowper	w	Mrs B Pratt, Frogmore, near Kingsbridge, Devon	*Pyke* 1973, 56
83.	nd	Isaac Gosset jnr	w	VAM 414:1369-1885	*Pyke* 1973, 57
84.	nd	John Seldon	w	Academisch Historisch Museum der Rijksuniversiteit, Leiden	*Pyke* 1973, 57; *Strien* 2000, 12, 14 (repr)
85.	nd	John, 1st Earl Granville	w	Bowood House, Wilts	*Gunnis* 1968, 176; *Pyke* 1973, 57
86.	nd	John, 1st Earl Spencer	w	Althorp, Northants	*Pyke* 1973, 57
87.	nd	John, 3rd Duke of Rutland	w	Chicago A I	*Pyke* 1973, 57
88.	nd	John, Lord Willoughby de Broke	w	Met NY	*Pyke* 1973, 57
89.	nd	Julius Caesar	w	Mrs R Pinney, Canterbury, New Zealand	*Pyke* 1973, 56
90.	nd	King George I	w	Windsor Castle, library Other versions: VAM 414:1352-1885 Wedgwood Museum, Barlaston, Staffs	*Gunnis* 1968, 176; *Pyke* 1973, 56
91.	nd	?King George II	w	J Glanz, London	*Pyke* 1981, 19
92.	nd	King George II (as Prince of Wales)	w	VAM 414:1353-1885	*Vertue* III, 160; *Gunnis* 1968, 176; *Pyke* 1973, 56
93.	nd	King George III	w	Windsor Castle Other versions: VAM A.57-1970 coll Miss H Curwen, Chewton Mendip, Somerset coll Miss M Gosset, Newbury, Berks coll Mrs AE Hamill, Lake Forest, Illinois, USA coll CL Gosset, East Grinstead, West Sussex BM Delhom Gallery and Institute, Mint Museum of Art, Charlotte, North Carolina Christie, 24 June 1975, lot 1; untraced reproduced by Wedgwood	*Pyke* 1973, 56, 57; *Pyke* 1981, 18, 19; *Reilly* 1995, 206
94.	nd	?King George III		J Glanz, London	*Pyke* 1981, 19
95.	nd	King William IV (as Duke of Clarence)	w	C L Gosset, East Grinstead, West Sussex	*Pyke* 1973, 57; *Ormond* 1973, 515
96.	nd	King William IV, Prince of Orange	w	Windsor Castle Other versions: VAM A.53-1970	*Pyke* 1973, 56, 57
97.	nd	?Lady Dacre	w	Mrs B Pratt, Frogmore, near Kingsbridge, Devon	*Pyke* 1973, 56
98.	nd	Lady Mary Coke	w	[Strawberry Hill, Twickenham, Middx]; sold Robins 14 May 1847, lot 82; untraced	*Gunnis* 1968, 176
99.	nd	Lepidus	w	Dr H Gosset, Christchurch, New Zealand	*Pyke* 1973, 56
100.	nd	Livia	w	Dr H Gosset, Christchurch, New Zealand	*Pyke* 1973, 56
101.	nd	Lord Anson	w	J Glanz, London	*Pyke* 1981, 18
102.	nd	Lord Bathurst	w	Untraced	*Gunnis* 1968, 176
103.	nd	Lord George Manners	w	Chicago A I	*Pyke* 1973, 57
104.	nd	Lord Maynard	w	Untraced	*Gunnis* 1968, 176
105.	nd	Lord Thurlow	w	Dr H Gosset, Christchurch, New Zealand	*Pyke* 1973, 56
106.	nd	Louth, Bishop of London	w	Untraced	*Gunnis* 1968, 176
107.	nd	Marie Anne of Bavaria	w	VAM	*Pyke* 1973, 57
108.	nd	Marie Antoinette	w	Philadelphia Museum of Art, USA	*Pyke* 1973, 57
109.	nd	Mr Dean	w	sold Sotheby, 2 June 1975, lot 132; untraced	*Pyke* 1981, 19
110.	nd	Mr I Hunter	w	sold Christie, 24 June 1975, lot 2; untraced	*Pyke* 1981, 19
111.	nd	?Mr Summer	w	D Wyndham Payne, Sidmouth, Devon	*Pyke* 1973, 57
112.	nd	Mrs Hume	w	sold Sotheby, 1975, lot 137; untraced	*Pyke* 1981, 19
113.	nd	?Mrs Summer	w	D Wyndham Payne, Sidmouth, Devon	*Pyke* 1973, 57
114.	nd	Pompeia [?]	w	Dr H Gosset, Christchurch, New Zealand	*Pyke* 1973, 56
115.	nd	Pope Clement XIV	w	Windsor Castle Other versions: ex coll Lieutenant-Colonel H H E Gosset, Watlington, Oxon	*Pyke* 1973, 56
116.	nd	Pope Innocent XII	w	V J Murrell, London	*Pyke* 1981, 19
117.	nd	President Montesquieu	w	Untraced	*Pyke* 1973, 58
118.	nd	Prince Charles Edward Stuart	w	D Nicholas, Goring-on-Thames, Oxon	*Pyke* 1973, 57
119.	nd	Prince James Francis Edward Stuart	w	D Nicholas, Goring-on-Thames, Oxon	*Pyke* 1973, 57
120.	nd	Prince Octavius	w	Hartlebury Castle, Kidderminster, Worcs	*Gunnis* 1968, 176; *Pyke* 1973, 57
121.	nd	Princess Augusta of Saxe-Gotha	w	Windsor Castle, library Other versions: VAM 414:1356-1885 Mrs IH Gosset, Northampton, Northants Sotheby, 2 June 1975, lot 136 Sotheby, 15 Dec 1975, lot 1 Reproducted by Wedgwood	*Gunnis* 1968, 176; *Pyke* 1973, 56; *Reilly* 1995, 206; C Lib (VAM version repr)

122.	nd	Princess Charlotte	w	VAM A.70-1970 Other versions: coll Mr and Mrs Chapman-Purchase, Warnford Thoralby, Yorks Delhom Gallery and Institute, Mint Museum of Art, Charlotte, Carolina	*Pyke* 1973, 56; *Pyke* 1981, 18
123.	nd	Princess Sophia	w	VAM A.71-1970	*Pyke* 1973, 57; *Pyke* 1981, 19
124.	nd	Professor Francis Hutcheson	w	Untraced Other versions: reproduced in enamel paste by James Tassie	*DNB;* *Pyke* 1973, 58
125.	nd	Queen Caroline	w	VAM 414:1354-1885	*Gunnis* 1968, 176; *Pyke* 1973, 56
126.	nd	Queen Charlotte	w	VAM 414:1370-1885 Other versions: coll Miss M Gosset, Newbury, Berks coll C C Sellers, Carlisle, USA coll Mrs A E Hamill, Lake Forest, Illinois, USA, Reproduced by Wedgwood	*Pyke* 1973, 56; *Reilly* 1995, 206
127.	nd	Ralph Allen	w	Hartlebury Castle, Kidderminster, Worcs	*Gunnis* 1968, 176; *Pyke* 1973, 56; C Lib (repr)
128.	nd	Rev Isaac Gosset	w	Windsor Castle Other versions: coll Mrs I H Gosset, Northampton, Northants	*Pyke* 1973, 56
129.	nd	Rev Nicholas Hill	w	VAM A.40-1970	*Pyke* 1973, 57; *Pyke* 1981, 19
130.	nd	Several unidentified subjects Payment(s): average price, £1 each	w	Stourhead, Wilts, small drawing room	*Gunnis* 1968, 176 citing Stourhead archives
131.	nd	Sir Walter Raleigh	w	Academisch Historisch Museum der Rijksuniversiteit, Leiden	*Pyke* 1973, 57; *Strien* 2000, 12 (repr)
132.	nd	The Duke of Sussex	w	Untraced	*Gunnis* 1968, 176
133.	nd	Thomas Townshend		Untraced	*Gunnis* 1968, 176
134.	nd	Tonton (Mme Duffand's dog)		Lewis Walpole Library, Conn, USA	*Pyke* 1981, 19
135.	nd	Unidentified divine	w	[Sotheby, 24th July 1978, lot 55]; untraced	*Pyke* 1981, 19
136.	nd	Unidentified female subject	w	Chicago A I	*Pyke* 1973, 57
137.	nd	Unidentified female subject	w	Jersey Museum	*Pyke* 1973, 57
138.	nd	Unidentified female subject	w	J Glanz, London	*Pyke* 1981, 19
139.	nd	Unidentified male subject	w	Dr H Gosset, Christchurch, New Zealand	*Pyke* 1973, 56
140.	nd	Unidentified male subject	w	VAM A.66-1970	*Pyke* 1973, 57; *Pyke* 1981, 19
141.	nd	Unidentified male subject	w	Westerham, Kent	*Pyke* 1973, 57
142.	nd	Unidentified male subject	w	Mrs C A H Gosset, Jamaica	*Pyke* 1973, 57
143.	nd	Unidentified male subject	w	Jersey Museum	*Pyke* 1973, 57
144.	nd	Unidentified male subject	w	Colonial Williamsburg Foundation, Virginia	*Pyke* 1981, 19
145.	nd	Unidentified male subject	w	[Sotheby, 24 July 1978, lot 55]; untraced	*Pyke* 1981, 19
146.	nd	Unidentified male subjects (three)	w	Mrs B Pratt, Frogmore, near Kingsbridge, Devon	*Pyke* 1973, 57
147.	nd	Unspecified male subject	w	J Glanz, London	*Pyke* 1981, 19
148.	nd	?William Pitt, 1st Earl Chatham	w	Dr H Gosset, Christchurch, New Zealand	*Pyke* 1973, 56
149.	nd	William Pitt, 1st Earl of Chatham	w	VAM 414:1361-1885 Other versions: Chevening, Kent	*Pyke* 1973, 57
150.	nd	William Winn	w	Nostell Priory, W R Yorks	RG/JP, 4, 606
151.	nd	William, Lord Mansfield (two)	w	Hartlebury Castle, Kidderminster, Worcs	*DNB; Gunnis* 1968, 176; *Pyke* 1973, 57
152.	nd	Zeno	w	Dr H Gosset, Christchurch, New Zealand	*Pyke* 1973, 56

GOSSET, James fl 1736–63

In 1736 he made frames costing £25 and £35 for two paintings of Frederick, Prince of Wales by Jacopo Amigoni (GPC). Mortimer lists him as a 'Modeller of portraits in wax, and carver in wood. Berwick-street, Soho' (*Mortimer* 1763, 12).

GOSSET, Matthew 1683–1744

A sculptor, wax-modeller and picture frame maker, he was the uncle of **Isaac Gosset**. He was French by birth but fled with his family from Normandy and settled in England where he became naturalized. He married Jeanne Ester le Touzay in 1700 and they had one child, Angelique-Elizabeth, who was born on 10 May 1709. Gosset's yard was at St Anne's, Westminster where in 1714, he bound apprentice 'Rodney, son of Joseph Stone' (Apprenticeship Lists, TNA I.R.1/3).

In 1718 Lady Arabella Furnese noted in her account book a payment to Gosset of £10 for 'a frame for the fine picture' (2). The next recorded payment was to Sir Godfrey Kneller for portraits of herself and her husband, so the frame may have been for one of these. Gossett was employed by Earl Fitzwalter at Moulsham Hall, Essex, in 1732. His work there included 'a Carv'd frame for a marble table', 'a Large frame of a Table' and 'Two frames for my wife's and my picture at full length' (3).

Sir J Percival was probably referring to Matthew Gosset when he wrote in his diary for 13 March 1730, 'Today I went to see Mr Gosset's representation of ye Court of France in wax, as big as the life, and clothed in ye habits ye

Court of France wore last year, being given to him for that purpose. Nothing can be finer done or more like, tho' only the Duke of Bourbon's face was taken off in plaster of Paris. He was so content he gave Mr Gosset a complete suit and 80 Louis Dores' (BL Add MS 47061, cited by *Pyke* 1973, 59) (1). Four oval wax plaques which belonged to Augusta, the widow of Arthur Gosset RA, in the late-19th century were thought to be Matthew Gosset's work. They depicted *A Caledonian boar hunt, Perseus with Medusa's head, The wars of the Titans against the gods* and *Ganymede in the palace of Jupiter* and were 'beautifully finished' (*Gosset* 1888–91, 551).

Gosset was elected a member of the Spalding Society in 1728 and was later one of the Band of Pensioners of George II. He was buried in St Marylebone, where, according to the epitaph, his monument 'had on it a specimen of his work' (*Gosset* 1888–91, 545). In his will Gosset left bequests to his wife Esther, his brother Henry and his nephews Gideon and Isaac. A house on the east side of Berwick Street was part of his estate. Vertue later noted that Gosset was 'much esteemd for his works, casting in wax all sorts of small figures from Ivory – carvings – antient and modern, statues, busts, medallions etc by which he gaind a considerable fortune and dyd rich' (*Vertue*, III, 160).

Literary References: *Gosset* 1888–91, 540–68; *Gunnis* 1968, 176; *Pyke* 1973, 59; *Murdoch and Hebditch* 1985, 313–4; *ODNB* (Craske)

Archival References: GPC

Will: PROB 11/732 (29 March 1744)

Statues

1.	1730	Members of the French royal court	w	Untraced		*Pyke* 1973, 59

Architectural Sculpture

2.	1718	'a frame for the fine picture' Payment(s): £10		Untraced		Archives, Earl of Guildford, in GPC
3.	1731–1732	Various frames for tables and pictures		[Moulsham Hall, Essex]; untraced		Mildmay Accts, Hants RO 15M50/31, in GPC

Reliefs

4.	1730	A man wearing a foreign order (oval)	w	Walker, Liverpool	SD	Walker, Liverpool, *Annual Reports*, vols II–IV, 1971–4, 32
5.	1741	Queen Caroline	w	Museum of Art, Carnegie Institute, Pittsburgh, Pennsylvania, USA		*Pyke* 1973, 59
6.	nd	George II	w	Museum of Art, Carnegie Institute, Pittsburgh, Pennsylvania, USA		*Pyke* 1973, 59 (pl 114); *Pyke* 1981, 19
7.	nd	George II	w	Colonial Williamsburg Foundation, Virginia, USA		*Pyke* 1981, 19
8.	nd	King George I (reproduced by Wedgwood)	w	Untraced		*Reilly* 1995, 206
9.	nd	King George II (reproduced by Wedgwood)	w	Untraced		*Reilly* 1995, 206
10.	nd	Lord North (reproduced by Wedgwood)	w	Untraced		*Gunnis* 1968, 176; *Reilly* 1995, 206

GOTT, Joseph 1785?–1860

A sculptor best known for his work on a small scale, he spent much of his career in Rome catering for his compatriots' taste for portraiture and figures of animals. His work contrasts markedly with the austere neo-Greek works of his English contemporaries in the city, **John Gibson RA** and **R J Wyatt**.

Gott was born in London, the son of John Gott of 31 Ogle St, Marylebone, whose family came from Calverley near Leeds. His second cousin and foremost patron, Benjamin Gott, was a leading Yorkshire wool manufacturer. Joseph had some early schooling in Calverley, where he stayed with his paternal uncle Joseph Coates. He was apprenticed to **John Flaxman RA** in 1798, when he was 12. He left Flaxman in 1802 and entered the Royal Academy Schools on 29 March 1805, giving his profession as sculptor. The following year he won the RA silver medal for the best model of an *Academic figure* (**20**) and in 1808 the Society of Arts awarded him their greater silver palette for a plaster group, *Samson slaying the Philistines* (**159**). At this time he was living in Upper Norton Street, near Buckingham Street, Fitzroy Square, where Flaxman had his studio. Nothing is known of his activities in the decade from 1808, but he took a wife, Ann Maria, and their first daughter was born in the parish of St Giles, Camberwell in 1815. By 1819, he had moved to Lower Belgrave Place, Pimlico, where a second daughter was born in 1821. Eventually they had a son, Benjamin, whose lazy self-indulgence later caused his father considerable concern. In 1819 Gott won the RA gold medal for *Jacob wrestling with the angel* (**21**). Thereafter he became a regular exhibitor at the Academy, showing an eclectic range of works including ideas for monuments, statues of classical, biblical and Shakespearian subjects, animal groups, portrait busts and profile reliefs. Several of his early RA exhibition works appeared a year or so later at British Institution shows (**21, 24, 26, 28**).

Gott was helped at the outset of his career by the president of the Royal Academy, Sir Thomas Lawrence, who met him around 1820. Lawrence noticed his talent and in 1822 provided a pension so that Gott might travel with his family to Rome. He also gave Gott a letter of introduction to **Antonio Canova**, though Canova died before he could be of assistance. The Gott family stayed with the artist Joseph Severn at 18, Via Isidoro, where Mrs Gott took over the housekeeping, providing Severn with 'an english pudding every day' (*Friedman and Stevens*, 1972, 8). These comfortable domestic arrangements evidently suited Gott's temperament, for there is no evidence that he fraternised with the group of British sculptors frequenting the cafés of Rome. Gott and Severn together designed monuments for the poets John Keats (†1821) and Percy Byshe Shelley (†1822), neither of which appears to have been executed (**4, 5**).

Gott's first year in Rome was difficult for he had financial problems and contracted a fever which laid him low for several months. Lawrence again assisted him by recommending distinguished English tourists to visit his studio. Among the first were Elizabeth, Duchess of Devonshire and her step-son, the 6th Duke. The Duke, who was commissioning works for a sculpture gallery at Chatsworth, gave Gott an early lesson in the foibles of patrons. He went to the studio early in 1823, when the sculptor 'was not recover'd from the fever, consequently had only sketches to show him, of which he spoke very favourably . . . but he said it was an invariable rule not to order Sculpture unless finish'd' (Gott Letters, 27 February 1823, quoted by *Friedman and Stevens* 1972, 58). The patron's approach softened when he returned to Rome at the end of the year, and he commissioned a bust. Gott took it upon himself to make it a colossal head of a *Bacchante* (**126**) intending it to match a head of *Achilles* which **George Rennie** was making for Chatsworth. Gott also sold the Duke one of his first groups of hearthside animals, *A greyhound with her two puppies suckling* (**37**).

Gott's imagination was at its most fertile in his early Rome years. He appears to have been the only British sculptor in the city making terracotta models, many of which are likely to have been sold as independent works of art. He had difficulties in translating his small models into full-size marbles: in July 1822 he wrote to Lawrence that he was hiring a studio in the Via Gregoriana so that he might have space to translate a model of *Venus dissuading Adonis from the chase* to a full-size work (**30**). This failed to materialise and the studio was soon taken over by **Richard Westmacott III**. Another casualty in the translation process was an ambitious group, *The madness of Athamas*, a composition of at least 4 figures. The small model, which was later owned by Lawrence, was made in 1825 and was translated to a life-size working model and plaster cast, but had eventually to be abandoned (**68**).

Gott was particularly successful with his 'fancy' groups of children and animals, especially dogs, depicted in playful attitudes. Though inspired by Antique representations in the Vatican Museums, Gott's animals were clearly modelled from life for they show considerable knowledge of canine anatomy. The repertoire was broadened to include foxes and kittens (**92, 67**), and his groups combining animals and children enjoyed particular popularity. His masterpiece in this genre, a series of four reliefs of putti with goats and greyhounds, was commissioned for the dairy at Syon House (**144**).

Gott travelled frequently to England to meet his patrons, secure new commissions and supervise the installation of monuments. In 1827 he assembled one of his first memorials, to Mary Williams at Walton-on-Thames (**7**). He went on to Leeds to meet Benjamin Gott and to discuss a monument for Gott's sons, Benjamin and Henry (**14**), left unexecuted by Flaxman when he died in 1826. The two monuments are virtually identical, each having a seated mourning figure and a standing image of *Faith* holding a cross. Benjamin and Elizabeth Gott introduced the sculptor to their friends, the Banks, Fairfax and Ferrand families, all of whom followed Benjamin's example by giving him commissions (**9, 15, 50**). Over the next decade Joseph was to complete 24 well-characterised images of Gott family members, including a memorable group of young Benjamin Gott with an Italian greyhound (**54**), another of Margaret and Jane Gott as *Babes in the wood* (**57**), seated and standing statues of Benjamin Gott (**48, 112**) and also his monument, a naturalistic reclining image in contemporary dress, which was commissioned by the subject in 1827, 14 years before his death (**10**). The sculptor's series of profile medallion portraits of Gott family members in terracotta, plaster and marble, are particularly penetrating: he took pains to reproduce the elaborate hair styles paraded by his fashion-conscious patrons, but did not idealise their determined faces.

Returning to Rome in 1828, Gott took a studio at 155, Via Babuino, which he kept for the rest of his life. The early 1830s were his busiest years, with busts, fancy groups and several monuments in hand, principally for Yorkshire patrons. He was back in Leeds in 1833 to install the monument to Thomas Lloyd in Leeds Parish Church, a dignified military memorial with a portrait-bust and an inscription tablet flanked by two finely cut figures of officers in full regimentals (**12**). While in Yorkshire he received further commissions, including a monument to a Bradford philanthropist, William Sharp, which has a draped female carved in the round, leaning against a pedestal supporting Sharp's relief portrait (**13**). Gott was a confirmed supporter of exhibitions as a means of advertisement: on this visit he arranged to show several works, advertised as being for sale, at the Carlisle Academy (**65–67**) and exhibited 7 more at Royal Northern Society in Leeds (**69–73, 75, 76**).

He returned to Rome via Paris and was visited shortly afterwards by friends of the Benjamin Gotts, Mr and Mrs William Allan, who ordered four ideal subjects for Benjamin Gott (**78, 79, 81, 82**). These included a statue of a *Vintager* (**79**) which was dispatched from Rome in December 1837 with the intention of exhibiting it at the Royal Academy in the following spring, but was shipwrecked on its voyage to England.

Gott's period of great success ended abruptly around 1836; on 17 November 1838 he wrote to Benjamin Gott 'I have had no orders for two years past, but perhaps that has been owing to the Cholera few people having visited Rome' (Gott Letters, quoted by *Friedman and Stevens* 1972, 67). The epidemic had a terrible effect on his family, causing the death of two of his daughters and inevitably affecting his own work. The shock apparently made his wife lose her memory.

The sculptor visited England again in 1839, 1841, 1845 and 1847 and it was soon after this last-known visit that he took on his most ambitious achievement in funerary art, the monument to Colonel Edward Cheney of the Scots Greys (**19**). Cheney had died heroically at the battle of Waterloo after four horses had been killed under him. Gott chose to portray the moment when the Colonel's fifth horse sank beneath him with a bullet-wound in its throat.

His work was now less distinguished and he began to receive hostile criticism. A *dancing nymph*, exhibited at the Royal Academy in 1845 (**91**), was badly received and a letter to his daughter Ann, sent from Leeds on 24 August 1845, refers to bills and lawsuits. His last Academy submission, a *Mary Magdalene*, 1848, again drew unfavourable reports (**94**). He nonetheless showed a figure of *Ceres* at the Great Exhibition of 1851 (**96**) and *Ruth Gleaning* at the Paris Universal Exhibition in 1855 (**56**).

He died in Rome on 8 January 1860 and was buried in the Protestant Cemetery 'followed to his last home. . .by most of the English, and several of the foreign artists resident in Rome' (*Leeds Intelligencer*). Gott's obituary in the *Athenaeum* said, 'Every visitor to Rome, this half century past, has looked in at the studios of Mr Gott – no sculptor of genius, but one of grace, whose figures of rustics oftentimes combined with animals, pleased us better than furniture art, though not high sculpture'. Today he is particularly appreciated for his highly finished terra cotta figures and groups. They were made as studies for larger works in marble, often in the hope of obtaining commissions, but were also regarded as finished works of art in their own right.

Interest in Gott was revived in the 1970s as a result of a well-researched exhibition held in Leeds and Liverpool (*Friedman and Stevens* 1972). The catalogue, which includes much Gott correspondence from the years 1822 to 1849, is the most comprehensive source for the sculptor's work.

IR

Literary References: RSA, *Transactions*, vol 26, 1808, 18; *Graves* II, 1905–6, 279–80; *Gunnis* 1968, 176–8; *Friedman and Stevens* 1972; *JKB* 1972 (3), 327–9, 331; *Lovell* 1986, 177–221; *Grove* 13, 213 (Friedman); *Sicca and Yarrington* 2000, 16; *ODNB* (Friedman); IGI

Archival Material: HMI Archive (album of photographs of the Banks family, patrons of Gott, and their home, St Catherine's House, near Doncaster)

Funerary Monuments

1.	1820	'an idea of a monument to the memory of the late President of the Royal Academy', Benjamin West PRA		[Exhib RA, London, 1019]; untraced		*Graves* II, 1905–6, 279
2.	†1820	Lady Elizabeth, Lady Julia (†1812) and Lady Frances Percy (†1803)		Stanwick, N R Yorks	S	*Friedman and Stevens* 1972, 36
3.	1821	'idea of a monument' to the Duke of York		[Exhib RA, London, 1102]; untraced		*Graves* II, 1905–6, 280
4.	†1821	John Keats, design only (with Joseph Severn)		Probably not executed		*Friedman and Stevens* 1972, 43
5.	†1822	Percy Bysshe Shelley, design only (with Joseph Severn)		Probably not executed		*Friedman and Stevens* 1972, 43
6.	†1827	Esther and Anne (†1814) Smith		Puritan Chapel, Bramhope, Leeds, W R Yorks	S	*Friedman and Stevens* 1972, 36
7.	1827	Lady Mary Williams (†1824)		Walton-on-Thames, Surrey	SD	*Friedman and Stevens* 1972, 35
8.	c1827	William Ewart (†1825)		St James's Mortuary Chapel, Liverpool	SD	*Friedman and Stevens* 1972, 24 (repr)
9.	1830	Thomas and Mary Fairfax (†1828)		Gilling, N R Yorks	S	*Friedman and Stevens* 1972, 34, 35–36 (repr)
10.	1827–1831	Benjamin Gott (†1840)		[Armley Chapel, W R Yorks]; St Bartholomew, Armley	S	*Friedman and Stevens*, 1972, 18–19 (repr)
11.	†1833	Samuel (†1826) and Mary Hartley		Bradford Cathedral, W R Yorks	S	*Friedman and Stevens* 1972, 37
12.	1826–1834	Lt Col Thomas Lloyd (†1828)		St Peter, Leeds, W R Yorks	S	*Gunnis* 1968, 177; *Friedman and Stevens* 1972, 34, 36–37 (repr); Pullan 2006, 24 (repr)
13.	c1834	William Sharp (†1833)		Bradford Cathedral, W R Yorks		*Friedman and Stevens* 1972, 34, 37 (repr)
14.	1828–1835	Benjamin (†1817) and Henry Gott		[Armley Chapel, Leeds, W R Yorks]; St Bartholomew, Armley, W R Yorks	S	*Friedman and Stevens*, 1972, 18 (repr)
15.	†1835	Walker Ferrand		All Saints, Bingley, W R Yorks	S	*Friedman and Stevens* 1972, 37
16.	?1838	Design for a monument (perhaps to Elizabeth and Louisa Gott)	tc	Giuseppina Sgambati, by descent from the sculptor (1972)		*Friedman and Stevens* 1972, 43
17.	†1843	Emily Cadogan		Durham Cathedral		*Friedman and Stevens* 1972, 38
18.	†1847	Jonathan Akroyd		[All Souls' Mortuary Chapel, Halifax, W R Yorks]; destroyed		*Friedman and Stevens* 1972, 39
19.	1848	Colonel Edward Cheney (†1815)		[Gaddesby Hall, Leics]; St Luke, Gaddesby, Leics	S	*Gunnis* 1968, 177; *Friedman and Stevens* 1972, 34, 38 (repr); *Cavanagh* 2000, 51–3 (repr)

Statues

20.	1806	Academic figure		[RA, London, silver medal]; untraced		*Friedman and Stevens*, 1972, 12
21.	1819	Jacob wrestling with the angel, model		[Exhib RA, London, 1820, (1028), RA Gold Medal]; untraced		*Graves* 1875, 222; *Graves* II, 1905–6, 280; *Friedman and Stevens* 1972, 14
22.	1820	The dying Spartacus, group	p	SJSM M 1140	SD	*Graves* 1875, 222; *Graves* II, 1905–6, 280; *Friedman and Stevens* 1972, 14
23.	?post-1820	Three small nymphs carrying Cupid in triumph	m	[coll Brookeborough family, Brookeborough, Ireland]; LMG, W R Yorks 8/72	S	*Friedman and Stevens* 1972, 42–43 (repr); *Leeds* 1996, 6 (repr)
24.	1821	David rescuing the lamb from the lion, sketch		[Exhib RA, London, 1154]; untraced		*Graves* 1875, 222; *Graves* II, 1905–6, 280
25.	1821	Faun and nymph, sketch		[Exhib RA, London, 1103]; untraced		*Graves* II, 1905–6, 280
26.	1821	Sisyphus, sketch		[Exhib RA, London, 1124]; untraced		*Graves* 1875, 222; *Graves* II, 1905–6, 280
27.	1821	The babes in the wood, sketch		[Exhib RA, London, 1100]; untraced		*Graves* II, 1905–6, 280
28.	1821	The brazen age, sketch		[Exhib RA, London, 1124]; untraced		*Graves* 1875, 222; *Graves* II, 1905–6, 280
29.	1822	Fawn		[Exhib Free Soc, 339]; untraced		*Graves* 1875, 222
30.	c1822	Venus dissuading Adonis from the chase, statuette	tc	LMG, W R Yorks 23/70	S	*Graves* II, 1905–6, 280; *Leeds* 1996, 6 (repr)
31.	1823	Titania and the changeling boy, model	tc	Untraced		*Friedman and Stevens* 1972, 44
32.	1824	Bacchus with grapes, statuette	tc	Dick Coates (1972)	S	

No.	Date	Title	Mat	Location		Literary References
33.	1824	Sleeping Venus, model	tc	[Sir Thomas Lawrence; Lawrence sale, 1830, lot 370]; untraced		*Friedman and Stevens* 1972, 44
34.	1824	The penitent Magdalen, statuette	tc	LMG, W R Yorks 19/82		*Leeds* 1996, 6 (repr)
35.	1822–1824	Venus playing with Cupid	tc	Angela Mathias (1972) Other versions: Venus and Cupid, marble, nd, coll Guy Read (1972) Venus embracing Cupid, model, 1826, Julian, London, (1969)	S	*Friedman and Stevens* 1972, 40, 42, 45 (repr)
36.	c1824	Young Apollo		Untraced		*Friedman and Stevens* 1972, 44
37.	1824–1825	A greyhound with her two puppies suckling	m	Chatsworth, Derbys Other versions: smaller version sold Sotheby, 11 Dec 1986, lot 191 'A greyhound bitch with two puppies on a grassy mound' sold Sotheby, 27 June 1958, lot 21, bt Poynter	SD	*Friedman and Stevens* 1972, 49, 50, 51; *JKB* 1972 (3), 331
38.	1826	Diana with a greyhound	m	[coll Dr Nevinson, 1847]; Mrs John Wintersteen, USA	SD	*Friedman and Stevens* 1972, 45 (repr); *Read* 1982, 141
39.	by 1826	Girl with a basket		[coll Peter Norton of Soho Square, London]; untraced		*Friedman and Stevens* 1972, 45
40.	1826	Gleaner		[Exhib RA, London, 1053]; untraced		*Graves* II, 1905–6, 280; *Friedman and Stevens* 1972, 45
41.	1826	Group of dogs		[coll Mr Raine]; untraced		*Friedman and Stevens* 1972, 50
42.	1826	Sleeping nymph		[Exhib RA, London, 1052]; untraced Other versions: Exhib RA, London, 1838, 1261, marble		*Graves* II, 1905–6, 280; *Friedman and Stevens* 1972, 45, 47
43.	1827	Greyhound	m	LMG, W R Yorks 30/71	SD	*Friedman and Stevens* 1972, 49 (repr)
44.	1827	Musidora	m	Chatsworth, Derbys	SD	*Friedman and Stevens* 1972, 45–46; *JKB* 1972 (3), 331 (repr)
45.	c1827	Pastoral Apollo Model(s): LMG, W R Yorks 29/71, 1827, clay	m	[coll George Banks]; destroyed		*Friedman and Stevens* 1972, 32, 33; *Leeds* 1996, 7 (repr)
46.	1828	A pug dog and cat on a footstool with the Doria and Shrewsbury arms	m	[coll Earl of Shrewsbury, Alton Towers]; untraced		*Friedman and Stevens* 1972, 51
47.	c1828	An Italian greyhound and puppies, model		[First Exhib of Paintings and Sculpture by British Artists, New Assembly Rooms, Dumfries, Feb 1828 (253)]; untraced		*Friedman and Stevens* 1972, 50
48.	c1828	Benjamin Gott, seated	tc	Mr and Mrs John Gott (1972)	S	*Friedman and Stevens,* 1972, 19 (repr)
49.	1828	Elizabeth Goodman Banks seated, model	p	[coll George Banks]; LMG, W R Yorks 9/73	SD	*Friedman and Stevens* 1972, 32; *Leeds* 1996, 8 (repr)
50.	1827–1828	George Banks seated Model(s): Leeds Art Galls, 8/73 (1828)	m	[coll Banks family]; LMG, W R Yorks 3.1/28	S	*Friedman and Stevens* 1972, 32 (repr)
51.	?1828	Two Greek wrestlers, statuette	tc	City Art Gall and Museum, Nottingham	S	*Friedman and Stevens* 1972, 42 (repr)
52.	c1829	Young Forbes with a dog, model		[coll Mr Forbes]; untraced		*Friedman and Stevens* 1972, 53
53.	1830	A boy leaning on a footstool playing with an Italian greyhound, statuette	tc	Giuseppina Sgambati, by descent from the sculptor (1972)	SD	*Friedman and Stevens* 1972, 53
54.	1827–1830	Benjamin Gott with an Italian greyhound	m	[coll Mr and Mrs William Gott]; untraced		*Friedman and Stevens* 1972, 30
55.	1830	Devotion		[Exhib RA, London, 1172]; untraced		*Graves* II, 1905–6, 280; *Friedman and Stevens* 1972, 46
56.	c1830	Ruth gleaning		[coll Lord Francis Gower]; untraced Other versions: exhib Paris Universal Exhib, Exhibition, 1855 (class 29, Sculpture, 1133)		*Friedman and Stevens* 1972, 46 (repr)
57.	1829–1831	'Babes in the Wood', Margaret and Jane Gott Model(s): Leeds Museums and Galls 15/77 (1829)	m	Untraced		*Graves* II, 1905–6, 280; *Friedman and Stevens* 1972, 29–30
58.	1831	Boy and greyhound		[RA London, 1163]; untraced		*Friedman and Stevens* 1972, 53
59.	pre-1832	A bather, model		[coll Sir Thomas Lawrence PRA]; untraced		*Friedman and Stevens* 1972, 44; GPC
60.	by 1832	Boy and dog	m	Alnwick Castle, Northumbs Other versions: *Il Ragazzo e Cane*, 1860, ex coll Lord Prudhoe; M E A Hampton (1960)		*Friedman and Stevens* 1972, 11, 53–54
61.	c1832	Infant piety, statuette	tc	Giuseppina Sgambati, by descent from the sculptor		*Friedman and Stevens* 1972, 46 (repr)
62.	1827–1832	Little Red Riding Hood	tc	[coll Lord Francis Gower]; VAM A.30-1975	S	*Friedman and Stevens* 1972, 53; *Bilbey* 2002, 288–9 (repr)

63.	1832	Peasant boy feeding a rabbit	m	[coll Richard Vaughan Yates]; destroyed		*Gunnis* 1968, 177; *Friedman and Stevens* 1972, 52
64.	c1832	The deluge		[coll Matthieu Kessels]; untraced		*Friedman and Stevens* 1972, 46
65.	1833	Cupid	m	[Exhib Carlisle Acad, 253]; untraced		*Friedman and Stevens* 1972, 46
66.	1833	Dog and sandal		[Exhib Carlisle Acad, 255]; untraced		*Friedman and Stevens* 1972, 51
67.	1833	Kittens	m	[Exhib Carlisle Acad, 264]; untraced		*Friedman and Stevens* 1972, 51
68.	1825–1833	The madness of Athamas Model(s): 1st model, 1825, clay, ex coll Sir Thomas Lawrence; untraced	m	Untraced		Lawrence sale cat, Christie, 17–19 June 1830, lot 372; *Gunnis* 1968, 177; *Friedman and Stevens* 1972, 25–7
69.	1834	Boy with a bird		[Exhib Royal Northern Soc, Leeds, 455]; untraced		*Friedman and Stevens* 1972, 54
70.	1834	Female devotion, model	tc	[Exhib Royal Northern Soc, Leeds, 456]; untraced		*Friedman and Stevens* 1972, 47
71.	pre-1834	Hagar and Ishmael, statuette	m	[Exhib Royal Northern Soc, Leeds, coll George Banks]; private coll	S	*Friedman and Stevens* 1972, 33 (repr); *Read* 1982, 206
72.	1834	Infant Bacchus	tc	[Exhib Royal Northern Soc, Leeds, 463]; untraced		*Friedman and Stevens* 1972, 47
73.	1834	Italian greyhound		[Exhib Royal Northern Soc, Leeds, 446]; untraced Other versions: private coll (formerly Messrs Mallett)		*Friedman and Stevens* 1972, 51, 52
74.	1834	Nymph and greyhound, statuette	m	LMG, W R Yorks 30/72	S	*Friedman and Stevens* 1972, 33 (repr)
75.	1834	Peasant girl	tc	[Exhib Royal Northern Soc, Leeds, 448]; untraced		*Friedman and Stevens* 1972, 46
76.	1834	Spaniel and pups, statuette		[Exhib Royal Northern Soc, Leeds, 450]; untraced		*Friedman and Stevens,* 1972, 51
77.	1835	Spaniel, statuette		[coll General Ramsay]; untraced		*Friedman and Stevens* 1972, 51
78.	1837	Sylvia and the wounded stag	m	[Exhib RA, London, 1170; Christie 1 Dec 1894, lot 116]; untraced		*Graves* II, 1905–6, 280; *Friedman and Stevens* 1972, 28
79.	1837	Vintager	p	Untraced Other versions: Marble exhib RA, London, 1847 (1408)		*Graves* II, 1905–6, 280; *Friedman and Stevens* 1972, 28–9; *Sicca and Yarrington*, 2000, 16
80.	c1838	Dog playing with a ball		Untraced		*Friedman and Stevens* 1972, 51
81.	1836–1838	Greek boxer awaiting his turn, statuette Model(s): Leeds Museums and Galls, 9/71, 1828, clay	m	[coll Mr and Mrs Benjamin Gott]; Prof James Holderbaum, Smith College, Mass, USA Other versions: Greek boxer awaiting his turn, 1836–1838, YCBA B 1980.34, marble	SD	*Graves* II, 1905–6, 280; *Friedman and Stevens* 1972, 21–2, 29; *Leeds* 1996, 8 (repr)
82.	?1838	Hylas at the fountain, model		Untraced		*Friedman and Stevens* 1972, 25–6 (repr)
83.	1838	Sleeping nymph		[Exhib RA, London, 1261]; untraced		*Graves* II, 1905–6, 280; *Friedman and Stevens* 1972, 47
84.	c1839	Bacchus and the Nymphs	p	Untraced		*Friedman and Stevens* 1972, 47
85.	c1839	Miss Dame embracing a Maltese dog	p	Untraced		*Friedman and Stevens* 1972, 54
86.	1841	Dog scratching for a rat	m	[Exhib RA, London, 1253, coll Earl of Cadogan]; untraced		*Graves* II, 1905–6, 280; *Friedman and Stevens* 1972, 51
87.	1841	Rebecca (companion to Ruth)	m	York City Art Gall	S	*Friedman and Stevens* 1972, 39
88.	1841	Ruth (companion to Rebecca)	m	[Exhib RA, London, 1264]; York City Art Gall (1890)	S	*Friedman and Stevens* 1972, 38 (repr)
89.	1844	Fawn and child Payment(s): £120		[coll Lord Grosvenor]; untraced		RG/JP, 4, 609
90.	1844	Sleeping bacchante Payment(s): £200 Model(s): 1823, clay, untraced	m	[coll Lord Grosvenor]; untraced		*Friedman and Stevens* 1972, 44
91.	1845	Dancing nymph		[Exhib RA, London, 133; Bicknell 1863, lot 141]; untraced		*AU*, 1845, 195; *Friedman and Stevens* 1972, 47
92.	1848	Fox and cubs		[Exhib RA, London, 1324, coll Benjamin Gott]; untraced Other versions: Fox and two cubs exhib Int Exhib, 1862		*Friedman and Stevens* 1972, 51–2
93.	c1848	Hindu girl placing her lamp upon the Ganges	m	[coll Rawson of Nidd Hall]; Guy Reed (1972) Other versions: reduced copy sold Sotheby, 19 July 1972, lot 339	S	*Friedman and Stevens* 1972, 38–9, 40 (repr)
94.	1848	Mary Magdalene	m	[coll George Banks]; destroyed		*Graves* II, 1905–6, 280; *Friedman and Stevens* 1972, 33; *Read* 1982, 203, 206

95.	1848	St Catherine	m	[coll George Banks]; destroyed		*Friedman and Stevens* 1972, 33–4
96.	1851	Ceres		[Gt Exhib, Foreign States, Papal section]; untraced		*Friedman and Stevens* 1972, 48
97.	1853	A boy with a basket playing with a greyhound	m	[coll J E Duboys]; Musées des Beaux Arts, Angers, 1882 Other versions: ex coll Mr and Mrs John Gott, before 1841, untraced	SD	*Friedman and Stevens* 1972, 54
98.	by 1854	A greyhound and two smaller dogs	m	[coll Howard Galton, 1854]; untraced		*Friedman and Stevens* 1972, 52
99.	1823–1860	A dog	m	[coll John Jones]; VAM 1183-1882	S	*Friedman and Stevens* 1972, 52 (repr); *Bilbey* 2002, 288 (repr)
100.	pre-1860	Flora	m	Nat Gall of Victoria, Melbourne, Australia (1885)		*Friedman and Stevens* 1972, 48
101.	nd	A bacchante dancing		[Peper Harow, Surrey; Christie, 31 July 1851, lot 92]; untraced		*Friedman and Stevens* 1972, 48
102.	nd	A boy snatching a greyhound puppy from its mother		Untraced		*Friedman and Stevens* 1972, 54
103.	nd	A boy with a ball and dog, statuette	m	[coll Rawson of Nidd Hall]; Guy Reed (1972)	S	*Friedman and Stevens* 1972, 50 (repr)
104.	nd	A boy, statuette	tc	Giuseppina Sgambati, by descent from the sculptor (1972)	S	*Friedman and Stevens* 1972, 53
105.	nd	A female at the bath, model	tc	[Sir Thomas Lawrence; Christie, 6 July 1830, lot 57]; untraced		*Friedman and Stevens* 1972, 44
106.	nd	A girl holding a terrier puppy, statuette	m	[Sotheby, 19 July 1972, lot 33]; untraced	S	*Friedman and Stevens* 1972, 54
107.	nd	A greyhound bitch playing with her puppy, statuette		[coll Rawson of Nidd Hall]; Guy Reed (1972) Other versions: sold Sotheby, 27 June 1958, lot 22, bt Poynter	S	*Friedman and Stevens* 1972, 50 (repr), 52
108.	nd	A greyhound with her three puppies, statuette	m	Private coll		*Friedman and Stevens* 1972, 50, 52
109.	nd	A partly draped girl carrying a basket of grapes on her head, statuette	m	[Jackson-Stops, 8–10 Jan 1968, lot 680]; untraced	S	*Friedman and Stevens* 1972, 48
110.	nd	A spaniel and a kitten with a basket of fruit, statuette	m	[coll Rawson of Nidd Hall]; Guy Reed, 1972 Other versions: Alnwick Castle, Northumbs	S	*Friedman and Stevens* 1972, 50, 51 (repr)
111.	nd	A spaniel with two puppies, model	tc	Sotheby, 27 June 1958, lot 22; untraced	S	*Friedman and Stevens* 1972, 52
112.	nd	Benjamin Gott, standing	p	Mr and Mrs W H E Gott (1972)	S	*Friedman and Stevens,* 1972, 19 (repr)
113.	nd	Boy defending his sister from a snake	m	[coll William Jones; Christie, 2 June 1852, lot 83]; untraced		*Friedman and Stevens* 1972, 54
114.	nd	Boy holding a puppy with two other puppies and a bitch, model	tc	[Sotheby, 27 June 1958, lot 20, by Levin]; untraced		*Friedman and Stevens* 1972, 54
115.	nd	Boy playing with a spaniel	m	Musées des Beaux Arts, Angers	S	*Friedman and Stevens* 1972, 54
116.	nd	'Crossing the Brook Cedron' (companion to 'Jeptha's Daughter', 120)	m	York City Art Gall	S	*Friedman and Stevens* 1972, 39
117.	nd	Diana		Philadelphia Museum of Art, USA	S	
118.	nd	Dog, cat and fruit		Alnwick Castle, Northumbs		*Worsley* 1988 (3), 174–8 (repr)
119.	nd	Ino teaching Bacchus to dance	m	[coll Rawson of Nidd Hall]; coll Guy Read, 1972	S	*Friedman and Stevens* 1972, 40 (repr)
120.	nd	'Jeptha's daughter' (companion to 'Crossing the Brook Cedron')	m	York City Art Gall	S	*Friedman and Stevens* 1972, 39–40
121.	nd	Nymph on a rustic couch, statuette	tc	Untraced	S	*Friedman and Stevens* 1972, 44 (repr)
122.	nd	Sleeping child	m	Tommaso Brothers, Leeds, 2000	S	
123.	nd	Susannah	m	[coll Rawson of Nidd Hall]; untraced		*Friedman and Stevens* 1972, 40 (repr)
124.	nd	Ulysses and his dog	m	[coll Rawson of Nidd Hall]; Guy Read (1972)	S	*Friedman and Stevens* 1972, 40
125.	nd	Vixen and two puppies	tc	[Sotheby 27 June, 1958, lot 21, bt Poynter]; untraced	S	*Friedman and Stevens* 1972, 51

Busts

126.	1823–1825	Bacchante	m	Chatsworth, Derbys	SD	*Friedman and Stevens* 1972, 44; *JKB* 1972 (3), 327, 329, 331 (repr)
127.	1828	Elizabeth Goodman Banks	m	LMG, W R Yorks 1/28 Other versions: LMG 10/73, plaster on marble base	S	*Friedman and Stevens* 1972, 32; *Ret to Life,* 2000, 17, 63 (repr)
128.	1828	George Banks	m	LMG, W R Yorks, 3/28		*Friedman and Stevens* 1972, 32; *Ret to Life,* 2000, 9, 61 (repr)
129.	*c*1828	William Ewart		[coll Mr and Mrs William Gott]; untraced		*Friedman and Stevens* 1972, 30
130.	1829	A satyr	m	LMG, W R Yorks 21/28	SD	*Friedman and Stevens* 1972, 32–3; *Leeds* 1996, 8 (repr)
131.	1827–1829	Benjamin Gott	m	[Leeds Philosophical and Literary Soc]; LMG, W R Yorks 2000.0021.T Other versions: LMG, W R Yorks 1.4/67	SD	*Friedman and Stevens* 1972, 19–20 (repr); *Carr* 1975, 173–4 (repr)

132.	1834–1835	John Gott	m	LMG, W R Yorks 1971.0002.T	S	*Friedman and Stevens* 1972, 22
133.	1834–1835	William Gott	m	LMG, W R Yorks 1971.0003.T	S	*Friedman and Stevens* 1972, 23–4 (repr)
134.	1830–1840	Unidentified man	m	VAM A.16-1982	S	*Friedman and Stevens* 1972, 47 (repr); *Bilbey* 2002, 289
135.	1844	Bacchus and Ariadne (two busts) Payment(s): £80		[coll Lord Grosvenor]; untraced		RG/JP, 4, 609
136.	nd	Christopher Columbus		Capitoline Museum, Rome	S	*Gunnis* 1968, 177
137.	nd	Cupid (after Amore or Eros of Centocelle)	m	[Hill House, Stanmore]; Ashmolean WA 1899, CDEF S35	S	*Friedman and Stevens* 1972, 46; *Penny* 1992, III, 94 (repr)
138.	nd	Eros	m	LMG, W R Yorks 2/28	S	*Friedman and Stevens* 1972, 33; *Leeds* 1996, 8 (repr)
139.	nd	George Banks		Private coll, Dublin		RG/JP, 4, 611
140.	nd	Isis, after the antique	m	[Hill House, Stanmore]; Ashmolean WA 1899, CDEF S34	S	*Friedman and Stevens* 1972, 43 (repr); *Penny* 1992, III, 95 (repr)
141.	nd	Napoleon Bonaparte	m	[coll Benjamin Gott]; LMG		*Friedman and Stevens* 1972, 29

Architectural Sculpture

142.	1834	Urn	m	[Exhib Royal Northern Soc, Leeds, 445]; untraced		*Friedman and Stevens* 1972, 46
143.	1835–1838	Cupid and Psyche, relief	m	[Armley House, Leeds, drawing room]; Lotherton Hall, W R Yorks		*Friedman and Stevens* 1972, 22 (repr); *Leeds* 1996, 9 (repr)
144.	nd	Putti milking goats, putti racing greyhounds, putti harvesting grapes and playing with a goat and dog, putti harvesting grapes and playing with goats, reliefs	p	Syon House, Middx, dairy	S	*Friedman and Stevens* 1972, 55

Reliefs

145.	1823	Aurora while praying met by Zephyrus and Zepherus and Aurora, relief models		Untraced		*Friedman and Stevens* 1972, 44
146.	1828–1830	Metobus and Camilla	m	[coll George Banks]; Lotherton Hall, W R Yorks 3.2/28	S	*Friedman and Stevens* 1972, 32 (repr)
147.	1834	Elizabeth Allan, née Gott, portrait medallion	m	LMG, W R Yorks 1.5/67 Other versions: LMG 1.2/67, s	S	*Friedman and Stevens* 1972, 21, 23, 25 (repr)
148.	c1834	John Edward Brooke, portrait medallion		[coll John Edward Brooke]; untraced		*Friedman and Stevens* 1972, 30
149.	1834–1838	Benjamin Gott, portrait medallion	m	[coll Benjamin Gott]; LMG, W R Yorks 1.4/67	S	*Friedman and Stevens* 1972, 20–21, 25 (repr)
150.	1834–1838	Elizabeth Gott, née Rhodes, portrait medallion	m	LMG, W R Yorks 1.2/67	S	*Friedman and Stevens* 1972, 21, 25 (repr)
151.	1834–1838	Harriet Gott, portrait medallion	m	LMG 1.1/67	S	*Friedman and Stevens* 1972, 23 (repr)
152.	1834–1838	Margaret Gott, née Ewart, portrait medallion	m	LMG 1.3/67	S	*Friedman and Stevens* 1972, 24 (repr); *Leeds* 1996, 10 (repr)
153.	1841	Mrs John Edward Brooke, portrait medallion Payment(s): £16	m	Charles Gott (1972)	S	*Friedman and Stevens* 1972, 25 (repr)
154.	nd	John Gott, portrait medallion	p	[coll Mr and Mrs Benjamin Gott]; Mr and Mrs John Gott (1972)		*Friedman and Stevens* 1972, 22 (repr)
155.	nd	John Joseph MacBraire, portrait medallion	p	[coll Benjamin Gott]; Mr and Mrs John Gott (1972)		*Friedman and Stevens* 1972, 25 (repr)
156.	nd	Mrs John Gott, portrait medallion	p	[coll Mr and Mrs Benjamin Gott]; Mr and Mrs John Gott (1972)		*Friedman and Stevens* 1972, 22 (repr)
157.	nd	Mrs John MacBraire, portrait medallion	p	[coll Benjamin Gott]; Mr and Mrs John Gott		*Friedman and Stevens* 1972, 25 (repr)
158.	nd	William Gott, portrait medallion	m	Mr and Mrs John Gott (1972)		*Friedman and Stevens* 1972, 24 (repr)

Miscellaneous

159.	1808	Samson slaying the Philistines	p	[Soc of Arts, greater silver palette]; untraced		RSA, *Transactions*, vol 26, 1808, 18; *Friedman and Stevens*, 1972, 13
160.	1820	Young bacchante		[Exhib RA, London, 1027]; untraced		*Graves* 1875, 222; *Graves* II, 1905–6, 280
161.	1821	Faun		[Exhib RA, London, 1153]; untraced		*Graves* II, 1905–6, 280
162.	1826	Nymph		[Exhib RA, London, 1052]; untraced		*Graves* II, 1905–6, 280
163.	1834	Design from 'The Lady of the Lake'	tc	[Exhib Royal Northern Soc, Leeds, 449]; untraced		*Friedman and Stevens* 1972, 47
164.	1834	Scipio's tomb, model	m	[Exhib Royal Northern Soc, Leeds, 444]; untraced		*Friedman and Stevens* 1972, 46
165.	1839	Clytie		[Exhib RA, London, 1366]; untraced		*Graves* II, 1905–6, 280; *Friedman and Stevens* 1972, 47
166.	1841	Bacchante		[Exhib RA, London, 1267]; untraced		*Graves* II, 1905–6, 280; *Friedman and Stevens* 1972, 47
167.	1844	Pan Payment(s): £120		[coll Lord Grosvenor]; untraced		RG/JP, 4, 609

GOUDE, Anthony, of Chelmsford fl *c*1726–before 1774

Anthony Goude was an assistant to **Christopher Cass I** before setting up for himself as a mason at Springfield, near Chelmsford, some time before 1726. In 1726–1731 he was working at Boreham House, Essex and in 1729–1741 for Earl Fitzwalter at Moulsham Hall. His work there included chimneypieces and stone capitals (1–4). He also supplied a 'purple marble slab for a table of 5 foot 10 inches long and 2 foot 7 inches wide, at 7s 6d per foot £5 13s 2d', paved the kitchen with Purbeck Stone for £28 11s 9d in May 1733, supervised the stone-coping of the stables in 1736–7 and squared and laid the 'Newcastle stone before the dairy and laundry at 2d per foot &c, in full' for £6 8s 6d in 1740 (*Edwards* 1977, 50, 57, 62, 103). An inscription tablet commemorates the fact that he rebuilt the tower at Terling church, Essex, in 1732. In 1741 he covenanted to erect eight substantial brick houses on land he had leased in Duke Street, Chelmsford, and was paid £7 13s 6d for the 6 milestones between Ingatestone and Chelmsford. He subsequently moved to Chatham in Kent, where he died some time before 1774.

Literary References: *Gunnis* 1968, 178; *Edwards* 1977, *passim*; *Colvin* 1995, 419

Archival References: Hoare partnership ledger, *passim*

Chimneypieces

1.	1732	for the hall		Moulsham Hall, Essex	*Gunnis* 1968, 179 citing Fitzwalter archives
2.	1732	Hall chimneypiece		[Moulsham Hall, Essex]; untraced	Fitzwalter archives, cited by *Gunnis* 1968, 178
3.	1733	'veined-marble'		Moulsham Hall, Essex	*Gunnis* 1968, 179 citing Fitzwalter archives

Architectural Sculpture

4.	1737	Capitals for the piers Payment(s): £45	s	[Moulsham Hall, Essex, stable court]; untraced	*Edwards* 1977, 58–9
5.	1737	Stone capitals for the piers		Moulsham Hall, Essex	*Edwards* 1977, 58–9

GOULD, I, of Barnstaple fl *c*1800–35

Gunnis considered his tablet to Thomas Gay, at George Nympton, which has 'a most unusual relief of butterflies leaving the chrysalis', the best of his monumental works (*Gunnis* 1968, 178) (2).

Funerary Monuments

1.	?1800	Ann Newbold	Shirwell, Devon		*Gunnis* 1968, 178
2.	†1802	Thomas Gay	George Nympton, Devon	S	Pevsner, *Devon*, 1989, 455
3.	?1818	Walter Robins	South Molton, Devon		*Gunnis* 1968, 178
4.	?1828	Major Glaze	Bishops Tawton, Devon		*Gunnis* 1968, 178
5.	†1832	Thomas Stevens	Little Torrington, Devon	S	Pevsner, *Devon*, 1989, 539
6.	?1835	Thomas Hogg	Northam, Devon		*Gunnis* 1968, 178

GOWAN, Alexander, of Edinburgh –1803

According to one 19th-century source Alexander Gowan spent some time in the studio of **Louis François Roubiliac** (*Scott* 1880, 13, cited by *Pearson* 1990, 50). He had established himself as a marble cutter at Abbey Hill, Edinburgh by 1780. In 1784 he entered into a partnership with **James Gowan** and in 1793 his two sons Charles and **William Gowan** joined the business. In 1856 a speaker at the Royal Association for the Promotion of the Fine Arts in Scotland recalled that around 1800 the 'marble yard at Abbey Hill . . . was then and long after the only *studio* in Edinburgh where marble was cut' (*RAPFAS* 1856, cited by Pearson 1991, 46). Gowan died at Edinburgh on 30 March 1803. An elaborately decorated tablet commemorating John Fullerton, at Inveresk, which is signed 'Gowan' is probably by this sculptor (1).

Literary References: *Woodward* 1977 (vol 1, pt 2), 82; *Pearson* 1991, 46, 50

Funerary Monuments

1.	1775	John Fullerton	Inveresk, East Lothian	SD	*Woodward* 1977, vol 1, pt 2, 82
2.	1776	Lady Catherine Drummond (†1774) (designed by James 'Athenian' Stuart)	Greyfriars churchyard, Edinburgh		*Pearson* 1991, 50 n9; *Colvin* 1995, 942

Statues

3.	nd	Peasant with a sheep, figure	[Gowan's marble yard, Abbey Hill, Edinburgh]; untraced	*Pearson* 1991, 46, 50 n9

Miscellaneous

4.	nd	Fiddler	[Gowan's marble yard, Abbey Hill, Edinburgh]; untraced	*Pearson* 1991, 46, 50 n9

GOWAN, James fl 1781–*c*1819

Gowan was a marble cutter at Abbey Hill, Edinburgh from 1781 until at least 1797. From 1784 he worked in partnership with **Alexander Gowan**, who probably was his brother. His monument to Peter Norns in the Old Calton Burying Ground, Edinburgh, incorporates a relief carving of figures and dates from about 1819 (1).

Literary References: *Woodward* 1977 (vol 1, pt 2), 82–3

Funerary Monuments

1.	*c*1819	Peter Norns	Old Calton Burying Ground, Edinburgh	S	*Woodward* 1977, vol 1, pt 2, 82–3

GOWAN (or GOWANS), William –1828

He was the son of the marble cutter **Alexander Gowan**. In 1793 William and his brother Charles formed a business partnership with their father which lasted until 1821. In that year William established his own business at 2 Bland Place, Edinburgh; the following year he moved to 4 Shrub Place and in 1827 to Easter Road. He died on 25 January 1828 leaving an estate worth £1,207. He was buried in the churchyard of the parish church of St Michael at Inveresk. His wife Catherine Grieg died on 16 August 1836 aged 58.

Literary References: *Woodward* 1977 (vol 1, pt 2), 83

Busts

1.	*c*1773	Professor Cullen	m	University of Edinburgh	*Woodward* 1977, vol 1, pt 2, 83; *Pearson* 1991, unpag.

GRAHAM, William I fl 1769–70

He was a pupil of **John Nost III**, who in 1769 brought to the attention of the Dublin Society, 'the very extraordinary genius for sculpture and the Fine Arts in general in William Graham, a poor country boy of the age of sixteen, who is now in his apprenticeship'. The Society accordingly voted him £10 towards his maintenance and clothing. The following year Graham exhibited a marble bas-relief (1). Nothing more is known of him.

Literary References: *Strickland* 1, 1913, 404; *Potterton* 1975, 85

Reliefs

1.	1770	Unidentified subject		[Exhib Dublin Soc]; untraced	*Strickland* I, 1913, 404

GRAHAM, William II fl 1845–72

He exhibited at the Royal Academy between 1845 and 1872 from various London addresses. His works included a bust of Sir Robert Peel, which the *Art Union* thought 'unlike, and in every way much too heavy' (*AU*, 1847, 200) (5). In 1864 the *Carlisle Patriot* reported a visit to Graham at 39 Stanhope Street, Regent's Park to see a bust of Lord Brougham 'with a view to its being executed in marble and placed in the Town Hall, Appleby, in commemoration of his Lordship having cut the first turf of the Eden Valley Railway on 14 August 1858'. 'Having been supplied with the mask taken from Lord Brougham's face some 25 years ago the sculptor commenced work' but not satisfied with this Mr Graham sought letters of introduction and from the necessary sittings was highly pleased with the likeness (13). The newspaper said of Appleby that it was 'supporting local talent Mr Graham being a native of the locality' and added 'it is perhaps not known that it was this rising artist who gave the finishing touches to the much-admired bas-relief on the Wellington monument in the Guild Hall of the City of London representing the final charge of the British Guards at the Battle of Waterloo'. In 1868 the RA Council awarded him an annual pension of £10, increased to £15 in 1878.

Literary References: *Gunnis* 1968, 178

Archival References: RA/GA *passim*

Statues					
1.	1845	Lieutenant-General Sir E Barnes		[Exhib Westminster Hall, London, 133]; untraced	*Westminster* 1845, 16
2.	1868	Children in the wood	m	[Exhib RA, London, 940]; untraced	*Graves* III, 1905–6, 290
Busts					
3.	1845	Unidentified gentleman		[Exhib RA, London, 1413]; untraced	*Graves* III, 1905–6, 290
4.	1845	Unidentified gentleman		[Exhib RA, London, 1415]; untraced	*Graves* III, 1905–6, 290
5.	1846	Sir Robert Peel		[Exhib RA, London, 1505]; untraced Other versions: exhib RA, London, 1847, 1379, marble; untraced	*AU*, 1847, 200; *Graves* III, 1905–6, 290
6.	1851	Unidentified gentleman		[Exhib RA, London, 1339]; untraced	*Graves* III, 1905–6, 290
7.	1853	Unidentified subject		[Exhib RA, London, 1430]; untraced	*Graves* III, 1905–6, 290
8.	1855	Unidentified lady		[Exhib RA, London, 1503]; untraced	*Graves* III, 1905–6, 290
9.	1856	Unidentified lady	m	[Exhib RA, London, 1318]; untraced	*Graves* III, 1905–6, 290
10.	1857	Unidentified lady		[Exhib RA, London, 1324]; untraced	*Graves* III, 1905–6, 290
11.	1863	Colonel Wilkinson	m	[Exhib RA, London, 1145]; untraced	*Graves* III, 1905–6, 290
12.	1863	R P Wilson	m	[Exhib RA, London, 1168]; untraced	*Graves* III, 1905–6, 290
13.	1868	Lord Brougham		[Exhib RA, London, 1121]; untraced	*Carlisle Pat*, 17 Sept 1864, 5; *Graves* III, 1905–6, 290
Reliefs					
14.	1854	Ceres	m	[Exhib RA, London, 1454]; untraced	*Graves* III, 1905–6, 290
15.	1860	M Webster, medallion		[Exhib RA, London, 1031]; untraced	*Graves* III, 1905–6, 290
Miscellaneous					
16.	1850	David		[Exhib RA, London, 1324]; untraced	*Graves* III, 1905–6, 290
17.	1854	Bacchante		[Exhib RA, London, 1427]; untraced	*Graves* III, 1905–6, 290
18.	1865	Colonel Wilkinson		[Exhib RA, London, 1009]; untraced	*Graves* III, 1905–6, 290
19.	1867	George Peabody (executed by Claudet's photo-sculpture process)		[Exhib RA, London, 1063]; untraced	*Graves* III, 1905–6, 290
20.	1867	Thomas Hankey MP		[Exhib RA, London, 1023]; untraced	*Graves* III, 1905–6, 290
21.	1867	W J R Cotton		[Exhib RA, London, 1097]; untraced	*Graves* III, 1905–6, 290
22.	1872	Rev H W Burrows		[Exhib RA, London, 1442]; untraced	*Graves* III, 1905–6, 290

GRANT, Benjamin fl 1775–1809

An advertisement in the *London Evening Press* for 10–12 December 1751 states that Grant was one of 4 apprentices employed by **John Cheere**. He appears to have been appointed Cheere's foreman by 1762 when he signed a receipt on behalf of Cheere acknowledging payment for a *Mercury* for Burton Constable. By 1774 he had formed a partnership with **James Hoskins** and together they supplied the firm of Wedgwood and Bentley with a large number of plaster busts and other items, which were subsequently manufactured in black basaltware.

In November 1789 Grant wrote to the Society of Arts claiming to have developed improved methods of bronze casting and requesting its patronage. His address at that time was 76 Tottenham Court Road, London. The Society contacted **John Bacon RA** requesting further information, since Grant had worked in his studio, assisting in casting the monumental bronze group of *King George III and the River Thames* for Somerset House. Bacon wrote back on 6 April 1790, stating that although some technical innovations might have been developed in his workshop, on the whole the methods described by Grant were recommended by a founder 'Mr Saville, now of the Minories' (RSA, Archive, PR AR/103/10/165, and PR AR/103/10/40). He did not get a premium.

As the partner of Hoskins, Grant was also a plaster-figure maker to the Royal Academy. He apparently got into difficulties, for the Academy Minute-book recorded in 1808 that a letter had been received 'from Mr **Flaxman** with a petition from Mr Benjamin Grant praying assistance from the President and Council'. On this occasion the Council gave him 10 guineas, but when Grant wrote to them again later in the same year 'stating his wretched situation', they added a further 10 guineas with a letter stipulating that he 'was not to expect any relief in the future'. This display of firmness seems to have made no impression, for Grant petitioned twice for help in 1809 and each time the Academy relented and gave him 10 guineas.

Literary References: *Cox-Johnson* 1962, 708; *Gunnis* 1968, 178; *Friedman and Clifford* 1974, appendix H; *Clifford* 1985, 294; *Clifford* 1992, 39–65; *Fulton* 2001, 11, appendix D, 79

Statues

1.	1775	'2 figures of Mk Antony & Cleopatre' (models for Wedgwood & Bentley) (co-sculptor: James Hoskins)	p	Untraced	*Clifford* 1992, 59
2.	1799	'2 Figures Zingara & Chrispagnia', 'a Setting Figure of Venus', 'a Setting Figure of Mercury' (models for Wedgwood & Bentley) (co-sculptor: James Hoskins)	p	Untraced	*Clifford* 1992, 60

Busts

3.	1774	19 classical subjects and Inigo Jones and Palladio (models for Wedgwood & Bentley) (co-sculptor: James Hoskins)	p	Untraced	*Clifford* 1992, 59
4.	1775	31 classical and English writers, largely paired, 'Sir Walter Raleigh, 'Harvey & Newton', (models for Wedgwood & Bentley) (co-sculptor: James Hoskins)	p	Untraced	*Clifford* 1992, 59
5.	1799	Large busts of Bacchus, Ariadne, Mercury, Alexander, and busts of Shakespeare Garrick and Julius Caesar (models for Wedgwood & Bentley) (co-sculptor: James Hoskins)	p	Untraced	*Clifford* 1992, 59–60

Reliefs

6.	1774	Ovals of the Elements, Psyche and Cupid and a sphinx with lyre (models for Wedgwood & Bentley) (co-sculptor: James Hoskins)	p	Untraced	*Clifford* 1992, 59
7.	1775	'Tablet of Adonis & Venus' (model for Wedgwood & Bentley) (co-sculptor: James Hoskins)	p	Untraced	*Clifford* 1992, 59
8.	1799	'6 Basrelevo Figures', 'Cast of an Oval Pshyche & Cupid', 'a Cast of the Aurora & a smale Tablit' (models of Wedgwood & Bentley) (co-sculptor: James Hoskins)	p	Untraced	*Clifford* 1992, 60

Miscellaneous

9.	1774	'2 mould of a Copper meddal of Charles the third' and 'a mould of little seal' (for Wedgwood & Bentley) (co-sculptor: James Hoskins)	p	Untraced	*Clifford* 1992, 59
10.	1774	'2 Moulds from a Sulpher Cast of Sr Robert Walpole', four other moulds and '2 Scrole Bracketts' (models for Wedgwood & Bentley) (co-sculptor: James Hoskins)	p	Untraced	*Clifford* 1992, 59
11.	1799	'Mould of Sterne' (for Wedgwood & Bentley) (co-sculptor: James Hoskins)	p	Untraced	*Clifford* 1992, 60

GRAVENOR (or GRAVENER), James fl 1741–68

The son of another James Gravenor, he was apprenticed to Thomas Adey 'Citizen and joiner' in 1741 (Apprenticeship Lists, TNA I.R. 16/170, in GPC). He was the head of a team of 12 craftsmen who carried out wood and stone carving at Kedleston Hall, Derbys between 1759 and 1765. As well as doors, doorcases, chair rails, shutters, mirror frames, girandoles and other fittings, they made several important pieces of furniture such as the curved sideboards and pedestals in the dining room niche, the large mahogany writing desk in the library, the carved organ-case in the music room and the state bed, which has posts carved to resemble full-size palmtrees and was completed in 1768 (3). In about 1761 Gravenor spent eight days carving the wooden model for the Corinthian capitals in the marble hall and in 1763 he made another model for 'four medallions' on the exterior (1, 2). In the same year a payment of £54 was made to **Joseph Hall** for 'carving two medallions' for the outside of the house, which may relate to the same ornaments. Gunnis comments, 'It seems hardly likely that he could have modelled the great circular plaques on the exterior of the main front', before adding they they were 'in any case' executed by **William Collins**. Gravenor also received payments of £16 for 'altering' four alabaster capitals and £5 9s 6d for 'altering' figures on the drawing-room chimneypiece (Curzon Archives, in *Gunnis* 1968, 178).

Literary References: *Gunnis* 1968, 178; *Hardy* 1978, 203–4, 207; *Hardy and Hayward* 1978, 264; *Beard and Gilbert* 1986, 364–5; *Harris* 1987, 12, 63

Archival References: GPC

Architectural Sculpture

1.	1761	Corinthian capitals for the Marble Hall, Kedleston, model	Untraced	*Harris* 1987, 12, 63
2.	1763	Four medallions for the exterior of Kedleston, model	Untraced	*Gunnis* 1968, 178
3.	1760–1768	Decorative carving in wood and stone	Kedleston Hall, Derbys	*Beard and Gilbert* 1986, 364–5; *Harris* 1987, 12, 63; *Kedleston* 1998, *passim* (repr)

GRAY, of Weymouth fl c1814–18

Funerary Monuments

1.	?1814	Priscilla Awdry	Wyke Regis, Dorset	S	*Gunnis* 1968, 178
2.	?1818	Robert Cope	Weymouth, Dorset	S	*Gunnis* 1968, 178

GRAY, William 1818–

Gray was admitted to the Royal Academy Schools in 1839 on the recommendation of **William Behnes**. He showed sculpture and paintings at the Academy, 1841–57, and at the British Institution, 1848–60, from addresses in London, the Isle of Wight and Manchester. In 1845 he received a medal from the Society of Arts for a bust of the Rev John Williams, a missionary killed by Eromangan islanders in 1839, which Gray had previously exhibited at the Academy (2).

Literary References: *Gunnis* 1968, 178

Archival References: RA Admissions

Busts

1.	1841	J C Evans	[Exhib RA, London, 1316]; untraced	*Graves* III, 1905–6, 307
2.	1841	Rev John Williams	[Exhib RA, London, 1259]; untraced	*Graves* III, 1905–6, 307; RSA, *Transactions*, 1845, 30, xv
3.	1845	Unidentified lady	[Exhib RA, London, 1375]; untraced	*Graves* III, 1905–6, 307
4.	1851	Sir Robert Peel	[Exhib RA, London, 1295]; untraced	*Graves* III, 1905–6, 307

Reliefs

5.	1854	Sir Augustus Clifford, medallion	[Exhib RA, London, 1526]; untraced	*Graves* III, 1905–6, 307

Miscellaneous

6.	1847	Ianthe	[Exhib RA, London, 1450]; untraced	*Graves* 1875, 226; *Graves* III, 1905–6, 307

GREAVES, L, of Sheffield fl 1833–37

Funerary Monuments

1.	†1833	William Patten	Ecclesall, W R Yorks	S
2.	†1837	Rowland Hodgson	Ecclesall, W R Yorks	S

GREEN, G, of Newcastle fl 1824–50

He signed a number of 'undistinguished tablets' (Pevsner).

Funerary Monuments

1.	?1824	Mrs Grey	Howick, Northumbs	S	GPC
2.	†1828	Thomas Ayer	Ushaw College, Co Durham	S	
3.	†1831	G Gibson	Ushaw College, Co Durham	S	
4.	?1836	Edward Blackburn	Alnwick, Northumbs	S	GPC
5.	1837	Unidentified subject, tablet	Christ Church, North Shields, Northumbs		Pevsner, *Northumbs*, 1992, 526
6.	?1839	Grey family	Warkworth, Northumbs	S	GPC
7.	1841	Unidentified subject	St Oswald, Bellingham, Northumbs		Pevsner, *Northumbs*, 1992, 165
8.	1830–1850	Unidentified subjects, tablets	St Nicholas, Gosforth, Northumbs		Pevsner, *Northumbs*, 1992, 501

GREEN, I

Funerary Monuments

1.	nd	Elizabeth Allat	Onibury, Salop	S	GPC

GREEN, James, of Denton fl 1800–25

One of a family of remarkable country masons who still provide monuments today. James is known to have provided 41 engraved slate headstones in Lincolnshire between 1800 and 1825.

Literary References: *Neave and Heron* 1969, 11

GREEN, John Hippisley 1753–

He was born on 30 June 1753, the son of Jane Hippisley, later Mrs Green, a noted actress. He entered the Royal Academy Schools in 1774, gained a silver medal in 1780 and was later employed by **Joseph Nollekens**, being 'among his best workmen' (*Smith* 1920, I, 97). He exhibited at the Academy between 1775 and 1820, but around the turn of the century he gave up sculpture and concentrated instead on landscape painting.

Literary References: *Hutchison* 1960–62, 140; *Gunnis* 1968, 179

Funerary Monuments

1.	1793	'a design for a monument to a late comic actress to be erected in St Paul's, Covent Garden'	[Exhib RA, London, 784]; untraced	*Graves* III, 1905–6, 313

Busts

2.	1800	Portrait of Miss Green	[Exhib RA, London, 976]; untraced	*Graves* III, 1905–6, 313

Reliefs

3.	1791	Rev J Wesley, medallion	[Exhib RA, London, 669]; untraced	*Graves* III, 1905–6, 313

Miscellaneous

4.	1776	Jacob meeting Rachel	[Exhib RA, London, 118]; untraced	*Graves* III, 1905–6, 313
5.	1788	Hercules and Omphale Model(s): exhib RA, London 1775, 136	[Exhib RA, London, 621]; untraced	*Graves* III, 1905–6, 313
6.	1789	Bacchus	[Exhib RA, London, 576]; untraced	*Graves* III, 1905–6, 313

GREEN, of Warwick –1817

The *Northampton Mercury* of 18 January 1817 reported that 'Mr Green, statuary and stone mason, of Warwick' had died on 'Tuesday se'nnight' aged 31.

Literary References: *Gunnis* 1968, 178

Archival References: GPC

Funerary Monuments

1.	?1814	John Knightley	Offchurch, Warks	S	*Gunnis* 1968, 178

GREEN, Thomas, of Camberwell c1659–c1730?

Green is something of a mystery figure since his common surname makes it difficult to identify him from contemporary records. He was the son of a tailor, Edward Greene of St Giles, Cripplegate, in the City of London, and was probably born c1659, since he is likely to have been about 14 when he was apprenticed to a London mason, **John Fitch**, on 27 March 1673. He was made free of the Masons' Company on 19 April 1681, listed as being 'by service' to Fitch. He later worked for **William Holland.** The general search of 1694, a record of masons then living in the City, lists 'Journeyman Thomas Green Mason', living with **Thomas Cartwright I**, whose assistant he had become. His first known work, the monument to Sir Richard Earle (†1697) was signed 'Tho: Green of Camberwell, Serr fecit' (**1**). It is not clear why Green had moved to a Surrey village more than two miles south of the River Thames and without a navigable waterway, nor whether he had a working relationship with a younger sculptor, **James Fisher of Camberwell.** Green's rural domicile evidently had no adverse impact on potential clients, for during the next 2 decades he sent elaborate monuments as far afield as Lincolnshire, Suffolk, Kent and Gloucester.

Twenty of his monuments have been identified, either because he advertised his authorship with a prominent signature or because he transcribed the inscriptions for publication in John Le Neve's *Monumenta Anglicana*, 1717–19. Green clearly considered no commission too trivial or too ambitious, for the works range from ledger stones (**6, 15**) and a chest-tomb in a country churchyard (**4**), to plain architectural wall tablets (**8, 10, 12**), wall monuments with cherubs (**7, 14, 18**) and others with portrait busts (**1, 13**). He was responsible for two confidently-handled monuments with standing effigies in contemporary dress inside architectural surrounds (**5, 9**). Two others, one of which commemorated a Lord Chief Justice and the other a land-owner of substance, were as ambitious as any monuments of the period (**3, 16**).

Green's first known work, the monument to Sir Richard Earle, was commissioned by the mother of the deceased, Eleanor Payne, née Welby, and was probably completed around 1700 (**1**). It has two busts flanking a tablet with distinctive consoles and above is a segmental pediment, with a heavy curtain drawn up over it to reveal a panel with four winged cherub heads. The use of a curtain as a dramatic framing device is a recurring feature in later 17th-century monuments, but Green's arrangement is inventive, if cumbrous.

The large memorial to Lord Chief Justice Sir John Holt, carved about a decade later, shows a knowledge of classical quotations becoming fashionable in metropolitan work (**3**). It has a tri-partite frame, divided by Corinthian columns and framed with pilasters. The seated judge looks to the left and gesticulates to the right in a gesture which implies that he hears all and judges impartially. He is flanked by standing allegorical Virtues, *Justice* and *Truth*, who have an unconvincing *contrapposto* pose, indicating that the sculptor's anatomical knowledge was too slender for full mastery of the baroque style. Their pose, each with one arm clasped to the breast and the other displaying identifying attributes, echoes Antique precedents. In the upper tier are six lively *putti* derived from Duquesnoy's famous groups of quarrelling and embracing infants.

The other grandiose monument, to Sir Henry Furnese (**16**), 'rises like a wedding-cake tier by tier to the very ceiling of the chapel built to contain it' (*Gunnis*). The lowest stage of this free-standing, rectangular composition has life-sized mourning female figures seated at the corners, flanking four large inscription tablets. Above them on the second stage are four joyful *putti* on pedestals, interspersed with armorial shields, and the edifice is crowned by an urn balanced on colossal volutes. The account book of Arabella Furnese details payments totalling £405 7s 6d made to 'Mr Green stone:cutter' during the years 1715–17.

Green was at his most successful when he worked on less ambitious schemes. The elegant effigy of Sir John Powell (†1713), another eminent judge, stands in an authoritative manner, his cloak clasped at the neck and folded back over his shoulders (**5**). The statue is set off by a restrained, architectural frame with finely carved pilasters and capitals. Green used a similar compositional formula for the near-contemporary monument to Richard Welby (**9**), a kinsman of Sir Richard Earle, but introduced subsidiary figures to give it a more dramatic character. The full-length effigy, fashionably dressed in the square-cut coat and square-toed shoes of the period, is attended by cherubs who reach down from puff-ball clouds to place a crown of immortality on Welby's head. They are reminiscent of *putti* on **Grinling Gibbons**'s monuments carved a decade or more earlier.

When he was working on his last known monuments *c*1717–18, Green was also employed as a carver of large armorial shields for government buildings (**19, 20, 22, 24**). In the previous generation architectural ornaments had often been the province of mason-sculptors, but there is no evidence that Green was directly involved in building work. An agreement made with the War Office Board for the King's arms to be fixed over the Royal Brass Foundry at Woolwich (**20**), describes him as a 'Stone Cutter' (Minutes of the War Office Board, PRO WO 47/3000 and WO 47/31, quoted by *Easter* 2001, 78 nn 12, 13).

Green did not take apprentices under the auspices of the Masons' Company, but since he lived outside the City boundaries he could employ assistants without permission from the Company. Gunnis suggests that he died around 1730, but since nothing is known of his activities after 1718, his death may have occured a decade or so earlier. (Inf. Geoffrey Fisher)

IR

Literary References: *Le Neve*; *Knoop and Jones* 1935, 74; *Esdaile* 1942, 176–97; *Gunnis* 1968, 179; Pevsner, *Suffolk*, 1974, 400; *Whinney* 1988, 141–2; *Grove* 13, 614 (Friedman); *Bailey* 1996, 158; *Webb* 1999, 14; *Craske* 2000 (2), 95; *Easter* 2001, 65–78

Archival References: Masons' Co, *Freemen*, fol 24, 19 April 1681 (listed as by service to John Fitch); Furnese Accounts, General Expenditure, 1715–17

Funerary Monuments

1.	†1697	Sir Richard Earle, 4th Bt	Stragglethorpe, Lincs	S	*Le Neve* 1680–1699, 182; *Lord* 1986 (2), 88–90; *Easter* 2001, 67–8 (repr)
2.	†1706	Edward Blunt	['Sisson, Lincs' (perhaps Syston)]; untraced		*Le Neve* 1650–1718, 211
3.	†1709	Lord Chief Justice Sir John Holt	Redgrave, Suffolk	S	*Whinney* 1988, 141–2 (repr); *Grove* 13, 614; *Easter* 2001, 68–71 (repr)
4.	†1713	Henry Framlingham (†1710) and wife, Bridgett	Twyford, Norfolk, churchyard		*Le Neve* 1650–1718, 240; *Easter* 2001, 75 (repr)
5.	†1713	Sir John Powell	Gloucester Cathedral	S	*Easter* 2001, 71–3 (repr)
6.	†1713	Walter Cock	Camberwell, London, churchyard		*Le Neve* 1650–1718, 250–1
7.	†1713	William Chew	Dunstable, Beds		*Le Neve* 1650–1718, 251; *Easter* 2001, 75–6 (repr)

8.	1714	John Bridges (†1712)	Barton Seagrave, Northants	S	
9.	†1714	Richard Welby	Denton, Lincs	S	*Le Neve* 1650–1718, 252–3; *Lord* 1986 (2), 90; *Easter* 2001, 72–4 (repr)
10.	1715	George Courthop (†1714)	Ticehurst, Sussex		*Le Neve* 1650–1718, 259; *Easter* 2001, 75
11.	†1715	Maynard Colchester	Westbury, Glos		*Le Neve* 1650–1718, 264–6; Pevsner, *Glos: Vale & Forest of Dean*, 1976, 400
12.	†1715	Rev Gustavus Hawes	[for Aylestone, Leics]; untraced		*Le Neve* 1650–1718, 272; *Easter* 2001, 76–7 (repr)
13.	†1715	Sir Peter Seaman	St Gregory, Norwich, Norfolk	S	*Le Neve* 1650–1718, 270; *Easter* 2001, 72–4 (repr)
14.	†1715	Thomas Hall	St George Colegate, Norwich, Norfolk		*Easter* 2001, 76–7 (repr)
15.	†1716	Benjamin Poole	Waltham Abbey, Essex, churchyard		*Le Neve* 1650–1718, 261–2
16.	1715–1716	Sir Henry Furnese Bt (†1712) and his wife (†1713) Payment(s): £405 or more	Waldershare, Kent	S	*Le Neve* 1650–1718, 249–50; *Gunnis* 1968, 614; *Whinney* 1988, 142; *Easter* 2001, 71–2 (repr)
17.	†1717	Anthony Bowyer (†1709) and wife, Catherine	[for Camberwell, Surrey]; untraced		*Le Neve* 1650–1718, 228
18.	†1718	Bishop Richard Cumberland	Peterborough Cathedral	S	*Bailey* 1996, 158 (repr); *Easter* 2001, 74–5 (repr)

Architectural Sculpture

19.	1717	Duke of Marlborough's arms on a keystone Payment(s): £7	s	[Royal foundry, Woolwich, London, on the keystone beneath the royal arms]; untraced	*Gunnis* 1968, 179 citing PRO, W 47/3000; GPC
20.	1717	Royal arms Payment(s): £26	s	Royal foundry, Woolwich, London, principal front	*Gunnis* 1968, 179; *Easter* 2001, 66, 78 n12; GPC
21.	1717	Royal arms Payment(s): £36		St Martin's tower, Tower of London	*Easter* 2001 66, 78 n13; GPC
22.	*c*1717	Royal arms and other work including perhaps the royal heraldry over the main gate Payment(s): £43		New storehouse, Chatham, Kent	*Gunnis* 1968, 179; GPC
23.	1718	Keystones with the king's cypher and crown Payment(s): £50		[Gun wharfe, Portsmouth, over the main gate]; destroyed	*Gunnis* 1968, 179
24.	1718	Royal arms Payment(s): £34		[New storehouse, Portsmouth]; destroyed	*Gunnis* 1968, 179; GPC
25.	1719	Four carved corbel stones		[New storehouse, Portsmouth]; destroyed	GPC

GREEN, W fl 1731–37?

Green, who worked in the Rotherham area of Yorkshire, was responsible for a number of monuments, mostly of stone. Gunnis notes that the designs are based on London work of the period, with cartouche inscription tablets, architectural details and mourning cherubs, but the carving is far above the level of the ordinary provincial statuary and an unusual touch is given to each monument by a curious and individual emblem in the centre of the gadrooned base. On the monument to John Spencer this takes the form of a skull, with a snake holding an apple in its mouth crawling out of one eye-socket (**2**). The memorial to Thomas Beaumont, at Darton, features a seated cherub with its arm resting on an hour-glass (**1**). Green painted his signature on his works and in some cases it has become so faded as to be almost indecipherable.

Literary References: *Gunnis* 1968, 179–80

Funerary Monuments

1.	?1731	Thomas Beaumont	Darton, W R Yorks	S	*Gunnis* 1968, 179
2.	?1732	John Spencer	Cawthorne, W R Yorks	S	*Gunnis* 1968, 179
3.	?1733	Lord Darcy of Navan	Gilling, N R Yorks	S	*Gunnis* 1968, 179
4.	?1733	Richard Green	Cawthorne, W R Yorks	S	*Gunnis* 1968, 180
5.	?1737	Christiana Spencer	Cawthorne, Yorks	S	*Gunnis* 1968, 180

GREENE, Alexander *c*1670–

He was the son of Richard Green of Ducklington, Oxon, a husbandman, and was apprenticed to Peter Powell, of London on 19 July 1676. In 1691 he became free of the Masons' Company. He was employed in 1713 with **Thomas Davies** in building Lord Ashburnham's house in St James's Square (Ashburnham Archives, cited by *Gunnis* 1968, 178).

Literary References: *Gunnis* 1968, 178; *Webb* 1999, 14

GREENSHIELDS, John, of Lanark 1795–1835

A Scottish mason-sculptor, he became famous when his work was promoted by Sir Walter Scott. He born at Lesmaghow, near Lanark in 1795, the eldest of 6 sons of James Greenshields and his wife Betty Jack. When he was young the family moved to Willans, near Carluke, on the Clyde, and he began his career as an apprentice mason in the neighbouring village of Crossford. He made his first attempts at sculpture during his leisure hours, carving a figure of a dog in stone and modelling portraits of his father and one of his brothers in clay (**17, 18**). When he was about 30 he went to work for **Robert Forrest**, who was then engaged on a statue of Lord Melville for Edinburgh. Greenshields' friendship with Forrest stimulated his interest in sculpture and while working as a journeyman in Glasgow, he devoted much of his free time to artistic studies.

During the first years of his independent practice Greenshields was employed principally on commissions for gravestones, architectural decoration and ornamental figures for gateposts and gardens. However he also worked on a speculative project, a small stone statue of Lord Byron (**3**). This was sent to **John Flaxman** whose positive response encouraged Greenshields to produce a life-sized version and to carve several more figures including a statue of the politician George Canning, executed in 1827, which attracted much attention when it was exhibited in Edinburgh and led to extensive patronage, particularly in Scottish literary circles (**2**).

His early patrons included several influential Scottish landowners and the publisher William Blackwood. William Lockhart of Cambusnethan provided the sculptor with blocks of freestone for statues of the Duke of York and King George IV, and when the Duke of York's statue was completed James Stewart of Allanbank arranged for it to be displayed to potential patrons at Brompton (**1, 4**). Blackwood was a regular advisor to the sculptor, particularly in matters relating to the sale of his work and he may have provided financial assistance as well as business guidance when Greenshields began to market small plaster reproductions of his statues. The 8th Earl of Elgin invited Greenshields to his estate, Broomhall in Fife, to study his art treasures and both he and James Stewart recommended Greenshields to Sir Walter Scott. While staying with William Lockhart in 1829 Scott visited Greenshields' studio on Lockhart's estate. He was greatly impressed by the sculptor's work and proposed providing financial assistance to enable him to study in London, but the offer was declined.

Greenshields received considerable publicity from the meeting with Scott and from his visits to Broomhall and to Blackwood's house in Edinburgh. There he met Professor John Wilson who, under the name Christopher North, wrote a long-running column in *Blackwood's Magazine* in which he parodied well-known literary figures. Wilson called the sculptor an original genius. His workshop in Willans soon became such a fashionable visiting place that he was obliged to restrict visitors to one day a week to enable him to work undisturbed.

In the early 1830s Greenshields, impressed by the popularity of the work of **James Thom**, began to produce figures based on the writings of Robert Burns. His group *The Jolly Beggars* was a particular success (**11**): it was exhibited in several cities, including London, where it was on display in 1836, when Greenshields died. The previous year he had won the competition for the Glasgow statue of Sir Walter Scott, a work that was unfinished at his death and was completed by **John Ritchie** (**12**).

Literary References: *Gunnis* 1968, 180; *Woodward* 1977, vol 1, pt 2, 87–90

Statues

1.	1828	Frederick-Augustus, Duke of York and Albany	s	[coll Mr Greenwood of Charing Cross]; untraced	*Gunnis* 1968, 180
2.	c1829	George Canning		[Exhib at Edinburgh]; untraced	*Gunnis* 1968, 180; *Woodward* 1977, vol 1, pt 2, 88
3.	c1829	George Lord Byron, statuette		Untraced	*Woodward* 1977, vol 1, pt 2, 88
4.	c1829	King George IV	s	Untraced	*Woodward* 1977, vol 1, pt 2, 88
5.	c1829	Pugilist		Untraced	*Woodward* 1977, vol 1, pt 2, 88
6.	c1829	Two figures of cherubs		Untraced	*Woodward* 1977, vol 1, pt 2, 88
7.	1832	Mr Morris	s	Abbotsford House, Roxburgh	*Woodward* 1977, vol 1, pt 2, 90 (pl 66)
8.	1832	Sir Walter Scott, small model		Powderham Castle, Devon	*Gunnis* 1968, 180
9.	1834	Prince Charles Edward Stuart	s	[Glenaladale, Inverness]; Glenfinnan	*Gunnis* 1968, 180; *Woodward* 1977, vol 1, pt 2, 90
10.	1835	Sir Walter Scott	s	Faculty of Advocates, Edinburgh Other versions: Abbotsford, Roxburghshire, p, nd ex coll Mr Cadell; untraced	*Gunnis* 1968, 180; *Pearson* 1991, 156 (repr); *Pearson* 1991, unpag
11.	1836	The Jolly Beggars		[Exhib London]; untraced	*Gunnis* 1968, 180; *Woodward* 1977, vol 1, pt 2, 89
12.	1834–1837	Sir Walter Scott (co-sculptor: John Ritchie) Payment(s): £1,710 13s	s	George Square, Glasgow, Lanarks	*Read* 1982, 116–7 (repr); *McKenzie* 2002, 124–6 (repr)
13.	nd	Lord Byron	s	Untraced	*Gunnis* 1968, 180
14.	nd	Sir John Sinclair of Ulbster, statuette	p	Royal Society of Edinburgh	*Pearson* 1991, unpag
15.	nd	Sir Walter Scott, statuette	p	Royal High School, Edinburgh	*Woodward* 1977, vol 1, pt 2, 90

Miscellaneous

16.	1810–1820	A greyhound	s	Untraced	*Gunnis* 1968, 180; *Woodward* 1977, vol 1, pt 2, 87–8
17.	1810–1820	James Greenshields (the sculptor's father)	tc	Untraced	*Gunnis* 1968, 180; *Woodward* 1977, vol 1, pt 2, 87–8
18.	1810–1820	The sculptor's brother	tc	Untraced	*Gunnis* 1968, 180; *Woodward* 1977, vol 1, pt 2, 87–8
19.	1835	Sir Walter Scott		[coll Mr Cadell]; untraced	*Gunnis* 1968, 180

GREENWAY FAMILY, of Bath

Thomas Greenway	fl 1704–1730
Benjamin and Daniel Greenway	fl 1740–1752
Joseph Greenway	fl 1757

They were a family of architects, masons and carvers with premises in Claverton Street, Widcombe, near Bath. Around 1704 **Thomas Greenway** designed the Cold Bath House at Widcombe, 'one of the earliest examples in Bath to show a competent use of Renaissance detail' (*Ison* 1948, 116). In 1720 he built a number of houses in St John's Court. According to the architect John Wood one of these was 'so profuse in ornament as to tempt the King to Bath to make part of it his palace' and, encouraged by this success, Greenway 'particularly applied himself to small ornaments in freestone, such as crests, vases, fruits, etc., and several that served their apprenticeship to him pursued the business till they brought it to such a perfection as to merit publick encouragement and render their work a rising branch of the trade of Bath' (*Wood* 1729, 424, cited by *Gunnis* 1968, 180). In 1730 he visited Dublin, taking with him for sale 'a large number of Flower Potts, urns and vases' (*Faulkner's Dublin Journal*, 15–19 December 1730).

Benjamin and **Daniel Greenway**, who are described as 'marble and free-stone masons, carvers and vase-makers', supplied ornaments for John Wood's Bristol Exchange in 1740–41 (**3**) and sold garden ornaments to the Duke of Atholl in 1752 (*Wood* 1745, cited by *Gunnis* 1968, 180) (**4–7**). Daniel married Anne Winslow of Bath in 1747. **Joseph Greenway** and **Robert Parsons** supplied garden ornaments to Robert Dundas of Arniston in 1757 (Arniston Accounts, quoted by *Friedman* 1974 (2), 31) (**8**). One of Joseph's tradecards, with engraved illustrations of seven vases and a pedestal based on engravings in popular pattern books of the day, survives in the papers of the

Bagshawe family of Oakes Hall, Norton, Sheffield. It states that 'Joseph Greenway carver at the Cold-Bath, in Bath, executes the above Designs or any other Ornamental Work in Bath Stone which may be sent safe to any part of Europe' and that 'He will wait on Gentlemen and Ladies at their Lodgings with Variety of Draughts'. Some of the illustrations are annotated by hand with dimensions and prices (repr *Friedman* 1974 (2), 29).

Literary References: *Gunnis* 1968, 180; *Friedman* 1974 (2), 29–32; *Colvin* 1995, 431

Architectural Sculpture

1.	1723–1725	Two urns (by Thomas Greenway, from a design by James Gibbs)		Cliveden, Bucks, Octagon Temple	Pevsner, *Bucks*, 1994, 257
2.	1725	Vase and pedestal (by Thomas Greenway, from a design by James Gibbs)		[Cliveden, Bucks]; untraced	*Friedman* 1984, 262
3.	1745	Carving and vases (by Benjamin and Daniel Greenway)		Bristol Exchange	*Gunnis* 1968, 180
4.	1752	'4 jars and 2 Flowerpots' (by Benjamin and Daniel Greenway)	s	[Blair Castle, Perths, gardens]; untraced	Atholl archives in GPC
5.	1752	An eagle (by Benjamin and Daniel Greenway)		Blair Castle, Perths, gardens	Atholl archives in GPC
6.	1752	Two vases 'from the patern of Lord Burlington' (by Benjamin and Daniel Greenway) Payment(s): £4	s	['for each side of the Gate going into the Lawn', Northsides, Atholl House]; Blair Castle, Perths, gardens	Atholl archives in GPC
7.	1752	Vase with a bird (by Benjamin and Daniel Greenway)	s	Blair Castle, Perths, gardens	Atholl archives in GPC
8.	1757	'1 Lyons head Vase 1 Moasack Do. 5 Baskets and 1 Box' (by Joseph Greenway) (co-sculptor: Robert Parsons) Payment(s): £4, £2 5s, 13s		[for Robert Dundas, of Arniston House, Midlothian]; untraced	*Friedman* 1974 (2), 31

GREENWAY FAMILY, of Bristol fl *c*1791–1839

Olive, John Tripp and Francis Howard Greenway were sons of Francis Greenway, or Grinway, a mason of Mangotsfield, Glos. The youngest son, Francis (1777–1837), trained as an architect under John Nash. Around 1805 the three brothers opened a yard in Bristol and announced their intention of doing business as 'stonemasons, architects, builders, etc', while Francis took the opportunity of 'offering his services to the public in the capacity of Architect, Statuary and Landscape-Gardener' (*Colvin* 1995, 430). In 1806 he designed the hotel and assembly rooms in the Mall at Clifton, which his brothers contracted to build. During the same period the brothers were buying unfinished houses in Clifton in a speculative capacity, which they completed and then sold. In 1809 they became bankrupt and the assembly rooms were completed by Joseph Kay. Some time after the failure Francis Greenway was accused of forgery and in 1812 he was sentenced to death at Bristol Assizes. His motive appears to have been to benefit his creditors rather than himself and the sentence was commuted to transportation for life. He was sent to Australia, where he found a patron and protector in Governor Lachlan Macquarie, who employed him on ambitious plans for public works in the colony. In 1816 he was appointed government architect and in this capacity designed many of the public buildings in Sydney, including St James's Church. Meanwhile, Olive and John Greenway recovered from their bankruptcy and continued business in Bristol. As well as executing monuments, Olive probably designed and certainly built Downend church, Glos, in 1831, 'in a feeble Gothic style' (*Colvin loc cit*).

Literary References: *Gunnis* 1968, 180; *Colvin* 1995, 430–1

Funerary Monuments

1.	†1791	Coppleston Bampfylde (by John Greenway)	Kingstone, Somerset	S	Pevsner, *Somerset: S & W*, 1958, 214
2.	†1804	Robert Sandford	Leonard Stanley, Glos	S	Pevsner, *Glos: Cotswolds*, 1999, 445
3.	?1818	Samuel Prosset (by John Greenway)	Mathern, Monmouths		*Gunnis* 1968, 180
4.	†1819	William Willcox (by Olive Greenway)	Stoke Gifford, Glos	S	Pevsner, *Glos: Vale & Forest of Dean*, 1976, 350
5.	†1826	Unidentified subject, tablet (by John Greenway)	Timsbury, Somerset	S	Pevsner, *Somerset: N & Bristol*, 1958, 271
6.	?1828	Caleb Pointing (by John Greenway)	Midsomer Norton, Somerset	S	*Gunnis* 1968, 180
7.	?1830	Elizabeth Palmer (by Olive Greenway)	Paulton, Somerset	S	*Gunnis* 1968, 180
8.	?1833	Benjamin Millard (by John Greenway)	Keynsham, Somerset	S	Pevsner, *Somerset: N & Bristol*, 1958, 212; *Gunnis* 1968, 180
9.	†1834	William Richards (†1827) and Thomas Whitfield (by Olive Greenway)	Winterbourne, Glos	S	Pevsner, *Glos: Vale & Forest of Dean*, 1976, 409
10.	†1836	Bluett Jones (by Olive Greenway)	Iron Acton, Glos	S	Pevsner, *Glos: Vale & Forest of Dean*, 1976, 277

GREENWOOD, John fl 1791

Chimneypieces

1.	1791	Several Payment(s): £116 15s	Somerset House, London	*Gunnis* 1968, 180; *Colvin* 1973–76, V, 467

GREENWOOD, John Danforth fl 1837

He took over the **Coade Factory**, with his partner **Thomas Routledge**, in 1837.

GREGG, Sidney, of Ledbury fl 1821–38

Funerary Monuments

1.	†1821	Richard Cooks	Castlemorton, Worcs	S	
2.	†1824	Charlotte Ballard	Ledbury, Herefs	S	*Gunnis* 1968, 180
3.	†1834	John Spencer	Ledbury, Herefs	S	*Gunnis* 1968, 180
4.	†1838	Francis Cross	Castlemorton, Worcs	S	

GREY & JOYNES, of London fl 1805

The firm's yard was in Park Lane, London.

Literary References: *Gunnis* 1968, 180

Funerary Monuments

1.	†1805	Hester Manning	Ormesby St Michael, Norfolk	Pevsner, *Norfolk: NE & Norwich*, 1997, 295

GRICE, Elias 1630–

He was baptised at St Alkmund, Derby, on 14 June 1630, the son of a mason of the same name from Borrowash, who settled in Derby before 1630. In addition to the font at All Saints, Derby (1), he rebuilt the east gable end of the north aisle in 1676, for which he was paid £26.

Literary References: *Cox* 1875–78, vol IV, 95

Architectural Sculpture

1.	1662	Octagonal font	All Saints, Derby	*Cox* 1875–9, 4, 95; *Gunnis* 1968, 180

GRICE, Philip fl 1671–84

The Minute Book of Blacknall's Charity at Abingdon, Berks records in 1671 that 'Philip Grice should have seaven pounds for setting up Mr. Blacknall's statue, his wife and children, and if he did them well with gilt and good colors to their liking, he was then to have eight pounds' (quoted by *Gunnis* 1968, 181) (1). The monument was not set up until 1684 and Grice received £17 11s from the Charity in the same year, perhaps because the work was on a larger scale than had at first been intended. Gunnis notes that since Blacknall had died as early as 1625, a Jacobean design was chosen for the monument. He and his wife are depicted kneeling face to face, while the two daughters kneel behind their mother.

Literary References: *Gunnis* 1968, 180–1

Funerary Monuments

1.	?1684	Mr Blacknall (†1625) his wife and children Payment(s): £17 11s	St Nicholas, Abingdon, Berks	*Gunnis* 1968, 180–1

GRIGGS, William fl 1830–40

Griggs was called as a witness in the court case which **John Edward Carew** initiated against the executors of the Earl of Egremont. After being sworn in, he identified himself as a sculptor, and said he was currently employed as an assistant to **Sir Richard Westmacott**, but had formerly worked for Carew (*Carew v Burrell* 1840, 66). He exhibited at the Royal Academy and the Society of British Artists, 1830–1835, from 80 High Street, Marylebone and 53 Paddington Street.

Literary References: *Graves* III, 1905–6, 326; *Gunnis* 1968, 181

Busts

1.	1832	King William IV, cabinet bust	[Exhib Soc of BA, London, 878]; untraced	*Johnson* 1975, 195
2.	1833	Rev Dr Morris, Bishop of Troy	[Exhib Soc of BA, London, 821]; untraced	*Johnson* 1975, 195
3.	1835	Rev J Jones	[Exhib Soc of BA, London, 773]; untraced	*Johnson* 1975, 195
4.	1835	Unidentified child	[Exhib RA, London, 1122]; untraced	*Graves* III, 1905–6, 326
5.	nd	Barbara Towneley	Burnley Corporation Museum, Lancs	GPC

Reliefs

6.	1832	Unidentified subject, medallic portrait	[Exhib RA, London, 1052]; untraced	*Graves* III, 1905–6, 326
7.	1833	General Charles Fitzroy, medallion	[Exhib RA, London, 807]; untraced	*Graves* III, 1905–6, 326

Miscellaneous

8.	1830	Prometheus	[Exhib RA, London, 1229]; untraced	*Graves* III, 1905–6, 326
9.	1831	Celadon and Amelia	[Exhib RA, London, 1233]; untraced	*Graves* III, 1905–6, 326
10.	1831	Flight of the soul	[Exhib RA, London, 1078]; untraced	*Graves* III, 1905–6, 326
11.	1832	The bull's eye	[Exhib RA, London, 1135]; untraced	*Graves* III, 1905–6, 326
12.	1835	The archer	[Exhib Soc of BA, London, 789]; untraced	*Johnson* 1975, 195

GRIMBALSTON, William fl 1769–78

He lived at 'Silver Street opposite Great Pulteney Street' when he exhibited wax portraits at the Free Society, 1769–78.

Literary References: *Gunnis* 1968, 181; *Pyke* 1973, 60

Miscellaneous

1.	1769	Unidentified lady		[Exhib Free Soc, London, 105]; untraced	*Graves* 1907, 107
2.	1769	William Grimbalston, self-portrait		[Exhib Free Soc, London, 104]; untraced	*Graves* 1907, 107
3.	1770	Unidentified gentleman	w	[Exhib Free Soc, London, 114]; untraced	*Graves* 1907, 107
4.	1770	Unidentified lady in antique dress	w	[Exhib Free Soc, London, 115]; untraced	*Graves* 1907, 107
5.	1771	Unidentified gentleman	w	[Exhib Free Soc, London, 112]; untraced	*Graves* 1907, 107
6.	1771	Unidentified lady	w	[Exhib Free Soc, London, 113]; untraced	*Graves* 1907, 107

7.	1772	Unidentified child	w	[Exhib Free Soc, London, 76]; untraced	*Graves* 1907, 107
8.	1773	A favourite horse, from life		[Exhib Free Soc, London, 78]; untraced	*Graves* 1907, 107
9.	1774	Unidentified gentleman	w	[Exhib Free Soc, London, 113]; untraced	*Graves* 1907, 107
10.	1776	Unidentified gentleman	w	[Exhib Free Soc, London, 99]; untraced	*Graves* 1907, 107
11.	1778	Unidentified gentleman	w	[Exhib Free Soc, London, 68]; untraced	*Graves* 1907, 107

GRIMSLEY, Thomas fl 1827–60

Grimsley exhibited at the Royal Academy, 1827–40, from several addresses in the Edgware Road area and from Oxford. In 1829 he received £220 for 6 vases for Buckingham Palace (**16**). In 1844 he sent a figure of Cardinal Wolsey to the Westminster Hall Exhibition, which the *Literary Gazette* described as suggesting 'more idea of the butcher's son than of the great Cardinal' (*Lit Gaz*, 1844, 482) (**10**). In the same year he provided a colossal figure of Thomas Rowney, a local MP who had contributed a large sum towards the construction of Oxford town hall in 1752 (**9**). The statue, carved from a block of Caen stone weighing more than three tons, was erected in the central niche of the town hall's façade. The *Gentleman's Magazine* commented, 'The costume is managed into considerable artistical effect. The flowing peruke, the brocaded vest, and the formal cut of the coat, are represented faithfully, and yet without stiffness' (*GM* 1844, ii, 630).

Literary References: *Gunnis* 1968, 181

Funerary Monuments					
1.	?1843	Viscountess Valentia		Bletchington, Oxon	*Gunnis* 1968, 181
2.	?1846	Brett family		Ambrosden, Oxon	GPC
3.	†1847	George Morgan		Biddlesden Park House, Bucks, chapel	Pevsner, *Bucks*, 1994, 179
4.	?1847	Rev Robert Brown		Bletchington, Oxon	*Gunnis* 1968, 181
5.	†1853	Edward Batt		St Mary, Witney, Oxon	Pevsner, *Oxon*, 1974, 845
6.	†1860	David Williams		New College, Oxford, chapel	RG/HMC
Statues					
7.	1831	Unidentified child		[Exhib Soc of BA, London, 883]; untraced	*Johnson* 1975, 195
8.	1832	Unidentified child		[Exhib RA, London, 1216]; untraced	*Graves* III, 1905–6, 329
9.	1844	Thomas Rowney (†1759)	s	[Oxford Town Hall, façade]; demol 1893	*GM*, 1844, ii, 630; *Gunnis* 1968, 181
10.	1844	Thomas Wolsey (†1530)		[Exhib Westminster Hall, London]; untraced	*Gunnis* 1968, 181
Busts					
11.	1827	Unidentified child		[Exhib RA, London, 1827]; untraced	*Graves* III, 1905–6, 329
12.	1830	Arthur, 1st Duke of Wellington		Stratfield Saye, Hants	*Gunnis* 1968, 181
13.	1831	King George IV	m	[Exhib RA, London, 1167]; untraced	*Graves* III, 1905–6, 329
14.	1840	Unidentified youth		[Exhib RA, London, 1136]; untraced	*Graves* III, 1905–6, 329
15.	1843	Christopher Codrington (after Sir Henry Cheere's statue at All Souls', Oxford)	m	Codrington College, Barbados	*Gunnis* 1968, 181
Architectural Sculpture					
16.	1829	'Six sculptured vases' Payment(s): £220		[Buckingham Palace, London]; untraced	*Gunnis* 1968, 181 incorrectly cites PRO Works 19/3
17.	1844	Thomas Rowney's coat of arms		[Oxford Town Hall, pediment]; demol 1893	*GM*, 1844, ii, 630
Miscellaneous					
18.	1830	Hannah		[Exhib RA, London, 1187]; untraced	*Graves* III, 1905–6, 329

GRINDROD, Timothy, of Liverpool –1817

Grindrod came from Rochdale, but was in partnership with **William Hetherington** in Liverpool when they built the New Exchange there in 1803. He died in 1817. His widow, who died the following year, is buried in the churchyard of St Nicholas, Liverpool. Their son, Robert, who acted as his father's assistant, died in 1820, aged about 32.

Literary References: *Gunnis* 1968, 181

Funerary Monuments					
1.	?1797	John Cooper	Runcorn, Cheshire	S	*Gunnis* 1968, 181
2.	?1817	John Bankes	Runcorn, Cheshire	S	*Gunnis* 1968, 181

GRINWAY, of Downend fl *c*1796

Funerary Monuments					
1.	*c*1796	Richard Brooke	Old Sodbury, Glos	S	Pevsner, *Glos: Cotswolds*, 1999, 535

GROCE, John fl 1748

He is noted as a 'statuary' living in the Hyde Park Road in the Westminster Poll Book of 1748. No works have been identified.

Archival References: GPC

GROVES, William 1809–

He first exhibited at the Royal Academy in 1834, showing a statue of *Psyche at the fountain of youth*, described as 'full of lively and appropriate expression' (*Lit Gaz*, 1834, 361) (**7**). He joined the RA Schools three years later on the recommendation of J T Smith, and continued to exhibit there until 1861, from 25 Charlotte Street. In 1839 he competed unsuccessfully for the commission for the national monument to Admiral Lord Nelson (**15**). One commentator was scathing about his design, which included a great deal of symbolic sculptural decoration: 'a vast superabundance of animals are made to mean anything or everything amongst these monuments. Had the design been by Noah, who saved their progenitors in the ark, they may have been more applicable' (*Lit Gaz*, 8 June 1839, 363).

Literary References: *Gunnis* 1968, 181; *Yarrington* 1988, 307

Funerary Monuments

1.	†1836	Lieutenant-Colonel John Jordan		Holy Trinity, Cheltenham, Glos	S	
2.	?1840	Samuel White		St John, Hampstead, London	S	*Gunnis* 1968, 181
3.	†1841	Thomas Allen		Shouldham, Norfolk	S	*Graves* III, 1905–6, 333; Pevsner, *Norfolk: N W & S*, 1999, 651
4.	1842	Unidentified subject, to be erected at St Benet Finck, Threadneedle Street		[Exhib RA, London, 1284]; untraced		*Graves* III, 1905–6, 333
5.	?1843	Hannah Cooper		St Michael, Cornhill, London		*Gunnis* 1968, 181
6.	?1848	Lieutenant Thomas Cubitt		Catfield, Norfolk		*Gunnis* 1968, 181
Statues						
7.	1834	Psyche at the fountain of youth	m	[Exhib RA, London, 1077]; untraced		*Graves* III, 1905–6, 333
Busts						
8.	1837	John Abernethy	m	St Bartholomew's Hospital, London		*Graves* III, 1905–6, 333; *Gunnis* 1968, 181
9.	1837	Unidentified gentleman	m	[Exhib RA, London, 1209]; untraced		*Graves* III, 1905–6, 333
10.	1838	Unidentified young lady		[Exhib RA, London, 1322]; untraced		*Graves* III, 1905–6, 333
11.	1839	Benjamin Sharpe RN	p	[Exhib RA, London, 1340]; untraced		*Graves* III, 1905–6, 333
12.	1846	Unidentified young lady		[Exhib RA, London, 1490]; untraced		*Graves* III, 1905–6, 334
13.	1857	Charlotte Gaskell	m	[Exhib RA, London, 1316]; untraced		*Graves* III, 1905–6, 334
Miscellaneous						
14.	1835	Hebe degraded		[Exhib RA, London, 1058]; untraced		*Graves* III, 1905–6, 333
15.	1839	Horatio, Admiral Lord Nelson, design for national monument (commission awarded to Railton and Baily)		[Exhib St James's Bazaar, London]; untraced		*Yarrington* 1988, 307
16.	1845	A flower girl		[Exhib RA, London, 1342]; untraced		*Graves* III, 1905–6, 333
17.	1861	The first plunge		[Exhib RA, London, 1095]; untraced		*Graves* III, 1905–6, 334

GRUBB, Edward, of Birmingham 1740–1826

He was probably born at Towcester, but early in life he moved to Stratford-upon-Avon with his 2 brothers, one of whom, **Samuel Grubb**, was a stonemason. Edward Grubb trained and worked as a stone carver and statuary but later turned to portrait-painting, 'and his numerous paintings on canvas, however coarse in execution, show his success in delineating the human face' (*Colvile* 1869, 303). He moved to Birmingham before 1769 where he rented a house near the top of Henley Street from the Corporation. That year he and his brother Samuel carved figures of a boy and girl for the front of the Birmingham Bluecoat School, taking 'likenesses of two children then residing in the establishment' (*ibid*) (5). The Birmingham historian William Hutton wrote that they were executed 'with a degree of excellence that a Roman statuary would not blush to own' (*Hutton* 1783, cited by *Noszlopy* 1998, 119–20). When the school moved to Edgbaston in 1932 replicas of the statues were made for the façade of the building and the originals were moved inside. Grubb died at Stratford-upon-Avon on 8 April, 1816. His son George, who was also a portrait-painter, predeceased him.

Literary References: *GM*, 1816, i, 475; *Gunnis* 1968, 181–2; *Noszlopy* 1998, xiii, 119–20, 194

Funerary Monuments

1.	†1787	Simon, 1st Earl of Carhampton	Kingsbury, Warks	S	*Gunnis* 1968, 182; Pevsner, *Warks*, 1966, 327
2.	?1789	William Ash	Sutton Coldfield, Warks	S	*Gunnis* 1968, 182
3.	?1796	Peter Judd	Stratford-on-Avon, Warks	S	*Gunnis* 1968, 182
4.	?1797	Edward Taylor	Steeple Aston, Oxon	S	*Gunnis* 1968, 182
Statues					
5.	1769–1770	Bluecoat boy and girl (co-sculptor: Samuel Grubb)	[Old Bluecoat School, St Philip's churchyard, Birmingham, niches above porch]; Bluecoat School, Harborne, Birmingham, main hall Other versions: replicas by William Bloye, 1930, Bluecoat School, Harborne, Birmingham, above entrance		Pevsner, *Warks*, 1966, 186; *Noszlopy* 1998, xiii, 119–120 (repr)

GRUBB, Samuel fl 1753–70

The *Northampton Mercury* for 25 June 1753 carries the advertisement 'Samuel Grubb, late apprentice to Mr John Austin of Stratford, stone-carver, deceased, has bought the Stock and Effects in trade belonging to his late Master'. He was the brother of **Edward Grubb**, with whom he worked on figures of a boy and girl for the Birmingham Bluecoat School in 1769–70.

Literary References: *Gunnis* 1968, 181–2; *Noszlopy* 1998, xiii

Archival References: GPC (inf: Bruce Bailey)

Statues

1.	1769–1770	Bluecoat boy and girl (co-sculptor: Edward Grubb)	[Old Bluecoat School, St Philip's churchyard, Birmingham, niches above porch]; Bluecoat School, Harborne, Birmingham, main hall Other versions: replicas by William Bloye, 1930, Bluecoat School, Harborne, Birmingham, above entrance	Pevsner, *Warks*, 1966, 186; *Noszlopy* 1998, xiii, 119–120 (repr)

GRUMBOLD, Robert 1639–1720

Grumbold was the best-known member of a family of freemasons who practised their trade in Northamptonshire and Cambridgeshire in the 16th, 17th and 18th centuries. As a master-mason he was responsible for a great deal of building work at Cambridge during his long life. His works there include the library and the rebuilding of the great fountain at Trinity College, the north range of Clare Hall, containing the hall and buttery, and the bridge at

St John's College. Gunnis notes that he also received several payments for carved work at Houghton House and Wrest Park. M I Webb pointed out that these bills 'show that Grumbold was responsible for work in those houses but do not prove him to have been a sculptor' (*Webb/Gunnis* 1954, 25).

Literary References: *Webb/Gunnis* 1954, 25; *Gunnis* 1968, 182; *Colvin* 1995, 434–5

Chimneypieces

1.	1687–1688	Several for the great hall	[Houghton House, Ampthill, Beds]; untraced	Archives, Marquess of Ailesbury, cited by *Gunnis* 1968, 182

Architectural Sculpture

2.	1687–1688	Doorcase for the great hall	[Earl of Elgin, Houghton House, Ampthill]; untraced	Archives Marquess of Ailesbury, cited by *Gunnis* 1968, 182
3.	1694	'a pair of stone piers with Wyverns on them' Payment(s): £69	[Wrest Park, Beds]; untraced	Archives Lady Lucas and Dingwall, cited by *Gunnis* 1968, 182
4.	1695	Two fountains Payment(s): £86	[Wrest Park, Beds, garden]; untraced	Archives Lady Lucas and Dingwall, cited by *Gunnis* 1968, 182

GRUNDY, Thomas –1829

Grundy, who became free of the Masons' Company by redemption in 1802, was much employed as a master-mason by the architect Sir John Soane. In 1807 he provided the sarcophagus for a mausoleum designed by Soane for Sir Francis Bourgeois, one of the founders of the Dulwich Picture Gallery (**1**). It commemorated Bourgeois' friend and business partner Noel Joseph Desenfans and was erected behind the house they shared in Charlotte Street, Portland Place (now Hallam Street). Grundy worked under Soane at the Bank of England from 1807 until his death, and was in partnership with **James Nelson** until 1811 (**4**). The abstracts of bills for his mason's work for 1812 lists many marble chimneypieces at the Bank and elsewhere (Soane cupboard F/35/29, 118). He was employed by Soane between 1825 and 1828 at the New Courts of Justice, Pelwall House and Freemasons' Hall (**7, 8, 9, 11**). In 1814 and 1817 he carved monuments to Soane's designs commemorating the naval commander Viscount Bridport and the singer Anna Storace (**2, 3**). Gunnis notes a bill in the Soane archives, dated 1818, 'to the executors of Signora Storace for a statuary marble wall-piece fixed in Lambeth Church, £30' (Soane Bill Book H f 169).

As a master mason he worked at Moggerhanger, Beds, 1809–12, providing also large quantities of stone. For the labour and materials he was paid £1,785 in 1809. He was also responsible for alterations to the homes of Lord St Germans and Samuel Thornton in St James's Square, and in 1818 and 1819 to Fife House, Whitehall, the home of Lord Liverpool, the Prime Minister. In 1821 he built 4 houses in Regent Street and, between 1827 and 1830, branches of the Bank of England at Bristol, Hull, Liverpool, Newcastle and Norwich, all designed by Soane. He may have worked in partnership with a craftsman named Wright at Grosvenor House, London, for payments of £1,046 are recorded to Wright and Grundy for masonry work. After Grundy's death in 1829 his widow Jane continued the business. His will gives his address as Earl Street, Horseferry Road.

Literary References: *Gunnis* 1968, 182

Archival References: Soane Bank Account, vol 8, (1808–9), fol 246 (Bank of England); Soane Bill Book G fols 185–6 (building work at Moggerhanger); Soane Bill Book G fols 423–4 (mason at Dulwich College); Soane Bill Book 1, fols 188–90 (mason's work, Earl St Germans's house, St James's Square, London); Soane Bill Book 1, fols 306–7 (mason for Messrs Grote, Prescott & Grote, 62 Threadneedle St, London); Soane Bill Book 1 fol 394 (removing, reworking and resetting staircase, Freemasons' Hall, London); Soane Bill Book K, fols 1–10 (mason for 8 houses built for Mr Robins in Regent St and King St); RG/JP, 4, 628

Will: PROB 11/1774

Funerary Monuments

1.	1807	Sarcophagus for Sir Francis Bourgeois (designed by Sir John Soane)	s	Charlotte Street Graveyard, Portland Place, London	*Gunnis* 1968, 182
2.	1814	Alexander, 1st Viscount Bridport (†1814) (designed by Sir John Soane) Payment(s): £250		Cricket St Thomas, Somerset	*Colvin* 1995, 912
3.	1817	Anna Storace (†1817) (designed by Sir John Soane) Payment(s): £30		[Lambeth, London]; destroyed	*Gunnis* 1968, 182; *Colvin* 1995, 912

Chimneypieces

4.	1809	Two veined marble chimneypieces (designed by Sir John Soane) (co-sculptor: James Nelson) Payment(s): £48	m	[Bank of England, London]; untraced	Soane bank acct, vol 8, fol 246; *Gunnis* 1968, 182
5.	1812–1814	of statuary marble Payment(s): £40		[Marquess of Buckingham's house, Pall Mall]; untraced	Soane bill book G fol 383
6.	1813–1824	Several (designed by Sir John Soane)		SJSM	RG/JP, 4, 628
7.	1825	Three (designed by Sir John Soane) Payment(s): £78	m	[Courts of Justice, Westminster, London]; untraced	TNA WORK 5/125 f75; *Gunnis* 1968, 182
8.	1826	Black and gold (designed by Sir John Soane) Payment(s): £49		[Pelwall House, Market Drayton, Salop, dining room]; untraced	*Gunnis* 1968, 182
9.	1826	Carved marble (designed by Sir John Soane) Payment(s): £140	m	[Pelwall House, Market Drayton, Salop, large drawing room]; untraced	*Gunnis* 1968, 182
10.	1826	Statuary marble and gold (designed by Sir John Soane) Payment(s): £58	m	[Pelwall House, Market Drayton, Salop, small drawing room]; untraced	*Gunnis* 1968, 182
11.	1828	Four veined marble chimneypieces (designed by Sir John Soane) Payment(s): £100	m	[Freemasons' Hall, London, council chamber]; untraced	*Gunnis* 1968, 182

Architectural Sculpture

12.	1818–1819	Ornaments, including balusters, runs of mouldings and carved laurel and honeysuckle Payment(s): £585	[for C G Thornton at Marden Hill, Herts]; untraced	Soane Bill Book H fols 370–2
13.	1825	Sixteen corbel heads; twenty-four bosses and cornice (designed by Sir John Soane) Payment(s): £51; £38	[Courts of Justice, Westminster, London]; destroyed	TNA WORK 5/125 f75; *Gunnis* 1968, 182
14.	1828	Four Ionic columns and capitals (designed by Sir John Soane) Payment(s): £50	[Freemasons' Hall, London, new council chamber]; demolished	*Gunnis* 1968, 182

Miscellaneous

15.	1828–1829	Masons' work, Ionic columns and chimneypieces	[Freemasons' Hall, City of London]; untraced	Soane Bill Book, K fols 237–40

GRYLLS, of Devonport fl *c*1823–27

He signs two large wall-tablets (1, 2).

Funerary Monuments

1.	?1823	Gertrude Hawkins	Saltash, Cornwall	S	*Gunnis* 1968, 182–3
2.	?1827	John Newton	Bridestowe, Devon	S	*Gunnis* 1968, 183

GUELFI (or GUELPHI), Giovanni Battista *c*1690/91–after 1734

An Italian sculptor, he spent a long period in England where he enjoyed the protection of Lord Burlington, the 'architect earl' for about 14 years. Vertue's short account of the sculptor, which suggests an irritation with the Italian's imperious manners, provides the best insights into the English phase of his career.

John Bridges, the Northamptonshire antiquary, recorded that Guelfi's family came from Bergamo in Lombardy and that he was trained in Rome under Camillo Rusconi (1658–1728). Rusconi was a leading practitioner of the late baroque style and under him Guelfi must have developed his skills as a modeller, and was perhaps employed on the lucrative business of restoring antique sculpture. His name is recorded during the years 1714–1720 in the *Stato delle Anime*, S Andrea delle Fratte, Rome, the area around the Spanish Steps favoured by artists and English collectors. Vertue suggests that he was 'encouragd. or brought to England' by Burlington (*Vertue* III, 50–51), but it is possible that Lord Leominster, later 1st Earl Pomfret, who was in Rome in 1718 and became his first certain patron in England, was responsible for Guelfi's journey north. William Kent, the painter and architect most closely associated with Burlington, was also in Rome in 1718 and that year painted a canvas for Leominster. Kent may have acted as an intermediary between Burlington and Guelfi. The patron was back in England by July 1720 and Guelfi followed a few months later.

Leominster had inherited a number of the ancient Arundel Marbles, which he displayed in the gardens of his Northamptonshire seat, Easton Neston, and Guelfi was given the task of restoring them (**8**). Bridges visited Easton Neston in July 1721 and noted 'In a corridor or room adjoining to ye South end of ye H[ouse] I saw 15 statues . . . I found an Italian employ[e]d by this pre[sent] Lord L[eominster] in making perfect those statues maimed. Si chiama Gio. Battista Guelfi . . .' (Bodleian, Bridges, Top. Northants f.1.60a). Horace Walpole condemned the results: 'the best of the collection are those which he restored the least. He misconceived the original character of almost every statue which he attempted to make perfect, and ruined the greater number of those he was permitted to touch' (*Anecdotes*, 1876, III, 40).

It is not clear what other sculpture Guelfi provided for Burlington. Vertue wrote that he was 'continually almost employed for him several years' (*Vertue* III, 73–4) working both at Burlington's London house and at Chiswick Villa where he carved many statues (**10**). Faulkner's guide, published in 1845, mentions that Guelfi's statues of *Venus* and *Mercury* were then in the Gallery (**11**), together with two little heads (**18**).

Guelfi's most influential work, the monument to Secretary of State, James Craggs, in Westminster Abbey (**1**) was overseen by Alexander Pope, a member of Burlington's inner circle. It was designed by the architect, James Gibbs, and broke new ground with its standing, cross-legged effigy, leaning against an urn. The pose, which has antique precedents, was later taken up by a number of other sculptors, notably **William Woodman II**, **Michael Rysbrack**, **Peter Scheemakers**, **Henry Cheere** and **John Bacon RA**. Pope superintended the design and its execution as well as providing the epitaph. In a letter to the patron, Craggs's sister, he pointed out that Guelfi was at a great disadvantage in not being able to work from the life since her brother had died before the commission came about. The critic, James Ralph, was uncharacteristically charitable about the result, admiring the 'simple and elegant taste' of the composition, but he felt that 'if the face and head had been more finish'd, the whole [would have] been without blemish' (*Ralph* 1734, 73). A curious terracotta statuette of Craggs with a detachable wax face has survived and appears to be the model for the effigy (SJSM).

Guelfi worked on a number of monuments for patrons linked to Burlington by family ties or a shared interest in Palladian architecture. Several of these memorials were designed by Kent (**3, 5, 7**), and most of Guelfi's monuments had busts set off by a variety of architectural grounds (**4–7**). In at least one case Guelfi was responsible only for the bust (**7**), of characteristically elongated form, with the 'vacuous expression common to all Guelfi's portraits' (*Grove* 13, 782). The sculptor's most ambitious and successful monument outside London, to Thomas Watson Wentworth (**3**), is undocumented, but signed *Guelfi Romanus fecit*. Kent's elegant design made use of a pyramidal ground (now missing) above a double plinth: a satisfying inner triangle is formed by his effigy, which stands to the left of a central urn and his wife's seated image at the right. A number of other monuments have been attributed to Guelfi by Margaret Webb, notably three to members of the Halsey family at Great Gaddesden, Herts, Thomas (†1715), Anne (†1714) and Jane (†1725). She also credits him with the memorial to Brigadier Michael Richards (†1721) at St Luke, Chalton, London.

Among Guelfi's documented memorials is the trio raised under the terms of the will of Katherine, 6th Countess of Westmorland (†Feb 1730) to members of her family (**4–6**). These were probably made in 1731 and they all have portrait busts, set either in an architectural frame (**5**) or more elaborately treated with a tent-like canopy (**4**, **6**). The first of the series was probably that commemorating Lady Westmorland's parents, Thomas and Katherine Stringer (**5**) and was the subject of correspondence from John Fane of Mereworth, who negotiated prices on Westmorland's behalf. Fane approached Guelfi and also Rysbrack, the Italian's chief rival in London, for estimates calculated on a design by Kent. Guelfi indicated that the two proposed busts would cost about £30 each; Rysbrack apparently rejected Kent's drawing, substituting 'a very bad one' of his own with an estimate of £155. Guelfi won the contract despite raising his price in a detailed estimate communicated by Fane on 5 September 1730, which set a fee of £70 for the busts and £100 for 'the back part' (Westmorland Papers fol 99). Westmorland's accounts itemise a first payment of £150 to Guelfi on 26 March 1731 and three weeks later, on 16 April 1731, another first payment of £100, for the monument to Lady Westmorland's first husband, Richard Beaumont (**4**) (*ibid*, fol. 95). The success of these monuments probably led the Duke of Richmond, whose Northamptonshire estates adjoined Westmorland's, to commission a monument for his mother (**7**), again designed by Kent, with a bust by Guelfi, conspicuously signed *Joannes Baptista Guelfi, Romanus fecit*. The delicate terracotta model survives as evidence of Guelfi's skill with the medium. It is not clear why the less familiar London sculptor **John Boson** (or Bossom), was called in to carve the surround.

Guelfi was probably introduced to the court by Kent, who was master carpenter in the office of works from 1726. In 1727 the sculptor received an unusual commission, to carve chandeliers for the sumptuous festivities which were held in Westminster Hall at the coronation of George II (**20**). A number of other payments are recorded to him in the royal accounts between 1730 and 1733, all associated with Richmond Lodge, a favourite summer residence of the King and particularly of Queen Caroline. In 1730 a library was added to the Lodge with a chimneypiece decorated on the cross-member with three masks by Guelfi. New work was under way late in 1730 on a rustic grotto in the gardens containing 3 graceful rooms, one of them a library dedicated to quiet meditation. Here Queen Caroline planned to install a series of busts of her particular pantheon of scientists and philosophers, Newton, Locke, Clarke, Woolaston and Boyle (**14**). Four were destined for niches and the fifth, Boyle, was to be on a pedestal in the farthest recess. In 1731 Vertue noted that 4 (he did not list the Boyle) were to be carved in stone by Guelfi and a payment of £160 4s, made in December 1731, probably relates to the 4 terracotta models, which later came into Kent's possession and were bequeathed to Lady Isabella Finch. A stone bust of Newton which belonged to Pope (**13**) was probably part of this commission but was rejected when the Queen changed her mind and decided to have the busts carved in marble. The bust of Sir Francis Bacon, whose authorship is undertain, was the last addition, provided in 1733. An assertion by Sir Francis Walsingham in the *Free Briton* that Rysbrack was the sculptor of the busts was vigorously refuted in the *Grub-Street Journal*: 'For in order to do honour to Mr Rysbrack, he [Walsingham] has attributed to him the bustoes in *her Majesty's* Grotto; which unfortunately happen to be the Work of another, and as Some think, a much inferior Hand' (*G-St J* 193, 6 Sept 1733).

Burlington's patronage of Guelfi came to an abrupt halt, and in 1734 the sculptor left England. Vertue reports a general view that 'Burlington had parted with him very willingly' and implies that his personality was the reason, describing him as 'a man of slow speech. much opinionated, [who] as an Italian thought no body coud be equal to himself. in skill in this country'. (*Vertue* III, 74). Nothing more is known of him except that by 1756 he was dead.

Guelfi had arrived in London without assistants and he left no followers behind him. His success no doubt hinged on his glamorous background as an Italian, trained by Rusconi, championed by Burlington, the great arbiter of English taste, and lucky enough to work to designs by the two leading architects of the day. In 1720 there was a shortage of able sculptors in this country, but by the early 1730s the situation had changed and patrons no longer needed to rely on a man of difficult temperament, whose skills could be now matched by other immigrant sculptors who had settled in London.

IR

Literary References: *Vertue* III, 51, 73–4; *Faulkner* 1845, 412; *Anecdotes* 1876, 3, 40; *Esdaile* 1948 (2), 317–21; *Webb* 1955 (1), 139–45; *Gunnis* 1968, 183; *Physick* 1969, 69; *Friedman* 1984, 102; *Whinney* 1988, 155–61; *Penny* 1992, 96; RG/JP, 4, 629–33; *Bailey* 1996, 54; *Ingamells* 1997, 780–1; *Grove* 13, 1996, 582–3 (Eustace); *Giometti* 1999, 26–43; *Giometti* 2000, 79–95

Archival References: Westmorland Papers, misc vol 1, fol 94, 26 March 1731, fol 95, 16 April 1731

Wills: William Kent, PROB 11/761

Funerary Monuments

No.	Date	Subject	Location		References
1.	1724–1727	James Craggs (†1721) (designed by James Gibbs) (co-sculptor: Francis Bird) Drawing(s): VAM E. 3641-1913 (repr *Physick* 1969, 70–1); Ashm vol ii, 13; VAM 3641-1913 (*Colvin* 1995, 406) Model(s): SJSM MP 190	Westminster Abbey, London, nave, window ledge under south west tower (architectural elements largely in lapidarium); formerly nave, south aisle		*Webb* 1955 (1), 139–45; 1955 (2), 261; *Sherburn* 1956, II, 242–3, 246, 266, 456–7, 463, 484; *Friedman* 1984, 101, 102, 313 (repr); *Physick* 1969, 69 (repr), *Thornton and Dorey*, 1992, 27 (tc repr); *Giometti* 1999, 29
2.	1730	Edward, Earl of Warwick and Holland (†1727) Payment(s): £100	[St Mary Abbotts, old church]; St Mary Abbots, Kensington, London		Charlotte, Lady Warwick, *Tradesmen's and other Accounts*, 1703/4–1732 BL, MS, Eg.1,973; *Whinney* 1988, 161; *Grove* 13, 782
3.	1725–1730	Thomas Watson Wentworth, Lord Malton (†1723) and his wife Alice (designed by William Kent)	York Minster, north choir aisle; formerly south choir aisle	S	*Aylmer* 1977, 449–51 (repr); *Colvin* 1995, 586; *Baker* 2000, 11, 12–15 (repr)
4.	1731	Richard Beaumont (†1704) Payment(s): £100, part-payment, 1731	Kirkheaton, W R Yorks		*Gunnis* 1968, 183

5.	1731	Thomas and Katherine Stringer (designed by William Kent) Payment(s): £150, part-payment, 1731		Kirkthorpe, W R Yorks		*Webb* 1955 (1), 143–4, (repr); *Gunnis* 1968, 183; *Colvin* 1995, 586
6.	c1731	Thomas Stringer (†1706)		Enfield, Middx		*Webb* 1955 (1), 143–4 (repr)
7.	by 1734	Anne, Duchess of Richmond (†1722), bust only (monument designed by William Kent; frame carved by John Boson) Model(s): VAM A.19-1947, clay		Deene, Northants	S	*Esdaile* 1948 (2), 317–21 (repr); Webb 1955 (2), 143; *Whinney* 1971, 68–9 (repr)

Statues

8.	1721	Arundel Marbles (restoration only)		[Easton Neston, Northants]; Ashmolean		*Whinney* 1988, 159, 449 n7; *Giometti* 1999, 30–35
9.	1732	'repairing the antique statue of Venus'		[coll King George III]; untraced		*Giometti* 1999, 39–40
10.	1727–1734	'many', perhaps including sphinxes for the gardens	s	Chiswick Villa, Middx (sphinxes)		*Vertue* III, 73–4; *Davis* 1991, 95–7 (repr)
11.	1727–1734	Venus and Mercury		[Chiswick House, Middx, Gallery, niches]; untraced		*Faulkner* 1845, 412; *Gunnis* 1968, 183

Busts

12.	1729	Palladio and Inigo Jones Payment(s): £50		[coll Lord Burlington]; Chatsworth, Derbys		Burlington Misc Box 3, Misc bills, 30 Oct 1729; *Hewlings* 2003, 3–4
13.	c1731	Sir Isaac Newton	s	[coll Alexander Pope]; Scone Palace, Perths		*GM* 1744, 313; *Webb* 1952, 216–8 (repr); *Giometti* 1999, 38–9 (repr)
14.	1732	British Scientists and Philosophers: Samuel Clarke, John Locke, William Woolaston, Sir Isaac Newton, Hon Robert Boyle Model(s): Newton, Locke, Woolaston and Clarke in William Kent's will, 1743 and i the codicil, 10 April 1748 (prob 11/761) bequeathed to Lady Isabella Finch, clay; untraced	m	[The hermitage, Queen Caroline's grotto, Old Lodge, Richmond, Surrey]; Locke, Clarke, Woollaston, Newton, Boyle, Royal Coll, Kensington Palace, London; Windsor Castle (Bacon only) Other versions: Boyle: Hilary Chelminski Antiques, exhib Sept–Oct 2002		TNA AO 1/2454/166; *GM* II, 1732, 922, III, 1733, *passim*; IV, 1734, 158, 1735, 532–35; *Webb* 1952, 216–8 (Newton repr); *Webb* 1954, 148, 153; *Sherburn* 1956, IV, 244; *Colvin* 1973–6, V, 224 n4; *Colton* 1974, pt 2, 181–91; *Colton* 1976, 1 –20; *Giometti* 1999, 38–9 (repr); *Balderston* 2008
15.	1733	John Locke, with tunic collar fastened	m	[Queen Caroline's Grove]; Kensington Palace, London, RCIN 1395	S	*Webb* 1952, 216–8 (repr), Ingamells forthcoming
16.	1733	Sir Isaac Newton	m	[Queen Caroline's Grotto, Richmond]; Kensington Palace, London		*Webb* 1952, 216–8 (repr); *Webb* 1954, 144, 222 (repr)
17.	1733	William Wollaston	m	[Queen Caroline's Grotto, Richmond]; Royal Coll, Kensington Palace, London, RCIN 1390	S	*Webb* 1954, 143, 147, 148, 153, 227 (repr)
18.	1727–1734	Two little heads of children		[Chiswick Villa, Middx]; Chatsworth, Derbys A 113		*Faulkner* 1845, 412; *Esdaile* 1948 (2) 318; *Giometti* 1999, 33, 35 (repr)

Chimneypieces

19.	1730	Three heads for a chimneypiece Payment(s): £16 5s 6d	m	[Richmond Lodge, Surrey, library]; untraced		*Giometti* 1999, 37, n72 (repr)

Miscellaneous

20.	1727	Chandeliers for the coronation of King George II Payment(s): £57 15s		[Westminster Hall, London]; untraced		*Giometti* 1999, 36, 42 n69
21.	1729	Portland terms and vases	s	[coll Lord Burlington]; untraced		*Hewlings* 2003, 3–4

GUTHRIE fl 1748

Architectural Sculpture

1.	1748	Ord family Arms		Fenham Hall, Northumbs, south front		Pevsner, *Northumbs*, 1992, 517

GVD

Signatory of an ivory portrait medallion of Queen Elizabeth in the Victoria and Albert Museum (1). The work is based on a bust by **Michael Rysbrack**, and it seems likely that the sculptor was also a Flemish artist working in England. It is possible that the sculptor is identical with '**GVDR**.'

Reliefs

1.	nd	Queen Elizabeth	i	VAM (Loan 11)	S	

GVDR fl 1734–40

A mysterious signatory of several ivory medallions. The profile portrait of the youthful Henry Wooton, portrayed with curls falling onto his shoulders and an intricately carved cravat, is the earliest known work of the sculptor and is of very high quality (1). So to are the full-face portrait *en negligé* of the artist and dealer Hamlet Winstanley and the historicising portrait of John Roe, presented in a loosely curled wig (2, 3). The signature differs slightly on each: Winstanley is signed 'G.V.D.R.,' John Roe 'G.V.D.R', and Henry Wootton 'G. VDR.' The identity of the sculptor has not yet been discovered, but affinities with the work of **Gasper Van Der Hagen**, who appears also on one occasion, to have signed his works with a oblique monogram, suggests that GVDR was one of a circle of Flemish sculptors working in London and connected with **Michael Rysbrack**. He may perhaps be identified with the sculptor who signs himself '**GVD**.'

Literary References: *Acquisitions* 1981, 63; *Theuerkauff* 1984, 105–7

Reliefs

1.	1734	Henry Wooton	i	BM n428	S	
2.	1740	Hamlet Winstanley	i	Solds Sotheby, 17 July 1980; VAM A.96-1980	SD	*Acquisitions* 1981, 63 (repr); *Theuerkauff* 1984, 105–7
3.	nd	John Roe	i	VAM A.122-1937	S	

GVR

Mysterious signatory of an ivory carving of Oliver Cromwell (VAM). It is possible that the author is identical with the carver who signs himself 'GVDR'.

HACKER, James fl 1826–39

In 1826, while living at 42 Park Street, Camden Town, he won an award from the Society of Arts (**1**). He exhibited at the Royal Academy for the last time in 1839 from 8 Gray's Inn Square.

Literary References: RSA *Transactions*, vol 44, 1826, xliii; *Graves* III, 1905–6, 345

Busts

1.	1826	Unidentified subject	[Soc of A, silver palette]; untraced	RSA, *Transactions*, vol 44, 1826, xliii
2.	1829	Unidentified artist	[Exhib RA, London, 1151]; untraced	*Graves* III, 1905–6, 345
3.	1839	Mr Back	[Exhib RA, London, 1325]; untraced	*Graves* III, 1905–6, 345
4.	1839	Rev Lancelot Sharpe	[Exhib RA, London, 1334]; untraced	*Graves* III, 1905–6, 345

HACKER, John, of Canterbury fl 1789–1831

He was probably the son of James Hacker of Canterbury, a mason, who was paid £407 in 1789 for building the market-place in Canterbury (City Archives). John signs a number of 'dull' tablets in Kent. That to William Price is signed 'J. and C. Hacker fecit London and Canterbury'.

Literary References: *Gunnis* 1968, 184

Funerary Monuments

1.	?1803	Rev William Gregory	Canterbury Cathedral, Kent	S	*Gunnis* 1968, 184
2.	?1806	Robert Stains	Holy Cross, Canterbury, Kent	S	*Gunnis* 1968, 184
3.	?1814	Vincent Wood	Chilham, Kent	S	*Gunnis* 1968, 184
4.	?1826	William Price (co-sculptor: C Hacker)	Allesley, Coventry	S	*Gunnis* 1968, 184
5.	†1830	Anthony Jennings	Fordwich, Canterbury, Kent	S	
6.	†1831	Rev Robert Croft	Rowley, E R Yorks	S	Pevsner, *Yorks: E R & York*, 1995, 662

HACKWOOD, William 1753–1839

He was one of Josiah Wedgwood's best modellers, hired in 1769, initially for 5 years. Wedgwood wrote to Bentley on 20 September describing Hackwood as an 'ingenious boy', who had 'modelled at nights in his way for three years past, has never had the least instruction, which circumstances considered he does things amazingly, and will be a valuable acquisition'. By 1776 Wedgwood was writing that he wished the firm had 'half a dozen more Hackwoods' (quoted in *Bindman* 1979, 67). He agreed to work for the firm for another 4 years on 11 November 1778, at a wage of one and a half guineas a week, with a rent-free house. He was probably the most prolific of the modellers employed by Wedgwood and was responsible for many heads in such series as 'Illustrious Moderns'. He modelled a medallion of Wedgwood himself, of which an impression, dated 1782, is in the British Museum. He remained in employment there until 1832. He also modelled for James Tassie.

Literary References: *Gunnis* 1968, 184; *Pyke* 1973, 61; *Bindman* 1979, 67; *Pyke* 1981, 20; *Tattersall* 1985, 37; *Dawson* 1981, repr 15

Archival References: Hackwood/Wedgwood MSS E2/1353A; E2/1353–1394, L1/54 (William Hackwood Accounts 1735–1831)

Miscellaneous

1.	nd	Classical-mythological works	w	Chicago AI	*Pyke* 1973, 61 (pl 118)

HADLOW, A T fl 1829

Funerary Monuments

1.	1829	Greet family	Queenborough, Kent, churchyard	Pevsner, *Kent: N E & E*, 1983, 420

HAGBOLT, Jacob Hermann 1775–1849

Principally known as a wax modeller, he was also responsible for one monument with a bust in London (**1**). He was born in Uerdingen in the Rhineland, trained under Caspar Hardy, and travelled in Holland and lower Germany. He executed portraits in wax of British sitters, and was certainly in England by 1826 when he exhibited at the Royal Academy from 53 Newman Street. He subsequently lived in Berwick Street and Frith Street, Soho, and was at 71 Princes Street, Leicester Square, in 1833.

His wax statuette of Lady Caroline Gordon is a tiny figure of a child in a white dress, with pink shoes. She holds a tabby cat under her left arm and a brown jug is at her side (**2**). Hagbolt appears also to have modelled for William Tassie, and took his portrait (**6**).

In 1840 he returned to Germany, where he stayed for the remainder of his life. He died in Cologne.

Literary References: *Graves* III, 1905–6, 347; *Gunnis* 1968, 184; *Pyke* 1973, 61–2; *Pyke* 1981, 20

Funerary Monuments

1.	1831	Major James Rennell		[Exhib RA, London, 1169]; Westminster Abbey, London, north west tower		*Graves* III, 1905–6, 347; *MacMichael* 1977, 22

Statues

2.	1829	Lady Caroline Gordon, statuette	w	VAM A.21-1939	D	*Gunnis* 1968, 184; *Pyke* 1973, 61 (pl 121)

Busts

3.	1826	Hon Lady Cust	[Exhib RA, London, 946]; untraced	*Graves* III, 1905–6, 347
4.	1830	Rt Hon John Sullivan	[Exhib RA, London, 1090]; untraced	*Graves* III, 1905–6, 347

Reliefs

5.	1831	Major Rennell, medallic portrait		[Exhib RA, London, 1043]; untraced	*Graves* III, 1905–6, 347
6.	1833	William Tassie, medallic portrait		[Exhib RA, London, 1082]; untraced Other versions: Private coll	*Graves* III, 1905–6, 347

Miscellaneous

7.	1796	Erasmus Darwin		Brighton AG and Museum Other versions: Private coll	*Pyke* 1981, 20
8.	1820	James Mure		Private coll, USA	*Pyke* 1981, 20
9.	1825	Anna Penelope Gordon	w	Private coll	*Pyke* 1973, 61
10.	1825	Anne Gordon	w	Private coll	*Pyke* 1973, 61
11.	1825	Charles David Gordon, Laird of Abergeldie	w	Private coll Other versions: private coll	*Pyke* 1973, 61
12.	1825	David Gordon	w	Private coll	*Pyke* 1973, 61
13.	1825	Michael Francis Gordon	w	Private coll	*Pyke* 1973, 61
14.	1832	Leigh Thomas		[Exhib RA, London, 1082]; untraced	*Graves* III, 1905–6, 1082
15.	nd	Alexander, 4th Duke of Gordon	w	Private coll	*Pyke* 1973, 61; *Pyke* 1981, 20

HAINES, Edward fl 1743

Chimneypieces

1.	1743	For the 'new hall and the eating room'		Hampden House, Bucks	Archives, Earl of Buckinghamshire cited in *Gunnis* 1968, 184; Pevsner, *Bucks*, 1994, 348

Architectural Sculpture

2.	1743	Carvings in the 'alcove'	wd	[Hampden House, Bucks]; untraced	Archives, Earl of Buckinghamshire cited in *Gunnis* 1968, 184

HAINES, John –1828

The son of another John Haines, who was apprenticed in 1743 and died in 1782. John II became a prominent mason and builder of Stamford, but was made bankrupt in 1794. He was probably the brother of **Robert Haines**.

Archival References: RG/JP, 4, 634v.

Funerary Monuments

1.	†1780	Elizabeth Lafargue	All Saints, Stamford, Lincs	S	RG/JP, 4, 634v
2.	†1788	John Bushby	St John the Baptist, Stamford, Lincs		RG/JP, 4, 634v

HAINES, Robert fl 1788–92

A builder and mason of Stamford, he was probably the brother of **John Haines**. He rebuilt Tickencote church in 1792 and in 1788 set up the monument to Elizabeth, widow of William 2nd Earl of Exeter, in Tinwell church after its removal from Clerkenwell.

Archival References: RG/JP, 4, 634v.

HAKEWILL, Henry James 1813–34

Hakewill was born at Grove Road, St John's Wood on 11 May, 1813 and christened on 5 June at St Marylebone. He was the third son of the architect, James Hakewill (1778–1843) and Maria Catherine Hakewill, a painter who exhibited portraits of her offspring at the Royal Academy. His brothers Henry and James Hakewill both became architects, and Henry James too was intended for the profession, training under Richard Sass. According to the *Literary Gazette*, Sass taught Hakewill drawing and modelling, whereupon the boy decided that his 'taste and inclination' were for sculpture rather than architecture (*Lit Gaz* 1834, 249). On 14 June 1830 he enrolled at the Royal Academy Schools to study sculpture. In the following year he won a silver medal for a figure of *Apollino* (1) and was admitted to the Life Academy.

In 1832 Hakewill first exhibited at the Royal Academy, giving his address as 9 Manchester Street, then the family home. He showed a full-length model of Sir Richard Beaumont, the founder of the Almshouses at Waltham Cross, in 'armour of the time of Richard the First' (*Lit Gaz* 1834, 250) (3). In the same year, capitalising on the successful passage of the Great Reform Act, Hakewill modelled a small figure of the Prime Minister, Lord Grey (2). A committee under the chairmanship of Lord Duncannon was formed to raise funds to have it carved in marble and erected in Marylebone. The project attracted the patronage of the Earl of Bedford, who was sceptical about the sculptor's abilities until he saw the model. Another subscriber was Earl Pomfret, who sent **E H Baily** to assess its quality. Baily's report was 'so favourable to the talent of the artist' that Pomfret increased the size of his subscription from £5 to £10 (*Lit Gaz* 1834, 250). Despite these endorsements the public subscription failed to raise enough funds and the project had to be abandoned.

Late in 1833 Hakewill fell ill and he died of consumption on 13 March 1834. His last exhibited work was a bust of Lord Brougham, modelled when the subject was dispensing justice in the assize courts (7). Hakewill's obituary described him as 'tall and elegant, and his face eminently beautiful; his manners and address were of the most prepossessing character – modest, unassuming but collected'. The writer considered it almost certain that had Hakewill lived 'his name would have ranked among the sculptors who have done honour to the country' (*Lit Gaz* 1834, 250).

Literary References: *Lit Gaz* 1834, 249–50; *Graves* III, 1905–6, 352; *Hutchison* 1960–62, 181; *Colvin* 1995, 446

Archival References: IGI

Statues

1.	1831	Figure of Apollino, model	[RA, London, silver medal]; untraced	RA Premium list; *Lit Gaz* 1834, 250; *Gunnis* 1968, 184
2.	1832	Charles, 2nd Earl Grey, model for unexecuted public statue in Marylebone, London	Untraced	*Lit Gaz* 1834, 250; *Gunnis* 1968, 184

No.	Date	Subject		Location		References
3.	1832	Sir Richard and Lady Beaumont, models for statues for Beaumont Almshouses, Waltham Cross Model(s): Sir Richard Beaumont, full-length, exhib RA, London, 1125; untraced		Untraced		*Lit Gaz* 1834, 250; *Graves* III, 1905–6, 351; *Gunnis* 1968, 184
Busts						
4.	1832	Unidentified gentleman		[Exhib Soc of BA, London, 877]; untraced		*Johnson* 1975, 199
5.	1833	James Wadmore		[Exhib RA, London, 1223]; untraced		*Lit Gaz* 1834, 250; *Graves* III, 1905–6, 351; *Johnson* 1975, 199
6.	1833	'Young gentleman' (perhaps Hakewill's younger brother)		[Exhib RA, London, 1111]; untraced		*Graves* III, 1905–6, 351; *Lit Gaz* 1834, 250
7.	1832–1834	Lord Chancellor Brougham		[Exhib RA, London, 1834, 1069]; untraced		*Lit Gaz* 1834, 250; *Graves* III, 1905–6, 351; *Gunnis* 1968, 184
Reliefs						
8.	1833	Mazeppa ('To me the desert born was led' – Lord Byron), bas-relief		[Exhib RA, London, 1115]; untraced		*Lit Gaz* 1834, 250; *Graves* III, 1905–6, 351; *Johnson* 1975, 199

HALE, J fl 1815

No.	Date	Subject		Location		References
Funerary Monuments						
1.	†1815	Long family member		Swindon, Glos	S	Pevsner, *Glos: Vale & Forest of Dean*, 1976, 354

HALE, William fl 1850

No.	Date	Subject		Location		References
Miscellaneous						
1.	1850	Model after the antique		[RA, London, gold medal]; untraced		RA Premium list

HALFPENNY, William –1786

Halfpenny was mason to Lincoln's Inn, 1752–85. He built the north wing of Stone Buildings, 1782–85. Mortimer gives Halfpenny's address as Red Lion Street, Holborn in 1763, and there he remained to the end of his life. He died in 1786 and his will was proved on 17 November that year. Gunnis confused him with the cabinetmaker, architect and writer, William Halfpenny, who built the Redland Chapel in Bristol and who died in 1755. A William Halfpenny signs a very fine monument with a portrait bust of Ann Dash, her head covered with a scarf. Beneath her are two portrait medallions (1).

Literary References: *Mortimer* 1763, 49; *Gunnis* 1968, 184; *Whinney* 1988, 249, 459n15

Archival References: Archives, Lincoln's Inn, cited in *Gunnis* 1968, 184

Will: PROB 11/1147

No.	Date	Subject		Location		References
Funerary Monuments						
1.	†1750	Anne Dash		All Saints, Isleworth	S	*Whinney* 1988, 249; Pevsner, *London: N W*, 1991, 430
Architectural Sculpture						
2.	1757	Sundial Payment(s): £21		[Garden Row, Lincon's Inn, London]; untraced		Archives, Lincoln's Inn, cited *in Gunnis* 1968, 184

HALL, J, of Sleaford fl 1776

No.	Date	Subject		Location		References
Funerary Monuments						
1.	1776	Robert Cranwell		Ruskington, Lincs	S	GPC

HALL, John fl *c*1814–38

He was the mason responsible for the sandstone Tuscan column at Swansfield House, built to commemorate British success in the Napoleonic Wars (2).

No.	Date	Subject		Location		References
Funerary Monuments						
1.	†1838	Mary Patterson		Chennai (Madras) Cathedral	S	
Miscellaneous						
2.	*c*1814	Peace Column	s	Alnwick golf course (formerly grounds of Swansfield House, Northumbs)		*Usherwood* 2000, 5–6 (repr)

HALL, Joseph I, of Derby –1766

The son of **William Hall of Derby**, he was the master-mason at Kedleston and was responsible for nearly all the carved stone, alabaster and woodwork in the house (7). In 1761 Hall went into a partnership for a short time with a Mr Chambers and together they built the east wing, but he was working on his own in 1763, when he was responsible for the west wing and for the main staircase. In June 1757 he produced carved work for Tissington Hall, including a chimneypiece (5). There his bill was overseen by **Daniel Sephton** and **Henry Watson**.

He was buried at St Werburgh's, Derby on 14 January 1766. He or his father is probably the 'Hall of Derby' who supplied works to Calke Abbey in the 1720s and 1730s (**2, 3, 10**).

Literary References: *Gunnis* 1968, 185

Archival References: RG/JP, 4, 635v (inf, Maxwell Craven)

No.	Date	Subject		Location		References
Funerary Monuments						
1.	1852	Archbishop Sandys, repairs only		Southwell Cathedral, Notts		*Gunnis* 1968, 185; Pevsner *Notts* 1979, 328
Chimneypieces						
2.	1724	Description unavailable Payment(s): £17	m	[Calke Abbey, Derbys]; untraced		GPC
3.	1733	Description unavailable Payment(s): £28	m	[Calke Abbey, Derbys, hall]; untraced		GPC
4.	1745	For 'the great dineing room' Payment(s): £31 10s	m	[Melbourne Hall, Derbys]; untraced		Archives, Marquess of Lothian quoted in *Gunnis* 1968, 185

5.	1757	Gothick, after an engraving by Batty Langley		Tissington Hall, Derbys	RG/HMC
6.	c1760	For Lord Scarsdale's dressing room and Lady Scarsdale's bedroom Payment(s): £21, £37		[Kedleston Hall, Derbys]; untraced	*Gunnis* 1968, 185
Architectural Sculpture					
7.	1760–1763	Including alabaster columns in the great hall; capitals and pilasters for the portico and Corinthian capitals for the drawing room Payment(s): £1,645		Kedleston Hall, Derbys	*Gunnis* 1968, 185
8.	1763	Pedestal for a statue of Venus	s	[Kedleston Hall, Derbys]; untraced	*Gunnis* 1968, 185
9.	1763	Piers for the churchyard gate		[Kedleston Hall, Derbys]; untraced	*Gunnis* 1968, 185
Miscellaneous					
10.	1723	Sideboard table	m	[Calke Abbey, Derbys]; untraced	GPC

HALL, Joseph II, of Derby 1789–

The grandson of **Joseph Hall I,** he was baptised on 6 December 1789 at All Saints, Derby, the son of Elias and Mary Hall. He appears to have spent his early career in the metropolis, since he is described in the marriage register of St Werburgh, Derby, as 'of London, Mineralist'. His bride, whom he married on 1 January 1816, was Ann Pitman, the granddaughter of **Richard Brown II**, who owned the Derbyshire Marble Works. In 1829 Hall succeeded **Richard Brown III** as proprietor of these works. In his *History and Gazeteer of the County of Derby* Glover wrote that Hall was 'a person well qualified from his knowledge of mineralogy and long experience in the business, to continue improving in taste and elegance the innumerable articles he manufactures'. He was also apparently a benefactor to his native town, responsible for building 'swimming and other baths for the accommodation of the inhabitants' some time before 1830 (*Glover* 1831–3, 2, 606).

Hall exhibited a statue of a faun at the Royal Academy in 1838 (**22**). He must have used an unusual material for an additional note in the catalogue assured the viewer that 'the colour of the marble' was 'entirely natural' (*Graves* III, 1905–6, 356). He was assisted by his sons Joseph (baptised on 19 November 1818 at St Alkmund's, Derby) and Thomas (baptised in 1825). They may have taken over the business by 1849, when the firm was listed in a local directory as 'Joseph and Thomas Hall'. The business was on the site of the ancient monastery of St Helen in St Helen's Street, with a showroom in Railway Terrace. The firm also owned premises at various times in King Street and Barlow Street.

The Halls manufactured monuments and ornaments in Derbyshire 'black marble'. Those to George Robinson and John Macauley have well-carved reliefs (**12, 15**), whilst the architectural monument to the Earl of Leicester (which was noted by the London press) incorporated a bust by **John Francis** and a ceramic crest executed at the Derby China Works (**19**). A selection of the firm's works, illustrating the polishing process from rough block to the finished article, was shown at the Great Exhibition in 1851 (**23–26**). That year the *Art Journal* wrote that 'Mr Hall is the most extensive and certainly the most meritorious manufacturer of these peculiarly native works' (quoted in *Tomlinson* 1996, 43). Four years later the firm were the only exhibitors showing ornaments in a Derbyshire black stone at the Exposition Universelle in Paris. It was taken over by a former manager, **R G Lomas** of 37 King Street, Derby, who advertised his succession to the business in 1860.

Literary References: *Builder* 1844, 554; *Gunnis* 1968, 185; *Tomlinson* 1996, 19, 43, 58, 67

Archival References: IGI; GPC; RG/JP, 4, 636 v

Funerary Monuments						
1.	†1819	John Hope		Derby Cathedral	S	*Gunnis* 1968, 185; Pevsner, *Derbys*, 1978, 171
2.	1822	Francis Launder		Elton, Notts		*Gunnis* 1968, 185; Pevsner, *Notts*, 1979, 123
3.	?1826	Granville family		Ellastone, Staffs		GPC
4.	†1826	Lady Welby		Allington, Lincs	S	*Gunnis* 1968, 185; Pevsner, *Lincs*, 1989, 97
5.	?1827	Martha Twigge		Bakewell, Derbys	S	*Gunnis* 1968, 185
6.	?1831	Thomas Grosvenor		Leek, Staffs	S	*Gunnis* 1968, 185
7.	†1834	Elizabeth Woodcock		Caythorpe, Lincs	S	Pevsner, *Lincs*, 1989, 217
8.	?1834	Rev John Mosley		Rolleston, Staffs	S	*Gunnis* 1968, 185
9.	†1836	John Browne		Tutbury, Staffs, churchyard	S	
10.	†1836	Joseph Cantrell		Melbourne, Derbys	S	
11.	?1836	Josiah Crammer		Heanor, Derbys	S	*Gunnis* 1968, 185
12.	†1837	Rev George Robinson		Tutbury, Staffs	S	*Gunnis* 1968, 185; Pevsner, *Staffs*, 1974, 289
13.	?1838	Samuel Allsopp		Burton-on-Trent Parish Church, Staffs	S	*Gunnis* 1968, 185
14.	†1839	Walter Evans		Darley Abbey, Derbys	S	Pevsner, *Derbys*, 1978, 193
15.	†1840	John Macaulay		Repton, Derbys	S	*Gunnis* 1968, 185; Pevsner, *Derbys*, 1978, 305
16.	†1841	Cecilia Cantrell		Melbourne, Derbys	S	
17.	?1841	Rev Charles Hope		Derby Cathedral, vault		GPC
18.	?1842	WA Shirley, Bishop of Sodor and Man		Shirley, Derbys	S	*Gunnis* 1968, 185
19.	1844	Thomas, 1st Earl of Leicester (†1842), bust by John Francis (design by Henry Stevens)		Longford, Derbys	S	*Builder* 1844, 554; *Penny* 1977 (1), 188; Pevsner, *Derbys*, 1978, 268
20.	?1845	Miss Linwood		St Margaret, Leicester		*Gunnis* 1968, 185
21.	†1846	Marianne, Sarah and Joseph Briggs		Melbourne, Derbys	S	
Statues						
22.	1838	A faun	m	[Exhib RA, London, 1352]; untraced		*Graves* III, 1905–6, 356; *Gunnis* 1968, 185
Chimneypieces						
23.	1851	'of black marble, from the quarries of the Duke of Devonshire'		[Gt Exhib]; untraced		*Tomlinson* 1996, 59

Miscellaneous

24.	1851	Tazza of Derbyshire rosewood marble; black marble with handles	[Gt Exhib]; untraced	*Tomlinson* 1996, 59
25.	1851	Tripod, carved in black marble	[Gt Exhib]; untraced	*Tomlinson* 1996, 59
26.	1851	Vases, in black marble	[Gt Exhib]; untraced	*Tomlinson* 1996, 59

HALL, Richard, of Nottingham –1680

Hall is said to have had his workshop in or near Stoney Street. Most of his work consists of alabaster monuments in the Midlands tradition. An early example erected in 1642 at Nottingham St Peter to George Cotes survived the destruction of the chancel during the Civil War, only to disintegrate in the 1680s (1). His later work is recorded in letters he wrote to Sir William Dugdale following his engagement as Dugdales's deputy for the Nottinghamshire and Derbyshire visitations of the early 1660s. It includes monuments in Derbyshire to Francis Cavendish (3), Jonathan Sacheverell (4), Sir John Curzon (6), and the replacement of the inscription on the monument of Elizabeth Countess of Shrewsbury (Bess of Hardwick) at Derby (9), and others to Richard Draycott (5), to Richard Mansfield (8) and to Dame Mary Middleton (7). A visit in 1663 to Lady Shirley must surely have been in connection with the inscription and sculpture over the west porch at Staunton Harrold church, Leics, for which she paid an unnamed Nottingham carver. Dugdale encouraged Hall to make drawings of Southwell Minster, which were engraved by Hollar and published in Dugdale's *Monasticon Anglicanum*. Thoroton's *Nottinghamshire* was largely illustrated by Hall and Hollar, including a plate of the monument at West Leake.

Jon Bayliss

Literary References: *Dugdale* 1987; *Transactions of the Thoroton Society*, 91; NT Guide, Staunton Harrold

Funerary Monuments

1.	1642	George Cotes	[St Peter, Nottingham]; destroyed	Inf. Jon Bayliss
2.	†1649	Countess of Kingston	Holme Pierrepont, Notts	C Lib (repr)
3.	†1658	Francis Cavendish	Doveridge, Derbys	Inf. Jon Bayliss
4.	†1662	Jonathan Sacheverell	Morley, Derbys	Inf. Jon Bayliss
5.	†1662	Richard Draycott	Draycott-le-Moors, North Staffs	Inf. Jon Bayliss
6.	1664	Sir John Curzon	Kedleston, Derbys	Inf. Jon Bayliss
7.	†1667	Dame Mary Middleton	Rawmarsh, Morley, W R Yorks	Harleian Soc NS VI, 1987
8.	1668	Richard Mansfield	West Leake, Notts	Inf. Jon Bayliss
9.	c1669	Elizabeth, Countes of Shrewbsury, inscription only	All Saints, Derby	Harleian Soc NS VI, 1987

HALL, W, of Alnwick fl c1814

The monument to Stanton Neale is described by Gunnis as a 'pretty wall tablet' (1).

Funerary Monuments

1.	?1814	Stanton Neale	Alnwick, Northumbs	S	GPC

HALL, William, of Derby –1744?

He was responsible for marble work at All Saints, Derby (2) and is presumably the 'marble-cutter' of that name who married Rebecca Webster at St Alkmund, Derby on 19 November 1724 and was buried at St Westburgh's on 23 October 1744. His father William Hall senior had been buried at the same church on 9 March 1732. His son was **Joseph Hall I of Derby.**

Archival References: RG/JP, 4, 635v (inf, Maxwell Craven)

Chimneypieces

1.	1731	'Urnes and scroles' Payment(s): £6		[All Saints, Derby]; untraced	Cathedral archives in GPC

Miscellaneous

2.	1730–1731	Altarpiece Payment(s): £126	m	All Saints, Derby	Cathedral archives in GPC

HALLEY, of Shrewsbury fl 1765

He was employed by **T F Pritchard.**

Chimneypieces

1.	1765	Baroque chimney frame (designed by Thomas Farnolls Pritchard) (co-sculptor: Nelson and Van der Hagen) Drawing(s): Pritchard drawing book (AIA 3)	wd	Shipton Hall, Salop, library	*Ionides* 1999, 122, 123, 327, 353 (repr)

HAMES, John, of Stamford –1828

He was a prominent mason and builder of Stamford, established by 1775. His career was only temporarily disturbed by bankruptcy in 1794.

Archival References: JP, Misc Corr

Funerary Monuments

1.	†1788	John Bushby	St John, Stamford, Lincs	S	Pevsner, *Lincs*, 1989, 691

HAMILTON, David and Sons, of Glasgow fl c1800–40

The Hamilton family had a marble cutting business in Buchanan Street, Glasgow in the first four decades of the 19th century.

Literary References: *Gunnis* 1968, 185; *Woodward* 1977 (vol 1, pt 2), 92

Funerary Monuments

1.	1816	Lieutenant-Colonel Cadogan (†1813) and sons	Glasgow Cathedral	S	Pevsner, *Glasgow*, 1990, 134
2.	?1817	Colonel Cunynghane	Kirkmichael, Ayrshire	S	*Gunnis* 1968, 185

HAMILTON, J fl c1844

A tablet at Otterden is signed 'J.Hamilton successor to Peter Rouw' (**Peter Rouw II**). A 'Jas Hamilton statuary &c' was listed in Thompson's *Commercial Directory* for 1844 at 80 Portland Road, Marylebone.

Literary References: *Gunnis* 1968, 185

Funerary Monuments

1.	?1844	Sibylla Wheeler	Otterden, Kent	S	*Gunnis* 1968, 185

HAMILTON, James, of Weymouth –1849?

A mason and architect of Weymouth, in 1784 he designed and erected an obelisk to the memory of James Frampton, engraved with 'an explanatory description' for the *Gentleman's Magazine* (*GM* 1787, 49). The obelisk, which is now in poor condition, is surmounted by an urn that weighs around 4 tons (**2**).

Hamilton was the mason responsible for building Bridport town hall in 1785 (Town Archives cited in *Gunnis* 1968, 185). In 1795 he rebuilt the south-east wall of the Cobb at Lyme Regis (Town Archives cited in *Gunnis* 1968, 185), and in 1796 contracted to rebuild the County Hall at Dorchester for £3,100 (Dorset County Archives). In 1803 he designed the statue of George III for Weymouth, which was executed in artificial stone by the **Coade Factory of Lambeth.** He provided a Greek Revival monument to commemorate the passengers and crew of the East Indiaman, *Alexander*, lost between London and Bombay, with 140 casualties (**1**). It was described it as 'a noble monument' (*New Monthly Mag* 1816, 5, 80).

The will of a James Hamilton, Builder of Weymouth was proved on 6 June 1849 (PROB 11/2094).

Literary References: *Gunnis* 1968, 185–6; *Colvin* 1995, 452–3

Archival References: GPC

Funerary Monuments

1.	1815	Passengers and crew of the *Alexander*	Wyke Regis, Dorset, churchyard		*New Monthly Mag* 1816, 5, 80; *Gunnis* 1968, 185; *Colvin* 1995, 453

Architectural Sculpture

2.	1785–1786	James Frampton (†1784), obelisk Drawing(s): Bodleian, Gough Maps 6 ff79, 105v	Moreton, Dorset		*GM* 1787, 57, 1, 49 (repr); *Colvin* 1995, 453

HAMILTON, John fl c1699

The architectural monument to Sir Robert Napier (**1**) is signed 'Johannes Hamiltonus Scoto-Britannus fecit'.

Funerary Monuments

1.	c1699	Sir Robert Napier	Puncknowle, Dorset	S	*Gunnis* 1968, 186; Pevsner, *Dorset*, 1972, 353

HAMILTON, of London fl 1803?

Funerary Monuments

1.	?1803	David Mitchell	Aberdeen Cathedral	S	GPC

HAMILTON, William fl 1782

He was employed under Sir John Soane in 1782 to assist in building a house for William Tollemache, later Earl of Dysart at Hyde Park Corner.

Archival References: Soane Journal, 1781–97, f 19v; Abstract of Bills 1, f 1 (both small payments)

HAMLET, Thomas fl 1823–27

A wax modeller and painter on glass and ivory.

Literary References: *Pyke* 1973, 62

Busts

1.	1823	Frederick-Augustus, Duke of York and Albany	w	Canberra Public Library, Australia Other versions: Stanton Harcourt, Oxon, dated 1827, Pyke 1973, 62 (pl 123)	SD	GPC

Miscellaneous

2.	1826	King George IV	w	Hove Museum, Sussex	D	*Pyke* 1973, 62
3.	1827	Ernest Augustus, Duke of Cumberland	w	Hove Museum, Sussex		GPC

HAMLETT, John, of Stroud fl 1826–54

He was in partnership at one time with a mason called Freebury (**3**).

Funerary Monuments

1.	†1835	Robert Griffin	s	Eastington, Glos	S	Pevsner, *Glos: Vale & Forest of Dean*, 1976, 178
2.	†1854	Elizabeth Dimock		St Cyr, Stonehouse, Glos	S	Pevsner, *Glos: Vale & Forest of Dean*, 1976, 352
3.	†1854	John Little (co-sculptor: Freebury)		Pitchcombe, Glos	S	Pevsner, *Glos: Cotswolds*, 1999, 561
4.	nd	Unidentified subject, tablet		St Mary (New), Woodchester, Glos	S	Pevsner, *Glos: Cotswolds*, 1999, 744

Busts

5.	1826	Augustus Frederick, Duke of Sussex	b	Ombersley Court, Worcs	SD	*Gunnis* 1968, 186

HAMMOND, H fl 1850–52

His address in 1850–1 was 111 Stanhope Street, London.

Literary References: *Graves* III, 1905–6, 370

Busts

1.	1850	The village maiden	[Exhib RA, London, 1452 BI, London, 1851, 535]; untraced	*Graves* 1875, 240; *Graves* III, 1905–6, 370
2.	1852	Dr Cholmondeley	[Exhib RA, London, 1434]; untraced	*Graves* III, 1905–6, 370

HAMMOND (or HAMON), William fl 1652–87

Probably the 'William Hamon' who was apprenticed to the chief bridge mason, Henry Wilson, he was working at London Bridge in October 1652 at 9s a week. A William Adams was apprenticed to Hammond on 4 August 1660. He was admitted to the livery of the Masons' Company in 1669. Between 1670 and 1679 he was employed in rebuilding Vintners' Hall and was paid £200 in 1669, £150 in 1672, £100 in 1674 and 1675 and £200 in 1676. He also worked at the Royal College of Physicians on projects that included a gateway, for which he earned £210 in 1675. Robert Hooke has the brusque entry in his diary for April 1675: 'Back to Physicians' College. Met Hammond. Disliked carvings' (*Robinson and Adams* 1935, 157). He was employed as a mason in the City churches of St Michael, Crooked Lane (1684–1690); St Anne and St Agnes (1676–87) and All Hallows the Great (1677–87) and provided the staircase at Montagu House, Bloomsbury, in 1678.

Hammond joined the Court of Assistants of the Masons' Company in 1672, was renter warden in 1680 and 1683, and was still a member of the Court in 1687. He probably died before 1696 since his name does not appear on the list of assistants for that year. His daughter, Mary, 'Spinster, about 25' married Richard Miller, a mason of St Saviour, Southwark, Surrey in 1687. Her father is described as 'of All Hallows the Less, Cit & Mason' (*Armytage* 1892, vol 31, 1687–1694, 21).

Literary References: *Knoop and Jones* 1935, 31; *Robinson and Adams* 1935, 364, 365; *Gunnis* 1968, 186; *Webb* 1999, 1

Archival References: Masons' Co, Masters and Wardens; Masons' Co, Freemen, fol 1; Vintners, RW Accts, vol 5; GPC

Architectural Sculpture

1.	nd	Carved stonework, including 'six pilasters with capitals' Payment(s): £107 for pilasters and capitals	s	[All Hallows the Great, London]; destroyed		*Gunnis* 1968, 186

Miscellaneous

2.	1675	Gateway Payment(s): £210		[R C Physic, London]; untraced		Archives, R C Physic, cited in *Gunnis* 1968, 186

HAMSTON, J S, of Kensington fl 1825

He is known only for one gothic tablet.

Funerary Monuments

1.	†1825	Major John Samuel Torriano		St Mary Abbots, Kensington, London	S	*Gunnis* 1968, 186

HANCOCK, John fl 1703–18

He was probably a York mason. The Mellish monument is about 18 feet high and features a stiff, semi-reclining figure in contemporary dress (**1**). The Pashley is a large architectural work with a central urn (**2**). The grandest of his works commemorates Sir Edward Blackett (**3**). This 24 feet high edifice has an architectural ground forming a backdrop to the reclining figure of Sir Edward, who is flanked by life-size figures of his two wives.

Gunnis wrote of the three monuments that they are 'on the grand scale, with life-size figures and architectural backgrounds. Though they may have a slight air of country clumsiness, they are nevertheless impressive witnesses to the high standard of craftsmanship attained by good provincial work in the first quarter of the eighteenth century. It was extremely difficult to find Hancock's signature on any of these works; indeed, in the case of the Mellish monument I was only able to discover it by climbing a ladder, for it was tucked away at the top of the right-hand Corinthian pilaster supporting the carved pediment' (*Gunnis* 1968, 186).

Funerary Monuments

1.	†1703	Edward Mellish	St Mary and St Martin, Blyth, Notts	S	*Gunnis* 1968, 186; Pevsner, *Notts*, 1979, 79
2.	?1708	George Pashley	Stainton, Yorks	S	*Gunnis* 1968, 186
3.	†1718	Sir Edward Blackett	Ripon Cathedral, W R Yorks		Pevsner, *Yorks: W R*, 1967, 411; *Gunnis* 1968, 186

HANCOCK, John, of London 1825–69

Hancock was closely associated with the Pre-Raphaelites during the 1840s and 1850s. A number of his statues and reliefs received critical acclaim but he appears to have produced only a small number of works and may have given up sculpture when he was in his late thirties. He was born at Fulham in West London in 1825. After his father's death in 1835 he and his eight brothers and sisters were brought up by their uncle, Thomas Hancock, at Marlborough Cottage, Stoke Newington. Thomas Hancock had patented a process for the vulcanization of rubber which he and his family exploited commercially. An affluent background made it possible for John to his pursue artistic interests as a young man free from financial constraints. He was largely self-taught but he attended the Royal Academy Schools briefly in 1842 and may have received encouragement from his uncle, Charles Hancock, who had trained as a painter in London and Norwich (although he eventually abandoned art in order to concentrate on entrepreneurial activities). He exhibited *The Prodigal Son* at the Royal Academy in 1843 (**31**) and the following year sent a statue of Chaucer to the exhibition held at Westminster Hall, to select artists for the new Palace of Westminster (**2**). The work was not well-received: the *Art Union* thought that it showed some originality but was 'not in good taste' (*AU*, 1844, 215), whilst the *Literary Gazette* suggested that 'Mephistopheles would have been a better title' (*Lit Gaz* 1844, 466).

He became involved with the group of artists who later formed the Pre-Raphaelite Brotherhood, *c*1844. He probably met **Thomas Woolner** at the RA Schools and went on to share a studio with him at 101, Stanhope Street, in the late 1840s. He was also friendly with Dante Gabriel Rossetti and prepared a portrait medallion of him in 1846 (**24**). He joined the Cyclographic Society, whose members included Rossetti, John Everett Millais, William Holman Hunt and **Alexander Munro** and was involved in setting-up the Pre-Raphaelite publication, *The Germ*, in 1849–50. He did not, however, become a fully-fledged member of the Brotherhood and his request to sign his works 'PRB' was refused. William Michael Rossetti seems particularly to have disliked Hancock: he expressed great surprise when Hancock was appointed one of the commissioners responsible for selecting sculpture for the Great Exhibition of 1851 and later described him as 'an ungainly little man, wizened, with a long thin nose and a squeaky voice' (*Rossetti* 1906, cited by *James* 1991, 72). His appearance not withstanding, on 30 August 1851 he married Eliza Ann Fernley at St Pancras Old Church, London.

Hancock's first public success was a relief of *Christ's journey to Jerusalem*, which was awarded a prize and issued as a print by the Art Union of London in 1849 (**26**). The relief is related to Pre-Raphaelite works of the same date, particularly in its religious subject matter and the depiction of the disciples as a series of receding profiles, a convention used in paintings by Rossetti and Millais. In 1853 Hancock exhibited a companion piece, *Christ led to crucifixion*, which was also engraved by the Art Union (**27**). His most successful work was a statue of *Beatrice*, shown at the RA in 1850 and at the Great Exhibition the following year (**7**). Again Hancock's choice of subject was clearly influenced by his Pre-Raphaelite connections. The statue was exhibited with a passage from a sonnet by Rossetti entitled *Of Beatrice de'Portinari, on All Saints' Day*, written to accompany *La Vita Nuova*, which describes Dante's first encounter with Beatrice. Rossetti had completed his translation of *La Vita Nuova* in 1848 and made his first drawings of Dante and Beatrice in the late 1840s. Alexander Munro's sculpture of another subject from Dante, *Paolo and Francesca*, is a contemporary work. Henry Weekes, who saw *Beatrice* at the Great Exhibition, wrote 'Will he [the visitor] not stop before the beautiful spiritualised figure of Beatrice . . . and become for a moment absorbed in expression as is the plaster itself?' (*Weekes* 1851, 101, cited by *Read and Barnes* 1991, 106). It was shown again at the Paris Exhibition of 1855, together with a figure of *Maidenhood* (**11**). Of this a French critic said 'the expression and movement in it are remarkable', but he also added that it was 'covered by a thick coat of paint which is barbarous' (*Gunnis* 1968, 186). Hancock sent sculpture to the London International Exhibition of 1862 and continued to exhibit at the RA until 1864, showing largely ideal works, including a bronze figure of *Ariel released from the tree*, which was described as 'of infinite grace and lightness' and 'full of action' (*AJ*, 1858, 172).

Unlike most sculptors of the period Hancock does not seem to have ventured far into the financially profitable areas of portraiture and funerary memorials. His only known monument commemorates Edward Colston, who died aged 10: it has a relief of the boy on his death bed visited by 3 child angels who guide his soul towards Heaven (**1**). A group of 3 mourning children at the foot of the bed is reminiscent of child groups by Munro and the naturalistically represented wild flowers, which decorate the scroll behind the dead boy's head and the corbel beneath the inscription panel, have a precedent in Woolner's monument to William Wordsworth at Grasmere. At least three of his portraits were relief medallions (**24, 29, 30**), a format which particularly appealed to the Pre-Raphaelites.

In 1861 Hancock was commissioned by the Corporation of London to carve a figure of *Penserosa*, based on Milton's poem *Il Penseroso* (**17**). It was one of an important series of 16 statues of subjects from British history and literature commissioned for the Egyptian Hall of the Mansion House in an unusual act of municipal patronage of poetic sculpture. Several years earlier Hancock had modelled a bust of the same subject, which was bought by Prince Albert in 1857 as a Christmas present for Queen Victoria (**19**). The statue was completed in December 1862 and Hancock exhibited a version of it (probably the plaster model) at the RA in 1864. The *Art Journal* considered it genuinely poetic but advised the sculptor to 'revise his drapery, which at present, in its too definite folds, militates against the force of the head' (*AJ*, 1864, 168). A second important commission for a City institution came from the National Provincial Bank in 1864–5. Hancock carved a series of six reliefs for their office in Bishopsgate, designed by the architect John Gibson (**23**). Each of the panels, representing *Agriculture, Navigation, Science, Manufacture, Commerce* and *The Arts*, has an angel holding symbolic objects flanked by appropriate scenes. The series is the most substantial of all Hancock's works but it may also have been his last.

Hancock exhibited for the final time in 1864 (when he showed *Penserosa* at the RA) and little is known of the last few years of his life. WM Rossetti later recorded that 'owing partly to unfortunate circumstances into which it is not my affair to enter, he gradually sank out of observation, and he died in middle age' (*Rossetti* 1906, cited by *James* 1991, 74). He seems to have been in financial difficulties. On his uncle's death in 1865 Hancock was left £4,000 but it was noted in a codicil that he had already received £1,000, and he had also borrowed from Woolner in 1864. Towards the end of his life he lived at South Norwood, but died on 17 October 1869 at 35 Grafton Street, off Tottenham Court Road. His will was administered by his widow and his assets amounted to just £20.

No individual pupils or studio assistants have been identified, but Hancock is mentioned in the records of the Science and Art Department of the South Kensington Museum and appears to have taught for them. Although his association with the Pre-Raphaelites has generated some interest in his life and work in recent years, he remains a shadowy figure. Few of his works survive and it is unlikely that many of them were executed in a more permanent medium than plaster, though some were reproduced as engravings (**26, 27**) or in Parian ware (**8, 9, 22**).

EH

Literary References: *Builder* 1856, 406; 1870, 44; *Palgrave* 1866, 38, 82; *Athenaeum*, 23 Oct 1869, 535; *DNB*, XXIV, 1890, 274 (Cust); *Gunnis* 1968, 186–7; *Read* 1982, 179, 206, 222; *Read* 1984, 97, 99–100, 109; *Read and Barnes*, 1991, 71–6, 104–8 (TB James); *Bilbey* 2003, 290–1; *ODNB* (Greenwood)

Portraits of the Sculptor: J E Millais, canvas, 1849, untraced; photograph of John Hancock's studio, with a woman and two men, one of whom may be Hancock (repr *Read and Barnes* 1991, 71)

Will: PPR, will, 28 December 1869, fol 767, effects valued at under £20

Funerary Monuments

1.	†1859	Edward Colston		St James the Great, Southbroom, Devizes, Wilts	S	*Read and Barnes* 1991, 74, 104 (repr)

Statues

2.	1844	Geoffrey Chaucer		[Exhib Westminster Hall, London, 111]; untraced	*AU*, 1844, 215; *Read and Barnes* 1991, 72
3.	1845	Comus listening to the singing of the benighted lady, a small sedentary plaster figure	p	[Exhib RA, London, 1347]; untraced	*AU* 1845, 196; *Graves* III, 1905–6, 373
4.	1845	The creation of Adam		[Exhib Westminster Hall, London, 137]; untraced	*Westminster* 1845, 16
5.	1847	Youth and joy		[Exhib RA, London, 1319]; untraced	*Graves* III, 1905–6, 373
6.	1848	Una and the lion, sketch		[Exhib RA, London, 1340]; untraced	*Graves* III, 1905–6, 373

7.	1850	Beatrice	p	VAM (anonymous loan) Other versions: ex coll Baroness Burdett Coutts, m; untraced reproduced as a bronze statuette by Elkington and Co	S	*Graves* III, 1905–6, 373; *Bilbey* 2002, 290–1 (repr)
8.	1851	Undine		[Exhib RA, London, 1263]; untraced Other versions: reproduced in Parian ware c1855		*Graves* III, 1905–6, 373; *Atterbury* 1989, 249 (repr 843); *Read and Barnes* 1991, 107 (repr)
9.	1852	The first impulse of love; an angel teaching two children to kiss (perhaps synonymous with Christ and John the Baptist), model for Parian ware		[Exhib RA, London, 1320]; untraced		*Graves* III, 1905–6, 373; *Read and Barnes* 1991, 76; *Atterbury* 1989, 255 (repr 882)
10.	1854	Miranda 'figure. . .attitude extravagant. .'		[Exhib RA, London, 1375]; untraced		*Athaneum* 1854, 656; *Graves* III, 1905–6, 373
11.	1855	Maidenhood Payment(s): 300 gns (marble) 15 gns (plaster)		[Int Exhib, Paris]; untraced		*AJ*, 1859 (repr); *Graves* 1875, 241; *Graves* III, 1905–6, 373; *Read and Barnes* 1991, 73; *Morris and Roberts* 1998, 278
12.	1858	Angel's mission Payment(s): £40	tc	[Exhib RA, London, 1276]; untraced		*Graves* 1875, 241; *Graves* III, 1905–6, 373
13.	1858	Ariel released from the tree	b	[Exhib RA, London, 1196]; untraced		*AJ*, 1858, 172; *Graves Graves* III, 1905–6, 373
14.	1858	Ophelia, statuette	tc	[Exhib RA, London, 1217]; untraced		*Graves* III, 1905–6, 373; *Morris and Roberts* 1998, 278
15.	1858	Temperantia, statuette	tc	[Exhib RA, London, 1283]; untraced		*Graves* III, 1905–6, 373; *Morris and Roberts* 1998, 278
16.	1859	Happiness, 'a light figure of a girl dancing or skipping'		[Exhib RA, London, 1256]; untraced		*AJ* 1859, 172; *Graves* III, 1905–6, 373
17.	1861–1862	Penserosa Model(s): C of L Coll, Mansion House, plaster, acc 140	m	CL Coll, Mansion House, City of London, Egyptian Hall, acc 139 Other versions: small marble sold Sotheby, London, 12 May 1995, lot 170	SD	*Graves* 1875, 241; *Graves* III, 1905–6, 373; *Read and Barnes* 1991, 108; *Ward-Jackson* 2003, 256 (repr)
Busts						
18.	1855	Head of a girl, study		[Exhib RA, London, 1504]; untraced		*Graves* III, 1905–6, 373
19.	1857	Penserosa	p	Royal Coll, Osborne House, I of W Other versions: clay, 1858, untraced family coll		*Graves* III, 1905–6, 373; *Read and Barnes* 1991, 74, 108; *Morris and Roberts* 1998, 278
20.	1859	Unidentified lady		[Exhib RA, London, 1340]; untraced		*Graves* III, 1905–6, 373
21.	1862	Beatrice	m	[Exhib RA, London, 1054]; untraced		*Graves* III, 1905–6, 373
22.	nd	Una, model for Copeland Parian ware		Untraced		*Atterbury* 1989, 181 (repr 591)
Architectural Sculpture						
23.	1864–1865	Agriculture, Navigation, Science, Manufacture, Commerce, the Arts, reliefs	s	National Westminster Bank (former National and Provincial Bank), Bishopsgate, City of London, façade		*Read* 1982, 222, 224–5 (repr); *Ward-Jackson* 2003, 38–9 (repr)
Reliefs						
24.	1846	Dante Gabriel Rossetti, portrait medallion		Untraced		*Mag of Art*, 12, 1889, 24 (repr); *Read and Barnes* 1991, 72 (repr)
25.	1846	The Hours leading out the horses of the sun		[Exhib RA, London, 1417]; untraced		*Graves* III, 1905–6, 373
26.	1849	Christ's journey to Jerusalem (The entry into Jerusalem)	p	[Art Union of London Exhib]; untraced Other versions: engraving issued by the Art Union of London		*Graves* III, 1905–6, 373; *Read and Barnes* 1991, 104–5 (repr)
27.	1853	Christ led to crucifixion	p	[Exhib RA, London, 1456]; untraced Other versions: Engraving issued by the Art Union of London		*Graves* III, 1905–6, 373; *Read and Barnes* 1991, 104–5 (repr)
28.	1853	Undine, medallion	m	[Exhib RA, London, 1459]; untraced		*Graves* III, 1905–6, 373; *Read and Barnes* 1991, 107
29.	1858	Female head, portrait medallion	tc	[Exhib RA, London, 1268]; untraced		*Graves* III, 1905–6, 373
30.	1858	John Ferneley, portrait medallion	tc	[Exhib RA, London, 1269]; untraced		*Graves* III, 1905–6, 373
Miscellaneous						
31.	1843	The Prodigal Son		[Exhib RA, London, 1459]; untraced		*Graves* III, 1905–6, 372
32.	1848	The poet in solitude		[Exhib RA, London, 1350]; untraced		*Graves* III, 1905–6, 373
33.	1858	Viola	tc	[Exhib Liverpool Ac, 966]; untraced		*Morris and Roberts* 1998, 278
34.	1859	Mrs Winn Knight	m	[Exhib RA, London, 1286]; untraced		*Graves* III, 1905–6, 373
35.	1860	Melancholy and mirth		[Exhib RA, London, 951]; untraced		*Graves* III, 1905–6, 373
36.	1862	Simplicity, sketch from nature		[Exhib RA, London, 1038]; untraced		*Graves* III, 1905–6, 373
37.	1863	Mirth, study for the head of a statue		[Exhib RA, London, 1082]; untraced		*Graves* III, 1905–6, 373

HANDYSIDE, Alexander fl later 18th century

A fisherman and self-taught sculptor. His work, dating from the second quarter of the 18th century, is represented in Inveresk churchyard.

Literary References: *Wrinch* 1969, 380

HANN, Robert, of Carlisle fl 1833

Reliefs

1.	1833	Lord Brougham, medallion portrait	[Exhib Carlisle Acad, 287]; untraced	*Carlisle Ac Exhibs*, 1973

HANSON, Job, of Newbury *c*1789–1874

He died in 1874, aged 85, and is buried in the churchyard of Speen.

Literary References: GPC

Funerary Monuments

1.	?1829	Rev Henry Hall	Chalton, Hants	S	*Gunnis* 1968, 187
2.	?1831	Mary Wyld	Speen, Berks	S	*Gunnis* 1968, 187

HARBORD, of Stratford-upon-Avon fl 1737

George Vertue, who made a trip to Warwickshire in 1737, noted that 'Mr Harbord, Statuary, lives there at Stratford and I commissioned him to make me a cast from the Bust of Shakespeare's head on his Mont' (*Vertue* VI, 83).

HARDCASTLE, Henry fl 1743

The apprenticeship lists record that 'Henry Hardcastle of St James's, Clerkenwell Carver' took Benjamin, son of Francis Saunders, apprentice on 25 October 1743 for seven years at a fee of 15 guineas (*Webb* 1957 (3), 116).

HARDCASTLE, Robert fl 1739–63

He became bankrupt in 1739. In a list of assistants compiled around 1740 by the Masons' Company he was recorded as working in Golden Square. The Westminster poll-book of 1748 describes him as 'mason of John Street, Westminster' (quoted in *Gunnis* 1968, 187). However the 'List of Artists' in Mortimer's *Universal Director* of 1763, lists him as a 'carver in wood and stone', living on the 'Surry side of Westminster Bridge' (*Mortimer* 1763, p13). No works by him have been recorded. Another Robert Hardcastle, perhaps a relation, became free of the Masons' Company by redemption on 29 November 1749.

Literary References: *Gunnis* 1968, 187

Archival References: Masons' Co, *Assistants*, fol 3; Masons' Co, *Freemen*, fol 31

HARDEN, T, of Burton-on-Trent fl *c*1818

He is known only for one large classical tablet.

Funerary Monuments

1.	?1818	George Hutchinson	Tutbury, Staffs	S	*Gunnis* 1968, 187

HARDENBERG, Francis –1852

He was a modeller and a sculptor. Nothing is known of his background or training, but a letter from an employee at the Derby China Works refers to him as a German. He worked at Turner's porcelain factory at Caughley, Salop, before commencing work at Derby in January 1789. He appears to have irritated fellow workers, for J Stables wrote to William Duesbury that **Thomas Mason**, a modeller, 'never can speak with patience of him' (*Bricknell* 1995, 24). The cause may have been Hardenberg's laziness: an undated note records that he had lost more than 18 days of work during the few months in which he was employed. By the end of the year he had aroused the ire of William Duesbury, who dismissed him on 6 December 1789 in an angry letter: 'I am not satisfied with your adding idleness to ignorance – & as to a hope of you ever being able to do me the justice of finishing your engagement with me is I now perceive intirely out of the question – A man that I have found out neither can (or ever cou'd) write or read is not a likely person to execute such an engagement as you had the audacity to make with me & therefore the sooner I put a stop to your picking my pocket in this way I think the better' (quoted in *Bricknell* 1995, 27). On 8 December he received £11 0s 6d in full for his work, and he was subsequently replaced by **J J Spängler**.

Hardenberg, who had married Hannah Woodward at St Alkmund, Derby on 16 November 1789, subsequently moved to London. In 1800 he exhibited at the Royal Academy (**17**), giving his address as 19 Mount Street, Grosvenor Square. He remained there until 1831. His business appears to have been diverse. In 1802 he was listed in a London directory as a 'Petrification manufacturer', presumably supplying ornaments in a variety of marbles (*Clifford* 1992, 56). In 1805 he supplied statues in plaster for Heaton Hall (**3**).

He went into partnership with **Federico Nicoli** in 1817 and was subsequently described in Johnstone's *London Commercial Guide* as 'sculptor and dealer in foreign china' (quoted in *Clifford* 1992, 56). He was paid in 1818 for the bust of Blücher signed by Nicoli for Carlton House (**8**). When William Stuart, Archbishop of Armagh, died in 1822, the *Gentlemans' Magazine* reported that 'a cast was taken from his face by Mr Hardenberg, the sculptor, by desire of Mrs Stuart' (*GM*, 1822, 1, 470).

He died in 1852 at a residence at Hollywood Place, Little Chelsea, where he had lived since 1831. In his will he asked to be buried in the cemetery at St George, Hanover Square. He left all his assets to his two daughters.

Literary References: *Clifford* 1992, 55–6; *Bricknell* 1995, *passim*; *Bricknell* 1998, 11, 73–5, 79

Will: PROB 11/2154

Funerary Monuments						
1.	†1820	Thomas Brooke		All Saints, Runcorn, Cheshire	S	*Gunnis* 1968, 187; Pevsner, *Cheshire*, 1971, 325
2.	†1822	William Stuart, Archbishop of Armagh		Luton, Beds		*Gunnis* 1968, 187
Statues						
3.	1805	Vestal virgins, Comedy and Tragedy	p	Heaton Hall, Lancs	S	*Clifford* 1992, 56
4.	1820	King George III, statuette		NPG, London 4383 Other versions: Several recorded, private colls	SD	*Clifford* 1992, 56
5.	nd	Arthur, 1st Duke of Wellington, statuette	b	Stratfield Saye, Hants	SD	*Gunnis* 1968, 187; *Clifford* 1992, 56
6.	nd	Unidentified figures	p	[for Mr Mundy, Markeaton Hall, Derbys]; untraced		*Clifford* 1992, 56
7.	nd	Vestal	p	Untraced (formerly Athenaeum room, Derby)		*Clifford* 1992, 56
Busts						
8.	1817	Field-Marshal Gebhard Lebrecht von Blücher (co-sculptor: Federico Nicoli) Payment(s): £150		[Carlton House, London]; Royal Coll, Windsor Castle	SD	TNA, L.C.9/367 fol 12; *Gunnis* 1968, 187; *Clifford* 1992, 56

9.	1818	Princess Charlotte (co-sculptor: Federico Nicoli)		Royal Coll		*Gunnis* 1968, 187; *Clifford* 1992, 56
10.	1820	Edward, Lord Ellenborough	m	Royal Coll, RCIN 35427 Other versions: plaster copy, Maidstone Museum	SD	*Gunnis* 1968, 187; *Clifford* 1992, 56
11.	1820	King George III	m	[coll Sir Philip William of Bridehead, Dorset]; Christie, 10 May 2006, lot 111 (repr)	SD	*CL*, 3 June 1999, 145 (repr)
12.	1819–1820	Three Roman Emperors: Nero, Vespasian and Claudius		[Kimbolton Castle, Hunts]; untraced		*Gunnis* 1968, 187
13.	1821	General Charles Morgan		Corsham Court, Wilts	SD	*Gunnis* 1968, 187
14.	1821	Marquess of Hertford		Noailles coll		*Clifford* 1992, 56
15.	nd	King George IV	p	Brynkinalt, Denbighs		*Gunnis* 1968, 187
16.	nd	Robert, 2nd Earl of Liverpool		Ickworth Park, Suffolk	S	*Gunnis* 1968, 187
Architectural Sculpture						
17.	1800	'The four seasons decorating an urn, intended for the centre of a green room'		[Exhib RA, London, 1094]; untraced		*Graves* III, 1905–6, 378
Miscellaneous						
18.	1822	Death mask of William Stuart, Archbishop of Armagh		Untraced		*GM* 1822, 1, 470; *Gunnis* 1968, 187

HARDING, Charles, of Sudbury fl *c*1830–37

He signs a number of tablets in Suffolk. Harding's wife, Charlotte, died in 1831 at the age of 43.

Literary References: *Gunnis* 1968, 187

Funerary Monuments					
1.	*c*1830	Rev John Bigg	Glemsford, Suffolk	S	*Gunnis* 1968, 187
2.	?1834	Captain Rodney Wentworth Sims and Mary Gibbon Sims	St Gregory, Sudbury, Suffolk	S	*Gunnis* 1968, 187
3.	?1834	Mrs Pemberton	Belchamp St Paul, Essex	S	*Gunnis* 1968, 187
4.	?1837	Walter Westropp	Long Melford, Suffolk	S	*Gunnis* 1968, 187

HARDING, James, of Farnham fl 1816–37

Funerary Monuments					
1.	?1823	Rev Thomas Butler	Bramshott, Hants	S	GPC
2.	1816–1837	Unidentified subjects, 'four undistinguished tablets'	St Andrew, Farnham, Surrey	S	*Gunnis* 1968, 187

HARDMAN, John, of Birmingham 1812–67

Hardman made a variety of metal fittings for buildings designed by A W N Pugin, including the Palace of Westminster. His firm also supplied brass tablets and memorial brasses. With his partner, a Mr Iliffe, he provided a brass monument to Reverend Hopkinson, designed in the Gothic style by Pugin (1). The firm also made stained glass and other church furnishings such as a chalice for the medieval court at the Great Exhibition, now in the Victoria and Albert Museum.

Literary References: *Meara* 1991; *Grove* 1996, 14, 167

Funerary Monuments					
1.	†1841	Rev Samuel Hopkinson (co-sculptor: Iliffe)	Hacconby, Lincs		*GM*, 1842, I, 266 (repr); *Gunnis* 1968, 187
2.	†1851	Father Lingard	St Margaret, Hornby, Lancs		Pevsner, *Lancs: N*, 1969, 147
3.	†1857	Archdeacon Richard Newcome	Ruthin, Denbighs	S	Pevsner, *Clwyd*, 1986, 275

HARDWICK, Thomas, of New Brentford fl 1761–80

He was the master-mason appointed to restore Syon House in 1761–3, receiving £571, a sum that included some carving (1). As a mason he was employed by Lord Paget, afterwards Earl of Uxbridge, on the rebuilding of Dawly House, Hayes, Middx, in 1770 (2). In 1766 Paget pulled down his house at Drayton. His steward wrote to him that Hardwick had tried to buy up some of the materials, including the 'Marble which was taken up in the Marble Hall', and added 'I signified I could not tell if your Lordship would part with the marble. Mr. Hardwick values the common chimneypieces at wherry [*sic*] little money'. His son was the architect Thomas Hardwick (1752–1829).

Archival References: GPC

Chimneypieces				
1.	1761–1763	Several, small	[Syon House, Middx]; untraced	Archives, Duke of Northumberland, Alnwick, U.III.6 in GPC
2.	1770	and 'moulded work' Payment(s): £95	[Dawly House, Hayes, Middx]; untraced	Archives, Marquess of Anglesey in GPC
3.	1780	Description unavailable	[Robert Child's house, Norwood, Middx]; untraced	Archives, Earl of Jersey in GPC
Architectural Sculpture				
4.	1767	Capitals	[Syon Park, Middx]; untraced	GPC

HARDY, James *c*1652–

The son of William Hardy of Kirby, Northumberland, he was apprenticed to Robert Bridles, citizen and mason of London, in 1669, becoming free in 1676. Two years later he was an as assistant to **Jasper Latham**. He married Elizabeth Johnson 'of Ebisham, Surrey, Spinster, abt. 30' in January 1688 at the Temple Church, London. Hardy is described in the register as being 'of St Giles in the Fields, Mason, Widr. abt. 36'. In 1696 his name was recorded in the general search of the Masons' Company as a master-mason, with an apprentice nearing the end of his time and a journeyman called Robert Rogers. He was steward of the Masons' Company in 1691, renter warden in 1705, upper warden in 1707 and master in 1711.

In 1706 Hardy was approached by a Mr Lanion, steward to the first Lord Ashburnham, to offer a quotation for statues for the 'attick' of Ampthill House. Lord Ashburnham commented in a letter to his steward that he had 'considered the papers in yours of the 26th and do find Mr Hardy more reasonable in his demands than Mr Nost [**John Nost I**]. Perhaps you may yet happen upon some other more reasonable than Mr Hardy, if not, you will please bring Hardy as much lower as you can and to strike a bargaine with him to perform in a month or six weeks' time' (Ashburnham Letterbook 28 Sept 1706, ASH 846). Ashburnham intended to employ Hardy as well as the ironworker Jean Tijou and the painter Louis Laguerre, but did not live to complete his house.

Hardy did not sign his monuments, but fortunately gave to his friend, John Le Neve, a list of several of his works for his publication, *Monumenta Anglicana* (1717–1719). Hardy's yard was in Piccadilly at this time. The works which he listed for Le Neve included a simple gravestone to Henry Puckering (**1**), a mural monument with drapery swags to Elizabeth Cradock (**2**) and two bust monuments, to Reynolds Calthorpe and his wife, both with fluted pilasters and a looped *baldacchino* (**11, 12**).

Hardy's grandson, another James, was born in 1717. The younger James Hardy was apprenticed to William Hale, citizen and mason, in 1733, but subsequently served a James (or Joseph) Manning. He was freed in March 1744. Hardy the Younger's address was given as New Bond Street in a list of assistants compiled by the Masons' Company c1740. In 1755, according to a Minute in the Court Book of the Masons' Company, he was summoned before the lord Mayor 'to show cause why he should not serve the office of Livery and Steward of the Company to which he had been duly elected.'

Literary References: *Le Neve* 1700–1715, xix; *Knoop and Jones* 1935, 68, 83; *Esdaile* 1942, 182; *Gunnis* 1968, 187–8; *Whinney* 1988, 246, 458 n7

Archival References: Masons' Co, Masters and Wardens; Assistants, fol 4; Freemen, fol 30; Court Book, 1722–51 (1733, 1738); Court Book, 1751–96 (2 Oct 1755); GPC; IGI

Funerary Monuments

1.	†1701	Sir Henry Puckering Bt		St Mary, Warwick	*Le Neve* 1700–1715, 6; *Esdaile* 1942, 182; *Gunnis* 1968, 188
2.	†1704	Elizabeth Cradock		St Peter, Berkhamstead, Herts	*Le Neve* 1700–1715, 86–7; *Esdaile* 1942, 182; Pevsner, *Herts*, 1977, 97
3.	†1705	Olive Duncomb		St Mary, Horsham, Sussex	*Le Neve* 1700–1715, 98; *Esdaile* 1942, 182; Pevsner, *Sussex*, 1965, 244
4.	†1710	Robert, Viscount Kilmorey		Adderley, Salop	*Le Neve* 1700–1715, 183; *Esdaile* 1942, 182; *Gunnis* 1968, 188; C Lib (repr)
5.	†1711	Alicia Stede		Harrietsham, Kent	*Le Neve* 1700–1715, 197; *Esdaile* 1942, 182; *Gunnis* 1968, 188; Pevsner *Kent: NE and E*, 1983, 343
6.	†1712	John Milner, ledger stone		All Saints, Kingston-upon-Thames, Surrey	*Le Neve* 1700–1715, 242
7.	†1712	Thomas Cockayne		Untraced	*Le Neve* 1700–1715, 227
8.	†1712	Viscount Ikerrin		Silchester, Hants	*Le Neve* 1700–1715, 235; *Esdaile* 1942, 182; Pevsner, *Hants & Isle of Wight*, 1967, 505
9.	†1713	John Postlethwayt		Untraced	*Le Neve* (MS only); *Esdaile* 1942, 182
10.	†1714	Constance Stede		Harrietsham, Kent	*Le Neve* 1700–1715, 284; *Esdaile* 1942, 183; Pevsner, *Kent: NE and E*, 1983, 343
11.	?†1714	Priscilla Calthorpe		Elvetham, Hants	Pevsner, *Hants & Isle of Wight*, 1967, 211
12.	†1714	Reynolds Calthorpe (†1714)		Elvetham, Hants	*Le Neve* 1700–1715, 282–3; *Esdaile* 1942, 183 (repr XXIII); Pevsner, *Hants & Isle of Wight*, 1967, 211
13.	†1715	Thomas Maule, monument and ledger stone		All Saints, Edmonton, Middx	*Le Neve* 1700–1715, 281; Pevsner, *London: N*, 1998, 423

Chimneypieces

14.	1703	Two ('and two slabes') Payment(s): £8 10s	m	[for Hon Richard Hill]; untraced	Hill family, personal & household bills (Richmond), Salop RO archives 112/1/2188

Miscellaneous

15.	1696	Unspecified work		[Gray's Inn, London]; untraced	Treasurer's Accounts in GPC
16.	1716	Unspecified work, possibly chimneypieces		[coll Lady Arabella Furnese]; untraced	Archives, Earl of Guilford, in GPC
17.	1719	Unspecified work, perhaps for statues on the façade Payment(s): Part payment of £30		[Burlington House, London]; untraced	GPC

HARDY, John fl 1800

Architectural Sculpture

1.	1800	Sundial, with cherub heads at the corners	m	Horne, Surrey, south wall	*Gunnis* 1968, 188

HARDY, William, of Norwich fl 1816–54?

This signature appears on a number of tablets in Norfolk. Given the date span of these works it seems possible that there were two masons of this name, probably different generations of the same family. The Watts monument (**2**), which was ordered by a Miss Yallop, was noticed in the *Norfolk Chronicle* of 15 January 1825. Hardy's address was given as St Stephen's Road. An earlier notice in the *Bury Post* of 13 May 1815 records the marriage of a Norwich stonemason of that name at Mulbarton, to Miss Howlett, also of Mulbarton.

Literary References: *Gunnis* 1968, 188

Archival References: GPC; RG/JP, 4, 646v

Funerary Monuments

1.	1816	Thomas (†1816) Penrice and wife (†1829)	Little Plumstead, Norfolk	S	Pevsner, *Norfolk: Norwich and N.E.*, 1997, 589
2.	1825	James Watts (†1788), Mary Watts, Lydia Watts and other family members	St John de Sepulchre, Norwich, Norfolk	S	Pevsner, *Norfolk: N.E. & Norwich* 1997, 240
3.	†1854	Smyth family member	Topcroft, Norfolk	S	Pevsner, *Norfolk: N W & S*, 1999, 738

HARGRAVE, Jeremiah, of Hull 1726–86

He and his son **Joseph Hargrave** were architects, architectural carvers, furniture makers, restorers and book illustrators, often working in collaboration with architects such as the Lightolers and James Wyatt. Like many provincial practitioners in the luxury trades, they were obliged to diversify rather than specialise in order to survive. The family came from Beverley Parks, and many are buried in York Minster.

An advertisement in the *York Courant* for 9 April 1751 (p3) read: CARVING IN MARBLE, WOOD and STONE/According to the newest Taste. . . .Manner, and at /the most reasonable Prices, by/JEREMIAH HARGRAVE,/At his Shop in High-Street, High Church lanne, Hull/where the following Work will be perform'd with . . . /most exactness and expedition, viz/Monuments, Tomb Stones, Arms &c. Chimney Pieces, Look-/ing Glasses, Table and Picture Frames &c. Trusses for Busto.s/and all Ornaments appertaining to Architecture &c. /N.B. Likewise ship-carving executed as well and cheap as in London'.

Jeremiah became a tenant of Trinity House, Whitefriargate, Hull, but left in 1754. He carried out unspecified work for the brethren in 1753, and he may have been the architect of Trinity House. He certainly carved the fine, large rococo relief in the building's pediment (**2**). In his *History of Hull*, Hadley describes the iconography: 'On the pediment is a carving, representing the King's Arms, on one side of which is Britannia, with her foot on an anchor, reclining on a cornucopia; on the other a figure of Neptune with Trident. It is a bas-relief, finely executed in stone' (*Hadley* 1788, 821).

In 1756 Hargrave supplied goods to the Langdales of Holme Hall, who perhaps mistrusted him for they asked John Carr of York to check his bill. A letter to the Langdales' steward signed by Hargrave survives in the Hull University archives (DDHA/14, 27). In it he apologises that 'one of ye pieces was done to wrong dimensions'. The nature of the misshapen work is not stipulated (*Hall* 1976 (2), 58). Hargrave also carried out a good deal of carved work at Burton Constable Hall (**1, 5, 6, 7**). He shared premises in Scale Lane with **George Earle I**, who married his daughter Mary in 1781. Two apprentices are recorded, E Cowham and William Clark, who subsequently set up in business on their own.

David Alexander

Literary References: *Gunnis* 1968, 188; *Hall* 1976 (1), 1476–80; *Hall* 1976 (2), 51–8

Architectural Sculpture

1.	1780	'Carving the Ornament & Moulding for three chimney pieces' Payment(s): 13 gns	[Burton Constable Hall, E R Yorks]; untraced	Constable Accounts, ERAO, DDCC/2/56
2.	1753–1759	Rococo tympanum relief	Trinity House, Hull, E R Yorks	*Hadley* 1788, 821; *Gunnis* 1968, 188; *Hall* 1976 (2), 52
3.	1773	Adamesque decoration	Trinity House, Hull, E R Yorks	*Hall* 1976 (2), 56 n5
4.	nd	Tympanum relief	Burton Constable, E R Yorks, west front, over central pediment (fragment only)	*Hall* 1976 (2), 54

Miscellaneous

5.	1767	Decorative carving in the great hall, ribbands and flowers 'in the Base' in the dining room, a 'Pedestal for Bacchus [by William Collins]', 'cutting & Vitruvian scroll round the Edges of the Marble Tables' and a large amethyst vase Payment(s): £94 2s 4d	Burton Constable Hall, E R Yorks	Constable Accounts, ERAO, DDCC/2/77; *Hall* 1976 (1), 1478 (repr); *Hall* 1976 (2), 56–7
6.	1769–1770	'Carving', vases, a sarcophagus and mahogany tables Payment(s): £164	[Burton Constable Hall, E R Yorks]; untraced	*Hall* 1976 (2), 56

HARGRAVE, Joseph fl 1771–85

He was the son of **Jeremiah Hargrave of Hull**. Hadley describes Joseph Hargrave as 'an ingenious artist, who designed the drawings in this book' (*Hadley* 1788, 821). He was employed at Burton Constable (**1**) and was paid for drawing designs for 2 chimneypieces for the same house in 1771 (Chichester-Constable Archives in GPC).

Architectural Sculpture

1.	1784–1785	Unspecified carving Payment(s): £42	[Burton Constable Hall, E R Yorks]; untraced	Chichester-Constable archives in GPC

HARGRAVES, Isaac, of Lewes fl 1792

He signs a large wall-tablet with an oval inscription panel (**1**).

Funerary Monuments

1.	?1792	Elizabeth Scrase	Stanmer, Sussex	S	*Gunnis* 1968, 188

HARLING, T fl 1823

Pevsner lists one monument, decorated with 'the usual female figure by an urn.'

Funerary Monuments

1.	1823	Unidentified subject	Nazeing, Essex	Pevsner, *Essex*, 1965, 305

HARMER, James fl 1851

His workshop was in Pentonville, London. The *Art Journal* wrote of his frieze shown at the Great Exhibition: 'shows considerable taste in the art of design as well as skill in the manipulation. The scroll is judiciously ornamented with flowers, leaves and wheat-ears, and a variety of other natural objects, and it encloses some admirably arranged groups of fruit, &c.' The journal describes him as 'Mr J Harmer, Jun' (*AJ Cat* 1851, 201).

Reliefs

1.	1851	Frieze	p	[Gt Exhib, London]; untraced	*AJ Cat* 1851, 201 (repr)

HARMER, Jonathan, of Heathfield 1762–1849

He was the son of Jonathan Harmer I, a mason and land surveyor of Heathfield. In 1796 the younger Jonathan Harmer went to America where he followed the same calling, working as a journeyman in New York, where he was employed chiefly among the Quaker community and became an ardent Republican. His father died in 1800 and left his stone, utensils and stock-in-trade to the sculptor and his brothers, with houses, buildings, gardens and tenements. Harmer returned to England that year with his wife and children, and began to manufacture small terracotta bas-reliefs, which he used principally in his monumental work, inserting them into the upper part of a tablet or tombstone. He also applied them as ornaments on the exterior of houses (**57**). There is a record of his purchasing Portland stone from Parsons and May, a firm of masons in Lewes, who are perhaps to be identified with the workshop run by **Latter Parsons, of Lewes**.

Harmer's favourite designs were vases or basket of flowers, urns with rams' heads, angels, baskets of fruit and figure groups. In February 1808 a Mr William Sinden bought composition flower baskets from him at 8s each, urns at 10s each, and tablets with impressions of *Charity*, (billed as 'the first impression'), *Faith* and *Hope* (*Harmer* 1962, 142).

Gunnis considered the best examples of his clay reliefs to be those in Cade Street Chapel, Sussex (**7, 25, 28, 34, 35, 40, 41**). There is a collection of his works in Sussex Archaeological Museum at Lewes, together with some of his moulds.

He died in 1849, aged 86, and was buried in the yard of Cade Street Chapel. He left his business to his sons Edwin and Sylvan, who also received properties, including shops in Heathfield and Portland Square. They must have continued to ply the family trade, presumably using the same moulds, for examples of Harmer terracottas are dated as late as 1878.

Literary References: *Lucas* 1910, 104–108; *Remnant* 1962, 142–8; *Remnant* 1964, 52–4; Pevsner, *Sussex*, 1965, *passim*; *Gunnis* 1968, 188

Funerary Monuments

1.	†1750	Edward Burgis	tc	Wadhurst, Sussex		*Remnant* 1964, 54
2.	†1780	Elizabeth Dadswell	tc	Mayfield, Sussex		*Remnant* 1962, 147
3.	†1802	Joseph Waters	tc	Salehurst, Sussex		*Remnant* 1962, 148
4.	†1803	Edward Russell	tc	Mayfield, Sussex		*Remnant* 1962, 147
5.	†1806	Edward Osmond	tc	Heathfield, Sussex		*Remnant* 1962, 146
6.	†1806	John Bassett	tc	Mayfield, Sussex		*Remnant* 1962, 147
7.	†1806	Lydia Huggett	tc	Cade Street Independent Chapel, Sussex		*Remnant* 1962, 146
8.	†1806	Maria Making	tc	Herstmonceux, Sussex		*Remnant* 1962, 147
9.	†1806	Stephen Hilder	tc	Mayfield, Sussex		*Remnant* 1962, 147
10.	†1807	Elizabeth Cole	tc	Mayfield, Sussex		*Remnant* 1962, 147
11.	†1807	John Paine	tc	Mayfield, Sussex		*Remnant* 1962, 147
12.	†1809	Ann Rogester	tc	Mayfield, Sussex		*Remnant* 1962, 147
13.	†1809	Sarah Smith	tc	Heathfield, Sussex		*Remnant* 1962, 146
14.	†1810	Elizabeth Hallaway	tc	Brightling, Sussex		*Remnant* 1962, 145
15.	†1810	John Buss	tc	Mayfield, Sussex		*Remnant* 1962, 147
16.	†1810	Judith Curtis	tc	Mayfield, Sussex		*Remnant* 1962, 147 (repr IV)
17.	†1810	Mary Krause	tc	Mayfield, Sussex		*Remnant* 1962, 147
18.	†1811	John Pursglove	tc	Herstmonceux, Sussex		*Remnant* 1962, 147
19.	†1811	Marianne New	tc	Glynde, Sussex, churchyard		*Remnant* 1962, 146 (repr IV); Pevsner, *Sussex*, 1965, 510
20.	†1811	Mary Rogester	tc	Mayfield, Sussex		*Remnant* 1962, 147
21.	†1812	John Arkcoll	tc	Herstmonceux, Sussex		*Remnant* 1962, 147
22.	†1812	Sarah Dawes	tc	Salehurst, Sussex		*Remnant* 1962, 148
23.	†1813	Sarah Kemp	tc	Warbleton, Sussex		*Lucas* 1910, 105; *Remnant* 1962, 148
24.	†1814	John Bray	tc	Chiddingly, Sussex, churchyard		Pevsner, *Sussex*, 1965, 471; *Remnant* 1962, 146
25.	†1815	Hannah Goldsmith	tc	Cade Street Independent Chapel, Sussex		*Remnant* 1962, 146
26.	†1815	John Fox	tc	Warbleton, Sussex, churchyard		*Remnant* 1964, 54 (repr IIIB)
27.	†1815	Walter Jenner	tc	Hailsham, Sussex		*Remnant* 1962, 146
28.	†1816	William Errey	tc	Cade Street Independent Chapel, Sussex		*Remnant* 1962, 146
29.	†1816	William Hilder	tc	Salehurst, Sussex		*Remnant* 1962, 148
30.	†1817	Mary Luck, and family members	m	Wadhurst, Sussex		*Remnant* 1964, 53 (repr I)
31.	†1817	Richard Gibbs, altar tomb	tc	Herstmonceux, Sussex		*Remnant* 1962, 147
32.	†1817	William Gilbert	tc	Mayfield, Sussex		*Remnant* 1962, 147
33.	†1818	Mary Hall	tc	Heathfield, Sussex		*Remnant* 1962, 146 (repr VIA)
34.	†1819	Hannah Stevens	tc	Cade Street Independent Chapel, Sussex		*Remnant* 1962, 146
35.	†1820	Elizabeth Pettitt	tc	Cade Street Independent Chapel, Sussex		*Remnant* 1962, 146
36.	†1820	John Tompsett	tc	Wadhurst, Sussex		*Remnant* 1964, 54 (repr IIIA)
37.	†1821	William Durrant	tc	East Grinstead, Sussex	S	*Remnant* 1964, 53 (repr 11A)
38.	†1822	John Miller	tc	Heathfield, Sussex		*Remnant* 1962, 146
39.	†1825	Ann Leadner	tc	Framfield, Sussex, churchyard		Pevsner, *Sussex*, 1965, 506; *Remnant* 1962, 146
40.	†1825	Sarah Smith	tc	Cade Street Independent Chapel, Sussex		*Remnant* 1962, 146
41.	†1827	Rev George Gilbert	tc	Cade Street Independent Chapel		*Remnant* 1962, (repr V)
42.	†1829	James and Ellis Newington	tc	Burwash, Sussex		*Remnant* 1962, 145
43.	†1831	Thomas Tomlinson	tc	Herstmonceux, Sussex		*Remnant* 1962, 147
44.	†1836	Marta Oliver	tc	Burwash, Sussex		*Remnant* 1962, 145
45.	†1837	Francis Ashfield Meek	m	Warbleton, Sussex		*Remnant* 1964, 54 (repr IIB)
46.	†1838	Ann Carey	tc	Herstmonceux, Sussex		*Remnant* 1962, 147

47.	†1851	Maria Smith	tc	Herstmonceux, Sussex	*Remnant* 1962, 147
48.	nd	Charles Woods	tc	Salehurst, Sussex	*Remnant* 1962, 148
49.	nd	Cornwall family members	tc	Salehurst, Sussex	*Remnant* 1962, 148
50.	nd	Elizabeth Attwood	tc	Salehurst, Sussex	*Remnant* 1962, 148
51.	nd	George Goldsmith	tc	Hellingly, Sussex	*Remnant* 1962, 146
52.	nd	Lewes Alsop	tc	Herstmonceux, Sussex	*Remnant* 1962, 147
53.	nd	Mary Parker	tc	Hellingly, Sussex	*Remnant* 1962, 146
54.	nd	Sarah Parsons	tc	Heathfield, Sussex	*Remnant* 1962, 146
55.	nd	Thomas Hicks, altar tomb	tc	Salehurst, Sussex	*Remnant* 1962, 148 (repr VI)
56.	nd	Will Mawman	tc	Hellingly, Sussex	*Remnant* 1962, 146

Architectural Sculpture

57.	nd	2nd Duke of Newcastle's arms	tc	Untraced	*Remnant* 1962, 144; *Gunnis* 1968, 188

HARMER, T, of Snettisham fl *c*1830

He is known only for one large wall-tablet in coloured marbles.

Funerary Monuments

1.	?1830	Nicholas Styleman	Heacham, Norfolk	S	*Gunnis* 1968, 188

HARPER, R, of London fl 1833

He gave his address as 41 James Street, New Cut, Lambeth, when he exhibited at the Society of British Artists in 1833.

Busts

1.	1833	Lord Brougham	[Exhib Soc of BA, London]; untraced	*Gunnis* 1968, 188
2.	1833	Rowland Hill	[Exhib Soc of BA, London, 838]; untraced	*Johnson* 1975, 207

HARRE fl –1753

The sale of the effects of Mr Harre, a 'statuary and carver,' was noticed in the *Public Advertiser* of 5 November 1753. The models in wax and terracotta that were sold included those for 'bustos, chimneypieces, girandoles and consoles . . . basso and alto relievos, monuments, terms, friezes etc, large frames for glasses, picture frames of various sizes, festoons of fruit and flowers, and other ornaments finished' (quoted in *Baker* 2000, 107).

HARRIS, Augustine fl 1688

A 'carver in stone', he was employed at Chatsworth.

Statues

1.	1688	Seven Payment(s): £44 18s 6d	[Chatsworth, Derbys, gardens]; untraced	*Hall* 1839, 398

HARRIS, Charles, of the Strand, London –1795

He was the son of William and Ann Harris, landowners of Painswick, Glos. By 1776 he had entered into partnership with **Richard Parker** and their premises were established in Strand, London, 'opposite the new church', with second premises in Bond Street, Bath. Their practice was diverse, offering 'Statues, Bas-reliefs, Bustos, Vases, Urns &c proper to introduce in the Decoration of Rooms, Chimney-pieces, Stair-cases, Halls, &c.' Samples and catalogues were available, and repairs and bronzing could be carried out. The store also stocked imported alabaster vases from Italy and obelisks of Derbyshire Spar (Cumbria Records Office D/Lons/C/13/1, copyright Lord Lonsdale). An undated trade card giving his address as 'At the Alfred's Head, opposite the New Church, Strand, London' offers to the public statues, bas-reliefs, busts, vases, urns, and chimneypieces in a range of marbles, as well as general mason's work. He also bought, sold and repaired antiques.

Harris's printed bill in the Croome accounts, dated June 1781, lists him alone at the same address (**26**). A catalogue of his stock, now in the National Art Library, lists 'the Statues, Bass Reliefs, Bustos etc of Charles Harris, Statuary'. A trade card boasts that he supplied elegant decoration in the 'newest taste' (Esdaile Papers, Huntington Library). He also offered 'the finest' reproductions in plaster of classical statuary (**24**).

Harris was also responsible for monumental sculpture, including tablets in the Greek and Adamesque styles (**6, 2**). One press report described the monument to the Templar sisters, with a relief of the shipwreck in which they perished, as a 'cenotaph of elegant sculpture' (**14**) (*Univ Mag* 1786, 78, 214). Gunnis thought highly of Harris's memorials, writing that 'his monuments have great charm, being in the best eighteenth-century tradition, with a lavish use of coloured marbles and reliefs. His most important work is that to the third and fourth Dukes of Ancaster (**5**), which has a life-size standing figure of the third Duke in Roman costume, while the fourth Duke is seated, dressed in full peer's robes and holding a medallion portrait of his wife'.

The business was still listed in the *London Directory* in 1793, 2 years before his death. In his will, which describes him as a statuary, he left his goods, chattels and stock in trade to his wife Elizabeth. She also received land in Painswick, inherited from Harris's father (PROB 11/1260/342).

Literary References: *Gunnis* 1968, 188–9; *Clifford* 1992, 56; *Beard* 1993, 106

Archival References: GPC; Esdaile Papers, Huntington

Tradecard: Heal Collection, BM 32.43; BM 106.15

Will: PROB 11/1260/342

Sales Catalogues: Harris Sale *c*1790

Funerary Monuments

1.	?1775	Barbara Reepington	Stony Stratford, Bucks	S	*Gunnis* 1968, 189
2.	†1778	Rev Thomas Wrench	Stedham, Sussex	S	Pevsner, *Sussex*, 1965, 337; *Gunnis* 1968, 189
3.	*c*1779	Francis Stonehouse	Hungerford, Berks	S	*Gunnis* 1968, 189
4.	?1779	Henry Allcraft	Mitcham, Surrey	S	*Gunnis* 1968, 189
5.	*c*1779	Peregrine, 3rd Duke (†1778), and Robert, 4th Duke of Ancaster (†1779)	Edenham, Lincs	S	*Gunnis* 1968, 188–9; *Whinney* 1988, 273–4 (repr)
6.	†1780	Captain Timothy Edwards	Llangian, Carnarvon	S	GPC
7.	†1780	Sophia Tate	St Peter and St Paul, Mitcham, Surrey		*Gunnis* 1968, 189

8.	†1781	Captain Thomas Allen	Chichester Cathedral, Sussex		Pevsner, *Sussex*, 1965, 153
9.	†1782	Lieutenant George Pigot Alms	Chichester Cathedral, Sussex	S	Pevsner, *Sussex*, 1965, 153
10.	†1784	Sarah Peckham	Chichester Cathedral, Sussex	S	Pevsner, *Sussex*, 1965, 156; *Gunnis* 1968, 189
11.	?1784	William Jennens	Long Wittenham, Berks	S	*Gunnis* 1968, 189
12.	†1785	George Gregory	Harlaxton, Lincs		Pevsner, *Lincs*, 1989, 361
13.	†1785	Henry Hoare Payment(s): £75	Stourton, Wilts	S	Stourhead archives, cited in *Gunnis* 1968, 189; Pevsner, *Wilts*, 1975, 494; *Whinney* 1988, 274
14.	1786	Anne and Mary Templar (both †1786)	Teigngrace, Devon		*Universal Magazine*, 1786, 78, 214; GPC
15.	?1786	George Dewer	Knights' Enham, Hants	S	*Gunnis* 1968, 189
16.	†1787	James Tamesz Grieve	Bath Abbey, Somerset		Pevsner, *Somerset: N. & Bristol*, 1958, 105
17.	?1787	Robert Palmer	Hurst, Berks	S	*Gunnis* 1968, 189
18.	†1788	Agnes Tucker	Kilmington, Devon	S	Pevsner, *Devon*, 1989, 519
19.	?1790	Benjamin Tate	Mitcham, Surrey	S	*Gunnis* 1968, 189
20.	†1790	Rev George Farhill	Chichester Cathedral, Sussex	S	Pevsner, *Sussex*, 1965, 157; *Gunnis* 1968, 189
21.	?1792	Henry Lloyd	Christchurch, Hants	S	*Gunnis* 1968, 189
22.	1793	Lady Fletcher (†1791)	Cheam, Surrey, Lumley Chapel	S	*Gunnis* 1968, 189
Statues					
23.	1776	Antinous, Sitting Venus, and Venus de Medici Payment(s): £6 14s 9d	[for 'Metcalfe Esq']; untraced		Cumbria RO D/Lons/C/13/1
24.	nd	Casts of classical statuary, including the Wild Boar, Cupid and Psyche, Marcus Aurelius, the Wrestlers and Zingara	p [Sculptor's premises, the Strand, London]; untraced		*Haskell and Penny* 1991, *passim*
Busts					
25.	1777	Hadrian Payment(s): 20 gns	[coll Charles, 2nd Marquess of Rockingham]; untraced		*Penny* 1991 (2), 19
Architectural Sculpture					
26.	1781	A pair of spar vases Payment(s): £8 8s	[Croome Court, Worcs]; untraced		*Beard* 1993, 106
Miscellaneous					
27.	c1790	John Locke, statuette, offered with busts of three sizes	[Offered from stock]; untraced		Ingamells forthcoming

HARRIS, Charles, of Wallingford fl 1766–76?

In 1797 he took his son, another Charles, as his apprentice. The tablet to Edward (†1766) and Elizabeth (†1752) Chaloner at Steeple Claydon, Bucks is signed 'HARRIS, BISTER'. This is perhaps Charles Harris, who may earlier have lived in Bicester (inf: Alastair Laing).

Literary References: *Gunnis* 1968, 189

Funerary Monuments					
1.	?1776	Richard Mason	Hambleden, Bucks	S	*Gunnis* 1968, 189

HARRIS, H, of Poole fl 1825

The *Gentleman's Magazine* recorded the erection of a 'handsome' work at Canford Magna in 1825 (**1**): 'It consists of a large tablet of statuary marble, raised on a dove coloured ground, surmounted by appropriate naval trophies, and with admiral's arms, and motto "Che sara sara", below. It was executed by Mr. H. Harris, of Poole, and is highly creditable to his abilities'.

Funerary Monuments					
1.	?1825	Admiral Russell	Canford Magna, Dorset		*GM* 1825, 2, 135; *Gunnis* 1968, 189

HARRIS, Joseph, of Bath fl 1779–1836?

Harris signed a number of monuments and tablets. A press report noted the erection of the Parish monument in Bath Abbey (**15**) and described Harris as 'a native and resident artist, of growing celebrity' (*New Monthly Mag*, 1829, 27, 461). There are other signs of Harris's success: the Baskerville monument (**7**) has the inscription 'J. Harris, Sculptor to her Majesty, Bath', as do the urns, with writhing snakes at Frogmore (**20**). Gunnis had a less charitable view of the sculptor's abilities, describing him as 'one of the least successful of the Bath school of statuaries. His absurd monument to Henry Haffey (**19**) has, for its chief decoration, a marble copy of the large silver trophy presented to Haffey by the inhabitants of Jamaica' (*Gunnis* 1968, 189).

Archival References: GPC

Funerary Monuments					
1.	†1779	Captain George Maxwell	Twyning, Glos	S	Pevsner, *Glos: Vale & Forest of Dean*, 1976, 393
2.	†1790	Richard Riche and family	St Peter and St Paul, Marlborough, Wilts		RG/JP, 4, 651
3.	†1790	Richard Samuel Wyche	Warminster, Wilts	S	
4.	†1808	John Butt	Warminster, Wilts	S	*Gunnis* 1968, 189
5.	†1813	Elizabeth and Susanna Bennett	St Nicholas, Cork	S	*Potterton* 1975, 47
6.	?1818	Josiah Patrick	St John in Bedwardine, Worcs	S	*Gunnis* 1968, 189
7.	1818	Thomas (†1817) and Jane (†1809) Baskerville, Charles Francis (†1830) and General John Calcrot (†1821)	Mildenhall, Wilts	SD	Pevsner, *Wilts*, 1975, 349
8.	?1819	Emily Roe	Walcot, Berks	S	*Gunnis* 1968, 189
9.	†1821	Charles Francis	St John Baptist, Mildenhall, Wilts		Pevsner, *Wilts*, 1975, 349
10.	†1823	Deborah (†1813) and Cuthbert Armstrong	Warminster, Wilts	S	

11.	?1823	Rev John Selwyn		Salisbury Cathedral, Wilts	S	*Gunnis* 1968, 189
12.	†1823	Sarah Knollis		Winscombe, Somerset		Pevsner, *Somerset: N. & Bristol*, 1958, 341
13.	†1824	Rev Michael Rowlandson		Warminster, Wilts	S	
14.	†1825	James Alfred Tayler		Warminster, Wilts	S	
15.	†1829	John Parish		Bath Abbey, Somerset		*New Monthly Mag* 1829, 27, 461
16.	?1831	Mr and Mrs Selwyn		Beaumaris, Anglesey		GPC
17.	?1833	Henry Griffiths		St Peter and St Paul, Marlborough, Wilts		RG/JP, 4, 652
18.	?1835	Adam Wrags		Seend, Wilts	S	*Gunnis* 1968, 189
19.	?1836	Henry Haffey		Bathampton, Somerset		*Gunnis* 1968, 189
Architectural Sculpture						
20.	nd	Urns, a pair	s	Royal Coll (Frogmore, Berks)	S	

HARRIS, M and P fl 1737

They were responsible for one known monument, with a bust, and were presumably Dublin sculptors.

Funerary Monuments

1.	†1737	Rev John Magee	Drogheda Parish Church, Ireland	S	GPC

HARRIS, Samuel, of Jacobstow fl 1712?

He is known only for one ledger with a fine coat of arms.

Funerary Monuments

1.	?1712	Thomas Cogcombe, ledger stone	Whitstone, Cornwall		*Gunnis* 1968, 189

HARRISON, Daniel fl 1801–12

He was the principal master-mason rebuilding Eaton Hall, Chester, 1808–12 (Grosvenor Archives). He became a freeman of Chester in 1801.

Archival References: GPC

HARRISON, Elizabeth, of Chester fl 1827–35?

She was perhaps the widow or daughter of Daniel Harrison who became a freeman of Chester in 1801. She signs a Hellenistic wall-monument to John Colley (2), and a work executed in partnership with **John Wright of Chester** is of similar design (1).

Funerary Monuments

1.	?1827	John Edgworth (co-sculptor: John Wright of Chester)	Marchwiel, Flint	S	*Gunnis* 1968, 189
2.	?1835	John Colley	Bruera, Chester	S	*Gunnis* 1968, 189

HARRISON, James, of Chester fl 1839–55

Funerary Monuments

1.	†1839	John Boydell	Gresford, Denbighs		Pevsner, *Clwyd*, 1994, 172
2.	†1855	John (†1800) and Grace (†1855) Parsons	Iscoed, Flint	S	Pevsner, *Clwyd*, 1994, 379

HARRISON, James, of Devizes fl 1811–43

He was responsible for several signed tablets. The Wragg monument, which is signed 'Harrison, sculp, Melksham', is possibly by this sculptor (8).

Funerary Monuments

1.	?1811	Thomas Pike	Pewsey, Berks	S	*Gunnis* 1968, 189
2.	†1816	Sir Andrew Baynton Rolt	Bromham, Wilts	S	*Gunnis* 1968, 189
3.	†1829	Francis (†1825) and Hannah (†1829) Ferris	Potterne, Wilts	S	
4.	†1829	John (†1824) and Ann Banks	Bromham, Wilts	S	
5.	†1829	Mary and Ralph Gaby	Chippenham, Wilts		RG/JP, 4, 652
6.	†1830	Ann Brown	St Peter and St Paul, Marlborough, Wilts		RG/JP, 4, 652
7.	†1837	John Madocks	Gresford, Denbighs		Pevsner, *Clwyd* 1994, 172
8.	† to 1843	Ann (†1831), Phebe (†1827), Adam (†1836) and Mary (†1843) Wragg	Seend, Wilts	S	

HARRISON, John fl 1831

He carved a monument for his wife (1) with decorative details similar to those on local door lintels.

Funerary Monuments

1.	†1831	Jane Harrison	s	Pateley Bridge, W R Yorks, churchyard	Pevsner, *Yorks: W R*, 1967, 390

HARRISON, of Marlborough fl 1823–32

He signs himself 'sculptor of Marlborough' (2).

Funerary Monuments

1.	†1823	Henry Woodman and family	Mildenhall, Wilts	S
2.	†1832	William Young and family	Mildenhall, Wilts	S

HARRISON, Richard, of Buckingham fl 1817–36

He signs several Buckinghamshire tablets.

Funerary Monuments

1.	?1817	Mary Aubrey	Middle Claydon, Bucks	S	*Gunnis* 1968, 189
2.	?1832	Rev John Dayrell	Lillingstone Darell, Bucks	S	*Gunnis* 1968, 189
3.	?1836	Richard Dayrell	Lillingstone Darell, Bucks	S	*Gunnis* 1968, 189

HARRISON, Thomas 1815–41

In 1836 he attended the Royal Academy Schools on the recommendation of **J C F Rossi**. His given address at that time was 4 Orchard Street, Portman Square. He died at Old Windsor in 1841.

Literary References: *Gunnis* 1968, 189

Archival References: RA Admissions

Busts

1.	1837	J Harrison	p	RIBA, London	GPC
2.	1838	Unidentified gentleman		[Exhib RA, London, 1302]; untraced	*Graves* IV, 1905–6, 8
3.	1840	Mrs Hinton Baverstock		[Exhib RA, London, 1177]; untraced	*Graves* IV, 1905–6, 8

HARRISON, William, of Stamford *c*1776–1845?

Harrison was apprenticed to John Cole of Stamford in 1790 and became a freeman of that town in 1797. He ran a stonemason's and builder's business, working at Browne's Hospital after 1800, where he rebuilt the 15th-century porch in 1808. It is not certain whether he is the stonecutter of the same name who died in 1845 and was buried at St Martin, Stamford.

Archival References: JP, Misc Corr

Funerary Monuments

1.	†1806	Elizabeth Plumptree	St Martin, Stamford, Lincs		Pevsner, *Lincs*, 1989, 692
2.	1808	Thomas Stevenson (†1806) and his wife (†1812)	St Mary, Stamford, Lincs	S	*Gunnis* 1968, 189
3.	†1810	Thomas Truman	St Martin, Stamford, Lincs		Pevsner, *Lincs*, 1989, 692

HARSTON, H fl 1795?

Harston is known only for one small monument. In 1811 the firm was known as 'Harston, Marshall and Co'.

Literary References: *Gunnis* 1968, 190

Funerary Monuments

1.	?1795	Garret Ordoyne	St Mary Magdalen, Newark, Notts	S	*Gunnis* 1968, 190

HART, Anthony fl 1686–1734

The son of Anthony Hart, a citizen and brewer of London, he served his apprenticeship under **Abraham Storey** and became free of the Masons' Company on 29 April 1686. He became chief assistant to **John Nost I**: in 1708 he is described in the archives of the Masons' Company as working 'with Mr. Nost a carver at Hide Park Corner' (Masons' Co, *List of Company Members*, 12).

In 1723 his chief assistant, **John Doe**, carved chimneypieces for Dudley North of Glenham Hall, Suffolk. North wrote to Hart in 1727: 'I have at last examined Mr. Doe's late bills and reduced the articles where they differ from my agreement with him'. North went on to quote from the contract and added: 'You have in some places charged more. I have with due help measured out all the chimney-pieces which I hope are very exactly done' (North Archives quoted in *Gunnis* 1968, 190). In 1734 Hart was living in Cripplegate.

Archival References: Masons' Co, *Freemen*, fol 28

HART, Joseph fl 1724–65

The son of Edward Hart, of Hackney, a husbandman, he was apprenticed to **John Annis** on 7 January 1724. Joseph Hart is noted as a 'journeyman with Mr Walker, a mason in Queen Street' *c*1740 (Masons' Co Assistants f4). Gunnis was unable to discover whether he was related to Clement Hart, who was apprenticed in 1719 to Thomas West, and who became renter warden of the Masons' Company in 1751, the year of his death.

Literary References: *Gunnis* 1968, 190

Archival References: Masons' Co, Court Book, 1722–51 (1725)

Funerary Monuments

1.	†1765	Lydia Mabletoft	St James, Weybridge, Surrey	S	*Gunnis* 1968, 190

HART, of Cheltenham fl 1830

Funerary Monuments

1.	†1830	Amelia Hicks	Coberley, Glos	S	Pevsner, *Glos: Cotswolds*, 1999, 289

HARTLEY, Henry Robert fl 1822–26?

He signs a number of monuments including one to Anne Brocas, which has a life-size kneeling figure of *Faith* with a cross and shield (2). It is signed 'Jos. Gwilt, arch. S.A.S. London invt. H. R. Hartley excud'.

Literary References: *Gunnis* 1968, 190

Funerary Monuments

1.	?1822	Susan Pigeon	St George-the-Martyr, Southwark, London		*Gunnis* 1968, 190
2.	?1824	Anne Brocas (designed by Joseph Gwilt)	Banbury, Oxon	S	*Gunnis* 1968, 190
3.	?1826	William Toulmin	St George-the-Martyr, Southwark, London		*Gunnis* 1968, 190

HARTLEY, Robert fl 1771

He was described as a 'stone-cutter from Kingston upon Hull' in an advertisement of September 30, 1771 published in the *New York Gazette and the Weekly Mercury*. His workshop in New York was at 'Hunter's-Quay, near the Merchants' coffee-house'. Hartley's practice encompassed 'all sorts of Marble Monuments, tombs, grave stones, head-stones, and marble chimney pieces', made and finished 'in the newest and most genteal fashion.'

Literary References: *Gottesman* 1970, 230

HARTLEY, Thomas Henry fl 1844

He was listed in Thompson's *Commercial Directory* for 1844 as a sculptor of 1 Earl Street, Westminster.

HARTSHORNE FAMILY, of London fl 1704–21

Robert Hartshorne I †1721
Rachel Hartshorne
Robert Hartshorne II

Robert Hartshorne I was an assistant to **William** and **Edward Stanton** and was described as 'Cit and Joyner' in the apprenticeship books (*Webb* 1957 (3), 116). He married Rachel Busbie on 18 June 1704 at St James, Westminster, and had a workshop at St Martin-in-the-Fields. He executed a number of monuments, including the tablet to Mark Kirkby, which has an inscription on carved drapery, hanging from a canopy in an architectural setting (5). His most notable work, the monument to Thomas Powys, has a semi-reclining figure of the deceased in judicial robes and statues of *Justice* and *Truth* flanking the effigy (6). The architectural frame is 20 feet high, and features fluted Corinthian columns holding up a segmental arch on which putti are seen in the act of pulling back a drapery curtain. Webb considered the work to be 'as fine a baroque example as can be found in England', but nonetheless considered the cutting of the figures coarse.

On 3 December 1718, Hartshorne apprenticed **Henry Cheere** at a fee of £20. Around the same time he unsuccessfully competed with Edward Stanton for the commission to carve the statue of George I for the Royal Exchange. His patrons at this time included the Earl of Lichfield, who paid him £26 for unspecified work at Ditchley Park on 23 May 1718, and Sir John Fellowes, one of the Directors of the South Sea Company who paid him £59 and then £99 16s in October and December 1720. A payment of £149 was made to Hartshorne by Fellowes between October and December 1720. This was either for work carried out at Sir John's house at Carshalton, Surrey, or possibly for a monument erected in Carshalton church.

Robert Hartshorne I died in 1721. In his will, proved in December that year, he described himself as a 'mason', though elsewhere he is given the status of 'statuary' (*Fellowes Inventory* 1721, 10). In his will he left two thirds of his estate to his wife **Rachel Hartshorne**, and a third to be divided equally among his four children. His 'modalls, drawings and prints' were to be shared equally between his wife and his son, **Robert Hartshorne II**, and it was presumably mother and son who continued the family business, providing chimneypieces at Ditchley Park (7). Rachel Hartshorne and John Earley, a carpenter of Broad Street, were his executors. Intriguingly, one of the witnesses was **Katherine Nost**, which suggests a possible professional relationship with the Nost workshop, hitherto unrecorded (PROB 11/582/224).

Literary References: *Gunnis* 1968, 190; *Douglas Stewart* 1978, 219; *Craske* 2000 (2), 95, 97

Archival References: Dillon DIL I/p/41; S S Co (Fellowes) no 9 in 1, p 10; IGI; GPC

Funerary Monuments

1.	†1712	Benet family member		Wroughton, Wilts		Pevsner, *Wilts*, 1975, 600
2.	1712	Sir John Button		Wroughton, Wilts		Pevsner, *Wilts*, 1975, 600
3.	†1715	Gilbert Burnet, Bishop of Salisbury		St James, Finsbury, London	S	Pevsner, *London: N*, 1998, 604
4.	?1715	John Rogers		St Mary, Leicester	S	*Gunnis* 1968, 190
5.	†1718	Mark Kirkby and daughter		Holy Trinity, Hull, E R Yorks	S	*Gunnis* 1968, 190; Pevsner, *Yorks: E R & York*, 1995, 508
6.	1720	Sir Thomas Powys (†1719) Drawing(s): Avery Library, Columbia University, NY		[Lilford, Northants]; Thorpe Achurch, Northants	S	*Webb* (3), 1957, 116–7, 119 (repr); *Gunnis* 1968, 190; *Whinney* 1988, 453

Chimneypieces

7.	1718	Two or more (by Robert Hartshorne) Payment(s): 12 gns on acct		Ditchley Park, Oxon		Dillon, DIL I/p/41; *Gunnis* 1968, 190

Architectural Sculpture

8.	1721	Frames for bas-reliefs	m	[coll Matthew Prior]; untraced		*Wright and Montgomery* 1945, 199

HARVEY, Frederick, of Ipswich and Diss fl *c*1836

He was the mason responsible for a 'very handsome mansion' for a Major Charles Walker at Lavington, Suffolk (*Clarke* 1830, 377). He also carved two tablets.

Funerary Monuments

1.	?1836	Elizabeth Bunny		Diss, Norfolk	S	*Gunnis* 1968, 191
2.	?1836	Sharan Shorting		Brome, Suffolk	S	*Gunnis* 1968, 191

HARVEY, of Fairford fl *c*1844

His only identified work is a large Gothic tablet in Gloucestershire (1).

Funerary Monuments

1.	*c*1844	Unidentified subject	s	Eastleach Turville, Glos		Pevsner, *Glos: Cotswolds*, 1999, 350

HARVEY, Samuel, of London fl 1762–65

He executed three life-size marble statues for the Society of Arts in 1762–5, for which he received premiums each time. Mortimer's *Director* for 1763 lists 'Samuel Harvey, Statuary. The upper end of Masham-Street, Westminster'.

Literary References: *Mortimer* 1763, 13; *Dossie* 1782, 440

Statues

1.	1762	Ceres, life-size	m	[Soc of A, premium, 50 gns]; untraced		*Dossie* 1782, 440
2.	1763	Bacchus and a young satyr		[Soc of A, premium, 70 gns]; untraced		RSA *Minutes*, 1762–63, seq 2 f 71; *Dossie* 1782, 440
3.	1765	Victory, a figure	m	[Soc of A, premium, 80 gns]; untraced		RSA *Minutes*, 1764–65 seq 3 f 62; *Dossie* 1782, 440

HARVEY (or HAVRE), of London –1755

The *York Courant* of 26 August 1755 carried an account of the monument by Harvey and **Charles Mitley** to Mrs Ramsden (1), stating that Harvey came from London.

With the aid of Mitley, he provided a monument to Sir Tancred Robinson in 1755, dying before it was completed (2). Mitley's sister, Diana Carr, petitioned a member of the Robinson family to transfer the commission to Mitley. She wrote 'Sir William Robinson has bespoke a monument for Sir Tancred here at York of one Mr Havre, he was taken ill and died 2 or 3 days ago, this man my brother sent for from London a year and a half ago and he have workt for him ever since, now as Sir Tancred's monument is not half finished Mr. Havre's widow must have somebody to compleat it and as my Brother has assisted Mr. Havre in making the Drawing and have furnished him with hands in Doing the work thus far, he beggs you'll Recommend hm to Sir Wm. that he may compleat it . . . and see it carefully put up. I beg Madm. that you'll speake to Sir Wm. Directly or Perhaps Mrs Havre may pick up some local tramper and spoil the work, as she is for London as soon as possible' (Compton Newby Archives). Carr was unsuccessful in her plea and the commission was completed by **Robert Avray**.

Archival References: GPC

Funerary Monuments

1.	†1745	Mrs Ramsden (co-sculptor: Charles Mitley)		Adlingfleet, W R Yorks		Pevsner, *Yorks: W R*, 1967, 73; *Whinney* 1988, 256; GPC
2.	†1754	Sir Tancred Robinson (completed by Robert Avray) (co-sculptor: Charles Mitley)		St Crux parish room, York		Pevsner, *Yorks: E R & York*, 1995, 164; GPC

HARVEY (or HERVE), Daniel, of York 1683–1733

Harvey (Hervé) was born in France and anglicized his name soon after arriving in England. He was responsible for a great deal of work at Castle Howard (**3, 6, 8, 9, 10**), where his compatriots included **Nadauld** and **Gideon du Chaime** (or **Duchesne**). His work included stone vases which must have been gilded as there are various payments for 'gold for ye vase' (**6**). In 1720 he agreed with the Earl of Strafford 'to carve, perform and finish 4 capitals after ye Corinthian order which are to be fitted in just proportions to 4 marble columns which have already been shewn to the said Daniel Harvey' (**4**). In 1730 Harvey provided a monument to Hugh Ripley (**1**). This was evidently a substitute or restoration of the original, for the inscription on it read 'the former monument having been defaced in the times of the Civil Wars, this new one was erected by the Corporation 1730'. One of his last works must have been the 'highly competent' wall-tablet to John Atkins (**2**). He died on 11 December 1733, aged 50, and was buried in St Olave's, York, where his epitaph describes him as '*sculptor. architector etiam peritus, ingenio acer*' (*Drake* 1736, 1, 260).

Literary References: *Gunnis* 1968, 190–1; *Murdoch and Hebditch* 1985, 276; Pevsner, *E R & York*, 1995, 445

Archival References: Castle Howard bills, G2/2/27, 22 Oct 1706, p 13 £30 12s 4d; G2/2/36, Jan 1710–July 1712, £239 17s; G2/2/50, 29 June 1721, £17 17s; G2/2/53, 3 Feb 1726, £276 15s 5d; G2/2/55, 1729, £66 10s 5d; CH Acct Book G2/1/1 fols 95, 96; G2/1/2, fols 32, 44, 60, 84, 119, 130–61 (summaries)

Funerary Monuments

1.	1730	Hugh Ripley (†1637)		Ripon Cathedral, W R Yorks		Ripon, Mayors Accts, cited in *Gunnis* 1968, 191; Pevsner, *Yorks: W R*, 1967, 410
2.	†1732	John Atkins		Great Givendale, E R Yorks	S	Pevsner, *Yorks: E R & York*, 1995, 445

Architectural Sculpture

3.	1709–1712	Sundry work Payment(s): £239 17s	s	Castle Howard, N R Yorks, north front		Castle Howard bills
4.	1720	Four Corinthian capitals, of Roche Abbey stone Payment(s): £50	s	Wentworth Castle, W R Yorks, gallery		BL Ad MS 22241, fol 11; *Gunnis* 1968, 190–1; *Friedman* 1984, 125, 321–2 (repr)
5.	1732–1723	Royal arms of King George II and city arms of York		Mansion House, York, state room		Pevsner, *Yorks: E R & York*, 1995, 195
6.	1721–1724	Vases and frostwork pedestals	s	Castle Howard, N R Yorks, parterre, south front		Castle Howard bills; *Saumarez-Smith*, 138–9
7.	1725	Four capitals	wd	Wentworth Castle, W R Yorks		BL Ad MS 22241, fol 29; *Gunnis* 1968, 191
8.	1726–1727	Carved stonework, including twenty-eight capitals and twelve vases Payment(s): £276, including £56 for the 28 capitals; £21 for the 12 vases	s	Castle Howard, N R Yorks, Temple of the Winds		Castle Howard bills

Miscellaneous

9.	1706	'frame for my Lds bed Chamber, Lords Cabinett Chimney peece, Glass frames for ye Cabinett, frames for pictures above ye glasses in ye cabinett'		Castle Howard, N R Yorks, east wing		*Saumarez-Smith*, 62
10.	1721	Unidentified 'sculpture' Payment(s): £89		[Castle Howard, N R Yorks]; untraced		*Gunnis* 1968, 191

HARVEY & SON, of Stonehouse fl 1830–50

They sign a number of 'uninteresting tablets' in Devon (*Gunnis* 1968, 190).

Funerary Monuments

1.	?1836	Edward Hockin		Hartland, Devon	S	*Gunnis* 1968, 190
2.	?1837	Catherine Butter		Woodbury, Devon	S	*Gunnis* 1968, 190
3.	?1837	Charlotte Pierce		Ipplepen, Devon	S	*Gunnis* 1968, 190
4.	?1837	Hugh Hockin		Stoke Climsland, Cornwall		*Gunnis* 1968, 190
5.	†1843	Major Jackson		Stoke Damerel, Devon	S	GPC

HARVEY FAMILY, of Bath fl 1687–after 1719

John Harvey I
John Harvey II †1742

The Harveys of Bath followed a variety of callings, as architects, statuaries, painter-stainers and stone-cutters. **John Harvey I** built the first Bath pump room in 1706. He may also have been the 'Mr Harvey' who carved the staircase at Badminton House, Glos (Beaufort Accts, FmF 3/3, December 1663). **John Harvey II** was responsible in 1734 for building St Michael-extra-Muros, Bath.

The elder Harvey was employed several times at Longleat in the years 1687–1702. In 1687 he was paid for carving a rock-work pedestal, 'Heads for ye Nessis', and trophies and other enrichments for one of the gate piers (**9**). Before 7 July 1687 he provided an ambitious design for a fountain incorporating three basons, the lowest supported by sea-horses, the second by mermen and the third by dolphins, with a merman blowing a conch shell at the top (**8**). The accompanying contract specified that the fountain was to cost £70 and a final clause directed that Harvey should add coats of arms with reindeer crests.

He was still alive in 1719, when Claver Morris noted in his *Diary*: 'When at Bath sent for the stone cutter Mr Harvey and discours'd with him and agreed to give for his son's cutting a coat of arms in my brother's farewell tombstone'. The work was to cost 40 shillings and Morris was 'to send an horse for him to Wells, and to supply him with diet and lodging; if he did it within a month from this time' (*Hobhouse* 1934, 69). The family's monuments include one with a bust to Dorothy Hobart (**4**).

Harvey II carved ornaments for the Lansdowne monument (**12**). According to the local historian John Wood, he was known for his parsimony. He used an excuse that Lord Lansdowne had never paid for the monument to delay on payments to his workmen, particularly John Pitcher, a freestone mason. Harvey stalled Pitcher 'to the day of his death with a promise of payment as soon as he should receive his money from Lord Lansdowne, protesting he had not received a shilling when in truth he had had the full value of the monument from him in three blocks or more of fine marble which his Lordship procured him from abroad' (*Wood* 1749, 1, 231). His will, in which he is described as a 'carver' of Bath, was proved on 13 November 1742 (PROB 11/721).

Literary References: *Gunnis* 1968, 191

Archival References: Longleat HA

Funerary Monuments

1.	?1703	John Tiley	St Mary Redcliffe, Bristol	S	*Gunnis* 1968, 191
2.	1711	Mary Blathwayt and her parents, John and Frances Wynter Payment(s): £90	St Peter, Dyrham, Glos	S	Glos RO 1799 F91; Pevsner, *Glos: Cotswolds*, 1999, 341
3.	†1717	Elizabeth Incledon	Barnstaple, Devon	S	*Gunnis* 1968, 191
4.	†1722	Dorothy Hobart	Bath Abbey, Som	S	
5.	?1733	Mary Coghill	St Peter and St Paul, Marlborough, Wilts	S	*Gunnis* 1968, 191

Statues

6.	1694	13 boys, and 2 shields (by James Harvey I)	Longleat, Wilts		Longleat HA 275, 14/11/1694
7.	1701	A boy, billed with repairs to a dolphin and birds (by John Harvey I) Payment(s): £6 5s	Longleat, Wilts		Longleat HA 275, 19/10/1701

Architectural Sculpture

8.	*c*1687	Fountain (by John Harvey I) Payment(s): £70 Drawing(s): Longleat HA 275, 06/07/1687	Longleat, Wilts		Longleat HA 275, 06/07/1687
9.	*c*1687	Sundry works including trophies and enrichments on gate piers, 12 heads of emperors, four figures, coats of arms on flower pots, four fowls, a sphinx and painting work in the garden (by John Harvey I) Payment(s): £270 for carving in 1687; £6 for each 'figure of a boy' on the fountain	Longleat, Wilts		Longleat HA 275 01/01/1687; 275 07/07/1687
10.	1693	Urns and scrolls (by John Harvey I)	Dyrham Park, Glos on balustrade and balcony		Pevsner, *Glos: Cotswolds*, 1999, 342
11.	1705	Eagle (by John Harvey I)	Dyrham Park, Glos, centre of east parapet		Pevsner, *Glos: Cotswolds*, 1999, 342
12.	1720	Trophy of arms on the Lansdowne monument (by John Harvey II)	['above Bath', Somerset]; untraced		*Wood* 1749, 2, 1, 231; *Gunnis* 1968, 191

Miscellaneous

13.	1704	Chimneypiece and water niche (by John Harvey I)	Swangrove Lodge, Badminton, Glos		Beaufort Accounts, 1704
14.	1714	Sculpture for the 2nd Duke of Beaufort's funeral (by John Harvey I)	Untraced		Beaufort Accounts, 1714

HARWOOD, Francis 1726/27–83

Best remembered as a superior copyist of the antique, Harwood lived and worked in Florence throughout most of his professional life. Nothing is known of his background. He was recorded as being in Rome by Easter 1752 when he was living in the Palazzo Zuccari on the Strada Felice with Joshua Reynolds and **Simon Vierpyl**. The following year he travelled to Florence where he met **Joseph Wilton**, who refers to Harwood in a surviving notebook and whose bust of the physician, Dr Cocchi, was later copied by Harwood (**17**). On 12 January 1755 he was admitted to the Florentine Academy and must have worked to gain a reputation over the following three years for in September 1758 he was involved in a notable public commission, the Arch of the Porta San Gallo (**28**). He worked on the edifice with **Giovanni Battista Piamontini**, whose studio in the Via della Sapienza near SS Annunziata Harwood acquired in August 1762 after Piamontini's death.

Work on the arch brought Harwood to prominence in the British community in Italy. Horace Mann, the British envoy, wrote to George Bubb Dodington in December 1759, remarking on the sculptor's ingenuity and his growing number of commissions for British clients, notably the 7th Earl Northampton of Castle Ashby (**2, 6–9, 11, 13, 14**). Harwood's works for Northampton, subsequently replicated for Sir Lawrence Dundas of Moor Park and others (**8, 11, 13**), are reproductions of classical prototypes, although the carving is of a very high quality and the poses and treatment often vary intentionally from the originals. Not all his works are based on classical precedents: the bust of Oliver Cromwell appears to be of his own invention, albeit an amalgam of many other printed and carved depictions of the Protector (**12**), whilst his muscular bust of a man in black limestone appears, almost uniquely, to be a portrait of a specific black sitter rather than a stereotytype (**10**).

Harwood's assistants included Pietro Pisani (who had been his pupil), Pietro Bastianelli and Niccolo Kindermann. In addition to classical copies, such as the *Apollo* for Syon commissioned by James and Robert Adam (**3**), the workshop produced a large range of carved chimneypieces, vases and urns after classical designs and also tables of polychrome Italian marbles (**29–34**). Harwood's only confirmed monument, to Earl Cowper (**1**), is a well-executed work with a life-size statue of an angel gesturing to a *gloria* and a putto with a portrait-medallion. A detailed report of its iconography and materials was published in the *Gazzetta Toscana* when it left Italy in 1770. In 1769 Joseph Nollekens remarked of Harwood, whom he referred to as 'FH' in a characteristically ill-spelt letter to **Thomas Banks**, that he was 'knocking the marbil about like feway & belive he as got more work to do than any One Sculptor in England' (*Whitley* 1930, 41). Harwood was depicted around this time (as a short fat man) by Thomas Patch, who produced a series of caricatures of English expatriates.

In October 1779 the young **Antonio Canova** visited Harwood's studio, which must by then have been on the tourist itinerary. Canova made a lengthy note in his diary of the numerous assistants and many plaster works of sculpture in the studio and of Harwood's copious use of coloured marbles. In 1780 Horace Mann, who had earlier lauded Harwood, now described him as the best of the indifferent practitioners in Florence, 'a drunken Englishman' whose sole employment was to make chimney-pieces for the Palazzo Pitti (**21**) and for the undiscerning agents of Catherine the Great (**22**; *Fleming and Honour* 1968, 514). Mann must have been in a temporary bad humour, or Florence genuinely offered few alternative sculptors, for he subsequently directed in his will, made in March 1781, that his monument was to be made by Harwood. It was to be a large sepulchral urn, intended for the church at Linton, Kent, to be sited near Richard Bentley and **James Lovell**'s monument to Galfridus Mann, the envoy's brother. By 1782 the memorial had reached the design stage, but Harwood died before it could be executed. He died in Florence on 5 December 1783. The entry in the Florence register of deaths records that shortly before his death Harwood converted to the Catholic faith. In his will, which described him as 'an Englishman by nation and sculptor of marble,' he left 169 zecchini to his servants and everything else to Donato, the son of Giusto Corsi.

Interest in Harwood has revived since Gunnis's terse paragraphs in the original edition of his *Dictionary*. A much fuller account was published by John Fleming and Hugh Honour, who nonetheless treated Harwood as a minor sculptor and copyist, such stuff 'as footnotes are made on' (*Fleming and Honour* 1968, 510). More recently Cremoncini has provided a more sympathetic reading of Harwood's abilities as an interpreter of the antique, and it seems likely that interest will continue to increase in this rare and early example of a capable British sculptor, who not only visited Italy but, unlike most of his contemporaries, forged a successful life and career there.

MGS

Literary References: *Gunnis* 1968, 191; *Fleming and Honour* 1968, 510–16; *Roani Villani* 1975, 53–85; *Belsey* 1980, 65–66; *O'Connor* 1986, 670–2; *Garstang* 1988, 179–81; *Salmon* 1990, 199–214; *Roani Villani* 1991, 68–74; *Roani Villani* 1993, 108–115; *Cremoncini* 1994, 68–73; *Ingamells* 1997, 472–3; *Bilbey* 2002, 88–89

Representations of the Sculptor: Thomas Patch, caricature, engraving, BM (*Watson* 1939–40, 44)

Miscellaneous Drawings: 14 sketches of urns, with prices, 1772, Audley End, library, *Fleming and Honour* 1968, 513, *Belsey* 1980, 65

Will: PROB 11/1112/189–90

Funerary Monuments						
1.	1770	William, 2nd Earl Cowper (†1764)		Hertingfordbury, Herts	S	*Belsey* 1980, 65–6 (repr)
Statues						
2.	c1758	Medici Venus	m	Castle Ashby, Northants, figures room (formerly great hall) Other versions: Spencer House, London		*McKay* 1992–3, 267; *Roani Villani* 1993, 110–3 (repr); *Ingamells* 1997, 472
3.	1762	Uffizi Apollo Payment(s): £150	m	Syon Park, Middx		*Fleming and Honour* 1968, 512; *Belsey* 1980, 65
4.	1765	Apollo Belvedere	m	[Gordon Castle, Morayshire]; Anglesey Abbey, Cambs	SD	*Roani Villani* 1991, 70 (repr); Pevsner; *Cambs*, 1970, 293
5.	1765	Marine Venus		[Gordon Castle, Morayshire]; untraced		*Gunnis* 1968, 191; *Belsey* 1980, 65
Busts						
6.	1758	Cicero	m	Castle Ashby, Northants Other versions: 1768, Crowthers' of Isleworth, 1950; untraced	SD	*Gunnis* 1968, 191; *McKay* 1992–3, 267; *Roani Villani* 1993, 110–3 (repr)
7.	1758	Julius Caesar	m	Castle Ashby, Northants Other versions: ex coll CW Beaumont, George Street, SD, 1756 Rainer Zietz, London, marble, SD, 1764	SD	*McKay* 1992–3, 267; *Roani Villani* 1993, 110–3 (repr); *Cremoncini* 1994, 73n11
8.	1758	Marcus Aurelius		Castle Ashby, Northants Other versions: Gordon Castle, Morayshire, 1762 Rainer Zietz, London, 1764, marble, SD Sotheby, London 2 July 1997, SD, 1764, marble; untraced ex Moor Park, Herts, bought 1767 for 50 zecchini, Marquess of Zetland sale, April 1934, lot 59, marble	SD	*Fleming and Honour* 1968, 512–3; *McKay* 1992–3, 267; *Roani Villani* 1993, 110, 111 (repr); *Cremoncini* 1994, 70, 73 n9

9.	1758	Sappho	m	Castle Ashby, Northants	SD	*McKay* 1992–3, 267; *Roani Villani* 1993, 110–3 (repr)
10.	1758	Unidentified man in black stone	s	[Stanwick Hall, N R Yorks]; Getty, Los Angeles 88.SA.114 Other versions: ex coll Paul Mellon, YCBA, unsigned, nd	SD	*Roani Villani* 1991, 68–74; *McKay* 1992–3, 268; *Fusco* 1998, 92–3 (repr); *Baker* 2000, 143 (repr)
11.	1759	Faustina	m	Castle Ashby, Northants Other versions: ex Moor Park, Herts, bought 1767 for 50 zecchini; Marquess of Zetland sale April 1934, lot 58, marble	SD	*Fleming and Honour* 1968, 512–3; *McKay* 1993–4, 267, 269 (repr); *Cremoncini* 1994, 73 n9
12.	1759	Oliver Cromwell	m	[Castle Forbes, Ireland Sold Sotheby NY, 10th July 1995, lot 66]; untraced	SD	*Cremoncini* 1994, 73 n13; *Dawson* 1999, 77; GPS
13.	1759	Seneca	m	Castle Ashby, Northants Other versions: VAM A.26-1948, ex Gordon Castle, Morayshire, marble, SD 1763 ex Moor Park, Herts, bought for 50 zecchini in 1767, Marquess of Zetland Sale, Christie, 16 April 1934, lot 58	SD	*Fleming and Honour* 1968, 512–3, 515 n12; *McKay* 1992–3, 267, 268 (repr); *Cremoncini* 1994, 73 n9; *Bilbey* 2002, 88–9 (repr)
14.	1760	Homer	m	Castle Ashby, Northants Other versions: VAM A.8-1958, SD 1764, ex Gordon Castle, Morayshire, marble	SD	*Fleming and Honour* 1968, 515 n12; *McKay* 1992–3, 267; *Roani Villani* 1993, 110–3 (repr); *Bilbey* 2002, 89 (repr)
15.	1762	Caracalla		Finchcox, Kent Other versions: Danny Katz Ltd (2004), marble, SD		*Gunnis* 1968, 191
16.	1765	Vestal		[Gordon Castle, Morayshire]; untraced Other versions: ex Moor Park, Herts, bought for 50 zecchini in 1767; Marquess of Zetland sale, Christie, 16 April 1934, lot 58		*Gunnis* 1968, 191; *Fleming and Honour* 1968, 512–3; *Cremoncini* 1994, 73 n9
17.	nd	Antonio Cocchi (after Joseph Wilton RA)	m	Private coll, Florence		*Roani Villani* 1991, 70 (repr); *Roani Villani* 1993, 109
Chimneypieces						
18.	1767	Four, lavishly carved Payment(s): 100; 25; 80; 80 zecchini	m	[Moor Park, Herts]; untraced		*Fleming and Honour* 1968, 512–3; *Cremoncini* 1994, 73 n9; GPC
19.	1768	with two terms, a ram's head and laurel festoons Payment(s): 258 zecchini, including carriage		[for Earl of Charlemont, perhaps for the Casino, Marino, Dublin]; untraced		*O'Connor* 1986, 670
20.	1774–1775	Description unavailable		[coll Patrick Home]; untraced		*Ingamells* 1997, 473
21.	1776–1780	Several, including one with eagle decoration	m	Palazzo Pitti, Florence		*Fleming and Honour* 1968, 514; *Roani Villani* 1975, 58
22.	nd	Description unavailable		[Tsarskoe Selo, Russia]; untraced		*Fleming and Honour* 1968, 514; *Ingamells* 1997, 472
23.	nd	(designed by George Dance the Younger)		[for Sir Henry Mainwaring, Over Peover, Cheshire]; untraced		*O'Connor* 1986, 670; *Ingamells* 1997, 473–4
24.	nd	Polychrome	m	Poggio Imperiale, Florence		*Roani Villani* 1975, 58
25.	nd	Polychrome	m	Fabbrica della Querce, Florence		*Roani Villani* 1975, 58
26.	nd	Polychrome	m	Casino di San Marco, Florence		*Roani Villani* 1975, 58
27.	nd	Polychrome	m	Villa di Poggio, Caiano, Tuscany		*Roani Villani* 1975, 58
Architectural Sculpture						
28.	1758	Statue of Equity, and a trophy		Arch of the Porta San Gallo, Florence		*Fleming and Honour* 1968, 511; *McKay* 1992–3, 267; *Roani Villani* 1993, 109; *Cremoncini* 1994, 68
29.	1767	Three lavish polychrome tables and 11 pairs of small alabaster vases, one of Siena marble ('to put on the chimney') Payment(s): 24; 50; 20; 20; 12 zecchini		[Moor Park, Herts]; untraced		*Fleming and Honour* 1968, 512–3; *Cremoncini* 1994, 73 n9; GPC
30.	1768	Two vases	a	[for Charles Townley]; untraced		*Cremoncini* 1994, 73 n10
31.	1768	Vases, 12 pieces of marble shaped like books, and a marble chequer table		[coll Sir Watkin Williams Wynn]; untraced		*Ingamells* 1997, 472
32.	1772	A garniture of vases		[coll Lord Shelburne]; untraced		*Ingamells* 1997, 472
33.	1772	Pair of vases and 'one urn to put between the pair' with '3 pieces of black marble to put at the foot of the vases and lick them of Lord Spencer'		[Bowood, Wilts]; untraced		*Belsey* 1980, 65
34.	1772	Vases Drawing(s): Audley End Archives		Audley End, Essex		*Fleming and Honour* 1968, 513; *Ingamells* 1997, 472
35.	1776	Copy of a monster on the balustrade of the Vasca dell'Isolotto, Boboli Gardens, Florence		[coll Grand Duke of Tuscany]; untraced		*Fleming and Honour* 1968, 514
Miscellaneous						
36.	1770–1771	Unspecified work, possibly chimneypieces		[for 3rd Earl of Bute, possibly for Luton Hoo, Beds]; untraced		*Ingamells* 1997, 473

HASELGROVE, of Luton and St Albans fl 1811–46

Funerary Monuments

1.	†1811	John Benthall		St Mary, Totnes, Devon		RG/JP, 4, 658v.
2.	†1846	John Prince and Octavius Benthall		St Mary, Totnes, Devon		RG/JP, 4, 658v.

HASKOLL, J S fl 1824–36

In 1824, when he first exhibited at the Royal Academy, he was living on the Isle of Wight. By 1829 he was in London, in Charterhouse Square, and the following year he moved to Pimlico. In 1835, while living in Covent Garden, he applied to the AGBI stating that 'he had passed many years on the Continent and had made a bas-relief for a church in the Isle of Wight'. Gunnis suggests that this bas-relief is probably part of the monument to Sir Leonard Worsley Holmes (1), which depicts the deceased's wife seated like a Grecian matron by a wreathed urn and pedestal, mourning with her children.

Literary References: *Graves* IV, 1905–6, 20; *Gunnis* 1968, 191–2; *Johnson* 1975, 210

Archival References: AGBI, vol 3, 52, 152, 183

Funerary Monuments

1.	1829	Sir Leonard Worsley Holmes (†1825), relief only Model(s): exhib Soc of BA, London, 1829, 861		Arreton, I of W	S	Pevsner, *Hants & Isle of Wight*, 1967, 731; *Johnson* 1975, 210

Busts

2.	1824	Unidentified lady		[Exhib RA, London, 993]; untraced		*Graves* IV, 1905–6, 20
3.	1830	Algernon Jones	m	[Exhib RA, London, 1233]; untraced		*Graves* IV, 1905–6, 20
4.	1830	Unidentified gentleman		[Exhib RA, London, 1198]; untraced		*Graves* IV, 1905–6, 20
5.	1831	A Jones	m	[Exhib RA, London, 1181]; untraced		*Graves* IV, 1905–6, 20
6.	1831	Unidentified subject	m	[Exhib RA, London, 1188]; untraced		*Graves* IV, 1905–6, 20
7.	1832	Augustus S Perkins	m	[Exhib RA, London, 1128]; untraced		*Graves* IV, 1905–6, 20
8.	1832	Colonel Jones		[Exhib Soc of BA, London, 885]; untraced		*Johnson* 1975, 210
9.	1834	Isaac Newton		Lincoln Public Library	D	*Gunnis* 1968, 192
10.	1835	Benson Hill		[Exhib RA, London, 1055]; untraced		*Graves* IV, 1905–6, 21
11.	1836	Countess of Yarborough		Brocklesby Park, Lincs		*Gunnis* 1968, 192

HASLEWOOD, Richard c1743–

Apprenticed to Mouchet, a chaser, on 18 May 1764, he received a premium from the Society of Arts for a model by a sculptor aged under 22. His address was Great Queen Street, Lincoln's Inn Fields.

Literary References: RSA *Premiums* 1763, 37; *Dossie* 1782, 437

Archival References: RSA *Minutes*, 1763–64 seq 3 f 83

Miscellaneous

1.	1764	Model of ornaments in clay		[Soc of A, premium (3gns)]; untraced		RSA *Minutes*, 1763–64, seq 3 f 83; RSA *Premiums* 1763, 37

HASWELL, George, of Chester fl c1840–52

He carved a coat of arms with wyverns, sword and wheatsheafs surrounded with foliage, for the lunatic Asylum in Chester (2).

Funerary Monuments

1.	1852	William Thackery, memorial cross		Chester Cemetery, Cheshire	S	

Architectural Sculpture

2.	c1840	County coat of arms		[Chester Lunatic Asylum, pediment]; untraced		*Builder*, 1850, 94; *Gunnis* 1968, 192

HATCHARD, James 1793–

In 1811 he exhibited at the Royal Academy, giving his address as Queen Street, Westminster. He entered the Royal Academy Schools on 21 January 1814. The monument to Elizabeth Fleming, a tablet with a draped urn on a sarcophagus, is signed 'James Hatchard of Pimlico' (2).

Literary References: *Gunnis* 1968, 192; *Hutchison* 1960–62, 167

Funerary Monuments

1.	?1823	Captain Thomas Fraser		Checkheaton, Oxon	S	*Gunnis* 1968, 192
2.	†1831	Elizabeth Fleming		St Mary, Llanfair Talhaearn, Denbighs	S	Pevsner, *Clwyd*, 1986, 210
3.	?1835	Sarah Smith		Holy Trinity, Marylebone, London	S	*Gunnis* 1968, 192

Busts

4.	1811	Mr Hatchard, architect (possibly the sculptor's father)		[Exhib RA, London, 930]; untraced		*Graves* IV, 1905–6, 24; *Gunnis* 1968, 192

HATCHARD, Samuel fl 1829

In 1829, while living at 44 Holywell Street, Millbank, he was awarded a silver medal from the Society of Arts.

Architectural Sculpture

1.	1829	An architectural ornament from Rochester Cathedral		[Soc of A, large silver medal]; untraced		RSA *Transactions*, vol 47, 1829, xxiii

HATFIELD, John fl 1844

He was listed in Thompson's *Commercial Directory* for 1844 as an 'artist in bronze', living at 20 Cumberland Street, by the Middlesex Hospital.

HATLEY

For further information the reader is referred to *Pyke* 1973, 65.

HATTON, Edward fl 1777–85

Samuel Smiles in his *Lives of the Engineers* quotes a letter from Thomas Telford written in July 1783 when he was working as a journeyman mason at Somerset House. Telford says of Edward Hatton that: 'He has been six years at Somerset House and is esteemed the finest workman in London and consequently in England. He works equally in stone and marble. He has excelled the professed carvers in cutting Corinthian capitals and other ornaments about this edifice, many of which will stand as a monument to his honour. He understands drawing thoroughly, and the master he works under looks on him as the principal support of his business. . . He may be half-a-dozen years older than myself at most [Telford was then 26]. He is honesty and good-nature itself and is adored by both his master and fellow-workmen. Not withstanding his extraordinary skill and abilities, he has been working all this time as a common journeyman, contented with a few shillings a week more than the rest' (*Smiles* 1861, 2, 311).

Literary References: *Gunnis* 1968, 192

Architectural Sculpture

1.	1779–1785	'Corinthian capitals and other ornaments'		Somerset House, London	*Gunnis* 1968, 192

HAWKE, Joseph fl 1777–84

He was one of the master-masons and builders at Gorhambury, Herts, 1777–84. The house was built to the designs of **Sir Robert Taylor** by Hawke, **John Wildsmith** and **Richard Westmacott I**. Hawke supplied Tottenhoe stone to Woburn Abbey in the years 1789–91.

Literary References: *Binney* 1984, 86

Archival References: Woburn Building Accts 1789–1791, May – Oct 1791, £119 11s 6d; Nov 1791, £30; 1791, £37 1s

Architectural Sculpture

1.	1777–1784	Carved stonework Payment(s): £2,621 including other masonry and building work		[Gorhambury, Herts]; untraced	Hertford county archives, B.XI.66 cited in *Gunnis* 1968, 192

HAWKE, William fl 1785–90

He was extensively employed during the rebuilding of Woburn Abbey, 1785–90, providing masonry and carving in Portland stone.

Architectural Sculpture

1.	1789–1790	Carved stonework Payment(s): £900 with other masonry work		Woburn Abbey, Beds	Woburn Building Accts, BLARS 1785–86, R5/1102; 1789–91, R3/2114/498–502

HAWKES, Thomas fl 1791

In July 1791 Thomas Hawkes, 'carver and Sculptor, Brownlow St., St Giles in the Fields', took as an apprentice **William Collet**, a pupil at the Westminster French Protestant Charity School.

Literary References: *le May* 2001, 570

HAWKINS fl 1766

Hawkins supplied a chimneypiece at Kirkleatham (1). Gunnis conjectured that this was the one of white stone with a woman's head in the centre, which is still in one of the rooms on the ground floor.

Archival References: GPC

Chimneypieces

1.	1766	Description unavailable	s	[Kirkleatham Hall, N R Yorks]; untraced	GPC

HAWKINS, Benjamin Waterhouse 1807–89?

He was born in London, educated at St Aloysius College, and trained under **William Behnes**. He may have been the 'Hawkins' who was listed by Jouin as a pupil of **David D'Angers** (*Jouin* 1878, 1, 581). He specialised in painting and modelling subjects from natural history, and in 1847 exhibited at the Royal Academy giving his address as 57 Cambridge Street, Hyde Park. He was elected a member of the Society of Arts in 1846, and in 1851 became assistant superintendent at the Great Exhibition, where he also showed (1). The work was subsequently presented by the Zoological Society of London to the Emperor of Russia.

In September 1852 he was appointed director of the fossil department of the Crystal Palace and, with the anatomist Richard Owen (1804–1892), he constructed a display of life-size models of extinct animals (2). The iguanodon was constructed of four iron columns, 600 bricks, 38 casks of cement and 90 casks of broken stone, altogether comprising 640 bushels of artificial stone.

Hawkins travelled to the United States in 1868, where he worked on a commission that aborted, to construct models of extinct animals in Central Park, New York. The date and place of his death are not certain.

Literary References: *Gunnis* 1968, 192; *Smith* 2000, 42–3; *ODNB* (McCarthy)

Statues					
1.	1851	European bison	b	[Gt Exhib]; untraced	*Gunnis* 1968, 192
2.	1854	Prehistoric monsters		Crystal Palace Park, London	*McCarthy* 1994; *Smith* 2000 (repr)
3.	nd	Animal sculpture		[Biddulph Grange, Staffs]; untraced	*ODNB*
Reliefs					
4.	1847	Miss Lea		[Exhib RA, London, 1406]; untraced	*Graves* IV, 1905–6, 32
5.	1847	Study of a head		[Exhib RA, London, 1407]; untraced	*Graves* IV, 1905–6, 32
Miscellaneous					
6.	1848	Model of the aurochs		[Exhib RA, London, 1383]; untraced	*Graves* IV, 1905–6, 32
7.	1849	Model from life of the jaguar		[Exhib RA, London, 1275]; untraced	*Graves* IV, 1905–6, 32

HAWKINS, J B fl 1842–45

The *Literary Gazette* said of his *Hesitation of Pandora* 'an accurate copy of bad nature, or a cast filled up, cannot be worth anything' (1). A sculptor of that name was a pupil of **David D'Angers**.

Literary References: *Jouin* 1878, 1, 581

Statues					
1.	1844	Hesitation of Pandora		[Exhib Westminster Hall, London]; untraced	*Lit Gaz*, 1844, 466; *Gunnis* 1968, 192
2.	1845	The infant St John		[Exhib Westminster Hall, London, 118]; untraced	*Westminster* 1845, 15
Reliefs					
3.	1842	Unidentified lady, medallion	m	[Exhib RA, London, 1392]; untraced	*Graves* IV, 1905–6, 32

HAWLEY, John, of Colsterworth 1767–

He came from a family of masons. Most of the 75 engraved slate headstones in Lincolnshire signed 'Hawley of Colsterworth', were carved 1790–1825, probably by this craftsman.

Literary References: *Neave and Heron* 1969, 12

HAWORTH, Henry 1760–81

A younger brother of **William Haworth**, he was born on 14 September 1760, the son of **Samuel Haworth**. He joined the Royal Academy Schools on the same day as his brother, 31 March 1777, giving his age as 16. He was appointed resident woodcarver to the Carron Company of Scotland in 1779. He died of pneumonia, contracted after attending a late ball in Linlithgow.

Literary References: *Hutchison* 1960–62, 142; *Brown* 1963, 21–3

Portrait of the Sculptor: Samuel de Wilde, oil on canvas (*Brown* 1963, 21, repr)

HAWORTH, Samuel –1779

He was a 'Carver and Gilder' of Denmark-Street, St Giles', London (*Mortimer* 1763, 13) and the father of **Henry** and **Samuel Haworth**. His workshop employed 30 assistants, many from the Dutch and Flemish Netherlands, and carried out some work for the Carron Company of Scotland. The workshop was visited by King George III.

Literary References: *Brown* 1963, 142

HAWORTH, William 1759–1838

He was born on 21 June 1759, the son of **Samuel Haworth** and the brother of **Henry Haworth**. He joined the Royal Academy Schools on 31 March 1777 giving his age as 17. Four years later he exhibited at the Academy (1) from 46 New Compton Street. When his brother died in 1781 he took over as resident carver at the Carron Company of Scotland. He married at Carron and remained there for 56 years. He was buried beside his brother in Larbert Churchyard, near Carron. A number of woodcarvings by the brothers were used as models for the decorative ironwork for which the firm was noted.

Literary References: *Graves* IV, 1905–6, 33; *Hutchison* 1960–62, 142; *Brown* 1963, 21–4; *Gunnis* 1968, 192

Portrait of the Sculptor: John Kerr, William Haworth, pencil, *Brown* 1963, 23 (repr)

Busts

1.	1781	Rev Dr Giffard	tc	[Exhib RA, London, 506]; untraced	*Graves* IV, 1905–6, 33

HAY, James I, of Portsea fl 1781?–after 1810

In 1765 he was apprenticed to John Mitchell, 'mason of St Anne's, Westminster' (TNA, I.R. 24/180). His most ambitious work is the monument 'in a pyramidal form ornamented, with marine trophies, arms, sculptured urns &c', erected in Portsea churchyard to the memory of Admiral Kempenfelt and the crew of the *Royal George* (**2**). This was unveiled in March 1783, and was described and illustrated in the *Gentleman's Magazine* (*GM* 1783, 357–8). Other monuments are more standard fare: the Bonham is a large neoclassical square tomb, and the Norris tablet features a draped urn (**6, 10**). He was the father of **James Hay II** and survived his son. The press notice of his son's death describes Hay I as 'an eminent naturalist and a fellow of the Linnaean Society' (*Monthly Mag* 1810, 29, 613).

Literary References: *Gunnis* 1968, 192

Archival References: GPC

Funerary Monuments

1.	?1781	Hans Flower	Holy Trinity, Gosport, Hants		GPC
2.	?1783	Admiral Kempenfelt and the crew of the *Royal George*	Portsea churchyard		*GM* 1782, 1, 357–8; *Gunnis* 1968, 192
3.	?1785	Mrs Sarah Reid	Fareham, Hants, churchyard	S	*Gunnis* 1968, 192
4.	?1789	William Feilding	Portsmouth Cathedral, Hants	S	*Gunnis* 1968, 192
5.	?1797	John Thomas	Porchester, Hants		GPC
6.	*c*1800	Bonham family	East Meon, Hants, churchyard	S	GPC
7.	?1802	Catherine Moody	Porchester, Hants	S	*Gunnis* 1968, 192
8.	?1807	James Clarenbould	Holy Trinity, Gosport, Hants		GPC
9.	?1810	Gavin Kempt	Bishops Waltham, Hants	S	*Gunnis* 1968, 192
10.	†1811	Rev James (†1782) and Anne (†1811) Norris	Warblington, Hants	S	*Gunnis* 1968, 192
11.	†1813	Captain Alexander Cameron	Warblington, Hants	S	*Gunnis* 1968, 192
12.	?1813	David Renaud	Havant, Hants	S	*Gunnis* 1968, 192

HAY, James II, of Portsea 1772–1810

The son of **James Hay I**, he had enthusiasm from an early age for the study of natural history, acquiring such a proficiency in draughtsmanship that he was sent to study painting under Benjamin West. Finding a preference for sculpture he soon became a pupil of **John Flaxman RA**, under whom he studied for two years. In addition he studied anatomy and physiology under Sheldon and Brookes. At the time of his death at Portsea in 1810, Hay was acting as assistant to his father. According to one obituary 'his too intense applications to the various branches of science brought on a lingering disease which terminated by a premature death, the life and labours of a rising genius who might have proved an honour and an ornament to his country' (*GM* 1810, 1, 498).

The *Monthly Magazine* adds that 'he left many drawings of the most remarkable antiquities in Hampshire; and a much greater number of almost the whole zoology of Great Britain, particularly a complete arrangement of all the shells, beautifully drawn and coloured from nature which were intended for publication'. He was 'much beloved for the virtues of the mind, as he was admired for his superior talents' (*Monthly Mag* 1810, 613). No independent works by him have come to light.

Literary References: *Euro Mag* 1810, 57, 393; *GM* 1810, 1, 498; *Monthly Mag* 1810, 612–3; *Gunnis* 1968, 193

HAYDON, Samuel James Bouverie 1815–91

Haydon was born at Heavitree, near Exeter, on 29 April 1815, the son of Samuel and Elizabeth Haydon and was christened on 17 October 1821 at Crediton, Devon. He went to Mount Radford School and was subsequently articled to a lawyer, who appears to have died in 1835, before Haydon completed his training. Haydon's father appealed to his contacts, including Duncombe Bouverie (**26**), and must have successfully placed the youth with another firm for Haydon went on to practise on his own account in Exeter. The love of art apparently proved too strong, however, and Haydon abandoned the law and went to London, where he studied sculpture under **E H Baily**. A letter from Baily to the young man, dated 22 November 1838, invites him to a meeting, and it seems that Haydon began his training around this time. He was certainly in London by 1840 when he exhibited at the Royal Academy, giving his address as 14 Compton Street, Brunswick Square.

He apparently showed great promise in his new profession. Benjamin Robert Haydon, the painter, whose kinship, if any, with the sculptor, has not been established, endorsed his work in October 1841, saying that the sculptor had a 'great feeling for nature and simplicity, the basis of fine portraiture' (*Wills* 1962, 787). B R Haydon later said of his namesake that he was 'capable of taking the place of Chantrey' (*Pycroft* 1883, 58). Haydon exhibited a large number of busts, in wax, bronze and marble. The *Art Union* said of his portrait *all'antica* of Sir Robert Newman (**8**) that it was 'a work treated with becoming simplicity. The features are modelled with infinite care, and are marked by passages of nice execution in parts which are often too much neglected' (*AU*, 1846, 189). The sitter himself felt that the work was 'a very strong specimen' and also commended the bust of his brother, Thomas Newman (**9**), as 'very like' (*Wills* 1962, 787). It is questionable how astute Haydon was in his business practice since Newman had to press him to send his final account three years after the busts were executed.

Haydon also tried his hand at poetic subjects. In 1844 he exhibited *Hermia and Helena* at the RA, endorsed by the *Art Union* as 'graceful and skilfully composed' (**2**; *AU*, 1844, 170). In 1847 his *Perdita* was declared 'a graceful and successful realization of the character' (*AU*, 1847, 200).

Haydon seems to have had a crisis in his career in 1849, when Duncombe Bouverie wrote to him: 'I know not whether you persevere in your intention of abandoning your professional pursuits in which you have executed so many striking likenesses: if you do, I think the public will have much reason to regret it' (*Wills* 1962, 787). Haydon continued to exhibit in the 1850s but showed few works and no portraits. In the 1860s, however, he returned to portraiture, carving a fine posthumous bust of a child, with a carved book acting as a plinth for the portrait (**30**). In 1870 he intended to apply for the curatorship of the Antique School at the Royal Academy, and acquired testimonials from **J H Foley, E B Stephens** and Frederick Leighton. Either he have changed his mind or was not selected for the post. He last exhibited at the Academy in 1876, giving his address as 6 Parkside, Knightsbridge.

Haydon married before 1860, and had a child called Flaxman. His death was announced in *The Art Journal* of 1891. Pyecroft wrote that his works were 'so good that it is more the pity they are so few. It was not from want of genius, power or personal merit that he failed to make for himself a far greater name' (*Pycroft* 1883, 58). A number of Haydon's letters came to light in 1962 when they were published by their owner, Geoffrey Wills, but much still remains unknown about the career of this talented sculptor.

MGS

Literary References: *Pycroft* 1883, 58; *AJ* 1891, 352; *Wills* 1962, 785–7

Archival References: IGI

Funerary Monuments

1.	1848	Sketch for a monument		[Exhib RA, London, 1417]; untraced		*Graves* IV, 1905–6, 37

Statues

2.	1844	Hermia and Helena, seated group	m	[Exhib RA, London, 1279]; untraced		*AU*, 1844, 170; *Graves* IV, 1905–6, 37
3.	1847–1850	Perdita Model(s): small plaster exhib RA, London, 1847, 1335	m	[Exhib RA, London, 1328]; untraced		*AU*, 1847, 200; *Graves* IV, 1905–6, 37
4.	1862	Charity, group	m	[Exhib RA, London, 1122]; untraced		*Graves* IV, 1905–6, 37
5.	1865	Ophelia, 'figure'	m	[Exhib RA, London, 905]; untraced		*Graves* IV, 1905–6, 37; *Pycroft* 1883, 60
6.	1873	King Charles I, statuette Payment(s): £60	m	[Exhib Soc of BA, London, 925]; untraced		*Johnson* 1975, 215

Busts

7.	1840	Captain Carslake		[Exhib RA, London, 1086]; untraced		*Graves* IV, 1905–6, 36
8.	1840	Sir Robert Newman	m	Untraced Other versions: private coll, marble, SD 1846 private coll, 1846 (different drapery)		*AU*, 1846, 189; *Graves* IV, 1905–6, 37; *Wills* 1962, 785 (repr)
9.	1840	Thomas Newman	m	Untraced Other versions: private coll, SD 1846		*Graves* IV, 1905–6, 37; *Wills* 1962, 787
10.	1841	Unidentified gentleman	m	[Exhib RA, London, 1301]; untraced		*Graves* IV, 1905–6, 36
11.	1842	Edward Divett MP		[Exhib RA, London, 1402]; untraced		*Graves* IV, 1905–6, 36
12.	1842	Sir Henry Goldfinch		[Exhib RA, London, 1383]; untraced		*Graves* IV, 1905–6, 36
13.	1843	John Dickens		[Exhib RA, London, 1476]; untraced		*Graves* IV, 1905–6, 37
14.	1843	Rev John Martin		[Exhib RA, London, 1451]; untraced		*Graves* IV, 1905–6, 37
15.	1843	Rev W Elliot	m	Untraced		*Pycroft* 1883, 58
16.	1843	Samuel Barnes		Devon and Exeter Institution, Exeter, Devon		*Pycroft* 1883, 60; GPC
17.	1843	Unidentified man	w	VAM A.44-1937 Other versions: VAM A.2-1918, bronze	SD	*Wills* 1963, 786–7 (bronze repr); *Gunnis* 1968, 193; *Pyke* 1973, 65 (repr 127); *Bilbey* 2002, 300 (bronze repr)
18.	1844	Cordelia	b	[Exhib RA, London, 1360]; untraced		*Graves* IV, 1905–6, 37
19.	1845	John Saywell	m	[Exhib RA, London, 1461]; untraced		*Graves* IV, 1905–6, 37
20.	1845	Unidentified lady	i	[Exhib RA, London, 1314]; untraced		*Graves* IV, 1905–6, 37
21.	1846	Rev J W Gleadall		Foundling Hospital, London, office		*Graves* IV, 1905–6, 37; *Gunnis* 1968, 193
22.	1846	William Denne	m	[Exhib RA, London, 1438]; untraced		*Graves* IV, 1905–6, 37
23.	1847	George Thompson		[Exhib RA, London, 1375]; untraced		*Graves* IV, 1905–6, 37
24.	1847	Unidentified lady		[Exhib RA, London, 1368]; untraced		*Graves* IV, 1905–6, 37

25.	1848	Mary Agnes Deane		[Exhib RA, London, 1446]; untraced		*Graves* IV, 1905–6, 37
26.	1849	Hon Duncombe Bouverie	m	[Longford Castle, Wilts]; untraced		*Graves* IV, 1905–6, 37
27.	1849	William, 3rd Earl of Radnor	m	[Longford Castle, Wilts]; untraced		*Graves* IV, 1905–6, 37
28.	1860	H Bridges	m	[Exhib RA, London, 1057]; untraced		*Graves* IV, 1905–6, 37
29.	1861	Unidentified child	m	VAM A.7-1970	SD	*Bilbey* 2002, 301 (repr)
30.	1862	Child of the Rev F Fanshawe	m	[Exhib RA, London, 1041]; untraced		*Graves* IV, 1905–6, 37
31.	1864	Lady Mason	m	[Exhib RA, London, 1060]; untraced		*Graves* IV, 1905–6, 37
32.	1876	Unidentified gentleman	m	[Exhib RA, London, 1446]; untraced		*Graves* IV, 1905–6, 37
33.	nd	G Boyer	m	Untraced		*Pycroft* 1883, 60
Reliefs						
34.	1848	Girl at confession, bas-relief	m	[Exhib Soc of BA, London, 797 Exhib RA, London, 1849, 1255]; untraced		*Graves* IV, 1905–6, 37; *Johnson* 1975, 215
35.	1848	Mrs George Read, medallion	b	[Exhib RA, London, 1474]; untraced		*Graves* IV, 1905–6, 37
Miscellaneous						
36.	1841	Captain William Symonds		[Exhib RA, London, 1303]; untraced		*Graves* IV, 1905–6, 36
37.	1845	Nell asleep		[Exhib RA, London, 1358]; untraced		*Graves* IV, 1905–6, 37
38.	1847	Sappho's fifth fragment		[Exhib BI, London, 556]; untraced		*Graves* 1875, 251
39.	1848	Belinda		[Exhib Soc of BA, London, 795]; untraced		*Johnson* 1975, 215
40.	1852	The rose		[Exhib RA, London, 1368]; untraced		*Graves* IV, 1905–6, 37
41.	1858	The travellers' club house		[Exhib RA, London, 229]; untraced		*Graves* IV, 1905–6, 37
42.	1861	Sir Henry Goldfinch		[Exhib RA, London, 1006]; untraced		*Graves* IV, 1905–6, 37
43.	1863	'She dwelt among the untrodden ways'		[Exhib RA, London, 1086]; untraced		*Graves* IV, 1905–6, 37
44.	1864	Mrs T Sheffield of Exeter	m	[Exhib RA, London, 1019]; untraced		*Graves* IV, 1905–6, 37; *Pycroft* 1883, 60

HAYES, James fl 1709

In the accounts of John Hervey, 1st Earl of Bristol is the record of a payment of £31 made in 1709 to 'James Hayes ye stone cutter' in full, for '98 foot of marble at 5s 6d for ye beufette & for other work.'

Literary References: *Hervey* 1894, 148

HAYES, T, of Beverley fl 1811–45

He signs a number of tablets in and around Beverley, including a large Gothic one to James Atkinson (**13**). He described himself as a 'stonemason' on the monument to Robert Dobson (**1**). He was presumably related to **W M Hayes.**

Funerary Monuments					
1.	†1811	Rev Robert Dobson and family members	Beverley Minster, E R Yorks	S	
2.	†1820	Alexander Shaw	Beverley Minster, E R Yorks	S	
3.	†1820	William Bradley	All Saints, Market Weighton, E R Yorks		Pevsner, *Yorks: E R & York*, 1995, 610
4.	1832	John Frith Soane (†1830) and his wife Mary (†1832)	Beverley Minster, E R Yorks	S	*Gunnis* 1968, 193
5.	†1834	Harriet Fox	Beverley Minster, E R Yorks	S	
6.	†1836	Jane Fawsitt	North Dalton, E R Yorks	S	Pevsner, *Yorks: E R & York*, 1995, 628
7.	†1837	Rev Joseph Coltman	Beverley Minster, E R Yorks	S	
8.	†1837	Thomas Ruesbury	St Mary, Beverley, E R Yorks	S	
9.	1837	William Beswick (†1829) and family	St Oswald, Filey, E R Yorks		Pevsner, *Yorks: E R & York*, 1995, 416
10.	†1842	Harriet and William Mickleton	St Mary, Beverley, E R Yorks	S	
11.	†1844	James Brown	Skirlaugh, E R Yorks	S	Pevsner, *Yorks: E R & York*, 1995, 690
12.	†1844	Matilda Smith	Routh, E R Yorks	S	Pevsner, *Yorks: E R & York*, 1995, 661
13.	1845	James Atkinson (†1839)	St Helen, York	S	Pevsner, *Yorks: E R & York*, 1995, 167

HAYES, W M, of Beverley fl 1846

Funerary Monuments				
1.	†1846	Henry John Hutton	Beverley Minster, E R Yorks	S

HAYLER, Henry 1825–

He joined the Royal Academy Schools in 1841, on the recommendation of **Sir Richard Westmacott RA.** At that time he was living at 129 Gawford Street, Baker Street. He began to exhibit at the Academy in 1849, from an address in Compton Street. By 1857 he had moved to 20 Bloomfield Terrace, Pimlico.

Literary References: *Graves* IV, 1905–6, 41

Archival References: RA Admissions

Reliefs				
1.	1852	Mr and Mrs Benedict J A Angel, cameo portraits	[Exhib RA, London, 648]; untraced	*Graves* IV, 1905–6, 41
2.	1854	George Godwin, cameo portrait	[Exhib RA, London, 1275]; untraced	*Graves* IV, 1905–6, 41
3.	1856	Mr and Mrs Eames, medallions	[Exhib RA, London, 1280]; untraced	*Graves* IV, 1905–6, 41
4.	1858	Unidentified sitter, cameo portrait	[Exhib RA, London, 1115]; untraced	*Graves* IV, 1905–6, 41
5.	1859	Unidentified subject, medallion portrait	[Exhib RA, London, 1382]; untraced	*Graves* IV, 1905–6, 41
Miscellaneous				
6.	1849	Sketch of St Peter, figure for an architectural setting	[Exhib RA, London, 1301]; untraced	*Graves* IV, 1905–6, 41
7.	1853	The wrecked	[Exhib RA, London, 1369]; untraced	*Graves* IV, 1905–6, 41
8.	1857	Cupid sleeping	[Exhib RA, London, 1239]; untraced	*Graves* IV, 1905–6, 41

HAYLEY, Thomas Alphonso 1780–1800

Hayley, who was described by Gunnis as a young man of much ability, was the natural (and only) son of William Hayley, the poet. He was placed under **John Flaxman RA** *c*1795 to study sculpture. William Hayley had been instrumental in securing Flaxman the commission for a monument to William Collins and he was also to supply verses for inscription on several of Flaxman's monuments. Thomas Hayley appeared in a painting by George Romney in 1795, showing Flaxman modelling a bust of William Hayley. The young man is depicted leaning in a *contrapposto* pose against a pedestal, watching the creative process. Flaxman provided his pupil with a classical education: in 1796 he gave the youth his tracings from James Stuart's *Antiquities of Athens* and set him to copy fragments of the Parthenon frieze.

Hayley died before he could establish himself as a sculptor, on 2 May 1800. He was buried at Eartham, Sussex, where there is a monument to his memory, carved and erected by Flaxman. The monument takes the form of a mandorla featuring a relief of an angel holding a crown. It has the inscription 'John Flaxman sculptor dedicates this stone to the virtues and talents of his beloved scholar.'

A *Memoir* of William Hayley and his son was published in 1823, edited by John Johnson. This comprised two volumes of nearly 1,000 pages: the *Literary Gazette* remarked that 'the Genius of Humbug never produced a more gross piece of absurdity' (*Lit Gaz*, 1823, 405).

Literary References: *Horsfield* 1835, 61–2; *Whinney* 1988, 359, 463 n29, 467 n12

Representations of the Sculptor: George Romney, *Flaxman modelling the bust of William Hayley*, 1795, oil on canvas, YCBA (*Bindman* 1979, 36, repr and NPG, 101)

Busts

1.	nd	J S Clarke	Untraced		*Gunnis* 1968, 193
2.	nd	Lord Thurlow	Untraced		*Gunnis* 1968, 193

Reliefs

3.	nd	George Romney, portrait medallion	Untraced		GPC

HAYNES, S, of Bristol fl 1769

He is known only for one tablet with a small relief of a seated female figure by an urn (1).

Funerary Monuments

1.	†1769	Mary Tutton	Bleadon, Somerset	S	Pevsner, *Somerset: N & Bristol*, 1958, 145

HAYNES, Thomas, of Witney fl 1766

Funerary Monuments

1.	?1766	William Brooks	Cogges, Oxon	S	GPC

HAYNES, William, of Bury St Edmunds fl 1729

In October 1729 John, 1st Earl of Bristol recorded that he had paid 10 guineas to 'William Haynes ye Bury Stone-Cutter in full for dear Babbs tomb-stone, altering ye coronet on my own etc., and removing some others in ye church' (*Hervey* 1894, 130). 'Dear Babbs' was Bristol's wife (1).

Funerary Monuments

1.	1729	Barbara, Countess of Bristol, ledger stone	Ickworth, Suffolk		*Gunnis* 1968, 193

HAYTER, Sir George 1792–1871

Hayter is chiefly remembered as a fashionable portrait-painter of the period, and his work as such is outside the scope of this book. He was responsible for some sculpture and exhibited his bust of Lady Hunloke (1) at the International Exhibition of 1862.

Busts

1.	1856–1857	Lady Hunloke as Atalanta	m	Chatsworth, Derbys		*Gunnis* 1968, 193–4; *Chatsworth Handlist*, 8
2.	1858	William, 6th Duke of Devonshire	m	Chatsworth, Derbys	S	*Gunnis* 1968, 193

HAYWARD, John, of Lincoln 1742–1817

Hayward was a mason, who twice held the post of Mayor of Lincoln. He came from a large family of masons and architects. His father, John (1708–1778) and uncle, Abraham (1692–1747) were both masons and builders from Whitchurch, Salop, who had settled in Lincoln. His brother, William (*c*1740–84) established himself as an architect in Shrewsbury and his son William (†1823/5) was surveyor to Lincoln Cathedral, 1799–1823. His sister, Ann, married into the Carline family and **John Carline I** was her son. The elder John Hayward designed and built St Mary's Bridge, Lincoln in 1853 (Lincoln Corp Minutes 1710–1800, 341, 342, cited by *Colvin* 1995 483) and either he or his son carried out building work at Burton Hall, Lincs, 1767–71 (Archives, Lord Monson, cited by *Gunnis* 1968, 194). As master-mason to Lincoln Cathedral the younger John Hayward oversaw repairs to that building and in 1787 was paid £867 for restoration work on the west front and elsewhere (Lincoln Cathedral Archives, in *Gunnis* 1968, 194).

Literary References: *Colvin* 1995, 483–5; *Gunnis* 1968, 194

Archival References: GPC

Funerary Monuments

1.	?1793	John Greenham	Billingborough, Lincs	GPC
2.	†1796	Peter Hallilay	Carlton-le-Moorland, Lincs	Pevsner, *Lincs*, 1989, 213

Architectural Sculpture

3.	1787	Restoration of stonework	Lincoln Cathedral	*Gunnis* 1968, 194

HAYWARD, Richard 1728–1800

Best remembered by art historians as a chronicler of British visitors to Rome and as a collector of sculptors' sales catalogues, Hayward was also a successful sculptor with a diverse practice. He was christened at Bulkington, Warks, on 13 May 1725, the son of Richard and Mary Hayward from nearby Weston-in-Arden. He seems to have been apprenticed first to **Christopher Horsnaile I**, a relation by marriage, at whose house in St Andrew, Holborn, he was living *c*1740 (Masons' Co Assistants, f4, 7). In June 1742 however he was apprenticed to **Sir Henry Cheere** for a full seven year term at the customary rate of £105.

Hayward appears quickly to have become a pivotal figure in Cheere's workshop. Cheere's accounts show payments of £1,901 made to Hayward between February 1744 and June 1747, though there is no information on the precise nature of Hayward's work. Webb has suggested that he may have been running the workshop, and that workshop products such as the monument to William Pole, 1746, may confidently be attributed to Hayward rather than Cheere (**2**). In February 1748, before he finished his apprenticeship, Hayward, who was then still living in St Andrew, Holborn, made his will, which was witnessed by three members of the Horsnaile family (FRC PROB 11/1347/p279). The document reveals that he already owned estates in Weston-in-Arden and Bulkington, which he intended to leave to his sisters, Mary and Anne.

Unlike Cheere and most members of his workshop, Hayward played an active part in the affairs of the Masons' Company after gaining his freedom in 1749. In 1752 he was in a position of authority as renter warden. In June 1753 he went to Rome, where he stayed until April 1754. Little is known of Hayward's Rome years but his list of visitors to Italy, beginning with his own arrival and updated via contacts in Rome over the next 20 years, has become an indispensable source for historians of 18th-century artistic tourism. The connections Hayward made in Rome benefited his career: the English banker and dealer, Thomas Jenkins, wrote to the Earl of Dartmouth from Rome on 30 March 1755: 'It is said here that your Lordship is about building a house at Westminster. If such a person as Mr. Hayward, a sculptor, should be recommended to your Lordship, I believe I may venture to say that he is a deserving young man; I knew him sometime here and he behaved well' (HMC 1896, 170).

Like Cheere, he was involved in the Society of Arts, becoming a member in November 1757 and replacing **Louis François Roubiliac** on the committee after his death in 1762. He exhibited what appear to be relief tablets for chimneypieces at the Society of Artists exhibitions in 1761, 1764 and 1766 (**60, 61, 62**), and he supplied chimneypieces at the same period for Kedleston and to the Jacobite, William Burrell Massingberd at Ormesby (**31, 32**). He was also negotiating with Massingberd for a monument: in 1762 three designs were sent up to Ormesby with a scale of prices ranging from £28–£80, depending on the material selected. The designs, which were not executed, have a neo-classical simplicity which shows the influence of his Rome experience. Hayward appears to have had a secondary business as a dealer, for he supplied the antiquarian, Thomas Hollis, with a copy of *Antichita di Roma*, imported from Rome in 1764. Hayward apparently also brought other Italian goods and materials (**46–8**). Two figures by Hayward 'after the antique' were listed at Charles Jennens's house in Great Ormond Street in Dodsley's guide to London (**26, 27**).

Jennens, the non-juring writer and collector, was a supportive patron. In 1764 Hayward carved a cenotaph to the scholar Edward Holdsworth for Jennens's park at Gopsall, Leics (**3**). This work, executed in 'fine statuary marble of Luna', was noted in two accounts published during Hayward's lifetime (*Nichols* 1795–1815, vol 4, 858; *GM*, 1791, pt 1, 305). It was placed in a temple surmounted by Roubiliac's emblematic figure of *Fides Christiana*. Hayward would use a version of this figure of *Religion* more than a decade later on his monument to Samuel Phillipps (**11**). When Jennens died in 1773 it was Hayward who provided his monument, drawing on Roubiliac's iconography for an ambitious composition in coloured marbles with a grieving female figure before a crumbling pyramid (**10**). Jennens was one of several patrons in the Midlands. Sir Roger Newdigate also commissioned extensively (**37, 43, 56**). A bill for £70 in the Newdigate archives relates to Hayward's monument (again with a figure of *Religion*) to Elizabeth and Sophia Newdigate (**13**), and the sculptor also carved a remarkable gothic chimneypiece for the drawing room at Arbury (**33**). Letters about both commissions survive and suggest that there may have been two separate monuments to the Newdigate ladies.

In 1763 Hayward was listed in Mortimer's *Director* as a 'Statuary. Near Dover-Street, Piccadilly' (*Mortimer* 1763, 13). His property was rated at £12 and his workshop remained at that address for 35 years. His neighbours included **John Cheere** and the **Carters** (**Benjamin** and **Thomas II**). It was around this time that **Thomas Banks** was recorded by **Joseph Nollekens** as 'at Mr Hayward's' (*Whitley* 1930, 40), presumably as an assistant. Another workshop member was **Peter Séguier**, who served his apprenticeship with Hayward. Though the rates on his property were modest, Hayward appears to have developed a good business, for he provided a succession of small monuments in Westminster Abbey (**5, 6, 7, 12, 15, 17, 18**). The most notable of these was to William Strode (**12**): it has a relief of the *Weeping Dacia* set into a segmental pediment, above an austere classical tablet and apron. The tablet is mounted on a slab of unusual 'bianco e nero' marble. Hayward was a regular buyer of marbles and other materials at sculptors' auctions from the 1750s until the 1780s. To the lasting benefit of sculpture historians he preserved the catalogues of sales, which now form a valuable archive in the British Museum. His most notable purchase was almost half of Henry Cheere's stock, auctioned when Cheere retired in 1770.

In 1772 John Norton, a London-based merchant from Virginia, was assigned the task of finding a suitable sculptor for a statue of the late Governor of the Province, Lord Botetourt, sponsored by the House of Burgesses (**28**). Norton, with the assistance of Botetourt's nephew, the 5th Duke of Beaufort, fixed upon Hayward as the sculptor. Norton announced the decision to a relative in Yorktown, adding 'he's to be finished in 12 months completely with iron rails, packages &ca, and to be put on ship for £700' (*Mason* 1937, 224). Hayward worked to schedule and the statue arrived in Virginia in May 1773. Apparently 'very apprehensive' about accidents befalling his work, Hayward sent his own mason **John Hirst** to America to set it up. It is the oldest surviving public statue in North America, and the figure, with classically-derived reliefs of *Britannia* and *America* on the base, was 'universally admired', according to one of the burgesses (*Mason* 1937, 332). Judging from Norton's correspondence, its particular merit was its verisimilitude, achieved by reference to a wax medallion by **Isaac Gosset**.

Hayward worked with the architects James Paine, Henry Keene, Robert Adam and Sir William Chambers as a purveyor of chimneypieces and architectural sculpture. Under Chambers's direction he supplied work in the 1770s and 1780s for Woburn Abbey, Ingress Abbey and Blenheim (**39, 49, 53**). In January 1774 the Duke of Marlborough wrote to Chambers that he wanted 'much to have this fountain settled. . . you must let Hayward or one of his foremen meet you here and I'll have the parts of the fountain put out ready for him to see'. This allusion is almost certainly to the famous Bernini fountain (**53**), which was set up by the 4th Duke in the park at Blenheim and later repaired and re-located by the 9th Duke in a place of honour on the terrace below the west front of the palace (Chambers's Letters-Book, 41136, fol 1). Hayward does not appear to have been much involved with the setting up of the Royal Academy but Chambers employed him extensively on chimneypieces at Somerset House, paying him a total of £835 0s 3d for his work on the building (**40–42**). Among the effects itemised in Hayward's posthumous sale was a 'large portfolio' of designs by Chambers.

Hayward's workshop appears to have expanded in the 1780s. His rates more than doubled to £33 in 1784, and after a few fluctuations, remained at £26 from 1787 until his death. He had attracted the patronage of the Carter-Thelwall family of Redbourne Hall, Lincs (**14, 16, 50, 55**) for whom he executed some innovative work including a relief of an oriental harbour on the monument to Roger Carter (**16**). Another innovative work was the large triptych monument to William Wyldbore (**22**). But on the whole, Hayward's monuments of the 1780s, though always delicately carved and detailed, were relatively unambitious and repetitive. The memorials to Mary Milles and George Ogden (**20, 24**) have almost identical reliefs of a woman grieving over a sarcophagus above a tablet, set into a coloured marble surround with bowed sides. Numerous other works which follow this pattern, occasionally with a *putto* extinguishing a very long torch (as on the Holdsworth monument), can be seen all over the country and may well come from Hayward's workshop.

He reserved what are probably his finest works for his family church in Bulkington, advertising his skill both as a sculptor and as a marble merchant with a font, which carries the inscription, a 'fragment of ancient numidian marble . . . imported from Rome by Richard Hayward'. The bowl has reliefs of religious subjects, which are lightly handled and have been compared by Whinney to the pretty genre scenes of Francis Wheatley (**57**). Hayward's retable relief of *The Last Supper* (**58**) is a more condensed composition with animated figures. In 1781 Hayward erected a monument in the church to his parents, with another *Weeping Dacia* crying over a ruined landscape, together with an inscription recording Hayward's role as a benefactor, and the material, Carrara marble (**21**).

He died in London on 11 August 1800, and his will was proved that September. His sister Mary had died in 1788, leaving Anne Hayward (now Debary) as his sole heir. She erected a monument to her brother and sister in Bulkington, with an epitaph identifying the donor, 'the surviving sister of Richard and Mary Hayward [who] placed this marble as a memorial of the taste and genius of one, of the virtue and affection of both'. Since this is virtually identical to the Milles and Ogden monuments, it seems probable that it too came from the workshop.

Anne authorised a sale of her brother's 'marble chimneypieces, alto and basso-relievos, ornaments, paintings, books on architecture, and valuable stock of marble' which took place in November at his premises 'opposite the Old White Horse Cellar' in Piccadilly. There were numerous lots of antique alabaster and marble as well as recently quarried specimens from Italy, Spain, Germany and Ireland. The catalogue also suggests that Hayward was a notable collector, for he owned paintings identified by the auctioneer as being by Wilson, Poussin, Heemskirk, Ruysdael, Correggio and Elsheimer.

Hayward's obituary described him as 'a kind, intelligent, and warm friend, to many who will long deplore his loss', and added of his work that his 'performances in the line of his profession, dispersed throughout the kingdom, shew him to have been an admirable master of the old school' (*GM*, pt 2, 1800, 909). Modern scholarship has tended to concur with this judgement, seeing Hayward as a relic of the mason-sculptor tradition in an age when sculpture was increasingly seeking recognition as a polite art. Lord has also pointed out that in his enthusiasm for Rome, his utilisation of objects and motifs from antiquity, and his possible influence on Thomas Banks, he can also be seen as a progenitor of the neoclassical taste.

MGS

Literary References: *Dodsley* 1761, 5, 97; *Mortimer* 1763, 13; *GM*, 1791, 1, 305; *GM*, 1800, 2, 909; *Nichols* 1795–1815, 4, 858; HMC 1896, 170; *Graves* 1907, 115; *Cust* 1909, 158; *Whitley* 1930, 40; *Mason* 1937, 149, 224–6, 264–6, 294, 308–13, 331–2; *Webb* 1958 (2), 232–40, 274–9; *Gunnis* 1968, 194–5; *Colvin* V 1973–76, 467; *Penny* 1977 (1), 6–8, 204, n 1; *Haskell and Penny* 1981, 194; *Stainton* 1983, 3–36; *Whinney* 1988, 240–1, 274–5, 461 n47 ff; *Hood* 1991, 978–85; *Allan and Abbott* 1992, 116; *Lord* 1997, 67–76; *Ingamells* 1997, 478; *Craske* 2000, 103; *Sullivan* 2006, 402–3

Archival References: Masons' Co, *Assistants*, fol 4, 7; *Freemen*, fol 31; Hayward's List and Sales Catalogues MS; Rate-Books, WCA, 1764, 1784, 1785, 1787, 1796 (Poor Rates C307, C361, C362, C367, C444); Chambers's Letter-Books 41133, fol 42, fol 50, fol 98; 41136, fol 1; *London Marriage Licenses*, 15 September 1740; Hayward/Newdigate; Newdigate Archives, letters, CR 136/B1736; IGI

Will: PROB 11/1347/279

Miscellaneous Drawings: Designs for a monument to members of the Massingberd family of South Ormesby, Lincs, 1762, Lincs RO MM7/1A/15–17 (*Lord* 1997, 68–9 (repr); *Craske* 1992, 53)

Auction Catalogues: *Hayward* 1783; *Hayward* 1800

Funerary Monuments

1.	†1745	Lieutenant William Bowyer	Denham, Bucks		Newdigate archives (letter), CR 136/B1736
2.	1746	William Pole (†1741) (workshop of Sir Henry Cheere) Payment(s): £345 Drawing(s): VAM 93 E27 c:8933/171	Shute, Devon		ATTRIB *Webb* 1958 (2), 235, 277; *Rococo* 1984, 279 (repr)
3.	1764	Edward Holdsworth (†1746) (designed by James Paine)	[Gopsall Hall, Leics, Ionic Temple]; Belgrave Hall (Leicester City Museum), monument garden		*Lord* 1997, 70; *Cavanagh* 2000, 187–9 (repr)
4.	†1764	Harriot Whitbread, with relief of children	Cardington, Beds	S	*Gunnis* 1968, 195; C Lib (repr)
5.	†1765	William Levinz	Westminster Abbey, London, nave, north aisle		*Gunnis* 1968, 195
6.	†1767	Susannah Davidson	[Westminster Abbey, London, Chapel of St Andrew]; dismantled; marble relief of 'Death with his Dart' now in lapidarium		WAM, June 1768; *MacMichael* 1977, 55

7.	†1768	Hannah Pritchard		Westminster Abbey, London, triforium		*MacMichael* 1977, 98
8.	1770	Diana Ball Payment(s): £10		Harefield, Middx		*Lysons* 1792–1811, vol 5, 116–7; Newdigate archives in GPC
9.	1772	Rev Stephen Slaughter Clarke and his wife Rachel		Theddingworth, Leics	S	Pevsner, *Leics & Rutland*, 1984, 404; *Whinney* 1988, 274
10.	1773	Charles Jennens		Nether Whitacre, Warks	S	*Lord* 1997, 70
11.	†1774	Samuel Phillipps		Shepshed, Leics		Pevsner, *Leics & Rutland*, 1984, 376
12.	†1776	General William Strode		Westminster Abbey, London, nave, north aisle		Pevsner, *London: Westminster*, 1973, 459; *Penny* 1977 (1), 6–8 (repr)
13.	1776	Lady Elizabeth (†1765) and Sophia (†1774) Newdigate Payment(s): £70		Harefield, Middx	S	Newdigate archives, (letters), CR 136/B1736; *Whinney* 1988, 462; Pevsner, *London: NW*, 1991, 317
14.	1776	William (†1744) and Susannah (†1752) Carter, with relief of three figures planting trees		Redbourne, Lincs		*Lord* 1997, 71, 72 (repr)
15.	*c*1777	John Roberts (†1772)		Westminster Abbey, London, south transept	S	*MacMichael* 1977, 93; *Penny* 1977 (1), 208, n26
16.	1777–1779	Roger Carter (†1774), with a relief of an oriental harbour with ships		Redbourne, Lincs		*Lord* 1997, 171–73 (repr)
17.	1779	William Wragg (†1777)		Westminster Abbey, London, nave, south choir aisle		Pevsner, *London: Westminster*, 1973, 443; *Sullivan* 2006, 403 (repr)
18.	†1780	General Sir James Oughton		Westminster Abbey, London, sanctuary, north ambulatory		*Gunnis* 1968, 195
19.	?1781	John Hamilton		Chester Cathedral	S	*Gunnis* 1968, 195
20.	†1781	Mary Milles		Nackington, Kent	S	Pevsner, *Kent: N E & E*, 1983, 400
21.	1781	Richard and Mary Hayward (the sculptor's parents)		Bulkington, Warks	S	Pevsner, *Warks*, 1966, 220
22.	†1781	William Wyldbore		St John the Baptist, Peterborough, Northants		Pevsner, *Beds, Hunts & Peterborough*, 1968, 325
23.	1788	Captain James Cook (†1779)	s	[Manby, Lincs]; Brocklesby Park, Lincs		*Lord* 1997, 74–5 (repr)
24.	1788	George Ogden (†1788) and his wife, Elizabeth (†1781)		Chester Cathedral, Cheshire	S	Pevsner, *Cheshire*, 1971, 144
Statues						
25.	1757–1758	Cast of Lord Bateman's Mercury	p	Kedleston Hall, Derbys		*Kedleston* 1998, 15; *Harris* 2001, 338 n71
26.	pre-1761	A Bacchanalian Boy (after Camillo Rusconi)		[Charles Jennens's house, Great Ormond St, London]; untraced		*Dodsley* 1761, vol. 5, 97
27.	pre-1761	A Vestal, after the antique	m	[Charles Jennens's house, Great Ormond St, London]; untraced		*Dodsley* 1761, vol. 5, 97
28.	1773	Norborne, Baron de Botetourt (†1770)		College of William and Mary, Williamsburg, Virginia, USA		*Mason* 1937, 149, 170, 224–6, 264–6, 294, 313, 331–2, 343; *Hood* 1991, 983–5 (repr); *Sullivan* 2006. 403 (repr)
29.	1773	Venus (possibly a statuette) Payment(s): 8 gns		[Grosvenor Square, London, coll Charles, 2nd Marquess of Rockingham]; untraced		*Penny* 1991 (2), 19
Busts						
30.	pre-1761	Aratus, after the antique	m	[Charles Jennens's house, Great Ormond Street]; untraced		*Dodsley* 1761, vol 5, 97
Chimneypieces						
31.	1760	'For ye Drawing-Room' Payment(s): £35 14s		South Ormesby Manor, Lincs		*Lord* 1997, 67
32.	1760	One		[Kedleston Hall, Derbys]; untraced		*Gunnis* 1968, 194
33.	1764	Derived from the tomb of Aymer de Vallance in Westminster Abbey, with circular relief Payment(s): £90		Arbury Hall, Warks, drawing room		Newdigate archives, (letters), CR 136/B1730–1736; *Nares* 1953 (2), 1212–3 (repr); Pevsner, *Warks*, 1966, 71
34.	1765	Description unavailable	m	[Croome Court, Worcs]; untraced		*Beard* 1993, 93
35.	1766	'two white marble chimneypieces with blue and white slabs . . . Architraves figur'd with Siena' Payment(s): £30 each	m	[Edward Knight, Wolverley, Worcs]; untraced		Account book, Kidderminster MSS.285–292, Worcs RO
36.	1767	Description unavailable		[Alscot Park, Warks, unidentified room]; untraced		*Girouard* 1958, 1184
37.	1767	Two Payment(s): £112		[Sir Robert Burdett, Bt, Foremark Hall, Derbys]; untraced		Berks CAO D/EBU.A/9/1
38.	1770	Gothic, with a medallion of King Alfred Payment(s): £150 Drawing(s): by Henry Keene, VAM E.903, 1921		University College, Oxford, hall		Newdigate Papers in GPC
39.	1771	'Well done and very large'	m	[Woburn Abbey, library]; untraced		William Chambers's Letter-Book, (BL Ad MS 41133 fol 50)

40.	1778	Two Payment(s): £212		Somerset House, London		*Gunnis* 1968, 194
41.	1784	Two, one of statuary and Sicilian jasper marble, the other of statuary & Spanish marble Payment(s): £51 5s each	m	Somerset House, London, Stamp Office and board room of Salt Office		Chambers/Somerset Hse, box 7, CHA 3/2/4, fo 145
42.	1790	Several including one with 'a frieze of Persia marble, three small ovals and broad flutes' (£60) and another with a 'long frieze carved with two oval flowers and three small figures' (£60), another with frieze carved with laurel leaves and flower (£30), another with three medallions and vases on breaks (£40), another with water leaves and small figures on breaks (£42)		Somerset House, London		Chambers/Somerset Hse, box 8, CHA 3/3/3, fo 200, 201
43.	nd	More than one		[Sir Roger Newdigate's house, Spring Gardens, London]; untraced		*Nares* 1953 (2), 1212

Architectural Sculpture

44.	1757	Wine-cooler of Sicilian Jasper		Kedleston Hall, Derbys, dining room		*Kedleston* 1998, 46–7 (repr); *Harris* 2001, 33, 338 n71
45.	1760	Two 'Italian Volterza Vases' Payment(s): 4 gns		[South Ormesby Manor, Lincs]; untraced		*Lord* 1997, 67
46.	1764	'A pair of Vulterra vases' and 'one pair of elegant bronze vases' Payment(s): £25 4s		[Croome Court, Worcs]; untraced		*Beard* 1993, 98
47.	1767	Two jasper tables Payment(s): £15 17s 4d		[Croome Court, Worcs]; untraced		*Beard* 1993, 100
48.	1768	Alabaster table		[Croome Court, Worcs]; untraced		*Beard* 1993, 101
49.	1771	A large slab (purpose unknown)		[Ingress Abbey, Kent]; untraced		William Chambers's Letters-Book, BL Ad MS 41133, fol 42
50.	1773	'Slab table' Payment(s): £4 10s		[Redbourne Hall, Lincs]; untraced		*Lord* 1997, 70
51.	1773	Terms for hall arcades	m	Blenheim Palace, Oxon (now moved into exedra)		William Chambers's Letters-Book, BL, Ad MS 41133, fol 98; Pevsner, *Oxon*, 1974, 475
52.	1773	'transparent Tuscan vases'		[coll Charles, 2nd Marquess of Rockingham]; untraced		*Penny* 1991 (2), 33 n20
53.	1774	Bernini Fountain (restoration only)		Blenheim Palace, Oxon		William Chambers's Letters-Book, BL Ad MS 41136, fol 1
54.	1774	'Puozelli marble vases' Payment(s): 8 gns	a	[Croome Court, Worcs]; untraced		*Beard* 1993, 104
55.	1775	Font, fluted bowl with anthemia on a fluted baluster Payment(s): £26 10s		Redbourne, Lincs		*Lord* 1986, 103; Pevsner, *Lincs*, 1989, 608
56.	1776	Marble bases with inscriptions for antique Roman candelabra Payment(s): £28	m	[Arbury Park, Warks; Radcliffe Library, Oxford]; Ashmolean		*Gunnis* 1968, 194; Newdigate archives in GPC
57.	1789	Font bowl carved with 'Baptism of Christ and Girls bringing flowers to the Virgin'	m	Bulkington, Warks	SD	Pevsner, *Warks* 1966, 220; *Whinney* 1988, 274 (repr)
58.	c1789	The Last Supper, retable		Bulkington, Warks		Pevsner, *Warks*, 1966, 220
59.	by 1800	'A neat modern font of statuary marble'		Swithland, Leics		*Nichols* 1795–1815, III, pt 2, 1050

Reliefs

60.	1761	Somnes, or sleep	m	[Exhib Soc of Artists, 148]; untraced		*Graves* 1907, 115
61.	1764	A sleeping boy		[Exhib Soc of Artists, 156]; untraced		*Graves* 1907, 115
62.	1766	'A basso-relievo of boys'		[Exhib Soc of Artists, 206]; untraced		*Graves* 1907, 115

HAYWARD, Samuel, of Lichfield fl 1799–1822

He signs some 'unimportant tablets' (*Gunnis* 1968, 195).

Funerary Monuments

1.	†1799	Lieutenant-Colonel Philip Bainbridge	Ashbourne, Derbys	S	*Gunnis* 1968, 195; Pevsner, *Derbys*, 1978, 62
2.	?1812	William Booth	Ecclesfield, W R Yorks	S	*Gunnis* 1968, 195
3.	1816	Rev William Vyse (†1770)	Lichfield Cathedral, Staffs	S	*Gunnis* 1968, 195; Pevsner, *Staffs*, 1974, 186
4.	?1826	Mercy Woodhouse	Lichfield Cathedral, Staffs	S	*Gunnis* 1968, 195

HAYWARD, William fl 1820–25

His yard was first at Pentonville and later in the borough. He signs a large wall-monument with a draped urn (1).

Literary References: *Gunnis* 1968, 195

Funerary Monuments

1.	?1822	Hon Michael Nolan	Bradwell, Essex	S	*Gunnis* 1968, 195

HEADLAND & WATSON fl 1787

Probably local masons, in 1787 they were responsible for alterations to Mulgrave Hall, working under Sir John Soane.

Archival References: Soane Bill Book 1, fols 64–8

HEALEY, Henry fl 1826

Funerary Monuments

1.	†1826	Archdeacon Sandiford	Awre, Glos	S	Pevsner, *Glos: Vale & Forest of Dean*, 1976, 93

HEAP, William, of Manchester fl 1810–28?

Heap advertised for stone and marble masons in the *Carlisle Journal* on 2 June 1810. The entry gave the address of his 'counting house' as Falkner Street, Manchester (RG/JP, 4 670v, inf, Dennis Perriam). As a master mason he submitted tenders in 1822 for some of the churches built by the Parliamentary Commissioners. These included St Thomas, Stockport, Cheshire; All Saints, Prestwick, Lancs and St Matthew, Campfield, Manchester (Minute Book, HM commission for building new churches, 1822, Lambeth Palace library). He signs a tablet with 'well-carved details' at Middleton (**2**). In 1825 *Baines's Gazetteer* gave his address as 31 Falkner Street.

Literary References: *Gunnis* 1968, 195

Archival References: GPC; NP/RG

Funerary Monuments

1.	?1819	Holland Watson	Congleton, Cheshire	S	*Gunnis* 1968, 195
2.	?1828	Rev John Haughton	Middleton, Lancs	S	*Gunnis* 1968, 195

HEARNDEN, John fl 1726

In 1726 he repaired Aylesford Bridge, Kent. His bill for the work itemised 'erecting a pillar on and repairing Aylesford Bridge, cutting an oval to place ye marble inscription in, cutting ye old inscription a new, consisting of 43 letters' (Kent county records, quoted in *Gunnis* 1968, 195).

HEDGES, Nathaniel –c1784

In 1772 the court of assistants of the Masons' Company upraided Hedges since 'not being a Freeman of' this Company he did 'use or exercise the Art or Mistery of Masonary, within the City of London or Liberties of thereof'. He was directed to attend the next court in order to accept and 'take upon you the Freedom and be made a Freeman of the Company under penalty of £10' (Masons' Co, *Court Book*, 1751–96, 7 Aug 1772).

From 1734 he was mason to Gray's Inn, receiving £93 in 1750 for work on their hall. In 1752–4 he received £156 for work at Holborn Court, and in 1755 was paid £40 for masonry at the chapel (Treasurer's Accounts, Gray's Inn, in GPC). He worked at Stationers' Hall from 20 December 1738, when he was paid 8/- for masonry work, until 1784, in which year he must have died, for the last payment was made to his widow. He was replaced by a Mr Golden. He was also mason to Hoare's Bank, 1764–75, and was employed by both Henry and Richard Hoare. His monument to Moses Ashley has a fine portrait-bust (**4**). That to Sir Thomas Denison consists of a sarcophagus with curious rococo legs on which stands a bust of the deceased (**5**). The Joseph Ashley is a tablet with three heads of *putti* (**2**).

Literary References: *Gunnis* 1968, 195

Archival References: Stationers, Accts, 20 Dec 1727–1787, *passim* (microfilm reel 76); Stationers, Supp documents, series I, box G, envelope 4

Funerary Monuments

1.	†1723	Higham Beamish	St Mary Magdalene, East Ham, Essex	S	Pevsner, *Essex*, 1965, 165; *Gunnis* 1968, 195
2.	†1738	Joseph Ashley	Ashby St Ledgers, Northants	S	*Gunnis* 1968, 195; Pevsner, *Northants*, 1973, 90
3.	†1740	Ephraim Chambers	Westminster Abbey, cloisters; formerly south walk	S	*Gunnis* 1968, 195; *MacMichael* 1977, 102
4.	†1749	Moses Ashley	Ashby St Ledgers, Northants	S	*Gunnis* 1968, 195; Pevsner, *Northants*, 1973, 90
5.	†1765	Sir Thomas Denison	Harewood, W R Yorks	S	Pevsner, *Yorks: W R*, 1967, 244; *Gunnis* 1968, 195

Chimneypieces

6.	1753–1757	Several	[Stourhead, Wilts]; untraced		*Gunnis* 1968, 195
7.	1767	Several	[Boreham Hall, Essex]; untraced		*Gunnis* 1968, 195

HEFFERNAN, James 1788–1847

He was born in Londonderry, the son of John Heffernan. His father worked for the Cork architect Michael Shanahan and is known to have been employed as a plasterer in 1791 at Downhill, the home of Frederick, Earl of Bristol and Bishop of Derry. After his father's death, Heffernan was apprenticed to Shanahan at the instigation of the Earl-Bishop. He was taken to Cork, where Shanahan owned a marble works and was employed in carving chimneypieces and tombstones.

Strickland writes that Heffernan left Ireland for London at the age of 22, and after brief spells working in the studios of **J C F Rossi** and **Sir Francis Chantrey**, he joined the Royal Academy schools to study sculpture. His name is recorded in the entry books in February 1811. He won silver medals in 1815 and 1817 (**5, 6**) and was beaten to the gold, first by **Samuel Joseph** and then by **William Scoular**. In 1816 he exhibited for the first time at the Royal Academy, giving his address as 27 St George's Row, Chelsea Bridge (**25**). He completed his education with a visit to Rome.

After returning to England he was again employed by Chantrey, but also continued to exhibit in his own right at the Royal Academy, where he showed a series of ideal works of subjects from Ovid (**26, 31, 33**), Homer (**28**) and Thomson (**30**). In 1823 he carved the monument to the Bishop of Cloyne, the 'chief promoter of Christianity among the American Indians' (*Graves* IV, 1905–6, 62). It presents a kneeling figure with curious braided hair and a loincloth, praying over a Bible in front of a palm-tree. Though the iconography is conventional, the monument is carved with considerable ability (**2**). Heffernan's talent was soon noted in the press. In 1825 a review of the Academy exhibition praised his bust of Miss Hill of Norfolk (**12**) and his *Susannah at the bath* (**32**) as works 'full of promise'. The critic suggested that this 'young and rising artist of considerable genius' was 'standing fair for the highest rank of his profession' (anon press report quoted at length in *Strickland* 1, 1913, 469–70).

Heffernan moved to 1 Ranelagh Grove, Islington in 1827. In 1830 he was at 5 Belgrave Place and in 1832 at 35 Coleshill Street. He does not seem to have established his own practice and when he exhibited the model of a

Girl caressing a child at the Royal Academy in 1831 (**36**), a journal of the arts expressed irritation that Heffernan did not produce his own works in marble: 'Why is it that we never, or so rarely, see the productions of this gentleman's chisel. . seeing that working in the marble is understood to be his peculiar province?' They feared that he was 'wasting the summer of his life, like so many other talented men in this town, to increase the already overgrown reputation of another' (*Library of Fine Arts* 1831, vol 1, 432).

Strickland writes that Chantrey actively dissuaded Heffernan from pursuing an independent career, in part by making the vain promise of a bequest in his will. Heffernan remained in Chantrey's studio until the death of the latter in 1841 and became indispensable to the business. *The Gentleman's Magazine* recorded that he carved 'almost every one of Chantrey's busts literally from the first to the last' (*GM* 1842, part I, 103) and Peter Cunningham credited Heffernan with breathing life into the finished works. He was a 'consummate master in transferring a look from dull, dead clay to semi-transparent Carrara marble; he saw and caught and translated Chantrey into another material' (*Builder*, 1863, 112). After Chantrey's death Heffernan completed many of his master's works and also carved a memorial with a portrait relief in his memory (**4**).

Heffernan's health failed soon after Chantrey's death and he retired to Cork where he took a cottage on the banks of the Lee. He died there of dysentery on 21 October 1847. Little is known of his family, though his wife was described by Peter Cunningham as 'dear old Mrs Heffernan'. Cunningham also left a thumbnail character sketch of the sculptor: he remembered Heffernan as a jovial character with a 'Cove of Cork' laugh, who combined merriment in the studio with considerable skill and certainty of touch (*Builder*, 1863, 112). Strickland's more sober tribute was to a man of good humour, who had industry, talent and a love of art, but whose advancement in life was 'marred by diffidence, a want of reliance upon himself, and broken health' (*Strickland* 1, 1913, 470).

MGS

Literary References: *Graves* 1875, 257; *Graves* IV, 1905–6, 62; *Strickland* 1, 1913, 468–471; *Hutchison* 1960–2, 166; *Gunnis* 1968, 195–6; *Potterton* 1975, 47–48

Will: Sir Francis Chantrey PROB 11/1954/343–347

Funerary Monuments						
1.	1808	Dr MacCarthy		St Finbarr's chapel, Cork	S	*Strickland* 1, 1913, 470; *Potterton* 1975, 47
2.	1823	William Bennett, Bishop of Cloyne (†1820)		Cloyne cathedral	S	*Graves* IV, 1905–6, 62; *Strickland* 1, 1913, 470; *Potterton* 1975, 48
3.	1834	William Forrester		All Saints, Leicester	S	Pevsner, *Leics & Rutland*, 1984, 210
4.	1842	Sir Francis Chantrey (†1841)		Norton, Sheffield, W R Yorks	S	*Strickland* 1, 1913, 470; Pevsner, *Yorks: W R*, 1967, 479
Statues						
5.	1815	'Model from the Antique Academy'		[RA, London, silver medal]; untraced		RA Premium list
6.	1817	'Model from the Life Academy'		[RA, London, silver medal]; untraced		RA Premium list
Busts						
7.	1818	J Stark		[Exhib RA, London, 1048]; untraced		*Graves* IV, 1905–6, 62
8.	1821	B O'Meara		[Exhib RA, London, 1159; 1827, 1079]; untraced		*Graves* IV, 1905–6, 62
9.	1824	G S Newton		[Exhib RA, London, 1017]; untraced		*Graves* IV, 1905–6, 62
10.	1824	J T Morton		[Exhib RA, London, 1004]; untraced		*Graves* IV, 1905–6, 62
11.	1824	Unidentified lady		[Exhib RA, London, 1021]; untraced		*Graves* IV, 1905–6, 62
12.	1825	Miss E W Hill		[Exhib RA, London, 1028]; untraced		*Graves* IV, 1905–6, 62; *Strickland* 1, 1913, 469–70
13.	1827	Unidentified lady		[Exhib Soc of BA, London, 843]; untraced		*Johnson* 1975, 220
14.	1828	H P Briggs ARA		[Exhib RA, London, 1154]; untraced		*Graves* IV, 1905–6, 62; *Johnson* 1975, 220
15.	1829	William Foy		[Exhib RA, London, 1156]; untraced		*Graves* IV, 1905–6, 62; *Johnson* 1975, 220
16.	1831	Dr Haslam		[Exhib RA, London, 1143]; untraced		*Graves* IV, 1905–6, 62
17.	1832	Dr Haglam		[Exhib Soc of BA, London, 840]; untraced		*Johnson* 1975, 220
18.	1832	James Morrah		[Exhib RA, London, 1218]; untraced		*Graves* IV, 1905–6, 62; *Johnson* 1975, 220
19.	1834	James Watt (after Sir Francis Chantrey)		Royal Society		*Manchester Art Treasures* 1857, 136; *Strickland* 1, 1913, 470; *Gunnis* 1968, 196
20.	1834	T Coombe		[Exhib Soc of BA, London, 816]; untraced		*Johnson* 1975, 220
21.	1835	Unidentified lady		[Exhib Soc of BA, London, 784]; untraced		*Johnson* 1975, 220
22.	1837	Mrs James Morrah, posthumous		[Exhib RA, London, 1242]; untraced		*Graves* IV, 1905–6, 62
23.	1843	Sir Francis Chantrey (after F W Smith)	m	NGI	SD	*le Harivel* 1988, 566 (repr)
Reliefs						
24.	1842	Sir Francis Chantrey, portrait medallion		SNPG, Edinburgh		*Strickland* 1, 1913, 470; *Gunnis* 1968, 196
Miscellaneous						
25.	1816	Prometheus chained		[Exhib RA, London, 917]; untraced		*Graves* 1875, 257; *Graves* IV, 1905–6, 62
26.	1817	The rape of Proserpine		[Exhib RA, London, 1031]; untraced		*Graves* 1875, 257; *Graves* IV, 1905–6, 62
27.	1818	The judgement of Paris		[Exhib BI, London, 304]; untraced		*Graves* 1875, 257
28.	1819	Achilles attacked by the waves of Scamander		[Exhib RA, London, 1196]; untraced		*Graves* 1875, 257; *Graves* IV, 1905–6, 62
29.	1820	Nymph playing with Cupid		[Exhib RA, London, 1022]; untraced		*Graves* 1875, 257; *Graves* IV, 1905–6, 62

30.	1821	Musidora		[Exhib RA, London, 1157]; untraced		*Graves* 1875, 257; *Graves* IV, 1905–6, 62
31.	1823	Ino with the infant Bacchus		[Exhib RA, London, 1125]; untraced		*Graves* IV, 1905–6, 62
32.	1825	Susannah at the bath	p	[coll Mrs Heffernan]; Crawford MAG, Cork	S	*Graves* IV, 1905–6, 62; *Strickland* 1, 1913, 469–70, 471; *Barrett* 1971 (1), 84; *Johnson* 1975, 220
33.	1827	Salmacis		[Exhib RA, London, 1117]; untraced		*Graves* IV, 1905–6, 62; *Johnson* 1975, 220
34.	1828	Cupid and Psyche		[Exhib RA, London, 1176]; untraced		*Graves* IV, 1905–6, 62
35.	1830	The deserted mother		[Exhib RA, London, 1178 School of Art, Cork]; untraced		*Graves* IV, 1905–6, 62; *Strickland* 1, 1913, 471; *Johnson* 1975, 220
36.	1831	Girl caressing a child	p	[coll Mrs Heffernan]; Crawford MAG, Cork	S	*Library of Fine Arts* 1831, vol 1, 432; *Graves* IV, 1905–6, 62; *Barrett* 1971 (1), 84; *Johnson* 1975, 220
37.	1837	Nymphs bathing		[Exhib Soc of BA, London, 577]; untraced		*Johnson* 1975, 220
38.	nd	Hermon sustaining the dead body of Antigone		untraced		*Strickland* 1, 1913, 471

HELBY, Joseph fl 1662–1700

He was apprenticed to Thomas Fletcher in 1662, became free of the Joiners' Company in 1670 and was Master in 1706. Helby carved a 'very fine' cartouche-tablet to Ann Papillon (1). The 'mort' or skull at the base of it has a wreath of ivy-leaves, which is most unusual (*Gunnis* 1968, 196). A Robert Helby was apprenticed to Joseph Helby in 1670 and was made free of the Joiners' Company in 1678.

Archival References: Joiners, Freedoms, vol 1 f 88r, f 110v; Joiners, Minutes, 25 July 1706

Funerary Monuments

1.	†1693	Ann Papillon		Acrise, Kent	S	*Gunnis* 1968, 196; Pevsner, *Kent: NE and E*, 1983, 125

Architectural Sculpture

2.	1700	Carved work Payment(s): £45 8s		[London customs house]; untraced		TNA T.11/4 cited in *Gunnis* 1968, 196

HELLYER, Isaac, of Dorchester and Weymouth fl 1820–34

He may have practised as a ship's carver for Gunnis quotes an unspecified source (possibly a newspaper report), which stated that 'a Mr Hellyer of H. M.'s Dockyard' carved the royal statue in Portsmouth (4, GPC).

Literary References: *Gunnis* 1968, 196

Funerary Monuments

1.	?1820	Jane Love		Weymouth, Dorset	S	*Gunnis* 1968, 196
2.	?1825	John Swaffield		Wyke Regis, Dorset	S	*Gunnis* 1968, 196
3.	?1834	Sarah Perkins		Melbury Osmond, Dorset	S	*Gunnis* 1968, 196

Statues

4.	1827	King George III	wd	[Jubilee Terrace, Portsmouth]; untraced		GPC (inf. Portsmouth Public Library)

HEMING, J fl 1845–46

Architectural Sculpture

1.	1845–1846	Thick garlands on stone piers	s	Royal Botanic Gardens, Kew, main entrance gates		Pevsner, *London: S*, 1983, 509

HEMMENS, of Regent Street fl 1837

He is known only for one neoclassical monument consisting of a Portland Stone urn on a pedestal.

Literary References: *Curl* 2001, 195

Funerary Monuments

1.	†1837	Amelia Jane Richman	s	Kensal Green Cemetery, London	S	*Curl* 2001, 195

HENDERSON, John –1829

He was a dentist, a collector, and an amateur carver and modeller. When he exhibited works in ivory at the Society of Artists in 1782 he gave his address as Duke's Court, St Martin's Lane. In 1783 he was at 7 Little St Martin's Lane, an address he shared with **H Cornman** and by 1786 he had moved to 14 Frith Street. A portrait-bust of 'Mr Henderson, modeller in London, cut on a sardonyx' is mentioned by James Tassie in his *Engraved Gems* (*Tassie* 1791, 743).

Literary References: *Graves* IV, 1905–6, 66; *Graves* 1907, 117; *Gunnis* 1968, 196; *Pyke* 1973, 66; *Young* 1996, 481

Reliefs

1.	nd	Mrs William Power (?)	w	Met NY		*Pyke* 1973, 66

Miscellaneous

2.	1782	Unidentified portraits	i	[Exhib Free Soc, London, 246]; untraced		*Graves* 1907, 117
3.	1783	Unidentified portraits	i	[Exhib Soc of Artists, London, 116]; untraced		*Graves* 1907, 117
4.	1786	Unidentified boy, portrait in paste		[Exhib RA, London, 257]; untraced		*Graves* IV, 1905–6, 66
5.	1787	Unidentified gentleman, model	w	[Exhib RA, London, 637]; untraced		*Graves* IV, 1905–6, 66
6.	1788	Unidentified gentleman, model	w	[Exhib RA, London, 633]; untraced		*Graves* IV, 1905–6, 66
7.	1788	Unidentified gentleman, portrait in paste		[Exhib RA, London, 627]; untraced		*Graves* IV, 1905–6, 66
8.	1788	Unidentified lady, portrait in paste		[Exhib RA, London, 625]; untraced		*Graves* IV, 1905–6, 66
9.	1789	Unidentified gentleman		[Exhib RA, London, 602]; untraced		*Graves* IV, 1905–6, 66
10.	1789	Unidentified lady		[Exhib RA, London, 590]; untraced		*Graves* IV, 1905–6, 66
11.	1789	Unidentified lady		[Exhib RA, London, 601]; untraced		*Graves* IV, 1905–6, 66
12.	1790	A celebrated actor		[Exhib RA, London, 686]; untraced		*Graves* IV, 1905–6, 66
13.	1790	Unidentified lady		[Exhib RA, London, 381]; untraced		*Graves* IV, 1905–6, 66

14.	1791	Unidentified gentleman	w	[Exhib RA, London, 654]; untraced		*Graves* IV, 1905–6, 66
15.	1793	Unidentified young gentleman	w	[Exhib RA, London, 375]; untraced		*Graves* IV, 1905–6, 66
16.	1794	Mr Morceau	w	[Exhib RA, London, 573]; untraced		*Graves* IV, 1905–6, 67
17.	1797	Unidentified subject, portrait model	w	[Exhib RA, London, 1042]; untraced		*Graves* IV, 1905–6, 67

HENDERSON, Joseph and Benjamin fl 1823

Funerary Monuments

1.	†1823	William Henderson		Penang Cathedral		RG/JP, 4, 676

HENDERSON, Robert fl 1821–32

He exhibited several bronze works at the Royal Academy, giving his address as 32 Charlotte Street in 1820 and 21 Great Russell Street in 1832. His statuettes of favourite racehorses found approval with their owners. C R Leslie remarked of him in a letter to John Constable that 'Little Bob Henderson' was 'a good judge of a horse' (6 September 1834, quoted in *Bilbey* 2002, 301).

Literary References: *Gunnis* 1968, 196

Statues

1.	1821	King George III, equestrian statuette	b	VAM A.4-1937	SD	*Graves* IV, 1905–6, 68; *Bilbey* 2002, 301
2.	1825	King George IV, equestrian statuette		[Exhib RA, London, 1014]; untraced		*Graves* IV, 1905–6, 68
3.	1826	Frederick-Augustus, Duke of York and Albany, statuette	b	[Exhib RA, London, 1085]; untraced		*Graves* IV, 1905–6, 68
4.	nd	'Whalebone', the 3rd Earl of Egremont's racehorse, statuette	b	Petworth House, Sussex, north gallery		*Rowell* 2000 (2), 46

Miscellaneous

5.	1820	Cart horse		[Exhib RA, London, 1059]; untraced		*Graves* IV, 1905–6, 68
6.	1820	Trotting horse startled by a dog		[Exhib RA, London, 1055]; untraced		*Graves* IV, 1905–6, 68
7.	1822	'Donkies,' after nature	b	[Exhib RA, London, 1020]; untraced		*Graves* IV, 1905–6, 68
8.	1822	'Donkies'	b	[Exhib RA, London, 1020]; untraced		*Graves* IV, 1905–6, 68
9.	1822	Goats	b	[Exhib RA, London, 1018]; untraced		*Graves* IV, 1905–6, 68
10.	1823	'Risk', a racehorse		[Exhib RA, London, 1109]; untraced		*Graves* IV, 1905–6, 68
11.	1824	'Sober Robin', a racehorse		[Exhib RA, London, 1002]; untraced		*Graves* IV, 1905–6, 68
12.	1825	Model of a horse	b	[Exhib BI, London, 414]; untraced		*Graves* 1875, 258
13.	1827	Race horse	b	[Exhib RA, London, 1109]; untraced		*Graves* 1875, 258; *Graves* IV, 1905–6, 68
14.	1832	'Skim'	b	[Exhib RA, London, 1193]; untraced		*Graves* IV, 1905–6, 68

HENNEKIN, Simon fl 1763

Mortimer's directory notes that he was a 'Carver and Gilder' of 'Edward Street, near Broad-street, Golden Square. This artist is eminent for making laymen for painters etc' (*Mortimer* 1763, 14).

HENNING, John I 1771–1851

A self-taught Scottish modeller, he was renowned in his day for his miniature copies of the Parthenon frieze sculpture. Henning was born at 56 High Street, Paisley on 2 May 1771, the son of Samuel Henning, a carpenter and builder, and Agnes, née Robertson. After attending the Commercial School, Henning he joined his father's business, aged 12, and worked with him on renovations to Caldwell House for Colonel William Mure. The young Henning was keen to educate himself and was encouraged by Mure, who allowed him access to the library at Caldwell. Like his father, he was also a political radical. In 1794 he was one of 185 suspects on a list of political subversives who were to be imprisoned under the suspension of *habeas corpus*. Popular feeling in Paisley deterred the Sheriff from carrying out the arrests.

By his own account, Henning's epiphany as a graphic artist occurred in 1799 when he visited a travelling exhibition of wax busts and other curiosities which so offended his eye that he resolved to produce better works himself. Three of his earliest were portrait medallions of a teacher (**20**), a work-mate (**17**) and his wife, Katherine Sunter, whom he married in Paisley high church in September that year (**11**). The failure of his father's business and some local acclaim for his waxes encouraged Henning to jettison joinery and move to Glasgow in 1801, where he found many customers for his portrait medallions in various materials, the mainstay of his later career. His Glasgow clients included the managers of the Royal Bank of Scotland (**39, 22**), and the Duke of Hamilton (**57**), who found the sculptor several new commissions.

In 1803, with the encouragement of Francis, Lord Jeffrey (**19**), Henning moved to Edinburgh, where he found a clientele amongst 'the galaxy of literary talent which burst forth so conspicuously' in the city at that time (*Art Journal* 1851, 212). His sitters included the philosopher Adam Fergusson (**49**) and Sir Walter Scott (**55**), with both of whom he subsequently corresponded on learned subjects. He replicated a medallion of Scott many times, charging four guineas for each image. Henning was encouraged in his art by the portrait painter Archibald Skirving and in November 1803 gained admission to the Trustees' Academy to study drawing. He exhibited at the exhibition of the Associated Society of Artists of Edinburgh in 1808 from an address in Rose Street. Many of his exhibits were in a translucent white enamel paste, probably intended to imitate alabaster, which Henning invented in 1800 after much experiment.

In July 1811 Henning went to London, where the sight of the Parthenon sculpture, recently imported by Lord Elgin from Greece, changed the course of his career. He applied for permission from Lord Elgin to draw the marbles, a request granted against the wishes of the President of the Royal Academy, Benjamin West, who believed that Henning was insufficiently trained to appreciate them. Henning's triumph did not endear him to the Academy's professors who subsequently denied him entry to life-classes. Apart from participating in exhibitions, Henning always remained aloof from the institution, which he later decried for its 'selfish spirit of exclusion' (*Art Journal*, 1849, 113). He appears to have supported himself at this time with portraiture and his sitters included Princess Charlotte. He arranged to have two portraits of the princess, one of them in the manner of a figure from the Elgin marbles, cast at Josiah Wedgwood's manufactory (**105, 111**). Wedgwood was sufficiently impressed by Henning's work to issue reproductions of several of his major portraits (**80, 88, 97, 102, 106**). Around 1810–12 Henning charged between seven and ten guineas for a wax.

His principal employment between 1811 and 1820 was on a commercial scheme of his own devising, a set of miniature copies of the entire Parthenon frieze (**128**). He told Wedgwood in October 1813 that he had begun to draw from the frieze because he felt his 'mind transfixed with admiration' for the reliefs, although it soon struck him forcibly that 'models of them while they might be improving to myself might become subjects of pecuniary advantage' (Henning I/Wedgwood). By 1820, after considerable and protracted labour, Henning was able to offer entire sets for sale from his home at 35 Lower Thornhaugh Street. These plaster reproductions were in six parts and on a scale of 1:20, and included imaginary restorations of the missing sections of the frieze. His customers included George IV, who bought a full set for £37 16s. Henning also made miniature reproductions of the Phygaleian marbles, which arrived in London in 1814 (**127**). These were followed in 1820 by copies of the Raphael Cartoons (**125**), which one journal described as works of 'transcendent merit, in which is faithfully preserved the truth of the original' and which elicited encomiums from **John Flaxman RA** and **Antonio Canova** (*Builder* 1851, 297).

In 1820 the *New Monthly Magazine* published a long account of Henning, calling him an 'extraordinary individual, who, from the humble station of a mechanic in Paisley, has risen to eminence as a British artist.' Henning was presented as a triumph of application over deprivation and as an illustration of the educational potential of the Elgin marbles, which for Henning had 'supplied the want of previous instruction and cultivation' (*New Monthly Mag* 1820, pt 1, 455, 457–8). He was quick to realise the economic potential of his knowledge of the marbles and in 1822 wrote to Sir Walter Scott offering to carve a Parthenaic frieze around the Carlton Hill monument in Edinburgh, then being erected by a committee led by Scott. This offer was not accepted but Henning was commissioned to execute similar friezes for the Athenaeum Club, Terling Place, the College of Surgeons, and for Decimus Burton's entrance arch to Hyde Park (**9**). He was assisted in these works by **John Henning II**, one of his eight children, who signed the contract with Decimus Burton for the frieze of the Athenaeum. In 1824 he was marketing miniature bas-reliefs of the Parthenon and Phygaleian Marbles from 2 Sommers Place west, opposite St Pancras Church (Flaxman Papers BL Ad MS 39791, f231).

Henning's friezes won him some celebrity, but not the financial rewards he had hoped for. Soon after they appeared they were pirated by Italian and French firms, whose inferior casts from Henning's own casts flooded the market. By 1830 Henning's work had become so devalued that, as a last resort, he reduced the price of the whole series to £8. In 1841 he complained of piracy in an advertisement in which he questioned the absence of a copyright law to protect such property. Over the following years he wrote to many members of parliament and found sympathisers to his cause. He argued aggressively to one peer that 'these sculptures are the creation of my mind and the work of my hands and therefore are truly my veritable property more truly so than your lordship's acres' (Henning I/David Murray). In 1846 he was given a dinner in his native Paisley: a report of it published in the *Art Union* described his Parthenon frieze as a 'source of enjoyment and instruction to hundreds and thousands' which had brought him little reward, but had made for Italian salesmen of plaster casts 'a sum that would have been a fortune to the producer' (*AU*, vol 8, 1846, 91).

He continued to produce portrait medallions and to design and model compositions for monuments, though there are few known examples of his sepulchral work. He did not find enough employment to save him from poverty and in 1848 wrote for assistance to the AGBI, citing piracy as the chief reason for his distress. In 1849 he was subsisting on a tiny pension from the Spalding Club of Edinburgh, and that year the *Art Journal*, moved by his plight, proposed a charitable scheme to pay for the publication of a series of engravings of his friezes. It was hoped that the sculptor could recoup at least some of the profits of which piracy had robbed him.

His last home was in Thorn Hill, Caledonia Road, London and in his later years he learnt Latin, Greek and Hebrew and corresponded extensively on theological matters with the Paisley theologian, Andrew Symington. He also wrote detailed and colourful memoirs of his life in letters to William Mure. He was a founder member of the Society of British Artists and an honorary member of the Royal Scottish Academy. In 1846 he was given the freedom of the burgh of Paisley.

Henning died in London on 8 April 1851 and was buried in St Pancras cemetery at Finchley. Both the *Art Journal* and the *Builder* marked his passing with obituaries which praised his innate abilities, his application, and the invaluable contribution he had made to taste and learning through his reproductions of Greek and Italian art. In 1977 John Malden's extensively-researched monograph made available a wealth of primary material which gives a detailed picture of Henning's life, reputation and career.

MGS

Literary References: *New Monthly Mag* 1820, Pt 1, 455–459; *AJ* 1849, 112–4, 1851, 212; *Builder* 1851, 297; *Graves* IV, 1905–6, 71; *Rinder and McKay* 1917, 158; *Gunnis* 1968, 196–8; *Pyke* 1973, 67; *Malden* 1977; *Wall* 2008

Archival References: Flaxman Papers BL Ad MS 39791, fol 231; Henning I/David Murray; AGBI, vol 2, 87

Miscellaneous Drawings: John Cartwright, pencil, s&d, private coll, (*Malden* 1977, unpag, repr); Thomas Dundas, exhib ASA 1809, untraced; H Sinclair Erskine, exhib ASA 1809, untraced; Charles 2nd Earl Grey, pencil, signed, private coll (*Malden* 1977, unpag, repr); Archibald Henning, chalk, Paisley MAG (*Malden* 1977, unpag, repr); Captain Jones, exhib ASA 1809, untraced; Professor Sir John Leslie, chalk, SNPG 660 (*Malden* 1977, unpag, repr); Louis XVIII, drawing, signed, private coll (*Malden* 1977, unpag, repr); Dr James Millar, drawing, SNPG 879, (*Malden* 1977, unpag, repr); Rev Morehead, exhib ASA 1811, untraced; Captain Jones, exhib ASA, 1809, 45; Master John Henning, exhib ASA 1810, 33; Mr S Henning, exhib ASA 1811, 4

Miscellaneous models: plaster casts of the sculptor's miniature reproduction of the Parthenon, BM PDB 1913, 1112.1; plaster cast set of the sculptor's miniature reproductions of the Parthenon and Phygaleian friezes, BM PDB 1913, 1112.1; thirty seven slate moulds of the sculptor's miniature reproductions of the Parthenon and Phigalia Marbles, BM PDB 1913, 1112.1; 1118.13-9

Portraits of the sculptor: Robert Adamson and David Octavius Hill, *c*1843–1848, NPG (P6/24), another (P6/31); another (P6/32); another (P6/92); another (P6/98); another (P6/151); another (P6/156); another (P6/158); another (P6/237); another (P6/238); John Henning II, bust, marble, 1848; Robert Scott Lauder *John Henning*, oil on canvas, 23.5 x 19.7cm, SNPG, (repr *Malden* 1977, frontispiece; engraving, *AJ* 1849, 112, repr); Photograph, *Malden* 1977, unpag (endpiece)

Funerary Monuments						
1.	?1818	John Heaton		Havering-atte-Bower, Essex	S	*Gunnis* 1968, 198
2.	?1836	John Ellis		Wyddial, Herts	S	*Gunnis* 1968, 198
Statues						
3.	1810	'A sitting statue in clay' Model(s): sketch, plaster, exhib ASA, 28		[Exhib ASA, 22]; untraced		*Rinder and Mackay* 1917, 159
4.	1816	Arthur, 1st Duke of Wellington, model for an equestrian statue		[Exhib BI, London, 265]; untraced		*Graves* 1875, 259
Busts						
5.	1809	Colonel John Campbell		[coll Lady Charlotte Campbell]; untraced		*Rinder and Mackay* 1917, 159; *Malden* 1977, unpag
6.	1809	Sarah Siddons		[Exhib North Soc, Leeds ASA 1810, 23 (cast)]; untraced		*Rinder and Mackay* 1917, 159; *Malden* 1977, unpag; GPC
7.	1810	Robert, 2nd Viscount Melville		Untraced		*Malden* 1977, unpag
Chimneypieces						
8.	1829	More than one Payment(s): £125	m	[Addington Palace, Surrey]; untraced		GPC
Architectural Sculpture						
9.	1828	Frieze based on the Parthenon and Phygaleian friezes (co-sculptor: John Henning II)		Hyde Park Corner, London, entrance arch Other versions: Athenaeum Club, Pall Mall, London Terling Place, Essex RCS, London, staircase hall		*AJ* 1866 (repr); Pevsner, *Essex*, 1965, 379; *Gunnis* 1968, 197; Pevsner, *London: Westminster*, 1973, 668; *Malden* 1977, unpag (repr); *Whinney* 1988, 382 (repr)
Reliefs						
10.	1799	A Woodrow, medallion	w	Untraced		*Malden* 1977, unpag
11.	1799	Katherine Sunter Henning, medallion	w	Paisley MAG		*Malden* 1977, unpag (repr)
12.	c1800	Henry, 3rd Duke of Buccleuch, medallion		Untraced		*Malden* 1977, unpag
13.	1800	John Hamilton, medallion		Untraced		*Malden* 1977, unpag
14.	1800	John Watt, medallion	p	Paisley MAG	SD	*Malden* 1977, unpag (repr)
15.	1800	Mr and Mrs Harvey, medallions		Untraced		*Malden* 1977, unpag (repr)
16.	c1800	Mr Bell, medallion		Untraced		*Malden* 1977, unpag (repr)
17.	1801	Andrew Stirling of Drumpeler, medallion	p	Paisley MAG	SD	*Malden* 1977, unpag (repr)
18.	1801	Ebenezer Macome, medallion		SNPG 1358 Other versions: Paisley MAG	SD	*Gunnis* 1968, 197; *Malden* 1977, unpag (repr)
19.	1801	Francis Lord Jeffrey, medallion Drawing(s): pencil, SD, private coll	w	SNPG 532 Other versions: SNPG 1539, enamel VAM 100-1065, wax, SD 1807 Glasgow Mitchell Library, wax		*Rinder and Mackay* 1917, 160; *Gunnis* 1968, 197; *Pyke* 1973, 67; *Malden* 1977, unpag (repr); *Pearson* 1991, unpag.
20.	1801	George Anderson, medallion		Hunterian Other versions: SNPG, plaster, SD	SD	*Malden* 1977, unpag (repr)
21.	1801	George Jeffrey, medallion	p	SNPG 530	SD	*Malden* 1977, unpag (repr)
22.	1801	James Smith, medallion		Untraced		*Malden* 1977, unpag
23.	1801	Mr Scott-Moncrieff, medallion	p	Paisley MAG	SD	*Malden* 1977, unpag (repr)
24.	1801	Thomas Bisland, medallion		Paisley MAG	SD	*Malden* 1977, unpag (repr)
25.	1802	Dr William Dunlop, medallion	p	SNPG 1945	SD	*Malden* 1977, unpag (repr)
26.	1802	Eliza Dawson Fletcher, medallion Drawing(s): Exhib ASA 1809	w	Paisley MAG Other versions: SNPG, 418, 696, two, plaster and enamel	SD	*Rinder and McKay* 1917, 159; *Gunnis* 1968, 197–8; *Malden* 1977, unpag (repr)
27.	1802	Grace Wilson Henning, medallion	p	Paisley MAG	SD	*Graves* IV, 1905–6, 71; *Malden* 1977, unpag (repr)
28.	1802	Hector MacNeil, medallion	p	SNPG 387, 2357 Other versions: Paisley MAG, two, enamel and plaster	SD	*Gunnis* 1968, 198; *Malden* 1977, unpag (repr)
29.	1802	Jane Graham, medallion	p	Paisley MAG	SD	*Malden* 1977, unpag (repr)
30.	1802	John Berry, medallion	p	Paisley MAG	SD	*Malden* 1977, unpag (repr)
31.	1802	Lady Elizabeth Douglas, medallion		Untraced		*Malden* 1977, unpag
32.	1802	Mrs K Struthers, medallion		Paisley MAG, copper mould	SD	*Malden* 1977, unpag (repr)
33.	1802	Mrs R Ferrie, medallion		Paisley MAG	SD	*Malden* 1977, unpag (repr)
34.	1802	Rev Alexander Carlyle, medallion	p	Paisley MAG, mould, wax, and small enamel Other versions: SNPG 245, enamel, SD 1805 and small plaster, 407, SD 1805		*Graves* IV, 1905–6, 71; *Rinder and McKay* 1917, 158; *Gunnis* 1968, 197–8; *Malden* 1977, unpag (repr)
35.	1802	Rev Archibald Alison, medallion		SNPG, Edinburgh	S	*Rinder and McKay* 1917, 159; *Gunnis* 1968, 198; *Malden* 1977, unpag (repr)
36.	1802	Sir William Forbes, medallion	p	Paisley MAG, mould and an enamel Other versions: SNPG 142, enamel	SD	*Rinder and McKay* 1917, 159; *Gunnis* 1968, 197, 198; *Malden* 1977, unpag (repr)
37.	1802	William Kelly, medallion		Private coll	SD	*Malden* 1977, unpag (repr)
38.	1803	A Bruce, medallion		Untraced	SD	*Malden* 1977, unpag (repr)
39.	1803	David Dale, medallion		NPG, London 5810	SD	
40.	1803	General Vyse, medallion		[Exhib ASA 1808 Exhib North Soc, Leeds 1809]; untraced		*Rinder and McKay* 1917, 159; *Malden* 1977, unpag; GPC

41.	1803	Rev Sydney Smith, medallion		SNPG 528, 1948 Other versions: Paisley MAG, enamel and plaster versions	SD	*Pearson* 1991, unpag; *Malden* 1977, unpag (repr)
42.	1803	Richard Lovell Edgeworth, medallion	p	Paisley MAG Other versions: SNPG, 2135, enamel	SD	*Rinder and Mackay* 1917, 160; *Malden* 1977, unpag (repr)
43.	1804	Colonel John Campbell, medallion	p	Paisley MAG, mould Other versions: private coll, enamel, SD 1806	SD	*Malden* 1977, unpag (repr)
44.	1804	Sir James Stewart, medallion		Paisley MAG	SD	*Rinder and Mackay* 1917, 159; *Malden* 1977, unpag (repr)
45.	1806	Francis Horner, medallion Drawing(s): NPG 2677, pencil and chalk; Parliament Hall, Edinburgh, chalk	w	NPG, London, 2678 Other versions: Paisley MAG, enamel and copper mould SNPG 533, plaster and enamel versions	SD	*Rinder and McKay* 1917, 159; *Gunnis* 1968, 197, 198; *Malden* 1977, unpag (repr)
46.	1806	James, 1st Earl of Lauderdale, medallion Drawing(s): SNPG acc 119, signed, pencil; SNPG acc 397, pencil		SNPG 1538 Other versions: Paisley MAG, enamel Private coll, enamel		*Graves* IV, 1905–6, 71; *Rinder and Mackay* 1917, 159; *Gunnis* 1968, 197; *Malden* 1977, unpag (repr)
47.	1807	John Henning II, medallion	p	Paisley MAG	SD	*Rinder and McKay* 1917, 159, 160; *Malden* 1977, unpag (repr)
48.	1807	Lord Webb Seymour, medallion		SNPG 1540	SD	*Rinder and McKay* 1917, 159; *Gunnis* 1968, 197, 198; *Malden* 1977, unpag (repr)
49.	1807	Professor Adam Ferguson, medallion Drawing(s): private coll, chalk, signed		[Exhib ASA, 1808, 13 Exhib RA, London, 1812, 682]; untraced	SD	*Graves* IV, 1905–6, 71; *Rinder and McKay* 1917, 159; *Malden* 1977, unpag (repr and drawing repr); GPC
50.	1807	Robert Burns, medallion	p	Paisley MAG Other versions: SNPG, 1275, enamel Burns Club, Paisley, copper mould	SD	*Rinder and McKay* 1917, 159; *Malden* 1977, unpag (repr)
51.	1807	Robert Gray, medallion		Paisley MAG, copper mould	SD	*Malden* 1977, unpag (repr)
52.	1807	Sarah Siddons, medallion Drawing(s): private coll, pencil, signed	p	SNPG 537 Other versions: Paisley MAG, plaster and copper mould	SD	*AJ* 1849, 113; *Rinder and McKay* 1917, 159; *Gunnis* 1968, 197, 198; *Malden* 1977, unpag (repr)
53.	1808	Lady Charlotte Campbell, medallion Drawing(s): chalk; untraced		Paisley MAG	SD	*Graves* IV, 1905–6, 71; *Rinder and Mackay* 1917, 159; *Malden* 1977, unpag (repr)
54.	1808	Lord Sylvester Glenbervie, medallion Drawing(s): SNPG, 2032, chalk	w	Paisley MAG Other versions: SNPG, 1276, enamel, SD		*Rinder and Mackay* 1917, 160; *Gunnis* 1968, 197; *Malden* 1977, unpag (repr)
55.	1808	Sir Walter Scott, medallion Drawing(s): private coll, pencil	w	Paisley MAG Other versions: SNPG, plaster, SD Reproduced by Wedgwood, 1815		*Graves* IV, 1905–6, 71; *Rinder and Mackay* 1917, 159; *Malden* 1977, unpag (repr)
56.	1809	Alexander, 10th Duke of Hamilton, medallion		Paisley MAG	SD	*Malden* 1977, unpag (repr)
57.	1809	Archibald 9th Duke of Hamilton, medallion		Untraced		*Gunnis* 1968, 197; *Malden* 1977, unpag
58.	1809	David, 11th Earl of Buchan, medallion	w	Paisley MAG	SD	*Rinder and Mackay* 1917, 159; *Malden* 1977, unpag (repr)
59.	1809	H Sinclair Erskine, medallion		[Exhib ASA, 51]; untraced		*Rinder and Mackay* 1917, 159
60.	1809	Henrietta, Countess of Rosslyn, medallion		Paisley MAG	SD	*Malden* 1977, unpag (repr)
61.	1809	James Francis Erskine of Mar, medallion	p	Paisley MAG (mould)	SD	*Graves* IV, 1905–6, 71; *Rinder and McKay* 1917, 159; *Malden* 1977, unpag (repr)
62.	1809	James Watt, medallion Drawing(s): SNPG, 294, chalk, signed		SNPG 419		*Rinder and Mackay* 1917, 159; *Malden* 1977, unpag (repr); *Pearson* 1991, unpag
63.	1809	John Erskine, medallion		[Exhib ASA 1808, 7; 1809, 3]; untraced		*Rinder and McKay* 1917, 158; *Malden* 1977, unpag (repr)
64.	1809	Lady Jean Hunter-Blair, medallion		[Exhib ASA, 4]; untraced		*Rinder and Mackay* 1917, 159; *Malden* 1977, unpag
65.	1809	Lord Frederick Campbell, portrait medallion	p	SNPG, Edinburgh, 409 Other versions: Paisley MAG, plaster mould	SD	*Graves* IV, 1905–6, 71; *Rinder and Mackay* 1917, 159; *Gunnis* 1968, 197; *Malden* 1977, unpag (repr)
66.	1809	Mrs Burnet, medallion		[Exhib ASA, 10]; untraced		*Rinder and Mackay* 1917, 159; *Malden* 1977, unpag
67.	1809	Mrs Trotter, medallion		[Exhib ASA, 7]; untraced		*Rinder and Mackay* 1917, 159; *Malden* 1977, unpag
68.	1809	Patrick Miller of Dalswinton, medallion	p	Paisley MAG	SD	*Rinder and Mackay* 1917, 159; *Malden* 1977, unpag (repr)
69.	1809	Robert, Lord Dundas, medallion	p	SNPG 408		*Gunnis* 1968, 198; *Malden* 1977, unpag (repr)
70.	1809	Sir Alexander Gordon, medallion		NPG 1801 Other versions: Sotheby Olympia 25 June 2003, lot 149, SD 1809	SD	*Gunnis* 1968, 198

No.	Date	Subject		Location		Bibliography
71.	1809	Sir Henry Moncrieff Wellwood, medallion Drawing(s): private coll, pencil; private coll, chalk		SNPG 527 Other versions: Paisley MAG, two, enamel and copper	SD	*Rinder and Mackay* 1917, 159; *Gunnis* 1968, 198; *Malden* 1977, unpag (repr)
72.	1809	Thomas Dundas of Carron Hall, medallion		[Exhib ASA, 225]; untraced		*Rinder and Mackay* 1917, 159
73.	1809	W Keir, medallion		[Exhib ASA, 12]; untraced		*Rinder and Mackay* 1917, 159; *Malden* 1977, unpag
74.	1809	William, Lord Craig, medallion		[Exhib ASA, 11]; untraced		*Rinder and Mackay* 1917, 159; *Malden* 1977, unpag (repr)
75.	1810	Alexander, 4th Duke of Gordon, medallion		[Exhib ASA, 1810]; Sotheby 28 Feb 1977, lot 22		*Rinder and Mackay* 1917, 159; *Gunnis* 1968, 197; *Malden* 1977, unpag
76.	1810	Anne Grant, medallion	p	Paisley MAG, mould	SD	*Malden* 1977, unpag (repr)
77.	1810	Colonel Henry Cadogan, medallion	p	Paisley MAG	SD	*Gunnis* 1968, 197; *Malden* 1977, unpag (repr)
78.	1810	D H Rucker and wife, medallions		Untraced		*Rinder and Mackay* 1917, 160; *Malden* 1977, unpag
79.	1810	Earl of Rosslyn, medallion		[Exhib ASA, 9]; untraced		*Rinder and Mackay* 1917, 159
80.	c1810	Henry Brougham, medallion	p	SNPG 520 Other versions: Reproduced by Wedgwood, 1815		*Rinder and Mackay* 1917, 159, 160; *Gunnis* 1968, 197; *Malden* 1977, unpag (repr)
81.	1810	James, 2nd Earl of Rosslyn, medallion		[Exhib ASA]; untraced		*Gunnis* 1968, 197; *Malden* 1977, unpag
82.	1810	Mary Smeaton Dixon, medallion		Untraced Other versions: Paisley MAG, slate mould, SD 1820		*Rinder and Mackay* 1917, 160; *Malden* 1977, unpag
83.	1810	Miss de Visme, medallion Drawing(s): exhib ASA 1809, 26		[Exhib ASA, 3]; untraced		*Rinder and McKay* 1917, 159; *Malden* 1977, unpag
84.	1810	Mr Meadows, medallion		Sotheby 15 Jan 1968, lot 113		*Malden* 1977, unpag
85.	1810	Mrs MacVicar, medallion	w	Paisley MAG	SD	*Malden* 1977, unpag (repr)
86.	1810	Mrs Maxwell, medallion		[Exhib ASA, 2]; untraced		*Rinder and Mackay* 1917, 159; *Malden* 1977, unpag
87.	1810	R Jaffray, medallion	p	Paisley MAG	SD	*Rinder and Mackay* 1917, 159; *Malden* 1977, unpag (repr)
88.	1810	Rev James Grahame, medallion		SNPG, Edinburgh Other versions: Paisley MAG, SD, enamel reproduced by Wedgwood	SD	*Rinder and Mackay* 1917, 160; *Gunnis* 1968, 198
89.	1810	Samuel Henning (†1809), medallion Drawing(s): Exhib ASA	i	Paisley MAG	SD	*Malden* 1977, unpag (repr)
90.	1810	Sir Humphry Davy, medallion Drawing(s): private coll, SD, pencil		Untraced		*Gunnis* 1968, 197; *Malden* 1977, unpag (repr)
91.	1810	William Anderson, medallion		Paisley MAG	SD	*Malden* 1977, unpag (repr)
92.	1810	William, Marquess of Douglas (?), medallion		[Exhib ASA, 8]; untraced		*Rinder and Mackay* 1917, 159; *Gunnis* 1968, 197
93.	1811	Countess of Rosslyn, medallion		[Exhib ASA, 1]; untraced		*Rinder and Mackay* 1917, 160
94.	1811	Hugh, 14th Baron Semphill, medallion		[Exhib ASA 1811, 4]; untraced		*Rinder and Mackay* 1917, 160; *Malden* 1977, unpag
95.	1811	Margaret Carfray, medallion	p	Paisley MAG (mould)	SD	*Malden* 1977, unpag (repr)
96.	1811	Mrs Dundas, medallion		[Exhib ASA, 10]; untraced		*Rinder and Mackay* 1917, 160; *Malden* 1977, unpag (repr)
97.	1811	Professor Dugald Stewart, medallion Drawing(s): SNPG L.36, chalk; NPG, chalk	p	SNPG 416 Other versions: Paisley MAG, enamel and copper versions Reproduced by Wedgwood	SD	*Rinder and Mackay* 1917, 160; *Malden* 1977, unpag (repr); *Pearson* 1991, unpag
98.	1811	Rev Mr Morehead		[Exhib ASA, 4]; untraced		*Rinder and Mackay* 1917, 159
99.	1811	Thomas Hamilton Miller, medallion		[ASA 1811, 3]; untraced		*Rinder and Mackay* 1917, 160; *Malden* 1977, unpag
100.	1811	William Oliphant, medallion		[Exhib ASA]; untraced		*Rinder and Mackay* 1917, 160; *Malden* 1977, unpag
101.	1812	Alexander Tilloch, medallion Drawing(s): SNPG, acc 336, pencil		Paisley MAG		*Malden* 1977, unpag (repr)
102.	1812	Arthur, 1st Duke of Wellington, medallion	w	[Exhib RA, London, 657 Exhib ASA 1813]; untraced Other versions: reproduced by Wedgwood, 1815 medal, published by S Parker, with battle scene on verso, SNPG, 538		*Graves* IV, 1905–6, 71; *Rinder and Mackay* 1917, 160; *Malden* 1977, unpag
103.	1812	Lord Archibald Hamilton MP, son of 9th Duke, medallion		Untraced		*Malden* 1977, unpag
104.	1812	Mr Mackie, medallion		[Exhib ASA, 30]; untraced		*Rinder and Mackay* 1917, 160; *Malden* 1977, unpag
105.	1812	Princess Charlotte Augusta, full-length seated figure	w	Paisley MAG, with copper mould Other versions: SNPG, plaster, SD 1812	SD	*Malden* 1977, unpag (repr); *Pearson* 1991, 150 (repr)
106.	1812	Sir Samuel Romilly, medallion		Paisley MAG Other versions: reproduced by Wedgwood, 1815	SD	*Rinder and Mackay* 1917, 160; *Gunnis* 1968, 197; *Malden* 1977, unpag (repr)
107.	1812	Unidentified woman	w	Private coll		*Pearson* 1991, unpag
108.	1813	Duke of Devonshire, medallion		[Exhib RA, London, 1814, 396]; untraced		*Graves* IV, 1905–6, 72; *Gunnis* 1968, 197; *Malden* 1977, unpag (repr)
109.	1813	Hugh Crawford, medallion		[Exhib ASA, 106]; untraced		*Rinder and Mackay* 1917, 160; *Malden* 1977, unpag (repr)

110.	1813	Miss S Smith, of Drury Lane Theatre, medallion Drawing(s): exhib RA 1813, 677		Untraced		*Gunnis* 1968, 197; *Malden* 1977, unpag
111.	1813	Princess Charlotte Augusta, medallion Drawing(s): private coll, pencil	p	SNPG, 535, 536 Other versions: Paisley MAG, enamel, copper	SD	Henning the Elder/Wedgwood; *Graves* IV, 1905–6, 71; *Rinder and Mackay* 1917, 160; *Malden* 1977, unpag (repr); *Pearson* 1991, unpag
112.	1813	Queen Caroline, medallion	p	Paisley MAG (mould. Also enamel, copper and plaster versions) Other versions: SNPG, 410, plaster, SD 1813		*Gunnis* 1968, 198; *Malden* 1977, unpag (repr)
113.	1813	Sir Robert Henry Inglis, medallion		Paisley MAG		*Malden* 1977, unpag (repr)
114.	1813	Thomas Campbell, medallion Drawing(s): NPG, chalk, SD		[Wedgwood archives]; untraced		*Gunnis* 1968, 197; *Malden* 1977, unpag (drawing repr)
115.	1813	Unidentified man	sl	Royal Coll RCIN 70003	S	
116.	1813	Unidentified woman		Royal Coll RCIN 70004		
117.	1814	R P Glenn, medallion		Paisley MAG	SD	*Malden* 1977, unpag (repr)
118.	1814	Thomas, 20th Baron Dacre, medallion	p	Paisley MAG	SD	*Malden* 1977, unpag (repr)
119.	1815	Archibald Skirving, medallion		untraced		*Malden* 1977, unpag
120.	1815	George Chalmers, medallion		Paisley MAG	SD	*Malden* 1977, unpag (repr)
121.	1816	Sir Thomas George Apreece Bt, medallion		Sotheby 28.8.1975, lot 88	SD	*Malden* 1977, unpag (repr)
122.	1817	Mrs Napier, medallion	p	Paisley MAG	SD	*Malden* 1977, unpag (repr)
123.	†1818	Lady Anne Romilly, medallion		untraced		*Malden* 1977, unpag
124.	1819	Thomas Dick, medallion	p	Paisley MAG (mould)	SD	*Malden* 1977, unpag (repr)
125.	1820–1822	A series of small plaster copies of the Raphael cartoons	p	untraced Other versions: Palace, Bishops Auckland ex coll Rupert Gunnis; untraced Brownsholme Hall, Clitheroe, wax, 1821	SD	*AJ* 1849, 114; *Builder* 1851, 297; *Gunnis* 1968, 197; *Pyke* 1973, 67; *Malden* 1977, unpag (repr)
126.	1822	Dr Furnival, medallion	p	Paisley MAG	SD	*Malden* 1977, unpag (repr)
127.	1822	Miniature copy of part of the Frieze of the Temple of Bassae (the 'Phygaleian marbles') (carved for reproduction in plaster)	sl	BM Other versions: numerous plaster reproductions	SD	*Neoclassicism* 1972, 243; *Malden* 1977, unpag
128.	1811–1823	Miniature copy of the Parthenon frieze (carved for reproduction in plaster) Payment(s): Plaster series, framed, 30g	sl	Untraced Other versions: Lever, SD ex coll Sir Thomas Lawrence, sold Christie, London; 17–19 June 1830, lot 380, £6 18s Perth Museum and Art Gallery, plaster Manchester CAG 1981.8 a-f numerous other plaster copies		*AJ* 1849, 112–4 (repr); *Rinder and Mackay* 1917, 160; *Malden* 1977, *passim* (repr); *Pearson* 1991, unpag
129.	1827	King William IV, medallion Drawing(s): private coll, SD, pencil	p	SNPG 534 Other versions: BM, medal		*Rinder and Mackay* 1917, 160; *Ormond* 1973, 512; *Malden* 1977, unpag (repr)
130.	1830	Lady Sydney Morgan, medallion	w	Paisley MAG		*Malden* 1977, unpag (repr)
131.	1836	George, 6th Lord Byron, medallion	p	Paisley MAG	SD	*Malden* 1977, unpag (repr)
132.	1837	John Macdonald, medallion		Paisley MAG	SD	*Malden* 1977, unpag (repr)
133.	1840	James Marinale, medallion		Paisley MAG		*Malden* 1977, unpag (repr)
134.	1840	Rev Dr Maltby, medallion		Paisley MAG	SD	*Malden* 1977, unpag (repr)
135.	1840	Rev Robert Fellowes, medallion	p	Paisley MAG (also a copper version and copper mould)	SD	*Malden* 1977, unpag (repr)
136.	1840	Sophia Jane, medallion		Paisley MAG	SD	*Malden* 1977, unpag (repr)
137.	1841	Admiral Sir Charles Napier, medallion	p	SNPG 85 Other versions: Paisley MAG, copper mould	SD	*Ormond* 1973, 332; *Malden* 1977, unpag (repr)
138.	1842	Dr Kaye, medallion		Paisley MAG	S	*Malden* 1977, unpag (repr)
139.	1842	R Murray, medallion		Paisley MAG	SD	*Malden* 1977, unpag (repr)
140.	1842	Thomas Eliot, medallion		Paisley MAG	SD	*Malden* 1977, unpag (repr)
141.	1843	Self-portrait, medallion	p	Paisley MAG Other versions: SNPG, plaster	SD	*Malden* 1977, unpag (repr)
142.	1847	J S Street, medallion	p	Paisley MAG	SD	*Malden* 1977, unpag (repr)
143.	nd	Helen D'Arcy Stewart, medallion	p	Paisley MAG Other versions: SNPG, plaster		*Malden* 1977, unpag (repr)
144.	nd	Hon Keppel Craven, medallion		Untraced		*Malden* 1977, unpag (repr)
145.	nd	Lord William Robertson, medallion		SNPG	SD	*Rinder and Mackay* 1917, 160; *Gunnis* 1968, 198; *Malden* 1977, unpag (repr)
146.	nd	Marchioness of Lansdowne, medallion		Untraced		*Gunnis* 1968, 197; *Malden* 1977, unpag
147.	nd	Thomas Telford, medallion		Untraced		*Gunnis* 1968, 197; *Malden* 1977, unpag
148.	nd	Thomas, Viscount Hampden and Catherine, Viscountess Hampden, medallions		Untraced		*Gunnis* 1968, 197; *Malden* 1977, unpag
149.	nd	William Carlile, medallion		Untraced		*Malden* 1977, unpag (repr)
Miscellaneous						
150.	1808	Cast of a model of a boy's head at six years of age	p	[Exhib ASA, 168]; untraced		*Rinder and McKay* 1917, 159
151.	1808	Cast of a model of a girl's head, four years of age	p	[Exhib ASA, 1808]; untraced		*Rinder and McKay* 1917, 159

152.	1808	Clay model of a boy's head at three years of age		[Exhib ASA, 167]; untraced	*Rinder and McKay* 1917, 159
153.	nd	Portraits of the Duke of Hamilton, his wife and daughters	w	Untraced	*Gunnis* 1968, 197

HENNING, John II 1802–57

He was born in Glasgow on 8 August 1802, the eldest son of **John Henning I** and Katherine, née Sunter. His father exhibited a drawing of the eight-year-old boy at the Associated Society of Artists in Edinburgh in 1810. The family moved to London in 1811, where young John continued to be educated by his father, who could not afford proper schooling for his family. Clearly something of a prodigy, Henning designed a scene for the obverse of a medal commemorating the battle of Waterloo in 1815, later exhibited at the Royal Academy, and in 1816, while living with his father in Glasshouse Street, Piccadilly, he won the silver Isis medal from the Society of Arts for his relief of *The Good Samaritan* (**31**). The following year he exhibited a biblical subject at the British Institution (**36**).

Henning had already come to the attention of the press by 1820 when the *New Monthly Magazine* published an article on the young man, noting that Henning I had discovered his son's 'decided talent' for sculpture, 'which he has since given proofs in many admirable productions' (*New Monthly Mag*, pt I, 1820, 455–59). In 1824 he exhibited a bust of Benjamin West's biographer, John Galt at the RA (**8**) and in 1825 he was employed in carrying out repairs to the statue of Queen Anne by **Francis Bird** at St Paul's Cathedral, which had been assaulted by a lunatic.

In July 1828 young Henning signed a contract with the architect Decimus Burton to assist his father in producing a frieze based on the Parthenon marbles for the exterior of the Athenaeum Club (**18**). Henning's part in making his father's famous copies of the Marbles supposedly began in the early 1810s, when his absent-minded scratching on a slate board during lessons provided the inspiration for using carved slate moulds. He worked with his father and his brother **Samuel Henning** to produce the 260-foot long reproduction for the Athenaeum in Bath stone and the family provided another version for Burton's archway entrance to Hyde Park (**17**).

In 1830 the family moved from 2 Somers Place, New Road to Lower Belgrave Place, Pimlico. Henning won the commission independently to execute bas-reliefs on the exterior of the Manchester Institution (now the City Art Gallery) in 1836, in competition with **Charles R Smith**. Sir Charles Barry had 'no hesitation in giving a decided preferrence' to Henning's designs, which the sculptor offered to execute for £30 a panel (**19**). Henning arrived in Manchester to put the finishing touches to his workman's carving the following summer, and also coated the finished works with wax, believing that this would prevent decay. He was ill at this time and also pleaded that he was 'hard up for some cash' in a letter to the Institution. In the same text he unsuccessfully attempted to sell them the models for his relief panels (corr: Manchester City Archives, transcribed in *Malden* 1977, unpag).

While travelling to Manchester in October 1837 Henning stayed at Trentham Hall, the home of the Duke of Sutherland, who the following month paid Henning for a marble chimneypiece for Stafford House, his London home (**16**). The architect of Stafford House at that time was Barry, who presumably recommended the sculptor, and Henning went on to produce two elaborate lunettes to be placed above paintings by the Spanish painter Murillo (**20**), which Sutherland had recently bought. Henning also designed and probably executed several embossed glass panels in the Italian mannerist style at a princely cost of about 1,000 guineas. The design was praised in the *Art Union* in 1846.

In 1844 Henning exhibited at Westminster Hall, where his work received a lukewarm reception from the *Literary Gazette*, who commented of his statue of Lord Bacon (**3**) that the head was 'full of character; but the figure is poor and the drapery unmeaning'. His group of *Boadicea* (**2**) was considered spirited but 'the pelvis is large enough for the life-size; and one of the daughters is Eve, à la **E H Baily**' (*Lit Gaz*, 1844, 466).

His most remarkable work was perhaps the carving on the column erected to commemorate Lord Leicester at Holkham, designed by the architect William Donthorn. The iconography reflected Leicester's pride in his agricultural achievements. In addition to the statues of animals and farming equipment and reliefs of Leicester engaged in acts of rustic improvement (**25**), Henning was responsible for the wheatsheaf finial and the decorative foliage, based, according to a very detailed account in the *Illustrated London News*, on the mangel-wurzel and the turnip. The same journal ran a feature on Henning's 'Homeric table' for Lord Northwick (**38**) and in 1852 said of his two bas-reliefs intended for the Mansion House (**28, 29**) that 'both are compositions of great merit, in classic treatment and feeling; and we hope to see them executed in marble, and placed in the positions for which they were designed, as a portion of enlightened patronage of art' (*ILN*, 30 October 1852, 365).

Henning produced a number of busts, including one of his father (**12**), only two of which have been located. The bust of Anna Maria, Duchess of Bedford (**14**), in a tiara and her hair in ringlets, is carved in broad shallow planes, whilst that of the 1st Duke of Marlborough, in armour, cravat, drapery and a full wig with drilled curls, is in the 18th-century style (**15**).

Henning died in 1857, six years after his father. He appears never to have established himself as an independent artist, despite producing several fine works alone. Five years before his death the *Illustrated London News* still prefaced their account of one of Henning's works with reference to his father's miniature reproductions of the Parthenon and Phygaleian marbles. He must have died in straitened circumstances for his widow received an annual pension of £10, rising to £15, from the Council of the Royal Academy in the years 1860–1875.

MGS

Literary References: RSA *Transactions*, vol 34, 1816, 29; *ILN*, 30 October 1852, 365; *Graves* 1875, 259; *Graves* IV, 1905–6, 72; *Gunnis* 1968, 197–8; *Malden* 1977, *passim*; *CIIA* 4/1/iii–iv; *Yorke* 1999, 44–8

Archival References: IGI; RA/GA *passim*

Portraits of the Sculptor: John Henning II, exhib ASA 1810, 33, untraced

Funerary Monuments

1.	?1857	Charles Heaton Ellis	Wyddial, Herts	*Gunnis* 1968, 198

Statues

2.	1844	Boadicea, Queen of the Iceni, group	[Exhib Westminster Hall, London, 113]; untraced	*Lit Gaz* 1844, 466; *Gunnis* 1968, 198; GPC
3.	1844	Lord Bacon	[Exhib Westminster Hall, London]; untraced	*Lit Gaz* 1844, 466; *Gunnis* 1968, 198

No.	Date	Work		Location		Reference
4.	1845	Alfred the Great		[Exhib Westminster Hall, London, 126]; untraced		*Westminster* 1845, 15
5.	1845	'Joan Plantagenet, Princess of Wales and Countess of Kent, surnamed the Fair Maid of Kent, with King Richard the Second, at the Shrine of the Virgin'		[Exhib Westminster Hall, London]; untraced		*Westminster Hall* 1845, 17
6.	nd	The triumph of Bacchus		[Exhib Colosseum, Regents Park, London]; untraced		GPC

Busts

No.	Date	Work		Location		Reference
7.	1824	Dr Maltby		[Exhib Suffolk St, London]; untraced		*Gunnis* 1968, 198
8.	1824	John Galt		[Exhib Suffolk St, London Exhib RA, London, 1830, 1184]; untraced		*Graves* IV, 1905–6, 72; *Gunnis* 1968, 198
9.	1825	Achilles		[Exhib Soc of BA, London]; untraced		*Gunnis* 1968, 198
10.	1834	Dr James		[Exhib Suffolk St, London]; untraced		*Gunnis* 1968, 198
11.	1845	'Agnes'		[Exhib RA, London, 1419]; untraced		*Graves* IV, 1905–6, 72
12.	1848	John Henning I		[Exhib RA, London, 1048]; destroyed		*Graves* IV, 1905–6, 72; *Malden* 1977, unpag
13.	1849	George Rigby	m	[Exhib RA, London, 1293]; untraced		*Graves* IV, 1905–6, 72
14.	nd	Anna Maria, Duchess of Bedford	m	Woburn Abbey, Beds	S	*Gunnis* 1968, 198; C Lib (repr)
15.	nd	John, 1st Duke of Marlborough	m	Windsor Castle, RCIN 35333	S	*Malden* 1977, unpag (repr)

Chimneypieces

No.	Date	Work		Location		Reference
16.	1837	With panels showing a serpent entwined around a tree		Stafford House, London, duchess's room		*Yorke* 1999, 45, 48 (repr)

Architectural Sculpture

No.	Date	Work		Location		Reference
17.	1828	Frieze based on the Parthenon and Phygaleian friezes (co-sculptor: John Henning I)		Hyde Park Corner, London, entrance arch		*Whinney* 1988, 382 (repr)
18.	1828	Frieze based on the Parthenon and Phygaleian friezes (designed by Decimus Burton) (co-sculptor: John Henning I) Payment(s): £1,300	s	Athenaeum Club, City of Westminster, London, exterior		*AJ* 1866 (repr); *Gunnis* 1968, 197; Pevsner, *London: Westminster*, 1973, 668; *Malden* 1977, unpag (repr)
19.	1836–1837	Architecture, Painting, Sculpture, Wisdom, Astronomy and Mathematics, high-reliefs Payment(s): £30 per relief Model(s): offered to the institution for £14 in Nov 1837; untraced	s	Manchester CAG, exterior		*CIIA* 4/6/85–91 (repr); *Malden* 1977, unpag (repr); *Read* 1982, 222–5 (repr)
20.	1840	Winged figures holding portrait medallions, two lunettes in alto-relievo above paintings by Murillo Payment(s): £150	p	Stafford House, London, picture gallery		*Yorke* 1999, 44, 45 (repr)
21.	1839–1841	Models for sidetables with marble tops, and wooden supports in the form of *putti* holding dolphins (executed by George Jackson and Co) Payment(s): £118		Stafford House, London, banqueting room		*Yorke* 1999, 45, 48 (repr)
22.	1845	'Groups of Cupid and Psyche supporting candelabra in the form of palm-trees, the figures being white and the draperies, leaves and plumes, etc. being gilded'		[Colosseum, Regents Park, London]; untraced		GPC
23.	1845	Reliefs		[Colosseum, Regents Park, London]; untraced		*Gunnis* 1968, 198
24.	1846	Gate piers and vases (designed by Decimus Burton)		Kew Gardens, London, 'new entrance'		*ILN* 21 March 1846, 193; *Builder* 1846, 175; GPC; C Lib (repr)
25.	1845–1848	Statues and three reliefs representing Thomas Coke, 1st Earl of Leicester superintending agricultural improvements and caring for tenants, with other decorative carving	s	Holkham Park, Norfolk, column commemorating the Earl of Leicester		*ILN* 16 Aug 1875, 111–2 (repr); *Penny* 1977 (1), 188–9 (repr); *Read* 1982, 159, 161 (repr)
26.	1850	Reliefs based on 'The industrious and the idle apprentices' by William Hogarth		[Freeman's Orphan School, Brixton, London]; untraced		*Gunnis* 1968, 198
27.	1850	Table decorated with the shield of Achilles		[Thirlstane House, Cheltenham (sold 1859, lot 657)]; untraced		*ILN* 12 Jan 1850, 21 (repr); Northwick Sale 1859; C Lib (repr)
28.	1852	Music and Painting, bas-relief	p	[Mansion House, London, intended for the long parlour]; untraced		*ILN* 30 Oct 1852, 365 (repr); *Gunnis* 1968, 198
29.	1852	The vintage, bas-relief	p	[Mansion House, London, intended for the drawing room]; untraced		*ILN* 30 Oct 1852, 365 (repr); *Gunnis* 1968, 198
30.	1854	Arms of the City of London and supporters	s	[City of London Freemen's Orphan School, Ferndale Road, London, principal front]; untraced		*Cavanagh* forthcoming 2007 ('lost or removed works')

Reliefs

No.	Date	Work		Location		Reference
31.	1816	The Good Samaritan		[Soc of A, silver Isis medal]; untraced		RSA *Transactions*, vol 34, 1816, 29
32.	1835	Unidentified subject, high relief		[Exhib RA, London, 1060]; untraced		*Graves* IV, 1905–6, 72

33.	1836	The vintage, high-relief	[Exhib BI, London, 501 Exhib RA, London, 1844, 1292]; untraced	*Graves* 1875, 259; *Graves* IV, 1905–6, 72
34.	1837	Death of the stag, high-relief	[Exhib BI, London, 449]; untraced	*Graves* 1875, 259
35.	1854	After Hogarth's 'Industrious and Idle Apprentices'	[City of London Freemen's Orphan School, Ferndale Road, London, dining hall]; untraced	*Cavanagh* forthcoming 2007 ('lost or removed works')
Miscellaneous				
36.	1817	'Composition, A mighty man is not delivered by much strength, an hero is a vain thing for safety, etc – Psalm xxxiii, 16, 17 . . .'	[Exhib BI, London, 234]; untraced	*Graves* 1875, 259
37.	1818	Meeting between Israel and his son Joseph	[Exhib BI, London, 305]; untraced	*Graves* 1875, 259
38.	1820	Design from the Iliad for a table	[Exhib BI, London, 319]; untraced	*Graves* 1875, 259
39.	1820	'Sketch of an encounter between the Life Guards and French Cuirassiers at Waterloo'	[Exhib BI, London, 320]; untraced	*Graves* 1875, 259
40.	1828	Obverse of a medal of the Duke of Wellington	[Exhib RA, London, 493]; untraced	*Graves* IV, 1905–6, 72; *Malden* 1977, unpag
41.	1834	'Sketch from nature'	[Exhib RA, London, 1067]; untraced	*Graves* IV, 1905–6, 72
42.	1837	The shield of Achilles, model	[Exhib RA, London, 1185]; untraced	*Graves* IV, 1905–6, 72
43.	1839	Love, Wine and Music	[Exhib RA, London, 1328]; untraced	*Graves* IV, 1905–6, 72
44.	1844	A group – the sisters	[Exhib RA, London, 1284]; untraced	*Graves* IV, 1905–6, 72
45.	1846	'Laressa softly stept and seized the boy'	[Exhib RA, London, 1411]; untraced	*Graves* IV, 1905–6, 72
46.	1847	The snake in the grass	[Exhib RA, London, 1340]; untraced	*Graves* IV, 1905–6, 72
47.	1850	Child with shells	[Exhib RA, London, 1352]; untraced	*Graves* IV, 1905–6, 72
48.	1852	Captain Thomas Coram, design for a group	[Exhib RA, London, 1366]; untraced	*Graves* IV, 1905–6, 72
49.	1852	Pandora attired	[Exhib RA, London, 1376]; untraced	*Graves* IV, 1905–6, 72
50.	1852	The last drop	[Exhib RA, London, 1355]; untraced	*Graves* IV, 1905–6, 72

HENNING, Samuel –1832

He was the younger son of **John Henning I** and the brother of **John Henning II**. In 1818, while living in Queen's Row, Pentonville, London, he received a silver palette 'for an original intaglio' from the Society of Arts. An 'A S Henning' and a 'J Henning,' presumably his siblings, were awarded prizes for a copy of an intaglio on the same occasion. Henning was awarded a silver Isis medal in 1819 for another intaglio and the large silver medal in 1820 for 'five intaglios' (RSA, *Transactions*, vol 36, 1818, xxxii; vol 37, 1819, xxxiii; vol 38, 1820, xxxv). In 1823 he exhibited at the Royal Academy, giving his address as 34 Lower Thornhaugh Street, and showing intaglios from ancient and modern subjects.

He assisted his father in reproducing the Raphael cartoons on slate in 1820–22. In 1825 and 1826 he exhibited 'restorations' of the Parthenon frieze (**2, 4, 5**) and he was clearly involved in the family business in reproductions of the celebrated marbles. He assisted his father and his brother, John in carving friezes for the Athenaeum and the entrance to Hyde Park. He seems chiefly, however, to have worked on a small scale, exhibiting numerous intaglios at the Academy and at the Society of British Artists, where he was elected a member in 1827.

In 1828 J T Smith described Henning as 'a young artist of promising abilities as a medallist', who took impressions of the best Italian medals in **John Flaxman RA**'s collection. Flaxman helped him to choose a selection of the most interesting and beautiful, which included that of Don Inigo de Davalos and Benedictus Depastis. From these Henning made casts which he sold 'at a price accommodated to the limited resources of the economical student' (*Smith* 1828, 318–9). His last work was a sarcophagus monument (**1**).

He died of cholera at his home at 40 Belgrave Place on 2 November 1832, apparently in poor circumstances, for his widow, Ann, was granted a pension by the Royal Academy, which she continued to draw until 1851. In 1834 Mrs Henning had a stall at the Soho Bazaar, selling 'Patent candle lamps and bronze articles.'

Literary References: *Graves* IV, 1905–6, 72; *Gunnis* 1968, 198; *Johnson* 1975, 223; *Malden* 1977, *passim*

Funerary Monuments				
1.	*c*1832	Duncan Sinclair, sarcophagus	Kensal Green Cemetery, London	*Gunnis* 1968, 198
Reliefs				
2.	1825	Restoration of the west frieze of the Parthenon	[Exhib BI, London, 412]; untraced	*Graves* 1875, 259
3.	1826	A case containing twelve medallions	[Exhib Soc of BA, London, 729]; untraced	*Johnson* 1975, 223
4.	1826	Restoration from the east frieze of the cella of the Parthenon	[Exhib BI, London, 411]; untraced	*Graves* 1875, 259
5.	1827	Restoration of part of the north frieze of the Parthenon	[Exhib RA, London, 72]; untraced	*Graves* IV, 1905–6, 72
Miscellaneous				
6.	1826	Copies from the antique	[Exhib Soc of BA, London, 731]; untraced	*Johnson* 1975, 223
7.	1826	Frame containing five heads	[Exhib Soc of BA, London, 732]; untraced	*Johnson* 1975, 223
8.	1827	The Canterbury pilgrimage	[Exhib Soc of BA, London, 860]; untraced	*Johnson* 1975, 223
9.	1828	Cavalcade proceeding to the tournament	[Exhib Soc of BA, London, 917]; untraced	*Johnson* 1975, 223
10.	1829	Aurora, after Guido	[Exhib Soc of BA, London, 831]; untraced	*Johnson* 1975, 223
11.	1829	Head of Hector	[Exhib RA, London, 1070]; untraced	*Graves* IV, 1905–6, 72
12.	nd	'two tablets for the New Buckingham Gate'	Untraced	*Gunnis* 1968, 198

HENRY, E fl 1802?

Funerary Monuments

1.	?†1802	Eliza Tupper	St Peter Port, Guernsey	S	

HENSHALL, William, of London –1820

Henshall became a liveryman of the Masons' Company in 1802. He lived in Mortimer Street and was a neighbour of **Joseph Nollekens.** In the 1818 draft of Nollekens' will, he left £100 to Henshall, 'stone mason,' and his wife (PROB 11/1673/276). Henshall however predeceased his neighbour and his death was reported in the *Gentleman's Magazine* on 27 November 1820. He is described as 'Mr. Wm. Henshall, many years statuary and mason to the Admiralty' (*GM*, 1820, 2, 571). He carved a large tablet with an Adamesque semi-urn against a pyramid to Joseph Ashley (1).

Literary References: *Gunnis* 1968, 198

Archival References: GPC

Funerary Monuments

1.	?1798	Joseph Ashley	Ashby St Ledgers, Northants	S	*Gunnis* 1968, 198
2.	?1799	Sir Peter Nugent	Stanwell, Middx, churchyard		GPC

Chimneypieces

3.	1806	Description unavailable Payment(s): £45	[Atherstone Hall, Warks, drawing room]; untraced		Bracebridge archives in GPC

HENSON, of Spalding fl 1794

Funerary Monuments

1.	†1794	Philip Ashby	All Saints, Holbeach, Lincs		Pevsner, *Lincs*, 1989, 384

HENSON, W, of Kettering fl c1841–43

He signs a 'pretty little tablet' to Sir George Robinson (1), and 'a plainer one' to the Rev William Layng (2).

Funerary Monuments

1.	?1841	Sir George Robinson	Cranford St John, Northants	S	*Gunnis* 1968, 199
2.	?1843	Rev William Laying	Great Harrowden, Northants	S	*Gunnis* 1968, 199

HENWOOD, John, of Plymouth fl 1815–30

He signs an anchor-shaped tablet in Devon (1).

Funerary Monuments

1.	†1815	Arthur Edgcumbe	Milton Abbot, Devon	S	*Gunnis* 1968, 199; Pevsner, *Devon*, 1989, 568

HERMANN, Joseph, of Dresden 1800–69

Born in Dresden, the son of a sculptor of the same name, he visited Rome in 1820 and spent a decade in Italy, mostly in the workshop of **Bertel Thorvaldsen**. He worked in Dresden, Berlin and St Petersburg. His only known English work is a stele decorated with a genius seated on a sarcophagus (1). Gunnis gave the sculptor's forename as 'Carl.'

Literary References: *Thieme Becker*, 499; *Gunnis* 1968, 199

Archival References: GPC

Funerary Monuments

1.	†1831	Charles Lucas	Filby, Norfolk		*Gunnis* 1968, 199; Pevsner, *Norfolk: N.E. & Norwich*, 1997, 469

HERRING, Richard fl 1661–65

Architectural Sculpture

1.	1661–1665	Sundry carving	s	Bishop's Palace, Bishop Auckland, Durham, chapel		Pevsner, *Durham*, 1983, 104

HERRMAN, Carl, of Dresden fl 1831?

Funerary Monuments

1.	?1831	Charles Lucas	Filby, Norfolk	S	*Gunnis* 1968, 199

HERTZ, B fl 1844

He was listed in Thompson's *Commercial Directory* for 1844 as a sculptor of 11 Great Marlborough Street, London.

HETHERINGTON, William, of Liverpool fl 1803–10

With his partner, **Timothy Grindrod**, he built the New Exchange at Liverpool in 1803.

Funerary Monuments

1.	?1808	Anne Walmley	Runcorn, Cheshire	S	*Gunnis* 1968, 199

HEWETSON, Christopher 1737–99

An Irish sculptor, who spent 33 years in Rome, he was considered the leading portrait sculptor in that city during the 1770s and early 1780s. He was the son of an officer, Lieutenant Christopher Hewetson, whose ancestry has been traced back to an Elizabethan clergyman, who moved to Ireland from Yorkshire. The family was well established among the Protestant gentry of County Kilkenny, where the sculptor was born, at Thomastown, in 1737. His father died in 1744 leaving a widow, Eleanor, with four young children. Hewetson received the best education that money could buy at Kilkenny College, where his uncle the Rev Dr Thomas Hewetson was the Master. Nothing more is known of him before the late 1750s, when he was working with or under the sculptor **John Nost III**, executing statues for the Rotunda Gardens, Dublin. With the possible exception of a bust, thought to be of Richard Rigby, who was Secretary to the Lord Lieutenant of Ireland between 1758 and 1765 (6), no record survives of work by Hewetson undertaken before he left his native land.

Richard Hayward recorded Hewetson's arrival in Rome in 1765 with Henry Benbridge, a young painter from Philadelphia. The sculptor took lodgings and a studio in the Strada Vittoria. In September 1779 he was living 'opposite Margherita's' (*Pembroke Papers*, 1734–1780, 273 quoted by *Ingamells* 1997, 494), and in 1790 in the Vicolo delle Orsoline. He appears to have left Rome only twice, to travel to Naples in 1766 and 1797. Hewetson forged valuable contacts with the principal English dealers and guides in Rome, among them James Byres and particularly

Thomas Jenkins, who supported him throughout his Rome career and introduced him to several patrons. Another influential ally was Don José Nicola d'Azara, the Spanish Ambassador to Rome (**19**). Hewetson's circle included some of the most talented artists of his day. He was on familiar terms with the neo-classical painters Anton Raffael Mengs, Gavin Hamilton, and the engraver, Johannes Pichler, and modelled or carved their portraits (**20, 22, 26, 34**). He is very likely also to have carved a head of Angelica Kauffman, now in Schwarzenberg church, Austria. His sculptor associates included **Nathaniel Marchant, Thomas Banks**, Johan Tobias Sergel from Sweden and the Italian, Giovanni Battista Capizzoldi. The Irish sculptor **Michael Foy**, another former associate of John Nost III, in due course followed Hewetson to Rome and was with him in 1776 when they met the English painter, Thomas Jones, at the Caffe degli Inglesi in the Piazza di Spagna (*Jones Memoirs* 1951, 53).

The sculptor's first two securely dated busts, carved in 1769, were of the antiquary, Charles Townley (**8**) and the collector, Sir Watkin Williams Wynn (**9**). On 7 January 1769 Sir Watkin 'Pd. Mr Hewson for a Bust in Clay of Sir Watkin and some casts from it'. The bust evidently pleased Wynn for five years later, in 1775, **Joseph Nollekens** would cast 'three busts of Sir Watkin from Mr. Hewson's mold' at a cost of £7 17s 6d (Nat Lib of Wales, Wynnstay MSS, Box 115/1, 7 quoted by *Potterton* 1974, 142–5). Another early client of consequence was the Earl Bishop of Derry, whose bust was carved *c*1770 (**10**).

Hewetson's great early coup, the work that spread his fame abroad, was a bust of Pope Clement XIV Gagnanelli, 1771 (**12**). This was perhaps initially a speculative exercise and it seems likely that Jenkins was involved, for the dealer was occupied in supplying antiquities at this time to the Pope for a planned extension to the Vatican galleries (now the Museo Pio-Clementino). The portrait is a confident, well-characterised representation and the sculptor rendered the rich embroidered fabric, buttoned shirt and twisted laces of the papal vestments with skill. Four signed versions in marble made their way into English collections, two of them as papal gifts. A fifth, dated 1773, was bought by Talbot, who himself sat that year to Hewetson (**14**). The collector was prepared to give £140 for his papal bust, £72 more than he paid for his own head.

Distinguished patrons from all quarters of Europe sat for the sculptor. His British clients included George III's brother, the Duke of Gloucester (**13**), whose head, modelled in clay, was mentioned in the *London Chronicle* for 30 April–2 May 1772. He is credited also with the Duchess of Gloucester's bust, now in the royal collection (RCIN 35403; *de Breffny* 1986, 53, repr). Hewetson was introduced to Baron Cawdor through Jenkins and carved his bust in marble (**27**). Models of a trio of visitors, Sir Thomas Gascoigne and Henry and Mary Swinburne were almost certainly prepared by Hewetson in 1778–9, and were cast in bronze by the Rome goldsmith, Luigi Valadier (LMG 7.123/68; *Friedman* 1976 (1), 16–23, repr; *Bowron and Rishel* 2000, 254). While they were in Rome, the Swinburnes' young daughter, Martha, died: Hewetson was brought in to carve her monument, a delicate profile relief in a frame of oak leaves, erected in the English College (**1**).

The Spanish ambassador, d'Azara, sat for Hewetson in 1779, when his bust was modelled 'under the direction' of Anton Rafael Mengs (**19**). Mengs's reputation as an arbiter of aesthetic standards resulted from his close association with Johann Joachim Winckelmann (†1768), the great advocate of classical Greek sculpture and a central figure in the Greek Revival. Hewetson arrived in Rome three years before Winckelmann's death. Mengs died in 1779 and Azaro placed his bronze bust by Hewetson, cast from a model again executed under Mengs's supervision, in the Pantheon, beside the tomb of Raphael. It was replaced in 1783 with a marble bust, also by Hewetson (**20, 22**).

The sculptor was responsible for two major church monuments. In 1771 he received a commission from Dublin for a memorial to a former Provost of Trinity College, Richard Baldwin, to be erected in the 'theatre' of his university college (**3**). This was Hewetson's most ambitious work and the first neoclassical ensemble ever seen in Ireland, a graceful tableau of three figures supported by a sarcophagus and set against a pyramidal background. According to the sculptor, the group represented 'Dr Baldwin . . . near his end . . . his will dropping from his hand [attended by] an angel [and] a muse, the simbol of science' (*Hodgkinson* 1952–4, 56). The pyramid of red granite was a source of pride to the sculptor, who claimed that he was the first to use the material in that context. The monument took 12 years to complete: in February 1781 James Irvine, a Scottish painter and dealer in Rome, wrote that the work was in progress and 'very clever' (BM Add MS. 36493). It was exhibited in Rome in July 1783 and in the following month an application was made to export the work. It was finally erected in Trinity College in 1784. Hewetson was apparently paid £1,000.

Following the death of Cardinal Giambattista Rezzonico (a nephew of Clement XIII), his brothers commissioned a monument from Hewetson (**2**). This has a portrait bust flanked by seated boys, one rejoicing and the other grieving, raised on an austere table-like sarcophagus. The monument had a mixed reception. A contemporary account dwelt on the verisimilitude and nobility of the bust and the lifelike character of the children (*Memorie per le Belle Arti: Hodgkinson* 1952–4, 47). An English visitor, Henry Quin, dismissed it as 'not a great work, but two Cupids and a Bust' (*Quin Journal*, MS 2226/1, Trinity College, Dublin, 14 January 1786; *Ingamells* 1997, 494). A similar composition, but minus the boys, was used for another monument in preparation at this time, commemorating Duke Frederick August von Oldenburg (**4**).

Quin noted that Hewetson was still the best sculptor in Rome in 1784. Important commissions continued to come to the studio, including a portrait of the Grand Duchess Maria Fedorovna, future Tsarina of Russia (**24**) and a severe herm bust of Gavin Hamilton (**26**). But his supremacy was under challenge from **Antonio Canova**, who had arrived in Rome in 1779 and at once became a serious rival. Canova noted his appreciation of Hewetson's 'multi buoni ritratti' in his diary on 12 June 1780 (Canova's Diary, fol 71v, transcribed in *Honour* ed, 1994, 141). Both sculptors competed in 1787 and again in 1790, for contracts to carve monuments for Pope Clement XIV and Clement XIII, and each time Canova won. Accounts of Hewetson's magnanimity in defeat reveals a remarkably generous spirit. While other sculptors, particularly the Romans, were jealous of Canova's success, Hewetson not only praised his work, which he saw in the studio, but also gave a dinner in Canova's honour in May 1787, attended by many fellow artists.

In 1787 Hewetson agreed to carve a colossal marble bust of the philosopher Leibniz for the Leibniz Temple in Waterlooplatz, Hanover, financed by public subscription (**32**). News of its completion was reported in a letter to the

Dublin Chronicle, dated 7 July 1788 and published 21–23 April 1789. The correspondent claimed that the newly completed bust surpassed any comparable work executed over the last few years. The reflective, wrinkled face and severe herm-like truncation of the upper torso apparently suggested 'the bust of a philosopher immersed in the subtility of metaphysics'. Hewetson's reputation was however waning. In 1789 the Earl Bishop of Derry, whose portrait head had been an early commission (**10**), wrote to his daughter in Rome asking whether Hewetson was currently employed and on what. Soon after, he commissioned a statue of 'Mr Pitt'; it is unclear whether this was Lord Chatham, Pitt the Younger or even George Pitt of Stratfield Saye, Hants, who had been in Italy in 1771 together with Edward Salter, whose bust is also credited to Hewetson (*Balderston* 2000, 193, repr). It was probably not completed, perhaps because of the imminence of a French invasion.

In May 1791 Hewetson wrote to George Cumberland that patrons had recently neglected him. But though commissions were drying up he clearly had an active social life and was enchanted that year by Emma Hart (the future Lady Hamilton) performing her 'attitudes'. He was still able to excite envy amongst rival sculptors. In 1794 **John Deare** was referring to Hewetson and Jenkins when he maintained that antiquaries were in league with artists in the city to the exclusion of outsiders.

By 1796 the invasion of Rome by Napoleon's armies was becoming inevitable and tourists and settlers were leaving the city. Hewetson did not leave Italy, but in June 1797, Robert Fagan, the Irish painter-dealer, reported that he had gone to Naples to carve busts of Sir William and Lady Hamilton, which were perhaps not completed, since there is no further record of them (**37, 38**). He was expected back in Rome by the end of 1797.

French troops finally arrived in 1798 and Jenkins fled to England, but died just after arriving at Great Yarmouth. He left Hewetson a ring in memory of their friendship. Deare died in Rome in August and 'Mr Christopher. Sculptor' was one of the few friends invited to his funeral (*Smith* II, 1828, 327). Hewetson himself died soon after, whether of age or anxiety in difficult times is not clear, and he was buried near a famous classical landmark, the tomb of Caius Sestius. His will is in the Archivo Capitoline in the Vallineliana at Rome.

The list of Hewetson's commissions is no doubt incomplete since his busts were dispatched all over Europe. Malcolm Baker has noted the variety of conventions and formats which he employed in response to the character, professional and social position of his subjects and the changing fashions of the time (*Bowron and Rishel* 2000, 254–5). The papal portraits are in the baroque tradition, whereas that of Gavin Hamilton, the protagonist of neoclassicism, conforms strictly to Antique precedent, and the heads of Lord Cawdor, the marble version of Mengs and the Pichler are archaeological in character. The bronze heads of Mengs and Azara, which have short, but not cropped hair and bare necklines, read as romantic images and constitute a relatively new type of portrait. Common to all is a marked care in the realisation of the hair and features and these qualities no doubt brought him many patrons, directed the studio by an influential group of supporters.

IR

Literary References: *Jones Memoirs* 1951, 53; *Hodgkinson* XXXIV, 1952–1954, 42–54; *Neoclassicism* 1972, 244–5; *Ramallo* 1973, 181–7; *Potterton* 1974, 242–5; *Friedman* 1976 (1), 17–23; *Stainton* 1983, 13; *de Breffny* 1986, 52–75, *Deuter* 1989, 161–93; *Ingamells* 1997, 494–5, 543–4; *Bowron and Rishel* 2000, 254–5; *Bilbey* 2002, 90–92; *ODNB* (Myrone)

Portraits of the Sculptor: Henry Bunbury [or Henry Benbridge?], pencil drawing, inscribed 'Christopher Hewetson, Sculptor /HB Rome del. 1769', formerly private coll, Bury St Edmunds'; Stefano Tofanelli, *Christopher Hewetson, Sculptor, with his bust of Gawen Hamilton*, nd, oil on canvas, Wallraf-Richartz Museum, Cologne (*de Breffny* 1986, 52)

Funerary Monuments

1.	†1779	Martha Swinburne, a child of nine		Venerable English College, Rome	S	*Friedman* 1976 (1), 20; *de Breffny* 1986, 53, cat 28 (repr)
2.	1783–1784	Cardinal Giovanni Battista Rezzonico (†1783)		S Nicola in Carcere, Rome	S	*Hodgkinson* 1952–54, 46–48 (repr); *de Breffny* 1986, 53, cat 22 (repr); *Ingamells* 1997, 494
3.	1771–1784	Provost Richard Baldwin (†1758) Payment(s): £1,000 + £416 transport costs		Trinity College, Dublin, examination hall		*Hodgkinson* 1952–54, 45–6 (repr); *de Breffny* 1986, 53, cat 2 (repr)
4.	1792–1793	Duke Frederick August von Oldenburg (co-sculptor: Angelo Uggeri and Luigi Antonio Acquisti)		St Lambert, Oldenburg, Germany		*Deuter* 1989, 161–93 (repr)
5.	nd	Count Anton Günther von Oldenburg		St Lambert, Oldenburg, Germany	S	*Deuter* 1989, 161–93 (repr)

Busts

6.	?1758–1765	Richard Rigby (?), later Master of the Rolls for Ireland	m	Provost's house, Trinity College, Dublin	S	*McParland* 1976, 1106–9; *de Breffny* 1986, 52, cat 23 (repr)
7.	?1767–1769	Catharine, Viscountess Sudley (†1770)	m	[coll 2nd Earl of Arran]; private coll	S	*de Breffny* 1986, cat 26 (repr)
8.	1769	Charles Townley	m	[coll Townley family, Lancs]; BM MLA 1995, 4-2, 1	SD	*de Breffny* 1986, 53, cat 31; *Dawson* 1999, 218–20 (repr)
9.	1769	Sir Watkin Williams Wynn Bt Payment(s): 20 sequeens 410 paoli (casts included)	tc	[coll Watkin Williams Wynn, Wynnstay]; NGI 8063 Other versions: casts provided with the clay model	SD	*Potterton* 1974 (2), 142, 143 (repr); *de Breffny* 1986, 53, cat 33 (repr)
10.	c1770	Frederick Augustus Hervey, Bishop of Derry and 4th Earl of Bristol	m	NPG, London 3895	S	*de Breffny* 1986, cat 13 (repr)
11.	1771	John Henderson of Fordell (previously thought to be Prince Hoare)	tc	RABASF, Madrid, E-204	SD	*Ramallo* 1973, 185; *Brea* 1994, 256–7 (repr); *Sanchez-Jauregui* 2001, 420–5; *Westmorland* 2003, 334–36, cat 70 (repr)

12.	1771	Pope Clement XIV Ganganelli	m	Beningbrough Hall, N R Yorks Other versions: Museo Civico, Bassano, inv 98, plaster, nd Gorhambury, Herts, marble, SD, 1772 Ammerdown Park, Somerset, marble, SD 1772 SNG, Edinburgh VAM A.22-1948, marble, ex coll Thomas Mansel Talbot, SD 1776 YCBA, B 1977.14.14, nd	D	*Hodgkinson* 1952–4, 43 n6; *Whinney* 1971, 109–10; *Treasure Houses* 1975, 71–9; *Bowron and Rishel* 2000, 255 (repr)
13.	1772	William Henry, 1st Duke of Gloucester Model(s): clay mentioned in the *London Chronicle*, 30 April–2 May 1772	m	Windsor Castle, RCIN. 316616	SD	*Hodgkinson* 1952–4, 43 (repr); *de Breffny* 1986, 53, cat 8 (repr)
14.	1773	Thomas Mansel Talbot	m	[Margam Castle, Glamorgan]; VAM, A.41-1953 Other versions: Penrice, Glamorgan	S	*de Breffny* 1986, 53, cat 29a (repr); *Bowron and Rishel* 2000, 254
15.	1776	Maria Maddalena Morelli	m	[Arcadian Academy, Rome]; Palazzo Braschi, Rome	SD	*de Breffny* 1986, cat 19 (repr)
16.	1776	Prince Luigi Gonzaga	m	[Arcadian Academy, Rome]; Palazzo Braschi, Rome	SD	*Hodgkinson* 1952–4, 45; *de Breffny* 1986, cat 9 (repr)
17.	1777	Unidentified subject	tc	RABASF, Madrid (duplicated in plaster)	SD	*Ramallo* 1973, 183
18.	1777–1778	Francis Basset, later Ist Baron Dunstanville, two	tc	RABASF, Madrid E-474 Other versions: RABASF, plaster		*Brea* 1994, 362 (repr); *Sanchez-Jauregui* 2001, 420–5 (repr); *Westmorland* 2003, 137 (repr), 301–3, cat 52
19.	1778	José Nicolas d'Azara, Marques de Nibiano	b	Bib Mazarine, Paris, on loan from Azara family Other versions: several in bronze and plaster	SD	*Hodgkinson* 1952–54, 44 (repr) *Ramallo* 1973, 186–7
20.	1778–1779	Anton Rafael Mengs	b	[Pantheon, Rome, until 1782]; Bib Mazarine, Paris, inv 1850 Other versions: marble, 1783, Pantheon, Rome RABASF, plaster	SD	*de Breffny* 1986, 53, cat 18a (repr); *Brea* 1994, 257–8; *Sanchez-Jauregui* 2001, 420–5; *Westmorland* 2003, 358–60, cat 87 (repr)
21.	c1782	Franiszek Saleby Potocki, Palatine of Kiev		Lancut Castle, Poland		*Barnes* 1996, 166–9
22.	1783	Anton Rafael Mengs	m	[Pantheon, Rome]; Protomoteca Capitolina, Rome, 1820	SD	*de Breffny* 1986, 53, cat 18b (repr); *Ingamells* 1997, 494
23.	1782–1783	Frau von Kniphausen	m	[Schloss Tamsel, near Cüstrin, Brandenburg, until 1945]; untraced Other versions: private coll, Berlin, bronze copy by F Righetti, 1788, private coll, plaster		*de Breffny* 1986, cat 16a, b; *Deuter* 1989, 170; C Lib (repr)
24.	1783	Grand Duchess Maria Fyodorovna, later Tsarina of Russia	m	[Palace of Gatchina, 1914]; untraced	SD	*de Breffny* 1986, 53, cat 24 (repr)
25.	1782–1783	Herr von Kniphausen	m	[Schloss Tamsel, near Cüstrin, Brandenburg, until 1945]; untraced Other versions: private coll, Berlin, bronze	SD	*de Breffny* 1986, cat 15; *Deuter* 1989, 170; C Lib (repr)
26.	1784	Gavin Hamilton	m	[coll Mr Greville]; Hunterian Art Gall, Glasgow Univ	SD	*Graves* IV, 1905–6, 91; *de Breffny* 1986, cat 10 (repr); *Whinney* 1988, 318 (repr)
27.	c1784	John Campbell, 1st Baron Cawdor FRS	m	[Cawdor Castle, Nairn]; NGS	S	*de Breffny* 1986, cat 3 (repr); *Bowron and Rishel* 2000, 254
28.	1784	Thomas Giffard	m	[coll Giffard family]; Chillington Hall, Wolverhampton, Staffs	SD	*de Breffny* 1986, cat 7 (repr); *Ingamells* 1997, 400
29.	c1789	Andrew Stuart of Craigthorn and Castlemilk	m	[coll Andrew Stuart]; Signet Library, Edinburgh	S	*de Breffny* 1986, cat 25 (repr); *Bouron and Rishel* 2000, 254
30.	1789	Thomas Westfaling, on a monument with a relief by William Theed I	m	St Mary, Ross-on-Wye, Herefs Other versions: Louvre, Paris, marble		*Esdaile* 1947 (3), 135; *de Breffny* 1986, cat 32; C Lib (repr)
31.	1790	A nobleman		[Exhib RA, London, 520]; Cyril Humphris, 1995		*Graves* IV, 1905–6, 91; *de Breffny* 1986, cat 36; C Lib (repr)
32.	1789–1790	Gottfried Wilhelm Leibniz	m	[Waterlooplatz, Hanover, Leibniz Temple]; Leibniz Haus, Hanover (copied in plaster)	S	*Hodgkinson* 1952–54, 50 (repr); *de Breffny* 1986, 53, cat 17a (repr)
33.	1786–1790	Lady Caroline Crichton	m	Private coll, Belfast	S	*de Breffny* 1986, cat 5 (repr)
34.	†1791	Johannes Pichler	m	[Pantheon, Rome, 1797]; Protomoteca Capitolina, Rome, 1820	S	*de Breffny* 1986, cat 20 (repr)
35.	1794	Augustus Frederick, Duke of Sussex		Untraced		*Esdaile* 1947 II (3), 135; *de Breffny* 1986, cat 27
36.	c1796	'Mr Pitt', colossal	m	Untraced		*Esdaile* 1947 (3), 135; *Ingamells* 1997, 495
37.	c1797	Lady Hamilton		Untraced		*de Breffny* 1986, cat 12
38.	c1797	Sir William Hamilton, FRS, FSA		Untraced		*de Breffny* 1986, cat 11
39.	1800	'Anonimo' (co-sculptor: Christopher Prosperi)		Private coll, a 'Noble Lord', England	SD	*de Breffny* 1986, cat 37

40.	1800	Sir John Throckmorton, 5th Bt, two clay models		[coll Throckmorton family]; Coughton Court, Alcester, Warks Other versions: marble from Hewetson's model by Christopher Prosperi, 1800; untraced	SD	*de Breffny* 1986, cat 30a and b (repr)
41.	nd	Unidentified gentleman	m	(coll Mrs R M Blacknell, Surrey)	S	*de Breffny* 1986, cat 35 (repr)
42.	nd	Unidentified gentleman, perhaps Charles, 11th Duke of Norfolk	m	[Holme Lacy, Herefs]; Richard Herner, London	S	*de Breffny* 1986, cat 34 (repr)
43.	nd	Unidentified man	m	Christie 5 Dec 95: private coll	S	*de Breffny* 1986, cat 35
44.	nd	Unidentified man, previously thought to be John Scudamore the younger		Musée du Louvre, Paris		*Louvre* 1988, 101–4, no 28; C Lib (repr)

HEWETT, of Camberwell fl 1820?

He signs a 'pretty wall-tablet in coloured marbles' (2) and a sarcophagus (1) (*Gunnis* 1968, 199).

Funerary Monuments						
1.	?1820	M Bentley McLeod		Brixton Parish Church, London, churchyard	S	*Gunnis* 1968, 199
2.	?1820	Maria Hammond		Brixton Parish Church, London	S	*Gunnis* 1968, 199

HEWITT, of Shrewsbury fl 1853

He is known only for a stele-form tablet in Yorkshire signed 'HEWITT / SALOP.'

Funerary Monuments						
1.	†1853	Francis Peacock		Easingwold, NR Yorks	S	

HEWITT & WORTH, of Retford fl 1806

Funerary Monuments						
1.	†1806	John and Alice (†1795) Kippax	m	St Swithun, East Retford, Notts	S	

HEWLETT, D fl 1847–60

He exhibited at the Royal Academy and the Society of British Artists. His first and last given address, presumably a family home, was 4 Gloucester Terrace, Vauxhall Road, Pimlico.

Statues						
1.	1854	Penelope	p	[Exhib Soc of BA, London, 742]; untraced		*Johnson* 1975, 227
Busts						
2.	1847	Captain M F F Berkeley RN		[Exhib RA, London, 1416]; untraced		*Graves* IV, 1905–6, 92
3.	1853	Lieutenant-General Sir Charles James Napier		[Exhib Soc of BA, London, 749]; untraced		*Johnson* 1975, 227
4.	1854	Arthur, 1st Duke of Wellington	m	[Exhib Soc of BA, London, 741]; untraced		*Johnson* 1975, 227
5.	1854	Queen Victoria		[Exhib Soc of BA, London, 743]; untraced		*Johnson* 1975, 227
6.	1854	Sir Robert Peel		[Exhib Soc of BA, London, 744]; untraced		*Johnson* 1975, 227
7.	1860	W Reeve		[Exhib Soc of BA, London, 865]; untraced		*Johnson* 1975, 227
Reliefs						
8.	1856	Thomas Babington, Baron Macaulay, medallion		[Exhib RA, London, 1276]; untraced		*Graves* IV, 1905–6, 92
Miscellaneous						
9.	1850	A time of peace		[Exhib Soc of BA, London, 731]; untraced		*Johnson* 1975, 227
10.	1850	Hon Admiral Berkeley MP		[Exhib Soc of BA, London, 730]; untraced		*Johnson* 1975, 227
11.	1851	Religious hope		[Exhib RA, London, 1264]; untraced		*Graves* IV, 1905–6, 92

HEWLETT, Daniel, of Gloucester fl 1808–38?

Presumably the 'Hewlett of Frampton' who signs the monument to Thomas Miles (3), he also signs two other tablets in Gloucestershire villages (1, 2).

Funerary Monuments						
1.	†1808	William Roberts		Brockworth, Glos	S	Pevsner, *Glos: Vale & Forest of Dean*, 1976, 115
2.	†1829	Francis Walker		Staunton, Glos	S	Pevsner, *Glos: Vale & Forest of Dean*, 1976, 347
3.	†1838	Thomas Miles		Leonard Stanley, Glos	S	Pevsner, *Glos: Cotswolds*, 1999, 445

HEWS, T fl 1785–87

'T Hews' signs a large tablet, with a relief of a female with urn and angels, which Pevsner describes as 'halfway between Palladian strictness and sentimentality' (1). It is presumably the same 'Hews' who signs a near-contemporary 'circular wall-tablet of good workmanship' to Mary Greetham (2).

Funerary Monuments						
1.	†1785	William Middlefield		Hascombe, Surrey	S	*Gunnis* 1968, 387; Pevsner, *Surrey*, 1971, 303
2.	?1787	Mary Greetham		Petersfield, Hants	S	*Gunnis* 1968, 199

HIBBINS FAMILY

William Hibbins I fl 1686
William Hibbins II fl 1755
Thomas Hibbins I fl 1754
Thomas Hibbins II fl *c*1834–5
Robert Hibbins fl *c*1852

The large Hibbins family, of Ketton in Rutland, worked as masons and stone-carvers for over 200 years. The first family member traced by Gunnis was **William Hibbins I**, who became a freeman of Stamford in 1686. **William II** was paid for work at the Town Hall in 1755 (Chamberlain's Accts) and was the father of **Thomas Hibbins I**, who became a freeman of Stamford by patrimony in 1754.

Thomas I signs a tablet at Langtoft, Lincs (**1**). Thomas II signs tablets in Ketton Church (**2**). William Hibbins II, who died young, is commemorated in Ketton churchyard by a tombstone decorated with the tools of the mason's craft. The only known work by **Robert Hibbins** is a sarcophagus-shaped white tablet set in a black frame with a carved family crest and ribbon above (**3**). His own gravestone is in the churchyard at Ketton. A member of this family was still working as a mason in the early 20th century.

Literary References: *Gunnis* 1968, 199

Funerary Monuments

1.	?1755	Mrs Handley (by Thomas Hibbins I)	Langtoft, Lincs	S	*Gunnis* 1968, 199
2.	1834–1835	Unidentified subjects, tablets (by Thomas Hibbins II)	Ketton, Rutland	S	*Gunnis* 1968, 199
3.	†1852	Cotton (†1835), Frances and Frances (†1877) Thompson (by Robert Hibbins)	Ketton, Rutland	S	

HICKEY, John 1751–95

Hickey was born in Dublin, the fourth son of Noah Hickey, a confectioner in Capel Street, and the brother of the painter, Thomas Hickey. He entered the Royal Dublin Society Schools in 1764, where he gained several prizes before he left to become a pupil of **Richard Cranfield**. Hickey may have worked for a cabinetmaker for he exhibited a group of dead game intended for a girandole in 1768 at the Society of Artists in William Street (**35**).

In 1772 he went to England, where on 20 January he joined the Royal Academy Schools, giving his date of birth as 7 November 1751 (not 1756, as stated in *Strickland*). In 1777 he exhibited a tablet for a chimneypiece at the Royal Academy from 34 Gerrard Street, Soho (**26**), and in 1778 won the Academy's gold medal for his relief of *The slaughter of the innocents* (**33**).

Hickey was living at Union Street, New Palace Yard in 1780 and was working on church monuments: that year and in 1781 he exhibited models for monuments at the Royal Academy (**4, 5**). The Elizabeth Hawkins, 1782, which Gunnis considered his finest, is a sophisticated wall monument with four stern neoclassical busts, a weeping cherub and a full-sized personification of *Faith*, leaning against a portrait medallion of the deceased (**6**). It incorporates a wealth of decorative detail, including an ornate rococo sarcophagus and branches and is carved in polychrome marbles.

In 1782 it was proposed to erect a monument in Dublin to the politician, Henry Grattan, and Hickey applied for the commission. He was supported by Edmund Burke, who wrote from Whitehall to Lord Charlemont: 'it will be a pleasure to you to know that at this time a young man of Ireland is here, who I really think, as far as my judgment goes, is fully equal to our best statuaries both in taste and execution. If you employ him, you will encourage the rising arts in the decoration of the rising virtue of Ireland. . . . The young man's name who wishes to be employed is Hickey' (HMC 1891, 1, 61). Though the project fell through and the monument was never erected, Burke continued to do all in his power for his fellow-countryman. He sat to Hickey for two portrait-busts (**19, 20**). One, with rounded drapery, was bought by Lord Fitzwilliam and engraved by William Ward. The other, in stern herm form, is in the British Museum.

Another of Hickey's patrons was Lord Loughborough, whose bust was carved in 1785 (**21**). Loughborough, too, seems to have been anxious to help Hickey, for in the same year he recommended the sculptor to Lord Berwick as a carver of chimney-pieces, adding in his letter that he had 'employed Hickey on work of that nature with complete satisfaction'. Here again Hickey was unfortunate, for Lord Berwick replied that he had already engaged another artist (Berwick Archives). Hickey did, however, execute a number of other chimneypieces, one at least under Sir John Soane (**30**).

In 1785 or 1786 he moved from Poland Street to lodgings at 128 Oxford Street. In 1786 he was appointed Sculptor to the Prince of Wales, and two years later he provided a figure for a Carlton House clock designed by Jutin Vulliamy (**37**). Two important commissions for Irish monuments came around this time: in 1787 *Freeman's Journal* reported the impending arrival of a monument to the Chief Justice of Ireland, Henry Singleton, at Drogheda (**12**), and the completion of the monument to David Latouche, a member of the Huguenot banking family (**15**). The former has a portrait bust and a large relief representing *Justice*, whilst the latter is an ambitious work with a standing figure of Latouche above a sarcophagus, at the foot of which are mourning figures of his three sons, David, John and Peter. The work is dramatically top-lit. *Freeman's Journal* said of the two monuments that 'Fame speaks loudly of both, but the latter more especially' and congratulated Ireland for employing one of her sons to perpetuate the memory of its deceased (July 31–August 2, quoted in *Potterton* 1975, 49). These successes failed to bring Hickey recognition among his fellow artists in London and in November 1794 he stood unsuccessfully for election as an Associate Royal Academician.

Strickland writes that Hickey was chosen by Irish Roman Catholics in 1794 to execute a statue of King George III for Dublin. He went over to the city to receive instruction from the committee but the project appears to have aborted. At this time Hickey also received one of the most notable commissions of the day, the monument to David Garrick for Westminster Abbey. The work was commissioned by Albany Wallis, a friend of Garrick, who chose Hickey on the recommendation of Edmund Burke. Burke described Hickey as 'one well qualified' who 'would do it on reasonable terms' (*Farington* II, 292), and the commission was thought to be worth £600.

Hickey was not able to execute the commission for he died on 13 January 1795 at his lodgings in Oxford Street. Burke wrote to Albany Wallis two days later that 'Death is in close pursuit of us . . . if poor Hickey had been spared to us, I should not have preferred any sculptor living to him [for the Garrick monument]' (quoted in *Strickland* 1, 1913, 482). Burke felt the only proper replacement for the commission was **Thomas Banks**, although **J C F Rossi** was also keen to take on the work. In the event it went to **Henry Webber**, who was a close associate of the deceased sculptor, and attended his funeral, held on 19 January. At the service an 'Ode on a young sculptor' penned by the architect William Porden was sung. The *Hibernian Magazine* commented that year that Hickey's death 'is a public loss, as he was an ingenious, deserving young man and an excellent artist' (quoted in *Potterton* 1975, 49).

Farington noted that Hickey died 'after an illness of 3–4 days only owing to having lain in a damp bed' (II 292), though the satirist Pasquin commented that Hickey died because 'intemperance abolished his powers and eclipsed his glory' (quoted in *Potterton* 1975, 49). He certainly died in debt. His will, dictated in a state of 'weakness and suffering' only a day before his death, asked that bequests should be made from the profits of a masque which he had written and sent to the managers of Covent Garden. Henry Webber and Thomas Hickey were appointed as executors, though Webber asked to be excused the responsibility. In the event Hickey's estate was insufficiently extensive to pay off the sculptor's debts, whilst the masque was rejected by the Covent Garden managers as 'not fit for representation'.

MGS

Literary References: *Farington*, I, 220, 225, 249; II, 292, 294; *Graves* IV, 1905–6, 93; *Strickland* I, 1913, 480–2; *Hutchison* 1960–62, 137; *Crookshank* 1966, 306, 308; *Gunnis* 1968, 199–200; *Potterton* 1975, 49; *Whinney* 1988, 316

Archival References: GPC

Will: PROB 11/1272/218–9

Funerary Monuments

1.	†1775	William Dowdeswell		Bushley, Worcs	S	*Gunnis* 1968, 200; Pevsner, *Worcs*, 1968, 114
2.	†1778	Lord Archer		Tamworth-in-Arden, Warks	S	*Gunnis* 1968, 200; Pevsner, *Warks*, 1966, 431
3.	1778	Samuel Foster (†1776)		St Wulfram, Grantham, Lincs	S	*Gunnis* 1968, 200; Pevsner, *Lincs*, 1989, 320
4.	1780	'Model of a monumental figure'		[Exhib RA, London, 429]; untraced		*Graves* IV, 1905–6, 94
5.	1781	'Model of a monument executing in marble'		[Exhib RA, London, 543]; unidentified		*Graves* IV, 1905–6, 94
6.	1782	Elizabeth Hawkins (†1780)		St Helen, Abingdon, Berks	S	*Gunnis* 1968, 200; Pevsner, *Berks*, 1988, 53; *Whinney* 1988, 316–7 (repr)
7.	†1782	Mary Child		St Nicholas, Abingdon, Berks	S	*Gunnis* 1968, 200
8.	†1784	General William Haviland		Penn, Bucks	S	*Gunnis* 1968, 200
9.	†1786	John Spencer		Cawthorne, W R Yorks	S	*Gunnis* 1968, 200
10.	†1787	John Story		Leyton, Essex	S	Pevsner, *Essex*, 1965, 268; *Gunnis* 1968, 200
11.	†1787	Sir Richard Hoare		St Mary, Barnes, London	S	*Gunnis* 1968, 200; Pevsner, *London: S.*, 1983, 468
12.	1788	Chief Justice Henry Singleton (†1787)		Drogheda, Ireland	SD	*Potterton* 1975, 49
13.	†1789	Joseph Baker		Chichester Cathedral, Sussex	S	Pevsner, *Sussex*, 1965, 153; *Gunnis* 1968, 200
14.	1790	Amy Burrell		St George, Beckenham, London	S	*Gunnis* 1968, 200; Pevsner, *London: S*, 1983, 159
15.	1787–1790	David Latouche (†1785)	m	Delgany, Co Wicklow	SD	*Gunnis* 1961, 9–1 (repr); *Crookshank* 1966, 306 (repr); *Potterton* 1975, 49

Statues

16.	1785	A tragic figure of Mrs Siddons in the character of Cassandra Model(s): Exhib RA, London, 637		[for Earl Fitzwilliam]; untraced Other versions: sold Christie 15 March 1798, marble, 'small' sold Christie, 15 July 1986, lot 92		*Graves* IV, 1905–6, 94; *Gunnis* 1968, 200; *Dawson* 1999, 49
17.	1789	Thalia, Tragic Muse Model(s): Exhib RA, London, 1787, 666		[Exhib RA, London, 615]; untraced		*Graves* IV, 1905–6, 94

Busts

18.	1782	A nobleman		[Exhib RA, London, 502]; untraced		*Graves* IV, 1905–6, 94
19.	c1785	Edmund Burke	m	[Wentworth Woodhouse, W R Yorks, mausoleum]; private coll (perhaps destroyed)		*Graves* IV, 1905–6, 94; *Strickland* 1, 1913, 482; *Gunnis* 1968, 200; *Dawson* 1999, 48)
20.	c1785	Edmund Burke	m	BM		*Graves* IV, 1905–6, 94; *Strickland* 1, 1913, 482; *Gunnis* 1968, 200; *Dawson* 1999, 48 (repr)
21.	1785	Lord Loughborough		[Exhib RA, London, 636]; untraced		*Graves* IV, 1905–6, 94
22.	1786	Mrs Siddons in the character of Cassandra		[Exhib RA, London, 616]; untraced		*Graves* IV, 1905–6, 94
23.	1789	Unidentified gentleman		[Exhib RA, London, 570]; untraced		*Graves* IV, 1905–6, 94
24.	1792	George Thicknesse	m	[Exhib RA, London, 722]; private coll		*Graves* IV, 1905–6, 94; *Gunnis* 1968, 200
25.	1794	Mrs Latouche		[Exhib RA, London, 600]; untraced		*Graves* IV, 1905–6, 94

Chimneypieces

26.	1777	Foliate tablet for a chimneypiece	m	[Exhib RA, London, 166]; untraced		*Graves* IV, 1905–6, 93
27.	1778	Description unavailable Payment(s): £45		Cannon Hall, Barnsley, W R Yorks		*Stirling* 1911, 2, 113
28.	1783	Description unavailable Payment(s): £54		[for Mr Branthwayt of Norfolk]; untraced		*Gunnis* 1968, 200
29.	pre-1785	Description unavailable		[for Lord Loughborough]; untraced		*Gunnis* 1968, 200
30.	1791	Black and veined marble	m	[Messrs Ransome and Morland of Pall Mall, London]; untraced		Soane bill book 3, fols 56–57; *Gunnis* 1968, 200

Reliefs

31.	1770	Unidentified subject	wd	[Exhib Society of Artists, Dublin]; untraced		*Strickland* 1, 1913, 480
32.	1777	'A monumental figure,' bas-relief	m	[Exhib RA, London, 165]; untraced		*Graves* IV, 1905–6, 93

33.	1778	The slaughter of the Innocents		[RA Gold Medal Sold Christie 15.03.1798]; untraced	*Strickland* 1, 1913, 482; *Gunnis* 1968, 199
34.	1781	Ariadne, bas-relief	m	[Exhib RA, London, 487]; untraced	*Graves* IV, 1905–6, 94
Miscellaneous					
35.	1768	'Group of dead game designed for a Girandole'		[Exhib Society of Artists, Dublin]; untraced	*Strickland* 1, 1913, 480
36.	1787	'Monumental figure of Fame'		[Exhib RA, London, 497]; untraced	*Graves* IV, 1905–6, 94
37.	1788	Figures of Time and Atlas for a clock Payment(s): £105 Model(s): Time, exhib RA, London, 1788, 598	p	[Carlton House, London, grand staircase]; untraced	*Carlton House* 1991–2, 226

HICKS, John, of Newbury 1726–68

Possibly a son of **Jonathan Hicks**, he is buried at Speen, Berks.

Literary References: *Gunnis* 1968, 200

Funerary Monuments					
1.	?1750	Rev Joseph Wells	Hungerford, Berks	S	*Gunnis* 1968, 200
2.	?1765	Sainsbury family	Market Lavington, Wilts	S	*Gunnis* 1968, 200
3.	?1768	Robert Hayward	Market Lavington, Wilts	S	*Gunnis* 1968, 200

HICKS, Jonathan *c*1685–1742

He was employed by Henry, Viscount Bolingbroke in 1712–13, who paid him £63 in all for his work (**2, 3**). Like **John Hicks of Newbury**, he is buried at Speen Church, Berks, where his monument in the chancel describes him as 'Freemason and carver.' He is commemorated with his wife, the daughter of John Boddington of Leics, who died in 1713. This monument, a very fine cartouche tablet with garlands, putti, a skull and an hour-glass, is possibly his own work.

Literary References: *Dormer* 1934, 148–9; Pevsner, *Berks*, 1966, 224; *Gunnis* 1968, 200

Funerary Monuments						
1.	nd	John Smith		Shalbourne, Wilts	S	
Chimneypieces						
2.	1712–1713	Description unavailable	m	[Bucklesbury House, Berks]; untraced		Berks CRO, D/E.H.7 in GPC
Miscellaneous						
3.	1712–1713	'New Flower Pott' Payment(s): £4	s	[Bucklesbury House, Berks]; untraced		Berks CRO, D/E.H.7 in GPC

HICKS, of Portsea fl 1823–59?

He is probably the John Hicks who lived at various addresses in Portsmouth between 1823 and 1859.

Archival References: RG/JP, 4, 689v

Funerary Monuments				
1.	†1828	Mrs S Cookson	Colemore, Hants	RG/JP, 4, 689v.

HIGGINS, William fl 1775

Miscellaneous				
1.	1775	An academy figure or a bas-relief	[RA, London, silver medal]; untraced	RA Premium list

HIGH & CRABTREE fl 1834

They advertised in the *Norwich Mercury* of 18 October 1834 as stone and marble masons of St George's Colegate, Middle Street. They supplied marble chimneypieces, wall pieces, tombs and headstones: 'Gentlemen will be waited on if required, with Designs made by an eminent Architect, for Chimney Pieces, Tombs, Monuments. . .' (Inf. David Cubitt)

HILL, Amelia Robertson Paton 1820–1904

She was born in Dunfermline, Fife to Joseph Neil Paton, a damask designer, and Catherine, née McDiarmid, a folklorist. Although one of a family of artists, Hill claimed to have received no formal art training. Instead, she learned the rudiments of drawing by watching her father and brother, Noel. Her initial efforts at sculpture were made with domestic implements (a crochet hook and a knife) until a sympathetic family friend equipped her with proper modelling tools. Portrait medallions of herself (**1**), Noel Paton and D O Hill are her earliest recorded works (**2, 3**). In 1860 she moved to Edinburgh, making her professional debut at the Royal Glasgow Institute of the Fine Arts in 1861. Her marriage the following year to D O Hill, secretary of the RSA, resulted in a mutually beneficial artistic alliance. She exhibited over 60 portraits and imaginative works at the Royal Academies and other prestigious venues in England and Scotland before her retirement *c*1882. Her monument to David Livingstone in Princes Street, Edinburgh was unveiled to loud cheers on 15 August 1876 and received resounding praise from eminent fellow artists and critics for its 'original design . . . perfect execution', and vigorous likeness to life. Assuming this to be the first public statue in Scotland by a female artist, the *Englishwoman's Yearbook* (*EY*) recorded the event as one of the landmarks of the 19th-century women's movement. Since the sculptor's opus falls very largely outside the perameters of this publication, the few works produced before 1851 are the only ones listed.

Shannon Hunter Hurtado

Literary References: *Glasgow Herald*, 8 June 1875, 3, col 3; *Tooley* 1895, 361–7; *EY* 1901, 348; 'Notable Victorians', *Weekly Scotsman*, 13 February, 1932, 6; *Pyke* 1973, 68; *Pyke* 1981, 22; *Smailes* 1990, 144–5, 147, 232, 233; *Bilcliffe* II, 1992, 232; *de Montfort* 1993, 8; *Hurtado* 2002

Reliefs					
1.	1849	Self-portrait (unsigned, but with handwritten label on verso: 'Miss Paten [sic], by herself, 1849')	w	Dunfermline Museum (1965)	
2.	*c*1851	D O Hill (wax and plaster)		SNPG Other versions: ex coll Rupert Gunnis; untraced	*Graves* IV, 1905–6, 102; *Pyke* 1981, 22
3.	*c*1851	Nöel Paton		SNPG (1970) Other versions: ex coll Mrs Halahan, Haslemere, wax; untraced	*Pyke* 1981, 22; *Pearson* 1991, 75, 76 (repr)

HILL, Edward, of Hill Street, Berkeley Square –1799

In the years 1790–91 he and his partner, Thomas Oldfield, received sums totalling nearly £2,300 for sundry work at Woburn Abbey (**1, 3**). As contractors Hill and Oldfield built houses in Sloane Street in 1789 (Middlesex Building Affidavits, quoted by *Gunnis* 1968, 201). Hill died on 25 December 1799: a short notice in the *Gentleman's Magazine* describes him as 'of Hill-street, Berkeley-square'

Literary References: *GM* 1799, pt 2, 1094

Archival References: Woburn Building Accts, detailed bill & loose receipts, 1790–91, BLARS R3/2114/496 BLARS R5/1297

Chimneypieces					
1.	1791–1792	Several, including one for the south-front west bedroom and one for the eating room (co-sculptor: Thomas Oldfield) Payment(s): £449	m	Woburn Abbey, Beds	Woburn Building Accts, BLARS R5/1105
2.	1795	Several (co-sculptor: Thomas Oldfield) Payment(s): £72		[146 Piccadilly, London]; untraced	Soane archives in GPC
Architectural Sculpture					
3.	1790	Carved work Payment(s): £719 for 'mason's work including carved Portland stone'	s	Woburn Abbey, Beds	*Gunnis* 1968, 200
Miscellaneous					
4.	1797	'Statuary work' (co-sculptor: Thomas Oldfield) Payment(s): £27 13s		[Castle Howard, N R Yorks]; untraced	GPC

HILL, George, of London fl 1733–47

He carried out a good deal of work for the partners of Hoare's Bank. Hill figures as a 'carver in wood and stone' in the *London Directory* (*Gunnis* 1968, 201).

Architectural Sculpture					
1.	1747	Festoons Payment(s): £4 4s		[for Christopher Arnold]; untraced	Hoare Partnership Ledger, 1742–1751, f362; *Gunnis* 1968, 201
Miscellaneous					
2.	1731–1733	Unidentified carving (chimneypieces?) Payment(s): £127 7s		[for Benjamin Hoare, Boreham Hall, Essex]; untraced	Hoare Partnership Ledger, 1725–34, ff225, 233, 237, 291; *Gunnis* 1968, 201
3.	1744–1745	Unidentified carving Payment(s): £20		[for Christopher Arnold]; untraced	Hoare Partnership Ledger, 1742–1751, f346

HILL, J, of Barnet fl 1818–32

Gunnis refers to three 'dull tablets' signed by this sculptor at Monken Hadleigh, Herts, the earliest of which is here listed (*Gunnis* 1968, 201).

Funerary Monuments					
1.	†1818	James and Mary Anne Quilter		Monken Hadley, Herts	S

HILL, James, of London fl 1762–70

He is noted in Mortimer's *Director* as 'statuary. Durham-yard, in the Strand' (*Mortimer* 1763, 14). He exhibited at the Society of Artists in 1765, giving a new address in Long Acre (**10**). Two of his works appeared in a special exhibition held by the Society of Artists on 30 September 1768, in honour of the King of Denmark's visit (**4, 5**).

Literary References: *Graves* 1907, 118; *Gunnis* 1968, 201

Chimneypieces					
1.	1768	Two marble chimneypieces for bedrooms and one in Portland stone for the hall Payment(s): £59 Drawing(s): Hall, Soane, Adam, 22:116		[Lansdowne House, London]; untraced	*Harris* 2001, 346 n26; GPC
Reliefs					
2.	1764	Unidentified subject, 'a large basso-relievo'		[Exhib Soc of Artists, London, 163]; untraced	*Graves* 1907, 118
3.	1766	Alexander refusing the water		[Exhib Soc of Artists, London, 207]; untraced	*Graves* 1907, 118
4.	1768	Diana and Endymion		[Soc of Artists special exhib, London, 151]; untraced	*Graves* 1907, 118
5.	1768	Marcus Curius		[Soc of Artists special exhib, London, 152]; untraced	*Graves* 1907, 118
Miscellaneous					
6.	1761	Britannia, emblematical model		[Exhib Soc of Artists, London, 149]; untraced	*Graves* 1907, 118
7.	1762	The Good Samaritan	w	[Exhib Soc of Artists, London, 142]; untraced	*Graves* 1907, 118
8.	1762	Unidentified poet	w	[Exhib Soc of Artists, London, 143]; untraced	*Graves* 1907, 118
9.	1763	Roman Charity		[Exhib Soc of Artists, London, 142]; untraced	*Graves* 1907, 118
10.	1765	Diana and Endymion, model		[Exhib Soc of Artists, London, 175]; untraced	*Graves* 1907, 118
11.	1767	Esther and Haman, model		[Exhib Soc of Artists, London, 207]; untraced	*Graves* 1907, 118
12.	1769	Europa, model		[Exhib Soc of Artists, London, 168]; untraced	*Graves* 1907, 118
13.	1770	An allegorical model		[Exhib Soc of Artists, London, 168]; untraced	*Graves* 1907, 118

HILL, John, of Reading fl 1786–88

An advertisement in the *Reading Mercury* of 9 January 1786, reads 'John Hill, stone-mason, and carver, on the High Bridge, London Street executes Monuments, chimney-pieces in different kinds of coloured marbles in the most elegant and modern taste – tombs and headstones, and all kinds of ornaments in stone.' In the voters' lists of 1782 his name is given as 'John Flewell Hill, stone-mason' (*Gunnis* 1968, 201).

Funerary Monuments

1.	?1788	Edward Waite	Shinfield, Berks	S	*Gunnis* 1968, 201

Architectural Sculpture

2.	nd	Font (designed by Rev George Bellas)	Basildon, Berks		*Gunnis* 1968, 201

HILL, of Leicester fl *c*1835

Funerary Monuments

1.	†1835	Katherine (†1830) and Robert Dale	Ashbourne, Derbys	S

HILL, Robert fl 1749–51

He was one of the principal masons building Ragley Hall.

Architectural Sculpture

1.	1749–1751	'Ashlering and mouldings,' columns, pilasters and entablature Payment(s): £274	Ragley Hall, Warks	Archives, Marquess of Hertford in GPC

HILL, Thomas I –1713

A mason-sculptor, he provided chimneypieces in exotic materials for the royal palaces. Hill became free of the Masons' Company by redemption on 17 November 1670 and held the office of warden in 1695 and master in 1699. Little is known of his early career and his name does not appear in the general search of 1678. An insight into his personality in middle age is provided by a letter from Sir John Vanbrugh to Lord Godolphin in which Sir Christopher Wren is quoted as calling him 'a whimsical man and a piece of an astrologer and would venture upon nothing till he had consulted the stars' (*Wren Soc* VII 140).

Hill was the mason employed by the vestries in fitting up St Michael, Wood St (1677) and St Anne and St Agnes, Gresham Street (1680–81), for both of which he provided fonts (**9, 10**). He worked at Chelsea Hospital in association with **Thomas Wise I** in 1685 and perhaps earlier, for after Wise's death that year he took over Wise's contract at St Paul's Cathedral in partnership with **Thomas Wise II** (**14**). The general search of September 1694 gives 12 names under the heading 'Mr Hills & Mr Wise's men'. From 1698 onwards he and Wise held the contract for the south-west quarter of the dome and Hill continued to work at the cathedral until 1707.

He was employed at several royal palaces. Between 1685 and 1693 he worked at Whitehall, where he provided chimneypieces in 'Egyptian', 'black and yellow' (Siena) and other lavish marbles at a cost of about £20 each (TNA WORK 5/47 fol 42,49, 57, 66, 81, 88), and at least one in Portland stone for the survey office (**5**, TNA WORK 5/46 fol 50). At Kensington Palace, he and two other partners, **John Thompson** and **Richard Walters**, were responsible for 25 marble chimney-pieces and 221 of Portland stone for lesser rooms (**6**, TNA E 351/3466). Payment for these and for several carved door-cases was made to them between 1689 and 1700 (**11, 12**). Among the items for which the partners charged £269 in 1700 were a white and veined marble chimneypiece in the King's Eating Room, a rance chimneypiece in the Drawing Room and for taking down, polishing and resetting an 'Egyptian' chimneypiece in the privy chamber (TNA WORK 5/50 f 317,333). Hill was also involved in substantial work at Hampton Court, 1689–96, particularly on the south range and in the quadrangle court, for which he charged some £7,000. Again he was responsible for several rich marble chimneypieces, as well as a pair of carved piers surmounted by urns (**7, 8, 13**). Other contracts took him to the Royal Hospital at Chelsea, 1686–1702 (**4**), the House of Commons, 1692, and the Tower of London, 1702 (**15**).

Only three monuments have been identified, one of which went to the West Indies (**3**). That to William Levinz, †1698, at St John's College, Oxford, is prominently signed and dated on the sill (**1**). It is an architectural wall-monument with a concave inscription tablet, flanked by composite columns. Above is a segmental broken pediment containing an armorial shield, set off by rich foliage. Skulls are suspended from the brackets below the sill.

Hill ran a large business and took on a number of apprentices. It was probably his son **Thomas Hill II**, who was bound to him in 1695 but was later turned over to **William Stanton**. Other obscure names in the Masons' Company Apprenticeship Registers include Richard Blackley (1671), Thomas Redwood (1673), William Collier (1684), William Pebworth (1701) and Joseph Hewit (1703). Hill perhaps came from an extended family of masons. A Thomas Hill, son of William Hill, 'citizen and mason', was apprenticed to Edward Maslin in 1710, becoming free on 1 April 1720 (Masons' Co, *Freemen*, fol 29). Another Thomas Hill was apprenticed to **Joseph Rose** in 1737 and was made free of the Company on 3 October 1745 (Masons' Co *Freemen*, fol 30).

The 'sentence' [will] of a Thomas Hill of Chelsea, Middx, was proved on 5 February 1714 and since Hill's address was given as 'Chelsea' in 1708 in the books of the Masons' Company, it seems likely that this is our sculptor. It mentions two beneficiaries by name, Thomas II and a daughter, Isabella.

IR

Literary References: *Knoop and Jones* 1935, 32, 77; *Wren Soc*, IV, VI, VII, X, XIV, XV, XVIII, XIX, *passim*; *Gunnis* 1968, 201; *Colvin* V 1973–76, *passim*; *Webb* 1999, *passim*

Archival References: Masons' Co, Masters and Wardens, 1695, 1699

Will: PROB 11/542, proved 1714

Funerary Monuments

1.	1699	William Levinz (†1698)	St John's College, Oxford, chapel	SD	Pevsner, *Oxon*, 1974, 197; C Lib (repr)
2.	†1704	Frances Ball	Hampton, Middx	S	*Gunnis* 1968, 201; C Lib (repr)
3.	†1706	Mr Jordan	[Barbados Cathedral, Bridgetown]; untraced	S	*Gunnis* 1968, 201

Chimneypieces					
4.	1687	for the Council Chamber		[Chelsea Hospital, London]; untraced	*Gunnis* 1968, 201
5.	1685–1693	Several, in coloured marbles and Portland stone		[Whitehall Palace, London, Duchess of Mazarin's apartments, Queen Mary's bedroom, survey office and other rooms]; untraced	*Wren Soc* VII, 109; *Gunnis* 1968, 201
6.	1689–1700	25 or more in coloured marbles and 221 in Portland stone (co-sculptor: John Thompson and Richard Walters)		[Kensington Palace, London, Queen's apartment, Queen's gallery, Lord Albemarle's lodgings and other rooms]; untraced	*Wren Soc* VII, 165; *Gunnis* 1968, 201; *Colvin* 1973–76, V, 184, 187
7.	1700	Black and yellow marble		[Hampton Court Palace, Middx, presence chamber]; untraced	*Gunnis* 1968, 201
8.	1701	More than one	m	[Hampton Court Palace, Middx, pavilions]; untraced	*Colvin* 1973–76, V, 168
Architectural Sculpture					
9.	1677	Font Payment(s): £8	m	[St Michael, Wood St, City of London]; untraced	*Wren Soc* XIX, 43; X, 124
10.	1680–1681	Font Payment(s): £8	m	St Anne and St Agnes, Gresham St, City of London	*Wren Soc* XIX, 5
11.	1689–1695	Doorcase, with shield, festoons and scrolls Payment(s): £46 2s 11 1/2d		Kensington Palace, Queen's private apartment, north end of east wall	*Colvin* 1973–76, V, 187
12.	1689–1695	Two entrance doorcases, with rusticated pilasters and arches with keystones carved with 'huskes and scrowles'		[Kensington Palace, London]; untraced	*Colvin* 1973–76, V, 184
13.	1699	'two large urns with festoons and 4 mask faces', set on piers Payment(s): £52 14s 8d		[Hampton Court Palace, Middx, adjoining the house before the Princesses' lodgings]; untraced	*Wren Soc* IV, 37
14.	1686–1707	Extensive stone carving (co-sculptor: Thomas Wise)		St Paul's Cathedral, London	*Gunnis* 1968, 201
Miscellaneous					
15.	1701	Four troughs for the lions	s	[Tower of London]; untraced	*Gunnis* 1968, 201

HILL, Thomas II –1724

He was apprenticed to his father, **Thomas Hill I**, in 1695, but was later turned over to **William Stanton**. He became free of the Masons' Company on 16 October 1702.

Literary References: *Gunnis* 1968, 210

Archival References: Masons' Co, *Freemen*, f28

HILL, Thomas III fl *c*1820

Funerary Monuments				
1.	*c*1820	Stephen Tempest	Rome	NP/RG

HILL, William I fl 1656–58

Between 1656–1658 he built Brasenose College Chapel (College Archives, cited in *Gunnis* 1968, 203).

HILL, William II fl 1805

His tradecard of 1805 carries the information 'Wm Hill,/Stone Mason & Carver,/Executes in the neatest manner all kinds of MONUMENTS/ Chimney Pieces & Tables/at the Original Shop and Yard/London Street, Reading' (Banks 106.14).

HILL & SON fl *c*1842

Funerary Monuments				
1.	†1842	Catherine Puget	Totteridge, Herts	S

HILL & WATSON fl 1699

Masons paid £75 3s 2d in 1699 for building Caister Lighthouse.

Archival References: RG/JP, 4, 689, quoting Trinity House archives

HILLS, Arthur fl 1800

Miscellaneous				
1.	1800	A girl with a bird	LMG, W R Yorks	D

HILLS, S fl *c*1836

He signs a large and elaborate Gothic monument, 15 feet high (1).

Funerary Monuments					
1.	†1836	Dugdale Dugdale	Merevale, Warks	S	*Gunnis* 1968, 202

HINCHLIFFE (or HINCHLIFF), Family

John Hinchliffe (or Hinchliff) I †1796
William Hinchliffe (or Hinchliff) fl 1777
John Hinchliffe (or Hinchliff) II fl 1801
John Hinchliffe (or Hinchliff) III fl 1791–6

John Hinchliffe I was the son of William Hinchliffe, a barber of the parish of St George, Bloomsbury. He was apprenticed to Lewis Cockram, citizen and mason, in 1748, was turned over to **Richard Buddle** in 1751 and gained his freedom on 26 June 1755. In 1768 he was experimenting with new inlay techniques, and exhibited at the Society of Artists (14). A trade cards of 1774 advertises 'Monuments, Chimney-pieces and MASONRY IN GENERAL BY John Hinchcliffe in Long Acre near St Martin's Lane LONDON' (Heal 66.13). Hinchliffe ran a diverse mason's business: as a contractor he built houses in Tottenham Court Road in 1777 and, with his son, **William Hinchliffe**, 11–19 Hereford Street, working under the architect John Crunden. He was responsible also for houses in Gower Street and Devonshire Place in 1785 and 1793 respectively (Middlesex Building Affidavits). His monument to Ann Herney (1) was described by Gunnis as 'a curious work, in the form of a large wreathed triumphal column'. In 1790 he became upper warden of the Masons' Company and was master in 1791. The family lived 'at the King's Place Farm near the Baldfaced Stag, Epping Forest,' and it was here that the elder Hinchliffe died in 1796.

John Hinchliffe II was apprenticed to his father in 1774. He signs a handful of monuments and tablets (**1, 3–5**). He was still living in 1801 for in that year his nephew Samuel, son of William Hinchliffe, was apprenticed to him. **John Hinchliffe III**, the son of John Hinchliffe II, was apprenticed to his father in 1791, and became free on 9 November 1796. **John Ely Hinchliffe** was probably a family member.

Archival References: Masons' Co *Assistants*, fol 7; *Apprentices*, 1791; *Freemen*, 26 June 1755, 9 November 1796, fol 31; *Court book*, 1751–96, 14 June 1790, 14 June 1791; *Apprentice binding book* (2), 1774

Literary References: *S of L*, vol 40 (1980), 174

Tradecard: BM Heal 106.16, nd, with asymetrical acanthus scrolled frame

Funerary Monuments

1.	?1771	Ann Herney (by John Hinchliffe (or Hinchliff) I)		Bristol Cathedral, triforium	S	*Gunnis* 1968, 202
2.	1784	Mausoleum with sarcophagus for Elizabeth Johnstone, designed by Sir John Soane (by John Hinchliffe (or Hinchliff) I) Payment(s): £129 3s 8d		St Mary Abbotts, Kensington, London, churchyard		Soane, Copies of Bills 1785, ff 1–2; *Gunnis* 1968, 202; *Colvin* 1995, 912
3.	†1795	Mrs A Worral (by John Hinchliffe (or Hinchliff) II)		Wisbech, Cambs	S	Pevsner, *Cambs*, 1970, 559
4.	?1795	Rev Richard Southgate (by John Hinchliffe (or Hinchliff) II)		St Giles-in-the-Fields, London	S	*Gunnis* 1968, 202
5.	?1804	Milward Row (by John Hinchliffe (or Hinchliff) II)		Tillington, Sussex	S	*Gunnis* 1968, 202

Chimneypieces

6.	1768	Three, for bedrooms (by John Hinchliffe (or Hinchliff) I) Payment(s): £54		[Lansdowne House, London]; untraced		Archives, Marquess of Lansdowne in GPC
7.	1769	Several (by John Hinchliffe (or Hinchliff) I) Payment(s): £112 10s		[Alscot Park, Warks, drawing room]; untraced		West of Alscot archives in GPC
8.	1772	Statuary marble, designed by Robert Adam with a Wedgwood tablet and inlay by Domenico Bartoli (by John Hinchliffe (or Hinchliff) I) Payment(s): £150 estimate Drawing(s): by Adam, Soane 23:13	m	20 St James' Square, London, dressing room		*Harris* 2001, 265, 266, 360 n48 (repr)
9.	1773	With frieze of vases, festoons and paterae (by John Hinchliffe (or Hinchliff) I) Payment(s): £150 Drawing(s): Adam, Soane SM 23:9	m	20 St James' Square, London, ante-room		*Harris* 2001, 261, 360 n21
10.	1776	'Statuary architrave' (by John Hinchliffe (or Hinchliff) I) Payment(s): £42	m	[20 St James' Square, London, 'Sr Watkins' dressing room']; untraced		NLW Wynnstay MSS in GPC
11.	1776	'Statuary architrave' (by John Hinchliffe (or Hinchliff) I)	m	[20 St James' Square, London, 'Sr Watkins' Bedchamber']; untraced		NLW Wynnstay MSS in GPC

Architectural Sculpture

12.	1772	'A statuary marble table, inlaid with scagliola' (by John Hinchliffe (or Hinchliff) I)	m	[Exhib Soc of Artists, London, 147]; untraced		*Graves* 1907, 118
13.	1772	Font, designed by Robert Adam (by John Hinchliffe (or Hinchliff) I) (co-sculptor: Sefferin Nelson) Payment(s): 13 gns (bowl only)		Ruabon, Denbighs		NLW Wynnstay Coll 115/5 a/c 1773

Miscellaneous

14.	1768	'specimen of a new manner of ornamenting chimney-pieces, tables, etc., with scagliola inlaid with marble' (by John Hinchliffe (or Hinchliff) I)		[Exhib Soc of Artists, London, 203]; untraced		*Graves* 1907, 118

HINCHLIFFE (or HINCHLIFF), John Ely 1777–1867

Best remembered as an assistant to **John Flaxman RA**, he was christened on 29 April 1777 at St Martin-in-the-Fields, the son of William and Mary Hinchliff. He was probably one of the extensive Hinchliffe family of masons. In January 1808, at the age of 30, he enrolled as a student at the Royal Academy.

In 1805 he began employment with John Flaxman and for the last 20 years of that sculptor's life acted as his faithful, devoted and confidential assistant. In 1817–18 Flaxman's accounts show that Hinchliffe was receiving a wage of around £5 per week. He was a witness to his employer's will in 1820, when his address was given as 5 Mornington Place, Hampstead Road. When Flaxman died in 1826 Hinchliffe helped to complete his unfinished works in the studio, including the statue of John Philip Kemble. Hinchliffe continued to receive a wage until January 1828, no doubt paid by Flaxman's relatives, **Ann Flaxman** and **Maria Denman**.

Hinchliffe exhibited works in his own right at the Royal Academy from 1814. He carved a number of busts and Flaxmanesque literary and religious subjects, often for unidentified monuments. His monument to Lieutenant-Colonel Burr depicts a pensive officer reading an inscription, behind which is a draped flag. To the right stands a sepoy in an attitude of mourning (**6**). A press report said of another, unidentified, 'monumental figure' exhibited at the Royal Academy in 1831 that it was 'a monumental figure with almost no body – though otherwise not deficient in talent' (*Library of Fine Arts*, I, 1831, 430). The *Art Journal* remarked of his sepulchral work that it was executed with a 'purity and simplicity of style' (*AJ*, 1868, 48). Gunnis, however, was of the opinion that

Hinchliffe's monuments, most of them in the neo-Hellenic tradition, were not, 'in spite of the years he spent with Flaxman, very inspired or exciting works'.

Hinchliffe's last known exhibit was a bust of his former employer (**48**), of whom he apparently 'never spoke but with the profoundest veneration' (*AJ*, 1868, 48). He died at his home at 185 Hampstead Road on 23 November 1867. His will, proved on 9 December 1867, revealed that his effects were valued at less than £1,000. He was the father of the engraver John James Hinchliffe (1805–1875). The *Art Journal* obituary noted of the long-lived sculptor that he was 'one of the last links connecting the present with the last generation of artists'. He was clearly an admirable man for 'in private life he had long enjoyed the sincere regard of a large number of friends, who found in the integrity of his nature many of the highest social qualities' (*AJ* 1868, 48).

MGS

Literary References: *Graves* IV, 1905–6, 108; *Hutchison* 1960–62, 164; *Gunnis* 1968, 202

Archival References: Flaxman Papers Ad MS 39, 784 X; 39,784 T; 39784 M; 39,784AA fol 22; IGI

Wills: PPR, will, 9 December 1867, fol 792; John Flaxman RA PROB 11/1720/129

Funerary Monuments

No.	Date	Subject	Medium	Location		Reference
1.	†1678	Sir Philip Monkton		Newbald, E R Yorks		Pevsner, *Yorks: E R and York*, 1995, 622
2.	†1812	Henry Rice		Great Holland, Essex		Pevsner, *Essex*, 1965, 204
3.	1819	'Then shall the righteous shine forth as the sun', monumental bas-relief		[Exhib RA, London, 1189]; untraced		*Graves* IV, 1905–6, 108
4.	1820	'Enter thou into the joy of thy Lord', monumental bas-relief		[Exhib BI, London, 318]; untraced		*Graves* 1875, 270
5.	†1820	John Quantock		Chichester Cathedral, Sussex	S	*Gunnis* 1968, 202
6.	†1821	Lieutenant-Colonel Charles Barton Burr		Mumbai (Bombay) Cathedral, India	S	
7.	?1822	John Pusey Edwardes		Grosvenor Chapel, London	S	*Gunnis* 1968, 202
8.	1822	Resignation, for a monument		[Exhib RA, London, 1040]; untraced		*Graves* IV, 1905–6, 108
9.	†1822	Seven members of the Brightmore family (†1815–22)		Eyam, Derbys	S	
10.	1824	'He that believeth in the son', sketch for a relief for a monument		[Exhib RA, London, 1026]; untraced		*Graves* V, 1905–6, 108
11.	?1824	Sir Harry Goring		Washington, Sussex	S	*Gunnis* 1968, 202
12.	1826–1827	John Philip Kemble (†1823) (co-sculptor: John Flaxman RA)		Westminster Abbey, London, Chapel of St Andrew; formerly north transept	S	Pevsner, *London: Westminster*, 1973, 449
13.	1827	'Thy will be done', part of a monument		[Exhib RA, London, 1119]; untraced		*Graves* IV, 1905–6, 108
14.	1828	'I shall go to him', part of a monument		[Exhib RA, London, 1157]; untraced		*Graves* IV, 1905–6, 108
15.	1828	'My hope hath been in thee', part of a monument		[Exhib RA, London, 1185]; untraced		*Graves* IV, 1905–6, 108
16.	1829	'I shall go to him', part of a monument		[Exhib RA, London, 1148]; untraced		*Graves* IV, 1905–6, 108
17.	?1829	Joseph Watson		Bermondsey Parish Church, London	S	*Gunnis* 1968, 202
18.	1830	Monumental figure		[Exhib RA, London, 1272]; untraced		*Graves* IV, 1905–6, 108
19.	1831	Monumental figure		[Exhib RA, London, 1161]; untraced		*Library of Fine Arts*, vol I, 1831, 430; *Graves* IV, 1905–6, 108
20.	?1832	James Smith		Udimore, Sussex	S	*Gunnis* 1968, 202
21.	?1833	Edward Biggs		All Hallows, Barking, City of London	S	*Gunnis* 1968, 202
22.	1833	Figure, part of a monument		[Exhib RA, London, 1156]; untraced		*Graves* IV, 1905–6, 108
23.	†1833	John Horatio Cotterill		Oakamoor, Staffs		Pevsner, *Staffs*, 1974, 214
24.	?1833	Lord Gambier		Iver, Bucks	S	*Gunnis* 1968, 202
25.	?1833	Margaretta Ewbank		St Mary, St Marylebone, London	S	*Gunnis* 1968, 202
26.	1834	Figure, part of a monument		[Exhib RA, London, 1046]; untraced		*Graves* IV, 1905–6, 108
27.	?1837	General Sir George Cooke		Harefield, Middx	S	*Gunnis* 1968, 202
28.	1837	Mary Norris		[Exhib RA, London, 1200]; Taunton, Somerset	S	*Graves* IV, 1905–6, 108
29.	?1837	Sir Mark Wood		Gatton, Surrey		GPC
30.	1838	A kneeling figure, part of a monument		[Exhib RA, London, 1273]; untraced		*Graves* IV, 1905–6, 108
31.	1838	'She is not dead', sketch for part of a monument		[Exhib RA, London, 1293]; untraced		*Graves* V, 1905–6, 108
32.	1839	Affection, part of a monument		[Exhib RA, London, 1370]; untraced		*Graves* IV, 1905–6, 108
33.	†1840	William Wickham		York Minster, south choir aisle	S	*Aylmer* 1977, 466; *Pattison and Murray* 2001, 117–9
34.	†1843	Mary Graves		St Margaret Pattens, City of London	S	Pevsner, *London: City*, 1997, 236
35.	1843	Thomas Lewis (†1822)		Lewes, Sussex		RG/JP, 4, 696
36.	1845	'The Lord gave', part of a monument		[Exhib RA, London, 1346]; untraced		*Graves* IV, 1905–6, 108
37.	†1846	General Charles Taylor		Canterbury Cathedral, Kent	S	*Gunnis* 1968, 202
38.	1847	Faith, figure for part of a monument		[Exhib RA, London, 1399]; untraced		*Graves* IV, 1905–6, 108

Statues

No.	Date	Subject	Medium	Location		Reference
39.	1835	Faith	m	[Exhib RA, London, 1130]; untraced		*Graves* IV, 1905–6, 108
40.	1835	Resignation	m	[Exhib RA, London, 1115]; untraced		*Graves* IV, 1905–6, 108
41.	1836	Hope	m	[Exhib RA, London, 1116]; untraced		*Graves* IV, 1905–6, 108

Busts

No.	Date	Subject	Medium	Location		Reference
42.	1817	Unidentified gentleman		[Exhib RA, London, 1014]; untraced		*Graves* IV, 1905–6, 108
43.	1817	Unidentified lady		[Exhib RA, London, 1013]; untraced		*Graves* IV, 1905–6, 108
44.	1818	Dr Clough		[Exhib RA, London, 1094]; untraced		*Graves* IV, 1905–6, 108
45.	1818	Unidentified gentleman		[Exhib RA, London, 1084]; untraced		*Graves* IV, 1905–6, 108
46.	1822	Unidentified gentleman		[Exhib RA, London, 1039]; untraced		*Graves* IV, 1905–6, 108
47.	1839	Unidentified gentleman	m	[Exhib RA, London, 1307]; untraced		*Graves* IV, 1905–6, 108
48.	1849	John Flaxman		[Exhib BI, London, 513]; untraced		*Graves* 1875, 270

Architectural Sculpture

No.	Date	Subject	Medium	Location		Reference
49.	1832	'Pity the sorrows of a poor old man', model for a candelabrum	pm	[Exhib RA, London, 1134]; untraced		*Graves* IV, 1905–6, 108

Reliefs

No.	Date	Subject	Medium	Location		Reference
50.	1823	Hope		[Exhib RA, London, 1080]; untraced		*Graves* IV, 1905–6, 108

Miscellaneous

51.	1814	Christian fighting with Apollyon	[Exhib RA, London, 802]; untraced	*Graves* 1875, 270; *Graves* IV, 1905–6, 108
52.	1815	Leonides opposing the Persians at the straits of Thermopylæ	[Exhib RA, London, 871]; untraced	*Graves* 1875, 270; *Graves* IV, 1905–6, 108
53.	1816	The combat between Menelaus and Paris	[Exhib RA, London, 915]; untraced	*Graves* 1875, 270; *Graves* IV, 1905–6, 108
54.	1817	Theseus throwing Sciron down the rocks	[Exhib RA, London, 1074]; untraced	*Graves* 1875, 270; *Graves* IV, 1905–6, 108
55.	1818	Aurora, as the morning star taking off the veil of night	[Exhib RA, London, 1074]; untraced	*Graves* 1875, 270; *Graves* IV, 1905–6, 108
56.	1818	Venus, as the evening star putting on the veil of night	[Exhib RA, London, 1076]; untraced	*Graves* 1875, 270; *Graves* IV, 1905–6, 108
57.	1820	Theseus rescuing Hippodamia from Eurytus	[Exhib RA, London, 1007]; untraced	*Graves* 1875, 270; *Graves* IV, 1905–6, 108
58.	1821	Night producing aether and the day – Theogony of Hesiod	[Exhib RA, London, 1152]; untraced	*Graves* IV, 1905–6, 108

HIND FAMILY, of Swithland

John Hind I fl 1718–61?
John Hind II fl *c*1779–94

John Hind I, who was one of the best of the Leicestershire slate-carvers, was apprenticed to William Heafford, a slater of Leicester, in 1718. He signs a large number of works in grave yards of the county, two of the best of which are listed here (**2, 3**). His finest monument, to Sir Joseph Danvers (**1**), is a large tomb-chest with scrolls and two reliefs of an agricultural landscape and an African sea-port. Pevsner describes its decoration as 'splendid'.

He was succeeded by his son, **John II**, who signs a free-standing urn on a black plinth to Edward Dawson (**4**). John II was apprenticed to his father and later became a freeman of Leicester.

Literary References: *Gunnis* 1968, 202

Archival References: GPC

Funerary Monuments

1.	†1753	Sir Joseph Danvers (by John Hind I)	sl	Swithland, Leics		Pevsner, *Leics & Rutland*, 1984, 401
2.	?1754	Robert Hall (by John Hind I)	sl	St Margaret, Leicester, churchyard		*Gunnis* 1968, 202
3.	?1761	Armston family (by John Hind I)	sl	Cosby, Leics, churchyard		*Gunnis* 1968, 202
4.	†1779	Edward and Mary Dawson (by John Hind II)	sl	Long Whatton, Leics	S	Pevsner, *Leics & Rutland*, 1984, 279
5.	?1792	George Doughty (by John Hind II)	sl	Mountsorrel, Leics	S	*Gunnis* 1968, 203
6.	†1794	William Hunt (by John Hind II)	sl	Rothley, Leics, churchyard		Pevsner, *Leics & Rutland*, 1984, 364
7.	nd	John Illston (by John Hind II)	sl	Whetstone, Leics, churchyard		Pevsner, *Leics & Rutland*, 1984, 421

HINDLE (or HINDLEY), John fl 1682–83

Chimneypieces

1.	1682	'two marble chimneypieces' and a 'white marble chimneypiece' Payment(s): £12	m	[Henderskelfe Castle, N R Yorks]; destroyed	GPC
2.	1683	Several Payment(s): £20		[Henderskelfe Castle, N R Yorks]; destroyed	GPC

HINDSON, William fl 1840–42

A local builder's son, he was employed by Sara Losh as a stone carver at St Mary, Wreay.

Architectural Sculpture

1.	1840–1842	Decorative stone carving (designed by Sara Losh)	St Mary, Wreay, Cumberland	*ODNB*

HIORN, John, of Warwick fl 1724–27

He was no doubt related to John Hiorne, a mason of Tew and to **William Hiorne**, the mason and architect who collaborated more than once in Oxfordshire with **Francis Smith of Warwick**. Between 1724 and 1727 John worked under Smith's direction on building Ditchley Park for the second Earl of Lichfield (Dillon Archives). During the same period he was also employed under Smith at Ombersley, Worcs (Archives, Lord Sandys).

Literary References: *Gunnis* 1968, 203

HIORNE, Francis, of Warwick 1744–89

A mason and architect, he was the elder son of **William Hiorne of Warwick**. In 1771 he was paid £42 for building the gateway at Wroxton Abbey for Lord Guilford. He succeeded to the family business on the death of his father in 1776. He specialised in an elegant, decorative Gothic style, notably at St Mary, Tetbury, Glos, which he rebuilt in 1777–1781. He was also employed as a mason at St Mary, Warwick, where he took down and rebuilt 14 pinnacles in January 1779. Later that year he was paid £158 16s for 'workmanship and materials employed in entirely new working, faceing, repairing, and painting the western compartment of the said chapel, taking out the whole window, and rebuilding it' (*Churches of Warwicks* 1847, 1, 64).

Hiorne was elected an alderman of Warwick in October 1773 and was mayor in 1773–4, 1782–3 and 1787–8. He became a fellow of the Society of Antiquaries in 1784 and bequeathed his coins and medals to the Society on his death, which occurred on 9 December 1789. He left his bust of **Francis Smith, of Warwick**, carved by **Michael Rysbrack**, to the Radcliffe Library, Oxford. His house, Kyte's Nest, at Beausale, near Warwick, went to his wife Elizabeth. Hiorne is commemorated by a tablet in St Mary, Warwick.

Literary References: *Anecdotes* 1937, 188; *Colvin* 1995, 495–6

Archival References: Bodl MS, North c 64, fols 174, 196

Will: PROB 11/1187, proved 27 January 1790

Funerary Monuments

1.	†1770	Sir Richard Lyttleton	Hagley, Worcs	*Colvin* 1995, 495

HIORNE (or HIORNS), William, of Warwick 1712–76

He and his brother, David (1715–1758) established themselves as the leading architects and master-builders of Warwick in the mid-18th century. They came from a family of masons of Great Tew, Oxon. First employed by the Smith family of Warwick, they succeeded to the business on the death of **William Smith of Warwick**. They designed and built churches and country houses all over the Midlands, largely in the Palladian style. John Hiorne, who must have been a relative, worked under Francis Smith between 1723 and 1727 on building work at Ditchley Park, Oxon.

William Hiorne was responsible for a number of chimneypieces, including some for Stoneleigh Abbey (**6**). A design for one is inscribed in Hiorne's hand 'this design estimated to be done in Panswick stone p Wm Hiorn at 35L the two chimney pieces'. A note to Hiorne from Lord Leigh, preserved with his final bill, reprimands the architect: 'Mr Hiorn, you are acquainted that my servants are never allow'd to take any money as vails, acknowledgements, or presents. Upon discovery of bribes both tradesman & servant will be turn'd off' (SBT RO DR/18/5/4203). It is not clear what Hiorne had done to receive this rebuke.

He died on 22 April 1776, leaving two sons by his wife Mary, née Duncalfe. The elder, **Francis Hiorne**, became a renowned architect. There is a tablet to his memory at St Mary, Warwick.

Literary References: *Gunnis* 1968, 203; *Gomme* 1971, 246–251; *Gomme* 1988, 276; *Colvin* 1995, 496–8

Archival References: Dillon (1) DIL I/p/i and k,p; (2) DIL I/p/q (John Hiorne)

Will: William Hiorns, or Hiorne, 23 June 1781, PROB 11/1079

Funerary Monuments						
1.	†1744	Thomas Crossfield		Rugby parish church, Warks	S	*Gunnis* 1968, 203; *Colvin* 1995, 496
2.	†1747	Edward Acton (designed by William Baker) Payment(s): £100		Acton Scott, Church Stretton, Salop	S	*Gunnis* 1968, 203; *Colvin* 1995, 95
Chimneypieces						
3.	1748	Description unavailable		[for Mr Weaver, Morville Hall, Salop]; untraced		*Gunnis* 1968, 203
4.	?1751	Description unavailable		[Arbury Park, Warks, dressing room]; untraced		Newdigate Accts, 1751–2, CR 136/V156
5.	1752	Seven	m	[for Edward Pytts, Kyre Wyard, Worcs]; untraced		Ass. Art Soc. Report 28, 1905–1906 cited by *Gunnis* 1968, 203
6.	1764	Several, plain Payment(s): £189 0s 2d Drawing(s): SBT RO DR/18/5/4192 (for library)		Stoneleigh Abbey, Warks		*Gomme* 1988, 276
Architectural Sculpture						
7.	1751	Carving		[Arbury Park, Warks]; untraced		Newdigate archives, cited in *Gunnis* 1968, 203
Miscellaneous						
8.	1749–1750	Altarpiece		[St Bartholomew, Birmingham]; destroyed		*Colvin* 1995, 497

HIRST, John fl 1773

Hirst was a mason in **Richard Hayward**'s workshop. In March 1773 Hayward, who was 'very apprehensive' about the safe carriage of his statue of Lord Botetourt to Williamsburg, Virginia, sent Hirst to America with the statue, in order that it might be set up properly. Robert C Nicholas, a member of the House of Burgesses wrote to John Norton, who acted for the Virginians in London on 21 June 1773: 'you will receive this by John Hirst, the mason, who came over to set up Lord Botetourt's statue, which he has done in a most expeditious and faithful manner. Every gentleman, whom I have conversed with, happily approves of your sending him over, indeed I know not what we should have done without such a man'. Hirst's efficiency may have been due to his desire to rush home, for he was anxious about the effects of the hot weather and wanted to see his family. His expenses came to £50.

Literary References: *Mason* 1937, 313, 331–2

HISCOCK, J S, of Blandford fl 1805?–27

Hiscock, a stone mason with yards in Poole and Blandford Forum, was declared a bankrupt in July 1827 (*New Monthly Mag* 1827, 360). His known tablets are all in Dorset.

Funerary Monuments				
1.	?1805	Mary Wright	Wareham, Dorset	*Gunnis* 1968, 203
2.	?1809	John Bastard	Blandford, Dorset	*Gunnis* 1968, 203
3.	†1809	Spurrier family member	Poole, Dorset	Pevsner, *Dorset*, 1972, 319
4.	?1814	George Churchill	St Peter, Dorchester, Dorset	*Gunnis* 1968, 203
5.	?1816	Mary Slade	Poole, Dorset	*Gunnis* 1968, 203

HISCOCK, William, of Christchurch *c*1763–1851

A builder and monumental sculptor, he was employed in 1809 on repairs to Christchurch Priory, Hants. All his known tablets are in that building. In 1825 he designed Hamworthy church, Dorset and in 1831, Milton church, Hants. He died in January 1851 and is buried in the graveyard of Christchurch Priory, where there is a large tomb to the memory of Hiscock and his wife Elizabeth, who died on 21 November 1830, aged 66.

Literary References: *Gunnis* 1968, 203; *Colvin* 1995, 498

Archival References: GPC

Funerary Monuments				
1.	†1797	John Cook and wife	Christchurch Priory, Hants	RG/JP, 4, 698A
2.	?1798	Augusta Bullock	Christchurch Priory, Hants	*Gunnis* 1968, 203
3.	?1806	Philip Norris	Christchurch Priory, Hants	*Gunnis* 1968, 203
4.	†1818	Rt Hon George Rose	Christchurch Priory, Hants	RG/JP, 4, 698v.
5.	?1819	J Penleaze	Christchurch Priory, Hants	*Gunnis* 1968, 203
6.	†1819	James Sympson	Christchurch Priory, Hants	RG/JP, 4, 698A
7.	†1801–1836	Jane Monatt and others	Christchurch Priory, Hants	RG/JP, 4, 698v.

HITCH, F

Busts

1.	nd	Admiral Lord Nelson	MOD Art Collection, 15903 (ID655)

HITCH, William Coles, of Hertford 1793–1832

He died on 13 September 1832, and was buried in the graveyard of St Andrew, Hertford.

Archival References: GPC

Funerary Monuments

1.	†1821	Samuel and Mary Pritchett	Bramfield, Herts	S	
2.	?1824	Unidentified subjects, tablets	Datchworth, Herts	S	*Gunnis* 1968, 203
3.	?1829	Poor family, obelisk	Hertingfordbury, Herts, churchyard	S	GPC
4.	?1821–1829	Unidentified subjects, tablets	Ware, Herts	S	*Gunnis* 1968, 203

HOARE, Prince, of Bath 1711–69

He was the younger brother of the portraitist and printmaker, William Hoare RA (1707/8–1792), who secured him a number of patrons in Bath. Hoare was probably born at Eye, in Suffolk, and may have been a student at Dr Ward's school in Moorfields. Vertue however says he 'was educated' under **Peter Scheemakers**. If 'educated' means that he was an apprentice, the training took place before 1728, when Scheemakers and William Hoare left for Italy. Alternatively Hoare may have served with Scheemakers after his return from Rome in 1730.

William Hoare was back in England by 1738 and he settled in Bath, where Prince Hoare spent a period *c*1740. On 15 February 1741 Lord Chesterfield wrote to the Bishop of Waterford: 'Lady Chesterfield has sent you from Bristol a busto of your humble servant, cast from a marble one done by Mr. Hoare at Bath' (**23**) (*Chesterfield* 1777, IV, 241). Prince Hoare went to Italy himself *c*1742, where he spent seven or eight years, visiting Rome and Florence. By January 1749 he had made 'an admirable copy' of an *Antinous* relief belonging to Cardinal Albani (**30**), who thought him 'very clever and anxious to succeed' (*Lewis* 1961, 155). In August 1749 Hoare wrote to Albani, thanking him for an introduction to Horace Mann, with whom he stayed in Florence. He added that he was thinking of leaving Italy shortly, but since he hoped to return in six or seven months he was leaving many of his principal works in Florence. Mann considered him able but lazy, judging him: 'very clever in copying, but I have seen nothing original of his doing. . . . Had he application equal to his skill, I believe he would make a great figure, at least in England, where sculpture is not at any great pitch' (*HWC*, 20, 86, 26 Aug 1749). Hoare had copied a bust of Cicero from the Uffizi (**27**) and was making a marble version of the antique *Ganymede* for an English client (**18**). He was elected to the Florentine Academy on 3 September 1749.

In January 1750 Vertue recorded his return to England, describing him as 'a tall handsom agreeable person and somewhat skilld in musick' adding that he 'bids fair for a great man' (*Vertue* III, 152). He noted that Hoare had advertised his return to Bath, where some citizens were proposing to subscribe to a statue of the great arbiter of sartorial taste, 'Beau' Nash, whose presence in the town had contributed for 40 years to its fashionable reputation. Hoare's statue in the pump room does not appear to have been unveiled until about 1752 and may possibly have been the work of his assistant, **Giovanni Baptista Plura** (**19**). Hoare carved a bust of Nash in 1761 (**25**).

Hoare made an advantageous marriage on 4 May 1751, to a Miss Coulthurst of Melksham, who had a fortune of £6,000 (*GM*, 1751, 284). This may have allowed him to choose his commissions rather than having to take what was available, as was the case with so many contemporaries.

His practice was largely in monuments that were typical of the period and lavishly adorned with coloured marbles. The finest is perhaps to Bishop Maddox, which has a standing female statue in classical draperies holding a long inverted torch, leaning on a sarcophagus with a relief of the *Good Samaritan* (**11**). The wall-monument to Lord Trevor presents a profile relief of a seated, classically-robed woman holding an urn and a large hollow ring symbolising *Eternity*, all set within an architectural frame (**15**). That to Alexander Pope, erected 17 years after his death by his friend William Warburton, is a restrained obelisk with a portrait medallion (**12**). A bust of Pope was ancillary to the more important commission, as had been the case with Beau Nash's bust (**26**). Hoare's use of coloured marbles extended to chimneypieces for Corsham Court, Wilts, where he provided several, including one with white marble flowers against a yellow-veined ground (**28, 29**).

He died at Bath on 8 November 1769. He left an annuity of £140 to his wife, Mary (presumably the heiress). He asked to be buried near the children of his brother, William Hoare, at Walcot, near Bath. A marble copy of the *Minerva*, then in his parlour, and a marble *Zingara* were both left to Henry Hoare of Stourhead, a former patron, and perhaps a kinsman (**21, 22**). Other works, including all the plaster figures in the shop, were left to William Hoare. Apart from a modest charitable bequest, the residue was left in trust for his nieces and nephews.

IR

Literary References: *Vertue* III, 85, 152; *London Mag*, 1769, 593; Pevsner, *Beds, Hunts & Peterborough*, 1968, 59; *Ramallo* 1973, 181–7; *Penny* 1977 (1), 136, 219, n 2; *Newby* 1986, 97, 126; *Whinney* 1988, 457 n 20; *Grove* 1996, 14, 599 (Newby), *Ingamells* 1997, 503; *Sullivan* 2006, 403–5

Additional MS Sources: BL Ad MS.50857

Will: PROB 11/952, made 20 July 1769, proved 13 Nov 1769

Funerary Monuments

1.	?†1730	Jacob Selfe	Melksham, Wilts	S	*Gunnis* 1968, 204
2.	?†1730	Sir Edward Mansel	Llangyndeyrn, Carmarthen	S	*Dale-Jones and Lloyd*, 1989, 50
3.	?1745	Mary Hilliard	Kilmerdown, Somerset	S	*Gunnis* 1968, 204
4.	?1746	John Long	Hedington, Wilts	S	*Gunnis* 1968, 204
5.	†1747	Thomas Chaplin	Tathwell, Lincs		Pevsner, *Lincs*, 1989, 742
6.	†1749	Dame Ann Cobb	Newton St Loe, Somerset	S	Pevsner, *Somerset: N & Bristol*, 1958, 233
7.	†1750	Canon James Barclay	Weston, Somerset	S	
8.	†1752	Dr and Mrs Cheyne	Weston, Somerset	S	GPC
9.	?1757	Eyles family	St John, Devizes, Wilts	S	*Gunnis* 1968, 204
10.	?1758	Thomas Dawtrey	Petworth, Sussex	S	*Gunnis* 1968, 204

11.	†1759	Bishop Maddox of Worcester	Worcester Cathedral	S	Pevsner, *Worcs*, 1968, 312; Penny 1977 (1), 136, 219 n2; *Bindman and Baker* 1995, 281
12.	1761	Alexander Pope (†1744)	St Mary, Twickenham, London	S	Pevsner, *London: S*, 1983, 539
13.	†1761	Thomas Collins	St Leonard, Exeter, Devon	S	Pevsner, *Devon*, 1989, 391
14.	?1762	Anne Carey	Steeple Aston, Wilts	S	*Gunnis* 1968, 204
15.	†1764	John, 3rd Baron Trevor	Bromham, Beds	S	Pevsner, *Beds, Hunts & Peterborough*, 1968, 59; *Sullivan* 2006, 404 (repr)
16.	†1766	Elizabeth Jenkins	Priston, Somerset	S	Pevsner, *Somerset: N. & Bristol*, 1958, 247
17.	*c*1769		Walcot, near Bath		RG/JP, suppl 4

Statues

18.	pre-1749	Ganymede	[for Lewis Monson Watson]; untraced		*HWC*, 20, 86
19.	1752	Richard 'Beau' Nash	[Pump Room, Bath]; untraced		*Gunnis* 1968, 203
20.	1759	Helen, Paris, Diana and Venus	[Stourhead, Wilts]; untraced		*Gunnis* 1968, 203
21.	nd	Minerva	[The sculptor's parlour, 1769]; untraced		Hoare's will
22.	nd	Zingara	[The sculptor's coll 1769]; untraced		Hoare's will

Busts

23.	pre-1741	Lord Chesterfield	Joanna Barnes (1990)		*Gunnis* 1968, 203
24.	1749	Plautilla	Untraced	SD	*Newby* 1986, 97 (pl 3)
25.	1761	Richard 'Beau' Nash	Guildhall, Bath, Somerset		*Gunnis* 1968, 204
26.	nd	Alexander Pope	Victoria Art Gallery, Bath BATVG: M:1983.590	S	*Gunnis* 1968, 204
27.	nd	Cicero	Untraced		HWC, 20, 86

Chimneypieces

28.	1760–1762	For the library and a bedroom	Corsham Court, Wilts		*Gunnis* 1968, 203–4
29.	1765	Several Payment(s): £75	Corsham Court, Wilts		*Gunnis* 1968, 204

Reliefs

30.	by 1749	Antinous	Untraced		*Lewis* 1961, 155

Miscellaneous

31.	1754	Bust of a Vestal	[coll Sir Robert Throckmorton]; untraced		*Gunnis* 1968, 204
32.	1754	Copy of the Wild Boar at Florence	[coll Sir Robert Throckmorton]; untraced		*Gunnis* 1968, 204
33.	1776	Unidentified work for Henry Hoare Payment(s): £100	untraced		Hoare Private Accounts, 1752–78, 28 Aug 1776

HOB, Samuel fl *c*1792–93

Pevsner notes that three low-relief headstones at Dumbleton with pictorial compositions of the Resurrection, are 'said to be by Samuel Hob,' who was presumably a local carver (1–3).

Funerary Monuments

1.	†1792	Hester Clayton	Dumbleton, Glos		Pevsner, *Glos: Vale & Forest of Dean*, 1976, 175
2.	†1792	Robert Straight	Dumbleton, Glos		Pevsner, *Glos: Vale & Forest of Dean*, 1976, 175
3.	†1793	Richard Clayton	Dumbleton, Glos		Pevsner, *Glos: Vale & Forest of Dean*, 1976, 175

HOBDAY, Samuel, of Evesham fl *c*1816

Funerary Monuments

1.	†1816	Bernard Baldwin	Ashton-under-Hill, Glos	S	*Gunnis* 1968, 204

HOBSON, Aaron, of Enfield fl 1826–30

His yard was in London Lane, from where he supplied a large wall tablet commemorating James Meyer (1). He was also a dealer in 'Welch black marble.'

Literary References: *Gunnis* 1968, 204

Funerary Monuments

1.	?1826	James Meyer	Enfield parish church, Middx	S	*Gunnis* 1968, 204

HOCKLEY, Daniel fl 1819?

Funerary Monuments

1.	?1819	Thomas Wolfe, large tablet	Arkesden, Essex	S	*Gunnis* 1968, 204

HOCKLEY, John, of London fl 1745–74

He was a son of Thomas Hockley, a tallow-chandler of Godalming, Surrey, and was apprenticed to **Thomas Bull** in 1745. Five years later he was turned over to another mason of the same name. He finally became free in 1753. By 1761 Hockley had set up on his own 'Old Broad Street, opposite the Pay Office' (Masons' Company *Court Book*, 1751–95 (9 Nov 1761). In 1774 he succeeded to the post of Assistant to the Company on the death of **John Deval I**. He signs two 'large and curious monuments of an architectural type' (*Gunnis* 1968, 204).

Literary References: *Gunnis* 1968, 204

Archival References: Masons' Co, Freemen, fol 31 (11 Jan 1753)

Funerary Monuments

1.	1758	Elizabeth Gildart	St Andrew, Totteridge, London, churchyard	S	Pevsner, *London: N*, 1998, 188
2.	?1763	John Hayley	Hendon, Middx, churchyard	S	*Gunnis* 1968, 204

HODGES, William fl 1759

His father, Robert Hodges, became free of the Masons' Company in 1738, having served under **Robert Taylor I** since 1731. The younger Hodges received a premium awarded anonymously from the Society of Arts on 22 March 1759 for a festoon. Dossie states that he was since 'a pupil of Wilson'.

Literary References: *Dossie* 1782, 437

Archival References: Masons' Co, Court Book, 1722–51 (29 June 1738); RSA Minutes 1758–60, seq 1 fol 78,80

HODGSON, J, of Driffield fl 1805?

Funerary Monuments

1.	?1805	William Schoolcroft, large wall tablet	Hovingham, N R Yorks	S	*Gunnis* 1968, 204

HOFFMAN, Karl 1815–86

Pevsner records three works by Hoffmann in British Roman Catholic churches. The sculptor was born in Wiesbaden, Germany and worked in Munich under Ludwig von Schwanthaler before studying in Rome. He was in Cologne from 1845 to 1850, and became a specialist in religious subject matter. His works can be found in Rome and Germany. He died near Rome in July 1886.

Literary References: *Grove* 1996, 14, 631 (Puls)

Statues

1.	*c*1848	'Our Lady'	Clifford, W R Yorks	Pevsner, *Yorks: W R*, 1967, 164
2.	post-1850	'Our Lady'	Mount St Bernard Abbey, Leics	Pevsner, *Leics & Rutland*, 1984, 325

Architectural Sculpture

3.	post-1844	Unidentified sculpture	St Cuthbert's College, Ushaw, Durham, chapel and St Joseph's Chapel	Pevsner, *Durham*, 1983, 479

HOGAN, H fl 1828

In 1828, while living at 12 Park Street, Dorset Square, he was awarded a medal from the Society of Arts.

Architectural Sculpture

1.	1828	Copy in plaster of an architectural ornament	[Soc of A, large silver medal]; untraced	RSA, *Transactions*, vol 46, 1828, xxvii

HOGAN, John 1800–58

Ireland's foremost neoclassical sculptor, he spent most of his career in Rome, though his patrons were predominantly Irish. He was born at Tallow, County Waterford, on 14 October 1800. His mother, Frances Cox, came from a privileged Protestant background and her family disinherited her when she married a Roman Catholic builder, another John Hogan. Hogan was the third of their six children. Soon after his birth the family moved to Cork and at the age of eight John was sent to a school at Tallow run by his father's friend, John Cangley, where he remained five years and apparently excelled at mathematics and history. He was articled to a solicitor in Cork in 1816 but had little enthusiasm for the law and later recalled 'even at school and in the office of my deceased master, Michael Foot, Attorney, I constantly availed myself of every opportunity to amuse myself with sketching the different orders of architecture and everything related to it' (Hogan to Carey, 26 November 1823, Hogan Papers, letter 28 addendum cited by *Turpin* 1982 (2), 98). In 1818–20 he was employed by the leading Cork architect, Thomas Deane, who set him to work making models and carving decorative details for his buildings, including a figure of *Minerva* for the Life and Fire Assurance Company offices (**16**). Hogan later wrote, 'undoubtedly it is to Mr. Deane that I am indebted for my being a sculptor, as my mind was never bent on that art. Until he placed the chisel in my hands, it was entirely given over to that of architecture' (*ibid*).

In 1818 a collection of casts of the marbles at the Vatican, made under the supervision of **Antonio Canova** and given by Pope Pius VII to the Prince Regent, was presented to the Cork Society for the Promotion of the Fine Arts, so forming the basis of the city's first art academy. Hogan was one of the early students who benefited from this gift and he began to draw from the casts in his spare time almost as soon as they were available. He studied sculpture virtually full-time between 1821 and 1823 and attended anatomy lectures given by Dr Woodruffe, the surgeon at Cork's South Infirmary, carving a number of anatomical studies, including a life-size skeleton, which Woodruffe used to illustrate a subsequent lecture (**85**). He soon began to exhibit his work in public, showing two studies at the Cork Society for the Promotion of the Fine Arts in 1821. His first patron was George Newenham, a banker, who commissioned his portrait bust in marble (**38**). The detailed, realistic carving shows that even at this early date Hogan had achieved a high level of technical competence. In 1822, he undertook his first ecclesiastical commission, a series of 27 small wood statues of saints and a relief of 'The Last Supper' to decorate St Mary's Pro-Cathedral in Cork (**75, 76**).

In August 1823 William Carey, a picture dealer and art critic, visited the cast collection at Cork and saw examples of Hogan's carving. He was sufficiently impressed to publicise Hogan's work in articles for the Cork and Dublin press and to campaign for a fund to send Hogan to Rome to continue his studies. Hogan also won support from other sources, including the collector Sir John Fleming-Leicester of Nether Tabley House, Knutsford, the Royal Irish Institution, William Crawford, a successful brewer, and the Royal Dublin Society, who bought a number of Hogan's studies (**86**). Early in 1824 Hogan set off for Rome, first briefly visiting London, where he called on **Francis Chantrey** and Sir Thomas Lawrence, to whom he had letters of introduction from Fleming-Leicester. He also visited the Royal Academy, where he met **John Flaxman RA**, dismissed by Hogan as a 'mean looking decrepit man' (*Atkinson* 1858, 517ff cited by *Turpin* 1982 (2), 98). He failed to be impressed by the Elgin Marbles in the British Museum, writing 'I know if they were in my possession I should throw half of them into the Thames' (*ibid*). He did however admire an eclectic range of monuments in Westminster Abbey by **L F Roubiliac, Michael Rysbrack, John Bacon RA, Joseph Nollekens** and **Sir Richard Westmacott**.

Hogan arrived in Rome on Palm Sunday, 1824. He joined the English Academy and spent much of his time drawing from the life or from antiquities in the museums. He soon made contact with other artists, including **Richard James Wyatt, Joseph Gott, Lawrence Macdonald** and **John Gibson**, who allowed Hogan to work in his studio. Within a few months he had become an advocate of the neo-classical style dominating artistic production in Rome and in December 1824 he enthusiastically described Canova and **Bertel Thorvaldsen** as the men who had 'completely reformed the heavy Gothic overcharged style of Donatello, Bernini and all those of that period to the beautiful simplicity of the antique' (Hogan to Crawford, 4 December 1824, Hogan Papers, letter 56, cited by *Turpin* 1982 (2), 99). He progressed well in his studies and was clearly confident in his ability for he wrote home, 'I feel myself gaining ground rapidly, and say from conviction that I can furnish the hands and extremities of the human figure, as well if not better that Gibson, Westmacott or any English Sculptor' (*Atkinson* 1858, cited by *Turpin* 1982 (1), 50). Late in 1825 he was running out of funds but a further £150 was forthcoming from his British supporters which enabled him to rent a studio in Vicola degli Incurabile, Vicino al Corso. Soon after, he took over part of Canova's old studio in Via di San Giacomo, a small street running from the Corso to Ripetta.

Hogan's first major work executed in Rome, *Italian shepherd boy* (**18**), a reclining male nude, was influenced by Canova's *Sleeping Endymion* and Gibson's recently completed *Sleeping shepherd*. This was followed by a *Drunken faun* (**19**) which Hogan executed in response to a challenge from the Italian painter, Vincenzo Camuccini, to produce an original work in the classical style. The figure's pose is unusual and effectively conveys the strength and drunkenness of the faun within a controlled triangular composition. Hogan soon turned his attention from mythological themes to religious subjects, such as the *Dead Christ* (**20**), which has an austere quality, perhaps derived from Thorvaldsen's religious works, though the subtly idealised modelling of the figure owes much to Canova. These early works were acclaimed by Hogan's fellow artists including Thorvaldsen, who is reputed to have said to him, 'My son, you are the best sculptor I leave after me in Rome' (*Atkinson* 1858, cited by *Turpin* 1982 (2), 100).

In 1829 Hogan returned briefly to Ireland, and exhibited his works in the board room of the Royal Irish Institution. The *Dead Christ* was purchased for the Carmelite Friary in Clarendon Street, Dublin and a *Pietà* was commissioned for the church of St Nicholas of Myra (**21**). During a second visit in 1832 he was awarded a medal by the Cork Society for the Promotion of the Fine Arts in recognition of his achievements and he obtained his first commission for a funerary monument (**1**). In 1833 he showed a modified version of his *Dead Christ*, a marble intended for Finbar, Cork at the Royal Academy in London (**23**). The work was badly displayed and 'it is said that he was so disgusted with the reception which his first great work met in England, that he determined on never submitting again to the judgement of so unfair a tribunal' (*Cork Mag*, March 1848, cited by *Turpin* 1982 (1), 64). He showed little subsequent inclination to exhibit in London or to court English patrons.

By 1837 Hogan was well established in his profession and sufficiently secure financially to marry Cornelia Bevignani, a cultured and beautiful Roman woman 15 years his junior. They lived at 24 Vicolo dei Greci for some years and moved in 1842 to 156 Via Babuino with their growing family. Between 1837 and 1849 Hogan worked principally on funerary monuments, statues and busts commemorating eminent Irishmen. One visitor to his studio described it as 'a sort of Hibernian Walhalla' (*Savanarola* 1847, quoted in *Atkinson* 1858, 562, cited by *Turpin* 1982 (1), 92). He made visits home in 1840, 1843 and 1846 to see works installed, meet patrons and collect payments. The monument to James, Bishop of Kildare and Leighlin (**4**), a champion of Catholic emancipation, gave Hogan the opportunity to explore for the first time a specifically Irish theme. The bishop is presented gazing heavenwards, exhorting a kneeling allegorical personification of Ireland to rise. Full recognition of Hogan's importance as a sculptor came soon after completing this group when in 1839 he was elected a member of the Virtuosi of the Pantheon.

His public statues included heroic, idealised images of Thomas Drummond (**28**), William Crawford (**30**) and Daniel O'Connell (**31**). He also continued to produce works for the Catholic church, for instance altarpieces commissioned by the Loreto order (**77, 78**). His finest work was perhaps another allegorical representation of Ireland, *Hibernia with the bust of Lord Cloncurry* (**29**), completed in 1844. Cloncurry wrote to Hogan in 1848, 'Every day gains new admirers for *Hibernia*. I really have not seen anything more perfect as to the marble or the execution' (Cloncurry to Hogan, 29 Oct 1848 quoted by *Fitzpatrick* 1855, cited by *Turpin* 1982 (1), 79). In a later version Hogan depicted *Hibernia* with the Irish king, Brian Boroimhe as a young boy (**36**). Hogan employed a number of assistants in his busy studio: Lorenzo Sassi, Marchucia, Bablone, G Malpieri and Restaldi are all listed as modellers or carvers in his account books. Later, in Dublin, he employed William Burnell and **James Cahill**.

In 1849 Hogan left Rome with his family, alarmed by political upheavals in the city. They settled in Dublin at 14 Wentworth Place (now Hogan Place). He exhibited at the RA once more in 1850 and at the Royal Hibernian Academy on several occasions. Examples of his work were displayed at the Cork, Dublin and Paris International Exhibitions, of 1852, 1853 and 1855 and *Eve startled by the sight of death* (**17**), executed at the beginning of his career for Sir John Fleming-Leicester, was lent to the Manchester Art Treasures Exhibition in 1857. He was responsible for a number of new works, including a statue of Thomas Davis (**34**), a founding member of the Young Ireland movement, which promoted Irish cultural regeneration. A second statue of Daniel O'Connell went to Limerick (**37**) and two monuments to the Roman Catholic Cathedral at St John's, Newfoundland (**11, 12**). He was greatly disappointed however by his failure to secure two important commissions: **Thomas Farrell** won the competition for the memorial to Daniel Murray, Archbishop of Dublin, with a design for a free-standing group much grander than Hogan's proposed relief (**10**) and **Christopher Moore** was chosen to execute a statue of the Irish national poet, Thomas Moore, though Hogan's design was generally thought far superior (**35**).

In 1855 Hogan 'was seized with an attack of paralysis, perhaps brought on by stress, which rendered his right, working arm useless for several months' (*O'Donoghue* 1896, 269 cited by *Turpin* 1982 (1), 108). Over the next 3 years his health deteriorated and he died on 27 March 1858, aged 57. He was buried a few days later at Glasnevin cemetery. A large number of mourners, including some 200 students from Trinity College, participated in the funeral procession. A Hogan testimonial fund raised £300 for his widow and she was awarded a civil list pension of £100 a year. At his death Hogan left unfinished a huge relief symbolising *Civil and religious liberty* for the Wellington Testimonial in Phoenix Park, Dublin (**82**). It had been commissioned in 1857, with reliefs by **Thomas Farrell** and **Joseph Kirk**, and Hogan had completed the plaster sketch model. The work was finished in Rome by his 17 year-old son, John Valentine Hogan, under the direction of his former assistant **Giovanni Maria Benzoni**. John Valentine Hogan went on to have a successful career as a sculptor in Rome, where he died in 1920.

Hogan believed that he was treated badly by his countrymen, particularly in his later years and this view of him as a neglected genius informs many early accounts of his life. Sydney, Lady Morgan wrote shortly after his death, that 'his reputation fell into the sere and yellow leaf of utter neglect from the want of patronage, the patronage of party, which he had no means or did not seek to entertain. He worked on hopelessly and helplessly in that country of all Europe, the one where talent is least noticed and the least rewarded' (*Athenaeum*, 10 April, 1858 cited by *Turpin* 1982 (1), 114). As a young man, however, Hogan received considerable encouragement and financial help from Irish supporters and as his career progressed his patrons included Irish Catholics, nationalists and the Protestant aristocracy. Ireland's depressed economic state after the famine, a growing preference for a more realistic style in portrait sculpture, Hogan's departure from Rome and his over-sensitive, sometimes abrasive personality, may all have affected his ability to attract commissions at the end of his career. A contemporary commentator considered him 'both original and powerful' and highlighted his 'intellectual vigour and depth of thought' (*AJ*, 1850, 376 cited by *Turpin* 1982 (2), 103). More recently John Turpin has reinforced this view, writing 'Hogan was a sculptor of ideas, and one of his strengths was his ability to give sculptural form to abstract concepts and to conceive a powerful, yet controlled religious art' (*Turpin* 1982 (1), 12).

EH

Literary References: *DNB* XXVII, 1891, 81–2; *Cork Hist Soc Journal* 1895, 207–18; *Strickland* I, 1913, 489–96; *Crookshank* 1966, 311; *Gunnis* 1968, 204–5; *Barrett* 1971 (1), 85; *Harbison, Potterton and Sheehy*, 1978, 218, 222; *Sheehy* 1980, 24–7; *Turpin* 1982 (1), *passim*; *Turpin* 1982 (2), 98–103; *Grove* 14, 1996, 636 (Turpin)

Additional MS Sources: Hogan Papers

Portraits of the Sculptor: B Mulrenin, drawing, NGI (*Turpin* 1982 (1), 21, repr); etching after C Grey, *Dublin University Magazine*, XXXV, 1850; woodcut, *AJ*, 1850, 376

Funerary Monuments

No.	Date	Work		Location		References
1.	c1833	Michael Collins, Bishop of Cloyne and Ross (†1832)		Skibbereen, Co Cork	S	*Potterton* 1975, 51; *Turpin* 1982 (1), 128
2.	†1835	Rev Fr Justin McNamara		Kinsale, Co Cork		*Potterton* 1975, 51; *Turpin* 1982 (1), 93, 94, 137–8 (repr)
3.	c1838	Patrick Murphy (†1837)		St Joseph's Cemetery, Cork		*Turpin* 1982 (1), 128–9
4.	1837–1839	James Warren Doyle, RC Bishop of Kildare and Leighlin (†1834)		Carlow Cathedral	S	*Potterton* 1975, 50; *Turpin* 1982 (1), 67, 129–31 (repr)
5.	c1843	Jeanette Mary Farrell (†1838)		St Andrew, Westland Row, Dublin	S	*Potterton* 1975, 32, 50 (repr); *Turpin* 1982 (1), 74, 131 (repr)
6.	1841–1844	William Beamish (†1828) Payment(s): £650 Model(s): Crawford MAG, Cork, 1842–3, plaster		St Michael, Blackrock, Co Cork	S	*Potterton* 1975, 50; *Turpin* 1982 (1), 75, 131–4 (repr)
7.	1845	Rev John Brinkley, Bishop of Cloyne (†1835)		Trinity College, Dublin		*Potterton* 1975, 51, 67 (repr); *Turpin* 1982 (1), 90, 134–5 (repr)
8.	1848	Amelia Curran (†1847)		S Isidro, Rome, Italy		*Turpin* 1982 (1), 136–7
9.	1846–1849	Peter Purcell (†1846) Model(s): Crawford MAG, Cork, 1847, plaster,		Pro-Cathedral, Dublin		*Graves* IV, 1905–6, 123; *Potterton* 1975, 51, 68 (repr); *Turpin* 1982 (1), 91, 135–6 (repr)
10.	1852	Daniel Murray, Archbishop of Dublin (†1852), two competition models only (Monument executed by Thomas Farrell)	pm	NMI, Dublin		*Turpin* 1982 (1), 138
11.	1853	Michael Fleming, Bishop of Newfoundland Model(s): Crawford MAG, Cork, c1852, plaster		Basilica of St John the Baptist, St John's, Newfoundland, Canada	SD	*Turpin* 1982 (1), 138–40
12.	1853	Rev Dr Thomas Scallan (†1830) Model(s): Crawford MAG, Cork, c1852, plaster		Basilica of St John the Baptist, St John's, Newfoundland, Canada		*Turpin* 1982 (1), 140–1
13.	c1857	Archdeacon Matthew Flanagan (†1856)		St Nicholas of Myra, Dublin	S	*Turpin* 1982 (1), 141–2
14.	1857	John Murphy, Bishop of Cork		[St Mary's Pro-Cathedral, Cork]; untraced		*Potterton* 1975, 50; *Turpin* 1982 (1), 141
15.	1874	Carolan Morgan (†1738)		St Patrick's Cathedral, Dublin		C Lib (repr)

Statues

No.	Date	Work		Location		References
16.	c1820	Minerva		[Life and Fire Assurance Co, Parnell Place, Cork]; Crawford MAG, Cork		*Turpin* 1982 (1), 175; *Hill* 1998, 74
17.	1825	Eve startled at the sight of death Payment(s): £74	m	[Exhib Manc Art Treas Exhib, 1857, 12, coll Lord de Tabley]; untraced		*Manchester Art Treasures* 1857, 133; *Gunnis* 1968, 205; *Turpin* 1982 (1), 177–8
18.	1824–1825	Italian shepherd boy Payment(s): £100	m	[Powerscourt House, Co Wicklow, gardens]; untraced Other versions: Iveagh House, Dublin, SD 1846, marble ex coll Sydney Lady Morgan, plaster miniature, nd; untraced	SD	*Turpin* 1982 (1), 48, 98, 176, 178–9 (repr); *Stewart* II, 1985, 92; *Grove* 14, 1996, 636
19.	1826	The drunken faun	p	[Royal Irish Institution, Dublin]; Crawford MAG, Cork Other versions: Destr, ex UCD, pl, c1850–1851	S	*Turpin* 1982 (1), 53, 177, 179 (repr); *Murray* 1991, 146 (f'piece repr)
20.	1829	Dead Christ Payment(s): £400	m	Carmelite Friary, Clarendon Street, Dublin		*Crookshank* 1966, 311; *Turpin* 1982 (1), 57, 164 (repr)
21.	c1831	Pietà	p	St Nicholas of Myra, Francis Street, Dublin		*Turpin* 1982 (1), 60, 63, 164–5 (repr)
22.	c1831	Two angels	m	St Nicholas of Myra, Francis Street, Dublin		*Turpin* 1982 (1), 60, 63, 165 (repr)
23.	1832	Dead Christ, with the instruments of the Passion Payment(s): £500 Model(s): Crawford MAG, 1832, plaster	m	St Finbar (South Chapel), Cork Other versions: Basilica of St John the Baptist, St John's, Newfoundland, Canada, 1853, marble		*Graves* IV, 1905–6, 123; *Lewis* 1837, I, 424; *Turpin* 1982 (1), 167–8, 172

No.	Date	Subject	Medium	Location		Literature
24.	1830–1839	The Judgement of Paris		[coll General Sir James Riall]; untraced		*Turpin* 1982 (1), 178
25.	c1840	Monsignor Hyacinth Quelen, statuette	m	[coll Lord de Clifford]; untraced		*Turpin* 1982 (1), 142
26.	?c1843	Madonna and child ('Our Lady of Victories')	p	Untraced		*Turpin* 1982 (1), 170
27.	1843	St Stanislas; the Madonna ('Immaculate Conception')		Convent of Villa Lanti, Rome		*Turpin* 1982 (1), 169–70; *Kane* 2000, 152 (repr)
28.	1840–1843	Thomas Drummond	m	City Hall, Dublin	S	*ILN*, 2 Dec 1843, 365; *Read* 1982, 118, 120 (repr); *Turpin* 1982 (1), 71, 143–4 (repr)
29.	1841–1844	Hibernia with the bust of Lord Cloncurry Model(s): bust of Lord Cloncurry, NMI, 1841, plaster; head and torso of Erin, NMI, ? 1844, plaster	m	[Lyons House, Co Kildare]; NGI		*Turpin* 1982 (1), 77, 78, 146, 153, 179–80 (repr); *Murphy* 1999, 69–70 (repr)
30.	1845	William Crawford	m	[The Savings Bank, Cork, Ireland]; Crawford MAG, Cork	S	*Barrett* 1971 (1), 85; *Turpin* 1982 (1), 71, 142–3 (repr)
31.	1843–1846	Daniel O'Connell	m	City Hall, Dublin	SD	ILN, 1846, 288 (repr); *Ormond* 1973, 348; *Read* 1982, 120; *Turpin* 1982 (1), 83, 144–5 (repr); *Hill* 1998, 89–90
32.	1848	Two kneeling angels	m	Loreto Abbey, Rathfarnham, Dublin Other versions: Loreto convent, Fermoy, c1853, marble		*Turpin* 1982 (1), 86, 171, 174 (repr)
33.	1849	Transfiguration	m	Convent of the Irish Sisters of Charity, Clarinbridge, Co Galway Other versions: Glanmire church, Cork, 1851, marble St Andrew Westland Row, c1858, marble ex Powerscourt House, c1858, marble; untraced		*Barrett* 1971 (1), 85; *Turpin* 1982 (1), 89, 171–2, 174–5 (repr); *Stewart* II, 1985, 92
34.	1853	Thomas Davis Payment(s): £525 Model(s): Crawford MAG, Cork, 1853, plaster		[Mount Jerome Cemetery, Dublin]; City Hall, Dublin	SD	*Read* 1982, 120; *Turpin* 1982 (1), 100, 145–7 (repr); *Stewart* II, 1985, 92
35.	1853	Thomas Moore, two alternative competition models only (statue executed by Christopher Moore)	p	NGI 8061, 8284		*Turpin* 1982 (1), 104, 147–8 (repr); *le Harivel* 1988, 567–8 (repr); *Hill* 1998, 97–8
36.	1855	Hibernia and Brian Boroimhe	p	Crawford MAG, Cork	SD	*Turpin* 1982 (1), 106, 107, 181–3 (repr)
37.	1857	Daniel O'Connell Payment(s): £1,000	b	The Crescent, Limerick		*Turpin* 1982 (1), 109, 148–9 (repr); *Hill* 1998, 90–1
Busts						
38.	c1821	George Newenham	m	Waterford AG		*Turpin* 1982 (1), 150
39.	1823	St Leger Aldworth	m	[coll Richard Aldworth]; untraced		*Turpin* 1982 (1), 150
40.	1828	Rev Fr Justin McNamara	m	Convent of Mercy, Kinsale	SD	*Turpin* 1982 (1), 150–1
41.	1833	Elizabeth Hogan, the sculptor's sister	p	NMI	SD	*Turpin* 1982 (1), 133, 151 (repr)
42.	1834	Daniel Murphy	m	Untraced	S	*Turpin* 1982 (1), 153
43.	1834	James Murphy	m	Sotheby, 1996 (formerly on loan Crawford MAG, Cork)	SD	*Turpin* 1982 (1), 139, 151 (repr)
44.	1834	Rev Dr John Murphy Model(s): Crawford MAG, Cork, 1834, plaster	m	Crawford MAG, Cork	SD	*Turpin* 1982 (1), 151
45.	1841	Fr Theobald Mathew Model(s): Capuchin Friary, Church Street, Dublin, 1841, plaster	m	[Capuchin Friary, Church Street, Dublin]; untraced Other versions: coll Séan O Criadáin, 1841, marble; untraced	S	*Graves* IV, 1905–6, 123; *Turpin* 1982 (1), 152, 153–4 (repr); *Stewart* II, 1985, 92
46.	c1841	Rev Peter Kenny	m	Loreto Abbey, Rathfarnham, Dublin		*Turpin* 1982 (1), 154
47.	1841	William Beamish	m	Untraced		*Athenaeum*, 1858, 174, 175; *Turpin* 1982 (1), 153
48.	1843	Daniel O'Connell	p	Loreto Abbey, Rathfarnham, Dublin		*Turpin* 1982 (1), 155
49.	1843	Mary, Lady Berehaven and Countess of Bantry	m	Bantry House, Cork		*Turpin* 1982 (1), 155
50.	1843	Richard, Viscount Berehaven and Earl of Bantry	m	Bantry House, Cork		*Turpin* 1982 (1), 154–5
51.	1844	Daniel O'Connell	m	coll D O'Connell Miley, Dublin	S	*Graves* IV, 1905–6, 123; *Turpin* 1982 (1), 156, 161 (repr); *Stewart* II, 1985, 92
52.	1844	Dominick O'Reilly	m	Untraced		*Turpin* 1982 (1), 157
53.	1844	Dr Daniel Murray, Archbishop of Dublin Model(s): Loreto Abbey, Rathfarnham, 1844, plaster	m	NGI 8034 Other versions: coll Irish Sisters of Charity, Elm Park, Dublin, 1844, marble	S	*Turpin* 1982 (1), 156–7, 165 (repr); *le Harivel* 1988, 567 (repr)
54.	?1844	'Erin' (? Cornelia Bevignani, the sculptor's wife)	p	NMI, Dublin Other versions: National College of Art and Design, Dublin, ?1844, plaster		*Turpin* 1982 (1), 181, 182
55.	1843–1844	James Power MP	m	Untraced		*Turpin* 1982 (1), 156
56.	1843–1844	Robert Batt	m	Untraced		*Turpin* 1982 (1), 156
57.	1844	Thomas Steele	p	NMI, Dublin		*Turpin* 1982 (1), 157–8, 173 (repr); *Stewart* II, 1985, 92

58.	1845	Thomas Farrell	m	Untraced		*Turpin* 1982 (1), 158
59.	1846	Mr Pike	m	Untraced		*Turpin* 1982 (1), 158
60.	?1844–1847	Samuel Kyle DD, Bishop of Cork	m	Untraced		*Turpin* 1982 (1), 159
61.	1848	Rev Francis Mahony ('Fr Prout')	m	Crawford MAG, Cork	S	*Turpin* 1982 (1), 158–9
62.	1850–1852	Head of Minerva	p	Royal Irish Academy		*Turpin* 1982 (1), 183
63.	1852	Thomas Higgs	m	Untraced		*Turpin* 1982 (1), 159
64.	1853	Dr Scanlon	m	[Dublin Int Exhib, 1070]; untraced		*Turpin* 1982 (1), 159
65.	1853	Mr Kennedy	m	[coll Charles Kennedy]; untraced		*Turpin* 1982 (1), 159
66.	1854	Dr Robert Graves Model(s): Meath Hospital, Dublin, 1854, plaster	m	RC Physic, Dublin	SD	*Turpin* 1982 (1), 159–60; *Stewart* II, 1985, 92
67.	1854	John Banim Payment(s): £100	m	Thosel, Kilkenny	D	*Turpin* 1982 (1), 160
68.	1855	Dr Daniel Corbett	m	Crawford MAG, Cork		*Turpin* 1982 (1), 160–2; *Stewart* II, 1985, 92
69.	1855	Miss Hart Payment(s): £20	p	[coll Andrew Hart]; untraced		*Turpin* 1982 (1), 160
70.	1855	Sir James Grattan Model(s): Crawford MAG, Cork, 1855, plaster	m	[The Infirmary, Maryborough (Portlaoise)]; untraced		*Turpin* 1982 (1), 160–2
71.	1855	William Carleton	p	NGI 8196	S	*Turpin* 1982 (1), 162; *le Harivel* 1988, 568 (repr)
72.	nd	Sir John and Lady Ennis	m	Sotheby, 5 July 2000, lot 142	S	
73.	nd	Unidentified man	m	NGI 8024	S	*Turpin* 1982 (1), 162; *le Harivel* 1988, 567 (repr)

Architectural Sculpture

74.	c1819	Shop front	wd	[Patrick Street, Cork]; destroyed		*Turpin* 1982 (1), 184
75.	1823	Apostles and Saints, 27 figures	wd	[St Mary's Pro-Cathedral, Cork]; untraced		*Turpin* 1982 (1), 163
76.	1823	'The Last Supper', altar frontal	wd	[St Mary's Pro-Cathedral, Cork]; Crawford MAG, Cork Other versions: ex Holy Trinity, Cork, 1823, wood (higher relief); untraced		*Turpin* 1982 (1), 163
77.	1843	Pietà, altar frontal Model(s): Crawford MAG, Cork, 1842, plaster	m	Loreto Abbey, Rathfarnham, Dublin Other versions: Ballymarn church, Crossabeg, Co Wexford, marble, 1843 St Saviour, Dominick Street, Dublin, SD 1857, marble St John the Baptist, Blackrock, Co Dublin Sts Peter and Paul, Balbriggan, Co Dublin Dungarvan church, Co Waterford (made by Scannell) Loreto Abbey, Balbriggan (reputed to be by Parnell)		*Crookshank* 1966, 311, 312 (repr); *Turpin* 1982 (1), 84, 168–9, 174 (repr); *Stewart* II, 1985, 92
78.	1844	'The Nativity', altar frontal Model(s): Crawford MAG, Cork, 1844, plaster	m	Loreto Abbey, Dalkey, Co Dublin		*Turpin* 1982 (1), 85, 170–1 (repr)

Reliefs

79.	c1823	Bacchanal (or Triumph of Silenus)	wd	Untraced		*Turpin* 1982 (1), 176
80.	1822–1823	Silenus and satyrs	s	Untraced		*Turpin* 1982 (1), 175
81.	c1842	Head of Christ	m	At Mary's Priory, Pope Quay, Cork		*Turpin* 1982 (1), 168
82.	1858–1860	Civil and religious liberty (co-sculptor: Giovanni Benzoni)	b	Wellington Testimonial, Phoenix Park, Dublin		*Harbison, Potterton and Sheehy* 1978, 233; *Turpin* 1982 (1), 110, 149–50 (repr); *Hill* 1998, 256 n77
83.	nd	John Hogan, the sculptor's father, portrait medallion	p	NMI, Dublin		*Turpin* 1982 (1), 162–3
84.	nd	The sculptor's daughters, portrait medallion	p	NMI, Dublin	S	*Turpin* 1982 (1), 162–3

Miscellaneous

85.	c1819	Female skeleton, anatomical study	wd	[coll Dr Woodroffe]; Crawford MAG, Cork		*Turpin* 1982 (1), 183–4
86.	1820–1821	Mask of Michelangelo's Moses, leg of Mercury, hand and staff, an arm showing muscles, hand and arm, hand holding a sword hilt, studies	wd	[RDS, Dublin]; Crawford MAG, Cork		*Turpin* 1982 (1), 184–5
87.	c1823	Adonis	wd	[coll Thomas Deane, Blackrock, Cork]; untraced		*Turpin* 1982 (1), 176
88.	1820–1823	Anatomical study, a human figure showing muscles and sinews	a	NGI 8047	S	*Turpin* 1982 (1), 25, 185 (repr); *le Harivel* 1988, 567 (repr)
89.	1820–1823	Head and torso of an Apostle, studies	wd	[coll J Fleming-Leicester]; untraced		*Turpin* 1982 (1), 184
90.	1822–1823	The young Augustus (model of a Roman soldier)		Untraced		*Turpin* 1982 (1), 175–6
91.	1841	Foot of Lady Cloncurry	m	Lyons House, Co Kildare		*Janson* 1981, 300–1 (repr); *Turpin* 1982 (1), 186
92.	nd	Anatomical study of a head in profile	wd	NGI 8253	S	*le Harivel* 1988, 568 (repr)
93.	nd	Anatomical study of a leg	wd	NGI 8291		*le Harivel* 1988, 568 (repr)
94.	nd	Four hands	p	[coll Hogan family]; NMI, Dublin		*Turpin* 1982 (1), 186
95.	nd	Infant Jesus		St John's Cathedral, Newfoundland, Canada, basilica museum		www.stjohnsarchdiocese.nf.ca
96.	nd	James Warren Doyle, RC Bishop of Kildare and Leighlin, deathmask	p	NGI 8131		*le Harivel* 1988, 567 (repr)
97.	nd	The maturity		[Crawford MAG, Cork, 1953]; untraced		*Turpin* 1982 (1), 183

HOLBERT fl 1701

Holbert was an assistant to **John Nost I**. In addition to the chimneypiece for Hampton Court (1), he was paid for eight days work as a carver, and £1 12s for work in the gardens, where he took down pedestals in the privy garden and removed two vases.

Archival References: TNA WORK 5/52 fol 301

Chimneypieces

1.	1701	Purple marble	m	[Hampton Court Palace, Middx, long gallery]; untraced	TNA WORK 5/52 f301; *Gunnis* 1968, 205

HOLBROW, Isaac fl 1705–06

Chimneypieces

1.	1705–1706	English marble	Swangrove Lodge, Badminton, Glos, closet	Beaufort Accounts, 1705–6

HOLDER, James, of Emsworth fl 1818?–c1824

Gunnis considered his best tablet, 'in a delightful neo-Hellenic style' was to John Campbell (1). The monument to John Walker is a tablet surmounted by an urn on a black background (3).

Literary References: *Gunnis* 1968, 205

Funerary Monuments

1.	?1818	John Campbell	Westbourne, Sussex		*Gunnis* 1968, 205
2.	?1821	Miles Monk	Funtington, Sussex	S	*Gunnis* 1968, 205
3.	†1824	Commander John Walker	Warblington, Hants	S	*Gunnis* 1968, 205

HOLDER, T, of Tewkesbury fl c1793–1820

He signs two known tablets, one with the architect John Mullins.

Funerary Monuments

1.	†1793	Thomas Hill	All Saints, Evesham	S	*Gunnis* 1968, 205
2.	†1820	William Dredge (designed by John Mullins)	Orpington, Kent	S	*Colvin* 1995, 673

HOLDERNESS, William fl c1799

He is known only for one wall-tablet with Adamesque details.

Funerary Monuments

1.	†1799	Rachel Elliott	Bridlington Priory, E R Yorks	S	Pevsner, *Yorks: E R & York*, 1995, 346

HOLDFORTH, Thomas fl 1771

In 1771 he built a 'Gothick' temple at Gilling Castle, N R Yorks (Wombwell Archives, in GPC). In the same year he was paid for carved work in York (1).

Architectural Sculpture

1.	1771	'Moulded masonry in the cornices, architraves and battlements' Payment(s): £55	[Fairfax House, York]; untraced	GPC

HOLL, Edward, of Norwich and Beccles fl 1778–89

Holl entered into partnership with **John Brewer** in 1778. The notice of their union in the *Norfolk Mercury* mentions that Holl 'for several years had conducted the business of the late **Robert Page, of Norwich**'. The partnership was dissolved in 1789, when it was announced that Holl, who was described as a stone and marble mason, would carry on the business alone. In 1793 the same newspaper reported that, on the previous Thursday, Holl had married 'Miss Beckwith, only daughter of Mr John Beckwith of the Close [Norwich]'.

Gunnis said of the large pyramidal wall monument in coloured marbles to Caleb Elwin that the 'carving and workmanship are excellent, especially the angel's heads at the base' (1). An unsigned replica of this monument, to Thomas Newton, is in St Martin at Oak, Norwich.

Literary References: *Norwich Mercury*, 24 October 1778, 10 January 1789, 12 January 1793

Funerary Monuments

1.	†1776	Caleb Elwin	Thurning, Norfolk	S	GPC; Pevsner, *Norfolk: N E & Norwich*, 1997, 696

HOLL, John 1808–

He entered the Royal Academy Schools to study sculpture on 8 December 1830. Gunnis mis-transcribed his name from the archives, as 'John Holt'.

Literary References: *Gunnis* 1968, 208; *Hutchison* 1960–62, 182

HOLLAND, William fl c1704–18

The Eyre family monument carries the signature 'William Holland, of London' (1). In 1712 Dudley North made a payment to Holland of £20, possibly for chimneypieces at Glenham Hall, Suffolk. Four years later, in the same account book, North noted another payment, to 'Mr Holland, stone-cutter' for the monument to his wife, Catherine North (2), (Earl of Guilford Archives, in GPC).

Two masons named William Holland were made free of the Company in the late-17th century. William, son of Thomas of White Cross Street, St Giles Cripplegate, was apprenticed to **John Martin** on 13 March 1668 and became free of the Masons' Company on 5 October 1680. William, son of Samuel, of St Botolph, Bishopsgate, also became free via service, to John Pursor on 21 March 1691. A 'William Holland Mason' was recorded at the workshop of **William Stanton** in the company search of September 1694 (*Knoop and Jones* 1935, 78). This is probably the mason who became master of the Masons' Company in 1717.

Literary References: *Webb* 1999, 17

Archival References: Masons' Co, Court Book, 1695–1722, fol 157v; Masons' Co, Freemen, fol 28

Funerary Monuments

1.	1704	Gervase (†1703) and Catherine Eyre	Rampton, Notts	S	*Lord* 1986, 103–4 (repr)
2.	1717–1718	Catherine North (†1715) Payment(s): £59 2s 6d	Little Glemham, Suffolk		*CL*, 6 Sept 1956, 480, (repr); Pevsner, *Suffolk*, 1974, 336

HOLLINS, of Rochester

His one known tablet is inscribed 'Hollins Eng. Rocester.'

Miscellaneous

1.	nd	'Large tablet set in a gothic frame'	Ellastone church, Staffs, exterior wall	S	GPC

HOLLINS, Peter 1800–86

Peter Hollins was Birmingham's leading mid-19th century sculptor. He spent part of his career in London but despite early critical success, he failed to gain a national reputation. He was born on 1 May 1800 in Great Hampton Street, Birmingham, the fourth surviving son of the sculptor and architect **William Hollins**. Several members of his family were involved in artistic pursuits, including a cousin, John Hollins, the son of a Birmingham glass painter, who became a successful painter of portraits and historical subjects. Peter began his own artistic training in his father's studio. In an untraced manuscript memoir Hollins later recalled walking to Warwick Castle with his father at the age of 15 to model details of the Warwick vase and described assisting his father in his work at Alton Towers (*Hill and Midgley* 1929, 42). He also attended John Vincent Barber's drawing school.

In 1822 William and Peter Hollins exhibited three busts at the RA as joint works (**77, 78, 80**). At about the same time Peter went to London to work under **Sir Francis Chantrey**. It is not clear how long Hollins stayed but in 1824 he was in Birmingham, helping to install Chantrey's statue of James Watt in St Mary, Handsworth. Hollins praised the statue for its 'qualities of conception, and beauty of effect in light and shade', which he considered unequalled anywhere (*Hill and Midgley* 1929, 42). This opinion has tended to be confirmed by posterity for the Watt statue remains widely regarded as one of Chantrey's masterpieces.

Hollins's bust of Edward Grainger, the anatomist (**79**) was an early independent work. A correspondent in *Aris's Birmingham Gazette* applauded its verisimilitude, its realistic rendering of skin textures and animation and considered it an extraordinary achievement for such a young sculptor.

Hollins returned to London around 1828 and he shared a studio with the portrait painter Henry Room, at 17 Old Bond Street. He held an exhibition in the studio in 1831, showing groups of *The murder of the innocents* (**62**), *Conrad and Medora* (**59**) and *Aurora and Zephyr* (**61**), as well as three plaster busts (**87–89**). He was awarded the Sir Robert Lawley prize by the Birmingham Society of Arts for *Conrad and Medora*. A critic in the *Spectator* described *The murder of the innocents* (later shown at the 1851 Great Exhibition) as 'a noble composition and a work of art of the highest class, and of superior merit' despite some faults and concluded that Hollins was a promising young sculptor who seemed likely to distinguish himself in the future (*Spectator*, 14 May 1831, vol 4, no 150, 478).

Hollins was in Italy in the years 1835–36. He returned to London, where he spent the next few years and produced two of his most important church monuments, to Sophia Thompson (**28**) and Georgina, Countess of Bradford (**30**). The Thompson effigy, reclining on a couch greeting a celestial apparition, owes debts to Chantrey's monument to Elizabeth Digby, 1825, but Hollins's turning figure has a sense of vitality and drama that is absent from the Chantrey image. The Bradford monument, which has a reclining effigy in front of a relief of angels about to bear her soul to heaven, is influenced by the work of **Sir Richard Westmacott**.

In 1839 Hollins unsuccessfully competed for the commission for the national monument to Admiral Lord Nelson, to be erected in Trafalgar Square, London. His design (**146**) featured a statue of *Britannia* 120 feet high and was probably influenced by John Flaxman's proposal for a monumental *Britannia* with a lion, intended to commemorate British naval victories and to be placed in Greenwich Park.

Hollins appears to have maintained close links with the Midlands while he was in London, continuing for instance to exhibit with the Birmingham Society of Artists, and it is possible that he worked with his father on several occasions before William Hollins's death in 1843. This collaboration provides problems in identifying authorship of works produced during the 1820s and 1830s: many are signed simply 'Hollins' and may be by the father or the son, or possibly both. After his father's death in 1843 he returned to Birmingham to oversee the family business. There he produced numerous monuments, mostly for churches in the Midlands, and many busts of local dignitaries.

Hollins was also responsible for a number of portrait statues, including the figure of Dr Samuel Wilson Warneford, which has a prime position in the entrance of the Warneford Psychiatric Hospital, Oxford (**68**). He also submitted designs in competition for statues of Lord George Bentinck to be erected in Mansfield and of Sir Robert Peel, for Manchester, both of which Hollins mentioned in letters to the Warneford Hospital authorities. He did not win the contracts. Hollins provided two prestigious statues for Birmingham, of Peel and the City Recorder, Sir Rowland Hill (**72, 75**) but evidently felt that he should have been employed more extensively in works for his native city. He later darkly commented, 'I wish to draw a veil over my labours for my native town as they were a grievous disappointment to me, and the more than Egyptian darkness and ignorance of that branch of art which I had chosen was simply appalling' (*Hill and Midgley* 1929, 43). Among his few ideal works was a statue of *Sabrina* for the 2nd Earl of Bradford, which was later presented to the city of Shrewsbury (**69**).

Despite his complaints about the city's philistinism Hollins was a leading figure in Birmingham's artistic community. He was vice-president of Birmingham Society of Artists for 37 years and was instrumental in obtaining its royal charter. He was also an active supporter of numerous local educational and philanthropic institutions, including the School of Design and the Birmingham and Midland Institute. A tablet in St Philip's Cathedral, Birmingham, states that in 1859 he paid for restoration work on the west end of the cathedral in memory of his father. His contribution to the city was acknowledged in 1872 when a testimonial portrait by William T Roden was commissioned by subscription. It is now in the collection of Birmingham Museum and Art Gallery.

Hollins died 16 August 1886, in the house of his birth. He had stopped working some years earlier, having suffered from rheumatism, perhaps caused by prolonged working with wet clay in a cold studio. He is commemorated by a monument in St Paul's, Birmingham. He is not well known in comparison with near-contemporaries such as **Edward Hodges Baily, Joseph Durham** or **William Theed II**. The fact that he spent much of his career in an artistically unfashionable, if economically and technologically dynamic provincial centre helps explain his relative neglect. Yet his sculpture, which ranges from a baroque drama in the monumental effigies to more sober Victorian realism in his portraiture, has elicited retrospective admiration. Gunnis wrote of him, 'Hollins at his best was a very great artist and his monuments to Lady Bradford and Sophia Thompson are as fine as anything by Chantrey' (*Gunnis* 1968, 205).

EH

Literary References: *Langford* 1873, *passim*; *Birmingham Daily Post*, 18 August 1886, 4; *DNB* 27, 1891, 174; *Hill and Midgley* 1929, *passim*; *Physick* 1969, 40, 181; *Penny* 1977 (1), 89–92, 214 n48; *Parry-Jones* 1981, 24–32; *Grove* 14, 1996, 686 (Stocker); *ODNB* (Fisher)

Archival References: *Hollins Notebook*

Additional Manuscript Sources: *Peel Papers*, 1844, Add MS 40544 fol 144

Wills and Administrations: Birmingham district probate registry, will with two codicils, 22 November 1886, (personal estate £24,219 1s 6d), re-sworn February 1888, (£24,389 7s 5d), re-sworn May 1888, (£25,089 7s 5d)

Portraits of the Sculptor: William Thomas Roden, oil on canvas, BMAG

Funerary Monuments

1.	†1817	Samuel Addison	St Bartholomew, Wednesbury, Staffs	S	Pevsner, *Staffs*, 1974, 299
2.	†1823	James Hereford	Mordiford, Herefs		Pevsner, *Herefs*, 1963, 256
3.	†1824	John Smith	Wolverley, Worcs	S	Pevsner, *Worcs*, 1968, 291
4.	?1826	Charles Adderley	Lea Marston, Warks		*Gunnis* 1968, 206
5.	?1826	Edward Guest	St John, Dudley, Worcs		RG/JP, 4, 710
6.	†1827	Mary Essington	Birmingham Cathedral		RG/JP, 4, 710
7.	?1828	John Home	St Martin, Birmingham, Warks		*Gunnis* 1968, 206
8.	†1829	John and Thomas (†1831) Pargeter	Park Lane Unitarian Chapel, Cradley, Halesowen, Worcs		RG/JP, 4, 710
9.	†1829	Rev George Breay	Birmingham Cathedral		Pevsner, *Warks*, 1966, 109
10.	?1830	John Hankins	Wormley, Herts		RG/JP, 4, 710
11.	?1830	Rev John Newling	Lichfield Cathedral, Staffs		*Gunnis* 1968, 206
12.	†1831	Sir Henry Wakeman	North Claines, Worcs		Pevsner, *Worcs*, 1968, 225
13.	1832	Edward Crowther	St Bartholomew, Wednesbury, Staffs		*Gunnis* 1968, 206; Pevsner, *Staffs*, 1974, 299
14.	†1833	James Woolley	Birmingham Cathedral	S	
15.	?1833	Rev John Stubbs	Market Drayton, Salop		*Gunnis* 1968, 206
16.	1833	Thomas Clarke	St Mary, Handsworth, Warks		Pevsner, *Warks*, 1966, 180
17.	?1834	Robert Cheshire	Hinckley, Leics		RG/JP, 4, 711
18.	†1835	Edward Wilkes	Birmingham Cathedral		Pevsner, *Warks*, 1966, 109
19.	?1835	John Booth	Ecclesfield, W R Yorks		*Gunnis* 1968, 206
20.	?1835	Samuel Bennitt	Dudley, Worcs		*Gunnis* 1968, 206
21.	†1836	Edward Greswolde	St Edburgha, Yardley, Warks		Pevsner, *Warks*, 1966, 212
22.	?1837	Elizabeth Buchanan	Chester Cathedral, Cheshire		*Gunnis* 1968, 206
23.	?1838	Thomas Unett	Stone, Staffs		*Gunnis* 1968, 206
24.	†1839	John Wilson	Hanbury, Staffs	S	Pevsner, *Staffs*, 1974, 141
25.	†1839	Martha Oliver	Wellington, Salop		Pevsner, *Salop*, 1958, 309
26.	?1840	William Simons and family	Kinver, Salop		RG/JP, 4, 711
27.	†1841	Francis and Anne (†1842) Walker	St Mary, Old Swinford, Worcs		RG/JP, 4, 711
28.	1841	Sophia Thompson (†1838)	Malvern Priory, Great Malvern, Worcs		*Graves* IV, 1905–6, 133; Pevsner, *Worcs*, 1968, 163; *Penny* 1977 (1), 89–90 (repr)
29.	†1841	Thomas Woodyatt	Malvern Priory, Great Malvern, Worcs	S	Pevsner, *Worcs*, 1968, 163
30.	†1842	Georgina, Countess of Bradford and Lady Georgiana Bridgeman (†1843)	St Andrew, Weston-under-Lizard, Staffs		*Graves* IV, 1905–6, 133; *Penny* 1977 (1), 91–2 (repr)
31.	†1842	Sarah Lane Freer	Bishopstone, Herefs	S	*Graves* IV, 1905–6, 133; Pevsner, *Herefs*, 1963, 76
32.	†1844	Anna Amery	Amblecote, Staffs		RG/JP, 4, 710v
33.	†1844	Anne Whittingham	Birmingham Cathedral		RG/JP, 4, 710v
34.	†1846	Henry Shaw	Park Lane Unitarian Chapel, Cradley, Halesowen, Worcs		RG/JP, 4, 711
35.	1848	William Hutton (†1815)	St Margaret, Ward End, Birmingham, Warks		Pevsner, *Warks*, 1966, 208
36.	†1849	Thomas Pargeter	Park Lane Unitarian Chapel, Cradley, Halesowen, Worcs		RG/JP, 4, 711
37.	1850	Officers and men of the 80th Regiment of Foot (Staffordshire Volunteers) killed during the Sutlej campaign	Lichfield Cathedral, Staffs		*ILN*, 10 Aug 1850, 112 (repr); Pevsner, *Staffs*, 1974, 186
38.	†1850	William Russell	St Mary, Moseley, Warks		Pevsner, *Warks*, 1966, 192
39.	†1852	Henry, 16th Baron Willoughby de Broke	Compton Verney, Warks, Chapel		Pevsner, *Warks*, 1966, 241
40.	†1852	Samuel (†1829) and Frances Taylor	St Leonard, Bilston, Staffs		RG/JP, 4, 711
41.	?1852	Sir Edward Hartopp	Aston Flamville, Leics		*Gunnis* 1968, 206
42.	†1853	James Foster	Old Swinford, Worcs		Pevsner, *Worcs*, 1968, 228
43.	†1854	C S Foster	Longdon, Staffs	S	Pevsner, *Staffs*, 1974, 197
44.	†1855	Bentinck Gilby Model(s): exhib RBSA, 1859, 189 (model of part of monument)	St James, Cheltenham, Glos	S	*RBSA Index*; Pevsner, *Glos: Vale & Forest of Dean*, 1976, 129 (repr 89)
45.	†1855	John Hollins	Kensal Green Cemetery, London		*Curl* 2001, 237
46.	c1856	Colonel Thomas Unett (†1855)	St Philip's Square, Birmingham	S	*Noszlopy* 1998, 128
47.	†1856	Thomas Badger	St Edmund, Dudley, Worcs		Pevsner, *Staffs*, 1974, 121
48.	1858	Lyndon J Grier	Amblecote, Staffs		*ILN*, 9 Oct 1858, 341 (repr)
49.	†1859	Mary Burd	Shrewsbury Abbey, Salop	S	C Lib (repr)
50.	?1860	Frances Ram	Ellastone, Staffs		RG/JP, 4, 711
51.	†1860	Rev Isaac Clarkson	St Bartholomew, Wednesbury, Staffs		Pevsner, *Staffs*, 1974, 299
52.	†1861	Phoebe and Charles (†1865) Shaw	St George, Birmingham, Warks		C Lib (repr)
53.	†1863	Benjamin Gibbons	Stone, Worcs	S	RG/JP, 4, 711
54.	†1864	Caroline Pargeter	Park Lane Unitarian Chapel, Cradley, Halesowen, Worcs		RG/JP, 4, 711
55.	†1865	Elizabeth Kinnersly	Ashley, Staffs		*Gunnis* 1968, 206
56.	†1870	Elizabeth Cameron	Oddingley, Worcs	S	
57.	?1870	John Badley	Dudley, Worcs		*Gunnis* 1968, 206

Statues

No.	Date	Subject	Material	Location		Sources
58.	1825	Henry, 1st Marquess of Anglesey		[Exhib RA, London, 1016]; untraced		*Graves* IV, 1905–6, 133; *RBSA Index*
59.	1830	Conrad and Medora	p	[Exhib RBSA, 1830, 459]; untraced		*Spectator*, 14 May 1831, 478; *RBSA Index*; *Gunnis* 1968, 205
60.	1830	Cupid and Psyche	m	Aston Hall, Birmingham, Warks		*Gunnis* 1968, 206
61.	1831	Aurora and Zephyr Model(s): exhib RBSA, 1827, 235 (unfinished model of Zephyrus and Aurora)	p	[Exhib sculptor's studio, London]; untraced		*Spectator*, 14 May 1831, 478; *RBSA Index*
62.	1831	The murder of the innocents	p	[Exhib sculptor's studio, London]; untraced		*Spectator*, 14 May 1831, 478; *Gunnis* 1968, 205
63.	1833	A young child		[Oakwood House, Boxhill, Surrey]; untraced	SD	C Lib (repr)
64.	1834	Daughter of Vincent Thompson	m	[Exhib RA, London, 1105]; untraced		*Graves* IV, 1905–6, 133; *RBSA Index*
65.	1841	Catherine Sarah Jenner, unfinished Model(s): exhib RBSA, 1840, 260	m	[Exhib RA, London, 1250]; untraced		*Graves* IV, 1905–6, 133; *RBSA Index*
66.	1841	Unidentified unfinished statue		[Exhib RBSA, 4A]; untraced		*RBSA Index*
67.	1841	Young girl with a straw hat	m	Reading Museum and Art Gallery, Berks	D	C Lib (repr)
68.	1846	Rev Dr Samuel Wilson Warneford	m	Warneford Hospital, Oxford, entrance hall		*AU*, 1846, 188; *Graves* IV, 1905–6, 133; Pevsner, *Oxon*, 1974, 338; *Parry-Jones* 1981, 24–32 (repr)
69.	1846	Sabrina		[Weston Park, Shifnal, Salop]; The Dingle, Quarry Park, Shrewsbury, Salop		*Graves* IV, 1905–6, 134; *RBSA Index*; Pevsner, *Salop*, 1958, 270; C Lib (repr)
70.	1849	Dr Henry Jephson	m	Jephson Gardens, Leamington, Warks, inside circular pavillion		*ILN*, 9 June 1849, 396 (repr); *Graves* IV, 1905–6, 133; *Noszlopy* 2003, 88–9 (repr)
71.	1853	'Dickie and Skye', portrait of Richard Crawshay Bailey	m	[Exhib RA, London, 1322]; untraced		*Graves* IV, 1905–6, 134; *RBSA Index*
72.	1855	Sir Robert Peel (†1850)	b	[Junction of Ann Street and Congreve Street, Birmingham, Warks]; Police training centre, Edgbaston, Birmingham, Warks		*Noszlopy* 1998, 103–4 (repr)
73.	1859	Faith	m	[Exhib RBSA, 191]; untraced		*RBSA Index*
74.	1859	Thomas Holloway	m	[Exhib RA, London, 1272]; untraced		*Graves* IV, 1905–6, 134; *RBSA Index*
75.	1868	Sir Rowland Hill	m	[Exchange buildings, Stephenson Place, Birmingham, Warks]; Post office, Hurst Street, Birmingham, Warks (in store 1998)		*Graves* IV, 1905–6, 134; *Noszlopy* 1998, 75–6 (repr)
76.	1870	The Playmates, a portrait of Gerald Marshall	m	[Exhib RBSA, 2]; untraced		*Graves* IV, 1905–6, 134; *RBSA Index*

Busts

No.	Date	Subject	Material	Location		Sources
77.	1822	E J Littleton (co-sculptor: William Hollins)		[Exhib RA, London, 1014]; untraced		*Graves* IV, 1905–6, 133, 134; *RBSA Index*
78.	1822	Henry, 1st Marquess of Anglesey (co-sculptor: William Hollins)		[Exhib RA, London, 1002]; untraced		*Graves* IV, 1905–6, 133, 134; *RBSA Index*
79.	1824	Edward Grainger Model(s): exhib RA, London, 1824, 972	m	RCS, London	S	*Graves* IV, 1905–6, 133
80.	1827	Charles, 15th Earl of Shrewsbury (co-sculptor: William Hollins)		[Exhib RA, London, 992]; untraced		*Graves* IV, 1905–6, 133, 134; *RBSA Index*
81.	1827	Emperor Nero		[Exhib RBSA, 246]; untraced		*RBSA Index*; *Gunnis* 1968, 206
82.	1827	L Gardner		[Exhib RBSA, 233]; untraced		*RBSA Index*
83.	1830	Charles Lloyd	m	Birmingham General Hospital, Warks		*Hill and Midgley* 1929, 16 (pl 10); *RBSA Index*; *Gunnis* 1968, 206
84.	1830	Miss Rhodes	m	[Exhib RBSA, 469]; untraced		*RBSA Index*
85.	1830	Mrs Edwards	m	[Exhib RBSA, 457]; untraced		*RBSA Index*
86.	1830	Thomas Bateman	m	[Exhib RBSA, 456]; untraced		*RBSA Index*; *Gunnis* 1968, 205
87.	1830	William Charles Macready as Cassius	p	Royal Shakespeare gallery, Stratford-upon-Avon, Warks		*Graves* IV, 1905–6, 133; *RBSA Index*; *Gunnis* 1968, 205
88.	1831	Caroline, Lady Stirling-Maxwell (Caroline Norton) Model(s): exhib RBSA, 1832, 443	p	[Exhib sculptor's studio, London]; untraced		*RBSA Index*; *Gunnis* 1968, 205
89.	1831	Thomas Telford	p	[Exhib sculptor's studio, London]; untraced		*Graves* IV, 1905–6, 133; *RBSA Index*; *Gunnis* 1968, 205
90.	1832	Dr De Lys	m	[Exhib RBSA, 477]; untraced		*RBSA Index*
91.	1832	John Reeve		[Exhib RA, London, 1141]; untraced		*Graves* IV, 1905–6, 133
92.	1832	Unidentified gentleman	m	[Exhib RBSA, 444]; untraced		*RBSA Index*
93.	1832	William Bedington		[Exhib RBSA, 480]; untraced		*RBSA Index*
94.	1834	John Bird	m	[Exhib RBSA, 532]; untraced		*RBSA Index*
95.	1835	H Earle		Institution of Civil Engineers		RG/JP, 4, 709; *RBSA Index*
96.	1835	Master Edward R Tindal		[Exhib RBSA, 211]; untraced		*RBSA Index*
97.	1835	T Villiers Lister as an infant	m	[Exhib RA, London, 1077]; untraced		*Graves* IV, 1905–6, 133; *RBSA Index*

98.	1836	Percival Pott	m	RCS, London	SD	*Graves* IV, 1905–6, 133; *Gunnis* 1968, 206; C Lib (repr)
99.	1839	John, 1st Earl Russell	m	[Exhib RA, London, 1384]; untraced		*Graves* IV, 1905–6, 133
100.	1839	William Phipson		[Exhib RBSA, 339]; untraced		*RBSA Index*; *Gunnis* 1968, 206
101.	1840	Benjamin St John Matthews		[Exhib RBSA, 253]; untraced		*Graves* IV, 1905–6, 133; *RBSA Index*
102.	1841	Rev Dr Samuel Warneford	m	[Queen's Hospital, Birmingham, Warks]; untraced		*AU*, 1842, 129; *Graves* IV, 1905–6, 133; *RBSA Index*; *Parry-Jones* 1981, 27, 32 n6
103.	1843	William Hollins		St Paul, Birmingham, Warks		*RBSA Index*; Pevsner, *Warks*, 1966, 138
104.	1844	George Baker		Birmingham General Hospital, Warks		*Graves* IV, 1905–6, 133; *RBSA Index*; *Gunnis* 1968, 206
105.	1845–1846	Rev Vaughan Thomas	p	Warneford Psychiatric Hospital, Oxford		*RBSA Index*; *Parry-Jones* 1981, 25, 27–8 (repr)
106.	1847	Unidentified man	m	VAM A.14-1982	SD	*Bilbey* 2002, 304 (repr)
107.	1848	Homer		[Exhib Colosseum, Regent's Park, London]; untraced		RG/JP, 4, 710
108.	1849	William Harding	m	[Exhib RBSA, 141D]; untraced		*RBSA Index*
109.	1849	William Sharpe	m	[Exhib RBSA, 141B]; untraced		*RBSA Index*
110.	1850	Felix Mendelssohn-Bartholdy	m	Birmingham MAG, inv 190'00	D	*Graves* IV, 1905–6, 133; *RBSA Index*; *Silber* 1987, 54, cat 158
111.	1850	George, 2nd Earl of Bradford		Weston Park, Salop	SD	C Lib (repr)
112.	1851	Mrs George Richmond Collis		[Exhib RBSA, 161]; untraced		*RBSA Index*
113.	1851	Robert Liston		[Exhib RA, London, 1381]; untraced		*Graves* IV, 1905–6, 133
114.	1851	Unidentified man (perhaps John Bright)	m	[Sotheby, 6 June 1997, lot 58]; untraced	SD	GPC
115.	1852	Colin Campbell		[Exhib Liverpool Ac, 601]; untraced		*Morris and Roberts* 1998, 323
116.	1852	Thomas Telford		Institution of Mechanical Engineers		RG/JP, 4, 710
117.	1853	Thomas Rhodes of Handsworth	m	[Exhib RA, London, 1399]; untraced		*Graves* IV, 1905–6, 134; *RBSA Index*
118.	1853	Unidentified man		Coll Ian Grant	SD	C Lib (repr)
119.	1853	William Congreve Russell	m	[Exhib RA, London, 1365]; untraced		*Graves* IV, 1905–6, 134; *RBSA Index*
120.	1854	Unidentified lady		[Exhib RA, London, 1478]; untraced		*Graves* IV, 1905–6, 134
121.	1855	John Rhodes	m	[Exhib RBSA, 1855]; untraced		*Graves* IV, 1905–6, 134; *RBSA Index*
122.	1860	David Cox	m	Birmingham MAG, inv 2622'85	D	*RBSA Index*; *Silber* 1987, 52–3, cat 155 (repr)
123.	1862	Unidentified lady	m	Private coll	SD	C Lib (repr)
124.	1863	Ada Thornton	m	[Exhib RA, London, 1021]; untraced		*Graves* IV, 1905–6, 134; *RBSA Index*
125.	1863	Mrs Henry Marten	m	[Exhib RBSA, 240c]; untraced		*RBSA Index*
126.	1867	Matthew Davenport Hill	m	Birmingham MAG, inv 2624'85		*Graves* IV, 1905–6, 134; *Silber* 1987, 52–3, cat 156 (repr)
127.	1868	William Scholefield	m	Birmingham MAG, inv 2625'85	D	*Silber* 1987, 52, cat 157; *Noszlopy* 1998, 35 (repr)
128.	1875	Samuel Timmins	m	[Birmingham reference library]; destroyed		*Birmingham Post*, 18 Aug 1886, 4; *RBSA Index*
129.	nd	Joseph Gillott	m	Birmingham MAG, inv P.11'73		*Silber* 1987, 54–5, cat 159 (repr)
Chimneypieces						
130.	1863	With Emblems of the Four Seasons		[for Samuel Messenger, Hallfield House, Edgbaston]; untraced		*RBSA Index*
Architectural Sculpture						
131.	1833	Group of figures		Bluecoat School, Birmingham, Warks, façade		*Graves* IV, 1905–6, 133; RG/JP, 4, 708, 710
132.	*c*1843	Carved window surround commemorating the Hollins family	m	St Paul, Birmingham, Warks		Pevsner, *Warks*, 1966, 138
133.	1848	Font		Darleston, Staffs		*Gunnis* 1968, 206
134.	1850	Fountain		Shrewsbury Market Square, Salop		*Builder*, 1860, 5
135.	1862	Font, with portrait statues of the daughters of Sir Hugh Williams Bt		Bodelwyddan, Clywd		*Graves* IV, 1905–6, 134; NP/RG
Reliefs						
136.	1835	Infant son of Henry Earle, medallion	m	[Exhib RBSA, 207]; untraced		*RBSA Index*
137.	1843	The pleasures of hope		[Exhib RA, London, 1422]; untraced		*Graves* IV, 1905–6, 133; *RBSA Index*
138.	1853	Two children, portrait medallion		coll Sir Timothy Clifford	SD	C Lib (repr)
139.	1857	Unidentified man, portrait medallion		Royal Holloway College, Egham, Surrey	SD	C Lib (repr)
Miscellaneous						
140.	1826	Susannah accused by the elders		[Exhib RA, London, 1047]; untraced		*Graves* IV, 1905–6, 133
141.	1827	The birth of Venus, model		[Exhib RBSA, 235]; untraced		*RBSA Index*
142.	1827	Wreath of flowers, model		[Exhib RBSA, 247]; untraced		*RBSA Index*
143.	1827	Zephyrs wafting Venus to the island of Cythera		[Exhib RA, London, 1070]; untraced		*Graves* IV, 1905–6, 133; *RBSA Index*
144.	1830	The lady of the lake, model	w	[Exhib RA, London, 1226]; untraced		*Graves* IV, 1905–6, 133; *Johnson* 1975, 236
145.	1834	Joshua Scholefield		[Exhib RBSA, 510]; untraced		*RBSA Index*
146.	1839	Admiral Lord Nelson, national memorial for Trafalgar Square, London, design only (monument executed by Baily, Railton and others)		Untraced		*Physick* 1969, 40, 181
147.	1839	'Thy will be done'		[Exhib RBSA, 344]; untraced		*RBSA Index*
148.	1846	Edward VI presenting the charter of the Birmingham Free Grammar School to Archbishop Cranmer		[Exhib RBSA, 158]; untraced		*RBSA Index*

HOLLINS, William 1763–1843

William Hollins was a successful Birmingham architect and sculptor and the father of **Peter Hollins**. He was born on 18 March 1763, the son of John and Mary Hollins of Shifnal, Salop. The family moved to Birmingham when he was a boy and he remained there throughout his life, eventually settling in Great Hampton Street, near the city centre. Hollins began his training as a stonemason but taught himself drawing and perspective.

In 1793 he assisted the London architect, George Saunders with working drawings for the Theatre Royal, New Street, Birmingham. Hollins went on to design several significant public buildings in the city including the old library, the general dispensary and the Athenaeum, now all demolished. These were in a competent Greek Revival style. He also carried out work in the gothic idiom at St Mary, Handsworth and was employed by the Charles, 15th Earl of Shrewsbury to design picturesque garden buildings for Alton Towers, Staffs. His obituary says that he declined an opportunity to go to St Petersburg to work for Catherine the Great, Empress of Russia, but he did work with Matthew Boulton, the famous Birmingham manufacturer, on a commission to supply machinery for the St Petersburg mint (*AU*, 1843, 37).

In 1806 Hollins submitted a design for the Nelson memorial in Birmingham (**28**). His proposal was for a combined post office and dispensary with a column in front, decorated with reliefs of Nelson's victories and with a statue of the hero at its base. His design won some local support and was displayed in the offices of *Aris's Birmingham Gazette* during the week in July 1806 before the designs were judged. He was unsuccessful in the competition, perhaps because of the considerable expense involved in his scheme, and a memorial by **Sir Richard Westmacott** was instead erected in 1809. One of the city councillors, Richard Pratchett, was sufficiently impressed with Hollins's work to commission personally the Egyptian conduit, an elaborate water pump of pyramidal form, which stood in the Bull Ring near Westmacott's statue of Nelson. This was known locally as Pratchett's Folly and 'must have convinced the subscribers that their decision to employ Westmacott had been wise' (*Yarrington* 1983, 321).

Hollins's practice as a sculptor was principally in church monuments. His obituary, which has a parochial note, told that in his later years he concentrated on 'introducing a more correct taste into mural monuments, upon which he spared no cost in collecting information from Italy, France, and this country'. The article paid tribute to his 'purity of taste and propriety of character rarely to be met with in a metropolitan studio' (*AU*, 1843, 37). Gunnis considered his monuments inferior to those of his son Peter, but commended 'a fine classical stele' commemorating Alexander Forrester in All Saints, Leicester (**6**).

Hollins carved ornaments for a few public buildings in central Birmingham, including a tympanum relief in artificial stone of *Hygeia*, goddess of health, for the general dispensary (**29**) and an impressive polychrome trophy of ancient and modern arms over the doorway of the Gun Barrel Proof house (**30**). He exhibited nationally and locally, at the Royal Academy, 1821–25 and at the Birmingham Society of Artists, 1827–140, showing largely portrait busts and medallions. He is reported to have been a skilled wax-modeller (*AU*, 1843, 37). Hollins was also interested in lettering and published *The British Standard of the Capital Letters contained in the Roman Alphabet* in 1813.

The versatile Hollins, who had a marked success in a provincial milieu, died on 12 January 1843, at his home in Great Hampton Street. He is buried in the churchyard of St Paul, Birmingham, where a granite obelisk marks his grave. Hollins is also commemorated inside the church by a bust and window. The window surround is carved with flowing foliage, forming cartouches which contain the names and dates of various family members. The bust is by Peter Hollins, who was probably also responsible for the carved window surround.

EH

Literary References: *AU*, 1843, 37; *DNB* 27, 1891, 174; *Edwards* 1951, 1626–7; *Gunnis* 1968, 206–7; *Yarrington* 1983, 320–1; *Yarrington* 1988, 109–10; *Colvin* 1995, 505–6; *ODNB* (Fisher)

Additional Manuscript Sources: tradecard, 1795, inscr, 'Hollins del. Pye sc.', Banks coll, BM 106.15

Miscellaneous Drawings: designs for the St Petersburg Mint, Birmingham ref lib, MS 1381

Portraits of the sculptor: Peter Hollins, bust, St Paul, Birmingham

Funerary Monuments

1.	†1802	Dr James Johnstone	Worcester Cathedral	S	*Edwards* 1951, 1627
2.	1808	John Freer (†1793)	St Mary, Handsworth, Warks	S	Pevsner, *Warks*, 1966, 180
3.	1808	William Withering (†1799)	St Bartholomew, Edgbaston, Warks	S	Pevsner, *Warks*, 1966, 164–5
4.	?1810	Joseph Wainwright	Dudley, Worcs	S	*Gunnis* 1968, 207
5.	†1810	Mary Elwell	Sedgley, Staffs		RG/JP, 4, 713
6.	?1817	Alexander Forrester	All Saints, Leicester		*Gunnis* 1968, 207
7.	†1817	Henry Perkins	Birmingham Cathedral	S	
8.	†1818	Edward Palmer	Birmingham Cathedral	S	
9.	?1818	Thomas Cooper	Birmingham Cathedral		*Gunnis* 1968, 207
10.	†1821	Archdeacon Edmund Outram of Birmingham	Birmingham Cathedral	S	Pevsner, *Warks*, 1966, 109
11.	†1821	James Goddington	St Peter and St Paul, Aston, Birmingham, Warks		Pevsner, *Warks*, 1966, 148
12.	?1821	Rev Thomas Best	St Peter, Cradley, Worcs		RG/JP, 4, 713
13.	?1823	Benjamin Spencer	St Peter and St Paul, Aston, Birmingham, Warks		*Gunnis* 1968, 207
14.	†1823	Mary Sayer	St Mary, Moseley, Birmingham, Warks	S	Pevsner, *Warks*, 1966, 192
15.	1829	John Newdigate Ladford	Ansley, Warks		Pevsner, *Warks*, 1966, 66
16.	†1831	David (†1823) and Mary Owen	Birmingham Cathedral		Pevsner, *Warks*, 1966, 109
17.	†1831	Gabriel Jean Marie de Lys	St Bartholomew, Edgbaston, Birmingham, Warks	S	Pevsner, *Warks*, 1966, 165
18.	†1837	Thomas Wakefield	Curdworth, Warks		Pevsner, *Warks*, 1966, 285
19.	nd	Several, unidentified subjects, tablets	St Paul, Birmingham, Warks		Pevsner, *Warks*, 1966, 138

Busts

20.	1821	Archdeacon Edmund Outram of Birmingham	[Exhib RA, London, 1115]; untraced		*Graves* IV, 1905–6, 134
21.	1822	Charles, 15th Earl of Shrewsbury (co-sculptor: Peter Hollins)	[Exhib RA, London, 992]; untraced		*Graves* IV, 1905–6, 133, 134; *RBSA Index*
22.	1822	E J Littleton (co-sculptor: Peter Hollins)	[Exhib RA, London, 1014]; untraced		*Graves* IV, 1905–6, 133, 134; *RBSA Index*

23.	1822	Henry, 1st Marquess of Anglesey (co-sculptor: Peter Hollins)		[Exhib RA, London, 1002]; untraced	*Graves* IV, 1905–6, 133, 134; *RBSA Index*
24.	1823	Christ		[Exhib RA, London, 1040]; untraced	*Graves* IV, 1905–6, 134; *RBSA Index*
25.	1823	Thetis		[Exhib RA, London, 1035]; untraced	*Graves* IV, 1905–6, 134; *RBSA Index*; *Gunnis* 1968, 207
26.	1827	Homer		[Exhib RBSA, 227]; untraced	*RBSA Index*
27.	1830	King George IV		[Exhib RBSA, 452]; untraced	*RBSA Index*; *Gunnis* 1968, 207
Architectural Sculpture					
28.	1806	Memorial to Admiral Lord Nelson, for Birmingham, design only (monument by Sir Richard Westmacott)		Untraced	*Yarrington* 1983, 320–1; *Yarrington* 1988, 109–10
29.	*c*1808	Hygeia, tympanum relief	sa	[General Dispensary, Union Street, Birmingham, Warks]; Birmingham MAG, inv P.28'68	*Silber* 1987, 54, cat 160; *Noszlopy* 1998, 35–6 (repr)
30.	1813	Trophies over principal entrance	s	Gun Barrel Proof House, Banbury Street, Birmingham, Warks	*Noszlopy* 1998, 7 (repr)
Reliefs					
31.	1827	James Watt, portrait medallion		[Exhib RBSA, 236]; untraced	*RBSA Index*; *Gunnis* 1968, 207
32.	1830	King George IV, medallic portrait		[Exhib RBSA, 454]; untraced	*RBSA Index*
33.	1830	Young artist, medallic portrait		[Exhib RBSA, 453]; untraced	*RBSA Index*
Miscellaneous					
34.	1825	Garden of Gethsemane, model		[Exhib RA, London, 997]; untraced	*Graves* IV, 1905–6, 134

HOLLIS, J, of London fl 1821–36?

He had a difficult career, becoming bankrupt in 1821 and again in 1828. He signs a neo-Hellenic tablet at Clerkenwell (**1**). The tablet to Henry Ryder has a medallion portrait (**2**).

Literary References: *Gunnis* 1968, 207

Funerary Monuments					
1.	?1824	Thomas Greatrex	Clerkenwell, London	S	*Gunnis* 1968, 207
2.	?1836	Henry Ryder, Bishop of Lichfield	Lutterworth, Warks		*Gunnis* 1968, 207

HOLLOWAY, Thomas 1748–1827

He was born in London, and exhibited at the Royal Academy from 1773, when he gave his address as 74 Broad Street, near the Royal Exchange. He worked as a modeller (**1, 2**), medallist and gem engraver. His exhibits in the last category included a 'portrait of the Rev. Mr. Wesley, impression of a seal from life' (*Graves* IV, 1905–6, 135). In 1784 his address was City Road, Hoxton. He died in Coltishall.

Literary References: *Gunnis* 1968, 207; *Pyke* 1973, 70

Miscellaneous					
1.	1775	Unidentified gentleman, portrait model	w	[Exhib RA, London, 136]; untraced	*Graves* IV, 1905–6, 135
2.	1775	Unidentified subject, portrait model	w	[Exhib RA, London, 156]; untraced	*Graves* IV, 1905–6, 135

HOLM (or HOLME), Lawrence Anderson fl 1759?–74

He came to Britain from Denmark some time before 1760. In 1762, according to a later report, he made the model for the state coach designed by Sir William Chambers (*Builder*, 1854, 72) (**22**). If this is true, it suggests a professional connection with **Joseph Wilton** and **Capizzoldi**, whose involvement in this venture is well documented. Two years later Holme was working as an assistant to **William Atkinson of London** and received a premium from the Society of Arts (**20**). In 1764 **Joseph Rose II** became his apprentice. Holm received further premiums from the Society for classical subjects in 1765, when he was living 'next door to the King's Arms, Hyde Park Corner' (*Graves* 1907, 122–3), and again in 1767 (**4, 5**). In the RSA Minutes for 1763–64 his name is incorrectly given as Lloyd Anderson Holmes.

In 1768 he participated in the special exhibition held by the Society of Artists in honour of the visit of the King of Denmark (**10, 11**). The following year he exhibited a bust of the Danish sovereign (**13**). In 1771 Holm received £408 for work on the 'Great Room near Exeter Exchange' which the Society of Artists were building as their own exhibition space (**18**). From 1776 to 1773 he lived in Cavendish Square. He appears to have returned to Denmark sometime around 1774.

His monuments include one with a life-size *putto* in front of an obelisk, celebrating Thomas Prowse (**3**). He signs the monument to Abigail Prowse with the words 'LAURENCE ANDERSON HOLM /INVENIT SCULPT' (**2**).

Literary References: *Dossie* 1782, 437; *Graves* 1907, 122–3; *Gunnis* 1968, 207; *Marsden and Hardy* 2001, 12 n31

Archival References: RSA, *Minutes*, 1764–65, seq 3 fol 62

Funerary Monuments						
1.	?1759	Sir Edward Hulse		Wilmington, Kent, churchyard	S	*Gunnis* 1968, 208
2.	†1763	Abigail Prowse		Axbridge, Somerset	S	*Gunnis* 1968, 208
3.	†1767	Thomas Prowse and seven family members		Axbridge, Somerset	S	Pevsner, *Somerset: N. & Bristol*, 1958, 81
Statues						
4.	1765	Oedipus expounding the riddle to the Sphinx	m	[Soc of A, premium, 140 gns]; untraced		RSA, *Minutes* 1764–65, seq 3 f 62; *Dossie* 1782, 440
5.	1767	Sophonisba with the cup of poison	m	[Soc of A, premium, 40 gns]; untraced		RSA, *Minutes of Premium Committees*, 1766–67, seq 3 f 34, 36; *Dossie* 1782, 440; *Graves* 1907, 123
6.	1773	Figure, sketch for a statue		[Exhib Soc of Artists, London, 137]; untraced		*Graves* 1907, 123

Busts

7.	1762	Unidentified gentleman, model		[Exhib Soc of Artists, London, 144]; untraced	*Graves* 1907, 122
8.	1763	Sir Edward Hulse		[Exhib Soc of Artists, London, 143]; untraced	*Graves* 1907, 122
9.	1766	Oliver Cromwell		[Exhib Soc of Artists, London, 208]; untraced	*Graves* 1907, 122
10.	1768	George Grenville	m	[Soc of Artists special exhib, London, 154]; untraced	*Graves* 1907, 122
11.	1768	Unidentified gentleman, model		[Soc of Artists special exhib, London, 155]; untraced	*Graves* 1907, 122
12.	1768	Unidentified lady	m	[Exhib Soc of Artists, London, 204]; untraced	*Graves* 1907, 122
13.	1769	The King of Denmark, model		[Exhib Soc of Artists, London, 235]; untraced	*Graves* 1907, 123
14.	1769	Unidentified gentleman	m	[Exhib Soc of Artists, London, 233]; untraced	*Graves* 1907, 123
15.	1769	Unidentified gentleman		[Exhib Soc of Artists, London, 234]; untraced	*Graves* 1907, 123
16.	1770	Unidentified nobleman		[Exhib Soc of Artists, London, 169]; untraced	*Graves* 1907, 123
17.	1772	Unidentified gentleman		[Exhib Soc of Artists, London, 144]; untraced	*Graves* 1907, 123

Architectural Sculpture

18.	1771	Decorative sculpture, supplied with chimneypiece Payment(s): £408		[Society of Arts, great room near Exeter Exchange, London]; untraced	Unidentified archives, Society of Arts, quoted in *Gunnis* 1968, 207

Reliefs

19.	1761	Æneas carrying his father Anchises		[Exhib Soc of Artists, London, 150]; untraced	*Graves* 1907, 122
20.	1763–1764	The parting of Hector and Andromache	m	[Soc of A, premium, 25 gns]; untraced	RSA *Minutes*, 1763–64, seq 3 f 76; *Press Cuttings* 1723–1800, f40; *Graves* 1907, 122; *Gunnis* 1968, 207
21.	1765	Adonis sleeping		[Exhib Soc of Artists, London, 176]; untraced	*Graves* 1907, 122

Miscellaneous

22.	1762	State coach, model (designed by Sir William Chambers)		Untraced	*Builder* 1854, 72
23.	1770	Model of a boy in the character of Adonis		[Exhib Soc of Artists, London, 170]; untraced	*Graves* 1907, 123
24.	1772	Hercules, model		[Exhib Soc of Artists, London, 145]; untraced	*Graves* 1907, 123
25.	1774	'carving and gilding large figures' Payment(s): £87		[Vintners' Company, London]; untraced	Archives, Vintners' Company, quoted in *Gunnis* 1968, 207–8

HOLMES, Lauret –1847

The will of Lauret Holmes, 'marble mason' of Turnham Green, Middlesex was proved on 19 July 1847 (PROB 11/2059).

HOLMES, of Pimlico fl *c*1842

The Wynne memorial tablet is in a neo-Jacobean style (2).

Funerary Monuments

1.	?1842	Helen Terry, tablet	Thornton-le-Dale, N R Yorks	S	GPC
2.	†1842	Robert William Wynne	Llanfair Talhaearn, Denbighs		Pevsner, *Clwyd*, 1986, 210

HOLMES, Sarah fl *c*1809–33?

She was described by Gunnis as 'of Brentford' and was responsible for a number of tablets. Gunnis said her work 'is dull and conventional and consists of a semi-urn or similar design'. The monument to Viscount Falkland, †1809, at Rudby-in-Cleveland, N R Yorks, signed 'Holmes of Edgware Road, may conceivably be by her, though it seems singular that it should be dispatched so far.'

Literary References: Pevsner, *Yorks, N R*, 1966, 314

Funerary Monuments

1.	?1811	Herbert Swyer	Isleworth, Middx	S	*Gunnis* 1968, 208
2.	?1818	John Howard	St Lawrence, Brentford, Middx	S	*Gunnis* 1968, 208
3.	?1823	Thomas Smith	St Mary, Ealing, Middx	S	*Gunnis* 1968, 208
4.	?1833	George Engleheart	East Bedfont, Middx	S	*Gunnis* 1968, 208

HOLMES, Thomas fl 1844

He was listed in Thompson's *Commercial Directory* for 1844 as 'builder, statuary & mason' of 11 Belgrave Street, Pimlico.

HOLT, John, of Brixworth and Spratton fl 1810–26

Holt signed a tablet at Spratton (1). On 17 November 1810 he advertised in the *Northampton Mercury* for two journeyman masons and an apprentice. He described himself as 'John Holt, Mason and Gravestone Cutter of Spratton' (GPC).

Funerary Monuments

1.	†1826	Thomas Chapman	Spratton, Northants	S	*Gunnis* 1968, 208

HOLT, Richard fl 1722–32

Richard Holt was a manufacturer of artificial stone. For a time he worked in competition with **Batty Langley**, whom Holt believed had stolen his formula. He began to make his material in the Lambeth area in the 1720s. In 1722 he took out a patent in conjunction with the architect, Thomas Ripley, for 'A certain Compound Liquid Metal never before known and used by the Ancients or Moderns, by which Artificial Stone and Marble is made by casting or running the metall into Moulds of any Form or Figure . . . which being petrified or vetrified and finished by Strong Fire, becomes more durable and harder than Stone and Marble . . .' (*Holt Patent*, cited by *Valpy* 1986, repr 125). Another document, written by Holt and signed by several of his friends who were sworn to secrecy, gives full details of his formula. It indicates that the composition was quite different from the material later developed by the **Coade Factory** since it included lead ore (*Holt Formula*, cited by *Valpy* 1986, 224–6, reprs 126–9). In 1730 he published a pamphlet, *A Short Treatise of Artificial Stone As 'tis now made, And converted into all Manner of Curious Embellishments, and Proper Ornaments of Architecture; containing The most Beautiful, the Strongest and the Cheapest Method, of Adorning Buildings of all Sorts. Being an Excellent and most useful Art, well known to the Ancients, but lost to the world for many Ages; now retriev'd by Richard Holt, Gent.* He claimed that the material he had developed was frost proof and that he could undercut the prices of the lead figure makers.

From early August 1729 he complained of being harassed by 'a certain pretending Architect, a meddling busy man' who said that he 'knowd how to elude and set aside any patent whatsoever' and was intending to use Holt's formula (*Holt* 1730, 41, 43). The 'pretending architect' was **Batty Langley**, who established a rival factory in Southwark. The two manufacturers placed rival advertisements in the *Daily Advertiser* throughout May, June and July 1731. Holt continued to advertise until 9 August 1732, boasting that 'the real lasting ARTIFICIAL STONE, is only made and converted into all manner of curious ORNAMENTS, consisting of various STATUES, Bustoes, Vases, Flower-Pots, Eagles, Stags, Lyons, Supporters of Arms, Foxes, Grey-hounds, Ballustrades, etc, by me RICHARD HOLT, The true Inventor thereof' and that these items could be purchased from his warehouse 'near Cuper's Bridge in Lambeth . . . at a very cheap Rate for ready Money' (*Daily Ad*, 12 April–9 Aug 1732, cited by *Valpy* 1986, 208).

It is not known when Holt died, but **Daniel Pincot** noted that the business flourished for a time before 'the projector dying, the whole affair died also'. Pincot was critical of Holt's work and felt 'there was neither taste in the designs, nor neatness in the execution' although he conceded that 'time has proved the materials durable in the severest trials' (*Pincot* 1790, 46–6). No examples of it have been discovered. Holt made many of the architectural features produced by the Coade factory and it has been suggested that Mrs Coade later took over the site of his factory (*Esdaile* 1940 (2), 95). This assertion is open to question since Holt's premises were immediately adjacent to the river and Coade's factory was a couple of hundred yards inland.

Literary References: *Holt* 1730, *passim*; *Pincot* 1790, 46–7; *Esdaile* 1940 (2), 94–5; *Valpy* 1986, 206–9, 223–6, reprs 124–9; *Kelly* 1990, 31–3, 37, 55, 313
Additional Manuscript Sources: *Holt patent; Holt formula*

HONE, Alfred 1810–

He was probably the son of the bookseller, parodist, writer, and political radical William Hone (1780–1842), whose bust he exhibited at the Suffolk Street Galleries (3). Hone also showed a bust of Joseph Parkes (1), an eminent antiquarian and close friend of William Hone. William Hone's eldest son, Alfred, was born 2 January 1810, and baptised at St Mary Street, Lambeth. He first exhibited at the Royal Academy in 1836, giving his address as 34 Grafton Street East. He was later recorded at addresses in George Street, Euston Square in the 1840s, and at 12 London Street in 1852. For many years he was an assistant to **J H Foley**. Graves lists a medallion portrait by 'A Hone Junr' shown at the Royal Academy in 1856. There is, however, confusion here, since the name was recorded as 'Hone' in the index, but as 'A Howe' in the catalogue.

Literary References: *Graves* IV, 1905–6, 140–1; *Gunnis* 1968, 208
Archival References: GPC; IGI

Busts						
1.	1836	Joseph Parkes		[Exhib RA, London, 1070]; untraced		*Graves* IV, 1905–6, 140
2.	1836	'Rev T B'		[Exhib RA, London, 1083]; untraced		*Graves* IV, 1905–6, 140
3.	1836	William Hone		[Exhib Soc of BA, London, 878]; untraced		*Johnson* 1975, 239
4.	1837	Sir William Molesworth Bt	m	[Exhib RA, London, 1211]; untraced		*Graves* IV, 1905–6, 140; *Ormond* 1973, 323
5.	1837	Unidentified subject		[Exhib RA, London, 1253]; untraced		*Graves* IV, 1905–6, 140
6.	1838	Dr Thomas Addison	m	R C Physic, London	SD	*Wolstenholme* 1964, 20–1 (repr)
7.	1838	Rev John Pye Smith DD		[Exhib RA, London, 1299]; untraced		*Graves* IV, 1905–6, 141
8.	1839	Mrs Duppa		Sharsted Court, Kent		*Graves* IV, 1905–6, 141
9.	1840	Rev J Burnet		[Exhib RA, London, 1133]; untraced		*Graves* IV, 1905–6, 141
10.	1840	Rev Joseph Fletcher DD		[Exhib RA, London, 1118]; untraced Other versions: exhib RA, London, 1841, 1316; untraced		*Graves* IV, 1905–6, 141
11.	1841	Bryan Edward Duppa		[Exhib RA, London, 1308]; untraced		*Graves* IV, 1905–6, 141
12.	1841	John Ramsbotham MD		[Exhib RA, London, 1272]; untraced		*Graves* IV, 1905–6, 141
13.	1843	Thomas Slingsby Duncombe MP		[Exhib RA, London, 1452]; untraced		*Graves* IV, 1905–6, 141
14.	1852	T Pollock		[Exhib RA, London, 1450]; untraced		*Graves* IV, 1905–6, 141
Reliefs						
15.	1836	Unidentified gentleman, medallion		[Exhib Soc of BA, London, 874]; untraced		*Johnson* 1975, 239
16.	1844	Unidentified child, medallic portrait to be executed in marble		[Exhib RA, London, 1345]; untraced		*Graves* IV, 1905–6, 141

HONEY, J, of South Molton early 19th century

Pevsner notes some good slate tombstones and tombs in churchyards in Molland, Devon, dating from the first half of the 19th century, signed by this mason. Other inscribed slates at North Molton, in the same county, are signed 'Honey and Roberts of South Molton.'

Literary References: Pevsner, *Devon*, 1989, 572, 603

HONEYBONE, of Shrivenham fl c1808

He signs a tablet with a relief of *Faith* (1).

Funerary Monuments				
1.	†1808	Elizabeth Batson	Ramsbury, Wilts	*Gunnis* 1968, 208; Pevsner, *Wilts*, 1975, 379

HOOKEY, John, of Southampton fl c1792–1808?

He was the son of G G Hookey, a 'stone-mason and auctioneer' of Southampton, whose widow died in 1802 (*Monthly Mag* 1802, 14, 195). His large wall-tablets in coloured marbles are 'well above the average work of the provincial statuary of the period' (*Gunnis* 1968, 208).

Funerary Monuments

1.	†1792	Jeremiah Meylor	St Thomas, Lymington, Hants	S	*Gunnis* 1968, 208
2.	?1796	John Stewart	North Stoneham, Hants	S	*Gunnis* 1968, 208
3.	?1808	James Allen	Lymington, Hants	S	*Gunnis* 1968, 208

HOOPER, John fl 1761–69

He was employed at Audley End as a mason and a carver (2). In 1762 he built 'a Temple in Pleasure garding at Ditchley', Oxon, the seat of the Earl of Lichfield, for which he was paid £192 10s 8d for the stone, after the bill had been examined by Stiff Leadbetter (1). In 1768 he built 'a New Lodge' in the 'New Park' at Ditchley, for which he was paid £97 6s on 20 July 1769 (3).

Literary References: *Gunnis* 1968, 208

Archival References: Dillon, DIL I/p/3t and I/p/3u; Dillon (2) DIL I/p/3p and I/p/1/26f

Architectural Sculpture

1.	1762	Decorative features, including columns, capitals, pilasters and cornice (designed by Leadbetter)	s	Ditchley Park, Oxon, garden temple	*Colvin* 1995, 604
2.	1761–1764	Carved gothic stonework	s	[Audley End, Essex]; untraced	Essex RO D/DBY A243 quoted in *Gunnis* 1968, 208
3.	1768	Lodge		Ditchley Park, Oxon	*Gunnis* 1968, 208

HOPE FAMILY, of Manchester

Samuel Hope 1741–1817
John Hope c1744–1822

Samuel and John Hope were architects and statuary masons, the sons of Samuel Hope of Manchester, a bricklayer. They were involved in building the Piece Hall at Halifax in 1775–9 and High Legh Hall in Cheshire. Samuel died at Altrincham on 9 May 1817 and John on 29 August 1822.

Gunnis describes their monuments and tablets as 'well designed and quite ambitious works with well-carved details' (*Gunnis* 1968, 208). The Kenworthy monument depicts the deceased raising a coffin lid, the shroud leaving her face fully visible (1). Later works are signed only by Samuel Hope.

Literary References: *Gunnis* 1968, 208; *Colvin* 1995, 510

Funerary Monuments

1.	†1776	Catherine Kenworthy	Mossley, Lancs	S	
2.	c1780	Anna Legh	Rostherne, Cheshire		*Gunnis* 1968, 208
3.	?1781	Mary Sayer	St John, Halifax, W R Yorks		*Gunnis* 1968, 208
4.	?1787	John Caygill	St John, Halifax, W R Yorks		*Gunnis* 1968, 208
5.	?1788	Hugh Hall	Bowden, Cheshire		*Gunnis* 1968, 208
6.	?1789	John Glegg	Goostrey, Cheshire		*Gunnis* 1968, 208
7.	?1795	Margaret Toosey	Stockport, Cheshire		*Gunnis* 1968, 208
8.	?1797	Thomas Drinkwater	Salford, Lancs		*Gunnis* 1968, 208
9.	?1801	James Brown	St Michael, Ashton-under-Lyne, Staffs		*Gunnis* 1968, 208

HOPKINS, Jordan, of Swindon fl 1718?

The Stratton memorial has an oval inscription tablet in a square surround.

Funerary Monuments

1.	?1718	John Stratton	Brinkworth, Wilts	S	*Gunnis* 1968, 208

HOPKINS, of Bath fl c1804

Funerary Monuments

1.	?1804	Ann Bathurst	Lydney, Monmouths	S	*Gunnis* 1968, 208

HOPKINS, William Alexander 1815–

He attended the Royal Academy Schools in 1840 on the recommendation of Charles Eastlake and four years later exhibited at the Academy, giving his address as 25 Bedford Square (1).

Archival References: RA Admissions

Busts

1.	1844	Infant son of H E Kendall jnr	[Exhib RA, London, 1363]; untraced	*Graves* IV, 1905–6, 151

HOPKINSON, Joseph fl 1762–63

Chimneypieces

1.	1762–1763	Several		[Staunton Harold Hall, Leics]; untraced	Ferrers archives, Leicester Museum, 26.D.53/2506 in GPC

Architectural Sculpture

2.	1762–1763	Carved stonework	s	[Staunton Harold Hall, Leics]; untraced	Ferrers archives, Leicester Museum, 26.D.53/2506 in GPC

HOPPER, Humphrey 1765–1844

He was baptised on 22 March 1765 at Wolsingham, County Durham, the son of Humphrey and Margaret Hopper. Nothing is currently known of his training. His address was 55 Paddington Street in 1799, when he first exhibited at the Royal Academy (2). Farington wrote in 1802 that Hopper 'had, it was said, been a mason, but had industriously exerted himself to acquire a knowledge of art' (*Farington*, 5, 1944). He completed his education as a mature man of 36 by enrolling in the Royal Academy Schools in February 1801 to study sculpture. He was a successful student, winning a silver medal in December 1802 (**86**), after three competitors were apparently disqualified for receiving assistance with their entries from **Thomas Banks**. Hopper won a gold medal the following year (**87**), submitting a sketch of *Hercules Chaining Cerberus* with his winning entry.

His practice in the 1800s was conducted from 14 New Road, Fitzroy Square and then from 3 Edward Street, Portman Square. Part of his output at this time was tasteful decorative work in plaster, sometimes bronzed. This included graceful, classical nymphs and vestals designed to hold lamps. They are sometimes stamped and precisely dated (**108**), which suggests that Hopper had patented the works. The large number of surviving examples indicates that the sculptor was reproducing these on an extensive commercial scale.

His early known monuments make use of both the classical and gothic styles. In 1807 he competed for the monuments to Nelson and Pitt in the Guildhall (**10, 12**), and although unsuccessful on both occasions, he was subsequently awarded a government commission to carve the multi-figured monument to Major General Hay, who died at the siege of Bayonne (**14**). This depicts Hay in full uniform, expiring in the arms of an almost naked Hercules. Two central diagonals are created by the falling body of the General and his sword, which hangs from his limp arm to the ground. A standing sentry on the left looks ponderously away from the action, and on the right a flat, decorative panel shows figures of almost identical soldiers, marching away from the besieged castle. The monument, like many of those produced for St Paul's, combines the theatrical tradition of British monumental sculpture with militaristic realism. As with British history painting, which similarly combined the two, the union was often perplexing to viewers. Subsequent commentators have found much to criticise in the work. G L Smyth was distressed by the conversion of the historical event into an allegory, commending the modern dress and military detail, but condemning the inclusion of a naked figure. This was 'a most perverse licence, and what is more provoking, he seems to be placed as he is merely for the sake of a display of art and the effect of attitude. There is not an expression about him to indicate concern for the melancholy charge he happens to support' (*Smyth* 1839, 2, 762). Gunnis described the figure of the General as 'merely absurd,' and the work as a whole as a 'lamentable mass of marble' (*Gunnis* 1968, 209). He was more generous about Hopper's other monumental works which, he said, 'have charm and distinction and well-carved reliefs'. He exempted from this praise such works in 'spiky Gothic,' as the Orlebar, Simeon and Fellowes monuments (**49, 65, 68**). Among Hopper's finest works is that to Robert Packe (**15**), who died at Waterloo, which features a scene of the dying man, carved 'with great skill and some feeling' (*Boase* 1956, 22). Hopper also carved busts, including one of another deceased soldier, J F Johnstone, who died at Algiers (**101**). **Peter Skae** was one of his assistants.

From 1815 Hopper resided at 13 Wigmore Street, Marylebone, where he died on 27 May 1844, in the presence of William Hopper of the same address. He is buried at Kensal Green Cemetery, under a raised gabled ledger, now much eroded.

MGS

Literary References: *Farington*, 6, 2191; *DNB*; *Graves*: IV, 1905–6, 152; *Hutchison* 1960–62, 160; *Gunnis* 1968, 209; *Clifford* 1992, 57; *Curl* 2001, 242; *ODNB* (JKB)

Funerary Monuments

1.	†1787	William Watson	St Giles-in-the-Fields, London		RG/JP, 4, 720
2.	1799	A monumental figure	[Exhib RA, London, 1108]; untraced		*Graves* IV, 1905–6, 152
3.	†1800	Anne Busby, Lady Kemys Tynte (†1798) and her sister Jane Busby	Addington, Bucks		Pevsner, *Bucks*, 1994, 127
4.	?1800	Lady Tynte	Addington, Bucks		*Gunnis* 1968, 209
5.	1801	Design for a monument	[Exhib RA, London, 978]; untraced		*Graves* IV, 1905–6, 152
6.	†1802	General Adeane	Babraham, Cambs		Pevsner, *Cambs*, 1970, 294
7.	?1803	Esther Cook	Chingford, Essex		*Gunnis* 1968, 209
8.	1805	A monumental sketch	[Exhib RA, London, 691]; untraced		*Graves* IV, 1905–6, 152
9.	1805	Model of a monumental figure	[Exhib RA, London, 699]; untraced		*Graves* IV, 1905–6, 152
10.	1807	Admiral Lord Nelson, for Guildhall, model	[Exhib RA, London, 981]; untraced		*Graves* IV, 1905–6, 152;
11.	1807	Monumental figure, model	[Exhib RA, London, 1001]; untraced		*Graves* IV, 1905–6, 152
12.	1807	William Pitt, for Guildhall, model	[Exhib RA, London, 974]; untraced		*Graves* IV, 1905–6, 152
13.	?1810	Joseph Green	Etwall, Derbys		*Gunnis* 1968, 209
14.	†1814	Major-General Andrew Hay	St Paul's Cathedral, London	S	*Smyth* 1839, 2, 762; *Gunnis* 1968, 209; *ODNB*
15.	†1815	Major Robert Christopher Packe	St George's Chapel, Windsor, Berks	S	*Boase* 1956, 22 (pl V); Pevsner, *Berks*, 1966, 276; *Bond* 1999, 258
16.	†1817	J Holford	Hampstead Parish Church, London		RG/JP, 4, 720
17.	†1818	Sir Edward West	Hillington, Norfolk	S	
18.	†1819	Rev James Austin	Steveton, Hants		RG/JP, 4, 720
19.	?1821	Lady Ann Simpson	Merstham, Surrey		*Gunnis* 1968, 209
20.	1821	'My Soul doth magnify the Lord', marble figure for a monument	[Exhib RA, London, 1108]; untraced		*Graves* IV, 1905–6, 152
21.	1822	Marble figure, part of a monument	[Exhib RA, London, 1046]; untraced		*Graves* IV, 1905–6, 152
22.	?1823	Caroline Coney	Cookham, Berks		*Gunnis* 1968, 209
23.	?1824	William Chute	Sherborne St John, Hants		*Gunnis* 1968, 209
24.	†1826	Margaret Brooke	Runcorn, Cheshire		*Clifford* 1992, 57
25.	†1826	Susan Mangin	Aston Rowant, Oxon		Pevsner, *Oxon*, 1974, 427
26.	?1827	Josiah Spode	Stoke-on-Trent parish church, Staffs		*Gunnis* 1968, 209
27.	†1828	Lady Browne West	Hillington, Norfolk		Pevsner, *Norfolk: N W & S*, 1999, 403
28.	?1829	Captain Digby	Warfield, Berks		*Gunnis* 1968, 209
29.	†1829	Henrietta Magens	Brightlingsea, Essex	S	
30.	†1829	Joseph Palmer, Dean of Cashel	Exeter Cathedral, Devon		Pevsner, *Devon*, 1989, 383
31.	?1829	Sir William Curtis	Ramsgate, Kent		*Gunnis* 1968, 209
32.	†1830	Admiral Sir Eliab Harvey	Hempsted, Essex	S	*Gunnis* 1968, 209
33.	†1830	James Wilson	Sneaton, N R Yorks		Pevsner, *Yorks: N R*, 1966, 349
34.	?1830	Thomas Faussett	Ramsgate, Kent		RG/JP, 4, 721
35.	†1830	William Duncan	Great Amwell, Herts	S	*Gunnis* 1968, 209
36.	?1831	Charles Mitford	Tillington, Sussex		*Gunnis* 1968, 209
37.	†1831	John North	St Mary, Harrow-on-the-Hill, London		Pevsner, *London: N W*, 1991, 262
38.	?1831	Julia Coulson	Teddington, London		*Gunnis* 1968, 209
39.	?1831	Rev William Fawssett	Ashstead, Surrey		*Gunnis* 1968, 209
40.	†1831	Sir Thomas Carlyon	St Blazey, Cornwall	S	Pevsner, *Cornwall*, 1970, 159

41.	?1832	C. Musgrave		Sunbury, Middx		*Gunnis* 1968, 209
42.	?1832	Colonel Noel Hill		Maidstone, Kent		*Gunnis* 1968, 209
43.	?1832	Emily Wynyard		St Katherine, Regent's Park, London		*Gunnis* 1968, 209
44.	†1832	John, 2nd Baron Rendlesham		Rendlesham, Suffolk	S	Pevsner, *Suffolk*, 1974, 402
45.	?1832	Mrs Chichester		Dawlish, Devon		*Gunnis* 1968, 209
46.	?1832	Rev W Hartley		Bucklebury, Berks		*Gunnis* 1968, 209
47.	1832	Thomas Capron (†1829)		Stoke Doyle, Northants		RG/JP, 4, 721
48.	?1833	Charles Green		Spalding, Lincs		GPC
49.	†1833	Richard Orlebar		Podington, Beds		Pevsner, *Beds, Hunts & Peterborough*, 1968, 134
50.	1834	Marble figure, part of a monument		[Exhib RA, London, 1043]; untraced		*Graves* IV, 1905–6, 152
51.	?1834	Martha Best		Haselbury Plunckett, Dorset		*Gunnis* 1968, 209
52.	†1834	Rev Thomas Hume		Salisbury Cathedral, Wilts		Pevsner, *Wilts*, 1975, 415
53.	1835	Admiral Thomas Spry (†1828) and his wife (†1835)		St Anthony-in-Roseland, Cornwall		Pevsner, *Cornwall*, 1970, 156
54.	†1835	James Bourne		St Edmund, Dudley, Worcs		GPC
55.	?1835	Mary Hill		Goathurst, Somerset		GPC
56.	†1835	Mrs Frances Crosbie		Donnington, Sussex		RG/JP, 4, 721
57.	?1835	Rev William Coop		Worlington, Suffolk		*Gunnis* 1968, 209
58.	?1835	Robert Hooper		Shoreham, Sussex		*Gunnis* 1968, 209
59.	†1835	Sir William Medlycott		Milborne Port, Somerset		Pevsner, *Somerset: S & W*, 1958, 238
60.	†1836	Anne Kemeys Tynte		Goathurst, Somerset	S	
61.	†1836	Charles Burlson		New College, Oxford, chapel		*Gunnis* 1968, 209; Pevsner, *Oxon*, 1974, 172
62.	†1836	Elizabeth Kemeys Tynte		Goathurst, Somerset	S	*Gunnis* 1968, 209
63.	?1836	Hon Eileen Fletcher		St Mary, St Marylebone, London		*Gunnis* 1968, 209
64.	?1836	John Wilson		Whitkirk, W R Yorks		*Gunnis* 1968, 209
65.	†1836	Rev Charles Simeon		Holy Trinity, Cambridge	S	Pevsner, *Cambs*, 1970, 231
66.	†1837	C M Dinham Green		St Mary and St Nicholas, Spalding, Lincs		Pevsner, *Lincs*, 1989, 673
67.	†1837	John White		St Mary, Cottingham, E R Yorks		Pevsner, *Yorks: E R & York*, 1995, 387
68.	†1837	W H Fellowes		St Thomas of Canterbury, Ramsey, Huntingdon		Pevsner, *Beds, Hunts & Peterborough*, 1968, 334
69.	?1838	Admiral Sir John Hood		St Mary, St Marylebone, London		*Gunnis* 1968, 209
70.	†1838	John C Hill		Barbados Cathedral, Bridgetown	S	RG/JP, 4, 722
71.	?1838	John Campbell		Liston, Essex		*Gunnis* 1968, 209
72.	?1838	Rev George Wasey		Edgcote, Northants		*Gunnis* 1968, 209
73.	?1838	Rev Philip Hunt		Aylsham, Norfolk		*Gunnis* 1968, 209
74.	?1838	Sarah Poynder		Holy Trinity, Tunbridge Wells, Kent		*Gunnis* 1968, 209
75.	†1838	Thomas Hopkins		Tredington, Warks		Pevsner, *Warks*, 1966, 435
76.	†1839	Colonel Edward Webb		Gloucester Cathedral	S	Pevsner, *Glos: Vale & Forest of Dean*, 1976, 219; *CIIA* 4/4/49 (repr)
77.	?1840	Philippa Foukes		Billingborough, Lincs		GPC
78.	?1840	Sir Frederick Cooper		Corfe, Somerset		*Gunnis* 1968, 209
79.	†1841	Gould family member		St Laurence, Upwey, Dorset		Pevsner, *Dorset*, 1972, 434
80.	†1841	Mary Ann Honeywood		Elmsted, Kent	S	
81.	?1842	Matthew Lister		Burwell, Lincs		GPC
82.	?1842	Thomas Ravenshaw		All Saints, Fulham, London		*Gunnis* 1968, 209
83.	†1843	General Sir John Crosbie		Donnington, Sussex		RG/JP, 4, 722
84.	†1845	Rev Henry Parsons		Goathurst, Somerset	S	
85.	†1853	Thomas Bainbridge		Chobham, Surrey		Pevsner, *Surrey*, 1971, 158
Statues						
86.	1802	Model of an academy figure		[RA, London, premium]; untraced		RA Premium list
87.	1803	The death of Meleager, group		[RA, London, gold medal]; untraced		RA Premium list
88.	1806	Gilt figures of young ladies reclining on chaise-longues, pair supporting candelabra	p	Untraced Other versions: many recorded	SD	*Clifford* 1992, 57
89.	1808	Mercury, intended to support a lamp		[Exhib RA, London, 898]; untraced		*Graves* IV, 1905–6, 152
90.	1809	Pair of two-light lustres supporting vases	p	[formerly Gregory and Co, Bruton Street, London]; untraced Other versions: several recorded	SD	*Clifford* 1992, 58
91.	1809–1810	Two		White House of the Confederacy, Richmond, Virginia, USA	SD	
92.	1812	Four muses (in clay or plaster)		Lewes County Hall, Sussex, passages (ex ballroom)	SD	*Dell* 1962, 11; *Gunnis* 1968, 209; *Clifford* 1992, 58
93.	1816	Draped female figure, statuette	pb	Phillips, 1 March 1988, lot 72	SD	
94.	nd	Four	p	Lancaster House, London		
95.	nd	Four	p	[Hackwood House, Hants, dining room]; Christie, London 1998; untraced		
96.	nd	Standing maidens, classically draped	p	Sold Sotheby 25 Jan 1973		*Clifford* 1992, 58
Busts						
97.	1814	Lord Beresford		[Exhib RA, London, 1815, 890]; Curraghmore, Co Waterford		*Graves* IV, 1905–6, 152; GPC
98.	1815	Arthur, 1st Duke of Wellington		[Exhib RA, London, 904]; untraced Other versions: model, exhib RA, London, 1817 (1073)		*Graves* IV, 1905–6, 152
99.	1815	Dr Thornton		[Exhib RA, London, 883]; untraced		*Graves* IV, 1905–6, 152
100.	1815	Lord Hill		[Exhib RA, London, 905]; untraced		*Graves* IV, 1905–6, 152
101.	1817	John Frederick Johnstone	m	[Exhib RA, London, 1040]; untraced		*Graves* IV, 1905–6, 152
102.	1825	C C Western	m	[Exhib RA, London, 1042]; untraced		*Graves* IV, 1905–6, 152
103.	1828	Arthur, 1st Duke of Wellington	p	Lewes Town Hall, Sussex		*Gunnis* 1968, 209

Chimneypieces					
104.	1800	'Music', designed for a chimneypiece	[Exhib RA, London, 1055]; untraced		*Graves* IV, 1905–6, 152
105.	1800	Painting, design for a chimneypiece	[Exhib RA, London, 1057]; untraced		*Graves* IV, 1905–6, 152
Architectural Sculpture					
106.	1806	Lamp	Farnley Hall, W R Yorks	SD	GPC
107.	1812	Giltwood chandelier with eight foliate arms, supporting a plaster group of man, woman and cherub	Sotheby, 8 April 1982, lot 121	S	*Beard and Gilbert* 1986, 29; *Clifford* 1992, 58
108.	1813	Lamp figures, life-size	Lancaster House, London	SD	
109.	1818	Ebonised bracket with gadrooning	Sotheby, 9 Feb 1968, lot 151		*Beard and Gilbert* 1986, 29; *Clifford* 1992, 58
110.	1825	Wall bracket with female head wreathed in oak leaves and framed by a goatskin	Sotheby, 31 July 1970, lot 79	SD	*Beard and Gilbert* 1986, 29; *Clifford* 1992, 58
Miscellaneous					
111.	1803	Adam and Eve	[Exhib RA, London, 1020]; untraced		*Graves* IV, 1905–6, 152
112.	1804	Design for a naval pillar	[Exhib RA, London, 936]; untraced		*Graves* IV, 1905–6, 152
113.	1805	Hercules and Omphale	[Exhib RA, London, 790]; untraced		*Graves* IV, 1905–6, 152
114.	1807	A bacchante	[Exhib RA, London, 1079]; untraced		*Graves* IV, 1905–6, 152
115.	1807	A bacchante	[Exhib RA, London, 1101]; untraced		*Graves* IV, 1905–6, 152
116.	1807	A nymph	[Exhib RA, London, 1102]; untraced		*Graves* IV, 1905–6, 152
117.	1808	Torcheres	Sotheby 25 Jan 1974, lot 125		
118.	1811	Venus	[Exhib RA, London, 946]; untraced		*Graves* 1875, 282; *Graves* IV, 1905–6, 152
119.	1813	Bacchante	[Exhib RA, London, 945]; untraced		*Graves* IV, 1905–6, 152
120.	1813	Bacchus	[Exhib RA, London, 903]; untraced		*Graves* IV, 1905–6, 152
121.	1820	Lamp in the form of draped female figure with an eagle at her side	p ex coll Derek Sherborn; untraced		*Gunnis* 1968, 209
122.	1824	Ganymede	[Exhib RA, London, 1030]; untraced		*Graves* IV, 1905–6, 152
123.	1825	Salmacis, model	[Exhib RA, London, 1044]; untraced		*Graves* IV, 1905–6, 152; *Johnson* 1975, 240
124.	1827	Psyche	[Exhib BI, London, 469]; untraced		*Graves* 1875, 282

HOPPER, William, of London fl 1833

Statues				
1.	1833	Two models for a statue	[Exhib Carlisle Acad, 259, 262]; untraced	*Carlisle Ac Exhibs*, 1973

HOPSON, Sir Charles –1710

He was the master-joiner at Chelsea Hospital in 1682 with **Roger Davis** and **John Smallwell**, under **William Emmett** and **William Morgan**. At Whitehall he worked as joiner for the great chapel under **Grinling Gibbons**. In 1694 he became purveyor to the king's works and in 1706, master-joiner to Sir Christopher Wren at Chelsea Hospital, Eton College and the royal palaces. In 1708 he succeeded John Smallwell as master of the Joiners' Company. He was knighted in 1709, presumably in recognition of his contribution to City affairs. At St Paul's, his bills for the choir came to £1,638 14s 11d. He made models for the altar, great and chair organ cases, dean's- and choir-stalls. A bill of 1696 included the item 'for Glewing of Boards for Mr Tijou to draw ye Iron Screens etc. upon & ditto for Mr Gibbons to draw upon'. Another reference to a panel for Gibbons 'to draw upon' gives its measurements as six feet by five. In another bill, submitted in 1697, he charged for 'Glewing & Preparing 2,381 ft of Rt Wainscor for Carving, all thicknesses being reduced to 2 in. thick'. He and his son John (†1718) later worked at Chatsworth and Blenheim, where he is thought to have provided the carved wainscotting in the private apartments.

Literary References: *Green* 1964 (1), 57–8, 62, 91, 96, 126

Will: PROB 11/514

HOROBIN, John fl 1763–64

In 1763 he was listed as a mason of Windmill-street, Piccadilly. A John Horobin was made free of the Masons' Company by redemption on 28 June 1764.

Literary References: *Mortimer* 1763, 49

Archival References: Masons' Co, *Freemen*, fol 31

Chimneypieces				
1.	1763	Two with Siena tablets, one ornamented with griffins, another with female term figures (designed by James Stuart)	Wentworth Woodhouse, W R Yorks, dressing rooms, 'supping room' and drawing room	*Penny* 1991 (2), 11, 13 (repr)

HORSMAN, Philip, of Wolverhampton fl 1847?–c1854

His known monuments are in the Gothic style.

Funerary Monuments					
1.	?1847	Edward Crowther	Claverley, Salop		RG/JP, 4, 722
2.	?1852	Penelope Brettell	Kingswinford, Staffs	S	GPC
3.	*c*1854	Thomas Bache and family	Worfield, Salop	S	

HORSNAILE, Christopher I *c*1658–1742

Horsnaile worked in partnership with **Edward Stanton** for more than a decade as a monumental sculptor, but he was also responsible for several monuments alone and he worked independently as a mason-contractor. He was the son of William and Ann Horsenail of Warfield, Berks, but was born in the parish of St Andrew, Holborn. He married Hester Chilton of Warfield on 6 April 1686. On 29 October 1700 he became a freeman of the Masons' Company by service with Herbert Paine and eight years later he was living in the parish of St Ann Blackfriars, at the Bell in Glasshouse Yard. His son was **Christopher Horsnaile II**.

Nothing is known of Horsnaile's work before *c*1720, when he began to collaborate with Stanton on monuments signed by both partners, with Stanton's name preceding Horsnaile's. The most ambitious, to Thomas Vernon, has a life-sized reclining effigy flanked by seated figures of *Justice* and *Learning* (**4**). Most of the partnership memorials are architectural tablets, or standing monuments decorated with a conventional vocabulary of scrolls, vases, torches, *putti*, garlands and skulls with bat-wings (**1–3, 6–9, 12, 13, 15, 20**). For his work at Ditchley Park, Oxon, Horsnaile received seven payments between August 1725 to March 1730, of sums ranging from £9 10s to £64 13s (Dillon DIL I/p/4p-v). A cheque or note of hand from Lord Lichfield, dated 17 April 1725, instructed Francis Child to pay 'Mr Stanton/Mason/£21'. It is endorsed by Stanton and witnessed by 'Christo. Horsnaile' (Dillon DIL I/p/4ao). 'Horsenaile and Stanton Masons Next St Andrews Church Holburne' made a number of chimneypieces for Ditchley between 1734 and 1729 (**24, 25, 27, 28**). Stanton died in 1734 and left 'Mr. Christopher Horsnaile, my honest and industrious co-partner, £40'.

Horsnaile is not known to have worked independently on monuments before about 1730. He employed the figure arrangement of the Vernon monument (**4**) for Sir Jacob Garrard's memorial, substituting Garrard's two standing sons for the allegorical Virtues (**19**). They are lumpen figures, clad in unconvincing classical armour. Some of his work however shows an awareness of newer fashions, particularly the monument to Sir John Philipps (**22**), which has a bust within an architectural frame reminiscent of some of Edward Stanton's monuments, but perhaps also owes debts to James Gibbs's design for the monument to Matthew Prior, 1723, in Westminster Abbey. The monument to William East also has a portrait-bust (**14**).

He was responsible for much building work in London. In 1722 he was employed at the Royal College of Physicians in Warwick Lane, where he was paid £26 12s for masonry work, and in 1726–40 at Hoare's Bank, receiving sums not exceeding £18 on at least three occasions. He also worked for Henry Hoare at Stourhead, Wilts, earning £198 4s in 1738–39. In February 1729 Horsnaile joined Stanton as joint mason to Westminster Abbey, and from 1733 (when Stanton was ailing) to 1737 he held the lucrative post alone. In 1740 he was granted a coat of arms. He was succeeded at the Abbey by **Samuel Tuffnell.**

Horsnaile rebuilt the medieval Bishopsgate entrance to London in 1733–4 under the direction of the architect, John James, receiving £300 for the structure and an extra £80 for the city arms on the attic storey above the central arch (**30**). He was paid £214 in 1733 for work on the dormitory of Westminster School, where he was employed together with Edward Stanton (WAM 35400, 35401 A–C). Horsnaile was also mason to the Inner Temple from 1737 to 1742 in 1737 he encased the south side of the Temple church at an estimated cost of £94 14s 5d and in 1742 worked on the front of the hall, cutting windows and providing Purbeck paving for a sum of £767 12s 6d. In 1737, in partnership with **John Deval I** and working under the direction of the architect, Henry Flitcroft, he rebuilt St Olave, Southwark, charging £2,277 for masonry work. He also provided the communion table at a cost of 16 guineas, including the ironwork, polishing and fixing (**31**).

The names of several of Horsnaile's apprentices are recorded in the Masons' Company Registers. Christopher Horsnaile II joined his father in 1709 and Thomas Tufnell, who is likely to have been related to Horsnaile's successor at Westminster Abbey, in 1722. Nothing further is known of William Cranke, apprenticed in 1720, Francis Kent (1727) and George Butler (1729). Another Christopher Horsnaile, the son of a carpenter, joined the workforce in 1732 and **Richard Hayward**, a relation by marriage, lived in Horsnaile's house in St Andrew, Holborn from 1740 and was perhaps about to be apprenticed formally when Horsnaile died in 1742.

Gunnis's claim that Horsnaile was 'important' as a sculptor is a curious statement since his solo output is limited, and he was neither markedly innovative nor singularly skilful as a carver. His successful business as a contractor was inherited by his son.

IR

Literary References: *Builder*, 2 May 1844, 252–3; *Roberts* 1933, IV, 348, 453; *Gunnis* 1968, 209–10; *Friedman* 1979–1980, 75–90; *Whinney* 1988, 139, 240–1, 248, 446 n.12; *Webb* 1999, *passim*; *Craske* 2000 (2), 103, 105; *Colvin* 1995, 916; IGI 445929

Archival References: Masons' Co, *Freemen*, f28, 29 Oct 1700; RC Physic, Cash Book 1664–1726, p 369; Westminster Abbey, masonry bills, 1729–1737, WA Muniments 45933A, 34514 ff; Hoare Private Accts 1734–49; Hoare Partnership Ledger, 1724–34, fol 123, 149; Hoare Partnership Ledger 1734–42, Shop Acct, fol 81

Will: PROB 11/665, fol 368–9 (Edward Stanton)

Funerary Monuments

1.	†1719	Anne, Lady Hodgson (co-sculptor: Edward Stanton)	Marston, Lincs	S	Pevsner, *Lincs*, 1989, 558
2.	†1719	Robert Pleydell (co-sculptor: Edward Stanton)	Ampney Crucis, Glos	S	Pevsner, *Glos: Cotswolds*, 1999, 140
3.	†1721	Alice, Lady Brownlow (co-sculptor: Edward Stanton)	Belton, Lincs	S	Pevsner, *Lincs*, 1989, 134
4.	†1721	Thomas Vernon (co-sculptor: Edward Stanton)	Hanbury, Worcs	S	*Gunnis* 1968, 210; Pevsner, *Worcs*, 1968, 184; *Whinney* 1988, 139
5.	† to 1722	Cressener family (co-sculptor: Edward Stanton)	Earls Colne, Essex	S	*Gunnis* 1968, 210
6.	†1722	George (†1712) and Judith Ayliffe (co-sculptor: Edward Stanton)	Foxley, Wilts	S	
7.	†1722	Thomas Renda (co-sculptor: Edward Stanton)	Wallingford, Berks	S	Pevsner, *Berks*, 1966, 248
8.	†1723	Bishop Fleetwood (co-sculptor: Edward Stanton)	Ely Cathedral, Cambs	S	Pevsner, *Cambs*, 1970, 365
9.	†1723	Gregory Geering (co-sculptor: Edward Stanton)	Denchworth, Berks	S	
10.	†1723	Sir James Wishart (co-sculptor: Edward Stanton)	Leatherhead, Surrey	S	Pevsner, *Surrey*, 1971, 339; *Whinney* 1988, 139
11.	†1724	Sir John Sherard (co-sculptor: Edward Stanton)	North Witham, Lincs	S	*Lord* 1986, 103; Pevsner, *Lincs*, 1989, 589
12.	†1726	Sir John Blencowe (co-sculptor: Edward Stanton)	Marston St Lawrence, Northants	S	Pevsner, *Northants*, 1973, 302

No.	Date	Work		Location		Reference
13.	†1726	William Brownlow (co-sculptor: Edward Stanton)		Belton, Lincs	S	*Lord* 1986, 103; Pevsner, *Lincs*, 1989, 134
14.	†1726	William East (co-sculptor: Edward Stanton)		Witham, Essex	S	*Gunnis* 1968, 210; Pevsner, *Essex*, 1965, 429
15.	†1727	Elizabeth, Lady Benet (co-sculptor: Edward Stanton)		Warminghurst, Sussex	S	Pevsner, *Sussex*, 1965, 363
16.	1729	William Beaumont (†1718) (co-sculptor: Edward Stanton)		Great Dunmow, Essex	S	Pevsner, *Essex*, 1965, 202
17.	1720–1730	Bartholomew Layton (†1702) (co-sculptor: Edward Stanton)		Ringwood, Hants	S	*Gunnis* 1968, 210
18.	1720–1730	Maude family († to 1703) (co-sculptor: Edward Stanton)		St Mary, Kilkenny	S	*Potterton* 1975, 83
19.	†1730	Sir Jacob Garrard		Langford, Norfolk	S	Pevsner, *Norfolk: N W & S*, 1999, 509–10
20.	†1730	Sir Richard Sherard (co-sculptor: Edward Stanton)		North Witham, Lincs	S	Pevsner, *Lincs*, 1989, 589; *Lord* 1986, 103
21.	†1731	William Rogers		Dowdeswell, Glos	S	*Gunnis* 1968, 210; Pevsner, *Glos: Cotswolds*, 1999, 323; C Lib (repr)
22.	†1736	Sir John Philipps		Haverfordwest, Pembrokes	S	*Whinney* 1988, 248; C Lib (repr)
23.	1738	Sir Brownlowe Sherard Bt (†1736) Payment(s): £142 7s 11d		North Witham, Lincs		Lincs RO, Misc. Dep. 45/3/14, 169; Pevsner, *Lincs*, 1989, 589
Chimneypieces						
24.	1726	Two for the library, one of black and yellow marble (£60 with a reduction of £2 on the bill), the other of purple marble (reduced from £38 to £36) (co-sculptor: Edward Stanton)		Ditchley Park, Oxon		Dillon DIL I/p/3bi; *Gunnis* 1968, 210
25.	1726	Two, with black fluted Corinthian columns and white capitals (co-sculptor: Edward Stanton)		Ditchley Park, Oxon, library		Pevsner, *Oxon*, 1974, 575
26.	1727	Description unavailable Payment(s): £17 16s 6d		[Lord Folkestone's London house]; untraced		*Gunnis* 1968, 210
27.	*c*1727	with cross-member carved with mask and garlands and term supports (designed by William Kent?) (co-sculptor: Edward Stanton) Payment(s): £64 15s	m	Ditchley Park, Oxon, hall		*Friedman* 1984, 121, 318–9; *Gomme* 1989, 89–90 (repr 9)
28.	1725–1729	Several, including one of 'a fine Agate Marble' (£27); another, for the hall, elaborately carved with terms and frieze (£52) (co-sculptor: Edward Stanton)		Ditchley Park, Oxon		Dillon DILI/p/3bh; 1/p/3bg; *Gunnis* 1968, 210
29.	1736	With pilasters, carved capitals, freeze and cornice, in purple and black and yellow marble Payment(s): £31 10s		[Okeover Hall, Staffs]; untraced		*Oswald* 1964, 226–7; GPC
Architectural Sculpture						
30.	1733	Keystone for central arch with a bishop's mitre and city arms above the arch, flanked by heraldic beasts Payment(s): £80		[Bishopsgate, London]; destroyed		*Gunnis* 1968, 210; *Friedman* 1979, 75–90
31.	1739	Communion table		[St Olave, Southwark, London]; untraced		*Builder*, 1844, 253
Miscellaneous						
32.	?*c*1725	Two agate tables (co-sculptor: Edward Stanton)		[Ditchley Park, Oxon]; untraced		*Gunnis* 1968, 210
33.	1725–1729	'Two fine Agate Marble Pallasters with their Bases & Caps Curiously wrot. And Glas'd for the front of a Beaufett [buffet]' (co-sculptor: Edward Stanton)		[Ditchley Park, Oxon]; untraced		Dillon DIL 1/p/3bg

HORSNAILE, Christopher II *c*1689–1760

The mason son of **Christopher Horsnaile I**, he was apprenticed to his father on 24 January 1708 for the customary seven years, but did not become free of the Masons' Company until 8 January 1719, the same day as **William Stanton**, the son of his father's partner, **Edward Stanton**. His premises were in the parish of St Andrew, Holborn and he was City Mason from 1734 until his death. He was also a freemason, a member of the court of common council in the years 1735–46 and deputy of the court of common council from 1747 until 1759. He had two wives, Mary, and then a widow, Ann Hayward (†1771), whom he married in 1740.

Horsnaile was given considerable employment at the Mansion House in London under the architect, George Dance the elder. On 16 May 1738 he tendered for the building contract in partnership with **Robert Taylor I** and **John Townshend II**, but as a rival bid by **Thomas Dunn** and **John Deval I** came in at the same price, £18,000, the Mansion House Council resolved to give the work to all five of them with a proviso that the total cost should not exceed £17,000. They received a further contract for work costing £325 in the dancing gallery in February 1742 and Horsnaile alone provided mason's work on the obelisks, plinths and paving at the front of the building in October 1744, at a sum of £134. A substantial contract went to Horsnaile for chimneypieces, produced to designs by Dance. These ranged from a costly statuary work with purple marble plinths (in the parlour) and another with a carved relief of the scales of justice, to a simple Portland stone chimneypiece in the Servants' Hall (**1**). Some of the designs have close similarities to drawings by **Sir Henry Cheere** and Jeffery has mooted the possibility that Horsnaile may have sub-contracted some of the work to him. Horsnaile also tendered in June 1751 for chimneypieces for the second floor and attic, quoting a sum of £690, but lost the contract to **William Barlow**, whose estimate was only £350.

Horsnaile's working relationship with the Mansion House committee and the architect was not always harmonious. In June 1752 he was called before the committee because work was progressing too slowly and in a report of 1753, Dance was critical of its quality. Dance wrote that 'the slabs of the chimney-pieces are not entire, but made out with some little pieces in the breaks thereof', and also that 'the marble of two of the chimneypieces is pretty much stained and the carving but indifferently performed'. Dance was also dissatisfied with other aspects of Horsnaile's work. There had been a discussion in 1752 about 'the regalia at the front of the Mansion House' which had apparently failed to follow Dance's pattern (**2**). Horsnaile refused to alter anything except the handle of the sword but a year later agreed that if Dance would redraw the shield, he would make the model. This was accordingly done and the new model was laid before the Committee, who found that the mace was too low in relief and ordered Horsnaile to make it bolder 'by raising the said mace three-quarters of its substance'. In 1755 Horsenaile received a payment of £450 for fluting the pillars in the Egyptian Hall although once again he was tardy, having failed to finish the work in May 1756 when he received another reprimand from the committee (**3**). He was paid for further paving in 1758 (**4**).

Horsnaile succeeded his father as mason at Stourhead, where he received payments totalling £51 18s between June 1743 and June 1750. In 1748 he was paid £256 11s 5d for masonry work on four houses in Cornhill being built by Earl Cowper, including the Rainbow tavern, and that year he was also employed by John Nicholl, the father of Lady Carnarvon, at his house in Red Lion Square. He was for many years mason to Christ's Hospital. The notice of his death on 31 January 1760 was published in the *London Magazine*, which described him as 'Deputy of the ward of Farringdon without' (*London Mag* 1760, 107). Horsnaile died a wealthy man. He left £10,000 to his daughter Ann and the residue of his estate to his wife, after setting aside £100 for good causes including charity schools in the parish of St Andrew, Holborn.

Richard Hayward lived with Christopher Horsnaile in the 1740s and appears to have been Horsnaile's apprentice. Hayward may also have been a step-son. In 1749 Hayward's estate at Weston in Arden, Bulkington was transferred to Horsnaile who became a tenant to the freehold of the property. In 1747 another Christopher Horsnaile became free of the Masons' Company, by service with his father. This may have been Christopher Horsnaile the younger's son.

MGS

Literary References: *Gunnis* 1968, 210–1; *Jeffery* 1993, 71, 49–50, 67, 125–6, 300; RG/JP, 4, 725–61; *Webb* 1999, 17; IGI

Archival References: Masons' Co, *Freemen*, 8 January 1729, fol 29; 7 Jan 1747, fol 30; *London Marriage Licences*, 1740–45; Hoare Private Accounts, 1734–49, 1750–61; Hayward/Horsnaile lease; Chandos Archives, 1748 (Red Lion Square); MHCM 01/01/2, 764, 774, 789, 792

Additional MS Sources: Panshanger Archives, 1748 (Cornhill); Christ's Hospital archives

Will: PROB 11/855/32, 1 April 1760

Chimneypieces

1.	1749	Six in fine statuary, one in white and veined marble for the Housekeeper's Room, and seven of Portland Stone (designed by George Dance the Elder) Payment(s): £900, including fluting of some columns in the withdrawing room, and making stone staircases to the vaults Drawing(s): by Dance, Soane 1:12–13		Mansion House, City of London, ground and principal floors (most survive)	MHCM Box 2, 1749; *Gunnis* 1968, 210; *Jeffery* 1993, 125–6, 301 (repr)

Architectural Sculpture

2.	*c*1752	Relief ornaments for the principal front		Mansion House, City of London	*Gunnis* 1968, 210
3.	1755	Columns (fluting only) Payment(s): £450		Mansion House, City of London, Egyptian hall	MHCM, 9 July; *Jeffery* 1993, 137, 301
4.	1757–1758	Paving Payment(s): £233 7s 10d		Mansion House, City of London, Egyptian hall	*Jeffery* 1993, 139

Miscellaneous

5.	1752	Eight marble slabs for table-tops, four of fine white and veined, two of Saravezza and two of Siena Payment(s): Max £120	m	Mansion House, City of London	*Gunnis* 1968, 210; *Jeffery* 1993, 168

HORSON, Ezra fl 1686

He was a mason, in partnership with **Joseph Warrington.**

Architectural Sculpture

1.	1686	Windows, cornices, chimney-panels and a doorcase (co-sculptor: Joseph Warrington)	s	[Grimsthorpe Castle, Lincs]; untraced	Wentworth Woodhouse archives cited in *Gunnis* 1968, 211

HORWELL, Charles 1754–

He was born on 1 April 1754, and joined the Royal Academy Schools on 31 March 1777, giving his age as 17. He lived at 3 Tottenham Court Road in 1784, the year he won a silver medal (**23**). A gold followed in 1788 for a group of *Achilles and Patroclus* (**13**). With this group he also submitted a sketch, possibly in pencil, of *David cutting off the head of Goliath.* He won an award from the Society of Arts in 1787 (**20**).

In the summer of 1787 he was employed by Joseph Lygo and William Duesbury of the Derby manufactory to produce figures of *Zephyrus* and *Flora*, presumably the models he showed at the Royal Academy the same year (**26**). Lygo called on Horwell in August but did not 'find him getting forward with the figures. . . he is busy working in marble'. In October he visited again and found that Horwell was 'getting forward very slow indeed' (*Bricknell* 1995, 18). Horwell was eventually paid five guineas for his work. The business relationship did not develop further, but one of Horwell's employees, **Sartine**, who worked on the figures, was subsequently employed by the Derby firm.

In 1798 Horwell's house or yard was at 16 Grenville Street, near the Foundling Hospital. He was responsible for some monuments, including one with a portrait-medallion to Robert Boyd (**3**) and appears to have competed for the commission to carve a monument to Nelson in 1806–7 (**12**). He continued to exhibit at the Academy until 1807.

In 1809 his daughter Ann married the engraver, Richard Woodman. Horwell's date of death has not been ascertained, but his son, also Charles Horwell, died in 1830. By this son's will Charles Horwell senior's portrait and his silver medal went to the sculptor's illegitimate son, William Haiskins. A portfolio of drawings by the sculptor and his prints of the Farnese collection were left to Richard Woodman.

Literary References: *AJ* 1860, 47; *Graves* IV, 1905–6, 163; *Hutchison* 1960–62, 142; *Gunnis* 1968, 211; *Bricknell* 1995, 18, 24

Will: PROB 11/1770/77 'Charles Horwell Jr, Gentleman of Somers Town'

Funerary Monuments						
1.	1788	Part of a monument		[Exhib RA, London, 492]; untraced		*Graves* IV, 1905–6, 163
2.	1789	Grief at the tomb of a friend, sketch for a monument		[Exhib RA, London, 573]; untraced		*Graves* IV, 1905–6, 163
3.	†1794	General Sir Robert Boyd		King's Chapel, Gibraltar	S	GPC
4.	1801	Monumental figure		[Exhib RA, London, 984]; untraced		*Graves* IV, 1905–6, 163
5.	1802	Design for a monument		[Exhib RA, London, 954]; untraced		*Graves* IV, 1905–6, 163
6.	1803	Design for a monument		[Exhib RA, London, 902]; untraced		*Graves* IV, 1905–6, 163
7.	1804	A general falling in the lap of Victory, design for a monument		[Exhib RA, London, 833]; untraced		*Graves* IV, 1905–6, 163
8.	1804	Naval monument for the Guildhall, design		[Exhib RA, London, 908]; untraced		*Graves* IV, 1905–6, 163
9.	1805	Hope supporting, and Faith directing a dying man, for the entablature of a monument		[Exhib RA, London, 769]; untraced		*Graves* IV, 1905–6, 163
10.	1805	Ocean receiving a lost mariner, design for a monument		[Exhib RA, London, 788]; untraced		*Graves* IV, 1905–6, 163
11.	*c*1807	Christopher Anstey (†1805)		Westminster Abbey, London, south transept	S	*MacMichael* 1977, 95
12.	1807	Design for a monument to Admiral Lord Nelson		[Exhib RA, London, 1008]; untraced		*Graves* IV, 1905–6, 163
Statues						
13.	1788	'Achilles' Grief at the Death of Patroclus', group		[RA, London, gold medal]; untraced		RA Premium list
Busts						
14.	1790	Unidentified nobleman's son		[Exhib RA, London, 559]; untraced		*Graves* IV, 1905–6, 163
15.	1799	The sculptor's daughter		[Exhib RA, London, 1114]; untraced		*Graves* IV, 1905–6, 163
16.	1799	The sculptor's son		[Exhib RA, London, 1113]; untraced		*Graves* IV, 1905–6, 163
17.	1800	Ariadne		[Exhib RA, London, 977]; untraced		*Graves* IV, 1905–6, 163
18.	1802	Rev Arthur O' Leary		[Exhib RA, London, 1056]; untraced		*Graves* IV, 1905–6, 163
Chimneypieces						
19.	1786	Psyche, for a chimneypiece tablet	m	[Exhib RA, London, 580]; untraced		*Graves* IV, 1905–6, 163
20.	1787	Recumbent Psyche, figure for a chimneypiece		[Soc of A, greater silver palette]; untraced		RSA, *Transactions*, vol 6, 1788, 216
Architectural Sculpture						
21.	1790	Bellerophon thrown from Pegasus		[Exhib RA, London, 552]; untraced		*Graves* IV, 1905–6, 163
22.	1796–1797	Decorative work		[Lord Mornington's house, Park Lane, London]; untraced		Soane bill book 1794–7, fols 183v–184v; *Gunnis* 1968, 211
Miscellaneous						
23.	1784	Model of an academy figure, or a bas-relief		[RA, London, silver medal]; untraced		RA Premium list
24.	1785	Friendship, model		[Exhib RA, London, 593]; untraced		*Graves* IV, 1905–6, 163
25.	1786	Spirits on the lake		[Exhib RA, London, 501]; untraced		*Graves* IV, 1905–6, 163
26.	1787	Zephyrus and Flora, model (for reproduction in Derby porcelain)		[Exhib RA, London, 621]; untraced		*Graves* IV, 1905–6, 163; *Bricknell* 1995, 17
27.	1789	Cupid and Psyche		[Exhib RA, London, 467]; untraced		*Graves* IV, 1905–6, 163
28.	1790	Design for a Bacchus, model		[Exhib RA, London, 521]; untraced		*Graves* IV, 1905–6, 163
29.	1790	Design for a Hebe, model		[Exhib RA, London, 558]; untraced		*Graves* IV, 1905–6, 163
30.	1791	The murder of Duncan		[Exhib RA, London, 672]; untraced		*Graves* IV, 1905–6, 163
31.	1798	Andromeda		[Exhib RA, London, 1054]; untraced		*Graves* IV, 1905–6, 163
32.	1803	Sketches		[Exhib RA, London, 905, 906, 913]; untraced		*Graves* IV, 1905–6, 163
33.	1804	Sleeping cupid		[Exhib RA, London, 896]; untraced		*Graves* IV, 1905–6, 163
34.	1805	Birth of a sea nymph		[Exhib RA, London, 696]; untraced		*Graves* IV, 1905–6, 163

HOSKINS, James –1791

Hoskins was apprenticed to **John Cheere** in 1747. He seems to have progressed in his employment at some speed: a note in the *London Evening Post* of December 1751 concerning the successful treatment of **William Collins**'s leg ulcer with 'Iron Pear Tree Water' described Hoskins, a witness to the recovery, as 'Foreman to Mr Cheere' (*Friedman and Clifford* 1974, appendix C).

By 1770 Hoskins had set up in business with **Samuel Euclid Oliver**, and together they supplied works for Mersham Hatch (**1, 2**) and a good many reliefs, busts and other works for Wedgwood (**4, 8–11**). Hoskins also held the post of 'moulder and caster in plaster' to the Royal Academy from its foundation. In July 1773 he provided two casts of lions for the Academy (**3**). A group of academicians, including **Agostino Carlini**, George Moser and Benjamin West went to Slaughters coffee-house to inspect the casts, which they found acceptable.

By 1775 he had entered into partnership with **Benjamin Grant**, another of John Cheere's apprentices. They together supplied Wedgwood with more items (**5, 6**). An invoice in the Wedgwood archives for a large number of moulds, dated 16 January 1773, came to 11s 6d. Another invoice of March 21, 1774, from Hoskins and Grant, was for 'plaister casts prepaird to mould' which included busts of Zeno, Pindar, Faustina, Inigo Jones and Palladio, at what appears to be a standard price of a guinea a bust, and moulds of antique stone. The whole bill came to £29 13s 2d. Another Hoskins and Grant invoice of January 1775 notes the supply of many more busts, including a Galen and Hippocrates, and British worthies such as Ben Jonson, 'Sir W Reigle', Fletcher and Beaumont, Harvey and Newton. This bill came to £23 17s 4d, and was signed 'for self and partner Benj Grant'. In 1779 they were paid £26 6s 6d for items including figures of *Zingara* and *Chrispagnia* at £2 2s (*Meteyard* 1866, 1, 324–5). Hoskins was still active in 1790, when he provided small works for Lord Delaval (**12**).

Literary References: *Meteyard* 1866, 1, 324–5; *Gunnis* 1968, 211; *Pyke* 1973, 70; *Friedman and Clifford* 1974, appendix H; *Clifford* 1992, 58

Archival References: RA Council Minutes, 1, ff160–1 June 1773; Wedgwood/Hoskins

Statues					
1.	1772	Apollo (co-sculptor: Samuel Euclid Oliver)	p	[Mersham Hatch, Kent, parlour]; untraced	Archives, Lord Brabourne, quoted in *Gunnis* 1968, 211
2.	1772	Mercury (co-sculptor: Samuel Euclid Oliver)	l	[Mersham Hatch, Kent, the 'mount']; untraced	Archives, Lord Brabourne, quoted in *Gunnis* 1968, 211
3.	1773	'casts of two lions' Payment(s): £21		[RA, London]; untraced	RA Council Minutes, vol 1, ff160–1
Busts					
4.	1770–1771	Cicero and Horace (models for Josiah Wedgwood) (co-sculptor: Samuel Euclid Oliver)		Untraced	Wedgwood MSS E2/30950-1
5.	1775	Swift, Milton, Spenser, Chaucer, Addison, Pope, Locke, Dryden, Dr Johnson, Ben Jonson, Sir William Reigley, Prior, Congreve, Fletcher, Beaumont, Bacon, Boyle, Harvey and Newton (models for Josiah Wedgwood) (co-sculptor: Benjamin Grant)		Untraced	Wedgwood MSS L1/115
6.	1779	David Garrick and Lawrence Sterne (models for Josiah Wedgwood) (co-sculptor: Benjamin Grant)		Untraced	Wedgwood MSS L1/116
7.	pre-1818	Robert Adam		[Adam Sale 1818, lot 10]; untraced	Adam Sale 1818, 1; *Gunnis* 1968, 211
Reliefs					
8.	1770–1771	16 round basso relievos (models for Josiah Wedgwood) (co-sculptor: Samuel Euclid Oliver)		Untraced	Wedgwood MSS E2/30950–1
9.	1770–1771	Ganymede and Bacchus (models for Josiah Wedgwood) (co-sculptor: Samuel Euclid Oliver)		Untraced	Wedgwood MSS E2/30950–1
Miscellaneous					
10.	1770–1771	'the rock for the Neptune' (model for Josiah Wedgwood) (co-sculptor: Samuel Euclid Oliver)		Untraced	Wedgwood MSS E2/30950–1
11.	1770–1771	'the tail of the dolphin' (model for Josiah Wedgwood) (co-sculptor: Samuel Euclid Oliver)		Untraced	Wedgwood MSS E2/30950–1
12.	1790	Four enriched Etruscan vases and eight small bronze figures		[Lord Delaval's house, Portland Place, London]; untraced	*Gunnis* 1968, 211

HOUGHTON, John fl 1739–75

Houghton was a carver working in Dublin, who won premiums from the Dublin Society in 1741 and 1742. He was assisted in his work for Lord Kildare by **John Kelly**, who appears to have been his pupil (1). He also worked with **David Sheehan**. He was responsible for the angels above the entablature on the monument to Lord Barrymore. For details of these works see the entry for Sheehan. He lived in Duke Street *c*1761–75.

Literary References: *Strickland* 1, 1913, 525; *Potterton* 1975, 79

Architectural Sculptor					
1.	1739	Pediment decoration, including arms, boys and cornucopiae (co-sculptor: John Kelly) Payment(s): £600		[Carton, Co Kildare]; untraced	*Strickland* 1, 1913, 525
Reliefs					
2.	1742	St Paul preaching at Athens	wd	[Dublin Society, premium]; untraced	*Strickland* 1, 1913, 525
Miscellaneous					
3.	1741	Unidentified subject		[Dublin Society, premium]; untraced	*Strickland* 1, 1913, 525

HOW, John

Chimneypieces					
1.	nd	Several		[East India House, Leadenhall St, London, façade]; untraced	*Gunnis* 1968, 59
Architectural Sculpture					
2.	nd	Sundry carving (co-sculptor: John Boson)	wd	[East India House, Leadenhall St, London, façade]; untraced	Archives, E I Co, cited in *Gunnis* 1968, 59; *Archer* 1965, 405

HOW, William fl 1755

How and **John Nicholl** were awarded the contract for all the carving designed by George Dance senior for the Mansion House, City of London in 1755, in preference to **John Vardy**, whose estimate was £450. How and Nicholl submitted a quotation of £437 (Mansion House Comm 01/01/2 p 764).

HOWARD, Isaac fl 1699

In 1699 he made several figures in 'brass' for Thomas Coke.

Statues					
1.	1699	Mercury, 'figure'	b	[for Thomas Coke, Melbourne Hall, Derbys]; untraced	Archives, Marquess of Lothian quoted in *Gunnis* 1968, 211
2.	1699	Tartar on horseback, 'figure'	b	[for Thomas Coke, Melbourne Hall, Derbys]; untraced	Archives, Marquess of Lothian quoted in *Gunnis* 1968, 211
Busts					
3.	1699	Oliver Cromwell, 'head'	b	[for Thomas Coke, Melbourne Hall, Derbys]; untraced	Archives, Marquess of Lothian quoted in *Gunnis* 1968, 211

HOWE fl 1732

In December 1732 Richard Hoare paid 'Mr. Howe, carver' £23 12s 6d for work on one of his houses, possibly Stourhead, Wilts (Hoare Partnership Ledger, 1725–34, fol 357).

HOWE, James fl 1824–42

He was awarded a medal from the Society of Arts in 1824 (7), while living in Little Tufton Street, London. By 1831 he had moved to 22 Sutton Street. Between 1829 and 1842 he exhibited busts and medallic portraits at the Royal Academy (**1–5**).

Literary References: *Gunnis* 1968, 211; *Pyke* 1973, 70

Busts					
1.	1829	H Phillips		[Exhib RA, London, 1189]; untraced	*Graves* IV, 1905–6, 173
2.	1831	Unidentified gentleman	w	[Exhib RA, London, 1179]; untraced	*Graves* IV, 1905–6, 173
3.	1842	Andrew Ducrow		[Exhib RA, London, 1186]; untraced	*Graves* IV, 1905–6, 173
Reliefs					
4.	1829	Mr Gardener, medallic portrait		[Exhib RA, London, 1112]; untraced	*Graves* IV, 1905–6, 173
5.	1831	Unidentified gentleman, medallic portrait		[Exhib RA, London, 1032]; untraced	*Graves* IV, 1905–6, 173
6.	nd	William Penn	w	Private coll	*Pyke* 1973, 70
Miscellaneous					
7.	1824	Original whole-length miniature	w	[Soc of A, silver Isis medal]; untraced	RSA, *Transactions*, vol 42, 1824, xlvii

HOWIE, John fl 1846–60

Most of his known work is in the Cupar area of Fife. He was one of a family of stonemasons who had lived at Saughtree Cottage, Ceres, since the late- 18th century. He was born and brought up there and was entirely self-taught as a sculptor. By 1846 he was working in marble as well as freestone and in 1859 received his most important commission, for a statue of Dr Maitland MacGill Crichton for Cupar (**2**). Between 1846 and 1873 he lived at Brandon Street, Edinburgh. He exhibited a bust at the Royal Academy in 1846 (**7**) and showed several works at the Royal Scottish Academy between 1846 and 1852 (**5, 6, 9, 10**).

Literary References: *Woodward* 1977 (vol 1, pt 2), 97

Statues					
1.	1852	HRH the Prince of Wales	m	[Exhib R Sc A, Edinburgh, 685]; untraced	*Laperriere* 2, 1991, 319
2.	1860	Dr Maitland MacGill Crichton		Cupar, Fife	*Woodward* 1977, vol 1, pt 2, 98
3.	nd	Rev Thomas Buchanan, 'Provost of Ceres', toby jug figure	s	Ceres, Fife	*Woodward* 1977, vol 1, pt 2, 98
4.	nd	Two men playing the bagpipes	s	Saughtree Cottage, Ceres, Fife, roof	*Woodward* 1977, vol 1, pt 2, 98
Busts					
5.	1846	J Maitland Macgill Crichton		[Exhib R Sc A, Edinburgh, 573]; untraced	*Laperriere* 2, 1991, 319
6.	1846	Major Playfair, Provost of St Andrews	m	[Exhib R Sc A, Edinburgh, 567]; untraced	*Laperriere* 2, 1991, 319
7.	1846	Unidentified subject		[Exhib RA, London]; untraced	*Woodward* 1977, vol 1, pt 2, 97
8.	1847	Dr David Brewster	m	Wallace national monument, Stirling	*Woodward* 1977, vol 1, pt 2, 98; *Laperriere* 2, 1991, 319
9.	1850	Major Barclay	m	[Exhib R Sc A, Edinburgh, 466]; untraced	*Laperriere* 2, 1991, 319
10.	1850	O Tyndal Bruce	m	[Exhib R Sc A, Edinburgh, 469]; untraced	*Laperriere* 2, 1991, 319

HUBBARD, J P fl 1812

His elaborate tradecard, designed by himself, gives the information 'J.P. HUBBARD'S / British Marble Works / near / Babicomb, Devon'. It has a figure of *Britannia* in front of a temple with *Neptune* standing on a giant scallop shell to right, *Time* sitting on a rock before him and a female, who looks like *Venus* displaced from the shell, face-down under *Time*'s foot. The firm had a London repository at 14 Parliament Street and a manufactury at 6 Millbank, Westminster (Banks 106.16). A second card of 1812 adds 'The warehouse in London. No 5 Grand junction Wharf, Whitefriars' (Banks 106.17).

HUDSON, Mrs fl 1774–96

A wax modeller and miniature painter, for further information the reader is referred to *Pyke* 1973, 71.

HUGGINS, William 1756–

He was born in March 1756 and joined the Royal Academy Schools in 1773 winning a silver medal two years later. In 1790 he exhibited at the Royal Academy, giving his address as Chapel Street, Westminster.

Literary References: *Hutchison* 1960–62, 139

Reliefs					
1.	1775	Unidentified subject, bas-relief		[RA, London, silver medal]; untraced	RA Premium list
2.	1790	Commerce presenting abundance from the four quarters of the world to Britannia, bas-relief		[Exhib RA, London, 545]; untraced	*Graves* IV, 1905–6, 182

HUGH, John, of Laugharne

He came from a well-established Laugharne family and tombs to many of his forebears are in the local churchyard. He is listed in Pigot's *Directory* of 1831. He carved the 'plain but elegant oval tablet' to William Laugharne (**4**), and other tombstones (**2, 3**). The monument to William Graffitt noted by Gunnis now appears to be missing (**1**). A footing in the transept carved with the sculptor's name may be the remains of the monument (*Dale-Jones and Lloyd* 1989, 50).

Funerary Monuments

1.	?1799	William Graffitt	[Laugharne, Carmarthen]; untraced	S	*Gunnis* 1968, 211; *Dale-Jones and Lloyd* 1989, 50
2.	†1850	Julia Dickinson	Laugharne, Carmarthen, graveyard		*Dale-Jones and Lloyd* 1989, 50
3.	†1856	Mary Tilly	Laugharne, Carmarthen, graveyard		*Dale-Jones and Lloyd* 1989, 50
4.	nd	William Laugharne	Laugharne, Carmarthen		*Dale-Jones and Lloyd* 1989, 50

HUGHES, of Llanvillo

Funerary Monuments

1.	†1786	William Davies	Llanelieu, Brecon	S	Pevsner, *Powys*, 1979, 334

HUGHES, Robert Ball 1804–68

He was born on 19 January 1804, the son of John Hallett Hughes and his wife Amelia Susannah and was baptised at St Martin-in-the-Fields on 17 February that year. **Thomas Hughes** was his elder brother. Robert's father apparently recognised his talent at an early age, and young Hughes attended the Royal Academy Schools in 1818, winning two silver medals and a gold within five years (**27, 47, 28**). In 1820 he received a medal from the Society of Arts (**3**). On leaving the schools he entered the studio of **E H Baily**, where he studied and worked for seven years.

He first exhibited at the Royal Academy in 1822, showing a family portrait (**13**) and giving his address as 59 Long Acre. Six years later he was at 13 Carnaby Street. In 1829, at the instigation of American friends, he left England for New York. He soon became acquainted with the history painter and president of the American Academy of Fine Arts, John Trumbull, with whom he maintained a lifelong friendship. A letter dated August 1830 from Hughes to Trumbull includes a request for a loan of $20, to be repaid when Hughes completed a commission. Several more letters, published by Thomas Brumbaugh in 1957, include similar requests, which suggests that Hughes, in common with other immigrant English sculptors such as **W J Coffee**, found it difficult to sustain a career in the United States. A letter relates that at one time all his studio works were seized by his landlord in lieu of rent totalling $62.

Hughes appears nonetheless to have eked out a living from wax portraits, cameos, busts and, later, 'poker drawings' (portraits drawn with a hot poker). He executed one graceful monument in the best London sculptural tradition, with a relief of a draped female directing the expiring figure of Bishop Hobart to Heaven (**1**). It was probably through Trumbull that he was engaged to repair **Joseph Wilton**'s statue of William Pitt, then in a state of disrepair and used as a support for a shed in the New York almshouses. The sculptor maintained that after 'bestowing on it months of arduous exertion', he 'restored it to its former state' (*Fehl* 1972, 11). On the strength of Hughes's performance, and the prestige resulting from his medals from the London schools, Trumbull and others recommended that he be awarded the commission to restore **Antonio Canova**'s statue of George Washington, damaged in 1831 by a fire in the State House in North Carolina. Hughes wrote to the governor's secretary 'I shall consider my visit to this country most fortunate should I be the means of preserving to the world the statue of your immortal Washington and the work of that great artist Canova' (*Fehl* 1972, 7). The General Assembly accepted Hughes's estimate in January 1832, but having received $2,800 on commencement of the work, he left Carolina to bring his family from New York and failed to return. Instead he removed to New Jersey and requested that the moulds and casts necessary for repairing the statue be sent to him to complete at his new address. This was forbidden by the contract and the statue was never restored.

Hughes received some highly significant commissions, including the first portrait-statue to be produced in the USA, of Alexander Hamilton (**7**). Typically, his relative, E B Hughes, had to solicit help from Trumbull so that the sculptor could get a suit for the unveiling ceremony; he was 'really so abominably shabby that he will be ashamed to be seen there' (*Brumbaugh* 1957, 427). Unfortunately, the statue was destroyed when the Merchants' Exchange was burnt to the ground a mere eight months later. A pattern of ill luck seemed to have followed the sculptor: in 1840 he won the commission for an equestrian statue of George Washington for Philadelphia, for which he probably used the model he had earlier recommended to the city of New York (**6**). He moved to the city, but the project aborted when the Bank of the United States failed to find the necessary funding.

In 1831 he became an honorary member (professional) of the National Academy of Design and in 1833 he was appointed a member of the board of directors of the American Academy of Fine Arts. In the 1840s he exhibited at the early American shows, and received a commission to model the statue of the navigator, Nathaniel Bowditch (**2**). This was the first full-size statue to be cast in bronze in America, but the material was so inferior that the family had to have it re-cast in 1886 by 'Gruet Jne' of Paris.

Hughes exhibited a work in the American section of the Great Exhibition in London in 1851 (**8**). He died at Dorchester, near Boston, on 5 March 1868. The English *Art Journal* carried his obituary, remarking that his reputation was 'almost exclusively limited to America' (*AJ* 1868, 128). He appears to have impressed the public in his adopted country: Christopher Baldwin remarked of *Uncle Toby and the widow Wadman*, from Sterne's *Tristam Shandy* (**11**) 'was there ever any statuary to equal this? Uncle Toby is inimitable. Such benevolence and perfect honesty as appear in his face! How well this is contrasted with the wicked looks of the frisky and lecherous widow! . . . no-one can look but with pleasure' (*Brumbaugh* 1958, 427).

The list of his commissions, together with his pioneering use of American marble and native casting technology, marks him out as one of the most notable of America's early sculptors. In the 20th century one scholar wrote admiringly of Hughes's portraiture, finding character, refinement, sensitivity and 'penetration of character' in his busts *all'antica* of Henry Inman, John Trumbull, John Watts, and others (*Chamberlain* 1957, 383) (**24, 25, 26**). Others have seen him as an undeniably significant but hapless sculptural pioneer, who, through bad luck and poor judgement, failed to realise his potential. Philipp Fehl, who provides a sensitive analysis of Hughes's combination of neo-classicism and naturalistic detail, summarised his reputation thus: 'At present Hughes's art is neither old enough to be considered interesting nor modern enough to be 'relevant' but, he added, 'these things are subject to change' (*Fehl* 1972, 22).

MGS

Literary References: *AJ* 1868, 128; *Graves* IV, 1905–6, 187; *Taft* 1930, 94; *Lovejoy* 1946, 175; *Mag Antiq*, 1947, 58; *Chamberlain* 1957, 383–7; *Brumbaugh* 1958, 423–7; *Gunnis* 1968, 211–2; *Fehl* 1972, 7–28; *Pyke* 1973, 71; *Wainwright* 1975, 963

Archival References: IGI

Portraits of the Sculptor: John Trumbull, private coll (*Fehl* 1972, 28, repr)

Funerary Monuments

No.	Date	Work		Location		References
1.	c1831	Bishop John Henry Hobart (†1830)		[Second Trinity Church, Broadway at Wall St]; 3rd Trinity Church, New York, USA, verger's office (1846)		*Gunnis* 1968, 212; *Fehl* 1972, 22 (repr)
2.	1847	Nathaniel Bowditch Model(s): Boston Athenaeum, plaster	b	Mount Auburn Cemetery, Cambridge, Massachusetts, USA	SD	*Taft* 1930, 98; *Sharf* 1961, 80, 82, 86 (repr); *Fehl* 1972, 23 (model repr); *Adams* 1991, 23 (model repr)

Statues

No.	Date	Work		Location		References
3.	1820	Barberini Faun		[Soc of A, London, silver medal]; untraced		RSA, *Transactions*, vol 38, 1820, xxxv
4.	1828	Shepherd boy		[Exhib RA, London, 1136]; untraced		*Graves* IV, 1905–6, 187
5.	1830	De Witt Clinton		[for the Clinton-Hall Association]; untraced		*Chamberlain* 1957, 383
6.	1833	George Washington, equestrian model		Museum of Fine Arts, Boston		*Taft* 1930, 98; *Lovejoy* 1946, 175; *Fehl* 1972, 21
7.	1835	Alexander Hamilton Model(s): Boston Athenaeum, USA; Detroit Institute of Arts; Museum of the City of NY, plaster	m	[Merchants' Exchange, New York, USA]; destroyed		*Brumbaugh* 1958, 422 (model repr); Fehl 1972, 22 (model repr); *Adams* 1991, 22 (model repr)
8.	1851	Oliver Twist		[Gt Exhib 1851, purchased by Duke of Devonshire]; untraced		*Gunnis* 1968, 212
9.	nd	Little Nell		Boston Athenaeum, USA		*Taft* 1930, 97; *Brumbaugh* 1958, 422, 423 (repr); *Fehl* 1972, 24 (repr)
10.	nd	Patrick Henry, model		Norfolk Museum of Arts and Sciences, Norfolk, Virginia		*Mag Antiq* 1955, 76 (repr)
11.	nd	Uncle Toby and the widow Wadman		Boston Athenaeum, USA		*Taft* 1930, 98; *Brumbaugh* 1958, 423, 425–6, 427; *Gunnis* 1968, 212
12.	nd	Washington Irving, statuette		Untraced		*Taft* 1930, 98

Busts

No.	Date	Work		Location		References
13.	1822	The sculptor's father		[Exhib RA, London, 1004]; untraced		*Graves* IV, 1905–6, 187
14.	1826	Arthur, 1st Duke of Wellington		[Exhib RA, London]; untraced		*Gunnis* 1968, 212
15.	1826	Augustus Frederick, Duke of Sussex		[Exhib RA, London]; untraced		*Gunnis* 1968, 212
16.	1832	Thomas Handasyd Perkins Model(s): exhib American Academy of Fine Arts, 1833		[Exhib Boston Athenaeum]; untraced		*Chamberlain* 1957, 384
17.	1833	Hon David B Ogden, model 'to be executed in marble'		[Exhib American Acad of Fine Arts]; untraced		*Chamberlain* 1957, 384
18.	1835	Hon William Gaston		[Exhib American Acad of Fine Arts]; untraced		*Chamberlain* 1957, 384
19.	1836	Washington Irving		Untraced Other versions: plaster copies sold for $15, several extant		*Taft* 1930, 98; *Chamberlain* 1957, 384
20.	pre-1839	Edward Livingston		Boston Atheneaum		*Chamberlain* 1957, 384, 387 (repr)
21.	1840	Dr Nathaniel Bowditch, model 'now being executed in marble'	p	[Exhib Boston Athenaeum, 'property of N I Bowditch']; untraced		*Chamberlain* 1957, 385
22.	1840	George W Bethune		[Exhib Artists' Fund Society, Philadelphia]; untraced		*Chamberlain* 1957, 385
23.	1840	Nicholas Biddle, 'now being executed in marble'	p	[Exhib, Artists' Fund Society, coll the sitter]; untraced		*Chamberlain* 1957, 385; *Wainwright* 1975, 962 (repr)
24.	1841	Henry Inman		National Academy of Design, NY		*Chamberlain* 1957, 385, 387 (repr)
25.	nd	John Trumbull		YCBA		*Chamberlain* 1957, 382, 385 (repr); *Fehl* 1972, 24, 26 (repr)
26.	nd	John Watts	b	Met NY Other versions: NY City Hall, bronze		*Chamberlain* 1957, 382, 384 (repr)

Reliefs

No.	Date	Work		Location		References
27.	1819	Apollo, model in the Antique Academy		[RA, London, silver medal]; untraced		RA Premium list; *AJ* 1868, 128–9
28.	1823	Mercury bringing Pandora to Epimetheus, from Hesiod's Theogony		[RA, London, gold medal]; untraced		RA Premium list
29.	1824	Pandora is brought by Mercury to Epimetheus		[Exhib RA, London, 975]; untraced		*Graves* IV, 1905–6, 187
30.	1829	Chief Justice John Marshall	w	Supreme Court Building, Washington DC		*Pyke* 1973, 71
31.	1830	Charles Wilkes, president of the Bank of New York	w	NYHS	SD	*Chamberlain* 1957, 383; *Pyke* 1973, 71
32.	1840	I R Jackson, medallion		[Exhib Artists' Fund Society, Philadelphia]; untraced		*Chamberlain* 1957, 385
33.	1840	Mrs C Ingersoll, medallion		[Exhib Artists' Fund Society, Philadelphia]; untraced		*Chamberlain* 1957, 385
34.	1840	Mrs John Butler, medallion		[Exhib Artists' Fund Society, Philadelphia]; untraced		*Chamberlain* 1957, 385
35.	1840	Rev George W Bethune, medallion		[Exhib Artists' Fund Society, Philadelphia]; untraced		*Chamberlain* 1957, 385

36.	1840	Van Rensselaer, medallion		[Exhib Artists' Fund Society, Philadelphia]; untraced	*Chamberlain* 1957, 385
37.	1841	I P Davis, cameo		[Exhib Boston Athenaeum]; untraced	*Chamberlain* 1957, 385
38.	1841	Mrs John Butler, cameo		[Exhib Boston Athenaeum]; untraced	*Chamberlain* 1957, 385
39.	1841	N I Bowditch, cameo		[Exhib Boston Athenaeum]; untraced	*Chamberlain* 1957, 385
40.	1841	W Rotch, cameo		[Exhib Boston Athenaeum]; untraced	*Chamberlain* 1957, 385
41.	1841	William Henry Harrison	w	Museum of Fine Arts, Boston	*Chamberlain* 1957, 385, 386; *Pyke* 1973, 71 (repr 144)
42.	nd	Elizabeth Rodman	w	Private coll	*Pyke* 1973, 71
43.	nd	Mary Jane Quincy	w	Private coll	*Pyke* 1973, 71
44.	nd	Robert Charles Winthrop	w	Parke-Bernet, NY, 10–12 Jan 1951	*Chamberlain* 1957, 385
45.	nd	Unidentified woman	w	Philadelphia Museum of Art S44-63-29	*Mag Antiq* 1947, 58 (repr); *Pyke* 1973, 71
46.	nd	Unidentified youth	w	Philadelphia Museum of Art S43-95-63	*Pyke* 1973, 71; *Mag Antiq* 1947, 58 (repr)
Miscellaneous					
47.	1822	Model in the life Academy		[RA, London, silver medal]; untraced	RA Premium list
48.	1825	Achilles		[Exhib RA, London, 1064]; untraced	*Graves* IV, 1905–6, 187
49.	pre-1829	George IV, 'statuettes and busts'		Untraced	*Taft* 1930, 94
50.	1830	'An eminent member of the NY Bar'		[Exhib Artists' Fund Society of Philadelphia]; untraced	*Chamberlain* 1957, 384
51.	nd	Mary Magdalen		Untraced	*Taft* 1930, 98

HUGHES, Thomas 1809–

In 1825, while living at 59 Long Acre, London, he received a medal from the Society of Arts (2). That year, aged 16, he joined the Royal Academy Schools on the recommendation of **E H Baily**, in whose studio his brother, **Robert Ball Hughes**, was then working. He exhibited at the Academy in 1836, giving his address as 37 Long Acre, and showing a bust of T Thompson 'the celebrated representative of the Grecian statues' (7).

Literary References: *Gunnis* 1968, 212

Archival References: RA Admissions, 1825

Statues				
1.	1851	Eve, figure	[Gt Exhib]; untraced	*Gunnis* 1968, 212
Busts				
2.	1825	Model of a bust after the antique	[Soc of A, silver medal]; untraced	RSA, *Transactions*, vol 43, 1825, xlvii
3.	1826	J H Hughes	[Exhib RA, London, 1013]; untraced	*Graves* IV, 1905–6, 188
4.	1828	Unidentified gentleman	[Exhib Soc of BA, London, 899]; untraced	*Johnson* 1975, 244
5.	1829	Theodore von Holst	[Exhib Soc of BA, London, 880]; untraced	*Johnson* 1975, 244
6.	1830	Unidentified gentleman	[Exhib RA, London, 1189]; untraced	*Graves* IV, 1905–6, 188
7.	1836	T Thompson	[Exhib RA, London, 1147]; untraced	*Graves* IV, 1905–6, 188
Miscellaneous				
8.	1828	Eve	[Exhib RA, London, 1138]; untraced	*Graves* IV, 1905–6, 188; *Johnson* 1975, 244
9.	1829	Cupid	[Exhib RA, London, 1149]; untraced	*Graves* IV, 1905–6, 188
10.	1830	Choice of Hercules	[Exhib RA, London, 1245]; untraced	*Graves* IV, 1905–6, 188

HULBERT FAMILY, of Cleeve, Salop fl 1728–1825

T Hulbert, of Cleeve, Salop signed a plain tablet with a pediment at Inkberrow (1). In the same church is a tablet with an obelisk and an urn erected a century later, signed by a sculptor of the same surname, and presumably from the same family. (Inf. Mike Wall)

Funerary Monuments				
1.	†1728	Thomas Dyson	Inkberrow, Worcs	S
2.	†1825	Henry Harvey	Inkberrow, Worcs	S

HULL, Samuel, of Leicester fl 1816?–*c*1842

Hull's monuments, whether signed alone or with his partner, **Thomas Pollard**, are nearly always neo-Hellenic in design, the best being to Stephen Peet, which has a relief of a cherub with an extinguished torch (**12**). They were presumably members of the firm of **Shenton, Hull and Pollard**, whose signature appears on a number of monuments in Leicestershire at around the same time.

Hull and Pollard put in a successful tender for the masonry work at St George, Leicester (Minute Book HM Commission for building New Churches, Lambeth Palace Library). In 1827 Samuel Hull was the master mason responsible for building Caythorpe Hall, Lincs (**18**). Hull, or possibly another family member, designed and built the pedestal for a statue in the city of the 5th Duke of Rutland (**19**).

Literary References: *Gunnis* 1968, 212

Funerary Monuments					
1.	?1816	Elizabeth Prickett (co-sculptor: Thomas Pollard)	Bridlington, E R Yorks		GPC
2.	?1818	Elizabeth Corrance (co-sculptor: Thomas Pollard)	Foxton, Leics	S	*Gunnis* 1968, 212
3.	?1818	Rev Auley Macaulay	Rothley, Leics	S	*Gunnis* 1968, 212
4.	?1820	Henry Bickley	Peckleton, Leics, churchyard	S	*Gunnis* 1968, 212
5.	?1822	John Heyrick (co-sculptor: Thomas Pollard)	Leicester Cathedral	S	*Gunnis* 1968, 212
6.	?1825	Colonel William Hulse (co-sculptor: Thomas Pollard)	Cossington, Leics	S	*Gunnis* 1968, 212
7.	1828	Charles Packe (co-sculptor: Thomas Pollard)	Prestwold, Leics	S	*Gunnis* 1968, 349
8.	?1828	Mary Wood (co-sculptor: Thomas Pollard)	St Mary, Leicester	S	*Gunnis* 1968, 212
9.	?1831	George Pochin	Barkby, Leics	S	*Gunnis* 1968, 212

10.	?1831	James Swan	Ridlington, Rutland	S	*Gunnis* 1968, 212
11.	?1832	Rev Robert Radcliffe	Ashby-de-la-Zouche, Leics		GPC
12.	?1834	Stephen Peet	Mount Sorel, Leics	S	*Gunnis* 1968, 212
13.	?1837	Mary Miles	Cosby, Leics	S	*Gunnis* 1968, 212
14.	?1838	Mary Clare	Cosby, Leics	S	*Gunnis* 1968, 212
15.	†1840	Rev Henry Sheild	Preston, Rutland	S	*Gunnis* 1968, 212
16.	?1840	Rev Samuel Heyrich	Brampton Ash, Leics	S	*Gunnis* 1968, 212
17.	†1842	Jane Sheild	Preston, Rutland	S	Leics & Rutland Notes and Queries

Chimneypieces

18.	1827	Several	[Caythorpe Hall, Lincs]; untraced		Leics county archives, Packe, DE.258 in GPC

Architectural Sculpture

19.	1852	Pedestal for statue of John, 5th Duke of Rutland by Edward Davis	[Cheapside, Leicester]; Leicester marketplace, in front of Corn Exchange		*Cavanagh* 2000, 142

HUME, Robert –1869?

He was a gilder and carver. Pigot's London directories of 1825–29 give his address as 4 Little Portland Street, Cavendish Square and then 22 Golden Square. In the 1830 *Directory*, Robert Hume and Son were listed at 65 Berners Street. The property was rated at £100 in 1840. Hume's name disappeared from the rate-books in 1869, presumably the year of his death.

Literary References: GPC (Inf. GW Addleshaw and Ann Saunders)

Architectural Sculpture

1.	1829–1834	Canopies over choir stalls (designed by Robert Smirke)	wd	York Minster	GPC

HUMPHREY, Thomas, of London fl 1786–c1815

Humphrey, who was apprenticed to **William Vere** in 1786, signed two tablets in memory of the same man, John Charrington (**1, 2**).

Literary References: *Gunnis* 1968, 212

Funerary Monuments

1.	†1815	John Charrington	St Dunstan, Stepney, London	S	*Gunnis* 1968, 212
2.	†1815	John Charrington	Aldenham, Herts	S	*Gunnis* 1968, 212

HUMPHREYS, Thomas fl 1801

Chimneypieces

1.	1701	Description unavailable	Dyrham Park, Glos, great room	Pevsner, *Glos: Cotswolds*, 1999, 344

HUNT, John, of Northampton –1754

John Hunt, who signed numerous monuments in and around Northampton, was apprenticed to Grinling Gibbons. The records of the Drapers' Company however list two pupils of that name as Gibbons's apprentices, the first in 1675 and the second in 1696. If the Northamptonshire monuments are the work of only one of these sculptors, which seems likely given their homogeneity, then they probably belong to the younger Hunt, who evidently settled and prospered in Northampton.

On 25 September 1712 a John Hunt became a freeman of Northampton, admitted 'gratis for carving King Charles's statue' (Northants town archives). The image in Roman armour is similar to statues of the king by Gibbons, but has a full wig (**32**). It was gilded by Hunt for £3 and was erected in gratitude for the king's help in rebuilding the church. Two years previously Hunt carved the large tympanum relief of *Diana and her cortège* for the garden front of Hinwick House, Beds (**33**). This portrays the goddess in her chariot and is 'a spirited work, though perhaps a little rustic and naive in treatment' (*Gunnis* 1968, 212).

In 1714 Sir Justinian Isham visited Hunt to enquire about the cost of executing a monument to Elizabeth Isham at Lamport, Northants. Isham considered Hunt's estimate of £60 too high and gave the commission to the London sculptor **Edward Stanton**. In a letter to his son, Isham wrote of Hunt's charges 'tho he is accounted a good workman, being apprentice to Gibbons ye carver yet I think it is very unreasonable'. Isham's judgement was based on his assessment that a much larger wall-monument could be had from Stanton for only £8 more (NRO, Isham corr quoted in *Isham* 1951, 440).

Hunt had no shortage of other patrons for his funerary monuments, which are varied and show the influence of his master. These include the monument to Mary Dolben, which has a relief profile medallion (**2**). The memorial to her kinswoman, Elizabeth Dolben, has a bust in a rounded arch niche, framed by carved curtains (**21**) and a similar design was used for the monument to the 12-year old Cilena l'Anson Bradley (**13**), which Gunnis considered the sculptor's best work, 'quite equal to London craftsmanship of the period' (*Gunnis* 1968, 212). His most complex achievement is the monument to Sir William and Lady Boughton which has stiffly standing figures with their hands on their hearts, beneath a broken, scrolled arch. Skulls lie by their feet (**4**). That to Diana Orlebar has two standing putti again with one hand to the heart while the other wipes away tears. A large skull is carved in profile on the apron (**3**).

Later monuments show a knowledge of fashionable trends by incorporating rococo decoration, such as the shell work on the wall-tablet to Lieutenant William Roberts (**30**) and the scrolls on the polychrome monument to John Nicolls Raynsford, a relative of the Ishams, at Faxton, which was given to the Victoria and Albert Museum when the church was demolished in 1965 (**28**). Terence Hodgkinson wrote that it 'has charm; but the parts of the design cannot be said to form a convincing unity; the capitals of the pilasters, for instance, are awkwardly cut away to accommodate the slab bearing the inscription'. Works such as the memorial to Rebecca Ivory, make use of a small putto holding a drape on which is carved the inscription (**6**).

On 1 July 1751 Hunt advertised himself in the *Northampton Mercury*, as a 'Statuary and carver in wood and stone, who served his apprenticeship with the noted and famous Mr Grinling Gibbons', that he 'makes monuments and all sorts of ornaments for houses and gardens'.

John Hunt died on 25 September 1754. Five days later the *Northampton Mercury* reported 'On Wednesday Morning last Mr John Hunt, of this town, an eminent statuary, was found dead in his bed; he ate a hearty supper the evening before and went to bed seemingly in good Health, not complaining of any illness' (GPC). The antiquary George Baker noted a small bust of Hunt (erroneously called 'Henry') at Upton Hall, Northants in 1822. He described the sitter as 'formerly of Northampton, a provincial statuary of some celebrity, and a pupil of Grinling Gibbons' (*Baker* 1822–30, 1, 226).

MGS

Literary References: *Isham* 1951, 441; *Lewis* 1953, 21; *Green* 1964, 54; *Hodgkinson* 1971–2, 334; *Bailey* 1996, 20, 125; *Esterly* 1998 174–6; *Bilbey* 2002, 93

Archival References: *Register of Freemen*, Northampton borough records, Northants RO 6/1, fol 140; GPC

Representations of the Sculptor: small bust, formerly at Upton Hall, Northants, untraced (*Baker* 1822–30, 1, 226)

Funerary Monuments

1.	†1707	Sophia Whitwell		Oundle, Northants, outside wall	S	*Gunnis* 1968, 213
2.	†1710	Mary Dolben, bust		Finedon, Northants	S	Pevsner, *Northants*, 1973, 217
3.	†1716	Diana Orlebar		Podington, Beds	S	*Gunnis* 1968, 213; Pevsner, *Beds, Hunts & Peterborough*, 1968, 134
4.	†1716	Sir William (†1716) and Lady Boughton		Newbold-on-Avon, Warks	S	*Gunnis* 1968, 213; Pevsner, *Warks*, 1966, 361
5.	†1717	Frances Stratford		Overstone, Northants		*Gunnis* 1968, 213; Pevsner, *Northants*, 1973, 368
6.	†1720	Rebecca Ivory		All Saints, Northampton	S	*Gunnis* 1968, 213
7.	†1721	Edward Stratford		Overstone, Northants	S	*Gunnis* 1968, 213; Pevsner, *Northants*, 1973, 368
8.	?1721	Samuel Knight		Wellingborough, Northants	S	*Gunnis* 1968, 213
9.	†1721	Sir Robert Hesilrige		Noseley, Leics	S	
10.	?1721	William Wykes		Hazelbeech, Northants	S	*Gunnis* 1968, 213
11.	†1724	John Bridges		Barton Seagrave, Northants		Pevsner, *Northants*, 1973, 104; *Bailey* 1996, 20
12.	†1724	Sir John Shuckburgh		Upper Shuckburgh, Warks	S	Pevsner, *Warks*, 1966, 439; *Gunnis* 1968, 213
13.	†1726	Cilena I'Anson Bradley	a	Long Buckby, Northants	S	*Gunnis* 1968, 212; Pevsner, *Northants*, 1973, 296
14.	†1726	Joseph Spinnall		Paulerspury, Northants		Pevsner, *Northants*, 1973, 371
15.	†1728	John and Samuel (†1718) Perkins		Kislingbury, Northants	S	*Gunnis* 1968, 213
16.	?1731	Benjamin Kidd		All Saints, Northampton	S	*Gunnis* 1968, 213
17.	?1731	Richard Cumberland		Peakirk, Northants	S	*Gunnis* 1968, 213
18.	†1731	William (†1728), Catherine (†1728) and Thomas Carter		Turvey, Beds	S	*Gunnis* 1968, 213
19.	?1732	Mary Shortgrave		St Peter, Northampton	S	*Gunnis* 1968, 213
20.	?1732	Thomas Peace		Hardingstone, Northants	S	*Gunnis* 1968, 213
21.	†1736	Elizabeth Dolben		Finedon, Northants	S	Pevsner, *Northants*, 1973, 217
22.	?1737	Elizabeth Trimmell		Brockhall, Northants	S	*Gunnis* 1968, 213
23.	?1738	William Watson		Spratton, Northants	S	*Gunnis* 1968, 213
24.	?1741	Anthony Eynead		All Saints, Northampton	S	*Gunnis* 1968, 213
25.	†1742	John Smith		St Peter, Northampton	S	*Gunnis* 1968, 213; Pevsner, *Northants*, 1973, 322
26.	?1743	Samuel Pennington		St Giles, Northampton	S	*Gunnis* 1968, 213; Pevsner, *Northants*, 1973, 320
27.	?1744	Dorcas Stratford		All Saints, Northampton	S	*Gunnis* 1968, 213
28.	†1746	John Nichols Raynsford		[St Dennis, Faxton, Northants]; VAM A.11-1965	S	*Gunnis* 1968, 213; *Hodgkinson* 1971–2, 336, 339 (repr); *Bilbey* 2002, 92–3 (repr)
29.	†1747	Anne Stonhouse		Untraced		*Hervey* I, 1749, 30, opp 104 (repr)
30.	†1747	William Roberts		Finedon, Northants	S	Pevsner, *Northants*, 1973, 217
31.	†1751	Philip Doddridge		Doddridge Street Congregational church, Northampton		Pevsner, *Northants*, 1973, 325

Statues

32.	1711–1712	King Charles II	s	All Saints, Northampton, above portico		*Isham* 1951, 441; *Gunnis* 1968, 213; *Gibson* 1997 (1), 374

Architectural Sculpture

33.	1710	Diana and her cortège, pediment sculpture		Hinwick House, Beds		*Gunnis* 1968, 212, citing Orlebar archives; Pevsner, *Beds, Hunts & Peterborough*, 1968, 99
34.	1712	Coat of Arms Payment(s): £9		All Saints, Northampton, portico		*Isham* 1951, 441

Miscellaneous

35.	by 1714	'a very good piece of carving done by Hunt'		[William Emmett's house, Bromley, Kent, hall]; untraced		*Gunnis* 1968, 212 citing archives, General Norman of Bromley, 1714 Inventory

HUNT, W fl *c*1794

He is known only for one carved Swithland slate tombstone. This has a relief of a skeleton rising from a grave in a country churchyard, whilst the church steeple crumbles in the background. In the heavens an angel blows the last trump, beside a *gloria* of cherubs emerging from ice-cream clouds.

Funerary Monuments

1.	1794	Unidentified subject, with a relief of the Day of Judgement	sl	Rothley, Leics, churchyard	GPC

HUNT, William, of London fl 1668–1718

He was apprenticed to 'William Stanborow' (presumably **William Stanborough**) in 1668 and became free in January 1677. Gunnis suggested that the mason of that name who carved the doorcase of Aylesbury Free School 40 years later was probably the same man (1).

Literary References: *Gunnis* 1968, 213

Archival References: Masons' Co *Freemen*, f28

Architectural Sculpture

1.	1718	Doorcase Payment(s): £30	s	Aylesbury Museum, Bucks	Aylesbury free school archives, cited in *Gunnis* 1968, 213

Miscellaneous

2.	1692	Sundial Payment(s): 10 gns		[for Sir Charles Kemeys]; untraced	Kemeys's Account book, cited in *Gunnis* 1968, 213 (ex coll Gunnis)

HUNTER, Hugh, of London fl c1781–96

His large tablets have finely carved details (1–3).

Funerary Monuments

1.	†1781	Dr Josiah Nisbet		Stratford-sub-Castle, Wilts	S	
2.	?1782	William Lyne		All Hallows, Twickenham, Middx	S	*Gunnis* 1968, 213
3.	?1791	Thomas Bush		Broxted, Essex	S	*Gunnis* 1968, 213

Chimneypieces

4.	1796	Portland stone, more than one	s	[Cleveland House, London]; untraced	Archives, Lord Brownlow, cited in *Gunnis* 1968, 213

Architectural Sculpture

5.	1796	Carved stonework	s	[Cleveland House, London]; untraced	Archives, Lord Brownlow, cited in *Gunnis* 1968, 213

HUNTER, Robert fl 1846–73

A carver of decorative stonework who lived in Edinburgh between 1847 and 1873. He first worked from 96 Abbey Hill, moved to Nottingham Place in 1855 and five years later to 30 Clerk Street. In 1867 he established a studio at Grange Road where he worked until 1873. He signs several elaborate gravestones in the Dalry and Grange Cemeteries, in Edinburgh, the most significant of which commemorate David Wright, Harriet Baird and Bernard Barker (1–3). He carved the tracery on the Celtic cross erected as the 78th Highlanders' Indian War Memorial on the Castle esplanade (4). It was designed by the architect Robert Rowand Anderson and featured relief sculpture by George MacCallum.

Literary References: *Woodward* 1977 (vol 1, pt 2), 98–9

Funerary Monuments

1.	1846	David Wright, gravestone		Grange Cemetery, Edinburgh	*Woodward* 1977, vol 1, pt 2, 98
2.	1864	Harriet Baird, gravestone		Grange Cemetery, Edinburgh	*Woodward* 1977, vol 1, pt 2, 98
3.	1866	Bernard Barker, gravestone		Grange Cemetery, Edinburgh	*Woodward* 1977, vol 1, pt 2, 98

Architectural Sculpture

4.	1862	Tracery for the Celtic Cross (monument to the 78th Highlanders) (designed by Robert Rowand Anderson)	s	Castle esplanade, Edinburgh	*Woodward* 1977, vol 1, pt 2, 98

HUNTINGTON (or HUNTINGDON), John –1748

His premises were at St Giles in the Fields. In 1735 he took an apprentice, Thomas Simmonds of St James, Westminster. Between 1737 and 1740 he was working at Lord North's London house, from an address in Henrietta Street (Bodl. MS. North C.58). He signs the large and imposing architectural monument to Elizabeth Cromwell, with George Sampson, the architect of the first Bank of England (1).

The accounts of Grace, Countess of Dysart include a part-payment to a 'Mr Huntington' for a monument at Helmingham, Surrey, costing £230. This is probably the work dated 1729, erected to Dysart's late husband, the 3rd Earl, †1727. It depicts him *all'antica*, in a semi-reclining pose before an architectural frame, mourned over by his wife.

In Huntington's will, proved on 26 November 1748, he asked to be commemorated by a flat Purbeck or Portland stone gravestone and requested that his estate, including his shop and warehouse goods, be divided between his wife, Margaret, and their three daughters. When Margaret Huntington died in 1762 it was reported that her husband's estate was 'reputedly worth £30,000' (*Court Magazine* 1762, 730). (Inf. Sally Jeffery)

Literary References: *Gunnis* 1968, 213

Archival References: Dysart Accounts, Buckminster, Lincs MS 765, f13r; GPC

Wills: John Huntington PROB 11/765; Margaret Huntington PROB 11/881

Funerary Monuments

1.	†1731	Elizabeth Cromwell (designed by G Sampson)	Hursley, Hants	S	Pevsner, *Hants & Isle of Wight*, 1967, 300; *Gunnis* 1968, 213

HURLE, J, of Frome fl 1808?

Funerary Monuments

1.	?1808	Elizabeth Hooper	Westbury, Wilts	S	*Gunnis* 1968, 213

HURST, Edward fl c1691–1714

Hurst's practice was, like many of his contemporaries, conducted from Hyde Park Corner. He had a property rated at £12 in Portugal Row in 1699, where his neighbours included **John Nost I** and **Josias Ibach**. His business must have developed well, since by 1714 he had two properties in the area. In 1716 **John Nost II** took over one of these properties, and in the following year Hurst took over a separate property from **Richard Osgood**. He was still living in the area in 1720.

Hurst signs the monument with portrait-busts to John and Mary Bohun and their daughter Mary (1) and to Elizabeth Saunderson (3). The Saunderson is a large architectural wall monument in veined grey and white marbles with three heads of cherubs under a white *baldacchino* carved in high relief. Two statues of standing *putti* flank the columns. A similar design was used for the large baroque monument to Sir Gilbert Lort (2). This was dismantled, but an illustration in Dart's *Westmonasterium* shows that it also had an architectural scheme with a canopy and mourning boys.

Literary References: *Gunnis* 1968, 213

Archival References: PR, CWAC, F1245, F3597, F3602, F452

Funerary Monuments

1.	†1691	John Bohun (†1691), his wife and daughter		Holy Trinity, Coventry, Warks	S	Pevsner, *Warks*, 1966, 261
2.	†1698	Sir Gilbert Lort		[Westminster Abbey, London]; untraced		*Dart* 1723, 2, 121 (repr); *Gunnis* 1968, 213
3.	†1714	Elizabeth Saunderson		Glentworth, Lincs	S	*Lord* 1986, 100; Pevsner, *Lincs*, 1989, 309

HUSKINSON (or HUSKISSON), Samuel, of London *c*1706–

He was a son of William Huskinson, of Little Appleby, Leics, and was apprenticed to Francis Commins of London in 1720, becoming free seven years later. His monuments are large, architectural works, the most important being that to Catherine Joliffe (1), which is about 14 feet high.

Literary References: *Gunnis* 1968, 213

Funerary Monuments

1.	†1731	Catherine Jolliffe		St Peter, Petersfield, Hants		Pevsner, *Hants & Isle of Wight*, 1967, 372; *Gunnis* 1968, 213
2.	†1734	Geoffrey Clarke		Brampton, Derbys	S	Pevsner, *Derbys*, 1978, 106
3.	1736	Maria Craven		Winwick, Northants	S	Pevsner, *Northants*, 1973, 464
4.	?1738	Ann Thirkell		Kinsbury, Warks	S	*Gunnis* 1968, 213
5.	?1742	Hester Probert		Denham, Bucks	S	*Gunnis* 1968, 213

HUSSEY, Richard Charles, of Birmingham 1802–

He trained as an architect and entered into partnership with Thomas Rickman in 1835. Together they built or made alterations to five churches, one asylum and two houses, one of which was Castle Bromwich Hall. Rickman retired in 1838 leaving the practice entirely to Hussey. On Rickman's death in 1841 Hussey erected a simple architectural monument to his memory, which is now very dilapidated (1).

Literary References: *Noszlopy* 1998, 196

Funerary Monuments

1.	1845	Thomas Rickman (†1841)	s	St George's Gardens (formerly St George's churchyard), Great Hampton Row, Hockley, Birmingham		*Noszlopy* 1998, 65 (repr)
2.	†1853	Sophia Bridges		Orlingbury, Northants		Pevsner, *Northants*, 1973, 361

HUTCHINSON, Edmund, of Spalding fl *c*1751

He was a pupil of William Sandes, an architect and freemason, and carved the monument to his master (1).

Funerary Monuments

1.	†1751	William Sands		[Spalding, Lincs]; untraced		*Nichols* 1812–15, 6, 72

HUTCHINSON, R, of Edinburgh fl *c*1835?

Funerary Monuments

1.	nd	Sir Walter Scott, with bust after Sir Francis Chantrey		Westminster Abbey, London, south transept	S	

IBACK, Josias fl 1679–1710

Iback signed the equestrian brass statue of Charles II at Windsor with the cryptic words '*Josias Jback Stadti Blarensis 1679 Fudit*,' cut into the horse's hoofs (1). Vertue and Evelyn record that this statue was by **Grinling Gibbons**, but it appears that the production process (as was often the case with Gibbons's large-scale work) involved many other hands. In 1682 Sir Christopher Wren referred to the Windsor statue in a letter to the Bishop of Oxford on the subject of a bronze statue for Tom Tower, Christ Church: 'the horse at Windsor was at first cut in wood by a German and then cast by one Ibeck a founder in London, but this is the dearer way, if wee can find a good statuary for brasse it will be better' (*Wren Soc* V, 22). The words cut into the hoofs are cryptic: Hope speculates that they may indicate that Iback came from Bever in Hanover.

Iback's name appears in the list of denizations for 22 June 1694 and in April 1709 he was listed in the rate-books, as a 'Figure maker', paying £20 pa on a property at Stone Bridge, Hyde Park Corner (CWAC F1291). His neighbours included **John Nost I**, **Andrew Carpenter**, **Edward Hurst**, **Richard Osgood** and the ironworker Jean Tijou. Iback carried out decorative work in brass at Chatsworth and Hampton Court (2–5), but his output appears to have extended beyond metalwork. On 14 June 1710 he signed an agreement with the 1st Earl of Cromartie for a projected, but ultimately unrealised, monument to the Earl's much younger second wife, known as the Countess of Wemyss.

His date of death is not known, but a 'Heyback' was still paying rates in Stone Bridge in September 1719 (Poor Rate CWAC F3613).

Literary References: *Shaw* 1911, 234; *Hope* 1913, 552, 555; *Gunnis* 1968, 214; *Colvin* 1973–76, 171; *Whinney* 1988, 442 n30; *Sullivan* 2005, 7–8

Archival References: CWAC F5311–2; Cromartie Muniments, National Archives of Scotland GD 305/1/147, 85 and 86

Statues

1.	1679	King Charles II, equestrian, casting only Payment(s): £1,300	b	Windsor Castle, brick court	SD	*Vertue* 1, 126; *Evelyn* 1959, 686, 24 July 1680; *Beard* 1989, 59–60, 188; *Gibson* 1997 (1), 368–9

Architectural Sculpture

2.	1692	'13 brass Vauses guilt' (£13) and '4 brass vauses more' (£4)	b	[Chatsworth, Derbys]; untraced	Chatsworth Building Accts, 1686–94, 97d
3.	1692	'an artificicall tree of brass for a Fountaine at Chatsworth' Payment(s): £60, part payment		Chatsworth, Derbys	Chatsworth Building Accts, 1686–94, 88

Miscellaneous

4.	1689–1694	'Brasse worke done about the [Diana] ffountain & for 4 large brasse shells. new casting & repairing'	b	[Hampton Court, Middx, privy garden]; Bushey Park, Hampton Court, Middx	*Harris* 1969, 444
5.	c1700	Fanelli's fountain (repairs and recasting of brass shells) Payment(s): £121 19s	b	Hampton Court, Middx, privy garden,	*Colvin* 1973–76, V, 171

INCE, Anthony fl 1753–69

He was probably a Mansfield mason and may perhaps have been a son of Thomas Ince of Mansfield, who was one of the master-masons at Welbeck Abbey in 1743 in partnership with **James Osborne** (Archives, Duke of Portland). In 1768–9 Ince was employed in building Thoresby Park, Notts, for the Duke of Kingston (Archives, Earl Manvers, 4420, Nottingham Univ Lib).

Literary References: *Gunnis* 1968, 214

Archival References: GPC

Funerary Monuments

1.	?1753	Peter Bayston	Tuxford, Notts	S	*Gunnis* 1968, 214

INSOM fl 1839

Busts

1.	1839	Captain George Gosset, cabinet bust	a	Tew Park, Oxon	SD	GPC
2.	1839	Miss Gosset, cabinet bust	a	Tew Park, Oxon	SD	GPC

IRELAND, Samuel, of London fl 1768–1805

The son of John Ireland, a carpenter from Horsham, on 31 March 1768 he was apprenticed to **William Ireland**, who was probably a relative. In 1775 he became free of the Masons' Company. He later set up in Cannon Street and then in Hackney. In 1800 Ireland was working at Vintners' Hall and five years later he became master of the Masons' Company. He was mason to the Cordwainers Company from 1788–1798 and again from 1800–1805. In 1801 he was the mason responsible for building the banking house of Messrs Down, Thornton and Free in St Bartholomew's Lane, working under Sir John Soane.

Literary References: *Gunnis* 1968, 214, citing Vintners' Co, Cordwainers' Co and Soane Archives; *Webb* 1999, 18

Archival References: GPC

IRELAND, William, of London fl 1769

Ireland, who was a freeman of the Masons' Company, exhibited a figure at the Society of Artists in 1769, giving his address as 'At Mr Taylor's, Porter Street, Newport Market'. Graves records that Ireland also showed a number of pictures with the society between 1764 and 1783. It is unclear whether the painter and sculptor are the same person.

Literary References: *Gunnis* 1968, 214

Miscellaneous

1.	1769	The Young Bacchus	[Exhib Soc of Artists, London, 236]; untraced	*Graves* 1907, 127

IREMONGER, Thomas fl 1751

In 1744 he was appointed master-mason at Hampden House, Bucks, where he provided carved stone work.

Architectural Sculpture

1.	1751	Stone carving	s	[Hampden House, Bucks, gothic porch]; untraced	Archives, Earl of Buckinghamshire, cited in *Gunnis* 1968, 214

IRESON, Nathaniel, of Wincanton 1672–1769

A native of Warwickshire, he was apprenticed to **Francis Smith of Warwick**. In 1720 he was described as 'Nathaniel Ireson of Coleshill' when he took as an apprentice Matthew, son of William Percy of Pentridge, Dorset (TNA, INL/1/7). He subsequently moved to Wiltshire, and in about 1726 settled in Wincanton. He was the master-builder at Redlynch House and Berkley House in Somerset, and from 1744 onwards, worked in the same capacity at Stourhead, Wilts (Stourhead Archives cited by *Gunnis*). At Berkley House he worked in co-partnership with **John Plimer of Bodmington**, but Ireson was clearly the driving force. In 1748 he gave an altar-piece to Wincanton church (**3**) and in the churchyard is his own monument which he 'executed in his lifetime and kept it ready to be erected after his death' (*Phelps* 1839, 1, 162, 167). It has a crude, life-size statue of the sculptor (**2**). Gunnis suggests that Ireson almost certainly carved the cartouche in memory of his daughter at Stourton, and according to Frederick Rhead, examples of his carved memorial tablets can also be seen at Gillingham, Hornblotton and Brewham. He died on 18 April 1769.

Literary References: *Rhead* 1924, 147–153; *Gunnis* 1968, 214; *Worsley* 1988, 168–171

Funerary Monuments

1.	?1748	Robert Kingston	St Cuthbert, Wells, Somerset	S	*Gunnis* 1968, 214
2.	†1769	Nathaniel Ireson	Wincanton, Somerset, churchyard		*Phelps* 1839, 1, 162, 167; *Rhead* 1924, 149, 152 (repr); *Gunnis* 1968, 214

Architectural Sculpture

3.	1748	Altarpiece	Wincanton, Somerset	*Gunnis* 1968, 214

ISBELL FAMILY, of Stonehouse and Truro

Digory Isbell fl 1739–59

James Isbell I fl 1759

Richard Isbell, of Stonehouse 1759–
Robert Isbell, of Stonehouse fl 1769–1824
James Isbell, of Truro fl 1808–21

Digory Isbell, a stone mason of Trewint, Altarnun, Cornwall, married Elizabeth Burnard, (who may have been a forebear of **N N Burnard**), at Altarnun in 1739. The following year Isbell played host to John Wesley at his cottage on Bodmin Moor and later he built an annexe onto this cottage as a resting-place for Wesley and his helpers whenever they came to Cornwall. Digory had a son, **James Isbell I**, who built Dartmoor Prison, and was the father of **Richard Isbell of Stonehouse**, baptised on 17 January 1759. He signs five monuments in Devon (**12, 14, 16, 28, 30**).

Robert Isbell of Stonehouse was responsible for numerous signed monuments and tablets in Cornwall. Gunnis writes 'his monuments are delicately carved, while a favourite type of tablet is oval in shape and carried out in coloured marbles. His most unusual work is the monument to Joseph Sawle (**1**), which has a delightful black-and-white marble Adam-style urn, set on a square base. Gunnis notes that the reliefs on some of his tablets somewhat resemble the work of **Thomas King and Sons of Bath**'. In 1793 he was paid for improvements to Antony House by Reginald Pole-Carew, who had earlier commissioned a monument from the sculptor (**4**). He was the father of **James Isbell of Truro**.

James Isbell of Truro was responsible for a number of monuments and tablets in Cornwall, including one to Viscount Falmouth, inscribed 'Falmouth invent. Isbell sculpt' (**21**). His monument to James Bull features a standing woman mourning by an urn against a dark obelisk (**31**). It is a reverse image of the monument to Richard Lockyer in the same church by **William Paty of Bristol**.

Literary References: *Gunnis* 1968, 214–5

Archival References: GPC; IGI

Funerary Monuments

No.	Date	Subject	Location		References
1.	†1769	Joseph Sawle (by Robert Isbell)	St Austell, Cornwall		*Gunnis* 1968, 214–5; Pevsner, *Cornwall*, 1970, 158
2.	†1785	William Williams (by Robert Isbell)	St Ewe, Cornwall	S	*Gunnis* 1968, 215; Pevsner, *Cornwall*, 1970, 173
3.	†1791	J Lyne	St Ives, Cornwall	S	Pevsner, *Cornwall*, 1970, 179
4.	1791	Mary Collings (by Robert Isbell) Payment(s): £10 18s 10d	Untraced		Archives Sir John Pole-Carew Bt in GPC
5.	†1792	Thomas Holliday (by Robert Isbell)	St Peter, Carmarthen	S	*Gunnis* 1968, 215; *Dale-Jones and Lloyd*, 1989, 40, 50 (repr)
6.	?1794	Admiral Cotton (by Robert Isbell)	Plympton St Maurice, Devon	S	*Gunnis* 1968, 215
7.	?1794	Lieutenant Buller (by Robert Isbell)	Stoke Damerel, Devon		GPC
8.	†1795	Thomas (†1792) and John (†1795) King (by Richard Isbell)	Ugborough, Devon	S	Pevsner, *Devon*, 1989, 879
9.	1796	Edmund Hearle (by Robert Isbell)	St Columb Major, Cornwall	S	*Gunnis* 1968, 215; Pevsner, *Cornwall*, 1970, 166
10.	?1796	Louisa Barlow (by Robert Isbell)	St Nicholas, Saltash, Cornwall	S	*Gunnis* 1968, 215
11.	?1797	John Wallis (by James Isbell, of Truro)	Sheviocke, Cornwall		*Gunnis* 1968, 214
12.	?1801	Elizabeth Docton (by Robert Isbell)	St Budeaux, Devon	S	*Gunnis* 1968, 215
13.	?1802	Silvanus Jenkins (by James Isbell, of Truro)	St Michael Penkevil, Cornwall		*Gunnis* 1968, 214
14.	†1803	Agnes Allen (by Richard Isbell)	Stokenham, Devon	S	
15.	†1804	Nicholas and Mary Connock	St Cleer, Cornwall	S	Pevsner, *Cornwall*, 1970, 163
16.	?1805	Radcliffe family (by Robert Isbell)	Tamerton Folliott, Devon	S	*Gunnis* 1968, 215
17.	?1806	Edward Bewes (by Robert Isbell)	Duloe, Cornwall	S	*Gunnis* 1968, 215
18.	?1806	Sarah Traill (by Robert Isbell)	St Stephen, Saltash, Cornwall	S	*Gunnis* 1968, 215; Pevsner, *Cornwall*, 1970, 202
19.	?1806	Thomas Hall (by Robert Isbell)	Lostwithiel, Cornwall	S	*Gunnis* 1968, 215
20.	†1808	George Evelyn Boscawen (by James Isbell, of Truro)	St Michael Penkevil, Cornwall		Pevsner, *Cornwall*, 1970, 193
21.	?1808	Viscount Falmouth (designed by the subject) (by James Isbell, of Truro)	St Michael Penkevil, Cornwall	S	*Gunnis* 1968, 214
22.	†1809	Lieutenant Hawkey (by Robert Isbell)	Liskeard, Cornwall	S	*Gunnis* 1968, 215; Pevsner, *Cornwall*, 1970, 104
23.	?1810	Grace Marrack (by James Isbell, of Truro)	Paul, Cornwall		Pevsner, *Cornwall*, 1970, 131
24.	†1810	I N Macomb (by James Isbell, of Truro)	Falmouth, Cornwall		RG/JP, 5, 738
25.	†1810	John Hoskin (by James Isbell, of Truro)	Cubert, Cornwall		Pevsner, *Cornwall*, 1970, 61
26.	?1811	Captain John Haswell (by James Isbell, of Truro)	Mylor, Cornwall		*Gunnis* 1968, 214
27.	†1812	Jane Nesbitt (by James Isbell, of Truro)	Falmouth, Cornwall		RG/JP, 5, 738
28.	?1814	Murrey family (by Robert Isbell)	Stoke Damerel, Devon		GPC
29.	†1815	William Inch	Lanteglos-by-Camelford, Cornwall	S	Pevsner, *Cornwall*, 1970, 93
30.	?1817	Thomas Strode (by Robert Isbell)	Plympton, Devon	S	*Gunnis* 1968, 215

31.	†1821	Captain James Bull (by James Isbell, of Truro)		King Charles the Martyr, Falmouth, Cornwall		Pevsner, *Cornwall*, 1970, 67
32.	?1824	Sir Edward Buller (by Robert Isbell)		Duloe, Cornwall	S	*Gunnis* 1968, 215
Architectural Sculpture						
33.	1837	Coat of arms (by James Isbell, of Truro)	s	Market House, Penzance, Cornwall		Town archives, cited in *Gunnis* 1968, 214

ISEPPONI, Luigi fl 1830–35

He lived at 15 James Square, Edinburgh and was an active contributor of sculpture to the Royal Scottish Academy exhibitions, 1830–35. He may well have been involved with the Garnkirk Fireclay Company, which was established on the estate of Mark Sprot of Garnkirk House in 1832, for four of these works were executed in Garnkirk terracotta (**7, 8, 9, 12**).

Literary References: *Woodward* 1977 (vol 1, pt 2), 104

Busts					
1.	1830	George Rowland		[Exhib R Sc A, Edinburgh, 326]; untraced	*Laperriere* 2, 1991, 357
2.	1830	Unidentified lady		[Exhib R Sc A, Edinburgh, 339]; untraced	*Laperriere* 2, 1991, 357
3.	1830	Unidentified young lady		[Exhib R Sc A, Edinburgh, 322]; untraced	*Laperriere* 2, 1991, 357
4.	1830	Unidentified young man		[Exhib R Sc A, Edinburgh, 334]; untraced	*Laperriere* 2, 1991, 357
5.	1831	Master Lewis Campbell		[Exhib R Sc A, Edinburgh, 373]; untraced	*Laperriere* 2, 1991, 357
6.	1831	Rt Hon Sir John Sinclair		[Exhib R Sc A, Edinburgh, 374]; untraced	*Laperriere* 2, 1991, 357
7.	1834	Mark Sprott, in Garnkirk terracotta	tc	[Exhib R Sc A, Edinburgh, 333]; untraced	*Laperriere* 2, 1991, 357
Architectural Sculpture					
8.	1834	Copy of the Florence vase, in Garnkirk terracotta	tc	[Exhib R Sc A, Edinburgh, 333]; untraced	*Laperriere* 2, 1991, 357
9.	1835	Sir Walter Scott vase, in Garnkirk terracotta	tc	[Exhib R Sc A, Edinburgh, 355]; untraced	*Laperriere* 2, 1991, 357
Miscellaneous					
10.	1831	Charles Galli		[Exhib R Sc A, Edinburgh, 385]; untraced	*Laperriere* 2, 1991, 357
11.	1831	George Bell		[Exhib R Sc A, Edinburgh, 370]; untraced	*Laperriere* 2, 1991, 357
12.	1835	Master G Sprott and North Pole dog, in Garnkirk terracotta		[Exhib R Sc A, Edinburgh, 355]; untraced	*Laperriere* 2, 1991, 357

IVORY, John, of Norwich –1805

John Ivory worked in Norwich as a stone mason and carver throughout the second half of the 18th century. He was apprenticed in 1741 to **Robert Page**, a Norwich mason who produced monuments in a style reminiscent of **Sir Henry Cheere**. Since the name of his mother, Elizabeth Ivory, appears alone in the apprenticeship records, it is likely that his father died before that date. After completing his apprenticeship he went into business, advertising that he had 'taken the Shop on Tombland near the Popinjay, late in the occupation of **Francis Stafford**' and 'laid in a considerable Stock of all Sorts of Marble' (*Norwich Mercury*, 24 September 1748). He advertised again in 1751, stating that he could provide carving 'in all its ornamental branches as Tables, Pier-Glasses, Porcelain & China Stands, Consoles, Girandoles, Chimney Pieces &c. performed either in the English, French, Italian or Chinese Taste, by proper Artists in each kind' at reasonable prices (*Norwich Mercury*, 7 September 1751). The following year he became a freeman of Norwich.

On 26 May 1753 the *Norwich Mercury* reported a fire at Ivory's workshop the previous day. It cannot have been serious for Ivory remained there until 1767, when he gave notice that he intended to let the Tombland workshop because he was moving to new premises in Upper Conisford Street (now King Street), near the Griffin public house (*Norwich Mercury*, 25 July 1767). He evidently moved again seven years later, for on 5 February 1774 **John Blackburn I** announced that he had taken over Ivory's premises in Upper Conisford Street (*Norwich Mercury*).

In April 1776 Ivory went into business with his former apprentice, **John de Carle**. Ivory was de Carle's partner for a period of 11 years, in return for a payment of £50, with £171 7s for a half share of the stock in his shop. They agreed to share all expenses and profits and that the accounts would be audited annually (*Ivory Stock Valuation; Ivory/de Carle Indentures*). A few months later the partners advertised that they could provide marble chimneypieces and monuments executed 'in the neatest manner' (*Linnell and Wearing* 1952, 26). The partners' expenditure for the period 1776–1789 is documented in a cash book in the Bury St Edmunds and West Suffolk Record Office (*De Carle Cash Book*) and they sign several monuments together (**8, 11, 12, 13**).

Ivory's wife died in 1805 at the age of 74 'after fifty-five years of married life' and Ivory did not long survive her, dying 'suddenly of a fit' in the same year (*Monthly Mag*, cited by *Gunnis* 1968 215). On 13 and 14 October 1806 a sale was conducted of his tools and stock of 'excellent statuary and veined marbles, very fine Sienna, in slabs and veneers, broca, hela, jaspar, and dove marble slabs and slips, drawings and drawing books, black marble, gravestones, Portland blocks, slabs and gravestones, thirteen Portland mile posts, a quantity of plaister ornaments and models, capital jack hand cut and barrow, a large quantity of packing cases, handspokes, iron crows, saw, poles, &c.' (*Norfolk Chronicle* 4 Oct 1806).

He may have been related to another marble and stone mason in the area, Thomas Ivory, who married Mrs Shewell of Blofield in April 1797 (*Bury and Norwich Post*, 26 April 1797).

Literary References: *Gunnis* 1968, 215; RG/JP, 5, 739–40

Archival References: Apprenticeship records PRO IR 50/63, in GPC

Wills: PROB 11/1546 (proved 27 July 1813)

Auction Catalogues: *Forrest* 1876

Funerary Monuments					
1.	?1746	Rev Thomas Scott	Old Meeting House, Norwich	S	*Gunnis* 1968, 215
2.	†1747	Charles (†1727) and Mary Mackerell	St Stephen, Norwich, Norfolk	S	Pevsner, *Norfolk: N E & Norwich*, 1997, 253

3.	?1748	Mary Slater	Hingham, Norfolk	S	*Gunnis* 1968, 215
4.	?1752	William Clarke	St George, Norwich, Norfolk	S	*Gunnis* 1968, 215
5.	†1753	Thomas Hurnard	St Mary Coslany, Norwich, Norfolk	S	Pevsner, *Norfolk: N E & Norwich*, 1997, 245
6.	?1756	John Dawson	Old Meeting House, Norwich	S	*Gunnis* 1968, 215
7.	1759	Unidentified subject, tablet	South Pickenham, Norfolk	S	Pevsner, *Norfolk: N W & S*, 1999, 665
8.	†1762	Sir Randall Ward Bt (co-sculptor: John De Carle)	Bixley, Norfolk	S	RG/JP, 5, 740; Pevsner, *Norfolk: N W & S*, 1999, 208
9.	1768	Elizabeth Wiggett	South Pickenham, Norfolk	S	*Gunnis* 1968, 215
10.	†1777	John Towne of Lynn	[Gunthorpe, Norfolk]; untraced		Norfolk RO MC 37/135–8
11.	†1779	Thomas Moore (co-sculptor: John de Carle)	Norwich Cathedral, Norfolk	S	Pevsner, *Norfolk: N E & Norwich*, 1997, 210
12.	†1780	Cyril Wyche (co-sculptor: John de Carle)	Hockwold, Norfolk	S	Pevsner, *Norfolk: N W & S*, 1999, 410
13.	†1787	Sarah Norris (co-sculptor: John de Carle)	Barton Turf, Norfolk	S	Pevsner, *Norfolk: N E & Norwich*, 1997, 380
14.	†1788	John Chamber	Norwich Cathedral, Norfolk	S	Pevsner, *Norfolk: N E & Norwich*, 1997, 210
15.	?1789	Martha Wilson	St Mary Coslany, Norwich, Norfolk	S	GPC
16.	1790	Unidentified subject, tablet	South Pickenham, Norfolk		Pevsner, *Norfolk: N E & S*, 1999, 665
17.	1791	Dean Philip Lloyd (†1790)	Norwich Cathedral, Norfolk	S	Pevsner, *Norfolk: N E & Norwich*, 1997, 210
18.	†1792	Clement Francis	Aylsham, Norfolk	S	Pevsner, *Norfolk: N E & Norwich*, 1997, 364
19.	1792	Ralph Caldwell	Hillborough, Norfolk	S	*Gunnis* 1968, 215
20.	†1798	Mary Evans	Salle, Norfolk	S	Pevsner, *Norfolk: N E & Norwich*, 1997, 655
Chimneypieces					
21.	1778	For the Peter-the-Great room	Blickling Hall, Norfolk	S	Pevsner, *Norfolk: N E & Norwich*, 1997, 405
22.	1793–1805	Several	[Heydon, Norfolk]; untraced		Norfolk RO BUL 11/208

JACK, J

For further information the reader is referred to *Pyke* 1973, 72.

JACKSON fl 1764–70

The master-mason responsible for building Lord Petre's seat, Thorndon Hall, Essex, 1764–70, he was also responsible for carved stonework, including capitals.

Literary References: *Gunnis* 1968, 21

Architectural Sculpture

1.	1764–1770	Carved stonework	s	Thorndon Hall, Essex	*Gunnis* 1968, 216 citing archives, Lord Petre

JACKSON, Benjamin –1719

He was a native of Grove, near Retford, Notts, and was appointed master-mason at Chatsworth in 1687, where he provided chimneypieces and worked on the bathing rooms and grotto (**1, 2, 4, 5**). Two payments of £100 each were made on his behalf to **Robert Kirker** for the grotto (Chatsworth Building Accts, 1687–94, 30A,31). In 1699 he was dismissed by the Duke of Devonshire, who was dissatisfied with the slow progress of work. The dismissal led to litigation.

Jackson was engaged in work at Hampton Court Gardens from the 1690s and petitioned for a debt for work done there as late as 1705. He was paid a large sum for constructing the basin at the centre of the Fountain Garden intended to hold a fountain designed by **John Nost I** and for its grey marble coping. Between 1689 and 1700 he carried out extensive masonry work at Whitehall, earning more than £3,000. In 1703 he received £443 for work at St James's Palace.

He was employed by Sir John Germain at Drayton House, Northants. His contract, dated 24 August 1702, shows him working 'according to what Mr. Tallman hath ordered', that is under the direction of the architect, William Talman (Drayton Archive MM/A/483). The contract makes it clear that Jackson was in charge of the building programme, but he also provided carved work, being directed 'to finish ye front of ye house against ye comeing into Drayton Hall with heads, vauses and fflames on pine Aples upon pedistalls in all points according to ye draft or designe drawn by Mr. Talman and to perform all his work, well rought, strong and fine'. The elaborate façade with its carving forms the front of the hall at Drayton, within the inner courtyard. The contract has on its verso records of payments, and Jackson's name occurs until April 1703, when the clerk of works, John Woodall, took command. Gunnis was fulsome in his appreciation of the result: 'His carved-stone work in the Inner Courtyard is beyond praise; how admirable is the cutting of the capitals, busts, vases, caryatids, heraldry, pineapples and trophy of arms which adorn and decorate the doorway and centre of the façade designed by Talman' (*Gunnis* 1968, 216; inf, Bruce Bailey).

In December 1701 Jackson succeeded **John Oliver** as master mason to King William III, an appointment he held until his death. That year he became free of the Masons' Company. Jackson was a protégé of William Talman, then comptroller of the Office of the Board of Works and this brought him into conflict with Talman's successor, Sir John Vanbrugh. There had been a long-standing practice whereby the master mason, though supposedly an independent guardian of the Crown's interests, would continue to undertake contracts, sometimes under the name of an employee. Vanbrugh drew attention to the conflict of interests represented by this practice and revealed a strong personal dislike of Jackson in a letter to Lord Godolphin of 1704, referring to Jackson's work on the greenhouse at Kensington: 'As for Jackson my Lord, besides this Crime, the highest the nature of his Office will admit of; I must acquaint your L'dship he is so villainous a Fellow and so Scandalous in every part of his Character; and that in the unanimous opinion of all Sorts of People he is known to; that he is indeed a disgrace to the Queen's service and to everybody that is oblig'd to be concer'd with him' (*Knoop and Jones* 1935, 37). Jackson received £1,651 for his work at Kensington Palace and although the rules were changed in 1705 to forbid the master mason from taking crown contracts, Jackson remained on the Board of Works until his death.

Colvin describes Jackson as 'a truculent character who did not suffer from undue deference to his superiors' (*Colvin* V, 1973–76, 20), a trait revealed in 1719 when Jackson was instrumental in securing the dismissal of the surveyor-general, William Benson, and his deputy, Colen Campbell, on grounds of incompetence. Benson had prepared a report outlining extensive problems with the fabric of the House of Lords, which Jackson, with the support of the architects James Gibbs and John James, revealed to be mythical.

He died in May 1719. In his will he left over £4,000. An inventory of his house in Hampton gives a vivid account of his household possessions, including 'ten modalls of boys & head of King William gilt' and two paintings by Sir James Thornhill (PROB 3/18/26 in *Boynton* 1990, 22). He seems also to have had property in Bolton Street and in his hometown of Grove.

MGS

Literary References: *Knoop and Jones* 1935, 36, 37; *Gunnis* 1968, 216; *Colvin* V, 1973–76, *passim*; *Friedman* 1984, 33; *Boynton* 1990, 20–6;
Archival References: TNA Work 5/52 fol 453 (Hampton Court); Masons' Co, Court Book, 1695–1722, (1701) fol 53r
Will: PROB 10/1573

Chimneypieces

1.	1687–1699	for the Queen of Scots' closet Payment(s): £25	m	[Chatsworth, Derbys]; untraced	Chatsworth Building Accts, 1695–96, 36
2.	1687–1699	Four Payment(s): £50		[Chatsworth, Derbys]; untraced	Chatsworth Building Accts, 1695–96, 37
3.	1702	White and veined	m	[Whitehall Palace, London, Sir John Stanley's room]; untraced	TNA Work 5/53; *Gunnis* 1968, 216

Architectural Sculpture

4.	1694	Marble works for the bathing rooms and grotto Payment(s): £100		[Chatsworth, Derbys]; untraced	Chatsworth Building Accts, 1687–94, 31
5.	1687–1699	'four vases upon ye East side' Payment(s): £60		[Chatsworth, Derbys]; untraced	Chatsworth Building Accts, 1695–96, 55
6.	1700	81 capitals	s	[Hampton Court Palace, Middx, Fountain Yard]; untraced	*Gunnis* 1968, 216
7.	c1700	Piers in Portland stone	s	[Hampton Court Palace, Middx]; untraced	*Colvin* V, 1973–76, 172
8.	1701–1702	Four fountains Payment(s): £622		[Hampton Court Palace, Middx]; untraced	*Colvin* V, 1973–76, 172–3
9.	1702	'ten new Doric columns with capitals and bases for the same palace'	s	[Whitehall Palace, London]; untraced	TNA Work 5/53; *Gunnis* 1968, 216
10.	1702–1703	Ten columns Payment(s): £8 10s each		[St James' Palace, London, colonnade]; untraced	*Colvin* V, 1973–76, 238
11.	1702–1704	Capitals, beads, vases, caryatids, heraldic motifs, trophies of arms and 'fflames on pine Aples upon pedistall's' (to designs by William Talman)		Drayton House, Northants, inner courtyard façade	*Gunnis* 1968, 216

Miscellaneous

12.	1700	'building and workmanship of the great basin in the Fountain Garden' Payment(s): £719 12s		[Hampton Court Palace, Middx]; untraced	*Gunnis* 1968, 216; *Colvin* V, 1973–76, 172

JACKSON, Benjamin and William, of Reading fl 1776–1809

Between 1776 and 1786 they built Caversham Park, near Reading, Berks, principally under Sir John Soane (Soane, Journal II, fols 81r, 85v, 1776).

Literary References: *Gunnis* 1968, 216
Archival References: GPC

Funerary Monuments

1.	1805	Unidentified subject, tablet	Shinfield, Berks	S	*Gunnis* 1968, 216
2.	1809	Unidentified subject, tablet	Shinfield, Berks	S	*Gunnis* 1968, 216

JACKSON, Edward, of Doncaster fl 1768–70

An agreement dated 1768 survives in the Monson Archives between Edward Jackson and **John Hayward II** made with Thomas Carleton, on behalf of Lord Monson (Lincs RO MON 19/2/19). On 2 May 1769 the Corporation of Doncaster ordered that Jackson should 'be admitted his freedom for his trouble in drawing a plan of the gaol and for his attendance to see the work properly executed' (Doncaster Corp Archives, in *Gunnis* 1968, 216).

Literary References: *Gunnis* 1968, 216

Chimneypieces

1.	1770	Description unavailable	[Nostell Priory, Wakefield, W R Yorks, alcove bedroom]; untraced	GPC

Architectural Sculpture

2.	1779	Corinthian capitals	[Nostell Priory, Wakefield, W R Yorks]; untraced	GPC

Miscellaneous

3.	1770	Cross	[Marketplace, Doncaster, W R Yorks]; untraced	*Gunnis* 1968, 216

JACKSON, Henry, of Lincoln fl c1816

He is known only for one tablet of coloured marbles.

Funerary Monuments

1.	†1816	George Wakefield	East Stoke, Notts	*Gunnis* 1968, 216; Pevsner, *Notts*, 1979, 117

JACKSON, Isaac, of Liverpool fl 1828–60

Gunnis notes that Jackson lived in Liverpool until c1850, when he appears to have gone to Rome. He exhibited in Liverpool, 1828–60, at Manchester in 1833 and at the Royal Academy in 1836 and 1837. He may have lived in London for a short period during the 1830s for his address in 1836 was given as 2 Royal Oak Place, Eaton Square.

Literary References: *Graves* IV, 1905–6, 226; *Gunnis* 1968, 216–7

Statues

1.	1831	Narcissus	[Exhib Liverpool Ac, 393]; untraced	*Gunnis* 1968, 217; *Morris and Roberts* 1998, 346
2.	1832	Study from the Elgin 'Theseus'	[Exhib Liverpool Ac, 392]; untraced	*Morris and Roberts* 1998, 346
3.	1833	Psyche	[Exhib Manchester]; untraced	*Gunnis* 1968, 217; *Morris and Roberts* 1998, 346
4.	1834	'Copy of the Colossal Statue of the late W Roscoe, Esq'	[Exhib Liverpool Ac, 439]; untraced	*Morris and Roberts* 1998, 346
5.	1838	Hygeia, design	[Exhib Liverpool Ac, 671]; untraced	*Morris and Roberts* 1998, 346
6.	1838	Roscoe's nurse, design	[Exhib Liverpool Ac, 674]; untraced	*Morris and Roberts* 1998, 346
7.	1845	Narcissus, study for a statue	[Exhib Liverpool Ac, 803]; untraced	*Morris and Roberts* 1998, 347
8.	1848	A domestic servant, model for a small bronze	[Exhib Liverpool Ac, 676]; untraced	*Morris and Roberts* 1998, 347
9.	1848	A gleaner, model for a small bronze	[Exhib Liverpool Ac, 673]; untraced	*Morris and Roberts* 1998, 347
10.	1848	A reaper, model for a small bronze	[Exhib Liverpool Ac, 675]; untraced	*Morris and Roberts* 1998, 347
11.	1848	An English peasant, model for a small bronze	[Exhib Liverpool Ac, 677]; untraced	*Morris and Roberts* 1998, 347

Busts

12.	1831	Admiral Murray	[Exhib Liverpool Ac, 394]; untraced	*Morris and Roberts* 1998, 346
13.	1831	John Johnson	[Exhib Liverpool Ac, 404]; untraced	*Morris and Roberts* 1998, 346
14.	1832	Charles Tayleur	[Exhib Liverpool Ac, 372]; untraced	*Morris and Roberts* 1998, 346
15.	1834	J Ackers	[Exhib Liverpool Ac, 446]; untraced	*Morris and Roberts* 1998, 346
16.	1834	Rev A Campbell	[Exhib Liverpool Ac, 442]; untraced	*Morris and Roberts* 1998, 346
17.	1834	Rev Dr Shepherd	[Exhib Liverpool Ac, 438]; untraced	*Morris and Roberts* 1998, 346
18.	1836	J A Paris MD FRS	[Exhib RA, London, 1087]; untraced	*Graves* IV, 1905–6, 226
19.	1836	James Smith	[Exhib RA, London, 1124]; untraced	*Graves* IV, 1905–6, 226
20.	1837	Unidentified subject	[Exhib RA, London, 1225]; untraced	*Graves* IV, 1905–6, 226
21.	1838	William Rathbone	[Exhib Liverpool Ac, 668]; untraced	*Morris and Roberts* 1998, 346
22.	1839	Rev Augustus Campbell	[Exhib Liverpool Ac, 708]; untraced	*Morris and Roberts* 1998, 346
23.	1839	Right Hon Lord Viscount Sandon	[Exhib Liverpool Ac, 707]; untraced	*Morris and Roberts* 1998, 346
24.	1839	T Brandreth MD	[Exhib Liverpool Ac, 709]; untraced	*Morris and Roberts* 1998, 346
25.	1840	D Macrorie MD	[Exhib Liverpool Ac, 693]; untraced	*Morris and Roberts* 1998, 346
26.	1840	George Syers	[Exhib Liverpool Ac, 702]; untraced	*Morris and Roberts* 1998, 346
27.	1840	John Bostock MD	[Exhib Liverpool Ac, 691]; untraced	*Morris and Roberts* 1998, 346
28.	1840	Miss S Macrorie	[Exhib Liverpool Ac, 685]; untraced	*Morris and Roberts* 1998, 346
29.	1840	Mrs Hughes	[Exhib Liverpool Ac, 680]; untraced	*Morris and Roberts* 1998, 346
30.	1840	Rev R Cardwell	[Exhib Liverpool Ac, 681]; untraced	*Morris and Roberts* 1998, 346
31.	1841	Gordon Grant	[Exhib Liverpool Ac, 652]; untraced	*Morris and Roberts* 1998, 346
32.	1841	Richard Formby	[Exhib Liverpool Ac, 666]; untraced	*Morris and Roberts* 1998, 346
33.	1841	Thomas Bolton	[Exhib Liverpool Ac, 665]; untraced	*Morris and Roberts* 1998, 346
34.	1841	Thomas Rodick	[Exhib Liverpool Ac, 667]; untraced	*Morris and Roberts* 1998, 346
35.	1841	William Fawcett	[Exhib Liverpool Ac, 653]; untraced	*Morris and Roberts* 1998, 346
36.	1841	William Maddie	[Exhib Liverpool Ac, 655]; untraced	*Morris and Roberts* 1998, 346
37.	1842	A child	[Exhib Liverpool Ac, 589]; untraced	*Morris and Roberts* 1998, 346
38.	1842	J Johnson	[Exhib Liverpool Ac, 587]; untraced	*Morris and Roberts* 1998, 346
39.	1842	M M G Dowling	[Exhib Liverpool Ac, 578]; untraced	*Morris and Roberts* 1998, 346
40.	1842	Richard Johnson MD	[Exhib Liverpool Ac, 585]; untraced	*Morris and Roberts* 1998, 346
41.	1842	Todd Naylor	[Exhib Liverpool Ac, 575]; untraced	*Morris and Roberts* 1998, 346
42.	1843	Archdeacon Robinson	[Exhib Liverpool Ac, 565]; untraced	*Morris and Roberts* 1998, 347
43.	1843	Mrs William Brown	[Exhib Liverpool Ac, 556]; untraced	*Morris and Roberts* 1998, 346
44.	1843	Samuel Turner	[Exhib Liverpool Ac, 566]; untraced	*Morris and Roberts* 1998, 347
45.	1843	Thomas H Illidge	[Exhib Liverpool Ac, 564]; untraced	*Morris and Roberts* 1998, 346
46.	1843	William Brown	[Exhib Liverpool Ac, 557]; untraced	*Morris and Roberts* 1998, 346
47.	1844	A child	[Exhib Liverpool Ac, 559]; untraced	*Morris and Roberts* 1998, 347
48.	1844	John Cunningham	[Exhib Liverpool Ac, 571]; untraced	*Morris and Roberts* 1998, 347
49.	1844	Thomas Sands, model	[Exhib Liverpool Ac, 558]; untraced	*Morris and Roberts* 1998, 347
50.	1845	A lady	[Exhib Liverpool Ac, 804]; untraced	*Morris and Roberts* 1998, 347
51.	1845	Dr Anson, Dean of Chester	[Exhib Liverpool Ac, 809]; untraced	*Morris and Roberts* 1998, 347
52.	1847	David Hodgson	[Exhib Liverpool Ac, 750]; untraced	*Morris and Roberts* 1998, 347
53.	1848	A child	[Exhib Liverpool Ac, 670]; untraced	*Morris and Roberts* 1998, 347
54.	1848	A town councillor	[Exhib Liverpool Ac, 683]; untraced	*Morris and Roberts* 1998, 347
55.	1848	Rev W Pollock MA	[Exhib Liverpool Ac, 681]; untraced	*Morris and Roberts* 1998, 347
56.	1848	William M'Millan	[Exhib Liverpool Ac, 652]; untraced	*Morris and Roberts* 1998, 347
57.	1849	Dr Harbord	[Exhib Liverpool Ac, 655]; untraced	*Morris and Roberts* 1998, 347
58.	1849	John Holden	[Exhib Liverpool Ac, 650]; untraced	*Morris and Roberts* 1998, 347
59.	1849	John Smith and wife	Untraced	*Morris and Roberts* 1998, 347
60.	1849	John Tyrer	[Exhib Liverpool Ac, 651]; untraced	*Morris and Roberts* 1998, 347
61.	1849	Rees Jeffreys	[Exhib Liverpool Ac, 653]; untraced	*Morris and Roberts* 1998, 347
62.	1849	Robert Henderson	[Exhib Liverpool Ac, 656]; untraced	*Morris and Roberts* 1998, 347
63.	1849	Thomas Campbell Foster	[Exhib Liverpool Ac, 654]; untraced	*Morris and Roberts* 1998, 347
64.	1850	Mrs John Smith	[Exhib Liverpool Ac, 526]; untraced	*Morris and Roberts* 1998, 347
65.	1850	Rev S I Phillips	[Exhib Liverpool Ac, 525]; untraced	*Morris and Roberts* 1998, 347
66.	1860	Head of Diana	[Exhib LSFA, Liverpool, 896]; untraced	*Morris and Roberts* 1998, 347
67.	nd	Rev Thomas Raffles	Walker, Liverpool Other versions: 'Rev Dr Raffles' exhib Liverpool Ac, 1832, 383; untraced 'Dr Raffles' exhib Liverpool Ac, 1849, 658; untraced exhib LSFA, Liverpool, 1860, 886; untraced	*Gunnis* 1968, 217; *Morris and Roberts* 1998, 346, 347

Architectural Sculpture				
68.	1846	Design for the enrichment of the pediment of St George's Hall	[Exhib Liverpool Ac, 815]; untraced	*Morris and Roberts* 1998, 347
Reliefs				
69.	1839	'By the waters of Babylon we sat down and wept . . .'	[Exhib Liverpool Ac, 710]; untraced	*Gunnis* 1968, 217; *Morris and Roberts* 1998, 346
70.	1844	Charity	[Exhib Liverpool Ac, 574]; untraced	*Morris and Roberts* 1998, 347
71.	1844	Rev Augustus Campbell, portrait medallion, with a relief representing Charity	[Exhib Liverpool Ac, 562]; untraced	*Morris and Roberts* 1998, 347
72.	1844	Rev Jonathan Brooks, portrait medallion	[Exhib Liverpool Ac, 561]; untraced	*Morris and Roberts* 1998, 347
73.	1847	Science and Commerce united by Wisdom, design	[Exhib Liverpool Ac, 748]; untraced	*Morris and Roberts* 1998, 347
74.	1848	Christ raising the daughter of Jairus, design	[Exhib Liverpool Ac, 669]; untraced	*Morris and Roberts* 1998, 347
Miscellaneous				
75.	1828	Greek youth playing a harp	[Exhib ALRI, Liverpool, 213]; untraced	*Morris and Roberts* 1998, 346
76.	1829	Venus and Adonis	[Exhib ALRI, Liverpool, 341]; untraced	*Morris and Roberts* 1998, 346
77.	1841	A muse	[Exhib Liverpool Ac, 670]; untraced	*Morris and Roberts* 1998, 346
78.	1841	Andromache	[Exhib Liverpool Ac, 654]; untraced	*Morris and Roberts* 1998, 346
79.	1842	Nidia on her mission from Glaucus to Ion	[Exhib Liverpool Ac, 576]; untraced	*Morris and Roberts* 1998, 346
80.	1842	Nidia's approach to Glaucus	[Exhib Liverpool Ac, 582]; untraced	*Morris and Roberts* 1998, 346
81.	1843	Cupid's caution to old age	[Exhib Liverpool Ac, 555]; untraced	*Morris and Roberts* 1998, 346
82.	1843	Venus and Cupid	[Exhib Liverpool Ac, 561]; untraced	*Morris and Roberts* 1998, 346
83.	1848	Christ teaching humility	[Exhib Liverpool Ac, 668]; untraced	*Morris and Roberts* 1998, 347
84.	1849	A naiad	[Exhib Liverpool Ac, 649]; untraced	*Morris and Roberts* 1998, 347
85.	1860	Devotion	[Exhib LSFA, Liverpool, 895]; untraced	*Morris and Roberts* 1998, 347

JACKSON, John I, of Oxford *c*1602–63

Jackson was a master mason much employed in Oxford in the mid-17th century. He moved to Oxford from London in 1634 to superintend the building of the Canterbury Quadrangle at St John's College, begun by **William Hill**. The decorative carving, which is such an important feature of the quadrangle, was shared between Jackson and a number of specialist carvers (**1**). Jackson was personally responsible for the great shields displaying the arms of the King, Queen and Archbishop Laud and certain other features of the two frontispieces including two heraldic shields over the new doorways in the front quadrangle. He also carved a series of 16 busts symbolising Virtues and the liberal arts, together with decorative reliefs of their attributes for the spandrels of the arcade. Jackson remained in Oxford after the building was completed in 1636.

In 1635–6 he was paid 10s for his advice on the new tower and gateway under construction at University College and in 1637–8 he provided designs for the wooden gates. He built the porch of St Mary's church in 1637 and was paid £112 for building a wall near the Convocation House in 1637–8. In 1641–2 he built the gabled extension to the cook's building over the kitchen at St John's College and in 1641 received £6 for making the niche for the bust of Charles I in the Bodleian library. In 1650 he was paid £1 10s for making '3 dials in the Guildhall Court' (*Hobson and Salter* 1933, 435) and was paid in 1656 for 'worke done about the pulpitt in St Maries' (*Clark* 1891–90, IV, 63). Between 1655 and 1659 he designed and built Brasenose College Chapel, the library and cloisters, receiving a payment for the carved decoration over the cloister door in the latter year (**2**). He was subsequently employed in 'clensing and polishing' the antique marbles, given to the university by John Seddon in 1660 (*Clark* 1891–90, I, 320 n3). He probably also built Welford Park, Berks, *c*1660. In 1663 he made a model for completing the great gate at Christ Church but nothing was done until nearly 20 years later, when Tom Tower was built to the designs of Sir Christopher Wren.

Jackson died on 22 December 1663 and was buried in the church of St Mary Magdalen where his epitaph stated that he was a 'stone-carver, an ingenious artist, a loyall subject, an honest man and a good neighbour' (*Clark* 1889–99, III, 1899). His will, dated 7 December 1663, was witnessed by **John Stone** and **Simon White**. The vice-chancellor's accounts for 1663/64 show a payment of £10 19s 3d to 'Mrs. Jackson, the stone-cutter's widow for work done by her husband'.

Literary References: *Gunnis* 1968, 217; *Colvin* 1988, 8, 9, 33n, 38, 58, 84, 119; *Mowl* 1994, 51–4; *Colvin* 1995, 532–33

Archival References: GPC

Will: Oxon CRO, Oxford Archdeaconry Wills 136/4/9

Architectural Sculpture					
1.	1634–1636	Decorative carving	s	Canterbury quadrangle, St John's College, Oxford	*Colvin* 1988, 9, 33n, 38, 40–2, 84 (repr)
2.	1659	'the frontispiece over the cloyster door, being of Burford stone, with ye King's arms on a shield'		Brasenose College, Oxford	*Allfrey* 1909, 22

JACKSON, John II, of Oxford fl 1749–97?

Funerary Monuments				
1.	†1789	Eleanor Rusbridge	St Mary, Oxford	*Gunnis* 1968, 217
2.	?1797	Richard Smith	St Giles, Reading, Berks	*Gunnis* 1968, 217
Reliefs				
3.	1749	Sir Isaac Newton, two profile medallions	[coll Sir Hans Sloane]; BM, MLA SL 2101	Keynes nd, 36

JACKSON, of Hagley fl *c*1833

Funerary Monuments				
1.	*c*1833	Marston family	Cardley, Warks	S

JACKSON, of Uley fl *c*1845

Miscellaneous

1.	*c*1845	Eleanor cross	Kingscote, Glos, churchyard	S	Pevsner, *Glos: Cotswolds*, 1999, 429

JACKSON, of Windrush fl 1772

He may perhaps be identified with **John Jackson II, of Oxford.** He signs the crude monument to William Bateman.

Archival References: RG/JP, 5, 744

Funerary Monuments

1.	1772	William Bateman	Asthall, Oxon	RG/JP, 5, 744

JACKSON, Philip, of Edensor fl 1695

In 1695 he received £456 for building the bowling green house at Chatsworth. This payment included the carved stonework and also 'four Potts standing upon ye front of ye battlement at forty shilling each'.

Archival References: Chatsworth Building Accts, 1686–94, 22–5

JACKSON, Robert fl 1851–78

He was chief assistant to **John Thomas**, with whom he executed statues and ornamental sculpture for the Houses of Parliament (**30**). In 1860 he was working in Rome, but he had returned to England three years later when he provided the monument to Robert Anderson in Glasgow Cathedral (**1**). It has 'the warrior's arms and accoutrements [in bronze] . . . most artistically grouped' on a marble slab (*AJ*, 1863, 157). In 1863 he was responsible for a drinking-fountain with a seated figure of a boy in St James's Park (**31**). The *Art Journal* commented 'The figure is very easy and natural in its position, and the whole design most creditable to the taste and judgement of the sculptor', but the journal disapproved of a spout in the form of a mask or animal's head, since 'the association of ideas is far from agreeable' (*AJ*, 1863, 167). Jackson's statue of the Prime Minister, Palmerston, was commissioned by the government and erected in Westminster Abbey in 1870 (**2**). The *Illustrated London News* commented that it presented 'a marked contrast in its simple, natural, unaffected, yet dignified attitude to some recent constrained and pretentious representations of the same personage' and suggested that it could not fail to raise the artist's reputation (*ILN*, 16 July 1870, 76). Jackson exhibited at the Royal Academy between 1851 and 1869, from 2 Dorchester Place, Blandford Square; 16 Maida Vale; 17 Newman Street; 16 Maida Hill and 29 Maida Hill.

Literary References: *Graves* IV, 1905–6, 229; *Gunnis* 1968, 217

Funerary Monuments

1.	1863	Lieutenant Robert Burn Anderson (†1860)		Glasgow Cathedral, crypt	*AJ*, 1863, 157; Pevsner, *Glasgow*, 1990, 131
2.	1865–1870	Henry, 3rd Viscount Palmerston (†1865) Model(s): death mask, formerly in the Hutton coll; untraced		Westminster Abbey, London, north transept	*ILN*, 16 July 1870, 76 (repr); *Ormond* 1973, 360
3.	?1872	James Rogers		St Margaret, City of Westminster, London	GPC

Busts

4.	1851	Miss Laura Amy Langley		[Exhib RA, London, 1292]; untraced	*Graves* IV, 1905–6, 229
5.	1854	Miss J A Jackson		[Exhib RA, London, 1477]; untraced	*Graves* IV, 1905–6, 229
6.	1858	Mrs W A Tollemache		[Exhib RA, London, 1232]; untraced	*Graves* IV, 1905–6, 229
7.	1860	Henry Edmund Gurney	m	[Exhib RA, London, 1002]; untraced	*Graves* IV, 1905–6, 229
8.	1860	Lady Mount-Temple		Broadlands, Hants	GPC
9.	1860	Mrs W Cowper	m	[Exhib RA, London, 1027]; untraced	*Graves* IV, 1905–6, 229
10.	1860	Rev Dr Raffles		Liverpool Public Library, Lancs	*Gunnis* 1968, 217
11.	1861	Master Henry Gurney		[Exhib RA, London, 1005]; untraced	*Graves* IV, 1905–6, 229
12.	1861	Mrs Lachlan M Rate		[Exhib RA, London, 1014]; untraced	*Graves* IV, 1905–6, 229
13.	1861	Rt Hon W Cowper		[Exhib RA, London, 1060]; untraced	*Graves* IV, 1905–6, 229
14.	1862	Autumn	m	[Exhib RA, London, 1035]; untraced	*Graves* IV, 1905–6, 229
15.	1862	Lord Mount-Temple		Broadlands, Hants	GPC
16.	1862	Mrs Lachlan M Rate	m	[Exhib RA, London, 1051]; untraced	*Graves* IV, 1905–6, 229
17.	1862	Rt Hon F W Cowper	m	[Exhib RA, London, 1026]; untraced	*Graves* IV, 1905–6, 229
18.	1863	J Gregory Crace		[Exhib RA, London, 1171]; untraced	*Graves* IV, 1905–6, 229
19.	1864	Mrs J Gibson	m	[Exhib RA, London, 928]; untraced	*Graves* IV, 1905–6, 229
20.	1865	Master Hulse		[Exhib RA, London, 946]; untraced	*Graves* IV, 1905–6, 229
21.	1865	Miss Seymour	m	[Exhib RA, London, 1068]; untraced	*Graves* IV, 1905–6, 229
22.	1865	Sir John Login		[Exhib RA, London, 1072]; untraced	*Graves* IV, 1905–6, 229
23.	1867	Hon A Campbell		[Exhib RA, London, 1062]; untraced	*Graves* IV, 1905–6, 229
24.	1867	William Cory		[Exhib RA, London, 1045]; untraced	*Graves* IV, 1905–6, 229
25.	1869	Angelique, daughter of Charles and Margaret Candy	m	[Exhib RA, London, 1153]; untraced Other versions: Exhib RA, London, 1869, 1312	*Graves* IV, 1905–6, 229
26.	1869	Earl of Cawdor	m	[Exhib RA, London, 1157]; untraced	*Graves* IV, 1905–6, 229
27.	1870	Henry, 3rd Viscount Palmerston		Harrow School, speech room	*ILN*, 16 July 1870, 76; *Ormond* 1973, 361
28.	1874	Henry Irving	m	[Exhib RA, London, 1650]; untraced	*Graves* IV, 1905–6, 229
29.	1877	H L Bateman	m	[Exhib RA, London, 1402]; untraced	*Graves* IV, 1905–6, 230

Architectural Sculpture

30.	1843–1851	Statues and ornamental sculpture (as chief assistant to John Thomas)	Palace of Westminster, London	*Gunnis* 1968, 217
31.	1863	Fountain (cast by Elkington & Co)	[St James's Park, London, south side]; untraced	*AJ*, 1863, 167; *Gunnis* 1968, 217
32.	nd	Fountain	[Regent's Park, London, near Gloucester Gate]; untraced	*Gunnis* 1968, 217

Reliefs

33.	1865	Unidentified lady, medallion	[Exhib RA, London, 983]; untraced	*Graves* IV, 1905–6, 229

Miscellaneous

34.	1865	Mischief	m	[Exhib RA, London, 943]; untraced		*Graves* IV, 1905–6, 229
35.	1869	Spring		[Exhib RA, London, 1253]; untraced		*Graves* IV, 1905–6, 229
36.	1869	Summer		[Exhib RA, London, 1306]; untraced		*Graves* IV, 1905–6, 229
37.	1874	'Waiting for the wave' (Mary, youngest daughter of J Macvicar Anderson)	m	[Exhib RA, London, 1502]; untraced		*Graves* IV, 1905–6, 230
38.	1877	Agnes (daughter of J Macvicar Anderson, with her pet dog, Gyp)	m	[Exhib RA, London, 1509]; untraced		*Graves* IV, 1905–6, 230
39.	1878	Favourite dogs of the Baroness Burdett-Coutts	m	[Exhib RA, London, 1469]; untraced		*Graves* IV, 1905–6, 230

JACKSON, T, of Regent Street and Pimlico, London fl *c*1854–55

Funerary Monuments

1.	†1854	Richard Kenner		Elmsted, Kent	S	
2.	†1855	James Burton		Warblington, Hants	S	

JACKSON, Thomas fl 1825

Baines's Gazetteer gave his address as 48 Mason St, Manchester, in 1825.

Archival References: NP/RG

JACKSON, William 1820–

He attended the Royal Academy Schools in 1844 and in the same year showed a statue of Newton at the Westminster Hall Exhibition (3). The *Art Union* noted 'the proportions of this figure do not appear to be sufficiently just and the drapery is mannered and untrue' (*AU*, 1844, 215). In 1848 he won a silver medal for a model of an academy figure in the round (4).

Jackson exhibited at the Royal Academy, 1848–54, from addresses in Upper Ebury Street and King's Row, Pimlico. In 1852 he was selected from about 40 competitors to carve a memorial tablet with a bust of Rev John Fawcett for St Cuthert, Carlisle (1). A local newspaper stated that the sculptor came from Cockermouth, had received two medals from the RA for modelling and had been employed in the studio of **Henry Weekes** for several years (*Carlisle Journal*, 7 May and 10 December 1852). Gunnis suggests that he may be identified with the 'Mr Jackson' who carved two caryatid figures for a marble chimneypiece, otherwise carved by Messrs Edwardes, Brothers & Burkey for Dorchester House in 1862 (*Builder*, 1862, 574).

Literary References: *Gunnis* 1968, 217

Funerary Monuments

1.	†1851	Rev John Fawcett		St Cuthbert, Carlisle, Cumberland	S	Pevsner, *Cumberland & Westmorland*, 1967, 96
2.	†1861	John Thornton, wall-tablet		Holy Trinity, Clapham Common, London	S	

Statues

3.	1844	Sir Isaac Newton		[Exhib Westminster Hall, London, 215]; untraced		*AU*, 1844, 215
4.	1848	Academy figure, model		[RA silver medal]; untraced		RA Premium list
5.	1848	The lamentation of Hagar, an unfinished group	m	[Exhib RA, London, 1344]; untraced		*Graves* IV, 1905–6, 231
6.	1848	The Murder of the Innocents	p	[Exhib RA, London, 1347]; untraced		*Graves* IV, 1905–6, 231
7.	1875	Sir Robert Clifton		[Nottingham]; untraced		*Gunnis* 1968, 217

Busts

8.	1849	Aurora	m	[Exhib RA, London, 1284]; untraced		*Graves* IV, 1905–6, 231
9.	nd	Admiral Lord Nelson		[W J Broderip; sold 1859]; untraced		*Gunnis* 1968, 217
10.	nd	General Napier		[W J Broderip; sold 1859]; untraced		*Gunnis* 1968, 217

Miscellaneous

11.	1849	Sleeping innocence		[Exhib RA, London, 1263]; untraced		*Graves* IV, 1905–6, 231
12.	1854	Aurora		[Exhib RA, London, 1422]; untraced		*Graves* IV, 1905–6, 231

JACKSON, William, of Melton Mowbray fl 1716–44

The son of Daniel Jackson of Oakham, Rutland, he was apprenticed to Edward Sharp of Stamford, Lincs, 'Freemason' in 1716 (PRO, I.R. 44/120, in GPC). He received payments of £1,500 as the master-mason rebuilding Melbourne Hall, Derbys (Archives, Marquis of Lothian, in *Gunnis* 1968, 217).

Literary References: *Gunnis* 1968, 217

Archival References: GPC

JAMES, C fl 1792

A wax modeller, his address was given as 15 Titchfield Street, Mortimer Street, when he exhibited at the Royal Academy in 1792.

Literary References: *Pyke* 1973, 72

Miscellaneous

1.	1792	Unidentified gentleman	w	[Exhib RA, London, 774]; untraced		*Graves* IV, 1905–6, 234

JAMES, David, of Carmarthen 1781–1859

Born at Llangynog, he was the foreman at **Daniel Mainwaring**'s yard. He signs two monuments at Llannon with his elder brother **John James** (1, 2). The Sarah Thomas memorial is a copy of Mainwaring's architectural memorial to Rees Goring Thomas in the same church. That to Morgan Thomas is a 'small and insignificant' tablet (*Dale-Jones and Lloyd* 1989, 50). David James probably continued to work for **John Mainwaring I** after he inherited his uncle's business in 1839 for his own name does not appear in the directories until 1849, when Mainwaring went to America. In 1847 the *Carmarthen Journal* reported that 'Mr David James, of Lammas Street, who was foreman to the late Mr Mainwaring when the present Picton monument was built, has taken the contract for the new one, which will be proceeded with, immediately the present building is removed' (cited by *Dale-Jones and Lloyd* 1989, 50).

James married twice and had six children. His youngest son, Charles, was a stone-mason and judging from his frequent appearances before the magistrates he was a wild young man. Family members are buried in St David's churchyard.

Literary References: *Dale-Jones and Lloyd* 1989, 50–51

Funerary Monuments

1.	†1836	Morgan Thomas Jnr (co-sculptor: John James)	Llannon, Carmarthen	S	*Dale-Jones and Lloyd* 1989, 51
2.	†1838	Sarah Thomas (co-sculptor: John James)	Llannon, Carmarthen	S	*Dale-Jones and Lloyd* 1989, 51
3.	†1848	Frederick George Philipps	Abergwili, Carmarthen	S	*Dale-Jones and Lloyd* 1989, 51
4.	†1848	Thomas Jones MD	Llanllwch, Carmarthen	S	*Dale-Jones and Lloyd* 1989, 51
5.	†1854	Philipps family (co-sculptor: Evan Harries)	Abergwili, Carmarthen	S	*Dale-Jones and Lloyd* 1989, 51

JAMES, H fl *c*1793–97

Funerary Monuments

1.	†1793	John Gwilliam	Skenfrith, Monmouths	S
2.	1796	David Powell and family	Grosmont, Monmouths	SD
3.	1797	Austen family	Skenfrith, Monmouths	SD

JAMES, John fl 1738

He was a 'carver' who worked for **Henry Watson** in the 1730s. Watson's account book shows that in 1738 he was paid £1 11s 6d 'at London' in order 'to carry him into Yorkshire' (Bodleian MS Eng Misc f383, f77). He also worked with Watson at Trentham Hall, Staffs in November 1738.

Literary References: *Brighton* 2001, 70, 72

JAMES, John, of Carmarthen *c*1780–1850

Like his brother, **David James**, he worked for **Daniel Mainwaring.** Of the two brothers John was 'the minor figure' and the only tablet signed by him alone has been described as 'a modest rectangle' (*Dale-Jones and Lloyd* 1989, 50) (**4**). His business was principally in gravestones and a large table tomb in Langunnor churchyard is his work (**1**). He may also be responsible for an identical tombstone in St Peter's churchyard, which commemorates Eliza and Elizabeth Thornton. In 1847 he received £18 5s 6d for unspecified work at the Fish Market.

Literary References: *Dale-Jones and Lloyd* 1989, 50–51

Funerary Monuments

1.	†1834	Rev David Charles	Llangunnor, Carmarthen, churchyard	S	*Dale-Jones and Lloyd* 1989, 50
2.	†1836	Morgan Thomas Jnr (co-sculptor: David James, of Carmarthen)	Llannon, Carmarthen	S	*Dale-Jones and Lloyd* 1989, 51
3.	†1838	Sarah Thomas (co-sculptor: David James, of Carmarthen)	Llannon, Carmarthen	S	*Dale-Jones and Lloyd* 1989, 51
4.	†1840	Mary Llewellyn	Tabernacle, Carmarthen	S	*Dale-Jones and Lloyd* 1989, 51

JAMESON, William fl 1781

Funerary Monuments

1.	1781	John Dalrymple (†1779)	Greyfriars churchyard, Edinburgh		Pevsner, *Edinburgh*, 1991, 161

JAQUES, John I and II fl 1781–96

They carved a number of tablets for chimneypieces and, in 1781–1782, made 'artificial ornaments' for Inverary Castle (**2, 3**). The firm was employed at Cordwainers' Hall in 1786 (Company Archives, cited by *Gunnis* 1968, 217). They became bankrupt in 1795, but in the following year Jaques was working in Holborn and he advertised 'chimney-pieces and composition ornaments of the newest designs, suitably adapted for rooms of every denomination, from the greatest elegance to the neatest simplicity' (*Aris's Birmingham Gazette*, 28 November 1896, cited by *Gunnis* 1968, 217).

Literary References: *Gunnis* 1968, 217

Chimneypieces				
1.	1785	Description unavailable	[Robert Mylne's house, Bridge Street, London]; untraced	*Journals of Robert Mylne*, in GPC
2.	nd	Tablets for chimneypieces	Inverary Castle, Argyll	*Gunnis* 1968, 217
Architectural Sculpture				
3.	1781–1782	'Artificial ornaments' Payment(s): £6 15s 8d	Inverary Castle, Argyll	*Mylne* 1893, 277
4.	nd	'Composition ornaments'	[Shottisham Hall, Norfolk]; untraced	Soane archives, in GPC

JARVIS, C, of Birmingham fl 1807–37?

In 1807 he was paid £83 for repairs to Atherstone Hall, Warks (Bracebridge Archives, in GPC).

Funerary Monuments

1.	?1830	Unidentified subject, tablet	Packwood, Warks	S	*Gunnis* 1968, 218
2.	?1832	Unidentified subject, tablet	Coleshill, Warks	S	*Gunnis* 1968, 218
3.	?1837	Sarah Taylor	Aston Cantlow, Warwicks	S	GPC

JEANS, William, of Edinburgh –1796

William or Willie Jeans, who signed himself Guglielmo Jehnes, carved two allegorical statues for Penicuik House in 1776 (**1**). He can probably be identified with a sculptor called Jeans who exhibited three models at the Free Society in London, giving his address as 'At Mr Kennedy's, George Street, York Buildings' in 1769 and 'Edinburgh' in 1770–71 (**3–5**). He lived at Gentles Close, Edinburgh, from 1782 to 1784 and was apparently dead by 11 October 1796, when the

Cumberland Pacquet reported that an 'urn of Parian marble cut by the late Mr. Jeans the statuary, was dedicated to the memory of Robert Burns and placed by the Earl of Buchan' in the chapter house at Dryburgh Abbey (2).

He may have been in Rome in 1767 when **Richard Hayward** noted the arrival of 'Mr. Jeans, a Scotch sculptor'. However, it is possible that Hayward was referring to John Jeans, whose collection of 'Specimens of Natural History from the North of Scotland' was sold in London on 3 and 4 June 1766. A copy of that sale catalogue is bound into the volume of Hayward's list of visitors to Rome (*Hayward's List and Sales Catalogues MS*, BM, P&D). The sculptor may be responsible for a drawing of the Scottish draughtsman and printmaker John Brown (1752–1787) in the SNPG, which is signed Jeans. A painting by Brown of Jeans in the robes of a Capuchin monk was included in the Earl of Buchan's sale on 10 December 1859 (lot 383, untraced).

Literary References: *Gunnis* 1968, 218; *Woodward* 1977, vol 1, pt 2, 104–5; *Stainton* 1983, 13, 26

Statues						
1.	1776	Dacian captives (or druids) two	s	Penicuik House, Midlothian	S	*Gunnis* 1968, 218; *Rowan* 1968, 384 (repr); *Pearson* 1991, 14, 144 (repr)
Architectural Sculpture						
2.	1796	Urn commemorating Robert Burns	m	[Dryburgh Abbey, Berwicks]; untraced		*CP*, 11 Oct 1796
Miscellaneous						
3.	1769	Laocoon and his sons, model	tc	[Exhib Free Soc, London, 115]; untraced		*Graves* 1907, 129
4.	1770	'Silenus and Ægle'		[Exhib Free Soc, London, 131]; untraced		*Graves* 1907, 129
5.	1771	Unidentified subject, model	tc	[Exhib Free Soc, London, 134]; untraced		*Graves* 1907, 129

JELFE, Andrews –1759

Jelfe was the son of William Jelfe of South Weald, Essex. His mother's maiden name was Andrews. He was apprenticed to a mason, John Keene, on 2 August 1704 and became free of the Masons' Company on 4 September 1711. He subsequently went into partnership with **Edward Strong II** and **Christopher Cass I**, working with both until December 1728 when Strong withdrew. Jelfe continued with Cass until the latter's death in 1734, after which he took over the business. Jelfe and Cass had contracts for masonry work for some of the fifty new churches: a petition for payment, dated 20 April 1732 is among the papers of the church commission in Lambeth Palace Library. Jelfe was also for a time in partnership with **George Mercer**.

He received a number of appointments from the office of works. On 13 August 1715 he became clerk of works at Newmarket, a position he held until 1718. He was clerk itinerant from 1715 to 1728, with a salary of £50 pa. In January 1719 he was appointed architect and clerk of the works for all garrisons, fortifications and castles in Great Britain. He was posted to Scotland where he built barracks at Ruthven and Bernara, and in 1720 went to Plymouth to supervise the construction of a new gun-wharf. Some of his drawings for these works survive. He also received contracts for masonry work on the Hermitage, Richmond (1730), where he was employed by Henry Flitcroft; on the Royal Mews, Charing Cross (1733); the library at St James's Palace (1737); the treasury in Whitehall (by 1737); Hampton Court (1732/3) and the Horse Guards in Whitehall, where he worked with his nephew **William Jelfe** and **John Carr** (1751). He was evidently in high demand, which is no doubt why he paid a fine to be excused serving as sheriff in 1744 (*GM* 1744, 14, 333).

Jelfe was principally a master-mason, though his letter-book shows that he also had a practice in church monuments and provided decorative carving. He made the black marble tombstone commemorating Nicholas Hawksmoor in the churchyard at Shenley (2) and was responsible for the monument in sarcophagus form to his parents at South Weald (1). In 1742 he carved a shield and festoon for Holkham Hall, Norfolk, where his friend, the architect Matthew Brettingham, was then working (5). In 1744 he made two friezes for Houghton Hall, Norfolk (6).

He worked for Lord Macclesfield at Sherborn Castle and built a house (now demolished) for Sir John Evelyn in St James's Place. In 1741–43 he was responsible for 13 houses near Palace Yard, Westminster, and in 1742 he was paid nearly £100 for mason's work at Warren House, for Frederick, Prince of Wales. In 1750 he worked at the India House, Kew, also commissioned by the Prince. In 1751 Henry Flitcroft paid him £550, presumably for houses designed by Flitcroft. He rebuilt Waresley church, Hunts, and carried out work at Abington Lodge, Cambs for Colonel Vachell.

His most notable work as an architect was probably the court house or town hall at Rye, Sussex, though he is best remembered for building Westminster Bridge. The contract, signed in June 1738, was executed in conjunction with **Samuel Tufnell**. It was completed in 1747, the year he was made a director of the Westminster Fire Office. **Sir Henry Cheere** was involved in the Westminster bridge project, as was the antiquarian William Stukeley, who suggested innovative engineering techniques to Jelfe. Stukeley, who was a friend of Jelfe, owned several of Jelfe's drawings and himself drew the mason's portrait.

Jelfe's yard and wharf were in New Palace Yard, Westminster. He was recorded there in the Masons' Company list of *c*1740, with an assistant named George Banks. There were several apprentices over the years, taken under the auspices of the Masons' Company: they included Peter Phillips (1727/8); Charles Pauling, who began his training with the elder Cass and completed it with Jelfe; Joseph Garnett, first apprenticed to **Joseph Rose**, but turned over to Jelfe in 1735/6 and George Banks and Thomas Waterfall, who joined Jelfe in 1739.

Jelfe clearly had gentlemanly pretensions. In 1747 he bought a country residence, Pendrell House, at Bletchingley in Surrey, which he left to his elder son, Andrew Jelfe RN, whom Jelfe had attempted to establish as a naval officer. The elder Jelfe wrote to a friend in 1741 'My son Andrew wrote me from St Helena. I am afraid he is a great distance from a Captain's commission. It hath already cost me an incredible sum to carry him on in the Service' (Jelfe Letter-Book, BL, Ad MS 27587). Jelfe left his stone-built dwelling house in New Palace Yard to his daughter, Elizabeth, with £10,000.

A similar sum went to his son William, 'who has proved very idle and extravagant' (PROB 11/846). He died on 26 April 1759 and left instructions that he wished to be buried at South Weald with his parents.

MGS

Literary References: *Gunnis* 1968, 218; *Stell* 1973, 20–30; *Colvin* V, 1973–76, *passim*; *Craske* 1992, 69; *Colvin* 1995, 542–3; *Webb* 1999, *passim*; *Craske* 2000 (2), 101

Archival References: Masons' Co, Freemen, fol 32; Assistants, fols 1, 5; Court Book, 1695–1722, MS 5305/2, fol 71r; Lambeth Palace Library, Commission for 50 New Churches, MSS/2690–2750/2723, fol 96; Jelfe Letter-Book, BL Ad MS 27587, fol 106, 141; WFO, MB, 343/8, 15 Oct 1747; GPC

Miscellaneous Drawings: Scottish fortifications, NLS Z2/2, 2a, 10, 26a; Library of the Wiltshire Archeological Society, Devizes; Bodleian MS Top. Gen. D.14, p59

Portrait of the Sculptor: William Stukeley, 1722/3, Bodleian, MS Eng Misc e 136 fol 30

Funerary Monuments

1.	?1726	Jelfe family		South Weald, Essex	*Gunnis* 1968, 218; *Colvin* 1995, 543
2.	†1736	Nicholas Hawksmoor		Shenley, Herts, churchyard	*Gunnis* 1968, 218; Pevsner, *Herts*, 1977, 337

Architectural Sculpture

3.	1734	Sundial		[Gogmagog, Cambs, for Lord Godolphin]; untraced	*Gunnis* 1968, 218
4.	1735	Carved doorcase	s	[for Mr Francis Sheppard, Exning House, Sussex]; untraced	*Gunnis* 1968, 218; *Colvin* 1995, 542
5.	1742	Shield and festoons Payment(s): 13s 4d		[Holkham Hall, Norfolk]; untraced	BL Ad MS 27587, fol 141; *Gunnis* 1968, 218
6.	1744	'two enriched pieces of frieze'		[Houghton Hall, Norfolk]; untraced	BL Ad MS 27587; *Gunnis* 1968, 218

JELFE, William –1772

Possibly a son of Robert Jelfe, a master carpenter, he was apprenticed to his uncle, **Andrews Jelfe**, on 10 January 1740, worked with him until the latter's death in April 1759 and joined the Masons' Company a few months later (Masons' Co, *Freemen*, fol 32, 3 August 1759). He continued to operate from the yard and wharf at New Palace Yard which Andrews Jelfe had left to his daughter Eliza in his will, and established secondary premises in Lambeth some time before 1763 when a directory listed him 'at the foot of Westminster-bridge' (*Mortimer* 1763, 49). He became a director of the Westminster Fire Office in 1762 (Westminster Fire Office, MB, 343/11, 14 Oct 1762).

In 1750–8 William Jelfe was employed with Andrews Jelfe and **John Carr** at the Horse Guards in Whitehall. In 1752 he was paid £180 for work for Augusta, Princess of Wales, including a summer house in the gardens of Leicester House, and in 1753 received a further £133 11s 6d, mostly for work at Leicester House (GPC). Like his uncle, Jelfe worked with the architect Henry Flitcroft. In 1753–4 he built a house to Flitcroft's designs on the north side of Clapham Common for the banker Henry Hoare. He later worked at Stourhead, Hoare's country house in Wiltshire, making a pavement for Flitcroft's Temple of Apollo in 1766 (Hoare Partnership Ledger 1751–1764, fol 66, 9 April 1753; Hoare Private Accts, 1750–66). In addition, the architect paid Jelfe £279 for unidentified work in 1764 (Flitcroft's bank account, Drummonds Bank Archives, in GPC). He took two apprentices through the Masons' Company, Thomas Phillips (1759) and John Cornwall (1768).

In 1767–9 Jelfe was paid £566 for work on the interior of Lansdowne House including the grand staircase (Archives, Marquess of Lansdowne, in GPC), and as the mason responsible for building the excise office, begun in 1769, he received £4,433. He held the office of stonemason to King George III, and was employed in that capacity on rebuilding Greenwich Palace in 1770. That year he was also employed at Hovingham Hall, N R Yorks, by the surveyor general, Sir William Worsley (Worsley Archives in GPC) and was awarded the masonry contract for rebuilding the Fleet Prison. In 1771 he was paid £68 for repairing the Queen's House at Kew as a home for the young princes. He may have worked with Sir William Chambers some time between 1769 and his death for a 'Mr Jelfe' is mentioned in connection with obelisks in a letter in Chambers's Letters-Book, (BL Ad MS 41133, fol 54). One of his last commissions was to build a new gateway at Hampton Court. A payment of £315 was made to his executors (PRO Works 5/46, in GPC). He died on 3 September 1771 and a sale of his stock in trade was held on 9 January 1772 at his yards in New Palace Yard, St Margaret's Street, and near Westminster Bridge, Lambeth. The catalogue states that these premises were taken over by Messrs Life and Saunders, stonemasons. This firm completed Jelfe's Fleet Prison contract.

Literary References: *London Mag*, vol 40 (1771), 472; *Gunnis* 1968, 218; *Colvin* 1973–76, 349, 353, 429, 430, 438; *Colvin* 1995, 543; *Webb* 1999, 8, 26

Archival References: Masons' Co, Court Book, 1722–51 (1740); GPC

Chimneypieces

2.	nd	Several	[Jelfe sale, 9 Jan 1772]; untraced	GPC

JENKINS, John fl c1744

Gunnis describes his only known work, a tablet to Uvedale King, as 'pretty'.

Literary References: *Gunnis* 1968, 218

Funerary Monuments

1.	1774	Uvedale King	Byford, Herefs	S	Pevsner, *Herefs*, 1963, 97

JENKINSON, Edward fl 1796

Gunnis suggests that he was perhaps a son of **Matthew Jenkinson**.

Literary References: *Gunnis* 1968, 218

Chimneypieces

1.	1796	Veined marble	St James's Palace, London	*Gunnis* 1968, 218

JENKINSON, Matthew fl 1790–1808

He was mason for the Tower of London, Greenwich Palace and the King's Mews in 1790, in which year he also built a colonnade at St James's Palace at a total cost of £398 (2). In 1808 he was paid £148 for work at the Duke of Clarence's apartments in St James's Palace and a further £26 for a marble chimneypiece (1).

Literary References: *Gunnis* 1968, 218

Chimneypieces

1.	1808	Description unavailable	m	[St James's Palace, London, Duke of Clarence's apartments]; untraced	*Gunnis* 1968, 218

Architectural Sculpture

2.	1790	'all carved and moulded work'	St James's Palace, London, colonnade	*Gunnis* 1968, 218

JENNINGS

A 'Jennings' is listed amongst the students of David d'Angers.

Literary References: *Jouin* 1878, 581

JENNINGS, Benjamin I, of Hereford fl c1800–46

Possibly a son of James Jennings, a mason of Hereford, he signs a number of tablets in that county and Gunnis comments that none of them are of any particular interest. That to the Davies family at Nantuel is signed 'Jennings, late Wood, Hereford' suggesting that he was an assistant to **T Wood** before he set up on his own account (3). In 1846 he 'extensively repaired and restored' the 15th-century altar monument to Sir Thomas Vaughan at Kington (*Builder*, 1846, 440) (**12**).

Literary References: *Gunnis* 1968, 218

Archival References: GPC

Funerary Monuments

1.	c1800	Hon Mrs Dew	Sellack, Herefs	S	*Gunnis* 1968, 218
2.	†1810	Unidentified subject, tablet	Linton-by-Ross, Herefs	S	Pevsner, *Herefs*, 1963, 234
3.	?1815	Davies family	Nantuel, Radnor	S	GPC
4.	?1821	John Griffiths	Sutton St Michael, Herefs		RG/JP, 5, 751
5.	†1830	Rev Harry Williams	Goodrich, Herefs	S	Pevsner, *Herefs*, 1963, 137
6.	1830	Rev John Clutton	Hereford Cathedral	S	*Gunnis* 1968, 218
7.	1831	John Collins	Walford, Herefs	S	*Gunnis* 1968, 218
8.	?1833	Rev Thomas Powell	Nantuel, Radnor		GPC
9.	1838	John Clutton	Hereford Cathedral	S	*Gunnis* 1968, 218
10.	1843	Sir James Kyrle Money	Much Marcle, Herefs	S	*Gunnis* 1968, 218
11.	1846	Rev George Woodhouse	Leominster, Herefs	S	*Gunnis* 1968, 218
12.	1846	Sir Thomas Vaughan (†1469) (restoration only)	Kington, Herefs		*Builder*, 1846, 440–1

JENNINGS, Benjamin II, of Hereford –1875

The son of **Benjamin Jennings I**, he studied in Rome under **John Gibson**. He exhibited at the Royal Academy in 1849 and 1850 showing two busts and a statue of Cupid entitled *The birth of the rose* (4) This ideal work illustrates a poem by Sappho in which Cupid argues that the rose should be named the queen of flowers. It gained immediate popularity and was illustrated in the *Art Journal* and in books on contemporary sculpture. Jennings lent it to the exhibition of Art Treasures held at Manchester in 1857, and at a sale held after his death it was purchased by a gentleman from Gloucester, then acquired by Hereford Museum. The same Gloucester gentleman purchased a head of the Madonna, which may have been the bust which the sculptor sent to the RA in 1850 (6). Gunnis also notes that Jennings exhibited at the Great Exhibition.

Literary References: *Gunnis* 1968, 219

Funerary Monuments

1.	1855	William Thompson	Kirkby, Westmorland	S	*Gunnis* 1968, 219
2.	1860	Major Lumley	Brecon Cathedral churchyard		*Builder*, 1860, 95
3.	1867	Rev John Price	Bleddfa, Radnor		GPC

Statues

4.	1850	The birth of the rose	Hereford Museum	*AJ*, 1850, 384 (repr); *Manchester Art Treasures* 1857, 134; *Graves* IV, 1905–6, 245

Busts

5.	1849	Thomas Elliotson	[Exhib RA, London, 1307]; untraced	*Graves* IV, 1905–6, 245
6.	1850	Madonna	[Exhib RA, London, 1356]; untraced	*Graves* IV, 1905–6, 245

JEPHSON, Surplice fl c1815

Funerary Monuments

1.	†1815	G Coldham	St Mary, Nottingham	NP/RG

JEWELL, Thomas I, of Barnstaple –1728

He signs a tablet to Lady Rolle at Tawstock (1). Gunnis described this as 'a very lovely cartouche tablet' adding that the work, 'with its swags of flowers in the Grinling Gibbons manner, is almost worthy of the master himself' (*Gunnis* 1968, 219). He attributed to Jewell three other unsigned cartouche tablets in the same church, all practically identical in design to the one to Lady Rolle. They commemorate Sir Boucher Wrey (1696), Florence, Lady Wrey (1726) and Robert Lovett (1710). Neighbouring churches contain similar tablets. At Braunton, for example, there is a 'delightful cartouche' with 'winged cherubs at the top' in memory of Margaret Allen (†1709).

Literary References: *Gunnis* 1968, 219

Funerary Monuments

1.	†1705	Lady Rolle	Tawstock, Devon	S	Pevsner, *Devon*, 1989, 790

JEWELL, Thomas II, of Barnstaple 1676–1758

He was presumably a son of **Thomas Jewell I** and became a freeman of Exeter in 1734. Gunnis comments of his large monument to Sir Henry Northcote at Tawstock, 'the workmanship, which can only be called provincial, already shows a deterioration from the carefully carved details and delicate cutting of his father' (*Gunnis* 1968, 219) (1). He also states that Jewell died, aged 82, on 29 September 1758, and his wife Joanna followed him on 1 September 1762, aged 77, citing a manuscript list of tombstones formerly in the churchyard of Barnstaple parish church. This list states that the tomb was situated in the south-eastern corner. Gunnis was unable to find any trace of it.

Literary References: *Gunnis* 1968, 219

Funerary Monuments

1.	†1729	Sir Henry Northcote	Tawstock, Devon	S	Pevsner, *Devon*, 1989, 790
2.	?1740	Robert Hales	Braunton, Devon	S	*Gunnis* 1968, 219
3.	?1750	Richard Bennett	Bishops Tawton, Devon	S	*Gunnis* 1968, 219

JEWELL, Thomas III, of Barnstaple fl 1761

According to the Barnstaple parish registers, there was a third Thomas Jewell, a mason and maker of tombstones, and presumably a son of **Thomas Jewell II**. He became a freeman of Exeter in 1761 (City Archives, cited by *Gunnis* 1968, 219).

Architectural Sculpture

1.	1771	Font	Buckland Brewer, Devon		Pevsner, *Devon*, 1989, 230

JOANES, John, of Worthing fl 1813–14

A stone mason, he was probably the son of **Ralph Joanes** and lived at 16 Warwick Street, Worthing, having a yard and shop in Ann Street. He was appointed Surveyor to the Board of Commissioners in 1813, and was succeeded by his son Ralph in 1826. The tablet to Elinor Newcome (†1844) at Broadwater, Sussex, is signed 'Joanes', but may be by another member of the family.

Literary References: *Gunnis* 1968, 219

Archival References: GPC; RG/JP, 5, 753

Funerary Monuments

1.	†1814	Thomas Nash	St George, Bloomsbury, London	S	*Gunnis* 1968, 219

JOANES, Ralph, of Horsham fl 1760–1801

In 1760 he was paid for repairs to Lewes prison and in 1778–79 received £393 for building the gaoler's house at Horsham, which was designed by Henry Joanes of Horsham, very likely a relative. Gunnis describes the box-tomb erected in memory of George Hutchinson, as a 'curious work' with 'relief panels of Christ with the woman of Samaria, and of angels bearing an urn heavenwards', surmounted by an urn produced by the **Coade Factory** (*Gunnis* 1968, 219) (1). In 1787 Joanes supplied stone to the Duke of Norfolk for his house at Horsham (Horsham Archives, cited by *Gunnis* 1968, 219).

Literary References: *Gunnis* 1968, 219

Funerary Monuments

1.	1801	George Hutchinson	Ifield, Sussex	S	*Gunnis* 1968, 219

JOHNSON, A fl 1848–52

He exhibited works at the Royal Academy, 1848–52, from 5 Hudson's Terrace, Westminster; 29 Clarence Gardens, Regent's Park; 15 Buckingham Street and 69 Regent Street.

Literary References: *Graves* IV, 1905–6, 250; *Gunnis* 1968, 219

Statues					
1.	1850	Early affection	m	[Exhib RA, London, 1300]; untraced	*Graves* IV, 1905–6, 250
2.	1852	Early joy Model(s): exhib RA, London, 1849, 1339	m	[Exhib RA, London, 1374]; untraced	*Graves* IV, 1905–6, 250
3.	1852	Sir Robert Peel, statuette		[Exhib RA, London, 1363]; untraced	*Graves* IV, 1905–6, 250
Busts					
4.	1848	George Trower	m	[Exhib RA, London, 1396]; untraced	*Graves* IV, 1905–6, 250
5.	1849	Unidentified lady		[Exhib RA, London, 1338]; untraced	*Graves* IV, 1905–6, 250
6.	1850	Henry Melton		[Exhib RA, London, 1411]; untraced	*Graves* IV, 1905–6, 250
7.	1852	Mrs G J Trower	m	[Exhib RA, London, 1412]; untraced	*Graves* IV, 1905–6, 250
Miscellaneous					
8.	1848	Infant sorrow		[Exhib RA, London, 1252]; untraced	*Graves* IV, 1905–6, 250

JOHNSON, Blucher 1816–72

An Irish sculptor and draughtsman, he was born in Dublin, where his father, George, held a post in the military accounts office in Merrion Street. He entered the Royal Dublin Society Schools in 1828 and won a number of prizes for modelling. He exhibited portrait busts at the Royal Hibernian Society in 1837, 1849, 1854 and 1862. Johnson was a shy and retiring character and after his father's death in 1844 he 'shut himself off altogether from the world and lived the life of an eccentric recluse' (*Daily Independent*, 29 December 1904, quoted by *Strickland* I, 1913, 554). An anonymous account published more than 30 years after his death, states that Johnson 'would often reject or neglect commissions of value and importance, in order to attend some surgeon in one or other of the city hospitals, and there take casts of broken or distorted limbs, to furnish illustrations for medical books' (*ibid*). As well as sculpture, Johnson practised painting and engraving and was employed as a designer and modeller by the Dublin silversmiths. He died in obscurity at the Mater Misericordiae Hospital in October 1872 and was buried in Mount Jerome cemetery.

Literary References: *Strickland* I, 1913, 553–555

Busts

1.	1837	Dr Handcock	[Exhib RHA, Dublin]; untraced	*Strickland* I, 1913, 554
2.	1849	Robert Smyth	[Exhib RHA, Dublin, 439]; untraced	*Stewart* 2, 1985, 121
3.	1849	Robert Smyth Furlong	[Exhib RHA, Dublin, 438]; untraced	*Stewart* 2, 1985, 121
4.	1854	Maurice Collis MD	[Exhib RHA, Dublin, 287]; untraced	*Stewart* 2, 1985, 121
5.	1854	Unidentified gentleman, posthumous	[Exhib RHA, Dublin, 288]; untraced	*Stewart* 2, 1985, 121
6.	1862	Edward L Dillon	[Exhib RHA, Dublin, 461]; untraced	*Stewart* 2, 1985, 121

JOHNSON, J, of Belfast fl 1838–41

His monument to Dr John Boyd is signed 'J. Johnson sc. Belfast Steam Marble Works' (2).

Literary References: *Potterton* 1975, 52

Funerary Monuments

1.	1838	Rev Ralph Bridge	Lisburn, Co Antrim		*Potterton* 1975, 52
2.	†1841	Dr John Boyd	Ballycastle Presbyterian churchyard, Co Antrim	S	*Potterton* 1975, 52

JOHNSON, James, of Stamfordham 1699–1777

His gravestone in the churchyard at Stamfordham, Northumbs indicates that Johnson was one of a family of stonemasons. His most important works are a series of life-size figures 'cut in stone according to the taste of the Normans', representing men 'in the act of defense, wielding such arms as were then used' on the battlements of Alnwick Castle (*Mackenzie* 1825, I, 450) (**1**). These were installed by the 1st Duke of Northumberland as part of his refurbishment of the castle in the gothic style, under the direction of James Paine and Robert Adam. They replaced earlier figures which had become decayed and they are said to have taken the sculptor at least 20 years to complete. It is likely that the statue of St Paulinus at Lady's Well, Holystone, Northumbs, and the summer house designed by Adam for the Duke of Northumberland at Hulne Priory were also executed by Johnson.

Literary References: *Gunnis* 1968, 219; *Usherwood* 2000, 326–7

Statues

1.	1750–1770	Battlement figures	s	Alnwick Castle, Northumbs	*Usherwood* 2000, 6–7 (repr)

Architectural Sculpture

2.	1755	St Michael lancing a winged dragon, for a fountain Payment(s): £5 7s 6d	s	St Michael's Pant, Clayport Street, Alnwick, Northumbs	*Usherwood* 2000, 5 (repr)

JOHNSON, John I fl 1710

There is a lengthy agreement, dated 1710, in the Kimbolton Archives, between the Earl of Manchester (later the 1st Duke) and John Johnson 'free mason of London'. In it Johnson agrees to carry out considerable work at Kimbolton Castle, including the carving of decorative details and ciphers and coronets on the keystones above the 'windows of the inner court'.

Literary References: *Gunnis* 1968, 219–20

JOHNSON, John II 1732–1814

This architect exhibited 'a tablet of the dining-room chimney-piece at the Jockey club-room, Newmarket' at the Royal Academy in 1773. It was described as 'absurd' by Horace Walpole (*Graves* IV, 1905–6, 255). It is not known who actually executed the work.

Literary References: *Gunnis* 1968, 220; *Colvin* 1995, 548–9

JOHNSON, Matthew Wharton, of London fl 1820–82

Gunnis says that Johnson was active between 1820 and 1860 and describes him as 'a prolific but dull statuary whose work may be found all over England'. Since monuments signed by Johnson span most of the 19th century, it seems likely that the firm extended to a second generation. The works can be found as far afield as the West Indies, Ireland and Australia (**18, 19, 21, 46**). Gunnis considered the monument to Joseph Somes, which has 'an amusing relief of merchant-ships moored at a quay', to be Johnson's most successful work and condemned the Augustus Clevland memorial with its 'relief of a woman lying prone at the foot of an impossible weeping-willow' as his worst (**32, 34**). He was responsible for the grey granite tomb of the Duke of Sussex in Kensal Green cemetery, completed in 1845 (**30**). It has a raised hipped ledger on a massive podium with bollards in the form of capped, unfluted Greek Doric columns that once supported bronze chains.

In 1829 Johnson was employed by the Archbishop of Canterbury on repairs and additions to Addington Palace, Surrey, earning over £1,500 (Lambeth Palace Archives in GPC).

In addition to monuments, Johnson produced decorative garden sculpture in artificial stone and he publicised this branch of his business by sending out brochures to clients, with line engravings illustrating available works. Several examples survive, each illustrating popular favourites and also offering limited new designs. The title page of the 1856 catalogue describes him as 'MATTHEW. W. JOHNSON / SCULPTOR AND MASON / MARBLE, STONE, AND ARTIFICIAL STONE WORKS / NEW ROAD FITZROY SQUARE, LONDON / MANUFACTURER OF FIGURES, FOUNTAINS, VASES &c. / WARRANTED TO RESIST FROST, / ALSO OF TOMBS, MONUMENTS, CHIMNEYPIECES &c. / IN MARBLE OR STONE'. From this publication Sir Clifford Constable of Burton Constable ordered a fountain with a boy and dolphin, measuring 12 feet in diameter and costing £16 (**52**). Other items illustrated with dimensions and prices, include classical figures, such as *Time with hour glass and scythe* (5 feet, £8), *Roman Flora* (5 feet 8 inches, £7 10s) and *Apollo and the Muses* (5 feet, £10), vases, seated dogs, a fox at £7, a stork at £2 10s and a stag at £6, as well as various fountains.

His address was recorded as Southampton Street, Fitzroy Square, when he was named as an executor in the will of **Richard Maile**, which was proved on 8 July 1850 (PROB 11/2116/290–1).

Literary References: *Gunnis* 1968, 220; *Curl* 2001, 116, 210

Funerary Monuments

1.	†1804	Rev William Gilpin	Boldre, Hants	S	Pevsner, *Hants & Isle of Wight*, 1967, 113
2.	†1810	Frances Burgoyne	Sutton, Beds	S	
3.	†1818	Frances Elizabeth Campbell	Sutton, Beds	S	
4.	?1822	Rev Holford Cotton	Adderbury, Oxon	S	*Gunnis* 1968, 220
5.	†1822	Rev P M Procter	Berry Hill, Glos	S	Pevsner, *Glos: Vale & Forest of Dean*, 1976, 104
6.	?1823	Sarah Holroyd	St Mary, Walthamstow, Essex	S	*Gunnis* 1968, 220
7.	†1826	Robert Nichols	Witham-on-the-Hill, Lincs	S	Pevsner, *Lincs*, 1989, 807
8.	†1827	John Jones	Shipston-on-Stour, Warwicks	S	
9.	?1829	Elizabeth Price	Llandovery, Carmarthen	S	*Gunnis* 1968, 220
10.	†1829	Mrs Hele	Brede, Sussex	S	Pevsner, *Sussex*, 1965, 423
11.	?1831	Hon Frederick Robinson	Flitton, Beds	S	*Gunnis* 1968, 220
12.	†1831	Samuel and Mercy Drayton	St George, Bridgetown, Barbados	S	
13.	?1831	Sir John Farnaby	West Wickham, Kent	S	*Gunnis* 1968, 220
14.	1831	Sir Roger (†1780) and Lady Frances (†1788) Burgoyne	Sutton, Beds	SD	
15.	†1832	Richard and Deborah (†1835) Hooton	Holy Trinity, Clapham Common, London	S	

16.	?1834	Rev James Sedgwick	Currey Rivel, Somerset	S	*Gunnis* 1968, 220
17.	?1834	Samuel Greg	Wilmslow, Cheshire	S	*Gunnis* 1968, 220
18.	†1835	Georgiana Hicks	St George, Gingerland, Nevis	S	
19.	†1836	Richard Hicks	St George, Gingerland, Nevis	S	
20.	†1838	Rowland Cooper	Cobham, Surrey, churchyard		C Lib (repr)
21.	†1839	Captain John Maitland Ross	Chennai (Madras) Cathedral, India	S	
22.	†1839	James Verschonner	Kensal Green Cemetery, London, catacombs		
23.	†1839	John Weatherall Smith	St Luke, Charlton, Middx	S	
24.	?1839	R H S Hele	Brede, Sussex	S	
25.	†1842	David Heusch	Kensal Green Cemetery, London, catacombs	S	
26.	?1842	General Thornton	Brockhall, Northants	S	*Gunnis* 1968, 220
27.	†1842	Rev Henry Plimley (†1764) and Mary Plimley	Cuckfield, Sussex	S	
28.	?1842	William Vale	Mathon, Herefs		RG/JP, 5, 755
29.	†1844	John and Sarah Smith	Oundle, Northants	S	
30.	1845	Augustus Frederick, Duke of Sussex (†1843)	Kensal Green Cemetery, London		*Curl* 2001, 115, 116, 210 (repr)
31.	†1845	John Brown	Wolverley, Worcs	S	
32.	†1845	Joseph Somes	St Dunstan, Stepney, London	S	*Gunnis* 1968, 220
33.	†1848	Skynner George Woodroffe	Farthinghoe, Northants		*CIIA* 4/3/76 (repr)
34.	†1849	Augustus Clevland	Westleigh, Devon	S	Pevsner, *Devon*, 1989, 901
35.	?1850	Commander Arthur Grant	Cluny, Aberdeen		GPC
36.	?1850	Sir Francis Hammond	Whepstead, Suffolk	S	*Gunnis* 1968, 220
37.	†1851	George Rush	Farthinghoe, Northants		C Lib (repr)
38.	†1853	Jane Sawbridge Erle Drax	Charborough, Dorset	S	Pevsner, *Dorset*, 1972, 140
39.	†1855	John Ledsam	St George's Chapel, Windsor Castle	S	*Bond* 1999, 204
40.	†1856	Robert, 1st Lord Carew	Christ Church Cathedral, Waterford		*Potterton* 1975, 52
41.	†1856	Thomas Worthington and parents	St Wilfred, Northenden, Manchester, Lancs	S	*CIIA* 4/8/56–7 (repr)
42.	†1857	John Jackson Blencowe	Marston St Lawrence, Northants	S	*Read* 1982, 190 (repr)
43.	*c*1858	Challoner (†1750) and Charles Ogle (†1858)	Ponteland, Northumbs	S	Pevsner, *Northumbs*, 1992, 542
44.	†1795–1859	Smith family members	Avening, Glos		C Lib (repr)
45.	†1860	Charles Howarth	Horwich, Lancs		C Lib (repr)
46.	†1866	John Campbell	Cobbitty, NSW, Australia		GPC
47.	†1871	Ellen (†1841), Christopher (†1851), Mary (†1870) and Herbert Packe	St Martin, Ruislip, Middx	S	
48.	†1880	Martha Savory	Kensal Green Cemetery, London, catacombs	S	
49.	†1882	Major Henry Savory	Kensal Green Cemetery, London, catacombs	S	
50.	nd	Rev L Smith	Passenham, Northants	S	
51.	nd	Unidentified subject	Northam, Devon	S	Pevsner, *Devon*, 1989, 598

Architectural Sculpture

52.	*c*1856	Fountain with a boy and dolphin	Burton Constable Hall, E R Yorks, west front		LMG, Burton Constable, 1589 (annotated brochure)

JOHNSON, Robert, of Westminster –1845

A mason, he signs the monument to Sir Francis Freeling in Kensal Green Cemetery, a severe Carrara marble column on an inscribed square sandstone base (1). It is one of the earliest monuments in the cemetery and is 'characteristic of the more severe tendencies in late-Neoclassical design' (*Curl* 2001, 189). Johnson is also buried at Kensal Green Cemetery.

Literary References: *Curl* 2001, 189

Funerary Monuments

1.	†1836	Sir Francis Freeling	Kensal Green Cemetery, London	S	*Curl* 2001, 189

JOHNSON, Thomas fl 1763

He is listed in a directory of 1763 as 'Carver, teacher of drawing and modelling', and the author of 'A book of designs for chimney-pieces and other ornaments and of several other pieces. Grafton-Street, Soho.'

Literary References: *Mortimer* 1763, 16

JOHNSON, William fl 1712

Chimneypieces

1.	1712	Description unavailable	[for Lord Stafford]; untraced	BL Add MS 22,257, vol 1, fol 447, in GPC

JOHNSTON, of Belfast fl 1845

He may possibly be identified with **J Johnson, of Belfast.**

Statues

1.	1845	Sir Robert Gillespie	Comber, Ulster	*Gunnis* 1968, 220

JOHNSTON (or JOHNSON), J, of Lichfield fl 1836–45

He exhibited a bust at the Liverpool Academy in 1836 (2) and is otherwise known only for one neo-Hellenic wall-tablet (1).

Funerary Monuments

1.	1845	Edward Gore	Shenstone, Staffs	S	*Gunnis* 1968, 220

Busts

2.	1836	John Rosson	[Exhib Liverpool Ac]; untraced		*Gunnis* 1968, 220

JOHNSTONE, A fl 1848–50

He may possibly be identified with **A Johnson.**

Busts

1.	1848	Unidentified man	coll Mr Lloyd, Great Bedwyn, Wilts	GPC
2.	1850	Jenny Lind	coll Mr Lloyd, Great Bedwyn, Wilts	GPC

JOHNSTONE, Charles fl 1824

His address was recorded as 25 Norfolk Street, Middlesex Hospital, when he exhibited with the Society of British Artists at the Suffolk Street Gallery in 1824.

Busts

1.	1824	Unidentified child	[Exhib Soc of BA, London, 347]; untraced	*Johnson* 1975, 260

JONES, Benjamin fl 1844

He was listed in Thompson's Commercial Directory for 1844 as a statuary and mason of Burser Street and Tooley Street.

JONES, Henry, of Bristol

He was the partner of **John Dunn** and **William Drewett**. The works of the firm are listed under the entry for William Drewett.

Literary References: *Dale-Jones and Lloyd* 1989, 49

JONES, Henry, of Canterbury fl 1808–44

He advertised in the *Kentish Gazette* on 24 June 1808: 'H. JONES, STATUARY AND MASON, Respectfully returns thanks to those friends who have honoured him with their commands, and begs to inform the Publick and Builders in general, that he has now for inspection a variety of ELEGANT MARBLE CHIMNEY PIECES, MONUMENTS &c at his MANUFACTORY in BRIDGE-STREET, and hopes by strict attention and moderate charges, to merit a continuance of that patronage which he has experienced since his commencement of business'.

The monument to William Hopson has two cherubic figures, one of whom holds a flaming heart (**1**). Gunnis, who considered this the best of Jones's monuments, noted that it was a very late example of imagery popular during the 17th and early-18th centuries, but which had gone out of fashion in the rest of England long before 1800. Jones was the mason employed in building the church at Seasalter, Kent in 1844 (*Builder*, 1844, 461).

Literary References: *Gunnis* 1968, 220

Archival References: GPC

Funerary Monuments

1.	†1819	William Hopson	Milton Regis, Kent	S	Pevsner, *Kent: NE & E*, 1983, 390
2.	?1839	John McDivitt	Bishopsbourne, Kent	S	*Gunnis* 1968, 220
3.	?1844	Hannah Woolley	Smarden, Kent	S	*Gunnis* 1968, 220

JONES, James, of Abergavenny fl 1781?

Funerary Monuments

1.	?1781	Mrs Jenkings	Abergavenny, Monmouths	*Gunnis* 1968, 220

JONES, James, of Bristol fl 1774–94

The son of William Jones, a mason of Bristol, he became a freeman of that city on 6 December 1774. In 1782 he received £18 from Lord Radnor for work at Longford Castle (Archives, Earl of Radnor, in *Gunnis* 1968, 220). He signs two monuments in Somerset. Gunnis suggests that may have been one of the partners in the firms of **Jones, Dunn and Tyley** and **Jones, Dunn and Drewett**. However, Dale-Jones and Lloyd indicate that it was **Henry Jones** who worked with **John Dunn** and **William Drewett.**

Literary References: *Gunnis* 1968, 220; *Dale-Jones and Lloyd* 1989, 49

Archival References: BRO, Burgess Books 04359, microfiche FC/BB/1(t) 4, fol 114

Funerary Monuments

1.	?1788	Sarah Exon	Creech St Michael, Somerset	S	*Gunnis* 1968, 220
2.	†1794	Peter Coates	Stanton Drew, Somerset	S	Pevsner, *Somerset: N & Bristol*, 1958, 262

JONES, John Edward 1806–62

Jones was born in Dublin on 2 May, 1806, the son of Edward Jones, a miniature-painter. He trained as a civil engineer under Alexander Nimmo and was employed with him on various important works in Ireland, including the building of Waterford Bridge, 1829–32. He later went to London to work as an engineer, a profession he abandoned for sculpture in 1840, making 'within a marvellously short space of time wonderful progress in that art' (*Lit Gaz*, 16 Nov 1844, 738).

Jones exhibited at the Royal Hibernian Academy between 1847 and 1854 and at the Royal Academy in London, 1842–62, showing more than 100 works, most of them portrait busts. Several of these received favourable reviews. When he showed a bust of Sir Henry Pottinger (**31**) in 1846, the *Art Union* critic wrote: 'The features bear a very marked resemblance to the life; they are endowed with an energy and firmness of purpose which sort most perfectly with the known character of Sir Henry Pottinger. There are few works of this kind which, in severe eloquence, are at all compatible with this bust' (*AU*, 1846, 189). Jones sent *The favourite*, a seated statue of a girl with a dog, to the Great Exhibition in 1851 (**2**). It was praised in the *Art Journal Catalogue*, which noted 'a natural simplicity about the figure that renders it extremely pleasing . . . the drapery is tastefully disposed, and the entire composition is altogether graceful and attractive' (*AJ Cat* 1851, 279). The sculptor also sent works to the Dublin Exhibition of 1853 and the International Exhibition held in London in 1862. His only recorded public statue is a figure of Sir Robert Ferguson erected in Londonderry in 1862 (**8**).

He died whilst on a visit to Finglas, near Dublin, on 25 July 1862. He was described as possessing 'a kind, courteous and generous disposition', while 'in wit, humour and vivacity he was a thorough Irishman' (*AJ*, 1862, 207).

Literary References: *Strickland* 1, 1913, 557–60; *Gunnis* 1968, 220–1

Statues

1.	1851	Countess of Landsfelt	m	[Exhib RA, London, 1302]; untraced	*Graves* IV, 1905–6, 275
2.	1851	The favourite (a portrait)		[Gt Exhib, London]; untraced	*AJ Cat* 1851, 279 (repr)
3.	1853	William Dargan		[Industrial Exhib, Dublin]; untraced	*ILN*, 4 June 1853, 464 (repr)
4.	1854	Arthur, 1st Duke of Wellington, model for an equestrian statue		[Exhib RHA, Dublin, 317]; untraced	*Stewart* 2, 1985, 126
5.	1855	Duke of Cambridge, sketch		[Exhib RA, London, 1428]; untraced	*Graves* IV, 1905–6, 276

6.	1855	Lord Jocelyn, sketch		[Exhib RA, London, 1438]; untraced		*Graves* IV, 1905–6, 276
7.	post-1860	Unidentified figure, statuette	p	NGI 8208	SD	*le Harivel* 1988, 572 (repr);
8.	1862	Sir Robert Ferguson MP		Londonderry		*Strickland* I, 1913, 558, 559; *Gunnis* 1968, 221

Busts

9.	1842	James Walker		[Exhib RA, London, 1353]; untraced		*Graves* IV, 1905–6, 274
10.	1843	J S Moore		Edinburgh University Library	SD	C Lib (repr)
11.	1844	Dr McNeil		[Exhib RA, London, 1316]; untraced		*Graves* IV, 1905–6, 275; *Strickland* I, 1913, 559
12.	1844	Espartero		[Exhib RA, London, 1401]; untraced		*AU*, 1844, 171; *Graves* IV, 1905–6, 275
13.	1844	G Roe		[Exhib RA, London, 1362]; untraced		*Graves* IV, 1905–6, 275; *Strickland* I, 1913, 559
14.	1844	J Tenier		[Exhib RA, London, 1338]; untraced		*Graves* IV, 1905–6, 275
15.	1844	King Louis Philippe		[Exhib RA, London, 1339]; untraced		*Graves* IV, 1905–6, 275
16.	1844	Lady Talbot de Malahide		[Exhib RA, London, 1370]; untraced		*Graves* IV, 1905–6, 275
17.	1844	Rev Hugh McNeil		[Exhib RA, London, 1366]; untraced		*Graves* IV, 1905–6, 275; *Strickland* I, 1913, 559
18.	1844	Sir William Magnay Model(s): RA, London, 1845, 1385	m	Palace of Versailles, France		*Graves* IV, 1905–6, 275; *Strickland* I, 1913, 559
19.	1845	Alexander Nimmo	m	RDS, Dublin	SD	*White and Bright* 1998, 55
20.	1845	Dr D W Cooke Taylor		[Exhib RA, London, 1417]; untraced		*Graves* IV, 1905–6, 275
21.	1845	Henry, 3rd Lord Rossmore, model		[Exhib RA, London, 1371]; untraced		*Graves* IV, 1905–6, 275; *Strickland* I, 1913, 560
22.	1845	John, 8th Earl of Scarborough	m	[Exhib RA, London, 1364]; untraced		*Graves* IV, 1905–6, 275
23.	1845	Lord Denman	m	Lincoln's Inn, London	SD	*Graves* IV, 1905–6, 275
24.	1845	Signora Favanti		[Exhib RA, London, 1393]; untraced		*Graves* IV, 1905–6, 275; *Gunnis* 1968, 221
25.	1846	A Anderson	m	[Exhib RA, London, 1448]; untraced		*Graves* IV, 1905–6, 275
26.	1846	Baboo Dwarkanaght Tagore	m	[Exhib RA, London, 1458]; untraced		*AU*, 1846, 189; *Graves* IV, 1905–6, 275
27.	1846	Daniel O'Connell	m	NGI 8071 Other versions: NPG, 1843 Reform Club, London, 1846	SD	*AU*, 1844, 171; *Graves* IV, 1905–6, 275; *Ormond* 1973, 348 (repr 682); *Wynne and White* 1975, 23
28.	1846	Michael William Balfe, model		[Exhib RA, London, 1508]; untraced		*Strickland* I, 1913, 558; *Graves* IV, 1905–6, 275
29.	1846	Mrs Thomas Saunders	m	[Exhib RA, London, 1487]; untraced		*Graves* IV, 1905–6, 275
30.	1846	Pierce Mahony	m	[Exhib RA, London, 1467]; untraced		*AU*, 1846, 189; *Graves* IV, 1905–6, 275; *Stewart* 2, 1985, 126
31.	1846	Sir Henry Pottinger, model		[Exhib RA, London, 1450]; untraced		*AU*, 1846, 189; *Graves* IV, 1905–6, 275
32.	1846	Sir William Betham	m	Office of Arms, Dublin Castle		*Graves* IV, 1905–6, 275; *Strickland* I, 1913, 558
33.	1846	Thomas Saunders	m	[Exhib RA, London, 1445]; untraced		*Graves* IV, 1905–6, 275
34.	1847	Dr Alderson (to be placed in the hospital at Hull)	m	[Exhib RA, London, 1400]; untraced		*Graves* IV, 1905–6, 275
35.	1847	Hon Miss Copley	m	[Exhib RA, London, 1361]; untraced		*Graves* IV, 1905–6, 275
36.	1847	Mr Parker	m	[Exhib RA, London, 1349]; untraced		*AU*, 1847, 200; *Graves* IV, 1905–6, 275
37.	1847	Richard Paterson	m	[Exhib RA, London, 1358]; untraced		*AU*, 1847, 200; *Graves* IV, 1905–6, 275
38.	1847	Unidentified gentleman	m	[Exhib RHA, Dublin, 475]; untraced		*Stewart* 2, 1985, 126
39.	1848	J Fisher	m	[Exhib RA, London, 1387]; untraced		*Graves* IV, 1905–6, 275
40.	1848	James Thompson	m	[Exhib RA, London, 1425]; untraced		*Graves* IV, 1905–6, 275
41.	1848	King of Holland		[Exhib RA, London, 1374]; untraced		*Graves* IV, 1905–6, 275
42.	1848	Lord Hyde, model		[Exhib RA, London, 1333]; untraced		*Graves* IV, 1905–6, 275
43.	1848	Sir John MacNeil	m	[Exhib RA, London, 1454]; untraced		*Graves* IV, 1905–6, 275
44.	1849	Sir Richard Morrison, model		[Exhib RA, London, 1278]; untraced		*Graves* IV, 1905–6, 275; *Strickland* I, 1913, 559
45.	1850	Countess of Landsfelt	m	[Exhib RA, London, 1354]; untraced		*Graves* IV, 1905–6, 275
46.	1850	Sir Herbert Edwardes CB		[Exhib RA, London, 1384]; untraced		*Graves* IV, 1905–6, 275; *Ormond* 1973, 157
47.	1850	Thomas Brassy	m	[Exhib RA, London, 1397]; untraced		*Graves* IV, 1905–6, 275
48.	1850	Unidentified gentleman	m	[Exhib RA, London, 1423]; untraced		*Graves* IV, 1905–6, 275
49.	1850	Unidentified lady	m	[Exhib RA, London, 1355]; untraced		*Graves* IV, 1905–6, 275
50.	1851	Bryan Waller Procter		[Exhib RA, London, 1363]; untraced		*Graves* IV, 1905–6, 275
51.	1851	'His Excellency the Ambassador from the Court of Nepaul'		[Exhib RA, London, 1367]; untraced		*Graves* IV, 1905–6, 275
52.	1851	James Wallack		[Exhib RA, London, 1368]; untraced		*Graves* IV, 1905–6, 275
53.	1851	Sir Elkanah Armitage		[Exhib RA, London, 1357]; untraced		*Graves* IV, 1905–6, 275
54.	1851	Unidentified artist		[Exhib RA, London, 1365]; untraced		*Graves* IV, 1905–6, 275
55.	1851	Unidentified gentleman	m	[Sotheby, London, 16 May 1996, lot 300]; untraced	SD	
56.	1852	Arthur L Guinness		[Exhib RHA, Dublin, 352]; untraced		*Stewart* 2, 1985, 126
57.	1852	Captain Robert Williams		[Exhib RHA, Dublin, 370]; untraced		*Stewart* 2, 1985, 126
58.	1852	Edward Jones		[Exhib RHA, Dublin, 388]; untraced		*Stewart* 2, 1985, 126
59.	1852	George, 4th Earl of Clarendon		[coll William Dargan]; coll Earl of Bessborough (1913)		*ILN*, 19 June 1852, 494 (repr); *Graves* IV, 1905–6, 275, 276; *Stewart* 2, 1985, 126
60.	1852	James Gwynne	m	[Exhib RA, London, 1482]; untraced		*Graves* IV, 1905–6, 275
61.	1852	James Perry		[Exhib RHA, Dublin, 386]; untraced		*Stewart* 2, 1985, 126
62.	1852	John Day Barry	m	[Exhib RA, London, 1420]; untraced		*Graves* IV, 1905–6, 275
63.	1852	Prince Louis Napoleon		[Exhib RA, London, 1404]; untraced		*Graves* IV, 1905–6, 275
64.	1852	Sir Charles Fox	m	[Exhib RA, London, 1380]; untraced		*Graves* IV, 1905–6, 275

No.	Date	Subject		Details		Literary references
65.	1852	Unidentified child		[Exhib RHA, Dublin, 389]; untraced		*Stewart* 2, 1985, 126
66.	1852	William Anketel	m	[Exhib RA, London, 1417]; untraced		*Strickland* I, 1913, 558; *Graves* IV, 1905–6, 275
67.	1852	William Fairbairn	m	[Exhib RA, London, 1487]; untraced		*Graves* IV, 1905–6, 275
68.	1853	Albert Smith		[Exhib RA, London, 1384]; untraced		*Graves* IV, 1905–6, 275
69.	1853	Alfred Pett MD		[Exhib RA, London, 1381]; untraced		*Graves* IV, 1905–6, 275
70.	1853	Archibald, 13th Earl of Eglinton		coll Earl of Bessborough (1913) Other versions: exhib RA, London, 1854, 1442, marble; untraced		*Graves* IV, 1905–6, 275, 276; *Strickland* I, 1913, 559
71.	1853	Charles Lever		[Dublin Int Exhib]; untraced		*Strickland* I, 1913, 559
72.	1853	Colley Grattan		[Dublin Int Exhib]; untraced		*Strickland* I, 1913, 559
73.	1853	Dr Lyons		[Dublin Int Exhib]; untraced		*Strickland* I, 1913, 559
74.	1853	Dr Waller		[Dublin Int Exhib]; untraced		*Strickland* I, 1913, 560
75.	1853	Duke of Cambridge		[Exhib RA, London, 1429]; untraced		*Graves* IV, 1905–6, 276
76.	pre-1853	Earl of St Germans		[coll William Dargan]; coll Earl of Bessborough (1913)		*Strickland* I, 1913, 560
77.	1853	George Petrie		[Exhib RHA, Dublin, 468]; untraced		*Stewart* 2, 1985, 126
78.	1853	J M'Glashen		[Dublin Int Exhib]; untraced		*Strickland* I, 1913, 559
79.	1853	Lady McNeil		[Dublin Int Exhib]; untraced		*Strickland* I, 1913, 559
80.	1853	Master Telford Tennent Jones		[Exhib RA, London, 1386]; untraced		*Graves* IV, 1905–6, 275
81.	1853	Miss Gernon		[Dublin Int Exhib]; untraced		*Strickland* I, 1913, 559
82.	1853	Mrs Cogan		[Dublin Int Exhib]; untraced		*Strickland* I, 1913, 559
83.	1853	Mrs Dargan		[coll William Dargan]; untraced		*Strickland* I, 1913, 559
84.	1853	Rev Dr Henry		[Dublin Int Exhib]; untraced		*Strickland* I, 1913, 559
85.	pre-1853	Rev Dr W D Sadleir		coll Rev F Sadleir (1913)		*Strickland* I, 1913, 560
86.	1853	Rev Peter Daly		[Dublin Int Exhib]; untraced		*Strickland* I, 1913, 559
87.	1853	Sir Henry Marsh		[Dublin Int Exhib]; untraced		*Strickland* I, 1913, 559
88.	1853	Sir Robert Kane		[Dublin Int Exhib]; untraced		*Strickland* I, 1913, 559
89.	1853	Sir Thomas Deane		[Dublin Int Exhib]; untraced		*Strickland* I, 1913, 559
90.	1853	Sir William Barrington		[Dublin Int Exhib]; untraced		*Strickland* I, 1913, 558
91.	1853	Sir William Hackett		[Dublin Int Exhib]; untraced		*Strickland* I, 1913, 559
92.	1853	Surgeon Cusack		[Dublin Int Exhib]; untraced		*Strickland* I, 1913, 559
93.	1853	Surgeon Rynd		[Dublin Int Exhib]; untraced		*Strickland* I, 1913, 560
94.	1853	William H Ford Cogan		[Exhib RHA, Dublin, 461]; untraced		*Stewart* 2, 1985, 126
95.	1854	Albert, the Prince Consort, model		[Exhib RA, London, 1367]; untraced Other versions: executed in marble for presentation to William Dargan exhib RHA, Dublin, 1854, 293, marble		*Graves* IV, 1905–6, 276; *Ormond* 1973, 13; *Stewart* 2, 1985, 126
96.	1854	Countess of Eglinton	m	coll Earl of Bessborough (1913)		*ILN*, 19 June 1852, 494 (repr); *Graves* IV, 1905–6, 276; *Strickland* I, 1913, 559
97.	1854	Hon Lewis Wingfield	m	coll Viscount Powerscourt (1913)		*Graves* IV, 1905–6, 276; *Strickland* I, 1913, 560
98.	1854	Hugh, Viscount Gough	m	[Exhib RHA, Dublin, 264]; untraced		*Stewart* 2, 1985, 126
99.	1854	Queen Victoria		National Gallery of Ireland, Dublin Other versions: model exhib RA, London, 1854, 1366 (executed in marble for presentation to William Dargan) exhib RHA, Dublin, 1854, 294, marble		*Graves* IV, 1905–6, 276; *Gunnis* 1968, 221; *Stewart* 2, 1985, 126
100.	1854	Sir John Patterson		[Exhib RA, London, 1438]; untraced		*Graves* IV, 1905–6, 276
101.	1854	Unidentified lady	m	[Exhib RHA, Dublin, 265]; untraced		*Stewart* 2, 1985, 126
102.	1854	William Dargan	m	[Given to Dargan by Queen Victoria]; NGI 8204 Other versions: NGI 8111, plaster	SD	*le Harivel* 1988, 572 (repr); *Wynne and White* 1975, 23
103.	1855	Madame Grisi		[Exhib RA, London, 1531]; untraced		*Graves* IV, 1905–6, 276
104.	1855	Miss Blyth		[Exhib RA, London, 1483]; untraced		*Graves* IV, 1905–6, 276
105.	1855	Mrs Turquand		[Exhib RA, London, 1466]; untraced		*Graves* IV, 1905–6, 276
106.	1855	Thomas Haliburton		[Exhib RA, London, 1526]; untraced		*Graves* IV, 1905–6, 276
107.	1855	William Keogh	m	[Exhib RA, London, 1473]; untraced		*Graves* IV, 1905–6, 276
108.	1856	J P Giustiani	m	[Exhib RA, London, 1362]; untraced		*Graves* IV, 1905–6, 276
109.	1856	Sir Alexander Cockburn Bt	m	[Exhib RA, London, 1355]; untraced		*Graves* IV, 1905–6, 276; *Ormond* 1973, 109
110.	1856	Unidentified young lady		[Exhib RA, London, 1350]; untraced		*Graves* IV, 1905–6, 276
111.	1857	Colonel Brownrigg		[Exhib RA, London, 1255]; untraced		*Graves* IV, 1905–6, 276
112.	1857	Colonel J Macdonald		[Exhib RA, London, 1332]; untraced		*Graves* IV, 1905–6, 276
113.	1857	General Sir George Browne	m	[Exhib RA, London, 1339]; untraced		*Graves* IV, 1905–6, 276
114.	1857	Hugh, Viscount Gough KG		[Exhib RA, London, 1328]; untraced		*Graves* IV, 1905–6, 276; *Ormond* 1973, 192
115.	1857	John Gibson	b	[Exhib RA, London, 1347]; untraced		*Graves* IV, 1905–6, 276; *Ormond* 1973, 187
116.	1857	Sir Samuel Martin		[Exhib RA, London, 1283]; untraced		*Graves* IV, 1905–6, 276
117.	1858	Colonel Caulfield	m	[Exhib RA, London, 1243]; untraced		*Graves* IV, 1905–6, 276
118.	1858	Colonel Cust	m	[Exhib RA, London, 1300]; untraced		*Graves* IV, 1905–6, 276
119.	1858	George Waddington	m	Durham Cathedral, Dean and Chapter Library		Pevsner, *Durham*, 1983, 204
120.	1858	Lord Adolphus Vane Tempest	m	[Exhib RA, London, 1299]; untraced		*Graves* IV, 1905–6, 276
121.	1858	Miss Foster		[Exhib RA, London, 1208]; untraced		*Graves* IV, 1905–6, 276; *Ormond* 1973, 187
122.	1858	Miss Ingram	m	[Exhib RA, London, 1314]; untraced		*Graves* IV, 1905–6, 276
123.	1858	Rev Mr Bellew		[Exhib RA, London, 1215]; untraced		*Graves* IV, 1905–6, 276
124.	1858	Shirley Brooks		[Exhib RA, London, 1288]; untraced		*Graves* IV, 1905–6, 276
125.	1858	William Henry Russell		[Exhib RA, London, 1285]; untraced		*Graves* IV, 1905–6, 276; *Strickland* I, 1913, 560

126. 1859	Arthur, 4th Marquess of Downshire		[Exhib RA, London, 1289]; untraced		*Graves* IV, 1905–6, 276; *Strickland* I, 1913, 559
127. 1859	Henry, 1st Lord Brougham and Vaux	p	Castle Howard, N R Yorks Other versions: exhib RA, London, 1859, 1299 exhib RA, London, 1860, 973, marble	S	*Graves* IV, 1905–6, 276
128. 1859	S Bateson		[Exhib RA, London, 1369]; untraced		*Graves* IV, 1905–6, 276; *Strickland* I, 1913, 558
129. 1860	E N Dennys		[Exhib RA, London, 966]; untraced		*Graves* IV, 1905–6, 276
130. 1860	Henry Allsop	m	[Exhib RA, London, 969]; untraced		*Graves* IV, 1905–6, 276
131. 1860	Lord Arthur Hay		[Exhib RA, London, 964]; untraced		*Graves* IV, 1905–6, 276
132. 1860	Mrs Henry Allsop	m	[Exhib RA, London, 1024]; untraced		*Graves* IV, 1905–6, 276
133. 1860	Unidentified gentleman	m	[Exhib RA, London, 1040]; untraced		*Graves* IV, 1905–6, 276
134. 1861	Frederick Slight	m	[Exhib RA, London, 1043]; untraced		*Graves* IV, 1905–6, 276
135. 1861	Henry, 3rd Viscount Palmerston		[Exhib RA, London, 1094]; untraced		*Graves* IV, 1905–6, 276
136. 1861	Thomas Bateson		[Exhib RA, London, 1074]; untraced		*Graves* IV, 1905–6, 276; *Strickland* I, 1913, 558
137. 1861	Torrens M'Cullagh		[Exhib RA, London, 1087]; untraced		*Graves* IV, 1905–6, 276
138. 1862	A K Bristow MP		[Exhib RA, London, 1100]; untraced		*Graves* IV, 1905–6, 276
139. 1862	Charles, 3rd Marquess of Londonderry		[Exhib RA, London, 1096]; untraced		*Graves* IV, 1905–6, 276; *Strickland* I, 1913, 559
140. pre-1862	George, 7th Earl of Carlisle		[coll William Dargan]; coll Earl of Bessborough (1913)		*Gunnis* 1968, 221
141. 1862	John Adam Malet		Trinity College, Dublin, Long Room		*Crookshank* 1986, 25
142. 1862	S Kincaid		[Exhib RA, London, 1090]; untraced		*Graves* IV, 1905–6, 276
143. nd	John Fitch Jnr	m	Walker, Liverpool		*Gunnis* 1968, 221
144. nd	Sir Robert Peel	b	Birmingham Art Gall		*Ormond* 1973, 373
Miscellaneous					
145. 1847	Morning visitors (portraits)		[Exhib RA, London, 1332]; untraced		*Graves* IV, 1905–6, 275
146. 1847	The guardian (portraits of the children of W McCormick of Bootle Hall, Liverpool)		[Exhib RA, London, 1389]; untraced		*Graves* IV, 1905–6, 275
147. 1850	Children and animals (portraits of the sons of Thomas Brassy)		[Exhib RA, London, 1310]; untraced		*Graves* IV, 1905–6, 275; *Gunnis* 1968, 221
148. 1851	Baron Meyer de Rothschild on his hunter Oscar		[Exhib RA, London, 1303]; untraced		*Graves* IV, 1905–6, 275
149. 1851	'Twenty-eighth of June 1815' (portrait of Arthur, 1st Duke of Wellington)		[Exhib RA, London, 1280]; untraced		*Graves* IV, 1905–6, 275

JONES, John, of Carmarthen 1753–1831

Jones appears to have been in business at premises 'near the church' in Church Street, Carmarthen, by 1796, when his name appears in a rate assessment. His only known work is a plain black marble casket in Llangunnor church. A worn and barely legible tombstone in St Peter's churchyard commemorates his two sons and his wife, Mary, who died in 1809 aged 66. Jones appears to have been quietly successful in his craft. His house was surveyed at £6 10s in the 1819 rate book, while a ledger of the first Carmarthen Savings Bank shows that he had £50 in his account in 1822 and that this had increased to £196 by 1828. He contributed small sums to the subscriptions for **E H Baily**'s Picton monument and St Paul's church. He was described as 'A man much respected by all who knew him' after his death, aged 78, in 1831 (*Carmarthen Journal*, cited by *Dale-Jones and Lloyd* 1989, 51).

Literary References: *Dale-Jones and Lloyd* 1989, 51

Funerary Monuments

1. †1823	Harriet James		Llangunnor, Carmarthen		*Dale-Jones and Lloyd* 1989, 51

JONES, R, of Swindon fl 1778–80

Jones is currently known only for one wall-tablet in coloured marbles. In 1780 he was working as a mason at Longford Castle (Archives, Earl of Radnor, in *Gunnis* 1968, 221).

Funerary Monuments

1. 1778	Thomas Cox		Shrivenham, Berks	S	*Gunnis* 1968, 221

JONES, Richard, of Wapping fl 1718–20

A citizen and mason of Mark Lane, Wapping, he worked at St Alphege, Greenwich, 1718–20. An Oliver Jones, son of Richard Jones of Mark Lane, 'Citizen and Mason', was apprenticed to his father in 1773.

Literary References: *Gunnis* 1968, 221

Archival References: Masons' Co, Court Book 1751–96 (30 Sept 1773)

Architectural Sculpture

1. 1718–1720	Capitals	s	St Alfege, Greenwich, London		*Gunnis* 1968, 221

JONES, Robert –1722

In 1696 Jones was paid £232 for 'carving in Portland stone and Marble' at Trinity Almshouses, Stepney (**1**). There was a much ornamental work at the almshouses, which were badly damaged during the Second World War. **John Waring** was also employed there and it is impossible to know which sculptor was responsible for the various decorative details, but Jones may have executed the magnificent carving for the pediment of the central bay on the east side, which has a coat of arms surrounded by swags of foliage and nautical instruments. In 1711 he was paid £50 3s 9d for further work at the almshouses (Trinity House Archives in GPC).

From 1698 until his death 24 years later he was employed at the Royal Hospital, Greenwich, where he was responsible for all the significant decorative carving on the King William and Queen Anne Buildings (**3**). Among the major items were, in 1698, 'a large ornament, being festoons of drapery and flowers on the west front of the new building' and 'a large pediment in basso-relievo over the west entrance containing the King's Arms held up by two genii with trophies and ornaments relating to marine affairs, 30 ft. long and 7 ft. 9 in. high imbosst'. For the latter

Jones received £80 (TNA ADM 68/672). In 1702 he provided four large Ionic capitals for the east front of the west dormitory 'with large festoons hanging out of the scrolls cut with several sorts of shellfish containing eight sides at £20 a side, and also four large keystones over the entrance into the vestibule of the hall and south dormitory', costing £44, 'being riverheads dressed with flags and water-flowers'. In the following year he was paid £51 for the cornice inside the cupola 'cut with sprigs of foliage, water leaves and husks' and £20 for the two large spandrels in the cupola (TNA ADM 68/676). Further payments for capitals, columns, pilasters, scrolls, festoons, ornaments for chimneypieces, coats of arms and other ornaments followed (TNA ADM 68/677–699). Between 1700 and 1704 he carved a series of relief heads for the upper window sills of the Painted Hall, which were not finally needed (2). Two have been set into a chimneypiece in the Dining Room under the Chapel but the rest are in store.

Jones died in 1722 and his will, which was proved on 9 May that year, describes him as a 'Carver of Stepney, Middlesex'. He was a captain in the City trained bands.

Literary References: *Gunnis* 1968, 221; *Bold* 2000, 48–9

Archival References: GPC

Will: PROB 11/585

Architectural Sculpture

1.	1696	Carved work Payment(s): £332	Trinity Almshouses, Stepney, London		Trinity House archives in GPC
2.	1700–1704	Neptune, Galatea and lions, relief heads	Royal Hospital, Greenwich, London, undercroft store (two incorporated into dining room chimneypiece)		*Bold* 2000, 48–9 (repr)
3.	1698–1722	Decorative carving	Royal Hospital, Greenwich, London, King William and Queen Anne buildings		*Gunnis* 1968, 221

JONES, T fl *c*1780–82

Funerary Monuments

1.	†1780	Thomas Williams	Llanfrynach, Brecon	S	Pevsner, *Powys*, 1979, 346
2.	†1782	William Lewis	Llangattock, Brecon	S	Pevsner, *Powys*, 1979, 346

JONES, T, of Cusop fl *c*1816

Funerary Monuments

1.	†1816	Mary Price	Llanstephan, Radnor	S	Pevsner, *Powys*, 1979, 235

JONES, Watkin D fl 1846–52

He was born at Merthyr in Wales, the son of the parish clerk. He exhibited at the Royal Academy between 1846 and 1859 from 27 Clipstone Street, 14 Carburton Street, 42 Cirencester Place and 39 Arlington Street, Mornington Crescent.

Literary References: *Graves* IV, 1905–6, 281; *Gunnis* 1968, 221

Busts

1.	1854	T E Evans		[Exhib RA, London, 1404]; untraced	*Graves* IV, 1905–6, 281; *Gunnis* 1968, 221
2.	1858	Unidentified lady		[Exhib RA, London, 1235]; untraced	*Graves* IV, 1905–6, 281
3.	1859	Ideal bust of a warrior	m	[Exhib RA, London, 1235]; untraced	*Graves* IV, 1905–6, 281
4.	1859	Unidentified subject		[Exhib LSFA, Liverpool, 775]; untraced	*Morris and Roberts* 1998, 356

Reliefs

5.	1846	Rev James Bennett, medallion		[Exhib RA, London, 1462]; untraced	*Graves* IV, 1905–6, 281
6.	1853	Unidentified gentleman, medallion		[Exhib RA, London, 1455]; untraced	*Graves* IV, 1905–6, 281

Miscellaneous

7.	1852	Pity		[Exhib RA, London, 1372]; untraced	*Graves* IV, 1905–6, 281
8.	1854	G V Brooke		[Exhib RA, London, 1405]; untraced	*Graves* IV, 1905–6, 281
9.	1854	Infant Napoleon		[Exhib RA, London, 1387]; untraced	*Graves* IV, 1905–6, 281
10.	1856	Infant Napoleon and eagle		[Exhib RA, London, 1237]; untraced	*Graves* IV, 1905–6, 281
11.	1859	Little Jessie		[Exhib RA, London, 1237]; untraced	*Graves* IV, 1905–6, 281

JONES, William fl 1843–47

The brother of **Watkin Jones.** After leaving Merthyr for London he found employment in the studio of **Joseph Edwards.** He exhibited at the Royal Academy, 1843–47, and carved a statue of *The Prince of Bards* for the Eisteddfod of 1845, at Abergavenny (1). His address was 27 Clipstone Street, London.

Literary References: *Graves* IV, 1905–6, 281; *Gunnis* 1968, 221

Statues

1.	1845	Taliesin pen Beirdd (Prince of the Bards)		[Exhib Eisteddfod, Abergavenny]; untraced	*ILN*, 25 Oct 1845, 265 (repr); *Graves* IV, 1905–6, 281

Busts

2.	1843	Caswallon	m	[Exhib RA, London, 1433]; untraced	*Graves* IV, 1905–6, 281
3.	1844	Thomas Bevan MD		[Exhib RA, London, 1369]; untraced	*Graves* IV, 1905–6, 281
4.	1845	John Fothergill MD	m	[Exhib RA, London, 1401]; untraced	*Graves* IV, 1905–6, 281
5.	1845	Rev James Bennett		[Exhib RA, London, 1390]; untraced Other versions: exhib RA, London, 1847, 1443, marble	*Graves* IV, 1905–6, 281
6.	1846	James Risdon Bennett MD		[Exhib RA, London, 1472]; untraced	*Graves* IV, 1905–6, 281
7.	1846	Joseph Gurney (son of Thomas Bevan) Model(s): exhib RA, London, 1845, 1376	m	[Exhib RA, London, 1469]; untraced	*Graves* IV, 1905–6, 281
8.	1846	Mohun Lall		[Exhib RA, London, 1493]; untraced	*Graves* IV, 1905–6, 281
9.	1847	Elizabeth Jane, daughter of David Evans	m	[Exhib RA, London, 1353]; untraced	*Graves* IV, 1905–6, 281
10.	1847	Ralph Brown		[Exhib RA, London, 1354]; untraced	*Graves* IV, 1905–6, 281
11.	1847	Ralph Lindsay		[Exhib RA, London, 1440]; untraced	*Graves* IV, 1905–6, 281

Reliefs

12.	1845	Jacob's vision		[Exhib RA, London, 1360]; untraced		*Graves* IV, 1905–6, 281

JONES, William, of Llanstephan fl *c*1787

Funerary Monuments

1.	†1787	Mary Price		Glascwm, Powys	S	Pevsner, *Powys*, 1979, 235

JONES, DUNN & DREWETT, of Bristol

See **William Drewett of Bristol**

JONES, DUNN & TYLEY, of Bristol fl 1786?–*c*1803

Funerary Monuments

1.	?1786	Ann Hillhouse		St Philip and St Jacob, Bristol	S	*Gunnis* 1968, 220
2.	†1803	John Savage		St Mary, Tetbury, Glos	S	Pevsner, *Glos: Cotswolds*, 1999, 686

JOPLING, Joseph and Isaac, of Gateshead fl *c*1776–1824

Joseph Jopling was 'a stonecutter', described as being of Newcastle, when his death at Richmond, N R Yorks, at the age of 36 was reported in the *Cumberland Pacquet* on 24 September 1811. His son Isaac won a silver palette from the Society of Arts for a plaster cast, 'a copy of the Gladiator' in 1811 (17). Isaac Jopling assisted his father and signed some of the later monuments and tablets, which are pleasant, simple works with good details.

Literary References: RSA Transactions, vol 29, 1811, 23; *Gunnis* 1968, 221–2

Funerary Monuments

1.	†1776	Rev T Orde and Sarah Orde (by Isaac Jopling)		Kirknewton, Northumbs	S	Pevsner, *Northumbs*, 1992, 367
2.	1782	Anne Williamson		Whickham, Durham		Pevsner, *Durham*, 1983, 502
3.	1792	Jacob Clavering		Whickham, Co Durham		Pevsner, *Durham*, 1983, 502
4.	1796	Percy Clennell		Alwinton, Northumbs		Pevsner, *Northumbs*, 1992, 145
5.	?1797	Richard Brewster		Greatham, Durham	S	*Gunnis* 1968, 222
6.	?1799	Anne Musgrave		Chester-le-Street, Durham	S	*Gunnis* 1968, 222
7.	?*c*1800	Richard Dawes		Heworth, Durham	S	*Gunnis* 1968, 222
8.	†1800	William Alder		Norham, Northumbs		Pevsner, *Northumbs*, 1992, 524
9.	?1806	Ralph Carr		Ponteland, Durham		*Gunnis* 1968, 222
10.	?1807	Margaret Maxwell		Bishop Auckland, Durham	S	*Gunnis* 1968, 222
11.	†1810	Mary Orde		Norham, Northumbs	S	Pevsner, *Northumbs*, 1992, 524
12.	†1817	John Carr (by Isaac Jopling)		Whickham, Durham	S	Pevsner, *Durham*, 1983, 502
13.	?1820	Hon Mary Smith (by Isaac Jopling)		Gateshead, Durham	S	*Gunnis* 1968, 222
14.	?1821	Thomas Headlam (by Isaac Jopling)		Gateshead, Durham		*Gunnis* 1968, 222
15.	1822	Unidentified subject, tablet (by Isaac Jopling)		Christ Church, North Shields, Northumbs		Pevsner, *Northumbs*, 1992, 526
16.	1824	Unidentified subject, tablet (by Isaac Jopling)		Wooler, Northumbs		Pevsner, *Northumbs*, 1992, 634

Statues

17.	1811	The gladiator (by Isaac Jopling)	p	[Soc of A, silver palette]; untraced	S	RSA *Transactions*, vol 29, 1811, 23

JORDAN, John fl 1699–1706

Probably a local mason, he was responsible for stonework in the gardens of Melbourne Hall, Derbys in 1699.

Literary References: *Gunnis* 1968, 222

Miscellaneous

1.	1699	Pedestals, pilasters, staircases and other work	s	Melbourne Hall, Derbys		*Gunnis* 1968, 222, citing archives, Marquess of Lothian

JORDEN, G fl 1835–42

He exhibited at the Royal Academy, 1835–42, and showed a wax miniature at the Society of British Artists in 1839 (4). His given address was Woburn Terrace, New Road, London.

Literary References: *Strickland* 1, 1913, 566; *Johnson* 1975, 262

Reliefs

1.	1835	E Jackson, 'medallic portrait'		[Exhib RA, London, 1024]; untraced		*Graves* IV, 1905–6, 284
2.	1836	Miss Stanhope, 'medallic portrait'		[Exhib RA, London, 989]; untraced		*Graves* IV, 1905–6, 284
3.	1842	Unidentified gentleman, 'medallic portrait'		[Exhib RA, London, 1191]; untraced		*Graves* IV, 1905–6, 284

Miscellaneous

4.	1839	Mrs Jackson	w	[Exhib Soc of BA, London, 762]; untraced		*Johnson* 1975, 262
5.	1841	J Flower Jackson		[Exhib RA, London, 1132]; untraced		*Graves* IV, 1905–6, 284

JORDEN, J S fl 1828

He exhibited 'models in composition' of Daniel O'Connell and the Duke of York at the Royal Hibernian Academy in 1828 (1, 2). Replicas of the O'Connell were issued and there are two of these small scale reliefs in coloured wax on glass in the National Gallery of Ireland. On the back of one of them is a cutting (probably from the *Morning Register*, 7 January 1827) advertising a 'Facsimile of a commissioned model'. Nothing further is known of the artist but he was probably related to **G Jorden**. A Robert Jorden, artist, was living in Sandymount Lane, Dublin, *c*1821.

Literary References: *Strickland* 1, 1913, 566; *Pyke* 1973, 73

Reliefs

1.	1828	Daniel O'Connell, model in composition	[Exhib RHA, Dublin, 281]; untraced Other versions: NGI 183-1944, wax, S (with newspaper cutting) NGI 684-'93, wax, S	*Stewart* 2, 1985, 131; *Pyke* 1973, 72 (pl 146); *le Harivel* 1988, 572 (repr)
2.	1828	Duke of York, model in composition	[Exhib RHA, Dublin, 288]; untraced	*Stewart* 2, 1985, 131

JOSEPH, Samuel 1791–1850

An innovative and individualistic portrait sculptor, he never received proper recognition during his lifetime and died bankrupt. Joseph was born in London, the son of Richard and Lucy Joseph and was christened at St Ann, Blackfriars on 8 April 1791. He became a pupil of **Peter Rouw I** and his first exhibited work at the Royal Academy appears to have been a portrait of his master's child which he showed from 22 Carmarthen Street (**17**). The naturalism and characterisation which distinguishes Joseph's later work may have been a result of this early training in the wax modelling tradition. Joseph entered the Royal Academy Schools in 1811 and won silver medals in 1811 and 1812. In 1815 he was awarded a gold medal for an ideal subject (**145**), and in July 1817 he and another Gold medallist, **E H Baily**, offered themselves unsuccessfully as candidates for the RA travelling scholarship to Rome. In January 1819 Farington noted that Joseph had begun working with a silversmith, Green of Ludgate Hill, producing models after military portraits by Sir Thomas Lawrence. From 1815–21 and perhaps later, his studio was at 68 Newman Street. He appears to have specialised in portrait busts, though few of his early heads have been traced. He evidently found it difficult to break into a market dominated by **Joseph Nollekens** and **Sir Francis Chantrey**, for in 1821 he moved to Edinburgh.

Living first in St George's Square, then in George Street, and finally in Windsor Street, Joseph built up a list of clients composed of Edinburgh's distinguished scientists, writers and academics. Notable early sitters included the eminent theologian Thomas Chalmers (**48**), and the essayist Henry Mackenzie (**52**), whose fragile, shrivelled and bony visage was pitilessly delineated. In 1822 Joseph became involved in the newly-founded Edinburgh Phrenological Society, which was dedicated to the pseudo-science of reading character through cranial bumps. Joseph supplied the society with casts of the heads of several interesting characters, including the murderers Burke and Hare. He also carved busts of two of the society's members, Sir George Mackenzie and Robert Buchan (**54, 70**).

Joseph's sculptural style was individual and sophisticated. Among his recurring interests was the herm form, and he enjoyed exploring the texture of thick, curled, braided or exuberant hair. His heads almost all show an intelligent and innovative engagement with the accepted conventions of the portrait bust and its potential to embody individual character. The head of the surgeon John Barclay, with its thick bushy hair and eyebrows, juts out from his shoulders and twists slightly, as if engaging the viewer in conversation (**67**). Its socle, a plain slab with rectangular grooves, is one of many innovative and unusual forms utilised by the artist. Lady Belhaven, her braided hair forming a halo, tilts her head forward and half-closes her eyes, resembling (but for her patterned shawl) a high renaissance madonna (**79**). For the bust of John Leslie, Joseph chose a strictly frontal pose and uncluttered lines, allowing the bulk of the enormous Professor of Natural Sciences to speak for itself (**53**). The herm bust of Sir Walter Scott, casting his eyes dramatically heavenwards, is a more vital embodiment of Scott's creativity than Chantrey's more famous depiction (**63**).

Joseph continued to exhibit at the Royal Academy in London, and in 1822 he sent six busts to the Northern Society for the Encouragement of the Fine Arts in Leeds. In Edinburgh he exhibited from 1821 at the Institution for the Encouragement of the Fine Arts in Scotland, and it was at his studio that some of the early discussions took place among artists interested in forming a Scottish Academy. When the Academy was opened in 1826 Joseph was a founder member. He attracted extensive patronage and produced busts described by John Murray Graham as 'superior to any examples of sculptural art that had been produced in Scotland previous to his practice' (*Graham* 1871, 448). He failed nonetheless to make a living in Edinburgh, and in 1828 he returned to London, in debt.

In London, Joseph continued to be supported by Scottish clients: he executed naturalistic busts of the grim-faced educationalists Andrew Bell (**106**) and GH Baird, Principal of Edinburgh University (**104**). He also carved busts of famous Englishmen, such as Sir William Huskisson, a posthumous representation of the politician who had recently been crushed to death at the opening of the Liverpool-Manchester railway (**102**). Another notable subject was the President of the Royal Academy, Sir Thomas Lawrence (**97**). He attracted royal patronage, winning the commission for a colossal, excessively flamboyant portrait of the recently deceased George IV (**100**), which was followed by a more staid image of the new king, William IV (**113**).

His most remarkable bust was perhaps of William Wilberforce, which has drawn comparisons with J-A Houdon's celebrated bust of Voltaire (**111**). Joseph made no attempt to idealise the head of the slave trade abolitionist, who had died that year. Instead, Wilberforce's face, with its sagging bottom lip and arched eyebrows, borders on the caricatural. When it was decided to erect a monument to Wilberforce in Westminster Abbey Joseph was selected as sculptor, although he had produced few monuments (**12**). The full-length, cross-legged statue is now considered his masterpiece. The naturalism of the portrait attracted praise and censure: William Bell Scott, writing on the British school of sculpture, felt the work showed 'the peculiar nervous action of the original' (*Scott* 1871, 81). The *Art Journal* considered it to have no pretensions as a work of art 'beyond its remarkable verisimilitude' (*AJ* 1858, 190).

In the early 1840s, whilst living in Upper Charlotte Street, London, Joseph produced a series of commemorative representations of the Scots painter, Sir David Wilkie, whom he had known in Edinburgh. The monument, which has a portrait-medallion (**13**) and the Byronic herm bust (**126**) were followed by a statue funded by subscription, with a pronounced *contrapposto* pose (**14**). Joseph won the commission in competition with **Musgrave Lewthwaite Watson**, though the decision to employ him was not universally popular. The statue itself received a mixed reception. W B Scott regarded it as a 'very able work of art' (*Scott* 1871, 81–2), but another unnamed viewer inverted the criticism levelled at the Wilberforce monument, by condemning the work as 'severely . . . wanting in truth to the personal characteristics of the original' (*Scott, ibid*).

It was perhaps during the 1840s that Joseph sought publicity by staging an exhibition in London 'chiefly of Eminent Scotch Characters executed during his late Residence in Edinburgh' in London, for which he commissioned a catalogue. Tickets were available at his house. The exhibition comprised 67 busts and four sketches or designs for monuments, to the Earl of Hopetoun, William Pitt, the Duke of York and Professor Dugald Stewart (**5–8**). There were also 10 small busts of eminent characters including King George IV, **John Flaxman RA**, and Thomas Stothard, all intended for execution in bronze (**134, 91, 137**) (*Notes and Queries*, 30 July 1910, 81–2).

Joseph and his more successful contemporaries **John Carew** and **William Behnes** all provided sculpture for the Royal Exchange (**139**). Joseph failed to find recognition and never enjoyed a secure income. He exhibited for the last time at the Royal Academy in 1846, and in 1848 became bankrupt, with a debt of £450, which led to a forced sale of his belongings. In 1848 the Council of the Royal Academy awarded him a pension of £30, repeated the following year. He died of cancer on 1 July 1850 at Ryecroft Lodge, Gibson's Hill, Norwood, and is commemorated with an unremarkable tomb-chest in Kensal Green Cemetery. Obituaries were not plentiful, but the *Literary Gazette* paid tribute to his busts, 'of considerable merit' and noted the high esteem in which he was held in Edinburgh (*Lit Gaz*, 27 July 1850, 508). Joseph left seven children and very little money. The Royal Academy granted an annual pension of £10 to his widow, Jane, which continued until her death 13 years later. Dr George Combe's phrenological reading of Joseph's character has survived, but so little is known of the sculptor's life and character that it is impossible to say whether the cranial assessment is close to the truth. The judgment that 'he ought to be no artist' suggests that Combe's exegesis is not a reliable guide (*Friedman* 1980 (1), 20–8).

In 1871 W B Scott noted the curious lack of contemporary accounts of Joseph's life and work, and it remains a mystery why a sculptor of such obvious talent, with a string of notable commissions, should have failed to attain the reputation accorded to his peers. In the late-20th century this neglect has begun to be reversed and articles by Friedman and Pearson have started to revive interest in this undervalued artist.

MGS

Literary References: *Farington*, vol 14, 5061; *Farington*, vol 15, 5311; *Graham* 1871, 448; *Graves* II, 1905–6, 286–8; *Rinder and McKay* 1917, 194–5; *Gunnis* 1968, 332; *Friedman* 1972, 18–25; *Friedman* 1980 (1), 20–8; *Pyke* 1981, 23; *Pearson* 1981, 14–23; *Friedman* 1991, 59–63; *Curl* 2001, 242

Archival References: RA/GA, 1848–49, 1859; AGBI, vol 5, 100 (application made by Jane Joseph, 1860); death certificate of Samuel Joseph; IGI

Portraits of the Sculptor: T Smith, wax, exhib RA, 1828, 1087, untraced; anon, pencil and wash, c1827–28, private coll (*Friedman* 1980 (1), 21,22 repr); anon, pencil and wash, coll Caroline Scott (exhib *Virtue and Vision*, 1991)

No.	Date	Subject		Location		References
Funerary Monuments						
1.	†1812	Rev John Tattershall		Otterden, Kent		*Gunnis* 1968, 223
2.	1818	Sir Samuel Hood, model of a statue 'to be erected in St Paul's Cathedral'		[Exhib RA, London, 1114]; untraced		*Graves* IV, 1905–6, 287
3.	†1819	William Vassall (†1800) and his daughter Margaret		St Mary, Battersea, London		*Gunnis* 1968, 223
4.	c1820	Rev Granville Wheler		Otterden, Kent		*Gunnis* 1968, 223
5.	1825	Earl of Hopetoun, sketch		[Exhib IEFAS, 9]; untraced		*Rinder and McKay* 1917, 194
6.	1829	Duke of York, sketch		[Exhib R Sc A, 293]; untraced		*Rinder and McKay* 1917, 194
7.	1829	Professor Dugald Stewart, sketch		[Exhib R Sc A, 294]; untraced		*Rinder and McKay* 1917, 194
8.	1829	William Pitt, sketch		[Exhib R Sc A, 290]; untraced		*Rinder and McKay* 1917, 194
9.	†1833	Rev Latham Wainwright		Great Brickhill, Bucks		*Gunnis* 1968, 223
10.	†1834	Agnes Wilberforce		East Farleigh, Kent	S	Pevsner, *Kent: W & Weald*, 1976, 264
11.	1837	Sir William Franklin (†1833)		Rochester Cathedral, Kent		Pevsner, *Kent: W & Weald*, 1976, 484; *Friedman* 1991, 59
12.	1838–1840	William Wilberforce (†1833)		Westminster Abbey, London, nave, north aisle Other versions: **St John's College, Cambridge, plaster**	SD	*Scott* 1871, 78b (repr); WAM (84); *Gunnis* 1968, 222; *Friedman* 1980 (1), 24, 26 (repr)
13.	1844	Sir David Wilkie RA (†1841)		Cults, Fife		C Lib (repr)
Statues						
14.	1843	Sir David Wilkie RA Model(s): plaster, Ashm	m	Tate Gall, London NO1764		*Cunningham* 1843, vol 3, 516–23; *Scott* 1871, 81–2; *Gunnis* 1968, 222
15.	1844	Hon Elizabeth Harriet Elliott	m	Port Eliot, Cornwall	SD	*AU*, 1844, 170; *Graves* IV, 1905–6, 288; *AU* 1844, 170
16.	1845	Sir Hugh Myddelton Payment(s): £430	s	Royal Exchange, City of London, north side	S	*Read* 1982, 216, 218 (repr); *Leith* 1997, 340, 341 (repr)
Busts						
17.	1811	Master T Rouw		[Exhib RA, London, 908]; untraced		*Graves* IV, 1905–6, 286
18.	1811	Rev R Cecil AM		[Exhib RA, London, 931]; untraced		*Graves* IV, 1905–6, 286
19.	1812	'Portrait of an old gentleman'		[Exhib RA, London, 939]; untraced		*Graves* IV, 1905–6, 286
20.	1812	R Clutterbuck		[Exhib RA, London, 923]; untraced		*Graves* IV, 1905–6, 286
21.	1814	J Renton		[Exhib RA, London, 793]; untraced		*Graves* IV, 1905–6, 286
22.	1814	'Portrait of a lady'		[Exhib RA, London, 761]; untraced		*Graves* IV, 1905–6, 286
23.	1815	Edmund Kean		Drury Lane Theatre, London		*Graves* IV, 1905–6, 287; *Gunnis* 1968, 222; *Friedman* 1980 (1), 20
24.	1815	'Portrait of a lady'		[Exhib RA, London, 829]; untraced		*Graves* IV, 1905–6, 286
25.	1815	'Portrait of a lady'		[Exhib RA, London, 841]; untraced		*Graves* IV, 1905–6, 287
26.	1815	'The Principal of Bernard's Inn for the Society'		[Exhib RA, London, 903]; untraced		*Graves* IV, 1905–6, 287
27.	1816	Prof J Brookes		[Exhib RA, London, 923]; untraced		*Graves* IV, 1905–6, 287
28.	1818	J Bartleman		[Exhib RA, London, 1068]; untraced		*Graves* IV, 1905–6, 287
29.	1818	R W Coxe		[Exhib RA, London, 1066]; untraced		*Graves* IV, 1905–6, 287
30.	1818	Rev Mr Goode		[Exhib RA, London, 1054]; untraced		*Graves* IV, 1905–6, 287

No.	Date	Subject		Location		Literature
31.	1818	Richard Allott, Dean of Raphoe		[Exhib RA, London, 1077]; untraced		*Graves* IV, 1905–6, 287
32.	1819	Daughter of General Sir George Walker GCB		[Exhib RA, London, 1210]; untraced		*Graves* IV, 1905–6, 287
33.	1819	Field-Marshal William, Viscount Beresford, GCB		Private coll		*Graves* IV, 1905–6, 287
34.	1819	General Sir George Walker GCB		[Exhib RA, London, 1195]; untraced		*Graves* IV, 1905–6, 287
35.	1819	General Sir Lowry Cole, GCB		[Exhib RA, London, 1207, coll Lady Cole, presented by the officers of Sir Lowry's staff (1844)]; untraced		*Graves* IV, 1905–6, 287
36.	1819	George Bullock		[Exhib RA, London, 1219]; untraced		*Graves* IV, 1905–6, 287
37.	1819	J Abernethy FRS		[Exhib RA, London, 1200]; untraced		*Graves* IV, 1905–6, 287
38.	1820	E Bates		[Exhib RA, London, 1053]; untraced		*Graves* IV, 1905–6, 287
39.	1820	H R Bishop		[Exhib RA, London, 1052]; untraced		*Graves* IV, 1905–6, 287
40.	1820	Lieutenant-General Sir Ronald Ferguson GCB		[Exhib RA, London, 1009 Exhib IEFAS, 1821, 2]; untraced		*Graves* IV, 1905–6, 287; *Rinder and McKay* 1917, 194
41.	1820	Mrs R C Barnett		[Exhib RA, London, 1069]; untraced		*Graves* IV, 1905–6, 287
42.	1820	R C Barnett		[Exhib RA, London, 1035]; untraced		*Graves* IV, 1905–6, 287
43.	1820	Robert Ferguson of Raith		[Exhib RA, London, 1050 Exhib IEFAS, 1821, 4; 1825, 3 Exhib R Sc A, 1827, 62, marble]; untraced		*Graves* IV, 1905–6, 287; *Rinder and McKay* 1917, 194
44.	1820	William Collins RA		[Exhib RA, London, 1020]; untraced		*Graves* IV, 1905–6, 287
45.	1821	H Perkins		[Exhib RA, London, 1121 Exhib IEFAS, 1821, 6]; untraced		*Graves* IV, 1905–6, 287; *Rinder and McKay* 1917, 194
46.	1821	J F Williams, mask		[to be presented to the Edinburgh Phrenological Society]; untraced		*Pearson* 1981, 14
47.	1821	Michael Angelo Taylor	m	[Exhib IEFAS, 194]; untraced		*Rinder and McKay* 1917, 194
48.	1821	Thomas Chalmers	p	Edinburgh University, Faculty of Divinity	SD	*Rinder and McKay* 1917, 194; *Pearson* 1981, 16, 17 (repr); *Pearson* 1991, 59
49.	1822	Charles Mathews	p	NPG 1710	SD	Joseph/Mathews; *Gunnis* 1968, 222; *Friedman* 1972, 25
50.	1822	Francis Jeffrey	p	SNPG Other versions: Green's Bookshop, High Street, Edinburgh, signed plaster	D	*Smailes* 1990, 160
51.	1822	Head of a lady		[Exhib RA, London, 1022]; untraced		*Graves* IV, 1905–6, 287
52.	1822	Henry Mackenzie Drawing(s): model, exhib RA, London, 1822, 1044	m	SNPG (254) Other versions: **high relief bust portrait, bronze, published 1830, Ashm** **exhib Joseph's private gall, nd, intended for execution in bronze**		*Graves* IV, 1905–6, 287; *Notes and Queries*, 30 July 1910, 82; *Rinder and McKay* 1917, 195; *Smailes* 1990, 192–3 (repr); *Friedman* 1991, 59–60, 63 (repr); *Penny* 1992, 107 (repr)
53.	1822	Prof John Leslie of Edinburgh		[Exhib RA, London, 1001 (model) Exhib IEFAS, 1822, 232 Exhib North Soc, 1822, 218]; untraced Other versions: executed by Sir John Steell, marble, Edinburgh University executed by John Rhind, marble, SNPG (291) exhib Samuel Joseph's private gall, nd, to be executed in bronze		*Graves* IV, 1905–6, 287; *Notes and Queries*, 30 July 1910, 82; *Rinder and McKay* 1917, 194; *Friedman* 1972, 25; *Smailes* 1990, 176
54.	1822	Sir George Mackenzie Bt	p	[Sent to George Combe, Edinburgh Phrenological Society]; untraced		*Rinder and McKay* 1917, 194; *Pearson* 1981, 16
55.	c1822	Sir Humphrey Davy	m	Royal Institution of Great Britain, London		C Lib (repr)
56.	1822	Sir William Fettes Bt Model(s): plaster, SNPG (334)		[Exhib RA, London, 1009 Exhib IEFAS, 1822, 235]; untraced		*Graves* IV, 1905–6, 287; *Rinder and McKay* 1917, 194, 195; *Smailes* 1990, 106
57.	1822	Unidentified male sitter	p	Private coll	SD	C Lib (repr)
58.	1823	James Hamilton, of Holmhead Model(s): Exhib RA, London, 1824, 1033	m	GAGM	SD	*Graves* IV, 1905–6, 287
59.	1823	Lord Sir James Wellwood Moncrieff	p	SNPG L51 (on loan from family)		*Smailes* 1990, 210
60.	1824	Dr James Hamilton Snr of Edinburgh Model(s): Exhib RA, London, 1822, 1007	m	RCP Scotland, Edinburgh	SD	*Graves* IV, 1905–6, 287; *Rinder and McKay* 1917, 194
61.	1824	Lord John Campbell		[Exhib RA, London, 1003]; untraced		*Graves* IV, 1905–6, 287
62.	1824	Mr Liston		[Exhib RA, London, 995 Exhib IEFAS, 1825, 12]; untraced Other versions: exhib Samuel Joseph's private gall, nd, to be executed in bronze		*Graves* IV, 1905–6, 287; *Notes and Queries*, 30 July 1910, 82; *Rinder and McKay* 1917, 194
63.	1824	Sir Walter Scott	m	Preston Hall, Midlothian Other versions: **private coll, 1824, marble** **private coll, nd, bronze reduction,** **exhib Samuel Joseph's private gall, nd, intended for execution in bronze**		*Notes and Queries*, 30 July 1910, 82; *Friedman* 1980 (1), 20 (repr); *Friedman* 1991, 59, 60 (repr); *Pearson* 1991, unpag
64.	1821–1825	Dr James Gregory of Edinburgh Model(s): Plaster, SNPG (287), dated 1821		University of Edinburgh, old library	SD	*Graves* IV, 1905–6, 287; *Rinder and McKay* 1917, 194; *Friedman* 1972, 25; *Pearson* 1981, 18 (repr); *Smailes* 1990, 129

No.	Date	Subject		Location		Literature
65.	1825	Dr McCulloch		[Exhib IEFAS, 1]; untraced		*Rinder and McKay* 1917, 194
66.	1825	Earl of Morton		[Exhib IEFAS, 2]; untraced		*Rinder and McKay* 1917, 194
67.	1825	John Barclay MD	m	RCS Scotland, Edinburgh	SD	*Rinder and McKay* 1917, 194; *Friedman* 1991, 59, 61
68.	1825	Rev Archibald Alison	m	**Fitz M.4-1974** Other versions: SNPG (1219), 1841, signed and dated, marble		*Gunnis* 1968, 223; *Friedman* 1980 (1), 20; *Smailes* 1990, 16–17 (repr); *Friedman* 1991, 59
69.	1825	Rev Sir Henry Wellwood Moncrieff	m	SNPG L151 (loan from family) Other versions: plaster, dated 1822, PGL 48 (on loan from family)	SD	*Graves* IV, 1905–6, 287; *Rinder and McKay* 1917, 194; *Friedman* 1980 (1), 24–5 (repr); *Smailes* 1990, 306; *Friedman* 1991, 59, 60, 61 (repr)
70.	1825	Robert Buchan		[Exhib IEFAS, 4]; untraced		*Rinder and McKay* 1917, 194
71.	1825	Sir Benjamin Bloomfield, Bt		[Exhib IEFAS, 1825, 15]; untraced		*Rinder and McKay* 1917, 194
72.	1825	Susannah Gott Kinnear	m	LMG	SD	*Friedman* 1972, 21, 22, 25 n29 (repr); *Friedman* 1991, 60; *Leeds* 1996, 6 (repr)
73.	1826	Robert, 8th Lord Belhaven and Stenton	m	VAM A.67-1965	SD	*Knox* 1998, 88 (repr); *Bilbey* 2002, 311 (repr)
74.	1826	Walter Fergus of Edinburgh		[Exhib RA, London, 1041 Exhib R Sc A, 64, marble]; untraced		*Graves* IV, 1905–6, 287; *Rinder and McKay* 1917, 194
75.	1826	William Allan		[Exhib RA, London, 1079]; untraced		*Graves* IV, 1905–6, 287
76.	1827	Alexander Allan of Hillside, Edinburgh	m	[Exhib RA, London, 1114 Exhib R Sc A, 1828, 308]; untraced		*Graves* IV, 1905–6, 287; *Rinder and McKay* 1917, 194
77.	1827	General Hamilton, of Dalziel		[Exhib R Sc A, 69]; untraced		*Rinder and McKay* 1917, 194
78.	1827	George Veitch, of Ratho Bank		Signet Library, Edinburgh	SD	
79.	1827	Hamilton, Lady Belhaven and Stenton	m	VAM A.68-1965	SD	*Friedman* 1980 (1), 22, 23; *Knox* 1998, 88 (repr); *Bilbey* 2002, 312
80.	1827	Mary Anne Gott		Untraced		*Friedman* 1972, 22
81.	1827	Miss Emma Campbell	m	[Exhib RA, London, 1107]; untraced		*Graves* IV, 1905–6, 287; *Rinder and McKay* 1917, 194
82.	1827	Miss Ramsay	m	[Exhib R Sc A, 72]; untraced		*Rinder and McKay* 1917, 194
83.	1827	Professor Dugald Stewart, FRSS	m	Edinburgh University, old library Other versions: SNPG (209), bronze, signed R Sc A, bronze exhib Samuel Joseph's private gall, nd, intended for execution in bronze	S	*Graves* IV, 1905–6, 287; *Rinder and Notes and Queries*, 30 July 1910, 82; *McKay* 1917, 194, 195; *Smailes* 1990, 278; *Pearson* 1991, 60 (repr); *Friedman* 1991, 59, 61
84.	1827	Robert Stevenson FRSE Model(s): exhib R Sc A, 71; Nat Museums Scotland	m	[Bell Rock Lighthouse, library]; Northern Lighthouse Board, George Street, Edinburgh, reception hall	SD	*Rinder and McKay* 1917, 194; *Smailes* 1990, 276; *Pearson* 1991, unpag
85.	1827	Stuart Menteath, of Closeburn	m	[Exhib R Sc A, 67]; untraced		*Rinder and McKay* 1917, 194
86.	1822–1827	Thomas Allan Model(s): exhib RA, London, 1822, 1047	m	Laurieston Castle, Edinburgh	SD	*Rinder and McKay* 1917, 194; *Graves* IV, 1905–6, 287
87.	1827	Unidentified young female sitter	m	LMG, W R Yorks	SD	*Friedman* 1980 (1), 22, 24, 28 n17 (repr); *Friedman* 1991, 60 (repr); *Curtis* 2000, 58, 61 (repr)
88.	1828	Robert Ramsay	m	[Exhib R Sc A, 309]; untraced		*Rinder and McKay* 1917, 194
89.	1830	George Charteris, third son of 9th Earl of Wemyss Model(s): Exhib RA, London, 1222	m	Gosford House, East Lothian		*Graves* IV, 1905–6, 288; *Pearson* 1991, unpag
90.	1830	George, 6th Duke of Argyll		Inverary Castle, Argyll	S	*Graves* IV, 1905–6, 287; *Gunnis* 1968, 222; *Friedman* 1980 (1), 26–7
91.	1830	John Flaxman	b	Lady Lever, LL 2706 Other versions: YCAG exhib Joseph's Private Gallery, nd, intended for execution in bronze	SD	*Notes and Queries*, 30 July 1910, 82; *Lady Lever* 1999, 63–4 (repr)
92.	1830	Lieutenant-General Sir Herbert Taylor		[Exhib RA, London, 1239]; untraced		*Graves* IV, 1905–6, 288
93.	1830	Margaret Alison		[Exhib RA, London, 1263]; untraced		*Graves* IV, 1905–6, 288
94.	1830	Mrs Fyler		[Exhib RA, London, 1218]; untraced		*Graves* IV, 1905–6, 287
95.	1830	Rev Dr Peddie		[Exhib R Sc A, 331]; untraced		*Rinder and McKay* 1917, 194
96.	1830	Robert Ferguson of Raith		[Exhib RA, London, 1208]; untraced		*Graves* IV, 1905–6, 287
97.	1830	Sir Thomas Lawrence PRA, model		[Exhib RA, London, 1205]; untraced Other versions: exhib Samuel Joseph's private gallery, nd, to be executed in bronze		*Graves* IV, 1905–6, 287; *Notes and Queries*, 30 July 1910, 82
98.	1831	Davies Gilbert, MP		[Exhib RA, London, 1199]; untraced		*Graves* IV, 1905–6, 288
99.	1831	Hon Mrs William Russell		[Exhib Suffolk St, London]; untraced		RG/JP, 5, 765
100.	1831	King George IV	m	VAM A.12-1956 Other versions: exhib Samuel Joseph's Private Gallery, nd, to be executed in bronze	SD	*Notes and Queries*, 30 July 1910, 82; *Whinney* 1971, 160–1 (repr); *Friedman* 1991, 59; *Bilbey* 2002, 312 (repr)
101.	1831	Lady Eleanor Campbell		[Exhib Suffolk St, London]; untraced		RG/JP, 5, 765
102.	1831	Rt Hon William Huskisson MP	m	Petworth House, Sussex	SD	*Gunnis* 1968, 223
103.	1831	William Trotter, of Ballindean	m	[Exhib R Sc A, 362]; untraced		*Rinder and McKay* 1917, 194
104.	1832	George Husband Baird, Principal of Edinburgh University	m	Edinburgh University, old library		*Graves* IV, 1905–6, 288; *Rinder and McKay* 1917, 195
105.	1832	James Laing		[Exhib RA, London, 1145]; untraced		*Graves* IV, 1905–6, 288

106.	1832	Rev Andrew Bell	m	Madras College, St Andrew's, Fife, rector's room	SD	*Graves* IV, 1905–6, 288; *Rinder and McKay* 1917, 195
107.	1832	Rev Jonathan Brooks	m	[Exhib Liverpool Ac, 381]; untraced		*Morris and Roberts* 1998, 357
108.	1833	Miss Trotter of Ballindean	m	[Exhib RA, London, 1202]; untraced		*Graves* IV, 1905–6, 288
109.	1833	Sir John Poulett Orde Bt		[Exhib RA, London, 1172]; untraced		*Graves* IV, 1905–6, 288
110.	1833	Unidentified lady	m	Gov Art Coll (1853)	S	Gov Art Coll archives
111.	1833	William Wilberforce	m	Wilberforce Residential Home for the Multiple-Handicapped Blind, York Other versions: Gov Art Coll, marble, bought 1953 United Services Club, London, dated 1835	SD	*Friedman* 1972, 25, n25; *Friedman* 1980 (1), 24, 28 n22, 23; *Friedman* 1991, 59; Gov Art Coll archives
112.	1834	Ernest Augustus, Duke of Cumberland		House of Dun, Angus		RG/JP, 5, 769
113.	1834	King William IV	m	Penshurst Place, Kent Other versions: United Service Club, London, 1835, marble Lord de L'Isle and Dudley, 1835, marble	SD	*Gunnis* 1968, 222; *Ormond* 1973, 514;
114.	1834	Robert Buchanan, model (marble executed by Alexander Handyside Ritchie)		untraced		*Rinder and McKay* 1917, 195
115.	1835	Lord Brougham, Chancellor of Great Britain	m	R Sc A, diploma work		*Graves* IV, 1905–6, 288; *Rinder and McKay* 1917, 195; *Pearson* 1991, unpag
116.	1836	John MacCulloch MD FGS	m	Geological Society, London	SD	
117.	1837	Sam Cartwright		[Exhib RA, London, 1217]; untraced		*Graves* IV, 1905–6, 288
118.	1838	Sophia, Lady De L'Isle and Dudley	m	Penshurst Place, Kent	SD	*British Portraits* 1956–7, 127; *Gunnis* 1968, 223; *Friedman* 1972, 22
119.	1840	Captain Basil Hall RN	m	Stirling Maxwell Coll, Pollok House, Glasgow PSL.08	SD	*Graves* II, 1905–6, 288
120.	1840	Colonel John Gurwood CB	m	Apsley House, London WM.1451-1948	SD	*Gunnis* 1968, 223
121.	1841	Henry Harvey of Hill House, Streatham		[Exhib RA, London, 1337]; untraced		*Graves* IV, 1905–6, 288
122.	1841	Robert Gray of Carntyne	m	Private coll, Fife		C Lib (repr)
123.	1842	David Barclay	m	[Exhib RA, London, 1375]; untraced		*AU*, 1842, 129; *Graves* IV, 1905–6, 288
124.	1842	John Gray of Carntyne Model(s): Exhib R Sc A, 1827, 314; untraced	m	[Exhib RA, London, 1842, 1319]; untraced		*Graves* IV, 1905–6, 288; *Rinder and McKay* 1917, 288
125.	1842	Mrs Burge		[Exhib RA, London, 1325]; untraced		*Graves* IV, 1905–6, 288
126.	1842	Sir David Wilkie RA	m	SNPG (1220) Other versions: exhib Samuel Joseph's Private gallery, nd, intended for execution in bronze	SD	*Notes and Queries*, 30 July 1910, 82; *Rinder and McKay* 1917, 195; *Smailes* 1990, 305, 307 (repr); *Friedman* 1991, 58, 60 (repr)
127.	1843	Joseph Wilson of Highbury		[Exhib RA, London, 1448]; untraced		*Graves* IV, 1905–6, 288
128.	1844	General Sir George Townshend Walker Bt	m	Royal Hospital, Chelsea		*Graves* IV, 1905–6, 288
129.	1844	Henry, 3rd Earl of Shannon (+1842)		[Exhib RA, London, 1385]; untraced		*Graves* IV, 1905–6, 288
130.	1844	Sir Francis Burdett Bt, MP	m	[Exhib RA, London, 1398]; untraced		*Graves* IV, 1905–6, 288
131.	1846	Maria Hamilton Gray		Private coll, Fife	SD	
132.	1846	W Strickland Cookson		[Exhib RA, London, 1498]; untraced		*Graves* IV, 1905–6, 288
133.	nd	John Clerk, Lord Eldin	p	SNPG		*Smailes* 1990, 210
134.	nd	King George IV, to be executed in bronze		[Samuel Joseph's Private Gallery]; untraced		*Notes and Queries*, 30 July 1910, 82
135.	nd	Mr and Mrs Cartwright		[Christie, 28 Feb 1865]; untraced		Christie, London, 28 Feb 1865
136.	nd	Mrs John Hamilton Gray	m	Private coll, Fife		C Lib (repr)
137.	nd	Thomas Stothard, to be executed in bronze		[Samuel Joseph's private gallery]; untraced		*Notes and Queries*, 30 July 1910, 82
138.	nd	Voltaire	m	Elvetham Hall, Hants		*Gunnis* 1968, 223; *Friedman* 1980 (1), 24

Architectural Sculpture

139.	1844	Design for the pediment of the Royal Exchange		[Exhib RA, London, 1146]; untraced		*Graves* IV, 1905–6, 288; *Leith* 1997, 338

Reliefs

140.	1816	A young lady, medallion		[Exhib RA, London, 870]; untraced		*Graves* IV, 1905–6, 287
141.	1816	Mrs Percival White, medallion		[Exhib RA, London, 892]; untraced		*Graves* IV, 1905–6, 287
142.	1817	E Kean, medallion		[Exhib RA, London, 980]; untraced		*Graves* IV, 1905–6, 287
143.	1818	E Lombe and E Lombe Jnr, medallions exhibited in a case		[Exhib RA, London, 979]; untraced		*Graves* IV, 1905–6, 287
144.	1822	Sir Walter Scott, high relief bust portrait	b	Ashmolean (published 1830) Other versions: Private Coll, herm bust, signed and dated 1830	SD	*Penny* 1992, 106 (repr)

Miscellaneous

145.	1815	Eve entreating forgiveness of Adam, 'group'		[RA, London, gold medal]; untraced		RA Premium list; *Graves* IV, 1905–6, 287; *Gunnis* 1968, 222
146.	1815	J Pugh		[Exhib RA, London, 839]; untraced		*Graves* IV, 1905–6, 287
147.	1815	Mrs Rickford		[Exhib RA, London, 832]; untraced		*Graves* IV, 1905–6, 287
148.	1815	Portrait of a clergyman		[Exhib RA, London, 834]; untraced		*Graves* IV, 1905–6, 287

JOYNES, Henry

See **Dance**, Giles

K, of Church Street, Edmonton fl 1836?–39

He can very likely be identified with W H King, of Church Street, Edmonton, who was described as a sculptor when he exhibited an *Arch of Constantine* at the Society of British Artists in 1836 (*Johnson* 1975, 271, cat 896).

Miscellaneous

1.	1839	Model (forming a time piece by removing the figure) partly based the porch of St Mary, Bury St Edmunds	[Exhib Soc of BA, London, 265]; untraced	*Johnson* 1975, 265

KACHLER, H fl 1837–44

'H Kachler' exhibited at the Royal Academy, 1837–44 and at the Society of British Artists in 1839. This was probably the German sculptor Johann Heinrich Daniel Kaehler. Born in Rostock in 1804, he studied under Johan Gottfried Schadow in Berlin and **Bertel Thorvaldsen** in Rome. He was in London 1834–47 and on 28 April 1838 he married a niece of the dramatist James Sheridan Knowles (inf. Marjorie Trusted).

Literary References: *Gunnis* 1968, 224

Statues

1.	1839	F Sheridan Knowles	[Exhib Soc of BA, London, 751]; untraced	*Johnson* 1975, 265
2.	1843	A boy, part of a group	[Exhib RA, London, 1501]; untraced	*Graves* IV, 1905–6, 299
Busts				
3.	1837	H Kachler, self portrait	[Exhib RA, London, 1233]; untraced	*Graves* IV, 1905–6, 299
4.	1837	Mademoiselle Schultse	[Exhib RA, London, 1239]; untraced	*Graves* IV, 1905–6, 299
5.	1839	Miss Elphinstone	[Exhib RA, London, 1381]; untraced	*Graves* IV, 1905–6, 299
6.	1842	James Sheridan Knowles	[Exhib RA, London, 1370]; untraced	*Graves* IV, 1905–6, 299
Miscellaneous				
7.	1838	A nymph	[Exhib RA, London, 1278]; untraced	*Graves* IV, 1905–6, 299
8.	1838	Group of children playing with a dog	[Exhib RA, London, 1272]; untraced	*Graves* IV, 1905–6, 299
9.	1844	The mother's face is turned upon her girl	[Exhib RA, London, 1285]; untraced	*Graves* IV, 1905–6, 299

KARN, George, of Chichester fl *c*1830

Funerary Monuments

1.	†1830	Charles Cullen	Chichester Cathedral, Sussex	S	*Gunnis* 1968, 224
2.	†1830	Georgiana Parker	Warblington, Hants	S	*Gunnis* 1968, 224

KAY, Richard fl 1748–49

He was employed by **Thomas Carter I** as a mason and carver at Welbeck and Okeover.

Architectural Sculpture

1.	1748–9	Work on the gate-piers and the arcade	[Okeover Hall, Staffs]; untraced	*Oswald* 1964, 175, 176

KEARNE (or KARNE), Andrew (or Andreas) fl 1627–76

A German sculptor, he married Nicholas Stone's sister, Grace, in 1627, and worked as Stone's assistant. The Masons' Company account book for 1628–9 gives an entry under the heading 'old debts', 'Andreas Kerne, iii*s*. vi*d*', which may have represented arrears of a foreign mason's contributions to the common box. Nearly 50 years later 'Andre Karne' was paid £272 for mason's work, including 12 marble chimneypieces, for Sir Cecil Wyche's London house (**3**). The premises of a 'Mr Kerne' were included in the general search on 16 April 1678 and a 'Mr Andrew Kerne' was one of the foreigners who appeared before the Court on 25 April that year. These later references suggest that either Kearne continued working into his 70s or that he was succeeded by a relative with the same name. The only known son was called Thomas. Vertue, writing *c*1721, stated that Kearne had 'carv'd many Statues' for Justinian Isham of Lamport, and figures of *Apollo* and *Venus* for the Countess of Mulgrave' (**1, 2**). He noted that Kearne 'livd and dyd in England & left a son that dy'd not many years agoe' (*Vertue* I, 98).

In addition to the listed works, Mrs Esdaile has suggested that Kearne may have been responsible for a statue of King Charles I which once stood on the porch of the Guildhall chapel and Gunnis has attributed to him two statues, of *Aeneas and Anchises* and *Hercules and Cacus*, which were once at Boughton Hall but are now in the gardens at Glendon Hall, Northants.

Literary References: *Knoop and Jones* 1935, 20 n1, 24 n4; Pevsner, *Northants*, 1973, 226; *Whinney* 1988, 435 n19

Archival References: GPC

Statues

1.	*c*1670	Wax figures		[Lamport Hall, Northants, music hall]; untraced	*Vertue*, I, 98; Pevsner, *Northants*, 1973, 287
2.	nd	Apollo and Venus		[coll Countess of Mulgrave]; untraced	*Vertue*, I, 98
Chimneypieces					
3.	1675–1676	Twelve Payment(s): £130	m	[Sir Cecil Wyche's house, St James's Square, London]; untraced	Wyche Archive, Norwich public library, in GPC

KEARNE (or KARNE), Hans Jacob fl 1660

He was probably a kinsman of **Andrew Kearne** and **John Stone**. Vertue may have been referring to this sculptor when he stated that Andrew Kerne 'left a son that dy'd noyt many years agoe' (*Vertue*, I, 98). He succeeded Stone as court sculptor to King Charles II in 1660 but apparently had little talent and was replaced by **C G Cibber** in 1667.

Literary References: *Gibson* 1997 (1), 162–3

Archival References: PRO LC3/25, 113

KEEBLE, Henry fl *c*1740

He is listed *c*1740 as working for 'Mr. Chair, Westminster' (**Sir Henry Cheere**) (Masons' Co Assistants, fol 7).

KEGWORTH, W Wooton fl *c*1763

Funerary Monuments

1.	†1763	Clare Taylor and family members	St George's Gardens, Holborn	S	Pevsner, *London: N*, 1998, 263

KEITH & Co, of London fl *c*1818

Funerary Monuments

1.	†1818	William Ramshaw (†1818)		St Mary, Beverley, E R Yorks	S	

KELLOW, James, of Winchester fl 1830?–*c*1850

Kellow of Winchester may be a member of the same family as 'Kellow, stone-mason', who was employed at Salisbury Cathedral in 1785 (Cathedral Archives in *Gunnis* 1968, 224). In 1839 he provided the monument to Sir Thomas Dyer (5). This 'elegant tomb', designed by Owen Carter, took the form of a sarcophagus decorated with 'arms and military trophies' and was considered of 'highly creditable workmanship' (*GM*, 1839, ii, 160). Kellow can presumably be identified with Kellow of Winton, near Bournemouth, who signs a plain tablet commemorating Edward and Delitia Salter in Winchester Cathedral (2).

Literary References: *Gunnis* 1968, 224

Funerary Monuments

1.	?1830	Sarah Rennell		Winchester Cathedral	S	*Gunnis* 1968, 224
2.	†1833	Edward (†1813) and Delitia Salter (†1833)		Winchester Cathedral, nave aisle	S	*Balderston* 2000, 199, n.64
3.	†1834	William, 8th Earl of Banbury		Winchester Cathedral	S	*Gunnis* 1968, 224
4.	1836	Elizabeth Gomm		Bramsdean, Hants	S	*Gunnis* 1968, 224
5.	1839	Sir Thomas Dyer Bt (†1838) (designed by Owen Carter)		Ovington, Hants, churchyard		*Colvin* 1995, 231
6.	†1850	William (†1831) and Matilda Nevill		Titchfield, Hants		*Gunnis* 1968, 224

KELLY, C fl 1818

Busts

1.	1818	Unidentified woman	i	VAM A.24-1938	SD	VAM SCP, colls list, ivories

KELLY, J

Reliefs

1.	nd	Princess Charlotte Augusta	i	VAM A.21-138		VAM SCP, colls list, ivories

KELLY, John fl 1739–73

An Irish carver, he was probably a pupil of John Houghton, whom he assisted in carving the pediment at Carton House (1). He worked chiefly as a wood carver, executing the fine carved doorways, window casings, cornices and staircase in the house which Doctor Mosse, the founder of the Rotunda Hospital, built for himself *c*1756 (2). He also made a bedstead for Mosse (6). His address was Eustace Street, Dublin, in 1765, when he exhibited two bas-reliefs with the Society of Artists (3, 4). He showed again at the Society's exhibitions in 1768, 1769 and 1773 and was awarded a premium for a relief by the Dublin Society in 1768 (5). There is no mention of him after 1773.

Literary References: *Strickland* I, 1913, 571

Architectural Sculpture

1.	1739	Coat of arms and other decorations	s	Carton House, Maynooth, Co Kildare, pediment		*Strickland* I, 1913, 571
2.	*c*1756	Carved woodwork		Dr Mosse's house, 9 Cavendish Row (formerly Rutland/Parnell Square), Dublin		*Strickland* I, 1913, 571, citing receipts at the Rotunda Hospital (1913)

Reliefs

3.	1765	Hibernia	wd	[Exhib Society of Artists, George's Lane, Dublin]; untraced		*Strickland* I, 1913, 571
4.	1765	The element of fire	wd	[Exhib Society of Artists, George's Lane, Dublin]; untraced		*Strickland* I, 1913, 571
5.	1768	Unidentified bas relief		[Dublin Society premium]; untraced		*Strickland* I, 1913, 571

Miscellaneous

6.	1759	Carved mahogany bedstead Payment(s): £19 8s 6 1/2 d		[for Dr Mosse]; coll Lady Stokes, of Carrigbreac, Howth (1913)		*Strickland* I, 1913, 571
7.	1768	Carving(s)		[Exhib Society of Artists, William Street, Dublin]; untraced		*Strickland* I, 1913, 571
8.	1769	Carving(s)		[Exhib Society of Artists, William Street, Dublin]; untraced		*Strickland* I, 1913, 571
9.	1773	Carving(s)		[Exhib Society of Artists, William Street, Dublin]; untraced		*Strickland* I, 1913, 571

KELLY, Thomas, of Chester fl 1821?–36

In 1826 he was employed in building Chester Bridge, and three years later was responsible for a 'marble monument handsomely executed' to Thomas Egerton, Viscount Brackley, who served as Lord Chancellor during the reign of James I (5).

Literary References: *Hemingway* 1831, I, 373; *Gunnis* 1968, 224

Funerary Monuments

1.	?1821	Emily Hamer		Bangor Cathedral	S	GPC
2.	1827	Sir John Grey Egerton (†1823)		Chester Cathedral, Cheshire	S	
3.	†1829	L W Halstead		Chester Cathedral, Cheshire	S	Pevsner, *Cheshire*, 1971, 143
4.	?1829	Mrs Drake		Thornton-le-Moors, Cheshire	S	*Gunnis* 1968, 224
5.	1829	Thomas, 1st Viscount Brackley (†1617) Payment(s): £100		Dodleston, Cheshire		*GM*, 1829, ii, 495
6.	†1832	Thomas Tarleton		Malpas, Cheshire	S	
7.	1833	Ann Truslove		St John the Baptist, Chester, Cheshire	S	*Gunnis* 1968, 224
8.	*c*1835	Ford family		Chester Cathedral, Cheshire	S	
9.	†1836	Thomas Tarleton		Malpas, Cheshire	S	

KELSEY, Charles Samuel 1820–

The records of the Clothworkers' Company indicate that Kelsey was apprenticed to John Kelsey of Paradise Street, Rotherhithe, a bricklayer, in November 1834 and became free of the Company in 1845, when his address was Anne Cottage, Commercial Road, Lambeth. The sculptor's own account asserts that he started work as an assistant to his sculptor father, **James Kelsey**, helping to make full-size models in London for the Corinthian capitals and other portions of architectural sculpture of St George's Hall, Liverpool (**11**) (*Builder*, vol 43, 1882, 126).

Kelsey entered the Royal Academy Schools in 1843 on the recommendation of the painter William Etty and won a silver medal in 1845. He was an occasional exhibitor at the Royal Academy between 1840 and 1877 and sent figures of the Earl of Shrewsbury and the Venerable Bede to the Westminster Hall exhibition of 1844 (**4, 6**). The Shrewsbury was described as 'a portrait of a suit of armour carefully put on' and the Bede as 'very heavy and unmeaning' (*Lit Gaz* 1844, 466). In 1846 Kelsey was awarded a silver medal by the Society of Arts for a design for an admission ticket to the Society's rooms. His large Gothic monument to William Rolls and a tablet with a medallion portrait of Henry Corbould date from the same period (**2, 3**).

In the late 1840s and 1850s he was again employed on architectural work for Liverpool. In 1848 he carved a relief for the Royal Insurance Office which included the Liverpool and royal arms, firemen's axes and helmets, and the ancient crest of the city, the liver (**12**). In 1849 he was engaged to execute models for interior ornaments in St George's Hall (**13**). By that date the building's architect, Harvey Lonsdale Elmes, was dead and Kelsey completed 'the various models and works required' under the supervision of C R Cockerell, 'having two of the rooms in the building for a studio' (*Builder*, vol 43, 1882, 126). Whilst residing in Liverpool he exhibited at the Liverpool Academy (**19–21, 28, 29**).

Kelsey's other works include allegorical figures for Smithfield Market and a 'poor relief' on the monument which replaced Temple Bar (*Gunnis* 1968, 224) (**16, 18**). He was last heard of in 1882 when, as an unsuccessful entrant in the competition for the reliefs on the east façade of St George's Hall, he wrote to the *Builder* describing his involvement in the building to date (*Builder, op cit*).

Literary References: *Gunnis* 1968, 224; *Cavanagh* 1997, 292, 331; *Wickham* 2000, 316

Archival References: RA Admissions, 1843

Funerary Monuments

1.	1840	St Michael, one of seven figures forming part of a monument		[Exhib RA, London, 1078]; untraced	*Graves* IV, 1905–6, 308
2.	†1840	William Rolls		St George, Bloomsbury, London	*Gunnis* 1968, 224
3.	†1844	Henry Corbould	S	Etchingham, Sussex	Pevsner, *Sussex*, 1965, 497

Statues

4.	1844	Earl of Shrewsbury		[Exhib Westminster Hall, London, 115]; untraced	*AU*, 1844, 215
5.	1844	Mischief		[Exhib RA, London, 1298]; untraced	*Graves* IV, 1905–6, 308
6.	1844	Venerable Bede		[Exhib Westminster Hall, London, 135]; untraced	*AU*, 1844, 216
7.	1845	One of the barons, the costume taken from the effigy of Robert de Roos in the Temple Church, London		[Exhib RA, London, 1345]; untraced	*Graves* IV, 1905–6, 308
8.	1846	Greek youth examining his sword	m	[Exhib RA, London, 1435]; untraced	*AU*, 1846, 189; *Graves* IV, 1905–6, 309; *Morris and Roberts* 1998, 363
9.	1863	Model for a group in bronze		[Exhib RA, London, 891]; untraced	*Graves* IV, 1905–6, 308

Busts

10.	*c*1859	Evening	m	Destroyed	Clothworkers' Company archives (photo)

Architectural Sculpture

11.	1842–1847	Architectural ornaments for the exterior of St George's Hall, Liverpool, models (as assistant to James Kelsey)		Untraced	*Builder*, vol 43, 1882, 126; *Cavanagh* 1997, 292
12.	1848	Overdoor relief		[Royal Insurance Office, North John Street, Liverpool, Lancs]; demol 1896	*Builder*, 1848, 614; *Cavanagh* 1997, 303
13.	1849–1856	Architectural decoration for the interior of St George's Hall, Liverpool, models		Untraced	*Cavanagh* 1997, 292, 295–6
14.	*c*1859	Firemens' helmets and other ornaments		Law Fire Office (now Law Society), City of London, overdoor	Pevsner, *London: City*, 1997, 450
15.	*c*1859	Loyalty, Integrity, Industry, Charity, reliefs	s	[Clothworkers' Hall, City of London]; destroyed	*Wickham* 2000, 316
16.	1868	Female figures representing Ireland, England, Wales and Scotland	s	Smithfield Market, London, attic	*CIIA* 4/5/5–8 (repr)
17.	1870	Tripod on Lord Carlisle's memorial column	s	Bulmer Hill, Castle Howard, N R Yorks	*Builder*, 1870, 347, 349 (repr)
18.	1880	Queen Victoria and Prince of Wales attending a thanksgiving service in St Paul's following the latter's recovery from typhoid, relief		Temple Bar memorial, Strand, London	*Gunnis* 1968, 224

Reliefs

19.	1853	A lady, portrait medallion		[Exhib Liverpool Ac, 233]; untraced	*Morris and Roberts* 1998, 363
20.	1853	Queen Victoria, medallion portrait		[Exhib Liverpool Ac, 703]; untraced	*Morris and Roberts* 1998, 363
21.	1854	Portrait		[Exhib Liverpool Ac, 757]; untraced	*Morris and Roberts* 1998, 363
22.	*c*1859	Samuel Pepys, oval	m	[Clothworkers' Hall, City of London]; destroyed (1941)	*Wickham* 2000, 316
23.	*c*1859	William Hewer, oval	m	[Clothworkers' Hall, City of London]; destroyed (1941)	*Wickham* 2000, 316
24.	1867	Christ blessing little children		[Exhib RA, London, 1092]; untraced	*Graves* IV, 1905–6, 309
25.	1877	Music	m	[Exhib RA, London, 1497]; untraced	*Graves* IV, 1905–6, 309

Miscellaneous

26.	1841	Marble hand		[Exhib RA, London, 1255]; untraced	*Graves* IV, 1905–6, 308
27.	1843	Rev James Sherman		[Exhib RA, London, 1370]; untraced	*Graves* IV, 1905–6, 308
28.	1851	Oberon		[Exhib Liverpool Ac, 586]; untraced	*Morris and Roberts* 1998, 363
29.	1851	Prometheus bound		[Exhib Liverpool Ac, 585]; untraced	*Morris and Roberts* 1998, 363
30.	1857	Study of a head, for a large relief of war		[Exhib RA, London, 1233]; untraced	*Graves* IV, 1905–6, 308

KELSEY, James fl 1840–46

He was the father of **Charles Samuel Kelsey**. Thompson's *Commercial Directory* for 1844 lists 'Kelsey Jas Statuary' in Commercial Street, Lambeth, London.

Chimneypieces

1.	1840–1846	Two, of green Irish marble	[Wyndham's Club, London]; untraced	*Builder* 1846, 477

Architectural Sculpture

2.	1843–1846	'the whole of the external architectural sculpture' (assisted by Charles Samuel Kelsey)	St George's Hall, Liverpool	*Builder*, vol 43, 1882, 126; *Cavanagh* 1997, 292

KELSEY, W T, of Brompton fl 1830–46

He signs a pair of 'eccentric' monuments in the de Grey mortuary chapel at Flitton, Beds, which 'revive, and unwittingly parody, the rococo style of the early eighteenth century' (**1, 2**). The Grantham is a cartouche with swagged curtains drawn back by a cherub. It was commissioned Lady Grantham's son, Thomas Philip, 2nd Earl de Grey, who rebuilt Wrest Park in the style of Louis XV during the same period and it is likely that he designed these tablets.

Literary References: *Gunnis* 1968, 224

Funerary Monuments

1.	1830	Lady Grantham	Flitton, Beds	S	*Penny* 1977 (1), 23–4 (repr)
2.	1833	Countess de Grey	Flitton, Beds	S	*Penny* 1977 (1), 23–4

KEMPSTER, Christopher 1627–1715

Kempster was one of the leading master masons employed in rebuilding the City churches after the Great Fire of London. The Burford baptismal records give the entry 'Christopher son of Christopher' christened on 25 March 1628, so refuting Gunnis's claim that his father's name was William. He married Joan, a Burford girl, around 1646, a partnership, (according to his epitaph), 'of perfect love and amity' which lasted nearly 60 years and produced five sons and seven daughters, including Christopher (1647–99), who was apprenticed to his father in 1684, and **William Kempster**. Kempster was made free of the Masons' Company by redemption in 1670, became renter warden 1685, upper warden 1688 and was twice master, in 1691 and 1700.

He owned quarries in Burford from which stone was sent to London as early as 1668, and entries in his daybook indicate that he was in London himself by January or February that year, possibly selling stone or working on buildings. He established a workshop on Garlick Hill. His first known metropolitan contract, received jointly with **Thomas Strong**, was as mason-contractor for St Stephen, Walbrook, where he worked from 1672–87 under Sir Christopher Wren (**2**). Their work evidently satisfied the patrons for on 27 May 1679 Wren, Strong, Kempster and several craftsmen were invited to the vestry dinner at the Bull's Head Tavern.

He also worked under Wren at St James, Garlickhythe, 1674–87 (**4**), St Mary Abchurch, 1681–7 (**5**), St Mary Somerset, 1686–94 (**6**) and St Mary at Hill, 1694–5. Miscellaneous bills indicate that he received many orders for gravestones throughout his London years and that he also worked at St Mary-le-Bow, in St Bride's churchyard and on several secular buildings including the Mitre tavern and the Anchor and Crown in Fish Street before 1716, and at the Dog tavern in 1717 (TNA C106/145). Outside London, he 'wrought the Town house' at Abingdon, 1678–80, which Wren mentioned in a letter to the Bishop of Oxford recommending Kempster for work on Tom Tower at Christ Church, Oxford. Wren wrote 'I have thought of a very able Man, modest, honest and Treatable, and one that Your masons wille submit to worke with because of his interest in the Quarries at Burford . . . His name is Xtopher Kempster. . .I have used him in goode workes he is very careful to worke trew to his designe and strong well bonded work' (Wren to Bishop Fell, 26 May 1681, quoted in *Wren Soc* V, 18). He and **Edward Strong I** worked on the west front of Winchester Palace in 1683–5, where they employed eighteen masons and nine labourers (**3**). In 1687 Kempster built the Perrot chapel on the north side of North Leigh church, Oxon.

Kempster was one of the principal masons at St Paul's Cathedral, where he was employed almost continuously from 1691–2 until 1707, in partnership with **Ephraim Beauchamp**. The team, which included 23 assistants, worked first on the legs of the dome and then on the dome itself. In October 1694 their work included composite capitals for the south wall, circular window splays and 77 foot 8 inches of 'great leaves and lace in the chaptring at bottom covering of the church' as well as a chimneypiece (TNA C106/145) (**1**). From 1707 to 1709 Kempster was employed on his own account, chiefly repairing the vaults.

The indentures of a number of Kempster's apprentices are recorded in the Masons' Company Apprenticeship Registers. They include William Greene (1671), Richard Cornell (1674), Thomas Hands (1674), George Whitehead, who was turned over to Kempster in 1686, Robert Mosley (1691), **Edward Tuffnell** (1692) and Joseph Henson (1693). Thomas Hands became his son-in-law.

Around 1698 Kempster went to live at 'Kitt's Quarry', a home he built or re-fronted for himself at the entrance to the quarry at Upton, near Burford. One of the window architraves has the inscription 'Christopher Kempster built this in 1698'. Both the house and quarry were bequeathed to his second son, John. He appears to have retired from business in 1709. His wife died in 1701 at the age of 82, and his own death took place on 12 August 1715 in his 89th year. He was buried in Burford church, where his son William provided a wall tablet to his memory surmounted by an armorial shield (*Wren Soc* XIX, repr LIX). The epitaph describes him as 'a person eminent in his profession and built several churches in the said City [London] . . . was many years employed in building the Cathedral and Dome of St. Paul's'. A ledger in the church also commemorates his son John who died on 21 February 1739. (Inf. Melody Mobus)

IR

Literary References: *Knoop and Jones* 1935, *passim*; Wren Soc V, VII, XV, XIX, *passim*; *Bolton* 1942, 90–1, 100–2; *Gunnis* 1968, 224–5; *Colvin* V, 1973–76, 309; *Colvin* 1995, 576–7; *Whitehead* 1999, 49; *Webb* 1999, *passim*; *Mobus* 2003; IGI

Archival References: Kempster Misc Bills

Additional Manuscript Sources: Christopher Kempster and family members, Day Book, *c*1667–80, Burford Local History Museum, Oxford; Day Book and Accounts, Chancery Masters' Exhibits, PRO C 106/145

Wills: PRO C.106/145 (dated 1712)

Chimneypieces

No.	Date	Work		Location	Reference
1.	by 1694	'a Portland chimneypiece. . .with an Italian moulding the jambs' (co-sculptor: Ephraim Beauchamp)		St Paul's Cathedral, London	TNA C106/145

Architectural Sculpture

No.	Date	Work		Location	Reference
2.	1672–1679	Capitals, small cherubim heads, scrolls, carved festoons and other ornaments (co-sculptor: Thomas Strong)		St Stephen Walbrook, City of London	*Wren Soc* X, 85–9
3.	1682–1683	Capitals, pilasters and other ornaments (co-sculptor: Edward Strong I)		[Winchester Palace, west front]; destroyed	*Wren Soc* VII, 40
4.	*c*1683	Font, five cherubim heads in windows and a door; shield on keystone of inward door in porch Payment(s): £20	m	St James Garlickhythe, City of London	Guildhall MS 25539/3; *Wren Soc* XIX, 21; *Gunnis* 1968, 225
5.	*c*1686	Font and seven pilaster-capitals and corbels, 12 cherubim heads in windows, three shields in the great windows		St Mary Abchurch, City of London	Guildhall MS 25539/4; Pevsner, *London* I, 1973, 167
6.	1686–1694	Cherub heads and keystones for outward doors, mask heads, festoons, vases and ornaments around the pinacles		St Mary Somerset, City of London	Guildhall MS 25539/4; *Gunnis* 1968, 225
7.	By 1694	Decorative carving including capitals and 'great leaves and lace in the chaptring' (co-sculptor: Ephraim Beauchamp)		St Paul's Cathedral, London	TNA C106/145

KEMPSTER, William 1651–1719

The son of **Christopher Kempster**, he was one of a large family of masons and assisted his father in his later works, particularly at St Paul's Cathedral. Christopher's baptism is recorded in the Burford parish records for 1651 and he was made free of the Masons' Company by redemption on 11 December 1677, became renter warden in 1700, upper warden in 1701 and master in 1705. His son, another William, was made free of the Company by patrimony on 17 January 1714. A family member, Edmund Kempster, became a freeman of the Company, having served under Christopher, on 12 April 1692 and another Christopher Kempster joined the freedom on 22 October 1701, having served under William.

Kempster was paid £20 10s for work as a mason at St Michael, Queenhythe in 1704, but by 1700 he was already at St Paul's Cathedral, where his father was a master mason. That year he spent four days modelling the scroll for a pilaster in the library at a rate of 2/6 per day and in 1703 he was paid £10 for making a stone cistern to hold water for making mortar. In 1704 he made a model for the geometrical staircase in the south-west tower; and he received just over £463 in June 1705 for the staircase itself. He continued to work at St Paul's after his father's death in 1715 and in 1717 was in charge of re-casing the great piers in the crypt, described as 'very confidential work' (*Wren Soc* XIX, 102). His burial is recorded in the Garlickhythe parish register for 13 March 1719.

Literary References: *Wren Soc* XIX, 102; XV, *passim*; *Mobus* 2003, *passim*

Archival References: Masons' Co, *Freemen*, fol 36

Architectural Sculpture

No.	Date	Work	Location	Reference
1.	*c*1705	Ornaments, including lacework for 20 panels, flowers, branches, scrolls, festoons, cherubs' heads and leatherwork	St Paul's Cathedral, London, geometrical staircase, south-west tower	*Wren Soc* XV, 123

KENDALL (or KENDAL), Edward, of Exeter –1796

Kendall, who was the mason responsible for building Exeter Guildhall, 1776–92, died on 28 November 1796, 'at an advanced age' (*GM*, 1796, ii, 1059). Gunnis notes that his monuments 'have charm and are usually carried out in coloured marbles'.

Literary References: *Gunnis* 1968, 225

Funerary Monuments

No.	Date	Subject	Location		Reference
1.	?1761	Joseph Hunt	Maker, Cornwall	S	*Gunnis* 1968, 225
2.	†1763	Paul Orchard (†1740) and wife	St Nectan, Hartland, Devon	S	Pevsner, *Devon*, 1989, 473
3.	?1767	Edward Hanbury	Dartmouth, Devon		*Gunnis* 1968, 225
4.	?1778	Thomas Morrison	Torrington, Devon		*Gunnis* 1968, 225
5.	?1785	Mary Cross	Cullompton, Devon		*Gunnis* 1968, 225
6.	?1785	Mrs Churchill	Dawlish, Devon		*Gunnis* 1968, 225
7.	?1787	Edward Hunt	Maker, Cornwall	S	*Gunnis* 1968, 225
8.	?1791	Charlotte Morrison	Alwington, Devon		*Gunnis* 1968, 225
9.	?1791	Mary Heathfield	Woodbury, Devon		*Gunnis* 1968, 225
10.	?1792	Rev John Newte	Tiverton, Devon		*Gunnis* 1968, 225

KENDALL (or KENDAL), John, of Exeter 1766–1829

The son of **Edward Kendall**, he can probably be identified with the John Kendall who became a pupil of James Paine, the architect, and exhibited architectural drawings at the Royal Academy in 1781–4. In 1796 he succeeded his father as stonemason to Exeter Cathedral, a post which he retained until his death in 1829 at the age of 63. He was more or less continuously employed on repairs and embellishments to that building from about 1805. His work included the refacing of the chapter-house and Chapel of the Holy Ghost, restoration of the west front, additions to the organ screen, a new gallery screen at the west end of the chapter house, the refitting of the Lady Chapel and various external repairs. Colvin comments, 'Like a medieval master mason he himself designed all the works that he executed, and he was one of the last men of his trade in whom these two capacities were thus combined' (*Colvin* 1995, 579).

It is possible that Kendall worked for **John Flaxman** for in 1799 he signed a tablet to George Speke at White Lackington, Somerset 'I: KENDALL, EXON'. This was designed by Flaxman and a payment is recorded to

Flaxman (Flaxman Account Book 1794–1810, 66). Alternatively Kendall may have been the mason who erected the work and signed it.

In 1818 Kendal published *An Elucidation of the Principles of Gothic Architecture, usually denominated Gothic* (reissued 1842) with plates illustrating examples in Exeter Cathedral. He was probably responsible for the new gothic altar piece, screen and pulpit for Haccombe church, Devon, in 1822. A contemporary source states that they were by 'Mr Nicholas Kendall' but this is almost certainly an error (Lysons, *Magna Britannia*, vol VI, part 2, 1822, 250, cited by *Colvin* 1995, 579).

Gunnis considered Kendall's monuments 'less ambitious than those of his father though some of them have quite pleasant reliefs' (*Gunnis* 1968, 225). Some feature pilasters with capitals in the form of rams' heads, a motif he probably copied from the work of Robert Adam. The monument to Humphrey Sibthorp features a wreath of sibthorpia (**12**), the Lyne has a pretty relief of a woman wreathing an urn (**18**) and the Brutton a relief of a mourning youth (**28**).

Literary References: *Gunnis* 1968, 225; *Colvin* 1995, 579

Funerary Monuments

1.	†1787	Sir Richard Hunt	Maker, Cornwall	S	Pevsner, *Cornwall*, 1970, 112
2.	†1791	Robert Harvey	Exeter Cathedral, Devon	S	GPC
3.	†1793	Andrew Quicke	Newton St Cyres, Devon	S	Pevsner, *Devon*, 1989, 597
4.	†1793	Edward Drew	Exeter Cathedral, Devon	S	RG/JP, 5, 775
5.	†1796	Philip Barton	Exeter Cathedral, Devon	S	RG/JP, 5, 775
6.	†1796	William Buller DD	Exeter Cathedral, Devon		RG/JP, 5, 774v
7.	†1798	Lady Southampton	Exeter Cathedral, Devon	S	GPC
8.	†1798	Rev Thomas Tarrant	St Petroch, Exeter, Devon	S	RG/JP, 5, 775
9.	†1798	Susannah Bealey	Exeter Cathedral, Devon	S	RG/JP, 5, 775
10.	†1799	Mary Irvine	Exeter Cathedral, Devon		RG/JP, 5, 774v
11.	†1800	Rachel O'Brien	Exeter Cathedral, Devon	S	Pevsner, *Devon*, 1989, 381
12.	1801	Humphrey Sibthorp (†1797)	Instow, Devon	S	Pevsner, *Devon*, 1989, 508; *Penny* 1977 (1), 208 n18
13.	†1801	Sarah Clarke	Exeter Cathedral, Devon	S	RG/JP, 5, 775
14.	?1803	Lord Hawarden	Teigngrace, Devon	S	*Gunnis* 1968, 225
15.	?1805	George Buck	Bideford, Devon	S	*Gunnis* 1968, 225
16.	?1805	Henry Downe	Northam, Devon	S	*Gunnis* 1968, 225
17.	?1805	James Rudman	Exeter Cathedral, Devon	S	*Gunnis* 1968, 225
18.	?1805	Lyne family	Launceston, Cornwall	S	*Gunnis* 1968, 225
19.	?1805	Thomas Galsworthy	Hartland, Devon	S	*Gunnis* 1968, 225
20.	?1807	Cann family	Spreyton, Devon	S	*Gunnis* 1968, 225
21.	1807	Unidentified subject, wall monument	Drewsteignton, Devon	S	Pevsner, *Devon*, 1989, 340
22.	?1809	Elizabeth Marshall	Barnstaple, Devon	S	*Gunnis* 1968, 225
23.	?1813	Lucretia Putt	Trent, Somerset	S	*Gunnis* 1968, 225
24.	†1813	Samuel Trancott Gruttner of Elbing, Prussia	St Swithin, Woodbury, Devon	S	Pevsner, *Devon*, 1989, 918
25.	†1814	Richard Ivyleafe	Siston, Glos	S	Pevsner, *Glos: Vale & Forest of Dean*, 1976, 338
26.	?1814	William Matterface	Dawlish, Devon	S	*Gunnis* 1968, 225
27.	†1816	Harriet Brooke	Tor, Devon		RG/JP, 5, 774v
28.	?1816	Henry Brutton	Cullompton, Devon	S	*Gunnis* 1968, 225
29.	†1816	Richard Kingdom	Holsworthy, Devon	S	Pevsner, *Devon*, 1989, 492
30.	?1819	John Barker	Wareham, Hants		*Gunnis* 1968, 225
31.	†1821	Edmund and Eliza Peel	Tor, Devon		RG/JP, 5, 774v
32.	†1821	Rev John Swete	Kenton, Devon	S	Pevsner, *Devon*, 1989, 517
33.	†1824	William Cuming	South Brent, Devon	S	Pevsner, *Devon*, 1989, 746
34.	†1825	Mary Peel	Littleham, Devon	S	Pevsner, *Devon*, 1989, 538
35.	†1826	Archdeacon Thomas Johnes	Exeter Cathedral, Devon		RG/JP, 5, 774v
36.	nd	Unidentified subjects, tablets	Northam, Devon	S	Pevsner, *Devon*, 1989, 598

Statues

37.	1817	Edward III, Alfred the Great, and other figures (restoration only)	Exeter Cathedral, Devon, West Front		*GM*, 1817, ii, 358

Chimneypieces

38.	1821	No description available	Exeter Cathedral, Devon, Chapter House		*Colvin* 1995, 579

Architectural Sculpture

39.	*c*1779	Altar	Torre Abbey, Devon, chapel		Pevsner, *Devon*, 1989, 853
40.	1818	Reredos	[Exeter Cathedral, Devon]; removed during later restoration		*Colvin* 1995, 579

KENDRICK, Edward –1812

The monument commemorating Elizabeth Howis signed 'E. KENDRICK Sculp., St Georges Square, Portsea'. Gunnis described it as a 'delightful work' with 'a pretty relief which resembles the work of Flaxman', but thought that it was by **Joseph Kendrick**. The will of 'Edward Kendrick, Statuary Carver of Portsea, Hampshire' was proved on 19 December 1812.

Literary References: *Gunnis* 1968, 226

Will: PROB 11/1539

Funerary Monuments

1.	†1806	Elizabeth How	Warblington, Hants	S

KENDRICK, Joseph 1754/5–

Joseph Kendrick signs several monuments and tablets. He was apprenticed to **Nicholas Read**, of St Martin-in-the-Fields, in 1770 (PRO, I R 26/145) and joined the Royal Academy schools on 18 December 1771, giving his age as 17. He may have had some connection with the village of Wateringbury in Kent for he signs a pedestal in the churchyard there, which once supported a sundial made by Thomas Crow, a local craftsman (7). One of Crow's children was christened 'Kendrick'. Gunnis thought that Joseph Kendrick was responsible for the monument to Elizabeth How at Warblington, Hants, but this was signed by **Edward Kendrick**, a carver of Portsea. Joseph's daughter, Emma Eleanor Kendrick (1789–1871) was a successful miniaturist and his son **Josephus John Pinnix Kendrick** was a sculptor. Both were christened at St Marylebone, London.

Literary References: *Hutchison* 1960–62, 137; *Gunnis* 1968, 226; RG/JP, 5, 775–6

Archival References: IGI

Funerary Monuments

1.	?1774	Charles Style	Wateringbury, Kent	S	*Gunnis* 1968, 226
2.	†1800	Frances Champneys	Boxley, Kent	S	Pevsner, *Kent: NE & E*, 1983, 153
3.	?1801	Geoffrey Hornby	Samelsbury, Lancs	S	*Gunnis* 1968, 226; Pevsner, *Lancs: N*, 1969, 216
4.	†1803	William Bleamire	St John, Hampstead, Middx	S	Pevsner, *London: N*, 1998, 202
5.	†1805	William St Quintin	Harpham, E R Yorks	S	Pevsner, *Yorks: E R & York*, 1995, 450
6.	?1811	George Grigby	Drinkstone, Suffolk	S	*Gunnis* 1968, 226

Architectural Sculpture

7.	nd	Sundial pedestal	Wateringbury, Kent, churchyard		*Gunnis* 1968, 226

KENDRICK, Josephus John Pinnix 1790–1832

The son of **Joseph Kendrick**, he was born on 15 April 1790 and baptised on 22 August at St Mary, St Marylebone Road, London. He joined the Royal Academy schools on 27 January 1808. There he was awarded silver medals in 1809 and 1811, the second for 'a model from the Antique Gallery' (**49**), and a gold medal in 1813 for a relief of *Adam and Eve lamenting over the dead body of Abel* (**46**). He received the Society of Arts' silver Isis medal in 1811 for a plaster cast, *Gladiator moriens*, a work which he exhibited two years later at the Liverpool Academy (**25**). His address at this time was 5 Upper Marylebone Street. He exhibited at the Royal Academy, 1813–29, and at the British Institution in 1819 and 1820, showing portrait busts, models for monuments and ideal works. His address throughout this period was 6 Upper Marylebone Street, London.

Gunnis later described Kendrick as 'a competent minor sculptor whose smaller monuments and bas-reliefs are harmless and even pleasing'. Examples include the monument to Sir George Murray which has a relief of the Battle of Copenhagen (**12**) and another commemorating Lord and Lady Henniker, which takes the form of two female allegorical figures flanking an urn bearing two medallion portraits (**13**). Gunnis was critical of Kendrick's most elaborate work, the national monument to Sir William Myers, which he called 'one of the most unfortunate memorials in the whole building', arguing that such a significant commission was far beyond the sculptor's capabilities (**10**). The design, which depicts *Hercules* and *Minerva* warmly shaking hands in front of a tomb surmounted by a bust of Myers, is derived from the monuments to Admiral Sir Peter Warren and General James Fleming in Westminster Abbey, both by **Louis François Roubiliac**. Gunnis was also unimpressed by Kendrick's melodramatic monument to Brigadier General Robert Ross, where 'Valour lays an American flag on the tomb of the departed warrior, on which Britannia is recumbent in tears, while fame is descending with a laurel to crown his bust' (*Graves* IV, 1905–6, 314) (**15**).

Kendrick seems to have been ambitious but was repeatedly disappointed in his attempts to secure commissions for public statues. In 1826 he exhibited a figure of Sir James Leith 'for Barbados' at the RA (**26**). Some years earlier, in 1819, the sculptor had written to the Dean and Chapter of Westminster Abbey stating that the subscribers, who were inhabitants of Barbados, wished to erect the statue 'immediately against the next column of the church to that where Mr. Addison's stands being of the same dimensions' (*Kendrick/Westm Abbey*). His application was rejected (*Westm Abbey Notes* 1819). The statue has not been traced and may never have progressed beyond the model stage. In 1827 and 1828 he showed a model for a proposed statue of the composer Carl Maria von Weber at the RA and the Suffolk Street Galleries but this scheme also apparently aborted (**27**). He then submitted a design for a statue in competition for the national monument to the Duke of York, but the commission was awarded to **Sir Richard Westmacott RA** (**29**).

Towards the end of his life Kendrick had serious financial problems. In 1831 he applied to the Artists General Benevolent Institution asking for money 'to enable him to complete some marble busts ordered by Lord Minto, Lord Selsey and gentlemen of the highest class of society' adding that 'his financial difficulty had arisen from gentlemen not honouring their accounts'. Soon after his death, early in 1832, Kendrick's widow, Frances, also applied for help, saying that 'the many disappointments which chequered his unfortunate career preying upon his mind caused his early decease'. In the same year Thomas Phillips RA wrote to tell Sir John Soane that he had given Soane's charitable donation to 'Widow Kendrick'. He thought it 'certainly a very distressing case to see so seemingly respectable a Woman's fall from the most reasonable expectations of success in life which her husband's talent promised her, to so very destitute a condition as she seems to be left in' (Soane Priv Corr, II P 8/4). She was granted a pension by the Royal Academy which continued until 1851. Kendrick's only son, born in 1828, emigrated to Australia in 1852.

EH

Literary References: *Gunnis* 1968, 226–7; *Whinney* 1988, 371–2; *Yarrington* 1988, 266 n1, 348; *Bindman and Baker* 1995, 313

Archival References: AGBI, vol 2, 70, 71; IGI

Funerary Monuments

1.	†1795	Katharine Page	Donnington, Sussex		RG/JP, 5, 775
2.	1812	Sir Francis Molyneux	Teversal, Notts	S	Pevsner, *Notts*, 1979, 347
3.	†1815	Lieutenant-Colonel Stables	Great Hormead, Herts	S	Pevsner, *Herts*, 1977, 152
4.	?1815	Sir George Thomas	Madehurst, Sussex	S	*Gunnis* 1968, 226
5.	†1816	Charles, 3rd Earl Stanhope	Chevening, Kent	S	*Gunnis* 1968, 226
6.	†1816	John, Baron Selsey	Barkway, Herts	S	Pevsner, *Herts*, 1977, 88
7.	†1816	Zachariah Foxall	Ashford, Middx	S	
8.	?1817	Major-General Churchill	St Mary, Lewisham, London	S	*Gunnis* 1968, 226
9.	†1816–1817	Officers of the 2nd or Queen's Regiment of Foot	Barbados Cathedral, Bridgetown	S	
10.	1817	Sir William Myers Drawing(s): PRO MPD 78, with agreement and bond Model(s): exhib RA, London, 1815, 875 (half-size)	St Paul's Cathedral, London		*Graves* IV, 1905–6, 314; *Gunnis* 1968, 226; *Whinney* 1988, 371, 372 (repr)
11.	1819	James Bindley	[St Mary-le-Strand, London]; destroyed		*Gunnis* 1968, 226
12.	†1819	Sir George Murray	Chichester Cathedral, Sussex	S	*Gunnis* 1968, 226; Pevsner, *Sussex*, 1965, 153

13.	†1821	John, Baron Henniker and Lady Emily Henniker (†1819)		Thornham Magna, Suffolk	S	*Gunnis* 1968, 226; Pevsner, *Suffolk*, 1974, 463
14.	?1822	Sir Thomas Bloomfield		St Nicholas, Plumstead, London	S	*Gunnis* 1968, 226
15.	1823	Brigadier General Robert Ross (†1814) Model(s): exhib RA, London, 1819, 1198 (sketch); exhib RA, London, 1821, 1095 (half-size); Soc of BA, London, 1829 (small sketch)		St Paul's Cathedral, London, south transept		*Graves* IV, 1905–6, 314; *Gunnis* 1968, 226; Pevsner, *London: City*, 1997, 173; *Johnson* 1975, 267
16.	?1823	Martha Rudding		St Mary, Hampton, Middx	S	*Gunnis* 1968, 226
17.	1824	Admiral Lord Duncan, for St Paul's Cathedral, small model only		[Exhib RA, London, 981]; untraced		*Graves* IV, 1905–6, 314; *Johnson* 1975, 267
18.	?1824	George Pring		St Paul, Hammersmith, London	S	*Gunnis* 1968, 226
19.	†1824	Janet Maude		Wakefield Cathedral, W R Yorks	S	Pevsner, *Yorks: W R*, 1967, 529
20.	†1825	Henry Nash		Stanstead Abbots, Herts	S	Pevsner, *Herts*, 1977, 342
21.	?1826	Lady Bloomfield		St Nicholas, Plumstead, London	S	*Gunnis* 1968, 226
22.	1828	Thomas Leverton (†1824)		Chipping Barnet, Essex		*Graves* IV, 1905–6, 314; Pevsner, *Essex*, 1965, 405; *Johnson* 1975, 267; Pevsner, *London: N*, 1998, 170
23.	1829	Dr Kitchener, executed by order of his son, W B Kitchener		[Exhib Soc of BA, London, 848]; untraced		*Johnson* 1975, 267
24.	?1829	Thomas Hardwick		St Lawrence, Brentford, Middx		*Gunnis* 1968, 227
Statues						
25.	1811	Gladiator moriens	p	[Soc of A, silver Isis medal]; untraced		RSA *Transactions*, vol 29, 1811, 23; *Morris and Roberts* 1998, 363
26.	1826	Lieutenant-General Sir James Leith		[Exhib RA, London, 1104]; untraced		*Graves* IV, 1905–6, 314; *Gunnis* 1968, 226; *Johnson* 1975, 266–7
27.	1827	Carl Maria von Weber, for St Paul's Cathedral, model only		[Exhib RA, London, 1087]; untraced		*Graves* IV, 1905–6, 314; *Johnson* 1975, 266
28.	1828	Britannia offering peace to the world, small model (for the Nelson column, Yarmouth)		[Exhib Soc of BA, London, 919]; untraced		*Johnson* 1975, 267
29.	*c*1829	Frederick Augustus, Duke of York and Albany, design only		PRO Work 20 5/1, 61–121		*Yarrington* 1988, 348
Busts						
30.	1813	G Smart		[Exhib RA, London, 905]; untraced		*Graves* IV, 1905–6, 314
31.	1813	John Fisher, Bishop of Salisbury		[Exhib RA, London, 930]; untraced		*Graves* IV, 1905–6, 314; *Johnson* 1975, 267
32.	1813	Unidentified gentleman		[Exhib RA, London, 896]; untraced		*Graves* IV, 1905–6, 314
33.	1815	Dr W Kitchener MD		[Exhib RA, London, 891]; untraced		*Graves* IV, 1905–6, 314; *Johnson* 1975, 267
34.	1818	Hon W Lamb		[Exhib RA, London, 1050]; untraced		*Graves* IV, 1905–6, 314
35.	1823	J Stewart		[Exhib RA, London, 1059]; untraced		*Graves* IV, 1905–6, 314
36.	1824	Alexander Davison		[Exhib RA, London, 979]; untraced		*Graves* IV, 1905–6, 314; *Johnson* 1975, 267
37.	1825	Lord Henniker		[Exhib RA, London, 1059]; untraced		*Graves* IV, 1905–6, 314
38.	1825	Lord Selsey		[Exhib RA, London, 1017]; untraced		*Graves* IV, 1905–6, 314; *Johnson* 1975, 267
39.	1825	Unidentified gentleman	m	Knox/Longstaffe-Gowan coll (acq 1995)	SD	
40.	1825	Unidentified lady		[Exhib RA, London, 1011]; untraced		*Graves* IV, 1905–6, 314
41.	1827	John Adams Bethune	m	[Exhib RA, London, 1080]; untraced		*Graves* IV, 1905–6, 314
42.	1829	A F C Kollman		[Exhib RA, London, 1133]; untraced		*Graves* IV, 1905–6, 314; *Johnson* 1975, 267
43.	1829	Miss Turner		[Exhib RA, London, 1150]; untraced		*Graves* IV, 1905–6, 314
44.	1830	Unidentified subject		[Exhib Soc of BA, London, 860]; untraced		*Johnson* 1975, 267
45.	1830	Unidentified subject		[Exhib Soc of BA, London, 861]; untraced		*Johnson* 1975, 267
Reliefs						
46.	1813	Adam and Eve lamenting over the dead body of Abel		[RA Gold Medal]; untraced		*Graves* IV, 1905–6, 314; *Gunnis* 1968, 226; *Johnson* 1975, 267
47.	1826	Lord Henniker, medallion		[Exhib RA, London, 1062]; untraced		*Graves* IV, 1905–6, 314
Miscellaneous						
48.	1811	Model from the antique gallery		[RA silver medal]; untraced		RA Premium list
49.	1817	Prometheus chained		[Exhib RA, London, 1015]; untraced		*Graves* IV, 1905–6, 314
50.	1819	Adam and Eve		[Exhib RA, London, 1187]; untraced		*Graves* IV, 1905–6, 314
51.	1822	Eve tempted by the serpent, small sketch		[Exhib RA, London, 1019]; untraced		*Graves* IV, 1905–6, 314
52.	1826	Eve's troublesome dream		[Exhib RA, London, 1038]; untraced		*Graves* IV, 1905–6, 314; *Johnson* 1975, 266

KENNEDY, E fl 1842

In 1842 she exhibited a relief entitled *Scenes at a Fair in the North of Ireland* at the Royal Academy. This work, which included 30 figures, 'many of them chiselled out of the mass with a boldness of relief truly surprising', was considered 'full of vigour, life and character'. Mrs Kennedy was described as an Irish lady 'not of the profession – whose station in society has made the cultivation of taste a source of enjoyment to herself – and now, to others' (*AU*, 1842, 129).

Literary References: *Gunnis* 1968, 227

Reliefs				
1.	1842	Scenes at a fair in the north of Ireland	[Exhib RA, London, 1348]; untraced	*AU*, 1842, 129; *Graves* IV, 1905–6, 315

KENT, of Boston, Lincs fl 1823?

Funerary Monuments

1.	?1823	Mary Millington	Gedney, Lincs	S	GPC

KENT, of London fl 1840?

His one recorded work is a large neo-Hellenic monument with a figure of *Hope*. He may perhaps be identified with the 'J Kent' who signed several designs for monuments in a scrapbook largely containing drawings by **Robert Shout** (VAM P&D 93-H-137). J Kent's designs include one of a woman mourning over a sarcophagus under an urn and weeping willow, and another with a large urn on a rectangular sarcophagus with lion's feet and gothic tracery.

Literary References: *Gunnis* 1968, 227

Funerary Monuments

1.	?1840	Ann Elverson	Oadby, Leics	S	*Gunnis* 1968, 227

KENT, Thomas Wickham 1744–1817

Kent was born at Bradwell, Derbys, and was believed to be 'the natural son of a peer, the grandfather of a Duke'. He was apprenticed to **Joseph Wilton**, and later studied in Rome. He was 'employed in the shops of several of our first artists' for many years, but *c*1795 he joined the band of the 101st Regiment, with whom he remained for five years. After this he kept a plaster figure shop at Whetstone Park, near Holborn. In 1816 he became infirm and entered St Giles's workhouse, where he died (*Annual Biography*, 2, 1818, 459). None of Kent's works have been identified, but Glover lists him among the 'Eminent Natives of the County of Derby' (*Glover* 1831–3, vol I, pt I, appendix 105).

Literary References: GPC

KESSELS, Mathieu (or Matthaus) 1784–1836

He was a Belgian sculptor who studied under **Thorvaldsen.** The 6th Duke of Devonshire visited his studio in Rome in December 1822 and a year later ordered a life-sized statue of the *Discobolus* for Chatsworth (**2**). A smaller version, dated 1826, was bequeathed to the Royal Dublin Society by Mrs Ann Putland in 1856. Another work destined for Britain was the monument to Georgiana Naylor, with its relief of a deathbed scene (**1**). The first version was lost at sea and the Hare family ordered another from the sculptor. The monument to Thomas Otway Cave (†1830) at St Nicholas, Stanford, Northants may also be by the sculptor. It was erected in 1832 and has a relief of the dying man, attended by his wife and a figure with an extinguished torch.

Literary References: *Gunnis* 1968, 227; *JKB* 1972 (3), 326–9, 330, 331; Pevsner, *Northants*, 1973, 410

Funerary Monuments						
1.	1829	Georgiana Hare-Naylor (†1806)		Herstmonceux, Sussex		Pevsner, *Sussex*, 1965, 534
Statues						
2.	1828	Discobolus Payment(s): 2,000 scudi	m	Chatsworth, Derbys, sculpture gallery Other versions: RDS, Dublin, m, SD 1826	SD	*JKB* 1972 (3), 326, 327–8, 329, 331 (repr); *White and Bright* 1998, 26 (repr)

KESTART fl *c*1833–36

He signs several 'Norman style' black marble tablets in the north aisle of Southwell Minster (NP/RG).

Funerary Monuments

1.	†1833	William Lawson	Southwell Minster, Notts	S
2.	†1836	William Barron	Southwell Minster, Notts	S
3.	†1838	Richard Barrow	Southwell Minster, Notts	S

KETT, George 1809–72

A mason from Norfolk, in 1843 he went into partnership with a joiner, **James Rattee**, to form the firm of Rattee and Kett, which specialised in architectural stonework and woodcarving. The business, which still exists as a subsidiary of a large construction company, carried out work on the Houses of Parliament, several Cambridge colleges and numerous British cathedrals and churches.

KEYWORTH, William Day I, of Hull 1817–97

He was born in Kingston-upon-Hull, the eldest son of Joseph Keyworth, a stone and marble mason. Joseph's two younger sons, Joseph Milburn (b 1825) and Edward John (b 1833), were trained as mason-sculptors, but no known works survive by either. In 1826 the family moved to London where Joseph was employed by **Sir Francis Chantrey** and in 1831 William was taken on as an apprentice by **Henry Weekes.** Joseph failed to establish himself in London and returned with his family to Hull *c*1834, where he resumed work as a marble mason. He never owned his own workshop.

William's first recorded commission, *c*1834, was for architectural ornaments for the Assembly rooms in Kingston Square, Hull (**67**). His name appeared in the *Trades' Directory* for 1838, where he was listed as a stone and marble-mason and modeller, working from 28 Junction Dock Street. He had already begun to practice as a sculptor, showing his first known busts at the Royal Academy in 1837, from an address in Arthur Street, Chelsea (**42, 43**). The portrait of Sarah Stickney (**43**), was singled out as a 'successful representation' in the *Eastern Counties Herald* on 30 January 1840. He exhibited five other busts at the Academy before 1845, all sent down from Hull, and courted local patrons by exhibiting at **John Earle**'s sculpture rooms in Hull.

By 1851 Keyworth was working as an architect and sculptor from new rooms at 54 Savile Street. His activities as an architect involved little more than restoration work on local churches and he was chiefly engaged on commissions for busts and church monuments. Portraiture features in a number of his most successful funerary works, such as the monument to William Woolley (**2**) which the local press described as an 'excellent work of art' (*Hull Advertiser*, 23 Aug 1839).

In 1849 Keyworth was initiated as a member of the Humber lodge of freemasons, where he became grand master in 1867. He was a committed freemason throughout his life and several of his commissions resulted from membership of the lodge. These include a chaste memorial with a cross and masonic emblems commemorating the benevolence of A O Arden, who had established a fund for the relief of distressed freemasons and their widows (**35**).

Keyworth admired medieval sculpture and took a delight in the gothic revival which he believed would redeem monumental sculpture from the 'nonsense' that had prevailed since the Reformation (*Hull Advertiser*, 3 April 1846). He contributed a series of casts from local medieval buildings to the medieval court at the Crystal Palace, Sydenham, in 1854, including canopies and canopied niches from Beverley Minster and a complete cast of the font at Walsingham in Norfolk (**69, 70**). Some of these were later donated to the Hull Museums. Several of his finest monuments were in the gothic style, including a 'highly-decorated' one to Major Thomas Northcliffe Dalton, reported in the *Illustrated London News* on 17 November 1855 (**20**).

By the mid 1850s William Day Keyworth II (1843–1902) was working with his father and supplementing his training by attending art classes at the Mechanics' Institute. Since there was no school of art in Hull, he moved to London in 1860 to join the South Kensington schools, later registering as a student at the Royal Academy schools.

The elder Keyworth was one of several active lobbyists for a school of art in Hull. In January 1861 a committee was appointed to this end. The Hull School of Art was opened in Jarratt Street later that year and the elder Keyworth became a leading member of the executive committee. The first exhibition was held in the spring of 1862. Both Keyworths were active participants in later exhibitions.

The younger Keyworth retained ties with Hull and was rewarded with a series of major commissions. Though he kept a studio in Buckingham Palace Road, London, by 1888 he also he was also working in partnership with his father. In 1892 W D Keyworth & Son of Hull had stone and marble works at 54 Savile Street and 244 Spring Bank, with a studio on Paragon Street. They employed at least one other man and 14 apprentices at the workshop in Savile Street during the 1880s and probably expanded their workforce in the 1890s when they acquired an additional studio on Paragon Street.

Keyworth I died in April 1897 leaving his interest in the partnership to his son. The firm was perhaps by then in decline for the younger Keyworth fell into debt and he committed suicide in 1902.

Gerardine Mulcahy

Literary References: *William White's General Directory of the Town and Port of Kingston-upon-Hull*, 1838; Hull School of Art, prospectus, 1862–63 (NAL & A. 97.E. Box 0180); *Sheahan* 1868, *passim*; census records, Kingston-upon-Hull, 1881; *Graves* IV, 1905–6, 321–2; *Shaw* 1935, *passim; Gunnis* 1968, 227; *Mulcahy* 2000 (2)

Will: W D Keyworth, proved 18 May 1897, district probate registry, York

Portraits of the Sculptor: Thomas Brookes (attrib), oil on canvas, *c*1847, Ferens Art Gallery, Kingston-upon-Hull (*Mulcahy* 2000 repr 99)

Funerary Monuments

1.	†1837	Samuel Welton	Municipal gardens, Trippet St, Hull, E R Yorks	S	*Mulcahy* 2000 (1), cat 233
2.	†1837	William Woolley	Holy Trinity, Hull, E R Yorks	S	Pevsner, *Yorks: E R & York*, 1995, 508; *Mulcahy* 2000 (1), cat 234 (repr)
3.	†1840	John Wallis and John Lambert	Cottingham, E R Yorks	S	Pevsner, *Yorks: E R & York*, 1995, 387; *Mulcahy* 2000 (1), cat 235
4.	†1840	Simon Horner	Cottingham, E R Yorks	S	*Mulcahy* 2000 (1), cat 236
5.	†1841	George Codd	Cottingham, E R Yorks	S	Pevsner, *Yorks: E R & York*, 1995, 387; *Mulcahy* 2000 (1), cat 238 (repr)
6.	†1841	John Cowham Parker	Holy Trinity, Hull, E R Yorks	S	*Gunnis* 1968, 227; *Mulcahy* 2000 (1), cat 238 (repr)
7.	†1842	Archdeacon F Wrangham	Hunmanby, E R Yorks	S	Pevsner, *Yorks: E R & York*, 1995, 569; *Mulcahy* 2000 (1), cat 239
8.	†1846	Isaac Raines	Burton Pidsea, E R Yorks	S	*Mulcahy* 2000 (1), cat 241; *Mulcahy* 2001, 127 (repr)
9.	†1846	Rev Henry Earl	Burstwick, E R Yorks	S	*Mulcahy* 2000 (1), cat 240 (repr)
10.	*c*1846	Samuel King	[Christ Church, Hull, E R Yorks]; destroyed		*Mulcahy* 2000 (1), cat 242
11.	†1847	Rev Thomas Dykes	[St John, Hull, E R Yorks]; untraced		*Gunnis* 1968, 227; *Mulcahy* 2000 (1), cat 243
12.	†1847	William West	St Mary, Sculcoates, Hull, E R Yorks		*Mulcahy* 2000 (1), cat 246
13.	†1848	Charles Louis Brett	Bridlington Priory, E R Yorks	S	*Mulcahy* 2000 (1), cat 247
14.	†1849	Rev George Carrick	Charterhouse Hospital chapel, Hull, E R Yorks		Pevsner, *Yorks: E R & York*, 1995, 560; *Mulcahy* 2000, cat 248
15.	†1850	John Wade	St Nicholas, Hornsea, E R Yorks	S	*Mulcahy* 2000 (1), cat 250
16.	†1850	Rheuban Craven	[Christ Church, Hull, E R Yorks]; destroyed	S	*Gunnis* 1968, 227; *Mulcahy* 2000 (1), cat 249
17.	†1850	Thomas Binnington	North Dalton, E R Yorks	S	Pevsner, *Yorks: E R & York*, 1995, 628; *Mulcahy* 2000 (1), cat 248
18.	1852	Darley family	Hunmanby, E R Yorks	S	*Mulcahy* 2000 (1), cat 251
19.	†1854	James Henwood	[Wesleyan chapel, Humber St, Hull, E R Yorks]; destroyed		*Mulcahy* 2000 (1), cat 253
20.	†1854	Major Thomas Northcliffe Dalton	Fillingham, Lincs, churchyard		*Mulcahy* 2000 (1), cat 254 (repr); *Mulcahy* 2001, 127–8
21.	1854	Sir William Lowthrop (†1853)	[Albion chapel, Humber St, Hull, E R Yorks]; destroyed		*Mulcahy* 2000 (1), cat 252
22.	†1855	Robert Roach	[St James, Hull, E R Yorks]; destroyed	S	*Mulcahy* 2000 (1), cat 255
23.	†1856	Andrew Fitzgerald Reynolds	Welton, E R Yorks	S	*Mulcahy* 2000 (1), cat 258
24.	†1856	Isaac Staveley	Kirkburn, E R Yorks	S	Pevsner, *Yorks: E R & York*, 1995, 583; *Mulcahy* 2000 (1), cat 256

No.	Date	Subject		Location		Bibliography
25.	†1856	Mary Heslewood		All Saints, Preston, E R Yorks	S	Pevsner, *Yorks: E R & York*, 1995, 652; *Mulcahy* 2000 (1), cat 257 (repr)
26.	†1857	John Ford Acey		All Saints, Preston, Lancs		*Mulcahy* 2000 (1), cat 259 (repr)
27.	†1857	Joseph Sykes		Kirk Ella, E R Yorks	S	Pevsner, *Yorks: E R & York*, 1995, 585; *Mulcahy* 2000 (1), cat 260 (repr)
28.	†1858	John King		[Christ Church, Hull, E R Yorks]; destroyed		*Sheahan* 1868, 648; *Mulcahy* 2000 (1), cat 262
29.	†1858	Olivia Grimston		Kilnwick-on-the-Wolds, E R Yorks	S	*Mulcahy* 2000 (1), cat 262; *Mulcahy* 2001, 127–8 (repr)
30.	†1859	Charles Grimston		All Saints, Kilnwick-on-the-Wolds, E R Yorks	S	*Mulcahy* 2000 (1), cat 263
31.	†1860	Mary Heath		[Christ Church, Hull, E R Yorks]; destroyed		*Sheahan* 1868, 524; *Mulcahy* 2000 (1), cat 264
32.	†1861	J H Wolfenden		[Spring Bank Cemetery, Hull, E R Yorks]; untraced		*Hull Packet and East Riding Times*, 16 May, 1862; *Mulcahy* 2000 (1), cat 265
33.	†1863	John Lee Smith		Sutton, Hull, E R Yorks	S	*Mulcahy* 2000 (1), cat 266
34.	†1863	Robert Glossop		[St Paul, Hull, E R Yorks]; destroyed		*Mulcahy* 2000 (1), cat 267
35.	†1865	A O Arden		Spring Bank Cemetery, Hull, E R Yorks		*Sheahan* 1868, 681; *Mulcahy* 2000 (1), cat 268
36.	†1866	John Gravill		Spring Bank Cemetery, Hull, E R Yorks		*Mulcahy* 2000 (1), cat 269 (repr)
37.	†1874	Henry Cautley		Hedon, E R Yorks	S	*Mulcahy* 2000 (1), cat 270
38.	†1884	Jemima Shutt Bell		St Peter's churchyard, Hambleton, E R Yorks	S	*Mulcahy* 2000 (1), cat 274 (repr)
39.	nd	Ann Mell		At Andrew's churchyard, Kirk Ella, E R Yorks	S	*Mulcahy* 2000 (1), cat 273
40.	nd	Harrison family		[St Mary, Sculcoates, Hull, E R Yorks]; untraced		*Sheahan* 1868, 506; *Mulcahy* 2000 (1), cat 271
41.	nd	Mr Skelton		[Christ Church, Hull, E R Yorks]; destroyed		*Sheahan* 1868, 524; *Mulcahy* 2000 (1), cat 272
Busts						
42.	1837	Dr Ayre MD, of Hull	m	Guildhall, Hull, E R Yorks		*Graves* IV, 1905–6, 321; *Gunnis* 1968, 227; *Mulcahy* 2000 (1), cat 275
43.	1837	Sarah Stickney		[Exhib RA, London, 1246]; untraced		*Graves* IV, 1905–6, 321; *Mulcahy* 2000 (1), cat 301
44.	1838	Rev George Lee	m	[Mechanics Institute, Hull, E R Yorks]; untraced Other versions: clay model, ex coll Mrs Lee; untraced		*Hull Advertiser*, 5 June 1846; *Graves* IV, 1905–6, 321; *Mulcahy* 2000 (1), cat 277, 278
45.	1839	Rev A Tideman		[Exhib Soc of BA, London, 759]; untraced		*Johnson* 1975, 268
46.	1839	Rev William Ellis		[Exhib RA, London, 339]; untraced		*Graves* IV, 1905–6, 321; *Gunnis* 1968, 227; *Mulcahy* 2000 (1), cat 279
47.	1840	Rev Thomas Dykes	m	[Exhib RA, London, 1185]; untraced Other versions: miniature, Ferens Art Gall, Hull, acq S105, marble, SD museum stores, Hull, plaster, nd, s		*Graves* IV, 1905–6, 321; *Mulcahy* 2000 (1), cat 280–2 (repr)
48.	1840	William Hutt	m	Untraced		*Mulcahy* 2000 (1), cat 283
49.	1841	John Cowham Parker		Untraced		*Mulcahy* 2000 (1), cat 284
50.	1844	Rev J Galland	m	[Exhib RA, London, 1333]; untraced		*Graves* IV, 1905–6, 321; *Mulcahy* 2000 (1), cat 288
51.	1844	Rev Walter Farquhar Hook	m	Leeds Civic Hall, W R Yorks		*Graves* IV, 1905–6, 321; *Gunnis* 1968, 227; *Mulcahy* 2000 (1), cat 286 (repr)
52.	c1847	An Eskimo and his wife, brought to Hull on a whaling-ship	p	Hull Maritime Museum, E R Yorks		*Gunnis* 1968, 227; *Mulcahy* 2000 (1), 297, 298 (repr)
53.	c1847	Captain Parker, cast	p	Hull Maritime Museum, E R Yorks		*Mulcahy* 2000 (1), cat 299 (repr)
54.	1848	Dr George Fielding	m	[Infirmary, Hull, E R Yorks]; untraced		*Gunnis* 1968, 227; *Mulcahy* 2000 (1), cat 288
55.	1848	Thomas Wilkinson Wallis, cast	p	Untraced		*Mulcahy* 2000 (1), cat 296
56.	1860	Henry Blundell	m	Guildhall, Hull, E R Yorks		*Gunnis* 1968, 227; *Mulcahy* 2000 (1), cat 294
57.	1860	John Fountain	m	Guildhall, Hull, E R Yorks	SD	*Mulcahy* 2000 (1), cat 293 (repr)
58.	1867	Samuel Solly		St Thomas's Hospital, London	SD	*Cavanagh* forthcoming 2007 (Lambeth 2)
59.	nd	Australian aborigine	p	[Museum, Kingston-upon-Hull]; destroyed		*Mulcahy* 2000 (1), cat 300
60.	nd	Charles Frost		[RI, London]; untraced		*Mulcahy* 2000 (1), cat 292
61.	nd	Dr Horner		[RI, London]; untraced		*Mulcahy* 2000 (1), cat 236
62.	nd	Edward Gibson		[Guildhall, Hull, E R Yorks]; untraced		*Mulcahy* 2000 (1), cat 285
63.	nd	Frank Huntington	p	[Royal Infirmary, Hull, E R Yorks]; untraced		*Mulcahy* 2000 (1), cat 289
64.	nd	J P Bell	p	Minerva lodge of freemasons, Hull, E R Yorks		*Mulcahy* 2000 (1), cat 295 (repr)
65.	nd	John Higsom		[Royal Infirmary, Hull, E R Yorks]; untraced		*Mulcahy* 2000 (1), cat 290
66.	nd	Sir William Wright	m	Maritime Museum, Hull, E R Yorks		*Mulcahy* 2000 (1), cat 301 (repr)

Architectural Sculpture

67.	c1834	Classical ornaments		[Assembly Rooms, Hull, E R Yorks]; untraced	*Mulcahy* 2000 (1), cat 228
68.	1847–1848	Lions guarding Pelham's pillar		Cabourne, Lincs	*Mulcahy* 2000 (1), cat 229 (repr)
69.	c1854	Cast of the Walsingham font	p	[Crystal Palace, Sydenham, Medieval court]; Norwich Nuseum, Norfolk, stores	*Mulcahy* 2000 (1), cat 231 (repr)
70.	c1854	Casts of medieval architecture	p	[Crystal Palace, Sydenham, Medieval court]; Hull Museums, stores	*Mulcahy* 2000 (1), cat 230
71.	c1865	Britannia		Lowgate, Hull, E R Yorks	*Mulcahy* 2000 (1), cat 232 (repr)

KIDWELL, Robert *c*1675–1747

He was apprenticed to his brother **William Kidwell** in 1689, becoming free of the Masons' Company in April 1703. He married Eleanor Elliby of the parish of St Giles Cripplegate, on 3 March 1697 and lived in Channel Row, Westminster in 1716. Kidwell was employed as a mason at Lord Ashburnham's house in St James's Square in 1713 (Ashburnham Archives, in *Gunnis* 1968, 227). In 1717 he was the sixth person to insure with the newly-founded Westminster Fire Office, taking out a seven year policy for £150 on 24 September on premises on the south side of Moors Alley, St Margaret, Westminster. He was elected a director of the Fire Office on 11 October 1722. In 1719 Vanbrugh engaged Kidwell as a mason for additions to Claremont, which he was then building for the Duke of Newcastle. Vanbrugh wrote to the Duke: 'I then explain'd matters with Kidwell, and finding there was really nothing in his declining the Work, but the fear of offending you, by not getting ready in time, I told he shou'd yet do it if he cou'd find means: Upon which he exerted; got men for his business, and next day cheerfully undertook it' (*Whistler* 1954, 147).

'Robert Kidwell *Mason*' subscribed to John Dart's *Westminasterium* in 1723 and to his *History of the Cathedral Church of Canterbury* in 1726. On 7 September 1733, he wrote to the Duke of Newcastle about the post of mason to Westminster Abbey, then held by **Edward Stanton**: 'Captain Stanton . . . is either Dead or Dying, so if a Vacancy should happen by that means, I am sure yr Grace has interest sufficient by a Recommendation to Robert Walpole to do much in my favour' (BL Add MS 32,688 in GPC). Kidwell's opportunism went unrewarded: Stanton was succeeded by his partner **Christopher Horsnaile I**. Kidwell worked at the London house of the Duke of Newcastle in 1738 and 1742, receiving more than £220 (Pelham Papers, BL Add MS 33,322 fo 2–7). He was also employed at Canons, the seat of the Duke of Chandos.

On 8 July 1747 the *Daily Advertiser* reported, 'Yesterday morning died upwards of 70, at his Seat at Wallham Green, Mr Kidwell, formerly a eminent Stone mason, whereby he had acquired a very plentiful fortune, and has retired from Business many years'. He was interred in a vault at St Margaret, Westminster, and in his will directed that a marble altar tomb then in his stoneyard in Cannon Row, Westminster, was to be put over his vault in the new chapel yard. He left the rents from his considerable property in the parish of St Margaret, Westminster, to his wife Jane and then to his grandchildren Katherine and Thomas Kidwell, the children of his son, Robert. The will also mentions tenements in Isleworth and Brentford Bridge.

Kidwell had two sons, Oliver and Robert Kidwell, who were apprenticed to him in 1713 and 1715 respectively. Oliver became free in 1723 (Masons' Co, *Freemen*, fol 36, 6 Sept 1723), was warden of the Masons' Company in 1734, and died in 1739, when his address was recorded as Channel Row, Westminster (Masons' Co *Assistants*, fol 7). The younger Robert's son, Thomas, was apprenticed to his grandfather in 1741. The names of several other apprentices who trained under Kidwell are recorded in the Masons' Company registers: Christopher Heisenbuttall (1705), Humphrey Jones (1708, turned over to Richard Lissiman (1710), Thomas Tripett (1711), Charles Pearce (1719) and Thomas Swinerton (1724). Nothing more is known of them.

Literary References: *Daily Ad*, 8 July 1747, 1 (obit); *Gunnis* 1968, 227; *Webb* 1999, 19

Archival References: Masons' Co, *Freemen*, fol 36, 22 April 1703; WFO, PR, no 6(1717); WFO DMB 343/2 (1722); GPC; IGI

Will: PROB 11/755 (proved 10 July 1747)

Funerary Monuments

1.	†1712	Francis Godfrey	Canterbury Cathedral	*Potterton* 1972 (3), repr 21 (engraving from Dart, *Canterbury Cathedral*, 1726)

KIDWELL, William *c*1664–1736

Kidwell was responsible for several monuments in England and Ireland which incorporate elements from the baroque repertoire with a somewhat heavy hand. The son of Robert Kidwell, 'gentleman', of Walton-on-Thames, Surrey, he was apprenticed to **John Bumpstead** under the auspices of the Joiners' Company on 26 March 1678. He was turned over to **Edward Pearce**, liveryman of the Painter-Stainers' Company, with whom he gained his freedom on 6 June 1687. Two of his brothers were apprenticed as joiners, Thomas and **Robert Kidwell**, who became William's apprentice on 6 August 1689. William appears to have been a bachelor most of his life, but he married a widow, Letitia Moore of Dublin, on 14 September 1733, when he was approaching the age of 70. In 1690 he was domiciled at Longditch, Westminster, and he remained a rate-payer in the parish of St Margaret, Westminster, until 1711, living in various properties until 1701 when he settled in Clincard's Alley and Pensioners Alley. Presumably one of these properties was his workshop and the other his dwelling. His brother Robert took over both the business and London residence when Kidwell left London for Ireland in 1711. He was made a freeman of Dublin at Christmas that year.

Soon after his arrival in Ireland he was employed by Sir John Perceval (later Lord Egmont), to execute marble tables and chimneypieces, probably of marble from Perceval's quarries in County Cork. There is no evidence to suggest (contra Gunnis) that Kidwell actually worked in Cork or that he trained Irish workers there. He probably worked in Dublin, since by 1733 he had a yard on the Strand in Dublin, where marble was sent to him from Cork. Kidwell remained in Ireland for the rest of his life, making occasional visits to London. Perceval notes in his account book that in 1712 he advanced Kidwell £2 15s 6d for 'going to England for work'. In 1713 he was back in Ireland with a number of orders and made two marble chimney-pieces and some marble tables for his patron's house at Duncarrey (**26**). In 1713 he provided chimneypieces of Irish marble for Edward Southwell's house at Kings Weston, near Bristol (**19**). One of these is probably the subject of a letter from Southwell, who was Perceval's uncle, to his nephew, dated

6 December 1713: 'I have almost forgot what I wrote about the two chimneypieces; but if I remember aright I desired one according to the wooden model I sent which being large was to go into the Great Parlour' (BM Add MD 47027, 735 D). Chimneypieces for other patrons of marble from Egmont's Cork quarries followed by *c*1719 (**20–25**).

Kidwell was responsible for several signed memorials in England. His first known monument, to John Bernard, has a characterised portrait bust in a full-bottomed wig above a richly carved inscription tablet (**1**). Francis Coventry's wall-monument, considered by Potterton to be his finest work, is elaborately framed by two male caryatid figures supporting a pediment and cornice with their upraised arms (**2**). Henry Herringman's wall-monument is a cartouche encrusted with garlands and surmounted by a *baldacchino*, its curtains held back by cherubs (**6**). Two of Kidwell's Irish monuments are signed 'Kidwell, London fecit', suggesting that he made them whilst in that city (**15, 16**). One of these, to Viscount Duncannon, †1724, had fashionable Gibbsian details (**15**). His most elegant work is perhaps the black and white standing monument to Sir Donat O'Brian, which has a reclining effigy in contemporary dress within a frame of composite fluted columns; above the cornice is a *baldacchino* with looped curtains, held by kneeling cherubs who point up to heaven (**12**).

Kidwell died in Dublin in 1736. His will, in which he describes himself as 'of the city of Dublin, Stonecutter' was signed on 7 August 1736 and proved on the following 13 September. (Add inf. Geoffrey Fisher)

IR

Literary References: *Strickland* 1, 1913, 579; *Gunnis* 1968 227–8; *Potterton* 1972 (1), 864–7; *Potterton* 1972 (3), 80–124; *Potterton* 1975, 52–54

Archival References: Joiners' Apprentices, 1678, fol 143r; 8052, fol 56v; Poor Rate Books, St Margaret Westminster, MSS E.305-25, 35, 48; Perceval Accts BM MS 4,7047 fol 3,13,28 (2 Oct 1712–6 Feb 1714)

Will: destroyed (briefly mentioned in Betham's *Genealogical Abstracts*, PRO, Dublin)

Funerary Monuments

1.	*c*1690	Sir Robert Bernard Bt (†1679)		Brampton, Hunts	S	*Gunnis* 1968, 228; *Potterton* 1972 (1), 867
2.	†1699	Hon Francis Coventry		Mortlake, Surrey	S	*Potterton* 1972 (1), 864–7; *Potterton* 1972 (3), cat 2 (repr 5)
3.	†1700	John Harvey		St Mary-at-Hill, City of London	S	Pevsner, *London: City*, 1997, 246
4.	+1700	Sir William Flower (†1681) and Thomas Flower		Finglas, Co Dublin	S	*Potterton* 1972 (3), repr 6; *Potterton* 1975, 53 (repr)
5.	†1702	Archbishop Boyle		Blessington, Co Wicklow	S	*Potterton* 1975, 52
6.	†1704	Henry Herringman and his wife Alice		Carshalton, Surrey	S	Pevsner, *London: S*, 1983, 645
7.	†1706	William King		Kilpeacon, Co Limerick	S	*Potterton* 1975, 54
8.	†1707	Bishop Foy		Waterford Cathedral	S	*Potterton* 1972 (3), (cat 8, repr 11); *Potterton* 1975, 54
9.	†1713	Mary Ponsonby		Fiddown, Co Kilkenny	S	*Potterton* 1972 (3), (cat 9, repr 13); *Potterton* 1975, 53
10.	†1715	Lady Mary Cox		Dunmanway, Co Cork	S	*Potterton* 1975, 53
11.	†1716	Rev Dillon Ashe		Trim, Co Meath	S	*Potterton* 1975, 54
12.	†1717	Sir Donat O'Brien		Kilnasoolagh, Co Clare	S	*Potterton* 1972 (3), repr 2, 3, 4; *Potterton* 1975, 21, 53–54 (repr)
13.	†1721	Francis Palmer		Killalla, Co Mayo	S	*Potterton* 1975, 53 (repr)
14.	†1721	Margaret Corker		Cloyne Cathedral, Co Cork	S	*Potterton* 1975, 52
15.	†1724	Viscount Duncannon		Fiddown, Co Kilkenny	S	*Potterton* 1972 (3), cat 15, repr 8; *Potterton* 1975, 53 (repr)
16.	†1728	Garret Wesley		Laracor, Co Meath	S	*Potterton* 1972 (1), 866–7; *Potterton* 1972 (3), cat 16, (repr 12); *Potterton* 1975, 20, 54 (repr)
17.	nd	Ordered by Mr Floyd of Newcastle		Untraced		*Gunnis* 1968, 228
18.	nd	Ordered by Mr Thornwell		Untraced		*Gunnis* 1968, 228

Chimneypieces

19.	1713–1714	Two, for Edward Southwell, ordered by Sir John Perceval Payment(s): £2 15s 6d and £4 19s (part payments)	m	Kings Weston, Bristol		Perceval Accts fo 28; *Gunnis* 1968, 227–8; *Potterton* 1972 (3), repr 9, design)
20.	by 1719	For Alderman Edward Hoare		Untraced		*Gunnis* 1968, 228
21.	by 1719	For Lord Barrymore		Untraced		*Gunnis* 1968, 228
22.	by 1719	For Lord Doneraile		Untraced		*Gunnis* 1968, 228
23.	by 1719	For Lord St George		Untraced		*Gunnis* 1968, 228
24.	by 1719	For Sir Matthew Deane		Untraced		*Gunnis* 1968, 228
25.	by *c*1719	For Sir Richard Meade		Untraced		*Gunnis* 1968, 228

Miscellaneous

26.	1713	Two marble chimneypieces and marble tables		for Sir John Perceval, Duncarrey, Ireland		Perceval Accts BM MS 47,047, fol 13; *Gunnis* 1968, 227

KILBY, of Bristol fl late 17th century

Funerary Monuments

1.	late C17	Sir Leoline Jenkins		Llanblethian, Glamorgan	S	Pevsner, *Glamorgan*, 1995, 371

KIMBERLEY FAMILY, of Dublin

Edward Kimberley I –1783
Edward Kimberley II
John Kimberley
Edward Kimberley III fl 1822–27
F C Kimberley fl 1829

Edward Kimberley I worked as a 'stone-cutter' in Dublin during the latter half of the 18th century, living in James's Street. His sons, **Edward Kimberley II** and **John Kimberley**, followed his trade. **Edward Kimberley III** entered the Royal Dublin Society Schools in 1822 and was awarded prizes, including one for a group of boys in high relief (**3**). An **F C Kimberley**, who lived at Blackrock, exhibited a bust at the Royal Hibernian Academy in 1829 (**2**).

Literary References: *Strickland* I, 1913, 579–580

Busts

1.	1827	Edward Kimberley III (self-portrait)	[Exhib RHA, Dublin, 305]; untraced	*Strickland* I, 1913, 580; *Stewart* 2, 1985, 159
2.	1829	John Comerford (by F C Kimberley)	[Exhib RHA, Dublin, 278]; untraced	*Strickland* I, 1913, 580; *Stewart* 2, 1985, 159

Reliefs

3.	1825	Group of boys (by Edward Kimberley III)	[RDS prize]; untraced	*Strickland* I, 1913, 580

KINDLESIDE fl 1763

He is listed as a mason at London Bridge in Mortimer's *Director* of 1763 (p 49).

KING fl 1692–1700

As a 'stonecutter' he was employed by Lord Fauconberg on work at Sutton Court, Chiswick, and in 1699 at his London House in Soho Square (Wombwell Archives in GPC). In 1698 he was paid for work at the London house of the 3rd Earl of Carlisle (Castle Howard Archives in GPC).

KING, Benjamin fl 1729–83

The son of Joseph King, he was apprenticed to John Barnes, of Sutton, Warwick, 'Stone-carver' in 1728 (PRO IR 49/17 in GPC). When the vault in the Beauchamp Chapel, Warwick, was opened in 1849, it was found that previous visitors had inscribed their names inside, including 'Benjamin King, carver 1729'. It is thought that King probably repaired the Earl of Warwick's tomb that year (*Transactions and Proceedings of the Birmingham Archaeological Soc*, LXI, 7, in GPC). In 1744 he was paid £17 4s 8d for 'Carvers work' in the chapel at Stoneleigh Abbey, Warks (Archives Lord Leigh, in GPC) and in 1755 he was employed at Arbury Hall, Warks, where he earned £39 9s 6d for work in the library.

In 1755–58 he provided all the stone-carving on the exterior and interior of the Warwick Shire Hall (**1**). Apparently there were difficulties with the pediment carving, for **David Hiorn**, the mason in charge, wrote to the architect, Sanderson Miller, on 3 February, 1758: 'I was a little surprised one even as came in Mr. Lightholder and Mr. Lowe and desired I would get them up a scaffold to do the pediment, for that you had given them orders so to do, which I hope is not true. For as I shall be glad of yours and Mr. Prowses approbation in the disposition of ye ornaments, and what they should be, but own I shall be very sorry to have any other persons come to do the work, unless it cannot be done by the people who have been already concerned; and as I a little doubt the veracity of Mr. Lightholder, I ask my Lord Brooke, who said something of the kind had been shown to him, but that he thought it was doing Mr. King a great injury if it [the pediment] was executed by others' (Warks Co Records, ACCR 125/33 in *Gunnis* 1968, 228).

In 1760–1 King worked at Egginton Hall, Derbys, receiving £85 (Archives Sir Richard Every Bt in GPC). He was also employed at Ragley Hall, Warks, receiving payments of £18 and £31 5s in 1779 and 1783 (**2**).

Literary References: *Gunnis* 1968, 228

Archival References: Newdigate Accts, 1755, CR 136/V156; GPC

Architectural Sculpture

1.	1755–1758	Interior and exterior stone carving	Shire Hall, Warwick	*Gunnis* 1968, 228
2.	1783	'3 friezes and do. capitals to the Cove Room and Room adjoining and three ditto for the saloon' Payment(s): £31 5s	Ragley Hall, Warks	Archives, Marquess of Hertford, in GPC

KING, Charles, of London fl 1800–46

He was probably a junior partner in the firm of **King and Sons** since in both cases the address of the yard is given as Chenies Street. He was paid £77 for alterations to Dr Pemberton's house in George Street, Hanover Square in 1800 (Soane, Abstract of Bills 3, f58) and in 1823 was employed as a mason on repairs to the tower at St Anne, Soho (WPL, A.2312 in *Gunnis* 1968, 228). Gunnis notes that his tablets are dull.

Literary References: *Gunnis* 1968, 228; *Potterton* 1975, 54

Funerary Monuments

1.	†1800	Rev L Smyth	Southill, Beds		Pevsner, *Beds, Hunts & Peterborough*, 1968, 145
2.	?1809	Douce family	West Malling, Kent	S	*Gunnis* 1968, 228
3.	?1813	John Martin	Plumstead, London	S	*Gunnis* 1968, 228
4.	?1815	Joseph Kirkwood	St George, Bloomsbury, London	S	*Gunnis* 1968, 228
5.	†1819	Rev Stringer Belcher and family	Ulcombe, Kent	S	Pevsner, *Kent: W & Weald*, 1976, 588
6.	?1825	John Wardle	Wardington, Oxon	S	*Gunnis* 1968, 228
7.	†1825	Nicholas Harry Charrington	Aldenham, Herts	S	
8.	?1825	Pierre Fournié, 'clerc tonsure'	St Pancras new parish church, London	S	*Gunnis* 1968, 228
9.	?1826	Rev Peregrine Bingham	Berwick St John, Wilts	S	*Gunnis* 1968, 228
10.	†1826	Sir William Bellingham	Castlebellingham, Co Louth		*Potterton* 1975, 54
11.	?1826	William Micklefield	West Tilbury, Essex	S	*Gunnis* 1968, 228
12.	†1827	Edward Parry	St George, Bloomsbury, London	S	
13.	?1833	Peter Gilkes	St James, Piccadilly, London	S	*Gunnis* 1968, 228
14.	†1833	Sir William Rush	St Mary the Virgin, Wimbledon, Surrey	S	*Gunnis* 1968, 228
15.	†1833	Thomas and Elizabeth Neale	St George, Bloomsbury, London	S	
16.	†1834	Luke Hansard (†1828) and others	St Giles-in-the-Fields, London		RG/JP, 5, 784
17.	†1840	Henrietta Pearce Sharp	St John, Hackleton's Cliff, Barbados	S	
18.	†1846	Rev James Moore	St Pancras new parish church, London	S	

KING, G E, of Ware fl 1826?

Funerary Monuments

1.	?1826	Adams family		Ware, Herts	S	*Gunnis* 1968, 228

KING, George fl 1771–76

The brother of **William King**, he exhibited at the Free Society between 1771 and 1776, describing himself as 'Mr King, Junr at Mr King's, 54 Wells Street, Oxford Road'.

Archival References: GPC

Funerary Monuments						
1.	1775	Samuel Harding		Little Stanmore, Middx	S	GPC
Statues						
2.	1774	A lion, after the antique		[Exhib Free Soc, London, 152]; untraced		*Graves* 1907, 137
Busts						
3.	1771	'A Mask of the Venus de Medicis; from plaister'		[Exhib Free Soc, London, 138]; untraced		*Graves* 1907, 137
4.	1778	Unidentified gentleman		[Exhib Soc of Artists, London, 101]; untraced		*Graves* 1907, 137
Miscellaneous						
5.	1772	'A sketch in clay; after the antique'		[Exhib Free Soc, London, 96]; untraced		*Graves* 1907, 137
6.	1773	'The head of Plato; after Plaister, a drawing'		[Exhib Free Soc, London, 106]; untraced		*Graves* 1907, 137
7.	1775	Madonna, model		[Exhib Free Soc, London, 136]; untraced		*Graves* 1907, 137
8.	1776	'An Academy; figures in chalk'		[Exhib Free Soc, London, 246]; untraced		*Graves* 1907, 137

KING, H fl 1828–45

Funerary Monuments					
1.	†1838	Rev Dawson Warren		All Saints, Edmonton, Middx	Pevsner, *London: N*, 1998, 423
Busts					
2.	1828	Unidentified boy, model		[Exhib RA, London, 1182]; untraced	*Graves* IV, 1905–6, 326
3.	1829	Unidentified gentleman		[Exhib RA, London, 1137]; untraced	*Graves* IV, 1905–6, 326
4.	1830	Unidentified gentleman		[Exhib RA, London, 1223]; untraced	*Graves* IV, 1905–6, 326
5.	1831	Unidentified gentleman	m	[Exhib RA, London, 1173]; untraced	*Graves* IV, 1905–6, 326
6.	1832	Unidentified gentleman		[Exhib RA, London, 1111]; untraced	*Graves* IV, 1905–6, 326
7.	1832	Unidentified gentleman		[Exhib RA, London, 1229]; untraced	*Graves* IV, 1905–6, 326
8.	1845	Unidentified child	m	[Exhib RA, London, 1396]; untraced	*Graves* IV, 1905–6, 326
9.	1845	Unidentified gentleman		[Exhib RA, London, 1447]; untraced	*Graves* IV, 1905–6, 326

KING, Henry

In 1789 Walter Fawkes purchased marble chimneypieces from King for Farnley Hall, W R Yorks (**1**). A 'Henry King, stonecutter' was employed on repairs and additions to Newburgh Priory, N R Yorks, 1742–44 (Wombwell Archives in GPC).

Chimneypieces

1.	1789	Several	m	[Farnley Hall, W R Yorks]; untraced	Farnley archives in GPC

KING, John Crookshanks 1806–82

Born in Kilwinning, Ayrshire, on 11 October 1806, he trained as a practical machinist. He emigrated to the United States in 1829 where he was employed for several years as superintendent of factories in Cincinnati and Louisville. In 1834, at the suggestion of the American neoclassical sculptor Hiram Powers (1805–73), he made a clay model of Mrs Powers's head, and his success encouraged him to adopt the profession of sculptor. From 1837 until 1840 he worked in New Orleans, modelling busts of public figures and making cameo likenesses. He later moved to Boston where he executed busts of local worthies and the monument, with a bust, to the Rev F W P Greenwood which was erected in King's Chapel, Boston, about 1853. His works are not listed since the America was no longer a colony at this date.

Archival References: RG/JP, 5, 789v citing *Appleton's Cyclopaedia*

KING, John, of Ripon and York fl 1792–1834?

His father, Henry King a 'foreigner', had become a freeman of Ripon in 1784 and King became a freeman too in 1792 (Ripon freemen list, Ripon Town Hall, in GPC). He signs a large neo-Hellenic wall-tablet to Marmaduke Hodgson, in the Cathedral. Gunnis notes that there are various other tablets by him in the cathedral but they are 'either insignificant or of the same design as the one already mentioned'.

Literary References: *Gunnis* 1968, 228

Archival References: GPC

Funerary Monuments

1.	?1834	Marmaduke Hodgson	Ripon Cathedral, W R Yorks	*Gunnis* 1968, 228–9

KING, S, of Castle Combe fl *c*1820

Funerary Monuments

1.	†1820	John Hitchcock	Kington St Michael, Wilts	Pevsner, *Wilts*, 1975, 281

KING, Thomas and Sons, of Bath fl *c*1760–1860

Thomas King (1741–1804), the founder of one of the most popular west country firms of monumental masons, was the son of Henry King, a clockmaker of St Dunstan-in-the-West in the City of London. He was apprenticed on 26 March 1752 to Charles Saunders, a London mason, but settled in Bath soon after becoming free. He married Elizabeth, the daughter of **Thomas Paty of Bristol** on 6 May 1779 at St Augustine the Less, Bristol. King maintained cordial relations with the Paty family and was left £250 in his father-in-law's will. When his brother-in-law, **William Paty**, died, clients were instructed to forward outstanding debts to King (*Felix Farley's Bristol Journal*, 4 April 1801).

King had three children, Thomas and Charles, who came into the business, and Mary, who did not marry during his lifetime.

The firm produced small, well-designed wall monuments, often incorporating coloured marbles in an elegant oval, rectangular or inverted shield frame. Most were sold to clients from stock. He used the customary range of neoclassical motifs: urns, sarcophagi, willow trees, mourning women, crumpled scrolls held by cherubs and broken columns. Though the designs were repeated without much variation, each memorial is a craftsmanly performance, not a mechanical replica.

King also worked on bespoke commissions. He provided memorials with portrait medallions for the actor James Quin in Bath Abbey and for Prebendary Adams in Gloucester Cathedral (**2, 41**). The philanthropic character of Nathaniel Stephens and William Pyke was suggested by elegant relief depictions of the *Good Samaritan* (**50, 58**) and Thomas Linley's talent as a composer, by the musical instruments on his tablet in Wells Cathedral (**64**). The memorial to Robert Walsh in Bath Abbey has a relief of a broken Ionic column clad with yew on an oval ground of streaked grey marble (**34**). Penny has suggested that this was the first time the broken column, a traditional symbol of *Fortitude*, was employed alone on a monument. Richard Warner, in his *History of Bath*, 1801, considered the monument the 'most remarkable for happiness of design in the whole Abbey' (*Penny* 1977 (1), 29). The monument to Walter Long (**107**), which was probably prepared by his sons, is idiosyncratic: it is a tri-partite composition with slender urns surrounded by rays on the side-panels and a long inscription in the central panel. Above are two long torches in the round and garlands. Pevsner unjustly called this King's *magnum opus*, 'magnum certainly in size, though in style both a little bleak and a little pompous' (*Pevsner*). Another unusual monument by the sons, to Elizabeth Smith, has a standing Virtue with a dove above her, holding a scroll (**116**). Like other leading workshop proprietors in the Bath and Bristol areas, King appears to have diversed: Thomas Gainsborough's account at Hoare's Bank records a payment of 18 guineas made to King in May 1771, perhaps for a picture frame.

King died in prosperity and left his widow a number of properties in Bath and Walcot, including offices, a garden and a yard 'now in my own occupation' at Beaufort Place, Walcot. His three children received generous bequests. He is buried at Woolley, where a modest tablet, for which he earmarked 20 guineas in his will, bears the epitaph: 'Many Years an eminent statuary in the parish of Walcot, who after sustaining a long and painful illness with exemplary fortitude and resignation, calmly departed this life December the 5th, 1804, in his 63rd. year'.

The business continued for a century and so is likely to have involved three generations: Philip King, who was perhaps a grandson of Thomas, signed two monuments credited to the King workshop (**65, 153**). Monuments were habitually signed 'King' or 'Thomas King of Bath' throughout the period. One sent to Ireland around 1790 has the fine-sounding but inaccurate inscription 'T King Ft. R.A. of England' (**42**). The high quality of the firm's earlier output was not sustained in the 19th century. An absence of known commissions between 1826 and 1844 suggests a break in production and the output during the firm's final years was very limited.

In addition to the monuments listed below, King and Sons produced a large number of plain memorial tablets, often of white marble on a black or grey ground, but occasionally coloured. These are principally in the southwest of England.

IR

Literary References: *Grigson* 1960, 1182, 1184; *Gunnis* 1968, 229; *Potterton* 1975, 54; Pevsner, *Wilts*, 1975, 571; *Penny* 1977 (1), 29; *Whinney* 1988, 319; *Dale-Jones and Lloyd* 1989, 51

Will: of 'Thomas King, Gentleman of Walcot, Somerset', PROB 11/1427, proved July 1805

Funerary Monuments

1.	*c*1760	Thomas Brocas	Bath Abbey, Somerset	S	*Gunnis* 1968, 229
2.	1761	James Quin (†1766)	Bath Abbey, Somerset	S	*Gunnis* 1968, 229; *Whinney* 1988, 319; C Lib (repr)
3.	†1764	Elizabeth Vanhattem	Dinton, Bucks	S	Pevsner, *Bucks*, 1994, 276
4.	†1764	William Brydges	Tyberton, Herefs	S	Pevsner, *Herefs*, 1963, 302; C Lib (repr)
5.	†1768	Chardin Musgrove	Chaddleworth, Berks	S	Pevsner, *Berks*, 1966, 112
6.	†1768	Maria Heathcote	St John, Devizes, Wilts	S	Pevsner, *Wilts*, 1975, 207
7.	?1768	Philip Allen	Bathampton, Somerset	S	RG/JP, 5, 792
8.	1769	Dr Butt	Bath Abbey, Somerset	S	*Gunnis* 1968, 229
9.	†1769	William Karslake	George Nympton, Devon	S	Pevsner, *Devon*, 1989, 455
10.	?1770	Mrs Baxter	Hilton Charterhouse, Somerset	S	*Gunnis* 1968, 229
11.	†1771	John Crofts	Sompting, Sussex	S	Pevsner, *Sussex*, 1965, 332
12.	?1771	Thomas Beach	Steeple Ashton, Wilts	S	*Gunnis* 1968, 229
13.	†1772	John (†1758) Burgess and wife	North Molton, Devon	S	*Gunnis* 1968, 229; Pevsner, *Devon*, 1989, 603
14.	†1772	Richard Chiswell	Debden, Essex	S	*Gunnis* 1968, 229
15.	†1776	Collingwood Foster	Alnwick, Northumbs	S	Pevsner, *Northumbs*, 1992, 133; GPC
16.	†1778	Henry Singer	St Andrew, Chippenham, Wilts	S	RG/JP, 5, 794
17.	†1778	John Key	Fulford, York	S	RG/JP, 5, 792
18.	†1779	Sir Thomas Lawley	Hinton, Staffs		
19.	†1780	Bridget Jones	Llandybie, Carmarthen	S	*Dale-Jones and Lloyd* 1989, 51
20.	†1780	T Camplin	Brompton Ralph, Somerset	S	Pevsner, *Somerset: S & W*, 1958, 101
21.	†1781	Fitz Foy	Buckland Newton, Dorset	S	Pevsner, *Dorset*, 1972, 122
22.	†1782	Bishop John Hume	Salisbury Cathedral, Wilts	S	Pevsner, *Wilts*, 1975, 415
23.	†1782	Rebecca Lewes	Llandybie, Carmarthen	S	*Dale-Jones and Lloyd* 1989, 51
24.	†1782	Theodore Sheere	St Petroch, Exeter, Devon	S	
25.	?1783	Elizabeth Lyde	Stanton Drew, Somerset	S	*Gunnis* 1968, 229
26.	†1783	George White	Long Newnton, Glos	S	Pevsner, *Glos: Cotswolds*, 1999, 459
27.	†1783	William Veel	Wotton-under-Edge, Glos	S	Pevsner, *Glos: Cotswolds*, 1999, 757

28.	†1784	Matthew Hale	Alderley, Glos	S	Pevsner, *Glos: Cotswolds*, 1999, 133
29.	†1785	Peter Muilman	Debden, Essex	S	
30.	†1785	Samuel Withers	Sherston, Wilts	S	C Lib (repr)
31.	†1787	John Paul	St Mary, Tetbury, Glos	S	Pevsner, *Glos: Cotswolds*, 1999, 686
32.	†1787	Robert Veel	Wotton-under-Edge, Glos	S	Pevsner, *Glos: Cotswolds*, 1999, 756
33.	?1787	Sir Nigel Gresley	Bath Abbey, Somerset	S	*Gunnis* 1968, 229
34.	†1788	Lieutenant-Colonel Robert Walsh	Bath Abbey, Somerset	S	*Penny* 1977 (1), 29 (repr)
35.	†1788	Samuel Trotman	Siston, Glos	S	Pevsner, *Glos: Vale & Forest of Dean*, 1976, 338
36.	†1789	Brydges Bryen Gordon	Hinxworth, Herts	S	
37.	†1789	Daniel Lysons and family	Hempsted, Glos	S	Pevsner, *Glos: Vale & Forest of Dean*, 1976, 268
38.	†1789	G Marten	East Pennard, Somerset	S	Pevsner, *Somerset: S & W*, 1958, 164
39.	†1789	John Moreton	Redmarley d'Abitot, Glos	S	Pevsner, *Glos: Vale & Forest of Dean*, 1976, 328
40.	†1789	John Wilkinson	Ossington, Notts	S	C Lib (repr)
41.	†1789	Prebendary William Adams DD	Gloucester Cathedral	S	Pevsner, *Glos: Vale & Forest of Dean*, 1976, 218; C Lib (repr)
42.	†1789	Rev John Quinn	Adare, Co Limerick	S	*Potterton* 1975, 54
43.	*c*1790	John Walford	Birdbrook, Essex	S	Pevsner, *Essex*, 1965, 88
44.	†1790	Peter and Mary (†1785) Muilman	Debden, Essex	S	*Gunnis* 1968, 229
45.	†1791	Alworth Merewether	Marshfield, Glos	S	Pevsner, *Glos: Cotswolds*, 1999, 469
46.	†1791	Anne, Lady Wrey	Tawstock, Devon	S	Pevsner, *Devon*, 1989, 790
47.	†1791	Leonard Beridge	Algarkirk, Lincs	S	Pevsner, *Lincs*, 1989, 95
48.	?1792	Dodington Sherston	Wells Cathedral, Somerset	S	*Gunnis* 1968, 229
49.	†1792	Margaret Heathcote	St John, Devizes, Wilts	S	
50.	1792	Nathaniel Stephens	Eastington, Glos	S	Pevsner, *Glos: Vale & Forest of Dean*, 1976, 178
51.	†1792	Obadiah Paul	King's Stanley, Glos	S	Pevsner, *Glos: Cotswolds*, 1999, 430; C Lib (repr)
52.	†1792	Poole Bathurst	Lydney, Glos	S	Pevsner, *Glos: Vale & Forest of Dean*, 1976, 293
53.	†1793	Charlotte, Lady Gordon	Hinxworth, Herts	S	
54.	†1793	Frances Brydges	Tyberton, Herefs	S	*Gunnis* 1968, 229
55.	†1793	J Harvey	Northill, Beds	S	Pevsner, *Beds, Hunts & Peterborough*, 1968, 128
56.	†1793	Rev Robert Henry Dingley	Camerton, Somerset	S	
57.	†1794	Henry Willis	Eastington, Glos	S	Pevsner, *Glos: Vale and Forest of Dean*, 1976, 178
58.	†1794	William Pyke	Great Somerford, Wilts	S	Pevsner, *Wilts*, 1975, 260
59.	†1794	William Smythe	Acton Burnell, Salop	S	RG/JP, 5, 792
60.	?1795	Andrew and Alexander Sutherland	Bath Abbey, Somerset	S	*Gunnis* 1968, 229
61.	†1795	Henry Stephens	Eastington, Glos	S	
62.	1795	Mrs Knatchbull Payment(s): £70	[Babington, Somerset (?)]; untraced		Knatchbull of Babington archives in RG/JP, 5, 791
63.	†1795	Thomas Cooper	St Mary Magdalene, Rodborough, Glos	S	Pevsner, *Glos: Cotswolds*, 1999, 579
64.	†1795	Thomas Linley	Wells Cathedral, Somerset	S	Pevsner, *Somerset: N & Bristol*, 1958, 312; C Lib (repr)
65.	†1796	Admiral William Lloyd (by Philip King)	Llangadog, Carmarthen	S	*Dale-Jones and Lloyd* 1989, 51
66.	?1796	Edward Baker	St Martin, Salisbury, Wilts	S	*Gunnis* 1968, 229
67.	†1796	Emma Long	Edington Priory, Wilts	S	
68.	†1796	John, Elizabeth (†1765) and William (†1775) Roe	Ancaster, Lincs	S	Pevsner, *Lincs*, 1989, 100; C Lib (repr)
69.	1796	Peter Shakerley	Astbury, Cheshire	S	Pevsner, *Cheshire*, 1971, 67; C Lib (repr)
70.	†1796	Richmond Moore	Monken Hadley, Herts	S	Pevsner, *Herts*, 1977, 249; C Lib (repr)
71.	†1797	Lady Hamlyn	Clovelly, Devon	S	Pevsner, *Devon*, 1989, 269
72.	†1797	Mary Burdett	Ramsbury, Wilts	S	Pevsner, *Wilts*, 1975, 378
73.	†1797	Rev Robert Taunton	Bradford-on-Avon, Wilts	S	
74.	†1797	William Jauncey	Stretton Grandison, Herefs	S	Pevsner, *Herefs*, 1963, 295
75.	?1797	William Pyke	Great Somerford, Wilts	S	*Gunnis* 1968, 229
76.	†1798	Elizabeth Smith	Great Somerford, Wilts	S	Pevsner, *Wilts*, 1975, 260
77.	†1798	John Oatway	Nettlecombe, Somerset	S	Pevsner, *Somerset: S & W*, 1958, 253
78.	†1798	Lord Calthorpe	St Bartholomew, Edgbaston, Birmingham, Warks	S	Pevsner, *Warks*, 1966, 164
79.	†1799	Berkeley Napier	East Pennard, Somerset	S	Pevsner, *Somerset: S and W*, 1958, 164
80.	†1799	Dorothea Patten	Warrington, Lancs	S	*CIIA* 4/8/129–30 (repr)
81.	†1799	James Matravers	Semington, Wilts	S	Pevsner, *Wilts*, 1975, 466
82.	†1799	Jane Fendall	Gloucester Cathedral	S	Pevsner, *Glos: Vale & Forest of Dean*, 1976, 219
83.	†1800	Martha Musgrave	West Monkton, Somerset	S	
84.	†1800	Robert Lisle	Felton, Northumbs	S	Pevsner, *Northumbs*, 1992, 280
85.	†1800	Sir Edward and Dame Mary Baynton Rolt (†1799)	Bromham, Wilts	S	
86.	†1801	Catherine Seymour	Wells Cathedral, Somerset, cloisters	S	RG/JP, 5, 793

87.	?1801	Harry Edgell	Beckington, Wilts	S	*Gunnis* 1968, 229
88.	†1801	Rev John Tattersall	St Mary the Virgin, Wotton under Edge, Glos	S	Pevsner, *Glos: Cotswolds*, 1999, 756
89.	†1801	Rev Philip Morris	Clun, Salop	S	*Grigson* 1960, 1184 (repr)
90.	†1801	Sir John Call	Stoke Climsland, Cornwall	S	Pevsner, *Cornwall*, 1970, 216
91.	†1801	Thomas Slocombe	Bishop's Lydeard, Somerset	S	Pevsner, *Somerset: S & W*, 1958, 89
92.	?1802	John Enys	St Gluvias, Cornwall	S	*Gunnis* 1968, 229
93.	†1803	Thomas Daunt	Owlpen, Glos	S	Pevsner, *Glos: Cotswolds*, 1999, 537
94.	†1803	William Jenkins	Sherston, Wilts	S	Pevsner, *Wilts*, 1975, 470; C Lib (repr)
95.	?1804	Jane Clootwyk	Bath Abbey, Somerset	S	*Gunnis* 1968, 229
96.	†1804	Rev Nathaniel Hume	Bremhill, Wilts	S	
97.	†1805	Arthur Price William Jones	Llandybie, Carmarthen	S	*Dale-Jones and Lloyd* 1989, 44, 51
98.	†1805	Catherine Clutterbuck	Ozleworth, Glos	S	Pevsner, *Glos: Cotswolds*, 1999, 539
99.	†1805	Sir James Tylney Long	Draycot Cerne, Wilts	S	*Gunnis* 1968, 229; C Lib (repr)
100.	†1806	John Walker Heneage	Lyneham, Wilts	S	Pevsner, *Wilts*, 1975, 319
101.	†1806	Samuel Angel	St Olaf, Exeter, Devon	S	RG/JP, 5, 793
102.	†1806	Samuel, Henrietta (†1795) and Ann (†1844) Shute	Wootton, I of W	S	
103.	†1806	Thomas Brand Hollis	Ingatestone, Essex	S	GPC
104.	†1806	William Barry Wade	Langford Budville, Somerset	S	Pevsner, *Somerset: S & W*, 1958, 216
105.	†1807	Edward Dixon	St Edmund, Dudley, Staffs	S	Pevsner, *Staffs*, 1974, 121
106.	†1807	Rev Dr Randolph Marriott	Worcester Cathedral	S	Pevsner, *Worcs*, 1968, 312; C Lib (repr)
107.	†1807	Walter Long	Whaddon, Wilts	S	Pevsner, *Wilts*, 1975, 571
108.	†1807	William Long	Edington Priory, Wilts	S	
109.	†1808	Anne Methuen	North Wraxall, Wilts	S	C Lib (repr)
110.	†1808	John Hickes	Berkeley, Glos	S	Pevsner, *Glos: Vale & Forest of Dean*, 1976, 101
111.	†1808	Rhoda Browne	Wolverley, Worcs	S	Colvin/Gunnis corresp box file, HMI
112.	†1807–1809	Caroline and other Ince children	Marshfield, Glos	S	Pevsner, *Glos and Cotswolds*, 1999, 469
113.	†1809	John, Elizabeth (†1805) and Ann (†1809) Perry	Montego Bay, Jamaica	S	C Lib (repr)
114.	†1810	Augusta Bradshaw	Yate, Glos	S	Pevsner, *Glos: Vale & Forest of Dean*, 1976, 414
115.	†1811	Edward Cottle	St George, Gingerland, Nevis	S	
116.	†1811	Elizabeth Smith	Sydling St Nicholas, Dorset	S	Pevsner, *Dorset*, 1972, 414; C Lib (repr)
117.	†1811	Sir James Hamlyn Bt	Clovelly, Devon	S	C Lib (repr)
118.	1812	Rev H T Ellacombe and his three wives	Bitton, Glos	S	Pevsner, *Glos: Vale & Forest of Dean*, 1976, 110
119.	†1813	Ann Tyres	St Laurence, Stroud, Glos	S	Pevsner, *Glos: Cotswolds*, 1999, 650
120.	†1813	Henry Barnard	Frampton-on-Severn, Glos	S	Pevsner, *Glos: Vale & Forest of Dean*, 1976, 191
121.	†1813	Henry Campbell	Charlton Kings, Glos	S	
122.	†1813	Mrs Dodington Hunt	Charlton Kings, Glos	S	Pevsner, *Glos: Vale & Forest of Dean*, 1976, 120
123.	†1813	Susannah Holcombe	St Peter and St Paul, Marlborough, Wilts	S	RG/JP, 5, 794
124.	1815	Daubeney and Herbert families	Bishops Caundle, Dorset	S	Pevsner, *Dorset*, 1972, 95
125.	†1815	Mawbey Tugwell	Bradford-on-Avon, Wilts	S	
126.	†1815	Thomas Timbrell	Bradford-on-Avon, Wilts	S	
127.	†1815	William Willes	Christian Malford, Wilts	S	Pevsner, *Wilts*, 1975, 178
128.	†1816	Elizabeth Whittington	Cold Ashton, Glos	S	*Grigson* 1960, 1182 (repr); Pevsner, *Glos: Cotswolds*, 1999, 291
129.	†1818	Edward Lambert	Bremhill, Wilts	S	
130.	†1818	Rev John Green	Poole Keynes, Glos	S	Pevsner, *Glos: Cotswolds*, 1999, 562
131.	†1818	Richard Martin	Hardwicke, Glos	S	Pevsner, *Glos: Vale & Forest of Dean*, 1976, 262
132.	†1818	Richard Singer	North Wraxall, Wilts	S	C Lib (repr)
133.	†1820	Isabella Eridge	St Andrew, Chippenham, Wilts	S	RG/JP, 5, 794
134.	?1820	Peter Sherston	Wells Cathedral, Somerset	S	*Gunnis* 1968, 229
135.	†1820	Rev Lewis Clutterbuck	Ozleworth, Glos	S	Pevsner, *Glos: Cotswolds*, 1999, 539
136.	†1821	Charles Timbrell	Bradford-on-Avon, Wilts	S	
137.	†1821	Harry Lancelot Lee	Alveley, Salop	S	RG/JP, 5, 794
138.	†1821	John Langley (†1799), John Masklyn (†1790) and James Filkes	Warminster, Wilts	S	
139.	†1821	Thomas Veel	Eastington, Glos	S	Pevsner, *Glos: Vale and Forest of Dean*, 1976, 178
140.	?1821	William Prinn	Charlton Kings, Glos	S	*Gunnis* 1968, 229
141.	†1822	Mary Long	Edington Priory, Wilts	S	
142.	†1823	Lady Catherine Tylney Long	Draycot Cerne, Wilts	S	Pevsner, *Wilts*, 1975, 226
143.	?1823	Thermuthis Ashe	Langley Burrell, Wilts	S	*Gunnis* 1968, 229
144.	†1824	Procter Anderton	Ruishton, Somerset	S	Pevsner, *Somerset: S & W*, 1958, 283
145.	?1824	Richard Bendyshe	Woolley, Somerset	S	*Gunnis* 1968, 229

146.	†1824	Sarah Fisher Ancram	Weelington, Somerset	S	
147.	†1825	Nathaniel Merriman	St Peter and St Paul, Marlborough, Wilts	S	RG/JP, 5, 794
148.	?1826	Lieutenant-Colonel North	Bath Abbey, Somerset	S	*New Monthly Mag*, 1826, 168; *Gunnis* 1968, 229
149.	†1839	Wadham (†1799) and Anne Locke	Seend, Wilts	S	
150.	†1844	John Tyrwhitt	Scrivelsby, Lincs		Pevsner, *Lincs*, 1989, 630
151.	†1844	Nicholas (†1805), William Clark (†1806), Elizabeth (†1844) and Winifred Pitts	Stokenham, Devon	S	
152.	†1857	William Coles Bennett	Corsham, Wilts	S	
153.	†1858	John Lewis Phillips (by Philip King)	Llangynin, Carmarthen		*Dale-Jones and Lloyd* 1989, 51
154.	†1860	Lewis Purbrick	St Andrew, Chippenham, Wilts	S	RG/JP, 5, 794
155.	nd	James Lind	Porchester, Hants	S	RG/JP, 5, 794
156.	nd	Robert Codrington	Cromhall, Glos	S	Pevsner, *Glos: Vale & Forest of Dean*, 1976, 166

Chimneypieces

157.	1795	One Payment(s): £39 12s	[Babington Court, Somerset]; untraced	Knatchbull of Babington archives in RG/JP, 5, 791
158.	1810	Several, of marble	Longleat, Wilts	Longleat HA, 1800–1818
159.	1812	Several, 'of Keinton stone' Payment(s): £28	Longleat, Wilts	Longleat HA, 1800–1818
160.	1810–1820	Several	Dodington Park, Glos	Pevsner, *Glos: Cotswolds*, 1999, 318

Miscellaneous

161.	1809–1811	Unidentified work Payment(s): £335	Dodington Park, Glos	Codrington Archives in GPC

KING, W and Son fl 1777

Chimneypieces

1.	1777	Description unavailable	[Croome Court, Worcs]; untraced	*Beard* 1993, 93

KING, W H, of Church Street, Edmonton

See **K, of Church Street, Edmonton**, Middx.

KING, William fl 1769–97

The brother of **George King**, he exhibited at the Free Society, 1769–82, from 48 Wells Street, Oxford Street. In 1797, when he made a chimneypiece for the Earl of Coventry, his address was recorded as 61 Wells Street (2).

Literary References: *Gunnis* 1968, 229

Archival References: GPC

Funerary Monuments

1.	1782	Monumental figure, of marble		[Exhib Free Soc, London, 243]; untraced	*Graves* 1907, 138

Chimneypieces

2.	1797	'Statuary Marble, Sunk pannells in Frieses and Pillasters' Payment(s): £23		Untraced	Archives, Earl of Coventry, in GPC

Reliefs

3.	1771	Holy Family		[Exhib Free Soc, London, 137]; untraced	*Graves* 1907, 138

Miscellaneous

4.	1769	Thetis dipping Achilles, model		[Exhib Free Soc, London, 120]; untraced	*Graves* 1907, 138
5.	1770	The graces crowning the arts, model		[Exhib Free Soc, London, 138]; untraced	*Graves* 1907, 138
6.	1772	Sketch after the antique	tc	[Exhib Free Soc, London, 1772]; untraced	*Graves* 1907, 138
7.	1773	'The portrait of a negro'	tc	[Exhib Free Soc, London, 105]; untraced	*Graves* 1907, 138
8.	1774	Unidentified gentleman		[Exhib Free Soc, London, 151]; untraced	*Graves* 1907, 138

KING, William, of Islington fl *c*1836

Gunnis describes his monument to Aeneas Barkly as 'a large tablet with carefully cut details' (*Gunnis* 1968, 229).

Funerary Monuments

1.	†1836	Aeneas Barkly	St Mary, Holloway, London	S	*Gunnis* 1968, 229

KING, William, of Oxford fl 1704–68

The son of William King of Wimbledon, a yeoman, he was apprenticed to **John Townesend I** for seven years from 1 May 1704. On 15 April 1734 he signed an agreement with All Souls College to finish 'the Gate Leading out of the North Quadrangle, to Finish the Cloysters on the Southside of the Gate' and to carve 'the Arms of the benefactors upon the shields in the gateway' according to drawings he had himself endorsed (Bodl MS D.D., All Souls Drawings a 15) (1). He received £796 for mason's work in the hall and buttery of the same college between 1735 and 1741. From 1757 until 1768 he was working with **John Townesend III** building the east wing of the Queen's College. They were paid £2,122 for this work (College Archives in GPC).

Literary References: *Gunnis* 1968, 229–30; *Graham* ed, fol 45

Archival References: GPC

Architectural Sculpture

1.	1734	Coats of arms Drawing(s): All Souls drawings a 15	[All Souls College, Oxford, gateway]; untraced	Bodl MS D.D.

KING & SONS, of London fl *c*1779–1835

The firm was based in Chenies Street. Gunnis notes that their monuments to Sir Robert and Lady Lawley and Lord Calthorp have 'charming' reliefs (*Gunnis* 1968, 228) (1, 4).

Funerary Monuments

1.	†1779	Sir Robert and Lady Lawley	Hints, Staffs	S	Pevsner, *Staffs*, 1974, 148
2.	†1795	Frances Cattell	Barford, Warks	S	Pevsner, *Warks*, 1966, 85
3.	?1797	Sir John Croft	Highworth, Wilts	S	*Gunnis* 1968, 228
4.	?1798	Lord Calthorp	Edgbaston, Birmingham		*Gunnis* 1968, 228
5.	†1802	George Schutz	Holton, Oxon	S	Pevsner, *Oxon*, 1974, 650
6.	†1807	Mrs John Mills	Barford, Warks	S	RG/JP, 5, 787
7.	†1830	J T Smoult	St George, Bloomsbury, London	S	
8.	1835	James Quilter	St John's Cathedral, Belize (formerly British Honduras)	S	*Hammond* 2000, 89–90, 90 (repr)

KINGSLAND, Richard fl *c*1732

Funerary Monuments

1.	†1732	Thomas Owen	Presteigne, Radnor	S	Pevsner, *Powys*, 1979, 270

KINGWILL, William, of Sidmouth fl 1809–44

From 1809–11 he was master-mason building Lord Despencer's house in Sidmouth (Soane Archives in GPC). The monument to Charlotte Temperence has a relief of *Hope* (3).

Literary References: *Gunnis* 1968, 230

Funerary Monuments						
1.	†1809	Henry Digby		Sidmouth, Devon	S	RG/JP, 5, 795
2.	†1810	Ambrose Crawley		Sidmouth, Devon	S	RG/JP, 5, 795
3.	†1810	Charlotte Temperance		Sidmouth, Devon	S	*Gunnis* 1968, 230
4.	†1832	Rev David Parker		Sidmouth congregational church, Devon		RG/JP, 5, 795
5.	†1844	Lady Audley		Sidmouth, Devon		RG/JP, 5, 795
Chimneypieces						
6.	1809–1811	Eleven, supplied with steps for the 'cottage' Payment(s): £132	m	[Lord Le Despencer's house, Sidmouth, Devon]; untraced		Soane bill book G fols 105–7

KINSON, Thomas A fl *c*1797

Gunnis notes that his wall-tablet to Elizabeth Scarisbrick is 'in coloured marbles with a charmingly carved design'.

Funerary Monuments

1.	†1797	Elizabeth Scarisbrook	Holy Trinity, Hull, E R Yorks	*Gunnis* 1968, 230

KIRK, Eliza 1812–

She was the second of the four daughters of **Thomas Kirk**. She worked in her father's studio and sent a number of works, mostly miniature busts, to the Royal Hibernian Academy exhibitions between 1838 and 1859. Her *Infant Bacchus* was shown at the Dublin Exhibition of 1853 (1).

Literary References: *Strickland* I, 1913, 582

Statues					
1.	1841	Infant Bacchus, model	p	[Exhib RHA, Dublin, 387]; untraced	*Strickland* I, 1913, 582; *Stewart* II, 1985, 162
2.	1848	Maternal love		[Exhib RHA, Dublin, 313]; untraced	*Stewart* II, 1985, 161, 162
Busts					
3.	1837	Frederick Shaw MP, miniature bust		[Exhib RHA, Dublin, 244]; untraced	*Stewart* II, 1985, 161, 162
4.	1837	King William III, miniature bust		[Exhib RHA, Dublin, 246]; untraced	*Stewart* II, 1985, 161
5.	1838	Unidentified lady, miniature bust		[Exhib RHA, Dublin, 216]; untraced	*Stewart* II, 1985, 161
6.	1839	Unidentified gentleman		[Exhib Liverpool Ac, 689]; untraced	*Morris and Roberts* 1998, 367
7.	1840	Robert Marshall		[Exhib RHA, Dublin, 364]; untraced	*Stewart* II, 1985, 161
8.	1840	Unidentified gentleman		[Exhib RHA, Dublin, 366]; untraced	*Stewart* II, 1985, 161
9.	1840	Unidentified lady		[Exhib RHA, Dublin, 362]; untraced	*Stewart* II, 1985, 161
10.	1842	Unidentified gentleman, miniature bust	m	[Exhib RHA, Dublin, 478]; untraced	*Stewart* II, 1985, 162
11.	1844	Unidentified gentleman, miniature bust		[Exhib RHA, Dublin, 418]; untraced	*Stewart* II, 1985, 162
12.	1844	Unidentified lady, miniature bust		[Exhib RHA, Dublin, 429]; untraced	*Stewart* II, 1985, 162
13.	1847	Unidentified lady	m	[Exhib RHA, Dublin, 459]; untraced	*Stewart* II, 1985, 162
14.	nd	Thomas Kirk Stewart (the sculptor's nephew)		coll Frank Stewart (Kansas City, USA)	*Strickland* I, 1913, 582
Miscellaneous					
15.	1846	'The juvenile recreations of an anti-teetotaller deity'		[Exhib RHA, Dublin, 470]; untraced	*Stewart* II, 1985, 162
16.	1856	Child and butterfly		[Exhib RHA, Dublin, 405]; untraced	*Stewart* II, 1985, 162
17.	1856	Sleeping child		[Exhib RHA, Dublin, 403 and RHA, Dublin, 1859, 349]; untraced	*Stewart* II, 1985, 162

KIRK, John, of Dumfries 1832–

He joined the Royal Academy Schools in 1847, and won a silver medal for a model the following year (4). In 1850 he was working at the Birmingham School of Design. Kirk exhibited at the Royal Academy, 1847–54, and the British Institution, 1849–54, from addresses in Dumfries, London and Birmingham.

Literary References: *Gunnis* 1968, 230

Statues					
1.	1851	Samson in his agony of thirst, statuette		[Exhib BI, London, 586]; untraced	*Graves* 1875, 323
Busts					
2.	1850	Thomas Clark	p	[Exhib RA, London, 1405]; untraced	*Graves* IV, 1905–6, 332

Miscellaneous

3.	1847	Mr John Craik		[Exhib RA, London, 674]; untraced	*Graves* IV, 1905–6, 332
4.	1848	Model in the antique academy		[RA Premium]; untraced	RA Premium list
5.	1849	Cephalus		[Exhib BI, London, 516]; untraced	*Graves* 1875, 323
6.	1851	Recollections of home		[Exhib BI, London, 528]; untraced	*Graves* 1875, 323
7.	1852	The golden age		[Exhib RA, London, 1285]; untraced	*Graves* IV, 1905–6, 332
8.	1853	Feeding time	m	[Exhib RA, London, 1328]; untraced	*Graves* IV, 1905–6, 332
9.	1854	Innocence petted	pm	[Exhib RA, London, 576]; untraced	*Graves* 1875, 323
10.	1854	Unidentified artist		[Exhib RA, London, 1283]; untraced	*Graves* IV, 1905–6, 332

KIRK, Joseph Robinson RHA 1821–94

He was born in 1821, the fifth child and eldest son of **Thomas Kirk** and his wife Eliza, née Robinson. Kirk entered Trinity College, Dublin in 1838 and took his degree in 1843. He had begun to study sculpture in his father's studio whilst still a boy and in 1840 he sent two busts to the Royal Hibernian Academy (**53, 54**). He continued to exhibit there regularly until 1871, as well as sending a few works to the Royal Academy in London (1846–62), the Liverpool Academy (1842, 1845–6) and the Liverpool Society of Fine Arts (1858). In 1843 he won the second prize of £5 from the Royal Irish Art Union for *Andromeda*, a figure study from the life, and was commissioned to execute it in marble (**34**). With the money thus earned he travelled to Rome, where he studied for a year. The Royal Irish Art Union later purchased Kirk's statues of *A child listening to the noise in a shell, Ruth and Naomi* and *The creation of the dimple* as prizes for their subscribers (**35, 36, 38**). He was elected an associate of the Royal Hibernian Academy in 1845 and became a full member in 1854. In 1852 he succeeded **Constantine Panormo** as master of the Royal Dublin Society Modelling School, a post he held for two years.

Kirk followed very much in his father's footsteps as a sculptor and like him obtained many commissions for public monuments, busts and church memorials. He is best known for his relief of *The siege of Seringapatam* on the base of the Wellington monument in Phoenix Park and for the monument to Captain Francis Crozier, a member of Sir John Franklin's ill-fated expedition to find the North West Passage, in Banbridge (**136, 22**). Crookshank comments that the latter is 'on altogether too big a scale for his talents', adding that he was 'apparently not familiar with the appearance of polar bears, which he used to surround the base' (*Crookshank* 1966, 311). Other public works include two statues of the 3rd Marquis of Downshire at Edenderry and Hillsborough and the figures of *Divinity, Law, Medicine* and *Science* on the campanile at Trinity College, Dublin (**37, 39, 127**). His most unusual composition was perhaps the monument to the eminent surgeon Sir Philip Crampton (**128**). This took the form of a fountain with a large bronze bust surrounded by exotic foliage. It was removed in 1959 after parts of the foliage began to become disengaged from the work and pose a danger to passers by.

Kirk's church monuments range from simple wall plaques, such as the Winter memorial in Agher, Co Meath, to an elaborate gothic canopied tomb with reclining effigy erected in memory of Viscount Massereene (**32, 26**). He continued to make use of the *Good Samaritan* reliefs with which his father had commemorated numerous clerics and divines throughout Ireland. Examples can be found in Limerick Cathedral and at Thurles, Co Tipperary (**28, 23**). The relief commemorating Captain Crozier at Seapatrick, illustrates the two ships used on his arctic voyage, the *Erebus* and the *Terror*, stranded in the ice-flows (**22**).

Kirk died at his home in Milward Terrace, Bray, on 30 August 1894 and was buried in the Mount Jerome cemetery. He had retired from his profession some years earlier due to ill-health. His wife, Jane Rachel, née Murray, whom he had married in 1845, survived him.

EH

Literary References: *Strickland* 1, 1913, 583–587; *Crookshank* 1966, 311; *Gunnis* 1968, 230; *Potterton* 1975, 54–5; *Penny* 1977 (1), 137, 219 n 5; *Crookshank* 1986, 24

Funerary Monuments

1.	†1845	Captain John Lucas (designed by A K Young)	Monaghan, Co Monaghan		*Potterton* 1975, 55
2.	†1845	John Synge	Killiskey, Co Wicklow		*Potterton* 1975, 55
3.	1845	'Model of a choir boy, designed to finish the monument of Sir John Stephenson, erected in Christ Church Cathedral'	[Exhib RHA, Dublin, 447]; untraced		*Stewart* II, 1985, 162
4.	1845	Patrick Sarsfield, model of a proposed monument for Limerick	Untraced		*Hill* 1998, 111
5.	†1845	Thomas Kirk (the sculptor's father)	Mount Jerome Cemetery, Dublin		*Strickland* I, 1913, 586
6.	1847	'And the spirit shall return to God who gave it', relief, part of a monument	[Exhib RHA, Dublin, 470]; untraced		*Stewart* II, 1985, 162
7.	1847	Hon C D Lindsay, Bishop of Kildare (†1846) Model(s): exhib RHA, Dublin, 1847, 471	Christchurch Cathedral, Dublin		*Strickland* I, 1913, 583, 585; *Potterton* 1975, 55; *Stewart* II, 1985, 162
8.	1848	'The trumpet shall sound, and the dead shall be raised', relief, part of a monument to be erected in the military chapel, Corfu	[Exhib RHA, Dublin, 326]; untraced		*Stewart* II, 1985, 162
9.	†1850	Children of Lady Caroline Burgess	Castlecaulfield, Co Tyrone	S	*Potterton* 1975, 55
10.	†1851	Alexander Shekelton	Dundalk, Co Louth		*Potterton* 1975, 55
11.	1851	Bluntish family member	Athlone, Co Westmeath		*Potterton* 1975, 55
12.	1851	Samuel Warren	Mount Jerome Cemetery, Dublin		*Strickland* I, 1913, 585; *Stewart* II, 1985, 163
13.	†1852	Elizabeth Cosby	St George, Dublin		*Potterton* 1975, 55
14.	1853	Design for a monument	[Exhib RHA, Dublin, 479]; untraced		*Stewart* II, 1985, 163
15.	†1853	Richard Ponsonby, Bishop of Derry	Londonderry Cathedral		*Potterton* 1975, 55
16.	1854	'Design for a monument to the Poet, Moore'	[Exhib RHA, Dublin, 296]; untraced		*Stewart* II, 1985, 163

17.	†1854	Dr Francis Rogan		Londonderry Cathedral	*Potterton* 1975, 55
18.	†1854	Rev Elias Thackeray		Dundalk, Co Louth	*Potterton* 1975, 55
19.	†1855	Anna Somerville		Kentstown, Co Meath	*Potterton* 1975, 55
20.	1855	Design for a monument to Lieutenant Kidd		[Exhib RHA, Dublin, 384]; untraced	*Stewart* II, 1985, 164
21.	†1855	Lt William Somerville		Kentstown, Co Meath	*Potterton* 1975, 55
22.	1856	Captain Francis Crozier RN (†1848) Model(s): working model exhib RHA, Dublin, 1855, 388; untraced		Seapatrick, Banbridge, Co Down	*Strickland* I, 1913, 584; *Potterton* 1975, 55; *Stewart* II, 1985, 164
23.	†1861	William Bradshaw		Thurles, Co Tipperary	*Potterton* 1975, 55
24.	1862	Sir Henry Marsh		Mount Jerome Cemetery, Dublin	*Strickland* I, 1913, 585; *Stewart* II, 1985, 164
25.	1863	Allegorical figure, part of a monument		[Exhib RHA, Dublin, 480]; untraced	*Stewart* II, 1985, 164
26.	†1863	John, Viscount Masserene	s	Antrim, Ulster	*Strickland* I, 1913, 585; *Potterton* 1975, 55, 69 (repr)
27.	1864	Rev James Robert Moffatt Payment(s): £200		Athlone, Co Westmeath	*Potterton* 1975, 55
28.	nd	Denis Mahony		Limerick Cathedral	*Potterton* 1975, 55
29.	nd	Thomas Gough		Londonderry Cathedral	*Potterton* 1975, 55
30.	nd	Unidentified subject		St Laserian's Cathedral, Old Leighlin, Co Carlow	*Potterton* 1975, 55
31.	nd	Vice Admiral Sir Josias Coghill Bt		Drumcondra, Co Dublin	*Strickland* I, 1913, 584; *Potterton* 1975, 55
32.	nd	Winter family member		Agher, Co Meath	*Potterton* 1975, 55
Statues					
33.	1842	A faun and a monkey	m	[Exhib RHA, Dublin, 472]; untraced	*Stewart* II, 1985, 162; *Morris and Roberts* 1998, 367
34.	1843	Andromeda Payment(s): £70 Model(s): awarded Royal Irish Art Union 2nd prize, 1843; exhib RHA, Dublin, 1843, 665; untraced	m	[Royal Irish Art Union prize awarded to Mrs Mounsell, of Ballymore, Westmeath]; untraced	*Strickland* I, 1913, 583, 586; *Stewart* II, 1985, 162
35.	1845	A child listening to the noise in a shell		[Royal Irish Art Union prize awarded to a subscriber]; untraced	*Strickland* I, 1913, 583; *Stewart* II, 1985, 162; *Morris and Roberts* 1998, 367
36.	1845	Ruth and Naomi Payment(s): £80	m	[Royal Irish Art Union prize awarded to W Hall, of Warrington]; untraced	*Graves* IV, 1905–6, 332; *Stewart* II, 1985, 162, 163; *Morris and Roberts* 1998, 367
37.	1846	Arthur, 3rd Marquess of Downshire Model(s): exhib RHA, Dublin, 1846, 478		Edenderry, Co Offaly	*Strickland* I, 1913, 584; *Stewart* II, 1985, 162
38.	1846	The creation of the dimple Payment(s): £100	m	[Royal Irish Art Union prize awarded to Henry Stuart, of Dame Street, Dublin]; untraced	*AU*, 1846, 188; *Graves* IV, 1905–6, 332; *Stewart* II, 1985, 162; *Morris and Roberts* 1998, 367
39.	1848	Arthur, 3rd Marquess of Downshire Model(s): quarter-sized model exhib RHA, Dublin, 1849, 435; untraced	s	Hillsborough, Co Down	*Strickland* I, 1913, 583, 585; *Stewart* II, 1985, 163; *Hill* 1998, 257 n108
40.	1848	Cassandra, statuette	m	[Exhib RHA, Dublin, 317]; untraced Other versions: £20 prize in the Shilling Art Union, won as a prize by John Leonard, Paris; untraced exhib RHA, Dublin, 1855, 400, marble statue; untraced exhib RHA, Dublin, 1860, 517, marble figure; untraced	*Graves* IV, 1905–6, 332; *Strickland* I, 1913, 586; *Stewart* II, 1985, 162, 163
41.	1848	Olivia raising the veil	m	[Exhib RHA, Dublin, 315]; untraced	*Graves* IV, 1905–6, 332; *Stewart* II, 1985, 162
42.	1848	Unidentified lady, statuette		[Exhib RHA, Dublin, 314]; untraced	*Stewart* II, 1985, 162
43.	1850	Sir Michael O'Loghlen Model(s): sketch model, clay, exhib RHA, Dublin, 1845, 461, untraced; half-sized model exhib RHA, Dublin, 1851, 346, untraced		Courthouse, Ennis, Co Clare	*Strickland* I, 1913, 585; *Stewart* II, 1985, 162, 163
44.	1852	Ariadne deploring the departure of Theseus, statuette		[Exhib RHA, Dublin, 383]; untraced	*Stewart* II, 1985, 163
45.	1852	Moses with the tablets of the law, designed to surmount a court house, sketch model		[Exhib RHA, Dublin, 381]; untraced	*Stewart* II, 1985, 163
46.	1853	Rachel weeping for her children		[Exhib RHA, Dublin, 452]; untraced	*Stewart* II, 1985, 163
47.	1854	Children at play	m	[Exhib RHA, Dublin, 280]; untraced	*Stewart* II, 1985, 163
48.	1856	Children and dog	m	[Exhib RA, London, 1257]; untraced	*Graves* IV, 1905–6, 333
49.	1858	The sisters (two daughters of John Vance MP)	m	[ex coll J Vance]; untraced	*Strickland* I, 1913, 585; *Morris and Roberts* 1998, 367
50.	1860	St John and the Virgin at the Crucifixion	m	[Exhib RHA, Dublin, 515]; untraced	*Graves* IV, 1905–6, 333; *Stewart* II, 1985, 164
51.	1862	Captain Francis Crozier	s	Town Square, Banbridge, Co Down	*Crookshank* 1966, 311; *Stewart* II, 1985, 164
52.	nd	Sappho	m	[for Sir B A Guinness]; coll Lord Iveagh Other versions: coll Lord Gough, marble exhib RHA, Dublin, 1855, 400, marble; untraced	*Strickland* I, 1913, 586; *Stewart* II, 1985, 164

Busts

No.	Date	Subject		Location		Bibliography
53.	1840	Hugh Ferguson		[Exhib RHA, Dublin, 353]; untraced		*Stewart* II, 1985, 162
54.	1840	Unidentified young lady		[Exhib RHA, Dublin, 384]; untraced		*Stewart* II, 1985, 162
55.	1841	Major Henry C Sirr		[Exhib RHA, Dublin, 404]; untraced		*Stewart* II, 1985, 162
56.	1841	Unidentified gentleman		[Exhib RHA, Dublin, 407]; untraced		*Stewart* II, 1985, 162
57.	1841	Unidentified lady		[Exhib RHA, Dublin, 405]; untraced		*Stewart* II, 1985, 162
58.	1843	Unidentified young lady, miniature bust		[Exhib RHA, Dublin, 663]; untraced		*Stewart* II, 1985, 162
59.	1844	Unidentified lady, miniature bust	m	[Exhib RHA, Dublin, 419]; untraced		*Stewart* II, 1985, 162
60.	1845	John Adair		[Exhib RHA, Dublin, 442]; untraced		*Stewart* II, 1985, 162
61.	1845	Unidentified gentleman, posthumous	m	[Exhib RHA, Dublin, 439]; untraced		*Stewart* II, 1985, 162
62.	1845	Unidentified lady	m	[Exhib RHA, Dublin, 449]; untraced		*Stewart* II, 1985, 162
63.	1846	Arthur, 3rd Marquess of Downshire		[Exhib RHA, Dublin, 463]; untraced		*Stewart* II, 1985, 162
64.	1846	Unidentified lady		[Exhib RHA, Dublin, 464]; untraced		*Stewart* II, 1985, 162
65.	1846	Unidentified lady, posthumous		[Exhib RHA, Dublin, 465]; untraced		*Stewart* II, 1985, 162
66.	1846	William O'Reilly	m	[Exhib RHA, Dublin, 484]; untraced		*Stewart* II, 1985, 162
67.	1847	Rev Mr Newland		[Exhib RHA, Dublin, 472]; untraced		*Stewart* II, 1985, 162
68.	1847	Unidentified gentleman	m	[Exhib RHA, Dublin, 458]; untraced		*Stewart* II, 1985, 162
69.	1847	Unidentified lady	m	[Exhib RHA, Dublin, 474]; untraced		*Stewart* II, 1985, 162
70.	1847	Unidentified lady	m	[Exhib RHA, Dublin, 478]; untraced		*Stewart* II, 1985, 162
71.	1847	Unidentified young lady		[Exhib RHA, Dublin, 480]; untraced		*Stewart* II, 1985, 162
72.	1848	Hon and Very Rev H Pakenham DD		[Exhib RHA, Dublin, 318]; untraced		*Strickland* I, 1913, 585; *Stewart* II, 1985, 162
73.	1848	John Mitchell, miniature bust		[Exhib RHA, Dublin, 332]; untraced		*Stewart* II, 1985, 162
74.	1848	Robert Howe Gould		[Exhib RHA, Dublin, 310]; untraced		*Stewart* II, 1985, 162
75.	1848	Unidentified gentleman, miniature bust		[Exhib RHA, Dublin, 320]; untraced		*Stewart* II, 1985, 162
76.	1848	Unidentified gentleman, posthumous		[Exhib RHA, Dublin, 327]; untraced		*Stewart* II, 1985, 162
77.	1849	E Geraghty		[Exhib RHA, Dublin, 437]; untraced		*Stewart* II, 1985, 163
78.	1849	Mrs G Stanley Murray, miniature bust		[Exhib RHA, Dublin, 420]; untraced		*Stewart* II, 1985, 163
79.	1849	Rev Elias Thackery		[Exhib RHA, Dublin, 412]; untraced		*Stewart* II, 1985, 163
80.	1849	Unidentified young lady		[Exhib RHA, Dublin, 426]; untraced		*Stewart* II, 1985, 163
81.	1849	William Boyton Kirk		[Exhib RHA, Dublin, 436]; untraced		*Stewart* II, 1985, 163
82.	1851	James, 13th Lord Dunboyne		[Exhib RHA, Dublin, 353]; untraced Other versions: miniature bust exhib RHA, Dublin, 1851, 363; untraced		*Strickland* I, 1913, 585; *Stewart* II, 1985, 163
83.	1851	Rev Charles Elrington		[Exhib RHA, Dublin, 343]; untraced		*Stewart* II, 1985, 163
84.	1851	Rev Dr Bisset, Lord Bishop of Raphoe		[Exhib RHA, Dublin, 344]; untraced		*Stewart* II, 1985, 163
85.	1851	Sir Michael O'Loghlen		[Exhib RHA, Dublin, 374]; untraced		*Stewart* II, 1985, 163
86.	1851	Unidentified lady, miniature bust		[Exhib RHA, Dublin, 368]; untraced		*Stewart* II, 1985, 163
87.	1852	Rev Dr Todd	m	Trinity College, Dublin		*Strickland* I, 1913, 585; *Stewart* II, 1985, 163
88.	1853	Rev Dr Macdonnell		[Exhib RHA, Dublin, 456]; untraced		*Stewart* II, 1985, 163
89.	1853	William Magee, Bishop of Dublin		[Dublin Int Exhib]; untraced		*Strickland* I, 1913, 585
90.	1853	Wills Hill Macready		[Exhib RHA, Dublin, 459]; untraced		*Stewart* II, 1985, 163
91.	1854	Augusta, Lady Langford	m	Castletown, Co Louth		*Strickland* I, 1913, 585; *Stewart* II, 1985, 163, 164
92.	1854	Colonel Layard		[Exhib RHA, Dublin, 292]; untraced		*Stewart* II, 1985, 163
93.	1854	Unidentified lady		[Exhib RHA, Dublin, 274]; untraced		*Stewart* II, 1985, 163
94.	1855	Infant son of Bertie Watkin Williams Wynn	m	[Exhib RA, London, 1450]; untraced		*Graves* IV, 1905–6, 333
95.	1855	Unidentified lady		[Exhib RHA, Dublin, 293]; untraced		*Stewart* II, 1985, 164
96.	1859	A O'Bryan Bellingham	m	RCS, Dublin		*Strickland* I, 1913, 584; *Stewart* II, 1985, 164
97.	1859	Rev Dr Manning		[Exhib RHA, Dublin, 327]; untraced		*Stewart* II, 1985, 164
98.	1859	Sir Philip Crampton	m	RCS, Dublin		*Strickland* I, 1913, 584; *Stewart* II, 1985, 164
99.	1860	Mortimer O'Sullivan DD		[Exhib RHA, Dublin, 519]; untraced		*Stewart* II, 1985, 164
100.	1860	T White		[Exhib RHA, Dublin, 518]; untraced		*Stewart* II, 1985, 164
101.	1860	Unidentified gentleman		[Exhib RHA, Dublin, 520]; untraced		*Stewart* II, 1985, 164
102.	1862	Arthur Armstrong (aged nine years)		[Exhib RHA, Dublin, 476]; untraced		*Stewart* II, 1985, 164
103.	1862	Arthur Jacob MD		[Exhib RHA, Dublin, 481]; untraced		*Stewart* II, 1985, 164
104.	1862	Edward Hayes RHA		[Exhib RHA, Dublin, 487]; untraced		*Stewart* II, 1985, 164
105.	1862	J W Cusack	m	RCS, Dublin		*Strickland* I, 1913, 584; *Stewart* II, 1985, 164
106.	1862	'- Loftie Esq'		[Exhib RHA, Dublin, 475]; untraced		*Stewart* II, 1985, 164
107.	1862	Paulus Emilius Singer		[Exhib RHA, Dublin, 485]; untraced		*Stewart* II, 1985, 164
108.	1862	Sir Leopold McClintock	m	RDS, Dublin	S	*Strickland* I, 1913, 585; *Stewart* II, 1985, 164; *White and Bright* 1998, 53–4
109.	1862	W H Porter	m	RCS, Dublin		*Strickland* I, 1913, 585; *Stewart* II, 1985, 164
110.	1863	Charles Sugrue	m	[Exhib RHA, Dublin, 484]; untraced		*Stewart* II, 1985, 164
111.	1864	Mrs John Brinton	m	[Exhib RHA, Dublin, 424]; untraced		*Stewart* II, 1985, 164
112.	1864	Mrs Richard Lawless	m	[Exhib RHA, Dublin, 442]; untraced		*Stewart* II, 1985, 164
113.	1864	Prof Rudolph Thomas Siegfried		Trinity College, Dublin, Long Room		*Stewart* II, 1985, 164; *Crookshank* 1986, 24
114.	1864	Rev Thomas Moffett	m	[Exhib RHA, Dublin, 448]; untraced		*Stewart* II, 1985, 164
115.	1864	Thomas Macksey		[Exhib RHA, Dublin, 436]; untraced		*Stewart* II, 1985, 164
116.	1864	Unidentified lady		[Exhib RHA, Dublin, 452]; untraced		*Stewart* II, 1985, 164
117.	1865	Miss Harriet Sanger		[Exhib RHA, Dublin, 470]; untraced		*Stewart* II, 1985, 164
118.	1865	Unidentified lady		[Exhib RHA, Dublin, 473]; untraced		*Stewart* II, 1985, 164

119. 1868	Thomas, 4th Viscount Southwell		[Exhib RHA, Dublin, 428]; untraced	*Strickland* I, 1913, 585; *Stewart* II, 1985, 164, 165
120. 1868	Unidentified child, posthumous	m	[Exhib RHA, Dublin, 430]; untraced	*Stewart* II, 1985, 164
121. 1871	Charlotte, Viscountess Southwell		[Exhib RHA, Dublin, 362]; untraced	*Strickland* I, 1913, 585; *Stewart* II, 1985, 165
122. 1872	Julia, Viscountess Powerscourt		[Dublin Int Exhib]; untraced	*Strickland* I, 1913, 585
123. nd	Arthur Guinness	m	Coll Lord Iveagh Other versions: bust 'from the marble' exhib RHA, Dublin, 1855, 392	*Strickland* I, 1913, 585; *Stewart* II, 1985, 164
124. nd	Francis Burton (after Chantrey)		Christ Church Cathedral, Oxford	*Gunnis* 1968, 230
125. nd	R Carlisle Williams MD	m	RCS, Dublin	*Strickland* I, 1913, 586
126. nd	Sir Henry Marsh	m	RCS, Dublin	*Strickland* I, 1913, 585
Architectural Sculpture				
127. 1849	Divinity, Law, Medicine and Science, four allegorical figures on the campanile Model(s): sketch models exhib RHA, Dublin, 1854, 281, 282, 285 and 286		Trinity College, Dublin	*Stewart* II, 1985, 163; *Crookshank* 1986, 24
128. 1862	Sir Philip Crampton, memorial fountain	b	[Pearse Street, Dublin]; removed 1959	*Strickland* I, 1913, 584; *Stewart* II, 1985, 164; *Murphy* 2001, 39 (repr)
129. 1870	St Peter and St Patrick, two statues Model(s): St Peter exhib RHA, Dublin, 1870, 395		St Paul, Arran Quay	*Strickland* I, 1913, 586; *Stewart* II, 1985, 164
130. nd	Military trophy	s	Parliament House, Dublin, above west gateway	*Strickland* I, 1913, 586
Reliefs				
131. 1849	'Suffer little children to come unto me . . .'		[Exhib RHA, Dublin, 417]; untraced	*Stewart* II, 1985, 163
132. 1849	'The Slaughter of the Innocents'		[Exhib RHA, Dublin, 418]; untraced	*Stewart* II, 1985, 163
133. 1852	Bernard Mullins (part of a monument lately erected in Dublin)		[Exhib RHA, Dublin, 380]; untraced	*Stewart* II, 1985, 163
134. 1852	Mrs Mullins (part of a monument lately erected in Dublin)		[Exhib RHA, Dublin, 382]; untraced	*Stewart* II, 1985, 163
135. 1852	The visit to the tomb	m	[Exhib RHA, Dublin, 354]; untraced	*Stewart* II, 1985, 163
136. *c*1860	The siege of Seringapatam Drawing(s): sketch in watercolours exhib RHA, Dublin, 1860, 528; untraced	b	Wellington monument, Phoenix Park, Dublin	*Harbison, Potterton and Sheehy* 1987, 233
137. 1868	Alderman Atkinson, medallion		[Exhib RHA, Dublin, 404]; untraced	*Stewart* II, 1985, 164
138. 1868	Hon Mrs Wood, medallion		[Exhib RHA, Dublin, 403]; untraced	*Stewart* II, 1985, 164
139. 1868	Viscountess Powerscourt		[Exhib RHA, Dublin, 462]; untraced	*Stewart* II, 1985, 164
Miscellaneous				
140. 1844	The young bird-catcher		[Exhib RHA, Dublin, 425]; untraced	*Stewart* II, 1985, 162
141. 1846	A child		[Exhib RA, London, 1483]; untraced	*Graves* IV, 1905–6, 332
142. 1846	Model for a gold fibula, from a design by W F Burton, presented to Miss Helen Faucit	w	[Exhib RHA, Dublin, 468]; untraced	*Stewart* II, 1985, 162
143. 1851	Unidentified lady, a 'miniature'		[Exhib RHA, Dublin, 364]; untraced	*Stewart* II, 1985, 163
144. 1853	Design for a centrepiece in metal emblematic of the Great Exhibition of 1851		[Exhib RHA, Dublin, 476]; untraced	*Stewart* II, 1985, 163
145. 1865	Sleeping child	m	[Exhib RHA, Dublin, 470]; untraced	*Stewart* II, 1985, 164

KIRK, Thomas RHA 1781–1845

One of the most important sculptors working in Ireland in the first half of the 19th century, he was born in Cork, the only son of William Kirk, a native of Edinburgh, and his wife, Elizabeth, née Bible. He studied at the Royal Dublin Society schools, where he won prizes in 1797 and 1800, and worked for **Henry Darley** before establishing his own studio at 21 Jervis Street, Dublin. In 1808 he married Eliza Robinson, the daughter of a Dublin builder. They had 12 children, including **Eliza, Joseph Robinson** and **William Boyton Kirk**.

In 1810 Kirk exhibited a relief of *Piety and Charity*, part of a monument erected in the Pro-Cathedral in memory of Rev Thomas Clark, at the Society of Artists in Hawkins Street (**2**). He sent further works to the Society of Artists over the next decade and was a founder member of the Royal Hibernian Academy, exhibiting there from 1826 onwards. He also exhibited a small number of works in England at the Royal Academy (1825–45), the British Institution (1840), the Society of British Artists (1832) and in Liverpool (1822–42).

His first major commission was the colossal statue of Nelson which stood at the top of the memorial column erected in Sackville Street in 1808 (**31**). He subsequently carved statues of the Duke of Wellington, Thomas Spring-Rice and the Earl of Caledon to surmount columns in Trim, Limerick and Caledon (**34, 42, 48**). He supplied the model for the statue of George III at the Bank of Ireland, in Dublin, which was carved by **John Bacon II** in 1812 and he later executed a statue of George IV commemorating the King's visit to the Dublin linen hall in 1821 (**32, 36**). His most significant work in England is the statue of the political reformer Admiral Sidney Smith, which was commissioned by parliament for the Royal Naval Hospital, Greenwich (**54**).

Kirk executed a large number of portrait busts, examples of which can be found at Trinity College, the Royal Dublin Society, the Royal College of Surgeons and elsewhere in Dublin. Whilst Cust writes that these were 'considered remarkable for the delicate handling of the marble and for distinctness of detail' (DNB), Gunnis comments that they 'can be lifeless' although some, including those of the lawyer T P Filgate and Professor Lloyd, are 'of high quality' (**91, 123**). He also exhibited ideal works, including *The young champion* and *The young suppliant* which were executed for the 2nd Earl de Grey, the Lord Lieutenant of Ireland (**49, 52**). *The young dog-stealer* was carved in marble for Lord Powerscourt and duplicated for the Royal Irish Art Union who awarded it as a prize to one of their subscribers as well as issuing fifteen casts (**50**).

Kirk is probably best known for his numerous church monuments, many of which include small-scale relief panels. His favourite relief subject was the *Good Samaritan*, which was appropriate for memorials to doctors and clergymen. Examples can be seen at Dundalk, Comber and Rosscarbery (**5, 17, 18**). The monument to Lady Rossmore has a relief entitled *The parting glance*, which shows her on her death bed, visited for the last time by her anguished husband who is pulled away by their son (**23**). Thomas Abbott's memorial in Christ Church Cathedral, Dublin has a figure of a weeping orphan girl (**10**). In the crypt of the same church is the tomb of Nathaniel Sneyd who was shot by 'an unhappy maniac' in 1833 (**15**). It features a figure of the dying man, with a female figure weeping over him, and Strickland describes it as 'a fine piece of work, Kirk's masterpiece' (*Strickland* I, 1913, 591). In addition to the works listed below, Kirk is also thought to have been responsible for monuments to Thomas Routledge (nd), at Ballinrobe, Co Down; Thomas Dillon (†1828), in the Pro-Cathedral, Dublin; Nathaniel Sneyd (†1833), at Cavan; William and Anne Bayley (nd), in the Pro-Cathedral, and George Pentland (†1844), at Kilruch, Co Clare (*Potterton* 1975, 56–7).

He died in Dublin on 19 April 1845 and was buried in Mount Jerome cemetery in Dublin. On his tomb is a life-size female figure, the work of his son, Joseph Robinson Kirk. He was subsequently described as 'a man of simple manners, honourable and upright in all his dealings, and scrupulously exact and punctual in carrying out his contracts' (*Strickland* I, 1913, 588). **Terence Farrell** was his pupil.

EH

Literary References: *DNB* (Cust); *Strickland* 1, 1913, 587–592; *Crookshank* 1966, 310; *Gunnis* 1968, 230; *Potterton* 1975, 55–57; *Penny* 1977, 137, 215 n56, 219 n5; *Harbison, Potterton and Sheehy* 1978, 217, 222; *ODNB* (Turpin)

Portraits of the Sculptor: anon, photograph (repr *Strickland* I, 1913, pl xxxvi)

Funerary Monuments

1.	†1800	John Chamber	St George, Dublin	S	*Potterton* 1975, 56
2.	1810	Rev Thomas Clark	Pro-Cathedral, Dublin		*Strickland* I, 1913, 587, 589; *Potterton* 1975, 56–7
3.	†1817	James Wright	Newry, Co Down	S	*Potterton* 1975, 57
4.	†1819	Countess Talbot	Ingestre, Staffs		Pevsner, *Staffs*, 1974, 156
5.	1819	Dr George Gillichan	Dundalk, Co Louth		*Potterton* 1975, 57
6.	†1822	Sir Samuel Auchmuty	Christ Church Cathedral, Dublin		*Strickland* I, 1913, 588; *Potterton* 1975, 56
7.	†1827	Dr Spray	St Patrick's Cathedral, Dublin		*Potterton* 1975, 56; *Stewart* II, 1985, 165
8.	c1828	Thomas Ball (†1826) Model(s): exhib RHA, Dublin, 1828, 355	St Patrick's Cathedral, Dublin		*Potterton* 1975, 55–56; *Stewart* II, 1985, 165
9.	1829	Jane Vernon (†1827) Model(s): exhib RHA, Dublin, 1828, 350	Carlow, Co Leinster		*Strickland* I, 1913, 591; *Potterton* 1975, 56; *Stewart* II, 1985, 165
10.	?1829	Thomas Abbott	Christ Church Cathedral, Dublin		*Strickland* I, 1913, 588; *Johnson* 1975, 272; *Potterton* 1975, 56; *Morris and Roberts* 1998, 367; *Stewart* II, 1985, 166
11.	1830	Rt Hon John Ormesby Vandeleur (†1828)	Kilruch, Co Clare		*Potterton* 1975, 57; *Stewart* II, 1985, 166
12.	†1831	William Montgomery	Greyabbey, Co Down		*Potterton* 1975, 57
13.	†1833	Francis Cole	Monaghan, Co Monaghan		*Potterton* 1975, 57
14.	†1834	Richard Jackson	Monaghan, Co Monaghan		*Potterton* 1975, 57
15.	c1835	Nathaniel Sneyd (†1833) Model(s): exhib RHA, Dublin, 1838, 207	Christ Church Cathedral, Dublin, crypt		*Potterton* 1975, 56; *Stewart* II, 1985, 166, 167
16.	1837	Rev Dr Doyle, model in pipeclay	[Exhib RHA, Dublin, 252]; untraced		*Stewart* II, 1985, 167
17.	†1837	Rev George Hill	Comber, Co Down		*Potterton* 1975, 56
18.	†1837	Rev Horatio Townsend	Rosscarbery, Co Cork		*Potterton* 1975, 57
19.	†1838	Rev Joseph Storey	Cavan, Co Cavan		*Potterton* 1975, 56
20.	1839	'Statue and pedestal, designed for a monument to the late Chief Baron Joy', sketch model	[Exhib RHA, Dublin, 369]; untraced		*Stewart* II, 1985, 167
21.	1841	Sepulchral tablet, a widow and orphans weeping over the tomb of their benefactor, part of a monument erected in memory of a clergyman	[Exhib RHA, Dublin, 389]; untraced		*Stewart* II, 1985, 167
22.	1843	Hon Charles Westenra Model(s): exhib Liverpool Ac, 1842, 580	Monaghan, Co Monaghan		*Potterton* 1975, 57, 68 (repr); *Stewart* II, 1985, 167; *Morris and Roberts* 1998, 367
23.	1843	Mary Anne, Lady Rossmore (†1807)	Monaghan, Co Monaghan		*Potterton* 1975, 31, 57 (repr); *Harbison, Potterton and Sheehy* 1978, 217 (repr); *Stewart* II, 1985, 167
24.	1843	Sir John Stevenson (unfinished)	Christ Church Cathedral, Dublin		*Potterton* 1975, 56; *Stewart* II, 1985, 167
25.	nd	Charles Dickinson, Bishop of Meath	St Anne, Dublin		*Strickland* I, 1913, 589; *Potterton* 1975, 56
26.	nd	Daniel McKay	St Anne, Dublin		*Strickland* I, 1913, 590; *Potterton* 1975, 56
27.	nd	Elizabeth Grogan	Rathaspeck, Co Wexford, churchyard		*Strickland* I, 1913, 590
28.	nd	Lieutenant-Colonel Seymour Vandeleur	Kilruch, Co Clare		*Potterton* 1975, 57
29.	nd	Rev G W Cotton	St Anne, Dublin		*Strickland* I, 1913, 589; *Potterton* 1975, 56
30.	nd	Rev Robert Fowler, Bishop of Ossory	Kilkenny Cathedral		*Potterton* 1975, 57

Statues

No.	Date	Subject		Location		Literary references
31.	1808	Horatio, Admiral Lord Nelson Payment(s): £300	s	[Memorial column, Sackville Street (O'Connell Street), Dublin]; destroyed 1966 (head in Dublin Civic Museum)		*Strickland* I, 1913, 587, 590; *Murray* 1991, 176; *Hill* 1998, 64–5 (repr)
32.	1812	King George III, model only (executed for the Bank of Ireland by John Bacon RA)		Untraced		*Strickland* I, 1913, 589
33.	1817	'A British tar'		Untraced Other versions: four colossal figures cast in metal 1819: one at Rosses Point, Sligo Harbour; another at Great Newtown Head, Tramore Bay, Co Waterford; two untraced		*Strickland* I, 1913, 592
34.	1817	Arthur, 1st Duke of Wellington		Trim, Co Meath		*Hill* 1998, 75–7 (repr)
35.	1818	Sleeping child	m	Crawford Municipal Gall, Cork		*Murray* 1991, 148 (repr); *Morris and Roberts* 1998, 367
36.	1821	King George IV Model(s): exhib RHA, Dublin, 1827, 289, half-size	m	[Linen Hall, Dublin]; RDS, Dublin		*Stewart* II, 1985, 165; *White and Bright* 1998, 86
37.	1824	Boy and dog		[Exhib ALRI, Liverpool, 179]; untraced		*Morris and Roberts* 1998, 367
38.	1826	Child asleep upon a Greek chair		[for W Mageogh Bond]; untraced		*Stewart* II, 1985, 165
39.	1827	Boy catching a butterfly		[for W Mageough Bond]; untraced		*Stewart* II, 1985, 165
40.	1827	Pop, a favourite dog of Sir Francis Johnston, model		[Exhib RHA, Dublin, 303]; untraced		*Stewart* II, 1985, 165
41.	1828	A favourite dog, full length portrait	m	[Exhib RHA, Dublin, 348]; untraced		*Stewart* II, 1985, 165
42.	1831	Thomas Spring Rice Model(s): exhib RHA, Dublin, 1826, 400		Pery Square (formerly New Square), Limerick		*Strickland* I, 1913, 591; *Stewart* II, 1985, 165; *Hill* 1998, 78
43.	1837	Unidentified child		[Exhib RA, London, 1205]; untraced		*Graves* IV, 1905–6, 333
44.	1838	Sleeping child, model		[Exhib RHA, Dublin, 224]; untraced		*Stewart* II, 1985, 165
45.	1839	A man roused from his sleep in the coil of a serpent, design for a statue		[Exhib RHA, Dublin, 385]; untraced		*Stewart* II, 1985, 167
46.	1839	Boy and dogs	m	[Exhib RHA, Dublin, 367]; untraced		*Stewart* II, 1985, 165
47.	1839	Group	m	[Exhib RA, London, 1390]; untraced		*Graves* IV, 1905–6, 333
48.	1840	Du Pré, 2nd Earl of Caledon Model(s): exhib RHA, Dublin, 1841, 401		Caledon, Co Tyrone		*Strickland* I, 1913, 589; *Stewart* II, 1985, 167; *Hill* 1998, 257, n 108
49.	1840	The young champion Model(s): exhib RHA, Dublin, 1838, 226, plaster	m	Wrest Park, Beds Other versions: purchased by the Royal Irish Art Union for £90 and lent to the Dublin Int Exhib, 1872, by W B Smythe, marble; untraced		*Graves* 1875, 323; *Strickland* I, 1913, 592; *Gunnis* 1968, 230; *Stewart* II, 1985, 167
50.	1840	The young dog-stealer	m	[Royal Irish Art Union prize awarded to Mr Hamilton of Rostrevor]; untraced Other versions: ex coll Viscount Powerscourt, marble; untraced 15 casts awarded as prizes by the Royal Irish Art Union		*Strickland* I, 1913, 592; *Stewart* II, 1985, 166
51.	1842	Eve, design for a statue		[Exhib RHA, Dublin, 463]; untraced		*Stewart* II, 1985, 167
52.	1843	The young suppliant	m	Wrest Park, Beds		*Gunnis* 1968, 230; *Stewart* II, 1985, 167
53.	1844	General O'Malley Drawing(s): RHA, Dublin, 1844, 433		Castlebar, Co Mayo		*Strickland* I, 1913, 591; *Stewart* II, 1985, 167
54.	1845	Admiral Sir William Sidney Smith Model(s): RHA, Dublin, 1844, 432, full-size	m	NMM, Greenwich, SCU0051	S	*AU*, 1845, 195; *Graves* IV, 1905–6, 333; *Gunnis* 1968, 230; *Stewart* II, 1985, 167

Busts

No.	Date	Subject		Location		Literary references
55.	1817	Professor Gregor von Feinagle	m	RDS, Dublin		*Strickland* I, 1913, 589; *White and Bright* 1998, 54
56.	1818	Arabella, Duchess of Dorset		Knole, Kent	S	*Strickland* I, 1913, 589; *Gunnis* 1968, 230
57.	1819	Ariadne		Coll Lord Powerscourt		*Graves* IV, 1905–6, 333; *Stewart* II, 1985, 167
58.	1819	John Wilson Croker		[Sir Robert Peel; Peel heirlooms sale, 1900]; untraced		*Graves* IV, 1905–6, 333; *Gunnis* 1968, 230; *Stewart* II, 1985, 165
59.	1821	Charles, 2nd Earl Talbot and his wife, Frances		Falconhurst, Hever, Kent	D	*Strickland* I, 1913, 591; *Stewart* II, 1985, 165
60.	1821	Classical head	a	NGI 8096	SD	*le Harivel* 1988, 573 (repr)
61.	1821	Edward Dalton	m	[Exhib Royal Arcade, Dublin]; untraced		*Strickland* I, 1913, 589
62.	1821	Judge Charles Burton	m	NGI 8052	SD	*Strickland* I, 1913, 589; *le Harivel* 1988, 573 (repr)
63.	1821	Rev Charles Boyton		[Exhib Royal Arcade, Dublin]; untraced		*Strickland* I, 1913, 589
64.	1822	King George IV		[Exhib ALRI, Liverpool, 190]; untraced		*Morris and Roberts* 1998, 367
65.	1822	Thomas Moore		[Exhib ALRI, Liverpool, 193]; untraced		*Morris and Roberts* 1998, 367
66.	1824	Angelica Catalani	m	Irish Georgian Soc, Longfield	SD	*Strickland* I, 1913, 589; *Barrett* 1971 (1), 88; *Stewart* II, 1985, 165, 166

67.	1824	Richard Brinsley Sheridan	m	NGI 8000	SD	*le Harivel* 1988, 573 (repr)
68.	1825	Miss Croker	m	[Exhib RA, London, 1003]; untraced Other versions: 'Cast for a bust of Miss Croker' exhib RHA, Dublin, 1826, 381; untraced		*Graves* IV, 1905–6, 333; *Stewart* II, 1985, 165
69.	1825	Unidentified gentleman		[Exhib RA, London, 1021]; untraced		*Graves* IV, 1905–6, 333
70.	1826	Countess of Bective	m	[Exhib RHA, Dublin, 378]; untraced		*Strickland* I, 1913, 589; *Stewart* II, 1985, 165
71.	1826	Earl of Bective	m	[Exhib RHA, Dublin, 379]; untraced		*Strickland* I, 1913, 589; *Stewart* II, 1985, 165
72.	1826	James Corry	m	[Exhib RHA, Dublin, 380]; untraced		*Strickland* I, 1913, 589; *Stewart* II, 1985, 165
73.	1826	King George IV (for the Bank of Ireland, Dublin)	m	[Exhib RHA, Dublin, 372]; untraced		*Stewart* II, 1985, 165
74.	1826	Lord Norbury	m	[Exhib RHA, Dublin, 377]; untraced		*Stewart* II, 1985, 165
75.	1826	W H Archer	m	[Exhib RHA, Dublin, 385]; untraced		*Strickland* I, 1913, 588; *Stewart* II, 1985, 165
76.	1826	William Gregory	m	[Exhib RHA, Dublin, 376]; untraced		*Strickland* I, 1913, 590; *Stewart* II, 1985, 165
77.	1826	William Magee, Archbishop of Dublin, model for a marble bust		[Exhib RHA, Dublin, 374]; untraced		*Stewart* II, 1985, 165
78.	1827	Colonel Verner	m	[Exhib RHA, Dublin, 302]; untraced		*Stewart* II, 1985, 165
79.	1827	Dr Hanneman		[Exhib RHA, Dublin, 296]; untraced		*Stewart* II, 1985, 165
80.	1827	Dr Matthew Young		Trinity College, Dublin, Long Room	D	*Crookshank* 1986, 24; *Stewart* II, 1985, 165
81.	1827	Francis Johnston PRHA	m	RHA, Dublin (presented by the sculptor) Other versions: several exhib RHA, Dublin, 1827–45		*Strickland* I, 1913, 590; *Stewart* II, 1985, 165, 166, 167
82.	1827	Frederick Kalkbrenner	m	[Exhib RHA, Dublin, 308]; untraced		*Stewart* II, 1985, 165
83.	1827	Mrs Johnston	m	[Exhib RHA, Dublin, 292]; untraced Other versions: several exhib RHA, Dublin, 1828–45, including one for the RHA Council Room; all untraced		*Stewart* II, 1985, 165, 166, 167
84.	1827	Rev Charles Bardin		[Exhib RHA, Dublin, 309]; untraced		*Stewart* II, 1985, 165
85.	1827	Richard Dease		[Exhib RHA, Dublin, 298]; untraced		*Stewart* II, 1985, 165
86.	1827	Sir John Stevenson		[Exhib RHA, Dublin, 299]; untraced		*Stewart* II, 1985, 165
87.	1827	Thomas Findlay	m	[Exhib RHA, Dublin, 294]; untraced		*Stewart* II, 1985, 165
88.	1827	Thomas Spring-Rice	m	[for Sir Aubrey De Vere Hunt Bt]; untraced Other versions: Limerick public library, 1828		*Stewart* II, 1985, 165, 166
89.	1827	William Magan	m	[Exhib RHA, Dublin, 301]; untraced		*Stewart* II, 1985, 165
90.	1829	Col James Cuffe		[Exhib RHA, Dublin, 288]; untraced		*Stewart* II, 1985, 166
91.	1829	T P Filgate		Royal Ulster Museum		*Strickland* I, 1913, 589; *Crookshank* 1966, 310; *Stewart* II, 1985, 165
92.	1829	Thomas Moore		[Exhib RHA, Dublin, 274]; untraced		*Stewart* II, 1985, 165; 166
93.	1829	Unidentified lady		[Exhib RHA, Dublin, 289]; untraced		*Stewart* II, 1985, 166
94.	1830	Edward Houghton	m	RHA, Dublin (presented by the sculptor)		*Strickland* I, 1913, 590; *Stewart* II, 1985, 166, 167
95.	1830	Lord George Hill	m	[Exhib RHA, Dublin, 286]; untraced		*Stewart* II, 1985, 166, 167
96.	1830	Mrs Verner	m	[Exhib RHA, Dublin, 282]; untraced		*Stewart* II, 1985, 166
97.	1830	Owen Phibbs		[Exhib RHA, Dublin, 288]; untraced		*Stewart* II, 1985, 166
98.	1830	Richard Cane		[Exhib RHA, Dublin, 289]; untraced		*Stewart* II, 1985, 166
99.	1830	Sir William Rowan Hamilton, Astronomer Royal Model(s): exhib RHA, Dublin, 1831, 277 'executed in marble' by order of the Earl of Dunraven); exhib RHA, Dublin, 1835, 293 (model bust . . . from which a marble bust has been executed for the Earl of Dunraven)	m	NGI Other versions: Dunraven-Limerick Estates Co	SD	*Crookshank* 1966, 309 (repr); *Stewart* II, 1985, 166; *le Harivel* 1988, 574 (repr)
100.	1830	Unidentified gentleman		[Exhib RHA, Dublin, 300]; untraced		*Stewart* II, 1985, 166
101.	c1830	W H, 2nd Earl of Dunraven Model(s): exhib RHA, Dublin, 1830, 299	m	untraced		*Stewart* II, 1985, 166
102.	1831	Captain Charles Hastings Boyle		[Exhib RHA, Dublin, 280]; untraced		*Stewart* II, 1985, 166
103.	1831	Captain Dallas		[Exhib RHA, Dublin, 283]; untraced		*Stewart* II, 1985, 166
104.	1831	George IV		[for the Marquess of Headfort]; untraced Other versions: commissioned by the Duke of Montrose for the Royal Archers' Society, Edinburgh		*Stewart* II, 1985, 166
105.	1831	Hugh, 3rd Duke of Northumberland		[Exhib RHA, Dublin, 270]; untraced		*Strickland* I, 1913, 591; *Stewart* II, 1985, 166
106.	1832	Charlotte, Duchess of Northumberland		[Exhib RHA, Dublin, 277]; untraced		*Stewart* II, 1985, 166
107.	1832	Miles O'Reilly		[Exhib RHA, Dublin, 270]; untraced		*Stewart* II, 1985, 166
108.	1832	Nathaniel Callwell		[Exhib RHA, Dublin]; untraced		*Strickland* I, 1913, 589
109.	1832	Unidentified lady		[Exhib RHA, Dublin, 272]; untraced		*Stewart* II, 1985, 166
110.	1832	William Cuming PRHA		[Exhib RHA, Dublin, 280]; untraced		*Stewart* II, 1985, 166, 167
111.	1834	Bertram Mitford		[Exhib RHA, Dublin]; untraced		*Strickland* I, 1913, 590
112.	1834	Dr J Kirkby		RCS, Dublin		*Strickland* I, 1913, 590
113.	1834	Hon Mrs Caulfield		[Exhib RHA, Dublin, 282]; untraced		*Stewart* II, 1985, 166

No.	Date	Subject		Location		Literature
114.	1834	Sir Capel Molyneux Bt		[Exhib RHA, Dublin]; untraced		*Strickland* I, 1913, 590
115.	1835	Lord Norbury, model		[Exhib RHA, Dublin, 298]; untraced Other versions: several marble busts executed; all untraced		*Stewart* II, 1985, 166
116.	1835	Master Francis Johnston Kirk		[Exhib RHA, Dublin, 290]; untraced		*Stewart* II, 1985, 166
117.	1835	The surgeon general, miniature bust		[Exhib RHA, Dublin, 307]; untraced		*Stewart* II, 1985, 166
118.	1835	Thomas Moore		Royal Irish Academy, Dublin Other versions: exhib RHA, Dublin, 1835, 288 and 1836, 247		*Strickland* I, 1913, 590; *Stewart* II, 1985, 166
119.	1835	Thomas Spring-Rice, model		[Exhib RHA, Dublin, 286]; untraced Other versions: several marble busts executed; all untraced miniature bust exhib RHA, Dublin, 1835, 292; untraced		*Stewart* II, 1985, 166
120.	1836	Sir Frederick Shaw	m	Coll Sir Frederick Shaw Bt (1913)		*Strickland* I, 1913, 591; *Stewart* II, 1985, 166, 167
121.	1836	Unidentified young lady		[Exhib RHA, Dublin, 263]; untraced		*Stewart* II, 1985, 166
122.	1837	Abraham Colles	m	RCS, Dublin		*Strickland* I, 1913, 589; *Stewart* II, 1985, 167
123.	1830–1837	Bartholomew Lloyd	m	NGI 8043 Other versions: Trinity College, Dublin	S	*Crookshank* 1966, 309, 310 (repr); *Stewart* II, 1985, 167; *le Harivel* 1988, 573 (repr)
124.	1837	Fleming O'Reilly	m	[Exhib RHA, Dublin, 248]; untraced		*Stewart* II, 1985, 167
125.	1837	Henrietta Blackwood, model		[Exhib RHA, Dublin, 247]; untraced		*Stewart* II, 1985, 166
126.	1837	Mrs Fleming O'Reilly	m	[Exhib RHA, Dublin, 256]; untraced		*Stewart* II, 1985, 167
127.	1837	Unidentified gentleman		[Exhib RHA, Dublin, 249]; untraced		*Stewart* II, 1985, 167
128.	1838	Rev Charles Boyton		[Exhib RHA, Dublin, 213]; untraced		*Stewart* II, 1985, 167
129.	1839	Lord Bishop of Kildare	m	[Exhib RHA, Dublin, 361]; untraced		*Stewart* II, 1985, 167
130.	1839	Unidentified child	m	[Exhib RHA, Dublin, 388]; untraced		*Stewart* II, 1985, 167
131.	1839	Unidentified subject		[Exhib RA, London, 1377]; untraced		*Graves* IV, 1905–6, 333
132.	1840	Charles W Wall		Trinity College, Dublin, Long Room		*Crookshank* 1986, 24
133.	1840	William Magee, Archbishop of Dublin		Trinity College, Dublin, Long Room		*Crookshank* 1986, 24; *Stewart* II, 1985, 166, 167
134.	1842	Samuel Kyle, Bishop of Cork		Trinity College, Dublin, Long Room		*Stewart* II, 1985, 167; *Crookshank* 1986, 24
135.	1843	Col Henry John Clements MP	m	NGI	SD	*Stewart* II, 1985, 167; *le Harivel* 1988, 574 (repr)
136.	1844	John Wilson Croker, model		[Exhib RHA, Dublin, 435]; untraced		*Stewart* II, 1985, 167
137.	1844	Rev Dr Miller, of Armagh, model for a bust in marble		[Exhib RHA, Dublin, 437]; untraced		*Stewart* II, 1985, 167
138.	1844	Unidentified lady in ancient costume (posthumous)		[Exhib RHA, Dublin, 434]; untraced		*Stewart* II, 1985, 167
139.	1845	Arthur Hume		[Exhib RHA, Dublin, 437]; untraced		*Stewart* II, 1985, 167
140.	?1845	Thomas Elrington		Trinity College, Dublin, Long Room		*Stewart* II, 1985, 167; *Crookshank* 1986, 24
141.	nd	George Millar		Trinity College, Dublin, Long Room		*Crookshank* 1986, 24
142.	nd	Horatio, Admiral Lord Nelson		Bank of Ireland, Dublin		*Strickland* I, 1913, 591
143.	nd	Lord Castlereagh	m	Untraced		*Strickland* I, 1913, 589
144.	nd	Mrs Lambert		Untraced		*Strickland* I, 1913, 590
Chimneypieces						
145.	*c*1805	Carvings for chimneypieces (as assistant to Henry Darley)		Untraced		*Strickland* I, 1913, 587
Architectural Sculpture						
146.	*c*1817	Justice and Mercy, two statues	s	Courthouse, Londonderry		*Strickland* I, 1913, 592
147.	nd	Hibernia, Justice and Commerce, three statues		[City and county courthouse, Cork]; untraced		*Strickland* I, 1913, 592; *Hill* 1998, 74
148.	nd	Hibernia, Mercury and Fidelity, three statues		General Post Office, Dublin, pediment		*Strickland* I, 1913, 592
Reliefs						
149.	1809	Cave scene (Drunken Banditti, Spanish Banditti)	m	RDS, Dublin		*Strickland* I, 1913, 592; *White and Bright* 1998, 28
Miscellaneous						
150.	1829	'Model of a monument to be executed in marble' (possibly the Wellington monument at Trim?)		[Exhib RHA, Dublin, 287]; untraced		*Strickland* I, 1913, 591; *Stewart* II, 1985, 166
151.	1829	The attraction of love		[Exhib RHA, Dublin, 389]; untraced		*Strickland* I, 1913, 592; *Stewart* II, 1985, 165
152.	1831	'Piece of Monumental Sculpture'		[Exhib RHA, Dublin, 286]; untraced		*Stewart* II, 1985, 166
153.	1840	Affection		[Exhib Liverpool Ac, 679]; untraced		*Morris and Roberts* 1998, 367

KIRK, William Boyton ARHA 1824–1900

He was born on 29 May 1824, the second son of **Thomas Kirk**. As a boy he showed a marked talent for sculpture and his father wished to place him as an apprentice with **Sir Francis Chantrey**. Chantrey however refused to take him, saying that his father would be his best teacher. He attended the Royal Dublin Society Schools in 1839 and also worked in his father's studio in Jervis Street. In 1845 he entered Trinity College, but he left without taking his degree. He made his first appearance as an exhibitor at the Royal Hibernian Academy in 1844. His 1846 exhibit *Iris ascending* received an enthusiastic public response: 'For a young man and his first public attempt it is astonishing; a lightness almost atmospheric is given to solid matter and a classic grace and feeling which evince great promise' (*AU*, 1846, 231) (2). It was purchased by the Royal Irish Institution and reproduced in bronze by the Art Union of London.

In 1848 Kirk moved to England and for several years lived and worked in Worcester. During this period he was employed by the Royal Worcester factory making models for the famous Shakespeare dessert service, exhibited at the Dublin Exhibition of 1853 and for parian ware figures and busts (**4–14, 20, 25, 26**). He exhibited at the Royal Academy between 1848 and 1857 and was elected ARHA in 1850.

In 1860 Kirk entered the church and he later held livings at Birkenhead and Ashton-under-Lyme. He resigned as an associate of the RHA in 1873 and was made an honorary member in the same year. After his ordination he occasionally made busts including those of Dr Ellicot, Bishop of Gloucester, Dr Ryle, Bishop of Liverpool and Lord James Butler (**21, 22, 23**). His last work, a figure of Jael, was exhibited in Dublin 1874 (**41**). Kirk also wrote poetry and a work about the antiquities of the Ashton-under-Lyme area. He died there on 5 July 1900.

Literary References: *Strickland* 1, 1913, 593–594; *Crookshank* 1966, 311; *Gunnis* 1968, 230; *Avery and Marsh* 1985, 328–37; *Atterbury* 1989, 262

Funerary Monuments					
1.	1851	Hope, figure designed for a monument		[Exhib RA, London, 1275]; untraced	*Graves* IV, 1905–6, 333
Statues					
2.	1844	Iris ascending Payment(s): £15		[Royal Irish Institution]; Marlborough House, London Other versions: bronze statuettes issued by the Art Union of London, 1847; all untraced	*Gunnis* 1968, 230; *Stewart* II, 1985, 168; *Avery and Marsh* 1985, 332 (repr)
3.	1845	Children frightened by a lizard		[Exhib RHA, Dublin, 459]; untraced	*Stewart* II, 1985, 168
4.	c1853	Ariadne, model for Worcester Parian ware statuette		Untraced	*Atterbury* 1989, 208 (repr 685)
5.	c1853	Comedy, model for a Worcester Parian ware statuette		Untraced	*Stewart* II, 1985, 168; *Atterbury* 1989, 215 (repr 705)
6.	c1853	Dr Hahnemann, model for Worcester Parian ware statuette		Untraced	*Atterbury* 1989, 209 (repr 687)
7.	c1853	Evangeline reclining, model for Worcester Parian ware statuette		Untraced	*Atterbury* 1989, 208 (repr 683)
8.	c1853	Lady Macbeth, model for Worcester Parian ware statuette		Untraced	*Atterbury* 1989, 214 (repr 702)
9.	c1853	Tragedy, model for a Worcester Parian ware statuette		Untraced	*Stewart* II, 1985, 168; *Atterbury* 1989, 215 (repr 705)
10.	c1855	Faust and Margaret, model for a Worcester Parian ware statuette		Untraced	*Graves* IV, 1905–6, 333; *Atterbury* 1989, 210 (repr 689)
11.	c1855	Henda and Hafed, model for Worcester Parian ware statuette		Untraced	*Atterbury* 1989, 210 (repr 689)
12.	c1855	Mary and Christ, model for a Worcester Parian ware statuette		Untraced	*Stewart* II, 1985, 168; *Atterbury* 1989, 212 (repr 697)
13.	1857	Summer, model for Worcester Parian ware statuette		Untraced	*Atterbury* 1989, 209 (repr 688)
14.	1857	Water nymph, model for Worcester Parian ware statuette		Untraced	*Atterbury* 1989, 213 (repr 699)
Busts					
15.	1844	Rev William Bushe		[Exhib RHA, Dublin, 416]; untraced	*Stewart* II, 1985, 168
16.	1845	Rev Dr Douglas		[Exhib RHA, Dublin, 441]; untraced	*Stewart* II, 1985, 168
17.	1846	Unidentified young gentleman		[Exhib RHA, Dublin, 467]; untraced	*Stewart* II, 1985, 168
18.	1846	Unidentified young lady		[Exhib RHA, Dublin, 471]; untraced	*Stewart* II, 1985, 168
19.	1849	Joseph R Kirk (the sculptor's brother)		[Exhib RHA, Dublin, 432]; untraced	*Stewart* II, 1985, 168
20.	1854	Unidentified gentleman, model for Worcester Parian ware		Untraced	*Atterbury* 1989, 204 (repr 678)
21.	post-1860	Dr Ellicot, Bishop of Gloucester		Untraced	*Strickland* I, 1913, 594
22.	post-1860	Dr Ryle, Bishop of Liverpool		Untraced	*Strickland* I, 1913, 594
23.	post-1860	Lord James Butler		Untraced	*Strickland* I, 1913, 594
24.	1875	Mrs Coles		[Exhib RHA, Dublin, 377]; untraced	*Stewart* II, 1985, 168
25.	nd	General Havelock, model for Worcester Parian ware		Untraced	*Atterbury* 1989, 203 (repr 674)
26.	nd	Unidentified gentleman, model for Worcester Parian ware		Untraced	*Atterbury* 1989, 203 (repr 673)
Architectural Sculpture					
27.	nd	Justice, statue		Courthouse, Belfast	*Strickland* I, 1913, 593
Miscellaneous					
28.	1844	An angel ascending with a celestial crown		[Exhib RHA, Dublin, 427]; untraced	*Stewart* II, 1985, 168
29.	1846	Pleasant thoughts		[Exhib RHA, Dublin, 320]; untraced	*Stewart* II, 1985, 168
30.	1848	Bacchante		[Exhib RA, London, 1359]; untraced	*Graves* IV, 1905–6, 333
31.	1848	Lear and Cordelia		[Exhib RA, London, 1336]; untraced	*Graves* IV, 1905–6, 333; *Stewart* II, 1985, 168
32.	1849	Bottom and Titania	m	[Exhib RHA, Dublin, 423]; untraced	*Stewart* II, 1985, 168
33.	1849	Hesione		[Exhib RHA, Dublin, 419]; untraced	*Stewart* II, 1985, 168
34.	1849	Paul and Virginia crossing a brook, unfinished sketch model		[Exhib RHA, Dublin, 430]; untraced	*Stewart* II, 1985, 168
35.	1851	The pastoral age	m	[Exhib RHA, Dublin, 356]; untraced	*Stewart* II, 1985, 168
36.	1856	Boy and dolphin		[Exhib RHA, Dublin, 407]; untraced	*Stewart* II, 1985, 168
37.	1856	'Design for a monument in bronze to the late Lord Fitzgibbon'		[Exhib RHA, Dublin, 385]; untraced	*Stewart* II, 1985, 168
38.	1856	The guardian angel		[Exhib RHA, Dublin, 396]; untraced	*Stewart* II, 1985, 168
39.	1857	Lady Georgiana Raglan		[Exhib RA, London, 1257]; untraced	*Graves* IV, 1905–6, 333
40.	1857	Mrs Coxwell		[Exhib RA, London, 1333]; untraced	*Graves* IV, 1905–6, 333
41.	1874	Jael		[Exhib RHA, Dublin, 339]; untraced	*Stewart* II, 1985, 168

KIRKBRIDE, John, of Carlisle 1786–1856

He was a sculptor and mason of Carlisle. He is probably the John Kirkbride, son of James Kirkbride and Elizabeth Sunderland, who was christened at St Cuthbert, Carlisle on 30 December 1786. He became chief foreman to **Paul Nixson**.

When Nixson went bankrupt in 1837 the Marble Works in Finkle Street were taken over by Kirkbride. At that time the premises were also home to the Carlisle Academy of Fine Art, though the committee of the Academy did not renew the lease with the new proprietor. Kirkbride's monument to W G Thurnham in Carlisle Cathedral takes the form of a stele with a profile portrait of the brigade major in uniform (5). Kirkbride died before 21 March 1856, when the *Carlisle Journal* reported that his executors were to sell his stock-in-trade including upwards of 20 new chimneypieces. Only a year later, on 19 June 1857 the same newspaper reported the death of his son, James, who, 'since the decease of his respected father conducted along with his brothers the marble and stone works in Finkle Street'. An advertisement in 1855 informed the public that J, I and J Kirkbride supplied 'marble chimneypieces etc' from the City Marble Works, still in Finkle Street (*CJ*, 9 Feb 1855). On 14 November 1857 and 17 April 1958 the *Carlisle Express* reported the bankruptcy of Isaac and John Kirkbride, stone and marble masons, because of a discrepancy in their accounts. The firm's premises, which were designed and built by Nixon and decorated by **David Dunbar I**, were demolished in 1929, but a painting of the building by Thomas Bushby, 1895, survives in Carlisle Art Gallery.

Literary References: *Perriam* 1975, 301, 305 n34

Archival References: IGI

Funerary Monuments

1.	†1805	Brisco family members, several tablets	Thursby, Cumberland		Pevsner, *Cumberland & Westmorland*, 1967, 193
2.	+1816	Robert Ferguson	St Michael, Carlisle, Cumberland		Pevsner, *Cumberland & Westmorland*, 1967, 97
3.	+1838	Edward Grave	Penrith, Cumberland	S	*Gunnis* 1968, 230
4.	1839	George Mounsey (†1838)	St Cuthbert, Carlisle, Cumberland	S	*Carlisle Journal*, 13 April 1839; *Gunnis* 1968, 230
5.	1843	Lieutenant William Graham Thurnam (+1823)	Carlisle Cathedral, Cumberland	S	*CJ*, 9 Sept 1843; *Gunnis* 1968, 230
6.	†1846	John Lambert	Alnwick, Northumbs		RG/JP, 5, 798
7.	†1848	John Steward	Hensingham, Cumberland		Pevsner, *Cumberland & Westmorland*, 1967, 137

KIRKER, Robert fl *c*1694

Kirker worked under **Benjamin Jackson** at Chatsworth where he was employed on carved ornaments in the bathing rooms and grotto.

Archival References: Chatsworth Building Accts, 1687–95, 31

KNAPP, John, of London fl *c*1810–39

Knapp's yard was in Foley Street. His monument to Urban Vigors in Marylebone Parish Church, has a medallion-portrait (3). Potterton describes the 'sober draped sarcophagus' erected in memory of St George Caulfield at Donamon as dull (2).

Literary References: *Gunnis* 1968, 230

Funerary Monuments

1.	*c*1810	John de Coussmaker	Staines, Middx	S	*Gunnis* 1968, 230
2.	†1810	St George Caulfield	Donamon, Co Roscommon		*Potterton* 1975, 57
3.	?1815	Urban Vigors	St Mary, St Marylebone, London		*Gunnis* 1968, 230
4.	†1820	Gilbert Hare	St Mary, St Marylebone, London	S	*Gunnis* 1968, 230
5.	†1828	Sir Andrew Hammond	Terrington St Clement, Norfolk	S	*Gunnis* 1968, 230
6.	†1830	Richard Uniacke (co-sculptor: H Knapp)	Halifax Cathedral, Nova Scotia	S	GPC
7.	†1835	Hon Charles Grantley (co-sculptor: H Knapp)	Halifax Cathedral, Nova Scotia	S	GPC
8.	†1838	Hon William Crofton (co-sculptor: H Knapp)	Halifax Cathedral, Nova Scotia	S	GPC
9.	†1839	Jared Chipman (co-sculptor: H Knapp)	Halifax Cathedral, Nova Scotia	S	GPC

KNIGHT, L and M fl 1799

In 1799 the Misses Knight, of Sticken, Bucks, sent to the Society of Arts 'two busts modelled in clay, and two casts in plaster of paris . . . hardened by wax in such manner that those in clay represent bronze, and those in plaster, Marble'. The greater silver palette of the Society of Arts was presented to 'these ingenious young ladies'. The busts were conveyed by a Samuel More. Two of them-one in each medium-were self-portraits of the Misses Knight themselves. Their method for producing 'an improvement in producing likeness, with a diminution of labour and expence [*sic*]' consisted of 'making the clay model moderately hot, and then pouring melted bees-wax on it . . . till such time as the colour becomes conveniently dark'. Plaster casts were heated less, then dipped into purer wax.

Literary References: RSA, *Transactions*, vol 17, 1799, 301–3, 366

KNIGHT, Samuel, of Exeter fl *c*1836–43

In 1841 he made furnishings for St Mary, Bickleigh, Devon (2). The *Gentleman's Magazine* noted that these were 'all of stone, beautifully carved and otherwise enriched' and that Knight had previously worked at Honiton new church, and other ecclesiastical edifices (*GM*, 1841, i, 87).

Literary References: *Gunnis* 1968, 230–1

Funerary Monuments

1.	?1836	James Coleridge		Ottery St Mary, Devon	S	*Gunnis* 1968, 231

Architectural Sculpture

2.	1841	Altarpiece, altar-table and pulpit	s	Bickleigh, Devon		*GM*, 1841, i, 87; *Gunnis* 1968, 230–1
3.	1843	Altar, reredos and font	s	Uffculme, Devon		Pevsner, *Devon*, 1989, 877

KNIGHT, Thomas I, of London 1637–80

Knight was apprenticed to Henry Wilson, who had a workshop at London Bridge in October 1656. He was made free of the Masons' Company on 12 November 1663, was admitted to the livery on 5 May 1665 and to the court in 1674–75.

He was renter warden in 1679 and warden in 1680 but died during his year of office. Knight was described as a mason and pavier and his name was included in a list of those who dealt in building stone, entered in the Masons' Company court book between 14 June and 6 July 1680. He took on several apprentices, Thomas Prigmore (1665), John Compton (1667), Henry Culliford (1667), Robert Parish (1667), Thomas Moore (1671) and John Robinson (1676).

He was appointed City Mason in 1667 and between then and 1675 he had an active hand in the re-erection of a number of municipal buildings destroyed by the Great Fire, including the Guildhall and Newgate. He received some £6,700 on his own account, £700 jointly with **Joshua Marshall** for work on Temple Bar and £238 jointly with **Thomas Shadbolt** in connection with the Sessions House. In 1679 he cut the lettering on the Monument. Robert Hooke noted, in his diary for 10 April, that 'Knight cut wrong R for P' on the 'Fish Street Piller' (*Robinson and Adams* 1935, 406).

Knight was described as of St Giles, Cripplegate 'Cit, and Free Mason, Bachr', aged about 31 in August 1669, when he married Sarah Collard, of the same parish, aged about 30 (Lic Vic Gen, Aug 24 1669, in GPC). He died on 11 June 1680 and left bequests to his widow and daughter Sarah, the latter receiving £2,500. Included in the estate was a house in St Giles, Cripplegate. He was buried at Sanderstead, Surrey, under a 'black coarse marble tomb', inscribed with verses that began, 'Stay Reader here, and leave one groan, / If not for my sake, for thy own. / Since impartiall Death that mee / Hath overtaken, followes thee./ Hast thou wealth, strength, art and industry / Yet dye thou must, for those had I. . . .' (*Manning and Bray*, 1804–14, II, 576–7).

Literary References: *Knoop and Jones*, 31; *Gunnis* 1968, 231; *Webb* 1999, 8, 9, 23, 25, 27, 28
Archival References: Guildhall MSS 184/4, *passim*; GPC
Will: PROB 11/363

KNIGHT, Thomas, of Thatcham fl 1666

Thomas Knight of Thatcham was apprenticed to **John Shorthose** on 12 February 1666 (*Webb* 1999, 20).

KNOLTON, S fl *c*1750

Funerary Monuments

1.	*c*1750	Edward Austen	Bexley, Kent	*Gunnis* 1968, 231

KNOWLES, John fl 1773

Statues

1.	1773	Percy lion (an heraldic beast)	l	Lion bridge, Alnwick, Northumbs	*Usherwood* 2000, 3 (repr)

KNOWLES, of Manchester fl *c*1791–1855

He signs several monuments in the north of England. He can perhaps be identified with John Knowles, who was listed in a Manchester directory of 1838 as a specialist marble chimneypiece-maker with premises at Ducie Street, Piccadilly, and 10 London Road (*Pigot* 1838, 38).

Funerary Monuments

1.	†1791	Richard Orford	St Mary, Disley, Cheshire	S	Pevsner, *Cheshire*, 1971, 198
2.	?1835	Richard Woodyeare	Conisborough, W R Yorks	S	GPC
3.	†1842	William Grant	St Andrew, Ramsbottom, Lancs	S	
4.	†1844	James (†1841) and John Ashton	St Mary, Hyde, Cheshire	S	Pevsner, *Cheshire*, 1971, 246
5.	†1855	John Grant and wife	St Andrew, Ramsbottom, Lancs	S	

KNOWLES, Robert fl 1825

Baines's Gazetteer lists him as a statuary of 11 Birdport Street, Liverpool, in 1825.

KNOWLES, Thomas I and II, of Oxford

Thomas Knowles I (1754–1826)
Thomas Knowles II (1781–1856)

Thomas Knowles I was foreman to **Stephen Townesend of Oxford**. He bought his master's business in 1797 and re-established it under his own name in a new yard in Holywell, Oxford in 1799. His son, **Thomas Knowles II**, became a partner in the firm in 1816. The business, which still exists today as Knowles and Son, was principally employed in building work for the Oxford colleges. As a sideline they made funerary monuments and gravestones. In 1843 the younger Knowles was paid £8 for erecting a monument to the memory of Dr Edward Tatham, carved by **Henry Weekes**, in All Saints, Oxford.

Literary References: *Gunnis* 1968, 231; *Sturdy* 1997, *passim*

Funerary Monuments

1.	?1799	Mapletoft family (by Thomas Knowles I)	Byfield, Northants	S	*Sturdy* 1997, 40
2.	?1802	Mr Kipling (by Thomas Knowles I)	Chilton, Bucks	S	*Sturdy* 1997, 40
3.	?1804	Rev W Breeres (by Thomas Knowles I)	Hampton Gay, Oxon		*Sturdy* 1997, 40
4.	†1806	Thomas Emsworth	All Souls College, Oxford		RG/JP, 5, 860
5.	†1809	Rev Samuel Stockford	St Aldate, Oxford		GPC
6.	1817	Earl and Countess of Banbury (both †1771) (by Thomas Knowles I) Payment(s): £22	Burford, Oxon	S	*Sturdy* 1997, 39, 40
7.	1820	Lord Charles Spencer (†1820) (by Thomas Knowles I) Payment(s): £25	Wheatfield, Oxon		*Sturdy* 1997, 39, 40, 47
8.	1822	Lady Elizabeth Spencer (†1812) (by Thomas Knowles I and II) Payment(s): £24	Wheatfield, Oxon		*Sturdy* 1997, 39, 40
9.	1824	Mrs Turner (by Thomas Knowles I) Payment(s): £22	Spelsbury, Oxon		*Sturdy* 1997, 40
10.	†1825	Ebenezer Robertson	Beverley Minster, E R Yorks	S	Pevsner, *Yorks: E R & York*, 1995, 293
11.	1820–1828	William Fletcher (†1828), altar tomb (by Thomas Knowles I, with modifications by Thomas Knowles II) Payment(s): £48	Yarnton, Oxon		*Sturdy* 1997, 39, 40, 47

12.	1828	William Fletcher (†1828), wall-tablet (by Thomas Knowles II)		Yarnton, Oxon	*Sturdy* 1997, 47
13.	1831	Hitchcock family member (By Thomas Knowles II) Payment(s): £15		Kidlington, Oxon	*Sturdy* 1997, 47
14.	1832	Mrs Roberts (by Thomas Knowles II) Payment(s): £21		Yarnton, Oxon	*Sturdy* 1997, 47
15.	1833	Dr Williams (by Thomas Knowles II) Payment(s): £30		Corpus Christi College, Oxford, cloisters	*Sturdy* 1997, 47
16.	1838–1839	J Pinfold (by Thomas Knowles II)		Holywell, Oxford, churchyard	*Sturdy* 1997, 47
17.	1841	Unidentified subject (by Thomas Knowles II)		Blenheim Palace, Oxford, chapel	*Sturdy* 1997, 47
18.	1842	Charles Stewart, Bishop of Quebec (†1837) (by Thomas Knowles II)		Corpus Christi College, Oxford, cloister	*Sturdy* 1997, 47
19.	1853	J Kensall (by Thomas Knowles II)		Holywell, Oxford, churchyard	*Sturdy* 1997, 47

Architectural Sculpture

20.	1847	Eagles and other ornaments including three Portland figures of Theology, Philosophy and Mathematics Payment(s): £135		The Queen's Coll, Oxford	QC, FIR; *Gunnis* 1968, 231

KÜCHLER, Conrad Heinrich

For further information the reader is referred to *Pyke* 1973, 75

KUMMEL, H fl 1839

The medallions to Sir Harry and Lady Verney, signed 'H Kümmel f. Rom. 1839', must have been commissioned during a tour which took them to Rome a little after their marriage and were presumably put up in Steeple Claydon church, which was built during their lifetimes, by their son. (Inf. Alastair Laing)

Reliefs

1.	1839	Sir Harry Verney, 2nd Bt and Eliza, his first wife	Steeple Claydon, Bucks	S	

LA MOTT

The catalogue of household furniture of the late Earl of Halifax at Horton, Northants, auctioned by Edward Cox of Northampton in June 1781, listed under day seven, in the section 'Menagery', 'Four vases, bronz'd with the trophies of the four quarters of the globe, executed by that ingenious Italian La Mott' (inf. John Harris).

LADD, of Pinchbeck fl *c*1827

He is known only for one tablet with a tiny relief of a seated woman by a broken column.

Funerary Monuments

1.	†1827	Ann Elsdaile	Surfleet, Lincs	S	Pevsner, *Lincs*, 1989, 730

LAFOND, Pierre C fl 1753

He was described as a sculptor when he took Jean Nadal, a pupil of the Westminster French Protestant Charity School, as an apprentice in July 1753.

Literary References: *le May* 2001, 563

LAING, Henry

For further information the reader is referred to *Pyke* 1973, 76.

LAKE, J fl *c*1728

The monument to Gilbert White is a marble cartouche tablet.

Funerary Monuments

1.	†1728	Gilbert White	Selborne, Hants	S	*Gunnis* 1968, 232

LAMB, Francis, of Bottesford 1705–89

He specialised in slate headstones featuring ogee panels, scrolls and rococo details. Over 40 of these can be found in churchyards in the Kesteven region of Lincolnshire. His son was **George Lamb**.

Literary References: *Neave and Heron* 1969, 5, 17

Funerary Monuments

1.	1728	Unidentified subject, headstone	sl	Denton, Lincs, churchyard		*Neave and Heron* 1969, 5, 17
2.	?1749	Edward Solomon, ledger		Grantham, Lincs	S	*Gunnis* 1968, 232
3.	?1756	Unidentified subject, tombstone	sl	Grantham, Lincs, churchyard	S	*Gunnis* 1968, 232
4.	nd	Unidentified subject	sl	Barrowby, Lincs		*Neave and Heron* 1969, 17
5.	nd	Unidentified subject	sl	Claypole, Lincs		*Neave and Heron* 1969, 17
6.	nd	Unidentified subject	sl	Hougham, Lincs		*Neave and Heron* 1969, 17
7.	nd	Unidentified subject	sl	Londonthorpe, Lincs		*Neave and Heron* 1969, 17
8.	nd	Unidentified subject	sl	Marston, Lincs		*Neave and Heron* 1969, 17
9.	nd	Unidentified subject	sl	Grantham, Lincs		*Neave and Heron* 1969, 17
10.	nd	Unidentified subject(s)	sl	Orston, Notts, churchyard		Pevsner, *Notts*, 1979, 283
11.	nd	Unidentified subjects, eleven gravestones	sl	Woolsthorpe, Lincs		*Neave and Heron* 1969, 17
12.	nd	Unidentified subjects, four gravestones	sl	Sedgebrook, Lincs		*Neave and Heron* 1969, 17
13.	nd	Unidentified subjects, seven headstones	sl	Foston, Lincs		*Neave and Heron* 1969, 17
14.	nd	Unidentified subjects, three gravestones	sl	Westborough, Lincs		*Neave and Heron* 1969, 17
15.	nd	Unidentified subjects, three headstones	sl	Folkingham, Lincs		*Neave and Heron* 1969, 17
16.	nd	Unidentified subjects, two headstones	sl	Great Gonerby, Lincs		*Neave and Heron* 1969, 17

LAMB, Frederick Herbert –1852

When his widow Ann applied for assistance to the AGBI in 1854, she said that her husband had worked for Hunt and Roskell, the silversmiths, and had modelled a number of original works for Queen Victoria. Lamb was responsible for one known bust (1). He also designed and executed a figure for the top of a flower stand, for which he was awarded a prize medal at the Great Exhibition of 1851 (2). Mrs Lamb stated that her husband had exhibited at the Royal Academy, which is open to doubt since he is not listed in the catalogues. He died on 31 October, 1852.

Literary References: *Gunnis* 1968, 232

Archival References: AGBI, vol 5, 243

Busts

1.	nd	Mr Fisk		[for General Goodfellow]; untraced		*Gunnis* 1968, 232

Architectural Sculpture

2.	1851	Figure for top of flower stand		[Gt Exhib prize medal]; untraced		*Gunnis* 1968, 232

LAMB, George, of Bottesford 1743–70

Like his father, **Francis Lamb**, he carved headstones of slate.

Literary References: *Neave and Heron* 1969, 5, 17

Funerary Monuments

1.	nd	Unidentified subject	sl	Hougham, Lincs		*Neave and Heron* 1969, 17
2.	nd	Unidentified subject	sl	Sedgebrook, Lincs		*Neave and Heron* 1969, 17
3.	nd	Unidentified subject(s)	sl	Orston, Notts, churchyard		Pevsner, *Notts*, 1979, 283

LAMBERT, James fl 1763?

He was probably the 'Mr Lambert' who was a pupil of **Louis François Roubiliac** and a member of the Academy of Painting and Sculpture in St Martin's Lane (*Pyne* I, 1823, 179).

Busts

1.	1763	Unidentified gentleman		[Soc of Artists, London]; untraced		*Gunnis* 1968, 232

LANCASHIRE, Francis and Son, of Bath fl c1770–1829?

Francis Lancashire (1740–1814) was described as 'an ingenious statuary' in his obituary (*GM*, 1814, i, 204) and his firm sent at least two wall-monuments to the West Indies (**5**, **22**). He was apparently assisted at one time by his elder brother, **Richard Lancashire**, and was succeeded by his son William. Gunnis states that William went into partnership with **Tyley of Bristol**, then with a Mr Walker of the same city, and that Queen Charlotte paid a visit to the firm when she was staying in Bath in 1817. He adds that the Lancashires' tablets 'are not as good as those of their rivals, the **Kings of Bath**'. It is possible that some of the works listed for this firm are actually by **Lancaster of Bristol** or **Lancaster and Walker** of Bristol.

Literary References: *Gunnis* 1968, 232

Funerary Monuments

1.	†1770	Rev Richard Eaton		Ringwould, Kent		RG/JP, 5, 802
2.	†1777	Ann Tubb		Ringwould, Kent		Pevsner, *Kent: N E & E*, 1983, 434
3.	†1784	James Cleare		Hawkesbury, Glos		RG/JP, 5, 802
4.	†1784	Thomas Curtis (signed by W Lancashire)		St Mary, Hawkesbury, Glos	S	Pevsner, *Glos: Cotswolds*, 1999, 409
5.	post-1790	Dames Christian and Jane Abel Alleyne and John Gay Newton Alleyne (perhaps by William Lancashire)		St James, Holetown, Barbados		*Coutu* 1997, 79–82 (repr)
6.	?1790	Mrs Jubb		Ringwould, Kent		*Gunnis* 1968, 232
7.	?1792	John Seare		Marsworth, Bucks		*Gunnis* 1968, 232
8.	?1792	Mary Parsloe		Great Somerford, Wilts		*Gunnis* 1968, 232
9.	?1793	Elizabeth Curtis		Sydling St Nicholas, Dorset		*Gunnis* 1968, 232
10.	†1793	Rev J Thomas		St Peter, Carmarthen		*Dale-Jones and Lloyd* 1989, 51
11.	?1795	James (†1763) and Mary Bishop		Worle, Somerset		GPC
12.	?1797	John Dowson		Greystock, Cumberland		*Gunnis* 1968, 232
13.	†1798	Francis, 7th Earl of Cork		Frome, Somerset		*Gunnis* 1968, 232
14.	?1798	James Montague		Lacock, Wilts		*Gunnis* 1968, 232
15.	†1798	John Gunning (signed by W Lancashire)		Cold Ashton, Glos	S	Pevsner, *Glos: Cotswolds*, 1999, 291
16.	†1798	Unidentified subject, tablet		Priston, Somerset		Pevsner, *Somerset: N & Bristol*, 1958, 247
17.	?1798	William Moody		Steeple Langford, Wilts		*Gunnis* 1968, 232
18.	†1799	Edward Read		St Mary, Gillingham, Dorset		Pevsner, *Dorset*, 1972, 215
19.	†1802	Sir John Smyth		Long Ashton, Somerset		*Gunnis* 1968, 232
20.	?1807	Leman family		Worle, Somerset		GPC
21.	†1814	Unidentified subject		Timsbury, Somerset		Pevsner, *Somerset: N & Bristol*, 1958, 271
22.	†1816	Michael Howard (signed by W Lancashire)		St Peter, Speightstown, Barbados	S	
23.	?1822	John Croft (co-sculptor: Walker)		Worle, Somerset		GPC
24.	?1822	Rev R W Howell		Mere, Wilts		*Gunnis* 1968, 232
25.	?1825	Rev Joseph Smith (co-sculptor: Walker)		Hutton, Somerset		GPC
26.	?1829	David Dallas (co-sculptor: Walker)		Bathampton, Somerset	S	GPC

Chimneypieces

27.	1794 & 1796	Marble Payment(s): £6 5s, supplied with unspecified items costing £42		Leadenham House, Lincs		*Oswald* 1965, 1594–5

LANCASHIRE, Richard 1736–1813

The elder brother of **Francis Lancashire**, he endorsed a receipt 'for carving 8 Ionic Capitals at £2:12:6 each capital' dated 11 July 1763 for Ditchley Park, Oxon (1). In 1809 he succeeded **Thomas Engleheart** as one of the carvers at Dodington Park, then being built by James Wyatt for Christopher Codrington (2). He was described as 'formerly a statuary, and pupil of **Mr Prince Hoare**' when he died in 1813 at the age of 77 (*GM*, 1813, ii, 502).

Literary References: *Gunnis* 1968, 232

Archival References: Dillon, DIL 1/p/3

Architectural Sculpture

1.	1763	Eight Ionic capitals Payment(s): 20 gns	s	Ditchley Park, Oxon	*Gunnis* 1968, 232 citing Dillon Archives
2.	1809–1811	Corinthian capitals (designed by James Wyatt)		Dodington Park, Glos, west portico	Codrington Archives in GPC; Pevsner, *Glos: Cotswolds*, 1999, 317

LANCASTER, of Bristol fl c1795–1832?

He may have been one of the partners in the firm **Lancaster & Walker of Bristol**.

Funerary Monuments

1.	†1795	Eleanora Roberts	Wiston, Pembrokes	S	RG/JP, 5, 803
2.	†1803	Rev Thomas Pearce	Wotton-under-Edge, Glos	S	Pevsner, *Glos: Cotswolds*, 1999, 757
3.	†1803	Thomas Edwards	St John Aberdare, Glamorgan	S	Pevsner, *Glamorgan*, 1995, 133
4.	†1809	Henry Long	Worle, Somerset		RG/JP, 5, 802v
5.	†1812	Anna Camplin	St Mary, Tidenham, Glos	S	Pevsner, *Glos: Vale & Forest of Dean*, 1976, 384
6.	†1812	Sarah Jones	Hill, Glos	S	Pevsner, *Glos: Vale & Forest of Dean*, 1976, 272
7.	?1832	Joseph and Mary Carde	St Andrew, Burnham-on-Sea, Somerset		RG/JP, 5, 802v

LANCASTER & WALKER, of Bristol fl c1821–24

Funerary Monuments

1.	†1821	Rev Charles Gally	St Brides Major, Glam, St Bridget	S	*Gunnis* 1968, 232
2.	†1823	Samuel King	Bridgetown Cathedral, Barbados	S	
3.	†1824	Joseph Brazier	St George, Gingerland, Nevis	S	
4.	nd	Saunders family	Tetbury, Glos	S	Pevsner, *Glos: Cotswolds*, 1999, 686

LANDER, E M fl c1837–78

A firm of monumental masons, they were closely associated with Kensal Green cemetery. The Lander family business got under way at Kensal Green in the 1830s, soon after the cemetery opened, and it still has premises outside the gates. Several of the family are buried in the cemetery, including **George Lander** (c1799–1861), who undertook building work for the cemetery in 1838, and **Edward Manuel Lander** (1836–1910). There was probably another **E M Lander** for some of the monuments signed Lander are clearly too early to be by Edward Manuel. Of all of their monuments, that commemorating Sir William Casement is the most extraordinary (3). Executed in Portland and artificial stone, it consists of a sarcophagus, draped with Casement's cloak and topped with his hat and sword. This is placed beneath a canopy with an Egyptian-style cornice, which is supported by four telamones in the form of turbaned Indians wrapped in long cloaks. Gunnis comments, 'Fantastic as the tomb appears at first sight, it must be admitted that the details, especially the modelling of the figures of the Indians, are well carried out. One cannot, however, say as much of all Lander's work in the cemetery'.

Literary References: *Gunnis* 1968, 232; *Curl* 2001, *passim*

Funerary Monuments

1.	1837	Huth family mausoleum	Kensal Green Cemetery, London		*Curl* 2001, 234 n 11
2.	1844	Emma (†1841) and Alexis Benoist Soyer (†1858) (co-sculptor: Pierre Puyenbroeck, of Brussels)	Kensal Green Cemetery, London	S	*Curl* 2001, 234 n 11
3.	†1844	Major-General Sir William Casement	Kensal Green Cemetery, London		*Gunnis* 1968, 232; *Curl* 2001, 184, 234, 283 (repr)
4.	†1861	Sarah Smedley	Kensal Green Cemetery, London, catacombs	S	
5.	†1869	John, Baron Broughton de Gyfford	Kensal Green Cemetery, London	S	*Curl* 2001, 181, 229 (repr)
6.	†1871	Charles Babbage	Kensal Green Cemetery, London	S	*Curl* 2001, 193
7.	†1871	John Savory	Kensal Green Cemetery, London, catacombs	S	
8.	†1877	Rev Francis Say	Braughing, Herts	S	
9.	†1878	Grace Bethel	Kensal Green Cemetery, London, catacombs	S	

LANDRE, John –1765

He was probably a nephew of Peter Landré, a Frenchman who had a house and nursery gardens on the east side of St Stephen's Green, Dublin, and died in 1747. It is not known whether he worked as a sculptor in Dublin but Strickland suggests that he may perhaps have been a pupil of **John Nost III**. He established a business in London: an undated tradecard states 'John Landre/ at ye corner of KING Street/ BLOOMSBURY, HIGH HOLBORN Makes and Sells all Manner of/ Figures Bustos Basso and Altorelievos in Brass Lead Plaster and all COMPOSITIONS OF WAX NB at the same shop may be had, all sorts of Horn Mold & Gilt Paper For Medals, or Small Bassorelievo' (Banks Coll, BM, 106.18). In his will, dated 16 November 1765, he described himself as a statuary of the Parish of St Giles and bequeathed his house in Dublin to his wife Mary.

Literary References: *Strickland* II, 1913, 2

Will: PROB 11/914 (proved 23 December 1765)

LANDRE (or LANDS), Mary fl 1769–74

Mary Landré was the proprietor of a London plaster shop who specialised in making casts after bronze reliefs. Little is known about her but she may have been the widow of **John Landré**. Invoices in the Wedgwood Archives show that she supplied Josiah Wedgwood with models in 1769 and 1774. She was, apparently, a formidable businesswoman for Wedgwood wrote to his partner, Thomas Bentley, on 31 October 1768, 'What shall I do – I dare not write to her, Mrs Landre, from hence and in my own name, **Voyez** says she is the D. . .1 at finding out *Pirates*, and if she once finds me out, I shall never be able to get a cast from her' (*Clifford* 1992, 60). Clifford suggests that she may have been related to Ami Jean Jaques Landry (1800–56), a medallist and watch-case engraver of Neuchâtel, Switzerland.

Literary References: *Gunnis* 1968, 232; *Clifford* 1992, 44, 60–1

Archival References: Wedgwood MSS L1/57, Mary Landré acct, 15 June 1774

Miscellaneous

1.	1769	21 classical, Biblical and other groups Payment(s): £16 11s 9d (including packing case)	[for Josiah Wedgwood]; untraced	*Clifford* 1992, 60
2.	1774	9 groups and reliefs Payment(s): £7 7s	[for Josiah Wedgwood]; untraced	*Clifford* 1992, 60–1

LANE, George fl 1778–1808

In 1778 George Lane, a mason and carver, took over the business of the late Mr Norman of Swaffham (*Norwich Mercury*, 21 June 1778). He was still there in 1804 when he advertised in the *Norwich Mercury* for a journeyman stonemason. On 21 November 1807 he advised the public that he had moved to new premises near the brickyard at Swaffham. In the *Norwich Mercury* for 7 May 1808, there is a notice of a creditors' meeting. George Lane's wife died at Swaffham in 1820.

Literary References: RG/JP, 5, 804

LANE, John fl 1722

Architectural Sculpture

1.	1722	Four 'solid vauses like ye Earl of Burlington's porphry' Payment(s): 6 gns	[coll Thomas Coke, of Melbourne Hall, Derbys]; untraced	Archives Marquess of Lothian in *Gunnis* 1968, 232

LANE, R, of Campden fl *c*1795

Funerary Monuments

1.	†1795	James Izod	sl	Chipping Campden, Glos	S	Pevsner, *Glos: Cotswolds*, 1999, 232

LANE, Richard James 1800–72

Best known as an engraver and lithographer, he was also a sculptor. He was employed as an assistant by **John Edward Carew** and gave evidence for his master in the lawsuit of 1840. He is known only for two representations of his brother, one of them a life-sized seated statue in Egyptian dress (1).

Literary References: *Gunnis* 1968, 233

Statues					
1.	1829	Edward Lane	p	NPG, London	*Ormond* 1973, 258 (pl 940)
Busts					
2.	*c*1833	Edward Lane		Bodleian	*Ormond* 1973, 258

LANE, William I and II, of Norwich

William Lane I (1729–1798)

William Lane II (1756–1806)

William Lane I became a freeman of Norwich in 1769. He or his son, William Lane II, advertised the opening of a yard (formerly Dobson's) in Bridge Street, St Andrew's in the *Norfolk Chronicle* of 30 April 1796. The elder Lane and his wife died within a few days of one another in 1798, and the business was taken over by the son (*Monthly Magazine*, 1798, 234). He seems to have had financial problems as he assigned property to his creditors in November 1802 and an auction of the stock in trade of Mr Lane, stone and marble mason, was held in Norwich on 15 December in the same year (*Norwich Mercury*, 6 November 1802; *Norfolk Chronicle*, 11 December 1802).

Literary References: *Gunnis* 1968, 233

Archival References: GPC; RG/JP, 803v

Funerary Monuments					
1.	†1767	Jeremiah Berry (by William Lane I)	Acle, Norfolk	S	Pevsner, *Norfolk: N E & Norwich*, 1997, 358
2.	?1773	P Browne (by William Lane I)	Bungay, Suffolk		*Gunnis* 1968, 233
3.	?1783	William Foster (signed by Lane and Son)	St Stephen, Norwich, Norfolk	S	*Gunnis* 1968, 233
4.	?1784	John Marks (signed by Lane and Son)	St Simon and St Jude, Norwich, Norfolk	S	*Gunnis* 1968, 233
Chimneypieces					
5.	1788	Several (by William Lane I)	[Mr Dillingham's House, Letton, Norfolk]; untraced		Soane Notebooks in *Gunnis* 1968, 233

LANG fl *c*1816

Funerary Monuments

1.	1816	William (†1816) and Mary Tash (†1812)	New Southgate, Middx	S	RG/JP, 5, 804

LANGLEY, Batty 1696–1751

An architect and writer, he is best known for his numerous manuals and pattern books for artisans and craftsmen. He also manufactured statues, busts and architectural ornaments in an artificial stone and provided designs for the pediment as part of his architectural scheme for London's new Mansion House.

Langley was evidently making artificial stone before 1730 for he staged a demonstration in London on 11 November 1729, when a comparison was made between the weight-bearing capacity of his product and natural Portland stone. It was reported in the *Northampton Mercury* that the Portland stone broke when the weight placed on it exceeded 168 lbs, whilst Langley's formidable artificial stone only collapsed when the weight was increased to 276 lbs. Vertue described Langley's product as 'a New invention of casting in stone or a hard composition – busts, statues, columns &c. or any frize or cornish workes for building. in immitation of free stone. & said to be more durable . . . made near Lambeth and sold by one Batty Langley', whom he described disparagingly as 'a bold face undertaker' (*Vertue* III, 51). The material may not indeed have been of Langley's own invention since a similar substance had been patented by **Richard Holt** in 1722 and Holt maintained that Langley obtained the formula by foul means.

During the spring and summer of 1831 Langley advertised that 'Sculptured or Carved Ornaments', including statues, busts, 'all manner of curious Vases, Urns, Pine Apples, Pedestals for Sundials, Balustrades, Key-Stones to the Arches of Windows and Doors, Bases and Capital for Piers of Gates, Columns and Pilasters' were available from his warehouse at 'the Hercules Head, near the Faulcon-Stairs on the Bank-side in Southwark' (*Daily Ad*, 25 May-6 July 1731). Holt retaliated with a notice stating that 'it appears from three several Affidavits, how and by what means [Langley] has come at any Insight into the Art of making *Artificial Stone*; and how very defective and short of *Holt's* true *Secret*, his Discoveries (by tampering with Workmen) must needs be' (*Daily Ad*, 28 May-1 June 1731). None of Langley's artificial stone products have been identified and no information about the composition has been discovered but it is possible that a fired clay portrait medallion of Sir Isaac Newton, formerly in Langley's possession, is one of his products (BM MLA SL 1984). If so, Langley's material was not strictly an artificial stone and was not related to the formulae developed by Holt or the **Coade Factory** since it contained neither lead nor glass.

Langley was one of the architects who unsuccessfully entered the competition to design a new Mansion House for the City of London in 1735–37. He was apparently the only architect to include a design for the pediment, depicting *Britannia with the Arms of the City*, attended by numerous allegorical figures. The architect George Dance the Elder won the competition and the tympanum sculpture was executed by **Sir Robert Taylor.**

Gunnis notes payments for work supplied to Lord Folkestone at Longford Castle by 'Langley', some of them paid for seven years after Batty Langley's death, and he suggests that either the business was carried on after his demise or that there were two Langleys. The items included a sundial, for which Folkestone paid £1 13s in 1748, carved capitals at £10 15s 6d (1757), 'stucco ornaments to ye Venetian seat' at 7 guineas (1758), four shields on gate piers at 12 guineas (1758) and a carved head in the passage at £4 12s 6d (1758).

EH

Literary References: *Esdaile* 1940 (2), 95; *Gunnis* 1968, 233; *Valpy* 1986, 206–9; *Kelly* 1990, 32–3; *Colvin* 1995, 597–8; *Grove* 18, 1996, 742–3 (White); *Dawson* 1999, 154–6; *Ward-Jackson* 2003, 239–40; *ODNB* (Harris)

Engraving: Langley's design for the Mansion House pediment, Guildhall Lib Print Room, cat q6918957

LANGLEY, William fl 1681–1724

William Langley carved the monument to Sir William Dugdale, Garter King of Arms, erected, some five years before his death, at Shustoke, Warks (1). The bill reads, 'Payd to Wm. Langley, 17 Feb., 1681 for worke done by him in making the monument in the chancell of Shustoke Church (excepting the tablet of marble, and the armes which were done at London), and setting in up, £3 12s' (*Hamper* 1827, 145). He is otherwise known only for two large figures of charity school children, carved 43 years later (2).

Literary References: *Gunnis* 1968, 233

Funerary Monuments

1.	1681	Sir William Dugdale (†1686) Payment(s): £3 12s		Shustoke, Warks	*Hamper* 1827, 145

Statues

2.	1724	Figures of a boy and girl known as 'Nancy Guy' and 'Billy Ball' Payment(s): £12 8s	s	Charity School, Frome, Somerset, front	Ch W in *Gunnis* 1968, 233

LANGSTAFF, Thomas I fl *c*1685

Funerary Monuments

1.	1685	King Edward I (†1307)	[Burgh Marsh, Cumberland]; untraced	SD	Todd MS 7/3F191, St Edmund Hall Oxford

LANGSTAFF, Thomas II fl –1778

A 'carver and mason of Edward Street, Marylebone', he became bankrupt and a sale of the contents of his yard was held on 10 March 1778.

Literary References: *Gunnis* 1968, 233

Auction catalogues: Langstaff 1778

Chimneypieces

1.	1778	Several including two 'in green and Sienna marble' and one 'very beautiful and highly finished, with dentals fitted with green, carved tablet'	[Langstaff sale, 1778]; untraced	*Gunnis* 1968, 233

LARSON, William fl 1673–89

Virtually nothing is known of Larson's background and career, but he was responsible for one of the most important lost royal monuments produced in 17th-century England. It is likely that he was the son of William Larson, an Anglo-Dutch carver of St Martin-in-the-Fields, who died *c*1661. In his will the elder Larson mentioned a son, also William, whom he praised as 'very industrious and helpful . . . in the time of my late long sickness', and to whom he left all his 'plaister moulds and brass moulds whatsoever'. Larson also left his son a share of land that he owned in Holland.

It may be either the father or son who was paid £12 for repairing statues at Northumberland House, Charing Cross in 1655. By August 1673 Larson had become statuary in ordinary to the Crown and in April 1686 he was commissioned to make and cast an equestrian statue in cannon brass of James II to stand on the Sandhill in the centre of Newcastle-upon-Tyne. The work was completed by 1688 under the supervision of Sir Christopher Wren, then the surveyor-general (2). It appears to be the first English royal statue to present a horse in the *levade* position, showing the King exercising mastery over the animal with its front hoofs off the ground. It was therefore a notable technical feat. Gibson attributes to Larson another royal statue in Newcastle, of King Charles II, 1680–85. This was set up on the Magazine Gate crossing the River Tyne and is now at the Guildhall (*Gibson* 1997 (1), 372).

During the Glorious Revolution of November 1688, Newcastle declared its allegiance to the Prince of Orange and the Protestant cause and the statue was symbolically dragged from its carved marble pedestal to the quayside, where it was toppled into the Tyne. The horse was subsequently melted down and in 1695 the bronze was given by the common council to two local churches, All Saints' and All Hallows', for the repair of their church bells. A print was subsequently produced, and an edition printed in 1742 is in the Royal Collection.

Literary References: *Brand* 1789, vol 1, 30–1; *Mackenzie* 1827, 161–2 n; *White* 1999, 76 n1; *Gibson* 2000, 10, 13 nn 63–5; *Usherwood* 2000, 328

Archival References: 1655 Archives, Duke of Northumberland, Alnwick

Will: William Larson the elder, proved 5 March 1661, PROB 11/303/82

Statues

1.	c1683	King Charles II, statuette (possibly designed by Jan Wyck)	b	NGI 8095	*le Harivel* 1988, 574 (repr); *Gibson* 1997 (1) 369; *Usherwood* 2000, 219 (repr); *Gibson* 2000, 10
2.	1686–1688	King James II, equestrian Payment(s): £800	b	[Newcastle-upon-Tyne, Northumbs, Sandhill]; destroyed	*Bourne* 1736, 126, 244; *Brand* 1789, vol 1, 30–1; *Usherwood* 2000, 219; *Gibson* 2000, 10, 13 nn63–5; *Sullivan* 2005, 32–5 (repr)
3.	1689	Four figures Payment(s): £8		[Sutton House, Chiswick, London]; untraced	Bellasis/Wombwell Archives, NYCRO ZDV

LASONS fl 1703

In 1703 William Wynde wrote to Lady Mary Bridgwater about lead figures: 'Madam since my laste I have enquired about a statue fitt for yr Ladys garden, and in order thereunto I was at Mr Nostes [**John Nost I**]; Mr Lasons, Mr **Varigne** and Mr Ansgood [**Richard Osgood** ?]; who has the best Leaden figures 3 of wch I picked on. . .a Venus and Cupide wch will cost about 12 pound, if single, withe out a Cupid 8 pound, the next is Juno . . . about 10 but ye best figure is an Extraordinary figure but one or two of ye moulds have been [illegible] very good pieces with fine mantel or drapery caste very loosely over him . . . this is the best of all the figures, they are moderne . . .' (Weston Hall, Staffs, Earl of Bradford MSS 18/4).

LATHAM, Jasper c1636–93

Latham was one of the City of London's leading mason contractors in the years after the Great Fire. As a sculptor he is remembered principally for his monument to Archbishop Sheldon at Croydon.

He was probably the son of another Jasper Latham, who was apprenticed to a mason, James Gilder, in 1621. He was married at St Giles-in-the-Fields by special licence on 21 December 1661, at which time he was described as a bachelor of about 25, and a mason and freeman of London. His wife was Elizabeth Sweete of St Giles Cripplegate (conceivably the daughter of **W Sweet**), 'aged about nineteen' (*Armytage* ed, 1890–92, 18). A son, Robert, joined the family business. In 1663 Latham's name was added to the yeomanry list of the Masons' Company, but it was not until October 1678 that, at his own request, he came on to the livery and court of assistants. He became a renter warden of the company in 1689 but was never master.

Latham worked under Sir Christopher Wren as mason contractor for the rebuilding of St Mildred, Poultry in 1670–79, receiving Portland stone to the value of £324 5s 3d in part payment, besides £2909 11s 6d for masonry work and carved ornaments (8). Wren employed him again as one of his master masons at St Paul's Cathedral, where he worked with **Joshua Marshall, Thomas Wise I, Edward Pearce** and **Edward Strong I** (10). Between 1679 and 1690, Latham received over £10,000 in regular payments for masonry and carved ornaments, largely on the south side of the choir and on the north side of the nave. He was also one of the masons under Wren as surveyor-general at Hampton Court when, in December 1689, part of the new buildings collapsed, killing two workmen and injuring 11 more. William Talman, the comptroller of works, sought to blame his superior and Latham, who appears to been the mason responsible, weighed in with Talman to blame Wren for the tragedy. In 1690, when Wren dispensed with Latham's services both at St Paul's and at Hampton Court, Wren objected 'against Mr Latham for a madman' in the matter of a certificate relating to new building at Hampton Court (Cal. Treasury Books, 1689–92, 355, quoted by *Knoop and Jones*, 20).

His work as a sculptor first came to public attention in 1672, when he was living near Fleet Street on the fringe of the City of London. On 29 May 1672 the most conspicuous outdoor statue of the time was unveiled by the new water conduit at the Stocks Market near Lombard Street. It was an equestrian figure of Charles II on a lofty pedestal with a prostrate figure beneath the horse's hooves (5). It was described on the following day in the *London Gazette* as 'an Excellent Figure of His present Majesty on Horseback having a Turk or Enemy underfoot. . .of White Genova Marble, and bigger than the Life'. The statue appears to have started life as a representation of the Polish King, Jan Sobieski, carved in Italy by an unidentified sculptor. It was shipped to England and acquired by a London merchant, Sir Thomas Vyner, whose nephew, Robert, probably conceived the idea of transforming it into a statue of Charles II trampling on Oliver Cromwell. Latham carved the new head. According to George Vertue, 'the head of the King was not done. Only a block fitt to carve. & was cutt by . . . Latham a sculptor near fleet ditch' (*Vertue* I, 129). The statue was first offered to the Joint Gresham Committee to stand in the centre of the Royal Exchange, but was declined because of its size, after which an alternative site was found in the Stocks Market. It was lampooned in a number of poems including *A Dialogue between two Horses imagining the Royal horses in Charing Cross and the Stocks market in conversation*. A later critic, James Ralph, condemned it as 'a thing in itself so exceedingly ridiculous and absurd, that 'tis not in one's power to look upon it without reflecting on the taste of those who set it up' (*Ralph* 1734, 12). It was removed to make way for the Mansion House in 1737 and lay neglected for 40 years in a yard before eventually finding its way to Newby Hall in Yorkshire.

Only four funerary monuments by Latham are known, three of them without figures. The Grandison has an urn flanked by trophies above a pedestal, the Brome is a simple architectural tablet and the Chare is a graceful cartouche with a backing of feigned drapery, knotted at the upper corners (**1–3**). The monument to Gilbert Sheldon, Archbishop of Canterbury at Croydon, 1683, is of another order (**4**). The reclining effigy in mitre and clerical robes was originally set against a lofty architectural backdrop, decorated with *putti* and garlands. The frame was badly damaged when the church was destroyed by fire in 1867, but the effigy survives, together with the tomb chest which incorporates an intricate relief panel of skulls and bones. In the 1730s Vertue noted 'Sheldons Monument his statue in Marble. A noble Mont. . .' (*Vertue* IV, 49). It was admired by a 19th-century antiquarian visitor to the church: 'There is a great individuality in the physiognomy of the prelate, which, together with the mitre, is very nicely sculptured . . . the skulls in the central compartment . . . for manipulation, would successfully vie with the most renowned sculpture . . .' (*Anderson* 1855, 16–18). Sheldon's niece married John Dolben, Archbishop of York, whose monument by **Grinling Gibbons** in York Minster, 1687–88, has close debts to Latham's memorial.

In 1681 Latham completed a statue in lead of Captain Richard Maples, a benefactor of Trinity House, for which he was paid £45 (**6**). This was originally placed in the Trinity Almshouses at Deptford, but was moved in 1873 to the corporation's almshouses in the Mile End Road and then to Trinity House itself during World War II. The imposing figure, originally posed on an inscribed pedestal, is presented in uniform with naval instruments at his feet. It was one of the first lead portrait statues in London and was painted to simulate stone.

Several of the City companies vied for the privilege of sponsoring a statue of Charles II for the line of kings in the quadrangle of the Royal Exchange. In 1684 the Grocers' Company claimed the privilege since they had elected the King a freeman at the Restoration, but this did not prevent the Founders from commissioning the royal statue and Latham was their choice of artist. He had already begun work when the Grocers appealed that this was 'an affront and wrong' to their Company and he was forced to abandon his efforts (Grocers' Co Minutes, Guildhall MS 11588, f.673, 6 June 1684, quoted by *Gibson* 1997 (2), 160). The King's statue was eventually provided by **Arnold Quellin** in 1686.

Latham was employed on building schemes in the City until shortly before his death. Between June 1670 and December 1671 he received regular payments totalling over £850 from the bankers Clayton and Morris for stonework at their offices in Cornhill and Old Jewry and in 1672 he carried out masonry work at their banking house in Hand Alley (Clayton & Morris fols 136v, 137v, 241v). He received small payments for stone-cutting from the Joiners' Company, 1679–82. He became mason to the Mercers' Company in 1682 and was City mason from 1687 until his death. He worked at the Royal Exchange between 1691 and 1693, assisted by his son, Robert, who continued at the Exchange after his father's death and prepared the double niche for statues of William III and Mary II in 1695 by **John Nost I**, for which he was paid £40. Robert succeeded his father as City Mason and held the post until 1696. His appointments of a clerk, Edmund Poynter, and a mason, John Newton, in 1694 and 1695 respectively, are recorded in the Masons' Company apprenticeship lists. Robert left England and was living in Port Mahon, Minorca, in 1713. Elizabeth Latham continued her husband's business, executing masonry work for Newgate and the Council Chamber at Moorfields, for which she was paid £26 18s in 1696, and receiving payments from the Mercers' Company until 1697.

Several of Latham's apprentices, none of whom appears to have had a successful career as a sculptor, are listed in the records of the Masons' Company. They include Richard Mapletoft, who was bound in 1664, James Burne, who may have been the 'Bonne' working on the Sheldon monument, bound in 1668, John Brookes (1689), William Heckford (1670) and **James Broomhall** (1679). The 1678 general search conducted by the Masons' Company lists Latham as a 'shopkeeper' employing three men, one of whom was **James Hardy**.

In his will Latham left his widow Elizabeth 'all my houses tenements Rents goods and Chattels' which suggests that he died reasonably affluent. **Abraham Storey** was one of his executors. The quantity of memorials authenticated as Latham's work is small. However, a considerable number of such works have been attributed to him, most of them swagged tablets, cartouche memorials and standing monuments surmounted by urns or portrait busts, but also several with crudely cut reclining, seated or standing effigies (C Lib repr). It seems likely that orders for sculpture formed an important part of a successful building practice.

IR

Literary References: *Vertue* IV, 49; *Weaver* 1915, 18; *Wren Soc* X, 1933, *passim; Knoop and Jones* 1935, 20; *Wren Soc* XIII, XIV, XV, *passim; Gunnis* 1968, 187, 234; *Colvin* V, 1973–76, 34; *Whinney* 1988, 138, 446 n 6; *Grove* 18, 829 (Friedman); *Gibson* 1997 (2), 158; *Roscoe* 1997, 175; *Gibson* 1998, 174–5; *Webb* 1999, 5, 6, 16, 21, 25; *Ward-Jackson* 2002, xv–xvi, xix

Archival References: *Clayton & Morris*, 1 (1669–1672); Joiners' Co, Master and Wardens, 1679–82; Masons' Co, Masters and Wardens, 1689; GPC; City Cash Accts 01/22 fol 51v (Royal Exchange niches), 01/22 fol 51r (Elizabeth Latham, work at Newgate and Moorfields)

Will: Commissary Court of London, register of wills, 1693, April: MS 9171, register 45, fol 107 v

Miscellaneous Drawings (all attrib): Burton Constable LDS 5275, 5278, 5280, 5281, 5282, 5284; Bodleian MS Tanner 89*, fol 271 (C Lib repr)

Portraits of the sculptor: 'Latham (statuary). His head painted by *Fuller* leaning his hand on a bust' (*Vertue* II, 59); untraced

Funerary Monuments

1.	†1673	Thomas Brome	Farnborough, Kent	S	Pevsner, *London: S*, 1983, 185; C Lib (repr)
2.	?c1675	William, 2nd Viscount Grandison of Limerick (†1643)	Christ Church Cathedral, Oxford	S	*Gunnis* 1968, 234; Pevsner, *Oxon*, 1974, 121; C Lib (repr)
3.	†1677	George Chare	Trinity College, Cambridge, chapel	S	Pevsner, *Cambs*, 1970, 168; C Lib (repr)
4.	1683	Archbishop Gilbert Sheldon (†1677) (co-sculptor: Bonne)	St John the Baptist, Croydon, Surrey	S	*Vertue* IV, 49; V 77; *Anderson* 1855, 16–18 (repr); *Gunnis* 1968, 234

Statues

5.	1672	King Charles II, equestrian (adapted from a statue of 'Jan Sobieski trampling the Turk', sculptor unknown)	s	[Stocks Market, London, until 1737]; Newby Hall, W R Yorks, since 1883	*Vertue* I, 129; *Perks* 1922, 125–31; *Gibson* 1997 (1), 174; *Ward-Jackson* 2002, XVI (repr)
6.	1681	Captain Richard Maples (†1680) Payment(s): £45	l	[Trinity Almshouses, Deptford, London]; Trinity House, City of London, entrance hall	Trinity House Court Minutes, 22 May, 1683; Corporation Cash Book, 22 Dec 1684; *Blackwood* 1989, 80–81 (repr); *Grove* 18, 829

Chimneypieces

7.	1667	Description unavailable Payment(s): £31		[Cobham Hall, Kent]; untraced	GPC citing PRO C.108/53

Architectural Sculpture

8.	1670–1679	Masonry work including a door with 'scrolls, cherubin-heads, deathsheads and bones' and other work	s	St Mildred, Poultry, City of London	*Wren Soc* X, 50; *Gunnis* 1968, 234
9.	1679–1680	Gateway, with 'two statues of demi-men' on either side		Joiners' Hall, City of London	Joiners' Company Archives in GPC
10.	1679–1690	Masonry work and ornaments Payment(s): Over £10 000	s	St Paul's Cathedral, London, north side of nave and south choir	*Wren Soc* XIII, *passim*; XIV, *passim*; *Gunnis* 1968, 234

LAUGHTON, Henry fl 1756

Henry Laughton, sculptor and gilder, bound Jacques Maillet, a pupil of the Westminster Protestant charity school, in October 1756.

Literary References: *le May* 2001, 563

LAUGHTON FAMILY, of Priors Cleeve fl 1741–85?

Several members of the Laughton family were masons by trade. They include John Laughton (1711–1754), his sons, William and Thomas, and another Thomas Laughton, statuary and mason (1790–1852).

Literary References: *Gunnis* 1968, 234–5

Funerary Monuments

1.	1741–1746	Several unidentified subjects, tombstones (by John Laughton)	Bretforton, Worcs	S	*Gunnis* 1968, 234
2.	?1750	Unidentified subject, tombstone (by John Laughton)	Welford-on-Avon, Warwicks	S	*Gunnis* 1968, 234
3.	†1755	Philip Fincher (signed by John Laughton)	Hambleton, Worcs	S	
4.	?1769	Thomas Vale (by William Laughton)	Elmley Castle, Worcs	S	*Gunnis* 1968, 234–5
5.	?1785	John Slatter (by Thomas Laughton)	Bidford, Warwicks	S	*Gunnis* 1968, 235

LAURIE, W fl *c*1846–49

He exhibited at the Royal Academy from 1 Addington Place, Lambeth, in 1846 and 1847 but was living at Downham Market, Norfolk, by 1849, when he published a book of designs for Gothic tombstones.

Literary References: *Gunnis* 1968, 235

Funerary Monuments

1.	1846	Lord Haddington, model	[Exhib RA, London, 1369]; untraced	*Graves* IV, 1905–6, 393
2.	1847	Design for a memorial to Shakespeare	[Exhib RA, London, 1133]; untraced	*Graves* IV, 1905–6, 393

LAW, Edward, of Sheffield 1798–1838

He was born on 9 December 1798, the fourth child of John Law of Sheffield and a grandson of Thomas Law, a well-known silversmith of that town. He began work as a sculptor when he was about 20. He received help and encouragement from **Sir Francis Chantrey** who, in declining a commission to execute a marble bust of Hugh Parker, Senior Magistrate of Sheffield, suggested that a committee should employ Law 'who has shown much talent and may require proper encouragement to bring that talent to maturity' (*Hoole* 1924, 382). Unfortunately for Law the committee ignored this recommendation and commissioned a painting instead. Besides being a sculptor and wax-modeller, Law was a designer of some skill, working for Sheffield silversmiths and iron-founders, including Hoole and Robson, who employed **Alfred Stevens** some years later. In 1825, for example, Law designed a bronze hexagonal stove with ormolu mounts for the registrar's office in Edinburgh. One of his last works was the gothic monument to Mrs Beard Holy, which was completed by his pupils, Morton and Bacon, after his death (5).

Literary References: *Hoole* 1924, 382–3; *Gunnis* 1968, 235; *Pyke* 1973, 76–7

Funerary Monuments

1.	1827	Thomas Rawson	St Mary, Ecclesfield, W R Yorks		Pevsner, *Yorks: W R*, 1967, 191
2.	?1828	John Greaves	Sheffield Cathedral, W R Yorks	S	*Hoole* 1924, 383
3.	1832	Thomas Holy	Carver Street Chapel, Sheffield, W R Yorks		*Hoole* 1924, 383
4.	1835	Thomas Watson	Sheffield Cathedral, W R Yorks		*Hoole* 1924, 383
5.	1838	Mrs Beard Holy	Carver Street Chapel, Sheffield, W R Yorks	S	*Hoole* 1924, 383

Busts

6.	*c*1818	Unidentified child's head, model	High Hazels Museum, Sheffield, W R Yorks	*Hoole* 1924, 382
7.	1821	John Rimington	Cutlers' Hall, Sheffield, W R Yorks	*Hoole* 1924, 382

8.	1826	Edward Rawson		Weston Park Museum, Sheffield, W R Yorks	*Gunnis* 1968, 235
9.	1826	Frank Stone		Weston Park Museum, Sheffield, W R Yorks	*Gunnis* 1968, 235
10.	1827	Thomas Rawson		Royal Infirmary, Sheffield, W R Yorks	*Hoole* 1924, 383
11.	1828	William, 2nd Earl Fitzwilliam		[Wentworth Woodhouse, W R Yorks]; untraced Other versions: Cutlers' Hall, Sheffield, W R Yorks, 1834	*Graves* IV, 1905–6, 394; *Hoole* 1924, 383
12.	1829	The late Thomas Rawson of Sheffield	m	[Exhib RA, London, 1193]; untraced	*Graves* IV, 1905–6, 394
13.	1831	Thomas Waterhouse		Sheffield University, W R Yorks	*Hoole* 1924, 383
14.	1832	Hall Overend		School of Medicine, Sheffield University, W R Yorks Other versions: Literary and Philosophical Society, Sheffield, W R Yorks	*Hoole* 1924, 383; *ODNB*
Reliefs					
15.	1826–1827	George Canning	w	coll Laurel G Blair (Toledo, Ohio) Other versions: Christie, 5 Oct 1976, lot 15	*Gunnis* 1968, 235; *Pyke* 1981, 25
16.	1826–1827	William Shakespeare	w	VAM Other versions: Christie, 5 Oct 1976, lot 15	*Pyke* 1973, 77; *Pyke* 1981, 25
17.	1826–1827	William Wilson	w	Untraced	*Gunnis* 1968, 235
18.	1829	Henry R Howard, medallic portrait		[Exhib RA, London, 1102]; untraced	*Graves* IV, 1905–6, 394
19.	1829	Unidentified gentleman, medallic portrait		[Exhib RA, London, 1111]; untraced	*Graves* IV, 1905–6, 394
20.	1832	William Wilson, medallic portrait		[Exhib RA, London, 1076]; untraced	*Graves* IV, 1905–6, 394
21.	1835	William Staniforth		Royal Infirmary, Sheffield, W R Yorks	*Gunnis* 1968, 235
22.	1838	John Law		Free Masons' Hall, Sheffield, W R Yorks	*Gunnis* 1968, 235
23.	nd	Sir Isaac Newton	w	VAM A.47-1970	*Pyke* 1973, 77; *Pyke* 1981, 25
24.	nd	Unidentified man	w	VAM	*Pyke* 1973, 77; *Pyke* 1981, 25
25.	nd	Unidentified man	w	NGI, Dublin, 554-1923	*Pyke* 1973, 77

LAW, John fl *c*1820–58

Funerary Monuments

1.	†1820	Alexander Stewart	Chennai (Madras) Cathedral, India	S
2.	†1825	Andrew Scott	Chennai (Madras) Cathedral, India	S
3.	†1829	Sarah Cooper	Chennai (Madras) Cathedral, India	S
4.	†1854	Lieutenant-Colonel John Johnstone	Chennai (Madras) Cathedral, India	S
5.	†1857	Clarence Colbeck	Chennai (Madras) Cathedral, India	S
6.	†1858	Emma Christian Mudge	Chennai (Madras) Cathedral, India	S

LAW, William, of Camberwell fl ?1775–95

He is known only for two large tablets in coloured marbles.

Literary References: *Gunnis* 1968, 235

Funerary Monuments

1.	?1775	Sarah Gretton	Birchington, Kent	S	*Gunnis* 1968, 234
2.	?1795	William Cody	St George-the-Martyr, Southwark, London	S	*Gunnis* 1968, 234

LAWLOR, John 1822–1901

Lawlor was an Irish sculptor who spent most of his working life in London, where he specialised in poetic subjects and portrait busts. He was born in Dublin in 1822 and received his early training at the Royal Dublin Society schools, studying sculpture under **John Smyth**. One of his early works, *Cupid pressing grapes into the glass of Time*, was purchased by the Royal Irish Art Union and awarded as a prize to the Countess of Ranfurly in 1843 (**80**). The following year he exhibited for the first time at the Royal Hibernian Academy (RHA), showing a group entitled *Boy and dog* (**81**) and in 1845 he moved to London, where he found employment modelling statues for the new Palace of Westminster, under the direction of **John Thomas**. Two years later he joined the Royal Academy schools on Thomas's recommendation.

Lawlor exhibited at the RA for the first time in 1848 (**1**) and he continued to show ideal works and portrait busts at the Academy until 1879, when he became involved in a dispute with the committee. He was also a frequent exhibitor at the RHA, becoming an associate member in 1861, and he showed at the British Institution (**42–44, 84**). His most successful work was perhaps *A bather*, a nude female figure which was awarded a prize medal when it was shown at the Great Exhibition of 1851 (**5**). **Henry Weekes** considered the statue 'not surpassed by any in the exhibition for the modelling of female flesh' and he recognised Lawlor as 'a rising sculptor' (*Weeks* 1851, cited by *Murphy* 1999, 72). The statue was displayed at the Dublin Exhibition of 1853, the Paris Exhibition of 1855 and the London International Exhibition of 1862. Prince Albert commissioned a version in marble as Queen Victoria's birthday present in 1855.

Royal approval helped Lawlor to secure a major public commission: in 1864 he was invited to sculpt a group representing *Engineering* for the Albert Memorial in Kensington Gardens, London (**9**). The committee found much to censure in the work from the outset: Doyne Bell described the first model as 'a signal failure' (Royal Archives Ad H2/973, cited by *Bayley* 1981, 88), while Sir Charles Eastlake commented that it hardly seemed to be the work of a practised artist (Royal Archives Ad H2/944, cited by *Brooks* 2000, 177). The second model was little better and Lawlor sought to excuse his poor performance by professing 'a natural inaptitude for minute modelling' (Royal Archives Ad H2/1080, cited by *Bayley* 1981, 89). There were problems also with the large-scale marble: in March 1870, when it was nearing completion, it was judged 'most unsatisfactory, bad in design and coarse in execution' and damaged as a result of careless workmanship (W Newton, Report, Royal Archives Ad H12, cited by *Bayley* 1981, 91). It was nonetheless completed and in position by March 1871. The group combines the ideal and the realistic, presenting an emblematic figure of *Engineering* presiding over three labourers and various items of industrial machinery. Lawlor's convincing depiction of a contemporary working man, a navvy, shovel in hand, dressed in a fur hat, loose necktie and tied trousers, was unusual in sculpture of the period.

In 1881 Lawlor provided a public statue for Limerick in his native Ireland (**12**). Patrick Sarsfield, the General who had attempted to defended the city against the army of William of Orange, was vigorously interpreted in flamboyant 17th-century costume. It has been described as 'one of the most attractive [statues] of the period' in Ireland (*Hill* 1995, 113). Five years later Lawlor went to America, though he soon returned to England. Although he had retired from exhibiting he continued to work for some years, executing a bust of Denny Lane in 1889 (**74**) and statue of Dr Delaney for Cork in 1890 (**14**). He died in 1901 aged 79. His nephew, Michael Lawlor, was his pupil and exhibited sculpture at the RA and RHA between 1877 and 1913.

Lawlor never married, but lived with his mother and other family members at 15 Hawley Road West, Camden Town, London (1881 Census). Walter Strickland later described him as 'well-known and popular in artistic and literary society in London; his tall, handsome figure, his fund of witty anecdotes and his fine baritone voice making him a welcome guest and a favourite with all who knew him'. His easy-going nature may in part explain his failure to make a significant contribution as a sculptor. Strickland noted that he was irregular in his profession, 'working only when he felt inclined or when necessity compelled him; and thus was unable to make provision for his old age.' (*Strickland* II, 1913, 9)

EH

Literary References: *Strickland* II, 1913, 8–10; *Gunnis* 1968, 235–6; *Bayley* 1981, 55, 74, 87–91; *Read* 1982, 19, 100, 349; *Hill* 1998, 111–3; *Brooks* 2000, *passim*

Additional Manuscript Sources: *Layard Papers*, 1866, Add 38993

Statues

No.	Date	Subject	Material	Location		References
1.	1848	The mourners		[Exhib RA, London, 1413]; untraced		*Graves* IV, 1905–6, 395
2.	1851	Christ blessing little children (Suffer little children to come unto me)		[Gt Exhib, London]; untraced Other versions: reproduced in Minton Parian ware		*Strickland* II, 1913, 9; *Stewart* II, 1985, 182; *Atterbury* 1989, 108 (repr 335)
3.	1851	Solitude, statuette		[Gt Exhib, London]; untraced Other versions: reproduced in Minton Parian ware (issued as a prize by the Art Union of London in 1852)		*Strickland* II, 1913, 9, 10; *Atterbury* 1989, 72 (repr 106)
4.	1853	The emigrant		[Exhib RA, London, 1350]; untraced		*Graves* IV, 1905–6, 395; *Murphy* 1999, 72
5.	1855	A bather (girl bathing)	m	Windsor Castle		*AJ Cat* 1851, 301 (repr); *Graves* IV, 1905–6, 395; *Holland Park* 1957, unpag (repr); *Johnson* 1975, 281; *Stewart* II, 1985, 182; *Morris and Roberts* 1998, 380; *Murphy* 1999, 71–2 (repr)
6.	1856	Titania Payment(s): £200 in marble; £10 in plaster	p	[Exhib RA, London, 1230]; untraced		*Graves* 1875, 337; *Graves* IV, 1905–6, 395, 396; *Johnson* 1975, 281; *Stewart* II, 1985, 182
7.	1862	Clio Payment(s): £250 in marble; £20 in plaster	p	[Exhib RHA, Dublin, 460]; untraced		*Stewart* II, 1985, 182
8.	1867	The wrestlers	m	[Exhib RA, London, 1181]; untraced		*Graves* IV, 1905–6, 396; *Johnson* 1975, 281
9.	1864–1870	Engineering	m	Albert Memorial, Kensington Gardens, London	S	*Bayley* 1981, 55, 74, 87–91, reprs 50–2; *Read* 1982, 100 (repr); *Brooks* 2000, *passim* (repr)
10.	1870	Poetry		[Manley Park, Manchester, Lancs]; untraced		*Gunnis* 1968, 235
11.	1872	The itinerant, statuette Payment(s): £200		[Exhib RA, London, 1498]; untraced		*Graves* IV, 1905–6, 396; *Stewart* II, 1985, 182
12.	1881	Patrick Sarsfield	b	Limerick, Ireland	SD	*Hill* 1998, 111–3 (repr)
13.	1881–82	Grief, statuette Payment(s): £35	m	[Exhib soc of BA, London, 834]; untraced		*Johnson* 1975, 282
14.	1890	Dr Delaney		Cork, Ireland		*Gunnis* 1968, 235

Busts

No.	Date	Subject	Material	Location		References
15.	1846	Unidentified subject		[Exhib RHA, Dublin, 485]; untraced		*Stewart* II, 1985, 182
16.	1850	Unidentified gentleman		[Exhib RA, London, 1417]; untraced		*Graves* IV, 1905–6, 395
17.	1852	George Sharp		[Exhib RHA, Dublin, 369]; untraced		*Stewart* II, 1985, 182
18.	1853	Dr J M Gully	m	[Exhib RA, London, 1405]; untraced		*Graves* IV, 1905–6, 395
19.	1853	Unidentified lady		[Exhib RA, London, 1433]; untraced		*Graves* IV, 1905–6, 395
20.	1854	Miss Cushman		[Exhib RA, London, 1494]; untraced		*Graves* IV, 1905–6, 395
21.	1854	T Kennedy MP		[Exhib RA, London, 1432]; untraced		*Graves* IV, 1905–6, 395
22.	1855	Unidentified lady		[Exhib RA, London, 1522]; untraced		*Graves* IV, 1905–6, 395
23.	1858	C Donovan		[Exhib RA, London, 1272]; untraced		*Graves* IV, 1905–6, 395
24.	1858	C Lindley		[Exhib RA, London, 1286]; untraced		*Graves* IV, 1905–6, 395
25.	1858	J H Parson		[Exhib RA, London, 1295]; untraced		*Graves* IV, 1905–6, 395
26.	1858	Miss Rosa Thomas		[Exhib RA, London, 1297]; untraced		*Graves* IV, 1905–6, 395
27.	1858	Mrs H White		[Exhib RA, London, 1290]; untraced		*Graves* IV, 1905–6, 395
28.	1859	Dr R Tuthill Massy		[Exhib RA, London, 1308]; untraced		*Graves* IV, 1905–6, 395
29.	1859	Unidentified lady		[Exhib RA, London, 1370]; untraced		*Graves* IV, 1905–6, 395

No.	Date	Title	Material	Location		Literary References
30.	1859	Unidentified subject		[Exhib RHA, Dublin, 334]; untraced		*Stewart* II, 1985, 182
31.	1860	Unidentified lady		[Exhib RA, London, 1046]; untraced		*Graves* IV, 1905–6, 395
32.	1861	A child Payment(s): £8	p	[Exhib RHA, Dublin, 589]; untraced		*Stewart* II, 1985, 182
33.	1861	A lady		[Exhib RHA, Dublin, 586]; untraced		*Stewart* II, 1985, 182
34.	1861	Head of our Saviour Payment(s): £80		[Exhib RA, London, 1103]; untraced		*Graves* IV, 1905–6, 395; *Stewart* II, 1985, 182
35.	1863	'A young gentleman'		[Exhib RA, London, 1154]; untraced		*Graves* IV, 1905–6, 395
36.	1863	A youth		[Exhib RHA, Dublin, 482]; untraced		*Stewart* II, 1985, 182
37.	1863	Unidentified gentleman		[Exhib RA, London, 1150]; untraced		*Graves* IV, 1905–6, 395
38.	1863	Unidentified subject	m	[Exhib RHA, Dublin, 481]; untraced		*Stewart* II, 1985, 182
39.	1863	Unidentified subject		[Exhib RHA, Dublin, 485]; untraced		*Stewart* II, 1985, 182
40.	1864	A young sculptor		[Exhib RHA, Dublin, 453]; untraced		*Stewart* II, 1985, 182
41.	1864	Clio		[Christie, 10 June 1904]; untraced		*Gunnis* 1968, 235
42.	1864	Summer Payment(s): £40	m	[Exhib BI, London, 647]; untraced		*Graves* 1875, 337; *Gunnis* 1968, 235; *Johnson* 1975, 281
43.	1865	Flora Payment(s): £40	m	[Exhib BI, London, 634]; untraced		*Graves* 1875, 337
44.	1865	Hermione Payment(s): £40	m	[Exhib BI, London, 641]; untraced		*Graves* 1875, 337; *Gunnis* 1968, 236; *Johnson* 1975, 281
45.	1865	M Lawlor		[Exhib RHA, Dublin, 472]; untraced		*Stewart* II, 1985, 182
46.	1865	Unidentified subject		[Exhib RA, London, 1058]; untraced		*Graves* IV, 1905–6, 395
47.	1866	Unidentified lady	m	[Exhib RA, London, 923]; untraced		*Graves* IV, 1905–6, 396
48.	1868	Unidentified gentleman		[Exhib RA, London, 1152]; untraced		*Graves* IV, 1905–6, 396
49.	1869	A young girl (?The rose)	m	NGI	SD	*Graves* IV, 1905–6, 396; *le Harivel* 1988, 575 (repr)
50.	1870	Unidentified gentleman		[Exhib RA, London, 1099]; untraced		*Graves* IV, 1905–6, 396
51.	1870	Unidentified lady		[Exhib RA, London, 1042]; untraced		*Graves* IV, 1905–6, 396
52.	1872	F Underhill		[Exhib Soc of BA, London, 872]; untraced		*Johnson* 1975, 281
53.	1872	H F B	m	[Exhib RA, London, 1533]; untraced		*Graves* IV, 1905–6, 396
54.	1872	R Waller		[Exhib Soc of BA, London, 873]; untraced		*Johnson* 1975, 281
55.	1872	W V Bromley		[Exhib RA, London, 1424]; untraced		*Graves* IV, 1905–6, 396
56.	1873	C Cattermole		[Exhib RA, London, 1445]; untraced		*Graves* IV, 1905–6, 396
57.	1873	J Danby		[Exhib RA, London, 1441]; untraced		*Graves* IV, 1905–6, 396
58.	1874	Florence Hardy		[Exhib RA, London, 1564]; untraced		*Graves* IV, 1905–6, 396
59.	1874	Master F Danby		[Exhib RA, London, 1574]; untraced		*Graves* IV, 1905–6, 396
60.	1876	The blind girl at Castle Cuille	m	NGI 8083	SD	*Graves* IV, 1905–6, 396; *Johnson* 1975, 281; *le Harivel* 1988, 574 (repr)
61.	1878	Unidentified gentleman		[Exhib RA, London, 1503]; untraced		*Graves* IV, 1905–6, 396
62.	1879	Meditation	m	[Exhib RA, London, 1543]; untraced		*Graves* IV, 1905–6, 396
63.	1881	O'Connor Power		untraced		*Strickland* II, 1913, 9, 10
64.	1882	John Jones	m	[Rogers, John Jones Ltd, 33 Bruton St, London]; VAM A.79-1970	SD	*Bilbey* 2002, 317 (repr)
65.	1882–1883	Henry Pettitt	p	[Exhib Soc of BA, London, 847]; untraced		*Stewart* II, 1985, 182
66.	1883	Miss K T		[Exhib Soc of BA, London, 769]; untraced		*Johnson* 1975, 282
67.	1882–1883	Unidentified gentleman	tc	[Exhib Soc of BA, London, 845]; untraced		*Johnson* 1975, 282
68.	1883	Unidentified subject		[Exhib RHA, Dublin, 650]; untraced		*Stewart* II, 1985, 182
69.	1883	Unidentified subject		[Exhib RHA, Dublin, 651]; untraced		*Stewart* II, 1985, 182
70.	1883–1884	N Vert		[Exhib Soc of BA, London, 828]; untraced		*Johnson* 1975, 282
71.	1884	P Merritt		[Exhib RHA, Dublin, 639]; untraced		*Stewart* II, 1985, 182
72.	1884	T Lloyd		[Exhib RHA, Dublin, 637]; untraced		*Stewart* II, 1985, 182
73.	1885	John O'Leary		[Exhib RHA, Dublin, 565]; untraced		*Stewart* II, 1985, 182
74.	1889	Denny Lane	p	NGI 8150	SD	*le Harivel* 1988, 574 (repr)
75.	nd	Daniel O'Connell		Untraced		*Strickland* II, 1913, 9, 10
76.	nd	James O'Kelly MP		Untraced		*Strickland* II, 1913, 9
77.	nd	W Smith O'Brien		Untraced		*Strickland* II, 1913, 9, 10

Architectural Sculpture

No.	Date	Title	Material	Location		Literary References
78.	post-1845	Statues		Palace of Westminster, London		*Gunnis* 1968, 235

Reliefs

No.	Date	Title	Material	Location		Literary References
79.	1852	Mrs Vandenhoff, medallion		[Exhib RA, London, 1383]; untraced		*Graves* IV, 1905–6, 395

Miscellaneous

No.	Date	Title	Material	Location		Literary References
80.	1843	Cupid pressing grapes into the glass of time		[Royal Irish Art Union prize won by Countess of Ranfurly]; untraced		*Strickland* II, 1913, 8
81.	1844	Boy and dog		[Exhib RHA, Dublin, 431]; untraced		*Stewart* II, 1985, 182
82.	1845	Gulnare		[Exhib RHA, Dublin, 445]; untraced		*Stewart* II, 1985, 182
83.	1848	Physical force		[Exhib RHA, Dublin, 59]; untraced		*Stewart* II, 1985, 182
84.	1848	Playmates		[Exhib BI, London, 462]; untraced		*Graves* 1875, 337
85.	1848	Punch and Pincher		[Exhib RHA, Dublin, 120]; untraced		*Stewart* II, 1985, 182
86.	1852	The disputed prize		[Exhib RA, London, 1345]; untraced		*Graves* IV, 1905–6, 395
87.	1859	Hermione	m	[Exhib RA, London, 1268]; untraced		*Graves* IV, 1905–6, 395
88.	1859	Surgeon Cusack		[Exhib RHA, Dublin, 333]; untraced		*Stewart* II, 1985, 182
89.	1860	Miranda		[Exhib RA, London, 980]; untraced		*Graves* IV, 1905–6, 395
90.	1862	Faith		[Exhib RA, London, 1093]; untraced		*Graves* IV, 1905–6, 395
91.	1862	Horatia		[Exhib RA, London, 1019]; untraced		*Graves* IV, 1905–6, 395
92.	1862	Medora		[Exhib RA, London, 1018]; untraced		*Graves* IV, 1905–6, 395, 396; *Johnson* 1975, 282
93.	1864	Fairies' frolic		[Exhib RHA, Dublin, 433]; untraced		*Stewart* II, 1985, 182
94.	1864	The captive		[Exhib RA, London, 922]; untraced		*Graves* IV, 1905–6, 395
95.	1864	The fugitive		[Exhib RA, London, 887]; untraced		*Graves* IV, 1905–6, 395; *Stewart* II, 1985, 182

96.	1864	The wayworn		[Exhib RA, London, 872]; untraced	*Graves* IV, 1905–6, 395
97.	1865	The mother's care		[Exhib RHA, Dublin, 467]; untraced	*Stewart* II, 1985, 182
98.	1868	Artemisia		[Exhib RA, London, 989]; untraced	*Graves* IV, 1905–6, 396; *Johnson* 1975, 281
99.	1869	Dante in exile Payment(s): £20		[Exhib RA, London, 1247]; untraced	*Graves* IV, 1905–6, 396; *Stewart* II, 1985, 182
100.	1869	Lashed to the helm Payment(s): £20		[Exhib RA, London, 1212]; untraced	*Graves* IV, 1905–6, 396; *Johnson* 1975, 281; *Stewart* II, 1985, 182
101.	1869	Musing Payment(s): £20		[Exhib RA, London, 1214]; untraced	*Graves* IV, 1905–6, 396; *Johnson* 1975, 281; *Stewart* II, 1985, 182
102.	1870	Eve		[Exhib RA, London, 1134]; untraced	*Graves* IV, 1905–6, 396
103.	1871	Reflection	m	[Exhib RA, London, 1260]; untraced	*Graves* IV, 1905–6, 396
104.	1872	E Hayes		[Exhib RA, London, 1441]; untraced	*Graves* IV, 1905–6, 396
105.	1872	The willow wreath Payment(s): £40	m	[Exhib Soc of BA, London, 868]; untraced	*Johnson* 1975, 281
106.	1874	Argyra	m	[Exhib RA, London, 1608]; untraced	*Graves* IV, 1905–6, 396
107.	1874	Maria		[Exhib RA, London, 1510]; untraced	*Graves* IV, 1905–6, 396
108.	1876	Mater dolorosa		[Exhib RA, London, 1468]; untraced	*Graves* IV, 1905–6, 396; *Stewart* II, 1985, 182
109.	1877–1878	Charles Baxter		[Exhib Soc of BA, London, 760]; untraced	*Johnson* 1975, 282
110.	1877–1878	Prospero Payment(s): £15	m	[Exhib Soc of BA, London, 761]; untraced	*Johnson* 1975, 282
111.	1883–1884	Two faces under a hood Payment(s): £5		[Exhib Soc of BA, London, 813]; untraced	*Stewart* II, 1985, 182; *Johnson* 1975, 282
112.	1885	Penseroso		[Exhib RHA, Dublin, 566]; untraced	*Stewart* II, 1985, 182

LAWRENCE, Peter –1846

Lawrence worked as a sculptor in Glasgow from 1837 until his death in 1846. His grave in the Glasgow necropolis is marked by a freestone statue of a naked youth bearing an extinguished torch, carved by **John G Mossman**. None of his works have been identified.

Literary References: *Woodward* 1977 (vol 1, pt 2), 114

LAWRENCE, Richard I fl 1746–95

He was probably the son of a carver, also Richard Lawrence, who provided furniture for the Duke of Montrose in 1732 and worked with **James Richards** on the Queen's Library at St James's Palace in 1737. Young Lawrence was apprenticed to **Sefferin Alken** in 1746. As 'Surveyor and Repairer of Carved Work' at Windsor Castle, he was responsible for maintaining the **Grinling Gibbons** carvings in the royal apartments in 1760–1. **George Murray**, the recently appointed master sculptor and master carver to the Crown, complained bitterly that the care of 'the Limetree work at His Majesty's Palace at Windsor' had been taken from him without his knowledge and 'given to one Lawrence a Carver who never had any Concern with His Majesty's work on any Acct' (Archives West of Alscot Park in *Gunnis* 1968, 236). Lawrence was paid £50 a year for this work, which Murray felt belonged to him.

By 1763 Lawrence was established at premises in Wardour-street, near Oxford Road and at about that time he went into partnership with Alken. He must have been a close friend of the family, for when **Oliver Alken**, Sefferin's brother, died in 1769, Lawrence, and the carver James Thorne of Westminster, were entrusted with the care of his children.

He was employed as a carver in stone and wood at several royal palaces and government buildings. In 1773 he was paid for work at Greenwich Palace on the King Charles building (**3**) and in 1784 he provided embellishments for Queen Mary's building, working with **John Deval II** (**11**). He had a major contract in the chapel, then being rebuilt after a disastrous fire (**10, 12, 14–16, 21, 22**). In 1778 he carved portico ornaments at the Queen's Lodge, Windsor (**6**). In the previous year he had begun to work at Somerset House, and continued there until 1791, carving in both wood and stone (**17**). Lawrence also worked at a number of private homes (**4, 7, 9, 19, 20**) and in 1791 provided part of the column commemorating Philip Hills at Colne Park, Essex (**18**).

Literary References: *Mortimer* 1763, 17, *Gunnis* 1968, 236; *Colvin* V, 1973–76, 479; *Beard* 1985, 690, 693

Statues					
1.	c1784	Two angels	m	Royal Hospital, Greenwich (ORNC), chapel	*Bold* 2000 (2), 176
Architectural Sculpture					
2.	1769	Carved work Payment(s): £40		[Excise office, London]; untraced	*Colvin* 1973–76, V, 349
3.	1773	74 large medallions; lion's head and foliage around circular window; Corinthian capitals to pilasters; capitals to Venetian window Payment(s): £102		Royal Hospital, Greenwich (ORNC), King Charles building	TNA ADM 68/876
4.	1764–1773	Carved work		[Manor House, Milton, Berks]; untraced	*Gunnis* 1968, 236
5.	1778	39 cantilevers for the gallery, 'a large rich foliage leaf and moulding with a beed carved in front, on the side a scrowl worm'd with a Stork flooroon and pead cods and two foliage flowers in spandrels' Payment(s): £140	wd	[Whitehall Palace, London, chapel]; untraced	RG/JP, 5, 816 citing PRO Work 5/64
6.	1778	Flowers, stars and ciphers, and two large stars and garters (£12 10s); twelve very rich flowers for the door post (£13) Payment(s): £12 10s	s	[Queen's Lodge, Windsor, Berks, gothic porch]; untraced	TNA Work 5/66; *Colvin* 1973–76, V, 340

7.	1780	Unidentified work Payment(s): £23 13s 6d		Hovingham Hall, N R Yorks	GPC citing Worsley Archives
8.	1781	Carved work		[St James's Palace, London, French chapel]; untraced	RG/JP, 5, 816 citing PRO Work 5/64
9.	1781–1782	Carved work		[Inverary Castle]; untraced	*Gunnis* 1968, 236
10.	1784	321 feet of ovolo; rich facia with honeysuckles, bands and other ornament Payment(s): £243 12s 6d; £502 14s 4d		Royal Hospital, Greenwich (ORNC), chapel	TNA ADM 68/813
11.	1784	Eight large mask heads; 83 faces of Corinthian capitals; 11 old capitals and five old pilasters recarved Payment(s): £66 16s; £58 16s		Royal Hospital, Greenwich (ORNC), Queen Mary's building	TNA ADM 68/813
12.	1784	Ten faces for eight capitals, east and west end Payment(s): £96 15s per capital	m	Royal Hospital, Greenwich (ORNC), chapel	*Gunnis* 1968, 236
13.	1785	Console decorated with a shell, cross, five birds and lions, and over the console a Gothic cornice	s	Westminster Hall, London	*Gunnis* 1968, 236
14.	1786	Ornaments including 24 faces of Ionic capitals for six columns in the the organ gallery	m	Royal Hospital, Greenwich (ORNC), chapel	TNA ADM 68/819; *Gunnis* 1968, 236
15.	?1786	Two richly carved pilaster capitals under the organ gallery and four ornaments to the pedestals in front of the Governor's and Lieutenant Governor's pews Payment(s): £49 10s 3d; £7 4s		Royal Hospital, Greenwich (ORNC), chapel	TNA ADM 68/819
16.	1787	Thirty-two cantilivers with rich foliate carving Payment(s): £528		Royal Hospital, Greenwich (ORNC), chapel	*Gunnis* 1968, 236 citing PRO Ad MS 68/819
17.	1777–1791	Capitals, flowers in soffits, and goats' heads over principal floor windows (wood and stone) Payment(s): £1,489 14s 7d		Somerset House, London	*Colvin* V, 1973–76, 467
18.	1791	Part of memorial column (designed by Sir John Soane)		Colne Park, Essex	*Gunnis* 1968, 236 citing Soane Notebooks
19.	1795	Carved work		[Buckingham House, Pall Mall, London]; untraced	*Gunnis* 1968, 236
20.	nd	Carved work Payment(s): £64		[Strawberry Hill, Twickenham, Middx, great north bedchamber]; untraced	*Toynbee* 1927, 147
Miscellaneous					
21.	post-1781	Carved and gilt frame for Benjamin West's altarpiece	wd	Royal Hospital, Greenwich (ORNC), chapel	*Bold* 2000 (2), 173, 176 (repr)
22.	*c*1784	Eight candelabra with dolphins, lions' heads, festoons of oak and laurel leaves		Royal Hospital, Greenwich (ORNC), chapel	*Bold* 2000 (2), 176

LAWRENCE, Richard II fl 1815–1839?

He exhibited from 9 Great Marlborough Street, London.

Literary References: *Gunnis* 1968, 236

Funerary Monuments					
1.	?1839	J Alexander	Broadstairs, Kent	S	*Gunnis* 1968, 236
Statues					
2.	1815	A Greek equestrian vaulting on his horse	[Exhib BI, London, 240]; untraced		*Graves* 1875, 337
3.	1816	An Arabian horse, model for part of an equestrian statue of the Duke of Wellington	[Exhib BI, London, 270]; untraced		*Graves* 1875, 337
4.	1829	Duke of York, equestrian statue	[Exhib Soc of BA, London, 846]; untraced		*Johnson* 1975, 282
Miscellaneous					
5.	1815	Restoration of a horse's head from Lord Elgin's marbles, cast	[Purchased by RA]; untraced		*Graves* 1875, 337; RA Archives in *Gunnis* 1968, 236
6.	1827	Hyperion rising from the ocean	[Exhib Soc of BA, London, 842]; untraced		*Johnson* 1975, 282
7.	1830	Horse swimming	[Exhib Soc of BA, London, 870]; untraced		*Johnson* 1975, 282

LAWRIE & FERGUSON, of Edinburgh fl *c*1849

Funerary Monuments				
1.	†1849	John Wilson	Kensal Green Cemetery, London	*Curl* 2001, 243–4 (repr)

LAWSON fl 1692

Statues				
1.	1692	Diana Payment(s): £16	[Chatsworth, Derbys]; untraced	Chatsworth Building Accts, 1686–94, 97D

LE GRAND, William

For further information the reader is referred to *Pyke* 1973, 77.

LE MARCHAND, David 1674–1726

Le Marchand was a Huguenot immigrant who made his living by ivory carving, a craft for which his native city of Dieppe was renowned. He was born on 12 October 1674, the son of Guillaume Le Marchand, a painter of altarpieces, and Madeleine Levasseur. One of his brothers, Guillaume, became a painter and other family members are thought to have worked in ivory.

His early life is undocumented, but two signed portrait reliefs which may be his work survive from the years before he came to Britain. These are a fluent, three-quarter-face image of Sebastien, Maréchal de Vaubon, signed 'Le Marchand Fecit. Anno 1689', at which date the sculptor was only 15, and an undated low-relief profile head of King Louis XIV, signed 'D.L.M.F'. Charles Avery, whose publications provide the principal source for Le Marchand's work, has suggested that the royal medallion may be a specimen of his carving taken into exile as evidence of his capabilities (*Avery* 1996, 52).

Le Marchand is thought to have been one of the Huguenots who fled from Dieppe after the revocation of the Edict of Nantes in 1685. Alternatively, he may have escaped in 1694, when the Anglo-Dutch fleet fired the city. His presence in Britain is first recorded in February 1696, when he was given permission to practise his craft and open a shop in Edinburgh, provided he took on children of local burghers as apprentices. The first known, indubitably signed portrait medallion, of Sir James Mackenzie, is dated 1696 (**23**), and a miniature portrait bust and three low-relief portraits of other Mackenzie family members were carved before 1700 (**32, 34, 35**). The sculptor's Protestant background was evidently not important to his clients, for other patrons included members of the Jacobite Drummond family (**24, 27, 33**), as well as the Earl of Leven, a protestant supporter of William III (**26, 30**). With the exception of one miniature bust (**7**) and the allegorical scene thought to celebrate the birth of the Old Pretender (**22**), all Le Marchand's Scottish works are small reliefs, carved from thin plaques of ivory, which may have been all that was available to him in Edinburgh.

He probably arrived in England *c*1700, soon after the death of **Jean Cavalier**, who had perhaps brought the courtly continental fashion for ivory carving to England and had created a metropolitan market for ivory portrait reliefs in the late-17th century. Le Marchand's movements in London are difficult to follow because of his relatively common French surname: a 'David lemarchant' was entered in the parish register of the French church in Swallow Street on 27 May 1705 as godfather to the daughter of Alexandre Sigournay, a cobbler of Newport Alley. The name appeared again in October 1709 in the oath roll of naturalizations, King's Bench list, which granted British citizenship to immigrants. A later record provides firm evidence of Le Marchand's whereabouts in the autumn of 1721: Edward, Lord Harley jotted in a pocket-book that Le Marchand 'Frenchman Merchant carver in Ivory [was to be found] in Barthol lane behind the Royal Exchange' (BL Add. MS.70456).

Le Marchand carved a few mythological or religious statuettes (**1–6**) but portraiture was his speciality. His talent for capturing the essence of his sitters in a rare material quickly brought him to the attention of the leaders of London society. These included members of the court and nobility, businessmen and particularly intellectuals at the forefront of science and literature. As his reputation grew he pioneered the use of much thicker plaques of ivory for his oval profile medallions, so that the head and shoulders projected to almost half their natural depth at the scale to which he was working. He also experimented successfully with full-face portrait reliefs, with shoulders cut almost to the waist (**44, 45, 49, 52, 65–67, 75**). The dominant character of each sitter is forcefully emphasised by frontal presentation and the lavish slice of ivory gave an opportunity to exhibit skills in realising the varied textures of a heavy curled wig, the fluid lines of a lawn shirt and particularly the quality of skin. The relief of Sir Isaac Newton (**44**), which succeeds in conveying both abstraction and piercing intelligence, was carved after a sitting from Newton and was considered by George Vertue to be the best of Le Marchand's four images of the astronomer. Sir John Houblon, Governor of the Bank of England (**45**) looks out from a voluminous wig with a direct, unflinching expression, and the determined character of Thomas Guy (**75**), businessman and founder of a London hospital, is evident from the drawn brows, thin-lips and heavy jowls of his portrait.

Le Marchand's most adventurous departure was a series of busts carved from the cylinder of a tusk, which gave him the opportunity to create a fully three-dimensional representation. He introduced the latest European stylistic fashions for these costly commissions. Two portraits of unidentified aristocrats, dated 1700 and 1701, (**9, 10**) are his first known large busts, each about 15 cm high. The man is wigged, but garbed *all'antica*, a representational compromise that paid lip-service to the fashionable interest in the classical world without obscuring the identity of the sitter. The woman's image is ground-breaking: her direct gaze challenges the coy femininity expected of female portraits, and satisfying contrasts are provided by her near-diaphanous chemise and crisply curled locks falling onto the bare flesh of her shoulder. Another innovative bust, of an unidentified nobleman, measures 23.5cm in height and was carved from a whole cylinder of ivory (**13**). The unbuttoned coat and open-necked shirt give a casual air, pre-figuring the rococo movement in England. Le Marchand exploited eye-catching realistic details like twin button-holes, but the salient feature of the portrait is the stern, unflinching gaze, made emphatic by a severe downturn of the mouth.

The sculptor counted the Duke of Marlborough's family among his aristocratic patrons and carved three busts of Marlborough's daughter, Anne Churchill, Countess of Sutherland, around the time of her marriage in 1699 (**8**). She was an acknowledged beauty and the opportunity to carve this image of femininity and youthful charm must have provided a welcome change from the grandiose representations which were his usual fare, as well as providing an endorsement from the most powerful family at Queen Anne's Court. A charming relief plaque of a seated noblewoman with her daughter and a pet whippet, *c*1710 (**41**), is thought to represent Anne Sunderland and her child. The sculptor also carved an authoritative profile relief of the Duke (**39**).

Le Marchand's most enthusiastic patrons came from a mercantile background: the Raper family were prosperous silk merchants, closely involved in the emerging institutions of the City of London, particularly the Bank of England. In the years 1716–20 Le Marchand carved a number of reliefs and busts for the Rapers, including three profile medallions of family members (**58, 59, 62**) and an ambitious rectangular full length portrait relief of young Mathew Raper III, standing in a library, demonstrating a geometrical proposition (**60**). Raper later became a mathematician, scholar and fellow of the Royal Society and was involved in the foundation of the British Museum, to which he presented a work by Le Marchand (**20**). The Rapers are thought to have commissioned the medallion portrait of Thomas Guy (**75**) and the only surviving religious narrative relief by the sculptor, *The miracle of Christ healing the man with the withered hand* (**64**). They were also almost certainly behind two of the sculptor's masterpieces, busts of John Locke (**19**) and Sir Isaac Newton (**52**). The Locke, which is now lost, was a posthumous representation owing superficial debts to Sir Godfrey Kneller's portrait, but Le Marchand's interpretation had greater conviction, for it conveyed the physical frailty of the sitter, evident in the deep-set eyes and lines about the mouth. By contrast, Newton's head is a forceful image taken from the life, which makes full play of the sitter's features, a square skull, receding hairline, strong jaw and wide-set eyes. When the Rapers commissioned Le Marchand's portrait by Joseph Highmore, *c*1723, the sculptor chose to be represented with this or another wigless head of Newton on the table before him.

Where possible Le Marchand is thought to have prepared a wax model from the life, which was then translated to ivory on the premises. The privilege of a personal sitting was recorded with the words *ad vivum*, sometimes in abbreviated form, added to the sculptor's initials on the back of the work. Le Marchand's images of famous men were rare or unique contemporary, three-dimensional records, and Avery has suggested that they, or wax impressions of them, were an important influence on sculptors of the next generation (*Avery* 1999, 33–4). He believes that Le Marchand's busts of Locke and Newton were a source for **G-B Guelfi**'s heads of worthies for Queen Caroline's Hermitage, 1732, and that **Michael Rysbrack**'s bust of Newton for John Conduitt, *c*1727–30, has affinities with a lost medallion by Le Marchand. Other definitive images, like the profile of Sir Christopher Wren (**74**) and of the antiquarian, William Stukeley, presented *all'antica* with a wreath circling his cropped head (**73**), were both later reproduced in bronze as commemorative medallions. The commercially-minded ceramic manufacturers Wedgwood and Bentley, clearly recognised the decorative value of Le Marchand's portraits and acquired plaster moulds of at least three sitters (**58, 59, 62**), as well as some wax casts (**28, 29, 31**). At least one of his reliefs (**59**) was translated to vitreous paste, perhaps by the Scot, James Tassie.

Le Marchand's commissions dwindled after 1720 and George Vertue's assessment of the sculptor's achievement, written in 1722, has perhaps a retrospective tone: 'an Ingenious man for carving in Ivory . . . has been many years in England. Done a vast number of heads from ye life in basso relief some statues in Ivory' (*Vertue* III, 13). The sculptor died in poverty on 17 March 1726 at the French Hospital in London, at the expense of the charity. William Stukeley, whose relief portrait (**73**) is the last securely dated work by Le Marchand, noted the death of 'the famous cutter in ivory Monsr. Marchand, who cut my profile' (William Stukeley, *Family Memoirs*, June 1726, quoted by *Avery* 1985, 1564). His best-known successor as a carver of busts in ivory was **Gaspar Van der Hagen**.

Le Marchand's portrait reliefs followed in the tradition of Cavalier, but they became increasingly less medallic and more sculptural and sensual during the course of his career. Avery, whose exhibition of Le Marchand's work in 1996 brought the sculptor's achievement into new focus, considers his 'brilliantly characterised portraits' to be among the most impressive ever carved in ivory.

IR

Literary References: *Vertue* II, 69–70; *Hodgkinson* 1965 (2), 29–32; *Whinney* 1971, 25–30; *Avery* 1984, 113–118; *Murdoch and Hebditch* 1985, 208–12; *Avery* 1985, 1562–64; *Grove* 19, 1996, 130 (Avery); *Avery* 1996; *Avery* 1999, 27–34; *Dawson* 1999, 150–2

Additional MS Sources: Edward Harley, Corr and Papers, BL Add. MS.70456

Portraits of the Sculptor: self-portrait (?), *c*1710, ivory, private coll; Joseph Highmore, *c*1723, oil on canvas, NPG, 6142

Statues

1.	?post-1700	Crucified Christ, statuette	i	[Tyttenhanger House, Herts]; VAM A.42-1983		Christie's *Review of the Year*, 1983, 14,16; *Avery* 1996, 104–5 (repr)
2.	1700–1720	Apollo with his lyre, a bow and quiver of arrows, statuette	i	Alnwick Castle, Northumbs		*Avery* 1996, 106–7 (repr)
3.	1700–1720	Apollo, statuette	i	Hessisches Landesmuseum, Darmstadt inv PL.36:58		*Avery* 1996, 107 (repr)
4.	1700–1720	Saturn abducting Cybele ('Time and Opportunity and Penitence'), statuette, after Thomas Regnaudin	i	VAM A.1-1935	S	*Whinney* 1971, 38–9 (repr); *Avery* 1996, 52–3 (pl 9, repr 3)
5.	1710–1720	Venus and Cupid, statuette	i	VAM A.69-1926	S	*Avery* 1996, 106 (pl 7)
6.	nd	Virgin and Child, statuette	i	Museum of Art and Archaeology, Missouri, Columbia 69.1023		*Avery* 1984, 1116 (xix b); *Avery* 1996, 104–5 (repr)

Busts

7.	post-1696	John, 2nd Earl of Cromartie, miniature bust	i	[coll Mackenzie family]; private coll		*Avery* 1996, 55–6 (repr)
8.	*c*1699	Anne, Countess of Sunderland	i	VAM A.67-1926 Other versions: Met, NY 1974.28.148, c1699 Althorp, Northants, *c*1699–1710		*Avery* 1996, 66–7 (repr); *Avery* 1999, 27–34
9.	1700	Unidentified nobleman	i	NT, Anglesey Abbey, Cambs, Fairhaven coll	SD	*Avery* 1996, 68–9 (pl 16); *Avery* 1999, 27–34 (repr)
10.	1701	Unidentified lady, previously thought to be Anne Nelthorpe	i	[coll Nelthorpe family]; private coll	SD	*Murdoch and Hebditch* 1985, 210–1 (repr); *Avery* 1996, 99 (repr); *Avery* 1999, 27–34 (repr)
11.	1702	John Vesey, Archbishop of Tuam	i	[coll Vesey family]; private coll	SD	*Avery* 1996, 73–4 (pl 3); *Avery* 1999, 27–34
12.	1704	Francis Sambrooke	i	Lord Thomson of Fleet, Toronto	SD	*Avery* 1996, 84–5 (repr 2); *Zock* 2002, 126 (repr)
13.	1704	Unidentified gentleman	i	Private coll	SD	*Avery* 1996, 99–100 (repr); *Avery* 1999, 27–34 (repr)
14.	1706	John, Lord Somers	i	[coll Lord Somers]; Wimpole Hall, Cambs (NT)	SD	*Vertue* IV, 166; *Avery* 1996, 72–3 (repr)
15.	1704–1710	Unidentified gentleman, conceivably Joseph Addison	i	Daniel Katz, 2002		*Avery* 1996, 100 (repr); *Zock* 2002, 122–7 (repr)
16.	*c*1714	King George I	i	VAM A.12-1931		*Snodin and Styles* 2001, 160 (colour repr)
17.	1714	Sir Isaac Newton PRS, without a wig	i	[coll Lord Halifax]; Nat Gall of Victoria, Melbourne	SD	*Avery* 1996, 78 (repr); *Dawson* 1999, 150–2; *Avery* 1999, 27–34 (repr)
18.	1716	King George I	i	[Basildon Park, Berks]; VAM A.12-1931	S	*Grove* 19, 1996, 130; *Avery* 1996, 70–1 (repr)

No.	Date	Subject		Location		Literature
19.	?c1718	John Locke	i	[coll Raper family]; untraced	S	*Avery* 1985, 1562–4; *Avery* 1996, 91–2 (repr); *Avery* 1999, 27–34
20.	1718	Sir Isaac Newton PRS, without a wig	i	BM 455	SD	*Vertue* II, 69; *Avery* 1996, 91 (repr); *Dawson* 1999, 150–2; *Avery* 1999, 27–34 (repr)
21.	1716–1720	Sir Humphry Morice, Governor of the Bank of England	i	Lord Thomson of Fleet, London	S	*Avery* 1996, 94–5 (repr & pl 8)
Reliefs						
22.	c1696	An allegorical scene probably celebrating the birth of Prince James Francis Edward Stewart, very likely the lid of a counter-box	i	Private coll		*Avery* 1996, 61–2 (repr)
23.	1696	Sir James Mackenzie of Royston, later Lord Royston, profile portrait	i	[coll Mackenzie family]; private coll		*Avery* 1996, 56–7 (repr)
24.	?c1696	Unidentified lady of the Drummond family, profile portrait	i	[coll Drummond family]; Grimsthorpe and Drummond Castle Trust		*Avery* 1996, 58–9 (repr)
25.	?pre-1699	Unidentified gentleman in a banyan, profile portrait	i	National Museum, Stockholm		*Avery* 1996, 64 (repr)
26.	1696–1700	Anna, Countess of Leven, profile portrait	i	VAM A.124-1956		*Pearson* 1991 (repr 137); *Avery* 1996, 54–5 (repr)
27.	1696–1700	Arms of the Duke of Perth, circular medallion	i	[coll Drummond family]; Grimsthorpe and Drummond Castle Trust		*Avery* 1996, 59–60 (repr)
28.	1700	Charles Chester Eyre aged seven, profile portrait	i	VAM A.19-1974 Other versions: Wedgwood Museum, Barlaston, wax medallion	SD	*Avery* 1996, 98 (repr)
29.	?c1700	Charles Nicholas Eyre	i	Untraced Other versions: Wegwood Museum, Barlaston, wax (repr)		*Avery* 1996, 97–8
30.	1696–1700	David, 3th Earl of Leven and 2nd Earl of of Melville, profile portrait	i	VAM A.123-1956		*Pearson* 1991 (repr 137); *Avery* 1996, 53–4 (repr)
31.	1700	Elizabeth Eyre, profile portrait	i	Fitzwilliam Other versions: Wedgwood Museum, Barlaston, wax medallion	SD	*Avery* 1996, 97 (repr)
32.	1696–1700	George Mackenzie of Rosehaugh, profile portrait	i	[coll Mackenzie family]; private coll		*Avery* 1996, 57–8 (repr)
33.	1696–1700	James, 2nd titular Duke of Perth, profile portrait	i	[coll Drummond family]; Grimsthorpe and Drummond Castle Trust	S	*Avery* 1996, 58 (repr)
34.	1696–1700	Lady Mackenzie of Rosehaugh, profile portrait	i	[coll Mackenzie family]; private coll		*Avery* 1996, 57 (repr)
35.	1696–1700	Sir George Mackenzie Bt, Viscount Tarbat, later 1st Earl of Cromartie, profile portrait	i	[coll Mackenzie family]; private coll		*Avery* 1996, 55 (repr)
36.	?c1700	Unidentified lady, possibly of the Eyre family, profile portrait	i	Reiner Winkler, Wiesbaden		*Avery* 1996, 98–9 (repr)
37.	1696–1700	Unidentified nobleman in armour, profile portrait	i	Lord Thomson of Fleet, Toronto		*Avery* 1996, 63 (repr)
38.	1700–1705	Samuel Pepys, profile portrait	i	BM 458	S	*Murdoch and Hebditch* 1985, 208; *Avery* 1996, 74–5 (repr 12)
39.	1700–1710	John, 1st Duke of Marlborough, profile portrait	i	VAM A.5-1950	S	*Murdoch and Hebditch* 1985, 307 (repr); *Avery* 1996, 64–5 (repr)
40.	1700–1710	King James II of England and VII of Scotland, profile portrait	i	[coll Drummond family]; Grimsthorpe and Drummond Castle Trust		*Avery* 1996, 60–61 (repr)
41.	c1710	Noblewoman, perhaps Anne, Countess of Sunderland, sitting with her daughter and a pet whippet, rectangular relief	i	[coll Dukes of Newcastle, Clumber, by 1879]; private coll	S	*Avery* 1996, 68 (pl 5); *Avery* 2002, 28–34 (repr)
42.	c1710	Self-portrait (?), profile portrait	i	[coll 'Mr T West' (possibly James West of Alscot Park, Warwicks)]; private coll		*Vertue* IV, 61; *Avery* 1984, 114 (repr); *Avery* 1996, 86 (repr)
43.	1700–1710	Sir Godfrey Kneller, profile portrait	i	Lord Thomson of Fleet, Toronto		*Avery* 1996, 74 (repr)
44.	1702–1710	Sir Isaac Newton PRS, in a full-bottomed wig, rectangular portrait plaque Model(s): full frontal high relief, 1702–10, Corsham Court, Wilts, wax	i	[coll Dr Richard Mead]; Lord Thomson of Fleet, Toronto	S	*Vertue* II, 69–70; Mead sale (2), 1755, lot 40; *Avery* 1985, 1564 (repr); *Avery* 1996, 76–7 (repr)
45.	c1710	Sir John Houblon, Lord Mayor of London (?), full-face portrait	i	Fondation d'Art du Docteur Rau, Embrach, Switzerland		*Avery* 1996, 93–4 (pl 8)
46.	1712	Gamaliel Voyce, profile portrait	i	VAM A.18-1936		*Avery* 1996, 85 (repr)
47.	?c1712	Mary Voyce, profile portrait	i	VAM A.19-1936		*Avery* 1996, 85 (repr)
48.	1702–1712	Queen Anne, profile portrait	i	Lord Thomson of Fleet, Toronto		*Avery* 1996, 64 (pl 13)
49.	1704–1713	Charles, 3rd Earl of Peterborough and 1st Earl of Monmouth, full-face portrait	i	Lord Thomson of Fleet, Toronto		*Avery* 1996, 69 (repr)
50.	c1715	Sir Richard Steele MP, profile portrait, cast in steel		BM, Coins and Medals, M.8277		ATTRIB. *Avery* 1996, 81 (repr)
51.	?c1718	John Locke, profile portrait	i	[Ince Blundell Hall, Lancs]; Christie, 13 Dec 1994, lot 30; NPG		*Avery* 1984, 113–18 (repr); *Avery* 1996, 75 (repr); Ingamells forthcoming

52.	1718	Sir Isaac Newton FRS, three-quarter profile portrait	i	[Christie, 18 April 1864, lot 2035]; untraced	SD	*Avery* 1996, 77–8 (repr)
53.	1715–1719	George, 10th Earl Marischal, full-face portrait	i	BM MLA 1960, 4-1, 1		*Kerslake* 1977, 1, 182–3 (repr 526); *Avery* 1996, 63–4 (repr)
54.	1719	John Flamsteed, profile portrait	i	[coll John Belchier FRS, who presented it to the Observatory]; Royal Greenwich Observatory, Cambridge	D	*Avery* 1996, 80–81 (repr)
55.	1700–1720	Charles Marbury, profile portrait	i	VAM A.43-1931 Other versions: Reiner Winkler, Wiesbaden, oval profile set in a looking-glass		*Vertue* IV, 50; *Avery* 1996, 79–80 (repr)
56.	1700–1720	Christopher Wren MP, profile portrait	i	[coll Mr Wilet c1763 ?]; Lord Thomson of Fleet, Toronto	S	*Anecdotes* 1876, II, 625; *Avery* 1996, 79 (repr)
57.	1714–1720	King George I, rectangular profile portrait	i	BM 456 Other versions: rectangular portrait plaque, 1714–20, private coll Portrait medallion, Herzog Anton Ulrich-Museum, Braunschweig Elf.351 (393) portrait medallion, 1714, Lord Thomson of Fleet, Toronto		*Avery* 1996, 70–1 (repr)
58.	*c*1720	Mary Elizabeth Raper, profile portrait	i	[coll Raper family]; untraced Other versions: Wedgwood Museum, Barlaston, modern ceramic (repr)		*Avery* 1996, 87–8
59.	*c*1720	Mathew Raper II (†1748), profile portrait	i	[coll Raper family]; untraced Other versions: Wedgwood Museum, Barlaston, modern ceramic (repr) attrib James Tassie, glass-paste medallion, *c*1770		*Avery* 1984, 115; *Avery* 1996, 86–7
60.	1720	Mathew Raper III FRS, rectangular full length portrait	i	VAM A.20-1959	SD	*Hodgkinson* 1965 (2), 29–32; *Whinney* 1971, 26–7 (repr); *Avery* 1996, 88 (repr)
61.	1700–1720	Michael Garnault of Chatellerault, profile portrait	i	Lord Thomson of Fleet, Toronto		*Murdoch and Hebditch* 1985, 210; *Avery* 1996, 84 (repr)
62.	1716–1720	Moses Raper (?), profile portrait	i	Untraced Other versions: Wedgwood Museum, Barlaston, modern ceramic portrait medallion (repr)		*Avery* 1996, 88–9
63.	1714–1720	Rt Hon Thomas Brodrick PC, profile portrait	i	BM 460	S	*Murdoch and Hebditch* 1985, 208; *Avery* 1996, 72 (repr)
64.	*c*1720	The miracle of Christ healing the man with the withered hand, rectangular relief	i	Nat Museum of Wales, Cardiff	S	*Avery* 1984, 113–8; *Murdoch and Hebditch* 1985, 208–9 (repr); *Avery* 1996, 89–90 (repr)
65.	1700–1720	Unidentified man, full-face portrait	i	Fitzwilliam M.5.1945	S	*Avery* 1996, 101 (repr)
66.	1700–1720	Unidentified lady, full-face portrait	i	Fitzwilliam M.6.1945	S	*Avery* 1996, 101 (repr)
67.	1700–1720	Unidentified man, nearly-frontal portrait	i	BM 459		*Avery* 1996, 100 (repr)
68.	1700–1720	Unidentified man, profile portrait	i	BM 461	S	*Avery* 1996, 100–1 (repr)
69.	1700–1720	Unidentified man, profile portrait	i	(coll David T Owsley, New York)		*Avery* 1996, 102 (repr)
70.	1700–1720	Unidentified nobleman, profile portrait	i	(coll R T Gwynn)		*Avery* 1996, 102 (repr)
71.	*c*1720	Unidentified young lady, circular profile portrait	i	(coll Eric Van Vredenburgh)		*Avery* 1996, 101–2 (repr)
72.	1712–1722	Elizabeth, Lady Cathcart, profile portrait	i	RMS, Edinburgh		*Avery* 1996, 96–7 (repr)
73.	1722	Rev William Stukeley MD, FRS, profile portrait	i	[coll William Stukeley]; Michael Hall, London		*Avery* 1996, 81–2 (repr)
74.	*c*1723	Sir Christopher Wren, profile portrait	i	[coll Margaret Willett, the sitter's daughter]; NPG, London 4500 Other versions: ex coll Matthew Raper III; BM 457	S	*Colvin* V, 1973–76, V (repr 1); *Murdoch and Hebditch* 1985, 211–2 (repr); *Avery* 1996, 78–9, 90–1 (repr)
75.	1700–1726	Thomas Guy, after a wax model perhaps by François le Pipre, rectangular portrait plaque	i	VAM A.1-1936	S	*Avery* 1996, 75–6 (pl 15)
76.	nd	Anne Dacier, profile portrait	i	BM 462 Other versions: Plaster mould, Wedgwood Museum, Barlaston		*Avery* 1996, 83 (repr)
77.	nd	'Diomedes with the Palladium and Inigo Jones's head ditto'		Untraced		Mead sale (2), 1755, lot 323; *Avery* 1985, 1564
78.	nd	Socrates, Homer, Cicero, Medusa (two), low relief portraits, after the Antique		[Dr Richard Mead]; untraced	S	Mead sale (2), 1755, lot 32; Avery 1985, 1564
79.	nd	Unidentified man, possibly André Dacier, profile portrait	i	Royal Coll RCIN 37078 Other versions: Plaster mould, Wedgwood Museum, Barlaston	S	*Avery* 1996, 83–4 (repr)

LE MASON (or LE MASSON), of Paris and London fl 1790

Le Mason, who was French Academician, exhibited a bust of the architect Sir William Chambers and medallions of his two daughters at the Royal Academy in 1790 (**1, 4, 5**). In the same year he made two reliefs for the exterior of the sculpture gallery at Woburn (**3**). In a letter to the Duke of Bedford Le Mason explained that he could not charge less than 25 guineas for the pair, 'seeing that I shall have to pay for fresh fruit and flowers and other indispensable articles' (Woburn Abbey Archives in *Gunnis* 1968, 238). His address in London was recorded as 33 Oxford Street.

Literary References: *Graves* V, 1905–6, 35; *Gunnis* 1968, 238

Busts

1.	1790	Sir William Chambers	[Exhib RA, London, 534]; untraced	*Graves* V, 1905–6, 35
2.	1790	Unidentified lady	[Exhib RA, London, 664]; untraced	*Graves* V, 1905–6, 35

Architectural Sculpture

3.	1790	'Spring sacrificing flowers presented to her by Zephyr' and 'Summer leaning on a sheaf of corn and receiving flowers from a child', two reliefs Payment(s): 25 gns	Woburn, Beds, sculpture gallery exterior	Woburn Building Accts, BLARS R5/1105

Reliefs

4.	1790	Miss Chambers, medallion	[Exhib RA, London, 536]; untraced	*Graves* V, 1905–6, 35
5.	1790	Miss L Chambers, medallion	[Exhib RA, London, 546]; untraced	*Graves* V, 1905–6, 35

LE PIPER (or LEPIPRE), Francis 1640–98

Le Piper was the son of a wealthy merchant who, having substantial private means, took up art as an amusement. Most of his works were drawings, paintings and engravings, but 'in the latter part of his life he apply'd himself to the Study and Practice of Modelling in wax, in *basso-relievo*, in which he did abundance of things with good success. He often said he wish'd he had thought of it sooner, for that sort of work suited better with his genius than any. Had he lived longer he would have arriv'd to a great Perfection in it'.

Literary References: *Buckeridge* 1706, 453–7; *Gunnis* 1968, 238–9; *Pyke* 1973, 79; *ODNB* (Cust rev. Griffiths)

LEA, William 1776–

Lea entered the Royal Academy schools in 1797. He had exhibited at the Academy three years previously, giving his address as 12 New Road, opposite Fitzroy Square.

Literary References: *Graves* V, 1905–6, 9; *Gunnis* 1968, 236

Miscellaneous

1.	1794	Cupid, model	[Exhib RA, London, 599]; untraced	*Graves* V, 1905–6, 9

LEADER, George fl 1785–1804

A medallist and wax modeller, his address was given as 188 Oxford Street, London. In addition to the relief portraits listed below, Leader exhibited seals of George II and George III at the Royal Academy in 1799.

Literary References: *Gunnis* 1968, 236; *Pyke* 1973, 77

Reliefs

1.	1785	General James Oglethorpe	w	Coll Mrs S Gaspar (Brighton)	*Pyke* 1973, 77
2.	1792	George Stubbs	w	[Exhib RA, London, 773]; untraced	*Graves* V, 1905–6, 11
3.	1792	Paul Sandby	w	[Exhib RA, London, 779]; untraced	*Graves* V, 1905–6, 11
4.	1797	Unidentified subject, portrait	w	[Exhib RA, London, 1039]; untraced	*Graves* V, 1905–6, 11
5.	1797	Unidentified subject, portrait	w	[Exhib RA, London, 1048]; untraced	*Graves* V, 1905–6, 11
6.	1801	Admiral William Bligh	w	[Exhib RA, London, 1026]; untraced	*Graves* V, 1905–6, 11
7.	1802	J K Powell MP		[Exhib RA, London, 1078]; untraced	*Graves* V, 1905–6, 11
8.	1802	Mr Ascough		[Exhib RA, London, 1079]; untraced	*Graves* V, 1905–6, 11
9.	1802	Mr Stevens		[Exhib RA, London, 1077]; untraced	*Graves* V, 1905–6, 11
10.	1804	Unidentified lady	i	[Exhib RA, London, 942]; untraced	*Graves* V, 1905–6, 11

LEADER, P H fl 1790–1800

He gave his address as New Brentford when he exhibited two wax models at the Royal Academy in 1797 (**2**).

Literary References: *Gunnis* 1968, 236–7; *Pyke* 1973, 77

Reliefs

1.	1790–1800	Unidentified man (possibly George Washington) boxwood portrait medallion		VAM A.24-1939	S	*Gunnis* 1968, 236–237

Miscellaneous

2.	1797	Models	w	[Exhib RA, London, 921 and 956]; untraced	*Graves* V, 1905–6, 11

LEARMOUTH, J fl 1836

His address was given as 9 Lower Belgrave Place when he exhibited at the Royal Academy in 1836.

Literary References: *Gunnis* 1968, 237

Busts

1.	1836	George Murray, Bishop of Rochester	[Exhib RA, London, 1089]; untraced	*Graves* V, 1905–6, 13
2.	1836	Master D Hanbury	[Exhib RA, London, 1069]; untraced	*Graves* V, 1905–6, 13

LEAVY, Michael fl 1810–49

He was born about 1787 and entered the Dublin Society's schools in 1810. There he studied under **Edward Smyth** and won several prizes for modelling and drawing. He does not seem to have found success as a sculptor since nothing more is heard of him, except that in 1849 he failed to obtain the mastership of the Dublin Society's modelling school. At that time his address was given as North King Street.

Literary References: *Strickland* II, 1913, 15

Busts

1.	1814	Unidentified subject	tc	[Exhib Hawkins Street, Dublin]; untraced	*Strickland* II, 1913, 15

LECUEL, William fl 1763

He is listed as a mason in Union Street, Berkeley Square in *Mortimer* 1763, 49.

LEDSHAM, Edward fl 1679

He was probably a Llanfair craftsman.

Literary References: *Gunnis* 1968, 237

Architectural Sculpture

1.	1679	Coat of arms Payment(s): £10 12s	s	Chirk Castle, Denbigh, over hall door	Myddelton Archives in *Gunnis* 1968, 237

LEE, Dennis, of Leeds fl c1852–67

There are references in the Leeds Town Hall committee minutes to work by **Lee and Welsh, Walsh & Lee** and **Dennis, Lee and Welsh**, who were clearly interconnected. They read as follows: '26 Nov 1858. Lee and Welsh paid £33 4s for marble pedestals; 18 June 1865 Lee and Walsh paid £4 10s for a marble mantle piece; 27 Feb 1865. Dennis Lee and Welsh paid £7 15s 6d for cleaning statues; 1 Feb 1867. Dennis Lee and Welsh paid £29 9s for cleaning statues and marrble' (HMI, misc file).

Funerary Monuments					
1.	†1852	Unidentified subject, tablet	All Saints, Kirkby Moorside, N R Yorks	S	Pevsner, *Yorks: N R*, 1966, 215
2.	†1854	Mary Holt	North Dalton, E R Yorks		Pevsner, *Yorks: E R & York*, 1995, 628
3.	†1855	Thomas Weddill	Claverley, Salop	S	RG/JP, 5, 818
Statues					
4.	1857	Robert Hall	Leeds Town Hall, W R Yorks		*Hall* 1995, 12 (repr)
Busts					
5.	1857	Robert Hall MD	Leeds Town Hall, W R Yorks	D	RG/JP, 5, 818
6.	nd	Edward Baines	Leeds Town Hall, W R Yorks		RG/JP, 5, 818

LEE, John, of Odiham fl 1797?–c1840

Funerary Monuments

1.	?1797	William Burgess	Odiham, Hants	S	*Gunnis* 1968, 237
2.	?1812	Richard Harrison	South Warnston, Hants	S	*Gunnis* 1968, 237
3.	?1821	Mrs Nichols	Odiham, Hants	S	*Gunnis* 1968, 237
4.	†1840	Elizabeth Rush	Odiham, Hants	S	RG/JP, 5, 818

LEE, W fl c1825–43

Funerary Monuments

1.	†1825	Caroline Gylby	s	St Swithun, East Retford, Notts	S
2.	†1843	Joshua Cottam	s	St Swithun, East Retford, Notts	S

LEE, Walter –1766

The son of a cook named Walter Lee, he was apprenticed to **James Hardy** in January 1706, completed his training in 1720, and then set up his yard in Oxford Road. In the same year he took a lease on 56 Grosvenor Square and in 1728 leased a site in the same square, scheduled for development. In 1726 he presented bills to the Westminster Fire Office for repairs to the house of a Mr DuCrox, which had recently been damaged by fire. Two years later he became a director of the fire office. In June 1728 he signed a contract for £500 with Francis Seymour, to erect a monument to Sir Edward Seymour, designed by James Gibbs (1). The contract is detailed and gives directions on materials, including a purple marble for the ground and architectural features and veined marble for the circular frame surrounding the urn. Lee was responsible only for the architectural work: 'the figure and carving about the said monument should be carved and finished by **Michael Rysbrack**' (TNA Chancery Masters' Exhibits C107/126).

This was one of several collaborations with Gibbs. Between 1733 and 1736 Lee and a carpenter, Robert Wanmer, worked on an unidentified house built by Gibbs. In 1742 Lee and a local builder, John Lane, agreed to build Marylebone Chapel for £1,000 (Archives, West of Alscot Park). Their designs were subject to Gibbs's approval. Lee was also responsible for a modest mural tablet erected in the same chapel in memory of Gibbs, who died in 1754 (2). The architect stated in his will that he wished to be buried at Marylebone and 'that a small monument of marble, to be made by Mr Walter Lee, mason, be put up against the wall within the said church, with a short inscription on it, as shall be thought fit by my executors' (*Euro Mag* 1789, 16, 169).

As a mason Lee built a house in Marylebone for Thomas Warren in 1731 (Inventory of Directors of the South Sea Company). About three years later he was working at Canons, where he received a payment of £90. In 1740–41 he was paid £114 for work at Canons for the second Duke of Chandos (Ipswich Record Office, SI/2/100). He was also paid £84 for mason's work for Sir Matthew Featherstonehaugh, who was then building a house in Whitehall. He was listed c1740 as 'Lee, Walter, Mason, near Cavendish Square' on the livery list of the Masons' Company (Masons' Co Assistants, fol 3).

The will of 'Walter Lee, Mason of St Marylebone' was proved on 7 November 1766. In it he requested that he should be buried, at 2 o'clock in the afternoon, 'without pomp or feathered hearse' near to his family in Marylebone burial-ground. He appointed his wife Clarentia as sole executor. Lee was succeeded in the business by his son, George (†1767), who was apprenticed to him in 1740. George became a member of the Masons' Company in January 1758, was made free on 12 January 1758 and died in 1766. In the year before his death, George's son, another Walter, was bound apprentice to him.

Literary References: *Baker* 1949, 199; *Gunnis* 1968, 237; *Friedman* 1984, 80, 95, 207, 305, 310, 325

Archival References: Masons' Co, Apprentices, 1694–1795 (1740); Freemen, 1677–95, fol 40; fol 41; Court Book, 1685–1722, fol 76r; Court Book, 1751–96 (1766); WFO, DM, 343/4, 3 Oct 1728; Glyn, Mills & Co archives, Uppark Archives, both in GPC; IGI

Will: PROB 11/923

Funerary Monuments

1.	1728–1730	Sir Edward Seymour Bt (†1707), masonry work only Payment(s): £500 (£400 paid in Oct 1729) Drawing(s): Ashm, Gibbs 52b and a	Maiden Bradley, Wilts	TNA Chancery Masters' Exhibits C.107/126; *Eustace* 1982, 80–81 (repr); *Friedman* 1984, 95, 96, 325 (repr); *Colvin* 1995, 407
2.	c1754	James Gibbs (†1754)	St Mary, St Marylebone, London	*Friedman* 1984, 20, 310

LEGÉ, F A 1779–1837

A Prussian immigrant, in the early 1800s he was principal carver in the workshops of **Samuel and Thomas Franceys** in Liverpool, where he was assisted by **John Gibson**. In 1805 he carved a coat of arms for the Union News room in Liverpool (**20**) and in 1814 be exhibited a colossal figure of *Satan* in Edinburgh where it apparently aroused hostility for in 1815 it was reported that 'some intrusive Goth has dared to mutilate it' (*Scots Magazine*, 1815, 334) (**4**). Around that time he moved to London and found employment in the studio of **Francis Chantrey**. There he worked on a small model of Satan (**8**) and carved the monument known as *The sleeping children* from Chantrey's model (**2**). After Chantrey's death questions were raised about the extent of Legé's involvement in the creation of some of his Chantrey's famous works, including *The sleeping children*.

Legé exhibited at the Royal Academy, 1814–25, showing ideal works and portraits, including busts of Chantrey and **Charles Harriott Smith** (**13, 14**). Gunnis particularly admired a small marble figure of a lady reclining on a couch (**11**), commenting 'This enchanting and delicate work might at first sight be taken for contemporary French sculpture, for it has all the charm of that country. On closer examination, however, it shows that curious virginal English frigidity which seems to add to its beauty' (*Gunnis* 1968, 237).

The sculptor's son, **George Legé**, was awarded a Society of Arts prize for a work of sculpture in 1826 but he does not seem to have exhibited, and died before his father. Legé himself died on 4 April 1837, leaving two children, Ann, a governess in Russia, and Frederick, a private soldier. He had providently joined the Artists' Annuity Fund in 1813 and his widow received payments from the fund from 1837 to 1844.

Literary References: *Notes and Queries*, 6 July 1850, 94; *Gunnis* 1968, 237; *Curtis* 1989, 23, 50; *Sicca and Yarrington* 2000, 135, 141

Archival References: AAF, Proposals, 10; AAF, AB

Funerary Monuments

1.	1810	Devotion, design for a monument		[Exhib Liverpool Ac, 188]; untraced		*Morris and Roberts* 1998, 384
2.	1815–1817	Ellen Jane and Mary Anne Robinson ('the sleeping children')	m	Lichfield Cathedral, Staffs		*Notes and Queries*, 1850, 94; *Gunnis* 1968, 237; *Yarrington* 2000, 141
3.	1827	Thomas Bridge (†1826)		Piddletrenthide, Dorset		GPC

Statues

4.	1814	Satan		[Exhib Edinburgh]; untraced		*Graves* 1875, 342; *Graves* V, 1905–6, 23; *Gunnis* 1968, 237
5.	1817	Satan, model		Untraced		*Yarrington* 2000, 135
6.	1818	Marquess of Anglesey, sketch for a half-size statue		[Exhib RA, London, 1082]; untraced		*Graves* V, 1905–6, 23
7.	1822	Miss S Wright		[Exhib BI, London, 337]; untraced		*Graves* 1875, 342
8.	1822	Satan		[Exhib BI, London, 334]; untraced		*Graves* 1875, 342; *Yarrington* 2000, 135
9.	1823	Unidentified child	m	[Exhib RA, London, 1118]; untraced		*Graves* V, 1905–6, 23
10.	1824	Psyche	m	[Exhib RA, London, 1025]; untraced		*Graves* V, 1905–6, 23
11.	1828	Lady reclining on a couch	m	Private coll	SD	*Gunnis* 1968, 237
12.	nd	Lady Louisa Russell (miniature copy after Chantrey)		[M Zachery sale, Christie, London, 30 March 1838]; untraced		GPC

Busts

13.	1815	Sir Francis Chantrey		[Exhib RA, London, 882]; untraced		*Graves* V, 1905–6, 23
14.	1822	Charles Harriot Smith		[Exhib RA, London, 1021]; untraced		*Graves* V, 1905–6, 23
15.	1822	G Williams		[Exhib RA, London, 1048]; untraced		*Graves* V, 1905–6, 23
16.	1825	John Crossley		[Exhib RA, London, 988]; untraced		*Graves* V, 1905–6, 23
17.	1829	Rev Robert Hawker		[St Andrew, Plymouth, Devon]; untraced		*Gunnis* 1968, 237
18.	1830–1839	Unidentified subject, on a pedestal	m	Joanna Barnes, London (1993)	S	

Architectural Sculpture

19.	1800–1802	Navigation, the Arts and Commerce, reliefs	s	Lyceum post office (formerly the Lyceum), Liverpool, Lancs		*Cananagh* 2000, 4 (repr)
20.	1805	Union arms	s	Union News room, Liverpool, Lancs		*Stranger in Liverpool*, 1812, 76

Miscellaneous

21.	1812	Model of a female hand holding a pen		Salford Museum, Lancs	SD	GPC
22.	1821	Sleeping infant		[Exhib RA, London, 1118]; untraced		*Graves* 1875, 342; *Graves* V, 1905–6, 23
23.	1825	Lady and child, sketch		[Exhib RA, London, 1012]; untraced		*Graves* V, 1905–6, 23

LEGE, George fl 1826

Legé was living at 41 Foley Street, Portland Place in 1826, when he won a silver medal from the Society of Arts.

Statues

1.	1826	Figure in the round, a copy	[Soc of A, large silver medal]; untraced		RSA *Transactions*, vol 44, 1826, xliii

LEGGE, W

For further information the reader is referred to *Pyke* 1973, 77.

LEGREW, James 1803–57

James Legrew was a sculptor, a scholar proficient in several ancient languages and deeply religious. He combined these passions in *A Few Remarks on the Sculpture of the Nations referred to in the Old Testament*, 1845.

He was born on 5 October 1803 in Caterham, Surrey, the second son the Rev James Legrew, the Rector of St Lawrence's and his wife Elizabeth. The family were descended from Huguenot refugees, who had settled in Spitalfields, London.

Legrew showed an early talent for sculpture and after completing a first class classical education his father sent him in 1821 to study under **Sir Francis Chantrey**. In 1822 he enrolled at the Royal Academy Schools where he gained the silver medal in 1824 and a gold in 1829 for *Ajax tearing Cassandra from the altar of Minerva* (**15**). In 1822, while living at 7 Palace Street, Pimlico, he was awarded the silver palette by the Society of Arts for a plaster copy of a single figure (**14**). Having acquired some training and experience, Legrew travelled extensively in Italy, working and studying for a period in Rome.

He executed several portrait busts and a number of church monuments, including several in his native Surrey. He also carved ideal figures drawn from the Bible, literature and classical mythology. In 1844 he sent two works to the Westminster Hall competition, *The last prayer of Ajax* (**20**) and *Milton dictating to his daughters* (**19**). Other ideal works include *Samson about to burst his bonds* (**18**), described as a 'fine and vigorous conception' (*AJ*, 1857, 348) and *Rachel mourning her children*, an emotional subject also known as *The murder of the innocents* (**49**). Both these were exhibited at the Crystal Palace in 1851. Legrew was responsible for some architectural sculpture, a group decorating the front of the Asylum for Orphan Girls in Lambeth and a statue of *London* for Somerset House (**35, 37**).

The sculptor wrote a short life of Flaxman and in 1845 published his major literary opus, *A Few Remarks on the Sculpture of the Nations*. He hoped this would be the precursor of a larger second volume, which did not materialise. *A Few Remarks* was poorly reviewed in the *Athenaeum* by T K Hervey, who considered it a deeply flawed work. Hervey described Legrew as a sculptor 'whom we have had occasion to commend for his promise, rather than its adequate redemption; and the work before us indicates that he is a man of learning and research – not, in this instance, turned to the most useful account' (*Athenaeum* 1845, 1106–7). Legrew also received adverse criticism for some of his sculpture: the *Literary Gazette* felt his work to be 'finely proportioned' but 'too smooth' and the composition of his figures 'liable to question' (*Lit Gaz*, cited in *Gunnis* 1968, 237–8). The *Art Journal* noted that Legrew's career was 'not successful' but that the sculptor did not allow this 'to affect his feelings towards his professional brethren' (*AJ* 1863, 348).

Following a period of mental illness the sculptor took his own life in 1857. He had experienced 'mental delusions' for some time (*Redgrave* 1878, 266) and these were exacerbated by the deaths of his father in 1856 and brother, Arthur in March 1857. Legrew died at his home in Kensington on 15 September 1857, aged 53. He never married. The *Art Journal* described him as a religious and charitable man 'of a most affectionate disposition' (*AJ*, 1863, 348). In addition to his talent for sculpture and languages, he was noted as having considerable skill as a musician, particularly on the organ. He exhibited at the Royal Academy over a period of 27 years. Few of his works have been identified and it may that many, particularly his female figures, were plaster models never executed in marble, a suggestion made in his obituary in the *Art Journal*. Fortunately, one of Legrew's earliest works, *A sleeping boy* survives and can perhaps be identified with *A sleeping child*, his first exhibit at the RA (**38**). This charming infant study suggests that Legrew's talent did not receive the encouragement it deserved.

Caroline Jordan

Literary References: *Builder*, 27 July 1844, 367; *AJ*, 1863, 348 (*obit*); *Redgrave* 1878, 266; *DNB*, 1892, XXXII, 422; *Graves* V, 1905–6, 24; *Gunnis*, 1968, 238

No.	Date	Subject		Location		References
Funerary Monuments						
1.	?1828	Henry Hoare		Morden, Surrey		*Gunnis* 1968, 238
2.	†1828	William (†1815) and Martha Lambert (†1828)		Barnstead, Surrey	S	
3.	1832	A monumental figure		[Exhib RA, London, 1143]; untraced		*Graves* V, 1905–6, 24
4.	1832	Elizabeth Legrew (†1825)		St Lawrence, Caterham, Surrey	SD	Pevsner, *Surrey*, 1971, 137–8
5.	?1832	Robert Wright		St Mary the Virgin, Wimbledon, Surrey		*Gunnis* 1968, 238
6.	?1836	George Smith		Sanderstead, Surrey		*Gunnis* 1968, 238
7.	†1836	Lieutenant Blackwood Gore Currie RN		St Mary the Virgin, Wimbledon, Surrey	S	
8.	1837	Blackwood Currie		St Mary the Virgin, Wimbledon, Surrey	S	
9.	†1839	Sarah Elizabeth Moore		St Luke, Liverpool, New South Wales	S	
10.	†1840	John Alleyne Beckles		Barbados Cathedral, Bridgetown	S	
11.	†1841	Edward and Harriet (†1861) Cranston		East Grinstead, Sussex	S	*AJ*, 1857, 348; *Gunnis* 1968, 238
12.	?1845	Bishop Allen		Ely Cathedral, Cambs		*Gunnis* 1968, 238
13.	nd	Rev J Kendrick		Bletchingley, Surrey		*Gunnis* 1968, 238
Statues						
14.	1822	'Plaster copy of a single figure'		[Soc of A, silver palette]; untraced		RSA, *Transactions*, vol 40, 1822, xxxviii
15.	1830	Ajax tearing Cassandra from the altar of Minerva		[Exhib RA, London, 1830, 1194, gold medal]; untraced		*Graves* V, 1905–6, 24; *Gunnis* 1968, 237
16.	1839	Cupid		[Exhib Birmingham Soc of A]; untraced Other versions: exhib RA, London, 1833, 1180; untraced		*Gunnis* 1968, 238; *Johnson* 1975, 284
17.	1843	Posthumous marble figure of the infant daughter of S Courtauld	m	[Exhib RA, London, 1401]; untraced		*Graves* V, 1905–6, 24
18.	1843	Samson about to burst his bonds		[Exhib RA, London, 1424]; untraced		*AJ* 1857, 348; *Graves* V, 1905–6, 24
19.	1844	Milton dictating his 'Address to Light' to his two daughters		[Exhib Westminster Hall, London]; untraced		*Lit Gaz*, 1435, 20 July 1844, 466; *Graves* V, 1905–6, 24; *Gunnis* 1968, 237
20.	1844	The last prayer of Ajax		[Exhib Westminster Hall, London, 97]; untraced		*AU*, 1844, 215; *ILN*, 13 July 1844, 21
21.	1851	The murder of the innocents		[Gt Exhib]; untraced		*Gunnis* 1968, 238
Busts						
22.	1829	Unidentified gentleman		[Exhib RA, London, 1172]; untraced		*Graves* V, 1905–6, 24
23.	1831	Mr Rosenthberg		[Exhib RA, London, 1148]; untraced		*Graves* V, 1905–6, 24
24.	1832	HRH Prince George of Cumberland		[Exhib RA, London, 1167]; untraced		*Graves* V, 1905–6, 24

25.	1833	Mrs George Smith of Sanderstead Park	[Exhib RA, London, 1208]; untraced	*Graves* V, 1905–6, 24
26.	1834	Rev C Rawlins	[Exhib Soc of BA, London, 834]; untraced	*Johnson* 1975, 284
27.	1834	Unidentified gentleman	[Exhib Soc of BA, London, 838]; untraced	*Johnson* 1975, 284
28.	1835	W Skelton	[Exhib Soc of BA, London, 1835, 790]; untraced	*Gunnis* 1968, 238; *Johnson* 1975, 790
29.	1836	Unidentified gentleman	[Exhib RA, London, 1074]; untraced	*Graves* V, 1905–6, 24
30.	1837	James Baily	[Exhib RA, London, 1243]; untraced	*Graves* V, 1905–6, 24
31.	1838	George Davys, Dean of Chester	[Exhib RA, London, 1379]; untraced	*AJ*, 1857, 348; *Graves* V, 1905–6, 24
32.	1843	Sketch of Sir Francis Chantrey	[Exhib RA, London, 1492]; untraced	*Graves* V, 1905–6, 24
33.	1857	Sir Bartle Frere	[Exhib RA, London, 1264]; untraced	*Graves* V, 1905–6, 24
34.		Study of a head of Ajax during his last prayer	[Exhib RA, London, 1361]	*Graves* V, 1905–6, 24

Architectural Sculpture

35.	*c*1826	A group of figures	Asylum for Orphan Girls, Lambeth, London	Brayley, *Surrey*, III, 344
36.	1850	Font	Morden, Surrey	*Gunnis* 1968, 238
37.	1856	London	Somerset House, London	*ILN*, 14 Feb 1857, 135 (repr)

Miscellaneous

38.	1826	A sleeping child	[Exhib RA, London, 1036]; 'Sleeping boy' sold Christie, 24 Sept 1987, lot 150	*Graves* V, 1905–6, 24
39.	1828	Study of a child	[Exhib RA, London, 1203]; untraced	*Graves* V, 1905–6, 24
40.	1829	Infancy	[Exhib BI, 539]; untraced	
41.	1829	The Spartan youth	[Exhib RA, London, 1220]; untraced	*Graves* V, 1905–6, 24
42.	1834	Innocence	[Exhib RA, London, 1106]; untraced	*Graves* V, 1905–6, 24; *Johnson* 1975, 284
43.	1836	Sleeping girl	[Exhib BI, 502]; untraced	
44.	1839	Ajax 'O Jove! Father of my ancestors'	[Exhib RA, London, 1279]; untraced	*ILN* 1844, 21; *Graves* V, 1905–6, 24
45.	1846	A youth about to bathe	[Exhib RA, London, 1407]; untraced	*Graves* V, 1905–6, 24
46.	1848	A sea nymph listening to a shell	[Exhib RA, London, 1352]; untraced	*Graves* V, 1905–6, 24
47.	1849	Venus 'A little winged serpent, see, Has pierced me'	[Exhib RA, London, 1215]; untraced	*Graves* V, 1905–6, 24
48.	1850	Musidora 'At the doubtful breeze alarmed'	[Exhib RA, London, 1309]; untraced	*Graves* V, 1905–6, 24
49.	1851	'In Rama there was a noise heard . . . Rachel weeping for her children'	[Exhib RA, London, 1261]; untraced	*Graves* V, 1905–6, 24
50.	1852	Contemplation 'By thoughts inspiring visions, blest'	[Exhib RA, London, 1328]; untraced	*Graves* V, 1905–6, 24
51.	1853	The deserted nest	[Exhib RA, London, 1325]; untraced	*Graves* V, 1905–6, 24
52.	1854	Castle building	[Exhib RA, London, 1372]; untraced	*Graves* V, 1905–6, 24
53.	1855	The mirror	[Exhib RA, London, 1440]; untraced	*Graves* V, 1905–6, 24

LEGTERIN (or LOGTERIN), J V fl 1685–1708

Statues

1.	*c*1700	Apollo, Artemis, Hera and Diana	Woburn Abbey, Beds, courtyard	Pevsner, *Beds, Hunts & Peterborough*, 1968, 168

LEIFCHILD, Henry Stormouth 1823–84

Born in Moorgate, London, he was the fourth son of William Gerard Leifchild of Moorgate and The Elms, Wanstead, Essex. He studied in the sculpture galleries of the British Museum and at the Royal Academy Schools, which he joined in 1844 on the recommendation of F S Cary. In 1848 he went to Rome, where he for three years he fell 'under the influence of **Thorwaldsen, Gibson**, and the classical school' (*Sparkes* 1891, 322).

Leifchild exhibited at the RA between 1844 and 1882, showing ideal works and portrait busts. In 1851 he sent a figure of *Rizpah watching over the dead bodies of her sons* to the Great Exhibition, where 'it attracted notice and then the young sculptor was recognised as a man destined to make his mark' (*Sparkes, op cit*, 322) (**5**). He was unsuccessful in the competition for the memorial to the Great Exhibition (**7**), but his model won the competition for the Guards' memorial in front of Chelsea Hospital (**31**). He also designed the gothic Robertson mausolem, which stands near the entrance gates of Warreston Cemetery in Edinburgh, and executed the incised panels depicting The Lord's Prayer which ornament the exterior and the effigy of Mrs Robertson which lies within (**2**).

Leifchild lived throughout most of his life in Stanhope Street, Regents Park, London, and died at 15 Kirkstall Road, Streatham, on 11 November 1884. After his death his widow presented the models of his more important works, including a group of *Athene repressing the fury of Achilles*, a figure of *Lot's wife* and a design for a memorial to Lord Byron, to Nottingham Museum (**12, 13, 16**). All except *Jacob and the Angel* (**44**) were destroyed before 1929.

Literary References: *Sparkes* 1891, 322–4; *Gunnis* 1968, 238; *Read* 1982, 34, 187–8; *ODNB* (Cust rev Whitehead)

Archival References: RA Admissions

Funerary Monuments

1.	1864	Officers and men of the 8th Regiment of Foot who died during the Indian Mutiny, monumental cross	Portsmouth, Hants	GPC
2.	*c*1865	Robertson mausoleum	Warriston Cemetery, Edinburgh	*Sparkes* 1891, 322–3; Pevsner, *Edinburgh*, 1991, 576; *Read* 1982, 187, 188 (repr)
3.	1867	Memorial effigy of a lady	[Exhib RA, London, 1099]; untraced	*Graves* V, 1905–6, 27

Statues

4.	1844	The mother of Moses leaving him on the banks of the Nile, sketch		[Exhib RA, London, 1287]; untraced		*AU*, 1844, 170; *Graves* V, 1905–6, 27
5.	1851	Rizpah watching over the dead bodies of her sons		[Gt Exhib, London]; untraced		*Sparkes* 1891, 332 (repr)
6.	1857	The fugitive slave (slave hunted like a beast by bloodhounds)		[Exhib RA, London, 1227]; untraced		*Sparkes* 1891, 322; *Graves* V, 1905–6, 27
7.	?1858	Torch-bearer handing on the light to the fresh runner, a memorial to the Great Exhibition, model only (commission awarded to Joseph Durham)		Untraced		*Graves* V, 1905–6, 27; *Morris and Roberts* 1998, 771
8.	1859	Oliver Cromwell	m	[Exhib RA, London, 1282]; untraced		*Graves* V, 1905–6, 27
9.	1860	Erinna		Holloway College, London	D	*Palgrave* 1866, 83; *Sparkes* 1891, 323, 324 (repr); *Graves* V, 1905–6, 27;
10.	1863	Go and sin no more, statuette		[Exhib RA, London, 1041]; untraced		*Palgrave* 1866, 38; *Graves* V, 1905–6, 27
11.	1863	The mother of Moses, statuette		[Exhib RA, London, 1038]; untraced		*Palgrave* 1866, 38; *Graves* V, 1905–6, 27
12.	1865	Athene repressing the fury of Achilles (Minerva repressing the wrath of Achilles)		[Nottingham Museum]; destroyed		*Graves* V, 1905–6, 27; *Gunnis* 1968, 238
13.	1866	Lot's wife, model		[Nottingham Museum]; destroyed		*Graves* V, 1905–6, 27; *Gunnis* 1968, 238
14.	1874	Wrecked		[Exhib RA, London, 1517]; untraced		*Sparkes* 1891, 323 (repr); *Graves* V, 1905–6, 27
15.	1881	Opportunity		[Exhib RA, London, 1482]; untraced		*Sparkes* 1891, 323 (repr); *Graves* V, 1905–6, 27
16.	nd	George, Lord Byron, design for a memorial		[Nottingham Museum]; destroyed		*Gunnis* 1968, 238

Busts

17.	1851	A J Scott		[Exhib RA, London, 1316]; untraced	*Graves* V, 1905–6, 27
18.	1852	Rev J Baldwin Brown BA		[Exhib RA, London, 1405]; untraced	*Graves* V, 1905–6, 27; *Morris and Roberts* 1998, 384
19.	1852	Rev J Leifchild DD		[Exhib RA, London, 1466]; untraced	*Graves* V, 1905–6, 27
20.	1856	Rev J Graham		[Exhib RA, London, 1305]; untraced	*Graves* V, 1905–6, 27
21.	1858	H Bidgood		[Exhib RA, London, 1212]; untraced	*Graves* V, 1905–6, 27
22.	1859	Oliver Cromwell		[Exhib RA, London, 1374]; untraced	*Graves* V, 1905–6, 27; *Morris and Roberts* 1998, 384
23.	1860	Prof A J Scott		[Exhib RA, London, 1013]; untraced	*Graves* V, 1905–6, 27
24.	1868	Rev Thomas Jones		[Exhib RA, London, 1194]; untraced Other versions: exhib RA, London, 1870, 1109	*Graves* V, 1905–6, 27
25.	1871	George Wilson RA	m	Manchester Town Hall, Lancs	*Graves* V, 1905–6, 27; *Read* 1982, 110, 112, 171 (repr)
26.	1871	Helen Macdonald		[Exhib RA, London, 1179]; untraced	*Graves* V, 1905–6, 27
27.	1873	H M Stanley		[Exhib RA, London, 1419]; untraced	*Graves* V, 1905–6, 27
28.	1876	J Bryce		[Exhib RA, London, 1480]; untraced	*Graves* V, 1905–6, 27
29.	1876	Jane Alexander	m	[Exhib RA, London, 1459]; untraced	*Graves* V, 1905–6, 27
30.	1876	Mrs W Danson		[Exhib RA, London, 1362]; untraced	*Gunnis* 1968, 238

Architectural Sculpture

31.	nd	Guards' memorial	Chelsea Hospital, London	*Sparkes* 1891, 322; *Gunnis* 1968, 238

Reliefs

32.	1845	Blessed are they that mourn	[Exhib RA, London, 1348]; untraced	*Graves* V, 1905–6, 27
33.	1882	Bacchus and Ariadne	[Exhib RA, London, 1636]; untraced	*Graves* V, 1905–6, 27

Miscellaneous

34.	1852	Bacchus awakening Ariadne	[Exhib RA, London, 1348]; untraced	*Graves* V, 1905–6, 27
35.	1854	Paolo and Francesca di Rimini	[Exhib RA, London, 1391]; untraced	*Graves* V, 1905–6, 27
36.	1859	'But Mary kept all these things, and pondered them in her heart'	[Exhib LSFA, Liverpool, 783]; untraced	*Graves* V, 1905–6, 27; *Morris and Roberts* 1998, 384
37.	1859	Dora	[Exhib RA, London, 1242]; untraced	*Graves* V, 1905–6, 27; *Morris and Roberts* 1998, 384
38.	1860	Paolo and Francesca	[Exhib RA, London, 952]; untraced	*Graves* V, 1905–6, 27
39.	1861	Don, a study	[Exhib RA, London, 1023]; untraced	*Graves* V, 1905–6, 27
40.	1861	The mother's last watch, a portrait	[Exhib RA, London, 1034]; untraced	*Graves* V, 1905–6, 27
41.	1865	Il pensiero	[Exhib RA, London, 912]; untraced	*Palgrave* 1866, 122; *Graves* V, 1905–6, 27
42.	1868	The dawn	[Exhib RA, London, 987]; untraced	*Graves* V, 1905–6, 27
43.	1869	Head and torso for a figure of Andromeda	[Exhib RA, London, 1230]; untraced	*Graves* V, 1905–6, 27
44.	nd	Jacob and the angel, model	Nottingham Museum	*Gunnis* 1968, 238

LEMOYNE, J B 1704–78

A Parisian sculptor, he carved portraits of the Duke and Duchess of Arygll when they were in Italy.

Busts

1.	post-1759	Elizabeth, wife of the 5th Duke of Argyll	Untraced	*Pearson* 1991, 45
2.	post-1759	John, 5th Duke of Argyll	Untraced	*Pearson* 1991, 45

LEQUINE, Claude François fl *c*1845

A plaster relief in the Corporation of London Collection is inscribed 'ALDERMAN MOON/ The Original in the possession of his Majesty Louis Phillippe King of the French./ Fr. Lequine ft. Londres 1845'.

Literary References: *Knight* 1986, 340

Reliefs

1.	1845	Alderman Moon	p	City of London Coll, acc 2222	*Knight* 1986, 340 (repr)

LESLIE, Robert ?1802–27

In the Protestant Cemetery at Rome is a tomb by **Thomas Campbell** commemorating Robert Leslie, a young Scottish sculptor who died there on 11 June 1827, aged nearly 25.

Archival Reference: GPC

LESOW (or LESSOW), William –1738

The son of Nicholas Lesow, of Wandswoth, a coppersmith, he was apprenticed to **Thomas Dunn** on 14 December 1716, becoming free in 1723. In 1734 he had a yard at 'the Bridgehouse' in Bermondsey. He was mason to St Thomas's Hospital from 1729 till his death in 1738, receiving £229 for the masonry of 'the new building' in 1734. His widow, Ursula, carried on the business until her death in 1741 (Hospital Archives in *Gunnis* 1968, 239). Lesow was employed in building work at Guy's Hospital at the time of his death.

Literary References: *Gunnis* 1968, 239; *Webb* 1999, 20

Archival References: GPC

LESTER, Edward, of Dorchester fl 1827–37?

In 1827 he was paid £26 for repairs to the 'County House', or Shire Hall, at Dorchester (Dorset County Archives in GPC).

Funerary Monuments

1.	?1827	Robert Pearson	Maiden Newton, Dorset	S	*Gunnis* 1968, 239
2.	?1830	Joseph Symes	Long Bredy, Dorset	S	*Gunnis* 1968, 239
3.	?1837	Rev Middleton Onslow	Bradford Peverell, Dorset	S	*Gunnis* 1968, 239

LEVEROTTI, G fl 1838

In 1838 his address was 45 Chapel Street, Lisson Grove, London.

Busts

1.	1838	A daughter of Lord Burghersh	m	[Exhib RA, London, 1360]; untraced	*Graves* V, 1905–6, 47

LEVERSUCH (or LEAVERSUCH), Richard fl 1725–32?

Known principally for his monument to Robert Pescod at Winchester (1), he was succeeded by his son, **Thomas Leversuch**. From 1709–15 he was one of the masons working for **William Townesend** on the chapel and kitchen at the Queen's College, Oxford. In 1719 a Richard Leaverett or Leveret received payments for work at the college. A large altar tomb at Bishops Waltham is signed 'W. Russell invenit, Leversuch, Winton, fecit' (3). At St John's, Winchester is a tablet to a Richard Leversuch who died in 1759 aged 67. No indication is given of his profession.

Literary References: *Gunnis* 1968, 239

Archival References: QCA Wm Townesend Accts II, hall and chapel, 1717–21, fols 10, 24); GPC

Funerary Monuments

1.	?1725	Robert Pescod	Winchester Cathedral, Hants		*Gunnis* 1968, 239
2.	†1730	William (†1727) and Grace Davies	Twyford, Hants	S	
3.	?1732	Unidentified subject	Bishops Waltham, Hants, churchyard	S	GPC

LEVERSUCH (or LEAVERSUCH), Thomas fl 1753–55

The son of **Richard Leversuch**, when he became bankrupt in 1755 he was described as 'of Fareham, Hants, stonemason' (*London Mag*, 1755, 301).

Literary References: *Gunnis* 1968, 239

Funerary Monuments

1.	†1753	Rev John Parke	Amport, Hants	S	GPC

LEWETT fl 1727?

His tablet to William Clarke at Warminster has an arched pediment, urn and flaming lamps.

Funerary Monuments

1.	?1727	William Clarke	Warminster, Wilts	S	*Gunnis* 1968, 239

LEWIS, John fl 1803

A sculptor and gilder of Lambs Buildings, Bunhill Row, in July 1803 he took as his apprentice Pierre Guillaume Schweyer of the Westminster French Protestant charity school.

Literary References: *le May* 2001, 571

LEWIS, John and family, of Gloucester and Cheltenham fl *c*1790–*c*1865

Although tablets by this firm 'are in no way outstanding in design, rarely showing anything more ambitious than the conventional figure of a mourning widow or a fluted semi-urn against a pyramid' (*Gunnis* 1968, 239) some have 'a certain charm' (*Potterton* 1975, 57). The monument to Rev Richard Buck is copied from a design by **John Flaxman** and that to Augusta Rossmore shows the depairing Lord Rossmore seated beside his wife's vacant chair (**70, 84**). Another at Cilycwm, is a 'fine work' with a mourning woman leaning on a broken pillar (*Dale-Jones and Lloyd* 1989, 51) (**100**).

Literary References: *Gunnis* 1968, 239

Funerary Monuments

1.	†1790	Lawrence Glover (†1790) and family	Northleach, Glos	S	Pevsner, *Glos: Cotswolds*, 1999, 514
2.	*c*1794	Naylor family member	St John, Northgate, Gloucester		RG/JP, 5, 828
3.	?1796	Richard Morgan	Lydney, Monmouths		*Gunnis* 1968, 239
4.	†1801	Cleaver Burland (by J Lewis, of Gloucester)	Bromsberrow, Glos	S	Pevsner, *Glos: Vale & Forest of Dean*, 1976, 116
5.	†1801	Richard Mytton (by G Lewis)	Guilsfield, Montgomery	S	Pevsner, *Powis*, 1979, 107
6.	?1802	Henry Parry	St Mary the Virgin, Monmouth		*Gunnis* 1968, 239
7.	†1803	John Humphreys (by G Lewis)	Fairford, Glos	S	Pevsner, *Glos: Cotswolds*, 1999, 368
8.	†1803	John Yarnton	Sapperton, Glos	S	Pevsner, *Glos: Cotswolds*, 1999, 591
9.	†1807	John Herbert (by C Lewis)	Kerry, Montgomery		Pevsner, *Powis*, 1979, 114
10.	†1807	Joseph Pearce	Staverton, Glos	S	Pevsner, *Glos: Vale & Forest of Dean*, 1976, 348
11.	†1807	Robert Pinckney	St Peter and St Paul, Marlborough, Wilts		RG/JP, 5, 828

No.	Date	Subject	Location		Reference
12.	†1808	Thomas Pearce (by J Lewis, of Gloucester)	Staverton, Glos	S	Pevsner, *Glos: Vale & Forest of Dean*, 1976, 348
13.	?1810	General Barnes	Queenhill, Worcs		*Gunnis* 1968, 239
14.	?1816	Francis and Elizabeth Choreley	Holy Trinity, Leeds, W R Yorks		GPC
15.	†1816	John Maggs (by G Lewis)	Winchcombe, Glos	S	Pevsner, *Glos: Cotswolds*, 1999, 729
16.	†1819	Richard Orlebar	Podington, Beds		*Gunnis* 1968, 239
17.	?1821	John Rose	St Mary the Virgin, Cheltenham, Glos		*Gunnis* 1968, 239
18.	†1821	Thomas de la Bere (by G Lewis)	Prestbury, Glos	S	Pevsner, *Glos: Vale & Forest of Dean*, 1976, 322
19.	?1822	Robert Phillips	Lugwardine, Herefs		*Gunnis* 1968, 239
20.	†1823	Colonel Thomas Ormsby	St Munchin, Limerick	S	*Potterton* 1975, 57
21.	†1823	Henry Campbell (by G Lewis)	St Mary, Charlton Kings, Glos		Pevsner, *Glos: Vale & Forest of Dean*, 1976, 120
22.	1823	Unidentified subject (by J Lewis, of Gloucester)	Christ Church, Gloucester		Pevsner, *Glos: Vale and Forest of Dean*, 1976, 230
23.	?1824	Peter Hunt	St Mary the Virgin, Cheltenham, Glos		*Gunnis* 1968, 239
24.	†1824	Thomas Philipps	Llangathen, Carmarthen		*Dale-Jones and Lloyd* 1989, 51
25.	c1825	Shekell family (by C Lewis, of Cheltenham)	Pebworth, Worcs		Pevsner, *Worcs*, 1968, 233
26.	†1826	John Jackson (by J Lewis)	Northleach, Glos	S	Pevsner, *Glos: Cotswolds*, 1999, 514
27.	†1827	Eliza Sproule (by G Lewis)	Holy Trinity, Cheltenham, Glos		RG/JP, 5, 827v
28.	†1827	Mary Christie (by G Lewis)	Prestbury, Glos	S	Pevsner, *Glos: Vale & Forest of Dean*, 1976, 322
29.	†1828	Benjamin Grisdale (by G Lewis)	Withington, Glos		Pevsner, *Glos: Cotswolds*, 1979, 484
30.	†1828	John Hincksman (by G Lewis)	Sevenhampton, Glos	S	Pevsner, *Glos: Cotswolds*, 1999, 597
31.	†1829	Dr Samuel Sproule (by G Lewis)	Holy Trinity, Cheltenham, Glos		RG/JP, 5, 827v
32.	†1829	Rev Charles Coxwell	Bibury, Glos	S	Pevsner, *Glos: Cotswolds*, 1999, 170
33.	†1830	Anne Orlebar	Podington, Beds	S	
34.	†1830	John Hornidge Green (by C Lewis)	Great Witcombe, Glos	S	
35.	1830	Robert Chaffey (by G Lewis)	Martock, Somerset	S	Pevsner, *Somerset: S & W*, 1958, 232
36.	†1831	Ann Westenra	Monaghan, Co Monaghan		*Potterton* 1975, 57
37.	†1831	Hon Robert Moore	Holy Trinity, Cheltenham, Glos		RG/JP, 5, 829
38.	c1832	Unidentified subjects, two neo-Greek tablets (by G Lewis)	Blockley, Glos		Pevsner, *Glos: Cotswolds*, 1979, 123
39.	†1833	Caroline Frobisher (by G Lewis)	Holy Trinity, Cheltenham, Glos		RG/JP, 5, 827v
40.	†1833	William Welch (†1833) (by C Lewis)	Dowdeswell, Glos	S	Pevsner, *Glos: Cotswolds*, 1999, 323
41.	†1834	Rosina Heyman (by G Lewis)	Holy Trinity, Cheltenham, Glos		RG/JP, 5, 827v
42.	†1835	Lieutenant-General George Prole	Holy Trinity, Cheltenham, Glos		RG/JP, 5, 829
43.	†1835	Thomas Gray (by C Lewis)	St Mary, Cheltenham, Glos		Pevsner, *Glos: Vale & Forest of Dean*, 1976, 126: *CIIA* 4/4/12 (repr)
44.	†1836	Colonel Augustus Warburton (by G Lewis, of Clarence Street, Cheltenham)	Holy Trinity, Cheltenham, Glos	S	Pevsner, *Glos: Vale & Forest of Dean*, 1976, 131
45.	†1838	Arthur Stephen Fryer (by C Lewis)	Coates, Glos	S	
46.	†1838	Commander Charles Timmins RN	Holy Trinity, Cheltenham, Glos		RG/JP, 5, 829
47.	†1838	Henrietta Ricketts (by G Lewis, of Cheltenham)	Swindon, Glos	S	Pevsner, *Glos: Vale & Forest of Dean*, 1976, 354
48.	†1838	Sarah Elliott (by G Lewis)	Swindon, Glos		Pevsner, *Glos: Vale & Forest of Dean*, 1976, 354
49.	†1838	Watkin Williams Massie (by G Lewis, of Clarence Street, Cheltenham)	Holy Trinity, Cheltenham, Glos	S	Pevsner, *Glos: Vale & Forest of Dean*, 1976, 131
50.	†1839	Caroline Lloyd	Llangadog, Carmarthen		*Dale-Jones and Lloyd* 1989, 51
51.	†1839	Elizabeth Robinson (by G Lewis)	Holy Trinity, Cheltenham, Glos		RG/JP, 5, 827v
52.	†1839	Sir William (†1834) and Lady Ann Hicks (by C or G Lewis)	Great Witcombe, Glos	S	Pevsner, *Glos: Vale & Forest of Dean*, 1976, 257
53.	†1839	William Proby	Seaton, Devon		RG/JP, 5, 828v
54.	†1840	Arthur Lewis	Monaghan, Co Monaghan		*Potterton* 1975, 57
55.	†1840	Major Thomas Billamore	Fladbury, Worcs	S	
56.	†1840	Rev Charles Evatt	Monaghan, Co Monaghan		*Potterton* 1975, 57
57.	†1841	Devereux Mytton (by G Lewis)	Guilsfield, Montgomery	S	Pevsner, *Powis*, 1979, 107
58.	†1841	Emily Carpenter	Wotton-under-Edge, Glos	S	*CIIA* 4/4/177 (repr); Pevsner, *Glos: Cotswolds*, 1999, 756
59.	†1841	Francis Paul Stratford (by G Lewis)	Farmcote, Glos	S	Pevsner, *Glos: Cotswolds*, 1999, 375
60.	†1841	Lieutenant Wenman Wynniatt	Guiting Power, Glos	S	Pevsner, *Glos: Cotswolds*, 1999, 395
61.	†1842	Emily Mellersh (by G Lewis)	Shipton Oliffe, Glos		Pevsner, *Glos: Cotswolds*, 1999, 400
62.	†1842	Jane Backhouse	Upper Slaughter, Glos	S	Pevsner, *Glos: Cotswolds*, 1999, 708
63.	†1842	Lydia and Mary Clunes	Holy Trinity, Cheltenham, Glos		RG/JP, 5, 829
64.	†1842	Mary Walker (by G Lewis)	Compton Abdale, Glos		Pevsner, *Glos: Cotswolds*, 1999, 201
65.	1842	Ruthetta Smithson	Holy Trinity, Leeds, W R Yorks		GPC
66.	†1844	Colonel George Knapton	Christ Church, Cork	S	*Potterton* 1975, 57
67.	†1844	Hon Mary Ann Gist (by G Lewis)	Wormington, Glos	S	Pevsner, *Glos: Vale & Forest of Dean*, 1976, 413

68.	1844	Unidentified subject (by G Lewis, of Cheltenham)	Christ Church, Gloucester		Pevsner, *Glos: Vale and Forest of Dean*, 1976, 230
69.	†1845	Emily Dryden	Broadwell, Glos	S	Pevsner, *Glos: Cotswolds*, 1999, 201
70.	†1845	Rev Richard Buck (by C Lewis, of Cheltenham, after a design by John Flaxman)	Poulton-le-Fylde, Lancs		*Gunnis* 1968, 239; Pevsner, *Lancs: N*, 1969, 192
71.	†1845	Samuel MacDowell	Monaghan, Co Monaghan		*Potterton* 1975, 57
72.	†1845	Thomas Hooper (by C L Lewis)	Elkstone, Glos	S	Pevsner, *Glos: Cotswolds*, 1999, 358
73.	†1846	John Lewes	Llangeler, Carmarthen		*Dale-Jones and Lloyd* 1989, 51
74.	†1846	William (†1844) and George Hetherington (by C Lewis)	St Mary, Birkenhead, Cheshire		Pevsner, *Cheshire*, 1971, 81
75.	†1847	Rev J Moseley (by G Lewis)	St Mary, Painswick, Glos	S	Pevsner, *Glos: Cotswolds*, 1999, 543
76.	†1847	Rev Samuel Montgomery (by G Lewis)	St Peter, Upper Gornal, Staffs		RG/JP, 5, 827v
77.	†1848	Ann Philipps	Llangathen, Carmarthen		*Dale-Jones and Lloyd* 1989, 51
78.	†1848	Elizabeth Home (by G Lewis)	Staverton, Glos	S	Pevsner, *Glos: Vale & Forest of Dean*, 1976, 348
79.	†1848	Joseph Durbin	Holy Trinity, Cheltenham, Glos		RG/JP, 5, 829
80.	†1848	Sir Maurice O'Connell	St James, King Street, Sydney, NSW		GPC
81.	†1848	Thomas Beck (by G Lewis)	Guilsfield, Montgomery		RG/JP, 5, 827v
82.	†1848	William Lewes	Llangeler, Carmarthen		*Dale-Jones and Lloyd* 1989, 51
83.	†1849	Celia, Ann and John Fereday (by G Lewis)	Sedgley, Staffs	S	RG/JP, 5, 828
84.	†1850	Augusta, 2nd Lady Rossmore	Monaghan, Co Monaghan		*Potterton* 1975, 57, 67 (repr)
85.	*c*1850	Unidentified subjects, several (by G Lewis, of Cheltenham)	Wolstone, Glos		Pevsner, *Glos: Vale and Forest of Dean*, 1976, 412
86.	*c*1851	Dorothy Freeman (†1818) and sisters (by G Lewis)	St Peter, Winchcombe, Glos	S	Pevsner, *Glos: Cotswolds*, 1999, 729
87.	†1851	James Barker (by C Lewis, of Cheltenham)	Severn Stoke, Worcs		Pevsner, *Worcs*, 1968, 259
88.	†1854	Mary Milbourne Swinnerton (by G Lewis & Co, of Cheltenham)	St Thomas, Butterton, Staffs		Pevsner, *Staffs*, 1974, 92
89.	†1855	Charles Proby (by G Lewis)	Seaton, Devon		RG/JP, 5, 827v
90.	†1855	E H Webb	St Mary, Donnington, Herefs		Pevsner, *Herefs*, 1963, 115
91.	†1855	Sir George Robinson	Dyrham, Glos	S	Pevsner, *Glos: Cotswolds*, 1999, 341
92.	†1855	Sir William Pilkington (by G Lewis & Co, of Cheltenham)	St Thomas, Butterton, Staffs		Pevsner, *Staffs*, 1974, 92
93.	†1857	Emily (†1842) and Isabella Peachey	Shipton Oliffe, Glos	S	Pevsner, *Glos: Cotswolds*, 1999, 607
94.	†1857	William Henry Baldwyn (by C Lewis)	Ashton-under-Hill, Worcs	S	
95.	†1858	Elizabeth Baker (by G Lewis)	St Michael, Dowdeswell, Glos	S	Pevsner, *Glos: Cotswolds*, 1999, 323
96.	†1859	Charles Greenaway (by G Lewis)	Little Barrington, Glos	S	Pevsner, *Glos: Cotswolds*, 1999, 449
97.	†1860	Anne Jones (by Lewis and Son, of Cheltenham)	Leigh, Glos		Pevsner, *Glos: Vale and Forest of Dean*, 1976, 252
98.	1861	Charlotte Walker (by G Lewis)	Farmington, Glos		Pevsner, *Glos: Cotswolds*, 1999, 252
99.	†1861	General Edward Showers	Holy Trinity, Cheltenham, Glos		RG/JP, 5, 829
100.	1862	Daniel (†1847) and Ann Jones	Cilycwm, Carmarthen		*Dale-Jones and Lloyd* 1989, 42, 51
101.	†1862	John, Katharine (†1833) and John (†1833) Mills (by C Lewis)	Miserden, Glos	S	
102.	†1865	Eliza Lewes	Llangeler, Carmarthen		*Dale-Jones and Lloyd* 1989, 51
103.	nd	Unidentified subject, tablet	St James, Trowbridge, Wilts		Pevsner, *Wilts*, 1975, 533
104.	nd	Unidentified subjects, several (by G Lewis)	Elmstone Hardwicke, Glos		Pevsner, *Glos: Vale and Forest of Dean*, 1976, 182
105.	nd	Unidentified subjects, several tablets	Christ Church, Malvern Road, Cheltenham		Pevsner, *Glos: Vale and Forest of Dean*, 1976, 128
106.	nd	Unidentified subjects, several tablets (by G Lewis, of Cheltenham)	St James, Suffolk Square, Cheltenham		Pevsner, *Glos: Vale and Forest of Dean*, 1976, 129
Architectural Sculpture					
107.	?1847	Column commemorating of the British forces in India (by Mr Lewis of Cheltenham)	Southam, Glos		*Builder*, 1847, 29

LEY, of Bristol fl *c*1810

His only known work is a monument with a 'well-carved arrangement of sword, guns and spears in small scale' (*Dale-Jones and Lloyd*, 1989, 52) (**1**).

Funerary Monuments

1.	†1808	Captain Thomas Edwards	Llangathen, Carmarthen	*Dale-Jones and Lloyd* 1989, 52

LEYLAND, Joseph Bentley, of Halifax 1811–51

He was born in Halifax in the West Riding on 31 March, 1811, the second son of Roberts Leyland, a bookseller, publisher and naturalist, and his wife Susannah Bentley. He was educated at the school kept by his uncle and grandfather in Wade Street, Halifax, and in his later teens attended drawing classes at the Mechanics' Institute. At the age of 16 he began modelling, and attracted the attention of a wealthy collector, Christopher Rawson of Hope Hall, Halifax, who allowed him to study his collection of ancient Greek marbles.

In 1831 Leyland exhibited a model, *An Italian greyhound*, at the Royal Manchester Institution, and the following year he showed a statue of *Spartacus* at the same venue (**15, 17**). These were followed by a colossal head of *Satan*, sent to the Royal Northern Society in Leeds (**28**). They works were well received and, encouraged by this success, Leyland moved to London in 1834. There he lodged with the Bradford engraver William Overend Geller and worked in a studio in Queen Street, off Oxford Street. Through his friend and patron, the portrait painter T H Illidge, he met **Francis Chantrey** and **Richard Westmacott** and he studied anatomy with the painter B R Haydon, who promoted his work.

Leyland enjoyed some success in London, receiving consistently favourable notices in the press, particularly for *Warrior listening to a prior reading* and *English greyhounds* (**18, 16**). His most famous work was the group, *African bloodhounds* (**21**), which Edwin Landseer considered 'the noblest modern work of its kind' (*DNB*). It was presented to Peel Park Museum, Salford, together with a *Thracian falconer* (**22**), after the sculptor's death, but both were subsequently destroyed.

In 1838 he returned to Halifax, where he largely abandoned the ambitious ideal subjects which had dominated his early career but had not proved profitable, and concentrated increasingly on church monuments and ornamental sculpture. His most important monumental commission was the recumbent effigy of Stephen Beckwith in York Minster (**7**). During this period Leyland formed a close friendship with the writer and artist Patrick Branwell Brontë and today he is chiefly remembered for the Brontë family connection.

Leyland's later years were blighted by his heavy drinking, debts and ill-health. He had difficulties in completing commissions and frequently quarrelled with clients. Mary Leyland described him as, 'self-opinionated, sarcastic, and unreliable, scornful of religion and of anyone who disagreed with him, only working when the spirit moved him' (*Leyland* 1954, 37). However, his friends considered him good natured and generous, with a remarkable, though largely unfulfilled, talent. He was arrested for debt in 1850 and sent to Manor gaol in Halifax, where he remained until he died of dropsy on 28 January 1851. He was buried three days later in the Salem Chapel churchyard in Halifax.

Literary References: *AJ*, 1851, 140; *DNB* (Cust); *Leyland* 1954, 29–48; *Leyland* 1963, 91–107; *Gunnis* 1968, 239–40; *ODNB* (Greenwood)

Additional MS Sources: Leyland MSS

Funerary Monuments

1.	1838	Christopher Rawson and wife		Holy Trinity, Halifax, W R Yorks		*Leyland* 1954, 39
2.	1838	John Rawson and wife		Holy Trinity, Halifax, W R Yorks	S	*Leyland* 1954, 39; *ODNB*
3.	†1841	Dr George Birkbeck (co-sculptor: Bromley)		Giggleswick, W R Yorks		Pevsner, *Yorks: W R*, 1967, 217
4.	1842	Dr Thomas Andrew		Haworth, W R Yorks		*Leyland* 1954, 40
5.	?1843	James Fawthorpe		Thornton, W R Yorks		*Gunnis* 1968, 239–40
6.	c1845	Alfred Camm		St Martin, Brighouse, W R Yorks		*Leyland* 1954, 40
7.	1845	Dr Stephen Beckwith (†1843)		York Minster, north choir aisle (formerly north transept)	S	*Aylmer* 1977, 467, 469
8.	c1845	Rev John Murray (†1842) Payment(s): £68		St John, Halifax, W R Yorks		*Leyland* 1954, 40
9.	1845	Rev William Weightman		Howarth, W R Yorks		*Leyland* 1954, 40
10.	1847	Bishop Ferrar		St John, Halifax, W R Yorks	S	*Leyland* 1954, 40; *ODNB*
11.	nd	Dan Holgate Sugden		[St John, Halifax, W R Yorks]; destroyed (1926)		*Leyland* 1954, 43
12.	nd	J H Beswicke		Holy Trinity, Littleborough, Lancs		*Leyland* 1954, 43
13.	nd	Joseph Midgley and family		Haworth, W R Yorks		*Leyland* 1954, 40
14.	nd	William Haworth		St Martin, Brighouse, W R Yorks		*Leyland* 1954, 43

Statues

15.	1831	An Italian greyhound, model		[Exhib Royal Manchester Institution]; untraced		*ODNB*
16.	1834	English greyhounds		[Exhib Soc of BA, London, 866]; untraced		*Johnson* 1975, 284; *ODNB*
17.	1834	Spartacus		[Exhib Royal Manchester Institution]; untraced		*ODNB*
18.	c1834	Warrior listening to a prior reading		Untraced		*Leyland* 1954, 38; *ODNB*
19.	c1835	Greyhounds		[coll Thomas Illidge]; untraced		*Leyland* 1954, 38; GPC
20.	1835	Kilmeny		[coll Halifax Literary and Philosophical Society]; destroyed		*Leyland* 1954, 38; *ODNB*
21.	1837	African bloodhounds		[Salford AG, Lancs]; destroyed		*Leyland* 1954, 38–9; *ODNB*
22.	c1838	Thracian falcolner (also known as Anglo Saxon chief; the listener; Goliath and Hercules)	pm	[Salford AG, Lancs]; destroyed Other versions: The Hollins, Warley, W R Yorks, cast iron		*AJ*, 1851, 140; *Leyland* 1954, 44; *ODNB*
23.	1839	The lady of Kirklees		[Exhib Sowerby Bridge, W R Yorks]; untraced		*Leyland* 1954, 39
24.	c1840	Theseus		Untraced		*Leyland* 1954, 39
25.	c1840	Warriors		[Exhib Manchester; purchased by Lord Ribblesdale, and broken in transit from the exhibition]; destroyed		*AJ*, 1851, 140; *Leyland* 1954, 40

Busts

26.	1827	Unidentified veteran soldier, model		Untraced		*Leyland* 1954, 38
27.	1830	Rev William Turner	p	Northgate End Chapel, Halifax, W R Yorks, Schoolroom		*Leyland* 1954, 38
28.	1834	Satan		[Exhib North Soc, Leeds]; untraced		*Leyland* 1954, 38; *ODNB*
29.	1845	Dr Stephen Beckwith		Yorkshire Museum, York Other versions: York Dispensary		*Leyland* 1954, 43, in GPC
30.	nd	Dan Holgate Sugden		Literary and Philosophical Society, Halifax, W R Yorks		*Leyland* 1954, 43
31.	nd	Mrs Sunderland, the Yorkshire queen of song		Literary and Philosophical Society, Halifax, W R Yorks		*Leyland* 1954, 43

Architectural Sculpture

32.	nd	Bosses		Oxenhope, W R Yorks		*Leyland* 1954, 43

Reliefs

33.	1846	Patrick Branwell Brontë	p	Brontë Parsonage Museum, Haworth, W R Yorks		*Leyland* 1954, 40–1; *ODNB*
34.	nd	An African greyhound	m	Brontë Parsonage Museum, Haworth, W R Yorks	S	
35.	nd	Thomas Illidge (portrait medallion)		[coll Thomas Illidge]; untraced		*Leyland* 1963, 106–7

Miscellaneous

36.	*c*1845	Dr George Birkbeck, 'monument'		Mechanics Institute, Settle, N R Yorks		*Leyland* 1954, 40

LIGHTFOOT fl 1763

He is Listed as a 'Carver. Opposite St George's Church, Southwark' in *Mortimer*, 1763, 17.

LINCOLN, Samuel fl 1793

An advertisement in the *Norfolk Chronicle* on 28 September 1793 announced that Samuel Lincoln, stone-mason, of St Andrew's, Bridge Street, had taken over the stock and premises of **John Dobson**.

LINDSEY, James fl 1763

A mason of Bishopsgate-street, London (*Mortimer* 1763, 49).

LINES, Edward fl 1827–29

The brother of **W R Lines**.

Literary References: *Gunnis* 1968, 240

Statues

1.	1827	Eve	[Exhib Birmingham Soc of A]; untraced	*Gunnis* 1968, 240
2.	1829	Musidora	[Exhib Birmingham Soc of A]; untraced	*Gunnis* 1968, 240

LINES, W R, of Birmingham 1801–46

Lines was the second son of Samuel Lines (1778–1863), a Birmingham artist and drawing-master. He exhibited sculpture at the Birmingham Society of Artists in 1827 and 1829 (1–3). He died on 27 July 1846 (*Birmingham Gaz*, 3 Aug 1846).

Literary References: *Gunnis* 1968, 240

Statues

1.	1827	Belisarius	[Exhib Soc of A, Birmingham]; untraced	*Gunnis* 1968, 240

Busts

2.	1829	An infant son of Mr Rice Harris	[Exhib Soc of A, Birmingham]; untraced	*Gunnis* 1968, 240
3.	1829	Thomas Hill	[Exhib Soc of A, Birmingham]; untraced	*Gunnis* 1968, 240

LINNELL, John 1792–1882

John Linnell, the painter, was awarded a prize for sculpture at the Royal Academy Schools in 1810. Story relates 'The question was raised among the students as to whether the sculptors could draw as well as the painters, or the painters model as well as the sculptors. Our artist was chosen to compete with **Thomas Wyon**, the medallist, in modelling in bas-relief a back-view from life . . . and Linnell came off in triumph, beating the sculptor on his own ground' (*Story* I, 1892, 50–1). The model was still with the artist's family in 1892.

LINNELL, William and John fl 1739–1810

The well-known Georgian cabinet-makers were responsible for a considerable amount of decorative carving. William Linnell (*c*1703–1764) was trained as a carver and *c*1730 he set up a business based which later expanded into cabinet making and upholstery. After his death he was succeeded by his son, John Linnell (1729–1796), who became one of the leading cabinet-makers of the period. Commissions for carved work, particularly frames, overmantles and girandoles, constituted an important part of the firm's work during the 1770s and 1780s.

Literary References: *Hayward and Kirkham* 1980, *passim*

Chimneypieces

1.	*c*1749	Several		[Oakley House, Beds]; untraced	*Hayward and Kirkham* 1980, 19
2.	*c*1750	Several, including one with a pedimented overmantle with an eagle		Woburn Abbey, Beds	*Hayward and Kirkham* 1980, 19, 72 (colour pl 1)
3.	1758–1759	Several, including one 'in the French taste with a lions face in the frieze'		Croome Court, Worcs	*Hayward and Kirkham* 1980, 61, 104, 150
4.	*c*1764	Elaborate rococo, with overmantel		Osterley Park, London, Mrs Child's dressing room	*Kirkham and Hayward* 1980, 62, 117 (reprs 27, 128)
5.	1763–1765	Six of carved wood		[Bowood, Wilts, bedrooms]; demol	*Hayward and Kirkham* 1980, 123–4
6.	1776	Overmantle mirror		Dyrham Park, Glos	*Hayward and Kirkham* 1980, 91 (reps 132, 133)

Architectural Sculpture

7.	1739–1745	Frames, consoles, brackets, cornices, mouldings and other carvings	wd	[for Richard Hoare]; untraced	*Hayward and Kirkham* 1980, 16–17, 72
8.	1745–1747	Architectural mouldings and structural features	wd	Radcliffe Library, Oxford	*Friedman* 1984, 250, 320
9.	1749	Carved ornaments, including two dragons for the handrails at the entrance	wd	[Chinese house, Woburn Abbey, Beds]; destroyed	*Hayward and Kirkham* 1980, 19–20
10.	*c*1749	Ornaments and frames	wd	[Oakley house, Beds]; untraced	*Hayward and Kirkham* 1980, 19
11.	1749–1752	Friezes, mouldings, frames, doorcases and other carving	wd	Woburn Abbey, Beds	*Hayward and Kirkham* 1980, 18–19

12.	1758–1759	Mouldings and other carved ornaments	wd	Croome Court, Worcs	*Hayward and Kirkham* 1980, 104
13.	1763–1765	Doorcases, mouldings and balustrading	wd	[Bowood, Wilts]; demol	*Hayward and Kirkham* 1980, 123
Reliefs					
14.	1810	Academy figure, model		[RA silver medal]; untraced	RA Premium list; *Story* 1892, 50–1

LINTON, William, of Norwich fl 1675–c1719

Nothing is known of his origins or training. On 22 June 1675 in Norwich he married Ursula Wright. She died in 1679, being buried on 22 December. On her floor slab, presumed to be William's work (2), he is described as a sculptor. The Offley monument (1) is suggestive of a working visit by him to London in 1680(?) involving a link of some kind with William Stanton, a design by whom was used for that monument. By 1681 Linton had a new wife, Elizabeth, and was presumably back in Norwich, where two of their children were baptised, Elizabeth in 1681 and John in 1683. A further child of one of William's marriages, also William, was buried in 1685. A land indenture of 1688 (Norfolk Record Office, AG 87, 233X3) names 'William Lynton of Norwich, carver'.

In addition to authenticated works, listed below, a number of late 17th and early 18th-century Norfolk church monuments are attributable to Linton on grounds of style. His works outside London provide stylistic confirmation that 'W. Linton' who signs the Offley monument and William Linton of Norwich are one and the same. Characteristic of Linton are wall monuments with convex inscription tablets, pilasters, side scrolls, and foliate aprons incorporating skulls and bones. The attributed monument to John Greene, +1684, at East Bradenham, Norfolk, includes two indifferent busts. The workmanship of the Offley monument does not match the quality of its design which is due to Stanton.

Jon Bayliss, Geoffrey Fisher

Funerary Monuments					
1.	† to 1678	John Offley and family Drawing(s): VAM D.1132-1898 by William Stanton	St Pancras old parish church, London	S	Pevsner, *London: N*, 1998, 348
2.	†1679	Ursula Linton (floor slab)	St Etheldreda, Norwich, Norfolk		GF
3.	†1685	Anthony Sparrow	Bishop's Palace chapel, Norwich, Norfolk	S	*Gunnis* 1968, 240
4.	1680–1690	Edmond Hobart (†1666)	Holt, Norfolk	S	Pevsner, *Norfolk: N-E & Norwich*, 1997, 555
5.	†1719	Elizabeth Scrope	Lincoln Cathedral	S	Pevsner, *Lincs*, 1989, 479
6.	nd	John Hall	[St Nicholas, Yarmouth, Hants]; destroyed	S	*Gunnis* 1968, 240

LISSEMORE –1773

In November 1773 *The London Magazine* announced the death of 'Mr. Lissemore, an eminent Stone-Cutter and Master-Builder, possessed of an estate of £1,500 per Ann' (p 587).

Archival References: GPC

LITANEER, Charles fl 1757

On 18 February 1757 the Berwick-upon-Tweed works committee 'Called before them Mr. Charles Litaneer the carver and endeavoured to know from him the lowest price he could carve the Town Arms upon stone and also upon wood' for the town hall. Just over a month later his model was rejected and **Christopher Richardson** was appointed to carry out the work (Guildbook, 18 February, 22 March 1757, in *Gunnis* 1968, 320).

LITTLE, J S fl 1843

He exhibited at the Royal Academy in 1843 from 14 Gloucester Road, London.

Busts				
1.	1843	Tyrone Power	[Exhib RA, London, 1380]; untraced	*Graves* V, 1905–6, 72

LOADMAN, Mark, of London fl 1761–72

He received nearly £4,000 for mason's work at Audley End between 1761 and 1767, a sum which included £855 for building the bridge in 1763 (Essex Records, D/DBY.243 in *Gunnis* 1968, 240). He was declared bankrupt in 1772, when his address was Lamb's Conduit Street, Holborn (*London Mag*, vol 41, 1772, 346).

Literary References: *Gunnis* 1968, 240

LOBB, Joel fl 1691–92

He was working on woodcarving at Chatsworth under **Thomas Young** and **Samuel Watson** by 1691 and again in 1692, when he agreed with **William Davis** and Watson to carve ornaments in limewood for the great chamber. Like the others he was influenced by Gibbons's work in limewood.

Literary References: *Green* 1964 (1), 119, 120–3

Archival References: Chatsworth Building Accts, 1687–94, 79–81

LOCATELLI, Giovanni Battista 1734–1805

Locatelli was born on 17 November 1734 in San Tommaso Cantauriense, Verona, the son of Giovanni Antonio Locatelli. He trained in the studio of GA Finali, and his earliest known works are statues of *Faith* and *Charity* for the Madonna del Popolo Chapel in Verona Cathedral, executed in 1756. Locatelli subsequently worked in Venice, where he received patronage from English travellers. He appears to have come to the attention of Sir Robert Strange, the British Resident in Venice, amongst whose papers is a receipt for a work by Locatelli (17). The sculptor also worked in Milan, where, by his own account, he was employed by Count Firmin, M Tilot and Cardinal Crescenzi and also executed upwards of 70 statues and groups for the Battoni brothers. In 1777 he carved a statue in the mannerist style of the 13th century astrologer, Pietro d'Abano for the Prato delle Valle, Padua.

By 1778 Locatelli was in England, where, according to JT Smith, he first lodged with **JCF Rossi**'s father in the Haymarket, though the catalogue of the Royal Academy exhibition for that year gives his address as 9 Bentinck Street, Soho. His submission in 1779, a Venus on a couch, was probably the model for the *Reclining Venus* now at

Lochée also provided the models for 10 cameos produced in paste by James Tassie. These are listed in R E Raspe's descriptive catalogue of Tassie's works, published in 1791. They include several subjects that Lochée had previously modelled for Wedgwood, including Count O'Kelly, Mrs Barwell, and the Princess de Lamballe (**15, 38, 40**).

His abilities extended beyond small-scale wax portraiture. Between 1788 and 1790 he exhibited six busts at the Royal Academy. In 1787 he carved a marble portrait of the Duke of York and Albany, with ermine, sash and lace cravat (**5**). This was the subject in two contemporary prints, a medium that Lochée also utilised to publicise his bust of the Duke of Clarence in 1788 (**8**). His bust of Sir William Herschel, commissioned by Sir William Watson and taken from a plaster life-mask, was exhibited at the Royal Academy in 1788 (**9**), and the bust of the playwright R B Sheridan, 1790 (**14**), was engraved in 1794. Busts of Sheridan, thought to be by the sculptor, are in the royal collection, the Victoria and Albert Museum, Harrow School and Pittsburgh Museum of Art.

In 1789 Lochée was awarded a silver medallion by the Society of Arts for his bust of George, Prince of Wales (**11**). This was engraved by Sharp as the frontispiece for volume 10 of the Society's *Transactions* in 1792, and shows the prince in cravat and full wig, his torso decorated with star and medal. Curiously the extant marble version lacks some of these embellishments and, as it is inscribed 'Logee', it is possible that this is a later copy.

Despite these apparent successes Lochée was declared bankrupt in March 1791 (*Univ Mag* 1791, 238). There appear to be no further records of his artistic activities in England.

MGS

Literary References: RSA, *Transactions*, vol 2, 1784, 126; vol 8, 1790, 231; vol 10, 1792, frontispiece; *Graves* V, 1905–6, 79; *Gunnis* 1968, 241; *Hodgkinson* 1969, 152–160; *Pyke* 1973, 80–1; *Bindman* 1979, 68; *Pyke* 1981, 25–6

Archival References: RA Premium list; Wedgwood/Lochée

No.	Date	Subject		Location	References
Statues					
1.	1775	'An Infant Representing Statuary', cast, 5 feet or more in height		[Soc of A, premium, 30 gns]; untraced	*Dossie* 1782, 439; RSA, *Transactions*, vol 2, 1784, 126
Busts					
2.	1776	A boy		[Exhib RA, London, 172]; untraced	*Graves* V, 1905–6, 79
3.	1776	Unidentified gentleman		[Exhib RA, London, 171]; untraced	*Graves* V, 1905–6, 79
4.	1785	'Portrait of a lady'		[Exhib RA, London, 358]; untraced	*Graves* V, 1905–6, 79
5.	1787	Frederick-Augustus, Duke of York and Albany	m	Windsor Castle, RCIN 31624 Other versions: plaster, coll Lord Sherwood, on loan to the Brighton Pavilion	*Gunnis* 1968, 241; *Hodgkinson* 1969, 154 (repr)
6.	1787	Prince Charles of Mecklenburg		[Exhib RA, London, 631]; untraced	*Graves* V, 1905–6, 79
7.	1787	Prince Edward		[Exhib RA, London, 642]; untraced	*Graves* V, 1905–6, 79
8.	1787	Prince William Henry, Duke of Clarence Payment(s): 10 gns Model(s): ?Exhib RA, London, 1786, 302	w	[for George, Prince of Wales]; untraced	*Hodgkinson* 1969, 152, 155
9.	1787	Sir William Herschel	p	[Exhib RA, London, 1788, 653]; NPG, London 4055	*Graves* V, 1905–6, 79; *Hodgkinson* 1969, 155 (repr); GPC
10.	1788	Admiral Lord Hood		[Exhib RA, London, 643]; ?Loders Court, Bridport	*Graves* V, 1905–6, 79; *Hodgkinson* 1969, 156
11.	1789	George, Prince of Wales	m	[Soc of A, silver medallion]; Wildenstein and Company, Paris Other versions: cast, Great Room, RSA, 1789	RSA, *Transactions*, vol 8, 1790, 231; vol 10, 1792 (frontispiece repr); *Graves* V, 1905–6, 79; *Gunnis* 1968, 241; *Hodgkinson* 1969, 157–8 (repr)
12.	1789	Unidentified gentleman		[Exhib RA, London, 579]; untraced	*Graves* V, 1905–6, 79
13.	1789	Unidentified gentleman		[Exhib RA, London, 614]; untraced	*Graves* V, 1905–6, 79
14.	1790	Richard Brinsley Sheridan (†1816)		[Exhib RA, London, 547]; untraced	*Graves* V, 1905–6, 79; *Hodgkinson* 1969, 156; *Bilbey* 2002, 94
15.	nd	Count O'Kelly (modelled for Wedgwood)		Untraced	*Gunnis* 1968, 241
16.	nd	Mrs Barwell (modelled for Wedgwood)		Untraced	*Gunnis* 1968, 241
17.	nd	Princesse de Lamballe (modelled for Wedgwood)		Untraced	*Gunnis* 1968, 241
Reliefs					
18.	1787	Admiral Lord Hood (medallion portrait, modelled for Wedgwood)		Untraced	*Gunnis* 1968, 241
19.	1787	Count Pinto, Portuguese Ambassador (medallion portrait, modelled for Wedgwood)		Untraced	*Gunnis* 1968, 241
20.	1787	Dr Denman 'the famous midwife' (medallion portrait, modelled for Wedgwood)		Untraced	*Gunnis* 1968, 241
21.	1787	Duke of Brunswick (medallion portrait, modelled for Wedgwood)		Untraced	*Gunnis* 1968, 241
22.	1787	Duke of York, cameo mounted in gold Payment(s): £3 13s 6d		[for George, Prince of Wales]; untraced	*Hodgkinson* 1969, 152
23.	1787	George, 1st Marquis of Buckingham (medallion portrait, modelled for Wedgwood)		Untraced	*Gunnis* 1968, 241; *Bindman* 1979, 68 (Wedgwood repr)

24.	1787	Hon Keith Elphinstone (medallion portrait, modelled for Wedgwood)		Untraced		*Gunnis* 1968, 241
25.	1787	King William IV (medallion portrait, modelled for Wedgwood)		Wedgwood Museum, Barlaston		*Ormond* 1973, 510
26.	1787	Mary, Marchioness of Buckingham (medallion portrait, modelled for Wedgwood)		Untraced		*Gunnis* 1968, 241; *Bindman* 1979, 68 (Wedgwood repr)
27.	1787	Dennis O'Kelly (medallion portrait, modelled for Wedgwood)		Untraced		*Gunnis* 1968, 241
28.	1787	Prince Adolphus Frederick Duke of Cambridge (medallion portrait, modelled for Wedgwood)		Untraced		*Gunnis* 1968, 241
29.	1787	Prince Augustus Frederick, Duke of Sussex (medallion portrait, modelled for Wedgwood)		Untraced		*Gunnis* 1968, 241
30.	1787	Prince Ernest Augustus, Duke of Cumberland (medallion portrait, modelled for Wedgwood)		Untraced		*Gunnis* 1968, 241
31.	1787	Princess de Ligne (medallion portrait, modelled for Wedgwood)		Untraced		*Gunnis* 1968, 241
32.	1787	William Pitt the Younger (medallion portrait, modelled for Wedgwood)		Untraced		*Gunnis* 1968, 241; *Bindman* 1979, 68 (repr Wedgwood)
33.	1789	Unidentified sitter	w	Christie 5 Sept 1976, lot 40	SD	*Pyke* 1981, 26
34.	by 1791	Count O'Kelly (modelled for James Tassie)		Untraced		*Tassie* 1791, 746; *Hodgkinson* 1969, 159
35.	by 1791	Count Pinto, Portuguese Ambassador (modelled for James Tassie)		Untraced		*Tassie* 1791, 747; *Hodgkinson* 1969, 159
36.	by 1791	Duke of York (modelled for James Tassie)		Untraced		*Hodgkinson* 1969, 159
37.	by 1791	George, Prince of Wales (modelled for a cameo by James Tassie)		Untraced		*Tassie* 1791, 736; *Hodgkinson* 1969, 159
38.	by 1791	Mrs Barwell (modelled for James Tassie)		Untraced		*Tassie* 1791, 738; *Hodgkinson* 1969, 159
39.	by 1791	Prince William Henry, Duke of Clarence (two), (modelled for a cameo by James Tassie)		Untraced		*Tassie* 1791, 736; *Hodgkinson* 1969, 159
40.	by 1791	Princesse de Lamballe (modelled for James Tassie)		Untraced		*Tassie* 1791, 744; *Hodgkinson* 1969, 159
41.	by 1791	Sarah Siddons (modelled for James Tassie)		Untraced		*Tassie* 1791, 749; *Hodgkinson* 1969, 159
42.	by 1791	Unidentified female 'in the head-dress of the present times' (modelled for James Tassie)		Untraced		*Tassie* 1791, 760; *Hodgkinson* 1969, 159
43.	nd	Frederick Augustus, Duke of York	w	BM		*Hodgkinson* 1969, 154, 159 (repr)
44.	nd	George, Prince of Wales	w	BM		*Hodgkinson* 1969, 152, 153, 159 (repr)
45.	nd	Henry, 2nd Earl Bathurst	w	Sotheby, 25 July 1977, lot 4		*Pyke* 1981, 25
46.	nd	King George III	w	BM		*Hodgkinson* 1969, 159
47.	nd	Prince Adolphus Frederick, Duke of Cambridge	w	BM		*Hodgkinson* 1969, 159
48.	nd	Prince Augustus Frederick, Duke of Sussex	w	BM		*Hodgkinson* 1969, 159; *Pyke* 1973, 81 (repr pl 175)
49.	nd	Prince Charles de Ligne	w	Sotheby, 27 May 1975, lot 35		*Pyke* 1981, 25
50.	nd	Prince Edward Augustus, Duke of Kent	w	BM		*Hodgkinson* 1969, 152, 153, 159 (repr)
51.	nd	Prince Ernest Augustus, Duke of Cumberland		BM		*Hodgkinson* 1969, 159
52.	nd	Prince William Henry, Duke of Clarence Model(s): ?Exhib RA, London, 1786, 302	w	BM		*Graves* V, 1905–6, 79; *Hodgkinson* 1969, 152, 153, 159 (repr)
53.	nd	Unidentified male sitter	w	VAM (A.56-1930)		*Hodgkinson* 1969, 153; *Bilbey* 2002, 94
54.	nd	Unidentified man	w	Phillips, 8 July 1975, lot 35		*Pyke* 1981, 26
55.	nd	Unidentified sitters (two)	w	Christie, 16 Sept 1973, lot 19		*Pyke* 1981, 26
Miscellaneous						
56.	1772	An academy figure or a bas-relief		[RA, London, silver medal]; untraced		RA Premium list
57.	1785	Admiral Lord Hood, model		[Exhib RA, London, 493]; untraced		*Graves* V, 1905–6, 79
58.	1785	'Portrait of a gentleman'		[Exhib RA, London, 355]; untraced		*Graves* V, 1905–6, 79
59.	1785	'Portrait of a gentleman'		[Exhib RA, London, 356]; untraced		*Graves* V, 1905–6, 79
60.	1787	George, Prince of Wales, original model Payment(s): £6 12s	w	[for George Prince of Wales]; untraced Other versions: For George, Prince of Wales, copy, wax, 4 gns; untraced		*Hodgkinson* 1969, 152

61.	1787	Models of the Royal Princes Payment(s): £29 8s		[for George, Prince of Wales]; untraced	*Hodgkinson* 1969, 152
62.	1787	Prince Charles de Ligne		[Exhib RA, London, 634]; untraced	*Graves* V, 1905–6, 79
63.	1788	Portrait of a clergyman		[Exhib RA, London, 618]; untraced	*Graves* V, 1905–6, 79
64.	nd	Thomas Baldwin	w	Sotheby, 4 March 1958, untraced	GPC

LOCK, J, of Abingdon fl *c*1822

Funerary Monuments

1.	*c*1822	Davis family	Radley, Berks	S	Pevsner, *Berks*, 1966, 196

LOCK, of Norwich fl 1761

He was a carver and gilder of St Andrew's, Norwich. On 26 September 1761 his foreman, **John Woons** announced that he had set up 'on his own account'.

Literary References: RG/JP, 5, 834v

LOCKWOOD, Joseph, of Doncaster 1759–1837

He became a freeman of Doncaster on 21 November 1794, on payment of 20 guineas. In 1807 he was elected to the town council and he was later twice elected mayor (Corporation Archives in *Gunnis* 1968, 241). He died on 14 February 1837. His son, also Joseph, became a freeman of Doncaster on 5 January, 1808. Gunnis notes that most of his tablets are neo-Hellenic in design and that the Samuel Tooker has a relief of fasces (*Gunnis* 1968, 241) (**4**).

Literary References: *Gunnis* 1968, 241

Funerary Monuments

1.	*c*1800	John Woodruff	Crowle, Lincs	S	*Gunnis* 1968, 241
2.	*c*1800	Rev Thomas Denton	Ashtead, Surrey	S	*Gunnis* 1968, 241
3.	?1804	John Neville	Badsworth, W R Yorks		*Gunnis* 1968, 241
4.	?1819	Samuel Tooker	All Saints, Rotherham, W R Yorks		*Gunnis* 1968, 241
5.	?1820	Charles Thellusson	Brodsworth, W R Yorks		*Gunnis* 1968, 241
6.	?1820	William Kent	Hooton Roberts, W R Yorks		GPC
7.	?1823	John Crosham	Barnby-on-Don, W R Yorks		*Gunnis* 1968, 241
8.	?1827	Gilbert Hill	Bawtry, W R Yorks		*Gunnis* 1968, 241
9.	?1827	Thomas Peacock	Crowle, Lincs	S	*Gunnis* 1968, 241
10.	?1830	Bartholomew Hodgetts	Barnsley, W R Yorks		*Gunnis* 1968, 241
11.	†1834	Rev John Rudd	St Mary and St Martin, Blyth, Notts	S	
12.	?1836	John Yarborough	Campsall, W R Yorks		*Gunnis* 1968, 241
13.	nd	Robert Popplewell Steer	Belton, Lincs		Pevsner, *Lincs*, 1989, 140

Busts

14.	1809	Unidentified subject	[Exhib North Soc, Leeds]; untraced		GPC

LODGE, William and Ann, of Birmingham fl 1806?–*c*1840

Ann was William's wife and signed some monuments on her own.

Literary References: *Gunnis* 1968, 241

Funerary Monuments

1.	?1806	Charles Richards (by William Lodge)	St Paul, Birmingham		*Gunnis* 1968, 241
2.	?1822	Daniel Mathews (by Ann Lodge)	Hagley, Worcs	S	*Gunnis* 1968, 241
3.	†1822	Samuel Tomlinson (by Ann Lodge)	St Leonard, Bridgnorth, Salop	S	GPC
4.	?1823	William Clare (by Ann Lodge)	Quatt, Salop	S	*Gunnis* 1968, 241
5.	†1827	John Mander	Queen Street Congregational Church, Bridgnorth, Salop		RG/JP, 5, 836
6.	†1832	John and Sarah (†1836) Scott	Stourbridge Unitarian Chapel	S	GPC
7.	†1834	Elizabeth and William (†1844) Hancocks (by Ann Lodge)	Wolverley, Worcs	S	GPC
8.	†1840	Rev Henry Hill	Rock, Worcs		RG/JP, 5, 836

LOFT, James *c*1800–89

Gunnis indicates that Loft was originally from Hull but the 1851 and 1861 census returns show that he was born at Binbrook, near Louth, in 1801 or 1802. At twenty he went to London, where he became a pupil of **Francis Chantrey** and attended the Royal Academy schools, winning a silver medal for a model of an academy figure (**29**). He exhibited at the Royal Academy between 1825 and 1867 and at the Society of British Artists in 1832 and 1837, from addresses at 73 Upper Ebury Street; 91 Dean Street, Soho; Chelsea and 29 Clipstone Street. His exhibits included a a statue of Daniel Sykes, reviewed in *The Athenaeum*, who noted 'There is some good drapery on this statue but the posture is a little restrained' (**10**). His group, *The Graces*, was discussed by the *Art Union* who commented, 'The figure are so individualized that each in the group yet not of it: such a want of correlation is always fatal to the subject. With respect to the disposition of the figures, it may be remarked that a mere departure from a normal propriety is not originality' (*AU*, 1842, 128) (**11**).

When he gave evidence before the National Gallery parliamentary commission in 1853, Loft stated that he had for many years run a plaster figure shop in Dean Street, which he had taken over from **Sarti**, and that he had the contract for making moulds from the statues at the British Museum. An unsigned terracotta bust of Oliver Cromwell belonged to Loft before it was acquired by the National Portrait Gallery in 1861 (NPG 132). It was probably made during the 19th century and is based on a marble in the Ashmolean which probably dates from the 18th century, but was once thought to be the work of **Edward Pearce**. (Inf. Gerardine Mulcahy)

Literary References: *Gunnis* 1968, 242; *Pyke* 1973, 81; *Penny* 1992, 142; *Jenkins* 1992, 34

Archival References: GPC

Funerary Monuments

1.	†1808	General Nott	St Peter, Carmarthen		*Dale-Jones and Lloyd* 1989, 52
2.	1829	HRH the late Duke of York	[2nd Exhibition, Hull Institution, 223]; untraced		Exhibition cat
3.	1829	King George IV	[2nd Exhibition, Hull Institution, 222]; untraced		Exhibition cat
4.	1829	Major Rook	[2nd Exhibition, Hull Institution, 224]; untraced		Exhibition cat
5.	?1834	Samuel Russell	Shepperton, Middx	S	*Gunnis* 1968, 242

6.	1835	Rev John Scott (†1834)		St Mary, Hull, E R Yorks		Pevsner, *Yorks: E R & York*, 1995, 512
7.	†1838	Major William Mills		St Mary, Bedford	S	Pevsner, *Beds, Hunts & Peterborough*, 1968, 48
8.	1839	Edmund Kean		St Mary Magdalene, Richmond, London		Pevsner, *London: S.*, 1983, 518
9.	?1848	James Rawlinson		Derby Cathedral		GPC
Statues						
10.	1833	Daniel Sykes	m	[Exhib RA, London, 1138]; Mechanics Institute, Hull, E R Yorks		*The Athenaeum*, 1830, 330; *Graves* V, 1905–6, 81
11.	1842	The Graces	m	[Exhib RA, London, 1281]; untraced		*AU*, 1842, 128; *Graves* V, 1905–6, 82
Busts						
12.	1825	Unidentified gentleman		[Exhib RA, London, 1000]; untraced		*Graves* V, 1905–6, 81
13.	1831	W Graham		[Exhib RA, London, 1203]; untraced		*Graves* V, 1905–6, 81; *Gunnis* 1968, 242; *Johnson* 1975, 292
14.	1832	Unidentified lady		[Exhib RA, London, 1124]; untraced		*Graves* V, 1905–6, 81
15.	1852	Unidentified lady	m	[Exhib RA, London, 1387]; untraced		*Graves* V, 1905–6, 82
16.	1854	J Knight		[Exhib RA, London, 1488]; untraced		*Graves* V, 1905–6, 82
17.	1855	Admiral Sir Charles Napier	m	[Exhib RA, London, 1513]; untraced		*Graves* V, 1905–6, 82
18.	1856	Edmund, Baron Lyons	m	[Exhib RA, London, 1353]; untraced		*Graves* V, 1905–6, 82
19.	1867	Edward Somerset, 2nd Marquess of Worcester (†1657)		[Exhib RA, London, 1193]; untraced		*Graves* V, 1905–6, 82
Reliefs						
20.	1836	Entombment of Christ		[Exhib RA, London, 1094]; untraced		*Graves* V, 1905–6, 82
21.	1841	Abbé Voyaux de Fransus, medallion		[Exhib RA, London, 1124]; untraced		*Graves* V, 1905–6, 82
22.	1851	Unidentified lady, medallion		[Exhib RA, London, 1294]; untraced		*Graves* V, 1905–6, 82
23.	1859	Unidentified gentleman, medallion		[Exhib RA, London, 1337]; untraced		*Graves* V, 1905–6, 82
24.	1862	Lord Brougham, medallion		[Exhib RA, London, 1114]; untraced		*Graves* V, 1905–6, 82
Miscellaneous						
25.	1832	Unidentified subject, portrait	w	[Exhib RA, London, 1079]; untraced		*Graves* V, 1905–6, 81
26.	1835	Unidentified gentleman	w	[Exhib RA, London, 1021]; untraced		*Graves* V, 1905–6, 81
27.	1837	Unidentified gentleman	w	[Exhib Soc of BA, London, 593*]; untraced		*Johnson* 1975, 292
28.	1853	The sisters		[Exhib RA, London, 1417]; untraced		*Graves* V, 1905–6, 82
29.	nd	Academy figure, model		[RA silver medal]; untraced		RA Premium list

LOGDON, of Great Yarmouth fl *c*1817–32

He was in partnership with **Henry Croskill of Great Yarmouth** or his descendant. He signs one known tablet alone (**2**).

Funerary Monuments					
1.	†1817	Mary Custen (co-sculptor: Henry Croskill, of Great Yarmouth)	Gorleston-on-Sea, Norfolk	S	RG/JP, 3, 392v; 5, 836v.
2.	†1832	Rev Thomas Browne	Gorleston-on-Sea, Norfolk	S	RG/JP, 5, 836v

LOMAS, John and Sons, of Bakewell fl 1827–81

They were a firm of Derbyshire marble masons. A number of such local firms flourished from the early 19th century, when steam-powered mills were introduced and new veins of marbles were discovered. John Lomas and his sons operated the Bakewell Marble Works, which were owned by the Duke of Rutland, throughout most of the century. Local directories list John Lomas at Ashford in 1827–9 and in Bakewell in 1828–84; a directory of 1846 has 'John Lomas and Son, Wye Mill, Bakewell' and in an advertisement of 1881 they are described as 'John Lomas & sons, manufacturers of chimneypieces, monuments, tables etc' (*Tomlinson* 1996, 43). Lomas also worked the entrochial marble quarries at Monyash with **Richard Brown and Sons** in the 1830s and Lomas showed Derbyshire marble pedestals for busts and coloured marble chimneypieces at the Great Exhibition of 1851 (**2, 3**). The firm also produced standard white statuary marble memorial tablets.

Literary References: *Glover* 1831–3, 72; *Penny* 1977 (1), 9–10; *Tomlinson* 1996, 19, 43, 62, 65, 82

Funerary Monuments					
1.	†1853	Nine members of the Walthall family (†1727–1853)	Bakewell, Derbys	S	
Chimneypieces					
2.	1851	Derbyshire black and Siena marbles, inlaid with a design in mosaic	[Gt Exhib prize medal]; untraced		*Tomlinson* 1996, 62, 65
3.	1851	Derbyshire rosewood marble, partly sculptured	[Gt Exhib]; untraced		*Tomlinson* 1996, 62

LOMAS, R G fl 1860

In 1860 R G Lomas, of 37 King Street, Derby, advertised that he had succeeded **Joseph Hall II** as the proprietor of the Derby Marble Works and was using steam power for all kinds of work in marble, alabaster and stone.

Literary References: *Glover* 1831–3, 72; *Tomlinson* 1996, 19

LONDON MARBLE WORKS fl 1829–52

They are perhaps synonymous with the **Patent Marble Works**, since they appear to have worked from the same address. Kelly's *Directory* for 1852 lists the 'London Marble and Stone Working Company, modellers, sculptors, stone and marble masons, stone and marble merchants, Esher Street, Holywell Street, Millbank, Wstmnstr'.

Funerary Monuments				
1.	†1845	Samuel Hiron	St James, Chipping Campden, Glos	Pevsner, *Glos: Cotswolds*, 1999, 232
Chimneypieces				
2.	1829	Several Payment(s): £134	[Lambeth Palace, London]; untraced	Account Book, Lambeth Palace, in GPC

LONG, Henry fl 1690

He was apparently a worker in terra-cotta, for in 1690 he received £6 5s for 'a large vase of earth wrought with handles and festoon: painted and gilt,' for Kensington Palace (TNA E 351/3466).

Architectural Sculpture

1.	?1690	'a large vase of earth wrought with handles and festoons, painted and gilt' Payment(s): £6 5s	tc	Kensington Palace, London		*Gunnis* 1968, 242

LONG, John fl 1797

Architectural Sculpture

1.	1797	Font	St Peter, Petersham, Surrey	SD	Pevsner, *Surrey*, 1971, 410

LONG, Joseph fl 1743?

His only recorded work is a monument with a relief of a cherub blowing a trumpet, which Gunnis describes as a naive but rather charming work.

Funerary Monuments

1.	?1743	Elizabeth Long	Ancaster, Lincs		GPC

LONG, Mark and family, of Taunton fl *c*1790–1853

The firm was founded by Mark Long, who was later joined by his wife, Maria. She and a son, Robert, carried on the business after Mark's death, and Robert eventually became the sole proprietor. Tablets made by the firm are signed 'M Long', 'M and M Long', or 'R Long'.

Literary References: *Gunnis* 1968, 242

Funerary Monuments

1.	*c*1790	John Tripp	St James, Taunton, Somerset		*Gunnis* 1968, 242
2.	?1809	Rev Thomas Tucker	Kingsdon, Somerset		*Gunnis* 1968, 242
3.	?1811	Elizabeth Corfield	St James, Taunton, Somerset		*Gunnis* 1968, 242
4.	?1813	George Hart	Taunton parish church, Somerset		*Gunnis* 1968, 242
5.	?1815	William Fraunciss	Taunton parish church, Somerset		*Gunnis* 1968, 242
6.	†1816	Henry Bell	Weelington, Somerset	S	
7.	†1817	William Paulson	Seaton, Devon		RG/JP, 5, 838
8.	?1824	Bridge Hamilton	Broomfield, Somerset		*Gunnis* 1968, 242
9.	†1827	Lieutenant-Colonel James Meredith	Pitminster, Somerset	S	
10.	†1830	William Jones	Weelington, Somerset	S	
11.	1831	Isaac Welman (†1715) and descendants († to 1831)	Pitminster, Somerset	S	
12.	?1838	Hooker Bartelot	Bishop's Hull, Somerset		*Gunnis* 1968, 242
13.	†1840	Margaretta Hazeland	Pitminster, Somerset	S	
14.	†1853	Thomas (†1830) and Mary Pulman	Watchett, Somerset	S	

Architectural Sculpture

15.	1842	Font (by Robert Long)	Holy Trinity, Taunton, Somerset		*GM* 1842, ii, 190

LONG, Mrs fl 1747

In 1747 the *Gentleman's Magazine* published an article on marble-staining and its practice before 1660 by **William Bird, of Oxford**. The author stated that the art was not a lost one, 'for we have lately been informed that the wife of Mr Long, stonecutter at Bow Bridge, Essex, performs it in a very curious manner' (*GM*, vol XVII, Sept 1747, 599). In 1769 a Mrs Long was paid for mason's work at Trinity House (Trinity House Archives in GPC).

Literary References: *Gunnis* 1968, 242

LONG, William fl 1759–61

He was 'bred a mason' (TNA C12 1287/20), but subsequently became a carver and gilder with his own business in Long Acre. He subcontracted work for **Samuel Norman**, and oversaw Norman's brief and unsuccessful venture into the masonry business in June 1759. He brought a successful action against Norman in the Court of King's Bench in 1760. Norman was ordered to pay damages of £140 although he swiftly retaliated with a counter-action in Chancery in 1761.

Literary References: *Kirkham* 1969, 502

LONGFIELD, J, of Liverpool fl *c*1719

Funerary Monuments

1.	*c*1719	Rev and Mrs Nathaniel Brownell	Halsall, Lancs	S	GPC

LONGLEY, Thomas White, of Canterbury fl *c*1782–1838

Gunnis describes Longley as 'the best of the nineteenth-century Canterbury statuaries' (*Gunnis* 1968, 242). He was the nephew of **Thomas White** and in 1799 he announced that he had taken over his uncle's business and intended 'carrying on that branch only, at the old established Stone Yard, near St George's Gate', where he would provide 'Monuments, Tombs, Wallpieces, Tablets, Chimney-pieces, Gravestones, Head and Body-stones, or any article in the above branch; executed in the neatest manner, on the shortest notice, and on the most reasonable terms' (*Kentish Gazette*, 6 May 1799, in GPC). Three years later he succeeded White as master-mason at the Cathedral. He may also be the 'Longley' who was employed on carved work for the library of Lambeth Palace in 1829 (Cambridge Univ MS 3928 in *Gunnis* 1968, 242). His monument to Major Cairns in Canterbury Cathedral is also signed by a 'Robert and Mary Rushbrook', who may have designed it (3). The Lady Sondes at Nackington is a copy of the monument to Mary Milles by **Richard Hayward** in the same church (4). After Longley's death his son John continued the business.

Literary References: *Gunnis* 1968, 242

Funerary Monuments

1.	†1782	Rev William Tatton, Sarah (†1777) and William (†1775) Tatton	Staple, Kent	S	
2.	?1809	Edward Brydges	Wooton, Kent		*Gunnis* 1968, 242
3.	†1815	Major Robert-Macpherson Cairnes	Canterbury Cathedral, Kent	S	*Gunnis* 1968, 242
4.	†1818	Mary Elizabeth, Lady Sondes	Nackington, Kent	S	Pevsner, *Kent: N E & E*, 1983, 400

5.	†1818	Mary Elizabeth, Lady Sondes	Rockingham, Northants		*Gunnis* 1968, 242
6.	†1822	Christopher Milles	Nackington, Kent		*Gunnis* 1968, 242
7.	†1823	Mary (†1822) and Catherine Elizabeth Milles	Nackington, Kent	S	Pevsner, *Kent: N E & E*, 1983, 400
8.	†1823	William Lasey	Hoath, Kent	S	
9.	†1827	Thomas Real	Sturry, Kent	S	
10.	†to 1828	William (†1727), Mary (†1750) and Elizabeth Belsey and family members	Minster-in-Thanet, Kent	S	
11.	?1828	William Hougham	St Martin, Canterbury, Kent		*Gunnis* 1968, 242
12.	†1830	Terry (†1789) and Olive Terry Marsh	Staple, Kent	S	
13.	†1831	Charlotte and George (†1855) Hannam	Minster-in-Thanet, Kent	S	*Gunnis* 1968, 242
14.	1832	Thomas Gillow and family (†1824)	St Nicholas-at-Wade, Kent	SD	
15.	†1835	Sir William Inglis	Canterbury Cathedral, Kent	S	
16.	?1836	Lord Sondes	Sheldwich, Kent		*Gunnis* 1968, 242
17.	†1838	Henry Boswell Bennet	Canterbury Cathedral, Kent	S	
18.	†1838	Robert Chisholm	Canterbury Cathedral, Kent	S	

Architectural Sculpture

19.	?1829	Unspecified carving	Lambeth Palace, London, library		*Gunnis* 1968, 242

LONGSTAFFE, John, of Bishop Auckland fl 1663–65

In 1663 he agreed to undertake mason's work and to make chimneypieces for Bishop Auckland palace, then being repaired by Bishop Cosin ('Corr of John Cosin', *Surtees Soc*, vol 2). Two years later he was paid for building the porter's lodge (*Durham Cathedral Lib*, Sharp, 163, in GPC). He may also have erected the pillar commemorating King Edward I (†1307) at Sands End, near Burgh by Sands, Cumberland, which was executed in 1685 by a mason named Thomas or John Langstaff, or Longstaff.

Literary References: *Darke* 1991, 235–6

Archival References: Todd MS 7/3F191, St Edmund Hall Oxford (inf. Denis Perriam); GPC

Chimneypieces

1.	1663	Several	Bishop Auckland Palace, Co Durham	GPC

LOSCOMB, of Reading fl 1818?

Funerary Monuments

1.	?1818	Sarah Terry	Warfield, Berks	S	*Gunnis* 1968, 242

LOSH, Sara 1786–1853

She was the architect of the singular church of St Mary, Wreay, in Cumberland. She designed the prolific and expressive naturalistic decoration and a local builder's son, William Hindson, provided the stone carving while her gardener executed the carved woodwork. Sara and her cousin William carved the font (**2**). She was also responsible for an irregularly shaped slab with a carved pine cone erected in the churchyard as a memorial to her schoolfellow, Major Thain, who was killed by a poisoned arrow in the Khyber Pass (**1**).

Literary References: *ODNB* (Plouviez)

Funerary Monuments

1.	†1842	Major Thain		Wreay, Cumberland, churchyard	*ODNB*

Architectural Sculpture

2.	1840–1842	Font (co-sculptor: William S Losh)	a	Wreay, Cumberland	*ODNB*

LOSH, William S fl 1840–42

Architectural Sculpture

1.	1840–1842	Font (co-sculptor: Sara Losh)	a	Wreay, Cumberland	*ODNB*

LOUGH, John Graham 1798–1876

Lough came of rural stock, but established himself as a successful metropolitan sculptor and was hailed as a genius early in his career. His work is eclectic, drawing upon classical, Renaissance and Gothic sources.

He was born in the hamlet of Greenhead, Northumberland, on 8 January 1798, the third son of William Lough, a blacksmith, and his wife Barbara Clemitson. Accounts of his early life are inconsistent because Lough embellished his story on moving to London. He took several years from his age and described himself as a farmer's son, an occupation his father only took up after March 1812. He also added Graham, his paternal grandmother's maiden name, to his own name.

Lough's talents for drawing and modelling were evident as a school boy and were encouraged by George Silvertop, the local squire, who allowed Lough access to his art collection. He was apprenticed for some years to a stonemason at Shotley Field and in the early 1820s worked on decorative sculpture for the Newcastle Literary and Philosophical Society building (**170**). He also executed a few minor monuments in the north-east (**1–4**).

In February 1825 he went to London on a coal ship and on his arrival visited the Parthenon Marbles at the British Museum. The following year he exhibited his first work at the Royal Academy (**173**) and was accepted as a student at the RA Schools on the recommendation of JT Smith, Keeper of Prints and Drawings at the British Museum and the biographer of **Joseph Nollekens**. He may have worked for **William Behnes** at this time, for Palgrave includes him in a list of Behnes's pupils. Lough's first major work was a colossal statue of *Milo* (**36**), inspired by the Parthenon sculpture, which he carved in his room above a greengrocer's shop in an alley off Strand. A story, which may be apochryphal, tells that Lough made a hole in his ceiling to accommodate the statue, so causing his landlord to threaten legal proceedings. The publicity apparently made his name.

At this time Lough came to know the painter, Benjamin Haydon. Haydon was impressed by Lough, praised his work in a letter published in the *Carlisle Journal* on 9 February 1828, and was instrumental in organising two shows of his work. In June 1827 *Milo* and *Samson slaying the Philistine* (**37**) were put on display in the great rooms, Maddox Street. The exhibition was a considerable success, a number of celebrities including the Duke of Wellington and Sarah Siddons attended the private day and Lough received several commissions. Nine months later he showed these works again, with two new ones, *Iris waking Somnus* (**38**) and *Musidora* (**39**), from rooms in Regent Street.

In January 1832 Lough made an advantageous marriage to Mary North, a daughter of the Duke of Kent's chaplain. They had two daughters, Mary Rebecca and Georgina. In 1834, shortly after Georgina's birth, the whole family left for Rome, where they remained for three years. The *Art Journal* for 1876 noted that the Duke of Northumberland and Lady Guildford had subsidised the journey. Whilst in Rome Lough carved a statue of James Losh, the Recorder of Newcastle, for the Literary and Philosophical Society (**49**), depicting him in classical pose and dress. Early in 1837 Lough wrote to the Duke of Northumberland asking for financial help, explaining that the visit had not been entirely successful. An outbreak of cholera had kept potential patrons away from Rome and other sculptors without families were able to undercut his prices. Lough then travelled to Naples on his doctor's instructions only to be trapped there by a further outbreak of the disease. In August 1837 the Loughs left Rome, travelling briefly on the Continent before returning to London.

By 1846 Lough was renting a house at 42 Harewood Square, in the area now occupied by Maylebone Station, where he remained for the rest of his life. He exhibited at the Royal Academy and the British Institution until 1863 but never became an Academician. He also sent works to the Westminster Hall Exhibition in 1844 and to the Great Exhibition in 1851. One of his most celebrated compositions, *The mourners* (**60**) was shown at both. It depicts an incident during the English Civil War, where a wife has found her husband dead on the battle field, his horse standing over him. The *Literary Gazette* was of the opinion that 'if visitors to the hall were asked to vote, nineteen out of twenty would prefer it to any other among its competitors' (*Lit Gaz*, 27 July 1844, 482)

Lough maintained lifelong connections with the north-east, which he clearly exploited. Among his most important northern patrons were the Ridley family of Blagdon in Northumberland. In 1832 the 3rd baronet bought a cast of *Duncan's Horses* (**43**) and commissioned an *Orpheus* (**44**). From 1836 onwards, his elder son, Matthew, began ordering works for his London house, 10 Carlton House Terrace. These included a series of statues of Shakespearean characters (**56, 59, 62, 66–73**), a group of *St Michael triumphing over Satan* (**77**) which cost £2,000, and a bronze version of *Milo*. Lough charged Ridley another £2,000 for a marble frieze of William Shakespeare surrounded by figures from *Macbeth* and *The Tempest* (**171**). He also executed busts of a number of Ridley family members (**104, 111, 112, 117, 121, 164**). A last commission from the family was a series of four statues for a bridge at Blagdon (**85**). Lough clearly depended on Ridley's patronage at times of financial hardship. In 1843 Lady Ridley wrote to her father of a 'melancholy letter' received from the Loughs, relating that he was penniless and obliged to borrow to pay his men. 'Literally now he lives on what he gets from Matt, who pays him every now and then as much as he can, and Lough hurries on his things much more than we wish really because he has no other hope' (*Ridley* 1958, 144–5). Charles Hanbury-Tracy, later Baron Sudeley, was another supportive patron. He was building a Gothic mansion at Toddington, Glos, and obtained a statue of a monk for a staircase niche (**46**) and then four nymphs and hunters for garden terraces (**89**).

Lough was also involved in a number of public commissions. In 1845 he was paid £1,050 for a statue of Queen Victoria for which she gave sittings, conceived as the marble centrepiece for the courtyard of the new Royal Exchange (**63**). The statue was not popular, Lough was criticised for his choice of a veined marble, and its exposed position led to degradation of the material. In 1896 it had to be replaced with a new statue by William Hamo Thornycroft. Lough's second Exchange commission fared better; this was a statue for Lloyd's Rooms of Prince Albert (**65**), ordered in 1845 to commemorate his laying of the foundation stone of the new building and it may be the earliest surviving representation of Prince Albert. A companion figure, *Queen Victoria as the Island Queen* (**64**) was not realised. Lough's connections with the Ridley family perhaps led to the statue of Admiral Cuthbert Collingwood at Tynemouth (**61**). The sculptor was among the many unsuccessful entrants in the competition for a national monument to Horatio, Viscount Nelson and was at one time invited to sculpt the lions at the column's base, but this plan was thwarted when the memorial committee was reconstituted. He had the wit to adapt his Nelson memorial design for the memorial to George Stephenson in Newcastle (**81**), an ambitious composition with four supporting figures of engineering workers represented in the classical style.

Although Lough preferred heroic subjects, patrons' demands led to a large number of busts and funerary monuments. He executed busts of several famous men including the Duke of Northumberland (**115**), Robert Southey, the Poet Laureate (**120**), Professor Edward Forbes, the naturalist (**135**) and Richard Twining, the tea merchant, who was Lough's brother-in-law (**138**). These were carved in a broad, smooth, generalised style. His monuments were more varied, ranging from neoclassical tablets, for instance to William Fermor (**5**), which has a relief of a mourning female figure leaning against an urn, to more elaborate Gothic tomb chests with effigies, particularly to Robert Southey (**18**) and Lord and Lady Sudeley (**35**). The monument to Emma Constance Methuen (**32**) takes the form of a young child sleeping on a marble bed, and owes debts to Thomas Banks's admired monument to Penelope Boothby. The Thomas Middleton monument is a large, freestanding image of the bishop blessing two kneeling Indian converts (**7**).

Lough continued to work into old age, though he ceased to exhibit in 1863. Ideal works, such as *The lost Pleiad* (**84**) and *Night's swift dragon* (**177**) were occasionally illustrated in the *Art Journal*. His daughter Georgina died in 1868 and he carved her monument for the mausoleum at Kensal Green Cemetery (**34**). This is a reclining effigy on a tomb chest decorated with medallion profile portraits of Lough, his wife and elder daughter and with mourning angels at either side. Mary Rebecca's name was added when she died three years later. Lough survived both his daughters, dying of bronchitis at his home in Harewood Square on 8 April 1876, at the age of 78.

His life is better documented that almost all his contemporaries and provides a good insight into what it must have been like to struggle as a sculptor with ambitions of gentility in the mid-19th century. Martin Greenwood comments that Lough's work 'reflected an impulse towards novelty in form and subject matter, and an eclectic mixture of sources . . . which mark him as a "transitional" sculptor, seeking to break the mould of neo-classicism' (*ODNB*). During his lifetime his work elicited extreme responses from the press: the *Literary Gazette* hailed him as an 'extraordinary genius', whose works were of 'perfectly miraculous power' (*Lit Gaz*, 12 May 1827, 299) whilst in 1844 the *Art Union* condemned *The mourners* (**60**) as 'maudlin sentimentality rarely outdone in the most drivelling essays' (*Art U*, 1844, 215). Attitudes changed however and the *Art Journal* gave him a favourable obituary (*AJ*, 1876, 202–3). In 1877 his studio models and several marble statues were given to Newcastle Corporation by his widow and displayed at Elswick Hall. This was closed in 1932 and later demolished. The hapless sculpture was dispersed and in due course largely destroyed and Lough was forgotten. The recent monograph by Lough and Merson has helped rehabilitate him.

EH

Literary References: *Palgrave* 1866, 41, 225; *AJ* 1869, 320; 1870, 192; 1876, 203; *Hall* II, 1883, 241–2; *Allen* 1958; *Ridley* 1958, 52, 144–6; *Boase* 1960, 277–90; *Gunnis* 1968, 242–4; *Physick* 1969, 42, 181; *Penny* 1977, *passim*; *Read* 1982, *passim*; *Lough and Merson*, 1987; *Stocker* 1989, 435–6; *Ellison* 1989, 240–241; *Groseclose* 1995, 95, 115–17; *Grove* 19, 1996, 720 (Greenwood); *Leith* 1997, 340–2, 345; *Usherwood* 2000, 328–9; *ODNB* (Greenwood)

Archival References: RA Admissions

Additional MS Sources: *Lough/Howard; Lough/Forster; Peel Papers*, 1844, 1846, Add MSS 40548 fol 375, 40591 fol 266

Wills and Administrations: PPR, will, 20 May 1878, effects under £7,000

Portraits of the Sculptor: self-portrait, bust (119); self-portrait profile relief, part of monument to Georgina Bourchier, née Lough (34); Benjamin Haydon, sketch, *Haydon Diary*, Houghton Library, Harvard (repr *Lough and Merson* 1987, repr 3); anon canvas, coll B Etherington (repr *Lough and Merson* 1987, repr 4); photo (*Lough and Merson* 1987, repr 6); Ralph Hedley, canvas, Lough in his studio at work on *Milo*, 1881 (sold Christie 31 July 1987, cat repr)

Funerary Monuments

1.	†1803–1819	Mayor family, headstone		Muggleswick, Co Durham, churchyard	S	*Lough and Merson* 1987, 6, 62, 85
2.	†1820	Robert Gibson, headstone		Shotley, Northumbs, churchyard		*Lough and Merson* 1987, 6, 85
3.	†1815–1822	Chatt family, headstone		Shotley, Northumbs, churchyard		*Lough and Merson* 1987, 6, 85; Pevsner, *Northumbs*, 1992, 292
4.	†1813–1823	Thompson family, headstone		Shotley, Northumbs, churchyard		*Lough and Merson* 1987, 6, 85; Pevsner, *Northumbs*, 1992, 292
5.	†1828	William Fermor		Somerton, Oxon		*Lough and Merson* 1987, 22, 62, 85 (pl 20)
6.	*c*1830	Mrs Ann Stephenson (†1823)	s	Allendale Town, Northumbs		*Lough and Merson* 1987, 6, 85; Pevsner, *Northumbs*, 1992, 126
7.	1832	Thomas Fanshaw Middleton, Bishop of Calcutta (†1822) Model(s): plaster exhib Egyptian Hall, 15 May 1830 (*Athenaeum*, 1830, 300)		St Paul's Cathedral, London, nave, south aisle	SD	*Lough and Merson* 1987, 22, 63 (repr 23); *Penny* 1977 (1), 221 n60; C Lib (repr)
8.	†1833	George Fennell Robson		St Mary-le-Bow, Durham		*Lough and Merson* 1987, 22, 85
9.	†1839	John James Watson		St John, Hackney, London	S	
10.	†1840	James Ramsay		Somerton, Oxon	S	Pevsner, *Oxon*, 1974, 768; *Lough and Merson* 1987, 62, 85 (repr 21)
11.	†1840	Rev William Ainger		St Bees, Cumberland		Pevsner, *Cumberland & Westmorland*, 1967, 184
12.	†1841	Ann Everard		Burnham Thorpe, Norfolk		*Lough* 1984, 85
13.	†1841	William Hay Macnaughton		St Paul's Cathedral, Kolkata (Calcutta)		*Groseclose* 1995, 115–6 (repr)
14.	†1841	William Macnaughton		Chennai (Madras) Cathedral	S	
15.	†1842	Thomas Singleton	s	St Michael, Alnwick, Northumbs, churchyard		*Lough* 1984, 85
16.	1843	Benjamin Malkin (†1842)		Bury St Edmunds Cathedral, Suffolk	SD	
17.	1844	Nelson monument, design only		[Exhib RA, London, 1299]; untraced Other versions: model or cast ex Elswick Hall, Newcastle; untraced		*Robinson* 1886, 26, cat 75; *Graves* V, 1905–6, 95;
18.	1846	Robert Southey (†1843)		St Kentigern, Crosthwaite, Cumberland Other versions: model or cast ex Elswick Hall, Newcastle; untraced	D	*Robinson* 1886, 13, cat 33; *Graves* V, 1905–6, 95; *Read* 1982, 103–4, 191 (repr)
19.	1847	General Sir Robert Dick (†1846)		Dunkeld Cathedral, Tayside, Scotland		*ILN*, 1848, 379 (repr)
20.	†1847	William Everard		Burnham Thorpe, Norfolk		*Lough and Merson* 1987, 86
21.	1848	Francis, 1st Marquess of Hastings (†1826)		Hastings Gardens, Valetta, Malta, mausoleum		*Graves* V, 1905–6, 95; *Lough and Merson* 1987, 40–1, 69, 88–9
22.	†1848	James Alexander		St Peter and St Paul, Tonbridge, Kent		Pevsner, *Kent: W & Weald*, 1976, 569; *Lough and Merson* 1987, 86
23.	1850	Hon Anne Rushout (†1849)		Blockley, Glos	S	*Graves* V, 1905–6, 95; *Lough and Merson* 1987, 63, 86 (repr 25)
24.	1851	The Rt Hon and Rev Lord Frederick Beauclerk (†1850)		Winchfield, Hants	S	Pevsner, *Hants & Isle of Wight*, 1967, 722; *Lough and Merson* 1987, 63–4, 86
25.	1851	William, 9th Duke of St Albans (†1849)		Redbourne, Lincs	S	*Graves* V, 1905–6, 95; *Lough and Merson* 1987, 86; Pevsner, *Lincs*, 1989, 608
26.	†1853	Philippa Dewar		Somerton, Oxon	S	Pevsner, *Oxon*, 1974, 768; *Lough and Merson* 1987, 62, 86 (pl 22)
27.	1855	Bishop William Broughton		Canterbury Cathedral, Kent Other versions: model or cast ex Elswick Hall, Newcastle; untraced	SD	*Robinson* 1886, 13, cat 32; Pevsner, *Kent: N E & E*, 1983, 214
28.	1856	Lieutenant-Colonel Frederick Mackeson		Canterbury Cathedral, Kent	SD	Pevsner, *Kent: N E & E*, 1983, 214; C Lib (repr)
29.	†1857	Edward and Mary (†1828) Moulton Barrett		Ledbury, Herefs		*Lough and Merson* 1987, 64, 86 (pl 26)

30.	†1857	Rev William Gilly Model(s): RA, London, 1858, 1197 (model for figure)		Norham, Northumbs		*Graves* V, 1905–6, 95; Pevsner, *Northumbs*, 1992, 524; C Lib (repr)
31.	†1858	Grace Emma Webber		Hamble, Hants		RG/JP, 5, 846
32.	1861	Emma Constance Methuen (†1859) Payment(s): £235, with the bust of Marie Cicely Methuen		Corsham, Wilts	S	*Graves* 1875, 354; *Lough and Merson* 1987, 64, 86 (repr 27)
33.	1862	Sir Henry Lawrence (†1857)		St Paul's Cathedral, London Other versions: model or cast ex Elswick Hall, Newcastle; untraced	SD	*Lough and Merson* 1987, 64, 86 (repr 28)
34.	†1868	Georgina Bourchier (née Lough)		Kensal Green Cemetery, London Other versions: model or cast ex Elswick Hall, Newcastle; untraced		*Robinson* 1886, 8, cat 13; *Lough and Merson* 1987, 45, 65, 86 (repr 31)
35.	1872	Charles, 1st Baron Sudeley (†1858) and Lady Sudeley		Toddington, Glos	SD	*Read* 1982, 193, 194 (repr)
Statues						
36.	1827	Milo	p	[Exhib Maddox Street, London]; destroyed Other versions: Blagdon, Northumbs, bronze		*Lough and Merson* 1987, 36, 81 (reprs 2, 7)
37.	1827	Samson slaying the Philistine	p	[Exhib Maddox Street, London]; untraced Other versions: model or cast ex Elswick Hall, Newcastle; untraced		*Robinson* 1886, 31, cat 100; *Lough and Merson* 1987, 11–3, 35, 81
38.	1828	Iris waking Somnus		[Exhib Regent Street, London]; untraced		*Lough and Merson* 1987, 13–4, 81
39.	1828	Musidora		[Exhib Regent Street, London]; untraced Other versions: model or cast ex Elswick Hall, Newcastle; untraced		*Lough and Merson* 1987, 13–4, 81
40.	1829	David	m	[Howick Hall, Northumbs]; Walker, Liverpool Other versions: model or cast ex Elswick Hall, Newcastle; untraced		*Graves* 1875, 354; *Robinson* 1886, 22, cat 61; *Lough and Merson* 1987, 21, 36, 54, 81 (pl 8)
41.	1829	The battle of the standard (Edward I creating a knight banneret) Payment(s): 750 gns	p	[coll Hugh, 3rd Duke of Northumberland]; untraced Other versions: model or cast ex Elswick Hall, Newcastle; untraced		*Robinson* 1886, 40, cat 133; *Read* 1982, 208–9; *Lough and Merson* 1987, 17–8, 81
42.	by 1830	A sleeping child, son of Mr Manning		Untraced		*Lough and Merson* 1987, 88
43.	1832	Duncan's horses	p	Los Angeles County Museum, California, USA M.81.263 Other versions: private coll, m VAM 92-1889, c1834, bronze private coll, p	S	*Graves* V, 1905–6, 94; *Lough and Merson* 1987, 36, 57, 84 (repr 15); *Schaefer and Fusco* 1987, 143 (repr); *Bilbey* 2002, 323–4 (repr)
44.	1832	Orpheus	m	[coll Sir Matthew White Ridley, 3rd Bt]; Blagdon, Northumbs Other versions: model or cast ex Elswick Hall, Newcastle; untraced		*Robinson* 1886, 29, cat 92; *Lough and Merson* 1987, 22, 81
45.	1832	Satan, model or cast	p	[Elswick Hall, Newcastle, Northumbs]; untraced		*Lough and Merson* 1987, 31–2, 35, 81 (repr 5)
46.	1833	A monk (St Bruno)	s	Toddington Manor, Glos, grand staircase	S	*Graves* 1875, 353; *Lough and Merson* 1987, 81 (pl 9)
47.	1834	Mercury and Argus	m	[coll Henry, 1st Baron Brougham]; untraced		*Lough and Merson* 1987, 20, 82
48.	1834	Milton invoking the muse, statuette	m	[Howick Hall, Northumbs]; Walker, Liverpool		*Graves* 1875, 353; *Lough and Merson* 1987, 21, 82
49.	1836	James Losh	m	Newcastle Lit and Phil Soc, Northumbs		*CJ*, 1 Feb 1834; *Lough and Merson* 1987, 22, 24–5, 68, 88 (repr 36)
50.	1837	Boy giving water to a dolphin (Boy riding a fish)	m	[coll Hugh, 3rd Duke of Northumberland]; Hatton Art Gallery, University of Newcastle Other versions: Blagdon, Northumbs	S	*Graves* V, 1905–6, 94; *Lough and Merson* 1987, 35, 56, 82
51.	1837	The infant lyrist taming Cerberus	m	[coll Charlotte Florentia, 3rd Duchess of Northumberland]; Hatton Art Gallery, University of Newcastle, Northumbs S.0006	S	*Graves* 1875, 353; *Lough and Merson* 1987, 56, 82 (repr 13)
52.	1839	Cupid and Psyche	m	[coll Hugh, 3rd Duke of Northumberland]; Hatton Art Gallery, University of Newcastle, Northumbs Other versions: model or cast ex Elswick Hall, Newcastle; untraced	S	*Graves* 1875, 354; *Lough and Merson* 1987, 82
53.	1840	Bacchanalian revel	m	[coll Sir Matthew White Ridley, 4th Bt]; untraced Other versions: model or cast ex Elswick Hall, Newcastle; untraced		*Graves* V, 1905–6, 94; *Lough and Merson* 1987, 82; *Lady Lever* 1999, 81

54.	1840	Infant son of P Bennett	m	[Exhib RA, London, 1107]; untraced		*Graves* V, 1905–6, 94
55.	1841	Boy conquering a bull	m	[coll Sir Matthew White Ridley, 4th Bt]; Blagdon, Northumbs Other versions: model or cast ex Elswick Hall, Newcastle; untraced		*Robinson* 1886, 20, cat 54; *Lough and Merson* 1987, 56, 82
56.	By 1841	Ophelia	m	[coll Sir Matthew White Ridley, 4th Bt, 10 Carlton House Terrace, London]; Blagdon, Northumbs, garden Other versions: model or cast ex Elswick Hall, Newcastle; untraced		*Robinson* 1886, 11, cat 25; *Graves* V, 1905–6, 94; *Lough and Merson* 1987, 56, 84
57.	1843	Eldest son of R Hedley, in the character of a young falconer	m	[Exhib RA, London, 1403]; untraced		*Graves* V, 1905–6, 94
58.	1844	Hebe banished	m	[Exhib RA, London, 1270]; untraced		*AU*, 1844, 170; *Graves* V, 1905–6, 95
59.	1844	Iago	m	[coll Sir Matthew White Ridley, 4th Bt, 10 Carlton House Terrace, London]; Destroyed		*Graves* V, 1905–6, 95; *Lough and Merson* 1987, 58, 84
60.	1844	The mourners, group	p	[Exhib Westminster Hall, London, 129]; destroyed		*Lit Gaz*, 27 July 1844, 482; *Lough and Merson* 1987, 36, 55, 82 (pl 11)
61.	1845	Cuthbert, Baron Collingwood (pedestal by John Dobson)	s	Pier Road, Tynemouth, Northumbs Other versions: model or cast ex Elswick Hall, Newcastle; untraced	SD	*Robinson* 1886, 38–9, cat 127; *Usherwood* 2000, 207–9 (repr)
62.	1845	Lady Macbeth	m	[coll Sir Matthew White Ridley, 4th Bt, 10 Carlton House Terrace, London]; Destroyed		*Graves* V, 1905–6, 95; *Lough and Merson* 1987, 79, 84
63.	1845	Queen Victoria Payment(s): 1,000 gns	m	[Royal Exchange, London]; removed due to disintegration, 1896		*Graves* V, 1905–6, 95; *Grove* 19, 1996, 720, *Leith* 1997, 340–1
64.	c1846	'Queen Victoria as the Island Queen' ('Queen of the Ocean'), model only	p	[Royal Exchange, London, Lloyds rooms]; untraced Other versions: model or cast ex Elswick Hall, Newcastle; untraced		*Robinson* 1886, 38, cat 124
65.	1845–1847	Albert, the Prince Consort	m	[Royal Exchange, London, Lloyds rooms]; Royal Exchange, City of London Other versions: model or cast ex Elswick Hall, Newcastle; untraced	SD	*Robinson* 1886, 17–8, 38 cats 44, 126; *Leith* 1997, 340, 342–3 (repr); *Ward-Jackson* 2003, 326–7 (repr)
66.	1847	Hamlet	m	[coll Sir Matthew White Ridley, 4th Bt; 10 Carlton House Terrace, London]; untraced		*Lough and Merson* 1987, 84
67.	by 1847	Oberon		[coll Sir Matthew White Ridley, 4th Bt, 10 Carlton House Terrace, London]; untraced Other versions: model or cast ex Elswick Hall, Newcastle		*Read* 1982, 140; *Lough and Merson* 1987, 36, 84
68.	by 1847	Puck	m	[coll W Minshull Bigg]; VAM 323-1867 Other versions: commissioned by Sir Matthew White Ridley, 4th Bt, later acquired by W H Lever, whose collection included another version; both untraced Model or cast ex Elswick Hall, Newcastle; untraced	S	*Graves* 1875, 354; *Lough and Merson* 1987, 36, 59, 84 (repr 17); *Bilbey* 2002, 324–5 (repr)
69.	by 1847	Titania and the ass's head	m	[coll W Minshull Bigg]; VAM 324-1867 Other versions: (ex coll Sir Matthew White Ridley, 4th Bt, acquired W H Lever; London art market 1989; untraced model or cast ex Elswick Hall, Newcastle; untraced	SD	*Graves* 1875, 354; *Lough and Merson* 1987, 36–7, 59, 84; *Victorian Nude*, 74–5 (repr); *Bilbey* 2002, 325 (repr)
70.	1848	Ariel	m	[coll Duchess of Sutherland]; untraced Other versions: Sir Matthew White Ridley, 4th Bt, marble another ex Elswick Hall, Newcastle, model or cast; untraced		*Robinson* 1886, 31, 33, cats 102, 109; *Graves* V, 1905–6, 95; *Lough and Merson* 1987, 37, 84
71.	1848	Edgar	m	[coll Sir Matthew White Ridley, 4th Bt; 10 Carlton House Terrace, London]; untraced		*Lough and Merson* 1987, 77, 84
72.	1848	Macbeth	m	[coll Sir Matthew White Ridley, 4th Bt, 10 Carlton House Terrace, London]; untraced		*Lough and Merson* 1987, 77, 84
73.	1848	Portia	m	[coll Sir Matthew White Ridley, 4th Bt, 10 Carlton House Terrace, London]; Blagdon, Northumbs, garden Other versions: model or cast ex Elswick Hall, Newcastle		*Robinson* 1886, 37, cat 122; *Lough and Merson* 1987, 58–9, 84 (repr 16)

No.	Date	Title	Medium	Location		Literary references
74.	c1850	Mercury and Pandora		[coll Sir Augustus Clifford]; untraced		*Gunnis* 1968, 244
75.	1850	Somnus	m	[coll Sir Matthew White Ridley, 4th Bt, 10 Carlton House Terrace, London]; Blagdon, Northumbs Other versions: model or cast ex Elswick Hall, Newcastle; untraced		*Robinson* 1886, 16, cat 41; *Read* 1982, 139–40 (repr); *Lough and Merson* 1987, 82
76.	pre-1851	Mercury and Hebe		[Phillips, 29 Jan 1851]; untraced		RG/JP, 5, 843
77.	1851	St Michael triumphing over Satan Payment(s): £2000 Model(s): Gt Exhib	m	[coll Sir Matthew White Ridley, 4th Bt; 10 Carlton House Terrace, London]; Destroyed		*Boase* 1960, 282–3, 287, 288 (repr 37c); *Lough and Merson* 1987, 36, 79, 82
78.	1853	Lady Diana Beauclerk		[Exhib RA, London, 1332]; untraced Other versions: model or cast ex Elswick Hall, Newcastle; untraced		*Robinson* 1886, 24, 36, cats 66, 116; *Graves* V, 1905–6, 95
79.	1853–1856	Comus Model(s): C L coll, 130, plaster	m	CL Coll, Mansion House, City of London, acc 129 Other versions: model or cast ex Elswick Hall, Newcastle; untraced	SD	*Robinson* 1886, 14, cat 37; *Knight* 1986, 341 (repr); *Ward-Jackson* 2003, 247–8 (repr)
80.	1857	Orlando, statuette	b	Christie, 13 April 1983, lot 170; untraced	SD	*Lough and Merson* 1987, 83; C Lib (repr)
81.	1862	George Stephenson	b	Newcastle, Northumbs	SD	*Usherwood* 2000, xvii, xix, 149–52 (repr)
82.	1863	Infant son of Sir John Lawrence		[Exhib BI, London, 613]; untraced Other versions: model or cast ex Elswick Hall, Newcastle, Northumbs; untraced		*Graves* 1875, 354; *Robinson* 1886, 36, cat 118
83.	1865	Jacques, from 'As You Like It'	m	[coll W Minshull Bigg]; VAM 325-1867 Other versions: model or cast ex Elswick Hall, Newcastle; untraced	SD	*Robinson* 1886, 12, cat 28; *Lough and Merson* 1987, 84; *Bilbey* 2002, 326 (repr)
84.	1869	The lost Pleiad	m	untraced Other versions: model or cast ex Elswick Hall, Newcastle; untraced		*Robinson* 1886, 33–4, cat 110; *Read* 1982, 206; *Lough and Merson* 1987, 41, 83
85.	1869–1871	Four statues: deer slayer, boar hunter, shepherd, eagle slayer Payment(s): £1,000 each	m	[coll Sir Matthew White Ridley, 4th Bt]; Blagdon, Northumbs, bridge		*Read* 1982, 140; *Lough and Merson* 1987, 37, 83 (reps 10, 14)
86.	nd	A fairy, model or cast		[Elswick Hall, Newcastle, Northumbs]; untraced		*Lough and Merson* 1987, 84
87.	nd	Boy and heron, model or cast		[Elswick Hall, Newcastle, Northumbs]; untraced		*Robinson* 1886, 41, cat 139
88.	nd	Daughter of R N Philip MP		Untraced		*Lough and Merson* 1987, 88
89.	nd	Four statues: Hunter and boar, Hunter and stag, Nymph and goats, Nymph and ram	m	[coll Charles, 1st Baron Sudeley]; Toddington Manor, Glos, grounds		*Lough and Merson* 1987, 83
90.	nd	Girl and dog		[Elswick Hall, Newcastle, Northumbs]; untraced		*Robinson* 1886, 36, cat 115
91.	nd	Horse and man, model or cast		[Elswick Hall, Newcastle, Northumbs]; untraced		*Lough and Merson* 1987, 83
92.	nd	Infant son of Mary Rebecca Scully (née Lough), model or cast		[Elswick Hall, Newcastle, Northumbs]; untraced		*Lough and Merson* 1987, 88
93.	nd	Infant son of Thomas Powell, model or cast		[Elswick Hall, Newcastle, Northumbs]; untraced		*Lough and Merson* 1987, 88
94.	nd	Morn Payment(s): £700	m	[coll Sir Matthew White Ridley, 4th Bt]; Blagdon, Northumbs Other versions: model or cast ex Elswick Hall, Newcastle; untraced		*Robinson* 1886, 21, cat 59; *Lough and Merson* 1987, 37, 83
95.	nd	Pan	m	untraced		*Lady Lever* 1999, 81
96.	nd	Peace, model or cast		[Elswick Hall, Newcastle, Northumbs]; untraced		*Lough and Merson* 1987, 83
97.	nd	Sabrina ('Kneeling Venus')	m	[coll Hugh, 3rd Duke of Northumberland ?]; Hatton Art Gallery, University of Newcastle, Northumbs		
98.	nd	Sir Henry Lawrence		Lahore, Pakistan		*Ormond* 1973, 263
99.	nd	Sir Henry Lawrence		Old India Office Building, City of London		*Ormond* 1973, 263
100.	nd	The descent of Satan	m	untraced Other versions: model or cast ex Elswick Hall, Newcastle; untraced		*Robinson* 1886, 37, cat 120; *Lough and Merson* 1987, 83
101.	nd	The mountain nymph	m	Laing Art Gallery, Newcastle, Northumbs		*Lough and Merson* 1987, 77, 83
102.	nd	Victory, model or cast		[Elswick Hall, Newcastle, Northumbs]; untraced		*Lough and Merson* 1987, 41, 83

Busts

No.	Date	Title	Medium	Location		Literary references
103.	1826	Duchess of Buckingham		[coll Duchess of Buckingham]; untraced		*Gunnis* 1968, 242; *Lough and Merson* 1987, 20, 77
104.	1833	Sir Matthew White Ridley, 3rd Bt	m	Blagdon, Northumbs		*Read* 1982, 139
105.	1838	Mrs Holcomb		[Exhib Newcastle, Northumbs]; untraced		*Lough and Merson* 1987, 87
106.	1838	Unidentified lady	m	[Exhib RA, London, 1362]; untraced		*Graves* V, 1905–6, 94
107.	1839	Eric, 7th Lord Reay	m	[Exhib RA, London, 1337]; untraced		*Graves* V, 1905–6, 94
108.	1839	Unidentified gentleman		[Exhib RA, London, 1358]; untraced		*Graves* V, 1905–6, 94

No.	Date	Subject		Location		Sources
109.	1840	Unidentified lady		[Exhib RA, London, 1154]; untraced		*Graves* V, 1905–6, 94
110.	1841	Mrs Thompson	m	[Exhib RA, London, 1294]; untraced		*Graves* V, 1905–6, 94
111.	1841	Sir Matthew White Ridley, 4th Bt	m	Blagdon, Northumbs Other versions: replicated 1863 model or cast ex Elswick Hall, Newcastle; untraced		*Robinson* 1886, 24–5, cat 71; *Graves* V, 1905–6, 94; *Read* 1982, 139; *Lough and Merson* 1987, 87
112.	1842	Cecelia, Lady Ridley	m	Blagdon, Northumbs Other versions: replicated 1846 model or cast ex Elswick Hall, Newcastle; untraced		*Robinson* 1886, 24, cat 70; *Graves* V, 1905–6, 95; *Lough and Merson* 1987, 66–7, 87 (repr 33)
113.	1842	D Blaine	m	[Exhib RA, London, 1360]; untraced Other versions: model or cast ex Elswick Hall, Newcastle; untraced		*AU*, 1842, 129; *Robinson* 1886, 19, cat 51; *Graves* V, 1905–6, 94
114.	1842	J Thompson	m	[Exhib RA, London, 1320]; untraced		*Graves* V, 1905–6, 94
115.	1843	Hugh, 3rd Duke of Northumberland	m	Alnwick, Northumbs Other versions: Laing Art Gallery, Newcastle upon Tyne, plaster		*Graves* V, 1905–6, 94; *Gunnis* 1968, 243; *Lough and Merson* 1987, 87
116.	1843	Mrs Thomas Powell		[Exhib RA, London, 1446]; untraced Other versions: model or cast ex Elswick Hall, Newcastle; untraced		*Robinson* 1886, 19, cat 48; *Graves* V, 1905–6, 94
117.	1844	Mary Howard (Lady Ridley's sister)	m	[Exhib RA, London, 1349]; untraced		*AU*, 1844, 171; *Graves* V, 1905–6, 95; *Boase* 1960, 282
118.	1845	Cuthbert, Baron Collingwood	m	NPG, London (attrib) Other versions: Laing Art Gallery, Newcastle upon Tyne, plaster		*Graves* V, 1905–6, 95; *Lough and Merson* 1987, 87
119.	*c*1845	John Graham Lough (self-portrait)	m	Laing Art Gallery, Newcastle upon Tyne Other versions: Laing Art Gall, plaster		*Read* 1982, 34 (repr); *Lough and Merson* 1987, 66, 77, 87 (repr 32)
120.	1845	Robert Southey	m	NPG, London	SD	*Graves* V, 1905–6, 95; *Lough and Merson* 1987, 87 (repr 34)
121.	1846	Matthew, 1st Viscount Ridley	m	Blagdon, Northumbs		*Read* 1982, 139; *Lough and Merson* 1987, 87
122.	1848	Charles, 2nd Baron Vivian		Oldway, Paignton, Devon		RG/JP, 5, 845
123.	†1848	Howel Gwyn		Oldway, Paignton, Devon		RG/JP, 5, 845
124.	1848	Lord Talbot de Malahide		Oldway, Paignton, Devon		RG/JP, 5, 845
125.	1848	Samuel Solly		[Exhib RA, London, 1377]; untraced		*Graves* V, 1905–6, 95
126.	1849	Ernest Durant		[Exhib RA, London, 1331]; untraced		*Graves* V, 1905–6, 95
127.	1849	R Durant		[Exhib RA, London, 1309]; untraced		*Graves* V, 1905–6, 95
128.	1849	R Durant Jnr		[Exhib RA, London, 1308]; untraced		*Graves* V, 1905–6, 95
129.	1849	W Vaughan		[Exhib RA, London, 1303]; untraced Other versions: model or cast ex Elswick Hall, Newcastle; untraced		*Robinson* 1886, 30, cat 96; *Graves* V, 1905–6, 95
130.	1850	J H Pope	m	[Exhib RA, London, 1427]; untraced Other versions: model or cast ex Elswick Hall, Newcastle; untraced		*Robinson* 1886, 18, cat 45; *Graves* V, 1905–6, 95
131.	1851	William Giles		Durham Cathedral Library		RG/JP, 5, 845
132.	1852	'A young lady'		[Exhib RA, London, 1414]; untraced		*Graves* V, 1905–6, 95
133.	1855	Sir Thomas Noon Talfourd	m	Crown Court, Stafford		*Lough and Merson* 1987, 39–40, 67, 87
134.	1856	Joseph Burnley Hume		[Exhib RA, London, 1338]; untraced		*Graves* V, 1905–6, 95
135.	1856	Professor Edward Forbes	m	Geological Museum, London Other versions: King's College, London model or cast formerly at Elswick Hall, Newcastle; untraced		*Graves* V, 1905–6, 95; *Lough and Merson* 1987, 87
136.	1857	Rev Dr William S Gilly	m	Durham Cathedral, Dean and Chapter Library Other versions: model or cast ex Elswick Hall, Newcastle; untraced	S	*Robinson* 1886, 26, cat 79; Pevsner, *Durham*, 1983, 204
137.	1857	Rev T Faithfull, vicar of Hatfield		[Exhib RA, London, 1327]; untraced		*Graves* V, 1905–6, 95
138.	1858	Richard Twining	m	[Exhib RA, London, 1271]; untraced Other versions: model or cast ex Elswick Hall, Newcastle; untraced		*Robinson* 1886, 26 cat 78; *Graves* V, 1905–6, 95
139.	1861	Marie Cicely Methuen Payment(s): £235 with effigy in Corsham church		Corsham Court, Wilts	SD	*Lough and Merson* 1987, 67, 87
140.	1862	Edward Stanley	p	St Bartholomew's Hospital, City of London		*Lough and Merson* 1987, 87
141.	1863	The Captain	m	[Exhib RA, London, 1159]; untraced		*Graves* V, 1905–6, 95
142.	1875	Dr Campbell de Morgan	m	Middlesex Hospital, London		*Lough and Merson* 1987, 45, 67, 87
143.	nd	Alexander Sim		Untraced		*Lough and Merson* 1987, 88
144.	nd	Charles, 1st Baron Sudeley	m	Private coll		*Lough and Merson* 1987, 87
145.	nd	Colonel Beresford, cast or model		[Elswick Hall, Newcastle, Northumbs]; untraced		*Lough and Merson* 1987, 88
146.	nd	Georgina Lough		Untraced		*Lough and Merson* 1987, 88

147.	nd	Henrietta, Lady Sudeley	m	Private coll	*Lough and Merson* 1987, 87
148.	nd	James Sewell White, model or cast		[Elswick Hall, Newcastle, Northumbs]; untraced	*Lough and Merson* 1987, 88
149.	nd	Joshua Watson, cast or model		[Elswick Hall, Newcastle, Northumbs]; untraced Other versions: Church House, Westminster, signed	*Lough and Merson* 1987, 88
150.	nd	Judge Knox, cast or model		[Elswick Hall, Newcastle, Northumbs]; untraced	*Lough and Merson* 1987, 88
151.	nd	Lady Bowen, cast or model		[Elswick Hall, Newcastle, Northumbs]; untraced	*Lough and Merson* 1987, 88
152.	nd	Lady Clementina Villiers, cast or model		[Elswick Hall, Newcastle, Northumbs]; untraced	*Lough and Merson* 1987, 88
153.	nd	Lady Diana Huddleston, cast or model		[Elswick Hall, Newcastle, Northumbs]; untraced	RG/JP, 5, 843
154.	nd	Lady Rothschild, cast or model	p	[Elswick Hall, Newcastle, Northumbs]; untraced	*Lough and Merson* 1987, 77, 88
155.	nd	Mrs Crawshaw, cast or model		[Elswick Hall, Newcastle, Northumbs]; untraced	*Lough and Merson* 1987, 88
156.	nd	Mrs Edward James, model or cast		[Elswick Hall, Newcastle, Northumbs]; untraced	*Lough and Merson* 1987, 88
157.	nd	Mrs John Sim, model or cast		[Elswick Hall, Newcastle, Northumbs]; untraced	*Lough and Merson* 1987, 88
158.	nd	Mrs Joseph Hume, model or cast		[Elswick Hall, Newcastle, Northumbs]; untraced	*Lough and Merson* 1987, 88
159.	nd	Mrs Lough		[Elswick Hall, Newcastle, Northumbs]; untraced	*Robinson* 1886, 5–6, cat 2
160.	nd	Mrs Sewell	p	[Elswick Hall, Newcastle, Northumbs]; untraced	*Lough and Merson* 1987, 88
161.	nd	Mrs Wardlaw, model or cast		[Elswick Hall, Newcastle, Northumbs]; untraced	*Lough and Merson* 1987, 88
162.	nd	Rev M Munro, model or cast		[Elswick Hall, Newcastle, Northumbs]; untraced	*Lough and Merson* 1987, 88
163.	nd	Sir James Paget, model or cast		[Elswick Hall, Newcastle, Northumbs]; untraced	*Lough and Merson* 1987, 88
164.	nd	Sir Matthew White Ridley, 2nd Bt		Blagdon, Northumbs	*Read* 1982, 139; *Lough and Merson* 1987, 87
165.	nd	Sir Probey Couteley, model or cast		[Elswick Hall, Newcastle, Northumbs]; untraced	*Lough and Merson* 1987, 88
166.	nd	Stuart Rendel, Baron Rendel of Hatchlands, cast or model		[Elswick Hall, Newcastle, Northumbs]; untraced	*Lough and Merson* 1987, 88
167.	nd	Thomas, 2nd Baron Sudeley		[Elswick Hall, Newcastle, Northumbs]; untraced	*Robinson* 1886, 27, cat 82; *Lough and Merson* 1987, 88
168.	nd	Young woman	m	Private coll	*Lough and Merson* 1987, 87 (repr 35)
Chimneypieces					
169.	nd	Several, carved		Minsteracres, Northumbs	Pevsner, *Northumbs*, 1992, 390
Architectural Sculpture					
170.	pre-1825	Carved ornaments		Newcastle Lit and Phil Soc, Northumbs	*Lough and Merson* 1987, 5
171.	1855	Shakespearean frieze, with scenes from *Macbeth* and *The Tempest* Payment(s): £2,000	m	[10 Carlton House Terrace, London, coll Sir Matthew White Ridley, 4th Bt]; Blagdon, Northumbs	*Read* 1982, 140; *Lough and Merson* 1987, 60, 84 (pl 18)
172.	nd	The Milton shield, model or cast		[Elswick Hall, Newcastle, Northumbs]; untraced	*Lough and Merson* 1987, 83
Reliefs					
173.	1826	The death of Turnus		[Exhib RA, London, 1028]; untraced	*Graves* V, 1905–6, 94; *Lough and Merson* 1987, 60, 85
174.	1841	'Basso-relievo forming part of a monument going out to India for a Light Cavalry Officer'		[Exhib RA, London, 1322]; untraced	*Graves* V, 1905–6, 94
175.	By 1841	Scenes from Homer		[Exhib RA, London, 1843, 1425]; untraced	*Graves* V, 1905–6, 94; *Lough and Merson* 1987, 85
176.	post-1851	Fall of Phaeton, plaque	b	[coll Sir Matthew White Ridley, 4th Bt]; 10 Carlton House Terrace, London Other versions: model or cast ex Elswick Hall, Newcastle	*Robinson* 1886, 29, cat 91; *Read* 1982, 140; *Lough and Merson* 1987, 60–1, 85
177.	by 1870	Night's swift dragon		Untraced	*Lough and Merson* 1987, 85
178.	nd	John Towlerton Leather's achievements	m	[Middleton Hall, Belford, Northumbs]; Laing Art Gallery, Newcastle, Northumbs	*Lough and Merson* 1987, 60, 85 (pl 19)
Miscellaneous					
179.	1831	Mazeppa bound to the wild horses		[Exhib BI, London, 1835]; untraced	*Lough and Merson* 1987, 81
180.	by 1832	Elijah		Untraced	*Lough and Merson* 1987, 82
181.	by 1832	The Death of Nessus		Untraced	*Lough and Merson* 1987, 81
182.	by 1832	The expulsion of Adam and Eve		[Elswick Hall, Newcastle, Northumbs]; untraced	*Lough and Merson* 1987, 81
183.	1834	Centaurs and Lapithae		Untraced	*Lough and Merson* 1987, 82
184.	1835	Hercules and Deianira		[Exhib BI, London]; untraced	*Lough and Merson* 1987, 82
185.	1839	Italian fishing boy		[Exhib BI, London, 430]; untraced	*Graves* 1875, 354
186.	1840	A Roman fruit girl		[Exhib RA, London, 1096]; untraced Other versions: model or cast ex Elswick Hall, Newcastle	*Graves* V, 1905–6, 94; *Robinson* 1886, 41, cat 136

187.	1840	The captive ('The Captive Maid')		[Exhib BI, London, 463]; untraced Other versions: model or cast ex Elswick Hall, Newcastle; untraced	*Graves* 1875, 354; *Robinson* 1886, 40, cat 134
188.	1851	Ganymede, model		[Exhib BI, London, 524]; untraced Other versions: model or cast ex Elswick Hall, Newcastle; untraced	*Graves* 1875, 354; *Lough* 1987, 82
189.	1854	The usurper		[Exhib BI, London, 574]; untraced	*Graves* 1875, 354
190.	1862	Mrs Alexander Sim		[Exhib RA, London, 1098]; untraced Other versions: model or cast ex Elswick Hall, Newcastle; untraced	*Robinson* 1886, 30, cat 98; *Graves* V, 1905–6, 95
191.	1863	Jeannie Deans		[Exhib BI, London, 615]; untraced Other versions: model or cast ex Elswick Hall, Newcastle; untraced	*Graves* 1875, 354; *Robinson* 1886, 40, cat 132
192.	nd	A little touch of Harry, model or cast		[Elswick Hall, Newcastle, Northumbs]; untraced	*Lough and Merson* 1987, 84
193.	nd	A pet, model or cast		[Elswick Hall, Newcastle, Northumbs]; untraced	*Robinson* 1886, 38, cat 125
194.	nd	Angels and apostles		untraced	*Lough and Merson* 1987, 83
195.	nd	Bacchus, the wine crusher		[Elswick Hall, Newcastle, Northumbs]; untraced	*Robinson* 1886, 15, cat 38; *Lough and Merson* 1987, 83
196.	nd	Boy and mermaid, model or cast		[Elswick Hall, Newcastle, Northumbs]; untraced	*Lough and Merson* 1987, 83
197.	nd	Cupid in the nest, model or cast		[Elswick Hall, Newcastle, Northumbs]; untraced	*Lough and Merson* 1987, 36, 83
198.	nd	Eros	m	untraced	*Lady Lever* 1999, 81
199.	nd	Group, 'Fame triumphing over death and crushing Cerberus'		[Elswick Hall, Newcastle, Northumbs]; untraced	*Robinson* 1886, 27 cat 87
200.	nd	Horses and tigers, model or cast		[Elswick Hall, Newcastle, Northumbs]; untraced	*Lough and Merson* 1987, 83
201.	nd	John, 1st Baron Lawrence, model or cast		[Elswick Hall, Newcastle, Northumbs]; untraced	*Robinson* 1886, 24, cat 69
202.	nd	Leda and the swan		untraced	*Lough and Merson* 1987, 83
203.	nd	Mary Rebecca and Georgina Lough, model or cast		[Elswick Hall, Newcastle, Northumbs]; untraced	*Lough and Merson* 1987, 88
204.	nd	Sabrina, model or cast		[Elswick Hall, Newcastle, Northumbs]; untraced	*Lough and Merson* 1987, 83
205.	nd	The Bat Slayer, model or cast		[Elswick Hall, Newcastle, Northumbs]; untraced	*Lough and Merson* 1987, 37, 84
206.	nd	The prophet Ezekiel		untraced	*Lough and Merson* 1987, 83
207.	nd	The spirit, model or cast		[Elswick Hall, Newcastle, Northumbs]; untraced	*Lough and Merson* 1987, 83
208.	nd	Una and the Lion		untraced	*Lough and Merson* 1987, 83

LOVE, Nicholas fl 1754–73

He signs a large, extremely competent, wall-monument in coloured marbles at Wellingborough (**1**). Henry Campion paid him £100 for repairing his London house in 1754, and a further £80 in 1757 (Archives, Campion of Danny, Sussex, in *Gunnis* 1968, 244).

Literary References: *Gunnis* 1968, 244

Funerary Monuments

1.	†1773	John Frederick	All Hallows, Wellingborough, Northants	S	Pevsner, *Northants*, 1973, 452

LOVELL, James fl 1747–77

Nothing is known of Lovell's background or training, but McCarthy suggests that he may have been a pupil in the studio of **Peter Scheemakers** and **Laurent Delvaux**. The earliest evidence of his activities dates from 16 January 1747, when he received a payment of £100 from Sir James Dashwood, perhaps for decorative work at West Wycombe Park. He was then working at Stowe where on 31 January he was paid £8 14s 'on balance for a year's carving', followed by another payment of two guineas on 23 May (Stowe Building and Repair Accounts in *McCarthy* 1973, 222). Over the course of the next 30 years Lovell executed a considerable amount of carving at Stowe, including chimneypieces, architectural ornaments in various materials, reliefs and statues (**15, 17, 20, 23–30**).

Lovell was seen by Gunnis as a protégé of Horace Walpole because of two linked commissions. In 1756 Lovell carved the Montagu family monument at Horton (**3**). Walpole apparently designed this and supervised Lovell's work, for he wrote to Frederick Montagu on 28 August 1756, 'I saw Lovel today, he is very far advanced, and executes to perfection; you will be quite satisfied; I am not discontent with my design now I see how well it succeeds' (HWC, vol 9, 195). Two years later Lovell carved the monument to Galfridus Mann (**4**), designed by Walpole's friend Richard Bentley. There is no evidence of further patronage by Walpole. Other monuments by the sculptor include the Fitzwalter, a 'large and magnificent architectural work, with a white-marble urn set in an alcove of green marble' (*Gunnis* 1968, 244) (**2**).

He worked with the architect Sanderson Miller on a number of occasions, for instance at Wroxted Abbey, Belhus and Hagley Hall. He supplied a rococo chimneypiece for the hall at Hagley (**13**) and one in the dining room is also thought to be his work because it has terms identical to those of the state dressing room chimneypiece at Stowe (**15**). Furthermore, Lovell appears to have supervised the decorative work at Hagley. For Miller's own house, Radway Grange, Warks, he made a statue which Bishop Pococke described as, 'Caractacus in chains, modelled, under Mr Miller's directions, by a countryman of great genius now established in London' (*Dickins and Stanton* 1910, 270) (**8**). Lovell worked in conjunction with the London carpenter and builder John Hobcraft at Stowe, Belhus, Croome Court and at Newton Paddox, Warks, where he received a payment of £293 17s for unidentified work in 1768.

Walpole noted that Lovell had his premises in 'Mortimer Street near Oxford Road' (HWC, vol 35, 644) but by September 1766, when one of Lovell's employees, a Thomas Austin, was tried for stealing a piece of Siena marble from his master, he had moved to Charles Street. Another assistant, John Marsden of Titchfield Street, Marylebone, gave evidence in the case (*The Proceedings of the Old Bailey*, ref t17660903-20, 3 September 1766). Two years later 'James Lovell, of St Mary le Bonne, carver and mason' became bankrupt (*London Mag*, 1768, vol 37, 711), because of his over-reliance on a narrow circle of aristocratic patrons. He was obliged to move to premises in Wall Street, which he rented from Lord Temple for £20 a year. In spite of these difficulties he continued in business until 1777 or later.

EH

Literary References: *Gunnis* 1968, 244; *McCarthy* 1973, 220–32; *Cornforth* 1989, 152–5; *Beard* 1993, 88–110; *Craske* 2000 (2), 113 n35

No.	Date	Work		Location		Reference
Funerary Monuments						
1.	c1754	Sir Thomas Lyttelton Bt (†1751) (designed by Sanderson Miller)		[Hagley Hall, Worcs]; destroyed		*Colvin* 1995, 654
2.	†1756	Benjamin, Earl Fitzwalter		Chelmsford Cathedral, Essex		Pevsner, *Essex*, 1965, 116
3.	1756	Edward and Henrietta Montagu		Horton, Northants	S	Pevsner, *Northants*, 1973, 264
4.	1758	Galfridus Mann (†1756) (designed by Richard Bentley)		Linton, Kent		Pevsner, *Kent: W and Weald*, 1976, 381; *Penny* 1977 (1), 112 (repr)
5.	1760	General James Wolfe		Westerham Church, Kent		*Gunnis* 1968, 244
6.	†1764	Bishop Richard Osbaldeston		Hutton Buscel, N R Yorks	S	Pevsner, *Yorks: N R*, 1966, 198
7.	?1777	Thomas Trotman		Bucknell, Oxon	S	*Gunnis* 1968, 244
Statues						
8.	nd	Caractacus (or 'Ancient Briton') (designed by Sanderson Miller)		Radway Grange, Warwicks, gardens		*McCarthy* 1973 (2), 222
Chimneypieces						
9.	1754–1757	Several	m	[Belhus, Essex]; demol 1956		*McCarthy* 1973 (2), 221–2, 231
10.	1758	'A new French chimney piece, all of statuary marble, black coves' Payment(s): £45		Croome Court, Worcs, lady's dressing room		Archives, Earl of Coventry, in GPC
11.	1758	'Statry Marble with three mouldings' Payment(s): £32		Croome Court, Worcs, 'dressing room over lord Coventry's dressing room'		Archives, Earl of Coventry, in GPC
12.	1758	'Two Marble Chimney Pieces Black Marble Coves' Payment(s): £190		Croome Court, Worcs, saloon		Archives, Earl of Coventry, in GPC
13.	c1760	Rococo		Hagley Hall, Worcs, hall		*McCarthy* 1973 (2), 221
14.	?1767	Two Payment(s): £52		[Sir Richard Lyttelton's house, Piccadilly, London]; untraced		Archives, Lord Brownlow, in *Gunnis* 1968, 244; *McCarthy* 1973 (1), 226
15.	1752–1777	Several, including those in the state dining room and state bedroom		Stowe, Bucks		*Gunnis* 1968, 244; *McCarthy* 1973 (1), 231
Architectural Sculpture						
16.	1751	Ornaments for ceilings	p	Wroxton Abbey, Oxon		*McCarthy* 1973 (2), 231
17.	1752	'two cupids with branches in their hands'		Stowe, Bucks		*Gunnis* 1968, 244
18.	1754	Capitals (designed by Thomas Prowse and Sanderson Miller)		Warwick Shire Hall		*McCarthy* 1973 (2), 222
19.	1754	Gothic ornaments	p	[Belhus, Essex, north drawing room]; demol 1956		*McCarthy* 1973 (2), 221, 231
20.	1752–1754	Ornaments	p	Temple of Concord and Victory, Stowe, Bucks, interior		*McCarthy* 1973 (1), 229, 231
21.	1757	Gothic ornaments	p	[Belhus, Essex, Lady Dacre's bedroom and dressing room]; demol 1956		*McCarthy* 1973 (2), 221–2, 231
22.	1758–1761	Marble and wood carving		Croome Court, Worcs		*Beard* 1993, 88, 91, 92
23.	c1762	Four muses		[Temple of Concord and Victory, Stowe, Bucks, principal front, above the pediment]; Anglesey Abbey, Cambs		inf Tim Knox
24.	1763	Twenty-one medallions commemorating the Seven Years War (from designs by James Stuart)	tc	Temple of Concord and Victory, Stowe, Bucks, pronaos and cella		*Plumptre* 1996, 70 (repr); *Eyres* 2001, 31–50 (repr)
25.	c1767	Festoons and other ornaments		Corinthian Arch, Stowe, Bucks, gardens		*McCarthy* 1973 (1), 220, 222 (repr); Pevsner, *Bucks*, 1994, 674
26.	c1774	Religion and Liberty; Ceres and Flora, two pairs of figures Payment(s): £200		Stowe, Bucks, south front parapet		*McCarthy* 1973 (1), 224, 225, 229 (repr)
27.	1775	Six roundel reliefs Payment(s): £120		Stowe, Bucks, east and west wing window lunettes		*McCarthy* 1973 (1), 223, 225, 229 (repr)
28.	1775–1776	Composite capitals		Queen's Temple, Stowe, Bucks		*McCarthy* 1973 (1), 225, 228 (repr)
29.	1776	Two roundel reliefs of dancing figures representing the seasons, frieze depicting the 'sacrifice of Bacchus', doorcase and ornamental details		Stowe, Bucks, south front portico		*McCarthy* 1973 (1), 225, 227, 228 (repr)
30.	1773–1777	Plaster reliefs and ornaments		Stowe, Bucks, interiors		*McCarthy* 1973 (1), 231
31.	nd	Tabernacle		St Jaques, Douai, France	S	*CL*, 5 June 1969, 1452 (repr)

LOVETT, Thomas, of Bath fl 1766?–95

He was declared bankrupt in 1795 (*Univ Mag*, May 1795, 380).

Literary References: *Gunnis* 1968, 244

Funerary Monuments

1.	?1766	Charles Shoare	Warminster, Wilts	S	*Gunnis* 1968, 244

LUCAS, Richard Cockle 1800–83

Lucas was a versatile artist who worked in a diverse range of media but particularly specialised in small scale wax models and ivory carvings. He was born at Harnham Mill, near Salisbury, on 24 October 1800, the grandson of a woollen manufacturer. At the age of 12 he was apprenticed to an uncle who worked as a cutler in Winchester and he soon became skilled in intricate, small-scale carving. He later recalled, 'I made twelve pairs of scissors so small that they were enclosed in a peach stone; this I elaborately carved . . . made hinges to it, wrote on its polished insides the Lord's Prayer so that it could be magnified and read, and sold it to a lady for a golden guinea' (*Lucas Autobiography*, cited by *Bilbey* 2002, 327). In 1828 he moved to 3 Pickering Terrace, London and at the age of 25, entered the Royal Academy Schools, where he trained under **Sir Richard Westmacott**. He was awarded silver medals in 1828 and 1829.

Lucas worked from a number of London addresses before 1849, when he moved to Otterbourne, near Winchester, and then to Chilworth, near Southampton, where he settled in 1854. He exhibited at the Royal Academy, 1829–59, showing principally busts, medallions and mythological subjects. In 1844 he sent two ideal works to the Westminster Hall Exhibition organised by the Royal Fine Art Commissioners, who were responsible for commissioning paintings and sculpture for the new Palace of Westminster. His statue of *Canute rebuking his flatterers* was not well received (**29**). One reviewer commented, 'it is deficient of all those aids and graces which, with much propriety, might have entered into the treatment. The work, on the whole, is heavy and appears not to have been sufficiently studied' (*AU*, 1844, 215). The second entry, a group entitled *Lilla by his own death preserves the life of Edwin*, was more successful (**30**). The *Literary Gazette* considered that it 'embodies original ideas, is ably treated and the group of the three figures tells well in several view points' (*Lit Gaz*, 20 July 1844, 466). Lucas showed ivory carvings and imitation bronzes, chiefly of classical subjects, at the Great Exhibition of 1851.

In the course of his career he received a number of significant commissions for funeral monuments and public statues. His monument to the Count de Salis has a recumbent effigy (**1**) whilst that to Sir Richard Colt Hoare takes the form of a seated portrait statue (**3**). He provided figures of Samuel Johnson for Lichfield and Isaac Watts, the nonconformist scholar and writer, for Southampton (**22, 33**). Both have reliefs depicting scenes from the subject's life on the pedestal.

Unfortunately Lucas is remembered principally for his involvement in the controversy surrounding a wax bust of *Flora* at the Bodemuseum, formerly the Kaiser Friedrich Museum, in Berlin (**89**). The bust was acquired for the museum by the respected Renaissance scholar Wilhelm von Bode in 1909 as an important work by Leonardo da Vinci. Authorship was called into question when Lucas's son, Albert Dürer Lucas, claimed that his father had made the bust in 1846. The evidence is contradictory and the debate has continued intermittently ever since without being fully resolved. It seems possible that the bust was restored, rather than modelled by Lucas.

He devoted much time to the study of ancient monuments and in 1845 made two models of the Parthenon, showing it both as he thought it might have appeared when newly erected, and also after it was damaged in an explosion in 1687 (**268, 269**). Each measured 12 feet in length and was constructed in wood, with the sculptural parts modelled in wax. They were purchased for the British Museum and displayed in the Elgin Room with the Parthenon sculpture. In the same year he published his findings as *Remarks on the Parthenon: being the results of studies and inquiries connected with the production of two models of that noble building*. The *Builder* welcomed the introduction of the models to the Elgin Room and praised Lucas for the scholarship, taste and sound judgement displayed in his reconstruction of the ancient edifice, enthusiastically declaring, 'A new world of art seems disclosed to us. For the first time we behold the true character of Greek architecture' (*Builder*, 1845, 593). Charles Newton, keeper of Greek and Roman antiquities at the British Museum, disliked Lucas and was less impressed by his archaeological efforts. After Lucas visited him in August 1859 with plans for a similar 'restoration' of the recently excavated mausoleum at Halicarnassus, Newton wrote to a colleague, 'He [Lucas] is evidently mad but as he persuaded the late Sir R. Peel to buy his rubbishy restored model of the Parthenon contrary to every person qualified to judge in the matter, he may succeed in his present object if not watched' (*Newton/Panizzi*, cited by *Jenkins* 1992, 192). Lucas was permitted to study the marbles from Halicarnassus at the museum and wrote a report on the mausoleum, but the museum authorities turned down his offer to sell them models and diagrams.

Lucas pursued his interest in architecture, painting, illustration and photography. In 1854 he designed and built himself a house, Chilworth Tower, and two years later published an account of it, illustrated with 17 plates, entitled, *An Artist's Dream Realized*. The house was sold some years later and Lucas built another nearby, called 'The Tower of the Winds', in homage to the original on the Acropolis. Neither building has survived. He produced large numbers of etchings, including illustrations to Thomas Gray's *Elegy written in a Country Churchyard*, Oliver Goldsmith's *The Deserted Village* and Robert Burns's *Tam O'Shanter*, as well as biblical subjects and representations of his own works. His writings range from art-historical studies, such as *An essay on ancient glass painting* published in 1877, to a whimsical unpublished fairy-tale called *Hetty Lottie and the Proceedings of Little Dick, showing how he woo'd and won a fairy* (Hartley Library, University of Southampton). A contemporary described him as 'a man of great conversational powers and a prolific writer in the periodical press' (*DNB*, XXXIV, 1893, 240).

With the support of Lord Palmerston, who was a friend and patron, in 1865 Lucas secured a civil list pension of £150, in return for donating 22 ivories, 12 waxes and a marble group to the South Kensington Museum. Lucas was proud to have his works displayed at such a prestigious institution and later wrote, 'it is a comfort to me to live and yet be exhibited as an old master' (*Lucas* 1870, cited by *Bilbey* 2002, 327). He died at his home at Chilworth on 18 January 1883 and was buried at the local church, where he is commemorated by a portrait medallion of himself, carved in 1840 (**2**).

His only son, Albert Dürer Lucas, was a flower painter who exhibited works at the British Institution and the Suffolk Street Galleries between 1859 and 1874.

EH

Literary References: *Builder*, 1845, 593–4, 619; *Athenaeum*, 27 Jan 1883, 127–8; *DNB*, XXXIV, 1893, 240 (O'Donoghue); *Sparrow* 1926, 220; *Gunnis* 1968, 244–5; *Ormond* 1973, 276–7; *Pyke* 1973, 82–6; *Jones* 1990, 303–7 (Kratz and Bloc); *Jenkins* 1992, 93, 97, 192–3; *Dawson* 1999, 118–20; *Bilbey* 2002, 327–8; *ODNB* (Rev. Edwards); *Willows* 2004, 56–62

Archival References: RA Admissions; RA Premium list; IGI

Additional MS Sources: Lucas Fragment; Lucas Miscellanea; Lucas Monument; Lucas/Granville; Lucas/Owen; Lucas/Peel

Wills and Administrations: Winchester probate registry, 13 June 1883, personal estate valued at £173 6s 6d; resworn August 1883 at £573 6s 6d

Collections of Drawings, Prints and Photographs: album of 24 drawings of the life of Christ, 1842 (HMI Archive Luc II); 49 drawings and 26 etchings including studies of Westminster Abbey and illustrations to the Book of Ruth, some in albums, many dating from the 1840s (HMI Archive Luc); etched illustrations to *Tam O'Shanter*, 1841 (Edinburgh University lib Ve.5.5); 'Facsimiles of Nature', a series of coloured impressions of leaves, etc, 1858 (BL Tab.442.a.12); 'My Album', 269 etchings and 3 photographs of Chilworth Tower (BM P&D 1859-8-6-946-1218); photographic studies, portraits, landscapes and groups, with MS explanations by the artist, 1859 (BL Tab.442.a.13); 'book of photographs done by R. C. Lucas, sculptor, made on Lord Palmerston confering [*sic*] him a pension from the Royal bounty', 1865 (Hartley lib, University of Southampton, rare books Cope 73 LUC); 'some of the works and phases of R. C. Lucas, sculptor, of the Tower of the Winds, Chilworth, Hants', 1865 (Hartley lib, Univ of Southampton, rare books Cope 73 LUC); album of 33 photographs (VAM P&D E.646-1998)

Miscellaneous Drawings, Prints and Photographs: 'Life, death and fancy', an allegorical etching (Wellcome Institute Library)

Portraits of the Sculptor: two self-portraits, busts (**88, 90**); self-portrait medallion, the sculptor's funeral monument (**2**); self-portrait etching, with pen and wash, 1858, NPG 1651b; self-portrait etching, BM P&D; 'Some of the phases and works of R C Lucas Sculptor done to show the great range of his expression', a collection of largely self-portrait photographs, c1858, NPG Album 62; '50 Studies of Expressions', an album of self-portrait photographs, 1865 (George Eastman House International Museum of Photography and Film, Rochester, NY, 81:1265:0000); self-portrait photo, BM P&D

Funerary Monuments

1.	†1836	Count de Salis Drawing(s): VAM NAL 86. WW.1		St Peter and St Paul, Harlington, Middx	S	Pevsner, *London: N W*, 1991, 323
2.	1840	Richard Cockle Lucas (†1883)		Chilworth, Hants	S	Pevsner, *Hants & Isle of Wight*, 1967, 166
3.	†1841	Sir Richard Colt Hoare Model(s): plaster, Stourhead, Wilts; study in marble exhib Soc of BA, London, 1842, 800		Salisbury Cathedral, Wilts		*Graves* V, 1905–6, 106; Pevsner, *Wilts*, 1975, 415; *Johnson* 1975, 295
4.	†1844	John Fleming		North Stoneham, Hants	S	Pevsner, *Hants & Isle of Wight*, 1967, 359
5.	?1855	Hon Charles Welbore-Ellis		Harrow School, chapel	S	*Gunnis* 1968, 245
6.	?1864	William of Wickham		Winchester Cathedral, Hants		*Willows* 2004, 56

Statues

7.	1830	Love enchained by the Graces, model for an ivory group	i	[Exhib RA, London, 1253]; untraced		*Graves* V, 1905–6, 106
8.	1832	Jane, Marchioness of Blandford, a doll	w	Mrs A H Sanborn, Lakewood, California, USA		*Pyke* 1973, 82
9.	1833	The captive		[Exhib RA, London, 1222]; untraced		*Graves* V, 1905–6, 106
10.	1834	A female and a boy		[Exhib RA, London, 1090]; untraced		*Graves* V, 1905–6, 106
11.	1835	Lady Charlotte Bury		[Exhib RA, London, 903]; untraced		*Graves* V, 1905–6, 106; *Johnson* 1975, 295
12.	1835	Mater Dolorum		[Exhib RA, London, 904]; untraced		*Graves* V, 1905–6, 106; *Johnson* 1975, 295
13.	*c*1835	Sleep (mother and child), statuette	m	VAM 209-1865		*Graves* 1875, 355; *Graves* V, 1905–6, 106; *Johnson* 1975, 295; *Bilbey* 2002, 327 (repr)
14.	1835	Thomas Burgess, Bishop of Salisbury		[Exhib RA, London, 1119]; untraced		*Graves* V, 1905–6, 106
15.	1836	Catherine, Lady Stepney, small full-length portrait	w	[coll Lady Stepney's family]; VAM A.9-1964		*Graves* V, 1905–6, 106; *Pyke* 1973, 82; *Bilbey* 2002, 328
16.	1836	Lady Adelaide Lennox		[Exhib RA, London, 1132]; untraced		*Graves* V, 1905–6, 106
17.	1836	Playfulness, group		[Exhib Soc of BA, London, 882]; untraced		*Johnson* 1975, 295
18.	1836	The young student (son of Rev J T Lait)		[Exhib BI, London, 491]; untraced		*Graves* 1875, 355; *Johnson* 1975, 295
19.	1837	Marquess of Douglas, statuette		[Exhib RA, London, 1153]; untraced		*AU*, 1844, 170; *Graves* V, 1905–6, 106
20.	1838	Anne Seymour Damer		[Exhib RA, London, 1346]; untraced		*Graves* V, 1905–6, 106
21.	1838	David		[Exhib Soc of BA, London, 639]; untraced		*Johnson* 1975, 295
22.	1838	Dr Samuel Johnson Model(s): exhib Soc of BA, London, 1839, 752		Market Square, Lichfield, Staffs		*Johnson* 1975, 295; *Darke* 1991, 167–8 (repr)
23.	1838	Lady Seymour and her son		[Exhib RA, London, 1353]; untraced		*Graves* V, 1905–6, 106; *Johnson* 1975, 295
24.	1839	The Hon Misses Thellusson		[Exhib RA, London, 1347]; untraced		*Graves* V, 1905–6, 106
25.	1840	Christ rejected	m	[Exhib BI, London, 460]; untraced		*Graves* 1875, 355
26.	1840	Mrs Henry Hoare	m	[Exhib Soc of BA, London, 733]; untraced		*Johnson* 1975, 295
27.	1843	Love taught by the Graces	p	[Exhib Soc of BA, London, 736:2]; untraced		*Johnson* 1975, 295
28.	1843	Venus and Adonis	w	[Exhib Soc of BA, London, 736:1]; untraced		*Johnson* 1975, 295
29.	1844	Canute rebuking his flatterers		[Exhib Westminster Hall, London, 98]; untraced		*AU*, 1844, 215; *Lit Gaz*, 1435, 20 July 1855, 466
30.	1844	Lilla by his own death preserves the life of Edwin		[Exhib Westminster Hall, London, 99]; untraced		*AU*, 1844, 215
31.	1844	Richard Whittington		[Exhib Soc of BA, London, 759]; untraced		*Johnson* 1975, 295

32.	1854	Sir Thomas Fleming, Lord Chief Justice of England	p	[Guildhall, Newport, I of W]; Destroyed	D	RG/JP, 5, 850
33.	1858	Isaac Watts		Watts Park, Southampton, Hants		*Gunnis* 1968, 245; *Darke* 1991, 93
34.	1859	Henry, 3rd Viscount Palmerston, statuette	m	[Exhib RA, London, 1240]; untraced		*Graves* V, 1905–6, 107; *Ormond* 1973, 360
35.	nd	Boy extracting a thorn from his foot, statuette	i	VAM 195-1865		VAM SCP colls list, ivories
36.	nd	Cupid seated, statuette	i	VAM 196-1865		VAM SCP colls list, ivories
Busts						
37.	1829	Mr Cockle		[Exhib RA, London, 1136]; untraced		*Graves* V, 1905–6, 105
38.	1829	Mrs Lucas		[Exhib RA, London, 1144]; untraced		*Graves* V, 1905–6, 105
39.	1830	Henry, 3rd Viscount Palmerston	m	Broadlands, Hants		*Graves* V, 1905–6, 107; *Ormond* 1973, 359
40.	1831	Rev Dr Fisher, Master of the Charterhouse		[Exhib RA, London, 1116]; untraced		*Graves* V, 1905–6, 106
41.	1831	Thomas Burgess, Bishop of Salisbury		[Exhib RA, London, 1137]; untraced		*Graves* V, 1905–6, 106
42.	1831	Unidentified gentleman		[Exhib RA, London, 1118]; untraced		*Graves* V, 1905–6, 106
43.	1832	George Law, Bishop of Bath and Wells		[Exhib RA, London, 1190]; untraced		*Graves* V, 1905–6, 106
44.	1832	John Woodhouse, Dean of Lichfield		[Exhib RA, London, 1156]; untraced		*Graves* V, 1905–6, 106
45.	1832	Sir J Burrough		[Exhib RA, London, 1189]; untraced		*Graves* V, 1905–6, 106
46.	1833	Henry, 1st Baron Brougham and Vaux, Sir William Horne and Mrs Denman		[Exhib RA, London, 1164]; untraced		*Graves* V, 1905–6, 106
47.	1833	Miss Bury		[Exhib RA, London, 1196]; untraced		*Graves* V, 1905–6, 106; *Johnson* 1975, 295
48.	1834	A B Lambert	p	Linnaean Soc, London		*Graves* V, 1905–6, 106; *Johnson* 1975, 295
49.	1834	'A shade with Busts of the Lord Chief Chancellor, the Lord Chief Justice, and the Ex-Attorney-General, Sir Wm. Horne'		[Exhib Soc of BA, London, 843]; untraced		*Johnson* 1975, 295
50.	1834	Hon Mrs Perceval		[Exhib RA, London, 1063]; untraced		*Graves* V, 1905–6, 106
51.	1834	Rev E Bury		[Exhib RA, London, 1092]; untraced		*Graves* V, 1905–6, 106; *Johnson* 1975, 295
52.	1835	'Bust of Mrs. Denman the Earl of Stamford, Mrs Read and R. Cockle Esq.'		[Exhib Soc of BA, London, 765]; untraced		*Johnson* 1975, 295
53.	1835	George, Lord Grey of Groby		[Exhib RA, London, 1137]; untraced		*Graves* V, 1905–6, 106; *Johnson* 1975, 295
54.	1835	Hon Miss Grey of Groby		[Exhib Soc of BA, London, 876]; untraced		*Johnson* 1975, 295
55.	1835	Katharine, Lady Grey of Groby		[Exhib RA, London, 1135]; untraced		*Graves* V, 1905–6, 106; *Johnson* 1975, 295
56.	1835	Lucien Bonaparte		[Exhib RA, London, 1097]; untraced		*Graves* V, 1905–6, 106
57.	1835	P Williams		[Exhib RA, London, 1095]; untraced		*Graves* V, 1905–6, 106
58.	*c*1836	Catherine, Lady Stepney, as Cleopatra	m	[coll Lady Stepney's family]; VAM A.8-1964		*Graves* V, 1905–6, 106; *Bilbey* 2002, 327–8 (repr)
59.	1836	Hon Mrs Warburton	m	[Exhib Soc of BA, London, 881]; untraced		*Johnson* 1975, 295
60.	1836	Lady Gray Egerton	m	[Exhib RA, London, 1106]; untraced		*Graves* V, 1905–6, 106
61.	1836	Louisa Bingham, Lady Elcho	m	[Exhib RA, London, 1152]; untraced		*Graves* V, 1905–6, 106; *Johnson* 1975, 295
62.	1836	Sir David Baird		[Exhib RA, London, 1090]; untraced		*Graves* V, 1905–6, 106; *Johnson* 1975, 295
63.	1836	Venerable Archdeacon Bayley		[Exhib RA, London, 1129]; untraced		*Graves* V, 1905–6, 106
64.	1837	Daughter of Lord Elcho	m	[Exhib RA, London, 1247]; untraced		*Graves* V, 1905–6, 106
65.	1837	Lord Elcho	m	[Exhib RA, London, 1244]; untraced		*Graves* V, 1905–6, 106
66.	1837	Richard Cockle		[Exhib Soc of BA, London, 579]; untraced		*Johnson* 1975, 295
67.	1838	Miss Carteris		[Exhib Soc of BA, London, 597]; untraced		*Johnson* 1975, 295
68.	1839	J R Parker		[Exhib Soc of BA, London, 753]; untraced		*Johnson* 1975, 295
69.	1839	Mrs R Green		[Exhib Soc of BA, London, 754]; untraced		*Johnson* 1975, 295
70.	1839	R Green		[Exhib Soc of BA, London, 755]; untraced		*Johnson* 1975, 295
71.	1840	James Campbell		[Exhib Soc of BA, London, 737]; untraced		*Johnson* 1975, 295
72.	1840	'Lady Georgiana Cholomeley'	m	[Exhib Soc of BA, London, 734]; untraced		*Johnson* 1975, 295
73.	1840	R Greene Senior		[Exhib Soc of BA, London, 736]; untraced		*Johnson* 1975, 295
74.	1840	Son of Sir Montague Cholomeley	m	[Exhib Soc of BA, London, 735]; untraced		*Johnson* 1975, 295
75.	1842	General George Michell		Mr Lloyd, Great Bedwyn, Wilts		*Graves* V, 1905–6, 106; *Johnson* 1975, 295
76.	1843	F C Meyer		[Exhib Soc of BA, London, 736:4]; untraced		*Johnson* 1975, 295
77.	1843	George Rokewood		[Exhib Soc of BA, London, 747]; untraced		*Johnson* 1975, 295
78.	1843	William, 1st Baron Wynford, Thomas, 1st Baron Denman and Mrs Denman		[Exhib RA, London, 1382]; untraced		*Graves* V, 1905–6, 106

79.	1844	Charles Carisbrook		[Exhib Soc of BA, London, 765]; untraced		*Johnson* 1975, 295
80.	1844	Miss Prince		[Exhib Soc of BA, London, 766]; untraced		*Johnson* 1975, 295
81.	1844	Unidentified lady		[Exhib Soc of BA, London, 768]; untraced		*Johnson* 1975, 295
82.	1849	Charles Sheridan		[Exhib for sale Colosseum, Regent's Park, London]; untraced		RG/JP, 5, 850
83.	1849	General Wyndham		[Exhib for sale Colosseum, Regent's Park, London]; untraced		RG/JP, 5, 850
84.	1849	Mr and Mrs Campbell		[Exhib for sale Colosseum, Regent's Park, London]; untraced		RG/JP, 5, 850
85.	1849	Mr Lucas		[Exhib for sale Colosseum, Regent's Park, London]; untraced		RG/JP, 5, 850
86.	1849	Sir Richard Colt Hoare		[Exhib for sale Colosseum, Regent's Park, London]; untraced		RG/JP, 5, 850
87.	1851	Edward Hawkins FRS, FSA	p	BM	SD	*Dawson* 1999, 118–20 (repr)
88.	1858	'The architect of Chilworth Tower' (Richard Cockle Lucas)		[Exhib RA, London, 1294]; untraced		*Graves* V, 1905–6, 107
89.	1846–1860	Flora (probably restoration only)	w	Kaiser Friedrich Museum, Berlin		*Jones* 1990, 303–7, cat no 335
90.	1868	Richard Cockle Lucas, self portrait	p	NPG 1783	SD	*Ormond* 1973, 276–7 (pl 548)
91.	nd	A boy	w	Ashmolean WA 1939.40		*Penny* 1992, III, 115 (repr)
92.	nd	D C Read	p	Ashmolean WA 1855.568 Other versions: ex coll D C Read, small wax (untr)		*Johnson* 1975, 295; *Penny* 1992, III, 116 (repr)
93.	nd	George, 7th Earl of Stamford	w	VAM A.78-1937 Other versions: ex Enville, Staffs, 1832, w; untraced		*Graves* V, 1905–6, 106; inf: VAM
Reliefs						
94.	1830	W Daking		[Exhib RA, London, 1088]; untraced		*Graves* V, 1905–6, 106
95.	1832	Children of George and Katharine, Lord and Lady Grey of Groby	w	[Enville, Staffs]; untraced		*Graves* V, 1905–6, 106; *Gunnis* 1968, 245
96.	1833	Mr I Hunter	w	Sold Christie, 24 June 1975, lot 2		*Pyke* 1981, 26
97.	1836	Countess of Wemyss and her daughters, Lady Jane and Lady Caroline Charteris, medallion		[Exhib Soc of BA, London, 875]; untraced		*Johnson* 1975, 295
98.	1836	Shakespeare, 'the poet of nature', frieze of seven scenes	w	Philadelphia Museum of Art, USA		*Pyke* 1973, 82; *Johnson* 1975, 295
99.	1837	Dr Edward Denison, Bishop of Salisbury	w	Wilton House, Wilts Other versions: VAM Knox / Longstaffe-Gowan coll, SD 1853, wax ex coll Sir Harry R Page, Manchester, 1853, wax; untraced coll Derek Sherborn, *c* 1985 wax (1854) Salisbury Museum, Wilts, SC1, 1854, wax Laurel G Blair, Toledo, Ohio, USA wax		*Pyke* 1973, 82; *Pyke* 1981, 26
100.	1840	Mrs Case Bunnel	w	Laurel G Blair, Toledo, Ohio, USA		*Pyke* 1981, 26
101.	1846	Cleopatra	w	E J Pyke, 1973		*Pyke* 1973, 82
102.	1847	Athena of the Parthenon	w	E J Pyke, 1973		*Graves* V, 1905–6, 106; *Pyke* 1973, 82
103.	1847	Jupiter (with bronzed finish)	w	Salisbury Museum, Wilts, SC3 Other versions: Salisbury museum, Wilts, SC4, copy in plain wax		*Graves* V, 1905–6, 106; *Pyke* 1973, 82
104.	1849	Arthur, 1st Duke of Wellington	w	[Exhib for sale Colosseum, Regent's Park, London]; untraced		RG/JP, 5, 850
105.	1849	Lady Madden	w	NPG D7202		*Graves* V, 1905–6, 107; *Ormond* 1973, 299
106.	1849	Mr le Normonte		[Exhib RA, London, 635]; untraced		*Graves* V, 1905–6, 107
107.	?1849	Proserpine, head and shoulders, low relief	i	VAM 186-1865		*Graves* V, 1905–6, 107
108.	1849	Sir Frederic Madden	w	NPG 1979	SD	*Ormond* 1973, 299 (pl 593); *Pyke* 1973, 82
109.	1849	William Richard Hamilton	w	Soc Antiq, London Other versions: V Claydon, Chelmsford, Essex, w		*Graves* V, 1905–6, 107; *Pyke* 1973, 82
110.	1850	Albert Way	w	Derek Sherborn, Bedfont, Middx Other versions: VAM, 185?, w Soc Antiq, London, w		*Pyke* 1973, 83
111.	1850	Edward Hawkins	w	[coll Sir Philip Malpas de Grey Egerton]; VAM 27-1867 Other versions: Soc Antiq, London, 1850, wax S C Grimes, Tunbridge Wells, Kent, wax ex coll Rupert Gunnis, wax; untraced		*Graves* V, 1905–6, 107; *Pyke* 1973, 82; *Dawson* 1999, 118
112.	1850	Edward Maltby, Bishop of Durham	w	R Wilson, Creve Coeur, MO, USA		*Pyke* 1973, 82
113.	1850	Emily Mary, Viscountess Palmerston	w	Stanton Harcourt Manor, Oxon Other versions: Angus, Kirriemuir (Countess Airlie of Cortachy Castle), w		*Pyke* 1973, 82; *Pyke* 1981, 26

No.	Date	Subject		Location		Literature
114.	1850	General Charles Fox	w	Untraced Other versions: S J Balston, Covington, Hunts, w		*Pyke* 1973, 82; *Pyke* 19781, 26
115.	c1850	Head of a girl	w	LMG, W R Yorks, 716/27		*Leeds* 1996, 11 (repr)
116.	1850	Henry George Liddell	w	Knox/Longstaffe-Gowan coll	SD	*Graves* V, 1905–6, 107; *Gunnis* 1968, 254; *Ormond* 1973, 271
117.	1850	Henry, 3rd Viscount Palmerston		Broadlands, Hants Other versions: Duke of Richmond and Gordon, London, 1851, wax BGM, 1851, wax Christie, 13 April 1983, lot 155, SD 1855, wax NPG 2226, 1856, wax J L Engel, Vancouver, Canada, 1858, wax BGM (three heads), 1863, wax VAM 201-1865, nd, ivory Brooks's Club, London, wax coll E J Pyke, wax coll Lord Faringdon, wax Countess Airlie of Cortachy Castle, Angus, Kirriemuirw Laurel G Blair, Toledo, Ohio, USA, wax		*Graves* V, 1905–6, 107; *Gunnis* 1968, 245; *Ormond* 1973, 358 (repr 708); *Pyke* 1973, 82; *Pyke* 1981, 26
118.	1850	Lieutenant-Colonel William Martin Leake	w	Soc Antiq, London		*Graves* V, 1905–6, 107; *Pyke* 1973, 82
119.	1850	Rev J T Law		[Exhib RA, London, 1158]; untraced		*Graves* V, 1905–6, 107
120.	1850	S Birch and his wife		[Exhib RA, London, 1426]; untraced		*Graves* V, 1905–6, 107
121.	1850	Sir Anthony Panizzi	w	NPG 2187 Other versions: BM, 1850, w coll Mrs Betty St John	SD	*Ormond* 1973, 363 (repr 712); *Pyke* 1973, 82
122.	1850	Sir Henry Rawlinson, 1st Bt	w	NPG 1714 Other versions: Sotheby, 27 April 1959, lot 126, 1850, wax Sotheby, 2 June 1975, lot 135, 1850, wax Ashmolean, S, wax	SD	*Gunnis* 1968, 245; *Pyke* 1973, 82; *Pyke* 1981, 26; *Penny* 1992, III, 118 (repr)
123.	1850	Sir Richard Major	w	BM		*Gunnis* 1968, 245; *Pyke* 1973, 82
124.	1850	Thomas Garnier, Dean of Winchester	w	NPG 4844 Other versions: Mrs A Garnier, Mayfield (Sussex?), 1851, wax Winchester City Museum (two), 1851, wax Carnegie Museum of Art, Pittsburgh, USA, 1851, wax Winchester Guildhall, wax Hon K R Thomson, Toronto, Canada, wax ex coll E J Pyke, London, w; untraced	SD	*Ormond* 1973, 184 (repr 346); *Pyke* 1973, 82 (repr 178)
125.	1850	Vernon Smith, Baron Lyveden	w	Laurel G Blair, Toledo, Ohio, USA		*Pyke* 1981, 26
126.	c1850	William, 3rd Earl of Enniskillen and his first wife, Jane	w	Saighton Grange, Cheshire		RG/JP, 5, 850
127.	1851	Abbott Laurence		[Exhib RA, London, 1386]; untraced		*Graves* V, 1905–6, 107
128.	1851	Alderman Willis, of Winton and Winchester	w	Sheffield, W R Yorks (A J Willis)		*Pyke* 1981, 26
129.	1851	Archdeacon Charles James Hoare and his wife, Jane Isabella	w	Sotheby, 27 April 1959, lot 125	SD	
130.	1851	Benjamin Vulliamy	w	Worshipful Company of Clockmakers, Guildhall, City of London, library, acc 1087 Other versions: Private coll, 1850, wax		*Gunnis* 1968, 245
131.	1851	Chevalier Bunsen	w	VAM		*Graves* V, 1905–6, 107; *Gunnis* 1968, 245; *Pyke* 1973, 82
132.	1851	Graeme Winton	w	Christie, 24 Oct 1967, lot 90		*Pyke* 1973, 82
133.	1851	H Raper RN and his wife		Sotheby, 24 Oct 1960, lot 92	SD	
134.	1851	Henry Hallam	w	[coll Mrs Malcolm Young]; NPG 3119 Other versions: coll Sir Henry Leonard (1929)	SD	*Ormond* 1973, 208 (repr 390); *Pyke* 1973, 82
135.	1851	Henry, 1st Marquess of Anglesey	w	NPG 5270 Other versions: NMW, Cardiff, w, 1851		*Graves* V, 1905–6, 107; *Pyke* 1973, 82
136.	1851	Lady Caroline Garnier	w	Mrs A Garnier, Mayfield (Sussex?)		*Pyke* 1973, 82
137.	1851	Lady Jocelyn		[Exhib RA, London, 1310]; untraced		*Graves* V, 1905–6, 107
138.	1851	Lord Stanley	w	Stanton Harcourt Manor, Oxon		*Pyke* 1973, 82
139.	1851	R H Layard	w	Stanton Harcourt Manor, Oxon		*Pyke* 1973, 82
140.	1851	Rev Dr Chandler	w	Carnegie Museum of Art, Pittsburgh, USA		*Pyke* 1973, 82

141.	1852	Caroline, Lady Stirling-Maxwell (Caroline Norton)	w	Stanton Harcourt Manor, Oxon Other versions: Christie, 5 Oct 1975, lot 13, 1852, w Laurel G Blair, Toledo, Ohio, USA w Countess Airlie, Cortachy Castle, Angus, Kirriemuir, w Philadelphia Museum of Art, USA, w		*Ormond* 1973, 433; *Pyke* 1973, 82; *Pyke* 1981, 26
142.	1852	Charles Richard Sumner, Bishop of Winchester	w	Stanton Harcourt Manor, Oxon Other versions: ex coll R Gunnis; VAM A.142-1965 1856, w		*Gunnis* 1968, 245; *Pyke* 1973, 83; inf: VAM
143.	1852	George Atkins	w	Worshipful Company of Clockmakers, Guildhall, City of London, library, acc 1087		
144.	1852	James Meadows Rendel and Lewis Rendel	w	Welholme Galleries, Grimsby, Lincs	SD	RG/JP, 5, 853v; *Pyke* 1981, 26
145.	1852	John Bullar	w	Hon K R Thomson, Toronto, Canada		*Pyke* 1973, 82
146.	1852	Lieutenant General Frederick	w	Stanton Harcourt Manor, Oxon Other versions: Bonham, 16 March 1976, lot 160		*Pyke* 1973, 82; *Pyke* 1981, 26
147.	1852	Miss Grenville Smith	w	Stanton Harcourt Manor, Oxon		*Pyke* 1973, 82
148.	1852	Rev Canon Caris	w	Untraced		*Gunnis* 1968, 245; *Pyke* 1973, 82
149.	1852	Robert Brown	w	Royal Botanic Gardens, Kew, Richmond, Surrey		*Pyke* 1973, 82
150.	1852	Sir Richard Colt Hoare	w	Stourhead, Wilts (NT)		*Pyke* 1973, 82
151.	1853	Thomas Willis Fleming	m	VAM A.7-1982	SD	*Bilbey* 2002, 328 (repr)
152.	1854	John Buller	w	Sotheby, 26 July 1976, lot 11 Other versions: Sotheby, 24 Jan 1974, lot 42		*Pyke* 1981, 26
153.	1855	Fox Maule, 2nd Baron Panmure	w	Stanton Harcourt Manor, Oxon		*Pyke* 1973, 82
154.	1855	Sir Arthur Helps	w	Sotheby, 13 April 1981, lot 7		*Pyke* 1981, 26
155.	1856	Abbot Lawrence	w	BGM		*Pyke* 1973, 82
156.	1856	Mrs William Gray	w	[ex coll Dame Jane Colt]; Earl of Stamford, Altrincham, Cheshire		*Pyke* 1973, 82
157.	1856	P Linn	w	Stanton Harcourt Manor, Oxon		*Pyke* 1973, 82
158.	1856	Sidney Herbert	w	Meiford, Montgomery (Sir Simon Meade)		*Pyke* 1973, 82
159.	1856	Thomas Winter Jones	w	BM		*Ormond* 1973, 363; *Pyke* 1973, 82
160.	1858	John Singleton Copley, Baron Lyndhurst	w	Knox/Longstaffe-Gowan coll Other versions: Sir Harry Page, Manchester, 1857, w Stanton Harcourt Manor, Oxon two, 1857, w BGM, 1863, w	SD	*Graves* V, 1905–6, 107; *Ormond* 1973, 283; *Pyke* 1973, 82
161.	1858	Mrs William Rogers	w	Philadelphia Museum of Art, USA		*Pyke* 1973, 82
162.	1858	Rev C Moore	w	Untraced		*Gunnis* 1968, 245; *Pyke* 1973, 82
163.	1858	Vernon Smith	w	J L Engel, Vancouver, Canada		*Graves* V, 1905–6, 107; *Pyke* 1973, 82
164.	1859	Samuel Wilberforce, Bishop of Oxford	w	VAM 175-1865		inf: VAM
165.	1860	Miss Holloway	w	VAM A.141-1965		inf: VAM
166.	1860	Rev Richard Croker	w	Anglesey Abbey, Cambs (NT) Other versions: T D Baxandale, London		*Pyke* 1973, 82
167.	nd	A J Wigram	w	Philadelphia Museum of Art, USA		*Pyke* 1973, 83
168.	nd	A Roman emperor, low relief	i	VAM 202-1865		VAM SCP colls list, ivory
169.	nd	Alderman Hoare and his wife	w	Delhom Gallery and Institute, Mint Museum of Art, Charlotte, KC, USA		*Pyke* 1981, 26
170.		Alexander the Great with the horns of Ammon	i	VAM 205-1865		VAM SCP colls list, ivory
171.	nd	Alfred, Lord Tennyson	w	[Rackstrow's Museum, London]; untraced		*Pyke* 1981, 26
172.	nd	Benjamin Disraeli	w	[Rackstrow's Museum, London]; untraced		*Pyke* 1981, 26
173.	nd	Bishop Gilbert	w	[Chichester Cathedral, Sussex]; untraced		RG/JP, 5, 855
174.	nd	C H S Bailey and W P Bailey	w	Sold Christie 11 Dec 1978, lot 137		*Pyke* 1981, 26
175.	nd	Captain Sir John Franklin RN	w	NMM, Greenwich		*Pyke* 1981, 26
176.	nd	Charles Tucker	w	Soc Antiq, London Other versions: Mr and Mrs Gardener, London		*Pyke* 1973, 83; *Pyke* 1981, 26
177.	nd	Christ blessing the little children	i	VAM 194-1865		VAM SCP colls list, ivories
178.	nd	Classical head (Iris?)	i	VAM 187-1865		VAM SCP colls list, ivories
179.	nd	Classical/mythological subject	w	Sotheby, 7 Nov 1980, lot 15		*Pyke* 1981, 26
180.	nd	Cleopatra with an asp	i	VAM 189-1865		VAM SCP colls list, ivories
181.	nd	Crouching Venus, oval	i	VAM 199-1865		VAM SCP colls list, ivories
182.	nd	D Z Watts	w	Thomas Duncan, London		*Pyke* 1981, 26
183.	nd	Daniel O'Connell	w	Stanton Harcourt Manor, Oxon		*Pyke* 1973, 82
184.	nd	Descent from the Cross, coloured ivory	i	VAM 190-1865		VAM SCP colls list, ivories
185.	nd	Dr William Hyde Wollaston FRS	w	N Wollaston, Stoke-by-Nayland, nr Colchester, Essex		*Pyke* 1981, 26
186.	nd	G M Pickard	w	Mr and Mrs Gardner, London		*Pyke* 1981, 26
187.	nd	G Winter	w	Laurel G Blair, Toledo, Ohio, USA		*Pyke* 1981, 26
188.	nd	George Washington	w	Stanton Harcourt Manor, Oxon		*Pyke* 1973, 83

189.	nd	George, Lord Byron	w	[Rackstrow's Museum, London]; untraced	*Pyke* 1981, 26
190.	nd	Head of Ariadne	i	VAM 200-1865	VAM SCP colls list, ivories
191.	nd	Henry, 1st Baron Brougham and Vaux	w	Stanton Harcourt Manor, Oxon	*Pyke* 1973, 82
192.	nd	Henry, 1st Marquis of Anglesey (?)	w	Stanton Harcourt Manor, Oxon	*Pyke* 1973, 82
193.	nd	Iris descending, coloured ivory	i	VAM 188-1865	VAM SCP colls list, ivories
194.	nd	J Brown	w	Sotheby, 11 Oct 1973	*Pyke* 1981, 26
195.	nd	J E Fitzgerald	w	Delhom Gallery and Institute, Mint Museum of Art, Charlotte, KC, USA	*Pyke* 1981, 26
196.	nd	James McGregor	w	Glasgow Chamber of Commerce, Lanarks	*Pyke* 1981, 26
197.	nd	John Constable	w	Anglesey Abbey, Cambs (NT)	*Pyke* 1973, 82
198.	nd	John Fisher, Bishop of Salisbury	w	Salisbury Museum, Wilts, SC2	inf: Salisbury Museum
199.	nd	John Hill	w	Untraced	*Pyke* 1973, 82
200.	nd	John Holmes	w	Soc Antiq, London	inf: Soc Antiq
201.	nd	John Lock	w	Sudeley Castle, Glos	*Pyke* 1981, 26
202.	nd	Julius Caesar	i	VAM 204-1865	VAM SCP colls list, ivory
203.	nd	Jupiter, head and shoulders, high relief	i	VAM 185-1865	VAM SCP colls list, ivories
204.	nd	Leda and the Swan	w	VAM 176-1865	inf: VAM
205.	nd	Marquess of Douglas	w	Stanton Harcourt Manor, Oxon	*Pyke* 1973, 82
206.	nd	Mrs Stey	w	NMM, Greenwich	*Pyke* 1981, 26
207.	nd	Pallas Athene, head and shoulders	i	VAM 184-1865	VAM SCP colls list, ivories
208.	nd	Religious subject	w	Laurel G Blair, Toledo, Ohio, USA	*Pyke* 1981, 26
209.	nd	Rev Dr Williams	w	Hon K R Thomson, Toronto, Canada	*Pyke* 1973, 83
210.	nd	Richard Pearson	w	R Allen, Surbiton, Surrey	*Pyke* 1981, 26
211.	nd	Robert Carr, Bishop of Chichester (?)	w	Carnegie Museum of Art, Pittsburgh, USA	*Pyke* 1973, 82
212.	nd	Robert, Earl of Leicester	w	Lady Elizabeth Longman, London	*Pyke* 1981, 26
213.	nd	Samuel Rogers	w	Stanton Harcourt Manor, Oxon	*Pyke* 1973, 82
214.	nd	The naming of St John the Baptist (after Georg Schweigger)	i	VAM 191-1865	*Jones* 1990, 125, cat 129b
215.	nd	The nativity, high relief	i	VAM 192-1865	VAM SCP colls list, ivories
216.	nd	The raising of Lazarus	i	VAM 193-1865	VAM SCP colls list, ivories
217.	nd	The three graces (after Canova)	i	VAM 197-1865 Other versions: VAM 198-1865, i	VAM SCP colls list, ivories
218.	nd	Thomas Carlyle	w	[Rackstrow's Museum, London]; untraced	*Pyke* 1981, 26
219.	nd	Two classical works	w	BGM 177/8-1865	*Pyke* 1973, 82
220.	nd	Two religious works	w	BGM 179 & 180-1865	*Pyke* 1973, 82
221.	nd	Two unidentified men	w	Stanton Harcourt Manor, Oxon	*Pyke* 1973, 83
222.	nd	Unidentified man	w	Philadelphia Museum of Art, USA S43-95-69	*Pyke* 1973, 83
223.	nd	Unidentified man	w	Christie, 14 Oct 1975, lot 9	*Pyke* 1981, 26
224.	nd	Unidentified woman	w	Stanton Harcourt Manor, Oxon	*Pyke* 1973, 83
225.	nd	Unidentified woman	w	Laurel G Blair, Toledo, Ohio, USA	*Pyke* 1981, 26
226.	nd	Unidentified woman	w	Mrs F A Simmonds, Pirbright, Surrey	*Pyke* 1981, 26
227.	nd	Victorian statesman	w	Christie, 15 Feb 1966, lot 177	*Pyke* 1973, 83
228.	nd	Warrior and Amazon	w	VAM 181-1865 Other versions: VAM 182-1865, w VAM A.83-1965, w	inf: VAM
229.	nd	William Ewart Gladstone		[Rackstrow's Museum, London]; untraced	*Pyke* 1981, 26
230.	nd	William Long		Caroline Rogers, London	*Pyke* 1981, 26
231.	nd	William, 3rd Earl of Radnor (?)	w	Stanton Harcourt Manor, Oxon	*Pyke* 1973, 82
Miscellaneous					
232.	1829	Cleopatra and her women		[Exhib RA, London, 1145]; untraced	*Graves* V, 1905–6, 105
233.	1830	A child, model		[Exhib RA, London, 1130]; untraced	*Graves* V, 1905–6, 106
234.	1830	Mrs Cockle, model		[Exhib RA, London, 1128]; untraced	*Graves* V, 1905–6, 106
235.	1830	The Hours bringing forth the horses of Apollo		[Exhib RA, London, 1215]; untraced	*Graves* V, 1905–6, 106
236.	1831	Daughters of the Earl of Carlisle, model		[Exhib RA, London, 1083]; untraced	*Graves* V, 1905–6, 106
237.	1831	Daughters of the Earl of Radnor, model		[Exhib RA, London, 1076]; untraced	*Graves* V, 1905–6, 106
238.	1831	Earl of Radnor, model for an ivory carving		[Exhib RA, London, 1084]; untraced	*Graves* V, 1905–6, 106
239.	1831	Mischief		[Exhib RA, London, 1124]; untraced	*Graves* V, 1905–6, 106
240.	1831	Venus and Adonis		[Exhib RA, London, 1122]; untraced	*Graves* V, 1905–6, 106
241.	1832	Charity		[Exhib RA, London, 1160]; untraced	*Graves* V, 1905–6, 106
242.	1832	Girl at a bath		[Exhib RA, London, 1157]; untraced	*Graves* V, 1905–6, 106; *Johnson* 1975, 295
243.	1833	An early Christian		[Exhib RA, London, 1160]; untraced	*Graves* V, 1905–6, 106
244.	1833	Samson killing the lion		[Exhib RA, London, 1195]; untraced	*Graves* V, 1905–6, 106
245.	1833	Sea nymph		[Exhib RA, London, 1159]; untraced	*Graves* V, 1905–6, 106; *Johnson* 1975, 295
246.	1834	Confirmation (portraits of the Henry Law, Bishop of Bath and Wells and his grand-daughter, Miss Powell)		[Exhib RA, London, 1044]; untraced	*Graves* V, 1905–6, 106; *Johnson* 1975, 295
247.	1836	The inspiration of Milton		[Exhib BI, London, 497]; untraced	*Graves* 1875, 355
248.	1837	Dr Samuel Johnson		[Exhib Soc of BA, London, 591]; untraced	*Johnson* 1975, 295
249.	1837	John Milton		[Exhib Soc of BA, London, 592]; untraced	*Johnson* 1975, 295

250.	1837	Milo		[Exhib Soc of BA, London, 597]; untraced	*Johnson* 1975, 295
251.	1837	Nymph and Cupid		[Exhib Soc of BA, London, 598]; untraced	*Johnson* 1975, 295
252.	1837	Psyche born by zephyrs		[Exhib Soc of BA, London, 596]; untraced	*Johnson* 1975, 295
253.	1837	Romeo and Juliet		[Exhib BI, London, 447]; untraced	*Graves* 1875, 355
254.	1837	William Shakespeare		[Exhib Soc of BA, London, 590]; untraced	*Johnson* 1975, 295
255.	1838	Adonis watching the chase		[Exhib Soc of BA, London, 640]; untraced	*Johnson* 1975, 295
256.	1838	The divine		[Exhib BI, London, 492]; untraced	*Graves* 1875, 355
257.	1838	The philosopher		[Exhib BI, London, 493]; untraced	*Graves* 1875, 355
258.	1838	The poet		[Exhib BI, London, 491]; untraced	*Graves* 1875, 355
259.	1839	A young sailor		[Exhib BI, London, 433]; untraced	*Graves* 1875, 355
260.	1839	Unidentified lady and child		[Exhib BI, London, 432]; untraced	*Graves* 1875, 355
261.	1839	Unidentified lady and her children		[Exhib BI, London, 436]; untraced	*Graves* 1875, 355
262.	1840	Hercules slaying the Nemaean lion		[Exhib BI, London, 453]; untraced	*Graves* 1875, 355; *Johnson* 1975, 295
263.	1840	The princes in the tower		[Exhib Soc of BA, London, 732]; untraced	*Johnson* 1975, 295
264.	1843	A druidical high priest		[Exhib Soc of BA, London, 748]; untraced	*Johnson* 1975, 295
265.	1843	A martyr	w	[Exhib Soc of BA, London, 736:3]; untraced	*Johnson* 1975, 295
266.	1843	Christ bearing his cross	p	[Exhib Soc of BA, London, 745]; untraced	*Johnson* 1975, 295
267.	1844	Ruth		[Exhib RA, London, 1335]; untraced	*Graves* V, 1905–6, 106
268.	1845	The Parthenon, immediately after the explosion of 1687, model		BM	*Builder* 1845, 619; *Gunnis* 1968, 245; *Jenkins* 1992, 97 (pl 26)
269.	1845	The Parthenon, in its original state, model		BM	*Builder* 1845, 593, 619; *Gunnis* 1968, 245; *Pyke* 1973, 82; *Jenkins* 1992, 97 (pl 26)
270.	1849	Canon Cureton	w	V Claydon, Chelmsford, Essex	RG/JP, 5, 854
271.	1849	'The Minerva Pallas of the Parthenon'	i	[Exhib RA, London, 624]; untraced	*Graves* V, 1905–6, 107
272.	1849	Trio, the messenger	i	[Exhib RA, London, 632]; untraced	*Graves* V, 1905–6, 107
273.	1849	Unidentified ivory carving	i	[Exhib RA, London, 621]; untraced	*Graves* V, 1905–6, 107
274.	1850	Restoration of the bronzes of Siris, in the British Museum		[Exhib RA, London, 1160]; untraced	*Graves* V, 1905–6, 107
275.	1850	The Ascension		[Exhib RA, London, 1148]; untraced	*Graves* V, 1905–6, 107
276.	1851	Neptune and Minerva, from the western pediment of the Parthenon		[Exhib RA, London, 1276]; untraced	*Graves* V, 1905–6, 107
277.	1857	Mrs Adelaide Cumming		[Exhib RA, London, 1290]; untraced	*Graves* V, 1905–6, 107
278.	1858	Minerva, of the Parthenon (cameo), Lady Jocelyn (ivory), Miss Hussey (ivory)		[Exhib RA, London, 1114]; untraced	*Graves* V, 1905–6, 107
279.	nd	Portland vase	w	BGM 173-1865	*Pyke* 1973, 82

LUDBY, William fl *c*1740

He was on the livery of the Masons' Company as 'Mason in Piccadilly' *c*1740 (Masons' Co, *Assistants*, fol 3). He, or another mason of the same name, served his apprenticeship under **James Hardy**, becoming free on 7 January 1742/3 (Masons' Co, *Freemen*, fol 41).

LUFKIN, George and Henry, of Colchester fl *c*1812–57

George Lufkin was responsible for a number of funerary tablets. At one time he was in partnership with **Slyth** and they signed a monument together in 1826 (**2**). The elder Lufkin was succeeded by his son Henry, who provided the altarpiece for St James, Colchester in 1855 (**14**) as well as signing a number of tablets in Essex. Gunnis notes that these are 'all extremely dull' (*Gunnis* 1968, 246).

Literary References: *Gunnis* 1968, 246

Funerary Monuments

1.	†1812	William Hawkins (by George Lufkin)	St Leonard-at-Hythe, Essex		*Gunnis* 1968, 245
2.	?1826	John Manistre (by George Lufkin) (co-sculptor: Slyth)	Halstead, Essex	S	*Gunnis* 1968, 245–246
3.	†1833	Thomas Walford (by George Lufkin)	St Augustine of Canterbury, Birdbrook, Essex		Pevsner, *Essex*, 1965, 88
4.	†1835	Anthony Merry (by Henry Lufkin)	Dedham, Essex	S	GPC
5.	1838	Elizabeth Cooke and family (by Henry Lufkin)	Lexden, Essex	S	
6.	?1839	Rev Peter Wright (by Henry Lufkin)	Mark's Tey, Essex		*Gunnis* 1968, 246
7.	?1839	Rev Robert Miller (by Henry Lufkin)	Dedham, Essex	S	GPC
8.	†1840	Susannah Kelso (by Henry Lufkin)	Layer Marney, Essex	S	
9.	?1843	Rev Josias Robinson (by Henry Lufkin)	Alresford, Essex		*Gunnis* 1968, 246
10.	?1844	Rev Edward Green (by Henry Lufkin)	Lawford, Essex		*Gunnis* 1968, 246
11.	†1845	Frederick Nassau (by Henry Lufkin)	St Osyth, Essex	S	

12.	†1851	Frances Wix (by Henry Lufkin)	St Bartholomew the Less, City of London	S	
13.	†1857	William Frederick Nassau (by Henry Lufkin)	St Osyth, Essex	S	

Architectural Sculpture

14.	1855	Altarpiece (by Henry Lufkin)	St James, Colchester, Essex		*Builder*, 1855, 417

LUMLEY, John, of Northampton 1654–1721

He was the only son of John Lumley of Harlestone, Northants, where his family had been masons since the middle ages. In 1686 he was made free of the London Masons' Company as a 'foreign member' (Masons' Co, *Freemen*, fol 40, 29 April) and in 1703 he became a freeman of Northampton 'gratis', in repayment of a debt owed to him by the corporation (Town Archives in GPC). He established a yard in Northampton and worked there as a surveyor and master mason until his death in November 1721.

The 2nd Earl of Nottingham employed Lumley to supervise the building of Burley-on-the-Hill, Rutland, between 1697 and 1705 and then, on Lord Nottingham's recommendation, his friend, the 1st Lord Ashburnham, employed him as surveyor at Great Park House, Ampthill, Beds, 1704–7. A letter from Ashburnham to Lumley of November 1706 expressed anxiety at the non-arrival of alabaster 'promised' by Lumley and asked for the carrier's name. There can have been no further frustrations for in the following year Ashburnham recommended Lumley to a neighbour, John Chester, 'as a friend and very able workman' (Ashburnham letterbook, 7 Nov 1706, 13 April 1707, ASH 846, ASH 847). Lumley drew up plans for rebuilding the south range of the front court at Emmanuel College, Cambridge, in 1719 and superintended the work until his death two years later. He surveyed Aynho Park, Northants, in 1698 (although no structural work was carried out at that time), undertook unspecified work at Cottesbrook Hall from 1702 onwards and examined the defective spire at Greens Norton church in 1718.

In his will, dated 10 November 1721, Lumley left half his marble and alabaster and all his working tools to his apprentice William Swann and the other half to the stonecarver **Samuel Cox I**, whom he described as 'my loving kinsman'.

Literary References: *Gunnis* 1968, 246; *Harris* 1956, 1239; *Houfe* 1971, 1086; *Colvin* 1995, 628

Archival References: GPC

Architectural Sculpture

1.	1706–1708	Marble and stone urns	Great Park House, Ampthill, Beds		*Gunnis* 1968, 246

LUPTON, George 1792–

Gunnis states that Lupton was born in 1792, citing as evidence the Artists Annuity Fund archives. However, it is possible that this Lupton was the engraver Thomas Goff Lupton (1791–1873). George Lupton worked as an assistant to **Joseph Nollekens** and was sent to Cambridge in 1812 to erect his master's statue of William Pitt. J T Smith later wrote, 'It is said that Nollekens charged one thousand pounds for Pitt's pedestal; but Lupton assured me that he had only twelve pounds for the working expenses' (*Smith* 1920, I, 369). Lupton seems to have set up on his own account before Nollekens's death but nonetheless received £100 under the sculptor's will. His workshop was in Keppel Row, New Road, London. Gunnis notes that his tablets are not very distinguished.

Literary References: *Gunnis* 1968, 246

Funerary Monuments

1.	†1812	Francis Shorey (†1808) and Sarah Bayley	St John, Hackleton's Cliff, Barbados	S	
2.	?1814	John Eligé	Nutfield, Surrey		*Gunnis* 1968, 246
3.	c1815	Elizabeth Blake	Swanton Abbots, Norfolk		*Gunnis* 1968, 246
4.	?1817	Lettice Patten	St Mary, St Marylebone, London		*Gunnis* 1968, 246
5.	?1817	Sarah Combe	Wincanton, Somerset		*Gunnis* 1968, 246
6.	?1819	General Charles Reynolds	St John's Wood Chapel, Marylebone, London		*Gunnis* 1968, 246
7.	†1819	Jane Arbuthnot	St John's Wood Chapel, Marylebone, London		RG/JP, 857
8.	?1821	Drake Clerk	Winchelsea, Sussex		*Gunnis* 1968, 246
9.	?1821	Hon Mrs George Montagu	Bishopsbourne, Kent		*Gunnis* 1968, 246
10.	?1821	Isabella Bartlett	St John's Wood Chapel, Marylebone, London		*Gunnis* 1968, 246
11.	†1822	Charles Binney	St John's Wood Chapel, Marylebone, London		RG/JP, 857
12.	?1822	John Pepper	Great Dunmow, Essex		*Gunnis* 1968, 246
13.	?1824	Andrew Crawford	Winchester Cathedral, Hants		*Gunnis* 1968, 246
14.	?1826	John Lloyd	Cowden, Kent		*Gunnis* 1968, 246
15.	?1827	Mary Tritton	Beddington, Surrey		*Gunnis* 1968, 246

LYDYARD, William, of Keynsham fl *c*1735

Funerary Monuments

1.	1735	Holbeach family	Whitchurch, Somerset	S	Pevsner, *Somerset: N & Bristol*, 1958, 339

LYNN & SHARP(E) fl 1780

In February 1780 Arnold and Co informed the public that they had opened an artificial stone manufactory at 1 Upper James Street, Golden Square, London 'on an improved and reduced Plan, where Gentlemen, Builders and others, may be accommodated with every necessary Decoration for external and internal Parts of Buildings, finished in the most elegant Stile, such as Capitals, Pedestals, Statues, Vases, Doorcases, Pateras, Tablets, Medallions, with a Variety of Chimney-Piece Ornaments, Festoons of Flowers ditto, of Vines etc' (*Daily Ad*, 3–4 February 1780). Two months later they announced that the partnership between John Lynn, Samuel Arnold and Thomas Sharp had been dissolved and that in future it would be conducted by John Lynn and Thomas Sharpe only. The firm's trade card, dated 1780, is in Banks Collection at the British Museum (BM, 106.19)

Literary References: *Daily Ad*, 12–14 April 1780; *Valpy* 1986, 218–9, 222–3

LYON, Edwin *c*1806–53

Lyon was a native of Liverpool, where his father, George Lyon, had a business listed in local directories as 'house, sign and ornamental painters, glass stainers, winder, etc'. He was admitted to drawing classes at the Liverpool Academy in January 1824 and was in London in 1826, returning to Liverpool in the following year, where he attended drawing classes in 1827–28. Lyon became an associate member of the Liverpool Academy by 1828 and was elected a full member in 1832. In 1829 he provided the drawings and commentary for a book on the sculpture of the Temple of Aphaia on the Greek island of Aegina, based on plaster casts in the Liverpool Royal Institution. The following year, on 21 January, he married his first wife, Elizabeth Sanderson, at St George, Everton. Lyon exhibited at the Liverpool Academy in most years between 1824 and 1832, showing portrait busts and a few ideal works. He sent one of these, a figure of *Diomed going to meet the council of the Grecians*, to the British Institution in London in 1827 (**2**).

Between 1834 and 1836–37 the sculptor was in Dublin. He never exhibited at the Royal Hibernian Academy, but was nonetheless elected an associate member on 18 January 1836. While there he executed two miniature wax busts (**21, 22**). Returning home, he attended meetings and exhibited at the Liverpool Academy in 1837 and 1838. He did not remain in Liverpool long, for the Academy records state that on 25 February 1840 it was resolved that 'owing to the number of absenses of Mr E Lyon who has removed to America he be no longer a member of the Academy and therefore be excluded' (Liverpool Academy Minute Book, Walker Art Gallery, in *Bacot and Lambdin* 1977, 555).

By April 1844 Lyon was living and working in Natchez, Mississippi, where he appears to have remained until his death, nine years later. A number of reports in the New Orleans newspapers indicate that he also had a studio in that city for a brief period towards the end of 1846. One report read 'Mr Edwin Lyon, an artist of great skill, taste and ingenuity has visited our city for the purpose of modelling numerous busts. By an original process the model is first moulded in clay, and an accurate likeness taken, and then completed by being cast in a species of composition of which the principal ingredient is wax, and which gradually hardens, assuming the finest of polish and having the appearance of purest marble. Specimens may be seen at Mr. Lyon's Studio, No. 6 Carondelet Street . . .' (*New Orleans Bee*, 20 October 1846, in *Bacot and Lambdin* 1977, 557 n1). On 17 August 1848 he married his second wife, Caroline Polkinghorn Bray, widow of Isaiah Bray, in Natchez. In 1850–52 he worked from a rented shop on Main Street, at the corner of Canal Street, and on 27 February 1852 he bought a large lot on Lower Frankin Street. He moved his business there by 1853 and renamed it the Natchez Marble Yard.

During his time in America Lyon seems to have come close to securing a prestigious public commission. In 1851 a Louisiana newspaper announced 'We are happy for the honour of Mississippi, to state, that one of their own resident artists, Edwin Lyon, of Natchez, has been selected by the "Monument Association" to build the marble monument to be erected at the State Capitol in honour of the Mississippi Volunteers . . . who lost their lives, in their country's cause, in the late Mexican War. The Model sent by Mr Lyon, we understand, was adopted by the committee in preference to all others, and thus he has become the architect of his own design . . .' (*Concordia Intelligencia*, 9 November 1851, in *Bacot and Lambdin* 1977, 556–7) (**4**). Sadly, the memorial sculpture appears not to have been executed for no further references to it have been traced and the model itself is lost.

Lyon died of yellow fever, on 29 August 1853 and was buried in Natchez Cemetery. His widow clearly continued the business for a time after his death for several monuments in that cemetery are signed 'Mrs Lyon'. Bacot and Lambdin suggest that she may have directed skilled slaves in this operation since she is known to have inherited one, named Clifton, from her husband, and to have hired three more, one of them a stonecutter, from a Mr Linder. The inventories of Lyon's business and personal estate, made after his death, suggest that in addition to carving he may have practiced other arts learned in his father's workshop in Liverpool, after he moved to America. Besides 'block Italian', 'American stone' and other materials for sculpture, he had items such as 'lights glass', 'gold leaf', paints and brushes. No examples of stained glass or paintings by him have been traced.

EH

Literary References: *Strickland* II, 1913, 35–6; *Pyke* 1973, 86; *Bacot and Lambdin* 1977, 554–9

Funerary Monuments						
1.	nd	Several, unidentified		Natchez Cemetery, Mississippi, USA		*Bacot and Lambdin* 1977, 557
Statues						
2.	1825	Diomed going to meet the council of the Grecians		[Exhib ALRI, Liverpool, 162]; untraced		*Graves* 1875, 358; *Gunnis* 1968, 246; *Morris and Roberts* 1998, 400
3.	1835	Maxwell Blacker, statuette	w	Coll Lord Dunally (Kilboy, Co Tipperary)	SD	*Strickland* II, 1913, 35
4.	1851	Mississippi volunteers of the first and second regiments of rifles, Mexican war memorial for the state Capitol, Jackson, Mississippi, model only		Untraced		*Bacot and Lambdin* 1977, 556–7
Busts						
5.	1824	Unidentified boy		[Exhib ALRI, Liverpool, 166]; untraced		*Morris and Roberts* 1998, 400
6.	1824	Unidentified gentleman		[Exhib ALRI, Liverpool, 167]; untraced		*Morris and Roberts* 1998, 400
7.	1825	Four unidentified gentleman		[Exhib ALRI, Liverpool, 172–4, 178]; untraced		*Morris and Roberts* 1998, 400
8.	1825	Pity		[Exhib ALRI, Liverpool, 181]; untraced		*Morris and Roberts* 1998, 400
9.	1825	Unidentified infant		[Exhib ALRI, Liverpool, 182]; untraced		*Morris and Roberts* 1998, 400
10.	1825	Unidentified lady		[Exhib ALRI, Liverpool, 175]; untraced		*Morris and Roberts* 1998, 400
11.	1827	Alexander Mosses	p	[Exhib ALRI, Liverpool, 279]; untraced		*Bacot and Lambdin* 1977, 555 (repr); *Morris and Roberts* 1998, 401

12.	1827	George Mosses	p	[Exhib ALRI, Liverpool, 284]; untraced		*Bacot and Lambdin* 1977, 555 (repr); *Morris and Roberts* 1998, 401
13.	1827	The sculptor's father		[Exhib ALRI, Liverpool, 272]; untraced		*Morris and Roberts* 1998, 400
14.	1827	Three unidentified sitters		[Exhib ALRI, Liverpool, 270, 282–3]; untraced		*Morris and Roberts* 1998, 400–1
15.	1828	An artist		[Exhib ALRI, Liverpool, 224]; untraced		*Morris and Roberts* 1998, 401
16.	1828	John Ashton Yates	w	[Exhib ALRI, Liverpool, 214]; untraced		*Gunnis* 1968, 246; *Morris and Roberts* 1998, 401
17.	1828	Thomas Stewart Traill MD	w	[Exhib ALRI, Liverpool, 237]; untraced		*Gunnis* 1968, 246; *Morris and Roberts* 1998, 401
18.	1828	Unidentified gentleman		[Exhib ALRI, Liverpool, 230]; untraced		*Morris and Roberts* 1998, 401
19.	1831	John Wright		[Exhib Liverpool Ac, 400]; untraced		*Morris and Roberts* 1998, 401
20.	1832	Unidentified gentleman		[Exhib Liverpool Ac, 394]; untraced		*Morris and Roberts* 1998, 401
21.	1834	Sir William Cusack-Smith	w	VAM	SD	*Bacot and Lambdin* 1977, 555 (repr); *Morris and Roberts* 1998, 401
22.	1835	Mrs Francis Beetham	w	VAM	SD	*Bacot and Lambdin* 1977, 555, 556 (repr)
23.	1837	A friend		[Exhib Liverpool Ac, 698]; untraced		*Morris and Roberts* 1998, 401
24.	1837	Charles Whitmore		[Exhib Liverpool Ac, 697]; untraced		*Morris and Roberts* 1998, 401
25.	1837	John Leigh	w	[Exhib Liverpool Ac, 705]; untraced		*Gunnis* 1968, 246; *Morris and Roberts* 1998, 401
26.	1837	Joseph Lyon	w	[Exhib Liverpool Ac, 696]; untraced		*Gunnis* 1968, 246; *Morris and Roberts* 1998, 401
27.	1837	Miss Eliza Leigh	w	[Exhib Liverpool Ac, 706]; untraced		*Gunnis* 1968, 246; *Morris and Roberts* 1998, 401
28.	1837	Mrs H Leigh	w	[Exhib Liverpool Ac, 704]; untraced		*Gunnis* 1968, 246; *Morris and Roberts* 1998, 401
29.	1837	Rev H McNeile	w	[Exhib Liverpool Ac, 715]; untraced		*Gunnis* 1968, 246; *Morris and Roberts* 1998, 401
30.	1837	Richard Buttler	w	[Exhib Liverpool Ac, 695]; untraced		*Gunnis* 1968, 246; *Morris and Roberts* 1998, 401
31.	1838	Samuel Eglington	tc	[Exhib Liverpool Ac, 662]; untraced		*Morris and Roberts* 1998, 401
32.	post-1844	Ruth Henry	w	Private coll	S	*Bacot and Lambdin* 1977, 556, 557 (repr)
33.	1845	Rev C Page	w	Private coll	SD	*Bacot and Lambdin* 1977, 556 (repr)
34.	1848	General Zachary Taylor	m	[coll General John A Quitman]; Auburn, Natchez, Mississippi, USA Other versions: Exhib Pennsylvania Academy, miniatures section, 480, probably wax; untraced	SD	*Bacot and Lambdin* 1977, 556, 559 (repr)
35.	1848	James Reid Lambdin		[Exhib Pennsylvania Academy, Miniatures Section, 481]; untraced		*Bacot and Lambdin* 1977, 556
36.	1848	Rev Joseph Buck Stratton	w	Private coll		*Bacot and Lambdin* 1977, 556, 557 (repr)
37.	1851	Hon George Winchester	w	Trinity Church, Natchez, Mississippi, USA	SD	*Bacot and Lambdin* 1977, 556, 558 (repr)
38.	nd	Dr Stephen Duncan	w	[Oakland, Natchez, Mississippi, USA]; untraced	S	*Bacot and Lambdin* 1977, 556
Reliefs						
39.	1825	The education of Bacchus		[Exhib ALRI, Liverpool, 165]; untraced		*Morris and Roberts* 1998, 400
40.	1853	General Zachary Taylor, medallion		[coll James Reid Lambdin]; untraced		*Bacot and Lambdin* 1977, 556
Miscellaneous						
41.	1824	Ajax, from a gem		[Exhib ALRI, Liverpool, 186]; untraced		*Morris and Roberts* 1998, 400
42.	1824	Head of Diomed, from a gem		[Exhib ALRI, Liverpool, 169]; untraced		*Morris and Roberts* 1998, 400
43.	1825	Innocence		[Exhib ALRI, Liverpool, 176]; untraced		*Morris and Roberts* 1998, 400
44.	1825	Seraph Abdiel		[Exhib ALRI, Liverpool, 160]; untraced		*Morris and Roberts* 1998, 400
45.	1837	Portrait of John Leigh, his gamekeeper and two favourite dogs		[Exhib Liverpool Ac, 682]; untraced		*Morris and Roberts* 1998, 401

LYON, J fl 1827

His address was recorded as Brownlow Hill, Liverpool, when he exhibited in that city in 1827. He was probably Joseph Lyon, the brother of **Edwin Lyon**.

Literary References: *Bacot and Lambdin* 1977, 554

Miscellaneous

1.	1827	Skeleton of a lion	[Exhib ALRI, Liverpool, 228]; untraced	*Morris and Roberts* 1998, 401

M'CARTHY, T fl 1831

M'Carthy [*sic*] was living at 3 Trellick Terrace, Vauxhall Road in 1831, when he won a medal from the Society of Arts.

Miscellaneous

1.	1831	Carving of a horse	i	[Soc of A, silver Isis medal]; untraced	RSA *Transactions*, vol 48, 1831, 550

MABEY, James fl 1842

He was the foreman modeller at the Palace of Westminster, engaged by **John Thomas** in 1842.

Literary References: *Read* 1982, 234

MACAULEY, Alexander fl 1832–38

He was one of several sculptors who attempted to establish practices in Edinburgh during the 1830s. From 1832 he had a studio at 12 Windmill Street and after 1837 he also worked from 12 Thanet Place, London. He settled in London in 1844.

Literary References: *Woodward* 1977 (vol 1, pt 2), 119

Busts

1.	1832	Alexander MacAuley (self-portrait)	[Exhib R Sc A, Edinburgh, 310]; untraced	*Laperriere* 3, 1991, 89
2.	1836	Dr Bowring MP	[Exhib R Sc A, Edinburgh, 349]; untraced	*Laperriere* 3, 1991, 89
3.	1836	Louis Herslett	[Exhib R Sc A, Edinburgh, 348]; untraced	*Laperriere* 3, 1991, 89
4.	1836	Unidentified gentleman	[Exhib R Sc A, Edinburgh, 350]; untraced	*Laperriere* 3, 1991, 89
5.	1836	Unidentified lady	[Exhib R Sc A, Edinburgh, 351]; untraced	*Laperriere* 3, 1991, 89
6.	1837	Mrs Fraser	[Exhib R Sc A, Edinburgh, 365]; untraced	*Laperriere* 3, 1991, 89
7.	1837	Rev Archibald Bennie, model	[Exhib R Sc A, Edinburgh, 375]; untraced	*Laperriere* 3, 1991, 90
8.	1837	Sir John Graham Dalziell	[Exhib R Sc A, Edinburgh, 366]; untraced	*Laperriere* 3, 1991, 89
9.	1837	Unidentified young lady	[Exhib R Sc A, Edinburgh, 382]; untraced	*Laperriere* 3, 1991, 90
10.	1837	William Williamson	[Exhib R Sc A, Edinburgh, 372]; untraced	*Laperriere* 3, 1991, 90

Miscellaneous

11.	1832	Study from nature	[Exhib R Sc A, Edinburgh, 315]; untraced	*Laperriere* 3, 1991, 89
12.	1838	Contemplation	[Exhib R Sc A, Edinburgh, 417]; untraced	*Laperriere* 3, 1991, 90

MACBRIDE, John Alexander Paterson, of Liverpool 1819–90

He was born on 27 February 1819, the son of Archibald MacBride of Campbelltown, Argyll and was christened at Oldham Street presbyterian chapel, Liverpool on 21 March. MacBride trained under **William Spence** and at the age of 16 exhibited at the Liverpool Academy, giving his address as 7 Finch Street, Liverpool. He went to London *c*1841, and in 1844 exhibited a group of *Margaret of Anjou and her son* at Westminster Hall (4). The *Literary Gazette* considered it 'a good subject poorly treated'. Margaret, they said, appeared 'a virago' instead of a 'sorrowing, yet dignified queen,' and her son 'a poor attenuated, impudent lad'. **Samuel Joseph** was however so impressed with the work that he took the sculptor into his studio as a pupil without charging his usual fee of 500 guineas. MacBride later became Joseph's chief assistant.

He seems, nonetheless, to have kept an address in Russell Street, Liverpool, from where he exhibited at the Liverpool Academy, 1847–65. He became an enthusiastic supporter of the Pre-Raphaelite School: as secretary of the Liverpool Academy in 1851–2, he was instrumental in awarding the annual prize of 50 guineas on two occasions to Holman Hunt and J E Millais. He competed unsuccessfully for the commission to provide a statue in Liverpool for the Wellington Column (54), but was more successful elsewhere, winning the contract for the statue of the biblical commentator Adam Clarke at Portrush (11), and providing numerous busts of local and national worthies. His monument to Dr Stevenson, one of his few funerary memorials, depicts the doctor attending to patrons in classical draperies (2). He prepared at least one model for the Minton pottery (13), and models of his Lady Godiva were awarded by the Liverpool Art Union as one of their prizes in 1850 (53). His death, on 10 April 1890, was reported the following day in the *Liverpool Daily Post.*

Literary References: *Graves* V, 1905–6, 128; *Gunnis* 1968, 247; *Cavanagh* 1997, 332; *Morris and Roberts* 1998, 401–2

Archival References: IGI

Funerary Monuments

1.	*c*1848	Rev James Appleton	[Exhib Liverpool Ac, 1848, 685 (relief)]; untraced	*Morris and Roberts* 1998, 401
2.	1854	Dr William Stevenson Model(s): exhib Liverpool Ac, 1855, 833	[St Mary, Birkenhead, Cheshire]; Oratory, St James Cemetery, Liverpool	Pevsner, *Cheshire*, 1971, 81; *Read* 1982, 186; *Cavanagh* 1997, 333; *Morris and Roberts* 1998, 402
3.	1854	Unidentified subject, 'Come ye Blessed', monumental bas relief Model(s): exhib Liverpool Ac, 1854, 772	[for Rock Ferry church]; untraced	*Morris and Roberts* 1998, 402

Statues

4.	1844	Margaret of Anjou and her son	[Exhib Westminster Hall, London]; untraced	*Lit Gaz* 1844, 482; *Gunnis* 1968, 247
5.	1846	Griselda, small sketch model	[Exhib Liverpool Ac, 814]; untraced	*Morris and Roberts* 1998, 401
6.	1848	A Merionethshire peasant girl, study for a statue	[Exhib Liverpool Ac, 671]; untraced	*Morris and Roberts* 1998, 401
7.	1851	Sir Robert Peel, 'model statuette'	[Exhib Liverpool Ac, 580]; untraced	*Morris and Roberts* 1998, 401
8.	1852	John Wycliffe Model(s): 'small model sketch' exhib Liverpool Ac, 1852, 600	[for Rev Dr Vaughan]; untraced	*Morris and Roberts* 1998, 401
9.	1856	Archdeacon Brooks, in archdeacon's garb, statuette	[Exhib Liverpool Ac, 880]; untraced	*Morris and Roberts* 1998, 402
10.	1856	Archdeacon Brooks, in full canonicals, statuette	[Exhib Liverpool Ac, 881]; untraced	*Morris and Roberts* 1998, 402
11.	1857	Dr Adam Clarke	Portrush, Northern Ireland	*Gunnis* 1968, 247
12.	1862	Albert, the Prince Consort, proof copy of a Parian statuette	[Exhib Liverpool Ac, 923]; untraced	*Morris and Roberts* 1998, 402

13.	nd	H M Stanley, statuette		Untraced Other versions: replicas made by Minton of Stoke-on-Trent	*Gunnis* 1968, 247
14.	nd	Seated Cybele, the four seasons, a miner and an agricultural worker Model(s): 2 statuettes exhib Liverpool Ac, 1851, 577		['Executed heroic size for Major Sir John Gerrard Bt, New Hall']; untraced	*Gunnis* 1968, 247; *Morris and Roberts* 1998, 401
Busts					
15.	1835	C M Seddon		[Exhib Liverpool Ac, 560]; untraced	*Morris and Roberts* 1998, 401
16.	1836	Unidentified young lady		[Exhib Liverpool Ac, 655]; untraced	*Morris and Roberts* 1998, 401
17.	1837	Lady Macbeth		[Exhib Liverpool Ac, 679]; untraced	*Morris and Roberts* 1998, 401
18.	1837	Rev Hugh Ralph		[Exhib Liverpool Ac, 686]; untraced	*Morris and Roberts* 1998, 401
19.	1837	Rev John Parke		[Exhib Liverpool Ac, 685]; untraced	*Morris and Roberts* 1998, 401
20.	1844	Two unidentified gentlemen		[Exhib Liverpool Ac, 570, 572]; untraced	*Morris and Roberts* 1998, 401
21.	1846	John S Leyland		[Exhib Liverpool Ac, 810]; untraced	*Morris and Roberts* 1998, 401
22.	c1846	Philip Bailey Model(s): exhib Liverpool Ac, 1846, 811		SNPG, Edinburgh, Scotland	*Gunnis* 1968, 247; *Morris and Roberts* 1998, 401
23.	1847	John Miller		[Exhib Liverpool Ac, 755]; untraced	*Graves* V, 1905–6, 128; *Morris and Roberts* 1998, 401
24.	1847	Rev Patrick Ross		[Exhib Liverpool Ac, 761]; untraced	*Morris and Roberts* 1998, 401
25.	1847	Richard Ansdell		[Exhib Liverpool Ac, 749]; untraced	*Morris and Roberts* 1998, 401
26.	1848	Hardman Earle		[Exhib Liverpool Ac, 679]; untraced	*Morris and Roberts* 1998, 401
27.	1849	Dr Laytham		[Exhib Liverpool Ac, 667]; untraced	*Morris and Roberts* 1998, 401
28.	1849	Samuel Clegg		[Exhib Liverpool Ac, 666]; untraced	*Morris and Roberts* 1998, 401
29.	1853	Field-Marshal Lord Combermere	m	[Exhib RA, London, 1401]; untraced	*Graves* V, 1905–6, 128; *Gunnis* 1968, 247; *Morris and Roberts* 1998, 401–2
30.	1853	Unidentified lady		[Exhib Liverpool Ac, 700]; untraced	*Morris and Roberts* 1998, 401
31.	1854	Soloque I, Emperor of Haiti Model(s): exhib Liverpool Ac, 1854, 773		[Imperial Palace, Haiti]; untraced	*Morris and Roberts* 1998, 402
32.	1855	Archdeacon Brooks, model		[Exhib Liverpool Ac, 828]; untraced	*Morris and Roberts* 1998, 402
33.	1856	Master Robert Pemberton, model		[Exhib Liverpool Ac, 882]; untraced	*Morris and Roberts* 1998, 402
34.	1857	Unidentified lady	m	[Exhib Liverpool Ac, 882]; untraced	*Morris and Roberts* 1998, 402
35.	1858	Mrs John Lightbody in Bernese costume, model		[Exhib Liverpool Ac, 969]; untraced	*Morris and Roberts* 1998, 402
36.	1858	William Rennie Model(s): exhib Liverpool Ac, 1857, 880		[Exhib Liverpool Ac, 968]; untraced	*Morris and Roberts* 1998, 402
37.	1860	Charles Verelst, model		[Exhib Liverpool Ac, 887]; untraced	*Morris and Roberts* 1998, 402
38.	1860	Launcelot Graham	m	[Exhib Liverpool Ac, 885]; untraced	*Morris and Roberts* 1998, 402
39.	1861	George Holt	m	[Exhib Liverpool Ac, 1098]; untraced	*Morris and Roberts* 1998, 402
40.	1861	Peter Denny, model		[Exhib Liverpool Ac, 1103]; untraced	*Morris and Roberts* 1998, 402
41.	1861	'Samuelson', model		[Exhib Liverpool Ac, 1101]; untraced	*Morris and Roberts* 1998, 402
42.	1863	John Laird		Birkenhead hospital, Cheshire	*Ormond* 1973, 252
43.	c1865	Rev Thomas Raffles	m	Great George Street chapel, Liverpool	*Gunnis* 1968, 247; *Morris and Roberts* 1998, 402
44.	nd	Colonel Peter Thomson		Untraced	*Gunnis* 1968, 247
45.	nd	Michael Whitby		Untraced	*Gunnis* 1968, 247
46.	nd	Sir A B Walker		Untraced	*Gunnis* 1968, 247
47.	nd	Sir James Allanson Picton	m	Picton Reference Library, William Brown Street, Liverpool, Lancs, reading room	*Cavanagh* 1997, 250–1 (repr)
48.	nd	Sir William Brown		Untraced	*Gunnis* 1968, 247
Reliefs					
49.	1846	Horatio R Roberts, portrait medallion		[Exhib Liverpool Ac, 812]; untraced	*Morris and Roberts* 1998, 401
50.	1851	Brother and sister, medallion		[Exhib Liverpool Ac, 581]; untraced	*Morris and Roberts* 1998, 401
51.	1860	Mother and child, alto-relievo		[Exhib Liverpool Ac, 886]; untraced	*Morris and Roberts* 1998, 402
Miscellaneous					
52.	1848	J Bailey		[Exhib RA, London, 1400]; untraced	*Graves* V, 1905–6, 128
53.	pre-1850	Lady Godiva		Untraced Other versions: models awarded as prizes by the Liverpool Art Union	*Gunnis* 1968, 247
54.	1862	Arthur, 1st Duke of Wellington, for the public memorial, Liverpool, bronzed model		[Exhib Liverpool Ac, 923]; untraced	*Morris and Roberts* 1998, 402
55.	1862	The Last of the Guanches		[Exhib LSFA, Liverpool, 779]; untraced	*Morris and Roberts* 1998, 402

MACCARTHY, Amelia fl 1843

The daughter of **J J A MacCarthy**, she exhibited two works, executed in conjunction with her sister, **Gertrude MacCarthy**, at the Royal Academy in 1843 (**1**, **2**). Her address was 21 Soho Square, London.

Literary References: *Gunnis* 1968, 247

Statues				
1.	1843	Miss Blanch Kelly, miniature full-length figure (co-sculptor: Gertrude MacCarthy)	[Exhib RA, London, 1488]; untraced	*Graves* V, 1905–6, 130
Busts				
2.	1843	Mrs Finch (co-sculptor: Gertrude MacCarthy)	[Exhib RA, London, 1379]; untraced	*Graves* V, 1905–6, 130

MACCARTHY, Carlton M 1817–

The son of **John James Alexander MacCarthy**, he was born in Scotland. Most of his works were executed in collaboration with his elder brother **Hamilton MacCarthy**. The two specialised in modelling animals and exhibited together at the Royal Academy, 1838–44, at the Westminster Hall Exhibition of 1844 and at the British Institution and Manchester Institution in 1846. Carlton showed independently at the RA and the British Institution 1852–66.

Literary References: *Gunnis* 1968, 247–8; *Woodward* 1977, vol 1, pt 2, 124

Statues

1.	1839	Queen Victoria, equestrian (co-sculptor: Hamilton W MacCarthy)	[Exhib RA, London, 1276]; untraced	*Graves* V, 1905–6, 130
2.	1842	A favourite horse, the property of Lady Dallas (co-sculptor: Hamilton MacCarthy)	[Exhib RA, London, 1305]; untraced	*AU*, 1842, 128; *Graves* V, 1905–6, 130
3.	1842	Deer and dogs (co-sculptor: Hamilton W MacCarthy)	[Exhib RA, London, 1306]; untraced	*Graves* V, 1905–6, 130
4.	1844	St George and the dragon (co-sculptor: Hamilton W MacCarthy)	[Exhib Westminster Hall, London, 93]; untraced	*AU*, 1844, 214–5
5.	1846	Deer and dogs (co-sculptor: Hamilton W MacCarthy)	[Exhib BI, London, 485]; untraced	*Graves* 1875, 360
6.	1846	King Charles XII (co-sculptor: Hamilton W MacCarthy)	[Exhib Manc Inst]; untraced	*Gunnis* 1968, 247
7.	1856	Marquis of Anglesey, national statue, design only	[Exhib RA, London, 1265]; untraced	*Graves* V, 1905–6, 130
8.	1859	Mare and deerhound	[Exhib RA, London, 1246]; untraced	*Graves* V, 1905–6, 130

Miscellaneous

9.	1838	Unidentified lady (co-sculptor: Hamilton W MacCarthy)	[Exhib RA, London, 1049]; untraced	*Graves* V, 1905–6, 130
10.	1839	A favourite mare, the property of - Williams Esq (co-sculptor: Hamilton W MacCarthy)	[Exhib RA, London, 1351]; untraced	*Graves* V, 1905–6, 130
11.	1841	Marmion, the property of Lord William Beresford (co-sculptor: Hamilton W MacCarthy)	[Exhib RA, London, 1276]; untraced	*Graves* V, 1905–6, 130
12.	1841	Nancy, the property of Mr Meyrick (co-sculptor: Hamilton W MacCarthy)	[Exhib RA, London, 1285]; untraced	*Graves* V, 1905–6, 130
13.	1841	Tam o' Shanter, the property of Colonel Copeland (co-sculptor: Hamilton W MacCarthy)	[Exhib RA, London, 1254]; untraced	*Graves* V, 1905–6, 130
14.	1842	A favourite horse, the property of Sir Robert Dallas (co-sculptor: Hamilton W MacCarthy)	[Exhib RA, London, 1326]; untraced	*Graves* V, 1905–6, 130
15.	1842	A horse, study (co-sculptor: Hamilton W MacCarthy)	[Exhib RA, London, 130]; untraced	*Graves* V, 1905–6, 130
16.	1842	Bucephalus (co-sculptor: Hamilton W MacCarthy)	[Exhib RA, London, 1332]; untraced	*Graves* V, 1905–6, 130
17.	1844	A favourite horse of the Count Baltiany (co-sculptor: Hamilton W MacCarthy)	[Exhib RA, London, 1320]; untraced	*Graves* V, 1905–6, 130
18.	1846	A horse (co-sculptor: Hamilton W MacCarthy)	[Exhib BI, London, 486]; untraced	*Graves* 1875, 360
19.	1846	A horse in a lassoo (co-sculptor: Hamilton W MacCarthy)	[Exhib Manc Inst]; untraced	*Gunnis* 1968, 247
20.	1846	A red deer (co-sculptor: Hamilton W MacCarthy)	[Exhib Manc Inst]; untraced	*Gunnis* 1968, 247
21.	1852	La Sentinelle	[Exhib BI, London, 536]; untraced	*Graves* V, 1875, 359
22.	1853	Study from life	[Exhib BI, London, 581]; untraced	*Graves* V, 1875, 359
23.	1853	Study from life	[Exhib BI, London, 584]; untraced	*Graves* V, 1875, 359
24.	1854	Mason and Lottery Payment(s): 3 gns with shade, 15 gns in bronze	[Exhib BI, London, 583]; untraced	*Graves* V, 1875, 359
25.	1855	Nero	[Exhib BI, London, 558]; untraced	*Graves* V, 1875, 359
26.	1856	Rival favourites, an alpine mastiff and deer hound	[Exhib BI, London, 551]; untraced	*Graves* V, 1875, 359
27.	1857	England's hope	[Exhib BI, London, 572]; untraced	*Graves* V, 1875, 359
28.	1862	Nursing mother, a brood mare and foal Payment(s): £5, or £1 5s for a cast	[Exhib BI, London, 639]; untraced	*Graves* V, 1875, 359
29.	1866	Belle du Village, the best greyhound in England	[Exhib BI, London, 641]; untraced	*Graves* V, 1875, 359

MACCARTHY, Gertrude fl 1838–53

The daughter of **J J A MacCarthy**, she exhibited at the Royal Academy, giving her address as 32 Great Marlborough Street in 1838 and 10b Argyll Place between 1839 and 1843. He sister was **Amelia MacCarthy**.

Literary References: *Gunnis* 1968, 247

Statues

1.	1843	Miss Blanch Kelly, miniature full-length figure (co-sculptor: Amelia MacCarthy)	[Exhib RA, London, 1488]; untraced	*Graves* V, 1905–6, 130

Busts

2.	1843	Mrs Col Finch (co-sculptor: Amelia MacCarthy)	[Exhib RA, London, 1379]; untraced	*Graves* V, 1905–6, 130

Miscellaneous

3.	1838	Miss Matilda Panermo	[Exhib RA, London, 257]; untraced	*Graves* V, 1905–6, 130
4.	1839	Portrait of a Blenheim spaniel	[Exhib RA, London, 1312]; untraced	*Graves* V, 1905–6, 130
5.	1853	Study from nature	[Exhib BI, London, 576]; untraced	*Graves* 1875, 360

MACCARTHY, Hamilton W 1809–

A son of **John James Alexander MacCarthy**, he was born in Scotland but by 1838 he and his younger brother **Carlton MacCarthy** had settled in London, where they remained for the rest of their lives. The brothers collaborated on many of their works and exhibited together at the Royal Academy from 1838 until 1844, showing mainly models of horses and other animals. They appear to have been particularly successful in modelling racehorses. They were employed by various owners, including Colonel Copeland, Lord William Beresford, Lady Dallas and Count Bathiany, and in 1846 their address was given as Tattersalls, the equestrian auctioneers in Grosvenor Place, near Hyde Park Corner.

In 1844 they sent a group of *St George and the dragon* to the Westminster Hall Exhibition (**3**). One reviewer described it as 'a bold equestrian group and deserving of much praise', while another considered it on the whole 'a most spirited work', exhibiting 'many of the finest points of sculpture' and predicted that although the artists were not well known, a few works of this kind would 'place them high in the esteem of all lovers of art' (*Lit Gaz*, 1435, 20 July 1844, 466; *AU*, 1844, 214–5). Their collaboration continued until at least 1846, when they exhibited together at the British Institution and the Manchester Institution, showing a figure of Charles XII as well as a group of deer and dogs (**5, 6**).

Hamilton MacCarthy exhibited independent works at the Royal Academy and the British Institution in 1838 and between 1846 and 1867. They included a number of portrait busts (**10–12**). He contributed to the Great Exhibition a group of a deer hunt, consisting of a Scottish huntsman about to blow his horn, with a felled stag and two dogs 'executed in silver for ornamental purposes' (**7**). It was praised as 'a spirited performance, well composed' and was considered 'a credit to the designer' (*AJ Cat*, 1851, 146). His wife exhibited a statuette of a famous racehorse, 'Pyrrhus the First', at the BI in 1857 (554). Their son, Hamilton P MacCarthy, was also a sculptor and he exhibited portraiture and ideal works at the RA between 1875 and 1884.

Literary References: *Graves* 1875, 360; *Gunnis* 1968, 247–8; *Woodward* 1977 (vol 1, pt 2), 124

Statues					
1.	1839	Queen Victoria, equestrian (co-sculptor: Carlton M MacCarthy)		[Exhib RA, London, 1276]; untraced	*Graves* V, 1905–6, 131
2.	1842	A favourite horse, the property of Lady Dallas, model (co-sculptor: Carlton M MacCarthy)	pm	[Exhib RA, London, 1305]; untraced	*AU*, 1842, 128; *Graves* V, 1905–6, 131
3.	1844	St George and the dragon (co-sculptor: Carlton M MacCarthy)		[Exhib Westminster Hall, London, 93]; untraced	*AU*, 1844, 214–5
4.	1846	A stag, small model		[Exhib RA, London, 1446]; untraced	*AU*, 1846, 189; *Graves* V, 1905–6, 131
5.	1846	Deer and dogs (co-sculptor: Carlton M MacCarthy)		[Exhib BI, London, 485]; untraced	*Graves* 1875, 360
6.	1846	King Charles XII (co-sculptor: Carlton M MacCarthy)		[Exhib Manc Inst]; untraced	*Gunnis* 1968, 247
7.	1851	A deer hunt 'executed in silver for ornamental purposes'		[Gt Exhib, London]; untraced	*AJ Cat* 1851, 146 (repr)
8.	1853	Nimrod the mighty hunter		[Exhib RA, London, 1324]; untraced	*Graves* V, 1905–6, 131
9.	1857	Emperor Napoleon III, statuette		[Exhib BI, London, 575]; untraced	*Graves* 1875, 360
Busts					
10.	1851	Mrs Capron		[Exhib RA, London, 1374]; untraced	*Graves* V, 1905–6, 131; *Gunnis* 1968, 248
11.	1864	Mrs Rae	m	[Exhib RA, London, 992]; untraced	*Graves* V, 1905–6, 131; *Gunnis* 1968, 248
12.	1867	Rev Edward Irving	m	[Exhib RA, London, 1867]; untraced	*Graves* V, 1905–6, 131; *Gunnis* 1968, 248
Miscellaneous					
13.	1838	A horse		[Exhib RA, London, 1348]; untraced	*Graves* V, 1905–6, 131
14.	1838	Unidentified lady (co-sculptor: Carlton M MacCarthy)		[Exhib RA, London, 1049]; untraced	*Graves* V, 1905–6, 131
15.	1839	A favourite mare, the property of - Williams Esq (co-sculptor: Carlton M MacCarthy)		[Exhib RA, London, 1351]; untraced	*Graves* V, 1905–6, 131
16.	1841	Marmion, the property of Lord William Beresford (co-sculptor: Carlton M MacCarthy)		[Exhib RA, London, 1276]; untraced	*Graves* V, 1905–6, 131
17.	1841	Nancy, the property of Mr Mwyrick (co-sculptor: Carlton M MacCarthy)		[Exhib RA, London, 1285]; untraced	*Graves* V, 1905–6, 131
18.	1841	Tam o' Shanter, the property of Colonel Copeland (co-sculptor: Carlton M MacCarthy)		[Exhib RA, London, 1254]; untraced	*Graves* V, 1905–6, 131
19.	1842	A favourite horse, the property of Sir Robert Dallas (co-sculptor: Carlton M MacCarthy)		[Exhib RA, London, 1326]; untraced	*Graves* V, 1905–6, 131
20.	1842	A horse, study (co-sculptor: Carlton M MacCarthy)		[Exhib RA, London, 1308]; untraced	*Graves* V, 1905–6, 131
21.	1842	Bucephalus (co-sculptor: Carlton M MacCarthy)		[Exhib RA, London, 1332]; untraced	*Graves* V, 1905–6, 131
22.	1842	Deer and dogs (co-sculptor: Carlton M MacCarthy)		[Exhib RA, London, 1306]; untraced	*Graves* V, 1905–6, 131
23.	1844	A favourite horse of the Count Baltiany (co-sculptor: Carlton M MacCarthy)		[Exhib RA, London, 1320]; untraced	*Graves* V, 1905–6, 131
24.	1846	A horse (co-sculptor: Carlton M MacCarthy)		[Exhib BI, London, 486]; untraced	*Graves* 1875, 360
25.	1846	A horse in a lassoo (co-sculptor: Carlton M MacCarthy)		[Exhib Manc Inst]; untraced	*Gunnis* 1968, 247
26.	1846	A red deer (co-sculptor: Carlton M MacCarthy)		[Exhib Manc Inst]; untraced	*Gunnis* 1968, 247
27.	1850	St George and the dragon		[Exhib RA, London, 1311]; untraced	*Graves* V, 1905–6, 131
28.	1852	A scene from the hippodrome		[Exhib BI, London, 538]; untraced	*Graves* 1875, 360

29.	1853	Mare and foal, study Payment(s): 4 gns, or 6 gns in bronze	[Exhib BI, London, 577]; untraced	*Graves* 1875, 360
30.	1853	'The Great Duke' Payment(s): 4 gns, or 6 gns in bronze	[Exhib BI, London, 580]; untraced Other versions: exhib BI, London, 1859, 584; untraced	*Graves* 1875, 360
31.	1854	Wild horse and python, sketch	[Exhib RA, London, 1407]; untraced	*Graves* V, 1905–6, 131
32.	1855	A grenadier guard, model	[Exhib BI, London, 548]; untraced	*Graves* 1875, 360
33.	1855	Neptune striking the ground with his trident - a fiery and beautiful horse sprang forth	[Exhib RA, London, 131]; untraced	*Graves* V, 1905–6, 131
34.	1856	Hubert de Burgh on a Crimean pony	[Exhib BI, London, 555]; untraced	*Graves* 1875, 360
35.	1856	Omar Pasha	[Exhib BI, London, 555]; untraced	*Graves* 1875, 360
36.	1858	Study of a horse	[Exhib BI, London, 583]; untraced	*Graves* 1875, 360
37.	1858	Study of a horse rampant	[Exhib BI, London, 579]; untraced	*Graves* 1875, 360
38.	1859	A startled horse Payment(s): 5 gns, or £25 in bronze	[Exhib BI, London, 585]; untraced	*Graves* 1875, 360
39.	1862	An old racer	[Exhib BI, London, 637]; untraced	*Graves* 1875, 360
40.	1865	Bucephalus	[Exhib RA, London, 970]; untraced	*Graves* V, 1905–6, 131

MACCARTHY, John James Alexander 1776–

In 1853 when he applied to the AGBI for assistance under the name John James MacCarthy Sexon, he gave a resumé of past activities. In 1805 he had held a lieutenancy in the 1st royal regiment 'expecting to prosecute the Army as a profession, but an increase of twins to the family' just as he was embarking for Cadiz induced his Colonel, the Duke of Kent, to send for him at Kensington Palace. Here in the course of conversation the Duke discovered MacCarthy's flair for art, and advised him to abandon the Army and turn to sculpture and painting. MacCarthy, by his own account, painted pictures of his patron and King George III and prepared many models (1). He had a large family, most of whom were artists. They included **S J J MacCarthy, H W MacCarthy, Carlton MacCarthy** and **Amelia** and **Gertrude MacCarthy**.

Literary References: *Gunnis* 1968, 247

Archival References: AGBI, vol 5, 221

Miscellaneous

1.	nd	'many subjects from the marbles at Christ Church College'	Untraced	*Gunnis* 1968, 247

MACCARTHY, S fl 1839

Busts

1.	1839	Arthur, 1st Duke of Wellington	[Exhib RA, London, 1323]; untraced	*Graves* V, 1905–6, 131; *Gunnis* 1968, 248

MACCARTHY, Sexon John James 1807–

The son of **John James Alexander MacCarthy**, he exhibited at the Society of British Artists in 1833, giving his address as 44 Coleshill Street, Chelsea.

Literary References: *Gunnis* 1968, 247

Statues

1.	1833	'Beauty', King William IV's horse	[Exhib Soc of BA, London, 848]; untraced	*Johnson* 1975, 301

MACDANIELL fl *c*1801

The Hare monument has a large, well-carved relief of *Hope* mourning over an urn (1).

Funerary Monuments

1.	†1801	Mary Hare	Stow Bardolph, Norfolk	S	Pevsner, *Norfolk: N W & S*, 1999, 674

MACDONALD, James fl 1831–33

In 1833 James MacDonald moved into the studio at 10 Cumberland Street, Edinburgh, left vacant when **Lawrence MacDonald** returned to Rome. The kinship, if any, between the two sculptors is unknown.

Literary References: *Woodward* 1977 (vol 1, pt 2), 125

Busts

1.	1831	John Wood		[Exhib R Sc A, Edinburgh, 386]; untraced	*Laperriere* 3, 1991, 112
2.	1831	Unidentified female head		[Exhib R Sc A, Edinburgh, 396]; untraced	*Laperriere* 3, 1991, 112
3.	1833	Unidentified officer	m	[Exhib R Sc A, Edinburgh, 324]; untraced	*Laperriere* 3, 1991, 112

Reliefs

4.	1833	Moses descending from Mount Sinai with the two tables of testimony, study	[Exhib R Sc A, Edinburgh, 315]; untraced	*Laperriere* 3, 1991, 112

MACDONALD, John fl 1844–

He was the older brother of **Lawrence MacDonald** and assisted him in Rome.

Literary References: *Woodward* 1977 (vol 1, pt 2), 126; *ODNB* (Greenwood)

Busts

1.	nd	J Crawford	Hospitalfield, Arbroath, Angus	*Woodward* 1977, vol 1, pt 2, 126

MACDONALD, Lawrence 1799–1878

A Scottish neoclassical sculptor, MacDonald spent most of his working life in Rome. He was born at Bonnyview, Findo-Gask, Perthshire, on 15 February 1799, the son of Alexander MacDonald and Margaret, née Morison. His father was an impoverished, half-blind violinist, his mother a nurse. MacDonald was schooled in Gask and apprenticed to a local mason, Thomas Gibson. An early commission was for carved decorative work for Robert Graeme of Garvock House (**192**). P R Drummond, a local historian, met MacDonald in 1816 and subsequently wrote a long memoir of the sculptor. His impression was that the young man was 'naturally somewhat impassioned and self-asserting' (*Drummond* 1879, 112).

MacDonald went to Edinburgh in 1822 and enrolled at the Trustees' Academy. Whilst studying he also worked for the architect James Gillespie Graham as a decorative carver. That winter he left Scotland for France in the company of the Oliphant family of Gask. MacDonald and the young laird of Oliphant continued on to Rome, where MacDonald set up a studio in the Corso. He stayed for three years, becoming an early member of the British Academy of Arts in Rome (founded 1821) and attracting the patronage of Scottish visitors, such as the Duke of Atholl and Sir Evan McGregor (**45, 47**). Scottish tourists apparently regarded the commissioning of a bust by MacDonald as 'an indispensable corollary to a short stay in the city' (*Drummond* 1879, 116).

He returned to Edinburgh in 1826 and exhibited a number of works at the Institution for the Encouragement of the Fine Arts in Scotland (later to become the Scottish Academy). His exhibits included several busts of notable patrons and friends, and the statue of a *Boy slinging*, carved in Rome in 1823 (**4**). In 1827 he succeeded **Samuel Joseph** as the most influential sculptor involved in the Edinburgh Phrenological Society. MacDonald carved a bust *all'antica* of its founder, George Combe (**64**), who acknowledged a great debt to Macdonald for directing his quasi-scientific studies towards the philosophy of art. MacDonald received his own phrenological analysis and Combe subsequently drew comparisons between the sculptor's cranial development and that of Raphael.

Many of Edinburgh's leading scientific and literary figures were absorbed with cranio-psychology, and MacDonald's connections with this group no doubt encouraged the Edinburgh journals to give him enthusiastic notices. In 1829, when Macdonald held a special exhibition of his *Ajax and Patroclus* (**6**), an engraving of the work featured on the front page of the *Scotsman*. When Charles Maclaren, the newspaper's editor, fought a duel with the editor of the *Caledonian Mercury*, Macdonald acted as his second. Their dispute was partly occasioned by a heated response in the *Scotsman* to criticism of MacDonald's work in the *Caledonian Mercury*. Macdonald made his own contribution to the world of letters with a couple of competent poems, published in Edinburgh journals.

In 1830 he held another special exhibition of ideal statuary and portraits at 70 Princes Street, which led the *Edinburgh Literary Journal* to compare him to Canova. This was followed by yet another special exhibition the following year in Pall Mall, London, again featuring busts and ideal subjects. This received favourable reviews in the *New Monthly Magazine* and the *Literary Gazette:* the *Gazette* opined that MacDonald 'promises to be – or, rather, he already is – one of the most distinguished ornaments of the British school of sculpture' and that his busts 'are full of character; and are executed in a most bold and masterly manner' (*Lit Gaz* 1831, 187). In spite of his high reputation in Edinburgh and London, MacDonald returned to Rome in September 1832, where he worked for the rest of his career. His journey appears to have been supported by a subscription fund organised by George Combe. Drummond later expressed his opinion that the sculptor's departure was dictated by the Scottish preference for less elevated works of popular literary subjects, particularly by **James Thom** and **John Greenshields**. In Scotland at this time a sculptor with MacDonald's ambition would certainly have found it difficult to procure either the patronage or the necessary workshop assistance to conduct a career founded exclusively on ideal works.

In Rome, where skilled labour and marble were cheaper, MacDonald met a steady stream of touring patrons for his classicising portrait busts. With these works he hoped to extend his connections and find patrons for ideal sculpture. This policy had some success, for Macdonald executed several ideal subjects for patrons who also commissioned busts. These included a statue for Viscount Powerscourt of *Eurydice stung by a viper*, a disrobing female attempting to fend off the attentions of a thin snake coiled around her ankle (**17**). MacDonald also carved a statue of a young girl attaching a letter to the leg of a small bird for John Marshall (**16**).

In 1844 **Bertel Thorvaldsen** died and Lawrence took over his studio in the Palazzo Barberini. His brother, **John MacDonald**, worked as an assistant. Lawrence sent work regularly to the Academy exhibitions in Edinburgh and London and maintained a clientele among the ever-increasing numbers of well-heeled British visitors to Rome. Apparently he was a man of tireless energy, often to be seen taking his coffee at 5.30am. He is known to have turned out nearly 100 busts in the years before his death, most of them classical in style. The female sitters are often robed in shifts and have hair plaited in a bun on the crown of the head, sometimes with ringlets falling onto their shoulders. In 1850 Macdonald carved the statue of Emily, Countess of Winchelsea and Nottingham (**1**), regarded by Gunnis and Greenwood as his most successful work. She is a classically dressed, elegant figure reclining on a day-bed, perusing a manuscript. When Macdonald visited Scotland in 1853 Drummond recalled that the sculptor moved with the air of a rich and successful man, his fingers 'bedizened with gems, the gifts of his admirers' (*Drummond* 1879, 126).

MacDonald's work was not admired universally. In 1854 a writer signing himself 'Fiorentia' visited his studio during his tour of the Roman workshops and compared the 'insipid' works of MacDonald unfavourably with those of **John Gibson**. Fiorentia noted that the studio contained images principally of 'the peerage done into marble, a plaster galaxy of rank and fashion' in which a 'potent family likeness' pervaded all. He found 'no flights of genius, no rude bones or vulgar sinews, but nature toned down to suit the fastidious notions of sickly countesses'. Even the handful of statues had an 'abominably genteel ball-room look'. The writer concluded: 'had Macdonald devoted himself to ideal works he might probably have achieved a very fair success, although by no means commensurate with the reputation with which that stupid flock of sheep, English [sic] tourists, have endowed him' (*AJ* 1854, 351–2).

In 1867 MacDonald was made an honorary member of the Royal Scottish Academy and in 1872 the Prince and Princess of Wales visited his studio in Rome. He seems in later years to have become a favourite sculptor of American visitors to the Eternal City. On 4 March 1878 he died and the *Art Journal* reported that 'A large number of American artists and other gentlemen attended the funeral of the deceased sculptor at the cemetery near the Porta San Paolo.' The marble medallion portrait on his tombstone in the Protestant cemetery was carved by his son, Alexander MacDonald, who was born in Rome in 1847 and assisted his father before pursuing his own successful career as a sculptor.

A year after his death Drummond wrote that MacDonald had left 'a world of uninterrupted successes' (*Drummond* 1879, 126). This verdict appears to be close to the truth. MacDonald enjoyed a good reputation with fellow Scots, who held him in high esteem, both before and after his permanent immigration to Rome. He continually offered assistance to young Scottish sculptors such as **Patric Park**, John Hutchison (1833–1910), who modelled his bust, and **William Brodie**. In addition he won the regard of English, Italian and American patrons. Although Gunnis was inclined to agree with Fiorentia, and felt that MacDonald flattered his sitters until they appeared 'too noble, too handsome and too distinguished to be true' (*Gunnis* 1968, 248–9), more recent writers have concentrated on the reasons for MacDonald's success. Greenwood has drawn attention to the careful execution, idealised form and high finish of the works, which are characteristic of the late neoclassical movement and reflect a move from severity to 'measured elegance' (*Grove* 1996, 878).

MGS

Literary References: *Lit Gaz* 1831, 187; *Passavant* 1836, vol 2, 283–4; *Le Grice* 1844, I, 77–82; II, 201–17; *AJ* 1854, 350–55; *Builder* 1866, 92; *AJ* 1878, 136; *Drummond* 1879, 109–126; *Gunnis* 1968, 248–9; *Pearson* 1981, 14–23; *Busiri Vici* 1981, 96–100; *Read* 1982, 132–3, 171, 199; *Pearson* 1991, 65–71 (Smailes); *Grove* 1996, 878 (Greenwood); *ODNB* (Greenwood); *JKB* 2006, 180

Archival References: GPC

Portraits of the sculptor: John Hutchison, marble bust, 1860, Royal Scottish Academy (repr ODNB); Alexander MacDonald, marble bust, 1870–1878, Accademia Nazionale di San Luca, Rome; Alexander Macdonald, marble medallion on tombstone, 1878, Protestant cemetery, Rome

No.	Date	Subject		Location		References
Funerary Monuments						
1.	1850	Emily, Countess of Winchilsea and Nottingham		[Eastwell, Kent]; VAM A.188-1969	SD	Pevsner, *Kent: NE & E*, 1983, 310; *Bilbey* 2002, 329 (repr)
2.	1863	Watts Russell		Ilam, Staffs		*Gunnis* 1968, 249
Statues						
3.	pre-1822	Boy supporting a vase upon his head		[Moncreiffe, Perths, gardens]; untraced		*Gunnis* 1968, 248; *Pearson* 1991, 69 n20
4.	1823	Boy slinging		Anatomy Department, Edinburgh University		*Lit Gaz* 1831, 187; *Gunnis* 1968, 248; *Pearson* 1991, 67 n18
5.	1827	Unidentified child	m	[Exhib IEFAS, 260]; untraced		*Rinder and McKay* 1917, 234
6.	1829	Ajax bearing the body of Patroclus, group		[Exhib Royal Institution, Edinburgh (model) Macdonald's exhibition of sculpture, Pall Mall 1831 (?)]; untraced		*Lit Gaz*, 19 March 1831, 187; *Passavant* 1836, 2, 283–4; *Drummond* 1879, 119; *DNB*; *Pearson* 1991, 67, 68
7.	1829	Unidentified child, 'to be executed in marble'		[Exhib IEFAS, 275]; untraced		*Rinder and McKay* 1917, 234
8.	1831	Ajax		Powerscourt House, Co Wicklow		*Gunnis* 1968, 248
9.	1831	Supplicating virgin		[MacDonald's exhibition of sculpture, Pall Mall, 1831]; untraced		*Lit Gaz*, 19 March 1831, 187; *Graves* V, 1905–6, 134; GPC
10.	1831	The youthful slinger		[MacDonald's exhibition of sculpture, Pall Mall, 1831]; untraced		*Lit Gaz*, 19 March 1831, 187
11.	1831	Thetis and Achilles, group		[MacDonald's exhibition of sculpture, Pall Mall, 1831]; untraced		*Lit Gaz*, 19 March 1831, 187; *Passavant* 1836, 2, 283; *Drummond* 1879, 119
12.	1831	Unidentified child	m	[Exhib RA, London, 1232]; untraced		*Graves* V, 1905–6, 134; *Library of Fine Arts* 1831, 1, 432; *Passavant* 1836, 2, 283
13.	1832	Bacchante	m	[coll Charles Jenner]; untraced		*Gunnis* 1968, 248; *Rinder and McKay* 1917, 234
14.	1832	Nereid, or sea nymph	b	[Exhib Scottish Acad, 330]; untraced		*Rinder and McKay* 1917, 234
15.	1832	Penelope	b	[Exhib Scottish Acad, 329]; untraced		*Rinder and McKay* 1917, 234; *Gunnis* 1968, 248
16.	1833	Girl with a carrier pigeon		Russell-Cotes AG, Bournemouth, Dorset		*Graves* V, 1905–6, 134; *Johnson* 1975, 302
17.	1836	Eurydice stung by a viper	m	[Powerscourt House, Co Wicklow]; NGI	SD	*AJ*, 1848, 50; *AJ*, 1878, 136; *Pearson* 1991, 68; *le Harivel* 1988, 575 (repr)
18.	1839	Maria Hamilton Gray as Psyche		[Charlton House, Fife]; private coll, Texas	SD	GPC
19.	*c*1840	Elizabeth, Viscountess Powerscourt		Powerscourt House, Co Wicklow		*Gunnis* 1968, 248; *Pearson* 1991, 68
20.	pre-1841	Ulysses and his dog Argus		[coll Sir Arthur Brook, Bt]; untraced		*AJ* 1855 (repr); *AJ*, 1878, 136; *DNB*; GPC
21.	1842	Andromeda chained	m	Christie 12 Feb 1976, lot 40	SD	*Graves* V, 1905–6, 134; *Read* 1982, 199 (repr)
22.	1842	Bacchante	m	Private coll, Scotland		*AU*, 1842, 128; *Graves* V, 1905–6, 134; *Pearson* 1991, unpag, 71 (repr)
23.	1846	A goat, group	m	[Exhib RA, London, 1419]; untraced		*Graves* V, 1905–6, 134
24.	1846	Nymph	m	Christie 28 Jan 1988, lot 180	SD	C Lib (repr)
25.	1848	Andromeda chained		[coll Earl of Aberdeen]; untraced		*Gunnis* 1968, 248
26.	1848	Lord Baltimore's son		untraced		*AJ* 1848, 50
27.	1849	Arethusa	m	[coll Lord Ward]; untraced		*AJ*, 1878, 136; *Graves* V, 1905–6, 135; *Manchester Art Treasures* 1857, 134; RG/JP, 5, 862, 863
28.	1850	Andromeda	m	[coll Marquess of Abercorn]; untraced		*Manchester Art Treasures*, 133; *Gunnis* 1968, 248
29.	1850	Lord Kilmorey, dressed as a Grecian warrior		Mourne Park, Newry		*AJ* 1854, 351; *Pearson* 1991, 68; *Urwin* 1997, 7
30.	1850	Ulysses		[coll Earl of Kilmorey]; untraced		*AJ* 1854, 352; *Gunnis* 1968, 248
31.	by 1854	Andromeda		[coll Lord Kilmorey]; untraced		*AJ* 1854, 352
32.	1854	Venus	m	[coll Hon A D Willoughby]; untraced		*Graves* V, 1905–6, 135; *Manchester Art Treasures* 1857, 133

No.	Date	Subject		Location		Literature
33.	pre-1857	Bacchante	m	[coll Lord Ward]; untraced Other versions: ex coll Wentworth Woodhouse, Yorks, 1874; untraced		*Manchester Art Treasures* 1857, 133; *Gunnis* 1968, 248; GPC
34.	pre-1857	Eurydice	m	[coll Lord Ward]; untraced		*Manchester Art Treasures* 1857, 133
35.	1857	Venus	m	Private coll, Scotland	D	C Lib (repr)
36.	1863	Albinia Gibbs ('the little maid')		Tyntesfield, Somerset		C Lib (repr)
37.	1877	Young fisherman		[coll Earl Fitzwilliam]; untraced		*Gunnis* 1968, 248; *Read* 1982, 132
38.	nd	Heroic nude statue (Captain Barclay Allardice as Hercules?)		Untraced		*Pearson* 1991, 68
39.	nd	Sir Michael O'Loghlen		[Four courts, Dublin]; untraced		GPC
Busts						
40.	c1822	Mr and Mrs MacDonald, the sculptor's parents		Untraced		*Drummond* 1879, 112
41.	1827	Charles Stirling	m	[Exhib IEFAS, 270]; untraced		*Rinder and McKay* 1917, 234
42.	1827	General Alexander Murray MacGregor		[Exhib IEFAS, 271]; untraced		*Rinder and McKay* 1917, 234
43.	1827	J Graham Stirling of Airth		[Exhib IEFAS, 275]; untraced		*Rinder and McKay* 1917, 234
44.	1827	James Gillespie Graham		[Exhib IEFAS, 263]; untraced		*Drummond* 1879, 117; *Rinder and McKay* 1917, 234
45.	1827	John, 4th Duke of Atholl		Blair Castle, Perths		*Gunnis* 1968, 248; *Pearson* 1991, 67; GPC
46.	1827	Miss Graham	m	[Exhib IEFAS, 261]; untraced		*Rinder and McKay* 1917, 234
47.	1827	Sir Evan Murray MacGregor		[Exhib IEFAS, 265]; untraced		*Drummond* 1879, 116; *Rinder and McKay* 1917, 234
48.	1828	Alexander Macleod of Muiravonside	m	[Exhib IEFAS, 276]; untraced		*Rinder and McKay* 1917, 234
49.	1828	General Sir David Baird		[Exhib RA, London, 1196]; untraced		*Drummond* 1879, 112; *Graves* V, 1905–6, 134
50.	1828	Miss Eliza Paton		[Exhib IEFAS, 274]; untraced		*Rinder and McKay* 1917, 234
51.	1828	Miss Stephens		[Exhib IEFAS, 280]; untraced		*Rinder and McKay* 1917, 234
52.	1828	Mr Balfour of Fernie Model(s): exhib IEFAS, 277	m	[Exhib IEFAS, 1829, 271]; untraced		*Rinder and McKay* 1917, 234
53.	1828	Mrs Smyth	m	[Exhib IEFAS, 279]; untraced		*Rinder and McKay* 1917, 234
54.	1828	Unidentified gentleman	m	[Exhib IEFAS, 278]; untraced		*Rinder and McKay* 1917, 234
55.	1828	Unidentified lady, posthumous	m	[Exhib IEFAS, 275]; untraced		*Rinder and McKay* 1917, 234
56.	1829	A lady	m	[Exhib IEFAS, 269]; untraced		*Rinder and McKay* 1917, 234
57.	1829	Forrest Alexander	m	[Exhib IEFAS, 272]; untraced		*Rinder and McKay* 1917, 234
58.	1829	James L'Amy	m	[Exhib IEFAS, 270]; untraced		*Rinder and McKay* 1917, 234
59.	1829	John Marshall MP		Leeds Lit and Phil Soc, W R Yorks		*Graves* V, 1905–6, 134; GPC
60.	1829	Robert Philips		[Exhib Manc Acad]; untraced		*Gunnis* 1968, 248
61.	1829	Unidentified child	m	[Exhib IEFAS, 286]; untraced		*Rinder and McKay* 1917, 234
62.	1829	Unidentified lady	m	[Exhib IEFAS, 273]; untraced		*Rinder and McKay* 1917, 234
63.	1829	Unidentified lady	m	[Exhib IEFAS, 282]; untraced		*Rinder and McKay* 1917, 234
64.	c1830	George Combe	m	SNPG, Edinburgh		*Drummond* 1879, 117; *Pearson* 1991, unpag, 67 (repr); *Ret. to Life*, 2000, 63 (repr)
65.	1830	Marjorie, Duchess of Atholl	m	Blair Castle, Perths		*Pearson* 1991, 67; GPC; C Lib (repr)
66.	c1830	Two Miss Wilsons (daughters of Professor Wilson)		Untraced		*Drummond* 1879, 117
67.	1831	Charles Kemble		[MacDonald's exhibition of sculpture, Pall Mall, 1831]; untraced		*Lit Gaz*, no 739, 19 March 1831, 187; *New Monthly Mag* 1831, 33, 172
68.	1831	Fanny Kemble, Charles Kemble's daughter		[MacDonald's exhibition of sculpture, Pall Mall, 1831]; untraced		*New Monthly Mag* 33, 1831, 172; *Drummond* 1879, 121
69.	1831	Mr James, author		[MacDonald's exhibition of sculpture, Pall Mall, 1831]; untraced		*New Monthly Mag*, 1831, 33, 172
70.	1831	Mr Sykes MP		[MacDonald's exhibition of sculpture, Pall Mall, 1831]; untraced		*New Monthly Mag* 1831, 33, 172
71.	1831	Mrs Balfour, of Fernie		[Exhib RA, London, 1216]; untraced		*Graves* V, 1905–6, 134
72.	1831	Mrs Brougham, of Brougham Hall		[Exhib RA, London, 1205]; untraced Other versions: exhib Scottish Academy, 1832, 325 'from the original marble in the possession of the Lord Chancellor'; untraced		*Lit Gaz*, no 739, 19 March 1831, 187; *Passavant* 1836, 2, 283; *Graves* V, 1905–6, 134; *Rinder and McKay* 1917, 234
73.	1831	Mrs Nairne		[MacDonald's exhibition of sculpture, Pall Mall, 1831]; untraced		*Lit Gaz*, no 739, 19 March 1831, 187; *Passavant* 1836, 2, 283–4
74.	1831	Professor John Wilson		[MacDonald's exhibition of sculpture, Pall Mall, 1831]; untraced		*New Monthly Mag*, 33, 1831, 172; *Lit Gaz* 1831, 187; *Passavant* 1836, 2, 283–4; *Drummond* 1879, 117
75.	1831	Sir John Sinclair		[MacDonald's exhibition of sculpture, Pall Mall, 1831]; untraced		*Lit Gaz*, 19 March 1831, 187
76.	1831	Sir Walter Scott		Untraced		*DNB*
77.	1832	'A head from a statue'		[Exhib Scottish Acad, 328]; untraced		*Rinder and McKay* 1917, 234
78.	1832	Earl of Errol	m	[Exhib Scottish Acad, 326]; untraced		*Rinder and McKay* 1917, 234
79.	1832	John G Lockhart ('to be cast in bronze')		[Exhib Scottish Acad, 327]; untraced		*Rinder and McKay* 1917, 234
80.	1832	John Gladstone	m	[Exhib Scottish Acad, 323]; untraced		*Rinder and McKay* 1917, 234; *Pearson* 1991, 68
81.	post-1836	6th Viscount Powerscourt		Untraced		*Pearson* 1991, 68
82.	1836	6th Viscount Powerscourt's mother		Untraced		*Pearson* 1991, 68

83.	pre-1836	Lord Brougham		Untraced		*Passavant* 1836, 2, 283–4
84.	1837	Psyche		[Exhib Scottish Acad, 360 'lent by George Dundas']; untraced		*Rinder and McKay* 1917, 234
85.	1838	3rd Earl of Mansfield's daughter	m	Scone Palace, Perths	S	
86.	1838	Emily Murray, later Marchioness of Hertford	m	Ragley Hall, Warks	SD	GPC
87.	1838	Marchioness of Waterford		Highcliffe Castle, Hants		*Gunnis* 1968, 248
88.	1838	Miss Coutts Trotter	m	[Exhib RA, London, 1303]; untraced		*Graves* V, 1905–6, 134; GPC
89.	1838	Miss Webber		[Exhib RA, London, 1324]; untraced		*Graves* V, 1905–6, 134
90.	1838	Viscountess Canning		Highcliffe Castle, Hants		*AJ* 1878, 136; *Graves* V, 1905–6, 134;
91.	1838	Young woman	m	NGS	SD	
92.	1839	Catherine and Mary Glynne		Hawarden Castle, Flints		*Pointon* 1975–1976, 90; GPC
93.	1839	Colonel Thomas Hunter-Blair	m	Blairquhan, Ayrshire		*Graves* V, 1905–6, 134; *Rinder and McKay* 1917, 234
94.	1839	Lady Ebury		Apsley House, London		*Gunnis* 1968, 248
95.	1839	Lady Hereford	m	Scone Palace, Perths	S	
96.	1839	Lady James		Betteshanger House, Kent		*Gunnis* 1968, 248
97.	1839	Lord Alexander Russell		Woburn Abbey, Beds	SD	*Gunnis* 1968, 248
98.	1839	Miss Stuart		[Exhib RA, London, 1378]; untraced		*Graves* V, 1905–6, 134
99.	1839	Unidentified woman	m	Cyril Humphris, 1972	SD	
100.	1840	A young lady (? Miss Edmonstone)		Willingdon, Sussex		RG/JP, 5, 864
101.	1840	Lady Emily Seymour		[Exhib RA, London, 1140]; untraced		*Graves* V, 1905–6, 134
102.	1840	Lady Sarah Villiers		[Exhib RA, London, 1129]; untraced		*Graves* V, 1905–6, 134
103.	1840	Lord Charles Montagu		Kimbolton Castle, Hunts		*Gunnis* 1968, 249
104.	1840	Miss Ellison		[Exhib RA, London, 1149]; untraced		*Graves* V, 1905–6, 134
105.	1840	Unidentified physician		[Exhib RA, London, 1195]; untraced		*Graves* V, 1905–6, 134
106.	1840	Viscount Strathallen		[Exhib RA, London, 1134]; untraced		*Drummond* 1879, 116; *Graves* V, 1905–6, 134
107.	by 1841	James, 1st Duke of Abercorn		Althorp, Northants		GPC
108.	1841	John, Viscount FitzGibbon		Prestwold Hall, Leics		GPC
109.	1841	Lord Crewe		[Exhib RA, London, 1298]; untraced		*Graves* V, 1905–6, 134; GPC
110.	1841	Lucy Towneley		Towneley, Burnley	SD	GPC
111.	1841	Miss Leycester	m	Manchester CAG 1978.314		
112.	pre-1841	Princess Mary of Cambridge		Untraced		*AJ* 1878, 136; GPC
113.	1841	Unidentified young girl	m	Sotheby 8 July 2003, lot 179	SD	
114.	1842	Charles John, Earl Canning	m	[Exhib RA, London, 1388]; untraced		*AJ* 1878, 136; *Graves* V, 1905–6, 134; GPC
115.	1842	Lady Baker	m	[Exhib RA, London, 1376]; untraced		*AU*, 1842, 129; *Graves* V, 1905–6, 134
116.	1842	Mrs Eyre	m	[Exhib RA, London, 1364]; untraced		*Graves* V, 1905–6, 134
117.	1843	Flora	m	Walker, Liverpool Other versions: Royal Coll, Osborne, I of W, SD, 1849	SD	Walker, Liverpool, *Annual Reports*, II–IV, 1971–4, 32
118.	1843	Lord Compton	m	Castle Ashby, Northants		*Graves* V, 1905–6, 134
119.	1843	Sir Henry Taylor	m	[coll Sir Henry Taylor]; NPG, London Other versions: Foreign and Commonwealth Office, London	SD	*Graves* V, 1905–6, 134; *Ormond* 1973, 445 (repr 887); GPC
120.	1843	Thomas Spring Rice, 1st Baron Monteagle (1790–1866)	m	NGI 8203	SD	*AJ* 1878, 136; *Graves* V, 1905–6, 134; *Wynne and White* 1975, 26; *le Harivel* 1988, 575 (repr)
121.	1844	George, 5th Earl of Aberdeen		Haddo House, Aberdeenshire		GPC
122.	1844	Helen Mackay, Lady Moncrieffe	m	Private coll		*Pearson* 1991, unpag, 68, 70 (repr)
123.	1844	Henry, Marquess of Worcester (afterwards Duke of Beaufort)		Badminton House, Glos	SD	
124.	1844	Louisa, Duchess of Abercorn	m	Althorp, Northants		C Lib (repr)
125.	1844	Mary Somerville	m	R I, London		*AJ* 1878, 136; *Graves* V, 1905–6, 134; *Ormond* 1973, 424; *Pearson* 1991, unpag, 68
126.	1844	Rev Walter Halliday		[W H Halliday, Glenthorne, Devon]; untraced		GPC
127.	1844	Unidentified lady		[Exhib RA, London, 1337]; untraced		*Graves* V, 1905–6, 134
128.	1844	Unidentified young woman	m	Sotheby 2 Nov 1989, bt R Bird	SD	
129.	1845	Lady Adela Villiers		Osterley Park, Middx		GPC
130.	1845	Maria Adelaide, 2nd Countess of Yarborough		Brocklesby Park, Lincs	S	GPC
131.	1845	Unidentified woman	m	Lacock Abbey, Wilts	SD	
132.	1846	Adolphus, 1st Duke of Cambridge	m	Windsor Castle RCIN 31611	SD	*Grove* 1996, 19, 878; C Lib (repr)
133.	1846	Charles Henry Higginson	m	Christie 18 March 1993, lot 23	SD	
134.	1846	Emily, Marchioness of Lansdowne	m	Meikleour, Scotland	SD	GPC
135.	1846	Hon A Willoughby		[Exhib RA, London, 1468]; untraced		*AJ* 1878, 136; *Graves* V, 1905–6, 134
136.	1846	John, 4th Marquess of Waterford	m	Curraghmore, Ireland	SD	GPC
137.	1846	William, Marquess of Douglas	m	[Exhib RA, London, 1513]; untraced		*AJ* 1878, 136; *Graves* V, 1905–6, 134; GPC
138.	1847	Lady Clementina Villiers		Osterley Park, Middx		*Graves* V, 1905–6, 135; GPC
139.	1848	Charles, 2nd Earl of Yarborough		Brocklesby Park, Lincs Other versions: Brocklesby Park, Lincs, SD, 1854		GPC
140.	1848	Charles, 3rd Earl of Yarborough		Brocklesby Park, Lincs Other versions: Brocklesby Hall, Lincs, 1854	SD	GPC
141.	1848	Countess of Eglinton		Brocklesby Park, Lincs		GPC
142.	1848	George Granville Harcourt	m	Private coll	SD	

No.	Date	Subject	Medium	Location		Literature
143.	1848	Lady Frances Waldegrave	m	Private coll	SD	
144.	1848	Lady Herbert of Lea	m	Wilton House, Wilts	SD	*Gunnis* 1968, 249; *Grove* 1996, 19, 87
145.	1848	Lady Sophia Pelham		Brocklesby Park, Lincs	S	GPC
146.	c1848	Lord Kilmorey		Mourne Park, Newry		*Urwin* 1997, 7
147.	1848	Louisa, Duchess of Northumberland		Syon House, Isleworth, Middx		GPC
148.	1848	Miss Waterton (or Miss Edmonstone?)		Walton Hall, W R Yorks		*Gunnis* 1968, 249
149.	1848	Unidentified lady		[Exhib RA, London, 1444]; untraced		*Graves* V, 1905–6, 134
150.	1848	Viscountess Milton		[Wentworth Woodhouse, W R Yorks]; untraced		*Gunnis* 1968, 249
151.	1849	Earl of Shelbourne		Bowood, Wilts		RG/JP, 5, 865
152.	1849	Lord Walpole	m	[Exhib RA, London, 1280]; untraced		*AJ* 1878, 136; *Graves* V, 1905–6, 135
153.	1849	Psyche	m	Royal Coll RCIN 41027 Other versions: Syon House, Isleworth, Middx, nd	SD	C Lib (repr)
154.	1849	Unidentified gentleman		[Exhib RA, London, 1241]; untraced		*Graves* V, 1905–6, 135
155.	1849	Unidentified lady		[Exhib RA, London, 1239]; untraced		*Graves* V, 1905–6, 135
156.	1850	Henry, 5th Duke of Newcastle	m	Sotheby, Gleneagles Hotel, 26 Aug 1997, lot 1372	SD	
157.	1851	A woman (?Lydia Dashwood)	m	Birmingham MAG, inv P.22'80	SD	*Silber* 1987 62–3, cat no 191 (repr)
158.	1851	Victoria, 3rd Countess of Yarborough		Brocklesby Park, Lincs	S	GPC
159.	1853	Lady Packenham		[Exhib RA, London, 1444]; untraced		*AJ* 1878, 136; *Graves* V, 1905–6, 135
160.	1854	Algernon, 4th Duke of Northumberland		Syon House, Isleworth, Middx		GPC
161.	1854	Algernon, 4th Duke of Northumberland and his Duchess		Alnwick Castle, Northumbs		*AJ*, 1854, 351; GPC
162.	1854	Emily, Countess Stanhope		Chevening, Kent	SD	*Gunnis* 1968, 249; GPC
163.	by 1854	Lady Walpole		[Sculptor's studio, Rome]; untraced		*AJ* 1854, 351
164.	by 1854	Mrs Denison		[Sculptor's studio, Rome]; untraced		*AJ* 1854, 351; *Graves* V, 1905–6, 135;
165.	1854	Mrs Thistlethwaite		[Exhib RA, London, 1447]; untraced		*Graves* V, 1905–6, 135
166.	1854	Philip Henry, 5th Earl Stanhope		Chevening, Kent	SD	*Gunnis* 1968, 249; GPC
167.	1854	Sir Robert Keith Arbuthnot	m	[Exhib RA, London, 1444 Exhib R Sc A, 1855, 781]; untraced		*Graves* V, 1905–6, 135; *Rinder and McKay* 1917, 234
168.	1855	James, 7th Earl of Cardigan	m	Gov Art Coll (1984)	SD	*Gawsworth Guide*, 47; Gov Art Coll archives
169.	1855	Miss C May		[Exhib RA, London, 1545]; untraced		*Graves* V, 1905–6, 135
170.	1855	Miss May		[Exhib RA, London, 1521]; untraced		*Graves* V, 1905–6, 135
171.	1855	Unidentified lady		[Exhib RA, London, 1506]; untraced		*Graves* V, 1905–6, 135
172.	1856	Henry, 5th Marquess of Londonderry		Londonderry House, London	SD	*Read* 1982, 171; *Pearson* 1991, 68
173.	1856	Thomas Stewart Gladstone of Capernoch	m	coll John Gladstone Esq of Capernoch	SD	
174.	1857	Hon Adelbert Wellington Brownlow	m	[Exhib RA, London, 1308]; untraced		*Graves* V, 1905–6, 135
175.	1858	Isabella Malcolm		[Poltalloch House, Argyll]; untraced		GPC
176.	1858	John Malcolm of Poltalloch	m	[coll Poltalloch House, Argyll]; Manchester CAG 1978.90	SD	
177.	1858	Unidentified man and woman	m	Christie, Wrotham Park, Herts, 21 June 1994, lots 185–6	SD	
178.	1859	Lady Charlotte Lane-Fox		Brocklesby Park, Lincs		GPC
179.	1861	Eleanor Watt (†1904)	m	BGM 252-1904, London	SD	*Gunnis* 1968, 249; *Bilbey* 2002, 330 (repr)
180.	nd	2nd Earl of Clare		Prestwold Hall, Leics		GPC
181.	nd	3rd Earl of Clare		Prestwold Hall, Leics		GPC
182.	nd	Andrew Dundas		Royal Coll Physic, Edinburgh	S	
183.	nd	Charlotte, Duchess of Leeds		Brocklesby Park, Lincs		GPC
184.	nd	Duke of Hamilton		Untraced		*AJ* 1878, 136
185.	nd	Elizabeth, Duchess of Argyll		Inverary Castle, Argyllshire	S	
186.	nd	Harriott, Countess of Meath		Kilruddery Castle, Co Wicklow		GPC
187.	nd	Henry, 4th Duke of Newcastle (†1851)	m	[Clumber House, Notts]; untraced		*Ormond* 1973, 338
188.	nd	John Gibson RA		[Crystal Palace, Sydenham, portrait gall, 1854]; untraced		*Ormond* 1973, 188
189.	nd	Sidney, Baron Herbert of Lea		[Crystal Palace, portrait gall, 1854]; untraced		*Ormond* 1973, 223
190.	nd	Sir George Cayley Bt		(coll Sir Kenelm Cayley, 1973)		*Ormond* 1973, 97
191.	nd	William Dyce		Untraced		*Ormond* 1973, 153–4
Architectural Sculpture						
192.	pre-1822	Coat of arms Payment(s): £5		[coll Robert Graeme, Garvock House, Perths]; untraced		*Drummond* 1879, 112
193.	post-1836	Ornamental works		[Powerscourt House, Co Wicklow, house and gardens]; untraced		*Pearson* 1991, 68
Reliefs						
194.	c1843	Lady Jean Ogilvie	m	Cortachy Castle, Forfarshire		*Pearson* 1991, unpag, 67 (repr)
195.	1844	Mary Somerville, medallion	b	Somerville College, Oxford		*Ormond* 1973, 424
196.	1855–1856	The dying Priscilla Hoste lying on a day-bed with the 2nd Earl of Kilmorey kneeling at its foot and their son Charles standing at the head	m	Kilmorey Mausoleum, Gordon House, Twickenham, Middx	S	*Urwin* 1997, 7

Miscellaneous

197.	1827	A boy singing	[Exhib IEFAS, 273]; untraced	*Rinder and McKay* 1917, 234
198.	c1831	William Wordsworth as a Grecian worthy	Untraced	*Pearson* 1991, 67–8, 69
199.	pre-1841	Hyacinthus	[coll John Gladstone]; untraced Other versions: 1852, Royal Coll, SD, marble nd, Crowther of Syon Lodge, 1991, marble, signed exhib RA, London, 1294; untraced	*AU*, 1842, 128; *Graves* V, 1905–6, 134; *Read* 1982, 132–3 (repr Royal Coll version); *Pearson* 1991, 68; GPC
200.	nd	Clytie	Manchester CAG M10984	

MACDONELL, Francis

A deaf-and-dumb artist, he studied at the Royal Dublin Society's School, and exhibited at the Royal Academy, giving his address as 24 Allen Street, Lambeth in 1846 and 5 Howland Street in 1852.

Literary References: *Gunnis* 1968, 249

Busts

1.	1846	Mrs Yearsley	[Exhib RA, London, 1495]; untraced	*Graves* V, 1905–6, 135

Miscellaneous

2.	1852	'The first born'	[Exhib RA, London, 1367]; untraced	*Graves* V, 1905–6, 135

MACDOWELL, Patrick RA 1799–1870

MacDowell was a largely self-taught sculptor of Irish origins who worked throughout his career in London and is best known for his poetic female figures. He was born in Belfast on 12 August 1799. MacDowell described his father as a tradesman who lost his livelihood when he sold his business and properties to invest in an unsuccessful commercial venture. He died soon after, when Patrick was still very young, leaving his widow 'in possession of little more than the house she lived in' (*AJ*, 1850, 8). In 1807 MacDowell was sent to a boarding school in Belfast run by an engraver called Gordon, who encouraged his early interest in drawing, allowing him to study his collection of prints. His mother brought him to England in 1811 and during the next two years he continued his education with a clergyman in Hampshire, before being apprenticed to a coach builder in London. This craft had little appeal for him, but MacDowell was not allowed to pursue his interest in art since his family considered it too precarious a way of making a living.

His opportunity for a more congenial career came after he had served four and a half years of his apprenticeship, when his master became bankrupt. MacDowell took lodgings in the house of **Peter Francis Chenu** in Charles Street, Mayfair and there he made sketches from Chenu's collection of casts. The coach builder then decided to move to Ireland and tried to pressurise MacDowell into leaving with him. MacDowell refused and finally succeeded in having his indentures cancelled. After leaving Chenu's house he continued to draw and model the human figure and eventually executed a small figure of *Venus holding a mirror* (**10**). MacDowell showed this work to Chenu, who was so delighted with it that he bought it. Chenu's encouragement spurred him to further efforts and he continued to model small figures, some of which he was able to sell.

In 1822 MacDowell exhibited for the first time at the Royal Academy (**42**). By 1826 he had set up a studio at 57 Seymour Street, near Euston Square, and submitted a design in the competition for a public statue commemorating the naval officer and political reformer John Cartwright (**11**). MacDowell's model was selected but he did not execute the work because the subscription failed to raise sufficient funds. A statue from MacDowell's model was produced by **George Clarke of Birmingham**, who agreed to carry out the work for the sum which had been raised, but became bankrupt soon after. The Cartwright family were much taken with MacDowell's work and gave him patronage. MacDowell later wrote, 'I can never forget the great kindness of that benevolent and amiable family, who were unwearied in their efforts to serve me in my profession at a time in my life when their kindness was most useful to me' (*AJ*, 1851, 8). In 1830 he entered the Royal Academy Schools on the recommendation of John Constable.

When not occupied with portrait commissions, MacDowell turned to ideal subjects. His first attempt, a small group, *The loves of the angels* (**12**), was inspired by a poem by a fellow Irishman, Thomas Moore, was followed by a subject from Ovid, *Cephalus and Procris* (**14**), which was commissioned in marble by E S Cooper, the MP for Sligo. His *Girl reading* (**15**), a charming, sentimental genre work, first exhibited at the Royal Academy in 1837, attracted considerable attention and made his name. MacDowell later recalled that **Sir Francis Chantrey** was impressed by the work and ensured that it was prominently displayed in the exhibition. After seeing it, Sir James Emmerson Tennent, a Belfast politician and writer, commissioned busts of himself and his wife (**61, 96**) and introduced MacDowell to Sir Thomas Wentworth Beaumont. Beaumont, a wealthy politician and art collector, became MacDowell's most important patron. He commissioned several major new ideal works (**16–19, 25**), as well as a marble version of *Girl reading*. (It was probably this version which appeared in the RA exhibition of 1868). In return, MacDowell agreed not to accept outside commissions over the next three years without first consulting Beaumont. He carved another marble version of *Girl reading* for Sir Francis Egerton, later the Earl of Ellesmere, with Beaumont's permission. Around this time MacDowell moved to a new studio at 75 Margaret Street, Westminster, where he remained for the rest of his life.

He continued to prosper during the 1840s and 1850s. In 1841 he was elected an associate of the Royal Academy. He then travelled, at Beaumont's expense, to Rome, where he remained for eight months 'visiting every church, palace, and museum, famed for its treasures, whether in painting or sculpture' (*AJ*, 1850, 9). In 1846 he was elected an Academician, submitting a *Nymph* as his diploma work (**21**). This draped female figure has been seen as typical of MacDowell's 'sweet, soft manner – infinitely pretty and ladylike' (*Crookshank* 1966, 312). In 1844 he exhibited *Girl at Prayer* (**17**) at the Westminster Hall exhibition organised to select artists to decorate the new Palace of Westminster. MacDowell won commissions for four statues of historical figures, Almeric and William de Warrenne for the chamber of the House of Lords (**34, 36**), and William Pitt the Elder and Younger for St Stephen's Hall (**32, 33**). In 1853 the Corporation of London commissioned a statue of *Lea* (**29**), a subject from Moore's *Loves of the Angels*, as one of the series of figures from English literature to decorate the Egyptian Hall in the Mansion House.

Despite his success, MacDowell appears to have felt, like many others, that public patronage of sculpture was too limited. In 1855 he was one of twenty-two sculptors who signed an open letter addressed to the first commissioner of works, objecting to the way in which the first Wellington memorial competition had been handled and complaining of a general lack of opportunities for talented British sculptors.

Works by MacDowell were displayed at the Great Exhibition of 1851 and at the international exhibitions held in Dublin (1853), Paris (1855) and in London (1862). Four of his works were lent by collectors to the Manchester Art Treasures Exhibition in 1857 (**17, 25, 26, 31**). The statue of *Eve* (**23**) was one of several works shown more than once. It appeared at the Great Exhibition and at the Dublin Exhibition two years later and was admired by many commentators as a chaste depiction of nude female form.

Like most successful sculptors of the mid-century MacDowell was responsible for large numbers of portrait busts, many of them exhibited at the RA, and a number of statues of major public figures, including several for Irish cities (**28, 35, 39, 41**). None of these has survived. Late in his career he provided statues of Leibniz, Cuvier and Linnaeus (**99**) for the façade of 6 Burlington Gardens in London, which was built as the headquarters of the University of London. It was designed by Sir James Pennethorne in a renaissance revival style and decorated with statues by **Joseph Durham, William Theed II, Matthew Noble** and others.

MacDowell's most important work is the colossal group of *Europe* on the Albert Memorial in Kensington Gardens, London (**40**). He was originally to have provided one of the smaller groups and was asked to execute *Europe* only after the elderly **John Gibson** turned down the opportunity. A first model was completed in November 1864 and found to be generally satisfactory, though some modifications were required. MacDowell's suggestion for figures of France and England holding between them an olive branch or festoon symbolising peace was rejected, for practical and intellectual reasons: it was felt that an olive branch would be difficult to realize in stone and that the symbolism did not reflect contemporary political reality. An improved model was approved in 1865. In October 1867 MacDowell completed the full-size model and was recorded as making progress in carving the central figure of Europe.

On 7 December 1870, soon after work on *Europe* was completed, MacDowell died. He had recently retired as an Academician, but had received honorary retired status. Two other members of his family, possibly sons, appear to have followed the same career, for a P MacDowell junior and R C MacDowell exhibited a few works at the RA between 1858 and 1865. They have fallen into obscurity.

Contemporary critical responses to MacDowell's work varied greatly. **Henry Weekes** enthusiastically described him as 'an artist that England may well be proud of' who appeals 'to our best and noblest feelings' (*Weekes* 1851–2, 65). J M Graham did not value his talents so highly, declaring that 'without any very elevated sentiment or feeling, MacDowell's works in poetic sculpture were mostly devoted to the representation of the female form. They were not equal to the masterpieces of Baily or Wyatt, but sufficiently attractive to the popular eye' (*Graham* 1871, 459). The writer of his obituary in *The Athenaeum* observed 'his designs were generally graceful, occasionally charming; but some of them were rather trite' (*Athenaeum*, 24 December 1870, 847). Writing in the early-20th century Strickland considered MacDowell's works within the context of his generation. He judged them among the best in a period dominated by a devitalised neoclassical style. His works were neither as original nor as influential as those of his near contemporary, **John Henry Foley**. More recently the scholars Potterton and Penny have both singled out for praise his monument to the Earl of Belfast, in Belfast Castle Chapel, a moving depiction of a bereaved mother at her young son's deathbed (**9**).

EH

Literary References: *AJ*, 1850, 8–9; 1871, 41; *ILN*, 31 Dec 1870, 681; *DNB*, XXXV, 1893, 66–7; *Weekes* 1880, 297–8; *Strickland* II, 1913, 59–63; *Crookshank* 1966, 309, 311–12; *Physick* 1969, 41–2, 193; *Potterton* 1975, 58; *Harbison, Potterton and Sheehy* 1978, 219–24; *Ormond and Rogers* 2, 1979–81, 140; *Bayley* 1981, 55, 100–113; *Read* 1982, *passim*; *Grove* 19, 1996, 879 (Turpin); *Murphy* 1999, 64–73; *Brooks* 2000, *passim*; *ODNB* (Turpin)

Additional MS Sources: *Biography Handbook Papers*, 1860, Add MS 28511 fols 100, 102; *Layard Papers*, 1866, Add MS 38993 fol 26; *Peel Papers*, 1842–1846. Add MSS 40520 fols 102, 104, 40581 fol 236, 40589 f. 199; *Manc Inst Letter Book*, 1849–50, 89, 101, 135, 219, 224

Will: PPR, 21 January 1871, fol 41, effects under £300

Portraits of the Sculptor: woodcut, *AJ*, 1850, 9; woodcut after a photograph, *ILN*, 31 Dec 1870, 681; Maull and Polyblank, photograph, NPG album of photos, 1949

Auction Catalogues: MacDowell 1871

Funerary Monuments

1.	†1832	William Tennent	First Presbyterian church, Belfast, Northern Ireland	S	*Potterton* 1975, 31, 58 (repr); *Grove* 19, 1996, 879
2.	†1834	Robert Wesley Hall	Barking, Essex		*Graves* V, 1905–6, 136; *Gunnis* 1968, 250
3.	†1845	Catherine Spurway	Milverton, Somerset	S	Pevsner, *Somerset: S & W*, 1958, 239
4.	†1845	Clement Delves Hill	Holy Trinity, Mahatma Gandhi Road, Bangalore	SD	
5.	†1846	Sir James Rivett Carnac, 1st Bt	Milford-on-Sea, Hants	S	
6.	†1851	Joseph Mallord William Turner	St Paul's Cathedral, London, crossing	S	Pevsner, *London: City*, 1997, 173
7.	†1853	Frederick Richard, Earl of Belfast	Memorial Chapel, Belfast Castle, Northern Ireland	S	*Potterton* 1975, 58 (repr); *Penny* 1977 (1), 123; *Harbison, Potterton and Sheehy* 1978, 220–1 (repr); *Grove* 19, 1996, 879
8.	1855	Anna, Marchioness of Donegall (†1849)	Memorial Chapel, Belfast Castle, Northern Ireland	S	*Gunnis* 1968, 249
9.	1855	Frederick Richard, Earl of Belfast (†1853)	Wimborne St Giles, Dorset		*Graves* V, 1905–6, 137; *Gunnis* 1968, 250

Statues

10.	1817–1822	Venus holding a mirror, statuette	[coll Peter Francis Chenu]; untraced		*AJ*, 1850, 8
11.	1826	Major John Cartwright, design only (executed by George Clarke of Birmingham from MacDowell's design)	Untraced		*AJ*, 1850, 8–9; *Graves* V, 1905–6, 136

12.	1827	'And looking into eyes where blue . . .', a group from Moore's 'Loves of the angels'		[coll George Davison of Belfast]; untraced		*AJ*, 1850, 9; *Graves* V, 1905–6, 136; *Johnson* 1975, 302
13.	1829	Bacchus and a satyr		[Exhib RA, London, 1223]; untraced		*AJ*, 1859, 9; *Graves* V, 1905–6, 136; *Johnson* 1975, 302
14.	?1827–1829	Cephalus and Procris	m	[Markree Castle, Sligo]; untraced		*Strickland* II, 1913, 90, 92; *Johnson* 1975, 302
15.	1838	Girl reading	m	NGI Other versions: RDS, Dublin, plaster Brynkinalt, Denbigh, replica reproduced in Parian ware		*Westminster* 1845, 16; *Graves* 1875, 360; *Graves* V, 1905–6, 136, 137; *Graves* I, 1913–15, 731; *Read* 1982, 20, 129, 209 (repr); *le Harivel* 1988, 575 (repr); *Murphy* 1999, 70
16.	1840	Girl going to bathe	m	[coll T Wentworth Beaumont]; untraced		*AJ*, 1850, 9; *Graves* V, 1905–6, 136
17.	1841	Girl at prayer	m	[coll T Wentworth Beaumont]; untraced		*AJ*, 1850, 9; *AJ Cat* 1851, 325 (repr); *Graves* 1875, 360; *Graves* V, 1905–6, 136; *Manchester Art Treasures* 1857, 134; *Murphy* 1999, 71, 73 n72
18.	1844	Love triumphant	m	[coll T Wentworth Beaumont]; untraced		*AU*, 1844, 170; *Westminster* 1845, 16; *AJ*, 1850, 8, 9 (repr); *Graves* V, 1905–6, 136
19.	1845	Cupid drawing an arrow		[coll T Wentworth Beaumont]; untraced		*AJ*, 1850, 9; *AJ Cat* 1851, 81 (repr); *Graves* V, 1905–6, 136, 137; *Graves* I, 1913–15, 731; *Murphy* 1999, 71, 73 n70
20.	1846	Admiral Edward, Lord Exmouth	m	[Greenwich, Naval Coll, painted hall]; NMM, Greenwich, London, Upper Court SCCUOO41	SD	*AU*, 1846, 188; *AJ*, 1850, 9; *Graves* V, 1905–6, 137; NMM newsletter, 2004
21.	1846	Nymph (RA diploma work)		RA, London		*Holland Park* 1957, unpag (repr); *Gunnis* 1968, 249
22.	1847	Early sorrow	p	Ulster Museum, Belfast		*AJ*, 1850, 9; *Graves* V, 1905–6, 137; *Harbison, Potterton and Sheehy* 1978, 221 (repr); *Murphy* 1999, 71, 73 n68
23.	1850	Eve Model(s): Royal Coll, plaster	m	VAM 29-1886 Other versions: Salford AG, Lancs Bendigo, Victoria, Australia sold Christie, London, 7 July 1877; untraced ex Glasgow Museums S.113, 1849, plaster; destr	SD	*Gunnis* 1968, 250; *Murphy* 1999, 71 (repr); *Wells* 1999, 54; *Bilbey* 2002, 331–2 (repr)
24.	1850	Psyche abandoned	m	[coll T Baring]; untraced		*ILN*, 31 Dec 1870, 681; *Graves* V, 1905–6, 137; *Graves* I, 1913–15, 731
25.	1850	Virginius and his daughter	m	[coll G W Beaumont]; untraced		*Manchester Art Treasures* 1857, 134; *Graves* V, 1905–6, 137; *Murphy* 1999, 71, 73 n69
26.	1851	The slumbering student		[coll S Ashton]; untraced		*Manchester Art Treasures* 1857, 134; *Graves* V, 1905–6, 137
27.	1853	The daydream		Ny Carlsberg Glyptotek, Copenhagen Other versions: Destr (ex Glasgow Museums S.114) 1853, pl		*Graves* V, 1905–6, 137; *Graves* I, 1913–15, 731; *AJ Cat* 1862, f.232 (repr); *Gunnis* 1968, 250
28.	1855	Frederick Richard, Earl of Belfast Model(s): Belfast Castle, chapel, plaster	b	[Royal Acad Institute, Belfast, exterior]; City Hall, Belfast		*ILN*, 31 Dec 1870, 681; *Graves* V, 1905–6, 137; *Strickland* II, 1913, 61; *Potterton* 1975, 58
29.	1853–1855	Lea	m	CL Coll, Mansion House, City of London, Egyptian Hall, acc 141	SD	*Graves* I, 1913–15, 731; *Knight* 1986, 341 (repr); *Ward-Jackson* 2003, 248 (repr)
30.	1856	The first thorn in life	m	[coll Thomas Baring]; untraced		*Graves* V, 1905–6, 137
31.	pre-1857	The summer reverie	m	[coll S Ashton]; untraced		*Manchester Art Treasures* 1857, 134
32.	1857	William Pitt the Younger (†1806)	m	Palace of Westminster, London, St Stephen's Hall	S	*Walker* 1961, 56, cat 61
33.	1857	William Pitt, Earl of Chatham (†1778) Model(s): exhib RA, London, 1857, 1220	m	Palace of Westminster, London, St Stephen's Hall	S	*Graves* V, 1905–6, 137; *Walker* 1961, 13, cat 16
34.	1847–1858	Almeric		Palace of Westminster, London, House of Lords		*Walker* 1961, 1, 97–8, cat 2
35.	1858	John, Viscount Fitzgibbon ('The young hussar') Model(s): exhib RA, London, 1858, 1171	b	[Limerick, Ireland]; destroyed		*Graves* V, 1905–6, 137; *Hill* 1998, 113

36.	1847–1858	William de Warenne, Earl of Surrey (†1240) Model(s): exhib RA, London, 1850, 1331		Palace of Westminster, London, House of Lords		*Graves* V, 1905–6, 137; *Walker* 1961, 70, 97–8, cat no 73
37.	1858–1860	Sir William Brown	m	St George's Hall, Liverpool, Lancs	S	*Cavanagh* 1997, 273–4 (repr)
38.	1863	William, Lord Plunket		[Four Courts, Dublin, Ireland]; destroyed		*Gunnis* 1968, 250; *Potterton* 1974 (3), 1305
39.	1866	Archibald, 13th Earl of Eglinton		[St Stephen's Green, Dublin]; destroyed		*Gunnis* 1968, 250; *Potterton* 1974 (3), 1305
40.	1870	Europe		Albert Memorial, Kensington Gardens, London		*Bayley* 1981, 55, 100–113 (repr); *Read* 1982, 100, 155, 160 (repr); *Brooks* 2000, *passim* (repr)
41.	nd	Sir Michael O'Loghlen		[Four Courts, Dublin, Ireland]; destroyed		*ILN*, 31 Dec 1870, 681; *Strickland* II, 1913, 62; *Potterton* 1974 (3), 1305
Busts						
42.	1822	Girl at prayer		[Exhib RA, London]; untraced		*Graves* V, 1905–6, 136
43.	1822	J Andrews		[Exhib RA, London, 1000]; untraced		*Graves* V, 1905–6, 136
44.	1824	Unidentified gentleman		[Exhib Soc of BA, London, 354]; untraced		*Johnson* 1975, 302
45.	1826	A Spanish gentleman		[Exhib RA, London, 1101]; untraced		*Graves* V, 1905–6, 136
46.	1826	Edmund Cartwright		[Exhib RA, London, 1017]; untraced		*Graves* V, 1905–6, 136
47.	1826	General Pepe		[Exhib RA, London, 1031]; untraced		*Graves* V, 1905–6, 136
48.	1826	Mr Imry, of Glasgow		[Exhib RA, London, 1032]; untraced		*Graves* V, 1905–6, 136
49.	1826	Thomas Campbell		[Exhib RA, London, 1021]; untraced		*Graves* V, 1905–6, 136
50.	1828	J Morice		[Exhib RA, London, 1207]; untraced		*Graves* V, 1905–6, 136
51.	1828	John Keats	p	Keats's House Museum, Hampstead, London		*Richardson* 1980, 79 (repr)
52.	1828	Lieutenant-General Bell		[Exhib Soc of BA, London, 887]; untraced		*Johnson* 1975, 302
53.	1828	Unidentified gentleman		[Exhib Soc of BA, London, 910]; untraced		*Johnson* 1975, 302
54.	1829	Canon Riego		[Exhib Soc of BA, London, 871]; untraced		*Johnson* 1975, 302
55.	1829	Master Rankin		[Exhib RA, London, 1191]; untraced		*Graves* V, 1905–6, 136
56.	1832	Colonel Rankin	m	[Exhib RA, London, 1201]; untraced		*Graves* V, 1905–6, 136
57.	1833	James Sheridan Knowles		[Exhib Soc of BA, London, 827]; untraced		*Johnson* 1975, 302
58.	1835	G Cartwright RN		[Exhib RA, London, 1128]; untraced		*Graves* V, 1905–6, 136
59.	1835	Unidentified gentleman	m	[Exhib RA, London, 1099]; untraced		*Graves* V, 1905–6, 136
60.	1837	Mrs Davenport		[Exhib RA, London, 1274]; untraced		*Graves* V, 1905–6, 136
61.	1838	Lady Tennent (two)		[Exhib RA, London, 1374, 1376]; untraced		*Graves* V, 1905–6, 136
62.	1838	Rev Dr Cooke, of Belfast		[Exhib RA, London, 1317]; untraced		*Graves* V, 1905–6, 136
63.	1840	Rev S Cook		[Exhib RA, London, 1186]; untraced		*Graves* V, 1905–6, 136
64.	1844	A gentleman, perhaps Sir James Rivett Carnac	m	Asiatic Society, Mumbai (Bombay), India (formerly Town Hall)	SD	
65.	1844	Alexander, 1st Baron Ashburton		Christie, 5 Dec 1950; untraced		*Gunnis* 1968, 250
66.	1844	G Rudall		[Exhib RA, London, 1405]; untraced		*Graves* V, 1905–6, 136
67.	1844	Master Liscombe		[Exhib RA, London, 1404]; untraced		*Graves* V, 1905–6, 136
68.	1844	Sir James Rivett Carnac, 1st Bt	m	NPG, London, 5128		*Graves* V, 1905–6, 136; *Gunnis* 1968, 250
69.	1845	James Hartley	m	[Exhib RA, London, 1452]; untraced		*Graves* V, 1905–6, 136, 137
70.	1846	Mrs Hartley	m	[Exhib RA, London, 1510]; untraced		*Graves* V, 1905–6, 137
71.	1848	J Barneby	m	[Exhib RA, London, 1452]; untraced		*Graves* V, 1905–6, 137
72.	1848	T Wentworth Beaumont	m	[Exhib RA, London, 1455]; untraced		*Graves* V, 1905–6, 137
73.	1852	Percy Boyd		[Exhib RA, London, 1436]; untraced		*Graves* V, 1905–6, 136
74.	c1854	Jonathan Pereira	p	Linnaean Soc		*Graves* V, 1905–6, 137
75.	1855	Miles Thomas, 8th Lord Beaumont	m	Carlton Towers, N R Yorks		*Graves* V, 1905–6, 137; *Gunnis* 1968, 250
76.	c1856	La Penserosa	m	Royal Coll, Osborne House, I of W, RCIN 41011	S	JM
77.	1856	Thomas Cubitt	m	[Exhib RA, London, 1368]; Denbies, Dorking, Surrey		*Graves* V, 1905–6, 137; *Ormond* 1973, 126
78.	1857	Sir Henry Stracey Bt		[Exhib RA, London, 1342]; untraced		*Graves* V, 1905–6, 137
79.	1858	Frederick, 1st Marquess of Dufferin		[Exhib RA, London, 1307]; untraced		*Graves* V, 1905–6, 137
80.	1859	George M Jones	m	[Exhib RA, London, 1346]; untraced		*Graves* V, 1905–6, 137
81.	1860	Andrew Cuthell	m	[Exhib RA, London, 1077]; untraced		*Graves* V, 1905–6, 137
82.	1860	T B Crompton	m	[Exhib RA, London, 1079]; untraced		*Graves* V, 1905–6, 137
83.	1861	Rt Hon James Whiteside MP	m	Trinity College, Dublin, Long Room		*Graves* V, 1905–6, 137; *Crookshank* 1986, 24
84.	1861	Rt Hon William Cubitt, Lord Mayor of London	m	[Exhib RA, London, 1064]; untraced		*Graves* V, 1905–6, 137
85.	1861	W J Rideout		[Exhib RA, London, 1013]; untraced		*Graves* V, 1905–6, 137
86.	1863	Jeremiah Lodge	m	[Exhib RA, London, 1030]; untraced		*Graves* V, 1905–6, 137
87.	1864	A youth		[Exhib RA, London, 898]; untraced		*Graves* V, 1905–6, 137
88.	c1865	Sir Joshua Jebb	m	VAM 550-1883		*Graves* V, 1905–6, 137; *Bilbey* 2002, 332–3 (repr)
89.	1866	H Hughes	m	[Exhib RA, London, 873]; untraced		*Graves* V, 1905–6, 137
90.	1868	R Lodge	m	[Exhib RA, London, 1010]; untraced		*Graves* V, 1905–6, 138
91.	1870	Mr and Mrs Richard Perrott	m	VAM 718 & 719-1902	SD	*Bilbey* 2002, 333 (repr)
92.	1870	Mrs Walter Hughes	m	[Exhib RA, London, 1206]; untraced		*Graves* V, 1905–6, 138
93.	nd	A gentleman, perhaps Charles, 5th Duke of Richmond	m	Sold Gorringe, Lewes, 21–23 Oct 2003; untraced	S	
94.	nd	Dr Disney		Dr Williams Library, Gordon Square, London		RG/JP, 5, 871
95.	nd	Isabella Dawson (afterwards Mrs Cane)		St Wolstan's, Cellbridge		*Strickland* II, 1913, 61

96.	nd	Sir James Emmerson Tennent	m	City Hall, Belfast	S	*Crookshank* 1966, 309 (repr); *Potterton* 1975, 58
97.	nd	T Jarvis		Dr Williams Library, Gordon Square, London		RG/JP, 5, 871
98.	nd	Unidentified woman	m	Russell-Cotes AG, Bournemouth, Dorset	S	

Architectural Sculpture

99.	1869	Gottfried Leibniz (†1716), Georges Cuvier (†1832) and Carl Linnaeus (†1778), statues		6 Burlington Gardens, London		*Read* 1982, 226

Reliefs

100.	1849	Cupid and Psyche		[Exhib RA, London, 1197]; untraced		*Graves* V, 1905–6, 137
101.	nd	Mrs Tennent and children	w	(coll Mrs Marshall of Belfast, 1913)		*Strickland* II, 1913, 62

Miscellaneous

102.	1843	A guitar player		[Exhib RHA]; untraced		*Strickland* II, 1913, 63
103.	1852	Love in idleness, model		[Exhib RA, London, 1332]; untraced		*Graves* V, 1905–6, 137
104.	1864	John Pender MP		[Exhib RA, London, 902]; untraced		*Graves* V, 1905–6, 137
105.	1866	Children of John Pender		[Exhib RA, London, 846]; untraced		*Graves* V, 1905–6, 137
106.	1867	The young mother		[Exhib RA, London, 995]; untraced		*Graves* V, 1905–6, 138
107.	nd	A seated lady	m	coll Lord Dunleath		*Barrett* 1971 (1), 89
108.	nd	The infant Samuel	m	coll Lord Dunleath		*Barrett* 1971 (1), 89

MACE, Frederick, of London ?1811–

He was perhaps the son of Robert and Mary Mace, christened on 12 May 1811 at South Moreton, Berks. He enrolled at the Royal Academy Schools, aged 16, in March 1818. On 28 February 1843, a notice in the *Norwich Mercury*, described him as a pupil of **Sir Francis Chantrey**. In 1820, while living in Queen's Row, Pimlico, he was awarded a medal from the Society of Arts (**24**) and another followed in 1821 (**25**).

Mace signed a handful of monuments but chiefly exhibited busts. He lived in Pimlico, near Chantrey, 1826–39, changing his address five times in the period.

Literary References: *Graves* V, 1905–6, 138; *Hutchison* 1960–62, 171; *Gunnis* 1968, 250; *Johnson* 1975, 302

Archival References: IGI; RSA, Transactions, vol 38, 1820, xxxv; vol 39, 1821, xxix; RG/JP, 5 870v

Funerary Monuments

1.	?1827	Rev Thomas Chute		South Pickenham, Norfolk	S	*Gunnis* 1968, 250
2.	†1829	Rev W Tattersall and Elizabeth Ward (†1825)		Westbourne, Sussex	S	
3.	c1840	Thomas Keeton		[Exhib RA, London, 1840, 1117 (medallic portrait); St Thomas, Bermondsey, London	S	*Graves* V, 1905–6, 138; *Gunnis* 1968, 250
4.	1843	Robert Peel (†1842) (designed by W J Donthorn)		South Runcton, Norfolk		Pevsner, *Norfolk: N W & S*, 1999, 666

Busts

5.	1820	Unidentified artist		[Exhib RA, London, 1017]; untraced		*Graves* V, 1905–6, 138
6.	1823	Unidentified artist		[Exhib RA, London, 1119]; untraced		*Graves* V, 1905–6, 138
7.	1825	Unidentified artist		[Exhib Soc of BA, London, 336]; untraced		*Johnson* 1975, 302
8.	1826	S Favell		[Exhib RA, London, 1024]; untraced		*Graves* V, 1905–6, 138
9.	1827	J Hurcombe		[Exhib Soc of BA, London, 847]; untraced		*Johnson* 1975, 302
10.	1827	J Mould		[Exhib RA, London, 1081]; untraced		*Graves* V, 1905–6, 138
11.	1827	T Favell		[Exhib Soc of BA, London, 845]; untraced		*Johnson* 1975, 302
12.	1828	W Hartley		[Exhib Soc of BA, London, 898]; untraced		*Johnson* 1975, 302
13.	1830	J G Middleton		[Exhib Soc of BA, London, 845]; untraced		*Johnson* 1975, 302
14.	1830	Rev S Crowther		[Exhib Soc of BA, London, 831]; untraced		*Johnson* 1975, 302
15.	1830	T Scandrett		[Exhib Soc of BA, London, 833]; untraced		*Johnson* 1975, 302
16.	1831	William Henry Poland		[Exhib RA, London, 1128]; untraced		*Graves* V, 1905–6, 138
17.	1832	Francis Read		[Exhib Soc of BA, London, 860]; untraced		*Johnson* 1975, 302
18.	1833	Alderman Harmer		[Exhib Soc of BA, London, 851]; untraced		*Johnson* 1975, 303
19.	1833	Henry Southam		[Exhib Soc of BA, London, 843]; untraced		*Johnson* 1975, 302
20.	1834	Unidentified gentleman		[Exhib Soc of BA, London, 836]; untraced		*Johnson* 1975, 303
21.	1835	Unidentified clergyman		[Exhib RA, London, 1063]; untraced		*Graves* V, 1905–6, 138
22.	1836	Daniel Higley Richardson		[Exhib Soc of BA, London, 869]; untraced		*Johnson* 1975, 303
23.	1838	John Reeve		[Exhib RA, London, 1315]; untraced		*Graves* V, 1905–6, 138; *Johnson* 1975, 303

Miscellaneous

24.	1820	Restored model of the Ilissus from the Elgin collection		[Soc of A, silver Isis medal]; untraced		RSA, *Transactions*, vol 39, 1821, xxxix
25.	1821	Bacchanalian figure		[Soc of A, large silver medal]; untraced		RSA, *Transactions*, vol 39, 1821, xxxix
26.	1820–1840	Busts and a bas-relief		[for the library of the Duke of Leeds]; untraced		*Graves* V, 1905–6, 138; *Gunnis* 1968, 250; *Johnson* 1975, 303

MACEWAN, Thomas fl 1847–91

In 1847–48 Thomas MacEwan exhibited portrait and subject pieces at the Royal Scottish Academy but in later years he specialised in church monuments. From 1849 to 1859 he worked in partnership with his father at 82 South Clerk Street,

Edinburgh; then, in 1860, he established his own business in Lothian Road where he worked until 1891. In 1861 he designed a monument to John Aitkin, for the Dean Street Cemetery, which was carved from his model by W Keith, of King Street, Aberdeen (3). In 1877 he was employed by William Brodie to carved the base for a statue of Sir James Simpson (6).

Literary References: *Woodward* 1977 (vol 1, pt 2), 130–1

Funerary Monuments					
1.	1861	Alexander Black	s	Dean Cemetery, Edinburgh	*Woodward* 1977, vol 1, pt 2, 131
2.	1861	Hugh Williams		Canongate churchyard, Edinburgh	*Woodward* 1977, vol 1, pt 2, 131
3.	1861	John Aitken (co-sculptor: W Keith)		Dean Cemetery, Edinburgh	*Woodward* 1977, vol 1, pt 2, 131
4.	1861	Wemyss family member	s	Dean Cemetery, Edinburgh	*Woodward* 1977, vol 1, pt 2, 131
Statues					
5.	1848	Dr Chalmers, statuette		[Exhib R Sc A, Edinburgh, 608]; untraced	*Laperriere* 3, 1991, 124
Architectural Sculpture					
6.	1877	Pedestal		for Sir James Simpson statue, West Princes St gardens, Edinburgh	*Woodward* 1977, vol 1, pt 2, 131
Miscellaneous					
7.	1847	A child and pigeon, sketch		[Exhib R Sc A, Edinburgh, 625]; untraced	*Laperriere* 3, 1991, 124
8.	1848	Early aversion		[Exhib R Sc A, Edinburgh, 603]; untraced	*Laperriere* 3, 1991, 124
9.	1848	Innocent amusement		[Exhib R Sc A, Edinburgh, 609]; untraced	*Laperriere* 3, 1991, 124

MACK, Robert fl 1761–75

In 1761 he was living in James's Street, Dublin, and was described as a mason. Mack is thought to have designed Powerscourt House in South William Street, Dublin in 1771, after Lord Powerscourt approved his plan and agreed to pay him 'at the rate of five pr cent for conducting the whole of the sd works'. He was also to execute all the work in stone on the house.

Literary References: *Potterton* 1975, 58, 72

Funerary Monuments					
1.	†1775	Lady Catherine Somerville	Kentstown, Co Meath	S	*Potterton* 1975, 72

MACKENZIE, A fl *c*1843–55

Funerary Monuments					
1.	†1843	Catherine Ross	Old St Duthus church, Tain	S	*Woodward* 1977, vol 1, pt 2, 145
2.	†1855	Catherine Duncan	Old St Duthus church, Tain	S	*Woodward* 1977, vol 1, pt 2, 145

MACKENZIE, Alexander, of London fl 1777–99

He exhibited wax portraits at the Royal Academy and at the Free Society. He lived at 'Mrs Beaufort's', Cross Street, near King Street, Golden Square in 1777, at 4 Walker's Court, Berwick Street in 1782, and at 101 Berwick Street in 1784.

Literary References: *Gunnis* 1968, 250; *Pyke* 1973, 87

Busts					
1.	1790	Unidentified nobleman		[Exhib RA, London, 662]; untraced	*Graves* V, 1905–6, 146
Reliefs					
2.	nd	William Shakespeare	w	VAM L178 (Bate loan coll)	*Pyke* 1973, 87 (repr 181)
Miscellaneous					
3.	1777	Unidentified subject, wax portrait	w	[Exhib RA, London, 198]; untraced	*Graves* V, 1905–6, 145
4.	1778	Four portrait models	w	[Exhib RA, London, 197]; untraced	*Graves* V, 1905–6, 145
5.	1779	Two models	w	[Exhib RA, London, 186]; untraced	*Graves* V, 1905–6, 145
6.	1779	Two models in paste		[Exhib RA, London, 187]; untraced	*Graves* V, 1905–6, 145
7.	1780	Unidentified gentleman	w	[Exhib RA, London, 299]; untraced	*Graves* V, 1905–6, 145
8.	1780	Unidentified lady	w	[Exhib RA, London, 298]; untraced	*Graves* V, 1905–6, 145
9.	1781	Unidentified gentleman	w	[Exhib RA, London, 123]; untraced	*Graves* V, 1905–6, 145
10.	1781	Unidentified lady	w	[Exhib RA, London, 122]; untraced	*Graves* V, 1905–6, 145
11.	1781	Unidentified lady	w	[Exhib RA, London, 124]; untraced	*Graves* V, 1905–6, 145
12.	1782	Unidentified lady, model		[Exhib RA, London, 346]; untraced	*Graves* V, 1905–6, 145
13.	1782	Unidentified young lady, model		[Exhib RA, London, 344]; untraced	*Graves* V, 1905–6, 145
14.	1784	Unidentified gentleman and lady	w	[Exhib RA, London, 320]; untraced	*Graves* V, 1905–6, 145
15.	1785	Unidentified gentleman		[Exhib RA, London, 612]; untraced	*Graves* V, 1905–6, 145
16.	1785	Unidentified nobleman		[Exhib RA, London, 263]; untraced	*Graves* V, 1905–6, 145
17.	1786	Unidentified lady	w	[Exhib RA, London, 272]; untraced	*Graves* V, 1905–6, 145
18.	1787	Portrait of a gentleman, model in wax	w	[Exhib RA, London, 644]; untraced	*Graves* V, 1905–6, 146
19.	1788	'Portrait of a young lady'	w	[Exhib RA, London, 636]; untraced	*Graves* V, 1905–6, 146
20.	1789	Model in wax	w	[Exhib RA, London, 589]; untraced	*Graves* V, 1905–6, 146
21.	1789	Portrait in wax	w	[Exhib RA, London, 572]; untraced	*Graves* V, 1905–6, 146
22.	1793	Portrait of an officer		[Exhib RA, London, 415]; untraced	*Graves* V, 1905–6, 146
23.	1799	Colonel Skelly		[Exhib RA, London, 1091]; untraced	*Graves* V, 1905–6, 146
24.	1799	Unidentified general officer killed at Lucknow		[Exhib RA, London, 1093]; untraced	*Graves* V, 1905–6, 146

MACKENZIE, Samuel RSA –1847

Although Mackenzie was successful principally as a painter and received academic recognition for his work in that branch of the arts, he began his career as a sculptor. He was born at Kilmuir in 1785, became an orphan at an early age and was brought up by an uncle. As a young man he helped on the farm before spending several years working in the north of Scotland supervising large teams of stonemasons for the engineer Thomas Telford. His son James records that after his father moved to Edinburgh in the early-19th century he worked first for **James Dalziel**, who taught him to model in clay and carve in marble. This assertion is questionable since Dalziel did not establish a business until 1820 by which year Mackenzie was devoting much of his time to painting. Mackenzie was a close friend of **Samuel Joseph** during the 1820s and both artists were among the first members of the Scottish Academy. He knew

Alexander Handyside Ritchie well and the two men worked together on the monument to David Dickson in Edinburgh, for which Mackenzie modelled the portrait (1). Although he retained his interest in modelling until his death in 1847, from 1810 onwards he worked principally as a painter.

Literary References: *Woodward* 1977 (vol 1, pt 2), 145–7

Additional Manuscript Sources: *Mackenzie Reminiscences*

Funerary Monuments

1.	1844	Rev David Dickson (co-sculptor: Alexander Handyside Ritchie)	St Cuthbert, Edinburgh		*Woodward* 1977, vol 1, pt 2, 146

Statues

2.	1800–1820	Sphinxes (co-sculptor: John D Marshall)	Charlotte Square, Edinburgh		*Woodward* 1977, vol 1, pt 2, 146
3.	1800–1820	Sphinxes (co-sculptor: John D Marshall)	Parliament Hill, Parliament Square, Edinburgh		*Woodward* 1977, vol 1, pt 2, 146

Architectural Sculpture

4.	1802–1806	Central group and coat of arms (co-sculptor: John D Marshall)	Bank of Scotland, Bank Street, Edinburgh		*Woodward* 1977, vol 1, pt 2, 146

MACSWINEY fl later 18th century

He signs a work which appears to be of later-18th century appearance, with an urn and weeping willow branch (1).

Funerary Monuments

1.	nd	Curteis family member	Wartling, Sussex		Pevsner, *Sussex*, 1965, 621

MADDOX fl *c*1817

His one known monument is signed '*Maddox*, Undertaker, Welbeck Street'.

Funeral Monument

1.	†1817	Henry Bosanquet	Weyhill, Hants	S	Pevsner, *Hants & Isle of Wight*, 1967, 649

MAGNUS, of London fl 1811?

Funerary Monuments

1.	?1811	Henry Bunbury	Great Barton, Suffolk	S	*Gunnis* 1968, 250

MAILE, Richard –1787

An advertisement in the *Public Advertiser* for 15 February 1774 (p3) reads 'CHIMNEY PIECES The Nobility and Gentry who have occasion for elegant Marble Chimney Pieces have now an opportunity of seeing several suitable for the most elegant Rooms, just completed by Maile, and set up in a large Room for Inspection at his House, No. 6 Riding-house Lane, near Portland-Street Chapel, Marylebone'.

In 1773, when redecoration of the drawing room at Drayton House, Northants was in progress under the direction of the plasterer and decorator William Rhodes, Richard Maile was paid for a chimneypiece (1). Rhodes also supervised redecoration of the dining room in 1771 and since many of the same craftsmen were involved in both schemes it is likely that 'The Chimney piece as Pr Agreement' for that room, with a relief of *Belisarius*, which was charged at £130, is also by Maile (Drayton Archive, GG/74/81). Both chimneypieces are still at Drayton and that in the dining room is the more elaborate. There is a copy of it at Serlby Hall, Lincs.

Maile's will, proved on 11 September 1787, left instructions for the disposal of an extensive estate, comprising property in Willesden Green, a house in Southwark, and a large residence in Norton Street, Marylebone, which included 'shops, stables, coach houses and other buildings'. He left shares worth over £1,200 and annuities to his wife Mary and his brothers Joseph, George and William. His nephews Richard and Joseph inherited the house in Norton Street. One of Maile's executors was his neighbour and friend **Peter Matthias Vangelder**, who was asked to organise a sale of Maile's stock in trade, furniture, horses and carriages (PROB 11/1157/134–7). (Inf. David Alexander and Bruce Bailey)

Chimneypieces

1.	1773	'A Large Chimney Piece Richly Carved and Ornamented compleat' Payment(s): £120	Drayton House, Northants, drawing room		Drayton Archive GG/71/136

MAILE FAMILY, of London

C Maile fl after 1786
Richard Maile –1850
George Maile fl 1850

The family was probably related to **Richard Maile**, though that mason made no provision for a continuation of the family business in his will. A '**C Maile**' had a yard in the New Road from 1786, and supplied a chimneypiece for Ryston, then being rebuilt for Mr E R Pratt by Sir John Soane (11). Robert Mylne, the architect, noted in his diary, 'Called at Mr. Maile's and directed alterations on a chimney-piece of Dressing Room at Argyll House, Aug. 21 1786' (GPC, quoting a diary coll Miss Mylne).

'Maile and Son of New Road, London' signed a number of tablets in the 19th century (**3, 5–9**). **Richard Maile**, 'Statuary and Mason of St Pancras' died in 1850. He is presumably the 'R Maile' who signed a tablet in Carmarthen (**4**). In his will he left his leasehold house and premises 'with the show room and workshop' in Keppel Row, New Road, to his son, **George Maile** (PROB 11/2116/290–1). **Matthew Johnson** was one of his executors. George Maile signed a standard New Road monument with a draped urn to Anthony Musgrave (**9**). The firm continued to produce memorial plaques as late as 1952.

Literary References: *Dale-Jones and Lloyd* 1989, 52

Archival References: GPC

Funerary Monuments

1.	†1802	Ethel Duncombe (by C Maile)	Langford, Notts	S	GPC
2.	†1818	Charlotte Tunnard (by C Maile)	Frampton, Lincs	S	
3.	†1830	Christopher Faulkner (by Maile & Son, of New Road, London)	Burford, Oxon	S	

4.	†1840	John Shickle (by R Maile)		Laugharne, Carmarthen		*Dale-Jones and Lloyd* 1989, 52
5.	†1842	Hannah Rawlinson (by Maile & Son, of New Road, London)		Lancaster Priory	S	
6.	†1843	William Faulkner (by Maile & Son, of New Road, London)		Burford, Oxon	S	
7.	†1846	Elizabeth Booth (by Maile & Son, of New Road, London)		Catworth, Hunts	S	Pevsner, *Beds, Hunts & Peterborough*, 1968, 230
8.	?1848	Emma and Henry Gould (by Maile & Son, of New Road, London)		St John the Baptist, Windsor, Berks	S	GPC
9.	†1852	Anthony Musgrave MD (by G Maile, New Road)		Antigua Cathedral, WI	S	
10.	1883	Large white marble sarcophagus containing the coffin of William Harvey (†1657) (by Maile & Son, of Euston Road, London)		Hempstead, Essex	S	
Chimneypieces						
11.	1789	Description unavailable Payment(s): £40	m	[Ryston Hall, Downham Market, Norfolk]; untraced		GPC

MAINE (or MAYNE), Jonathan fl 1680–1709

Maine was one of the most prominent woodcarvers of his day, much employed by Wren in rebuilding work on the London churches after the Great Fire. He came from Oxford and worked in the Midlands at Burghley, Sudbury and Chatsworth during the 1680s and 1690s, perhaps largely on limewood overmantels. His work is not easy to distinguish from that of **Thomas Young** or **Samuel Watson**, who worked alongside him in these great houses. Esterly suggests he may have had a hand in the rich overdoors for the First George Room at Burghley, carved with imbrocation and oak foliage and credited to **Grinling Gibbons**.

He became a liveryman of the Joiners' Company in 1694, and from 1696 to 1709 carried out extensive carving at St Paul's Cathedral for which he was paid £1,252 6s 11d (**4, 6–8, 10–16**). His carving there is rich and sophisticated: the drops in the consistory are ornamented with an inkpot, quills, skull, hourglass and portrait medallion. Elsewhere in the same chapel he carved naturalistic details including peapods, blackberries, lilies of the valley and half-open horse-chestnut fruit.

Maine's work on seven of the City churches was carried out under the supervision of the surveyor, **John Oliver**. He also worked at Eton and at Christ's Hospital, where in 1697 he was paid £7 12s for work about 'the Neech in the New Writing Schoole for Sr John Moores figure' (carved by Gibbons). In Oxford he provided carving at Trinity College and at Corpus Christi (**3, 9**), where some of his correspondence with the president of the college survives. There were difficulties, for the president suspected Maine of overcharging. Maine wrote on 19 February 1702 that he had worked under Oliver who 'hath passed several of my bills for ye perokel churches and hath not bated me one.' Maine concluded that 'having a great occasion for moneys I would desire you would not be long before I have your order for the rest of my money.' The President was later to tell his banker that 'Mayn ye carver . . . has already received above £20 more than his due according to our valuation. That I would be contented to lose, and a little more, if need be, but not much, rather than have any more to do with such a sawcy rascal as you see him to be; his reckoning at Trinity College was near twice as much as he received; so very a knave he is; and yet he will be a knave still in denying us too' (*Hiscock* 1948, 1398–9).

By 1701 Maine was working with his son, Jonathan Maine II, whose name appears in the accounts of the Earl of Bristol (**18**). Maine junior also designed a chimneypiece for Corpus Christi, which his father offered to the President with the words 'if you do your altar piece like this drawing enclosed you will have as pretty a one as any in Oxford, and the whole joiners and carvers work may be done for £150 or £160 fixed in its place' (*Hiscock, op cit*). Given the earlier antagonism it is not surprising that the college rejected Maine's design, following instead a pattern by **William Townesend.**

Maine's work is frequently confused with that of his more famous contemporary, **Grinling Gibbons**, who also provided carved work at St Paul's, Trinity College, Oxford and in the city churches.

Literary References: *Hervey* 1894, 146; *Green* 1964 (1), 28, 99–101, 1329, 84, 112, 112; *Gunnis* 1968, 250; *Beard* 1985, 686–94; *Beard* 1989 (1), 30, 36, 43; *Esterly* 1998, 22, 28, 92, 96–7, 150

Archival References: Christ's H, TAB, MS 12819/12, 78; GPC

Architectural Sculpture

1.	c1687	Font, octagonal	m	St Clement, Eastcheap, City of London	Pevsner, *London I*, 1997, 213
2.	1682–1691	Carved work (co-sculptor: Thomas Young) Payment(s): £730	wd	Burghley, Northants	*Green* 1964 (1), 112; *Beard* 1985, 689 (repr 32)
3.	1695	Carved work Payment(s): £5 8s		Trinity College, Oxford, chapel	*Hiscock* 1948, 1398; *Green* 1964 (1), 84
4.	1696	Extensive carved work Payment(s): £66 2s 5d	wd	St Paul's Cathedral, London, south-east and north-east vestries	*Wren Society* XV, 26
5.	1697	Work about the 'Neech . . . for Sr John Moores figure' Payment(s): £7 12s		[Christ's Hospital, London, new writing school]; untraced	Guildhall MS 12819/12, p78; Christ's Hospital, Treasurer's Account Book, 1695–1717
6.	1698	Extensive carved work Payment(s): £263 1s 1d		St Paul's Cathedral, London, morning prayer chapel	*Wren Society* XV, 40–1; *Green* 1964 (1), 100 (repr 143); *Beard* 1985, 690, 691 (repr)
7.	1701	Bishop's coat of arms and mitre with mantling and other ornaments Payment(s): £13		St Paul's Cathedral, London, consistory exterior, under window	*Wren Society* XV, 72; *Gunnis* 1968, 250; *Green* 1964 (1), 100

8.	1701	Capital of a composite pilaster in free stone Payment(s): £5	s	St Paul's Cathedral, London, inside dome	*Wren Society* XV, 72; *Gunnis* 1968, 250
9.	1700–1701	Chapel screen Payment(s): £100		Corpus Christi, Oxford	*Hiscock* 1948, 1398–9 (repr)
10.	1703	Cornice	s	St Paul's Cathedral, London, interior, above Whispering Gallery	*Wren Society* XV, 99 *Gunnis* 1968, 250
11.	c1705	Carved frieze	s	St Paul's Cathedral, London, interior, under the windows	*Wren Society* XV, 129; Pevsner, *London: City*, 1997, 164
12.	c1705	Exterior carving below windows	s	St Paul's Cathedral, London	Pevsner, *London: City*, 1997, 164
13.	1706	Carved work including 8 Composite capitals and two large shields with cherubs Payment(s): £234 0s 3d	wd	St Paul's Cathedral, London, consistory chapel (now chapel of St Michael and St George)	*Wren Society* XV, 137–8; *Green* 1964 (1), 100 repr 142–3); *Gunnis* 1968, 250
14.	1708–1709	Carved work		St Paul's Cathedral, London, Bishop of London's seat	*Wren Soc* XV, 175–6
15.	1708–1709	Carved work in oak Payment(s): £208 for cantilevers, £3 3s 6d for moulding	wd	St Paul's Cathedral, London, south library	*Malcolm* 1803–7, 3, 126; *Wren Soc* XV, 175; *Green* 1964 (1), 101
16.	1708–1709	Drops on pilasters, of flowers and fruit and books Payment(s): £6 10s each	s	St Paul's Cathedral, London, south library	*Wren Soc* XV, 175; *Green* 1964 (1), 101
17.	nd	Carved work		[Kiveton, W R Yorks]; destroyed	*Green* 1964 (1), 112
Miscellaneous					
18.	1701	'Carv'd work' in the 'closett'		[for John, 1st Earl of Bristol, unidentified residence]; untraced	*Hervey* 1894, 146

MAINI, Giovanni Battista 1690–1752

He was a pupil of **Camillo Rusconi**. After make a copy from the antique for Lord Malton (1), he was commissioned to prepare a series of Roman busts for Lord Charlemont, but died in 1752 before he could begin them.

Literary References: *Honour* 1958, 224

Statues				
1.	1749–1750	Callipygian Venus	Wentworth Woodhouse, W R Yorks, marble saloon	*Honour* 1958, 224; Pevsner, *Yorks W R*, 1967, 652

MAINWARING, Daniel, of Carmarthen 1776–1839

Mainwaring was the pre-eminent stone and marble mason of his day in West Wales. He was born in 1776, but nothing is known of his parentage, early life or apprenticeship. In March 1803 he married Mary Rees, a well-connected widow with three children and a sizeable inheritance, at St Peter, Carmarthen. Mainwaring advertised his business in the *Carmarthen Journal* in September 1810, reminding customers that 'he continues to work black and other marble chimney pieces, monuments, tombstones etc in a neat and expeditious manner, equal if not superior to those manufactured in London and Bristol' (*Dale-Jones* 1989, 64). In 1804–26 he lived in King Street, Carmarthen, and he owned or leased a number of other properties. He was rated in 1804 on a building on the quay, formerly the property of his wife's deceased husband, and in June 1818 he purchased Parade House, a substantial property in the town.

Mainwaring won a number of major commissions for building work in the region. He was employed at St David's College, Lampeter, and was chosen in 1824 to build John Nash's church of St Paul, Carmarthen, a project that aborted. That year he won the commission to build the town's monument, with a statue on a column, to Sir Thomas Picton. This was designed by Nash and **E H Baily** was responsible for the statue and reliefs. Mainwaring laid the foundation stone on 16 August 1825, and was paid £1,500 for his work, which was completed two years later. The *Gentleman's Magazine* carried news of the structure's erection, which 'in its general design. resembles Trajan's Pillar in Rome: and for the durability of the materials (black marble) promises to survive the wreck of as many ages as that mouldering but interesting relic of antiquity' (*GM* 1828, 2, 264–5). In fact the work deteriorated within a few years, largely because Baily used a sub-standard Roman cement for the figurative work. The structure was demolished by **David James**, Mainwaring's foreman, in 1846.

Mainwaring died of water on the lungs on 29 March 1839 in his house in Spilman Street, where he had lived since 1827, a property with stables, a garden, outhouses and five cottages to the rear. He left his marble business to his nephew John, together with his 'working tools . . . saws tables books plans desks chests trucks scales and all other implements . . . and all my stock of marble stone and other materials.' His estate was worth over £2,000. Two workmen were mentioned in his will, David James and John Thomas. The *Carmarthen Journal* carried his obituary, describing him as a man 'of the strictest integrity and probity.' He was buried in St Peter's churchyard and his gravestone was inscribed 'Daniel Mainwaring, Statuary and Marble Sculptor of this town' (*Dale-Jones* 1989, 72–4).

Mainwaring's monumental work consisted almost exclusively of elegant tablets, such as that to John Laugharne, which has an urn, swags and Adamesque details (27). The monument to John Picton has a lion and appears to be his only attempt to carve in the round (8). Gunnis regarded his work as 'above the usual provincial average' (*Gunnis* 1968, 250–1) and a substantial account of Mainwaring's life and work was published by Edna Dale-Jones in 1989.

Literary References: *Gunnis* 1968, 250–1; *Dale-Jones and Lloyd* 1989, 52–54; *Dale-Jones* 1989, 61–75

Funerary Monuments					
1.	1791	Two, unidentified subjects	Llandygwydd, Cardigans	SD	*Dale-Jones* 1989, 66
2.	†1801	William Rees	St Peter, Carmarthen		*Dale-Jones* 1989, 66
3.	†1809	Catherine Thomas	Kidwelly, Carmarthen		*Dale-Jones and Lloyd* 1989, 53
4.	1809	Mary Ann and George Humphreys	St Ishmael, Carmarthen		*Dale-Jones and Lloyd* 1989, 53; *Dale-Jones* 1989, 66
5.	†1810	Thomas Jones and family, of Job's Well	St Peter, Carmarthen	S	*Gunnis* 1968, 250; *Dale-Jones and Lloyd* 1989, 53; *Dale-Jones* 1989, 66
6.	†1813	Edwardes family of Rhydgors	Llanllwych, Carmarthen	S	*Dale-Jones and Lloyd* 1989, 53

7.	†1816	John George Philipps	Abergwili, Carmarthen		*Dale-Jones and Lloyd*, 1989, 53
8.	1816	Major-General John Picton (†1815)	Rudbaxton, Pembrokes		*Gunnis* 1968, 250; *Dale-Jones and Lloyd* 1989, 54; *Dale-Jones* 1989, 66–7
9.	†1821	George Day DD	Tenby, Pembrokes		*Dale-Jones and Lloyd* 1989, 44, 54
10.	†1821	Rees Goring Thomas	Llannon, Carmarthen		*Dale-Jones and Lloyd* 1989, 53
11.	†1822	David Lloyd of Alltyrodin	Llandyssul, Cardigan		*Dale-Jones and Lloyd* 1989, 44, 54
12.	†1822	Griffith Griffiths	Cilgerran, Pembrokes		*Dale-Jones and Lloyd* 1989, 44, 54
13.	†1822	Henry Lewis of Galtygog	Llanegwad, Carmarthen		*Dale-Jones and Lloyd* 1989, 53
14.	†1823	Mary Jones	Capel Colman, Pembrokes		*Dale-Jones and Lloyd* 1989, 44, 54
15.	†1825	Lady Sarah Champion de Crespigny	Pencarreg, Carmarthen	S	*Dale-Jones and Lloyd* 1989, 53
16.	†1825	Rev Thomas Griffiths	Llandygwydd, Cardigan		*Dale-Jones and Lloyd* 1989, 44, 54
17.	1826	Richard Phillips (†1823)	St Peter, Carmarthen	S	*Dale-Jones and Lloyd* 1989, 53; *Dale-Jones* 1989, 67
18.	†1826	William Howell Thomas	Laugharne, Carmarthen		*Dale-Jones and Lloyd* 1989, 53
19.	†1826	William Howell Thomas	Llaugharne, Carmarthen	S	*Dale-Jones and Lloyd* 1989, 53
20.	†1828	John Smith of Bloomfield	Narberth, Pembrokes		*Dale-Jones and Lloyd* 1989, 44, 54
21.	†1829	Edward Warren Jones	Nevern, Pembrokes		*Dale-Jones and Lloyd* 1989, 44, 54
22.	†1829	Rev Charles Bowen Payment(s): £50	Kidwelly, Carmarthen	S	*Gunnis* 1968, 250; *Dale-Jones and Lloyd* 1989, 44, 54
23.	†1829	Rev John Williams	Laugharne, Carmarthen	S	*Gunnis* 1968, 250; *Dale-Jones and Lloyd* 1989, 53
24.	†1829	Sir James Hamlyn Williams	St Peter, Carmarthen	S	*Dale-Jones and Lloyd* 1989, 53
25.	†1831	Rev David Davies	Abergwili, Carmarthen	S	*Dale-Jones and Lloyd* 1989, 44, 54
26.	†1831	William Owen Brigstocke	Llandygwydd, Cardigan		*Dale-Jones and Lloyd* 1989, 44, 54
27.	†1832	Vice-Admiral John Laugharne and relatives	Laugharne, Carmarthen		*Gunnis* 1968, 250; *Dale-Jones and Lloyd* 1989, 38, 54 (repr)
28.	†1833	Archdeacon Thomas Beynon	Llandeilo, Carmarthen	S	*Dale-Jones and Lloyd* 1989, 44, 54
29.	1833	Family of John Jones	Capel Colman, Pembrokes		*Dale-Jones and Lloyd* 1989, 44, 54
30.	†1834	Frances Bowen	Troedyraur, Carmarthen		*Dale-Jones and Lloyd* 1989, 54
31.	†1835	Mary Morris	Llanstephan, Carmarthen	S	*Dale-Jones and Lloyd* 1989, 54
32.	†1835	Rev Edward Picton	St Thomas, Ferryside, Carmarthen, new church, moved from the old		*Dale-Jones* 1989, 66; *Dale-Jones and Lloyd*, 1989, 54
33.	†1837	Rev David Peter	Heol Awst, Carm, Carmarthen		*Dale-Jones and Lloyd* 1989, 54
34.	nd	Eleven table-tombs, unidentified subjects	Llangunnor, Carmarthen, churchyard		*Dale-Jones* 1989, 66
35.	nd	John Daniel	Llangunnor, Carmarthen, churchyard		*Dale-Jones* 1989, 66
36.	nd	Madam Bridget Bevan	Llanddowror, Carmarthen		*Dale-Jones and Lloyd* 1989, 53; *Dale-Jones* 1989, 67
37.	nd	Mr and Mrs Edwardes of Rhydygors	Llanllwch, Carmarthen		*Dale-Jones and Lloyd*, 1989, 38 (repr); *Dale-Jones* 1989, 66
38.	nd	Philip Vaughan	St Peter, Carmarthen		*Dale-Jones* 1989, 66
39.	nd	Unidentified subject	Llanfallteg, Pembrokes		*Dale-Jones* 1989, 66
40.	nd	Unidentified subject	Uzmaston, Pembrokes	S	*Dale-Jones* 1989, 66

MAINWARING, John I 1793–1876

He was the nephew of **Daniel Mainwaring** and was born outside Carmarthen, possibly in Swansea, where he was recorded in a *Directory* of 1830. He married and baptised his three children, including **John Mainwaring II**, at St Mary, Swansea. From 1834 to 1839 he was in Edinburgh, employed as superintendent of masonry work on the Edinburgh, New Haven and Leith Railway. He inherited his uncle's stone and marble business in Carmarthen in 1839 and continued to work from the premises in Spilman Street until March 1841 when he moved to a grander house and premises in Lammas Street. An advertisement of April 1841 in the *Carmarthen Journal* states that his stock included 'a great variety of tombs and head stones, of all descriptions'. His monument to Thomas Lewis has a relief of an angel's head, with leaf decoration (1). After 1841 he became increasingly involved in important building projects in the town. He became a major contractor on the South Wales Railway in 1847, an endeavour that seems to have placed him in acute financial difficulties, for he emigrated to America in the spring of 1849. He became a farmer in Wisconsin and is buried in Indian Creek cemetery, Richland County.

Literary References: *Dale-Jones and Lloyd* 1989, 54

Funerary Monuments

1.	†1829	Thomas (†1829) and Catherine Lewis (†1840)	Llandeilo, Carmarthen		*Dale-Jones and Lloyd* 1989, 54
2.	†1841	James and Elizabeth Hughes and the Lawrence family	St Peter, Carmarthen	S	*Gunnis* 1968, 251; *Dale-Jones and Lloyd* 1989, 54
3.	†1843	William Sheild	Llandawke, Carmarthen		*Dale-Jones and Lloyd* 1989, 54
4.	†1844	Abiah Hill	Laugharne, Carmarthen		*Dale-Jones and Lloyd* 1989, 54

MAINWARING, John II 1821–87

A stone and marble mason, builder, engineer and surveyor, he was born in Swansea, the son of **John Mainwaring I**, and was educated in Swansea and Edinburgh. He worked with his father in Scotland and in the business in Lammas Street, Carmarthen and was probably responsible for monuments produced by the workshop in the 1840s. He supported his father in the ill-fated contracts for building the South Wales Railway and after the project was postponed, he emigrated with his father to Wisconsin. He returned in 1851 and continued the marble business from **Daniel Mainwaring**'s leasehold premises on Carmarthen quay. He advertised in local trade directories in 1849 and 1852 and signed a tablet, a tall rectangle enclosed in a white marble arch, around this time (1). He worked as a builder, surveyor and engineer on the resumed South Wales Railway contracts. Mainwaring married at St David, Carmarthen, where his four children were later baptised. In 1861 he returned to Wisconsin with his family, prospered as a farmer in Richland County, and wrote an autobiographical account for the *History of Wisconsin*, published in 1884.

Literary References: *Dale-Jones and Lloyd* 1989, 54

Funerary Monuments

1.	†1851	David and Ann Lewis	Abernant, Carmarthen		*Dale-Jones and Lloyd* 1989, 54

MALERBI, C, of London fl 1849

Busts

1.	1849	Mrs Milner-Gibson	Cullum Library, Bury St Edmunds, Suffolk	SD GPC

MALIPHANT, John, of Kidwelly 1751–1836

Maliphant's memorials, frequently signed 'JM', are often flat, undecorated slabs. He lived in Bower Street, Kidwelly and left six children, three of whom were also stone masons. Several further generations of the family pursued the craft. He appears to have had a connection with the **Paty** family of Bristol, for a design for a monument executed by Maliphant appears in the Paty copybook (3). He was probably related to Richard Maliphant, a builder and surveyor of London, active *c*1810, and to George Maliphant (*c*1788–1865) who became an architect and was responsible for a book, *Designs for Sepulchral Monuments* (*c*1830).

Literary References: *Dale-Jones and Lloyd* 1989, 55; *Colvin* 1995, 636; *Priest* 2003, 145

Funerary Monuments

1.	†1771	John Palmer, table tomb	Laugharne, Carmarthen, churchyard	*Dale-Jones and Lloyd* 1989, 55
2.	1775	Jane and Joshua Griffiths, tombstone	Llandyfaelog, Carmarthen, churchyard	*Dale-Jones and Lloyd* 1989, 55
3.	†1778	William and John Howell Drawing(s): (related) Paty Copybook, 10, apparently by Henry Wood the Elder	Eglwys Fair a Churig, Carmarthen	*Dale-Jones and Lloyd* 1989, 55; *Priest* 2003, 145
4.	†1780	Chapman family	St Clears, Carmarthen	*Dale-Jones and Lloyd*, 1989, 55
5.	†1794	Esther Davies	Llanfihangel-ar-arth, Carmarthen	*Dale-Jones and Lloyd* 1989, 55
6.	†1799	Charlotte Rees	Pembrey, Carmarthen	*Dale-Jones and Lloyd* 1989, 55
7.	†1799	John Hale	Kidwelly, Carmarthen	*Dale-Jones and Lloyd* 1989, 55
8.	†1800	Cartwright Morris	Kidwelly, Carmarthen	*Dale-Jones and Lloyd* 1989, 55
9.	†1803	Richard Davies	Laugharne, Carmarthen, churchyard	*Dale-Jones and Lloyd* 1989, 55

MALLCOTT (or MALCOTT), Family fl 1730–1862

John Mallcott I *c*1717–66
John Mallcott II 1742–
John Mallcott III *c*1777–1851

A family of stonemasons, they were responsible for masonry work, carved decoration and a number of funerary monuments. **John Mallcott I** was the son of William Mallcott, a carpenter of St James, Westminster. His father died before he was apprenticed in 1730 to **Robert Taylor I**. He became free on 9 September 1737. In the Masons' Company list of 1740 he is described as living at Grey Friars, but in the same list a 'John Mallcott, mason' is noted as working with 'Mr Taylor', which suggests that he continued to work for his former master (Masons' Co Freemen List, fol 45). He was mason to the Royal College of Physicians in Warwick Lane from 1743, perhaps until his death in 1766, though the last payment refers merely to payment of 'a mason's' bill. In 1765 he was elected renter warden of the Masons' Company, but was too ill to take up the post. He died in 1766, leaving properties in Leicester Street and Air Street, as well as his business and leasehold estate at Grey Friars in the City of London. His wife, Ann, and **Sir Robert Taylor** were his executors. His business, stock and utensils were left to his son, John Mallcott II.

John Mallcott II was christened at Grey Friars in December 1742. He was apprenticed to his father in 1757, and was freed from service on 4 October 1764. In 1766 he took his father's place as mason to the College of Physicians. The Mallcott tradecard, dated 1788, survives in the British Museum Print Room. The firm, which included a partner called Scrimshaw, worked under the architect Sir John Soane, rebuilding a house for William Cooke in Walthamstow in 1790, and they were building contractors for developments in Chelsea in 1804. In 1802 John II and 'E. Malcott' were appointed masons to the Ironmongers' Company. Mallcott was a warden of the Masons' Company in 1810–11 and became master in 1812. By 1809 he had taken a son, presumably John Mallcott III, into the business, for in Holden's *Directory* of 1811, the firm is described as 'Mallcott and Son' of 12 Newgate Street.

John Mallcott III was was apprenticed to **Samuel Ireland** in 1792 and became free in 1799. He married Louisa Susannah Grace at Grey Friars church on 30 August 1804. By 1809 he had been taken into the family business and in 1811 he received a press notice for his monumental tablet to William Hawes, founder of the Humane Society (4). The *Gentleman's Magazine* illustrated the work, described as a 'neat and elegant' slab with a 'small but correct' portrait-medallion of Hawes. The magazine hailed the sculptor as 'an ingenious young artist' (*GM* 1811 vol 81, pt I, 307, 313). The firm produced numerous monuments and tablets over the next 30 years, described by Gunnis as 'mostly dull', though he considered the monument to Sir Wharton Amcotts (3), designed by William Kinnaird, to be 'really rather a charming work'.

In 1821 the *Gentleman's Magazine* illustrated Mallcott's monument to Robert Wells (7), a Greek stele with palmette brackets and acroteria, and relief carvings of the two sides of a medal awarded to the deceased by the Royal Society. On the engraving Mallcott is described as a 'Statuary' of 12 Newgate Street, so he clearly took this aspect of the business seriously. In 1824, he provided carved ornaments for the new Post Office (**19**).

The firm continued to be involved principally in masonry work. Mallcott succeeded his forebears as mason to the College of Physicians, he became the principal mason working on the new National Gallery and the Insolvent Debtors' Court in Lincoln's Inn Fields, and in 1820 he was employed at Stationers' Hall. In 1823–4 he built the Lombard Street premises of the bankers, Glyn Mills and Co, at a cost of £2,278. In 1830–31, he was warden of the Masons' Company, and in 1832 he became master. In 1845 *The Builder* illustrated a view of St Bartholomew's Hospital, which the firm had cased in Portland stone ten years earlier, and referred to Mallcott as a 'practical mason who has been engaged for fifty years in repairing old Churches and raising new buildings' (*Builder* 1845, 78).

Mallcott's will was proved in January 1851. He left houses in Newgate Street and Streatham Hill, as well as a lease on stonemasonry premises in West Street in the parish of Saint Sepulchre. To his second wife, Mary Ann, he left household goods and 'detached articles of sculpture,' as well as 'all machinery, implements, utensils, plant, stock . . . employed by me in my business of a stone-mason'. His various premises were left in trust for the seven children of his second marriage.

His son by his first marriage, John Rowles Mallcott, was apprenticed to his father in 1823 and became a renter warden of the Masons' Company in 1840. In the 1830s the firm is known to have signed at least one tablet 'J Malcott & Son' (**16**) and it therefore seems likely that John Rowles Mallcott had joined it by this date. In 1841 father and son succeeded Thomas Burnell as masons for the restoration of the Temple church. The firm produced monumental work as late as 1862 (**18**), so either John Rowles Mallcott, one of his step-siblings, or his trustees must have chosen to continue the business after the death of John III.

One of the Mallcotts must have had talents beyond his skills as a stonemason for there exists, in private possession, a pen, ink, watercolour and body-colour *trompe-l'oeil* painting of playing cards, newspapers, pens, and other items signed 'JOHN MALCOTT Delint.' The painting includes Malcott's own tradecard marked 'MALLCOTT Mason . . . Newgate Street, London.'

MGS

Literary References: *Holden* 1811; *Condor* 1894, 297, 302; *Gunnis* 1968, 251

Archival References: IGI; Masons' Co, Freemen, fols 45, 75; Assistants fols 2, 7; RC Physic, Cash Book, 1726–78, 1743, p 4 (John Malcott I) 1766, p 335 (John Malcott II); Soane Bill Book 3, fols 8–9 (William Cooke's house, Walthamstow); GPC

Wills: John Mallcott I, 5 Feb 1766 PROB 11/916/144–5; John Mallcott III, 18 January 1851 PROB 11/2126/13–16

Tradecards: Banks Collection, BM, 106.20, dated 1788; Heal coll, BM 106.17, undated

Funerary Monuments

1.	†1807	Edward Pryce	St Stephen Walbrook, City of London	S	
2.	†1807	Frances Handley	Sleaford, Lincs	S	Pevsner, *Lincs*, 1989, 653
3.	†1807	Sir Wharton Amcotts (designed by William Kinnard)	St Swithun, Retford, Notts		Pevsner, *Notts*, 1979, 296; *Colvin* 1995, 587
4.	1811	William Hawes (†1808)	St Mary, Islington, London		*GM* 1811, vol 81, 307, 313 (repr); *Gunnis* 1968, 251
5.	?1815	Clement Kynnersley	Cheam, Surrey, Lumley chapel		*Gunnis* 1968, 251
6.	?1820	Catharine Langstaff	St Martin, Ludgate, City of London		*Gunnis* 1968, 251
7.	pre-1821	Dr Robert Wells (†1794) and wife, Mary (†1805)	[St Bride, Fleet Street, London]; untraced		*GM* 1821, 505 (repr); *Gunnis* 1968, 251
8.	?1821	James Carr	Cheshunt, Herts		*Gunnis* 1968, 251
9.	?1822	Benjamin Hawes	St Magnus-the-Martyr, London		*Gunnis* 1968, 251
10.	?1823	Philip Green	St Magnus-the-Martyr, London		*Gunnis* 1968, 251
11.	?1826	Margaret Donovan	Crowhurst, Surrey		*Gunnis* 1968, 251
12.	?1827	Thomas Dalton	Milton-by-Gravesend, Kent		*Gunnis* 1968, 251
13.	?1831	Nathaniel Proctor	Rye, Sussex		*Gunnis* 1968, 251
14.	†1836	Lieutenant-Colonel William Garrard	Chennai (Madras) Cathedral, India	S	
15.	?1837	Sarah Raven	St Leonard, Streatham		*Gunnis* 1968, 251
16.	*c*1837	Unidentified subject, tablet	Rodborough Tabernacle, Glos		Pevsner, *Glos: Cotswolds*, 1999, 579
17.	†1848	Mary Owen	St Bartholomew the Less, City of London	S	
18.	?1862	Allen Laing	Temple Church, London	S	*Gunnis* 1968, 251

Architectural Sculpture

19.	*c*1824	160 feet of 'egg and tongue, highly relieved on Grecian moulding' and 147 feet of 'antique Grecian leaf and dart' Payment(s): £203	[New Post Office, London]; untraced		*Gunnis* 1968, 251; *Colvin* VI, 1973–6, 434
20.	1851	Font	St James, Clerkenwell, London		*Gunnis* 1968, 251

MAN, Edward fl 1752

Man made the very fine stone globes at Greenwich Palace. They were inscribed with astronomical lines, with outlines of the land and sea, and with the track of the Centurion round the world.

Architectural Sculpture

1.	1752	Gate pier globes	s	Royal Naval College, Greenwich (ORNC)	*Drake* 1886, 68 n3; *Gunnis* 1968, 251

MANDERSON, of Dublin fl *c*1844

He signed a number of tablets. Potterton saw several, but dismissed them as 'too simple to be recorded' (*Potterton* 1975, 72).

Funerary Monuments

1.	†1844	Major P Carleton	Killyleagh, Co Down	S	*Potterton* 1975, 72
2.	nd	Charles Courtenay	Newry, Co Down	S	*Potterton* 1975, 72
3.	nd	George Lucas	Newry, Co Down	S	*Potterton* 1975, 72

MANLEY, of Bidford fl 1799?

Funerary Monuments

1.	?1799	William Brittain	Beoley, Worcs	S	GPC

MANNING, Charles ?1776–1812

Charles Manning worked in partnership with **John Bacon II**, 1808–12. Little is known of his family background, but in his will he mentioned a brother and a cousin, both called John Manning, whom he described as 'statuaries' living at 10 Arlington Street, Camden, London, and another brother, Samuel, who may have been the sculptor **Samuel Manning I**. He entered the Royal Academy Schools on 31 December 1794 and three years later was awarded a silver medal. He exhibited a number of portrait busts at the RA between 1801 and 1812 (**2, 4–6**) and showed ideal works at the British Institution in 1806 and 1807 (**7, 9**). As a young man he appears to have found employment in the studio of **John Bacon RA**, for a letter written by Bacon and still in the family's possession, refers to an employee called Manning.

In 1808 Manning went into business with John Bacon II, who had inherited his father's workshop in 1799. A contract discovered and published by Ann Saunders (née Cox-Johnson) in 1959 discloses that in return for an annual income of £300 and a quarter share of the profits, Manning took over the day-to-day management of Bacon's studio. This must have been a demanding task, for the workshop was extremely active, turning out large numbers of funeral monuments for locations all over Britain and in the Colonies. The working stock was valued at the substantial sum of £4,000, reflecting the scale of the business. Bacon and Manning agreed that the partnership would operate in Bacon's name from his premises at 17 Newman Street, near Fitzroy Square, London and that Manning would work there full-time, though Bacon would 'not be obliged to attend there further or otherwise than he shall think fit and proper' (*Bacon Property Papers*, cited by *Cox-Johnson* 1959, 239). It therefore seems likely that many of the monuments produced in Bacon's name during the period 1808–12 were executed by, or under the direction of Charles Manning, with little input from Bacon. Both sculptors are known to have collaborated on the monument to Sir William Staines at St Giles Cripplegate in the City of London, of which only the bust survives (**2**). Bacon designed the work and his drawing survives, but Manning exhibited the bust, plaster and marble at the Royal Academy in 1808 and 1809.

He undertook at least two independent commissions after 1808. The monument in St Paul's Cathedral to George Hardinge, a naval captain who died in a sea battle off Bombay in 1808, was a public commission, awarded by the Committee of Taste (**1**). It has figures of a grieving Hindu and *Fame* holding a victor's wreath, who flank a sarcophagus inscribed with a lengthy encomium. Gunnis noted that the monument has sometimes been erroneously attributed to Samuel Manning I, adding 'it is by no means a masterpiece, but is nevertheless a far better work than that sculptor ever produced' (*Gunnis* 1968, 251). Also in St Paul's is the monument to Major-General Mackenzie and Brigadier Langwerth, both of whom fell at Talavera in 1809, signed 'C. MANNING INVT' and 'S. MANNING FECT', presumably carved by Samuel Manning I (**3**).

When Manning died in 1812 John Bacon paid Manning's share of his profits to his heirs. The partnership had clearly been successful, for this amounted to £1,002 2s 11d. Manning left a widow, Sarah, who later published a print of his monument to Captain Hardinge.

EH

Literary References: *Cox-Johnson* 1959, 236–242; *Cox-Johnson* 1961, 42; *Gunnis* 1968, 251–2; *Whinney* 1988, 313, 371, 465 n21; *Groseclose* 1995, 59–60, 136 n42

Additional Manuscript Sources: Bacon Family Papers; Bacon Property Papers (used extensively in *Cox-Johnson* 1959, 236–242, and *Cox-Johnson* 1961)

Will: PROB 11/1537

Funerary Monuments					
1.	†1808	Captain George Hardinge Model(s): exhib RA, London, 1812, 916 (half-size)	St Paul's Cathedral, London		*Graves* V, 1905–6, 177; *Gunnis* 1968, 251; *Groseclose* 1995, 59–60; Pevsner, *London: City*, 1997, 173
2.	1808–1809	Sir William Staines (†1807) (co-sculptor: John Bacon II) Drawing(s): VAM E.1569-1931 Model(s): exhib RA, London, 1808, 964	St Giles Cripplegate, City of London (bust only)		*Graves* V, 1905–6, 177; Pevsner, *London: City*, 1997, 220
3.	1810	Major-General Mackenzie (†1809) and Brigadier-General Langwerth (†1809) (co-sculptor: Samuel Manning I)	St Paul's Cathedral, London	S	Pevsner, *London: City*, 1997, 174
Busts					
4.	1801	A clergyman	[Exhib RA, London, 888]; untraced		*Graves* V, 1905–6, 177
5.	1805	Dr Jenner	[Exhib RA, London, 723]; untraced		*Graves* V, 1905–6, 177
6.	1812	John Bacon II	[Exhib RA, London, 921]; untraced		*Graves* V, 1905–6, 177
Reliefs					
7.	1806	Chaining of Prometheus	[Exhib BI, London, 13]; untraced		*Graves* 1875, 366
Miscellaneous					
8.	1806	An eminent physician, model	[Exhib RA, London, 845]; untraced		*Graves* V, 1905–6, 177
9.	1807	Captivity, a juvenile study from nature	[Exhib BI, London, 240]; untraced		*Graves* 1875, 366

MANNING, Joshua 1810–

Gunnis, who erroneously states that Manning's father was **Samuel Manning I**, also maintains that Joshua was the son of John Manning of Newman Street (1753–1845). He attended the Royal Academy Schools in December 1830, having been recommended by J Ward, RA. He gave his address as 1 Holmes Terrace, Kentish Town. In 1830, whilst living at 183 Tottenham Court Road, he received a medal from the Society of Arts (**1**). He exhibited at the Academy two years later, but all trace of him is lost after that date.

Literary References: *GM* 1845, 563; *Gunnis* 1968, 252

Archival References: RA Admissions

Statues				
1.	1830	'an original model of a group'	[Soc of A, gold Isis medal]; untraced	RSA, *Transactions*, vol 48, 1831, xxiii
Miscellaneous				
2.	1832	Leonidas, a sketch	[Exhib RA, London, 1115]; untraced	*Graves* V, 1905–6, 177

MANNING, Samuel I 1786–1842

A prolific monumental sculptor, he frequently worked in collaboration with **John Bacon II**. He is generally thought to have been either the brother or the son of **Charles Manning**, but one source indicates that his father was a sculptor who died around 1845, at the age of 93, and was named either Samuel or John Manning (*ILN*, 30 June 1849, 436). A model of a young lady by 'S. Manning Jun.' of Little Charlotte Street, London exhibited at the Royal Academy in 1806 was presumably his work (**84**) and three years later he and Charles Manning together signed the monument to Major-General Mackenzie and Brigadier Langwerth in St Paul's Cathedral (**5**).

By 1819 Samuel Manning was working with John Bacon II, as Charles Manning had done before him, and he had taken up residence at Bacon's premises at 17 Newman Street, London. No documentary evidence of the terms of their partnership survives but the two men jointly signed a large number of monuments, including one to Christopher

Metcalfe, 1820, which is signed 'Bacon inv Manning fec', suggesting that Manning was responsible for executing works to Bacon's designs (**19**). In 1823 Bacon moved away from London and virtually retired from active work as a sculptor, although he continued to produce designs, while Manning still worked from the Newman Street studio.

Manning's monuments are largely prosaic tablets. Some, including those commemorating the Marquess of Ormonde and James Antrobus Newton, have conventional mourning or allegorical figures derived from designs by **John Bacon RA** (**23, 30**). Gunnis was harshly dismissive of them: 'All Manning's monumental work is dull and uninspired and specimens of it are only too prevalent in England'. He considered the best to be the monument to Charles Grant at St George, Bloomsbury, which has a sensitive portrait of the dying man with a supporting figure of *Faith* and is jointly signed by Manning and Bacon (**29**).

Manning's work was not, however, limited entirely to the production of standardised funeral monuments. He exhibited a number of portrait busts at the RA, including one of Warren Hastings, which forms part of his monument in Westminster Abbey, and a statue of Princess Charlotte (**25, 73**). A delicately carved bust of Margaret Blanshard appeared in a sale in 1996 (**80**). In 1825 he showed a model for a posthumous statue of John Wesley (**74**). This was based on a bust modelled from life by **Enoch Wood** of Burslem and was considered to be an excellent likeness. Joseph Butterworth, the MP for Dover, commissioned Manning to execute the statue in marble in 1828 for 1,000 guineas, but work was suspended when the patron died and the block of marble purchased for it was used instead for the Grant monument (**29**). Although a number of possible sites were proposed during Manning's lifetime, Butterworth's statue was only carved after his death, by his son **Samuel Manning II**.

Manning died at his home in Newman Street on 7 December 1842. He left his household goods, furniture and books to his wife Eliza, £200 to each of his four daughters Eliza, Ann, Abigail and Christiana Mary, and all his statues, materials, drawings, tools and stock-in-trade to his son.

Literary References: *ILN*, 30 June 1849, 436; *Redgrave* 1878, 285; *DNB*, XXXVI, 1893, 71 (Godwin); *Grant* 1953, 161; *Cox-Johnson* 1959, 236–242; *Gunnis* 1968, 252; *Whinney* 1988, 313; *Groseclose* 1995, 98; *ODNB* (Hardy)

Will: PROB 11/1973

Portraits of the Sculptor: Samuel Manning II, bust for monument, exhib RA, London, 1847

Funerary Monuments

1.	†1798	John and Charlotte (†1797) Mellish (co-sculptor: John Bacon II)	Braughing, Herts	S	
2.	†1801	Christopher Barton Metcalfe (co-sculptor: John Bacon II)	Hawstead, Suffolk	S	Pevsner, *Suffolk*, 1974, 256
3.	post-1807	George (†1738), Thomas (†1740) and George Fieschi Heneage (†1782)	Hainton, Lincs		*Lord* 1986, 101
4.	†1808	William Hutchinson (co-sculptor: John Bacon II)	St Mary, Beverley, E R Yorks	S	Pevsner, *Yorks: E R & York*, 1995, 299
5.	1810	Major-General Mackenzie (†1809) and Brigadier-General Langwerth (†1809) (co-sculptor: Charles Manning)	St Paul's Cathedral, London	S	Pevsner, *London: City*, 1997, 174
6.	†1813	John Bones (co-sculptor: John Bacon II)	Fen Ditton, Cambs	S	Pevsner, *Cambs*, 1970, 384
7.	†1814	Rev Thomas Coke	Wesley's Chapel, City Road, London	S	
8.	†1815	Lieutenant Peter Lawtie (co-sculptor: John Bacon II) Drawing(s): VAM E.1575-1931	Banff	S	
9.	†1817	Rev William Clerk (co-sculptor: John Bacon II)	Stretton-on-Dunsmore, Warks	S	Pevsner, *Warks*, 1966, 421
10.	†1818	Louisa Fullerton (co-sculptor: John Bacon II) Drawing(s): VAM E.1560-1931	Thrybergh, WR Yorks		Pevsner, *Yorks: W R*, 1967, 517
11.	†1818	Philip Booth and his wife Elizabeth (†1798) (co-sculptor: John Bacon II)	Stanstead Abbots, Herts	S	Pevsner, *Herts*, 1977, 342
12.	†1818	Philip Metcalfe (co-sculptor: John Bacon II)	Hawstead, Suffolk	S	Pevsner, *Suffolk*, 1974, 256
13.	†1818	Robert, Viscount Kilmorey (co-sculptor: John Bacon II)	Adderley, Salop	S	Pevsner, *Salop*, 1958, 53
14.	1818	Sir Jacob Astley (†1817)	Melton Constable, Norfolk		*Gunnis* 1968, 252
15.	?1818	Thomas Davies	St Mary, Fort St George, Chennai (Madras), India	S	*Gunnis* 1968, 252
16.	†1819	Abbot Upcher (co-sculptor: John Bacon II)	Upper Sheringham, Norfolk		Pevsner, *Norfolk: N E & Norwich*, 1997, 661 (repr 86)
17.	*c*1819	General Sir William Augustus Pitt (†1809) and his wife (†1819) (co-sculptor: John Bacon II) Drawing(s): VAM E.1572-1931	Heckfield, Hants	S	Pevsner, *Hants & Isle of Wight*, 1967, 287
18.	†1819	John Woollett (co-sculptor: John Bacon II)	Rye, Sussex	S	Pevsner, *Sussex*, 1965, 596
19.	1820	Christopher Metcalfe (†1794) (co-sculptor: John Bacon II)	Hawstead, Suffolk	SD	Pevsner, *Suffolk*, 1974, 256
20.	†1820	George Stainforth (co-sculptor: John Bacon II)	Holy Trinity, Clapham, London	S	
21.	†1820	Rev Browse Trist and family (co-sculptor: John Bacon II)	St Mary, Totnes, Devon		RG/JP, 1, 69
22.	†1820	Richard Terveys (co-sculptor: John Bacon II)	Britford, Wilts		RG/JP, 1, 69
23.	†1820	Walter, Marquess of Ormonde and his wife, Anna-Maria (co-sculptor: John Bacon II)	Ulcombe, Kent	S	Pevsner, *Kent: W & Weald*, 1976, 588
24.	?1821	John Addenbrooke	St George, Esher, Surrey		*Gunnis* 1968, 252

25.	1819–1821	Rt Hon Warren Hastings (†1818) (co-sculptor: John Bacon II)	m	Westminster Abbey, London, north transept		*Graves* V, 1905–6, 177; *Cox-Johnson* 1959, 241; *MacMichael* 1974, 87
26.	†1822	Frodsham Hodson		Brasenose College, Oxford, chapel	S	Pevsner, *Oxon*, 1974, 107
27.	†1822	William Godson (co-sculptor: John Bacon II)		Tenbury Wells, Worcs		Pevsner, *Worcs*, 1968, 278; *Gunnis* 1968, 32
28.	?1823	Arthur Pott (co-sculptor: John Bacon II)		Eltham, Kent		*Gunnis* 1968, 32
29.	†1823	Dr Charles Grant (co-sculptor: John Bacon II) Model(s): exhib RA, London, 1826, 1015		St George, Bloomsbury, London	S	*Graves* V, 1905–6, 177; Pevsner, *London: N*, 1998, 258
30.	†1823	James Antrobus Newton (co-sculptor: John Bacon II)		St Mary, Stockport, Cheshire	S	Pevsner, *Cheshire*, 1971, 340; *Penny* 1977 (1), 208 n24
31.	†1823	Sir Mark Masterman Sykes (co-sculptor: John Bacon II)		Sledmere, E R Yorks	S	Pevsner, *Yorks: E R & York*, 1995, 692
32.	†1824	Sarah Jenkins (co-sculptor: John Bacon II)		Stroud, Glos	S	Pevsner, *Glos: Cotswolds*, 1999, 650
33.	†1824	William Gurdon (co-sculptor: John Bacon II)		St Mary, St Marylebone, London		*Gunnis* 1968, 32
34.	†1825	Anne Smith (co-sculptor: John Bacon II)		St Thomas, Kingston, Jamaica	S	*Lewis* 1965–7, July 1966, 232–4
35.	†1825	Caroline Curteis (co-sculptor: John Bacon II)		Wartling, Sussex	S	*Gunnis* 1968, 32
36.	†1825	Sir John B Walsh (co-sculptor: John Bacon II)		Warfield, Berks	S	Pevsner, *Berks*, 1966, 257
37.	†1826	Bishop Charles Warburton and wife (†1826) (co-sculptor: John Bacon II)		Cloyne Cathedral, Co Cork	S	*Potterton* 1975, 72
38.	†1826	Joseph Butterworth		Wesley's Chapel, City Road, London	S	
39.	†1826	Keith Fraser		Langton, Long Blandford, Dorset	S	
40.	†1826	Samuel Twyford		Trotton, Sussex		*Gunnis* 1968, 252
41.	†1826	Sir John Wilmot Prideaux		Farway, Devon	S	Pevsner, *Devon*, 1989, 447
42.	?1827	Ann Dollond (co-sculptor: John Bacon II)		Tuxford, Notts		*Gunnis* 1968, 32
43.	†1827	Rebekah Gillam Williams (co-sculptor: John Bacon II)		Berrington, Salop		Pevsner, *Salop*, 1958, 73; RG/JP, 5, 577
44.	1828	Augustus Henry East (co-sculptor: John Bacon II)		Bisham, Berks	S	*Gunnis* 1968, 32
45.	†1828	Edward (†1818) and Frances Maxwell (co-sculptor: John Bacon II)		Rumboldswyke, Chichester, Sussex	S	
46.	†1830	Frances Jane Metcalfe (co-sculptor: John Bacon II)		Hawstead, Suffolk	S	Pevsner, *Suffolk*, 1974, 256
47.	?1830	Rev William Vivian		Bushey, Herts		*Gunnis* 1968, 252
48.	†1830	Sir Thomas Staines (co-sculptor: John Bacon II)		St John the Baptist, Margate, Kent		Pevsner, *Kent: N E & E*, 1983, 383
49.	†1830	William Dawson (co-sculptor: John Bacon II)		St George's Chapel, Windsor, Berks	S	*Bond* 1999, 89
50.	?1831	Matthew Isaake		Jamestown, St Helena		GPC
51.	†1831	Sir Thomas Stapleton (co-sculptor: John Bacon II)		Rotherfield Greys, Oxon	S	Pevsner, *Oxon*, 1974, 735
52.	†1832	Captain Richard Burton (co-sculptor: John Bacon II)		St Peter's-in-Thanet, Broadstairs, Kent	S	*Gunnis* 1968, 31
53.	†1832	Francis, 1st Earl of Kilmorey (co-sculptor: John Bacon II)		Adderley, Salop	S	*Gunnis* 1968, 32
54.	†1832	Sarah, Lady Staines		Frindsbury, Kent	S	Pevsner, *Kent: W & Weald*, 1976, 289
55.	†1833	George R Heneage (co-sculptor: John Bacon II)		Hainton, Lincs	S	Pevsner, *Lincs*, 1989, 356
56.	†1833	Margaret Maude (co-sculptor: John Bacon II)		Langham, Essex	S	*Gunnis* 1968, 32
57.	?1833	Octavia Harvey		Gillingham, Kent		*Gunnis* 1968, 252
58.	†1835	Elizabeth Isherwood		All Saints, Marple, Cheshire	S	Pevsner, *Cheshire*, 1971, 276
59.	†1835	John Wilson		Southborough, Kent		Pevsner, *Kent: W & Weald*, 1976, 537
60.	?1835	Lord Henry Fitzroy		Euston, Suffolk		GPC
61.	†1835	Mary King		Trotton, West Sussex	S	
62.	†1835	Mary, Lady Stapleton		Rotherfield Greys, Oxon		Pevsner, *Oxon*, 1974, 735
63.	†1835	Samuel Smith		Watton-at-Stone, Herts		Pevsner, *Herts*, 1977, 392
64.	†1836	John Sargent and sons (co-sculptor: John Bacon II)		East Lavington, Sussex		RG/JP, 1, 70
65.	†1836	Rev Isaac Saunders		St Andrew-by-the-Wardrobe, City of London		Pevsner, *London: City*, 1997, 195
66.	?1836	Robert Field		Sidney Sussex College, Cambridge, Chapel		*Gunnis* 1968, 252
67.	†1838	Lancelot Haslop		Wesley's Chapel, City Road, London	S	Pevsner, *London: N*, 1998, 606
68.	†1840	Colonel Robert Kingscote		Kingscote, Glos	S	Pevsner, *Glos: Cotswolds*, 1999, 428
69.	†1840	George Tyrwhitt Drake Clerk		St Mary, Old Amersham, Bucks	S	Pevsner, *Bucks*, 1994, 132
70.	†1838–1841	Kingscote children		Kingscote, Glos	S	Pevsner, *Glos: Cotswolds*, 1999, 429
71.	†1841	Sir Astley Paston Cooper and family members (co-sculptor: John Bacon II)		St Mary, Hemel Hempstead, Herts	S	Pevsner, *Herts*, 1977, 178
72.	nd	Rev John de Flechers		Wesley's Chapel, City Road, London	S	

Statues

73.	1820	Princess Charlotte		[Exhib RA, London, 1023]; untraced		*Graves* V, 1905–6, 177
74.	1825–1829	John Wesley, model only (marble by Samuel Manning II) Model(s): exhib RA, London, 1825, 1052		Untraced		*Graves* V, 1905–6, 177; *ILN*, 30 June 1849, 436; *Ward-Jackson* 2003, 381–3

Busts

75.	1819	Colonel Addenbrooke		[Exhib RA, London, 1212]; untraced		*Graves* V, 1905–6, 177
76.	1823	Dr Jenner		[Exhib RA, London, 1063]; untraced		*Graves* V, 1905–6, 177
77.	1831	'A young lady'		[Exhib RA, London, 1153]; untraced		*Graves* V, 1905–6, 177
78.	†1833	Richard Kennaway		[Escot, Devon]; untraced		GPC
79.	1833	Unidentified lady		[Exhib RA, London, 1216]; untraced		*Graves* V, 1905–6, 177
80.	*c*1835	Margaret Blanshard	m	Sotheby, 22 May 1996, lot 136	S	
81.	†1836	Sir John Kennaway Bt		[Escot, Devon]; untraced		GPC
82.	1839	Miss Hunter	m	[Exhib RA, London, 1367]; untraced		*Graves* V, 1905–6, 177
83.	1839	Thomas Hunter, model		[Exhib RA, London, 1364]; untraced		*Graves* V, 1905–6, 177

Miscellaneous

84.	1806	'A young lady', model		[Exhib RA, London, 862]; untraced		*Graves* V, 1905–6, 177

MANNING, Samuel II 1815–66

The son of **Samuel Manning I**, he continued his father's monumental practice into the early 1860s and exhibited portrait sculpture during the 1840s and 1850s. He was born on 28 May 1815 and baptised on 18 July 1819 at St Pancras Old Church, London. He probably received his early training in his father's studio and by 1831 he was sufficiently advanced in his studies to be awarded a medal by the Society of Arts (**42**). The following year he won another prize (**43**) and in 1833, when he was 17, the same institution awarded him a gold medal for a model of *Prometheus chained* (**38**). Further prizes came to him in 1838 and 1840 (**39, 44**).

Within two years of his father's death in 1842 Manning moved from 17 Newman Street, where he had spent his early life, to 75 Newman Street. In 1846 he was married in Marylebone to Honoria, daughter of Captain James Williams of Stoke Demerel in Devon. He soon established himself at 3 Union Place, Marylebone and the Studio, York Terrace. In 1845 his early work *Prometheus chained* was exhibited at the Royal Academy and two years later an engraving with a commentary appeared in the *Art Union*. The writer praised the work for its 'great boldness of thought and execution' but regretted that the sculptor had so far failed to produce further works of equal merit, probably because of the lack of patronage for such ambitious ideal works (*AU*, 1847, 284).

Manning's next significant commission was a statue of John Wesley, which he carved from a model made by his father more than 20 years earlier (**41**). It was erected at the Methodist theological college, Richmond, in 1849 and later moved to its current site, Methodist Central Hall, Westminster. One writer commended it as a good likeness carved in finest quality marble, but erroneously stated that the model was by the younger Manning's grandfather (*ILN*, 30 June 1849, 436). A recent copy in bronze now stands in the churchyard of St Paul's Cathedral.

Manning signed a large number of monuments, many of them very similar to those produced by his father in association with **John Bacon II**. The Susannah Perkins in Southwark Cathedral (**15**), has two allegorical female figures standing on either side of a draped urn and repeats a design which was first developed by **John Bacon RA** for his monument to Elizabeth Draper in Bristol Cathedral in 1780. He exhibited about 20 busts at the Royal Academy, including depictions of his father and John Bacon II (**48, 49**). Most of these have not been traced but his portraits of Joseph Williamson and Rev Charles Simeon survive, at Hull Guildhall and Cambridge University Library (**50, 66**). With his death, on 29 November 1866 at Victoria Road, Surbiton, the monumental sculpture business carried on by the Bacon and Manning families since the latter part of the 18th century seems finally to have come to an end.

Literary References: *Gents Mag*, XXVI, 528 (Nov 1846); *AU*, 1847, 284; *ILN*, June 30 1849, 436; *DNB*, XXXVI, 1893, 71 (Godwin); *ODNB* (EH)

Funerary Monuments

1.	†1842	Cornewall children	Kingscote, Glos		Pevsner, *Glos: Cotswolds*, 1999, 429
2.	†1842	Frances Heneage	Hainton, Lincs	S	
3.	1844	44th Regiment (Afghan War Memorial) (co-sculptor: John Bacon II)	Alverstoke, nr Gosport, Hants		*ILN*, 11 April 1846, 245 (repr)
4.	†1845	William (†1829) and Sophia Dawson (†1845) (co-sculptor: John Bacon II)	St George's Chapel, Windsor, Berks	S	*Bond* 1999, 88
5.	†1848	Mary Booth	Stanstead Abbots, Herts	S	Pevsner, *Herts*, 1977, 342
6.	†1849	Francis Ede	Sawbridgeworth, Herts	S	Pevsner, *Herts*, 1977, 335
7.	?1849	Henry Shute	Alverstoke, Hants		GPC
8.	†1850	Edward Weller	St Mary, Old Amersham, Bucks	S	Pevsner, *Bucks*, 1994, 132
9.	†1850	Mrs Winterton (†1830) and others	St Giles-in-the-Fields, London		GPC
10.	†1850	Sir Felix Booth FRS	Catworth, Hunts	S	Pevsner, *Beds, Hunts & Peterborough*, 1968, 230
11.	†1850	Sir Felix Booth FRS	Stanstead Abbots, Herts	S	Pevsner, *Herts*, 1977, 342
12.	†1850	Sir John Edwards	Machynlleth, Montgomery	S	Pevsner, *Powys*, 1979, 155
13.	†1850	Solomon P Cox	Limpsfield, Surrey	S	
14.	†1851	Highmore Skeats (†1835) and his daughter Harriet Elvey	St George's Chapel, Windsor Castle	S	*Bond* 1999, 303
15.	1851	Susannah Perkins	Southwark Cathedral, London		*Cox-Johnson* 1961, 16
16.	†1852	Anna Horlick Potts	Holy Trinity, Cambridge	S	
17.	†1852	Edward Knight	Godmersham, Kent		Pevsner, *Kent: N E & E*, 1983, 332
18.	1852	William Lee Warner	East Dereham, Norfolk	S	
19.	†1853	Edward Hodgson	St Mary Rickmansworth, Herts	S	
20.	†1853	Sarah, Lady Harris	Anglican Cathedral, Port of Spain, Trinidad	S	L Lewis, *CL*, 21 Aug 1969, 456
21.	1854	Edward Laws	Kensal Green Cemetery, catacombs	S	
22.	1855	Anne Reynardson (†1853)	Christchurch Priory, Hants		GPC

No.	Date	Subject	Medium	Location		Reference
23.	†1855	Sir Jacob Henry Astley		Melton Constable, Norfolk		Pevsner, *Norfolk: N E & Norwich*, 1997, 611
24.	?1856	General William Butterworth		Singapore Cathedral		RG/JP, 5, 879
25.	†1856	Joseph Allan Honnor		Great Missenden, Bucks	S	
26.	1856	Thomas Kingscote		Kingscote, Glos	S	Pevsner, *Glos: Cotswolds*, 1999, 429
27.	1857	Captain Herbert Vaughan		Llangoedmore, Cardigan		*ILN*, 12 Sept 1857, 261 (repr)
28.	†1857	German Wheatcroft		Crich, Derbys	S	Pevsner, *Derbys*, 1978, 157
29.	†1857	Oliver Simpson Bridges		Birch, Essex	S	
30.	?1858	Sophia and Ellen Metcalfe		Hawstead, Suffolk	S	*Gunnis* 1968, 253
31.	1859	90th Light Infantry (Crimean War Memorial)		St John the Baptist, Perth		*ILN*, 1 April 1859, 344 (repr)
32.	1860	53rd Regiment (Indian Mutiny Memorial)		St Chad, Shrewsbury, Salop	SD	*ILN*, 12 March 1864, 248 (repr)
33.	†1860	Charlotte Athanans		Christ Church, Kensington, London	S	
34.	?1860	Elizabeth Trecothick		Addington, Surrey	S	*Gunnis* 1968, 253
35.	†1860	Henry Butterfield		St Dunstan-in-the-West, London		RG/JP, 5, 879
36.	†1861	Thomas Henry Kingscote		Kingscote, Glos	S	Pevsner, *Glos: Cotswolds*, 1999, 429
37.	†1862	Frances Thornton		Blunham, Beds	S	*Gunnis* 1968, 253
Statues						
38.	1833	Prometheus chained Model(s): exhib RA, London, 1845, 1351 (plaster model)	p	[Soc of A, gold medal]; untraced		*AU*, 1847, 284 (repr); *Graves* V, 1905–6, 178; *Gunnis* 1968, 252
39.	1840	'Clay model of a group'		[Soc of A, silver medal]; untraced		RSA, *Transactions*, vol 53, 1840, xvi
40.	1843	A child of Henry Kingscote	m	[Exhib RA, London, 1390]; untraced		*Graves* V, 1905–6, 177
41.	1849	Rev John Wesley (after a model by Samuel Manning the Elder)		[Wesleyan Theological Institute, Richmond, Surrey]; Methodist Central Hall, Westminster, London		*Graves* V, 1905–6, 178; *ILN*, 30 June 1849, 436 (repr); *Ward-Jackson* 2003, 381–3
Busts						
42.	1831	after the antique		[Soc of A, silver medal]; untraced		RSA *Transactions*, vol 48, 1831, 550; *AU*, 1847, 284
43.	1832	Model of a bust from life		[Soc of A, silver medal]; untraced		RSA, *Transactions*, vol 49 pt 1, 1832, xxv; *AU*, 1847, 284
44.	1838	'Portrait bust in marble'		[Soc of A, silver medal]; untraced		RSA, *Transactions*, vol 52, 1838, xvi
45.	1843	Rev Charles Manning		[Exhib RA, London, 1508]; untraced		*Graves* V, 1905–6, 177
46.	1843	Unidentified lady	m	[Exhib RA, London, 1497]; untraced		*Graves* V, 1905–6, 177
47.	1844	H B Scott		[Exhib RA, London, 1324]; untraced		*Graves* V, 1905–6, 177
48.	1845	John Manning	m	[Exhib RA, London, 1463]; untraced		*Graves* V, 1905–6, 178
49.	1846	John Bacon II		[Exhib RA, London, 1474]; untraced		*Graves* V, 1905–6, 178
50.	1846	Joseph Williamson		Guildhall, Hull, E R Yorks		GPC
51.	1847	Samuel Manning	m	[Exhib RA, London, 1382]; untraced		*Graves* V, 1905–6, 178
52.	1849	Thomas Hawkins	m	[Exhib RA, London, 1242]; untraced		*Graves* V, 1905–6, 178
53.	1850	Mrs W H Jackson, model		[Exhib RA, London, 1399]; untraced		*Graves* V, 1905–6, 178
54.	1851	Rev John Wesley		[Exhib RA, London, 1307]; untraced		*Graves* V, 1905–6, 178
55.	1851	Thomas Farmer of Gunnersbury	m	[Exhib RA, London, 1326]; untraced		*Graves* V, 1905–6, 178
56.	1852	Lajos Kossuth		[Exhib RA, London, 1393]; untraced		*Graves* V, 1905–6, 178
57.	1852	Samuel Rogers		[Exhib RA, London, 1471]; untraced		*Graves* V, 1905–6, 178
58.	1853	Angus Fletcher		[Exhib RA, London, 1382]; untraced		*Graves* V, 1905–6, 178
59.	1853	Colonel Kingscote		[Exhib RA, London, 1432]; untraced		*Graves* V, 1905–6, 178
60.	1853	George Peabody		[Exhib RA, London, 1353]; untraced		*Graves* V, 1905–6, 178
61.	1853	Lord Bloomfield		[Exhib RA, London, 1385]; untraced		*Graves* V, 1905–6, 178
62.	1854	Mr Haggett, model		[Exhib RA, London, 1495]; untraced		*Graves* V, 1905–6, 178
63.	1855	Dr Hastings, model		[Exhib RA, London, 1455]; untraced		*Graves* V, 1905–6, 178
64.	1855	Frederick Perkins, of Chipstead Place, Kent	m	[Exhib RA, London, 1505]; untraced		*Graves* V, 1905–6, 178
65.	1855	John Jones		[Exhib RA, London, 1518]; untraced		*Graves* V, 1905–6, 178
66.	1855	Rev Charles Simeon		Cambridge University Library		*Graves* V, 1905–6, 178; RG/JP, 5, 879
Miscellaneous						
67.	1858	Mr Claudet		[Exhib RA, London, 1210]; untraced		*Graves* V, 1905–6, 178

MANNING, Thomas –1747

He was perhaps related to the **Manning family** of masons, but was a notable statuary in lead and artificial stone. He may be the 'Thomas Manning' who is described in **John Nost I**'s will of 1710 as 'my manservant,' and was left a suit of apparel (LMA AM/FW 1710/89). If so it is likely that he learned his craft with Nost. His earliest recorded works date from 1720 and were sent, at a cost of £1 17, by 'Waggon and car' to Gough Park (7).

In 1729 Manning moved into a property in Portugal Row next door to **Catherine Nost** and, from 1734, to **Thomas Carter I**. His premises were initially rated at £8, but his business must have expanded by 1737, when he had two properties in the street, rated at £10 and £12. He appears to have taken over the second premises from **Andrew Carpenter**, who died that year. By 1744 he had taken over another property, with tenants, in the street, renamed White Horse Street in 1737.

In 1735 Manning supplied a statue of *Britannia* to an insurance company in Westminster, one of the earliest recorded works in artificial stone produced in this country (5). Manning stood as a character witness in the trial of Mary Johnson, otherwise Sudley, otherwise Barker, on 5 December 1746, who was accused of the theft of a gold ring from a William Archer. Manning described himself as a 'Master Statuary of Hide-Park', and testified that the defendant had 'lived in two houses of mine for these two years'. The properties were in 'White-horse street, just as you go down the hill' (POB 1674–1834, ref t17461205-24).

Manning died in 1747. An obituary describes him as 'an ingenious statuary near Hyde Park Corner' (*GM* 1747, 545). In his will, proved on 19 November, he left his stock in trade, utensils, chattels, books, plate and his house on the corner of White Horse Street to his wife Mary. Another 'little house' in White Horse Street was left jointly to his wife and his mother, Elizabeth, together with the lease of three houses and a stable in the same road. He mentions two brothers, Edward and Arnold, and his nephews, Thomas and John Manning (PROB 11/758/6).

J T Smith noted that **John Cheere** took over two of Manning's properties in 1748. His widow Mary was still rated on the house on the corner of White Horse Street in December 1752.

Literary References: *Smith* 1846, 15–16; *Gunnis* 1968, 252; *Davis* 1991, 28, 31, 34

Archival References: Rate-books, CWAC, C106–7, C120–1, C126, C226, C234, C243; GPC

Statues

1.	1720	Fame	l	[Gough Park, Middx]; untraced	*Weaver* 1909, 194; *Gunnis* 1968, 252
2.	1720	Mercury	l	[Gough Park, Middx]; untraced	*Weaver* 1909, 194; *Gunnis* 1968, 252
3.	1720	Neptune	l	[Gough Park, Middx]; untraced	*Weaver* 1909, 194; *Gunnis* 1968, 252
4.	1720	Two boars Payment(s): £8 8s	l	[Gough Park, Middx, gate piers]; untraced	*Weaver* 1909, 194; *Gunnis* 1968, 252
5.	1735	Britannia Payment(s): £9	sa	London Assurance Company offices, King William Street, London	GPC
6.	1744	River God Payment(s): £18 15s		Stourhead, Wilts	Hoare Private Accounts 1734–49, 28 Jan 1744

Architectural Sculpture

7.	1720	Two large vases	l	[Gough Park, Middx]; untraced	*Weaver* 1909, 194; *Gunnis* 1968, 252

MANNING FAMILY, of London fl 1681

Many masons called Manning worked in 18th-century London, and were perhaps all inter-related. Bryan Manning was one of the chief masons working on extensions to Whitehall Palace, 1685–1687, and Christopher Manning was responsible for carving at Westminster Hall (1). A William Manning, son of John Manning of Ketton, Rutland, mason, was apprenticed to **John Young II** on 8 January 1684.

The will of a James Manning, 'mason of St Botolph Aldersgate, City of London' was proved on 2 January 1755 (PROB 11/813), and that of a mason of the same name and description, presumably a son, on 18 March 1802 (PROB 11/1371). It was probably the latter who worked as a mason and stone-carver at St Bartholomew's Hospital, 1752–58, and subscribed to *Vitruvius Britannicus* in 1767. It is possible that he may be the nephew of **Thomas Manning,** mentioned in the latter's will.

Literary References: *Gunnis* 1968, 252; *Webb* 1999, 21

Architectural Sculpture

1.	1681	Carved pinnacles (by Christopher Manning)	s	Westminster Hall, London, south end	*Gunnis* 1968, 252

MANTON, Thomas –1789

He was a prominent Stamford mason and builder, who was made a freeman in 1769 and had a shop in St Paul's Street by 1777.

Archival References: JP, Misc Corr

Funerary Monuments

1.	†1782	Robert (†1776) and Ann Frisby, headstone	Great Casterton, Rutland	S

MANZONI fl 1839

The firm bought many works from the auction of **Peter Turnerelli**'s workshop in 1839. They issued numerous plaster copies, sold cheaply, with 'published by Manzoni' stamped upon them.

Literary References: *Gilmartin* 1967, 15–16

MAPLETOFT, Richard, of London fl 1699–1702

Described as a 'stonecutter', he was paid £398 3s for sundry work when Winslow Hall, Bucks, was built by Sir Christopher Wren for William Lowndes.

Literary References: *Bolton and Hendry* 1940, 55

MARCELLI, Giuseppe, of Rome fl c1775

'Giuseppe Marcelli, Scultore Romano' signed the Taswell monument, executed in coloured marbles, and featuring a life-size figure of the youth *Thanatos*, emblematic of death, who leans on an urn and carries a down-turned torch in his hand (1). According to Gunnis 'local tradition insists that the monument was captured in a French ship by Mr. Taswell himself, who brought it home in triumph and kept it in readiness to be set up in the church after his death. A more probable and less romantic version of the story is that the figure was ordered direct from the sculptor by Mr. Taswell or his heir' (*Gunnis* 1968, 253).

Funerary Monuments

1.	†1775	William Taswell	Wotton-under-Edge, Glos	S	*Gunnis* 1968, 253; *CIIA* 4/4/178–9 (repr); Pevsner, *Glos: Cotswolds*, 1999, 756

MARCHANT, Nathaniel, RA 1739–1816

Marchant was primarily a gem-engraver but also produced a number of medals and works in wax. He was born in Mayfield, Sussex, possibly the son of a watchmaker. He appears to have had family connections with Pennsylvania and possibly lived there a short while himself as a child. He was apprenticed to the celebrated intaglio-maker **Edward Burch RA**, *c*1754–1765, and attended drawing classes for a short while at St Martin's Lane Academy, London. He won several prizes for gem-carving from the Society of Artists, including an interpretation of the *Apollo* from the Villa Medici and a head of *Homer* in 1762 and a *Dancing faun* and head of the *Apollo Belvedere* in 1764, all taken from originals and casts in the collection of the 3rd Duke of Richmond. Although it was disputed even at the time whether gem-carving constituted sculpture, in a letter written to the Society in 1768 Marchant requested that both he and Burch be described as sculptors. 'The word Sculptor', he wrote, 'is more applicable to our profession than Engraver' (RA, SA/34/14).

Although it was common for 18th-century intaglio and cameo carvers to work from antique examples of gemstone carving, Marchant made a name for himself by using antique sculpture as his predominant source material. This interest in classical sculpture led him to travel to Rome late in 1772, with the help of his first significant patron, the 4th Duke of Marlborough. He remained there until 1788, living first in Strada Paolina. In 1774 he moved to the artists' quarter of via Babuino, apparently sharing his studio with the painters Solomon Delane and Henry Tresham. In 1786 he took a house and studio in the more prosperous area of strada Felice (now via Sistina), not far from the Spanish Steps, which can be taken as a sign of his increasing success. Although Marchant made brief trips to Florence, Naples, Tivoli and Venice, most of his time was spent in Rome, where he specialised increasingly in intaglio sealstones with designs taken from the ancient sculpture he saw in the city, particularly in the newly-created Museo Pio Clementino. Marchant offered many of these intaglios to Marlborough who was a keen collector of his work, but he was in growing demand from the many aristocratic visitors who went to Italy from Britain and other parts of Europe on the Grand Tour. In Marchant's carved gemstones they found beautifully-made mementoes of the antiquities seen on their travels with the added advantage of portability. Although a minor part of his output, Marchant also produced a small number of portrait intaglios whilst in Italy, notably of Pope Pius VI in 1781, Emma Hamilton in 1786, and Catherine the Great of Russia in 1788.

Marchant exhibited regularly with the Society of Artists in London from 1765 to 1774, sending his work over from Italy in 1773 and 1774. In consequence he experienced at first hand the excessive import duty charged to overseas British artists when they sent their work home for exhibition, and he was asked to represent the British artists in Italy in a petition to the British government to reduce tariffs on the import of artworks. This was successful. After a gap of several years, when he worked mainly on commissions, Marchant began to exhibit in Britain again in 1781, this time sending work to the Royal Academy.

When he returned to Britain in 1788, Marchant settled in New Bond Street, London. Despite his feeling that his abilities as an artist and services to art deserved some recognition, official honours and public appointments were 'disappointingly slow to follow' (*Seidmann*, 1985, 152). An attempt to become keeper of the King's Pictures shortly after his return met with failure, and although he became an ARA in 1791, Marchant had to wait a further 18 years, until 1809, to be elected a full Academician. He was considered by some in the RA to be over-keen to claim a 'right' to be elected, particularly by the way he played on his success in reducing import tax on artworks. There remained a doubt also over whether gem-carving was a form of sculpture, particularly with the increasing emergence of mass-produced copies of inferior quality. In addition, Marchant's case was probably not helped by the jealousy of his former master, Burch, who had become an RA in 1772. Official recognition came, however, from overseas academies of art, for Marchant was elected a member of the Academies of Vienna in 1792, Stockholm in 1795 and Copenhagen in 1798.

In 1797 he began to work for the Royal Mint as an assistant engraver to **Lewis Pingo**, a post which brought a certain prestige, though it prompted Thomas Frankland to write that employing Marchant in this way 'made a mockery of his superior talents' (*Seidmann* 1987, 22). Certainly Marchant's designs for coins, medals and seals do not appear to have found particular favour with the royal household although he was diligent in producing them, often to the detriment of his professional career as an artist. In 1799 he was made the senior engraver at the Stamp Office, a post which allowed him to move into Somerset House on Strand.

Marchant was generally well-liked and admired both as a person and an artist, although Charles Long, 1st Baron Farnborough, dismissed him as 'a driveller' (*Ingamells* 1997, 641). Against Long's disdain must be set the overwhelming number of positive comments by Marchant's contemporaries, who praised him for his moral integrity as well as his artistic talent. Marchant counted the artists Joseph Farington, Henry Fuseli and **John Flaxman RA**, and the art-collector Charles Townley, among the many friends who regularly dined with him in his apartment in Somerset House. He died on 24 March 1816 after a long illness, and is buried at Stoke Poges, Bucks, where there is an inscribed memorial stone to him by Flaxman. Marchant never married and left a fortune of £24,000. The executors of his will were Flaxman and William Penn of Pennsylvania. The latter also oversaw his funeral.

Michael Paraskos

Literary References: *Lipscomb* 1847, 565; *Graves* 1905–6, V, 180–82; *Gunnis* 1968, 253; *RSA Journal*, vol 133, 1985, 150–53; *Seidmann* 1985, 152; *Seidmann* 1987, 5–27 (with comprehensive list of the engraved gems); *Grove* (Seidmann); *Ingamells* 1997, 641; *ODNB* (Seidmann)

Archive References: RA, SA/34/14; RG/JP, 5, 880–2; Soane Note Books, no.110, 39, Soane Museum

Portraits of the Sculptor: George Dance, 1794, pencil and chalk on paper, RA 03/3261; William Daniell, after George Dance, etching, NPG D12085; John Flaxman, pen and ink, MFAB 53.2618; Hugh Douglas Hamilton, *c*1779, oil on canvas, Soane Museum

Busts

1.	1791	Andromache		[Exhib RA, London, 627]; untraced	*Graves* V, 1905–6, 181; *Seidmann* 1987, 86
2.	1810	Lord Downe, model	tc	[Exhib RA, London, 760]; untraced	*Graves* V, 1905–6, 181

Miscellaneous

3.	1769	Model, from an antique bust of a daughter of Niobe	w	[Exhib Soc of Artists, London, 240]; untraced	*Graves* 1907, 155
4.	1769	Model, from an antique bust of Sappho	w	[Exhib Soc of Artists, London, 239]; untraced	*Graves* 1907, 155
5.	1772	Agrippina weeping over the ashes of Germanicus, model	w	[Exhib Soc of Artists, London, 207]; untraced	*Graves* 1907, 155
6.	1789	Emma		[Exhib RA, London, 344]; untraced	*Graves* V, 1905–6, 181
7.	1789	Head of a Bacchante		[Exhib RA, London, 280]; untraced	*Graves* V, 1905–6, 181
8.	1792	A nymph, model	w	[Exhib RA, London, 759]; untraced	*Graves* V, 1905–6, 181
9.	1792	Torquato Tasso, model from a cast in wax		[Exhib RA, London, 778]; untraced	*Graves* V, 1905–6, 181
10.	1793	Reconciliation of Venus to Cupid		[Exhib RA, London, 344]; untraced	*Graves* V, 1905–6, 181; *Seidmann* 1987, 87
11.	1795	Homer		[Exhib RA, London, 403]; untraced	*Graves* V, 1905–6, 181

12.	1795	Rt Hon William Wyndham		[Exhib RA, London, 402]; untraced	*Graves* V, 1905–6, 181
13.	1797	Pope Pius VI, modelled from life, for a gem in the Vatican Library		[Exhib RA, London, 885]; untraced	*Graves* V, 1905–6, 181
14.	1797	Sappho		[Exhib RA, London, 1126]; untraced	*Graves* V, 1905–6, 181
15.	1798	Britannia, model	w	[Exhib RA, London, 908]; untraced	*Graves* V, 1905–6, 181
16.	1798	Unidentified gentleman		[Exhib RA, London, 846]; untraced	*Graves* V, 1905–6, 181
17.	1798	Unidentified subject, portrait		[Exhib RA, London, 852]; untraced	*Graves* V, 1905–6, 181
18.	1799	Figure of the Nile, model, for the reverse of a medal of Lord Nelson	w	[Exhib RA, London, 871]; untraced	*Graves* V, 1905–6, 181
19.	1805	Jupiter Serapis, after an antique bust		[Exhib RA, London, 791]; untraced	*Graves* 1875, 367; *Graves* V, 1905–6, 181
20.	1806	Female, identity unknown	p	[Exhib BI, London, 92]; untraced	*Graves* 1875, 367
21.	1806	Hercules restoring Alcestes to Admetus		[Exhib BI, London, 18]; untraced	*Graves* 1875, 367
22.	1806	The Nile, emblematical figure, model		[Exhib BI, London, 12]; untraced	*Graves* 1875, 367
23.	1808	Duke of Norfolk (model, intended to be engraved on a steel die)	w	[Exhib RA, London, 697]; untraced	*Graves* V, 1905–6, 181
24.	nd	An 'ideal female head of my own invention'		[RA, London]; untraced	*Seidmann* 1987, 87

MARES, Henry 1813–

In 1831 he joined the Royal Academy Schools on the recommendation of a Mr Smith, whose initials are difficult to decipher but appear to be 'R W'. Gunnis construed him as **C H Smith**. Mares gave his address as 21 Lower Belgrave Street, where he was still to be found in 1838. He exhibited sculpture and pictures at the Royal Academy from 1839, when he had moved to 7 South Place, Belgrave Terrace.

In 1844 Mares exhibited a group of King *Charles I parting with his children* (**6**) and was censored by the *Art Union* who considered the modelling 'extremely careless and coarse' (*AU* 1844, 215). The *Literary Gazette* went further, remarking that the work was 'perhaps the most curious sculpture ever perpetrated, the thin monarch with the quaint countenance, and the young lady who seems to be intimating by a wink that it is not real but fun, are thoroughly grotesque' (*Lit Gaz* 1844, 482).

He appears to have produced a handful of monuments, including one to James Brook, which has a kneeling woman in relief, depicted in profile by an altar (**3**). In 1849 he exhibited *A View of the Trevi fountain at Rome* at the Royal Academy. In 1851 he was living at 31 Ebury Street (*Graves* V, 1905–6, 182).

Literary References: *Gunnis* 1968, 253; *Johnson* 1975, 310

Archival References: RA Admissions

Funerary Monuments						
1.	1840	Statue, 'part of a monument erected in the artists' ground at Kensal Green'	s	[Exhib RA, London, 1130 and 1146]; untraced		*Graves* V, 1905–6, 182
2.	†1827	Joseph Beaumont		Kirkheaton, W R Yorks		GPC
3.	†1836	James Brook		Meltham, W R Yorks		Pevsner, *Yorks: W R*, 1967, 363
4.	1839	Charity, model of a relief for a monument		[Exhib RA, London, 1310]; untraced		*Graves* V, 1905–6, 182
5.	?1847	Rev John Marshall		St Peter, Huddersfield, W R Yorks	S	*Gunnis* 1968, 253
Statues						
6.	1844	King Charles I parting with his children		[Exhib Westminster Hall, London, 130]; untraced		*AU*, 1844, 215; *Lit Gaz* 1844, 482
Busts						
7.	1835	Charles Mares		[Exhib Soc of BA, London, 787]; untraced		*Johnson* 1975, 310
8.	1838	Unidentified lady		[Exhib Soc of BA, London, 633]; untraced		*Johnson* 1975, 310
Reliefs						
9.	1841	Venus caressing Cupid, model		[Exhib RA, London, 1266]; untraced		*Graves* V, 1905–6, 182
Miscellaneous						
10.	1833	Sleeping nymph		[Exhib Soc of BA, London, 854]; untraced		*Johnson* 1975, 310
11.	1833	Sleeping shepherd		[Exhib Soc of BA, London, 846]; untraced		*Johnson* 1975, 310
12.	1851	Master Mainwaring		[Exhib RA, London, 673]; untraced		*Graves* V, 1905–6, 182
13.	1851	Nymph and Cupid, model	m	[Exhib RA, London, 1259]; untraced		*Graves* V, 1905–6, 182

MARMAN, Henry fl 1782

He was employed at Loseley House, and was presumably related to **John Marman, of Guildford**, who had worked for the Molyneux family over twenty years earlier.

Literary References: *Gunnis* 1968, 254

Chimneypieces					
1.	1782	Description unavailable	m	[Loseley House, Surrey]; untraced	*Gunnis* 1968, 254

MARMAN, John, of Guildford fl 1748–60

A Guildford statuary, he was responsible for the Molyneux monument. His bill included 5s for 'blacking the wall around the monument' (**1**). He was also employed as master-mason supervising repairs carried out between 1748 and 1753 by Sir Matthew Featherstonehaugh to Uppark, Sussex (Uppark Archives, in GPC).

Literary References: *Gunnis* 1968, 253–4

Funerary Monuments				
1.	1760	James More Molyneux Payment(s): £27 14s	Haslemere, Surrey	Surrey History Centre, Loseley MSS 1087/1796; *Gunnis* 1968, 253

MAROCHETTI, Carlo, Baron RA 1805–68

A Franco-Italian sculptor, he spent the last 17 years of his life in Britain. He was a controversial figure, admired by Queen Victoria and Prince Albert, but resented by many British sculptors and critics.

He was born in Turin, the capital of Piedmont, then a French possession, on 14 January 1805. His father Vincenzo Marochetti was a prominent civil servant and lawyer and a committed republican. The family moved to Paris soon after Carlo's birth and when Piedmont was restored to the Sardinian kingdom in 1814 Vincenzo obtained French citizenship for himself and his family. Carlo was educated at the Lycée Napoleon and studied sculpture under François-Joseph Bosio. At his father's death in 1820 Marochetti inherited the Chateau of Vaux, where he later set up his studio. For a time he lived in Paris with his father's friend, Carlo Botta, one of the leaders of Piedmont's short-lived republican regime. Although he failed to win the *Prix de Rome* of the *Ecole des Beaux Arts* he travelled to Italy in 1822 and spent some years studying in Rome.

On returning to France Marochetti began to exhibit at the Salon, showing a group, *Young girl with a dog* in 1827 and *Rebel angel* in 1831. Significant French commissions soon followed, including a marble relief, *The battle of Jemmapes* for the Arc de Triomphe in Paris, 1833–34, and a marble altarpiece for the Madeleine depicting the *Assumption of the Magdalen*, 1834–44. His reputation was established with a bronze equestrian statue of Duke Emanuele Filiberto of Savoy, presented to his native city, Turin, in 1837. In this work he brought romantic elements to a conventional mode of representation, including picturesque historical costume, a convincing sense of dramatic action and a vigorous style of modelling. In recognition of his donation to Turin he was created a baron of the Kingdom of Sardinia. Further commissions followed, including a bronze equestrian statue of Ferdinand Duc d'Orléans for the courtyard of the Louvre, 1844 (now at Chateau d'Eu, Seine-Maritime) and in 1839 he was awarded the *legion d'honneur*. He was given the commission for Napoleon's tomb at the Invalides but the choice of a foreign interloper to provide a memorial to France's great hero caused an outcry and after years of wrangling, the contract went elsewhere. Eventually Marochetti was invited to provide an equestrian statue of Napoleon for the Esplanade des Invalides, but it was never accorded a permanent site.

As he came increasingly under attack in France, Marochetti sought opportunities in England, submitting a model, which was rejected, in the competition of 1839 for a national monument to Admiral Nelson (**24**). His first British work was an equestrian statue of the Duke of Wellington for Glasgow, erected in 1844 (**25**). Critics questioned whether it was appropriate for Marochetti to work concurrently on monuments to Wellington and Napoleon and doubted whether his elaborate, energetic style would be acceptable to a British audience. Marochetti enlisted the help of influential friends to obtain the commission, which led to accusations of foul play. The statue is a restrained, naturalistic portrayal of the duke as he would have appeared at the time of his famous victories and it was generally well received, although one correspondent insisted that it looked 'too like a real man on horseback' and lacked the more elevated qualities of 'invention, grandeur, expression, beauty of form, purity of taste, simplicity of style' (*Art U*, Nov 1844, 337). Marochetti went on to provide Glasgow with three more public statues (**31, 35, 55**) and was responsible for a second, posthumous, statue of the Duke of Wellington for Leeds (**32**).

After the revolution of 1848 Marochetti settled in London, establishing his studio at 34 Onslow Square, Kensington. In 1853 he set up his own bronze foundry so that he could control every stage of the production process. He exhibited regularly at the Royal Academy from 1851 onwards and that year the plaster model for his equestrian statue of *Richard, Coeur de Lion* (**43**) was prominently displayed at the entrance to the Crystal Palace. One lively account relates that Marochetti hurriedly assembled a crowd of friends to help complete the statue in time for the exhibition and the resulting workmanship was so poor that the horse's tail fell off almost as soon as it was in position (*Hallé* 1909, 6). Marochetti's powerful depiction of the crusader-king met varied responses. When the bronze version was erected outside the Palace of Westminster in 1860 one writer claimed 'The designer of this Richard may, without presumption, claim for this work a place by the side of the terrible Bartolommeo Colleoni of Verocchio, or the statelier, if less living, Gattamelata of Donatello' (*The Times*, 7 Nov 1860, 7). Palgrave, however, dismissed it as 'an essentially vulgar and low-class work' (*Palgrave* 1866, 269). A proposal to erect a companion statue of the *Edward the Black Prince*, opposite the *Coeur de Lion* on the other side of the peers' entrance, never came to fruition and this work is known only in small-scale bronze and silver versions (**40**).

One of Marochetti's first important British patrons was William John Bankes, an influential collector, who spent many years renovating and furnishing his home at Kingston Lacy. He was instrumental in securing for Marochetti the Glasgow Wellington commission, but was obliged to flee abroad after a sexual misdemeanour and he completed the refurbishment of his Dorset home whilst living in exile. Bankes ordered several works from Marochetti, including a group of three statues commemorating King Charles I and his Royalist ancestors, Sir John and Lady Mary Bankes (**33**). The pedestal for the king's statue incorporates a relief of the siege of Corfe Castle, which Lady Mary Bankes and the women of her household held against the Commonwealth forces. The statues, like Charles Barry's additions to the building, are derived from 17th-century prototypes.

Marochetti became a favourite sculptor with the English Royal family, for whom he provided busts of Prince Albert and Queen Victoria and statuettes of the young princes, Alfred and Arthur (**71, 86, 66, 67**). Princess Louise later based her own bust of her father on Marochetti's and **William Theed II**'s representations. She apparently felt Marochetti's the better work of art, but Theed's the better likeness. The Queen also commissioned a work harking back to the Civil War period, the monument to Princess Elizabeth Stuart at Newport (**7**). The Princess had died aged 14, during her imprisonment at Carisbrook Castle. She is depicted in contemporary costume, with her head resting on an open bible, as her attendants apparently found her. The prison bars are indicated in relief within the niche containing the monument. The Queen found the work 'really beautiful' and 'very touching' (*Queen Victoria's Journal*, Royal Archives, Windsor, quoted in *Ward-Jackson* 1990 (2), 278).

His publicly-funded works caused controversy. He was accused of charging too much for casting the four lions modelled by **Sir Edwin Landseer** for the base of Nelson's Column in Trafalgar Square (**60**) and his Crimean War memorial for Scutari was much criticised (**9**). The design, for a granite obelisk with four identical winged female figures at the corners, was ridiculed and the cost, £17,500, was considered excessive. Rival sculptors were jealous that the commission had been awarded to a foreigner without the opportunity for native sculptors to compete. Marochetti was at the centre of the long-running controversy over the Wellington Memorial competition. Many sculptors were convinced that the competition was a sham and that Marochetti would be awarded the commission, regardless of the merit of other designs. The government had stipulated that the models should be no larger than quarter-size and that they must be submitted anonymously, so there was outrage when Marochetti ignored both conditions. He began work on a full-size version and *The Times* published a lengthy description of it a month before the competition, suggesting that he was confident of being selected. The resultant outcry caused Marochetti to withdraw from the competition. The episode was not closed: in 1859, after **Alfred Stevens** had been awarded the commission, Marochetti placed part of his design, an *Angel of Victory* (**38**), on full public view in the garden of the Duke of Wellington's London residence, Apsley House. Critics suspected that he was trying to override the official procedure even at this late stage.

Marochetti was employed continuously on memorials to Prince Albert after his death in 1861. The most important of these is perhaps the tomb at Frogmore (**21**). Marochetti sculpted marble effigies of Prince Albert and also Queen Victoria, together with four kneeling angels for the corners of the black granite sarcophagus. (The Queen's image was hidden at Windsor Castle and only added to the monument after her death in 1901). This intimate memorial presents the royal couple sleeping, with their heads turned towards one another, so reflecting the Queen's conviction of their reunion in an afterlife. Shortly before the Frogmore commission Marochetti provided his first public monument to the Prince Consort, for Aberdeen (**49**). This was much less successful. The seated figure is overwhelmed by 'military trappings and ribbands and bell-pull tassels and ornamental frippery' (*Aberdeen Herald*, 17 October 1863, 5 quoted in *Darby and Smith* 1983, 84) and it was considered a poor likeness. It was so unpopular that a replacement by **William Brodie** was proposed, though never commissioned. In Glasgow an equestrian statue (**55**), which complements an earlier one of Queen Victoria (**31**), was more favourably received. It was particularly admired by the Queen herself, who asked Joseph Edgar Boehm for a replica, erected in Windsor Great Park in 1887. Marochetti was also chosen as sculptor for the large statue of Prince Albert, the focal point of the national memorial in Kensington Gardens (**58**). However, his model of the enthroned figure was considered so unsatisfactory that after Marochetti's death **John Henry Foley** was called on to design and execute a new statue of the prince.

Marochetti was responsible for numerous public statues in England, including images of the engineers Isambard Kingdom Brunel (**45**) and Robert Stephenson (**47**) and Joseph Locke (**56**), which have been described as 'remarkable for mundane realism' (*Grove* 20, 1996, 455). They were executed during the early 1860s and intended as part of a series to be erected in a prominent site, the gardens of St Margaret's churchyard, Westminster, near the Institute of Civil Engineers, but were dispersed after approval for the scheme was withdrawn by the commissioner for public works. During the 1850s and 1860s he also worked on major commissions for France and Italy including a monument to the Comtesse de Lariboisière in Paris (**1**) and a second equestrian statue for Turin, of King Carlo Alberto (**46**). His works were exhibited internationally; an equestrian statue of George Washington (**29**), now destroyed, was sent to the New York Crystal Palace and another, of King Victor Emmanuel of Italy (**34**), was shown at the Paris exhibition of 1855.

Marochetti was an early champion of polychrome sculpture and in 1864 produced a coloured statuette of *Queen Victoria as queen of peace and commerce* (**52**). The Queen commissioned naturalistically painted busts of Princess Gauramma of Coorg (**92**) and the former Maharajah of the Punjab, Dalip Singh (**90**), but later asked Marochetti to remove the colour from the Maharajah's head. Fortunately coloured versions of both survived in Marochetti's own collection. It is thought that all three were painted by William Millais, the brother of the Pre-Raphaelite artist John Everett Millais. Marochetti is thought to have experimented with aluminium as a material for sculpture, long before the Alfred Gilbert used it in the 1890s. He made effective use of various reproductive media to promote his work. A number of his royal portraits were reproduced in parian ware by Copeland (**66, 67, 71, 86**) and some of his best-known works including the equestrian statue of Queen Victoria (**31**) were widely available as small bronzes. Other works were disseminated through photographs on *cartes de visite* taken by the society photographer, Camille Silvy. Marochetti also designed race cups, furniture and other decorative objects, including the Doncaster cup (Doncaster Art Gallery), a testimonial statuette of a knight holding a standard (private coll, Scotland), a sideboard made by Snell of London (Great Exhib, 1851) and an elaborate terracotta and parian ware flower vase, made by Minton (Great Exhibition 1851).

In Britain official recognition came late in his career. He became an ARA in 1861 and an Academician in 1867, when he deposited a bust of Sir Edwin Landseer as his diploma work (**122**). He died suddenly the following year, on 28 December, at Passy near Paris, of a heart attack, perhaps brought on by his extravagant lifestyle and was buried in the cemetery at Vaux-sur-Seine, where his grave is marked by a relief of an angel he modelled himself. In the spring of 1868 a sale of his collection of prints was held at Sotheby's, when the 687 lots fetched £2,960 12s 6d. The sale of his studio contents at Christie's on 7 May 1868 included a bronze bust of Napoleon, three bronze medals designed to commemorate the Great Exhibition of 1851 and a plaster statuette of Sir Robert Peel. The sculptor's widow lent a number of his works to the South Kensington Museum after his death, most were returned to the family during the 1930s and a few remained at the museum until 2001. Marochetti's English pupils included the painter, Charles Lutyens and the sculptor, Morton Edwards. **Robert Glassby** worked as an assistant in his studio and was commissioned to complete unfinished works after Marochetti's death, such as the effigy of the Prince Consort for the royal mausoleum at Frogmore.

Marochetti's work attracted much adverse criticism. The *Art Union* (and later the *Art Journal*) demonstrated its support for native British sculptors by attacking him. Palgrave was unimpressed by the 'clever effectism' of works such as the bust of William Marshall exhibited at the RA in 1859 (102). He felt that 'the features are made to tell, not by truth or subtlety of surface, but by suppressing all minor details in favour of those points which strike first the eye, and then by opposing to the flesh a coarse and heavily-handled mass of drapery.' These and other tricks were seen as compensating for a lack of 'mastery over form, insight into character, and power to put them into marble' (*Palgrave* 1866, 41–2). The writer of his obituary in the *Athenaeum* however stressed the popularity of such works as the statues to Richard the Lionheart and to Queen Victoria in Glasgow and understood the appeal of an artist 'who, if he did not satisfy the graver requirements of artists, made his figures look alive, if theatrical' (*Athenaeum*, 11 Jan 1868, 62). John Ruskin went much further, pronouncing Marochetti 'a thoroughly great sculptor' (*Ruskin* 1903–12, xii, 155). A biography, in Italian, was published in 1928 but a dismissive view of the sculptor persisted into the 20th century.

Gunnis so disliked his work that he chose not to list him in his *Dictionary of British Sculptors* (*Knox* 2001, 90). More recent studies, particularly by Philip Ward-Jackson, have located his work within a wider European political and artistic context and argued his ability to meet the varying requirements of patrons in Italy, France and Britain. Marochetti brought a radically different approach to modelling to Britain and it has been suggested that he can, therefore, be seen as a forerunner of the New Sculpture.

The following list includes all Marochetti's works executed while he was resident in Britain but only those commissions with British connections for the period up until 1848.

EH

Literary References: *Sandby* 1862, II, 352–3; *Palgrave* 1866, *passim*; *The Times*, 4 Jan 1868, 9; *Athenaeum*, 11 Jan 1868, 62; *Builder*, 11 Jan 1868, 35; *ILN*, 11 Jan 1868, 48; *Redgrave* 1868, 285–6; *Mag of Art*, 1883, 134; *DNB*, XXXVI, 1893, 193–4; *Calderini* 1928, *passim*; *Physick* 1970, *passim*; *RG/JP*, 5, 883–894; *RG/JP*, suppl 5; *Ormond* 1973, 301; *Read* 1982, *passim*; *Darby and Smith* 1983, *passim*; *Ward-Jackson* 1990 (1), 851–62; *Ward-Jackson* 1990 (2), 266–80; *Jenkins* 1992, 185, 200; *Read* 1992, 7; *Ward-Jackson* 1993, 63–83; *Ward-Jackson* 1994, 43–8; *Grove* 20, 1996, 454–5 (Ward-Jackson); *Ward-Jackson* 2000, 175–190; *Brooks* 2000, 167, 184–9; *Harrison* 2004, 62–8; *Ward-Jackson* 2004, 115–20; *ODNB* (Ward-Jackson)

Additional Manuscript Sources: Marochetti/Ashburton; misc corr, BL, Fitz, Getty Centre Library, Pierpoint Morgan Library; artist file, Frick Reference Library

Will: PPR, will with codicil, 5 February 1868, fol 119, effects in England, under £9,000

Auction References: Marochetti 1868 (1); Marochetti 1868 (2)

Miscellaneous Drawings: Marochetti family scrapbook, private coll, France (including drawings by the sculptor and other family members)

Portraits of the Sculptor: Drawing *c*1840 (repr *Calderini* 1928, f24); Louis Laurent Atthalim, *Studio of Carlo Marochetti at Vaux in 1843*, private coll, France (repr *Ward-Jackson* 2000, 181); Sir Anthony Coningham Sterling (attrib), photo, late 1840s, NPG P171 (34); two photos of the sculptor in fancy dress, 1856–7, private coll, France (one repr *Ward-Jackson* 2000, 175); photo, 1866 (repr *Calderini* 1928, f40); woodcut, after a photo by J Watkins, *ILN*, XXXVIII, 1868, 178; E Browning, painting, untraced (exhib RA, London, 1868, 820); Gabriele Ambrosio, bronze statuette, 1888, NPG 1038; G F Watts, painting, untraced (Victorians Exhib, 1892, 278); V Brooks, chromolithograph after painting of Marochetti in his studio by J Ballantyne (example NPG); Camille Silvy, photo, with a statuette, a reduced version of the Richard Coeur de Lion (repr *Ward-Jackson* 1994, 45); oil painting, private coll, France

Funerary Monuments

1.	*c*1853	Comtesse de Lariboisière (†1851)		Hôpital Lariboisière, Paris, France Other versions: Rennes Museum, France, plaster model	*Calderini* 1928, 56 (reprs XXXIV–XXXVI)
2.	†1853	Granville Gower Loch		St Paul's Cathedral, London, south aisle	Pevsner, *London: City*, 1997, 171–2; C Lib (repr)
3.	†1853	John, 1st Earl Brownlow		Belton, Lincs	Pevsner, *Lincs*, 1989, 135; *Knox* 1999, 49 (repr)
4.	†1853	William (†1848) and Frederick (†1853), Viscounts Melbourne		St Paul's Cathedral, London, north aisle	*Calderini* 1928, 57 (repr LX); Pevsner, *London: City*, 1997, 171
5.	†1854	Officers of the Coldstream Guards (Battle of Inkerman memorial)		St Paul's Cathedral, London	*ILN* 23 Aug 1856, 1999 (repr); *DNB*, XXXVI, 1893, 194; *Calderini* 1928, 57
6.	†1855	Captain Arthur Wellesley Torrens		St Paul's Cathedral, London, north aisle Other versions: Chelsea Hospital, London, plaster model	Pevsner, *London: City*, 1997, 170
7.	1854–1856	Princess Elizabeth Stuart (daughter of King Charles I) Model(s): untraced (ex Ashmolean)		St Thomas, Newport, I of W	*Ward-Jackson* 1990 (2), 267, 277–8 (repr 35a,c); *Penny* 1992, III, 125 (repr)
8.	*c*1857	Cavalry division (Crimean War memorial)		St Paul's Cathedral, London, north aisle	Pevsner, *London: City*, 1997, 171
9.	1856–1857	Crimean War memorial		British War Cemetery, Scutari, Turkey Other versions: ex Museum of Construction, South Kensington, small copy; untraced	*DNB*, XXXVI, 1893, 194; *Ward-Jackson* 2000, 186
10.	†1858	Lady Margaret Leveson Gower Model(s): plaster, private coll, France		Castle Ashby, Northants	*CIIA* 4/3/34–8 (repr)
11.	1858	Lieutenant-Colonel James Cowell (same design as the Coldstream Guards Inkerman Memorial, St Paul's Cathedral, London (5)	b	Llanelli, Carmarthen	*Dale-Jones and Lloyd* 1989, 43, 55
12.	†1859	Henry, 3rd Marquis of Waterford		Clonegam, Co Waterford	*Graves* V, 1905–6, 188
13.	*c*1860	9th Queen's Royal Lancers (Indian Mutiny memorial)		Exeter Cathedral, Devon	RG/JP, 5, 896
14.	†1861	Albert, the Prince Consort		St Thomas, Newport, I of W	Pevsner, *Hants*, 1967, 750; *Darby and Smith* 1983, 88, 89 (repr)
15.	1860–1862	Colonel Tommaso Morelli		[Duomo, Casale Monferrato]; Seminario della Curia Vescovile, Casale Monferrato, Italy	*Sgherzi* 2003, 204–8
16.	1862	Officers of the Royal Engineers who fell in the Indian Mutiny		St Paul's Cathedral, Kolkata (Calcutta)	*ILN*, 1 Aug 1863, 124 (repr)
17.	†1863	William Beckett		St Peter, Leeds, W R Yorks	*Leeds Man* 1868, 52; *Moore* 1877, 33; *Pullan* 2006, 24, 29 (repr)
18.	†1865	Admiral Henry Meynell		Yoxall, Staffs	Pevsner, *Staffs*, 1974, 331
19.	1865	Angel of the Resurrection, memorial to the women and children who died at Cawnpore		[Cawnpore, the Well]; All Souls memorial church, Cawnpore, India	*Steggles* 2000, 36–38 (repr)
20.	*c*1865	William Makepeace Thackeray (†1863) Payment(s): £600		Westminster Abbey, London, south transept	*Ormond* 1973, 465; *Read* 1982, 59, 171 (repr); *Bilbey* 2002, 334
21.	1864–1867	Albert, the Prince Consort (†1861) and Queen Victoria (†1901) Model(s): royal coll, full-size plaster		Royal mausoleum, Frogmore, Berks	*Darby and Smith* 1983, 25 (repr); *Ward-Jackson* 1993, 71–5, 76 (repr)

22.	†1867	Carlo, Baron Marochetti (the sculptor's own monument)	b	Vaux-sur-Seine Cemetery, France		C Lib (repr)
23.	1867	John, 4th Marquis of Waterford (†1866)		Clonegam, Co Waterford		C Lib (repr)
Statues						
24.	1839	National memorial to Admiral Lord Nelson, model only (monument executed by E H Baily and William Railton)		Untraced		*Yarrington* 1986, 356
25.	1840–1844	Arthur, 1st Duke of Wellington, equestrian figure on a pedestal with reliefs Drawing(s): Wellington coll, Stratfield Saye	b	Royal Exchange Square, Glasgow Other versions: reproduced as a small bronze		*Ward-Jackson* 1990 (1), 851–862 (repr); *McKenzie* 2002, 336–9 (repr)
26.	1850	Sappho	m	Untraced		*Calderini* 1928, 57, 58
27.	1851	Dead Christ		[Royal Manchester Institution Modern Artists Exhib, 549]; untraced		inf. PW-J
28.	1854	Child and greyhound (or Cupid and greyhound)	m	[Exhib RA, London, 1381]; Tuileries, Paris (1856) Other versions: sold Christie, 15 Feb 1990, bronze, SD 1853		*Graves* V, 1905–6, 187; *Morris and Roberts* 1998, 413
29.	1854	George Washington (standing figure)		[Crystal Palace, Sydenham]; destroyed		inf: PW-J
30.	1853–1854	George Washington, equestrian	p	[Crystal Palace, New York, USA]; destroyed Other versions: Chateau de Cheverny, France, bronze reduction		*ILN*, 6 Aug 1853, 72 (repr); *Calderini* 1828, 59
31.	1854	Queen Victoria, equestrian, with pedestal reliefs	b	[St Vincent Place, Glasgow]; George Square, Glasgow, Lanarks Other versions: Numerous small replicas, inc NGS		*Building Chronicle*, 16.9.1854, 78; *McKenzie* 2002, 126–131 (repr)
32.	1855	Arthur, 1st Duke of Wellington	b	[Victoria Square, Leeds]; Woodhouse Moor, Leeds, W R Yorks Other versions: Stratfield Saye, Hants, 1863		Pevsner, *Yorks: W. R.*, 1967, 331; *Ward-Jackson* 1990 (1), 861
33.	1853–1855	King Charles I (with pedestal relief of the siege of Corfe Castle), Sir John Bankes and Lady Mary Bankes	b	Kingston Lacy, Dorset (NT), staircase loggia Other versions: Dorchester museum, cast of pedestal relief		*Ward-Jackson* 1990 (2), 266–80 (repr 31a-c)
34.	1855	King Victor Emmanuel II, equestrian	b	[Paris Int Exhib, 5075]; untraced		*Lami* 1914–21, 398
35.	1856	James Oswald MP	b	[Sandyford Place, Sauchiehall St, Glasgow, Lanarks]; George Square, Glasgow, Lanarks		*McKenzie* 2002, 131–2 (repr)
36.	1856	Peace trophy		[Crystal Palace, Sydenham]; untraced		*Illustrated Times*, 17 May 1856 (repr)
37.	1858	Sir Jamsheti Jeejeebhoy Bt Payment(s): £4,000	m	Asiatic Society, Mumbai (Bombay), India (formerly Town Hall) Other versions: Bombay, full-size bronze (loaned to VAM 1868–1934) Bombay Hospital, small bronze Bronze version gifted by Marochetti's grandson, s side of Nariman Road, Bombay		*Graves* V, 1905–6, 187; *Groseclose* 1995, 36, 37 (repr); *Giara* 2000, 117–9, 121
38.	1859	Angel of Victory (project for the tomb of the Duke of Wellington)		[Exhib Apsley House, London, gardens]; untraced		*ILN*, 25 June 1859, 601 (repr); *Ward-Jackson* 2004, 124–5 (engraving repr)
39.	1859	Unidentified figure	b	[Exhib LSFA, Liverpool, 769]; untraced		*Morris and Roberts* 1998, 413
40.	*c*1860	Edward the Black Prince, equestrian statuette with two reliefs on pedestal	b	Private coll Other versions: Royal Coll RCIN 2121, bronze Anglia Television Company, silver, made by Garrard, 1849, altered by Asprey *c*1959 for use as television mascot	S	*Harrison* 2004, 62–8 (repr)
41.	*c*1860	Italy		[coll Marquess of Dufferin]; untraced		*The Times*, 7 Nov 1860, 7
42.	1860	Portrait, statuette	m	[Exhib RA, London, 949]; untraced		*Graves* V, 1905–6, 187
43.	1860	Richard Coeur de Lion Payment(s): over £3,000	b	Old Palace Yard, Westminster, London Other versions: Gt Exhib 1851, marble; untraced Royal Coll, Windsor Castle, *c*1853, small bronze private coll, France, small bronze		*ILN*, 12 Jan 1861, 41; *Read* 1982, 13, 59 (col repr 1); *Read* 2000, 266–8 (repr); *Harrison* 2004, 62–8 (repr)
44.	1860	Robert, Lord Clive	b	Market Square, Shrewsbury, Salop		*Read* 1982, 21 (repr)
45.	1859–1861	Isambard Kingdom Brunel Payment(s): £2,500	ir	Victoria Embankment Gardens, London (erected 1877)		*Blackwood* 1989, 160–1 (repr); *Grove* 20, 1996, 454; *Ward-Jackson* 2000, 186–7
46.	1861	King Carlo Alberto of Savoy	b	Piazzo Carlo Alberto, Turin, Italy Other versions: Arts Club, Dover St, London, small bronze (loaned to VAM 1869–1937)		*Calderini* 1928, 55 (pl XLIX, L); *Grove* 20, 1996, 455
47.	1861	Robert Stephenson	b	[Euston Square, erected 1871]; Euston Station, London		*Blackwood* 1989, 158–9 (repr); *Grove* 20, 1996, 455; *Ward-Jackson* 2000, 186–7

No.	Date	Subject	Material	Location		Literature
48.	post-1862	Jonas Webb	b	[Corn Exchange, Cambridge]; Babraham, Cambs		*Read* 1982, 167, 169 (repr); *Grove* 20, 1996, 455
49.	1863	Albert, the Prince Consort	b	Union Terrace, Aberdeen		*Darby and Smith* 1983, 84, 101, 107 n43 (repr)
50.	c1863	Sidney, Baron Herbert of Lea	b	Victoria Park, Salisbury, Wilts		*Calderini* 1928, 57; *Ormond* 1973, 223
51.	1864	Gioacchino (Antonio) Rossini Model(s): VAM 1153–1868, plaster	b	Liceo Musicale Rossini, Pesaro, Italy		*Calderini* 1928, 55 (pl XVIII); *Bilbey* 2002, 335 (repr)
52.	1864	Queen Victoria, as Queen of Peace and Commerce, statuette		Untraced		*Grove* 20, 1996, 455; C Lib (repr)
53.	1864	Sir George Cornewall Lewis Bt	b	Shire Hall, Hereford		*Ormond* 1973, 270
54.	1865	Field Marshal Lord Combermere		Chester (outside Castle gates)		*Graves* V, 1905–6, 188; RG/JP, 5, 895
55.	1863–1866	Albert, the Prince Consort, equestrian figure on a pedestal with reliefs Payment(s): £6,000	b	George Square, Glasgow, Lanarks Other versions: Windsor Great Park, replica by Joseph Edgar Boehm, 1887 reproduced as a small bronze (eg coll Duke of Argyle, Inverary Castle)		*Darby and Smith* 1983, 74, 75–6, 104–5 (repr); *McKenzie* 2002, 134–6 (repr)
56.	1866	Joseph Locke	b	Locke Park, Barnsley, W R Yorks		*Graves* V, 1905–6, 188; *Ward-Jackson* 2000, 186–7
57.	1866	Sir Mark Cubbon, equestrian	b	Cubbon Park, Bangalore, India		*Steggles* 2000, 70 (repr)
58.	1864–1867	Albert, the Prince Consort, for the Albert Memorial, three models (statue executed by John Henry Foley)		Untraced		*Darby and Smith* 1983, 51–2; *Brooks* 2000, 167, 184–9
59.	1867	Field Marshall Sir Colin Campbell, Baron Clyde	b	Waterloo Place, London		*ILN*, 18 Jan 1868, 76; *Blackwood* 1989, 260–1 (repr)
60.	1858–1867	Lions	b	Nelson's Column, Trafalgar Square, London		*Read* 1982, 89, 90 (repr)
61.	nd	Carlo Botta, statuette (formerly misidentified as Lord Eldon and William Bankes)	b	Kingston Lacy, Dorset (NT) Other versions: Private coll, France		*Ward-Jackson* 1990 (1), 856, 857 (repr)
62.	nd	Erin	m	[coll Duke of Sutherland]; untraced		*Read* 1982, 129; *Lady Lever* 1999, 81
63.	nd	Group of lions		Ivi, India		*Calderini* 1928, 59
64.	nd	Henry Lutyens	p	Private coll		inf: PW-J
65.	nd	India		Crystal Palace Park, Sydenham, London		C Lib (repr)
66.	nd	Prince Alfred, Duke of Edinburgh with his highland pony, statuette	b	Royal Coll, Osborne House, I of W Other versions: reproduced in Minton Parian ware (eg Royal Coll, Osborne House, I of W)		*Atterbury* 1989, 43, 44, 85 (repr 60, 62, 132)
67.	nd	Prince Arthur	m	Buckingham Palace, London RCIN 2076 Other versions: reproduced in bronze and Minton Parian ware		*Atterbury* 1989, 111 (repr 369)
68.	nd	Sir Robert Peel		[Parliament Square, London]; untraced		*Ormond* 1973, 373

Busts

No.	Date	Subject	Material	Location		Literature
69.	1841	Arthur, 1st Duke of Wellington (as a young man)	b	Private coll, France		*Ward-Jackson* 1990 (1), 857, 859 (repr)
70.	1841	Arthur, 1st Duke of Wellington (as an old man)		Stratfield Saye, Hants Other versions: ex coll George Marochetti, marble; untraced		*Ward-Jackson* 1990 (1), 857, 859
71.	1848–1849	Albert, the Prince Consort Payment(s): £120	m	Royal Coll, Windsor, RCIN 31628 Other versions: reproduced in bronze and Minton Parian ware (eg Royal Coll, Osborne House, I of W)	SD	*Graves* V, 1905–6, 187; *Ormond* 1973, 12; *Atterbury* 1989, 125 (repr 446); *Ward-Jackson* 1993, 68; *Roberts* 2002, 145 (repr)
72.	1849	Catherine Mathie Lamond	m	Glasgow Museums S.232		inf. PW-J
73.	1849	Young man		Private coll, Scotland	SD	inf. PW-J
74.	1850	Napoleon Bonaparte	m	Sotheby, 1995; untraced		inf. PW-J
75.	1851	Lady Constance Leveson Gower	m	[Exhib RA, London, 1378]; untraced Other versions: purchased by Royal family, 1855, bronze; untraced		*Graves* V, 1905–6, 187
76.	1851	Unidentified gentleman		[Royal Manchester Institution Modern Artists Exhib, 538]; untraced		inf. PW-J
77.	1851	Unidentified subject	p	[Royal Manchester Institution Modern Artists Exhib, 553]; untraced		inf. PW-J
78.	1852	Charles, 1st Earl of Cottenham	m	Peers Library corridor, Palace of Westminster		C Lib (repr)
79.	1852	Miss Baring		[Exhib RA, London, 1416]; untraced		*Graves* V, 1905–6, 187
80.	1852	Miss Tennant		[Exhib RA, London, 1423]; untraced		*Graves* V, 1905–6, 187
81.	1852	Miss Wadell		[Exhib RA, London, 1486]; untraced		*Graves* V, 1905–6, 187
82.	1851–1853	George Washington	p	VAM 1152-1868		*Bilbey* 2002, 334 (repr)
83.	1854	Unidentified lady	m	[Exhib RA, London, 1441]; untraced		*Graves* V, 1905–6, 187
84.	1854	Unidentified woman (? Eliza, 3rd Viscountess Clifdon)		Ickworth, Suffolk	SD	inf. PW-J
85.	1855	Lady Strathavon Payment(s): 5 gns	b	[Royal Coll]; untraced		inf. PW-J

No.	Date	Subject		Location		Literature
86.	1855	Queen Victoria	m	Buckingham Palace, London RCIN 2077 Other versions: Haddo House, Aberdeenshire (NT), nd, marble reproduced in Minton Parian ware (eg Royal Coll, Osborne)		*Graves* V, 1905–6, 187; *Ormond* 1973, 487; *Atterbury* 1989, 125 (repr 446); *Pearson* 1991, unpag
87.	1841–1855	Sir John Bankes (two, with different costumes)	b	Kingston Lacy, Dorset (NT)		*Ward-Jackson* 1990 (2), 270 (repr 32a-b)
88.	1855	The Hon Mrs G		[Exhib RA, London, 1480]; untraced		*Graves* V, 1905–6, 187
89.	c1855	Victor Emmanuel II	b	Private coll, France		C Lib (repr)
90.	c1856	Dalip Singh	m	Royal Coll, Osborne House, I of W Other versions: private coll, coloured marble		*Blühm* 1996, 168–9 (repr)
91.	1856	James Oswald MP		[Scottish exhib of arts and manufactures connected with architecture]; untraced		*McKenzie* 2002, 132
92.	1856	Princess Gauramma of Coorg	m	Royal Coll, Osborne House, I of W Other versions: private coll, France, coloured plaster		*Read* 1982, 174, 175 (repr); *Grove* 20, 1996, 455; *Blühm* 1996, 168–9 (repr)
93.	1855–1856	Sir Anthony (Antonio) Panizzi Model(s): private coll, on loan VAM, 1868–2001, plaster	m	BL		*Dawson* 1999, 161–164 (repr); *Bilbey* 2002, 334
94.	pre-1857	Adam Smith	m	Council Chamber, Kircaldy Other versions: private coll, France, bronze		*Calderini* 1928, 57 (repr LIV); *Manchester Art Treasures* 1857, 136
95.	1857	Charles Philippe Henri de Noailles, duc de Mouchy	b	Mouy, France		*Calderini* 1928, 57; *Lami* 1914–21, 398
96.	pre-1857	Henry Hallam	m	[Manc Art Treas exhib, 124]; untraced		*Manchester Art Treasures* 1857, 136
97.	1857	Rev William Sinclair		Philosophical Hall, Leeds, W R Yorks		*Leeds Phil and Lit Soc Report*, 1857–8, 12, 18
98.	1858	Duchesse de Nemours		[Royal Coll]; untraced		inf. PW-J
99.	?1858	John, 1st Earl Russell	m	[coll Russell family]; Clarendon Gallery, London (1984)	D	*Graves* V, 1905–6, 187; *Ormond* 1973, 407
100.	1858	Sir James Stephen	m	[coll Stephen family]; NPG, London, 1029		*Graves* V, 1905–6, 187; *Ormond* 1973, 430 (reprs 853, 854)
101.	1857–1858	William Ewart Gladstone		Untraced		*Gladstone Diaries* V, 1978, 63, 224, 225, 245, 282, 283
102.	1859	William Marshall	m	[Exhib RA, London, 1342]; untraced		*Graves* V, 1905–6, 187
103.	c1860	John, 1st Baron Hampton	m	Museum of Royal Naval Hospital, Haslar, Gosport, Hants		*Ormond* 1973, 210
104.	1861	Duchess of Manchester		[Exhib RA, London, 1026]; untraced		*Graves* V, 1905–6, 188
105.	1861	Effie Millais	m	Private coll		*Lutyens* 1968, 195, 196 (repr)
106.	1861	Louise, Lady Ashburton	m	Castle Ashby, Northants		*Graves* V, 1905–6, 188
107.	1861	Marquess of Abercorn		[Exhib RA, London, 1010]; untraced		*Graves* V, 1905–6, 187
108.	1862	James Thomas, 7th Earl of Cardigan	m	[coll Countess of Cardigan]; United Services club, London		*Graves* V, 1905–6, 188; *British Portraits* 1956–7, 133
109.	1862	Marshal Pelissier, Duke of Malakoff	m	[Exhib RA, London, 1015]; untraced		*Graves* V, 1905–6, 188
110.	1862	Unidentified lady	m	[Exhib RA, London, 1024]; untraced		*Graves* V, 1905–6, 188; *British Portraits* 1956–7, 133
111.	1862	William Spence (co-sculptor: E Panini)	m	Coll Ted Few, London, 1994–5	SD	*Graves* V, 1905–6, 188; Christie, Wrotham Park, 21 June 1994, lot 184; C Lib (repr)
112.	1863	H C Marshall	m	[Exhib RA, London, 1028]; untraced		*Graves* V, 1905–6, 188
113.	1864	Dr Blackwood		[Exhib RA, London, 914]; untraced		*Graves* V, 1905–6, 188
114.	1864	Mrs Hertz		[Exhib RA, London, 895]; untraced		*Graves* V, 1905–6, 188
115.	1864–1865	Sir John Charles Robinson	b	VAM A.202-1929 Other versions: Ashm, WA 1998.183, plaster bust		*Bilbey* 2002, 335 (repr)
116.	1866	Dr Gueneau de Mussy	m	Académie Nationale de Médicine, Paris, France	S	*Graves* V, 1905–6, 188
117.	1866	Lady Alice Hill		[Exhib RA, London, 879]; untraced		*Graves* V, 1905–6, 188
118.	1866	Marquis of Downshire	m	[Exhib RA, London, 888]; untraced		*Graves* V, 1905–6, 188
119.	1866	Rev Edward Goddard		[Exhib RA, London, 902]; untraced		*Graves* V, 1905–6, 188
120.	1866	Richard Cobden	m	[Exhib RA, London, 895]; untraced		*Graves* V, 1905–6, 188
121.	1867	Alice Silvy		Private coll, France	SD	
122.	1867	Sir Edwin Landseer (diploma work)	m	[Exhib RA, London, 1040]; RA, London		*Graves* V, 1905–6, 188; *Radcliffe* 1969, 51 (repr)
123.	nd	Andrew S Dalgliesh	m	Glasgow Museums S.202		
124.	nd	Augusta Bromley Davenport	m	Capesthorne Hall, Cheshire		C Lib (repr)
125.	nd	Daniel Robertson	m	National Westminster Bank (formerly National Provincial Bank of England), Bishopsgate, City of London		*Ward-Jackson* 2003, 35
126.	nd	Duchess of Sutherland		Untraced		*Calderini* 1928, 57
127.	nd	Duchess of Wellington		Untraced		*Calderini* 1928, 57
128.	nd	Duchess of Westminster		Untraced		*Calderini* 1928, 57
129.	nd	Duke of Hamilton		Untraced		*Calderini* 1928, 58
130.	nd	Duke of Manchester		Untraced		*Calderini* 1928, 57
131.	nd	Henry, Lord Langdale		PRO, London		C Lib (repr)
132.	nd	Julia Stephen	m	Charleston Farmhouse, Sussex		C Lib (repr)
133.	nd	Lady Caroline Gordon		Haddo House, Aberdeenshire (NT) Other versions: Royal Coll, 1855, plaster; untraced		inf. PW-J; C Lib (repr)
134.	nd	Lord Gifford		Untraced		*Calderini* 1928, 58
135.	nd	Lord Lansdowne		[on loan VAM c1869–1937]; private coll, France		inf. PW-J

136.	nd	Lord Stratford of Redcliffe	m	[on loan VAM c1869–1937]; untraced		*Calderini* 1928, 57
137.	nd	Miss Susan Vincent		Untraced		*Calderini* 1928, 57
138.	nd	Mrs Seymour		Untraced		*Calderini* 1928, 57
139.	nd	Mrs St Barbe Sladen	m	Russell-Cotes AG, Bournemouth, Dorset		C Lib (repr)
140.	nd	Princess Mary of Teck	m	Buckingham Palace, London RCIN 2080 Other versions: Christie, London, 10 Nov 1980, lot 28, marble		C Lib (repr)
141.	nd	Sir James Elphinstone		Untraced		*Calderini* 1928, 57
142.	nd	Sir Jamsheti Jeejeebhoy Bt	m	[on loan, VAM, c1869–1937]; Birmingham MAG, inv P.38'49		*Silber* 1987, 64, cat 194
143.	nd	Unidentified man (perhaps Charles Edward Trevelyan)	b	Wallington Hall, Northumbs, (NT)	S	C Lib (repr)
Architectural Sculpture						
144.	nd	Drinking fountain, replica of Germain Pillon's 'Three Graces'		Hampton Court Palace, Middx		*Calderini* 1928, 57
145.	nd	Two figures of Atlas (cast by Soyer)	b	Hamilton Palace, Lanarks		*ILN*, 19 Jan 1878, 60
Reliefs						
146.	1847–1848	James Oswald MP	p	Private coll, London		*McKenzie* 2002, 132
147.	1848	Thomas, 1st Baron Macaulay	b	NPG, London, 257 Other versions: Wallington, Northumbs SNPG	SD	*Ormond* 1973, 288–9 (repr 571)
148.	1851	Profiles of two gentlemen		[Exhib RA, London, 1305]; untraced		*Graves* V, 1905–6, 187
149.	1852	Massimo d'Azeglio, portrait medallion	b	Christie, 15 Oct 1981; private coll, Germany Other versions: Christie, 15 Oct 1981 (ex coll Henry Holiday)	SD	C Lib (repr)
150.	1853	Two roundels, after Jean Goujon	b	Kingston Lacy, Dorset (NT)		*Ward-Jackson* 1990 (2), 271–2; *Kingston Lacy*, NT guidebook, 1998, 46
151.	1854	La Tour d'Auvergne saves a wounded Spanish officer; La Tour d'Auvergne takes leave of le Brigant family	b	Monument to La Tour d'Auverge, Carhaix, Finistere, France		inf. PW-J
152.	1855–1860	The death of Richard Coeur de Lion	p	Private coll, France		C Lib (repr)
153.	nd	Lady Clementina Villiers, portrait medallion	m	Private coll, France Other versions: monument to Sarah Princess Nicolas Esterhazy (+1853) and Lady Clementina Villiers (+1858), Middleton Stoney, Oxon (monument perhaps by Marochetti?)		C Lib (repr)
154.	nd	Philibert and Maurice Marochetti, large medallion	b	Private coll, France Other versions: Private coll, France, plaster		*Calderini* 1928, 56 (repr XXXIX)
Miscellaneous						
155.	1851	The angel of sleep		[Gt Exhib, London]; untraced		*AJ Cat* 1851, 148 (repr)
156.	1856	Duchess of Argyll, figurehead for the yacht of Lord Dufferin	b	untraced		inf. PW-J
157.	nd	Tortoises (supporting urns)	b	Kingston Lacy, Dorset (NT)		C Lib (repr)

MARS, W, of Yarm fl 1835?

He is known only for one large Hellenic monument (1).

Funerary Monuments

1.	?1835	Mary Langley	Greatham, Durham	S	*Gunnis* 1968, 254

MARSDEN, James fl –1741–66

He was responsible for two chimneypieces at Holkham (1). A John Marsden, perhaps a relative, lived in Titchfield-Street, Marylebone, and worked for **James Lovell**. He gave evidence in September 1766 in the trial of another of Lovell's employees, Thomas Austin, for the theft of a piece of Siena marble.

Archival References: POB 1674-1834, t17660903-20

Chimneypieces

1.	pre-1741	Two	Holkham Hall, Norfolk, library and sitting room	Pevsner, *Norfolk: N W & S*, 1999, 419

MARSH, of Bristol and Ross fl 1776

The fine monument erected in 1776 to John Kyrle is signed 'Marsh of Ross.' Writing in 1799, Heath described its creator as 'Mr Marsh, Statuary, in Bristol' (1). It is executed in coloured marbles with a medallion portrait, and 'is so good that it gives the impression of being London, rather than local, work' (*Gunnis* 1968, 254).

Funerary Monuments

1.	1776	John Kyrle, the 'Man of Ross' (†1724)	St Mary, Ross-on-Wye, Herefs	S	*Heath* 1799, 34; Pevsner, *Herefs*, 1963, 278

MARSH, T, of London fl 1820?–c1854

His premises were at 20 New Road, where he produced a large number of monumental tablets. These included a tablet in a Gothic surround (1), another in the form of a Roman altar (12) and a polychrome wall monument (18). His memorials, 'though pleasant, are not very distinguished,' the best being that to Barbara Murphy (3) which takes the form of an amphora set in a niche, and to Hannah Allcroft (9), which has a figure of a mourning woman.

Literary References: *Dale-Jones and Lloyd* 1989, 55

Funerary Monuments

1.	†1845	Elizabeth Weyland	Woodrising, Norfolk		Pevsner, *Norfolk: N W & S*, 1999, 786
2.	?1820	Brampton Dillingham	Cranworth, Norfolk	S	*Gunnis* 1968, 254

3.	?1822	Barbara Murphy	St Mary, Paddington, London		*Gunnis* 1968, 254
4.	post-1822	Weyland family	Woodrising, Norfolk		Pevsner, *Norfolk: N W & S*, 1999, 786
5.	?1825	John Cope	St Paul, Birmingham	S	*Gunnis* 1968, 254
6.	†1827	James Wildman	Much Hadham, Herts	S	*Gunnis* 1968, 254
7.	†1828	Barwell Browne and family members	St George, Esher, Surrey		*Gunnis* 1968, 254
8.	†1828	Jacob Bosanquet (designed by T W Atkinson)	Broxbourne, Herts	S	*Gunnis* 1968, 254; Pevsner, *Herts*, 1977, 114
9.	†1831	Hannah Allcroft	St Peter the Great, Worcester		*Gunnis* 1968, 254; Pevsner, *Worcs*, 1968, 321
10.	†1835	Frances Woodhouse	St George, Esher, Surrey	S	
11.	†1836	1st Countess of Glengall	Cahir, Co Tipperary		*Potterton* 1975, 72
12.	†1837	Abel Gower	Cilgerran, Pembrokes		*Dale-Jones and Lloyd* 1989, 55
13.	?1838	William Vawdry	Gwinear, Cornwall	S	*Gunnis* 1968, 254
14.	c1840	Morgan Morgans	Llandovery, Carmarthen		*Dale-Jones and Lloyd* 1989, 55
15.	?1840	Thomas Farrer	Holy Trinity, Brompton, London	S	GPC
16.	?1841	Louisa King, large classical altar tomb	Ambrosden, Oxon, churchyard	S	GPC
17.	?1842	Captain William Tucker	East Wickham, Kent	S	*Gunnis* 1968, 254
18.	c1842	Nicholas Spencer (†1783) (designed by L B Lamb)	Ifield, Sussex	S	Pevsner, *Sussex*, 1965, 207
19.	†1842	Rev S J Lewin (designed by L B Lamb)	Ifield, Sussex	S	Pevsner, *Sussex*, 1965, 207
20.	?1844	Rebecca Cotton	Adderbury, Oxon	S	*Gunnis* 1968, 254
21.	†1845	Sir Thomas Foxwell Buxton	Overstrand, Norfolk	S	Pevsner, *Norfolk: N E & Norwich*, 1997, 632
22.	?1850	William King	Amblecote, Staffs	S	GPC
23.	†1852	William Hawkesworth	Barbados Cathedral, Bridgetown	S	
24.	†1854	Henry Hopkins	Christchurch Priory, Hants		RG/JP, 5, 897

MARSHALL, Edward 1597/98–1675

He was a successful mason-sculptor with a long and varied career. Nothing is known of his father's profession, but Marshall was apprenticed through the Masons' Company of London to John Clarke, who was probably responsible for building Lincoln's Inn chapel. He was made free of the Masons' Company in January 1627, joined the Livery in 1631, served as a warden in 1643 and became master in 1650. He married Anne James, who was almost certainly the daughter of the 'tomb maker', Isaac James, on 26 June 1627 at St Martin-in-the-Fields, Westminster. Early in 1629 the couple moved from Westminster to St Dunstan-in-the-West in the City of London where Marshall took a workshop apparently vacated by another mason-sculptor, Francis Grigs. He later moved to Pink's Alley, off Fetter Lane and then to Whitefriars, near Whitefriars Stairs, where in 1668 he took a 51 year lease on the site where he had been living and where he undertook to rebuild the houses destroyed by the Great Fire. There was a secondary home at Barn-Elms, Surrey, which, with its pleasant walks by the Thames side and its 'spring water brought to the house in leaden pipes', he advertised as being to let in 1659 (GPC). The inscription on Marshall's monument in St Dunstan-in-the-West relates that he and his wife Anne had 15 children, including **Joshua Marshall**, the eldest and the only one to survive him. It also proclaims his loyalty to the monarchy and established religion and his generosity to the poor of his parish. Anne died in 1673 and Marshall took a second wife, Margaret, who outlived him and was named in his will.

Marshall was a versatile artist. His earliest recorded works are all carved church monuments, but he is also known to have engraved at least one monumental brass (**3**) and was paid in 1644 for altering the inscriptions on several brasses in the parish of St Dunstan's. He worked as a mason-contractor under the architect John Webb at The Vyne, Hampshire between 1654 and 1656, where he built the portico, carved capitals, pilasters and a coat or arms and supplied ten chimneypieces in marble and stone (**25, 26**). He also worked as mason-contractor at Northumberland House, Strand, 1655–57, at Syon House, Middlesex in 1656, and at Gunnersbury House, Middlesex in 1658. In 1661–62 he was employed as architect for his church, St Dunstan's, which was extensively repaired and partly rebuilt under his direction. In 1662 he was one of those consulted by the vestry of St Martin-in-the-Fields about rebuilding the tower. He designed the new front and supervised the rebuilding of Aynho Park in Northants, c1660, a dramatic edifice with a tall, three-storey central block, and provided a design for a gallery in Aynho church.

Ten signed or documented monuments by 'Mr Marshall' survive (**3, 4, 6–10, 14, 15, 18**). Another five are merely signed 'Marshall' or documented as by 'Marshall', but the date of death of the persons commemorated argues against the authorship of either Joshua Marshall or the obscure John Marshall, who flourished in the 1650s (**11, 13, 20, 21, 24**). Three more are credited to Marshall on the testimony of the biographer, John Aubrey, who recorded obtaining the texts to be inscribed on the monuments from 'Mr Marshall' or 'Mr Marshall in Fetter-Lane' (**12, 16, 18**). Another 27 have been convincingly attributed to him by Adam White, largely on stylistic grounds (*White* 1999, 86–89, 92–94).

Marshall's monuments reflect the changing fashions of his day. The more conservative make use of heavily painted effigies and flamboyant heraldic motifs, but others incorporate classical references learnt, at least in part, from the work of Nicholas Stone (c1586–1647), master mason to the Crown, who had trained in Amsterdam and become conversant with European trends. His first securely dated monument, to the poet Michael Drayton, 1631, in Westminster Abbey, was commissioned by a prominent aristocrat, the Countess of Dorset, which suggests that Marshall already had a reputation at that date (**4**). The portrait bust reflects a knowledge of antique sculpture, for it is crowned with laurels and has a cloak draped *all'antica* over the jerkin. Several large figural works followed in the later 1630s. The memorial to George, Earl of Totnes at Stratford (**2**) is unsigned, but a contemporary, the antiquarian William Dugdale, noted in his diary in 1653 that it was the work of 'Mr. Marshall in Fetter-lane'. Marshall used the well-tried formula of a recumbent effigy with hands joined in prayer under an arched canopy, but added classical motifs. Whinney has described the small allegorical figures on the monument as 'clumsy cousins' of Stone's Virtues on monuments from the second decade of the 17th century. She suggests that the rosettes in coffered panels under the arch are such ill-understood quotations that they are 'almost Gothic pendants' and that the painted effigies and heraldic ornaments give the monument 'the gay but coarse effect typical of Jacobean tombs' (*Whinney* 1988, 80).

The near-contemporary monument to Lady Culpeper (7) is another recumbent effigy on a tomb-chest, but posed in more naturalistic manner, one finely carved hand resting on her breast and the other on her cloak. The textures of contrasting fabrics and particularly the folds of the dress and cloak proclaim a carver confident with marble. The effigy's pose is similar to that of Stone's monument to Lady Carey at Stowe-nine-churches, carved nearly twenty years earlier. Marshall's monument to Henry Curwen is more inventive (8). The composition again owes debts to Stone's work for it has tabernacle doors opened by angels to reveal a standing shrouded effigy, reminiscent of Stone's famous figure of John Donne in St Paul's Cathedral. Curwen's stance, however is novel: he stands with one foot resting on a skull, his head turned over the weight-bearing leg, his torso twisted in an ambitious *contrapposto* pose. The architectural frame, with its complex pediment is typical of Marshall's work.

For a number of other monuments sent out largely to country seats over the period 1639–51, Marshall reverted to familiar compositional formulae. The memorials to Thomas Playters and Francis Williamson both present figures kneeling at prayer (9, 10), while the Mary Barkham and Bridget Howe have two upright half-length effigies set in a recess, with their kneeling children beneath and much heraldry above (14, 15). The Barkham appears to be a naturalistic representation of a domineering woman and her timid husband. The monument to Lady Selby, another work identified through the writings of John Aubrey, has a coarsely cut bust flanked by curtains pulled back by angels, to reveal small relief figures of *Time* and *Death*. There is a detailed representation of an embroidery by the deceased in the background (12). The Verney (18), a large standing monument, presents four stiff portrait busts in oval niches flanking a central draped inscription tablet. Verney was Charles I's elderly standard-bearer at Edgehill. Two other monuments to distinguished men, the architect Inigo Jones and the anatomist, William Harvey, have or had portrait busts and inscriptions noted by John Aubrey (16, 22). Inigo Jones's monument was damaged during the Great Fire, after which Marshall salvaged the bust and other elements and took them home for safe-keeping. Later they disappeared.

The post of master mason to the Crown had been vacant since the death of Nicholas Stone in 1647. At the Restoration two rivals, Stone's son, **John Stone**, and Edward Marshall both sought the position. In his petition Marshall professed to have 'constantly endeavoured to promote His Majesty's interest in the late Common Council', a claim challenged by Stone who countered that Marshall was 'a Pretender . . . who in no kind served Your Majestie' (Cal State Papers Domestic 1660–1, 13, quoted by *Colvin* 1995, 641). Marshall, who was better equipped for the office, since his rival had recently suffered a stroke, was successful. He resigned as master mason in 1673 in favour of his son, Joshua. Edward died on 10 December 1675 and was buried in St Dunstan-in-the-West with his first wife. His daughter-in-law, Joshua's widow, eventually commissioned a memorial tablet celebrating father and son.

Marshall is known to have taken six apprentices under the auspices of the Masons' Company. These do not include his son, Joshua, although the latter almost certainly trained with his father. Henry Boughton is known to have had a workshop of his own before the Restoration and **Thomas Burman** established himself as an independent artist. Nothing is known of three others, Francis and William Harper, and a late-comer, Henry Turner, who began his training elsewhere and was turned over to Marshall in 1671.

Marshall left his son Joshua 'the ground I hold by lease from the Master of the Rolls, with all moveable goods on the said ground'. He also made bequests to his second wife, his son Edward (who must have died after his father made his will) and a son-in-law, Henry Parker.

IR

Literary References: *Knoop and Jones* 1935, 34; *Esdaile* 1943, 1094–5; *Gunnis* 1968, 254; *Whinney* 1988, 80–5, 437, n53; *Wood* 1993, 55–80; *Colvin* 1995, 641; *Bailey* 1996, 9; *Howard* 1998, 50–52; *White* 1999, 61, 83–95; *Webb* 1999, 33

Archival References: GPC

Will: PROB 11/349/128

Funerary Monuments

1.	†1625	Katherine Gildredge and two infant children	St Mary, Eastbourne, Sussex	S	
2.	†1629	George, Earl of Totnes	Holy Trinity, Stratford-on-Avon, Warks		*Whinney* 1988, 80; *White* 1999, 88
3.	†1629	Sir Edward Filmer and his wife (†1638), brass	East Sutton, Kent	S	*Physick* 1969, 12; *White* 1999, 84, 91 nn16, 17
4.	1631	Michael Drayton (†1631)	Westminster Abbey, London, south transept		*MacMichael* 1977, 94; *White* 1999, 85, 91 nn 42, 43
5.	*c*1635	Members of the Oxenham family	Untraced		*White* 1999, 85, 92 nn51, 52
6.	†1637	Henry Saunders	St Mary Magdalene, Canterbury, Kent	S	*White* 1999, 84, 91 nn18, 19
7.	†1638	Elizabeth, Lady Culpeper	Hollingbourne, Kent	S	*Gunnis* 1968, 254 (repr XVI); *Whinney* 1988, 81; *White* 1999, 84, 91 nn24, 25
8.	1638	Henry Curwen	Amersham, Bucks	SD	*Whinney* 1988, 81, 437 n51; *White* 1999, 84, 91 nn20, 21
9.	†1638	Thomas Playters	Sotterley, Suffolk	S	*Whinney* 1988, 437 n53
10.	1639	Francis Williamson and family	Walkeringham, Notts	SD	Pevsner, *Notts*, 1979, 362; *Whinney* 1988, 437 n53; *White* 1999, 84, 91 nn26, 27
11.	†1640	Richard Braham (†1619) and his wife (†1640) (signed 'Marshall')	St John the Baptist, Windsor, Berks	S	ATTRIB *White* 1999, 85, 91 nn38, 39
12.	†1642	Dorothy, Lady Selby (by 'Mr Marshall' according to John Aubrey)	Ightham, Kent		ATTRIB *Esdaile* 1943, 1094; *Whinney* 1988, 437 n53; *White* 1999, 86, 88, 93 nn 86, 87
13.	†1643	Edith Bostock (signed 'Marshall')	St John the Baptist, Windsor, Berks	S	ATTRIB *White* 1999, 85, 91 nn40, 41
14.	†1644	Lady Mary Barkham (†1644) and her husband Sir Robert	All Hallows, Tottenham, Haringay, London	S	*Whinney* 1988, 83–4 (repr); *White* 1999, 84, 91 nn28, 29

15.	1651	Bridget Howe (†1642) and her husband John (†1670)	Withington, Glos	SD	*White* 1999, 84, 91 nn30, 31; Pevsner, *Glos: Cotswolds*, 1999, 741
16.	†1652	Inigo Jones by ('Mr Marshall in Fetter-Lane' according to John Aubrey)	[St Benet Paul's Wharf, City of London]; destroyed		ATTRIB *White* 1999, 86, 89, 93 nn109, 110
17.	†1652	Lucy, Lady Nethersole	Polesworth, Warks	S	*White* 1999, 84, 91 nn33, 34
18.	1653	Sir Ralph Verney, his wife and parents	Middle Claydon, Bucks		*Stone* 1955–6, 67; *Whinney* 1988, 83, 437 n50; *White* 1999, 85, 91, nn44, 45
19.	†1654	Elizabeth Delves	St Mary, Horsham, Sussex		Pevsner, *Sussex*, 1965, 244; *White* 1999, 89
20.	*c*1655	John Selden, wall tablet and gravestone (documented as by 'Mr Marshall') Payment(s): £100	[Temple Church, London]; destroyed		ATTRIB *White* 1999, 85, 91–92 nn46–48
21.	1655	Sir Robert Cotton Bt (by 'Mr Marshall')	Conington, Cambs	S	ATTRIB *White* 1999, 85, 92 nn49, 50
22.	†1657	Dr William Harvey (by 'Mr Marshall' acc John Aubrey)	Hempstead, Essex		ATTRIB *White* 1999, 86, 89, 93 nn128, 129
23.	†1659	Sir Thomas Playters Bt (†1638) and his two wives	Sotterley, Suffolk	S	*Whinney* 1988, 437; *White* 1999, 84, 91 nn22, 23
24.	†1666	Mrs Nazareth Pagett (†1666), her second husband Zephaniah Sayers (†1628) and her first and third husbands (signed 'Marshall')	St John the Baptist, Windsor, Berks	S	ATTRIB *Gunnis* 1968, 254; *White* 1999, 85, 91 nn35–37
Chimneypieces					
25.	1656	Two white marble, six Portland stone, one 'Italian raunce' and another (designed by John Webb) Payment(s): £121	The Vyne, Hants		*Gunnis* 1968, 254; *Howard* 1998 30, 51 (repr)
Architectural Sculpture					
26.	1656	Coat of arms and architectural ornaments Payment(s): £3 (coat of arms), £13 (capitals), £11 (pilasters)	The Vyne, Hants, portico		*Gunnis* 1968, 254; *Howard* 1998, 4, 52
27.	1666	Large carved pedestal	[Northumberland House, Charing Cross]; untraced		GPC

MARSHALL, James W fl 1827–38

In October 1829 a special exhibition of sculpture by Marshall was held at 31 Andrew Square, Edinburgh. The exhibits included portraits of Napoleon and Lord Byron and a group of three figures illustrating *Willie Brew'd a Peck o' Maut*, a song by Robert Burns (**3, 4, 1**). The bust of Napoleon was 'executed under the immediate superintendence of Dr. Stroke who had the honour of attending the Emperor at St. Helena – assisted by a correct cast taken by Dr. Antomarchi immediately after death.' It was the bust of Byron which most appealed to a reviewer in the *Scotsman* of 28 October 1829 who wrote: 'how nobly intellectual in character, how natural, how classic'. The sculptor lived at 43 William Street, Edinburgh. He exhibited at the Royal Institution for the Encouragement of the Fine Arts in Scotland and the Royal Scottish Academy and was awarded a prize for his group *Maternal instruction* by the Association for the Promotion of the Fine Arts in Scotland in 1838 (**2**).

Literary References: *Woodward* 1977 (vol 1, pt 2), 150

Statues				
1.	1829	Willie Brew'd a Peck o' Maut	[Exhib 31 St Andrew Square, Edinburgh]; untraced	*Woodward* 1977, vol 1, pt 2, 150
2.	1838	Maternal instruction	[Awarded RAPFAS prize]; untraced	*Woodward* 1977, vol 1, pt 2, 150
Busts				
3.	1829	George, Lord Byron	[Exhib 31 St Andrew Square, Edinburgh]; untraced	*Woodward* 1977, vol 1, pt 2, 150
4.	1829	Napoleon Buonaparte	[Exhib 31 St Andrew Square, Edinburgh]; untraced	*Woodward* 1977, vol 1, pt 2, 150
5.	1831	John Fraser	[Exhib R Sc A, Edinburgh, 360]; untraced	*Laperriere* 3, 1991, 237
6.	1831	John Langford Pritchard in the character of Mark Antony	[Exhib R Sc A, Edinburgh, 383]; untraced	*Laperriere* 3, 1991, 237
7.	1831	Rev Dr Dickson	[Exhib R Sc A, Edinburgh, 360]; untraced	*Laperriere* 3, 1991, 237
Reliefs				
8.	1838	The anointment of David	[Exhib R Sc A, Edinburgh, 422]; untraced	*Laperriere* 3, 1991, 235
Miscellaneous				
9.	1831	Virgin and child	[Exhib R Sc A, Edinburgh, 310]; untraced	*Laperriere* 3, 1991, 237
10.	1832	Unidentified gentleman	[Exhib R Sc A, Edinburgh, 337]; untraced	*Laperriere* 3, 1991, 237

MARSHALL, John D fl 1802–49

He worked on a number of projects with **Samuel Mackenzie** in the first two decades of the 19th century and can probably be identified with the John Marshall who owned a marble cutting business in Leith Walk, Edinburgh from 1801 until 1820, when it was taken over by **James Dalziel**. In the 1830s and 1840s Marshall exhibited from 10 Archibald Place, Edinburgh, an address shared with his nephew **William Calder Marshall** from 1832 to 1837 and in 1838 after William's return from Rome. In 1849 John Marshall had rooms in Abercromby Place.

Literary References: *Woodward* 1977, vol 1, pt 2, 151

Additional Manuscript Sources: *Mackenzie Reminiscences*

Statues				
1.	1800–1820	Sphinxes (co-sculptor: Samuel Mackenzie)	Charlotte Square, Edinburgh	*Woodward* 1977, vol 1, pt 2, 151
2.	1800–1820	Sphinxes (co-sculptor: Samuel Mackenzie)	Parliament Hill, Parliament Square, Edinburgh	*Woodward* 1977, vol 1, pt 2, 151
Architectural Sculpture				
3.	1802–1806	Central group and coat of arms (co-sculptor: Samuel Mackenzie)	Bank of Scotland, Bank Street, Edinburgh	*Woodward* 1977, vol 1, pt 2, 151
Reliefs				
4.	1838	Maternal instruction	[Exhib R Sc A, Edinburgh, 427]; untraced	*Laperriere* 3, 1991, 235

MARSHALL, Joshua 1628–78

He was the eldest son of **Edward Marshall**, from whom he probably received his training. He was baptised on 24 June 1628 at St Martin-in-the-Fields, Westminster, but appears to have spent most of his life living off Fetter Lane in the City of London, where he and his father shared responsibility for a property for a number of years. Joshua married Catharine, the daughter of John George, a Londoner, and they had five children, two of whom, Ann and Edward, survived their father.

Like his father, Marshall held office in the Masons' Company, where he was admitted to the livery in 1655 and served as a warden in 1665–66 and again in 1668–69. He became master in 1670 and had the distinction of serving a second term in 1677–78. In 1667 he succeeded **John Stone** as master mason at Windsor Castle and in 1673 became master-mason to the Crown on his father's retirement from that office. He carried out much work at the royal palaces.

Marshall appears to have had a large practice as a maker of church monuments, particularly before the Great Fire of 1666, after which he concentrated principally on building projects in the City. Only ten of his memorials from the pre-Fire period are signed or documented though another 56 have been attributed to him by Adam White on stylistic or circumstantial grounds (*White* 1999, 96–104). The earliest identified memorial appears to be to Richard Brownlow and was probably erected in the late 1640s (**1**). Marshall made use of one his father's compositional formulae, a half-length figure in a swagged architectural niche. Sir John Cullum, writing in 1774 to Gough the antiquary, noted that the bust had admirable vitality and the hands and draperies were finely rendered: 'in short it would be no discredit to any of our most modern artists' (*Nichols* 1812–15, VIII, 674, quoted by *Gunnis* 1968, 255). The monument to John Whatton and his two wives (**3**), which also owes debts to his father's work, has three frontal busts in hemispherical niches. The busts are similar in style to fifteen other monuments attributed by White to Joshua Marshall. Elizabeth Sherard's monument takes the form of an oval inscription panel with a border of bay leaves set in a scrolly cartouche, surmounted by an open-topped baroque pediment (**4**). This pattern was repeated with variations of detail on the monument to John Turner (**5**), and six of White's attributed memorials are very similar. Another recurring formula makes use of a panel architrave with a segmental top surmounted by diminutive pediments and indented along the lower edge to make room for a winged cherub's head. The first recorded instance of its use is on the monument to Sir John Gore, it appears also on the near-contemporary monument to Henry Hammond and then a decade later on Richard Hale's memorial (**6, 7, 12**). The quirky composition is repeated on eleven other undocumented monuments listed by White.

There are doubts about authorship of the monument to Lady Frances Kniveton and Lady Anne Holbourne, *c*1663, which has been altered, but originally featured two shrouded full-length effigies under a pediment with mantling supported by two boys (**8**). It may possibly be the work of Edward Marshall, who was responsible for several memorials with figures in winding sheets, but it is conceivable that another, unidentified sculptor named Marshall was responsible. Holbourne's will has a codicil stating that she has contracted for the work with 'Mr Marshall a stonecutter in Shoe Lane' for a sum of £120 (FRC PROB 11/312/108, quoted by *Gunnis* 1968, 255). White notes that Shoe Lane is some way to the east of Fetter Lane, where the Marshalls worked (*White* 1999, 105, n2). Joshua Marshall was certainly responsible for another monument with shrouded figures, to Viscount Campden (**10**). He again borrowed from his father's work in presenting an open-doored sepulchre framing swathed standing figures. The doors of the monument were originally hinged. The contract for one of his last monuments, to a member of the Strangways family of Melbury, 1672, stipulates that Joshua Marshall, 'tombmaker of St Dunstan in the West', would, for the sum of £300, provide an architectural monument of the Corinthian order, 'with Capitals and Bosses and Archatrave and ffrieze', containing two tablets of white marble. It was to be topped by mantling with helmet and crest (Agreement between Giles Strangways IV and JM, Dorset RO D/FSI box 233ii, 1672). This can be identified with the monument to Sir John Strangways and family, part of which survives in the church (**13**). It was described in 1863 as being 'a stately monument of white marble with a canopy under which was a shield bearing the Strangways arms' (*Hutchins*). All that remains is the upper inscription in its immediate ornamental surround, surmounted by an open pediment with the coat of arms, the whole being raised on a bracket (inf. Adam White).

Marshall's work as a sculptor was not confined to monuments. During the 1660s he provided three or four chimneypieces for the Queen's House, Greenwich, which was enlarged for Charles II and Catherine of Braganza in 1661–62 (**18**), a considerable number for the Palace of Whitehall, destroyed in the fire of 1691 (**19–27**) and one for the presence chamber at St James's Palace (**36**). He also began to be employed regularly by the Crown as a mason. He worked at Horse Guards in 1663–64, at Whitehall 1666–67, where he received £465 for 'ye front next ye Thames' in 1666 (PRO Works 5/7 quoted by *Gunnis* 1968, 255) and at Greenwich Palace, where he worked as master mason with **John Young** from 1664–69 and was responsible with Young for the central portion of the building and the north pavilion. The itemised accounts record payments for foliate and egg and anchor ornaments to enrich the entrance arches of the east vestibule, as well as quantities for Portland stone for paving and other needs (TNA, A.1 2487/357 fol 3). Marshall alone provided figures of *Fortitude* and *Dominion of the sea* for the east pediment and *Mars* and *Fame* for the north pediment (**31**). Payments were made for scaffolding for the carvers. The four pediment figures were carved in a nearby shed, which had to be removed when they were ready to be set in position.

In his office as master mason at Windsor Castle, Marshall was involved in a continuous programme of work during the years 1674–78, during which period he was paid £10,545. He also worked at Hampton Court, where the King's first major project was the alignment of the long canal on the east front. The contract for masons' work at the ends of the canal went to Marshall in 1668 and it took six years to complete.

He must have employed a large work-force, for he was extensively involved in the City's rebuilding programme and handled large sums over a period of 17 years. He rebuilt or helped rebuild six of the City churches, largely under the supervision of Sir Christopher Wren: they were St Mary, Aldermanbury, 1670–86 (£3,190), St Stephen, Coleman Street, 1674–81 (£2,160), St Peter, Cornhill, 1677–87 (£741), St Mary-at-Hill, 1670–76 (£1,928), the tower of St Clement Dane's, 1682 (£2,525) and St Bride's, Fleet Street, 1670–84. His work at St Bride's brought in £8,964 between 1670 and 1684 (**35**). He was also employed at St Swithun's from 1677, but died before the building was finished and the payments were made to his executors **Henry Phillips** and **John Oliver** on 18 March 1680. In 1674 he began work as one of the mason contractors at St Paul's Cathedral, responsible initially for laying foundation walls. He was still working in the choir in 1678 at the time of his death, when he was due the sum of £2,391.

His secular commissions included the London Custom House, 1669 (**33**) and Temple Bar, the latter built with **Thomas Knight** in 1670 (£700). Both were designed by Wren. Marshall was the master mason for the Monument to the Great Fire, working under Wren and the architect Robert Hooke, a project that was delayed, according to Wren's son, by the difficulty Marshall experienced in obtaining stone of an appropriate size and shape. Over a four year period Marshall handled payments of more than £11,000 (Guildhall restoration, 8 April 1671–30 June 1675). Hooke mentions dining several times at London taverns with Marshall in 1673, on one occasion with **Abraham Storey** and on another with **C G Cibber**. On the second occasion Hooke noted 'Marshall plaid the Knave and conspird against me' (*Robinson and Adams* 1935, 66). He also worked out of London. He quoted for repairs to Rochester Cathedral in 1667 and was active at Bromley College, Kent, in 1670–72, where he provided the centrepiece for the colonnade in the quadrangle.

In October 1673 Marshall succeeded his father as master mason to the king, a life appointment. In 1675 he made the pedestal for Hubert le Sueur's statue of King Charles I at Charing Cross (**34**) and was commissioned by the King to provide a simple monument in memory of the 'Little Princes in the Tower', completed in 1678 (**17**). This too was designed by Wren. Marshall died shortly afterwards, on 6 April 1678. He was buried with his father and family members at St Dunstan-in-the-West in the City, where his widow raised a wall tablet to father and son, provided by the workshop. After Marshall's death Robert Hooke tried to help his widow get the money owing to her husband for work on the City churches. Marshall's probate inventory lists among other items in his yard, twenty-nine marble grave stones, five of 'purbeck and Irish', '4 Marble boyes sitting upon scroles unfinished', '2 little monuments', a large quantity of marble and other blocks and tables, marble heads and relief figures and '1 monument for ye princes Bones in ye Tower'. In the closet at the lower end of the yard were twenty-one capitals, five marble sets, '3 Reames of Drawinge paper and other Lumber' (PRO PROB 4/12829).

The workshop seems to have struggled on for a short period after his death. Few of his assistants have been identified and none had an independent reputation. William Springett became his clerk on 24 November 1664, John Marshall, the son of a glover, became an apprentice in 1668 and James Hutchinson in 1676.

Joshua Marshall's epitaph records that 'hee walked in ye steps of his father & succeeded not only in his office but vertues'. The link to Edward Marshall is appropriately made, for Joshua's success as a sculptor and mason-contractor owed much to his father's reputation. He is not remembered for any novel departures in funerary sculpture, but was evidently an able businessman, who benefited from the City's pressing need for competent masons in the 1670s.

IR

Literary References: *Weaver* 1915, 16–20; *Knoop and Jones* 1935, 35; *Robinson and Adams*, 1935, 30, 36, 66, 96, 120; *Gunnis* 1968, 254–6; *Colvin* V, 1973–76 *passim*; *Whinney* 1988, 135; *Colvin* 1995, 641; *White* 1999, 95–106; *Webb* 1999, 18, 31

Archival References: Lic Vic Gen, Feb 5, 1668/9; BM Harleian MS, 1618 fol 50, 55, 62, 95 (chimneypieces for Whitehall); TNA WORK 5/9 fol 298, 328, 329, 332, 335 (building work at Whitehall); TNA E 101/475/2 (2 payments totalling £1,500 for building work at the Monument, Sept and Oct 1674); Westminster Public Library MS B 13/A (tower of St Clement Dane's); Bodleian Rawlinson MSS, B 387 fol 235 (building work at St Swithin's); Rochester Cathedral Archives D 236 (estimate for repairs, £592 Masons' Co, Masters and Wardens, 1677; 10s); Guildhall restoration, 1670–1675, 30r (Temple Bar); City Lands, Rough Minutes 03/001 (warrant, 11 Nov 1672, for £400 for the 'Column Fishstreet-hill'. Further £400 granted 29 Jan 1673).

Additional MS Sources: PRO, Works 5/12 (chimneypieces and paving, Volary Building, Whitehall Palace); PRO Works 5/4 (chimneypiece and other work at St James's Palace); PRO Works 5/2 and 5/3 (chimneypieces at the Queen's House); PRO Works 5/9, April 1666; Works 5/9, Feb 1667 (building work at the Queen's House) PRO Works 5/149, p 9, Works 5/23, Oct 1674 (Hampton Court, Canal); PRO AO 1/2492/397 (enrolled account, London Custom House); PRO AO 1/2478/270 (E 351/3450) (building work, Windsor Castle): PRO Works 5/25, Extraord (pedestal for the statue of Charles I); PRO Works 5/30, fol 187 (Princes in the Tower monument)

Will: PROB 11/356/36

Funerary Monuments

1.	post-1641	Richard Brownlow (†1638)	a	Belton, Lincs	S	*Gunnis* 1968, 255; *White* 1999, 95, 96, 101 nn16, 17
2.	†1649	Sir John Backhouse		Swallowfield, Berks	S	*White* 1999, 95, 101 nn18, 19
3.	†1657	John Whatton (†1657) and his two wives		Leicester Cathedral	S	*Whinney* 1988, 135; *White* 1999, 95, 96, 101 nn20, 21
4.	†1659	Elizabeth Sherard		N Witham, Lincs	S	*Lord* 1986 (2), 1, 50; *White* 1999, 95, 96, 101 nn22, 23
5.	†1659	John Turner (†1643) and his wife		Kirkleatham, N R Yorks	S	*White* 1999, 95, 96, 101–2, nn24, 25; C Lib (repr)
6.	†1659	Sir John Gore		Gilston, Herts	S	*White* 1999, 95, 96, 102, nn26, 27
7.	1661	Henry Hammond (†1660)		Hampton Lovett, Worcs	SD	*White* 1999, 95, 96, 102, nn28, 29; C Lib (repr)
8.	*c*1663	Lady Frances Kniveton († before 1645) and Lady Anne Holbourne (monument perhaps by Edward Marshall) Payment(s): £120		St Giles-in-the-Fields, Holborn, London		*Gunnis* 1968, 255; *Whinney* 1988, 83, 437 n48; *White* 1999, 104, 105 nn1–3
9.	1663	Sir Heneage Proby (†1663), gravestone Payment(s): £13		Amersham, Bucks, Chapel		Elton Hall MS 96; GPC

10. 1664	Edward, Viscount Campden (†1642) and wife		Chipping Campden, Glos	S	*Kemp* 1985, 24 (repr); *Whinney* 1988, 81, 135; *White* 1999, 95, 102 nn30, 31
11. 1666	John Warner, Bishop of Rochester (†1666) Payment(s): £120		Rochester Cathedral, Kent	SD	Pevsner, *Kent: W & Weald*, 1976, 483; *White* 1999, 95, 96, 102, nn32, 33; C Lib (repr)
12. *c*1671	Richard Hale		[St Dunstan-in-the-East, City of London]; Destroyed		*White* 1999, 96, 102, nn33, 34, 35
13. *c*1672	Sir John Strangways (†1666)		[Melbury Sampford, Dorset]; dismantled *c*1901		Fox-Strangways Papers, Dorset RO; *Hutchins* II, 3rd ed, 1863, 679); C Lib (repr)
14. 1675	Sir Orlando Bridgeman Bt		St Mary, Teddington, Surrey	S	*White* 1999, 96–97 102 nn36, 37
15. 1670–1675	William Cleave, ledger stone Payment(s): £8	s	All Saints, Kingston-upon-Thames, Surrey		*Gunnis* 1968, 255; *White* 1999, 105, nn4,5
16. 1678	Catherine, Lady Leveson		St Mary, Warwick		*White* 1999, 96, 102, nn40, 41
17. 1678	King Edward V and Richard, Duke of York (†1483) (designed by Sir Christopher Wren)		Westminster Abbey, London, Henry VII's Chapel		Pevsner, *London I*, 1973, 441; *Colvin* 1973–76, V, 455 n7; *White* 1999, 96, 102, nn38, 39
Chimneypieces					
18. 1661–1662	Three, of marble, perhaps including one of 'enriched' white marble for the King's Bedchamber Payment(s): £78 (for three)		Queen's House, Greenwich		*Colvin* V, 1973–1976, 145–6
19. 1664	'of Italian . . . marble with a rich moulding'		[Whitehall Palace, London, Duke of York's bedchamber]; destroyed		MS Harleian 1618 fol 50
20. 1664	'white and Egyptian marble'	m	[Whitehall Palace, London, 'Mada (?) Steward's lodging']; destroyed		BM Harleian 1618 fo 62; *Gunnis* 1968, 255
21. 1664	'wrought after the Italian fashion . . . with a deep moulding'	s	[Whitehall Palace, London, Duke of York's closet]; destroyed		BM Harleian 1618, fo 95; *Gunnis* 1968, 255
22. ?1664–1667	Character unknown Payment(s): 15 gns		[Whitehall Palace, London, Miss Howard's lodgings]; destroyed		*Gunnis* 1968, 255
23. ?1664–1667	Egyptian marble	m	[Whitehall Palace, London, 'Queen's new closet']; destroyed		BM Harleian 1618 fo 55; *Gunnis* 1968, 255
24. *c*1667	Several, and paving		[Whitehall Palace, volary building]; destroyed		*Colvin* V, 1973–76, 270
25. ?1664–1667	Two		[Whitehall Palace, London, Duke of Monmouth's bedchamber and closet]; destroyed		*Gunnis* 1968, 255
26. ?1664–1667	White marble Payment(s): £17 5s	m	[Whitehall Palace, London, Countess of Castlemaine's lodgings]; destroyed		*Gunnis* 1968, 255 quoting PRO Works 5/10
27. 1668	'clean white marble' Payment(s): £16	m	[Whitehall Palace, London, 'Queen's little bedchamber']; destroyed		*Gunnis* 1968, 255 quoting PRO Works 5/145
28. 1671–1672	White marble	m	[Somerset House, London, Queen's Tribune]; untraced		*Colvin* V, 1973–76, 257
29. 1671–1674	Several, including one of black marble for the Council Chamber	m	[Custom House, London]; untraced		TNA AOI, 2492/397; *Gunnis* 1968, 255
Architectural Sculpture					
30. 1665–1667	Carved work including 'two capitals carved for 3 quarter coulmns' (£36) and 'flower stands over the keystones of the windows wrought with abacus moulding' (co-sculptor: John Young)		Greenwich Palace, London		TNA WORK 5/9 f332
31. 1664–1669	Pediment figures of Fortitude, Dominion of the Sea, Mars and Fame, and other decorative ornaments Payment(s): £18 each for capitals		Greenwich Palace, London, central portion of the building		*Gunnis* 1968, 255; *Colvin* V 1973–76, 148–9; *Bold* 2000 (2) 47 (repr)
32. 1670	Coat of arms		Cleaves Almshouses, Kingston upon Thames, Surrey		Pevsner, *London: S*, 1983, 318
33. 1671–1674	Carved work, including shields of arms and Ionic capitals Payment(s): £1,839		[Custom House, London]; untraced		TNA, AOI, 2492/397
34. 1675	Pedestal for Hubert le Sueur's statue of King Charles I, with shields, arms and trophies Payment(s): £230		Trafalgar Square, London, south side		*Gunnis* 1968, 255; *Colvin* V, 1973–76, 284; GPC
35. nd	Ten heads of cherubim, 12 shields and other ornaments		St Bride, Fleet Street, City of London		*Gunnis* 1968, 255
Miscellaneous					
36. 1663	Large Portland stone chimneypiece and a black marble table and cornice		[St James's Palace, London, Duke of York's Presence Chamber]; untraced		*Colvin* V, 1973–76, 235
37. 1678	Tablet recording Lady Katherine Leveson's benefactions to St Mary, Warwick Payment(s): £20		St Mary, Warwick		GPC

MARSHALL, of Blandford fl *c*1840

Funerary Monuments

1. †1840	Dorothy (†1835) and Thomas Rackett		Spetisbury, Dorset	S	

MARSHALL, R fl *c*1824–43?

He was in partnership with **James Wallis, of Newark**. Together they sign a number of tablets (listed in the entry for his partner). Marshall erected a large tomb to Wallis after the latter's death on 6 January 1824 (1), and continued the business.

Literary References: *Gunnis* 1968, 411

Funerary Monuments

1.	†1824	James Wallis, of Newark	Newark, Notts, churchyard		*Gunnis* 1968, 411
2.	†1826	William Ashton	Hough-on-the-Hill, Lincs		Pevsner, *Lincs*, 1989, 400
3.	†1831	Slingsby Duncombe	Langford, Notts	S	*Gunnis* 1968, 411; Pevsner, *Notts*, 1979, 163
4.	?1843	James and Mary Dyson	Newark, Notts	S	*Gunnis* 1968, 411

MARSHALL, T and G, of Deptford fl 1790–1832

They were among several masonry firms and minor statuaries, working from Deptford in the late 18th and early 19th centuries. Their earlier tablets have 'delightful details' (*Gunnis* 1968, 254).

Funerary Monuments

1.	*c*1790	Rayley family	Lee, Kent, churchyard	S	*Gunnis* 1968, 256
2.	?1790	William Board	Lindfield, Sussex	S	*Gunnis* 1968, 256
3.	?1809	Harriot Kruse	St Mary, Lewisham, London	S	*Gunnis* 1968, 256
4.	?1811	Oliver Stapleton	St Mary, Ealing, Middx	S	*Gunnis* 1968, 256
5.	?1816	Elizabeth Bland	Isleworth Parish Church, Middx	S	*Gunnis* 1968, 256
6.	?1831	Countess Winterton	Westerham, Kent	S	*Gunnis* 1968, 256
7.	?1832	Stephen Groombridge	Goudhurst, Kent	S	*Gunnis* 1968, 256

MARSHALL, W, of London fl 1817?–1828?

He signed a number of tablets, one of which was illustrated in the *Gentleman's Magazine* (4). The monument to Alexander Baron has a relief profile portrait (2). Marshall had yards in Westminster and Regent Street and although he was declared bankrupt in early 1821 he continued working for some years after that date.

Literary References: *New Monthly Mag* 1821, 3, 84; *Gunnis* 1968, 256

Funerary Monuments

1.	?1817	Captain Fothergill	St Paul's Walden, Herts	S	*Gunnis* 1968, 256
2.	†1819	Alexander Baron	First Presbyterian Church, Charleston, South Carolina, USA	S	*Hershey* 1970, 802 (repr)
3.	?1822	Sir John Silvester	Chingford, Essex	S	*Gunnis* 1968, 256
4.	?1828	Dr John Shaw	Magdalen College Chapel, Oxford	S	*GM* 1828, 1, 209 (repr); *Gunnis* 1968, 256

MARSHALL, William Calder RA 1813–94

Calder Marshall was a highly-regarded and prolific sculptor of poetic subjects. He was born in Gilmour Place, Edinburgh on 18 March 1813, the eldest son of William Marshall, the founder of a firm of jewellers in Princes Street, and his wife Annie Calder. He was educated at Edinburgh High School and then the University, and began his study of art at the Trustees' Academy in 1830. In 1834 he moved to London where he received tuition from **Francis Chantrey** and **E H Baily** and at the Royal Academy Schools, winning a silver medal in 1835. He was in Rome, 1836–38, studying the antiquities and contemporary neo-classical works. There he came into contact with British sculptors resident in the city, including **John Gibson, Lawrence MacDonald** and **R J Wyatt**, and under their influence, began to sculpt classical subjects, such as *Hebe rejected* (10). He nonetheless received few commissions in Rome and had to rely on his family for support. He returned to Britain in 1838 when he worked in Edinburgh for a short time before settling permanently in London in 1839.

Marshall came to prominence in 1844 when he sent statues of *Eve* and Geoffrey Chaucer to the Westminster Hall exhibition (21, 22). They were favourably received and one writer suggested that the Chaucer stood 'pre-eminently above any other contribution' (*Lit Gaz*, 1435, 20 July 1844, 466). His success led to commissions for statues of the Earl of Clarendon and Lord Somers for the House of Lords (27, 53). He subsequently executed a statue of *Griselda*, a subject from Chaucer's *The Clerk's Tale*, for the Egyptian hall in the Mansion House. It is one of an important series of statues celebrating heroes and heroines of English literature by some of the most successful artists of the day (52).

In 1857 he was awarded first prize in the competition for a national monument to the Duke of Wellington to be erected in St Paul's Cathedral. His design was for a portrait statue flanked by allegories of *Peace* and *War*, with reliefs depicting the hero's great victories on the pedestal (4). Opinions of Marshall's model were divided; some writers commended the technical and formal aspects of the design, but the iconography was considered over-complex and irrelevant. One critic asked, 'What has *so much* allegory to do with the Duke of Wellington, the simplest and plainest hero that the English people ever knew?' (*'One of the People'* 1857; see *Physick* 1970, 170). The competition results were discredited when the judges' report revealed that, having no specialist architectural or artistic knowledge, they had not even attempted to assess the suitability of the designs for the proposed site and that Charles Robert Cockerell, the only architect on the panel, had disassociated himself from his colleagues' choice. The commission was eventually awarded to **Alfred Stevens**, but Marshall and the second prize winner, **W F Woodington**, provided a series of reliefs for walls of the chapel housing the memorial (152).

Marshall executed a number of public commemorative works, including a statue of Sir Robert Peel with two supporting allegorical figures for Manchester (44) and a seated figure of Edward Jenner, the scientist who pioneered vaccination, originally erected in Trafalgar Square but later moved to a less prominent site in Kensington Gardens (59). He provided Bolton, Lancs, with statues of Samuel Crompton and the 7th Earl of Derby, both important personalities in the commercial development and history of the town, and also carved a tympanum relief for the town hall (66, 74, 140). His best known public work is the group representing *Agriculture* for the Albert Memorial (72). Surprisingly, he received only one commission for a public work in his native Scotland (62) and was unsuccessful in the competition for the Scottish national monument to the Prince Consort, which was won by **Sir John Steell**.

Marshall was responsible for a number of funerary monuments and portrait busts but he was chiefly concerned with ideal, or poetic works. He depicted subjects from a wide range of sources, including Shakespeare, Milton, English history, the Bible and fairy tales as well as classical mythology. Stylistically these works were strongly influenced by the neoclassical sculpture he had seen early in his career in Rome, but they were also 'characteristically Victorian in their narrative interest and sentimental appeal' (*Grove* 20, 1996, 479). Many were engraved for the *Art Journal* and reproduced in parian ware by Copeland and other factories. Reductions of *Rebecca at the well, The broken pitcher* and *The first whisper of love* were commissioned as prizes by the Art Union of London (**11, 17, 24**).

He was a regular exhibitor at the Royal Scottish Academy, the Royal Academy and the British Institution from the 1830s onwards. Examples of his work were displayed at the Great Exhibition of 1851 (**26, 31, 37**), the Paris Exposition Universelle, 1855 (**45, 31, 17, 51**), The Crystal Palace, Sydenham, 1854 (**22, 24, 26, 31, 37**), the Manchester Art Treasures Exhibition in 1857 (**13, 17, 23, 30, 31**) and at the 1862 London International Exhibition (**13, 26, 27, 31, 33, 42, 66**). He was elected an associate of the Royal Scottish Academy in 1840, but relinquished this honour in 1844 in order to accept associate membership of the RA. He became an academician in 1852 and an honorary member of the Scottish Academy towards the end of his career. As an established sculptor he played an active public role: with others he signed letters to the press objecting to the chaotic and unfair way in which the Wellington Memorial competition was organised and to the publication of F T Palgrave's controversial *Handbook to the Fine Art Collections in the International Exhibition of 1862* under official sanction of the exhibition commissioners. He was appointed a *chevalier du Legion d' Honneur* in recognition of his work as a member of the royal commission representing British exhibitors at the Paris International Exhibition of 1878. Marshall was also on the panel of judges who selected Edward Onslow Ford as sculptor of the statue commemorating Sir Rowland Hill, erected in London in 1881.

Marshall died on 16 June 1894 after an illness of only a few months and was buried at Kensal Green cemetery, where his grave is marked by a red granite slab. He had resigned from the RA in 1890 and completed his last work in 1893 (**104**). Many of his sculptures were displayed after his death in his studio at 115, Ebury Street. Catalogues were printed in 1894 and 1895, which stated that a large number of these works could be purchased privately, for the sculptor had particularly requested that his works should not be auctioned. His executors donated several pieces to public collections.

William Sandby praised Marshall's works in his history of the RA, published in 1862, writing, 'The originality of his conceptions, his elegant taste, his power of rendering expression with truth and sweetness, and of modelling the human figure, arranging drapery, and working his materials, combine to render his productions beautiful in themselves and excellent as specimens of works of art' (*Sandby* II, 1862, 315). However, within a few years of his death J L Caw, in the *Dictionary of National Biography*, could find few points in his favour: 'His style was of his time, and pseudo-classicism in his hands was informed by no richness of fancy or real power of technique. A certain elegance of design and type and conscientiousness of execution are the greatest merits his art possesses' (DNB, suppl III, 1901, 145).

EH

Literary References: *Sandby* II, 1862, 314–5; *AJ*, 1894, 286; *Weekly Scotsman*, 23 June 1894 (obit); *DNB*, suppl III, 1901, 144–5 (Caw); *Gunnis* 1968, 256–7; *Physick* 1969, 41, 193; *Physick* 1970, *passim*; *Read* 1982, *passim*; *Grove* 20, 1996, 478–9 (Greenwood); *Curl* 2001, 243; *ODNB* (Greenwood)

Archival References: RA Premium List

Additional MS Sources: biographical notice, 1860, *Biography Handbook Papers*, Add 28511, f. 133; *Marshall Journals*; *Marshall Papers (1)*; *Marshall Papers (2)*; *Marshall/Smirke*; *Marshall/Stephens*; letter to Sir Robert Peel, 1846, *Peel Papers*, Add 40591 f129; letter, 1884, *Sherborn Autographs*, Add 42576 f198; coll of platinotype photos of the sculptor's work taken by his son, NGS

Will: PPR, 3 August 1894, effects £48,709 7s 4d

Studio Exhibition Catalogues: *Marshall* 1894; *Marshall* 1895

Portraits of the Sculptor and Studio Photographs: self-portrait, bust, plaster, *c*1838 (**107**); *Marshall Album* (portrait and views of the studio and images of works); P Allan-Fraser, oil painting, RSA 1856, Hospitalfield House, Arbroath; photo of the sculptor as an old man, Conway Lib; *Weekly Scotsman*, 23 June 1894; four photographic images, NPG (*Ormond and Rogers* ed, 1979–81, 138)

Funerary Monuments

1.	1848	Thomas Campbell		Westminster Abbey, London, south transept	SD	*Graves* V, 1905–6, 196; Pevsner, *London: 1*, 1973, 444
2.	1849	'Model of a monument to William Cowper; to be erected in Poet's Corner, Westminster Abbey. The bas-relief represents Cowper in his study with Mrs. Unwin and Lady Austen.'		[Exhib RA, London, 1232]; untraced		*Graves* V, 1905–6, 196
3.	1852	Mary Blacklock (†1850)		St Michael, Charleston, South Carolina	SD	*Hershey* 1970, 807 (repr)
4.	1857	Arthur, 1st Duke of Wellington, national memorial, design only (monument executed by Alfred Stevens)		[Exhib Westminster Hall, London]; untraced		*Marshall* 1894, 7; *Physick* 1970, *passim* (repr)
5.	?1857	Mrs Adams		Newport, Salop	S	*Gunnis* 1968, 256
6.	†1859	Lady John Manners		Rowsley, Derbys		*Marshall* 1894, 6; Pevsner, *Derbys*, 1978, 312
7.	†1871	Louisa Foljambe	a	Tickhill, W R Yorks	S	*Gunnis* 1968, 256; Pevsner, *Yorks, WR*, 1967, 520
8.	†1877	John Miland		St Mary, Wimbledon		Pevsner, *London 2: S*, 1983, 452

Statues

9.	1836	Hero guiding Leander across the Hellespont	m	[Exhib RA, London, 1059]; untraced		*AU*, 1846, 188; *Graves* V, 1905–6, 195, 196; *Johnson* 1975, 313; *Laperriere* 3, 1991, 238
10.	1837	Hebe rejected	m	SNG, Edinburgh	SD	*Marshall Album*, 11 (repr); *Graves* V, 1905–6, 196, 198; *Grove* 20, 1996, 478; *Laperriere* 3, 1991, 238, 239; *Pearson* 1991 (cover repr)

11.	1839	Rebecca at the well		[Exhib BI, London, 434]; untraced Other versions: plaster models awarded to Art Union prizewinners		*Graves* 1875, 369; *Johnson* 1975, 313; *Marshall* 1895, 4; *Laperriere* 3, 1991, 238
12.	1840	Bacchus and Ino		[Exhib Soc of BA, London, 729]; untraced		*Gunnis* 1968, 256; *Johnson* 1975, 313
13.	1840	Ophelia	m	[Exhib RA, London, 1122]; untraced Other versions: reproduced in Parian ware by Copeland		*AJ Cat* 1862, 317, 323 (repr); *Marshall Album*, 20 (repr); *Marshall* 1894, 4, 11; *Graves* V, 1905–6, 195, 197; *Atterbury* 1989, 155 (repr 522); *Laperriere* 3, 1991, 238, 239
14.	1840	The creation of Adam		[Mansfield College, Oxford]; untraced		*Marshall Album*, 10 (repr); *Marshall* 1894, 5; *Graves* V, 1905–6, 195
15.	1841	Caractacus before Claudius		[Exhib RA, London, 1248]; untraced		*Marshall Album*, 12 (repr); *Marshall* 1894, 12; *Graves* V, 1905–6, 195, 196; *Johnson* 1975, 313; *Laperriere* 3, 1991, 238
16.	1841	Venus rescuing Aeneas from Diomed		[Awarded RA Gold Medal]; untraced		RA premium list; *Sandby* II, 1862, 314; *Graves* V, 1905–6, 196
17.	1842	The broken pitcher	m	[Exhib RA, London, 1270]; untraced Other versions: plaster statuettes awarded to Art Union prizewinners		*Marshall Album*, 39 (repr); *Marshall* 1894, 11; *Graves* V, 1905–6, 195, 196
18.	1842	The fountain glass	m	[Exhib RA, London, 1296]; untraced		*Graves* V, 1905–6, 196; *Laperriere* 3, 1991, 238
19.	1843	David with the head of Goliath, model		[Royal Scottish Museum, Edinburgh 1886.506]; untraced		*Marshall Album*, 13 (repr); *Graves* V, 1905–6, 196
20.	1844	Christ blessing little children		[Exhib RA, London, 1302]; untraced		*AU*, 1844, 171; *Graves* V, 1905–6, 196
21.	1844	Eve		[Exhib Westminster Hall, London, 165; sold Phillips 15 April 1851]; untraced		*AU*, 1844, 216; *AU*, 1846, 188; *Marshall* 1894, 14; *Graves* V, 1905–6, 196, 198
22.	1844	Geoffrey Chaucer		[Exhib Westminster Hall, London, 100]; untraced		*AU*, 1844, 215; *Lit Gaz*, 1435, 20 July 1844, 466
23.	1844	Little Red Riding Hood	m	[Exhib RA, London, 1278]; untraced		*AU*, 1844, 170; *Graves* V, 1905–6, 196; *Laperriere* 3, 1991, 238
24.	1845	The first whisper of love		[coll Sir Erskine Perry]; untraced Other versions: reproduction awarded to 1843 Art Union prizewinner RDS, Dublin, p, 1846		*Marshall*, 1894, 9; *Graves* V, 1905–6, 196; *Read* 1982, 208, 209 (repr); *Laperriere* 3, 1991, 239; *Grove* 20, 1996, 479
25.	1846	Ariadne	m	[Exhib BI, London, 492]; untraced		*Graves* 1875, 369; *Marshall* 1895, 14; *Laperriere* 3, 1991, 238
26.	c1846	Dancing girl reposing, model	p	Battersea Town Hall, Lavender Hill, London, (in niche beside entrance to bar) Other versions: reproduced in Parian ware by Copeland		*AJ Cat* 1862, f.32 (repr); *Graves* V, 1905–6, 196; *Gunnis* 1968, 256; *Atterbury* 1989, 33, 153 (repr 43, 518); *Laperriere* 3, 1991, 238; *Cavanagh* forthcoming 2007 (Wandsworth)
27.	1847	Edward Hyde, 1st Earl of Clarendon (†1674) Model(s): exhib Westm Hall, London, 1847 (unfinished)	m	Palace of Westminster, London, St Stephen's Hall	SD	*Marshall* 1894, 9; *Walker* 1961, 16, cat no 19; *Read* 2000, 259 (repr)
28.	c1847	Eurydice, model	p	[Battersea Town Hall, Lavender Hill, London]; untraced		*AU*, 1847, 200; *Marshall Album*, 16 (repr); *Graves* V, 1905–6, 196
29.	1847	Leander	m	[Exhib BI, London, 547]; untraced		*Graves* 1875, 369
30.	1847	Paul and Virginia		Glasgow Museums S.62 Other versions: Philips's sale, 18 Nov 1986, lot 106, marble; untraced		*Manchester Art Treasures* 1857, 133; *Marshall Album*, 14 (repr); *Marshall* 1894, 7; *Graves* V, 1905–6, 196; *Johnson* 1975, 313; *Laperriere* 3, 1991, 238, 239
31.	1847	Sabrina	m	[coll G Moore]; untraced Other versions: RDS, Dublin, plaster Royal Coll, bronze (cast by Robinson and Cottam), 1855 Reproduced in Parian ware by Copeland (eg Royal Coll) Amherst coll, Mass, bronze		*Graves* 1875, 369; *Marshall Album*, 15 (repr); *Marshall* 1894, 3; *Graves* V, 1905–6, 196; *Read* 1982, 205, 208 (repr); *Atterbury* 1989, 34, 143 (repr 46, 496); *Laperriere* 3, 1991, 238
32.	1847	The first step	p	[Exhib RA, London, 1323]; untraced		*AU*, 1847, 200; *ILN*, 8 May 1847, 297 (repr); *Graves* V, 1905–6, 196
33.	1848	Cupid captive		[Exhib RA, London, 1332]; untraced Other versions: reproduced in Parian ware by Copeland		*AJ Cat* 1862, 315 (repr); *Graves* V, 1905–6, 196; *Atterbury* 1989, 158 (repr 528)
34.	1848	Sir Thomas Fowell Buxton, sketch for a statue		[Exhib RA, London, 1348]; untraced		*Graves* V, 1905–6, 196

35.	1845–1849	Infant satyr ('The last drop'), diploma work	m	RA, London	S	*ILN*, 24 Feb 1849, 120 (repr); *Graves* 1875, 369; *Marshall Album*, 39 (repr); *Marshall* 1894, 15; *Graves* V, 1905–6, 196
36.	1849	The Grecian maid		[Exhib RA, London, 1210]; untraced		*Athenaeum* 1849, 603; *Graves* V, 1905–6, 196
37.	*c*1849	Zephyr and Aurora, model	p	Battersea Town Hall, London, (in niche beside entrance to bar)	S	*Marshall Album*, 17 (repr); *Graves* V, 1905–6, 196; Cavanagh forthcoming 2007 (Wandsworth)
38.	1850	A mermaid on a dolphin's back		[Exhib RA, London, 1350]; untraced		*AJ*, 1850, 178; *Graves* V, 1905–6, 196, 198
39.	1850	Two nymphs		[Exhib RA, London, 1305]; untraced		*AJ* 1852, 176; *Graves* V, 1905–6, 196
40.	1852	Captain Coram		[Foundling Hospital, Berkhamstead, Herts]; destroyed		*ILN*, 22 Nov 1856, 523 (repr); *Gunnis* 1968, 257; Pevsner, *Herts*, 1977, 100
41.	1852	The Hindoo girl	p	[Exhib RA, London, 1317]; untraced		*AJ* 1852, 176; *Graves* V, 1905–6, 196
42.	1853	Dick Whittington and Jeanie Deans		[City of London Freemen's orphan school, Ferndale Road, London, boys' and girls' staircases]; untraced		*Cavanagh* forthcoming 2007 ('lost or removed works')
43.	1853	Pandora	p	[Exhib RA, London, 1321]; untraced		*AJ* 1853, 152; *Marshall* 1895, 5; *Graves* V, 1905–6, 196
44.	1853	Sir Robert Peel	b	Manchester, Lancs, Piccadilly garden	SD	*Graves* V, 1905–6, 196; *Read* 1982, 107, 112, 149, 169 (repr); *Grove* 20, 1996, 478
45.	1854	Ajax praying for light		[R Sc A, Edinburgh]; destroyed		*Marshall Album*, 4 (repr); *Marshall* 1895, 10; *Graves* V, 1905–6, 197; *Laperriere* 3 1991, 239; info NGS
46.	1854	Bessie, a portrait in the nursery		[Exhib RA, London, 1369]; untraced		*AJ* 1855, 184; *ILN* 7 July 1855 (engraved); *Marshall* 1894, 7; *Graves* V, 1905–6, 197; *Laperriere* 3, 1991, 238
47.	1854	Glasgow		[Crystal Palace, Sydenham]; untraced		*Jameson* 1854, 85
48.	1854	Lady Godiva	p	St Mary's Hall, Coventry, Warks		*Marshall Album*, 19 (repr); *Marshall* 1894, 3; *Graves* V, 1905–6, 197
49.	1854	Psyche kneeling with a butterfly	m	[Exhib RA, London, 1837, 1198]; Hospitalfield House, Arbroath, Scotland	SD	*Graves* V, 1905–6, 195; *Laperriere* 3, 1991, 238
50.	1855	Ariel		[Exhib RA, London, 1422]; untraced		*Graves* 1875, 369; *Graves* V, 1905–6, 197; *Laperriere* 3, 1991, 239
51.	1855	Concordia		[Paris Int Exhib]; untraced		*Gunnis* 1968, 257
52.	1853–1855	Griselda	m	CL Coll, Mansion House, City of London, Egyptian hall, acc 136		*Marshall Album*, 18 (repr); *Marshall* 1894, 3; *Knight* 1986, 342 (repr); *Jeffery* 1993, 306; *Ward-Jackson* 2003, 243. 246–7 (repr)
53.	1855	John, Baron Somers (†1716) Payment(s): £1,000	m	Palace of Westminster, London, St Stephen's Hall	SD	*Walker* 1961, 68, cat 71; *Read* 1982, 83 (repr)
54.	1855	The mother's prayer		[Exhib RA, London, 1417]; untraced		*ILN*, 7 July 1855, 21 (engraving); *Graves* V, 1905–6, 197; *Laperriere* 3, 1991, 239
55.	1856	Hermia and Helena		[Exhib RA, London, 1241]; untraced		*Athenaeum* 1856, 687; *Marshall* 1894, 8; *Graves* V, 1905–6, 197, 198
56.	1856	Imogen asleep		[Exhib RA, London, 1232]; untraced		*Graves* V, 1905–6, 197; *Laperriere* 3, 1991, 239
57.	1856	The refuge	m	[R Sc A, Edinburgh, 1856, 749]; untraced		*Graves* 1875, 369; *Laperriere* 3, 1991, 239
58.	1857	The bather	p	[Exhib RA, London, 1216]; untraced		*AJ* 1857, 176; *Graves* V, 1905–6, 197
59.	1858	Edward Jenner	b	[Trafalgar Square, London]; Kensington Gardens, London	SD	Pevsner, *London: N W*, 1991, 477; *Read* 1982, 11–12, 14 (repr)
60.	1858	Ruth gleaning	m	Hospitalfield House, Arbroath, Scotland	S	*Graves* V, 1905–6, 197, 198; *Laperriere* 3, 1991, 239
61.	1859	Comus, model		Untraced Other versions: reproduced in Parian ware by Copeland		*Atterbury* 1989, 143 (repr 496)
62.	1859	Joseph Hume	m	High Street, Montrose, Angus, Scotland		*Gunnis* 1968, 257
63.	1859	The expulsion		[Exhib RA, London, 1249]; untraced		*Marshall Album*, 22 (repr); *Marshall* 1894, 9; *Graves* V, 1905–6, 197
64.	1860	Hermione, model		Untraced Other versions: reproduced in Parian ware by Copeland		*Atterbury* 1989, 161 (repr 536)

No.	Date	Subject	Medium	Location	Signed	Literary references
65.	1860	Lear and Cordelia, model		Untraced Other versions: reproduced in Parian ware by Copeland		*Marshall* 1894, 15; *Atterbury* 1989, 141 (repr 491)
66.	1862	Samuel Crompton (cast by Elkington & Co)	b	Nelson Square, Bolton, Lancs	SD	*Marshall Album*, 8 (repr); *Marshall* 1894, 13; *Read* 1982, 107
67.	1862	Sir George Grey		Cape Town, South Africa		*ILN*, 7 Jan 1865, 21 (repr); *Graves* V, 1905–6, 197
68.	1862	The young Briton		[Royal Scottish Museum, Edinburgh 1885.29]; untraced		*Marshall Album*, 21 (repr); *Graves* V, 1905–6, 197
69.	1863	Resignation, model		Untraced Other versions: reproduced in Parian ware by Copeland		*Atterbury* 1989, 76 (repr 113)
70.	1863	Undine	m	Walker, Liverpool	S	*Marshall Album*, 40 (repr); *Marshall* 1894, 10; *Graves* V, 1905–6, 197; *Laperriere* 3, 1991, 239
71.	1864	A summer cloud		[Exhib RA, London, 860]; untraced		*Marshall Album*, 23 (repr); *Marshall* 1894, 11; *Graves* V, 1905–6, 197; *Laperriere* 3, 1991, 239
72.	1864	Agriculture		Albert Memorial, Kensington Gardens, London	S	*Marshall* 1894, 6; *Marshall* 1895, 14; *CIIA* 4/1/78–81 (repr); *Read* 1982, 100
73.	c1865	Albert, the Prince Consort, Scottish National Monument, design only (executed by Sir John Steel)		Untraced		*Darby and Smith* 1983, 113 n39
74.	1865	James, 7th Earl of Derby (†1651)		Bolton, Lancs		*Marshall* 1895, 10; *Graves* V, 1905–6, 197; *Gunnis* 1968, 257
75.	c1865	The carrier pigeon	p	[Glasgow Museums S.63]; destroyed		*Marshall* 1894, 8; *Graves* V, 1905–6, 197; inf: Glasgow Museums
76.	1867	Jael		[Exhib RA, London, 998]; untraced		*AJ* 1867, 39; *Marshall* 1894, 8; *Graves* V, 1905–6, 197
77.	1867	Olinda and Sophronia		[Salford AG, Lancs]; destroyed		*Marshall Album*, 24 (repr); *Graves* V, 1905–6, 197
78.	1868	Psyche feeling Cupid's arrows		[Exhib RA, London, 958]; untraced		*Marshall Album*, 27 (repr); *Marshall* 1894, 6; *Graves* V, 1905–6, 197
79.	1868	The prehistoric artist		[Royal Scottish Museum, Edinburgh 1885.28]; untraced		*Marshall Album*, 25 (repr); *Graves* V, 1905–6, 197
80.	1868	The tryst	p	Hospitalfield House, Arbroath, Scotland	SD	*Marshall* 1894, 5; *Graves* V, 1905–6, 197; *Laperriere* 3, 1991, 239
81.	1871	A girl fishing	m	[Exhib RA, London, 1278]; untraced		*AJ* 1871, 179; *Graves* V, 1905–6, 197
82.	c1873	Tali players		[Glasgow Museums S.64]; destroyed		*Marshall Album*, 26 (repr); *Marshall* 1894, 15; *Graves* V, 1905–6, 198
83.	1874	The Venerable Bede translating the gospel of St John	p	[Salford AG, Lancs]; destroyed		*Marshall Album*, 41 (repr); *Marshall* 1894, 9, 12; *Graves* V, 1905–6, 197; *Laperriere* 3, 1991, 239; *Wells* 1999, 42; *Gunnis* 1968, 257
84.	1875	Convalescence		[Exhib RA, London, 1337]; untraced		*Marshall Album*, 29 (repr); *Marshall* 1894, 5; *Graves* V, 1905–6, 198
85.	1875	Marguerite		[Exhib RA, London, 1275]; untraced		*Marshall Album*, 28 (repr); *Marshall* 1894, 4; *Graves* V, 1905–6, 198
86.	1875	Nausicaa		[Exhib RA, London, 1326]; untraced		*Marshall Album*, 30 (repr); *Graves* V, 1905–6, 198
87.	1876	From stone to life, 'Pygmalion me fecit' (Pygmalion's statue)		[Exhib RA, London, 1414]; untraced		*Marshall Album*, 30 (repr); *Graves* V, 1905–6, 198
88.	1877	The prodigal son Payment(s): £735	m	Tate Britain, London (Chantrey Bequest)		*Marshall Album*, 34 (repr); *Graves* V, 1905–6, 198
89.	1878	Early troubles		[Exhib RA, London, 1472]; untraced		*AJ* 1878, 199; *Graves* V, 1905–6, 198
90.	1878	Whispering vows to Pan		[Exhib RA, London, 1480]; untraced		*Marshall Album*, 31 (repr); *Marshall* 1894, 8; *Graves* V, 1905–6, 198
91.	1880	Miranda		[Exhib RA, London, 1584]; untraced		*Marshall Album*, 33 (repr); *Marshall* 1894, 5; *Graves* V, 1905–6, 198
92.	1880	Sabrina thrown into the Severn	b	Worcester Art Gall	SD	*Marshall Album*, 37 (repr); *Marshall* 1894, 36; *Graves* V, 1905–6, 198; *Laperriere* 3, 1991, 239
93.	1880	Stepping stones	p	[Salford AG, Lancs]; destroyed Other versions: bronze exhib RA, 1879, 1528; untraced		*Marshall Album*, 32 (repr); *Marshall* 1894, 10; *Graves* V, 1905–6, 198; *Laperriere* 3, 1991, 239; *Wells* 1999, 42

94.	1881	Mother and child		[Exhib RA, London, 1508]; untraced		*AJ* 1878, 199; *Graves* V, 1905–6, 198
95.	1882	Cinderella	m	[Exhib RA, London, 1568]; untraced		*Marshall Album*, 35 (repr); *Marshall* 1894, 9, 14; *Graves* V, 1905–6, 198; *Laperriere* 3, 1991, 239
96.	1882	Oedipus at Colonus		[Exhib RA, London, 1601]; untraced		*Marshall Album*, 40 (repr); *Graves* V, 1905–6, 198
97.	1884	Little Bo Peep	m	[Exhib RA, London, 1728]; untraced		*Marshall Album*, 41 (repr); *Marshall* 1894, 11, 12; *Graves* V, 1905–6, 198; *Laperriere* 3, 1991, 239
98.	1885	The temptation of Eve		[Exhib RA, London, 2114]; untraced		*Marshall Album* 36; *Graves* V, 1905–6, 198; *Laperriere* 3, 1991, 239
99.	1886	Deborah, model		[Royal Scottish Museum, Edinburgh 1886.507]; untraced		*Marshall Album*, 36 (repr); *Graves* V, 1905–6, 198; *Laperriere* 3, 1991, 239
100.	*c*1886	Oenone	m	Art Gallery of New South Wales, Sydney	S	*Graves* V, 1905–6, 197
101.	1888	The foolish virgin, model		[Royal Scottish Museum, Edinburgh]; untraced		*Marshall Album*, 38 (repr); *Graves* V, 1905–6, 198; *Laperriere* 3, 1991, 239; RG/JP 5, 909, 913
102.	1888	The old, old story		[Exhib RA, London, 2069]; untraced		*Marshall* 1894, 16; *Graves* V, 1905–6, 198
103.	1890	Noon		[Exhib RA, London, 2040]; untraced		*Graves* V, 1905–6, 198
104.	1893	Echo		Untraced		*Marshall Album*, 42 (repr); *Marshall* 1894, 11
Busts						
105.	1835	Camilla		[Exhib RA, London, 1082]; untraced		*Graves* V, 1905–6, 195
106.	1838	Head of Italia	m	[Exhib R Sc A, Edinburgh, 407]; untraced		*Laperriere* 3, 1991, 238
107.	*c*1838	William Calder Marshall, self-portrait	p	SNPG, Edinburgh		*Marshall Album*, 3 (repr)
108.	1841	Dr S S Alison		[Exhib RA, London, 1279]; untraced		*Graves* V, 1905–6, 195
109.	1841	Ophelia		[Exhib RA, London, 1271]; untraced Other versions: reproduced in Parian ware by Copeland		*Graves* 1875, 369; *Graves* V, 1905–6, 195; *Johnson* 1975, 313; *Atterbury* 1989, 181 (repr 591); *Laperriere* 3, 1991, 238
110.	1841	Sappho	m	[Exhib BI, London, 396]; untraced		*Graves* 1875, 369; *Laperriere* 3, 1991, 238
111.	1842	Unidentified lady	m	[Exhib RA, London, 1397]; untraced		*AU*, 1842, 129; *Graves* V, 1905–6, 196
112.	1843	Francis Bennock		[Exhib RA, London, 1505]; untraced		*Graves* V, 1905–6, 196
113.	1843	Sir George Clerk		[Exhib RA, London, 1455]; untraced		*Graves* V, 1905–6, 196
114.	1844	Samuel Rogers		[Exhib RA, London, 1856, 1319]; untraced		*Marshall Album*, 8 (repr); *Marshall* 1894, 14; *Graves* V, 1905–6, 197; *Laperriere* 3, 1991, 239
115.	1845	Unidentified lady	m	[Exhib RA, London, 1441]; untraced		*Graves* V, 1905–6, 196
116.	1848	Miranda	m	[Exhib BI, London, 474]; untraced Other versions: reproduced in Parian ware by Copeland		*Graves* 1875, 369; *Atterbury* 1989, 181 (repr 593)
117.	1849	Innocence	m	[Exhib BI, London, 517]; untraced		*Graves* 1875, 369; *Marshall* 1894, 14
118.	1849	James Matheson MP	m	[Exhib RA, London, 1317]; untraced		*Graves* V, 1905–6, 196
119.	1849	Queen Victoria	m	Athenaeum, London	SD	
120.	1850	Sabrina	m	[Exhib BI, London, 500]; untraced		*Marshall* 1895, 14; *Graves* 1875, 369; *Laperriere* 3, 1991, 239
121.	1852	Henry		[Exhib R Sc A, Edinburgh, 674]; untraced		*Laperriere* 3, 1991, 238
122.	1852	Henry B H Beaufoy	m	CL Coll, City of London School, acc 114		*Graves* V, 1905–6, 196; *Knight* 1986, 342 (repr)
123.	1853	Mrs F		[Exhib RA, London, 1446]; untraced		*Graves* V, 1905–6, 196
124.	1853	Willie		[Exhib R Sc A, Edinburgh, 680]; untraced		*Laperriere* 3, 1991, 238
125.	1855	A lady	m	[Exhib R Sc A, Edinburgh, 780]; untraced		*Laperriere* 3, 1991, 239
126.	1855	Elizabeth Allan-Fraser Model(s): Hospitalfield House, Arbroath, plaster	m	Hospitalfield House, Arbroath	SD	
127.	1855	Patrick Allan-Fraser Model(s): Hospitalfield House, Arbroath, plaster	m	Hospitalfield House, Arbroath	SD	
128.	1858	Admiral Sir Hugh Pigot		[Exhib RA, London, 1303]; untraced		*Graves* V, 1905–6, 197
129.	1859	Lesbia, model		Untraced Other versions: reproduced in Parian ware by Copeland		*Atterbury* 1989, 180 (repr 587)
130.	1859	Oenone, model for Copeland Parian ware		Untraced Other versions: reproduced in Parian ware by Copeland		*Marshall Album* 1894, 15; *Atterbury* 1989, 180, 181 (repr 587, 592)
131.	1863	Dr Thomas Alexander	m	[Netley Hospital (Hants?)]; Millbank Hospital, London		*Graves* V, 1905–6, 197
132.	1864	Ideal bust, 'Kilmeny'	m	[Exhib R Sc A, Edinburgh, 731]; untraced		*Marshall* 1895, 16; *Laperriere* 3, 1991, 239

133.	1866	Cordelia	m	[Exhib R Sc A, Edinburgh, 873]; untraced		*Graves* V, 1905–6, 198; *Laperriere* 3, 1991, 239; *Wells* 1999, 42
134.	1869	Ideal bust of a Pompeian	m	[Exhib RA, London, 1221]; untraced		*Marshall* 1895, 12; *Graves* V, 1905–6, 197; *Laperriere* 3, 1991, 239
135.	1872	James Hopgood		[Royal Free Hospital, London]; untraced		*Graves* V, 1905–6, 197; *Gunnis* 1968, 257
136.	1874	Sir Isaac Newton	s	Leicester Square, London	S	*Read* 1982, 171
137.	nd	Hermione	m	Sotheby, 4 June 1998; untraced	S	
Chimneypieces						
138.	1848	With frieze representing 'the Seven Ages of Man', 'L'Allegro' and 'Il Penseroso' on the pilasters, the whole surmounted by statues of Cupid and Psyche		[Exhib RA, London, 1354]; untraced		*Marshall* 1895, 8; *Graves* V, 1905–6, 196
Architectural Sculpture						
139.	1839	Two fountains	m	Bowood, Wilts, east terrace		RG/JP, 5, 906
140.	1870	Pediment sculpture	s	Bolton Town Hall, Lancs		*Grove* 20, 1996, 479; CIIA, 4/9/1-3 Lancs
141.	1873–1874	Michelangelo, statue		Burlington House, London, courtyard		*Survey of London*, vol 32, 419–20 (repr)
142.	1873–1874	Titian, statue		Burlington House, London, courtyard		*Survey of London*, vol 32, 419–20 (repr)
143.	1878–1879	Justice, statue	s	Temple Gardens, London, south front		*Ward-Jackson* 2003, 399–400
144.	1878–1879	Learning, statue	s	Temple Gardens, London, south front		*Ward-Jackson* 2003, 399–400
Reliefs						
145.	1837	Sophronio and Olindo		[Exhib R Sc A, Edinburgh, 379]; untraced		*Laperriere* 3, 1991, 238
146.	1838	An interview between Hero and Leander, after his having swum across the Hellespont		[Exhib R Sc A, Edinburgh, 410]; untraced		*Laperriere* 3, 1991, 238
147.	1838	Head of Sterne's Maria, medallion		[Exhib R Sc A, Edinburgh, 423]; untraced		*Marshall* 1894, 12; *Graves* V, 1905–6, 195; *Johnson* 1975, 313; *Laperriere* 3, 1991, 238
148.	1840	Study of a head	m	[Exhib R Sc A, Edinburgh, 389]; untraced		*Laperriere* 3, 1991, 238
149.	1840	The five wise and five foolish virgins		[Exhib Soc of BA, London, 730]; untraced		*Johnson* 1975, 313
150.	1842	Psyche opening the box of cosmetics	m	[Exhib R Sc A, Edinburgh, 543]; untraced		*Marshall* 1895, 15; *Johnson* 1975, 313; *Laperriere* 3, 1991, 238
151.	1855	Psyche borne by zephyrs, medallion		[Exhib R Sc A, Edinburgh, 773]; untraced		*Laperriere* 3, 1991, 238
152.	1863	Series of reliefs Payment(s): £2,420	s	St Paul's Cathedral, London, Wellington Memorial Chapel	SD	*Marshall* 1894, 7; *Physick* 1970, 51, 54, 75, 81; *Ward-Jackson* 2004, 126–7 (repr)
153.	1863	W Caldwell Roscoe, medallion		[Exhib RA, London, 1047]; untraced		*Graves* V, 1905–6, 197
154.	1888	A summer cloud		[Exhib RA, London, 2041]; untraced		*Marshall* 1894, 14; *Graves* V, 1905–6, 198
155.	nd	The mourner	m	[Posthumous studio exhib]; untraced		*Marshall* 1895, 13
Miscellaneous						
156.	1833	'Sterne's 'Maria'	p	[Exhib R Sc A]; untraced		*Marshall* 1895, 12
157.	1836	Eve and the first born		[Exhib R Sc A, Edinburgh, 329]; untraced		*Graves* 1875, 369; *Graves* V, 1905–6, 195; *Laperriere* 3, 1991, 238
158.	1836	Hector and Andromache		[Exhib Soc of BA, London, 879]; untraced		*Johnson* 1975, 313
159.	1836	Innocence		[Exhib RA, London, 1061]; untraced		*Graves* V, 1905–6, 195; *Laperriere* 3, 1991, 238
160.	1836	Samson		[Exhib RA, London, 1068]; untraced		*Marshall* 1894, 9; *Graves* V, 1905–6, 195
161.	1837	The evening prayer		[Exhib R Sc A, Edinburgh, 373]; untraced		*Laperriere* 3, 1991, 238
162.	1838	Cupid feeding the doves of Venus	m	[Exhib R Sc A, Edinburgh, 416]; untraced		*Marshall* 1895, 15; *Graves* V, 1905–6, 195; *Johnson* 1975, 313; *Laperriere* 3, 1991, 238
163.	1839	Jacob		[Exhib R Sc A, Edinburgh, 499]; untraced		*Laperriere* 3, 1991, 238
164.	1839	The dead ass		[Exhib RA, London, 1336]; untraced		*Marshall* 1894, 13; *Graves* V, 1905–6, 195
165.	1840	Cupid and Psyche		[Exhib RA, London, 1101]; untraced		*Graves* V, 1905–6, 195
166.	1840	Hercules rescuing Hesione from the sea monster		[Exhib BI, London, 448]; untraced		*Graves* 1875, 369; *Laperriere* 3, 1991, 238
167.	1840	Una and the lion		[Exhib RA, London, 1103]; untraced		*Graves* V, 1905–6, 195
168.	1841	Atalanta and Hippomenes		[Exhib RA, London, 1256]; untraced		*Graves* V, 1905–6, 195
169.	1841	Instruction		[Exhib R Sc A, Edinburgh, 559]; untraced		*Laperriere* 3, 1991, 238
170.	1841	Puck 'on mischief bent'		[Exhib RA, London, 1258]; untraced		*Graves* V, 1905–6, 195; *Laperriere* 3, 1991, 238
171.	1841	The bath		[Exhib R Sc A, Edinburgh, 560]; untraced		*Laperriere* 3, 1991, 238
172.	1842	Design to commemorate the victories of Wellington		[Exhib R Sc A, Edinburgh, 545]; untraced		*Laperriere* 3, 1991, 238
173.	1843	May morning		[Exhib RA, London, 1483]; untraced		*Graves* V, 1905–6, 196; *Laperriere* 3, 1991, 238

174.	1843	The sick child		[Exhib BI, London, 435]; untraced	*Graves* 1875, 369
175.	1844	Holy Family	b	[Exhib Soc of BA, London, 774]; untraced	*Johnson* 1975, 313
176.	1844	Nature's mirror		[Exhib Soc of BA, London, 772]; untraced	*Johnson* 1975, 313
177.	1844	The lost breakfast		[Exhib R Sc A, Edinburgh, 568]; untraced	*Laperriere* 3, 1991, 238
178.	1845	Calypso		[Exhib BI, London, 513]; untraced	*Graves* 1875, 369
179.	1845	The evening star		[Exhib R Sc A, Edinburgh, 559]; untraced	*Laperriere* 3, 1991, 238
180.	1845	The morning star		[Exhib R Sc A, Edinburgh, 555]; untraced	*Laperriere* 3, 1991, 238
181.	1856	She never told her love		[Exhib RA, London, 1243]; untraced	*Graves* V, 1905–6, 197; *Laperriere* 3, 1991, 239
182.	1859	Frolic		[Exhib RA, London, 1243]; untraced	*Graves* V, 1905–6, 197
183.	1860	Fresh from the bath		[Exhib RA, London, 957]; untraced	*Graves* V, 1905–6, 197
184.	1868	Eve's dream		[Exhib RA, London, 954]; untraced	*Marshall* 1894, 4; *Graves* V, 1905–6, 197
185.	1869	The mother of Moses		[Exhib RA, London, 1284]; untraced	*Marshall* 1894, 5; *Graves* V, 1905–6, 197
186.	1871	A Christian martyr		[Exhib RA, London, 1225]; untraced	*Marshall* 1894, 13; *Graves* V, 1905–6, 197
187.	1872	Briseis		[Exhib RA, London, 1511]; untraced	*Graves* V, 1905–6, 197
188.	1872	Off the book		[Exhib RA, London, 1505]; untraced	*Graves* V, 1905–6, 197
189.	1873	Wilder'd fancies		[Exhib RA, London, 1527]; untraced	*Marshall* 1894, 6; *Graves* V, 1905–6, 197
190.	1874	The new story	tc	[Exhib RA, London, 1526]; untraced	*Marshall* 1894, 13; *Graves* V, 1905–6, 198; *Laperriere* 3, 1991, 239
191.	1874	The old story	tc	[Exhib RA, London, 1524]; untraced	*Marshall* 1894, 12; *Graves* V, 1905–6, 198; *Laperriere* 3, 1991, 239
192.	1875	Estia		[Exhib RA, London, 1245]; untraced	*Marshall* 1894, 59; *Graves* V, 1905–6, 198
193.	1879	The mother's kiss	tc	[Exhib RA, London, 1548]; untraced	*Graves* V, 1905–6, 198; *Laperriere* 3, 1991, 239
194.	1881	Noonday idleness		[Exhib RA, London, 1445]; untraced	*Marshall* 1894, 16; *Graves* V, 1905–6, 198
195.	1881	The last day of Pompeii		[Royal Scottish Museum, Edinburgh 1886, 203]; untraced	*Graves* V, 1905–6, 198; *Laperriere* 3, 1991, 239
196.	1883	Thetis dipping Achilles in the Styx		[Exhib RA, London, 1579]; untraced	*Marshall* 1894, 7; *Graves* V, 1905–6, 198
197.	1884	Psyche (the soul) indulging in forbidden curiosity, faints		[Exhib RA, London, 1811]; untraced	*Graves* V, 1905–6, 198
198.	1884	Youth		[Exhib RA, London, 1723]; untraced	*Marshall* 1894, 4; *Graves* V, 1905–6, 198
199.	1889	Lilith leaving the garden of Eden		[Exhib RA, London, 2194]; untraced	*Marshall* 1894, 15; *Graves* V, 1905–6, 198
200.	1891	A summer noon		[Exhib R Sc A, Edinburgh, 562]; untraced	*Laperriere* 3, 1991, 239
201.	nd	Hebe		[Elkanah Bicknell, of Herne Hill, London; sold 1863, lot 140, £315]; untraced	Bicknell sale cat, 1863, 23
202.	nd	Portraits of the sculptor's children		[Posthumous studio exhib]; untraced	*Marshall* 1895, 8
203.	nd	The death of the venerable Bede		[Posthumous studio exhib]; untraced	*Marshall* 1895, 14
204.	nd	The deluge		[Posthumous studio exhib]; untraced	*Marshall* 1894, 8
205.	nd	The gleaner		[Posthumous studio exhib]; untraced	*Marshall* 1894, 8
206.	nd	The toilet, model for Parian ware		[Posthumous studio exhib]; untraced	*Marshall* 1895, 6

MARSHALL & GRAY, of London fl 1804

The firm, whose studio was in Mortimer Street, sign a large wall-tablet to John Manning (1). The design takes the form of a semi-urn (the handles formed of writhing snakes), set against a pyramid.

Literary References: *Gunnis* 1968, 254

Funerary Monuments

1.	?1804	John Manning	St Stephen, Norwich, Norfolk	S	*Gunnis* 1968, 254

MARSTON, Robert, of Norwich fl 1770–1806

In 1770 he advertised 'Monuments in the most Modern Taste, Chimney Pieces of all Kinds, and every article of Masonry' to be had from his workshop, 'opposite Bethel' (*Norfolk Chronicle*, 29 September 1770). A similar advertisement appeared in the *Norwich Mercury* on 22 September 1770. He signs the large pyramidal tablet to Richard Boardman (1), carved with a fine *gloria* at the base. His widow, Sarah, died at Norwich on 12 November 1834, aged 84 (*Bury Post*).

Literary References: *Gunnis* 1968, 257

Archival References: GPC; RG/JP, 5, 912v (inf. David Cubitt)

Funerary Monuments

1.	?1785	Richard Boardman	St Michael Coslany, Norwich	S	*Gunnis* 1968, 257; GPC
2.	1806	Rev John Peele (†1804) (designed by A Browne)	St Peter Mancroft, Norwich, Norfolk		RG/JP, 6, 912v.

MARTEN, John, of Tenterden 1728–1814

He executed 'good provincial work in a pleasantly typical eighteenth-century style, his tablets in coloured marbles having the usual semi-urn set against a pyramid with flaming lamps.' Marten, who was married four times, is buried in Tenterden churchyard (*Gunnis* 1968, 257).

Funerary Monuments

1.	?1771	Rev Matthew Wallace	Tenterden, Kent	S	*Gunnis* 1968, 257
2.	?1779	Arnold Nesbitt	Icklesham, Sussex	S	*Gunnis* 1968, 257
3.	?1798	Thomas Holford	Rye, Sussex	S	*Gunnis* 1968, 257

MARTIN, George, of Highgate fl 1825–35

He was responsible for the monument to Coleridge, originally in the poet's local church. Coleridge was reinterred in 1961 (1).

Funerary Monuments

1.	†1834	Samuel Taylor Coleridge	[Old Highgate Chapel]; St Michael, Highgate, St Pancras, London		*Gunnis* 1968, 257; Pevsner, *London: N*, 1998, 348

MARTIN, John –1691

He was the mason employed in rebuilding Brewers' Hall, 1669–1673 (Archives, Brewers' Company). Martin became renter warden of the Masons' Company in 1678, upper warden in 1682 and master in 1687. His apprentices included John Child (bound in 1664), Thomas Fetch (1666), **William Holland** (1668), William Stevens (1669), Thomas Quarterman (1670), Daniel Farmer (1675), Nicholas Perring (1676), and John Turner (1684). He is buried in the graveyard of St Mary's Whitechapel, together with his wife, Mary (†1683), and ten of their children.

Literary References: *Seymour* 1735, 2, 709; *Gunnis* 1968, 257; *Webb* 1999, *passim*

Archival References: Masons' Co, Masters and Wardens

MARTIN, William

For further information the reader is referred to *Pyke* 1973, 88

MASON, Christopher fl *c*1727

He is known only for one cartouche tablet (1). He may be the Christopher Mason, the son of a labourer, who was apprenticed to **Joshua Fletcher** (probably II) on 2 January 1718 and became free of the Masons' Company on 5 February 1724.

Literary References: *Webb* 1999, 22

Archival References: Masons' Co, *Freemen*, fol 45

Funerary Monuments

1.	†1727	John Braddyll	St Mary, Ulverston, Lancs	S	Pevsner, *Lancs: N*, 1969, 251

MASON, John, of London fl 1702–26

He worked as an assistant to **William Stanton** and may be the John Mason who was made free of the Masons' Company on 9 March 1696 having served his apprenticeship with **Samuel Fulkes**. Under Stanton he was employed at various periods between 1702 and 1715 as a mason and stone-carver at Stonyhurst, Lancs. Mason is named as the craftsman who in 1703 built 'ye Stone Stares in ye Court' at a cost of £30, and in 1704, at the same price, carved 'ye unycornes Head and Helmet at ye Head of ye Stone Stairs' (1). In 1705 Mason he was paid 20/- a week 'wherof his Wife is to Receive 14s p. week for subsistance in her husband's Absence.' In 1707 he designed the Shireburn Almshouses at Stonyhurst, which were erected by Richard Rideing, a mason of Waddington, Yorks. John Mason was also at Stonyhurst in 1715, presumably working for Stanton, when he witnessed a Jacobite supper party on the eve of the Battle of Preston. He later testified that he was at the house on 10 November when the guests borrowed from him a 'lead pann' and about 20lbs of lead, which they used to cast bullets through the night. In his testimony, he identified himself as 'of the parish of St Sepulchre, City of London' (*Stonyhurst* 1964, 77, 480). In 1726 was paid 3/6 a day to set up chimneypieces by **Edward Stanton** and **Christopher Horsnaile I** who sent him down to Ditchley Park, Oxon to work on site.

A Thomas Mason, who may have been a brother, was apprenticed to William Stanton on 20 July 1697 and was made free in October 1707.

Literary References: *Stonyhurst* 1894, 77; *Payne* 1889, 144–5; *Stonyhurst* 1964, 480; *Gunnis* 1968, 257–8; *Colvin* 1995, 643; *Webb* 1999, 22

Archival References: Masons' Co *Freemen*, fol 44; Dillon, DIL I/p/3bi

Architectural Sculpture

1.	1704	Ornaments surmounting staircase	Stonyhurst Coll, Lancs, formerly main court, currently boys' refectory		*Stonyhurst* 1964, 480

MASON, John, of Twickenham fl *c*1802–42

Mason was awarded medals from the Society of Arts in 1827 and 1828 (**9**, **10**). He exhibited busts at the Royal Academy, 1827–33, and signed a small number of monuments.

Literary References: *Gunnis* 1968, 257

Funerary Monuments

1.	?1802	Lucia, Viscountess Clifden		St Mary, Twickenham, Middx	S	GPC
2.	?1814	Caroline Agar-Ellis		St Mary, Twickenham, Middx	S	GPC
3.	?1815	Lambert Blair		St Mary, Twickenham, Middx	S	GPC
4.	1827	'A Design for part of a Monument to be executed in Marble'		[Exhib Soc of BA, London, 838]; untraced		*Johnson* 1975, 316
5.	?1828	John Carr		St Mary, Twickenham, Middx	S	GPC
6.	?1837	Marie Espinasse		St Mary, Twickenham, Middx	S	*Gunnis* 1968, 257
7.	?1838	Elizabeth Palmer		Sunbury, Middx	S	*Gunnis* 1968, 257
8.	?1842	James Willis		Hampton, Middx	S	GPC

Busts

9.	1827	'copy of a bust from the antique'		[Soc of A, silver Isis medal]; untraced		RSA *Transactions*, vol 45, 1827, xxxi
10.	1828	'bust from life'		[Soc of A, large silver medal]; untraced		RSA *Transactions*, vol 46, 1828, xxvii
11.	1828	Unidentified gentleman		[Exhib Soc of BA, London, 902]; untraced		*Johnson* 1975, 316
12.	1828	Unidentified gentleman		[Exhib RA, London, 1189]; untraced		*Graves* V, 1905–6, 210
13.	1829	Sir Humphrey Davy, after Anne Seymour Damer	m	[Exhib Soc of BA, London, 850]; untraced		*Johnson* 1975, 316
14.	1830	Mr McKinsel, copy	p	Brynkinalt, Denbighs	D	*Gunnis* 1968, 257
15.	1830	Unidentified gentleman		[Exhib RA, London, 1190]; untraced		*Graves* V, 1905–6, 210
16.	1833	Two sons of Captain Probyn		[Exhib RA, London, 1109 and 1219]; untraced		*Graves* V, 1905–6, 210; *Gunnis* 1968, 257

Miscellaneous

17.	1829	Sleeping child		[Exhib Soc of BA, London, 862]; untraced		*Johnson* 1975, 316

MASON, of Sandwich fl 1835

Funerary Monuments

1.	†1835	Sarah Steward	s	Woodnesborough, Kent	S	

MASON, Robert, of London fl 1678

In 1678 he agreed with Richard Newdigate of Arbury, Warks, that he 'should well and finely carve the frontispiece of a Grotto according to a draught signed with both their hands', a work for which he was to receive £16 (1).

His son, Robert Mason II, became free of the Masons' Company by patrimony on 9 March 1696. A note in the margin of the Company records suggests that the elder Mason was dead by this date.

Literary References: *Gunnis* 1968, 258

Archival References: Masons' Co *Freemen*, fol 44; Newdigate Archives, CR 136/B2452 (agreement)

Miscellaneous

1.	1678	Frontispiece of a grotto Payment(s): £16		[Arbury, Warks, for Richard Newdigate]; untraced		Newdigate Archives cited by *Gunnis* 1968, 258

MASON, Thomas fl *c*1765–99

Mason was a long-serving repairer and modeller at the Derby manufactory, where he was employed for over thirty years from c1765. He became overlooker of the ornamental department in the 1780s and left *c*1799. As well as having the 'care and management of the moulds and models' he was employed by Duesbury to use a stopwatch to monitor other modellers' hours, and to report the results in a secret ledger. His replacement, Kean, said that Mason was 'overlooker of the claymen but he was old and ignorant, and did harm and I think no good' (*Bricknell* 1995, 97, 100).

Literary References: *Bricknell* 1995, 57, 75, 124; *Bricknell* 1998, 80

MASSART (or MASSARET), J, of Paris fl 1773–74

He was described as 'sculptor in bas-relief to the Dauphin' when he exhibited at the Society of Artists (3), giving his address as the home of a Mrs Duperte, 13 Little Chapel Street, Soho, opposite Hollen Street.

Reliefs

1.	1773	Two basso relievos	a	[Exhib RA, London, 193]; untraced		*Graves* V, 1905–6, 212
2.	1774	Bas relief	a	[Exhib Soc of A, London, 161]; untraced		*Graves* 1907, 160
3.	1774	Bas relief	a	[Exhib Soc of A, London, 162]; untraced		*Graves* 1907, 160
4.	1774	Bas relief	a	[Exhib RA, London, 177]; untraced		*Graves* V, 1905–6, 212

MASTLAND (or MASSELIN) fl 1720–21

On 26 December 1720 he was paid £150 by Francis Hawes for stone cutting at Purley Hall, Berks, and on 20 March 1721, a further £100. In the Declared Accounts of the South Sea Company there are, besides these payments, others of the same date to various workmen and artificers connected with building work at Hawes's house, so it seems likely that Mastland was the master mason in charge.

Literary References: S S Co (*Hawes*), no 7 in 3, p 69

MATHEWS, of Plymouth fl *c*1832–37

Funerary Monuments

1.	?1832	John Shearm		Kilkhampton, Cornwall	S	*Gunnis* 1968, 258
2.	?1837	Thomas Bond		St Martin, Cornwall	S	*Gunnis* 1968, 258

MATTHYSSENS fl 1738

In 1738 John Wood the elder engaged him to carve a relief in freestone for the pediment of the Mineral Water Hospital at Bath, for which he was to receive 25 guineas. The work never advanced beyond the preliminary drawings (1).

Architectural Sculpture

1.	1738	The good Samaritan, relief model Payment(s): 5s		Untraced		*Green* 1902, 104

MATZURA, P J fl 1816–17

His address was given as 7, Chapel Street, St Marylebone in 1817.

Literary References: *Annals of the Fine Arts* 1817, 437

Busts

1.	1816	Captain Hehl		[Exhib RA, London, 964]; untraced		*Graves* V, 1905–6, 214

MAUGE & CO, of Bath fl *c*1768–83

This firm signs a large wall-monument in coloured marbles to James Long (1), and a smaller one to members of the Bluett family, with two seated allegories by an urn, high above the inscription tablet (2).

Literary References: *Gunnis* 1968, 258

Funerary Monuments

1.	†1768	James Long		Urchfont, Wilts	S	Pevsner, *Wilts*, 1975, 545
2.	1783	Robert and Kerrenhappuch Bluett		Holcombe Rogus, Devon	S	Pevsner, *Devon*, 1989, 487

MAY fl 1797

Chimneypieces

1.	1797	Description unavailable Payment(s): £51		[Firle Place, Sussex, drawing room]; untraced		GPC

MAY, Edward fl 1804

In 1804 he and his partner, **Latter Parsons of Lewes**, were paid £346 for repairs to Firle Place, Sussex (Archives, Viscount Gage, in GPC).

MAY, George, of Romsey, Hants fl 1767–83

He exhibited wax portraits at the Free Society of Artists in 1767. A number of other exhibited waxes entered under 'Charles May' may well be his work (*Graves* 1907, 161).

Literary References: *Gunnis* 1968, 258; *Pyke* 1973, 89

Reliefs

1.	1782	William of Wykeham, model	w	[Exhib Free Soc, London, 166]; untraced	*Graves* 1907, 161
2.	1783	Unidentified lady, 'portrait in coloured wax'	w	[Exhib Free Soc, London, 81]; untraced	*Graves* 1907, 161

Miscellaneous

3.	1767	Unidentified lady	w	[Exhib Free Soc, London, 106]; untraced	*Graves* 1907, 161

MAY, Thomas, of Romsey, Hants fl 1766

He was presumably a relative of **George May** of the same town.

Miscellaneous

1.	1766	Wax Portrait	w	[Exhib Free Soc, London, 118]; untraced	*Graves* 1907, 161; *Gunnis* 1968, 258

MAZOTTI, P fl 1820

His tradecard, engraved in Norwich and decorated with a male bust, describes him as an 'Artist' who offered 'Busts taken from the living and dead and executed at the shortest notice/ Figures etc repaired, cleaned and bronzed in the neatest manner.' He also neatly repaired alabaster, china and marble ornaments (BM Heal 106.18).

Busts

1.	1820	Bishop Bathurst, 'painted terracotta'		Bonham's sale, Old Rectory, Banningham, Norfolk, 22–23 March 2004, lot 1182	SD
2.	nd	Unidentified judge or ecclesiastic, small, painted	p	Knox/Longstaffe Gowan coll	S

MAZZONI, J M fl 1817

He was listed in Johnstone's *Directory* of 1817 as a 'Modeller and figure maker' of 44 Old Compton Street, Soho. (Inf. Hilary Young)

MAZZONI, P, of Norwich fl c.1811

On 10 November 1811 he advertised in the *Norfolk Chronicle* that he had for sale 'Busts of the late Dr. Rigby, taken from Life. To be had of his Rooms adjoining the Catholic Chapel, of St. John's Maddermarket, where also may be had Busts of Capt. Parry and a variety of Casts from the Antique'.

Archival References: RG/JP, 5, 916v. (inf. David Cubitt)

MCDONALD, of Aberdeen fl 1834

In 1834 a Mr McDonald of King Street, Aberdeen, possibly a marble mason, sent two red granite columns costing £34 to Holkham Hall at **Sir Francis Chantrey**'s behest.

Archival References: NP/RG

MCDONELL, Alexander fl *c*1784

Funerary Monuments

1.	†1784	Archibald McCambridge	Ramoan old graveyard, Co Antrim	S	*Potterton* 1975, 58
2.	nd	Francis Boyd	Ramoan old graveyard, Co Antrim	S	*Potterton* 1975, 58

MCDONNELL, Alexander fl 1740–88

Probably a talented stone cutter rather than a sculptor, the monument to John Martin, †1740, at Rathlin is attributed to him and he was responsible for two graveyard tombstones in Antrim.

MCGAW, Alexander fl 1856

Architectural Sculpture

1.	1856	Royal arms	s	[General post office, George Square, Glasgow]; untraced	*McKenzie* 2002, 436–7

MCGLASHEN, Stewart and Co fl 1848–1901

In 1847 Stewart McGlashen established a marble cutting business at Canonmills, Edinburgh; in 1871 he formed a partnership with his son and the firm, which still exists, has remained a family concern ever since. McGlashen's practice consisted principally of funerary monuments and many of those executed between 1851 and 1901 incorporated particularly fine decorative carving or allegorical figures. McGlashen's work is represented in most Edinburgh graveyards.

Literary References: *Woodward* 1977, vol 1, pt 2, 144

MEADES, of Chipping Norton fl *c*1804–37

Funerary Monuments

1.	†1804	William Horton	Evenlode, Glos	S	Pevsner, *Glos: Cotswolds*, 1999, 359
2.	†1837	Anne Horton	Evenlode, Glos	S	Pevsner, *Glos: Cotswolds*, 1999, 359

MEATYARD, M, of Blandford fl 1773–75

He is known only for large tablets of 'good workmanship' (*Gunnis* 1968, 258). Meatyard was the master mason building Sadborow House, Dorset for John Bragge, 1773–75 (Archives, Dorset County Museum, 8871.A, in GPC).

Funerary Monuments

1.	?1773	Mary Russell	Wimborne St Giles, Dorset	S	*Gunnis* 1968, 258
2.	?1774	Sir William Phipard	Poole, Dorset	S	*Gunnis* 1968, 258

MEDCALF, T, of Liverpool fl 1838

Busts

1.	1838	A child	[Exhib Liverpool Ac, 681]; untraced	*Morris and Roberts* 1998, 424
2.	1838	John Finch	[Exhib Liverpool Ac, 667]; untraced	*Morris and Roberts* 1998, 424
3.	1838	Miss Dawson	[Exhib Liverpool Ac, 679]; untraced	*Morris and Roberts* 1998, 424
4.	1838	T Metcalf	[Exhib Liverpool Ac, 682]; untraced	*Morris and Roberts* 1998, 424
5.	1838	Two unidentified gentleman	[Exhib Liverpool Ac, 680, 683]; untraced	*Morris and Roberts* 1998, 424
6.	1838	W Dawson, two	[Exhib Liverpool Ac, 666, 676]; untraced	*Morris and Roberts* 1998, 424

MELLIAN, C Maximilian –by 1769

He exhibited bronzes at the Free Society (**1, 2**). He was dead by 1769 when the engraver P C Canot put forward his widow's name as an object of charity, 'in very low circumstances' (Archives, Society of Artists, Burlington House, in GPC).

Reliefs

1.	1763	Venus and Cupid being offered a coral by a marine deity	b	[Exhib Free Soc, London, 133]; untraced	*Graves* 1907, 163
2.	1764	Unidentified subject	b	[Exhib Free Soc, London, 120]; untraced	*Graves* 1907, 163

MELLING fl 1833

In 1833 he held an exhibition of sculpture in London which included the lively work here listed (**1**). In a foreword to the catalogue he questioned whether the introduction of a comic style was a national innovation, adding 'Why should the chisel lead a melancholy life? Why should gravity have it all its own way?' In its review of the exhibition the *Literary Gazette* said that the sculptor 'had at least kept within the bounds of good taste' and had 'not polluted his humour with vulgarity' (*Lit Gaz* 1833, 265). Since he never exhibited at the Royal Academy and nothing more is known of him 'it is to be feared that he was more comic than successful' (*Gunnis* 1968, 258).

Statues

1.	1833	Comic group of Falstaff, Mistress Doll and Bardolph	[Exhib London]; untraced	*Lit Gaz*, 27 April 1833

MERCER, George fl 1726–67

He was a subscriber to Kent's *Designs of Inigo Jones* and a member of the Society of Virtuosi. A close associate of James Gibbs, he worked as a mason at 16 Arlington Street, London with **William Wilton** and others in 1734, on the court house in Marylebone Lane in 1729, and on the Oxford market house in St Marylebone from 1726 to 1737. For a time he was in partnership with **Andrews Jelfe**.

In the Hartwell archives is Mercer's estimate of £106 11s 5d, dated 16 August 1740, for 'Portland paving for Hall' at Hartwell Park, Bucks, the home of Sir Thomas Lee. Mercer agreed to pay 'Water carriadge to Edgworth and Wharfe and his Honour to pay land carriadge after.' Mercer's address is given as 'near Cavendish Square' (Bucks CRO Lee Papers D/LE/A/2/1 p13 in *Friedman* 1984, 291). In the archives of Glynde Place, Sussex, are a number of drawings by Sir William Chambers for The Hoo, Herts, Lord Hampden's seat; among these is one for a gate pier on which is written 'Mr Mercer is desired to let me know what he will do them for at the lowest.' A note by Mr Mercer states that his price was £34 (GPC).

In 1748 he took Richard Gayfere, son of **Thomas Gayfere I**, as an apprentice. The Masons' Company lists record the apprenticeship of George, son of George Mercer, mason, to Walter Lee on 3 August, 1739 and he became free on 22 October 1746. The stock and utensils of a Mr Mercer were sold from premises in Bolsover Street and Chandos Street, Cavendish Square, on 20 May 1772.

Literary References: *Gunnis* 1968, 258; *Friedman* 1984, 24, 207, 291, 304, 306–7; *Webb* 1999, 22

Archival References: Masons' Co, *Freemen*, fol 45

Sales Catalogues: Mercer 1772

Chimneypieces

1.	1767	Several Payment(s): £144	[Milton Hall, Berks]; untraced	Hall archives cited in *Gunnis* 1968, 258

MERIER, William fl 1753–54

Architectural Sculpture

1.	1753–1754	'Carving' Payment(s): £218	[New Exchange, Liverpool, Lancs]; untraced	City Corp Cash Book in GPC

MERRETT, Thomas Henry 1823–

He entered the Royal Academy Schools in 1841, on the recommendation of **William Behnes**, giving his address as 6 Stepney Green. He won a prize that year and exhibited again three years later, when his name was given as 'Merritt' in the index, and 'Merrett' in the catalogue (**1**).

Literary References: *Gunnis* 1968, 258–9

Archival References: RA Admissions

Reliefs

1.	1844	Combat between the Centaurs and Lapithae	[Exhib RA, London, 1296]; untraced	*Graves* V, 1905–6, 230

Miscellaneous

2.	1841	Model	[RA, London, silver medal]; untraced	RA Premium list

MERRIFIELD, Thomas 1797–1833

He attended the Royal Academy Schools in 1815 and exhibited at the Academy from that year until 1822. In 1817, when living at 7 Prince's Street, Bedford Row, he gained a medal from the Society of Arts (**1**). Another followed in 1818 (**2**). In 1819 he was living at 53 Red Lion Square. Gunnis, citing the papers of the Artists' Annuity Fund, notes that he died on 1 May 1833, leaving a widow, Charlotte, and three children. The fund's archives have been searched, but the reference was not located.

Literary References: *Graves* V, 1905–6, 231; *Hutchison* 1960–62, 168; *Gunnis* 1968, 259

Statues						
1.	1817	Original model of a figure		[Soc of A, silver medal]; untraced		RSA *Transactions*, vol 35, 1817, 29
2.	1818	Original model of figure		[Soc of A, gold Isis medal]; untraced		RSA *Transactions*, vol 36, 1818, xxxii
Busts						
3.	1819	Unidentified child		[Exhib RA, London, 1192]; untraced		*Graves* V, 1905–6, 231
Reliefs						
4.	1818	Unidentified lady, medallion	w	[Exhib RA, London, 986]; untraced		*Graves* V, 1905–6, 231
5.	1821	Ganymede	w	[Exhib RA, London, 1051]; untraced		*Graves* V, 1905–6, 231
Miscellaneous						
6.	1815	Unidentified young lady		[Exhib RA, London, 845]; untraced		*Graves* V, 1905–6, 231
7.	1816	A sylphid sailing		[Exhib RA, London, 956]; untraced		*Graves* V, 1905–6, 231
8.	1816	Jupiter and Europa		[Exhib RA, London, 916]; untraced		*Graves* V, 1905–6, 231
9.	1816	Unidentified subject, a portrait		[Exhib RA, London, 885]; untraced		*Graves* V, 1905–6, 231
10.	1817	Miss Holdsworth		[Exhib RA, London, 975]; untraced		*Graves* V, 1905–6, 231
11.	1818	Satan calling up his legions		[Exhib BI, London, 302]; untraced		*Graves* 1875, 377
12.	1819	Hebe		[Exhib RA, London, 1208]; untraced		*Graves* V, 1905–6, 231
13.	1819	Mr Doyley		[Exhib RA, London, 1114]; untraced		*Graves* V, 1905–6, 231
14.	1819	Unidentified young lady		[Exhib RA, London, 1115]; untraced		*Graves* V, 1905–6, 231
15.	1820	Cupid and Psyche		[Exhib RA, London, 1012]; untraced		*Graves* V, 1905–6, 231
16.	1821	Cupid, a study	w	[Exhib RA, London, 1049]; untraced		*Graves* V, 1905–6, 231
17.	1822	Medusa		[Exhib RA, London, 963]; untraced		*Graves* V, 1905–6, 231
18.	1822	Model of the temple of Vesta at Tivoli		[Exhib RA, London, 984]; untraced		*Graves* V, 1905–6, 231
19.	1823	Cupid sleeping		[Exhib RA, London, 1108]; untraced		*Graves* V, 1905–6, 231

MERRYMAN, James, of Windsor –1838

The son of **John Merryman**, in 1805 he built the 'new Gothic portico' designed by Wyatt on the south side of St George's Chapel, receiving £249 for the work (*Hope* 1913, 408). His will, in which he is described as a 'stone mason of New Windsor, Berkshire' was proved on 13 January 1838 (PROB 11/1889).

Literary References: *Gunnis* 1968, 259

Funerary Monuments						
1.	†1811	Mary Gaskoin		St George's Chapel, Windsor Castle	S	*Bond* 1999, 133
2.	†1826	Major Thomas Stephenson Fairtlough		St George's Chapel, Windsor Castle	S	*Bond* 1999, 121
3.	?1830	William Bonsor		Upton, Bucks	S	*Gunnis* 1968, 259
4.	?1833	Louisa Legh		St John the Baptist, Windsor, Berks	S	*Gunnis* 1968, 259
5.	?1833	Rev Joseph Morris		Feltham, Middx	S	*Gunnis* 1968, 259
6.	†1833	William Henry Oram, Captain William Oram (†1836) and Anne Oram (†1852)		St George's Chapel, Windsor Castle	S	*Bond* 1999, 255

MERRYMAN, John, of Windsor 1773–1800

He was presumably the son of John Merryman of Windsor, the mason who built Baylies, Stoke Poges, for Francis Godolphin in 1735 (Archives, Duke of Leeds). The younger John was employed at St George's Chapel (1). His obituary in the *Reading Mercury* of 22 March, 1800 calls him a 'stone-cutter and sculptor.' He is buried at Stoke Poges.

Literary References: *Gunnis* 1968, 259

Will: PROB 11/1339

Architectural Sculpture						
1.	1785–1792	Stone carving	s	St George's Chapel, Windsor, Berks		*Gunnis* 1968, 259

MESSER, J, of Exeter fl c1765

The Hore tablet has 'excellently carved details' (*Gunnis* 1968, 259).

Funerary Monuments						
1.	?1765	Thomas Hore		Spreyton, Devon	S	*Gunnis* 1968, 259

MEYRICK, Thomas fl 1842–45

'A local gentleman', he 'naively' carved two fonts with sacred scenes (1, 2).

Architectural Sculpture						
1.	1842	Relief scenes against stem of font		Ramsbury, Wilts		Pevsner, *Wilts*, 1975, 377
2.	c1845	Carved octagonal font		Chilton Foliat, Wilts		Pevsner, *Wilts*, 1975, 166

MICALI FAMILY, of Leghorn fl 1787–1826

Their monument to Rear-Admiral Robert Reynolds has a medallion-portrait and below it, the relief of a young soldier pointing to a memorial with a depiction of a naval battle (1). The work, curiously, is signed '*Micali direxit Liburni 1816*' instead of the more usual '*fecit*.' The Micali family owned the largest alabaster workshop in Leghorn and specialised in copies from the antique. Many of their customers were visitors to Italy. They had long-standing connections with the British: in 1787 Josiah Wedgwood wrote to one of the family asking him to assist **John Flaxman RA**, a 'much-valued friend of mine who is going to make some residence in Italy' (*Smiles* 1894, 221). Equally strong connections were held with the French, including Empress Josephine who was a customer in 1810, and with American visitors. Charles Micali was charged with the execution of the important Tripoli monument to six American naval heroes, carved in Leghorn, 1806–7, and shipped to the Academy at Annapolis, where it still stands. The family was also active in Carrara and the workshop was still functioning in 1826.

Literary References: *Gunnis* 1968, 259; *Headley* 1994, 247–64; *Sicca and Yarrington* 2000, 12, 70, 165, 166, 168

Funerary Monuments						
1.	1816	Rear-Admiral Robert Courtenay Reynolds (†1811)		St Clement, Cornwall	S	Pevsner, *Cornwall*, 1970, 164

MICHELL, John fl 1723

He was probably a Plymouth mason.

Chimneypieces

1.	1723	Two	m	[Antony House, Cornwall]; untraced	Archives, Sir John Carew-Pole, Bt in GPC

MICHENDEN, Thomas fl 1718

Architectural Sculpture

1.	1718	'a architrave, arches in nib'd and gag'd work' Payment(s): £47	Langley, Essex	Account book, Samuel Tufnell, of Langley, quoted in *Gunnis* 1968, 259

MIDDLETON, Charles fl 1762–72

He was listed as 'Modeller, chaser in bronze, and Papier Maché Manufacturer. In Tottenham-court-road, near Windmill Street' (*Mortimer* 1763, 18). He exhibited at the Society of Artists, 1762–72.

Literary References: *Gunnis* 1968, 259; *Pyke* 1973, 92

Architectural Sculpture					
1.	1772	Model for the panel for a ceiling	w	[Exhib Soc of Artists, London, 230]; untraced	*Graves* 1907, 165
Reliefs					
2.	1762	Foliage frieze in the manner of Stefano Della Bella	w	[Exhib Soc of Artists, London, 145]; untraced	*Graves* 1907, 165
3.	1770	Model for a tablet		[Exhib Soc of Artists, London, 174]; untraced	*Graves* 1907, 165
Miscellaneous					
4.	1762	Red deer, after nature		[Exhib Soc of BA, London, 146]; untraced	*Graves* 1907, 165
5.	1766	An elephant, cast of a model designed for a bronze		[Exhib Soc of Artists, London, 210]; untraced	*Graves* 1907, 165
6.	1768	A lion and stag, model		[Exhib Soc of Artists, London, 206]; untraced	*Graves* 1907, 165
7.	1768	A stag, model		[Soc of Artists special exhib, London, 157]; untraced	*Graves* 1907, 165

MIDDLETON, John, of Towcester 1718–1801

He carved the large 'ambitious' monument to John Daye (**1**). His death was announced in the *Northampton Mercury* of 16 May 1801. On 6 June in the same newspaper, his son, John Middleton II thanked 'numerous friends and customers of himself and his late father in their partnership', adding that he had for sale 'a large quantity of carved headstones, the designs taken from some of the most capital monuments in the country' (GPC). The second Middleton died in 1805, aged 56.

Literary References: *Monthly Mag* 1805, 19, 191; *Gunnis* 1968, 259

Funerary Monuments

1.	†1757	John Daye	Stowe-Nine-Churches, Northants	S	*Gunnis* 1968, 259; Pevsner, *Northants*, 1973, 419
2.	?1759	Mary Hodges	Towcester, Northants	S	*Gunnis* 1968, 259

MIDDLETON, Thomas fl 1726–c1740

A mason originating from Hertford, he became a 'husbandman' to **William Holland** on 4 February 1726 and was made free of the Masons' Company on 10 January 1733. He is noted as living at 'Norton Folgate', Stepney in a Masons' Company list of *c*1740.

Literary References: *Webb* 1999, 22

Archival References: Masons' Co, *Freemen*, fol 45; *Assistants*, fol 6

MILES, M

See **SWEET, William**

MILLANE fl 1829

Funerary Monuments

1.	†1829	William Taylor	St Bartholomew, Smithfield, London	RG/JP, 5, 921v.

MILLAR, I fl 1819

Funerary Monuments

1.	†1819	Rebecca Guinness	St Werburgh, Dublin	S	*Potterton* 1975, 72

MILLARD, James, of Gloucester fl 1790–1820

He was apprenticed to John Bryan of the **Bryan family of Painswick and Gloucester**, in 1760. The *Gloucester Journal* of 24 December 1770 carries an advertisement for 'J. Millard, Carver and Gilder of St Mary's Square (late of London)', who is probably the sculptor under discussion. His monuments, like most of those executed by the Gloucester statuaries, are of 'excellent workmanship' (*Gunnis* 1968, 259). Examples include the tablet with a draped broken column to Sir John Guise (**1**) and another carved with a crown in heaven and inverted torches to John Holbrow (**3**). He also sometimes used polycrome marbles, as with the Adam-style tablet to John Niblett (**8**).

Millard later went into partnership with **James Cooke, of Gloucester** and together they signed a number of monuments, including a coloured tablet to Judith Hooper (**19**) and the Hotham monument, which has a carved inverted shield with two oval inscription tablets (**22**), a design also used in Millard's solo work (**26**).

Literary References: *Gunnis* 1968, 259

Archival References: GPC

Funerary Monuments

1.	†1794	Sir John Guise	Gloucester Cathedral	S	*Gunnis* 1968, 259; Pevsner, *Glos: Vale & Forest of Dean*, 1976, 218
2.	†1778	Rev Thomas Gregory (co-sculptor: James Cooke of Gloucester)	Uley, Glos	S	Pevsner, *Glos: Cotswolds*, 1999, 703
3.	†1780	John Holbrow	Leonard Stanley, Glos	S	Pevsner, *Glos: Cotswolds*, 1999, 445
4.	†1787	Judith Hicks	Redmarley d'Abitot, Glos	S	Pevsner, *Glos: Vale & Forest of Dean*, 1976, 328
5.	†1790	John James (co-sculptor: James Cooke, of Gloucester)	Eastington, Glos	S	*Gunnis* 1968, 259; Pevsner, *Glos: Vale & Forest of Dean*, 1976, 178
6.	†1793	Sarah Hawker	Kings Stanley, Glos	S	Pevsner, *Glos: Cotswolds*, 1999, 431
7.	?1793	Thomas Smith	Much Marcle, Hereford		*Gunnis* 1968, 259
8.	†1794	John Niblett	Haresfield, Glos	S	Pevsner, *Glos: Vale & Forest of Dean*, 1976, 264
9.	†1799	John Howe	Redmarley d'Abitot, Glos	S	Pevsner, *Glos: Vale & Forest of Dean*, 1976, 328
10.	†1801	John Jones	Brockworth, Glos	S	Pevsner, *Glos: Vale & Forest of Dean*, 1976, 115
11.	†1802	Robert Yate	Bromsberrow, Glos	S	Pevsner, *Glos: Vale & Forest of Dean*, 1976, 116
12.	†1802	Sir Howe (†1801) and Lady Hicks	Great Witcombe, Glos	S	Pevsner, *Glos: Vale & Forest of Dean*, 1976, 257
13.	†1803	Gilbert Elton	Tibberton, Glos	S	Pevsner, *Glos: Vale & Forest of Dean*, 1976, 383
14.	†1804	Elizabeth Head	Gloucester Cathedral	S	*Gunnis* 1968, 259
15.	†1805	Priscilla Bromwich	Arlingham, Glos	S	Pevsner, *Glos: Vale & Forest of Dean*, 1976, 87
16.	†1807	William White (co-sculptor: James Cooke, of Gloucester)	Chaceley, Glos	S	Pevsner, *Glos: Vale & Forest of Dean*, 1976, 119
17.	†1808	Joseph Clark (co-sculptor: James Cooke, of Gloucester)	Taynton, Glos	S	Pevsner, *Glos: Vale & Forest of Dean*, 1976, 355
18.	†1809	Anne (†1759) and Thomas (†1809) Rudge and family	Gloucester Cathedral	S	*Gunnis* 1968, 259
19.	†1809	Judith Hooper (co-sculptor: James Cooke, of Gloucester)	Elkstone, Glos	S	Pevsner, *Glos: Cotswolds*, 1999, 358
20.	†1810	Elizabeth Holder (co-sculptor: James Cooke, of Gloucester)	North Cerney, Glos	S	Pevsner, *Glos: Cotswolds*, 1999, 509
21.	†1811	Francis Donovan (co-sculptor: James Cooke, of Gloucester)	Tibberton, Glos	S	Pevsner, *Glos: Vale & Forest of Dean*, 1976, 383
22.	†1811	Sir Charles Hotham and his wife, Elizabeth (†1834) (co-sculptor: James Cooke, of Gloucester)	Gloucester Cathedral	S	*Gunnis* 1968, 259
23.	†1812	Mary Snell (co-sculptor: James Cooke, of Gloucester)	St Michael, Guiting Power, Glos	S	Pevsner, *Glos: Cotswolds*, 1999, 395
24.	†1812	Mary Stanford (co-sculptor: James Cooke, of Gloucester)	Gloucester Cathedral	S	*Gunnis* 1968, 259
25.	?1815	Mrs O'Malley (co-sculptor: James Cooke, of Gloucester)	St Mary, Cheltenham, Glos		*Gunnis* 1968, 259
26.	† to 1836	John Pitt MP (†1805)	Gloucester Cathedral	S	*Gunnis* 1968, 259
27.	nd	Lady Maria Price	North Cerney, Glos	S	Pevsner, *Glos: Cotswolds*, 1999, 509

Chimneypieces

28.	1790	Description unavailable	Barnsley Park, Glos, dining room		Pevsner, *Glos: Cotswolds*, 1999, 159

MILLER fl 1672–74

In 1672 a 'Mr Miller the Carver' was paid £15 10s for carving work about the Vintners' Company hall. In 1674 he was paid £8 for carved work around the door cases.

Archival References: Vintners, RW Accts, vol 5

MILLER, A fl 1825

Miss Miller was living in Dorset Street, Dublin, in 1825, when she won a medal from the London Society of Arts.

Miscellaneous

1.	1825	'Carvings in ivory of heads and figures'	[Soc of A, gold Isis medal]; untraced	RSA, *Transactions*, vol 43, 1825, xlviii

MILLER, Felix Martin 1819–

Miller was born on 8 February 1819 and christened on 11 September 1822 at Folkestone, Kent, the son of Martin and Sarah Miller. He was left fatherless at an early age and was brought up at the London orphan school. He joined the Royal Academy Schools in 1842 on the recommendation of **Henry Weekes**, giving his address as 6 Lower Eaton Street, Pimlico. At the exhibition of works of art for the Houses of Parliament, held three years later, he showed *The dying Briton* and *Orphans* (**6, 5**). The *Art Union* reported the progress of the former work in 1844, saying that it possessed 'no inconsiderable merit,' and a year later described the finished piece as 'composed of two figures, a boy and a girl, evidently all-in-all to each other. The boy holds his sister's hand and the bearing of both forcibly tells the tale of their joint bereavement'. Miller received many enthusiastic press notices. His *Spirit of the Calm* was described by the *Art Journal* as 'elegant' with 'much fancy and refined taste' (**4**), and his *Attendant spirit in Comus* as 'a highly poetic image' which 'reflects honour on the young sculptor who has so successfully executed it' (**26**).

In the 1850s he lived in Bloomfield Place, Pimlico, before taking up a post as master in the modelling class at South Kensington Museum in 1860 and moving to Drayton Terrace, West Brompton. He remained in the post until at least 1880. Miller executed several monuments, modelled for Minton and Copeland, and his busts include a study of Dr Livingstone *ad vivum* (**14**). Chiefly, however, he produced bas-reliefs of poetic subjects, notably from Shakespeare. These works were apparently small in scale and intended for the domestic market: Miller described one of his models, of *Titania* (**30**), as 'designed for a drawing room, etc' (*Graves* V, 1905–6, 250). The *Art Journal* commented of his *Ariel*: 'It is in subjects of playful and graceful imagination, like this, that Mr Miller peculiarly excels . . . they should be encouraged: there are many ways of using them for ornamental purposes' (**27**).

His fellow sculptor and friend, **J H Foley**, was an ardent admirer of Miller's sculpture and commissioned, among other works, a marble copy of *Titania asleep* (**30**). On the death of Foley, the *Art Journal* carried an obituary in which the author pays tribute to Miller: 'he is one of the few sculptors whose genius is manifest and who has produced works, chiefly *bas-reliefs*, that are unsurpassed by any productions of their class in modern art. . . but whose evil fortune it has been to obtain much praise with little recompense' (*AJ*, 1874, 306). Miller exhibited at the RA for the last time in 1880, giving his address as 16 Victoria Grove, Fulham Road. His date of death is uncertain. On 16 December 1953, lot 555 in the Sotheby sale catalogue was a volume of over 500 silhouettes of wild and domestic animals by the sculptor.

Literary References: *ILN* 26 May 1866, 512; *AJ*, 1874, 306; *Graves* 1875, 379; *Graves* 1905–6, 249–51; *Gunnis* 1968, 259–60; *Morris and Roberts* 1998, 427–8; *Bilbey* 2002, 337

Archival References: RA Admissions; GPC; IGI

Funerary Monuments						
1.	†1856	Sir James Morrison		Sutton, Surrey	S	
2.	1865	'Modelled sketch for the monument to Dr Andrew Reed in the London Orphan Asylum Clapton'		[Exhib RA, London, 968]; untraced		*Graves* V, 1905–6, 251
3.	1869	Edward Jordan		Kingston Cathedral, Jamaica		*Gunnis* 1968, 260
Statues						
4.	1843	'The spirit of the Calm, sketch for a small statue'		[Exhib RA, London, 1493]; untraced		*Graves* V, 1905–6, 249
5.	1844	Orphans Model(s): Exhib RA, London, 1844, 1303	m	London orphan asylum		*AU*, 1844, 171; *AU*, 1845, 258; *AU* 1847, 83; *Graves* 1875, 379; *Graves* V, 1905–6, 249
6.	1845	The dying Briton		[Exhib Westminster Hall, London, 123]; untraced		*Westminster* 1845, 15; *AU*, 1845, 258; *Graves* V, 1905–6, 249
7.	1848	Spring		[Exhib RA, London, 1364]; untraced		*AJ Cat* 1851, 260 (repr); *Graves* V, 1905–6, 249/50
8.	1852	Lycidas, sketch for a statue		[Exhib BI, London, 539]; untraced		*Graves* 1875, 379
9.	1854	Spring-flower seller, sketch for a statue		[Exhib RA, London, 1415]; untraced		*Graves* 1875, 379; *Graves* V, 1905–6, 250
10.	1866	Engineer's blacksmith, statuette	p	VAM 304-1876	S	*Bilbey* 2002, 339 (repr)
11.	nd	Nymph		Christie, 26 March 1858 (£62)		GPC
12.	nd	The Archer		[Sydney, Australia]; destroyed		*Gunnis* 1968, 260
Busts						
13.	1842	Ideal head of Pythagoras, sketch	p	[Exhib RA, London, 1359]; untraced		*Graves* V, 1905–6, 249
14.	1857	Dr David Livingstone	p	VAM 349-1872 Other versions: 'cabinet bust' exhib RA, London, 1858, 1287	SD	*Graves* V, 1905–6, 250; *Ormond* 1973, 273; *Johnson* 1975, 324; *Bilbey* 2002, 338 (repr)
15.	1861	'Sketch for a head of Viola, disguised as a page'		[Exhib RA, London, 1130 Exhib Liverpool Ac, 1099 (sold to Mr Tetley for £5 5s)]; untraced		*Graves* V, 1905–6, 250; *Morris and Roberts* 1998, 428, 699
16.	1862	Samuel Taylor Coleridge	p	VAM 348-1872	S	*Graves* V, 1905–6, 250; *Bilbey* 2002, 338 (repr)
17.	1864	'Shakespeare in Paris *plastique*'		[Exhib RA, London, 931]; untraced		*Graves* V, 1905–6, 250
18.	1865	Elaine		[Exhib RA, London, 1073]; untraced		*Graves* V, 1905–6, 251
19.	1868	Alexandra of Denmark, Princess of Wales	sa	[Crystal Palace Art Union]; Gov Art coll (1986)	S	Gov Art coll archives
Architectural Sculpture						
20.	1843	Hero and Leander, sketch for a relief		[Exhib RA, London, 1471]; untraced		*Graves* V, 1905–6, 249
21.	1853	Reredos Model(s): 'Christ and the Disciples at Emmaus; model for the altar-piece of S. Barnabus, Homerton' exhib RA, London, 1853, 1343		St Barnabus, Homerton, London		*Graves* V, 1905–6, 250; *Gunnis* 1968, 259–60
22.	1866	Group and two figures, models		Untraced Other versions: marble, carved by James Underwood, Natwest Bank, Bishopsgate, London		*Ward-Jackson* 2003, 35–39; GPC
Reliefs						
23.	1843	'A young lady', medallion	m	[Exhib RA, London, 1465]; untraced		*Graves* V, 1905–6, 249
24.	1847	The genius of the calm	m	[Exhib RA, London, 1435]; untraced		*AU*, 1847, 200; *Graves* V, 1905–6, 249

No.	Date	Title	Mat.	Location		Literary references
25.	1847	'The Translation of Milton'; sketch for a bas-relief, one of a series of 120 designs in outline from the works of Milton'		[Exhib RA, London, 1427]; untraced		*Graves* V, 1905–6, 249
26.	1848	The attendent spirit in Comus descending on a 'Glancing star'; one of a series of 40 designs		[Exhib RA, London, 1355]; untraced		*AJ Cat* 1851, 279 (repr); *Graves* V, 1905–6, 249
27.	1850	Ariel ('Merrily, merrily shall I live now Under the blossom that hangs from the bough')		[Exhib RA, London, 1335]; untraced Other versions: 1870, plaster, exhib RA, London, 1195 1871–2, exhib Soc of BA, London, 513, £15		*AJ* 1873, 28 (repr); *Graves* V, 1905–6, 251; *Gunnis* 1968, 260; *Johnson* 1975, 324
28.	1851	Lycidas, bas-relief		[Gt Exhib]; untraced		*Gunnis* 1968, 260
29.	1851	The spirit of calm, bas-relief		[Gt Exhib]; untraced		*Gunnis* 1968, 260
30.	1851	Titania asleep	m	Glasgow Museums S.198 Other versions: for **J H Foley RA**, 1853, marble; untraced exhib RA, London 1865, 981, relieve-electro-bronze; untraced		*AJ* 1856, 316 (repr); *Graves* V, 1905–6, 250, 251; *Gunnis* 1968, 260; *Morris and Roberts* 1998, 427, 682
31.	1852	Ariel, bas-relief	m	[Exhib RA, London, 1362]; untraced		*Graves* V, 1905–6, 250
32.	1852	'March, April, May; sketches for bas-reliefs'		[Exhib RA, London, 1361]; untraced		*Graves* V, 1905–6, 250
33.	1852	Peace, sketch for a relief		[Exhib RA, London, 1489]; untraced		*Graves* V, 1905–6, 250; *Morris and Roberts* 1998, 427, 684
34.	1852	War (the miseries of war), sketch for a relief		[Exhib RA, London, 1490]; untraced		*Graves* V, 1905–6, 250; *Morris and Roberts* 1998, 427, 682
35.	pre-1855	Ariel	m	VAM 2638-1856	S	*Bilbey* 2002, 337 (repr)
36.	1856	Emily and the white doe of Rylstone		[Exhib Liverpool Ac, 875 (sold to John Butterworth for 10 gns)]; untraced Other versions: ex coll J H Foley; untraced		*AJ*, 1859, 24 (repr); *Graves* V, 1905–6, 250–1; *Morris and Roberts* 1998, 427
37.	1857	Hindoo girl watching the progress of her love-lamp on the Ganges		[Exhib RA, London, 1295]; untraced		*Graves* V, 1905–6, 250; *Morris and Roberts* 1998, 428
38.	1858	Ariel on the mission to calm the tempest		[Exhib RA, London, 1323]; untraced		*Graves* V, 1905–6, 250; *Morris and Roberts* 1998, 428
39.	1859	Four reliefs illustrative of Industrial Science: Fine Arts, Machinery, Manufactures, Raw Materials		[Exhib LSFA, Liverpool, 748]; untraced		*Morris and Roberts* 1998, 428
40.	1860	Sappho		[Exhib RA, London, 1095]; untraced		*Graves* V, 1905–6, 250
41.	1864	Dr Raffles, of Liverpool, medallion portrait		[Exhib RA, London, 944]; untraced		*Graves* V, 1905–6, 250
42.	1868	A cruise amongst the water lilies		[Exhib RA, London, 985]; untraced		*AJ*, 1872, 124 (repr); *Graves* 1875, 379; *Graves* V, 1905–6, 251; *Gunnis* 1968, 260; *Morris and Roberts* 1998, 427
43.	1873	Hero signalling to Leander	p	VAM 114-1877	S	*Graves* V, 1905–6, 251; *Bilbey* 2002, 339 (repr)
Miscellaneous						
44.	1843	Viola's sister; study of a head		[Exhib RA, London, 1457]; untraced		*Graves* V, 1905–6, 249
45.	1846	Distress, a sketch		[Exhib RA, London, 1463]; untraced		*Graves* V, 1905–6, 249
46.	1848	A guardian angel		[Exhib RA, London, 1353]; untraced		*Graves* V, 1905–6, 249
47.	1848	Autumn		[Exhib RA, London, 1366]; untraced		*Graves* V, 1905–6, 249
48.	1848	Summer		[Exhib RA, London, 1365]; untraced		*Graves* V, 1905–6, 249
49.	1848	The lover overtasked (adaptable for a rose-stand)		[Exhib BI, London, 470 Exhib RA, London, 1850, 1367]; untraced		*Graves* 1875, 379; *Graves* V, 1905–6, 250
50.	1848	Winter		[Exhib RA, London, 1367]; untraced		*Graves* V, 1905–6, 249
51.	1849	Sabrina		[Exhib RA, London, 1216]; untraced		*Graves* V, 1905–6, 249
52.	1850	Childhood's happy hour		[Exhib RA, London, 1317]; untraced		*Graves* V, 1905–6, 249
53.	1850	'Lycidas is dead . . .'		[Exhib RA, London, 1334]; untraced		*Graves* V, 1905–6, 250
54.	1850	The Brother and Sister in 'Comus'		[Exhib RA, London, 1318]; untraced		*Graves* V, 1905–6, 249
55.	1850	The brothers in 'Comus'		[Exhib RA, London, 1329]; untraced		*Graves* V, 1905–6, 250
56.	1850	'Virtue may be assailed . . ., sketch'		[Exhib RA, London, 1326]; untraced		*Graves* V, 1905–6, 249
57.	1851	Elf of the brook		[Exhib BI, London, 527]; untraced		*Graves* 1875, 379; *Graves* V, 1905–6, 249
58.	1854	A calm spirit		[Exhib RA, London, 370]; untraced		*Graves* V, 1905–6, 250; *Morris and Roberts* 1998, 427
59.	1855	Ariel (two versions of the subject)		[Exhib Liverpool Ac, 328, 830 (830 sold to Charles Pemberton for 10 gns)]; untraced		*Morris and Roberts* 1998, 427, 684
60.	1855	Flower girl		[Exhib Liverpool Ac, 839 (sold to Mrs Avison for £7 10s)]; untraced		*Morris and Roberts* 1998, 427
61.	1855	Mechanical science adding speed to the wheel		[Exhib Liverpool Ac, 836]; untraced		*Graves* V, 1905–6, 250; *Morris and Roberts* 1998, 427
62.	1855	Medieval wayfarers receiving their evening benediction		[Exhib Liverpool Ac, 152]; untraced		*Morris and Roberts* 1998, 427
63.	1856	Ariel appeasing the tempest		[Exhib RA, London, 1272]; untraced		*Graves* V, 1905–6, 250; *Morris and Roberts* 1998, 427
64.	1856	Ariel, 'Where the bee sucks . . .'		[Exhib RA, London, 1274 Liverpool Ac, 1856, 874 (sold to W D Holt for £8)]; untraced		*Graves* V, 1905–6, 250; *Morris and Roberts* 1998, 427

65.	1856	We frolic while 'tis May, study for a group		[Exhib BI, London, 556]; untraced		*Graves* 1875, 379; *Morris and Roberts* 1998, 427, 428
66.	1856	Youth, a study for one of a series to illustrate 'Passages in the Voyage of Life'		[Exhib Liverpool Ac, 757]; untraced		*Morris and Roberts* 1998, 427
67.	1858	Allurements		[Exhib RA, London, 409]; untraced		*Graves* V, 1905–6, 250; *Morris and Roberts* 1998, 427
68.	1858	Designs for medals for the department of science and art		[Exhib RA, London, 1319]; untraced		*Graves* V, 1905–6, 250
69.	1859	Evangeline		[Exhib RA, London, 1266]; untraced		*Graves* V, 1905–6, 250; *Johnson* 1975, 324; *Morris and Roberts* 1998, 428
70.	1859	Oberon and Titania		[Exhib RA, London, 1373]; untraced		*Graves* V, 1905–6, 250
71.	1860	Michelangelo attending his sick servant		[Exhib RA, London, 1058]; untraced		*Graves* V, 1905–6, 250
72.	1860	Nature adorned		[Exhib RA, London, 1052]; untraced		*Graves* V, 1905–6, 250
73.	1860	Study of a head of Oenone		[Exhib RA, London, 1088]; untraced		*Graves* V, 1905–6, 250
74.	1861	Enid		[Exhib Liverpool Ac, 1100]; untraced		*Graves* 1875, 379; *Graves* V, 1905–6, 250/1; *Morris and Roberts* 1998, 428, 699
75.	1861	'Geraine, a sketch'		[Exhib RA, London, 1133]; untraced		*Graves* V, 1905–6, 250
76.	1861	Marble study of a head of Mechanical Science	m	[Exhib RA, London, 1086]; untraced		*Graves* V, 1905–6, 250
77.	1861	Mournful Oenone wandering for her love		[Exhib RA, London, 1117]; untraced		*Graves* V, 1905–6, 250
78.	1861	'Viola, a sketch'		[Exhib RA, London, 1132]; untraced		*Graves* V, 1905–6, 250
79.	1862	Excelsior, study of a head for a statue		[Exhib RA, London, 1052]; untraced		*Graves* V, 1905–6, 250; *Morris and Roberts* 1998, 428
80.	1863	Oenone	m	[Exhib BI, London, 603]; untraced		*Graves* 1875, 379
81.	1863	Stalking for a shot		[Exhib RA, London, 1084]; untraced		*Graves* V, 1905–6, 250
82.	1863	The lady in 'Comus' entranced by the enchanted chair		[Exhib RA, London, 1078]; untraced		*Graves* 1875, 379; *Graves* V, 1905–6, 250; *Johnson* 1975, 324
83.	1863	'There in the twilight cold and grey'		[Exhib RA, London, 1104]; untraced		*Graves* V, 1905–6, 250
84.	1865	'with Head upraised and Look intent'		[Exhib RA, London, 919]; untraced		*Graves* V, 1905–6, 250
85.	1866	Christabel Payment(s): £15		[Exhib Soc of BA, London, 518]; untraced		*Johnson* 1975, 324
86.	1866	'For since the Birth of Time'		[Exhib RA, London, 912]; untraced		*Graves* V, 1905–6, 251
87.	1866	The lady in 'Comus' benighted		[Exhib RA, London, 910]; untraced		*Graves* V, 1905–6, 251; *Johnson* 1975, 324
88.	1867	A blacksmith preparing to strike		[Exhib Soc of BA, London, 1072]; untraced		*Johnson* 1975, 324
89.	1868	'The Indian Siesta, a sketch'		[Exhib RA, London, 1103; Int Exhib 1872]; untraced		*Graves* V, 1905–6, 251; *Gunnis* 1968, 260
90.	1868	'The Launch, a sketch for a projected series of eight to represent passages in the voyage of life'		[Exhib RA, London, 996]; untraced		*Graves* V, 1905–6, 251
91.	1869	Viola	m	[Exhib RA, London, 1186]; untraced		*Graves* V, 1905–6, 251
92.	1870	'We frolic while 'tis Spring, sketch for a portrait group'		[Exhib RA, London, 1209]; untraced		*Graves* V, 1905–6, 251
93.	1871	'A yeoman of olden time training his sons as volunteers'		[Exhib RA, London, 1329]; untraced		*Graves* V, 1905–6, 251
94.	1871	Zephyr with Aurora playing		[Exhib RA, London, 1328]; untraced		*Graves* V, 1905–6, 251
95.	1875	Parental affection		[Exhib RA, London, 1297]; untraced		*Graves* V, 1905–6, 251
96.	1877	Portraits of Theodore and Herbert, infant sons of J J Mellor		[Exhib RA, London, 1401]; untraced		*Graves* V, 1905–6, 251
97.	1878	Miranda watching the shipwreck		[Exhib RA, London, 1505]; untraced		*Graves* V, 1905–6, 251
98.	1880	Defiance, study for a bust		[Exhib RA, London, 1644]; untraced		*Graves* V, 1905–6, 251

MILLER, George James Somerton –1876

He exhibited at the Royal Academy, giving his addresses as 20 Abingdon Street, Westminster in 1857, 1 Little College Street in 1862, and in 1876 at 10 Cowley Street.

Literary References: *Graves* V, 1905–6, 251

Busts

1.	1862	William Cureton DCL, FRS	p	BM	SD	*Graves* V, 1905–6, 251; *Dawson* 1999, 81–2 (repr)
2.	1864	Sir George Cornewall Lewis Bt		[Exhib RA, London, 1052]; untraced		*Graves* V, 1905–6, 251; *Ormond* 1973, 270

Miscellaneous

3.	1857	Aeneas		[Exhib RA, London, 1212]; untraced		*Graves* V, 1905–6, 251
4.	1858	The good Samaritan		[Exhib RA, London, 1219]; untraced		*Graves* V, 1905–6, 251
5.	1859	Sir Richard Mayne, KCB		[Exhib RA, London, 1323]; untraced		*Graves* V, 1905–6, 251
6.	1862	Griselda and Janicola		[Exhib RA, London, 1103]; untraced		*Graves* V, 1905–6, 251
7.	1862	Rev Henry Hutton, MA		[Exhib RA, London, 1112]; untraced		*Graves* V, 1905–6, 251
8.	1862	Rev James Lupton, MA		[Exhib RA, London, 1129]; untraced		*Graves* V, 1905–6, 251
9.	1863	Alfred Mellon		[Exhib RA, London, 1149]; untraced		*Graves* V, 1905–6, 251
10.	1864	Charles Santley		[Exhib RA, London, 1055]; untraced		*Graves* V, 1905–6, 251
11.	1864	Clemency, Bernard and Emily		[Exhib RA, London, 1026]; untraced		*Graves* V, 1905–6, 251
12.	1865	W Wreford Major		[Exhib RA, London, 1076]; untraced		*Graves* V, 1905–6, 251
13.	1866	Charles Major		[Exhib RA, London, 1039]; untraced		*Graves* V, 1905–6, 251
14.	1866	Rev Lord John Thynne, DD		[Exhib RA, London, 1041]; untraced		*Graves* V, 1905–6, 251
15.	1867	Rev William Talfourd, MA		[Exhib RA, London, 1187]; untraced		*Graves* V, 1905–6, 251
16.	1867	Robert Montague		[Exhib RA, London, 1080]; untraced		*Graves* V, 1905–6, 251
17.	1867	The Ven Archdeacon Wordsworth, DD		[Exhib RA, London, 1175]; untraced		*Graves* V, 1905–6, 251

18.	1868	Charles Vignoles, FRS		[Exhib RA, London, 980]; untraced	*Graves* V, 1905–6, 251
19.	1874	Sir George Musgrave, Bt		[Exhib RA, London, 1462]; untraced	*Graves* V, 1905–6, 251
20.	1876	Hilda		[Exhib RA, London, 1464]; untraced	*Graves* V, 1905–6, 252
21.	1876	Nora		[Exhib RA, London, 1466]; untraced	*Graves* V, 1905–6, 252
22.	1877	David Reid	m	[Exhib RA, London, 1517]; untraced	*Graves* V, 1905–6, 252

MILLER, George M –1819

For further information the reader is referred to *Pyke* 1973, 92 and *Pyke* 1981, 28

MILLER, George, of Bedford fl *c*1833

He is only known to have been responsible for one small wall-monument of sarcophagus form. A Samuel Miller of Bedford, 'free-mason', was the master-mason employed in 1710 for building Hinwick House, Beds (Orlebar Archives cited in *Gunnis* 1968, 260).

Funerary Monuments

1.	?1833	Philip Sanson	Sharnbrook, Beds	S	*Gunnis* 1968, 260

MILLER, John fl 1680

He was paid £16 in 1680 for 'Carving worke done in ye withdrawinge roome' of Mercers' Hall (Mercers S & R W Accts).

MILLER, Richard fl 1693

William Pett's executors paid 'Mr Richard Miller and partner' for 'setting up a monument' to the deceased (1). The monument has not been traced nor the partner identified.

Funerary Monuments

1.	1693	William Pett (†1692) Payment(s): £52 11s	Untraced		Hoare's Customer Ledger d.2, fols 217, 218

MILLER & BOUCOCK fl 1787–90

In the archives of Wanstead church, Essex, Gunnis located a contract for building that church made between the parishioners and William Miller and George Boucock of 'St Martin's, Ludgate'. They later received £9,000 for the work, which they carried out between 1787 and 1790 (*Gunnis* 1968, 260).

MILLER & DERKS, of Manchester fl *c*1836

They sign a tablet with a small figure of a pensive woman at the top.

Funerary Monuments

1.	†1836	Ellen Sandiford	Tottington, Lancs	S	Pevsner, *Lancs: N*, 1969, 247

MILLERS & CO, of Salford fl *c*1847

Only one monument has been identified. They may conceivably be identified with **Millers and Derome, of Manchester.**

Funerary Monuments

1.	†1847	Rev Isaac Robley	St Philip, Salford, Lancs	S	

MILLERS & DEROME, of Manchester fl *c*1830–38

Only one monument has been identified by the partners, who are described as manufacturers of 'chimneypieces etc' at 3, Stanley Street in *Pigot's Directory*, 1838 (p38).

Funerary Monuments

1.	†1830	William Johnson Edensor (†1829) and Joana Thomasine	St Giles, Wrexham, Denbighs	S	Pevsner, *Clwyd*, 1986, 301

MILLIGAN, J, of London fl 1817–34

He exhibited busts at the Royal Academy, 1817–24, giving addresses as 15 Nassau Street (1817), 'At Mr. Marshall, Regent Street' (1820), 21 Palace Place, Pimlico (1821), and 33 York Buildings (1824). He signed a number of monuments, the best being to the Rev John Currey which has 'a charming portrait-relief of a clergyman in a wig' (*Gunnis* 1968, 260) (1).

Literary References: *Graves* V, 1905–6, 255

Funerary Monuments

1.	†1824	Rev John Currey	Holy Trinity, Dartford, Kent	S	*Gunnis* 1968, 260; Pevsner, *Kent: W & Weald*, 1976, 256
2.	?1825	Robert and Mary Wright	Middle Claydon, Bucks	S	*Gunnis* 1968, 260
3.	†1833	Neville Somerville Cameron	Chennai (Madras) Cathedral, India	S	*Gunnis* 1968, 260
4.	†1834	Sophia and William Godfrey (†1833) Jervis	Old Woking, Surrey	S	*Gunnis* 1968, 260

Busts

5.	1817	E J Richardson, model	[Exhib RA, London, 1075]; untraced		*Graves* V, 1905–6, 255
6.	1818	Mr Kimlin	[Exhib RA, London, 1043]; untraced		*Graves* V, 1905–6, 255
7.	1820	Unidentified gentleman Model(s): RA, 1817, no. 1050	[Exhib RA, London, 1033]; untraced		*Graves* V, 1905–6, 255
8.	1821	Sir J Cotterell, model 'to be executed in marble'	[Exhib RA, London, 1142]; untraced		*Graves* V, 1905–6, 255
9.	1817–1824	H Cooper, of Canterbury	[Exhib RA, London, 1122]; untraced		*Graves* V, 1905–6, 255
10.	1824	Lady Mary Brownlow	[Exhib RA, London, 1027]; untraced		*Graves* V, 1905–6, 255; *Gunnis* 1968, 260

MILLIGAN, William, of London 1812–78

When he built the mausoleum for James Morison (1) at Kensal Green designed by **Robert and Benjamin Shout**, he was accused of 'improper conduct' towards the clerk and directors of the cemetery and was banned from entering the grounds. Milligan had to write a grovelling apology, expressing his sorrow and promising future good conduct (*Curl* 2001, 102). In 1850 he carved the seven foot high statues of Nelson and Wellington commissioned by Lord Frederick FitzClarence for Southsea Common (3). The works were unveiled on Waterloo Day, 18 June 1850, with a large display and a fete. The *Illustrated London News* described these figures as 'elegant' though the *Builder* felt that there had been a 'tasteless mistake' in 'placing the Duke's foot on the Gallic cock', and later added that 'the impression of looking at them is one of discomfort'.

Milligan also carved a bust of Nelson which realized £73 at a sale in 1900 (5) and he supplied historicising busts for the Vyne, which are well executed and convey considerable character (6, 7). His premises were in Old Cavendish Street, London. He is buried in Kensal Green Cemetery.

Literary References: *ILN* 18 May 1850, 357; 22 June 1850, 440; *Gunnis* 1968, 260; *Curl* 2001, 102, 183, 242

Funerary Monuments						
1.	1836–8	James Morison 'the Hygeist') Drawing(s): VAM E.3063-1980		Kensal Green Cemetery, London		*Curl* 2001, 102, 183 (repr)
2.	nd	Pakenham family member		Ballynadrentagh, Co Antrim	S	*Potterton* 1975, 72
Statues						
3.	1850	Admiral Lord Nelson and Arthur, 1st Duke of Wellington		[Southsea Common, Hants]; untraced		*Builder* 1850, 243, 317; *ILN* 18 May 1850, 357 (repr); *ILN* 22 June 1850, 440; *Gunnis* 1968, 260
4.	nd	Boy with a cat, statuette		[Phillips, 13 April 1885]; untraced		GPC
Busts						
5.	nd	Admiral Lord Nelson		Peel heirlooms sale, 1900, £73; untraced		*Gunnis* 1968, 260
6.	nd	Mary, Queen of Scots	m	The Vyne, Hants	S	*Gunnis* 1968, 260
7.	nd	William Shakespeare	m	The Vyne, Hants	S	

MILLS, J, of Cirencester fl *c*1771–1837

He signed a number of Gloucestershire tablets in slate and stone. Mills is probably related to, or perhaps synonomous with John Mills, who built Down Ampney House, Glos, for Lord Eliot in 1799–1800, under the architect Sir John Soane. Mills was responsible for the gothic windows and entrance porch, and the cornice of the south-east front.

Archival References: Soane Bill Book C fols 11r–12r

Funerary Monuments						
1.	†1804	Sarah Naish		Stratton, Glos	S	Pevsner, *Glos: Cotswolds*, 1999, 646
2.	†1771–1805	John Haines (†1771) and 7 family members	sl	Daglingworth, Glos	S	Pevsner, *Glos: Cotswolds*, 1999, 309
3.	†1806	John Howes		Winson, Glos	S	Pevsner, *Glos: Cotswolds*, 1999, 738
4.	†1817	William Kilmister		Rodmarton, Glos	S	Pevsner, *Glos: Cotswolds*, 1999, 582
5.	†1794–1821	Haines family members		Daglingworth, Glos	S	Pevsner, *Glos: Cotswolds*, 1999, 309
6.	†1830	James Pitt		Stratton, Glos	S	Pevsner, *Glos: Cotswolds*, 1999, 646
7.	†1837	Catherine Wace		Lechlade, Glos	S	Pevsner, *Glos: Cotswolds*, 1999, 438
8.	nd	Unidentified subjects, tablets		Horsley, Glos		Pevsner, *Glos: Cotswolds*, 1999, 416

MILLS, Mrs

For further information the reader is referred to *Pyke* 1973, 92

MILLS, of Cheltenham fl 1762

Funerary Monuments						
1.	†1762	Ralph Ollife		Bagendon, Glos	S	Pevsner, *Glos: Cotswolds*, 1999, 153

MILLS, Richard, of Cirencester fl *c*1784–1842

He was probably the son of **J Mills of Cirencester**, and he signed a number of simple tablets.

Literary References: *Gunnis* 1968, 260

Funerary Monuments						
1.	†1786	Daniel and Sarah (†1761) Mills		Miserden, Glos	S	
2.	†1802	Rev William Walbank (†1784) and his wife, Hester		Brimpsfield, Glos	S	Pevsner, *Glos: Cotswolds*, 1999, 196
3.	†1802	William Walbrook (†1782) and wife (†1802)		Brimpsfield [?], Glos		RG/JP, 5, 929
4.	†1812	Ann Watson		Duntisbourne Abbots, Glos	S	Pevsner, *Glos: Cotswolds*, 1999, 329
5.	?1812	William Adams		Cricklade, Wilts	S	*Gunnis* 1968, 260
6.	†1758–1813	Pitt family		Badgeworth, Glos	S	
7.	1814	Daniel Mills		Miserden, Glos	S	Pevsner, *Glos: Cotswolds*, 1999, 486
8.	†1814	William Davies		Withington, Glos	S	Pevsner, *Glos: Cotswolds*, 1999, 741
9.	†1816	Apsley Bathurst		St John the Baptist, Cirencester, Glos	S	Pevsner, *Glos: Cotswolds*, 1999, 255
10.	†1820	William Mill		Shorncote, Glos	S	Pevsner, *Glos: Cotswolds*, 1999, 610
11.	†1821	Elizabeth Tyndale		North Cerney, Glos		RG/JP, 5, 929
12.	1821–1823	Unidentified subjects, tablets		Cranham, Glos	S	Pevsner, *Glos: Cotswolds*, 1999, 306
13.	†1824	Sarah Buckoll		Siddington, Glos	S	Pevsner, *Glos: Cotswolds*, 1999, 611
14.	†1824	William Hall		Bibury, Glos	S	Pevsner, *Glos: Cotswolds*, 1999, 170
15.	†1825	Nathaniel (†1821) and Jane Sadler		Cranham, Glos	S	
16.	†1784–1828	Giles Haines (†1803) and five family members		Duntisbourne Rouse, Glos	S	Pevsner, *Glos: Cotswolds*, 1999, 332
17.	†1839	John Poole		Bourton-on-the-Water, Glos	S	Pevsner, *Glos: Cotswolds*, 1999, 189
18.	†1842	Daniel (†1834) and Rev Charles Mesman		Duntisbourne Abbots, Glos	S	Pevsner, *Glos: Cotswolds*, 1999, 329

MILLWARD, Charles, of Hereford fl c1788

Millward, who became a freeman of Hereford in 1761, signed the wall-tablet with an 'Adam' semi-urn to Henry Davies (1).

Funerary Monuments

1.	?1788	Henry Davies	Bredwardine, Hereford	S	*Gunnis* 1968, 260

MILLWARD FAMILY, of Hay-on-Wye fl c1793–1808

Members of the family, who sign monuments, include R and I Millward. John Millward is described in Pigot's *Directory* (1830) as a 'carpenter, joiner and stone-cutter' at Hay-on-Wye. In 1806–8 he remodelled Ridgebourne, near Kington, Herefs (*Colvin* 1995, 658).

Funerary Monuments

1.	†1793	Joan Jones (by R Millward, of Hay)	Aberedw, Radnor	S	Pevsner, *Powys*, 1979, 217
2.	†1797	Elizabeth Tuck (by I Millward, of Hay)	Llanbedr Painscastle, Radnor	S	Pevsner, *Powys*, 1979, 243
3.	?1806	Freeman family (by John Millward)	Bishops Frome, Herefs	S	

MILNES, R fl c1823

The monument to John Owen is neo-Greek and matches that of Owen's wife's by John Carline I, of the **Carline family of Shrewsbury**.

Funerary Monuments

1.	†1823	John Owen	Penrhos, Montgomery	S	Pevsner, *Powys*, 1979, 183

MILNES, Thomas 1813–88

He was born at Tickhill, near Doncaster, Yorks. In 1841 he joined the Royal Academy schools on the recommendation of **E H Baily**, giving his address as 3 Keppel Row. Three years later he exhibited at Westminster Hall a group entitled *The Death of Harold*, described by the **Literary Gazette** as 'the strangest collection of short trunks and consumptive legs ever congregated together. The same model (and that a bad one) must have sat for them all. The king is not falling from his horse, but turning aside to whisper' (14). Despite the adverse criticism Milnes won a number of important commissions. In 1847 he was paid 700 guineas for his seven foot high statue of Nelson erected at Norwich, and in the same year was selected to execute a broadly-carved statue of the Duke of Wellington, depicted in a cape, with his right arm across his chest. Both commissions were reported in the *Builder* (15, 16).

In 1858 Milnes was invited by the government to model four lions for the base of Nelson's column in Trafalgar Square (18). They were considered unsuitable and the First Commissioner of Works returned them to the sculptor. Titus Salt, who had earlier commissioned a stern, be-whiskered bust from the sculptor (31), bought the unwanted lions for his workers' village at Saltaire. The *Art Journal* reported the arrival of the beasts in Yorkshire, commenting 'The expression of the grand animal is almost human in watchfulness and wrath; yet nothing is sacrificed to effect that is not natural.' It added with some relish 'they are admirably modelled comparing by no means unfavourably with those in Trafalgar Square' (*AJ* 1869, 159).

Milnes executed a number of monuments, including one with a scroll and weeping willow to Lady Louisa Bunbury (1), a portrait medallion to Sir John Barrow (2), and another with a tympanum-shaped relief of a broken bridge (presumably relating to the manner of death) to George Knowles (8). His most ambitious work in this genre was the a monument in limestone to Alfred Cooke, a circus performer and horse breeder (6). The monument has been badly vandalised. Milnes died in 1888 and is buried in Kensal Green Cemetery.

Literary References: *Gunnis* 1968, 260–1; *Read* 1982, 90, 93; *Curl* 2001, 235

Archival References: RA Admissions; GPC

Funerary Monuments

1.	†1828	Lady Louisa Bunbury		Great Barton, Suffolk	S	GPC
2.	†1848	Sir John Barrow		Ulverston, Lancs	S	
3.	†1849	Captain John Simpson	s	Devonport House, Greenwich, grounds (formerly Old Greenwich Hospital, London, burial ground)	S	
4.	1851	Design for a monument to Lord George Bentinck		[Gt Exhib]; untraced		*Gunnis* 1968, 261
5.	?1853	Admiral Sir Francis Mason		Husbands Bosworth, Leics	S	GPC
6.	1854	Alfred Cooke, tomb with figures of a child and a horse		Kensal Green Cemetery, London		*Curl* 2001, 189, 235; *Gunnis* 1968, 261
7.	1855	Hon H A and Hon Grey Neville		Saffron Walden, Essex		*ILN* 1855, 17 Nov 593; GPC
8.	†1856	George Knowles		Sharow, W R Yorks		Pevsner, *Yorks: W R*, 1967, 44
9.	†1888	R Barker		Fairford, Glos	S	

Statues

10.	1843	Model of a stag		[Exhib RA, London, 1499]; untraced		*Graves* V, 1905–6, 259
11.	1843	The captured stag, group		[Exhib RA, London, 1498]; untraced		*Graves* V, 1905–6, 259
12.	1844	A favourite horse, model, the property of Captain Oliver, Royal Horse Guards Blue		[Exhib RA, London, 1321]; untraced		*Graves* V, 1905–6, 259
13.	1844	A game-keeper returning from deer-shooting, group		[Exhib RA, London, 1250]; untraced		*Graves* V, 1905–6, 259
14.	1844	The death of Harold at the Battle of Hastings		[Exhib Westminster Hall, London, 159]; untraced		*Lit Gaz* 1844, 483; *AU*, 1844, 216
15.	1847	Admiral Lord Nelson Payment(s): 700 gns	m	[Guildhall, Norwich]; Cathedral Close, Norwich, since 1856		*Builder* 1847, 5, 522; *Gunnis* 1968, 260–1; Barnes, *Norfolk*, 2001, 28 (repr)
16.	1848	Arthur, 1st Duke of Wellington		[Tower of London]; Royal Arsenal, Woolwich, London		*Builder* 1847, 5, 522; *ILN* 14 Oct, 232; *Gunnis* 1968, 261; *Read* 1982, 93 1848; *Blackwood* 1989, 248 (repr)
17.	1853	Dr Charlesworth		[Lincoln Lunatic Asylum]; Lincoln, junction of Union and Carline Road		*Gunnis* 1968, 261; Pevsner, *Lincs*, 1989, 511

18.	1858	Four lions, representing Peace, War, Vigilence and Fidelity, intended for the base of Nelson's Column, Trafalgar Square, London	s	Saltaire School, W R Yorks	S	*AJ* 1869, 159; *Athenaeum*, 1858, 240; *Physick* 1970, 20; *Gunnis* 1968, 261; *Read* 1982, 90
Busts						
19.	1843	B Hopkinson	m	[Exhib RA, London, 1473]; untraced		*Graves* V, 1905–6, 259
20.	1843	James Barston		[Exhib RA, London, 1447]; untraced		*Graves* V, 1905–6, 259
21.	1845	Sir Michael Gibbs, Lord Mayor of London		[Exhib RA, London, 1365]; untraced		*Graves* V, 1905–6, 259; *Gunnis* 1968, 261
22.	1845	Unidentified man		[Exhib RA, London, 1403]; untraced		*Graves* V, 1905–6, 259
23.	1847	Rev Armin Herring, of Thorpe near Norwich		[Exhib RA, London, 1371]; untraced		*Graves* V, 1905–6, 259
24.	1847	W Ross		[Exhib RA, London, 1442]; untraced		*Graves* V, 1905–6, 259
25.	1848	John Brine	m	[Exhib RA, London, 1386]; untraced		*Graves* V, 1905–6, 259
26.	1848	John Gurney	m	[Exhib RA, London, 1398]; untraced		*Graves* V, 1905–6, 259; *Gunnis* 1968, 261
27.	1848	Mrs Brine	m	[Exhib RA, London, 1394]; untraced		*Graves* V, 1905–6, 259
28.	1848	William Martin	m	[Exhib RA, London, 1453]; untraced		*Graves* V, 1905–6, 259; *Gunnis* 1968, 261
29.	1850	Admiral Lord Nelson		[Exhib RA, London, 1342]; untraced		*Gunnis* 1968, 261
30.	1854	W Cooper		[Exhib RA, London, 1434]; untraced		*Graves* V, 1905–6, 259
31.	1856	Titus Salt	m	Congregational church, Saltaire, W R Yorks		
32.	1857	Lieutenant William Rivers	m	[Exhib RA, London, 1284]; NMM, Greenwich, SCU0046	SD	*Graves* V, 1905–6, 259; *Gunnis* 1968, 261
33.	1857	Mrs H F Lockwood	m	[Exhib RA, London, 1312]; untraced		*Graves* V, 1905–6, 259
34.	c1863	Captain Francis Liardet	m	NMM SCU0035		
35.	†1864	Joseph Allen	p	NMM SCU0004		
36.	1866	Thomas Wormald		[Exhib RA, London, 1010]; untraced		*Graves* V, 1905–6, 259; *Gunnis* 1968, 261
Miscellaneous						
37.	pre-1842	Imuam, model		[Exhib RA, London, 1842, 1309, coll Albert, the Prince Consort]; untraced		*Graves* V, 1905–6, 259
38.	1843	Greyhound and hare, model		[Exhib RA, London, 1487]; untraced		*Graves* V, 1905–6, 259
39.	1845	'The Duke of Wellington in full regimentals on horseback'		[Exhib RA, London, 1424]; untraced		*Graves* V, 1905–6, 259
40.	1847	'Model of a fox's head, to be executed in marble'		[Exhib RA, London, 1357]; untraced		*Graves* V, 1905–6, 259
41.	1847	Models of a horse		[Exhib RA, London, 1396, 1403]; untraced		*Graves* V, 1905–6, 259
42.	1848	A study from nature		[Exhib RA, London, 1382]; untraced		*Graves* V, 1905–6, 259
43.	1862	Samson slaying the lion		[Int Exhib]; untraced		*Gunnis* 1968, 261

MILNES, William fl 1831–48

He was a marble mason, statuary and quarry owner of Ashford, Derbys. His works were listed in various local directories between 1831 and 1848: in Pigot's *Directory*, 1835, he was described as a 'Manufacturer of inlaid mosaic and tesselated marble tables, chimney pieces'. Bagshaw's *Directory* of 1846 notes that Milne's workshops were opposite the Rookery in Ashford, and that he submitted specimens of marble, presumably local Derbyshire marbles, for use at the Houses of Parliament. The same source states that various works were purchased for the royal palaces (*Tomlinson* 1996, 44).

MILTON, W fl *c*1773

Funerary Monuments						
1.	†1773	Henry Brace		Acton Beauchamp, Herefs	S	Pevsner, *Herefs*, 1963, 63

MINTORN, John and Horatio

For further information the reader is referred to *Pyke* 1973, 93

MITCHARD, John, of Salisbury fl *c*1812–16

Funerary Monuments						
1.	?1812	Charles Pole		Barford St Martin, Wilts	S	*Gunnis* 1968, 261
2.	?1816	Harriet Jukes		Tisbury, Wilts	S	*Gunnis* 1968, 261

MITCHELELE, F, of Path-head fl *c*1840

Nothing is known of this sculptor other than the work listed below. For some of the other sculptural contributors to the pseudo-science of phrenology, see the entries for **Samuel Joseph**, **Lawrence Macdonald** and **James Deville**. There are four settlements named 'Path-head', in Ayrshire, Midlothian, Kircaldy and Co Durham.

Busts						
1.	*c*1840	Phrenological head	p	NMS		*Pearson* 1991, unpag

MITCHELL, Edward fl 1692–1717

Mitchell, who was master of the Masons' Company in 1692, had a yard in St Anne's, Westminster. He was located on the Southwark side of the Thames at the time of the Company's general search of September 1694. In 1716–17, John, son of 'Joseph Kettidge of Ramsey, Hunts, inn-keeper,' was apprenticed to him (TNA IR 1/4). The will of a mason called Kettidge, 'of Wapping Stepney,' was proved on 13 July 1719 (PROB 11/569).

Literary References: *Knoop and Jones* 1935, 67, 70, 75, 82; *Gunnis* 1968, 261

MITCHELL, George 1815–

He joined the Royal Academy schools in 1835 and exhibited twice in the following year. He gave his address as 1 Graham Street, Chelsea.

Literary References: *Graves* V, 1905–6, 262

Statues						
1.	1836	Hector casting a stone at Ajax		[Exhib RA, London, 1072]; untraced		*Graves* V, 1905–6, 262; *Gunnis* 1968, 261

Miscellaneous

2.	1836	Model	[RA, London, silver medal]; untraced	RA Premium list

MITCHELL, Nicholas –1694

Mitchell was the son of Robert Mitchell, a mason of the Isle of Portland. He was apprenticed to **Stephen Switzer** on 17 September 1668. The Masons' Company general search of April 1678 listed him at 'St Peter's Cornhill Church'. The bracket signed 'N Mitchell,' thought by Mrs Esdaile to be part of the monument to Sir William Morton, was presumably his work (1). The will of Nicholas Mitchell, 'mason of St Dunstan in the West,' was proved on 29 January 1694 (PROB 11/418). He was very likely responsible for the monument to the wife of Claver Morris, the bill for which was paid to 'Mrs Mitchell in Sheare-Lane' in November 1694. Morris described the work in his ledger as a 'black marble tombstone of 6 1/2 feet long and 3 1/4 feet broad, with Armes, Mantling and Cress *(sic)* emboss'd and inscription cutt.' £1 6s 6d was added to the bill for 'bringing it up from London to Manston by land and sea' (**2**).

Another mason named Nicholas Mitchell, again, confusingly the son of Robert Mitchell of Portland, Dorset, was apprenticed to **John Deane** on 9 October 1694 and was recorded in the General Search of the Masons' Company in May 1696. Robert Hooke mentions in his diary that a mason called Mitchell was hired in July 1680 in connection with the building of a house for Lord Conway. Hooke noted that on 7 July 'Michell returned Draught of Portalls for Lord Conway' (*Robinson and Adams* 1935, 448).

Literary References: *Esdaile* 1933 (2), 32; *Knoop and Jones* 1935, 67, 70, 75, 82; *Webb* 1999, 23

Archival References: GPC

Funerary Monuments

1.	†1672	John Morton (†1668), Anne Morton (†1668) and Sir William Morton	Temple Church, London (damaged)	S	*Esdaile* 1933 (2), 32; *Gunnis* 1968, 261

Funeral Monument

2.	1694	Mrs Morris Payment(s): £9 8 6	[for Claver Morris, of Manston]; untraced		*Hobhouse* 1934, 149

MITCHELL, of Tamworth fl *c*1841

The monument to Ann Middleton has a relief of *Hope.*

Funerary Monuments

1.	?1841	Ann Middleton	sl	Armitage, Staffs	GPC

MITCHELL, William –1762

In 1762 he won a premium from the Society of Arts (1). The register of the Society carries a note that he died the same year.

Literary References: RSA, *Register*, 1778, 31; *Dossie* 1782, 438

Archival References: RSA, *Minutes*, 1761–62, seq 3 fol 49

Reliefs

1.	1762	Coriolanus and Volumnia, clay	[Soc of A, premium, 10 gns]; untraced	RSA *Minutes*, 1761–62 seq 3 fol 49; RSA *Register*, 1778, 31

MITLEY, Charles, of York 1705–58

The first located record of Mitley's work is at Castle Howard in 1736 where he was employed with **Edward Raper**. The two men must have had some form of partnership for both signed the monument to two members of the North family in St Michael-le-Belfry, York (3). Mitley provided a statue for the Market House at York in 1739, which was subsequently moved to the Guildhall and has now disappeared (**8**).

It is possible that the payment Mitley received from Lord Fauconberg in 1745 (**10**) was for two statues in niches on the façade of Newburgh Priory, which Fauconberg was then improving. In the same year Mitley became a freeman of York.

In 1753 or 1754 Mitley encouraged Mr **Harvey**, a London sculptor, to work with him in York. The two men signed the monument to Mrs Ramsden in Adlingfleet which incorporates amply draped, life-size figures, set off by fluted Corinthian columns in grey and pink marble, with festoons and cherubs' heads (5). This was described in the *York Courant* of 26 August 1755.

Mitley also had a hand in designing the monument to Sir Tancred Robinson in the St Crux Parish Room, York, which was executed by Harvey. When Harvey died in 1755 Mitley's sister, Diana Carr (who was married to a builder, William Carr of York), petitioned a member of the Robinson family to transfer the commission to Mitley. In the letter Mrs Carr writes of her brother, 'I hope his abilities need not be disputed in such an affair as he has had the Honr. to carve most of the nobility in the neighbourhood this 30 years' (Compton Verney Archives, quoted in GPC). Mrs Carr complained that Sir Tancred's agent, William Bowes, was prejudiced against her brother and had been responsible for Mitley being overlooked for the original commission. She was concerned that if Bowes should be involved in finding Harvey's successor, it was likely to be 'some local tramper' who would 'spoil the work' (*ibid*). Mitley was indeed overlooked again in favour of **Robert Avray**.

He died on 26 August 1758 and was buried at St Cuthbert, York, where there is a cartouche tablet to his memory. An advertisement in the *York Courant* for 4 March 1760 stated that marble blocks, chimneypieces and other goods belonging to 'Charles Mitley of Aldwark, deceased' were for sale. Mitley's daughter, Mary Mitley, married William Peckitt, the celebrated glass stainer, on 3 April 1763 at St Michael-le-Belfry, York.

Literary References: *Gunnis* 1968, 261; *Whinney* 1988, 256

Archival References: Castle Howard Building Accts, mausoleum, G2/2/68–9, 1735–37; G2/2/76–77, 1738–9 (Mitley and Raper); deed of partition, York City Archives department, 1775, acc 484; IGI

Funerary Monuments

1.	†1689	Sir Metcalfe Robinson Bt	Topcliffe, N R Yorks		GPC
2.	†1721	Lady Frances Graham	Holy Trinity, Goodramgate, York	S	*Gunnis* 1968, 261; Pevsner, *Yorks: E R & York*, 1995, 161

3.	†1734	Catherine and Christiana North (co-sculptor: Edward Raper)	St Michael-le-Belfrey, York	S	*Gunnis* 1968, 261; Pevsner, *Yorks: E R & York*, 1995, 173
4.	†1750	Beilby Thompson	Escrick, E R Yorks		*Myerscough* 1996, unpag; GPC
5.	1755	Mrs Ramsden (†1745) (co-sculptor: Mr Harvey) Payment(s): nearly £1,000	Adlingfleet, W R Yorks		Pevsner, *Yorks: W R*, 1967, 73; *Whinney* 1988, 256; GPC
6.	1755	Sargeant Agar	[Stockton, W R Yorks (?)]; untraced		GPC
7.	nd	Darcy Dawes	Long Marston, N R Yorks		GPC
Statues					
8.	1739	King George II	[Market House, York]; untraced		*Gunnis* 1968, 261; *Ingamells* 1972, 5
Miscellaneous					
9.	1736	Unidentified work	[Castle Howard, N R Yorks]; untraced		*Gunnis* 1968, 261
10.	1744–1745	Unidentified work Payment(s): £42	[for Lord Fauconberg]; untraced		GPC

MOCOCK, Thomas, of Leyton fl *c*1819

He is known only for one monument, an altar-tomb surmounted by an oval urn (1).

Funerary Monuments					
1.	?1819	Frances Sherburne	Leyton Parish Church, Essex, churchyard	S	*Gunnis* 1968, 261

MOFFITT, T, of Liverpool fl *c*1837–40

Funerary Monuments					
1.	†1837	Anna Maria Patten	St Elphin, Warrington, Lancs		*CIIA* 4/8/132 (repr)
2.	?1840	Peter Brooke	Rostherne, Cheshire	S	GPC

MOLE, Elizabeth fl 1840

In 1840, while living in Bury Road, Gosport, she won a medal from the Society of Arts.

Reliefs					
1.	1840	Five cameos	[Soc of A, silver medal]; untraced		RSA, *Transactions*, vol 53, 1840, xvi

MOLE, Leonard, of Worcester fl 1763–81

In 1763 he was apprenticed to his father, also Leonard Mole, a mason and bricklayer, who had become a freeman of Worcester in 1740. The younger Mole signs a large architectural wall-tablet (1).

Funerary Monuments					
1.	†1771	Benjamin Hook	St Helen, Worcester	S	
2.	?1781	Mrs Bodledge	All Saints, Evesham, Worcs	S	*Gunnis* 1968, 261

MOLTEN, R

For further information the reader is referred to *Pyke* 1973, 93

MONEYPENNY, George fl 1740–1807

Nothing is known of Moneypenny's birth and training. He had settled in Derby by September 1766, when he and his wife Mary christened their daughter at St Werburgh's. In 1776 he was working at Kedleston Hall, where he carved under the direction of the architect Joseph Pickford (2–5). The sculptor enjoyed a close professional relationship with the architect, working with him at Edensor Inn, Egginton, and Staunton Harold (6–8). Both were based at Nun's Green, Derby. Moneypenny organised the posthumous sale of Pickford's stock of marble chimneypieces in July 1782. It seems likely that Moneypenny was responsible for a good deal of other carving on buildings designed by Pickford, including the Moot Hall, Derby and Ashford Hall, Derbyshire. A number of monuments have been attributed to him by Edward Saunders in Derbys and Staffs.

The *Derby Mercury* reported the death of Mrs Moneypenny in August 1803 and of the sculptor in October 1807. His son, George Moneypenny II, worked with his father (both are listed as carvers in the 1792 *Derby Directory*), but subsequently became a noted architect. Moneypenny also engraved the plates for William Hutton's *History of Derby* (1791).

Literary References: *Saunders* 1993, *passim*; *Kedleston* 1998, 14

Archival References: GPC

Chimneypieces				
1.	*c*1778	Description unavailable	The Hall, Long Eaton, Derbys	Pevsner, *Derbys*, 1978, 266
Architectural Sculpture				
2.	1771	21 lions heads, 21 large husks and a Vitruvian scroll Payment(s): 8 gns for the lions heads; £6 10s for the husks and scroll	[Kedleston Hall, Derbys]; untraced	Kedleston Archives in GPC
3.	1771	Two medallions with boys and seahorses Payment(s): £10 0s	Kedleston, Derbys, fishing house	Kedleston Archives in GPC; *Kedleston* 1998, 70
4.	*c*1774	Ceiling entablature mouldings	Kedleston Hall, Derbys, hall	Pevsner, *Derbys*, 1978, 257
5.	1776	Base and sub-base mouldings, saloon door, side doors to the hall, picture frames Payment(s): £258 7s 10d	[Kedleston Hall, Derbys]; untraced	*Saunders* 1993, 158
6.	1777	Cavendish arms Payment(s): £6 6s	Edensor Inn, Chatsworth, Derbys	*Saunders* 1993, 140
7.	1782	'Door case for the new front door' and other unidentified carving Payment(s): £31 7s	[Egginton Hall, Derbys]; untraced	*Saunders* 1993, 151
Miscellaneous				
8.	1772	Unidentified carving Payment(s): £5 5s	[Staunton Harold Hall, Leics]; untraced	*Saunders* 1993, 151

MONKMAN, of Malton fl c1773

Funerary Monuments

1.	†1773	Rev G Walmsley	Settrington, E R Yorks	Pevsner, *Yorks: E R & York*, 1995, 676

MONNOT, Pierre-Etienne 1657–1733

One of the major European sculptors working in the decades around 1700, he carried out a number of commissions for the 5th Earl of Exeter and had an important influence on British commemorative sculpture. He was born in Orchamps-Vennes, France, on 9 August 1657, the son of Elizabeth Flegguerin and Etienne Monnot, a woodcarver. He trained under his father before departing for Dijon where he studied under Jean Dubois and spent a decade working in Paris before leaving for Rome c1687. From his studio in the Via Arco della Ciambella he produced copies of classical sculpture, carved two reliefs for the Capocaccia Chapel in S Maria della Vittoria and executed a monument to Pope Innocent XI. He also embarked on a commission to decorate the Marmorbad in Kassel, an extensive project on which he was employed intermittently from 1792 to the end of his career.

Monnot carved a monument with a bust to Cardinal Savo Millini for the family chapel in S Maria del Popolo before 1699, and it was this work that brought him to the attention of the Earl of Exeter, then visiting Rome. Monnot's biographer, Pascoli, recounted that Exeter was so impressed with the monument that he requested 'a monument with his portrait and that of his wife, with five other great statues and one little one' to be sent back to England (1). Monnot had other work on hand but prepared a model of the monument for translation to marble. Pascali relates that Exeter visited the sculptor's studio frequently but was obliged to leave Rome before its completion. 'Eventually the monument was packed into cases, loaded onto a boat at Ripa Grande and arrived safely in England to the delight and satisfaction of Lord Exeter' (*Pascoli* 1736, 2, 491).

Doubt has to be cast on Pascoli's account because surviving freight charges indicate that the statues arrived in England, 1702–04, after the earl's death in 1700. The monument (1) is dated 1704, and was erected by **William Palmer.** It has full-size reclining effigies of the earl and countess, leaning on their elbows, flanked by figures of *Wisdom* and *Science.* The antique prototype appears to be the tomb of Alexander Severus and Giulia Mammaea in the Capitoline Museum. The composition had an impact on **Michael Rysbrack**, whose drawing of the monument is in Plymouth Art Gallery, and echoes of the composition can be seen in the work of **Peter Scheemakers** and **Louis François Roubiliac.**

It has not proved possible to identify the 'five other great statues and one little one' mentioned by Pascoli, but a number of signed works are still at Burghley. The Earl's bust, with its close-cropped hair and Roman breastplate, is closely related to the effigy on the Exeter monument (3). The *Virgin and Child* (4), which Gunnis calls 'most lovely', is one of a series of similar subjects executed by the sculptor around the same date, one of which is in the Staatliches Museen, Berlin. An *Andromeda and Sea Monster*, formerly at Burghley, was identified as the sculptor's work from the mid-18th century, though the earliest known account, by George Vertue, identified the work as 'A fine marble statue. Andromeda & Monster. Italian. Carv'd by Dominico Guidi. Cost 4000 crowns. At 5s 6d' (*Vertue* II, 34). Other attributed works at Burghley are statuettes of a sleeping and waking child.

From 1706 Monnot's Rome studio was at Via delle Carozze 12. His later works include statues of St Peter and St Paul in San Giovanni in Laterano, 1708–13. He spent several years in Kassel, where his extravagant decorations for the Marmorbad eventually comprised 12 life-size statuary groups, eight enormous marble reliefs, eight smaller reliefs, and other polychrome marble decoration. He died on 24 August 1733 and was buried by the French community in S Claudio dei Borgognoni, Rome. He left over 30,000 scudi and a studio sale, which included a 'restoration' of the antique *Discobolus*, was held for the benefit of his wife, Cecilia Alberetti, and their three children. Pascoli described him as 'small in stature and well made . . . handsome and noble . . . tireless . . . he did the work of ten' (*Pascoli*, 2 1736, 497–8).

MGS

Literary References: *Pascoli* 1736, 2, 491; *Castan* 1888; *Francastel* 1933, 138–56; *Honour* 1958 (2), 220–6; *Seymour* 1962, 330–4; *Gunnis* 1968, 261–2; *Schlegal* 1974, 56–68; *Enggass* 1976 (1), 77–87; *Raggio* 1977, 364–75; *Enggass* 1981, 74–81; *Haskell and Penny* 1981, 200, 227; *Bershad* 1984, 72–75; *Fusco* 1988, 70–77; *Whinney* 1988, *passim*; *Johns* 1989 (1), 279–285; *Raggio* 1991, 231–52; *Walker* 1994; *Bacchi* 1994, 64–70; *Bacchi* 1995, 39–52; *Bindman and Baker* 1995, 60, 90, 384 n40; *Grove*, 21, 889–90 (Engass); *Bailey* 1996, 191; *Fuchs* 1997; *Loire* 1998, 18–19

Archival References: GPC

Funerary Monuments

1.	1700–1704	John, Earl of Exeter (†1700) and his wife (†1709)		St Martin, Stamford, Lincs	SD	*Honour* 1958 (2), 220–1 (repr); *Enggass* 1976 (1), 79; *Lord* 1986, 98–99; *Whinney* 1988, 146, 147 (repr); *Impey* 1998, 8

Busts

2.	1701	Anne, Countess of Exeter		Burghley House, Northants	SD	*Bacchi* 1994, 64
3.	1701	John, 5th Earl of Exeter	m	Burghley House, Northants	SD	*Honour* 1958 (2), 220, 221 (repr); *Whinney* 1988, 447 n24; *Impey* 1998, 8 (repr)

Reliefs

4.	1700	Virgin and child	m	Burghley House, Northants	SD	*Honour* 1958 (2), 220; *Gunnis* 1968, 261; *Shlegel* 1974, 66 (repr); *Enggass* 1976 (1), 78; *Impey* 1998, 148 (repr)
5.	1709	Madonna and child with St John		[Private house of the Jesuit General, Rome]; Wardour Castle, Wilts, chapel	SD	Pevsner, *Wilts*, 1975, 553

MONTEIRO, M L fl 1845

Statues

1.	1845	Boy with a pet bird, unfinished model	[Exhib Westminster Hall, London, 145]; untraced	*Westminster* 1845, 17

MONTGOMERY fl 1843

He is known only for one bust signed 'Montgomery 1843 ROMA' (1). An 'R Montgomery of Belfast' signs a tablet with a relief of a draped sarcophagus to Emily Hamilton (†1869) at Dundalk, Ireland, but there is no reason to assume that they are one and the same.

Literary References: *Potterton* 1975, 72

Busts

1.	1843	Duke of Manchester	Kimbolton Castle, Hunts	SD GPC

MONTI, Gaetano 1776–1847

An Italian pupil of **Bertel Thorvaldsen** in Rome, he sculpted busts of British sitters, including Henry Howard who was in the city *c*1819–21, and commissioned two busts and basso-relievos. Monti was papal sculptor to Pius VII. He was the father of **Raffaelle Monti**.

Busts

1.	1819–1820	Henry Howard	m	[Corby Castle, Cumberland]; Knox/Longstaffe-Gowan coll	RCHME NRA 7034

MONTI, Raffaelle 1818–81

An Italian sculptor who spent much of his life in Britain, Monti is best known for his illusionistic veiled figures in marble, but he also provided decorative sculpture for the Crystal Palace at Sydenham and worked as a designer, collaborating with firms specialising in metalwork and ceramics. He was born at Ticino, Switzerland, the son of **Gaetano Monti**, and grew up in Milan, studying with his father and at the Accademia di Belle Arti in Brera. His first successes were classically inspired sculptural groups, *Alexander training Bucephalus*, which won the Imperial Academy's gold medal (untraced) and *Ajax defending the body of Patroclus* (untraced), exhibited in 1838, which secured him an invitation to go to Vienna, where he stayed four years. He also worked on the frieze and pediment of the Hungarian National Museum in Budapest with the Munich sculptor Ludwig Schaller. The pediment relief represents *The Apotheosis of Pannonia* and was cast in zinc, a material chosen for its lightness. Monti returned to Milan in 1842 and four years later he travelled to England, where he carved a marble statue of a *Veiled vestal* for the 6th Duke of Devonshire (**6**). The nude figure is swathed in delicate draperies creating a semi-transparent effect. After completing the statue, Monti returned to Italy where he became a senior officer of the National Guard of Milan. When the Italian insurgents were defeated by the Austrian army at Custozza in 1848, Monti fled back to London, where he spent the rest of his life.

He established a studio at 45 Great Marlborough Street, near Oxford Circus and soon secured several commissions for funerary monuments. The most impressive commemorates Barbara, Lady de Mauley and is the focal point of a splendid gothic revival mortuary chapel at Hatherop, Glos (**2**). She is depicted in neo-medieval Victorian dress, peacefully at rest on a low tomb chest and flanked by two statues of kneeling angels on gothic-inspired pedestals. The figures are notable for their detailed, naturalistic carving. In 1851 Monti sent several works to the Great Exhibition, including variations on the theme of the veiled figure (**9, 10, 11**), and a statue of *Eve after the Fall*, for which the sculptor was awarded a prize medal (**8**). He exhibited at the Royal Academy in 1853, 1854 and 1860.

Monti's practice assumed industrial proportions when he became involved with the Crystal Palace Company, which transferred Joseph Paxton's Great Exhibition building to Sydenham in 1853. Monti provided allegorical statuary, together with decorative fountains, vases and tazzas, for the palace and the elaborate terraced gardens which were constructed around it (**14, 17, 19, 21–4, 49, 50**). He was also responsible for the installation and colouring of the reconstructions of the Parthenon marbles in the Grecian Court. Monti seems to have over-stretched himself and before the work was completed he was declared bankrupt. Fortunately, the bankruptcy court, convinced of Monti's determination to fulfil his obligations to the Crystal Palace Company and his creditors, allowed him to complete much of the contract instead of ordering the immediate sale of his stock-in-trade. Although much of the sculpture survived the fire which destroyed the building in 1936, most has subsequently been lost. The few surviving works include a cast concrete figure of *Thames* from one of the fountains, re-erected at Lechlade, Glos.

Meanwhile, Monti developed a sideline as a dealer in commercially produced Italian sculpture, acquiring 37 crudely finished pieces so that he could improve and resell them. About 20 of these 'statues and busts by modern Italian sculptors, to which the last finish has been given under Monti's eye' were sold at Christie's on 22 June 1855, together with 24 of the sculptor's original works. Towards the end of the decade Monti was involved in some significant architectural schemes. In 1857 he worked with Sir Joseph Paxton on embellishments for the great hall of the Rothschild country house, Mentmore, and the following year he designed and modelled the relief over the proscenium arch at the Royal Opera House, Covent Garden (**53**). In 1859–61 he published a series of 'Letters from London' in the newly established French art journal, *Gazette des Beaux-Arts*. In these he discussed idiosyncrasies of the British art world.

Monti was much in the public eye in the early 1860s. In December 1861 his colossal equestrian statue of Charles, 3rd Marquess of Londonderry in a hussar's uniform, was unveiled in Durham Market Square (**31**). This was said to be the largest ever cast by electrotype, a process with which Monti had experimented for several years. The following year he exhibited an exuberant neo-Baroque group entitled *The sleep of sorrow and the dream of joy* at the London International Exhibition (**32**). The composition, which has a sleeping figure beneath a rose bush and a second veiled figure floating serenely upwards above the flowers, can be read both as a poetic representation of 'the springing up of the soul to light and bliss, after prolonged suffering from grief and spiritual darkness' and as a political allegory of the Italian Risorgimento (*Waring* III, 1863, pl 231). Characteristically FT Palgrave condemned this extravagant work as a salutary example of 'how far sculpture must fall, when it has once admitted any taint of the sensational' (*Palgrave* 1866, 201).

Towards the end of his career Monti was increasingly preoccupied with the applied arts. He was closely associated with Elkington's, the Birmingham metal-working firm, in the early 1860s and provided them with models for reproduction in bronze. He designed yachting and racing trophies for the silversmith C F Hancock, as well as five large vases on the theme of British poets, which were displayed at the 1862 International Exhibition.

In 1878 he designed a silver centrepiece for the Mansion House for a rival firm, Garrards. Although the design was greatly admired by the director of the Guildhall Art Gallery, A G Temple, it was rejected by the London corporation authorities and therefore never executed. Parian ware statuettes and busts based on Monti's designs were produced by Copeland and Wedgwood (**32–38, 45–7**). Monti also collaborated with the sculptor James Forsyth to produce a relief of *Christ the Comforter* for St Joseph's Missionary College in Mill Hill, London (**54**). The two men became close friends and Forsyth's son, James Nesfield Forsyth, purchased Monti's models after his death.

In spite of all this commercial activity the sculptor was unable to resolve his financial problems and he passed the last years of his life in poverty, afraid to go out until after dark 'on account of his liabilities' and was even finally compelled to sell his tools (*Temple* 1918, 143). He died in London on 16 October 1881. His work attracted little posthumous interest until 1962, when his masterpiece, *The sleep of sorrow and the dream of joy*, which had been in private ownership for many years, was displayed in an exhibition marking the centenary of the 1862 International Exhibition. It was subsequently purchased by the Victoria and Albert Museum. An article by Anthony Radcliffe, published in 1965 and reissued in 1970, went some way towards reviving the sculptor's reputation.

EH

Literary References: *The Times*, 15 Nov 1854, 6; 25 Nov 1854, 11; 15 Feb 1855, 9; 29 March 1855, 10; 1 Nov 1855, 9; 26 Sept 1863, 6; 18 Oct 1881, 10; *AJ*, 1881, 352; *Temple* 1918, 142–3; *Gunnis* 1968, 262; *Radcliffe* 1970, *passim*; *Gerdts* 1971, 65; *Penny* 1977 (1), 131–4; *Grove* 22, 1996, 27–8 (Ward-Jackson); *Usherwood* 2000, 246–8; *Sicca and Yarrington* 2000, 10, 23 n55; *ODNB* (Ward-Jackson)

Auction Catalogue: Monti 1855

Portraits of the Sculptor: C Silvy, carte-de-visite photograph, NPG; wood-engraving (repr *ILN*, 25 Oct 1851, 536)

Funerary Monuments

1.	†1835	Isabella Anne Kemeys		Goathurst, Somerset	Pevsner, *Somerset: S & W*, 1958, 185; *Penny* 1977 (1), 116; C Lib (repr)
2.	1848	Barbara, Lady de Mauley (†1844)		Hatherop, Glos	*Penny* 1977 (1), 131–134 (repr); Pevsner, *Glos: Cotswolds*, 1999, 405
3.	1848	William Poyntz (†1840)		Eastbourne, Sussex	Pevsner, *Sussex*, 1965, 212
4.	†1860	Viney Vernon		Ardington, Berks	RG/JP, 5, 936v
5.	†1871	Mary James		Sidmouth, Devon	RG/JP, 5, 936v

Statues

6.	1847	Veiled vestal	m	[Chiswick House]; Chatsworth, Derbys, sculpture gallery	*Gunnis* 1968, 262; *Radcliffe* 1970, 7–8; *Chatsworth Handlist*, 24
7.	1848	Angelica and Medoro	m	[Monti sale, Christie, 22 June 1855]; McLean Museum and Art Gallery, Greenock, Strathclyde	*Radcliffe* 1970, 8; *Pearson* 1991, unpag, 161 (repr)
8.	1848	Eve after the Fall	m	[Grittleton House, Wilts]; untraced Other versions: coll H W Eaton, 1850; untraced	JKB 1966, 712 (repr); *Grittleton Marbles* 1966, 18 reor VIII); *Gunnis* 1968, 262; *Read* 1982, 141, 143 (repr)
9.	1851	A Georgian lady of the harem		[Gt Exhib, London]; untraced	*Radcliffe* 1970, 8
10.	1851	Circassian slave at the market place in Constantinople		[Gt Exhib, London]; untraced Other versions: Wallace coll, London, reduced marble, 1850	*ILN*, 5 July 1851, 32; *Gunnis* 1968, 262; *Radcliffe* 1970, 8 (repr 4)
11.	1851	Fisher girls (sister anglers)		[Gt Exhib; Christie, 20 July 1860]; untraced	*Gunnis* 1968, 262; *Radcliffe* 1970, 8
12.	1853	Boy with rabbit	m	[Exhib RA, London, 1337]; untraced	*Graves* V, 1905–6, 276
13.	1853	Truth unveiling herself	m	[Exhib RA, London, 1312]; untraced	*Graves* V, 1905–6, 276; *Gunnis* 1968, 262
14.	1853–1855	Atlantic, Pacific, Arctic and Indian Oceans		[Crystal Palace, Sydenham, fountains]; untraced Other versions: Atlantic Ocean sold Phillips, 20 May 1985	*The Times*, 25 Nov 1854, 11
15.	?1855	Christianity		[Monti sale, Christie, 22 June 1855]; untraced	*Radcliffe* 1970, 8
16.	?1855	Dead Christ		[Monti sale, Christie, 22 June 1855]; untraced	*Radcliffe* 1970, 8
17.	1853–1855	Hope, Joy, Friendship, Love, Modesty, Valour, Vigilance, Prudence		[Crystal Palace, Sydenham, fountains in the terrace gardens]; untraced	*The Times*, 25 Nov 1854, 11
18.	?1855	Margaret		[Monti sale, Christie, 22 June 1855]; untraced	*Radcliffe* 1970, 8
19.	1853–1855	Mercury and fortune		[Crystal Palace, Sydenham, cascade]; untraced	*The Times*, 25 Nov 1854, 11
20.	?1855	Modesty		[Monti sale, Christie, 22 June 1855]; untraced	*Radcliffe* 1970, 8
21.	1853–1855	Nile, Ganges, Amazon		[Crystal Palace, Sydenham, fountains]; untraced	*The Times*, 25 Nov 1854, 11
22.	1853–1855	Pacific ocean		[Crystal Palace, Sydenham, fountain]; Dacres Road, Lower Sydenham, London	*The Times*, 25 Nov 1854, 11; C Lib (repr)
23.	1853–1855	South America, Italy, Spain, Holland, the Zollverein		[Crystal Palace, Sydenham, upper terrace]; untraced	*Radcliffe* 1970, 7–8
24.	1853–1855	Thames		[Crystal Palace, Sydenham, fountain]; Lechlade, Glos	*Conc.* 1975, 23 (repr); *CIIA* 4/4/73–4 (repr); Pevsner, *Glos: Cotswolds*, 1999, 442
25.	?1855	The Graces (after Bertel Thorvaldsen)		[Monti sale, Christie, 22 June 1855]; untraced	*Radcliffe* 1970, 8

26.	?1855	Tired reaper		[Monti sale, Christie, 22 June 1855]; untraced Other versions: 'Tired reaper', Monti sale, Christie, 22 June 1855; untraced		*Radcliffe* 1970, 8
27.	pre-1857	Indian mother		[Sold Phillips, 7 March 1857]; untraced		Phillips archives
28.	pre-1857	Narina		[Sold Phillips, 7 March 1857]; untraced		Phillips archives
29.	pre-1857	The slave		[Sold Phillips, 7 March 1857]; untraced		Phillips archives
30.	pre-1857	Young girl holding a bird		[Sold Phillips, 7 March 1857]; untraced		Phillips archives
31.	1858–1861	Charles, 3rd Marquess of Londonderry, equestrian		Market Square, Durham		*Darke* 1991, 228–9 (repr); *Usherwood* 2000, 246–8 (repr)
32.	1861	The sleep of sorrow and the dream of joy	m	[Farnhams Hall, Ware, Herts]; VAM A.3-1964 Other versions: Copeland Parian ware repr issued by the Ceramic and Crystal Palace Art Union, 1875		*Graves* V, 1905–6, 276; *Radcliffe* 1970, passim (reprs 1, 11); *Atterbury* 1989, 148 (repr 507)
33.	1862	Morning (Day), statuette	m	Private coll Other versions: reproduced in Copeland Parian ware		*Radcliffe* 1970, 16 (repr 6); *Atterbury* 1989, 166 (repr 550); C Lib (repr)
34.	1862	Night, model		Untraced Other versions: reproduced in Copeland Parian ware		*Radcliffe* 1970, 16 (reprs 6, 10); *Atterbury* 1989, 167 (repr 552)
35.	1867	Lady Godiva	m	Sotheby, 21 Nov 1995 Other versions: reproduced in Copeland Parian ware, 1870	SD	*AJ*, 1881, 279; *Atterbury* 1989, 152 (repr 515)
36.	1870	Flute player, model		Untraced Other versions: reproduced in Copeland Parian ware		*Atterbury* 1989, 157 (repr 526A)
37.	1870	Nora Creina, model		untraced Other versions: reproduced in Copeland Parian ware		*Atterbury* 1989, 152 (repr 515)
38.	1871	Infancy of Jupiter, model		untraced Other versions: reproduced in Copeland Parian ware		*Atterbury* 1989, 155 (repr 523)
39.	nd	Sleeping harvester (sleeping girl), statuette	m	Shepherd Gallery, New York, USA (1973) Other versions: Shepherd gallery, New York (1973), bronze		
40.	nd	Venus de Medici (after the antique)	m	Birmingham MAG inv 2632'85		*Silber* 1987, 68, cat 208
Busts						
41.	1854	Dowager Marchioness of Downshire	m	[Exhib RA, London, 1501]; untraced		*Graves* V, 1905–6, 276
42.	1856	Elizabeth McArthur Caird	m	McLean Museum and Art Gallery, Greenock, Strathclyde 1978.238		
43.	1856	James Tennant Caird	m	McLean Museum and Art Gallery, Greenock, Strathclyde 1978.239		
44.	c1860	Veiled lady	m	Minneapolis Institute of Arts, Minnesota, USA 70.60		*Bull. MIA* 1970, 36–7 (repr)
45.	*c*1861	Veiled bride		Untraced Other versions: Copeland Parian ware repr issued by the Art Union *c*1861		*Atterbury* 1989, 35
46.	*c*1865	Thomas Henry Huxley, model		untraced Other versions: reproduced in Copeland Parian ware		*Atterbury* 1989, 198 (repr 660)
47.	1871	Love, model		untraced Other versions: Copeland Parian ware reproduction issued by the Ceramic and Crystal Palace Art Union 1882		*Atterbury* 1989, 186 (repr 618)
48.	nd	William Shakespeare	m	Private coll		C Lib (repr)
Architectural Sculpture						
49.	1853–1855	Decorative fountains, vases and tazzas		[Crystal Palace, Sydenham]; untraced		*The Times*, 25 Nov 1854, 11
50.	1853–1855	Two fountains symbolising the 'four races of men'		[Crystal Palace, Sydenham, north nave]; untraced		*Radcliffe* 1970, 7–8
51.	1857	Figurative motifs		Mentmore, Bucks, great hall, coving		*Builder*, 1857, 741; Pevsner, *Bucks*, 1994, 475
52.	1858	Figures over windows		St James's Hall, Piccadilly, London		*Builder*, 1858, 282
53.	1858	Medallion portrait of Queen Victoria flanked by Orpheus and Ossian, relief		Covent Garden Opera House, London, over proscenium arch		*The Times*, 18 May 1858, 11; *Builder* 1858, 347; *Grove* 22, 1996, 28
Reliefs						
54.	?1874	Christ the comforter (co-sculptor: James Forsyth)		[St Joseph's Missionary College, Mill Hill, London]; untraced		*Fosyth Album*, f65
Miscellaneous						
55.	1853	'Erma, portait of a lady'	m	[Exhib RA, London, 1360]; untraced		*Graves* V, 1905–6, 276
56.	pre-1856	Cupid peeping through the heart's-ease		[Sold Phillips, 4 July 1856]; untraced		Phillips Archives
57.	pre-1856	Female wearing a wreath of roses		[Sold Phillips, 4 July 1856]; untraced		Phillips archives
58.	pre-1857	Eloisa		[Sold Phillips, 30 June 1857]; untraced		Phillips Archives
59.	pre-1860	Guardian angel		[W O Hunt coll, Christie, 20 July 1860]; untraced		Auction cat
60.	1860	Piacere e dolore		[Exhib RA, London, 958]; untraced		*Graves* V, 1905–6, 276
61.	1860	Town and country ('A gossip on the borders of Senegal')		[Exhib RA, London, 954]; untraced		*Graves* V, 1905–6, 276

MOODY, Robert 1807–

He joined the Royal Academy Schools in 1830 on the recommendation of Sir T Tyrwhitt Bt, giving his address as 1 Parliament Place. He subsequently exhibited busts at the RA, from 6 King's Parade, Chelsea in 1836, 42 Cheyne Walk in 1837 and Sloane Street in 1841.

Literary References: *Graves* V, 1905–6, 277; *Gunnis* 1968, 262; *Pyke* 1973, 94

Archival References: RA Admissions

Statues					
1.	nd	Father Thames		[Coates, nr Cirencester, Glos, at the source of the Thames]; Lechlade, Glos	NP/RG
Busts					
2.	1836	Lord Shaftesbury		[Exhib RA, London, 1108]; untraced	*Graves* V, 1905–6, 277; *Gunnis* 1968, 262
3.	1837	Lord Eldon		[Exhib RA, London, 1158]; untraced	*Graves* V, 1905–6, 277; *Gunnis* 1968, 262
4.	1838	Arthur, 1st Duke of Wellington		[Exhib RA, London, 1323]; untraced	*Graves* V, 1905–6, 277; *Gunnis* 1968, 262
5.	1838	Major-General Dyson		[Exhib RA, London, 1332]; untraced	*Graves* V, 1905–6, 277
6.	1838	William, Viscount Melbourne		Royal Coll Other versions: Exhib RA, London, 1841, 1149	*Graves* V, 1905–6, 277; *Ormond* 1973, 314
Reliefs					
7.	1836	Arthur, 1st Duke of Wellington	w	Stanton Harcourt, Oxon	*Pyke* 1973, 94
8.	1836	John, Earl of Eldon	w	[coll Sir Robert Blundell]; untraced Other versions: Stanton Harcourt, wax	*Pyke* 1973, 94
Miscellaneous					
9.	1844	Sir Robert Peel Bt, model		[Exhib RA, London, 1251]; untraced	*Graves* V, 1905–6, 277; *Ormond* 1973, 372

MOON, Christopher fl *c*1766

Only one large wall-tablet by the sculptor has been identified.

Funerary Monuments					
1.	?1766	Thomas Ogden	Manchester Cathedral, Lancs	S	*Gunnis* 1968, 262

MOON, L, of Godalming fl *c*1824–45

He was responsible for a number of tablets and appears at one time to have been in partnership with **James Smart of Guildford.**

Funerary Monuments					
1.	†1824	William Sadler	Chiddingfold, Surrey	S	*Gunnis* 1968, 262
2.	†1842	John Watts de Belin (co-sculptor: James Smart, of Guildford)	Holy Trinity, Guildford, Surrey	S	
3.	†1845	Francis Annesley	Shalford, Surrey	S	*Gunnis* 1968, 262

MOORE, Christopher 1787–1863

Moore was born in Dublin and may perhaps be the plasterer paid £1,300 for ornaments in the dining room at Carton, County Kildare in 1819. He exhibited *Combat between the Archangel Michael and Satan* (**4**) in Dublin in 1819, giving his address as 2 Upper Gloucester Place, Dublin. Two years later he was in London, living at 178 Terrace, Tottenham Court Road. He enrolled at the Royal Academy schools in November 1821, giving his age as 34, and exhibited the Dublin *Combat* at the British Institution. He lived in Tottenham Court Road until 1829, when he moved to 23 Howland Street, where he remained until 1859 or later.

He was principally a portraitist, working in wax, plaster and marble, and had no shortage of clients, in part because he canvassed for commissions. Having completed a bust of Lord Morpeth (**69**) he wrote in 1840 requesting to make a likeness of his father, the 6th Earl of Carlisle. It is not known if this resulted in a commission (Castle Howard Archives J19/1/28/10, 7 Aug 1840). There was much contemporary appreciation of Moore's portraiture: the *Art Union* described the bust of J P Curran as 'the production of a mind capable of realizing its impressions with the most perfect success' (**140**), and commented on Moore's ability to convey the thoughtful characters of Matthew Evans and Sir Philip Crampton with simplicity (**91, 93**). The appreciation has persisted: Strickland felt that Moore was a talented portraitist, who created 'well modelled and expressive likenesses', and Crookshank described his busts as 'handled with simplicity and a lack of ostentation, qualities that were disappearing' (*Crookshank* 1966, 310).

Unfortunately, a consensus by like critics condemns Moore's lack of success in his larger works. Strickland remarks that 'in his statues and figure subjects he was not successful,' and his 'grotesque' effigy of the popular poet, Thomas Moore, whose bust he had earlier carved 'is an unfortunate memorial to the poet' (**11, 39**). More recently, Judith Hill has described the same work, the sculptor's only effort in bronze, as a 'kindly' depiction of Moore reading aloud from a book of his poems, but 'disappointingly lumpen' (*Hill* 1998, 98). Moore carved only a few monuments, but Gunnis thought his recumbent figure of a dead child, Isabella Cooper, 'lovely' (**1**).

He frequently visited Dublin, and had a house there from 1858. He exhibited at the Royal Hibernian Academy, 1829–61, was elected an associate of that institution on 26 May 1846 and was made a member on the same day. In October 1853 he resigned his membership and in the following year became an honorary member. He died at his house in 11 Dorset Street, Dublin on 17 March 1863, and was buried in Glasnevin.

Literary References: *Strickland* 2, 1913, 112; *Hutchison* 1960–62, 174; *Gunnis* 1968, 262–3; *Pyke* 1973, 94; *Potterton* 1975, 72; *Sheehy* 1980, 41; *Pyke* 1981, 29; *Read* 1982, 117; *Morris and Roberts* 1998, 432–3

Portrait of the Sculptor: John Doyle, unfinished sketch in oils, NGI

Funerary Monuments				
1.	?1835	Isabella Cooper	Goathurst church, Somerset	*Gunnis* 1968, 262
2.	1842	Rt Hon John Philpott Curran, Master of the Rolls in Ireland, bust	[Exhib RA, London, 1313]; St Patrick's Cathedral, Dublin	*AU*, 1842, 128; *Strickland* 2, 1913, 123; *Potterton* 1975, 72

3.	1845	T N Longman (†1842) Model(s): exhib RA, London, 1845, 1394		St John, Hampstead, London		*Graves* V, 1905–6, 281; Pevsner, *London: N*, 1998, 202
Statues						
4.	1819	Combat between the archangel Michael and Satan		[Exhib Dublin Society, Hawkins St]; untraced		*Graves* 1875, 384; *Strickland* 2, 1913, 122; *Potterton* 1975, 72
5.	1824	Nymph and Cupid, sketch for a group		[Exhib RA, London, 1001]; untraced		*Graves* 1875, 384; *Graves* V, 1905–6,
6.	1826	Model for a group		[Exhib Soc of BA, London, 744]; untraced		*Johnson* 1975, 329
7.	1826	Wounded hero		[Exhib Soc of BA, London, 742]; untraced		*Johnson* 1975, 329
8.	1833	Unidentified young lady, statuette	p	[Exhib Soc of BA, London, 817]; untraced		*Johnson* 1975, 329
9.	1839	A sleeping child – 'She passed away so sweetly . . .'	m	[Exhib RA, London, 1299]; untraced		*Graves* V, 1905–6, 280; *Strickland* 2, 1913, 125
10.	1850	Sir Michael O'Loghlie	m	Law Courts, Dublin, great room		*Strickland* 2, 1913, 124
11.	1857	Thomas Moore	b	College Street, Dublin		*Strickland* 2, 1913, 124; *Read* 1982, 117; *Hill* 1998, 97; *Murphy* 2001, 38 (repr)
12.	1858	Nursery legend, 'This little pig went to market . . .', small figures	p	[Exhib LSFA, Liverpool, 542]; untraced		*Graves* V, 1905–6, 282; *Morris and Roberts* 1998, 433
Busts						
13.	1819	Self-portrait		[Exhib Dublin Society, Hawkins St]; untraced		*Strickland* 2, 1913, 122; *Potterton* 1975, 72
14.	1821	An artist		[Exhib RA, London, 1101]; untraced		*Graves* V, 1905–6, 279
15.	1821	Charles Phillips		[Exhib RA, London, 1150]; untraced		*Graves* V, 1905–6, 279; *Strickland* 2, 1913, 124
16.	1821	Dr Daniel Murray, Archbishop of Dublin		[Exhib RHA, Dublin]; untraced		*Strickland* 2, 1913, 124
17.	1821	Infant daughter of G Beaufort		[Exhib RA, London, 1097]; untraced		*Graves* V, 1905–6, 279
18.	1821	Rt Hon H Grattan		[Exhib RA, London, 1105]; untraced		*Graves* V, 1905–6, 279; *Strickland* 2, 1913, 123
19.	1822	General Sir J Doyle Bt, GCB		[Exhib RA, London, 1008]; untraced		*Graves* V, 1905–6, 279;
20.	1822	Young Bacchanalian		[Exhib BI, London, 326]; untraced		*Graves* 1875, 384
21.	1823	A child		[Exhib RA, London, 1076]; untraced		*Graves* V, 1905–6, 279
22.	1823	Miss Grace Croft		[Family coll]; untraced		*Gunnis* 1968, 263
23.	1823	Mrs Woody		[Exhib RA, London, 1121]; untraced		*Graves* V, 1905–6, 279
24.	1824	Child's head		[Exhib BI, London, 381]; untraced		*Graves* 1875, 384
25.	1826	Augustus Frederick, Duke of Sussex	m	[Exhib RA, London, 1057]; untraced		*Graves* V, 1905–6, 280; *Gunnis* 1968, 263; *Johnson* 1975, 329
26.	1826	Child's head, study		[Exhib Soc of BA, London, 709]; untraced		*Johnson* 1975, 329
27.	1826	Master J W Papworth		[Exhib Soc of BA, London, 711]; untraced		*Johnson* 1975, 329
28.	1827	Francis Danby ARA	p	NGI 8059	SD	*Graves* V, 1905–6, 280; *Johnson* 1975, 329; *le Harivel* 1988, 576 (repr); *Morris and Roberts* 1998, 432
29.	1827	Jakob Götzenberger		[Exhib RA, London, 1067]; untraced		*Graves* V, 1905–6, 280; *Johnson* 1975, 329; *Morris and Roberts* 1998, 432
30.	1827	Master Edward Coke		[Exhib RA, London, 1077]; untraced		*Graves* V, 1905–6, 280; *Johnson* 1975, 329
31.	1827	Miss Valpy Burton Pettigrew, aged three		[Exhib RA, London, 1068]; untraced		*Graves* V, 1905–6, 280
32.	1827	Mrs Hudson Gurney	m	[Exhib RA, London, 1086]; untraced		*Graves* V, 1905–6, 280
33.	1827	Rev T J Judkin		[Exhib RA, London, 1097]; untraced		*Graves* V, 1905–6, 280; *Johnson* 1975, 329
34.	1827	Unidentified child		[Exhib RA, London, 1106]; untraced		*Graves* V, 1905–6, 280;
35.	1828	Child's head, two studies		[Exhib BI, London, 513, 520]; untraced		*Graves* 1875, 384
36.	1828	Fanny Denman, 3rd daughter of Thomas, 1st Baron Denman		[Exhib RA, London, 1145]; untraced		*Graves* V, 1905–6, 280; *Johnson* 1975, 329
37.	?1828	Lady Denman (†1852)	m	Chatsworth, Derbys, sculpture gallery Other versions: 1827, (Balcombe Place, Sussex, 1955), plaster, untraced		GPC; *Graves* V, 1905–6, 280; *Chatsworth Handlist*, 26
38.	1828	Lord Nugent	m	[Exhib RA, London, 1151]; untraced		*Graves* V, 1905–6, 280; *Morris and Roberts* 1998, 432
39.	1828	Thomas Moore		[Exhib ALRI, Liverpool, 229]; untraced Other versions: exhib RA 1834 (1049), marble exhib RA 1841 (1321), marble NGI 1842, for James, 3rd Earl of Charlemont, SD, marble, NPG London, 1842, SD exhib Liverpool Ac, 1854, 770 exhib LSFA, Liverpool, 1859, 779		*Graves* V, 1905–6, 280; *Strickland* 2, 1913, 124; *Gunnis* 1968, 263; *le Harivel* 1988, 577 (repr); *Morris and Roberts* 1998, 432, 433
40.	1828	Thomas, 1st Baron Denman	m	Chatsworth, Derbys, sculpture gallery Other versions: Balcombe Place, Sussex, 1827, plaster, SD	SD	*Gunnis* 1968, 263; *Chatsworth Handlist*, 25; *Johnson* 1975, 329; *Morris and Roberts* 1998, 432; GPC
41.	1829	A bacchante's head		[Exhib Soc of BA, London, 859]; untraced		*Johnson* 1975, 329

42.	1829	Charles Steedman		[Exhib RA, London, 1173]; untraced		*Graves* V, 1905–6, 280;
43.	1829	Head of a rabbi		[Exhib RA, London, 1132]; untraced		*Graves* V, 1905–6, 280
44.	1829	Sir James Mackintosh		[coll Lord Nugent]; untraced		*Graves* V, 1905–6, 280; *Gunnis* 1968, 263
45.	1829	T W Coke MP		[Exhib RA, London, 1174]; untraced		*Graves* V, 1905–6, 280; *Johnson* 1975, 329
46.	1829	Thomas Joseph Pettigrew FRS		[Exhib RA, London, 1143]; untraced		*Graves* V, 1905–6, 280; *Johnson* 1975, 329
47.	1830	A little girl	m	[Exhib RA, London, 1248]; untraced		*Graves* V, 1905–6, 280; *Johnson* 1975, 329
48.	1830	William Mulready RA		[Crystal Palace, portrait coll, 1854]; RHA, Dublin		*Strickland* 2, 1913, 124; *Ormond* 1973, 328; *Johnson* 1975, 329
49.	1831	Henry, 1st Lord Brougham and Vaux		[Exhib RA, London, 1230]; untraced		*Library of Fine Arts* 1831, vol 1, 433; *Graves* V, 1905–6, 280; *Johnson* 1975, 329
50.	1831	Sir Thomas Lawrence PRA		[Exhib RA, London, 1219]; untraced		*Graves* V, 1905–6, 280; *Gunnis* 1968, 263; *Johnson* 1975, 320
51.	1831	Unidentified lady	m	[Exhib RA, London, 1186]; untraced		*Graves* V, 1905–6, 280
52.	1832	Dr Thomas Denman		[Exhib Soc of BA, London, 868]; untraced		*Johnson* 1975, 329
53.	1832	George Evelyn	m	[Exhib Soc of BA, London, 890]; untraced		*Johnson* 1975, 329
54.	1832	George Stephenson		Newcastle Literary and Philosophical Society Other versions: Small bust, *c*1848 (?), cast iron, Knox/Longstaffe-Gowan coll Museum of Science and Industry, Birmingham Portobello Road, London, Feb 2000, plaster		*Graves* V, 1905–6, 280; *Gunnis* 1968, 263; *Johnson* 1975, 329; *Morris and Roberts* 1998, 432; *Usherwood* 2000, 150
55.	1832	Master Britiffe Skottowe	m	[Exhib RA, London, 1209]; untraced		*Graves* V, 1905–6, 280; *Johnson* 1975, 329
56.	1832	Mrs Boyce	m	[Exhib Soc of BA, London, 837]; untraced		*Johnson* 1975, 329
57.	1832	Simon McGillivray		[Soc of BA, London, 839]; untraced		*Johnson* 1975, 329
58.	1832	Unidentified boy		[Exhib Soc of BA, London, 867]; untraced		*Johnson* 1975, 329
59.	1832	Unidentified child		[Exhib Soc of BA, London, 848]; untraced		*Johnson* 1975, 329
60.	1833	Hon Sir Edward Cust		[Exhib Soc of BA, London, 815]; untraced		*Johnson* 1975, 329
61.	1833	Mrs Evelyn		Wotton, Surrey		*Graves* V, 1905–6, 280; *Gunnis* 1968, 263
62.	1834	G T Goodenough FRS	m	Lady Lever, LL 725	S	*Graves* V, 1905–6, 280; *Lady Lever* 1999, 65 (repr)
63.	1834	Head of a boy		[Exhib BI, London, 561]; untraced		*Graves* 1875, 384
64.	1836	Solomon Cox		Colonel E Goldsworthy		*Graves* V, 1905–6, 280; *Gunnis* 1968, 263
65.	1837	Daniel O'Connell MP	m	[Exhib RA, London, 1241]; untraced		*Graves* V, 1905–6, 280; *Ormond* 1973, 347; *Morris and Roberts* 1998, 432
66.	1837	Lord Denham	m	[Exhib RA, London, 1191]; untraced		*Graves* V, 1905–6, 280
67.	1838	Charles Phillips	m	[Exhib RA, London, 1372]; untraced		*Graves* V, 1905–6, 280
68.	1838	T S Goodenough		[Exhib Birmingham Soc of A]; untraced		*Gunnis* 1968, 263
69.	1839	George William, Lord Morpeth, later 7th Earl of Carlisle		Castle Howard, N R Yorks Other versions: NGI 8088, SD 1839, marble		Castle Howard archives in GPC; *Gunnis* 1968, 263; *le Harivel* 1988, 577 (repr)
70.	1839	Lord Stanley	m	[Exhib RA, London, 1374]; untraced		*Graves* V, 1905–6, 280; *Morris and Roberts* 1998, 432
71.	1840	Anthony, eldest son of General and Lady Charlotte Bacon	m	[Exhib RA, London, 1180]; untraced		*Graves* V, 1905–6, 280; *Morris and Roberts* 1998, 433
72.	1840	Lord Clements	m	[Exhib RA, London, 1188]; untraced		*Graves* V, 1905–6, 280
73.	1840	Thomas, 3rd Viscount Southwell	m	[Exhib RA, London, 1183]; untraced		*Graves* V, 1905–6, 280; *Strickland* 2, 1913, 124
74.	1841	Anne, Countess of Charlemont	m	Windsor Castle, RCIN 45142 Other versions: NGI, Dublin, nd, marble	SD	*Graves* V, 1905–6, 280; *le Harivel* 1988, 578 (repr); *Morris and Roberts* 1998, 433
75.	1841	Daughter of William Hunter Baillie	m	[Exhib RA, London, 1265]; untraced		*Graves* V, 1905–6, 280
76.	1841	Georgiana, Lady Dover	m	[Exhib RA, London, 1299]; Chatsworth, Derbys, orangery Other versions: 1842, Castle Howard, E R Yorks, SD		*Graves* V, 1905–6, 280; *Gunnis* 1968, 263; *Chatsworth Handlist*, 28
77.	1841	William, 1st Baron Plunket	m	NGI 8066 Other versions: Castle Howard, N R Yorks, 1841, plaster Trinity College, Dublin, Long Room, 1846	SD	*Graves* V, 1905–6, 280; *Crookshank* 1986, 24; *Gunnis* 1968, 263; *le Harivel* 1988, 577 (repr);
78.	1842	D C Golden, of New York	m	[Exhib RA, London, 1316]; untraced		*Graves* V, 1905–6, 280; *Gunnis* 1968, 263
79.	1842	Dr James McDonnell	m	Municipal gallery, Belfast		*Graves* V, 1905–6, 280; *Strickland* 2, 1913, 124

80.	1842	Hugh, 2nd Earl Fortescue	m	[Exhib RA, London, 1380]; untraced Other versions: exhib RA, London, 1845 (1455) marble; untraced Infirmary, Barnstaple, Devon, nd		*Graves* V, 1905–6, 280–1
81.	1842	Lord Charlemont		Untraced		*Hill* 1998, 97
82.	1842	Theobald Mathew	m	[Exhib RA, London, 1338]; untraced		*Strickland* 2, 1913, 124; *Ormond* 1973, 306
83.	1843	Augustus, 3rd Duke of Leinster	m	[Exhib RA, London, 1454 (family coll)]; untraced		*Graves* V, 1905–6, 281; *Strickland* 2, 1913, 124
84.	1843	Emily, daughter of James Henry Blake QC	m	[Exhib RA, London, 1509]; untraced		*Graves* V, 1905–6, 281
85.	1843	Judge Louis Perrin	m	NGI 8108	SD	*Graves* V, 1905–6, 280; *le Harivel* 1988, 577 (repr)
86.	1843	Matthew Baillie	m	[Exhib RA, London, 1512]; untraced		*Graves* V, 1905–6, 281;
87.	1843	Mr Justice Perrin	m	[Exhib RA, London, 1429]; untraced		*Graves* V, 1905–6, 280; *Strickland* 2, 1913, 124
88.	1843	Sir Henry Marsh Bt	m	[Exhib RA, London, 1431]; RC Physic, Dublin		*Graves* V, 1905–6, 281; *Strickland* 2, 1913, 124
89.	1843	Unidentified lady	m	[Exhib RA, London, 1478]; untraced		*Graves* V, 1905–6, 280
90.	1844	Henry, 1st Marquess of Anglesey		[Coll W H Curran]; untraced Other versions: exhib RA, London, 1845, 1368, marble; untraced		*Graves* V, 1905–6, 281; *Gunnis* 1968, 263
91.	1844	Matthew Evans	m	[Exhib RA, London, 1315]; untraced		*AU*, 1844, 171; *Graves* V, 1905–6, 281; *Morris and Roberts* 1998, 433
92.	1844	Sir Edward Blakeney, KCB		[Exhib RA, London, 1331]; untraced		*Graves* V, 1905–6, 281; *Strickland* 2, 1913, 123
93.	1844	Sir Philip Crampton		[Exhib RA, London, 1400]; untraced		*AU*, 1844, 171; *Graves* V, 1905–6, 281; *Strickland* 2, 1913, 123
94.	1844	William Elliott Hudson	m	[Exhib RA, London, 1336]; Royal Irish Academy		*Strickland* 2, 1913, 123
95.	1846	Josiah Dunne	m	[Exhib RA, London, 1440]; untraced		*Graves* V, 1905–6, 281; *Strickland* 2, 1913, 123
96.	1846	Lord Talbot de Malahide		[Exhib RHA, Dublin]; untraced		*Strickland* 2, 1913, 124
97.	1846	Maziere Brady, Chief Baron of Ireland	m	[Exhib RA, London, 1437]; untraced		*Graves* V, 1905–6, 281; *Strickland* 2, 1913, 123
98.	1847	Jonathan Henn, QC	m	[Exhib RA, London, 1404]; untraced		*Graves* V, 1905–6, 281; *Strickland* 2, 1913, 123
99.	1847	Lord Doneraile		Doneraile, Co Cork		GPC
100.	1847	Marble head of a bacchante	m	[Exhib RA, London, 1413]; untraced		*Graves* V, 1905–6, 281; *Morris and Roberts* 1998, 433
101.	1847	Richard Carmichael		[Exhib RA, London, 1410 (family coll)]; untraced Other versions: Copy, R C Surg, Dublin		*Graves* V, 1905–6, 281; *Strickland* 2, 1913, 123
102.	1847	Richard Lalor Sheil MP	m	[Commissioned by Henry Labouchère, 1st Baron Taunton]; NGI 8065	SD	*Graves* V, 1905–6, 280; *le Harivel* 1988, 577 (repr)
103.	1847	Robert Holmes	m	[The Bar messroom (Dublin?)]; Knox/Longstaffe-Gowan coll (1994)	SD	*Graves* V, 1905–6, 281; *Barrett* 1971 (1), 89–90
104.	1848	Henry, 3rd Viscount Palmerston		[Exhib RA, London, 1436]; untraced		*Graves* V, 1905–6, 281; *Strickland* 2, 1913, 124; *Gunnis* 1968, 263; *Morris and Roberts* 1998, 433
105.	1849	Emily Labouchère	m	[Exhib RA, London, 1287]; untraced		*Graves* V, 1905–6, 281
106.	1849	George, 4th Earl of Clarendon	p	RDS, Dublin	SD	*Graves* V, 1905–6, 281; *White and Bright* 1998, 73
107.	1849	James McCullagh	m	[Exhib RA, London, 1330]; Trinity College, Dublin		*Graves* V, 1905–6, 281; *Strickland* 2, 1913, 124
108.	1849	John Finlay, Senescal of Kilmainham	m	[Exhib RA, London, 1311]; untraced		*Graves* V, 1905–6, 281; *Strickland* 2, 1913, 123
109.	1849	Katherine, Countess of Clarendon	m	[Exhib RA, London, 1334]; untraced		*Graves* V, 1905–6, 281; *Strickland* 2, 1913, 123
110.	1849	Mary Labouchère	m	[Exhib RA, London, 1256]; untraced		*Graves* V, 1905–6, 281;
111.	1849	Mina Labouchère	m	[Exhib RA, London, 1249]; untraced		*Graves* V, 1905–6, 281
112.	1849	Rev Humphrey Lloyd	m	[Exhib RA, London, 1292]; untraced		*Strickland* 2, 1913, 124; *Graves* V, 1905–6, 281; *Morris and Roberts* 1998, 433
113.	1850	Cardinal Cullen	w	Dublin Civic Museum		GPC
114.	1850	Edmund Burke, model		[Crystal Palace, London]; untraced		*Graves* V, 1905–6, 281; *Gunnis* 1968, 263
115.	1850	John Doyle	m	[Exhib RA, London, 1369]; untraced		*Graves* V, 1905–6, 281
116.	1850	Mr Justice Burton, model		[Exhib RA, London, 1407]; untraced		*Graves* V, 1905–6, 281; *Strickland* 2, 1913, 123
117.	1851	Cardinal Nicholas Wiseman, 'cabinet bust'	p	Knox/Longstaffe-Gowan coll (acq 1989)		*Graves* V, 1905–6, 281; *Ormond* 1973, 518; *Morris and Roberts* 1998, 433
118.	1851	Unidentified gentleman		[Exhib RA, London, 1323]; untraced		*Graves* V, 1905–6, 281
119.	1852	Alderman Benjamin Lee Guinness, Lord Mayor of Dublin	m	[Exhib RA, London, 1484]; untraced		*Graves* V, 1905–6, 281; *Strickland* 2, 1913, 123
120.	1852	Dr Gartland, Bishop of Savannah, Georgia, model		[Exhib RA, London, 1400]; untraced		*Graves* V, 1905–6, 281
121.	1852	Edmund Burke, model		[Exhib RA, London, 1402]; untraced		*Graves* V, 1905–6, 281
122.	1852	Hon Mrs George Villiers		[Exhib RA, London, 1408]; untraced		*Graves* V, 1905–6, 281
123.	1852	William Henn	m	[Exhib RA, London, 1418]; untraced		*Graves* V, 1905–6, 281; *Strickland* 2, 1913, 123

124.	1853	Charles, 2nd Earl Grey		Eton College, Windsor, Berks		*Ormond* 1973, 203
125.	1853	Dr Daniel Murray, Archbishop of Dublin		[Exhib RA, London, 1387]; untraced		*Graves* V, 1905–6, 281; *Strickland* 2, 1913, 124
126.	1853	G T Braine	m	[Exhib RA, London, 1397]; untraced		*Graves* V, 1905–6, 281
127.	1853	Lord Jeffreys		[Exhib RA, London, 1418]; untraced		*Graves* V, 1905–6, 282
128.	1853	Mr Musurus, Turkish Ambassador	m	[Exhib RA, London, 1409]; untraced		*Graves* V, 1905–6, 282
129.	1853	Thomas, 1st Baron Denman		Law Institution, London		*Gunnis* 1968, 263
130.	1854	Annie Hutton	m	NGI 8060	SD	*Harbison, Potterton and Sheehy* 1978, 219 (repr); *le Harivel* 1988, 576 (repr)
131.	1854	Edmund, 14th Earl of Derby		[Crystal Palace, portrait gallery (coll Lord Skelmersdale)]; untraced		*Manchester Art Treasures* 1857, 136; *Ormond* 1973, 136
132.	1855	Unidentified lady, posthumous	m	[Exhib RA, London, 1537]; untraced		*Graves* V, 1905–6, 282
133.	1857	Unidentified gentleman	m	[Exhib RA, London, 1311]; untraced		*Graves* V, 1905–6, 282
134.	1858	Colonel Larcom, CB		[Exhib RHA]; untraced		*Strickland* 2, 1913, 124
135.	1859	A lady of the Caulfield or Clements family	m	NGI	SD	*le Harivel* 1988, 578 (repr)
136.	1859	The Rt Hon Thomas Lefroy		Trinity College, Dublin	SD	*Graves* V, 1905–6, 282; *Read* 1982, 125, 128 (repr); *Crookshank* 1986, 24
137.	1860	Sir Richard Griffith Bt	m	[Exhib RA, London, 1037]; untraced		*Graves* V, 1905–6, 282
138.	1860	Thomas Lefroy, Lord Chief Justice of Ireland	m	[Exhib RA, London, 1020]; untraced		*Graves* V, 1905–6, 282
139.	nd	John Doyle ('HB'), artist and political cartoonist	p	NGI	S	*le Harivel* 1988, 578 (repr)
140.	nd	John Philpott Curran	m	RDS, Dublin		*White and Bright* 1998, 53
141.	nd	Richard, 1st Viscount Wellesley	p	NGI 8202		*Wynne and White* 1975, 29
142.	nd	Unidentified man	p	NGI		*le Harivel* 1988, 578 (repr)
143.	nd	Unidentified sitter		Trinity College, Dublin, Long Room		*Crookshank* 1986, 24
Reliefs						
144.	1821	Frederick Augustus, Duke of York	w	Philadelphia Museum of Art		*Pyke* 1973, 94 (pl 195)
145.	1823	Dr Hill, portrait medallion	w	[Exhib RA, London, 1003]; untraced		*Graves* V, 1905–6, 281
146.	1823	'Sketch for a bas-relief to illustrate His Majesty's gracious Letter to the Irish People . . .'		[Exhib RA, London, 1116]; untraced		*Graves* V, 1905–6, 279
147.	1824	Unidentified lady, medallion	w	[Exhib RA, London, 911]; untraced		*Graves* V, 1905–6, 279
148.	1824	Unidentified man	w	Private coll		*Pyke* 1973, 94
149.	1823–1824	Unidentified men	w	VAM (A43-1970, A50-1970, Bate)		*Pyke* 1973, 94
150.	1825	Augustus Frederick, Duke of Sussex, medallion model		[Exhib RA, London, 937]; untraced Other versions: ?1826, Dublin Civic museum, wax		GPC; *Graves* V, 1905–6, 279; *Johnson* 1975, 329
151.	1825	Dr Bathurst, Bishop of Norwich, medallion		[Exhib RA, London, 965]; untraced		*Graves* V, 1905–6, 279; *Morris and Roberts* 1998, 432
152.	1825	J Galt, medallion		[Exhib Soc of BA, London, 369]; untraced		*Johnson* 1975, 329
153.	1825	Lieutenant-Colonel D'Este, medallion		[Exhib RA, London, 960]; untraced		*Graves* V, 1905–6, 279
154.	1825	Master Coke of Holkham, medallion		[Exhib RA, London, 936]; untraced		*Graves* V, 1905–6, 279; *Johnson* 1975, 329
155.	1825	Mrs Johnson, medallion		[Exhib RA, London, 935]; untraced		*Graves* V, 1905–6, 279
156.	1825	Sydney, Lady Morgan, medal		[Exhib RA, London, 1834, 966]; untraced		*Graves* V, 1905–6, 280; *Ormond* 1973, 325
157.	1826	Daughter of Colonel Hugh Baillie (medallic portrait)		[Exhib RA, London, 972]; untraced		*Graves* V, 1905–6, 279
158.	1826	Earl of Essex, medallion		[Exhib RA, London, 974]; untraced		*Graves* V, 1905–6, 279
159.	1826	Henry, 3rd Earl Bathurst (†1834), medallion		[Exhib RA, London, 967]; untraced		*Graves* V, 1905–6, 279
160.	1827	Mrs Grant, medallion portrait		[Exhib RA, London, 999]; untraced		*Graves* V, 1905–6, 280
161.	1828	S Woolrich, medallion portrait		[Exhib RA, London, 1089]; untraced		*Graves* V, 1905–6, 280
162.	1830	Daniel O'Connell MP, medallion		[Exhib RA, London, 1096]; untraced		*Strickland* 2, 1913, 124; *Ormond* 1973, 347; *Johnson* 1975, 329; *Morris and Roberts* 1998, 432
163.	*c*1840	George Papworth	w	National Museum of Ireland		*Strickland* 2, 1913, 124; *Pyke* 1973, 94
164.	nd	Unidentified youth		National Museum of Ireland (206: 1895)		*Pyke* 1973, 94
Miscellaneous						
165.	1821	Infant Orpheus		[Exhib RA, London, 1096]; untraced		*Graves* 1875, 384; *Strickland* 2, 1913, 122
166.	1822	Caresses declined		[Exhib BI, London, 336]; untraced		*Graves* 1875, 384
167.	1822	'Cupid and Psyche, a sketch'		[Exhib RA, London, 1029]; untraced		*Graves* V, 1905–6, 279
168.	1822	Infantine fear		[Exhib BI, London, 335]; untraced		*Graves* 1875, 384
169.	1822	Infantine group		[Exhib RA, London, 1028]; untraced		*Graves* 1875, 384; *Graves* V, 1905–6, 279
170.	1822	Venus at the bath		[Exhib RA, London, 1017]; untraced		*Graves* 1875, 384; *Graves* V, 1905–6, 279
171.	1823	Child and dog, sketch		[Exhib RA, London, 1110]; untraced		*Graves* V, 1905–6, 279; *Johnson* 1975, 329
172.	1824	Cupid and Psyche		[Exhib BI, London, 383]; untraced		*Graves* 1875, 384
173.	1824	General Sir J Doyle GCB (portrait)	w	[Exhib RA, London, 918]; untraced		*Graves* V, 1905–6, 279
174.	1824	J Abbott	w	[Exhib RA, London, 945]; untraced		*Graves* V, 1905–6, 279
175.	1824	J D Hunter	w	[Exhib RA, London, 944]; untraced		*Graves* V, 1905–6, 279
176.	1824	'Sketch, made in 1821, for a public testemonial to commemorate His Majesty's visit to Ireland . . .'		[Exhib RA, London, 1034]; untraced		*Graves* V, 1905–6, 279

177.	1826	The origin of fiction, sketch	tc	[Exhib RA, London, 1054]; untraced	*Graves* V, 1905–6, 279
178.	1827	Child playing with a dog		[Exhib BI, London, 474]; untraced	*Graves* 1875, 384; *Johnson* 1975, 329; *Morris and Roberts* 1998, 432
179.	1827	Mother and child		[Exhib BI, London, 475]; untraced	*Graves* 1875, 384; *Johnson* 1975, 329
180.	1829	Memorial of a departed infant		[Exhib RA, London, 1073]; untraced	*Graves* V, 1905–6, 280
181.	1831	Girl leading a blind man		[Exhib BI, London, 558]; untraced	*Graves* 1875, 384
182.	1832	The parting of Hector and Andromache, sketch	tc	[Exhib Soc of BA, London, 843]; untraced	*Johnson* 1975, 329
183.	1856	Cupid disarmed	p	[Exhib RA, London, 1244]; untraced	*Graves* V, 1905–6, 282
184.	1859	Group	p	[Exhib LSFA, Liverpool, 770]; untraced	*Morris and Roberts* 1998, 433

MOORE, John Francis –1809

Moore is remarkable for his fashionable use of colour at a time when monochrome memorials were considered the acme of good taste. He was born in Hanover and came to England about 1760, where he became a member of the Free Society of Artists. He exhibited with them, as 'James Moore', every year from 1766–76, giving as his address, Berners Street, London. Moore showed a variety of sculpture including models in clay and works in marble, designs for monuments, low reliefs (including some for chimneypieces), animals, portrait busts and statues and, in 1769, a statue of *Apollo* (**38**). In 1766 he presented to the Society of Arts a marble relief entitled *Britannia reviver of Antique and prompter to modern Arts* (**71**). Thanks were returned by letter. On 6 January 1769 'Francis More in Berner Street, Oxford Road', won the Society of Arts silver palette for unspecified accomplishments (RSA *Minutes*, 1767–68, seq 3 f11). Among his earliest known commissions were several chimneypieces for Audley End, Essex, supplied in 1763. For one with Doric columns, after a design by Robert Adam he was paid the large sum of £111 14s 3d in January 1764 (**60**).

His most valued patron was probably Alderman William Beckford (1709–70), the builder of Fonthill Splendens. Moore supplied several elaborate polychrome chimneypieces for the house, including one flanked by female figures for the banqueting hall (**56**) and another with piping fauns for the music room (**58**). A third, for the saloon (**57**), was seen in Moore's studio in 1765 by a French visitor, P T Grosley, who described it as 'remarkable on account of its high finishing . . . All the most remarkable deaths in the Iliad were presented . . . the figures protuberant and almost starting from the marble . . . intermixed with figures in basso-relievo representing the deaths of less consequence' (*A Tour to London*, 1772, 69). In 1765 Moore exhibited a marble statue at the Free Society, of Beckford in the livery of the Lord Mayor of London, delivering a speech (**37**). Gunnis described it as 'a dramatic essay in baroque which gives ample proof of the sculptor's talents' (*Gunnis* 1968, 263). When Beckford died in 1770 the City of London held a competition for a monument to be set up in Guildhall, for which they set aside £1,000. Among the 17 competitors were **Agostino Carlini** and **Nathaniel Smith**, but it seems that through influence Moore had already been chosen as the sculptor (**39**). The statue is a variant of the earlier figure and was priced at £1,300. It depicts Beckford delivering the impromptu remonstrance he had made in May 1770 which confused and angered King George III. Below are seated figures representing *Trade* and *Navigation*. J T Smith called it 'a glaring specimen of marble spoiled' (*J T Smith* II, 1828, 204).

Moore was responsible for a number of wall monuments with sarcophagi carrying figural roundel-reliefs, often with a Christian theme (**1, 2, 5, 6, 7, 19, 25, 27, 30**). Among his more ambitious memorials is the tribute to Field-Marshal Lord Ligonier, 1773, in Westminster Abbey, which has a figure of *Britannia* surrounded by martial trophies and a portrait medallion (**10**). The Ferrers memorial at Ettington has a stiff, reclining figure of George Shirley, the patron, flanked by more successful standing images of Lord and Lady Ferrers in 17th-century dress (**12**). A later work, raised at North Stoneham in 1781, commemorates Admiral Hawke with a spirited relief of his last victory at Quiberon Bay (**16**). Generally the figures on the monuments lack animation and the draperies are unconvincing, but the formal sculpture is well executed and he made good use of coloured marbles. Nineteen surviving drawings for monuments in the Victoria and Albert Museum would doubtless have attracted potential patrons by their good draughtsmanship and clear bright colouring.

A number of portrait busts by Moore were shown with the Free Society, most of them now lost. His head of the 2nd Earl of Bessborough, which is probably the 'bust of a Nobleman' exhibited at the Free Society in 1775 and at the Royal Academy in 1776, is now at Spencer House (**50**). For the sentimental Dr Thomas Wilson, Rector of St Stephen Walbrook, London, Moore provided a statue of his adored lodger, the blue-stocking, Catherine Macaulay, in the character of *History* (**15**). It was unveiled in that church on 8 September 1777, but without permission from the churchwardens, who had it removed since the inscription gave offence to the parishioners.

The sculptor had several children, one of whom, **John** (or **James**) **Moore II** became a sculptor and assisted his father. Together they signed the monument to Jonas Hanway (†1786) in Westminster Abbey, which has a relief of *Britannia clothing boys*, mounted on a sarcophagus (**26**). Shortly after, the son appears to have died and Moore took as a partner the unidentified 'J Smith', whose signature is on some late monuments (**31–4**). One of his pupils was **James Calvert**.

He died on 21 January 1809, at York Buildings, New Road, St Marylebone, London. Moore was clearly a man of substance for in his will, dated 21 November 1805, he left his wife, Barbara, his chattels and £100 'for her immediate sustenance' plus an annuity of £570. Everything else was to be sold for the benefit of his son and three unmarried daughters. Two houses in Welbeck Street, London, were left in trust for the daughters' benefit. P T Grosley, the French visitor to Moore's workshop, considered Moore and **Joseph Wilton** to be the leading statuaries of the day (*Grosley* 2, 1772, 67). The shortage of modern commentators on Moore's work denies this judgement, but he was certainly a skilful sculptor, particularly when working in relief, and his use of polychrome work brought him a steady flow of customers.

IR

Literary References: *Graves* 1907, 171–3; *Gunnis* 1968, 236–4; *Physick* 1969, 17n 37, 130–3, 140, 141; *Penny* 1977 (1), passim; *Whinney* 1988, 315–6, 465 n25; *Hardy* 1989, 40–2; *ODNB* (JKB)

Archival References: Audley End Archives, 1763–4

Collections of Drawings: 19, for monuments, including one for the Rev Harvey Spragg, 4910 VAM 4910, pen and ink and watercolour

Will: PROB 11/1491/371-2, proved 24 Jan 1809

Funerary Monuments

No.	Date	Subject	Location		References
1.	post-1760	Benedict Conquest (†1753)	Irnham, Lincs	S	Pevsner, *Lincs*, 1989, 408; C Lib (repr)
2.	†1767	Faith Sawrey	Bradford Cathedral, W R Yorks	S	Pevsner, *Yorks: W R*, 1967, 123
3.	†1767	James Brockman	Newington, Kent		Pevsner, *Kent: N E & E*, 1983, 400
4.	†1767	Mary Mason (designed by James Stuart)	Bristol Cathedral		*Colvin* 1995, 942
5.	†1770	William Baker Drawing(s): VAM 4910.16	Bath Abbey, Somerset		Pevsner, *Somerset: N & Bristol*, 1958, 104; *Penny* 1977 (1), 3, 5, 173–4 (repr)
6.	†1771	Hon Chaloner and Hon Catherine Harris	Saxton, W R Yorks	S	
7.	†1771	Robert Hucks	Aldenham, Herts	S	Pevsner, *Herts*, 1977, 67; C Lib (repr)
8.	1772	Margaret Rae Drawing(s): VAM 4910.	Worcester Cathedral	SD	Pevsner, *Worcs*, 1968, 311; *Whinney* 1988, 465 n25; C Lib (repr)
9.	†1772	Thomas Patten	St Elphin, Warrington, Lancs		Pevsner, *Lancs: S*, 1969, 412
10.	1773	Field-Marshal John Louis, 1st Earl Ligonier (†1770) Drawing(s): exhib Free Soc, 1771, 179 Model(s): exhib Free Soc, 1773, 121	Westminster Abbey, London, chancel ambulatory	S	FFB, 14 May 1771; *Graves* 1907, 172; Pevsner, *London: Westminster*, 1973, 431; *Whinney* 1988, 315–6; C Lib (repr)
11.	†1773	Mary Langham	Cottesbrooke, Northants		Pevsner, *Northants*, 1973, 162; *CIIA* 4/3/43 (repr)
12.	1775	Robert, 2nd Earl Ferrers (†1717) and his second wife, Selina (†1762) Model(s): Exhib Free Soc 1775, 160, 161, models of Robert Earl Ferrers and his lady	Ettington, Warks	SD	*Graves* 1907, 172; Pevsner, *Warks*, 1966, 290 (repr); *Whinney* 1988, 465 n25
13.	1775	William Jones Drawing(s): VAM 4910	Ramsbury, Wilts	SD	Pevsner, *Wilts*, 1975, 378; *Whinney* 1988, 465 n316
14.	†1776	Winefred Bridger and family members (designed by Stephen Riou)	St Mildred, Canterbury, Kent	S	Pevsner, *Kent: N E & E*, 1983, 243
15.	1777	Catharine Macaulay (†1791), as 'History'	[St Stephen, Walbrook, City of London]; Warrington Library, Lancs, (formerly Town Hall), foyer	S	*White* 1904, 387; *Pierpoint* 1908; *Gunnis* 1968, 264; *ODNB*
16.	†1781	Admiral Edward, 1st Baron Hawke Drawing(s): VAM 4910/4-5 two (*Physick* 1969, 133, repr)	North Stoneham, Hants	S	*Physick* 1969, 132–3 (repr)
17.	†1782	Edith Thew	Symondsbury, Dorset		Pevsner, *Dorset*, 1972, 415; C Lib (repr)
18.	?1782	Randolph Marriott	Darfield, W R Yorks	S	
19.	† to 1783	Lord Hawke's children	Saxton, W R Yorks	S	*Universal Mag*, 783, 264; Pevsner, *Yorks: WR*, 19azine67, 431
20.	†1784	Jane Affleck	Finedon, Northants	S	Pevsner, *Northants*, 1973, 217; C Lib (repr)
21.	1784	Rev Thomas and Mrs Wilson	St Stephen Walbrook, City of London		Pevsner, *London: City*, 1997, 264
22.	†1786	Hon Barbara Clifford	St Mary, Stafford		Pevsner, *Staffs*, 1974, 242; C Lib (repr)
23.	?1786	Lieutenant John Dalling	Earsham, Norfolk		*Gunnis* 1968, 264
24.	†1787	George, 14th Earl of Shrewsbury	Heythrop, Oxon	S	
25.	†1788	John Barrington	Hatfield Broad Oak, Essex	S	Pevsner, *Essex*, 1965, 235; C Lib (repr)
26.	*c*1788	Jonas Hanway (†1786) (co-sculptor: John Moore II) Drawing(s): VAM 4910-20, 4910-22 (*Physick* 1969, 130, repr)	Westminster Abbey, London, north transept	S	WAM 16 April 1788; *Physick* 1969, 130–31 (repr); *Penny* 1977 (1), 152, 220 n35 (repr)
27.	†1788	Thomas Halsey, father and son	Great Gaddesdon, Herts	S	
28.	†1789	Rt Hon Charles Cornwall	St Cross, Winchester, Hants	S	Pevsner, *Hants & Isle of Wight*, 1967, 711; C Lib (repr)
29.	*c*1790	Rushout family, including three busts, Lady Alice, Lady Ann and another (earlier busts by Rysbrack of Sir James and Sir John Rushout incorporated in the monument)	Blockley, Glos		Pevsner, *Glos: Cotswolds*, 1999, 183; C Lib (repr)
30.	†1791	Elizabeth (†1783) and Mary (†1791) Jones (co-sculptor: J Smith, of London)	Stowey, Somerset	S	Pevsner, *Somerset: N & Bristol*, 1958, 266; C Lib (repr)
31.	†1791	Mary Anne Chichester (co-sculptor: J Smith, of London)	Arlington, Devon	S	Pevsner, *Devon*, 1989, 130
32.	†1793	Joseph Blount (co-sculptor: J Smith, of London)	Mapledurham, Oxon	S	*Gunnis* 1968, 264; C Lib (repr)
33.	?1795	Peter Oliver (co-sculptor: J Smith, of London)	Marylebone Chapel, London	S	*Gunnis* 1968, 264
34.	†1795	Thomas Wildman (co-sculptor: J Smith, of London)	St Mary, Twickenham, Middx	S	*Gunnis* 1968, 264; C Lib (repr)

No.	Date	Subject	Material	Location	Signed	Reference
35.	?1797	Barbara, Countess of Scarborough		St John's Wood Chapel, Marylebone, London		*Gunnis* 1968, 264
36.	?1801	Lady Maria Churchill		St Mary, Lewisham, London		*Gunnis* 1968, 264
Statues						
37.	1767	William Beckford	m	[Fonthill, Wilts]; Ironmongers' Hall, City of London		*Graves* 1907, 171; *Gunnis* 1968, repr XV; *Whinney* 1988, 315; *ODNB*
38.	1769	Apollo	m	[Exhib Free Soc, 151]; untraced		*Graves* 1907, 172; *Gunnis* 1968, 264
39.	1770–1772	William Beckford Model(s): exhib Free Soc, 1772, 124	m	CL Coll, Guildhall, City of London, great hall, acc 41	SD	*Graves* 1907, 171, 172; *Knight* 1986, 343 (repr); *Whinney* 1988, 315 (repr); *Ward-Jackson* 2002, 371–7; *ODNB*
40.	1777	An Italian greyhound	m	[Exhib RA, London, 239]; untraced		*Graves* III, 1905–6, 286
Busts						
41.	1766	A child's head, model		[Exhib Free Soc, 207]; untraced		*Graves* 1907, 171
42.	1766	A lady's head, model		[Exhib Free Soc, 206]; untraced		*Graves* 1907, 171
43.	1766	Unidentified gentleman		[Exhib Free Soc, 209]; untraced		*Graves* 1907, 171
44.	1768	Unidentified subject	m	[Exhib Free Soc, 155]; untraced		*Graves* 1907, 172
45.	1769	Sir John Rushout		Worcester Infirmary		*Gunnis* 1968, 264
46.	1769	Unidentified subject	tc	[Exhib Free Soc, 154]; untraced		*Graves* 1907, 172
47.	1770	'Portrait of a gentleman'	m	[Exhib Free Soc, 173]; untraced		*Graves* 1907, 172
48.	1774	Portrait of a nobleman, clay model		[Exhib Free Soc, 179]; untraced		*Graves* 1907, 172
49.	1774	Portrait of a nobleman, clay model	tc	[Exhib Free Soc, 180]; untraced		*Graves* 1907, 172
50.	1775	A nobleman, probably William, 2nd Earl of Bessborough	m	Spencer House, London	S	*Graves* 1907, 172: *ODNB*
51.	1775	Unidentified nobleman		[Exhib Free Soc, 159]; untraced		*Graves* 1907, 172
52.	1776	'Portrait of a young gentleman'		[Exhib Free Soc, 167]; untraced		*Graves* 1907, 172
53.	1776	Portrait of a young lady		[Exhib Free Soc, 166]; untraced		*Graves* 1907, 172
54.	1776	Unidentified nobleman	m	[Exhib RA, London, 191]; untraced		*Graves* III, 1905–6, 286
55.	nd	Unidentified man in middle age		William Agnew, 2001	S	
Chimneypieces						
56.	post-1755	With female flanking figures and tablet of Apollo and the Muses Drawing(s): coll R J R Arundell (*Hardy* 1989, 42, repr)		[Fonthill Splendens, Wilts]; private coll		*Hardy* 1989, 40–2
57.	post-1755	'with the most remarkable death scenes from The Iliad, intermixed with figures in low relief'		[Fonthill Splendens, Wilts]; Manor House, Beaminster, Dorset		*Harris* 1966, 1373; *Whinney* 1988, 315, 465 n24; *ODNB*
58.	post-1755	With two figures of piping fauns and tablet of Vertumnus and Pomona flanked by oak garlands	m	[Fonthill Splendens, Wilts]; private coll		*Hardy* 1989, 40–2
59.	1761	Several		[Audley End, Essex; north room, fish room and gallery]; untraced		*Gunnis* 1968, 263
60.	1763	With Doric columns and relief scenes from The Iliad Payment(s): £111 14s 3d	m	[Audley End, Essex, library]; Carton House, Co Kildare		*ODNB*
61.	1764	With 'Terms and Festoons of Statuary' Payment(s): £140	m	Newburgh Priory, N R Yorks		Wombwell Archives ZDV X 15 (MIC 1271)
62.	1766	Green and red veined alabaster	a	Newburgh Priory, N R Yorks		Wombwell Archives ZDV X 15 (MIC 1271)
63.	1767	Description unavailable		[King's Weston, near Bristol]; untraced		RG/JP, 5, 947
64.	1770	Bacchanalians, tablet		[Exhib Free Soc, 175]; untraced		*Graves* 1907, 172
65.	1770	Somnus, tablet		[Exhib Free Soc, 176]; untraced		*Graves* 1907, 172
66.	1770	The Aldobrandini marriage, tablet		[Exhib Free Soc, 174]; untraced		*Graves* 1907, 172
67.	1767–1771	Neo-classical		Fawley Court, Bucks, saloon		Pevsner, *Bucks*, 1994, 327
68.	1773	A faun offering a sheep to Pomona, tablet		[Exhib Free Soc, 119]; untraced		*Graves* 1907, 172
69.	1773	The triumph of Bacchus, tablet		[Exhib Free Soc, 118]; untraced		*Graves* 1907, 172
Architectural Sculpture						
70.	pre-1788	Reredos (Wogan family memorial)		Redenhall, Norfolk, north chapel		*Gunnis* 1968, 264; Pevsner, *Norfolk: N W & S*, 1999, 610
Reliefs						
71.	1766	'Britannia reviver of Antique and prompter to modern Arts'	m	[Soc of A, presented by the artist]; Progress House, Coventry, Warks		*Dossie* 1782, 439; *ODNB*
72.	1766	Two bas-reliefs of cattle	m	[Exhib Free Soc, 210]; untraced		*Graves* 1907, 172
73.	1767	A centaur, from a painting in Herculaneum	m	[Exhib Free Soc, 192]; untraced		*Graves* 1907, 172
74.	1767	A shepherd and flock	m	[Exhib Free Soc, 191]; untraced		*Graves* 1907, 172
75.	1769	Medallion	m	[Exhib Free Soc, 153]; untraced		*Graves* 1907, 172
76.	1771	'Celestial Victory, a monumental medallion, after a drawing by Captain Roiv'		[Exhib Free Soc, 177]; untraced		*Graves* 1907, 172
77.	1771	'Commercial Justice; a monumental medallion, after a design of Captain Roiv'		[Exhib Free Soc, 178]; untraced		*Graves* 1907, 172
78.	1771	'Tablet of beavers, after nature; a model'		[Exhib Free Soc, 176]; untraced		*Graves* 1907, 172
79.	1772	King George I, medallion		[Exhib Free Soc, 260]; untraced		*Graves* 1907, 172
80.	1772	King George II, medallion		[Exhib Free Soc, 261]; untraced		*Graves* 1907, 172
81.	1772	King George III, medallion		[Exhib Free Soc, 262]; untraced		*Graves* 1907, 172
82.	1772	Portrait of a lady and gentleman, monumental medallion		[Exhib Free Soc, 126]; untraced		*Graves* 1907, 172

83.	1772	Portrait of a lady, monumental medallion		[Exhib Free Soc, 125]; untraced	*Graves* 1907, 172
84.	1773	Britannia		[Exhib Free Soc, 120]; untraced	*Graves* 1907, 172
85.	1773	Monumental medallion		[Exhib Free Soc, 123]; untraced	*Graves* 1907, 172
86.	1774	King George I, medallion		[Exhib Free Soc, 184]; untraced	*Graves* 1907, 172
87.	1774	Monumental medallion of a young gentleman, model		[Exhib Free Soc, 185]; untraced	*Graves* 1907, 172
88.	1774	Monumental medallion of King William III and Queen Mary II		[Exhib Free Soc, 183]; untraced	Graves 1907, 172
89.	1774	Monumental medallion representing piety	m	[Exhib Free Soc, 182]; untraced	*Graves* 1907, 172
90.	1775	'Alexander ordering the works of Homer to be deposited in a casket-a model, a tablet'		[Exhib Free Soc, 164]; untraced	*Graves* 1907, 172
91.	1775	'The soldiers rushing upon Archimedes in his study; a tablet, study'		[Exhib Free Soc, 163]; untraced	*Graves* 1907, 172
Miscellaneous					
92.	1766	Boys with a bird's nest		[Exhib Free Soc, 208]; untraced	*Graves* 1907, 171
93.	1767	A dog, model	tc	[Exhib Free Soc, 193]; untraced	*Graves* 1907, 171
94.	1767	Model in clay		[Exhib Free Soc, 190]; untraced	*Graves* 1907, 172
95.	1767	Model in clay		[Exhib Free Soc, 190]; untraced	*Graves* 1907, 172
96.	1768	A group of boys with a bird's nest and a cat		[Exhib Free Soc, 156]; untraced	*Graves* 1907, 172
97.	1769	A dog	m	[Exhib Free Soc, 152]; untraced	*Graves* 1907, 172
98.	1769	'A sketch in clay, from a drawing of Mr. Stuart'		[Exhib Free Soc, 155]; untraced	*Graves* 1907, 172
99.	1770	A dog, model in clay		[Exhib Free Soc, 176]; untraced	*Graves* 1907, 172
100.	1771	'An Elephant-after the Queen's', model		[Exhib Free Soc, 174]; untraced	*Graves* 1907, 172
101.	1771	Somnus, a model		[Exhib Free Soc, 175]; untraced	*Graves* 1907, 172
102.	1773	Aristotle, 'a deception for a library'	s	[Exhib Free Soc, 122]; untraced	*Graves* 1907, 172
103.	1774	Group of children, with a cat and bird's nest	m	[Exhib Free Soc, 181]; untraced	*Graves* 1907, 172

MOORE, John II fl 1767–88

John (or James) Moore was the son of **John Francis Moore**. Like his father he showed annually with the Free Society between 1767 and 1775, exhibiting drawings as well as models and a few marble medallions (**9, 10, 12, 14**). In 1768 he was described as 'Pupil to Mr Hodgson' (*Graves* 1907, 172). He assisted his father with the monument to the philanthropist, Jonas Hanway, 1786, in Westminster Abbey, which is signed by both sculptors (**1**). Hanway's involvement in the Marine Society and the Foundling Hospital is commemorated with a relief of *Britannia* giving sailors' clothes to three boys.

Literary References: *Graves* 1907, 172–3; *Gunnis* 1968, 263

Miscellaneous Drawings: two heads in red chalk, exhib Free Soc 1767 (214, 215), untraced; flowers in black lead, exhib Free Soc 1768 (157), untraced; group of boys with bird's nest and cat, exhib Free Soc 1769 (157), untraced; *Apollo*, exhib Free Soc, 1769 (158), untraced; portrait of a lady of quality, in black lead, exhib Free Soc 1770 (177), untraced; the Holy Family after Raphael, exhib Free Soc 1771 (180), untraced; two studies after Fiamingo, exhib Free Soc 1771 (181,182), untraced; *Susanna and the elders*, drawing, exhib Free Soc 1772 (127), untraced

Funerary Monuments						
1.	c1788	Jonas Hanway (co-sculptor: John Francis Moore) Drawing(s): VAM 4910-20, 4910-22 (*Physick* 1969, 130, repr)		Westminster Abbey, London, north transept	S	WAM 16 April 1788; *Physick* 1969, 130–31 (repr); *Penny* 1977 (1), 152, 220 n35 (repr)
Statues						
2.	1767	Boar and dog, model	tc	[Exhib Free Soc, 196]; untraced		*Graves* 1907, 172
3.	1767	Goats, model	tc	[Exhib Free Soc, 194]; untraced		*Graves* 1907, 172
4.	1767	Stag and dog, model	tc	[Exhib Free Soc, 195]; untraced		*Graves* 1907, 172
5.	1768	A beaver, rabbits etc, model	tc	[Exhib Free Soc, 158]; untraced		*Graves* 1907, 172
6.	1769	Mare and foal, model	tc	[Exhib Free Soc, 156]; untraced		*Graves* 1907, 172
7.	1770	Dog and duck, model	tc	[Exhib Free Soc, 178]; untraced		*Graves* 1907, 173
8.	1774	The good shepherd, model	tc	[Exhib Free Soc, 186]; untraced		*Graves* 1907, 173
Reliefs						
9.	1773	King George II, medallion	m	[Exhib Free Soc, 125]; untraced		*Graves* 1907, 173
10.	1773	Queen Anne, medallion	m	[Exhib Free Soc, 124]; untraced		*Graves* 1907, 173
11.	1773	Two boys		[Exhib Free Soc, 128]; untraced		*Graves* 1907, 173
12.	1775	Monumental medallion		[Exhib Free Soc, 165]; untraced		*Graves* 1907, 173
13.		'cast of Mr. Moore's Aldobrandini marriage'		[Exhib Free Soc, 125]; untraced		*Graves* 1907, 173
14.		King George III, medallion	m	[Exhib Free Soc, 125]; untraced		*Graves* 1907, 173
Miscellaneous						
15.	1770	Triumph of Bacchus, model		[Exhib Free Soc, 179]; untraced		*Graves* 1907, 173

MOORE, T, of Normanton fl c1803

His monument to Anthony Woodward is a wall-tablet with a terra-cotta urn.

Funerary Monuments						
1.	†1803	Anthony Woodward	tc	Smalley, Derbys	S	*Gunnis* 1968, 264; Pevsner, *Derbys*, 1978, 319

MOREHOUSE, James, of Greenwich fl 1759–61

He was employed as master-mason at Greenwich Palace from 1759 until 1761. His son, also James Morehouse, was apprenticed to Moses Waite on 30 September 1756, but was turned over to his father on 1 October 1761. A James Morehouse became free of the Masons' Company by redemption on 26 June 1760. It is unclear whether it is the father or the son who signs the large wall-monument at Shalford.

Literary References: *Gunnis* 1968, 264; *Webb* 1999, 23

Archival References: Masons' Co, *Freemen*, fol 45

Funerary Monuments				
1.	†1759	Robert Austen	Shalford, Surrey	*Gunnis* 1968, 264; Pevsner, *Surrey*, 1971, 452

MOREHOUSE, of Dover –1811

He carved an oval tablet in Kent. Nothing is known of him beyond the circumstances of his death, which occurred on 19 July 1811. According to the *Gentleman's Magazine* he 'dropped down in the market-place, Dover, and instantly expired, while going to his ordinary work' (*GM*, 1811, 2, 589).

Funerary Monuments

1.	1791	William Smythe (†1768)		Stanford, Kent	S	*Gunnis* 1968, 264

MOREHOUSE (or MOORHOUSE) fl 1742–44

He was the mason responsible for building Rye Town Hall between 1742 and 1744 (1). There is also a payment to him for a journey to London and 'Going to the Heraldry Offie to Examin for the Coat of Arms' (Tower Archives in GPC).

Architectural Sculpture

1.	1742–1744	'the Coat of Arms and the Rest of the Carvd Work in the Compartiment' Payment(s): £16		Rye Town Hall, Sussex		Town Archives in GPC

MOREY, J fl 1767–80

He carved two works at Warblington. The monument to Thomas Sone is a cartouche tablet with cherub-heads, wreaths and flowers (1). Gunnis, who mis-transcribed the sculptor's name as 'More' describes it as 'a good copy, in stone, of a typical early eighteenth-century marble cartouche' (*Gunnis* 1968, 264).

Funerary Monuments

1.	†1767	Thomas Sone	s	Warblington, Hants	S	*Gunnis* 1968, 264
2.	†1800	John Sone (†1767) and John Lellyett (†1800)	s	Warblington, Hants	S	

MORFITT (or MORPHITT) fl 1717–21

He made two fonts for churches in Cheshire. The earlier is classical in design (1).

Literary References: *Gunnis* 1968, 265

Architectural Sculpture

1.	1717	Font Payment(s): 35 s		Church Minshull, Cheshire		*Richards* 1947, 133
2.	1721	Font	s	Holme Chapel, St Luke, Cheshire		*Richards* 1947, 189

MORGAN, C F, of Chipping Sodbury fl 1825–34

He signed two tablets with urns.

Funerary Monuments

1.	†1825	Fitzherbert Brooke		Old Sodbury, Glos	S	Pevsner, *Glos: Cotswolds*, 1999, 535
2.	†1834	Laura d'Esterre	m	Old Sodbury, Glos	S	Pevsner, *Glos: Cotswolds*, 1999, 535

MORGAN, E, of Llandaff fl 1791–1824

Gunnis noted that a number of tablets signed by this sculptor between 1791 and 1822 are in Monmouthshire and Glamorganshire churches. He may possibly be identified with the 'E Morgan of Canton' who signed three contemporary tablets in the same region (1, 3, 4).

Funerary Monuments

1.	†1806	Catherine Price		Capel Lanilltern, Glamorgan	S	Pevsner, *Glamorgan*, 1995, 179
2.	?1817	Henry Beauchamp		Gwennap, Cornwall		*Gunnis* 1968, 265
3.	†1818	John Price		Capel Lanilltern, Glamorgan	S	Pevsner, *Glamorgan*, 1995, 179
4.	post-1824	Morgan Thomas		Coychurch, Glamorgan	S	Pevsner, *Glamorgan*, 1995, 334

MORGAN, F fl 1847–67

He is known only for two Gothic tablets.

Funerary Monuments

1.	†1847	Rev Henry Berkin	s	Holy Trinity, Drybrook, Glos	S	Pevsner, *Glos: Vale & Forest of Dean*, 1976, 174
2.	†1867	Rev Henry Nicholls	s	Drybrook, Glos	S	Pevsner, *Glos: Vale & Forest of Dean*, 1976, 174

MORGAN, Jacob, of Pontypridd fl *c*1860

Funerary Monuments

1.	*c*1860	Ann Davis (†1852) and Elizabeth Davis (†1860)		Glyntaff, Glamorgan		Pevsner, *Glamorgan*, 1995, 362

MORGAN, John –1797

The son of **Richard Morgan**, he trained at the Dublin Society's school, and after his father's death took over the carving business in Chequer Lane. He was employed with **Simon Vierpyl** on stone work at the Dublin Royal Exchange in 1766. In 1764 he married Rebecca Babington of Londonderry. He died in his house in Exchequer Street in January 1797.

Literary References: *Strickland* 2, 1913, 129

MORGAN, Richard –1765

He was a stone mason who resided in Chequer Lane, Dublin. He died there on 21 April 1765 and was buried at St Andrew's church six days later.

Literary References: *Strickland* 2, 1913, 129

MORGAN, W, of Exhall fl 1825

He signed a 'large Hellenic tablet with well-cut details' (1) (*Gunnis* 1968, 265).

Funerary Monuments

1.	†1839	Anne Brooks		St Giles, Exhall, Warks		Pevsner, *Warks*, 1966, 291

MORGAN, William fl 1682–1706

He was a liveryman of the Joiners Company and worked with William Emmett on wood carving at Chelsea Hospital, under the direction of Sir Christopher Wren.

Literary References: *Green* 1964 (1), 67–8; *Dunbar* 1977, 372–3

1.	1682	Eight festoons in the 'Capitall Freize' of the oak altarpiece Payment(s): £15		[Chelsea Hospital, London]; untraced	*Green* 1964 (1), 67–8

MORILL fl 1775–1802

He was probably a Reading statuary. Three of his large wall-tablets have been identified.

Funerary Monuments

1.	?1775	Elizabeth Shaw	Kintbury, Berks	S	*Gunnis* 1968, 265
2.	?1784	Admiral Fowke	Shaw, Berks	S	*Gunnis* 1968, 265
3.	†1786	Mary Hartley	Bucklebury, Berks	S	*Gunnis* 1968, 265

MORISON, Colin fl 1768–78

A painter, dealer and sculptor, he studied under Thomas Blackwell, a Greek scholar in Aberdeen, and went to Rome before 1778, sponsored by the Earl of Findlater. He is better known as a painter and an associate of Gavin Hamilton, Mengs and Winckelmann. Boswell apparently said that he was such an enormous man that his body would take six souls to animate it.

Literary References: *Graves* V, 1905–6, 304; *Pearson* 1991, 41

Funerary Monuments					
1.	nd	Unidentified subject		[Exported from Italy]; untraced	Export licence in *Pearson* 1991, 41
Statues					
2.	1769	Copy of the Apollo Belvedere		[Sent to RA, London]; untraced	*Pearson* 1991, 41
Miscellaneous					
3.	1778	Dying mother	m	[Exhib RA, London, 419]; untraced	*Graves* V, 1905–6, 304; *Pearson* 1991, 41
4.	nd	Galatea, figure		[Exported from Italy]; untraced	Export licence in *Pearson* 1991, 41

MORISON, M

For further information the reader is referred to *Pyke* 1973, 94 and *Pyke* 1981, 29

MORISON (or MORRISON), David fl 1793–1850

In 1826 he was appointed 'miniature modeller' to the Duke and Duchess of Gloucester, the Duchess of Cambridge and Princess Augusta. He exhibited at the Royal Academy, 1821–1850, and at the Carlisle Academy of Fine Arts where he principally showed miniature medallic portraits. His lived at 15 Mornington Crescent, Hampstead, and, in 1825, at 55 Newman Street. He was also a gem-engraver.

Literary References: *Gunnis* 1968, 265; *Pyke* 1973, 94–5; *Perriam* 1975, 300–5; *Johnson* 1975, 333–4; *Leeds* 1996, 6

Busts					
1.	1822	Sir John Sinclair Bt, model		[Exhib RA, London, 952]; untraced	*Graves* V, 1905–6, 293
2.	1822	Unidentified lady		[Exhib RA, London, 961]; untraced	*Graves* V, 1905–6, 293
3.	1823	Unidentified lady		[Exhib RA, London, 1005]; untraced	*Graves* V, 1905–6, 293
4.	1825	Charles O'Neal		[Exhib RA, London, 1031]; untraced	*Graves* V, 1905–6, 293
5.	c1825	James Kidd		United French Church, Aberdeen	GPC
6.	1826	Admiral Sir Benjamin Hallowell		[Exhib RA, London, 973]; untraced	*Graves* V, 1905–6, 294
7.	1827	King George IV	w	Private coll Other versions: several in private colls Christie, 19 April 1966, lot 186	*Gunnis* 1968, 265; *Pyke* 1973, 95; *Pyke* 1981, 29
8.	1827	Unidentified gentleman		[Exhib RA, London, 996]; untraced	*Graves* V, 1905–6, 294
9.	1832	Unidentified gentleman		[Exhib RA, London, 1053]; untraced	*Graves* V, 1905–6, 294
10.	1836	A child		[Exhib RA, London, 1079]; untraced	*Graves* V, 1905–6, 294
11.	1848	Lady Augusta Fielding		[Exhib RA, London, 1302]; untraced	*Graves* V, 1905–6, 294
Reliefs					
12.	1793	Unidentified woman	w	Private coll	*Pyke* 1973, 95
13.	c1820	Miss Macleod of Macleod	w	Carnegie Institute, Pittsburgh, USA	*Pyke* 1973, 95
14.	1824	Mrs Yeoman		[Exhib RA, London, 946]; untraced	*Graves* V, 1905–6, 293
15.	1824	Sir Everard Home Bt, 'medallic portrait'		[Exhib RA, London, 947]; untraced	*Graves* V, 1905–6, 293
16.	1825	Sir E Home, medallion		[Exhib Soc of BA, London, 370]; untraced	*Johnson* 1975, 334
17.	1825	Unidentified gentleman, medallion		[Exhib Soc of BA, London, 368]; untraced	*Johnson* 1975, 334
18.	1827	Frederick Augustus, Duke of York	w	Private coll Other versions: Stanton Harcourt, Oxon private coll, Rome Christie, 19 April 1966, lot 186 Christie, 10 Nov 1980, lot 74 Sotheby, 14 April 1980, lot 135 Sotheby, 5 Nov 1980, lot 9	*Pyke* 1973, 95; *Pyke* 1981, 29
19.	1827	Henry, Baron Brougham	w	Untraced (ex coll Derek Sherborn) Other versions: 1829, VAM A80-1965	*Pyke* 1973, 95
20.	1827	Unidentified man	w	Untraced (formerly coll Rupert Gunnis)	*Pyke* 1973, 95
21.	1831	King William IV	w	Private coll	*Pyke* 1973, 95
22.	1835	A child, medallic portrait		[Exhib RA, London, 1023]; untraced	*Graves* V, 1905–6, 294
23.	1836	'A young gentleman', medallic portrait		[Exhib RA, London, 988]; untraced	*Graves* V, 1905–6, 294
24.	1836	John Dawson	w	Private coll, USA	*Pyke* 1981, 29

25.	1838	Hon Lydia Whittaker	w	Private coll	*Pyke* 1973, 95
26.	1847	Mr and Mrs Ricketts	w	Private coll, USA	*Pyke* 1981, 29
27.	1848	Lord Montague, medallic portrait		[Exhib RA, London, 1472]; untraced	*Graves* V, 1905–6, 294
28.	1849	Edward Budd, medallic likeness		[Exhib RA, London, 637]; untraced	*Graves* V, 1905–6, 294
29.	1849	Hon Mrs Gerald Dillon, medallic portrait		[Exhib RA, London, 639]; untraced	*Graves* V, 1905–6, 294
30.	1849	Thomas, Earl of Ranfurley, 'medallic likeness'		[Exhib RA, London, 638]; untraced	*Graves* V, 1905–6, 294
31.	1849	Unidentified lady, medallic likeness		[Exhib RA, London, 636]; untraced	*Graves* V, 1905–6, 294
32.	nd	Abadon family	w	VAM L7-L10 Bate	*Pyke* 1973, 95
33.	nd	Charles Campbell	w	Private coll	*Pyke* 1981, 29
34.	nd	Dr Herb Mayo	w	Private coll	*Pyke* 1981, 29
35.	nd	Dr Williams of Llansantffrain-Ym Mehhan	w	Private coll, USA	*Pyke* 1981, 29
36.	nd	Dr Wollaston		VAM	*Pyke* 1973, 95
37.	nd	George Canning	w	Sotheby, 2 June 1975, lot 138	*Pyke* 1981, 29
38.	nd	George Hooper and wife	w	Christie, 25 Nov 1970, lot 1	*Pyke* 1973, 95
39.	nd	Liverpool Agricultural Society		Private coll, USA	*Pyke* 1981, 29
40.	nd	Mr and Mrs Simpson		Private coll, USA	*Pyke* 1981, 29
41.	nd	Mrs William (later Mrs Dawson)	w	Private coll, USA	*Pyke* 1981, 29
42.	nd	Nathaniel Whitehouse	w	Private coll	*Pyke* 1981, 29
43.	nd	Robert Paterson	w	Private coll, USA	*Pyke* 1981, 29
44.	nd	Thomas Carlyle	w	Private coll, USA	*Pyke* 1981, 29
45.	nd	Unidentified man	w	Stanton Harcourt, Oxon	*Pyke* 1973, 95
46.	nd	Unidentified man	w	VAM A24-1960	*Pyke* 1973, 95 (repr 197)
47.	nd	Unidentified man	w	VAM A107-1965 Other versions: private coll	*Pyke* 1981, 29
48.	nd	Unidentified man and son	w	Private coll, USA	*Pyke* 1981, 29
49.	nd	Unidentified woman	w	Stanton Harcourt, Oxon	*Pyke* 1973, 95
50.	nd	Unidentified woman	w	Private coll	*Pyke* 1973, 95
51.	nd	Unidentified woman	w	Untraced (ex coll Mrs AE Hamill)	*Pyke* 1973, 95
52.	nd	Unidentified woman	w	Private coll	*Pyke* 1981, 29
53.	nd	Unidentified women	w	VAM (L11-12, L62 Bate)	*Pyke* 1973, 95
54.	nd	Unidentified youth	w	Private coll	*Pyke* 1973, 95
55.	nd	W Murdoch FRS	w	Private coll	*Pyke* 1981, 29
56.	nd	William IV on a sofa		Untraced (ex coll B Hill)	*Pyke* 1981, 29
Miscellaneous					
57.	1821	A clergyman, model		[Exhib RA, London, 1054]; untraced	*Graves* V, 1905–6, 293
58.	1821	Lady Clifford, model		[Exhib RA, London, 1050]; untraced	*Graves* V, 1905–6, 293
59.	1821	Miss Murray, model		[Exhib RA, London, 1059]; untraced	*Graves* V, 1905–6, 293
60.	1822	Two children		[Exhib RA, London, 955]; untraced	*Graves* V, 1905–6, 293
61.	1823	W Stark		[Exhib RA, London, 1001]; untraced	*Graves* V, 1905–6, 293
62.	1824	Miss M Henderson		[Exhib RA, London, 940]; untraced	*Graves* V, 1905–6, 293
63.	1826	Duchess of Gloucester		[Exhib RA, London, 935]; untraced	*Graves* V, 1905–6, 293
64.	1826	'Princess Augusta, in enamel for a bracelet'		[Exhib RA, London, 940]; untraced	*Graves* V, 1905–6, 293
65.	1826	The Duchess of Cambridge		[Exhib RA, London, 942]; untraced	*Graves* V, 1905–6, 294
66.	1827	Ernest Augustus, Duke of Cumberland	w	Hove Museum, Sussex	GPC; *Pyke* 1973, 95
67.	1828	The guardian angel		[Exhib RA, London, 1057]; untraced	*Graves* V, 1905–6, 294
68.	1832	Model of a Gothic mansion		[Exhib RA, London, 957]; untraced	*Graves* V, 1905–6, 294
69.	1833	A nobleman		[Exhib RA, London, 1051]; untraced	*Graves* V, 1905–6, 294
70.	1848	J Baker		[Exhib RA, London, 1306]; untraced	*Graves* V, 1905–6, 294
71.	1848	The Marquess of Bath		[Exhib RA, London, 1313]; untraced	*Graves* V, 1905–6, 294
72.	1850	Dr Turnbull		[Exhib RA, London, 713]; untraced	*Graves* V, 1905–6, 294
73.	1850	Two children		[Exhib RA, London, 687]; untraced	*Graves* V, 1905–6, 294
74.	nd	Abadon family, four wax portraits	w	VAM (Bate loan)	*Gunnis* 1968, 265

MORLEY, Martin fl 1653–69

He became a freeman of Norwich in 1653. Only one monument by him has been identified, though numerous others in the county have been attributed to him on the basis of stylistic similarity.

Funerary Monuments

1.	1669	Thomas Windham (†1654) Payment(s): £45	s	Felbrigg, Norfolk	Archives, Felbrigg Hall in *Gunnis* 1968, 265; Pevsner, *Norfolk: NE & Norwich*, 1997, 461

MORRELL, Mark fl 1732

Morrell advertised in the *Stamford Mercury* on 22 February 1732 that he was a marble mason from London and had set up in St Martin's, Stamford.

Archival References: JP, Misc corr

MORRIS, Arthur, of Lewes –1744

He was the son of Arthur Morris, also a mason of Lewes. He applied to become a 'foreign member' of the London Masons' Company in 1712 and was admitted on payment of £1 16s (Masons' Co Court Books 1695–1722, fol 19v). He built Lewes bridge in 1727, carried out improvements to Coombe Place, near Lewes, and acted for Colen Campbell at Compton Place. Between 1738 and 1743 the trustees of the Duke of Newcastle paid 'Arthur Morris, Stonecutter' £592, a sum likely to have been for building the duke's house in Lewes (BL, Ad MS 33, 321). Morris died in Lewes in September 1744 (parish register, All Saints, Lewes).

Literary References: *SAC* 1929, 70, 222; *Gunnis* 1968, 265; *Brock* 1996, 74–84

Archival References: GPC

Funerary Monuments

1.	1731	Mr Beard, altar-tomb		[Newhaven churchyard]; untraced	Streatfield Archives in GPC

MORRIS, John, of Lewes 1716–92

He was the son of **Arthur Morris**, and, like his father, a mason and builder of Lewes. He signs only one known wall monument (1). He did much work for Richard Trevor, Bishop of Durham, at Glynde in Sussex and between 1755 and 1760 he was the mason responsible for building the east front of the house (2–5). At about the same time he built the stables and in the early 1760s, the chapel, to designs by Sir Thomas Robinson (Archives, Brand of Glynde in *Gunnis* 1968, 265). He was paid a further £145 for masonry work in 1775 when Glynde bridge was rebuilt.

From 1757 until 1761 he was employed in rebuilding Ashburnham Place, Sussex (Ashburnham Archives in *Gunnis* 1968, 265). In 1761–1763 he was paid £646 for building Lewes Sessions house, described by Gunnis as a charming building with a cupola. In 1786 he received £100 for rebuilding Riverhall bridge (Town Archives in *Gunnis* 1968, 265). Sir John Bridger employed Morris to rebuild Coombe Place, near Lewes: in 1768 he was paid for building a Gothic Temple in Down Field and a further payment of £247 5s 8d was made to him in 1776. In 1777 he was paid £160 4s 9d for a new stable and in 1778, £60 14s 5d for a new pigeon house.

He was buried on 3 August 1792 (parish registers, All Saints, Lewes in GPC). In his will, proved on 15 August 1792, he mentions his wife, Elizabeth, and his nephews John and Joseph, the sons of his brother Joseph.

Literary References: *Hussey* 1953, 1246, 1249; *Gunnis* 1968, 265; *Brock* 1996, 74–84

Archival Reference: GPC

Funerary Monuments

1.	?1775	Mary Lushington		St Mary, Eastbourne, Sussex	S	*Gunnis* 1968, 265

Chimneypieces

2.	1755	Description unavailable		Glynde Place, Sussex, library		Archives Mrs Humphrey Brand, in GPC
3.	1759	Description unavailable	s	Glynde Place, Sussex, hall		Archives Mrs Humphrey Brand, in GPC
4.	1772	Description unavailable Payment(s): £134	m	Glynde Place, Sussex, drawing room		Archives Mrs Humphrey Brand, in GPC

Architectural Sculpture

5.	1755–1760	Carved stonework	s	Glynde Place, Sussex		*Gunnis* 1968, 265

MORRIS, S, of Hay fl *c*1834

Funerary Monuments

1.	†1834	Hugh Evans		Glascwm, Powys		Pevsner, *Powys*, 1979, 235

MORRIS, Thomas fl 1760–71

Morris was employed on building work at Woburn Abbey in 1749–50, receiving a payment of £75, and further payments were made to him between 1753 and 1756. In June 1760 Sir Roger Newdigate signed an agreement with Morris and his partners Andrew Hardy and Thomas Cheshire 'to erect a stone Bow window at Arbury in the same form and with all the carvings and ornaments as that of the Library, only the whole to be six inches wider in diameter . . . by the first of June 1761'. Work on the parlour is recorded in 1761 and on a room over the same in 1762. In 1762 Morris was paid for work in the drawing room and in 1771 he was employed in rebuilding the hall.

Archival References: Woburn Building Accts 1748–62 BLARS R5/1092; Newdigate Archives CR 136/B2419 (agreement); CR 136/V156 (account); Newdigate Accts CR 136/V119 (1771)

MORRIS, Tom, of Pendine 1804–86

He was apprenticed to **James Rogers of Tenby**, before returning to Morfa Bychan, Pendine, to set up his home and workshop near to the Pwll quarry. There are numerous ornamentally lettered gravestones by him in local graveyards. Morris was a musician as well as a mason, he won local celebrity during his day and was accorded a biography by George Traherne.

Literary References: *Dale-Jones and Lloyd* 1989, 55

Funerary Monuments

1.	†1852	James Eastment		Llandawke, Carmarthen	S	*Dale-Jones and Lloyd* 1989, 55
2.	nd	Rev Joshua Lewis		Henllan Amgoed Chapel		*Dale-Jones and Lloyd* 1989, 55

MORRISON, D, of London fl 1823–26

Reliefs

1.	1825	A lady, medallion	w	[Exhib Carlisle Acad, 285]; untraced	*Carlisle Ac Exhibs*, 1973; *Perriam* 1975, 300–5
2.	1825	Sir Everard Horne, medallion	w	[Exhib Carlisle Acad, 134]; untraced	*Carlisle Ac Exhibs*, 1973; *Perriam* 1975, 300–5
3.	1826	A child, medallion		[Exhib Carlisle Acad, 172]; untraced	*Carlisle Ac Exhibs*, 1973; *Perriam* 1975, 300–5
4.	1826	Duchess of Gloucester, medallion		[Exhib Carlisle Acad, 171]; untraced	*Carlisle Ac Exhibs*, 1973; *Perriam* 1975, 300–5

Miscellaneous

5.	1823	Sir John Sinclair, model	w	[Exhib Carlisle Acad, 150]; untraced	*Carlisle Ac Exhibs*, 1973; *Perriam* 1975, 300–5
6.	1823	W. Starke, model	w	[Exhib Carlisle Acad, 151]; untraced	*Carlisle Ac Exhibs*, 1973

MORRISON (or MORISON), Michael fl 1810–37

Michael Morrison executed wax portraits of the Hon James Forbes and Lord Charles Murray for the Duke of Atholl in 1810 (**5, 6**). He can probably be identified with the artist who exhibited at the Royal Scottish Academy between 1829 and 1837, showing portraits and a representation of *The Transfiguration* chased in silver (**8**). He lived at 11 Drummond Street, Edinburgh and was listed in the Edinburgh Post Office Directory as a modeller and chaser.

Literary References: *Woodward* 1977 (vol 1, pt 2), 158; RG/JP, 6, 956

Busts

1.	1831	Unidentified gentleman, miniature bust		[Exhib R Sc A, Edinburgh, 372]; untraced	*Laperriere* 3, 1991, 313
2.	1836	Unidentified gentleman, miniature bust		[Exhib R Sc A, Edinburgh, 341]; untraced	*Laperriere* 3, 1991, 307

3.	1836	Unidentified gentleman, miniature bust		[Exhib R Sc A, Edinburgh, 341]; untraced		*Laperriere* 3, 1991, 313
4.	1837	Unidentified gentleman		[Exhib R Sc A, Edinburgh, 364]; untraced		*Laperriere* 3, 1991, 313
Miscellaneous						
5.	1810	Hon James Forbes	w	[coll 4th Duke of Atholl]; untraced		Archives, Duke of Atholl in GPC
6.	1810	Lord Charles Murray	w	[coll 4th Duke of Atholl]; untraced		Archives, Duke of Atholl in GPC
7.	1827	Mr Fulton, four models in wax and one in metal		[Exhib R Sc A, Edinburgh, 133]; untraced		*Laperriere* 3, 1991, 313
8.	1829	Transfiguration, chased in silver		[Exhib R Sc A, Edinburgh, 265]; untraced		*Laperriere* 3, 1991, 313
9.	1834	George Combe, model		[Exhib R Sc A, Edinburgh, 292]; untraced		*Laperriere* 3, 1991, 313

MORSE, Samuel Finley Breese 1791–1872

The American history painter, portraitist and inventor of the telegraph was responsible for one notable work of sculpture during his stay in London. The son of a clergyman, he trained at Phillips Academy in Andover and at Yale, where he began painting miniatures. He studied with the painter Washington Allston, attended anatomy lectures, and decided to further his artistic studies in London, leaving America on 13 July 1811. He lived in Fitzroy Square, and seems to have attended drawing classes at the Royal Academy later that year.

Morse's cast of the *Dying Hercules*, after his own clay model, was made as an aid for his history painting of the subject which was exhibited to acclaim at the Royal Academy. The model was also received enthusiastically and won him a prize from the Society of Arts (1). Morse's countryman Benjamin West saw the work and is said to have been 'extremely delighted with it. He said it was not merely an academical figure, but displayed mind and thought.' Showing the work to his son Raphael, West remarked 'look there sir, I have always told you any painter can make a sculptor' (*Kloss* 1988, 26). The model, painting and Morse's winning medal are preserved at Yale, New Haven.

He left London in 1815, and his well-documented later career appears not to have included any further ventures into sculptural art. He attempted to perfect a marble-carving machine in New Hampshire in 1816, but his fame derives principally from his invention of the telegraph, first demonstrated in 1844. He died of pneumonia in New York on 2 April 1872.

Literary References: RSA, *Transactions*, vol 31, 1813, 23; *Larkin* 1954; *Gunnis* 1968, 265; *Kloss* 1988; *Staiti* 1989; *Grove* 1996, 22, 150 (Staiti)

Statues						
1.	1812	Dying Hercules	p	[Soc of A, lesser gold medal 1813]; YCBA	S	RSA *Transactions*, vol 31, 1813, 23; *Kloss* 1988, 26 (repr); *Staiti* 1989, 18, 20, 261 (repr)

MORSSE, Symon fl 1671

Chimneypieces						
1.	1671	Description unavailable Payment(s): £31 17s	m	[Clayton and Morris's bank, Old Jewry, London]; untraced		*Clayton & Morris*, 1671; *Gunnis* 1968, 265

MORTIN, Ellis, of Leicester fl 1785–99

He is known only for one signed tablet. He became a freeman of Leicester in 1799 as 'a stranger' practising as a 'stone mason and builder'. His son Robert was apprenticed to **William Firmadge** in 1800, but was assigned to his father in 1804. Two other sons, Thomas and John, who were apprenticed to their father, became freemen of Leicester in 1816 and 1824 respectively.

Literary References: *Gunnis* 1968, 265

Funerary Monuments						
1.	†1785	Jonathan Foster		Aylestone, Leics	S	*Gunnis* 1968, 265

MOSELEY, John fl c1750–65

He was the mason responsible for additions to Cusworth Hall in the West Riding of Yorkshire in 1750–1753 under the architect James Paine. He built the library and chapel, for which he received £280. His contract with Paine for the south front of the hall is dated 17 May 1750 (Leeds Public Library, Cusworth Hall, BW/A/320, in GPC).

MOSER, Joseph fl 1762–65

The nephew of George Michael Moser, keeper of the Royal Academy, he won several premiums for models in wax from the Society of Arts between 1762 and 1765 (1–3).

Literary References: *Dossie* 1782, 435–6

Statues						
1.	1763	Allegory of Hawke's victory over the Spanish fleet, ornamental model	w	[Soc of A, premium, 7 gns]; untraced		*Dossie* 1782, 436
2.	1767	Ornamental model of a dog seizing a duck	w	[Soc of A, premium, 7 gns]; untraced		*Dossie* 1782, 436
Miscellaneous						
3.	1765	Stem of a candelstick depicting the young Hercules		[Soc of A, premium, 4 gns]; untraced		FRSA *Minutes*, 1764–65, seq 3 f61; *Dossie* 1782, 436

MOSS, W, of Canterbury fl c1780–1800

He signed a number of tablets in Kent. The two which Gunnis considered his best are listed below.

Funerary Monuments						
1.	?1780	Elizabeth Denne		Littlebourne, Kent	S	*Gunnis* 1968, 265–266
2.	?1800	John Foote		Bishopsbourne, Kent	S	*Gunnis* 1968, 265–266

MOSSMAN, George 1823–63

The youngest son of **William Mossman**, he was born in 1823 in Edinburgh, where his father had a marble cutting business. The family moved to Glasgow when he was about eight, where he began to learn his craft, tutored by his father and at one of the local schools of art. In 1844 he moved to London where on 15 December he was admitted to the Royal Academy Schools, recommended by **William Behnes.** The following year he won a silver medal for a model in the Antique Academy (**19**). He studied under Behnes and **John Henry Foley** and is said to have 'received the most flattering recognition of his powers' from his teachers and fellow-pupils, including **Thomas Woolner** and the painter John Everett Millais (*AJ*, 1864, 12). Ill-health forced him to return to Glasgow before 1847. He took on no independent work for the next four or five years, but joined the studio of his elder brother John at 83 North Frederick Street and worked for him when his health permitted.

Mossman's output consisted chiefly of subject pieces but he also received several commissions for portrait sculpture. He exhibited at the West of Scotland Academy (1843, 1845–1853), the RA (1846), the Royal Scottish Academy (1847–1863) and the Royal Glasgow Institute of the Fine Arts (1861, 1862 and 1864). He became an associate of the West of Scotland Academy in 1851. Mossman died in 1863 and was survived by a son, John, who continued the family business for a brief period after the death of his uncle, **John Mossman.** His obituary in the *Art Journal* suggested that if he had survived Mossman 'would have had a fair chance of rising to fame in the higher regions of ideal sculpture' (*AJ*, 1864, 12).

Literary References: *AJ*, 1864, 12; *Gunnis* 1968, 266; *Woodward* 1977, vol 1, pt 2, 158–60; *Read* 1982, 69

Archival References: RA Admissions; RA Premium list

No.	Date	Subject	Material	Location		References
Funerary Monuments						
1.	1850	J Fleming	b	Duncan Street burying ground, Greenock		*Woodward* 1977, vol 1, pt 2, 160
Statues						
2.	1846	Prince Charles Edward Stuart, statuette		[Exhib RA, London, 1480]; untraced		*Graves* V, 1905–6, 313; *Billcliffe* 3, 1990–92, 262; *Laperriere* 3, 1991, 320
3.	1849	The wayside flower		[Exhib R Sc A, Edinburgh, 630]; untraced		*AJ*, 1864, 12; *Laperriere* 3, 1991, 320
4.	1862	The bather ('girl bathing') Payment(s): £110	m	[Exhib RGIFA, Glasgow, 677]; untraced		*AJ*, 1864, 12; *Billcliffe* 3, 1990–92, 262
5.	1862–1863	Alexander Wilson (co-sculptor: John G Mossman)	b	Paisley, Renfrewshire		*Woodward* 1977, vol 1, pt 2, 160
6.	c1863	Hope		Untraced		*AJ*, 1864, 12
7.	nd	Jeannie Morrison (group based on Motherwell's poem)		Untraced		*AJ*, 1864, 12
8.	nd	Kilmeny		Untraced		*AJ*, 1864, 12
Busts						
9.	1850	Unidentified boy	m	[Exhib R Sc A, Edinburgh, 471]; untraced		*Laperriere* 3, 1991, 320
10.	1855	A grand-daughter of Dr Buchanan of Greenock	m	[Exhib R Sc A, Edinburgh, 754]; untraced		*Laperriere* 3, 1991, 320
11.	1855	Unidentified lady		[Exhib R Sc A, Edinburgh, 753]; untraced		*Laperriere* 3, 1991, 320
12.	1861	Unidentified boy		[Exhib RGIFA, Glasgow, 876]; untraced		*Billcliffe* 3, 1990–92, 262
13.	1861	Unidentified lady		[Exhib RGIFA, Glasgow, 873]; untraced		*Billcliffe* 3, 1990–92, 262
14.	1862	Unidentified man	m	Ayr Public Library		*Woodward* 1977, vol 1, pt 2, 160
15.	1863	Unidentified lady		[Exhib R Sc A, Edinburgh, 813]; untraced		*Laperriere* 3, 1991, 320
Reliefs						
16.	1846	The guardian angels foresaking Paradise after the Fall		[Exhib RA, London, 1422]; untraced		*Graves* V, 1905–6, 313; *Laperriere* 3, 1991, 320
17.	1862	Sound asleep Payment(s): £42 or £95 in marble		[Exhib RGIFA, Glasgow, 683]; untraced		*Billcliffe* 3, 1990–92, 262
18.	nd	John Wesley	w	Philadelphia Museum of Art	S	*Pyke* 1973, 95
Miscellaneous						
19.	1845	Model after the antique		[RA, silver medal]; untraced		RA Premium list
20.	1861	The martyrdom of Margaret Wilson		[Exhib R Sc A, Edinburgh, 780]; untraced		*Billcliffe* 3, 1990–92, 262; *Laperriere* 3, 1991, 320

MOSSMAN, John 1817–90

John Mossman ran the firm of J & G Mossman, which was responsible for large numbers of funerary monuments in the Glasgow necropolis and dominated architectural sculpture in the city during the second half of the 19th century. He was born in 1817 in London where his father **William Mossman** was employed by **Sir Francis Chantrey.** In the early 1820s the family moved to Edinburgh and then to Glasgow. John received his first instruction in sculpture from his father and then studied in Edinburgh and later in London, where for a time he was employed by **Carlo, Baron Marochetti.** In 1847 he returned to Glasgow, where he worked almost exclusively for his father until the latter's death in 1851. John then took over control of the family firm, which he ran with assistance from his brothers **George Mossman** and William Mossman II. He had a studio at 83 North Frederick Street from 1850 until 1878, when he moved to 21 Elmbank Crescent.

Mossman's earliest recorded independent work is the monument commemorating the sculptor **Peter Lawrence** which once stood in Glasgow necropolis (1). It is probably the first example of a free standing figure carved in the west of Scotland by a sculptor, not a mason. The statue of a winged youth bearing an extinguished torch was badly vandalised in 1996 and its headless remains are now in a City Council store, though the pedestal with its profile portrait of Lawrence remains *in situ.*

He provided architectural sculpture for many prominent Glasgow buildings, including St Andrew's halls and the Athenaeum, both of which have extensive sculptural programmes incorporating life-size figures and allegorical groups (**105, 114**). Although some of his best work was architectural sculpture, a significant part of his practice was in portraiture. He exhibited large numbers of busts, only a few of which have been traced, and he provided several public monuments. His statue of Sir Robert Peel, erected in Glasgow in 1859, is noteworthy because it was the first major public commission awarded to a sculptor living in the west of Scotland (**29**). Further statues for Glasgow, Paisley and Bombay followed (**30, 33, 34, 35, 37, 39, 40**). He also set up the first foundry for casting bronze sculpture in Glasgow, though he continued to send his large public statues to English founders for casting.

Mossman was one of the founders of the Glasgow School of Art in 1844, where he taught modelling and served as a visiting master and member of the Committee of Management until 1890. A number of sculptors were trained or employed as assistants in his workshop, including **Walter Buchan**, James Young, James Pittendrigh Macgillivray, Francis Leslie and Daniel Ferguson. He died at Port Bannatyne on the Isle of Bute on 22 September 1890 and is buried at Sighthill cemetery, Springburn, north Glasgow. His estate was valued at more than £7,245. Since his son, William Mossman III, had died in 1877, the family business passed to his nephew John, the son of George Mossman. It was sold soon after but still exists under its original name and specialises in monumental masonry.

The list of works includes sculpture produced by the Mossman firm between 1851 and 1890.

Literary References: *Gunnis* 1968, 266; *Woodward* 1977, vol 1, pt 1, 137–8, vol 1, pt 2, 160–4; *Pearson* 1991, 92–3 (Woodward); *Grove* 28, 1996, 242 (Johnston); *McKenzie* 2002, 492–3

Additional MS Sources: Mossman & Co Papers

Will: NLS SC36/51/102, SC36/48/130 and 136, GSC will, 2 December 1890, inventory, 8 December 1890 and 5 April 1892

Funerary Monuments

1.	c1840	Peter Lawrence	s	Glasgow Necropolis		*McKenzie* 2002, 443
2.	†1847	William Smith		Mauchline parish churchyard		*Woodward* 1977, vol 1, pt 2, 163
3.	1850	Ann Sparkwood		Western Cemetery, Glasgow		*Woodward* 1977, vol 1, pt 2, 164
4.	c1851	Esther Ritchie Cooper	s	Glasgow Necropolis	S	*McKenzie* 2002, 458
5.	c1851	Pastor William Black (designed by J T Emmet)		Glasgow Necropolis		*McKenzie* 2002, 459 (repr)
6.	†1852	James Fillans (after a model of Grief by James Fillans)		Woodside Cemetery, Paisley, Renfrewshire		*Gildard* 1892, 294
7.	†1853	James Ewing	b	Glasgow Necropolis		*Woodward* 1977, vol 1, pt 2, 163
8.	1853	Rev Ralph Wardlaw		Glasgow Necropolis		*McKenzie* 1999, 12, no 2.13; *McKenzie* 2002, 460
9.	1854	Henry Monteith		Glasgow Necropolis		*Gunnis* 1968, 266; *Woodward* 1977, vol 1, pt 2, 163
10.	pre-1856	Mrs Matthew Montgomerie (designed by Charles Wilson)		Glasgow Necropolis		Pevsner, *Glasgow*, 1990, 141
11.	1858	Rev A O Beattie (designed by Alexander Thomson)		Glasgow Necropolis		Pevsner, *Glasgow*, 1990, 139
12.	†1859	Major William Middleton		Glasgow Cathedral		Pevsner, *Glasgow*, 1990, 134
13.	1863	Rev Patrick Brewster	s	Woodside Cemetery, Paisley, Renfrewshire		*Gunnis* 1968, 266; *Woodward* 1977, vol 1, pt 2, 162; *Billcliffe* 3, 1990–92, 262
14.	1863	Rigby family	s	Glasgow Necropolis		*Woodward* 1977, vol 1, pt 2, 163
15.	1863	William, 11th Duke of Hamilton		Hamilton monument, Cadzow, Scotland		*Gunnis* 1968, 266
16.	†1864	William Munsie	b	Glasgow Necropolis		*Woodward* 1977, vol 1, pt 2, 163
17.	1866	James Sheridan Knowles	s	Glasgow Necropolis	S	*McKenzie* 1999, 10–11, no 2.4 (repr); *McKenzie* 2002, 460
18.	1866	Rev George M Middleton		Glasgow Necropolis		*Woodward* 1977, vol 1, pt 2, 163
19.	†1872	David Runciman	b	Glasgow Necropolis		*Woodward* 1977, vol 1, pt 2, 163
20.	1872	Highland Mary (Mary Campbell †1786)	s	Greenock Cemetery, Renfrewshire		*Woodward* 1977, vol 1, pt 2, 163
21.	†1872	William Miller	b	Glasgow Necropolis		*Woodward* 1977, vol 1, pt 2, 163
22.	†1873	George Baillie		Glasgow Necropolis		*Woodward* 1977, vol 1, pt 2, 163
23.	1873	Thomas Pointer	s	Glasgow Necropolis		*Woodward* 1977, vol 1, pt 2, 163
24.	1876	Henry Dubs		Glasgow Necropolis		*Woodward* 1977, vol 1, pt 2, 163
25.	1878	Duncan Turner	b	Glasgow Necropolis	SD	*McKenzie* 2002, 458
26.	1882	Rev Samuel Miller DD		Glasgow Necropolis		*Woodward* 1977, vol 1, pt 2, 163
27.	†1885	Lachlan McBean		Glasgow Necropolis		*Woodward* 1977, vol 1, pt 2, 163
28.	nd	Andrew Park	b	Woodside Cemetery, Paisley, Renfrewshire		*Woodward* 1977, vol 1, pt 2, 163

Statues

29.	1859	Sir Robert Peel (cast by Robinson & Cottam)	b	George Square, Glasgow	SD	*McKenzie* 2002, 132–3 (repr)
30.	1859–1862	Lord Provost James Lumsden	b	Cathedral precinct, Glasgow		*McKenzie* 2002, 61–2 (repr)
31.	1866	Cupid, statuette	m	[Exhib RGIFA, Glasgow, 878]; untraced		*Billcliffe* 3, 1990–92, 262
32.	1866	Homer, statuette	m	[Exhib RGIFA, Glasgow, 877]; untraced		*Billcliffe* 3, 1990–92, 262
33.	1872	Rev Alexander Wilson (co-sculptor: George Mossman)	b	Paisley, Renfrewshire		*Woodward* 1977, vol 1, pt 2, 162 (pl 79)
34.	1875–1877	Thomas Campbell (cast by Cox and Sons of Thames Ditton) (co-sculptor: James Pittendrigh Macgillivray) Payment(s): approx £1,400	b	George Square, Glasgow Other versions: marble statuette exhib RGIFA, Glasgow, 1879, 685, £158; untraced	SD	*Billcliffe* 3, 1990–92, 262; *McKenzie* 2002, 143–4 (repr)
35.	1875–1879	Dr David Livingstone (cast by Cox and Sons of Thames Ditton) (co-sculptor: Francis Leslie) Payment(s): £2,000	b	[George Square, Glasgow]; Cathedral precinct, Glasgow		*McKenzie* 2002, 62–4 (repr)
36.	1880	Unidentified subject, statuette		[Exhib RGIFA, Glasgow, 764a]; untraced		*Billcliffe* 3, 1990–92, 262
37.	1881	Rev Dr Norman Macleod	b	Cathedral precinct, Glasgow	SD	*McKenzie* 2002, 71–2 (repr)
38.	1884	Alexander Bannatyne Stewart	b	Rothesay, Isle of Bute, esplanade		*Gildard* 1892, 292; *Billcliffe* 3, 1990–92, 262
39.	1885	George A Clark	b	Paisley, Renfrewshire		*Woodward* 1977, vol 1, pt 2, 162

40.	1888	Thomas Ormiston	m	University gardens, Mumbai (Bombay), India	*Steggles* 2000, 152–3 (repr)
41.	1891	Robert Burns, model only, for Ayr Burns Monument (commission awarded to George Lawson) Payment(s): £130 in bronze or £40 in plaster		[Exhib RGIFA, Glasgow, 815]; untraced	*Billcliffe* 3, 1990–92, 262
42.	nd	Godiva, equestrian figure, model	p	Untraced	*Gildard* 1892, 294
Busts					
43.	1840	James Lumsden	m	[Exhib R Sc A, Edinburgh, 382]; untraced Other versions: another exhib RGIFA, Glasgow, 1871, 635	*Billcliffe* 3, 1990–92, 262; *Laperriere* 3, 1991, 320
44.	1853	Unidentified gentleman		[Exhib R Sc A, Edinburgh, 695]; untraced	*Laperriere* 3, 1991, 320
45.	1853	Unidentified gentleman		[Exhib R Sc A, Edinburgh, 699]; untraced	*Laperriere* 3, 1991, 320
46.	1853	Unidentified young lady		[Exhib R Sc A, Edinburgh, 692]; untraced	*Laperriere* 3, 1991, 320
47.	1854	Queen Victoria		McLellan Galleries, Sauchiehall Street, Glasgow	*McKenzie* 2002, 346 (repr)
48.	1856	William Connal	m	Glasgow Museums S.52	*Gunnis* 1968, 266; *Laperriere* 3, 1991, 321
49.	1859	Margaret, daughter of James Campbell		[Exhib R Sc A, Edinburgh, 737]; untraced	*Billcliffe* 3, 1990–92, 262; *Laperriere* 3, 1991, 320
50.	1861	Archibald Orr Ewing	m	[Exhib RGIFA, Glasgow, 863]; untraced	*Billcliffe* 3, 1990–92, 262
51.	1861	Mrs Archibald Orr Ewing	m	[Exhib RGIFA, Glasgow, 865]; untraced	*Billcliffe* 3, 1990–92, 262
52.	1861	Rev Norman Macleod		[Exhib RGIFA, Glasgow, 886]; untraced	*Graves* V, 1905–6, 313; *Billcliffe* 3, 1990–92, 262; *Laperriere* 3, 1991, 321
53.	1861	Unidentified gentleman		[Exhib RGIFA, Glasgow, 871]; untraced	*Billcliffe* 3, 1990–92, 262
54.	1861	Unidentified lady		[Exhib RGIFA, Glasgow, 861]; untraced	*Billcliffe* 3, 1990–92, 262
55.	1863	Principal William Cunningham (after Patric Park)	p	New College, Edinburgh Other versions: ex coll M A Denniston, marble; untraced	*Woodward* 1977, vol 1, pt 2, 163; *Laperriere* 3, 1991, 321
56.	1863	Unidentified lady		[Exhib R Sc A, Edinburgh, 816]; untraced	*Laperriere* 3, 1991, 321
57.	1863	Unidentified subject	m	[Exhib RGIFA, Glasgow, 907]; untraced	*Billcliffe* 3, 1990–92, 262
58.	1863	Unidentified subject	m	[Exhib RGIFA, Glasgow, 914]; untraced	*Billcliffe* 3, 1990–92, 262
59.	1863	Unidentified subject		[Exhib RGIFA, Glasgow, 917]; untraced	*Billcliffe* 3, 1990–92, 262
60.	1865	Charles Heath Wilson (to be executed in bronze)		[Exhib RGIFA, Glasgow, 686a]; untraced	*Billcliffe* 3, 1990–92, 262
61.	1865	Mary, daughter of John Cowan	m	[Exhib RGIFA, Glasgow, 674]; untraced	*Billcliffe* 3, 1990–92, 262
62.	1867	Unidentified girl		[Exhib RGIFA, Glasgow, 911]; untraced	*Billcliffe* 3, 1990–92, 262
63.	1869	George Baillie		[Exhib RGIFA, Glasgow, 714]; untraced	*Billcliffe* 3, 1990–92, 262
64.	1869	William Tait	m	[Exhib RGIFA, Glasgow, 731]; untraced	*Billcliffe* 3, 1990–92, 262
65.	1871	Sir Michael Shaw Stewart	m	Grand lodge of Scotland, Edinburgh	*Woodward* 1977, vol 1, pt 2, 163; *Billcliffe* 3, 1990–92, 262; *Laperriere* 3, 1991, 321
66.	1872	William Towers Clark	m	Faculty of procurators, Glasgow	*Woodward* 1977, vol 1, pt 2, 163 (repr 77)
67.	1873	Charlie		[Exhib RGIFA, Glasgow, 693]; untraced	*Billcliffe* 3, 1990–92, 262
68.	1873	Unidentified lady		[Exhib RGIFA, Glasgow, 687]; untraced	*Billcliffe* 3, 1990–92, 262
69.	1874	Henry Glassford Bell, Sheriff of Lanarkshire		SNPG, Edinburgh	*Graves* V, 1905–6, 313; *Woodward* 1977, vol 1, pt 2, 163; *Laperriere* 3, 1991, 321
70.	1874	Unidentified subject		[Exhib RGIFA, Glasgow, 640]; untraced	*Billcliffe* 3, 1990–92, 262
71.	1874	Unidentified subject		[Exhib RGIFA, Glasgow, 650]; untraced	*Billcliffe* 3, 1990–92, 262
72.	1875	William Towers-Clark (†1870)		Faculty of Advocates Library, Glasgow	RG/JP, 6, 958
73.	*c*1877	Alexander Thomson	m	Glasgow Museums S.39	*Graves* V, 1905–6, 313; *Billcliffe* 3, 1990–92, 262; *Laperriere* 3, 1991, 321
74.	*c*1877	Rosalind	m	Glasgow Museums SNR.40	*Graves* V, 1905–6, 313; *Billcliffe* 3, 1990–92, 262; *Laperriere* 3, 1991, 321
75.	1877	Unidentified young man	m	Glasgow Museums SNR.46	inf: Glasgow Museums
76.	1878	Mrs Tillie	m	[Exhib RGIFA, Glasgow, 662]; untraced	*Billcliffe* 3, 1990–92, 262
77.	1878	Rev John Eadie DD		[Exhib RA, London, 1487]; untraced	*Graves* V, 1905–6, 313; *Laperriere* 3, 1991, 321
78.	1878	Unidentified subject		[Exhib RGIFA, Glasgow, 666]; untraced	*Billcliffe* 3, 1990–92, 262

79.	1879	D Y Stewart	m	[Exhib RGIFA, Glasgow, 699]; untraced	*Billcliffe* 3, 1990–92, 262
80.	1879	James Reid	m	[Exhib RGIFA, Glasgow, 687]; untraced	*Billcliffe* 3, 1990–92, 262
81.	1879	Little Red Riding Hood	m	[Exhib RA, London, 1580]; untraced	*Graves* V, 1905–6, 313; *Billcliffe* 3, 1990–92, 262
82.	1880	Unidentified child		[Exhib RGIFA, Glasgow, 779]; untraced	*Billcliffe* 3, 1990–92, 262
83.	1880	Unidentified gentleman		[Exhib RGIFA, Glasgow, 794]; untraced	*Billcliffe* 3, 1990–92, 262
84.	1880	Unidentified young man	m	Glasgow Museums SNR.47	inf: Glasgow Museums
85.	*c*1881	Portia	m	[coll Glasgow Corporation]; untraced	*Billcliffe* 3, 1990–92, 262; *Laperriere* 3, 1991, 321
86.	1881	Sir Archibald Campbell	m	Glasgow Museums S.184.[1]	*Laperriere* 3, 1991, 321
87.	1881	Stephen Mitchell	m	Mitchell Library, Glasgow, vestibule	*McKenzie* 2002, 312
88.	1884	Miss McGown		[Exhib RGIFA, Glasgow, 987]; untraced	*Billcliffe* 3, 1990–92, 262
89.	1884	Unidentified lady		[Exhib RGIFA, Glasgow, 989]; untraced	*Billcliffe* 3, 1990–92, 262
90.	1885	Unidentified subject		[Exhib RGIFA, Glasgow, 970]; untraced	*Billcliffe* 3, 1990–92, 262
91.	1885	Unidentified subject		[Exhib RGIFA, Glasgow, 972]; untraced	*Billcliffe* 3, 1990–92, 262
92.	1886	Henry Moore		[Exhib RGIFA, Glasgow, 780]; untraced	*Billcliffe* 3, 1990–92, 262
93.	1886	Unidentified lady		[Exhib R Sc A, Edinburgh, 824]; untraced	*Laperriere* 3, 1991, 321
94.	1890	Unidentified subject		[Exhib RGIFA, Glasgow, 1011]; untraced	*Billcliffe* 3, 1990–92, 262
95.	nd	Lady Augusta Campbell	m	Glasgow Museums S.185 [1]	inf: Glasgow Museums
Architectural Sculpture					
96.	1839–1840	Statues of John Henry Alexander, David Garrick, Thalia and Melpomene		[Theatre Royal, Dunlop Street, Glasgow, Lanarks, façade]; destroyed	*McKenzie* 2002, 436
97.	1854	Royal arms and 'Tobacco Warehouse' inscription		Tobacco warehouse, James Watt St, Glasgow	Pevsner, *Glasgow*, 1990, 258; *McKenzie* 2002, 464
98.	1857–1858	Frieze and portrait roundels (co-sculptor: Walter Buchan)		Hindu Temple (former Queen's rooms and Christian Science church), 1 La Belle Place, Glasgow	*McKenzie* 2002, 270–2 (repr)
99.	1862–1863	Carved stonework	s	Lansdowne parish church, Glasgow	Pevsner, *Glasgow*, 1990, 300
100.	1870–1871	Pulpit	s	St Mary's Episcopal chapel, Glasgow	*Woodward* 1977, vol 1, pt 2, 164
101.	1872	MacDonald Fountain	b	Paisley, Renfrewshire	*Woodward* 1977, vol 1, pt 2, 163
102.	1871–1872	Stewart Memorial Fountain (designed by James Sellars)		Kelvingrove Park, Glasgow	*Billcliffe* 3, 1990–92, 262; *McKenzie* 2002, 222–7 (repr)
103.	1871–1874	Allegorical groups: Trade and Industry		Clydesdale Bank, 30–40 St Vincent Place, Glasgow	*CIIA* 4/11/121–7 (repr); *McKenzie* 2002, 367–8 (repr)
104.	1871–1876	Allegorical statues, reliefs panel, coats of arms, masks in roundels (co-sculptor: William Mossman II)		[Municipal buildings, Ingram Street, Glasgow, Lanarks]; destroyed	*McKenzie* 2002, 429, 439
105.	1875–1877	Four allegorical groups, caryatids, atlantes (co-sculptor: William Mossman II)	s	[St Andrew's Halls, Glasgow]; Mitchell theatre, Granville Street, Glasgow	*McKenzie* 2002, 190–5 (repr)
106.	1878	Cicero, Galileo, James Watt and Homer, statues	s	Strathclyde house, 94 Elmbank Street, Glasgow (Cicero a modern replacement)	*McKenzie* 2002, 107–9 (repr)
107.	*c*1878	William Shakespeare, Music, Dance, Comedy, Tragedy and Robert Burns, statues	s	Citizen's theatre, Gorbels Street, Glasgow, foyer (formerly on the roof)	*McKenzie* 2002, 174–6 (repr)
108.	1841–1879	Allegorical statues, narrative tympana and decorative carving		Corinthian (formerly Union) bank, 191 Ingram Street, Glasgow	*McKenzie* 2002, 212–4 (repr)
109.	1878–1879	Group of Minerva and putti; friezes illustrating the Arts, Industry and Science (co-sculptor: William Mossman II)		[Fine Art Institute, Sauchiehall Street, Glasgow, Lanarks]; untraced	*McKenzie* 2002, 444–5
110.	1879–1880	William Caxton and Johannes Gutenberg, statues	s	63–69 Buchanan Street, Glasgow (former Glasgow Herald office)	*McKenzie* 2002, 38–40 (repr)
111.	*c*1882	Allegorical pediment relief; Poseidon and Triton group; pairs of putti symbolising various agricultural and industrial occupations; pair of ships' prows		Clydeport building, Glasgow	*McKenzie* 2002, 331–336 (repr)
112.	1881–1882	Sir William Collins memorial fountain		Glasgow Green, Glasgow	SD *McKenzie* 2002, 165–6 (repr)
113.	1883–1888	Allegorical figure groups, putti and associated decorative carving		Glasgow City Chambers, north façade	*McKenzie* 2002, 159–60 (repr)
114.	1886–1888	Allegorical groups: scientific education and literary education Statues: John Flaxman, Sir Christopher Wren, Henry Purcell and Sir Joshua Reynolds		8 Nelson Mandela Place (formerly Athenaeum) Glasgow	*McKenzie* 2002, 305–6 (repr)
115.	1883–1888	Spandrel carvings representing the trades and industries of Glasgow		Glasgow City Chambers, west façade	*McKenzie* 2002, 154–5 (repr)
116.	1883–1888	Two pairs of caryatids		Glasgow City Chambers, George Square entrance loggia	*McKenzie* 2002, 158–9 (repr)
117.	nd	Figure of Commerce, busts of the Seasons, reliefs of Vulcan and Neptune		Municipal buildings, Greenock, Renfrewshire	*Gildard* 1892, 293

Reliefs					
118.	1850	The finding of Moses		[Exhib R Sc A, Edinburgh, 474]; untraced	*Laperriere* 3, 1991, 320
119.	1871	Unidentified subject(s), medallion portraits		[Exhib RGIFA, Glasgow, 733]; untraced	*Billcliffe* 3, 1990–92, 262
120.	1878	Unidentified subject(s), medallion portraits		[Exhib RGIFA, Glasgow, 671]; untraced	*Billcliffe* 3, 1990–92, 262
Miscellaneous					
121.	1862	Chasing the butterfly ('the butterfly chase') Payment(s): £130	m	[Exhib RGIFA, Glasgow, 675]; untraced	*Billcliffe* 3, 1990–92, 262; *Laperriere* 3, 1991, 321
122.	1881	Unidentified subject		[Exhib RGIFA, Glasgow, 1006]; untraced	*Billcliffe* 3, 1990–92, 262
123.	1881	Unidentified subject		[Exhib RGIFA, Glasgow, 1007]; untraced	*Billcliffe* 3, 1990–92, 262
124.	1882	George H B MacLeod		[Exhib RGIFA, Glasgow, 990]; untraced	*Billcliffe* 3, 1990–92, 262
125.	1882	John McGavin		[Exhib RGIFA, Glasgow, 972]; untraced	*Billcliffe* 3, 1990–92, 262
126.	1883	A Arrol		[Exhib RGIFA, Glasgow, 888]; untraced	*Billcliffe* 3, 1990–92, 262
127.	1883	Mrs A Arrol		[Exhib RGIFA, Glasgow, 882]; untraced	*Billcliffe* 3, 1990–92, 262
128.	1884	Stewart Clark		[Exhib RGIFA, Glasgow, 988]; untraced	*Billcliffe* 3, 1990–92, 262
129.	1889	Moses		[Exhib RGIFA, Glasgow, 1014]; untraced	*Billcliffe* 3, 1990–92, 262
130.	nd	Child's hands and foot	m	Glasgow Museums S.172 and S.172.a	inf: Glasgow Museums

MOSSMAN, William 1793–1851

William Mossman was a carver and monumental mason who established a firm, later known as J & G Mossman, which dominated the sculpture trade in Glasgow in the second half of the 19th century. Little is known of his early life but he was born in Glasgow in 1793 and is thought to have been a descendant of James Mossman, goldsmith to Mary, Queen of Scots. He studied at the Trustees School of Design in Edinburgh and in the studio of **Sir Francis Chantrey** in London and worked for a time in London before moving to Edinburgh in the early 1820s, where he started a marble cutting business in Leith Walk. Around 1830 he returned to Glasgow, where he worked for a brief period for a firm of marble masons, either **David Hamilton and Sons** or **Clelands and Co.** In 1832, he established his own business at 172 Upper Nile Street, the city's first sculpture studio of any significance.

Mossman exhibited at the Royal Institution for the Encouragement of the Fine Arts in Scotland in 1829 and at the Royal Scottish Academy in 1829, 1831 and 1833. His bust of James Cleland, exhibited in 1831, was reputedly the first marble bust professionally carved in Glasgow (**4**). He sent several works to the exhibition arranged by the Glasgow Dilettanti Society in 1835 which were not well received (**7, 8, 15**). An anonymous critic derided one of the busts as 'a clay man', adding that the features had 'all the frigidity they could have, had the original been made of stone instead of flesh and blood'. He dismissed another as 'a horrid bad bust – of a horrid bad subject', before concluding, 'We are sorry to be this severe on Mr. Mossman but truth compels us to say that he has mistaken his trade when he took to modelling busts' (*Glasgow Exhibition* 1835, quoted by *Woodward* 1977, vol 1, pt 1, 138).

Mossman seems to have taken this criticism to heart and he exhibited his work only once more, at the West of Scotland Academy exhibition of 1846. Instead he confined his activities as a sculptor to the production of funerary monuments and the carving of architectural decoration. In 1842 he was employed by the architect Edward Blore to restore ornaments at Glasgow Cathedral (**14**). He was also responsible for the gothic monument to Lord Cathcart erected in Paisley Abbey in 1848 (**2**). After William's death in 1851, his sons **John Mossman, George Mossman** and William Mossman II (1824–1884), who had all begun their training with the family firm, continued and expanded the business.

The list of works includes sculpture produced by the Mossman firm during William Mossman's lifetime.

Literary References: *Gunnis* 1968, 266; *Woodward* 1977, vol 1, pt 1, 137–8, vol 1, pt 2, 166–7; *Pearson* 1991, 92 (Woodward); *McKenzie* 1999, 109; *McKenzie* 2002, 493

Additional MS Sources: Mossman Job Book

Wills: NAS SC36/51/30 and SC36/48/38, GSC will and inventory (22 October 1851)

Funerary Monuments					
1.	†1842	Mrs Lockhart		Glasgow Necropolis	*McKenzie* 2002, 458 (repr)
2.	1848	Lord Cathcart		Paisley Abbey, Renfrewshire	*Gunnis* 1968, 266; *Woodward* 1977, vol 1, pt 2, 165
Statues					
3.	nd	The deluge	m	Glasgow Museums S.153	*Gildard* 1892, 295; *Woodward* 1977 (vol 1, pt 2), 162
Busts					
4.	1831	James Cleland		[Exhib R Sc A, Edinburgh, 394]; untraced	*Woodward* 1977, vol 1, pt 2, 165; *Pearson* 1991, 92; *Laperriere* 3, 1991, 321
5.	1831	Unidentified gentleman		[Exhib R Sc A, Edinburgh, 358]; untraced	*Laperriere* 3, 1991, 321
6.	1833	Thomas Muir	m	[Exhib R Sc A, Edinburgh, 323]; untraced	*Laperriere* 3, 1991, 321
7.	1835	Unidentified gentleman		[Glasgow Dilettanti Soc exhib, 306]; untraced	*Woodward* 1977, vol, pt 1, 138
8.	1835	Unidentified gentleman	m	[Glasgow Dilettanti Soc exhib, 309]; untraced	*Woodward* 1977, vol, pt 1, 138
9.	nd	David Hamilton		Untraced	*Gildard* 1892, 291; *McKenzie* 2002, 493

Architectural Sculpture					
10.	1829	Medicean vase, copy		[Exhib R Sc A, Edinburgh, 361]; untraced	*Laperriere* 3, 1991, 321
11.	1835–1836	Coat of arms	s	Cleland Testimonial building, Glasgow, Lanarks	*McKenzie* 2002, 46 (repr)
12.	1836	Decorative carving		[St Paul, John Street, Glasgow]; demol 1906	*McKenzie* 2002, 493
13.	1838	Decorative carving		Mosesfield House, Springburn, Glasgow	*McKenzie* 2002, 493
14.	1842	Restoration of medieval carving and corbel heads		Glasgow Cathedral, Lanarks, west front	*Woodward* 1977, vol 1, pt 2, 165; *McKenzie* 1999, 3, no 1.1
Miscellaneous					
15.	1835	Unidentified subject		[Glasgow Dilettanti Soc exhib, 312]; untraced	*Woodward* 1977, vol, pt 1, 138

MOSSOP, William 1751–1805

A medallist, he used wax as a preliminary medium. For more information the reader is directed to *Pyke* 1973, 95 and *Pyke* 1981, 30.

MOTLEY, Frederick

For further information the reader is referred to *Pyke* 1973, 96

MOTTLEY, R fl *c*1740

The Holman monument has Corinthian columns of variegated marble supporting a curved pediment, below which are angels' heads.

Funerary Monuments					
1.	†1740	William Holman	Warkworth, Northants	S	Pevsner, *Northants*, 1973, 444

MOUNTAIN, R, of York fl *c*1787

Funerary Monuments				
1.	†1787	Rev C S Brearey	Middleton-on-the-Wolds, E R Yorks	Pevsner, *Yorks: E R & York*, 1995, 615

MOUNTSTEVEN, Eley George fl 1782–92

Born in County Meath, he was in London by 1782, when he exhibited at the Royal Academy, giving an address 'at Mr Charron's' in Little Marlborough Street, Argyle Buildings (**1, 2, 17**). He carried out work for both Josiah Wedgwood and James Tassie. His wax portraits included one of a fellow modeller **John Henderson**. By 1786 he was living at 26 Buckingham Street, York Buildings. He last exhibited at the Academy in 1792, from 6 Carlisle Street.

Mountsteven is probably the wax modeller of the same name who held an exhibition in Manchester in the 1790s. According to an early biographical sketch he left England for the Continent, where he died aged 30. 'He was supposed to have brought this inferior department of statuary art' (ie wax modelling) 'to a higher degree of perfection than ever it had attained before' (*Warburton, Whitelaw and Walsh* 1818, 2, 1187).

Literary References: *Gunnis* 1968, 266; *Pyke* 1973, 96

Busts					
1.	1782	Unidentified gentleman, portrait		[Exhib RA, London, 352]; untraced	*Graves* V, 1905–6, 316
2.	1782	Unidentified gentleman, portrait		[Exhib RA, London, 355]; untraced	*Graves* V, 1905–6, 316
3.	1788	Unidentified lady, portrait		[Exhib RA, London, 635]; untraced	*Graves* V, 1905–6, 316
4.	1789	Unidentified gentleman, portrait		[Exhib RA, London, 606]; untraced	*Graves* V, 1905–6, 316
5.	1790	Unidentified gentleman, portrait		[Exhib RA, London, 689]; untraced	*Graves* V, 1905–6, 316
6.	1790	Unidentified lady, portrait		[Exhib RA, London, 691]; untraced	*Graves* V, 1905–6, 316
Reliefs					
7.	nd	Charles James Fox	w	Untraced	*Pyke* 1973, 96
8.	nd	Duke of York	w	Untraced	*Pyke* 1973, 96
9.	nd	Edmund Burke	w	Untraced	*Pyke* 1973, 96
10.	nd	Lord Cremorne	w	Untraced	*Pyke* 1973, 96
11.	nd	Mr Cosway	w	Untraced	*Pyke* 1973, 96
12.	nd	Mr Patch	w	VAM (Bate)	*Pyke* 1973, 96
13.	nd	Mr Sharpe	w	Untraced	*Pyke* 1973, 96
14.	nd	Mrs Abington	w	Untraced	*Pyke* 1973, 96
15.	nd	Unidentified man	w	Private coll	*Pyke* 1973, 96
16.	nd	Unidentified man	w	Untraced (ex coll Rupert Gunnis)	*Pyke* 1973, 96
Miscellaneous					
17.	1782	A figure of Venus, model	w	[Exhib RA, London, 261]; untraced	*Graves* V, 1905–6, 316
18.	1782	Unidentified subject(s), portraits	w	[Exhib Free Soc, London, 258]; untraced	*Graves* 1907, 180
19.	1785	Unidentified gentleman	w	[Exhib RA, London, 264]; untraced	*Graves* V, 1905–6, 316
20.	1786	'Portrait of a young lady', model	w	[Exhib RA, London, 274]; untraced	*Graves* V, 1905–6, 316
21.	1786	Portrait of Dr Rowley, model	w	[Exhib RA, London, 250]; untraced	*Graves* V, 1905–6, 316
22.	1786	Shute Barrington, Bishop of Salisbury	w	[Exhib RA, London, 247]; untraced	*Graves* V, 1905–6, 316; *Gunnis* 1968, 266
23.	1787	'Portrait of a lady', model	w	[Exhib RA, London, 628]; untraced	*Graves* V, 1905–6, 316
24.	1788	George, Prince of Wales	w	[Exhib RA, London, 619]; untraced	*Graves* V, 1905–6, 316; *Gunnis* 1968, 266
25.	1788	Lord and Lady Auckland (for Josiah Wedgwood)		Untraced Other versions: Wax, *c*1790, Sotheby 1975	*Gunnis* 1968, 266; *Pyke* 1981, 30
26.	?1788	Sir Eyre Coote (for Josiah Wedgwood)		Untraced	*Gunnis* 1968, 266
27.	1789	Duke of Orleans	w	[Exhib RA, London, 599]; untraced	*Warburton, Whitelaw and Walsh* 1818, 1187; *Graves* V, 1905–6, 316; *Gunnis* 1968, 266
28.	1790	A nobleman, portrait		[Exhib RA, London, 680]; untraced	*Graves* V, 1905–6, 316
29.	1790	Unidentified lady, portrait		[Exhib RA, London, 701]; untraced	*Graves* V, 1905–6, 316

30.	1791	Benjamin West	w	Private coll	D	*Gunnis* 1968, 266
31.	1791	Unidentified gentleman, portrait	w	[Exhib RA, London, 641]; untraced		*Graves* V, 1905–6, 317
32.	1791	Unidentified gentleman, portrait	w	[Exhib RA, London, 650]		*Graves* V, 1905–6, 317
33.	1791	Unidentified lady, portrait	w	[Exhib RA, London, 644]; untraced		*Graves* V, 1905–6, 317
34.	1792	Sir Joshua Reynolds	w	RA, London		*Graves* V, 1905–6, 317; *Gunnis* 1968, 266; *Pyke* 1973, 96 (pl 200)
35.	nd	John Henderson		VAM (Schreiber coll)		*Gunnis* 1968, 266; *Pyke* 1973, 96

MOYER (or MAYER), Humphrey –1661

Moyer, who was apprenticed to Thomas Kingsfield and was made free of the Masons' Company in 1627, became an assistant to Nicholas Stone. He was admitted to the livery in 1634 and served as warden in 1645 and 1649, as master in 1653 and an auditor of the Company's accounts in 1655–6 and 1656–7. He assisted Stone in carving the famous monument to Dr Donne with its shrouded figure, one of the few which survived when Old St Paul's was destroyed in the Great Fire. Only one signed monument has survived, to Simon and Bridget Coston (1), but White attributes to the sculptor the monument to Simon Coston's parents and sister at St Botolph Aldersgate, *c*1637. Among his obituaries 'Remembrancer' Smith has the entry '5 September, 1661, Mr. Moyer, stonecutter in Little Britain, buried' (*Gunnis* 1968, 266–7). Smith noted the death of Mrs Moyer on 11 November 1659. The sculptor was buried in the City church of St Botolph Aldersgate on 3 September.

Literary References: *Knoop and Jones* 1935, 23 n9; *Gunnis* 1968, 266–7; *White* 1999, 106–7

Funerary Monuments

1.	†1637	Bridget Coston (†1637) and her husband Simon	Holy Cross, Greenford, Middx	S	*White* 1999, 106

MOYLE, John fl 1716–24

Probably a Plymouth mason, he built Antony House, Cornwall, for Sir William Carew between 1716 and 1724 (Archives Sir John Carew-Pole, Bt, in GPC).

MOYSEN, of Birmingham fl *c*1842

He is known only for one elaborate gothic tablet.

Funerary Monuments

1.	†1842	Brooks Forester	Elmley Lovett, Worcs	S	GPC

MULLANE, W fl *c*1820–38

Gunnis lists a selection of 'ordinary and dull' tablets by W Mullane of the New Road. There were other family members involved in the business, for the will of John Mullane 'statuary and mason of 5 Palace Row, New Road' was proved on 3 June 1837 (PROB 11/1880).

Funerary Monuments					
1.	†1820	Lewis Dymoke	Scrivelsby, Lincs	S	Pevsner, *Lincs*, 1989, 630
2.	†1824	Robert Mackintosh	St Pancras new parish church, London (in store)	S	*Gunnis* 1968, 267
3.	?1826	Elizabeth Gulston	West Clandon, Surrey		*Gunnis* 1968, 267
4.	?1830	William Dawson	St Paul, Hammersmith, London		*Gunnis* 1968, 267
5.	?1832	Miss Belcher	St Martin, Ludgate, London		*Gunnis* 1968, 267
6.	?1838	Rev Ellis Burroughs	Stratton, Norfolk		*Gunnis* 1968, 267
Chimneypieces					
7.	1829	Several	[Addington Place, Surrey]; untraced		Account book, Lambeth Pal library in GPC

MULLEY

See **Barlow & Mulley**, of London.

MUNDEN, Charles, of Windsor fl *c*1762–77

He was employed as a mason at Windsor Castle from 1772 until 1777. He signs a large tablet in coloured marbles to Ann Bidleson (1). This has 'good details and is above the level of the ordinary provincial statuary's work' (*Gunnis* 1968, 267).

Funerary Monuments

1.	?1762	Ann Bidleson	m	Bray, Berks	S	*Gunnis* 1968, 267

MUNRO, Alexander 1825–71

Munro was closely associated with the Pre-Raphaelites and is best known for his charming and fanciful portraits of women and children. He was born in Inverness on 26 October 1825, the eldest son of John Munro, a dyer, and was educated at the local grammar school, Inverness Academy. There the headmaster fostered Munro's artistic talents and introduced him to influential future patrons, perhaps including the Duke and Duchess of Sutherland, who employed Charles Barry to enlarge the family seat, Dunrobin, Sutherland, in 1845. The Sutherlands used their connections to find Munro work in London and paid his fare south.

In 1844 Munro began his London career as a stone carver at the new Houses of Parliament (**110**), working under Barry, AWN Pugin and **John Thomas**. Two years later he applied to join the Royal Academy Schools, submitting a relief model (**118**), which was rejected. **E H Baily RA**, the only sculptor on the admissions board, encouraged him however and taught him in his studio. **Patric Park** also allowed the young man to use his workshop. Munro applied for admission to the Academy a second time in January 1847 and was admitted after a three-month probationary period. The Sutherlands continued to support him by commissioning an elaborate chimneypiece that year for Dunrobin (**109**). In 1849 he began to exhibit at the Royal Academy, where he showed regularly for the next 20 years.

At the Academy schools Munro met Dante Gabriel Rossetti and his Pre-Raphaelite associates. Although he was not a member of the Brotherhood, Munro's sculpture had strong affinities with their work: the group of *Paolo and Francesca* (**5**), a subject from Dante's *Divine Comedy*, has a strong Pre-Raphaelite flavour, both in its poetic subject matter and its mood of restrained but intense eroticism. It was shown in plaster at the Great Exhibition of 1851 and subsequently commissioned in marble by W E Gladstone. In 1857 Munro worked to a design by Rossetti for a tympanum relief of *King Arthur and the knights of the round table* (**112**) on the portico of the Oxford Union building. He also executed a number of sentimental genre works (**7, 10, 28**) similar in theme and mood to paintings by his friend Arthur Hughes, another Pre-Raphaelite associate.

Munro carved few works for public spaces, but was responsible for a colossal head of Sir Robert Peel for the Peel memorial in Oldham (**40**) and a statue of James Watt for Ratcliffe Place, a square in Birmingham (**24**). He provided a series of six statues of scientists for the Oxford University museum (**19**). Several Pre-Raphaelite artists were involved in work for this innovative building, remarkable for its extensive and coherent programme of Gothic Revival decoration. A stiffness in the drapery treatment of Munro's statues provides a gothic aura, appropriate to the setting.

Munro was in considerable demand for idealised portrait sculpture, particularly charming and informal busts, relief medallions and groups of women and children. A bust of Josephine Butler depicts her with loose shoulder-length hair decorated with a band of stars (**41**) and a profile medallion shows her locks entwined with morning glory (**130**). Munro carved several representations of boys with pet dogs or birds in the countryside among lush ferns (**20, 21, 26, 171**) and a group entitled *Measurement by foxglove* (**12**), now lost, a portrait of two girls, Edith Gathorne Hardy and her little sister Emily, whose height is measured 'in an exuberant swirl of foxglove, skirt, hair and ferns' (*Read and Barnes* 1991, 60). Another group of Arthur and Edmund Hardy (**16**), a posthumous representation, presents them reading together with toys lying beside them. It was placed in the church after the family left Chilham Castle in Kent. The monument to Julian Harcourt (**3**), who died at the age of two, has the child sleeping on a bed of ferns and bluebells. Munro was, however, also capable of producing powerful portraits of men such as his bust of William Henry Hunt (**72**) and the high-relief portrait medallion of Benjamin Woodward (**151**). Munro made the sub-genre of the high-relief medallion very much his own, other examples include those of little Eva Butler, who was killed tragically, a subject well-suited to his sensitive approach (**152–4**).

In his introduction to the official handbook for the 1862 International Exhibition F T Palgrave attacked Munro's sculpture, comparing it unfavourably with **Thomas Woolner RA**'s work. The critic's comments lost currency however when it was revealed that he and Woolner were close friends and shared a number of patrons, for instance W E Gladstone. Munro himself dismissed Palgrave in a letter to a well-wisher with the words 'the bark of a cur is preferable to his slaver' (*Read and Barnes* 1991, 64) and the demand for his work appears to have been little affected.

Towards the end of his life Munro suffered from cancer and he spent the winter months in Cannes, where he built a house and studio and continued to work. His French commissions included several portraits, among them a head of the writer, Prosper Mérimée (**158**). There was a demand for copies of his sculpture and his friend Clement Massier at Vallauris reproduced some of his works in terracotta or pottery. One of Munro's assistants, Wallace Martin, made a version of *Maternal Joy* (**14**) now in the Victoria and Albert Museum. Munro died in Cannes on 1 January 1871.

EH

Literary References: *The Times*, 13 Jan 1871, 3; *AJ*, 1871, 79; *Redgrave* 1878, 303; *DNB* XIII, 1202; *Gere* 1963, 508–10; *Ormond* 1967, 25–7; *Gunnis* 1968, 267–8; *Pointon* 1975–6, 89–92; *Simon* 1981, 115; *Macdonald* 1982, 190–7; *Read* 1982, *passim*; *Read* 1984, 97–110; *Read and Barnes* 1991, 46–65, 94, 111–30; *Penny* 1992, 130–6; *Parris* 1994, 35; *Grove* 22, 1996, 314 (Stocker); *ODNB* (Macdonald)

Archival References: *Munro Papers*

Additional MS Sources: *Munro/Trevelyan; Oxford Univ Museum Papers; Munro/Gladstone; Gladstone Papers*, 1852–63, Add MSS 44371 fols 60, 252, 44385 fol 297, 44386, fols 83, 153, 255, 44397 fol 32, 44401 fols 1, 67; *Munro/Hamilton; Munro/Brown*

Will: PPR, will with a codicil, 10 October 1871, effects under £5,000

Miscellaneous Drawings: *Paolo and Francesco*, study after D G Rossetti, BM, PDB, 1992, 1003.146

Portraits of the Sculptor: John Everett Millais, pencil drawing, 12 April 1853, William Morris House, Walthamstow (*Ormond* 1967, 26, 27 repr); Lewis Carroll, the sculptor at work on *Measurement by Foxglove*, photo, summer 1859 (*Taylor and Wakeling* 2002, 58 repr); Lewis Carroll, photo, Alexander and Mary Munro, summer 1859, Munro family coll; John Brett, pencil drawing, 1861 (repr *Read and Barnes* 1991, 94); after John Brett, cameo, ex Munro family coll; anon, woodcut after a photograph, for *ILN*, 28 January 1871, BM (*Ormond and Rogers* 3, 1979–81, 148); two albums of studio photos (coll B Read and Munro family coll)

Funerary Monuments

1.	1854	Sir John and Lady Gladstone		Fasque, Kincardine, Scotland		*Read and Barnes* 1991, 61, 62
2.	1860	David Scott		Dean Cemetery, Edinburgh		*Macdonald* 1982, 193 (repr); *Pearson* 1991, unpag (repr)
3.	†1862	Julian Harcourt		All Saints old church, Nuneham Courtenay, Oxon		*Read and Barnes* 1991, 61, 63 (repr)
4.	1869	M D Hill family headstone (design only)		Arnos Vale, Bristol		*Read and Barnes* 1991, 61

Statues

5.	1851–1852	Paolo and Francesca	m	[coll W E Gladstone]; Birmingham MAG, P.29'60 Other versions: Wallington Hall, Northumbs, plaster	SD	*AJ Cat* 1851, 203 (repr); *Read and Barnes* 1991, 48, 62, 111–2 (repr); *Laperriere* 3, 1991, 329
6.	1853	'The Brothers' Little Pet', the Ingram Children (Child Play)	m	[coll Herbert Ingram]; untraced		*Manchester Art Treasures* 1857, 133; *Graves* 1875, 392; *Graves* V, 1905–6, 326; *Read and Barnes* 1991, 60; *Laperriere* 3, 1991, 329
7.	1855	Lovers' Walk, sketch	pm	[Exhib RA, London, 1452]; untraced Other versions: later produced in Parian ware		*Read and Barnes* 1991, 119 (repr)
8.	1856	Undine	m	[Exhib BI, London, 545]; untraced		*Manchester Art Treasures* 1857, 134; *Graves* 1875, 392; *Graves* V, 1905–6, 327
9.	1857	The Sisters, group	m	[Exhib RA, London, 1309]; untraced Other versions: small ceramic, private coll		*Graves* 1875, 392; *Graves* V, 1905–6, 327; *Laperriere* 3, 1991, 329; *Taylor and Wakeling* 2002, 59, 117 n148, 154 (repr)

No.	Date	Subject	Medium	Location		Literature
10.	1858	Lovers' walk	m	[Exhib RA, London, 1213]; untraced		*Read* 1982, 209; *Macdonald* 1982, 191, 195 (repr); *Read and Barnes* 1991, 119; *Laperriere* 3, 1991, 329; *Morris and Roberts* 1998, 441; *Taylor and Wakeling* 2002, 156 (repr)
11.	By 1859	Hope, statuette		Untraced		*Taylor and Wakeling* 2002, 157 (repr)
12.	1859	Measurement by foxglove, the Gathorne Hardy children		[Exhib RA, London, 1251]; untraced		*Graves* V, 1905–6, 327; *Taylor and Wakeling* 2002, 48, 59, 117 n147, 151, 158 (repr)
13.	c1860	Henry Hallam	pm	Christ Church, Oxford		*Read and Barnes* 1991, 118–9 (repr)
14.	1861	Maternal joy (Mother's Joy)		[Exhib BI, London, 643]; untraced		*ILN*, 30 March 1861, 290 (repr); *Graves* 1875, 392
15.	1861	'The Sound of the Shell', Mary and Kenneth Matheson	m	[Exhib RA, London, 993]; private coll		*AJ Cat* 1862, 321, 324 (repr); *Read and Barnes* 1991, 120
16.	1862	Arthur and Edmund Hardy		[Chilham Castle, Kent]; Chilham, Kent		*Graves* V, 1905–6, 327; *Read and Barnes* 1991, 60, 61 (repr)
17.	1862	Herbert Ingram		Marketplace, Boston, Lincs		*Read and Barnes* 1991, 57, 125
18.	c1863	Fountain nymph	p	VAM A.15-2000		*Bilbey* 2002, 343 (repr)
19.	1856–1863	Watt, Leibnitz, Hippocrates, Newton, Galileo and Davy Model(s): Galileo and Hippocrates, plaster, Ashm		Oxford University Museum		*Read* 1982, 235, 236 (repr); *Read and Barnes* 1991, 58–9, 115 (repr)
20.	c1863	Young Romilly	m	NGS, Edinburgh, 2571 Other versions: private coll, plaster	S	*Read and Barnes* 1991, 126–7 (repr)
21.	1865	Gillie and hound		[coll Lord Leverhulme]; private coll		*Read and Barnes* 1991, 57
22.	c1865	Three children, the Gilstrop family, small group	p	[coll Boulton or Robb family]; private coll	S	*Graves* V, 1905–6, 328; *Read and Barnes* 1991, 129 (repr)
23.	1865	Violet and Henry, the Crompton Roberts Children, group		[Exhib RA, London, 906]; untraced		*ILN* 17 June 1865, 581; *Graves* V, 1905–6, 327; *Read* 1982, 21
24.	1868	James Watt Model(s): plaster bust, BMAG, inv no 2631'85	m	[Ratcliffe Place, Birmingham, Warks]; Chamberlain Square, Birmingham, Warks		*Noszlopy* 1998, 32–3 (repr)
25.	1862–1868	Queen Mary II	m	[Exhib Westminster Hall, London]; Central Criminal Court (Old Bailey), City of London		*Read* 1982, 121 (repr); *Ward-Jackson* 2003, 75–6 (repr)
26.	1868	'The Baffled Hawk', Ronald Munro Fergusson	m	Private coll		*Graves* V, 1905–6, 328; *Read and Barnes* 1991, 60 (repr)
27.	c1869	Undine	m	Cragside, Northumbs		*Graves* V, 1905–6, 328; *Read and Barnes* 1991, 57, col pl 5
28.	nd	'Another Reading'		Untraced		*Read* 1982, 61–2, 209 (repr); *Read and Barnes* 1991, 119
29.	nd	Rorie Matheson as an infant Bacchus	m	Inverness Art Gallery		*Read and Barnes* 1991, 120
30.	nd	The Gladstone children	m	Hawarden, Flint Other versions: private coll, plaster		*Read and Barnes* 1991, 65, 114
Busts						
31.	1839	The infant St John the Baptist	m	[Exhib R Sc A, 509]; untraced		*Laperriere* 3, 1991, 329
32.	1849	Mrs W Banks, model		[Exhib RA, London, 1279]; untraced		*Graves* V, 1905–6, 326
33.	1850	'A lady, unfinished'	m	[Exhib RA, London, 1420]; untraced		*Graves* V, 1905–6, 326
34.	1850	Innocence	m	[Model exhib RA, London, 1392]; untraced		*Graves* 1875, 392; *Graves* V, 1905–6, 326; *Morris and Roberts* 1998, 441
35.	1850	James Loch		Stoke College, Suffolk		*Graves* V, 1905–6, 326; *Gunnis* 1968, 267
36.	1851	A boy	p	[Exhib BI, London, 526]; untraced		*Graves* 1875, 392
37.	1851	Angus B Reach		[Exhib RA, London, 1313]; untraced		*Graves* V, 1905–6, 326
38.	1851	Unidentified lady		[Exhib RA, London, 1371]; untraced		*Graves* V, 1905–6, 326
39.	1853	Unidentified lady		[Exhib RA, London, 1422]; untraced		*Graves* V, 1905–6, 326
40.	1854	Sir Robert Peel		[Peel memorial, Oldham, Lancs]; Swimming Pool, Oldham, Lancs, entrance lobby		*Graves* V, 1905–6, 326, *Read and Barnes* 1991, 65
41.	1855	Josephine Butler	m	Girton College, Cambridge	S	*Read and Barnes* 1991, 113–4 (repr)
42.	1855	William Allingham	p	NGI 8116		*Graves* V, 1905–6, 327; *le Harivel* 1988, 579 (repr)
43.	1855	William Ewart Gladstone	m	[Exhib RA, London, 1481]; untraced		*Read and Barnes* 1991, 114
44.	1856	A boy	m	[Exhib RA, London, 1365]; untraced		*Graves* V, 1905–6, 327
45.	1856	Dante Alighieri	m	Girton College, Cambridge		*Graves* V, 1905–6, 327; *Read and Barnes* 1991, 48 (repr); *Taylor and Wakeling* 2002, 159 (repr)
46.	1856	Unidentified gentleman	m	[Exhib RA, London, 1336]; untraced		*Graves* V, 1905–6, 327
47.	1857	Beatrice	m	[coll George Butler]; untraced		*Graves* V, 1905–6, 327
48.	1857	Giuseppe Mazzini		[Exhib R Sc A, Edinburgh, 1858, 766]; untraced		*Laperriere* 3, 1991, 329; *Taylor and Wakeling* 2002, 164 (repr)
49.	1857	Henry Wentworth Acland	m	[coll Sarah Acland]; Acland nursing home, Woodstock Road, Oxford Other versions: Ashm, plaster Wallington Northumbs, plaster Hawarten, Kent, plaster	SD	*Graves* V, 1905–6, 327; *Read and Barnes* 1991, 116 (repr); *Penny* 1992, III, 132 (repr)

50.	1858	A child	m	[Exhib LSFA, Liverpool, 558]; untraced		*Graves* 1875, 392; *Morris and Roberts* 1998, 441
51.	1858	Adelaide Ristori	m	[Exhib RA, London, 1247]; untraced		*Graves* V, 1905–6, 327; *Taylor and Wakeling* 2002, 151 (repr)
52.	1858	Bianca, child of Adelaide Ristori	m	[Exhib RA, London, 1248]; untraced		*Graves* V, 1905–6, 327; *Taylor and Wakeling* 2002, 151 (repr)
53.	pre-1858	Robert Hussey		Untraced		*Taylor and Wakeling* 2002, 144 (repr)
54.	1855–1859	Aurelio Saffi		Untraced		*Taylor and Wakeling* 2002, 171 (repr)
55.	1859	Hon Admiral Campbell	m	[Exhib RA, London, 1328]; untraced		*Graves* V, 1905–6, 327
56.	By 1859	Ida Wilson		untraced		*Taylor and Wakeling* 2002, 154 (repr)
57.	1859	Robert Wiedeman Barrett (Pen) Browning	m	Armstrong Browning Library, Waco, Texas		*Graves* V, 1905–6, 327
58.	1860	A little girl	m	[Exhib RA, London, 968]; untraced		*Graves* 1875, 392; *Graves* V, 1905–6, 327
59.	1860	Kenneth Matheson, 2nd Baronet of Lochalsh	m	Inverness art gall		*Read and Barnes* 1991, 120 (repr)
60.	1860	Louis Huth	m	[Exhib RA, London, 1041]; untraced		*Graves* V, 1905–6, 327
61.	1860	Mary Isabella Matheson	m	Inverness art gall		*Read and Barnes* 1991, 120 (repr)
62.	1860	Mrs Louis Huth	m	[Exhib RA, London, 986]; untraced		*Graves* V, 1905–6, 327
63.	1860	Sir William Armstrong		Newcastle Lit and Phil soc, Northumbs Other versions: Cragside, Northumbs		*Graves* V, 1905–6, 327; *Read* 1982, 122–3 (repr), 180
64.	1860	William, 2nd Baron Ashburton	m	Castle Ashby, Northants	SD	*ILN*, 2 April, 1864, 352; *Graves* V, 1905–6, 327; *Read and Barnes* 1991, 117–8 (repr)
65.	1861	Frederick Robb	m	Private coll		*Gunnis* 1968, 267
66.	1861	Hon Mrs Stewart-Mackenzie, of Seaforth	m	[Exhib RA, London, 1036]; untraced		*Graves* V, 1905–6, 327
67.	1861	John Hardy, MP	m	[Exhib RA, London, 1004]; untraced		*Graves* V, 1905–6, 327
68.	1861	Josephine Butler	m	Walker, Liverpool Other versions: several plaster casts		*Read and Barnes* 1991, 114
69.	c1861	Mary Munro (the sculptor's wife)	m	Private coll		*Graves* V, 1905–6, 328; *Read and Barnes* 1991, 124 (repr)
70.	1861	Unidentified lady	m	[Exhib RA, London, 1009]; untraced		*Graves* V, 1905–6, 327
71.	1861	Unidentified woman	m	Christie, 29 Sept 1988, lot 303	SD	
72.	1861	William Henry Hunt	m	[coll Barbara Leigh Smith Bodichon]; Royal Watercolour Society	SD	*Read and Barnes* 1991, 122–4 (repr)
73.	c1861	William Pole Carew		Private coll		*Read and Barnes* 1991, 122 (repr)
74.	1862	Joan of Arc (Helen Beyer)	m	[Exhib RA, London, 1004]; untraced		*Graves* V, 1905–6, 327; *Read and Barnes* 1991, 48
75.	1862	Mrs Bowen	m	[Exhib RA, London, 1068]; untraced		*Graves* V, 1905–6, 327
76.	1862	Mrs Edward Watkin	m	[Exhib RA, London, 1006]; untraced		*Graves* V, 1905–6, 327
77.	1863	General Shirreff		[Exhib RA, London, 1169]; untraced		*Graves* V, 1905–6, 327
78.	1863	Lieutenant-Colonel Adam Steuart Gladstone		[Exhib RA, London, 1033]; untraced		*Graves* V, 1905–6, 327; *Read and Barnes* 1991, 62
79.	1863	Miss Annie Leigh Smith		[Exhib RA, London, 1151]; untraced		*Graves* V, 1905–6, 327
80.	1863	Mrs Ludlow		[Exhib RA, London, 1158]; untraced		*Graves* V, 1905–6, 327
81.	1863	Pippa, study of a head	m	[Exhib BI, London, 605]; untraced		*Graves* 1875, 392
82.	1864	Henry, 5th Duke of Newcastle		[Hawarden, Flint]; private coll		*Graves* V, 1905–6, 327; *Ormond* 1973, 338
83.	1864	Rev T Barker		[Exhib RA, London, 1022]; untraced		*Graves* V, 1905–6, 327
84.	1864	Sir Henry Taylor DCL		[Exhib RA, London, 996]; untraced		*Graves* V, 1905–6, 327
85.	1864	Virginia, study of a head	m	[Exhib RA, London, 879]; untraced		*Graves* V, 1905–6, 327
86.	1865	Arthur Bosanquet		[Exhib RA, London, 932]; untraced		*Graves* V, 1905–6, 327
87.	1865	Rt Hon W Hutt, MP		[Exhib RA, London, 1047]; untraced		*Graves* V, 1905–6, 327
88.	1866	Master Walter Ingram	m	[Exhib RA, London, 1030]; untraced		*Graves* V, 1905–6, 327
89.	c1866	Professor Goldwin Smith	m	Art Gallery of Ontario, Toronto Other versions: Ashm, plaster		*Penny* 1992, III, 136 (repr)
90.	1866	Rt Hon Sir James Stephen	m	Private coll Other versions: Gov Art Coll, plaster		*Graves* V, 1905–6, 327; *Ormond* 1973, 430
91.	1867	M Victor Cousin	m	[Institut de France, Paris]; untraced		*AJ* 1867, 114; *Gunnis* 1968, 267; *Read and Barnes* 1991, 59–60, 64
92.	1867	Mrs Stephen A Ralli		[Exhib RA, London, 1024]; untraced		*Graves* V, 1905–6, 327
93.	1867	Stephen A Ralli		[Exhib RA, London, 1026]; untraced		*Graves* V, 1905–6, 327
94.	1868	Joseph Mitchell		[Exhib RA, London, 968]; Inverness Town Hall		*Graves* V, 1905–6, 328; *Inverness Guide*, 6
95.	1868	Mrs Harcourt Griffin		[Exhib RA, London, 1116]; untraced		*Graves* V, 1905–6, 328
96.	1869	George, 1st Baron Wolverton		[Exhib RA, London, 1165]; untraced		*Graves* V, 1905–6, 328
97.	1870	Dr Robert Carruthers, the sculptor's father-in-law		Inverness Town Hall		*Inverness Guide*, 6
98.	1870	Fox, 11th Earl of Dalhousie		[Exhib RA, London, 1063]; untraced		*Graves* V, 1905–6, 328; *Ormond* 1973, 128
99.	1865–1870	Grand Duchess Alexandra of Russia		Untraced		*Read and Barnes* 1991, 64
100.	1865–1870	Odilon Barrot		Untraced		*Read and Barnes* 1991, 64
101.	1870	W Cosmo Gordon, of Fyvie		[Exhib RA, London, 1112]; untraced		*Graves* V, 1905–6, 328
102.	nd	Countess of Dudley		Untraced		GPC
103.	nd	Henry Gladstone		Untraced		*Read and Barnes* 1991, 60, 62
104.	nd	Master Dunbar		Untraced		*Read and Barnes* 1991, 60

No.	Date	Subject	Material	Location		Literature
105.	nd	Miss Cameroon	m	Private coll		
106.	nd	Mrs Cosmo Gordon	p	Inverness Museum		KM
107.	nd	Mrs Edward O'Brien	m	Private coll, Dublin		*Read and Barnes* 1991, 61
108.	nd	R Quain	p	Town Hall, Gravesend, Kent		*Gunnis* 1968, 267

Chimneypieces

No.	Date	Subject	Material	Location		Literature
109.	*c*1848	Two knights in full armour below the Duke of Sutherland's heraldic arms, perhaps provided with other chimneypieces Drawing(s): private coll		[Dunrobin Castle, Sutherland]; untraced		*Gunnis* 1964, 267; *Macdonald* 1982, 191, 195 (drawing repr)

Architectural Sculpture

No.	Date	Subject	Material	Location		Literature
110.	1844–1848	Decorative ornaments		Palace of Westminster, London		*Macdonald* 1982, 190–1
111.	1853	'Egeria, sketch for a statue for a fountain'		[Exhib RA, London, 1333]; untraced		*Graves* V, 1905–6, 326
112.	1857–1858	King Arthur and the knights of the round table (after a design by Dante Gabriel Rossetti)		Oxford Union, tympanum relief		*Read* 1982, 180–2 (repr)
113.	*c*1865	Boy with a dolphin, fountain		[Grovesnor gate, Hyde Park, London]; Regents Park, London		*Gunnis* 1968, 267; *Read and Barnes* 1991, 57, 65
114.	1865	Drinking fountain, nymph with a pitcher		Berkeley Square, London		*Read and Barnes* 1991, 57
115.	nd	Angel		[English Church, Cannes, France, chancel wall]; destroyed		*Read and Barnes* 1991, 58
116.	nd	'plasterwork and decorations'		Gravesend Town Hall, Kent		*Chatham Evening Post*, 28 Jan 1986

Reliefs

No.	Date	Subject	Material	Location		Literature
117.	1840	Unidentified subject	m	[Exhib R Sc A, 1840, 386]; untraced		*Laperriere* 3, 1991, 329
118.	1846	'a figure modelled in relief from an antique in the round'		Untraced		*Macdonald* 1982, 191
119.	*c*1853	Agnes Gladstone (aged 11)	m	Untraced		*Read and Barnes* 1991, 114; *Laperriere* 3, 1991, 329; *Taylor and Wakeling* 2002, 145 (repr)
120.	1853	Lady Constance Grosvenor (medallion)	m	[Cliveden, Berks]; untraced Other versions: Inverness art gall others recorded		*Read and Barnes* 1991, 112 (repr); *Laperriere* 3, 1991, 329
121.	1854	Chevalier Bunsen	b	Bonn, Germany		*Graves* V, 1905–6, 326; *Read and Barnes* 1991, 65; *Laperriere* 3, 1991, 329
122.	*c*1854	John Everett Millais Bt, medallion	p	Ashmolean Other versions: private coll, *c*1855, marble NPG 4959, nd, plaster private coll, nd, plaster	S	*Simon* 1981, 115 (repr); *Laperriere* 3, 1991, 329; *Penny* 1992, III, 130 (repr)
123.	1854	Lady Alwyne Compton, medallion portrait	m	Chatsworth, Derbys, sculpture gallery	S	*Graves* V, 1905–6, 326; *Macdonald* 1982, 191, 197 (model repr); *Laperriere* 3, 1991, 329; *Penny* 1992, 130
124.	1854	Mrs H D Macleod, portrait medallion		[Exhib RA, London, 1527]; untraced		*Graves* V, 1905–6, 326
125.	1854	Sarah Acland, portrait medallion		[coll Acland family]; Christ Church Cathedral, Oxford Other versions: Acland nursing home, Oxford, replica, marble		*Read and Barnes* 1991, 59; *Penny* 1992, 130
126.	1854	The Seasons, four reliefs	s	Cliveden, Bucks, terrace		*Read and Barnes* 1991, 46, 57; *Laperriere* 3, 1991, 329
127.	1854	William Bell Scott, medallion	b	[Penkill Castle, Ayrshire]; Penkill, Ayrshire, churchyard		*Graves* V, 1905–6, 326; *Laperriere* 3, 1991, 329
128.	*c*1855	Agnes Gladstone (b 1842, daughter of W E Gladstone)	p	Private coll	S	*Read and Barnes* 1991, 114 (repr)
129.	1855	Honora Glynne		Hawarden, Flint, churchyard		*Read and Barnes* 1991, 60, 62, 114
130.	*c*1855	Josephine Butler	p	Walker, Liverpool		*Read and Barnes* 1991, 114
131.	1855	Master Henry Acland, portrait medallion		[coll Acland family]; untraced		*Graves* V, 1905–6, 327; *Penny* 1992, 131
132.	1855	Sarah James, medallion	m	[Exhib RA, London, 1553]; untraced Other versions: private coll, plaster		*Graves* V, 1905–6, 327
133.	*c*1855	Walter James, medallion	p	Private coll		KM
134.	1856	Agnes and Herbert, W E Gladstone's children	m	[Exhib RA, London, 1352]; untraced Other versions: Agnes Gladstone, NGS, nd, plaster		*Graves* V, 1905–6, 327; *Read and Barnes*, 1991, 114
135.	*c*1856	Pauline, Lady Trevelyan	m	Wallington Hall, Northumbs		*Read and Barnes* 1991, 60, 64 (repr)
136.	1856	Repose, study of a baby	m	[Exhib RA, London, 1374]; untraced Other versions: BMAG 3162'85, plaster Wallington Hall, Northumberland		*Graves* 1875, 392; *Read and Barnes* 1991, 117 (repr)
137.	1856	Rev Dr Henry Wellesley, medallion	m	Ashmolean WA 1857.4		*Graves* V, 1905–6, 327; *Penny* 1992, III, 131 (repr)
138.	1856	Sir C Trevelyan, medallion portrait		[Exhib R Sc A, Edinburgh, 738]; untraced		*Laperriere* 3, 1991, 329
139.	1856	Unidentified subject, medallion		[Exhib R Sc A, Edinburgh, 722]; untraced		*Laperriere* 3, 1991, 329
140.	1858	'A sketch; bas relief'		[Exhib RA, London, 1318]; untraced		*Graves* V, 1905–6, 327
141.	1858	Bat-sprite		[Exhib R Sc A, Edinburgh, 780]; untraced		*Laperriere* 3, 1991, 329

142.	1858	Mrs John Gurney, medallion	m	[Exhib RA, London, 1266]; untraced		*Graves* V, 1905–6, 327
143.	1858	Study of a head		[Exhib R Sc A, Edinburgh, 777]; untraced		*Laperriere* 3, 1991, 329
144.	c1859	George Macdonald, medallion	b	SNPG, Edinburgh Other versions: Kings College, Aberdeen private coll, plaster (sold Sotheby, 16 April 2002)	S	*Read and Barnes* 1991, 59, 60 (repr)
145.	1859	Mrs George Smith, medallion	m	[Exhib RA, London, 1364]; untraced		*Graves* V, 1905–6, 327
146.	1859	Mrs Tom Hughes, portrait medallion		[Exhib RA, London, 1314]; Working Men's college, Camden Town, London		*Graves* V, 1905–6, 327
147.	1859	Unidentified lady, medallion	m	[Exhib RA, London, 1336]; untraced		*Graves* V, 1905–6, 327
148.	1860	A little boy, portrait medallion	m	[Exhib RA, London, 972]; untraced		*Graves* V, 1905–6, 327
149.	1860	Mrs George Stewart-Mackenzie, medallion	m	[Exhib RA, London, 1016]; untraced		*Read and Barnes* 1991, 118
150.	c1860	Sabrina	m	Ackland Art Museum, North Carolina, USA		*Graves* V, 1905–6, 327; *Read and Barnes* 1991, 57 (repr)
151.	1861	Benjamin Woodward, medallion	m	Oxford University Museum	S	*Read and Barnes* 1991, 121 (repr)
152.	c1864	Eva Butler with a butterfly		Untraced		*Read and Barnes* 1991, 127
153.	c1864	Eva Butler with a dead dove	m	Private coll		*Read and Barnes* 1991, 127
154.	c1864	Eva Butler with a live dove	m	Private coll Other versions: private coll, plaster	S	*Read and Barnes* 1991, 127 (repr; col repr 3)
155.	1865	Emily Ursula Hamilton	m	['set into the wall of the family home in Abingdon']; private coll (the sitter's descendants)		*Read and Barnes* 1991, 128–9 (repr)
156.	1867	Pauline, Duchess of Vallombrosa Payment(s): 100 gns	m	[coll Riccardo, Duke of Vallombrosa]; untraced Other versions: private coll, plaster		*Graves* V, 1905–6, 328; *Read and Barnes* 1991, 130 (repr)
157.	1868	Mary, Lady Molyneux, portrait medallion	m	Joanna Barnes Fine Art, London (1992)		
158.	1865–1870	Prosper Mérimée	b	Le Grand Jas Cemetery, Cannes, France		*Read and Barnes* 1991, 64, 65
159.	nd	Alexander Munro (self portrait)		Inverness Museum and Art Gallery	S	C Lib (repr)
160.	nd	Dante Alighieri and William Shakespeare, pair of portrait roundels	tc	Sotheby, 16 April 2002		
161.	nd	Mary Ann Matilda Roby, portrait medallion	m	Sotheby, Gleneagles Hotel, 26 Aug 1997, lot 1370	S	C Lib (repr)
162.	nd	Mother and child	b	NMW, Cardiff Other versions: coll Gabriel Summers, ceramic copy by Clement Massier		
163.	nd	Mrs Robb		[coll Bolton family]; untraced		*Read and Barnes* 1991, 60
164.	nd	Sir Walter Trevelyan		Wallington Hall, Northumbs		*Read* 1984, 109; *Read and Barnes* 1991, 62
165.	nd	Walter Carruthers	tc	Private coll		
Miscellaneous						
166.	1850	The child's playmate	p	[Exhib BI, London, 494]; untraced		*Graves* 1875, 392
167.	1851	The young Highlander	p	[Exhib BI, London, 531]; untraced		*Graves* 1875, 392
168.	1858	Study in marble		[Exhib BI, London, 584]; untraced		*Graves* 1875, 392
169.	1861	Babe asleep		[Exhib RA, London, 1001]; untraced		*Graves* V, 1905–6, 327
170.	1862	Master Herbert Ingram	m	[Exhib RA, London, 1104]; untraced		*Graves* V, 1905–6, 327
171.	1862	The young hunter		[Exhib RA, London, 999]; untraced		*Graves* V, 1905–6, 327
172.	1863	Group in aluminium		[Exhib RA, London, 1080]; untraced		*Graves* V, 1905–6, 327
173.	1864	Boy asleep	m	[Exhib RA, London, 1032]; untraced		*Graves* V, 1905–6, 327
174.	nd	Seal in the form of a bust of a bearded warrior	s	Ashmolean WA 1947.174	S	*Penny* 1992, III, 135 (repr)

MURRAY, George –1761

In 1747 he was described in the Moulsham Hall accounts as 'Geo. Murray, carver and cabinet-maker' (*Edwards* 1977, 111). Murray was a long-term assistant to **James Richards**, working with the latter at 17 Arlington Street and at the Horse Guards in the 1750s (**2, 4**). By 1754 Richards was incapacitated by ill health and in 1760 Murray succeeded him as master sculptor and master carver to the Crown. On 15 February 1760 Murray wrote to the Duke of Ancaster about the terms of this appointment, complaining that 'Your Honour was so good as to acquaint me with His Grace the Duke of Newcastle's promise that I was to enjoy the whole in the same manner as the Said James Richards which was by Pattent and a Warrant from the Lords of ye Treasury, for takeing care of the Limetree work [ie, the carving by **Grinling Gibbons**] at His Majestys Palace at Windsor, which is taken from me without my Knowledge and given to one Lawrence a Carver [**Richard Lawrence I**] who never had any Concern with His Majestys work on any Acct.' Murray pointed out also that if he were to receive the same salary as Richards had enjoyed he would have 'four score pounds a year.' From this, however, £50 was being deducted as payment for Lawrence, while in addition 'my pattent will cost me eighty pounds' (Archives, West of Alscot Park in *Gunnis* 1968, 236).

In 1760 he was paid £70 for work carried out at Ashburnham Place, Sussex (**6**), but died in the following year, and the last payment, amounting to £95, was made by Lord Ashburnham to his executors in February, 1762. His will, which describes him as a 'carver of St Martin in the Fields' was proved on 5 January 1761 (PROB 11/862).

Literary References: *Gunnis* 1968, 268

Chimneypieces						
1.	1754	Description unavailable Payment(s): £8		[Strawberry Hill, Twickenham, Middx; 'little parlour']; untraced		*Toynbee* 1927, 5, 70; *Gunnis* 1968, 268
2.	1757–1758	Statuary marble Payment(s): £23 6s 7d	m	Horse Guards, Whitehall, London, secretary of war's apartments		Board of Works/Horseguards HOR/1/3 i, fol 12; *Gunnis* 1968, 268

No.	Date	Work	S	Location	Source
Architectural Sculpture					
3.	1751	Carving		[New Lodge, Richmond, Surrey]; untraced	Archives, Viscount Galway in GPC
4.	1757–1758	2 pairs of trusses with scrolls and raised raffled leaves 'to Windows on each side of the venetian' Payment(s): £3 4s		Horse Guards, Whitehall, London, south pavilion, west front	Board of Works/Horseguards HOR/1/3 i, fol 2
Miscellaneous					
5.	1745–1747	Unidentified work Payment(s): £54 5s 8d in 1745; £48 17s 6d in 1747		[Moulsham Hall, Essex]; untraced	*Edwards* 1977, 63
6.	1760	Unidentified work Payment(s): £165		[Ashburnham Place, Sussex]; untraced	Ashburnham Archives in *Gunnis* 1968, 268

MURRAY, Patrick fl 1702–03

He signs the important architectural monument commemorating the Marquess of Atholl and family members, which has portrait busts and a large number of heraldic shields. The contract, dated 1702, for Murray to build the vault underneath, is in the Blair Castle archives.

Archival References: GPC

No.	Date	Work	Location	S	Source
Funerary Monuments					
1.	†1703	John, 1st Marquess of Atholl (designed by Alexander Edward)	Dunkeld Cathedral, Perth	S	*Colvin* 1995, 333

MUSCHAMP, W, of Liverpool fl *c*1799

He signs a large wall-tablet, with a relief of *The good Samaritan* (1).

No.	Date	Work	Location	S	Source
Funerary Monuments					
1.	†1799	Rev David Simpson	Christ Church, Macclesfield, Ches	S	*Gunnis* 1968, 268; *Penny* 1977 (1), 219 n5

MUSCO, Salvator fl 1678–1700

He worked for a 'Mr Sybert' (probably **C G Cibber**) in 1678, when he was listed in the general search of the Masons' Company as 'Salvator Musco an Italian'. In 1698 Musco carved a coat of arms for the Earl of Nottingham's seat at Burley-on-the Hill (1). Pearl Finch repeated a legend that the masons charged with erecting the arms were killed when the scaffolding gave way. A little later Musco probably worked at Great Park, Ampthill, for the owner, Lord Ashburnham, mentioned in a letter that he was thinking of employing the carver, who was then working for Lord Nottingham. It seems that most of the craftsmen at Burley entered Lord Ashburnham's service after leaving Nottingham (Ashburnham Archives). Musco's son, Joseph, was apprenticed to **John Young** in 1695, but was turned over to **Thomas Stayner** two years later.

Literary References: *Finch* 1901, 66; *Knoop and Jones* 1935, 69; *Gunnis* 1968, 268

Archival References: Masons' Company, *Court Book*, 1677–94, 16 April 1678; List of Apprentices, 1695

No.	Date	Work	Location	Source
Architectural Sculpture				
1.	1698	Coat of arms Payment(s): £10	Burley House, Rutland, north front	*Finch* 1901, 66; Pevsner, *Leics & Rutland*, 1984, 459

MYERS fl *c*1810

The *Gentleman's Magazine* notes that Myers was responsible for 'a very elegant monument of a pyramidical form' erected in Calcutta' (1) (*GM*, 1810, 2, 203–4).

No.	Date	Work	Location	Source
Funerary Monuments				
1.	1810	Hon John Hyde (†1796)	Kolkata (Calcutta), 'the new burying ground'	*GM* 1810, 2, 203–4; *Gunnis* 1968, 268

MYERS, George fl *c*1843–51

Myers executed a good deal of stonework, and at least one monument, to Lord Rolle, from designs by A W N Pugin (2). This is an elaborate tomb-chest with Gothic details. The *Art Journal* described the font he exhibited in 1851 as 'elaborately and beautifully enriched' (6). His monument to Major General Jones, is signed 'Myers of Lambeth' (1). A biography of Myers, entitled *Pugin's Builder*, was published by Patricia Spencer-Silver in 1993.

No.	Date	Work	S	Location	Source
Funerary Monuments					
1.	†1843	Major-General Sir John Thomas Jones		Sculthorpe, Norfolk	Pevsner, *Norfolk: N W & S*, 1999, 634
2.	1850	John, Lord Rolle (†1842) (designed by A W N Pugin)		Bicton, Devon, mausoleum	Pevsner, *Devon*, 1989, 173 (repr 161); *Read* 1982, 256
Chimneypieces					
3.	1845	With corbelled overmantel and quatrefoil frieze	s	Chirk Castle, Denbighs, Cromwell, hall	Pevsner, *Clwyd*, 1994, 124
Architectural Sculpture					
4.	*c*1843	Crucifixion (relief)	s	Ratcliffe College, Leics	Pevsner, *Leics & Rutland*, 1984, 359; *Cavanagh* 2000, 264–5 (repr)
5.	*c*1843	Virgin and Child (statue)	s	Ratcliffe College, Leics Other versions: St David, Pentasaph, N Wales St Augustine, Ramsgate, Kent, Pugin chantrey	*AJ Cat* 1851, 320 (repr); *Cavanagh* 2000, 264 (repr)
6.	1851	Font with rich gothic decoration		[Gt Exhib, London]; untraced	*AJ Cat* 1851, 320 (repr)
7.	*c*1859	Capitals		All Saints, Marylebone, London	Pevsner, *London: N W*, 1991, 597
8.	nd	Intricate stonework, including the figures of St Peter and St Paul on the w front, the sculptures of the spire and the complex finials on the Easter Sepulchre		St Giles, Cheadle, Cheshire	*Read* 1982, 256

MYERS, Thomas –1806

He was a Liverpool statuary.

Archival References: GPC

MYLNE, Robert I 1633–1710

The eldest son of Alexander Mylne, he was apprenticed to his uncle, John Mylne, in 1667, and succeeded him as master mason to the Scottish Crown the following year. He built Wood's hospital at Largo (1665), the market cross at Perth (1668), Leslie House, Fife, and made additions to Wemyss Castle, Fife (1669). In 1671 he worked on the rebuilding of Holyrood and around the same time, Thirlestane Castle, Berwickshire. In 1674 he built the west tower of South Leith parish church and between 1677 and 1685 he was employed on fortifications at Edinburgh Castle. Mylne was also a speculative builder and his profits enabled him to buy two estates, at Balfargie in Fife and Inveresk, near Edinburgh. He died on his Inveresk estate on 10 December 1710 and was buried in the family vault in Greyfriars churchyard.

His monument to his uncle and master, John Mylne, is a tall Corinthian aedicule with a mantled coat of arms and cherub supporters breaking a segmental pediment (1). The inscription tablet is held in the mouth and paws of a lion. Mylne utilised a similar design for his monument to Alexander Beatton (2).

Literary References: Pevsner, *Edinburgh*, 1991, 157; *Pearson* 1991, 28; *Colvin* 1995, 678–9

Funerary Monuments				
1.	†1667	John Mylne	Greyfriars churchyard, Edinburgh	Pevsner, *Edinburgh*, 1991, 162; *Colvin* 1995, 679
2.	1674–1675	Alexander Beatton (†1672)	Greyfriars churchyard, Edinburgh	Pevsner, *Edinburgh*, 1991, 157
Statues				
3.	late C17	George Heriot	George Heriot's school, Edinburgh, rear wall of the courtyard.	*Pearson* 1991, unpag

MYLNE, Robert II 1733–1811

He was born on 4 January 1733, the son of Thomas Mylne, a leading Edinburgh mason. In 1747 he was apprenticed for six years to Daniel Wright, a carpenter. He worked for a time as a woodcarver at Blair Atholl, but his wish was to qualify as an architect and in 1754 he departed for the Continent. He arrived in Rome that December, and in 1758 won a silver medal for a neoclassical building to house busts of eminent men at the Academy of St Luke, in the Concorso Clementino. After a period spent surveying the antiquities of Sicily for the connoisseur Richard Phelps he travelled back to London via the Rhineland and Holland, arriving in July 1759. Mylne became one of the most successful architects of his day, particularly noted for Blackfriars bridge. Its detailed masonry, elliptical arches and Ionic columns made it one of the major public works of the 18th century. It was replaced in 1868. Mylne went on to build several more bridges, and to design and renovate a number of country houses in Shropshire including Condover Hall, Halston Hall, Loton Park and Woodhouse. He held the post of surveyor to the New River Company (the precursor of the Metropolitan Water Board) and commemorated the founder of the company, Sir Hugh Myddelton, with an elegant urn near the source of the river (8). His other monuments include a tablet to his brother William (5), and the memorial to Elizabeth Berry, which has an urn on a column (1). Mylne's diaries record a number of dealings with sculptors such as **Joseph Dixon** (who worked on Blackfriars bridge), **Daniel Pinder** and **John Flaxman RA**, and it is quite possible that he only produced the designs for some of the monuments. The Berry is signed 'Mylne fecit' which suggests that he at least directed some of the work.

Mylne went on to become surveyor of St Paul's and Canterbury Cathedrals, clerk of the works at Greenwich Hospital, and surveyor to the Stationers' Company. He died on 5 May 1811, and was buried in the Crypt of St Paul's.

Literary References: *Stainton* 1983, 11, 28; *Colvin* 1995, 679–856

Funerary Monuments					
1.	1770	Elizabeth Berry (†1767)	Askham Richard, W R Yorks, churchyard	SD	*Colvin* 1995, 685
2.	1776	Barlow Trecothick (†1770)	Addington, Surrey		*Colvin* 1995, 685
3.	1778	St Aubyn family mausoleum	Clowance, Cornwall		*Colvin* 1995, 685
4.	1787–1789	Sir William Duncan Bt (†1774), mausoleum	Lundie, Angus		*Colvin* 1995, 685
5.	†1790	William Mylne	St Catherine, Dublin		*Colvin* 1995, 685
6.	1791–1793	William Berners (co-sculptor: Edward Tovell of Ipswich)	[Woolverstone Hall, Suffolk]; destroyed		*Colvin* 1995, 685
7.	1800	Mylne family mausoleum	Great Amwell, Herts		*Colvin* 1995, 685
8.	1800	Sir Hugh Myddelton, urn	Great Amwell, Herts, island in New River		*Colvin* 1995, 685
9.	1807	Sir Christopher Wren	St Paul's Cathedral, London, crypt		*Colvin* 1995, 685
Chimneypieces					
10.	1783	Description unavailable sa Payment(s): 6 1/2 gns	Argyll House, London		*Kelly* 1990, 392

NADAULD, Henri 1653–1724

He was a Huguenot sculptor and carver, responsible for sophisticated decorative carving and statues at two of the great English baroque houses. Nadauld was born in France and after the revocation of the Edict of Nantes fled to England, where he was active from 1698–1710. His son Pierre, born in 1685 in France, was naturalised in 1707 and is described in the records of the Huguenot church in West Street, London, as coming from 'l'Ile de Oléron', near La Rochelle. He became a surgeon and raised a family in Ashford, Derbys.

Nadauld worked at Hampton Court Palace in 1698, where he was paid £50 for plaster work in the Queen's closet in the water gallery (19). The shed provided for the 'Frenchman to burne his Plaister in' and the 'Squaring and laying two stones' for him 'to beat his plaster on' probably refer to Nadauld although the accounts spell his name 'Nadue'. Again he is almost certainly the 'Monsieur Noddo' who was rated on two houses in Portugal Street, Piccadilly, on 20 December 1697. His yard in Portugal Row, Piccadilly, was near to such other statuaries as **John Nost I**, **Edward Hurst** and **Richard Osgood**. He was named 'Nedos' in the Castle Howard accounts.

By 1700 Nadauld had moved to Chatsworth where in July the carpenter was paid for making a shed for him and where he worked, inside and out, until 1706. He produced ornamental details for the façades and garden sculpture under the supervision of Monsieur Huet, a Huguenot minister who acted as steward to the 1st Duke of Devonshire. Many of the other craftsmen were also Huguenot refugees. Nadauld worked also on the interior, providing a chimneypiece (**18**) and figures for niches on the west staircase (**10**). One of his finest achievements at Chatsworth was a plaster relief of *putti* on horseback and acanthus foliage, on the coving of the west subvestibule. Such ornamental carving was usually supervised by the architect in charge, but six working drawings by Nadauld at Chatsworth indicate that he was responsible for developing his own designs. The design for the frieze on the west front, in black chalk on paper, shows pairs of tritons blowing conch shells and pairs of winged sea horses, their tails entwined or tied with ribbons to three-pronged tridents (**20**). The drawing also relates to the great frieze on the south front at Castle Howard where Nadauld worked from 1704 (**30**). His work at Chatsworth was sometimes mundane (**21**) but he also produced a wealth of mythological and allegorical sculture (**2–9**). An account of work done in 1703 includes three figures for the inner court in 'Roach Abbey stone' (**5**), a building material considered by Wren to be second only to Portland stone. Nadauld's bill includes 'Charges to Roach Abbey' of 12/-, which suggests that he selected the stone himself. He was still working in the gardens in 1714, but largely on repairs to figures, cleaning statues before their repainting and on carving a pedestall and '2 Seafish heads for ye cascade', which sound as though they were replacements.

Meanwhile he retained his London yard and in 1704 won the commission to provide a mural monument to Lady Eland (grand-daughter of the Huguenot Marquis de la Tour de Gouvernet), in Westminster Abbey. Now dismantled, only the bas-relief survives, representing the deceased reclining on a plinth supported by cushions, with a mourning female figure in her left (**1**). It is signed 'Nadaud fecit'.

Nadauld was in Yorkshire working at Castle Howard from 1704–10 (**11–13, 25, 27–33**), so that his work there overlapped with Chatsworth. Indeed one of his bills to the Earl of Carlisle specifies 'foure little figures called the foure Sezons made at Chattworths' (**12**). Initially he was employed in Lord Carlisle's private apartments carving wooden architraves, cornices and friezes in the first closet and grand cabinet (**25**) and in 1710 he provided cornices in the saloon and dining room, now the tapestry and music room (**33**). He also had a considerable involvement in exterior carving on the south and north fronts (**30, 31**). Some of his sculpture for the garden has not survived but the figure of *Apollo* is intact, supported on a pyramidal base with a relief apparently representing a *Procession to the shrine of Apollo at Delphi* (**11**).

He retired to Derbyshire, dying at Ashford-in-the-Water, near Bakewell (on the Devonshire estate) in 1723 and his descendants continued to live there until the 19th century. His name features in the Ashford Court Rolls where it is recorded that his death had occurred by the time of the October court but not before the June court of 1724.

IR (Inf. Stuart Band, Christopher Ridgway)

Literary References: *Thompson* 1949, *passim*; *Murdoch* 1988, 240–1

Archival References: Poor Rates, F 1232 (1697); Castle Howard Building Accts, G2/2/27, 22 Oct 1706; G2/2/28, 22 Oct 1706; G2/2/31–34, nd; Chatsworth Building Accts vol vi, fol 1 (April 28–Aug 28, 1700); fol 16, Dec 1700–April 1701; fol 17, Feb 1701; fol 91 (1703); vol vii, fol 57 (1702); fol 63 (1703); fol 82 (1704); fol 93 (1706); vol C/21, fol 27 (1710–11); fol 40 (1713); fol 41 (1714)

Funerary Monuments

1.	1704	Esther, Lady Eland (†1694)	Westminster Abbey, London, triforium (bas-relief only); formerly chapel of St John	S	*Gunnis* 1968, 269; *Murdoch* 1988, 242

Statues

2.	1700	Cleopatra and other figures Payment(s): £22 (Cleopatra)	[Chatsworth, Derbys]; removed		Chatsworth Accts, vol 6, fol 91
3.	1700	'the Figure called Amphritite', with a pedestal Payment(s): £10; pedestal £2 3s	Chatsworth, Derbys		Chatsworth Accts, vol vi, fol 16
4.	1700–1703	'Antonius' Payment(s): £22	[Chatsworth, Derbys]; untraced		Chatsworth Accts, vol 6, fol 91; *Murdoch* 1988, 242
5.	1700–1703	Mars, fortitude and prudence Payment(s): £36	[Chatsworth, Derbys, inner court]; removed	s	Chatsworth Accts, vol 6, fol 91; *Murdoch* 1988, 240–1
6.	1700–1703	Phorsis and Pathos Payment(s): £22 each	[Chatsworth, Derbys]; untraced		Chatsworth Accts, vol 6, fol 91; *Murdoch* 1988, 242
7.	1700–1703	The muses Payment(s): £22	[Chatsworth, Derbys]; untraced		Chatsworth Accts, vol 6, fol 91; *Murdoch* 1988, 242
8.	1700–1703	Two rivers Payment(s): £22 each	Chatsworth, Derbys, Canal	s	Chatsworth Accts, vol 6, fol 91; *Murdoch* 1988, 242
9.	1704	Phorsis, father of the tritons Payment(s): £22	[Chatsworth, Derbys]; untraced		Chatsworth Accts, vol 6, fol 91; *Murdoch* 1988, 242
10.	1704	'two Figures for the Neeches in ye staircase in the West front' (niches by Samuel Watson) Payment(s): £24	Chatsworth, Derbys, west front staircase	s	Chatsworth Accts, vol 6, 9; *Murdoch* 1988, 240; *Chatsworth Handlist*, 17
11.	1705–1709	Apollo and rockwork pedestal	[Castle Howard, Ray Wood]; Castle Howard, N R Yorks, south parterre, sw corner	s	*Murdoch* 1988, 242; *Saumarez Smith* 1990, 125
12.	1705–1709	Four seasons, 'little figures'	[Castle Howard, N R Yorks]; untraced	s	*Murdoch* 1988, 242; *Saumarez Smith* 1990, 64
13.	1709–1710	Ceres, Flora, Pallas, four vestals, Seneca, Socrates, Cicero, Plato Payment(s): Ceres and Flora (£28); Seneca and Socrates £14 each	Castle Howard, N R Yorks, parapets etc	s	Castle Howard Building Accts, G2/2/33, £56 for 4 statues; G2/2/34, £42 for 3 figures on n front; *Murdoch* 1988, 242; *Saumarez Smith* 1990, (repr 18)

Busts

14.	1700	'2 Busto Heads set in the Neeches upon the Staircase before the West Front' Payment(s): £6	Chatsworth, Derbys, staircase, niches on west front		Chatsworth Accts, vol 6, fol 91; *Saumarez Smith* 1990, 64

No.	Date	Work	Material	Location	References
15.	1703	'A head of Lucretia, looking up'	m	Chatsworth, Derbys, west stairs	*Chatsworth Handlist*, 17
16.	1700–1703	Cleopatra Payment(s): £22	m	Chatsworth, Derbys	Building Accts, Chatsworth, cited in *Gunnis* 1968, 269; *Chatsworth Handlist*, 17
17.	1703	Several		Chatsworth, Derbys, courtyard	Building Accts, Chatsworth, cited in *Gunnis* 1968, 269
Chimneypieces					
18.	1701	In auricular style Payment(s): £20	s	Chatsworth, Derbys (formerly gallery, two corbels surviving between dining room and sculpture gallery)	Chatsworth Accts, vol 6, 91; *Murdoch* 1988, 240
Architectural Sculpture					
19.	1689–1692	Plasterwork Payment(s): £50		Hampton Court, Middx, Queen's closet, water gallery	*Colvin* 1973–76, 158, citing Hampton Court Accts AO 1/2482/296 *Saumarez Smith*, 1990, 64
20.	1702	Ornaments in frieze and around windows over entrance, cyphers and coronets on 4 keystones in middle windows Payment(s): £114 10s Drawing(s): frieze, black chalk on paper, Chatsworth Muniments, vol 6, p 1	s	Chatsworth, Derbys, west front	Chatsworth Accts, vol vii, fol 57; *Murdoch* 1988, 240 (drawing repr)
21.	1700–1703	'41 foot Superficiall of Frost worke about the Grotto under the Staircases' and '94 foot of ffrost workes for ye Cascades' Payment(s): £6 4s 6d; £14 6s	s	Chatsworth, Derbys	Chatsworth Accts, vol vi, fol 1; *Saumarez Smith* 1990, 64
22.	1700–1703	'the Figure of Fluvius, Two Dolphins and two Vauses For ye cascade' (designed by Thomas Archer) Payment(s): £40	s	Chatsworth, Derbys, cascade	Chatsworth Accts, vol vi, 91; *Murdoch* 1988, 242; *Devonshire* 1999, 16–17 (repr)
23.	1704	Carved ornaments (designed by Thomas Archer)		Chatsworth, Derbys, cascade house	Chatsworth Accts, vol vii, 82; *Devonshire* 1999, 16–17 (repr)
24.	?1704	'ornaments for the two gallerys on each side of the inner court' Payment(s): £60		Chatsworth, Derbys	Chatsworth Accts, vol vii, 82
25.	1705	Architraves, cornices and friezes	wd	[Castle Howard, N R Yorks, first closet and grand cabinet]; destroyed	*Murdoch* 1988, 242; *Saumarez Smith* 1990, 65
26.	1706	Relief of putti on horseback and acanthus foliage Payment(s): £14 10s	p	Chatsworth, Derbys, coving of west vestibule	Chatsworth Accts, vol 7, 82; *Murdoch* 1988, 240 (repr)
27.	1705–1709	Diana the huntress, relief	s	Castle Howard, N R Yorks, east end, beyond Lord Carlisle's apartment (formerly west front)	*Murdoch* 1988, 242; *Saumarez Smith* 1990, 65–66 (repr 21)
28.	1705–1709	External, including frieze of martial trophies, four keystones, boy and horse frieze, lion frieze, tritons, metopes Payment(s): £173 2s Drawing(s): (related to south front frieze) Chatsworth, black chalk on paper	s	Castle Howard, N R Yorks, north and south fronts and cupola	Castle Howard, Building Accts G2/2/17; *Saumarez Smith* 1990, 64–66 (reprs 18–19)
29.	1705–1709	Faun, urn, three-faced terms, sea horses and sea boy for the fountain, Bacchus	s	[Castle Howard, N R Yorks, Ray Wood]; untraced	*Saumarez Smith* 1990, 125
30.	1705–1709	Frieze of sea horses and seaboys, coat of arms in pediment with attendant figures and other ornaments		Castle Howard, N R Yorks, south front	*Saumarez Smith* 1990, 64–66 (repr); *Murdoch* 1988, 242
31.	1705–1709	Martial trophies, coronet and cyphers in keystones, putti on central window surround, four statues in niches and other ornaments Payment(s): £56	s	Castle Howard, N R Yorks, north front	*Saumarez Smith* 1990, 66 (repr)
32.	1705–1709	Scrolled ornaments, composite capitals, floral bosses, keystones, frieze around kerb of cupola and other ornaments	s	Castle Howard, N R Yorks, great hall	*Saumarez Smith* 1990, 66 (pl 26)
33.	1710	Cornices, supplied with two keystones for the hall		Castle Howard, N R Yorks, tapestry room, music room and saloon	Castle Howard Building Accts, G2/2/33; *Murdoch* 1988, 242

NAISMYTH, Mungo 1730–70

A master mason and sculptor, he built the parish church at St Andrew's, Fife, 1739–56 to designs by Allan Dreghorn and was in return given the freedom of the city. He carried out repairs to the spire of Glasgow Cathedral after it was struck by lightning in 1756 and is thought to have been responsible for five of the 'tontine faces', keystone masks formerly on the town hall at Trongate, Glasgow, and now in St Nicholas Garden, Glasgow (*McKenzie* 2002, 52–6). Naismyth had a workshop in Parnie Street. He is buried in the Merchant City at St David's Churchyard, Ingram Street.

His portrait forms part of the decoration of the façade of 'Cruise' at 178–82 Ingram Street, Glasgow, which was built by the architects Page and Park in 1994.

Literary References: *McKenzie* 1999, 109; *McKenzie* 2002, 211, 465, 493

NAPPER, George, of London 1754–1840

In 1828, when he applied to the AGBI for funds, he stated that he had worked 'for the late Mr. **John Bacon [I]** for forty years' and had also worked under **J E Carew** and **William Behnes**. Napper then apparently set up in business in Manchester and executed a number of monuments. Those to Mrs Trafford and the Reverend Samuel Bennett (**2, 3**) 'have the usual contemporary classical details' (*Gunnis* 1968, 269). His monument to Reverend Corker has a female figure mourning at an urn and a portrait medallion (**1**). Napper also executed several monuments for the West Indies.

Archival References: AGBI, vol 2, 11, 94, 164

Funerary Monuments

1.	†1795	Rev Chambre Corker		Clonmel, Co Tipperary		*Potterton* 1975, 73
2.	†1813	Elizabeth Trafford		Manchester Cathedral, Lancs		*CIIA* 4/8/53 (repr)
3.	?1823	Rev Samuel Bennett		Hatfield Peverel, Essex		*Gunnis* 1968, 269
4.	nd	Master Astley		Duckinfield, Cheshire		*Gunnis* 1968, 269
5.	nd	Rev Mr Lock		[Newcastle, Co Limerick]; destroyed		*Potterton* 1975, 73

NASMYTH, Patrick 1787–1831

Busts

1.	c1810	Self-portrait	wd	YCBA B 1977.14.15	S	

NAYLOR, Georgina fl mid 19th century

She was responsible for a mid-nineteenth century angel in the gothic family mausoleum in Montgomery, where her family were the local squires (**1**).

Statues

1.	nd	An Angel		Leighton, Montgomery	S	Pevsner, *Powys*, 1979, 114

NEALE, George, of Grantham fl 1798–1820

One of a large family of Lincs and Leics stone masons, he moved to Grantham by 1800 where he set up business in Whard Road at the end of the Grantham Canal. In addition to the monuments noted by Gunnis, there are at least 110 and probably 140 engraved slate headstones by him in Kesteven and they are of a very high standard. He appears to have had several partners, for tablets are signed 'Neale and Wilson,' and 'Neale and Johnston.' There are also headstones in Lincs signed 'G & R Neale' (Pevsner, *Lincs*, 1989, 284). Neale was succeeded in the firm by his son Joseph, who had a Mr Dunn as his partner.

Literary References: *Gunnis* 1968, 269; *Neale and Heron* 1969, 12–13

Funerary Monuments

1.	†1785	Richard Metheringham		Caythorpe, Lincs	S	Pevsner, *Lincs*, 1989, 217
2.	?1822	Beaumont Leeson		St Wulfram, Grantham, Lincs		*Gunnis* 1968, 269
3.	?1823	James Faithful		Eastwell, Lincs		*Gunnis* 1968, 269

NEILL, Henry fl c1728–43

He signs the monument to Benjamin Morris 'Henricus Neill Fecit' (**2**).

Funerary Monuments

1.	†1728	Alexander Castell and family		[Duncannon Port, Co Wexford]; untraced	S	*Strickland* 2, 1913, 165; *Potterton* 1975, 73
2.	†1743	Benjamin Morris		Waterford Cathedral	S	*Potterton* 1975, 73

NELSON, George 1810–88

He was related to **Thomas and James Nelson of Carlisle**, and as a young man became an assistant to **M L Watson**, who was also a native of Cumberland. He enrolled at the Royal Academy schools and won two premiums for his work (**13, 23**). In 1837 his address was 26 Carburton Street and during the following decade he lived in Belvedere Road, Lambeth and George Street, Euston Square.

After Watson's death in 1847 Nelson executed in marble those works that his master had only modelled in clay. These included the great group of Lords Eldon and Stowell and the statue of **John Flaxman RA** (**14, 18**). The latter was signed 'George Nelson from a sketch by the late M. L. Watson.' Nelson also carved a monument to his deceased master, whose imminent erection was recorded in the *Carlisle Journal* of 21 January 1859 (**7**).

His best-known independent work was a statue of *Musidora*, which appeared as an engraving in several Victorian art magazines (**15**). His monuments include that to James M'Laughlan, decorated with floral scrolls (**1**), the monument with a medallion portrait to Louis Petit (**4**), and that to the memory of the men of the 50th regiment of the line, who died at the battle of Sutlej in the Anglo-Sikh war (**2**).

Nelson died on 14 October 1888, probably at 275 Goldhawk Road, Shepherds Bush. His personal estate was valued at £3,190 13s 1d. He is commemorated on a tablet (which he carved himself) in memory of Mrs Blackmore and her father **Paul Nixon** (**12**). It would appear therefore that there must have been some sort of connection between Nixon and Nelson.

On 15 February 1889 the *Carlisle Journal* reported that clay models of statues bequeathed to the corporation of Carlisle by Edward [*sic*] Nelson had arrived in the city and were housed temporarily in the town hall. They numbered 60 and were all approximately a foot high, though a model of *Satan* was double that size. His full size model of M L Watson's Flaxman statue was difficult to house. It was put into the School of Art in Fisher Street where it was damaged by students, and appears not to have made the transition to Tullie House when the Society of Arts moved there in 1894. The models were intended for the use of the art students. (Inf. D Perriam)

Literary References: *CJ*, 14 Dec 1888, 4 (bequest to city of Carlisle); *Gunnis* 1968, 269; *Graves* V, 1905–6, 347/8; RG/JP, 6, 970v., 971

Archival References: GPC; RG/JP, 6, 970v-1

Will: PPR, 15 November 1888, fol 993

Funerary Monuments

1.	†1848	James M'Lauchlan		St Michael, Dumfries	S	*Gunnis* 1968, 270
2.	1848	Officers and men of the 50th Regiment (co-sculptor: M L Watson) Model(s): Gt Exhib, London, 1851		Canterbury Cathedral, Kent	SD	*AJ Cat* 1851, 121 (repr); *ILN* 11 Oct 1851, 465; Pevsner, *Kent: N E & E*, 1983, 211

3.	c1850	Clara Steel		Grinsdale, Cumberland	S	Pevsner, *Cumberland & Westmorland*, 1967, 134
4.	1850	Louis Petit (†1849)		St Michael, Lichfield, Staffs		Pevsner, *Staffs*, 1974, 190
5.	1856	Thomas Sheffield (†1853)		Carlisle Cathedral, Cumberland	SD	*Graves* V, 1905–6, 348; *Read* 1982, 190–1 (repr)
6.	†1857	John Dixon of Knells		Houghton, Cumberland		Pevsner, *Cumberland & Westmorland*, 1967, 139
7.	1859	Musgrave Lewis Watson		Carlisle Cathedral, Cumberland		*CJ*, 21 Jan 1859, 5; *Graves* V, 1905–6, 348
8.	?1859	Thomas Elliot		Carlisle Cathedral, Cumberland	S	*Gunnis* 1968, 270
9.	1872	Lord Stanley of Alderley		Untraced		*Gunnis* 1968, 270
10.	1883	Isaac Sheffield		St Michael, Dalston, Cumberland		*Carlisle Journal*, 16 Feb 1883
11.	†1885	Hannah Mylne		Great Amwell, Herts	S	
12.	†1888	Paul Nixon (†1850), Mrs Blackmore and the sculptor, George Nelson		Cowgill Church, W R Yorks		GPC
Statues						
13.	1841	Figure in the round from the life		[RA, London, silver medal]; untraced		RA Premium list
14.	c1847	Lord Eldon and Lord Stowell (co-sculptor: M L Watson)	m	University College, Oxford, library		Pevsner, *Oxon*, 1974, 212
15.	1847	Musidora, 'Warm in her cheek the sultry season glowed . . .'		[Exhib RA, London, 1331]; untraced		*Graves* V, 1905–6, 348;
16.	1847	The captive, 'The groaning captive washes her life away . . .'		[Exhib RA, London, 1393]; untraced		*Graves* V, 1905–6, 348
17.	1869	The bather		[Exhib RA, London, 1300]; untraced		*Graves* V, 1905–6, 348
18.	nd	John Flaxman RA (co-sculptor: Musgrave Lewthwaite Watson)	m	UCL, library		*Gunnis* 1968, 269
Busts						
19.	1840	Lord Western	m	[Exhib RA, London, 1137]; untraced		*Graves* V, 1905–6, 347
Reliefs						
20.	1840	A dream		[Exhib RA, London, 1093]; untraced		*Graves* V, 1905–6, 347
21.	1858	Colonel Petit, medallion	m	[Exhib RA, London, 1317]; untraced		*Graves* V, 1905–6, 348
22.	1859	Martin Lewthwaite Watson, medallion		[Exhib RA, London, 1378]; untraced		*Graves* V, 1905–6, 348
Miscellaneous						
23.	1837	Model		[RA, London, silver medal]; untraced		RA Premium list
24.	1837	The last interview		[Exhib RA, London, 1220]; untraced		*Graves* V, 1905–6, 347
25.	1839	H Gorges		[Exhib RA, London, 1173]; untraced		*Graves* V, 1905–6, 347
26.	1842	'Despair, a sketch'		[Exhib RA, London, 1341]; untraced		*Graves* V, 1905–6, 347
27.	1843	'A sketch'		[Exhib RA, London, 1440]; untraced		*Graves* V, 1905–6, 348
28.	1845	Combat between centaurs and lapithae		[Exhib RA, London, 1357]; untraced		*Graves* V, 1905–6, 348
29.	1861	Musidora, 'This cool retreat his Musidora sought . . .'		[Exhib RA, London, 1123]; untraced		*Graves* V, 1905–6, 348

NELSON, James –c1811

One of the principal master-masons of his day, he received much employment from the architects Henry Holland and Sir John Soane. In 1784 he supplied marble tables to Sir Philip Yorke, later Lord Hardwicke. He worked on the building of Fonthill in 1787 and in the same year he was master mason supervising alterations at Lees Court, Sheldwich, Kent, for Lewis Watson, later Lord Sondes.

In 1789–90 Nelson was the master-mason responsible for building or repair work for the Countess of Pembroke at Richmond, Sir Henry Peters in Park Street, and the Earl of Hardwicke in New Cavendish Street, London. In 1792–4 he was master-mason charged with rebuilding Wimpole, Cambs, for Lord Hardwicke. In 1793–95 he built a house for Wilbraham Tollemache, later Earl of Dysart, at Hyde Park Corner (148 Piccadilly). He was also chief mason at Peter Thelluson's house in Philpot Lane, London, where he was paid £204 *in toto*. Between 1794 and 1802 he built Tyringham, Bucks for William Praed and a bridge in the park, as well as the lodges and stables. For this he received a total of £4,552 9s 7d on 29 March 1802. He was the principal mason and supplier for the Marquess of Buckingham's house in Pall Mall where he was paid £2,003 for masonry work in 1795–96. In 1804 he received £61 from the Marquess of Buckingham for marble or ormolu tables (the ormolu by Dominique Jean) for the house in Pall Mall.

Nelson's most important commission was to build the Bank of England under Sir John Soane, where he was employed from 1791 until 1811. During the last five years **Thomas Grundy** was his partner. Nelson became a liveryman of the Mason's Company in 1801; a note in the Company's archive records, 'He owes £25, not to be wrote to any more' (GPC).

Literary References: *Builder*, 1850, 113; *Gunnis* 1968, 270

Archival References: Soane, Abstract of Bills I, fols 62–3, 92; 2, fol 35, 112; Soane, Wimpole Acct Bk, 1791–94, fols 43–50, 121–25; Soane Bill Book 5, fols 17–23, 171; Soane Bill Book 1794–7, fols 128–9v; Soane Accts, 1792–1805

Funerary Monuments					
1.	1796	Unidentified subject		[Ordered by the Marquess of Abercorn]; untraced	Soane Abstract of Bills 2, fol 116
2.	1807	Samuel Bosanquet (designed by Sir John Soane) Payment(s): £326		Leytonstone, Essex, churchyard	*Gunnis* 1968, 270; Soane Order Book 1787, pt 1, fol 130
Chimneypieces					
3.	1769	Coloured	m	[Lord Guilford's London house]; untraced	*Gunnis* 1968, 270
4.	1770	Description unavailable		[Lord Bristol's house, St James's Square, London]; untraced	*Gunnis* 1968, 270
5.	1787	Description unavailable Payment(s): £30		[Tendring Hall, Suffolk, Lady Rowley's room]; untraced	GPC
6.	c1787	For the south east Parlour (designed by Sir John Soane)		[Fonthill Splendens, Wilts]; untraced	Soane, Journal I, 33; *Woodward* 1998, 32

7.	1793	Two Payment(s): £75, £43	m	Bank of England, London, centre room and room adjoining	*Gunnis* 1968, 270
8.	1794	Description unavailable		[Thomas Lewis' house, Palmers' Green]; untraced	Soane bill book 5, fols 258–60
9.	1792–1794	Several, for Philip, Lord Hardwicke		[for Wimpole, Cambs and New Cavendish St, London]; untraced	Soane acct book 1791–4, fols 43–50, 121–25; abstract of bills I, fol 169; *Gunnis* 1968, 270
10.	1793–1794	Two, of enriched marble Payment(s): £75 and £43		[Bank of England, centre room and room adjoining]; untraced	Soane bank acct, vol 3, fol 32
11.	1786–1796	Description unavailable		[for Sir Alexander Hood, Cricket St Thomas, Somerset]; untraced	*Gunnis* 1968, 270
12.	1786–1796	Description unavailable		[for William Pitt 'at Hollwood']; untraced	*Gunnis* 1968, 270
13.	1786–1796	Description unavailable		[Lady Pembroke's house, Charles Street, London]; untraced	*Gunnis* 1968, 270
14.	1786–1796	Description unavailable		[Buckingham House, Pall Mall, London]; untraced	Soane bill book 5, fols 17–23
15.	1786–1796	Ornamented with flowers Payment(s): £32		[for Peter Thelluson, Philpot Lane, London]; untraced	Soane bill book 1794–7, fols 128–9v; *Gunnis* 1968, 270
16.	1801	With antique flowers (designed by Sir John Soane) Payment(s): £48	m	Bank of England, London	*Gunnis* 1968, 270
17.	1801–1802	Two, one with 'antique flowers' Payment(s): £48	m	[Bank of England, London]; untraced	Soane bank acct, vol 6, fol 177
18.	1803	Description unavailable Payment(s): £41	m	[Robert Knight's house, Charles Street, Grosvenor Square, London]; untraced	GPC
19.	1806	Description unavailable	m	[Lord Jersey's house, Berkeley Square, London]; untraced	Archives, Earl of Jersey in GPC
20.	1806	Two (designed by Sir John Soane)	m	[for W H Fellowes, Ramsey Abbey, Hunts]; untraced	GPC
Architectural Sculpture					
21.	1767	Decorative details	s	[Lord Bristol's house, St James's Square, London]; untraced	*Gunnis* 1968, 270
22.	1790	Greyhounds	s	Langley Park, Norfolk, Chedgrave lodges	Pevsner, *Norfolk: N W & S*, 1999, 513
23.	1791	Unidentified	s	Audley End, Essex, temple	Essex R O, D/DBy/A.222; *Gunnis* 1968, 270
24.	1795–1802	Mouldings, swags and other ornaments		[Bank of England]; destroyed	Soane bank act, vol 3, fol 132; fol 228; vol 6, fol 125
25.	1802–1811	Capitals, friezes, Vitruvian scrolls, swags and lion-mask		[Bank of England]; untraced	*Gunnis* 1968, 270

NELSON, John Henry 1800–47

An Irishman, born in Sligo, he began his career by painting portraits, many of which were exhibited at the Royal Hibernian Academy. They attracted the attention of two wealthy Irish landowners, Colonel Lloyd and Mr Wynne, who in 1833 sent him to study in Paris. After four years there, Nelson went to England and then to Wales, where he painted a number of portraits. From Wales he moved to Bristol and in about 1838 returned to Dublin.

It was not until 1844 that he turned his attention to sculpture. In 1846 he produced a statue of *Venus attiring*, modelled from life, which he exhibited in Dublin, at 13 D'Olier Street, hoping to get subscriptions to execute the work in marble (1). He took the statue to England in 1845, exhibiting it at the Egyptian Hall, London in 1847, and then in Manchester. The *Builder* remarked that it had 'cost him two years of unremitting toil' (*Builder* 1848, 53). The *Art Union* wrote that 'the great talent displayed in the execution of his figure attracted the notice of many patrons of art who expressed much interest in the future prospects of the sculptor' (*AU* 1848, page 52). It was while he was in Manchester that he died, on 26 December 1847, leaving a destitute widow and four children.

Literary References: *Strickland* 2, 1913, 165–166; *Gunnis* 1968, 271

Statues				
1.	1845	Venus attiring	[Royal Irish Art Union, £15 prize; exhib Egyptian Hall, London, 1847]; untraced	*Builder*, 1848, 53; *AU*, 1848, 52; *Strickland* 2, 1913, 166; *Gunnis* 1968, 271
Busts				
2.	1844	Sappho	[Royal Irish Art Union, £5 premium]; untraced	*Strickland* 2, 1913, 166
3.	1845	Unidentified gentleman	[Exhib RHA, Dublin]; untraced	*Strickland* 2, 1913, 166
4.	1846	Rev Alexander McDonnell of Trinity College	[Exhib RHA, Dublin]; untraced	*Strickland* 2, 1913, 166

NELSON, John, of Shrewsbury 1726–1812

John Nelson was a monumental mason in Shrewsbury, who was also employed as a carver by **Thomas Farnolls Pritchard.** He was baptised on 9 April 1726 at St Andrew, Penrith, Westmorland, the son of Richard and Ann Nelson, of whom nothing is otherwise known. He received a 'liberal education', possibly at Penrith grammar school, but from his birth until 1759, when he appears in the registers of St Anne, Soho, Westminster, with his wife, Hannah (†1802), whom he married *c*1751, details of his life are unrecorded. By 1759 he had become a skilled carver in wood and marble. He was recruited by Pritchard as a journeyman for Pritchard's Shrewsbury workshop *c*1762. His name appears frequently in an album of the architect's designs produced during the later 1760s (American Institute of Architects Library, Washington DC, reproduced in full by *Ionides* 1999) and his association with Pritchard may well have continued until his former master's death in 1777. Nelson was probably Pritchard's principal carver, because when Pritchard moved out of Shrewsbury in 1770 Nelson took a joint tenancy of his house and yard, and he became the sole tenant after Pritchard's death in 1777.

Whilst working for Pritchard, his fellow carvers included **van der Hagen, Swift, Danders** and **Halley**. They were employed in carving chimneypieces, picture frames and other decorative details, mostly in wood, for houses in Shropshire and the surrounding counties. His work for Pritchard also included monuments and at least one large-scale architectural feature. He spent 29 days carving a group of three winged cherubs' heads for the monument to Sir Richard Lyster (**3**). Although the monument remains *in situ* the cherubs' heads have been removed, presumably to make room for the small tablet commemorating Lyster's wife, which was added to the base of the monument by van der Hagen. Nelson worked with van der Hagen and Swift on the tablet commemorating Richard Ward Offley (**5**) and with Danders on a stone pediment for Hatton Grange, Salop, which has a coat of arms in a cartouche flanked by cornucopiae (**73**).

A brief reference to Richard Whinney 'Late Journeyman to Mr Nelson, Carver' in the *Shrewsbury Chronicle* for 12 December 1772 shows that Nelson employed studio assistants (*Ionides* 1999, 55). In the following year it was reported that 'Mr. Nelson, carver of this town, was putting up some pictures at Nicholas Smith's esq at Cundover [*sic*] when one of the rounds of the ladder on which he stood broke by which accident he unfortunately broke his right thigh' (*Shrewsbury Chronicle*, 17 July 1773, cited by *Ionides* 1999, 55–6). He must have been temporarily incapacitated by this injury but seems to have been working again by 1777, when he applied, as a 'statuary carver and stonemason', for the freedom of the Shrewsbury Guild of Bricklayers and Carpenters. He paid the £10 fee and it was immediately agreed that 'Mr Nelson shall make a drawing of a frontispiece with an estimate there annexed to put up in front of the Company's arbour' (C and B Company Roll). This building, which was on the site now occupied by Shrewsbury School, no longer exists.

In the same year Nelson sculpted the two lions outside the Lion Hotel, Wyle Cop, Shrewsbury (**74**). He later carved a statue of Sir Rowland Hill and two sphinxes for Hawkstone Park, Salop (**35, 76**) and in 1796 executed a statue of Roger de Montgomery for Shrewsbury Castle (**36**). This was subsequently removed from the castle and stored in a basement for some years. After an accident, in which it fell on a boy and broke his leg, it was moved again, to a corporation yard, where it disappeared. Nelson had a thriving monumental practice, often in coloured memorials, and his daybook for the period 1798–1805, now in Shrewsbury School Library, shows that he produced wall tablets, churchyard tombs, headstones and ledgers, including several for the new St Chad's burial ground in Shrewsbury. Surviving examples include Sarah Hurtle's polychrome marble monument, which has two winged boys praying and weeping at either side of an urn (**6**) and a simple oval tablet with two columns commemorating Thomas Hanmer (**25**).

As a masonry contractor Nelson built two curious round, domed toll-houses on Worcester Bridge in the late 1770s, to the design of John Gwynn. He was described as an architect both on his tombstone and on his contract and drawings for rebuilding a bridge over the Rea at Meole Brace near Shrewsbury in 1789. His contemporaries prefered to remember him as a sculptor. His tradecard of 1786 described him as a statuary of Shrewsbury working in marble and stone, who 'neatly executed monuments and Chimney pieces etc' (Banks 106.21).

Nelson died on 17 April 1812 at the house of correction Shut, Shrewsbury and was buried locally at St Mary's church five days later. When his death was announced the *Salopian Journal* remarked that Nelson's 'moral worth excited the esteem of all acquainted with him' (cited by *Gunnis* 1968, 270). His obituary in the *Gentleman's Magazine* asserted that his 'eminent abilities as a statuary will be long remembered in Shropshire and the neighbouring counties', before adding that, 'having had a liberal education and possessing a fund of lively anecdote, [he] was a very pleasant companion'. The article ends with some lines 'to the worthy and aged Nelson', in which he is asked why he has not carved a bust of himself. The question is answered in another verse, which concludes, 'In busts to *others* '*merits* raised / He has *his own* declared' (*GM*, 1812, i, 492).

EH

Literary References: *Gunnis* 1968, 270–1; *Ionides* 1999, *passim; ODNB* (Lawson)

Funerary Monuments

1.	†1733	Rev Richard Lloyd	St Mary, Shrewsbury, Salop		Pevsner, *Salop*, 19578, 256
2.	†1742	Brochwel Griffiths	Guilsfield, Montgomery	S	Pevsner, *Powis*, 1979, 107
3.	†1766	Group of three winged cherubs' heads for monument to Richard Lyster MP (designed by Thomas Farnolls Pritchard) Drawing(s): Pritchard drawing book (AIA 82)	[Alberbury, Salop]; untraced	S	*Ionides* 1999, 240–3 (repr)
4.	?1767	Beatrice Peck	Market Drayton, Salop	S	*Gunnis* 1968, 270
5.	1769	Richard Ward Offley (†1762) (designed by Thomas Farnolls Pritchard) (co-sculptor: Van der Hagen and Swift) Drawing(s): Pritchard drawing book (AIA 64)	Pontesbury, Salop		*Ionides* 1999, 236 (repr)
6.	†1771	Sarah Hurtle	Wolverley, Worcs	S	
7.	†1772	John Owen and Thomas Lloyd	Guilsfied, Montgomery	S	Pevsner, *Powis*, 1979, 107
8.	†1772	Rev James and Rev Juckes Egerton	Guilsfied, Montgomery	S	Pevsner, *Powis*, 1979, 107 (repr)
9.	†1774	John Dod	Cound, Salop	S	
10.	†1774	Mary Lea	Cound, Salop	S	
11.	†1777	Rev John (†1741) and Mrs Mary (†1777) Fletcher	Bangor, Flint	S	Pevsner, *Clwyd*, 1986, 321
12.	†1779	John Ashby	Westbury, Salop	S	
13.	?1779	M Dorsett	Llangedwyn, Denbighs	S	*Gunnis* 1968, 271
14.	1779	Severne family	Westbury, Salop	S	
15.	1784	Sir Rowland Hill (†1783)	Hodnet, Salop	S	*Gunnis* 1968, 271
16.	1785	Edward Lloyd and family members	St Mary, Shrewsbury, Salop	S	*Gunnis* 1968, 271; Pevsner, *Salop*, 1958, 256
17.	c1786	Dunne family (†1734–86)	Aymestrey, Herefs		Pevsner, *Herefs*, 1963, 69
18.	†1787	Canon David Evans	Llangynyw, Montgomery	S	Pevsner, *Powis*, 1979, 139
19.	?1788	Thomas Prostam	St Julian, Shrewsbury, Salop	S	*Gunnis* 1968, 271
20.	†1789	Catherine Corbet	Westbury, Salop	S	

21.	†1790	David Davis		Llanfair, Caereinon, Montgomery	S	Pevsner, *Powis*, 1979, 128
22.	?1790	Scarlett Lloyd		Fitz, Salop	S	*Gunnis* 1968, 271
23.	†1792	John Hurtle		Wolverley, Worcs	S	Pevsner, *Worcs*, 1968, 291
24.	1793	Milward and Dovaston families		West Felton, Salop	S	
25.	†1794	Thomas Hanmer		Overton, Flint	S	Pevsner, *Clwyd*, 1986, 411
26.	†1797	John (†1796) and Ann Bill		Llansantffraid-ym-Mechain, Montgomery	S	Pevsner, *Powis*, 1979, 150
27.	?1799	Jane Vernon		Chester Cathedral, Cheshire		*Gunnis* 1968, 271
28.	†1800	Hannah Worthington		Llansantffraid-ym-Mechain	S	Pevsner, *Powis*, 1979, 150
29.	?1800	Mrs Gardner		High Ercall, Salop	S	*Gunnis* 1968, 271
30.	?1800	Rev Robert Jeffreys		Baschurch, Salop	S	*Gunnis* 1968, 271
31.	?1800	William Davies		Montgomery Parish Church		*Gunnis* 1968, 271
32.	?1801	Ann Corser		Whitchurch, Salop	S	*Gunnis* 1968, 271
33.	?1801	Elizabeth Jones		Oswestry, Salop	S	*Gunnis* 1968, 271
34.	?1803	Mary Lea		Acton Burnell, Salop		RG/JP, 6, 975
Statues						
35.	1795	Sir Rowland Hill		[Hawkstone Park, Salop, Hill Column]; Destroyed		*Gents Mag*, 1812, i, 492; *Gunnis* 1968, 270; PMSA NRP database
36.	1796	Roger de Montgomery		[Shrewsbury Castle, Salop]; untraced		*Gents Mag*, 1812, i, 492; *Gunnis* 1968, 270
Chimneypieces						
37.	?1765	Baroque chimney frame (designed by Thomas Farnolls Pritchard) (co-sculptor: Van der Hagen and Halley) Drawing(s): Pritchard drawing book (AIA 3)	wd	Shipton Hall, Salop, library		*Ionides* 1999, 122, 123, 327, 353 (repr)
38.	?1765	Chimney frieze with oak branches and ribbon (designed by Thomas Farnolls Pritchard) Drawing(s): Pritchard drawing book (AIA 10)		[Croft Castle, Herefs, 'Bed Chamber South Front']; untraced		*Ionides* 1999, 52, 328, 360 (repr)
39.	?1765	Chimney frieze with wreath and leaves (designed by Thomas Farnolls Pritchard) (co-sculptor: Van der Hagen) Drawing(s): Pritchard drawing book (AIA 10)	wd	Croft Castle, Herefs, bishop's room		*Ionides* 1999, 52, 91, 328, 360 (repr)
40.	?1765	Gothic chimney frame (designed by Thomas Farnolls Pritchard) (co-sculptor: Van der Hagen) Drawing(s): Pritchard drawing book (AIA 4–5)	wd	[Croft Castle, Herefs, library]; Croft Castle, Herefs, ante-room		*Ionides* 1999, 47, 52, 91–2, 327, 354–5 (repr)
41.	1765	With cornucopia and phoenix heads in the frieze (designed by Thomas Farnolls Pritchard) (co-sculptor: Van der Hagen) Drawing(s): Pritchard drawing book (AIA 7)	wd	27 Broad Street, Ludlow, Salop		*Ionides* 1999, 166–9, 327, 357 (repr)
42.	1765–1766	Two, for the dining room and parlour (designed by Thomas Farnolls Pritchard) (co-sculptor: Van der Hagen) Drawing(s): Pritchard drawing book (AIA 12)		[for Mr Bather, of Mardol, Shrewsbury, Salop]; untraced		*Ionides* 1999, 328, 362 (repr)
43.	1765–1769	Six, for the drawing room, centre chamber, hall, dressing room, best chamber and dining parlour (designed by Thomas Farnolls Pritchard) (co-sculptor: Van der Hagen and Swift) Drawing(s): Pritchard drawing book (AIA 29, 30, 43, 58, 60, 62)		Hatton Grange, Salop		*Ionides* 1999, 130–3, 331–2, 334, 379, 380, 394, 409, 411, 423 (repr)
44.	1765–1769	Six, of various designs (designed by Thomas Farnolls Pritchard) (co-sculptor: Van der Hagen and Swift) Drawing(s): Pritchard drawing book (AIA 69, 72–77)		[Tern Hall, Salop]; untraced		*Ionides* 1999, 212, 335–7, 420, 423–8 (repr)
45.	1765–1769	Three, for the common parlour, Mr Freeman's chamber and the hall (designed by Thomas Farnolls Pritchard) (co-sculptor: Van der Hagen and Swift) Drawing(s): Pritchard drawing book (AIA 19, 21, 57)		[Gaines, Worcs]; untraced		*Ionides* 1999, 105–6, 329, 334, 369, 371, 408 (repr)
46.	1765–1769	Three, with classical, rococo and gothic decoration (designed by Thomas Farnolls Pritchard) (co-sculptor: Van der Hagen and Swift) Drawing(s): Pritchard drawing book (AIA 34, 47, 63)	wd	Bitterley Court, Salop		*Ionides* 1999, 126–7, 331, 333, 335, 384, 398, 414 (repr)

47.	1765–1769	Two (designed by Thomas Farnolls Pritchard) (co-sculptor: Van der Hagen and Swift) Drawing(s): Pritchard drawing book (AIA 36, 37)		[for John Ashby, High Street, Shrewsbury]; untraced	*Ionides* 1999, 158, 331, 387, 388 (repr)
48.	1765–1769	Two, including one for Miss Egerton's Room (designed by Thomas Farnolls Pritchard) (co-sculptor: Van der Hagen and Swift) Drawing(s): Pritchard Drawing Book (AIA 40, 41)		[for Samuel Egerton, of Tatton Park, Cheshire]; untraced	*Ionides* 1999, 47, 150, 332, 391, 392 (repr)
49.	1765–1769	Two, with rococo ornament, for Miss Leighton's bed chamber and dressing room (designed by Thomas Farnolls Pritchard) (co-sculptor: Van der Hagen and Danders) Drawing(s): Pritchard drawing book (AIA 13)		[Condover Hall, Salop]; untraced	*Ionides* 1999, 328, 363 (repr)
50.	February 1769	With 'laurell leafe and ribbon' frieze (designed by Thomas Farnolls Pritchard) (co-sculptor: Swift) Drawing(s): Pritchard drawing book (AIA 65)		[for Mr Good of Shrewsbury]; untraced	*Ionides* 1999, 23, 335, 416 (repr)
51.	1765–1769	With a scallop shell (designed by Thomas Farnolls Pritchard) (co-sculptor: Van der Hagen) Drawing(s): Pritchard drawing book (AIA 53)		[for Mr Bather, of Mardol, Shrewsbury, Salop]; untraced	*Ionides* 1999, 333, 404 (repr)
52.	1765–1769	With birds in the frieze (designed by Thomas Farnolls Pritchard) (co-sculptor: Van der Hagen and Swift) Drawing(s): Pritchard drawing book (AIA 17)		[for Mr Haycock in Wales]; untraced	*Ionides* 1999, 329, 367 (repr)
53.	1765–1769	With classical motifs (designed by Thomas Farnolls Pritchard) (co-sculptor: Van der Hagen and Swift) Drawing(s): Pritchard drawing book (AIA 46)		[for Bartholomew Barnaby, of Brockhampton House, Herefs]; untraced	*Ionides* 1999, 99, 333, 397 (repr)
54.	1765–1769	With classical mouldings (designed by Thomas Farnolls Pritchard) (co-sculptor: Van der Hagen) Drawing(s): Pritchard drawing book (AIA 11)		[for Mr Pritchard]; untraced	*Ionides* 1999, 328, 361 (repr)
55.	1765–1769	With classical mouldings (designed by Thomas Farnolls Pritchard) (co-sculptor: Van der Hagen and Swift) Drawing(s): Pritchard drawing book (AIA 79)		[for John Wilkinson of The Lawns, Broseley, Salop]; untraced	*Ionides* 1999, 172, 337, 430 (repr)
56.	1765–1769	With foliage in the frieze (designed by Thomas Farnolls Pritchard) (co-sculptor: Van der Hagen and Swift) Drawing(s): Pritchard drawing book (AIA 20)		[for Mr Burton, of Longner Hall, Salop]; untraced	*Ionides* 1999, 330, 370 (repr)
57.	1765–1769	With frieze of oak leaves and acorns (designed by Thomas Farnolls Pritchard) (co-sculptor: Van der Hagen) Drawing(s): Pritchard drawing book (AIA 80)	wd	High Hatton Hall, Salop	*Ionides* 1999, 135–6, 337, 431 (repr)
58.	1765–1769	With frieze of scrolling foliage (designed by Thomas Farnolls Pritchard) (co-sculptor: Swift) Drawing(s): Pritchard drawing book (AIA 27)	wd	[Kinsham Court, common parlour]; Kinsham Court, Herefs, dining room (now part of an overmantel)	*Ionides* 1999, 110–1, 330, 377 (repr)
59.	1765–1769	With frieze of scrolling foliage (designed by Thomas Farnolls Pritchard) (co-sculptor: Van der Hagen and Swift) Drawing(s): Pritchard drawing book (AIA 38)	wd	Broseley Hall, Salop	*Ionides* 1999, 171, 332, 389 (repr)
60.	1765–1769	With head of Apollo and sunburst (designed by Thomas Farnolls Pritchard) (co-sculptor: Van der Hagen) Drawing(s): Pritchard drawing book (AIA 33)		[Condover Hall, Salop]; untraced	*Ionides* 1999, 331, 383 (repr)

61.	1765–1769	With Jacobean style details (designed by Thomas Farnolls Pritchard) (co-sculptor: Van der Hagen and Swift) Drawing(s): Pritchard drawing book (AIA 24)	wd	Benthall Hall, Salop, drawing room	*Ionides* 1999, 172, 330, 374 (repr)
62.	1765–1769	With lion's head and grapes, for the best parlour (designed by Thomas Farnolls Pritchard) (co-sculptor: Van der Hagen and Swift) Drawing(s): Pritchard drawing book (AIA 35)	wd	Kinsham Court, Herefs	*Ionides* 1999, 10, 111, 331, 385 (repr)
63.	1765–1769	With mask of Diana the huntress and dogs (designed by Thomas Farnolls Pritchard) (co-sculptor: Van der Hagen) Drawing(s): Pritchard drawing book (AIA 14)		[for Bartholomew Barnaby, of Brockhampton House, Herefs]; untraced	*Ionides* 1999, 99, 328, 364 (repr)
64.	1765–1769	With oak leaf moulding (designed by Thomas Farnolls Pritchard) (co-sculptor: Van der Hagen) Drawing(s): Pritchard drawing book (AIA 9)		[for Mr Powis, Gravel Hill]; untraced	*Ionides* 1999, 327, 359 (repr)
65.	1765–1769	With palmette and garlands of husks (designed by Thomas Farnolls Pritchard) (co-sculptor: Van der Hagen and Swift) Drawing(s): Pritchard drawing book (AIA 22)	wd	[Gaines, Worcs, Bed Chamber]; Unidentified house, Sussex	*Ionides* 1999, 105–6, 330, 372 (repr)
66.	1765–1769	With scallop shell and scrolling foliage (designed by Thomas Farnolls Pritchard) (co-sculptor: Van der Hagen) Drawing(s): Pritchard drawing book (AIA 16)		[for Mr Scot Draper, Grope Lane, Shrewsbury, Salop]; untraced	*Ionides* 1999, 329, 366 (repr)
67.	1765–1769	With scrolls and flowers in the frieze (designed by Thomas Farnolls Pritchard) (co-sculptor: Van der Hagen and Swift) Drawing(s): Pritchard drawing book (AIA 78)		[for Mr Good of Shrewsbury]; untraced	*Ionides* 1999, 23, 337, 427 (repr)
68.	1765–1769	With waterleaf coving and frond-like branches (designed by Thomas Farnolls Pritchard) (co-sculptor: Van der Hagen and Swift) Drawing(s): Pritchard drawing book (AIA 41)	wd	[for Mr Harley]; Kinsham Court, Herefs, dining room (now part of an overmantel)	*Ionides* 1999, 110–1, 332, 392 (repr)

Architectural Sculpture

69.	?1765	Two door friezes with lion's head masks and branches (designed by Thomas Farnolls Pritchard) (co-sculptor: Van der Hagen) Drawing(s): Pritchard drawing book (AIA 10)		[Croft Castle, 'Mr Johnes dressing room']; Croft Castle, Herefs, saloon (one missing)	*Ionides* 1999, 52, 93–4, 328, 360 (repr)
70.	?1765	Two door friezes with scrolling foliage (designed by Thomas Farnolls Pritchard) (co-sculptor: Van der Hagen) Drawing(s): Pritchard drawing book (AIA 10)		Croft Castle, Herefs, saloon (one missing)	*Ionides* 1999, 52, 93, 328, 360 (repr)
71.	1765–1769	'29 Stair Case Brackets in Oak' (designed by Thomas Farnolls Pritchard) (co-sculptor: Swift) Drawing(s): Pritchard drawing book (AIA 42)	wd	Hatton Grange, Salop	*Ionides* 1999, 332, 393 (repr)
72.	1765–1769	Gothic columns, eight (designed by Thomas Farnolls in Pritchard) (co-sculptor: Van der Hagen and Swift) Drawing(s): Pritchard drawing book (AIA 54)		Gaines, Worcs	*Ionides* 1999, 106–8, 334, 405 (repr)
73.	1765–1769	Pediment (designed by Thomas Farnolls Pritchard) (co-sculptor: Danders) Drawing(s): Pritchard drawing book (AIA 31)	s	Hatton Grange, Salop	*Ionides* 1999, 128–9, 331, 381 (repr)
74.	1777	Lions, two		Lion Hotel, Shrewsbury, Salop	Pevsner, *Salop*, 1958, 284; *Gunnis* 1968, 270; *Ionides* 1999, 56, 157 (repr)

75.	c1790	Door frames carved with acanthus and rosettes	St Chad, Shrewsbury, Salop	*Friedman* 2004, pl 26
76.	c1795	Sphinxes, two	[Hawkstone House, Salop, west entrance]; untraced	*Gents Mag*, 1812, i, 492; *Gunnis* 1968, 270
Miscellaneous				
77.	1768	'2 Frames for Shell pieces' (designed by Thomas Farnolls Pritchard) (co-sculptor: Van der Hagen and Swift) Drawing(s): Pritchard drawing book (AIA 28)	[for Rev Mr Fowler, of Atcham Rectory, Salop]; untraced	*Ionides* 1999, 330–1, 378 (repr)
78.	1765–1769	Frame for Lord Bath's Picture (designed by Thomas Farnolls Pritchard) (co-sculptor: Van der Hagen) Drawing(s): Pritchard drawing book (AIA 6)	[Red Lion Inn, Wolverhampton]; demol c1960	*Ionides* 1999, 327, 356 (repr)
79.	1765–1769	Glass frame (executed under the direction of Thomas Farnolls Pritchard) (co-sculptor: Van der Hagen and Swift)	[for Mr Walcot, of Bitterley Hall, Salop]; untraced	*Ionides* 1999, 337, 432
80.	1765–1769	Model for an iron 'Machine Grate' at Shipton Hall, cast by the Coalbrookdale Co (designed by Thomas Farnolls Pritchard) Drawing(s): Pritchard drawing book (AIA 15)	untraced	*Ionides* 1999, 122–3, 329, 365 (repr)
81.	1765–1769	Rococo glass frame (designed by Thomas Farnolls Pritchard) (co-sculptor: Van der Hagen) Drawing(s): Pritchard drawing book (AIA 11)	[for Mr Pritchard]; untraced	*Ionides* 1999, 328, 361 (repr)
82.	1765–1769	'Three frames in Burnished Gold for a Dessart Table' (designed by Thomas Farnolls Pritchard) (co-sculptor: Van der Hagen) Drawing(s): Pritchard drawing book (AIA 55)	[for Mr Lee, of Coton Hall, Salop (?)]; untraced	*Ionides* 1999, 334, 406 (repr)
83.	1765–1769	Two candlestick brackets and a mahogany shield for a bookcase (designed by Thomas Farnolls Pritchard) (co-sculptor: Van der Hagen) Drawing(s): Pritchard drawing book (AIA 15)	[for Mr Bather, of Mardol, Shrewsbury, Salop]; untraced	*Ionides* 1999, 329, 365 (repr)

NELSON, Robert, of Melsonby fl 1752–67

A local mason, he rebuilt the spire of Darlington church assisted by **Robert Corney** for £105 in 1752. In 1767 he contracted to rebuild Darlington bridge in local stone for £860.

Literary References: *Longstaffe* 1854, 39, 218

NELSON, Sefferin 1739–97

He was a leading wood-carver in his day, employed on several projects by Robert Adam and Henry Holland. Nelson was christened at St Martin-in-the-Fields, Westminster on 1 September 1739 and later ran his business from Marshall Street, Golden Square. A trade card at the Victoria and Albert Museum has a mirror frame carved with swags, lion masks and a crest, and describes him as carver and frame maker to 'their royal highnesses the Prince of Wales and the Duke of Cumberland' (*Beard and Gilbert* 1986, 641). He married Mary Benson at St Mary Putney on 5 April 1764. In 1791 Nelson was the senior churchwarden at St James, Piccadilly, and he was also a trustee of the Girl's Charity School of St James in Boyle Street, Westminster (Middlesex Land Register, 1810/5/760 in GPC). His will, which describes him as a 'carver of St James Westminster' was proved on 18 May 1797 (PROB 11/1291).

Literary References: *Beard* 1981, 273; *Beard and Gilbert* 1986, 640–1

Chimneypieces					
1.	c1772	Four friezes, carved and gilded (designed by Robert Adam)		Kenwood House, London, Chinese room	*Harris* 2001, 192, 195
Architectural Sculpture					
2.	1769	Carving, including seven circular frames, ornamented pilasters, a jib door and seven mahogany doors		[Lansdowne House, London]; untraced	*Harris* 2001, 121
3.	1772	Curtain cornices, with tazze finials (designed by Robert Adam)		Nostell Priory, W R Yorks	*Harris* 2001, 206, 336 n80 (repr)
4.	1773	Carved gothic stand for a font Payment(s): £31 2s		Ruabon, Denbighs	Wynnstay coll, NLW in GPC
5.	1773	Round pedestals and vases for sideboards	wd	Nostell Priory, W R Yorks	*Harris* 2001, 109
6.	1773	Two oval frames Payment(s): £200 with glass		[Kenwood House, London]; untraced	*Harris* 2001, 191
7.	1776	Carved and gilt mirror frames, girandoles on columns (designed by Robert Adam) Payment(s): £109 2s 6d	wd	[Derby House, London, great drawing room]; untraced	*Beard and Gilbert* 1986, 640; *Harris* 2001, 287–8, 363 n37

8.	1781	Capitals to columns and two pilasters	wd	[Croome Court, Worcs]; untraced	*Beard and Gilbert* 1986, 640
9.	nd	Term (designed by Robert Adam)	wd	[Kenwood House, London, great staircase]; untraced	*Beard and Gilbert* 1986, 640; Harris 2001, 188–9

Miscellaneous

10.	*c*1773	Table, with fluted legs and frieze, vases on ram's head pedestals, and a mahogany wine cooler		Kenwood House, London, hall	*Harris* 2001, 191
11.	1783	Unidentified carving		[Croome Court, Worcs]; untraced	*Beard* 1993, 93
12.	1782–1784	Carved and gilt candelabras for the music room (£109 3s), glass frames for the drawing room (£76 12s), two tables (£58 each), three curtain cornices (£67 10s), 300 feet of border (£45 7s), carved window draperies in the music room		[Chatsworth, Derbys]; untraced	*Beard and Gilbert* 1986, 640
13.	1786	Unidentified carving Payment(s): £85		[Aston Clinton, Bucks]; untraced	*Beard and Gilbert* 1986, 640
14.	1789	Unidentified carving		[Carlton House, London]; untraced	*Beard and Gilbert* 1986, 641
15.	1787–1791	Miscellaneous carving work, including carving and gilding a gothic organ case in the chapel, work on the Temple of Concord, and picture frames	wd	[Audley End, Essex]; untraced	*Beard and Gilbert* 1986, 641
16.	1791–1792	Carving and gilding tops of chimney and pier glasses in red drawing room, six cabriole backstools and other furniture Payment(s): £100 paid in 1791, £50 in 1792	wd	[Althorp, Northants]; untraced	*Beard and Gilbert* 1986, 641
17.	1793	Unidentified carving work Payment(s): £1,376 2s	wd	[Woburn Abbey, Beds]; untraced	*Beard and Gilbert* 1986, 641
18.	1794	Unidentified carving work Payment(s): £823 13s	wd	[Drury Lane Theatre, London]; untraced	*Beard and Gilbert* 1986, 641

NELSON, Thomas and James, of Carlisle fl *c*1824–62

They were brothers and joint owners of the Carlisle Marble Works, where they produced monumental tablets, chimneypieces and other goods. In 1847 they operated from 18 Lowther Street. One of their advertisements stated that 'experienced workmen could be sent to any part of the kingdom to fix work at a reasonable rate' (*Builder* 1848, 515). By 1858 the business had moved to Mill Street.

Thomas Nelson (1807–1890) married a Miss Craig at St John, Hampstead, on 22 December 1835. They had 11 children. He exhibited architectural drawings at the Carlisle Academy of Fine Arts in 1830 and 1833, and carried out work at Wynyard Park for the Marquess of Londonderry. He was mayor of Carlisle in 1851–2. His obituary appeared in the *Carlisle Journal* of 23 September 1890.

Literary References: *Gunnis* 1968, 271

Archival References: GPC; RG/JP, 6, 975v

Funerary Monuments

1.	†1824	John Canning	Ilmington, Warks	S	*Gunnis* 1968, 271
2.	†1824	Mary Anne Canning	Ilmington, Warks	S	*Gunnis* 1968, 271
3.	?1849	Rev Christopher Hodgson	Marholm, Isle of Ely	S	*Gunnis* 1968, 271
4.	†1857	John Dixon	St John the Evangelist, Houghton		RG/JP, 6, 975v.
5.	†1862	Thomas Elliot	Carlisle Cathedral		RG/JP, 6, 975v.
6.	nd	Clara Steel	St Kentigern, Grimsdale		RG/JP, 6, 975v.

Architectural Sculpture

7.	1857	Decorative details	[Lowther, Westmorland, mausoleum]; untraced		*Gunnis* 1968, 271

NESS, David 1786–1852

He was born in Edinburgh in 1786 and owned a marble cutting business in Leith Walk from 1821 until his death on 19 October 1852. His memorial in the New Calton burying ground records that he was married to Katherine White and that they had thee children, Robert who died aged two in 1825, Esther who died at Trinidad in the West Indies in 1844 and Margaret. He was survived by his wife who died on 4 May 1860 and his daughter Margaret who died unmarried on 16 December 1885.

Literary References: *Woodward* 1977, vol 1, pt 2, 171

Funerary Monuments

1.	1838	Andrew MacCartney		East Preston Street graveyard, Edinburgh		*Woodward* 1977, vol 1, pt 2, 171
2.	†1840	Isabella Ransay (†1809) and John Thomson of Duddington		Duddingston parish church, Edinburgh	S	Pevsner, *Edinburgh*, 1991, 555
3.	1848	R Dick		St Giles's Cathedral, Edinburgh		*Woodward* 1977, vol 1, pt 2, 171

Chimneypieces

4.	*c*1830	Several	m	Hendersyde Park, Roxburghshire, main rooms		RG/JP, 6, 977

NEWMAN fl *c*1783

His monument to Samuel Crisp has an epitaph by Charles Burney.

Funerary Monuments

1.	?1783	Samuel Crisp	Chessington, Surrey	GPC

NEWMAN, James, of Sidmouth fl *c*1793–1850

He was responsible for a number of tablets.

Funerary Monuments

1.	†1793	James (†1789) and Mary Lyde	St Nicholas with St Giles, Sidmouth, Devon		RG/JP, 6, 976v
2.	†1816	Charlotte Storer	St Nicholas with St Giles, Sidmouth, Devon		RG/JP, 6, 976v
3.	?1817	Thomas Hopkins	Ottery St Mary, Devon	S	*Gunnis* 1968, 271
4.	†1822	Emma Robins	Sidmouth Congregational church, Devon		RG/JP, 6, 976v
5.	†1824	Thomas Lyde	St Nicholas with St Giles, Sidmouth, Devon		RG/JP, 6, 976v
6.	†1827	John Taylor	St Nicholas with St Giles, Sidmouth, Devon		RG/JP, 6, 976v
7.	†1850	H E Slessor (†1834) and Major-General John Slessor	St Nicholas with St Giles, Sidmouth, Devon		RG/JP, 6, 977

NICHOLL, A, of London fl c1793

He is known only for one large wall-monument of good workmanship.

Funerary Monuments

1.	?1793	John Hopkins	Harwell, Berks	*Gunnis* 1968, 271

NICHOLL, John fl 1763

He was a 'Carver [of] John-Street, Oxford-Market' (*Mortimer* 1763, 20).

NICHOLL, of Grafton Street, London fl 1823

He was awarded a medal by the Society of Arts in 1823 (**1**).

Statues

1.	1823	Carved wood figure	[Soc of A, gold Isis medal]; untraced	RSA *Transactions*, 1823, vol 41, xxxix

NICHOLL, William Grinsell 1796–1871

William Grinsell Nicholl signed a number of funerary monuments and occasionally exhibited portraits and ideal works but he worked principally as an architectural sculptor. Nothing is known of his background and early life but he seems to have struggled to make a living until he found employment with the architect, Charles Robert Cockerell. In 1821 Nicholl carved decorative details, including capitals decorated with palm branches and doves, for his first major building, the Hanover Chapel, Regent Street, London (**27**). Cockerell must have been impressed by Nicholl's work for he continued to employ him until the mid-1850s. After the sculptor's death his friend Henry Baker wrote 'I suspect that his progress was little better than a struggle for dear life until one day Cockerell, R.A., found him out, happily for both, one requiring most important work to be done, and well done, under his own eye, and the other sighing at once for fame and money, apparently so distant' (*Builder*, 1871, 1002).

Nicholl entered the Royal Academy Schools in November 1822, giving his age as 26. In the same year he exhibited at the RA for the first time, showing a bust of Henry Sass (**21**). Later contributions included a model for a colossal statue of *Satan*, inspired by a passage from Milton's *Paradise Lost* (**17**). This work failed to impress the critics: Passavant commented 'The tame and feeble proportions of the model are little calculated to express the terrors of his Satanic Majesty' (*Passavant* 1836, 2, 285). Nicholl's submission to the 1844 Westminster Hall exhibition, a model for a statue of Captain Cook, was equally badly received (**19**). The *Literary Gazette* described it as 'a tame, crabbed looking person' (cited by *Gunnis* 1968, 271) and the sculptor was awarded no commissions for the new Palace of Westminster. He was also unsuccessful in the competition for the national monument to Admiral Nelson in 1838, to which he submitted models for a column and commemorative medals (**43**).

Nicholl apparently worked for the goldsmiths Rundle and Bridge, probably as a modeller, for Cockerell noted in his diary for May 1826 that his recommendation had helped Nicholl to obtain employment, for which he would be paid eight guineas per week 'whenever he likes' (*Cockerell Diary*, cited by *Watkin* 1974, 42). At about the same time he began to attract commissions for funerary monuments. In June 1827 Henry, 4th Duke of Newcastle visited the studio of 'Mr Nichols the Sculptor' where work on his father's monument, designed by Robert Smirke for St George's Chapel, Windsor, was in progress (*Fletcher* 2001, 342). The monument was never erected at Windsor but was almost certainly installed, as a monument to the 4th Duke, in the Clinton family mausoleum built by Smirke for the 5th Duke at Markham Clinton, Notts (**3**).

Nicholl was particularly successful however as an architectural sculptor, notably at the Fitzwilliam Museum in Cambridge, where he carved decorative details for the frieze and capitals in 1837 under the direction of the architect George Basevi (**30**). In 1838 he sculpted a relief of *The Muses* for the pediment to the designs of Sir Charles Eastlake (**34**) and in 1840 he carved the four stone lions guarding the entrance steps of the museum (**18**). In 1845 he was at work on the extensive programme of sculptural decoration for Cockerell's Taylorian Institute and University Galleries (now the Ashmolean Museum) at Oxford (**35**). His work there includes a sculpted pediment with the arms of the university supported by a pair of torch-bearing genii, set against vigorous scrolling foliage. The pediment is surmounted by a figure of *Apollo*. The principal front of the Taylorian Institution is decorated with statues representing Italy, France, Germany and Spain, and ornamental panels carved with griffins and coats of arms.

In his day Nicholl was probably best known as the sculptor of the pediment for St George's Hall, Liverpool (**36**). This was based on a drawing by Cockerell entitled *Idea for the Frontispiece of a Public Building in England* (RIBA OS 5/5) which had greatly impressed the Hall's architect, Harry Elmes. It was an extraordinarily elaborate work consisting of 18 figures, a leopard and four horses, most of them carved fully in the round. At the centre was a figure of *Britannia*, with personifications of commerce and the four quarters of the globe to her left and images representing agriculture, industry, the sciences and domesticity on her right. Nicholl was obliged to extend his studio, at 1 Grafton Street, Piccadilly, to accommodate the work. During the 1880s there was controversy over whether either Sir Charles Eastlake or **Alfred Stevens** had contributed to the design and the debate, which raged in the letters pages of the *Daily Post* and *The Builder*, has never been satisfactorily resolved. The pediment was executed in Caen stone, which unfortunately proved unable to withstand Liverpool's polluted atmosphere. Its rapid deterioration was becoming apparent by 1856, when Nicholl was called in to examine the stonework and recommended the application of a protective layer of oil. By 1950 the sculpture had become dangerous and it was dismantled. Nicholl was also responsible for a set of four recumbent lions and models for four pairs of lamp-holders in the form of male and female tritons which are still outside the building (**20, 38**).

He died at his home, 2 Bell Terrace, Churchfield Road, Acton, on 8 December 1871, leaving property valued at under £200. Later that month Henry Baker wrote to the *Builder* that 'Too much praise cannot be given to Cockerell for selecting so able an assistant' and asking 'but who will mete out the praise to Nicholl for his suggestions, modellings and finished sculpture?' (*Builder*, 1871, 1002).

EH

Literary References: *Builder* 1846, 505; *Eastlake* 1870, 160; *Builder*, 1871, 1002; *Hutchison* 1960–2, 175; *Gunnis* 1968, 271–2; *Physick* 1969, 181; *Watkin* 1974, *passim*; *Penny* 1977 (1), 13; *Read* 1982, 15, 281, 220; *Yarrington* 1988, 357; *Penny* 1992, xvii–xxv; *Cavanagh* 1997, 305–8, 334

Will: PPR, 25 April 1872, fo 264

Funerary Monuments

1.	†1825	Bishop Jacob Mountain		Quebec Cathedral		GPC
2.	?1825	Sir John Hippisley		Temple Church, London	S	*Gunnis* 1968, 272
3.	c1827	Henry, 4th Duke of Newcastle (†1851) (designed by Robert Smirke)		Markham Clinton (Clinton Mausoleum), Notts		*Fletcher* 2001, 342 (repr)
4.	†1827	Jacob Theophilus Mountain		St Mary, Hemel Hempstead, Herts	S	
5.	†1827	Joseph (†1827) and Elizabeth (†1827) Planta		St George, Bloomsbury, London	S	
6.	?1829	John Turner		Cold Overton, Leics	S	*Gunnis* 1968, 272
7.	?1829	Robert Bourne		Worcester College, Oxford, library stairs		GPC
8.	?1832	Sir George Don (designed by George Basevi)		Garrison church, Gibraltar	S	*Gunnis* 1968, 272
9.	†1834	Robert Bridge (designed by C R Cockerell)		Piddletrenthide, Dorset		Pevsner, *Dorset*, 1972, 314; *Watkin* 1974, 245
10.	?1835	Joseph Bonsor		Great Bookham, Surrey	S	*Gunnis* 1968, 272
11.	†1837	Elizabeth Morley		St Mary, Walthamstow, Essex	S	Pevsner, *Essex*, 1965, 407
12.	?1837	Richard Stevenson		Trinity College, Cambridge, chapel	S	*Gunnis* 1968, 272
13.	?1841	Frederick Farquharson		Langton Long Blandford, Dorset		GPC
14.	†1853	Henry (†1821) and Mary Wootton		Minster-in-Thanet, Kent	S	*Gunnis* 1968, 272
15.	?1862	Rev J Murray		St Andrew, Well Street, London	S	*Gunnis* 1968, 272

Statues

16.	1830	Hercules Agonistes		[Exhib RA, London, 1169]; untraced		*Graves* V, 1905–6, 364
17.	1831	Satan, model		[Exhib RA, London, 1194]; untraced		*Library of Fine Arts* 1, 1831, 430; *Passavant* 2, 1836, 284–5; *Graves* V, 1905–6, 364
18.	1839	Lions, four		Fitzwilliam, Cambridge, foot of staircase		*Gunnis* 1968, 271
19.	1844	Captain Cook, model		[Exhib Westminster Hall, London, 90]; untraced		*AU*, 1844, 214
20.	1855	Four recumbent lions (designed by C R Cockerell) Payment(s): £1,820 17s 11d	s	St George's Plateau, Liverpool, Lancs		*Cavanagh* 1997, 90–1 (repr)

Busts

21.	1822	Henry Sass		[Exhib RA, London, 1012]; untraced		*Graves* V, 1905–6, 364; *Johnson* 1975, 341
22.	1827	Archdeacon Law		St Margaret, Rochester, Kent		*Gunnis* 1968, 272
23.	c1827	Philip Rundell	m	[Drapers' Hall, London]; VAM A.1-1995	S	*Bilbey* 2002, 344 (repr)
24.	†1829	Robert Brown		Worcester College, Oxford, outside library		RG/JP, 6, 977v.
25.	nd	Unidentified man		Mrs Baidoun, 53 Lonsdale Road, Oxford	S	NP/RG

Chimneypieces

26.	c1845	Reading room (marble parts only)		Taylorian Institute, Oxford		*Penny* 1992, xxiv (repr)

Architectural Sculpture

27.	1821	Decorative carving (designed by C R Cockerell)		Hanover Chapel, Regent Street, London		*Watkin* 1974, 42, 144 (repr 27); *Penny* 1992, xx
28.	c1828	Carved stonework Payment(s): £80		Customs House, City of London, exterior		Pevsner, *London: City*, 1997, 295
29.	1832–1833	Two figures flanking entrance Payment(s): £16 10s		[Truesdale's Hospital, Stamford, Lincs]; untraced		RG/JP, 6, 977v.
30.	1837	Capitals, frieze and decorative details (designed by George Basevi) Model(s): exhib RA, London, 1840, 910		Fitzwilliam, Cambridge		*Graves* V, 1905–6, 364; *Penny* 1992, xx
31.	c1838	Reliefs (designed by Sir Robert Smirke)		Oxford and Cambridge Club, Westminster, London		Pevsner, *London: Westminster*, 1973, 615
32.	1837–1838	'Westminster', statue (designed by C R Cockerell)		London and Westminster Bank, 41 Lothbury, City of London		*Watkin* 1974, 223
33.	1840	Model for proposed new Royal Exchange building, sculptural parts (designed by C R Cockerell)		Destroyed		*Watkin* 1974, 210
34.	1837–1840	The Muses, relief (designed by Charles Eastlake)		Fitzwilliam, Cambridge, pediment		*Read* 1982, 14–5, 218; *Penny* 1992, xx
35.	c1845	Pediment, statues, relief panels and architectural ornament (designed by C R Cockerell)		Ashmolean, Oxford, exterior		*Watkin* 1974, 200, 202, 204, (repr 107–114); *Penny* 1992, xvii–xxv (repr)
36.	1845–1854	Britannia with Commerce and the Arts (designed by C R Cockerell)	s	[St George's Hall, Liverpool, Lancs, pediment]; dismantled c1950		*Watkin* 1974, 42, 238 *Read* 1982, 220; *Cavanagh* 1997, 305–8 (repr)

37.	1855	Decorative carving (designed by C R Cockerell and Alfred Stevens)		Liverpool and London Insurance Office, Dale Road, Liverpool, Lancs	*Watkin* 1974, 231 (repr 143, 145)
38.	c1855	Triton lamp bearers, four pairs (designed by C R Cockerell)	s	St George's Hall, Liverpool, Lancs	*Cavanagh* 1997, 254–5 (repr)
39.	1861	A nymph, part of a group for a fountain		[Exhib RA, London, 1059]; untraced	*Graves* V, 1905–6, 365
40.	1866	Statues of Wisdom, Fidelity, Charity and Unity and architectural ornaments		Freemasons' Hall, Longacre, London	*ILN* 1866, 305
Miscellaneous					
41.	1825	Portrait of an Italian greyhound, the property of T B Lennard MP		[Exhib Soc of BA, London, 363]; untraced	*Johnson* 1975, 341
42.	1826	An eagle		[Exhib RA, London, 1099]; untraced	*Graves* V, 1905–6, 364
43.	1838	Admiral Lord Nelson, national monument, models only (monument executed by E H Baily and William Railton)		Untraced	*Yarrington* 1988, 357
44.	1840	Apollo		[Exhib RA, London, 1224]; untraced	*Graves* V, 1905–6, 365
45.	1861	'Ideal head of Australia seated on the Platycerium Grande, a plant indigenous to the tropical coast of New South Wales'		[Exhib RA, London, 1093]; untraced	*Graves* V, 1905–6, 365

NICHOLLS, Thomas, of Stamford fl 1771

In 1771 he was paid about £10 as a 'stonecarver' at Burghley House, Stamford (Day Books, Exeter Estate Office).

Archival References: JP, Misc Corr

NICHOLSON, George, of Durham 1726–1804

Nicholson was a Durham mason with premises in Bow Lane. He built one of the local bridges and was responsible for a good deal of controversial stone carving on Durham Cathedral from 1780. Ogle, a local diarist, wrote of Nicholson that 'to create a job for himself he made Dr Sharp and the Dean and Prebends believe he could greatly add to the beauty of the Church by new chiselling it over on the outside, and that he could add to the beauty of the ancient window by means of his own genius. This Nicholson is now going on with what he calls repairs in the year 1780.' Nicholson replaced ancient tracery in the cloisters with what Boyle calls his 'own poor and meaningless work' (2). He also carved an image of the Dun Cow for the exterior (3) (which Boyle says looks more like a Durham shorthorn) and figures of his own choice to replace ones said to represent Friars Fossor and Castell over the great window of the north transept (1) (*Boyle* 1892, 207, 209). At the time of his death in December 1804 he was sword-bearer to the Provincial Grand Lodge of Freemasons of County Durham.

Literary References: *Univ Mag* 1804, 2, 573; *Gunnis* 1968, 272

Statues				
1.	nd	Bishop Pudsey and a seated prior	Durham Cathedral, above great window of north transept	*Boyle* 1892, 209; *Gunnis* 1968, 272
Architectural Sculpture				
2.	1799	Carved work	Durham Cathedral, cloisters	*Boyle* 1892, 309
3.	1799	The Dun Cow	Durham Cathedral	*Boyle* 1892, 209; *Gunnis* 1968, 272

NICHOLSON, John fl c1839

He signs an Hellenic wall-monument with **Wood of Newark** (1).

Funerary Monuments					
1.	†1839	Hon Lady Bromley (co-sculptor: Wood, of Newark)	East Stoke, Notts	S	Pevsner, *Notts*, 1979, 117

NICHOLSON, Thomas Henry –1870

A modeller, draughtsman on wood, illustrator and oil painter, he distinguished himself as a young man with his models of horses, and when **William Behnes** needed the services of an artist who had experience of modelling animals for his group of *Lady Godiva*, Nicholson was recommended to him. The association was a success. The *Art Journal* noted that **Alfred, Count D'Orsay** visited Behnes's studio and was so struck by the modelling of the horse in the group that he engaged Nicholson to work for him on a number of statuettes. These included figures of the Duke of Wellington and the Marquis of Anglesey which were executed and cast in bronze and were 'among the most beautiful of their class' (*AJ* 1870, 204). Nicholson was later to claim that he alone was responsible for the models and that when visitors came to the studio he was hustled out of the room. He also complained that when D'Orsay did attempt to contribute to the modelling process, Nicholson would lose up to a week of his time rectifying the Count's mistakes.

Whilst working for D'Orsay, Nicholson exhibited his sketches of horses and historical subjects at the Royal Academy. He is probably to be identified with the 'H Nicholson' who showed a figure of Charles I in 1842. The *Art Union* remarked that 'this small figure is the result of much research into the costume of the cavalier period. It is "toileted" with exceeding care, and reminds us very much of the small portrait of Charles in the Louvre, painted by "that Antonio Vandyke" ' (1).

One of the most successful works modelled by Nicholson for D'Orsay was an equestrian statuette of Napoleon I. Prince Louis Napoleon, then an exile in London, and a close friend of the Count, would go to Gore House to give advice and make suggestions on details, for instance, of uniforms. Later, as Emperor of the French, he remembered Nicholson and asked him to come to Paris to work for him. The offer was declined, since after the Gore House sale of 1849 and D'Orsay's flight to France, Nicholson abandoned modelling.

He died on 8 March 1870 at Portland, Hants, where for some years he had produced drawings on wood, oil paintings and book illustrations. He illustrated Defoe's *Robinson Crusoe*, *The Six Sisters of the Valley* by W J B Moore and the *Complete Works of Shakespeare*. His obituary records that 'his works achieved a very extensive popularity, but without gaining for him the reputation he so richly merited. He was known only to a limited circle of artists and literary men, and so reserved were his habits of life that he seemed to shrink from public recognition. His merits lay in rich conception and power of hand generally, but he distinguished himself particularly in drawing and modelling horses, and for a long series of years certain of the illustrated journals were enriched by his works. His reserve and retired habits militated against the acquisition of that reputation which he ought to have enjoyed' (*AJ* 1870, 204). His will, proved on 6 April 1870, recorded effects valued at under £2000.

Literary References: *Gunnis* 1968, 272

Will: PPR, will, fol 284

Statues

1.	1842	King Charles I, sketch	[Exhib RA, London, 1347]; untraced	*AU*, 1842, 128–9; *Graves* V, 1905–6, 367
2.	1851	Lady Godiva, model of horse only (the remainder by William Behnes)	[Gt Exhib]; untraced	*AJ* 1870, 204; *Gunnis* 1968, 272

Miscellaneous

3.	1838	A cavalier	[Exhib RA, London, 1355]; untraced	*Graves* V, 1905–6, 367
4.	1838	The courier of St Petersburgh	[Exhib RA, London, 1340]; untraced	*Graves* V, 1905–6, 367
5.	1843	The death of William Rufus	[Exhib RA, London, 1470]; untraced	*Graves* V, 1905–6, 367

NICOLI, Frederico fl 1817–19

His workshop was in Mount Street, next door to that of **Sir Richard Westmacott RA**. He exhibited at the Royal Academy, showing in 1818 a bust of the Princess Charlotte modelled at Claremont (**2**). Gunnis described the bust of Marshal Blucher (**1**) as 'a very fine work' (*Gunnis* 1968, 273).

Literary References: *Graves* V, 1905–6, 369

Busts

1.	1817	Marshal Blücher Payment(s): £150	m	Windsor Castle, RCIN 31634	SD	TNA, L.C.9/367 f12; *Graves* V, 1905–6, 369; *Gunnis* 1968, 273; *Clifford* 1992, 56
2.	1818	Princess Charlotte		[Exhib RA, London, 1086]; untraced		*Graves* V, 1905–6, 369; *Gunnis* 1968, 273
3.	1819	Prince Leopold	m	[Exhib RA, London, 1185]; untraced		*Graves* V, 1905–6, 369; *Gunnis* 1968, 273
4.	1819	Princess Charlotte		[Exhib RA, London, 1233]; untraced		*Graves* V, 1905–6, 369
5.	nd	Charles James Fox	m	NMM, Greenwich, SCU0019	S	*Gunnis* 1968, 273

NIMMO, Claude fl 1824

He was probably a stone-carver local to Lancaster.

Statues

1.	1824	John of Gaunt	s	Lancaster Castle, above main gateway	GPC

NINI, Jean-Baptiste

For further information the reader is referred to *Pyke* 1973, 98 and *Pyke* 1981, 30.

NIXON, James Thomas 1826–

He was baptised on 17 August 1826, one of at least eight children born to James Henry Nixon (1802–1857) and his wife Frances. His father was an esteemed painter on glass, and his uncle was **Samuel Nixon**. He is listed in the 1851 census as a sculptor, living with his family at 7 Chalcott Villas, Hampstead.

Archival References: IGI; VAM inf file (compiled by Judith Pyle)

Architectural Sculpture

1.	c1845	Capitals of columns, corbels of foliage, a reredos representing the two disciples at Emmaus	St Barnabas, Homerton, London	*Godwin* 1850, 24

NIXON, Richard fl 1730–38

From 1730–38 he was the principal mason at Lamport Hall, Northants.

Chimneypieces

1.	1730–1738	Description unavailable	[Lamport Hall, Northants, front hall]; untraced	Isham Archives in *Gunnis* 1968, 273

Miscellaneous

2.	1730–1738	'dial for a pedestal'	Lamport Hall, Northants	Isham Archives in *Gunnis* 1968, 273

NIXON, Samuel 1803–54

Born in London on 30 June 1804, the seventh child of Thomas and Sarah Nixon, he was baptised at St Mary-at-Hill on 29 July. His elder brother was James Henry Nixon (1802–1857), a painter on glass, and he was the uncle of **James Thomas Nixon**. He does not appear to have studied at the Royal Academy and no details have been discovered about his training. In 1826 he exhibited at the RA (**25**), giving his address as 'The Shepherd,' 21 Little Eastcheap. He remained at this address for at least five years. During this period he exhibited a handful of literary and religious subjects (**25–28**), but must also have executed a number of portraits since in 1836 the German visitor, J G Passavant, listed Nixon amongst the British sculptors who were distinguished in portrait sculpture. The *Art Journal* later opined that Nixon's portraits were 'highly meritorious productions, if not of the most elevated character' (*AJ* 1854, 280).

In 1838 he carved the statue of Dr Richard Valpy, headmaster of Reading School, to a design by the architect Edward Charles Hakewill (**5**). Its erection was enthusiastically reported in the *Reading Mercury* on 15 December 1838. The journal liked the choice of Roche Abbey stone as a material that perfectly harmonised with its context and felt the design displayed 'sound judgement and refined taste'. Nixon's work was apparently 'highly approved by those who selected him' (GPC). Valpy is shown standing with his right hand raised in a supposedly oratorical gesture though the *Architectural Magazine* reported that this, in fact, stemmed from Valpy's habit of tracing his dead wife's initials in the air with his forefinger.

By 1838 Nixon had moved to 2 Whitehart Court, off Bishopsgate Street, where he kept premises for the remainder of his short career. In 1839 he was employed by the architect Philip Hardwick RA to design and execute statues representing the seasons for Goldsmiths' Hall (**12**). *Summer* was interpreted as a boy with a sheep and a festoon, the flowers apparently 'equal to anything of the kind we have seen in sculpture' (*AU* 1842, 128), and *Winter* as a girl shielding herself against a fierce wind, her figure outlined by tightly stretched drapery. When *Winter* was exhibited at the RA, the *Art Union*'s critic viewed the commission as 'the dawning of a new and brighter day for an art that has been permitted to languish in this country' (*AU* 1840, 2, 93–4). The *Art Journal* later recorded that Nixon was responsible for exterior carving on the hall, though the archives of the Goldsmiths' Company record detailed payments for this work to **Thomas Piper II** and his son.

In 1844 Nixon was selected to execute the colossal standing figure of William IV for the City of London (**14**). The statue's erection was celebrated with a dinner at the nearby Adelaide Tavern, where Nixon ate with 'a numerous assembly of the influential gentlemen of the wards of Bridge and Candlewick'. The statue, carved from twenty tons of Scottish granite, depicts the barrel-chested 'Sailor King' in a *contrapposto* pose, with a long cape falling in broad folds. The *Builder*'s reception was lukewarm: 'We are sorry that we cannot coincide in the flattering opinions of the statue which have been expressed. It is, to us coarse and clumsy and not likely to advance the reputation of the sculptor' (*Builder* 1845, 26). The *Art Journal* and *The Times* both wrote approvingly of the statue and the *Gentleman's Magazine* called it 'a striking and imposing object. . . a masterpiece of its kind' and 'one of the chief ornaments of the City of London.' It was, they wrote, 'admired by all who are capable of appreciating artistic genius' (*GM*, 1854, 42, 406).

Despite the acclaim, the work did not prove profitable. The tender was for £2,200, which did not cover Nixon's materials and expenses. It was recorded in the sculptor's obituary that the granite was 'a material difficult to work and the expenses attending the conscientious execution of the contract severely crippled the artist.' Nixon never recovered from the financial losses suffered through this commission (*GM* 1854, 2, 406). The statue itself was moved to Greenwich when an underpass was built in 1935 and the junction could no longer support its weight.

Nixon carved a number of varied sepulchral monuments. He produced memorials with busts to the clerics William Rodber and George Avery Hatch (**8, 4**). Several others have classical details: the monument to George Wynch has slender urns in the Greek style (**3**), the tablet to the Gillespie family takes the form of a stele with a high relief of three children in classical shifts, two of them crowning the third with laurels (**2**) and the monument to Dean Andrews (**11**) had a large weeping willow carved in marble. The *Art Journal* considered the work 'admirably executed' but suggested that a statue of the deceased could have been had for the same price, and questioned whether Nixon had in this case and others, sacrificed some of his artistic legacy to the whims of his clients. Nixon apparently maintained the view that 'a man had no right, artist though he might be, to enforce his own views to the subversion of those entertained by his patron' (*AJ* 1854, 280). The sculptor also executed monuments for export to Canada, though no specimens have been identified with certainty.

His later works included ornaments for the House of Lords (**20**), which the *Art Union* felt to give 'indubitable evidence of that which so many others lack, the mind and hand of AN ARTIST' (*AU* 1844, 111). His standing statue of John Carpenter, founder of the City of London School for Poor Scholars in 1442, was exhibited at Westminster Hall in 1844 (**13**). It depicts the balding founder, his beard trimmed below his chin, holding a bound book and quill. The sculptor has attempted period detail with an ornamented buckle and a purse hanging from the belt. Nixon's commissions for educational institutions continued with a relief in Darley Dale stone for the Ragged School in Lambeth, an institution founded by Henry Beaufoy to teach destitute children (**21**). He appears once again to have made his work more challenging by his choice of material: he added £91 16s to his bill of 11 November 1850 because 'in consequence of the extreme hardness and obdurate nature of the stone' he had been compelled 'to employ extra labour for which I am indebted to Messrs Lee' (Lambeth Archives, IV/71/22).

In the Shoreditch census of 1851, Nixon was listed at 1 Manley Place, Kennington Common. He died there after a severe illness on 2 August 1854, aged only fifty. In his will, proved on 19 October 1850, he left all his 'household furniture and all real and personal estate' to his wife, Maria (PROB 11/2199/135).

The *Art Journal*'s obituary concluded that 'Mr Nixon was a liberal master to those he employed, and held pecuniary profit in small estimation in comparison with the credit which he might derive from the excellence of his productions' (*AJ* 1854, 280). The *Gentlemans' Magazine* listed Nixon's finest productions, bemoaning the time he had spent on mere church monuments, and finding regret 'that a mind which could conceive and a hand which could execute such beautiful personifications, should have been so little employed. The reason is no doubt partly to be sought in the retiring manners and unselfish character which usually accompany true genius. These characteristics Mr Nixon possessed in an eminent degree' (*GM* 1854, 42, 405–6).

MGS

Literary References: *Passavant* 1836, 2, 284; *AJ* 1854, 280; *GM* 1854, 42, 405–6; *Graves* 1875, 403; *DNB*; *Graves* III, 1905–6, 374; *Gunnis* 1968, 273; *Read* 1982, 95; *Blackwood* 1989, 54; *ODNB* (Terry Cavanagh)

Archival References: Nixon/Brayley 1845; IGI; VAM information file (compiled by Judith Pyle); GPC

Additional MS Sources: Note describing model, letter describing statue 6.4.1841, and letter to Henry Howard 28.7.1841: Edinburgh City Library BRS/qwN 45; BRS/qwN 45/Box; BRS/qwN 45/Box

Funerary Monuments

1.	?1830	Philip Lucas		St John, Hackney, London	S	*Gunnis* 1968, 273
2.	†1833	Grace, Mary (both †1832) and Catherine Gillespie		St John's Wood Chapel, Marylebone, London	S	Pevsner, *London: N W*, 1991, 601
3.	†1836	George Wynch		Pett, Sussex	S	Pevsner, *Sussex*, 1965, 579
4.	†1837	Rev George Avery Hatch		[St Matthew, Friday St, City of London]; St Vedast alias Foster, City of London		Pevsner, *London: City*, 1997, 266
5.	1838	Dr Richard Valpy (†1836) (designed by E C Hakewill)	s	St Laurence, Reading, Berks		*Architectural Magazine*, 1838, 621; Pevsner, *Berks*, 1966, 200
6.	†1840	John Marshall		St Leonard, Shoreditch, City of London	S	Pevsner, *London: N*, 1998, 518
7.	?1843	Rev William Parker		St Ethelburga, Bishopsgate, City of London		*Gunnis* 1968, 273

No.	Date	Work		Location		References
8.	†1843	Rev William Rodber		St Mary-at-Hill, City of London		Pevsner, *London: City*, 1997, 246
9.	†1844	Thomas Reynolds		Boxmoor, Herts	S	
10.	†1847	Samuel Whiteway		Kingsteignton, Devon	S	Pevsner, *Devon*, 1989, 523
11.	nd	Dean Andrews		[Great Bookham, Surrey]; untraced		*AJ*, 1854, 280
Statues						
12.	1839–1843	Four statues representing the seasons Payment(s): £630	m	Goldsmiths' Hall, City of London, grand staircase		Goldsmiths Co, Committee Book 19, 1837–1846, 98–99, 154, 325; *AU* 1839, 1, 88; *AU* 1840, 2, 93–4; *GM* 1854, 42, 406; *Graves* III, 1905–6, 375; Pevsner, *London: City*, 1997, 390
13.	1843–1844	John Carpenter, town clerk and founder of the City of London School Payment(s): £150	s	[Old City of London School for Boys]; CL Coll, City of London School, acc 113		*GM*, vol 42, 1854, 405–6; *Knight* 1986, 344 (repr); *Ward-Jackson* 2002, 209–11
14.	1844	King William IV Payment(s): £2,200 (tender)		[King William Street, City of London (until 1935)]; Greenwich, London, King William's walk	S	*Builder* 1845, 26; *GM*, vol 42, 1854, 405–6; *Graves* III, 1905–6, 375; *Read* 1982, 95; *Blackwood* 1989, 54–5 (repr); *Bold* 2000 (2), 32–3 (repr)
15.	1844	The British warrior		[Exhib Westminster Hall, London]; untraced		*Lit Gaz* 1844, 483; *Gunnis* 1968, 273
16.	1845	Sir John Crosby		[Crosby Hall, Bishopsgate, London]; untraced		*DNB*; *Gunnis* 1968, 273
17.	1846	Marian, daughter of Thomas Powell		[Exhib RA, London, 1475]; untraced		*Graves* III, 1905–6, 375
Busts						
18.	1845	F Powell, model to be executed in marble		[Exhib RA, London, 1405]; untraced		*Graves* III, 1905–6, 375
19.	1845	The infant son of Thomas Cooke, model to be executed in marble		[Exhib RA, London, 1429]; untraced		*Graves* III, 1905–6, 375
Architectural Sculpture						
20.	1844	Carved doors		[House of Lords, London]; untraced		*AU* 1844, 111
21.	1849–1850	The Beaufoy arms, with foliage and flowers, and a relief of Education (schoolteacher with two children) Payment(s): £182 7s, and £91 16s additional labour costs	s	Beaufoy Institute, Black Prince Road, Lambeth (now Beaconsfield Art Gall)	S	Lambeth Archives, IV/21/22, 37; *ILN*, 8 March 1851, 192–3 (repr); *Cavanagh* forthcoming 2007 (Lambeth: Brixton)
22.	nd	The Shakespeare Vase (modelled for J M Blashfield)		Untraced		*Gunnis* 1968, 273
Reliefs						
23.	1846	A clergyman, medallion bust	m	[Exhib RA, London, 1457]; untraced		*Graves* III, 1905–6, 375
24.	nd	John Milton, medallion bust	m	Sotheby Olympia, 25 April 2002; private coll	S	C Lib (repr)
Miscellaneous						
25.	1826	The shepherd		[Exhib RA, London, 1030]; untraced		*Graves* III, 1905–6, 374
26.	1828	Reconciliation of Adam and Eve after the Fall, from Milton's *Paradise Lost*, book 10		[Exhib RA, London, 1208]; untraced		*Graves* III, 1905–6, 374
27.	1830	The birth of Venus, from Hesiod		[Exhib RA, London, 1185 Exhib BI, London, 1831, 551]; untraced		*Graves* 1875, 403; *Graves* III, 1905–6, 374
28.	1831	The infant Moses	m	[Exhib RA, London, 1226 Exhib BI, London, 591]; untraced		*Graves* 1875, 403; *Graves* III, 1905–6, 374
29.	1844	W D Saull, model to be executed in marble	p	[Exhib RA, London, 1391]; untraced		*Graves* III, 1905–6, 375; *AU* 1844, 171

NIXON & SONS fl *c*1840

They executed a tablet sent to Nova Scotia (1). It is possible that this work is by **Samuel Nixon**, who reportedly executed work for export to Canada. There is, however, no record of Samuel Nixon taking a son into partnership.

Literary References: *GM* 1854, 42, 405–6

No.	Date	Work	Location		References
Funerary Monuments					
1.	†1840	William Almon	Halifax Cathedral, Nova Scotia	S	GPC

NIXSON (or NIXON), Paul, of Carlisle 1768–1850

Nixson was the son of William Nixon, a stonemason of Cumdivock, Dalston, and his wife Mary, née Alcock, and was baptised at Dalston on 7 March 1768 (Dalston parish registers). He was the younger brother of the mason and bridge-master William Nixon (1760–1824). Although baptised Nixon he signed his name Nixson on drawings and documents. He married Jane Brisco, also of Cumdivock, on 7 February 1791, living in the family burgage plot in Castle Street, Carlisle (Trans CWAAS, NS, lxxxviii, 141, n58). His first wife appears to have died in childbirth, and was buried in Dalston on 3 December 1792 (Dalston parish registers). He married as his second wife Ann Slack at St Mary, Carlisle on 14 June 1795 and they had seven daughters, five of whom survived (St Mary's, typescript, Cumbria RO). He leased Glencrake quarry, Wetheral on 27 November 1799 (CRO D/MBS/Box 59) and was described as a marble cutter and stone mason in Jollie's *Directory*.

It was perhaps he, rather than his brother William, identified as 'Mr Nixon of Carlisle' who did work at Hutton-in-the-Forest and Greystoke Castle, both in Cumberland. His name appears in the accounts for Lowther Castle, rebuilt by the architect Robert Smirke, who employed him extensively before 1821, and he drew plans and elevations for alterations to the county gaol in Carlisle. He cut a new doorway and windows for the nave of Carlisle Cathedral, 1813–14, which also included interior alterations (St Mary's, contract, Cumbria RO). Payments were made to him for work on the new court houses and county gaol (CRO QS records). His design for St Cuthbert's Vicarage, Botchergate, Carlisle is dated 1814 (CRO DRC 12/18). Several houses in and around Carlisle have been attributed to him.

In 1822 Nixson designed and built his own marble works in Finkle Street, Carlisle, where he also housed the Carlisle Academy of Fine Art, founded that year. The secretary of the Academy was his employee, **David Dunbar I**. The *Carlisle Patriot* praised Nixson's public spirit in June 1823, saying 'his effort has nothing of self in it – he has no eye to remuneration – his only desire is to embellish the town and promote useful improvement' (quoted in *Perriam* 1975, 300).

He created chimneypieces, including several made in 1825 for the Council House, Bristol, and provided monuments for churches in Cumberland. The memorial to Hugh Patrickson in Carlisle has a relief profile portrait with military trophies (**3**), and elsewhere he utilises the urn motif (**1, 4**).

By 1829 Nixson had a flourishing and diverse business, which he ran in partnership with William Smith Denton, who had married his daughter Sarah Nixson in January 1824 (*Carlisle Journal*, 24 Jan 1824). In addition to his marble works in Carlisle, he had premises in Leith Walk, Edinburgh and Osnaburgh Place, New Road, London. He owned the Stone House Marble Works near Sedburgh in the Valley of Dent, and imported white Carrara marble from Italy. In 1832 he employed more than 350 men in road construction work.

Nonetheless in 1837 the firm went bankrupt and the Finkle Street Marble Works was taken over by the chief foreman, **John Kirkbride**. The connection with the Carlisle Academy ceased, although during the institution's brief life Nixson's premises housed a large permanent collection of sculpture as well as holding distinguished temporary exhibitions. Parson and White's Cumberland *Directory* of 1829 gives a detailed description of the interior which contained works by **Joseph Gott** and others as well as numerous casts after antique and modern works.

Nixson moved to Dent in retirement. His death, at the age of 82, was recorded in the *Cumberland Pacquet* on 15 January 1850. He is commemorated on the tablet to his daughter, Anne Blackmore, at Cowgill in the West Riding of Yorkshire. The tablet may have been by **George Nelson**, who is also commemorated on the work. A portrait survives of Nixson, depicting him as an architect with dividers and plans. A list of his architectural and building works can be found in *Colvin*.

Denis Perriam and MGS

Literary References: Jollie, *Carlisle Directory*, 1811, xvii; *Parson and White* 1829, 146, 160, 166; *Gunnis* 1968, 273; *Perriam* 1975, 300–5; RG/JP, 6, 982, 983v; *Taylor* 1989, 92–7; *Perriam* 1992, 51; *Colvin* 1995, 707–8

Archival References: Cumbria RO D/Lons/Lowther Castle Accts; Cumbria RO DX/1357 (Carlisle County Gaol); IGI; Sir Robert Smirke/New Church Commission

Portrait of the Sculptor: Private coll, *Colvin* 1995, 707

Funerary Monuments

1.	†1797	William Giles (†1797) and wife (†1814)		St Cuthbert, Carlisle, Cumberland	Pevsner, *Cumberland & Westmorland*, 1967, 96
2.	†1814	Walter Vane		Bassenthwaite, Cumberland	Pevsner, *Cumberland & Westmorland*, 1967, 64
3.	†1821	Captain Hugh Patrickson		St Michael, Carlisle, Cumberland	Pevsner, *Cumberland & Westmorland*, 1967, 96
4.	1823	Unidentified subject		Aspatria, Cumberland	Pevsner, *Cumberland & Westmorland*, 1967, 63

Chimneypieces

5.	1825	Several Payment(s): £130 10s	m	Old Council House, Bristol	*Gunnis* 1968, 273 citing Bristol City Archives

NOAKES, of London fl *c*1809–56

He was in partnership with **Edward Pearce of London**. 'Like the majority of the New Road statuaries, their work is of little interest and the designs of their tablets uninspiring' (*Gunnis* 1968, 273–4). Their monumental designs include the white marble sarcophagus surmounted by an Adam-style urn to Sarah Heusch (**5**).

Funerary Monuments

1.	?1809	Robert Usherwood (co-sculptor: Edward Pearce, of London)	Whitby, N R Yorks		*Gunnis* 1968, 273
2.	?1813	John Pidcock and family (†1791–1813) (co-sculptor: Edward Pearce, of London)	St Michael, Brierley Hill, Staffs		GPC
3.	?1814	Sarah Ridehalgh (co-sculptor: Edward Pearce, of London)	Eccles, Cheshire		*Gunnis* 1968, 274
4.	?1816	Mrs Falconbridge (co-sculptor: Edward Pearce, of London)	St James, Garlickhithe, City of London		*Gunnis* 1968, 274
5.	†1845	Sarah Heusch (co-sculptor: Edward Pearce, of London)	Kensal Green Cemetery, London, catacombs	S	
6.	†1848	Charles Heusch (co-sculptor: Edward Pearce, of London)	Kensal Green Cemetery, London, catacombs	S	
7.	†1856	Rev Spencer Thornton (co-sculptor: Edward Pearce, of London)	Wendover, Bucks		Pevsner, *Bucks*, 1994, 717

NOBLE, I, of London fl 1851

Funerary Monuments

1.	1851	Jenkin (†1797) and Ann (†1808) Phillips	Myddfai, Carmarthen	S	*Dale-Jones and Lloyd*, 1989, 55

NOBLE, Matthew 1817–76

Matthew Noble was one of the leading portrait sculptors in mid-19th century England. He came from Yorkshire and lived in London throughout his career, but his extensive practice was largely founded on patronage in the newly rich and powerful industrial centres of Manchester and Salford. He was born at Hackness, near Scarborough, on 23 March 1817, the son of Robert Noble, a local stonemason, and his wife Elizabeth. He was apprenticed to his father and his talent as a sculptor soon attracted the attention of a local landowner, Sir John Johnstone of Hackness Hall, who arranged for him to study in London. Noble became a pupil in the studio of **John Francis** and lived in the Francis family home at 56 Albany Street, near Regent's Park. In 1855 he married Frances Mary Claxton, who is thought to have been his master's granddaughter or niece, and moved to premises in Bruton Street, Mayfair. He exhibited at the Royal Academy, 1845–76, showing over 100 works, most of them portrait busts.

Noble's first major commission for the north west of England was a statue of Sir Robert Peel, erected by public subscription in Peel Park, Salford, in 1852 (**52**). It was both Salford's first public statue and the first in the country commemorating the statesman, who had died in 1850 (it predated statues by **William Behnes** and **E H Baily RA** in Leeds and Bury respectively by just a few months). Noble went on to execute three more statues of Peel for Tamworth, Liverpool and London (**54, 55, 97**) as well as several portrait busts (**115**). Noble came to public prominence in 1853, when he was awarded the commission for a memorial to the Duke of Wellington outside the Town Hall in Manchester (**56**). He provided a bronze statue of Wellington speaking in the House of Lords, but dressed in a military frock coat and with a pile of his published military dispatches at his foot. The seated allegorical figures at the base, *Minerva, Mars, Victory* and *Peace* reflect Wellington's two careers as military commander and statesman. The representation was not universally admired. One critic condemned Noble as 'an artist of very third-rate power and ability' (*AJ*, 1853, 321) and others argued that an equestrian statue reflecting Wellington's military achievements without drawing attention to his controversial political views, would have been more appropriate. Furthermore, there were allegations of serious irregularities in the management of the competition and it was suggested that Noble's supporters had ensured that he would be selected even before the other models were submitted. Work on the monument proceeded in spite of calls for a new competition and it was inaugurated with great ceremony in August 1856. The committee's choice of sculptor was finally vindicated and Noble's reputation was established through numerous favourable notices of the completed statue in the national press. A string of commissions for the Manchester area followed, including statues of Queen Victoria, Joseph Brotherton and Richard Cobden for Peel Park, Salford (**57, 58, 78**), a series of busts of worthies for Manchester Town Hall (**134, 141, 142, 143, 166**) and a statue of Oliver Cromwell, now in Wythenshawe Park (**94**).

Noble was one of 22 sculptors who signed an open letter complaining of unfairness in the competition for the national memorial to the Duke of Wellington (*Daily News*, 31 May 1856, cited by *Physick* 1970, 29). On this occasion public criticism resulted in a second competition and Noble submitted a design for a portrait statue with four supporting symbolic figures, reminiscent of his Manchester statue of the Duke (**10**). He did not win the commission (which eventually went to **Alfred Stevens**) but was awarded the seventh premium of £100. Noble did, however, provide London with several important public works. His statue of Sir John Franklin in Waterloo Place depicts the explorer in realistic contemporary dress, telling his crew that the North West Passage, the object of their voyage, has been discovered (**75**). He also executed statues of Lieutenant-General Sir James Outram, the 14th Earl of Derby and Sir Robert Peel for prominent sites in the capital (**83, 89, 97**).

After Prince Albert's death in 1861, Noble provided commemorative statues of him for Salford, Manchester, Leeds and Bombay (**68, 70, 76, 79**). The statue in Manchester is housed in a magnificent gothic canopy designed by the Manchester architect, Thomas Worthington. Noble's portraits of the Prince did not find favour with the Queen, who is known to preferred images by **William Theed II** and **Carlo, Baron Marochetti**. She rejected a suggestion by the Duke of Newcastle that Noble should execute a statue for Sydney, Australia (which was eventually commissioned from Theed) and because of her low opinion of his work he was not invited to carve a group for the Albert Memorial.

In addition to portraiture and a few ideal works (**63, 227**), Noble was responsible for many funerary monuments, which vary greatly in scale, complexity and style. A portrait bust set in an ornate architectural niche commemorates Sir James Yorke Scarlett at Burnley (**44**). The monument to Edward Brown at Ashton-under-Lyme is a more elaborate composition: Brown's dignified bust is set on an inscribed pedestal with a naturalistic medallion portrait of his wife at the base. Seven figures of different ages in gradated relief cluster round the pedestal (**11**). Mrs van den Bempde Johnstone's monument at Hackness shows her greeted by angels in very low relief, who give the work an ethereal effect (**5**). The most familiar of Noble's monuments is perhaps Lieutenant-General Sir James Outram's in Westminster Abbey (**28**). The authoritative but naturalistic portrait bust is set on herm-type square shoulders and the pedestal below has an incongruous quatrefoil relief. Two cowed Indian figures lean against the pedestal. The idiosyncratic combination of styles has an incoherent effect.

Noble died on 23 June 1876 and was buried in Brompton Cemetery. His obituary records that he was always 'a man of exceedingly delicate constitution' and suggests that his death may have been hastened by grief at the loss of two sons, one of whom had also shown great promise as a sculptor. The writer continues: 'Few men have been more esteemed and regarded, not alone for his great abilities, the manifestations of talent that very closely approximated to genius, but for rare kindly qualities of mind and heart. Generous in his acts and in his sympathies, amiable in his disposition, his nature was essentially kind and good. He was a gentleman of high rectitude, irreproachable in all the relations of life' (*AJ*, 1876, 275–6). The unfinished works in his studio were completed by his assistant **Joseph Edwards**.

Despite his successful career, Noble was not elected to the Royal Academy, partly because more exciting rivals were emerging in **John Henry Foley** and later Woolner, both of whom became Academicians. Noble was not alone among leading sculptors in being passed over: **John Bell** and William Theed II were among those who also never achieved the distinction.

The critic FT Palgrave condemned Noble as an inferior follower of 'the founder of that coarse and careless style in modelling and execution' **Sir Francis Chantrey RA** and wrote that his work had done 'much to disfigure Manchester'.

Thomas Woolner RA (who was a close friend of Palgrave) accused Noble of using friends in high places to obtain commissions and described him as 'a person who never touches the work that goes under his name' (*Woolner/Trevelyan*, 23 Dec 1860 cited by *Read* 1982, 24). It was not however unusual for sculptors to cultivate influential contacts or to rely to a large degree on studio assistants and Woolner's views may well have been coloured by his keenly developed sense of professional rivalry. During the 20th century regard for Noble's work diminished further. Many of his works in plaster, which were given to the city of Newcastle by Noble's widow and were displayed at nearby Elswick Hall, were destroyed during the 1950s. Other statues and busts in the care of Salford's local authority were sold. Although interest in 19th century sculpture has increased in recent years, no attempt has been made to provide a full assessment of Noble's contribution to the art. He should perhaps be seen as a no-nonsense mid-Victorian realist, sometimes prosaic, sometimes surprisingly vigorous and generally competent.

EH

Literary References: *Palgrave* 1866, *passim*; *DNB*, XLI, 1895, 83 (Nicholson); *Physick* 1969, 41; *Physick* 1970, 31–2, 41, 141–2; *Penny* 1977 (1), 101, 134; *Read* 1982, *passim*; *Darby and Smith* 1983, 81, 114 nn98, 99; *Read* 1992, 7; *Grove* 23, 1996, 171–2 (Stocker); *ODNB* (Greenwood)

Additional MS Sources: *Gladstone Papers*, Add 44431 fol 143, 1871; *Noble/Gladstone*, 1875; *Noble Letter*, 1876

Wills and Administrations: PPR, will, 17 July 1876, effects under £2,000

Auction Reference: Noble and others, 1879

Portraits of the Sculptor: woodcut after photo by Charles Watkins, *ILN*, July 1876; W Walker & Sons, *carte de visite* photo, NPG AX7565; John and Charles Watkins, *carte de visite* photo, NPG AX11932

Funerary Monuments

1.	†1839	William Smith	St Peter, Northampton	S	Pevsner, *Northants*, 1973, 322
2.	†1844	Anne Harland	All Saints, Brompton, N R Yorks		Pevsner, *Yorks: N R*, 1966, 89
3.	†1851	Joseph Kay	St Philip, Salford, Lancs		NP/RG
4.	†1852	John Marsland	Stockport, Cheshire		*Gunnis* 1968, 275
5.	†1853	Mrs van den Bempde Johnstone	Hackness, N R Yorks		Pevsner, *Yorks: N R*, 1966, 180; *Penny* 1977 (1), 101
6.	1854	Thomas Hood (†1845)	Kensal Green Cemetery, London		*Graves* V, 1905–6, 377; *Morris and Roberts* 1998, 453, 682; *Mellor* 1999, 197; *Curl* 2001, 188–9 (repr)
7.	1855	Edward Vernon Harcourt, Archbishop of York (†1847)	York Minster, north choir aisle	SD	*Aylmer* 1979, 467–8 (repr); *Pattison and Murray* 2001, 120–1
8.	1856	Captain Edmund Mowbray Lyons (†1855)	St Paul's Cathedral, London		Pevsner, *London: City*, 1997, 171
9.	1856	Officers and Men of the 77th East Middlesex Regiment (Crimea Memorial) (co-sculptor: Forsyth)	St Paul's Cathedral, London		Pevsner, *London: City*, 1997, 171
10.	1857	Arthur, 1st Duke of Wellington, national memorial, design only (monument executed by Alfred Stevens)	Untraced		*Physick* 1970, 141–2, 45 (repr)
11.	†1857	Edward Brown and wife (†1867)	St Michael, Ashton-under-Lyne, Lancs Other versions: model or cast ex Elswick Hall, Newcastle; untraced		*Robinson* 1886, 43, cat 4; *Read* 1982, 191, 192 (repr)
12.	†1857	Francis, 1st Earl of Ellesmere, effigy only (monument designed by Sir G G Scott, tomb chest carved by John Birnie Philip)	Worsley, Lancs		*Penny* 1977 (1), 134; *CIIA* 4/8/148-50 (repr)
13.	1858	Edward Vernon Harcourt, Archbishop of York (†1847)	Stanton Harcourt, Oxon	SD	Pevsner, *Oxon*, 1974, 781
14.	1858	Isaac Barrow Model(s): exhib RA, London, 1859, 1258	Trinity College, Cambridge, chapel Other versions: model or cast ex Elswick Hall, Newcastle; untraced	S	*Robinson* 1886, 56, cat 67; *Graves* V, 1905–6, 377; *Read* 1982, 125 (repr), 128
15.	1859	Thomas Kinnersley	Ashley, Staffs		Pevsner, *Staffs*, 1974, 33, 63
16.	†1859	Thomas Philip de Grey, Lord Lucas	Flitton, Beds, de Grey mausoleum	S	Pevsner, *Beds, Hunts & Peterborough*, 1968, 91
17.	†1859	William, 8th Earl Waldegrave	Navestock, Essex	S	*Read* 1982, 190
18.	†1860	George, 4th Earl of Aberdeen	Westminster Abbey, London, north transept		*Read* 1982, 172–3 (repr)
19.	†1860	John, 13th Baron Elphinstone	Limpsfield, Surrey	S	Pevsner, *Surrey*, 1971, 343; *Ormond and Rogers* 3, 1979–81, 64
20.	?1860	Thomas Carr, Bishop of Bombay	Mumbai (Bombay) Cathedral, India		*Gunnis* 1968, 275
21.	†1861	George Granville Harcourt	Stanton Harcourt, Oxon		Pevsner, *Oxon*, 1974, 781
22.	1861	Mary Scudamore Stanhope (†1859)	Holme Lacy, Herefs Other versions: model or cast ex Elswick Hall, Newcastle; untraced		*Robinson* 1886, 49, cat 24; Pevsner, *Herefs*, 1962, 193; *Read* 1982, 191
23.	1862	Edmund, Baron Lyons (†1858)	St Paul's Cathedral, London	SD	*Ormond* 1973, 284; C Lib (repr)
24.	1862	Hannah Maria, Lady Chetwynd (†1860) Drawing(s): VAM E.205-1982	Colwich, Staffs	SD	Pevsner, *Staffs*, 1974, 33, 107; C Lib (repr)
25.	1863	Archbishop Thomas Musgrave (†1860)	York Minster, north choir aisle	SD	*Aylmer* 1977, 472; *Pattison and Murray* 2001, 127

26.	1863	Frederick, 1st Earl of Ripon (†1859) (effigy on a tomb chest designed by George Gilbert Scott)		Nocton, Lincs		Pevsner, *Lincs*, 1989, 578
27.	1863	John Pearson, Bishop of Chester (†1686), effigy only (designed by Sir A W Blomfield) (co-sculptor: Nicholas Earp)		Chester Cathedral		C Lib (repr)
28.	†1863	Lieutenant-General Sir James Outram		Westminster Abbey, London, nave	S	*Read* 1982, 171, 172 (repr); *Groseclose* 1990, 507; *Groseclose* 1995, 17, 121–2
29.	1863	Mountstuart Elphinstone (†1859)		St Paul's Cathedral, London, crypt	SD	Pevsner, *London: City*, 1997, 182
30.	1864	Thomas, 2nd Earl de Grey (†1859)		Flitton, Beds		*Gunnis* 1968, 275
31.	?1867	Lady Charlotte Dundas		Richmond, N R Yorks		*Gunnis* 1968, 275
32.	†1868	Harriet, Duchess of Sutherland		Trentham, Staffs		Pevsner, *Staffs*, 1974, 286
33.	?1868	Mr and Mrs Allgood		Simonburn, Northumbs		Pevsner, *Northumbs*, 1957, 292
34.	1869	Richard Dawes, Dean of Hereford (†1867) (effigy on a tomb chest designed by George Gilbert Scott)		Hereford Cathedral		Pevsner, *Herefs*, 1962, 162; *Ormond and Rogers* 2, 1979–81, 60
35.	†1870	Christopher Pemberton		Newton, Cambs		Pevsner, *Cambs*, 1970, 443
36.	†1870	John Balston Walter		Bear Wood, Berks		Pevsner, *Berks*, 1966, 79
37.	†1871	Chandos Scudamore-Stanhope		Holme Lacy, Herefs		Pevsner, *Herefs*, 1962, 194; *Gunnis* 1968, 275
38.	†1871	William Harcourt		Nuneham Courtenay, Oxon		Pevsner, *Oxon*, 1974, 726
39.	1872	Edward, 14th Earl of Derby (†1869)		Knowsley, Lancs Other versions: model or cast ex Elswick Hall, Newcastle; untraced		*Robinson* 1886, 50, cat 29; Pevsner, *Lancs: S*, 1969, 132; *Ormond* 1973, 137
40.	†1872	Emily Leveson-Gower (née Doyle)		Titsey, Surrey		Pevsner, *Surrey*, 1971, 489
41.	†1872	Richard, 6th Earl of Mayo		Malta Other versions: model or cast ex Elswick Hall, Newcastle; untraced		*Robinson* 1886, 62–3, cat 102
42.	?1872	William and Mary Heath		Biddulph, Staffs Other versions: model or cast ex Elswick Hall, Newcastle; untraced		*Robinson* 1886, 49, cat 25; Pevsner, *Staffs*, 1974, 33, 69; C Lib (repr)
43.	†1874	A S Leveson-Gower		Trentham, Staffs		Pevsner, *Staffs*, 1974, 286
44.	1874	Sir James Yorke Scarlett (†1871)		St Peter, Burnley, Lancs	SD	*Read* 1982, 190, 192 (repr)
45.	†1874	Sir Stephen Glynne		Hawarden, Flint	S	Pevsner, *Clwyd*, 1986, 367
46.	1874	Sir Thomas Fermor-Hesketh (†1872) Payment(s): £1,000		Rufford, Lancs		Pevsner, *Lancs: N*, 1969, 214
47.	1875	Rev Henry Venn		St Paul's Cathedral, London, crypt		*Graves* V, 1905–6, 378; Pevsner, *London: City*, 1997, 179; C Lib (repr)
48.	1875	Sir John Franklin (†1847)		Westminster Abbey, London, Chapel of St John the Evangelist	D	*Ormond* 1973, 182
49.	1876	Robert, Baron Lyveden (†1873)		Brigstock, Northants		Pevsner, *Northants*, 1973, 123; *CIIA* 4/3/19–23 (repr)

Statues

50.	1849	Edward Vernon Harcourt, Archbishop of York, statuette		[Exhib RA, London, 1299]; untraced		*Graves* V, 1905–6, 377
51.	1852	Arthur, 1st Duke of Wellington	b	Apsley House, London	SD	
52.	1852	Sir Robert Peel	b	[Peel Park, Salford, Lancs]; Gawsworth Hall, Cheshire Other versions: model or cast ex Elswick Hall, Newcastle; untraced		*Robinson* 1886, 47–8, cat 20; *Cavanagh*, 1997, 271; *Wells* 1999, 13–7 (repr); *Morris* 2002, 29–30
53.	1853	Arthur, 1st Duke of Wellington		[East India House, Leadenhall Street, City of London]; Foreign and Commonwealth Office, Whitehall, London		*Archer* 1965, 407; Pevsner, *London: 1*, 1973, 548; C Lib (repr)
54.	1853	Sir Robert Peel	b	Tamworth, Staffs		Pevsner, *Staffs*, 1974, 278; *Cavanagh* 1997, 271
55.	1854	Sir Robert Peel	m	St George's Hall, Liverpool, Lancs	SD	*Graves* V, 1905–6, 377; *Cavanagh* 1997, 270–2 (repr)
56.	1856	Arthur, 1st Duke of Wellington	b	Piccadilly, Manchester, Lancs Other versions: models or casts of statue and reliefs ex Elswick Hall, Newcastle; untraced	SD	*Robinson* 1886, 54–5, cat nos 59–63; *Read* 1982, 109, 112, 149–151 (repr)
57.	1857	Queen Victoria Payment(s): 1,000 gns	m	Salford AG, Lancs, forecourt		*Ormond* 1973, 488; *Read* 1982, 106–7, 369 (repr)
58.	1858	Joseph Brotherton MP Payment(s): £1,500	b	[Peel Park, Salford, Lancs]; Bridge Street, Manchester, Lancs	SD	*Gunnis* 1968, 274; *Wells* 1999, 26–8 (repr)
59.	1858	Queen Victoria		Leeds Town Hall, W R Yorks, entrance		Pevsner, *Yorks: W R*, 1967, 315; *Hall* 1995, 11 (repr)
60.	1859	Brigadier-General James Neill	m	Ayr, Scotland Other versions: Madras Museum, India, bronze, 1860		*Gunnis* 1968, 274; *Steggles* 2000, 145–6 (repr)
61.	1859	Captain Pechell		[Brighton Pavilion, Sussex, vestibule]; untraced		RG/JP, 6, 989
62.	1859	Frances, Countess of Waldegrave, statuette	m	[Exhib RA, London, 1300]; untraced		*Graves* V, 1905–6, 377
63.	1859	Purity		[Int Exhib, London, 1862]; untraced Other versions: model or cast ex Elswick Hall, Newcastle; untraced reproduced in Parian ware by Copeland as a bust and a statuette, 1860, 1865		*AJ Cat* 1862, f.120 (repr); *Robinson* 1886, 56, cat 68; *Atterbury* 1989, 151, 182 (repr 513, 595)

64.	1860	Henry, 1st Marquess of Anglesey, on a column		Llanfair, Anglesey, North Wales		*Darke* 1991, 119–20 (repr)
65.	1861	George, 2nd Duke of Sutherland	m	Dunrobin Castle, Sutherland Other versions: Cliveden, Bucks, 1865 model or cast ex Elswick Hall, Newcastle		*Robinson* 1886, 61, cat 96; *Gunnis* 1968, 274
66.	1860–1861	King Arthur, model only		Untraced		*Ward-Jackson* 2003, 244
67.	1862	Dr Robert Bentley Todd Model(s): exhib RA, London, 1861, 1091	m	[King's College Hospital, Strand, London]; King's College Hospital, Denmark Hill, London		*Graves* V, 1905–6, 377; *Blackwood* 1989, 154 (repr); *Cavanagh* forthcoming 2007 (Lambeth: Brixton)
68.	1864	Albert, the Prince Consort Payment(s): £1,100	m	Salford AG, Lancs, forecourt Other versions: model or cast ex Elswick Hall, Newcastle; untraced		*Robinson* 1886, 48, cat 22; *Read* 1982, 95, 147 (repr); *Darby and Smith* 1983, 76, 80–1, 82 (repr)
69.	1864	Lord Brougham Model(s): model RA, London, 1864, 892		Brown's Institute, Liverpool		*Graves* V, 1905–6, 378; *Gunnis* 1968, 274
70.	1865	Albert, the Prince Consort		Leeds Town Hall, W R Yorks, entrance hall		Pevsner, *Yorks: W R*, 1967, 315; *Darby and Smith* 1983, 81; *Hall* 1995, 11 (repr)
71.	1865	Archibald, 13th Earl of Eglinton		Wellington Square, Ayr, Scotland		*Gunnis* 1968, 274; *Ormond and Rogers* 3, 1979–81, 62
72.	1865	J Foster		Assize Court, Manchester, Lancs		*Gunnis* 1968, 274
73.	1865	Jagannath Shankarshet		Asiatic Soc, Mumbai (Bombay), India Other versions: model or cast ex Elswick Hall, Newcastle; untraced		*Robinson* 1886, 47, 56 cats 19, 65; *Gunnis* 1968, 274
74.	1865	Sir James McGrigor Bt, MD	b	[Chelsea Hospital, grounds]; Royal Army Medical Corps barracks, Atterbury Street, Millbank, London		*Blackwood* 1989, 155 (repr)
75.	1866	Sir John Franklin Payment(s): £1,950	b	Waterloo Place, London		*Blackwood* 1989, 298–9 (repr)
76.	1867	Albert, the Prince Consort	m	Albert Memorial, Albert Square, Manchester, Lancs		*Read* 1982, 109, 112, 153, 154 (repr); *Darke* 1991, 243 (repr)
77.	1867	Henry, 3rd Viscount Palmerston	b	Marketplace, Romsey, Hants		Pevsner, *Hants & Isle of Wight*, 1967, 487; *Ormond* 1973, 361
78.	1867	Richard Cobden	m	[Peel Park, Salford, Lancs]; untraced Other versions: model or cast ex Elswick Hall, Newcastle; untraced		*Robinson* 1886, 62, cat 98; *Gunnis* 1968, 274; *Wells* 1999, 29–31 (repr)
79.	1869	Albert, the Prince Consort Payment(s): £3,000	m	Dr Bhau Daji Lad Museum, Mumbai (Bombay), India	D	*Darby and Smith* 1983, 81 (repr); *Steggles* 2000, 32–3 (repr); *Steggles* 2002, 17–18 (repr)
80.	1869	Harriet, Duchess of Sutherland		Dunrobin Castle, Sutherland		*Gunnis* 1968, 274
81.	1869	Sir Peter Fairbairn Model(s): Thoresby Soc, Leeds, W R Yorks (plaster)		Woodhouse Square, Leeds, W R Yorks		*Read* 1982, 29
82.	1870	Dr James Lee, Bishop of Manchester		John Rylands Library, University of Manchester, Lancs		*Graves* V, 1905–6, 378; *Gunnis* 1968, 274
83.	1871	Lieutenant-General Sir James Outram	b	[Whitehall, London]; Victoria Embankment Gardens, London		*Blackwood* 1989, 262–3 (repr)
84.	1871	William, 2nd Baron Feversham		Helmsley, N R Yorks		Pevsner, *Yorks: N R*, 1966, 187
85.	1872	James Ramsden, 1st Mayor of Barrow Model(s): Dock Museum, Barrow-in-Furness (statue); Tyne and Wear Museums (reliefs)		Ramsden Square, Barrow-in-Furness, Cumbria Other versions: facsimile by Matthew Noble to be presented to Mrs Ramsden (*C E & E*, 25 May 1872, 2)		*Carlisle Express & Examiner*, 25 May 1872, 7; *Graves* V, 1905–6, 378
86.	1869–1872	Queen Victoria, seated beneath a Gothic canopy Payment(s): £15,500 Model(s): head and shoulders, Foreign and Commonwealth Office	m	[intersection of Mahatma Gandhi and Mayo roads, Bombay]; Dr Bhau Daji Lad Museum, Mumbai (Bombay), India Other versions: model or cast ex Elswick Hall, Newcastle; untraced	D	*Robinson* 1886, 62, cat 97; *Steggles* 2000, 178–80 (repr); *Steggles* 2002, 1318–19, 23 (repr)
87.	1872	Rev William Vernon Harcourt, statuette	m	[Exhib RA, London, 1583]; untraced		*Graves* V, 1905–6, 378
88.	post-1872	Richard, 6th Earl of Mayo Payment(s): £1,189 4s 8d inclusive	m	[Ajmer, in front of Ajmer Club]; Mayo Coll, Ajmer, India		*Steggles* 2000, 134–6 (repr)
89.	1873	Edward, 14th Earl of Derby		Avenham Park, Preston, Lancs		*Read* 1982, 107–112, 147 (repr)
90.	1873	Oliver Cromwell, statuette	m	[Exhib RA, London, 1581]; untraced		*Graves* V, 1905–6, 378
91.	1874	Edward, 14th Earl of Derby	b	Parliament Square, London Other versions: models or casts ex Elswick Hall, Newcastle; untraced	S	*Robinson* 1886, 48, 52, cats 21, 46–9; *Walker* 1961, 105; *Blackwood* 1989, 190–1 (repr)
92.	1874	Maharajah Kali Krishna		Kolkata (Calcutta), India Other versions: model or cast, ex Elswick Hall, Newcastle; untraced		*Robinson* 1886, 63, cat 103
93.	1874	Queen Victoria		St Thomas's Hospital, London	SD	*Graves* V, 1905–6, 378; *Ormond* 1973, 489; Cavanagh forthcoming 2007 (Lambeth 2); C Lib (repr)

No.	Date	Subject	Material	Location		Literary References
94.	1875	Oliver Cromwell	b	[Junction of Cateaton Street and Deansgate, Manchester]; Wythenshawe Park, Manchester, Lancs		*Read* 1982, 112, 113 (repr)
95.	1875	Samuel, Lord Masham of Swinton	m	Lister Park, Bradford, W R Yorks	SD	*Darke* 1991, 220–1 (repr)
96.	1876	Rowland, Viscount Hill of Hawkstone and Harwicke	m	[Hawkstone Park, Salop]; Abbey gardens, Shrewsbury, Salop Other versions: model or cast ex Elswick Hall, Newcastle; untraced	SD	*Robinson* 1886, 48–9, cat 23; *Gunnis* 1968, 274
97.	1876	Sir Robert Peel	b	[Palace Yard, London]; Parliament Square, London	SD	*Walker* 1961, 105; *Blackwood* 1989, 185 (repr)
Busts						
98.	1845	Alice Johnstone		[Exhib RA, London, 1379]; untraced		*Graves* V, 1905–6, 376
99.	1845	Edward Vernon Harcourt, Archbishop of York		Eridge Castle, Sussex		*Graves* V, 1905–6, 376
100.	1847	George Hudson MP	m	[Exhib RA, London, 1362]; untraced		*Graves* V, 1905–6, 376
101.	1847	John Francis		[Exhib RA, London, 1417]; untraced		*Graves* V, 1905–6, 376
102.	1848	Countess of Galloway		[Exhib RA, London, 1407]; untraced Other versions: model or cast ex Elswick Hall, Newcastle; untraced		*Robinson* 1886, 59, cat 83; *Graves* V, 1905–6, 376
103.	1848	Hon Alexander Stuart		[Exhib RA, London, 1409]; untraced		*Graves* V, 1905–6, 376
104.	c1848	Joseph Paxton		Private coll, by descent		Inf: JKB
105.	1848	Professor Lyon Playfair (1st Lord Playfair)		Geological Museum, London		RG/JP, 6, 990
106.	1848	William Smith	m	Oxford University Museum	SD	*Graves* V, 1905–6, 376; *Read* 1982, 172
107.	1849	Angus MacDonell	m	[Exhib RA, London, 1265]; untraced		*Graves* V, 1905–6, 377
108.	1849	Charles James Blomfield, Bishop of London	m	[Exhib RA, London, 1253]; untraced Other versions: model or cast ex Elswick Hall, Newcastle; untraced		*Robinson* 1886, 50, cat 31; *Graves* V, 1905–6, 377; *Ormond* 1973, 41
109.	1849	John Phillips		Oxford University Museum		*Graves* V, 1905–6, 377; *Read* 1982, 172; *Morris and Roberts* 1998, 453
110.	1850	Alexander Halley	m	[Exhib RA, London, 1439]; untraced		*Graves* V, 1905–6, 377
111.	1850	Colonel Sir John Malcolm	m	[Exhib RA, London, 1402]; untraced Other versions: model or cast ex Elswick Hall, Newcastle; untraced		*Robinson* 1886, 44, cat 9; *Graves* V, 1905–6, 377
112.	1850	Lady Feversham	m	[Exhib RA, London, 1395]; untraced		*Graves* V, 1905–6, 377
113.	1850	Lord Feversham	m	[Exhib RA, London, 1440]; untraced		*Graves* V, 1905–6, 377
114.	1850	Lord Neville		Eridge Castle, Sussex Other versions: model or cast ex Elswick Hall, Newcastle; untraced		*Robinson* 1886, 58, cat 76; *Graves* V, 1905–6, 377; *Gunnis* 1968, 275
115.	1850	Sir Robert Peel	m	Palace of Westminster, London, committee stairs (loan from Earl Peel) Other versions: War Memorial Building, Harrow School, Middx coll Earl Peel, small marble, 1850 NPG 596, full-size marble, 1851 NPG 596a, small marble, 1851 Royal Coll RCIN 35727, ivory, nd		*Manchester Art Treasures* 1857, 136; *Graves* V, 1905–6, 377; *Walker* 1961, 52, cat 57; *Ormond* 1973, 370–1 repr 729); *Morris and Roberts* 1998, 453
116.	1850	William Etty RA	m	NPG 595 Other versions: model or cast ex Elswick Hall, Newcastle; untraced	SD	*Manchester Art Treasures* 1857, 136; *Robinson* 1886, 58, cat 77; *Graves* V, 1905–6, 377; *Ormond* 1973, 165 (pl 313); *Morris and Roberts* 1998, 453
117.	1852	Admiral Lord Nelson		Grocers' Hall, City of London Other versions: Newcastle Museum, Northumbs (ex Elswick Hall, Newcastle), plaster		*Robinson* 1886 62, cat no 100; *Gunnis* 1968, 275
118.	1852	Arthur, 1st Duke of Wellington		Grocers' Hall, City of London Other versions: Gov Art Coll, bronze, 1852 Walker, Liverpool, marble, nd		*Manchester Art Treasures* 1857, 136; *Graves* V, 1905–6, 377; *Morris and Roberts* 1998, 453
119.	1852	Charles, Earl Canning		Highcliffe Castle, Hants Other versions: coll Lord Allendale, 1860; untraced coll Brian Hills, Birmingham (1991), SD 1862 Victoria Memorial Hall, Calcutta, India ex Guildhall, London; destr model or cast ex Elswick Hall, Newcastle; untraced		*Robinson* 1886, 50–51, cat 34; *Graves* V, 1905–6, 378; *Gunnis* 1968, 275; *Ormond* 1973, 85
120.	1852	Countess Canning		Highcliffe Castle, Hants Other versions: model or cast ex Elswick Hall, Newcastle; untraced		*Robinson* 1886, 50–51, cat 34; *Gunnis* 1968, 275
121.	1853	Bryan Donkin FRS	p	[Exhib RA, London, 1426]; untraced Other versions: model or cast ex Elswick Hall, Newcastle; untraced		*Robinson* 1886, 52; *Graves* V, 1905–6, 377

122.	1853	James Walker		Institution of Civil Engineers, London		*Graves* V, 1905–6, 377; *Morris and Roberts* 1998, 453, 682
123.	1853	Miss S J Donkin	p	[Exhib RA, London, 1423]; untraced		*Graves* V, 1905–6, 377
124.	1854	George Stephenson		[Exhib RA, London, 1489]; untraced		*Graves* V, 1905–6, 377
125.	1854	Henry, 1st Marquess of Anglesey	m	Plas Newydd, Anglesey		*Graves* V, 1905–6, 377
126.	1854	Michael Faraday		R Soc, London Other versions: R I, London, marble R I, London, small ivory model or cast ex Elswick Hall, Newcastle; untraced		*Manchester Art Treasures* 1857, 136; *Robinson* 1886, 54, cat no 56; *Graves* V, 1905–6, 377; *Ormond* 1973, 170
127.	1855	Lady Willoughby de Broke		St Margaret, Bodelwyddan, Clywd Other versions: model or cast ex Elswick Hall, Newcastle; untraced	SD	*Robinson* 1886, 60, cat 85; Pevsner, *Clwyd*, 1986, 324n
128.	1855	Lucy Mildmay	m	[Exhib RA, London, 1516]; untraced		*Graves* V, 1905–6, 377
129.	1855	Master James Boyle	m	[Exhib RA, London, 1461]; untraced		*Graves* V, 1905–6, 377
130.	1856	Edmund, Baron Lyons	m	Arundel Castle, Sussex Other versions: model or cast ex Elswick Hall, Newcastle; untraced	SD	*Robinson* 1886, 45, cat 14; *Graves* V, 1905–6, 377
131.	1856	Harcourt Johnstone		Eridge Castle, Sussex		*Graves* V, 1905–6, 377
132.	1856	Joseph Brotherton MP	m	[Salford AG, Lancs, 1860]; Gawsworth Hall, Cheshire Other versions: Manchester City Hall, Lancs, SD 1860 Salford AG, Lancs (acquired 1937)	SD	*Graves* V, 1905–6, 377; *Gawsworth Guide*, 47; *Gunnis* 1968, 275; *Wells* 1999, 39, 45, 46, 61 (repr)
133.	1856	Master Agnew		[Exhib RA, London, 1294]; untraced		*Graves* V, 1905–6, 377
134.	1856	Queen Victoria	m	Manchester Town Hall, Lancs Other versions: Royal Coll RCIN 27487, ivory, 1856 RCIN 2082, marble, SD 1857 Palace of Westminster, London, Peer's Library, marble, SD, 1856 Cecil Higgins Art Gallery, Bedford, ivory model or cast ex Elswick Hall, Newcastle; untraced reproduced in Copeland Parian ware (eg Bristol AG)		*Robinson* 1886, 44, cat no 7; *Graves* V, 1905–6, 377; *Walker* 1961, 76, cat no 78; *Ormond* 1973, 487–8; *Atterbury* 1989, 182 (repr 598)
135.	1856	William Cotton	m	[Exhib RA, London, 1306]; untraced Other versions: model or cast ex Elswick Hall, Newcastle; untraced		*Robinson* 1886, 60, cat 87; *Graves* V, 1905–6, 377
136.	1857	Francis, 1st Earl of Ellesmere	m	Arundel Castle, Sussex Other versions: NPG 2203, small marble	SD	*Graves* V, 1905–6, 377; *Ormond* 1973, 159 (pl 304)
137.	1857	General Sir W F Williams of Kars, MP		[Exhib RA, London, 1258]; untraced		*Graves* V, 1905–6, 377
138.	1857	Henry, 5th Duke of Newcastle		[coll Earl Waldegrave]; untraced		*Graves* V, 1905–6, 377; *Ormond* 1973, 338
139.	1857	Lady M Poe		Tramore, Waterford		RG/JP, 6, 991
140.	1858	Miss Domville		[Exhib RA, London, 1249]; untraced		*Graves* V, 1905–6, 377
141.	1858	Sir Joseph Heron	m	Manchester Town Hall, Lancs Other versions: model or cast ex Elswick Hall, Newcastle; untraced	SD	*Robinson* 1886, 58, cat 74; *Read* 1982, 172; C Lib (repr)
142.	1859	Albert Edward, Prince of Wales (later King Edward VII)	m	Manchester Town Hall, Lancs Other versions: ex Salford AG and Gawsworth Hall, Cheshire, marble, SD 1868; untraced Town Hall, Leeds, W R Yorks, marble, 1872 Forbes Magazine coll, New York, USA, marble model or cast ex Elswick Hall, Newcastle; untraced		*Robinson* 1886, 43, cat 5; *Gawsworth Guide*, 46, 47 (repr); *Hall* 1995, 11 (repr); *Wells* 1999, 40, 45, 46
143.	1859	Albert, the Prince Consort Model(s): exhib RA, London, 1858, 1162	m	Manchester Town Hall, Lancs Other versions: Forbes Mag Coll, New York, USA, marble, nd VAM A.221-1969, ivory, nd model or cast ex Elswick Hall, Newcastle; untraced		*Robinson* 1886, 44, cat 8; *Graves* V, 1905–6, 377; *Ormond* 1973, 13
144.	1859	Anthony, 7th Earl of Shaftesbury	m	Wimborne St Giles, Dorset		*Graves* V, 1905–6, 377; *Gunnis* 1968, 275; *Ormond* 1973, 417
145.	1859	The eldest son of Rear-Admiral Lord Clarence Paget	m	Plas Newydd, Anglesey Other versions: Reform Club, London	SD	*Graves* V, 1905–6, 377
146.	1860	Alderman Thomas Goadsby	m	[Salford AG, Lancs]; Sotheby, 9 Dec 1993; untraced Other versions: Manchester Town Hall, Lancs, SD 1862	SD	*Read* 1982, 112; *Gawsworth Guide*, 45; *Wells* 1999, 39, 45 (repr)
147.	1860	Dr Robert Bentley Todd, small scale	m	R C Physic, London Other versions: RC Surg, London	SD	*Wolstenholme* 1964, 408–9 (repr)

No.	Date	Subject	Medium	Location	Signed	Literature
148.	?1860	Henry, 3rd Viscount Palmerston	m	Palace of Westminster, London, committee stairs Other versions: Reform Club, London Trinity House, London model or cast ex Elswick Hall, Newcastle; untraced	SD	*Robinson* 1886, 46, cat no 17; *Graves* V, 1905–6, 377; *Walker* 1961, 51, cat 56; *Ormond* 1973, 361
149.	1860	J F Foster	m	[Exhib RA, London, 1025]; untraced		*Graves* V, 1905–6, 377
150.	1860	Mrs W A Fairbairn		[Exhib RA, London, 1051]; untraced Other versions: model or cast ex Elswick Hall, Newcastle; untraced		*Robinson* 1886, 52, cat 39; *Graves* V, 1905–6, 377
151.	1860	Oliver Cromwell	m	VAM 448-1884 Other versions: Reform Club, London, 1860 sold Tennant, 22 Nov 2001, ivory, SD 1860 Manchester Town Hall, Lancs, marble, SD 1861 ex Reform Club, London, 1864; untraced coll Brian Hills, Birmingham (1991), clay	SD	*Graves* V, 1905–6, 377; *Gunnis* 1968, 275; *Bilbey* 2002, 346 (repr)
152.	1860	William Fairbairn	m	[Exhib RA, London, 1054]; untraced		*Graves* V, 1905–6, 377
153.	1861	Jessie Hartley	m	Liverpool Town Hall, Lancs Other versions: model or cast ex Elswick Hall, Newcastle; untraced		*Robinson* 1886, 54, cat 57; *Graves* V, 1905–6, 378
154.	1861	John, 13th Baron Elphinstone	m	[coll Lord Elphinstone]; Carberry Tower Sale, 1961 Other versions: model or cast ex Elswick Hall, Newcastle; untraced		*Robinson* 1886, 51, cat 37; *Graves* V, 1905–6, 377
155.	1861	Mrs T Potter	m	[Exhib RA, London, 1035]; untraced Other versions: model or cast ex Elswick Hall, Newcastle; untraced		*Robinson* 1886, 52, cat 42; *Graves* V, 1905–6, 377
156.	1861	Thomas Bayley Potter	m	[Exhib RA, London, 1031]; untraced		*Graves* V, 1905–6, 377
157.	*c*1862	Albert, the Prince Consort		[Bath Royal United Hospital]; untraced		*Darby and Smith* 1983, 63, 112 n22 (repr)
158.	1862	Joseph Bell		Untraced		RG/JP, 6, 991
159.	1862	Margaret Harriet Beaumont		[Exhib RA, London, 1000]; untraced		*Graves* V, 1905–6, 377
160.	1862	Master Walter Francis Clinton		[Exhib RA, London, 1105]; untraced Other versions: model or cast ex Elswick Hall, Newcastle; untraced		*Robinson* 1886, 44, cat 11; *Graves* V, 1905–6, 378
161.	1863	George, 2nd Duke of Sutherland		Millmeece Pumping Station, Staffs Other versions: Castle Howard, N R Yorks, marble, *c*1863 ex coll Dukes of Sutherland and Ellesmere; untraced reproduced in Minton Parian ware		*Gunnis* 1968, 275; *Read* 1982, 129; *Atterbury* 1989, 129 (repr 479)
162.	1863	James, 8th Earl of Elgin	m	[Exhib RA, London, 1059]; untraced		*Graves* V, 1905–6, 378
163.	1863	Richard Pennefather		Chevening, Kent	S	C Lib (repr)
164.	1864	Count de Flahault	m	Meikleour House, Perth Other versions: model or cast ex Elswick Hall, Newcastle; untraced	SD	*Robinson* 1886, 53, cat 54; *Graves* V, 1905–6, 378; C Lib (repr)
165.	1864	Lieutenant-General Sir James Outram		[Exhib RA, London, 1010]; untraced		*Graves* V, 1905–6, 378; *Ormond* 1973, 351
166.	1864	Sir Thomas Potter		[coll Sir Thomas Potter]; Manchester Town Hall, Lancs	SD	*Read* 1982, 111, 113, 172 (repr)
167.	1864	Unidentified subject		King's College, London	S	RG/JP, 6, 991
168.	1865	George Langworthy		[Salford AG, Lancs]; untraced	S	*Gawsworth Guide*, 44, 46 (repr); *Wells* 1999, 40 (repr)
169.	1865	James Heald		[RA, London, 1866, 897]; untraced		*Graves* V, 1905–6, 378
170.	1865	John Milton, model for Copeland Parian ware		Untraced		*Atterbury* 1989, 184 (repr 609)
171.	1865	Lady Frere		Mumbai (Bombay), India		*Gunnis* 1968, 275
172.	1865	Richard Cobden	m	Gov Art Coll Other versions: Dunford Museum, Midhurst, 1865 Reform Club, London, 1866 ex Guildhall, London, 1869; destr	SD	Gov Art Coll archives; *Ormond* 1973, 106, 108
173.	1866	Alexandra, Princess of Wales	m	[Salford AG, Lancs, 1870]; untraced Other versions: Leeds Town Hall, W R Yorks, marble, 1872 Forbes Magazine Coll, New York, USA, marble model or cast ex Elswick Hall, Newcastle; untraced	SD	*Robinson* 1886, 43, cat 6; *Gawsworth Guide*, 46, 47 (repr); *Hall* 1995, 11 (repr); *Wells* 1999, 40, 45
174.	1866	Sir Compton Domville		Tramore, Waterford Other versions: model or cast ex Elswick Hall, Newcastle; untraced		*Robinson* 1886, 53, cat 55
175.	1867	Charles Seeley MP	m	[Exhib RA, London, 1135]; untraced		*Graves* V, 1905–6, 378

176.	1867	General Giuseppe Garibaldi		VAM 449-1884	SD	*Graves* V, 1905–6, 378; *Bilbey* 2002, 346 (repr)
177.	1867	Master C Manners	m	[Exhib RA, London, 1086]; untraced		*Graves* V, 1905–6, 378
178.	1868	Frances Geraldine Manners	m	[Exhib RA, London, 953]; untraced		*Graves* V, 1905–6, 378
179.	1868	John Allen	m	[Exhib RA, London, 1005]; untraced		*Graves* V, 1905–6, 378
180.	1869	Frederick Dawes Danvers	m	[Exhib RA, London, 1264]; untraced		*Graves* V, 1905–6, 378
181.	1869	Harriet, Duchess of Sutherland		Castle Howard, N R Yorks Other versions: NPG 808, plaster, SD 1869 Chatsworth, Derbys, Orangery, marble, *c*1870 ex coll Dukes of Sutherland and Ellesmere; untraced reproduced in Minton Parian ware, 1871	SD	*Graves* V, 1905–6, 378; *Chatsworth Handlist*, 28; *Ormond* 1973, 440 (repr 880); *Read* 1982, 129; *Atterbury* 1989, 129 (repr 480)
182.	1869	Mrs Catherine Hill		[Exhib RA, London, 1159]; untraced		*Graves* V, 1905–6, 378
183.	1870	Alexina Napier	m	[Exhib RA, London, 1181]; untraced		*Graves* V, 1905–6, 378
184.	1870	Edward, 14th Earl of Derby	m	(coll Mrs M Kershaw) Other versions: ex Guildhall, London, 1871; destr		*Ormond* 1973, 137 (repr 254)
185.	1870	John Champley, Mayor of Scarborough		[Exhib RA, London, 1120]; untraced Other versions: model or cast ex Elswick Hall, Newcastle; untraced		*Robinson* 1886, 44, cat 12; *Graves* V, 1905–6, 378
186.	1871	David Napier	m	Glasgow Museums S.32		*Graves* V, 1905–6, 378; *Gunnis* 1968, 275
187.	1871	John Hartley		Liverpool Town Hall, Lancs Other versions: model or cast ex Elswick Hall, Newcastle; untraced		*Robinson* 1886, 58, cat 71; *Graves* V, 1905–6, 378
188.	1871	Miss A Beaumont		[Exhib RA, London, 1243]; untraced		*Graves* V, 1905–6, 378
189.	1871	Mr Sargeant Spinks, of Brinley House, Kent	m	[Exhib RA, London, 1190]; untraced		*Graves* V, 1905–6, 378
190.	1871	Wentworth Blackett Beaumont MP	m	[Exhib RA, London, 1213]; untraced		*Graves* V, 1905–6, 378
191.	1872	Captain Francis Lean RN		Seamen's Home, Belvedere, Erith, Kent Other versions: model or cast ex Elswick Hall, Newcastle; untraced		*Robinson* 1886, 61, cat 93
192.	1872	Edward Vernon Harcourt, Archbishop of York (after Sir Francis Chantrey)		All Saints, Nuneham Park, Oxon	SD	Pevsner, *Oxon*, 1974, 726
193.	1872	Hon Mrs Stourton	m	[Exhib RA, London, 1538]; untraced Other versions: model or cast ex Elswick Hall, Newcastle; untraced		*Robinson* 1886, 53, cat 51; *Graves* V, 1905–6, 378
194.	1872	James Ramsden	m	Christie, 24 Sept 1987, lot 147		
195.	?1872	William Vernon Harcourt	p	NPG 5300	SD	
196.	1873	Captain Francis Maude		Seamen's Home, Belvedere, Erith, Kent Other versions: model or cast ex Elswick Hall, Newcastle; untraced		*Robinson* 1886, cat 95
197.	1873	Edith, Countess of Winchilsea		Private coll	SD	*Graves* V, 1905–6, 378
198.	1873	General Sir James Yorke Scarlett	m	Townley Hall and Art Gall, Burnley, Lancs Other versions: NPG 807, plaster coll Mrs M Kershaw, marble	SD	*Graves* V, 1905–6, 378; *Ormond* 1973, 410–1 (repr 813)
199.	1873	James Robert Hope Scott QC	m	Luffnell House, East Lothian Other versions: model or cast ex Elswick Hall, Newcastle; untraced		*Graves* V, 1905–6, 378; *Robinson* 1886, 59, cat 79; C Lib (repr)
200.	1873	Mrs White	m	[Exhib RA, London, 1573]; untraced		*Graves* V, 1905–6, 378
201.	1874	Contessa Teresa Caracciolo		[Exhib RA, London, 1551]; untraced		*Graves* V, 1905–6, 378
202.	1874	Hon Mrs Ellis	m	[Exhib RA, London, 1578]; untraced		*Graves* V, 1905–6, 378
203.	1874	Lord Southampton	m	[Exhib RA, London, 1459]; untraced		*Graves* V, 1905–6, 378
204.	1875	Edward Wood		[Exhib RA, London, 1360]; untraced Other versions: model or cast ex Elswick Hall, Newcastle; untraced		*Robinson* 1886, 47, cat 18; *Graves* V, 1905–6, 378
205.	1876	Hon John Bright MP	m	Sotheby, 15 Dec 1982, lot 33 Other versions: model or cast ex Elswick Hall, Newcastle; untraced	SD	*Robinson* 1886, 43, cat 2; C Lib (repr)
206.	1876	Hon Mrs Lionel Ashley	m	[Exhib RA, London, 1350]; untraced		*Graves* V, 1905–6, 378
207.	nd	Albert, the Prince Consort, on a Siena marble base	i	Royal Coll RCIN 27488		JM
208.	nd	Brigadier-General James Neill	m	Victoria Memorial Hall, Kolkata (Calcutta)		*Steggles* 2000, 145
209.	nd	Dr William Harland		Scarborough Museum, N R Yorks		RG/JP, 6, 992
210.	nd	Duncan McLaren MP		[Elswick Hall, Newcastle, Northumbs]; Newcastle Museum, Northumbs		*Robinson* 1886, 57–8, cat 70; *Graves* V, 1905–6, 378
211.	nd	Edward Venables		Dalhousie Institute, Kolkata (Calcutta)		RG/JP, 6, 992
212.	nd	General Bruce		[Elswick Hall, Newcastle, Northumbs]; untraced		*Robinson* 1886, 52, cat 38

213.	nd	? George, 8th Earl of Strafford (†1898)		[Elswick Hall, Newcastle, Northumbs]; untraced	*Robinson* 1886, 51, cat 36
214.	nd	Henry, 3rd Viscount Clifden		[Elswick Hall, Newcastle, Northumbs]; untraced	*Robinson* 1886, 52, cat 40
215.	nd	Lord Albert Gower		[Elswick Hall, Newcastle, Northumbs]; untraced	*Robinson* 1886, 60, cat 84
216.	nd	Seth Merwangee Framjee Panday	m	Panday Sanatorium, Colaba, Mumbai (Bombay), India	*Giara* 2000, 189
217.	nd	Sir Francis Grant		Untraced	*Ormond* 1973, 194
218.	nd	Sir Henry Havelock	m	Victoria Memorial Hall, Kolkata (Calcutta) Other versions: model or cast ex Elswick Hall, Newcastle	*Robinson* 1886, 56, cat 66; *Ormond* 1973, 218
219.	nd	Sir James Grant		untraced	*Ormond* 1973, 196
220.	nd	Sir John Franklin, model	pm	[Elswick Hall, Newcastle, Northumbs]; Newcastle Museum of Science and Engineering, Northumbs	*Robinson* 1886, 61, cat 94; *Read* 1982, 34 (repr)
221.	nd	W M Stopford-Sackville		[Elswick Hall, Newcastle, Northumbs]; untraced	*Robinson* 1886, 59, cat 81
Architectural Sculpture					
222.	1870	Dr John Hunter, Joseph Hume and Sir Humphrey Davy		Former University of London Headquarters, Burlington Gardens, London, façade	*Read* 1982, 226
223.	c1872	The Last Supper, reredos		Ugglebarnby, N R Yorks	Pevsner, *Yorks: N R*, 1966, 376
Reliefs					
224.	1860	Matthew Henry, portrait medallion		Henry Monument, castle roundabout, Chester	SD
225.	1867	Alice Danvers		[Exhib RA, London, 1025]; untraced	*Graves* V, 1905–6, 378
226.	nd	Cotton Spinning, five reliefs	pm	[Elswick Hall, Newcastle, Northumbs]; (coll Tyne and Wear Museums)	*Robinson* 1886, 57, cat 69; *Read* 1982, 34 (repr)
Miscellaneous					
227.	1869	Amy and her pet fawn		[Exhib RA, London, 1207]; untraced	*Graves* V, 1905–6, 378
228.	nd	Alderman Kinahan JP		[Elswick Hall, Newcastle, Northumbs]; untraced	*Robinson* 1886, 52, cat 45
229.	nd	C Clinton		[Elswick Hall, Newcastle, Northumbs]; untraced	*Robinson* 1886, 44, cat 10
230.	nd	Charles Tindal RN		[Elswick Hall, Newcastle, Northumbs]; untraced	*Robinson* 1886, 54, cat 58
231.	nd	Hon Mr Lionel Ashbey		[Elswick Hall, Newcastle, Northumbs]; untraced	*Robinson* 1886, 53, cat 53
232.	nd	Infant sleeping		[Elswick Hall, Newcastle, Northumbs]; untraced	*Robinson* 1886, 52, cat 41
233.	nd	Infant sleeping		[Elswick Hall, Newcastle, Northumbs]; untraced	*Robinson* 1886, 52, cat 44
234.	nd	J J Forster		[Elswick Hall, Newcastle, Northumbs]; untraced	*Robinson* 1886, 61, cat 92
235.	nd	Lady Edward Howard		[Elswick Hall, Newcastle, Northumbs]; untraced	*Robinson* 1886, 58, cat 75
236.	nd	Lord Stourton		[Elswick Hall, Newcastle, Northumbs]; untraced	*Robinson* 1886, 53, cat 50
237.	nd	Maude Domville, asleep		Tramore, Waterford	RG/JP, 6, 990
238.	nd	Mr Turner		[Elswick Hall, Newcastle, Northumbs]; untraced	*Robinson* 1886, 50, cat 33
239.	nd	Mrs Higgins		[Elswick Hall, Newcastle, Northumbs]; untraced	*Robinson* 1886, 62, cat 101
240.	nd	Rev George W Barker		[Elswick Hall, Newcastle, Northumbs]; untraced	*Robinson* 1886, 59, cat 80
241.	nd	Rev John Hodgson		[Elswick Hall, Newcastle, Northumbs]; untraced	*Robinson* 1886, 45, cat 15
242.	nd	Richard Harris		[Elswick Hall, Newcastle, Northumbs]; untraced	*Robinson* 1886, 58, cat 78
243.	nd	Robert Barnes		[Elswick Hall, Newcastle, Northumbs]; untraced	*Robinson* 1886, 53, cat 52
244.	nd	Sir Charles Douglas		[Elswick Hall, Newcastle, Northumbs]; untraced	*Robinson* 1886, 59, cat 82
245.	nd	William Ewart Gladstone		[Elswick Hall, Newcastle, Northumbs]; untraced	*Robinson* 1886, 49–50, cat 26
246.	nd	Wright Turner		[Elswick Hall, Newcastle, Northumbs]; untraced	*Robinson* 1886, 50, cat 32

NOLLEKENS, Joseph RA 1737–1823

Nollekens was Britain's foremost portrait-sculptor in the years 1770–1815. His highly successful workshop also produced monuments and some ideal works. He was born on 11 August 1737 in Dean Street, Soho, and baptised at the Roman Catholic Chapel in Duke Street, Lincoln's Inn, the second son of Joseph Francis Nollekens (1702–1748) and Mary Anne, née Le Sacq. His father, 'Old Nollekens,' was a painter from Antwerp who settled in London in 1733 and specialised in *fetes galantes* and conversation pieces. His French mother remarried after her husband died in 1748 and went to live in Wales. Joseph remained in London and was apprenticed to **Peter Scheemakers** in 1750.

Nollekens remained in Scheemakers's workshop in Vine Street as an apprentice and then a journeyman for 12 years. He also had drawing lessons from **Michael Henry Spang** and took full advantage of burgeoning art institutions in the capital. He attended William Shipley's drawing school in the Strand, drew from casts in the Duke of Richmond's Gallery and in 1757/8 submitted an entry for the modelling prize awarded by the Society of Arts. On 27 February 1759 the Society awarded him a premium in the category 'Drawings and Figures from Models and Casts by Youths under the age of 22'. The subject was not specified. Two further premiums followed, for a *Bacchus* (**143**) and *Abraham entertaining the angels* (**409**), but on 24 March 1759, the committee withdrew the award for *Bacchus* after it was shown that Nollekens had been assisted by 'Mr Wilton' in 'touching' the clay model and was therefore in breach of the terms of the advertisement. The award for *Abraham* was also investigated and Nollekens protested that 'the model was done from a thought of his own, that no person touched it afterwards' and that his source was 'from the print in Raphael's bible and . . . La Fage's drawing (RSA, *Minutes*, 1758–60 seq 1 fols 79–80). On 29 March the second award was upheld, but the following month he was invited to 'give proof of his abilities' by seketching a composition and drawing a head from the subject *Lot and his daughters*, while locked in a room to ensure he received no assistance. This test was completed successfully (RSA *Minutes*, 1758–60, seq 1 ff82, 95). Several premiums followed, for models of figures and reliefs. The subjects were all historical and won him high praise from the judges. In awarding the young sculptor 50 guineas for his relief of *Timocles conducted before Alexander* (**412**) they declared that Nollekens had 'eminently distinguished himself' (RSA *Minutes*, 1761–62 seq 3 fol 59). By May 1762 Nollekens was able to finance a visit to Rome himself.

He travelled through Paris, Lyons, Turin, Venice, Bologna and Florence. **Richard Hayward** recorded his arrival in Rome on 11 August 1762, accompanied by the son of the Swiss-born engraver, Johann Jacob Frey. Nollekens was to remain in Italy for eight years, where he successfully made a reputation and amassed a fortune. His sketchbooks, some of which survive, show that he was an assiduous student, who visited the great collections and steadily became familiar with antique and modern sculpture. By 1764 he had numerous patrons among the travelling British *cognoscenti*. His earliest known portraits, of David Garrick and the Duke of York, are assured in technique and already distinctive in style. The Garrick is shoulderless, bare-chested, and classical (**185**) and the York, bulky and baroque in feeling (**186**). In 1764 the sculptor carved copies of *Boy on a dolphin* for Viscount Palmerston, Lord Spencer and the Earl of Exeter (**146**). The original for this work, supposedly designed by Raphael, belonged to **Bartolommeo Cavaceppi**, the antiquarian and restorer, whose studio Nollekens entered before 1764. There he learnt many dubious restoration techniques of which he was to boast in later life.

He kept his own workshop off the Via del Babuino, 1765–70, where he lived with the landscape painter James Forrester. Working, sometimes in partnership, with the dealer Thomas Jenkins, Nollekens made 'considerable sums of money' buying, restoring and selling antiques (*Euro Mag* 1788, 387), many of which were exported to clients in England such as William Weddell of Newby Hall, who paid £1,000 for a headless statue of Minerva fitted with an alien head. Nollekens's copies after the antique also found British buyers. Lord Exeter purchased a copy of the *Rondanini Medusa* (**184**), and Thomas Anson of Shugborough Hall a fine copy of *Castor and Pollux* (**147**). Anson's patronage was secured through James 'Athenian' Stuart, who appears to have acted as an agent for Nollekens in England. Stuart was also entrusted with installing Nollekens's work at exhibitions organised by the Society of Arts, including a bust of the author Laurence Sterne (**189**), which the sculptor sent to him from Rome in 1767.

Nollekens appears to have been acquainted with members of elevated intellectual circles. His bust of the architect and neoclassical theoretician, G B Piranesi, is one of his most dynamic portraits (**192**). He also received some official recognition. He apparently had the patronage of Cardinal Albani, who saved Nollekens from censure when he neglected his religious duties. In 1768 he won a gold medal at the Concorso Balestra (**148**) and in June 1770 became a member of the Academy of St Luke in Florence. Nonetheless, in September 1770, Nollekens chose to return home, taking back antiquities, books, prints, paintings and *cinquecento* terracottas. He later boasted that he also smuggled lace ruffles through customs, concealed in his plaster casts. His sketchbooks show that he returned home via Genoa, Vienne and Paris. He must have become relatively affluent, for in Paris he settled a £40 annual allowance on a penniless uncle (*Euro Mag* 1788, 13, 387). He arrived in England on 24 December 1770.

During the 1770s Nollekens established himself in London in business and social circles. Within a few months he took a property at 9, Mortimer Street, Marylebone, rated annually at £33. The house doubled in rateable value before 1782. His early assistants included **Giuseppe Angelini**, whom he knew in Rome, and **Nathaniel Smith**. On 25 October 1771 he was elected an Associate of the Royal Academy, and on 9 February 1772 a full Academician. On 5 February 1774, dressed in ostentatious Italian finery, he married Mary, the younger daughter of Saunders Welch JP, of Westminster. His wife was tall, graceful and well-connected. A family friend of Samuel Johnson, she liked to move in the best intellectual and artistic circles (Angelica Kaufmann painted her as *Innocence*), and despite the Nollekens's preference for simple food, the couple played host to many guests from high society in the property in Mortimer Street.

Nollekens could boast numerous members of the Society of Dilettanti among his acquaintances and patrons. The collector Charles Townley bought antiques from Nollekens and always spoke of him as 'the first sculptor of his day' (*Smith* 1828, 1, 263). Nollekens secured the enlightened patronage of Lord Rockingham and Lord Yarborough who commissioned busts (**220, 200**) and poetic works. Rockingham ordered three statues to be juxtaposed with a restored antique figure to form *The judgment of Paris* (**157–9**), one of the most ambitious compositional groups ever created by a British sculptor. Yarborough ordered a *Venus chiding Cupid* and a *Mercury* (**160, 163**).

Nolleken's first monuments combined styles and motifs from various sources. Those to Lady Henrietta Williams Wynn (**7**) and to Bishop Trevor (**10**) make use of full-size statues, the former a female figure of *Hope*, the latter the seated Bishop. Nollekens's monument to Sir Thomas and Lady Salusbury (**14**) depicts the couple together clasping a myrtle wreath in front of a finely carved oak tree, reminiscent of Flemish baroque pulpit sculpture.

The mainstay of Nollekens's business and the source of his reputation was his portrait busts of public figures. He was on close terms with Henry Fox, Lord Holland, then under scrutiny for his alleged embezzlement as paymaster-general. Nollekens went 'every Sunday morning to Holland-House' (*Farington*, 6, 2244, 14 Feb, 1804) and his first entry at a Royal Academy exhibition was a bust of the statesman, the last work Nollekens had carved in Rome (**191**). Horace Walpole admired the likeness achieved with Holland's bust, and later expressed appreciation for the heads of Lord Chancellor Bathurst and the Marquess of Rockingham (**206, 220**). A skill in accurate and lively portrayal was the reason for Nollekens's success. His busts are typically bare-chested or have only simple draperies, and poses are rarely complex. Little attempt is made to dignify features into an ideal form. Attention, as Smith later noted, was focussed on the eyes (which were usually incised), nose and mouth. Nollekens became to contemporary sculpture what Reynolds was to painting. He attracted royal patronage, although George III was apparently uncomfortable with the stern image chosen for his bust (**198**).

In 1782 Nollekens received his only public commission, the monument in Westminster Abbey to three naval captains, who had died that year in the Battle of the Saints (**24**). He submitted a design for a spiralling, freestanding monument, evocative of the sculpture of Bernini and Giambologna, which would have been one of the most remarkable English monuments of the 18th century. His estimates were however considered too high and this design was abandoned for a flatter, less energetic composition, created in collaboration with a Royal Academy committee. Flaxman called it 'a very moderate performance' (*Farington*, 2, 638). The unveiling of the monument and payments to the sculptor were delayed for several years, while the Treasury failed to provide a text for the inscription.

Nollekens's experience with the vagaries of state sponsorship no doubt inhibited him from competing for future public works and he later told Farington that he had refused subsequent government commissions (*Farington* 8, 2853, 19 Sept 1806). In fact Nollekens had little need of the public exposure attendant on such commissions, for he already had a considerable reputation. Sophie von la Roche visited the studio of this 'clever, modest man' in September 1786 and declared his talent 'equal to that of the ancients,' (*la Roche* 1933, 233–4). An extensive notice in the *European Magazine* for 1788 said of Nollekens's works that they were 'sufficiently known' to 'transmit his name to posterity as an artist equal to any of the present times' (*Euro Mag* 13, 387).

In 1791 Nollekens carved his first bust of Charles James Fox, the leader of the Whig party (**226**). This was executed for Lord Fitzwilliam and passed on to Catherine the Great to mark the start of diplomatic relations between the Russian government and the Foxite opposition, and it was a notable coup for Nollekens. It was copied for a number of Fox's Whig colleagues. In 1802 the 5th Duke of Bedford ordered a second version, this time portraying Fox with the close-cropped hair then fashionable among radical Whigs, to be placed in the Temple of Liberty at Woburn Abbey (**248**). In 1807 Nollekens told Farington that he had executed twenty-one marble copies and had orders for 8 more, for which he was charging 100 guineas apiece (*Farington* 8, 3059–60).

Nollekens was quick to capitalise on the death of Fox's great rival, the prime minister, William Pitt the Younger, who died in 1806 (**272**). He was asked to take a death mask (a regular practice for Nollekens) from Pitt's face and within a year boasted that he had orders for 52 marble busts (*Farington*, 8, 3059–60). The astute Nollekens well understood the adverse effect that the market for plaster multiples would have on his sales of marble copies and he refused to sell casts of his bust until he had exhausted interest in marble versions (*Farington* 8, 2853, 19 Sept 1806). According to his biographer, J T Smith, the sculptor sold 74 replicas in marbles of the Pitt, and then 600 casts at 6 guineas each (*Smith* 1828, 2, 48). The busts of Fox and Pitt became stock pieces and brought his work before an even wider public. When the senate of the University of Cambridge voted to erect a statue to the deceased prime minister, Nollekens was chosen as sculptor, although it was widely thought that the commission was intended for **Antonio Canova**. The *Gentleman's Magazine* reported that the statue was 'esteemed a good likeness and the figure a fine piece of statuary' (*GM*, 82, June 1812, 659).

Funerary sculpture had remained a major workshop activity. During the course of his career Nollekens produced about 140 monuments. The early ones were innovative but he turned increasingly to the production of formulaic and repetitive designs, often incorporating a mourning woman in high relief, putti extinguishing torches or grieving over urns, portrait busts or medallions of the deceased. He nonetheless took considerable care with these minor works, monitoring, for instance, work in progress and the installation of the modest slab to Lord Southampton (**76**, *Farington*, 12, 4157). His monument to Mrs Coke, is atypical, for it has an angel hovering over a tide of ice-cream clouds, extending a hand to escort the deceased up to heaven (**32**). The memorial to Mrs Howard, who died during childbirth, is his monumental masterpiece (**30**). Described by Robert Smirke as 'excellent – sensible and beautiful,' (*Farington*, 3, 961) it represents Religion comforting Mrs Howard, dying with her lifeless infant on her lap. After its erection Benjamin West declared that he had recently seen works by Canova, 'which could not be compared with Nollekens's monument to Mrs Howard' (*Farington*, 8, 2796, 25 June 1806).

Nollekens was still recognised as Britain's premier portraitist in 1815. When the banker Thomas Coutts asked Fuseli to whom he should go for a bust, he was told that 'although Nollekens is superannuated in many particulars, yet in a bust he is unrivalled. . . [for] a group of figures, I should have recommended Flaxman; but for a bust, give me Nollekens (*Smith* 1828, 2, 50). Nollekens's price had now risen to 150 guineas for a marble bust with shoulders and 100 guineas without, and he could command 75 guineas for a plaster (*Farington*, 13, 4555). His prices did not deter customers, who continued to sit for the 16 or so hours which Nollekens needed to model their features. Among the notable later busts were those of Arthur, Duke of Wellington, Spencer Perceval and the Reverend Charles Burney (**320, 327, 337**). Nollekens commented that people seemed most pleased with his busts of Benjamin West and Lady Charlemont (**307, 290**). The bust of Thomas Coutts (**343**) is believed to be the last which Nollekens modelled, and is not his finest. Cunningham felt it deficient in likeness and deplored its air of poverty and sickness, neither of which seemed appropriate in the sitter (*Cunningham* 1829–33, 3, 171).

After a long period of infirmity Mrs Nollekens died in August 1817 (*GM*, 87, 190), and it was commonly expected that her husband would soon follow. The sculptor had collapsed in St Albans Street in July 1813 and had since become deaf and gout-ridden. Although no longer capable of modelling from life, he 'amused himself by working on smaller matters' (*Farington*, 14, 5022), presumably the small models in clay (*pensieri*) which he had been producing and exhibiting since about 1800. Cunningham noted that some felt these little works to be superior to Nollekens's marbles, and in 1839 one commentator maintained that his tiny sketch of *The Graces* (**170**) was superior Canova's interpretation of the subject (Thomas Medwin, quoted in *JKB* 1998, 75).

Cunningham remembered seeing Nollekens, infirm and carried in a sedan chair, at the Royal Academy exhibition in 1819, and in September that year Farington saw the sculptor bed-bound, swathed in bandages and 'in a state of great debility. His look was ghastly' (*Farington* 15, 5404). Despite the predictions of his surgeon, Dr Carlisle, Nollekens lived on until 1823, cared for by his lifelong servants and his assistant **L A Goblet.** He died at Mortimer Street on 23 April and was buried at St Mary's, Paddington, where a monument by **William Behnes** was erected to his memory. It incorporates a relief image of Nollekens's monument to Mrs Howard.

In his will (which had 14 codicils) Nollekens left money and property worth about £200,000. He had no children and small bequests were made to dozens of friends and family members, as well as his assistants, including **George Gahagan**, his doctor and even his hairdresser. The principal beneficiaries were the three legatees, Rev Thomas Kerrich, librarian of Cambridge University, the antiquary Francis Douce, and Francis Russell Palmer, the natural son of the 5th Duke of Bedford, whose mother was one of Nollekens's close friends.

Goblet, who was left an annuity of £30, was instructed to sell the sculptor's remaining works, stock and antiques, and auctions duly took place in July and December 1823. Nollekens's sale included several busts and statues, numerous *pensieri*, and a large collection of terracotta figures, said to be by such illustrious sculptors as Giambologna, Fiammingo and Michelangelo. Nollekens also owned sketches by **Louis François Roubiliac, Michael Rysbrack** and **Agostino Carlini.** The buyers included many of a new generation of sculptors, whose sculpture would reflect the influence of Nollekens, including **E H Baily**, William Behnes, **Sir Richard Westmacott** and **Francis Chantrey**. Nollekens had praised and promoted the young Chantrey, and in return the latter always mentioned Nollekens 'with tenderness and respect' (*Cunningham* 1829–33, 3, 190).

Nollekens was admired by many of his fellow academicians. Benjamin West called him 'a very honest man' and a firm supporter of the Royal Academy (*Farington*, 6, 2331). There are numerous recorded instances of Nollekens providing advice and financial support to fellow artists, either personally, as in the case of the architect George Richardson, or through beneficiary funds. His professionalism and his talent were universally recognised: **Nathaniel Marchant** considered him to be unrivalled by any contemporary in the practice and execution of sculpture. Nollekens's concentration on portraiture however suggested to a younger generation of neo-classical sculptors a lack of poetic ambition. Flaxman said that Nollekens 'wanted mind' (*Farington*, 2, 2511). Allan Cunningham believed his genius to be limited to the close observation of 'the visible and earthly' rather than the higher reaches of art (*Cunningham* 1829–33, 3, 199).

He was also an eccentric character and his personal foibles received greater attention after his death than his sculptural achievements. Wordsworth had commented in 1800 that Nollekens 'was a strange and grotesque figure' (*Selincourt and Darbyshire* 1947, 4, 409) and Farington had noted a 'narrow disposition' in some of his dealings in property (*Farington* 2, 638). In 1828 these quirks were given a full public airing in *Nollekens and his Times*, a petty-minded, vindictive and entertaining biography by John Thomas Smith, the son of Nollekens's assistant **Nathaniel Smith.** J T Smith was virtually brought up in Nollekens's studio and had been assured by the sculptor that he would benefit substantially through Nollekens's will. He received only £100 as an executor. His response was to give a pitiless insight into the 'pecuniary and domestic habits' of the sculptor and his wife (*Smith* 1828, 1, iii), who, despite their wealth and position, practised economies close to self-degradation. Despite its vengeful motives and numerous factual inaccuracies, the book is one of the first full-length biographies of a British sculptor, and the second volume contains numerous vignettes of other sculptors' lives, making it one of the most important printed sources for the study of 18th-century sculpture.

Smith's account of Nollekens did not go unchallenged. The *Gentleman's Magazine* considered the book to be born of unworthy motives and gratifying only to 'the most malevolent feelings.' It predicted that 'the fruits of [Nollekens's] talents will survive the memory of his faults' (*GM*, December 1828, 98, 536–40). In 1830 Allan Cunningham sought to rescue the character of 'this remarkable man' from his 'ungentle executor'. Cunningham rebutted Smith's suggestion that Nollekens underpaid his assistants, and he replaced Smith's caricature of the sculptor, at 'one remove from an idiot', with the image of a blunt, but well-liked and sincere man (*Cunningham* 1829–33, 3, 122, 186; *Smith* 1828, 1, 118).

Regardless of Nollekens's perceived limitations as a poetic sculptor, or of his domestic eccentricities, it has long been recognised that he was the unchallenged master of British portrait sculpture for nearly 50 years. Despite the less-elevated position of this genre in the traditional hierarchies of academic art, it is nevertheless an achievement which distinguishes Nollekens as one of Britain's foremost sculptors.

MGS

Literary References: *Hayward's List*, 12; *Euro Mag*, 1788, 387; *Farington, passim*; *GM*, 1817, vol 87, 190; *MS Inscriptions*; *Smith* 1828, *passim*; *GM*, December 1828, vol 98, 536–40; *Cunningham* 1829–33, vol 3, 122–199; *Selincourt and Darbyshire* 1947, vol 4, 409; *Howard* 1964, 177–89; *Wilton Ely* 1976, 592–5; *Penny* 1977 (2), 1336–7; *JKB* 1977 (1), 180–2; *JKB* 1979, 1844–8, 1930–1; *Lord* 1988, 915–9; *JKB* 1989, 27–32; *Penny* 1991 (2), 5–34; *Grove* 1996, 196 (JKB); *Mitchell* 1992, 117–8; *Ingamells* 1997, 709–11; *ODNB* (JKB); *JKB* 1998, 72–84; *Bilbey* 2002, 95–107; *Coltman* 2004, 35–56; *Wilson* 2006 (3), 17–24; *Sullivan* 2006, 401–2

Archival References: St Marylebone Rate Books, Reel 14, 1771, p 60; reel 20, 1782, p 244; RA Council Minutes, vol 1, 25 Oct 1771, fol 111; Nollekens Family Papers; Nollekens/Polley; Nollekens Corr, BL; Nollekens Corr, Yale; letter to Thomas Banks, 1762–3, untraced, (transcribed in *Whitley* 1930, 40); RA/GA, I Nov 1779, report of JN's election as Associate; Nollekens lecture ticket; Nollekens leasehold assignments; Nollekens' note on Cowper bust; IGI

Will: Joseph Nollekens, 1823, FRC PROB 11/1673 p275–278v, proved 1 July 1723 (transcribed in *Smith* 1828, 2, 17–34)

Collections of Drawings: VAM, E.4343-4442-1920 (100 sheets of designs); E.547-663-1950 (117 sheets); two complete sketch books of sculpture in Rome, Genoa, Vienna, Paris, c1765, Ashm 1462 (*Ingamells* 1997, 710); designs for monuments and drawings, sketches of Roubiliac's busts, Harris P 437–442, P 504–510; 229 loose drawings, Sackler coll, USA; untraced, sold at Abbott and Holder, Feb–March 1989, lot 214, the folder entitled 'Nollekens/Proportions of celebrated statues in Italy, measured by himself in 1770', including two large drawings of Laöcoon and one of statues of women; Soane, vol 19

Miscellaneous Drawings: Design for a monument, 1799, sgd, BM 1901-4-17-11; design for a tablet monument, BM 1920-12-14-9; pencil drawing of the Laocoon, BM 1901-4-17-10; a faun with kid, 1759, Soc of Arts, London, *Allan* 1979, opp 161 (repr); figure of *Ocean* and drawing(s) for monuments and/or chimneypieces, HMI, Henry Wood of Bristol Archive; drawings of antiquities, apparently for sale, RIBA, c1769, Soane (*Ingamells* 1997, 710)

Auction Catalogues: *Nollekens* 1823 (1); *Nollekens* 1823 (2); *Nollekens* 1823 (3)

Portraits of the sculptor: James Barry attrib, Rome c1769, oil on canvas, YCBA (*JKB* 1979, 1931 repr); Johann Zoffany *Life Class at the Royal Academy* 1771–2, oil on canvas, Royal coll; John Francis Rigaud, exhib RA 1772, oil on canvas, untraced (Christie, 23 March 1979, lot 113 repr);

Charles Grignion, *c*1780, chalk and bodycolour, Huntington (59.55.624); Thomas Rowlandson *Joseph Nollekens modelling a female nude*, caricature, engraving, *c*1780 (*Baker* 2000, 36, repr); Lemuel Francis Abbott, *c*1791, oil, NPG, acc 30; Henry Singleton, *The Royal Academicians under the Presidentship of Benjamin West*, 1793–5, RA; H Edridge, January 1807, pencil and watercolour, BM; G H Harlow, *c*1810, oil on canvas, private coll; G Dance, 17 Feb 1810, black chalk, RA; Sir William Beechey, exhib RA 1812, oil on canvas, Tate acc N00120; James Lonsdale, *c*1816, oil on canvas, NPG, acc 360; Lewis Alexander Goblet, herm bust, exhib 1816, plaster, Ashm, 1821 and marble, VAM A.70-1965 (*Bilbey* 2002, 287 repr); J Jackson, pencil and watercolour, *c*1818, BM; Sir Francis Chantrey, 1818, marble, Woburn Abbey, Beds (another version: marble, 1819–20, BM. Original model Ashm, prelim drawing, pencil, Huntingdon); James Northcote, *c*1820, oil on canvas, Fitz; William Behnes, marble bas-relief on a monumental tablet, after 1823, St Mary, Paddington Green, London

Note on MS Inscriptions (Osborn coll, Beinecke Library, Yale d.174)

This document, lot 284 in Nollekens's sale, 19 Dec 1823, gives the complete text of the epitaphs, i.e. the inscriptions that were cut on some 134 funeral monuments, and underneath 14 portrait busts.

The epitaphs were written out in copperplate hand by professional scribes, with occasional notes added by Nollekens himself. On his visit to the studio, the scribe will have had a batch of epitaphs to copy. Thus, the order of the texts in the manuscript is approximately the order in which the monuments were completed.

The inscribed pages are numbered from 1 to 131, with four more unnumbered; there is also an index, which runs only to page 131. From page 4 to page 92 (from the 1770s to the early 1790s) one scribe only was employed. After that different hands are evident, and the calligraphy is of less fine quality. Evidently the new scribe was told by Nollekens to fill in blank spaces on the earlier pages. Eleven texts, thus interpolated, are out of order. They are indicated in the list below by asterisks.

The following list of works was prepared by John Kenworthy-Browne.

Funerary Monuments

No.	Date	Work	Location		References
1.		Jonathan Shipley, Bishop of St Asaph (†1788) Drawing(s): BM PDL 1920-12-14-6, marked '3 foot 6'	Twyford, Hants	S	*MS Inscriptions*, 85; *Smith* 1828, vol 2, 71
2.		Welbore Ellis, Bishop of Meath (†1733), Diana Ellis (†1739) and six of their children Drawing(s): VAM E.4383-1920; 4404-1920; E.4353-1920 (bust only)	Christ Church Cathedral, Dublin (dismantled)		*MS Inscriptions*, 86; *Smith* 1828, vol 2, 74; *Potterton* 1975, 73
3.		George Keate (†1797)	[Isleworth, Middx]; destroyed		*MS Inscriptions*, 102; *Smith* 1828, vol 2, 74
4.		Colonel David Woodburn (†1804)	Untraced		*MS Inscriptions*, 117; *Smith* 1828, vol 2, 75
5.		Maria, Countess of Dysart (†1804) Drawing(s): VAM E.4360-1920; Harris Art Gallery, Preston P442 (drawing attrib, to John Taylor)	Helmingham, Suffolk	S	*MS Inscriptions*, 119; *Smith* 1828, vol 2, 72
6.		Elizabeth Maude (†1796)	Great Offley, Herts	S	*Smith* 1828, vol 2, 74
7.	1773	Lady Henrietta Williams Wynn (†1769) Drawing(s): VAM E.610-1950, E.4382-1920 (preliminary), 609-1950; Soane vol 37, fol 42 (as executed) Model(s): **?Exhib RA, London, 1773, 213 ('Hope leaning on an Urn'), *Graves* 1905–6, 381; untraced**	Ruabon, Denbighs	SD	*MS Inscriptions*, 4
8.	1774	Henry Leslie and Peter Leslie	Hillsborough, Co Down	S	*MS Inscriptions*, 18; *Potterton* 1975, 62, 73 (repr)
9.	1775	Giles Earle (†1758)	Hankerton, Wilts	SD	Pevsner, *Wilts*, 1975, 263
10.	1775	Richard Trevor, Bishop of Durham (†1771) (designed by Lord Trevor, brother) Drawing(s): Sackler Priv Coll, 21 (niche only); VAM E.956-1965 Model(s): 'A bishop, model' exhib RA, London, 1774, 193, untraced	Bishop Auckland, Durham, Bishop's chapel	SD	*MS Inscriptions*, 5; *Smith* 1828, vol 2, 75; *Graves* V, 1905–6, 381; Pevsner, *Durham*, 1983, 105 (repr 83); *ODNB*; JKB, *Geo Gp J*, forthcoming 2008
11.	1777	Elizabeth Ellis (†1761) Drawing(s): VAM E.4422-1920 (only the bracket)	Shelford, Notts	SD	*MS Inscriptions*, 88
12.	1777	Oliver Goldsmith (†1774) Drawing(s): VAM E.4406-1920; Sackler Priv Coll 23r, 24	Westminster Abbey, London, above door to Chapel of St Faith	S	*MS Inscriptions*, 46; *Smith* 1828, vol 2, 73
13.	1777	Sir Septimus Robinson (†1765)	Rokeby, Durham	S	*MS Inscriptions*, 7
14.	1777	Sir Thomas Salusbury (†1773) Drawing(s): VAM E.601, 602-1950 (preliminary designs); E.603-1950 (tree and shroud); E.4371-1920 (final design)	Great Offley, Herts	SD	*MS Inscriptions*, 17; *Smith* 1828, vol 2, 75; *Whinney* 1988, 291 (repr)
15.	*c*1778	Allen, 1st Earl Bathurst (†1776) and Countess Bathurst (†1768) (busts possibly not by Nollekens) Drawing(s): VAM E.4388-1920; rejected designs: VAM E.4364-1920; Soane vol 19, fol 45	Cirencester, Glos		*CIIA* 4/4/25, 28–9 (repr)
16.	1778	Samuel Burroughs (†1761)	Great Offley, Herts	S	*MS Inscriptions*, 16
17.	1783	Sir John Pringle Bt (†1782)	Westminster Abbey, London, south transept	S	*MS Inscriptions*, 45; *Smith* 1828, vol 2, 74

18.	1786	Henry Barwell (†1785)	Westbourne, Sussex	S	*MS Inscriptions*, 58
19.	1787	Lt-Gen Bennett Noel (†1766)	Exton, Rutland	SD	*MS Inscriptions*, 61
20.	1787	Robert Denison (†1785) Payment(s): £921	Ossington, Notts	S	*MS Inscriptions*, 69; *Penny* 1977 (1), 65, 66 (repr)
21.	1790	Baptist, 4th Earl of Gainsborough (†1751), Countess of Gainsborough (†1771) and Thomas Noel (†1788) Drawing(s): Soane vol 19, fol 32	Exton, Rutland	S	*MS Inscriptions*, 76; *Whinney* 1988, 292–3 (repr)
22.	1790	Dr John Crossley (†1789)	St Helen, Abingdon, Berks	SD	*MS Inscriptions*, 90
23.	?1792	Giovanni Battista Cipriani (†1785), 'intended for the cloisters at Westminster' (epitaph composed by Reynolds)	Untraced		*Farington* VII, 2524; *MS Inscriptions*, 92
24.	1793	Captains William Bayne, William Blair and Lord Robert Manners (†1782) Payment(s): £4,000 Drawing(s): 1st design: BM PDL 1920-12-14-10; VAM E.4379-1920; Soane vol 19, fol 44; Sackler Priv Coll, 1, 2, 1v (two rear views); Ashmolean 149-2N (40) Intermediate design: Sackler 3, 3v, 4 Contract drawing: YCBA Model(s): **?Exhib RA, London, 1788, 647 ('Britannia') *Graves* 1905–6, 381; untraced**	Westminster Abbey, London, north transept	SD	*MS Inscriptions*, 89; *JKB* 1977 (1), 180–2 (reprs)
25.	1795	John Lee (†1793) Drawing(s): VAM E.4408-1920	Staindrop, Durham	S	*MS Inscriptions*, 97
26.	1795	William Weddell (†1789) (the portrait bust s&d) Drawing(s): VAM E.4427-1920	Ripon Cathedral, W R Yorks	SD	
27.	c1797	Mary Willis (†1797)	Greatford, Lincs		
28.	1801	James Stewart Mackenzie (†1800)	Westminster Abbey, London, south transept	S	*MS Inscriptions*, 106
29.	1802	John Frederick, 3rd Duke of Dorset (†1799) Drawing(s): **VAM E.4378-1920 (preliminary) *Physick* 1969, 152 (repr); BM PDL 1920–12-14-8** ('approved'); VAM **E.4400-1920 (measured)**	Wythyam, Sussex	SD	*MS Inscriptions*, 108; *Smith* 1828, vol 2, 72
30.	1803	Hon Maria Howard of Corby (†1789) Drawing(s): **VAM E.957, 958-1965 (*Neoclassicism* 1972, 704); Harris Art Gallery, Preston P443 (drawing attrib. to John Taylor)** Model(s): **t-c, VAM A.5-1944, *Bilbey* 2002, 103–4 (repr)**	Wetheral, Cumberland	S	*MS Inscriptions*, 121; *Whinney* 1971, 17, 120–1 (repr); *JKB* 1998, 74, 77, 80
31.	1804	John, Viscount Bateman (†1802)	Shobden, Herefs	S	*MS Inscriptions*, 113
32.	1805	Jane, Mrs Coke (†1800) Payment(s): 'About £2000' (JT Smith) Drawing(s): **VAM E.636-1950, E.4358-1920; Soane vol 19, f37; Ashmolean 149-2N; Harris Art Gallery, Preston P441 (drawing attrib. to John Taylor), *JKB* 1989, 81 (repr)**	Tittleshall, Norfolk	SD	*MS Inscriptions*, 116; *Penny* 1977 (1), 54–5 (repr)
33.	1806	Hon Frances Boscawen (†1805) (similar design to Viscountess Falmouth; 'designed by Viscount Falmouth')	St Michael, Penkevil, Cornwall	SD	*MS Inscriptions*, 118
34.	c1807	Rev Francis Willis (†1807)	Greatford, Lincs	S	
35.	1808	Cecilia Towneley (†1778), and Edward Towneley Standish (†1807)	Standish, Lancs	S	*MS Inscriptions*, 124
36.	1810	Viscount Irwin (†1778) and Lady Irwin (†1807) Drawing(s): Sackler Priv Coll, 19	Whitkirk, W R Yorks	S	*MS Inscriptions*, 127
37.	c1810	William Offley (†1789) (portrait bust, unsigned, with tablet)	Great Offley, Herts		*Farington* X, 3689
38.	1812	Clement Saxton (†1810) Drawing(s): VAM E.4405-1920	St Helen's, Abingdon, Berks	S	*MS Inscriptions*, 130
39.	1813	William Windham (†1810) Drawing(s): VAM E.4384-1920; Soane vol 19, fol 47 (with a herm bust)	Felbrigg, Norfolk	S	*MS Inscriptions*, 133
40.	1815	Isabella, Countess of Beverley (†1812)	Westminster Abbey, London, Chapel of St Nicholas	S	*MS Inscriptions*, 135
41.		1st Lord Ashburton (†1783)	Ashburton, Devon		*MS Inscriptions*, 71
42.		Admiral Robert Biggs (†1803)	Untraced		*MS Inscriptions*, 115
43.		Admiral Sir George Bowyer (†1800) Drawing(s): VAM 4436, 4389-1920	Radley, Berks	S	*MS Inscriptions*, 108
44.		Andrew Ramsay Karr (†1799)	Cobham, Surrey	S	*MS Inscriptions*, 130

No.	Subject	Location		Source
45.	Ann Simpson (†1785)	St Margaret, Lothbury	S	*MS Inscriptions*, 53
46.	Anne Delmé, Lady Robert Seymour (†1804)	Taliaris, Carmarthen		*MS Inscriptions*, 115; *Dale-Jones and Lloyd* 1989, 42, 55
47.	Anne Parker (†1780)	Untraced		*MS Inscriptions*, 19
48.	Anne Purefoy Jervoise (†1782), Caroline (†1789) and Catherine (†1795) Drawing(s): VAM E.4430-1920	Shalstone, Bucks	S	*MS Inscriptions*, 121
49.	Anthony Morris Storer (†1800?)	Purley, Berks		*MS Inscriptions*, 103
50.	Archbishop John Tillotson (†1694) (inscription only; the marble figure by Wilton)	Sowerby, W R Yorks		*MS Inscriptions*, 91
51.	Bodvell family: Lloyd (†1731), Anne (†1757), Peter (†1711), William MP (†1757) et al	Llandwrog, Gwynnedd		*MS Inscriptions*, 29
52.	Captain John Urry (†1802) Drawing(s): VAM E.4392-1920	Untraced		*MS Inscriptions*, 105
53.	Charles Long (†1812) Drawing(s): VAM E.4367 -1920; Sackler Priv Coll, 29	Saxmundham, Suffolk	S	*MS Inscriptions*, 135
54.	Charles Townley (†1805)	Burnley, Lancs	S	*MS Inscriptions*, 117
55.	Charlotte, Duchess of Somerset (†1773)	St Nicholas, Chiswick		*MS Inscriptions*, 95
56.	Christian Methuen (†1779) and son Thomas (†1774)	North Wraxall, Wilts		*MS Inscriptions*, 23
57.	Col Alexander Champion (†1793) Drawing(s): VAM E.4421-1920 (preliminary)	Bath Abbey	S	*MS Inscriptions*, 98
58.	Dame Arabella Boyd (†1791)			*MS Inscriptions*, 94
59.	Daniel Minet (†1790)	Bengeo, Herts	S	*MS Inscriptions*, 79
60.	David Ramsay Karr (†1794)	Titchfield, Hants		*MS Inscriptions*, 63*
61.	Dr Samuel Arnold, MD (†1802)	Westminster Abbey, north choir aisle		*MS Inscriptions*, loose
62.	Earl of Bessborough (†1793) Drawing(s): VAM E.4357-1920	Derby Cathedral	S	*MS Inscriptions*, 2*
63.	Edward Greathead (†1803) Drawing(s): VAM E.4397, 4420-1920	Hampreston, Dorset	S	*MS Inscriptions*, 110
64.	Edward Hugh Boscawen (†1774) (probably designed by Viscount Falmouth)	St Michael Penkevil, Cornwall	S	*MS Inscriptions*, 48
65.	Edward Southwell (†1787)	Wisbech, Cambs	S	*MS Inscriptions*, 77
66.	Edward, 5th Lord Leigh (†1786) Drawing(s): VAM E.4399-1920	Stoneleigh, Warks		*MS Inscriptions*, 63
67.	Edwin, 2nd Lord Sandys (†1797)	Ombersley, Worcs	S	*MS Inscriptions*, 101
68.	Elizabeth Grigg (†1792) and her two daughters, Anne Winne (†1786) and Mary Grigg (†1792) Drawing(s): VAM E.4367-1920	St Katherine, Regents Park, London	S	*MS Inscriptions*, 51*
69.	Elizabeth Johnson (†1792) (the inscription was altered for John Johnson †1800) Drawing(s): VAM E.4363-1920	Carlisle Cathedral	S	*MS Inscriptions*, 101
70.	Elizabeth Johnston (†1784)	Untraced		*MS Inscriptions*, 65
71.	Elizabeth, Viscountess Falmouth (†1793) Drawing(s): VAM 4395-1920	St Michael, Penkevil, Cornwall		*MS Inscriptions*, 94
72.	Ezekial Wallis (†1735) and Cecilia Wallis (†1760)	North Wraxall, Wilts		*MS Inscriptions*, 25
73.	Frances Cust (†1785), aged 8	Belton, Lincs		*MS Inscriptions*, 56
74.	Gen the Hon Charles Stuart (†1801) Drawing(s): VAM E.4445 (?)-1920v	Westminster Abbey, London, Chapel of St Andrew	S	*MS Inscriptions*, 111
75.	George Dashwood (†1801) Drawing(s): VAM E.4439-1920	West Wycombe, Bucks	S	*MS Inscriptions*, 110
76.	George, Lord Southampton (†1810) Drawing(s): VAM E.4393-1920 (same as J P Jervoise)	[St James, Hampstead Road]; in store	S	*MS Inscriptions*, 130
77.	H W B Portman (†1796)	Old church, Bryanston, Dorset		*MS Inscriptions*, 28*
78.	Hannah, Countess of Exeter (†1765)	Burghley House, Lincs, garden		*MS Inscriptions*, 49
79.	Harry, 6th Duke of Bolton (†1794)	St Mary, Basing, Hants		*MS Inscriptions*, 124
80.	Henry Kent (†1759), Christian (†1763), Joanna (†1743), Christian (†1774) and Henry Kent DD (†1799)	Potterne, Wilts	S	*MS Inscriptions*, 107
81.	Henry, 2nd Earl Bathurst (†1794) (portrait bust s&d 1777)	Cirencester, Glos		*CIIA* 4/4/30-1 (repr)
82.	Hester Elwes (†1770) and Cary Elwes (†1782)	Throcking, Herts	S	*MS Inscriptions*, 35
83.	Hon Mary Leigh (†1806)	Stoneleigh, Warks	S	*MS Inscriptions*, 125
84.	Hugo Meynell (†1800)	Ashley, Staffs		*MS Inscriptions*, 111
85.	Jacob Gosett (†1788), inscribed tomb-chest	[St John, Church Row, Hampstead, London]; untraced		*MS Inscriptions*, 75
86.	James Johnson, Bishop of Worcester (†1774) (designed by Robert Adam) Drawing(s): Soane, Adam vol 19/13.36, vol 21/174	Worcester Cathedral	S	*MS Inscriptions*, 13
87.	Johann Zoffany (†1810)	Kew churchyard, London (tomb inscription)		*MS Inscriptions*, 129

88.	John Bird (†1772)	Kenilworth, Warks		*MS Inscriptions*, 32
89.	John Came (†1796)	[Cordwainers's Hall, London]; destroyed		*MS Inscriptions*, 109
90.	John Charlesworth (†1781, at 4 months)	Untraced		*MS Inscriptions*, 66
91.	John Fuller (†1810) Drawing(s): VAM E.4418 (preliminary), 4386-1920	Catsfield, Sussex	S	*MS Inscriptions*, 129
92.	John Gordon (†1774)	Untraced		*MS Inscriptions*, 15
93.	John Thompson (†1799) Drawing(s): VAM E.4368-1920	Petham, Kent		*MS Inscriptions*, 105
94.	John, 1st Earl Spencer (†1783) (made to the designs of G-B Cipriani) Drawing(s): (by Cipriani) Ashmolean; Sotheby, 31 March 1999, lot 93	Great Brington, Northants	S	*MS Inscriptions*, 60; *Smith* 1828, vol 2, 75; *Penny* 1977 (1), 98–100 (repr)
95.	Joseph Hill (†1811)	Untraced		*MS Inscriptions*, 134
96.	Leonard Robinson (†1788)	Untraced		*MS Inscriptions*, 26*
97.	Lionel Robert Tollemache (†1793) Drawing(s): Sackler Priv Coll, 25, 25v (preliminary), 26 (as executed)	Helmingham, Suffolk		*MS Inscriptions*, 126
98.	Lord Robert Manners (†1782)	Bottesford, Leics		*MS Inscriptions*, 96
99.	Mary Ainslie (†1767)	Untraced		*MS Inscriptions*, 44
100.	Mary Irby (†1792) Drawing(s): VAM 4361-1920; Soane vol 19, f34; Sackler Priv Coll, 28	Whiston, Northants	S	*MS Inscriptions*, 93; *CIIA* 4/3/151-2 (repr)
101.	Mary Jane Wilkinson (†1803)	Untraced		*MS Inscriptions*, 112
102.	Mary Lee (†1812) Drawing(s): VAM E.4408-1920	Staindrop, Durham	S	*MS Inscriptions*, 132
103.	Mary Yate (†1777)	Arlingham, Glos	S	*MS Inscriptions*, 31; *CIIA* 4/4/3 (repr)
104.	Mary, Countess Talbot (†1787) Drawing(s): VAM E.4420-1920; Sackler Priv Coll, 13	Great Barrington, Glos	S	*MS Inscriptions*, 72; Pevsner, *Glos: Cotswolds*, 1999, 390 (repr 86)
105.	Mrs Francis Leevers (†1785)	Untraced		*MS Inscriptions*, 64
106.	Patrick Grant (†1783) and others	Untraced		*MS Inscriptions*, 41
107.	Rev Arthur Collier, LLD (†1777)	Untraced		*MS Inscriptions*, 90
108.	Rev Edward Buckworth (†1792)	Untraced		*MS Inscriptions*, 59*
109.	Rev George Purefoy Jervoise (†1805) Drawing(s): VAM E.4426-1920	Shalstone, Bucks	S	*MS Inscriptions*, 120
110.	Rev Jervoise Purefoy Jervoise (†1808) Drawing(s): VAM E.4393-1920 (same as Southampton monument)	Shalstone, Bucks	S	*MS Inscriptions*, 125
111.	Rev Joseph Disney (†1777); Ann Disney (†1785) and Rev Matthew Disney (†1763)	Cranbrook, Kent		*MS Inscriptions*, 50
112.	Rev Robert Pool Finch (†1803)	[St John, Smith Square, London]; destroyed		*MS Inscriptions*, 113
113.	Rev Thomas Jones (†1807)	Trinity College, Cambridge, chapel	S	*MS Inscriptions*, 130
114.	Richard Barwell (†1804)	Westbourne, Sussex	S	*MS Inscriptions*, 131
115.	Richard Davenport (†1799) Drawing(s): VAM 4411, 4413-1920	Great Marlow, Bucks		*MS Inscriptions*, 104
116.	Richard Jackson (†1786), and three of his children	Untraced		*MS Inscriptions*, 73
117.	Richard Salter (†1776) Drawing(s): VAM E.4387-1950; Sackler Priv Coll, 27	St George, Bridgetown, Barbados	S	*MS Inscriptions*, 33; *Perowne* 1951 1941–2 (repr)
118.	Robert Cooper Lee	Untraced		*MS Inscriptions*, 10*
119.	Roger Hesketh (†1791)	Churchtown, Lancs	S	*MS Inscriptions*, 55*
120.	Samuel Peploe (†1781)	Chester Cathedral	S	*MS Inscriptions*, 40
121.	Sarah Mitford (†1776) Drawing(s): BM PDL 1920-12-14-7; VAM E.4366-1920; Sackler Priv Coll 31 (preliminary?)	Chipping Ongar, Essex	S	*MS Inscriptions*, 34
122.	Sir Charles Booth (†1795) Drawing(s): VAM E.4261-1920	Maidstone, Kent	S	*MS Inscriptions*, 2*
123.	Sir Charles Kemeys Tynte (†1785)	Goathurst, Somerset	S	*MS Inscriptions*, 57
124.	Sir Henry Mildmay Bt (†1808)	Dogmersfield, Hants	S	*MS Inscriptions*, 129
125.	Sir John Dashwood King (†1793), his wife Sarah Moore (†1777), and six of their children	West Wycombe, Bucks	S	*MS Inscriptions*, 109
126.	Sir John Mordaunt (†1780)	Untraced		*MS Inscriptions*, 1*
127.	Sir John Tyrrell Bt (†1766) Drawing(s): Sackler private coll 34	[East Horndon, Essex]; VAM A.92-1970	S	*MS Inscriptions*, 70; *Bilbey* 2002, 95 (repr)
128.	Sir John Wynn Bt (†1773)	Boduan, Gwynnedd		*MS Inscriptions*, 38
129.	Sir Richard Levett (†1721), Abraham Blackborne (†1721), Frances Blackborne (†1795) and others	Untraced		*MS Inscriptions*, 99
130.	Sir Robert Chambers (†1803)	[Temple Church, London]; destroyed		*MS Inscriptions*, 131
131.	Sir Robert Cunliffe Bt (†1778) Drawing(s): **VAM E.4354-1920 (*Physick* 1969, 144 repr)**	Bruera, Cheshire	S	*MS Inscriptions*, 42; *Whinney* 1988, 291 (repr)
132.	Sir Thomas Pinfold (†1701)	Walton, Bucks	S	*MS Inscriptions*, 52
133.	Sir Wadham Wyndham (†1668) and family	[St Edmund's College, Salisbury, Wilts]; untraced		*MS Inscriptions*, 27
134.	Sir William Wynn (†1754)	Boduan, Gwynnedd		*MS Inscriptions*, 39
135.	Thomas Bridges of Binham Abbey (†1768)	Untraced		*MS Inscriptions*, 74
136.	Thomas Chase (†1788)	Untraced		*MS Inscriptions*, 78

137.		Thomas Edward Freeman (†1808) Drawing(s): VAM E.4390, 4374, 4410-1920		Batsford, Glos	S	*MS Inscriptions*, 122
138.		Vice-Admiral Sayer (†1776) Drawing(s): VAM E.4429-1920 (wall monument); Sackler Priv Coll, 33 (standing monument)		St Paul, Deptford, London	S	*MS Inscriptions*, 11
139.		William Denison (†1782) Payment(s): £416		Ossington, Notts	S	*MS Inscriptions*, 67; *Penny* 1977 (1), 52, 180–1 (repr); *Wilson* 1971, 213–4
140.		William Greig (†1795)		Untraced		*MS Inscriptions*, 3*
141.		William Hogarth (†1764)		Chiswick churchyard, inscription on tombstone		*MS Inscriptions*, 43
142.		William, Lord Boston (†1775) and Albinia, Lady Boston (†1769) Drawing(s): **VAM E.4365-1920 (*Neoclassicism* 1972, 703)**		Whiston, Northants	S	*MS Inscriptions*, 21; *CIIA* 4/3/146–7 (repr)
Statues						
143.	1759	Bacchus, model in clay after Michelangelo		[Soc of A, premium, 10 gns]; untraced		RSA, *Minutes*, 1758–60, seq 1 f77; RSA *Premiums*, 1758, 16
144.	1760	Dancing faun	tc	[Soc of A, premium, 20 gns, with additional gratuity of 10 gns]; untraced		RSA *Minutes*, 1758–60, seq 4 f49, seq 4 f54; *Graves* 1907, 183
145.	1761	Bacchus and a young satyr, statuette after Michelangelo or Sansovino	tc	[Exhib Free Soc, London, 95]; untraced		*Graves* 1907, 183
146.	1764	Boy on a dolphin (half size) Payment(s): £30 Model(s): t-c, Garrick Sale, 23rd June 1823, lot 76; untraced	m	[for Henry Temple, 2nd Viscount Palmerston]; Broadlands, Hants Other versions: replica, Althorp, for Lord Spencer, marble full size, for Brownlow Cecil, 9th Earl of Exeter, Burghley House, c1768, marble		*Howard* 1964, 177–189 (repr); *JKB* 1979, 1844
147.	1767	Castor and Pollux	m	[for Thomas Anson, Shugborough, sold 9 Aug 1842, lot 9]; VAM A.59 -1940	SD	*Bilbey* 2002, 96 (repr); *Coltman* 2004, 36–7 (repr)
148.	1767	Jupiter, Juno and Io Drawing(s): (x2) Fondation Custodia, Institut Néerlandais, Paris 1971-T.20 recto	tc	[Concorso Balestra, Rome, gold medal]; untraced		*JKB* 1979, 1931 (drawing repr)
149.	c1770	Juno Pronuba, statuette	tc	[Nollekens sale, 4 July 1823, lot 71, bt by Mr Rouw]; VAM A.10-1944		*JKB* 1998, 73, 77, 79 (repr)
150.	c1770	Paetus and Arria, statuette	tc	[Exhib RA, London, 1771, 141]; Arthur M Sackler Coll, USA, 77.5.59		*Graves* V, 1905–6, 381; *JKB* 1998, 74, 77, 80 (repr); *Avery and Laing* 1981, 268–9 (repr)
151.	1770	Paris, model	tc	[Exhib Free Soc, London, 191]; untraced		*Graves* 1907, 183
152.	c1770	Seated Mercury, statuette	tc	Private coll		*JKB* 1998, 73, 77, 79 (repr)
153.	1771	Bacchus, a model		[Exhib RA, London, 140]; untraced		*Graves* V, 1905–6, 381
154.	1772	Bacchus, after Michelangelo		[Exhib RA, London, 169]; untraced		*Graves* V, 1905–6, 381
155.	1771–1772	The King; the Queen; Britannia; Liberty		[for P E Turst, Pantheon, Oxford Street, London]; destroyed		*Survey of London*, vol 30, 1963, 271
156.	1773	Venus taking off her sandal Payment(s): £210 Drawing(s): VAM E.643-1950; E.644-1950	m	[Rockingham House, London, Wentworth Woodhouse, Yorks, sculpture gall, by 1801]; Getty, Los Angeles 87.SA.106 Other versions: replica, exhib BI, 53, 1806, marble, SD; private coll	SD	*Graves* V, 1905–6, 381; *Penny* 1991 (2), 5–34 (repr); *Baker* 2000, 36–40 (repr); *Fusco* 1998, 97–8 (repr)
157.	1775	Minerva Payment(s): £210 Drawing(s): VAM E.593-1950	m	[Rockingham House, London; Wentworth Woodhouse, Yorks, sculpture gall, by 1801]; Getty, Los Angeles 87.SA.107	SD	*Penny* 1991 (2), 5–34; *Baker* 2000, 38 (repr)
158.	1776	Juno Payment(s): £210 Drawing(s): VAM E.644-1950	m	[Rockingham House, London; Wentworth Woodhouse, Yorks, sculpture gall, by 1801]; Getty, Los Angeles 87.SA.108	SD	*Penny* 1991 (2), 5–34; *Baker* 2000, 36–40 (repr)
159.	1778	Diana Payment(s): 300 gns Drawing(s): VAM E.643-1950	m	[Rockingham House, London, Wentworth Woodhouse, Yorks, sculpture gall, by 1801]; VAM A.5-1986	SD	*Penny* 1991 (2), 5–34 (repr); *Baker* 2000, 15–18; *Bilbey* 2002, 96–7 (repr)
160.	1778	Venus chiding Cupid Drawing(s): VAM E.581-1950 Model(s): **Exhib RA, London, 209 ('Venus chiding Cupid; a model'), *Graves* 1905–6, 381**	m	[for Lord Yarborough; exhib RA, London, 216]; Usher Art Gallery, Lincoln	S	*Graves* V, 1905–6, 381; *Whinney* 1988, 290 (repr); *Lord* 1988, 917 (repr)
161.	c1780	Apollo or Bacchus, statuette	tc	Private coll		*JKB* 1998, 74–5, 78–9, 82 (repr)
162.	1782	'Cupid sharpening his arrow'	m	[Exhib RA, London, 556; exhib BI, London, 1806, 52]; untraced		*Graves* 1875, 403; *Graves* V, 1905–6, 381
163.	1783	Mercury Payment(s): £262 10s	m	[for Lord Yarborough; exhib RA, London, 464]; Usher Art Gallery, Lincoln	S	*Graves* V, 1905–6, 381; *Lord* 1988, 915 (repr); *JKB* 1998, 73
164.	c1790	Hero dying in the arms of Victory, statuette	tc	VAM A.7-1944		*JKB* 1998, 77, 80 (repr); *Bilbey* 2002, 102–3 (repr)
165.	c1790	Sophia Aufrere Pelham (†1786)	m	Brocklesby Park, Lincs, mausoleum		*Penny* 1977 (1), 50–55 (repr); *Lord* 1992, 85–96 (repr)

No.	Date	Subject	Medium	Location		Literature
166.	1790–1792	Charles, 2nd Marquess of Rockingham (†1782)	m	Wentworth Woodhouse, W R Yorks, mausoleum	S	*MS Inscriptions*, 80; *Penny* 1977 (1), 62 (repr)
167.	post-1800	Seated Nymph combing her hair, statuette	tc	Philip Ward-Jackson		*JKB* 1998, 75, 78, 83 (repr)
168.	1800	Venus anointing her hair		[Exhib RA, London, 1031 Exhib BI, London, 1808, 141 Nollekens sale, 5 July 1823, lot 104 Hertford House (inventories 1870–90)]; untraced		*Graves* 1875, 403; *Graves* V, 1905–6, 382
169.	c1801	Religion (or Mrs Coke of Holkham), statuette	tc	VAM A.8-1944		*JKB* 1998, 74, 77, 81 (repr); *Bilbey* 2002, 103 (repr)
170.	1802	The Graces, seated, statuette	tc	[Exhib RA, London, 1064]; VAM A.1-2000		*Graves* V, 1905–6, 382; *JKB* 1998, 75, 78, 83 (repr); *Bilbey* 2002, 104 (repr)
171.	1803	Lot and his two daughters, statuette	tc	[Exhib RA, London, 930]; private coll		*Graves* V, 1905–6, 382; *JKB* 1998, 75, 78, 83 (repr)
172.	1803	The judgment of Paris, statuette	tc	[Exhib RA, London, 932]; VAM A.21-1955		*Graves* V, 1905–6, 382; *JKB* 1998, 73, 78, 84 (repr); *Bilbey* 2002, 105–6 (repr)
173.	1805	Laocoon and his sons, statuette	tc	[Exhib RA, London, 694]; VAM A.12-1966		*Graves* V, 1905–6, 382; *JKB* 1998, 75–6, 78, 84 (repr); *Bilbey* 2002, 106
174.	c1810	Venus and Adonis, statuettes, a pair	tc	VAM A.6-1944		*JKB* 1998, 76, 78, 84 (repr); *Bilbey* 2002, 106–7 (repr)
175.	1812	William Pitt (executed by Sebastian Gahagan) Payment(s): £3,000 Drawing(s): Ashm 149-2N 23, 26; BM PDL 1901-4-17-9 ('Pitt'); Soane vol 37, f49; VAM E.606-1950 (rear view) Model(s): Fitz, plaster	m	Senate House, Cambridge	SD	*Penny* 1977 (2), 1336–7 (repr)
176.	nd	Adam and Eve, Venus at the bath, dancing Nymph, Susannah and the elders, statuettes	tc	Peter Norton sale, Christie, 11 Jan 1869; untraced		*JKB* 1998, 73, n13
177.	nd	Adonis, statuette	tc	YCBA, B197714, 18		*JKB* 1998, 82 (repr)
178.	nd	Eve bewailing the death of Abel, statuette	tc	Private coll		*JKB* 1998, 75, 78, 83 (repr)
179.	nd	Marine Venus (statuette)	tc	Christie, 23 Feb, 1883, lot 144; untraced		*Heseltine* 1916, no 26 (repr); *JKB* 1998, 72
180.	nd	Sitting Venus (model only, the marble carved by John Charles Felix Rossi RA for Petworth House, Sussex)	p	[Exhib BI, London, 1807, 87 Nollekens sale, 5 July 1823, lot 21, bt Earl of Egremont]; private coll		*Smith* 1828, vol 2, 63; *Graves* 1875, 403
181.	nd	Venus standing on a shell, statuette	tc	VAM A.9-1944		*JKB* 1998, 75, 78, 84 (repr); *Bilbey* 2002, 103 (repr)
182.	nd	Venus, statuette	tc	YCBA, B197714, 17		*JKB* 1998, 74–5, 78–9, 82 (repr)
Busts						
183.	1759	Head from 'Lot and his daughters'		[Soc of A, submitted as a test of his abilities]; untraced		RSA *Minutes* seq 1 f95
184.	1764	Copy of the Rondanini Medusa (after the antique now in the Glyptothek, Munich)	m	Burleigh House, Northants		*Horn* 1797, 132
185.	1764	David Garrick Payment(s): 12 gns (tc model)	m	Althorp, Northants		*JKB* 1979, 1847 (repr)
186.	1764	Edward Augustus, Duke of York and Albany	m	Windsor Castle		*JKB* 1979, 1847 (repr)
187.	1764	John Richards of North House, Horndean, Hants	m	Untraced		*Ingamells* 1997, 709, 711
188.	1764	Sir John Wodehouse Bt (later 1st Baron Wodehouse)	m	Untraced		*Ingamells* 1997, 709, 711
189.	1767	Laurence Sterne (tc?)		[Exhib Free Soc, London, 309]; untraced Other versions: replica, NPG, London, 1891, marble		*Graves* 1907, 183; *JKB* 1979, 1848 (repr)
190.	1768	Frederick, 5th Earl of Carlisle	m	Castle Howard, N R Yorks		*JKB* 1979, 1848 (repr)
191.	1768	Henry Fox, 1st Lord Holland	m	[Exhib RA, London, 139; Holland House, Kensington, London]; private coll		Nollekens to Thomas Anson, 19 April 1768 (Staffs Ro D615/) (S) /1/6/6, inf JKB); *Graves* V, 1905–6, 381
192.	c1769	Giovanni Battista Piranesi	m	Accademia di San Luca, Rome		*Wilton Ely* 1976, 593–5; *JKB* 1979, 1848 (repr)
193.	c1770	Head of young Bacchus		Private coll		
194.	1772	Charles Drummond, lord provost of Edinburgh	m	Royal Infirmary, Edinburgh		*Pearson* 1991, unpag, 18, 23 (repr)
195.	1772	Thomas Wynn (later Lord Newborough)	m	[Holland House, Kensington, London]; English Heritage	S	JKB forthcoming
196.	c1772	Wills Hill, Lord Hillsborough, 1st Marquess of Downshire	m	Hillsborough Castle, Co Down		*Cornforth* 1994, 64
197.	c1773	Empress Catherine II of Russia		[for James Cox's museum]; untraced		*Cox* 1773, unpag
198.	1773	King George III	m	[Exhib RA, London, 1774, 190]; Royal Soc, London	SD	*Graves* V, 1905–6, 381; *Whinney* 1988, 296–7 (repr)
199.	1774	Robert Orme	p	[India Office library, Downing Street]; India coll, BL		*Archer* 1965, 407 (repr); *ODNB*
200.	1775	Charles Pelham, later 1st Lord Yarborough	m	Private coll Other versions: replica, private coll, marble	SD	

201.	1775	John Manners, Marquess of Granby	m	[Exhib RA, London, 208]; Belvoir Castle, Leics Other versions: replica, Windsor Castle, marble, SD another, 1814, Windsor Castle, RCIN 45143, SD	SD	*Graves* V, 1905–6, 381; *Carlton House*, 1991–2, 54 (repr)
202.	1775	Sir William Stanhope	m	[5th Earl of Chesterfield]; Carnarvon sale, Christie, 3 June, 1918, 192 Christie, 3 April, 1985, 71; YCBA	SD	*The British Face*, 1986, 128–9 (repr)
203.	1776	Anna Manzolini	p	[Peterhof, Russia]; untraced	S	Inf Sergei Androssov, Hermitage
204.	1776	Charles, 6th Duke of Somerset (after Michael Rysbrack)	m	Belvoir Castle, Leics	SD	
205.	1776	Dr Richard Robinson, later 1st Baron Rokeby	m	[Exhib RA, London, 1775, 210; 1776, 200]; untraced		*Graves* V, 1905–6, 381
206.	1776	Henry, 2nd Earl Bathurst	m	[Exhib RA, London, 201; 1777, 249]; Palace of Westminster, London Other versions: replica, Cirencester church, 1777, SD (see monuments)	SD	*Graves* V, 1905–6, 381
207.	1776	King George II	m	Belvoir Castle, Leics	SD	
208.	1777	A man in early middle age	m	[Sotheby, 10 Dec 2002, lot 142]; untraced	SD	
209.	1777	Dr Samuel Johnson	m	untraced Other versions: replicas, Johnson's Birthplace Museum, Lichfield, one plaster (2000.282), one bronzed plaster (2000.283) YCBA, B1990.1.63, plaster VAM A-1926, lead		*Bilbey* 2002, 107 (repr)
210.	1777	George Aufrere		Brocklesby Park, Lincs, mausoleum	SD	*Lord* 1988, 918 (repr); Pevsner, *Lincs*, 1989, 191
211.	1777	King William III	m	Belvoir Castle, Leics	SD	
212.	c1777	Oliver Cromwell	m	Belvoir Castle, Leics		
213.	1777	Sir Thomas Salusbury	m	[Sotheby, 6 Nov 1995, lot 94]; Private coll	SD	
214.	1779	Jacques Mathias	m	Private coll	SD	
215.	1779	Sir Eyre Coote	m	[Possibly exhib RA, London, 218 ('a general') Queniborough Old Hall, Leics Sotheby; Lane Fine Art Ltd (1994)]; NAM	SD	*NACF Annual Review*, 1996, 124 (repr)
216.	1779	William, 1st Earl of Mansfield	m	[Exhib RA, London, 217]; Iveagh Bequest, Kenwood, Hampstead, London Other versions: replica, Belvoir Castle, Leics, marble, SD copy, Trinity Hall, Cambs, unsigned	SD	
217.	1780	King Charles II	m	Royal Soc, London	SD	
218.	c1780	William Weddell	m	Newby Hall, W R Yorks Other versions: replica, Ripon Cathedral, SD 1795 (see monuments)	S	
219.	post-1782	Lord Robert Manners		Belvoir Castle, Leics	S	
220.	1784	Charles, 2nd Marquess of Rockingham	m	[Exhib RA, London, 498]; Muncaster Castle, Cumberland Other versions: replica, BMAG, marble, ns, inv P.17'56 second version, Dalmeny, Lothian, 1788, marble, s replica, Althorp, Northants, 1793, marble, s third version (in peer's robes), House of Lords (loan), marble, s replica: Goodwood, Sussex, s	S	*Graves* V, 1905–6, 381; *Silber* 1987, 72–3, cat no 220 (repr)
221.	1784	Louisa, Countess of Aylesford	m	[Exhib RA, London, 497]; Packington Hall, Warks	S	*Graves* V, 1905–6, 381; Nollekens's Sale 1823, lots 20–3, 78 ('Lady Aylesbury'); *Gunnis* 1968, 278
222.	1784	Sir George Savile	m	[Exhib RA, London, 1785, 635]; VAM A.16-1942 Other versions: replicas: Fitz, marble, S ex Wentworth Woodhouse; private coll Holdernesse House, Hull, marble, S ex Osberton Hall, sold Christie 6 Dec 1988, 134; private coll, marble, S	SD	*Graves* V, 1905–6, 381; *la Roche* 1933, 233–4; *Gunnis* 1968, 278; *Bilbey* 2002, 97–8 (repr)
223.	c1785	Sir Joseph Banks	p	Burleigh House, Northants Other versions: ex coll Lord Yarborough, London, marble; untraced		*Smith* 1846, vol 1, 42
224.	c1785	Sophia Aufrere, Mrs Pelham (†1786), two busts (replicas) of different dates	m	Brocklesby Park, Lincs	S	*Neoclassicism* 1972, 266–7 (repr); *Whinney* 1988, 297 (repr)

225.	c1790	Frederick Montagu	m	[Wentworth Woodhouse, W R Yorks]; private coll	S	
226.	1791	Charles James Fox (first version)	m	[Exhib RA, London, 632]; State Hermitage, St Petersburg H. ck.13 Other versions: ex Wentworth Woodhouse, W R Yorks, mausoleum, marble, S; private coll, ex coll Lord Robert Spencer; YCBA, marble, S Althorp, Northants, 1793, marble, SD at least six other replicas	SD	*Graves* V, 1905–6, 381; *Allen and Dukelskaya* 1996–7, 26 (repr); *Neverov*, 2000–1, 125 (repr); *Wilson* 2003, 65–70; *Wilson* 2006 (1), 4–11; *Wilson* 2006 (2), 20–25
227.	1793	Hon Frances Knight Drawing(s): VAM E.548-1950 (reversed)	m	Philadelphia Museum of Art, USA	SD	
228.	1793	Mrs Bradyll	m	[Exhib RA, London, 1792, 498]; Huntington coll, San Marino	SD	*Graves* V, 1905–6, 381
229.	1793	William Windham (with curled hair)	m	[Exhib RA, London, 652]; Holkham Hall, Norfolk	S	*Graves* V, 1905–6, 381
230.	1795	Catherine Grey, Lady Manners Drawing(s): VAM E.549-1950	m	Private coll	SD	
231.	c1795	John Lee	m	[Wentworth Woodhouse, W R Yorks, mausoleum]; private coll Other versions: replica: see monuments	S	
232.	1795	William Windham, second version with short hair	m	Althorp, Northants	S	
233.	1796	Miss Le Clerc	m	Untraced		*Farington* II, 480
234.	1796	Unidentified child	m	[Sold G. Sloan & Co Inc, Washington, 27–30 April 1978]; (coll Cyril Humphris)	SD	
235.	1797	William, 4th Earl Fitzwilliam, first version (with curled hair)	m	Untraced	SD	
236.	1797	William, 4th Earl Fitzwilliam, second version (with short hair)	m	[Coll Lord Yarborough]; private coll	SD	
237.	1797–1798	Maria Stella Chiappini, Lady Newborough	m	Nationalmuseum, Stockholm	S	*Farington* III, 967; JKB forthcoming
238.	1799	Henry Richard Fox, 3rd Lord Holland	m	[Holland House, Kensington, London]; private coll Other versions: replica, Woburn Abbey, Beds, marble, head only, SD	SD	*JKB* 1989, 31 (repr)
239.	1800	Arthur Chichester, 1st Marquess of Donegal	m	Anthony Roth, 1985	SD	
240.	1795–1800	Caroline, Princess of Wales, as Isis	m	Untraced		*Euro Mag*, May 1813
241.	1800	Francis Egerton, 3rd Duke of Bridgewater	m	[Sotheby, 15 Dec 1977 (as C J Fox)]; private coll	SD	
242.	1800	John Carr (architect)	m	YCAG	SD	*British Portraits* 1956–7, 98
243.	post-1800	William Le Marchant (†1799)	m	YCBA B1979.36.2	S	*MS Inscriptions*, 104
244.	1801	Francis Russell, 5th Duke of Bedford Drawing(s): VAM E.4350-1920 (bust on pedestal)	m	[Holland House, Kensington, London]; private coll Other versions: replicas, Woburn Abbey, and perhaps 25–30 other examples elsewhere, sometimes without shoulders	SD	*Clifford* 1995, 63 (repr)
245.	1801	John Towneley (herm bust)	m	[Exhib RA, London, 999]; Towneley, Burnley, (loan)		
246.	1801	Louisa Hervey, Countess of Liverpool	m	[Exhib RA, London, 1007 ('Lady Hawkesbury')]; NMW	S	*Graves* V, 1905–6, 382; *JKB* 1975, 1509 (repr of plaster cast)
247.	1801	Robert, Lord Petre	m	[Exhib RA, London, 1009]; untraced		*Graves* V, 1905–6, 382
248.	1802	Charles James Fox (second version)	m	[Exhib RA, London, 1073]; Woburn Abbey, Beds Other versions: **replicas, NMGM** **Lady Lever, LL 726 many others (about 30 examples) recorded, some without shoulders**	SD	*Graves* V, 1905–6, 382; *Penny* 1976 (3), 94–5; *JKB* 1989, 27–32 (repr); *Carlton House* 1991–2, 52; *Lady Lever* 1999, 66 (repr); *Wilson* 2003, 65–70; *Wilson* 2006 (1), 4–11; *Wilson* 2006 (2), 20–25
249.	1802	Dr Charles Burney, MD	m	[Exhib RA, London, 1802, 382]; BL	SD	*Dawson* 1999, 50–52 (repr)
250.	1802	Francis, 1st Marquess of Hastings	m	[Exhib RA, London, 1803, 1024 ('Lord Moira')]; Holkham Hall, Norfolk Other versions: replica, Windsor Castle, 1810, marble, SD	SD	*Graves* V, 1905–6, 382
251.	c1802	Mrs Howard of Corby	m	Ashmolean WA 1965.10		*Penny* 1992, vol 3, 140–1 (repr)
252.	1803	Charles, 2nd Earl Grey	m	[Exhib RA, London, 1804, 947]; Woburn Abbey, Beds Other versions: replica, private coll, 1805, marble, SD	SD	*Graves* V, 1905–6, 382; *Ormond* 1973, 202
253.	1803	General Richard Fitzpatrick	m	[Exhib RA, London, 1804, 949]; Woburn Abbey, Beds	SD	*Graves* V, 1905–6, 382; *JKB* 1989, 31 (repr)
254.	1803	James, 6th Earl of Lauderdale (†1839)	m	[Exhib RA, London, 1804, 950]; SNPG	SD	*Graves* V, 1905–6, 382; *Ret to Life*, 2000, 19, 63 (repr); *JKB* 1989, 31 (repr)
255.	1803	Lord Robert Spencer	m	[Exhib RA, London, 1804, 951]; Woburn Abbey, Beds	SD	*Graves* V, 1905–6, 382; *JKB* 1989, 31 (repr)

No.	Date	Subject	Material	Location		References
256.	1803	Sir Christopher Sykes	m	Sledmere, E R Yorks Other versions: seven known plaster copies	SD	*Masterpieces* 1994, 113 (repr); *Ditner* 1988, 338, n11
257.	1803	Thomas Stonor	m	[Exhib RA, London, 925]; Walker, Liverpool	SD	*Graves* V, 1905–6, 382
258.	1804	James Hare	m	Woburn Abbey, Beds	SD	*JKB* 1989, 31 (repr)
259.	1804	Jane Coke, Countess of Andover	m	Untraced		*Farington* VI, 2356; Nollekens sale, 1823, lot 14
260.	1804	Miss Caroline Symmons	m	[Exhib RA, London, 948]; untraced		*Graves* V, 1905–6, 382; *MS Inscriptions*, 110
261.	1804	T W Coke (Coke of Norfolk, 1st Earl of Leicester)	m	[Exhib RA, London, 1805, 789]; untraced		*Graves* V, 1905–6, 382; *Farington* VI, 2356
262.	1805	Charles Townley		[Exhib RA, London, 783]; untraced Other versions: herm bust, Towneley Hall, Lancs (loan), 1807, marble, SD herm bust, BM, 1811, marble, SD; destroyed World War II head, BM, 1811, marble, SD		*Graves* V, 1905–6, 382; *Dawson* 1999, 18, 222 (repr)
263.	1805	Georgiana Gordon, Duchess of Bedford	m	Woburn Abbey, Beds	SD	
264.	1805	William Leveson-Gower, Marquess of Stafford, later 1st Duke of Sutherland	m	[Exhib RA, London, 695 ('Marquis of Stafford')]; YCBA Other versions: Castle Howard, E R Yorks, 1808, plaster	SD	*Graves* V, 1905–6, 382
265.	1806	Charles Pelham, later 1st Earl of Yarborough	m	Brocklesby Park, Lincs Other versions: replica exhib RA, London, 1808, 969, now VAM A.119-1929, marble, SD	SD	*Graves* V, 1905–6, 382; *Bilbey* 2002, 99–100 (repr)
266.	1806	Charlotte, Duchess of Beaufort	m	Birmingham Museum of Art, Alabama, USA		*Monthly Mag*, 1806, I, 67
267.	1806	Henry Edward Fox, 4th Lord Holland, as a child	m	[Holland House, Kensington, London]; private coll	SD	
268.	1806	John, 2nd Lord Boringdon, 1st Earl of Morley	m	Saltram, Devon	SD	
269.	1806	John, 4th Earl of Darnley	m	[Exhib RA, London, 1808, 970; Cobham Hall, Kent]; sold 23 Feb 1957, lot 408, £65; untraced		*Graves* V, 1905–6, 382
270.	1806	Peter Holford	m	Untraced		*Monthly Mag*, 1806, I, 67
271.	1806	Sir Mark Sykes	m	NGC, Ottawa 15754	SD	*Ditner* 1988, 335 (repr)
272.	1806	William Pitt the Younger		Dalmeny House, Lothian Other versions: at least 74 replicas		*Smith* 1828, vol 2, 48; *Gunnis* 1968, 278; *Bilbey* 2002, 99
273.	1807	Clytie (or Isis), copy after the antique in the BM	m	[sold to John Towneley]; private coll	SD	*Smith* 1828, vol 2, 264
274.	1807	Lady St Aubyn	m	St Michael's Mount, Cornwall	SD	
275.	1807	Louisa, wife of the 6th Duke of St Albans	m	NGC, Ottawa, 14929	SD	*Ditner* 1988, 338 n7
276.	1807	Sir John St Aubyn, 5th Bt	m	St Michael's Mount, Cornwall	SD	
277.	1808	Elizabeth Howard, Duchess of Rutland	m	[Exhib RA, London, 1810, 876]; Belvoir Castle, Leics Other versions: Castle Howard, E R Yorks	SD	*Graves* V, 1905–6, 382
278.	c1808	George, 5th Earl of Jersey	m	Gov Art Coll, Embassy, Rio de Janeiro		
279.	1808	Henrietta Pelham	m	[Exhib RA, London, 1810, 874 ('Hon Mrs Pelham')]; Brocklesby Park, Lincs Other versions: replica, VAM A.120-1929, 1810, marble, SD	SD	*Graves* V, 1905–6, 382; *Lord* 1988, 918 (repr); *Bilbey* 2002, 100 (repr)
280.	1808	John Russell, 6th Duke of Bedford	m	[Exhib RA, London, 972]; Woburn Abbey, Beds Other versions: **replica, Royal Coll, RCIN 35413, 1811, marble, SD**	SD	*Graves* V, 1905–6, 382; *Clifford* 1995, 19, 86 (repr)
281.	1808	King George IV, as Prince of Wales	m	[Holland House, Kensington, London]; BM (damaged) Other versions: replicas, Ragley Hall, Warks, marble, SD Belvoir Castle, Leics, 1815, marble, SD Ferens Art Gallery, Hull Acq S49 (studio copy)		*Dawson* 1999, 106
282.	1808	Male bust (formerly known as 'Earl Brownlow')	m	Belton House, Lincs	SD	
283.	1807–1808	Richard, Marquess Wellesley	m	[Exhib RA, London, 1807, 971]; Windsor Castle, RCIN 35428	SD	*Graves* V, 1905–6, 382
284.	1808	Sir Watkin Williams Wynn, 5th Bt	m	[Exhib RA, London, 979]; untraced		*Graves* V, 1905–6, 382
285.	1808	Unidentified girl aged about 18–20	m	Private coll	SD	
286.	1809	John Cust, 1st Earl Brownlow	m	[Exhib RA, London, 1810, 766]; Belton House, Lincs	SD	*Graves* V, 1905–6, 382
287.	1809	Lady Louisa Hartley	m	LMG	SD	
288.	1809	Robert Stewart, Viscount Castlereagh, later 2nd Marquess of Londonderry	m	Mount Stuart, Co Down Other versions: ex Bayham Abbey, Kent, 1812, marble, SD; private coll	SD	

No.	Date	Subject		Location		Bibliography
289.	1809	William Wyndham, Lord Grenville	m	House of Lords, London (loan) Other versions: Althorp, Northants, marble, SD replicas, Royal Coll, Windsor, marble, SD, Brasenose coll, Oxford, marble, SD Woburn Abbey, Beds, marble, nd	SD	*Graves* V, 1905–6, 382
290.	1810	Anne Bermingham, Countess of Charlemont	m	[Exhib RA, London, 885]; untraced		*Graves* V, 1905–6, 382
291.	1810	Francis, 2nd Earl of Moira Payment(s): 120 gns		Royal Coll	D	*Carlton House* 1991–2, 53 (repr)
292.	1810	George Canning	m	Wellington Museum, Apsley House, London 1450–1948	SD	*Graves* V, 1905–6, 382
293.	1810	George, Lord Gower, later 2nd Duke of Sutherland	m	Private coll	SD	
294.	1810	Henry Phipps, 3rd Baron Mulgrave	m	[Exhib RA, London, 886]; untraced		*Graves* V, 1905–6, 382
295.	1810	John Manners, 5th Duke of Rutland	m	[Exhib RA, London, 753]; Belvoir Castle, Leics	S	*Graves* V, 1905–6, 382
296.	1810	Lady Elizabeth Bingham (later Mrs Vernon-Harcourt)	m	San Francisco Museum of Art, USA	SD	
297.	1810	Young man (aged about 20)	m	Private coll (Simon Houfe)	SD	
298.	1811	Admiral Sir J Colpoys	m	[Exhib RA, London, 952]; untraced		*Graves* V, 1905–6, 382
299.	1811	Granville Leveson-Gower, Viscount Granville	m	[Exhib RA, London, 941 ('Lord Granville Leveson-Gower')]; YCBA	SD	*Graves* V, 1905–6, 382
300.	1811	Lady Elizabeth Monck	m	[Lord Oranmore and Browne]; untraced		Sotheby, 3 March 1961, lot 51
301.	1811	Richard Arkwright	m	Ferens Art Gallery, Hull	SD	
302.	1811	Sir John Pitt, 2nd Earl of Chatham	m	[Exhib RA, London, 940]; untraced Other versions: replica, private coll, 1814, marble, SD		*Graves* V, 1905–6, 382
303.	1811	Sir John Rous, 1st Earl of Stradbroke	m	[Exhib RA, London, 949 ('Lord Rous'); Henham church, Suffolk]; YCBA	SD	*Graves* V, 1905–6, 382
304.	1811	William, 2nd Earl of Mornington	m	[Exhib RA, London, 948]; NPG 5060	SD	*Graves* V, 1905–6, 382
305.	c1811	Wriothesley Digby	m	Forest Hall, Meriden, Warks	SD	Pevsner, *Warks*, 1966, 354
306.	1812	Bateman Dashwood	m	Private coll	SD	Christie, South Kensington, 18 Sept 2002
307.	1812	Benjamin West PRA	m	[Exhib RA, London, 934]; RHS	SD	*Graves* V, 1905–6, 382
308.	1812	Charlotte Gordon, 4th Duchess of Richmond	m	Goodwood, Sussex Other versions: ex coll Jonathan Harris, bronze; private coll	SD	
309.	1812	Dr Matthew Baillie		RCS, London	SD	
310.	1812	Du Pré Alexander, 2nd Earl of Caledon	m	[Tyttenhanger, Herts]; SANG	SD	
311.	1812	Dudley Long North (?)	m	MMAG	SD	
312.	1812	Female, aged about 35–40 (sold incorrectly as Charlotte, 4th Duchess of Richmond)		YCBA B 1977.14.19	SD	Sotheby, 2 July 1973, lot 138
313.	1812	Henry, 3rd Earl of Warwick	m	[Exhib RA, London, 936 ('Lord Brooke')]; Warwick Castle, Warks	SD	
314.	1812	Lord George Augustus Henry Cavendish, later 1st Earl of Burlington of the 2nd creation (1754–1834)	m	[Exhib RA, London, 1813, 925]; Chatsworth, Derbys	SD	*Graves* V, 1905–6, 382; *Chatsworth Handlist*, 28
315.	1812	'Princess Charlotte' (?)	m	Braunschweigisches landesmuseum, Germany	SD	
316.	1812	Robert Gregory	m	[family poss; sold Sotheby 20 April 1989, 193]; untraced	SD	
317.	1812	Thomas Finch	m	Taylorian Institute, Oxford	SD	
318.	1812	William, 5th Duke of Devonshire	m	Chatsworth, Derbys Other versions: replicas, royal coll RCIN 35410, marble, SD North Carolina Museum, Raleigh, USA, marble, SD Chiswick House, Middx, marble, SD	SD	*JKB* 1977 (3), 1–13
319.	1813	Alexander, 4th Duke of Gordon (?)	m	Institute of Arts, Detroit, USA	SD	
320.	1813	Arthur, 1st Duke of Wellington	m	[Exhib RA, London, 935]; Wellington Museum, Apsley House, London, 1446–1948 Other versions: replica (head), Woburn Abbey, Beds, marble, SD Castle Howard, E R Yorks, marble, SD 1815 Sledmere House, E R Yorks, marble, c1813	SD	*Graves* V, 1905–6, 382; *Whinney* 1988, 302; *Mulcahy* 2006, 61 (repr)
321.	1813	Francis, 2nd Earl of Charlemont	m	[Exhib RA, London, 1814, 789]; Crowther of Isleworth; untraced		*Graves* V, 1905–6, 382
322.	1813	Frederick-Augustus, Duke of York and Albany Payment(s): £157	m	[Exhib RA, London, 926]; Windsor Castle, RCIN 31621	SD	*Graves* V, 1905–6, 382
323.	1813	George, 4th Duke of Grafton	m	[Exhib RA, London, 1814, 792; Euston Hall, Suffolk]; Castle Howard, N R Yorks	SD	*Graves* V, 1905–6, 382
324.	1813	Peter, 5th Earl Cowper	m	[Exhib RA, London, 1814, 789]; Firle Place, Sussex	SD	*Graves* V, 1905–6, 382
325.	1813	Richard Roberts	m	Private coll	SD	
326.	1813	Sir Peter Burrell, 1st Baron Gwydir	m	[Exhib RA, London, 1812, 937]; St Michael, Edenham, Lincs	SD	*Graves* V, 1905–6, 382

No.	Date	Subject	Material	Location	Marks	Literature
327.	1813	Spencer Perceval	m	[Exhib RA, London, 919]; untraced Other versions: 15 traced		*Graves* V, 1905–6, 382; *Smith* 1828, vol 2, 74
328.	1813	William Windham, as second version but head only	m	Woburn Abbey, Beds	SD	
329.	1814	George, 4th Earl of Aberdeen	m	[Exhib RA, London, 801]; private coll	SD	*Graves* V, 1905–6, 382; *Ormond* 1973, 3; *George Bullock* cat, 1988, (70)
330.	1814	Gerard, 1st Viscount Lake Payment(s): £157	m	Windsor Castle, RCIN 20747	SD	
331.	1814	Henry, 13th Viscount Dillon	m	Untraced		*Farington* XIII, 4515
332.	1814	Lady ffolkes	m	Untraced		*Farington* XIII, 4555
333.	1814	Samuel Whitbread		[Exhib RA, London, 781]; Southill, Beds Other versions: replica, Theatre Royal, Drury Lane, London, marble, SD	SD	*Graves* V, 1905–6, 382; *Webb* 1951 (3), 56 (repr); *Deuchar* 1984, 102–3 (repr)
334.	1814	Sophia Hume, Lady Brownlow	m	VAM A.60-1965 Other versions: Replica, Belton House, Lincs BEL/SC/4, 1815, marble, SD	SD	*Bilbey* 2002, 100–1 (repr)
335.	1814	William Augustus, Duke of Cumberland (after Rysbrack) Payment(s): £157	m	Windsor Castle, RCIN 31627	SD	
336.	1815	George, 3rd Earl of Egremont	m	[Exhib RA, London, 895]; Petworth, Sussex	SD	*Graves* V, 1905–6, 383; *JKB* 1977 (2), 369, 371
337.	1815	Rev Charles Burney DD, FSA	m	[Exhib RA, London, 889]; BL Other versions: replicas, BM, plaster; St Paul, Deptford, plaster	SD	*Graves* V, 1905–6, 383; *Dawson* 1999, 53–56 (repr)
338.	1815	Thomas, Lord Erskine	m	[Exhib RA, London, 888]; Windsor Castle RCIN 45143	SD	*Graves* V, 1905–6, 382
339.	1816	Alleyne FitzHerbert, Lord St Helens	m	[Exhib RA, London, 932]; Tissington Hall, Derbys	SD	*Graves* V, 1905–6, 383; *Gunnis* 1968, 278
340.	1816	Henry, 4th Duke of Newcastle	m	[Exhib RA, London, 961]; Grantham Town Hall, Lincs		*Graves* V, 1905–6, 383
341.	1816	Mrs Arkwright	m	Sold Amsterdam, Nov 1985, bt R Feigen	SD	
342.	1816	Robert, 2nd Earl of Liverpool	m	[Exhib RA, London, 951]; Windsor Castle RCIN 31318	SD	*Graves* V, 1905–6, 383
343.	1816	Thomas Coutts	m	[Exhib RA, London, 950]; private coll Other versions: Burdett-Coutts Foundation, London, marble, SD	SD	*Graves* V, 1905–6, 383
344.	nd	'a Cardinal'		Untraced		Nollekens sale 1823, lot 50
345.	nd	A laughing child	m	State Hermitage, St Petersburg	S	*Dukelskaya* 1979, 228–9 (repr)
346.	nd	Admiral Burney	m	Untraced		*Smith* 1828, vol 2, 71
347.	nd	Admiral King	m	Untraced		*Smith* 1828, vol 2, 74
348.	nd	Alexander Pope (after Roubiliac)	m	Met NY Other versions: Sotheby Parke Bernet, 18 June 1965, lot 82, marble		
349.	nd	Anthony Malone	m	Untraced		*Smith* 1828, vol 2, 74
350.	nd	Colonel Sotheby		Untraced		Nollekens sale 1823, lot 14
351.	nd	Count Parr	m	Untraced		*Smith* 1828, vol 2, 74
352.	nd	Dr Chambers	m	Untraced		*Smith* 1828, vol 2, 71
353.	nd	Duke of Bolton		Untraced		Nollekens sale 1823, lot 74
354.	nd	Duke of Manchester		Untraced		Nollekens sale 1823, lot 62
355.	nd	Galley Knight		Untraced		Nollekens sale 1823, lot 67
356.	nd	General Neal	m	Untraced		*Smith* 1828, vol 2, 74
357.	nd	General Paoli	m	Untraced		*Smith* 1828, vol 2, 74
358.	nd	General Stroonlof	m	Untraced		*Smith* 1828, vol 2, 75
359.	nd	Head of a woman, from a model by Mrs Damer		Rhode Island School of Design, USA		
360.	nd	Head of an unidentified sitter (Sir John Wodehouse Bt, later 1st Baron Wodehouse)	m	[Colnaghi]; untraced	S	*The British Face*, 1986, 126–7 (repr)
361.	nd	Hon Edward Farr	m	Untraced		*Smith* 1828, vol 2, 72
362.	nd	Hon Thomas Anson	m	Untraced		*Smith* 1828, vol 2, 71
363.	nd	Hon Thomas Greville	m	Untraced		*Smith* 1828, vol 2, 73
364.	nd	HRH Duchess of York	m	Untraced		*Smith* 1828, vol 2, 75
365.	nd	Julius Caesar, after the antique	m	Eaton Hall, Cheshire	S	
366.	nd	Lady Berwick	m	Untraced		*Smith* 1828, vol 2, 71
367.	nd	Lady Brook		Untraced		Nollekens sale 1823, lot 47
368.	nd	Lady Darnley	m	Untraced		*Smith* 1828, vol 2, 72
369.	nd	Lady Gower	m	Untraced		*Smith* 1828, vol 2, 73
370.	nd	Lady Hood		Untraced		Nollekens sale 1823, lot 45
371.	nd	Lord Barrington (Lord Borringdon?)	m	Untraced		*Smith* 1828, vol 2, 71
372.	nd	Lord Frederick Cavendish	m	Untraced		*Smith* 1828, vol 2, 71
373.	nd	Lord Henry Stuart	m	Untraced		*Smith* 1828, vol 2, 75
374.	nd	Lord Keith	m	Untraced		*Smith* 1828, vol 2, 74
375.	nd	Lord Leitrim		Untraced		Nollekens sale 1823, lot 24
376.	nd	Lord Milton		[Nollekens sale 1823, lot 40]; untraced		*Smith* 1828, vol 2, 74
377.	nd	Lord Mulgrave	m	Untraced		*Smith* 1828, vol 2, 74
378.	nd	Lord Percy	m	Untraced		*Smith* 1828, vol 2, 74
379.	nd	Master Borrows	m	Untraced		*Smith* 1828, vol 2, 71
380.	nd	Master Mitford	m	Untraced		*Smith* 1828, vol 2, 74
381.	nd	Miss Starkie		Untraced		Nollekens sale 1823, lot 145

382. nd	Moses Levi	m	Untraced		*Smith* 1828, vol 2, 74
383. nd	Mr Adam	m	Untraced		*Smith* 1828, vol 2, 71
384. nd	Mr Busk		Untraced		Nollekens sale 1823, lot 20
385. nd	Mr Dunning	m	Untraced		*Smith* 1828, vol 2, 72
386. nd	Mr Foley	m	Untraced		*Smith* 1828, vol 2, 72
387. nd	Mr Fraine	m	Untraced		*Smith* 1828, vol 2, 73
388. nd	Mr Hamilton	m	Untraced		*Smith* 1828, vol 2, 73
389. nd	Mr Harringdon	m	Untraced		*Smith* 1828, vol 2, 73
390. nd	Mr Keebel	m	Untraced		*Smith* 1828, vol 2, 74
391. nd	Mr Maddocks		Untraced		Nollekens sale 1823, lot 72
392. nd	Mr Maud	m	Untraced		*Smith* 1828, vol 2, 74
393. nd	Mr Popham	m	Untraced		*Smith* 1828, vol 2, 74
394. nd	Mr Saunders Welch	m	Untraced		*Smith* 1828, vol 2, 75
395. nd	Mr Stonehewer		Untraced		Nollekens sale 1823, lot 53
396. nd	Mr Taylor	m	Untraced		*Smith* 1828, vol 2, 75
397. nd	Mr Tulmarsh	m	Untraced		*Smith* 1828, vol 2, 75
398. nd	Mrs Cornelli	m	Untraced		*Smith* 1828, vol 2, 72
399. nd	Mrs Ellis	m	Untraced		*Smith* 1828, vol 2, 72
400. nd	Mrs Kirby	m	Untraced		*Smith* 1828, vol 2, 74
401. nd	Mrs Welch (wife of Mr Saunders Welch)	m	Untraced		*Smith* 1828, vol 2, 75
402. nd	Rev Mr Key	m	Untraced		*Smith* 1828, vol 2, 74
403. nd	Simon Fraser	m	Untraced		*Smith* 1828, vol 2, 73
404. nd	Sir John Stuart	m	Untraced		*Smith* 1828, vol 2, 75
405. nd	Sir William Robinson	m	Untraced		*Smith* 1828, vol 2, 75
Architectural Sculpture					
406. 1775	Bas reliefs for two ceilings (designed by George Richardson) Payment(s): £280	p	[Drapers's Hall, London]; destroyed		*Richardson* 1776; *GM* 1778, vol 48, 585; Draper's Court Book, f133
407. 1778	Five identical keystones of Portland stone ('lares, or tutelar deities of the place,' £21 each)	s	Somerset House, London, back front		RIBA Library 335A; *Colvin* 1973–76, V, 372–3, 467; *Jenkins* 2000–1, 27
408. c1780	Medallions representing Justice and Mercy (modelled by Nollekens, passed to Locatelli, who had his pupil J C F Rossi do the carving) Payment(s): £100	s	Middlesex Sessions House, Clerkenwell, London		Sessions House Minutes, MA/S/21-373, MES 160, 163, 172; *Smith* 1828, vol 2, 126
Reliefs					
409. 1759	Abraham entertaining the angels		[Soc of A, premium, 15 gns]; untraced		RSA *Minutes*, 1758–60, seq 1 fol 77; RSA *Premiums*, 1758, 17
410. 1760	Jephtha's rash vow	tc	[Soc of A, premium, 30 gns]; untraced		RSA *Minutes*, 1758–60, seq 4 f49, 53; *Dossie* 1782, 438; *Knight* 1843, 534
411. 1761	Regulus returned to Carthage, bas relief in Portland stone	s	[Soc of A, premium, 10 gns]; untraced		RSA *Minutes*, 1760–61, seq 3 f48, 52; *Dossie* 1782, 439; *Graves* 1907, 183
412. 1762	Timocles conducted before Alexander	m	[Soc of A, premium, 50 gns]; untraced		RSA *Minutes*, 1761–62, seq 3 f59; *Dossie* 1782, 439; *Graves* 1907, 183; *ODNB*
413. 1773	Cupid and Psyche, bas-relief (RA Diploma work)	m	[Exhib RA, London, 212]; RA	SD	RA Council Minutes, vol 1, 1st Feb 1773, f153; *Graves* V, 1905–6, 381
414. 1805	Miss Ackland, medallion		[Exhib RA, London, 693]; untraced		*Graves* V, 1905–6, 382
Miscellaneous					
415. 1766	Two Victors in the Panathenian Games		[Exhib Free Soc, London, 126]; untraced		*Graves* 1907, 183

NORMAN, Robert fl 1782

On 24 August 1782 he advertised in the *Norwich Mercury* that he had entered into partnership with C Bottomley (presumably Charles, of the **Bottomley family**), and that their premises were near St Margaret's, King's Lynn and at Wells-next-the-Sea, Norfolk. They offered inlaid marbles and other kinds of stone for monuments, tombs and chimneypieces.

Archival References: RG/JP, 6, 1016v

NORMAN, Samuel fl 1760–82

A carver, gilder and cabinet-maker, Norman was one of the leading craftsmen in London in the 1750s and 1760s. He was apprenticed to Thomas Woodin, 1746–53, at a premium of 15 guineas. Soon after completing his articles he set up his own carving and gilding business in King Street, Soho, with financial help from his uncle, the cabinet-maker William Hallett (1707–1781). Norman is known to have taken John Haynes as an apprentice in July 1754, for £30. With the support of his uncle, he married Ann, the daughter of another carver, **James Whittle**, on 24 April 1755. Hallett paid the marriage portion of £700. Norman entered into a lucrative partnership with Whittle, supplying work at a cost of over £1,000 to the Earl of Egremont at Petworth (7) and carving at Woburn, for which detailed accounts survive (1, 2). From 1758 the pair expanded into cabinet-making and upholstery and went briefly into partnership with John Mayhew. In June 1759 Whittle and Norman considered expanding into the masonry business and bought a large piece of marble. This was inspected by their subcontractor, **William Long**, and taken into the King Street premises. It was there cut and worked by their own workmen into chimneypieces and slabs for tables.

The venture proved short-lived since the material was soon destroyed. Whittle died on 10 December 1759 and Norman succeeded to a business and an estate worth around £6,000. On 23 December 1759 Norman's house, warehouses, goods, books and effects were destroyed in a large fire that razed over 30 houses. The following day the *Public Advertiser* reported the blaze at the house of Norman, an 'eminent cabinet maker, carver and gilder'. He and his wife 'escaped from the said fire with their lives almost naked' (*Kirkham* 1969, 503). After this catastrophe Norman set up a small business in rooms above the Exeter Exchange. His fire insurance policy with the Sun Company covered household goods at a mere £350.

In May 1760 he entered into negotiations to take over Paul Saunders's premises at the Royal Tapestry factory in Sutton Street. This included Saunders's furniture, stock and materials, valued at £1,270, and it enabled Norman to re-establish himself with clients inherited from Saunders such as Theresa Cornelys of Carlisle House (5). He increased his insurance on household goods and stock-in-trade to £1,100 plus £500 for china, plate and glass, and £800 for stock in the yard. Norman's prices appear to have been high, and he entered into a number of long wrangles with clients over payments. The Duke of Bedford sought independent assessments of Norman's bills on two separate occasions.

On 4 December 1761 he was appointed master-sculptor and carver in wood to the Office of Works, a post he held until 1782. From 30 October 1761 he was also surveyor and repairer of carved work. In the list of artists given in Mortimer's *Director* he is described as 'sculptor and carver to Their Majesties and surveyor of the curious carvings in Windsor Castle. Soho Square' (*Mortimer* 1763, 20). Around the same time he was paid £4 3s 4d 'for looking after and repairing the carved work' in Windsor Castle (TNA WORK 5/66). Norman's premises and business continued to grow: in March 1764 he had £3,600 worth of stock and goods in trade.

Despite his extensive contracts, clientele and public reputation Norman became bankrupt in 1767. His bankruptcy was reported in the *London Gazette* the following October, and no major works are known by him after this date. A sale of his stock was held before January 1768, when an ornate rococo bed was bought by James Cullen on behalf of the Earl of Hopetoun (11). Norman appears to have had a number of legal and financial problems. Disputes over payment with the Earls of Dundas and Holderness and Sir Herbert Packington seem to have contributed to the demise of his business.

EH

Literary References: *Thomson* 1949, 63; *Coleridge* 1964, 122–8; *Gunnis* 1968, 279; *Kirkham* 1969, 501–10; *Colvin* 1973–76, 5, 473, 479; *Jackson-Stops* 1977, 362; *Beard* 1981, 273; *Beard and Gilbert* 1986, 651–2; *Kirkham* 1988, 6–7, 62–3, 75; *Beard and Hayward* 1988, 393–400

Chimneypieces

1.	1756	'With Apollo's head & Glory & foliage leaves and flowers' (marble by John Deval I) (co-sculptor: James Whittle) Payment(s): £29 8s	wd	Woburn Abbey, Beds, state dining room	*Beard and Hayward* 1988, 396, 398 (repr)

Architectural Sculpture

2.	1755–1760	Decorative ornaments, including glass frames with eagles, a decorated head of Flora and a grand state bed (co-sculptor: James Whittle)		Woburn Abbey, Beds, state rooms	*Coleridge* 1964, 125, 127 (repr); *Kirkham* 1969, 504 (repr 32); *Jackson-Stops* 1977, 362; *Beard and Hayward* 1988, 394–5 (repr)
3.	1771	Cornice Payment(s): Nearly £200		[Buckingham House, London]; untraced	*Beard and Gilbert* 1986, 652

Miscellaneous

4.	1760–1761	Fourteen parcel-gilt walnut chairs, with two elbow chairs, an easy chair and a sofa Payment(s): £122 13s 7d		[Bedford House, London]; untraced	*Beard and Gilbert* 1986, 652
5.	1760–1761	Papier-mâché pier frame, girandoles with richly carved bird, boys heads and sheep		[Carlisle House, London]; untraced	*Beard and Gilbert* 1986, 653
6.	1761	Unidentified carver's work		[Ashburnham Place, Sussex]; untraced	Ashburnham Archives in GPC
7.	1763	Carved work, including a picture frame, carved with palm branches and laurels; foliage additions to a gilt wood pier table Payment(s): Frame £23 2s	wd	Petworth House, Sussex	*Jackson-Stops* 1977, 362, 364 (repr); *Rowell* 2000 (2), *passim*
8.	1764	Two gilt frames		[Chevening, Kent]; untraced	*Beard and Gilbert* 1986, 653
9.	1764–1765	Pair of gilt frames Payment(s): £82 7s and £75 17s		[Windsor Castle, Berks]; untraced	*Kirkham* 1969, 504; *Beard and Gilbert* 1986, 652
10.	1763–1766	Chest of drawers and other carved work Payment(s): £2410		[for Sir Lawrence Dundas (Moor Park, Aske Hall, and Arlington Street, London)]; untraced	*Beard and Gilbert* 1986, 652, 653
11.	pre-1767	State bed		Coll Earl of Hopetoun	*Kirkham* 1969, 504 (repr 34–5)
12.	1760–1768	Unidentified carving Payment(s): £648		[for the Earl of Holderness]; untraced	*Beard and Gilbert* 1986, 652
13.	nd	Unidentified carving		[for Sir Herbert Packington]; untraced	*Beard and Gilbert* 1986, 652

NORRIS fl 1677

In 1677 Robert Hooke 'agreed for seven chimney-pieces for £80' for Montagu House, London, with Norris, whom he described as a stonecutter (1). He may be identical with or related to **George Norris**.

Chimneypieces

1.	1677	Seven Payment(s): £80		[Montagu House, London]; untraced	*Robinson and Adams* 1935, 301; *Gunnis* 1968, 279

NORRIS, George fl 1713

A George Norris was employed on stone-carving work at Lord Ashburnham's house in St James's Square in 1713 (Ashburnham Archives). He may be identical with or related to **Norris**.

Architectural Sculpture

1.	1713	Carving	s	[Lord Ashburnham's house, St James Square, London]; untraced	*Gunnis* 1968, 279

NORRIS, William fl 1774–88

In 1788 he built the Freemasons' Tavern, London. He worked in partnership with **William Pinder**, 1774–84, when he joined **Daniel Pinder**.

Literary References: *Gunnis* 1968, 279

Architectural Sculpture

1.	1788	Carving	s	[Freemasons' Tavern, London]; untraced	Freemasons' Archives in *Gunnis* 1968, 279

NOSEDA, Joseph –1779

The death of this statuary of Fishamble Street, Dublin, was recorded in *Faulkner's Journal* in December 1779.

Literary References: *Strickland* 2, 1913, 175

NOST, Adam I fl 1724

Described as 'Cit & Mason', on 20 May 1724 he took **Samuel Dunage**, the son of Daniel Dunage 'Cit. and Weaver' as an apprentice at a fee of £4 10s (*Webb* (3), 1957, 115).

NOST, Adam II fl 1779

Graves lists a bust of George III in marble exhibited at the Royal Academy by the sculptor Adam Nost of Pimlico in 1779. It seems likely, however, that the work in question was by **John Nost III**, the royal sculptor, whose workshop was in Pimlico at this time.

Literary References: *Graves* 1905–6, 391; *Gunnis* 1968, 282

NOST, Catherine fl 1708–35

Catherine Cheesborough became the wife of **John Nost II** on 25 April 1708 and appears to have run the workshop in Portugal Row after the death of her husband in May 1729. They married at St Martin-in-the-Fields, London and had two children by 1710, both of whom received bequests in the will of **John Nost I**. Their son, **John Nost III**, was born in July 1713. A daughter, Frances, received £100 in the will of Frances Nost (Nost I's wife) in 1716.

After the death of Nost II in 1729 Catherine Nost continued to pay rates on the premises in Portugal Row, at the same figure, £20. The rates rose to £40 in 1734, around the time that the workshop supplied a royal statue to Glasgow (**1**), and dropped to £14 in April 1735. From December 1735, rates were paid by Anthony Nost (†1738), whose role in the workshop is unclear, but who surrendered the premises to **John Cheere** between April and November 1737.

Archival References: CWAC Poor Rate C106–7; C120–1; C122; C123; C127

Wills: John Nost I LMA AM/PW 1710/89; Frances Nost PROB 11/555/fols 195v–196v; Anthony Nost 3rd July 1738, LMA AM/PBA/13/322

Statues

1.	1735	King William III, equestrian	[The Cross, Glasgow]; Cathedral Square, Glasgow	C Lib (repr)

NOST (or VAN OST), John I –1710

John Nost carved several magnificent baroque monuments but his principal activity was the design, manufacture and supply of lead garden statues. He was a native of Mechelen (Malines) in Belgium, but nothing is known of his training or family, except that he had a sister, Mary, mentioned in his will. He arrived in England some time before 1686, and was 'foreman' to **Arnold Quellin** before the latter's death in London that year (*Vertue* IV, 35). Nost subsequently married his master's widow and sole heiress, Frances, née Siberechts, a daughter of the landscape painter, Jan Siberechts.

He seems to have established himself quickly with influential patrons. In the 1690s he supplied marble tables to the Duke of Devonshire (**71**), wooden equestrian figures of monarchs for the 'line of Kings' at the Tower of London (**7**) and in 1695, statues of King William and Queen Mary for the Royal Exchange, for which he received £120 (**9, 11**). In 1697 the agent for one patron, Lady Noel (Lord Irwin's widow: **2**), described Nost as 'one of the best hands in England' (*Gilbert* 1962–3, 5).

He acquired a property in the Haymarket in 1692, rated at £60, which remained in the family until the death of his widow in 1716. His affluent neighbours included the Dutch ambassador and Lord Orrery. In 1698 Nost took another property in Portugal Row. Here, and in neighbouring Stone Bridge, both on Hyde Park Corner, the Nost family owned premises until 1737, when **John Cheere** took them over. **Richard Osgood, Edward Hurst** and **Josias Iback** were all neighbours. Nost's visitors included the architect William Wynde, who in 1703 wrote to Lady Mary Bridgeman that he was searching for 'a statue fitt for yr Ladys garden' and 'in order thereunto I was at Mr Nostes . . . and Mr Ansgood' (presumably Osgood). The architect appears to have recommended Osgood's work (Wynde/Bridgeman). Nost's apprentices and assistants included **William Colebourne, William Palmer** and **Andrew Carpenter**, who according to Vertue was 'for some years principal assistant (to Mr. Nost Senr, Carver) in Modelling. & Carving. . .' (*Vertue* III, 83).

By 1700 Nost was occupied with an extensive contract at Hampton Court. This included several marble chimney-pieces, two of which were costed at £235 and £275 (**55, 57**). Both are intricately carved and count among his finest works, the first with a relief of a reclining Venus in her chariot and the second with a relief of two intertwined doves. In 1701 he provided 'several drawings of the King's statue for the marble fountain', charged at £2 and clay models for a fountain (**64**). One had four mermaids seated on dolphins and four shells between them, whilst the alternative had four figures of young men on dolphins and four swans between them (TNA WORK 5/52 fol 32). A third model had shells, dolphins, a sea-horse and 11 other figures (TNA WORK 5/51 fol 506). He was also responsible for the statue of a blackamoor and submitted accounts 'for modelling a figure of a Blackamore kneeling being 5 ft high holding up a sundial' and then for 'casting the said Balackamore in hard metal and repainting' (**14**). Pedestals of Portland stone were provided by Nost for statues of the *Gladiator*, *Diana*, *Hercules* and *Apollo* (**68**) (TNA WORK 5/51 fol 506; 5/52 fol 340).

His sculpture was evidently noticed by members of the Court, for one of Nost's most discerning and extensive patrons was Thomas Coke of Melbourne Hall, vice-chamberlain to Queen Anne. Among Coke's many purchases were the stupendous *Four Seasons* vase (**67**), dramatic figures of *Perseus* and *Andromeda* (**29**) and copies of the *Blackamoor* and *Indian* which Nost had originally supplied to Hampton Court (**24**). A letter to Coke in the Melbourne archives suggests that there were problems with the casting process and that the sculptor was under pressure: 'Hon.red Sir, I hope you will pardon my not answering your desires sooner. I had set up 2 moulds of boys but thay weare not to my minde and having had some Exterordinary brake which Call'd me out of towne which hath beene a great hindrance to me in my Buisines. But I wish now with all speed Dispatch y.or Boys' (Nost I/Coke). Enclosed with the letter were his prices for lead figures: 'The Sabine Rape, £90', 'Hercules and Centoure, £70,' and 'Hercules and Anteus, £80'. Nost claimed that he 'made as nice a calculation as can be and find it cannot be done under the prises that is rated above', but Coke, who was a demanding client, found them too expensive (Melbourne Hall archives, quoted in *Gunnis* 1968, 280). In the library at Melbourne Hall is Nost's copy of Serlio's *Five Books of Architecture*, 'Englished by Robert Peake', 1611, bought by the sculptor in 1696, and later purchased by Coke for 15s at the sale of Nost's effects.

In 1706 Lord Ashburnham asked Brian Fairfax to ascertain Nost's charges for the 'statues for the attic of the Duke of Buckingham's London house' (**66**). They had cost £27 each. In a later letter Lord Ashburnham complained that Nost had raised his prices, which were now so excessive that he would have to find another sculptor for his house at Ampthill (Letter-book of the 1st Lord Ashburnham in *Gunnis* 1968, 280). His complaint sounds unjustified: with the exception of the Melbourne commission, Nost's charges appear to have remained stable, and comparable to those later proposed by Carpentiere: his 'Prices of Statues and Flowerpotes proposed for the Earl of Hoptone' submitted in 1709 included a six foot high *Hercules and his Mistress*, a *Venus and Adonis* and a *Bacchus and Ceres*, all at £30, as well as two figures of *Hope, a Flying Horse & Fame, Four statues about the fountain*, and four six foot high urns at £25 each (Nost/Hopetoun MS). What, if anything, was purchased from this list, prepared for Charles, 1st Earl of Hopetoun, is unknown. Eight years later, in 1718, his cousin, **John Nost II**, who had taken over his business, signed two contracts to supply the earl with a total of eight 'Mettle statues'.

Nost provided several important monuments, though many attributed to him have not been fully established as his work. The identified memorials range from a relatively modest wall-tablet, costing £50 (**5**) to the monument to Viscount Irwin, at £600, which has a tabernacle frame enclosing a full sized effigy and grieving widow (**2**). The monument to the Duke and Duchess of Buccleuch at Durisdeer, his most elaborate work, has an inner segmental frame surrounded by a rectangular frame with Corinthian capitals and urns at its corners and above that a richly swagged baldacchino. Putti carrying a scroll hover above the two effigies. The design, model and monument survive and indicate that the patron expected few changes to the proposed composition (**4**).

Nost died, apparently childless, in August 1710, and 'left behind him a good fortune' (*Vertue* IV, 35). In his will, signed on 2 August, he bequeathed half of all 'money, stocks, rights, credits, effects and estate whatsoever' to his wife, Frances, and one third of the other half to his sister, Mary. He also left £60 to his cousin, John Nost II, £10 of which was to go 'towards discharging his debts'. The rates for Stone Bridge continued to be paid after 1710 by a John Nost, which suggests that his cousin took over the running of the yard.

In 1712 a sale of Nost's effects was held 'at his late Dwelling House in Hyde-Park-Road (near the Queen's Mead-house)'. The catalogue's title-page described the collection as 'the most Valuable that ever was Exposed to Sale in this Kingdom'. A year later an advertisement in *The Guardian* (no 60, 20 May 1713) informed the public that there remained 'several extraordinary fine things belonging to the late famous sculptor Mr John Nost . . . fine inlaid tables, marble chimneypieces, figures etc' and that Mrs Nost 'designing to go beyond seas, will dispose of them at reasonable prices at her house near Hyde Park Corner where attendance will daily be given'. When she died in 1716 she left over £1,460 and various chattels, including a bequest to 'my cousin John Nost [of] all the marble goods and figures which belongs to me'. She also left her share in an unidentified business to her partner and cousin, Mary Macadam. This may have been the yard, or perhaps a separate business run from the Haymarket property, where 'Widow Mackadam' continued to pay the rates.

Nost was an influential figure in the history of garden sculpture. Versions of his *Blackamoor*, for instance, were being produced until the late-18th century. Many of his garden ornaments must have perished, including the leadwork at Stonyhurst, which was apparently melted down by a Jesuit father to mend the roofs. The few known facts of his life offer little insight into Nost's character. Until recently he and his cousin, John Nost II, were thought to be one person, and this, coupled with countless attributions, has prevented any conclusive evaluation of his oeuvre.

MGS

Literary References: *Vertue* IV, 35; *Webb/Gunnis* 1954, 25; *Blakiston* 1957, 54–58; *Croft-Murray and Hulton* 1960, 476–7; *Gilbert* 1962–3, 4–5; *Stonyhurst* 1964, 478–481; *Gunnis* 1968, 279–82; *O'Connell* 1987, 802–6; *Whinney* 1988, *passim*; *Davis* 1991 (1), *passim*; *Schellekens* 1995, 80–94; *Grove* 23, 1996, 253–4 (Murdoch); *Spencer-Longhurst* 1998, 33, n26–29; *ODNB* (Sullivan); *Sullivan* 2005, 8

Archival References: WCA, Poor Rates 1692 (F1176), 1694 (F422), 1696 (F1222), 1698 (F1241), 1699 (F1245), 1706 (F1281), 1711 (F440-1), 1717 (F3602), 1737 (C126); Wynde/Bridgeman; Nost I/Coke; Nost/Hopetoun MS

Wills: Arnold Quellin (proved 3 September 1686, PROB 11/384/fol 332); John Nost (proved 12 August 1710 LMA, Archdeaconry of Middlesex, AM/PW 1710/89); Frances Nost (proved December 1716, PROB 11/555/fols 195v–196v)

Drawings: Attributed design for the monument to William Douglas, Earl of Selkirk and 3rd Duke of Hamilton (†1694), HMI, Leeds; four attributed drawings of putti (VAM Box H10); 'Design of the Two Pedestalls for the two Statues' [Bacchus and Ceres] in the Inner Court at Hopetoun-house 1709/10, Linlithgow NRA (S) 888 Bundle 630

Auction Catalogues: Nost I, 1712 (1); Nost I, 1712 (2); Nost I, 1713

Funerary Monuments

1.	1692	Sir Hugh Windham (†1684)	Silton, Dorset		*Longridge* 1954, 2–3 (repr); *Beard* 1952 (3), 1411, Pevsner, *Dorset*, 1972, 392; *Whinney* 1988, 130
2.	1697	Edward, Viscount Irwin (†1688), and his wife (co-sculptor: Edward Pearce?) Payment(s): £600	Whitkirk, W R Yorks		*Gilbert* 1962–3, 4 (repr); *Whinney* 1988, 130, 445 n69, n70; *Guide to Leeds Archives*, 1988, 71; *Friedman* 1997, 46
3.	†1698	John Digby, 3rd Earl of Bristol and his two wives	Sherborne Abbey, Dorset	S	*Whinney* 1988, 130–1 (repr)

4.	1695–1711	Duke (†1711) and Duchess (†1709) of Buccleuch and Queensberry Drawing(s): Bodl., MS Gough Drawings a.2.f.132, *Physick* 1969, 18 (repr); Model(s): Duke of Buccleuch, Drumlanrig, wood and clay		Durisdeer, Dumfries, mortuary chapel		*Friedman* 1987, 22–31 (repr); *Pearson* 1991, 29–30, 36–37 (repr)
5.	†1711	John Pierrepont Payment(s): £50		Lucton, Herefs		Herefs RO BD 13/27/28; 13/27/33; 13/28/15; C Lib (repr)
Statues						
6.	1688–1689	Horse, for the horse armoury Payment(s): £20	wd	[Royal Armoury, Tower of London]; untraced		War Office, Ordnance, Accounts, Ledgers 48/28, 28 Sept 1687; *Blakiston* 1957, 57; *Borg* 1975, 321
7.	1691	Five figures with carved faces, carrying sceptres and five horses Payment(s): £100	wd	[Royal Armoury, Tower of London]; untraced		TNA 48/30; *Blakiston* 1957, 57; *Borg* 1975, 321
8.	1694	Two, Prometheus and Ceres Payment(s): £30 each		[Chatsworth, Derbys]; untraced		Chatsworth Building Accts, 1697–98, 25
9.	1695	King William III Payment(s): £120 with Queen Mary Model(s): attrib, VAM A.35-1939, clay	s	[Royal Exchange, London, line of kings on the façade of the piazza]; untraced		City Cash Accts 01/22 fol 51 v; *Roscoe* 1997, 175–6, 178 (model repr); *Bilbey* 2002, 7–9 (repr)
10.	1695	Two flower pots		Cholmondeley Castle, Cheshire		Cheshire R O, DCH 137; *Davis* 1991 (1), 29
11.	1696	Queen Mary II Payment(s): £120 with William III Model(s): Attrib VAM, A.208-1946, c1695, clay	s	[Royal Exchange, London, line of kings on the façade of the piazza]; untraced		City Cash Accts 01/22 fol 51 v; *Roscoe* 1997, 175–6, 178 (model repr); *Bilbey* 2002, 7–9 (repr)
12.	1698	Two, a boy and girl Payment(s): £30		[Chatsworth, Derbys]; untraced		Chatsworth Building Accts, 1697–98, 25
13.	1700	'a young Triton with a brass pipe in the middle' Payment(s): £6 9s	l	[Melbourne Hall, Derbys]; untraced		*Weaver* 1909, 160; *Schellekens* 1995, 84
14.	c1700	Blackamoor Payment(s): £30		[Hampton Court Palace, Middx]; untraced		TNA WORK 5/52 f339
15.	c1700	'for making new ye best part of both ye hands of a figure called the Susannah or creeping Venus, mending ye nose, eyelids, mouth, ears and legs'	m	[Hampton Court Palace, Middx]; untraced		TNA WORK 5/51 f506
16.	1700	Pegasus and Fame Payment(s): £150	l	[Stonyhurst, Lancs]; untraced		*Stoneyhurst* 1964
17.	c1700	Two sphinxes, Samson defeating a Philistine	l	[Stowe, Bucks]; Trent Park, Southgate		Pevsner, *London: N*, 1998, 472
18.	1701	Several, including Pan and a Faun	l	Rousham Hall, Oxon	D	*Woodbridge* 1974 (2), 288, 291 n18 (repr); *Whinney* 1988, 134, 445 n.80
19.	1701	Two little figures Payment(s): £15		[Chatsworth House, Derbys]; untraced		Chatsworth Building Accts, 1701, 24
20.	1701	Two sundials 'in hard metal', one in the form of a blackamoor, the other an Indian slave Payment(s): £30, £35	l	[Hampton Court Palace, Middx, gardens]; untraced		*Colvin* 1973–76, V, 173; *Davis* 1991 (1), 48–9
21.	1702	Crouching Venus	m	Umberslade, Warks, entrance hall		Pevsner, *Warks*, 1966, 438
22.	1699–1705	Cupid shaping his bow and Cupid with a curling horn	l	Melbourne Hall, Derbys, gardens		*Weaver* 1909, 162–4 (repr); *Whinney* 1988, 133
23.	?c1705	Two flying Cupids Model(s): Melbourne House, Derbys	l	[Nost sale, lot 181]; Melbourne House, Derbys		*O'Connell* 1987, 805–6
24.	1706	Blackamoor and Indian slave, each supporting a tray above the head Payment(s): £30	l	Melbourne Hall, Derbys, gardens		*Davis* 1991 (1), 48–9; *Schellekens* 1995, 80–94 (repr)
25.	c1706	Boy playing with a swan Payment(s): 10 gns	l	Melbourne Hall, Derbys, gardens		*Schellekens* 1995, 85
26.	c1706	Flying Mercury	l	Melbourne Hall, Derbys, gardens		*Schellekens* 1995, 80–94 (repr)
27.	1706	Four pairs of Amorini	l	Melbourne Hall, Derbys, gardens		*Whinney* 1988, 133–4 (repr); *Davis* 1991 (1), 29, 36–9 (repr); *Schellekens* 1995, 80–94 (repr)
28.	c1706	Group of Mercury and Syca (Psyche) Payment(s): £50	l	[Melbourne Hall, Derbys, gardens]; untraced		*Davis* 1991 (1), 28–9, 36–41 (repr); *Schellekens* 1995, 80–94 (repr);
29.	c1706	Perseus and Andromeda Payment(s): £45	l	Melbourne Hall, Derbys, gardens		*Davis* 1991 (1), 28–9, 36–41 (repr); *Schellekens* 1995, 80–94 (repr) (repr); *Baker* 2000 121 (repr)
30.	c1706	Swan in its nest, and a duck Payment(s): £8	l	[Melbourne Hall, Derbys]; untraced		*Schellekens* 1995, 85
31.	1707	Diana on horseback and other statues Payment(s): £30 (part payment)	l	[Stonyhurst, Lancs]; untraced		*Stoneyhurst* 1964, 479
32.	1708	'Statues in ye garden and before ye Stabeles' (a captive and two kneeling figures) Payment(s): £100		Stonyhurst, Lancs		*Stoneyhurst* 1964, 479

No.	Date	Subject	Material	Location	Literature
33.	c1710	Hercules with a club		[Hopetoun House, Lothian]; Goldney House, now Bristol University (since c1738)	Linlithgow NRA (S) 888, Bundle 2964
34.	1703–1710	Several, probably including Venus and a Satyr, large as life Payment(s): £127	l	Ray Wood, Castle Howard, N R Yorks	Castle Howard, H1/1/5, f49, 60, 62, 70, 72, 74, 77; *Saumarez Smith* 1990, 124–5
35.	pre-1712	King William 'with a very good pedestal . . . of Mr Nost'	l	[Nost sale 1712 (2), lot 50]; YCBA B 1977.14.6	*O'Connell* 1987, 806; *Whinney* 1988, 445–6 n80
36.	nd	'A dancing boy . . . of Mr Nost'	m	[Nost sale, lot 99]; untraced	*O'Connell* 1987, 806
37.	nd	'A Girl curiously carved [two] . . . of Mr Nost'	m	[Nost sale, 1712 (2), lots 94 and 95]; untraced	*O'Connell* 1987, 806
38.	nd	Apollo and the Muses		[Stowe, Bucks]; untraced	*Davis* 1991 (1), 52, 371 n87
39.	nd	Crouching Venus	m	[Coll Mr Joye of the South Sea Company]; untraced	SSC Directors' sale, Feb 1722, lot 180
40.	nd	Cupid 'of Mr Nost'	m	[Nost sale 1712 (2), lot 100]; untraced	*O'Connell* 1987, 806
41.	nd	Cupid playing on a viol 'of Mr Nost'	l	[Nost sale 1712 (2) lot 98]; untraced	*O'Connell* 1987, 806
42.	nd	Garden statues and groups	l	Seaton Delaval, Northumbs	*Gunnis* 1968, 281, citing Seaton Delaval archives
43.	nd	Garden statues and groups	l	Chirk Castle, Denbigh	*Gunnis* 1968, 281
44.	nd	Mr Secretary Johnson's two bulldogs (conceivably by John Nost II)	l	[Orleans House, Twickenham]; Chantilly, Musée Condé, France	*Meslay* 2004
45.	nd	Pan	l	[Painswick House, gardens]; Painswick House, Glos, house	Pevsner, *Glos: Cotswolds*, 1999, 553; *The Times*, 1 Aug 2001 (repr)
46.	nd	Queen Mary 'of Mr Nost'	l	[Nost sale, 1712 (2) lot 51]; untraced	*O'Connell* 1987, 806; *Whinney* 1988, 445–6 n80
47.	nd	Two figures representing Painting and Sculpture	l	Hardwick Hall, Derbys	*Davis* 1991 (1), 52
48.	nd	Two, a boy and a girl		Stourhead, Wilts	Stourhead Archives
49.	nd	Young Orpheus 'of Mr Nost'	m	[Nost sale, 1712 (2), lot 97]; untraced	*O'Connell* 1987, 806
Busts					
50.	1699	Two marble heads, paid for in London by Mr Kinton on behalf of the 1st Duke of Devonshire Payment(s): £18		[Chatsworth House, Derbys]; untraced	Chatsworth Building Accts, 1699–1700, 8
51.	nd	'A Fine Marble Bust . . . of Mr Nost'	m	[Nost sale, 1712 (2), lot 101]; untraced	*O'Connell* 1987, 806
52.	nd	'A Woman and Bust . . . of Mr Nost'	m	[Nost sale, 1712 (2), lot 102]; untraced	*O'Connell* 1987, 806
Chimneypieces					
53.	1698	'Marbles for ye Gallery Chimny' Payment(s): £6 5s	m	[Chatsworth, Derbys]; untraced	Chatsworth Building Accts, 1697–98, 25
54.	1699	Description unavailable Payment(s): £50		[Thomas Coke's house, St James's Place, London]; untraced	*Gunnis* 1968, 280, citing archives, Marquess of Lothian
55.	1699	Purple and dove marble, with central female bust, garlands, two doves and two reclining putti on scrolls Drawing(s): VAM 3436.330	m	[Hampton Court, Middx, King's state apartments (until 1701)]; Hampton Court Palace, Middx, Queen's gallery	*Physick* 1969, 61–63 (repr); *Colvin* 1973–76, V, 165; *Whinney* 1988, 131
56.	1700	Dove-coloured		Hampton Court Palace, Middx, Queen's gallery	TNA WORK 5/52
57.	c1700	Purple, black and white with 'frieze of the triumph of Venus and mask-heads each side cast in bronze'	m	[Hampton Court Palace, Middx, King's gallery]; Hampton Court Palace, Middx, cartoon gall, inv 1222	TNA WORK 5/50 f327, 5/52; *Colvin* 1973–76, V, 164–5; *Whinney* 1988, 131, 133 (repr)
58.	1690–1701	Dove-coloured, and for 'takeing down a purple marble chimney peice in the long Gallery . . . and putting up the Venus' Payment(s): £30		Hampton Court Palace, Middx, Queen's gallery	*Colvin* 1973–76, V, 169; Pevsner, *London: S.*, 1983, 494
59.	1701	Several Payment(s): £40		[Chatsworth House, Derbys]; untraced	Chatsworth Building Accts, 1701, 24
60.	1701	Several, including one of 'rich purple marble with freeze and cornish and pallasters of white marble'	m	[Melbourne Hall, Derbys]; untraced	RG/JP, suppl. 6; *Gunnis* 1968, 280 – Melbourne Hall Archives, 00
61.	1707	'for the Pendilum room, the Clossett and stone-room'		[Melbourne Hall, Derbys]; untraced	*Gunnis* 1968, 280 citing archives, Marquess of Lothian
Architectural Sculpture					
62.	1700	'for fluting ye foot of ye vases that came from Mr. Pearce and polishing the plinth and moulding step'		[Hampton Court Palace, Middx]; Windsor Castle	TNA WORK 5/51; *Whinney* 1988, 130
63.	1701	24 Urns (modelled by Nost, cast by Osgood) (co-sculptor: Richard Osgood)		[Hampton Court Palace, Middx, bowling-green pavilions]; untraced	*Colvin* 1973–76, V, 168
64.	1701	Three models for fountains, one to re-use the base of the Diana Fountain Drawing(s): VAM 9145; BM PDL 1964-12-12-7, unsigned, attrib	l	[for Hampton Court Palace, Middx, gardens]; untraced	*Physick* 1969, 56–7 (attrib drawings repr); *Colvin* 1973–76, V, 172, 17
65.	1701	Two pedestals of black marble for sundials Payment(s): £45 each	m	[Hampton Court Palace, Middx, gardens]; untraced	*Colvin* 1973–76, V, 173
66.	c1703	Apollo, Equity, Liberty, Mercury, Secret, Truth and four seasons Payment(s): £27 each		[Buckingham House, London, pediment figures]; untraced	*New View of London*, 1708, vol 2, 623
67.	1705	Four seasons vase, with four busts and a bas-relief of putti at play Payment(s): £100	l	Melbourne Hall, Derbys, gardens	*Jackson-Stops* 1987 (1), 782–97 (reprs); *Davis* 1991 (1), 29, 32, 37, 41 (repr); *Schellekens* 1995, 80–94 (repr)

68.	nd	Pedestals of Portland stone for Hubert le Sueur's bronze figures of the Gladiator, Diana, Hercules and Apollo		[Hampton Court Palace, Middx, gardens]; untraced	*Whinney* 1988, 445 n77
Miscellaneous					
69.	1686	Unspecified items Payment(s): £18 9s		[probably for Thoresby Hall, Notts]; untraced	Archives, Earl Manvers
70.	*c*1692	A table of Italian marble, marble window seats and lead garden figures		[Castle Bromwich Hall, Warks]; untraced	*Beard* 1952 (3), 1411
71.	1692	Garden figures and marble tables		[Chatsworth, Derbys]; untraced	*Whinney* 1988, 130
72.	1688–1695	Garden figures or chimneypieces		[Lowther Castle, Westmorland]; untraced	Archives, Earl of Lonsdale, Lowther Castle
73.	1694–1695	Unspecified work		[coll Richard Norton]; untraced	Richard Norton Account
74.	1698	'a table of Italian marble'		[coll Duke of Devonshire]; untraced	Wynde/Bridgeman 16th Jan 1698/9; *Beard* 1952 (3), 1411
75.	1699	'ffor marble bought of Mr Nost 35.0.0.' paid for in London by Mr Kinton on behalf of the 1st Duke of Devonshire		Untraced	Chatsworth Building Accts, 1699–1700, 27
76.	1700	Relief panels, and statues of basket-bearing putti	l	Hampton Court Palace, Middx, gardens, end of the broad walk	TNA WORK 5/51; *Colvin* 1973–76, V, 172; *Whinney* 1988, 445; C Lib (repr)
77.	?1701	Carving of the 'great vauses' and 'eight panels and the pedestals of the said two vauses with emblems relating thereunto' Payment(s): £86		[Hampton Court Palace, Middx]; untraced	TNA WORK 5/52; *Gunnis* 1968, 280
78.	1701	Fountain and probably 16 statues representing the months and elements		Cholmondeley Castle, Cheshire	Cheshire RO, DCH L37
79.	1702	Pedestal for a statue of Apollo		[Hampton Court Palace, Middx, gardens]; untraced	*Colvin* 1973–76, V, 173
80.	1702	Three chimneypieces and a black table Payment(s): £17 10s	m	[James Sotheby's house, near High Beach, Sewardston, Essex]; untraced	*Sotheby MSS*, L2715-1955
81.	1702	'Work and materialls' including a 'Door Case of Portland Stone' Payment(s): £28 4s		[James Sotheby's House, near High Beach, Sewardston, Essex]; untraced	*Sotheby MSS*, L2715-1955
82.	1704	Marble basin with brass socket and wooden pedestal Payment(s): £8 10s		[Thomas Coke's apartments, St James's Palace, London]; untraced	Archives, Marquess of Lothian
83.	1704	'Marble inlayed table upon a carved guilded fframe' Payment(s): £80		[Kensington Palace, London, library]; untraced	TNA WORK 6/14; *Colvin* 1973–76, V, 194
84.	nd	Blackamoor sundial		[Cowdray Park, Sussex]; Crowther & Son, 12 Oct 1992; untraced	RG/JP, 6, 1020v.
85.	nd	Unspecified work		[Boreham, Essex]; untraced	*Gunnis* 1968, 281 citing Boreham Archives

NOST (or VAN OST), John II –1729

John Nost II was the cousin of **John Nost I**, and ran the family workshop until 1729. His business was chiefly in lead garden figures, but also included a number of large-scale equestrian statues of George I.

Nost I left his cousin £50 in his will and an extra £10 'towards discharging' his debts, which suggests that the young man began his adult life inauspiciously. Nost II continued to pay rates for the property previously occupied by Nost I in Stone Bridge, near Hyde Park, from September 1710, and he managed to retain some of Nost I's patrons, including Sir Nicholas Shireburn of Stonyhurst, who bought several garden figures in 1714 and 1716 (**3, 4**). Among his new clients was Edward Dryden of Canons Ashby (**2**), who owed the sculptor £65 5s for a gilt gladiator in 1713 (Nost II/Dryden).

Little is known of his family background, except that he had a sister called Mary Butler (or Buller), who was mentioned in Nost I's will. He married Catherine Cheesborough at St Martin-in-the-Fields in 1708 and they already had two children in 1710, both of whom received £5 in his will. One of these, another Catherine, was baptised at St Martin's on 27 March 1710.

Frances Nost, the widow of Nost I, died in 1716, leaving Nost II 'all the marble goods and figures at his house which belongs to me'. She also released him from 'all debts and moneys from him to me due and owing at the time of my decease', which suggests that his fortunes had not improved.

By 1717 the business was evidently prospering, for Nost received a commission for a bronze statue of King George I from the corporation of Dublin (**12**). They agreed in that year to pay the sculptor £1,500, and a part-payment of £500 to 'Mr John Noast of London, statuary' was made in August 1721. Nost cast the figure of the horse from moulds made from Le Sueur's statue of King Charles I at Charing Cross, and went on to use the cast to produce several more lead versions for other patrons, including the extravagant Duke of Chandos, whose gilded statue with a handsome pedestal carved with trophies of war, was erected at Canons (*Canons Grand Inventory*). The statue, which terminated a vista in the gardens, was singled out for appreciative comment by an anonymous Frenchman visiting in 1728. Nost may have provided several other figures for Canons: the 1725 inventory includes, for instance, such parapet figures as *Courage represented by Hercules with his club, History with a table & pen in her hand*, and *Fame sounding a trumpet*, all subjects associated with the Nost workshop. Several Whig patrons followed the Duke's example and Nost's workshop became associated with equestrian figures of George I, presented as a conquering hero in plate armour and crowned with laurels. A very similar image in lead appeared outside the market hall in Gosport (**8**), there was a gilt version in Grosvenor Square that cost £260 19s (**17**), and two leading figures in the Whig ministry, Lord Cobham and the Duke of Bolton, advertised their political allegiance with versions of the statue sited in pivotal positions at Hackwood and Stowe (**11, 16**).

In 1716 Nost took over another property from the sculptor **Edward Hurst**, next to his premises in Stone Bridge. The two buildings were rated at £12 and £18 respectively. By 1720 one of them was vacant and in 1722, Nost's name disappeared from the Stone Bridge rate books. He paid annual rates of £20 from 1720 until his death in 1729 on another property, a yard in neighbouring Portugal Row.

In April 1718 Nost made an agreement with Sir John Germaine to supply to Drayton House, Northants 'two leading Statues Six footh hey from the plint, one a [. . .] for a [. . .] and the Other figur a backus according to the patrons showed to the Sd. Sr. John, and also to make three Leadin Vasis upwards of four footh high of two Severall Sorts' (**24**). He also agreed that 'the Sayd figurs and Vasis Shal be painted twice over with a White Stone colour'. The price set for this commission was £40 and Nost's signed receipt, dated 27 May 1718, records the supply (Drayton Archive MM/A/723). Another paper in the same archive headed 'quitance de Mr. Nost Statuaire' records the above payment and date as well as other charges for porterage, with an intriguing payment of one guinea 'a la femme francaise'. An earlier receipt in the Drayton Archive labelled 'Quitance des vases' headed London and dated 6 October 1710 but with an indecipherable signature is for twelve vases costing £60 (*ibid*, MM/A/675). This almost certainly refers to lead vases above colonnades in the courtyard at Drayton, for which there are bills, also dated 1710, which the mason John Woodall, who had earlier worked there for the architect William Talman, was building. Today there are only eight vases. The London heading for the receipt suggests that this also refers to the Nost yard.

Further evidence of John Nost's ability to retain Nost I's patrons comes from two contracts drawn up eight years after his elder cousin's death. These were for lead statues for the 1st Earl of Hopetoun's gardens at Hopetoun House, near Edinburgh. The first contract, dated 24 May 1718, was for four metal statues, *Cain and Abel*, *Diana*, a *Gladiator* and *Hercules with a club*, at a cost of £86. The second, dated 20 June 1718, was for *Adonis with a greyhound*, *Venus with Cupid*, *Venus coming out of the bath*, and *Phaon playing on a pipe* (**7**). These were to cost £56 (Nost/Hopetoun MS). The contract says Nost was to deliver the first statues to Scotland 'by the latter end of July next' and the second batch was to arrive by 1 October. Surprisingly, the goods did not arrive until 16 September 1719 and this is confirmed by a shipping order, dated 28 February 1719, for 'fave larg' casses of Leaden status' with a freight charge of one guinea to cover the journey from London to Leith (Nost/Hopetoun MS) and a receipt accepted by 'Mr. John Nost' for the total of the two contracts, £142, dated 14 September 1719 (Nost/Hopetoun MS). The only statues from the large number named in the 1709 estimate sent by John Nost I were the *Bacchus* and *Ceres*. None of these works remain at Hopetoun.

The Duke of Chandos called him back to Canons in 1723 to inspect some vases which appeared to be in danger of falling from the parapet. Chandos paid him £480 10s between 1722 and 1725, probably for vases and lead figures in the extensive pleasure-grounds. He also provided a statue of George II, ordered at the time of the King's accession in 1727. This was sold at the Canons auction in 1747 and erected in Golden Square in 1753 (**18**).

One of Nost's last works, his only known monument, celebrates Joseph Banks and was erected at Revesby, Lincs, shortly before the sculptor's death (1). A letter from Nost to Banks's son refers to an order for chimneypieces and concludes 'I desire to know whether I can have the picture of your father, for I am going on with the monument, and the head will take more time in finishing, for the more time I take in doing itt the better it will be completed' (*Hill* 1952, 93).

He died in April 1729, and two obituaries survive. The *Political State of Great Britain* recorded 'Sunday the 27th, died Mr Nost, a famous Statuary, at his House near Hyde-Park Corner' and *The Historical Register* announced 'Dyd Mr Nost, a noted Statuary'. The administration of his will was granted to his widow **Catherine Nost** on 23 May 1729. His son, **John Nost III** (often known as 'the younger') was at that time apprenticed to **Henry Scheemakers**.

Nost appears to have been the man referred to by Vertue as a nephew of Nost I, 'who drove on the business but never studied – nor did himself anything tolerable' (*Vertue* IV, 35). If so, this is a harsh judgement to pass on a sculptor who successfully ran the family workshop for 19 years and provided memorable iconic portraits of the first Hanoverian king. Nost was confused with his cousin John Nost until the recent discovery of his will and posthumous sale catalogue. To add to the confusion Musgrave's *Obituary* mistakenly indexed him with the forename Gerard.

BB/MGS

Literary References: *Northampton Mercury*, 13 Dec 1725; *PSGB*, v38 (1729), 425; *Voyage d'Angleterre*, 1728; *Hist Reg*, v14, (1729), 28; *Vertue* IV, 35; *Musgrave* 1899–1901, IV, 309; *Hill* 1952, 93; *Webb* 1957 (3), 119; *Stonyhurst* 1964, 479; *O'Connell* 1987, 802–6; *Davis* 1991 (1), *passim*; *Grove* 23, 1996, 253–4 (Murdoch); *Spencer-Longhurst* 1998, 31–40; *Jenkins* 2005, 64; *Sullivan* 2005, 8

Archival References: WCA, Highways Rate, 1710 (F5311-2); Poor Rate 1712, (F3574); Poor Rate 1716, (F3597), Highways, 1722 (F5550); Nost II/Dryden; Nost II casting warrant; *Voyage d'Angleterre*, 1728; Canons, *Accounts with Tradesmen*; Nost/Hopetoun MS; *Canons Grand Inventory*; Chandos catalogue, June 19, lot 57, June 26, lots 54–61; IGI

Wills: John Nost I (proved 12 August 1710 LMA, Archdeaconry of Middlesex, AM/PW 1710/89); Frances Nost (proved December 1716, FRC PROB 11/555/fols 195v–196v); John Nost's Admin, 23 May 1729 (FRC PROB 6/105 fol 95)

Funerary Monuments

1.	†1729	Joseph Banks		Revesby, Lincs	*Hill* 1952, frontispiece, xxxvii, 93; *Lord* 1994, 84

Statues

2.	1713	A gladiator and other figures	l	Canons Ashby, Northants, gardens	*Davis* 1991 (1), 25, 47, 370 n2; 371 n75
3.	1714	'4 Thermes and 3 whole Statues' Payment(s): £120		[Stonyhurst, Lancs]; untraced	*Stoneyhurst* 1964, 479
4.	1716	'two Vauces, 2 Groops of Infants, peace and abundance' Payment(s): £40		[Stonyhurst, Lancs]; untraced	*Stoneyhurst* 1964, 479
5.	1716	Two, shepherd and shepherdess Payment(s): £26 with Portland stone pedestals	m	[Park House, Gateshead, coll William Ramsay jnr]; untraced	*Hughes* 1952, 49
6.	1717	Unidentified figures	l	[Moulsham Hall, Essex]; untraced	*Gunnis* 1968, 281 citing archives, Moulsham Hall

7.	1718	Cain and Abel, Diana, Gladiator, Hercules with a club, Adonis with greyhound, Venus with Cupid, Venus coming out of the bath, Phaon playing on a pipe Payment(s): £142	l	[Hopetoun House, Lothian]; untraced	Nost II-Hopetoun contract; account for shipping, NRA (S) 888
8.	1718	King George I	l	[Gosport, Hants, market hall]; untraced	*Roscoe* 1997, 179
9.	1719	Two unidentified statues, a gladiator, and Diana and Actaeon Payment(s): £39 5s	l	[Castle Bromwich Hall, Staffs]; untraced	Sir John Bridgeman Accounts, Staffs RO, D1287/4/4; *Davis* 1991 (1), 30
10.	1720	Queen Mary		University College, Oxford	*Gunnis* 1968, 281
11.	1722	King George I, equestrian	l	Hackwood Park, Hants	*Spencer-Longhurst* 1998, 32–33 (repr)
12.	1717–1722	King George I, equestrian Payment(s): £1,500	b	[Essex Bridge, Dublin]; Barber Institute, Birmingham University, Warks	TNA LC/5157 p241; *Kelly* 1995, 103–7; *Spencer-Longurst* 1998, 31–40 (repr)
13.	c1723	King George I, equestrian (co-sculptor: C Buchard) Payment(s): £171	l	[Canons, Middx, north garden]; untraced	*O'Connell* 1987, 803–4 (repr); *Spencer-Longhurst* 1998, 32–3; *Jenkins* 2005, 168, 192, n39
14.	1723	Sir Robert Geffrye (†1703)	l	[Ironmongers' Almshouses, Shoreditch, City of London (replica in situ)]; Ironmongers' Almshouses, Mottingham, Kent	*Gunnis* 1968, 281; *Pevsner, Kent: W & Weald*, 1976, 427
15.	1724	'2 estridges 6 ft. high' and '2 Cocketresses' Payment(s): £27	l	[Gough Park]; untraced	*Weaver* 1972, 194; *Davis* 1991 (1), 30
16.	1723–1724	King George I, equestrian Payment(s): £150	l	[Stowe, Bucks, far end of canal]; Stowe, principal front	*Davis* 1991 (1), 131, 139, 149, 372 n3 (repr); *O'Connell* 1987, 803 (repr); *Spencer-Longhurst* 1998, 32
17.	1725–1726	King George I, equestrian Payment(s): £262 10s	l	[Grosvenor Square, London]; untraced	*Gatty* 1921, 2, 209; *Spencer-Longhurst* 1998, 32, n1
18.	c1727	King George II	s	[Canons, Middx]; Golden Square, London (1753)	*O'Connell* 1987, 805; *Whinney* 1988, 134
Chimneypieces					
19.	1728	Several		[Revesby Hall, Lincs]; untraced	*Hill* 1952, 93
Architectural Sculpture					
20.	1722	Five vases		[Canons, Middx, s and e fronts]; untraced	*Collins Baker* 1949, 141
21.	1731	Unidentified work, perhaps a bason Payment(s): £83 16s 6d		[Canons, Middx]; untraced	Canons, *Accounts with Tradesmen*
Miscellaneous					
22.	1711	Unidentified work		[House in the Privy Gardens, Whitehall, London]; untraced	*Friedman* 1984 (1), 307
23.	1716	Six statues, two vases, two groups of infants, 'peace and abundence. . .' Payment(s): £40		[Stonyhurst, Lancs]; untraced	*Stonyhurst* 1964, 479
24.	1718	Flora, Bacchus and three lead vases		[Drayton House, Northants]; untraced	Drayton Archive MM/A/723
25.	1725–1727	Two large vases and eight heads	l	[coll Duke of Kent]; Wrest Park, Beds, gardens	Wrest (Lucas) Hoare's *Customer Ledger*, 1725–1728, vol I, 371, 460; Hoare's *Customer Ledger*, 1728–1731, vol K, f91 Archive (1), *Account Book* L31/199; *Davis* 1991 (1), 45, 371

NOST (or VAN OST), John III –1780

Nost was born and trained in London, but made his name in Dublin, where he was the pre-eminent sculptor of the 1750s and 1760s, known particularly for his public statues of Hanoverian monarchs. He appears to have been the son of **John Nost II** and **Catherine Nost**, born on 22 June 1713 and christened at St Martin-in-the-Fields two days later. An entry in the Apprenticeship Books for 17 October 1726 records that 'Jn Son of Jn Nost of St. Geo: Hanov: Square' was bound to **Henry Scheemakers** for seven years, at a cost of £40.

Nothing is known of his career before 1749 when he presented a terracotta bust to the Dublin Society (**24**). His move to Dublin appears to have been dictated by a lack of competition in that city, where there was a considerable demand for sculpture and relatively few Irish practitioners to take advantage of it. He soon established an extensive practice in busts, monuments and royal statues.

Nost played an active role in the Dublin Society, an institution founded to promote 'Husbandry and Other Useful Arts', and the forerunner of the Society of Arts in London. In 1751 he carved a marble bust of its founder, Dr Samuel Madden, and in 1760, another senior member, Thomas Prior (**25, 36**). These and a bust in the Society's rooms of the 4th Earl of Chesterfield, Lord Lieutenant of Ireland (**44**), demonstrate that Nost was a highly accomplished portrait sculptor. Although Prior is portrayed *all'antica*, his sagging flesh and wrinkled brow are naturalistic, and Chesterfield has a bulbous nose and open mouth. Nost's growing reputation for verisimilitude is confirmed by a letter from Mary Delaney to her sister, Mrs Dewes of 14 March 1752: 'We called on a famous statuary, who has been here about two years – Vanhost. He served his time with Scheemaker and seems an ingenious man, and a great artist in his way: he takes as strong a likeness as ever I saw taken in marble – his price is forty guineas for the model and bust' (*Llanover* 1861, III, 95–6). Delaney also noted that the sculptor was selling highly varnished plaster library busts, and making others to order. In this capacity he aided the Society by supplying plaster busts for students to work from, and he taught in the Society's Figure Drawing School, providing tuition for numerous pupils including **Patrick Cunningham, John Crawley, William Graham, Michael Foy** and **Christopher Hewetson.**

Nost was fortunate to arrive in Dublin at a time of civic expansion. In 1752 he answered an advertisement issued by the Corporation by providing two proposals for an equestrian statue of George II. These were estimated at £1,200 and £1,730, the latter to include a stone plinth decorated with trophies. The Corporation chose Nost's more costly design (12), noting that the sculptor was 'the most knowing and skilful statuary in this kingdom' and also that it would benefit 'the honour and reputation of the city' to have the work made in Dublin, rather than imported. A model was prepared by 1754 and the work was cast in 1756. It was placed in a focal position in the centre of St Stephen's Green, and according to the Corporation was 'allowed by persons of skill and judgement to be a complete and curious piece of workmanship' (*Hill* 1998, 50).

During the 1750s Nost also continued the family tradition of lead ornament manufacture, though with less success. The philanthropist Dr Bartholomew Mosse, who founded Dublin's first lying-in hospital, commissioned six classical figures (11) for the hospital's new gardens. Nost had difficulties in obtaining payments from the governors of the Hospital and wrote to them on 24 October 1757: 'My present distress compels me immediately to dispose of them, and am very willing to sell them many pounds cheaper at this juncture than at any other time I could afford them, being just now in misfortune, and must, this instant, raise a large sum to extricate me'. He later removed the works altogether and failed to deliver further gilt lead statues of George II and Frederick, Prince of Wales, which Mosse had ordered. (*Strickland* 1913, vol 2, 483).

In 1756 the Friendly Brothers of St Patrick, a masonic group, commissioned a gilt bronze statue of General William Blakeney (13), an octogenarian hero of the Seven Years War, who had been made an Irish peer for his defence of Minorca against the French. The statue was unveiled on St Patrick's Day, 1759, after being carried from the sculptor's house in Aungier Street to the affluent residential square at the end of the mall where it was erected. In 1760 a commission followed from the fiercely loyal Corporation of Cork, who chose to commemorate the end of George II's reign with an equestrian statue erected to his memory (15). A temporary foundry was set up in a lane off South Main Street, and the statue was cast under Nost's supervision.

The new reign was soon to be commemorated in Dublin by a statue of George III (17), commissioned and paid for, at a cost of 700 guineas, by another Lord Lieutenant, the Earl of Northumberland. In May 1765 the English press reported that 'Mr Van Nost, Statuary from Dublin' had modelled 'an elegant design for a statue in brass,' a 'striking testimony' to the Lord Lieutenant's 'loyalty and munificence'. Further notices in June reported 'His majesty has most graciously condescended to sit three times to Mr Van Nost who came from Ireland on purpose' (*Press Cuttings 1723–1800*, fols 54, 61).

Although it is less well-documented, Nost appears to have had a career in London as well as Dublin. In 1763 he was listed in Mortimer's *Universal Director* 'at Mr Clarke's, St Martin's-lane, opposite May's-buildings' (p 28; Rate-Books 1763, Cleansing Street Rates, F6007). J T Smith later recollected that Nost had lived at 104 St Martin's Lane, in a large house once inhabited and decorated by King George I's sergeant painter, Sir James Thornhill. Smith considered Nost's most noteworthy work to be 'the famous mask of Garrick from his face' (55) which had been in **Nathaniel Smith's** collection, but had finished up in a 'gallery of theatrical pictures, busts &c' owned by a Mr Mathews of Highgate Hill. According to the actor, Macklin, Nost's bust of Garrick was 'in every barber's shop-window, as a block for wigs' (*Smith* 1828, v.2, 228, 275) (44). Nost appears to have had other connections with Garrick. The great actor owned a marble bust of George III executed in 1764 (41?), and on 17 June 1778 an advertisement was placed in *The Morning Post* for a statuette of 'GARRICK represented in the Figure of ROSCIUS, By JOHN VAN NOST' (19). The prolix text described Roscius 'studying the Character of Phaedria in the Eunuch of Terence,' and the statuette could be had on subscription for two guineas. Sir Watkin Williams Wynn was one of those who took advantage of the offer. The advertisement called Nost 'Statuary to their Majesties', and now gave his address as Chelsea-Road, Pimlico.

Nost had a steady flow of patrons for monuments throughout his Irish career and new stylistic trends from London manifested themselves in these works. His memorial to Judge George Gore (3) is close in concept and composition to **Louis François Roubiliac**'s near-contemporaneous Last Judgement monuments to Mary Myddelton and General Hargrave. Nost borrowed the image of the deceased casting off a winding sheet at the Last Trump and included a medallion portrait of Gore's predeceased wife among the heavenly clouds. Roubiliac's theatricality is also evident in Nost's monument to Nicholas and John Fitzgerald in Waterford Cathedral (8), erected through a bequest of £600 by Richard Fitzgerald of London (†1763), an Anglo-Irish landowner with large estates, who wished to honour his father and uncle (PROB 11/893 f505). A winged figure of *Time* with a broken hourglass approaches a weeping woman, leaning on a portrait medallion of the deceased men. Nost's figures are carved with anatomical intensity, and *Time*'s muscles and veins and the small rolls of flesh above the navel are precisely rendered. The profile portraits have flabby chins and mis-shapen noses. Damage to the monument has upset the composition, but its original appearance is known from a description and an engraving for Smith's *Waterford*, 1774.

Towards the end of his life Nost began to lose his monopoly on on Irish public statues. In 1771 the commission for a figure of Dr Charles Lucas for the Dublin Exchange went instead to the young **Edward Smyth**. A 19th-century source tells that Nost challenged the decision that his model was too large, and begged to be allowed to resubmit: 'In the interval he cut his model in two, and omitted part of the centre, and thus presented it a second time for judgement; but this alteration had so cheated every other part of the figure of its fair proportions, that Smyth's model was immediately chosen' (*Wright* 1821, 320–1). Nost's last monument, to Archbishop Smyth (9), a grand architectural piece with a large urn in a niche, was completed by **Henry Darley** of Abbey Street (*Hibern Mag*, April 1775, 193). Nost may have been in failing health by 1778, for a letter from Frederick Hervey, the Earl Bishop of Derry to his daughter mentions 'Van Oost . . . if he is able' as the intended sculptor for a life sized statue of Hervey's brother for a mausoleum (20) (*Childe-Pemberton* 1925, vol 1, 181).

The *Gentleman's Magazine* recorded the death in Dublin, late in 1780, of 'Mr John van Nost, statuary to his majesty' (vol 50, 494). His will, dated 24 October 1779, from an address in Mecklenburgh Street suggests that the sculptor left considerable assets. His wife, Ann ('otherwise Armstrong') inherited 'all and every of his houses, estate, leasehold, interests, lands, household furniture, goods, chattels and effects.' His sister Catherine Legross, widow, and his nephew, Richard Lynd, each received the proverbial shilling.

Nost was a versatile sculptor. He appears to have designed commemorative medals during the 1760s, including one showing the bloated profile of the victor of Culloden, William Augustus, Duke of Cumberland (**56**). His public works had a turbulent later life. The statue of General Blakeney survived only six years before being pulled down and removed to a new location, after which it disappeared. The royal statues suffered, like so many other statues in Ireland proclaiming loyalty to the English government. The equestrian George II in Cork was assaulted in 1849 by two men with staves, and after numerous other attacks and repairs it was destroyed. On the 13 May 1937 the Dublin statue fell a victim to dynamite. The poet W. B. Yeats wrote the following day 'I would go into mourning, but the suit I kept for funerals is worn out. Our tomfools have blown up the equestrian statue of George II in St Stephen's Green, the only Dublin statue that has delighted me by beauty and elegance' (*Irish Times*, 14 May 1937).

MGS

Literary References: *Press Cuttings* 1723–1800, fols 54, 61; *Mortimer* 1763, 28; *Smith* 1774, 177; *Hibernian Mag*, April 1775, 193; *Morning Post*, 17 June 1778; *GM* vol 50, 1780, 494; *Wright* 1825, 181–2; *Smith* II, 1828, 228, 275; *Llanover* 1861, III, 95–6; *Strickland* 1913, vol 2, 478–487; *Childe-Pemberton* 1925, vol 1, 181; *Webb* 1957 (3), 119; *Potterton* 1974 (1), 260; *Potterton* 1975, *passim*; *Hill* 1998, *passim*; *Sullivan* 2005, 8–9

Archival References: Parish register, St Martin-in-the-Fields, vols 9–10, 1713; Cleansing street rates 1763, WCA, F6007

Wills: 'A memorial of the last will and testament of John Van Nost' registered 3 Feb 1781, Registry of Deeds, Dublin (338.145.226588); Richard Fitzgerald, PROB 11/893 fol 505

Auctions: *Strickland*, vol 2, 485 notes that when Nost moved from his home in Aungier Street to a residence on the property of the Right Hon Anthony Malone on the east side of St Stephen's Green (1763), he held a sale of his moulds and models; no reference to a surviving catalogue or source is included.

Funerary Monuments

No.	Date	Subject		Location		References
1.	†1749	Sir Arthur Acheson		Mullaghbrack, Co Armagh		*Potterton* 1975, 86
2.	†1752	Susanna Mason		Waterford Cathedral		*Smith* 1774, 176; *Potterton* 1975, 86; C Lib (repr)
3.	†1753	Judge George Gore, with medallion of his wife Bridget Sankey (†1748)		Tashinny, Co Longford	S	*Gunnis* 1963, 1174, 1176 (repr); *Potterton* 1975, 27, 86 (repr)
4.	1756	Thomas Prior, with relief showing 'Prior introducing Ceres to Hibernia'		Christ Church Cathedral, Dublin	SD	*Pool and Cash* 1780, 102 (repr); *Potterton* 1975, 30, 86 (repr)
5.	1764	Charles Moore, Lord Charleville, with bust of his nephew John Bury of Shannongrove (†1764) [designed by the same John Bury]		Tullamore, North Offaly	SD	*Potterton* 1975, 60, 61, 86 (repr)
6.	†1767	Lord Chancellor John Bowes Payment(s): £500		Christ Church Cathedral, Dublin		*Pool and Cash* 1780, 107 (repr); *Potterton* 1975, 86
7.	†1768	Anne, Viscountess Loftus		New Ross, Co Wexford		*Potterton* 1975, 86; C Lib (repr)
8.	1770	Nicholas and John Fitzgerald		Waterford Cathedral		*Smith* 1774, 177 (repr); *Potterton* 1975, 59, 86 (repr)
9.	1775	Archbishop Arthur Smyth (†1771) (co-sculptor: Henry Darley) Payment(s): £1,500		St Patrick's Cathedral, Dublin		*Pool and Cash* 1780, 95–7 (repr); *Potterton* 1975, 85–6

Statues

No.	Date	Subject		Location		References
10.	1754	Catherine Poer, Countess of Tyrone		Curraghmore, Co Waterford, shell house	D	*Strickland* 1913, vol 2, 487; *Loeber* 1970, 24
11.	1757	Antinous, Venus de Medici, Sitting Venus, Mercury, Apollo and Faunus	l	[New Gardens, Dublin]; untraced		*Strickland* 1913, vol 2, 480;
12.	1753–1758	King George II, equestrian Payment(s): £1,730 incl pedestal	b	[St Stephen's Green, Dublin]; destroyed		*Gilbert* 1889–1922, vol X, 21–2, 82–4, 212; *Hill* 1998, 49–51 (repr)
13.	1756–1759	General Blakeney	b	[Dublin, Mall, Sackville Street, coll Friendly Brothers of St Patrick]; untraced		*GM*, March 1759, v.29, 144; *Strickland* 1913, vol 2, 480;
14.	1750–1760	Several		Rotonda Gardens, Dublin		*Potterton* 1975, 85; *Dawson* 1999, 218
15.	1760–1761	King George II, equestrian		[Cork, Tuckey's Bridge]; destroyed		*Strickland* 1913, vol 2, 484; *Hill* 1998, 72–3
16.	1764	Sir Edward Hawke		[Rostellan Castle, Cork]; untraced		*Walpole* 1760–1795, 155
17.	1765	King George III Payment(s): 700 gns	b	Mansion House, Dublin		*Harbison, Potterton and Sheehy* 1978, 140, 173 (repr); *O'Connell* 1987, 805 (repr);
18.	1771	Dr Charles Lucas, unsuccessful model for Exchange statue	wd	Untraced		*Wright* 1821, 320–1
19.	1778	Garrick represented as Roscius, statuette (multiple by subscription)		[Curraghmore, Co Waterford]; untraced		*Morning Post*, 17 June 1778; *Potterton* 1974 (1), 260
20.	1778	George, 5th Earl of Bristol (†1775)		[Down Hill, Northern Ireland, mausoleum]; destroyed		*Childe-Pemberton* 1925, vol 1, 155, 181
21.	1779	Hugh Lawton (later Mayor of Cork)		[Cork]; untraced		*Strickland* 1913, vol 2, 485
22.	nd	King George III		Mansion House, Dublin		*O'Connell* 1987, 805 (repr)
23.	nd	Lion couchant		86, St Stephen's Green, Dublin, portico		*Loeber* 1970, 26 (repr); *Hill* 1998, 48

Busts

No.	Date	Subject		Location		References
24.	1749	A bust in clay	tc	[Royal Dublin Society, presented for approval]; untraced		*Potterton* 1975, 85
25.	1751	Dr Samuel Madden	m	RDS, Dublin		*White and Bright* 1998, 36
26.	post-1752	Dean Patrick Delany, DD		Trinity College, Dublin, library		*Crookshank* 1986, 23, 27 (repr)

27.	1752	Library busts, including Seneca, Aristotle, Galen and Horace	p	[coll Dr Patrick Delany, Dean of Down]; untraced		*Llandover* 1861, vol 3, 95–6
28.	1753	Marcus, 1st Earl of Tyrone		Curraghmore, Co Waterford		RG/JP, 6, 1028
29.	1753	Sir Marcus Beresford	m	Private coll	SD	
30.	1754	Henry Boyle, Speaker of the House of Commons		Farmer's Club, Munster		*Strickland* 1913, vol 2, 480
31.	1754	King William III		Untraced Other versions: several, for subscribers		*Faulkner's Journal*, 13 April 1754; *Strickland* 1913, vol 2, 480, 487
32.	1755	Lord Kingsborough		Untraced		*Strickland* 1913, vol 2, 487
33.	1755	William, 4th Earl of Inchiquin		Untraced		*Strickland* 1913, vol 2, 487
34.	c1757	Arthur, 1st Earl of Arran		[Assembly Rooms, Dublin]; Rotunda, Dublin		*de Breffny* 1986, cat 26
35.	1759	Robert Clayton, Bishop of Clogher and Henry, 1st Earl of Shannon	m	Assembly Rooms, Dublin, entrance hall		*Strickland* 1913, vol 2, 483
36.	1760	Thomas Prior	m	RDS, Dublin	D	*White and Bright* 1998, 30–2
37.	1762	David Garrick		[Exhib Free Soc, 178]; untraced		*Graves* 1907, 266
38.	1762	George, 2nd Earl of Halifax Payment(s): Subscriptions at 3g each		[Mr Clarkes, St Martin's Lane]; untraced		*Walpole* 1760–1795, 155; *Strickland* 1913, vol 2, 484, 487
39.	1763	Lord Chancellor John Bowes		Untraced		*Strickland* 1913, vol 2, 486
40.	1763	Sir Edward Hawke		Untraced		*Strickland* 1913, vol 2, 484, 487
41.	1764	King George III	m	YCBA B 1977.14.22 Other versions: VAM, copy	SD	Garrick's posthumous sale, 23 June, 1823, lot 74; *Waterhouse* 1977, 352 (repr)
42.	?1765	David Garrick	p	Garrick Club, London, inv 22 or 67 Other versions: many		*Smith* 1828, vol 2, 275; *Ashton* 1997, 511 (repr)
43.	1767	King George III	m	VAM	SD	*Mag Antiq* 1958, 73 (repr)
44.	1769	Philip Stanhope, 4th Earl of Chesterfield Payment(s): 35 gns		RDS, Dublin, members' room		*Strickland* 1913, vol 2, 486; *White and Bright* 1998, 36
45.	1779	King George III		[Exhib RA, London, 220]; untraced		*Graves* V, 1905–6, 391 (where listed as Adam Nost); *Gunnis* 1968, 282
46.	nd	David Garrick		Curraghmore, Co Waterford		*Loeber* 1970, 24
47.	nd	Dr Bartholomew Mosse		Rotunda Hospital, Dublin		*Strickland* 1913, vol 2, 487
48.	nd	Earl of Tyrone		Curraghmore, Co Waterford		*Loeber* 1970, 24
49.	nd	Edward, 7th Earl of Meath		Kilruddery Castle, Co Wicklow		RG/JP, 6, 1028
50.	nd	James, 1st Duke of Leinster		[Carton, Co Kildare]; untraced		*Strickland* 1913, vol 2, 487
51.	nd	King George III		Curraghmore, Co Waterford		*Loeber* 1970, 24
52.	nd	Unidentified man	m	NGI	S	*le Harivel* 1988, 602 (repr)

Reliefs

53.	1762	David Garrick, medallion		[Mr Clarke's, St Martin's Lane]; untraced Other versions: sold by subscription at half a guinea each		*Walpole* 1760–1795, 155

Miscellaneous

54.	c1763	George II, memorial medal		Untraced		*Strickland* 1913, vol 2, 485
55.	?1765	David Garrick, mask		Untraced Other versions: plaster painted to resemble bronze, Garrick Club, London, inv 363		*Smith* 1828, vol 2, 228; *Ashton* 1997, 512
56.	c1765	Silver mortuary medal commemorating the death of William Augustus, Duke of Cumberland (†1765)		NAM (on the lid of the Cumberland tankard)	S	*Reid* 1971, 158–60 (repr)
57.	1766	Robert Clive, silver medal		NPG	S	NPG cat

NOWELL, Philip –1853

Nowell had a yard in Grosvenor Wharf, Pimlico. From 1806 until 1818 he worked under Sir Jeffry Wyatville on building work at Longleat and was described in the House Accounts as a stone mason. He leased houses adjoining the Castle Inn in Warminster from the 2nd Marquess of Bath. In 1824–25 he was employed extensively in restoration work at Windsor Castle (1), receiving over £9,300 for masonry and carving.

He was also the mason responsible for building the Duke of York's column, surmounted by the bronze statue by **Sir Richard Westmacott**. The column, an engineering feat, is cut from Yorkshire, Peterhead and Aberdeen granite, stands 94 feet high and has an internal staircase. Nowell completed it in 18 months and was paid £15,760. The *Architectural Magazine* carried a lengthy description of the structure, concluding with a commendation of Nowell's 'most substantial and workmanlike manner' (*Archit Mag* 1834, 192).

In 1828 he was employed on restoration work and additions to Apsley House, receiving £7,624. Ten years later he was again working for the Duke of Wellington as master-mason in charge of alterations to Stratfield Saye, where he was assisted by his son, Philip Nowell II (Archives, Duke of Wellington in *Gunnis* 1968, 282).

Literary References: *Archit Mag* 1834, 192

Archival References: TNA WORK 5/125 and 19–30/1, fol 385; Longleat HA, 1806–31, NMR o, WMR o; WMR 452; NMR 7499

Will: PROB 11/2169, proved 12 March 1853

Architectural Sculpture

1.	1824–1825	Carved gothic details, including '6 sunk gothic eyes, 28 moulded gothic eyes' and 'cutting large holes in grotesque heads'	[Windsor Castle]; untraced	TNA WORK 5/125 and 19–30/1, fol 385

NUGENT –1729

The *Northampton Mercury* for 23 June 1729, reported that members of a family named Nugent, who were Irish masons, were all killed in an accident.

Archival References: GPC

NURSEY FAMILY, of Beccles and Bungay fl c1827–55

They sign a large wall-tablet 'with excellent details' to Charlotte Windham (1). In 1855 the firm was located in Bungay, and was run by Henry and James Nursey who lived in Upper Olland Street and Lower Olland Street respectively.

Archival References: GPC

Funerary Monuments

1.	?1827	Hon Charlotte Windham	Earsham, Norfolk	S	*Gunnis* 1968, 282
2.	?1838	Rev Richard Dreyer	Thwaite, Norfolk	S	*Gunnis* 1968, 282

NUTCHER, J, of Swaythling fl c1753–94

Though Nutcher lived in a small Hampshire town, two of his signed monuments were considered by Gunnis to be of 'considerable importance'. That to Philemon Ewer (4), whose epitaph relates that 'during the late war with Spain [he] built seven large ships of war' and was 'an ingenious artist and an excellent workman' has, at its base, a high relief of a man-of-war in full sail. The other significant monument is to Anne Woodroffe (2). This is about nine feet high and has 'a curious design, embodying two cornucopiae from each of which springs a rose-tree in full bloom. The mantling of the coat of arms is elaborate and well-carved'.

Literary References: *Gunnis* 1968, 282

Funerary Monuments

1.	?1753	Imber family	St Lawrence, Winchester	S	GPC
2.	†1762	Anne Woodroffe	Seale, Surrey	S	Pevsner, *Surrey*, 1971, 449
3.	?1767	Matthew Imber	St Lawrence, Winchester	S	GPC
4.	†1794	Philemon Ewer	St Leonard, Bursledon, Hants	S	Pevsner, *Hants & Isle of Wight*, 1967, 156

NUTT, John, of Birmingham fl c1810–40

He was responsible for a number of tablets, including one to Richard Craddock which has two flaming lamps on either side of a pyramid (8).

Funerary Monuments

1.	?1810	Will Pearson	Sutton Coldfield, Warks	S	*Gunnis* 1968, 282
2.	?1814	Edward Bower	St Martin, Birmingham	S	*Gunnis* 1968, 282
3.	?1816	Rev Benjamin Carpenter	Stourbridge Unitarian chapel, Worcs	S	GPC
4.	?1824	Frances Kendall	Stourbridge Unitarian chapel, Worcs	S	GPC
5.	?1827	Rev John Scott	Stourbridge Unitarian chapel, Worcs	S	GPC
6.	?1833	Samuel Woollaston	Beoley, Worcs	S	GPC
7.	?1839	Thomas Mountford	Beoley, Worcs	S	GPC
8.	?1840	Richard Craddock	Eccleshall, Staffs		*Gunnis* 1968, 282

NUTTALL, Thomas fl 1814–16

He was responsible for much masonry work at Ashburnham Park, Sussex between 1814 and 1816, when it was being rebuilt under Dance the Younger. In 1814 he was paid £1,745 5s 7d for work including a bridge between the two lakes.

Archival References: Ashburnham Accts with Artificers, ASH 2854 (31 Dec 1814), ASH 2867 (1813–14)

NYS, Daniel fl 1707

Statues

1.	1707	Pallas Athene	Hall Barn, Beaconsfield, Bucks, niche on east front (formerly in gardens)	Pevsner, *Bucks*, 1994, 362

O'NEIL (or O'NEILL), Luke fl 1827–40

Luke O'Neil prepared the large scale clay model of the first Lord Melville from which **Robert Forrest** carved the Edinburgh statue in 1827 (1). He occupied a studio at 125 Canongate, Edinburgh from 1825 to 1840. Between 1825 and 1829 he worked in partnership with his father, whose profession was listed in the *Edinburgh Post Office Directories* as fire-worker and figure-maker. During the 1830s O'Neil continued the business but worked principally as a modeller and chaser. He was artist to the Edinburgh Phrenological Society from 1825 to 1840.

Literary References: *Woodward* 1977, vol 1, pt 2, 173

Statues

1.	1827	Lord Melville, model		Untraced	*Woodward* 1977, vol 1, pt 2, 173

Busts

2.	nd	Set of four idealised phrenological heads: boy, gentleman, girl, lady	p	Fyvie Castle, Aberdeenshire (NT)	*Pearson* 1991, unpag

OBRISSET, Jean fl 1705–27

The Obrisset family came from Dieppe, where in 1676 a Jean Aubrisset was recorded as an ivory worker with an open shop. He was probably related to Jean Obrisset who worked in London from 1705, specialising in pressed horn and tortoiseshell work. Pyke notes that **James Tassie** later based a paste medallion on a wax portrait of Queen Anne by this artist (1). In 1691, a Jean Obrisset, described as a turner in ivory, stood godfather to Judith, a daughter of Jean Obrisset, 'graveur' at the French church, Hungerford Market.

Literary References: *Pyke* 1973, 99; *Murdoch and Hebditch* 1985, 208

Reliefs

1.	1705	Queen Anne, oval portrait plaque in tortoiseshell		Museum of London	*Murdoch and Hebditch*, 1985, 208–9 (repr)
2.	nd	King Charles I, oval portrait plaque, horn		Museum of London	*Murdoch and Hebditch*, 1985, 208–9 (repr)
3.	nd	Queen Anne	w	Untraced	*Pyke* 1973, 99

OGILVIE AND MERCER fl 1725–26

Thomas Ogilvie and Mercer (whose first name is not recorded) were the masons employed on the 'New Building on the Mount' at Waldershare, Kent in 1725–6. It was erected by Sir Robert Furnese, who noted in the account-book that the first stone was 'lay'd by my son, August 16th 1725'. It must have been a sizeable building since the bill for it came to nearly £1,700 (Archives Earl of Guildford in GPC).

OLDFIELD fl 1767–69

He was probably dead by the end of 1769 as the bill for nine chimneypieces provided for James, 3rd Duke of Atholl, in 1769 was receipted by his partner **Edward Hill** on behalf of Mary Oldfield (Archives Duke of Atholl in GPC) (2).

Chimneypieces

1.	1767	'made of a piece of Gibraltar petrification given to His Grace by Captain George Oliphant'	[James, 3rd Duke of Atholl]; Dunkeld, Perths, dining room	Archives Duke of Atholl, in GPC
2.	1769	Nine, of various marbles including Plymouth, Derbyshire and Welsh	[for James, 3rd Duke of Atholl]; untraced	Archives Duke of Atholl, in GPC

OLDFIELD, G, of Ashford, Derbys fl 1829–55

Gunnis refers to him as C Oldfield and notes that he signs a 'very attractive classical monument' in the form of a small sarcophagus with a medallion-portrait in the centre (1). He was probably the founder of George Oldfield & Co (or 'Oldfield & Sons'), who were listed as marble masons and statuaries in Derby directories between 1829 and 1855, and operated from the Ashford Marble Works between 1831 and 1853. There was also an Elias Oldfield described as a 'Marble Mason and Statuary' in Pigot's *Directory* of 1831. Oldfield and Co exhibited columns of Derbyshire marble at the Great Exhibition in 1851.

Literary References: *Gunnis* 1968, 283; *Tomlinson* 1996, 16, 18, 39, 45, 59, 81

Funerary Monuments

1.	†1835	William Montagu Burgoyne	Sutton, Beds	S	Pevsner, *Beds, Hunts & Peterborough*, 1968, 152

OLDFIELD, James I fl 1708–17

He carried out work for Sir John Chester of Chicheley Hall, Bucks, and Chester's friend Burrell Massingberd of Ormsby, Lincs, between 1708 and 1717. In 1708 he was employed on the new chancel of Chicheley church, receiving a payment of £3 12s 'for 8 weeks at 9s per week in carving ye Capitals & Trophys for ye chancel at Chicheley' (3). Oldfield also provided monuments to the Chester family which Sir John set up in the chancel the following year, receiving payments of £3 17s 6d 'towards making ye Monuments & Sawing Marble' in March 1709 and £33 2s 6d for 'work abt. ye Monuments' that September (Chester Archives in GPC) (1). In 1716–7 Oldfield furnished a marble table and a bust for Massingberd (2) under Chester's supervision (Massingberd/Chester, 1716–17, in GPC).

Funerary Monuments

1.	1709	Chester family members	Chicheley, Bucks	Chester Archives, in GPC

Busts

2.	1717	Unidentified subject	[for Burrell Massingberd]; untraced	Letters from Sir John Chester to Burrell Massingberd, in GPC

Architectural Sculpture

3.	1708	Capitals and trophies	Chicheley, Bucks	Chester Archives, in GPC

OLDFIELD, James II fl 1800–11

James Oldfield was employed at Castle Howard, executing carved stonework in 1801 and making chimneypieces for the Long Gallery in 1802 (1, 2). He was probably the senior partner in the firm of **Oldfield and Turner**.

Literary References: *Gunnis* 1968, 263

Archival References: Castle Howard Building Accts, G5/1/1-2

Chimneypieces

1.	1802	Description unavailable	Castle Howard, N R Yorks, long gallery	Castle Howard archives in GPC

Architectural Sculpture

2.	1801	Carved stonework	[Castle Howard, N R Yorks]; untraced	Castle Howard archives, in *Gunnis* 1968, 283

OLDFIELD, Thomas fl 1789–91

A London mason, he worked in partnership with **Edward Hill** between 1789 and 1791, building houses in Sloane Street and carrying out various works at Woburn Abbey. In 1803, after his partner's death he carved the pedestal and inscription for the bust of Charles James Fox by **Joseph Nollekens** in the Temple of Liberty at Woburn. He also provided and polished the console brackets for Nollekens's other six busts of friends of the Duke of Bedford for the same location.

Literary References: *JKB* 1989, 30

OLDFIELD AND TURNER, of London fl *c*1810–11

See **Oldfield, James II**

Funerary Monuments

1.	†1811	Sir William Myers	St Mary, Cheltenham, Glos	S	Pevsner, *Glos: Vale & Forest of Dean*, 1976, 126; *CIIA* 4/4/10 (repr)

Chimneypieces

2.	1810	'dove-grey marble'	[Coventry House, Piccadilly, London, eating room]; untraced	Archives, Earl of Coventry, in *Gunnis* 1968, 283
3.	1810	'Porto Veneri' marble Payment(s): £36	[Coventry House, Piccadilly, London, back parlour]; untraced	Archives, Earl of Coventry, in *Gunnis* 1968, 283

OLIPHANT, James, of Durham fl 1662–64

In 1662–63 James Oliphant, **John Richardson** and **Christopher Wilkinson**, all of the 'citty of Durham, free-masons', agreed to carry out various works at Durham Castle for Bishop John Cosin. They undertook to 'artificially work in stone all the window-worke, chimney-worke, and door-worke' and agreed to build the classical doorway to the hall, which has carving at the top of an angel holding a coat of arms, with a mitre and a crested helm to right and left (1). In 1664 Oliphant also contracted to build a 'fountaine of fine free ashler worke' in the courtyard of the castle (*Cosin Letters* 1870, 358–74).

Archival References: GPC

Architectural Sculpture

1.	1662	Carved doorway (co-sculptor: John Richardson and Christopher Wilkinson)	Durham Castle, hall	*Cosin Letters* 1870, 360; GPC

OLIVER, John 1616/17–1701

Oliver was 'a glazier by trade, a surveyor by profession and a master-mason by virtue of office' (*Colvin* 1995, 714). The St Paul's Cathedral accounts include payments to him for glass and he left a small legacy to the Glaziers' Company in his will. He seems to have specialised in painted heraldic glass and an example of his work, a window painted in enamel colours with the Royal arms and those of the Grocers' Company, dating from *c*1664, survives in St Mary, Northill, Beds. A panel formerly at Christ Church, Oxford of *St Peter Delivered from Prison*, inscribed 'J. Oliver, aetat. suae lxxxiv, anno 1700' (untraced) establishes the year of his birth as 1616 or 1617.

Little is known of Oliver's architectural work but he supervised the erection of the Mercers' Company Hall and chapel in Cheapside and designed the Skinners' Company Hall on Dowgate Hill, completed *c*1670. He was involved in designing various new buildings for Christ's Hospital, an institution which he also served as a Governor and he left a sum of money in his will for an annual roast dinner for the boys. In 1676 Oliver and **Edward Pearce** made designs for the woodwork of the chapel of Emmanuel College, Cambridge, executed by **Cornelius Austin**, and in 1700 he designed the screen and other woodwork in the hall of Corpus Christi College, Oxford, executed in 1700–1 by Arthur Frogley with carving by **Jonathan Maine**.

Oliver was one of the four surveyors appointed to supervise the rebuilding of the City of London after the Great Fire and his name is frequently mentioned in connection with the rebuilding of the City churches. He was particularly closely involved in the rebuilding of St Mary Aldermary, in 1679–82, which was funded by a private benefactor. He also assisted in supervising the building of the Monument, and in January 1676 succeeded Edward Woodroffe as assistant surveyor of St Paul's Cathedral, a post he retained for over 20 years. On 2 March 1685/6 he took over from **Thomas Wise I** as master-mason to the Crown, in which capacity he worked at Hampton Court and Kensington Palace. In August 1701 he received a payment of £115 for 'imbossing and casting the imperiall supporters the Lyon and Unicorn in Hard Metall . . . and two imperiall shields' for the main gates at Hampton Court, and after his death that November, his wife received a further payment of £130 for trophies on the gate piers (TNA Work 5/52) (1).

Oliver was one of **Joshua Marshall**'s executors, together with **Henry Phillips**. In his own will, proved on 18 November 1701, Oliver left property in Ironmonger Lane and elsewhere in the City to his wife Susanna and stated that he wished to be buried under the choir of St Paul's Cathedral. According to Vertue a portrait of Oliver in crayons was the last work of William Faithorne, †1691.

Literary References: *Knoop and Jones* 1935, 36; *Wren Soc*, XVIII, 146; *Colvin* 1973–76, vol V, 165, 471; *Colvin* 1981, 24–31; *Colvin* 1995, 714–5; *ODNB* (Cust rev Koller)

Wills: PROB 11/462 (18 November 1701)

Architectural Sculpture

1.	1701	'Lyon and Unicorn, in Hard Metall', shields and trophies Payment(s): £115 and £130 after his death in November	[Hampton Court Palace, Middx, gate]; untraced	*Colvin* 1973–76, V, 173–4

OLIVER, Samuel Euclid fl 1769–74

In 1769 Oliver exhibited wax portraits at the Royal Academy and the Free Society giving his address as 'At Mr Hoskyn's, Golden Head, St Martin's Lane' (1, 2). The following year, 1770, he was in partnership with **James Hoskins** running a plaster shop (their joint works are listed in the entry for Hoskins). He remained in partnership with Hoskins until 1774, when Hoskins took another partner, **Benjamin Grant**.

Literary References: *Gunnis* 1968, 283; *Pyke* 1973, 99; *Clifford* 1992, 61

Miscellaneous

1.	1769	Unidentified nobleman	w	[Exhib RA, London, 76]; untraced	*Graves* V, 1905–6, 11
2.	1769	Unidentified subjects, two portraits	w	[Exhib Free Soc, London, 167 and 168]; untraced	*Graves* 1907, 184

OLIVER, Sanders *c*1719–

He was apprenticed to Thomas Bull in 1733 and had a workshop, 1741–86, at 62 Cannon Street, opposite the north end of Laurence Poultney Lane. He carried out masonry repairs at St Mary Abchurch during that period and had a minor role in building Ironmongers' Hall between 1748 and 1750 (Ironmongers WA, vol 12). In 1772 Oliver received a communication from the Court of Assistants of the Masons' Company informing him 'that not being a Freeman of the Company he did use or exercise Art or Mistery of Masonary within the City of London or Liberties thereof'. He was directed to attend the next Court 'in order to accept and take upon you the Freedom, and be made a Freeman' or face a penalty of £10 (Masons' Co, *Court Book*, 1751–96, 7 Aug 1772). His date of death is not known but in 1787 his yard was taken over by **Samuel Ireland**, who remained there until 1826. Gunnis notes that his monuments are 'of good workmanship' and include one with a portrait bust (5). The memorial to Benjamin and Elizabeth Eaton (1) has 'an inscription panel adorned with a charming group of cherubs heads and flanked by fluted pilasters' (*Smith* 1957, 727). He may have been related to a John Oliver who was admitted to the freedom of the Masons' Company on 4 September 1730, having served his apprenticeship with **Joseph Rose I** (Masons' Co, *Freemen List*, fol 52).

Literary References: *Mortimer* 1763, 49; *Smith* 1957, 727; *Gunnis* 1968, 283

Archival References: Masons' Co, Apprentices, 1733

Funerary Monuments

1.	post-1741	Benjamin Easton (†1730) and wife (†1741)	St Mary Abchurch, City of London	S	Pevsner, *London: City*, 1997, 239
2.	?1765	George Baker	Mayfield, Sussex		*Gunnis* 1968, 283

3.	1776	Deschamps family		St Stephen Walbrook, City of London	S	Pevsner, *London: City*, 1997, 264
4.	†1777	Matthew Perchard		St Mary Abchurch, City of London	S	Pevsner, *London: City*, 1997, 239
5.	?1779	Joseph Innes		St Mary, Lewisham, London		*Gunnis* 1968, 283
Architectural Sculpture						
6.	1767	Masonry, including ornamental stonework	s	Scotch Meeting House, London Wall		Guildhall MS 4976

OLIVIERI, P fl 1828

Busts

1.	1828	Mr Tucker	The Hall, Ashburton, Devon, entrance hall	Pevsner, *Devon*, 1989, 133

OLIVIERI (or OLIVERI), Dominick Andrew, of London fl 1823–35

Gunnis states that his studio was in Berkeley Street, Lambeth, but his address was recorded as 18 Wardour Street, Soho, when he exhibited at the Society of British Artists in 1833 and 1835.

Literary References: *Gunnis* 1968, 283

Busts

1.	1823	William Pitt the Younger (after Joseph Nollekens)	m	NPG 1240 Other versions: 10 Downing Street, London, 1825	SD	*Gunnis* 1968, 283
2.	1833	E R Colville		[Exhib Soc of BA, London, 811]; untraced		*Johnson* 1975, 348
3.	1833	Miss Malcolm		[Exhib Soc of BA, London, 842]; untraced		*Johnson* 1975, 348
4.	nd	Frederick-Augustus, Duke of York and Albany		[Thomas Robson sale, 1835]; untraced		*Gunnis* 1968, 283
5.	nd	George Washington		[Thomas Robson sale, 1835]; untraced		*Gunnis* 1968, 283
6.	nd	King George IV		[Thomas Robson sale, 1835]; untraced		*Gunnis* 1968, 283
Miscellaneous						
7.	1835	J Olivera		[Exhib Soc of BA, London, 842]; untraced		*Johnson* 1975, 348
8.	1835	T Googe		[Exhib Soc of BA, London, 772]; untraced		*Johnson* 1975, 348

OLVERS, Jacob and Thomas, of Falmouth fl *c*1811–47

The most significant of their works is a large Hellenic wall-monument to the Rev Lewis Mathias in Falmouth parish church (**3**).

Literary References: *Gunnis* 1968, 283–4

Funerary Monuments

1.	?1811	John Pellow		Mylor, Cornwall	S	*Gunnis* 1968, 283
2.	?1812	James Burke		Mylor, Cornwall	S	*Gunnis* 1968, 283
3.	1837	Rev Lewis Mathias		King Charles the Martyr, Falmouth, Cornwall		Pevsner, *Cornwall*, 1970, 67
4.	†1839	John Carne		King Charles the Martyr, Falmouth, Cornwall		RG/JP, 6, 1043
5.	†1840	Henry Williams		King Charles the Martyr, Falmouth, Cornwall		RG/JP, 6, 1043
6.	†1847	Ann Renfree	sl	King Charles the Martyr, Falmouth, Cornwall, old churchyard		RG/JP, 6, 1043

OSBORN, Esau, of Bristol fl *c*1742

Funerary Monuments

1.	*c*1742	Abrahall family (†1702–1742)	St Mary, Foy, Herefs	Pevsner, *Herefs*, 1963, 134

OSBORNE, James, of Bristol fl 1729–67

He became a freeman of Bristol in 1729 at the time of his marriage to Anne, daughter of George Britten, a woolcomber. His wall-tablets commemorating Humphrey Ash and John Eveleigh are large and 'of superior workmanship' (*Gunnis* 1968, 284) (**2, 3**).

Archival References: BRO Burgess Books 04359 microfiche FC/BB/1 (1)

Funerary Monuments

1.	?1763	John Hast	St James, Bristol	S	*Gunnis* 1968, 284
2.	†1767	Humphrey Ash	Chard, Somerset	S	*Gunnis* 1968, 284
3.	†1767	John Eveleigh	Chard, Somerset	S	*Gunnis* 1968, 284

OSBORNE, James, of Mansfield fl 1751–68

In 1743 he was in partnership with Thomas Ince, and they were responsible for much building work at Welbeck Abbey, Notts. Osborne was paid £93 for work in the great hall in 1751. By 1757 he was working on his own, but he then went into partnership with a Matthew Porter. Together they received payments amounting to £2,380 between 1767 and 1768 for building the bridge at Welbeck (Welbeck Abbey archives in *Gunnis* 1968, 284).

OSBORNE, John, of Bath –*c*1838

He taught himself to model in clay, and later, with the help of a local farmer, went to London, where he worked in the studio of **John Bacon RA**. He eventually settled in Bath where he carved a figure of the *Goddess of sculpture* and a colossal head of *Jupiter*, both of Bath stone (**3, 4**). The *Jupiter* weighed six tons and took the sculptor several years to complete. Walter Savage Landor wrote of it in a private letter 'Nothing of Michael Angelo's is nobler and nothing of **Thorwaldsen**'s finer' (*Gunnis* 1968, 284).

His widow was left destitute at his death, her only asset being the *Jupiter*. The corporation of Bath purchased this from her for £100 but it was left neglected until 1861 when Alderman Bush of Bath rescued both works and placed them in Victoria Park. He employed an architect named Wilson to design pedestals for them, later executed by H Treasure. Augustus Bozzi Granville wrote of him, 'Poor Osborne! Born in penury – a mere shepherd's boy – he died in misery – an admired genius and a statuary worthy of a place among the ablest chisels of either ancient or modern times' (*Granville* 1841, III, 424).

Literary References: *Gunnis* 1968, 284

Funerary Monuments

1.	?1821	Thomas Baines		Queenhill, Worcs	S	*Gunnis* 1968, 284
2.	?1831	Ann Tetherly		Northam, Devon	S	*Gunnis* 1968, 284

Statues

3.	*c*1835	Goddess of Sculpture	s	Victoria Park, Bath	*Gunnis* 1968, 284

Busts

4.	*c*1835	Jupiter	s	[coll sculptor's widow]; Victoria Park, Bath	*Gunnis* 1968, 284

OSBORNE, John, of Oxford –*c*1785

The Osborne family of masons were associated with Oxford for many years. The first John Osborne was apprenticed to William Townsend in 1706 and was perhaps the John Osborne made free of the Masons' Company by redemption on 23 January 1712 (Masons' Co, *Freemen*, fol 52). He was probably the father of John Osborne who signs two tablets, received a payment for a chimneypiece in 1780 and died about 1785 (**1–3**). He had two sons. 'William Osborne Eldest son of John Osborne Mason' paid his due of 3d and was sworn in as a freeman on 30 October 1775. The much younger second son, John Hodges Osborne, was apprenticed on 22 January 1787 to his mother, Jane, 'to learn her Art'. Jane had carried on the business since her husband's death. He paid his fees and was sworn in as a freeman on 2 July 1802.

Literary References: *Gunnis* 1968, 284

Archival References: Hanaster EB, L 5.5

Funerary Monuments

1.	†1771	Rev David Price	St John the Baptist, Stockton, Wilts	S	Pevsner, *Wilts*, 1975, 485
2.	?1784	Francis Emmett	Great Milton, Oxon	S	*Gunnis* 1968, 284

Chimneypieces

3.	1780	Description unavailable	[St John's College, Oxford]; untraced		*Gunnis* 1968, 284

OSGOOD, Richard –*c*1724?

A lead figure manufacturer, the first record of Osgood's work dates from 1691, when he supplied two heads for Kensington Palace (**15**). His name subsequently appears in the accounts of several country estates and royal palaces as the provider of a considerable amount of lead and other metal work. He must have made a good living prior to 1691 for on 1 January 1689, in partnership with Huntley Bigg, a scrivener, he bought 30 acres of land in Alkham, Kent from Mathias Shore of St Martin-in-the-Fields. In 1694 Osgood sent off statues for Sir Roger Hill at Denham Place, Bucks (**2, 25**). These do not appear to have survived but a topographical sketch of Denham shows several statues *in situ*, which may well be his work (repr *Harris* 1957–8, 192).

In 1700 Osgood was employed in mending statues at Hampton Court and his bill gives an insight into the practice of restoration at that time. He was paid £43 'for casting of new feet and part of ye legs of copper to the great Hercules' and another £40 'for casting a large piece of drapery of the great statue of Antineous and making good what was wanting of ye legs. . .' He also provided 'two new arms of copper and the great part of the drapery and a new quiver of arrows for the Diana that stands in the Quadrangle Court and burning altogether and mending several other parts. For rifling and cleaning the figure with aquafort to make it look bright all alike' (TNA WORK 5/51 fol 506). In 1709 he was responsible for further repairs at Hampton Court, supplying 'two new wings for the statue of Victory and two new trumpets for the statue of Fame'. In 1715 he was ordered 'to model and cast in hard metal two large sea-horses and two large Tritons to spout the water in the great bason' in Bushey Park (*Gunnis* 1968, 285, incorrectly cites PRO AO1.2447).

Osgood's premises were at Hyde Park Corner, close to the lead manufacturers **John Nost I, Edward Hurst** and **Josias Iback**. He collaborated with Nost at least once. The statues sent to Knole in 1697 were billed by Osgood but possibly supplied by Nost (**6–8, 18**) and in 1701 he certainly collaborated with Nost on a large order for twenty-four lead urns for Hampton Court (**20**) and he appears to have worked in partnership with another neighbour, the ironsmith Jean Tijou, at Sutton Court (**13**). He was rated on three houses in Portugal Row in 1697, two at £12 and one at £30. His premises were visited in 1703 by the architect William Winde, who was attempting to find a statue for the garden of Lady Mary Bridgwater. Winde reported that he had been to 'Mr Nostes' and 'Mr Ansgood' and that the latter 'has the best leaden figures . . . very good pieces with fine mantel or drapery caste very loosely . . . they are moderne' (Winde/Bridgeman).

The will of a Richard Osgood of St Martin-in-the-Fields was proved in April 1724, and though there is no mention of the profession of the deceased in the document, it is likely that this is the sculptor. He left his 'little house' in the 'high road leading to Piccadilly' to his daughter Elizabeth Osgood, and another property on Hyde Park Corner to his wife Anne, who also received houses in Knightsbridge, Chelmsford and Much Haddon. These properties continued in family possession until 1737.

MGS

Literary References: *Harris* 1957–8, 193–7; *Gunnis* 1968, 284–5; *Davis* 1991 (1), 34, 42, 52

Archival References: 'large Caesar's head for the Guard-room, 1691', TNA WORK E.351/1347 fol 9; Lincs RO Jarvis I/D/2/14; WCA; Poor Rate 1697, F1232; Highways Rate 1722 F5550; Poor Rate 1733–1737, C118–C127; GPC

Will: PROB 11/597/26-7

Statues

1.	1694	Mars and Minerva, two statues Payment(s): £34	[Sutton Court, Chiswick, coll Lord Fauconberg]; untraced	Bellasis/Wombwell Archives, NYCRO ZDV; *Harris* 1957–8, 194; GPC
2.	1694	Several, perhaps including a Neptune and Hercules	Denham Place, Bucks	*Harris* 1957–8, 192
3.	1695	'Cain and Abel' (Samson and the Philistine, after Giambologna) Payment(s): £42	[Sutton Court, Chiswick, coll Lord Fauconberg]; untraced	Bellasis/Wombwell Archives, NYCRO ZDV; *Harris* 1957–8, 194; *Davis* 1991 (1), 42; GPC

No.	Date	Subject		Location	Sources
4.	1696	Three figures for niches in the bowling green house Payment(s): £18	l	[Chatsworth, Derbys]; untraced	Chatsworth Building Accts, 1695–96, 57; *Gunnis* 1968, 284
5.	1696	'Two leaden ducks'	l	[Chatsworth, Derbys, gardens]; untraced	*Gunnis* 1968, 284
6.	by 1697	Crouching Venus		Knole, Kent	Sackville Archives, Kent RO, Maidstone U269 A198/6
7.	1697	Gladiator Payment(s): £18		Knole, Kent	Sackville Archives, Kent RO, Maidstone U269 A198/6
8.	1697	Susanna, 'of hard mettal' Payment(s): £25 for mould and cast	b	[Knole, Kent]; untraced	Sackville Archives, Kent RO, Maidstone U269 A198/6
9.	1699	Two, unspecified Payment(s): £15		[coll Lord Fauconberg]; untraced	Bellasis/Wombwell Archives, NYCRO ZDV; GPC
10.	1700	'a large piece of drapery of the great statue of Antinous' Payment(s): £40		[Hampton Court Palace, Middx]; untraced	TNA WORK 5/51 fol 506; *Gunnis* 1968, 284
11.	1703	Juno Payment(s): 'about £10'	l	[Sculptor's premises]; untraced	Wynde/Bridgman
12.	1703	Venus and Cupid Payment(s): £12, or £8 without the Cupid	l	[Sculptor's premises]; untraced	Wynde/Bridgman
13.	1704	'painting and mending all the statues in the garden'		[Sutton Court, Chiswick]; untraced	North Yorks CRO ZDV (V) 10 MIC 2793; GPC
14.	1709	Victory and Fame, two, repairs only (two new wings for the former and two new trumpets for latter)		[Hampton Court Palace, Middx]; untraced	PRO AO 1/2447; *Gunnis* 1968, 285; *Colvin* 1973–76, V, 173
Busts					
15.	1691	'a large Caesar's head & Busto broonsed sett up in the Guardroome' Payment(s): £6		[Kensington Palace, London, guard-room]; untraced	TNA WORK E.351/3467 fol 9; *Gunnis* 1968, 284; *Colvin* 1973–76, V, 189
16.	1698	'a head' Payment(s): £32 with the bas-relief		[Chatsworth, Derbys]; untraced	Chatsworth Building Accts, 1697–98, 25; *Gunnis* 1968, 284
17.	1704	'Two large Roman heads and bustoes of hard metal' Payment(s): £10	l	[coll Colonel Sir Francis Child]; untraced	Royal Bank of Scotland Archives GB 1502/CH/315/2, f43; GB 1502/CH/199; *Gunnis* 1968, 285
Architectural Sculpture					
18.	1697	Large stone plinth and Earl of Dorset's heraldic shield Payment(s): £2		Knole, Kent	Sackville Archives, Kent RO, Maidstone U269 A198/6
19.	1701	12 vases 'with flutes and gadurnes (sic) and other ornaments' Payment(s): £20 each		[Hampton Court Palace, Middx, for the top of the two pavilions by the bowling green]; untraced	TNA WORK 5/51 fol 506; *Gunnis* 1968, 284
20.	1701	24 urns (designed by John Nost I)		[Hampton Court, Middx, bowling-green pavilions]; untraced	*Colvin* 1973–76, V, 168
21.	1704	Eight large vases, five pairs of flower pots Payment(s): £26; £12 10s		[coll Colonel Sir Francis Child]; untraced	Royal Bank of Scotland Archives GB 1502/CH/315/2, fol 43; GB 1502/CH/199
22.	1704–1705	Fourteen vases (£1 10s each), two pairs of large flower pots (£5 10s), one pair of smaller pots (£1 10s), two pairs of smaller pots (£2), two pairs of 'sheild boys' (£6 a pair), 3 'Antick Romane Heads & Cartuzes (£3), pair of vases (£3)' Payment(s): £48		[coll Colonel Sir Francis Child]; untraced	Royal Bank of Scotland archives GB 1502/CH/315/2 fol 19; *Gunnis* 1968, 284; *Harris* 1957–8, 194
23.	1715	Two large sea-horses and two large Tritons, 'to spout the water in the fountain' Payment(s): £180 Model(s): one included in the price	l	[Bushey Park, Hampton Court, Middx]; untraced	PRO AO 1/2447; *Gunnis* 1968, 285
Reliefs					
24.	1698	Head and bas-relief Payment(s): £32 with the 'head'		[Chatsworth, Derbys]; untraced	Chatsworth Building Accts, 1697–98, 25; *Gunnis* 1968, 284
Miscellaneous					
25.	1693–1694	'figures on the great gates' (possibly statues of Gog and Magog) Payment(s): £40		[Denham Place, Bucks]; untraced	*Harris* 1957–8, 194
26.	1697–1698	Unspecified work Payment(s): £39 15s		[coll Charles, 3rd Earl of Carlisle]; untraced	Castle Howard archives; GPC
27.	1700	Diana (repairs and restoration only) Payment(s): £72	b	[Hampton Court, Middx]; untraced	TNA WORK 5/51; *Colvin* 1973–76, V, 166
28.	1700	Restoration of Hercules, which had 'been melted and broke by ye fire at Whitehall', casting new feet, part of the legs, hands and lion's skin		[Hampton Court Palace, Middx]; untraced	TNA WORK 5/51 fol 506; *Gunnis* 1968, 284
29.	1712	'Statuary worke'		[coll Richard Hill of Attingham, Salop]; untraced	Shrops Archives, Hill Papers, 112/1/2203

OSMOND, William, of Salisbury I 1791–1875

He worked as a stonemason and monumental sculptor in Salisbury for more than 50 years and the firm he established survived into the 1880s under the superintendence of his son, **William Osmond II**. Nothing is known of the elder Osmond's background before he was appointed mason to Salisbury Cathedral *c*1818. He first made new pinnacles for the south-east and north-east corners of the tower (**93**) and then, in about 1820, blocked the quartrefoils in the singers' gallery and began repointing the west front. Other work for the cathedral included the fixing of iron railings outside the west doors in 1822 and carving columns and capitals for the south walk of the cloister in 1843 (**95**). In 1856 he was responsible for renewing the decayed Purbeck shafts, capitals and bases around the west windows in Chilmark stone, later replaced during Sir George Gilbert Scott's restoration of the west front of 1866–69 (**96**). He also undertook maintenance work at the bishop's palace and restored the city's 15th-century poultry cross in 1852–54.

In about 1820 Osmond moved into a workshop at 13 St John Street, Salisbury, a building with an elegant neoclassical façade, conveniently situated opposite the St Anne's gate entrance to the cathedral close. From there he ran a thriving business, supplying funerary monuments of all sizes and in a variety of styles, most of them for the Cathedral and churches in Wiltshire and Dorset. Early in his career he produced classical tablets, such as those commemorating Sarah Hayter and the Arney family in Salisbury Cathedral (**11, 15**). However, he specialised increasingly in gothic monuments. An early example is the table tomb commemorating Bishop John Fisher which dates from 1828 and is derived from 15th-century prototypes (**19**). It is surmounted by a cushion, Bible and crozier, in place of an effigy. Most of his later wall monuments are in a hybrid thirteenth-century manner, described by Gunnis as 'the spikiest Gothic style'. The monument to Sir William and Lady Paxton, 1847, is unusual because it was erected far from Salisbury, at Llanarthne, Carmarthenshire and is neo-baroque in form (**69**). It has two large marble pillars with a black marble panel recessed in an arched opening. Beneath is a small medallion with the Paxtons' heads in relief.

Osmond was a friend of the influential gothic revival architect AWN Pugin, who apparently lived at Osmond's house for a time before moving into St Marie's Grange, outside Salisbury, which he built in 1835. In 1833–34 Pugin wrote several letters to Osmond describing his tour of cathedrals and abbeys in southern England. In one Pugin informed his friend that he would soon travel to France to study 'the splendid remains of every description of the middle ages' and he entreated his friend to 'Leave your blisters, leave your Doric porticos, leave all and follow me.' Pugin's biographer, Ferrey, explained that 'blister' was the term used by Pugin to describe the tablets which Osmond 'was in the habit of affixing to the walls of churches as memorials' (*Ferrey* 1978, 90–1). Gunnis suggests that Osmond's adoption of the gothic style may be the result of Pugin's influence, though it should be noted that Pugin was only 16 in 1828 when Osmond was already at work on Bishop Fisher's monument (**19**).

Osmond died in 1875 and is commemorated with a tablet in the cloisters of Salisbury Cathedral which records that he 'was many years a lay-preacher and mason to this Cathedral'.

EH

Literary References: *Gunnis* 1968, 285; *Ferrey* 1978, 74–91; *RCHME* 1980, 50, 116; *RCHME* 1987, 63, 76; *Dale-Jones and Lloyd* 1989, 55–6; *Atterbury and Wainwright* 1994, 185, 293 n1; *Brown* 1999, 141–3, 154; *Ayers* 2000, 90–2

Will: Salisbury probate registry, 11 August 1875, effects under £2,000

Funerary Monuments

1.	†1778	Robert Cooper and family	St Edmund, Salisbury, Wilts		RCHME 1980, 38
2.	†1807	Edward Hinxman and family	St Martin, Salisbury, Wilts		RCHME 1980, 35
3.	†1809	John White and family	Silton, Dorset		RCHME 1952–75, vol IV, 78
4.	†1810	Willoughby Vere Bertie (aged one year) and Willoughby Bertie (†1812)	Salisbury Cathedral, Wilts		*Brown* 1999, 152
5.	†1774–1818	Isaac Maggs and family	Silton, Dorset		RCHME 1952–75, vol IV, 78
6.	†1819	Anna Eliza Slade	Salisbury Cathedral, Wilts		*Brown* 1999, 141, 152
7.	†1819	William Douglas	Salisbury Cathedral, Wilts		*Brown* 1999, 152
8.	†1820	John and Hester (†1829) Matthews	Gillingham, Dorset		RCHME 1952–75, vol IV, 29
9.	†1821	Dorothy Cookson	Osmington, Wilts		RCHME 1952–75, vol II, pt I, 179
10.	†1821	John Mill	Shaftesbury, Dorset		RCHME 1952–75, vol IV, 64
11.	†1822	Sarah Hayter	Salisbury Cathedral, Wilts		*Gunnis* 1968, 285; *Brown* 1999, 141, 148
12.	†1824	Elizabeth Staines (†1808), her son Joseph and others	Wareham, Dorset		RCHME 1952–75, vol II, pt II, 308
13.	?1824	John Lampard	Barford St Martin, Wilts	S	*Gunnis* 1968, 285
14.	†1723–1824	Long family	St Thomas, Salisbury, Wilts		*Gunnis* 1968, 285; RCHME 1980, 30
15.	†1824	William and Maria (†1845) Arney and two sons	Salisbury Cathedral, Wilts, cloisters		*Brown* 1999, 154
16.	†1825	Richard Withers	Sixpenny Handley, Dorset		RCHME 1952–75, vol V, 65
17.	?1825	Thomas King	Alvediston, Wilts	S	*Gunnis* 1968, 285
18.	1826	Joan Popple (†1572)	St Thomas, Salisbury, Wilts		RCHME 1980, 30
19.	1828	Bishop John Fisher (†1825)	Salisbury Cathedral, Wilts		Pevsner, *Wilts*, 1975, 415; *Brown* 1999, 141, 142, 152 (repr)
20.	†1828	John Jacob	Salisbury Cathedral, Wilts		*Gunnis* 1968, 285
21.	†1828	John Woodward	St Clement, Salisbury, Wilts		RCHME 1980, 42
22.	†1828	Thomas Harrington	St Thomas, Salisbury, Wilts		RCHME 1980, 30
23.	†1828	William Cox and his wife Eleanor (†1830)	St Andrew, Salisbury, Wilts		RCHME 1980, 43
24.	†1830	Amelia Calder	St Clement, Salisbury, Wilts		RCHME 1980, 42
25.	?1830	Anne Kennicott	Windsor Parish Church, Berks		*Gunnis* 1968, 285
26.	?1830	Henry Eyre	Winchester Cathedral		*Gunnis* 1968, 285
27.	1830	Unidentified subject	Netherhampton, Wilts		RCHME 1987, 161
28.	1831	Anne Hussey	Lyme Regis, Dorset		RCHME 1952–75, vol I, 143
29.	†1831	Elizabeth White	St Edmund, Salisbury, Wilts		RCHME 1980, 38
30.	†1831	Harriet Sarjeant and family	St Lawrence, Salisbury, Wilts		RCHME 1980, 41
31.	†1831	Thomas Rendall	Tidcombe, Wilts	S	Pevsner, *Wilts*, 1975, 519
32.	†1832	John Chester Pern Tinney	St Martin, Salisbury, Wilts		RCHME 1980, 34

33.	†1832	John Edward Young		Salisbury Cathedral, Wilts, cloisters		*Brown* 1999, 154
34.	†1832	Rev John Fisher		Osmington, Dorset		Pevsner, *Dorset*, 1972, 308; RCHME 1952–75, vol II, pt I, 179
35.	†1833	Matilda Mill		Shaftesbury, Dorset		RCHME 1952–75, vol IV, 64
36.	?1833	Rev Daniel Williams		Woolston, Hants		*Gunnis* 1968, 285
37.	?1833	Rev James Shuckburgh		Downton, Wilts	S	*Gunnis* 1968, 285
38.	†1833	William Chapeau, Louise Chicheley (†1848), Francis Chicheley (†1831) and Louisa Elizabeth		Salisbury Cathedral, Wilts, cloisters		*Brown* 1999, 154
39.	†1834	Dame Betty Miles		Yateley, Hants		Pevsner, *Hants & Isle of Wight*, 1967, 727
40.	†1834	John Douglas		Salisbury Cathedral, Wilts		*Brown* 1999, 152
41.	†1835	Christopher Clarke		Salisbury Cathedral, Wilts, cloisters		*Brown* 1999, 154
42.	†1835	Rev Edmund and Anne (†1826) Benson	s	Salisbury Cathedral, Wilts		*Brown* 1999, 148
43.	†1835	W G Maton	s	Salisbury Cathedral, Wilts		*Brown* 1999, 148
44.	†1835	Wadham Wyndham and his wife Jane (†1856)		Salisbury Cathedral, Wilts, cloisters		*Gunnis* 1968, 285; *Brown* 1999, 154
45.	†1835	William Locke and family		Seend, Wilts	S	*Gunnis* 1968, 285
46.	†1836	Daniels Eyre		Salisbury Cathedral, Wilts, cloisters		*Brown* 1999, 155
47.	†1836	William Boucher		Stalbridge, Dorset		RCHME 1952–75, vol III, pt II, 249
48.	1836	William Chillingworth (†1643/4)		Salisbury Cathedral, Wilts		Pevsner, *Wilts*, 1975, 413; *Brown* 1999, 153
49.	1836	William Hooker (†1600)		Salisbury Cathedral, Wilts		Pevsner, *Wilts*, 1975, 413; *Brown* 1999, 152
50.	†1837	Bishop Thomas Burgess		Salisbury Cathedral, Wilts		Pevsner, *Wilts*, 1975, 413; *Brown* 1999, 153
51.	†1837	Margaret (†1820) and Herbert Hawes		St Andrew, Salisbury, Wilts		RCHME 1980, 43
52.	†1837	Rev Herbert Hawes		St Edmund, Salisbury, Wilts		*Gunnis* 1968, 285; RCHME 1980, 38
53.	†1837	Unidentified subject, gothic tablet		Laverstock, Wilts		Pevsner, *Wilts*, 1975, 294
54.	†1838	Thomas Atkinson and his wife Charlotte (†1845)		St Clement, Salisbury, Wilts		RCHME 1980, 42
55.	?1839	Samuel Marindin		Worfield, Salop		GPC
56.	1839	Thomas Nelson		Trafalgar House church, Wilts		Pevsner, *Wilts*, 1975, 531
57.	†1840	Matthew Marsh		Salisbury Cathedral, Wilts		*Brown* 1999, 153
58.	?1841	Henry Hinxman		Salisbury Cathedral, Wilts		*Gunnis* 1968, 285
59.	†1843	Silas Benjafield		Silton, Dorset		RCHME 1952–75, vol IV, 78
60.	†1844	Elizabeth Bassnett		Yateley, Hants		Pevsner, *Hants & Isle of Wight*, 1967, 727
61.	?1844	Henrietta Thornycroft		Bodenham, Hereford		*Gunnis* 1968, 285
62.	†1844	Louisa Moilliet		Stock Gaylard, nr Lydlinch, Dorset		RCHME 1952–75, vol III, pt I, 384
63.	†1845	Harriett Phipps	s	Osmington, Dorset		RCHME 1952–75, vol II, pt I, 180
64.	†1845	Lieut William Fisher		Salisbury Cathedral, Wilts		*Brown* 1999, 152
65.	†1846	Frederick and Augustus Frederick (†1854) Webb		Salisbury Cathedral, Wilts		*Brown* 1999, 149
66.	†1846	General George Michell		Salisbury Cathedral, Wilts		*Brown* 1999, 148
67.	†1846	Henry Hatcher	s	Salisbury Cathedral, Wilts		*Brown* 1999, 141–3
68.	†1846	Rev William England and his wife Elizabeth (†1874)	s	Winterbourne Came, Dorset		RCHME 1952–75, vol II, pt II, 384
69.	?1847	Sir William and Lady Paxton		Llantharne, Carmarthen		*Dale-Jones and Lloyd* 1989, 56
70.	†1840–1849	Richard Guy (?)		Salisbury Cathedral, Wilts, cloisters		*Brown* 1999, 154
71.	†1850	Elizabeth Eyre		Salisbury Cathedral, Wilts, cloisters		*Brown* 1999, 155
72.	?1850	Rev Edmund Davenport		Worfield, Salop		GPC
73.	†1850	Rev Sir Edward Bowyer Smith		Theydon Mount, Essex	S	Pevsner, *Essex*, 1965, 386
74.	*c*1850	Unidentified subject		South Newton, Wilts		RCHME 1987, 188
75.	†1850	William Lisle Bowles		Salisbury Cathedral, Wilts		*Builder*, 1851, 173; *Brown* 1999, 153
76.	1855	Unidentified subject, gothic tablet		Nunton, Wilts		Pevsner, *Wilts*, 1975, 362
77.	†1857	Rev William Scoresby		St Mary, Upton, Torquay, Devon		RG/JP, 6, 1039
78.	?1858	James Cobb		Salisbury Cathedral, Wilts		*Gunnis* 1968, 285
79.	†1858	Sergeant Major John Michael Peniston		Salisbury Cathedral, Wilts		*Brown* 1999, 148
80.	†1859	James Bennett		Salisbury Cathedral, Wilts		*Brown* 1999, 152
81.	*c*1861	Stephen Mills		Orcheston St George, Wilts		RCHME 1987, 172
82.	†1862	William Wadham Young		Salisbury Cathedral, Wilts, cloisters		*Brown* 1999, 154
83.	†1866	Arthur Corfe Anael (?)		Salisbury Cathedral, Wilts, cloisters		*Brown* 1999, 154
84.	†1867	Henry Stevens, Francis Margaret (†1879) and Henry Chicheley Chapeau (†1877)		Salisbury Cathedral, Wilts, cloisters		*Brown* 1999, 154
85.	†1867	Jane Louise Chapeau		Salisbury Cathedral, Wilts, cloisters		*Brown* 1999, 154
86.	†1868	Arthur Thomas Corfe and Frances (†1847)		Salisbury Cathedral, Wilts, cloisters		*Brown* 1999, 154
87.	†1872	Sarah Ann Louisa Middleton and Andrew Bogle Middleton (†1879)		Salisbury Cathedral, Wilts, cloisters		*Brown* 1999, 155
88.	†1874	The Rev William England (†1846) and his wife Elizabeth	s	Winterborne Came, Dorset	S	
89.	nd	David Charles Read, his wife Charlotte and their son Raphael (†1886)		Salisbury Cathedral, Wilts, cloisters		*Brown* 1999, 155
90.	nd	Henrietta Sophia Jacob		Salisbury Cathedral, Wilts, cloisters		*Brown* 1999, 154
91.	nd	Unidentified subjects, two gothic monuments		Wilsford, Wilts		RCHME 1987, 207
92.	nd	Unidentified subjects, two tablets		Berwick St James, Wilts		RCHME 1987, 109

Architectural Sculpture

93.	1819–1820	Pinnacles		Salisbury Cathedral, Wilts, south-east and north-east corners of the tower	*Gunnis* 1968, 285
94.	1820	Sundial	sl	St Peter and St Paul, Thruxton, Hants	*Gunnis* 1968, 285
95.	1843	Columns and capitals		Salisbury Cathedral, Wilts, south walk of the cloisters	*Gunnis* 1968, 285
96.	1856	Columns, bases and capitals	s	[Salisbury Cathedral, Wilts, west front windows]; destroyed	*Ayers* 2000, 90

OSMOND, William, of Salisbury II 1821–90

He was responsible for carving richly ornamented capitals and figures over them in T H Wyatt's Italian romanesque church at Wilton, built for Sidney, Lord Herbert of Lea in 1845 (1). He also published a monumental pattern book, *Christian Memorials*, in 1848. He later succeeded his father, **William Osmond I** as mason to Salisbury Cathedral and as head of the family firm. The 1881 census records that he lived at 113 Exeter Street, Salisbury, with his wife and two children and employed eight men and one boy. He died on 9 August 1890 at the age of sixty-nine and is commemorated by a tablet in the cloisters of Salisbury Cathedral.

Literary References: *Gunnis* 1968, 285; *RCHME* 1987, 215; *Brown* 1999, 155; *Ayers* 2000, 90–2

Archival References: IGI (1881 Census)

Will: Salisbury probate registry, 30 September 1890, personal estate valued at £1,151 0s 8d

Architectural Sculpture

1.	*c*1845	Capitals	s	St Mary and St Nicholas, Wilton, Wilts	Pevsner, *Wilts*, 1975, 578; RCHME 1987, 215

OUGHTIBRIDGE, Thomas 1699–1753

He was the younger son of a Yorkshire squire who worked principally as an engraver in London. Oughtibridge issued an allegorical trade card as 'Tho.s Oughtibridge Engraver Engraves Armes, Crests, or Cyphers, on gold or Silver plate-. Copper plates of all sorts, Stamps cutt in Brass, or Wood, for such as can't write Inscriptions in Brass, Stone, or Marble for Monuments, Shopkeepers bills, bills of Parcells, or Lading, allso Gentlemen's Seats, neatly drawn in perspective, and Engraven if Requir'd. &c'. The impression in the BM (Heal 59.119) has the added words in the blank central shield 'at ye Sign of ye Sun in Brooks Market near Holborn London'. He can be identified as Thomas, son of William Oughtibridge of Hatfield Woodhouse, near Doncaster and Sarah, née de Pryne.

He probably returned to Yorkshire after his father's death in 1728 and is presumably the Thomas who married Susannah Smith at Hatfield on 12 May 1734 and the father of Peter, baptized in Hatfield on 8 May 1745. He drew and engraved some Yorkshire views and also carved and signed two monuments in Hatfield church. That to William Oughtibridge, †1756, signed 'T.Oughtibridge Engraver' is described by Pevsner as 'attractive and rustic' (2). The memorial to Thomas Johnson (1) takes the form of a cartouche tablet. Thomas died on 26 December 1753 and his will was proved at York on 19 June 1754.

David Alexander

Funerary Monuments

1.	?1751	Thomas Johnson	Hatfield, W R Yorks	S	*Gunnis* 1968, 285
2.	†1756	William Oughtibridge	Hatfield, W R Yorks	S	Pevsner, *Yorks: W R*, 1967, 255

OUTRIDGE, A, of Petersfield fl *c*1777–82

The Mitford is a large wall-monument in coloured marbles and the Edward Patrick is an elaborate work decorated with putti, flowers and swags (1, 3).

Literary References: *Gunnis* 1968, 285

Archival References: GPC

Funerary Monuments

1.	†1777	William Mitford		Tillington, Sussex	S	Pevsner, *Sussex*, 1965, 351
2.	†1778	Joseph Patrick		Petersham, Hants	S	GPC
3.	†1782	Edward Patrick	s	Petersham, Hants	S	GPC

OUTRIDGE, Elizabeth fl 1823?

Funerary Monuments

1.	?1823	Harriet Godbold	Greatham, Sussex	S	*Gunnis* 1968, 285

OWEN, Thomas, of Liverpool fl 1812–29

He was an assistant of **George Bullock** and exhibited a statue of *Cupid sleeping* at the Liverpool Academy in 1812 as T Owen of 'Mr Bullock's, Bold Street, Liverpool' (1). The following year, when he showed figures of *Music* and *Pan*, he was listed as Thomas Owens of Vincent Street, Liverpool (2, 3). He can probably be identified with the Thomas Owen who was responsible for the extensive programme of gothic architectural sculpture at St Mary, Pleasington, Lancs, which was designed by John Palmer, of Manchester (4). Read comments that 'it would be rash perhaps to judge too harshly the almost unbelievable crudity of the Pleasington work', noting that it dates from an early stage in the development of gothic revival architecture and may have been influenced by the then prevalent view that gothic sculpture was crude and primitive.

Literary References: *Gunnis* 1968, 285; *Read* 1982, 254–5

Statues

1.	1812	Cupid sleeping	[Exhib Liverpool Ac, 265]; untraced	*Morris and Roberts* 1998, 462
2.	1813	Music	[Exhib Liverpool Ac, 319]; untraced	*Morris and Roberts* 1998, 462
3.	1813	Pan	[Exhib Liverpool Ac, 313]; untraced	*Morris and Roberts* 1998, 462

Architectural Sculpture

4.	1816–1829	Exterior statues and ornamentation; roof bosses with relief scenes from the life of Christ; large reliefs of the penitent St Mary Magdalen and the decollation of St John the Baptist on either side of the altar	s	St Mary and St John the Baptist, Pleasington, Lancs	*Read* 1982, 252–4 (repr)

OWEN, William fl 1730

A carver who worked for **Henry Watson** in the 1730s, payments to him of £1 4s 'at London' and 4s 'for his tools at Northampton' are recorded in Watson's account book (Bodleian MS Eng Misc fol 383, fol 76, *in Brighton* 2001, 70).

PACETTI, Camillo

For information the reader is referred to *Pyke* 1973, 100

PAGE, George –1853

A sculptor and painter, in 1831, while living at 7 Gerrard Street, Soho, he received a silver medal from the Society of Arts for a model of a bust (3). Page, who lived in Camden Town, 1846–48 and at 19 Albert Street, Regents Park, in 1849, exhibited sculpture at the Royal Academy between 1841 and 1849, and at the Society of British Artists in 1846. He also showed *Hebe* (1833), *Reconciliation* and *The soldier's return* (both 1851) at the Society of British Artists, all of which may have been paintings. In 1852 he became insane and was placed in Colney Hatch lunatic asylum, where he died in August 1853 (Archives, Artists' Annuity Fund, in *Gunnis* 1968, 286).

Literary References: *Graves* VI, 1905–6, 38; *Gunnis* 1968, 286

Statues				
1.	1846	King Charles I, original model of an equestrian statuette	[Exhib Soc of BA, London, 777]; untraced	*Johnson* 1975, 351
2.	1849	Unidentified child, statuette	[Exhib RA, London, 1244]; untraced	*Graves* VI, 1905–6, 38
Busts				
3.	1831	Unidentified subject, model from the life	[Soc of A, silver medal]; untraced	RSA *Transactions*, vol 48, pt 1, 1833, xxv
4.	1832	Model from the life	[Soc of A, silver medal]; untraced	RSA *Transactions*, 1833, vol 48, pt 1, xxv
Miscellaneous				
5.	1841	The esquire	[Exhib RA, London, 143]; untraced	*Graves* VI, 1905–6, 38
6.	1846	Maximillian, Emperor of Germany, model	[Exhib Soc of BA, London, 778]; untraced	*Johnson* 1975, 351
7.	1846	Virgin and Saviour, model	[Exhib Soc of BA, London, 779]; untraced	*Johnson* 1975, 351
8.	1848	A girl with a lyre	[Exhib RA, London, 1429]; untraced	*Graves* VI, 1905–6, 38
9.	1849	Lady rescued by her brothers	[Exhib RA, London, 1203]; untraced	*Graves* VI, 1905–6, 38

PAGE, Gregory, of Horsham 1773–1834

The Matthew Napper monument (1) consists of an urn and inscription and is 'still purely eighteenth century in spirit, a local job affectionately done'. Gunnis describes the Henry Napper as a 'wall-monument with a semi-urn against a rounded background' (2). Smith Whittby is commemorated by an oval tablet (3).

Literary References: Pevsner, *Sussex*, 1965, 364; *Gunnis* 1968, 286

Funerary Monuments					
1.	†1801	Matthew and Sarah (†1844) Napper	Warnham, Sussex	S	Pevsner, *Sussex*, 1965, 364
2.	?1803	Henry Napper	Wisborough Green, Sussex	S	*Gunnis* 1968, 286
3.	†1816	Smith Whitby	West Chiltington, Sussex	S	*Gunnis* 1968, 286

PAGE, Robert, of Norwich 1707–78

An East Anglian stone-mason and carver, his mother was named Ann Page and he was apprenticed to **Robert Singleton** in 1721. On 25 October 1729 the *Norwich Gazette* announced that 'Robert Page of the Back of the Inns in St Peter's parish, Norwich, Freestone-Mason' had imported 'a large stock of the best Italian marbles and Portland Stone', adding that he also performed 'all sorts of wood carving'. In December 1737 Page advertised that he had bought the stock in trade of **Robert Singleton** and **George Bottomley** (*Norwich Mercury*, December 1737). He was in partnership with **Matthew Cufaude** at Great Yarmouth, 1754–78, with **John Brewer** at Beccles to 1778, and he paid the fine to be excused serving the office of sheriff in 1765 (*Norwich Mercury*, 11 July 1778). Page died in July 1778, while visiting Rush, an architect at Battersea, London, and was buried in St John Timberhill, Norwich, where a monument, probably from his own yard, commemorates him and his wife Mellicent, who died on 17 May 1755. An advertisement in the *Norwich Mercury* of 3 November 1778, stated that **Matthew Cufaude**, who had been in partnership with Page for 24 years, was to carry on the business of stone mason and carver at the Old Yard upon the Quay, near the Custom House, Yarmouth. Page's assistants and apprentices included **Robert Marston** (1753), **Edward Holl**, who later 'for several years conducted the business', and **John Ivory**.

Gunnis commented that Page was 'the best of the Norfolk statuaries' adding that his monuments, with their skilful use of coloured marbles and details such as rococo shields and groups of angels' heads 'are very similar, and almost equal, to contemporary works by **Sir Henry Cheere**'. The monument to Sir Philip and Dame Elizabeth Astley features two portrait medallions and has two *putti* reclining on the pediment above, while that to Nathaniel Micklethwaite has a bust 'within the arms of an open scrolly pediment, in front of a pink marble obelisk' (Pevsner) (**10, 17**). (Add inf. John Bayliss)

Literary References: *Norfolk Chronicle*, 5 and 12 Sept 1778 (debts to Page to be paid Robert and Edmund Page, executors); *Gunnis* 1968, 286; Pevsner, *Norfolk: Norwich & N E*, 1997, 672

Archival References: GPC; RG/JP, 6, 1040v-1042

Funerary Monuments					
1.	†1725	John Moore	Norwich Cathedral, Norfolk		Pevsner, *Norfolk: NE & Norwich*, 1997, 210
2.	†1725	Rev Thomas Cowper	Bedingham, Norfolk		RG/JP, 6, 1040v, 1041
3.	?1727	Elizabeth Segrave	Gateley, Norfolk	S	*Gunnis* 1968, 286
4.	†1729	Mary Lubbock	St George Colegate, Norwich, Norfolk		Pevsner, *Norfolk: NE & Norwich*, 1997, 235
5.	?1730	Edward Coleburne	St Peter Mancroft, Norwich, Norfolk		*Gunnis* 1968, 286
6.	?1730	Robert Bene	St Martin at Oak, Norwich, Norfolk		*Gunnis* 1968, 286
7.	†1732	Elizabeth Pell	Dersingham, Norfolk		Pevsner, *Norfolk: NW & S*, 1999, 297
8.	†1734	Robert and Dorothy (†1747) Suckling	Woodton, Norfolk	S	
9.	?1738	Robert Snell	St Giles, Norwich, Norfolk		*Gunnis* 1968, 286

10.	†1739	Sir Philip and Dame Elizabeth (†1738) Astley	Melton Constable, Norfolk		Pevsner, *Norfolk: NE & Norwich*, 1997, 611
11.	?1740	Robert Daye	Scoulton, Norfolk		*Gunnis* 1968, 286
12.	?1741	Elizabeth Browne	Colton, Norfolk		*Gunnis* 1968, 286
13.	†1742	Sir Edward Ward	Bixley, Norfolk	S	Pevsner, *Norfolk: NW & S*, 1999, 208
14.	*c*1745	Bussy Greene and family	Old Catton, Norfolk		Pevsner, *Norfolk: NE & Norwich*, 1997, 627
15.	†1750	Edward Atkyns	Ketteringham, Norfolk		Pevsner, *Norfolk: NW & S*, 1999, 454–5
16.	†1751	Dr Thomas Crowe	St Andrew, Norwich, Norfolk		Pevsner, *Norfolk: NE & Norwich*, 1997, 232
17.	†1757	Nathaniel Micklethwaite	Sprowston, Norfolk		Pevsner, *Norfolk: NE & Norwich*, 1997, 672
18.	†1760	Sir Jacob, Dame Lucy (†1739) and Dame Judith (†1742) Astley	Melton Constable, Norfolk		Pevsner, *Norfolk: NE & Norwich*, 1997, 611
19.	†1778	Robert and Mellicent (†1755) Page	St John Timberhill, Norwich, Norfolk		Pevsner, *Norfolk: NE & Norwich*, 1997, 239

PAGET, James fl 1702–25

He was described as living in the parish of St Dunstan-in-the-West in 1702, when he agreed to erect a monument to Sir Thomas Jones in Shrewsbury (**1**). The contract specified that the design was to be taken from the monument to Sir Thomas Richardson (†1683) in the Temple Church, a work which Esdaile has attributed to **John Settle** because of its closely similarity to his monument to Sir Lumley Robinson (†1684) in Westminster Abbey.

From 1712 he was working at Petworth, Sussex, where he was paid £359 for unidentified mason's work (Archives, Duke of Northumberland, Alnwick, U.1.31, in GPC). Between 1720 and 1725 he was employed on the new house for the Master of the Rolls, designed by Colen Campbell and situated next to the Rolls Chapel in Chancery Lane. There he provided decorative carving and chimneypieces as well as undertaking general construction work (**2, 3**).

Other members of the family appear to have followed the same craft. In January 1712 James Paget II, who was apprenticed to his father on 10 January 1699, was made free of the Masons' Company and it is possible that it was this James Paget who was employed on the house for the Master of the Rolls. William Paget, son of James Paget became free of the Company by patrimony on 3 August 1722 and George Paget was made free, again by patrimony, on 22 November 1738.

Literary References: *Esdaile* 1933 (2), 78; *Beard* 1956, 289; *Gunnis* 1968, 286; *Colvin* V, 1973–76, 358; *Webb* 1999, 25

Archival References: Masons' Co, *Freemen*, fol 57 (12 January 1712; 3 August 1722; 22 November 1738); GPC; RG/JP, 6, 1042

Funerary Monuments

1.	1702	Sir Thomas Jones (†1692) Payment(s): £85	St Alkmund, Shrewsbury, Salop	S	*Beard* 1956, 289 (repr)

Chimneypieces

2.	1720–1725	Several	[House of the Master of the Rolls, Chancery Lane, London]; untraced		TNA AO1/2494/407

Architectural Sculpture

3.	1720–1725	The great door case, Ionic capitals, lions' heads and masks	[House of the Master of the Rolls, Chancery Lane, London]; untraced		TNA AO1/2494/407

PAIN, John fl 1801

Chimneypieces

1.	1801	'Gothic moulded chimney piece for the Dining Parlour' Payment(s): £17 2s 6d	[Wroxton Abbey, Oxon]; untraced		Archives, Earl of Guildford, in GPC

PAINE, James 1745–1829

Paine was born in Pontefract in August 1745, the son of James Paine, the architect (1717–1789). Throughout his career he produced paintings, architectural drawings and sculpture, including one large-scale monument and a number of elegant designs for chimneypieces. His father trained Paine in the architectural profession, employing him as clerk of works at Thorndon Hall, Essex. His earliest exhibits at the Society of Artists were however watercolours of Yorkshire and Derbyshire landscapes. He became a student at St Martin's Lane Academy by 1764, and, according to his own account, went to Paris in that year and to Rome for the first time in 1765 (*Farington* VI, 2117).

In January 1767 Paine was in Florence and a few months later he visited southern Italy. His sketchbook includes views of Tivoli, Capua, Naples and Vesuvius. His earliest datable work of sculpture was a model of *Venus and Adonis* (**16**) which, according to James Barry, 'got him no small degree of credit', on account of the 'novelty, genius and agreeable manner with which he has treated it' (*Ingamells* 1997, 731). Paine was clearly integrated into British society in Italy: Barry included a portrait of him in a self-portrait of 1767, and the influential diplomat and antiquarian, Sir William Hamilton, acquired Paine's work (**14**). In 1767 Paine described himself as 'sculptor' in the first volume of his father's *Plans, Elevations and Sections*. In 1769 he visited Venice before returning to London.

In London, Paine exhibited works at the Society of Artists (**5–9, 15**). Neither his bust of a lady nor his relief after the antique (**7, 15**), both exhibited in 1770, impressed Horace Walpole who described them as 'very poor' (*Graves* 1907, 187). Paine became a fellow of the Society of Antiquaries the following year. He exhibited 'stained drawings' of chimneypieces, several examples of which have been preserved. These make use of classical motifs, such as satyrs, paterae and strips of key pattern. Paine executed a parade room chimneypiece at Brocket Hall, which his father was then rebuilding (**10**). Sketches survive for chimneypieces for other clients, but it is not known if these were executed. They include one with grotesques for Lord Clifford of Ugbrook in Devon, another with floral decoration for Mr Kettle (possibly Tilly Kettle the painter, who was the husband of Paine's half-sister), and a third for Loyd Baxendale, which makes use of a design from James Stuart's *Antiquities of Athens*.

Paine's most notable funerary monument, to the Covent Garden actor, William Powell, dates from 1771 (**1**). The work, which is almost 17 feet high and neoclassical in style, presents a figure of *Fame* holding a profile portrait-medallion. Sketches survive for several other monuments, all classical in style, and again it is not known whether these were executed. A design for a monument to Thomas Richardson features a cylindrical altar with ram's head decoration and an urn. Another, intended to commemorate Thomas Hirst, has a relief of a seated boy releasing a butterfly and is inscribed 'Mortality rendered Immortal, in its escape from the body'. The relief was used as part of another monument, to Lady Sondes, which has an architectural pediment with Vitruvian scrolls and Corinthian pilasters decorated with floral grotesques (2).

Paine married Elizabeth Crow, the daughter of a land surveyor who was an associate of his father, on 16 August 1773 at St Martin-in-the-Fields. Later that year the couple left England for the Continent, staying in Lyons in December and Turin the following January. They arrived in Rome in February with the painter Joseph Wright of Derby. A second sketch book is inscribed 'I P St Rome 1774 Studies' and contains more than 50 drawings of painted, sculptural and architectural subjects. Paine made extremely detailed measured drawings of the *Venus de Medici*, the *Putti fighting with a swan*, *Dying Gaul* and the *Endymion* in the Capitoline museum as well as pencil sketches of numerous other works of sculpture. His architectural drawings included elevations of the Baths of Diocletian and a ground plan of the Palazzo Farnese. Several of these are signed 'J Paine Archt.', reflecting Paine's aspiration to be recognised as an architect. His son, John Thomas, was born in Rome.

By 1776 the couple were back in London, living in Upper Charlotte Street. They may have returned occasionally to Rome, for Gunnis records that Paine gave his address as 'Rome' until 1783 in various books to which he was a subscriber (*Gunnis* 1968, 286). He was certainly in Upper Charlotte Street in 1781 when he exhibited 'An idea of a geometrical elevation for a national monument to the late Earl of Chatham' at the Royal Academy (*Graves* VI, 1905–6, 42). Subsequent exhibited designs, which suggest that he was now determined on an architectural career, included a design for a prison and for a bridge across Lough Foyle at Derry, produced for the corporation of that city. Paine was also responsible for erecting a villa, Belmont, at Mill Hill, Middx, and he produced designs for building projects on the Marquess of Salisbury's London estates. In 1791 he became a member of the Architects' Club.

A good deal of incidental biographical information on Paine's later life is available in the diaries of Joseph Farington, who was a close friend of Paine and a drawing instructor to Paine's daughter. Farington, for instance, records Paine's stint as a juror in a court case, and his involvement in the campaign to elect Sir Alan Gardner as an MP in June 1796, in competition with Charles James Fox and Horne Tooke. Farington also records details of Paine's work. In Autumn 1797 he was working on the architecture of Stoke Park, where his costs were apparently high: Farington records that Paine's bill for flooring in one suite of rooms was £600, and that Paine too often seemed 'to leave workmen idle' (*Farington*, 3, 890–1). Farington also notes that he, Paine and **Nathaniel Marchant** dined at Stoke Park in August, when John Penn, the owner, proposed that a monument should be raised to the poet Thomas Gray, who was buried at nearby Stoke Poges. Farington records that Paine produced a design based on Nero's tomb, which was rejected, but later presented another design with an estimate of £450. Farington does not record whether the project materialised.

Paine was living at North End, near Hammersmith in 1788. By 1804 he had moved to Turnham Green, west London, where he and his wife played host to Farington many times, and served home-made blackcurrant wine to their guests. Farington writes that Paine had dealings with the Proby family in 1804, and it may be that his last known monument dates from around this time (3). In 1809 he moved with his family to an estate at Sunninghill, Berks, and held a sale of part of his collection of paintings at Christie's. Various illnesses forced the family to stay in Brighton in 1810, although the air could not prevent the death of Paine's daughter in May 1813 and his wife the following year. Paine himself underwent an emergency operation to remove a carbuncle from his neck in 1813, which required four incisions. He was directed to live well and drink a pint of port a day, which must have proved good advice for he survived another 16 years before passing away in May 1829. He left three surviving daughters, Elizabeth, Barbara and Mary.

In his will, proved in July, Paine requested to be buried under a slab carved with his monogram 'IP', in the family vault at Marylebone Church. He left freehold and leasehold lands in Berkshire, Yorkshire, Surrey, and Middlesex, as well as houses in Great Newport Street, Westminster and Castle Street, Leicester Square. In addition to other household items he also had an impressive art collection, including family portraits by Tilly Kettle, George Romney and a picture of himself and his father by Sir Joshua Reynolds, 'a painting of extraordinary merit', which was bequeathed to the Ashmolean Museum. Paine's daughter Mary inherited a portfolio of Paine's prints, drawings, memoranda and sketch-books as well as his 'sculptured marbles, models, Terra cottas and casts'. She also received rings, intaglios and casts from antique gems 'which I purchased whilst a student at Rome, together with all my implements for drawing, modelling and painting' (PROB 11/1758).

The remainder of his collection was sold at Christie's on 12 March 1830. The sale included a book of Paine's chimneypiece designs and several Italian, French and English books on architecture. There were also numerous casts after the antique, a terracotta model by **Thomas Banks**, and paintings by Murillo, Van Goyen, Stothard, Wilson, Farington, Romney, Reynolds and Stubbs. Among the lots were the account-books of the sculptor, Nicholas Stone, which had originally belonged to George Vertue and are now in Sir John Soane's Museum.

MGS

Literary References: *Farington, passim*; *Graves* VI, 1905–6, 42; *Gunnis* 1968, 286; *Stainton* 1983, 15, 30; *Laing* 1983, 186–188; *Colvin* 1995, 727; *Ingamells* 1997, 731

Archival References: IGI

Collections of Drawings: Studies made in Rome, 1774, VAM 93 E.26 3859 (1–57); designs for chimney-pieces VAM D.1540-7-1907

Miscellaneous Drawings: Monument to Thomas Richardson VAM D 1550-1907, pen and coloured wash, signed; monument to Thomas Hirst VAM D 1549-1907, signed; monument to unidentified subject, VAM D 1549-1907, pen and coloured wash of a relief of a standing child with caduceus; design for a stone bridge across Lough Foyle, 1793, tinted drawing, framed, VAM D213-1890 (sold with his elevation of a prison in India ink in 1830, lot 83, 14s); design for a memorial to Admiral Lord Nelson, proposed for St Paul's Cathedral, VAM 8520-10, pen and wash, signed 'J. Paine Archt' (*Physick* 1969, 164, repr)

Portraits of the Sculptor: James Barry, self-portrait with Dominique Lefevre and James Paine the Younger, oil on canvas, 1767, NPG 213; Sir Joshua Reynolds, Portrait of James Paine the Elder and James Paine the Younger, 1764, Ashmolean; Romney James Paine, half-length portrait, mentioned in Paine's will, untraced

Auction Catalogues: Paine Sale 1830

Funerary Monuments

1.	1771	William Powell (†1769)	Bristol Cathedral	SD	*Gunnis* 1968, 286; *Penny* 1977 (1), 100 (repr); *Colvin* 1995, 727
2.	†1777	Lady Sondes Drawing(s): VAM D.1551-1907	Rockingham, Northants	S	*Gunnis* 1968, 286; *Colvin* 1995, 727
3.	1783	Sarah Proby	St Mary, Chatham, Kent	S	*Gunnis* 1968, 286; *Colvin* 1995, 727

Statues

4.	1773	Narcissus, model 'to be worked in statuary marble life-size'	[Exhib Soc of Artists, London, 251]; untraced		*Graves* 1907, 187

Busts

5.	1769	Unidentified gentleman	[Exhib Soc of Artists, London, 243]; untraced		*Graves* 1907, 187
6.	1769	Unidentified gentleman	[Exhib Soc of Artists, London, 242]; untraced		*Graves* 1907, 187
7.	1770	Unidentified lady, model	[Exhib Soc of Artists, London, 175]; untraced		*Graves* 1907, 187
8.	1771	Sir John Fielding	[Exhib Soc of Artists, London, 224]; untraced		*Graves* 1907, 187
9.	1771	Unidentified subject	[Exhib Soc of Artists, London, 225]; untraced		*Graves* 1907, 187

Chimneypieces

10.	1771	With frieze representing 'The Rape of Europa' Drawing(s): Two, VAM D1546-1907; D1545-1907	[Brocket Hall, Herts, saloon]; untraced		*Gunnis* 1968, 286; *Colvin* 1995, 727
11.	1773	'A design for a chimneypiece of the cariatic order'	[Exhib Soc of Artists, London, 252]; untraced		*Graves* 1907, 187
12.	1773	Description unavailable	[for Lady Middleton, Peper Harow, Surrey]; untraced		*Gunnis* 1968, 286
13.	nd	With key pattern Drawing(s): two, pen and ink, D1544-1907	[The Grove, I of W]; untraced		

Reliefs

14.	1767–1769	Copy of a bas-relief from Portici, near Herculaneum	[Purchased by Sir William Hamilton]; untraced		*Ingamells* 1997, 731
15.	1770	Agrippina mourning over the ashes of Germanicus, sketch	[Exhib Soc of Artists, London, 176]; untraced		*Graves* 1907, 187

Miscellaneous

16.	1767	Venus and Adonis, model	[Prepared in Italy]; untraced		*Ingamells* 1997, 731

PAINE, W, of Stratford-on-Avon fl 1800–16

He was the son of a William Paine, of Stratford-on-Avon, mason, who died in 1800.

Literary References: *Gunnis* 1968, 287

Chimneypieces

1.	1816	Eight	[Judges' lodgings, Warwick]; untraced		Warks CRO QS 24/36 (plans), QS 24/37 (vouchers); *Gunnis* 1968, 287

PALMER, Benjamin fl c1712–78

After the death of his father, **William Palmer**, in 1739, he took over the yard in Bedford Row near Gray's Inn. Shortly before his death William had supplied Henry Purefoy of Shalstone, Bucks, with a purple marble mantelpiece and chimney slab, together with a black slab for another chimneypiece. Purefoy wrote a series of letters to William and then to Benjamin Palmer expressing his disatisfaction with various aspects of this work, particularly the purple marble slab, which he thought 'must be Counterfeit, for everywhere where it looks like mother of pearl it blisters & rises up, & where it is trod upon it breaks of[f] in a thin shell & underneath is a course stone like freestone' (*Eland* 1931, vol I, 58). After Benjamin sent a replacement slab to Shalstone in April 1841, Purefoy wrote to complain that the new one would probably peel too, that it had small cracks which might expand and that it was 'not near so good marble as the mantle piece itself' (*ibid*, 59). Purefoy's letters ceased after the new slab was laid so it seems that his fears were groundless.

Palmer's most ambitious work is the statue of Sir William Harpur over the old Grammar School at Bedford (**23**). He also provided the Harpur monument (**18**) which has medallion portraits and was paid £200 for both works in 1768 (Bedford School MS, account book, in *Gunnis* 1968, 287). Gunnis comments that 'as a statuary Palmer is not as good as his father, and his monuments, though large, are not particularly distinguished'. Those to Arthur O'Keefe and Sir Thomas Gage feature portrait busts (**15, 6**). Palmer retired in 1778, and a sale of his stock was held on 7 and 8 July that year.

Literary References: *Eland* 1931, vol I, pp 53–4, 58–60; *Gunnis* 1968, 287

Archival References: Harpur charity documents, Bedford School, fol 4c (bill for Harpur's monument and statue); fol 5a, (Palmer's bill for the above); fol 5b (letter from Palmer to the master), governors and trustees of the Bedford Charity, complaining about lack of payment

Auction Catalogue: Palmer 1778

Funerary Monuments

1.	†1712	William Middlemore	St Wulfram, Grantham, Lincs	S	Pevsner, *Lincs*, 1989, 320
2.	c1740	Frances Legh	St Elphin, Warrington, Lancs	S	*Gunnis* 1968, 287
3.	?1741	Stephen Master	Daventry, Northants	S	*Gunnis* 1968, 287
4.	c1742	Edward Payne (†1728)	Hough-on-the-Hill, Lincs		Pevsner, *Lincs*, 1989, 400
5.	post-1742	Sir Roger (†1738) and Lady Maria Meredith	St Nicholas, Leeds, Kent	S	Pevsner, *Kent: W & Weald*, 1976, 370
6.	?1742	Sir Thomas Gage	Hengrave, Suffolk		Pevsner, *Suffolk*, 1974, 262
7.	?1742	Thomas Master	Westminster Abbey, London	S	*Gunnis* 1968, 287
8.	†1742	Thomas Payne	Hough-on-the-Hill, Lincs		Pevsner, *Lincs*, 1989, 400

No.	Date	Subject	Location		References
9.	?1744	John Willis	Malmesbury, Wilts	S	*Gunnis* 1968, 287
10.	†1749	Arthur Bevan MP	Laugharne, Carmarthen	S	*Dale-Jones and Lloyd*, 1989, 56
11.	†1751	Sir Thomas Stepney	St Elli, Llanelli, Carmarthen	S	*Dale-Jones and Lloyd* 1989, 56
12.	?1753	Charles, Lord Stourton	Cheam, Surrey, Lumley Chapel	S	*Gunnis* 1968, 287
13.	†1753	William Rose	East Retford, Notts	S	*Gunnis* 1968, 287
14.	†1754	Thomas Price	Llangyfelach, Glamorgan	S	Pevsner, *Glamorgan*, 1995, 386
15.	†1756	Arthur O'Keefe	Westminster Abbey, London, cloisters		Pevsner, *London: Westminster*, 1973, 465
16.	†1757	Henry Uthwatt	Lathbury, Bucks	S	Pevsner, *Bucks*, 1994, 425
17.	†1761	Lieutenant-Colonel John Littlehales and wife (†1807)	St Leonard, Bridgnorth, Salop		RG/JP, 6, 1046
18.	†1768	Sir William Harpur (†1768) and Dame Alice Harpur Payment(s): £200 (included with the statue outside the Grammar School)	St Paul, Bedford		Harpur charity documents, Bedford School, fol 4cc, 2 July 1766; Pevsner, *Beds, Hunts & Peterborough*, 1968, 47
19.	?1769	Robert Johnson	Sandy, Beds	S	*Gunnis* 1968, 287
20.	†1770	Margaret Sparhauke	Graveley, Herts	S	Pevsner, *Herts*, 1977, 148
21.	?1771	Rev Louis Monoux	Sandy, Beds	S	*Gunnis* 1968, 287
22.	†1777	Samuel Prime	Temple Church, London	S	

Statues

No.	Date	Subject	Location	References
23.	1756	Sir William Harpur Payment(s): £200 with the monument to Harpur at St Paul's, Bedford (18)	Town Hall, Bedford	Harpur Charity Documents, Bedford School, fol 4cc, 2 July 1766; Pevsner, *Beds, Hunts & Peterborough*, 1968, 50

PALMER, J, of Manchester fl *c*1817

Palmer, whose address is given as Pump Street, London Road, in *Baines's Gazetteer*, signs a Hellenic wall-tablet at Bowden (1).

Literary References: *Gunnis* 1968, 287

Funerary Monuments

No.	Date	Subject	Location		References
1.	?1817	John Baldwin	Bowden, Cheshire	S	*Gunnis* 1968, 287

PALMER, Nathaniel fl 1829–44

He exhibited at the Royal Academy between 1829 and 1844, from various London addresses, and showed a figure of Charles I at Westminster Hall in the latter year (2). One critic described it as 'a poor thing, as if the king were going to dance a corrante' (*Lit Gaz*, 1844, 466). In 1846 he applied for assistance to the AGBI owing to 'accute inflammation of the eyes' (*Gunnis* 1968, 287) and in the same year he received £10 in assistance from the Council of the Royal Academy.

Literary References: *Gunnis* 1968, 287; *Pyke* 1973, 100

Archival References: AGBI, vol 4, 125

No.	Date	Subject	Material	Location	References
Statues					
1.	1837	Princess Victoria, cabinet statue		[Exhib RA, London, 1249]; untraced	*Graves* VI, 1905–6, 44
2.	1844	King Charles I		[Exhib Westminster Hall, London]; untraced	*Gunnis* 1968, 287
Busts					
3.	1829	Rev Roland Hill		[Exhib RA, London, 1169]; untraced	*Graves* VI, 1905–6, 44
4.	1838	Sir Robert Peel		[Soc of BA, London, 627]; untraced	*Johnson* 1975, 352
5.	1838	Unidentified child		[Exhib RA, London, 1343]; untraced	*Graves* VI, 1905–6, 44
6.	1838	Unidentified lady		[Exhib RA, London, 1330]; untraced	*Graves* VI, 1905–6, 44
7.	1840	Unidentified gentleman		[Exhib RA, London, 1164]; untraced	*Graves* VI, 1905–6, 44
8.	1840	Unidentified gentleman		[Exhib RA, London, 1176]; untraced	*Graves* VI, 1905–6, 44
9.	1843	Unidentified gentleman	m	[Exhib RA, London, 1502]; untraced	*Graves* VI, 1905–6, 44
10.	1844	Lavinia	m	[Exhib Soc of BA, London, 757]; untraced	*Graves* VI, 1905–6, 44; *Johnson* 1975, 352
11.	1844	Unidentified child		[Exhib RA, London, 1323]; untraced	*Graves* VI, 1905–6, 44
Reliefs					
12.	1835	Unidentified lady, medallic portrait		[Exhib RA, London, 995]; untraced	*Graves* VI, 1905–6, 44
13.	1836	Unidentified gentleman, medallic portrait		[Exhib RA, London, 978]; untraced	*Graves* VI, 1905–6, 44
14.	1838	Queen Victoria	w	VAM	*Pyke* 1973, 100 (repr pl 206)
15.	1838	Unidentified lady, medallion		[Exhib Soc of BA, London, 619]; untraced	*Johnson* 1975, 352
16.	1838	Unidentified lady, medallion		[Exhib Soc of BA, London, 620]; untraced	*Johnson* 1975, 352
17.	1842	Arthur, Duke of Wellington		[Exhib RA, London, 1333]; untraced	*Graves* VI, 1905–6, 44
18.	nd	Unidentified man	w	VAM	*Pyke* 1973, 100
Miscellaneous					
19.	1832	The sketch book		[Exhib RA, London, 1120]; untraced	*Graves* VI, 1905–6, 44

PALMER, William 1673–1739

Palmer was described by Whinney as a sculptor of modest potential who learnt a good deal from better works he had seen. The son of a coachman of St Giles in the Fields, he was apprenticed to **James Hardy** on 23 April 1687. In 1694 he became free of the Masons' Company, remaining with Hardy for a year or so before joining **John Nost I**. He may have worked for **Thomas Hill** since in November 1704 Sir John Vanburgh wrote to Lord Godolphin about Hill's shortcomings as master mason for the building of the Orangery at Kensington Palace and noted 'I ask'd one of his [Hill's] foreman who they work'd for, but he tould me One Palmer whom his master had made his Deputy' (*Wren Soc* VII, 140). In 1704 he was responsible for carving the inscription and for setting up **Pierre Monnot**'s Exeter monument at Stamford. He was working for **Edward Chapman** in Red Lion Square, London by 1706 and four years later had his own workshop in the Square, making chimneypieces and carrying out mason's work as well as tomb sculpture. Palmer gave a list of seven monuments he had 'set up' to Le Neve for inclusion in the latter's *Monumenta Anglicana*.

He is best known for the remarkable memorial to Margaret Watson at Rockingham (5). In about 1721 John Bridges, the Northamptonshire historian, described the 'handsome grey monument . . . Under the arms is a canopy supported by two pillars of the Corinthian order. Below the canopy, on a pedestal in full proportion a female figure in a winding-sheet, looking upward, and pointing to a skull at her feet' (John Bridges, MS notes, quoted by *Bailey* 1996, 181). Whinney wondered if Palmer was in fact responsible for the striking, twisted effigy with its small head and mannered gestures or whether he was again erecting imported work.

The monument to Lord and Lady Lexington (12), erected in 1726, is a singular composition, for two reclining figures are set back to back on a padded mattress. Whinney notes that Lord Lexington's figure in classical armour is reminiscent of the ducal effigy on the Buckingham monument, 1721–2, in Westminster Abbey, but the arrangement of the figures appears to be Palmer's own. In the executor's accounts of Bridget, Duchess of Rutland are payments totalling £346 6s made to Palmer for the monument, plus a bill for £13 19s for its carriage from London to Kelham.

Among his other works, either signed or on Le Neve's list, is the wall monument to Anna Crispe, which has a pretty bust enclosed in a restrained architectural frame with fluted pilasters (2). Charles Hussey's memorial also makes use of a bust, set this time within a heavy frame with a scrolled pediment above and consoles flanking the tablet below (15). Hussey is presented in a soft cap reminiscent of Coysevox's bust of Matthew Prior in Westminster Abbey, but lacks its vitality, since the head is almost frontal and the cap frames the face like a clumsy halo.

Palmer's building work included the post of mason to Lincoln's Inn, held from 1718 until his death. There he received £300 between 1730 and 1733 for his work in the chapel and elsewhere. A number of payments were also made to him at Gray's Inn between 1722 and 1727. He was responsible for unspecified work at Lord Folkestone's London house between 1727 and 1738 and was paid £65, again for unspecified work, at the Duke of Norfolk's house in St James's Square in 1737. He was still working, from a yard in Bedford Row, Holborn, at the time of his death, for several posthumous payments were made to his widow, Anne. In his uncomplicated will, in which he left all his real estate and personal chattels to his wife, he described himself as a 'stonecutter'.

IR

Literary References: *Esdaile* 1942, 177, 183–4; *Gunnis* 1968, 287–8; *Whinney* 1988, 246–7, 458 8–10; *Webb* 1999, 25
Archival References: BM Ad MS 34747 fol 113 (Bedford Row yard); GPC
Miscellaneous Drawings: design for a monument to Earl Fitzwilliam (†1719), attrib Palmer, BL Add MS 32467, fol 570-58R (monument executed by James Fisher of Camberwell)
Will: PROB 11/689, signed 13 April 1738

Funerary Monuments

1.	1704	5th Earl (†1700) and Countess of Exeter (†1703), set up by Palmer (carved in Rome by Pierre Monnot)		St Martin, Stamford, Lincs		*Le Neve* 1700–1715, 1–2; *Esdaile* 1942, 183; *Bailey* 1996, 191
2.	†1709	Anna Crispe		Birchington, Kent		*Le Neve* 1700–1715, 159; Pevsner, *Kent: N E & E*, 1983, 143
3.	†1712	Timothy (†1708) and Elizabeth Davison		Untraced		*Le Neve* 1700–1715, 244
4.	†1714	Andrew Giffard		St Pancras old parish church, London, churchyard		*Le Neve* 1700–1715, 280–1
5.	†1714	Hon Margaret Watson		Rockingham, Northants		*Le Neve* 1700–1715, 258; *Bailey* 1996, 181 (repr)
6.	†1715	Richard Walburge		Barholm, Lincs		*Le Neve* 1700–1715, 298–9; Pevsner, *Lincs*, 1989, 115
7.	†1716	Anne Gelsthorp		Hillington, Norfolk		*Le Neve* (MS only); *Gunnis* 1968, 288
8.	?†1717	William Martin		Nettleswell, Essex	S	GPC
9.	†1722	William Pigott		Horsted Keynes, Sussex	S	GPC
10.	†1724	Elizabeth Hatten		Lincoln Cathedral		Pevsner, *Lincs*, 1989, 479
11.	†1724	Richard Vaughan		St Peter, Carmarthen	S	*Dale-Jones and Lloyd* 1989, 56
12.	1726	Robert, 2nd Baron Lexington (†1723) and Lady Lexington (†1703) Payment(s): £345 6s		Kelham, Notts		*Whinney* 1988, 246–7, 458 n10 (repr)
13.	†1727	Ann Croftes		Little Saxham, Suffolk		Pevsner, *Suffolk*, 1974, 338
14.	†1727	James Fortrye		Northfleet, Kent	S	GPC
15.	?c1727	Sir Charles Hussey (†1664) and others		Caythorpe, Lincs	S	*Whinney* 1988, 246; Pevsner, *Lincs*, 1989, 217; GPC
16.	†1728	Sir Constantine Phipps		White Waltham, Berks		Pevsner, *Berks*, 1966, 265
17.	†1728	William Chamber		Great Offley, Herts	S	Pevsner, *Herts*, 1977, 264
18.	1730	John (+1723) and Lucy (+1716) Barham		Wadhurst, Sussex	S	Pevsner, *Sussex*, 1965, 617
19.	†1731	Henry Pawson		[St Mary Bishophill snr, York]; St Clement, York		Pevsner, *Yorks: E R & York*, 1995, 164
20.	+1731	William Games		Upton, Soke of Peterborough		*Gunnis* 1968, 288
21.	†1732	Edward Barkham		Wainfleet St Mary, Lincs		Pevsner, *Lincs*, 1989, 778
22.	†1733	Eleanor Stepney		St Elli, Llanelly, Carmarthen		*Dale-Jones and Lloyd* 1989, 56
23.	1734	Thomas Maire and wife		Romaldkirk, N R Yorks		GPC
24.	†1736	Barbara Cressett		Cound, Salop	S	GPC
25.	†1737	Gilbert Browne		North Mimms, Herts	S	Pevsner, *Herts*, 1977, 263
26.	†1738	Banastre Parker		Leyland, Lancs		GPC
27.	†1738	Stephen Everard		St Mary of Charity, Faversham, Kent	S	Pevsner, *Kent: N E & E*, 1983, 317

Chimneypieces

28.	1706	One		[Ashburnham House, Westminster, London, staircase-hall]; untraced		*Gunnis* 1968, 288
29.	1706	Two	m	[Lord Ashburnham's house at Ampthill, Beds]; untraced		*Gunnis* 1968, 288
30.	1719	Description unavailable		[Knowsley, Lancs]; untraced		*Gunnis* 1968, 288

31.	1738	Description unavailable		[Mr Edward Trotman's house at Shelswell]; untraced	*Gunnis* 1968, 288
32.	1739	Description unavailable		Shalstone House, Shalstone, Bucks	Pevsner, *Bucks*, 1994, 617

Miscellaneous

33.	1737	Unspecified work for the Duke of Norfolk, perhaps a chimneypiece Payment(s): £65		[Norfolk House, St James's Square, London]; untraced	Account Books, Frederick, Prince of Wales, Duchy of Cornwall, VII; GPC

PAMPALONI, Luigi 1791–1847

An Italian sculptor, he was born in Florence and studied under **Lorenzo Bartolini**. He caused a sensation in Italy in 1827 with a statue of a praying boy, part of a sepulchral group, which was repeatedly reproduced in plaster. His best-known works in Italy are the figures of Arnolfo dei Lapi and Brunelleschi on the eastern side of the Cathedral in Florence. He signed a monument for an English client with a relief of an angel bearing a mother and her child heavenwards (**1**).

Literary References: *Gunnis* 1968, 288; *Penny* 1977 (1), 73; *Panzetta* 1994, 178

Funerary Monuments

1.	1840	Mrs Gooch (†1838)	Benacre, Suffolk	S	Pevsner, *Suffolk*, 1974, 97

PANORMO, Constantine ARHA *c*1805–52

Panormo was born in London, the son of Francis Panormo, a professor of music from Dublin. He studied at the Royal Dublin Society's schools and distinguished himself by gaining numerous prizes. In 1824 **William Behnes**, who had himself been a pupil at the school, offered to take two boys and instruct them for two years at £60 a year each. The RDS accepted the offer and sent over Panormo and **John Gallagher**. As Behnes's pupil, Panormo attended the Royal Academy Schools, gaining silver medals in 1825 and 1826 (RA Premium list). In 1825, while living at 91 Dean Street, Soho, he also received a medal from the Society of Arts (**1**). He then spent a time in Rome at the expense of the RDS, returning to London in 1833. He exhibited at the Royal Academy in 1833 and 1834, giving his address as 4 Tottenham Court Road (**10–13, 24**).

By 1837 Panormo was living in Dublin, where he was appointed master of the RDS modelling school in June 1840. He exhibited at the Royal Hibernian Academy, 1837–49, and was elected an associate member in 1842. In the same year the Royal Irish Art Union awarded him a prize of £5 for his model, *The rescue*, describing it as 'one of the most classically conceived and ably executed groups for some time exhibited in this country' (*Strickland* II, 1913, 216) (**6**). They subsequently purchased a marble version and awarded it as a prize to one of their subscribers. In 1844 the sculptor sent a group of the *Liberation of Caractacus* (**7**) to the Westminster Hall exhibition which elicited an acid response from the *Literary Gazette*'s correspondent, who wrote 'And one group, not in the catalogue, The Liberation of Caractacus; and glad we were to be liberated from the sight of it' (*Lit Gaz* 1844, 483). He later completed a statue of George IV for the RDS, started by William Behnes but not finished due to financial difficulties (**8**). He died at his house in Queen's Square, Dublin, on 15 May 1852.

Literary References: RSA *Transactions*, 1825, vol 43, xlvii; *New Monthly Mag*, vol 18 (1826), 11; *Strickland* II, 1913, 215–7; *Gunnis* 1968, 288–9

Statues

1.	1825	'An entire figure', plaster copy in the round		[Soc of A, silver medal]; untraced	RSA *Transactions*, vol 43, 1825, xlvii
2.	1838	Bishop Doyle, sketch models		[Exhib RHA, Dublin, 218, 219]; untraced	*Stewart* III, 1985, 58
3.	1838	St Paul, for St Paul's church, Arran Quay, rough sketch model		[Exhib RHA, Dublin, 209]; untraced	*Stewart* III, 1985, 58
4.	1842	Mercury		National Museum, Kildare Street, Dublin (1913)	*Strickland* II, 1913, 216; *Stewart* III, 1985, 58
5.	1842	The young protector, a model submitted for an Art Union prize		[Exhib RHA, Dublin, 473]; untraced	*Stewart* III, 1985, 58
6.	1843	The rescue Model(s): awarded £5 prize by the Irish Art Union 1842; untraced	m	[Royal Irish Art Union prize awarded to Mrs Reddon, Clare Street, Limerick]; untraced	*Strickland* II, 1913, 216; *Stewart* III, 1985, 58
7.	1844	Liberation of Caractacus		RDS, Dublin (1913)	*Strickland* II, 1913, 216
8.	1822–1846	King George IV (co-sculptor: William Behnes)	m	RDS, Dublin	*White and Bright* 1998, 86–7
9.	nd	Theseus rescuing Hippodamia from the Centaur		RDS, Dublin (1913)	*Strickland* II, 1913, 216

Busts

10.	1833	Lady Mary Leslie		[Exhib RA, London, 1224]; untraced	*Graves* VI, 1905–6, 46
11.	1833	Sir Anthony Carlisle		[Exhib RA, London, 1147]; untraced	*Graves* VI, 1905–6, 46
12.	1833	Sir Edward Antrobus		[Exhib RA, London, 1143]; untraced	*Graves* VI, 1905–6, 46
13.	1834	Sir Richard Paul Joddrell		[Exhib RA, London, 1054]; untraced	*Graves* VI, 1905–6, 46
14.	1837	Robert Ball		[Exhib RHA, Dublin, 250]; untraced	*Stewart* III, 1985, 58
15.	1838	General Sir Barry Close Bt		[Exhib RHA, Dublin, 210]; untraced	*Stewart* III, 1985, 58
16.	1838	Mrs Fitzsimon		[Exhib RHA, Dublin, 220]; untraced	*Stewart* III, 1985, 58
17.	1838	Unidentified gentleman		[Exhib RHA, Dublin, 208]; untraced	*Stewart* III, 1985, 58
18.	1838	William Deane Freeman, model		[Exhib RHA, Dublin, 211]; untraced	*Stewart* III, 1985, 58
19.	1842	Richard Carmichael		[Exhib RHA, Dublin, 465]; untraced Other versions: exhib RHA, Dublin, 1849, 424, marble; untraced	*Stewart* III, 1985, 58
20.	1842	Unidentified lady		[Exhib RHA, Dublin, 474]; untraced	*Stewart* III, 1985, 58
21.	1843	Isaac M D'Olier		[Exhib RHA, Dublin, 653]; untraced	*Stewart* III, 1985, 58
22.	1843	John Harding	m	[Exhib RHA, Dublin, 651]; untraced	*Stewart* III, 1985, 58
23.	1844	Sir Edward Stanley	m	RDS, Dublin Other versions: exhib RHA, Dublin, 1842, 471; untraced NGI, Dublin, plaster	*Stewart* III, 1985, 58; *le Harivel* 1988, 580 (repr)

Miscellaneous

24.	1833	Cupid imploring Venus to return him his bow	[Exhib RA, London, 1126]; untraced	*Graves* VI, 1905–6, 46
25.	1842	Eurathe clipping the wings of love	[Exhib RHA, Dublin, 479]; untraced	*Stewart* III, 1985, 58
26.	1843	David throwing the sling at Goliath	[Exhib RHA, Dublin, 662]; untraced	*Stewart* III, 1985, 58
27.	1844	Ulysses and his dog	[Exhib RHA, Dublin, 414]; untraced	*Stewart* III, 1985, 58
28.	1846	The pet rabbit	[Exhib RHA, Dublin, 488]; untraced	*Stewart* III, 1985, 58
29.	1853	The pet dove	[Int Exhib, Dublin]; untraced	*Strickland* II, 1913, 217

PANTON (or PANTIN), L fl 1761–63

'PANTON, L, Carver' exhibited at the Free Society in 1761 (**2**). Two years later 'PANTIN, Carver', who was listed as, 'Jeweller, Southampton Court, Strand' showed a comparable work at the Society of Artists (**1**). Graves suggests that they were probably the same person.

Funerary Monuments

1.	1763	'A tomb, with Gothic Frontispiece'	[Exhib Soc of Artists, London, 200]; untraced	*Graves* 1907, 188

Miscellaneous

2.	1761	'A gothic temple carved in box'	[Exhib Free Soc, London, 103]; untraced	*Graves* 1907, 188

PANZETTA, Joseph fl *c*1787–1830

When he applied to the AGBI for assistance in 1830, Panzetta stated that he had been a pupil 'of Mr Joseph Wilton, who was also his godfather, and of J B Cipriani, and after a long residence in Italy for improvement returned to London in 1787'. He then gave a list of his principal works, which included 'A Monument in Westminster Abbey to Sir Archibald Campbell', 'Vases for Somerset House' and 'The Lions on the Terrace' (also for Somerset House), and the statue of Archbishop Tillotson in Yorkshire, which were all 'done for Mr Wilton' (**1, 11, 4, 5**). Panzetta also said that he had 'done in Portland stone for Mr Banks' the relief in front of the Shakespeare Gallery in Pall Mall and claimed that he was responsible for figures of *Hercules* and *Justice* on the Union Insurance Office (**12, 9**). Gunnis expresses some doubts about the sculptor's claims, writing, 'If all that Panzetta said was true it would appear that he did the work and more famous sculptors got the credit and the cash; but what is more likely is that he merely carved in stone or marble the works which others had modelled and designed'.

Panzetta also stated that he had worked for the **Coade Factory** for 26 years and his name appears frequently in the firm's records between 1813 and 1821. He modelled a statue of George III for Dunstan, Lincs, a figure of Britannia for Plymouth, a pediment relief commemorating Nelson for the Royal Hospital at Greenwich and the statue of Lord Hill for the column at Shrewsbury for the firm and it is likely that he undertook many other works for them too (**6, 8, 13, 7**).

He exhibited at the Royal Academy, 1789–1810, from addresses at 42 Great Titchfield Street; 9 Union Street, Middlesex Hospital; 40 James Street, Lambeth and the Artificial Stone Factory, Lambeth. In 1830, when he was clearly in financial difficulties, he was given a donation of £5 by the Council of the Royal Academy.

Literary References: *Gunnis* 1968, 289; *Kelly* 1990, *passim*

Archival References: RA/GA 1830; AGBI, vol 2, 59

Funerary Monuments

1.	1795	General Sir Archibald Campbell (†1791) (as assistant to Joseph Wilton RA)		Westminster Abbey, London, south transept	*Gunnis* 1968, 289
2.	1802	Part of a monument to a child		[Exhib RA, London, 960]; untraced	*Graves* VI, 1905–6, 46
3.	1808	Charles James Fox, model		[Exhib RA, London, 880]; untraced	*Graves* VI, 1905–6, 46

Statues

4.	?1790	Lions (as assistant to Joseph Wilton RA)		Somerset House, London, terrace	*Gunnis* 1968, 289
5.	1796	Archbishop John Tillotson (†1694) (as assistant to Joseph Wilton RA)		Sowerby, W R Yorks	*Gunnis* 1968, 289
6.	1810	King George III, model for Coade		Untraced Other versions: executed in artificial stone for Dunstan, Lincs (now at Lincoln Castle)	*Kelly* 1990, 233–4 (repr)
7.	1817	Rowland, Baron Hill of Almarez and Hawkstone, model for Coade Factory (designed by Edward Haycock)		Untraced Other versions: executed in artificial stone for Lord Hill column, Abbey foregate, Shrewsbury, Salop	*GM*, vol LXXXVII, Nov 1817, II, 393; *Kelly* 1990, 239 (repr)
8.	1835	Britannia, model for Coade		Untraced Other versions: executed in artificial stone for town hall, Devonport, Plymouth, Devon	Pevsner, *Devon*, 1989, 675
9.	nd	Hercules and Justice		[Union Insurance Office, London]; untraced	*Gunnis* 1968, 289

Busts

10.	1810	Rev W Jay		[Exhib RA, London, 899]; untraced	*Graves* VI, 1905–6, 46

Architectural Sculpture

11.	?1787	Vases (as assistant to Joseph Wilton RA) (co-sculptor: Joseph RA Wilton)		Somerset House, London	*Gunnis* 1968, 289
12.	1789	Shakespeare between the Dramatic Muse and the Genius of Painting (as assistant to Thomas Banks RA)	s	[Shakespeare gallery, Pall Mall, London (until 1868)]; New Place, Stratford-on-Avon, Warks, gardens	*Gunnis* 1968, 289
13.	1810–1812	Neptune handing over Nelson to Britannia, model for Coade (designed by Benjamin West)		Untraced Other versions: executed in artificial stone for Royal Hospital, Greenwich	*Kelly* 1990, 235–7 (repr)

Reliefs				
14.	1789	A fountain	[Exhib RA, London, 468]; untraced	*Graves* VI, 1905–6, 46
Miscellaneous				
15.	1791	Perseus going to cut off the Medusa's head	[Exhib RA, London, 631]; untraced	*Graves* VI, 1905–6, 46
16.	1791	Perseus transforming his enemies to stone	[Exhib RA, London, 628]; untraced	*Graves* VI, 1905–6, 46
17.	1791	Polyphemus, Acis and Galatea	[Exhib RA, London, 622]; untraced	*Graves* VI, 1905–6, 46
18.	1802	British Mars triumphant	[Exhib RA, London, 1049]; untraced	*Graves* VI, 1905–6, 46
19.	1802	The mother and her babe	[Exhib RA, London, 1048]; untraced	*Graves* VI, 1905–6, 46

PAPERA, Bartholomew –1815

The first record of Papera's activities dates from 1790, when he was listed in Wakefield's *London Directory* at Marylebone Street, Golden Square. In the Petworth House archives is a receipt dated 29 January 1801 from 'B Papera' for several models which included a '3 foot figure' at £3 12s' a 'Gladeator' and 'Hercules' at 16 shillings each, and a 'Laying Venus' which cost 8 shillings (1). The following year Wedgwood paid him for three busts and 'one vase with lamp' (Wedgwood MSS L108/20403, Papera acct, 12 June 1802) and in 1806, as 'Mr Papera figure-maker', he supplied busts to Lord Bridport (Soane, Abstract of Bills 3, fol 118) (5). An advertisement in *The Times* of 23 November 1805, announced that casts after the bust of Nelson by **Anne Seymour Damer** could be had at his shop (4) and his trade card of 1806 describes him as 'B. PAPERA Figure Maker TO HER MAJESTY No 16 Marylebone St, Golden Square' (BM, Banks Collection 106.22). Papera later sold a figure of *Hercules* to the clock and decorative metalwork manufacturer, Benjamin Vulliamy (2). A modified version of this figure, modelled by **James Smith**, was used for several sets of candelabra produced by the firm. The earliest examples were two pairs supplied to Thomas, Viscount Anson for Shugborough, Staffs, in 1812 and the model was still in use as late as 1821. In his will, which gives his christian name as Bartholomew, Papera left all his property to his wife Susannah. It mentioned his daughter **Louisa Papera** and a son called James, who may well have been **James Philip Papera**.

Literary References: *Gunnis* 1968, 289; *Clifford* 1992, 61; *Yarrington* 1997, 41, 43 n76; *Murdoch* 2004, 98–9

Archival References: GPC

Wills and Administrations: 'Bartholomew Papera, Figure Maker of st James, Westminster' PROB 11/1572 (8 August 1815)

Statues				
1.	1801	'3 foot figure', 'Gladeator', Hercules', 'Laying Venus' and three other items Payment(s): £18 7s 8d	Untraced	Petworth House Archives, PHA 7558
2.	c1812	Hercules	[coll Benjamin Vulliamy]; untraced	*Murdoch* 2004, 98–9 (repr)
Busts				
3.	1802	Mrs Siddons, Lord Nelson and Mrs Deamour	[for Josiah Wedgwood]; untraced	Wedgwood/Papera L108/20403
4.	1805	Horatio, Admiral Lord Nelson, casts after Anne Seymour Damer	Untraced	*Yarrington* 1997, 41, 43 n76
5.	1806	Several, unidentified	[coll Lord Bridport]; untraced	Soane, Abstract of Bills 3, f118
Architectural Sculpture				
6.	1802	'one vase with lamp'	[for Josiah Wedgwood]; untraced	Wedgwood/Papera L108/20403

PAPERA, James Philip fl 1829–51

Probably the son of **Bartholomew Papera**, he exhibited busts at the Royal Academy between 1829 and 1831 from 16 Marylebone Street. 20 years later, whilst living at Clarendon Street, Cambridge he sent several works to the Great Exhibition (**8**).

Literary References: *Gunnis* 1968, 289; *Clifford* 1992, 61

Funerary Monuments						
1.	†1829	Mary Cripps		Cirencester, Glos	S	*CIIA* 4/4/26 (repr); Pevsner, *Glos: Cotswolds*, 1999, 254
2.	†1845	Sir Arthur Brooke Faulkner		Staplestown, Co Carlow	S	*Potterton* 1975, 74
Statues						
3.	nd	Sleeping child	m	[Phillips, 3 June 1857]; untraced		GPC
4.	nd	The infant Saviour	m	[Phillips, 3 June 1857]; untraced		GPC
Busts						
5.	1829	A child		[Exhib RA, London, 1187]; untraced		*Graves* VI, 1905–6, 47
6.	1830	Unidentified lady		[Exhib RA, London, 1228]; untraced		*Graves* VI, 1905–6, 47
7.	1831	James Philip Papera, self-portrait		[Exhib RA, London, 1142]; untraced		*Graves* VI, 1905–6, 47
Miscellaneous						
8.	1851	'Queen Elizabeth, Sir Robert Peel, the Saviour, Rubens, Vandyke, Oliver Cromwell and King Charles I'		[Gt Exhib, London]; untraced		*Great Exhib* 1851 (2), 148

PAPERA, Louisa fl 1828

The daughter of **Bartholomew Papera**, she is noted in the *London Directory* of 1828 as a 'figure maker' of 16 Marylebone Street.

Literary References: *Gunnis* 1968, 289; *Clifford* 1992, 61

Busts				
1.	nd	Sir John Herschel	Timothy Millet Ltd	S

PAPWORTH, Edgar George 1809–66

Born on 20 August 1809 and baptised on 9 January 1810 at St Marylebone, London, he was the only son of **Thomas Papworth** and his wife Sarah. Papworth's grandfather, John (1750–1799), had been the leading stuccoist of his day, the first of a dynasty of stucco workers, architects and sculptors. His early master was **Edward Hodges Baily** and he married Baily's daughter, Caroline, on 10 February 1831. There were six children.

Papworth entered the Royal Academy Schools on 15 December 1826, aged 17. He was living at 16 Caroline Street, Bedford Square when he won a silver medal for a model from the antique in December 1829 and a second came in 1831 (**57, 11**). Two years later he achieved a gold for a group of *Leucothea presenting the scarf to Ulysses* (**12**). He was awarded the silver palette by the Society of Arts, in 1827 (**54**) and exhibited regularly at the Royal Academy from 1832 onwards, showing a wide range of works, including portrait busts and statuettes, designs for monuments, metalwork and medals, and ideal works making use of biblical, mythological, historical, literary and genre subject matter.

In 1834 he won the Royal Academy's travelling scholarship and went to Italy. There he began work on his *Original Sculptural Designs*, published as a book of engravings in 1840, and he made a model of *Psyche* (**61**). He also painted a watercolour panorama of Naples, now considered an invaluable record of the city's architecture, and he made preliminary sketches for another, of Rome, which was completed some years later and exhibited briefly at a gallery in Great Portland Street about 1844. Illness forced Papworth to return home in 1837 but he seems to have made a rapid recovery and he exhibited busts of *Flora* and *Psyche* the following year (**30, 31**).

He was disappointed repeatedly in attempts to secure prominent public commissions. In 1844 he sent figures of a *Sleeping girl* and of Lord Chancellor Brougham to the Westminster Hall exhibition (**17, 16**). The Brougham was commended in the *Art Journal* as 'very easy, very good and very like' (*Gunnis* 1968, 289), but Papworth was not selected to provide sculpture for the new Palace of Westminster. His elaborate design for the memorial to the Duke of Wellington in St Paul's Cathedral features a mausoleum surmounted by a statue of Wellington. An angel closes a pair of bronze doors at the front, whilst at the back *History* records the hero's deeds (**8**). Although the model was a popular success, praised for its 'eminently solemn and sepulchral character' and 'great poetic beauty' (*AJ*, 1857, 292), it was placed only third in the competition and the commission was eventually awarded to **Alfred Stevens**. Papworth also competed unsuccessfully for the national monuments to William Wordsworth and Admiral Lord Nelson (**6, 14**). One of his last commissions was the restoration in 1862 of John Bunyan's tomb in Bunhill Fields Cemetery, where he reconstructed the effigy and added reliefs depicting scenes from *The Pilgrim's Progress* (**10**).

Papworth's extravagant and careless habits led to financial difficulties in later life. He died at his home, 36 Milton Street, Dorset Square, London, on 26 September 1866 and was buried in Highgate cemetery. His death seems to have gone unnoticed by the press. Since then Papworth's work has received little scholarly attention and only a handful of his works have been traced. In 2001 one of his busts, of an unidentified man, featured in the an exhibition in Leeds (**52**). It was displayed as it was found in an art gallery store room, without cleaning or conservation, to demonstrate the extent to which the portrait bust, as an art form, has fallen out of favour. As well as being 'poorly regarded as a work of art' this particular bust 'no longer even functions as a likeness of a known individual' (*Return to Life*, 2000, 11).

Papworth is sometimes confused with his eldest son and namesake, Edgar George Papworth II (1832–1884), who also worked as a sculptor. This younger Papworth entered the RA Schools in 1848 and exhibited at the Academy between 1852 and 1882. His best known work is a figure of a *Startled Nymph* commissioned by Joseph Neeld of Grittleton Hall and lent to the Manchester Art Treasures Exhibition in 1857.

EH

Literary References: *AJ*, 1856, 250; *Redgrave* 1878, 320; *DNB* (Moriarty); *JKB* 1966, 712; *Gunnis* 1968, 289–9; *Physick* 1970, 33, 41, 149, 150; *Penny* 1977 (1), 12, 217 n38; *Read* 1982, 84; *Yarrington* 1988, 357; *De Seta* 1994, 97–126; *Grove* 34, 1996, 86–7 (Prout); *ODNB* (Stocker)

Additional MS Sources: *Papworth Letters*

Wills: PPR, will, 27 November 1866, fo 733 (effects valued at under £100)

Funerary Monuments

1.	1833	Part of a monument to the memory of a military officer	[Exhib Soc of BA, London, 857]; untraced		*Johnson* 1975, 352
2.	?1838	Alfred Tebbitt	St George, Camberwell, London	S	*Graves* VI, 1905–6, 47; *Gunnis* 1968, 290
3.	†1841	Thomas White, his wife Mary and son, Jonathan	Wethersfield, Essex	S	*Gunnis* 1968, 290
4.	1842	Lucy Fielding, part of a monument	[Exhib RA, London, 1300]; untraced		*Graves* VI, 1905–6, 47; *Johnson* 1975, 352
5.	?1846	John Mitchel	Mancetter, Warks	S	*Gunnis* 1968, 290
6.	1852	William Wordsworth, for Westminster Abbey, sketch only (monument executed by Frederick Thrupp)	[Exhib RA, London, 1359]; untraced		*Graves* VI, 1905–6, 48
7.	1856	Sisters; part of a monument	[Exhib RA, London, 1373]; untraced		*Graves* VI, 1905–6, 48
8.	1857	Arthur, 1st Duke of Wellington, national memorial, model only (monument executed by Alfred Stevens)	Untraced		*ILN*, 12 Sept 1857, 277; *Graves* VI, 1905–6, 48; *Physick* 1970, 33, 41, 149, 150 (repr 26)
9.	†1861	Rev Samuel Wix	St Batholomew the Less, City of London	S	
10.	1862	John Bunyan (†1688), restoration	Bunhill Fields, London		*Builder*, 1862, 393; *Graves* VI, 1905–6, 48; *Gunnis* 1968, 290; C Lib (repr)

Statues

11.	1831	Figure		[Awarded RA silver medal]; untraced	*DNB*
12.	1833	Leucothea presenting the scarf to Ulysses		[Awarded RA Gold Medal]; untraced	*Graves* VI, 1905–6, 47; *Gunnis* 1968, 289
13.	1838	Minerva	s	[Royal Polytechnic, Regent Street, London]; untraced	*Builder*, 1848, 174; *Johnson* 1975, 352
14.	1839	Admiral Lord Nelson, national monument, models only (monument executed by E H Baily and William Railton)		Untraced	*Graves* VI, 1905–6, 47; *Johnson* 1975, 352; *Yarrington* 1988, 357

No.	Date	Title		Location		Literature
15.	1840	Cupid and Psyche	m	[Exhib RA, London, 1201]; untraced		*Graves* VI, 1905–6, 47; *Gunnis* 1968, 290; *Morris and Roberts* 1998, 463
16.	1844	Henry, Lord Brougham and Vaux		[Exhib Westminster Hall, London, 167]; untraced		*AU*, 1844, 216; *Gunnis* 1968, 289
17.	1844	Sleeping girl		[Exhib Westminster Hall, London]; untraced		*Gunnis* 1968, 289
18.	1854	A nymph of Diana (perhaps by E G Papworth II)		[Crystal Palace, Sydenham]; untraced		*Gunnis* 1968, 290
19.	1854	Martino, for the Crystal Palace at Sydenham		[Exhib RA, London, 1380]; untraced		*Graves* VI, 1905–6, 48
20.	1856	Douglas Jerrold, statuette		[Exhib RA, London, 1287]; untraced		*Graves* VI, 1905–6, 48
21.	1856	Rev Robert Montgomery, statuette		[Exhib RA, London, 1270]; untraced		*Graves* VI, 1905–6, 48
22.	1856	Sir Robert Peel, statuette		[Exhib RA, London, 1290]; untraced		*Graves* VI, 1905–6, 48
23.	1857	Dr Latham, statuette		[Exhib RA, London, 1350]; untraced		*Graves* VI, 1905–6, 48
24.	1858	An incident in the siege of Lucknow, statuette		[Exhib RA, London, 1202]; untraced		*Graves* VI, 1905–6, 48; C Lib (repr)
25.	1859	The young emigrant		[Exhib RA, London, 1296]; untraced		*Graves* VI, 1905–6, 48
26.	nd	Summer (perhaps by E G Papworth the Younger)		Salford AG, Lancs		*Wells* 1999, 48, 52 (repr)
Busts						
27.	1833	Henry, Lord Brougham and Vaux		[Exhib Soc of BA, London, 832]; untraced		*Johnson* 1975, 352
28.	c1836	Charles Swain	m	Manchester, CAG 1902.8		*Ormond* 1973, 442
29.	1838	Capt Godfrey Bing Webster		[Exhib RA, London, 1324]; untraced		*Graves* VI, 1905–6, 47; *Johnson* 1975, 352
30.	1838	Flora		[Exhib RA, London, 1260]; untraced		*Graves* VI, 1905–6, 47; *Johnson* 1975, 352
31.	1838	Psyche	m	[Exhib RA, London, 1356]; untraced		*Graves* VI, 1905–6, 47
32.	1838	Unidentified gentleman		[Exhib Soc of BA, London, 626]; untraced		*Johnson* 1975, 352
33.	1839	William Murdock (after Sir Francis Chantrey)	m	Birmingham MAG 2633'85		*Silber* 1987, 74–5, cat 227 (repr)
34.	1841	Sir James Fellowes FRS		[Exhib RA, London, 1152]; untraced		*Graves* VI, 1905–6, 47; *Johnson* 1975, 352
35.	1849	Mrs Saxby Penfold	m	[Exhib RA, London, 1270]; untraced		*Graves* VI, 1905–6, 48
36.	1855	Ruth	m	Royal Coll, Osborne House, I of W, RCIN 41021	SD	*ODNB*; C Lib (repr)
37.	1857	Mr and Mrs James Watts		J Watts, of Manchester		GPC
38.	1860	Admiral Blake		Shire Hall, Taunton, Somerset		*Gunnis* 1968, 290
39.	1861	Elkanah Armitage (perhaps by E G Papworth II)	m	[Salford AG, Lancs, 1936]; untraced	SD	*Gawsworth Guide*, 47; *Wells* 1999, 39, 40–1, 43, 45 (repr)
40.	1861	Unidentified gentleman	m	[Exhib RA, London, 1073]; untraced		*Graves* VI, 1905–6, 48
41.	1862	Arthur, 1st Duke of Wellington (perhaps by E G Papworth II)		Rotherham Art Gall and Museum, W R Yorks		RG/JP, 6, 1053
42.	1862	John Locke		Shire Hall, Taunton, Somerset		*ILN*, 15 March 1862, 266; *Gunnis* 1968, 290
43.	1862	The infant son of James Strange		[Exhib RA, London, 1116]; untraced		*Graves* VI, 1905–6, 48
44.	1863	Henry, 3rd Viscount Palmerston (perhaps by E G Papworth II)		Rotherham Art Gall and Museum, W R Yorks		*Johnson* 1975, 353
45.	1864	William Dyce	m	RA, London Other versions: Aberdeen Art Gallery		*Graves* VI, 1905–6, 48; *Ormond* 1973, 153; *ODNB*; C Lib (repr)
46.	1865	John Hanning Speke		Shire Hall, Taunton, Somerset		*Graves* VI, 1905–6, 48; *Ormond* 1973, 426
47.	1865	Lady Burton		[Exhib RA, London, 1024]; untraced		*Graves* VI, 1905–6, 48
48.	1865	Sir Richard Burton		[Exhib RA, London, 979]; untraced		*Graves* VI, 1905–6, 48
49.	nd	Female head (perhaps by E G Papworth II)		Salford AG, Lancs		*Wells* 1999, 48, 53 (repr)
50.	nd	Richard Cobden (perhaps by E G Papworth II)		Manchester Reform Club, Lancs		*Ormond* 1973, 109
51.	nd	Sir Henry de la Beche (perhaps by E G Papworth II)		Geological Museum, London		*Ormond* 1973, 134
52.	nd	Unidentified man	s	LMG, W R Yorks		*Ret. to Life*, 2000, 9, 61
Architectural Sculpture						
53.	1840	'When the wicked man turneth away', part of an altarpiece		[Exhib RA, London, 1081]; untraced		*Graves* VI, 1905–6, 47; *Johnson* 1975, 352
Reliefs						
54.	1827	'Copy in bas-relief of an entire figure'		[Soc of A, silver palette]; untraced		RSA *Transactions*, 1827, vol 45, xxxi
55.	1840	Queen Victoria, profile	m	[Exhib RA, London, 1126]; untraced		*Graves* VI, 1905–6, 47; *Johnson* 1975, 352; *Morris and Roberts* 1998, 463
56.	c1849	King Richard II and Bolingbroke entering London Drawing(s): RA, London, 1849, 1201		Cecil Higgins Art Gallery, Bedford		*Graves* VI, 1905–6, 48
Miscellaneous						
57.	1829	Model from the antique		[Awarded RA silver medal]; untraced		*DNB*
58.	1832	The massacre of the Innocents		[Exhib RA, London, 1112]; untraced		*Graves* VI, 1905–6, 47; *Johnson* 1975, 352
59.	1833	Infant Hercules		[Exhib RA, London, 1125]; untraced		*Graves* VI, 1905–6, 47; *Johnson* 1975, 352
60.	1834	Pastoral Apollo		[Exhib RA, London, 1079]; untraced		*Graves* VI, 1905–6, 47; *Johnson* 1975, 352
61.	1836	Psyche, model		[Exhib RA, London, 1063]; untraced		*Graves* VI, 1905–6, 47; *Johnson* 1975, 352

62.	1839	The Emancipated, part of a centrepiece for the Marquess of Sligo, model(?)		[Exhib RA, London, 1268, 1275]; untraced Other versions: 'an idea of emancipation, sketch, exhib RA, London, 1849, 1326; untraced	*Graves* VI, 1905–6, 47, 48; *Johnson* 1975, 352
63.	1840	A greyhound, model	w	[Exhib Liverpool Ac, 687]; untraced	*Morris and Roberts* 1998, 463
64.	1840	Coronation shield, model		[Exhib RA, London, 1139]; untraced	*Graves* VI, 1905–6, 47; *Johnson* 1975, 352
65.	1841	Ceres		[Exhib RA, London, 1147]; untraced	*Graves* VI, 1905–6, 47
66.	1841	Poor little Nell		[Exhib RA, London, 1233]; untraced	*Graves* VI, 1905–6, 47; *Johnson* 1975, 352
67.	1841	The contention between the Archangel and Satan for the body of Moses		[Exhib RA, London, 1234]; untraced	*Graves* VI, 1905–6, 47
68.	1842	Cupid	m	[Exhib Soc of BA, London, 784]; untraced	*Johnson* 1975, 352
69.	1842	Model for a piece of plate to be presented to the Duke of Buckingham		[Exhib RA, London, 1310]; untraced	*Graves* VI, 1905–6, 47; *Johnson* 1975, 352
70.	1842	Sketch for a piece of plate, proposed to be presented to Mr Harmer		[Exhib Soc of BA, London, 790]; untraced	*Johnson* 1975, 352
71.	1843	Cupid with the attributes of Mars, unfinished sketch		[Exhib RA, London, 1408]; untraced	*Graves* VI, 1905–6, 47
72.	1843	Psyche		[Exhib RA, London, 1528]; untraced	*Graves* VI, 1905–6, 47
73.	1844	Deliver us from evil		[Exhib RA, London, 1294]; untraced	*AU*, 1844, 170; *Graves* VI, 1905–6, 47
74.	1847	Virginia		[Exhib RA, London, 1342]; untraced	*Graves* VI, 1905–6, 47
75.	1848	The slave		[Exhib Soc of BA, London, 800]; untraced	*Johnson* 1975, 352
76.	1848	Thetis conveying the arms to Achilles		[Exhib RA, London, 1334]; untraced	*Graves* VI, 1905–6, 48
77.	1849	An idea of slavery, sketch		[Exhib RA, London, 1328]; untraced	*Graves* VI, 1905–6, 48
78.	1849	Babel destroyed		[Exhib Soc of BA, London, 339]; untraced	*Johnson* 1975, 352
79.	1850	Moabitish maiden		[coll Albert, the Prince Consort]; untraced	*Graves* VI, 1905–6, 48
80.	1853	Eva		[Exhib RA, London, 1334]; untraced	*Graves* VI, 1905–6, 48
81.	1853	Wellington entering Madrid		[Exhib RA, London, 1314]; untraced	*Graves* VI, 1905–6, 48
82.	1857	Boy with a bird's nest Model(s): exhib RA, London, 1857, 1304		[coll Mr Joyce, of Tulse Hill, London]; untraced	*Graves* VI, 1905–6, 48; *Gunnis* 1968, 290; *Johnson* 1975, 352
83.	1859	Clarence Hewitt		[Exhib RA, London, 950]; untraced	*Graves* VI, 1905–6, 48
84.	1859	Maid of Athens	m	[coll Albert, the Prince Consort]; untraced Other versions: exhib Soc of BA, London, 1859, 923	*Johnson* 1975, 352
85.	1859	The love chase (perhaps by E G Papworth II)		[Exhib LSFA, Liverpool, 756]; untraced	*Morris and Roberts* 1998, 463
86.	1861	Sir Roderick Murchison FRS		[Exhib RA, London, 1061]; untraced	*Graves* VI, 1905–6, 48
87.	1862	George Offor		[Exhib RA, London, 1102]; untraced	*Graves* VI, 1905–6, 48
88.	1863	The woman of Samaria	m	[Exhib RA, London, 1061]; untraced	*Graves* VI, 1905–6, 48
89.	1865	Adam and Eve		[Exhib RA, London, 903]; untraced	*Graves* VI, 1905–6, 48
90.	1865	David Brand		[Exhib RA, London, 1070]; untraced	*Graves* VI, 1905–6, 48
91.	1866	Andromeda		[Exhib RA, London, 964]; untraced	*Graves* VI, 1905–6, 48

PAPWORTH, Thomas 1773–1814

Thomas Papworth was the eldest son of John Papworth (1750–1799), a stuccoist frequently employed by the office of works in the time of Sir William Chambers. John and his partner, Thomas Collins, received payments amounting to £7,915 2s 8d for plasterwork at Somerset House. Papworth continued his father's work and was the owner of the last major stucco and plastering business in London. He exhibited at the Royal Academy, 1794–1815, showing designs for ceilings and sketches of candelabra, as well as a number of busts. Thomas's brothers, J B Papworth (1775–1847) and George Papworth (1781–1855) both trained as architects and his son, **Edgar George Papworth**, became a sculptor.

Literary References: *Gunnis* 1968, 290; *Colvin* V, 1973–76, 466; *Grove* 34, 1996, 86–7 (Prout)

Busts

1.	1798	T Papworth		[Exhib RA, London, 976]; untraced	*Graves* VI, 1905–6, 51
2.	1801	Unidentified artist		[Exhib RA, London, 881]; untraced	*Graves* VI, 1905–6, 51
3.	1801	Unidentified deceased gentleman		[Exhib RA, London, 879]; untraced	*Graves* VI, 1905–6, 51
4.	1801	Unidentified gentleman		[Exhib RA, London, 880]; untraced	*Graves* VI, 1905–6, 51
5.	1807	John Buonarotti Papworth		[Exhib RA, London, 1015]; untraced	*Graves* VI, 1905–6, 51; *Ormond* 1973, 363
6.	1807	Miss Mellon		[Exhib RA, London, 1103]; untraced	*Graves* VI, 1905–6, 51
7.	1814	Daughter of a friend		[Exhib RA, London, 758]; untraced	*Graves* VI, 1905–6, 51
8.	1814	Unidentified gentleman		[Exhib RA, London, 760]; untraced	*Graves* VI, 1905–6, 51
9.	1815	Unidentified gentleman		[Exhib RA, London, 906]; untraced	*Graves* VI, 1905–6, 51

Miscellaneous

10.	1799	An ornamental column designed to commemorate a naval victory		[Exhib RA, London, 996]; untraced	*Graves* VI, 1905–6, 51
11.	1802	'An unfinished model of Mr Kemble in Cato'		[Exhib RA, London, 1085]; untraced	*Graves* VI, 1905–6, 51
12.	1805	Il Penseroso, a portrait of Mrs Papworth		[Exhib RA, London, 802]; untraced	*Graves* VI, 1905–6, 51
13.	1805	Miss F Holroyd	p	[Exhib RA, London, 809]; untraced	*Graves* VI, 1905–6, 51

PARBURY, George fl 1760–91

He was described by Dossie as a pupil of George Michael Moser, the Keeper of the Royal Academy, in 1760 and as a metal chaser of Islington in 1761 (*Dossie* 1782, 437). He was employed by Matthew Boulton, making models for coins and medals including two, of *French Liberty* and the *Sierra Leone lion*, for which he was paid £13 13s in 1762 (**3**). He exhibited at the Society of Artists, 1764–1771, and the Royal Academy, 1772–1791, from addresses at Salisbury Court, Fleet Street; Mr Pember's Paper Warehouse, 111 Fleet Street; 4 Bangor Court, Shoe Lane, Fleet Street; 4 Back Road Islington; Noowel's Buildings, Islington and Mount Row, Back Road, Islington.

Literary References: *Gunnis* 1968, 290; *Pyke* 1973, 100

Reliefs

1.	1766	Africa, model for a medallion	w	[Exhib Soc of Artists, London, 212]; untraced Other versions: Africa, a model in wax, Soc of Artists special exhib, London, 1768, 158; untraced	*Graves* 1907, 188
2.	1766	King George III and Minerva consuming the implements of war, models for a medallion	w	[Exhib Soc of Artists, London, 211]; untraced	*Graves* 1907, 188
3.	1792	French Liberty and the Sierra Leone lion, two models Payment(s): £13 13s	w	[for Matthew Boulton]; untraced	*Pyke* 1973, 100

Miscellaneous

4.	1760	Model of ornaments in clay		[Soc of A, premium]; untraced	RSA, *Minutes*, 1758–60, seq 4 fol 50
5.	1761	Model of ornaments in clay, under 22 class		[Soc of A premium, 6 gns]; untraced	RSA Minutes 1760–61, seq 3 fol 48
6.	1764	Perseus and Andromeda	w	[Exhib Soc of Artists, London, 158]; untraced	*Graves* VI, 1905–6, 52
7.	1765	Telemachus and Calypso	w	[Exhib Soc of Artists, London, 179]; untraced	*Graves* 1907, 188
8.	1767	Vertumnus and Pomona, model	w	[Exhib Soc of Artists, London, 209]; untraced	*Graves* VI, 1905–6, 51–2
9.	1769	Jupiter and Leda	w	[Exhib Soc of Artists, London, 244]; untraced	*Graves* 1907, 188
10.	1771	Diana, model	w	[Exhib Soc of Artists, London, 223]; untraced	*Graves* VI, 1905–6, 52
11.	1772	Artemesia, Queen of Caria, drinking the ashes of her husband Mausoleus, model	w	[Exhib RA, London, 178]; untraced	*Graves* VI, 1905–6, 51
12.	1773	The muse Clio, model	w	[Exhib RA, London, 219]; untraced	*Graves* VI, 1905–6, 51
13.	1774	Venus and Cupid, model	w	[Exhib RA, London, 197]; untraced	*Graves* VI, 1905–6, 51
14.	1776	Cybele, model	w	[Exhib RA, London, 209]; untraced Other versions: exhib RA, London, 1789, 571; untraced	*Graves* VI, 1905–6, 51
15.	1782	Faith, model	w	[Exhib RA, London, 359]; untraced	*Graves* VI, 1905–6, 52

PARK, Patric 1811–55

A Scottish sculptor who specialised in portrait busts, he was born on 12 February 1811 in Glasgow, where his grandfather and his father, Matthew Park, both worked as masons and builders. He went to Glasgow grammar school and was then apprenticed, aged 14, to John Cornell, the mason who was building Hamilton Palace for Alexander, 10th Duke of Hamilton. Having worked there as a stone-cutter for two years, Park's skill as a carver came to the attention of the Duke and he was entrusted with the execution of the coat of arms above the main entrance (**180**). In 1828 he went to work for the architect James Gillespie Graham and spent two years carving architectural ornaments at Murthly Castle, Perthshire (**181**). Whilst pursuing this practical training he also continued his studies in drawing, mathematics and French during his free time. In October 1831 he travelled to Rome, with financial help and a letter of introduction to **Bertel Thorvaldsen** from the Duke of Hamilton. During his two years of study under Thorvaldsen he developed an interest in the heroic nude, which influenced some later, ill-fated, projects. Apparently Park, who was always impetuous, left Rome very suddenly in 1833 after a model he had just completed was knocked over and destroyed in Thorvaldsen's studio (*DNB*, XLIII, 1895, 222).

On returning to Britain he began working independently, first from a studio in Glasgow, and soon after from 8, George Street, Euston, London, where he 'lived for the most part a bachelor existence with plenty of whiskey and emancipated talk' (*Bell Scott* 1892, 162). There were clearly financial pressures from the start: a letter to Park from a Mr W Smith Williams, 1841, referred to the sculptor's lifesize portrait of Dickens (**63**) and suggested that a smaller version could be cast for 5/- and would sell well as a multiple if Park would only bring himself to make small-size models, a practice he disliked (Williams/Park, NLS 100098). By the time of his marriage to Robina Roberts, daughter of the proprietor of the *Inverness Courier*, in August 1844, Park had moved to 13 Bruton Street, Berkeley Square, where for a brief period he shared a studio with his future brother-in-law, **Alexander Munro**.

Park exhibited regularly at the Royal Academy from 1836 and at the Royal Scottish Academy in Edinburgh from 1839, as well as showing a few works at the British Institution, the Society of British Artists, the West of Scotland Academy and the Royal Manchester Institution. He sent several works to the Westminster Hall exhibitions of 1844 and 1845, held to select suitable works of art for the new Palace of Westminster (**6, 20, 22, 23**). Two years later he entered a statue, *Modesty unveiled*, for the Art Union competition, but the organisers refused to exhibit the work, which they found shocking and distasteful (**24**). Park was reprimanded for his failure to idealise the female form and the statue was condemned as 'an offensive portraiture of a model, coarse in more than average degree . . . utterly deficient of that beauty and elegance which are the great charm of the nude figure' (*AU*, 1846, 263). Fortunately Park's portraiture was less controversial. He produced numerous busts, including depictions of such celebrities as Dickens, David Octavius Hill, Macaulay,

Emperor Napoleon III and Henry Austen Layard (**63, 71, 101, 156, 160**) and carved full-size commemorative statues of Charles Tennant for Glasgow necropolis and Michael Sadler for Leeds parish church (**4, 5**).

In spite of his large practice in portrait busts Park struggled to make a living and a number of his works, including portrait busts, remained as models in plaster or clay. His blunt manner and eccentric behaviour alienated potential clients and he was unable to secure prestigious public commissions. He competed unsuccessfully for the national monument to Admiral Nelson in 1839 (**12**). His design for a statue of the admiral in modern dress, holding his sword by both hilt and blade and supported by figures of *Manhood mourning the death of Nelson* and *Honour consoled by the glory of Nelson*, was ridiculed for its obscure symbolism (*Lit Gaz*, 8 June 1839, cited by *Yarrington* 1988, 307). In 1846 he wrote to the Duke of Wellington offering to complete four high-reliefs for the pedestal of the Nelson monument at his own cost, again without success. Another unsuccessful project was a statue in bronze of the poet, Thomas Campbell for Glasgow, to be supervised by a committee headed by Sir Robert Peel (**25**). Park wrote three times to Peel asking to show the Prime Minister the model for the colossal head, but nothing appears to have come of his entreaties.

In the mid-1840s Park secured an important commission, to carve twenty life-sized statues of characters from the writings of Sir Walter Scott for the Scott Monument in Edinburgh (**182**). 14 models were exhibited at Edinburgh's Waverley Hall in March 1846 and Park again wrote to Peel, asking him to view some of them. The work was already well advanced when Park was overtaken by his financial problems, and the commission ended in disaster. Although they were already paid for, Park sold the 20 models and 13 statues, at least seven of which were finished, to prevent their being seized to cover rent arrears. For a time they decorated a merchant's garden at Clapham Common in south London. Park considered going to India to escape his problems but instead fled to Scotland in the winter of 1848–9.

From 23 York Place, Edinburgh, Park submitted 13 busts to the 1849 Royal Scottish Academy exhibition. He was elected an associate of the Royal Scottish Academy in the same year and became a full member in 1851. In 1850 he was working on the model for a monument to the Scottish hero William Wallace, which he proposed to erect on the hillside near Edinburgh (**28**). The nude figure of Wallace with the lion of Scotland was 15 feet high and required ten tons of clay. In the end Park 'abandoned the idea of proceeding further from want of encouragement and destroyed with his own mallet the model which he had so ingeniously fashioned' (*Builder*, 6 Oct 1866, 733). He had already invested much money and hard work in this ambitious project, which aggravated his financial problems and may have contributed to ill-health towards the end of his life. Park also proposed a monument to commemorate the battle of Culloden in the form of a statue of a wounded highlander, intended to mark the site of the battlefield. This scheme was not realised, but the figure was displayed at the Inverness Exhibition of Art and Industry in 1867 (**35**). Following these failures he moved in 1852 to 104 King Street Manchester. There he submitted a design for the Manchester Wellington monument but the commission went to **Matthew Noble** (**31**).

He died, aged 44, on 16 August 1855 after bursting a blood vessel while helping a porter with a heavy trunk at Warrington railway station. One obituary writer considered that 'all his works were marked by a vigorous originality, a grace of style and a delicate beauty of finish which few ever equalled' (*Building Chronicle*, 1855, 236), but a later commentator wrote that 'Park's appreciation of beauty in subjects of a more ideal kind was not equalled to his appreciation of character in portrait busts' (*Graham* 1871, 449, cited by *Gunnis* 1968, 291).

In addition to his physical work, Park also wrote on art, expounding his views in the *The Scotsman*, the *Art Union*, pamphlets and lectures. His letter to Sheriff Alison 'on the Use of Drapery in Portrait Sculpture', dated 1864, was circulated privately and his 'Observations on Hay's Theory of Proportions' were included in Hay's published reply in 1851. The Park correspondence (NLS 10098) includes some items of technical interest, other than the letters themselves. There is verbose and slightly polemical paper dated 11 June 1855 entitled 'Mechanical and artist's operations of the Art of Sculpture' (No 60), which includes a description of waste moulding (casting of the first plaster from the clay model) as practised by Park and also of bronze casting.

EH

Literary References: *Hunt* 1846, *passim*; *Scotsman*, 28 July 1849 (Park writing on the comparative cost of bronze and marble); *DNB*, XLIII, 1895, 221–3 (Gray); *Barron* III, 1913, 334; *Simpson* 1925, 16–8; *Gunnis* 1968, 290–1; *Woodward* III, 1977, 173–78; *Read* 1982, 43–4, 62, 117; *Yarrington* 1988, 292 n1, 307; *Pearson* 1991, 91–2; *Dawson* 1999, 128–31; *ODNB* (rev King)

Additional MS Sources: Park/Peel; Park/Wellington; Park/Brown; Park/Napier; Smith Williams/Park; Hamilton Archives, Lennoxlove; Combe Papers NLS MS 7231 fol FO 68 (Lawrence Macdonald to his brother James re possible sale to Park of apparatus used by LM for a colossal figure)

Portraits of the Sculptor: Kenneth Macleay, watercolour, 1859, SNPG

Funerary Monuments

No.	Date	Work		Location		Reference
1.	†1835	Andrew Milne		New Calton burying ground, Edinburgh		Pevsner, *Edinburgh*, 1991, 438
2.	?1836	Andrew Skene		New Calton burying ground, Edinburgh	S	*Gunnis* 1968, 291
3.	†1839	Jane Richardson		Sigglesthorne, E R Yorks	S	Pevsner, *Yorks: E R & York*, 1995, 682
4.	1841	Charles Tennant (†1838)		Glasgow Necropolis		*Graves* VI, 1905–6, 53; *McKenzie* 2002, 300 (repr)
5.	1837–1841	Michael Sadler MP (†1835) Model(s): exhib RA, London, 1837, 1166; RA, London, 1842, 1282		[St Peter, Leeds, W R Yorks]; Leeds University cemetery, W R Yorks		*Graves* VI, 1905–6, 53; Pevsner, *Yorks: W R*, 1967, 312; *ODNB*
6.	1845	Design for a monument to Campbell, the poet		[Exhib Westminster Hall, London, 141]; untraced		*Westminster* 1845, 16–17; *Hunt* 1846, 141
7.	c1846	Johnstone mausoleum, with a bust on a pillar (perhaps not fully realised)		Alva House, Clackmannanshire		Park Corr, 74, NLS 10098

Statues

No.	Date	Work		Location		Reference
8.	c1833	Ixion on the wheel		Untraced		*DNB*, XLIII, 1895, 222
9.	1837	A sphaerobolos or ball-thrower, the son of Alcinous preparing to dance before Ulysses	p	[Exhib RA, London, 1172]; untraced		*Graves* VI, 1905–6, 53; *Laperriere* 4, 1991, 413; *Morris and Roberts* 1998, 463

No.	Date	Subject	Medium	Location		Literature
10.	1838	Robert McIan		[Exhib Soc of BA, London, 604]; untraced		*Johnson* 1975, 353
11.	1838	Sir Walter Scott, monument for Calton Hill, Edinburgh, design only		[Exhib RA, London, 1351]; untraced		*Graves* VI, 1905–6, 53
12.	1839	Admiral Lord Nelson, national monument, model only (monument executed by E H Baily and William Railton)		Untraced		*Graves* VI, 1905–6, 53; *Gunnis* 1968, 290; *Yarrington* 1988, 307
13.	1840	A child in the bath	m	Palm House, Sefton Park, Liverpool, Lancs	SD	*Graves* 1875, 414; *Read* 1982, 43–5 (repr); *Cavanagh* 1997, 204 (repr)
14.	1841	Genius bound		[Exhib Soc of BA, London, 817]; untraced		*Johnson* 1975, 353
15.	1841	Lord Lovelace's children		[coll Lady Noel Byron]; untraced		*DNB*, XLIII, 1895, 222; *Graves* VI, 1905–6, 53
16.	1842	A Greek warrior crouching, illustrative of caution and resolution		[Exhib RA, London, 1291]; untraced		*AU*, 1842, 128; *Graves* VI, 1905–6, 53; *Johnson* 1975, 353
17.	1842	Alexander Johnstone		[Exhib Soc of BA, London, 799]; untraced		*Johnson* 1975, 353
18.	1843	Eliza	m	[Exhib BI, London, 432]; untraced		*Graves* 1875, 414
19.	1843	Hector reflective	p	[Exhib RA, London, 1420]; untraced		*Graves* VI, 1905–6, 53
20.	1844	The descent of Mercury with the Cestus of Venus		[Exhib Westminster Hall, London, 86]; untraced		*AU*, 1844, 214; *DNB*, XLIII, 1895, 222; *Johnson* 1975, 353
21.	1845	Alexander	m	[Exhib BI, London, 520]; untraced		*Graves* 1875, 414
22.	1845	An attendant, Greek huntsman and dog		[Exhib Westminster Hall, London, 136]; untraced		*Westminster* 1845, 26; *AU*, 1845, 258; *Hunt* 1846, 185; *Gunnis* 1968, 290
23.	1845	Thomas Campbell, model for a monument	p	[Exhib Westminster Hall, London, 141]; untraced		*AU*, 1845, 258
24.	1846	Modesty unveiled		[Art Union Competition]; untraced		*AU*, 1846, 263; *Gunnis* 1968, 290
25.	1845–1846	Study for the head of a bronze statue of Thomas Campbell, to be erected in Glasgow		[Park's studio]; untraced		Park/Peel 30 Nov 1845 (fol 101); 2.12.1845 (fol 165); 22 May 1846 (fol 251)
26.	1847	Impartiality	m	[Exhib BI, London, 546]; untraced		*Graves* 1875, 414
27.	1850	Sir Charles James Napier addressing his troops, equestrian statuette		[Exhib R Sc A, Edinburgh, 480]; untraced		*Laperriere* 4, 1991, 414
28.	1850	William Wallace, model only	tc	Destroyed		*Scotsman*, 14 Aug 1850, 7 Sept 1850; *Builder*, 6 Oct 1866, 733; *DNB*, XLIII, 1895, 222; *Gunnis* 1968, 290
29.	1851	Francis Abbott, fragment		[Exhib R Sc A, Edinburgh, 666]; untraced		*Laperriere* 4, 1991, 414
30.	1851	Lieut-Col Spark commanding 93rd Highlanders, statuette		[Exhib R Sc A, Edinburgh, 646]; untraced		*Laperriere* 4, 1991, 414
31.	c1852	Arthur, 1st Duke of Wellington, monument for Manchester, design only (monument executed by Matthew Noble)		Untraced		*DNB*, XLIII, 1895, 222–3
32.	1853	Daughters of R N Philips	m	Untraced		*Laperriere* 4, 1991, 414
33.	1856	Child		[Exhib R Sc A, Edinburgh, 741]; untraced		*Laperriere* 4, 1991, 415
34.	nd	Two children with hound	m	[coll G Stuart Robertson, of London]; untraced		*Laperriere* 4, 1991, 415
35.	nd	Wounded highlander (a monument commemorating the Battle of Culloden)		[Art and Industry Exhib, Inverness, 1867]; untraced		*Simpson* 1925, 17
Busts						
36.	c1833	Alexander, Duke of Hamilton		Untraced		*DNB*, XLIII, 1895, 222
37.	post-1833	Sir William Allan		Untraced		*DNB*, XLIII, 1895, 222
38.	1834	'Mr Brown'		[Hamilton Palace, Lanarks]; untraced	SD	Hamilton Palace sale, 13 Nov 1919
39.	1836	Duke of Newcastle	m	[Exhib RA, London, 1115]; untraced		*Graves* VI, 1905–6, 53
40.	1836	Henry, Earl of Lincoln, later 5th Duke of Newcastle	m	[Exhib RA, London, 1101]; untraced		*Graves* VI, 1905–6, 53; *Ormond* 1973, 338
41.	1836	Lord Clinton	m	[Exhib RA, London, 1138]; untraced		*Graves* VI, 1905–6, 53
42.	1837	George Browne		[Exhib Soc of BA, London, 582]; untraced		*Johnson* 1975, 353
43.	1837	Robert Brown	m	[Exhib RA, London, 1240]; untraced		*Graves* VI, 1905–6, 53
44.	1838	Benjamin Robert Haydon		[Exhib Soc of BA, London, 610]; untraced		*Johnson* 1975, 353; *Laperriere* 4, 1991, 413
45.	c1838	Charles Tennant	p	Glasgow Museums S.103		*McKenzie* 2002, 300
46.	1838	Fanny McIan		[Exhib Soc of BA, London, 599]; untraced		*Johnson* 1975, 353
47.	1838	Michael Sadler MP		[Exhib Soc of BA, London, 631]; untraced		*Johnson* 1975, 353
48.	1838	Miss Rainsforth		[Exhib Soc of BA, London, 611]; untraced		*Johnson* 1975, 353
49.	1838	Sir John Bowring		[Exhib Soc of BA, London, 624]; untraced		*Johnson* 1975, 353
50.	1838	Theodore von Holst		[Exhib Soc of BA, London, 617]; untraced		*Johnson* 1975, 353
51.	1838	The sculptor's brother		[Exhib Soc of BA, London, 635]; untraced		*Johnson* 1975, 353

52.	1839	John Landseer ARA		[Exhib R Sc A, Edinburgh, 501]; untraced		*Johnson* 1975, 353; *Laperriere* 4, 1991, 413
53.	1839	Thomas Campbell		untraced		*Gunnis* 1968, 291
54.	1840	A lady		[Exhib R Sc A, Edinburgh, 369]; untraced		*Laperriere* 4, 1991, 413
55.	1840	David E Williams		[Exhib RA, London, 1132]; untraced		*Graves* VI, 1905–6, 53
56.	1840	Dr Walmsley, rector of Hanwell		[Exhib RA, London, 1157]; untraced		*Graves* VI, 1905–6, 53; *Johnson* 1975, 353
57.	1840	Edward Gibbon Wakefield		[Exhib RA, London, 1166]; untraced		*Graves* VI, 1905–6, 53
58.	1840	Francis, Lord Jeffrey		SNPG, Edinburgh Other versions: NPG 133 m 1840		*Gunnis* 1968, 291; *Laperriere* 4, 1991, 413, 414
59.	1840	John Black		[Exhib RA, London, 1165]; untraced		*Graves* VI, 1905–6, 53
60.	1840	Mr Rintoul		[Exhib RA, London, 1143]; untraced		*Graves* VI, 1905–6, 53
61.	1840	Sir Thomas Dick Lauder Bt		[Exhib R Sc A, Edinburgh, 377]; untraced		*Laperriere* 4, 1991, 413
62.	1840	Unidentified man	m	Glasgow Museums TEMP.11881		inf: Glasgow Museums
63.	1841	Charles Dickens	m	[Exhib Soc of BA, London, 820]; untraced Other versions: Two known		McCulloch sale, 1867, lot 553; *DNB*, XLIII, 1895, 222; *Graves* VI, 1905–6, 53; *Johnson* 1975, 353; *Laperriere* 4, 1991, 413
64.	1841	Daniel Maclise		[Exhib Soc of BA, London, 820]; untraced		*Johnson* 1975, 353
65.	1841	J Dodgson		[Exhib Soc of BA, London, 824]; untraced		*Johnson* 1975, 353
66.	*c*1841	Sir Charles Barry		Reform Club, City of Westminster, London, staircase	S	*Ormond* 1973, 29
67.	1841	Thomas Landseer		[Exhib Soc of BA, London, 822]; untraced		*Johnson* 1975, 353
68.	1841	Unidentified gentleman		[Exhib R Sc A, Edinburgh, 551]; untraced		*Laperriere* 4, 1991, 413
69.	1842	Admiral Sir George Cockburn		[Exhib RA, London, 1328]; untraced		*Graves* VI, 1905–6, 53; *Johnson* 1975, 353
70.	1842	Allan Fullarton	m	[Exhib RA, London, 1366]; untraced		*Graves* VI, 1905–6, 53
71.	1842	David Octavius Hill RSA, model only (executed in marble by John Hutchinson RSA in 1880)		SNPG, Edinburgh		*R Sc A Art Property*, 1883; *Laperriere* 4, 1991, 413, 414, 415; *Gunnis* 1968, 291
72.	1842	Dr Brown, of St John's, Glasgow		[Exhib Soc of BA, London, 797]; untraced		*Johnson* 1975, 353
73.	1842	Dr Norman McLeod		[Exhib RA, London, 1381]; untraced		*Graves* VI, 1905–6, 53
74.	1842	Dr S Dickson		[Exhib Soc of BA, London, 796]; untraced		*Johnson* 1975, 353
75.	1842	James Jardine	m	SNPG 1203	SD	*Laperriere* 4, 1991, 413, 414; *Ret to Life*, 2000, 19, 63 (repr)
76.	1842	James Miller		[Exhib R Sc A, Edinburgh, 527]; untraced		*Laperriere* 4, 1991, 413
77.	1842	James Oswald	m	Glasgow Museums S.70		*Gunnis* 1968, 291
78.	1842	John Forster		[Exhib Soc of BA, London, 798]; untraced		*Johnson* 1975, 353
79.	1842	Mrs Finlay		[Exhib R Sc A, Edinburgh, 528]; untraced		*Laperriere* 4, 1991, 413
80.	1842	Mrs Lees		[Exhib R Sc A, Edinburgh, 538]; untraced		*Laperriere* 4, 1991, 413
81.	1842	Patrick Robertson		[Exhib R Sc A, Edinburgh, 530]; untraced		*Laperriere* 4, 1991, 413
82.	1842	Sir Charles Napier		[Exhib Soc of BA, London, 795]; untraced		*Johnson* 1975, 353; *Laperriere* 4, 1991, 413
83.	1842	Thomas Duncan RSA, model only		[Exhib R Sc A, Edinburgh, 529]; NGS, Edinburgh		*R Sc A Art Property*, 1883; *Laperriere* 4, 1991, 413, 415
84.	1842	Unidentified gentleman		[Exhib R Sc A, Edinburgh, 526]; untraced		*Laperriere* 4, 1991, 413
85.	1842	W T Musgrave		[Exhib R Sc A, Edinburgh, 540]; untraced		*Laperriere* 4, 1991, 413
86.	1843	Master John Malcolm		[Exhib R Sc A, Edinburgh, 593]; untraced		*Laperriere* 4, 1991, 414
87.	1843	Mrs Robertson	m	[Exhib RA, London, 1466]; untraced		*Graves* VI, 1905–6, 53
88.	1843	William Scott	m	[Exhib R Sc A, Edinburgh, 578]; untraced		*Laperriere* 4, 1991, 414
89.	1844	Charles Brown	m	[Exhib RA, London, 1322]; untraced		*AU*, 1844, 171; *Graves* VI, 1905–6, 53
90.	1844	John Sands		[Exhib RA, London, 1365]; untraced		*Graves* VI, 1905–6, 53
91.	1844	M H Barker RN ('the old sailor')	p	[Exhib RA, London, 1350]; untraced		*Graves* VI, 1905–6, 53
92.	1844	Mrs Mackay	p	[Exhib RA, London, 1379]; untraced		*AU*, 1844, 171; *Graves* VI, 1905–6, 53
93.	1844	Sir William Ross RA	p	[Exhib RA, London, 1352]; untraced		*Graves* VI, 1905–6, 53
94.	1844	The Bairds of Gartsherrie		untraced		*DNB*, XLIII, 1895, 222
95.	1845	Adam Smith	m	Glasgow Museums S.11		*Gunnis* 1968, 291
96.	1845	John Heraud		[Exhib Soc of BA, London, 834]; untraced		*Johnson* 1975, 353
97.	1845	Rev Mr Antrobus		[Exhib RA, London, 1388]; untraced		*Graves* VI, 1905–6, 53
98.	1845	Thomas Wyse MP		[Exhib Soc of BA, London, 833]; untraced		*Johnson* 1975, 353
99.	1845	William Dixon		[Exhib RA, London, 1457]; untraced		*Graves* VI, 1905–6, 53
100.	1846	John Huggins		[Huggins College, Gravesend, Kent]; untraced Other versions: exhib Soc of BA, London, 1842, 794, marble; untraced		*Gunnis* 1968, 291; *Johnson* 1975, 353; *Knox* 1996, 92, 96 n50

No.	Date	Subject		Location	Literature
101.	1846	Thomas, 1st Baron Macaulay	p	Wallington, Northumbs (NT)	*Ormond* 1973, 289
102.	1847	James Reddie		Library of the Faculty of Advocates, Glasgow	*Laperriere* 4, 1991, 414
103.	1847	Major-General Sir Harry Smith		[Exhib R Sc A, Edinburgh, 1848, 618]; untraced	*Graves* VI, 1905–6, 53; *Ormond* 1973, 421; *Laperriere* 4, 1991, 414
104.	1848	Thomas, 10th Earl of Dundonald	m	[Exhib R Sc A, Edinburgh, 615]; untraced	*Graves* VI, 1905–6, 54; *Laperriere* 4, 1991, 414, 415
105.	1849	A young lady		[Exhib R Sc A, Edinburgh, 616]; untraced	*Laperriere* 4, 1991, 414
106.	1849	Alex Dunlop		[Exhib R Sc A, Edinburgh, 621]; untraced	*Laperriere* 4, 1991, 414
107.	1849	Hon John Jeffrey		[Exhib R Sc A, Edinburgh, 605]; untraced	*Laperriere* 4, 1991, 414
108.	1849	Horatio McCulloch RSA		R Sc A, Edinburgh	*Gunnis* 1968, 291; *Laperriere* 4, 1991, 414, 415
109.	1849	Lieut-Gen Sir Neil Douglas		[Exhib R Sc A, Edinburgh, 620]; untraced	*Laperriere* 4, 1991, 414
110.	1849	P S Fraser		[Exhib R Sc A, Edinburgh, 613]; untraced	*Laperriere* 4, 1991, 414
111.	1849	Rev Dr Begg		[Exhib R Sc A, Edinburgh, 603]; untraced	*Laperriere* 4, 1991, 414
112.	1849	Rev John Bruce		[Exhib R Sc A, Edinburgh, 604]; untraced	*Laperriere* 4, 1991, 414
113.	1849	Rev Samuel Miller		[Exhib R Sc A, Edinburgh, 607]; untraced	*Laperriere* 4, 1991, 414
114.	1849	Rev Thomas Guthrie		[Exhib R Sc A, Edinburgh, 606]; untraced	*Laperriere* 4, 1991, 414
115.	1849	Sir Charles James Napier		[Exhib R Sc A, Edinburgh, 612]; untraced	*Graves* VI, 1905–6, 53; *Laperriere* 4, 1991, 414
116.	*c*1849	The artist's wife	p	Glasgow Museums S.96	*Laperriere* 4, 1991, 414, 415
117.	1850	'A young gentleman'	m	[Exhib R Sc A, Edinburgh, 468]; untraced	*Laperriere* 4, 1991, 414
118.	1850	James Kinnear (cast by Mr Milne)	b	[Exhib R Sc A, Edinburgh, 479]; untraced	*Laperriere* 4, 1991, 414
119.	1850	John Miller	m	[Exhib R Sc A, Edinburgh, 467]; untraced	*Laperriere* 4, 1991, 414
120.	1850	Lady Anne Charteris		[Exhib R Sc A, Edinburgh, 463]; untraced	*Graves* VI, 1905–6, 54; *Laperriere* 4, 1991, 414
121.	1850	Oliver Cromwell	p	[Exhib R Sc A, Edinburgh, 465]; NGS, Edinburgh	*R Sc A annual report*, 1862, 11; *Graves* VI, 1905–6, 53; *Laperriere* 4, 1991, 414
122.	1850	Professor Simpson		SNPG, Edinburgh	*Graves* VI, 1905–6, 53; *Gunnis* 1968, 291; *Laperriere* 4, 1991, 414
123.	1851	Dr Malcolm		[Exhib R Sc A, Edinburgh, 651]; untraced	*Laperriere* 4, 1991, 414
124.	1851	James Stewart		[Exhib R Sc A, Edinburgh, 647]; untraced	*Laperriere* 4, 1991, 414
125.	1851	Kenneth Macleay RSA	p	[Exhib R Sc A, Edinburgh, 655]; destroyed	*R Sc A Art Property*, 1883; *Laperriere* 4, 1991, 414
126.	1851	Mrs W M Ellis	m	[Exhib R Sc A, Edinburgh, 648]; untraced	*Laperriere* 4, 1991, 414
127.	1851	Sir David Brewster		[Exhib R Sc A, Edinburgh, 658]; untraced	*Laperriere* 4, 1991, 414
128.	1851	Sir John Watson Gordon RA PRSA		R Sc A, Edinburgh	*R Sc A Art Property*, 1883; *Graves* VI, 1905–6, 54; *Gunnis* 1968, 291; *Laperriere* 4, 1991, 414, 415
129.	1851	The Very Rev Principal Lee		[Exhib R Sc A, Edinburgh, 645]; untraced	*Laperriere* 4, 1991, 414
130.	*c*1851	William Edmondstoune Aytoun	p	[coll William Edmondstoune Aytoun]; NPG 1544	*Laperriere* 4, 1991, 414, 415
131.	1852	A lady		[Exhib R Sc A, Edinburgh, 677]; untraced	*Laperriere* 4, 1991, 414
132.	1852	'An elderly lady'		[Exhib RA, London, 1433]; untraced	*Graves* VI, 1905–6, 54
133.	1852	David Ness		[Exhib R Sc A, Edinburgh, 676]; untraced	*Laperriere* 4, 1991, 414
134.	1852	Francis Carr Beard		[Exhib RA, London, 1470]; untraced	*Graves* VI, 1905–6, 54
135.	1852	Grant of Glen Morriston (a highland chieftain) Model(s): exhib R Sc A, Edinburgh, 1852, 678 (model of the marble bust for the family of Grant of Glenmorriston); RA, London, 1854, 1490		[Exhib Inverness Castle]; untraced	*Graves* VI, 1905–6, 54; *Simpson* 1925, 17–8; *Laperriere* 4, 1991, 414
136.	1852	John Inglis, study		[Exhib R Sc A, Edinburgh, 713]; untraced	*Laperriere* 4, 1991, 414
137.	1848–1852	Lady Elcho		Untraced	*DNB*, XLIII, 1895, 222
138.	1852	Master George Harrison Park		[Exhib RA, London, 1462]; untraced	*Graves* VI, 1905–6, 54
139.	1852	Mrs C D Young		[Exhib R Sc A, Edinburgh, 684]; untraced	*Laperriere* 4, 1991, 414
140.	1852	Mrs John Griffith Frith	m	[Exhib RA, London, 1454]; untraced	*Graves* VI, 1905–6, 54
141.	1852	Mrs John Sands	m	[Exhib RA, London, 1415]; untraced	*Graves* VI, 1905–6, 54
142.	1852	Mrs John Scott	m	[Exhib R Sc A, Edinburgh, 710]; untraced	*Graves* VI, 1905–6, 54; *Laperriere* 4, 1991, 414
143.	1852	Mrs Kenneth Macleay, model		[Exhib R Sc A, Edinburgh, 679]; untraced	*Laperriere* 4, 1991, 414

144.	1852	Rev Henry Grey	m	New College, Edinburgh University		*Pearson* 1991, unpag; *Laperriere* 4, 1991, 414
145.	?1852	The artist's mother	p	Glasgow Museums S.95		*Johnson* 1975, 353
146.	1852	Unidentified lady		[Exhib RA, London, 1435]; untraced		*Graves* VI, 1905–6, 54
147.	1853	Admiral Sir Charles Napier		[coll Emperor Napoleon III]; untraced		*Gunnis* 1968, 291
148.	1853	Countess of Zetland		[Exhib RA, London, 1403]; untraced		*Graves* VI, 1905–6, 54
149.	c1853	John Thomson Gordon		[coll Mrs Gordon]; untraced		*Graves* VI, 1905–6, 54; *Laperriere* 4, 1991, 415
150.	1854	Dr Charles Bell		[Exhib R Sc A, Edinburgh, 700]; untraced		*Laperriere* 4, 1991, 414
151.	1854	Lord Justice-General David Boyle		[coll Soc of Scottish Solicitors]; untraced		GPC; *Laperriere* 4, 1991, 414
152.	1854	Robert Shadwick		[Exhib RA, London, 1430]; untraced		*Graves* VI, 1905–6, 54
153.	1854	Sir James Bardsley MD		[Exhib RA, London, 1436]; untraced		*Graves* VI, 1905–6, 54
154.	1854	Sir John Potter		Manchester Free Library, Lancs		*Gunnis* 1968, 291
155.	1854	William Bevan		[Exhib R Sc A, Edinburgh, 714]; untraced		*Laperriere* 4, 1991, 415
156.	1855	Emperor Napoleon III Payment(s): £150	m	VAM 2637-1856 Other versions: ex Hamilton Palace, Lanarks, 1854, marble; untraced ex Glasgow Museums S.94; destr	SD	Park Corr 1854, NLS 10098; *Graves* VI, 1905–6, 54; *Gunnis* 1968, 291; *Laperriere* 4, 1991, 415; *Bilbey* 2002, 347 (repr)
157.	1855	Joseph Whitworth	m	Gawsworth Hall, Cheshire	SD	*Gawsworth Guide*, 44, 46 (repr)
158.	1855	Mark Phillips	m	[Exhib RA, London, 1469]; untraced		*Graves* VI, 1905–6, 54
159.	1855	Mrs Houldsworth	m	[Exhib R Sc A, Edinburgh, 748]; untraced		*Laperriere* 4, 1991, 415
160.	1855	Sir Austen Henry Layard CGB	m	BM	SD	*Manchester Art Treasures* 1857, 136; McCulloch sale, 1867, lot 555; *Laperriere* 4, 1991, 415; *Dawson* 1999, 128–31 (repr)
161.	c1855	Sir William Fairbairn		Royal Society, London		*Gunnis* 1968, 291; *Laperriere* 4, 1991, 415
162.	1855	Unidentified lady	m	[Exhib RA, London, 1476]; untraced		*Graves* VI, 1905–6, 54
163.	1855	William Fergusson		[Exhib R Sc A, Edinburgh, 769]; untraced		*Laperriere* 4, 1991, 415
164.	1856	A boy		[Exhib R Sc A, Edinburgh, 739]; untraced		*Laperriere* 4, 1991, 415
165.	c1856	A Scotch lassie, model (executed in marble by William Brodie)		NGS, Edinburgh Other versions: ex Glasgow Museums S.97, plaster; destroyed		*R Sc A Art Property*, 1883, 39; *Gunnis* 1968, 291; *Laperriere* 4, 1991, 415
166.	1856	Duke of Cambridge		[Exhib R Sc A, Edinburgh, 725, coll Horatio McCulloch]; untraced		*McCullouch* 1867, lot 554; *Laperriere* 4, 1991, 415
167.	nd	A child	p	[Glasgow Museums S.98]; destroyed		inf: Glasgow Museums
168.	nd	Andrew Dalglish		People's Palace, Glasgow		RG/JP, 6, 1062
169.	nd	Charles Mackay	p	Perth Art Gallery		GPC
170.	nd	David Hamilton	m	Glasgow Museums S.42 Other versions: SNPG, Edinburgh		*Gunnis* 1968, 291; *Laperriere* 4, 1991, 415
171.	nd	Empress Eugénie	m	[Hamilton Palace]; untraced		Hamilton Palace sale, 13 Nov 1919, lot 323
172.	nd	Horatio MacCulloch, model, only (commissioned by the Royal Scottish Academy and executed in marble by W G Stevenson, 1873)		NGS, Edinburgh		*R Sc A Art Property*, 1883
173.	nd	James Hutton		Geological Museum, London		*Gunnis* 1968, 291
174.	nd	Principal Cunninghame, model only (carved in marble by John G Mossman)		Untraced		*Laperriere* 4, 1991, 415
175.	nd	Sir Archibald Alison		SNPG, Edinburgh		*Gunnis* 1968, 291
176.	nd	Sir Francis Jeffery		John Fairrie sale, Christie, 22 April 1861		GPC
177.	nd	Sir James Hall		Geological Museum, London		*Gunnis* 1968, 291
178.	nd	Unidentified woman	m	Aske Hall, N R Yorks	S	
179.	nd	William Fraser-Tytler	m	[Duns Castle, Berwickshire]; Knox/Longstaffe-Gowan coll (acq 1998) Other versions: Inverness Castle		*Simpson* 1925, 17

Architectural Sculpture

180.	c1827	Coat of arms		[Hamilton Palace, Lanarks, above main entrance]; untraced		*Gunnis* 1968, 290
181.	1828	Decorative details (designed by James Graham Gillespie)		Murthly Castle, Perths		*Gunnis* 1968, 290
182.	1846	Seven statues of characters from Sir Walter Scott (originally intended for Scott Monument)		[Private garden, Clapham Common, London]; untraced		*Read* 1982, 117

Miscellaneous

183.	1837	Portrait of a celebrated Scottish greyhound		[Exhib Soc of BA, London, 615]; untraced		*Johnson* 1975, 353
184.	1837	Theseus slaying Coesus		[Exhib BI, London, 439]; untraced		*Graves* 1875, 414
185.	1838	Diomede, a youth submissive to counsel		[Exhib Soc of BA, London, 641]; untraced		*Johnson* 1975, 353; *Laperriere* 4, 1991, 413
186.	1838	Research		[Exhib BI, London, 488]; untraced		*Graves* 1875, 414
187.	1849	The artist's son		[Exhib R Sc A, Edinburgh, 619]; untraced		*Laperriere* 4, 1991, 414

188.	1850	Child, daughter of A S Logan		[Exhib R Sc A, Edinburgh, 475]; untraced	*Laperriere* 4, 1991, 414
189.	1850	Early efforts		[Exhib R Sc A, Edinburgh, 473]; untraced	*Laperriere* 4, 1991, 414
190.	1851	Mask	m	[Exhib R Sc A, Edinburgh, 659]; untraced	*Laperriere* 4, 1991, 414
191.	1852	Diomed before the lightning		[Exhib R Sc A, Edinburgh, 695]; untraced	*Laperriere* 4, 1991, 414
192.	1853	Dying child	m	[Exhib BI, London, 571]; untraced	*Graves* 1875, 414
193.	1854	A Huguenot leader		[Exhib R Sc A, Edinburgh, 715]; untraced	*Laperriere* 4, 1991, 415
194.	1854	Euphrosyne		[Exhib R Sc A, Edinburgh, 708]; untraced	*Laperriere* 4, 1991, 415
195.	1854	Sisterly affection and protection		[Exhib BI, London, 573]; untraced	*Graves* 1875, 414

PARK, William *c*1829–

For further information the reader is referred to *Pyke* 1973, 101

PARKER, G G

For further information the reader is referred to *Pyke* 1973, 101 and *Pyke* 1981, 31

PARKER, Richard fl 1768–74

Parker was employed by Wedgwood. The firm's archives contain a letter written about 1769 from William Cox, the London agent, in which he informs Wedgwood that 'Mr. Parker has cast the medallions off in the best manner him and I could well contrive. I should be glad of your notes respecting the propriety or Deserts of the Performance' (Wedgwood/Parker E5/30873, Cox to Wedgwood, undated).

He apparently specialized in making casts, for a bill sent to Wedgwood in 1774 has the following printed heading: 'SCAGLIOLA; / OR PLASTER CASTS OF ELEGANT SUBJECTS / Proper to introduce in the Decoration of ROOMS, STAIR-CASES, HALLS &c / RICHARD PARKER / OPPOSITE THE NEW CHURCH IN THE STRAND / HAVING obtained from Joseph Wilton Esq. Statuary to His Majesty, / various Moulds of Bas Reliefs and Busto's, made upon his Original models, / has the Honour to acquaint the Nobility and Gentry, that they may be accommodated with Casts at the Shortest Notice. Sundry Samples of which, with / their prices be seen at the above RICHARD PARKER'S. / N.B. These Original Casts, can be had at no other place; and although it may happen / that some Figure Makers may clandestinely make Moulds of any of those Casts, they can / produce at best, but an Impression void of every Original Touch' (Wedgwood/Parker L1/74, Richard Parker acct, 10 Feb 1774). In that year he supplied Wedgwood with three models (7). The last of these was a cast after **L F Roubiliac** of Hogarth's dog, Trump, which the potter used as the model for a version in black basaltware. It is possible that the celebrated Chelsea porcelain pug was also based on one of Parker's casts.

Gunnis notes that at Ashburnham Place there was a set of library busts by Parker based on works by well-known sculptors such as Roubiliac and **Michael Rysbrack** and that this set, which includes likenesses of Locke, Milton, Congreve, Prior and Inigo Jones, is similar to one in the possession of Lord Trevor, at Brynkinalt, Denbigh (1). Parker also made wax portraits, on one of which is a trade label reading 'Mr. Parker, modeller, 40 Kathleen Place, Oxford Street, medallions, busts, statuettes modelled' (*Pyke* 1973, 101).

Literary References: *Gunnis* 1968, 291; *Pyke* 1973, 101; *Clifford* 1992, 42–3, 62

Busts					
1.	*c*1770	Locke, Milton, Congreve, Prior, Inigo Jones and others, casts		Ashburnham Place, Sussex	*Gunnis* 1968, 291; Ingamells forthcoming
Reliefs					
2.	nd	Unidentified divine	w	ex coll Rupert Gunnis; untraced	*Pyke* 1973, 101
3.	nd	Unidentified man	w	Coll Sir Harry Page, Manchester (1973)	*Pyke* 1973, 101
4.	nd	William Pitt the Younger	w	Bristol City Art Gallery	*Pyke* 1973, 101 (repr 207)
Miscellaneous					
5.	1768	Anatomical statue		[coll 3rd Duke of Atholl]; untraced	Blair Castle Archives, in GPC
6.	1768	Group of Venus and Hercules		[coll 3rd Duke of Atholl]; untraced	Blair Castle Archives, in GPC
7.	1774	'Zingara', 'Vestal' and 'Pug Dog' Payment(s): £2 5s 6d (including packing case)		[for Josiah Wedgwood]; untraced	*Clifford* 1992, 62

PARKER, Samuel fl 1820–51

Parker was a London craftsman working principally in bronze. He was almost certainly the grandson of William Parker, a glass manufacturer, and the son of Samuel Parker, who took over the family business at 69 Fleet Street in 1798. William Parker and his successors were George IV's chief lighting suppliers, providing him with chandeliers, patent lamps, candlearms and lanterns. These were usually of cut glass and incorporated gilt-bronze fittings. The younger Samuel Parker worked with his father and brother for a time but by 1820 he had moved to 35 Argyll Street and set up on his own account as a bronze manufacturer. From 1824 onwards he had a workshop at 12 Argyll Place, in addition to the Argyll Street house.

In 1821–2 Parker made a marble chimneypiece with ormolu mounts to designs of Robert Jones, for the Royal Pavilion at Brighton (4). This sumptuous work features two large Chinese figures in niches, cast in metal by Parker and painted in imitation of enamel by Jones. Parker supplied the accompanying fender and fire irons, as well as decorative ormolu mounts for a clock plinth (the marble was provided by **Henry Westmacott**), a pair of candelabra, a pot-pourri tripod incorporating pieces of oriental porcelain and two cabinets, all designed by Jones for the same room. Not all his work there was of the expected standard. Deficiencies in the metal door handles he had supplied were later made good by **James de Ville**.

Parker's work clearly found favour with both George IV and his architect John Nash, for he was employed in the remodelling of Buckingham Palace during the 1820s and 1830s. For the exterior he provided railings and the grand gates of the marble arch. His internal work included gilt-bronze ornaments for doors and door-cases, Corinthian capitals for columns and three staircase balustrades, of which the most opulent and ambitious was the balustrade for the principal staircase. It cost £3,900 and has been described as 'probably the finest example of applied metal-work of the Regency period' (*Smith* 1931, 131–2).

On addition to his ornamental work, Parker was responsible for a number of small bronze busts. At the Great Exhibition of 1851 a Mr Peachey showed a bronze bust of Sir Thomas Lawrence by Parker, 'made in London from a model produced at great cost and afterwards destroyed' (*Great Exhib* 1851 (1), vol II, 841, in *Gunnis* 1968, 291) (**3**). A bronze high-relief portrait of Sir Walter Scott after **Samuel Joseph** in the Ashmolean is thought to be Parker's work because it is similar to the portrait of Henry Mackenzie, which is inscribed 'SAML JOSEPH SCULPSIT / S. PARKER FECIT XII ARGYLL PLACE / PUBLISHD / AS THE ACT DIRECTS / LONDON FEBY VI / MDCCCXXX' (**6**).

In spite of his apparent success Parker found himself in financial difficulties and he was declared bankrupt in 1832. At that time he was still executing work for Buckingham Palace and a considerable number of ornaments for the drawing room chimneypieces had yet to be cast. Parker refused to give up the models and these chimneypieces and overmantels appear to have been abandoned. He continued in business after the settlement of his debts in 1834, but possibly only as a lamp maker. In 1839 he was described in the *London Directory* as a 'Lamp and coffee pot manufacturer' and by the following year he had moved to the Egyptian Hall, Piccadilly, where he called himself a 'Lamp and patent steam fountain coffee pot manufacturer' (*De Bellaigue* 1997, 26). He is last recorded, at the Egyptian Hall, in 1843.

Literary References: *Gunnis* 1968, 291–2, *Colvin* 1973–76, 267 n4, 283, 296; *Mackay* 1995, 288; *De Bellaigue* 1997, 26–37

Busts						
1.	1831	King William IV	b	SNPG, Edinburgh Other versions: Knox / Longstaffe-Gowan coll, SD 1831 Christie, 5 May 1988, lot 1, SD 1831		*Gunnis* 1968, 291; *Penny* 1992, III, 107
2.	1831	Lord Brougham	b	SNPG, Edinburgh		*Gunnis* 1968, 291
3.	1851	Sir Thomas Lawrence	b	[Gt Exhib, London]; untraced		*Great Exhib* 1851 (2), 154
Chimneypieces						
4.	1822	With two Chinese figures and ornaments in gilt bronze Payment(s): 800 gns	m	[Royal Pavilion, Brighton, saloon]; Buckingham Palace, London, yellow drawing room		*De Bellaigue* 1997, 27–8 (repr)
Architectural Sculpture						
5.	1821–1822	Communion rail panels Payment(s): £220 10s	b	[St James, Piccadilly, London]; untraced		Vestry Minute Books and Church Wardens' Accts, in GPC
Reliefs						
6.	1830	Henry Mackenzie (after Samuel Joseph)	b	Ashmolean	SD	*Penny* 1992, III, 107 (repr)

PARKER, Theodore fl 1769

Gunnis suggests that he was probably the father of **Richard Parker**. He supplied Wedgwood with a number of casts in 1769.

Literary References: *Gunnis* 1968, 292; *Clifford* 1992, 42–3, 62

Statues				
1.	1769	'Flora', 'Seres', 'Spencer', 'Hercules', 'Seres Large', 'Juno', 'Prudence', 'Milton' and 'Shakespear'	[Supplied to Josiah Wedwood]; untraced	Wedgwood/Parker L1/73, Theodore Parker acct, Sept 1769–18 Dec 1769
Miscellaneous				
2.	1769	'Bracket Open Work', 'A Boy A Couch' and '3 Dogge'	[Supplied to Josiah Wedwood]; untraced	Wedgwood/Parker L1/73, Theodore Parker acct, Sept 1769–18 Dec 1769

PARKER AND HARRIS, of London and Bath fl 1776

See **Charles Harris** and **Richard Parker**

Architectural Sculpture				
1.	1776	Two lions and a vase Payment(s): Lions, 1 gn each	Lion Inn, Shrewsbury, Salop	TNA C109/71 (Chancery Masters, non-political no 32)

PARKES, Alexander

For further information the reader is referred to *Pyke* 1981, 31

PARKINSON, Robert, of Newmarket fl c1830–33

He was the son of William Parkinson, a 'statuary and mason' of Newmarket, who must have died before 1826 since his widow died in that year. In 1833 he married Jemima Well, a dressmaker of Grosvenor Square. John Parkinson, of Mildenhall 'mason', may have been a relative.

Literary References: *Gunnis* 1968, 292

Archival References: GPC

Funerary Monuments					
1.	?1830	John Isaacson	Burwell, Cambs	S	*Gunnis* 1968, 292

PARR, R fl c1674

The Douch family monument has a pediment supported by two Corinthian pillars.

Literary References: *Gunnis* 1968, 292

Funerary Monuments					
1.	†1674–1675	Douch family	Stalbridge, Dorset	S	*Hutchins* 1861–70, vol III, 679

PARRY, R, of Kilpeck fl 1812

Funerary Monuments					
1.	1812	Unidentified subject, tablet	sl	Bacton, Herefs	Pevsner, *Herefs*, 1963, 70

PARRY, T fl 1818

Funerary Monuments

1.	†1818	Sarah (†1817) and Joseph Thompson		Great Gaddesdon, Herts	S

PARS, Albert fl 1759–67

Born in London in the early-18th century, Pars was the son of Albertus Pars, a silver-chaser, and the brother of William Pars the portrait painter and Henry Pars the draughtsman and drawing master. In 1759, 1764 and 1765 he received premiums for models in wax from the Society of Arts, while in 1767 a further award was made to him for a bronze cast (1–4).

Literary References: *Gunnis* 1968, 292; *Mackay* 1995, 288

Miscellaneous

1.	1759	Wax model of flowers in festoons		[Soc of A, premium, 2 gns]; untraced	RSA, *Minutes*, 1758–60, seq 1 fol 78; *Dossie* 1782, 436
2.	1764	Horses in a landscape, wax model		[Soc of A, premium, 10 gns]; untraced	RSA *Minutes*, 1763–64, seq 3 fol 86; RSA, *Premiums* 1763, 37
3.	1765	Cows in a landscape, wax model		[Soc of A, premium, 8 gns]; untraced	RSA *Minutes*, 1763–64, seq 3 fols 57, 65
4.	1767	Cast of an anatomy figure after Spang	b	[Soc of A, premium, 10 gns]; untraced	RSA *Minutes*, 1763–64, seq 3 fol 26

PARS, William fl 1758–59

The brother of **Albert Pars**, he won premiums from the Society of Arts in the late 1750s, when he was under 17.

Miscellaneous

1.	1758	Wax ornaments, models	[Soc of A]; untraced	*Dossie* 1782, 436
2.	1759	Unidentified model	[Soc of A, premium]; untraced	RSA *Minutes*, 1758–60, seq 1 fol 65

PARSONS fl *c*1718–20

He was probably a Gloucestershire mason and his monuments are excellent copies of contemporary London work. The Millechamp and Roche monuments are charming cartouche tablets (**2, 3**) and the Gorges has an inscription-tablet in the form of a heavy fringed curtain (**1**).

Literary References: *Gunnis* 1968, 292

Funerary Monuments

1.	†1718	Ferdinando Gorges	s	Ashley, Glos	S	Pevsner, *Glos: Cotswolds*, 1999, 145
2.	†1719	Anne Millechamp		Long Newnton, Glos	S	Pevsner, *Glos: Cotswolds*, 1999, 459
3.	†1720	Deborah Roche		St Mary, Tetbury, Glos	S	Pevsner, *Glos: Cotswolds*, 1999, 686

PARSONS, C, of Lewes

See **Latter Parsons**, of Lewes.

PARSONS, Latter, of Lewes 1772–1848

He worked in partnership with **Edward May** from 1794 and his son, C Parsons, joined him in due course, and was responsible for some of the tablets listed below. In 1804 Parsons was the mason building County Hall, Lewes. In 1823 he bought the stone works in Eastgate Street, Lewes, which had been occupied by **Arthur** and **John Morris** (East Sussex RO HIL/6/28C/1–25).

Gunnis notes that Parsons's monuments and tablets derive from London work and are in excellent taste. The Durrant (**3**) is in the manner of the younger Bacon, while the cartouche tablet commemorating George Peckham (**1**) is 'far above the ordinary provincial level in design and workmanship' (*Gunnis* 1968, 292). Latter Parsons died on 22 October 1848, aged 76, and his wife Sarah in 1827. They are both buried in the churchyard of All Saints, Lewes.

The firm, which ultimately became Bridgeman Ltd, continued producing high quality monuments at their yard in Eastgate Street into the second half of the 20th century. Gunnis considered their later monuments, including the 'very dignified ledger' in memory Viscount Gort in Penshurst church (unveiled 1950), to be 'in the best manner and style'.

Literary References: *Gunnis* 1968, 292; *Remnant* 1962, 142

Archival References: GPC

Additional Manuscript Sources: Parsons accounts; Parsons records; Bridgeman records

Funerary Monuments

1.	?1788	George Peckham	Salehurst, Sussex		*Gunnis* 1968, 292
2.	†1794	John Challen	Shermanbury, Sussex	S	
3.	†1799	Robert Durrant	Framfield, Sussex		Pevsner, *Sussex*, 1965, 506
4.	?1808	William Chambers	East Blatchington, Sussex		*Gunnis* 1968, 292
5.	?1810	William Constable	Burwash, Sussex		*Gunnis* 1968, 292
6.	?1819	Odiarne Hooper	Beckley, Sussex		*Gunnis* 1968, 292
7.	?1824	Richard Stone	Mayfield, Sussex		*Gunnis* 1968, 292
8.	?1831	Mary Wright	Framfield, Sussex		*Gunnis* 1968, 292
9.	?1835	Rev James Capper	Wilmington, Sussex		*Gunnis* 1968, 292
10.	†1839	Ida Beauclerk	Cowfold, Lewes, Sussex	S	
11.	†1839	Rev Richard Constable	Cowfold, Lewes, Sussex	S	
12.	†1847	Mary Pringle (? by C Parsons)	Cowfold, Lewes, Sussex	S	
13.	?1849	Captain John Crofts (by C Parsons)	Sompting, Sussex	S	
14.	?1857	Bishop of Sierra Leone (by C Parsons)	Upper Dicker, Sussex		*Gunnis* 1968, 292
15.	†1876	Ven. William Bruere Otter (?by C Parsons)	Cowfold, Lewes, Sussex	S	

PARSONS FAMILY, of Bath

Robert Parsons 1717–1790
Thomas Parsons 1744–1790

Robert Parsons was employed in 1744 by John Wood the Elder as a free stone-mason and one of the house-carvers for the building of the Bristol Exchange, but he was chiefly known for his garden vases and ornaments carved from Bath stone, which he sent all over England.

In Parsons's manuscript commonplace book (private coll) is an account of how he went in 1764 to see Ralph Allen on the day before the latter's death, to show him designs for tombstones and memorials. Parsons, therefore, is presumably responsible for the pyramid in Claverton churchyard under which Allen lies buried (2). Parsons was responsible for at least one monument in partnership with **John Ford I**, the large architectural tablet to Winchcombe Packer, which is signed by both men (1).

In 1754–5 John Ivory Talbot employed the architect, Sanderson Miller, on work in the new gothic great hall at Lacock Abbey, Wilts. He wrote to Miller shortly beforehand stating that he intended to have the chimneypiece and doorcases 'finished [by Parsons] in the Painswick stone, having lately seen one done by him for Lord Egmont [at Enmore Castle, Somerset] in the Gothick Taste, which pleased me greatly' (Miller of Radway archives, Warks RO CR 125B/394).

Parsons became a Baptist minister about 1768, but 'from the congregation he received no remuneration for his services and never relinquished his business as a stone-carver. He was removed to the Eternal World, February, 1790, and was buried in the Baptist Chapel at Walcot' (*Cater* 1834, 292–3). His obituary in the *Bath Chronicle* of 4 March 1790 states that 'for forty [*sic*] years he had been Pastor of the Baptist Congregation in Garrard Street, and it is to his disinterested zeal that the Society owed its origin and establishment' (p 3, col 2). In 1772 he published *Letters of the Rev. Mr. Fletcher of Madely on the differences subsisting between him and the Hon. and Rev. Mr. Shirley.*

Thomas Parsons was Robert's son and, like his father, a carver of stone vases and chimney-pieces. His book of designs in Bath municipal library shows that he copied his vases from drawings by Hoare, Cipriani, Kent, Wedgwood, **Eleanor Coade** and others. He made the famous vase for Mrs Miller into which verses were dropped by the wits of Bath. These she would pick out and read to her assembled guests, an amusement which terminated on the unfortunate day when a most indelicate ode polluted the urn (11). Like his father, Thomas Parsons was a Baptist minister, and his published works include *Effusions of Paternal Affection on the Death of a Lovely Daughter* (1799) and *High Church Claims Exposed* (1808).

Literary References: *Gunnis* 1968, 292–3; *Colvin* 1995, 654 (Lacock Abbey)

Archival References: Thomas Parsons, *A Collection of Vases Terms etc*, Bath Central Library, B731.7 PAR 38:18

Funerary Monuments						
1.	?1747	Winchcombe Howard Packer (by Robert Parsons) (co-sculptor: Ford)		Bucklebury, Berks	S	*Gunnis* 1968, 293
2.	1764	Ralph Allen (by Robert Parsons; designed by Richard Jones)		Claverton, Somerset		*Gunnis* 1968, 292; *Colvin* 1995, 562
Chimneypieces						
3.	pre-1753	In the Gothic taste (by Robert Parsons)		Enmore Castle, Somerset		WCA, CR 125 B, letter 394
Architectural Sculpture						
4.	1748	Four pairs of vases (by Robert Parsons) Payment(s): £16 4s	s	[Moulsham Hall, Essex]; untraced		*Edwards* 1977, 64
5.	1748	Stone carving, including Corinthian capitals, pine apples, heads and festoons on the west front (by Robert Parsons)	s	Titan Barrow, Bathford, Somerset		GPC
6.	1745–1751	Vases (by Robert Parsons) Payment(s): £110		Stourhead, Wilts		*Gunnis* 1968, 292
7.	1759	Two vases (by Robert Parsons)		Longford Castle, Derbys		*Gunnis* 1968, 292
8.	1757–1763	Urns and eagles (by Robert Parsons)	s	Newbridge, Co Dublin, parapet		*Friedman* 1974, (2), 29–32; *Jackson-Stops* 1988 (2), 65 (repr 1)
9.	1766	Six vases (by Robert Parsons)		[Corsham Court, Wilts, front]; untraced		*Gunnis* 1968, 292
10.	nd	Twelve vases (by Robert Parsons) Payment(s): £2 15s each Drawing(s): Lord Fortescue		Castle Hill, Devon		*Gunnis* 1968, 292
11.	nd	Vase (by Thomas Parsons)		[coll Mrs (later Lady) Miller of Bath]; untraced		*Gunnis* 1968, 293

PASCO, Joseph fl *c*1728–65

He lived at Hackney, where he carried out repairs to the parish church in 1754, and in 1765 was became a churchwarden (Simpson's *Memorials of St John at Hackney*, in *Gunnis* 1968, 293).

Funerary Monuments					
1.	†1728	René Baudouin	St Mary Aldermary, City of London	S	Pevsner, *London: City*, 1997, 242
2.	?1758	Anne Meade	Great Easton, Essex	S	*Gunnis* 1968, 293
3.	?1765	Samuel Bosanquet	Leyton parish church, Essex	S	*Gunnis* 1968, 293

PASSEY, J, of Tillingdon fl *c*1821

He signs a stone wall-tablet painted to represent coloured marble (1).

Literary References: *Gunnis* 1968, 293

Funerary Monuments						
1.	?1821	Elizabeth Weaver	s	Mansall Lacy, Hereford	S	*Gunnis* 1968, 293

PATENT MARBLE WORKS, of Westminster fl 1809–53

The firm, which was established in 1809, appears to have had yards in Esher Street and Earl Street, Westminster, since both addresses appear on monuments signed by them. They may be synonymous with both the **London Marble Works**, who were based in Esher Street, and the **Westminster Marble Company**, whose address was recorded as Earl Street in 1852. They seem to have been mass-producers of chimneypieces and monuments. Gunnis comments of the latter that they are 'extremely dull and frequently ugly', although he concedes that 'one or two trained designers of taste must have been employed' since the firm 'occasionally turned out a good monument', the best of which can be compared with the work of contemporary sculptors. One example is the monument to Thomas Bennion at Overton, Flint, which has a 'fine, indeed noble, relief of three daughters mourning at a parent's tomb' (16). At the time of the Great Exhibition of 1851 the works were owned by a Mr Thomas Hartley, who showed 'a design for a Gothic monument'.

Literary References: *Gunnis* 1968, 293

Archival References: GPC

Funerary Monuments						
1.	†1800	1st Lord Rancliffe		Bunny, Notts		GPC
2.	†1832	John Bullivant		St Mary, Lambeth, London (now Museum of Garden History)	S	
3.	?1833	Admiral Windham		Felbrigg, Norfolk		*Gunnis* 1968, 293
4.	†1833	Elizabeth Walshman		St Mary, Lambeth, London (now Museum of Garden History)	S	
5.	†1833	Maria Mackennon		St Mary Abbots, Kensington	S	Pevsner, *London: N W*, 1991, 460
6.	†1833	Thomas Dentnick		Oldbury, Salop		GPC
7.	†1833	William Craddock		St Nicolas, Nuneaton, Warks		Pevsner, *Warks*, 1966, 364
8.	1834	Henry Hoare of Mitcham Grove (†1828)		Staplehurst, Kent	SD	
9.	?1834	James Seton		Byculla, India		*Gunnis* 1968, 293
10.	?1836	John Holford		St John's Wood Chapel, Marylebone, London		*Gunnis* 1968, 293
11.	†1836	Phyllis Byam Shirley		Holy Trinity (St Nicholas), Ettington, Warks		Pevsner, *Warks*, 1966, 290
12.	*c*1836	Thomas Lamplugh, Archbishop of York (†1691)		Thwing, E R Yorks	S	Pevsner, *Yorks: E R & York*, 1995, 724
13.	†1837	Frances Mingay Mountain		St Mary, Hemel Hempstead, Herts	S	
14.	*c*1837	Isaac Badger (†1836) and family		St Edmund, Dudley, Worcs		GPC
15.	†1837	Sophia (†1836) and Caroline Purton		Oldbury, Salop		GPC
16.	†1840	Thomas (†1803) and Mary Bennion (†1840)		Overton, Flint		Pevsner, *Clwyd*, 1986, 411
17.	?1841	Arthur Annesley		Bletchington, Oxon		*Gunnis* 1968, 293
18.	†1841	Carr, Bishop of Worcester		Hartlebury, Worcs		GPC
19.	†1841	Robert Peddie		Antigua Cathedral, WI	S	
20.	†1843	John Martyr		Holy Trinity, Guildford, Surrey	S	
21.	?1844	Francis Stewart-Mackenzie		St George, Grenada		*Gunnis* 1968, 293
22.	†1844	James (†1838) and Maria Wright		Walkern, Herts	S	
23.	†1845	John Willard		St Mary, Eastbourne, Sussex		RG/JP, 6, 1069
24.	†1846	George D'Oyley		St Mary, Lambeth, London (now Museum of Garden History)	S	
25.	?1847	John Richards		Hagley, Worcs		RG/JP, 6, 1069
26.	†1848	Sir Robert Harland		St Mary, Wherstead, Suffolk		Pevsner, *Suffolk*, 1974, 486
27.	†1850	2rd Lord Rancliffe		Bunny, Notts		GPC
28.	?1850	Colonel Joseph Bradshaw		Duffield, Derby		*Gunnis* 1968, 293
29.	†1852	John William		Cooling, Kent		RG/JP, 6, 1069
30.	†1853	Eleanor Chafy		Milstead, Kent		RG/JP, 6, 1069
Chimneypieces						
31.	1829	Several Payment(s): £122	m	Lambeth Palace, London		Cambridge University Library MS.3928, in *Gunnis* 1968, 293
32.	1830	Black and gold marble Payment(s): £23		[Hodsock Priory, Notts]; untraced		Hodsock Archives, in GPC

PATERSON, Robert 1716–1801

Paterson was the stonemason whose history inspired Sir Walter Scott's novel *Old Mortality*, and most accounts of his life are based on the author's introduction to this work. He was born at Haggisha, Hawick, and baptized on 25 April 1716, the youngest son of a farmer, Walter Paterson, and his wife Margaret née Scott. In his thirteenth year he was apprenticed to his brother Francis at the Corncockle quarry, Lochmaben. In 1743 he married Elizabeth, daughter of Robert Gray, gardener to Sir John Jardine, who had worked as cook-maid to Sir Thomas Kirkpatrick of Closeburn, Dumfries, for some considerable time. With Sir Thomas's assistance Robert obtained the lease of a freestone quarry at Gatelowbrigg, Morton, from the Duke of Queensberry and he built a house there shortly before 1746. Not long afterwards the Jacobite army retreating from England towards Glasgow plundered Paterson's house and arrested him. While one account has it that Paterson had unwisely expressed violent opinion against 'the bloody and wicked house of Stuart' and 'the abominable heresies of the church of Rome' (*DNB*) another suggests that he had done nothing to warrant this treatment.

Some time after his release Paterson joined the Cameronians, a sect of covenanters who followed the teachings of Richard Cameron (†1680). As well as attending Cameronian conventicles in Galloway, he erected gravestones to martyred members of the sect. His religious zeal appears to have become a mania and around 1758 he failed to return to his family, even after his wife sent his eldest son, Walter, and then his two daughters to fetch him home. Legend has it that he spent the next 40 years riding through the lowlands of Scotland on a white pony repairing Covenanter monuments without payment. Paterson died at Bankhill, near Lockerbie, on 14 February 1801 and was buried in the churchyard at Caerlaverock, where Scott's publishers later erected a monument to his memory carved by **John Currie**. Paterson's son Walter (1749–1812) was also a stone carver.

Literary References: *DNB* (Black); *Gunnis* 1968, 293; *ODNB* (Sherbo)

PATIENCE, T fl 1798–1800

He was probably related to the architects Joseph Patience (*c*1739–1797) and Joseph Patience (*c*1767–1835) of Wormwood Street, Bishopsgate. It seems likely that they were his father and elder brother and that he was the Thomas Patience who was christened at All Hallows, London Wall on 19 October 1777, the son of Joseph and Mary Patience. He exhibited at the Royal Academy in 1798, showing a bust and a bas-relief for a monument to the memory of the elder Joseph Patience (1). He exhibited there again in 1800 (2). His addresses were 23 Wormwood Street and 25 New Broad Street, City. It is possible that the T Patience who exhibited architectural designs in 1796 and 1797 and is described as an architect 'At Mr Patience' was the same man (*Graves* VI, 1905–6, 72). Patience was declared bankrupt in 1801 (*Universal Mag*, 1801, 381).

Literary References: *Gunnis* 1968, 293; *Colvin* 1995, 741–2

Archival References: IGI

Funerary Monuments

1.	c1798	Joseph Patience (†1797)	All Hallows London Wall, City of London	S	*Graves* VI, 1905–6, 72; Pevsner, *London: City*, 1997, 188

Architectural Sculpture

2.	1800	Two figures designed for holding lights	[Exhib RA, London, 1093 and 1095]; untraced		*Graves* VI, 1905–6, 73

PATTEN, C T, of Bristol fl c1792–96

The *Gentleman's Magazine* states that he was responsible for the very handsome marble monument erected to the memory of the Rev George Bridle at Hardwick, Bucks.

Funerary Monuments

1.	†1792	Rev George Bridle	Hardwick, Bucks	S	*GM*, vol LXVI, Oct 1796, II, 841

PATTEN, Francis, of Rochester fl 1791–1821

His father, Francis Smith Patten, purchased the freedom of Rochester in 1761, and became free of the Masons' Company in 1773. Patten himself, became a freeman of his native city by patrimony in 1791 and served as mayor four times between 1812 and 1821 (Archives, City of Rochester, in *Gunnis* 1968, 294). With his partner, **T Brisley**, he built the cloisters at Cobham Hall, Kent (Archives, Earl of Darnley, in *Gunnis* 1968, 294).

Literary References: *Gunnis* 1968, 294

Funerary Monuments

1.	?1818	Thomas Brenchley (co-sculptor: T Brisley)	Bredgar, Kent	S	*Gunnis* 1968, 294

PATTESON (or PATTERSON, PATTISON), James and Samuel, of Manchester fl 1792–1857

James Patteson was first in partnership with a Daniel Mathison, but the firm was declared bankrupt in 1792 (*Universal Mag*, 1792, 397) and after his discharge his son Samuel became his partner. As a master mason James Patteson built St Philip's, Salford, Lancs between 1822 and 1825 (Minute Book, HM Commission for Building New Churches, 1822, Lambeth Palace Library, in GPC). He was listed as of York Street and Oxford Street, Manchester in *Baines Gazeteer* in the latter year. The firm advertised themselves as manufacturers of marble mantelpieces in 1840.

Literary References: *Gunnis* 1968, 294

Archival References: GPC

Funerary Monuments

1.	?1818	Rev Thomas Whitaker (by Samuel Patteson)	Bowden, Cheshire	S	*Gunnis* 1968, 294
2.	?1832	Thomas Wilkinson	Middleton, Lancs	S	*Gunnis* 1968, 294
3.	?1833	Egerton Leigh	Rostherne, Cheshire		GPC
4.	?1834	William Greenwood	Burnley, Lancs	S	*Gunnis* 1968, 294
5.	†1834	William Vaughan	St Philip, Salford, Lancs		NP/RG
6.	†1842	Robert Tebbutt	St Paul, Didsbury, Lancs		Pevsner, *Lancs: S*, 1969, 319
7.	†1857	William Case	Dunton, Norfolk		Pevsner, *Norfolk: N W & S*, 1999, 315

PATY, James I, of Bristol –1748

Paty (or Patty) was the first of a dynasty of stone-masons, carvers and sculptors, who practised in Bristol throughout the 18th century. His cousins and descendants all worked independently or as a loose federation, supplying wall monuments, chimneypieces and architectural ornaments in wood, as well as dressed stone for many buildings in the city.

He came from Somerset and his earliest known work pre-dates his move to Bristol by several years. This is an elegant wall monument with a framed inscription tablet above an apron carved with a cherub's head (1). Paty's name was entered on the Bristol burgess list on 15 April 1721, when he paid a fine of £15 4s 6d and so became a freeman of the city, at liberty to work within its confines. He took a dwelling and workshop at 21 Merchant Street, Broadmead. That year he provided a large architectural wall monument with composite columns, consoles and an apron carved with rich swags for Richard Sandford (2). By 1722 he was sufficiently established to take an apprentice, Samuel Phillips, son of Maurice Phillips of Bursley, a clothier. Paty did not revise his designs to meet new fashions: the large monument to George Locke, 1735 at Frome is a finely executed adaptation of the Sandford memorial (5).

Paty appears to have worked on several Bristol buildings, some of which have been destroyed or damaged. He is credited with carving and painting the quarter-jacks on the tower of Christ Church, 1728, and a strong claim can be made for his authorship of the design for King Street library, 1739–41, which had superb civic arms in the pediment and charming panels depicting *Putti studying the arts and sciences* over the first-floor windows. These survived until 1951, when they were chiselled off to avoid the cost of repair. He is also thought to have been responsible for work on two other Bristol buildings decorated with carved panels, 32 College Green, which was built in the early 1740s, perhaps under Paty's direction, and had knotted and tasselled swags below two upper floor windows, and Redland Court, built c1735 by the architect John Strahan, who probably brought in Paty to carve the garlanded swags and a pair of quivers above the first floor windows. During the 1740s he appears to have worked on a number of houses in the centre of Bristol, particularly in College Green and Unity Street, and may also have designed and built a countryhouse of five bays, Earnshill, Somerset, where he perhaps supplied the saloon chimneypiece.

The first drawing in the Paty Copybook, a catalogue of designs by family members and other draughtsmen assembled over a long period, relates closely to the Barker monument, though the suggestion for a classicizing portrait bust and martial trophies above the tablet was not implemented. Several other unsigned designs in the Copybook for wall monuments with funerary urns or heraldic shields have been ascribed to Paty on stylistic grounds (nos 28, 37, 38, 39, 102).

Paty died in February 1748, two months after writing his will, at which time his wife Rachel was pregnant with their only child, **James Paty III**.

Literary References: *Gunnis* 1968, 294; *Priest* 2003, *passim*

Archival References: Bristol Burgess book, 15 April 1721; Paty Copybook, University of Bristol Library (*Priest* 2003, 139–86, repr)

Will: Bristol RO EP/J/4, proved 25 February 1747

Funerary Monuments

1.	1715	Joseph Barker Drawing(s): (related) Paty Copybook, 92	Evercreech, Somerset		*Priest* 2003, 16
2.	†1721	Rev Richard Sandford	St Mary Redcliffe, Bristol	S	*Gunnis* 1968, 294; *Priest* 2003, 16, 20 (repr)
3.	†1722	Richard Loucher	Newton Nottage, Glamogan	S	
4.	1726	Sir William Pendarves	Camborne, Cornwall		Pevsner, *Cornwall*, 1970, 50
5.	†1735	George Locke	Frome, Somerset		*Priest* 2003, 8, 16–19, 21 (repr)

PATY, James II, of Bristol 1718–79

His parentage is not known, but he was a nephew of **James Paty I** and was **Thomas Paty**'s younger brother and partner in building schemes. They worked together on major city developments in Bristol and on the first phases of the Clifton layout, but they also worked independently and their workshops always remained separate. Paty became a burgess of Bristol in 1755, by marriage to the daughter of another burgess, Peter Tonkin, a deceased mariner. His address was given as 21 Horse Street (now Host Street) and his occupation as carver.

Monuments signed 'James Paty' provided between 1755 and 1768 are given to James II, but those signed in the same manner between 1768 and 1775 may be by James II or III. James II's monuments are conservative compositions, competently carved: a profile medallion portrait is a feature of several (**2, 3, 5, 7**). The only building in which he is known to have been involved is Stoke Park, near Bristol, which was rebuilt in the 1760s. The architect was Thomas Wright, but Paty appears to have been site architect and contractor. Among designs attributed to James II in the Paty Copybook are two wall monuments with urns (nos 7, 8) and one with a profile medallion on a ribbon suspended from a pointed arch (no 89).

He is thought to have been responsible for the obelisk erected in 1762 to commemorate Lady Elizabeth Somerset at Stoke Park, Stapleton, Bristol, designed by Thomas Wright. This is now destroyed (PMSA national recording project, 1998–99).

Paty had a son, John Paty I, who became a burgess in 1778 and announced that he was continuing the business after his father's death. A notice in *Felix Farley's Journal* for February and March 1779 states that John 'intended to carry on the business at the Yard Under the Bank in all its branches – monuments, chimney pieces etc. N.B. Land surveying and plans accurately drawn, also measuring'. John had no known issue.

Literary References: *Gunnis* 1968, 294; *Priest* 2003, *passim*

Archival References: Paty Copybook, University of Bristol Library (*Priest* 2003, 139–86, repr)

Funerary Monuments

1.	†1757	Mary Rees	Llandyfaelog, Carmarthen	S	
2.	†1761	John Rich	St Thomas, Bristol	S	*Gunnis* 1968, 294
3.	?1763	Francis Colston	All Saints, Corn St, Bristol	S	*Gunnis* 1968, 294
4.	†1764	Freeman family member Drawing(s): (related) Paty Copybook, 38 (by James Paty I)	Henbury, Glos		*Priest* 2003, 154
5.	†1766	Francis Davis	Chepstow, Monmouths	S	*Gunnis* 1968, 294
6.	†1766	Freeman family member Drawing(s): (related) Paty Copybook, 38, by James Paty I	Henbury, Glos		*Priest* 2003, 154
7.	†1767	Henry Allen	Monmouth parish church	S	*Gunnis* 1968, 294
8.	†1769	William Paston (perhaps by James Paty III)	Horton, Glos	S	Pevsner, *Glos: Cotswolds*, 1999, 418; C Lib (repr)
9.	†1771	Henry Foy (perhaps by James Paty III)	St Philip and St Jacob, Bristol	S	Pevsner, *Somerset: N & Bristol*, 1958, 408; C Lib (repr)
10.	† to 1772	Thomas Holmes (†1761) and others (perhaps by James Paty III)	Christ Church, Broad Street, Bristol	S	Pevsner, *Somerset: N & Bristol*, 1958, 389

PATY, James III, of Bristol *c*1748–1807

James Paty (or Patty) III was the posthumous son of **James Paty I** and the first cousin of **Thomas Paty** and **James Paty II**. A lease dated August 1786 between Paty and the Bristol corporation for a small message in Well Court, near Castle Green, describes him as being about 38 years old. He worked principally as a carver and gilder, but may also have been responsible for a few monuments signed simply 'James Paty', erected between 1768 and 1775, when his cousin James Paty II died (**1–3**). His name was entered in the city apprentice book on 23 February 1760, when he was bound to Thomas Kilby, a mason. Paty became a burgess or freeman of Bristol on 9 March 1768, when his address was given as 32 Broadmead. He later moved to Merchant Street. Several designs in the Paty Copybook for wall monuments with urns or figures in relief have been ascribed to Paty on stylistic grounds (13, 53, 6, 88 and 90).

Felix Farley's Journal recorded the death of 'Mr Patty, Carver and Gilder' on 29 August 1807 in his sixtieth year.

Literary References: *Gunnis* 1968, 294; *Priest* 2003, *passim*

Archival References: Bristol Burgess book, 9 March 1768; Paty Copybook, University of Bristol library (*Priest* 2003, 139–86, repr)

Funerary Monuments

1.	†1769	William Paston (perhaps by James Paty II)	Horton, Glos	S	Pevsner, *Glos: Cotswolds*, 1999, 418
2.	†1772	Henry Foy (perhaps by James Paty II)	St Philip and St Jacob, Bristol	S	Pevsner, *Somerset: N & Bristol*, 1958, 389
3.	†to 1772	Thomas Holmes (†1761) and others (perhaps by James Paty II)	Christ Church, Broad Street, Bristol		Pevsner, *Somerset: N & Bristol*, 1958, 389

PATY, John 1754–89

Born on 10 December, 1754, the son of **Thomas Paty of Bristol**, he joined the Royal Academy Schools on 11 June 1772, giving his age as 17. He became a freeman of Bristol on 7 December 1778. He and his brother **William Paty** had an extensive business as monumental masons and tablets signed by them are to be found in many churches in Bristol and the neighbouring counties. After his premature death on 10 June 1789, his brother William continued the business alone.

Literary References: *Hutchison* 1960–62, 138; *Gunnis* 1968, 294

Archival References: Bristol Burgess Book (microfiche FC/BB/1 (t) 8 (279), 7 December 1778 (described as John Paty 'RA')

PATY, Thomas, of Bristol 1712/13–89

Thomas Paty is best known as an architect, but he also had a thriving practice as a monumental mason, was an accomplished carver in stone and wood. He worked with his brother, **James Paty II**, on a number of urban developments in Bristol. Nothing is known of his background and training, or of his wife, who probably predeceased him, for she is not mentioned in his will. There were three children, John Paty II, **William Paty** and Elizabeth, who married **Thomas King of Bath**. From 1777 onwards he worked in association with his sons, who returned from London after studying at the Royal Academy, John as a sculptor from 1772 and William as an architect. After their induction, the firm was known as Thomas Paty and Sons. The workshop and family home were in Limekiln Lane.

Paty was the only male member of the immediate family who did not become a freeman of Bristol. This clearly placed him at no disadvantage since the corporation consulted him regularly as an architect and employed him as a stone carver and mason. In 1741–2 he worked under the architect, John Wood the Elder, carving architectural ornaments on the Bristol Exchange (**50**), and at the same period he was employed at Redland Court, providing all the wood and stone carving in the chapel. A contemporary note on the chapel observes that Paty 'is generally esteemed one of the best Carvers in England, either in Wood or Stone', and that 'all the Ornaments in the Chapel were designed and carved' by him (Redland Chapel, Church Book, 18 October 1755, fol 29v). He was responsible for the dressed masonry and carving at Clifton Hill House, designed by Isaac Ware in 1746 (**55**), and at the Royal Fort House, designed by James Bridges, *c*1758–60, where Paty worked on interior schemes with the plasterer, Thomas Stocking, his next door neighbour and a regular member of his team. Paty was the superintending architect for the Theatre Royal, Bristol between 1764–66, a building inspired by Sir Christopher Wren's theatre in Drury Lane, London. This commission consisted largely of structural carpentry with appropriate embellishments (**54**). He was also the mason and carver at St George's, Kingswood, near Bristol, between 1752 and 1756 (**51**). In 1768 Henry Hoare engaged him to dismantle the famous Bristol Cross and to move it to Stourhead.

Most of Paty's wall monuments subscribe to late-18th century taste with their elegantly carved urns, floral swags, mourning women, reeded decoration and classical devices. The exception is the ambitious, but graceful monument to William Hilliard, executed around 1750 (**11**). This edifice is nearly 20 feet in height and is structured in three stages. The base is a rusticated archway leading into the vault. Above that is a small gadrooned sarcophagus flanked by *putti*, on which is set an imposing portrait bust, framed by a triangular pediment on consoles. The upper zone has a pyramid supporting an armorial shield.

A letter dated 24 April 1787 gives insights into Paty's marketing practice. A potential client, Charles Morgan, enquired about a tablet for a kinswoman, Mrs Parry of Herefordshire. Paty sent him two roughly similar designs for decorative urns, set on an oval ground of coloured marbles. He readily admitted that the simpler of the two, which he priced at £12, had already been used for another monument (**42**). The variant design 'will be £18 to £22 according to the relief given to the work but if the urn and part under it should be thought too plain it may be ornamented so as to make the monument look much better, which may be done from thirty shillings to five guineas' (Glamorgan Archive Service, Cardiff (D/D Xgc 54). The embellishments and price were variable, as the letter explained.

Between 1775 and 1779, when his brother died, Thomas and John Paty II worked on the development of a number of new streets in Bristol. Their workshops remained separate throughout. They played a major role in the development of the Georgian city, where their repetitive designs satisfied a market for quiet, conservative elegance. The Patys laid out Clare, High, Bridge, Union and Bath Streets. Between 1763 and 1769 Thomas rebuilt Bristol Bridge and the adjoining church of St Nicholas, where he designed and executed a gothic tower and a spire for the church.

Paty's assistants included **James Allen of Bristol**, who was apprenticed to him in 1752 and **Michael Sidnell**, who assisted him at the Redland chapel. His sons John and William no doubt received some training with him before joining the Academy schools.

He appears to have died in reasonably comfortable circumstances: his will, dated 2 May 1789, a couple of days before his death, specified that his daughter, Elizabeth, should received £800 and her husband, Thomas King, £250. John Paty was to receive a sum equivalent to the value of a house that Paty had already given to his other son, William. The sons continued the business from Limekiln Lane for a short time before John's premature death on 10 June 1789.

Paty appears to have been responsible for many of the designs in the Paty Copybook, though positive identification is impossible since they are unsigned and his technique is similar to his son, William's. They include 15 with funerary urns (nos 5, 9, 10, 22, 26, 29, 30, 42, 43, 44, 46, 48, 49, 60, 71), one with a *putto* leaning on an urn (no 87) and one with an heraldic shield (no 102). There is a proposal for the principal front of the Merchant Venturers' Hall (no 125) and a design for a chimneypiece in the gothic taste, inscribed 'Statuary; £40.0' (no 133). Several other attributed designs for monuments appear in Henry Wood's *Monumental Masonry*.

Paty's brief obituary in the *European Magazine* for May 1789 described him as an 'Architect and Statuary [of] Bristol' and the *Bristol Journal* called him an architect 'whose extensive virtues, professional abilities and strict integrity, will in this city ever be rever'd' (*BJ*, 9 May 1789). His great achievement as a carver is the interior of the Redland Chapel.

In addition to the monuments listed below there are modest memorials by Paty in a number of churches in the Bristol area.

IR

Literary References: *Euro Mag*, May 1789, 424; *Gunnis* 1964, 294–5; *Nason* 1983, 886–888; *Beard* 1981, 274; *Whinney* 1988, 256; *Dale-Jones and Lloyd* 1989, 56; *Lloyd* 1989, 44; *Colvin* 1995, 742–3; Priest 2003, *passim*

Archival References: Paty/Morgan, 1787 (quoted in *Lloyd* 1989, 44); Paty Copybook

Additional MS Sources: St George, Kingswood, Book of Commissioners, 1751–64; St George, Kingswood, Chamberlain's cash accounts, 1752–64

Collections of Drawings: Paty Copybook; Wood's *Monumental Masonry*, nos 153, 226, 227, 230, 234, 235 (some perhaps by William Paty)

1.	1753	Butler, Bishop of Durham, tombstone Payment(s): £14 1s 5d	Bristol Cathedral		BM MS.9815 f5; GPC

Funerary Monuments

2.	†1658	John Tilly	St Mary Redcliffe, Bristol	S	C Lib (repr)
3.	†1719	John Price	Brecon Cathedral	S	Pevsner, *Powys*, 1979, 291
4.	*c*1724	William Jones (†1718) and family	Stowey, Somerset	S	C Lib (repr)

5.	†1735	George and Susanna Locke		Frome, Somerset	S	*Gunnis* 1968, 295; C Lib (repr)
6.	†1741	George Hussey		Seend, Wilts	S	Pevsner, *Wilts*, 1975, 465
7.	†1745	Hon Rothesia Ann Barrington		Shrivenham, Berks	S	Pevsner, *Berks*, 1966, 218; C Lib (repr)
8.	†1748	Edward Gore		Barrow Gurney, Somerset	S	*Gunnis* 1968, 295
9.	†1748	Walter Jeffreys		Brecon Cathedral	S	Pevsner, *Powys*, 1979, 291
10.	†1749	Mary Garlick		Doulting, Somerset	S	*Gunnis* 1968, 295
11.	*c*1750	William Hilliard (†1735)		Lord Mayor's Chapel, Bristol	S	*Eustace* 1982, 17, 21–2 (repr); *Whinney* 1988, 256; *Priest* 2003, 36–7
12.	†1755	Edward Southwell		Henbury, Glos	S	*Gunnis* 1968, 295; C Lib (repr)
13.	†1758	George (†1741), George (†1758) and Mary Husey		Seend, Wilts	S	
14.	pre-1762	John and Martha (†1762) Cossins Drawing(s): BL K Top XIII 95d		Redland Chapel, Bristol	S	*Eustace* 1982, 94–5 (repr)
15.	†1763	Judith Alleyne Drawing(s): (related) Wood's Monumental Masonry f203 rt		Bristol Cathedral	S	*Gunnis* 1968, 295; C Lib (repr)
16.	?1763	William Rees		Laugharne, Carmarthen	S	*Gunnis* 1968, 295
17.	†1764	Thomas Bedingfield		St Mary, Bury St Edmunds, Suffolk	S	*Gunnis* 1968, 295
18.	†1765	Mrs Twyford		Kilmerdown, Somerset	S	*Gunnis* 1968, 295
19.	†1765	Sir Robert Cocks		Dumbleton, Glos	S	Pevsner, *Glos: Vale & Forest of Dean*, 1976, 174
20.	†1770	Edward and John (†1774) Peach		Woodchester, Glos	S	Pevsner, *Glos: Cotswolds*, 1999, 744; C Lib (repr)
21.	†1773	Rev John Rodgers		Brixton Deverill, Wilts	S	*Gunnis* 1968, 295
22.	†1775	Mrs Hallings		Ledbury, Herefs	S	*Gunnis* 1968, 295
23.	†1775	William and Mary Rees		Laugharne, Carmarthen	S	*Dale-Jones and Lloyd* 1989, 56
24.	1777	John Haviland		Langford Budville, Somerset	S	*Gunnis* 1968, 295
25.	†1777	Rev Thomas Payne AM Drawing(s): (related) Paty Copybook, 4		St James, Bristol		*Priest* 2003, 143
26.	1778	Elizabeth (†1713) and John Nelmes (†1742)		Wotton-under-Edge, Glos	S	Pevsner, *Glos: Cotswolds*, 1999, 757; C Lib (repr)
27.	†1779	Margaret Sherston		Wells Cathedral	S	*Gunnis* 1968, 295
28.	†1779	Morgan family		Chepstow, Monmouths	S	*Gunnis* 1968, 295
29.	†1779	Susanna Higfoot		Chepstow, Monmouths	S	*Gunnis* 1968, 295
30.	†1780	Christian Alleyne		St George, Barbados	S	*Gunnis* 1968, 295
31.	†1780	James Morgan Drawing(s): (related) Paty Copybook, 41		Westbury-on-Trym, Bristol	S	*Priest* 2003, 155
32.	†1780	Martha Travell		Upper Slaughter, Glos	S	Pevsner, *Glos: Cotswolds*, 1999, 708
33.	†1781	Rev Richard Thomas		Llangeler, Carmarthen	S	*Dale-Jones and Lloyd* 1989, 56
34.	†1781	Rev Thomas Merriot DD Drawing(s): (related) Paty Copybook, no 11, inscribed 'Ab't £28.10'		Bristol Cathedral		*Priest* 2003, 145
35.	†1781	Thomas Hobby		Hill, Glos	S	Pevsner, *Glos: Vale & Forest of Dean*, 1976, 272
36.	†1783	Daniel (†1778) and John Cox		Beaminster, Dorset	S	
37.	†1783	Elizabeth Holder		Hinton Charterhouse, Somerset	S	*Gunnis* 1968, 295
38.	†1783	Erasmus Williams		Myddfai, Carmarthen	S	*Dale-Jones and Lloyd* 1989, 56
39.	†1783	George Thorne		Swimbridge, Devon	S	*Gunnis* 1968, 295
40.	†1783	M Davis		Abbots Leigh, Somerset	S	*Gunnis* 1968, 295
41.	†1784	John Morgan		St Peter, Carmarthen	S	*Dale-Jones and Lloyd* 1989, 56
42.	†1784	Mrs Lowder of Cardiff		Untraced		*Lloyd* 1989, 44; *Dale-Jones and Lloyd* 1989, 44
43.	†1784	Sarah Paget		Shepton Mallet, Somerset	S	*Gunnis* 1968, 295
44.	†1785	Arthur Tucker		Winterbourne, Glos	S	Pevsner, *Glos: Vale & Forest of Dean*, 1976, 409
45.	†1785	Samuel Peach		Olveston, Glos	S	Pevsner, *Glos: Vale & Forest of Dean*, 1976, 316
46.	†1785	Thomas Rees		St Clears, Carmarthen	S	*Dale-Jones and Lloyd* 1989, 56
47.	†1785	William Paget		Shepton Mallet, Somerset	S	
48.	†1787	Peter Fry Drawing(s): Paty Copybook, 6, 14, 71		Axbridge, Somerset		*Priest* 2003, 144
Architectural Sculpture						
49.	1740–1743	Stone and wood carving, including ornaments for the chancel, a limewood pulpit, oak reading-desk and panelling Payment(s): £106 8s (chancel and pulpit)		Redland Chapel, Bristol		*Gunnis* 1968, 294; *Colvin* 1995, 742; C Lib (repr)
50.	1744	Ornamental carving, including three armorial shields for the pediments		The Exchange, Bristol		*Colvin* 1995, 742; *Priest* 2003, 37–8 (repr)
51.	1752–1755	Carving and dressed masonry		St George, Kingswood, Bristol		*Gunnis* 1968, 294–5
52.	1755	Font with carved eagle cover	wd	Redland Chapel, Bristol		*Gunnis* 1968, 294
53.	1758–1760	Tympanum carving and interior decorative schemes		Royal Fort House, Bristol		*Colvin* 1995, 743; *Priest* 2003, 51, 55–60 (repr)
54.	1764–1766	Decorative work		Theatre Royal, Bristol		*Little* 1966, 889–90
Miscellaneous						
55.	*c*1750	Carved monogram in west pediment, heraldic devices on garden front, chimneypieces and other interior ornaments		Clifton Hill House, Bristol		*Priest* 2003, 51, 54 (chimneypieces repr)

PATY, William, of Bristol 1758–1800

Like his father, **Thomas Paty**, William was an architect, who also supplied funerary monuments. He studied briefly at the Royal Academy Architectural Schools in 1775 and may have worked in the office of a London architect, but he was back in Bristol by 1777, when his father started to advertise his firm as Thomas Paty and Sons. After the death of his father and brother John in 1789 he continued the family business alone from Limekiln Lane and College Place. Paty married Sarah Hickes, the daughter of Alderman Hickes, a 'foreigner' from Gloucestershire in January 1784. The marriage did not give him free access to the burgess list and on 9 December 1790 he paid a fine of 15 guineas to become a freeman of Bristol. He had two children, George William Paty, who did not follow his father's profession and a daughter, Marie.

Paty was one of the three Bristol surveyors appointed under the act of 1788 and he played an important part in the development of Bristol, particularly Great George Street, where he designed a number of houses. He appears also to have designed many of the terraces in Clifton and was responsible for Blaise Castle House on the outskirts of Bristol, 1795–6. He rebuilt Christ Church, considered by Howard Colvin to be his best building, between 1785 and 1790.

Most of Paty's wall-monuments are in the south-west of England though he built up a connexion with the West Indies, sending several to Barbados (**6, 11, 22, 36**). Like his father, he employed a repertoire of elegantly carved classical motifs on his monuments, including urns, paterae, portrait medallions and mourning women garlanding obelisks. He used variegated marbles, indicated on his designs with colour-washes, and often backed his compositions with an inverted shield ground. A number of designs in the Paty copybook are thought to be by William: they include nine for wall tablets with urns (nos 3, 16, 25, 46, 47, 49, 63, 68, 69) and three with heraldic shields (nos 95, 97, 102). The Copybook also includes ground and first floor plans for an unidentified house (no 126) and several refined Adamesque chimneypieces (nos 128, 129, 131, 132, 135, 136).

Paty, who was the last surviving sculptor member of his family, died in December 1800, aged 48, and was commemorated with a tablet in St Augustine's, Bristol. His former pupil and assistant, **James Foster of Bristol**, was established in independent practice, so the workshop, Paty Copybook, architectural practice and goodwill were sold to an outsider, **Henry Wood**. In the business-like manner characteristic of the family, a notice in *Felix Farley's Bristol Journal* on Saturday 4 April 1801 directed all to whom Paty owed debts to take their demands to his banker, and those who owed sums to him to pay them to Paty's brother-in-law, **Thomas King of Bath**.

Literary References: *Gunnis* 1968, 295; *Whinney* 1988, 459 n.23; *Dale-Jones and Lloyd* 1989, 56; *Colvin* 1995, 372, 743–4, 1071–2; *Priest* 2003, *passim*

Will: PROB 11/1352

Collections of Drawings: Paty Copybook

Miscellaneous Drawings: sketches of proposals for monuments with some estimates of costs, including one signed by William Paty, Bristol RO, Ashton Court Papers AC/F/9/5

Funerary Monuments

1.	†1762	Thomas Stokes	Wickwar, Glos	S	Pevsner, *Glos: Vale & Forest of Dean*, 1976, 406
2.	†1773	Richard Street	Aust, Glos	S	Pevsner, *Glos: Vale & Forest of Dean*, 1976, 92
3.	†1775	Mary Hale	Alderley, Glos	S	Pevsner, *Glos: Cotswolds*, 1999, 133
4.	†1777	William Springett	Alderley, Glos	S	Pevsner, *Glos: Cotswolds*, 1999, 133
5.	1778	Adams family	Stanton Drew, Somerst	S	
6.	†1780	Christian Gibbes (née Alleyne)	St George, Bridgetown, Barbados	S	
7.	†1785	Daniel Cox	Beaminster, Dorset	S	*Gunnis* 1968, 295
8.	†1785	Samuel Phillimore	Upper Cam, Glos	S	Pevsner, *Glos: Cotswolds*, 1999, 210
9.	†1785	Thomas and Mary Jones	Llanegwad, Carmarthen	S	*Dale-Jones and Lloyd* 1989, 56
10.	†1786	Samuel and Mary Coxe	Cherington, Glos	S	Pevsner, *Glos: Cotswolds*, 1999, 226
11.	†1787	Edward Jordan	St James, Holetown, Barbados	S	*Gunnis* 1968, 295
12.	†1788	Richard Musgrave	Lismore, Co Waterford	S	*Potterton* 1975, 74
13.	†1789	Henry Harvey	St Mary, Tetbury, Glos	S	Pevsner, *Glos: Cotswolds*, 1999, 686
14.	†1789	Richard Lockyer	King Charles the Martyr, Falmouth, Cornwall	S	Pevsner, *Cornwall*, 1970, 67; C Lib (repr)
15.	†1789	Richard Nelmes	St Philip and St Jacob, Bristol		*Gunnis* 1968, 295
16.	†1790	James Cleare	Hawkesbury, Glos	S	Pevsner, *Glos: Cotswolds*, 1999, 409
17.	†1790	Richard Chapman and family members	Axbridge, Somerset	S	
18.	1791	James Cross Drawing(s): (related) Paty Copybook, no 16, signed	Westbury, Somerset	S	*Priest* 2003, 147
19.	†1791	James Lansdowne	Radstock, Somerset	S	
20.	†1791	Thomas Stokes	Wickwar, Glos	S	*Gunnis* 1968, 295
21.	†1792	Anne Pitt	Stratton, Glos	S	Pevsner, *Glos: Cotswolds*, 1999, 646
22.	†1792	Henry Frere	St George, Bridgetown, Barbados	S	
23.	†1792	Hester Prideaux Drawing(s): (related) Paty Copybook, 67	St Michael, Bristol		*Priest* 2003, 163
24.	1792	Unidentified subject, invoiced to Richard Tombs	[St Augustine, Bristol]; untraced		Bristol RO, Misc Papers 37160
25.	†1793	D Bull	Calne, Wilts	S	*Gunnis* 1968, 295
26.	†1793	Elizabeth Weston	Aust, Glos	S	Pevsner, *Glos: Vale & Forest of Dean*, 1976, 92
27.	†1793	Mary Hall	Benthall, Salop	S	
28.	†1793	Mrs Bragge	Lydney, Glos	S	Pevsner, *Glos: Vale & Forest of Dean*, 1976, 293

29.	†1794	Abraham Elton Drawing(s): (related) Paty Copybook, 40, signed by William Paty	Wells Cathedral	S	*Gunnis* 1968, 295; *Priest* 2003, 154
30.	†1794	John Taylor	St Andrew, Droitwich, Worcs	S	
31.	1794	Mary Stretton Drawing(s): (related) Paty Copybook, 87, 169, by Thomas Paty	St Michael, Bristol	SD	*Priest* 2003, 169 (repr)
32.	†1794	Rev Charles Selwyn	Blockley, Glos	S	Pevsner, *Glos: Cotswolds*, 1999, 183
33.	†1794	Robert Hughes	St Laurence, Stroud, Glos	S	Pevsner, *Glos: Cotswolds*, 1999, 650
34.	†1795	John Lewis Philipps	Llangynin, Carmarthen	S	*Dale-Jones and Lloyd* 1989, 56
35.	1796	Hugh Inglis	St Michael, Bristol	D	*Priest* 2003, 143
36.	†1796	Thomas (†1795) and Jane Griffith	Barbados Cathedral, Bridgetown		*Gunnis* 1968, 295
37.	†1797	Frances Diggle	St Peter, Carmarthen	S	*Dale-Jones and Lloyd* 1989, 44, 56
38.	†1797	Henry and Jane Savage	Ardkeen, Co Down	S	*Potterton* 1975, 74
39.	†1797	Thomas Harris	St Mark, Bristol, Somerset, Lord Mayor's chapel	S	*Gunnis* 1968, 295
40.	1797	William Keats Drawing(s): (related) Paty Copybook, 5, 68, inscribed £46.10s	St Michael, Bristol	S	*Priest* 2003, 143
41.	†1798	Agnes Chisholme	Cromhall, Glos	S	Pevsner, *Glos: Vale & Forest of Dean*, 1976, 166
42.	†1798	Nicholas Hickes	Berkeley, Glos	S	Pevsner, *Glos: Vale & Forest of Dean*, 1976, 101
43.	†1798	Sir Anthony Fitzherbert	Bristol Cathedral		*Gunnis* 1968, 295
44.	†1799	Julian Charnley	Lismore, Co Waterford		*Potterton* 1975, 74; C Lib (repr)
45.	†1799	Mary McTaggart	St Augustine, Bristol		*Gunnis* 1968, 295
46.	†1799	R Winpenny Drawing(s): (related) Paty Copybook, 3	Westbury, Somerset		*Priest* 2003, 143
47.	nd	Mr Berjew Drawing(s): (related) Paty Copybook no 16, signed by William Paty	Westbury, Somerset	S	*Priest* 2003, 147

PAUL, Nubboo Coomar fl 1845

Of Kolkata (Calcutta), he was awarded a medal from the Society of Arts in 1845.

Busts

1.	1845	The late Dr Carey, taken from an engraving	[Soc of A, silver Isis medal]; untraced	RSA, *Abstract of Proceedings*, 1845, 30, xv

PAYE, Richard Morton 1750–1821

A painter, engraver and sculptor, he specialised in subtly humorous depictions of children engaged in everyday activities. He was baptised at Botley, Kent, in 1750. Virtually nothing is known of his early life but he worked as a chaser from his youth. He was clearly a skilled metalworker for one account states that although George Michael Moser 'was at this time considered at the head of this class of art', Paye's works, particularly his small-scale models, were thought by many 'to possess more of the spirit of sculpture and less of the French flutter' (*Library of the Fine Arts*, 3, 1832, 96). He was in London by 1773 when he exhibited four wax models and two oil paintings at the Royal Academy from his lodgings in Leicester Fields (1). He showed two wax models at the RA the following year, exhibited a 'cast of an emblematical figure' in 1779 and produced a competition design for a monument to Lord Nelson in 1807 (2–5). None of the models have been traced. Throughout most of his career he concentrated on his paintings and engravings but critical success eluded him and he died in obscurity.

Literary References: *Clayton* 1913, 229–236; *Gunnis* 1968, 295; *Pyke* 1973, 102; *ODNB* (Bryant)

Miscellaneous

1.	1773	Four models	w	[Exhib RA, London, 218]; untraced	*Graves* VI, 1905–6, 84
2.	1774	Portrait of a beggar	w	[Exhib RA, London, 203]; untraced	*Graves* VI, 1905–6, 84
3.	1774	Unidentified lady, model	w	[Exhib RA, London, 202]; untraced	*Graves* VI, 1905–6, 84
4.	1779	'A cast of an emblematical figure'		[Exhib RA, London, 231]; untraced	*Graves* VI, 1905–6, 84
5.	1807	Design for a monument to Lord Nelson		Untraced	*ODNB*

PAYNE, of St Ives, Hunts fl *c*1792

He signs a tablet with 'an urn and cherub-heads' (*Gunnis* 1968, 295) (1).

Funerary Monuments

1.	†1792	Robert Underwood	Boxworth, Cambs	S	Pevsner, *Cambs*, 1970, 308

PAYTON, John Morris, of Bristol fl *c*1836–41

Payton probably had a flourishing business, though few of his works are recorded. The close commercial links between Bristol and the West Indies account for two monuments shipped to Nevis (1, 3).

Funerary Monuments

1.	†1836	Rev John Laurence	St Thomas, Lowland, Nevis	S	
2.	?1836	Sarah Major	Hungerford, Berks	S	*Gunnis* 1968, 295
3.	†1837	Frances Huggins	St Thomas, Lowland, Nevis	S	
4.	?1838	James Williams	Mathern, Monmouths	S	*Gunnis* 1968, 295
5.	?1839	John Purnell	Camerton, Somerset	S	*Gunnis* 1968, 295
6.	†1841	Flora Fust	Hill, Glos	S	Pevsner, *Glos: Vale & Forest of Dean*, 1976, 272

PEACHEY, Emma

For information the reader is referred to *Pyke* 1973, 102

PEACOCK, William fl 1810

In 1810 he was paid £150 'for mason's and statuary work' at the New Mint in London (TNA AOI/2500/443).

Literary References: *Gunnis* 1968, 296

PEARCE, Edward c1635–95

Pearce was a carver in stone and wood and also a designer and a mason-contractor with a thriving business in the construction industry. He was one of three sons of Edward Pearce, or Pierce (†1658), a history and landscape painter and a designer of ornaments. Pearce senior's drawings for friezes, engraved by Robert Peake, were published in 1640 and re-issued by his son Edward in 1668 and again around 1680. The family lived in the City of London in the parish of St Botolph, Aldersgate in 1641, and Pearce was still living in that area when he was granted a licence to marry Anne Smith of St Bride's, a widow, at St Michael, Bassishaw, on 22 October 1661. In 1678 the couple were domiciled in the parish of St Andrew, Holborn, and c1681 they moved to Arundel Street, immediately west of Temple Bar, where Pearce already had a workshop in 1678. They remained in that street for the rest of Pearce's life.

Nothing is known of his early training, but he became a freeman by patrimony of the Painter-Stainers' Company on 16 January 1656 and was admitted to the livery on 20 February 1668. He continued to serve the Company throughout his career and became its master in 1693.

Pearce was employed as an assistant or mason-carver by the leading architects of his day. In 1665 he worked as Sir Roger Pratt's clerk of works at Horseheath, at Lord Alington's house near Cambridge, and around the same date he provided carved work under the architect, William Wynde, at Hamstead Marshall, the 1st Earl of Craven's Berkshire seat (**15**). He became heavily involved in building work in the City after the Great Fire and was 'was much employd by Sr. Chr. Wren in his Carvings & designs' (*Vertue* V, 9). Pearce was the master mason for three of Wren's City churches (St Lawrence Jewry, St Matthew Friday Street, St Andrew, Holborn) and he supplied ornaments in wood for four of them (St Lawrence Jewry, St Matthew Friday Street, St Andrew, Holborn, St Benet Fink). He also carved the preliminary wooden model of a dragon for a copper weathervane above St Mary-le-Bow (**27**). He worked under Wren at St Paul's Cathedral as a mason from 1678 to 1690 and was responsible for work including carved ornamental details on the south side of the choir, the south-east quadrant of the dome and the whole of the south transept front (**38**). Among his City contracts was masonry work undertaken at Fishmongers Hall, 1669, with the otherwise unknown Thomas Bedford, for which the pair were paid £890. He also worked 'in front of Guildhall', perhaps on the frontispiece (**18**), which was billed in 1673 with a public cistern in Pancras Lane. In 1676 Pearce was involved in development of the site of Norfolk House, Strand, where he provided a design for the front of a mansion. The project was abandoned, but Pearce himself leased 45 feet of frontage on the east side of Arundel Street. He supplied a doorway with an armorial panel for the Fishmongers' Hall (**16**), another doorcase for his own Company Hall (**19**), and was responsible for sundry 'works done about ye hall' of the Grocers' Company in the years 1680–84 (**30**).

Pearce sent carved woodwork for domestic interiors out of London a number of times in the 1670s and early 1680s. Around 1677 his assistants set up panelling and carved ornaments in the dining-room at Wolseley Hall, Staffs (**25**). The work was singled out for praise a decade later in Robert Plot's history of the country: 'of all the joiner's work I have met with in this County there is none comparable to that of the new dining-room of Sir Charles Wolseley at Wolseley, the carved work therof is also very good, both done by one Pearce' (*Plot* 1686, 383). In 1675–78 he was working for George Vernon at nearby Sudbury Hall, where he provided carvings for the great staircase including a richly carved pine and limewood balustrade, which perhaps drew on his father's engraved designs for acanthus scrolls (**22**). He also supplied crisply carved floral and foliate festoons for the panelling and overdoors of the saloon (**24**). Beard and Knott have noted that that there is no indication in Vernon's *Creditor and Debtor Book* for 1675–78 that Pearce visited Sudbury himself. The carving was prepared in his London workshop, and an assistant, John Grew, to whom there are small payments in Vernon's account book, went down to Sudbury three times to install it with the help of a small team of local joiners. Whilst working on the Sudbury commission, Vernon's wife Margaret died, and Pearce provided her monument, his only known solo monument (**1, 3**). It consists of a gadrooned urn above a pedestal with carved consoles.

Whilst the Sudbury and Wolseley commissions were under way, Pearce was again working under Wren and with the architect, Robert Hooke, on the Monument commemorating the Great Fire in Pudding Lane. The principal contractor for the great column was **Joshua Marshall**, and the controlling sculptor, **Caius Gabriel Cibber**. Pearce is not mentioned in the surviving accounts, but Vertue, who had access to a manuscript statement of payments made in 1679, noted 'the four dragons at 50 pounds each dragon done by Edward Pierce' above the pedestal (**21**), (*Vertue* V, 80). The dragons and probably also the festoons linking them, are likely to have been sub-contracted to Pearce by Cibber. Pearce was one of the signatories endorsing costs after the death of Joshua Marshall in 1678 and he then inherited Marshall's position as joint mason, with **John Shorthose**, at St Clement Danes, where he remained from 1679 until the church's completion in 1682.

In 1676 he worked with Wren on the chapel at Emmanuel College, Cambridge, which was paid for largely by Archbishop Sancroft. Pearce supplied drawings for the ground plan, wainscot and seats and was paid £2 for his designs, which were executed by **Cornelius Austin** (**20**). It was probably through Sancroft's influence that Pearce obtained the commission in 1686 for the Bishop's Palace at Lichfield, the only complete building he is known to have designed. It is an elegant house of seven bays and has pedimental sculpture and piers topped with urns flanking the main entrance. The carved ornaments were supplied by the workshop (**34**). Colvin suggests that he may also have been responsible for a screen and panelling in the chapel at Winchester College, 1681.

Pearce may have been angling for contracts in 1674, when on New Year's Day he made a present of sack and claret to Robert Hooke, the architect of a new theatre at the Royal College of Physicians. In 1675 he discussed a possible statue of Sir John Cutler with Hooke, but the commission eventually went to **Arnold Quellin**. He was more successful in obtaining commissions from the City livery companies. In 1684 he carved a full-length figure in oak for the Fishmongers' Hall, of Sir William Walworth, the 14th-century lord mayor who stabbed Wat Tyler, leader of the Peasants' Revolt (**5**). The texture of the velvet bonnet and fur-lined gown are finely realised and Walworth's sharply turned head, which has considerable vitality, succeeds in indicating the agitation the uprising must have provoked in the mayor. Pearce also provided three stone figures of English sovereigns for the line of kings in the second Royal Exchange (**6–8**). He was considered by the Tallowchandlers in 1685 for their statue of Henry VII, together with **John Bushnell** and Cibber, but they were all passed over in favour of Arnold Quellin. Following the success of Walworth's statue, the Fishmongers, together with the Mercers, chose Pearce for the statue of Queen Elizabeth (**7**), which was modelled on her image in Westminster Abbey. Cibber provided a model and an estimate of £60 for the statue of Edward III for the Skinners, but he apparently passed the assignment on to Pearce (**6**), who also carved the figure of Henry V for the Goldsmiths, commissioned on 30 March 1686 (**8**).

Pearce's reputation as a sculptor is in need of some re-assessment since it rests principally on his portrait busts, several of which are insecure in their attribution. A clay head of the poet John Milton, which belonged to Vertue, who believed it was by Pearce, is now thought to be by the medallist and wax modeller, Abraham Simon (ODNB). A bronze bust of Oliver Cromwell in the Museum of London is signed and dated 1672 (**9**), but a marble version in the Ashmolean, Oxford, which is also signed, though with uncharacteristic lettering, is probably by an 18th-century sculptor (ODNB). The head of Sir Christopher Wren, *c*1673 (**10**), which was presented to Oxford University by Wren's son and is recognised as one of the most outstanding busts of the 17th century, may be a copy by Pearce after a lost bust by a French sculptor, perhaps Antoine Coysevox. Penny has drawn attention to the 'alert conviviality' of the face, the voluminous drapery across the chest, the loose shirt and disordered locks, all characteristic of Coysevox's work. The busts of Dr Baldwin Hamey and Thomas Evans are securely documented (**11, 12**). Robert Hooke noted in his diary on 19 February 1675 that he had ordered Hamey's bust for the Royal College of Physicians, and a payment of £50 is entered in their cash book for April 1684. The bust of Evans, a master of the Painter-Stainers, is recorded in the Company's terrier of 1723 as being 'carved by Mr Pierce at the Company's charge'. Both are assured portraits in marble and Pierce once again used his skills to suggest contrasting textures.

He worked on prestigious commissions during the last decade of his life. In 1689 the temperamental William Talman, who was or became a close friend, began rebuilding the south and east fronts at Chatsworth, using Pearce as a mason contractor (**35**). Estimates prepared by Pearce, Thomas Webb and **Edward Strong I** in April–May 1692, include a sum of nearly £8,000 'ffor workmanship and setting and his carvings' (*Wren Soc*, XVII, 35). In 1689 Pearce also began work on garden sculpture for Hampton Court. He made substantial alterations to Hubert le Sueur's *Diana Fountain*, erected at Somerset House in the 1630s and moved to the privy garden at Hampton Court *c*1690 (**39**). The bill for 'Carving in Portland stone two Dolphins and a cisterne for a fountain' and '8 scrowles and 4 festoons with shells and sevll foot of sup. in the gt. stones under the cornish' totalled £1,262 3s (PRO Works, December Accts, A.O. Roll 2981, bundle 2482, quoted in *Harris* 1969, 444). Pearce also provided two magnificent urns, both of which were unfinished at his death (**36, 37**). They were completed by **John Nost I**, who was paid in 1700, 'for fluting ye foot of ye vases that came from Mr Pearce and polishing the plinth and moulding atop' (PRO, Work 5/51). Pearce earned a substantial sum, £2,003, for his work at Hampton Court.

It is not known whether Nost worked for Pearce in the decade before the latter's death, but he may have taken over at least one of Pearce's unfinished contracts for monuments (**4**). Pearce prepared a design for a monument to a viscount, his wife and child (BL 1881-6-11-190), almost certainly for Viscount Irwin's monument at Whitkirk (**2**), begun and significantly progressed by Pearce, and completed by Nost in 1697.

In 1694 Pearce took on his last new commission, preparing the design and supervising the erection of the column at Seven Dials, Covent Garden, London (**40**). He died in March 1695 and was buried at St Clement Danes, where he had worked a little over a decade earlier. His will states that he supposed himself 'to be worth 2516 pounds', left to his widow, his son-in-law, John Killingworth, and his son, John. His widow was to receive ground rents on three properties adjoining their house in Arundel Street, and his son was left '[his] picture & my wife's of Mr [Isaac] Fuller's Painteing'. Pearce had collected a 'Clositt of Bookes, prints and drawings', and his 'very good friend' William Talman was given his choice of these. The residue was divided between his son and son-in-law and was sold at auction early in 1696.

Pearce's masonry contracts were sometimes undertaken in partnership, but he must also have had a large workforce of his own, and some of his apprentices and assistants have been identified. **Richard Crutcher**, who was put to the London mason, William King in 1674, completed his apprenticeship with Pearce. In July 1680 **William Beard** was bound to him and **William Kidwell**, who was originally apprenticed to **John Bumpstead**, was turned over to him, receiving his freedom in 1687. Thomas Grew, the son of John Grew, was an assistant at St Lawrence Jewry and also at Combe Abbey, Worcs, where Pearce was working in the 1680s (**13, 32**). Four 'foreigners' (who were not members of a London livery company) were named as working for 'Mr Pearse in Arundel Street' in the general search conducted by the Masons' Company in 1686.

It is tempting to see Pearce principally as a successful mason contractor, who made occasional but brilliant forays into portrait sculpture. This judgment is challenged by a frequently quoted letter sent in 1711 from John Talman to his father, William, describing the decoration of a banqueting room at an entertainment John had given in Rome. Portraits of Palladio, Raphael and Michelangelo had been sited on one wall and opposite them were images of Inigo Jones, Isaac Fuller, the portraitist, and Pearce. In this galaxy Pearce was evidently intended to represent modern sculpture. (Add inf. Geoffrey Fisher).

IR

Literary References: *Vertue* I, 69, V, 9; *Poole* 1922–3, 32–45; *Knoop and Jones* 1935, *passim*; *Robinson and Adams*, 1935, 78, 145; *Wren Soc* XIII, *passim*, XVII, 35; *Seymour* 1952, 10–18; *Colvin and Oswald* 1954, 2312–6; *Croft-Murray and Hilton* 1960, 451–5, pl 243; *Harris* 1969, 444–7; *Physick* 1969, 23, 46–7, 58; *Fisher & Newman* 1985, 531–2; *Whinney* 1988, 102–9; *Penny* 1992, III, 142–6; *Colvin* 1995, 754–5, 1094–5; *Grove* 24, 1996, 753–4 (Physick); *Jervis* 1996, 893–903; *Gibson* 1997 (2), 160, 161; *Beard and Knott* 2000, 26, 43–8; *Ward-Jackson* 2003, 473; *ODNB* (Eustace); *Higgott* 2004, 534–47

Archival References: Fishmongers' PW and W Accts, 1669, 1684, 1686; Guildhall Restoration 1671–73, 8r, 9v, 9r; R C Physic, Cash Book, MS 2041, 1684, 92; CWA, St Clement Danes, Dutchy Liberty, 1681, WCA B13.178; H and B, St Clement Danes, April 1681, December 1695, WCA; St Matthew, Friday St, Accounts, 1685, 72, 1686, 68; Painter-Stainers, 11505; GPC

Will: proved 20 April 1695 Archdeaconry Court of Middx, Middx CRO (abstract repr *Harvey* 1965, 127)

Miscellaneous drawings: Design for a palace, Cumbria RO, Lowther papers 11/4/1; design for a church monument, Chicago A I, 1922.1306; Kingston Lacy, elevation drawn for Pratt, at Kingston Lacy; designs for church monuments, SJSM W3/62 (to a divine), W3/64; design for a porch, SJSM W3/65; design for a church monument, Ashm, Gibbs III, 110; design for a church monument to George Villiers, 2nd Duke of Buckingham, BM, P&D 1881-6-11-176 (*Croft-Murray and Hilton* 452–3, repr 242); another, Ashm, smaller Talman album, fol 7v; design for a monument to a divine, BM, P&D 1881-6-11-189 (*Croft-Murray and Hilton*, 454); design for a church monument, BM 1881-6-11-189; two designs for a monument to a bishop, BM, P&D 1881-6-11-191, 1881-6-11-192 (*Croft-Murray and Hilton*, 455, reprs 244, 245); design for the parlour chamber chimneypiece at Combe Abbey, Warks nd, BL MS Gough drawings, a 2, fol 79; ground plan and elevation for the former bishop's palace at Lichfield, Staffs, BL MS, Tanner 217, fols 48, 53; misc drawings formerly attrib William Talman and others, VAM 3436, 318–20 (chimneypieces), 432, 433, 441 (church monuments: *Wren Soc* 17, repr XXII, XXIII); Talman album, sold Sotheby, 27 May 1989, lot 737, inc fol 2 (gate piers, 1675), fol 13 (church monument), fol 18a (door), fol 40 (door), fol 41 (door), fol 43 (St Clement Danes, door), fol 45 (door), fol 52 (door), fol 54 (door), fol 57 (wainscot), fol 98 Fishmongers' Hall, door (C Lib repr); design for an urban building, Lowther drawings *c*1680–90, Cumbria RO, Lowther Drawings, cat 2; design for a clock at St Stephen Walbrook, *c*1681–2, Guildhall Lib; design for a statue of King Charles I, VAM D.377-1885; design for a reredos, VAM. P&D, E.342-1937; design, perhaps for St Mary Abchurch, All Souls, Oxford, Wren drawings I.60; for St Edmund the King, Wren drawings II.44 (*Wren Soc*, IX, repr 15); for St Martin Ludgate, Wren drawings II.50; Wren drawings IV.90 (stalls); designs for frames, Ashm, smaller Talman album, fol 8R, fol 9R; design for a vase, Bodleian, Radcliffe, fol 172R; Sotheby, 16 July 1992, lot 40 & 31 March 1999, lot 97 (pulpit)

Auction Catalogues: Pearce 1696

Portraits of the sculptor: 'a head of . . . Pierce the Carver painted by Fuller in poses of Coll. Seymor . . . a part of a Statue before him' (*Vertue* 1, 135, IV, 114), before 1672, probably the version at Sudeley Castle, Glos (*Beard and Knott*, 46 repr). This identification is discounted by Eustace, who suggests this it perhaps represents Pearce's father (*ODNB*)

Funerary Monuments

No.	Date	Work		Location		References
1.	1676	Margaret Vernon (†1675) Payment(s): £70		Sudbury, Derbys		*Beard and Knott* 2000, 43–8 (repr); GPC
2.	†1688	Edward, Viscount Irwin (†1688), and his wife (completed by John Nost I in 1697) Drawing(s): BM 1881-6-11-190; Ashm, Gibbs III, 110; SJSM W3/61		Whitkirk, Leeds, W R Yorks		*Gilbert* 1962–3, 4 (repr); *Whinney* 1988, 130, 445 n69, n70; *Guide to Leeds Archives*, 1988, 71; *Friedman* 1997, 46
3.	†1692	John Withers (†1692) and his wife (co-sculptor: John Nost I ?) Drawing(s): Soane W3/60		Arkesden, Essex		*Wren Soc* 17, p19 (repr XXV); *Whinney* 1988, 130; *ODNB*
4.	†1694	Diana, Lady Warburton (co-sculptor: John Nost I ?) Drawing(s): VAM 3436.421		St John the Baptist, Chester, Cheshire		*Physick* 1969 23, 46–7 (repr)

Statues

No.	Date	Work		Location		References
5.	1684	Sir William Walworth	wd	Fishmongers' Hall, City of London, staircase		*Vertue* I, 106; *Whinney* 1988, 102–3 (repr)
6.	1685	King Edward III Payment(s): £60 Model(s): Skinners' Hall, City of London, attrib C G Cibber	s	[Royal Exchange, London, line of kings on the façade of the piazza]; untraced		*Vertue* I, 106; *Gibson* 1997 (2), 161, 170, 172, (repr 4b)
7.	*c*1685	Queen Elizabeth I Payment(s): £50	s	[Royal Exchange, London, line of kings on the façade of the piazza]; untraced		Fishmongers Accounts, 3, 1686; *Gibson*, 1997 (2), 160, 162, 172; *Ward-Jackson* 2003, 326
8.	1686	King Henry V Payment(s): £60	s	[Royal Exchange, London, line of kings on the façade of the piazza]; untraced		Goldsmiths Ct Bk 9, fol 146v; *Gibson* 1997 (2), 172

Busts

No.	Date	Work		Location		References
9.	1672	Oliver Cromwell	b	Museum of London Other versions: several bronze casts taken from the original, including one coll H Labouchere, exhib Manc Art Treas Exhib, 1857, 111 Wemyss coll, Gosford House, marble	SD	*Manchester Art Treasures* 1857, 135; *Penny* 1992, III, 142–3
10.	*c*1673	Sir Christopher Wren (perhaps after a model by a Continental sculptor)	m	Ashmolean WA 1916.74 Other versions: All Souls, Oxford, plaster		*Vertue* IV, 181; Vertue V, 9; *Whinney* 1988, 104–5 (repr); *Penny* 1992, III, 142–5 (repr); *ODNB*
11.	1675–1684	Dr Baldwin Hamey Payment(s): £50 Drawing(s): Ashm, Talman album fol 87R (repr *Wolstenholme* 1964, 201)	m	R C Physic, London, X122		R C Physic Cash Book, 1684; *Robinson and Adams* 1935, 148; *Wolstenholme* 1964, 198–200 (repr); *Whinney* 1988, 105–6, 441, n32 (repr); *Colvin* 1995, 755, n3
12.	1688	Thomas Evans	m	Painter-Stainers' Hall, City of London, court room		*Vertue* II, 30; *Whinney* 1988, 105, 107 (repr); *Simon* 1993, 48–9 (repr); *ODNB*

Chimneypieces

No.	Date	Work		Location		References
13.	1684–1685	Six, three of them ornamented Payment(s): £190 18s 2d	m	Combe Abbey, Warks		*Colvin* 1984, 300
14.	*c*1690	Four		[Castle Bromwich Hall, Warks]; untraced		*Gunnis* 1968, 296

Architectural Sculpture

No.	Date	Work		Location		References
15.	post-1663	Designs for a gate-pier and carved work on the house Drawing(s): for a gate-pier, insc 'E.Peirce Fct', Bodl MS, Gough Drawings, a.2, fol 12, 36 (gate piers); SJSM W4/68 (gate pier)		Hamstead Marshall, Berks (gate piers only extant)		*Colvin* 1995, 754, 1067
16.	*c*1669	Doorway with the Company's coat of arms Drawing(s): Talman album, Sotheby, 27 April 1989, lot 737, fol 98	s	[Old Fishmongers' Hall, Thames Street entrance]; Fishmongers' Hall, City of London, rear entrance (part surviving)		*Ward-Jackson* 2003, 473; C Lib (repr)

17.	c1673	Carved fittings	wd	[St Benet Fink, Threadneedle St, City of London]; dispersed	*Colvin* 1995, 1095
18.	1670–1673	Work on the principal front Payment(s): £662	s	Guildhall, City of London	Guildhall restoration, 8r, 9v, 9r; *Seymour* 1952, 10–11 (repr); *Gunnis* 1968, 296
19.	1675	Doorcase with capitals and drops		Painter-Stainers' Hall, City of London, door to the hall	*Croft-Murray and Hulton* 1960, 451
20.	1676	Designs for woodwork (executed by Cornelius Austin)	wd	Emmanuel College, Cambridge	*Colvin* 1995, 754
21.	c1676	Four dragons (designed by Robert Hooke) Payment(s): £200 Drawing(s): by Robert Hooke, BL Add. MS. 5238	s	The Monument, City of London	*Vertue* V, 80; *Ward-Jackson* 2003, 263, 473 (repr)
22.	1675–1677	Balustrade carving and other ornaments for the great staircase, and a panel in the stairhead chamber (the latter now lost) Payment(s): £112 15s 5d	wd	Sudbury Hall, Derbys	*Beard* 1981, 275; *Colvin* 1995, 754; *Beard and Knott* 2000, 43–8 (repr)
23.	c1677	Great staircase with pineapples on the newel posts	wd	[Wolseley Hall, Staffs]; untraced	*Beard and Knott* 2000, 44
24.	1677	Overmantel, overdoor festoons and swags and flourishes for the panelling Payment(s): £120	wd	Sudbury Hall, Derbys, saloon	*Beard and Knott* 2000, 44, 48 (repr)
25.	?c1677	Panelling and doorcases	wd	[Wolseley Hall, Staffs, dining room]; White House, Gawsworth, Cheshire	*Plot* 1686, 383; *Colvin* 1995, 754
26.	c1678	Sundry enrichments Payment(s): £971 12s 5d	wd	[St Lawrence Jewry, City of London]; destroyed	*Beard and Knott* 2000, 47; *ODNB*
27.	1680	Model for the dragon weathervane Payment(s): £4	wd	St Mary-le-Bow, City of London	*Colvin* 1995, 754; *Ward-Jackson* 2003, 473; C Lib (repr)
28.	1682–1683	Craven coat of arms and a rebus Payment(s): £91 9s 5d	s	Combe Abbey, Warks	*Gunnis* 1968, 296; *Colvin* 1984, 248–309; *ODNB*
29.	begun 1684	Mason's work and a pulpit carved with 'Rapehild leaves with flowers' [acanthus], lace, foliage, scrolls, six cherubim and festoons		[St Andrew, Holborn, London]; masonry surviving; pulpit destroyed World War II	*Cobb* 1948, 78; *Colvin* 1995, 754; *Beard and Knott* 2000, 47
30.	1680–1684	'works done about ye hall' Payment(s): £70 (1681); £105 (1682)		[Grocers' Hall, City of London]; destroyed	Grocers WA. 11571/16 and 17; *Seymour* 1952, 12
31.	c1685	Dial		[St Swithin, Cannon St, City of London]; untraced	*Colvin* 1995, 1097
32.	c1685	Great staircase with 21 balusters and other carving Payment(s): £353 5s 5d	wd	Combe Abbey, Warks	*Colvin* 1984, 300; *Beard and Knott* 2000, 44, 48 n5
33.	1682–1685	Marble font, carved work on an oak font cover, a communion table, an oak pulpit and sounding board, an oak reredos and ornaments surrounding windows and doors	wd	[St Matthew Friday Street, City of London]; font and cover and pulpit at St Andrew-by-the-Wardrobe, City of London; communion table at St Vedast, City of London; reredos at Polesden Lacey, Surrey	St Matthew, Friday St, Accts, Aug 1685, 75; *Seymour* 1952, 12–13 (repr); JKB 1977–78, 63–74 (repr)
34.	1685–1687	Cartouche for the pediment with diocesan arms and festoons; gate piers with urns and scrolls Payment(s): £20 Drawing(s): Bodleian MS Tanner 217, fol 48, fol 53	s	Bishop's Palace, Lichfield, principal front	*Tringham* 1985–86, 57–63; *Colvin* 1995, 754; C Lib (repr)
35.	from 1689	Mason's work, including carving		Chatsworth, Derbys, south and east fronts	*Wren Soc* XVII, 22–42
36.	post-1690	A great vase with a relief of 'Amphitrite and Nereids', companion to a vase by Caius Gabriel Cibber (completed by John Nost I, 1700) Payment(s): £250	m	[Hampton Court Palace, Middx, fountain garden; Portland stone pedestal still in situ]; Kensington Gardens, London, orangery	*Wren Soc* 17 (repr VII); *Colvin* 1973–76, V, 171; C Lib (repr)
37.	post-1690	'a great white marble urne with divers figures and other ornaments' (completed by John Nost I, 1700) Payment(s): £475 10s	m	[Hampton Court Palace, Middx, (the former at the entry to the parterre, the latter in the privy garden)]; Windsor Castle, east terrace	*Colvin* 1973–76, V, 171
38.	1678–1690	Extensive carved work and architectural ornaments including carved panels 'with their flowers and Inrichments' Drawing(s): Corinthian capital and cartouche and swag, St Paul's coll, Guildhall Lib KD 31, 128; misc elements, Downes coll (Guildhall)	s	St Paul's Cathedral, London, south side, south portico, south front and choir	*Wren Soc* XIII, XIV, *passim*; *Knoop and Jones* 1935, 46; *ODNB*; *Higgott* 2004 (repr)
39.	1689–1694	Scrolls, festoons, shells and other ornaments for the reassembled Diana (Arethusa) fountain Payment(s): £1,262 3s od Drawing(s): YCBA B1975.4.1707	s	[Hampton Court, Middx, privy garden]; Bushey Park, Hampton Court, Middx	*Harris* 1969, 444–7 (repr); *Colvin* 1973–76, V, 172; *Fisher & Newman* 1985, 531–2; *ODNB*

40.	1694	Seven Dials column (design and supervision of its erection) Drawing(s): BM PDL 1881-6-11-177	s	Weybridge, Surrey, Monument Green, since 1773	*Grenside* 1953–4, 143–5; *Croft-Murray and Hulton* 1960, 452–4 (repr 241); *Worsley* 1986, 78–9 (repr)
41.	1689–1695	'carving work done about ye fountain in ye Privy Garden', including shells, festoons and scrolls	s	[Whitehall Palace, London]; untraced	*Gunnis* 1968, 296
42.	*c*1695	Four large flowerpots, richly carved Payment(s): £187 10s	s	King's gallery, Hampton Court Palace, Middx, attic storey façade	*Colvin*, 1973–76, V, 190
43.	1689–1695	Garden seats		[Whitehall Palace, London]; untraced	*Gunnis* 1968, 296
44.	nd	'modeling and carving an Eagle' Payment(s): £2 10s		['for the Spire of St Swithun's']; untraced	MS Rawlinson B.389, f126; *ODNB*
45.	nd	'roses, festoons and other work about ye gates'		Clare College, Cambridge	*Willis and Clark* 1888, I, 104; *Gunnis* 1968, 296

PEARCE, Edward, of London fl *c*1809–64

Pearce worked in partnership with **Noakes of London** between *c*1809 and 1856 but he also signed several works independently. He was responsible for routine parts of the monument to Princess Sophia, the daughter of George III, in Kensal Green Cemetery (7). The elaborate carved sarcophagus which is its main feature was carved by **Bardi** to the designs of Professor Lüdwig Grüner. The monument to Ann Gregory in Barbados is signed by 'E Pearce of 163 & 165 Euston Road, London' (11).

Literary References: *Gunnis* 1968, 273–4, 296; *Curl* 2001, 123, 200

Funerary Monuments

1.	?1809	Robert Usherwood (co-sculptor: Noakes, of London)	Whitby, N R Yorks		*Gunnis* 1968, 273
2.	?1813	John Pidcock and family (†1791–1813) (co-sculptor: Noakes, of London)	St Michael, Brierley Hill, Staffs		GPC
3.	?1814	Sarah Ridehalgh (co-sculptor: Noakes, of London)	Eccles, Cheshire		*Gunnis* 1968, 274
4.	?1816	Mrs Falconbridge (co-sculptor: Noakes, of London)	St James, Garlickhithe, City of London		*Gunnis* 1968, 274
5.	†1845	Sarah Heusch (co-sculptor: Noakes, of London)	Kensal Green Cemetery, London, catacombs	S	
6.	†1848	Charles Heusch (co-sculptor: Noakes, of London)	Kensal Green Cemetery, London, catacombs	S	
7.	1848	Princess Sophia (co-sculptor: Signori, of Carrara Bardi)	Kensal Green Cemetery, London	SD	*Curl* 2001, 200–1, 223 (repr)
8.	†1856	Rev Spencer Thornton (co-sculptor: Noakes, of London)	Wendover, Bucks		Pevsner, *Bucks*, 1994, 717
9.	?1859	Anna Dethick	Oldbury, Salop	S	GPC
10.	†1859	Rev Henry Toller	Market Harborough Congregational chapel, Leics	S	
11.	†1864	Ann Gregory	St Martin, Barbados	S	

PEARCE, J, of Frampton-on-Severn fl *c*1763–1812

His tablets in Gloucestershire include a large one with 'delicate details' at Stone and 'a charming one with a relief of a violin and an open music-book' at Westbury-on-Severn (*Gunnis* 1968, 297) (5, 11). Another, at Longney, features a sarcophagus, urn and weeping willow (4).

Funerary Monuments

1.	†1763	Sarah Cowley	Slimbridge, Glos	S	Pevsner, *Glos: Vale & Forest of Dean*, 1976, 340
2.	†1763	Sarah Smith	Slimbridge, Glos	S	Pevsner, *Glos: Vale & Forest of Dean*, 1976, 340
3.	†1768	Daniel Willey	Moreton Valence, Glos	S	Pevsner, *Glos: Vale & Forest of Dean*, 1976, 302
4.	†1783	John Fryer	Longney, Glos	S	Pevsner, *Glos: Vale & Forest of Dean*, 1976, 292
5.	†1795	John Cox	Stone, Glos	S	Pevsner, *Glos: Vale & Forest of Dean*, 1976, 352
6.	†1797	Betty Wiltshire	Berkeley, Glos	S	Pevsner, *Glos: Vale & Forest of Dean*, 1976, 101
7.	†1797	John Bray	Whitminster, Glos	S	Pevsner, *Glos: Vale & Forest of Dean*, 1976, 403
8.	†1798	Nathaniel Rogers	Arlingham, Glos	S	Pevsner, *Glos: Vale & Forest of Dean*, 1976, 87
9.	†1798–1799	Samuel and John Pearce	Frampton-on-Severn, Glos	S	Pevsner, *Glos: Vale & Forest of Dean*, 1976, 191
10.	*c*1805	Unidentified subject, tablet	Christ Church, Painswick, Glos	S	Pevsner, *Glos: Cotswolds*, 1999, 545
11.	†1812	Thomas Sinderby	Westbury-on-Severn, Glos	S	Pevsner, *Glos: Vale & Forest of Dean*, 1976, 400
12.	nd	Unidentified subjects, several	Congregational Church, Upper Cam, Glos	S	Pevsner, *Glos: Cotswolds*, 1999, 210

PEARCE, W H, of Truro fl *c*1820–48

In 1848 he made two columns of serpentine and a pedestal of steatite, with a porphyry and jasper base, for Osborne House at the order of the Prince Consort (*Builder*, 1848, 416). Gunnis notes that his monuments are 'mostly neo-Hellenic' and that one, to Thomas Teague, has a medallion-portrait (*Gunnis* 1968, 297) (5).

Funerary Monuments

1.	?1821	Frances Bettesworth	St Michael Carhays, Cornwall	S	*Gunnis* 1968, 297
2.	?1826	Susannah Bayntun	Mylor, Cornwall	S	*Gunnis* 1968, 297
3.	?1833	Jonathan Passingham	Helston, Cornwall	S	*Gunnis* 1968, 297
4.	?1837	Colonel Pasmore	Helston, Cornwall	S	*Gunnis* 1968, 297

5.	?1837	Thomas Teague	Redruth, Cornwall	S	*Gunnis* 1968, 297
6.	?1840	Benjamin Sampson	Gwennap, Cornwall	S	*Gunnis* 1968, 297
7.	1820–1840	Unidentified subjects	Redruth, Cornwall		Pevsner, *Cornwall*, 1970, 150
8.	†1841	Edward, Earl of Falmouth	St Michael Penkevil, Cornwall		Pevsner, *Cornwall*, 1970, 193
9.	†1842	Caroline Rashleigh	Tywardreath, Cornwall	S	Pevsner, *Cornwall*, 1970, 237
Architectural Sculpture					
10.	?1848	Two serpentine columns and a steatite pedestal	[Osborne House, I of W]; untraced		*Builder* 1848, 416

PEARCE (or PIERCE), Robert fl 1694–1723

Pearce served his apprenticeship under John Davis and was made free of the Masons' Company on 20 October 1694. He succeeded **Thomas Cartwright II** as mason at St Thomas's Hospital, receiving payments from 1712 to 1723, including £10 16s on 4 December 1714 'for beautifying the statue of Sir Robt. Clayton' (St Thomas's Hospital Account Books, in RG/JP, 6, 1075v). His son Charles was apprenticed to **Robert Kidwell** in 1719.

Literary References: *Webb* 1999, 25

Archival References: Masons' Co, *Freemen*, fol 56 (29 October 1694)

PEARCE (or PIERCE), Thomas fl 1752

The *London Magazine* states that Pearce was responsible for the sculpture of Portland stone in the pediment of the naval hospital at Haslar (**1**). It is 48 feet long and 11 feet high, with a large carving of the Royal arms in the centre, figures of *Navigation* and *Trade* to left and right, and various subsidiary figures and emblems, including 'a sea-bird bringing an eel in its mouth to a sailor in distress' (*London Mag*, 1752, 575). Gunnis comments, 'One could think of a great many things a shipwrecked mariner would have infinitely preferred' (*Gunnis* 1968, 297).

Architectural Sculpture					
1.	1752	Pediment carving	s	Royal Naval Hospital (Haslar Hospital), Gosport, Hants	Pevsner, *Hants & Isle of Wight*, 1967, 244

PEARSON, William fl 1848

Pearson's trade card of 1848 gives his address as 4 Blagdon Street, Gibson Street, New Road, Newcastle on Tyne and advertises his competence with monuments, tombs, chimneypieces, head stones etc. It adds 'Lettering done in town or country' (Banks 106.24).

PEART, Charles 1759–98

Peart was born at English Newton, Monmouth, on 22 December 1759. He was in London by 1778, when he exhibited three wax models at the Royal Academy from Mr Abington's, Paulin Street, Hanover Square (**20**). He entered the Royal Academy Schools on 29 March 1781 and the following year was awarded a medal for a bas-relief of *Hercules and Omphale*, which he had submitted together with a sketch of *Apollo and Daphne* (**17**).

After leaving the Schools, Peart worked as an assistant to **John Charles Lochee**, and was employed as a modeller by Josiah Wedgwood and the Derby porcelain factory (**9, 18, 19, 33**). Much of his time seems to have been devoted to work for George Grenville, Marquess of Buckingham, at Stowe, where he made a set of four reliefs for the Queen's Temple (**16**). In 1788 he wrote to Wedgwood's agent, Bierly, from Stowe, apologising for his delay in completing a commission, explaining that he was obliged to 'work 14 Hours in a Day and which Sir, at present puts it quite out of my power to attend to anything else' (Wedgwood/Peart L1/59, Peart to Wedgwood, 2 June 1788). He sent a similar message to William Duesbury II at Derby in February 1790.

Peart exhibited regularly at the RA until the year of his death, from addresses in Paulin Street, Charlotte Street, Great Tichfield Street and the New Road. His early exhibits were all wax models but in the late 1780s he began to show larger-scale work, including designs for monuments and portrait busts. One of his first large commissions, the monument to Lieutenant-Colonel John Campbell in Bombay, may have been obtained through the influence of his wife, Elizabeth, whose sister's husband, Mr Woodcock, worked for the East India Company (**1**). It has life-sized figures of *Death* and *Hope* flanking an urn on a tall pedestal. This was followed in 1791 by the monument to Joseph Moorhouse, a colonel in the Company's coast artillery who was killed at the siege of Bangalore (**4**). This comprises a sarcophagus on lion's feet surmounted by flags and a medallion portrait of Moorhouse, hoisted aloft by a cherub to obtain the recognition of *Britannia*, who holds a laurel crown in readiness.

In 1792 Peart provided a statue of Henry V for Monmouth Shire Hall and three years later he carved a marble chimneypiece for the Marquess of Buckingham's London house (**10, 14**). At the same time he continued to work for Wedgwood. Writing to Bierly on 14 July 1794, he asked the agent to remit £20 on account, for 'at this time I have been laying in a large stock of stone to save the duty, which I am called on to pay of course immediately' (ODNB).

He died in 1798, leaving a widow and a young child. Farington records that in September 1799 Peart's affairs were not yet settled, but that Mrs Peart expected to receive little as he was 'much in arrears to the parish of St Pancrass having rec'd. money as Parish Officer' (*Farington*, vol 4, 1281). Gunnis notes that she was granted a small pension by the Academy in that year.

Literary References: *Hutchison* 1960–62, 145; *Gunnis* 1968, 298; *Pyke* 1973, 102; *Clifford* 1990, *passim*; *ODNB* (Graham-Vernon)

Funerary Monuments					
1.	†1784	Lieutenant-Colonel John Campbell	St Thomas's Cathedral, Mumbai (Bombay), India	S	*Groseclose* 1995, 55–6 (repr)
2.	1789	'Design for a monument'	[Exhib RA, London, 574]; untraced		*Graves* VI, 1905–6, 93
3.	?1791	John Finch	Dudley, Worcs	S	*Gunnis* 1968, 298
4.	†1791	Lieutenant-Colonel Joseph Moorhouse	St Mary, Fort St George, Chennai (Madras), India	S	*Groseclose* 1995, 51–4 (repr)
5.	1792	'Genius of Friendship; model for a monument'	[Exhib RA, London, 723]; untraced		*Graves* VI, 1905–6, 93
6.	1793	'A monumental figure'	[Exhib RA, London, 747]; untraced		*Graves* VI, 1905–6, 93
7.	†1795	Rev Henry Brownam	Upper Swell, Glos	S	Pevsner, *Glos: Cotswolds*, 1999, 711
8.	1797	'Britannia rewarding merit; a design for a monument; a sketch'	[Exhib RA, London, 1178]; untraced		*Graves* VI, 1905–6, 93

Statues

No.	Date	Work		Location		Reference
9.	1787	Clothed putti, two models		Untraced Other versions: reproduced in Derby biscuit porcelain for Vulliamy's clocks		*Clifford* 1990, 20–4 (repr)
10.	1792	King Henry V		Monmouth Shire Hall		*Gunnis* 1968, 298; *CL*, CXXVI, 3271, 12 Nov 1959, 846 (repr)

Busts

No.	Date	Work		Location		Reference
11.	1790	Unidentified nobleman		[Exhib RA, London, 659]; untraced		*Graves* VI, 1905–6, 93
12.	1796	Sir Samuel Marshall		[Exhib RA, London, 876]; untraced		*Graves* VI, 1905–6, 93
13.	1797	Unidentified officer		[Exhib RA, London, 1189]; untraced		*Graves* VI, 1905–6, 93

Chimneypieces

No.	Date	Work		Location		Reference
14.	1794	Description unavailable Payment(s): £51 16s		[Buckingham House, Pall Mall, London]; untraced		Soane bill book 5 fol 24
15.	1798	Figure for the front of a chimneypiece, two models 'to be executed in marble'		[Exhib RA, London, 1040 and 1044]; untraced		*Graves* VI, 1905–6, 93

Architectural Sculpture

No.	Date	Work		Location		Reference
16.	1790	Four medallions celebrating the patriotism of King George III	p	Stowe, Bucks, Queen's Temple		*Gibbon* 1969, 79, 80 (repr)

Reliefs

No.	Date	Work		Location		Reference
17.	1782	Hercules and Omphale (with a sketch of Apollo and Daphne)		[RA gold medal]; untraced		RA Premium list; *Gunnis* 1968, 298
18.	1787	Plaques after gems in the collection at Stowe		[Models for Wedgwood]; untraced		*ODNB*
19.	1787	Sir William Chambers, two sons of King George III, Hastings, Elliot and Lord Hillsborough, medallions		[Models for Wedgwood]; untraced		Wedgwood/Peart E2/931; *Gunnis* 1968, 298

Miscellaneous

No.	Date	Work		Location		Reference
20.	1778	Three models	w	[Exhib RA, London, 229]; untraced		*Graves* VI, 1905–6, 93
21.	1779	Unidentified lady, model	w	[Exhib RA, London, 234]; untraced		*Graves* VI, 1905–6, 93
22.	1780	Unidentified general, model		[Exhib RA, London, 468]; untraced		*Graves* VI, 1905–6, 93
23.	1780	Unidentified gentleman, model	w	[Exhib RA, London, 297]; untraced		*Graves* VI, 1905–6, 93
24.	1780	Unidentified lady, model	w	[Exhib RA, London, 296]; untraced		*Graves* VI, 1905–6, 93
25.	1781	Unidentified subjects, two portraits	w	[Exhib RA, London, 358 and 363]; untraced		*Graves* VI, 1905–6, 93
26.	1782	Unidentified subjects, four portraits	w	[Exhib RA, London, 341, 342, 343 and 345]; untraced		*Graves* VI, 1905–6, 93
27.	1784	Prometheus, model		[Exhib RA, London, 518]; untraced		*Graves* VI, 1905–6, 93
28.	1786	Hercules and Cacus		[Exhib RA, London, 500]; untraced		*Graves* VI, 1905–6, 93
29.	1786	Princess Amelia, 'composition'		[Exhib RA, London, 261]; untraced		*Graves* VI, 1905–6, 93
30.	1786	Unidentified subjects, two portraits	w	[Exhib RA, London, 263 and 345]; untraced		*Graves* VI, 1905–6, 93
31.	1787	Euphrosyne hiding the arrows from Cupid		[Exhib RA, London, 623]; untraced		*Graves* VI, 1905–6, 93
32.	1787	Neptune and Amphitryte		[Exhib RA, London, 619]; untraced		*Graves* VI, 1905–6, 93
33.	1789	'Cupid model'd by Peart'		[for Josiah Wedgwood]; untraced		Wedgwood/Peart E2/1358; E2/1358 (Wm Hackwood Acct)
34.	1789	Foscari, Doge of Venice		[Exhib RA, London, 575]; untraced		*Graves* VI, 1905–6, 93
35.	1789	King George III		[Exhib RA, London, 592]; untraced		*Graves* VI, 1905–6, 93
36.	1790	Britannia with a medallion of her Majesty, model		[Exhib RA, London, 657]; untraced		*Graves* VI, 1905–6, 93
37.	1792	Ambarvalia, or sacrifice before harvest		[Exhib RA, London, 721]; untraced		*Graves* VI, 1905–6, 93
38.	1792	Regulus's return to Carthage, sketch	tc	[Exhib RA, London, 740]; untraced		*Graves* VI, 1905–6, 93

PEATTS, of Nottingham fl 1827

He signs a large wall-tablet at Costock, Notts (1).

Literary References: *Gunnis* 1968, 298

Funerary Monuments

No.	Date	Work		Location		Reference
1.	1827	Rev William Wild		Costock, Notts	S	Pevsner, *Notts*, 1979, 107

PECK, George fl 1843–51

In 1843 he carved very fine pews with poppyheads for Holy Trinity, Hull (East Yorks CRO, Holy Trinity Acct Bks, 4 March 1843 – 'To cash. pd. George Peck for carving model. £1-7-6'). The *Hull Advertiser* of 2 May 1851 noted that he had emigrated to California (Inf. Gerardine Mulcahy)

Funerary Monuments

No.	Date	Work		Location		Reference
1.	1849	'Monument to Andrew Marvell'		Untraced		*Hull Advertiser*, 27 July 1849

Architectural Sculpture

No.	Date	Work		Location		Reference
2.	1843	Carved pews	wd	Holy Trinity, Hull, Yorks		Holy Trinity Accts, EYCRO

Reliefs

No.	Date	Work		Location		Reference
3.	1843	Woman and her child in a draped bed, limewood		Knox/Longstaffe-Gowan coll	SD	

Miscellaneous

No.	Date	Work		Location		Reference
4.	1847	'Carving of Jenny Lind'		Untraced		*Hull Advertiser*, 10 Sept 1847

PECK, Henry William fl 1816–21

In 1816, while living at Union Place, Shoreditch, Peck won a silver medal from the Society of Arts for a plaster-cast of *Adam and Eve*, a work he showed at the Royal Academy a year later (1). He continued exhibiting at the Academy until

1820 and also sent work to the British Institution in 1819–1821. In 1817 his address was 23 Gloucester Street, Hoxton, he was at 55 Exmouth Street, Spa Fields, two years later and had moved to St James's Place, Hampstead Road by 1821.

Literary References: RSA *Transactions*, vol 34, 1816, 29; *Gunnis* 1968, 298

Statues					
1.	1816	The Lord pronouncing judgement on Adam and Eve	p	[Soc of A, silver medal]; untraced	RSA *Transactions*, vol 34, 1816, 29; *Graves* VI, 1905–6, 94
Busts					
2.	1817	Unidentified gentleman		[Exhib RA, London, 1016]; untraced	*Graves* VI, 1905–6, 94
Miscellaneous					
3.	1818	Endymion visited by Cynthia		[Exhib RA, London, 1078]; untraced	*Graves* 1875, 421; *Graves* VI, 1905–6, 94
4.	1820	Instruction		[Exhib RA, London, 1021]; untraced	*Graves* 1875, 421; *Graves* VI, 1905–6, 94
5.	1821	Mercy		[Exhib BI, London, 306]; untraced	*Graves* 1875, 421

PECK, J, of Loughborough fl *c*1770–1804

He signs a number of architectural tablets, the best of which are listed below.

Literary References: *Gunnis* 1968, 298

Funerary Monuments					
1.	?1770	Benjamin Brookes	Loughborough, Leics	S	*Gunnis* 1968, 298
2.	?1798	Rev Francis Wilcox	Loughborough, Leics	S	*Gunnis* 1968, 298
3.	†1800	Elizabeth Cropper	Bunny, Notts	S	Pevsner, *Notts*, 1979, 85
4.	†1804	Rev T Hastings	West Leake, Notts	S	Pevsner, *Notts*, 1979, 375

PECK, John, of Bishop's Stortford –1834

His date of death is given by the *Essex and Herts Mercury* as 18 April 1834 (*Gunnis* 1968, 298).

Funerary Monuments					
1.	†1776	Rev Robert Tooke	Lambourne, Essex	S	*Gunnis* 1968, 298

PEDLEY, Joseph, of London fl 1717–21

He must have been established by 1717 for in that year 'Joshua, son of Edward Cale of St. James's' was apprenticed to him (PRO, INL/1/6). In 1720 he built a brick corner house on the west side of Bond Street which he insured for £450, and another on the corner of Bond Street and Pedley Street (the latter, presumably, was named after him). In the same year he built two little houses in Castle Street, St. Martin-in-the-Fields, for Sir Robert Chaplin (Declared Accounts of the Directors of the South Sea Company). In 1721 Pedley built several other houses in Pedley Street, which no longer exist, and those were insured with the Westminster Fire Office, together with two which he had built on the east side of St Martin's Lane and his own house and yard.

Archival References: WFO, PR, no 2223 (31 Dec 1720); GPC

PEDLEY, Joseph, of Warwick 1677–

As a young man Pedley lived in Rocester, Staffs, but he settled in Birmingham in 1703, and about four years later was employed in rebuilding King Edward's Grammar School. In 1713, when aged 36, he made a deposition regarding the mason's work he carried out there (*King Edward's School* 1924–74, vol 3, 93). He was apparently paid in instalments, receiving £268 in total.

In 1710 Pedley agreed to execute the stonework for Birmingham Cathedral, for '2 1/2 d. a foot and the mouldings at 7d. a foot, but if the Commissioners did find that 7d. per foot for the said mouldings be not enough, they to give something more' (1). The commissioners did decide that 7d. was insufficient, and three years later agreed to pay an extra 'six-and-thirty pounds in consideration of the hard bargain made' (*Gunnis* 1968, 298). William Shenstone, the poet and landscape gardener, later wrote that Pedley '. . . has been a great Sufferer by Undertaking Birmingham new-Church; wch was, I think, a Design of ye late Groom-Porters [i.e. Thomas Archer] Certain it is yt he has been a great sufferer by the Groom-porter himself; concerning which he relates a Story not much to ye Groom-porter's Honour' (*Williams* 1939, 247).

In 1749 Pedley and his son were working for Shenstone at his *ferme ornée*, The Leasowes, carving ornamental urns and constructing two 'Gothick' pinnacles for one of the buildings (2). Shenstone recommended Pedley to his friend, Henrietta, Lady Luxborough, writing, 'He desires me to mention him to your Ladyship; says he has workd you some Urns formerly and shou'd be glad to serve you hereafter. He is an honest man, will be *glad* to work *cheap*, & as to ye *manual operation*, I fancy works very well' (*Williams* 1939, 233). Lady Luxborough seems to have declined the invitation, employing another mason in Warwick to make an urn for her garden instead.

Literary References: *Williams* 1939, *passim*; *Gunnis* 1968, 298

Architectural Sculpture				
1.	1709–1715	Stonework, probably including decorative window surrounds (designed by Thomas Archer)	[St Philip's Cathedral, Birmingham, Warks]; building refaced 1864–1869	*Gunnis* 1968, 298; *Noszlopy* 1998, 114
2.	1749	Urns	[The Leasowes, Halesowen, Salop, gardens]; untraced	*Williams* 1939, 240, 244, 246

PEISLEY, Bartholomew I, II and III, of Oxford

Bartholomew Peisley I (1620–1692)
Bartholomew Peisley II (c1654–1715)
Bartholomew Peisley III (†1727)

A family of Oxford master masons, they supplied Headington stone for St Paul's Cathedral in 1686 and 1697 and so may have been quarry owners as well as builders. The family lived in a house in St Michael's Street, Oxford, which they re-fronted with a façade in the style of Vanbrugh *c*1721.

Bartholomew I built the senior common room at St John's College in 1673–6 and in 1685–6 he completed the library and chapel of St Edmund Hall, begun by Edmund Bird in 1680–2. In November 1681 he gave evidence in a lawsuit between Thomas Wood, mason, and Richard Frogley, carpenter, stating that he was 61 and that he had built 'a stone house in St Gyles's parish in the suburbs of Oxon where in Esqr. Bateman lately lived' (OU Chancellor's Ct Papers, fol 33). He died in December 1692 and was buried at St Giles's. His property was divided between his sons, Bartholomew and Charles, and his daughter, Miriam.

Bartholomew II was apprenticed to his father in 1669. By 1689 he had 'severall times been chief contriver of buildings of about £200 and £300 value' (OU Chancellors Ct Papers, 1689 Easter, bundle 54, in *Colvin* 1995, 746). He was the master mason responsible for Trinity College chapel in 1691–4 and the New Building at Wadham College in 1693–4. In 1697 he contracted to build Stones almshouses in St Clement's, Oxford. He was one of the principal contractors at Blenheim Palace, where he was responsible for building the great arch of the grand bridge. In his will he left £300 as a marriage settlement for his daughter Mary, who had married Henry Joynes, the comptroller at Blenheim. His property in Oxford went to his son Bartholomew III, and his daughter Elizabeth was to 'have and enjoy one of the chambers in the house where I nowe live'. To Joynes he left £300, 'to be pay'd within twelve months next, after the debt of Twelve Hundred pounds due to me for work done at Blenheim House at Woodstock shall be paid to my Executor, or as soon as Three Hundred pounds of that debt shall be payd him' (Peisley/Blenheim 23 May 1715, BL Ad MS 24327, fol 12). Apparently many of the craftsmen employed at Blenheim had difficulties in extracting payments, for Joynes himself, writing to a Mr Small in 1748, complained of his 'hard fate of not being paid the amounts remaining due to me', adding 'but the temper of the Duchess of Marlborough was such and I really know not for what or why, she would do everything that she could to prevent my being paid' (*ibid*, fol 65).

Bartholomew III appears to have entered into partnership with **William Townesend**, for they worked together on a number of important contracts and Thomas Hearne wrote that Peisley 'and one William Townsend carried (as it were) all the business in masonry before them, both in Oxford and in all the Parts about it' (*Hearne* 1914, 343). They built the Radcliffe quadrangle at University College (1717–9) and the Codrington library at All Souls (1715 onwards) and contracted for the erection of Radley Hall, Berks in June 1721. Like his father Peisley worked at Blenheim, where he and Townesend built the Woodstock gate to Hawksmoor's designs in 1722–3. He died, aged 44, on 29 August 1727 and was buried in St Giles's churchyard.

Literary References: *Gunnis* 1968, 298–9; *Colvin* 1995, 746–7

Architectural Sculpture

1.	1708	Capitals of columns (by Bartholomew Peisley II)		Blenheim Palace, Oxon	*Gunnis* 1968, 299
2.	1723	Door cases (by Bartholomew Peisley III) Payment(s): £350	m	Blenheim Palace, Oxon, gallery	*Gunnis* 1968, 299

PELLE, Honoré fl 1672–1706

A Franco-Italian sculptor working in northern Italy at the end of the 17th century, he may have visited Rome before becoming a pupil-assistant to Pierre Puget in Genoa. Examples of his work can be found in Genoa and Modena. He signs two busts of Charles II, but since the sculptor was still in Genoa in 1685, the year of the King's death, it is doubtful that he ever saw him in person (**2, 3**). The earlier bust is at Burghley where it was listed, together with another work by Pellé, in an inventory of 1688, as '2 Large figures of pollisht Marble being the late King Caro. the 2d head, & a Sibill on painted peddistalls' in 'The Marble Salloon Roome' (Burghley House inventory made by Culpepper Tanner, p 25). They were probably commissioned by the 5th Earl of Exeter, who may well have encountered Pellé on his travels in Italy, 1679–81. The 'painted peddistalls' are in fact of inlaid marble. The second bust is thought to have been inspired by Bernini's bust of Francesco d'Esté (Galleria Estense, Modena), since it shares the same turn of the head and horizontal swathe of drapery, together with the deeply cut straggling curls of the wig and the circular stump-like arms (**3**). It is thought that busts of King William III in the grand staircase hall at Petworth House and on the north wall of the town hall at Petworth, Sussex, may also be by Pellé.

Literary References: Pevsner, *Sussex*, 1965, 297; *Whinney* 1988, 440, n4; *Gibson* 1997(1), 192; *Rowell* 2000 (2), 22

Statues

1.	*c*1682	Sibyl, on a polchrome inlaid pedestal	m	Burghley House, Lincs, formerly marble saloon, now overlooking courtyard		*Gibson* 1997 (1), 193

Busts

2.	1682	King Charles II, on a polychrome inlaid pedestal	m	Burghley House, Lincs, formerly marble saloon, now overlooking courtyard	SD	*Gibson* 1997 (1), 193, 375
3.	1684	King Charles II	m	VAM 239-1881	SD	*Williamson* 1996, 135 (repr)

PENN, Francis fl 1751

Chimneypieces

1.	1751	Several Payment(s): £66	s	[Ragley Hall, Warks]; untraced	Archives Marquess of Hertford in GPC

PENNISTONE, Henry fl 1720

He was paid £83 in 1720 for the 'Balustrade' and other work at Temple Newsam House, W R Yorks, including a 'palisade, two pedestalls att the end of ye walk and ye Hall Door'.

Archival References: GPC

PEPPER, W fl *c*1767

A Lincolnshire statuary, he signs a wall-tablet at Rippingale.

Literary References: *Gunnis* 1968, 299

Funerary Monuments

1.	?1767	Richard Quincey	Rippingale, Lincs	S	*Gunnis* 1968, 299

PEPPER, William I, of Brighton fl *c*1831–54

In 1846 Pepper made the model for the 'delightful fountain with its three intertwined dolphins' which stands on the Steine at Brighton (*Gunnis* 1968, 299) (**11**). He exhibited busts at the Royal Academy, 1846–54, from Duke Street, Brighton and then 39 Western Road, Brighton. He signs a number of monuments, including one with a relief-bust of Joseph Allen and a 'charming miniature Gothic work to Mrs Crozier, with a small figure of a woman mourning by an urn' (*ibid*) (**3, 4**).

Literary References: *Gunnis* 1968, 299

Funerary Monuments						
1.	?1831	Lidbetter children		Bramber, Sussex	S	*Gunnis* 1968, 299
2.	?1838	Mary Marla		Bramber, Sussex	S	*Gunnis* 1968, 299
3.	?1851	Joseph Allen		St Peter, Brighton, Sussex	S	*Gunnis* 1968, 299
4.	nd	Mrs Crozier		St Nicholas, Brighton, Sussex	S	*Gunnis* 1968, 299
Busts						
5.	1846	J Cordy Burrows		[Exhib RA, London, 1476]; untraced		*Graves* VI, 1905–6, 105
6.	1846	Sir John Hare		[Exhib RA, London, 1441]; untraced		*Graves* VI, 1905–6, 105
7.	1847	Master Pilcher	m	[Exhib RA, London, 1367]; untraced		*Graves* VI, 1905–6, 105
8.	1850	William Seymour		Brighton Town Hall, Sussex		*Gunnis* 1968, 299
9.	1853	F W Robertson		Bodleian	D	*Gunnis* 1968, 299
10.	1854	James Golding	m	[Exhib RA, London, 1447]; untraced		*Graves* VI, 1905–6, 105
Architectural Sculpture						
11.	1846	Fountain with three intertwined dolphins, model		[The Steine, Brighton, Sussex]; untraced		*GM*, vol XXVI, Aug 1846, 193; *Gunnis* 1968, 299

PEPPER, William II, of Brighton fl 1852–68

The son of **William Pepper I**, he joined the Royal Academy Schools in 1852, and exhibited busts at the Academy, 1851–68, from addresses in Penzance, London and Brighton. Gunnis notes that 'his best monument', to Luke Flood, has 'a relief of a deathbed scene' (*Gunnis* 1968, 299) (**1**). The 'J. Pepper' who signs an undated bust of Sir Walter Scott in Brighton Art Gallery may have been another member of the family.

Literary References: *Gunnis* 1968, 299

Funerary Monuments						
1.	†1857	Luke Flood		St Luke, Chelsea, London		Pevsner, *London: N W*, 1991, 560
2.	?1864	William King		St George, Brighton, Sussex	S	*Gunnis* 1968, 299
3.	nd	Rev Richard Wake		Courteenhall, Northants	S	*Gunnis* 1968, 299
Busts						
4.	1851	Louis Philippe Paul		[Exhib RA, London, 1297]; untraced		*Graves* VI, 1905–6, 105
5.	1852	Unidentified lady, model 'for marble'	p	[Exhib RA, London, 1452]; untraced		*Graves* VI, 1905–6, 105
6.	1857	Unidentified infant	m	[Exhib RA, London, 1278]; untraced		*Graves* VI, 1905–6, 105
7.	1862	Sir James Prior	m	[Exhib RA, London, 1101]; untraced		*Graves* VI, 1905–6, 105
8.	1865	Lewis Slight		Brighton Town Hall, Sussex		*Gunnis* 1968, 299
9.	1868	Henry Collinson	m	[Exhib RA, London, 1160]; untraced		*Graves* VI, 1905–6, 105
Reliefs						
10.	1854	Rev F W Robertson		[Exhib RA, London, 1521]; untraced		*Graves* VI, 1905–6, 105

PERCIVALL AND RICKETTS, of Birmingham fl 1790–1800

They sign 'a large wall-tablet of simple, but good, design' at Walsall, and 'a smaller one' at Curdworth (*Gunnis* 1968, 299) (**1–2**).

Funerary Monuments						
1.	?1793	Mary Scott		Walsall, Staffs	S	*Gunnis* 1968, 299
2.	?1798	William Wakefield		Curdworth, Warks	S	*Gunnis* 1968, 299

PERCY, A

For information the reader is referred to *Pyke* 1973, 102 and *Pyke* 1981, 31

PERCY, Francis I fl 1676–87

Architectural Sculpture						
1.	1676–1679	Capitals, festoons, shields, 'thirteen great heads' and other ornaments		Trinity College, Cambridge		*Wren Society*, V, 39
2.	1687	Coat of arms		Clare Hall, Cambridge, above hall door		*Willis and Clarke*, I, 1886, 107, in *Gunnis* 1968, 299

PERCY, Francis II fl later 18th century

A statuary working in Dublin in the second half of the 18th century; nothing is known of his works, but administration of his effects was granted to his widow, Jane, on 3 March 1776.

Literary References: *Strickland* II, 1913, 226

PERCY, John Francis 1801–

Born in Dublin, the son of an artist, Edward H G Percy, he entered the Dublin Society's Schools in 1816 and won prizes for modelling in wax in 1819 and 1820. In 1821 he was living at 15 Lower Dorset Street and sent two wax models to an exhibition at the Royal Arcade in Dublin (**3, 8**). He showed at the Royal Academy, 1827–39, from addresses in Vauxhall Bridge Road, Middlesex Place and Munster Street. Percy worked as a designer and modeller of silver for a Dublin silversmith called West and for Elkington's in London *c*1835.

Literary References: *Strickland* II, 1913, 226; *Gunnis* 1968, 299; *Pyke* 1973, 102–3

Busts						
1.	1833	C F Schrader	w	[Exhib RA, London, 1200]; untraced		*Graves* VI, 1905–6, 105
2.	1833	Unidentified gentleman		[Exhib RA, London, 1199]; untraced		*Graves* VI, 1905–6, 105
Reliefs						
3.	1821	Unidentified gentleman	w	[Exhib Royal Arcade, Dublin]; untraced		*Strickland* II, 1913, 226
4.	1827	Bacchus and Ariadne	w	Bethnal Green Museum, London		*Graves* VI, 1905–6, 105; *Pyke* 1973, 103
5.	1831	Unidentified artist		[Exhib RA, London, 1046]; untraced		*Graves* VI, 1905–6, 105
6.	1834	Unidentified woman	w	Philadelphia Museum of Art, USA		*Pyke* 1973, 103
7.	nd	Unidentified woman	w	Philadelphia Museum of Art, USA		*Pyke* 1973, 103 (repr 213)

Miscellaneous

8.	1821	Unidentified subject, model	w	[Exhib Royal Arcade, Dublin]; untraced	*Strickland* II, 1913, 226
9.	1839	'This is the house that Jack built'		[Exhib RA, London, 1277]; untraced	*Graves* VI, 1905–6, 105

PERCY, Samuel 1750–1820

Percy, who was a Dubliner by birth, was one of the most celebrated wax-modellers of his day. By his own account he was 'thoroughly bred to every branch of the Statuary-business', including lead-casting (*Gore's Liverpool General Advertiser*, 1782, quoted in *Friedman* 1985, 20). He was a student at the Dublin Society's schools and first exhibited at the Society of Artists' exhibition in William Street in 1772 (**5**). By 1774 he was in London, but he paid frequent visits to Dublin, taking orders in December 1779 for profile-likenesses, whole-lengths and groups, all available via a Mr Moore of 1 Capel Street. He also promoted himself as a specialised copyist and restorer of mandarin figures. In advertisements in *Saunders's Newsletter*, 1780, he offered to execute portraits in coloured wax for one and a half guineas, or bracelet-sized waxes in the manner of Roman coins for one guinea. Such works, he promised his prospective buyers, were 'quite the style in France and Italy' (quoted in *Strickland* 1913, vol 2, 228). He also offered, at short notice, to take death masks from which he would produce portraits.

Percy appears to have worked as an itinerant modeller in England, visiting towns like Liverpool, Chester, Brighton and Doncaster and he often advertised his arrival in the local press. In 1786 he exhibited for the first time at the Royal Academy (**9**) giving his contact address as at 'Mr Dodd's, 57 St Martin's Lane', from where he soon moved to 26 Millman Row, Great Chelsea (*Graves* VI, 1905–6, 105). In 1787, on a working trip to Tunbridge Wells where he modelled portraits in the great rooms on the Walk, Percy confidently advertised himself as 'so well-known in . . . the kingdom at large it is unnecessary in this puffing age to spin out his own panegyric further' (handbill quoted in *Pyke* 1973, 104). From his advertisements it is clear that Percy sold himself on his ability to produce a realistic likeness with more speed than a painter in oils. The resultant works were accessible to those on a restricted budget and were particularly suitable for modest domestic environments. Some works, such as the three-quarter length relief of Mary Berry in her shawl (**152**), still carry Percy's instructions on the verso on how best to view the works against the light. According to Hughes, Percy had modelled 800 portraits by 1786.

Percy's portraits differ from the wax reliefs of predecessors such as **Isaac Gosset**, because they are cast in naturalistically coloured, or 'stained' liquid wax. In addition, though works such as a portrait of the scientist Joseph Priestley (**12**) and the dwarf Joseph Boruwlaski (**18**) are in profile, they are in much higher relief than Gosset's. Percy also produced characterised full-face portraits, for instance of the lugubrious-featured Quaker philanthropist, Richard Reynolds (**27**), or Percy's own beady-eyed, sharp-nosed visage (**177**). These four portraits are framed by Baroque curtains modelled in wax, which in the case of Reynolds, leak out of the picture plane over the gilt-wood frame.

On 31 January 1800, Mr Christie held a sale of Percy's wax portraits and groups, including Percy's portrait. The 48 lots were sold for a total of £172 (Archives, Messrs Christie). They included *Tinker's Family*, which sold for £36 15s (**205**), one of numerous tableaux modelled by the artist. Framed in recessed cases, they combine multiple fully rounded statuettes in coloured wax, often with the addition of real lace, hair and other ornaments, to give the figures a doll-like verisimilitude. His subjects were often rustic genre scenes, for instance *Gypsy Encampment* (**37**), in which nine figures, including a screaming infant, gesture furiously, creating a bustling composition of theatrical unrest. Others feature down-at-heel musicians, chimney-sweeps on donkeys, prize-fighters and quarrelling fishwives (**41, 42, 87, 200**). On occasion Percy would try his hand at more elevated subjects such as the *Death of Voltaire* or *Timandra covering with robes the body of Alcibiades* (**65, 204**), subjects which developed his art from genre studies to a sculptural parallel to history painting.

Percy continued to exhibit at the Royal Academy, showing in 1803 a series of portraits of leading political figures across the ideological spectrum (**19–23**), and in 1804 images of members of the Royal family, who were regular clients (**24, 25**). Percy clearly felt his skills worthy of leading national commissions, for in 1806 he submitted a model in competition for the Guildhall monument to Nelson, offering to carry out the work for £4,000. His design was not accepted, and the commission went to **James Smith** (City Corp Records, MSS 95.2).

His death was recorded in the *Annals of the Fine Arts* in 1820. It described him as 'well known for his exquisite models in miniature size' and added (conjuring up a dramatic tableau worthy of the artist himself), that he 'expired suddenly, of an apoplectic fit, whilst finishing a portrait of Prince Leopold' (*Annals of the Fine Arts* 1820, 177). He may have been the Samuel Percy of Bristol, Exeter and Chelsea Common, whose will was proved in December 1819. This Samuel Percy left all his possessions to his wife of 30 years, Annabel. Little is known of Percy's life and character, although a sense of humour and a delight in burlesque are clearly evident in his portraits and rustic scenes. Whether or not he was able to make a good living from his art is unclear, but the incorporation of a small box in his scene, *The three musicians* (**200**) bearing the inscription 'Voluntary Subscriptions for the Benefit of Percy, Artist' suggests that he probably had difficulties.

Wax portraits represented a significant bulwark of realism in a national art which largely promoted classical idealism and as such it had confirmed admirers. In 1857 more than 100 of Percy's works collected by the 15th Earl of Shrewsbury at Alton Towers, Staffs, were sold at Christie's. Gunnis, himself a collector of waxes, described Percy as 'one of the best, if not the best, of the English wax-modellers' (*Gunnis* 1968, 300). An exhibition of Percy's work was held at the Egyptian Hall in Piccadilly, London. Articles on the sculptor have appeared sporadically throughout the last century, testifying to the fascination which his technique and iconography still hold for scholars and collectors.

MGS

Literary References: *Graves* VI, 1905–6, 105; *Strickland* 1913, vol 2, 227–8; *Elwyn* 1934, 320–4; *Comstock* 1940 (2), 258–9; *Bull. PMA* 1947 (1), 49–63; *Hughes* 1955, 1255–7; *Gunnis* 1968, 299–300; *Pyke* 1973, 103–5; *Pyke* 1981, 31–2; *Grace* 1980, 175–82; *Friedman* 1985, 15–22

Will: PROB 11/1623/300

Portraits of the Sculptor: Self-portrait (177)

Funerary Monuments

1.	1806	Admiral Lord Nelson, for the Guildhall, City of London, model	Untraced	*Gunnis* 1968, 300

Busts

No.	Date	Subject	Medium	Location	SD	References
2.	nd	16 of the Royal families of Russia, Prussia and England (in two frames)		[Alton Towers sale 1857]; untraced		*Pyke* 1973, 104
3.	nd	Arthur, 1st Duke of Wellington (copy after an unspecified marble)	w	[Alton Towers sale 1857]; untraced		*Pyke* 1973, 104
4.	nd	King George III (copy after an unidentified marble)	w	[Alton Towers sale 1857]; untraced		*Pyke* 1973, 104

Reliefs

No.	Date	Subject	Medium	Location	SD	References
5.	1772	Abraham offering Isaac, alto-relief		[Exhib Society of Artists, Dublin]; untraced		*Hughes* 1955, 1255
6.	1773	'Likenesses in wax'	w	[Exhib Society of Artists, Dublin]; untraced		*Strickland* 1913, 2, 227
7.	1777	Unidentified man	w	Stanton Harcourt, Oxon		*Pyke* 1973, 104
8.	1779	Herbert Mackworth	w	VAM A.93-1965		*Pyke* 1973, 103
9.	1786	Portrait of a young gentleman		[Exhib RA, London, 256]; untraced		*Graves* VI, 1905–6, 105
10.	1788	Emperor and Empress of Russia	w	[Christie, 31 Jan 1800]; untraced		*Gunnis* 1968, 300
11.	1788	John Wesley	w	Methodist Archives and Research Centre, London Other versions: Christie 11 Dec 1978, lot 135		*Pyke* 1981, 32
12.	1788	Joseph Priestley	w	Science Museum, London Other versions: Alton Towers sale 1857	SD	*Pyke* 1973, 104, 105; *White* 1978, 63 (repr)
13.	1791	Mrs Henry King	w	Private coll		*Pyke* 1981, 32
14.	1795	King George III		Royal Coll Other versions: exhib RA, London, 1804, 957 Christie 31 Jan 1800 Alton Towers sale 1857 Brighton MAG Rackstrow's museum		*Graves* VI, 1905–6, 105; *Gunnis* 1968, 300; *Pyke* 1973, 103, 104; *Pyke* 1981, 32
15.	1795	Queen Charlotte	w	Windsor Castle		*Gunnis* 1968, 300; *Pyke* 1973, 103
16.	1795	Queen Charlotte, on a sofa with her dog	w	Private coll		*Pyke* 1981, 32
17.	1796	Richard Pearson, Doncaster haberdasher	w	Private coll		*Pyke* 1981, 32
18.	1798	Joseph Boruwlaski	w	Met NY	SD	*Grace* 1980, 175–182 (repr)
19.	1803	Charles James Fox	w	[Exhib RA, London, 1027]; untraced Other versions: VAM A.54:0-1940, *c*1809 Stanton Harcourt, Oxon Brighton MAG Prof Mario Praz, Rome Madame Tussaud's, London Delhom Gallery and Institute, Mint Museum of Art, Charlotte, USA		*Graves* VI, 1905–6, 105; *Elwyn* 1934, 321; *Hughes* 1955, 1257; *Pyke* 1973, 104; *Pyke* 1981, 32; GPC
20.	1803	Earl Stanhope	w	[Exhib RA, London, 1027]; untraced		*Graves* VI, 1905–6, 105
21.	1803	John Horne Tooke	w	[Exhib RA, London, 1027]; untraced Other versions: ex coll Mrs A E Hamill, 1815; untraced		*Graves* VI, 1905–6, 105; *Elwyn* 1934, 321; *Pyke* 1973, 104
22.	1803	Sir Francis Burdett	w	[Exhib RA, London, 1027]; untraced Other versions: Alton Towers sale 1857 ex coll E J Pyke; untraced VAM A.30-1970 (?) Delhom Gallery and Institute, Mint Museum of Art, Charlotte, USA		*Graves* VI, 1905–6, 105; *Pyke* 1973, 103, 105
23.	1803	William Pitt, 1st Earl of Chatham	w	[Exhib RA, London, 1027]; untraced Other versions: Christie, 31 Jan 1800 Alton Towers sale 1857 Sotheby 16 May 1957 lot 96 Brighton MAG Madame Tussaud's, London VAM A.15-1970; A.43-1940		*Graves* VI, 1905–6, 105; *Pyke* 1973, 104; *Pyke* 1981, 31; GPC
24.	1804	Frederick, Duke of York	w	[Exhib RA, London, 957]; untraced Other versions: Brighton MAG Sotheby 29 Oct 1973 lot 117		*Graves* VI, 1905–6, 105; *Pyke* 1981, 32
25.	1804	George, Prince of Wales	w	[Exhib RA, London, 957]; untraced		*Graves* VI, 1905–6, 105
26.	1809	Sir Arthur Paget	w	VAM A.56-1940		*Hughes* 1955, 1257; *Gunnis* 1968, 300; *Pyke* 1973, 104
27.	1810	Richard Reynolds	w	LMG, W R Yorks Other versions: Cedric Van (1985), SD 1810 Birmingham MAG inv P.126'80, SD 1811 NPG, London, *c*1817 NMM Alton Towers sale 1857	SD	*Friedman* 1985, 19, 20 (repr); *Silber* 1987, 76, cat 230; *Leeds* 1996, 5 (repr); *Pyke* 1973, 105; *Pyke* 1981, 32
28.	1811	Unidentified man	w	Philadelphia Museum of Art, USA, 43.95.36		*Pyke* 1973, 104
29.	1813	Unidentified man	w	Stanton Harcourt, Oxon		*Pyke* 1973, 104
30.	1814	Princess Charlotte Augusta of Wales (†1817)	w	NPG, London Other versions: Private coll	SD	*Gunnis* 1968, 300; *Pyke* 1981, 31

31.	1816	Unidentified man	w	Chicago A I (58.429)		*Pyke* 1973, 104
32.	1816	Unidentified women	w	Private coll		*Pyke* 1981, 32
33.	1817	Charlotte, Princess of Wales	w	Brighton Art Gall, Sussex		*Gunnis* 1968, 300
34.	1817	Princess Charlotte, daughter of the Prince Regent	w	Brighton MAG Other versions: Alton Towers sale, 1857 Stanton Harcourt, Oxon ex coll E J Pyke, 1817		*Gunnis* 1968, 300; *Pyke* 1973, 103, 104; *Grace* 1980, 177 (repr)
35.	1818	Elizabeth Fry	w	[coll Mrs A E Hamill]; untraced		*Pyke* 1973, 103
36.	1818	Unidentified man	w	Stanton Harcourt, Oxon		*Pyke* 1973, 104
37.	nd	A gypsy encampment, tableau	w	[Alton Towers sale 1857]; untraced		*Elwyn* 1934, 322, 324 (repr)
38.	nd	A huntsman and peasant family at a cottage door, tableau	w	[Alton Towers sale 1857]; untraced		*Elwyn* 1934, 322, 324 (? repr)
39.	nd	A pair of frames containing illustrious characters from Henry VIII to Cromwell	w	[Alton Towers sale 1857]; untraced		*Pyke* 1973, 104
40.	nd	A pair of frames containing poets and statesmen	w	[Alton Towers sale 1857]; untraced		*Pyke* 1973, 104
41.	nd	A prize fight, tableau	w	[Alton Towers sale 1857]; untraced		*Elwyn* 1934, 323 (repr)
42.	nd	A race of chimney-sweeps on donkeys, tableau	w	[Alton Towers sale 1857]; Private coll, USA		*Elwyn* 1934, 324
43.	nd	A soldier and peasants, tableau	w	[Alton Towers sale 1857]; untraced		*Elwyn* 1934, 320 (repr)
44.	nd	A struggle between a miller and a sweep interrupted by a schoolmaster, tableau	w	VAM 445-1882		*Elwyn* 1934, 324; *Pyke* 1973, 104
45.	nd	Admiral Lord Nelson	w	[Alton Towers sale 1857]; untraced Other versions: Brighton MAG		*Elwyn* 1934, 321; *Hughes* 1955, 1257; *Pyke* 1973, 104
46.	nd	Admiral Roddam	w	[Christie, 31 Jan 1800]; untraced		*Gunnis* 1968, 300
47.	nd	Agnes Berry	w	VAM A.13-1970		*Pyke* 1973, 103; *Pyke* 1981, 31
48.	nd	Alexander, 5th Earl of Antrim	w	Private coll		*Pyke* 1973, 103
49.	nd	'Algerines and Circassians'	w	[Christie, 31 Jan 1800]; untraced		*Pyke* 1973, 104
50.	nd	Arthur, 1st Duke of Wellington	w	Stanton Harcourt, Oxon		*Pyke* 1973, 104
51.	nd	Blind beggar	w	[Exhib Egyptian Hall, London]; untraced		*Gunnis* 1968, 300
52.	nd	Brutus	w	[Alton Towers sale 1857]; untraced		*Pyke* 1973, 104
53.	nd	Capt R N Gwynn	w	NMM		*Pyke* 1981, 32
54.	nd	Captured poacher	w	[Ackermann & Sons, NY]; untraced		*Pyke* 1973, 105
55.	nd	Cardinal Wolsey	w	Royal Coll Other versions: Christie, 31 Jan 1800		*Pyke* 1973, 104
56.	nd	Cassius	w	[Alton Towers sale 1857]; untraced		*Pyke* 1973, 104
57.	nd	Catherine of Aragon	w	[Christie, 31 Jan 1800]; untraced		*Pyke* 1973, 104
58.	nd	Charles Bernadotte	w	Stanton Harcourt, Oxon		*Pyke* 1973, 103
59.	nd	Charles, Archduke of Austria	w	Stanton Harcourt, Oxon		*Pyke* 1973, 103
60.	nd	Colin Maclaurin	w	Private coll		*Pyke* 1973, 103
61.	nd	Count Matvei Ivanovich Platov	w	Stanton Harcourt, Oxon		*Pyke* 1973, 104
62.	nd	Count Struenzee	w	[Christie, 31 Jan 1800]; untraced		*Gunnis* 1968, 300
63.	nd	Daniel O'Connell addressing an audience	w	Untraced		*Friedman* 1985, 17
64.	nd	Dead Christ	w	[Exhib Egyptian Hall, London]; VAM A.5-1960	S	*Pyke* 1973, 103 (repr); *Gunnis* 1968, 300
65.	nd	Death of Voltaire, tableau	w	VAM A.19-1932 Other versions: Musée Carnavalet		*Elwyn* 1934, 321; *Gunnis* 1968, 300; *Friedman* 1985, 17
66.	nd	Dr Charles Lucas	w	[Christie, 31 Jan 1800]; untraced		*Pyke* 1973, 104
67.	nd	Dr Cleghorn	w	[Christie, 31 Jan 1800]; untraced		*Pyke* 1973, 104
68.	nd	Dr Willis	w	[Christie, 31 Jan 1800]; untraced		*Pyke* 1973, 104
69.	nd	Duke of Leeds	w	[Christie, 31 Jan 1800]; untraced		*Gunnis* 1968, 300
70.	nd	Duke of Marlborough	w	[Christie, 31 Jan 1800]; untraced		*Pyke* 1973, 104
71.	nd	Duke of Norfolk	w	[Christie, 31 Jan 1800]; untraced		*Pyke* 1973, 104
72.	nd	Duke of Richmond	w	[Christie, 31 Jan 1800]; untraced		*Gunnis* 1968, 300
73.	nd	Edward Augustus, Duke of Kent	w	Brighton MAG		*Pyke* 1973, 103
74.	nd	Edward the Black Prince	w	[Christie, 31 Jan 1800]; untraced		*Pyke* 1973, 104
75.	nd	Edward VI	w	Royal Coll		*Pyke* 1973, 103
76.	nd	Edward, Duke of Somerset	w	Royal Coll		*Pyke* 1973, 104
77.	nd	Edward, Earl of Clarendon	w	Royal Coll		*Pyke* 1973, 103
78.	nd	Edward, Lord Thurlow	w	Brighton MAG Other versions: Christie, 31 Jan 1800 Alton Towers sale 1857		*Gunnis* 1968, 300; *Pyke* 1973, 104
79.	nd	'Eleven figures'	w	[Dr Köhler's sale, Vienna, 30 Jan 1917]; untraced		*Elwyn* 1934, 324
80.	nd	Elizabeth Best	w	VAM A.89-1965	S	*Pyke* 1973, 103
81.	nd	Emperor Alexander I of Russia	w	Stanton Harcourt, Oxon		*Pyke* 1973, 103
82.	nd	Emperor Joseph of Austria	w	[Christie, 31 Jan 1800]; untraced		*Pyke* 1973, 104
83.	nd	Emperor Napoleon I	w	Stanton Harcourt, Oxon Other versions: Alton Towers sale 1857 coll Prof Mario Praz, Rome		*Pyke* 1973, 104, 105
84.	nd	Empress Josephine	w	Stanton Harcourt, Oxon		*Pyke* 1973, 103
85.	nd	Ernest, Duke of Cumberland	w	VAM A.29-1970		*Pyke* 1973, 103
86.	nd	Field-Marshal Gebhard Lebrecht von Blücher	w	Stanton Harcourt, Oxon		*Pyke* 1973, 103
87.	nd	Fisherwomen quarrelling, tableau	w	[Alton Towers sale 1857]; untraced		*Elwyn* 1934, 323 (repr)
88.	nd	Frederick the Great in his last illness	w	[Exhib Egyptian Hall, London]; untraced		*Gunnis* 1968, 300; *Friedman* 1985, 17
89.	nd	Frederick, Duke of Sussex	w	Brighton MAG		*Pyke* 1973, 103

90.	nd	Frederick, Earl of Guilford	w	Christie 11 Dec 1978, lot 135	*Pyke* 1981, 32
91.	nd	G M Pickard	w	Private coll	*Pyke* 1981, 32
92.	nd	General Fleetwood	w	Royal Coll	*Pyke* 1973, 103
93.	nd	General Haviland	w	[Christie, 31 Jan 1800]; untraced	*Gunnis* 1968, 300
94.	nd	General Ireton	w	Royal Coll Other versions: Sudeley Castle, Glos	*Pyke* 1973, 103; *Pyke* 1981, 32
95.	nd	General Lambert	w	Royal Coll Other versions: Sudeley Castle, Glos	*Pyke* 1973, 103; *Pyke* 1981, 32
96.	nd	Geoffrey Chaucer	w	[Christie, 31 Jan 1800]; untraced	*Pyke* 1973, 104
97.	nd	George Buchanan	w	Royal Coll Other versions: Christie, 31 Jan 1800	*Pyke* 1973, 103, 104
98.	nd	George Canning	w	Brighton MAG	*Pyke* 1973, 103
99.	nd	George, Baron Rodney	w	Brighton MAG	*Pyke* 1973, 104
100.	nd	George, Lord Grafton	w	Christie 11 Dec 1978, lot 135	*Pyke* 1981, 32
101.	nd	George, Prince of Wales (later King George IV)	w	Royal Coll Other versions: 29 Nov 1975, lot 117	*Pyke* 1973, 103; *Pyke* 1981, 32
102.	nd	Gilbert Hamilton	w	Chamber of Commerce, Glasgow Other versions: Paisley MAG	*Pyke* 1981, 32
103.	nd	Gilbert, 1st Lord Minto	w	Christie 11 Dec 1978, lot 135	*Pyke* 1981, 32
104.	nd	Henderson, the actor	w	[Christie, 31 Jan 1800]; untraced	*Gunnis* 1968, 300
105.	nd	Henry Grattan	w	[Christie, 31 Jan 1800]; untraced Other versions: Private coll	*Pyke* 1973, 104; *Pyke* 1981, 32
106.	nd	Howard	w	[Christie, 31 Jan 1800]; untraced	*Pyke* 1973, 104
107.	nd	Inigo Jones	w	[Alton Towers sale 1857]; untraced	*Hughes* 1955, 1257
108.	nd	James McGregor	w	Chamber of Commerce, Glasgow Other versions: Paisley MAG	*Pyke* 1981, 32
109.	nd	Jane Shore	w	[Christie, 31 Jan 1800]; untraced	*Pyke* 1973, 104
110.	nd	Jérôme Bonaparte	w	Stanton Harcourt, Oxon	*Pyke* 1973, 103
111.	nd	John Locke	w	Stanton Harcourt, Oxon Other versions: Christie 31 Jan 1800 Sudeley Castle, Glos	*Pyke* 1973, 103; *Pyke* 1981, 32
112.	nd	John Milton	w	Stanton Harcourt, Oxon	*Pyke* 1973, 104
113.	nd	John Philip Kemble	w	Museum of London	*Pyke* 1973, 103
114.	nd	Joseph Bonaparte	w	Stanton Harcourt, Oxon	*Pyke* 1973, 103
115.	nd	Joseph Hanway (?)	w	[Christie, 31 Jan 1800]; untraced	*Pyke* 1973, 104
116.	nd	Judge Butler	w	[Christie, 31 Jan 1800]; untraced	*Gunnis* 1968, 300
117.	nd	Judge Eyre	w	[Christie, 31 Jan 1800]; untraced Other versions: Christie 11 Dec 1978, lot 135	*Gunnis* 1968, 300; *Pyke* 1981, 32
118.	nd	Judge Heath	w	[Christie, 31 Jan 1800]; untraced	*Pyke* 1973, 104
119.	nd	Judge Sir Francis Buller	w	[Christie, 31 Jan 1800]; untraced Other versions: Christie 11 Dec 1978, lot 135	*Pyke* 1973, 104; *Pyke* 1981, 31
120.	nd	Judge Wilson	w	[Christie, 31 Jan 1800]; untraced	*Gunnis* 1968, 300
121.	nd	King Charles I	w	Royal Coll Other versions: Christie, 31 Jan 1800 Sudeley Castle, Glos	*Pyke* 1973, 103, 104; *Pyke* 1981, 31
122.	nd	King Charles II	w	Royal Coll Other versions: Christie, 31 Jan 1800 Sudeley Castle, Glos	*Pyke* 1973, 103, 104; *Pyke* 1981, 31
123.	nd	King Charles XII of Sweden	w	[Christie, 31 Jan 1800]; untraced	*Pyke* 1973, 104
124.	nd	King George II	w	[Alton Towers sale 1857]; untraced	*Pyke* 1973, 104
125.	nd	King George IV	w	Royal Coll Other versions: Alton Towers sale 1857 Stanton Harcourt, Oxon Brighton MAG	*Pyke* 1973, 103, 104
126.	nd	King Henry VIII	w	Royal Coll Other versions: Christie, 31 Jan 1800	*Pyke* 1973, 103, 104
127.	nd	King James I	w	Royal Coll Other versions: Alton Towers sale 1857	*Pyke* 1973, 103, 104
128.	nd	King Louis XVI	w	[Christie, 31 Jan 1800]; VAM A.109–1965	*Gunnis* 1968, 300; *Pyke* 1973, 103
129.	nd	King Louis XVIII	w	Stanton Harcourt, Oxon	*Pyke* 1973, 103
130.	nd	Lady Barrington	w	VAM A.55-1940 Other versions: Brighton MAG	*Gunnis* 1968, 300; *Pyke* 1973, 103
131.	nd	Lady Carfax	w	Philadelphia Museum of Art, USA	*Pyke* 1973, 103
132.	nd	Lady Erskine	w	Chicago A I	*Pyke* 1973, 103
133.	nd	Lady Jane Grey	w	Royal Coll	*Pyke* 1973, 103
134.	nd	Lady Stuart Menteith	w	Mrs A E Hamill, 1934; untraced	*Lederer* 1934, 105; *Gunnis* 1968, 300; *Pyke* 1973, 104
135.	nd	Lady with three children gathering apples, tableau	w	VAM A.12-1970	*Pyke* 1973, 103
136.	nd	Lord Ankerville	w	[Christie, 31 Jan 1800]; untraced	*Pyke* 1973, 104
137.	nd	Lord Burleigh	w	[Christie, 31 Jan 1800]; untraced	*Pyke* 1973, 104

138.	nd	Lord Duncan	w	[Alton Towers Sale 1857]; untraced Other versions: Delhom Gallery and Institute, Mint Museum of Art, Charlotte, USA	*Pyke* 1973, 104; *Pyke* 1981, 32
139.	nd	Lord Ellicock	w	[Christie, 31 Jan 1800]; untraced	*Pyke* 1973, 104
140.	nd	Lord Heathfield	w	[Christie, 31 Jan 1800]; untraced Other versions: Christie 11 Dec 1978, lot 135	*Pyke* 1981, 32
141.	nd	Lord Keith	w	Brighton MAG	*Pyke* 1973, 103
142.	nd	Lord Kenyon	w	[Christie, 31 Jan 1800]; untraced	*Gunnis* 1968, 300
143.	nd	Lord Moira	w	[Christie, 31 Jan 1800]; untraced	*Pyke* 1973, 104
144.	nd	Lord Rockingham	w	Mrs A E Hamill, 1934; untraced	*Lederer* 1934, 105; *Gunnis* 1968, 300
145.	nd	Lord Romney	w	[Christie, 31 Jan 1800]; untraced	*Gunnis* 1968, 300
146.	nd	Louis Lucien Bonaparte	w	Stanton Harcourt, Oxon	*Pyke* 1973, 103
147.	nd	Major-General Dugald Campbell	w	Private coll	*Pyke* 1981, 31
148.	nd	'market figures.. modelled and coloured with wonderful truth to nature,' tableau	w	[Alton Towers sale, 1857]; untraced	*Elwyn* 1934, 320; *Hughes* 1955, 1257; *Gunnis* 1968, 300
149.	nd	Marquis of Granby	w	[Christie, 31 Jan 1800]; untraced	*Pyke* 1973, 104
150.	nd	Marquis of Montrose	w	Royal Coll	*Pyke* 1973, 104
151.	nd	Marquis of Worcester	w	[Christie, 31 Jan 1800]; untraced	*Pyke* 1973, 104
152.	nd	Mary Berry	w	VAM A.14-1970	*Pyke* 1973, 103; *Pyke* 1981, 31
153.	nd	Mary I, Queen of England	w	Private coll	*Pyke* 1981, 32
154.	nd	Mary, Queen of Scots	w	Royal Coll Other versions: Christie, 31 Jan 1800	*Pyke* 1973, 104
155.	nd	Misses Richardson, two	w	Private coll	*Pyke* 1981, 32
156.	nd	Mr Hastings	w	[Christie, 31 Jan 1800]; untraced	*Pyke* 1973, 104
157.	nd	Mr Reynolds	w	Private coll	*Pyke* 1973, 104
158.	nd	Mrs Carr	w	Private coll	*Pyke* 1973, 103
159.	nd	Mrs Timothy Shelley	w	Met NY	*Pyke* 1973, 104
160.	nd	Nell Gwynn	w	[Christie, 31 Jan 1800]; untraced	*Pyke* 1973, 104
161.	nd	Old Parr	w	[Christie, 31 Jan 1800]; untraced	*Pyke* 1973, 104
162.	nd	Oliver Cromwell	w	Royal Coll	*Pyke* 1973, 103, 104
163.	nd	Prince Leopold	w	Stanton Harcourt, Oxon Other versions: Alton Towers sale 1857 Brighton MAG	*Pyke* 1973, 103, 104
164.	nd	Priscilla Moon	w	Private coll	*Pyke* 1981, 32
165.	nd	Queen Caroline 'full-length'	w	[Alton Towers sale, 1857]; untraced	*Gunnis* 1968, 300; *Pyke* 1973, 104
166.	nd	Queen Charlotte	w	Stanton Harcourt, Oxon Other versions: Brighton MAG	*Pyke* 1973, 103
167.	nd	Queen Elizabeth I	w	Royal Coll Other versions: Christie 31 Jan 1800 Private coll	*Pyke* 1973, 103, 104; *Pyke* 1981, 2
168.	nd	Queen Marie Antoinette	w	Stanton Harcourt, Oxon	*Pyke* 1973, 104
169.	nd	Rachel, Countess of Antrim	w	Private coll	*Pyke* 1973, 104
170.	nd	Ralph Carr	w	Private coll	*Pyke* 1973, 103
171.	nd	Rev Lawrence Sterne	w	Brighton MAG Other versions: Christie, 31 Jan 1800 Alton Towers sale 1857	*Pyke* 1973, 104
172.	nd	Rev M Wesley	w	[Christie, 31 Jan 1800]; untraced	*Pyke* 1973, 104
173.	nd	Rev William Wesley	w	[Christie, 31 Jan 1800]; untraced	*Pyke* 1973, 104
174.	nd	Robert, 2nd Earl of Essex	w	Private coll	*Pyke* 1981, 32
175.	nd	Robert, Earl of Leicester	w	Royal Coll Other versions: Christie, 31 Jan 1800 Private coll	*Pyke* 1973, 103, 104; *Pyke* 1981, 32
176.	nd	Rt Hon Edward Carey	w	Chicago A I	*Pyke* 1973, 103
177.	nd	Samuel Percy, self-portrait	w	VAM A.57-1940	*Hughes* 1955, 1255; *Friedman* 1985, 17 (repr)
178.	nd	Sir Anthony More	w	Royal Coll	*Pyke* 1973, 104
179.	nd	Sir Christopher Wren	w	[Christie, 31 Jan 1800]; untraced	*Pyke* 1973, 104
180.	nd	Sir Francis Bacon	w	[Christie, 31 Jan 1800]; untraced	*Pyke* 1973, 104
181.	nd	Sir Francis Drake	w	[Christie, 31 Jan 1800]; untraced Other versions: Private coll	*Pyke* 1973, 104; *Pyke* 1981, 32
182.	nd	Sir Francis Walshingham	w	[Christie, 31 Jan 1800]; untraced	*Pyke* 1973, 104
183.	nd	Sir George Saville	w	[Christie, 31 Jan 1800]; untraced	GPC
184.	nd	Sir Gilbert Elliott	w	Lloyd's, London	*Pyke* 1981, 32
185.	nd	Sir Isaac Newton	w	Private coll	*Pyke* 1981, 32
186.	nd	Sir Joseph Banks	w	[Christie, 31 Jan 1800]; untraced	*Pyke* 1973, 104
187.	nd	Sir Nicholas Bacon	w	[Christie, 31 Jan 1800]; untraced	*Pyke* 1973, 104
188.	nd	Sir Samuel Romilly	w	Sotheby, 16 May 1957, lot 97 Other versions: Alton Towers sale 1857 Lord Ponsonby of Shulbrede, Lynchmere, Hants	*Pyke* 1973, 104, 105; GPC
189.	nd	Sir Thomas Fairfax	w	Royal Coll	*Pyke* 1973, 103
190.	nd	Sir Thomas More	w	Royal Coll Other versions: Christie, 31 Jan 1800	*Pyke* 1973, 104

191.	nd	Sir Walter Raleigh	w	Royal Coll Other versions: Private coll		*Pyke* 1973, 104; *Pyke* 1981, 32
192.	nd	Sir William Draper	w	Christie 11 Dec 1978, lot 135		*Pyke* 1981, 32
193.	nd	Spencer Perceval	w	Stanton Harcourt, Oxon		*Pyke* 1973, 104
194.	nd	Tableau	w	Private coll Other versions: Edinburgh, Royal College of Surgeons		*Pyke* 1981, 32
195.	nd	Tavern fight	w	Private coll		*Pyke* 1981, 32
196.	nd	Tavern group tableau	w	Museum of London		*Hughes* 1955, 1255 (repr); *Pyke* 1973, 104
197.	nd	The Greenwich pensioner, tableau	w	[Alton Towers Sale 1857 Ackermann & Sons, NY]; untraced		*Elwyn* 1934, 320, 321, 324 (repr)
198.	nd	The pirates, tableau	w	[Ackermann & Sons, NY]; untraced		*Pyke* 1973, 105
199.	nd	The progress of inebriety, group	w	[Exhib Egyptian Hall, London]; untraced Other versions: Christie 19.11.1970, lot 10		*Gunnis* 1968, 300; *Pyke* 1973, 104
200.	nd	The three musicians	w	VAM 446-1882		*Elwyn* 1934, 324; *Gunnis* 1968, 300; *Friedman* 1985, 17
201.	nd	Thomas Best	w	VAM A.88-1965	S	*Pyke* 1973, 103 (repr pl 214)
202.	nd	Thomas, Earl of Strafford	w	Royal Coll		*Pyke* 1973, 104
203.	nd	Three Admirals	w	Philadelphia Museum of Art, USA		*Pyke* 1973, 103
204.	nd	Timandra covering with robes the body of Alcibiades	w	[Christie, 31 Jan 1800]; untraced		*Pyke* 1973, 104
205.	nd	Tinker's family (group of eight figures) Payment(s): £36 15s in 1800	w	[Christie, 31 Jan 1800]; untraced		GPC
206.	nd	Tom Paine	w	[Christie, 31 Jan 1800]; untraced		*Gunnis* 1968, 300
207.	nd	Travelling gypsy family (seven figures) Payment(s): £36 15s in 1800	w	[Christie, 31 Jan 1800]; untraced		GPC
208.	nd	Two genre works	w	Private coll, USA		*Pyke* 1981, 32
209.	nd	Unidentified divine	w	Stanton Harcourt, Oxon		*Pyke* 1973, 104
210.	nd	Unidentified girl, presumably child of Thomas and Elizabeth Best	w	VAM A.91-1965		*Pyke* 1973, 104
211.	nd	Unidentified man	w	Private coll		*Pyke* 1973, 104
212.	nd	Unidentified man	w	Private coll		*Pyke* 1973, 104
213.	nd	Unidentified man	w	VAM A.92-1965		*Pyke* 1973, 104
214.	nd	Unidentified man	w	Chicago A I (58.425)		*Pyke* 1973, 104
215.	nd	Unidentified man	w	VAM A.23-1970		*Pyke* 1973, 104
216.	nd	Unidentified man and woman	w	Private coll		*Pyke* 1973, 104
217.	nd	Unidentified man and woman	w	Phillips, 8 July 1975, lots 33/34		*Pyke* 1981, 32
218.	nd	Unidentified men	w	Brighton MAG		*Pyke* 1973, 104
219.	nd	Unidentified men	w	Private coll		*Pyke* 1981, 32
220.	nd	Unidentified naval officer	w	Private coll		*Pyke* 1981, 32
221.	nd	Unidentified woman	w	Private coll		*Pyke* 1973, 104
222.	nd	Unidentified woman	w	Met NY (39.180.1)		*Pyke* 1973, 104
223.	nd	Unidentified youth	w	Philadelphia Museum of Art, USA (43–95–34)		*Pyke* 1973, 104
224.	nd	Unidentified youth	w	Sotheby 30 Nov 1964, lot 92		*Pyke* 1973, 104
225.	nd	Unidentified youth, presumably child of Thomas and Elizabeth Best	w	VAM A.90-1965	S	*Pyke* 1973, 104
226.	nd	William IV, Prince of Orange	w	Stanton Harcourt, Oxon Other versions: Brighton MAG		*Pyke* 1973, 104
227.	nd	William Roscoe	w	Sotheby, 16 May 1957, lot 97 Other versions: Alton Towers sale 1857		*Pyke* 1973, 105; GPC
228.	nd	William Shakespeare	w	[Christie, 31 Jan 1800]; untraced Other versions: Rackstrow's museum; untraced		*Pyke* 1973, 104; *Pyke* 1981, 32
229.	nd	William Sheridan	w	[Rackstrow's Museum]; untraced		*Pyke* 1981, 32
230.	nd	William, 4th Earl of Queensbury	w	Chicago A I Other versions: Christie, 31 Jan 1800		*Pyke* 1973, 104; GPC
231.	nd	William, Duke of Clarence (later King William IV)	w	Sotheby 17 Dec 1973, lot 61		*Pyke* 1981, 32
232.	nd	William, Earl of Mansfield	w	[Alton Towers sale 1857]; untraced Other versions: Brighton MAG Christie 31 Jan 1800		*Elwyn* 1934, 321; *Hughes* 1955, 1257; *Pyke* 1973, 103, 104

Miscellaneous

233.	1773	'Model in clay'		[Exhib Society of Artists, Dublin]; untraced		*Strickland* 1913, 2, 227
234.	1785	Sir Charles Morgan		Tredegar Park, Monmouth		*Gunnis* 1968, 300

PERRY, John, of Hackney fl 1797–1803

In 1797 he built the new lodge, Hyde Park, to designs by Soane (Soane, Abstract of Bills 3, fol 58). He was succeeded in the business by his son, Joseph William.

Literary References: *Gunnis* 1968, 300

Funerary Monuments

1.	?1803	Zipporah Sierra	St Albans Cathedral, Herts	S	*Gunnis* 1968, 300

PERRY, of Bewdley fl *c*1776–93

Funerary Monuments

1.	†1776	Rev John Adams	Arley Kings, Worcs	S	GPC
2.	†1793	Walter (†1793) and Mrs Moseley (†1771)	Enville, Staffs		GPC

PETHER, Thomas

For information the reader is referred to *Pyke* 1973, 105

PETTIGRUE & CO, of Dublin fl c1827

'Pettigrue, Dublin' signs a monument in Waterford Cathedral with 'a female figure kneeling amidst a swirl of drapery at an urn' and shows that the sculptor, 'though limited in his talents, had some ability at carving' (**1**) (*Potterton* 1975, 74). Two other tablets signed 'Pettigrue & Co' were, presumably, produced by the same workshop (**2, 3**).

Funerary Monuments

1.	†1827	Samuel Morgan	Waterford Cathedral	S	*Potterton* 1975, 74
2.	nd	Hungerford family	Rosscarbery, Co Cork	S	*Potterton* 1975, 74
3.	nd	Major William Cosby	St George, Dublin	S	*Potterton* 1975, 74

PEYMAN, Henry Prince, of Abingdon fl c1825–51

At the Great Exhibition of 1851 he showed 'a font executed in marble', which Gunnis suggests may be the one now in St Helen, Abingdon (**4**). He also signs two monuments at Abingdon.

Funerary Monuments

1.	?1825	Richard Galloway		St Helen, Abingdon, Berks	S	*Gunnis* 1968, 300
2.	?1825	Thomas Herbert		Farringdon, Berks	S	*Gunnis* 1968, 300
3.	?1841	Rev John Cleoburey		St Helen, Abingdon, Berks	S	*Gunnis* 1968, 300

Architectural Sculpture

4.	1851	Font	m	[Gt Exhib]; St Helen, Abingdon, Berks		Pevsner, *Berks*, 1966, 52

PHILIP, John Birnie 1824–75

A successful mid-Victorian architectural sculptor, he was born in London on 23 November 1824, the son of William and Elizabeth Philip. He entered the Government School of Design at Somerset House at the age of 17, where he studied under John Rogers Herbert, RA. Herbert later resigned from the Government School to open his own school in Maddox Street, London and Philip was one of the students who moved with him to the new school. Philip married Frances Black, of whom little is known, but one of their daughters became the wife successively of EW Godwin, the architect and designer, and James McNeil Whistler, the painter.

He was first employed in AWN Pugin's wood carving department at the House of Parliament, where he worked on gothic architectural ornament, but he was soon able to set up his own studio. His principal commissions were for architectural sculpture and church monuments, but he also carved several portrait statues and busts and at least one ideal work (**24**). He frequently worked with the architect George Gilbert Scott (1811–1878) and is best known for the sculpture he provided for Scott's Albert Memorial (**51**). The sculptor apparently held Scott in high regard, for it was at his suggestion that a portrait of Scott was included in the *Architects* frieze of the Albert Memorial podium.

Philip exhibited at the Royal Academy from 1858 until 1875. During the early part of his career he had a studio at Hans Place, Knightsbridge, but later he moved to Merton Villa, King's Road, Chelsea where he died of bronchitis on 2 March 1875. He is buried in Brompton cemetery.

A number of sculptors employed in Philip's workshop either went on to work for other established sculptors and architects or became independent sculptors in their own right. The best known is Edwin Roscoe Mullins (1848–1907). Robert Glassby (1835–1892), who assisted with the podium reliefs for the Albert Memorial, later worked as an assistant to **Henry Weekes, Carlo, Baron Marochetti** and Joseph Edgar Boehm (1834–1890) and after Boehm's death succeeded him as sculptor to the Queen. Philip's chief assistant modeller, Signor Fucigna, oversaw the completion of works which were in progress in Philip's studio at the time of his death, including the statue of Edward Akroyd for Halifax (**25**) and he subsequently worked for the architect William Burges at Cardiff Castle and Castel Coch.

Philip is not well known today, possibly because so much of his work was architectural, and thus subservient to the architect's designs. However, his podium frieze for the Albert Memorial was well received by contemporaries. The *Art Journal* of 1874 remarked 'he has so arranged the figures as to present a series of distinct groups, yet all forming one harmonious whole. There is not a single figure which will not repay close examination, while each leads the eye to a given point of special interest. All give evidence of close study, beauty of composition, and great artistic ability.' (*AJ*, 1874, 56)

EH

Literary References: *AJ*, 1874, 56; *DNB* 1896, XLV, 158; *Gunnis* 1968, 300–1; *Handley Read* 1970, 276–9; *CIIA* 4/2/iii; *Ormond and Rogers* 3, 1979–81, 165; *Read* 1982, *passim*; *Grove* 24, 1996, 604–5 (Stocker); *Trumble* 1999, 739–48; *Trumble* 2000, 20–8; *Brooks* 2000, *passim*; *ODNB* (Turpin)

Additional MS Sources: *Whistler Papers*, c1853–75, A194, B256, B258, B58–61, C136, C198, C200, D27, H230–1, L150, P282–299, P591, P706, S129, S300, W823, X64

Wills and Administrations: PPR, will, 17 April 1875, fol 341, effects under £3,000

Portraits of the Sculptor: RL, *John Philip Sculpting the Podium Frieze*, 1872, Museum of London (repr Brooks 2000, 195); two woodcuts after photographs, one for *ILN*, 13 March 1875, BM; several photos, *Whistler Papers*, c1853–75, PH1/163, PH1/27–29, PH8/1

Funerary Monuments

1.	1851	Model, reconstruction of the monument to Queen Philippa of Hainault (designed by Sir George Gilbert Scott) (co-sculptor: Samuel Cundy)	VAM A.15-1973	*Victorian Church Art*, 56; *Bilbey* 2002, 354–5 (repr)
2.	†1852	John, 2nd Earl Somers	Eastnor, Herefs	*Gunnis* 1968, 301
3.	†1853	Rev W Hodge Mill (designed by Sir George Gilbert Scott) Model(s): recumbent effigy exhib RA, London, 1860, 979	Ely Cathedral, Cambs	*Graves* VI, 1905–6, 118; Pevsner, *Cambs*, 1970, 365
4.	†1857	Dean Lyall (co-sculptor: H G Austin)	Canterbury Cathedral, Kent	
5.	?1857	Elston family	Christ Church, Doncaster, W R Yorks, churchyard	*Gunnis* 1968, 301
6.	†1857	Francis, 1st Earl of Ellesmere (designed by Sir George Gilbert Scott) (co-sculptor: Matthew Noble)	Worsley, Lancs	*CIIA* 4/8/148 (repr)

7.	1858	Lieutenant-Colonel Willoughby Moore and other members of the 6th Inniskillin Dragoons, lost in the *Europa*, 1854		York Minster, south choir aisle		*Aylmer* 1977, 470–1 (repr); *Pattison and Murray* 2001, 124–5
8.	1858	Scholars of Westminster School killed during the Crimean War (designed by George Gilbert Scott) (co-sculptor: Richard Clayton)	s	Westminster column, Broad Sanctuary, London		*CIIA* 4/7/100–107 (repr); *Read* 1982, 269 (repr)
9.	1857–1858	Sir Charles Hotham (†1855) (designed by Sir George Gilbert Scott)	s	Melbourne General Cemetery, Australia		*Trumble* 1999 (repr)
10.	1859	Eleanor, Duchess of Gloucester (†1399)		Westminster Abbey, London, Chapel of St Edmund		*Gunnis* 1968, 301
11.	post-1861	Sidney, Baron Herbert of Lea (†1861) and his mother, Katharine, Countess of Pembroke (†1856) (designed by T H Wyatt) Model(s): effigy exhib RA, London, 1863, 1193		Wilton, Wilts		*Graves* VI, 1905–6, 118; Pevsner, *Wilts*, 1975, 579; *Penny* 1977, 126
12.	1859–1862	Queen Katherine Parr (†1548) designed by Sir George Gilbert Scott)		Sudeley, Glos		*Graves* VI, 1905–6, 118; *CIIA* 4/4/130–8 (repr)
13.	1864	Charlotte, Countess Canning (†1861) (designed by Sir George Gilbert Scott)		[Barrackpore, India]; St John, Kolkata (Calcutta), north porch		*Trumble* 2000 (repr)
14.	?1864	Rebekah Foord		St Nicholas, Rochester, Kent		RG/JP, 6, 1089
15.	1867	Col Baird Smith		Kolkata (Calcutta) Cathedral		*ILN*, 6 April 1867, 336 (repr)
16.	1867	William (†1860) and Mary (†1856) Canning		St George's Chapel, Windsor, Berks	SD	*Bond* 1991, 61
17.	1868	James, 8th Earl of Elgin (†1863) (designed by Sir George Gilbert Scott) Model(s): 'Model of four bronze panels forming part of the monument exhib RA, London, 1869, 1251		Kolkata (Calcutta) Cathedral		*Trumble* 2000, 27–8 (repr); *Steggles* 2000, 88
18.	?1868	John Foord		St Nicholas, Rochester, Kent		RG/JP, 6, 1089
19.	1874	'Waiting'; statue for a monument		[Exhib RA, London, 1498]; untraced		*Graves* VI, 1905–6, 119

Statues

20.	1866	Richard Oastler Payment(s): £1,500	b	[Forster Square, Bradford, W R Yorks]; Northgate, Bradford, W R Yorks	S	*ILN*, 15 May 1869, 501 (repr); *Gunnis* 1968, 301
21.	1861–1869	Eight English monarchs: Alfred the Great, William I, Richard I, Edward III, Henry V, Queen Elizabeth, William III, Queen Anne	s	Palace of Westminster, London, Royal Gallery	S	*Walker* 1961, *passim*; *Read* 1982, 120, 121, 164 (repr)
22.	1870	Rev Robert Hall Payment(s): £1,077	m	De Montford Square, Leicester	SD	*Cavanagh* 2000, 89–91 (repr)
23.	1870	Sir David Baird Bt		Kolkata (Calcutta), India		*Ormond and Rogers* 2, 1979–81, 11
24.	1873	Narcissus		[Exhib RA, London, 1514]; untraced		*Graves* VI, 1905–6, 119
25.	1875	Colonel Edward Akroyd	b	Akroydon, Halifax, W R Yorks		*Read* 1982, 76 (repr)
26.	*c*1875	Sir Joshua Reynolds		[Chelsea Town Hall, London]; destroyed		*Read* 1982, 39

Busts

27.	1858	Dr Lyall, Dean of Canterbury		[Exhib RA, London, 1293]; untraced		*Graves* VI, 1905–6, 118
28.	1863	James S Blyth		[Exhib RA, London, 1182]; untraced		*Graves* VI, 1905–6, 119
29.	1863	Sidney, Baron Herbert of Lea		[Exhib RA, London, 1165]; untraced		*Graves* VI, 1905–6, 119
30.	1867	Richard Cobden		[Exhib RA, London, 1037]; untraced		*Graves* VI, 1905–6, 119
31.	1872	A Philanthropist	m	[Exhib RA, London, 1406]; untraced		*Graves* VI, 1905–6, 119

Architectural Sculpture

32.	1852	Arch over recumbent figure of Edward, 7th Earl Powis (by E Richardson) (designed by Sir George Gilbert Scott)	s	Welshpool, Montgomery		*Gunnis* 1968, 300
33.	1853	Reredos		Tamworth, Staffs		*Gunnis* 1968, 301
34.	1853	Wellington memorial, font cover		St Nicholas, Brighton, Sussex		Pevsner, *Sussex*, 1965, 428
35.	1854	Reredos		Ely Cathedral, Cambs		*Gunnis* 1968, 300
36.	*c*1856	Reredos (designed by Sir George Gilbert Scott)	a	Flaxley, Glos		*CIIA* 4/4/36–9 (repr)
37.	1856	Virtues and vices, figures (restoration of C13th work)		Salisbury Cathedral, Wilts, chapter house		Pevsner, *Wilts*, 1975, 421
38.	1854–1858	Decorative sculpture		St George, Doncaster, W R Yorks		Pevsner, *Yorks: W R*, 1967, 182
39.	1856–1858	St Michael disputing with Satan about the body of Moses, tympanum relief; gable roundel with Blessing Christ; spandrel roundels of adoring angels		St Michael, Cornhill, City of London		*Graves* VI, 1905–6, 118; *Read* 1982, 267 (repr); *Ward-Jackson* 2003, 89–90 (repr)
40.	*c*1859	Decorative ornaments		All Souls, Haley Hill, Halifax, W R Yorks		Pevsner, *Yorks: W.R.*, 1967, 234
41.	*c*1860	Pulpit		Frome, Somerset		RG/JP, 6, 1087
42.	1862	Reredos		St Olave, Hart Street, City of London		RG/JP, 6, 1087
43.	1863	Reredos (designed by Sir George Gilbert Scott) Model(s): Chelsea public library	a	St George's chapel, Windsor, Berks		*Redgrave* 1878, 330; *Graves* VI, 1905–6, 119
44.	1864	Five choir screen figures and reredos ornaments (co-sculptor: Francis Skidmore)		Lichfield Cathedral, Staffs		*Read* 1982, 267–9 (repr)
45.	1864	Memorial fountain commemorating the 3rd Marquess of Waterford		Ford, Northumbs		*Usherwood* 2000, 26–7 (repr)

46.	c1865	Font (designed by Sir George Gilbert Scott)		St Mary, Sudeley, Glos		*CIIA* 4/4/117–25 (repr)
47.	c1865	Reredos (designed by Sir George Gilbert Scott)		Sudeley, Glos		*CIIA* 4/4/126–9 (repr)
48.	1867	Races of the Indian empire, statues		Foreign and Commonwealth Office, Whitehall, London		*Gunnis* 1968, 301
49.	1860–1869	Four octagonal capitals	s	Blackfriars Bridge, City of London		*Ward-Jackson* 2003, 40–1 (repr)
50.	1870	Statues		Burlington House, London, façade		*Gunnis* 1968, 301
51.	1864–1872	Architects and sculptors friezes; figures of geometry, geology, physiology and philosophy; eight figures of angels Model(s): VAM		Albert Memorial, Kensington Gardens, London		*CIIA* 4/1/30–40, 68–77, 101, 103–4, 106, 112–6 (repr); *Brooks* 2000, passim
52.	1871–1873	'Peace' drinking fountain (cast by Elkington & Co) (co-sculptor: Farmer and Brindley)	b	West Smithfield gardens, City of London	SD	*Ward-Jackson* 2003, 436–8 (repr)
53.	1873–1874	Home secretaries, statues in niches on the upper storeys		Foreign and Commonwealth Office, Whitehall, London		*AJ*, 1874, 374
54.	1873–1874	Justice and Wisdom		Foreign and Commonwealth Office, Whitehall, London, statues at roof level		*AJ*, 1874, 350, 374
55.	1873–1874	Law, Art, Manufacture, Commerce, Science, Agriculture and Literature, spandrel reliefs		Foreign and Commonwealth Office, Whitehall, London		*Read* 1982, 269–72 (repr)
56.	nd	Decorative ornaments		Crewe Hall, Cheshire		*Gunnis* 1968, 301
57.	nd	Decorative Ornaments		[General Post Office, St Martin-le-Grand, London]; demol		*Gunnis* 1968, 301
58.	nd	Reredos		Christ Church, Reading, Berks		RG/JP, 6, 1087
59.	nd	Reredos		Crewe Hall, Cheshire, chapel		*Gunnis* 1968, 301
Reliefs						
60.	1874	'Suffer little children to come unto me'	m	[Exhib RA, London, 1544]; untraced		*Graves* VI, 1905–6, 119
Miscellaneous						
61.	1871	The wise virgin		[Exhib RA, London, 1280]; untraced		*Graves* VI, 1905–6, 119
62.	1875	Homeward bound		[Exhib RA, London, 1303]; untraced		*Graves* VI, 1905–6, 119

PHILLIPS, Henry fl 1661–78

Phillips was appointed master sculptor and carver in wood to the Crown in 1661. He was the first to hold this post and his warrant of appointment stated, 'Whereas the Art of Sculpture or Carving in Wood is an Art peculiar of it Selfe and not practised used or annexed with or in the Names Misteries Art or Occupations of Carpenters Joyners Masons or any other Art of manuall workemanship wherof Our Services are Already furnished, but an Art of more excellent Skill & Dexterity for the Adorning and Beautifyung of Our Pallaces Castles Manors houses & other Our buildings & workes whatsoever & wheras we have received good Testimony & proofe of the sufficient skill & rare knowledge of Henry Phillips in the Aforesaid Art of Sculpture & Carving in wood . . . The Fee or wages to be Eighteen pence by the Day . . . and One Robe yearely of the Suit of the other Esquires of our household' (TNA Work 6/2, 3 September 1661, in *Beard* 1989, 21). In 1676–8 Phillips and **Grinling Gibbons** were together paid for carving at Windsor Castle which suggests that they were working in partnership (**21, 23**). Phillips was a prominent member of the Joiners' Company and served as warden in 1668. He continued to take his fees as Master Carver until his death in 1693, when he was succeeded by Gibbons, although he actually retired some years earlier and his cousin, **William Emmett**, acted on his behalf between 1688 and 1692.

Literary References: *Colvin* 1973–76, V, 29, 275, 321, 473; *Beard* 1989 (1), 20–1, 187; *Gibson* 1999, 22, 178–95; *Beard* 2004, 73, 75

Chimneypieces				
1.	1666–1667	Large, ornamented with festoons, letters and a crown	[Whitehall Palace, London, Queen's apartments]; destroyed	*Colvin* 1973–76, V, 269
Architectural Sculpture				
2.	1660	Carved work	[Whitehall Palace, London, King's private apartments]; destroyed	*Colvin* 1973–76, V, 266
3.	post-1660	Festoons and trophies in the bed alcove	[St James's Palace, London, Duchess of York's bedchamber]; untraced	*Colvin* 1973–76, V, 233–4
4.	post-1660	'modern church worke in the canopy over the staules'	[St James's Palace, London, chapel]; untraced	*Colvin* 1973–76, V, 233
5.	1662	Decorative work, including festoons of tulips and 'two oval frames containing pedestals for heads to stand on'	[Whitehall Palace, London, Queen's bedchamber]; destroyed	*Colvin* 1973–76, V, 267
6.	1661–1662	Unidentified carving Payment(s): £10	[Somerset House, London]; untraced	*Colvin* 1973–76, V, 255
7.	1663–1664	'waved leaves and berries', ornaments for doorways	[St James's Palace, London, Queen's chapel]; untraced	*Colvin* 1973–76, V, 245
8.	1665	'Arcutts', 22 feet under the organ	[Whitehall Palace, London, chapel]; destroyed	*Colvin* 1973–76, V, 271
9.	1666–1667	Carving	[Whitehall Palace, London, Queen's oratory, bedchamber and alcove]; destroyed	*Colvin* 1973–76, V, 269
10.	1666–1667	Carving	[Whitehall Palace, London, 'Queen's room at the end of the Shield gallery']; destroyed	*Colvin* 1973–76, V, 269
11.	1667	Picture frame carved with 'french leaves', 'folding leaves', 'a knot of ribbon' and a 'foliage pannel'	[St James's Palace, London, Duke of York's withdrawing room, above chimneypiece]; untraced	*Colvin* 1973–76, V, 235
12.	1669	'Cartookes' for the frontispiece	[Whitehall Palace, London, brick gallery]; destroyed	*Colvin* 1973–76, V, 272

13.	1669	King's arms Payment(s): £23	[Custom House, London]; destroyed	*Colvin* 1973–76, V, 347
14.	1671–1672	Arms of Portugal	[Somerset House, London, Queen's great bedchamber]; untraced	*Colvin* 1973–76, V, 257
15.	1672	Enriched mouldings and mantel panels	[Whitehall Palace, two first floor rooms]; destroyed	*Colvin* 1973–76, V, 279
16.	1673	Carving in several rooms Payment(s): £106 1s 7d	[Hampton Court Palace, Middx]; untraced	*Colvin* 1973–76, V, 155
17.	1674	Altar rail with carved balusters and foliage panels, alterations to the canopy and throne, carving to the altarpiece	[Whitehall Palace, London, chapel]; destroyed	*Colvin* 1973–76, V, 274–5
18.	1676	Carving	[Whitehall Palace, London, duchess's dressing room]; destroyed	*Colvin* 1973–76, V, 277
19.	1675–1676	Decorative carving, including a shield with the king's arms, garter and crown	[Tower of London, chapel of St Peter ad Vincula]; untraced	*Colvin* 1973–76, V, 383
20.	1676	Four fluted pilasters with 'Compositive Capitalls' and 'a very Larg imbosement of drapery fruit and flowers about the chimney peece' Payment(s): £10	[Hampton Court Palace, Middx, 'Paradise']; untraced	*Colvin* 1973–76, V, 155
21.	1676–1677	'severall sorts of Carved workes. . . upon the Chimney peeces Pedestalls and picture frames' (co-sculptor: Grinling Gibbons) Payment(s): £625 14s	[Windsor Castle, Berks, several rooms]; some survivals	*Colvin* 1973–76, V, 321
22.	1678	Carved cantilever	Banqueting House, Whitehall, London	*Colvin* 1973–76, V, 300
23.	1678	Carved work on oak chimneypieces, doors, pedestals and pictures (co-sculptor: Grinling Gibbons) Payment(s): £614 17s 8d	[Windsor Castle, Berks, several rooms]; some survivals	*Colvin* 1973–76, V, 321
Miscellaneous				
24.	1660	Gnomons for the great sundial (to be cast in brass)	[Whitehall Palace, London, privy garden]; untraced	*Colvin* 1973–76, V, 266

PHILLIPS, J S fl 1826–39

He showed at the Society of British Artists from addresses in Kirby Street, Hatton Garden and Old Street, St Luke's, between 1826 and 1839. His exhibits included several intaglios, in addition to the two wax portraits listed below (1–2). In 1828 the Society of Arts awarded him a large silver medal for a cameo gem-engraving of a horse (RSA *Transactions*, 1828, vol 46, xxviii).

Reliefs

1.	1826	Antonio Canova	w	[Exhib Soc of BA, London, 728]; untraced	*Johnson* 1975, 367
2.	1839	Rev Dr Hawkes	w	[Exhib Soc of BA, London, 764]; untraced	*Johnson* 1975, 367

PHILLIPS, Joseph fl 1825

An entry in the Bristol Records Office cash book, 1819–26, reads '30 June 1825 Joseph Phillips Mason p Robert Smirke Esq. on account of statue £210:0:0. Samuel Snell for the carriage of the statue from London £21:0:0' (BRO 04030/8, fol.OR p 187).

PHILLIPS, T H fl 1845

Busts

1.	1845	Unidentified youth	p	Knox/Longstaffe-Gowan coll (acq 1994)	SD

PHILLIPS, Thomas, of Bourne 1767–1813

He was responsible for 75 engraved slate headstones in the Kesteven area and probably another 39.

Literary References: *Neave and Heron* 1969, 13

PHILLIPS FAMILY, of Haverfordwest fl *c*1764–1839

At least three generations of this family worked as sculptors and masons in Haverfordwest. The first was **Robert Phillips**, who signs a monument to Sir John Philipps in the local church (1). Gunnis felt that this work, 'with its composite pillars and recessed pilasters of the same order, supporting a broken pediment, has considerable merit'. He was succeeded by his son, **John Phillips**, whose monument to Lord Milford has 'Corinthian pillars, draped peers' robes, coronet, etc.' (2), who was in turn succeeded by his son, **Henry Phillips, of Cartlett, Haverfordwest** (*fl* 1830–60), who signs a monument with a well carved urn at Llangynin (3). Henry may have been the father of **James Phillips**, a mason buried in Carew churchyard, Pembrokes.

Literary References: *Gunnis* 1968, 301; *Dale-Jones and Lloyd* 1989, 56

Funerary Monuments

1.	?1764	Sir John Philipps Bt (by Robert Phillips of Haverfordwest)	Haverfordwest, Pembrokes	S	*Gunnis* 1968, 301
2.	?1823	Lord Milford (by John Phillips, of Haverfordwest)	Haverfordwest, Pembrokes	S	*Gunnis* 1968, 301
3.	†1839	Elizabeth Phillips (by Henry Phillips, of Cartlett, Haverfordwest)	Llangynin, Carmarthenshire		*Dale-Jones and Lloyd* 1989, 56
Chimneypieces					
4.	1796	Black marble (by John Phillips of Haverfordwest)	[Ffynone House, Pembroke]; untraced		Colby Archives, in *Gunnis* 1968, 301

PHILLIPSON, Thomas –1785

On 12 December, 1785, Mr Christie held a sale of the stock in trade of 'Mr. Phillipson, statuary, deceased, of Great Castle Street, Cavendish Square' (**2**). He can perhaps be identified with Thomas Phillipson who was paid 12 guineas for two busts for Temple Newsam House in February 1773 (**1**).

Busts

1.	1773	Unidentified subjects, two busts	[Temple Newsam House, W R Yorks]; untraced	Temple Newsam Archives (inf TF)

Miscellaneous

2.	pre-1785	Various works including 'a bas-relief of the Forge of Vulcan, a bronze bust of a satyr, a bas-relief of the Marriage of Tobias, figures of Shakespeare, Milton and Newton, and busts of Lord Holland, Lord Ligonier and Garrick'	[Phillipson sale, Christie, 12 Dec 1785]; untraced	*Gunnis* 1968, 301

PHILPOTT, C, of Bromyard fl *c*1747–1826?

Funerary Monuments

1.	†1747	Francis Badham	s	Bishop's Frome, Herefs	S	GPC
2.	†1753	Laetitia Pauncefoot	s	Bromyard, Herefs	S	GPC
3.	†1757	James Parlour		Grendon Bishop, Herefs		RG/JP, 6, 1090
4.	†1804	James Gardiner		Grendon Bishop, Herefs		RG/JP, 6, 1090
5.	†1806	John Jenks		Grendon Bishop, Herefs		RG/JP, 6, 1090
6.	†1826	Philip Ballard		Suckley, Worcs		

PHYFFERS, Theodore fl *c*1844–70

A native of Louvain and a pupil of **Charles Geerts**, he assisted his master in modelling sculpture put on display in the Byzantine court of the Crystal Palace, Sydenham, in 1856. Phyffers was invited to come to London and execute wood carvings for the Houses of Parliament by Sir Charles Barry in 1844 (**15**). He then settled in England and after completing his work at the Palace of Westminster was 'engaged in many of the ecclesiastical sculptures in the Crystal Palace, on the restorations of Carlisle Cathedral and the picture gallery of Lord Howe at Gospall Hall, Leicestershire' (*AJ*, 1858, 48) (**32, 17, 18**).

Phyffers exhibited at the Royal Academy, 1850–64, and at the British Institution in 1854, from addresses in Arthur Street, Chelsea; Lansdowne Yard, Guildford Street; Bennet's Yard, Westminster and 'Grosvenor Row SW'. He may have been linked to Beernaert and Phyffers, wood and stone carvers, at the New Catholic Church, Westminster Road, who exhibited a group of *Charity*, carved in wood, at the Society of British Artists in 1845 (cat 837) and to J B Phyffers, who exhibited a statuette at the British Institution in 1848.

Literary References: *Gunnis* 1968, 300–301

Funerary Monuments

1.	†1856	Henry, Viscount Hardinge (designed by Anthony Salvin)		Penshurst, Kent	Pevsner, *Kent: W & Weald*, 1976, 454
2.	1859	Unidentified subject		St Augustine's Coll, Canterbury, Kent, crypt chapel	*AJ*, 1859, 116; Pevsner, *Kent: N E and E*, 1983, 25

Statues

3.	1850	Unidentified subject, statuette		[Exhib Soc of BA, London, 733]; untraced	*Johnson* 19755, 368
4.	1858	Florence Nightingale supporting a wounded Crimean soldier in the Scutari hospital		[coll Mrs Bracebridge, a friend of Florence Nightingale]; untraced Other versions: reproduced in Copeland Parian ware	*AJ*, 1858, 48 (repr); *Graves* VI, 1905–6, 133; *Atterbury* 1989, 164 (repr)
5.	1867	Sir Henry Ward		Kandy, Sri Lanka	*Gunnis* 1968, 302
6.	1870	Crucifix and Virgin and child with elaborate canopy		St Francis, Pottery Lane, Kensington, London	Pevsner, *London: N W*, 1991, 465

Busts

7.	1850	John Watkins		[Exhib RA, London, 1365]; untraced	*Graves* VI, 1905–6, 133
8.	1850	Unidentified subject		[Exhib Soc of BA, London, 732]; untraced	*Johnson* 1975, 368
9.	1854	H S Parkman		[Exhib RA, London, 1475]; untraced	*Graves* VI, 1905–6, 133
10.	1854	J R Clayton		[Exhib RA, London, 1484]; untraced	*Graves* VI, 1905–6, 133
11.	1856	Ewan Christian		[Exhib RA, London, 1303]; untraced	*Graves* VI, 1905–6, 133
12.	1857	John Billing FRIBA		[Exhib RA, London, 1320]; untraced	*Graves* VI, 1905–6, 133
13.	1859	Mrs W B Philpot		[Exhib RA, London, 1304]; untraced	*Graves* VI, 1905–6, 133
14.	1863	Augustus de Rothschild		[Exhib RA, London, 1201]; untraced	*Graves* VI, 1905–6, 133

Architectural Sculpture

15.	*c*1844	Wood carving		Palace of Westminster, London	*Gunnis* 1968, 301
16.	1850	Reredos (designed by A W N Pugin)		St Marie, Sheffield, W R Yorks	Pevsner, *Yorks: W R*, 1967, 452
17.	*c*1855	Hammer beam roof, restoration		Carlisle Cathedral, Cumberland	*Gunnis* 1968, 301
18.	*c*1855	Unidentified work		Gospall Hall, Leics, picture gallery	*AJ*, 1858, 48
19.	*c*1864	Altar frontal, and other work including reredos in private chapel	b	Church of the Immaculate Conception, Farm Street, London	*Palgrave* 1866, 83; *Graves* VI, 1905–6, 133; Pevsner, *London* I, 1973, 489
20.	1865	Statues of historical figures Payment(s): £24 each	s	Canterbury Cathedral, Kent, south porch	*Builder*, 1865, 629
21.	1867	Warren Hastings and Lord Teignmouth, statues, and four panels representing incidents in Indian history		Foreign and Commonwealth Office, Whitehall, London	*Gunnis* 1968, 302; *Handley-Read* 1970, 111, 112 (repr)
22.	1868	Queen Victoria and Albert, the Prince Consort, statues	s	Canterbury Cathedral, Kent, west front	*Darby and Smith* 1983, 88–9 (repr)
23.	nd	Carved ornaments	s	St John the Baptist, Harleston, Norfolk	*Gunnis* 1968, 301

24.	nd	Carved ornaments		Salisbury Cathedral, Wilts, chapter house		*Read* 1982, 266
25.	nd	Corsham stone lectern	s	Birlingham, Worcs		*Gunnis* 1968, 301
26.	nd	The Virgin and St John, statues		St Mary, Rugby, Warks, exterior		*Gunnis* 1968, 301
Reliefs						
27.	1850	The first lesson of the Bible		[Exhib Soc of BA, London, 734]; untraced		*Johnson* 1975, 368
28.	1863	Admiral Sir Charles Napier, medallion portrait		Landport, Hants	D	*Gunnis* 1968, 302
29.	1863	Attack on the Taku ports (on column plinth)		HMS Chesapeake memorial, Southsea, Portsmouth, Hants		*Builder*, 1863, 862
Miscellaneous						
30.	1854	Holy Family		[Exhib RA, London, 1515]; untraced		*Graves* VI, 1905–6, 133
31.	1854	The heavenly chorus		[Exhib RA, London, 1510]; untraced		*Graves* VI, 1905–6, 133
32.	*c*1855	Ecclesiatical sculpture		Crystal Palace, Sydenham, London		*AJ*, 1858, 48
33.	1861	The child's first ride		[Exhib RA, London, 1131]; untraced		*Graves* VI, 1905–6, 133
34.	1862	'I'll not leave thee, thou lone one. . .'		[Exhib RA, London, 1094]; untraced		*Graves* VI, 1905–6, 133

PHYSICK FAMILY, of London

Edward Physick	active *c*1769
Edward William Physick	*c*1774–1862
Edward Gustavus Physick	1802–1875
Charles Physick	born 1810
Robert Physick	1815–1865/6
Edward James Physick	1829–1906

The Physick family hailed from villages of Cornwall on the Atlantic coast, north of Bodmin Moor, and along the Tamar Valley to Tavistock. The 19th century sculptors were descended from husbandmen in the area of Stoke Climsland. In 1769, **Edward Physick** settled land and property in Cornwall and Devon on his son, Edward William Physick, mason, of Downing Street, Middx. As Sir Henry Cheere leased many properties in the area from the Dean and Chapter of Westminster, there is a possibility that Physick was one of the workmen in Cheere's yard adjacent to St Margaret's church. For well over a century, the eldest son was named Edward, which sometimes makes identification problematic.

It is not known how **Edward William Physick** blossomed as a sculptor, but by 1810 he began to exhibit at the Royal Academy and continued regularly until 1842. Between 1824 and 1838 he also exhibited at the British Institution. Although most of his exhibited works seems to have been portrait busts, he also executed ideal subjects such as *The parting of Hector and Andromache*, 1824 (**165**) and *St John the Baptist preaching in the wilderness*, 1832 (**179**), and several church monuments from the 1820s to the 1840s. He lived from 1810–24 at 23 Spring Street, Portman Square and then at 16 Park Terrace, Regent's Park. He is buried at Kensal Green Cemetery.

Three of his sons, Charles, Robert and Edward Gustavus, exhibited from the same address. **Charles Physick** became a student at the Royal Academy Schools aged 21 in 1831, to which he had been recommended by **Samuel Joseph**. He exhibited at the Royal Academy, the British Institution and the Suffolk Street Galleries; **Robert Physick**, when aged 22, became a student in the Royal Academy Schools in 1837, sponsored by Thomas Maisey, where he won the silver medal in 1840, exhibiting at the Royal Academy from 1837–56.

Edward William's eldest son was **Edward Gustavus Physick**. In 1823, while living at 20 Spring Street, Portman Square, he received the silver medal from the Society of Arts for the figures of *Telemachus and Narcissus* (**80**), winning the same medal again in the following year. In 1825 he moved to 16 Park Terrace, Regent's Park and that year won the gold Isis medal and a year later the large gold medal. At the Society of Arts prize distribution in 1825, one report stated that 'We could not but smile at the good-natured observation of the Duke [of Sussex] when a candidate was announced by the name of Physick, who before had been rewarded by the Society and who is a very clever youth'. The President spoke of the nausea which the name treated, but added, 'what's in a name?'. Physick exhibited *Maternal playfulness* (**84**), first at the Royal Academy in 1835, and then at the Birmingham Society of Artists in 1839. He showed *Timidity* at Westminster Hall in 1844 (**90**) and *Head of the dying Saviour* (**134**) was first shown at the British Institution in 1850, and then at the Great Exhibition of 1851. He executed a group above the portico of the Female Orphans School in St John's Wood in 1854 (**94**). Physick exhibited at the Royal Academy 1822–1871, and at the British Institution from 1834 to 1866.

Edward James Physick, the eldest son of Edward Gustavus Physick attended the Royal Academy Schools in 1847, at the age of 18, on the recommendation of **Edward Hodges Baily**. In the same year he won a large silver medal for a figure of *Mercury* from the Society of Arts (**91**). In 1849 he was awarded the Royal Academy's gold medal for a high relief of the *Rape of Proserpine*, which he showed at the Royal Academy in 1850 and at the Great Exhibition of 1851. This was given to the Victoria and Albert Museum in 2004 (**158**). He exhibited at the Royal Academy, 1848–1863, and at the British Institution, 1849–1855. Among his many church monuments is that to Robert Campbell, (†1846), in St Philip's, Sydney, which has life-sized figures of *Faith, Hope* and *Charity*, and is said to be the largest in Australia (**36**). He is recognised as having thought up the idea of using lead letters and figures inserted into inscriptions, *c*1853. In 1848 he was living in his father's house at 20 Upper Gloucester Place, later at 6 Gloucester Place, and by 1863 settled permanently at 136 Marylebone Road. He is buried in Kensal Green Cemetery.

The PRO records of the 1857 competition for the monument in St Paul's Cathedral to the Duke of Wellington do not include entrants' names, but a contemporary journal noted that 'Mr Physick' had entered a model (*AJ*, Sept 1857, 293). This could have been either Edward James or his father Edward Gustavus.

His eldest son did not follow in his father's profession but became a poet and writer under the pen name of Edward Harold Visiak. A younger son Sidney Herbert Physick (1868–1961) gained a scholarship in sculpture to the South Kensington School, winning book prizes and a bronze medal. He then went on to the Royal Academy Schools, sponsored by his sister-in-law's brother, J W Waterhouse RA. Here he gained the Landseer scholarship (Sculpture) and the silver medal and was awarded the British Institution's scholarship for a bas-relief of the *Good Samaritan*. He exhibited at the Royal Academy and worked in the studios of Sir Thomas Brock and Sir Hamo Thornycroft. For the latter he modelled the clay effigy for the large bronze of Bishop Goodwin in Carlisle Cathedral in 1892.

A Robert Physick of 20 Carlton Street, who died on 2 November 1882, was probably a relative, and it is likely that he was the sculptor of the unidentified bust sold at Sotheby's in March 1989 (lot 329). His son, William Valentine Physick, born in 1843, was described as a marble carver and exhibited at the Royal Academy, 1864–71, and at the British Institution in 1868.

John Physick

Literary References: RSA *Transactions*, 1823–26; *Burgess* 1963, 247; *Gunnis*, 1968, 302, 303; *Physick* 1970, 45; *Manning* 1982, 202; *Curl* 2001, 215; *Physick* 2002, 9–11

Archival References: RA Admissions 1831, 1832, 1847; RA Premium list, *passim*

Funerary Monuments

1.	1811	Monumental figure (by Edward William Physick)	[Exhib RA, London, 900]; untraced		*Graves* VI, 1905–6, 133
2.	†1812	J T Hall (by Edward William Physick)	Somerton, Somerset	S	
3.	†1812	Rev Isaac King (by Edward William Physick)	All Saints, High Wycombe, Bucks	S	Pevsner, *Bucks*, 1994, 386
4.	1819	A monumental figure, to be executed in marble (by Edward William Physick)	[Exhib RA, London, 1246]; untraced		*Graves* VI, 1905–6, 133
5.	†1825	Lieutenant-General Thomas Trent (by Edward William Physick)	St Pancras new parish church, London	S	*Gunnis* 1968, 302
6.	?1826	James Bushel (by Edward William Physick)	St Mary, St Marylebone, London	S	*Gunnis* 1968, 302
7.	1828	Mrs Vaughan (by Edward William Physick)	[Exhib RA, London, 1828, 1143]; Sandal Magna, W R Yorks	S	*Graves* VI, 1905–6, 133; *Gunnis* 1968, 302
8.	1830	Part of a monument (by Edward William Physick)	[Exhib RA, London, 1207]; untraced		*Graves* VI, 1905–6, 133
9.	†1830	Patrick Bartlet (by Edward William Physick)	All Saints, St John's Wood, London		RG/JP, 6, 1094
10.	†1830	Rev William Woodall (by Edward William Physick)	St Mary, Scarborough, N R Yorks	S	Pevsner, *Yorks: NR*, 1966, 321
11.	?1830	Robert Fullerton (by Edward William Physick)	St Mary, St Marylebone, London	S	*Gunnis* 1968, 302
12.	†1831	Elizabeth Darnell (by Edward William Physick)	Thrapston, Northants	S	Pevsner, *Northants*, 1973, 430
13.	1831	Mrs Woodall (by Edward William Physick)	[Exhib RA, London, 1831, 1140]; St Mary, Scarborough, N R Yorks	S	*Graves* VI, 1905–6, 133; *Gunnis* 1968, 302
14.	1831	Part of a monument (by Edward William Physick)	[Exhib RA, London, 1150]; untraced		*Library of Fine Arts*, vol I, 1831, 430; *Graves* VI, 1905–6, 133; *Johnson* 1975, 368
15.	?1832	Lieutenant-General Gordon (by Edward William Physick)	St Mary, St Marylebone, London	S	*Gunnis* 1968, 302
16.	†1834	Benjamin Bond (by Edward William Physick)	St John's Wood Chapel, Marylebone, London	S	Pevsner, *London: N W*, 1991, 601
17.	†1835	Nathaniel Peach (by Edward William Physick)	Ketteringham, Norfolk	S	Pevsner, *Norfolk: N W & S*, 1999, 455
18.	†1836	Lady Janet Grant (by Edward William Physick)	Leigh, Glos	S	*Graves* VI, 1905–6, 135; Pevsner, *Glos: Vale & Forest of Dean*, 1976, 287
19.	†1836	Lieutenant-Colonel John By (by Edward William Physick) Model(s): part-model exhib RA, London, 1838, 1269	Frant, Sussex	S	*Graves* VI, 1905–6, 135; Pevsner, *Sussex*, 1965, 507
20.	†1836	Margaret Vaughan (by Edward William Physick)	Little Gaddesden, Herts	S	
21.	?1836	Richard Goodwin (by Edward William Physick)	St Mary, St Marylebone, London	S	*Gunnis* 1968, 302
22.	†1837	Michael Shepley (by Edward William Physick)	All Saints, Carshalton, Surrey	S	Pevsner, *Surrey*, 1971, 133; *Skelton* 1996, 14–15
23.	†1838	Esther By (by Edward William Physick) Model(s): part of monument exhib RA, London, 1838, 1269	Frant, Sussex		Pevsner, *Sussex*, 1965, 507
24.	1838	Miniature model of a monument to the late Major-General Hay (by Edward Gustavus Physick)	[Exhib RA, London, 1123]; untraced		*Graves* VI, 1905–6, 134
25.	1838	Miss Vaughan (by Edward William Physick)	[Model exhib R A London, 1838, 1277]; Sandal Magna, W R Yorks		RG/JP, 6, 1094
26.	?1838	Rev Charles Wood (by Edward William Physick)	Drayton Beauchamp, Bucks	S	*Gunnis* 1968, 302
27.	?1839	General Sir Henry King (by Edward William Physick)	Winkfield, Berks	S	*Gunnis* 1968, 302
28.	?1839	Lady Janet Grant (by Edward William Physick)	St Mary, Cheltenham, Glos		*Gunnis* 1968, 303
29.	c1839	Margaret Vaughan (†1826) (by Edward William Physick)	Little Gaddesden, Herts	S	*Graves* VI, 1905–6, 135; *Gunnis* 1968, 302
30.	?1840	Susanna Sheepley (by Edward William Physick)	All Saints, Carshalton, Surrey	S	*Gunnis* 1968, 302
31.	?1841	Captain Allen (by Edward William Physick)	Tenby, Pembrokes		*Gunnis* 1968, 302
32.	†1841	Hon George Berkeley Molyneux (by Edward William Physick)	St George, Hulme, Lancs	S	Pevsner, *Lancs: S*, 1969, 331

33.	†1841	Hon Henry Richard Molyneux (by Edward William Physick)	St George's Chapel, Windsor Castle		*Bond* 1958, 144, 236
34.	?1842	Margaret Bowes (by Edward William Physick)	Tooting parish church, London	S	*Gunnis* 1968, 303
35.	?1845	Charles Manners-Sutton (by Edward Gustavus Physick)	Addington, Surrey		*Gunnis* 1968, 302
36.	†1846	Robert Campbell (by Edward James Physick)	St Philip, Sydney, Australia		RG/JP, 6, 1098
37.	1847	James Brook (†1845) (by Edward Gustavus Physick) Model(s): Model, part of monument exhib RA, London, 1847, 1401	Meltham Mills, W R Yorks		*Graves* VI, 1905–6, 134; Pevsner, *Yorks: W R*, 1967, 363
38.	1847	Model of the bust of Charlotte Louisa Smith, for her monument (by Edward Gustavus Physick)	[Exhib RA, London, 1414]; untraced		*Graves* VI, 1905–6, 134
39.	?1848	Hon Esther Ashburnham (by Robert Physick)	Frant, Sussex	S	*Gunnis* 1968, 303
40.	?1848	John Lacon (by Robert Physick)	Ormesby St Margaret, Norfolk	S	*Gunnis* 1968, 303
41.	†1849	Edward Bromhead (by Edward James Physick)	Thurlby, Lincs		Pevsner, *Lincs*, 1989, 765
42.	†1849	Magens Dorrien Magens (by Robert Physick)	Brightlingsea, Essex	S	*Gunnis* 1968, 302
43.	?1850	Sir James Kempt (by Robert Physick)	Kensal Green Cemetery, London	S	*Gunnis* 1968, 303
44.	?1850	Thomas Brook (by Edward Gustavus Physick)	Goodrich, Herefs		*Gunnis* 1968, 302
45.	†1851	Henry Samuel Davis (by Robert Physick)	Kingham, Oxon	S	Pevsner, *Oxon*, 1974, 674
46.	†1851	Lady Harvey (by Robert Physick)	Halifax Cathedral, Nova Scotia		RG/JP, 6, 1101
47.	1852	Christopher Pemberton (†1850) (by Edward Gustavus Physick) Model(s): 'Small model of the figures' exhib RA London, 1852, 1335	Newton, Cambs		*Graves* VI, 1905–6, 135; Pevsner, *Cambs*, 1970, 443
48.	?1852	Louisa Eardly (by Edward James Physick)	Little Berkhamstead, Herts		*Gunnis* 1968, 303
49.	†1852	Mary Hughes (by Edward James Physick)	Meidrim, Carmarthen		*Dale-Jones and Lloyd* 1989, 56
50.	†1852	Sir John Harvey (by Robert Physick)	Halifax Cathedral, Nova Scotia		RG/JP, 6, 1101
51.	?1852	Thomas Brown (by Edward Gustavus Physick)	Brent Eleigh, Suffok		*Gunnis* 1968, 302
52.	?1853	Captain Colby (by Edward Gustavus Physick)	Manordivy, Cardigan		*Gunnis* 1968, 302
53.	?1853	Edward Jones (by Robert Physick)	Bayford, Herts	S	*Gunnis* 1968, 303
54.	?1854	Archibald Clevland (by Edward James Physick)	Westleigh, Devon		*Gunnis* 1968, 303
55.	1854	Lieutenant Bellot (by Robert Physick)	Beechey Island, Barrow Strait		RG/JP, 6, 1100
56.	†1857	7th Viscount Strangford (by Edward James Physick)	Kensal Green Cemetery, London		RG/JP, 6, 1098
57.	1857	'A father of the fatherless', model for a monument (by Edward James Physick)	[Exhib RA, London, 1234]; untraced		*Graves* VI, 1905–6, 135
58.	†1857	Children of Lord Poulett (by Edward James Physick)	Hinton St George, Somerset		Pevsner, *Somerset: S & W*, 1958, 198
59.	1858	Crimean War Memorial (by Edward James Physick)	Royal Naval School, New Cross, London		RG/JP, 6, 1098
60.	†1858	Lieutenant Louis Chichester (by Edward James Physick)	Arlington, Devon		Pevsner, *Devon*, 1989, 130
61.	1858	Model for a Crimean monument for Sheffield (by Edward Gustavus Physick)	[Exhib RA, London, 1201]; untraced		*Graves* VI, 1905–6, 135
62.	?1859	Admiral Grace (by Edward James Physick)	Kensal Green Cemetery, London		*Gunnis* 1968, 303
63.	†1859	Duchess of Cleveland (by Edward James Physick)	Staindrop, Co Durham		RG/JP, 6, 1098
64.	†1859	Edward Kemp (by Edward James Physick)	East Hoathly, Sussex		Pevsner, *Sussex*, 1965, 496
65.	†1860	Rev Henry Soames (by Edward James Physick)	Stapleford Tawney, Essex	S	
66.	?1860	Sir John Tullock (by Edward Gustavus Physick)	Kensal Green Cemetery, London		*Gunnis* 1968, 302
67.	?1863	Charles Vernon (by Edward James Physick)	Wherstead, Suffolk		*Gunnis* 1968, 303
68.	1863	Ida Lovatt Ayshford (by Edward James Physick)	Hanford, Staffs		RG/JP, 6, 1098
69.	1863	Mary Ann Gertrude Chichester (†1858) (by Edward James Physick)	Arlington, Devon	S	*Graves* VI, 1905–6, 135; Pevsner, *Devon*, 1989, 130
70.	†1866	Lieutenant-Colonel Louis Bazalgette and Major Thomas Clark (by Edward James Physick)	St Mary, Warwick		*Gunnis* 1968, 302; RG/JP, 6, 1097v.
71.	?1868	Mary Bolton (by Edward James Physick)	Instow, Devon, churchyard		*Gunnis* 1968, 303
72.	?1870	Blanch Astley (by Edward James Physick)	Melton Constable, Norfolk		*Gunnis* 1968, 303
73.	†1878	Henry Buckworth Montgomery (by Edward James Physick)	St Michael, Lyndhurst, Hants	S	
74.	†1878	Rev C Bigsby (by Edward James Physick)	Bidborough, Kent	S	

No.	Date	Subject	Material	Location		Reference
75.	†1878	Sophia Lloyd (by Edward James Physick)		Llangadog, Carmarthen		*Dale-Jones and Lloyd* 1989, 56
76.	†1883	Law family member (by Edward James Physick)		Bishop's Taunton, Devon	S	
77.	†1886	James and Richard (†1885) Musgrave (by Edward James Physick)		St Mary, Flint, Clwyd	S	
78.	†1886	Sir Charles Trevelyan (by Edward James Physick)		Cambo, Northumbs, churchyard		RG/JP, 6, 1098
79.	†1895	Law family member (by Edward James Physick)		Bishop's Taunton, Devon	S	
Statues						
80.	1823	Telemachus and Narcissus (by Edward Gustavus Physick)	p	[Soc of A large silver medal]; untraced		RSA *Transactions*, vol 41, 1823, xxix
81.	1824	Model of a group (by Edward Gustavus Physick)		[Soc of A, silver medal]; untraced		*Gunnis* 1968, 302
82.	1826	Original group of figures (by Edward Gustavus Physick)		[Soc of A, large gold medal]; untraced		RSA *Transactions*, vol 44, 1826, xliii
83.	1829	Venus and Adonis, sketch intended for a group (by Edward William Physick)		[Exhib BI, London, 534]; untraced		*Graves* 1875, 428; *Johnson* 1975, 368
84.	1835	Maternal Playfulness, group (by Edward Gustavus Physick)		[Exhib RA, London, 1072]; untraced		*Graves* 1875, 428; *Graves* VI, 1905–6, 134
85.	1839	John the Baptist preaching in the wilderness, sketch in clay (by Robert Physick)	tc	[Exhib RA, London, 1314]; untraced		*Graves* 1875, 428; *Graves* VI, 1905–6, 136
86.	1840	The captive prisoner, sketch in clay (by Edward Gustavus Physick)		[Exhib RA, London, 1108]; untraced		*Graves* VI, 1905–6, 134
87.	1841	Sleeping boy (by Robert Physick) Model(s): sleeping boy, sketch in clay exhib RA, London, 1840, 1121	m	[Exhib RA, London, 1396]; untraced		*Graves* VI, 1905–6, 136
88.	1843	My Darling Boy, group (by Edward Gustavus Physick)	m	[Exhib RA, London, 1435]; untraced		*Graves* VI, 1905–6, 134
89.	1844	Female and child, group (by Edward Gustavus Physick)	m	[Exhib BI, London, 431]; untraced		*Graves* 1875, 428; *Johnson* 1975, 368
90.	1844	Timidity (by Edward Gustavus Physick)		[Exhib Westminster Hall, London, 216]; untraced		*AU*, 1844, 216
91.	1847	Mercury, figure (by Edward James Physick)		[Soc of A silver medal]; untraced		*Gunnis* 1968, 302
92.	1852	Sketch for a statue of Wordsworth (by Edward Gustavus Physick)		[Exhib RA, London, 1377]; untraced		*Graves* VI, 1905–6, 135
93.	1853	Nature's mirror, model (by Edward Gustavus Physick)		[Exhib RA, London, 1373]; untraced		*Graves* 1875, 428; *Graves* VI, 1905–6, 135
94.	1854	Defend the fatherless, group (by Edward Gustavus Physick) Model(s): exhib RA, London, 1854, 1374; BI, London, 1856, 547	s	Female Orphans School, St John's Wood, London, above portico		*Graves* 1875, 428; *Graves* VI, 1905–6, 135; *Gunnis* 1968, 302
95.	1866	'Alarmed', statuette (by Edward Gustavus Physick) Payment(s): £80	m	[Exhib Soc of BA, London, 1092]; untraced		*Johnson* 1975, 368
96.	1871	Dying Saviour, figure (by Edward Gustavus Physick)	m	[Yorkshire Exhib, Leeds]; untraced		RG/JP, 6, 1094
Busts						
97.	1810	Unidentified gentleman (by Edward William Physick)		[Exhib RA, London, 770]; untraced		*Graves* VI, 1905–6, 133
98.	1813	Unidentified young lady (by Edward William Physick)		[Exhib RA, London, 904]; untraced		*Graves* VI, 1905–6, 133
99.	1814	One of the sculptor's sons (by Edward William Physick)		[Exhib RA, London, 809]; untraced		*Graves* VI, 1905–6, 133
100.	1815	Miss Freeman (by Edward William Physick)		[Exhib RA, London, 884]; untraced		*Graves* VI, 1905–6, 133
101.	1817	Miss Phillips (by Edward William Physick)		[Exhib RA, London, 1071]; untraced		*Graves* VI, 1905–6, 133
102.	1821	Unidentified young lady (by Edward William Physick)		[Exhib RA, London, 1821, 1163]; Untraced		*Graves* VI, 1905–6, 133
103.	1823	H G Clough (by Edward William Physick)		[Exhib RA, London, 1067]; untraced		*Graves* VI, 1905–6, 133
104.	1825	King George IV, cabinet bust (by Edward William Physick)	m	[Exhib RA, London, 1013]; untraced		*Graves* 1875, 428; *Graves* VI, 1905–6, 133; *Johnson* 1975, 368
105.	1826	'A young gentleman, to be executed in marble' (by Edward Gustavus Physick)		[Exhib RA, London, 1102]; untraced		*Graves* VI, 1905–6, 134
106.	1827	Carl Maria von Weber (by Edward William Physick)		[Exhib Soc of BA, London, 867]; untraced		*Johnson* 1975, 368
107.	1827	Master Robert Noble, model (by Edward Gustavus Physick)		[Exhib Soc of BA, London, 853]; untraced		*Johnson* 1975, 368
108.	1827	Miss Wilkinson (by Edward William Physick)		[Exhib RA, London, 1075]; untraced		*Graves* VI, 1905–6, 133; *Johnson* 1975, 368
109.	1829	H G Clough (by Edward William Physick)		[Exhib RA, London, 1146]; untraced		*Graves* VI, 1905–6, 133; *Johnson* 1975, 368
110.	1829	Miss E Lomax (by Edward Gustavus Physick)		[Exhib Soc of BA, London, 879]; untraced		*Johnson* 1975, 368
111.	1829	Rev Basil Wood (by Edward Gustavus Physick) Model(s): 'Small model of the head of Rev Basil Wood' exhib RA, London, 1833, 1161		[Exhib RA, London, 1147]; untraced		*Graves* VI, 1905–6, 134; *Johnson* 1975, 368
112.	1832	Arthur, 1st Duke of Wellington (by Edward William Physick)		[Exhib Soc of BA, London, 708]; untraced		*Johnson* 1975, 368

113.	1832	Lord Eldon (by Charles Physick)		[Exhib Soc of BA, London, 872]; untraced		*Johnson* 1975, 368
114.	1832	Mr Ewen (by Edward William Physick)		[Exhib RA, London, 1119]; untraced		*Graves* VI, 1905–6, 133; *Johnson* 1975, 368
115.	1833	Lieutenant-General Gordon (by Edward William Physick)		[Exhib RA, London, 1144]; untraced		*Graves* VI, 1905–6, 133
116.	1833	Mary Ann Haines (by Charles Physick)		[Exhib Soc of BA, London, 847]; untraced		*Johnson* 1975, 368
117.	1833	Master William Lomax, small model (by Edward Gustavus Physick)		[Exhib RA, London, 1218]; untraced		*Graves* VI, 1905–6, 134; *Johnson* 1975, 368
118.	1833	Miss Curwin (by Edward William Physick)		[Exhib RA, London, 1129]; untraced		*Graves* VI, 1905–6, 133; *Johnson* 1975, 368
119.	1834	Rev Sanderson Robins, model (by Edward Gustavus Physick)		[Exhib RA, London, 1038]; untraced Other versions: cabinet bust exhib RA, London, 1835, 1121 and Soc of BA, London, 1836, 860 model for a bust exhib RA, London, 1839, 1356		*Graves* VI, 1905–6, 134; *Johnson* 1975, 368
120.	1834	Unidentified young lady (by Edward William Physick)		[Exhib RA, London, 1110]; untraced		*Graves* VI, 1905–6, 133
121.	1836	Boy's head, a study in marble (by Robert Physick)		[Exhib BI, London, 493]; untraced		*Graves* 1875, 428
122.	1836	Child's head (by Robert Physick)		[Exhib BI, London, 495]; untraced		*Graves* 1875, 428
123.	1837	Boy's head (by Robert Physick)	m	[Exhib RA, London, 1194]; untraced		*Graves* VI, 1905–6, 1194
124.	1838	Posthumous bust of a child (by Edward Gustavus Physick)		[Exhib RA, London, 1329]; untraced		*Graves* VI, 1905–6, 134
125.	1840	Unidentified gentleman, model (by Edward Gustavus Physick)		[Exhib RA, London, 1087]; untraced		*Graves* VI, 1905–6, 134
126.	c1840	Unidentified woman (by Robert Physick)	m	Sotheby, 21 & 22 May 1996, 431 (repr)	S	
127.	1841	Joseph Whitehead, to be executed in marble (by Edward Gustavus Physick) Model(s): exhib RA, London, 1855, 1474		[Exhib RA, London, 1304]; untraced		*Graves* VI, 1905–6, 134
128.	1841	Lord Kingston, model (by Edward William Physick)		[Exhib RA, London, 1329]; untraced		*Graves* VI, 1905–6, 133
129.	1843	Arthur, 1st Duke of Wellington (by Edward William Physick)		[Exhib RA, London, 1472]; untraced		*Graves* VI, 1905–6, 136; *Gunnis* 1968, 303
130.	1845	Unidentified child, to be executed in marble (by Robert Physick)		[Exhib RA, London, 1420]; untraced		*Graves* VI, 1905–6, 136
131.	1845	Unidentified clergyman (by Edward Gustavus Physick)		[Exhib Soc of BA, London, 830]; untraced		*Johnson* 1975, 368
132.	1847	Lady Smith, model (by Edward Gustavus Physick)		[Exhib RA, London, 1374]; untraced		*Graves* VI, 1905–6, 134
133.	1848	Model of a child, to be executed in marble (by Edward Gustavus Physick)		[Exhib RA, London, 1381]; untraced		*Graves* VI, 1905–6, 134
134.	1850	Head of the dying Saviour (by Edward Gustavus Physick)	m	[Exhib Birmingham Soc of A]; untraced		*Graves* 1875, 428; *Graves* VI, 1905–6, 135; *Gunnis* 1968, 302; *Johnson* 1975, 368
135.	1850	Sir Robert Peel (by Robert Physick)		Merchant Taylors' Company, City of London		*Ormond* 1973, 372
136.	1850	William Westall ARA (by Edward James Physick)		[Exhib RA, London, 1391]; untraced		*Graves* VI, 1905–6, 135; *Gunnis* 1968, 302
137.	1851	Queen Victoria (by Robert Physick)	m	NPG, London	SD	
138.	1852	A head in marble (by Edward Gustavus Physick)		[Exhib BI, London, 540]; untraced		*Graves* 1875, 428
139.	1852	Arthur, 1st Duke of Wellington (by Robert Physick)		Royal United Services Museum, London Other versions: Arthur, 1st Duke of Wellington, SD 1853, (by Robert Physick)		*Gunnis* 1968, 303
140.	1853	Sir Lewis Grant (by Robert Physick)	m	[Exhib RA, London, 1362]; untraced		*Graves* VI, 1905–6, 136; *Gunnis* 1968, 303
141.	1854	J B Basham (by Edward James Physick)		[Exhib RA, London, 1440]; untraced		*Graves* VI, 1905–6, 135
142.	1854	R B Haydon 'for Philadelphia' (by Edward James Physick)		[Exhib RA, London, 1479]; untraced		*Graves* VI, 1905–6, 135;
143.	1854	Sir John Barrow Bt (†1898) (by Robert Physick)	m	[Exhib RA, London, 1445]; untraced Other versions: Exhib RA, London, 1855, 1445		*Graves* VI, 1905–6, 136; *Ormond* 1973, 28
144.	1856	Mrs H Montefiore (by Robert Physick)		[Exhib RA, London, 1298]; untraced		*Graves* VI, 1905–6, 136
145.	1857	Rev George Fisk (by Edward Gustavus Physick)		[Exhib RA, London, 1321]; untraced		*Graves* VI, 1905–6, 135
146.	1861	The bride, an ideal head (by Edward Gustavus Physick)	m	[Exhib RA, London, 1100]; untraced Other versions: 'The Bride' exhib RA, London, 1859, 1362		*Graves* VI, 1905–6, 135; *Johnson* 1975, 368
147.	1863	Cupid (by Edward Gustavus Physick) Payment(s): £15	m	[Exhib Soc of BA, London, 896]; untraced		*Graves* 1875, 428; *Johnson* 1975, 368
148.	1863	Joy (by Edward Gustavus Physick) Payment(s): £15	m	[Exhib Soc of BA, London, 897]; untraced		*Graves* 1875, 428; *Johnson* 1975, 368
149.	1864	Evening (by Edward Gustavus Physick)	m	[Exhib RA, London, 995]; untraced		*Graves* VI, 1905–6, 135; *Johnson* 1975, 368
150.	1865	Ideal head (by Edward Gustavus Physick)	m	[Exhib RA, London, 994]; untraced Other versions: Exhib RA, London, 1865, 995		*Graves* VI, 1905–6, 135

151.	1867	Little Red Riding Hood, ideal bust (by Edward Gustavus Physick)	m	[Exhib RA, London, 1082]; untraced	*Graves* VI, 1905–6, 135
152.	1871	'Peep', ideal head (by Edward Gustavus Physick)	m	[Exhib RA, London, 1872, 1211]; untraced	*Graves* VI, 1905–6, 1211
153.	nd	A nymph (by Robert Physick)		Christie, 3 Feb 1857; untraced	RG/JP, 6, 1100
154.	nd	Arthur, 1st Duke of Wellington (by Edward William Physick)		Merchant Taylors' Hall, City of London	Pevsner, *London: City*, 1997, 400
155.	nd	King Charles I, (perhaps after H le Sueur) (by Charles Physick)	m	Royal Coll, Windsor Castle, RCIN 31321	
156.	nd	Richard Cobden, after Matthew Noble (by Edward James Physick)	m	National Liberal Club, London	*Ormond* 1973, 108
Architectural Sculpture					
157.	1842	Font (by Charles Physick)		St Paul, Knightsbridge, London	Pevsner, *London: Westminster*, 1973, 498
Reliefs					
158.	1850	Rape of Proserpine (by Edward James Physick)		[Exhib RA, London, 1337, gold medal, coll the sculptor]; VAM	*Graves* VI, 1905–6, 135; *Gunnis* 1968, 302
159.	1854	F B Woodward, medallion portrait (by Edward James Physick)		[Exhib RA, London, 1520]; untraced	*Graves* VI, 1905–6, 135
Miscellaneous					
160.	1822	Narcissus, sketch in clay (by Edward Gustavus Physick)	tc	[Exhib RA, London, 1031]; untraced	*Graves* VI, 1905–6, 133
161.	1823	Minerva receiving the attack of Mars (by Edward Gustavus Physick)		[Exhib RA, London, 1107]; untraced	*Graves* 1875, 428; *Graves* VI, 1905–6, 133
162.	1823	Narcissus at the brook (by Edward Gustavus Physick)		[Exhib RA, London, 1131]; untraced	*Graves* 1875, 428; *Graves* VI, 1905–6, 133; *Johnson* 1975, 368
163.	1823	Ulysses compelling Circe to restore his transformed companions (by Edward William Physick)		[Exhib RA, London, 1073]; untraced	*Graves* 1875, 427; *Graves* VI, 1905–6, 133; *Johnson* 1975, 368
164.	1824	Original model of a group in plaster (by Edward Gustavus Physick)		[Soc of A, large silver medal]; untraced	RSA *Transactions*, vol 42, 1824, xlvi
165.	1824	The parting of Hector and Andromache (by Edward William Physick)		[Exhib RA, London, 977]; untraced	*Graves* 1875, 427; *Graves* VI, 1905–6, 133; *Johnson* 1975, 368
166.	1824	Theseus finding his father's sword and sandals (by Edward Gustavus Physick)		[Exhib RA, London, 974]; untraced	*Graves* 1875, 428; *Graves* VI, 1905–6, 133–4
167.	1825	Affection (by Edward Gustavus Physick)		[Exhib RA, London, 993]; untraced	*Graves* 1875, 428; *Graves* VI, 1905–6, 134; *Johnson* 1975, 368
168.	1825	Original plaster model of a group (by Edward Gustavus Physick)		[Soc of A, gold Isis medal]; untraced	RSA *Transactions*, vol 43, 1825, xlvii
169.	1826	Adam and Eve discovering the body of Abel (by Edward Gustavus Physick)		[Exhib RA, London, 1097]; untraced	*Graves* VI, 1905–6, 134; *Johnson* 1975, 368
170.	1826	The fair penitent (by Edward Gustavus Physick)		[Exhib Soc of BA, London, 752]; untraced	*Johnson* 1975, 368
171.	1827	Cupid and Psyche (by Edward William Physick)		[Exhib BI, London, 470]; untraced	*Graves* 1875, 428; *Johnson* 1975, 368
172.	1827	Summer, 'Robed in loose array she came, to the well-known pool to bathe . . .' (by Edward Gustavus Physick)		[Exhib RA, London, 1082]; untraced Other versions: Summer, 'In folds loose floating. . .' exhib RA, London, 1833, 1221	*Graves* 1875, 428; *Graves* VI, 1905–6, 134
173.	1827	The Captive, sketch in clay (by Edward Gustavus Physick)	tc	[Exhib RA, London, 1101]; untraced	*Graves* 1875, 428; *Graves* VI, 1905–6, 134; *Johnson* 1975, 368
174.	1830	Hymen giving advice to a married couple, 'When rosy Love . . .' (by Edward William Physick)		[Exhib RA, London, 1196]; untraced	*Graves* VI, 1905–6, 133; *Johnson* 1975, 368
175.	1830	The happy mother (by Edward William Physick)		[Exhib RA, London, 1201]; untraced	*Graves* VI, 1905–6, 133
176.	1830	The young robin (by Edward Gustavus Physick)		[Exhib RA, London, 1278]; untraced	*Graves* 1875, 428; *Graves* VI, 1905–6, 134
177.	1831	The serpent tempting Eve (by Edward Gustavus Physick)		[Exhib RA, London, 1144]; untraced	*Library of Fine Arts*, vol I, 1831, 431; *Graves* VI, 1905–6, 134; *Johnson* 1975, 368
178.	1832	A study in marble (by Charles Physick)	m	[Exhib RA, London, 1212]; untraced	*Graves* VI, 1905–6, 133
179.	1832	St John the Baptist preaching in the wilderness (by Edward William Physick)		[Exhib RA, London, 1129]; untraced	*Graves* VI, 1905–6, 133
180.	1833	The toilet; unfinished model (by Edward Gustavus Physick)		[Exhib RA, London, 1131]; untraced	*Graves* VI, 1905–6, 134
181.	1834	A girl fondling a rabbit (by Charles Physick)		[Exhib BI, London, 563]; untraced	*Graves* 1875, 427
182.	1834	'. . . a Jogi or Sanyasi, a Hindu religious mendicant', model (by Edward William Physick)	tc	[Exhib RA, London, 1117]; untraced	*Graves* VI, 1905–6, 133; *Johnson* 1975, 368
183.	1835	The bath, 'She with careful eye, around the banks surveyed, Ere from her fiar form the closing waves received', model (by Edward Gustavus Physick)		[Exhib RA, London, 1056]; untraced	*Graves* 1875, 428; *Graves* VI, 1905–6, 134

184.	1835	The nestling (by Edward William Physick) Model(s): exhib RA, London, 1827, 1110; BI, London, 1828, 515; RA, London, 1833, 1146; BI, London, 1834, 558	m	[Exhib Soc of BA, London, 802]; untraced	*Graves* 1875, 428; *Graves* VI, 1905–6, 133; *Johnson* 1975, 368
185.	1836	Girl at the brook (by Edward William Physick)		[Exhib BI, London, 496]; untraced	*Graves* 1875, 428; *Johnson* 1975, 368
186.	1837	Thetis dipping Achilles in the waters of the Styx, model (by Edward William Physick)	tc	[Exhib RA, London, 1181]; untraced	*Graves* 1875, 428; *Graves* VI, 1905–6, 133
187.	1838	Hope, 'With innocent delight the boy uplifts his eyes', model (by Edward Gustavus Physick)		[Exhib RA, London, 1286]; untraced	*Graves* VI, 1905–6, 134
188.	1838	Study from nature (by Robert Physick)		[Exhib BI, London, 490]; untraced	*Graves* 1875, 428
189.	1840	Grief, model (by Robert Physick)		[Exhib BI, London, 437]; untraced	*Graves* 1875, 428
190.	1841	Maternal affection (by Edward Gustavus Physick)		[Exhib RA, London, 1262]; untraced	*Graves* VI, 1905–6, 134
191.	1842	Nymph preparing to bathe, model (by Edward Gustavus Physick)		[Exhib RA, London, 1271]; untraced	*AU*, 1842, 127
192.	1842	'Venus and Adonis, sketch intended for a group' (by Edward William Physick)		[Exhib RA, London, 1344]; untraced	*Graves* VI, 1905–6, 133
193.	1848	'Prometheus watching the approach of the vulture, sketch' (by Edward James Physick)		[Exhib RA, London, 1360]; untraced	*Graves* 1875, 428; *Graves* VI, 1905–6, 135
194.	1852	The lesson, model (by Edward Gustavus Physick)		[Exhib RA, London, 1352]; untraced	*Graves* VI, 1905–6, 135
195.	1854	Hagar and Ishmael (by Edward James Physick)		[Exhib RA, London, 1409]; untraced	*Graves* 1875, 428; *Graves* VI, 1905–6, 135
196.	1854	Ida Lamb (by Edward James Physick)		[Exhib RA, London, 1428]; untraced	*Graves* VI, 1905–6, 135
197.	1854	Little Edward (by Edward James Physick)		[Exhib RA, London, 1483]; untraced	*Graves* VI, 1905–6, 135
198.	1862	The gipsy girl (by Edward Gustavus Physick) Payment(s): £10; in marble £80		[Exhib RA, London, 1120]; untraced	*Graves* 1875, 428; *Graves* VI, 1905–6, 135; *Johnson* 1975, 368
199.	1864	The shipwrecked mariner cast ashore, model (by Edward Gustavus Physick)		[Exhib RA, London, 1045]; untraced	*Graves* VI, 1905–6, 135
200.	1866	An incident after a storm at sea (by Edward Gustavus Physick) Payment(s): £220 (model £40)	m	[Exhib Soc of BA, London, 1092]; untraced	*Johnson* 1975, 368
201.	1866	Pleasant thought (pleasing thoughts), model (by Edward Gustavus Physick) Payment(s): £20		[Exhib Soc of BA, London, 895]; untraced	*Graves* 1875, 428; *Johnson* 1975, 368
202.	1868	The startled nymph (by Edward Gustavus Physick)	m	[Exhib RA, London, 1039]; untraced	*Graves* VI, 1905–6, 1039
203.	1874	Spring time (by Edward Gustavus Physick) Payment(s): £15 15s	m	[Exhib Soc of BA, London, 1020]; untraced	*Johnson* 1975, 368
204.	1899	Cross (by Edward James Physick)		Farnham Royal, Bucks, churchyard	*Building News*, 15 Sept 1899

PIAMONTINI, Giovanni Battista –1761

In 1754 he made full size copies of *The wrestlers* and *The listening slave* for Joseph Leeson (1). He appears to have shared a workshop in Florence, near SS Annunziata, with **Francis Harwood**, with whom he worked on the decoration of the Porta San Gallo, providing a statue of *il Dio Buon Evento* and a trophy. Piamontini died in 1761 and Harwood took over his studio.

Literary References: *Fleming and Honour* 1968, 511; *Ingamells* 1997, 472

Statues

1.	1754	The wrestlers and The listening slave, copies after the Antique	[coll Joseph Leeson]; NGI, Dublin	*Ingamells* 1997, 472

PICKERING, Joseph 1820–

The 1861 national census listed him in London Road, Carlisle, aged 41, having come from Blackburn, Lancs. **David Dunbar I** visited his studio on 13 January 1860 and spoke of his work in glowing terms, listing some of the works he had seen (*CJ*, 13 Jan 1860). The same journal referred in 1862 to a pair of monuments (**1, 2**). (Inf. D Perriam).

Funerary Monuments

1.	nd	Rev W Graham	Untraced	*CJ*, 21 Oct 1862
2.	nd	Sir James Graham	Untraced	*CJ*, 21 Oct 1862

PICKERSGILL, William Crellin fl 1832

Miscellaneous

1.	1832	Unidentified subject, model	[RA silver medal]; untraced	RA Premium list

PICKFORD, Joseph 1684–1762

Baptised in Badger, Salop, in March 1684, he was the son of a stonemason, William Pickford, and his wife Constance. Little is known of Joseph's early life and training but his three elder brothers established themselves as masons in Warwick and it seems likely that he joined them. In 1721 he worked with **Giovanni Battista Guelfi** at Easton Neston, Northants, on restoration work to the ancient Arundel marbles for Lord Leominster, later 1st Earl of Pomfret. When Lady Pomfret presented the marbles to Oxford University in 1755 Pickford wrote to Sir Roger Newdigate that he 'was at the placing and repairing of them with signor Guelfi when he first came from Italy, as well as moving them lately to Towcester, and I know it will be attended with a great deal of trouble and expense before they are properly fixed' (Newdigate Archives, CR 136/B2994).

Pickford settled in London by 1735, where he paid rates varying from £12 to £24 on property in Stone Bridge, Hyde Park Corner until his death. This was situated in Piccadilly, between Brick Street and Down Street, on the site now occupied by the Park Lane Hotel. He married Mary Atkinson, a widow, at St Bride's, Fleet Street, on 3 December 1734 and soon entered into partnership with **William Atkinson**, who was probably his step-son, though Pickford described him as a son-in-law in his will.

From the late 1730s onwards Pickford was much employed on building projects associated with the architect William Kent and his pupil Stephen Wright. Kent was the landscape architect at Claremont, Surrey, when in 1738–39 the Duke of Newcastle paid Pickford £160 for unidentified work. In the following years Kent employed him at London houses designed for Lady Isabella Finch and Henry Pelham and, very extensively, at Holkham Hall, Norfolk (**9, 10, 15–17**). Pickford and **Andrews Jelfe** were the principal contractors for the Horse Guards in Whitehall, designed by Kent but erected between 1751 and 1755 by his followers, John Vardy and Thomas Robinson. Between 1754 and 1758 Pickford and William Atkinson were employed in building the new university library in Cambridge, designed by Wright, for which they received nearly £5,000. Atkinson appears to have been responsible for most of the decorative stone carving.

Pickford also executed a number of monuments including one to Sir John and Lady Bendyshe at Steeple Bumpstead, which has medallion-portraits (**3**). This and the tablet to George Pyke at Birdbrook, is signed jointly with Atkinson (**1**). Around 1740 he made two busts to be added to the monument of Richard Hopkins at St Michael, Coventry, commemorating a son and daughter-in-law (**7**). He later carved the architectural parts of the monument to the 9th Earl of Huntingdon at Ashby-de-la-Zouche, which was designed by Kent and has a figure by **Michael Rysbrack** (**5**).

Pickford died in 1760, aged 76. His will, proved that December, directed that his stock in trade and moneys owed by creditors should be divided between his wife and step-son. Control of the yard and three houses at Hyde Park Corner passed to William Atkinson during his lifetime but the property then reverted to descendants of Pickford's brothers and sisters. This arrangement appears to have caused a dispute between the families which was only resolved when new letters of administration were granted 20 years later. Pickford's nephew, Joseph Pickford (1734–1782), served his apprenticeship with him between 1748 and 1855 and went on to establish a successful architectural practice in Derby.

EH

Literary References: *Gunnis* 1968, 303; *Saunders* 1993, *passim*; *White* 1995, 78–9; *Colvin* 1995, 752

Archival References: Poor Rates St George, Hanover Square, WCA C122 (1735), C220–222 (1741–3), C294 (1755) C304 (1761/2), C122, C304 (1735–1761/2); IGI

Will: PROB 11/861

Funerary Monuments

No.	Date	Subject		Location		Reference
1.	?1738	George Pyke (co-sculptor: William Atkinson)		Birdbrook, Essex	S	*Gunnis* 1968, 303
2.	1740	Roberts family		Cranbrook, Kent	S	Pevsner, *Kent: W & Weald*, 1976, 244
3.	c1740	Sir John Bendyshe Bt (†1707) and Lady Bendyshe (†1705) (co-sculptor: William Atkinson)		Steeple Bumpstead, Essex	S	Pevsner, *Essex*, 1965, 370
4.	1741	George Monson		[? South Carlton, Lincs, churchyard]; untraced		GPC
5.	†1746	Theophilus, 9th Earl of Huntingdon (designed by William Kent) (co-sculptor: Michael Rysbrack)		St Helen, Ashby-de-la-Zouch, Leics	S	Pevsner, *Leics & Rutland*, 1984, 79–80
6.	†1755	William Hanger		Farningham, Kent	S	Pevsner, *Kent: W & Weald*, 1976, 283

Busts

No.	Date	Subject		Location		Reference
7.	c1740	Richard Hopkins and Anna Maria Hopkins (added to monument to Richard Hopkins †1707)		[St Michael, Coventry, Warks]; destroyed		*Gunnis* 1968, 303

Chimneypieces

No.	Date	Subject		Location		Reference
8.	1738	For the drawing room (with other unspecified work) Payment(s): £18 0s 10d; £6 for sundries	m	[Earl Fitzwalter's house, Pall Mall, London]; untraced		RIBA MS 728–3; *Edwards* 1977, 74
9.	1742	Two in the saloon	m	44 Berkeley Square, London (for Lady Isabella Finch)		RIBA MS 728–3, *Gunnis* 1968, 30;
10.	1743	'rich marble column chimneypiece' Payment(s): £126		[for Henry Pelham, 22 Arlington Street, London, great room]; untraced		*Gunnis* 1968, 303
11.	1751	Several Payment(s): £528 (with other work)		[White Lodge, Richmond Park, Surrey]; untraced		GPC
12.	1762	For the dressing room		[Ashburnham Place, Sussex]; untraced		*Gunnis* 1968, 303, citing Ashburnham Archives
13.	nd	Description unavailable		[for Lord Duncannon]; untraced		*Gunnis* 1968, 303, citing Archives, Lord Falmouth
14.	nd	Description unavailable		[for Admiral Boscawen]; untraced		*Gunnis* 1968, 303, citing Archives, Lord Falmouth
15.	nd	Nine, of various designs	m	Holkham Hall, Norfolk		*Brettingham* 1773, 3, 15, 16, 17 (repr 17, 43, 51, 54, 55)

Architectural Sculpture

No.	Date	Subject		Location		Reference
16.	1743	Frieze with festoons of fruit and flowers Payment(s): £48		[Rt Hon Henry Pelham's house, Arlington Street, London]; untraced		RIBA MS 728–3; *Gunnis* 1968, 303
17.	nd	Including alabaster columns and capitals for the great hall and marble friezes		Holkham Hall, Norfolk		*Gunnis* 1968, 303

Miscellaneous

No.	Date	Subject		Location		Reference
18.	1734–1735	Unidentified statuary Payment(s): £23 12s		[Kew Palace, Surrey]; untraced		GPC
19.	1738–1739	Unspecified work		[Claremont, Surrey]; untraced		BL Add MS 33321

PICKMAN, W

He exhibited at the Royal Academy, 1825–44, and at the Suffolk Street Galleries in 1828 giving addresses at 79 Dean Street, Soho, 6 Albany Street and 30 Oxford Street.

Literary References: *Gunnis* 1968, 303; *Pyke* 1973, 106

Busts					
1.	1828	Frederick-Augustus, Duke of York and Albany	w	[Exhib Soc of BA, London, 916]; untraced	*Gunnis* 1968, 303; *Johnson* 1975, 369
2.	1828	King George IV	w	[Exhib Soc of BA, London, 914]; untraced	*Gunnis* 1968, 303; *Johnson* 1975, 369
3.	1828	Unidentified young lady		[Exhib Soc of BA, London, 906]; untraced	*Johnson* 1975, 369
4.	1831	An infant		[Exhib RA, London, 1117]; untraced	*Graves* VI, 1905–6, 149
5.	1832	Unidentified gentleman		[Exhib RA, London, 1158]; untraced	*Graves* VI, 1905–6, 149
6.	1832	Unidentified lady		[Exhib RA, London, 1162]; untraced	*Graves* VI, 1905–6, 149
7.	1833	Sir Francis Burdett		[Exhib RA, London, 1191]; untraced	*Graves* VI, 1905–6, 149
8.	1833	Unidentified gentleman		[Exhib RA, London, 1192]; untraced	*Graves* VI, 1905–6, 149
9.	1844	Unidentified lady	w	[Exhib RA, London, 1259]; untraced	*Graves* VI, 1905–6, 149
Reliefs					
10.	1825	J C Hobhouse		[Exhib RA, London, 932]; untraced	*Graves* VI, 1905–6, 149
11.	1825	Unidentified lady		[Exhib RA, London, 968]; untraced	*Graves* VI, 1905–6, 149
12.	1826	Unidentified lady		[Exhib RA, London, 938]; untraced	*Graves* VI, 1905–6, 149
13.	1826	Unidentified lady		[Exhib RA, London, 966]; untraced	*Graves* VI, 1905–6, 149
14.	1827	Unidentified lady		[Exhib RA, London, 1001]; untraced	*Graves* VI, 1905–6, 149
15.	1828	Unidentified lady	w	[Exhib RA, London, 1093]; untraced	*Graves* VI, 1905–6, 149
16.	1830	Unidentified lady		[Exhib RA, London, 1129]; untraced	*Graves* VI, 1905–6, 149
17.	1833	Unidentified lady		[Exhib RA, London, 1049]; untraced	*Graves* VI, 1905–6, 149
18.	1833	Unidentified lady, medallion		[Exhib Soc of BA, London, 861]; untraced	*Johnson* 1975, 369
19.	1841	Mr McKenzie, of Edinburgh, medallion	w	[Exhib RA, London, 1138]; untraced	*Graves* VI, 1905–6, 149
20.	1841	Unidentified lady		[Exhib RA, London, 1141]; untraced	*Graves* VI, 1905–6, 149
Miscellaneous					
21.	1829	Miss Byfield	w	[Exhib Soc of BA, London, 890]; untraced	*Johnson* 1975, 369
22.	1829	Unidentified 'Amateur'	w	[Exhib Soc of BA, London, 886]; untraced	*Johnson* 1975, 369
23.	1829	Unidentified lady		[Exhib RA, London, 1071]; untraced	*Graves* VI, 1905–6, 149
24.	1831	The nativity		[Exhib RA, London, 1045]; untraced	*Graves* VI, 1905–6, 149
25.	1840	Unidentified lady and child		[Exhib RA, London, 1086]; untraced	*Graves* VI, 1905–6, 149
26.	1842	Unidentified gentleman		[Exhib RA, London, 1185]; untraced	*Graves* VI, 1905–6, 149
27.	1842	Unidentified lady		[Exhib RA, London, 1183]; untraced	*Graves* VI, 1905–6, 149
28.	1843	Unidentified lady, model	w	[Exhib RA, London, 1372]; untraced	*Graves* VI, 1905–6, 149
29.	1843	Unidentified young lady, model	w	[Exhib RA, London, 1368]; untraced	*Graves* VI, 1905–6, 149

PIDDINGTON FAMILY, of Oxford

Anthony Piddington	fl 1657–1664
Richard Piddington I	–1724
John Piddington I	1682–1716
Richard Piddington II	–1752
John Piddington II	

A number of statuaries and masons called Piddington worked in Oxford during the 17th and 18th centuries. The first of them, Richard, son of Humphrey Piddington of Stanton St John, was probably the 'Piddington' who was in partnership with William Badger in 1639, when they were paid £32 10s for 'paving the passage of the Congregation House and pitching the gutters' (*Clark* 1891–90, vol IV, 55). **Anthony Piddington** was employed at Oriel College between 1657 and 1661. He was made free of the City of Oxford on 3 May 1664 and had a son, **Richard Piddington I**, whom he took as his apprentice. Richard worked in partnership with George Smith on the erection of the south building at New College in 1700. Gunnis notes that he seems to have been well known, for in 1718 a Richard Curtin, the son of an Oxford baker, was apprenticed to him (PRO, I.R. 1/6, in *Gunnis* 1968, 304). He died in 1724. **John Piddington I** was Richard's elder son and was apprenticed to his father in 1698. He signs several monuments including that to George Blackall at Great Haseley (1). This exuberant baroque work features a 'podgy bust' beneath 'trumpeting cherubs' on the pediment and is 'remarkably accomplished for a local sculptor' (Pevsner, *Oxon*, 1974, 619). **Richard Piddington II**, the second son of Richard I, was apprenticed to his father in 1715 and died in 1752. The last of the family, **John Piddington II**, was the son of John II. He was transported for seven years for stealing the club box of the Oxford Benefit Society (*Royal Magazine*, 1764).

Literary References: *Gunnis* 1968, 303–4

Archival References: Hanaster EB, L 5.4; Oriel Accts OCA L 5.5

Funerary Monuments					
1.	†1709	George Blackall (by John Piddington I)	Great Haseley, Oxon	S	Pevsner, *Oxon*, 1974, 619
2.	1709	Sir Thomas Coghill and family (by John Piddington I)	Bletchingdon, Oxon	S	Pevsner, *Oxon*, 1974, 476
3.	?1710	Edmund Fettiplace (by John Piddington I)	Kingston Bagpuize, Berks		*Gunnis* 1968, 304

PIDGEON, G F

For information the reader is referred to *Pyke* 1973, 106

PIERACHINI, Pietro fl 1835–39

Busts				
1.	1835	Signor de Val	[Exhib Liverpool Ac, 563]; untraced	*Morris and Roberts* 1998, 488
2.	1835	Signor Morani	[Exhib Liverpool Ac, 567]; untraced	*Morris and Roberts* 1998, 488

3.	1835	Unidentified gentleman	[Exhib Liverpool Ac, 562]; untraced	*Morris and Roberts* 1998, 488
4.	1836	Thomas Gresham	[Exhib Liverpool Ac, 663]; untraced	*Morris and Roberts* 1998, 488
5.	1836	William Ewart	[Exhib Liverpool Ac, 662]; untraced	*Morris and Roberts* 1998, 488
6.	1836	William Roscoe	[Exhib Liverpool Ac, 661]; untraced	*Morris and Roberts* 1998, 488
7.	1837	Unidentified gentleman	[Exhib Liverpool Ac, 688]; untraced	*Morris and Roberts* 1998, 488
8.	1838	Queen Victoria	[Exhib Liverpool Ac, 665]; untraced	*Morris and Roberts* 1998, 488
9.	1838	Unidentified lady	[Exhib Liverpool Ac, 669]; untraced	*Morris and Roberts* 1998, 488
10.	1839	George Tyrer	[Exhib Liverpool Ac, 692]; untraced	*Morris and Roberts* 1998, 488
11.	1839	Two unidentified gentlemen	[Exhib Liverpool Ac, 691, 705]; untraced	*Morris and Roberts* 1998, 488

PIERCE, Robert, of Exeter fl *c*1803–14

His works include a tablet in coloured marbles at Littleham, one with a relief of a mourning woman in Exeter Cathedral and another with a trophy of arms in Holy Trinity, Exeter (**1, 2, 4**). Pierce committed suicide in 1827 or 1829.

Literary References: *Gunnis* 1968, 304; *Devon and Cornwall Notes and Queries*, 33 (8), 1977 (HMC)

Funerary Monuments

1.	?1803	Peter Middleton	Littleham, Devon	S	*Gunnis* 1968, 304
2.	?1805	James Bell	Exeter Cathedral, Devon	S	*Gunnis* 1968, 304
3.	†1806	Shuldham family member	West Bagborough, Somerset		Pevsner, *Somerset: S & W*, 1958, 335
4.	?1814	William Burn	Holy Trinity, Exeter, Devon	S	*Gunnis* 1968, 304

PIERCE (or PEIRCE), Edward, of Deptford fl *c*1777–89

Pierce was a competent minor statuary who made use of 'Adam' details in some of his works.

Literary References: *Gunnis* 1968, 304

Funerary Monuments

1.	?1777	James Hawley	Leybourne, Kent		*Gunnis* 1968, 304
2.	1778	Viscountess Falkland (designed by George Gibson) Payment(s): £210	Widford, Essex, churchyard		*Gunnis* 1968, 304
3.	*c*1780	John Mittell (†1734)	East Hoathly, Sussex	S	Pevsner, *Sussex*, 1965, 496
4.	?1782	George Collard	St Martin, Dover, Kent		*Gunnis* 1968, 304
5.	?1784	William Hardyman	Farningham, Kent, churchyard		*Gunnis* 1968, 304
6.	†1787	Henry Woodgate	SS Peter and Paul, Tonbridge, Kent	S	
7.	†1789	Charles Brown (†1754) and wife (†1789)	Frant, Sussex	S	Pevsner, *Sussex*, 1965, 507
8.	?1789	John Staples	St Swithun, East Grinstead, Sussex	S	*Gunnis* 1968, 304
Chimneypieces					
9.	1782	Several	[for two houses built by James Adams at Eltham, Kent]; untraced		Adams Acc Book in GPC

PIGG, J, of Watford fl *c*1833

Funerary Monuments

1.	†1833	Hon Henry Watson	St Mary, Hemel Hempstead, Herts	S

PIGGOTT, of Richmond fl 1847

Funerary Monuments

1.	?1847	Caroline, Duchess of Montrose	Ham, Surrey	S	GPC
2.	†1847	Maria, Duchess of Montrose	Petersham, Surrey		RG/JP, 6, 1107v.

PILE, George fl 1686

Chimneypieces

1.	1686	Several, of white, yellow and black marble (co-sculptor: John Clarke)	[Windsor Castle, Queen's closets, bedchamber, bathing and dressing rooms]; untraced	*Hope* 1913, 328

PILLGREEN, Francis

The tradecard of 'Francis Pillgreen FIGURE MAKER Old Bolton Street Long Acre LONDON' is in the Print Room at the British Museum (Heal 32.45) (HY).

PINCOT, Daniel –1797

A 'Mr Pincot' was established as a sculptor in the east end of London by about 1765, for **John Bacon RA**'s trade card for that period states that he was working as a 'Stone-carver and modeller at Mr Pincot's in Paternoster Row, Spitalfields' (BM Banks Coll, 106.2).

In January 1767 Daniel Pincot (who is erroneously listed as 'Pincat' in *Graves* 1907, 199 and *Gunnis* 1968, 304) advertised that he had set up as an artificial-stone manufacturer in Goulston Square, Whitechapel. He offered 'all sorts of rich carved Ornaments used in Buildings, viz. Tablets, Frizes, Medalions, Ionic and Corinthian Capitals, Statues, Bustos, Vases, etc in several Compositions; some resembling Portland Stone, but much harder and more durable, others still more beautiful, approaching nearer to Marble; the Whole executed in a Manner far exceeding any Thing of the like Kind that has hitherto been offered to the Publick' (*Daily Ad*, 31 Jan 1767 cited by *Valpy* 1986, 210). On 7 July 1767 it was announced that 'the Proprietor of the Artificial Stone Manufactory in Goulston-Square, has now opened a Warehouse at No. 18, the Corner of Glastonbury Court, in Long Acre' (*Daily Ad*, 7 July 1767 cited by *Valpy* 1986, 210). This may not have been Pincot himself, for by October 1767 **George Davy** had taken over the Goulston Square premises and Pincot was trading from Narrow Wall, Lambeth. In the same year Pincot exhibited an 'antique basso-relievo, in artificial stone, unburned' (**2**) at the Free Society. In December 1767 there was a sale at Christie's of artificial stone produced at Goulston Square over the last year, presumably by both Pincot and Davy.

The **Coade Factory** was established at Pincot's premises in Narrow Wall, Lambeth, soon after. It appears that Eleanor Coade took over Pincot's business but kept him on for some years as her manager. She dated the foundation of her business to 1769, though Pincot was still advertising in his own name in March 1770 (*Public Ad*, 6 March 1770). It is not known how Mrs Coade came into contact with Pincot, but she and her family lived for some years at Hoxton, not far from Spitalfields and Whitechapel, and since they were both dissenters they may have met through non-conformist circles.

In 1770 Pincot published a pamphlet entitled *An Essay on the Origins, Nature, Use and Properties of Artificial Stone* promoting its use. He complained of the unwillingness of masons to use the material, which they considered 'but an imitation, a meer makeshift'. Pincot alleged that they were 'decrying the material and deterring modellers from working in the manufactory; telling them they will be despised by the whole trade as forwarding a work which it is in their interest to supress' (*Pincot* 1770, 77–8).

The following year Pincot submitted a copy of the *Borghese vase* (1) for exhibition at the Society of Artists. It was not displayed in the main exhibition since it was not an original design but being 'desirous of giving every encouragement in their power to merit and ingenuity' and 'in consideration of its being a very fine performance' the committee allowed it to be placed in the entrance lobby (*Graves* 1907, 199). He also solicited successfully 'for leave to place a vase of artificial stone, in the passage for two days' at the Royal Academy (Council Minutes, vol 1, fol 105, 13 April 1771).

Pincot made no reference to Mrs Coade in his pamphlet and he seems to have angered her by taking certain business transactions into his own hands, including an agreement to provide Borghese vases for Stourhead and Kedleston. On 11 September 1771 Mrs Coade placed advertisements stating, 'WHEREAS Mr Daniel Pincot has been represented as a Partner in the Manufactory which has been conducted by him; Eleanor Coade, the real Proprietor, finds it proper to inform the Publick that the said Mr Pincot has no Proprietry in this Affair; and no Contracts or Agreements, Purchases or Receipts, will be allowed by her unless signed or assented to by herself' (*Daily Ad*, 11 Sept 1771, cited by *Valpy* 1986, 215–6). Three days later she announced that Pincot was no longer employed by her. The Coade factory seems to have continued to use some of Pincot's moulds for many years after his dismissal, including the *Borghese Vase* and relief plaques depicting a *Phrygian Shepherd and Shepherdess* and the *Aldobrandini Marriage* (see **Coade Factory, of Lambeth** 150, 171).

Nothing further is known of Pincot, except that he died in 1797 and was buried in Bunhill Fields cemetery.

EH

Literary References: *Pincot* 1770, *passim*; *S of L*, XXIII, 1951, 58; *Hamilton* 1954, 295; *Gunnis* 1968, 304; *Clifford* 1985, 290; *Valpy* 1986, 209–216, 220–22; *Kelly* 1990, 33, 37–8, 41, 169, 189, 200

Auction catalogue: Pincot and Davy 1767

Architectural Sculpture

1.	1771	Borghese vase	sa	[Exhib Soc of Artists, 228]; untraced	*Graves* 1907, 199

Reliefs

2.	1767	An antique bas-relief in artificial stone	sa	[Exhib Free Soc, 224]; untraced	*Graves* 1907, 199

Miscellaneous

3.	1767	Several pieces of artificial stone		[Exhib Free Soc, 221–3]; untraced	*Graves* 1907, 199

PINDER, William –1784

The son of William Pinder, a merchant taylor and citizen of London, he was apprenticed in 1719 to **Thomas Broomhall**. In 1763 he was listed as a mason of Noble-Street, Foster-lane, Cheapside (*Mortimer* 1763, 49) and in 1766 he carried out general masonry work and made a chimneypiece for the vestry of St Matthew, Friday Street (4). He signs three monuments. In 1774 he made a chimneypiece for Bowood, Wilts (5) and a year later the steps for the great staircase. The payment for the chimneypiece is made out to William Pinder and **William Norris**, therefore Norris must have worked with Pinder until Pinder's death, after which he went into partnership with **Daniel Pinder**.

Pinder died in Falcon Square on 11 October 1784 (*GM* 1784, 798). His will, in which he is described as 'mason of St Giles without Cripplegate' was proved on 19 October 1784 (PROB 11/1122). A sale of his stock-in-trade was held on 26 and 27 April 1785. He had two sons, Samuel and William. The former was apprenticed to **Thomas Bull** in 1754, but was turned over to **William Bull** on his master's death two years later. The latter assisted his father and the pair worked as masons for the rebuilding of the Dyer's Hall in 1770. William Pinder the younger was declared bankrupt in 1789.

Literary References: *Gunnis* 1968, 305

Archival References: St Matthew, Friday-Street, Papers

Sales: Pinder 1785

Funerary Monuments

1.	†1777	John Seale of Mount Boone	Cornworthy, Devon	S	*Gunnis* 1968, 305; Pevsner, *Devon*, 1989, 291
2.	?1779	Daniel Sandford	Castle Hedingham, Essex	S	*Gunnis* 1968, 305
3.	†1787	Sarah Marwood	Widworthy, Devon	S	Pevsner, *Devon*, 1989, 910

Chimneypieces

4.	1766	Description unavailable	m	[St Matthew, Friday Street, London, vestry]; destroyed	St Matthew, Friday St, Accts, 24 Sept 1766, 31; *Gunnis* 1968, 305
5.	1774	Description unavailable (co-sculptor: William Norris)		[Bowood, Wilts]; untraced	GPC

PINDER (or PINDAR), Daniel 1734/5–1820

Mortimer listed Pinder as a mason of Blackfriars in 1763 (p 49), where in 1761 he was paid £51 for repairs to St Anne's church. Between 1766 and 1798 he worked as mason to the Ironmongers' Company and he had similar appointments with the Royal College of Physicians in 1768 and the Vintners' Company in 1769. In 1772 he and **William Pinder** were summoned by the Court of Assistants of the Masons' Company to take up their freedoms or pay a fine of £10.

He worked as mason to the Stationers' Company, 1782–89. In 1783 he received £202 for masonry work connected with **John Bacon RA**'s statue of Lord Chatham in Guildhall (Corporation of London Records, MS 55.28). Pinder built the house of Robert Mylne, the architect, in Bridge Street, in 1783–5. Mylne also employed him as a carver of chimneypieces and noted in his journal, 'March 15th. 1773. Gave Mr. Owen designs for three chimneypieces to be made by Pinder in town.' A year later there is a note that Pinder was to make the dining-room chimneypiece for Mr Owen's house at Brungwyn (4). In 1782 Pinder built two other houses designed by Mylne, for a Mr Donaldson and a Mr St John, both in Arundel Street (GPC).

Pinder was City Mason from 1782 to 1803. In 1784 he was paid £249 for building a house for Francis Adams, in Adams Place, Southwark. About this time he took **William Norris** into partnership. Norris appears to have worked with William Pinder until the death of the latter in 1784, when he joined forces with Daniel Pinder. In 1786 Pinder and Norris were masons at St Luke's Hospital, Old Street, then being built by George Dance. That year they received £211 for 'finishing the mason's work on the basement storey' and £325 for 'erecting the façade and entrance to the new hospital.' In 1788 they were paid £200 for the west wing of the hospital (Hospital Archives, in GPC). In 1788–90, working under Dance, they rebuilt the south front of the Guildhall for which they were paid £900 (*Journal City Lands*, vol 81). They were paid £82 13s in 1789 for repairs to a house Lord Carlisle was renting in Grosvenor Place. In 1791 a further £129 was paid to them for repairs to the steps of Surgeons' Hall. They carried out work at Peter Thellusson's house in Philpot Lane in 1795 under Sir John Soane, earning £76. They were also masons at Child's Bank, 1785–1804. In 1798 their bill for mason's work carried out during the rebuilding of East India House amounted to £6,770 (India Office Archives).

Pinder and Norris together signed the large monument to Richard Sorbell (2) and the monument erected by the Governors of Christ's Hospital in 1792 to the memory of Mr T Parr, who bequeathed a large part of his fortune to the hospital. Next to the tablet with its long inscription stands a life-sized and well-carved figure of a Bluecoat boy (3).

In 1765 Pinder was elected to the Common Council, where he sat for 55 years. In 1807 he became the senior member, and a body of his friends subscribed to his three-quarter length portrait, holding a scroll, by John Opie RA, which was presented to the Corporation. He died on 6 November 1820 and his will, in which he is described as being 'of Pilgrim Street, Blackfriars' was proved 2 December 1820 (PROB 11/1637). Pinder was married to the sister of **Sir William Staines.**

MGS

Literary References: *Gunnis* 1968, 304

Archival References: Masons' Co, Court Book, 1751–96 (7 Aug 1772); Stationers Accts, 1727–87, 1788–1837, *passim*; Ironmongers WA, vol 13; R C Physic, Cash Book 1726–1778 (1768, 9 357); Soane, Abstract of Bills Book 1, fol 52 (Francis Adams's house); Soane, Abstract of Bills, 2, fols 109–111 (Thelluson's house); Soane, Bill Book for 1794–1797, fols 128r–129v (Thellusson's house); GPC

Portrait of the Sculptor: John Opie RA, 1807, oil on canvas, Corporation of London (*Knight* 1986, 225, repr)

Funerary Monuments					
1.	?1781	Alexander Dalmahoy	Horsted Keynes, Sussex		GPC
2.	1784	Richard Sorbell (co-sculptor: William Norris)	Great Warley, Essex	S	*Gunnis* 1968, 305
3.	1792	Mr T Parr (co-sculptor: William Norris)	Lisbon Cemetery, Portugal, mortuary chapel	S	GPC
Chimneypieces					
4.	1774	Description unavailable	[Brungwyn, North Wales, dining room]; untraced		GPC
Miscellaneous					
5.	1783	Masonry work for the statue of Lord Chatham Payment(s): £202	Guildhall, City of London		*Gunnis* 1968, 304

PINGO fl 1765–74

His Christian name is unknown, but it is possible that he is the John Pingo, son of **Lewis Pingo**, who exhibited wax models and other work at the Free Society, 1765–1774. He was employed as a modeller by Wedgwood. In 1800 his wife, Theodosia, wrote to the firm as follows: 'My husband who has long laboured under a severe illness being now reduced to that state as not to be able to attend any longer to business and myself and family destitute, Mr. Silvester who's knowledge and diligence are well known has obligingly engaged to give every assistance in conducting the business on my account' (Wedgwood/Pingo, L1/24, Theodosia Pingo to Wedgwood and Co, Feb 1800). Mr. **Silvester** is presumably the modeller of that name who exhibited at the Royal Academy in 1788. Redgrave states that it was Thomas Pingo who worked for Wedgwood, but as he died in 1776 this must be a mistake. A Walter Pingo, who may be a relative, had a wife called Theodosia. They had a son, Thomas, christened at St Andrew Holborn on 13 May 1785.

Literary References: *Gunnis* 1968, 305; *Pyke* 1973, 107

Busts				
1.	nd	King George III, model	[for Josiah Wedgwood]; untraced	*Meteyard* I, 1866, 441
Reliefs				
2.	1769	Battle of Pondicherry, medallion	[for Josiah Wedgwood]; untraced	*Meteyard* I, 1866, 441
3.	1769	Battle of Plassey, medallion	[for Josiah Wedgwood]; untraced	*Meteyard* I, 1866, 441

PINGO, Lewis 1743–1830

He was a medallist who made preliminary models in wax. The fourth son of the medallist Thomas Pingo (1714–1776), he was baptized on 26 July 1743 at St Andrew, Holborn. He attended William Shipley's drawing school before entering the Royal Academy Schools in 1770. He was awarded several Society of Arts premiums for medal-making, gem-engraving, wax modelling, and drawing between 1756 and 1771 and exhibited medals and models at the Society of Artists and the Free Society between 1761 and 1782.

Pingo produced more than 15 portrait medals, including images of David Garrick (1772) and Captain James Cook (1783) and he provided prize medals for the Royal Humane Society (1776) and the Board of Admiralty (1796). He succeeded his father as third engraver at the Mint in 1776 and was appointed chief engraver in 1780. He and his brother John Pingo (1738–1827) began trading under their joint names around the time of their father's death, when they inherited his medal dies. A trade label in the British Museum (P&D) refers to 'J & L Pingo, Engravers to His Majesty' and gives their address as 101 Gray's Inn Lane (repr *Eimer* 1998, 26). They continued to produce medals until the mid-1790s. Lewis retired from his post as chief engraver at the Mint in 1815 and subsequently moved to Grove Lane, Camberwell, Surrey, where he died on 26 August 1830.

Gunnis erroneously states that a sculptor called Pingo was employed as a modeller by Josiah Wedgwood, citing Meteyard as his source. This mistake originated in the misreading of the word 'medal' for 'model' in an invoice from Thomas Pingo in the Wedgwood archives. Another member of the family, Walter Pingo, a customs officer, also had business connections with Wedgwood. It was his wife who sought the manufacturer's assistance in February 1800, her husband having 'long laboured under a severe illness' (Wedgwood/Pingo, L1/24, Theodosia Pingo to Wedgwood and Co).

Literary References: *Dossie* 1782, 441; *Meteyard* I, 1866, 441–2; *Gunnis* 1968, 305; *Pyke* 1973, 107; *Pyke* 1981, 33; *Eimer* 1998, *passim* (includes an illustrated catalogue of the family's works); *ODNB* (Eimer)

Reliefs

1.	1759	Liberty with her attributes and the barons obtaining Magna Carta, two models	w	Royal Society of Arts, London	*Eimer* 1998, 79
2.	1759–1760	Britannia and Louisburg, two models	w	[Soc of A premium, 10 gns]; untraced	*Eimer* 1998, 79
3.	c1760	King George III	w	BM, London	*Graves* 1907, 201; *Eimer* 1998, 79 (repr)
4.	1761	Unidentified subject, portrait	w	[Exhib Free Soc, London, 147]; untraced	*Graves* 1907, 201
5.	1762	Mr Pinchbeck		[Exhib Free Soc, London, 180]; untraced	*Graves* 1907, 201
6.	c1762	Penelope Pingo (?)	p	[Exhib Free Soc, London, 179]; private coll	*Graves* 1907, 201; *Eimer* 1998, 79 (repr)
7.	1763	Queen Charlotte		[Exhib Soc of Artists, London, 162]; untraced	*Graves* 1907, 201
8.	1763	Unidentified gentlemen, two models		[Exhib Free Soc, London, 163–4]; untraced	*Graves* 1907, 201
9.	1765	King Stanislas Augustus of Poland	w	Private coll	*Graves* 1907, 201; *Eimer* 1998, 79 (repr)
10.	1765	Unidentified gentleman		[Exhib Free Soc, London, 148]; untraced	*Graves* 1907, 201
11.	1766	Unidentified young gentleman	w	[Exhib Free Soc, London, 138]; untraced	*Graves* 1907, 201
12.	1767	Unidentified subjects, three models	w	[Exhib Free Soc, London, 226–8]; untraced	*Graves* 1907, 201
13.	1768	Unidentified young lady, two models	w	[Exhib Free Soc, London, 175 and 176]; untraced	*Graves* 1907, 201
14.	1767–1769	King George III and Liberty, two models	w	[Soc of A, London]; untraced	*Eimer* 1998, 80 (repr)
15.	1769	Unidentified gentleman	w	[Exhib Free Soc, London, 173]; untraced	*Graves* 1907, 201
16.	1770	King George III	w	[Exhib Free Soc, London, 204]; untraced	*Graves* 1907, 201
17.	1770	Victory at Cape Lagos	w	[Soc of A premium, gold palette]; untraced	*Eimer* 1998, 81
18.	1771	Surrender of Havannah	w	[Soc of A premium, gold palette]; untraced	*Eimer* 1998, 81
19.	1772	Unidentified gentleman	w	[Exhib Free Soc, London, 152]; untraced	*Graves* 1907, 201
20.	1772	Unidentified lady	w	[Exhib Free Soc, London, 153]; untraced	*Graves* 1907, 201
21.	1773	Dr Mead	w	[Exhib Free Soc, London, 170]; untraced	*Graves* 1907, 201
22.	1775	Justice	w	[Exhib Free Soc, London, 212]; untraced	*Graves* 1907, 201
23.	1775	Unidentified gentleman	w	[Exhib Free Soc, London, 210]; untraced	*Graves* 1907, 201
24.	1775	Unidentified subject, model of a medal	w	[Exhib Free Soc, London, 211]; untraced	*Graves* 1907, 201
25.	1779	Admiral Keppel	w	[Exhib Free Soc, London, 201]; untraced Other versions: exhib Free Soc, London, 1782, 167	*Graves* 1907, 201
26.	1782	Earl of Sandwich	w	[Exhib Free Soc, London, 159]; untraced	*Graves* 1907, 201

PINK, James, of Lincoln –1810

He either came from Bath or was working there before he settled in Lincoln, where he was employed on carving ornaments for the altarpiece in the cathedral in 1769. He later added the screen on either side of the altar-piece, and his signature is carved on the stonework of the southwest corner of the reredos. Pink was also responsible for the small figures on the rood-loft, and repaired a great deal of the stone-carving both inside and outside the cathedral (1). He had hoped to be appointed cathedral mason, but 'being a Dissenter in religion eclipsed all his merits and he was rejected' (*Milton* 1947, 213). He died in 1810 and was buried in the cemetery of the Old Baptist Chapel at Lincoln.

Literary References: *Milton* 1947, 212–4; *Gunnis* 1968, 305

Architectural Sculpture

1.	from 1769	Altarpiece ornaments, screen, reredos, figures on the rood loft and other stonework	Lincoln Cathedral	*Gunnis* 1968, 305

PINK, W, of London fl 1828–44

He exhibited busts at the Royal Academy, 1828–44, from 25 Crescent Street, Euston Square; 2 Hertford Street; 38 Windmill Street and 31 Mary Street.

Literary References: *Graves* VI, 1905–6, 154; *Gunnis* 1968, 305

Busts

1.	1828	Mr J Pink	[Exhib RA, London, 1141]; untraced	*Graves* VI, 1905–6, 154; *Gunnis* 1968, 305
2.	1829	Mr T Wright	[Exhib RA, London, 1135]; untraced	*Graves* VI, 1905–6, 154; *Gunnis* 1968, 305
3.	1829	Unidentified gentleman	[Exhib RA, London, 1142]; untraced	*Graves* VI, 1905–6, 154
4.	1830	Unidentified gentleman	[Exhib RA, London, 1199]; untraced	*Graves* VI, 1905–6, 154

5.	1838	Unidentified gentleman	[Exhib RA, London, 1300]; untraced	*Graves* VI, 1905–6, 154
6.	1839	Unidentified gentleman	[Exhib RA, London, 1349]; untraced	*Graves* VI, 1905–6, 154
7.	1841	Unidentified lady	[Exhib RA, London, 1332]; untraced	*Graves* VI, 1905–6, 154
8.	1844	Unidentified subject	[Exhib RA, London, 1330]; untraced	*Graves* VI, 1905–6, 154

PIPER FAMILY, of London

Thomas Piper I †1794
Elizabeth Piper fl 1794–1800
Thomas Piper II †1858
Thomas Piper III
William Piper fl 1833

Thomas Piper I was the son of a butcher, William Piper of Hampton, Middx. He was apprenticed to **Charles Easton** on 28 October 1767 and continued to work with Easton after he became free in 1774. In 1790 he had a yard at 43 Little Eastcheap. He was the chief mason employed in building Fishmongers' Hall from 1788 until his death in 1794. He also provided the carved stonework and supplied marble chimneypieces (**10, 8**). This work was completed by his widow, **Elizabeth Piper**, who took over the business. In 1799 and 1800 she executed orders for marble chimneypieces for the Mote, Maidstone, then being rebuilt by Lord Romney (Mote Building Accts, in *Gunnis* 1968, 306) (**9**).

Thomas Piper II, the son of of Thomas Piper I, inherited the business from his mother and was appointed mason to the Fishmongers' Company about 1800 (Fishmongers Co Archives, in *Gunnis* 1968, 306). He served as City Mason from 1803 until his death in 1858 and was the mason responsible for re-building Goldsmiths' Hall in 1830. He also worked on the building of the City prison for debtors in White Cross Street, and the military depot in Tooley Street.

Thomas II's son, another **Thomas Piper III**, was bound to his father in 1813 and became a partner in the firm soon after gaining his freedom in 1820. Father and son were the masons responsible for rebuilding the Customs House, 1825–1827, for which they were paid £1,752 9s 7d (TNA WORK 5/119 fol 17, and 5/125 fol 265). They restored the steeple of St Antholin's, Budge Row, in 1829. In 1840–1 they were paid about £1,500 for rebuilding Dyers' Hall and they sent in a tender, which was not accepted, for building the Company's almshouses at Kingsland (Dyers' Co Archives in GPC). According to his obituary in the *Builder* Thomas Piper II retired from business in 1844. He was described as 'a man of active benevolence' who served on the committees of Mill Hill School and New College and took a leading part in the management of the asylum for the deaf and dumb (*Builder* 1858, 650). **William Piper**, the son of Thomas Piper III, was apprenticed to his father in 1833.

Literary References: *Builder* 1858, 650; *Gunnis* 1968, 305–6; *Webb* 1999, 26

Archival References: Goldsmiths CB, bk 18, 326, 333–5; GPC

Funerary Monuments

1.	?1805	Sir Culling Smith		Monken Hadleigh, Herts	*Gunnis* 1968, 306
2.	?1822	Rev Charles Wakeman		Bocking, Essex	*Gunnis* 1968, 306
3.	?1823	Charles de Mauriel		Henley, Oxon	*Gunnis* 1968, 306
4.	?1825	Lady Mitchell		Halifax Cathedral, Nova Scotia	GPC
5.	?1840	Thomas Berrington		St John the Baptist, Croydon, Surrey, churchyard	GPC
6.	?1841	Russell family		Sanderstead, Surrey, churchyard	*Gunnis* 1968, 306
7.	?1849	Williams family		St Magnus the Martyr, London Bridge	*Gunnis* 1968, 306

Chimneypieces

8.	1788–1794	Several (by Thomas Piper I)	m	[Fishmongers' Hall, City of London]; untraced	*Gunnis* 1968, 305
9.	1799–1800	Description unavailable	m	The Mote, Maidstone, Kent	Mote Building Accts, cited by Gunnis 1968, 306; Pevsner, *Kent: W & Weald*, 1976, 413

Architectural Sculpture

10.	1788–1794	Carved stonework (by Thomas Piper I)		[Fishmongers' Hall, City of London]; untraced	*Gunnis* 1968, 305
11.	1831–1835	Extensive carved work including ten Corinthian capitals, 50 leopards' heads, a large leopard, 'trophies and coats of arms' on the entrance front and a chimneypiece Payment(s): £441 7s		Goldsmiths' Hall, City of London	Goldsmiths' Co, Committee Book 18, 1823–37, 326, 333–5; Abstract of Contractors Accounts, 1831–1835, E 1/2/48, fols 6r, 7r, 22r, 43v, 49r, 69r, 96v

PIRANESI, Giovanni Battista 1720–78

An Italian etcher, engraver, designer, architect, archaeologist and theorist, he is best known for his topographical engravings. Aided by his son, Francesco Piranesi (1759–1810), he manufactured ornamental chimneypieces incorporating classical fragments, several of which were exported to Britain (1–3). He was also involved in the restoration of antiquities for export during the 1770s.

Literary References: *Grove* 24, 1996, 841–7 (Wilton-Ely)

Chimneypieces

1.	1774	With cameos on amethyst and rosso antico reliefs Payment(s): 371 scudi	Wedderburn Castle, Berwicks, drawing room	*Rowan* 1974, 356 (repr)
2.	nd	With antique fragments	Burghley House, Cambs	*Grove* 24, 1996, 845
3.	nd	With antique fragments	Gorhambury House, Herts	*Grove* 24, 1996, 845

PISTELL, William, of London –1845

In 1816 Pistell worked with Robert Smirke, **John Flaxman RA** and **Sir Richard Westmacott** on the construction of two prefabricated galleries to house the Parthenon Marbles at the British Museum, then at Montagu House. When Lord Elgin first proposed moving the marbles to the museum he commented, 'Pistol the marble cutter in the New Road near Fitzroy Square, brought them in safety from Piccadilly (Park Lane) to Burlington House; and is much employed by Flaxman on such occasions' (*Smith* 1916, 319).

Although Gunnis considered many of Pistell's tablets 'dull and obvious', he noted that his monument to Maria Parratt has 'a very fine relief of a mother mourning at her daughter's deathbed, rather in the manner of **Chantrey**' (**21**). The monument to Joseph Priestley, the engineer, in Bradford Cathedral has 'an elegant neoclassical frame, and a neat assembly of globe, divider, quill, compass, ruler and set-square in the pediment and also a rather surprisingly naïve pictorial relief of an engineer supervising two navvies working on a canal tunnel' (*Penny* 1977 (1), 177) (**3**). Another, to John Ludlow, in Kolkata (Calcutta), has a relief of a sarcophagus flanked by a mourning soldier and a classically draped female figure (**8**).

Literary References: *Gunnis* 1968, 306; *Colvin* 1973–76, vol VI, 405

Funerary Monuments

1.	?1814	William Lee		Alton, Hants	S	*Gunnis* 1968, 306
2.	†1815	Edward Grose		St Helens, I of W	S	Pevsner, *Hants & Isle of Wight*, 1967, 767
3.	†1817	Joseph Priestley		Bradford Cathedral, W R Yorks	S	Pevsner, *Yorks: W R*, 1967, 123; *Penny* 1977 (1), 177–8 (repr)
4.	?1817	Major Balfour		St Mary, St Marylebone, London	S	*Gunnis* 1968, 306
5.	?1819	Jonathan Hammond		Penshurst, Kent	S	*Gunnis* 1968, 306
6.	?1820	Sir Archibald Grant		Cluny, Aberdeen		RG/JP, 6, 1114
7.	?1820	Theodosia Crawley		Luton, Beds	S	*Gunnis* 1968, 306
8.	†1821	Lieutenant-Colonel John Ludlow		St John, Kolkata (Calcutta)	S	*Groseclose* 1995, 70 (repr)
9.	?1821	William Hickman		Marlow, Bucks	S	*Gunnis* 1968, 306
10.	†1822	Rev Edward Balm		St Pancras new parish church, London	S	*Gunnis* 1968, 306
11.	†1823	G R Savage Nassau		Easton, Suffolk	S	Pevsner, *Suffolk*, 1974, 197
12.	†1823	John (†1781) and Catherine Cranston		St Swithun, East Grinstead, Sussex	S	*Gunnis* 1968, 306
13.	?1825	Richard Cray		St Mary, Ealing, London	S	*Gunnis* 1968, 306
14.	?1825	William Yates		Hanley, Staffs		RG/JP, 6, 1114
15.	†1826	William Phillips		St Pancras new parish church, London	S	*Gunnis* 1968, 306
16.	†1828	Frances Thruston		Pennal, Merioneth		RG/JP, 6, 1114
17.	?1828	Robert Denn		Shipdham, Norfolk	S	*Gunnis* 1968, 306
18.	?1830	Oddie family		Branwell, Northants		RG/JP, 6, 1114
19.	†1832	Jane Shee		Chippenham, Wilts		RG/JP, 6, 1114
20.	?1840	James Burnet		Chippenham, Wilts	S	*Gunnis* 1968, 306
21.	†1844	Maria Parratt		Effingham, Surrey		*Gunnis* 1968, 301; Pevsner, *Surrey*, 1971, 207

Chimneypieces

22.	1808	Several Payment(s): £65		[Royal Naval Asylum, Greenwich, London]; untraced		*Gunnis* 1968, 306 incorrectly cites PRO, Adm. 80/1 10
23.	1812	Description unavailable	m	[Eaton Hall, Cheshire, saloon]; untraced		RG/JP, 6, 1113

Architectural Sculpture

24.	1814–1817	Decorative carving Payment(s): £180		Ashridge Park, Herts		Archives Lord Brownlow in *Gunnis* 1968, 306

PISTRUCCI, Benedetto 1783–1855

Pistrucci was an Italian gem-engraver, medallist and sculptor who worked in Britain for many years. He was born in Rome on 24 May 1783, the son of a senior judge, Federico Pistrucci, and his wife Antonia Greco. The family repeatedly moved to escape Napoleon's advancing army and Benedetto attended schools in Bologna, Rome and Frosinone. He showed little aptitude for academic studies and later commented 'At length after the efforts of so many teachers, I acquired a little Latin, somewhat after the manner of a parrot' (*Pistrucci Autobiography*, cited by *Marsh* 1996, 2). Benedetto's talent as a modeller became apparent at an early age and his family eventually allowed him to pursue his artistic interests. At first he joined his elder brother Filippo in the studio of a landscape painter in Frosinone. Then, after the family returned to Rome, he studied under the painter's brother, Guiseppe Mango, a cameo cutter, and was later placed with the eminent gem engraver Nicola Morelli. In his spare time he attended the drawing academy of the Campidoglio, where he was awarded the first prize for sculpture in 1800.

After an argument with Morelli, Pistrucci, then aged nearly 16, decided to go into business on his own account and was soon 'loaded with commissions on all sides' (*Forrer* IV, 583). In 1802 he married Barbara Folchi, the daughter of a wealthy merchant, and between 1803 and 1838, the couple had nine children. They lived in Rome until 1814, where Pistrucci supplied neo-classical cameos and intaglios to dealers. He also spent a period with the Imperial Court in Florence and Pisa working for Napoleon's sister, the Grand-Duchess Baciocchi of Tuscany.

In 1814 Pistrucci moved to England in search of new opportunities and after a brief stay in Paris, arrived in London in January 1815. News of the newcomer's skill spread rapidly after he became involved in a dispute with the connoisseur and writer, Richard Payne Knight. Knight had recently bought a cameo head of *Flora*, which he believed to be 'the finest Greek cameo in existence' for £100 (*Pistrucci, op cit*, cited by *Marsh* 1996, 14). Pistrucci immediately recognised it as one of his own gems, carved for less than £5 and marked with his symbol, the Greek letter lambda. Knight continued to insist that it was an antique.

Pistrucci worked for the Royal Mint from 1816 and took over as chief engraver in 1817, after the death of **Thomas Wyon II**. He was never formally appointed since foreigners were debarred from the permanent staff, but he moved into an official residence at the Mint and was paid a salary of £500 p a. He made models and engraved dies for gold and silver coins and for official commemorative medals. His most famous design for the coinage was a representation of *St George slaying the Dragon*, first used on the obverse of the gold sovereign issued in 1817, and his works as a medallist included the coronation medals of King George IV and Queen Victoria.

Pistrucci began his first and most important medal commission soon after his arrival in Britain. In 1816 he was invited to submit designs for a medal commemorating the final defeat of Napoleon at Waterloo, to be struck in gold and presented to the allied sovereigns, their ministers and generals. In August 1819 authority came from the Treasury for work to begin. It was to be ambitious, measuring 5.3 inches in diameter and decorated with a large number of allegorical figures and profile portraits of the four sovereigns on the obverse, together with equestrian figures of the generals Wellington and Blucher on the reverse. Pistrucci estimated that the work involved would be equal to that required to produce 30 ordinary medals and agreed to a price of £2,400. A series of problems and delays meant that the dies were not ready until 1849, by which time many of the intended recipients were dead. When the dies were finally delivered, the technicians at the Mint decided that the hardening of dies of such unprecedented size was too hazardous and so the medal was never issued. Large numbers of electrotypes were however produced after the artist's death.

Pistrucci, who described himself as 'very excitable, and unfortunately very proud with the artists of my own era', was constantly involved in disputes with colleagues at the mint (*Pistrucci op cit*, cited by DNB). His concerns over the insecurity of his position were exacerbated by a bitter rivalry with **William Wyon**, who had held the post of second engraver since May 1816. Pistrucci's work on the coinage came to an end in the early 1820s, after he refused to produce designs based on a bust of King George IV by **Sir Francis Chantrey**, but he remained at the Mint and continued with his other duties. By 1824 he thought it necessary to send his family back to Rome for a time so that he would be more at liberty to 'carry on the war' with the Mint authorities (*Pistrucci, op cit*, cited in *Marsh* 1996, 33). A compromise over his status was reached in 1828 when he was appointed to the newly created post of chief medallist, with Wyon as chief engraver. However, the animosity between the two artists continued and a spasmodic but bitter campaign was conducted by their respective supporters through the newspapers.

Pistrucci undertook many private commissions for cameos and medals. His cameos were greatly admired and could command high prices: a large *Minerva* in oriental chalcedony onyx was sold for 500 guineas and a representation of *Augustus and Livia* in sapphirine fetched 800 guineas. Among his privately commissions were medals commemorating the Duke of York, Lord Maryborough, the Master of the Mint and the eminent physician Gilbert Blane.

He also produced a small number of large-scale works of sculpture. In 1830 he exhibited an unusual piece, *Capriccio*, at the Royal Academy (**16**). The *Gentleman's Magazine* described this as a block of marble 'chiselled by a most masterly hand into subjects without any connection with each other, we have Hercules, two or three busts on medallions, a female figure, above which there is a kind of grating through which are peeping fanciful and distorted heads' (*GM*, 1830, 543, cited in *Marsh* 1996, 39). He later sent to the Academy a design or model for a projected statue of George IV, a relief of *Thetis consoling Achilles* and a portrait bust of Count Pozzo di Borgo (**1, 15, 10**).

His most important sculptural work was a colossal bust of the Duke of Wellington, carved for the Duke in 1832 (**4**). When the art historian Dr Waagen saw it in the sculptor's studio he pronounced it 'by far the more like and the best I have seen and the more remarkable as the production of an artist accustomed to work on a very small scale' (*Gunnis* 1968, 306). The sculptor went on to produce several life-size replicas of this work and a number of other busts. His competition design for the national memorial to Lord Nelson was less well received (**2**). Pistrucci proposed a colossal trident, 89 feet high, rising from a segment of the globe on which were three reclining Victories carving memorials to the hero. It was ridiculed for its resemblance to a giant toasting fork.

In 1832 Pistrucci travelled to Rome, probably to seek an appointment at the papal Mint, but he returned to London a few months later. He lived at the Royal Mint until 1844, when he moved to Fine Arts Cottage, Old Windsor, moving again six years later to Flora Lodge, Englefield Green, near Windsor. The latter years of his life were 'tranquil and happy' (DNB) and he continued to take orders for gems until a few months before his death on 16 September 1855. He was buried in Christ Church cemetery, Virginia Water, Surrey.

Pistrucci was honoured by the Academy of St Luke at Rome, the Royal Academy of Arts at Copenhagen and the Institute of Arts during his lifetime and he was a member of the Athenaeum Club from 1842 onwards. After his death a street in Rome was named after him. Many of his original wax models for coins, medals, and cameos are preserved the Museo Numismatico della Zecca in Rome and several studies of his life and works have been published in recent years. Two of his daughters, Elena and Maria Elisa, became cameo cutters and his eldest son, Camillo, worked as a sculptor in Rome.

EH

Literary References: *AJ*, 1856, 27; *Redgrave* 1878, 334–5; *DNB* (Wroth); *Forrer* IV, 1904–30, 582–621; *Brooke* 1932, 52–3; *Numis* 1953, 457; *Pyke* 1973, 108–11; *Avery* 1975, 36–38; *Beulah* 1985, 12–4; *PBS* 1989, *passim; Marsh* 1996, *passim; Graves* 34, 1996, 887 (Pollard); *Dawson* 1999, 114–6; *ODNB* (Pollard)

Additional MS Sources: Pistrucci family papers, private coll; Pistrucci medal sketches; Pistrucci Mint papers; Pistrucci/Gladstone; Pistrucci/Hamilton; Pistrucci/Herschel; Waldeck diary

Will: PROB 11/2219

Auction Catalogues: Pistrucci 1855

Portraits of the Sculptor: self-portrait wax model, Museo della Zecca, Rome (repr *PBS* 1, 1989, 39, pl 1); C F Voigt, medallic plaque, 1826, examples Royal Mint, Llantrisant, Wales and coll M A Marsh (*Marsh* 1996, 82–3, reprs 17–8); self-portrait bust (**8**); A Busiri Vici, oil on canvas, 1839, Accademia Nazionale di San Luca, Rome (*PBS* 1, 1989, 40, pl 39d); A Busiri Vici, pencil drawing, 1839, Busiri Vici coll, Rome (*PBS* 1, 1989, 40, repr 8a); W R Hamilton, photo, 1853, examples Museo della Zecca, Rome and coll Signora Villavecchia Pistrucci (repr *PBS* 1, 1989, 40, pl 8d); M E Pistrucci, sardonyx cameo, untraced (repr PBS 1, 1989, 40 pl 8c); (?) cameo VAM A.5-1940 (repr *PBS* 1, 1989, 40 pl 8e)

Statues

1.	1832	Project for a statue of King George IV holding the globe with the figure of peace		[Exhib RA, London, 1113]; untraced		*Graves* VI, 1905–6, 156
2.	1839	Admiral Lord Nelson, model for national monument in Trafalgar Square, London (executed by Baily and Railton)		Untraced		*Lit Gaz*, no 1168, 8 June 1839, 363; *Gunnis* 1968, 306; *Read* 1982, 87; *PBS*, 1, 1989, 38
3.	1840	Maddalena		Untraced		*PBS* 1, 1989, 38

Busts

4.	1832	Arthur, 1st Duke of Wellington	m	Wellington Museum, Apsley House, London 1448–1948 Other versions: Stratfield Saye, Hants United Service Club, London ex coll W Hamilton; untraced Landes Bibliotek, Weimar	SD	*Avery* 1975, 36–8 (repr); *PBS* 1, 1989, 37, (repr 30a)

5.	1832	Nicolo Paganini, terracotta painted plaster		[Coll George Makins, Independent Assayer, Bank of England]; Sotheby, 7 July 2006 Other versions: Genoa municipality, town hall	SD	*PBS* 1, 1989, 37; Sotheby auction cat, 144–6, lot 154 (repr)
6.	1833	For Mrs Morrison		Untraced		*PBS* 1, 1989, 37
7.	1833	For the wife of a banker		Untraced		*PBS* 1, 1989, 37
8.	1835	Benedetto Pistrucci (self-portrait)	p	[Accademia di S Luca, Rome]; untraced Other versions: Protomoteca Capitolina, Rome, copy by Camillo Pistrucci, m, inscr 'BENEDETTO PISTRUCCI SE IPSUM FECIT LONDRA 1835' Museo della Zecca, Rome, copies in bronze and plaster coll Signora Giorgia Villavecchia Pistrucci, Rome, plaster Pontifica Bolognese Accademia di Belle Arti, Bologna		*PBS* 1, 1989, 37 (pl 7a)
9.	1839	Elena Pistrucci		Untraced		*PBS* 1, 1989, 38
10.	1839–1840	Carlo Andrea Pozzo di Borgo	b	Père-Lachaise Cemetery, Paris	S	*Graves* VI, 1905–6, 156; *PBS* 1, 1989, 38 (repr 7c)
11.	1842	Samuel Cartwright	m	NPG, London, 4883	S	*PBS* 1, 1989, 39 (repr 7d)
12.	1845	Archibald Billing	m	Private coll		*Billing* 1875, 208 (repr 187); *PBS* 1, 1989, 39 (pl 36b)
13.	1851	Unidentified man	m	Sold Christie, London, 16 July 1980, lot 73		*PBS* 1, 1989, 39 (pl 7b)
14.	nd	Giuditta Pasta		Untraced		*ODNB*
Reliefs						
15.	1839	Thetis consoling Achilles after his dispute with Agamemnon	p	[Exhib RA, London, 1309]; untraced		*Graves* VI, 1905–6, 156
Miscellaneous						
16.	1830	Capriccio (unfinished)	m	[Exhib RA, London, 1167]; untraced		*Graves* VI, 1905–6, 156

PITCHES, William fl 1732

Probably a local craftsman, he was master-mason at the University Schools, Cambridge, in 1732 (Vice-Chancellor's Accounts, in *Gunnis* 1968, 307).

Architectural Sculpture						
1.	1732	'two heads, corbels' and other decorative details		University Schools, Cambridge		*Gunnis* 1968, 307

PITT, T, of Gloucester fl *c*1816–18

Funerary Monuments						
1.	†1816	E and R Sayer		St John Northgate, Gloucester		RG/JP, 6, 1114v
2.	†1818	John Buckle		Elmstone Hardwicke, Glos	S	Pevsner, *Glos: Vale & Forest of Dean*, 1976, 182

PITTS, Joseph –*c*1870

He was the third son of **William Pitts**, but is a shadowy figure whose birth date is unknown. Joseph may have been baptised in 1821, but this is at odds with the date of 1831 when he won the Society of Arts' silver Isis medal for a bust of an unidentified sitter, suggesting either a late baptism or a precocious talent (**3**). In 1836 he won another Isis medal, this time for a bas-relief figure composition (**13**). He was initially an assistant to his father and following his father's suicide achieved a limited success as a sculptor. He worked from his father's last studio, at 5 Watkin's Terrace, Pimlico, until 1844, and then from Ebury Street, Pimlico. Pitts exhibited at the Royal Academy, 1842–46, showing mainly portrait busts. During the early 1850s he supplied models for parian ware groups and busts to John Rose and Co of Coalport. These included a series of statuettes based on Spencer's *The Faerie Queen* and a group of 'Puck throned on a mushroom' which the manufacturer sent to the Great Exhibition of 1851 (**2, 1**). The *Art Journal Catalogue* commented of the latter, 'It is a clever design and the figures are capitally modelled: it is we believe the work of the late admirable sculptor, Mr Pitts and finished by his son' (*AJ Cat* 1851, 259). After this little is known of his activities. He exhibited once more at the RA in 1870 from an address in Manchester Square, London, but his place and date of death are also a mystery.

Literary References: *Gunnis* 1968, 307; *ODNB* (McConnell)

Statues						
1.	1851	Puck throned on a mushroom, model (co-sculptor: William Pitts)		Untraced Other versions: Parian ware group by Rose & Co of Coalport, Gt Exhib, 1851		*AJ Cat* 1851, 259 (repr)
2.	1851–1852	Sir Celapine rescuing Serena; the vision of the Red Cross Knight; Britomartis unveiling Amoret; Britomartis releasing Amoret, models		Untraced Other versions: Parian ware statuettes manufactured by Rose & Co of Coalport		*Atterbury* 1989, 243–4 (repr)
Busts						
3.	1831	Unidentified subject		[Soc of A, silver Isis medal]; untraced		*Gunnis* 1968, 307
4.	1842	Arthur, 1st Duke of Wellington		[Exhib RA, London, 1176]; untraced		*Graves* VI, 1905–6, 159
5.	1843	Albert, the Prince Consort		[Exhib RA, London, 1377]; untraced Other versions: Exhib RA, London, 1846, 1425 Hughenden Manor, Bucks, tc, nd		*AU*, 1846, 189; *Graves* VI, 1905–6, 159; *Ormond* 1973, 11, 12
6.	1844	George Stephenson		[Exhib RA, London, 1317]; untraced Other versions: NPG 261, marble, SD 1846		*AU*, 1844, 171; *Graves* VI, 1905–6, 159
7.	1845	Miss Symes		[Exhib RA, London, 1406]; untraced		*Graves* VI, 1905–6, 159

8.	1850	Sir Robert Peel, model	Untraced Other versions: Parian ware busts manufactured by Rose & Co of Coalport	*Atterbury* 1989, 244
9.	1852	Arthur, Duke of Wellington, model	Untraced Other versions: Parian ware busts manufactured by Rose & Co of Coalport	*Atterbury* 1989, 244 (repr)
10.	1853	Horatio, Admiral Lord Nelson, models	Untraced Other versions: large and small Parian ware busts manufactured by Rose & Co of Coalport	*Atterbury* 1989, 244 (repr)
Architectural Sculpture				
11.	1870	Groups on gate lodges	Euston station, London	inf John Summerson, in GPC
Reliefs				
12.	1831	The outrage of the centaurs, alto-relievo	[Exhib RA, London, 1165]; untraced	*Library of Fine Arts*, vol I, 1831, 430
13.	1836	Group of figures	[Soc of A, silver medal]; untraced	*Gunnis* 1968, 307
Miscellaneous				
14.	1870	Startled by a windfall	[Exhib RA, London, 1073]; untraced	*Graves* VI, 1905–6, 159

PITTS, William 1789–1840

He was born in London on 9 November 1789 into a family of London silversmiths who specialised in small-scale tableware, larger épergnes and, during the Regency period, rococo-style candelabra. This background is significant since Pitts was to maintain a profile as both a silver-chaser and a sculptor throughout his career. Indeed, evidence suggests that it was not until 1818 that he ceased to be described simply as a silver-chaser, when an insurance document for 24 York Row in Kennington, south London, described him a modeller and chaser (Guildhall Lib MS 11936/437).

In 1806 Pitts was apprenticed to his father, also William, and he entered the Royal Academy Schools in 1811 before his apprenticeship was completed. Despite an early marriage, at the age of 18, and the rapid arrival of children, Pitts was clearly able to devote enough energy to his studies to win the Society of Arts gold Isis medal for a model in 1812 (**29**). Yet in his early career it is clear that the chasing in silver of works by other sculptors remained his dominant occupation, perhaps because it gave him a steady income. Notable commissions at this time included **Thomas Stothard**'s *Wellington Shield*, of 1814, and **John Flaxman**'s *Shield of Achilles* of 1818: in the latter work Pitts is said to have undertaken some of the modelling of the figures, a claim that coincides with his change of job description.

Between 1823 and 1840 he was a regular exhibitor at the Royal Academy and British Institution exhibitions, showing work ranging from drawings to bas-reliefs, and portrait busts to ideal pieces. He continued work as a silver-chaser, but also produced paintings and modelled his own designs for tableware in both precious metals and ceramics. In the late 1820s and early 1830s he was awarded several commissions for decorative sculpture at Buckingham Palace (**18, 20, 21**) and carved a relief of *St Martin and the Beggar* for the vestry-room pediment of St Martin-in-the-Fields (**19**). In 1839 he entered the competition for a monument to Lord Nelson in Trafalgar Square, producing a design described by the *Art Union* as 'a boldly arranged group, deserving of applause, although wanting of fitness and expression of purpose' (*AU*, March 1839, 18) (**13**). He was not successful.

Pitts was also commissioned to produce a number of church monuments, including one to Frederick, 2nd Baron Boston and his wife, which has a relief depicting a group of kneeling mourners with an angel floating above them (**8**). The Ricardo monument in Hardenhuish is on a much grander scale (**1**). David Ricardo, a self-made millionaire, economist and MP for the rotten borough of Portalington in Ireland, paid £2,000 for this monument which comprises four full-length free-standing classical figures in mourning. They are covered by a simple four-columned square structure in a neo-classical style that compliments well the austere neoclassicism of the Georgian church it stands beside. The work is imposing, though there appears to have been some deception in its production. Pitts was commissioned and paid to produce the four figures in marble but during the monument's restoration in the 1870s they were found 'to be made of composition' (*Wait* 1977, 258).

Despite his relative success, Pitts suffered long-term financial problems. In 1831 he was forced to write to the Lords of the Treasury to request that the balance of £550 be paid for his work at Buckingham Palace, claiming that without it 'I and my family will be ruined' (PRO T. 1/3489 in *Gunnis* 1968, 307). His problems came to a head on 6 April 1840 when worries over money led Pitts to take a fatal overdose of laudanum. This was doubly unfortunate as he was on the verge of securing a valuable contract to act as modeller for the London jewellers Mortimer and Hunt, which would probably have brought financial security. There is no doubt that Pitts was admired by many of the leading sculptors of the day, with the *Gentleman's Magazine* singling out **Flaxman, Chantrey** and **Westmacott** amongst his strongest supporters. His obituary states that 'in subjects of pure classical taste he stood unrivalled and his talents were highly appreciated' (*GM*, 1840, i, 661). Pitts left his widow, daughter Mary and the infant Frederick destitute and Chantrey helped organise a relief fund to save them from starvation. His elder sons, Thomas, William and **Joseph Pitts** had all been employed as assistants in his studio.

Michael Paraskos

Literary References: *AU*, 1839, 18; *AU* 1840, 101; *GM*, 1840, i, 661; *The Times*, 21 April 1840, 6; *DNB*, XLV, 1896, 388 (Cust); *Graves* VI, 1905–6, 159; *Jones* 1934, 248–50; *Gunnis* 1968, 307–8; *Pyke* 1973, 111; *Wait* 1977, 258; *Penny* 1977 (1) 11–13; *Penny* 1992, 64f; *ODNB* (McConnell)

Archival References: GPC; RG/JP, 6, 1117–9

Funerary Monuments				
1.	†1823	David Ricardo Payment(s): £2,000	Hardenhuish, Wilts, churchyard	Pevsner, *Wilts*, 1975, 264; GPC
2.	?1828	Matty Chilton	St Giles-in-the-Fields, Holborn, London	*Gunnis* 1968, 307
3.	†1828	P W Poore	St Giles-in-the-Fields, Holborn, London	Pevsner, *London: N*, 1998, 259
4.	†1830	Charles Yonge	Eton College, Windsor, Berks, upper chapel	Pevsner, *Bucks*, 1994, 307

5.	†1830	John Farhill		Chichester Cathedral, Sussex	S	*Gunnis* 1968, 307
6.	†1832	Elizabeth Bourke		St John, Paramatta, New South Wales, Australia	SD	HMI Archive, Esdaile & Gunnis (repr)
7.	†1832	Sir John Courtenay Honeywood		Elmsted, Kent	S	
8.	†1835	Frederick, Lord Boston, and Lady Boston (†1832)		Whiston, Northants	S	*CIIA* 4/3/150 (repr)
9.	?1835	Miss Wainwright		Sandgate, Kent		*Gunnis* 1968, 307
10.	?1836	Charles Irby		Morningthorpe, Norfolk		*Gunnis* 1968, 307
Statues						
11.	1832	Puck		[Exhib RA, London, 1211]; untraced		*Graves* 1875, 432; *Graves* VI, 1905–6, 159
12.	1833	Frederick-Augustus, Duke of York and Albany, part of a model of the Duke of York's column presented to the Duke of Wellington		Stratfield Saye, Hants		*Gunnis* 1968, 307
13.	1839	Horatio, Admiral Lord Nelson, design for national monument (commission awarded to E H Baily and William Railton)		Untraced		*AU*, March 1839, 18
Busts						
14.	1831	From the antique, model		[Soc of A, silver Isis medal]; untraced		RSA *Transactions*, vol 48, 1831, 550
15.	1838	Unidentified child		[Exhib Soc of BA, London, 609]; untraced		*Johnson* 1975, 373
16.	nd	Captain Fitzherbert, of Swinnerton		Untraced		*Gunnis* 1968, 307
17.	nd	Sir W Horne		Untraced		*Gunnis* 1968, 307
Architectural Sculpture						
18.	1828–1830	The progress of Rhetoric, reliefs Payment(s): £450		Buckingham Palace, London, bow room		*Colvin* VI, 1973–76, 302
19.	1831	St Martin and the beggar		St Martin-in-the-Fields, London, vestry room pediment		*Gunnis* 1968, 307
20.	1829–1832	The origin and progress of pleasure (sports of boys), series of 12 reliefs planned, six completed Payment(s): £720 (price agreed for full set of 12)		Buckingham Palace, London, north drawing room		*Colvin* VI, 1973–76, 302
21.	1833	Apotheoses of Shakespeare, Milton and Spenser, reliefs Payment(s): £315		Buckingham Palace, London, south drawing room		*Colvin* VI, 1973–76, 283, 302
22.	1837	Group of figures		[Soc of A, silver medal]; untraced		RSA *Transactions*, vol 52, 1838, xv
23.	1838	Muses between Greek and British poets, reliefs		[General news room and library, Belvoir Street, Leicester]; destroyed		*Cavanagh* 2000, 316–7 (repr)
Reliefs						
24.	1824	Pandora brought by Mercury to Epimethus		[Exhib Soc of BA, London, 345]; untraced		*Graves* 1875, 432; *Johnson* 1975, 372
25.	1829	The outrage of the centaurs at the nuptials of Pirithous and Hippodamia		[coll Mr Simons of Regent's Park, London]; untraced		*Graves* VI, 1905–6, 159; *Gunnis* 1968, 307; *Johnson* 1975, 372
26.	1829	The rape of Proserpine		[RA, London, 1829, 1160]; untraced		*Graves* VI, 1905–6, 159; *Gunnis* 1968, 307
27.	nd	Flora with the seasons; the pledges of virtue; the triumph of innocence		[coll George Harrison of Carlton Gardens, London]; untraced		*Gunnis* 1968, 307
28.	nd	Three bas-reliefs		[coll Sir W A Cooper of Isleworth House, Middx]; untraced		*Gunnis* 1968, 307
Miscellaneous						
29.	1812	Two warriors, wax model		[Soc of A, gold Isis medal]; untraced		RSA *Transactions*, vol 30, 1812, 25
30.	1823	Herod's cruelty, sketch		[Exhib RA, London, 1111]; untraced		*Graves* VI, 1905–6, 159
31.	1823	Samson killing the lion		[Exhib RA, London, 1064]; untraced		*Graves* 1875, 432; *Graves* VI, 1905–6, 159
32.	1823	The deluge, sketch		[Exhib RA, London, 1130]; untraced		*Graves* VI, 1905–6, 159
33.	1826	A chariot race, model	w	[Exhib RA, London, 1056]; untraced		*Graves* VI, 1905–6, 159
34.	1826	Model of a vase	w	[Exhib Soc of BA, London, 759]; untraced		*Johnson* 1975, 372
35.	1828	The shield of Æneas, 'to be executed in gold, after the style of Benvenuto Cellini'		[Exhib RA, London, 1180]; untraced		*Graves* VI, 1905–6, 159
36.	1829	Haemon and Antigone		[Exhib BI, London, 538]; untraced		*Graves* 1875, 432
37.	1830	The setting sun		[Exhib RA, London, 974]; untraced		*Graves* VI, 1905–6, 159
38.	1833	Love benighted		[Exhib Soc of BA, London, 825]; untraced		*Graves* 1875, 432; *Johnson* 1975, 372
39.	1833	The Pleiades adoring night		[Exhib RA, London, 1120]; untraced		*Graves* VI, 1905–6, 159
40.	1834	The shield of Hercules		[Exhib RA, London, 1027]; untraced		*Graves* VI, 1905–6, 159
41.	1835	The creation of Eve		[Exhib RA, London, 1138]; untraced		*Graves* VI, 1905–6, 159
42.	1836	The drama		[Exhib RA, London, 1149]; untraced		*Graves* VI, 1905–6, 159
43.	1837	The sovereigns of England, 'with a characteristic feeling and symbol to each'		[Exhib RA, London, 1193]; untraced		*Graves* VI, 1905–6, 159
44.	1838	Innocence		[Exhib Soc of BA, London, 603]; untraced		*Johnson* 1975, 373
45.	1838	The nine muses		[Exhib RA, London, 1271]; untraced		*Graves* VI, 1905–6, 159
46.	1839	Manlius defending the Capitol		[Exhib RA, London, 1263]; untraced		*Graves* VI, 1905–6, 159
47.	1840	The triumph of Ceres		[Exhib RA, London, 1089]; untraced		*Graves* VI, 1905–6, 159

PLACE, F, of Combe Martin fl *c*1821

Funerary Monuments

1.	?1821	Jane and William Ridd	Challacombe, Devon	S

PLATT, George and John, of Rotherham

Platt, George 1700–1743
Platt, John 1728–1810

The Platts were a family of quarrymen, builders and masons originating in Cheshire. Around 1730 **George Platt** settled in the Yorkshire village of Thrybergh, near Rotherham, where he bought a quarry and established a building firm, specialising in the restoration and construction of buildings. Little is known of his training but it is likely that he was apprenticed to an uncle, John Platt I, whilst still in Cheshire. It may indeed have been his uncle's commission to build St Paul's, Sheffield that originally brought George Platt to the Rotherham area.

The firm employed significant numbers and although most of George Platt's commissions were for building work, he appears also to have welcomed smaller-scale masonry carving that could be undertaken when outdoor conditions were difficult. The earliest recorded examples come from the 1740s when he was commissioned by the politician William Wrightson to build Cusworth Hall, a Palladian villa near Doncaster. As part of the contract, Wrightson ordered six marble chimneypieces in 1742, only five of which were completed by the time George Platt died from consumption the following year (**13–18**). The remaining chimneypiece was completed by the firm in 1744 under the direction of his son, **John Platt**, though at the time the firm was legally the property of George's wife, Elizabeth, since John was a minor (**18**).

John Platt engaged in a wide range of connected building enterprises. As well as restoration, building and carving work, he extended the quarrying business, developed a polished marble concern and in 1765 established the Rotherham Pottery with Samuel Walker. Sculptural work remained a small part of the firm's output but the number of recorded pieces increased under John, who took on commissions for funerary monuments and architectural sculpture as well as chimneypieces. The monuments include one to the Hopkins family in Lincolnshire (**1**), and eleven other known works for Yorkshire churches (**2–12**). Most of these relied for ornament on simple classical motifs such as urns with festoons.

The Platts met a considerable demand for architectural ornaments. In the 1750s and 1760s John worked for the 2nd Earl of Strafford at Wentworth Castle, first on restoration work and then in 1762 on 'carved work in ye pediment of the grand portico', which comprised a baroque roundel flanked by festoons (Wentworth Castle Papers, cited by *Gunnis*, 1968, 308) (**21**). He also provided a series of chimneypieces for which he received a payment of £129 17s 4 3/4 d in January 1765 (**19**). The family appear also to have acted as jobbing masons for other sculptors, for instance **Thomas Atkinson**, for whom they supplied carved work in 1798 for the Constable family mausoleum at Halsham (**22**).

John Platt made repeated efforts to encourage his sons to follow in his footsteps, apprenticing the three eldest to architects and sculptors. All three eventually joined the army. Only the youngest boy, William, retained a tangential connection with his father's profession by becoming an engraver with a workshop in Golden Square, London. John Platt died in Halifax, W R Yorks, in 1810 and was buried in the churchyard at Rotherham Minster.

Michael Paraskos

Literary References: *Potts* 1959, 6–20; *Gunnis* 1968, 308; *Hewlings* 1980, 397–406; *Friedman* 1981, 5–13; *Colvin* 1995, 759–60; *Tomlinson* 1996, 18, 45, 85
Archival References: GPC
Additional MSS References: Wentworth Castle papers; Platt Journal

Funerary Monuments

1.	*c*1748	Hopkins family		Gainsborough, Lincs	S	*Gunnis* 1968, 308
2.	1767	Mrs Bamford		['Sheffield Church']; untraced		*Gunnis* 1968, 308
3.	1769	Lionel Copley (†1766)		Sprotbrough, W R Yorks		*Gunnis* 1968, 308
4.	1769	Mr Wolrich		Leeds, W R Yorks		*Gunnis* 1968, 308
5.	1778	Lady Bute		Wortley, W R Yorks, chapel		*Gunnis* 1968, 308
6.	?1778	Mrs Catherine Buck		All Saints, Rotherham, W R Yorks	S	*Gunnis* 1968, 308
7.	?1783	Miss Freeman		Ecclesfield, W R Yorks		*Gunnis* 1968, 308
8.	1783	Mr Birk		Sheffield, WR Yorks		*Gunnis* 1968, 308
9.	?1785	Lieutenant-Colonel Downes		All Saints, Rotherham, W R Yorks	S	*Gunnis* 1968, 308
10.	1790	'Mr. Foljambe of Aldwark'		Untraced		*Gunnis* 1968, 308
11.	1793	Rev Francis Hall Payment(s): £60		Tankersley, W R Yorks		*Gunnis* 1968, 308
12.	?1799	Robert Cutforthay		All Saints, Rotherham, W R Yorks	S	*Gunnis* 1968, 308

Chimneypieces

13.	1742	Derbyshire marble	m	[Cusworth Hall, W R Yorks, Miss Wrightson's 'lodging room']; untraced		GPC
14.	1742	Derbyshire marble Payment(s): 'nearly £20'	m	[Cusworth Hall, W R Yorks]; untraced		GPC
15.	1742	'large panel'd . . . of statuary marble' Payment(s): £6		[Cusworth Hall, W R Yorks, 'ye common drawing room']; untraced		GPC
16.	1742	Statuary marble	m	[Cusworth Hall, W R Yorks, Miss Wrightson's dressing room]; untraced		GPC
17.	1742	Veined marble for the 'South East Chamber'; 'pannel'd' for 'ye best dressing room'; veined marble for the 'best chamber' Payment(s): £72 19s 2d		[Cusworth Hall, W R Yorks]; untraced		GPC
18.	1744	'a good Chimneypiece of Vein'd Marble for the best Drawing-room' Payment(s): £30	m	Cusworth Hall, W R Yorks		GPC
19.	1762	Several Payment(s): £110		Wentworth Castle, W R Yorks, library, 'My Lord's own room', 'my lady's own room' and their bedchamber		*Potts* 1959, 7; *Gunnis* 1968, 308

20.	1763	Two, including one for the library Payment(s): £21, £28	m	[Clumber Park, Notts]; untraced	GPC

Architectural Sculpture

21.	1762	'the carved work in ye pediment of the grand portico' Payment(s): £45	Wentworth Castle, W R Yorks	*Gunnis* 1968, 308
22.	1798	Urn and pedestal, columns and other masonry work (designed by Thomas Atkinson) Payment(s): £42 10s, £344	Constable mausoleum, Halsham, E R Yorks	Pevsner, *Yorks: E R & York*, 1972, 90; GPC

PLIMER, John, of Bodmington fl *c*1830

He was a carver who worked as co-partner to **Nathaniel Ireson, of Wincanton** on the building of Berkley House in Somerset in 1830.

PLOWS, T, of Hertford fl *c*1763–69

Gunnis notes that he signs three tablets of careful workmanship (**1–3**).

Funerary Monuments

1.	?1763	Margaret Lewin	Broxbourne, Herts	S	*Gunnis* 1968, 308
2.	?1765	Matthew Martin	Hunsdon, Herts	S	*Gunnis* 1968, 308
3.	?1769	Elizabeth Hutton	Broxbourne, Herts	S	*Gunnis* 1968, 308

PLOWS FAMILY, of York

Benjamin Plows	?1775–1824
William Abbey Plows	?1789–1865
Henry Plows	fl 1806–*c*1813
T Plows	fl *c*1840

In 1811 **Benjamin Plows** advertised that he had begun business as a marble mason in Coppergate, York (*York Courant*, 2 March 1811). The death of his widow, Rebecca, was announced in the *York Gazette* on 2 January 1830. Gunnis states that he was the father of **William Abbey Plows**, who was apprenticed to him in 1806. If this was the case Benjamin would only have been 14 when his son was born, so one of these birth dates is likely to be wrong. William married Miss E Abbey, late of Salton, at St Denis, Walmsgate, York, in 1828 (*York Gazette*, 26 April 1828). He showed a sarcophagus with a Gothic canopy, marble tables and a figure of David carved in stone at the Great Exhibition of 1851 (**28, 29**).

It is not clear how **Henry Plows** is related to to other family members. In 1806 he went into partnership with **Francis Cowgill** of Micklegate (*York Courant*, 6 Oct 1806). He continued with the yard after Cowgill's death in 1807, and he must have died himself about 1813, as his widow Jane announced that she was 'not declining business' that autumn (*York Courant*, 13 September 1813). On 18 April 1814 his stock of marble and stone was offered for sale in the *York Courant*.

The large wall monument to John Strangways, 1840, at Well is signed by a **T Plows**, who may well have been a member of the same family (**20**).

Literary References: *Gunnis* 1968, 308

Archival References: GPC

Funerary Monuments

1.	†1785	Unidentified subject, tablet	Hemingbrough, E R Yorks		Pevsner, *Yorks: E R & York*, 1995, 460
2.	†1800	Unidentified subject, tablet	Hemingbrough, E R Yorks	S	Pevsner, *Yorks: E R & York*, 1995, 460
3.	†1801	Sir Christopher Sykes	West Heslerton, E R Yorks	S	Pevsner, *Yorks: E R & York*, 1995, 745
4.	†1803	Thomas Court	St Crux parish room, York	S	Pevsner, *Yorks: E R & York*, 1995, 164
5.	?1815	Nicholas Smith	Selby Abbey, W R Yorks	S	RG/JP, 6, 1123
6.	†1819	Unidentified subject, tablet	St Michael, Malton, N R Yorks	S	Pevsner, *Yorks: N R*, 1966, 234
7.	?1821	Strangways family	Well, N R Yorks	S	GPC
8.	†1823	John Hunter (co-sculptor: Fisher family, of York)	Christ Church, Harrogate, W R Yorks	S	
9.	†1823	Unidentified subject, tablet	Hemingbrough, E R Yorks	S	Pevsner, *Yorks: E R & York*, 1995, 460
10.	?1824	Richard Spofforth	Howden, E R Yorks	S	*Gunnis* 1968, 309
11.	†1825	Unidentified subject, tablet	St Stephen, York	S	Pevsner, *Yorks: E R & York*, 1995, 177
12.	?1828	Mary Clayton	Kippax, W R Yorks	S	*Gunnis* 1968, 309
13.	†1829	Sergeant-Major Polety	All Saints, Pavement, York	S	*Gunnis* 1968, 309; Pevsner, *Yorks: E R & York*, 1995, 160
14.	†1830	John (†1809) and Jane (†1830) Andus (signed by W Plows)	Selby Abbey, W R Yorks	S	
15.	†1830	Seth Stables	Pocklington, E R Yorks	S	Pevsner, *Yorks: E R & York*, 1995, 649
16.	†1834	Samuel Woodhead	All Saints, Pavement, York	S	*Gunnis* 1968, 309; Pevsner, *Yorks: E R & York*, 1995, 160
17.	†1836	Mary Holtby	Little Driffield, E R Yorks	S	Pevsner, *Yorks: E R & York*, 1995, 598
18.	†1836	Unidentified subject, tablet	All Saints, Pavement, York	S	Pevsner, *Yorks: E R & York*, 1995, 160
19.	*c*1839	Butler family (signed by W Plows)	Hemingbrough, E R Yorks	S	
20.	?1840	John Strangways (signed by T Plows)	Well, N R Yorks	S	*Gunnis* 1968, 309
21.	†1842	Morley (†1797) and Elizabeth (†1842) Wharrey (signed by W Plows)	Selby Abbey, W R Yorks	S	
22.	?1843	Rev James Andrew	Whitby, N R Yorks	S	*Gunnis* 1968, 309
23.	†1846	Henry Darley	Buttercrambe, N R Yorks	S	Pevsner, *Yorks: N R*, 1966, 93
24.	†1848	Seth Stables	Pocklington, E R Yorks	S	*Gunnis* 1968, 309
25.	†1858	William Preston	Burythorpe, E R Yorks		Pevsner, *Yorks: E R & York*, 1995, 380

26.	nd	Unidentified subject, tablet		St Michael, Crambe, N R Yorks		Pevsner, *Yorks: N R*, 1966, 130
27.	nd	Unidentified subject, tablet		Gate Helmsley, N R Yorks	S	Pevsner, *Yorks: N R*, 1966, 165
Statues						
28.	1851	David (by William Abbey Plows)	s	[Gt Exhib, London]; untraced	S	*Gunnis* 1968, 308
Miscellaneous						
29.	1851	Sarcophagus with gothic canopy, 'model . . . in stone from the quarries at Heldenley, near Malton' (by William Abbey Plows)		[Gt Exhib, London]; untraced		*AJ Cat* 1851, 267 (repr)

PLUM, J

For information the reader is referred to *Pyke* 1973, 112 and *Pyke* 1981, 33

PLUMIER, Pierre-Denis 1688–1721

Plumier was an Antwerp-born sculptor who combined classical and naturalistic elements in an ambitious series of secular and sacred commissions in his native land. He was baptised in Antwerp Cathedral on 14 March 1688 and ten years later was admitted to the Guild of St Luke as a pupil of the sculptor Ludovic Willemssens (†1702). It is not certain where he completed his training. Among his most powerful works are two ambitious baroque groups in marble, *The Rape of Proserpine* and *Abundance supported by Science and Military Power*, both carved *c*1712 for the Palais d'Egmont-Arenberg, Brussels. He also responsible for the Spinola family monument in Notre-Dame de la Chapelle, Brussels, 1716–17, a dramatic triangular composition featuring a bearded figure of *Cronos* carrying a medallion portrait, a kneeling female mourner and an angel representing *Fame*. He also carved the magnificent oak pulpit for Notre-Dame de la Chapelle, Brussels, which features a naturalistic tableau of *Elias and the Angel* and was completed by his former assistants in Brussels, *c*1720.

Vertue notes that he came to England 'by the encouragement of my Lord Codogon for whom he was to make some Statues. & also for my Lord Castlemain' (*Vertue* I, 91). He arrived in London *c*1717 with a number of assistants, one of whom was his former apprentice, **Laurent Delvaux**. Plumier took premises in Long Ditch and **Peter Scheemakers** joined the workshop around 1720.

John Sheffield, Duke of Buckingham, considered commissioning his bust from Plumier but recoiled when he was given an estimate of 50 guineas, exclaiming 'then you had best return [to Flanders] . . . for here you are not like to get so much' (*Vertue* III, 106). The Duke was so disgusted at Plumier's prices that 'he evry where immediately went and spoke against him – and his extravagant prices' (*ibid*). He died early in 1721 and his widow, a woman of independent mind, invited Plumier to provide a design for her husband's monument (1). His proposal, a variation on the Spinola monument, was another triangular arrangement with a reclining ducal effigy in Roman armour attended by a kneeling spouse, whilst above, on a bracket, was a life-sized figure of *Cronos*, carrying away portrait medallions of dead Sheffield children. Plumier prepared the maquette for the kneeling duchess, but died of consumption soon after, leaving Delvaux and Scheemakers to complete the monument to Plumier's design. It received much attention for its novelty and the combination of classical quotations and high narrative drama. Vertue described Plumier's premature death as a cause for regret 'of all lovers of arts' (*Vertue* I, 91). A number of his models were auctioned with other works sold by Delvaux and Scheemakers in 1728.

Literary References: *Jacobs* 1999 (2), 113–70; *Roscoe* 1999, 178–80

Auction Catalogues: Scheemakers and Delvaux, 1728 (1)

Miscellaneous Drawings and Engravings: 8 'plates of Cacchanals Etch'd by Plimier', Scheemakers and Delvaux sale 1728, day 1, lot 86, untraced; 22 drawings, day 2, lot 4

Portraits of the Sculptor: P Baert, ink and wash, nd, Bibliotheque Royale, Brussels (repr *Jacobs* 1999 (2), 114)

Funerary Monuments						
1.	1721	John, 1st Duke of Buckingham (†1721), design and models (co-sculptor: Peter Scheemakers, Laurent Delvaux) Model(s): 'A Dutchess kneeling', lot 11, Scheemakers and Delvaux sale, 1728		Westminster Abbey, Henry VII's Chapel		*Vertue* I, 101; *Avery* 1980, 150–70; *Whinney* 1988, 157–9; *Bindman and Baker* 1995, 37–8, 384 n31, 386, n17 (repr); *Roscoe* 1999, 178–80 (repr)
Statues						
2.	1717	Reclining Venus		Cassiobury sale, June 1922, lot 1174; untraced	SD	*Gunnis* 1968, 309
3.	pre-1728	Diana hunting, Vulcan, Venus, Hercules, Omphale, Perseus and Andromeda, Apollo and Ceres, satyr, river god, autumn, spring, seven 'Academy figures', models		[Scheemakers's and Delvaux's sale, 1728, several lots]; untraced		*Gunnis* 1968, 309 (Hercules)
4.	pre-1728	Figures raising the cross, 'Gironimus', group of angels, models		[Scheemakers's and Delvaux's sale, 1728, lots 32, 87, 88]; untraced		
5.	nd	Hercules Model(s): Rysbrack's sale, 25 Jan 1766, lot 68		Untraced		*Gunnis* 1968, 309
6.	nd	'Time, taking up truth by the hair of ye head & a child in his Arms'		Untraced		*Vertue* I, 91
7.	nd	Two 'by Plomar'	m	[Canons, Middx, dining room]; untraced		Canons Grand Inventory, 1725, room 77
Busts						
8.	pre-1728	Two		[Scheemakers and Delvaux sale, 1728, lot 61]; untraced		
Architectural Sculpture						
9.	1717	Pair of urns		[Winslow Hall, Aylesbury, Bucks]; untraced	SD	*Gunnis* 1968, 309
Miscellaneous						
10.	nd	Time and Truth, casts in the style of Michaelangelo		Untraced		*Gunnis* 1968, 309

PLUMLEY, Thomas 1824–

He was 18 and living at 38 Lower Belgrave Place, Pimlico, in 1842, when he entered the Royal Academy Schools on the recommendation of **Richard Westmacott III**. Two years later he sent statues of Chaucer and Sir Thomas More to the Westminster Hall Exhibition (**1, 2**). They were not well received. The *Literary Gazette* condemned both as 'but feeble things' (*Lit Gaz*, 20 July 1844) and the *Art Union* commented that the portrait of More was 'by no means a favourable impersonation' (*AU*, 1844, 215). He carved ornaments for the church at Wootton St Lawrence (**3**) and exhibited a work at the Royal Academy, giving his address as 11 Dartmouth Street, Westminster (**4**).

Literary References: *Gunnis* 1968, 309

Archival References: RA Admissions

Statues					
1.	1844	Geoffrey Chaucer		[Exhib Westminster Hall, London, 87]; untraced	*AU*, 1844, 214
2.	1844	Sir Thomas More		[Exhib Westminster Hall, London, 109]; untraced	*AU*, 1844, 215
Architectural Sculpture					
3.	1864	Eighteen heads		Wootton St Lawrence, Hants	Ch W, in *Gunnis* 1968, 309
Miscellaneous					
4.	1865	Charles Conway		[Exhib RA, London, 1016]; untraced	*Graves* VI, 1905–6, 165

PLURA, Joseph I –1756

He was the son of Carlo Giuseppe Plura (†1737), an Italian sculptor and wood carver who worked in Turin and who may have been the Plura recorded as a stuccoist working at Castle Howard in 1711. He probably trained in Turin at the Carlo Emmanuele III Sculpture Academy and may have completed his studies in Paris. By 1749 he had settled in Bath and married the daughter of John Ford, a local building contractor. Plura probably worked as an assistant to **Prince Hoare** at Bath as there is some evidence that he carved Hoare's statue of Beau Nash in the pump room (**3**). This was completed in 1752 and the following year Plura set up business on his own, taking the lease on a statuary yard in Bath on 1 October 1753. By May that year he had carved the coat of arms for the pediment of the grammar school, for which his father in law was the contractor, and in 1755 he completed the five busts of worthies which surmount the façade of the building (**5, 6**).

His most significant work is a group of *Diana and Endymion*, inscribed 'Jos: Plura Taurinensis Fecit Bathoniae 1752' (**4**). This depicts Endymion asleep with his dog at his feet, while Diana gazes fondly at him, caressing his hand and shoulder. The protagonists are attended by two putti bearing torches of love. The work must have been on view in Plura's studio in Bath for Ivory Talbot of Lacock Abbey wrote to his friend the architect Sanderson Miller on 13 August 1754, 'When at Bath fail not to see a piece of sculpture of Endymion on Mount Patmos, the performance of Mr Plura, a statuary' (*Warwick County Archives*, CR.125.B, letter 405).

By April 1755 Plura had moved to London, taking a studio in Oxford Row, near Poland Street, where the *Diana and Endymion* group was displayed, together with two tables of 'Diaspero and Antico' marble. He was evidently disappointed by his progress in London for in April 1755 he approached the ambassador of the King of Sardinia about his prospects should he return to Turin. The following month word was sent from Turin that employment could be found for him in the service of the King, though the terms would be settled after his return when his abilities could be judged. Plura took some time to consider this offer but eventually decided to accept. The ambassador in London wrote to Turin on 18 March 1736 that Plura had intended to leave England for Piedmont in April but he had died that very morning 'd'une fievre maligne' leaving a widow and three young children, one of whom was **Joseph Plura II**.

Literary References: *Fleming* 1956, 178–81; *Gunnis* 1968, 309; *Sumner* 1996, 61

Funerary Monuments						
1.	†1748	William Bowles		Newchurch, I of W	S	GPC
2.	†1750	Rev William Alsop		West Littleton, Glos	S	Pevsner, *Glos: Cotswolds*, 1999, 713
Statues						
3.	*c*1750	Richard Nash (as assistant to Prince Hoare)		Pump room, Bath, Somerset		Pevsner, *Somerset: N & Bristol*, 1958, 112
4.	1752	Diana and Endymion	m	Holburne Museum, Bath, Somerset	SD	*Fleming* 1956, 179, 180 (repr); *Sumner* 1996, 61 (repr)
Architectural Sculpture						
5.	1753	Coat of arms		Grammar school, Bath, Somerset, pediment		*Fleming* 1956, 180
6.	1755	Five busts		Grammar school, Bath, Somerset, above façade (two are modern replacements)		*Fleming* 1956, 180

PLURA, Joseph II 1753–

The son of **Joseph Plura I**, he returned with his family from London to Bath after his father's death in 1756. He entered the Royal Academy Schools in 1773 and he may have worked in the studio of **Joseph Nollekens** for J T Smith mentions that a 'Plara' was 'among his best workmen' (*Smith* 1920, I, 97). He cannot have remained there long for in 1777 he went to Rome to continue his studies. In the autumn of 1778 he visited Naples with Thomas Jones and in the following September Lord Herbert included him in a list of artists in the city, giving his address as Strada Croce. In his diary for 24 September 1779 Lord Herbert mentions that he went with John Coxe Hippisley 'to see his Bust not yet finished, by a young English Artist, viz: Plura, but could not see it to advantage as he was then placing the cast upon it' (*ibid*) (**1**). In September 1780 he was in Florence, copying in the Uffizi and he was twice in Venice, on 11 February and 16 May 1781. Plura was back in London in 1782, when he exhibited two wax portraits and a bust at the RA, from an address in Broad Street, Soho (**5, 6, 2**). Four years later he sent a 'busto of the Abbé Grant at Rome' to the Academy, giving his address as 'At Mr. Dufour's, Litle Titchfield Street' (**3**).

Literary References: *Fleming* 1956, 181; *Gunnis* 1968, 309; *Pyke* 1973, 112; *Ingamells* 1997, 777–8

Busts

1.	1779	Sir John Coxe Hippisley		Untraced		*Fleming* 1956, 181
2.	1782	Unidentified nobleman		[Exhib RA, London, 516]; untraced		*Graves* VI, 1905–6, 165
3.	1786	Abbé Grant		[Exhib RA, London, 553]; untraced		*Graves* VI, 1905–6, 165

Reliefs

4.	1777	Joseph Baretti	w	[Coll Cavaliere Antonio Abrate of Turin, 1902]; untraced		*Fleming* 1956, 181
5.	1782	Unidentified gentleman	w	[Exhib RA, London, 264]; untraced		*Graves* VI, 1905–6, 165
6.	1782	Unidentified gentleman	w	[Exhib RA, London, 262]; untraced		*Graves* VI, 1905–6, 165
7.	1783	Mr Smith, of Bath	w	Coll T Sainsbury, Bournemouth, Hants		*Pyke* 1973, 112
8.	nd	Self-portrait	w	VAM (Bate Loan)		*Pyke* 1973, 112 (repr 223)

POBJE, A

For information the reader is referred to *Pyke* 1973, 112

POCOCKE, of Huntingdon fl *c*1834

Funerary Monuments

1.	?1834	Rev Edward Edwards		Offord Cluny, Hunts	S	GPC

POLLARD, of Quorn fl *c*1765

Funerary Monuments

1.	?1765	Benjamin Clarke		Hardingstone, Northants	S	*Gunnis* 1968, 309

POLLARD, of Taunton fl 1840–70

It is possible that he was George Pollard of Taunton, who was the contractor for building the Carmarthenshire, Pembrokeshire and Cardiganshire Counties lunatic asylum, at Carmarthen in 1863.

Literary References: *Dale-Jones and Lloyd* 1989, 56

Funerary Monuments

1.	1841	Gwenllian Bishop		Myddfai, Carmarthen		*Dale-Jones and Lloyd* 1989, 56
2.	†1852	Henry Burchell Peren		South Petherton, Somerset	S	

POLLARD, Thomas

The partner of **Samuel Hull of Leicester**: see Hull for a list of their works.

POND fl 1747

Busts

1.	1747	Unidentified subjects, 'Bustos' Payment(s): £5 11s 6d		[Rousham Hall, Oxon]; untraced		Cotterell-Dormer Archives in GPC

POOLE fl *c*1850

Funerary Monuments

1.	†1850	Colonel Thomas Weare		Hampton Bishop, Herefs		Pevsner, *Herefs*, 1963, 141

POOLE, of Westminster fl *c*1845–46

Funerary Monuments

1.	†1845	Vice-Admiral John Chambers White		Aldenham, Herts	S	Pevsner, *Herts*, 1977, 67
2.	†1846	Edward Richard (†1846) and Sophia (†1846) Barwell and their five children		Westbourne, Sussex	S	

POOLE, Thomas R fl *c*1788–1821

Poole, who became Modeller to the Prince of Wales, exhibited three portraits, presumably wax reliefs, at the Royal Academy in 1799 and 1800 (**5, 6, 8**). He worked from several London addresses, 19 Lambeth Road, Vauxhall; St James's Street, Piccadilly; 'At Egerton's', Whitehall and 27 (or possibly 7) Vere Street, Oxford Street. Two labels on the verso of his portrait of King George IV in the Philadelphia Museum of Art set out his prices (**8**). He charged 7 guineas for modelling a medallion portrait of a gentleman from life and 2 guineas each for copies, while portraits of clerics and ladies, which involved modelling more elaborate costume, cost 10 guineas, with copies at 3 guineas each. A note adds, 'Mr Poole continues to model, free of expense, the head of a Gentleman, on receiving a guarantee for twenty copies' (*Pyke* 1973, 113). He also made death masks, charging 2 guineas for this service.

Literary References: *Gunnis* 1968, 309; *Pyke* 1973, 112–3; *Pyke* 1981, 33

Reliefs

1.	?1788	Unidentified man	w	VAM A.104-1965		*Pyke* 1973, 113
2.	1791	Edmund Burke	w	NPG 1607 Other versions: coll G G Robinson, Wokingham, Berks, 1795 VAM Sotheby 24 July 1978, lot 57	D	*Pyke* 1973, 113; *Pyke* 1981, 33
3.	1795	Charles James Fox	w	Coll G G Robinson, Wokingham, Berks		*Pyke* 1973, 113
4.	1795	Frederick-Augustus, Duke of York and Albany and King George IV	w	NPG 3308	SD	*Pyke* 1973, 113
5.	1799	Frederick-Augustus, Duke of York and Albany	w	[Exhib RA, London, 1087]; untraced Other versions: Sotheby, 24 July, 1978, lot 57 coll R Margolis, Toledo, New Jersey, USA		*Graves* VI, 1905–6, 180; *Pyke* 1981, 33
6.	1799	Sir James Saunderson	w	[Exhib RA, London, 1072]; untraced		*Graves* VI, 1905–6, 180
7.	1799	Unidentified man	w	Phillips, 8 July 1975, lot 31		*Pyke* 1981, 33

8.	1800	King George IV	w	[Exhib RA, London, 444]; untraced Other versions: BM, London, 1807 VAM, 1821 Philadelphia Museum of Art, USA, 1821 Museum of London (on loan) Museum of London (on sofa) Christie, 18 April 1967, lot 129 Met NY Royal Coll (?) Blair Castle, Perthshire (?)		*Graves* VI, 1905–6, 180; GPC; *Gunnis* 1968, 309; *Pyke* 1973, 113
9.	c1805	Admiral Lord Nelson	w	Lloyds, London, Nelson room		*Pyke* 1973, 113
10.	1810	Rev John Sibree	w	Coll Miss E Sibree, Tunbridge Wells, Kent Other versions: Coll Viscount Harcourt, Stanton Harcourt, Oxon, 1811		*Pyke* 1973, 113
11.	1810	Rev William Jay	w	Coll Miss E Sibree, Tunbridge Wells, Kent Other versions: Christie, 5 Oct 1976, lot 33, 1810		*Pyke* 1973, 113; *Pyke* 1981, 33
12.	1810	Richard Barton	w	VAM		*Pyke* 1973, 113
13.	1812	James Arding	w	VAM		*Pyke* 1973, 112
14.	1812	Unidentified man	w	Coll J Glanz, London	SD	*Pyke* 1981, 33
15.	1814	Rev Robert Hall	w	NPG 5066 Other versions: SD 1814, Christie, 29 July 1975, lot 2 BM, London, 1815	SD	*Pyke* 1973, 113; *Pyke* 1981, 33
16.	1814	Rev Thomas Toller	w	VAM		*Pyke* 1973, 113
17.	1814	Unidentified man	w	Coll Hon Mrs John Mulholland, Upton Grey, Hants		*Pyke* 1981, 33
18.	1815	Rev R Aspland	w	VAM		*Pyke* 1973, 112 (repr 224)
19.	1815	Rev W B Collyer	w	Coll Mrs C Wilkinson, Harrogate, W R Yorks		*Pyke* 1973, 113
20.	1817	Rev John Griffin	w	Coll Mrs E M Page, Bury St Edmunds, Suffolk		*Pyke* 1973, 113
21.	1817	Rev Rowland Hill	w	VAM Other versions: Sotheby, 21 Oct 1968, lot 99		*Pyke* 1973, 113
22.	1817	Rev William Borrow	w	VAM		*Pyke* 1973, 113
23.	1817	Rev William Priestley	w	Lloyds, London		*Pyke* 1973, 113
24.	1817	Unidentified man	w	Coll Professor Mario Praz (Rome)		*Pyke* 1973, 113
25.	1817	Unidentified man	w	VAM		*Pyke* 1973, 113
26.	1818	John, Baron Teignmouth	w	NPG, London Other versions: Met NY	SD	*Pyke* 1973, 113; *Pyke* 1981, 33
27.	1818	Unidentified man	w	Coll G Pollard (Cambridge)		*Pyke* 1973, 113
28.	1818	Unidentified man	w	VAM		*Pyke* 1973, 113
29.	1819	Unidentified man	w	Christie, 16 Dec 1970, lot 3		*Pyke* 1973, 113
30.	1819	Unidentified woman	w	Coll Professor Mario Praz, Rome		*Pyke* 1973, 113
31.	1819	Unidentified woman	w	Christie, 16 Dec 1970, lot 3		*Pyke* 1973, 113
32.	1820	Philip Henry, 4th Earl Stanhope	w	Coll late Earl of Stanhope, Chevening, Kent		*Pyke* 1973, 113
33.	1820	Thomas Watson	w	VAM		*Pyke* 1973, 113
34.	1821	Mrs Byron	w	Coll Professor Mario Praz, Rome		*Pyke* 1973, 113
35.	nd	Admiral Keppel (?)	w	BM, London		*Pyke* 1973, 113
36.	nd	Charlotte, Princess of Wales	w	NPG		*Pyke* 1973, 113
37.	nd	General Lafayette	w	Met NY		*Pyke* 1973, 113
38.	nd	George Engleheart	w	Coll Viscount Harcourt, Stanton Harcourt, Oxon Other versions: Coll H Engleheart, Stoke-by-Nayland, Suffolk		*Pyke* 1973, 113; *Pyke* 1981, 33
39.	nd	King George IV (as Prince of Wales)	w	Windsor Castle Other versions: Met NY		*Pyke* 1973, 113
40.	nd	Mrs Mary Chatham	w	Met NY		*Pyke* 1973, 113
41.	nd	Mrs Shelley	w	Coll Mrs A E Hamill, Lake Forest, Illinois		*Pyke* 1973, 113
42.	nd	Napoleon I	w	Christie, 16 Oct 1973, lot 13		*Pyke* 1981, 33
43.	nd	O'Dwyer, Dean of Cashel	w	Museum of Lithophanes and Wax Miniatures, Toledo, Ohio		*Pyke* 1981, 33
44.	nd	Sir Charles Price	w	Met NY		*Pyke* 1973, 113
45.	nd	Sir Joshua Reynolds	w	Sotheby, 24 July 1978, lot 57		*Pyke* 1981, 33
46.	nd	Unidentified man	w	Coll Viscount Harcourt, Stanton Harcourt, Oxon		*Pyke* 1973, 113
47.	nd	Unidentified man	w	Sotheby, 2 June 1975, lot 23	S	*Pyke* 1981, 33
48.	nd	Unidentified man	w	Phillips, 8 July 1975, lot 32		*Pyke* 1981, 33
49.	nd	Unidentified men, two models	w	Philadelphia Museum of Art, USA		*Pyke* 1973, 113
50.	nd	Unidentified women, two	w	Coll D Mathias, Westerham, Kent		*Pyke* 1973, 113
51.	nd	William March (?)	w	Christie, 16 Oct 1973, lot 20		*Pyke* 1981, 33

POORE, Joseph, of Newport fl *c*1846

Funerary Monuments

1.	†1846	Mary (†1844) and Richard Cass		Newport, I of W	S	

POPE-STEVENS, Justin fl 1764–c1808

He worked for many years as a carver and gilder from 44 Stephen Street, Dublin. He was the son of the portrait painter Thomas Pope and the nephew of Justin Pope-Stevens, who is also thought to have been a portrait painter. He entered the Dublin Society Schools in 1764 and in 1768 won a prize for architectural drawing. He subsequently studied under the carver **Richard Cranfield** and exhibited 'An Elevation for a Temple' at the Society of Artists in William Street, in 1770. In 1800 the Dublin Society commissioned him to execute a model of the Giant's Causeway, for which he was to be paid £30. He died in or about 1808.

Literary References: *Strickland* II, 913, 257–258

PORTER, Thomas, of London fl c1821–43

Funerary Monuments

1.	?1821	George Parry	Haverfordwest, Pembrokes	S	*Gunnis* 1968, 309
2.	?1830	Jacob Jones	Wesley's chapel, City Road, London	S	*Gunnis* 1968, 309
3.	†1837	Maurice (†1814) Mary and Thomas (†1828) Budgett	St Andrew Cheddar, Somerset	S	*Gunnis* 1968, 309
4.	†1843	Anne Thomas	Llantrisant, Glamorgan	S	Pevsner, *Glamorgan*, 1995, 401

POWEL, of Talgarth fl c1779–80

Funerary Monuments

1.	†1779	Thomas Williams	Llandefalle, Brecon	S	Pevsner, *Powys*, 1979, 332
2.	†1780	Roderick Gwynne	Llandefalle, Brecon	S	Pevsner, *Powys*, 1979, 332

POWELL, Henry fl c1701

Funerary Monuments

1.	†1701	Sir Uvedale Corbet	Leebotwood, Salop	S	SRR, Corbett Accts (uncat); VCH *Salop* VIII, 1968, 106

POWELL, J fl c1759

This sculptor's identity is not established: he may be either James Powell, son of **William Powell, of Hampton**, or John Powell, who worked for **Robert Taylor I**.

Funerary Monuments

1.	†1759	Rev George Lilsley	Chipping Norton, Oxon		RG/JP, 6, 1125v

POWELL, Robert, of Bristol fl 1705

Chimneypieces

1.	1705	'the Chimney peece &c in the Councell Chamber' Payment(s): £7	m	[Bristol Council House]; untraced	Bristol Cash Books, fol OR p 78

POWELL, T, of Leominster fl c1763

He is known only for one 'large wall-tablet with good details' (1).

Funerary Monuments

1.	?1763	Eleanor Morgan	Bodenham, Herefs	S	*Gunnis* 1968, 309

POWELL, William, of Hampton fl c1731

He was the son of Thomas Powell, of Hampton, Middx (†1714), the mason for Hampton Court during the reign of William and Mary. William Powell was a pupil of **Sir Henry Cheere**. He signs the 'very fine' monument with two life-size figures, to Susannah Thomas at Hampton (1), though Gunnis suggests it is possible that much of the carving was actually done by his master, who allowed him to take the credit for it. The monument was perhaps designed by the architect, Thomas Archer, for Mrs Thomas's will directs him to erect it as her executor.

Powell's son, James, was apprenticed to William Perkins, citizen and mason of London, in 1743. Other masons of the same name, who may have been members of the family, are John Powell, who in 1743 received the balance owing to his late master, **Robert Taylor I**, for work done at the Royal College of Physicians; Joseph Powell, who was apprenticed to Robert Wright in 1700; and Roger Powell who was apprenticed to John Harris in 1717.

Literary References: *Gunnis* 1968, 310; *Colvin* 1995, 78

Funerary Monuments

1.	†1731	Susannah Thomas (design attributed to Thomas Archer)	Hampton, Middx	S	*Colvin* 1995, 78

POWERS, Hiram 1805–73

A leading American neoclassical sculptor, he lived and worked in Florence from 1837 until his death. He executed a number of busts of British sitters and received a large number of orders for replicas of ideal heads from British patrons from the 1840s onwards. Only works with British associations are listed.

The first marble version of his most famous work, *The Greek slave*, was purchased by an Englishman, Captain John Grant (1). Inspired by the Greek War of Independence, it is a full-length statue of a Greek maiden, captured by the Turks and forced to stand chained and naked in the slave market. To dispel objections to her nudity Powers explained that the girl's faith in God shielded her and kept her from shame. The subject also reflected the views of the growing anti-slavery lobby in America. It was exhibited in London at the gallery of Henry Graves, an art dealer in Pall Mall, in 1845 and at the Great Exhibition of 1851, where it appeared alongside the *Fisher boy* (2). Another version, purchased from the sculptor by William, 11th Baron Ward, was sent to the Manchester Art Treasures Exhibition in 1857. Although the figure was widely acclaimed in Britain it was only awarded a bronze medal (one of 83 for sculpture) at the Great Exhibition, an outcome which Powers attributed to the presence of a rival sculptor, **John Gibson**, among the judges.

Other works by Powers were exhibited at the Royal Academy between 1840 and 1850. In 1852–4 the Crystal Palace, which had housed the Great Exhibition, was re-erected at Sydenham, South London and Powers was asked to contribute to the display of contemporary sculpture a colossal plaster copy of his statue of *America* (Smithsonian, Washington DC, plaster). He hired an Italian sculptor, Odoardo Fantacchiotti, to make the copy, which was completed in January 1856, but it was so poor that Powers decided to have it destroyed rather than sending it to London. A figure of *California* (untraced; another version Met NY) was exhibited at the Graves gallery in 1860–62, then put on display at the International Exhibition, together with a bust of *Proserpine.* It was subsequently returned to the sculptor and finally found an American buyer in 1867.

Powers visited London for the first time in 1862 and returned to England in the summer of 1863, shortly after the marriage of his eldest daughter, Loulie, to the Sheffield industrialist Alfred Ibbotson. During his stay in Sheffield he started work on the model for a bust of *Ginevra*, completed in Florence that autumn (**20**).

Literary References: *Wunder* 1991, *passim*; *Grove* 1996, 25, 400–2 (Dimmick)

Statues

1.	1844	The Greek slave Model(s): Smithsonian, Washington DC, two full-size plasters	m	[coll Captain John Grant]; Raby Castle, Co Durham Other versions: coll William, 11th Baron Ward (1st Earl of Dudley), Whitley Court, Worcs (destroyed 1944) 1848 marble seven other versions recorded		*Wunder* II, 1991, 157–168 (repr)
2.	1844–6	Fisher boy Model(s): Smithsonian, Washington DC, USA, 1841–4	m	[coll Robert Stephenson, Newcastle-upon-Tyne, Northumbs]; private coll, Sweden Other versions: five replicas recorded		*Wunder* II, 1991, 146–8 (repr)

Busts

3.	1840	Gertrude Maria Rose Harrison Model(s): Toledo Museum of Art, Ohio, USA (destroyed after 1916)	m	coll Sir James Harwood Harrison, Woodbridge, Suffolk	S	*Wunder* II, 1991, 51–2 (repr)
4.	1840	Marianne Burlton Bennett Payment(s): $250	m	[coll the subject]; untraced		*Graves* VI, 1905–6, 195; *Wunder* II, 1991, 20
5.	1842	Edward Everett	m	National Portrait Gallery, Washington DC, USA Other versions: Chatsworth, Derbys (commissioned by William, 6th Duke of Devonshire) 1849 marble Detroit Institute of Arts, Mich, USA, 1855, marble Boston University, Mass, USA, 1857, marble		*Graves* VI, 1905–6, 195; *Wunder* II, 1991, 39–41 (repr)
6.	1843	Charles Lesingham Smith	m	Christ Church College Cambridge, library Other versions: ex coll Countess Maynard, 1845 marble; untraced	S	*Graves* VI, 1905–6, 1409; *Wunder* II, 1991, 91–2 (repr)
7.	1843	Infant Nero Model(s): Smithsonian American Art Museum, Washington DC, USA	m	[coll C Noel Wellman, Taunton, Somerset]; untraced		*Wunder* II, 1991, 180 (repr)
8.	1844	Captain John Grant Model(s): Smithsonian American Art Museum, Washington DC, USA	m	Private coll, Norwich, Norfolk		*Wunder* II, 1991, 45–6 (repr)
9.	1842–4	Ellen Julia Holland	m	[coll H Robert Holland]; untraced Other versions: second version for the patron, marble, 1844–7, and six casts of the original, 1842–4; all untraced		*Graves* VI, 1905–6, 1409; *Wunder* II, 1991, 53
10.	1843–4	Proserpine Model(s): Galleria, d'Arte Moderna, Florence, Italy; Smithsonian, Washington DC	m	[coll Edward L Carey]; Philadelphia Museum of Art, USA Other versions: over 100 replicas including large number for British patrons *c*1845–1870		*Wunder* II, 1991, 187–204 (repr)
11.	1845–6	Greek slave Model(s): Smithsonian, Washington DC, USA, two plasters		coll Louise Bruse, New York, USA Other versions: about 100 marble replicas, including a large number for British patrons, also plaster casts		*Wunder* II, 1991, 168–77 (repr)
12.	1845–1848	James Playfair Model(s): Smithsonian, Washington DC, USA	m	[coll James Playfair]; untraced Other versions: coll Lord and Lady Holland, Florence, 1845 (a cast?) Smithsonian, Washington DC, USA, plaster cast		*Wunder* II, 1991, 82–3 (repr)
13.	1848	Psyche Model(s): Smithsonian, Washington DC, USA	m	[coll Ignatius Sargent, Boston, Mass, USA]; untraced Other versions: several replicas recorded, including one for Lionel Lincoln, of London 1852, marble (sold Christie, London, 15 May 1986, lot 26)		*Wunder* II, 1991, 204–5 (repr)
14.	1849	Fisher boy		Cincinnati Art Museum, Ohio, USA Other versions: approx 15 known replicas, including several for British patrons		*Wunder* II, 1991, 148–9 (repr)
15.	1852	Diana Model(s): Smithsonian, Washington DC, two plasters	m	High Museum of Art, Atlanta, Georgia Other versions: approx 20 replicas recorded, including several for British patrons		*Wunder* II, 1991, 131–4 (repr)

16.	1850–2	Mrs Walpole Smith	m	[coll Martin Tucker Smith, London]; untraced		*Wunder* II, 1991, 92
17.	1858	Two young sons of Dr Henry Cusack of Dublin	p	[for Dr Cusack]; untraced		*Wunder* II, 1991, 32
18.	1859	Charlotte, Countess Spencer Model(s): Toledo Museum of Art, Ohio, USA (destroyed after 1916)	m	Althorp, Northants		*Wunder* II, 1991, 94 (repr)
19.	1862	Eve disconsolate	m	Museum of Art, Rhode Island School of Design, Providence, USA Other versions: approx 30 replicas recorded, including several for British patrons		*Wunder* II, 1991, 136–9 (repr)
20.	1863	Ginevra Model(s): Smithsonian, Washington DC, two plasters	m	[coll Ignatius Sargent, Boston, Mass, USA]; untraced Other versions: approx 20 known replicas including several for British patrons		*Wunder* II, 1991, 155–7 (repr)
21.	1863	Sir John Murray Naesmyth	m	[coll Sir J M Naesmyth]; Chambers Institution, Peebles	SD	*Wunder* II, 1991, 74–5 (repr)
22.	1863	Thomas Henry Sutton Sotheron Estcourt	m	[coll T H S S Estcourt]; untraced Other versions: coll Borough of Devizes, Wilts, 1865 (?), marble		*Wunder* II, 1991, 38–9 (repr)
23.	1863–5	Ida Firth	m	[coll Ida Firth, Sheffield, W R Yorks]; untraced		*Wunder* II, 1991, 42
24.	1864–5	Miss Warburton	m	[coll Dean William Warburton, Elphin, Ireland]; untraced Other versions: replica commissioned by Dean Warburton as a gift for his nephew; untraced		*Wunder* II, 1991, 102–3
25.	1866	John Williamson	m	[coll John Williamson]; untraced		*Wunder* II, 1991, 108–9
26.	1866	William Murphy Jnr	m	[coll Mrs Margaret Murphy, Dublin]; untraced		*Wunder* II, 1991, 73–4
27.	1866–7	Faith Model(s): Smithsonian American Art Museum, Washington DC, USA	m	[coll Marshall Woods]; Chrysler Museum, Norfolk, Va, USA Other versions: approx 20 known replicas including several for British patrons		*Wunder* II, 1991, 144–6 (repr)
28.	1867–8	Mary L Martin	m	[coll George Martin, Queen's Gate, London]; untraced		*Wunder* II, 1991, 72–3
29.	1868	Walter Richard Cassels	m	[coll W R Cassels, English poet]; coll Ian Grant, London	S	*Wunder* II, 1991, 28–9 (repr)
30.	1868–9	Mrs Jones Payment(s): £200 (and £10 for column) Model(s): Smithsonian, Washington DC, USA	m	[for H L Jones, Pontefract, W R Yorks]; untraced		*Wunder* II, 1991, 58 (repr)
31.	1872	John Elder Payment(s): £200 Model(s): Smithsonian, Washington DC, USA	m	[coll Mrs John Elder]; Glasgow Art Gallery	S	*Wunder* II, 1991, 38 (repr)
Miscellaneous						
32.	1839	Loulie's hand Model(s): Smithsonian, Washington DC, USA		[coll Elizabeth Powers]; Mr and Mrs Julian Ganz, Los Angeles, Cal Other versions: approx 20 known replicas including several for British patrons		*Wunder* II, 1991, 185–7 (repr)

POWLEY, Harris fl 1776

An advertisement in the *Norwich Mercury* of 6 April 1776 stated that Harris Powley, stonemason of Wells-next-the-Sea, Norfolk made marble, Portland stone and freestone chimneypieces, monuments, tombs and gravestones.

POWLEY, John fl 1757

On 9 July 1757 the *Norwich Mercury* reported, 'We hear from Wells that last week was erected in the Parish Church of Narford in this County, a Monument to the Memory of Sir Andrew Fountaine, consisting of various colour'd Marble, with a swelling statuary Table and ornamented with the bust of Sir Andrew, upon the top of a Pyramid highly finished, is a statuary Urn, in a chased antique Manner. The whole polished and completed to entire Satisfaction, by John Powley, of Wells next the Sea' (1). The bust is after a terracotta by **L F Roubiliac** and may not be Powley's work.

Literary References: *Gunnis* 1968, 310

Funerary Monuments

1.	1757	Sir Andrew Fountaine (†1753)	Narford, Norfolk	S	Pevsner, *Norfolk: N W & S*, 1999, 553

POWNALL, John, of Liverpool fl 1813

Busts

1.	1813	Unidentified Lady	[Exhib Liverpool Ac, 297]; untraced	*Morris and Roberts* 1998, 498

POYNTELL, Thomas, of London fl 1790

He is listed in the *London Directory* of 1790 as chimneypiece maker of 71 High Holborn (GPC).

POYNTON, Edward, of Nottingham –1737

One of the most accomplished local sculptors working in the Nottinghamshire area in the earlier 18th century, he was apprenticed to **Richard Saunders** in 1699 and later worked with the Warwick architect, Francis Smith, at Chicheley Hall, Bucks, Sutton Scarsdale, Derbys and Badminton House, Glos. He carried out decorative carving in both wood and stone (3–8). At Sutton Scarsdale an inscription on a lead plaque recorded 'This house was begun to be rebuilt in the year 1724 by order of the Right Honourable Nicholas Earl of Scarsdale. Francis Smith of Warwick Gent. architect' and listed the craftsmen employed there, including 'Edd Poynton of Nottingham Gent. Carver' (BL Add MS 6674, fol 179, in *Colvin* 1995, 888). The house is now a ruin and the plaque has been lost. Poynton's surviving works at Badminton include the mahogany overdoors in the parlour which were once thought to be by **Grinling Gibbons** and an unusual panel carved with forty different botanical specimens set within a guilloche scroll pattern (8).

As a statuary Poynton signs the large monument to William Huntingdon, a ship's carpenter, which has a life-size effigy, reclining on one elbow and holding in his hand a sheet of paper bearing a drawing of a ship (1). The monument to Ann Parkyns has an arched inscription panel framed by Corinthian columns, with winged cherubs' heads and deaths' heads at the base and a small kneeling figure at the top (2). Lord suggests that Poynton was probably also responsible for the monument to her kinsman, Sir Thomas Parkyns, (†1715), in the same church. Parkyns was a keen wrestler and he is depicted in a wrestling posture, standing with his knees bent and his hands held out, ready to take on an adversary. This monument also features a relief of a prostrate Parkyns cut down by a figure of *Time* with a scythe, which is carved in a more naïve style than the standing figure and the architectural surround. It is possible that this amateur work was by Poynton's brother, Rev Thomas Poynton, who is thought to have been the vicar of Bunny, since there is an early reference to the monument being 'wrought out of a fine piece of marble by his [Parkyns'] chaplain in a barn' (*Thoroton* 1790, in *Lord* 1990 (1), 65).

Literary References: *Gunnis* 1968, 310; *Gomme* 1984, 167–9; *Beard* 1989 (1), 42; *Lord* 1990 (1), 64–69; *Colvin* 1995, 884, 888

Archival References: GPC

Will: Notts CRO (2 Nov 1737)

Funerary Monuments

1.	†1714	William Huntingdon		West Stockwith, Notts	S	*Lord* 1990 (1), 65–8 (repr)
2.	†1725	Ann Parkyns		Bunny, Notts	S	*Lord* 1990 (1), 65–8 (repr)

Architectural Sculpture

3.	*c*1724	Arts and Sciences	wd	Chicheley Hall, Bucks, blue drawing room		Pevsner, *Bucks*, 1994, 246
4.	*c*1724	Capitals and frieze of cornucopiae Payment(s): £53 4s		Chicheley Hall, Bucks, south front		Pevsner, *Bucks*, 1994, 246
5.	1724–5	Carving, including Leake coat of arms in the pediment and Corinthian capitals on the principal front		Sutton Scarsdale House, Derbys		*Gunnis* 1968, 310
6.	*c*1730	Pediment and doorcase		Badminton House, Glos, east front		*Gomme* 1984, 169 (repr 4b)
7.	*c*1732	A 'pannel with Mathematical Instruments in it', 'Fryze with Emblems of peace & plenty' and other woodwork Payment(s): £9, £7 10s, £5 5s		[Badminton House, Glos]; untraced		*Gomme* 1984, 168
8.	*c*1732	Ornaments, including Corinthian capitals and friezes in the hall, overdoors in the parlour and the 'great Pannel with foldage and flowers' in the library	wd	Badminton House, Glos		*Gomme* 1984, 168 (reprs 3a-b); *Beard* 1989, 42

POZZI, Francesco 1790–1844

He was an Italian sculptor and wax modeller. William, 6th Duke of Devonshire commissioned a group of *Leto and her children at Delos, turning the shepherds into frogs* from him in January 1823 (2). The Duke had seen the plaster model, which he thought 'very superior and original', during a visit to Rome (*K-Browne* 1972 (3), 328). However when the marble version arrived at Chatsworth he was disappointed and he commented that Leto had 'made her enemies besides the shepherds' (*ibid*). Pozzi signs a monument with a relief of a mother and child at Davenham (1).

Literary References: *Gunnis* 1968, 310; *K-Browne* 1972 (3), 326, 328, 330; *Pyke* 1973, 115; *Pyke* 1981, 33; *Panzetta* 1994, 184–5

Funerary Monuments

1.	1833	Anne Harper		Davenham, Cheshire	S	Pevsner, *Cheshire*, 1971, 196

Statues

2.	1824	Leto and her children at Delos turning the shepherds into frogs Payment(s): 1,760 scudi	m	Chatsworth, Derbys, sculpture gallery	SD	*Chatsworth Handlist*, 26; *JKB* 1972 (3), 326, 328, 330, 331 (repr)

Busts

3.	1832	Youthful Hercules		The Vyne, Hants	SD	*Gunnis* 1968, 310

PRACNER, Peter fl 1770

Reliefs

1.	1770	'Academy Figure-Basso Relievo'		[RA silver medal]; untraced		RA Premium list

PRATT, J, of Nottingham fl *c*1817

Funerary Monuments

1.	?1817	John Entwisle		Rempstone, Notts	S	*Gunnis* 1968, 310

PREECE, J, of London fl 1821–22

Preece, of Upper Mary-le-bone Street, London, won two awards from the Society of Arts in 1821 and 1822. Nothing more is known of him.

Literary References: RSA Transactions, 1821, 1822

Statues

1.	1821	Laocoon, plaster copy		[Soc of A, silver palette]; untraced		RSA *Transactions*, vol 39, 1821, xxxix

Miscellaneous

2.	1822	'Copy of a group', plaster		[Soc of A, silver Isis medal]; untraced		RSA *Transactions*, vol 40, 1822, xxxviii

PREECE, John, of Hereford fl 1799–1815

He became a freeman of Hereford in 1814 and signs a number of tablets in the county.

Literary References: *Gunnis* 1968, 310

Funerary Monuments

1.	1799	Tablets, unidentified subjects	St Michael, Bodenham, Herefs		Pevsner, *Herefs*, 1963, 77
2.	?1809	Evan Lloyd	Weobley, Hereford	S	*Gunnis* 1968, 310
3.	?1811	Nicholas Mason	Bodenham, Hereford	S	*Gunnis* 1968, 310
4.	?1812	Joseph Clarke	Walford, Hereford	S	*Gunnis* 1968, 310
5.	?1815	William Money	Much Marcle, Hereford	S	*Gunnis* 1968, 310

PRESTAGE fl 1754–61

In 1754 he was employed by the Duke of Chandos, at both Winchendon House, Bucks and Grosvenor Square, receiving £82 (Stowe Archives, in *Gunnis* 1968, 310). In 1761 Lord Rockingham paid him £63 for two marble centaurs (**1**).

Statues

1.	1761	Two centaurs Payment(s): £63	m	[coll Charles, 2nd Marquess of Rockingham]; untraced	Wentworth Woodhouse Archives, in *Gunnis* 1968, 310

PRICE, Edward fl 1683

Probably a Chester craftsman, he was the mason responsible for building Erddig Park, Denbighs. In 1683 he agreed to set all the 'dress stonework, such as coigns, cornice, plinth and cresting', also the doorcases with pediments to the entrances, doorways on both the hall and saloon sides, and 'the bases, topp stones, heads and capitalls of chimneys' (*Tipping* 1920, 184).

PRICE, John –1736

John Price was the builder and architect responsible for rebuilding St Mary-at-the-Walls in 1713–14, for which he was paid £1,134. He received a further payment of £3 10s for the new font in the church in June 1715 (**1**). The church was rebuilt by A W Blomfield in 1871–2, who retained only the tower and font. Price also designed Isleworth church, Middx (1705–7) and St George, Southwark (*c*1734). He worked in partnership with his son John Price junior, designing and building St George's chapel (1714–6), the town hall (*c*1715) and the assembly rooms (*c*1715; demolished) in Yarmouth. His secular designs included a remarkably early project for a terraced residential development at Headley, in Surrey, which was never completed. He was employed by the Duke of Chandos at Canons, Middx, in 1720–1, but his design for a London mansion for the Duke was never realised.

Literary References: *Rickword* 1942–45, 311–20; *Gunnis* 1968, 310; *Colvin* 1995, 779–80

Architectural Sculpture

1.	1715	Font	St Mary-at-the-Wall, Colchester, Essex	*Rickword* 1942–45, 319

PRICE, of Builth fl *c*1796

Funerary Monuments

1.	†1796	John Davies	Disserth, Radnor	S	Pevsner, *Powys*, 1979, 230

PRICE, R fl *c*1848

Funerary Monuments

1.	?1848	Harriet Cotterell	Wormley, Herefs	GPC

PRICE, Thomas, of Ruthyn fl 1727

Chimneypieces

1.	1727	Of Welsh marble	[Chirk Castle, Denbigh]; untraced	Chirk Castle Accounts, in *Gunnis* 1968, 311

PRICE, William, of Chepstow fl *c*1832

Funerary Monuments

1.	†1832	George Watkins	Alvington, Glos	S	Pevsner, *Glos: Vale & Forest of Dean*, 1976, 85

PRITCHARD, Thomas Farnolls 1723–77

Pritchard was an architect with a successful practice in Shrewsbury, who designed funerary monuments, chimneypieces and architectural ornaments. He was born in Shrewsbury and baptised at St Julian, Shrewsbury on 11 May 1723, the son of a joiner, John Pritchard, and his wife Hannah, née Farnolls. His own background was also as a joiner, but from the late 1740s he developed a quite extensive professional practice in Shropshire and the neighbouring counties. In 1748 he started work on rebuilding St Julian, Shrewsbury, and during the next three decades he worked on houses, public buildings and churches. He is remembered primarily as the designer of the first cast-iron bridge, which was constructed, with some modifications, by Abraham Darby, over the river Severn at Coalbrookdale in 1777–79.

An album of Pritchard's drawings for chimneypieces and architectural details in the Library of the American Institute of Architects in Washington DC (reproduced in full by *Ionides* 1999) shows that he was a competent designer of decorative features in various styles. Many of these designs are annotated with the names of the carvers who executed them, details of the hours they worked and payments disbursed. Three carvers, **John Nelson, Gaspar Van Der Hagen of Shrewsbury** and **Swift of Shrewsbury** were regularly employed to work from his designs, while **Danders** and **Halley** were used occasionally. It was quite common for two or three carvers to co-operate on a single commission. For example Pritchard employed Nelson for six and a half days, van der Hagen for eleven and half days and Danders for one day, carving a rococo chimneypiece for Miss Leighton's dressing room at Condover Hall, Salop. The high quality of surviving ornaments at houses such as Hatton Grange and Bitterley Court, both in Shropshire, attests to the skill of Pritchard's team of craftsmen.

As well as decorative features for houses, the album includes designs for two funerary monuments (**6, 7**). The architect signed eight other known monuments: the Lloyd (**2**) is in the manner of James Gibbs and the Acton is in the gothic style (**4**). Several feature coloured marbles combined with delicate rococo decorative details, and that to Sir Richard Lyster, a Shropshire landowner and an MP, also includes a pair of mourning putti flanking an urn (**7**).

The largest and most elaborate, commemorating Sir Whitmore Acton, is decorated with an eclectic mixture of classical, rococo and gothic motifs (4). Pritchard's annotated design for Richard Ward Offley's monument is a tablet with a broken scrolled pediment enclosing a coat of arms in a rococo cartouche, decorated with bell-flower swags and crossed palm-fronds (8). A note on the drawing indicates that it took Nelson, van der Hagen and Swift more than ten weeks in total to complete the work. The other monuments are less well documented, but it seems likely that they were also executed by Pritchard's usual carvers.

He died on 23 December 1777 and was buried at St Julian, Shrewsbury, where there is a tablet to his memory. His wife, Eleanor Russell, and three of their four children predeceased him.

For works designed by Pritchard see separate entries for John Nelson of Shrewsbury, Gaspar van der Hagen, Swift, Danders and Halley, all of Shrewsbury.

EH

Literary References: *Gunnis* 1968, 311; *Harris* 1968, 17–24; *Colvin* 1995, 782–4; *Ionides* 1999, *passim; ODNB* (Leach)

Will: PROB 11/1043

Collections of Drawings: book of four designs for a house for Mr Good, RIBA Drawings Coll SD64/3(1–4); designs for chimneypieces including two for Condover Hall, Salop and a neoclassical pier glass frame, Pritchard Drawing Book (*Ionides* 1999, repr)

Pritchard Drawing Book, Portraits of the Sculptor: anon, canvas, Ironbridge Gorge Museum 1978.218.1

Funerary Monuments

1.	†1756	Ann Wilkinson	Wrexham, Denbighs	S	*Ionides* 1999, 233 (repr)
2.	†1758	Rev John Lloyd	St Mary, Shrewsbury, Salop	S	*Ionides* 1999, 233 (repr)
3.	1759	Dr Samuel Sprott	Ludford, Salop	SD	*Colvin* 1995, 784; *Ionides* 1999, 234–5 (repr)
4.	1763	Sir Whitmore Acton (†1732)	Acton Round Church, Salop	SD	*Colvin* 1995, 784; *Ionides* 1999, 238–40 (repr)
5.	†1765	Mary Morhall and family	St Mary, Shrewsbury, Salop	S	*Ionides* 1999, 233–4 (repr)
6.	†1765	Sir Edward Blount Bt Drawing(s): Pritchard Drawing Bookk AIA 48	Mamble, Worcs (fragment only)	S	*Colvin* 1995, 784; *Ionides* 1999, 237–8, 339 (repr)
7.	†1766	Sir Richard Lyster Drawing(s): Pritchard Drawing Book AIA 82–4	Alderbury, Salop	S	*Colvin* 1995, 784; *Ionides* 1999, 240–3, 433–5 (repr)
8.	1769	Sir Richard Ward Offley	Pontesbury, Salop	S	*Colvin* 1995, 784
9.	†1770	Richard Corbet	Morton Corbet, Salop	S	*Gunnis* 1968, 311
10.	nd	Richard Hollings	Old St Chad, Shrewsbury, Salop	S	*Colvin* 1995, 784; *Ionides* 1999, 234 (repr)

Chimneypieces

11.	1765–1769	With flower entwined columns Drawing(s): Pritchard Drawing Book AIA 52	Loton Park, Salop	*Ionides* 1999, 333, 403 (repr)
12.	1765–1789	With foliage in the frieze Drawing(s): Pritchard Drawing Book, AIA 39	Brodely Hall, Salop, bed chamber	*Ionides* 1999, 171–2, 332, 390 (repr)

Architectural Sculpture

13.	1765–1769	Two overdoors in the form of vases of flowers Drawing(s): Pritachrd Drawing Book AIA 31	Croft Castle, Herefs, dining room	*Ionides* 1999, 335, 419 (repr)

PRIVETT, William, of Chilmark fl 1726–70

Privett was employed as a builder and stonemason at Longleat, Stourhead and Longford Castle, all in Wiltshire. He is first mentioned in a conveyance of 28 May 1726, which granted 'William Privett the Younger of Chilmark, freemason', and a yeoman, Edward Moody the assignment of 'Cowleaze' and a way through 'Whales Coppice' on the Longleat estate. On 23 August 1743 £30 was paid to 'Messrs Wm. & Robert Privet and Moore in part of their Bill of Stone & Stone Work done at Long Leat Ano. 1739'. Privett received a further payment of £20 18s on 29 June 1745 (Longleat HA 18, 24/03/1736; Longleat HA 150, 26/02/1740).

At Stourhead, he not only erected but also carved the stone details of many of the buildings in the garden and grounds (2). These included the grotto in 1740; the obelisk in 1748, for which he was paid £349; and the bridge a year later. In 1753 he built the *Temple of Hercules* and in 1755 the Palladian temple, at a cost of £300 and £226 respectively. He was also responsible for masonry work at Stourhead House (Hoare Archives, in *Gunnis* 1968, 311). Henry Hoare paid 'Mr Privet ye Mason' £28 8s 1d 'in full of all Demands' on 3 November 1746; £30 'on Accot of Buildings' on 30 March 1747; £70 for the obelisk on 18 June 1747 and a further £50 on account on 24 November 1748 (Hoare Private Accounts, 1734–49). Five further payments of £50 and, on one occasion, £40, for unspecified work are recorded in 1748 and 1750 (Hoare Partnership Ledger, 1742–1751, fols 221, 223, 313, 314).

In 1742 he made a balustrade 'on ye walk', an obelisk and a pedestal for Lord Folkestone, at Longford Castle (1). In 1743 he built the summer-house known as the flintery and, in 1757, he received £52 for 'ye logio' and £50 for piers. In 1769 he carved the four columns supporting the cupola under which was placed **Rysbrack**'s statue of *Fame* (3). Privett also received £100 for repairs to the church at Britford, Wilts, in 1767 (Longford Castle Archives, in *Gunnis* 1968, 311).

Literary References: *Gunnis* 1968, 311

Architectural Sculpture

1.	1742	'balustrade on ye walk', 'ye obelisk and ye pedestal'	Longford Castle, Wilts	Longford Castle Archives, in *Gunnis* 1968, 311
2.	1740–1755	Stone details	Stourhead, Wilts, buildings in garden and grounds	Hoare Archives, in *Gunnis* 1968, 311
3.	1769	Four columns	Longford Castle, Wilts, cupola	Longford Castle Archives, in *Gunnis* 1968, 311

PROCTOR, Thomas 1753–94

Proctor was a sculptor and history painter. He was born at Settle, W R Yorks, on 22 April 1753, and was first apprenticed to a tobacconist in Manchester. Before 1777 he went to London, where he took a job in the counting-house of the merchants Messrs Harrison and Ansley. He enrolled at the Royal Academy Schools on 30 September 1777. Three years later he exhibited a portrait of a gentleman at the Royal Academy giving his address as 'Of Settle, or 8, New Inn' (*Graves* VI, 1905–6, 210).

In 1782 he was awarded a premium from the Society of Arts and the year after, whilst living at 144, Strand, won a Royal Academy medal in the category comprising models of academy figures and bas-reliefs (4). In 1784 he won a gold medal for a history painting, a scene from *The Tempest*. Proctor also submitted a sketch of *Atalanta and Hippomenes*. According to J T Smith, he was an excellent draughtsman and very popular with his fellow students, who paraded him on their shoulders around the quadrangle of Somerset House to celebrate his victory.

In 1785 Proctor exhibited a model of *Ixion* which depicted the ancient king of Thessaly, bound naked to a flaming wheel (1). A note in Horace Walpole's papers says the work pleased the George III so much that it was decided that Proctor should be sent abroad on a travelling scholarship for three years, a proposal that was not implemented by the Academicians until 1793. The model was to be retained in the Academy and a 'gratuity paid to the artist for his labor' (*Anecdotes* 1937, 150). Walpole himself was impressed: he wrote to Horace Mann the Younger in May 1785 that Proctor was 'marvellous. He has gained the prizes in drawing, painting and sculpture; and now exhibits a model in terra-cotta of 'Ixion' less than life, which is a prodigy of anatomy, with all the freedom of nature' (HWC, 25, 577). The work was praised so highly by Benjamin West, the future president of the Royal Academy, that it was purchased by Sir Abraham Hume.

Encouraged by his success, Proctor spent twelve months working on a larger work, *Diomedes devoured by his horses* (2). This attracted much attention at the Royal Academy but failed to find a purchaser, though the sculptor asked only 50 guineas for it. It was too large to store and, bitterly disappointed, Proctor destroyed the group in a fit of despondency. In 1789, whilst living at 6 Cecil Street, he exhibited a painted portrait, and he continued to exhibit paintings every year until his death, including a portrait of Thomas Chippendale. In 1792 he exhibited another model, building on the fame of his earlier work: *Pirithous, son of Ixion, destroyed by Cerberus* depicted the King of the Lapithae helplessly attempting to extricate himself from the paws of Pluto's dog (3). This work too also acquired by Abraham Hume.

In October 1793 Proctor competed for the Royal Academy scholarship to Rome, which carried an allowance of £100 a year for three years, plus 30 guineas for travelling costs. In November the sculptor called on Joseph Farington to solicit his vote. Farington recorded that he had 'promised him my vote in consequence of the very ingenious models which he had at different times made, and sent to the exhibition' (*Farington* 1, 90). Proctor was also supported by James Barry, Henry Fuseli, **Thomas Banks** and **Joseph Wilton**. He received 19 votes in the December ballot, 15 more than his nearest rival, Henry Howard.

On 3 June 1794 Farington reported that Proctor was due to leave England for Rome the following week. This was not to be: a little over a month later he died in London. Farington recorded on 22 July that 'Poor Proctor is supposed to have been overcome by anxiety of mind on acct. of his circumstances being deranged – so Rossi told Smirke – I afterwards learnt that he had broke a blood vessel in the night, and only lived a few hours' (*Farington* 1, 218, 22 July). Later accounts of the story add more detail: Proctor is said to have fallen into a deep depression at the prospect of being unable to pay a small bill. Benjamin West managed to find the impoverished sculptor, who exhibited at the RA without giving an address, at humble lodgings in Cider-cellar, Maiden Lane, Covent Garden. Despite feeding him, and promising letters of introduction to friends in Rome, West failed to revive Proctor's spirits. He was buried in Hampstead church-yard on 13 July 1794.

JT Smith left a graphic physical description of Proctor: he was 'short in stature, remarkably well-proportioned, and firmly built. His hair and whiskers were of a jet black, the latter of which he suffered to grow with a preposterous projection from his cheeks. His skin was swarthy, but his black eyes were piercingly energetic, particularly when a grand idea had struck his mind, which was well-stored with classical reading. He then instantly grappled with his clay; upon which he was sure to leave vigorous marks of superior genius' (*Smith* 1828, 2, 130).

Proctor's contemporaries had enduring memories of the quality of his work. West mentioned Proctor's *Ixion* in his annual *Discourse*, delivered in December 1794. **Sir Richard Westmacott RA**, when professor of sculpture at the Royal Academy, borrowed the *Ixion* and the *Pirithous* from Hume and told his students in a lecture that they were works 'of true genius and worthy of their deepest attention' (*Smith* 1828, 2, 132). Farington and his guests were still discussing Proctor's merits at a dinner party in March 1808. The *New Monthly Magazine* opined that although unremarkable as a painter, 'Proctor as a sculptor will ever be classed among the first, if not regarded as the very first, that ever appeared in this country. His *Ixion* is justly considered the finest piece of work ever produced by a Briton' (*New Monthly Mag*, 1816, 6, 423).

MGS

Literary References: *Farington*, 1, *passim*; IX, 3235; *Smith* 1828, *passim; Graves*, VI, 1905–6, 210; *ODNB* (Desmarais)

Statues

No.	Date	Title	Material	Location	References
1.	1785	Ixion	tc	[Exhib RA, London, 640, acquired by Sir Abraham Hume of Wormleybury, Herts]; untraced	*Hamilton* 1839, 3, 162 (repr); *Gunnis* 1968, 311; *HWC*, 25, 577
2.	1786	Diomedes devoured by his horses Payment(s): asking price 50 gns		[Exhib RA, London, 614]; destroyed	*Graves* VI, 1905–6, 210; *Gunnis* 1968, 311
3.	1792	Pirithous, son of Ixion, destroyed by Cerberus	p	[Exhib RA, London, 393, acquired by Sir Abraham Hume of Wormleybury, Herts]; untraced	*Hamilton* 1839, 3, 204 (repr); *Graves* VI, 1905–6, 210; *Gunnis* 1968, 312; *ODNB*

Miscellaneous

No.	Date	Title	Material	Location	References
4.	1783	Model of an academy figure or bas-relief		[RA Silver Medal]; untraced	RA Premium list

PROSPERI, Christopher fl 1800–16

Prosperi was in Italy in 1800 when he carved a bust of Sir George Throckmorton after a model by **Christopher Hewetson** (5). He exhibited at the Royal Academy, 1810–16, from a number of London addresses: 5 Edward Street,

Cavendish Square; 76 Portland Road and 76 Norton Street, Portland Road. He was an unsuccessful candidate for associate membership of the RA in 1811 and 1814. Gunnis comments that his bust of the Duke of Sussex at Woburn Abbey (11) is 'a very fine work'.

Literary References: *Farington*, vol 11, 4025; *Gunnis* 1968, 312; *Ingamells*, 2007, appendix II

Archival References: GPC

Funerary Monuments

1.	?1812	Edward Grant		Lichborough, Northants	S	*Gunnis* 1968, 312
2.	†1814	Captain Sir Peter Parker		St Margaret, Westminster, London	S	Pevsner, *London: Westminster*, 1973, 495

Statues

3.	c1812	Bacchus and Ariadne		[coll Arthur, 1st Duke of Wellington]; Stratfield Saye, Hants		*Gunnis* 1968, 312
4.	c1812	Venus and Cupid		[coll Arthur, 1st Duke of Wellington]; Stratfield Saye, Hants		*Gunnis* 1968, 312

Busts

5.	1800	Sir John Throckmorton (after a model by C Hewetson)	m	Coughton Court, Warks		*De Breffny* 1986, 59
6.	1810	J Symmons		[Exhib RA, London, 867]; untraced		*Graves* VI, 1905–6, 211
7.	1810	Lord Downe		[Exhib RA, London, 887]; untraced		*Graves* VI, 1905–6, 211
8.	1810	Mr Vestris		[Exhib RA, London, 868]; untraced		*Graves* VI, 1905–6, 211
9.	1810	V Pucitta		[Exhib RA, London, 768]; untraced		*Graves* VI, 1905–6, 211
10.	1810	William Pitt		Untraced		*Memorie Enciclopediche*, 1810, in RG/JP, 6, 1134
11.	1811	Augustus Frederick, Duke of Sussex	m	Woburn Abbey, Beds	SD	*Graves* VI, 1905–6, 211; *British Portraits* 1956–7, 161
12.	1811	Henry Hope		[Exhib RA, London, 937]; untraced		*Graves* VI, 1905–6, 211
13.	?1811	Horatia Nelson	m	NMM Greenwich, SCU0107		*Graves* VI, 1905–6, 211
14.	1811	Mr Bruce		[Exhib RA, London, 911]; untraced		*Graves* VI, 1905–6, 211
15.	1811	Unidentified gentleman		[Exhib RA, London, 923]; untraced		*Graves* VI, 1905–6, 211
16.	1812	Mrs Morse	m	[Exhib RA, London, 899]; untraced		*Graves* VI, 1905–6, 211
17.	1811–1812	Noel Desenfans	m	Dulwich Picture Gallery, London, mausoleum	S	*Ingamells* 2007, appendix II
18.	1811–1812	Sir Francis Bourgeois	m	Dulwich Picture Gallery, London, mausolem	S	*Ingamells* 2007, appendix II
19.	1813	Princess Pietrapersia of Naples		[Exhib RA, London, 921]; untraced		*Graves* VI, 1905–6, 211
20.	1813	William Shakespeare		[Exhib RA, London, 923]; untraced		*Graves* VI, 1905–6, 211
21.	1814	Diana		[Exhib RA, London, 777]; untraced		*Graves* VI, 1905–6, 211
22.	1814	George, Marquess of Blandford		[Exhib RA, London, 767]; untraced		*Graves* VI, 1905–6, 211
23.	1814	P Watkins		[Exhib RA, London, 799]; untraced		*Graves* VI, 1905–6, 211
24.	1814	Rev R Harington		[Exhib RA, London, 776]; untraced		*Graves* VI, 1905–6, 211
25.	1814	Rev T Watkins		[Exhib RA, London, 775]; untraced		*Graves* VI, 1905–6, 211
26.	1815	General Moreau		[Exhib RA, London, 873]; untraced		*Graves* VI, 1905–6, 211
27.	1816	J Forbes		[Exhib RA, London, 942]; untraced		*Graves* VI, 1905–6, 211
28.	nd	Frederick-Augustus, Duke of York and Albany		[Holland House, London]; untraced		*Gunnis* 1968, 312

Miscellaneous

29.	1813	Achilles lamenting the death of Patroclus		[Exhib RA, London, 906]; untraced		*Graves* VI, 1905–6, 211

PROST, V, of Dijon fl *c*1680–90

His original signed drawings for the trophies of armour on the main gates of Petworth House, Sussex, are in the Wyndham archives at Petworth. Gunnis comments that these 'superb baroque trophies' consisting of 'great cuirasses and plumed helm' are 'of their kind are almost without equal in England'. The house was built *c*1680–90 and the trophies are probably contemporary.

Literary References: *Gunnis* 1968, 312

Architectural Sculpture

1.	1680–1690	Trophies of armour, cuirasses and plumed helms Drawing(s): Wyndham Archives		Petworth House, Sussex, main gates		*Gunnis* 1968, 312

PUCKRIDGE fl 1666

Statues

1.	1666	The golden boy at Pye Corner		[The 'Fortune of War' public house, Giltspur St, façade]; Junction of Giltspur St and Cock Lane, City of London	S	C Lib (repr)

PUGH, W, of Bristol fl *c*1829–32

His monument to Elizabeth Calley is an accurate copy of the monument by **John Flaxman RA** to Agnes Cromwell (1798–1800) in Chichester Cathedral, Sussex (2). It has a relief of a draped female figure being borne heavenwards by three angels.

Funerary Monuments

1.	†1829	Rev John Price		Worle, Somerset	S	GPC
2.	†1832	Elizabeth Calley		Chiseldon, Wilts		*Penny* 1977 (1), 215 n52

PUJOLAS, Henry fl 1763

Mortimer's *Director* of 1763 lists him as a carver of Margaret-Street, Cavendish Square (p 23).

PULFORD, William fl *c*1836

The son of William Pulford, a mason, he is known only for one tablet in coloured marbles.

Literary References: *Gunnis* 1968, 312

Funerary Monuments

1.	?1836	William Kemp		Belton, Rutland	S	*Gunnis* 1968, 312

PULHAM, James I and II

Pulham, James I (1788–1838)
Pulham, James II (1820–1898)

James Pulham I was the eldest of ten children born in poverty at Woodbridge, Suffolk. With no formal education as a child, he and his younger brother, Obadiah, were apprenticed to John and William Lockwood, the owners of a successful building firm in Woodbridge. Pulham's ability to model in pipe clay was quickly recognised by the Lockwoods, and his models were soon being used as to make moulds for casting interior ornaments in plaster and exterior decorative details in concrete, terracotta and artificial stone. This latter material was to become a speciality of the firm, and was suitable not only for creating landscape features such as boulders, rockeries and water-pools, but also garden sculpture, particularly when a weathered appearance was desired.

Pulham was clearly a favourite with the Lockwoods, and soon rose to be foreman with responsibility for the 30 or so workers employed by the firm. In 1814, John Lockwood had built a house and garden in Woodbridge to show off the company's wares, and in this he made extensive use of Pulham's abilities as a modeller, employing him to produce a range of grotto figures of Greek gods and goddesses, allegorical statues and sculptures of exotic animals, as well as architectural ornaments for the house (1, 5).

The success of the Lockwood firm in Woodbridge caused them to establish a second yard in 1819 at 22 Elder Street, Spitalfields, London and the Pulham brothers moved to the city, where Pulham was given responsibility for producing a range of chimneypots, garden vases, fountains, animal figures and armorial insignia. Many of these appear to have been made of artificial stone, which the firm marketed increasingly under the name 'portland stone cement' (not to be confused with portland cement) and 'pulhamite', though the material had in reality been an invention of John Lockwood. Although the firm had by the mid-1820s expanded sufficiently to establish an additional sale room at Tottenham, Middx, in 1827 it split into two separate companies, with the Lockwoods retaining the Woodbridge business and Pulham taking ownership of the London operation. Pulham ran this successfully until his death at the age of 49 in 1838. It was then taken over by his eldest son, **James Pulham II**, and was renamed Pulham and Son. It soon relocated at Hoddesden, Herts. The reason for this move is not known, but in Hertfordshire the younger Pulham continued to produce architectural and garden sculpture using pulhamite. After his death in 1898 the firm still produced garden sculpture and landscape features until its closure during the Second World War.

Michael Paraskos

Literary References: *Burgess* 1960, 639; *Gunnis* 1968; *Festing* 1984, 138, 139; *Festing* 1988, 90; *Curl* 2001, 185, 225, 283

Statues				
1.	c1814	Rhinoceros, crocodile, boa constrictor and porcupine; Greek gods and goddesses; 'Old Time' (by James Pulham I)	[The Little Castle, Woodbridge, Suffolk]; untraced	*Gunnis* 1968, 312; *Festing* 1984, 138
2.	1825	Adam and Eve (by James Pulham I)	Untraced	*Gunnis* 1968, 312
3.	1825	Romeo and Juliet (by James Pulham I)	Private coll	*Gunnis* 1968, 312
Busts				
4.	1827	Alfred the Great, William Penn, John Milton and William Shakespeare (by James Pulham I)	Untraced	*Festing* 1984, 139
Architectural Sculpture				
5.	1806	Ornaments including two statues on the roof and works for the grotto (by James Pulham I)	The Castle, Woodbridge, Suffolk	Pevsner, *Suffolk*, 1974, 500
6.	1842	Neptune fountain (by James Pulham II)	[Hoddesdon Hall, Herts]; untraced	*Gardeners' Chronicle*, Sept 1842; *Festing* 1988, 90
7.	nd	Keystone heads in Roman cement	New Street, Woodbridge, Suffolk	*Burgess* 1960, 639 (repr)
Reliefs				
8.	nd	Christ and the woman of Samaria	Doric Place(?), Woodbridge, Suffolk Other versions: unidentified headstone, Wrentham, Suffolk	*Burgess* 1960, 639
Miscellaneous				
9.	nd	Inn sign	[The Black Bull, 122 Holborn, London]; untraced	*Gunnis* 1968, 312

PYCOCK, George, of Hull fl c1787–88

Funerary Monuments				
1.	†1787	Thomas Pitts	Bridlington Priory, E R Yorks	GPC; Pevsner, *Yorks: E R & York*, 1995, 346
2.	†1788	John Taylor	Bridlington Priory, E R Yorks	GPC; Pevsner, *Yorks: E R & York*, 1995, 346

QUELLIN, Arnold 1653–86

Artus Quellin was known as Arnold only whilst in England. His career in this country spanned eight years, during which he worked both independently and in partnership with **Grinling Gibbons**. Quellin is now known to have had a major hand in the commissions in stone executed by Gibbons in the years 1681–83 and 1686.

He was baptised in Antwerp on 13 September 1653, the first of eight children of Artus Quellin II (1625–1700), a distinguished Antwerp sculptor, and Anna Maria, née Gabron. He was the great-nephew of Artus Quellin I (1609–68), the classicising sculptor responsible for much work at Amsterdam Town Hall. Quellin trained in his father's workshop, which specialised in church furnishings in stone, marble and oak carved in a decorative baroque style, which were sent out to religious institutions throughout the Spanish Netherlands and also to Denmark. His younger brother **Thomas Quellin** also became a sculptor and worked briefly in England before settling in Copenhagen. Arnold, who was described by George Vertue as 'A tall well shaped man [who] wore his own hair' (*Vertue* III, 35) married Frances, the daughter of Jan Siberechts of Antwerp, the topographical painter, who was in England some time after 1672 and may have encouraged Quellin to join him.

The first record of Quellin's presence in England appears in a licence granted on 16 November 1678 to the stone-carver **John Vanderstaine**, who was permitted to work under Hugh May, the architect at Windsor Castle, and 'to remaine here wth out molestation together with **John Oastes [John Nost I]** and Arnold Luellan [Quellin] his servants' (PRO Domestic Entry Book, Car II, vol LI, 77, quoted in *Gunnis* 1968, 407). A few months later, on 21 May 1679, the privy council issued another permit granting certain painters and other craftsmen employed at Windsor Castle the right to move freely in London and Westminster. These included **Laurens Vandermeulen, Anthony Verhuke** and Quellin, all described as 'servants' of Grinling Gibbons. Gibbons's commission at Windsor included an equestrian statue of Charles II on a marble pedestal. Quellin is likely to have carved the relief panels for the pedestal, to designs by Gibbons. The complex composition of martial trophies, musical instruments, crustacea and fruit is carved with a delicacy associated with fruitwood carving, yet here finely realised in a much less tractable material. Gibbons charged £400 for the four panels in 1680 and included charges for a sundial pedestal, probably also Quellin's work, in the same invoice.

In about 1679 Gibbons accepted his first commission for a church monument and several others followed in 1680. There was a perennial demand for memorials and Gibbons evidently decided to broaden his practice by including work in this field, though it required knowledge of carving materials of which he had limited experience. He turned to Quellin and in 1681 he and Quellin entered a partnership 'for the undertaking & p'forming of all sort of Carvers works in Stone, joyntly to be undertaken between them' (Chancery document, Gibbons-Quellin partnership, 25 Oct 1683, PRO C9/415/250; quoted by *Beard* 1989 (1), 52–3). The two partners were to take equal responsibility for meeting the costs of marbles and stone and to share equally in any losses they might incur. Each would have 7/- a day while either or both of them were working on a contract.

Their most innovative collaborative monument, at Tamworth, Staffs, *c*1681, commemorates John Ferrers and his son, Sir Humphrey, who had drowned in 1678 (**1**). The precise role played by each sculptor in the commission is unclear, but Beard's suggestion that it was designed by Gibbons, and largely or entirely executed by Quellin, carries conviction. The life-sized effigies crouching at either side of the inscription tablet are tense, twisting figures with characterful faces, framed by sumptuous wigs. Above them is a gadrooned sarcophagus, draped with garlands held by cherubs.

The contract for a monument to Archbishop Richard Sterne in York Minster followed about two years later (**8**). The effigy reclines in a framed recess with looped curtains, his head on one hand. There was a 17th-century precedent for the anachronistic composition in York Minster, the monument to Archbishop Hutton. The deep folds of Sterne's gown and the band of lace across his chest are delicately rendered and point to Quellin's hand.

Quellin also took on independent commissions in the early 1680s, for Vertue writes that he 'made several great & valuable workes. besides Esqr. Thinns Monument Westminster' (*Vertue* IV, 35). The monument to Thomas Thynne (**4**), another *tour-de-force*, was celebrated in early Westminster Abbey guide books, both for its sensational narrative content and for its crisp execution. Thynne's semi-draped reclining figure is posed above a pedestal carved with a relief scene of his murder in the London thoroughfare of Pall Mall. A cherub at Thynne's feet points up to an inscribed reference to the event on a richly draped tablet behind the effigy. James Ralph, a prominent Opposition journalist usually given to acerbic comments, praised the 'languid dying posture' of the effigy, 'the inimitable boy at his feet', and 'the execution . . .equal to the design' (*Ralph* 1734, 74–5). The monument evidently pleased the Thynne family for a letter from Quellin to Lord Weymouth and an account book entry in the Thynne archives, both dated October 1685, refer to a later monument for a family member (**9**). It is possible that the sculptor also provided parapet statues of Boadicea, Alexander the Great, Queen Zenobia and King Henry V for the south front of Longleat.

Gibbons ended his partnership with Quellin acrimoniously in May 1683, and on 25 October he laid his case before the court of chancery, claiming that Quellin had failed to abide by his contractual obligations. A sum of £250 had been owing to the partners since December 1682 and Gibbons maintained that Quellin had collected 'several great sumes' of that debt but failed to pass on Gibbons's share. Furthermore Gibbons had recently been obliged to lay out £220 on marbles, stone and other essentials and Quellin had advanced very little of his agreed half share. Quellin had also proved unreliable in his work, 'neglecting the p'formance & fineshing' of contracts. (PRO C9/415/250: *Beard* 1989 (1), 52–3). The case seems not to have proceeded but the two sculptors went their separate ways.

Quellin's reputation cannot have been much harmed for he continued to find work without apparent difficulty in the City of London, where there was a considerable demand for statues on new buildings springing up after the Great Fire. His first City associations date from 1682, when he carved a marble statue of Sir John Cutler (**10**), a generous benefactor and several times master of the Grocers' Company, for the parlour of their hall. Cutler's livery company robes, lined in fur and worn over a deep lace collar and buttoned doublet, gave Quellin the opportunity to show his virtuoso skills. A second philanthropic gesture on Cutler's part, the gift of an anatomical theatre for the new College of Physicians, led the College to order commemorative statues in Portland stone of Cutler and the king from Quellin for niches on the external front of the Theatrum Cutlerianum (**11, 12**). Cutler is again depicted with assurance in his company robes. The companion statue of Charles II is a less convincing portrait: the king wears a full wig, Roman cuirass and medieval breeches and has an unconvincing *contrapposto* pose.

One of the most extensive City projects involving sculptors in the 1680s was the new Royal Exchange. In 1683–84, shortly after severing his partnership with Quellin, Gibbons provided a stone statue of Charles II, sponsored by the Merchant Adventurers, for the centre of the piazza. Contemporary commentators voiced no doubt over its authorship, but Vertue, writing 50 years later, alleged that this royal statue was 'actually the worke of Quelline' (*Vertue* IV, 52–53). The statue has been destroyed and no documentation survives but its date makes Quellin's involvement unlikely. A mayoral precept issued on 11 November 1684 urged the City livery companies each to sponsor a statue for the line of kings, to be sited in niches at first floor level in the piazza of the Exchange. The kings were to be represented 'in proper habits' and to be as close as possible in design to their predecessors on the first Exchange, destroyed in 1666 (CLRO, Court of Alderman, Repertory 90, fol 15b). Despite the stricture, London's leading sculptors **John Bushnell, Caius Gabriel Cibber, Edward Pearce**, Gibbons and Quellin were all prepared to be involved in the project. Quellin won the largest number of contracts, providing six of the first 14 in the space of two years

(**13–18**). The Tallow-Chandlers considered commissioning from Pearce, Bushnell and Cibber, before fixing on Quellin for the statue of Henry VII (**14**) and the statue of Edward IV (**13**), the Ironmongers' gift, was subcontracted to Quellin by **Thomas Cartwright I**, the contracting mason for the Exchange. The Grocers' Company, with whom Quellin already had associations, turned to him for their image of Charles II in garter robes (**16**). The terracotta model for this statue survives in the Soane Museum and is considered 'one of the best [portraits] . . .of the King's last years' (*Gibson* 1997 (2), 161).

In December 1685 Quellin signed a contract which shows his workshop was also making lead figures. The Earl of Strathmore ordered four statues of Stuart monarchs for Glamis Castle, cast in 'hardened' lead and painted to resemble 'brass' (**19**). The precise garb and height of each was clearly specified. The revealing part of the contract follows. Strathmore also required a portrait bust of himself, 'in Clay to the Life', which was to be cast in lead (**22**). Its dimensions were to be similar to those of a marble statue of Charles II, then in Quellin's house. This mention of a clay model for the bust makes it clear that it was a bespoke item, but since there is no reference to models for the statues, they were probably stock figures for which Quellin already had moulds. Vertue notes that John Nost I was Quellin's foreman and since Nost was to become a leading purveyor of lead figures after Quellin's death, the inference is that garden figures were in production and Nost was either superintending their manufacture and/or learning casting techniques. Lead figure making had the potential to be a lucrative sideline for Quellin: he was able to charge £160 for the Glamis contract, but only earned between £38 and £57 for his time-consuming work on each of the stone Exchange figures. Some time between 1683 and his death three years later, Quellin moved from a house in the parish of St Martin-in-the-Fields to an 'old great house in Tower Street <parish of St. Giles's> near (where is now) the Seaven dyals' (*Vertue* IV, 35). The business in lead multiples may well have provided the means to this improved standard of living.

Quellin and Gibbons came together briefly in 1686 for Quellin's most demanding commission, the altarpiece for the Roman Catholic chapel ordered by James II for the Palace of Whitehall (**23**). Wren provided the design for a large architectural edifice of several stages framing a painting by Benedetto Gennari. On the upper cornice was a central glory, flanked by four life-sized biblical figures, a pair of cherubs and two life-sized angels. The contract, signed by Gibbons and Quellin, allowed only five and a half months for the work, but it made allowance for 50 or so marblers, sculptors, sawyers, polishers and labourers working under the partners' control (PRO Works 5/145, fols 184–5). Quellin must have had a major hand in the figures on the upper cornice, particularly the graceful kneeling angels, who twist inwards, looking down towards the altar. The work survived the Whitehall fire of 1694, but was dismantled a year later. The elements were eventually dispersed.

Quellin fell ill before the altarpiece was complete. He made his will on 3 September 1686, but was already so weak that he signed the document with a mark. He left all his leases, goods and chattels, including several figures to his wife, Frances, who carried on the business and acknowledged the final payment for the Glamis commission. She married Quellin's foreman, John Nost I, and after his death in 1710, went into business with a cousin, Mary Macadam (or Maradam), to whom she left her share of the stock-in-trade. Frances was then in a position to leave bequests totalling over £2,000 to her relatives. Her marble goods and figures housed by her second husband's cousin, **John Nost II**, were left to him.

Quellin was a fluent and inventive stone-carver, he had City patrons and he was exploring the new market for lead figures at the time of his death. The success of his workshop must have seemed assured.

IR

Literary References: *Vertue* IV, 35; *Esdaile and Toynbee* 1958, 34–43; *Gunnis* 1968, 313; *Apted* 1984, 53–8 (repr); *Whinney* 1988, 118–29; *Beard* 1989 (1), *passim*, but esp 51–64, 197; *Grove* 25, 1996, 813 (Kockelbergh); *Gibson* 1997 (2), 154–6, 157, 160, 161, 164, 172; *Esterly* 1998, 45–6, 176, 209, *Bénezit* II, 243

Additional MS Sources: Letter from Quellin to 1st Viscount Weymouth refering to a monument at Longbridge Deverill, Wilts, 8 October 1685, Thynne Papers, XXII, fol 247, (quoted by *Gunnis* 1968, 313 and *Beard* 1989 (1), 58); payment for a monument at Longbridge Deverill, Thynne Papers, Account Book 176, 78, 28 October 1685 (quoted by *Beard* 1989 (1), 58)

Wills: Arnold Quellin, PROB 11/384 fol 332; Frances Nost, proved December 1716, PROB 11/555, fols 195v–196v

Funerary Monuments

1.	c1681	John (†1680) and Sir Humphrey (†1678) Ferrers (co-sculptor: Grinling Gibbons)	Tamworth, Staffs	*Beard* 1989 (1), 56–7, 195, 187 (reprs 68–70)
2.	1681	Robert Southwell (†1677) and his wife Helena (†1679) (co-sculptor: Grinling Gibbons)	St Multose, Kinsale, County Cork	*Loeber* 1983, 84–101 (repr 7); *Beard* 1989 (1), 55 (repr 75)
3.	1681–1682	Dame Catherine Perceval (née Southwell) (†1679) (co-sculptor: Grinling Gibbons)	St Multose, Kinsale, County Cork	*Loeber* 1983, 85, 86 (repr 4); *Beard* 1989 (1), 54–5
4.	†1682	Thomas Thynne	Westminster Abbey, London, south choir aisle	*Vertue* IV, 35; *Dart* 2, 1723, 84–5, 88 (repr); *Gunnis* 1968, 303; *Whinney* 1988, 119, 443 n36; *Beard* 1989, (1) 95 (repr 72)
5.	1683	Sir Philip Perceval, 2nd Bt (†1680)	[Burton, County Cork]; destroyed	*Loeber* 1983, 85 (repr 6); *Beard* 1989 (1), 54–5
6.	1683	Sir Richard Browne (co-sculptor: Grinling Gibbons)	[St Nicholas, Deptford, London]; destroyed	*Gunnis* 1968, 168; *Beard* 1989 (1), 57, 209
7.	1683–1684	German (†1683) and Anne (†1700) Pole (co-sculptor: Grinling Gibbons) Payment(s): £300	Radbourne, Derbys	*Whinney* 1988, 129; *Beard* 1989 (1), 57–9, 69, 106 (repr 76–8); GPC
8.	1683–1684	Richard Sterne, Archbishop of York (†1683) (co-sculptor: Grinling Gibbons)	York Minster, rested north choir aisle, 1949	*Douglas Stewart* 1976, 508–9; *Beard* 1989 (1), 59 (repr 79–80)
9.	1685	Sir John Thynne (†1580)	Longbridge Deverill, Wilts	*Gunnis* 1968, 313 (mis-identified as the Duchess of Somerset); *Beard* 1989 (1), 58

Statues

10.	1682	Sir John Cutler Bt Payment(s): £83	m	Grocers' Hall, City of London, vestibule	*Esdaile and Toynbee* 1958, 35–9 (repr); *Green* 1964 (1), 140–1; *Whinney* 1988, 119, 443 n35; *Beard* 1989 (1), 195
11.	1683	King Charles II Payment(s): £80 16s with statue of Cutler Model(s): SJSM, clay	s	[R C Physic, Warwick Lane, over main portal on façade]; CL Coll, Guildhall, City of London, art library, acc 1087	*Knight* 1986, 344 (repr); *Beard* 1989 (1), 60 (pl 82); *Gibson* 1997 (1), 187–8, 371
12.	1683	Sir John Cutler Bt Payment(s): £80 16s with statue of King Charles II	s	[R C Physic, Warwick Lane, London, façade]; CL Coll, Guildhall, London, acc 1088	*Whinney* 1988, 119, 443 n35; *Knight* 1986, 344 (repr)
13.	1685	King Edward IV Payment(s): £50 Model(s): one only, Ironmongers' Hall, City of London	s	[Royal Exchange, London, line of kings on the façade of the piazza]; destroyed	*Esdaile and Toynbee* 1958, 40–2; *Gibson* 1997 (2), 159, 161, 172 (colour repr IVc)
14.	1685	King Henry VII Payment(s): £57 3s	s	[Royal Exchange, London, line of kings on the façade of the piazza]; untraced	*Esdaile and Toynbee* 1958, 39; *Gibson* 1997 (2), 160, 162, 170, 172 (repr)
15.	1685	King Henry VIII Payment(s): £49 12s 6d	s	[Royal Exchange, London, line of kings on the façade of the piazza]; untraced	*Gibson* 1997 (2), 161–5, 170, 172 (repr)
16.	1685–1686	King Charles II Payment(s): £60 Model(s): SJSM MP 211, clay; bust, VAM, A.7-1945, clay	s	[Royal Exchange, London, line of kings on the façade of the piazza]; destroyed	*Whinney* 1988, 121 (repr); *Thornton and Dorey* 1992, 55 (repr); *Gibson* 1997, 159–60, 163, 170, 172 (repr); *Bilbey* 2002, 9–10 (repr)
17.	1685–1686	King Edward V Payment(s): £38	s	[Royal Exchange, London, line of kings on the façade of the piazza]; untraced	*Esdaile and Toynbee* 1957, 42; *Gibson* 1997 (2), 160, 172
18.	1686	King Henry VI Payment(s): £50	s	[Royal Exchange, London, line of kings on the façade of the piazza]; destroyed	*Gibson* 1997 (2), 167, 185, 172
19.	1685–1686	King James VI and I in 'Royall Robes'; King Charles I in complete armour; King Charles II and King James II 'in the Roman habitt', all on Portland stone pedestals	l	[Glamis Castle, Angus, principal front]; James I and Charles I extant at Glamis, gardens	Contract, Glamis Charter Room, Box 61, bundle 6 (*Apted* 1984, app. 1); *Apted* 1984, 53–61 (repr); *Pearson* 1991, unpag, 34 (repr)
20.	nd	'King James big as the life, in stone of Mr Quellin £6'	s	[Nost sale (1), 1712]; untraced	*O'Connell* 1987, 806; *Whinney* 1988, 443 n43
21.	nd	'Neptune in stone, large life, of Mr Quellin £5'	s	[Nost sale (1), 1712, lot 109]; untraced	*Whinney* 1988, 443 n43

Busts

22.	1685–1686	Patrick, 1st Earl of Strathmore and Kinghorne 'in Clay to the Life', then cast in lead		Glamis Castle, Angus, in circular recess over front entrance	Contract, Glamis Charter Room, Box 61, bundle 6; *Apted* 1984, 53–61 (repr); *Whinney* 1988, 443 n43

Architectural Sculpture

23.	1686	High altarpiece, with a glory flanked by statues of St Peter, St Paul and two others, two or more angels, a pair of cherubs; relief panels (designed by Sir Christopher Wren) (co-sculptor: Grinling Gibbons) Payment(s): £1,875 2s	m	[Whitehall Palace, London, Roman Catholic Chapel, dismantled 1695]; Canons' garden, Westminster (statues); Burnham, Somerset (angels and relief panels); dean's yard, Westminster and VAM (reliefs)	*Vivian-Neal* 1935, 127–32; *Green* 1964 (1), 164–6; *Gunnis* 1968, 313; *Colvin* 1973–76, V, 290–93 (plan repr); *Whinney* 1988, 121–3, 443 n (repr); *Bilbey* 2002, 10–11

QUELLIN, Thomas 1661–1709

One of the great Antwerp dynasty of 17th century sculptors, he was the son and pupil of Artus Quellin the Younger (1625–1700), who had a thriving practice in Copenhagen, and Anna Maria, née Gabron. There were seven other children, one of whom, **Arnold Quellin**, spent the latter part of his life working in London. After completing his apprenticeship, Thomas joined Arnold in London, where he married Anna Maria Cocques and remained until at least January 1688. On 19 July 1689 he was paid £20 for a 'horse statue of wood by him carv'd and delivered into his Majesty's Stores of Armoury. As also a statue of wood wheron a face is carved' (**1, 2**). This was the work of **Grinling Gibbons**, assisted by Quellin.

By mid-1689 he was in Copenhagen, where he oversaw the numerous commissions received in his father's studio, but also established himself as an independent artist. His workshop, which was staffed largely by sculptors from Flanders, specialised in funerary monuments for Danish and north German patrons. He died in Antwerp and was buried on 7 September 1709. Quellin's kinsman, **Peter Scheemakers**, spent about three years in Copenhagen *c*1717–20, very likely encouraged by the success his forebears had met in that city.

Literary References: *Green* 1964 (1), 136; *Bach-Nielson* 1985, 163–209; *Beard* 1989 (1), 198; *Grove* 32, 813–14 (Kockelbergh)

Statues

1.	1688–1689	Equestrian figure Payment(s): £20	wd	[Royal Armoury, London]; untraced	War Office, Ordnance, Accounts, Ledgers, 48/28; *Blakiston* 1957, 57
2.	1688–1689	Of wood, with a carved face		[Royal Armoury, London]; untraced	War Office, Ordnance, Accounts, Ledgers, 48/28; *Blakiston* 1957, 57

R-AN, Patrick fl 1816

He was probably a decorative sculptor since his only known monument, to Miss Tynte, in Dunlavin, is made up of simple decorative motifs including a small medallion portrait (1).

Literary References: *Potterton* 1975, 75

Funerary Monuments

1.	1816	Miss Tynte	Dunlavin, Co Wicklow	S	*Potterton* 1975, 75

RACKSTROW, Benjamin –1772

Rackstrow was a statuary and the proprietor of a museum which was a well known sight in 18th century London. It occupied two Tudor houses at the sign of the head of Sir Isaac Newton in Fleet Street, between Temple Bar and Chancery Lane. Among the exhibits were anatomical specimens and models but the display also included a miscellany of wax figures and curiosities, such as a whale's skeleton, a perpetual motion machine, two stuffed crocodiles, a rhinoceros hide, a pair of snow shoes and Cromwell's and Newton's death masks.

Rackstrow's sculptural activities were varied too and it is likely that he had to draw on specialist craftsmen within his workshop and probably from outside to produce all the varied works he advertised. His trade card of 1738 claimed that he 'takes off Faces from the Life and forms them into Busts to an exact likeness & with as little trouble as sitting to be shaved', that he supplied 'Chimney pieces in the neatest manner to represent either Marble, Stone or terracotta', that he made and mended 'leaden figures, vases &c for gardens and Fountains and erects Grottos' (*Baker* 1995 (1), 98; *Baker* 2000, 107). He also offered for sale 'to all lovers of their Country .. all sorts of busts, figures and Basso-Relievos, either in Plaister or Metal, and . . . several fine busts of the Ancient and Modern poets, Philosophers and Great Men' (*Baker* 1995 (3), 118).

On 25 April 1759 a bird-cage maker was convicted of stealing a small plaster figure of William Shakespeare, worth about 12s from Rackstrow's shop (3). Rackstrow told the court that he was 'gone out upon business' at the time of the theft but he was able to identify the figure as one of his 'by the manner of it's being repair'd'.

In 1763 he exhibited several works, including a particularly realistic coloured plaster figure of a seated elderly man, at the Free Society of Artists (4). In the same year Horace Walpole, writing of Anne Conway's 'progress in waxen statuary', predicted, perhaps not without humour, that 'by next winter she may rival Rackstrow's old man' (*HWC*, XXXVIII, 198–9).

William Wynn was a pupil of Rackstrow, as was a Mrs Clark, who showed 'a cucumber vine; in composition' at the Free Society in 1763. The sculptor died on 29 May 1772.

Literary References: *London Mag* 1772, vol 41, 293; *Anecdotes* 1937, 150–1; *Gunnis* 1968, 314; *Altick* 1978, 55–6; *Snodin* 1986, 86 (tradecard repr)

Statues					
1.	1749–1750	King George II		Weavers' Hall, Dublin, over entrance	*Dublin Courant*, 17 Oct, 14 Nov 1749; 18 Sept, 30 Oct 1750; *Black* c1872, 49
2.	1751	'a Figure of King Edward' Payment(s): 6 gns		[Ironmongers' Company]; untraced	Ironmongers WA, vol 13; *Gunnis* 1968, 314
3.	1759	Shakespeare, statuette	p	[Stolen from Rackstrow's shop, by Joseph Adams, 21 April 1759]; untraced	*Proceedings of the Old Bailey*
4.	1763	Unidentified gentleman, seated		[Exhib Free Soc, London, 172]; untraced	*Graves* 1907, 207
Busts					
5.	1748	Unidentified subjects, 'three bustos'		[for Arbury, Warks]; untraced	Newdigate Accts, 1748, CR 136/V156; *Gunnis* 1968, 314
6.	1750	Two, unidentified subjects Payment(s): £3 13s		[Ironmongers' Company]; untraced	Ironmongers, WA, vol 13; *Gunnis* 1968, 314
7.	1763	John, Marquess of Granby		[Exhib Free Soc, London, 169]; untraced	*Graves* 1907, 207
8.	1763	Mr Frye		[Exhib Free Soc, London, 170]; untraced	*Graves* 1907, 207
9.	1763	Unidentified 'doctor of laws'		[Exhib Free Soc, London, 171]; untraced	*Graves* 1907, 207
Miscellaneous					
10.	1748	Unidentified 'group'		[for Arbury, Warks]; untraced	Newdigate Accts, 1748, CR 136/V156; *Gunnis* 1968, 314

RADBURN, Stephen, of London fl c1823–35

His studio was at 44 South Audley Street.

Literary References: *Gunnis* 1968, 314

Funerary Monuments

1.	?1823	Sir William Smyth	Theydon Mount, Essex	S	*Gunnis* 1968, 314
2.	?1826	James Sutherland	St Mary, St Marylebone, London	S	*Gunnis* 1968, 314
3.	?1835	John Butcher	St Mary, Paddington, London	S	*Gunnis* 1968, 314

RADCLIFFE, F, of Nottingham fl c1758–77

His works include a monument with mourning cherubs at Lockington (2). After his death his yard was taken over by **William Stretton.**

Literary References: *Gunnis* 1968, 314

Funerary Monuments

1.	†1758	Elizabeth Cumberland	sl	Wilford, Notts, churchyard		Pevsner, *Notts*, 1979, 273
2.	†1769	Philip Bainbridge		Lockington, Leics	S	*Gunnis* 1968, 314
3.	†1777	William Adkinson		Basford, Notts, churchyard		Pevsner, *Notts*, 1979, 266

RAGGETT, Henry, of Weymouth fl c1819–39

Funerary Monuments

1.	?1819	John Ruddock	Weymouth, Dorset	S	*Gunnis* 1968, 314
2.	?1839	William Williams	Little Bredy, Dorset	S	*Gunnis* 1968, 314

RAGGI, Antonio 1624–86

An Italian Baroque sculptor and stuccoist. After arriving in Rome in 1645 he worked for Alessandro Algardi before joining the workshop of Gianlorenzo Bernini in 1647. He became Bernini's most trusted assistant and chief collaborator, working with him on such commissions as the the over-life-size marble group *Noli me tangere* (1649) for SS Domenico e Sisto and the Four Rivers Fountain in the Piazza Navona. He also worked with Carlo Fontana and executed independent works from the 1680s onwards.

The monument to Lady Jane Cheyne in Chelsea Old Church was commissioned by her husband, Charles Cheyne, later Viscount Newhaven, from Paolo Bernini, the architect son of Gianlorenzo Bernini, in 1670 (1). It has a life-sized effigy by Raggi in contemporary dress, reclining on a black marble sarcophagus and clutching one hand to her breast. The figure is housed within a 20 foot high temple-like structure featuring coloured marble columns and surmounted by a large cross and two flaming hearts. The monument attracted considerable attention and by 1705 was popularly said to be by Bernini himself. It is an important work because it was unusual for patrons to commission such substantial sculpture from abroad at that date. In her recent work on the monument Peck has highlighted the complex negotiations between artist and patron which were involved in producing a Roman baroque monument for an English Anglican church.

Literary References: *Grove* 25, 1996, 851–2 (Westin); *Peck* 2005, 277–310

Funerary Monuments

1.	1672	Lady Jane Cheyne (†1669) (designed by Paolo Bernini)	Chelsea Old Church (All Saints), London		*Peck* 2005, 277–310 (repr)

RANALOW, Daniel –1765

A Dublin carver, in 1742 he was awarded a premium of £10 for a carving of *Orpheus charming the brutes* (1). In the same year he married a Miss Clark from near Tullamore. A second wife, Jane Rutland, followed in 1756. He died at his house on St Stephen's Green in December 1765 and was buried in St Andrew's churchyard.

Literary References: *Strickland* II, 1913, 173

Miscellaneous

1.	1742	Orpheus charming the brutes	[£10 premium]; untraced		*Strickland* II, 1913, 173

RANDALL, Charles, of London fl *c*1807–27

One of the London 'New Road statuaries'. Gunnis comments that his tablets are neither better nor worse than those of his neighbours in the same street, adding that his best work is the monument to Edward Howard, which has a relief of two women mourning by an urn (*Gunnis* 1968, 314) (8).

Funerary Monuments

1.	?1807	Rev Isaac Bingham	Holy Trinity, Gosport, Hants		GPC
2.	?1807	William Young	St Mary, Battersea, London	S	*Gunnis* 1968, 314
3.	?1815	John Field	Barton, Beds	S	*Gunnis* 1968, 314
4.	?1822	James Payn	Cookham, Berks	S	*Gunnis* 1968, 314
5.	?1822	Robert Robinson	Denston, Suffolk	S	*Gunnis* 1968, 314
6.	?1826	Lady Smyth	Berechurch, Essex	S	*Gunnis* 1968, 314
7.	?1826	Walter Meller	Tuxford, Notts	S	*Gunnis* 1968, 314
8.	†1827	Edmund Howard	St Mary, St Marylebone, London		Pevsner, *London: N W*, 1991, 603

Chimneypieces

9.	1808	Several Payment(s): £30 8s 2d	[Royal Naval Asylum, Greenwich, London]; untraced		TNA, ADM.80/110, f21

RANDALL, John, of Bristol fl *c*1717

Funerary Monuments

1.	†1717	Catherine Rice	Llandeilo, Carmarthen	S	*Dale-Jones and Lloyd*, 1989, 36, 56

RANDALL, John, of Worcester fl *c*1735

Funerary Monuments

1.	†1735	Thomas Dangerfield	Mathon, Herts		GPC

RANDELL, William fl *c*1821–22

Funerary Monuments

1.	†1821	George Corbin	St Peter Port, Guernsey	S
2.	†1822	William Corbin	St Peter Port, Guernsey	S

RANDLE, John, of Gloucester fl 1709

An agreement dated 2 January 1709 between John Randle of Gloucester, stone-cutter, and John Digges of Newent specified that Randle would make 'a free-stone monument, full 6 feet high and 3 feet wide in which said monument there shall be fixed and placed in a workmanlike manner a good white oval marble table'. He would also supply a 'good Pryor Cleeve blew stone of 5ft and 10 inches in length and 34 [inches] in breadth' to be placed on the grave of John Digges's late wife. Digges, for his part, agreed to 'provide, entertain and accommodate' Randall, his servants and workmen, with 'good meat and drink and lodging' during the period taken in 'erecting fixing up and painting' the monument (1).

Literary References: *Gunnis* 1968, 314

Archival References: Glos RO D177 I/1 fol 22

Funerary Monuments

1.	1709	Mrs Digges, monument and ledger	[for Newent, Glos]; untraced		Digges/Randle Glos RO

RAPER, Edward, of York fl 1724–38

In 1724 he was working at Seaton Delaval with his partner, Wilcox (Archives, Lord Hastings, in GPC) (2). Three years later Edward and Henry Raper wrote to Sir William Robinson, who was then building Newby Hall, Yorks, 'Last night Mr. Carpenter came to my shop to know what share he has or ought to have for the work he and Mr. Harvey did all the Pannels finisht at Newby for which I cannot give your Honor a certain account only this: Mr. Carpenter declares that ten pounds is enough for both Pannels to boast and finish, so in our humble opinions the work that was done before' at ye Pannels deserves six pounds six shillings eight pence (Archives, Compton of Newby, in GPC). The craftsmen referred to were probably **Daniel Harvey** and **John Carpenter**. In 1736–38 Raper was working with **Charles Mitley** at Castle Howard. Raper was responsible for most of the decorative stonework for the mausoleum (3). He and Mitley jointly signed the North monument in St Michael-le-Belfry, York (1). He may have been related to another Edward Raper, son of Edward Raper of Leyburn, York, who was apprenticed to George White of York in 1724 (City Archives, in *Gunnis* 1968, 314).

Literary References: *Gunnis* 1968, 314

Archival References: Castle Howard Building Accts, mausoleum, G2/2/68–9, 1735–37; G2/2/76–77, 1738–9 (Mitley and Raper)

Funerary Monuments

1.	?1734	Catherine and Christiana North	St Michael-le-Belfrey, York	*Gunnis* 1968, 314

Architectural Sculpture

2.	1724	Unidentified (co-sculptor: Wilcox)	Seaton Delaval, Northumbs	Archives, Lord Hastings, in GPC
3.	1736–1738	Stonework, including 8 capitals; the entablature, modelling in the panels and the dome, 16 cherubim heads, 48 'flooroones' and 144 roses in the panels of the dome Payment(s): £64; £30; £27; £11; £25; £28	Castle Howard, N R Yorks, mausoleum	Castle Howard archives in *Gunnis* 1968, 314

RATHBONE, Richard fl 1780–86

He worked on decorative sculpture for Somerset House in the 1780s, receiving payments totalling £669 11s (**1–6**).

Literary References: *Gunnis* 1968, 314–5; *Colvin* V, 1973–76, 467

Architectural Sculpture

1.	1780	Large ornament in Portland stone carved with bows of ribbands, swags and drops of laurel leaves Payment(s): £30	s	Somerset House, London, water-front of the Lodge	Chambers/Somerset Hse, box 8, CHA 3/3/3 fol 202
2.	1784	Two seahorses with a figure of Amphitrite supporting naval arms Payment(s): £87	wd	Somerset House, London, north front pediment	Chambers/Somerset Hse, box 8, CHA 3/3/3 fol 144
3.	1786	16 faces of composite capitals Payment(s): £151	s	Somerset House, London, south front of loggia	*Gunnis* 1968, 315
4.	1786	20 trusses carved in wood under the Gallery with raffled leaves in front & ornaments on the sides Payment(s): £25	wd	Somerset House, London, sale room of the Naval Office	Chambers/Somerset Hse, box 8, CHA 3/3/3 fol 298
5.	1786	Large ornament in Portland stone over the arch next to the terrace, 'on the keystone the head of Neptune, with Dolphins, Sea Weeds, the Navy Arms, Swags and Laurel leaves, Crown &c, the greatest part carved all round' Payment(s): £140	s	Somerset House, London, west end of main building	Chambers/Somerset Hse, box 8, CHA 3/3/3 fol 28
6.	1786	'twelve flowers in soffit of arches leading to the terrace' Payment(s): £66	s	Somerset House, London	*Gunnis* 1968, 315

RATTEE, James 1820–55

A joiner from Norfolk and the partner of **George Kett** in the firm of Rattee and Kett.

RAWLINGS, John, of Bruton fl *c*1817

He signs a wall-monument with a draped urn (1).

Funerary Monuments

1.	?1817	George Prince	Bruton, Somerset	S	*Gunnis* 1968, 315

RAWLINGS, John, of Maidstone fl *c*1753

Funerary Monuments

1.	?1753	William Horsmonden Turner (†1753), ledger stone	All Saints, Maidstone, Kent	*Gunnis* 1968, 315

RAWLINGS, Samuel, of Bruton and Shepton Mallet fl *c*1809–47

Funerary Monuments

1.	†1809	Zachary Bayly and his wives Margaret (†1774) and Mary (†1798)	Shepton Mallet, Somerset	S	
2.	†1813	Hon Catherine Frankland	Wells Cathedral, Somerset		RG/JP, 7, 1146
3.	?1822	Rev William Provis	Shepton Mallet, Somerset	S	*Gunnis* 1968, 315
4.	?1823	Sarah Lock	Wells Cathedral, Somerset	S	*Gunnis* 1968, 315
5.	?1827	Mary Jellard	Milborne Port, Somerset	S	*Gunnis* 1968, 315
6.	†1830	Harriot Anne Steele	Shepton Mallet, Somerset	S	
7.	†1847	William Plumley	Shepton Mallet, Somerset	S	
8.	nd	Unidentified subject, tablet	Pitcombe, Somerset		Pevsner, *Somerset: S & W*, 1958, 273

RAWLINGS, William fl 1763–74

A local mason, he supplied much of the stone when Bowood, Wilts, was built between 1763 and 1774. He built the 'Gate way at Derry Hill' and was responsible for balustrades for the bridge and carved stonework for the house itself (1). He was succeeded by his son James (Archives, Marquess of Lansdowne, in GPC).

Architectural Sculpture

1.	1763–1774	Balustrades for the bridge and carved stonework for the house	s	Bowood, Wilts	Archives, Marquess of Lansdowne, in GPC

RAWLINGS FAMILY, of Box fl 1716–95

A West Country family of stone-masons and carvers. A 'Mr. Rawlings, freemason', was paid 'for stone and work about my Lady Dutchess's monument at Great Bedwin' in 1716 (1). It may be his son who signed three west country monuments (2–4). Gunnis comments that 'These are excellent copies in local stone of contemporary marble works by London statuaries, and Rawlings makes good use of the swags, draperies, flaming lamps and winged cherubs so typical of the period'. In 1799 a Rawlings was employed at Doddington Park, Glos, then being built by James Wyatt (Codrington Archives in GPC).

Literary References: *Gunnis* 1968, 315

Funerary Monuments

1.	?1716	2nd Duchess of Somerset		Great Bedwyn, Wilts		*Gunnis* 1968, 315
2.	?1760	Edward Baily	s	Bradford-on-Avon, Wilts	S	*Gunnis* 1968, 315
3.	?1785	Robert Fisher	s	Bathampton, Somerset	S	*Gunnis* 1968, 315
4.	?1795	Stephen Bowyer	s	South Wraxall, Somerset	S	*Gunnis* 1968, 315

RAWLINS, Nathaniel fl 1664–1707

The first record of his activities dates from July 1664 when he was employed as a mason at Greenwich at the rate of 2s 6d per day (BL Harley MS 1618, in *Knoop and Jones* 1935, 34). He was admitted to the freedom of the Haberdashers' Company by redemption on 28 October 1670. In the Masons' Company general search of 1678, he was noted as working with **Thomas Strong I** at St Paul's Cathedral. At the time of the 1694 Search he was working with **Edward Strong** 'At St Pauls Church' and about a year previously he had succeeded **Jasper Latham** as one of the master-masons at St Paul's Cathedral. By 1696 he had four apprentices. He was employed at St Paul's until 1707 and carrying out mason's work and stone carving, receiving a total sum of £15,751 (**1–5**).

Literary References: *Knoop and Jones* 1935, 34; *Wren Soc* XV, 11, 14, 53, 54, 67, 103; *Gunnis* 1968, 315

Archival References: Haberdashers, Freedom, 136; Masons Co, Court Book, 1677–94, fol 13v, fol 162v; Court Book 1695–1722, fol 13v

Architectural Sculpture

1.	1696	Extensive carved work including two key stones for the head of the Tribune Payment(s): £55 18s	St Paul's Cathedral, London	*Wren Soc*, XV, 11
2.	1697	Freestone wreaths in the ceiling of the north cross aisle and other carved ornaments Payment(s): £142 18s 8d	St Paul's Cathedral, London	*Wren Soc*, XV, 14
3.	1699	Work on the arch damaged by fire including mouldings, cornices, faces of capitals and scrolls Payment(s): £270 10s 6 1/2d	St Paul's Cathedral, London	*Wren Soc*, XV, 54
4.	1700	Work on the arch damaged by fire', including cross mouldings and other carving Payment(s): £245 18s 2 1/2d	St Paul's Cathedral, London	*Wren Soc*, XV, 67
5.	1703–4	'39 Faces of Portland Compositt Capitalls', '12 Faces of Freestone Capitalls', and several festoons Payment(s): £165 15s, £60, £15, £16	St Paul's Cathedral, London, dome	*Wren Soc*, XV, 103

RAWLINS, Thomas, of Norwich –1789

Rawlins ran a successful business as a monumental mason in Norwich *c*1743–81. He was the son of Thomas Rawlins, a worsted weaver of Norwich. He appears to have been trained by a London sculptor, for in 1753, he advertised that he had opened an establishment adjoining the Duke's Palace Yard, where he executed monuments and chimneypieces 'of the newest fashion . . . having work'd at the most eminent Carvers in London' (*Norwich Mercury*, 29 September 1753). On 1 May 1762 he offered 'Five Rooms on one Floor' to let in the parish of St John Maddermarket (*Norwich Mercury*) and two weeks later he advertised as a 'carver and mason at the Duke's Palace, Norwich', stating that he executed 'monuments and chimney pieces both ancient and modern' (*Norwich Mercury*, 15 May 1762).

Rawlins specialised in tablets of coloured marbles with 'delightful and delicately carved details' and Gunnis considered him to be 'in the front rank of the Norfolk statuaries', rivalled only by **Robert Page**. His monument to Sir Thomas Churchman, which has a medallion portrait and a relief of *Fame Overthrowing Time* 'compares favourably with the work of any London sculptor of the period' (*Gunnis* 1968, 315) (**18**).

He also practised as an architect, exhibiting designs at the Society of Artists in 1767, 1769 and 1770, and at the Royal Academy in 1773, 1774 and 1776 and competing for the Royal Exchange at Dublin in 1769. In 1765 the *Ipswich Journal* advertised a proposed work on architecture by Rawlins and in 1768 he published *Familiar Architecture: or Original Designs of Houses for Gentlemen and Tradesmen; Parsonages; Summer Retreats; Banqueting-Rooms; and Churches.* The designs are Palladian in style and further editions were issued in 1789 and 1795. His only documented architectural works are the entrance to St Andrew's Hall, Norwich (1774, subsequently rebuilt) and Weston House, Weston Longvill, Norfolk (1781, demol 1926). His reinforcement of the south aisle of the church of St John Maddermarket with ironwork was the subject of satirical verses published in the *Norfolk Chronicle* on 8 August 1772.

The *Norwich Mercury* for 3 September 1785, recorded the death of his wife. Rawlins died four years later, on Wednesday 18 March 1789, and is commemorated by a stone in the floor of St John Maddermarket (*Norwich Mercury*, 21 March 1789).

Literary References: *Gunnis* 1968, 315; *Colvin* 1995, 793

Funerary Monuments

1.	†1743	Peregrina Brown (†1743) and Charles Browne (†1753)	Bungay, Suffolk	RG/JP, 7, 1146v.
2.	†1743	William Rant	Mendham, Suffolk	Pevsner, *Suffolk*, 1974, 360
3.	?1744	Edward Cooper	Bungay, Suffolk	*Gunnis* 1968, 315

4.	?1747	Stannard Family	St Giles, Norwich, Norfolk		*Priestley* 1994, 4, 26 (repr)
5.	?1756	John Custance	St Andrew, Norwich, Norfolk		*Gunnis* 1968, 315
6.	1756	William Rolfe (†1754)	Norwich Cathedral, Norfolk		Pevsner, *Norfolk: N E & Norwich*, 1997, 209
7.	†1757	Hambleton Custance	St Andrew, Norwich, Norfolk		Pevsner, *Norfolk, N E and Norwich*, 1997, 232
8.	†1758	Gibson Lucas	East Bradenham, Norfolk		Pevsner, *Norfolk: N W & S*, 1999, 317
9.	†1759	John Drake	Wymondham Abbey, Norfolk		Pevsner, *Norfolk: N W & S*, 1999, 797
10.	?1762	Richard Oram	Smallburgh, Norfolk		*Gunnis* 1968, 315
11.	†1764	Timothy Balderstone	St George Colegate, Norwich, Norfolk		Pevsner, *Norfolk: N E & Norwich*, 1997, 235
12.	?1765	William Stone	Woodton, Norfolk		*Gunnis* 1968, 315
13.	?1765	William Woodcocks	St Swithin, Norwich, Norfolk		*Gunnis* 1968, 315
14.	†1767	Richard and Margaret (†1768) Dennison	St Andrew, Norwich, Norfolk		Pevsner, *Norfolk: N E & Norwich*, 1997, 232
15.	†1770	William Wilcocks	St Swithin, Norwich, Norfolk		Pevsner, *Norfolk: N E & Norwich*, 1997, 253
16.	†1772	Sir Horatio Pettus	Rackheath, Norfolk		Pevsner, *Norfolk: N E & Norwich*, 1997, 642
17.	†1781	Robert Rushbrook	St John Maddermarket, Norwich, Norfolk		Pevsner, *Norfolk: N E & Norwich*, 1997, 241
18.	†1781	Sir Thomas Churchman	St Giles, Norwich, Norfolk		Pevsner, *Norfolk: N E & Norwich* 1997, 237

RAY, Irving, of Wigton 1816–1906

A self-taught sculptor described in the *Carlisle Journal* of 13 June 1851 as having great ability. The journal noted his death, aged 90, on 6 March 1906. His estate was divided between his eleven children (*CJ*, 3 May 1907, 6) (Inf. D Perriam).

Funerary Monuments

1.	1851	Dr Carson	Wigton, Cumberland		*CJ*, 13 June 1851

Architectural Sculpture

2.	1851	Wisdom, Knowledge and Learning	[Mechanics' Institute, Wigton, Cumberland, pediment]; demol		Pevsner, *Cumberland & Westmorland*, 1967, 207

RAY, W, of Lincoln fl *c*1817–58

Funerary Monuments

1.	†1817	Mary Hale	Holton Beckering, Lincs		Pevsner, *Lincs*, 1989, 389
2.	†1858	Anna Ealand	Aisthorpe, Lincs		Pevsner, *Lincs*, 1989, 92

RAYSON, of Horncastle fl *c*1846

Funerary Monuments

1.	†1846	Unidentified subject, tablet	Asgarby, Lincs	S	Pevsner, *Lincs*, 1989, 104

READ, Nicholas –1787

A student and the self-appointed successor to **Louis François Roubiliac**, Read's monuments are characterised by drama and excess. He was probably the son of James and Anne Read, born 1 April 1730 and christened at St Martin-in-the-Fields ten days later. He was the eldest of three or more children. Read was first a student at the St Martin's Lane Academy and around 1746 he was apprenticed by his father to Roubiliac. A later account in the *Gentleman's Magazine* claims that Read became a favourite student of the French sculptor after covertly and successfully completing one of his master's busts. 'From that moment they continued inseparable friends ever after and all distinction was lost in the affection [Roubiliac] bore him' (*GM*, 1787, vol 57, pt II, 644).

George Vertue, who saw a drawing by Read of an 'academy figure' in 1750, recorded that it showed 'great skill & fire & spirit extraordinary' (*Vertue*, III, 152). Read is said to have worked on many of Roubiliac's major commissions, including the famous skeletal figure of Death on the monument to Mrs Nightingale, and he was left in charge of the business whilst his master was in Rome in 1752. When Roubiliac died, early in 1762, Read took over the workshop, advertising within a few days that, having been with Roubiliac for the last 16 years 'and executed great part of his most capital works' he now meant to succeed him (*Anecdotes* 1937, 151). It seems likely that Read completed some of Roubiliac's unfinished commissions, particularly the monument to Francis Hooper, which incorporates a bust by Roubiliac (**2**), and another to Lucretia Betenson at Wrotham, Kent (**1**). He repeated the Betenson emblem of a cut rose on the monument to John Kendall (**3**).

In March 1762 Read published an advertisement offering casts of several busts by Roubiliac including representations of Alexander Pope, Isaac Ware and David Garrick. These were to be had 'considerably cheaper than their usual price' since the contents of Roubiliac's studio were to be sold in May (*Anecdotes* 1937, 151–2). By this date Read was evidently an accomplished marble sculptor for on 27 April 1762 he won a premium of 100 guineas from the Society of Arts for his life-size figure of *Actaeon* (**19**). He married Mary Simmonds at about this time, and their child, Thomas James, was christened in December 1763. On 27 April 1764 he won another prize of 140 guineas from the Society of Arts for a figure of *Diana out of water by a rock* (**20**). These were the largest premiums for sculpture ever offered by the Society, and his achievement won him notices in the Press.

An anecdote by J T Smith relates that Read had once declared that when he finished his apprenticeship to Roubiliac 'he would show the world what a monument ought to be' (*Smith* 1828, vol 2, 240–1). His early independent works indicate that he aimed to make an impression with his innovative designs and powerful dramatic effects. His monument to Nicholas Magens, 1766, which was described in the *Ipswich Journal* that November (**5**), is an overpowering assembly of motifs. A statue of *Fame* with inappropriately large outstretched wings stands with a globe and cherub, in front of a Breccia marble pyramid. They are surrounded by emblems of trade, bales of merchandise, an anchor, rope and a bursting cornucopia, which pours forth a flood of fruits of the earth intermixed with golden guineas. The pyramid is encrusted with ice-cream clouds and numbers of twisting putti who threaten to overwhelm the figures below.

Soon after completing the Magens monument Read won the commission for Admiral Tyrrell's monument in Westminster Abbey (**6**), a Resurrection scene. This was partly dismantled in the 19th century when the figure of the Admiral was put into store, which is regrettable, for the work has received ridicule and high praise in equal measure. Its swelling clouds earned it the sobriquet 'the pancake monument,' and J T Smith considered it the vilest work in the Abbey. On the other hand, Mrs Esdaile later described the remaining figures as 'very beautiful' and the relief of Tyrrell's ship, the *Buckingham*, as 'technically among the most amazing things in English art' (*Esdaile* 1928, 214).

Although few in number, Read's monuments are ambitious and varied. The Northumberland memorial is built around the family vault in Westminster Abbey (**11**) and was carved to a neoclassical design by Robert Adam. It nonetheless incorporates a very naturalistic sarcophagus relief of *Charity giving alms*. The monument to Mrs Simons is an asymmetrical variant on a standard type, the portrait-medallion on a draped pyramid (**10**). The Finch monument incorporates two unusual urns (**7**) and Lady Margan's memorial, an x-shaped composition, has a figure of *Fame* with her head falling backwards in an ecstasy of grief (**8**).

In 1779 Read submitted an unsuccessful design for the monument to Lord Chatham, presenting Chatham standing on a sarcophagus in an oratorial pose, surrounded by figures of *Learning, Eloquence* and *History* (**13**). Like his friend **John Cheere**, who left him a small bequest to buy a mourning ring, Read appears to have had a high public profile, but he won little recognition amongst artists. He appears not to have sought any connection with the Royal Academy, unlike his co-apprentice in Roubiliac's studio, **William Tyler RA**, and he exhibited on only a couple of occasions at the Free Society.

The paucity of Read's known work supports Smith's claim that the mainstay of his business was not sculpture but property development. According to Smith, who clearly disliked Read intensely, the sculptor was able to increase his means tenfold by 'the trade of purchasing old houses, fitting them up, and then letting them at an immense increase of rent' (*Smith* 1828, vol 2, 240–1).

He died on 11 July 1787 at his house at 65, St Martin's Lane. His obituary noted 'his faculties were, from his great studies, impaired at a time of life when other men's are in their prime, and he became totally deprived of reason a short time before his death' (*GM*, 1787, vol 57, pt 2, 644–5). His will, proved that month, left all his 'real and personal estates' to his wife Mary, and an annuity of £100 per annum to his son, Thomas James. Further annuities went to three other family members. A sale of his stocks of marble and clay, his casts, tools and utensils was held at his workshop by William Booth on 2 August.

The *Gentleman's Magazine* claimed that Read 'received the highest wages given to any of his profession' (*GM*, 1787, vol 57, pt 2, 644–5). His contemporary success has not been matched by his posthumous reputation. Smith, whose father **Nathaniel Smith** also served his apprenticeship in Roubiliac's workshop, regarded Read's frequent self-promotion as the heir to Roubiliac as immodest and presumptuous. Other accounts, not coloured by personal antipathy, treat Read's sculptural bombast as an anticlimactic appendage to Roubiliac's career and a final and outdated flourish of the baroque tradition. The *Gentleman's Magazine* commented in 1818 that Read 'displayed more of concetto than his master, without his judgement or taste' (*GM*, vol 88, I, 597).

MGS

Literary References: *Press Cuttings* 1723–1800, fols 30, 40; *Mortimer* 1763, 24; *GM*, vol 57, pt 2, 644–5; *Smith* 1828, II, 240–1; *Esdaile* 1928, 213–4; *Anecdotes* 1937, 151–3; *Gunnis* 1968, 315–6; *Penny* 1977 (1), *passim*; *Whinney* 1988, 272–3, 400, 456 n49, 461 n44 and 46; *Bindman and Baker* 1995, *passim*; *ODNB* (Baker)

Archival References: IGI

Wills: John Cheere, 1787, FRC PROB 11/1155/104r; Louis-François Roubiliac 1762, FRC PROB 11/872/213r-4; Nicholas Read, FRC PROB 11/1155/294–5, proved 12 July 1787

Auction Catalogues: Read 1787

Funerary Monuments

1.	†1758	Lucretia Betenson (completing Roubiliac's work)		Wrotham, Kent		*Bindman and Baker* 1995, 354–5
2.	†1763	Francis Hooper (bust by L-F Roubiliac)		Trinity College, Cambridge, chapel	S	*Baker* 1995 (3), 123, 136; *Bindman and Baker* 1995, 357–8
3.	c1765	John Kendall (†1750)		West Horsley, Surrey	S	Pevsner, *Surrey*, 1971, 512; *Whinney* 1988, 273; *Bindman and Baker* 1995, 354
4.	†1766	Elizabeth (†1765) and Stephen Niblett		All Souls College, Oxford	S	*Gunnis* 1968, 316
5.	1766	Nicholas Magens (†1764)		Brightlingsea, Essex	S	*Penny* 1977 (1), 3, 4, 173, 222 n8 (repr); *Whinney* 1988, 273 (repr)
6.	†1766	Rear-Admiral Richard Tyrrell		Westminster Abbey, London, nave, south aisle		*Esdaile* 1928, 212; *Whinney* 1988, 273
7.	†1767	John Finch (†1739) and his wife Elizabeth		Thrybergh, WR Yorks	S	Pevsner, *Yorks: W R*, 1967, 517
8.	1767	Lady Anne Margan (†1764)		Kinnersley, Herefs	S	Pevsner, *Herefs*, 1963, 212
9.	†1768	Sir Gilbert Heathcote		Devizes, Wiltshire		*Whinney* 1988, 273
10.	†1769	Anne Simons		Lechlade, Glos		Pevsner, *Glos: Cotswolds*, 1999, 438
11.	†1776	Elizabeth, Duchess of Northumberland (designed by Robert Adam) Drawing(s): Soane, Adam Drawings, xix n.19, Box 4		Westminster Abbey, London, Chapel of St Nicholas	S	*Penny* 1977 (1), 151–152 (repr)
12.	?1776	Rev George Legh		Halifax Parish Church, Yorks		*Gunnis* 1968, 316
13.	1779	William Pitt, Earl of Chatham (†1778), model (commission won by John Bacon RA)		[Exhib Free Soc, London, 146]; untraced		*Graves* 1907, 210
14.	1780	A model for an unspecified monument	tc	[Exhib Soc of Artists, London, 209]; untraced		*Graves* 1907, 209
15.	1778–1782	Elizabeth, Duchess of Northumberland (†1776) (designed by Robert Adam) Payment(s): £240		[Alnwick Castle, Northumberland, chapel]; untraced		Alnwick Archives, U/I/46/59, 60; *Harris* 2001, 93, 344 n45

16.	?1785	James Poole		Budworth, Cheshire	*Gunnis* 1968, 316
17.	nd	'A small [unspecified] monument complete' Payment(s): £15 5s		[Sculptor's workshop, St Martin's Lane, sold 1787, lot 70]; untraced	Read sale 1787, 6
18.	nd	Models for unspecified monuments, including one 'in a case'		[Sculptor's workshop, St Martin's Lane, sold 1787, lots 56, 61–3, 91–2]; untraced	Read sale 1787, 5
Statues					
19.	1762	Actaeon and his dog Payment(s): 100 gns	m	[Soc of A, premium (100 gns)]; untraced	RSA *Minutes*, 1761–62, seq 3 fol 53; *Dossie* 1782,440; *Gunnis* 1968, 316
20.	1764	Diana out of water by a rock Payment(s): £147	m	[Soc of A, premium]; untraced	RSA *Minutes*, 1763–64, des 3 f76; *Dossie* 1782, 440; *Press Cuttings* 1723–1800, fols 30, 40; *Gunnis* 1968, 316; *Graves* 1907, 209
21.	nd	Atlanta		Earl of Wemyss, Gosford, Lothian	RG/JP, 7, 1149
Busts					
22.	nd	'A quantity of plaster busts, &c'	p	[Sculptor's workshop, St Martin's Lane, sold 1787, lots 57–8, 98, 100]; untraced	Read sale 1787, 5
Reliefs					
23.	nd	Unspecified bas-reliefs		[Sculptor's workshop, St Martin's Lane, sold 1787, lots 89, 94, 96]; untraced	Read sale 1787, 6
Miscellaneous					
24.	nd	'A statuary shield and four ornaments' Payment(s): £1 7s		[Sculptor's workshop, St Martin's Lane, sold 1787, lot 108]; untraced	Read sale 1787, 108

READING, John fl 1690

A 'stone-cutter', he was paid £108 by Thomas, Earl of Coventry, on 30 October 1690 (Child's Bank Archives in GPC).

REDDAWAY, of Exeter fl 1833

There is an identical pair of tablets to the daughters of James Pitman of Dunchideock House, the first to Lydia Astley, †1832 and her infant son, Edward. This is unsigned. The second commemorates Catharine Keats and her sister, Diana Pitman, aged 28 and 27, who both 'by the overset of a Boat in a gust of wind near Babbicombe were unfortunately droened. . .on the 8th June 1833' (1).

Funerary Monuments					
1.	†1833	Catharine Keats and Diana Portman	Dunchideock, Devon	S	RG/AL

REDFERN, of Ashford early 19th century

A firm of Derbyshire marble masons, they produced 'standard white statuary' memorial tablets and items such as tables and chimneypieces in local coloured marbles during the early nineteenth century (*Penny* 1977 (1), 9–10).

REEVE fl *c*1760–68

Possibly a Wiltshire stone-carver, he signs wall-tablets 'of quite good workmanship' in that county (*Gunnis* 1968, 316) (1–2).

Funerary Monuments					
1.	?1760	Lionel Seaman	Upton Scudamore, Wilts	S	*Gunnis* 1968, 316
2.	?1768	Alice Wayte	Dauntsey, Wilts	S	*Gunnis* 1968, 316

REEVE, George fl 1829–31

He was living at 21 Masham Street, Westminster, when he was awarded a medal by the Society of Arts in 1829.

Miscellaneous				
1.	1829	'an original model of foliage'	[Soc of A, large silver medal]; untraced	RSA *Transactions*, 1929, vol 47, xxiii
2.	1831	Foliage	[Exhib Soc of BA, London, 912]; untraced	*Johnson* 1975, 389

REEVE FAMILY, of Gloucester

Francis Reeve	*c*1639–1715
Stephen Reeve	1662–1724
Joseph Reeve	*c*1669–1716
Francis Reeve	before 1706–
Joseph Reeve	fl 1751
Nathaniel Reeve	fl 1761
Francis Reeve	fl 1768

A dynasty of Gloucestershire sculptors, they lived in the parish of St Nicholas, where several family members are commemorated on tombstones in the churchyard. These include Francis Reeve, 'mason and carver', who died on 7 February 1715, aged 76, Hannah, his wife, who died on 20 July 1680, aged 50, Joseph Reeve, a 'carver', who died on 10 March 1716, aged 47 and his wife Sarah, who died on 22 December 1714. Stephen Reeve is buried in the church of St John the Baptist, Gloucester.

Francis Reeve made his will on 16 August 1706 and it was proved on 16 November 1715, witnessed by Anne, his second wife. He left 'unto my son Stephen and my grandson Francis Reeve my moddels & drafts they being about thirty in number be they more or lesse, to be divided betwene them and to my son Stephen my Architecture book called Pallada and alsoe my Westminster Epitaps, one third part of my stock of stone unwrought free stone Weather stone, Alabaster & Marble & my working tooles to my son Stephen and Grandson Francis'. He also mentions a son, Francis, then living in Ross, Herefs.

Reeves of a later generation include Joseph, 'son of Joseph Reeve, stonecutter', who became free in 1751, and his two brothers, Nathaniel and Francis, who gained their freedom in 1761 and 1768 respectively (Corporation records, in *Gunnis* 1968, 317).

Literary References: *Gunnis* 1968, 316–7

Archival References: GPC; C Lib (repr)

Funerary Monuments

1.	1653	Sir William Guise (†1642)		Elmore, Glos	S	Pevsner, *Glos: Vale & Forest of Dean*, 1976, 180
2.	†1672	Jane Berkeley		Rendcomb, Glos		RG/JP, 7, 1151
3.	†1678	Thomas Price		St John the Baptist, Gloucester		Pevsner, *Glos: Vale & Forest of Dean*, 1976, 232
4.	†1681	Daniel Lysons		St Mary de Crypt, Gloucester, Glos	S	Pevsner, *Glos: Vale & Forest of Dean*, 1976, 234
5.	†1684	Sir Richard Cocks	s	St Peter, Dumbleton, Glos	S	Pevsner, *Glos: Vale & Forest of Dean*, 1976, 174
6.	†1691	Elizabeth Brydges (by Francis Reeve)		Tyberton, Herefs		C Lib (repr)
7.	†1693	Dorothy Price		St John the Baptist, Gloucester	S	Pevsner, *Glos: Vale & Forest of Dean*, 1976, 232
8.	†1696	Anne Brydges (by Stephen Reeve)		Tyberton, Herefs		C Lib (repr)
9.	†1698	John Rogers	s	Haresfield, Glos	S	Pevsner, *Glos: Vale & Forest of Dean*, 1976, 263
10.	†1722	Beata Johnson (by Stephen Reeve)		Barnwood, Glos	S	Pevsner, *Glos: Vale & Forest of Dean*, 1976, 97

Architectural Sculpture

11.	1719–21	Coat of arms above the windows and font (by Stephen Reeve)		Tyberton, Herefs		Archives, Brydges of Tyberton, in GPC

REEVES & SON, of Bath fl 1778–1860

The firm was responsible for hundreds of wall monuments in the south-west, particularly in Somerset. It was founded by William Reeves, who was succeeded by his son Charles, who took a Mr Holland briefly into partnership about 1825. Pigot's *Directory of Somerset*, *c*1844, lists Charles and William B Reeves as statuaries and marble masons with premises at 26 Charles St, Bath. An undated advertisement on the verso of a design in the **Paty family** Copybook reads 'Wm. Reeves and Son, Statuaries, Bath. Monuments, Chimneypieces, Tombs &c, &c'. The design in the Paty copybook could be by a member of the Reeves, Paty or another family, for it for is a standard shield-shaped memorial slab with beaded moulding and a cornice above on which is a gothic arch. There is a signature above the advertisement which appears to be that of **Henry Wood**: this has prompted Priest to suggest that the firm passed into Wood's ownership.

Like the **King family** of Bath, the firm was able to rely on a number of stock designs, and they made repeated use of relief ornaments such as draped urns, lamps, weeping willows and grieving figures, sometimes executed in polychrome marbles. One of their more lively tableaux was the monument to John Millward (†1822), which was sent out to Jamaica. It has two crudely executed standing females in draperies, their arms clasped about one another, one of them pointing to a pair of covered urns decorated with armorial shields (**45**). A more refined piece of carving, the memorial to Daniel Steigenberger (†1823) in Bath, presents a grieving draped woman perched on a sarcophagus with a weeping cherub at her knee (**46**).

In 1824 and 1833 the firm made marble chimney-pieces for Stourhead, Wilts, and in the latter year were also paid for shields for the gate piers at the same house. For these the material used was Bath stone, carved with the arms of Colt and Hoare.

Literary References: *Gunnis* 1968, 317; *Priest* 2003, 171–2

Archival References: GPC

Funerary Monuments

1.	†1706	Bernard Powlett (†1700) and Jane Brown	Atworth, Wilts	S	
2.	†1763	Mary Boyd	Bath Abbey, Somerset	S	
3.	† to 1776	Thomas (†1739), Thomas (†1753), Mary (†1762), Rachael (†1774) and Wadham (†1776) Locke	Seend, Wilts	S	
4.	?1778	Robert Perfect	Wincanton, Somerset	S	*Gunnis* 1968, 317
5.	†1780	Rev John Phillips and wife (†1786)	St David's Cathedral, Lampeter	S	
6.	†1785	John Deverell	Bradford-on-Avon, Wilts	S	
7.	†1786	Captain Thomas Stokes	Yate, Glos	S	Pevsner, *Glos: Vale & Forest of Dean*, 1976, 414
8.	?1786	Moulton Messiter	Wincanton, Somerset	S	*Gunnis* 1968, 317
9.	†1788	Elizabeth Jeane	Broomfield, Somerset		Pevsner, *Somerset: S & W*, 1958, 102
10.	†1790	Robert Davis	Bradford-on-Avon, Wilts	S	
11.	†1791	Elizabeth Moffat	Bath Abbey, Somerset	S	Pevsner, *Somerset: N & Bristol*, 1958, 104
12.	†1791	John Hay Balfour	Bath Abbey, Somerset	S	Pevsner, *Somerset: N & Bristol*, 1958, 104
13.	†1794	Jane Hyatt	Shepton Mallet, Somerset	S	
14.	?1797	John Long	Corhampton, Hants		*Gunnis* 1968, 317
15.	†1800	John Baskerville	Bradford-on-Avon, Wilts	S	
16.	†1802	Rev Edward Estcourt	Long Newnton, Glos	S	Pevsner, *Glos: Cotswolds*, 1999, 459
17.	†1803	Edward Bearpacker	St Mary the Virgin, Wotton-under-Edge, Glos	S	Pevsner, *Glos: Cotswolds*, 1999, 757
18.	*c*1804	Joanne Gooch	Wells Cathedral, Somerset	S	
19.	†1806	Charles Moss	Wells Cathedral, Somerset	S	
20.	†1807	Simon Wayte	St Mary, Swindon, Wilts		Pevsner, *Wilts*, 1975, 514
21.	†1808	Charles Coxe	Kemble, Glos	S	Pevsner, *Glos: Cotswolds*, 1999, 423
22.	†1808	Mary Gwynne	Gloucester Cathedral	S	Pevsner, *Glos: Vale & Forest of Dean*, 1976, 218

23.	†1812	Rev Thomas Eyre	Wells Cathedral, Somerset	S	
24.	†1813	Mary Goodden (†1812) and Rev John Culliford Goodden	Over Compton, Dorset	S	*Gunnis* 1968, 317; C Lib (repr)
25.	?1814	Harry Atwood	Batheaston, Somerset	S	*Gunnis* 1968, 317
26.	†1814	John Blagden Hale (†1808) and his wife, Ann	Alderley, Glos	S	Pevsner, *Glos: Cotswolds*, 1999, 133
27.	†1814	John Morris	Marshfield, Glos	S	Pevsner, *Glos: Cotswolds*, 1999, 469
28.	†1815	Jane Hughes	Llantilio Crossenny, Monmouths	S	
29.	†1815	John Hume	Bathampton, Somerset		Pevsner, *Somerset: N & Bristol*, 1958, 137
30.	†1816	Edward Witts	Chipping Norton, Oxon	S	
31.	?1817	Ann Gunning	Langridge, Somerset	S	*Gunnis* 1968, 317
32.	?1817	Anne, Lady Crosby	Bath Abbey, Somerset	S	*Gunnis* 1968, 317
33.	?1817	Archdeacon Turner	Wells Cathedral, Somerset	S	*Gunnis* 1968, 317
34.	†1817	Maria Anne Daniels	Barbados Cathedral, Bridgetown	S	
35.	†1818	Dame Jane Wilson	St Luke, Charlton, Middx	S	*Gunnis* 1968, 317
36.	†1818	Thomas Morris	Wingfield, Wilts		Pevsner, *Wilts*, 1975, 588
37.	†1818	William James	Stone, Glos	S	Pevsner, *Glos: Vale & Forest of Dean*, 1976, 352
38.	?1819	Alexander Luders	Widcombe, Somerset	S	*Gunnis* 1968, 317
39.	†1820	Edward Taylor	Hamble, Hants	S	
40.	†1820	Fanny Austin	St Mary the Virgin, Wotton-under-Edge, Glos	S	Pevsner, *Glos: Cotswolds*, 1999, 757
41.	†1821	Dr James Lee	Spanish Town Cathedral, Jamaica	S	*Gunnis* 1968, 317; C Lib (repr)
42.	†1821	John Dunning	St Mary, Bridgwater, Somerset		Pevsner, *Somerset: S & W*, 1958, 96
43.	?1821	Stephen Ram	South Stoneham, Hants		*Gunnis* 1968, 317; C Lib (repr)
44.	†1821	Thomas Stannard Penoyre	Clifford, Herefs		Pevsner, *Herefs*, 1963, 102
45.	†1822	John Millward	Spanish Town Cathedral, Jamaica	S	*Gunnis* 1968, 317
46.	†1823	Daniel Watson Steigenberger	Weston by Bath, Somerset	S	
47.	†1823	Rev Thomas Maddock	Chester Cathedral	S	
48.	†1823	Samuel Wood (†1801) and his wife Grace	Didmarton, Glos		Pevsner, *Glos: Cotswolds*, 1999, 314–5
49.	†1824	Samuel Dyer	Wotton-under-Edge, Glos	S	Pevsner, *Glos: Cotswolds*, 1999, 757
50.	†1825	Catherine, the Hon Mrs William Pole-Tylney-Long-Wellesley (co-sculptor: Holmes)	Draycot Cerne, Wilts		*Gunnis* 1968, 317
51.	?1825	Fridiswyde Broderip	Wells Cathedral, Somerset	S	*Gunnis* 1968, 317
52.	?1826	Admiral Holloway	St Cuthbert, Wells, Somerset	S	*Gunnis* 1968, 317
53.	†1826	Rev Roger Frankland	Wells Cathedral, Somerset	S	
54.	†1826	Sarah Jarrett	Camerton, Somerset	S	
55.	†1826	Thomas Preston	St Magnus the Martyr, City of London		Pevsner, *London: City*, 1997, 233
56.	?1827	James Wickens	Salisbury Cathedral, Wilts		*Gunnis* 1968, 317
57.	†1827	John Cooper	St Mary the Virgin, Wotton-under-Edge, Glos	S	Pevsner, *Glos: Cotswolds*, 1999, 756
58.	†1828	Elizabeth Wollen	Wedmore, Somerset	S	
59.	†1828	George Nutt	Siston, Glos	S	Pevsner, *Glos: Vale & Forest of Dean*, 1976, 338
60.	†1828	Rev George Wheelle	Shipton Moyne, Glos	S	
61.	†1829	James Phelps	Adderley, Glos	S	
62.	†1829	Rev Isaac Horlock	Marshfield, Glos	S	Pevsner, *Glos: Cotswolds*, 1999, 469
63.	†1830	John Frodsham (†1791) and his wife, Anne	Broadwell, Glos	S	Pevsner, *Glos: Cotswolds*, 1999, 201
64.	† to 1830	Legg family	Market Lavington, Wilts	S	
65.	†1831	Frances Morgan	Tidenham, Glos	S	Pevsner, *Glos: Vale & Forest of Dean*, 1976, 384
66.	†1831	James Bethell	Bradford-on-Avon, Wilts	S	
67.	†1831	Mary Littlewood	Edington Priory, Wilts	S	
68.	† to 1832	Hester (†1795), Frederick Seymour (†1803), Peter (†1826) and Elizabeth (†1832) Awdry	Seend, Wilts	S	
69.	?1832	Sir Henry Mathias	Haverfordwest, Pembrokes		*Gunnis* 1968, 317
70.	†1832	Thomas Mostyn Edwards	Cilcain, Flint	S	Pevsner, *Clwyd*, 1986, 337
71.	†1833	Thomas (†1816) and Martha Williams	Bredon, Worcs	S	
72.	†1834	Rev Martin Smith	Fladbury, Worcs	S	
73.	†1834	Sir Edward Thornborough	Exeter Cathedral, Devon	S	
74.	†1834	Thomas Thomas	Kingswood, Glos	S	Pevsner, *Glos: Vale & Forest of Dean*, 1976, 282
75.	†1835	Ann (†1796) and Joyce Mogg	Cameley, Somerset	S	
76.	†1835	Frances Levett	Croxall, Staffs		Pevsner, *Staffs*, 1974, 110
77.	†1836	Frances Clutterbuck	Ozleworth, Glos	S	Pevsner, *Glos: Cotswolds*, 1999, 539
78.	†1836	Rev Robert Foster	Wells Cathedral, Somerset	S	
79.	†1837	James Codrington	Olveston, Glos	S	
80.	†1837	Margaret Prinsep	Croxall, Staffs		Pevsner, *Staffs*, 1974, 110
81.	†1838	Rev George Wheeler	Shipton Moyne, Glos	S	Pevsner, *Glos: Cotswolds*, 1999, 605
82.	?1840	Lieutenant-Colonel Edward Woods	Byculla, India		*Gunnis* 1968, 317
83.	†1841	Henry Marshall	St Peter, Colombo, Sri Lanka (the garrison church)		*Gunnis* 1968, 317; GPC
84.	†1842	Frances Pottinger	St Saviour, Bath, Somerset		Pevsner, *Somerset: N & Bristol*, 1958, 108

85.	†1844	Robert Charleton		Olveston, Glos	S	Pevsner, *Glos: Vale & Forest of Dean*, 1976, 316
86.	†1846	Rev John Rees-Mogg (†1835) and Mary Rees-Mogg		Cameley, Somerset	S	
87.	†1846	Sarah Kilmister		Didmarton, Glos	S	Pevsner, *Glos: Cotswolds*, 1999, 315
88.	†1846	Susanna Williams		Cameley, Somerset	S	
89.	†1846	William Tanner Powell		Marshfield, Glos	S	Pevsner, *Glos: Cotswolds*, 1999, 469
90.	†1847	Rev Robert Molesworth		Christ Church, Bandon, Co Cork	S	
91.	?1849	Bishop Coleridge		Christ Church, Barbados		*Gunnis* 1968, 317
92.	†1851	General Paul Anderson		Christ Church Cathedral, Waterford	S	
93.	†1851	Hon Anne Noel		Alvington, Glos		Pevsner, *Glos: Vale & Forest of Dean*, 1976, 85
94.	†1851	Margaret and William Gwyn		Llangain, Carmarthen		*Dale-Jones and Lloyd* 1989, 56
95.	†1852	Rev Thomas Williams		Cameley, Somerset	S	
96.	†1855	Emily Garnons		Llanegwad, Carmarthen		*Dale-Jones and Lloyd* 1989, 56
97.	†1856	John (†1839) and Dinah (†1856)		Corsham, Wilts	S	
98.	1858	Fuller 55th regiment		[Lost in the Crimea]		CJ, 5 Feb 1858
Chimneypieces						
99.	?1824–25	Several		[Stourhead, Wilts]; untraced		*Gunnis* 1968, 317
Architectural Sculpture						
100.	?1825	Shields with the arms of Colt and Hoare	s	Stourhead, Wilts, gate piers		*Gunnis* 1968, 317
101.	1844	Large circular coat-of-arms		Bowood, Wilts, Golden Gates		Archives, Marquess of Lansdowne, in GPC

REGNART, Alexander fl early 19th century

Jane Regnart, widow of Alexander Regnart, stone-carver, died at Richmond, Surrey, in 1839, aged 71 (inf. Cornelius Willcock, in GPC).

REGNART, Charles, of London 1759–1844

Regnart was born in Bristol, the son of **Philip Regnart**. He was living at 12 Cleveland Street, Fitzroy Square by 1800 when his name was recorded in the Royal Academy Index but not in the Catalogue (*Graves* VI, 1905–6, 253). Gunnis describes him as an extremely competent monumental mason whose work may be found all over England. His masterpiece is the altar tomb with a recumbent figure of George Rush at Farthinghoe (**35**). It depicts Rush as 'an old, old, man, thin and emaciated, clad in a loose robe with slippers on his feet and his Bible in his hand . . . at the point of death', his eyes gazing towards heaven. Gunnis describes this effigy as 'one of the most remarkable and unusual executed in Britain during the early nineteenth century'. Regnart exhibited the tomb chest and a model of the figure at the RA in 1806.

Regnart was married twice, first to a Miss Hunter of Hexham and, after her death, to his cook. He had one son, Charles, born to his first wife in 1796. He died on 19 November 1844 and was buried in the Hampstead Road cemetery. In 1850 the Royal Academy made a charitable gift to 'Jane Regnart' who was probably his widow (RA Archives in *Gunnis* 1968, 317).

Literary References: *Gunnis* 1968, 317

Funerary Monuments

1.	†1750	Michael Baker and wife (†1796)	St Dunstan, Mayfield, Sussex	S	Pevsner, *Sussex*, 1965, 566
2.	†1775	Robert Welch	Caton, Lancs		Pevsner, *Lancs: N*, 1969, 92
3.	†1781	Henry Davidson	All Saints, Kingston upon Thames, London		Pevsner, *London: S*, 1983, 312
4.	?1784	Ann Robertson	Stoke, nr Guildford, Surrey		*Gunnis* 1968, 317
5.	†1790	Rachel Sandercock	Unitarian Chapel, York		Pevsner, *Yorks: E R & York*, 1995, 179
6.	†1791	Thomas Warry	West Coker, Somerset		RG/JP, 7, 1153
7.	†1793	Sarah Johnson	Hadleigh, Suffolk		Pevsner, *Suffolk*, 1974, 244
8.	†1794	Mary Wortley	Wortley, WR Yorks		Pevsner, *Yorks: W R*, 1967, 559
9.	†1795	Jane Pole	Tywardreath, Cornwall		Pevsner, *Cornwall*, 1970, 237
10.	?1795	Jane Rashleigh	Tywardreath, Cornwall		*Gunnis* 1968, 317
11.	1795	William Vachell	Hinxton, Cambs		*Gunnis* 1968, 317
12.	?1796	Ann Cox	Grays, Essex		*Gunnis* 1968, 317
13.	†1796	George Medley	Buxted, Sussex	S	Pevsner, *Sussex*, 1965, 465
14.	1796	Robert and William Marden	Thorpe Market, Norfolk		*Bartell* 1800, 45–6; Pevsner, *Norfolk: N E & Norwich*, 1997, 691
15.	?1796	Thomas Somers Cocks	Eastnor, Hereford		*Gunnis* 1968, 317
16.	1797	Bucknall family member	Oxhey Chapel, Oxhey, Herts		Pevsner, *Herts*, 1977, 268
17.	†1797	Captain Henry Newcome	St John, Hackney, London		Pevsner, *London: N*, 1998, 481
18.	†1797	John Finch	Kentish Town, London		Pevsner, *London: N*, 1998, 344
19.	†1797	Richard Bowen	Holy Trinity, Ilfracombe, Devon		Pevsner, *Devon*, 1989, 502
20.	†1797	William Sparkes	Aldeburgh, Suffolk	S	*Gunnis* 1968, 317
21.	†1798	Captain Cooke	Carnalway, Co Kildare	S	*Potterton* 1975, 74
22.	†1799	General Morrison	St Luke, Charlton, Middx		Pevsner, *London: S*, 1983, 247
23.	?1800	Edward Beynon	Carshalton, Surrey		*Gunnis* 1968, 317
24.	1800	Humphrey Cole (†1775)	Perranuthnoe, Cornwall	S	Pevsner, *Cornwall*, 1970, 140
25.	†1800	Michael Biddulph	Ledbury, Herefs		Pevsner, *Herefs*, 1963, 217
26.	1801	Elizabeth St Aubyn (†1796)	Orsett, Essex		*Gunnis* 1968, 317
27.	?1802	Elizabeth Surtees	Hambleden, Bucks		*Gunnis* 1968, 317
28.	?1802	Margaret Bearsley	St Mary, Aldermary, London		*Gunnis* 1968, 318
29.	*c*1803	Anne and Henrietta Wenyeve	Salisbury Cathedral, cloisters		
30.	?1803	Elizabeth French	Chesham, Bucks		*Gunnis* 1968, 318
31.	?1803	Thomas Astle	St Mary, Battersea, London		*Gunnis* 1968, 318
32.	?1804	Ann Corpe	Barnet, Herts		*Gunnis* 1968, 318
33.	?1804	Anthony Atcheson	Portsmouth Cathedral, Hants		*Gunnis* 1968, 318
34.	?1804	John André	Grosvenor Chapel, London		*Gunnis* 1968, 318

35.	†1806	George Rush Model(s): Exhib RA, London, with model, 1806, 821	Farthinghoe, Northants	S	*Graves* VI, 1905–6, 253; Pevsner, *Northants*, 1973, 212
36.	?1806	Sarah Pepys	Kentish Town, London		*Gunnis* 1968, 318
37.	†1807	Alston family	Alston, Cumberland		Pevsner, *Cumberland & Westmorland*, 1967, 60
38.	?1809	Charles Boycott	All Saints, Northampton		*Gunnis* 1968, 318
39.	?1810	Admiral White	Cookham, Berks		*Gunnis* 1968, 318
40.	†1810	John Heath	St Andrew, Chippenham, Wilts		RG/JP, 7, 1154
41.	†1811	Lieutenant Henry Sedgwick	St John, Hackney, London		Pevsner, *London: N*, 1998, 481
42.	†1811	Robert Hay	St Mary, Higham (nr Stratford St Mary), Suffolk		Pevsner, *Suffolk*, 1974, 271
43.	†1812	Thomas (†1785) and Jane (†1810) Punnett and Caroline Hodgson	Hunton, Kent	S	Pevsner, *Kent: W & Weald*, 1976, 340
44.	?1814	Lieutenant Andrew Hay	Fordingbridge, Hants		*Gunnis* 1968, 318
45.	†1815	John Birch	St Margaret Pattens, City of London		Pevsner, *London: City*, 1997, 236
46.	?1815	Rev George Harper	St Dunstan, Stepney, London		*Gunnis* 1968, 318
47.	pre-1815	Sir John Kemp and others	Gissing, Norfolk		*Gunnis* 1968, 318; Pevsner, *Norfolk: N W & S*, 1999, 360
48.	?1816	Richard Chilton	Mendlesham, Suffolk		*Gunnis* 1968, 318
49.	?1818	David Milligan	Spanish Town Cathedral, Jamaica, WI		*Gunnis* 1968, 318
50.	?1819	Frances Addington	Goldington, Beds		*Gunnis* 1968, 318
51.	1819	Hugh James (†1817)	Carlisle Cathedral		*CP*, 11 May 1819; Pevsner, *Cumberland & Westmorland*, 1967, 94
52.	?1820	Captain John Wood	Ickham, Kent		*Gunnis* 1968, 318
53.	?1821	Marie Herlock	Roxwell, Essex		*Gunnis* 1968, 318
54.	?1821	Sir Jonathan Miles	Ealing, London		*Gunnis* 1968, 318
55.	?1823	Richard Davies	Hartfield, Sussex		*Gunnis* 1968, 318
56.	†1823	William Noble	Bampton, Westmorland		Pevsner, *Cumberland & Westmorland*, 1967, 223
57.	?1827	Thomas Ashness	St Mary, Battersea, London		*Gunnis* 1968, 318
58.	?1834	Henry Smith	Kentish Town, London		*Gunnis* 1968, 318
59.	1842	John Lawford	St John's Wood Chapel, Marylebone, London		RG/JP, 7, 1155

REGNART, Philip 1745–

The family, whose badge was a fox, originally came from Flanders, and is said to be descended from Raginhart, a Gothic chief present with Alaric at the sack of Rome (*Gunnis* 1968, 318). The RSA *Minutes* state that Philip Regnart was born in the West Indies. He was taught by his father in 1760, became an apprentice carver in 1763, was with 'Mr Walsh' in 1764 and with 'Mr Rickert' in 1765 (*Dossie* 1782, 437–8). He won a premium on 22 February 1760 for a model of ornaments by a sculptor under 19 and four more by 1765. He became bankrupt in 1805. It is possible that he was responsible for some of the earlier monuments and tablets signed *Regnart* which Gunnis attributed to his son Charles.

Literary References: *Monthly Mag*, 1805, 1, 276; *Gunnis* 1968, 318

Archival References: RSA, *Minutes*, 1758–60; 1760–61, 1762–3, 1763–64, 1764–65

Miscellaneous

1.	1760	'model of ornaments'	[Soc of A, premium]; untraced	RSA, *Minutes*, 1758–1760, seq 4 fol 49; *Monthly Mag* 1805, I, 276
2.	1761	'ornamental composition in clay'	[Soc of A, premium]; untraced	RSA, *Minutes*, 1760–61, seq 3 fol 48
3.	1763	'model of ornaments in clay'	[Soc of A, premium]; untraced	RSA *Minutes*, 1762–63, seq 2 fol 71; RSA, *Premiums*, 1762, 33
4.	1764	'model of ornaments in clay'	[Soc of A, premium]; untraced	RSA *Minutes*, 1763–64, seq 3 fols 84, 90; RSA *Premiums*, 1763, 37 RSA,
5.	1765	'model of ornaments in clay'	[Soc of A, premium]; untraced	*Minutes*, 1764–65, seq 3 fol 61

REID, James fl 1803–06

J Reid of Glasgow carved the sandstone figure of William Wallace that stands in a niche on the façade of the Alliance Building Society office, High Street, Ayr (1). The statue appears to date from the early 19th century and is very probably the work of James Reid, a mason and carver who had a studio in Queen Street, Glasgow from 1803 to 1806.

Literary References: *Woodward* 1977, vol 1, pt 2, 182

Architectural Sculpture

1.	nd	William Wallace, statue	Alliance Building Society office, High S Street, Ayr	*Woodward* 1977, vol 1, pt 2, 182

RENDALL, Joseph, of Bristol fl 1723

A founder by trade, he made the large lead statue of *Neptune* which now stands near the Broad Quay in Bristol (*Latimer* 1893, 135–6) (1).

Statues

1.	1723	Neptune	l	[Temple Conduit, Temple Street, Bristol]; Broad Quay, Bristol	Pevsner, *Somerset: N & Bristol*, 1958, 425

RENE, Claudius fl *c*1675

Funerary Monuments

1.	†1675	Sir Thomas Wentworth and wife	Silkstone, W R Yorks	Pevsner, *Yorks: W R*, 1967, 483

RENNIE, George 1802–60

He was born at Phantassie, East Lothian, the son of George Rennie, the agriculturist (1749–1828) and the nephew of John Rennie, the engineer (1762–1821). After studying sculpture in Rome, possibly under **Bertel Thorvaldsen**, Rennie returned to England and he exhibited his most famous work, *The archer*, at the Royal Academy in 1828 (**3**). The *New Monthly Magazine* commented that the model of an almost naked figure, showed an 'admirable knowledge of anatomy', while the finish showed the influence of the Apollo Belvedere and both countenance and form were 'well worthy of one of those whom we might imagine a hero of a marathon'. The writer was surprised therefore to find that the 'very inferior' statue of a *Gleaner* in the same exhibition was 'from the chisel of the same artist' (*New Monthly Mag*, 1828, vol 24, 256) (**4**). Rennie exhibited at the RA in 1831–4 and in 1837, and his addresses were recorded in the Academy catalogues as George Street, Portman Square; Stafford Row, Pimlico and Chesham Place.

During the 1830s he turned his attention to politics, with the aim of improving the state of the arts in England. In 1836 he suggested to the Liberal politician William Ewart that a parliamentary committee should be formed, leading to the establishment of the School of Design at Somerset House. He also assisted the radical politician Joseph Hume in his efforts to obtain public freedom of access to all monuments and works of art in public buildings and museums. He was elected Liberal MP for Ipswich in 1841. The sculptor's collection of his own models, bronzes and marbles, together with models by Thorvaldsen and **Richard James Wyatt**, was sold in London on 9 June 1843. After retiring from Parliament in 1847, he was appointed governor of the Falkland Islands and in that position he won praise for his diplomatic skills and for encouraging the economic development of the islands. He returned to England in 1855 and died at his home, 32 York Terrace, Regent's Park, London, on 22 March 1860 and was buried in the catacombs of the Anglican chapel at Kensal Green cemetery. He left a widow, Jane, and two sons, William Hepburn Rennie, and Richard Temple Rennie, a barrister, of Shanghai, China and 113 Piccadilly.

Literary References: *Athenaeum*, 31 March, 1860, 445; *Physick* 1969, 22, 181; *Read* 1982, 50; *Curl* 2001, 242; *Bilbey* 2002, 350; *ODNB* (Dodgson rev Woodward)

Wills and Administrations: PPR, letters of administration, 7 April 1860, effects valued at under £3,000. 'Admon of Goods unadministered pasted at the Principal Probate Registry August 1867 / Admon of Goods twice unadministered pasted at the Princl. Regy. January 1875'

Auction Catalogues: Rennie 184

Funerary Monuments						
1.	†1832	John Mack		Chennai (Madras) Cathedral, India	S	
2.	1835	George, Ist Lord Harris		St Michael and All Angels, Throwley, Kent		Pevsner, *Kent: N E & E*, 1983, 477
Statues						
3.	1828	The archer		Athenaeum Club, London		*Graves* VI, 1905–6, 226; *Gunnis* 1968, 318
4.	1828	The gleaner		[Exhib RA, London, 1135]; untraced		*Graves* VI, 1905–6, 266
5.	c1831	Cupid kindling the torch of Hymen	m	VAM A.22-1936	S	*Library of Fine Arts* 1831, vol 1, 431; *Graves* VI, 1905–6, 266; *Bilbey* 2002, 350 (repr)
6.	1832	The conchologists	m	[Exhib RA, London, 1144]; untraced		*Graves* VI, 1905–6, 266
7.	1837	Group of four figures	m	[Exhib RA, London, 1188]; untraced		*Graves* VI, 1905–6, 266
8.	1838	Horatio, Admiral Lord Nelson, two competition models for the national monument (commission awarded to William Railton and E H Baily)		Untraced		*Yarrington* 1988, 358
9.	nd	A child at prayer		[Rennie sale, Christie, 9 July 1843]; untraced		Christies Archives in GPC
10.	nd	A draped female playing the mandolin		[Rennie sale, Christie, 9 July 1843]; untraced		Christies Archives in GPC
11.	nd	Greek water-bearer	m	Glasgow Museums S.15		inf: Glasgow Museums
12.	nd	Group of two children and a dog		[Rennie sale, Christie, 9 July 1843]; untraced		Christies Archives in GPC
13.	nd	Mars		Chatsworth, Derbys		*Gunnis* 1968, 318
Busts						
14.	1826	Achilles Payment(s): 60 louis	m	[coll William, 6th Duke of Devonshire]; Chatsworth, Derbys, sculpture gallery	SD	*JKB* 1972 (3), 327, 331
15.	pre-1828	Bertel Thorvaldsen (co-sculptor: Bertel Thorwaldsen)		[Rennie sale, Christie, London, 9 July 1843, lot 42]; untraced		*Graves* VI, 1905–6, 266; *Bilbey* 2002, 350
16.	1830	B Flanders		Ackworth School, W R Yorks		GPC
17.	1831	John Rennie		[Exhib RA, London, 1202]; untraced		*Graves* VI, 1905–6, 266
18.	1831	Sir Edward Banks		[Exhib RA, London, 1210]; Ammerdown Park, Somerset	SD	*Graves* VI, 1905–6, 266
19.	1832	Unidentified gentleman	m	[Exhib RA, London, 1152]		*Graves* VI, 1905–6, 266
20.	1832	William Jolliffe	m	Ammerdown, Somerset		*Graves* VI, 1905–6, 266; *Gunnis* 1968, 318
21.	1833	Sir David Wilkie RA	m	RA, London		*Graves* VI, 1905–6, 266
22.	?1849	King William IV	p	Burlington House, London		GPC
Architectural Sculpture						
23.	1834	Mercury, Britannia, Ceres, the Thames, Industry and Calculation, reliefs		Dividend Office, Bank of England, London		*Gunnis* 1968, 318
Miscellaneous						
24.	1834	Infantine devotion		[Exhib RA, London, 1108]; untraced		*Graves* VI, 1905–6, 266
25.	1834	The minstrel		[Exhib RA, London, 1048]; untraced		*Graves* VI, 1905–6, 266

REVITT, J, of Biggleswade and Linford fl c1802–03

Funerary Monuments					
1.	?1802	Mrs Pigott	Henlow, Beds	S	*Gunnis* 1968, 319
2.	?1803	Robert Callinson	Newport Pagnell, Bucks	S	*Gunnis* 1968, 319

REX, of Salisbury fl c1846

On 24 June 1848 the *Builder* reported that some 'ornamental figures surmounting the pillars at the gate entrance to Wilton House', recently executed by a local artist called Mr Rex, had been 'wantonly or maliciously destroyed' (*Builder*, 1848, 306).

Architectural Sculpture

1.	c1846	Ornamental figures 'surmounting the pillars'	[Wilton House, Wilts, gate entrance]; destroyed 1848	*Builder*, 1848, 306; *Gunnis* 1968, 319

REYNOLDS, Alfred John

A wax modeller: for further information the reader is referred to *Pyke* 1973, 119.

REYNOLDS, George 1746–

In 1764 Reynolds was apprenticed, but *Dossie* leaves the name of his master blank (*Gunnis*'s 'Mr Fest' is a misreading of 'festoon'). Dossie described him as a woodcarver. On 18 May 1764 he won a four guinea premium from the Society of Arts in the under-19 class (1) and on 24 May 1765, a 5 guinea premium, for a model by a youth aged nineteen (2). Nothing more is known of him.

Literary References: *Dossie* 1782, 437, 438; RSA, *Premiums*, 1763–64, 37; *Gunnis* 1968, 319

Archival References: RSA, *Minutes*, 1763–64, seq 3 fol 84; 1764–65, seq 3 fol 65

Reliefs

1.	1764	Clay festoon in bas-relief	[Soc of A, premium (4 gns)]; untraced	RSA, *Minutes*, 1763–64, seq 3 f84; RSA *Premiums*, 1763, 37

Miscellaneous

2.	1765	Model of ornaments in clay	[Soc of A, premium (5 gns)]; untraced	RSA, *Minutes*, 1764–65, seq 3 f65

RHODES, Robert, of Leeds fl 1757–1802

Rhodes was apprenticed to John Carr, an architect of York, in 1757 (City Archives in *Gunnis* 1968, 319). He signs a large wall-tablet in coloured marbles in Leeds Parish Church (1). He was succeeded in the business by his son Edward, who worked from 1817 to 1834. They may have been related to John Rhodes, one of the contractors for St Mary, Bridgnorth, Salop, in 1792 (Archives Lord Sandys in *Gunnis* 1968, 319) and to Mr R Rhodes, a stonemason whose widow died early in 1806 (*Monthly Mag*, 1806, 21).

Literary References: *Gunnis* 1968, 319

Funerary Monuments

1.	?1802	Thomas Close	St Peter, Leeds, W R Yorks	S	*Gunnis* 1968, 319

RICE, Thomas, of Brompton fl c1823–40

Funerary Monuments

1.	?1823	Rev Benjamin Wainewright	East Bergholt, Suffolk	S	*Gunnis* 1968, 319
2.	†1838	John Kennard	Holy Trinity, Clapham, London	S	*Gunnis* 1968, 319
3.	†1840	Rev John Hanley	Amberley, Sussex	S	*Gunnis* 1968, 319

RICE, W, of Barnstaple fl c1760

He signs a 'wall-tablet with pilasters supporting a plain pediment' (*Gunnis* 1968, 319) (1).

Funerary Monuments

1.	?1760	Mary Chichester	Georgeham, Devon	S	*Gunnis* 1968, 319

RICHARD (or RICKARD), Samuel fl 1748

A stone mason, he received payments at Woburn Abbey from November 1748.

Archival References: Woburn Building Accts, 1748–1762, R5/1092

RICHARDS, A fl c1832–40

Funerary Monuments

1.	†1832	Samuel White	Holy Trinity, Exeter, Devon		RG/JP, 7, 1157v.
2.	†1840	Frances Bellew	Holy Trinity, Exeter, Devon		RG/JP, 7, 1157v.

RICHARDS, J, of Exeter fl c1794–1830

Funerary Monuments

1.	†1794	John Saltren of Petticombe	Monkleigh, Devon		Pevsner, *Devon*, 1989, 573
2.	†1807	John Hanning	White Lackington, Somerset		Pevsner, *Somerset: S & W*, 1958, 344
3.	?1817	George Barbor	Fremington, Devon	S	*Gunnis* 1968, 319
4.	†1819	Edward Lee	Buckland Brewer, Devon		Pevsner, *Devon*, 1989, 230
5.	?1824	James Haynes	Hartbury, Devon	S	*Gunnis* 1968, 319
6.	†1830	George and Anne Bradshaw	St Nicholas with St Giles, Sidmouth, Devon		RG/JP, 7, 1158
7.	?1830	Hannah Beard	Lifton, Devon	S	*Gunnis* 1968, 319
8.	†1830	Susan Mordaunt	Shobrooke, Devon		GPC

RICHARDS, James 1671–1759

He was Carver to the King in wood, marble and stone. On 20 December 1721 he was appointed successor to **Grinling Gibbons** as master sculptor and master carver in wood to the crown, at a fee of 18 pence per day, plus all the 'Profits Rights Allowances Liberties Commodities and Advantages' enjoyed by his predecessor. He also received 'One Robe yearly' which was to be taken 'out of Our Great Wardrobe against the Feast of the Birth of Our Lord Jesus Christ by the hands of the Master Keeper or other Officer of Our said Wardrobe' (Account Book of Richard Arundel, quoted in *Gunnis* 1968, 319). On 20 May 1724 he was also appointed surveyor and repairer of carved wood to the crown. Richards kept both posts until his death.

By his own testimony he was made a freeman of the City of London as a mason before 1723, and he is recorded as a carver at several houses working under Colen Campbell (**7, 13, 18**) and William Kent (**1, 6, 14, 15, 27, 30**). He was responsible for much of the consummate carving on the royal barge in 1730–31, working to Kent's designs (**22**). Beard describes Richards as 'one of the most accomplished carvers of the Palladian years' (*Beard* 1985, 690).

Richards married a Miss Mary Morse (†1760). Their only son died 13 January 1739, aged 36. One daughter, Elizabeth, married the architect Isaac Ware at St James, Paddington, on 22 September 1729 and another, Mary, married the glazier Charles Carne. Richards was one of the subscribers to Ware's edition of Palladio's *Quattro Libri* published in 1738. Richards lent Ware and Carne £1,500, perhaps as an investment in their building projects, a sum that had still not been repaid at the time of his death. In 1739 Ware and Carne mortgaged their lease of 429 Strand to Richards as security for the loan.

Richards's employees included Ralph Kite, who was recorded as his 'man' at Houghton in 1729 and also his grandson **Walter James Ware.** Richards petitioned the Board of Works to employ him and Ware to carry out carved work for the Horse Guards building in August 1750 (**15**). He left £200 to Ware in his will (later reduced to £100) to discharge his debts, and £1,000 in securities.

In 1744 Richards became a director of the Westminster Fire Office. By 1754 he was ill and the Board of Works declared that he was 'by age and infirmity render'd incapable of performing the Duty of his Office.' They recommended that **George Murray** 'who hath been employed as his Assistant, be . . . continued in that Employment' (TNA Work 6/17, 128 quoted in *Colvin* 1973–76, vol V, 473). Murray seems to have been a long-term assistant: he had worked with Richards at 17 Arlington Street in 1742 (**30**) and provided carved work at the Horse Guards in 1750–1 (**15**). He succeeded to the office of master carver on Richards's death.

Richards died on 21 December 1759, and was buried at Sandon, Essex. In his will, proved in January 1760, he left nearly £2,800 in named gifts, which he estimated as half his estate; the money owed to him by Carne and Ware was to be counted as part of the portion left to his daughter, Mary Carne. A freehold estate near 'Westram', Kent was left to his granddaughter Margaret Millington, and his freehold estate, Woodhill 'or what other name it be called' passed to his daughter Mary Carne in a codicil. In another codicil the value of several of the gifts was slightly reduced, suggesting that Richards had overestimated the value of his estate.

MGS

Literary References: *Gunnis* 1968, 319; *S of L*, 36, 1970, 264; *Colvin* V, 1973–76, 438, 473, 479; *Beard* 1985, 690, 693; *Beard* 1986, 1278–91; *Beard and Gilbert* 1986, 742

Archival References: IGI; GPC

Chimneypieces

No.	Date	Description	Material	Location	References
1.	1724	Ornaments to a design ordered by the King and approved by the Board Payment(s): £45 exclusive of mouldings	m	Kensington Palace, London, King's drawing room	*Wren Soc* VII, 195; *Gunnis* 1968, 319; *Colvin* 1973–76, V, 200–1; Pevsner, *London: N W*, 1991, 475
2.	1727	Overmantel ornaments Payment(s): £7 and £6		Boynton Hall, E R Yorks, oak room and drawing room	*Beard* 1986, 1282; Pevsner, *Yorks: E R & York*, 1995, 335
3.	1734	Several	m	[Kew Palace]; untraced	GPC
4.	1736	Statuary marble with heads, foliage and scrolls Payment(s): £30		[Kew Palace, London]; untraced	GPC
5.	1740	Description unavailable Payment(s): £12 2s	wd	[for Earl Fitzwalter, Pall Mall, London]; untraced	*Beard and Gilbert* 1986, 742

Architectural Sculpture

No.	Date	Description	Material	Location	References
6.	1722	'for carving ye Tabernacle & ye Frontispiece for ye Hall'		Chicheley Hall, Bucks, entrance hall	*Beard and Gilbert* 1986, 742; Pevsner, *Bucks*, 1994, 247
7.	1717–1724	Carving		[Rolls House, Chancery Lane, London]; untraced	*Colvin* 1973–76, V, 358; *Beard* 1985, 690
8.	1728	Unidentified Payment(s): £233 5s 3d		[Admiralty, London]; untraced	GPC
9.	*c*1729	Unspecified woodwork		Eton College, Windsor, Berks, Cloister Court Library	Pevsner, *Bucks*, 1994, 312
10.	1731	Carving in bed chamber, dressing room and 'Long Blew Roome' Payment(s): £60 3s		[Kew Palace, London]; untraced	*Beard and Gilbert* 1986, 742; GPC
11.	1731	'Carving the King's Arms' Payment(s): £8		[St Margaret's, Westminster]; untraced	Vestry Minutes, 8 Nov 1731 (E2419)
12.	1731	Six carved and fluted Corinthian columns Payment(s): £53 8s 6d		[Sherborne House, Glos]; untraced	*Beard and Gilbert* 1986, 742
13.	1731	Unspecified decorative carving Payment(s): £290		[Compton Place, Eastbourne]; untraced	*Beard* 1985, 690; *Beard and Gilbert* 1986, 742; GPC
14.	1737	Carving		[Whitehall, London, Treasury]; untraced	*Colvin* 1973–76, V, 432
15.	1750–1751	Decorative ornaments, including small pineapples and fasces (co-sculptor: Walter James Ware) Payment(s): £41 4s 5 1/4d	s	Horse Guards, Whitehall, London, west front	Board of Works/Horseguards HOR/1/2 II; *Colvin* 1973–76, V, 438; *Gunnis* 1968, 319; *Beard and Gilbert* 1986, 742
16.	nd	Overdoor carving	wd	Chiswick House, London	*Beard* 1985, 692 (repr)

Miscellaneous

No.	Date	Description	Material	Location	References
17.	1720	Unspecified carving Payment(s): £14		[for Robert Chester, former Director of the South Sea Company, possibly for Briggens, Herts]; untraced	*Chester Inventory* 1721, 51; GPC
18.	1719–1721	Unspecified work Payment(s): £40 in Sept 1719, £55 in part payment of £115 in May 1720		[Burlington House, Piccadilly, London]; untraced	*Beard* 1985, 690; *Beard and Gilbert* 1986, 742; GPC
19.	1726	Carved frame Payment(s): £13		[for Earl Lichfield of Ditchley Park, Oxon]; untraced	Oxon RO, Dil/I/P/3aq; GPC
20.	1731	Carving, painting and gilding two table frames (made by James Moore) Payment(s): £19	wd	[Sherborne House, Glos, Banqueting House]; untraced	*Beard and Gilbert* 1986, 742
21.	1731	Chairs and settees Payment(s): £10.2.6.		[for Charles, Earl of Tankerville, 1–2 St James's Square, London, great room]; untraced	*Beard* 1986, 1282

22.	1731–1732	Ornaments for royal barge (designed by William Kent) Payment(s): £150 16s 6d	wd	[for Frederick, Prince of Wales]; NMM, Greenwich	*Beard* 1985, 690, 692 (repr); *Beard* 1986, 1282, 1286; *Beard and Gilbert* 1986, 742
23.	1732	Unspecified carving Payment(s): £150		[Kew Palace, London]; untraced	*Beard and Gilbert* 1986, 742; GPC
24.	1733	Settees, chairs, frames and architraves		[Kew Palace, London]; untraced	*Beard and Gilbert* 1986, 742; GPC
25.	1730–1733	Unidentified carving Payment(s): £47 5s 1d		[Westminster School, London, new dormitory]; untraced	*Wren Soc* XI, 44
26.	1733	Unspecified carving Payment(s): £130		[Kew Palace, London]; untraced	*Beard and Gilbert* 1986, 742; GPC
27.	1733–1737	Unidentified carving		[Treasury, Whitehall, London]; untraced	*Beard* 1985, 693
28.	1737	Unidentified work		[St James's Palace, London, Queen Caroline's library]; untraced	*Beard* 1985, 690
29.	1737	Unidentified work		[St James's Palace, library]; untraced	*Colvin* 1973–76, V, 243, n1
30.	1742	Unidentified carving		[for Henry Pelham, 17 Arlington Street, London]; untraced	*Beard* 1985, 693; *Beard and Gilbert* 1986, 742
31.	1749	Unidentified carving Payment(s): £106 19s		[Moulsham Hall, Chelmsford]; untraced	*Beard and Gilbert* 1986, 742
32.	1752	Unidentified carving		[Cleveland House, St James's, London]; untraced	*Beard and Gilbert* 1986, 742

RICHARDS, John fl 1721

John Richards, carver, was paid for unspecified work on 31 October 1721 by Robert Chester, one of the directors of the South Sea Company (*Chester Inventory* 1721, 51).

RICHARDS, John, of Bishopsgate fl *c*1772

He is known only for one rococo cartouche tablet, surmounted by a portrait bust (**1**). He was probably related to William and John Richards, masons of Bishopsgate Street, who are listed under the Livery of the Masons' Company *c*1740 (Masons' Co Assistants, fol 3).

Funerary Monuments

1.	†1772	John Clare	Buckland, Herts	Pevsner, *Herts*, 1977, 117

RICHARDS, L, of Hereford fl 1728

He signs an architectural wall monument about eight feet high with a semicircular pediment supported by four Corinthian pilasters. Gunnis says that it is above the usual provincial standard.

Funerary Monuments

1.	1728	Gilbert Abrahall (†1723)	Ross-on-Wye, Herefs	S	*Gunnis* 1968, 319

RICHARDS, of Birmingham fl *c*1847

Funerary Monuments

1.	?1847	Benjamin Sidaway and family	Cradley Heath, Staffs	S

RICHARDS, of London fl *c*1823

Funerary Monuments

1.	†1823	Joseph Benfield	St Charles the Martyr, Falmouth, Cornwall	S

RICHARDSON fl 1780

A man of this name appeared in the trial for highway robbery of William Harding on 13 September 1780. He described himself as 'a statuary and wood-carver' and gave a good character reference for the defendant. **Welch** appeared as a character witness in the same trial (Proceedings of the Old Bailey, t 17800913-11).

RICHARDSON, Christopher, of Doncaster 1709–81

A sculptor and maker of chimneypieces, Richardson worked on decorative carving at Welbeck Abbey for the 1st Duke of Portland, 1747–51 (**3, 5, 6, 7, 9**). In 1750–1 he was employed on various works at Cusworth Hall, then being extended under the direction of the architect James Paine (**4, 8, 10**). In 1756 he worked on the statue of *Liberty* for the top of the column at Gibside (**1**). The original design for this work is attributed to another architect, Daniel Garrett, but its completion was supervised by Paine, who probably designed the figure and recommended that Richardson be employed to carve it. A year later Richardson carved the coat-of arms for the town hall at Berwick-upon-Tweed, taking the place of **Charles Litaneer** who had originally been engaged to do the work (**11**). The Works Committee was authorised to employ him after they 'reported that they did not approve of the model Mr. Litaneer made of the Corporation Arms' and that 'Mr. Christopher Richardson, of Doncaster carver, a person of known character who is now carving at Alnwick Castle, for the Rt. Hon. the Earl of Northumberland and at other parts of the north, has offered to carve our Arms with the ornaments . . . on stone which the Guild has seen and approved of, £42 (the stone being fixed up at Corporation expense)' (Guildbook 22 March 1757, in *Gunnis* 1968, 320). In 1756–62 Richardson was working for the 2nd Marquess of Rockingham at Wentworth Woodhouse, Yorks (Wentworth Woodhouse Archives, in *Gunnis* 1968, 320), and two years later he was again at Welbeck, executing decorations for the cupola over the chapel clock (**12**). He carved capitals and a coat of arms at Burton Constable Hall in 1767–68 (**13, 14**). He died in November 1781 and was buried at Doncaster, his wife Sarah having predeceased him on 19 July 1771 (Doncaster Parish Church Registers, in *Gunnis* 1968, 320).

Literary References: *Gunnis* 1968, 319–20; *Hudson* 1979, 2460–2461; *Usherwood* 2000, 214–5, 333

Statues

1.	1756–1757	Liberty	s	Gibside Park, Co Durham, Column of British Liberty	*Usherwood* 2000, 214–5 (repr)
2.	nd	Two sphinxes		Harewood House, W R Yorks, entrance steps	*Jewell* 1822, 22

Chimneypieces

3.	1750	Description unavailable	[Welbeck Abbey, Notts, daylight room]; untraced	Archives Duke of Portland, in *Gunnis* 1968, 319

4.	1751	Description unavailable Payment(s): £7		[Cusworth Hall, W R Yorks]; untraced	GPC
5.	1748–1751	Gothic chimneypiece in Roach Abbey stone Payment(s): £44		[Welbeck Abbey, Notts, great hall]; untraced	Archives Duke of Portland, in *Gunnis* 1968, 319
6.	1757	White veined-marble Payment(s): £42	m	[Welbeck Abbey, Notts]; untraced	Archives Duke of Portland, in *Gunnis* 1968, 319
Architectural Sculpture					
7.	1747	Carving		[Welbeck Abbey, Notts, alcove room]; untraced	Archives Duke of Portland, in *Gunnis* 1968, 319
8.	1750	Eight Ionic capitals Payment(s): £10 4s	s	[Cusworth Hall, W R Yorks]; untraced	GPC
9.	1750	Six stags' heads	wd	[Welbeck Abbey, Notts, daylight room]; untraced	Archives Duke of Portland, in *Gunnis* 1968, 319
10.	1750	Unspecified woodwork Payment(s): £51	wd	[Cusworth Hall, W R Yorks]; untraced	GPC
11.	1757	Town arms Payment(s): £42	s	Town hall, Berwick-upon-Tweed, Northumbs	*Gunnis* 1968, 320
12.	1764	Ornaments		[Welbeck Abbey, Notts, cupola over chapel clock]; untraced	Archives Duke of Portland, in *Gunnis* 1968, 320
13.	1766–1767	Constable Coat of Arms Payment(s): £63	s	Burton Constable Hall, E R Yorks, east front	Constable Accounts, ERAO, DDCC/2/52; *Mulcahy* 2006, 31 (repr)
14.	1768	Two Ionic capitals Payment(s): 10 gns	m	[Burton Constable Hall, E R Yorks]; untraced	Constable Accounts, ERAO, DDCC/2/52

RICHARDSON, Edward 1812–69

Edward Richardson was a sculptor and archaeologist who specialised in the restoration of medieval tombs. He is thought to have been born in London but nothing is known of his parents and early life. In 1832 he entered the Royal Academy Schools on the recommendation of **Sir Francis Chantrey**. He may have been responsible for two classically inspired works and a study of a horse shown at the Academy by an artist called E Richardson between 1829 and 1832 and he certainly exhibited at the RA between 1836 and 1866, showing works based on mythological and literary subject matter, portrait busts and models for church monuments. He also sent works to the British Institution, the Society of British Artists in Suffolk Street and the Great Exhibition of 1851.

In 1842 Richardson was commissioned to restore the effigies of the Knights Templar in the Temple church (**2**). The figures had suffered considerable damage whilst stored in a damp shed the previous winter and extensive restoration was consequently needed. However, Richardson's intervention was considered insensitive by some experts and resulted in a chorus of disapproval. He was refused admission to the Society of Antiquaries and Augustus Hare condemned him as 'a charlatan who has planed down the effigies' (*Gunnis* 1968, 320). Two years later Richardson was under attack again, this time for a statue of the medieval poet John Gower which he sent to the Westminster Hall Exhibition (**39**). It was described as 'a mere strait furrowed mass of plaster' in the *Art Union* (1844, 217) and the art critic of the *Literary Gazette* remarked, 'how a man could be audacious enough to send such an abortion as this to a competition, must astonish everyone' (cited by *Gunnis* 1968, 320). He exhibited a more successful statue of *The inspired David meditating the destruction of Goliath* at the same venue the following year (**40**).

In spite of the controversy surrounding his work at the Temple Church, Richardson soon established himself as an expert restorer of medieval monuments. At Chichester Cathedral he restored two 14th-century monuments to the Earl and Countess of Arundel and Robert Stratford, Bishop of Chichester (**3, 6**). The Stratford monument was then thought to commemorate an earlier bishop, Richard of Wyche (†1253), who was canonized in 1262 after miracles were reported at his tomb. As well as repairing the effigy Richardson re-carved much of the tomb chest, adding seven statuettes representing figures associated with the life of St Richard. In 1848 he was employed on similar work at Elford Church, Staffs (**8**). The *Gentleman's Magazine* noted that the contract had been awarded to Richardson because of his reputation for 'intelligence and reverential accuracy in dealing with the productions of ancient art' (*GM*, 1852, ii, 66). In 1850 he was called in by the authorities at Wells Cathedral to repair the seated statue of the Saxon King, Edward the Elder, on the west front, after it fell from a height of 60 feet, narrowly missing the carriage of a judge (**53**). Three years later he was commissioned to make or procure many of the casts of sepulchral effigies for the Crystal Palace at Sydenham (**18**).

Meanwhile, Richardson developed an extensive practice as a sculptor of funerary monuments, executing a large number of military memorials. In 1848 he carved two for Canterbury Cathedral, commemorating the officers and men of the 16th Lancers and the 31st Regiment, killed during the First Sikh War (**10, 11**). Though the *Builder* considered them 'ably executed' it nevertheless felt 'bound to say the designs ought, in our opinion, to have been very different in character for the proposed situation' (*Builder*, 1848, 310). His monument to Major-General Sir Robert Dick, who died during the same conflict, has a relief portrait of the General in the uniform of the 42nd Royal Highlanders, with a Sikh shield and helmet at his feet (**12**). The *Gentleman's Magazine* thought it 'in one sense but a costume figure' but noted that it was treated 'with a chaste and classic feeling' and that the overall effect was 'pleasing and picturesque' (*GM*, 1850, i, 620). His monuments to John Abel Smith, the Earl of Powis, the Marquess of Ormonde and the Earl of Bandon all have gothic-inspired recumbent effigies (**9, 15, 23, 31**).

Richardson was an active member of the London and Middlesex Archaeological Society. He published accounts of *The monumental effigies of the Temple Church* (1843), *The ancient stone and leaden coffins, encaustic tiles, etc. recently discovered in the Temple Church* (1845) and *The monumental effigies and tombs in Elford Church, Staffordshire* (1852) and presented papers to the Archaeological Institute on English medieval alabaster sculpture (1852), the monuments in Chichester Cathedral (1853) and effigies of English Kings at Fontrevault and Le Mans (1854) He also contributed several articles to the *Archaeological Journal.* Richardson lived at 17 Melbury Terrace, Marylebone from 1847 onwards. After some years of ill-health he died of erysipelas on 17 May 1869 at 19 Egremont Place, Brighton, Sussex.

EH

Literary References: *Redgrave* 1878; *DNB* (Dodgson); *Grant* 1953, 203; *Gunnis* 1968, 320–1; *ODNB* (Rev. Edwards)

Wills: PPR, will, 14 June 1869, fol 423, effects valued at under £4,000

Funerary Monuments

1.	†1854–55	7th Royal Fusiliers (Crimean War Memorial)		Winchester Cathedral, Hants		*Builder*, 1859, 590
2.	1842	Effigies of the Knights Templar (restoration only)		[Temple Church, London]; destroyed		*ODNB*
3.	1843	Richard, 13th Earl of Arundel (†1376) and his wife Eleanor (†1372) (restoration only)	s	Chichester Cathedral, Sussex		*Tummers* 1988, 31–6 (repr)
4.	†1845	Major-General George Broadfoot		St George's Cathedral, Chennai (Madras), India	S	*Gunnis* 1968, 320; *Groseclose* 1995, 70–1 (repr)
5.	?1846	Catherine Lushington		Chennai (Madras) Cathedral, India	S	*Gunnis* 1968, 320
6.	1846	Robert Stratford, Bishop of Chichester (†1362) (restoration only)	s	Chichester Cathedral, Sussex		*GM*, 1847, i, 258–9 (repr); *Tummers* 1988, 10–14 (repr)
7.	1847	Two medallions, for monument of Sir Alexander Dickson	b	Woolwich, London		*GM*, 1850, i, 619; *Gunnis* 1968, 320
8.	1848	Ancient effigies (restoration only)		Elford, Staffs		*GM*, 1848, ii, 531; 1852, ii, 66–9; Pevsner, *Staffs*, 1974, 127
9.	1848	John Abel Smith Model(s): exhib RA, London, 1848, 1379		Chichester Cathedral, Sussex		*GM*, 1847, i, 259; *Graves* VI, 1905–6, 285; Pevsner, *Sussex*, 1965, 160
10.	1848	Officers and privates of the 16th Queen's Lancers		Canterbury Cathedral, Kent	SD	*Builder* 1848, 310; *GM*, 1848, ii, 83; Pevsner, *Kent: NE & E*, 1983, 214
11.	1848	Officers and privates of the Huntingdonshire 31st Regiment		Canterbury Cathedral, Kent	SD	*Builder* 1848, 310; *GM*, 1848, ii, 83
12.	1850	Major-General Sir Robert Dick (†1846)		Chennai (Madras) Cathedral, India	SD	*GM*, 1850, i, 619–20 (repr); *Gunnis* 1968, 320
13.	1851	Officers and men of the North Lincoln Regiment (Indian Wars)		Lincoln Cathedral	S	Pevsner, *Lincs*, 1989, 477
14.	†1852	Colonel McNeill		St Mary, Fort St George, Chennai (Madras), India	S	*Graves* VI, 1905–6, 285; *Gunnis* 1968, 320
15.	1852	Edward, Earl of Powis (†1848) (designed by Sir George Gilbert Scott) Model(s): exhib RA, London, 1853, 1347	a	St Mary, Welshpool, Montgomery	S	*Graves* VI, 1905–6, 285; Pevsner, *Powys*, 1979, 208
16.	1853	Hugh Montgomery (†1853)		Holy Trinity, Mahatma Gandhi Road, Bangalore	SD	
17.	1853	John Wylie MD (†1852)	m	St Andrew's Kirk, Chennai (Madras), India	SD	*Graves* VI, 1905–6, 285
18.	1853	Plaster casts of sepulchral effigies	p	[Crystal Palace, Sydenham]; untraced		*Gunnis* 1968, 320
19.	1854	Alicia Murray		Chichester Cathedral, Sussex	SD	
20.	1854	Sir Marmaduke Constable (restoration only)		Nuneaton, Warks		*Gunnis* 1968, 320
21.	1855	51st (King's Own) Light Infantry Regiment (†Burma 1852–3)		York Minster, St John's chapel	SD	*Aylmer* 1977, 469–71 (repr)
22.	?1855	Dean of Lincoln Model(s): exhib RA, London, 1855, 1447		St Peter Port, Guernsey	S	*Graves* VI, 1905–6, 285; *Gunnis* 1968, 320
23.	1855	John, 2nd Marquess of Ormonde (†1854) Model(s): exhib RA, London, 1860, 999	s	Kilkenny Cathedral		*Graves* VI, 1905–6, 285; *Potterton* 1975, 6, 74–75 (repr)
24.	1855	Lady Harriet Paget		All Saints, Hastings, Sussex, churchyard		GPC
25.	†1856	Edmund, 8th Earl of Cork		Frome, Somerset	S	*Gunnis* 1968, 320
26.	?1857	Sir George Napier		Geneva, Switzerland	S	*Gunnis* 1968, 320
27.	1859	2nd Batallion Military Train (Indian Rebellion monument)		Bristol Cathedral		*Builder* 1859, 590
28.	1859	33rd Regiment (Duke of Wellington's) Crimean War memorial		York Minster, All Saints chapel	S	*Aylmer* 1977, 470; *Pattison and Murray* 2001, 125–6
29.	1859	49th Regiment Crimean War memorial		All Saints, Hertford		GPC
30.	1859	Colonel Charles Chester (†1857)		Winchester Cathedral, Hants		*Builder*, 1859, 590
31.	1859	James, 2nd Earl of Bandon (†1856)		St Peter, Bandon, Co Cork	S	*Potterton* 1975, 74
32.	?1859	Royal Welch Fusiliers Crimean War Memorial		Carmarthen		*Gunnis* 1968, 320
33.	1860	General Sir James Law Lushington (†1859)		Kensal Green Cemetery, London	SD	*Curl* 2001, 217, 239, n73 (repr)
34.	?1861	Officers and men of the Duke of Cornwall's Light Infantry		Exeter Cathedral, Devon	S	*Gunnis* 1968, 321
35.	1863	101st Regiment		Winchester Cathedral, Hants		GPC
36.	?1867	Sir Richard Shakespear		St Anne, Indore, India	S	*Gunnis* 1968, 321

Statues

37.	1839	Mercury preparing for flight		[Exhib RA, London, 1282]; untraced		*Graves* VI, 1905–6, 284–5; *Gunnis* 1968, 320
38.	1842	Unidentified female, sketch for a statue		[Exhib RA, London, 1342]; untraced		*Graves* VI, 1905–6, 285
39.	1844	John Gower, the poet	p	[Exhib Westminster Hall, London, 179]; untraced		*AU*, 1844, 217; *Graves* 1875, 453; *Gunnis* 1968, 320
40.	1845	The inspired David meditating the destruction of Goliath		[Exhib Westminster Hall, London, 131]; untraced		*Westminster* 1845, 16; *AU*, 1845, 258; *Builder* 1845, 316
41.	1854	Bluecoat boy		Bluecoat school, Chester, niche over entrance		Pevsner, *Cheshire*, 1971, 161
42.	nd	Venus reposing		[Colosseum, Regent's Park, London]; untraced		GPC

No.	Date	Subject		Location	References
Busts					
43.	1840	Unidentified subject, study		[Exhib BI, London, 459]; untraced	*Graves* 1875, 453
44.	1847	Richard Rothwell		[Exhib RA, London, 1432]; untraced	*Graves* VI, 1905–6, 285
45.	1848	Master Puck		[Exhib RA, London, 1410]; untraced	*Graves* VI, 1905–6, 285
46.	1850	John Smith MP	m	[Exhib RA, London, 1400]; untraced	*Graves* VI, 1905–6, 285
47.	1855	Dr Gideon Mantell		[Exhib RA, London, 1533]; untraced	*Graves* VI, 1905–6, 285
48.	1856	Dr Thomas Watts	m	[Exhib RA, London, 1337]; untraced	*Graves* VI, 1905–6, 285
49.	1856	Earl of Powis		Powis Castle, Montgomery	*Graves* VI, 1905–6, 285; *Gunnis* 1968, 320
50.	1857	Sir Edward Tierney Bt	m	[Exhib RA, London, 1276]; untraced	*Graves* VI, 1905–6, 285
51.	1859	Unidentified subject	m	[Exhib RA, London, 1306]; untraced	*Graves* VI, 1905–6, 285
52.	1866	Colonel Sir Harry Colville Darell	m	[Exhib RA, London, 1038]; untraced	*Graves* VI, 1905–6, 285
53.	1866	Rev Sir Lionel Darell Bt		[Exhib RA, London, 1037]; untraced	*Graves* VI, 1905–6, 285
Architectural Sculpture					
54.	1850	King Edward the Elder (restoration only)		Wells Cathedral, Somerset, west front	*Builder* 1853, 560; *Gunnis* 1968, 320
55.	1853	Pulpit		St Mary, Shrewsbury	*Gunnis* 1968, 320
Reliefs					
56.	1837	Study of horses from nature		[Soc of BA, London, 595]; untraced	*Johnson* 1975, 391
57.	1852	Unidentified gentleman, medallic portrait		[Exhib RA, London, 1429]; untraced	*Graves* VI, 1905–6, 285
58.	1852	Unidentified subject, medallic portrait		[Exhib RA, London, 1430]; untraced	*Graves* VI, 1905–6, 285
Miscellaneous					
59.	1829	Impression from a die of the late Duke of York		[Exhib Soc of BA, London, 843]; untraced	*Johnson* 1975, 391
60.	1836	Mercury and Pandora		[Exhib RA, London, 1102]; untraced	*Graves* VI, 1905–6, 284
61.	1837	Il sogno (the dream)		[Exhib RA, London, 1174]; untraced	*Graves* VI, 1905–6, 284
62.	1840	Horse struck by lightning		[Exhib BI, London, 452]; untraced	*Graves* 1875, 453
63.	1841	Two fauns breaking in a wild horse		[Exhib RA, London, 1309]; untraced	*Graves* VI, 1905–6, 285
64.	1843	A sketch		[Exhib RA, London, 1500]; untraced	*Graves* VI, 1905–6, 285
65.	1845	The village Sayn, on the river Priestbach, Prussia		[Exhib RA, London, 1280]; untraced	*Graves* VI, 1905–6, 285
66.	1846	William Marshall, Earl of Pembroke		[Exhib BI, London, 488]; untraced	*Graves* 1875, 453
67.	1862	The youthful aspirant		[Exhib BI, London, 640]; untraced	*Graves* 1875, 453
68.	1863	Astronomy		[Exhib Soc of BA, London, 901]; untraced	*Johnson* 1975, 391

RICHARDSON, John, of Durham
See **James OLIPHANT, of Durham**.

RICHTER, John Augustus *c*1730–after 1809

One of the leading scagliola workers in England in the 18th century. He is reputed to have come from Dresden and was probably born about 1730, for a manuscript label on the reverse of a plaque by him in the Victoria and Albert Museum is dated 1809 and records his age as 79 (**18**). Richter was in England by 1767, when he formed a partnership with **Domenico Bartoli**, working from premises in Great Newport Street. He married Mary Haig and was the father of the painter Henry Richter, with whom he produced and published an illustrated edition of *Paradise Lost* in 1794.

In 1770 Richter took out a patent for 'his Method of inlaying Scagliola or Plaister in and upon Marble and Metals to imitate flowers, trees, fruits, birds. . .and all sorts of ornaments' (BL Patent 978). By this date he had already repaired and polished pillars in the north hall at Burghley House (**17**), provided scagliola columns in imitation of porphyry for the saloon at Holland House, Kingsgate, Kent (**11**) and a marble chimneypiece at Strawberry Hill which Horace Walpole described as 'taken from the tomb of Edward the Confessor (in Westminster Abbey), improved by Adam and beautifully executed in white marble inlaid with scagliola, by Richter' (*Walpole* 1784, 53). He attempted to reproduce Italian cosmati work (glass and stone mosaic) for the *Shrine of Capoccio*, also at Strawberry Hill (**1, 13**).

He appears to have worked in partnership with Bartoli for about a decade, during which time the two were particularly in demand for chimneypieces and scagliola table tops in houses designed by Robert Adam (**2, 3, 4, 19, 21, 23, 24, 25**). The firm must have had a good reputation, for Sir William Chambers, in a letter of October 13, 1773 to Mr Key, a master-builder in Edinburgh, recommended 'Messrs. Ritter Bartoli, Newport Street, near Newport Market, London' as the best makers of scagliola in England, who could 'imitate almost any sort of marble you please and also make very beautiful ornaments' (Sir William Chambers's Letter-Book, BL Ad.MS. 41133, fol 113). Chambers noted that the price of their scagliola was between 5–12 shillings per foot. In 1777 the firm received £158 6s from Sir Rowland Wynn for 'two statuary tables inlaid of scagliola according to Messrs. Adams disaing for Nostel at 75 guineas each' (Nostell Papers C3/1/5/4/5).

The partnership seems to have been dissolved about 1777 and by 1780 Richter was working on his own account at Burghley. List of payments to artificers at Burghley show that he was again at the house several times in the years 1799–1800 with his two assistants, supervising work on columns and installing a chimneypiece (**10**). There survives in the house archives a brass plaque engraved 'John Richter, Scagliolist, Newman Street, London'. One of his major later commissions was for the chapel at Greenwich (**15**), where in 1788 he provided 'Majestick columns on each side of the altarpiece' in yellow scagliola, and a scagliola pavement inlaid with an anchor (*General Magazine and Impartial Review*, March 1789, 108, 109).

He exhibited designs for scagliola with the Irish artist Edward Hodgson at the Free Society in 1782 and 1783. His last known work is the scagliola plaque in the Victoria and Albert Museum depicting a scene from *Ossian* (**18**).

Donald Cameron / IR

Literary References: *Graves* 1907, 121; *Gunnis* 1968, 321; *Beard* 1981, 277–8; *Beard* 1993, 101; *O'Neill* 1998, 152; *Harris* 2001 *passim*

Archival References: Letter from Sir William Chambers quoted by RB Wragg, *CL*, 10.10.1957, p719 (Newport Street premises); 9th Earl's notes from Abroad, Burghley Archives, 10 July 1768; Burghley Artificers, 1798–1803

Miscellaneous Drawings: Richter and Hodgson, 'Drawing in scagliola, in a new manner' exhib Free Soc 1782, 98, untraced; Richter and Hodgson, 'Drawing in scagliola, Roses, in a new manner' exhib Free Soc 1782, 99, untraced; Richter and Hodgson, 'Drawing, in scagliola, Landscape, in a new manner', exhib Free Soc 1782, 100, untraced

Chimneypieces

1.	1766–1767	'taken from the tomb of Edward the Confessor'	m	Strawberry Hill, Middx, round drawing room		*Gunnis* 1968, 321; *Harris* 2001, 9
2.	1771	Inlaid with scagliola (co-sculptor: Domenico Bartoli)		20, St James's Square, London		*Harris* 2001, 266
3.	1774	Inlaid with brown and fawn and red and black scagliola ornaments (surround by Thomas Carter II) (co-sculptor: Domenico Bartoli)		[Derby House, Grosvenor Square, London, dressing room]; Dartmouth House, London		*Harris* 2001, 293
4.	1774	Inlaid with scagliola (co-sculptor: Domenico Bartoli)		[Northumberland House, London, glass drawing room]; Syon House, London		DC
5.	1775	Inlaid with scagliola (co-sculptor: Domenico Bartoli)		Osterley Park, Middx		DC
6.	1776	Two, inlaid with scagliola (co-sculptor: Domenico Bartoli)		Home House, London		DC
7.	1777	Two, inlaid with scagliola (co-sculptor: Domenico Bartoli)		[Bolton House, London]; untraced		*Harris* 2001, 8
8.	1783	Statuary chimney-piece in flutes, in imitation of porphyry		[Exhib Free Soc, 54]; untraced		*Graves* 1907, 213
9.	1783	Statuary chimneypiece inlaid with scagliola		[Exhib Free Soc, 96]; untraced		*Graves* 1907, 213
10.	1799–1800	Neo-classical design inlaid with scagliola		Burghley House, Northants, state dressing room (first George room)		*Drakard* 1815, 73; *Gunnis* 1968, 321

Architectural Sculpture

11.	?post-1767	Scagliola columns in imitation of porphyry (co-sculptor: Domenico Bartoli)		Holland House, Kingsgate, Kent, saloon		*Gunnis* 1968, 321 citing Kent's *Ireland*, I, 528
12.	1772	Columns in imitation of *giallo antico* (co-sculptor: Domenico Bartoli)		[Pantheon, London]; untraced		RG/JP, 7, 1166
13.	1774	Mosaic work for the shrine of Capoccio		[Strawberry Hill, Twickenham, Middx]; St Mary and St Nicholas, Wilton, Wilts (columns only)		*Walpole* 1784, 53; *Gunnis* 1968, 321
14.	1782	Two scagliola pedestals in imitation of porphyry		[Exhib Free Soc, 241, 242]; untraced		*Graves* 1907, 213
15.	1788	'yellow antique' scagliola columns and a black and white scagliola pavement, inlaid with an anchor		Royal Naval Hospital, Greenwich, chapel		*GM and Impartial Review*, March 1789, 108, 109
16.	1790	Unspecified scagliola work Payment(s): £300		[Carlton House, London]; untraced		Kings Works RA Geo/31470
17.	1799–1800	Twelve scagliola columns		Burghley House, Northants, north hall		Burghley Artificers, July 1799–Aug 1800

Reliefs

18.	1809	Scene from *Ossian*, plaque		VAM A25-1932	S	

Miscellaneous

19.	1768	'Mosaic tables' with red and blue interlaced circles on a creamy ground (designed by Robert Adam) (co-sculptor: Domenico Bartoli) Payment(s): £134 5s Drawing(s): by Adam, Soane vol 5, 78		[Coventry House, London]; private coll		Croome Court archives 8/12/68; *Harris* 2001, 57
20.	1768	Two scagliola tables, each supplied with leather covers (co-sculptor: Domenico Bartoli) Payment(s): £65 each		[Croome Court, Worcs]; untraced		Croome Archives 8/12/68; *Beard* 1993, 41–3
21.	c1770	Ionic pilasters of *verde antico* scagliola (co-sculptor: Domenico Bartoli)		Kedleston, Derbys, saloon		*Harris* 2001, 39
22.	1771	Two white marble tables 'inlaid with roses and oak leaves in colour' Payment(s): £57		[for John, 3rd Duke of Atholl]; untraced		RG/JP 7, 1166 citing Atholl Archives
23.	1774	Table top inlaid with scagliola (co-sculptor: Domenico Bartoli) Drawing(s): Soane Adam Drawings, vol 39, pl 8		[Northumberland House, London]; Syon House, London		DC
24.	1775	Table top (co-sculptor: Domenico Bartoli)		Osterley Park, Middx		*Harris* 2001, 171
25.	1777	Two semi-circular tables, inlaid with eagle motifs in scagliola (designed by Robert Adam) (co-sculptor: Domenico Bartoli) Payment(s): £158		Nostell Priory, W R Yorks		*Gunnis* 1968, 321; *Harris* 2001, 206
26.	1783	Table inlaid with scagliola		[Exhib Free Soc, 316]; untraced		*Graves* 1907, 213
27.	nd	Two 'Marble Scariole' tables		[for Dudley, 1st Earl of Harrowby]; untraced		*Beard* 1981, 278

RICKETTS, John, of Bath fl 1787–96

Possibly related to the **Ricketts Family, of Gloucester**. He became bankrupt in 1793 (*Universal Mag*, 1793, 471) but continued to work after that date. Gunnis comments that 'his tablets are not outstanding, they have quite carefully carved details' (*Gunnis* 1968, 321).

Funerary Monuments

1.	†1756	Elizabeth Warneford	Bibury, Glos	S	Pevsner, *Glos: Cotswolds*, 1999, 170
2.	†1775	Cornelius Robbins	St Lawrence, Didmarton, Glos	S	Pevsner, *Glos: Cotswolds*, 1999, 314

3.	†1780	Thomas Hodges	Arlingham, Glos	S	Pevsner, *Glos: Vale & Forest of Dean*, 1976, 87
4.	†1787	Ann Trotman	St Peter, Winchcombe, Glos	S	*Universal Mag*, 1793, 471; Pevsner, *Glos: Cotswolazineds*, 1999, 729
5.	†1789	Charles Barrow	Minsterworth, Glos	S	Pevsner, *Glos: Vale & Forest of Dean*, 1976, 299
6.	1790	John Jenner (†1787)	Meysey Hampton, Glos	S	Pevsner, *Glos: Cotswolds*, 1999, 475
7.	†1791	Anne Cresswell	Bibury, Glos	S	Pevsner, *Glos: Cotswolds*, 1999, 170
8.	?1791	Jane Crosse	Compton, Berks	S	*Gunnis* 1968, 321
9.	†1795	Jane Bland	St Denys, Warminster, Wilts	S	
10.	†1795	John Scott	Longborough, Glos	S	Pevsner, *Glos: Cotswolds*, 1999, 458
11.	?1795	Thomas Crosse	Kintbury, Berks	S	*Gunnis* 1968, 321

RICKETTS FAMILY, of Gloucester

John Ricketts I –1734
Thomas Ricketts –1780
John Ricketts II 1740–1796/6

The Ricketts family of carvers and masons were active in Gloucester throughout most of the 18th century. **John Ricketts I**, the firm's founder, is thought to have come to Gloucester from Cheltenham *c*1710, for that year he petitioned the corporation to be made a freeman of the City, offering in return to execute a statue in stone of Queen Anne. The proposal was accepted and he became a freeman on 11 September 1711. In 1712 he received a part-payment of £23 for the statue, an iconic image representing the Queen in robes of state, carrying sceptre and orb, standing on a pedestal decorated with military trophies and cherubs supporting the arms of England, Ireland and Scotland (**35**). George Vertue visited Gloucester in 1729 and noted 'Mr . . . Rickett Stone Carver. At Glocestr a Son-a hopefull young man-' (*Vertue* II, 61). Ricketts appears to have worked on a considerable amount of stone carving in the city and district, including the wall monument to William Lisle in Gloucester Cathedral, which has a convincing portrait bust in wig and contemporary dress, set in an elaborate architectural surround (**5**). He died on 16 July 1734, leaving six children, including two sons, Thomas and William.

Thomas Ricketts, who was his father's executor, took on the business and lived in Eastgate Street. He was responsible for a number of elegant, crisply-carved wall-monuments, for instance the memorial to Lady Strachan, which has a convincing portrait medallion held by a grieving putto (**22**). He died on 20 June 1780 and was buried with his wife, Martha (†1773) in St Michael, Southgate Street.

John Ricketts II Thomas's son, was baptised at St Michael's on 2 June 1740. One of his finest monuments, to Elizabeth Charlett (†1746), has a lively portrait bust above a sarcophagus (**12**). A statue of William Beckford was exhibited at the Free Society in 1771, when he gave his address as 41 Ogle Street, Portland Chapel. In addition to his work as a sculptor, he was busily engaged in building work in Gloucester for some years and frequent mention is made of him in the corporation Minutes. On 27 May 1778 he submitted a proposal with a ground plan to the corporation for demolishing Eastgate and adjoining buildings. He appears to have been successful, for documents in private hands are said to show that he built and presumably designed Eastgate House, Gloucester, *c*1780. Ricketts appears to have designed the triumphal arch erected in Gloucester in 1777 in honour of William Bromley Chester, MP for that city. An engraving of the arch in Bishop Hooper's Museum is signed 'John Ricketts, Statuary at Gloucester'. In 1784 Ricketts was among those who surveyed the tower of St Nicholas, Gloucester, receiving £1 11s 6d for his plan. He probably had a son, Thomas, who joined the family firm. It is not known whether the Gloucester family were related to **John Ricketts of Bath**, whose known monuments all have 'Bath' or 'of Bath' after the signature.

In the following list of works monuments by the Gloucester family signed only 'Ricketts' are listed under John I until 1734, under Thomas if dated between 1734 and 1780, and under John II thereafter.

Literary References: *GM* 1839, vol 1, 631 (statue of Queen Anne); Gunnis Archive, Conway; *Gunnis* 1968, 321–2; RG/JP, 7, 1166–7; *Colvin* 1995, 811–2

Archival References: Gloucester Freemen, GBR c9/7; Gloucester Council Minutes GBR B3/8, B3/11, B3/9–10; GPC

Will: John Ricketts I, proved 31 Jan 1735, GBR wills 1734/13

Funerary Monuments

1.	†1709	Rev George Bull (by John Ricketts I)		Brecon Cathedral	S	Pevsner, *Powys*, 1979, 294
2.	†1716	William Guise (by John Ricketts I)	s	Elmore, Glos	S	Pevsner, *Glos: Vale & Forest of Dean*, 1976, 180; C Lib (repr)
3.	†1719	Nathaniel Peach (by John Ricketts I)		Woodchester, Glos	S	Pevsner, *Glos: Cotswolds*, 1999, 744
4.	†1722	Robert Bridges (by John Ricketts I)		Woodchester, Glos	S	Pevsner, *Glos: Cotswolds*, 1999, 744
5.	†1723	William Lisle (by John Ricketts I)		Gloucester Cathedral	S	Pevsner, *Glos: Vale and Forest of Dean*, 1976, 219
6.	†1723	William Little (by John Ricketts I)		Gloucester Cathedral	S	Pevsner, *Glos: Vale & Forest of Dean*, 1976, 219
7.	†1734	John Holder (by Thomas Ricketts)		Taynton, Glos	S	Pevsner, *Glos: Vale & Forest of Dean*, 1976, 355
8.	†1740	Henry Perrot (by Thomas Ricketts)		North Leigh, Oxon		Pevsner, *Oxon*, 1974, 721
9.	†1740	William Osbaldeston (by Thomas Ricketts)		Chadlington, Oxon		Pevsner, *Oxon*, 1974, 525
10.	†1742	John Probyn (by Thomas Ricketts)		Newland, Glos	S	Pevsner, *Glos: Vale & Forest of Dean*, 1976, 308
11.	†1745	Sir Thomas Snell (by Thomas Ricketts)		St Leonard, Upton St Leonard's, Glos	S	Pevsner, *Glos: Vale & Forest of Dean*, 1976, 396
12.	†1746	Elizabeth Charlett (by Thomas Ricketts)		Fladbury, Worcs	S	Pevsner, *Worcs*, 1968, 154

13.	?1748	Rev Prideaux Sutton (by Thomas Ricketts)		Bredon, Worcs		*Gunnis* 1968, 322
14.	?1751	Thomas Shaw (by Thomas Ricketts)		Bramley, Hants		*Gunnis* 1968, 322
15.	†1752	Thomas Pyrke (by Thomas Ricketts)		Little Dean, Glos	S	Pevsner, *Glos: Vale & Forest of Dean*, 1976, 288; C Lib (repr)
16.	†1754	John Coxwell (by Thomas Ricketts)		St Mary, Bibury, Glos	S	Pevsner, *Glos: Cotswolds*, 1999, 170
17.	†1754	Sir Thomas Snell (by Thomas Ricketts)		Upton St Leonards, Glos	S	*Gunnis* 1968, 322; C Lib (repr)
18.	?1756	Robert Thomas (by Thomas Ricketts)		St Bride's Major, Glamorgan		*Gunnis* 1968, 322
19.	†1761	Anthony Ellys, Bishop of St David's (by Thomas Ricketts)		Gloucester Cathedral		Pevsner, *Glos: Vale & Forest of Dean*, 1976, 218
20.	†1762	Sarah Bourchier (by Thomas Ricketts)		Barnsley, Glos	S	Pevsner, *Glos: Cotswolds*, 1999, 155
21.	?1767	Williams family (by Thomas Ricketts)		Llantwit, Glamorgan		*Gunnis* 1968, 322
22.	†1770	Lady Mary Strachan (by Thomas Ricketts)		Gloucester Cathedral	S	Pevsner, *Glos: Vale & Forest of Dean*, 1976, 218
23.	†1770	Samuel Sheppard (by Thomas Ricketts)		Minchinhampton, Glos	S	Pevsner, *Glos: Cotswolds*, 1999, 480
24.	†1771	Elizabeth Prinn (by Thomas Ricketts)		Charlton Kings, Glos	S	*Gunnis* 1968, 322; Pevsner, *Glos: Vale & Forest of Dean*, 1976, 120
25.	†1771	John Whithorne (by Thomas Ricketts)		St Mary, Charlton Kings, Glos	S	Pevsner, *Glos: Vale & Forest of Dean*, 1976, 120
26.	?1775	Captain Dansey (John Ricketts II)		Little Hereford, Herefs		*Gunnis* 1968, 322
27.	†1776	Admiral James Sayer (by Thomas Ricketts)		Sandford St Martin, Oxon	S	*Gunnis* 1968, 322
28.	†1776	Thomas (†1776) and Mary (†1774) Bush (by Thomas Ricketts)		South Cerney, Glos	S	Pevsner, *Glos: Cotswolds*, 1999, 619
29.	†1778	Edward Machen (by Thomas Ricketts)		English Bicknor, Glos	S	
30.	?1778	Henry Perrot (by Thomas Ricketts)		North Leigh, Oxon		*Gunnis* 1968, 322
31.	†1783	Elizabeth Coxe (by John Ricketts II)		Kemble, Glos	S	Pevsner, *Glos: Cotswolds*, 1999, 422
32.	?1785	James Benson (by John Ricketts II)		Gloucester Cathedral		*Gunnis* 1968, 322
33.	†1792	Susannah Warren (by John Ricketts II)		Worcester Cathedral	S	Pevsner, *Worcs*, 1968, 313
34.	?1797	John Whitehouse (by John Ricketts II)		Charlton Kings, Glos		*Gunnis* 1968, 322
Statues						
35.	1710	Queen Anne (by John Ricketts I)	s	[Southgate, Gloucester]; Spa Pleasure Ground, Gloucester		Gloucester Council Minutes 1710–16, GBR B3/8; *GM*, 1839, I, 631; Pevsner, *Glos: Vale & Forest of Dean*, 1976, 252
36.	1771	William Beckford (by John Ricketts II)		[Exhib Free Soc, London, 203]; untraced		*Graves* 1907, 213; *Gunnis* 1968, 322
Architectural Sculpture						
37.	1726	White marble mensa (by John Ricketts I)		Tewkesbury Abbey, Glos, St Margaret's chapel		Pevsner, *Glos: Vale & Forest of Dean*, 1976, 370
38.	1741	City arms and regalia and ornaments (by Thomas Ricketts)	s	Gloucester Guildhall	S	Gloucester Council Minutes 1716–60, GBR B3/9-10; *Gunnis* 1968, 322
39.	nd	City arms (by Thomas Ricketts)		[Booth Hall, Gloucester]; Corner of Three Cocks Lane and Westgate Street, Gloucester		Pevsner, *Glos: Vale & Forest of Dean*, 1976, 246
40.	nd	High relief figures (by John Ricketts I)		Bearland Lodge, Gloucester, tympanum		Pevsner, *Glos: Vale & Forest of Dean*, 1976, 252

RIDDELL, William fl 1690

Architectural Sculpture						
1.	1690	Lion and unicorn staircase, with carvings of seated beasts	s	Glasgow University		*McKenzie* 2002, 396–7 (repr)

RIGALI, G fl 1832–39

Rigali worked at 42 High Street, Edinburgh from 1832 to 1839, principally producing casts of the work of other sculptors, though two signed plaster busts by him are recorded (**2, 3**). The extent of his trade in copies is not known but he is recorded as having made plaster reproductions of the *Sleeping child* by **John Greenshields** (**1**).

Literary References: *Woodward* 1977, vol 1, pt 2, 199–200

Statues						
1.	nd	Sleeping child (copies of a work by John Greenshields)	p	Untraced		*Woodward* 1977, vol 1, pt 2, 200
Busts						
2.	1834	Unidentified man	p	St Andrews University	SD	*Woodward* 1977, vol 1, pt 2, 200
3.	nd	Unidentified man	p	Signet Library, Edinburgh	S	*Woodward* 1977, vol 1, pt 2, 200

RIGBY, Edward fl 1754

In 1754 he was paid £126 for carving at Liverpool Exchange, then being erected to designs by John Wood (City Corp Cash Book in GPC) (**1**).

Architectural Sculpture						
1.	1754	Unidentified 'carving' Payment(s): £126		Liverpool Exchange, Lancs		GPC

RINALDI, Rinaldo 1793–1873

William, 6th Duke of Devonshire was in Rome shortly after Canova's death in 1822. Amongst other works he ordered copies of Canova's famous lions on the monument to Pope Clement XIII Rezzonico in St Peter's, which were executed by Rinaldi and **Francesco Benaglia** (1). They were completed and set up at Chatsworth ten years later as a memorial to Canova, with busts of Canova (5) and the Duke in niches above them. Sir Arthur Guinness also owned a work by Rinaldi, which he lent to the 1872 Dublin Exhibition. The *Delphic Sybil* once presided over the stairs at Stafford House but is now in the gardens at Cliveden, Bucks (3). The sculptor also executed works for the Duchess of Sutherland and Lord Grosvenor (2–4).

Literary References: *Le Grice* 1844, I, 92–9; II, 218–25; *K-Browne* 1972 (3), 327; *Knox* 2001, 28–9; *Bryant* 2002, 20

Statues

1.	1825	Sleeping lions, a pair, after Canova (co-sculptor: Francesco Benaglia) Payment(s): 1,100 scudi		Chatsworth, Derbys, sculpture gallery		*JKB* 1972 (3), 327, 330, 331
2.	nd	Cephalus and Procris		[coll Lord Grosvenor]; untraced		*Le Grice* 1844, I, 97; II, 223–5
3.	nd	Delphic sybil		[Stafford House, London]; Cliveden, Bucks, gardens		*Le Grice* 1844, I, 92–6, 98; *Knox* 2001, 28–9 (repr)
4.	nd	Ulysses recognised by his dog		[coll Lord Grosvenor]; untraced		*Le Grice* 1844, I, 97

Busts

5.	1823	Antonio Canova, after Canova Payment(s): 40 louis		Chatsworth, Derbys, sculpture gallery		*JKB* 1972 (3), 327, 331
6.	pre-1823	Ceres Payment(s): 50 scudi		Chatsworth, Derbys, sculpture gallery		*JKB* 1972 (3), 331
7.	1869	Unidentified lady		Discovered in the Firth of Clyde, Scotland, 2007	S	*The Times*, 3 Feb 2007, 31
8.	nd	Bacchantes (two)	m	Chatsworth, Derbys		*Chatsworth Handlist*, 25

RING, James, of Reading fl 1741–66

The son of James Ring, he was apprenticed to **William Blake of Basingstoke** in 1741 (GPC). He signs several tablets of white and coloured marbles (1–3). He remained in Basingstoke and was dead by 20 October 1774, when his son, Moses, was apprenticed to **Thomas Burnell**.

Literary References: *Gunnis* 1968, 322; *Webb* 1999, 28

Funerary Monuments

1.	?1751	Thomas Shaw	m	Bramley, Hants	S	*Gunnis* 1968, 322
2.	?1760	John Baker	m	Farnham, Surrey	S	*Gunnis* 1968, 322
3.	?1766	Nathaniel Butler	m	Farnham, Surrey	S	*Gunnis* 1968, 322

RINGLEMAN fl c1806

Funerary Monuments

1.	†1806	Anne Porter	m	Southwell Minster, Notts	S	NP/RG

RINGWOOD, R fl 1836–43

His studio was at 26, Albany Street, London

Busts

1.	1836	Unidentified young lady	[Exhib RA, London, 1146]; untraced	*Graves* VI, 1905–6, 303

Reliefs

2.	1835	Unidentified 'noble lord and lady', medallion	[Exhib RA, London, 1106]; untraced	*Graves* VI, 1905–6, 303
3.	1843	Unidentified artist, medallion	[Exhib RA, London, 1462]; untraced	*Graves* VI, 1905–6, 303

RIPPINGILLE, Edward Villiers 1798–1859

He is chiefly known as a painter, but he exhibited two works of sculpture at the Birmingham Society of Artists in 1829 (1, 3). In the same year the newly founded Bristol Institution acquired a model by Rippingille, entitled *Sleep*, but only after insisting that the subject's bosom was covered with drapery (2).

Literary References: *Gunnis* 1968, 322; *Grove* 26, 1996, 418–9 (Morgan); *ODNB* (Greenacre)

Busts

1.	1829	Head of a sleeping child	[Exhib Birmingham Soc of A]; untraced	*Gunnis* 1968, 322

Miscellaneous

2.	1829	Sleep	[coll Bristol Institution]; untraced	*ODNB*
3.	1829	Sympathy	[Exhib Birmingham Soc of A]; untraced	*Gunnis* 1968, 322

RITCHIE, Alexander Handyside 1804–70

A Scottish sculptor, he specialised in portraiture and architectural sculpture. He was born on 15 April 1804 at Musselburgh, a fishing town near Edinburgh, the second son of James Ritchie and his wife Euphemia. His father was an ornamental plasterer and brickmaker and his mother was descended from **Alexander Handyside**. Ritchie was educated at the local parish school, where his talent for drawing and design soon became apparent. He continued his studies in Edinburgh, where he attended the School of Arts founded by Leonard Horner in 1821 as a college for working men, and Dr John Barclay's Anatomy School. In 1823, under the sponsorship of Walter, 5th Duke of Buccleuch, Ritchie obtained a place in the Edinburgh studio of **Samuel Joseph**. He remained with Joseph for two years and then, after a visit to London, entered the Trustees School of Design in Edinburgh, returning to London to model from the Elgin Marbles in the British Museum during the vacation.

In June 1826 he visited the Continent, staying in Paris for a few weeks, then studying in Carrara for four months before travelling to Rome, where he entered the studio of **Bertel Thorvaldsen**. He remained there for several years and is said to have been a favourite pupil of Thorvaldsen, who awarded him a gold medal. After his return to Scotland in 1830 he worked from his home at Musselburgh for 12 years before establishing a studio at 92 Princes Street, Edinburgh, in 1842. He was assisted by his younger brother **John Ritchie** and employed an Italian assistant, as well as taking pupils, including John Rhind, **Alexander Munro** and George Anderson Lawson.

Ritchie built up a considerable practice as a portrait sculptor from 1830 onwards, executing more than 70 busts and securing several commissions for public statues, including those of Sir Walter Scott in Selkirk, Sir Robert Peel in Montrose and the physician and writer David Moir in Musselburgh (16, 25, 26). He was particularly successful as an architectural sculptor, working on prominent buildings in Edinburgh and Glasgow during the 1840s and 1850s. These included the Commercial Bank in George Street, Edinburgh, where he carved an elaborate allegorical pediment group to designs by **James Wyatt** (**121**). This was praised by the *Art Union*, whose critic was particularly impressed by three figures of children, which 'would do credit to the chisel of any sculptor'. He suggested that Ritchie himself 'must be a man of fine sympathies and of gentle nature, as well as high genius, who can represent the innocence of childhood so successfully' (*AU*, 1846, 284). Ritchie was a regular exhibitor at the Royal Scottish Academy from 1831 and was elected an associate member in 1846. He showed work at the Royal Institution for the Encouragement of the Fine Arts in Scotland (1825–1827, 1830), the West of Scotland Academy (1831–1832) and the Royal Academy in London (1830–1868).

Beyond Scotland, Ritchie provided sculpture for the Houses of Parliament in London. In 1844 he sent a group of *Sophronia and Olinda at the stake* to the Westminster Hall Exhibition organised by the Royal Fine Art Commissioners to select artists to execute works for the new building (**20**). The *Literary Gazette* was sparing in its praise for the group, noting that 'while some parts have had great care bestowed upon them, there are others, for instance the drapery at the foot, as slovenly as any we have ever witnessed' (cited by *Gunnis* 1968, 323). In 1847 Ritchie was nonetheless commissioned to model figures of two signatories of the Magna Carta, Eustace de Vescy and William de Mowbray, for the Chamber of the House of Lords (**34, 38**). **John Thomas** employed him on decorative work for the same building in 1848 (**122**).

In 1854 Peter Denny, the Provost of Dumbarton, commissioned from Ritchie a colossal nude statue, which was to embody the passions of horror and despair (**27**). According to the *Scotsman*, this untraced work was the 'first bona fide commission given in Scotland for a work in sculpture free from all local conventionality of treatment and dependent entirely on its power of exciting universal sympathy' (11 Jan 1854, cited by *Woodward* 1977, vol 1, pt 2, 202). It was perhaps in connection with this work that Ritchie paid a second visit to Rome where he spent six months. On his return he moved his premises to Mound Place. There in the late 1850s he executed a series of statues of Scottish religious leaders and a group commemorating the martyred Covenanter Margaret Wilson and her sister Agnes for the Valley cemetery, Stirling (**36, 41**).

Ritchie retired from business in 1861 and the occasion was marked with a retrospective exhibition the following year at his studio, now at Coates Place. He moved back to the family home at Herkes Loan, Fisherrow, Musselburgh but retained his studio for several years and continued to exhibit at the Royal Scottish Academy. He died on 24 April 1870 and was buried in the churchyard of St Michael, Inveresk. He left all his property, which, apart from the money he was owed for a monument to James Morrison of Greenfield at Alloa, was valued at the meagre sum of £6 10s 6d, to his sister Euphemia who cared for him in the last years of his life. A contemporary later wrote that Ritchie's 'simple, guileless and kindly disposition' made him a favourite with all who knew him and suggested that 'Only greater restraint and power of steady application was required to have enabled him to win a very high place among the sculptors of this country' (J M Gray, cited by *Wrinch* 1969, 481).

EH

Literary References: *Builder*, 1870, 422; *Gunnis* 1968, 323; *Wrinch* 1969, 380–1; *Woodward* 1977, vol 1, pt 2, 200–7; *ODNB* (Woodward)

Archival References: IGI

Additional MS Sources: Ritchie/Wyatt

Wills: NAS SC70/4/127 and SC70/1/149, ESC general disposition and settlement and inventory

Portraits of the Sculptor: David Octavius Hill and Robert Adamson, 3 calotypes (including group portraits), 1843–8, NPG P6 (24), NPG P6(33), NPG P6(98); David Octavius Hill and Robert Adamson, calotype (group portrait), *c*1845, NPG x18781; David Octavius Hill, *The Disruption* (large group oil painting), 1843–65, Free Church Presbytery Hall, Edinburgh; David Octavius Hill, calotype, nd, R Sc A

Funerary Monuments

1.	1838	Rev John Brown Patterson Model(s): exhib R Sc A, Edinburgh, 1838, 409		Falkirk, Stirling		*Woodward* 1977, vol 1, pt 2, 207; *Laperriere* 4, 1991, 55
2.	1842	Wedderburn family member		St Michael, Inveresk, East Lothian, churchyard		*Woodward* 1977, vol 1, pt 2, 207
3.	†1844	George Meikle Kemp		St Cuthbert, Edinburgh, churchyard		*Colvin* 1995, 576
4.	1844	Rev David Dickson (†1842)	s	St Cuthbert, Edinburgh, churchyard	S	*Wrinch* 1969, 380–1 (repr); Pevsner, *Edinburgh*, 1991, 277
5.	1848	James Reoch (†1845) (designed by Thomas Hamilton)		South Leith, Edinburgh		Pevsner, *Edinburgh*, 1991, 458
6.	1848	Thomas Reid	s	Rosebank Cemetery, Edinburgh		*Woodward* 1977, vol 1, pt 2, 207
7.	1851	John Henry Alexander (designed by James Hamilton)	s	Glasgow Necropolis	S	*McKenzie* 1999, 12–13, no 2.11 (repr); *McKenzie* 2002, 459
8.	1853	Colonel James Gardiner	s	Tranent, East Lothian		*Woodward* 1977, vol 1, pt 2, 207
9.	1856	The fishermen's monument	s	Dunbar, East Lothian, near old pier		*Woodward* 1977, vol 1, pt 2, 207
10.	nd	Rev George D Cullen	s	Warriston Cemetery, Edinburgh		*Woodward* 1977, vol 1, pt 2, 206
11.	nd	Sir George Harvey	s	Warriston Cemetery, Edinburgh		*Woodward* 1977, vol 1, pt 2, 206

Statues

12.	1828	Ganymede and the eagle, copy after Thorwaldsen	m	[coll Henry Hallam]; untraced		*Wrinch* 1969, 380
13.	1832	Telemachus		[Exhib West of Scotland Academy]; untraced		*Woodward* 1977, vol 1, pt 2, 201; *Laperriere* 4, 1991, 56
14.	*c*1836	Charles Marjoribanks MP	s	[Coldstream, Berwicks]; destroyed		*Woodward* 1977, vol 1, pt 2, 205
15.	1839	Ralph Erskine	s	Church of Scotland, Dunfermline		*Woodward* 1977, vol 1, pt 2, 202, 205
16.	1839	Sir Walter Scott Drawing(s): NGS, Edinburgh, D2682, pen and ink, 1838 Model(s): exhib R Sc A, Edinburgh, 1843, 592	m	Market place, Selkirk		*Woodward* 1977, vol 1, pt 2, 205; *Laperriere* 4, 1991, 592
17.	1842	Robert Ferguson of Raith, competition design only (commission awarded to Robert Forrest)		[for Haddington]; untraced		*Woodward* 1977, vol 1, pt 2, 202

No.	Date	Subject	Material	Location		References
18.	1844	Meg Merrilees	s	Scott monument, Princes Street, Edinburgh		*Woodward* 1977, vol 1, pt 2, 205
19.	1844	Prince Charles Edward Stuart	s	Scott monument, Princes Street, Edinburgh		*Woodward* 1977, vol 1, pt 2, 205
20.	1844	Sophronia and Olinda at the stake		[Exhib Westminster Hall, London, 105]; untraced		*AU*, 1844, 215; *Laperriere* 4, 1991, 57
21.	1847	Joseph Hume, for Montrose, competition design only		Untraced		*Woodward* 1977, vol 1, pt 2, 202
22.	1849	Flower girl	m	[Exhib R Sc A, Edinburgh, 628]; untraced		*Laperriere* 4, 1991, 56
23.	1850	Unicorns	s	Middle Meadow Walk, Edinburgh		*Woodward* 1977, vol 1, pt 2, 207
24.	1851	Queen Victoria	s	[Palace of Holyroodhouse, Edinburgh]; destroyed		*Ormond* 1973, 487; *Woodward* 1977, vol 1, pt 2, 205
25.	1852	Sir Robert Peel	m	High Street, Montrose, Angus		*Ormond* 1973, 372; *Woodward* 1977, vol 1, pt 2, 205
26.	1853	Dr David Macbeath Moir Model(s): exhib R Sc A, Edinburgh, 1855, 799	s	High Street, Musselburgh, East Lothian		*Woodward* 1977, vol 1, pt 2, 205; *Laperriere* 4, 1991, 56
27.	1854	Horror and despair		[coll Peter Denny, of Dumbarton]; untraced		*ODNB*
28.	1855	A muse	m	[Exhib R Sc A, Edinburgh, 793]; untraced		*Laperriere* 4, 1991, 56
29.	1855	An archangel	m	[Exhib R Sc A, Edinburgh, 788]; untraced		*Laperriere* 4, 1991, 56
30.	1855	Unidentified young lady	m	[Exhib R Sc A, Edinburgh, 790]; untraced		*Laperriere* 4, 1991, 56
31.	1855	Venus	m	[Exhib R Sc A, Edinburgh, 794]; untraced		*Laperriere* 4, 1991, 56
32.	1857	Scotch lassie	m	[Exhib RA, London, 1250]; untraced		*Graves* VI, 1905–6, 307
33.	1858	Daughter of J Haig, part of a group, model, and pedestal		[Exhib R Sc A, Edinburgh, 767, 768]; untraced		*Laperriere* 4, 1991, 57
34.	1847–1858	Eustace de Vescy (†1216)		Palace of Westminster, London, House of Lords		*Walker* 1961, 72, 97–8, cat 75
35.	1858	Hugh Miller	s	Cromarty		*Woodward* 1977, vol 1, pt 2, 205
36.	1858	John Knox, Thomas Guthrie, Andrew Melville, Alexander Henderson, James Renwick and Ebenezer Erskine	s	Valley Cemetery, Stirling		*Woodward* 1977, vol 1, pt 2, 202, 205
37.	1858	Mungo Park, competition design only		[for Selkirk]; untraced		*Woodward* 1977, vol 1, pt 2, 202
38.	1847–1858	William de Mowbray (†1223/4)		Palace of Westminster, London, House of Lords		*Walker* 1961, 47, 97–8, cat 51; *Read* 1982, 120 (repr)
39.	1859	Daughters of an unidentified gentleman	m	[Exhib R Sc A, Edinburgh, 712]; untraced		*Laperriere* 4, 1991, 57
40.	1859	William Wallace	s	Athenaeum, King St, Stirling		*Woodward* 1977, vol 1, pt 2, 205
41.	By 1860	Margaret and Agnes Wilson with a guardian angel	m	Valley Cemetery, Stirling		*Woodward* 1977, vol 1, pt 2, 202–3, 205
42.	1871	Faith, statuette		[Exhib R Sc A, Edinburgh, 765]; untraced		*Laperriere* 4, 1991, 57
Busts						
43.	1830	Dr David Macbeath Moir	p	St Michael, Inveresk, East Lothian		*Woodward* 1977, vol 1, pt 2, 206
44.	1830	Joseph Hume		Palace of Westminster, London, House of Commons, library Other versions: Royal Scottish Museum, Edinburgh, marble, 1830	S	*Graves* VI, 1905–6, 307; *Ormond* 1973, 235 (pl 455); *Laperriere* 4, 1991, 56
45.	1831	Lady Ann Hope	m	[Exhib R Sc A, Edinburgh, 364]; untraced		*Laperriere* 4, 1991, 55
46.	1831	Lady Macdonald Lockhart	m	[Exhib R Sc A, Edinburgh, 378]; untraced		*Laperriere* 4, 1991, 55
47.	1831	Unidentified young lady		[Exhib R Sc A, Edinburgh, 391]; untraced		*Laperriere* 4, 1991, 55
48.	1831	William Aitchison	m	[Exhib R Sc A, Edinburgh, 366]; untraced		*Laperriere* 4, 1991, 55
49.	1834	James Stuart		[Exhib R Sc A, Edinburgh, 340]; untraced		*Laperriere* 4, 1991, 55
50.	1834	Robert Buchanan (after a model by Samuel Joseph)	m	New College, Edinburgh		*Woodward* 1977, vol 1, pt 2, 205; *Laperriere* 4, 1991, 55
51.	1834	William Rigby Murray	m	[Exhib R Sc A, Edinburgh, 344]; untraced		*Graves* VI, 1905–6, 307; *Laperriere* 4, 1991, 55
52.	1836	Dr Thomas McCrie		[Exhib R Sc A, Edinburgh, 335]; untraced		*Laperriere* 4, 1991, 55
53.	1836	James Abercrombie	m	[Exhib RA, London, 1091]; untraced Other versions: exhib R Sc A, Edinburgh, 1836, 334; untraced		*Graves* VI, 1905–6, 307; *Laperriere* 4, 1991, 55
54.	1836	Lady S H, aged 15		[Exhib RA, London, 1097]; untraced		*Graves* VI, 1905–6, 307
55.	1836	Major-General James Stirling		[Exhib R Sc A, Edinburgh, 336]; untraced		*Laperriere* 4, 1991, 55
56.	1836	Unidentified subject, miniature bust		[Exhib R Sc A, Edinburgh, 340]; untraced		*Laperriere* 4, 1991, 55
57.	1837	Bertel Thorvaldsen		[Exhib RA, London, 1284]; untraced		*Graves* VI, 1905–6, 307; *Gunnis* 1968, 322
58.	1837	Charles Craigie Halkett		[Exhib R Sc A, Edinburgh, 370]; untraced		*Laperriere* 4, 1991, 55
59.	1837	Countess of Lincoln	m	[coll Duchess of Buccleuch]; untraced		*Laperriere* 4, 1991, 55
60.	1837	Sir Thomas Haggerston		[Exhib R Sc A, Edinburgh, 376]; untraced		*Laperriere* 4, 1991, 55, 56

61.	1838	? George, Marquess of Huntly		[Exhib R Sc A, Edinburgh, 419]; untraced		*Laperriere* 4, 1991, 55
62.	1838	Master Suttie	m	[Exhib R Sc A, Edinburgh, 412]; untraced		*Laperriere* 4, 1991, 55
63.	1838	Miss Brown		[Exhib R Sc A, Edinburgh, 418]; untraced		*Laperriere* 4, 1991, 55
64.	1838	Mrs Thomas Bannerman		[Exhib RA, London, 1365]; untraced		*Graves* VI, 1905–6, 307; *Laperriere* 4, 1838, 424
65.	1838	Rev Andrew Thomson DD Model(s): exhib R Sc A, Edinburgh, 1836, 355 and RA, London, 1837, 1254	m	Highland Tolbooth church, Edinburgh		*Graves* VI, 1905–6, 307; *Woodward* 1977, vol 1, pt 2, 206; *Laperriere* 4, 1991, 55
66.	1838	Rev George Lee	m	[for the Hull Mechanics' Institute]; untraced		*Graves* VI, 1905–6, 307
67.	1838	Rev John Brown		[Exhib R Sc A, Edinburgh, 414]; untraced		*Laperriere* 4, 1991, 55
68.	1838	Unidentified lady		[Exhib R Sc A, Edinburgh, 420]; untraced		*Laperriere* 4, 1991, 55
69.	1838	W Paxton	m	[Exhib RA, London, 1325]; untraced		*Graves* VI, 1905–6, 307
70.	1839	Master William Aitchison	m	[Exhib R Sc A, Edinburgh, 488]; untraced		*Laperriere* 4, 1991, 55
71.	1839	Miss Anne Mary Aitchison	m	[Exhib R Sc A, Edinburgh, 489]; untraced		*Laperriere* 4, 1991, 55
72.	1839	Miss Helen Margaret Aitchison	m	[Exhib R Sc A, Edinburgh, 487]; untraced		*Laperriere* 4, 1991, 55
73.	1839	Miss Jane Aitchison	m	[Exhib R Sc A, Edinburgh, 490]; untraced		*Laperriere* 4, 1991, 55
74.	1839	Rev Charles Findlater	m	Tweeddale Museum, Peebles		*Woodward* 1977, vol 1, pt 2, 205; *Laperriere* 4, 1991, 55
75.	1840	Mrs J M McHardy		[Exhib R Sc A, Edinburgh, 372]; untraced		*Laperriere* 4, 1991, 55
76.	1840	Rt Hon Lord Dunfermline	m	[Exhib R Sc A, Edinburgh, 381]; untraced		*Laperriere* 4, 1991, 56
77.	1840	Unidentified subject	m	[Exhib R Sc A, Edinburgh, 378]; untraced		*Laperriere* 4, 1991, 55
78.	1840	William Bell	m	[Exhib R Sc A, Edinburgh, 366]; untraced		*Laperriere* 4, 1991, 55
79.	1843	James Callender		[Exhib R Sc A, Edinburgh, 588]; untraced		*Laperriere* 4, 1991, 56
80.	1843	Mrs D M Moir		[Exhib R Sc A, Edinburgh, 584]; untraced		*Laperriere* 4, 1991, 56
81.	1843	Sir David Wilkie		[Exhib R Sc A, Edinburgh, 585]; untraced		*Laperriere* 4, 1991, 56
82.	1844	Sir Ilay Campbell Bt		[Exhib R Sc A, Edinburgh, 561]; untraced		*Laperriere* 4, 1991, 56
83.	1844	Unidentified young lady, model for a marble bust		[Exhib R Sc A, Edinburgh, 565]; untraced		*Laperriere* 4, 1991, 56
84.	1845	George Meikle Kemp		SNPG, Edinburgh		*Gunnis* 1968, 323; *Woodward* 1977, vol 1, pt 2, 206; *Laperriere* 4, 1991, 56, 57
85.	1845	Unidentified gentleman		[Exhib R Sc A, Edinburgh, 558]; untraced		*Laperriere* 4, 1991, 56
86.	1846	Admiral Sir David Milne		[Exhib R Sc A, Edinburgh, 574]; untraced		*Laperriere* 4, 1991, 56
87.	1846	Unidentified child		[Exhib R Sc A, Edinburgh, 570]; untraced		*Laperriere* 4, 1991, 56
88.	1846	Unidentified lady	m	[Exhib R Sc A, Edinburgh, 571]; untraced		*Laperriere* 4, 1991, 56
89.	1847	Colonel Robert Winchester		[Exhib R Sc A, Edinburgh, 628]; untraced		*Laperriere* 4, 1991, 56
90.	1848	Henry, Lord Cockburn	m	NPG, London	SD	
91.	1848	Lady Caroline Wynford Menzies	m	[Exhib R Sc A, Edinburgh, 619]; untraced		*Laperriere* 4, 1991, 56
92.	1848	Maurice Henry Lothian		[Exhib R Sc A, Edinburgh, 605]; untraced		*Laperriere* 4, 1991, 56
93.	1849	Hon Mrs James Johnstone	m	[Exhib R Sc A, Edinburgh, 610]; untraced		*Laperriere* 4, 1991, 56
94.	1849	John Hay		[Exhib R Sc A, Edinburgh, 618]; untraced		*Laperriere* 4, 1991, 56
95.	1849	John Wilson		[Exhib R Sc A, Edinburgh, 614]; untraced		*Laperriere* 4, 1991, 56
96.	1850	Alexander Maclagan		[Exhib R Sc A, Edinburgh, 470]; untraced		*Laperriere* 4, 1991, 56
97.	1850	W B Scott		[Exhib R Sc A, Edinburgh, 477]; untraced		*Laperriere* 4, 1991, 56
98.	1851	David Stow Model(s): exhib R Sc A, Edinburgh, 1852, 681	m	Glasgow Museums S.66		*Woodward* 1977, vol 1, pt 2, 206; *Laperriere* 4, 1991, 56
99.	1851	Lieutenant Henry Veitch		[Exhib R Sc A, Edinburgh, 650]; untraced		*Laperriere* 4, 1991, 56
100.	1851	Unidentified young gentleman, model		[Exhib R Sc A, Edinburgh, 652]; untraced		*Laperriere* 4, 1991, 56
101.	1854	Stewart Marjoribanks	m	[Exhib R Sc A, Edinburgh, 718]; untraced		*Laperriere* 4, 1991, 56
102.	1854	Unidentified gentleman		[Exhib R Sc A, Edinburgh, 728]; untraced		*Laperriere* 4, 1991, 56
103.	1855	Head of a cherub	m	[Exhib R Sc A, Edinburgh, 791]; untraced		*Laperriere* 4, 1991, 56

No.	Date	Title	Material	Location	Literary References
104.	1855	Head of a cherub	m	[Exhib R Sc A, Edinburgh, 792]; untraced	*Laperriere* 4, 1991, 56
105.	1857	Agnes, daughter of David Rhind		[Exhib R Sc A, Edinburgh, 675]; untraced	*Laperriere* 4, 1991, 56
106.	1858	Unidentified sitter	p	[Exhib LSFA, Liverpool, 645]; untraced	*Morris and Roberts* 1998, 513
107.	1861	Arthur, 1st Duke of Wellington		[Exhib LSFA, Liverpool, 781]; untraced	*Morris and Roberts* 1998, 513
108.	1862	Unidentified lady		[Exhib R Sc A, Edinburgh, 844]; untraced	*Laperriere* 4, 1991, 57
109.	1864	Unidentified lady		[Exhib R Sc A, Edinburgh]; untraced	*Laperriere* 4, 1991, 57
110.	1866	James Bridges		[Exhib R Sc A, Edinburgh, 914]; untraced	*Laperriere* 4, 1991, 57
111.	1866	Unidentified lady, model		[Exhib R Sc A, Edinburgh, 884]; untraced	*Laperriere* 4, 1991, 57
112.	1867	Sir Charles Eastlake		[Exhib R Sc A, Edinburgh, 903]; untraced	*Laperriere* 4, 1991, 57
113.	1868	Unidentified artist		[Exhib RA, London, 1108]; untraced	*Graves* VI, 1905–6, 307
114.	1869	Thomas Handyside		[Exhib R Sc A, Edinburgh, 936]; untraced	*Laperriere* 4, 1991, 57
115.	1869	Unidentified gentleman, model		[Exhib R Sc A, Edinburgh, 949]; untraced	*Laperriere* 4, 1991, 57
116.	nd	Hugh Miller	m	Hugh Miller's cottage, Cromarty	*Woodward* 1977, vol 1, pt 2, 206
117.	nd	Margaret, the sculptor's sister		[coll James Taylor, of Musselburgh]; untraced	*Laperriere* 4, 1991, 57
118.	nd	Unidentified young woman	b	Sotheby, 16 April 2002, lot 69	
Architectural Sculpture					
119.	c1840	Caledonia with her children	s	3, Victoria St, Edinburgh, balconied doorpiece	Pevsner, *Edinburgh*, 1991, 226
120.	1844	Hippocrates, Aesculapius and Hygeia, statues	s	R C Physic, Queen St, Edinburgh, façade	*Woodward* 1977, vol 1, pt 2, 206; *Pearson* 1991, 156 (repr); Pevsner, *Edinburgh*, 1991, 288
121.	1843–1847	Fruitfulness flanked by Prudence, Agriculture, Commerce, Enterprise, Mechanical Science and Learning, pediment sculpture (designed by James Wyatt) Drawing(s): VAM E.1896-1948 (by Wyatt)	s	Royal Bank of Scotland (formerly Commercial Bank), George Street, Edinburgh	*Wrinch* 1969, 380–1 (repr); Pevsner, *Edinburgh*, 1991, 300
122.	1848	Decorative work		Palace of Westminster, London	*Gunnis* 1968, 322
123.	1848	Group of children		[Western Bank, St Andrew Square, Edinburgh]; demol 1962	*Builder* 1848, 325, 350; *Gunnis* 1968, 322
124.	1849	Arms of the Bank of Scotland (designed by William Burn) Payment(s): 30 gns	s	[Bank of Scotland, 174–6 Ingram Street, Glasgow]; untraced	*McKenzie* 2002, 438–9
125.	1852	Pair of lions		Hamilton Palace, Lanarks, mausoleum	*Woodward* 1977, vol 1, pt 2, 206
126.	1851–1852	Six statues and reliefs on the façade, and interior ornaments Drawing(s): Agriculture exhib R Sc A, Edinburgh, 1926, 62 (lent by D Birnie Rhind)	s	Bank of Scotland (formerly British Linen Bank), 37–8 St Andrew Square, Edinburgh	*Woodward* 1977, vol 1, pt 2, 201, 206; *Laperriere* 4, 1991, 57
127.	1854	Law lords, 14 keystone portrait heads, models only (carved by James Shanks)	s	Royal Faculty of Procurators' Hall, Glasgow	*McKenzie* 2002, 306–8 (repr)
128.	1854–1856	Decorative carving	s	Burgh planning offices (former High School), Academy Road, Stirling	*Woodward* 1977, vol 1, pt 2, 206
129.	1855–1856	Relief panels and pediment scenes of commercial activities, keystone heads (co-sculptor: John Thomas)	s	Former Commercial Bank of Scotland, 2–16 Gordon St, Glasgow	*McKenzie* 2002, 177–8 (repr)
130.	1859	Putti and decorative carving (modelled by John Thomas)		[Life Association of Scotland, 82 Princes St, Edinburgh, façade]; demol 1968 (only fragments survive)	*Builder*, 1859, 13; *Wrinch* 1969, 381 (repr)
131.	1863	Time, Death and Eternity, three heads Model(s): exhib R Sc A, Edinburgh, 1863, 831–2		Hamilton Palace, Lanarks, mausoleum	*Wrinch* 1969, 381 (repr); *Laperriere* 4, 1991, 57
132.	nd	Six allegorical figures	s	Bank of Scotland, High St, Inverness	*Woodward* 1977, vol 1, pt 2, 206
Reliefs					
133.	1844	Lady Campbell, medallion	m	[Exhib R Sc A, Edinburgh, 570]; untraced	*Laperriere* 4, 1991, 56
134.	1849	James Johnstone, medallion		[Exhib R Sc A, Edinburgh, 627]; untraced	*Laperriere* 4, 1991, 56
135.	1849	Mrs Johnstone, medallion	m	[Exhib R Sc A, Edinburgh, 629]; untraced	*Laperriere* 4, 1991, 56
136.	c1865	Two, symbolising war and peace (designed by Sir John Steell)	b	Albert Memorial, Charlotte Square, Edinburgh	Pevsner, *Edinburgh*, 1991, 294
137.	1866	Sir Charles Eastlake, medallion		[Exhib R Sc A, Edinburgh, 923]; untraced	*Ormond* 1973, 156; *Laperriere* 4, 1991, 57
Miscellaneous					
138.	1831	Shepherd boy		[Exhib R Sc A, Edinburgh, 381]; untraced	*Laperriere* 4, 1991, 55
139.	1831	Young infant		[Exhib R Sc A, Edinburgh, 388]; untraced	*Laperriere* 4, 1991, 55

140.	1838	Miss Menteith		[Exhib R Sc A, Edinburgh, 425]; untraced	*Laperriere* 4, 1991, 55
141.	1839	Infancy, study	m	[Exhib R Sc A, Edinburgh, 515]; untraced	*Laperriere* 4, 1991, 55
142.	1847	Childhood		[Exhib R Sc A, Edinburgh, 624]; untraced	*Laperriere* 4, 1991, 56
143.	1847	The bird catchers		[Exhib R Sc A, Edinburgh, 647]; untraced	*Laperriere* 4, 1991, 56
144.	1848	Alexander Stewart, youngest son of Robert Harrington		[Exhib R Sc A, Edinburgh, 601]; untraced	*Laperriere* 4, 1991, 56
145.	1852	Unidentified young lady		[Exhib R Sc A, Edinburgh, 674]; untraced	*Laperriere* 4, 1991, 56
146.	1863	Charity at the holy well, model		[Exhib R Sc A, Edinburgh, 803]; untraced	*Laperriere* 4, 1991, 57

RITCHIE, James fl 1834–55

He exhibited portrait studies and narrative pieces, often illustrating literary subjects, at the Royal Scottish Academy from 1834 to 1855. In these years he lived in Edinburgh and in the 1830s exhibited his work from 1 St John's Hill, an address he shared with Alexander Ritchie, a painter. His relationship to the Ritchie family of Musselburgh is not known and he may have been the father or elder brother of Alexander Handyside and of **John Ritchie**, whose work has sometimes been confused with his own. In 1838 his statue of an *Arcadian shepherd* was awarded as a prize by the Association for the Promotion of the Fine Arts in Scotland (5).

Literary References: *Woodward* 1977, vol 1, pt 2, 207–8

Funerary Monuments

1.	1837	Model of a figure, part of a monument to Rev Samuel Kennedy		[Exhib R Sc A, Edinburgh, 363]; untraced	*Laperriere* 4, 1991, 59
2.	†1845	Lieutenant-Colonel Martin	s	Warriston Cemetery, Edinburgh	*Woodward* 1977, vol 1, pt 2, 208
3.	1848	Design for a monument		[Exhib R Sc A, Edinburgh, 622]; untraced	*Laperriere* 4, 1991, 59

Statues

4.	1837	Cain and Mahala		[Exhib R Sc A, Edinburgh, 380]; untraced	*Laperriere* 4, 1991, 59
5.	1838	Arcadian shepherd listening to Echo		[Exhib R Sc A, Edinburgh, 415]; untraced	*Laperriere* 4, 1991, 59
6.	1844	The last minstrel	s	Scott Monument, Princes Street, Edinburgh	*Woodward* 1977, vol 1, pt 2, 208

Busts

7.	1834	Unidentified boy		[Exhib R Sc A, Edinburgh, 336]; untraced	*Laperriere* 4, 1991, 59
8.	1835	Unidentified gentleman		[Exhib R Sc A, Edinburgh, 347]; untraced	*Laperriere* 4, 1991, 59
9.	1836	Rev James Peddie DD, miniature bust		[Exhib R Sc A, Edinburgh, 368]; untraced	*Laperriere* 4, 1991, 59
10.	1836	Unidentified gentleman		[Exhib R Sc A, Edinburgh, 353]; untraced	*Laperriere* 4, 1991, 59
11.	1839	Robert Johnstone		[Exhib R Sc A, Edinburgh, 505]; untraced	*Laperriere* 4, 1991, 59
12.	1839	Unidentified gentleman		[Exhib R Sc A, Edinburgh, 507]; untraced	*Laperriere* 4, 1991, 59
13.	1840	Innocence	m	[Exhib R Sc A, Edinburgh, 380]; untraced	*Laperriere* 4, 1991, 59
14.	1841	Baron Cuvier		[Exhib R Sc A, Edinburgh, 555]; untraced	*Laperriere* 4, 1991, 59
15.	1842	Unidentified artist		[Exhib R Sc A, Edinburgh, 556]; untraced	*Laperriere* 4, 1991, 59
16.	1842	Unidentified gentleman		[Exhib R Sc A, Edinburgh, 520]; untraced	*Laperriere* 4, 1991, 59
17.	1843	Richard Elliot Graham		[Exhib R Sc A, Edinburgh, 582]; untraced	*Laperriere* 4, 1991, 59
18.	1847	Morning, model		[Exhib R Sc A, Edinburgh, 631]; untraced	*Laperriere* 4, 1991, 59
19.	1850	Unidentified gentleman		[Exhib R Sc A, Edinburgh, 484]; untraced	*Laperriere* 4, 1991, 59
20.	1853	Unidentified child, model		[Exhib R Sc A, Edinburgh, 684]; untraced	*Laperriere* 4, 1991, 59
21.	1855	Unidentified gentleman		[Exhib R Sc A, Edinburgh, 751]; untraced	*Laperriere* 4, 1991, 59

Architectural Sculpture

22.	1851	Design of a triumphal arch		[Exhib R Sc A, Edinburgh, 582]; untraced	*Laperriere* 4, 1991, 59

Reliefs

23.	1835	Hebe, model		[Exhib R Sc A, Edinburgh, 356]; untraced	*Laperriere* 4, 1991, 59
24.	1836	Cupids		[Exhib R Sc A, Edinburgh, 344]; untraced	*Laperriere* 4, 1991, 59
25.	1837	Hero guiding Leander across the Hellespont		[Exhib R Sc A, Edinburgh, 362]; untraced	*Laperriere* 4, 1991, 59
26.	1839	Genevra, medallion	m	[Exhib R Sc A, Edinburgh, 493]; untraced	*Laperriere* 4, 1991, 59

Miscellaneous

27.	1836	An old head, study		[Exhib R Sc A, Edinburgh, 343]; untraced	*Laperriere* 4, 1991, 59
28.	1836	Unidentified young lady, wax miniature		[Exhib R Sc A, Edinburgh, 256]; untraced	*Laperriere* 4, 1991, 59

RITCHIE, John 1809–50

John Ritchie, the younger brother of **Alexander Handyside Ritchie**, was born at Mill Hill, Fisherrow, Musselburgh, in 1809. He first studied sculpture at home, making models and exhibiting at the Royal Institution for the Encouragement of the Fine Arts in Scotland in 1821 and 1822, but he attracted little attention and went to work with his brother Alexander after the latter's return from Rome in 1830. The partnership lasted almost twenty years.

In 1837 he came second in the competition for the Glasgow statue of Sir Walter Scott (**6**) and after the death of the successful competitor, **John Greenshields**, in 1838, Ritchie took over execution of the work. The statue was completed in 1838 and is reputed to have been the first monument to Scott erected in Scotland. When it was unveiled it drew considerable criticism because the plaid was draped over the left shoulder rather than the right, as worn by Scott.

Ritchie had extraordinary dreams which he recounted to his friends and one of these provided the inspiration for his group *The deluge* (**3**). This was modelled in clay in 1832, exhibited at Edinburgh in 1837 and at the Royal Academy in 1840. Although it attracted much attention in Edinburgh, initially it brought Ritchie no major commissions in that city, It was then brought to the attention of a Mr Davidson of London, who was so impressed that he commissioned it in marble and so gave Ritchie the opportunity to fulfil a long-cherished wish to visit Rome. Ritchie left Scotland for Italy in September 1850, and began work on the marble group immediately after his arrival. It was never completed for Ritchie contracted malaria during an excursion to Ostia and after a few days' illness, he died on 30 November 1850. His marble statue of *A poetess* was shown after his death at the Great Exhibition of 1851 (**12**).

Literary References: *A J*, 1851, 44; *Gunnis* 1968, 323; *Woodward* 1977 (vol 1, pt 2), 208–210

Funerary Monuments					
1.	1838	Lieutenant-Colonel Alexander Hope Pattison (†1835)	s	Glasgow Necropolis	*McKenzie* 2002, 299–300 (repr)
2.	1840	The ascension, part of a monument to be executed in marble to Mrs Grant		[Exhib R Sc A, Edinburgh, 391]; untraced	*Laperriere* 4, 1991, 59
Statues					
3.	1832	The deluge	tc	[Exhib R Sc A, Edinburgh, 378]; untraced	*Graves* VI, 1905–6, 307; *Gunnis* 1968, 323; *Laperriere* 4, 1991, 59
4.	1833	George, Lord Byron		[Exhib Bond Street, London]; untraced	*Gunnis* 1968, 323
5.	1836	Sir Walter Scott, miniature figure		[Exhib R Sc A, Edinburgh, 347]; untraced	*Laperriere* 4, 1991, 59
6.	1837–1838	Sir Walter Scott (after a model by John Greenshields) (co-sculptor: John Greenshields) Payment(s): a little over £1,000	s	George Square, Glasgow, Lanarks	*McKenzie* 2002, 124–6 (repr)
7.	1839	Infant Hercules	m	[Exhib R Sc A, Edinburgh, 498]; untraced	*Laperriere* 4, 1991, 59
8.	1840	Arthur, 1st Duke of Wellington, statuette		[Exhib R Sc A, Edinburgh, 370]; untraced	*Laperriere* 4, 1991, 59
9.	1841	Duke of Gordon in Highland costume, statuette		[Exhib R Sc A, Edinburgh, 557]; untraced	*Laperriere* 4, 1991, 56
10.	1841	Master Veitch, statuette		[Exhib R Sc A, Edinburgh, 552]; untraced	*Laperriere* 4, 1991, 56
11.	1841	The meeting at Goshen		[Exhib R Sc A, Edinburgh, 554]; untraced	*Laperriere* 4, 1991, 59
12.	1851	A poetess	m	[Gt Exhib]; untraced	*Gunnis* 1968, 323
Busts					
13.	1826	Unidentified gentleman		[Exhib Carlisle Acad, 170]; untraced	*Carlisle Ac Exhibs*, 1973
14.	1841	H Veitch		[Exhib R Sc A, Edinburgh, 558]; untraced	*Laperriere* 4, 1991, 56
15.	1841	J S William RN		[Exhib R Sc A, Edinburgh, 562]; untraced	*Laperriere* 4, 1991, 56
16.	1842	Alexander Earle Monteath		[Exhib R Sc A, Edinburgh, 524]; untraced	*Laperriere* 4, 1991, 56
17.	1843	Walter Moir		[Exhib R Sc A, Edinburgh, 576]; untraced	*Laperriere* 4, 1991, 56
18.	1849	Infancy	m	[Exhib R Sc A, Edinburgh, 623]; untraced	*Laperriere* 4, 1991, 59
Reliefs					
19.	1832	Unidentified subject		[Exhib R Sc A, Edinburgh, 317]; untraced	*Laperriere* 4, 1991, 59
Miscellaneous					
20.	1832	Study	m	[Exhib R Sc A, Edinburgh, 319]; untraced	*Laperriere* 4, 1991, 59
21.	1836	Italian mask		[Exhib R Sc A, Edinburgh, 352]; untraced	*Laperriere* 4, 1991, 59
22.	1837	Flower nymph		[Exhib R Sc A, Edinburgh, 408]; untraced	*Laperriere* 4, 1991, 59
23.	1839	Sappho	m	[Exhib R Sc A, Edinburgh, 497]; untraced	*Graves* 1875, 457; *Laperriere* 4, 1991, 59
24.	1841	Shepherd boy of the Alps		[Exhib R Sc A, Edinburgh, 563]; untraced	*Laperriere* 4, 1991, 56
25.	1841	The young warrior's farewell		[Exhib R Sc A, Edinburgh, 546]; untraced	*Laperriere* 4, 1991, 56
26.	1842	Christ and the doctors, finished sketch		[Exhib R Sc A, Edinburgh, 317]; untraced	*Laperriere* 4, 1991, 56
27.	1850	Faith		[Exhib R Sc A, Edinburgh, 476]; untraced	*Laperriere* 4, 1991, 59

RITSON, Jonathan fl *c*1827–43

A local woodcarver, he worked at Petworth *c*1827–43 and was paid an average of £60 a year from 1827 to 1837. George, 3rd Earl of Egremont was proud of having 'discovered' Ritson and commissioned a portrait of him from

George Clint ARA (1770–1854), who also painted a portrait of **Grinling Gibbons** to hang next to it. Both are hung, in frames carved by Ritson, in the 3rd Earl's carved room. Ritson's life was one of intermittent industry and drunkenness: 'his only pleasures were his works and his cups' wrote a contemporary.

Literary References: *Rowell* 2000 (2), 13, 28–9

Architectural Sculpture

1.	1830–1837	Carved pelmets and pendants	wd	Petworth House, Sussex	*Rowell* 2000 (2), 13
2.	1827–1846	Ceiling carvings, festoons in the style of Gibbons	wd	Petworth House, Sussex, carved room	*Rowell* 2000 (2), 26
3.	1846	Extensive decorative carving	wd	[Petworth House, West Sussex, 3rd Earl's carved room]; mostly dismantled 1870–2 [in store at Petworth], ceilings and some frames still in situ	*Rowell* 2000 (2), 28–9

RIVERS, Charles Augustus 1811–

Rivers was 19 in 1830, when he entered the Royal Academy Schools on the recommendation of **E H Baily**. Two years later he was awarded a prize by the Society of Arts and in 1837 he received a silver medal from the Royal Academy (**2, 69**). He exhibited at the Society of British Artists, 1831–1838, and at the RA, 1831–1847, from the recorded addresses of 26 Derby Road, Kingsland, 11 Church Street, Islington and 3 Territt's Court, Islington. He sent figures of John Rennie and Richard I to the Westminster Hall Exhibition in 1844 (**6, 7**). The *Literary Gazette* dismissed them as 'half size figures of small merits' (*Lit Gaz*, 20 July 1844, 466) but the *Builder* described them respectively as 'a work of animation' and 'suitable' (*Builder* 1844, 367).

Literary References: RSA Transactions, 1832, vol 49, xxv; *Gunnis* 1968, 323

Archival References: RA Admissions

Funerary Monuments

1.	1835	Hannah Pattison and husband (†1832)		Witham, Essex	GPC

Statues

2.	1832	Original model of a group		[Soc of A, large silver medal]; untraced	RSA *Transactions*, 1832, vol 49, xxv
3.	1837	Elizabeth Fry		[Exhib RA, London, 1258]; untraced	*Graves* VI, 1905–6, 308
4.	1838	Sir Thomas Telford		[Exhib Soc of BA, London, 636]; untraced	*Johnson* 1975, 394
5.	1841	William Farren, in the character of the Spanish curate, cabinet statue		[Exhib RA, London, 1263]; untraced	*Graves* VI, 1905–6, 308
6.	1844	John Rennie		[Exhib Westminster Hall, London, 95]; untraced	*AU*, 1844, 215
7.	1844	King Richard I		[Exhib Westminster Hall, London, 91]; untraced	*AU*, 1844, 214
8.	1847	Charles Thomas		[Exhib RA, London, 1295]; untraced	*Graves* VI, 1905–6, 309
9.	nd	Benjamin Babington, cabinet statuette		R C Physic, London	*Gunnis* 1968, 323

Busts

10.	1831	Rev Daniel Wilson		[Exhib RA, London, 1126]; untraced	*Graves* VI, 1905–6, 308
11.	1831	Robert Edwards Broughton		[Exhib RA, London, 1177]; untraced	*Graves* VI, 1905–6, 308; *Johnson* 1975, 394
12.	1832	Elizabeth Fry		[Exhib Soc of BA, London, 873]; untraced	*Johnson* 1975, 394
13.	1832	Henry, Lord Brougham and Vaux		[Exhib Soc of BA, London, 879]; untraced Other versions: Stanton Harcourt, Oxon, wax	*Pyke* 1973, 120; *Johnson* 1975, 394
14.	1832	William Holden		[Exhib RA, London, 1188]; untraced	*Graves* VI, 1905–6, 308
15.	1833	Henry Arthur Broughton		[Exhib RA, London, 1165]; untraced	*Graves* VI, 1905–6, 308
16.	1833	John Andree MP		[Exhib RA, London, 1166]; untraced	*Graves* VI, 1905–6, 308
17.	1833	Sir Thomas Denman		[Exhib Soc of BA, London, 812]; untraced	*Johnson* 1975, 394
18.	1833	Sir Thomas Lawrence		[Exhib RA, London, 1162]; untraced	*Graves* VI, 1905–6, 308
19.	1833	William Henry Pattison		[Exhib RA, London, 1158]; untraced	*Graves* VI, 1905–6, 308
20.	1834	Rev John Lindsay		[Exhib RA, London, 1061]; untraced	*Graves* VI, 1905–6, 308
21.	1834	Unidentified child		[Exhib RA, London, 1065]; untraced	*Graves* VI, 1905–6, 308
22.	1834	Unidentified gentleman		[Exhib RA, London, 1062]; untraced	*Graves* VI, 1905–6, 308
23.	1834	Unidentified gentleman		[Exhib RA, London, 1091]; untraced	*Graves* VI, 1905–6, 308
24.	1834	Unidentified gentleman		[Exhib RA, London, 1093]; untraced	*Graves* VI, 1905–6, 308
25.	1834	Unidentified lady		[Exhib RA, London, 1060]; untraced	*Graves* VI, 1905–6, 308
26.	1834	Unidentified lady		[Exhib RA, London, 1064]; untraced	*Graves* VI, 1905–6, 308
27.	1835	Sir William Blizard		[Exhib RA, London, 1116]; untraced	*Graves* VI, 1905–6, 308; *Johnson* 1975, 394
28.	1835	Unidentified lady		[Exhib Soc of BA, London, 776]; untraced	*Johnson* 1975, 394
29.	1836	Mrs Fry	w	Coll Mrs Gervis (Sherborne, Dorset) Other versions: Coll Mrs Geoffrey Williams (London) 1836 Coll Dr Cavat (Guernsey)	*Pyke* 1973, 120 (repr pl 240); *Pyke* 1981, 34
30.	1836	Rev Ozias Linley		[Exhib RA, London, 1109]; untraced	*Graves* VI, 1905–6, 308
31.	1836	Rev William Yate		[Exhib RA, London, 1131]; untraced	*Graves* VI, 1905–6, 308
32.	1836	Sir F Fowke Bt		[Exhib RA, London, 1112]; untraced	*Graves* VI, 1905–6, 308
33.	1837	Daniel Wilson, Bishop of Calcutta		[Exhib RA, London, 1154]; untraced	*Graves* VI, 1905–6, 308
34.	1837	Jacob Perkins		[Exhib RA, London, 1156]; untraced	*Graves* VI, 1905–6, 308
35.	1837	Madame Malibran		[Exhib RA, London, 1150]; untraced	*Graves* VI, 1905–6, 308
36.	1837	Master A Perkins		[Exhib RA, London, 1147]; untraced	*Graves* VI, 1905–6, 308
37.	1837	Master L Perkins		[Exhib RA, London, 1144]; untraced	*Graves* VI, 1905–6, 308

38.	1838	Captain Joseph Huddart	w	Institution of Civil Engineers, London		*Pyke* 1981, 34
39.	1838	Dr Thomas Rees		[Exhib RA, London, 1337]; untraced		*Graves* VI, 1905–6, 308
40.	1838	John Barwise		[Exhib RA, London, 1328]; untraced		*Graves* VI, 1905–6, 308
41.	1838	John Hardy		[Exhib RA, London, 1333]; untraced		*Graves* VI, 1905–6, 308
42.	1838	Sir Isaac Newton	w	Institution of Civil Engineers, London	D	*Pyke* 1981, 34
43.	1838	Thomas Meux		[Exhib RA, London, 1354]; untraced		*Graves* VI, 1905–6, 308
44.	1838	Unidentified lady		[Exhib RA, London, 1335]; untraced		*Graves* VI, 1905–6, 308
45.	1839	Queen Victoria		[Exhib RA, London, 1320]; untraced		*Graves* VI, 1905–6, 308
46.	1839	William Cooke		[Exhib RA, London, 1389]; untraced		*Graves* VI, 1905–6, 308
47.	1840	S Samuel		[Exhib RA, London, 1109]; untraced		*Graves* VI, 1905–6, 308
48.	1840	Unidentified gentleman		[Exhib RA, London, 1113]; untraced		*Graves* VI, 1905–6, 308
49.	1840	Unidentified lady		[Exhib RA, London, 1115]; untraced		*Graves* VI, 1905–6, 308
50.	1841	Miss Helen Faucit		[Exhib RA, London, 1151]; untraced		*Graves* VI, 1905–6, 308
51.	1841	Sir Marc Brunel		[Exhib RA, London, 1148]; untraced		*Graves* VI, 1905–6, 308
52.	1842	R J Longbottom		[Exhib RA, London, 1169]; untraced		*Graves* VI, 1905–6, 308
53.	1842	Sir Astley Paston Cooper		[Exhib RA, London, 1192]; untraced		*Graves* VI, 1905–6, 308
54.	1842	Unidentified child		[Exhib RA, London, 1351]; untraced		*Graves* VI, 1905–6, 308
55.	1843	Dr George Robert Rowe FBA		[Exhib RA, London, 1481]; untraced		*Graves* VI, 1905–6, 308
56.	1843	Dr John Ryan		[Exhib RA, London, 1376]; untraced		*Graves* VI, 1905–6, 308
57.	1843	Prof Bachhoffner		[Exhib RA, London, 1386]; untraced		*Graves* VI, 1905–6, 308
58.	1845	Sir Isaac Newton	m	[Exhib RA, London, 1372]; untraced		*Graves* VI, 1905–6, 309
59.	1845	Sir William Follett		[Exhib RA, London, 1317]; untraced		*Graves* VI, 1905–6, 309; *Ormond* 1973, 176
60.	1846	Dr Thomas Wallis		[Exhib RA, London, 1389]; untraced		*Graves* VI, 1905–6, 309
61.	1847	John Bright		[Exhib RA, London, 1297]; untraced		*Graves* VI, 1905–6, 309
62.	1847	John Knight MP		[Exhib RA, London, 1297]; untraced		*Graves* VI, 1905–6, 309
63.	1847	Lady MacNab		[Exhib RA, London, 1415]; untraced		*Graves* VI, 1905–6, 309
64.	1847	Sir Allan Napier MacNab		[Exhib RA, London, 1376]; untraced		*Graves* VI, 1905–6, 309
65.	nd	Charles James Blomfield, Bishop of London	w	Viscount Harcourt (Stanton Harcourt, Oxon)		*Pyke* 1973, 120
Reliefs						
66.	1842	Mrs Sievier		[Exhib RA, London, 1198]; untraced		*Graves* VI, 1905–6, 308
67.	1842	R W Sievier		[Exhib RA, London, 1193]; untraced		*Graves* VI, 1905–6, 308
Miscellaneous						
68.	1831	Mars		[Exhib RA, London, 1151]; untraced		*Library of Fine Arts*, vol I, 1831, 430; *Graves* VI, 1905–6, 308
69.	1837	Unidentified subject, model		[RA silver medal]; untraced		RA Premium list
70.	1842	'Chessmen in the costume and armour of the time of the Battle of Agincourt, 1415'		[Exhib RA, London, 1201]; untraced		*Graves* VI, 1905–6, 308

RIVERS, J

For further information the reader is referred to *Pyke* 1973, 120

RIVERS, Mary Adeline fl 1841–44

In 1841, while living at 26 Charlotte Street, Fitzroy Square, she was awarded a silver medal by the Society of Arts. She was described as 'An Honorary Exhibitor' when she showed works at the Royal Academy between 1842 and 1844. Her address was 3 Territt's Place, Islington in 1844.

Literary References: RSA *Transactions*, 1843, vol 54, xv; *Graves* VI, 1905–6, 309

Busts				
1.	1841	A child, modelled in wax	[Soc of A, silver medal]; untraced	RSA *Transactions*, 1843, vol 54, xv
2.	1842	A child	[Exhib RA, London, 1182]; untraced	*Graves* VI, 1905–6, 309
3.	1843	Miss Louisa Tulley	[Exhib RA, London, 1375]; untraced	*Graves* VI, 1905–6, 309
4.	1844	Miss Cullen	[Exhib RA, London, 1263]; untraced	*Graves* VI, 1905–6, 309

ROACH, A fl 1830

Statues				
1.	1830	Lady Godiva	[Exhib RA, London, 1252]; untraced	*Graves* VI, 1905–6, 313

ROBANS, William fl 1687

In 1687 the Earl of Danby paid 'William Robans, stonecutter' £20 for unidentified works (Archives, Child's Bank, in GPC).

ROBERTS, C, of Sheffield fl c1800

His tombstone commemorating Richard Walker, a trumpeter, has 'finely cut military emblems' (*Gunnis* 1968, 323) (2).

Funerary Monuments					
1.	?1800	Mary Mort	St James, Sheffield, W R Yorks	S	*Gunnis* 1968, 323
2.	†1800	Richard Walker	Sheffield Cathedral, W R Yorks, churchyard	S	*Holland* 1869, 19; *Gunnis* 1968, 323
Architectural Sculpture					
3.	nd	Capitals of eight pillars	Carver Street Chapel, Sheffield, W R Yorks		*Gunnis* 1968, 323

ROBERTS, of Bramley fl c1841

Funerary Monuments					
1.	?1841	Ann Firth	Hooton Roberts, W R Yorks	S	GPC

ROBERTS, of Exeter fl c1813

He signs a wall-tablet with a relief of a mourning woman (1).

Funerary Monuments					
1.	?1813	Elizabeth Gartside	Topsham, Devon	S	*Gunnis* 1968, 323

ROBERTS, William fl c1741

Chimneypieces

1.	c1741	Description unavailable	Wolterton Hall, Norfolk		Pevsner, *Norfolk: N E & Norwich*, 1997, 73

ROBERTSON, J fl 1838

For further information the reader is referred to *Pyke* 1973, 120

ROBINS (or ROBBINS), Francis, of Bath fl c1755–96

He was described as a 'statuary, mason and penant man' when he was declared bankrupt in 1770 (*Universal Mag*, 1770, 335). Gunnis notes that his best work is the monument to Sir Bouchier Wray, which is a large square pedestal surmounted by an urn (4). He may be related to George Robins, a mason of Bristol, whose son Samuel, also a mason of that city, became free in 1739.

Literary References: *Gunnis* 1968, 323–4

Funerary Monuments

1.	?1755	Charles Biggs	Backwell, Somerset	S	*Gunnis* 1968, 324
2.	†1778	Rev Henry Lockett	Crowcombe, Somerset	S	Pevsner, *Somerset: S & W*, 1958, 142
3.	1780	Anne Acton	Camborne, Cornwall	S	Pevsner, *Cornwall*, 1970, 50
4.	†1784	Sir Bouchier Wray Bt	Tawstock, Devon	S	*Gunnis* 1968, 324
5.	†1789	Thomas Creed	Kingscote, Glos	S	Pevsner, *Glos: Cotswolds*, 1999, 428
6.	†1794	Sir James Tylney-Long Bt	Draycot Cerne, Wilts	S	*Gunnis* 1968, 324
7.	?1796	Henry Dickanson	Bathampton, Somerset	S	*Gunnis* 1968, 324

ROBINSON, Charles Backhouse, of Liverpool 1806–94

Robinson was born in Liverpool on 13 January 1806, the son of Nicholas Robinson, a wealthy corn merchant who built Sudley House and served as mayor of Liverpool in the 1820s. He exhibited at the Liverpool Academy between 1836 and 1852, at the Royal Hibernian Academy in 1843, at the Westminster Hall Exhibition of 1844, at Royal Manchester Institution in 1846 and at the Carlisle Academy in 1850. His addresses were recorded as Aigburth, near Liverpool; Renshaw Street, Liverpool; 79 Renshaw Street, Liverpool; Clark Street, Toxteth Park, Liverpool and 14 Myrtle Street, Liverpool.

Literary References: *Gunnis* 1968, 324

Archival References: GPC

Funerary Monuments					
1.	?1836	John Hodgkinson	Prescot, Lancs	S	*Gunnis* 1968, 324
2.	1841	Hope, monumental figure	[Exhib Liverpool Ac, 671]; untraced		*Morris and Roberts* 1998, 520
Statues					
3.	1844	King William IV	[Exhib Westminster Hall, London]; untraced		*Gunnis* 1968, 324
4.	1847	The Saviour	[Exhib Liverpool Ac, 760]; untraced	p	*Morris and Roberts* 1998, 520
5.	1848	Our Saviour and St Peter	[Exhib Liverpool Ac, 686]; untraced		*Morris and Roberts* 1998, 520
6.	1850	Christ	[Exhib Carlisle Acad, 296]; untraced		*Carlisle Ac Exhibs* 1973
7.	1850	Musidora	[Exhib Liverpool Ac, 524]; untraced	p	*Morris and Roberts* 1998, 520
8.	nd	Holy Family	[Frankton Grange, Ellesmere, Salop]; untraced		GPC
9.	nd	St Euphemia	[Frankton Grange, Ellesmere, Salop]; untraced		GPC
10.	nd	Woman with a pitcher	[Frankton Grange, Ellesmere, Salop]; untraced		GPC
Busts					
11.	c1836	Nicholas Robinson (the sculptor's father)	[Frankton Grange, Ellesmere, Salop]; untraced		GPC; *Morris and Roberts* 1998, 520
12.	1840	Unidentified lady	[Exhib Liverpool Ac, 697]; untraced		*Morris and Roberts* 1998, 520
13.	1843	Unidentified gentleman	[Exhib Liverpool Ac, 558]; untraced		*Morris and Roberts* 1998, 520
14.	1845	T Tobin	[Exhib Liverpool Ac, 794]; untraced		*Morris and Roberts* 1998, 520
15.	1846	W Hodgson	[Exhib Liverpool Ac, 813]; untraced		*Gunnis* 1968, 324; *Morris and Roberts* 1998, 520
16.	1846	William Lowe	[Exhib Royal Manc Institution]; untraced		*Gunnis* 1968, 324
17.	1851	Master James Rowe Danson	[Exhib Liverpool Ac, 584]; untraced		*Morris and Roberts* 1998, 520
18.	1851	R Stubbs	[Exhib Liverpool Ac, 582]; untraced		*Morris and Roberts* 1998, 520
19.	1851	W Danson	[Exhib Liverpool Ac, 583]; untraced		*Morris and Roberts* 1998, 520
20.	nd	R N Robinson (the sculptor's brother)	[Frankton Grange, Ellesmere, Salop]; untraced		GPC
Chimneypieces					
21.	nd	In the dining and drawing room	Frankton Grange, Ellesmere, Salop		GPC
Reliefs					
22.	1836	Rev N Robinson, portrait medallion	[Exhib Liverpool Ac, 660]; untraced		*Morris and Roberts* 1998, 520
23.	1842	Greek warrior and horse	[Exhib Liverpool Ac, 581]; untraced		*Stewart* III, 1985, 112; *Morris and Roberts* 1998, 520
24.	1843	Unidentified lady, portrait medallion	[Exhib Liverpool Ac, 562]; untraced		*Morris and Roberts* 1998, 520
25.	nd	Several, religious subjects	[Frankton Grange, Ellesmere, Salop]; untraced		GPC
Miscellaneous					
26.	1840	The break of day	[Exhib Liverpool Ac, 689]; untraced		*Morris and Roberts* 1998, 520
27.	1841	Dragoon and horse	[Exhib Liverpool Ac, 650]; untraced		*Morris and Roberts* 1998, 520
28.	1841	Return from coursing	[Exhib Liverpool Ac, 660]; untraced		*Morris and Roberts* 1998, 520
29.	1842	Highland shepherd boy	[Exhib Liverpool Ac, 577]; untraced		*Morris and Roberts* 1998, 520
30.	1846	Pouring out the sacred wine	[Exhib Liverpool Ac, 803]; untraced		*Morris and Roberts* 1998, 520
31.	1847	Red Riding Hood	[Exhib Liverpool Ac, 756]; untraced	p	*Morris and Roberts* 1998, 520

32.	1849	A virgin saint		[Exhib Liverpool Ac, 660]; untraced	*Morris and Roberts* 1998, 520
33.	1850	Unidentified subject		[Exhib Carlisle Acad, 294]; untraced	*Carlisle Ac Exhibs* 1973
34.	1852	Arab and horse		[Exhib Liverpool Ac, 602]; untraced	*Morris and Roberts* 1998, 520
35.	1852	Christianity triumphant over Satan		[Exhib Liverpool Ac, 597]; untraced	*Morris and Roberts* 1998, 520

ROBINSON, John fl 1834

Reliefs

1.	1834	Venus	m	[Exhib Royal Northern Soc, Leeds]; untraced Other versions: 'Figure of Venus' exhib Liverpool Academy, 1835, 553; untraced	*Gunnis* 1968, 324; *Morris and Roberts* 1998, 520

Miscellaneous

2.	1836	Unidentified lady		[Exhib Liverpool Ac, 422]; untraced	*Morris and Roberts* 1998, 520

ROBINSON, John, of London fl 1824–25

Architectural Sculpture

1.	1824	Font Payment(s): £36 15s	m	Tooting parish church, London	*Morden* 1897, 177
2.	1825	Ten Corinthian capitals and 'enrichment in the architrave' Payment(s): £400, £152 5s 10d		Privy Council offices, London	TNA WORK 5/125 fol 205
3.	1825	Two capitals, '10 pine apples', '12 pendant roses to coffers' and other ornaments Payment(s): £90 for the capitals, £6 for the pineapples		Board of Trade buildings, London	TNA WORK 5/125, fols 172, 205

ROBINSON, Joseph Barlow 1820–83

He was born at South Wingfield, Derbys, began work in Belper and when quite young moved to London, where for eight years he was employed on gothic carving at the Houses of Parliament (**3**). In 1847 he set up on his own account in London and in 1848–50 worked from premises at Savoy Way, Strand. In 1850 he returned to Derby and established monumental works in Derwent Street, specialising in funerary monuments and decorative carving for churches. His numerous publications include books of designs for monuments and gothic architectural carving, practical manuals for builders and sculptors and a work on Derbyshire history and topography. He died on 18 January 1883, at Derby.

Archival References: GPC (inf. Derby public library)

Funerary Monuments

1.	†1856	Rev William Cantrell and his wife Anne (†1852)		Melbourne, Derbys	S	

Statues

2.	1859	Feargus O'Connor	s	Nottingham arboretum	*Fry* 1999, 32–3 (repr)

Architectural Sculpture

3.	1839–1847	Ornamental carving		Palace of Westminster, London	GPC
4.	*c*1850	Unidentified		[Elvaston Castle, Derbys, south front]; untraced	RG/JP, 7, 1176v
5.	nd	Pulpit	s	[Armitage, Staffs]; untraced	RG/JP, 7, 1176v
6.	nd	Unidentified		[Aldingham Hall, Lincs]; untraced	RG/JP, 7, 1176v

ROBINSON, L, of Barnstaple fl 1801–02

Funerary Monuments

1.	?1801	Elizabeth Hale	South Molton, Devon	S	*Gunnis* 1968, 324
2.	?1802	Samuel Chappell	Fremington, Devon	S	*Gunnis* 1968, 324

ROBINSON, Lewis *c*1745–

He was apprenticed to Grepel of Rathbone Place in 1763, the year he won a premium in the under-19 class (**2**). In the RSA Minutes for 1762–63 he was described as an 'ornament carver'. On 18 May 1764 he was awarded a one guinea premium in the under-22 class (**1**).

Literary References: *Dossie* 1782, 437–8

Archival References: RSA *Minutes*, 1762–63, seq 2 fol 70

Architectural Sculpture

1.	1764	Model of ornaments in clay	tc	[Soc of A, premium]; untraced	*Dossie* 1782, 437

Miscellaneous

2.	1763	Clay festoon		[Soc of A, premium]; untraced	RSA *Minutes*, 1762–63; RSA *Premiums*, 1762, 33

ROBINSON, Mary *c*1744–

She won a 3 guinea premium from the Society of Arts in 1763 and another, of 10 guineas, on 18 May 1764 for a model in wax in the girls under-21 class (**1, 2**). Her given address was 'at Mr Robinson's in Beaufort Buildings, Strand'.

Literary References: RSA Premiums, 1763, 37; *Dossie* 1782, 436

Archival References: RSA Minutes, 1763–64, Pr/GE/112/12/5 seq 3 fol 84

Miscellaneous

1.	1763	Wax ornament of flowers and foliage	[Soc of A, premium]; untraced	*Dossie* 1782, 436
2.	1764	Model of ornaments in wax	[Soc of A, premium]; untraced	RSA Premiums; RSA Minutes

ROBINSON, of Redditch fl *c*1835

Funerary Monuments

1.	?1835	Charles Dowderswell	Beoley, Worcs	S	GPC

ROBINSON, of Saffron Walden fl *c*1791

Funerary Monuments

1.	†1791	Rev Nathaniel Salter	Ashdon, Essex	*GM*, 1791, ii, 780

ROBINSON, T, of Chudleigh fl c1805–09

He signs two pretty polychrome marble wall-tablets (1–2).

Funerary Monuments

1.	?1805	Robert Sutton	Littleham, Devon	S	*Gunnis* 1968, 324
2.	?1809	Edward Kershaw	Dawlish, Devon	S	*Gunnis* 1968, 324

ROBINSON, Thomas, of Oxford fl 1670–1709

He was possibly a son of the Thomas Robinson of Oxford who was employed on building the north side of Christ Church quadrangle in 1641 and was a master-mason at the Sheldonian, 1664–1669.

There are a number of payments to Robinson in the Vice-Chancellor's accounts. In 1670 he received £91 19s 4d for work 'about ye winter house for Plants for ye Physick Garden' (Oxford V-C's Accts fol 16) and a further £40 10s 8d 'upon the same account' (fol 20). In 1671–72 he received £23 5s 2d. for mason's work at the new printing house, with further entries in 1672 and 1674 (fols 25, 26). In 1675 and 1676 he was being paid 'for worke done in the Schooles' (fols 38, 40) and the physick garden and 'for the Stone Works and setting up of 40 Pinnacles about St Marie's Church at £2 10s, per pinnacle, together with other repairs to the University church' (fol 41). In 1686–87 he was paid £112 10s 10d for the Carfax conduit (unfol v) and in 1693–94, £122 8d 11d for work at the physick garden (unfol).

In 1681 Robinson and **Christopher Kempster** were the master-masons building Tom Tower. In 1709 Robinson was one of the master-masons at the Queen's College.

Literary References: *Clark* 1891–90, IV, 78, 81; *Hiscock* 1946, 148, 232; *Gunnis* 1968, 324

ROBINSON, William fl 1708–58

Probably a Yorkshire mason, Robinson worked at Castle Howard in 1708 as an assistant to **Henri Nadauld**, and he later worked there on his own account. He built the mausoleum, 1729–37, and provided carved stonework, assisted by two other masons, William Hodgson and Christopher Robson (not Robinson, as stated by Gunnis) (1). Robson and Hodgson received £109 for building the steps on the south front of the house. William Robinson was the mason responsible for building the 'New Wing' in 1753–58.

Literary References: *Gunnis* 1968, 324–5

Archival References: Castle Howard Building Accts, mausoleum, 1729–37 G2/2/72, Dec 1737 (William Robinson); G2/2/63, 1731; G2/2/67, 1736; G2/2/70, 1737 (Hodgson and Robson); south front steps, G2/2/71, 1737 (Robson and Hodgson); new wing, G3/1/2, 1753–58; G3/3/2–20, 1759–60 (William Robinson)

Architectural Sculpture

1.	1729–1737	Carved stonework	Castle Howard, N R Yorks, mausoleum		*Gunnis* 1968, 324

RODDIS, Thomas –1845

Roddis of Sutton Coldfield was the family firm of stonemasons employed by A W N Pugin in the building of Oscott College, Sutton Coldfield. Pugin also employed one of the family, Thomas Roddis, as a sculptor. His most important work was the ornamental carving at St Giles, Cheadle (2). It has been suggested that Roddis, a pupil of **Sir Francis Chantrey**, was brought to Birmingham to work on the town hall by the architect, Joseph Hansom, and that he also worked on the restoration of Perry Hall for John Gough, before Pugin persuaded him to relocate to Sutton Coldfield (*Thomson* 1931, in *Belcher* 2001, 135). He moved to Cheadle in 1842.

Literary References: *Thomson* 1931, 63–84; *Wedgwood* 1977, *passim*; *Read* 1982, 256; *Belcher* 2001, *passim*

Architectural Sculpture

1.	c1838	Altar, font, piscina and holy water stoups	St Augustine, Solihull, Warks		*Wedgwood* 1977, 81 n47
2.	1841	Carved details, including capitals	St Giles, Cheadle, Cheshire		*Read* 1982, 256

ROGERS, of Tavistock fl c1813

He signs a wall-tablet with a relief of a seated mourning woman (1).

Funerary Monuments

1.	?1813	John Carpenter	Tavistock, Devon	S	*Gunnis* 1968, 325

ROGERS, of Tenby fl c1834

Funerary Monuments

1.	†1834	Thomas Millard	Manorbier, Pembrokes	S	

ROGERS, Philip and Son, of Swansea fl 1826–70

Rogers ran a flourishing business from successive addresses in Swansea, advertising himself specifically as working in marble. He had a marble works in Wassail Street in 1844 and later opened premises in the High Street. He signs gravestones in the churchyard of St Mary, Swansea, and may have executed memorials for the interior of the church, which was destroyed by bombing in 1941. The *Gentleman's Magazine* describes his monument to Rev Edward Davies as a tablet in the Grecian style, with pilasters and a pediment, decorated with sprigs of oak and mistletoe in relief (2). Dale-Jones and Lloyd considered his work in Carmarthenshire 'rather ordinary'.

Literary References: *Gunnis* 1968, 325; *Dale-Jones and Lloyd* 1989, 57

Funerary Monuments

1.	†1826	Lewis Lewis	Gwynfe, Carmarthen		*Dale-Jones and Lloyd* 1989, 57
2.	1837	Rev Edward Davies (tablet and tombstone)	Bishopston, nr Swansea, Glamorgan		*GM*, 1838, i, 596–7
3.	†1838	Rev John Thomas	Llangennech, Carmarthen		*Dale-Jones and Lloyd* 1989, 57
4.	†1845	Bruce Knight, Dean of Llandaff	St Mary, Margam, Glamorgan	S	Pevsner, *Glamorgan*, 1995, 426
5.	†1846	John Wood	Llandeilo, Carmarthen		*Dale-Jones and Lloyd* 1989, 57
6.	†1856	Frances Mary Thomas	Laugharne, Carmarthen		*Dale-Jones and Lloyd* 1989, 57
7.	†1857	Catherine Lewis	St Clears, Carmarthen		*Dale-Jones and Lloyd* 1989, 57
8.	†1861	Anne Miller	Pembrey, Carmarthen		*Dale-Jones and Lloyd* 1989, 57
9.	†1861	Rev Thomas Davies	Llangadog, Carmarthen		*Dale-Jones and Lloyd* 1989, 57
10.	†1868	Rev George Green	Llangathen, Carmarthen		*Dale-Jones and Lloyd* 1989, 57
11.	†1868	Udea Thompson	Pembrey, Carmarthen		*Dale-Jones and Lloyd* 1989, 57

12.	†1870	Marguerite Thompson	Kidwelly, Carmarthen		*Dale-Jones and Lloyd* 1989, 57
13.	nd	At least ten, unidentified subjects	St May, Swansea, Glamorgan, churchyard		*Dale-Jones and Lloyd* 1989, 57

ROGERS, William Gibbs 1795–1875

His early taste for drawing and modelling led him to a life-long interest in the wood carving of **Grinling Gibbons**. He made an historical collection of wood carvings, devised a method of conserving woodwork of the Gibbons period and himself gained a high reputation as a wood carver. He was employed by the Royal family at Carlton House, Kensington Palace and the Brighton Pavilion, and at the 1851 Exhibition showed a boxwood cradle commissioned by the Queen. In 1872 he received a civil list pension. His church work included the furnishings inserted in Scott's restoration (1858–60) of St Michael, Cornhill.

Literary References: *Victorian Church Art*, VAM exhib, 1971–2, 62

ROGERSON, William, of London fl c1794–1800

Rogerson, whose yard was in Gerrard Street, was declared bankrupt in 1800. Gunnis says that his monument to John Madocks has a 'fine portrait-bust' (3).

Literary References: *The Times*, 26 February, 7 March, 7 April, 23 December 1800; 7 December 1801, 4; *Gunnis* 1968, 325

Funerary Monuments

1.	?1794	Captain James Thresher	Fareham, Hants	S	*Gunnis* 1968, 325
2.	?1794	John Bull	St Thomas, Lewes, Sussex	S	*Gunnis* 1968, 325
3.	†1794	John Madocks	Gresford, Denbighs		*Gunnis* 1968, 325; Pevsner, *Clwyd* 1994, 172
4.	†1795	William Kennaway	Winyard's Hospital, Exeter, Devon, chapel	S	GPC
5.	†1796	Michael Keane	Barbados Cathedral, Bridgetown		*Gunnis* 1968, 325

ROOME, Samuel fl 1738

He was a 'Carver at London' who worked for **Henry Watson**. A payment to him, of £1 1s, on 27 April 1738 is recorded in Watson's account book (Bodleian MS Eng Misc fols 383, 77, in *Brighton* 2001, 70).

ROPER, Roger, of Preston 1757–1838

The son of **William Roper**, he took over his father's masonry business. In 1816 the architect Lewis Wyatt wrote that 'he has the character of doing his work well and is considered to be a good general builder' (Lancs CRO, DDX 1564, in *Colvin* 1995, 834). As an architect he designed several churches and houses in Lancashire. His bill for erecting a monument to Rev Phillip Darrell survives amongst the papers of the Darrell family of Calehill, Kent, but the monument itself has not been identified (2).

Literary References: *Gunnis* 1968, 325; *Colvin* 1995, 834

Archival References: GPC

Funerary Monuments

1.	?1782	Edward Buckley	Penwortham, Lancs	S	*Gunnis* 1968, 325
2.	1814	Rev Philip Darrell Payment(s): £45	Untraced		CKS U.386.A.13, in RG/JP, 7, 1180

ROPER, William, of Preston fl 1782

A local mason, he died in the 1790s.

Literary References: *Gunnis* 1968, 325; *Colvin* 1995, 834

Architectural Sculpture

1.	1782	Obelisk	[Old market place, Preston, Lancs]; dismantled 1853		Borough Archives, in *Gunnis* 1968, 325

ROSE, Joseph I –before 1747

The son of John Rose, a gunsmith of Chipping Wycombe, Bucks, he was apprenticed to **James Paget** on 25 July 1710, becoming free of the Masons' Company in June 1721. On 1 March 1723 he took his first apprentice, John Oliver. Several others followed: John Lloyd joined him on 5 August 1726 and Joseph Garnett on 26 May 1731. Garnett was turned over to **Andrews Jelfe** in March 1736, when Rose was declared bankrupt. His yard was then at Cow Lane, West Smithfield. He evidently recovered for he took on Thomas, perhaps the son of **Thomas Hill II**, on 5 May 1738 and another apprentice, Richard or Edward Lowfield, on 14 June 1742. This last was turned over to Rose's widow, Elizabeth, on 25 June 1747.

Gunnis comments that Rose's two known monuments are 'grand and imposing works with life-size reclining figures and elaborate architectural settings' and that they 'place the sculptor in the front rank of early eighteenth-century statuaries' (*Gunnis* 1968, 325). The Packington memorial has a reclining figure in contemporary costume in front of an arched pediment, from which falls a curtain inscribed with the epitaph (1). The Ladbroke is a towering tripartite composition with a pedestal decorated with skulls and bones, a life-sized reclining figure in Roman dress flanked by statues of *Justice* and *Truth*, and above, two angels with trumpets and palm branches on either side of a resplendent sun. The inscription is on a pyramid forming part of the background and the whole is set within a rich but restrained architectural frame (2). This work is of 'very high quality, especially the humane, unaffected face of Ladbroke; not in the least academic and completely overcoming the disadvantage of the Roman dress' (Pevsner, *Surrey*, 1971, 425).

Literary References: *London Mag*, vol 4, 1735, 100; *Gunnis* 1968, 325; *Webb* 1999, 13, 16, 21, 24, 28

Archival References: Masons' Co, *Freemen*, fol 64 (30 June 1721)

Funerary Monuments

1.	†1727	Sir John Packington	St Mary, Hampton Lovett, Worcs	S	Pevsner, *Worcs*, 1968, 183
2.	†1730	Richard Ladbroke	St Mary, Reigate, Surrey	S	*London Mag* 1735, 100; Pevsner, *Surrey*, 1971, 425

ROSE, Joseph II 1744–99

A highly successful craftsman, he specialised in decorative plasterwork. He was born at Norton, Derbys, on 5 April 1745. His father and brother (both called Jonathan) and his uncle, Joseph, were all plasterers and together they formed the firm of Joseph Rose & Co and monopolised the most important plasterwork commissions of the Adam period.

Rose, was living with his father 'opposite Portland Chapel, Cavendish Square' when he was awarded a premium for a model from the Society of Arts in 1765 (**5**). He went to Rome in 1769, and in June he joined **Joseph Nollekens** and others on an 18-day expedition into the Roman campagna. In 1770 he exhibited a model of a bas-relief at the Royal Academy, giving his address as Rome (**2**). He returned to Britain later that year and enrolled as a student at the RA Schools. He went on to exhibit four more works at the RA between 1771 and 1798 from addresses in Queen Anne Street, where the Rose firm had its premises (**1, 3, 4, 6**).

During the 1790s, when Rose was working for Sir Christopher Sykes on plaster ornaments at Sledmere House, in the East Riding, he apparently also acted as an agent, interceding in the purchase of sculpture for his patron. In letters to Sykes, dated between May and June 1793, Rose referred to sculpture from Italy sent up to Yorkshire, including reliefs, capitals and a tripod, and noted that 'a satyr which Nollekens has taken to pieces and then reassembled cannot be shipped north for a fortnight' (Sykes/Rose).

Literary References: *Dossie* 1782, 438; *Gunnis* 1968, 325; *Beard* 1975, 237–244 (including a list of his plasterwork commissions); *Stainton* 1983, 13, 32; *Ingamells* 1997, 822

Busts					
1.	1798	Unidentified gentleman		[Exhib RA, London, 467]; untraced	*Graves* VI, 1905–6, 362
Chimneypieces					
2.	c1793	Two (co-sculptor: Peter Van Gelder)	m	Sledmere House, E R Yorks, library	*Mulcahy* 2006, 68–9 (repr)
Reliefs					
3.	1770	Unidentified subject, bas relief, model		[Exhib RA, London, 157]; untraced	*Graves* VI, 1905–6, 362
4.	1771	A sacrifice to Hymen, model		[Exhib RA, London, 169]; untraced	*Graves* VI, 1905–6, 362
Miscellaneous					
5.	1765	Model of ornaments in clay		[Soc of A, premium, under 22 class, 10 gns]; untraced	RSA *Minutes*, 1764–65, seq 3 f61
6.	1787	Design for a British Capital		[Exhib RA, London, 626]; untraced	*Graves* VI, 1905–6, 362

ROSE, of London fl c1848

Funerary Monuments					
1.	†1848	Nicholas Segar (†1828) and Mary Parry		Little Hadham, Herts	S

ROSS, Henry fl 1851–67

His works were exhibited at the Great Exhibition of 1851, the International Exhibition of 1862 and the Royal Academy, 1858–67. He may have been an assistant to **John Bell** as his address is recorded as 15 Douro Place, Kensington, in 1851 and 1858–9. He subsequently exhibited from 42 Lower Belgrave Place.

Literary References: *Gunnis* 1968, 325

Statues					
1.	1851	Arthur, 1st Duke of Wellington, statuette	w	[Gt Exhib]; untraced	*Gunnis* 1968, 325
2.	1851	Sir Robert Peel, statuette	w	[Gt Exhib]; untraced	*Great Exhib* 1851 (2), 151
3.	1859	A group of children		[Exhib RA, London, 1352]; untraced	*Graves* VI, 1905–6, 364
4.	1862	'Home Sweet Home'	w	[Int Exhib]; untraced	*Gunnis* 1968, 325
Busts					
5.	?1854	Arthur, 1st Duke of Wellington	m	[Crystal Palace, Sydenham]; untraced	*Gunnis* 1968, 325; *Johnson* 1975, 404
6.	1854	John Worsfold, for a monument		[Exhib Soc of BA, London, 740]; untraced	*Johnson* 1975, 404
7.	1866	Charles Waterton		[Exhib RA, London, 1048]; untraced	*Graves* VI, 1905–6, 364
8.	nd	Dr Joseph Hutton	p	Dr Williams's Library, Gordon Square, London	GPC
Miscellaneous					
9.	1858	Mrs Adams, of Charlton, Kent		[Exhib RA, London, 1284]; untraced	*Graves* VI, 1905–6, 364
10.	1867	'The foundress of St Saviour's, Clapham, to be executed in marble and placed in the new church'	m	[Exhib RA, London, 1124]; untraced	*Graves* VI, 1905–6, 364

ROSSETER, James Marmaduke, of the Borough fl 1777–1818

The son of 'Thomas Rosseter, Gentleman, of the Bank of England', he was apprenticed to Robert Clemens on 26 June 1777, becoming free of the Masons' Company in 1784. He was declared bankrupt in 1790 (*General Mag*, 1790, 524). However, he was soon back in business, taking his son, Richard Baker Rosseter, as an apprentice on 12 January 1792. At that time he described himself as a gentleman, of St Saviour, Southwark. His name continued to appear in local directories until 1818.

Literary References: *Gunnis* 1968, 325; *Webb* 1999, 28

Funerary Monuments					
1.	?1789	Roberts family	Southwark Cathedral, London		GPC
2.	?1799	Anthony Hall	St George the Martyr, Southwark, London	S	*Gunnis* 1968, 325

ROSSI, Charles –1826

The son of **JCF Rossi** and his first wife Mary, he was born on 12 November 1796 and baptised at St Pancras Old Church on 18 December that year. He emigrated to Barbados, where he set up as a monumental mason and executed a number of tablets between 1819 and 1830, four of which are listed by Gunnis. He married Elizabeth Mellows Henry Crofts on 13 February 1820, at St Michael, Barbados. Their son, also named Charles, was christened at St Michael's on 8 May 1823.

Literary References: *Gunnis* 1968, 327

Archival References: IGI

Funerary Monuments				
1.	?1819	Jane Edwards	Barbados Cathedral, WI	*Gunnis* 1968, 327
2.	?1820	A M Clinton	Barbados Cathedral, WI	*Gunnis* 1968, 327
3.	?1821	H J Lorraine	Barbados Cathedral, WI	*Gunnis* 1968, 327
4.	?1824	J W Fletcher	Barbados Cathedral, WI	*Gunnis* 1968, 327

ROSSI, Frederick Orton 1811–51

The son of **JCF Rossi** and Peggy Orton, he was christened on 20 November 1811 at St Mary, St Marylebone Road, London. He was probably trained by his father and in 1830, whilst living at Grove Street, Lisson Grove, he was awarded the silver Isis medal by the Society of Arts for a model of a figure (**2**). That year he exhibited a bust of his brother at the Royal Academy from the family home at Lisson Grove (**4**) and the following year he enrolled at the Royal Academy Schools. In his first year at the Schools he won a gold medal (**3**).

In 1838 Rossi exhibited a bust of his father, with whom he was now living at 12 Cochrane Street (**5**). JCF Rossi died the following year, leaving his entire estate to his wife, to be disposed of 'to the best advantage of herself and my dear children'. Rossi subsequently held a raffle of his father's work. From his new address at 27 Adam Street East, Rossi issued up to 500 subscription tickets, 24 of which would entitle the lucky holders to the original model for one of his father's works. Such innovative business techniques could not save Rossi from penury and towards the end of his life he was obliged to apply to the Royal Academy for poor relief. He was granted a number of small sums, £15 in 1847, 15 guineas in 1848, and £10 in 1851, the year of his death.

Literary References: *Graves* VI, 1905–6, 371; *Gunnis* 1968, 325–6

Archival References: RSA *Transactions*, 1831, vol 48, 550; RA Premium list; IGI

Wills: JCF Rossi PROB 11/1909/402

Funerary Monuments					
1.	†1838	Emma Chambers		Llanelli, Carmarthen	*Dale-Jones and Lloyd* 1989, 57
Statues					
2.	1830	Model of a figure from the antique		[Soc of A, silver Isis medal]; untraced	RSA *Transactions*, 1831, vol 48, xxiii
3.	1831	'Original model of an entire figure'		[Soc of A, gold Isis medal]; untraced	RSA *Transactions*, 1831, vol 48, xxiii
Busts					
4.	1830	F J O Rossi, the sculptor's brother		[Exhib RA, London, 1269]; untraced	*Graves* VI, 1905–6, 371; *Johnson* 1975, 404
5.	1838	J C F Rossi RA		[Exhib RA, London, 1321]; untraced	*Graves* VI, 1905–6, 371
Miscellaneous					
6.	1832	Study of a warrior		[Exhib Soc of BA, London, 897]; untraced	*Johnson* 1975, 404
7.	1836	Hercules rescuing Hesione from the sea monster, sketch	tc	[Exhib Soc of BA, London, 858]; untraced	*Johnson* 1975, 404
8.	1848	The vanquished, unfinished model		[Exhib RA, London, 1385]; untraced	*Graves* VI, 1905–6, 371

ROSSI, Henry 1791–?1844

Henry Rossi was a son of **JCF Rossi** and his first wife Mary. He joined the Royal Academy Schools in 1811, and was awarded a silver medal by the Society of Arts four years later (**13**). In 1818 he was sharing a house in Lisson Grove with his father, but he set up for himself in the New Road in 1820. He was elected to the livery of the Merchant Taylors' Company on 20 December 1814 (Merchants Taylors, Court Minutes, vols 16, 18, MS 34,010/16, 351) and first exhibited in 1813, when he showed a medallion of the Prince Regent at the Liverpool Academy (**11**). He exhibited at the Royal Academy between 1817 and 1827 and at the British Institution from 1820 to 1829. He was also a founder member of the Society of British Artists and sent works to their exhibitions until 1837. In 1819 Rossi assisted his father with the terracotta decoration of St Pancras Church, for which they received £4,300 (**10**). Three years later he was appointed sculptor to the Duke of Gloucester. Rossi is perhaps best known for his statues of cricketers which were first shown as models at the Academy in 1819 (**7, 8**). They were later executed in marble for the Duke of Bedford and replicated in plaster.

In 1820, through the intervention of Charles Long (later Lord Farnborough), Rossi was appointed to a clerkship at the Chelsea Hospital with a salary of £120 a year. Even with this regular income he found himself in financial difficulties and in 1825 he wrote to his father that he could not live on less than £200 a year. He added, 'tho' I was fortunate in getting some commissions last year, which have enabled me to pay my way, still that is not the case at present' (Soane Priv Corr, II R 8/7–9). A few years later he requested a loan of £80 or £100 from the Merchant Taylors' Company, offering as security the statues of the Cricketer and the Bowler, to be deposited at the Company's Hall. He was firmly refused (Merchant Taylors, Court Minutes, MS 34,010/18, 187, 197, inf. Ann Saunders).

In 1829 Rossi held a raffle of his figures of cricketers. He wrote to Sir John Soane asking him to take a ticket and informing him that there were to be 40 tickets at 5 guineas each (Soane Priv Corr, II P 8/4). In November 1837 he again sought assistance from the Merchant Taylors' Company, asking them to buy an 'original model' of *Mary washing the feet of Jesus*, which 'with my only remaining casts of the Cricketers the Bowler and the Batter I am now most anxious to dispose of' (Merchant Taylors, Court Minutes, 30 Nov 1837). He added that these were 'the last I shall have' and asked for 40 guineas in total. The matter was referred to the master and wardens and by 21 February 1838 they had decided to purchase all three for £42 (GL, MS 34010, 298–9). Gunnis suggests that Rossi probably died in 1844, since his name does not figure in the list of members of the Society of British Artists after that date.

Literary References: *Gunnis* 1968, 326

Archival References: GPC

Funerary Monuments				
1.	†1820	Mary Walter	Holmpton, E R Yorks, churchyard	Pevsner, *Yorks: E R & York*, 1995, 476
2.	1834	Major-General Andrew Hay (†1814), sketch (for a monument in St Paul's Cathedral, commission won by Humphrey Hopper)	[Exhib Soc of BA, London, 825]; untraced	*Johnson* 1975, 404
3.	1836	Major-General Arthur Gore (†1814) and Major-General John Byrne Skerett (†1814), design (for a monument in St Paul's Cathedral, commission won by Sir Francis Chantrey)	[Exhib Soc of BA, London, 859]; untraced	*Johnson* 1975, 404

4.	1837	Major-General Sir Robert Rollo Gillespie (†1814), sketch (for a monument in St Paul's Cathedral, commission won by Sir Francis Chantrey)		[Exhib Soc of BA, London, 613]; untraced	*Johnson* 1975, 404
5.	1838	Design for a monument to a military officer		[Exhib Soc of BA, London, 623]; untraced	*Graves* VI, 1905–6, 371; *Johnson* 1975, 404–5
Statues					
6.	*c*1818	Mary washing the feet of Jesus (Mary Magdalen anointing Christ's feet), model		[Merchant Taylors' Company, City of London]; untraced	*Court Minutes, Merchant Taylors*, 14 Dec 1837; *Graves* 1875, 467 *Graves* VI, 1905–6, 371; *Johnson* 1975, 404
7.	1823	A cricketer (batsman) Model(s): RA, London, 1819, 1182	m	[Sculpture gall, Woburn Abbey]; destroyed Other versions: cast bought by Merchant Taylors' Company, 1837; untraced	*Graves* 1875, 467; *Graves* 1905–6, 371; *Johnson* 1975, 404
8.	1825	The bowler Model(s): Stourhead, store-room, plaster, 2002		Woburn, Beds, sculpture gall Other versions: cast purchased by Merchant Taylors' Company, 1837; untraced Stourhead, Wilts, cast	*Court Minutes, Merchant Taylors*, 14 Dec 1837; *Graves* 1905–6, VI, 371; *Johnson* 1975, 404
Busts					
9.	1817	Antonio Canova		[Exhib RA, London, 1024]; untraced	*Graves* VI, 1905–6, 371; *Johnson* 1975, 404, 405
Architectural Sculpture					
10.	?1819–1822	Four colossal female caryatids, columns, friezes and other ornaments (co-sculptor: John Charles Felix Rossi) Payment(s): £4,300	tc	St Pancras new church, London	*Kelly* 1977 (2), 1432
Reliefs					
11.	1813	Prince Regent, medallion portrait		[Exhib Liverpool Ac, 317]; untraced	*Morris and Roberts* 1998, 527
12.	1820	Shipwrecked seaman		[Exhib RA, London, 1005]; untraced	*Graves* 1875, 467; *Graves* VI, 1905–6, 371; *Johnson* 1975, 404
Miscellaneous					
13.	1815	Copy of a plaster cast		[Soc of A, silver medal]; untraced	RSA *Transactions*, 1815, vol 33, 22
14.	1822	Ajax forcing Cassandra from the Temple of Minerva		[Exhib RA, London, 1043]; untraced	*Graves* 1875, 467; *Graves* VI, 1905–6, 371; *Johnson* 1975, 404
15.	1823	Hercules rescuing Hesione		[Exhib RA, London, 1066]; untraced	*Graves* VI, 1905–6, 371
16.	1825	Eve entreating forgiveness at the feet of Adam, sketch		[Exhib RA, London, 1033]; untraced	*Graves* VI, 1905–6, 371; *Johnson* 1975, 404
17.	1826	The heroism of James Fitzjames		[Exhib RA, London, 1080]; untraced	*Graves* 1875, 467; *Graves* VI, 1905–6, 371; *Johnson* 1975, 404
18.	1832	Adam and Eve lamenting over the body of Abel		[Exhib Soc of BA, London, 866]; untraced	*Johnson* 1975, 404
19.	1837	The sportsman		[Exhib Soc of BA, London, 500]; untraced	*Johnson* 1975, 404
20.	1838	Le Palissier, sketch		[Exhib Soc of BA, London, 760]; untraced	*Johnson* 1975, 405

ROSSI, John Charles Felix RA 1762–1839

Rossi was a talented, ambitious, but frequently poverty-stricken sculptor, best remembered for his monuments to national heroes in St Paul's Cathedral. He was born on 8 March 1762, at Nottingham, in 'humble circumstances'. His father, an Italian from Siena, is said to have been a sort of 'quack-doctor to the neighbourhood' (*AU*, 1839, 22), and Rossi himself described his father as a Roman Catholic who was 'irregular in his conduct' (*Farington* vol 9, 3240). Accounts of Rossi's early life vary, however, and other sources suggest that he spent his early life at Mountsorrel in Leicestershire, or even in Sheffield.

As a young man Rossi studied sculpture under **Locatelli** and after finishing his apprenticeship remained with his master for a short time at the meagre wage of eighteen shillings a week, apparently because he lacked confidence in his own abilities. On 29 March 1781 he enrolled at the Royal Academy Schools, giving his age as nineteen. In 1784 he was given a gold medal for the group, *Venus conducting Helen to Paris* (**162**).

In 1785 he and **John Deare** won Academy travelling studentships and he went to Rome for three years. Little is known of this period, but he is said to have 'studied closely' and to have carved a marble statue of *Mercury* (**47**) (*AU*, 1839, 22). Rossi also prepared a marble relief for the Academy exhibition, for which the RA defrayed the expenses of sending the work to England, but after its arrival at Burlington House he received a letter from the Council informing him that they were of the 'opinion that his time would be more properly employed in modelling than in working in marble', and that in future he should send 'only models' (RA Council Minutes, vol 2, December 1786, fol 33).

The sculptor appears to have taken this criticism to heart. He later told Farington that he had returned from Rome full of the desire to be a great sculptor, but that he 'wanted encouragement' (*Farington* vol 14, 4913). So instead he went to work at various manufacturing enterprises. In late 1788 he was modelling figures for Benjamin Vulliamy the clock-maker, produced in Derby porcelain (**165**). Rossi's erratic punctuality appears to have distressed Duesbury's London agent, but Vulliamy declared himself satisfied and Rossi received 13 guineas. He continued to work for Vulliamy until around 1810.

Rossi had a long-standing association with the firm of **Coade** at Lambeth, where he worked as a designer and modeller until 1798. He also made efforts to found a firm of his own, producing sculpture in terracotta.

According to the *Gentleman's Magazine* (1827, 2, 395), he invented a terracotta composition which 'it is hoped will rival in firmness and durability the same description of material of the ancients.'

Soon after his return to London the sculptor went into partnership with **John Bingley**, a venture in which 'he lost much money', according to his own account (*Farington* vol 14, 4913). In 1796 the partners modelled terracotta statues of *Music* and *Dancing* for the Assembly Rooms at Leicester (**129**). Later he began his own ceramic stone business, with a kiln, cottage and stables in Lisson Grove. Here he made the angels, now gilded, which surround the cupola of St Marylebone church, for which he was paid £300 in 1814 (**139**).

In 1790 Rossi had been paid £240 for 'modelling, moulding, casting in plaster and executing in Portland stone two colossal lions 10 ft. 3 in. long erected at the western water-gate' of Somerset House (**127**) (RIBA. Library MS. 335A), and that year he won a premium of 50 guineas from the Society of Arts for his group of *King Edward I and Queen Eleanor* (**50**) which **Nathaniel Marchant** called a 'work of great merit' (*Farington*, vol 7, 2715).

In 1794, with the support of the architect Sir Robert Smirke, Rossi made a model for the proposed monument to Captain Montagu in Westminster Abbey (*Farington* vol 1, 208), and in 1795 he hoped to take over the monument to the actor David Garrick, again for the Abbey, following the death of the sculptor **John Hickey** (*Farington* vol 2, 292). He was unsuccessful in both cases but for the next three decades was a perennial applicant for public commissions. Between 1802 and 1825 he was selected to design and execute several of the publicly funded monuments to national heroes in St. Paul's Cathedral. Unfortunately, despite the prestigious nature of these commissions Rossi's designs and works received a good deal of adverse criticism, both at the time and later. **John Flaxman RA** said of his monument to Captains Mosse and Riou (**13**), that 'it was rather mason's work than that of a sculptor.' Farington added that 'Rossi had by employing ordinary men at low wages got much money by it, but had greatly suffered in reputation' (*Farington* vol 7, 2770). The diarist also noted Marchant's opinion that the monument was 'very badly designed and executed. Rossi could do nothing without Smirke's designs' (*Farington* VII, 2715). A more generous view emerged in the *Gentleman's Magazine* (1839, 548) which praised the monuments to Marquess Cornwallis (**18**) and General Le Marchant (**19**) as being in a 'grand and tasteful style'. These efforts won him some reputation and in 1798 he was elected an associate of the Royal Academy and in 1802, a full member.

In 1806 Rossi sent in a design for the Guildhall monument to William Pitt the Younger, but to his chagrin the commission was awarded to his pupil, **J G Bubb**. Tactlessly the committee then wrote to Rossi asking him for his opinion of Bubb's capabilities. Smirke penned the reply for him with 'much spirit and humour justly ridiculing the ignorance, folly and illiberality of the Common Council in their conduct upon such occasions' (*Farington* vol 8, 2890). Rossi had received their letter with 'considerable mortification' and declined to pass comment on their choice of sculptor, since Bubb had worked on nothing comparable to the Guildhall commission whilst with Rossi, and Rossi knew nothing of his subsequent career (Guildhall Committee/J C F Rossi). The two sculptors must have made it up, however, because they went into partnership in 1816 to supply works in artificial stone for the Custom House.

Rossi consulted Joseph Farington regularly during these years about strategies for obtaining commissions, and as a result he features strongly in the latter's *Diaries*. The image that emerges of Rossi is of an insecure, and occasionally despairing figure. Flaxman described Rossi as possessing an 'anxious, unsettled temper' (*Farington* vol 6, 2404), and on one occasion Farington said that Rossi had 'the peevishness and discontent of a disappointed man', (*Farington* vol 14, 5021). This is perhaps not surprising as Rossi reportedly had a family of 16 children, a house which he could not afford to maintain, and, by his own admission, little financial acumen. This situation, coupled with the relatively few commissions on offer and the competition, not only from Flaxman but also from **Joseph Nollekens RA** and **Sir Richard Westmacott RA**, left him in a constantly precarious financial position.

In 1815 Rossi complained to Farington that changes in the prevailing architectural style had led to the introduction of such plain chimneypieces that sculptors could no longer get more than four to fifteen pounds for them, whereas formerly they could have had 50 or 60 (*Farington* vol 8, 3). Not surprisingly, apart from work at Shugborough, Longleat and Chatsworth between 1805–1820, Rossi's chimneypieces were few. By 1816 he was in such straitened circumstances, 'being without a professional commission for a year and a half past' (*Farington* vol 14, 4869), that he was considering taking up a post as assistant to another sculptor or leaving England altogether. That same year King Christophe of Haiti invited him to come out and execute sculpture for his palaces, then under construction. Rossi was tempted, but the terms of the contract seemed so uncertain that he decided to remain in England. The following year he thought of moving to America (*Farington* vol 14, 5021). Curiously enough, one of his sons, **Charles Rossi**, later emigrated to Barbados and set up as a monumental mason.

In 1817 he took in the temperamental painter Benjamin Robert Haydon as a tenant. Haydon called him 'a singular man' who 'had made by commissions £10,000, but he had such an appetite for bricks and mortar he would let no tenant repair his house'. Haydon had met Rossi in 1810 'and he received me then with great vulgarity and almost pushed me from the door; now he was glad to have me as tenant; appealed to me for an advance to help him to make the alterations, to which, out of sheer sympathy, I consented and advanced him £60, for he and his family were most wretchedly off' (*Haydon Autobiography.* I, 1926, 261).

He exhibited considerable enthusiasm for the Greek taste. In 1819 he and his son, **Henry Rossi**, entered into a contract to execute terracotta decorations for the new church of St. Pancras for £4,300, their contribution consisting principally of the four colossal female caryatids which form the porch on the north side of the building (**143**). These figures are closely based upon those brought back from the Erechtheum in Athens by Lord Elgin, and Rossi was among the sculptors consulted by Parliament about the state purchase of the marbles. The figures were made in pieces and then cemented round the cast-iron pillars which are the real supporters of the entablature (*Britton and Pugin* 1823–1828, v.1, 154, 160–161). The poet Byron said that they were 'a little heavy, but no less divine' (*Kelly* 1977 (2), 1432).

In the 1820s Rossi carried out a great deal of work for Buckingham Palace in artificial stone, receiving £1,000 from Treasury chambers on 25 June 1828, for work done with **E H Baily** (who received £1,500 (TNA WORK 19/3 and 5/119, fols 174–275, 307). Two friezes executed in this material depicted *The progress of navigation* and *The seasons* (**156**), the latter pleasing 'George IV so much that he directed Mr. Nash, the architect, to give Rossi [the commission for] any part of the sculpture he wanted'. Rossi showed some of his lack of financial sense by selecting only 'as much as came to £3,000' (*GM*, 1839, I, 548). He had been appointed sculptor to the Prince of Wales, afterwards George IV, in 1797, a post he held until the latter's death in 1830, when he became Sculptor-in-Ordinary to William IV. A bust of the George, Prince of Wales, later the Prince Regent (**103**) was apparently very successful, for Farington quotes Flaxman comparing Rossi favourably with Nollekens, saying that Rossi's bust of the Prince was 'worth all that the other had done'.

Rossi also attracted attention from another of the great patrons of the age, the third Earl of Egremont, for whom he executed the dramatic group of *Celadon and Amelia, overtaken by a thunderstorm* (**71**). The work was installed in the Earl's sculpture gallery at his country seat, Petworth House in Sussex. In 1828, again for Petworth, Rossi completed his *British pugilist*, which J T Smith called 'truly vigorous and masterful' and applauded the carving from a single piece of marble (**76**) (*JKB* 1977 (2), 369). Typically, however, Rossi found himself in financial difficulties when paying for the marble and applied to Lord Egremont for help. In reply the Earl told him that 'he had nothing to do with his marble, that [he] must finish his statue, and send it home, that in mode of application he forgot his, Lord E's, rank, as well as his own' (*K-Browne* 1977 (2), 369).

Rossi's financial situation did not improve in the 1830s. In 1834, Soane sent the sculptor £50 to help ease his financial difficulties (Soane Priv Corr II R 8/12, 14) and in the same year Rossi attempted to persuade the architect William Wilkins to employ him on a grand scheme of sculptural decoration for the National Gallery which never came to fruition. Instead, an earlier group by Rossi of two female figures holding a medallion of Wellington was adapted for the purpose and placed over the main arch (**78**). That year he was forced to write to the Royal Academy 'stating his great distress and urging the Council to afford him immediate assistance' and in 1835 was granted the pension of a superannuated member, 100 guineas a year (RA Archives).

In March 1835 Rossi was obliged to retire from business and to sell the contents of his studio at Grove Place, Lisson Grove, in the northern suburbs of London. The sale catalogue includes an address by Rossi, full of bitterness and pathos. In it he described how, throughout his career, he had devoted himself to 'the more elevated line of classical composition' and had expended 'several thousand pounds' on materials and assistants, under the illusion that the nation would encourage the highest form of native sculpture. Instead, the public commissions had ceased and the taste for works of 'poetic fancy' had not increased. Rossi, now in bad health, had 'advisedly relinquished all intention of again practising his profession'. On 21 February 1839 he died, and was buried in the same grave as his first wife, Mary (†1804), in St James's burial ground, Hampstead Road. His will, which gave his address as Wellington Road, St Marylebone, was executed by his second wife, Peggy Orton Rossi (PROB 11/1909/fol 402). In 1842 the Academy made a gift of £10 to his second wife, and in the following year one of £20 to his unmarried daughter (RA Archives). Rossi seems to have had numerous apprentices and assistants. **R J Wyatt, James Heffernan, James Smith** and **Richard Williams** all worked for him at different times. His sons, **Frederick Orton, Henry** and **Charles** all became sculptors.

Posthumous critical opinion has largely concurred with Rossi's own view of himself as a martyr suffering from a lack of enlightened patronage. After the sculptor's death the *Art Union* wrote that 'our Nobility have no space for masses of hewn stone and Mr. Rossi found but few patrons. . . and he bequeathed to his family nothing but his fame' (1839, 22). At his best, and when given the opportunity, Rossi could produce work to compete with the best of his contemporaries, although his circumstances never made it possible for him entirely to fulfil this potential.

MGS

Literary References: *GM* 1839, pt 1, 546; *Farington, passim*; *Holland* 1851, 183; *Gunnis* 1968, 326–9; *Martin* 1974, 48–53; *Kelly* 1977 (2), 1430–1432; *K-Browne* 1977 (2), 367–73; *Penny* 1977 (1), *passim*; *Whinney* 1988, *passim*; *Clifford* 1990, 226–37; *Kelly* 1990, *passim*; *RG/JP*, 7, 1183–93; *Bricknell* 1995, 20–24; *Grove* 1996, 24, 197 (Bryant)

Archival References: J C F Rossi Archive; J C F Rossi Catalogue 1833 (Guildh PMD); RA Council Minutes, vol 2, 1785, fl, f15; 1786, f22; TNA WORK 5/144 (Mason's work at Customs House, executants unidentified); J C F Rossi/Phillips; J C F Rossi/Balmano; J C F Rossi/Balfour; J C F Rossi/Rigaud; J C F Rossi/Beckford; Guildhall Committee/J C F Rossi

Will: PROB 11/1909/fol 402

Miscellaneous Drawings: Designs for monuments, projected monuments and architectural sculpture, Guildhall Library (uncatalogued)

Auction Catalogues: *Rossi* 1835; *Rossi* 1840

Funerary Monuments

1.	†1783	Thomas Tyndale	North Cerney, Glos	S	*CIIA* 4/4/80 (repr); Pevsner, *Glos: Cotswolds*, 1999, 509
2.	1791	A monumental figure	[Exhib RA, London, 661]; untraced		*Graves* VI, 1905–6, 371
3.	1792	'Design for a monument'	[Exhib RA, London, 742]; untraced		*Graves* VI, 1905–6, 371
4.	1793	Elizabeth, Countess of Pembroke Model(s): 'Model of part of a monument, in marble, for Wilton church, Wiltshire' exhib RA, London, 997	St Mary and St Nicholas, Wilton, Wilts		Pevsner, *Wilts*, 1975, 579; *Penny* 1977 (1), 95 (repr)
5.	†1796	Gibbs Crawfurd	St Swithun, East Grinstead, Sussex		Pevsner, *Sussex*, 1965, 492
6.	†1797	Sir John Dryden	Canons Ashby, Northants	S	*CIIA* 4/3/24, 26–7 (repr)
7.	†1798	Lady Charlotte Disbrowe	Walton-upon-Trent, Derbys	S	C Lib (repr)
8.	†1799	Elizabeth Chester	Almondsbury, Glos	S	Pevsner, *Glos: Vale & Forest of Dean*, 1976, 83
9.	†1800	Henry, 1st Lord Bradford	St Andrew, Weston-under-Lizard, Staffs	S	Pevsner, *Staffs*, 1974, 307; C Lib (repr)
10.	1803	Captain Robert Faulknor (†1795) (co-sculptor: John Bingley, of London) Payment(s): £5,250 (estimate) Drawing(s): PRO MPD 78 with agreement and bond; Guildhall Lib, identified as designed by Richard Smirke	St Paul's Cathedral, London	SD	*Whinney* 1988, 362, 363 (repr); *Yarrington* 1988, 64, 69–70 (repr 27)
11.	1803	'Sketch of a monument representing the death of Abercromby'	[Exhib RA, London, 938]; untraced		*Graves* VI, 1905–6, 372
12.	1805	Bishop of Down (epitaph by C J Fox)	Tottenham Court Road Cemetery, London		*GM* 1805, 1169

No.	Date	Subject		Location		References
13.	1803–1805	Captain James Robert Mosse and Captain Edward Riou (both †1801) Payment(s): £4,200	m	St Paul's Cathedral, London		*Farington* III, 238 and 182; *Whinney* 1988, 366–8 (repr); *Yarrington* 1988, 64–5
14.	?1807	Robert Cobb		Lydd, Kent		*Gunnis* 1968, 328
15.	1809	Edward, 1st Lord Thurlow (†1806), design 'for his monument in the Temple Church'		[Exhib RA, London, 875]; Bust, Inner Temple, London; pedestal, Temple Church,	S	*Graves* VI, 1905–6, 372; *Esdaile* 1933 (2), 32
16.	†1809	Francis Pemberton		Newton, Cambs	S	Pevsner, *Cambs*, 1970, 443
17.	1810	Colonel Thomas Vassal (†1807) (designed by John Flaxman RA)		St Paul, Bristol		Pevsner, *Somerset: N & Bristol*, 1958, 406
18.	1811	Charles, 1st Marquess Cornwallis (†1805) Model(s): Sketch for the monument exhib RA, London, 1810, 872: two models (half-size), exhib RA, London, 1811, 927		St Paul's Cathedral, London		*Gunnis* 1968, 328; Pevsner, *London: City*, 1997, 17; C Lib (repr)
19.	†1812	General John Le Marchant (designed by James Smith) Drawing(s): PRO MPD 78, by Smith, with agreement and bond		St Paul's Cathedral, London	S	Pevsner, *London: City*, 1997, 175
20.	†1812	Lt John Ayling		Tillington, Sussex	S	*Gunnis* 1968, 329; C Lib (repr)
21.	?1812	Rev Anthony Hamilton		Much Hadham, Herts		*Gunnis* 1968, 329
22.	†1813	Rev Thomas Leigh		St Mary Magdalene, Adlestrop, Glos		Pevsner, *Glos: Cotswolds*, 1999, 132
23.	†1814	Sir George Beaumont		St Mary, Great Dunmow, Essex		Pevsner, *Essex*, 1965, 202
24.	†1815	Anne Pemberton		Newton, Cambs	S	Pevsner, *Cambs*, 1970, 443
25.	†1815	Major Robert Packe Model(s): 'Cavalry Charging', bas-relief, Rossi 1840		Prestwold, Leics	S	Pevsner, *Leics & Rutland*, 1984, 349
26.	1811–1815	Vice-Admiral George, 1st Lord Rodney (†1792) Payment(s): £6,300	m	St Paul's Cathedral, London	SD	*Whinney* 1988, 368 (repr)
27.	1817	Ann Farington (†1816)		Broxbourne, Herts		*Farington* XIV, 4906
28.	†1817	Catherine Whalley		Ecton, Northants	S	*CIIA* 4/3/70 (repr)
29.	?1817	Elizabeth Harrington		Corsham, Wilts		*Gunnis*, 1968, 329
30.	†1818	John Edward Turner Dryden		Canons Ashby, Northants		*CIIA* 4/3/25, 28–9 (repr)
31.	1819	Admiral Cuthbert, Lord Collingwood (†1810) (designed by C R Cockerell) Model(s): bust exhib RA, London, 1820, 1060; model of monument, one third size, exhib RA, London, 1820, 1066		Newcastle Cathedral		Pevsner, *Northumbs*, 1992, 423; C Lib (repr)
32.	?1819	David Denne		Lydd, Kent		*Gunnis* 1968, 329
33.	†1819	Maria Master		St John the Baptist, Cirencester, Glos	S	*CIIA* 4/4/27 (repr); Pevsner, *Glos: Cotswolds*, 1999, 254
34.	?1821	Elizabeth Tyndale		Chelsea Old Church (all Saints), London, churchyard		*Gunnis* 1968, 329
35.	1821	John Deverell (designed by CR Cockerell)		[Hampton, Middx]; destroyed		*Colvin* 1995, 261
36.	1821	Miss F A Hamond (†1820)		West Acre, Norfolk		*Farington* XVI, 5585, 5613, 5621, 5624, 5653; Pevsner, *Norfolk: N W & S*, 1999, 760
37.	1822	Ferdinando Travell (†1808)		Upper Slaughter, Glos	S	*CIIA* 4/4/163 (repr); Pevsner, *Glos: Cotswolds*, 1999, 708
38.	†1822	Henry Charles Litchfield		Temple Church, London	S	*Esdaile* 1933 (2), 124
39.	c1822	Hippisley family		St Edward, Stow-on-the-Wold, Glos	S	Pevsner, *Glos: Cotswolds*, 1999, 640
40.	1823	Mrs H Battersby (designed by C R Cockerell)		Henbury, Glos		*Colvin* 1995, 261
41.	†1823	Sir Thomas Master		Cirencester, Glos	S	Pevsner, *Glos: Cotswolds*, 1999, 254
42.	1823–1825	George, 1st Lord Heathfield (†1790) Model(s): Half-size model, and model of the bas-relief on the pedestal, Rossi 1840		St Paul's Cathedral, London, south transept	SD	Pevsner, *London: City*, 1997, 174
43.	1830	'A Model. A design for an heroic monument as a commemorative tribute to national valour'		[Exhib RA, London, 1168]; untraced		*Graves* VI, 1905–6, 373
44.	1832	Rev Basil Wood, in relief, with figures of Faith, Hope and Charity		St Mary, Paddington, London, churchyard		*British Mag*, vol. 1, 418; C Lib (repr)
45.	†1834	John Bridge (designed by C R Cockerell)		Piddletrenthide, Dorset		*Colvin* 1995, 261
46.	?1837	Mary and Frances Swinney		St Mary, St Marylebone, London		*Gunnis* 1968, 329
Statues						
47.	1786	Mercury	m	Cawdor sale, 5–6 June, 1800, day 2, lot 78; untraced	SD	*AU* 1839, 22; C Lib (repr)
48.	1788	Hermes		Messrs Crowther, Isleworth, Middx, 1959; untraced	SD	Crowther, 1959
49.	1789	Mercury		[Exhib RA, London, 569]; untraced		*Graves* VI, 1905–6, 371

50.	1790	'A group representing the story of Queen Eleanora sucking the poison from the wound of her husband King Edward [I]' Payment(s): 50 gns Model(s): James Wyatt sale, Phillips, 6 June 1814	tc	[Soc of A, premium, 50 gns]; untraced		RSA *Transactions*, 1790, vol 8, 231; *Rossi Catalogue* 1833; *Graves* VI, 1905–6, vol 6, 372
51.	1792	Cupid		[Exhib RA, London, 738]; untraced		*Graves* VI, 1905–6, 371
52.	1796	Eve, model		[Exhib RA, London, 880]; untraced		*Graves* VI, 1905–61, 372; *Pasquin* 1796, 29
53.	1797	'Protection; study for a large group'		[Exhib RA, London, 1147]; untraced		*Graves* VI, 1905–6, 372
54.	1800	Sir Edward Coke, for a column designed by James Wyatt		Stoke Poges Park, Bucks		*Colvin* 1995, 1121
55.	1801–1802	Britannia / Minerva	sa	Town Hall, Liverpool, Lancs, dome		*Monthly Mag*, 1799, vol. 8, 904; *Cavanagh* 1997, 72–4 (repr)
56.	1802	King George IV, in regimental uniform	p	[Royal Crescent, Brighton, Sussex]; removed 1819		*Chantrey Ledger*, 171; *Monthly Mag.*, vol. 14, Aug. 1, 1802, 91
57.	1805	'Sketch of a group'		[Exhib RA, London, 710]; untraced		*Graves* VI, 1905–6, 372
58.	1806	Recumbent figure of Eve		[Exhib BI, London, 41]; untraced		*Graves* VI, 1905–6, 467
59.	1807	'Design in terracotta, of Lord Nelson, for Liverpool'		[Exhib RA, London, 1109]; untraced		*Graves* VI, 1905–6, 372
60.	1808	'Maternal Affection, exemplified in the character of Cornelia educating her Sons; for a larger group'		[Exhib RA, London, 878]; untraced		*Graves* VI, 1905–6, 372
61.	1809	William Shakespeare (on a pedestal of Siena marble) Model(s): t-c, head only, Rossi 1840		[Covent Garden Theatre, London, ante-room beyond the entrance hall from Bow Street]; untraced		*Lady's Mag*, vol. 40, Sept 1809, 386–7
62.	1811	Royal equestrian statue for Rio de Janeiro, model		[RA, London]; untraced		*Farington* XIII, 4667, 11 July 1815
63.	1812	'Saving his brother from drowning, sketch design for a group'		[Exhib, RA, London, 892]; untraced		*Graves* VI, 1905–6, 372
64.	pre-1812	St Anthony of Padua	a	[Fonthill, Beds; Beckford sale, 1830]; untraced		*Farington*, III, 880; *Storer* 1812, 23 (repr); *Beckford* 1976, frontispiece (repr)
65.	1814	'Design for a groupe, representing Venus persuading Mars to peace'		[Exhib RA, London, 772]; untraced		*Graves* VI, 1905–6, 372
66.	1814	'Lord Cornwallis, in Garter robes'		[Exhib RA, London, 764]; untraced		*Graves* VI, 1905–6, 372
67.	1815	'Monument to be erected in marble, to be erected in the Factory House at Canton. History giving to Posterity the Virtues of the gentleman it is intended to commemorate'		[Exhib RA, London, 901]; untraced		*Graves* VI, 1905–6, 372
68.	1817	Kings Henry II, Henry III and Edward II		[Inner Temple Hall, London]; destroyed World War II		*Gunnis* 1968, 328
69.	1819	'An Escape, sketch for a group'		[Exhib RA, London, 1203]; SJSM		*Graves* VI, 1905–6, 372; SJSM Inventory
70.	1819	'Benjamin West, sketch for a statue'		[Exhib RA, London, 1235]; untraced		*Rossi Catalogue* 1833; *Graves* VI, 1905–6, 372
71.	1820	Celadon and Amelia Model(s): half-size model exhib at Rossi Studio, 1833, Rossi Cat; first finished model, Rossi 1840		[Sketch exhib RA, London, 1820, 1067]; Petworth, Sussex		*Rossi Cat* 1833; *JKB* 1977 (2), 369 (repr)
72.	1821	'Benjamin West, model of a statue'		[Exhib RA, London, 1112]; untraced		*Graves* VI, 1905–6, 373
73.	c1823	Zephyrus and Aurora (group)		[Exhib RA 1823, 1098; Rossi sale, 1835 (£150); untraced		*Rossi Catalogue* 1833; *GM*, 1839, 1, 547–8; *Graves* 1875, 468; *Graves* VI, 1905–6, 373
74.	1825	'Sketch of a group of a Shepherd and Shepherdess'		[Exhib RA, London, 1032]; untraced		*Graves* VI, 1905–6, 373
75.	1826	'Model designed for an equestrian groupe of HRH the Duke of York'		[Exhib RA, London, 1068]; untraced		*Graves* VI, 1905–6, 373
76.	1828	British pugilist		Petworth House, Sussex	SD	*JKB* 1973 (3), 1641 (repr); *JKB* 1977 (2), 369 (repr)
77.	1829	Musidora	m	[Westfield, I of W, coll Sir Augustus Clifford]; untraced		*Gunnis* 1968, 328; *Graves* VI, 1905–6, 373
78.	c1830	Europe and Asia, group Payment(s): £2,500 Model(s): model, with a three-quarter bust of the Duke of Wellington, Rossi 1840		[Intended for the Marble Arch, London]; Nat Gall, London, façade		*Martin* 1974, 52; *Colvin* VI, 1976, 295, 296 n14, 467; *Yarrington* 1988, 229–45 (pl 87)
79.	1832	Mercury with the apple of discord		[Exhib RA, London, 1176]; untraced		*Rossi Catalogue* 1833; *Graves* VI, 1905–6, 374
80.	1832	The poet Thomson in his study	m	[Exhib RA, London, 1173; Rossi sale, 1835, £320]; untraced		Rossi sale, 1835; *Gunnis* 1968, 327; *Graves*, VI, 1905–6, 373
81.	1832	Two models for statues		[Exhib RA, London, 1174]; untraced		*Graves* VI, 1905–6, 374
82.	1833	'A group of a shepherd and shepherdess; a model'		[Exhib RA, London, 1140]; untraced		*Graves* VI, 1905–6, 374
83.	c1833	Eve at the fountain (from Milton) Model(s): life size, Rossi 1840	m	[Exhib sculptor's studio, 1833, 5; Rossi sale, 1835 200 gns]; untraced		*Rossi Catalogue* 1833

No.	Date	Work	Material	Location	S	Reference
84.	1833	Musidora, recumbent ('robed in loose array she came to bathe') Model(s): three, Rossi 1840	m	[Exhib sculptor's studio, 1833, 4]; untraced		*Rossi Cat* 1833
85.	1834	'[Arthur, 1st Duke of] Wellington Attended by Fame and Victory, equestrian figure' Model(s): sketch exhib RA, London, 1820, 1004	b	[Exhib BI, London, 567; Rossi sale, 1835, 96 gns]; untraced		Rossi sale, 1835 (96 gns); *Graves* 1875, 468
86.	1834	'George Washington, sketch for an equestrian statue'		[Exhib RA, London, 1041]; untraced		*Graves* VI, 1905–6, 374
87.	1834	'Recumbent group of Zephyrs and Aurora'		[Exhib BI, London, 569]; untraced		*Graves* 1875, 468
88.	nd	Acis and Galatea, a group	sa	[Exhib Coade's Gallery]; untraced		*Kelly* 1990, 48
89.	nd	Bacchanalian youth	tc	Sold by Jurich Properties Ltd 1981; untraced	S	
90.	nd	Mercury	m	[Rossi sale, 1835 (£190)]; untraced		*Gunnis* 1968, 327
91.	nd	'Parental Affection, a Father Protecting His Child from a Wolf'	tc	[Rossi sale, 1835 (£19 18s 6d)]; SJSM		*Gunnis* 1968, 327
92.	nd	Shepherd and shepherdess, a group	b	[Christie, 21 March 1850]; untraced		RG/JP, 7, 1190
93.	nd	Sitting Venus, from the model by Joseph Nollekens RA	m	Petworth House, Sussex		*JKB* 1973 (3), 1643; *JKB* 1977 (2), 371–2
Busts						
94.	1792	Sarah Siddons		[Exhib RA, London, 744]; untraced		*Graves* VI, 1905–6, 371
95.	1793	A clergyman		[Exhib RA, London, 801]; untraced		*Graves* VI, 1905–6, 372
96.	1796	'Prince of Wales, in the uniform of the 10th Regiment of the Dragoons'		untraced		RG/JP, 7, 1185
97.	1797	James Wyatt	b	[Phillips, 6 June 1814]; NPG, London, 344 Other versions: RIBA, cast, plaster, painted green	S	C Lib (repr)
98.	1798	Mrs Montgomery Campbell		[Exhib RA, London, 599]; untraced		*Graves* VI, 1905–6, 372
99.	1800	A nobleman		[Exhib RA, London, 637]; untraced		*Graves* VI, 1905–6, 372
100.	1801	Edward, Baron Thurlow	tc	RA, London, diploma work Other versions: Royal Coll, RCIN 2024 (£63) Royal Coll, RCIN 35183	S	RA Council Minutes, vol 3, 1802, fol 136; C Lib (repr)
101.	1802	George Dance		RA, London, diploma work		*Gunnis* 1968, 328; C Lib (repr)
102.	1802	Sir Elijah Impey Model(s): two, Rossi 1840		[Exhib RA, London, 1075; Rossi sale, 1835]; untraced		*Graves* VI, 1905–6, 372
103.	1804	George, Prince of Wales		[Exhib RA, London, 842]; untraced		*Graves* VI, 1905–6, 372
104.	1806	Admiral Lord Nelson		[Exhib RA, London, 827]; untraced		*Graves* VI, 1905–6, 372;
105.	1807	Edward Sexton, Viscount Perry	m	[Exhib RA, London, 1196]; Trinity College, Dublin		*Graves* VI, 1905–6, 372; *Crookshank* 1986, 24
106.	1809	Edward, Baron Thurlow (†1806)	sa	NPG, London	S	
107.	1815	'His Majesty' (King George III)	m	[Exhib RA 1815, 868]; Former Crown Court, English St, Carlisle		*Graves* VI, 1905–6, 372
108.	1817	Unidentified lady		[Exhib RA, London, 1060]; untraced		*Graves* VI, 1905–6, 372
109.	1822	Admiral Lord Nelson	m	[Exhib RA, London, 1024]; untraced		*Graves* VI, 1905–6, 372
110.	1823	John Nash	m	[Exhib RA, London, 1104]; untraced		*Graves* VI, 1905–6, 373
111.	1825	George Dance 'to be executed in marble'	p	[Exhib RA, London, 1024]; SJSM 50 Other versions: Exhib RA, London, 1826, 1060		*Graves* VI, 1905–6, 373; SJSM Inventory
112.	1826	George Dance	m	untraced		
113.	1832	King William IV		[Exhib RA, London, 1174]; untraced		*Rossi Cat* 1833; *Graves* VI, 1905–6, 374
114.	*c*1833	'of a lady'		[Exhib Studio 1833]; untraced		*Rossi Cat*, 1833
115.	nd	Admiral Lord Nelson	m	[Rossi sale, 1836, 45 gns]; untraced		*Gunnis* 1968, 327
116.	nd	Bennet Langton Model(s): Rossi 1840		Untraced		Rossi 1840
117.	nd	King George IV as Alexander		[Rossi, 1840]; untraced		RG/JP, 7, 1191
118.	nd	King George IV, in the uniform of a Colonel of the 10th Hussars		[Rossi, 1835]; untraced		RG/JP, 7, 1191
119.	nd	Unidentified gentleman		[Rossi, 1840]; untraced		Rossi 1840
120.	nd	Warren Hastings	sa	Melchet Park, Wilts		*Kelly* 1990, 48
Chimneypieces						
121.	1805	Two, of white metal and marble, in simple rectilinear style		Shugborough, Staffs, saloon		*Robinson* 1989, 39, 71 (repr)
122.	1813	Description unavailable Payment(s): £250		Longleat, Wilts		*Gunnis* 1968, 328
123.	1820	Description unavailable		Chatsworth, Derbys		*Gunnis* 1968, 328
124.	1821	Description unavailable		[Mr Robins, Warwick Street, London]; untraced		SJSM Archives, green folders
125.	*c*1833	'with bronze group of Shepherds and Nymphs' Model(s): Rossi 1840	m	[Exhib sculptor's studio, 1833, 7]; untraced		*Rossi Cat* 1833
Architectural Sculpture						
126.	*c*1780	Medallions representing Justice and Mercy (modelled by Nollekens, passed to Locatelli, who had his pupil JCF Rossi do the carving) Payment(s): £100	s	Middlesex Sessions House, Clerkenwell, London		Sessions House Minutes, MA/S/21-373, MES 160, 163, 172
127.	1790	Two lions Payment(s): £220 including a plaster model	s	Somerset House, London, western water gate		Chambers/Somerset Hse, box 8, CHA 3/3/3, fo 202; *Colvin* 1973–76, vol 5, 467; *Jenkins* 2000–1, 28

128.	c1794	Signs of the Zodiac and plaques of Morning, Noon and Evening	sa	Radcliffe Observatory, Oxford	Pevsner, *Oxon*, 1974, 271; *Kelly* 1990, 173–4 (repr)
129.	1796	Two statues: Music and Dancing (Comic Muse and Lyric Muse) (co-sculptor: John Bingley)	tc	Assembly Rooms, Leicester	*Cavanagh* 2000, 124–6 (repr)
130.	?1797	'King Alfred instituting Trial by Jury'		Arundel Castle, Sussex (fragment)	*Robinson* 1983, 46, 47 (repr); *Robinson* 1994, 28–31
131.	c1799	Justice and Mercy Drawing(s): pen, Guildhall Lib, print room		Shire Hall, Stafford, pediment	*Richardson* 1802–8, v.2, 2 (reprs 7, 8); Pevsner, *Staffs*, 1974, 243
132.	c1804	Battlements Payment(s): £56		Royal stables, Brighton	*Roberts* 1939, 28
133.	1809	Thalia		Covent Garden Theatre, London	*Gunnis* 1968, 328; C Lib (repr)
134.	1809	The Ancient Drama, relief (from a model by John Flaxman RA) Model(s): by Flaxman: UCL 1109, 1110; VAM A.8-1968, A.9-1968	s	Covent Garden Theatre, London, façade	Flaxman Account Book 1809–26, 8; *Lady's Mag*, vol 40, Sept 1809, 385–6 (repr); *Gunnis and Whinney* 1967, 60–1 (pl 21); *Bilbey* 2002, 82–4 (model repr)
135.	1809	The Modern Drama, relief (designs by John Flaxman RA) Drawing(s): by Flaxman: untraced; 10 gns received in Sept 1809 (Flaxman Account Book 1809–26, 8) Model(s): plaster, VAM A.10-1968, A.11-1968	s	Covent Garden Theatre, London, façade	*Lady's Mag*, vol 40, Sept 1809, 385–6 (repr); *Gunnis and Whinney* 1967, 60–1; *Bilbey* 2002, 82–4 (model repr)
136.	1809	Tragedy		Covent Garden Theatre, London, façade	*Gunnis* 1968, 328
137.	1810	Justice		Stamford Hotel, Lincs	Pevsner, *Lincs*, 1989, 709
138.	1811	Royal arms Payment(s): 300 gns		RCS, London	*Gunnis* 1968, 328
139.	1814	Angel caryatids		St Mary, St Marylebone, London, tower	RG/JP, 7, 1186; Pevsner, *London: N W*, 1991, 602
140.	1814	Four tripods Payment(s): 300 gns		RCS, London	*Gunnis* 1968, 328
141.	1818	Reliefs representing Commerce, Prosperity and Britannia, accompanied by allegorical figures, and large marine shell to surmount the clock (co-sculptor: James George Bubb) Payment(s): Over £5,000	tc	[Customs House, London, façade]; Destroyed	*New Monthly Mag*, 1818, 152–5; *Gunnis* 1968, 67; *Kelly* 1977 (2), 1430–2; *Kelly* 1990, 225–226
142.	1820	Two sphinxes		Chatsworth, Derbys, west entrance	RG/JP, 7, 1187
143.	?1819–1822	Four colossal female caryatids, columns, friezes and other ornaments (co-sculptor: Henry Rossi) Payment(s): £4,300	tc	St Pancras new church, London	*Kelly* 1977 (2), 1432
144.	1823	Coat of Arms Payment(s): £100		RCS, London, portico	*Gunnis* 1968, 328
145.	1827	Arts, Sciences and Manufactures, pediment relief Payment(s): £1,500	s	Buckingham Palace, London, east front, north wing	*Colvin* VI, 1976, 301
146.	1827–1828	Four military trophies Payment(s): £630	sa	Buckingham Palace, London, west front	*Colvin* VI, 1976, 301
147.	1827–1828	Six Virtues, statues Payment(s): £1,386	sa	[Buckingham Palace, London, west front around bow]; Buckingham Palace, London, behind royal mews	*Colvin* VI, 1976, 301
148.	1828–1829	The Seasons, relief Payment(s): £800		[Buckingham Palace, London, east front, north wing, under portico]; Buckingham Palace, London, west gallery, garden front	*Colvin* VI, 1976, 301
149.	1829	Two military and two naval trophies Payment(s): £693		Buckingham Palace, London, east front, north and south wing entrances	*Colvin* VI, 1976, 301
150.	1832	Apollo and Diana Model(s): 'Small finished model', Rossi 1840		[Exhib RA, London, 1175]; Buckingham Palace, London, pediment	*Graves* VI, 1905–6, 374
151.	1837	Royal Arms		Windsor Castle, private entrance	*Gunnis* 1968, 328
152.	c1840	Three caryatid figures between shop fascias (designed by W H Knight)	tc	Cheltenham, Glos	Pevsner, *Glos: Vale & Forest of Dean*, 1976, 140
153.	nd	Angel with a trumpet	tc	[Angel Inn, Sheffield, W Yorks]; untraced	*Holland* 1851, 183
154.	nd	Crests and arms on the lodges and gate-piers		Shugborough, Staffs	*Robinson* 1989, 41 (repr)
155.	nd	Gothic ornaments	ir	Eaton Hall, Cheshire	*Penny* 1977 (1), 11
156.	nd	Two friezes, The progress of navigation and The seasons Model(s): Four Seasons, offered for sale by raffle, Rossi 1840	sa	Buckingham Palace, London	*GM* 1839, 1, 548;

Reliefs

157.	1792	'The birth of Shakespeare'		[Exhib RA, London, 610]; untraced	*Graves* VI, 1905–6, 371
158.	1824	Frieze		Assembly rooms, York	*Allen* II, 1828–31, 305

Miscellaneous

159.	1781	Academy Figure or bas-relief, model		[RA silver medal]; untraced	RA Premium list
160.	1782	'Portrait in wax'		[Exhib RA, London, 263]; untraced	*Graves* VI, 1905–6, 371

161.	1783	'School for love, model'		[Exhib RA, London, 399]; untraced	*Graves* VI, 1905–6, 371
162.	1784	Venus conducting Helen to Paris		[RA, London, gold medal]; untraced	RA Premium list; *Gunnis* 1968, 326
163.	1785	Diana and Endymion		[Exhib RA, London, 513]; untraced	*Graves* VI, 1905–6, 371
164.	1787	'The Temptation of Ulysses'		[Exhib RA, London, 618]; untraced	Rossi/Newton 29 April 1784 and 7 Dec 1784; *Graves* VI, 1905–6, 371
165.	1788	Female sacrificial figure and a figure of Aesculapius, for a clock for Benjamin Vulliamy (female figure designed by Vulliamy, Aesculapius by William Duesbury) Payment(s): 13 gns		Untraced	*Clifford* 1990, 233; *Bricknell* 1995, *passim*
166.	1789	'A Rape by Castor and Pollux'		[Exhib RA, London, 489]; untraced	*Graves* VI, 1905–6, 371
167.	1791	'George III, with Genius and Judgement'		[Exhib RA, London, 630]; untraced	*Graves* VI, 1905–6, 371
168.	1792	'Study of the lion in Exeter Exchange'		[Exhib RA, London, 635]; untraced	*Graves* VI, 1905–6, 371
169.	1799	'Model, in marble, in memory of Sir John Dryden'	m	[Exhib RA, London, 1099]; untraced	*Graves* VI, 1905–6, 372
170.	1800	Hindu Temple		Melchet Park, Wilts	*GM* 1841, 2, 243 (repr); *Kelly* 1990, 209, 211
171.	1804	Avarice		[Exhib RA, London, 961]; untraced	*Graves* VI, 1905–6, 372
172.	1805	Embellishments for a clock		[Exhib RA, London, 709]; untraced	*Graves* VI, 1905–6, 372
173.	1808	'Content, a model, in the character of a cobbler' Model(s): offered for sale by raffle, Rossi 1840		[Exhib BI, London, 143]; untraced	*Graves* 1875, 468
174.	1808	Cupid and Psyche, for a clock	tc	[Exhib BI, London, 139]; untraced	*Graves* 1875, 467
175.	1820	'Sketch for a national memorial to George Washington'		[Exhib RA, London, 1024]; untraced	*Graves* VI, 1905–6, 372
176.	1822	Eve		[Exhib RA, London, 990]; untraced	*Graves* VI, 1905–6, 373
177.	1830	'Recumbent Venus and sleeping Cupid'	m	[Exhib RA, London, 1175]; untraced	*Rossi Catalogue* 1833; *Graves* VI, 1905–6, 373
178.	1831	The husbandman		[Exhib RA, London, 1192]; untraced	*Graves* VI, 1905–6, 373; *Library of Fine Arts*, vol I, 1831, 430
179.	*c*1833	'Model of a monumental group to the memory of Nelson'		[Exhib Studio 1833]; untraced	*Rossi Catalogue* 1833
180.	nd	Adam dropping the wreath on Eve, having tasted the fruit of the Forbidden Tree, model		[Offered for sale by raffle 1840]; untraced	Rossi 1840
181.	nd	Apollo Drawing his Bow, model	tc	[Offered for sale by raffle, 1840]; untraced	Rossi 1840
182.	nd	'Casts of Colossal Horse's Heads'		[Offered for sale by raffle, 1840]; untraced	Rossi 1840
183.	nd	Minerva (for Eleanor Coade)		untraced	RG/JP, 7, 1191
184.	nd	Pro Aris et Focis, finished sketch		[Offered for sale by raffle in 1840]; untraced	Rossi 1840
185.	nd	St Cecilia, model, after Sir Thomas Lawrence		[Offered for sale by raffle, Rossi 1840]; untraced	Rossi 1840
186.	nd	'Youth of the Vintage' (for Eleanor Coade)		Untraced	RG/JP, 7, 1191

ROTHERY fl *c*1722

The Rothery family were engaged in the building trade in Ireland from 1676 or earlier. It is not known which family member executed the monument to John Bury, which is simply signed 'Rothery fecit' (1). Potterton comments that the memorial owes much to **William Kidwell**, the most noticeable borrowings being the gadrooned base, the scrolls which flank the inscription and the cherub's head, although the executant had 'nothing of Kidwell's skill'. He also notes that the consoles, which should support the monument at its base, are now positioned at the top and suggests that this odd arrangement probably dates from a later restoration.

Literary References: *Potterton* 1975, 75

Funerary Monuments

1.	†1722	John Bury of Shannongrove	Adare, Co Limerick	S	*Potterton* 1975, 75

ROTTIERS, John

For further information the reader is referred to *Pyke* 1973, 122

ROUBILIAC, Louis François ?1705–62

Recognised by contemporaries as the outstanding sculptor of his age, Roubiliac was a pivotal figure not only in the development of both the monument and the bust but in the emergence in Britain of the sculptor as an independent inventive artist. His achievement was to give sculpture an equality with painting and to produce work that can compare with sculpture made anywhere in Europe during the 18th century. The son of Pierre Roubiliac, merchant, and his wife, Suzanne, he was born on 31 August 1702 in the parish of Saint-Nizier, Lyon, France into a well-established Lyon merchant family with connections with the silk industry. There is no clear evidence that his family was Protestant though Roubiliac was later to have close links with the Huguenot community in London. Roubiliac's training and early years are poorly documented but the evidence of J T Smith and an independent German source suggest that he went to Dresden around 1718–20, perhaps with the help of a relation who was a financial official at the Saxon court. In Dresden he probably worked for Balthasar Permoser, the sculptor responsible for the rich late baroque sculptural decoration of the Zwinger, Augustus the Strong's court Festspielplatz (parade-ground). Works such as the Montagu monuments (**29, 31**) hint at a familiarity with this distinctive northern version of late baroque. More important, however, was the training he received in Paris during the late 1720s when he was a pupil at the

Académie Royale, (probably under Guillaume Coustou and Robert le Lorrain), and won the second prize for sculpture in 1730. The usual pattern was for the winner of the second prize to be awarded the first prize in the following year, with a period at the French Academy in Rome. By 1731, however, Roubiliac had for unknown reasons already moved to London. The first record of him in England is the appearance of his name in a list of members of the White Bear masonic lodge in 1730, along with that of the Swiss engineer, Charles Labelye. By this date he seems already to have been associated with Huguenot circles in London and it was in the Huguenot church of St Martin Orgar that on 11 April 1735 that he married Catherine Magdalen Helot (b *c* 1709; † between 1744 and 1752), who was to bear him a daughter, Sophia.

According to 19th-century accounts, Roubiliac worked first for the sculptors Thomas Carter and Henry Cheere. Following contemporary practices of sub-contracting and collaboration, he may well have continued to work with Cheere at least into the 1740s. Already by the mid 1730s, however, Roubiliac was undertaking individual commissions. One of the earliest of these was probably a bust of Sir Isaac Newton, made for John Conduit (**59**). According to John Belchier who later bequeathed the terracotta model to the Royal Society, this was 'made under the Eyes of Mr. Conduit and several of Sir Isaac Newton's particular friends . . . and esteemed more like than anything extant of Sir Isaac' (Royal Society, Minute Book). These connections with those associated with the Royal Society (links made initially through Labelye and his friend John Theophilus Desaguliers) remained important for Roubiliac later in his career, not least in the case of the sculptural portraits commissioned by Robert Smith for Trinity College, Cambridge (**86–89, 91, 93, 94, 97–99**). By the mid 1730s, however, the sculptor was receiving commissions from patrons in other circles. Among these was the entrepreneur Charles Clay, for whose musical clock (called the Temple of the Monarchies) Roubiliac produced bronze figures of both the four Monarchies and Hercules and Atlas. Another early commission came from John, 2nd Duke of Argyll for whose library at Adderbury he executed busts of Turenne and the Prince Condé (**57, 58**). These were placed alongside portraits by **Michael Rysbrack**, the sculptor whom Roubiliac would rival and eventually outshine.

The turning point in Roubiliac's career came with the commission from Jonathan Tyers for the statue of Handel at Vauxhall Gardens (**47**). As a full-size statue of a composer, this work was exceptional in representing a living figure who was not a monarch, military leader or at least a nobleman, but it was probably just as striking for contemporary spectators in the casualness of its dress and pose which played upon the impression of the momentary. As well as becoming famous as the 'logo' of Tyers's pleasure gardens, the sculpture was, most unusually, celebrated not only on account of its subject but also for its aesthetic qualities. Praising the 'finish'd beauties of the sculptor's hand', one poem dedicated to the patron went so far as to claim that 'when times remote dwell on Roubillac's name, / They'll still be just to thee who gave him fame.' By 1740 two distinctive aspects of Roubiliac's career were already clear: firstly, his association with writers, thinkers and artists and, secondly, the claims he and his work were making for the status of both sculpture and the sculptor.

Roubiliac's practice during the late 1730s and early 1740s was primarily as a sculptor of busts. Unlike Rysbrack and **Peter Scheemakers**, his more established rivals, Roubiliac received relatively few portrait commissions from the nobility. His sitters were, above all, writers, professional figures and artists and creative figures, especially those associated with either the St Martin's Lane Academy or the Italian opera. They included the artists William Hogarth (**71**), Francis Hayman (**?84**), Isaac Ware (**70**) and the musicians Handel (**63, 64**) and Farinelli (**111**). To this group also belongs the bust of Alexander Pope, four marble versions of which he produced between 1738 and 1744 (**60, 61, 65, 69**). Of all the contemporary images of Pope, whether painted or sculpted, these became the most celebrated as well as the most frequently reproduced. Some of these multiple versions in plaster and terracotta were produced by Roubiliac's own workshop. The sculptor was evidently selling plasters as early as 1740 when the Earl of Marchmont purchased a plaster version of Lord Bolingbroke's bust (**67**) and the production of multiples, often of 'worthies', formed a distinctive aspect of his sculptural practice which continued throughout his career.

While Roubiliac's activity as a sculptor of portrait busts took advantage of the growing number of consumers for luxury commodities including sculpture, his busts in marble and terracotta from the late 1730s onwards show him making the bust into a more ambitious and serious genre. Already in the bust of Newton, Roubiliac had created an image which in its subtlety of execution and its quality of surface finish assumed that it would be looked at closely rather than glanced at from a distance. This characteristic feature of his portraits becomes even more marked in the busts produced during the 1740s, such as the marbles of Lord Chesterfield and Martin Folkes (**72, 80**). In such images Roubiliac took the conventions of sculptural portraiture – whether the classicising bust without drapery or the informal portrait with soft cap – and reworked them in original and striking ways. Frequently, these busts played off the enduring and commemorative function of the marble portrait against the immediate impression of an individual physiognomy. As well as representing contemporaries in this manner, Roubiliac succeeded in giving similar vividness of expression to his historicising portraits, most notably those produced during the 1750s for Trinity College, Cambridge, as part of a sculptural peopling of the college conceived by the master, Robert Smith, who referred to Roubiliac as 'our sculptor' (**86–89, 91, 93, 94, 97–99**). In this remarkable series, the bust format takes on a new grandeur, in part because of the larger scale employed. By the 1750s, however, Roubiliac's practice was no longer confined to the making of busts as he had become celebrated for monuments in which the conventions of a genre were reconfigured even more dramatically than in the case of the bust.

Roubiliac received his first major monument commission in 1744 when he was asked to design and make the memorial to Bishop Hough in Worcester Cathedral (**4**). Although this consists of familiar elements (the bishop reclines on a sarcophagus with *Religion* lifting back drapery from behind to reveal a relief) the monument is already strikingly different from the familiar types used by his principal rivals, Rysbrack and Scheemakers. Before the Hough monument was completed, Roubiliac had already been commissioned (in 1745) to execute the monument in Westminster Abbey to John, 2nd Duke of Argyll, perhaps the most prestigious sculptural commission of the 1740s (**11**). In this work – 'opened' in 1748 and described by Vertue as surpassing 'for nobleness and skill all those done before, by the best sculptors, this fifty years past' – the format of a sarcophagus with flanking figures (in this case *Eloquence* and *Minerva*) follows a well-established pattern, based ultimately on papal monuments. But the pose of *Eloquence*, lunging out into the spectator's space, and the organisation of the figural group above the sarcophagus offer something entirely new, as does the virtuoso carving of all the figures, but most especially *Eloquence*, as was indeed recognised by Vertue. Most notably, the action of *History* writing the inscription and the relationship between this figure and the Duke introduce a new narrative drama to the monument. Roubiliac's subsequent monuments develop this new mode of narrative monument which link figures together in the enactment of a central event, as on that to the Duke of Montagu where the figure of the mourning Duchess observes from below as Charity hangs a medallion of her deceased husband on the 'Temple of Fame'.

Such elaborate interactions between the protagonists usually means that the figures are not simply placed on an architectural structure but that the figural and architectural elements are fully integrated. Apart from involving complex and ambitious piecing of the component parts in the full-scale marble version, such compositions also required a distinctive design process. Rather than executing initial drawings and executing terracotta models of individual figures late in the development of a composition, as Scheemakers and Rysbrack usually did, Roubiliac seems from the start to have worked in clay and conceived the monument as a whole. Unlike his rivals, he appears not to have offered patrons a range of possibilities from which they might chose but instead seems to have negotiated on the basis of a single proposal which was subsequently developed. Here Roubiliac's practice corroborates anecdotal evidence that suggests his relationship with patrons differed from that of earlier 'statuaries' with theirs. Just as Hogarth was asserting the independent status of the painter, so Roubiliac was making a claim for the sculptor as someone to be valued for his inventiveness as well as for powers of execution.

The complexity and narrative quality of Roubiliac's relatively early monuments are developed still further in the major monuments created during the later 1750s. But costly undertakings though these were, Roubiliac's practice during this period also involved the making of a remarkable series of statues, as well as the continuing production of portrait busts. Among the statues, each of which inventively modifies the format of the standing or seated figure, were the unduly neglected image of Sir Thomas Molyneux (**21**) (yet another subject associated with the Royal Society) and the far better known figures of Lord President Forbes (**53**), with its dramatic thrusting gesture recalling that of *Eloquence* on the Argyll monument, and Sir Isaac Newton (**54**). Commissioned by Robert Smith for Trinity, Cambridge, the last was memorably described by Wordsworth as the 'marble index of a mind for ever/Voyaging through strange seas of thought alone'. Still more famous is the figure of Shakespeare commissioned by David Garrick for the temple in the grounds of his villa at Hampton (**55**). As well as executing both a bust of Garrick and a bronze relief (**100, 129**), one of a number of such reliefs executed late in his career – Roubiliac seems have had a particular kinship with Garrick whose acting style employed the same dramatic gestures used by Roubiliac for figures such as *Eloquence*. The statue for Garrick represents the playwright in the process of composition and evidently inspired in a way that was appropriate and meaningful for both patron and sculptor. It is thus unsurprising that in Carpentier's portrait of Roubiliac the sculptor is shown at a similar moment of creative frenzy while working on the model for this particular figure.

However original and striking these statues (some of them on monuments) are, Roubiliac's reputation for subsequent generations rests above all on the series of exceptional monuments without naturalistic depictions of the deceased, executed in the decade or so before his death in 1762. Unlike Rysbrack, Scheemakers and **Sir Henry Cheere**, Roubiliac and his workshop produced few smaller monuments and only rarely re-used earlier designs for these. Similarly, only a small number of his works were executed for parish churches outside London. Along with the monuments to the Duke and Duchess of Montagu (**29, 31**), intended for a chancel apparently designed by the sculptor himself, the major exceptions are the monuments to Mary Myddleton at Wrexham (**20**) and that to Viscount Shannon at Walton-on-Thames (**39**). As well as prompting one of the earliest extended critical accounts of a work of British sculpture (in the *London Magazine*) the latter was the subject of a legal dispute between the patron, Shannon's daughter, the Countess of Middlesex, and the parish, which provides telling evidence about how both sculpture and sculptor were regarded. Still more celebrated, however, are the monuments in Westminster Abbey. Several were designed for the newly developed area above the nave arcade. Following those commemorating Generals Wade and Fleming, Roubiliac exploited the dramatic potential offered by this setting still more effectively in the monument to General Hargrave, completed in 1757 (**13, 28, 34**). Here the devices of the pyramid collapsing at the end of the time and the emergence of Hargrave from his sarcophagus are used to create a monument which John Wesley considered 'the most Christian in the Abbey'. The other was the monument to Joseph and Elizabeth Nightingale, completed in 1761 (**42**), perhaps Roubiliac's single most celebrated work. With the husband attempting to ward off the skeletal figure of *Death* emerging from a sarcophagus in the vault below, Roubiliac heightens still further the potential of sculpture to represent dramatic narrative and creates a work that was both deeply imbued with evangelical Christian theology and admired for its inventiveness and virtuosity. The year before the erection of the Nightingale monument. Roubiliac competed unsuccessfully for the Wolfe monument commission (**40**) and his final monument in the Abbey was that to Handel, whose image had brought him fame almost a quarter of a century earlier (**44**).

Roubiliac's very few surviving letters are concerned with business matters and give no hint of his personality but various anecdotes about him suggest that he was a witty and and cultivated person, who had strong opinions which were expressed in an animated way. An alertness of mind as well as engagement with his creative endeavours is certainly indicated by Carpentiers' portrait of him modeling the statue of Shakespeare. Roubiliac married three times. His first wife was Catherine Magdalen Helot (b *c*1709) whom he married on 11 April 1735 in the Huguenot church of St Martin Orgar; she died between 1744 and 1752, having borne him a daughter, Sophie, to whom Nicholas Sprimont stood godfather. He then married on 12 January 1752 Elizabeth Crosby, 'a celebrated Beauty, with a fortune of Ten Thousand Pounds' (*General Advertiser*, 11 Jan 1752) and on her death in the late 1750s married the printseller, Celeste Regnier. She, their unborn child, together with his two daughters, Sophie and Amelia and his brother Thomas, were the beneficiaries of his will made on 6 January 1762, naming the goldsmith Thomas Harache as his executor. Despite the major monumental commissions received during his last decade, Roubiliac's financial circumstances were difficult in his late years and he died after along illness on 11 January 1762 leaving debts of £80. His assistant, Nicholas Read, made an unsuccessful attempt to continue the business by advertising plaster and terracotta multiples of Roubiliac's busts of celebrated sitters. In the event, the contents of the studio were sold by Langford in sales on 12 May and 12 June 1762.

Already in his lifetime Roubiliac enjoyed a reputation for his powers of invention which prompted him and Joseph Wilton to be regarded 'names as high/As Phidias of antiquity'. As a description in the *Gentleman's Magazine* in 1788 of the unsuccessful model for the Wolfe monument indicates, his terracottas continued to be esteemed while his monuments continued to be highly rated (and described at length) in accounts of Westminster Abbey, such as that in the 1783 edition of James Ralph's *Critical Review of Public Buildings*. Similarly his monuments were frequently engraved. Prints of the Hargrave monument, for instance, range from the modest etching in Thomas Johnson's *Summer Productions* of 1788 to Philip Dawe's dramatic mezzotint of 1806. Compositional devices seen in Roubiliac's monuments were appropriated by sculptors such as **John Bacon RA** and **John Nost III** and, according to Cunningham, Chantrey considered the busts at Trinity College, Cambridge, to be of 'such surpassing beauty' that 'no other works . . . may safely be compared to them' (*Cunningham*, III, 1830, 57). By this date, however, Walpole's criticism of Roubiliac's monuments for 'advancing into scenery' had become amplified in Flaxman's dislike of their 'epigrammatic conceits' and the sculptor's pictorial and illusionistic effects were seen as increasingly at odds with the taste for neo-classical idealism. With 19th-century attempts to restore the Abbey as a medieval building, Roubiliac's work at Westminster was less highly regarded, allowing the Warren monument (**22**) to be partially demolished. The re-appraisal of Roubiliac's achievement as a sculptor, though already apparent in Dean Stanley's *Historical Memorials of Westminster Abbey*, came with Katherine Arundel Esdaile's writings about 18th-century monuments and, in particular, her monograph of 1928. More recently, Roubiliac has been recognized as one of the major sculptors of 18th-century Europe and an artist who can stand alongside Hogarth and Reynolds in histories of British art.

Malcolm Baker

Literary References: *Vertue* III, 84, 85, 143, 127, 146, 152, 154, 161–2; *Smith* 1828, II, 3, 188, 241, 274; II, 55, 62; *Cunningham* III, 1829–33, 31–67; *Passavant* 1836, II, 56, 276; *Esdaile*, 1928; *Anecdotes* 1937, 151–2; *Whinney* 1971, 77–95; *Penny* 1977 (1), *passim; Murdoch* 1980, 40–6; *Baker* 1984 (1), 106–13; *Baker* 1986 (1); *Baker* 1995 (1); *Baker* 1995 (3), 110–37; *Bindman and Baker* 1995; *Grove*, vol 27, 242–45 [Murdoch]; *Baker* 1997, 222–225; *Bindman* 1997, 22–31; *Baker* 1998 (1), 41–45; *Baker* 1998 (2), 498–530; *Herding* 1998, 268–72; *Dawson* 1999, *passim*; *Baker* 2000, *passim; Bilbey* 2002, 112–26; *ODNB* vol 47, 930–33 (Baker)

Will: repr *Esdaile* 1928, 168

Auction Catalogues: Roubiliac 1762 (1); Roubiliac 1762 (2)

Portraits of the Sculptor: Andrea Soldi, canvas, 1751, Dulwich Picture Gall, London, (*Vertue* III, 159); Adriaen Carpentiers, canvas, *Louis François Roubiliac modelling his monument to Shakespeare*, 1761, YCBA (*Bindman and Baker* 1995, repr 43); another, NPG, 1762

Funerary Monuments

1.	†1721	Martha Manason		Tintinhull, Somerset	S	*Bindman and Baker* 1995, 339–40 (repr)
2.	†1728	Elizabeth Craven		St Mary, Scarborough, NR Yorks	S	*Bindman and Baker* 1995, 174, 340 (repr)
3.	†1740	Thomas Milles, Bishop of Waterford (designed by Sir Charles Frederick)		Highclere, Hants	S	*Bindman and Baker* 1995, 185, 340–1; *Colvin* 1995, 381
4.	1747	Bishop John Hough (†1743)		Worcester Cathedral	S	*Bindman and Baker* 1995, 43, 109–12, 216–18, 246–7, 279–285 (reprs I, 69–71, 173–6, 242–5)
5.	1747	George Baillie		Mellerstain, Berwicks		*Bindman and Baker* 1995, 358
6.	†1747	Jane (†1744) and Cecilia (†1747) Kerridge		Framlingham, Suffolk	S	*Bindman and Baker* 1995, 174, 341 (repr)
7.	1747	Lady Grisel Baillie		Mellerstain, Berwicks		*Bindman and Baker* 1995, 358
8.	†1747	Lucy Lyttelton (designed by Sir Charles Frederick)		Hagley, Worcs		*Bindman and Baker* 1995, 184, 341–3 (repr); *Colvin* 1995, 381
9.	1748	Colonel Francis Ligonier (†1745)		Westminster Abbey, London, south wall of cloisters		*Bindman and Baker* 1995, 174, 342
10.	†1749	Henry, 9th Earl of Pembroke Payment(s): £165		[Wilton, Wilts]; bust sold Christie 2 Dec 1997, lot 377		*Bindman and Baker* 1995, 343–4 (repr); *Wilson* 2006 (4), 141–84
11.	1745–1749	John, Duke of Argyll and Greenwich (†1743) Payment(s): £1,000 Drawing(s): VAM; 8381; coll Duke of Buccleuch and Queensberry Model(s): VAM 21-1999		Westminster Abbey, London, south transept	S	*Vertue* III, 143, 146, 148–9; *Physick* 1969, 117–21, (repr); *Baker* 1992, 785 –97; *Bindman and Baker* 1995, *passim* (repr II and *passim*)
12.	†1750	Elizabeth Smith		St Botolph, Aldersgate, City of London	S	*Bindman and Baker* 1995, 346–7 (repr)
13.	1750	Field-Marshal George Wade (†1748)		Westminster Abbey, London, nave, south aisle	S	*Vertue* III, 150; *Bindman and Baker* 1995, 22, 102–4, 247, 294–298 (reprs III, 121–4, 126, 228, 253 –4)
14.	†1750	James Sotheby		St John, Hackney, London	S	*Bindman and Baker* 1995, 174, 344 (repr)
15.	post-1750	Judge Spencer Cowper (†1727)		Hertingfordbury, Herts	S	*Vertue* III, 162; *Bindman and Baker* 1995, 174, 179, 232, 344 (repr XIV)
16.	?post-1750	Mary Cary (†1738)		St Mary, Putney, London		*Bindman and Baker* 1995, 174, 352 (repr)
17.	1745–1750	Robert, 8th Baron Petre (†1742)	p	[Denbies, nr Dorking, Surrey, coll Jonathan Tyers]; untraced		*Bindman and Baker* 1995, 29, 107–8, 254, 285–6
18.	1749–1750	Thomas Winnington (†1746)		Stanford-on-Teme, Warks		*Baker* 2000, 82, 83 (repr)

No.	Date	Subject	Material	Location		References
19.	post-1751	Henry, Earl of Shelburne (†1751), model only (monument by Peter Scheemakers)	tc	Royal Museum of Scotland, Edinburgh		Blanckley 1770, day 2, lot 38; *Bindman and Baker* 1995, 306–8 (repr)
20.	post-1751	Mary Myddelton (†1747) Payment(s): £300		St Giles, Wrexham, Denbighs	S	*Bindman and Baker,* 1995, 304–6 (repr V)
21.	1752	Sir Thomas Molyneux (†1733) Drawing(s): Soane, vol 37/22; BM PDL		Armagh Cathedral, Northern Ireland	S	*Potterton* 1975, 62, 75–6 (repr)
22.	1753	Admiral Sir Peter Warren (†1752)		Westminster Abbey, London, north transept	SD	*Bindman and Baker,* 318–323 (repr VIII)
23.	†1753	Dr William Stratford		St Mary, Lancaster	S	*Bindman and Baker* 1995, 181, 349–50 (repr)
24.	†1753	George Sawyer		Canon Pyon, Herefs	S	*Bindman and Baker* 1995, 350 (repr)
25.	1753	Henry, Viscount Bolingbroke (†1751) and his wife, Mary Clara (†1750)		St Mary, Battersea, London	S	*Bindman and Baker* 1995, 347–8 (repr)
26.	†1753	Richard Children		St Peter and St Paul, Tonbridge, Kent	S	*Bindman and Baker* 1995, 177, 348–9 (repr)
27.	†1754	Daniel Lock Drawing(s): VAM		Trinity College, Cambridge, chapel	S	*Bindman and Baker* 1995, 178, 350–1 (repr)
28.	1754	General James Fleming (†1750)		Westminster Abbey, London, nave, south aisle	S	*Bindman and Baker,* 308–310 (repr VII)
29.	1749–1754	John, 2nd Duke of Montagu (†1749) Model(s): t-c, VAM A.6-1947; wood and plaster, WA (on loan to VAM)		Warkton, Northants	S	*Murdoch* 1980, 40–46; *Bindman and Baker,* 298–304 (reprs IV, XVI); *Bilbey* 2002, 121 (model repr)
30.	†1754	Lieutenant William Stapleton Model(s): three auctioned 1762, day 2, lot 72		St Peter, Port Royal, Jamaica	S	*Bindman and Baker* 1995, 168–9, 351–2 (repr)
31.	1752–1754	Mary, Duchess of Montagu (†1751) Model(s): WA, on loan VAM, wood and plaster		Warkton, Northants	S	*Murdoch* 1980, 40–46; *Bindman and Baker,* 308–310, 360–1 (repr VI)
32.	†1756	Rev Thomas (†1754) and Arabella (†1756) Myddelton		St Giles, Wrexham, Denbighs	S	*Bindman and Baker* 1995, 177, 353 (repr)
33.	†1757	Anne Taylor		St Mary Magdalene, Newark, Notts	S	*Bindman and Baker* 1995, 174, 352–3 (repr)
34.	1757	General William Hargrave (†1751)		Westminster Abbey, London, nave, south aisle	SD	*Bindman and Baker,* 315–8 (repr IX)
35.	†1758	Henry Fynes		Wing, Bucks		*Bindman and Baker* 1995, 183, 355 (repr)
36.	†1758	Lucretia Betenson (completed by Nicholas Read)		Wrotham, Kent		*Bindman and Baker* 1995, 354–5
37.	1758	William (†1742) and Elizabeth (†1761) Harvey		Hempstead, Essex	S	*Bindman and Baker* 1995, 353–4 (repr XV)
38.	1759	George Lynn (†1758) Payment(s): £500		Southwick, Northants		*Bindman and Baker* 1995, 330–32 (repr XII)
39.	1756–1759	Richard, Viscount Shannon (†1740)		Walton-on-Thames, Surrey	S	*Bindman and Baker* 1995, 323–5 (repr X)
40.	1760	General James Wolfe (†1759), model		Untraced		*Bindman and Baker* 1995, 336–9
41.	†1761	John Wale		Earl's Colne, Essex	S	*Bindman and Baker* 1995, 355–6
42.	1761	Joseph (†1752) and Lady Elizabeth Nightingale (†1734) Model(s): WA		Westminster Abbey, London, Chapel of St Michael	SD	WAM, Feb 1768; *Bindman and Baker* 1995, 325–30 (repr XI)
43.	†1761	Matthew Cropton		[St John, Wapping, London]; destroyed	S	*Bindman and Baker* 1995, 355
44.	1759–1762	George Frederick Handel (†1759) Payment(s): £600 in Handel's will Model(s): Ashm; Gerald Coke coll		Westminster Abbey, London, south transept	S	*Penny* 1992, III, 153–4 (repr); *Bindman and Baker* 1995, 332–6 (repr XIII)
45.	nd	Two original sketches in terracotta, monuments, by Roubiliac, one bearing his autograph	tc	Sold Phillips 16 March 1860; untraced		Archives Phillips, Son and Neale in GPC
Statues						
46.	1730	Daniel saving Susannah when she was condemned to death		[Second grand prix, France]; untraced		*Gunnis* 1968, 329
47.	1738	George Frederick Handel Payment(s): 300 gns Drawing(s): VAM A.3-1965 Model(s): Fitz, clay (*Vertue* III, 157)	m	[Vauxhall Gardens, London, coll Jonathan Tyers]; VAM	S	*Vertue* III, 144, 157; *Rococo* 1984, 85–86 (repr); *Bindman* 1986 (1), 137–8, 140–1; *Baker* 1998 (1); Coke 2007, 5–22 (repr)
48.	1738	Tarquin and Lucretia, statuette	tc	[Christie, 29 March 1805]; untraced		*Gunnis* 1968, 330; *Rococo* 1984, 281
49.	1738	Venus	m	[coll Sir Andrew Fountaine]; untraced		*Rococo* 1984, 281
50.	1735–1740	Hercules and Atlas, statuette	b	Kensington Palace, London		*Baker* 2000, 90–91 (repr)
51.	pre-1747	Hogarth's dog Trump, model Model(s): t-c, Erlestoke sale 1832, lot 171		James Brindley's sale, 1819, lot 238; untraced		*Erlestoke* 1832, 167; *Gunnis* 1968, 330; *Rococo* 1984, 66
52.	1751	Sir John Cass Payment(s): £100	l	[Sir John Cass Foundation, Aldgate High Street, City of London]; Guildhall, City of London		*Rococo* 1984, 279–80 (repr); *Ward-Jackson* 2002, 475–8
53.	1748–1752	Lord President Duncan Forbes (†1747)		Outer Parliament House, Edinburgh (formerly faculty of advocates library)		*Pinkerton* 1973, 274–9 (reprs); *Whinney* 1988, 226, 456 n55; *Pearson* 1991, 47, 54 (repr)

No.	Date	Subject	Material	Location	Signed	Literature
54.	1755	Sir Isaac Newton	m	Trinity College, Cambridge, ante-chapel	SD	*Whinney* 1988, 225–226 (repr); *Baker* 1995 (3), 136 (repr 73)
55.	1758	William Shakespeare Payment(s): £300 Model(s): VAM, clay; Folger Shakespeare Library, Washington DC, clay	m	[Temple of Shakespeare, Hampton, Middx]; BM	SD	*Dawson* 1999, 192–204 (repr); *JKB* 2006, 196 (Crystal Palace cast)
56.	1761	Religion (Fides Christiana)	m	[Gopsall Hall, Leics, Ionic Temple]; Belgrave Hall (Leicester City Museum), walled garden	S	*Whinney* 1988, 226; *Cavanagh* 2000, 184–7 (repr)
Busts						
57.	1733	Marshal Turenne		Untraced		*Baker* 2000, 133
58.	1733	Prince de Condé		Untraced		*Baker* 2000, 133
59.	1737	Sir Isaac Newton Model(s): NMM ZBA 1640	m	Royal Society, London Other versions: several in various media	D	*Vertue* III, 84; *Whinney* 1971, 80 n2; *Baker* 1995 (3), 125; *Keynes* nd, 19–20
60.	1738	Alexander Pope	m	LMG 6/42	SD	*Leeds* 1996, 2 (repr)
61.	1738	Alexander Pope	tc	[Roubiliac sale (1), 1762, lot 76]; Barber Institute of Fine Arts, Birmingham		*Dawson* 1999, 166
62.	*c*1738	Jonathan Tyers	tc	VAM A.94-1927		*Whinney* 1971, 82–3 (repr); *Whinney* 1988, 199–200
63.	1739	George Frederick Handel	m	Windsor Castle, RCIN 35255	S	*Whinney* 1988, 200
64.	*c*1739	George Frederick Handel	tc	Thomas Coram foundation, Holborn, London		*Whinney* 1971, 82–3 (repr)
65.	1740	Alexander Pope	m	Milton Hall, Cambs		*Dawson* 1999, 165
66.	1740	James Thomson		Museum of London		RG/JP, 7, 1202
67.	pre-1740	Lord Bolingbroke		Untraced Other versions: several in plaster		Marchmont Inventory, NAL
68.	1741	Alexander Pope	m	[Lambton Castle, Durham]; Shipley Art Gallery, Gateshead	SD	*British Portraits* 1956–7, 202; *Whinney* 1988, 203
69.	1741	Alexander Pope	m	YCBA, B 1993.27	SD	*Wimsatt* 1965, 246; *Rococo* 1984, 290 (repr)
70.	*c*1741	Isaac Ware Model(s): *Vertue* III, 105	m	[coll Throckmorton family?]; Detroit Institute of Arts, USA Other versions: Buckland House, Berks Copy: NPG, London, 4982		*Rococo* 1984, 70–1 (repr)
71.	*c*1741	William Hogarth Model(s): *Vertue* III, 105	tc	[coll Mrs Hogarth]; NPG, London, 121		*Rococo* 1984, 65, 283 (repr)
72.	1745	Philip, 4th Earl of Chesterfield	m	NPG 5829, 1985 Other versions: YCBA B 1977.14.26, plaster St Patrick's Hall, Dublin, 1746, bronze Private coll	SD	*Whinney* 1971, 86–7 (repr); *Murdoch and Hebditch* 1985, 212–3 (repr); *Dawson* 1999, 63–5; *Baker* 2000, 92, 93 (repr)
73.	*c*1745	William Cheselden	tc	RCS, London		*Baker* 2000, 106 (repr)
74.	1746	Lady Grisel Baillie	m	Mellerstain, Berwicks		*Pearson* 1991, 48, 55 (repr); *Bindman and Baker* 1995, 358
75.	1747	Countess of Pembroke		Wilton, Wilts		*Gunnis* 1968, 330
76.	1747	Lady Murray of Stanhope	m	Mellerstain, Berwicks	D	*Rococo* 1984, 292 (repr); *Pearson* 1991, 48
77.	1747	Sir Andrew Fountaine	tc	Narford Hall, Norfolk Other versions: several marble and plaster versions		*Whinney* 1988, 214–5 (repr); *Moore* 1985, (2), 112–3 (repr)
78.	1748	Arabella Aufrère	m	[coll Earl of Yarborough]; Brocklesby Park, Lincs	SD	*British Portraits* 1956–7, 166; *Rococo* 1984, 292 (repr); *Murdoch and Hebditch* 1985, 212–3 (repr)
79.	1749	Dean Jonathan Swift	m	Trinity College, Dublin, Long Room		*Rococo* 1984, 293 (repr); *Crookshank* 1986, 22–3, 25 (repr); *Baker* 1995 (2), 821–31
80.	1749	Dr Martin Folkes	m	Wilton House, Wilts	SD	*Vertue* III, 152; *Rococo* 1984, 293–4 (repr)
81.	1750	Henry, 9th Earl of Pembroke Payment(s): £30 Model(s): Fitz, clay		Wilton House, Wilts Other versions: marble replica, BMAG, P.11'56	D	*Silber* 1987, 82, cat 245; *Whinney* 1988, 214–6, 456n (repr)
82.	*c*1750	John, 1st Earl Ligonier Model(s): NPG, London, clay	m	Windsor Castle, RCIN 35256		*Whinney* 1988, 220
83.	1745–1750	Jonathan Tyers	m	BMAG, P18'56		*Rococo* 1984, 82 (repr); *Silber* 1987, 82, cat 246 (repr)
84.	*c*1750	Unidentified man, perhaps Francis Hayman	tc	YCBA B 1977.14.25		*Waterhouse* 1977, 351–2 (repr)
85.	1751	Archbishop Chichele Payment(s): 50 gns		All Souls College, Oxford		Pevsner, *Oxon*, 1974, 97
86.	1751	Francis Willoughby Model(s): BM, clay	m	Trinity College, Cambridge, library	SD	*Baker* 1995 (3), 134 (repr 70); *Whinney* 1988, 224 (repr); *Dawson* 1999, 227–9 (repr)
87.	1751	John Ray Payment(s): £108 10s 10d Model(s): BM, clay	m	Trinity College, Cambridge, library	SD	*Baker* 1995 (3), 133 (repr 69); *Whinney* 1988, 224
88.	1751	Sir Francis Bacon	m	Trinity College, Cambridge, library	SD	*Baker* 1995 (3), 133 (repr 68)
89.	1751	Sir Isaac Newton	m	Trinity College, Cambridge, library Other versions: Mechanics Institute, Louth, Lincs, nd Wilton House, Wilts, nd, plaster Trinity College, Dublin, marble	SD	*Baker* 1995 (3), 133 (repr 67)

No.	Date	Subject	Material	Location	Signed/dated	Literature
90.	1755	Sir Mark Pleydell Payment(s): £86	m	[Coleshill House, Wilts, saloon]; VAM (National Trust loan 1)	SD	Pleydell-Bouverie Papers, D/EPB/E11; *Rococo* 1984, 300–1 (repr); *Bilbey* 2002, 116–7 (repr)
91.	1756	Dr Richard Bentley Model(s): BM, clay	m	Trinity College, Cambridge, library	SD	*Rococo* 1984, 301–2 (repr); *Baker* 1995 (3), 134 (repr 93)
92.	1756	Dr Richard Mead Model(s): BM, clay	m	R C Physic, London		*Wolstenholme* 1964, 290–1 (repr)
93.	1756	Isaac Barrow Model(s): BM, clay	m	Trinity College, Cambridge, library	SD	*Whinney* 1988, 224; *Baker* 1995 (3), 134
94.	1757	Charles, Lord Whitworth	m	Trinity College, Cambridge, library	SD	*Whinney* 1988, 224; *Baker* 1995 (3), 134 (repr 92)
95.	c1757	Colley Cibber		NPG, London		*Gunnis* 1968, 331
96.	1757	Dr Richard Frewen	m	Christ Church College, Oxford, library	SD	*Manchester Art Treasures* 1857, 136; *Webb* 1953 (1), 243, 245 (repr 14);
97.	1757	Sir Edward Coke	m	Trinity College, Cambridge, library	SD	*Whinney* 1988, 221–2; *Baker* 1995 (3), 134 (repr 91)
98.	1757	Sir Robert Cotton (1571–1631) Model(s): BM, clay	m	Trinity College, Cambridge, library	SD	*Rococo* 1984, 301–2 (repr); *Whinney* 1988, 223 (repr); Baker 1995 (3), 134 (fig. 90, 94); *Dawson* 1999, 74–6 (repr)
99.	1757	Thomas, Baron Trevor	m	Trinity College, Cambridge, library	SD	*Whinney* 1988, 224; *Baker* 1995 (3), 134 (repr 89)
100.	1758	David Garrick	b	Garrick Club, London		*Whinney* 1988, 224
101.	c1758	William Shakespeare	tc	Garrick Club, London, inv 139 Other versions: Barbican Centre, City of London, 1760 Royal Shakespeare Theatre, Stratford-on-Avon, plaster cast Shugborough Hall, Staffs, sold 1842, 36 gns, bt Lord Derby	S	*Gunnis* 1968, 330; *Ashton* 1997, 520–1 (colour repr 46)
102.	1759	King Charles I	m	Wallace Coll, London		*Dawson* 1999, 60 (repr)
103.	1760	Joseph Wilton	p	RA, London		*Whinney* 1988, 220–1 (repr)
104.	c1760	Thomas 1st Earl of Leicester (†1759) and Countess of Leicester (set on a monument signed by Charles Atkinson)		Tittleshall, Norfolk		*Bindman and Baker* 1995, 357
105.	c1761	John Wilkes	m	CL Coll, Guildhall, London, acc 1098		*Knight* 1986, 345 (repr)
106.	c1761	John, 1st Earl Ligonier	tc	NPG (1924)		*Whinney* 1988, 220
107.	nd	Admiral Peter Warren	m	Huntington Art Coll, San Marino, Cal		*Bindman and Baker*, 1995, 320 (repr)
108.	nd	Alexander Pope	tc	Barber Inst, Birmingham		*Whinney* 1988, 200–2 (repr)
109.	nd	Charles I, after Bernini		Courtauld Institute, London		RG/JP, 7, 1198v.
110.	nd	Dr John Belchier	m	RCS, London	S	*Whinney* 1988, 218, 220 (repr)
111.	nd	Farinelli Model(s): *Vertue* III, 84		untraced		*Rococo* 1984, 283
112.	nd	John Milton	tc	NPG, Scot		*Whinney* 1988, 224
113.	nd	John, Lord Ligonier	m	Royal Coll, RCIN 35256 (1817)	S	*Carlton House*, 1991–2, 210
114.	nd	King Charles I	tc	BM, 1762		*Gunnis* 1968, 329; *Whinney* 1988, 224
115.	nd	King Charles I, Oliver Cromwell and William Shakespeare; bt Dr Maty	tc	[Roubiliac sale 1762 (1); bt Dr Maty]; BM		*Vertue* III, 84; *Dawson* 1999, 61, 77–8, 190–2 (repr)
116.	nd	King Edward VI		King Edward VI Grammar School, Birmingham, Warks		Pevsner, *Warks*, 1966, 168
117.	nd	King George II (in armour) Model(s): Blanckley 1770, day 2, lot 37; untraced	m	Windsor Castle, RCIN 31614	S	*Whinney* 1988, 220; *Carlton House* 1991–2, 210
118.	nd	Marcus Aurelius from a cast brought from Rome		[Roubiliac sale 1762 (1), bt Dr Maty]; BM, London		*Gunnis* 1968, 329
119.	nd	Molière		[Peel heirlooms sale, 1900]; untraced		*Gunnis* 1968, 330
120.	nd	Oliver Cromwell (†1658)		BM, London		*Walker* 1961, 20
121.	nd	Princess Amelia	m	[coll Princess Amelia]; Fitz, Cambridge	S	*Rococo* 1984, 294
122.	nd	Self-portrait	tc	NPG, London		*Whinney* 1988, 219–20 (repr)
123.	nd	Socrates, Plato, Demosthenes, Tully from the antique		[Roubiliac 1762 (1); bt Dr Maty]; BM, London		*Gunnis* 1968, 329
124.	nd	Time		[Phillipson sale, 12 Dec 1785]; untraced		*Gunnis* 1968, 330
125.	nd	Unidentified subject		Crystal Palace sale, Phillips, 24 May 1852; untraced		RG/JP, 7, 1200 (Archives, Messrs Phillips, Son and Neale)
126.	nd	Voltaire		[Peel heirlooms sale, 1900]; untraced		*Gunnis* 1968, 330
Architectural Sculpture						
127.	1744	Mansion House pediment, 'model of a design'		Untraced		*Vertue* III, 122; *Baker* 2000, *passim*
128.	1760	Two models representing Painting and Sculpture for a pediment		[Exhib Soc of Artists, London, 87]; untraced		*Graves* VI, 1905–6, 373
Reliefs						
129.	1758	David Garrick	b	Garrick Club, London	SD	*Mallet* 1962, 153–8 (repr); *Ashton* 1997, 513 (colour repr 45), *Baker* 2000, 90
130.	1750–1760	Alexander Pope	b	YCBA B 1977.14.24		*Baker* 2000, 90, 91 (repr)
131.	1750–60	George Frederick Handel	b	(coll Cherg Huan)		*Rococo* 1984, 306

Miscellaneous

132.	1735–1740	Hercules and Atlas, for Temple of the Monarchies clock	b	Royal Coll, Kensington Palace Other versions: Leeds MAG Castletown House, Limerick BM	*Gilbert* 1978, I, 168–70; *Rococo* 1984, *cat S2, S3*; *Baker* 2000, 90, 91, 134 (repr); *Wilson* 2007, 73–83
133.	nd	John Milton, Alexander Pope, Dr Richard Mead, Martin Folkes, Philip, 4th Earl of Chesterfield	p	[Roubiliac sale (1), 1762; bt Dr Maty]; BM	*Murdoch and Hebditch* 1985, 213–4 (Folkes repr); *Dawson* 1999, 63, 99–101, 140–2, 142–144, 165–8 (repr)

ROUCH, Arthur 1779–1839

Rouch exhibited at the Royal Academy, 1818–1833, and at the British Institution, 1821–1832, from 9 Fitzroy Row, New Road and 9 Clarence Place, Pentonville. In 1824 he was elected to the Artists' Annuity Fund. As a widower he married Frances Moore, a widow, at St James, Clerkenwell, on 12 December 1833. He died on 11 August 1839 and his widow received payments from the Artists' Annuity Fund from 1840 to 1844.

Literary References: *Gunnis* 1968, 331; *Pyke* 1973, 122

Archival References: AAF, CM, 23667/4, 96; AAF, Proposals, 84; AAF, AB

Miscellaneous

1.	1818	Young lions, model	w	[Exhib RA, London, 1080]; untraced	*Graves* 1875, 469; *Graves* VI, 1905–6, 377
2.	1819	Study, from a young lion from the Cape of Good Hope		[Exhib RA, London, 1224]; untraced	*Graves* VI, 1905–6, 377
3.	1822	Search the scriptures, an allegory		[Exhib BI, London, 332]; untraced	*Graves* 1875, 469
4.	1823	Adam and Eve		[Exhib RA, London, 1124]; untraced	*Graves* VI, 1905–6, 377
5.	1824	Mercy and Truth, model	w	[Exhib RA, London, 1015]; untraced	*Graves* VI, 1905–6, 377
6.	1830	Godiva riding through Coventry		[Exhib RA, London, 1252]; untraced	*Graves* 1875; *Graves* VI, 1905–6, 377
7.	1831	Golgotha	w	[Exhib RA, London, 1123]; untraced	*Graves* VI, 1905–6, 377
8.	1831	The wise merchant		[Exhib RA, London, 1125]; untraced	*Graves* VI, 1905–6, 377
9.	1832	A group of brood mares		[Exhib RA, London, 1161]; untraced	*Graves* VI, 1905–6, 377
10.	1833	'Providential escape in hunting the tiger of a European who was torn from the back of an elephant and carried several miles by the ferocious animal'	w	[Exhib RA, London, 1198]; untraced	*Graves* VI, 1905–6, 377

ROUCHEAD, Alexander –1776

A mason by trade, he was much employed in London, but also worked at Wimpole, Cambs, where James Gibbs remodelled the house in 1713–32, and he supplied a number of chimneypieces for the Duke of Atholl at Blair Castle (1). Rouchead became free of the Masons' Company by redemption on 27 May 1728. At this date he was already active as a builder, for instance on the Harley estate in Oxford Street, where he took a plot in 1726, perhaps as a yard. As a result he was in contact with members of Lord Harley's circle of artists, including **Michael Rysbrack** and, more important, several architects, including Roger Morris, George Shakespeare and Gibbs himself. These were probably a fruitful source of commissions. He later moved to North Audley Street, where he remained until his death.

There are a large number of payments to Rouchead (or 'Roughhead') in the accounts of the Duke of Kent at Hoare's Bank between 1726 and 1728, and further payments in the 1730s. In 1748–50, under Matthew Brettingham, he was master-mason for building Norfolk House, St James's Square, receiving in total, over £1,800. In 1753 he was paid £49 17s 8d for 'marble work' at Euston Hall, Suffolk, then being extended by the same architect (PRO, c.108/362, in GPC). He appears to be identical with the 'Alexander Rovehead' of London, who perhaps designed and certainly superintended the erection of the naval hospital at Stonehouse, Plymouth, 1758–64. In 1764–66 he worked as a mason at 15 St James's Square under the architect, James Stuart, who mentioned his name in a letter written late in 1764 to the patron, Thomas Anson: 'the masons have proceeded but slowly but Rouchead is at length arrived in town & we shall unless I am greatly deceived cover in by Christmas' (Anson Papers, Staffs RO D.615 P(S)/1/6).

Several of his apprentices are recorded in the Masons' Company lists, including his son, Alexander, who was apprenticed to him on 29 October 1744. Four others joined him in the 1730s, John Bland (1733), William North (1737), Edward Beck (1736) and George Diorrell (1736).

Literary References: *Friedman* 1984, 24, 207, 295; *Roscoe* 1987, 181; *Colvin* 1995, 835–6; *Webb* 1999, 3, 4, 11, 24, 29

Archival References: Hoare's Customer Ledger, 1725–1728, vol I, fol 318; fol 371; fol 460; fol 73 (payments received 1726); fol 144 (1726, first name given as Alexander; fol 251 (July 1727); fol 284 (Oct 1727); Hoare's Customer Ledger, 1728–1731, vol K, fols 29, 91; GPC

Chimneypieces

1.	1744	Dove marble	m	[Blair Castle, Perths]; untraced	GPC

Architectural Sculpture

2.	1755	Six vases, Portland stone	s	[coll Duke of Atholl]; untraced	GPC

ROUSSE, Jean fl 1771

Jean Rousse, sculptor, bound Jacques Rousset, pupil of the Westminster French Protestant Charity School, in June 1771.

Literary References: *le May* 2001, 566

ROUTLEDGE, Thomas fl 1837

He and his partner **John Danforth Greenwood** took over the **Coade Factory** 1837.

Architectural Sculpture

1.	1841	Scagliola columns		[Dyers' Hall, London]; untraced	Archives, Dyers' Company, in GPC

ROUW, Henry c1780–1855

The son of **Peter Rouw I** and brother of **Peter Rouw II**, he is probably the 'H Rouw Junior' who exhibited paintings at the Royal Academy between 1796 and 1803. Pyke describes him as a wax modeller and painter but gives no examples of his works in wax. Gunnis felt that as a statuary Henry was not the equal of his brother. His most successful works are perhaps the monument to Jane Akers at Yalding, which has a relief of an angel bearing a child heavenwards, and that to the brothers Aubrey in Paddington which has a figure of *Victory* standing by a sarcophagus with medallion portraits of the two officers (**7, 10**). He is buried at All Souls, Kensal Green (inf. Bob Moulder).

Literary References: *Gunnis* 1968, 331–2; *Pyke* 1973, 123

Funerary Monuments

1.	1773	Unidentified subject, tablet	Bobbingworth, Essex		Pevsner, *Essex*, 1965, 90
2.	?1795	Mrs Gazeley	Hornsey, London	S	*Gunnis* 1968, 331
3.	?1798	Rev R Henning	Great Canford, Dorset	S	*Gunnis* 1968, 331
4.	†1801	Mary Christie Burton	North Cave, E R Yorks	S	Pevsner, *Yorks: E R & York*, 1995, 625
5.	?1803	Eleazar Davey	Yoxford, Suffolk	S	*Gunnis* 1968, 331
6.	?1804	Elizabeth and Joanna Cure	Bovinger, Essex	S	*Gunnis* 1968, 331
7.	†1804	Jane Charlotte Akers	Yalding, Kent		*Busco* 1994, 149 (repr)
8.	†1804	Thomas Percival	St Elphin, Warrington, Lancs		*CIIA* 4/8/131 (repr)
9.	?1805	Diana Miller	Exeter Cathedral, Devon	S	*Gunnis* 1968, 331
10.	?1806	Colonel Aubrey and Captain Thomas Aubrey	Paddington, London		*Gunnis* 1968, 331
11.	†1806	George Arnold	Niton, I of W	S	Pevsner, *Hants & Isle of Wight*, 1967, 754
12.	?1808	Charles Purvis	Darsham, Suffok	S	*Gunnis* 1968, 331
13.	?1811	John Tunnard	Frampton, Lincs	S	GPC
14.	?1813	Edward Pocock	St Mary, Twickenham, Middx	S	*Gunnis* 1968, 332
15.	?1814	James Hill	Uppingham, Rutland	S	*Gunnis* 1968, 332
16.	†1814	William Chavasse (†1784) and son William	Burford, Oxon	S	
17.	?1819	Rev George Burvill	Charing, Kent	S	*Gunnis* 1968, 332
18.	?1820	Elizabeth Fowke	Chelsworth, Suffolk	S	*Gunnis* 1968, 332
19.	†1834	John Fuller MP	Brightling, Sussex	S	Pevsner, *Sussex*, 1965, 425

ROUW, Peter I –1807

Rouw was a sculptor and wax modeller who worked in a similar style to his son **Peter Rouw II**.

Literary References: *Gunnis* 1968, 332; *Pyke* 1973, 123

Reliefs

1.	c1787	Frderick the Great	w	Untraced	*Pyke* 1973, 123
2.	nd	Matthew Boulton	w	Birmingham Assay Office	*Pyke* 1973, 123

ROUW, Peter II 1770–1852

A versatile artist who worked as a sculptor, modelled wax portraits, cut gems and cameos and designed medals. He was born on 17 April 1770, the son of **Peter Rouw I**, and entered the Royal Academy Schools in 1788. He exhibited at the RA between 1787 and 1838 from London addresses in Portland Row, Norton Street, Portland Road, Upper Titchfield Street, Carmarthen Street and the New Road, and he sent a collection of his wax portraits to the Great Exhibition of 1851. He was appointed 'sculptor-modeller of gems to HRH the Prince of Wales' in 1807. Gunnis notes that in 1816 he received £23 for carving the tablet designed by Soane recording the history of Daylesford church which had been rebuilt by Warren Hastings. The bill for this has not been traced (**219**).

Rouw was a friend of **Joseph Nollekens**, who left him £100 and a slab of marble in his will, while Mrs Rouw received a legacy of £20. When the contents of Nollekens's studio were sold after his death Rouw purchased several of his small terracotta models, perhaps including five presented to the Victoria and Albert Museum by Zoe Gordon-Smith.

He lost the sight of one eye in 1840 and by 1842 he seems to have been in financial difficulties, for the Royal Academy granted him £30 as a charitable gift. He died at Pentonville on 9 December 1852. Gunnis comments, 'Rouw's monuments are in the classic style; they are all well carved and a number of them have medallion portraits' (*Gunnis* 1968, 332).

Literary References: *Great Exhib* 1851 (2), 153; *Gunnis* 1968, 332; *Pyke* 1973, 123–4; *JKB* 1998, 73

Funerary Monuments

1.	1794	Figure for a monument	[Exhib RA, London, 591]; untraced		*Graves* VI, 1905–6, 379
2.	1799	Monumental figure	[Exhib RA, London, 1065]; untraced		*Graves* VI, 1905–6, 379
3.	?1799	Sir John de la Pole	Shute, Devon		*Gunnis* 1968, 332
4.	1800	General Joshua le Marchant Model(s): exhib RA, London, 1800, 1046	St Peter Port, Guernsey	S	*Graves* VI, 1905–6, 379
5.	†1801	Maximilian Western	Standlake, Oxon		Pevsner, *Oxon*, 1974, 777
6.	†1801	Sophia, Lady Pole	Shute, Devon		Pevsner, *Devon*, 1989, 731
7.	†1802	Henry Stevens of Cross	Little Torrington, Devon		Pevsner, *Devon*, 1989, 539
8.	†1804	Dr Francis Rogers	Birmingham Cathedral		Pevsner, *Warks*, 1966, 108
9.	?1804	Elizabeth Western	Standlake, Oxon		*Gunnis* 1968, 332
10.	†1804	Joseph Priestley	Church of the Messiah, Birmingham, Warks		GPC
11.	†1804	Moses Haughton Model(s): 'part of the model of a monument erected at Birmingham to an artist' exhib RA, London, 1810, 837	Birmingham Cathedral, Warks		*Graves* VI, 1905–6, 379, 380; Pevsner, *Warks*, 1966, 108
12.	?1804	Robert Coales	St Martin, Birmingham, Warks		*Gunnis* 1968, 332
13.	?1808	Lady de la Pole	Shute, Devon		*Gunnis* 1968, 332
14.	?1809	Marmaduke Pricket	Bridlington, E R Yorks		GPC
15.	?1809	Sir Elijah Impey	St Paul, Hammersmith, London		*Gunnis* 1968, 332
16.	?1810	Christopher Tower	Iver, Bucks		*Gunnis* 1968, 332
17.	?1810	John Hyde	Mitcham, Surrey		*Gunnis* 1968, 332
18.	†1810	Paul Prickett	Old Woking, Surrey	S	
19.	?1810	Thomas Brograve	Springfield, Essex		*Gunnis* 1968, 332
20.	?1811	Rev John Vardill	St Mary, St Marylebone, London		*Gunnis* 1968, 332
21.	†1811	Robert (†1783), Sarah (†1797) and James (†1811) Marwood	Widworthy, Devon		*Graves* VI, 1905–6, 380; Pevsner, *Devon*, 1989, 910
22.	†1812	Paul Orchard	St Nectan, Hartland, Devon		Pevsner, *Devon*, 1989, 473

No.	Date	Subject		Location		Reference
23.	†1813	Henrietta Masterman		Sledmere, E R Yorks		Pevsner, *Yorks: E R & York*, 1995, 692; *Mulcahy* 2006, 74 (repr)
24.	?1813	Lady Sykes		Sledmere, E R Yorks		GPC
25.	?1813	Thomas Ruggles		Finchingfield, Essex		*Gunnis* 1968, 332
26.	?1814	Joseph Green		Bocking, Essex		*Gunnis* 1968, 332
27.	†1814	Lieutenant-Colonel Thomas Aubrey		St Mary, Paddington Green, London		Pevsner, *London: N W*, 1991, 676
28.	†1816	Elizabeth Stewart Laing		St Leonard, Streatham, London		Pevsner, *London: S*, 1983, 391
29.	?1818	Granville Charles Wheler		Otterden, Kent		*Gunnis* 1968, 332
30.	†1819	Jane Micklethwait		Salehurst, Sussex		Pevsner, *Sussex*, 1965, 601
31.	?1820	Capel Cure		Bovinger, Essex		*Gunnis* 1968, 332
32.	†1820	John Pring of Ivedon		Awliscombe, Devon	S	Pevsner, *Devon*, 1989, 142
33.	1820	Model for part of a monument to Captain G B Westcott		[Exhib RA, London, 1064]; untraced		*Graves* VI, 1905–6, 380
34.	1820	Unidentified subject, tablet		Bobbingworth, Essex		Pevsner, *Essex*, 1965, 90
35.	†1821	Robert Sherson		Fetcham, Surrey		Pevsner, *Surrey*, 1971, 245
36.	?1821	William Bremner		Wokingham, Berks		GPC
37.	†1822	Robert Burton		North Cave, E R Yorks	S	Pevsner, *Yorks: E R & York*, 1995, 625
38.	†1822	William Merle		St James, Weybridge, Surrey	S	*Gunnis* 1968, 332
39.	†1823	Rev George Thorold		Hougham, Lincs		Pevsner, *Lincs*, 1989, 399
40.	†1825	Elizabeth Merle		St James, Weybridge, Surrey	S	*Gunnis* 1968, 332
41.	†1826	John Blades		St Bride, Fleet St, London, crypt (2005)	S	
42.	†1826	John Farquhar		St John's Wood Chapel, Marylebone, London		*Graves* VI, 1905–6, 381; Pevsner, *London: N W*, 1991, 601
43.	†1826	W Murvell		St Mary, Ware, Herts	S	Pevsner, *Herts*, 1977, 378
44.	?1827	Foster Pigott		Abington Piggotts, Cambs		*Graves* VI, 1905–6, 381; *Gunnis* 1968, 332
45.	?1827	Stephen Pellet		St Mary, Paddington, London		*Gunnis* 1968, 332
46.	?1828	Granville Wheler		Otterden, Kent		*Gunnis* 1968, 332
47.	?1828	Mrs Creswell		St George, Bloomsbury, London		*Gunnis* 1968, 332
48.	†1829	William Shield		Brightling, Sussex		*Graves* VI, 1905–6, 381; Pevsner, *Sussex*, 1965, 425
49.	†1830	Rev Thomas Tucker		Widworthy, Devon		Pevsner, *Devon*, 1989, 910
50.	?1832	Jemima Pigou		Whitchurch, Oxon		*Gunnis* 1968, 332
51.	?1832	Lady de la Pole		Shute, Devon		*Gunnis* 1968, 332
52.	?1832	Sarah Hawkins		Rivenhall, Essex		*Gunnis* 1968, 332
53.	?1833	Sir John Sewell		St Mary, St Marylebone, London		*Gunnis* 1968, 332
54.	†1834	John Manship Ewart		Worth, Sussex	S	*Gunnis* 1968, 332; Pevsner, *Sussex*, 1965, 642
55.	†1835	Catherine Ewart		Worth, Sussex	S	Pevsner, *Sussex*, 1965, 642
56.	†1835	Mary Harrison		Newton Purcell, Oxon	S	Pevsner, *Oxon*, 1974, 717
57.	1835	Sir Banastre Tarleton		St Mary Magdalene, Leintwardine, Herefs		Pevsner, *Herefs*, 1963, 223
58.	1836	John Henderson M D		St Vigeans, Arbroath		RG/JP, suppl. 2
59.	†1837	James and Mary (†1857) Norman		Worth, Sussex	S	
60.	?1837	Mrs Schemberg		Shute, Devon		*Gunnis* 1968, 332
61.	?1837	Mrs Tattershall		Otterden, Kent		*Gunnis* 1968, 332
62.	†1838	Thomas White		Widworthy, Devon		Pevsner, *Devon*, 1989, 910
63.	?1838	William Richardson		St John's Wood Chapel, Marylebone, London		*Gunnis* 1968, 332
64.	1839	Medallion for the monument of an unidentified officer		[Exhib RA, London, 1346]; untraced		*Graves* VI, 1905–6, 381
65.	1839	Sir Herbert Taylor		St Katherine, Regent's Park, London		*Gunnis* 1968, 332
66.	?1840	William Money		Kensal Green Cemetery, London		*Gunnis* 1968, 332
67.	†1846	Augustus Plinke		Witham-on-the-Hill, Lincs		Pevsner, *Lincs*, 1989, 807
Statues						
68.	1796	An archer		[Exhib RA, London, 816]; untraced		*Graves* VI, 1905–6, 379
Busts						
69.	1795	Unidentified gentleman		[Exhib RA, London, 735]; untraced		*Graves* VI, 1905–6, 379
70.	1797	Unidentified lady		[Exhib RA, London, 1111]; untraced		*Graves* VI, 1905–6, 379
71.	1812	'A gentleman's son, deceased'		[Exhib RA, London, 909]; untraced		*Graves* VI, 1905–6, 308
72.	1812	The late J Hyde		[Exhib RA, London, 888]; untraced		*Graves* VI, 1905–6, 380
73.	1825	Aldus Pius Romanus, for Syston Hall		[Exhib RA, London, 999, 1035]		*Graves* VI, 1905–6, 381
74.	1825	John Charles Thorold	m	[Exhib RA, London, 1029]; untraced		*Graves* VI, 1905–6, 381
75.	1828	Gutenberg, the printer, for the library of Syston Hall		[Exhib RA, London, 1148]; untraced		*Graves* VI, 1905–6, 381
76.	1825–1829	Aldus Paolus Manutius, Aldus Pius Romanus, Gutenberg and Caxton Model(s): Exhib RA, London, 1825, 999, 1035; 1828, 1148; 1829, 1167	b	[Syston New Hall, Lincs, library]; untraced		*Graves* VI, 1905–6, 391; *Gunnis* 1968, 332
77.	1829	Unidentified deceased lady, model		[Exhib RA, London, 1178]; untraced		*Graves* VI, 1905–6, 381
78.	1830	Mrs Webb		[Exhib RA, London, 1213]; untraced		*Graves* VI, 1905–6, 381
79.	1831	Lady Thorold	m	[Exhib RA, London, 1185]; untraced		*Graves* VI, 1905–6, 381
80.	1831	Thomas Robson		[Exhib RA, London, 1187]; untraced		*Graves* VI, 1905–6, 381
81.	1831	Unidentified gentleman	m	[Exhib Liverpool Ac, 398]; untraced		*Morris and Roberts* 1998, 528
82.	1832	C Flood		[Exhib RA, London, 1121]; untraced		*Graves* VI, 1905–6, 381
83.	1832	Mrs Litchfield, model		[Exhib RA, London, 1140]; untraced		*Graves* VI, 1905–6, 381
84.	1832	William Tucker	m	[Exhib RA, London, 1151]; untraced		*Graves* VI, 1905–6, 381
85.	1833	T White		[Exhib RA, London, 1142]; untraced		*Graves* VI, 1905–6, 381
86.	1838	C Calland		[Exhib RA, London, 1377]; untraced		*Graves* VI, 1905–6, 381
87.	1838	Unidentified lady		[Exhib RA, London, 1369]; untraced		*Graves* VI, 1905–6, 381
88.	1840	G Maclean	m	[Exhib RA, London, 1127]; untraced		*Graves* VI, 1905–6, 381

Chimneypieces

No.	Date	Subject		Location		Literature
89.	1792	Flora, figure for a chimneypiece		[Exhib RA, London, 614]; untraced		*Graves* VI, 1905–6, 379
90.	1794	Bacchantes, two chimneypiece figures		[Exhib RA, London, 586, 608]; untraced		*Graves* VI, 1905–6, 379
91.	1822	Description unavailable Payment(s): £70 9s		[Wootton House, Bucks]; untraced		RG/JP, 7, 1206

Reliefs

No.	Date	Subject		Location		Literature
92.	1787	The late King of Prussia	w	[Exhib RA, London, 648]; untraced		*Graves* VI, 1905–6, 379
93.	1788	Agostino Carlini RA	w	[Exhib RA, London, 639]; untraced		*Graves* VI, 1905–6, 379
94.	1791	Lord Fife	w	[Exhib RA, London, 651]; untraced		*Graves* VI, 1905–6, 379; *Gunnis* 1968, 332
95.	1792	Unidentified artist	w	[Exhib RA, London, 776]; untraced		*Graves* VI, 1905–6, 379
96.	1793	Unidentified ladies, two	w	[Exhib RA, London, 407, 409]; untraced		*Graves* VI, 1905–6, 379
97.	1793	Unidentified subjects, two portraits in a frame	w	[Exhib RA, London, 376]; untraced		*Graves* VI, 1905–6, 379
98.	1794	Unidentified lady	w	[Exhib RA, London, 464]; untraced		*Graves* VI, 1905–6, 379
99.	1794	Unidentified officer	w	[Exhib RA, London, 475]; untraced		*Graves* VI, 1905–6, 379
100.	1797	Unidentified lady	w	[Exhib RA, London, 850]; untraced		*Graves* VI, 1905–6, 379
101.	1797	William Davidson	w	Art Institute of Chicago, USA		*Pyke* 1973, 123
102.	1801	Mr Flood	w	Philadelphia Museum of Art, USA		*Pyke* 1973, 123
103.	1801	Mr Haley	w	[Exhib RA, London, 1015]; untraced		*Graves* VI, 1905–6, 379
104.	1801	Mr Tahourdin	w	[Exhib RA, London, 1016]; untraced		*Graves* VI, 1905–6, 379
105.	1801	Mrs Haley	w	[Exhib RA, London, 1019]; untraced		*Graves* VI, 1905–6, 379
106.	1802	James Watt	w	NPG 183 Other versions: Tew Park, Oxon, 1802 Sotheby, 21 Oct 1968, lot 103, 1803 Coll Thomas Duncan (London) 1803 VAM A.52-1970, 1804 coll Hon K R Thomson (Toronto)		*Graves* VI, 1905–6, 379; *Pyke* 1973, 124; *Pyke* 1981, 36; *Murrell* 1994, 44, 45 (repr)
107.	1802	Matthew Boulton	w	Tew Park, Oxon Other versions: Sotheby, 17 Dec 1979, lot 59, 1803 Birmingham Museum and Art Gallery, nd Sotheby, 23 July 1979, lot 8		*Graves* VI, 1905–6, 379, 380; *Pyke* 1973, 123 (repr 246); *Pyke* 1981, 35
108.	1803	M R Boulton	w	Tew Park, Oxon		*Graves* VI, 1905–6, 379
109.	1803	Major-General Burton	w	[Exhib RA, London, 762]; untraced		*Graves* VI, 1905–6, 379
110.	1803	Miss Burton	w	[Exhib RA, London, 835]; untraced		*Graves* VI, 1905–6, 379
111.	1803	William Boulton	w	Sotheby, 21 Oct 1968, lot 98		*Pyke* 1973, 123
112.	1804	Francis, 3rd Duke of Bridgewater	w	NPG 4276	SD	*Graves* VI, 1905–6, 379; *Pyke* 1973, 123
113.	1804	Mr Lawson	w	Coll T Sainsbury, Bournemouth, Hants		*Graves* VI, 1905–6, 380
114.	1805	Lieutenant-Colonel Imhoff	w	[Exhib RA, London, 796]; untraced		*Graves* VI, 1905–6, 379
115.	1805	Unidentified gentlemen	w	[Exhib RA, London, 797 and 799]; untraced		*Graves* VI, 1905–6, 379
116.	1806	Child of the Rolls family	w	Coll Hon K R Thomson, Toronto		*Pyke* 1973, 123
117.	1806	Unidentified man	w	Coll Hon K R Thomson, Toronto		*Pyke* 1973, 123
118.	1806	Warren Hastings	w	Christie, 16 Oct 1973, lot 21		*Graves* VI, 1905–6, 379; *Pyke* 1981, 36
119.	1807	James Woolley	w	Coll H Engleheart (Stoke-by-Nayland, Suffolk)		*Graves* VI, 1905–6, 379; *Pyke* 1973, 124
120.	1808	B Howard	w	Coll Miss Lapworth (Nuneaton)		*Graves* VI, 1905–6, 380; *Pyke* 1981, 36
121.	1808	Charles James Fox	w	VAM Other versions: 1802, coll Derek Sherborn c1985		*Graves* VI, 1905–6, 380; *Pyke* 1973, 123
122.	1808	William Pitt (the younger)	w	[RA, London, 1809, 677]; VAM Other versions: NPG 1747, SD 1809		*Graves* VI, 1905–6, 380; *Pyke* 1973, 123
123.	1808	William Wilberforce, for a medal commemorating the abolition of the slave trade		[Exhib RA, London, 755]; untraced		*Graves* VI, 1905–6, 380
124.	1810	King George IV	w	[RA, London, 1810, 646]; VAM Other versions: Sotheby, 30 Nov 1964, lot 94, 1812 coll E J Pyke, London, 1817 Sotheby, 24 Oct 1977, lot 46, c1825 Sotheby, 2 April 1979, lot 54, c1825 Christie, 16 July 1980, lot 8 Christie, 16 Oct 1973, lot 23		*Graves* VI, 1905–6, 380, 381; *Pyke* 1973, 123; *Pyke* 1981, 36; *Morris and Roberts* 1998, 528
125.	1810	Sir John Thorold Bt, two	w	Sotheby, 17 May 1971, lots 13 and 14		*Graves* VI, 1905–6, 380; *Pyke* 1981, 36
126.	1812	King George III	w	Coll Viscount Harcourt (Stanton Harcourt, Oxon) Other versions: exhib RA, London, 1820, 951 Christie, 16 Oct 1973, lot 23		*Graves* VI, 1905–6, 380; *Pyke* 1973, 123; *Pyke* 1981, 36
127.	1812	Thomas Sheldon	w	VAM		*Pyke* 1973, 123
128.	1813	William Egerton	w	Coll Viscount Harcourt (Stanton Harcourt, Oxon)		*Pyke* 1973, 123
129.	1814	Prince Lucien Bonaparte	w	VAM Other versions: Philips, 3 Dec 1974, lot 48, 1814 Christie, 5 Oct 1971, lot 4		*Pyke* 1973, 123; *Pyke* 1981, 35
130.	1815	Son of Sir Robert Williams	w	VAM		*Pyke* 1973, 124
131.	1815	William J R Clay	w	Christie, 26 Feb 1980, lot 101		*Pyke* 1981, 36

132.	1816	Henry Bathurst, Bishop of Norwich	w	Coll T Sainsbury (Bournemouth, Hants)	*Pyke* 1973, 123
133.	1817	Stephen Adisoffe	w	VAM Other versions: Walters Art Gallery, Baltimore, USA	*Graves* VI, 1905–6, 380; *Pyke* 1973, 123
134.	1818	Arthur, 1st Duke of Wellington	w	VAM Other versions: Christie, 16 Oct 1973, lot 18, 1818 VAM, 1822 Coll Hon Mrs John Mulholland (Upton Grey, Hants)	*Graves* VI, 1905–6, 380; *Pyke* 1973, 124; *Pyke* 1981, 36
135.	1818	Charlotte Augusta, Princess of Wales	w	VAM Other versions: Christie, 16 Oct 1979, lot 24, 1818	*Graves* VI, 1905–6, 380; *Pyke* 1973, 123; *Pyke* 1981, 36
136.	1819	Colonel Newport		[Exhib RA, London, 1140]; untraced	*Graves* VI, 1905–6, 380
137.	1819	John Hone	w	Coll T Sainsbury (Bournemouth, Hants)	*Graves* VI, 1905–6, 380; *Pyke* 1973, 123
138.	1819	Joshua Cristall		[Exhib RA, London, 1143]; untraced	*Graves* VI, 1905–6, 380; *Ormond* 1973, 121
139.	1819	Mrs Foster Pigott		[Exhib RA, London, 1142]; untraced	*Graves* VI, 1905–6, 380
140.	1819	Queen Charlotte	w	Coll E J Pyke (London) Other versions: Christie, 16 July 1980, lot 8	*Graves* VI, 1905–6, 380; *Pyke* 1973, 123; *Pyke* 1981, 36
141.	1819	Rev Dr Foster Pigott		[Exhib RA, London, 1144]; untraced	*Graves* VI, 1905–6, 380
142.	1819	Thomas, Lord Lyndoch	w	United Services Club, London	*Graves* VI, 1905–6, 380; *Pyke* 1981, 36
143.	1819	Unidentified lady		[Exhib RA, London, 1138]; untraced	*Graves* VI, 1905–6, 380
144.	1819	W H Merle	w	Antony House, Cornwall	*Graves* VI, 1905–6, 380; GPC
145.	1820	J Wadmore		[Exhib RA, London, 983]; untraced	*Graves* VI, 1905–6, 380
146.	1820	Rev George Edison	w	Christie, 11 Dec 1978, lot 136	*Graves* VI, 1905–6, 380; *Pyke* 1981, 36
147.	1821	J Burnett		[Exhib RA, London, 1060]; untraced	*Graves* VI, 1905–6, 380
148.	1821	Queen Caroline		[Exhib RA, London, 1055]; untraced Other versions: Christie, 16 Oct 1973, lot 29	*Graves* VI, 1905–6, 380; *Pyke* 1981, 36
149.	1821	R Aberdeen		[Exhib RA, London, 1016]; untraced	*Graves* VI, 1905–6, 380
150.	c1822	Jane Maria Pole	w	Antony House, Cornwall	GPC; *Graves* VI, 1905–6, 380
151.	1822	Lady Pole	w	Antony House, Cornwall	GPC
152.	1822	Miss Pole		[Exhib RA, London, 923]; untraced	*Graves* VI, 1905–6, 380
153.	1822	P Mules		[Exhib RA, London, 958]; untraced	*Graves* VI, 1905–6, 380
154.	1822	Rev R Lewis		[Exhib RA, London, 919]; untraced	*Graves* VI, 1905–6, 380
155.	c1822	William Pole	w	Antony House, Cornwall	*Graves* VI, 1905–6, 380; GPC;
156.	1823	A device proposed for an Indian coinage from a design by John Flaxman RA, model	w	[Exhib RA, London, 1004]; untraced	*Graves* VI, 1905–6, 380
157.	1823	J Boyick		[Exhib RA, London, 1009]; untraced	*Graves* VI, 1905–6, 380
158.	1823	J Hathorn RN		[Exhib RA, London, 998]; untraced	*Graves* VI, 1905–6, 380
159.	1824	Colonel Duncan		[Exhib RA, London, 912]; untraced	*Graves* VI, 1905–6, 380
160.	1824	Major Bowden		[Exhib RA, London, 913]; untraced	*Graves* VI, 1905–6, 380
161.	1825	Model for a medal die, for the Asiatic Society		[Exhib RA, London, 933]; untraced	*Graves* VI, 1905–6, 380
162.	1825	Son of John Hone (?)	w	Coll T Sainsbury, Bournemouth, Hants	*Pyke* 1973, 123
163.	1825	William Cobbett, 'for a medal die'		[Exhib RA, London, 964]; untraced	*Graves* VI, 1905–6, 381
164.	1826	Lord Mayor John Garratt and the Lady Mayoress, portraits for a medal		[Exhib RA, London, 934]; untraced	*Graves* VI, 1905–6, 381
165.	1827	Unidentified gentleman		[Exhib RA, London, 1034]; untraced	*Graves* VI, 1905–6, 381
166.	1828	Don Miguel, for a medal		[Exhib RA, London, 1096]; untraced	*Graves* VI, 1905–6, 381
167.	1828	Earl Ferrers		[Exhib RA, London, 1059]; untraced	*Graves* VI, 1905–6, 381
168.	1828	Rev R Tweddell		[Exhib RA, London, 1063]; untraced	*Graves* VI, 1905–6, 381
169.	1829	Captain Bradshaw RN MP	w	[Exhib RA, London, 1075]; untraced	*Graves* VI, 1905–6, 381
170.	1830	Mrs Progers	w	[Exhib RA, London, 1098]; untraced	*Graves* VI, 1905–6, 381
171.	1831	Rear-Admiral Sir Thomas Graves	w	[Exhib RA, London, 1039]; untraced	*Graves* VI, 1905–6, 381
172.	1832	Unidentified lady		[Exhib RA, London, 1047]; untraced	*Graves* VI, 1905–6, 381
173.	1833	Mrs Evans	w	[Exhib RA, London, 1075]; untraced	*Graves* VI, 1905–6, 381
174.	1834	Thomas Wheeler	w	VAM	*Graves* VI, 1905–6, 381; *Pyke* 1973, 124
175.	1835	J R Wheeler		[Exhib RA, London, 988]; untraced	*Graves* VI, 1905–6, 381
176.	1837	Unidentified gentleman		[Exhib RA, London, 1141]; untraced	*Graves* VI, 1905–6, 381
177.	1838	H Richards		[Exhib RA, London, 583]; untraced	*Graves* VI, 1905–6, 381
178.	1839	Margerit Georgiana Maclean	w	Christie, 19 May 1980, lot 67	*Pyke* 1981, 36
179.	nd	George John Montague	w	Philadelphia Museum of Art, USA	*Pyke* 1973, 123
180.	nd	George Whatley	w	Sotheby, 26 July 1976, lot 10	*Pyke* 1981, 36
181.	nd	James Rennell	w	VAM	*Pyke* 1973, 123
182.	nd	Unidentified man	w	Coll D Mathias (Westerham, Kent)	*Pyke* 1973, 123
183.	nd	Unidentified man	w	Sotheby, 17 July 1980, lot 227	*Pyke* 1981, 36
184.	nd	Unidentified woman	w	VAM 106-1871	*Pyke* 1973, 124
185.	nd	Unidentified woman	w	Coll J Glanz (London)	*Pyke* 1981, 36
186.	nd	Unidentified women, four	w	Coll D Mathias (Westerham, Kent)	*Pyke* 1973, 124
187.	nd	Woodbine Parish	w	Woodbine-Parish coll (London)	*Pyke* 1973, 123
Miscellaneous					
188.	1788	Unidentified gentleman		[Exhib RA, London, 637]; untraced	*Graves* VI, 1905–6, 379
189.	1790	Unidentified gentleman		[Exhib RA, London, 700]; untraced	*Graves* VI, 1905–6, 379
190.	1791	Sheldon		[Exhib RA, London, 637]; untraced	*Graves* VI, 1905–6, 379
191.	1791	Unidentified lady		[Exhib RA, London, 656]; untraced	*Graves* VI, 1905–6, 379

192.	1795	Admiral Sir Richard King	[Exhib RA, London, 544]; untraced	*Graves* VI, 1905–6, 379
193.	1795	Unidentified gentlemen, two portraits	[Exhib RA, London, 483, 534]; untraced	*Graves* VI, 1905–6, 379
194.	1797	Unidentified child	[Exhib RA, London, 1047]; untraced	*Graves* VI, 1905–6, 379
195.	1798	Unidentified 'gentleman of the faculty'	[Exhib RA, London, 836]; untraced	*Graves* VI, 1905–6, 379
196.	1799	Mr Joseph	[Exhib RA, London, 1085]; untraced	*Graves* VI, 1905–6, 379
197.	1800	Admiral Lord Nelson	[Exhib RA, London, 863]; untraced	*Graves* VI, 1905–6, 379
198.	1803	Mrs Gibbs	[Exhib RA, London, 826]; untraced	*Graves* VI, 1905–6, 379
199.	1803	Unidentified gentleman	[Exhib RA, London, 838]; untraced	*Graves* VI, 1905–6, 379
200.	1804	Mr Dumergue	[Exhib RA, London, 953]; untraced	*Graves* VI, 1905–6, 379
201.	1805	Rev Mr Weston	[Exhib RA, London, 792]; untraced	*Graves* VI, 1905–6, 379
202.	1805	Vestal, part of a candelabrum	[Exhib RA, London, 713]; untraced	*Graves* VI, 1905–6, 379
203.	1806	Mr Palmer	[Exhib RA, London, 626]; untraced	*Graves* VI, 1905–6, 379
204.	1806	Unidentified gentleman	[Exhib RA, London, 628]; untraced	*Graves* VI, 1905–6, 379
205.	1807	C White	[Exhib RA, London, 915]; untraced	*Graves* VI, 1905–6, 380
206.	1807	Mr Blades	[Exhib RA, London, 816]; untraced	*Graves* VI, 1905–6, 379
207.	1807	Mr Hoy	[Exhib RA, London, 899]; untraced	*Graves* VI, 1905–6, 380
208.	1807	P Marsland	[Exhib RA, London, 911]; untraced	*Graves* VI, 1905–6, 380
209.	1807	W Salte	[Exhib RA, London, 905]; untraced	*Graves* VI, 1905–6, 380
210.	1808	H Bone	[Exhib RA, London, 783]; untraced	*Graves* VI, 1905–6, 380
211.	1808	S Greg	[Exhib RA, London, 752]; untraced	*Graves* VI, 1905–6, 380
212.	1808	Unidentified officer in the Third Regiment of the Guards	[Exhib RA, London, 809]; untraced	*Graves* VI, 1905–6, 380
213.	1809	John Ainsley, Lord Mayor	[Exhib RA, London, 676]; untraced	*Graves* VI, 1905–6, 380
214.	1810	R J Harper	[Exhib RA, London, 643]; untraced	*Graves* VI, 1905–6, 380
215.	1810	W Thorold	[Exhib RA, London, 609]; untraced	*Graves* VI, 1905–6, 380
216.	1811	J Hyde	[Exhib RA, London, 703]; untraced	*Graves* VI, 1905–6, 380
217.	1811	The late J Hyde	[Exhib RA, London, 702]; untraced	*Graves* VI, 1905–6, 380
218.	1812	Rev W Butler	[Exhib RA, London, 639]; untraced	*Graves* VI, 1905–6, 380
219.	1816	Tablet recording the history of Daylesford church (designed by Sir John Soane) Payment(s): £23 (bill, SJSM)	Daylesford, Glos	Pevsner, *Glos: Cotswolds*, 1999, 311

ROWE, Simon, of Exeter fl *c*1799–1850

Contemporary press reports indicate that Rowe, whose workshop was in St Sidwell's, Exeter, was a skilled carver of architectural ornament and church fittings. He was responsible for 'the whole of the stonework' in the Exwick chapel, Devon, which he carried out 'in a manner highly creditable to him' (*GM*, 1842, ii, 523) (**12**). He carved a 'very superb and magnificent font of Caen stone' decorated with 'very close and elaborate carving' and a 'Latin inscription, engraved with singular neatness and precision' for Exeter Cathedral (*Builder*, 1843, 372) and his pulpit, reading desk and font at Holy Trinity, Barnstaple, are described as 'exquisite specimens of carving' (*GM*, 1845, ii, 186) (**14, 15**). He worked with John Hayward, the leading local gothic revival architect, on several occasions (**4, 14, 17**).

Literary References: *Gunnis* 1968, 333

Funerary Monuments

1.	†1799	Rev Thomas Comins	Exeter Cathedral, Devon		GPC
2.	†1835	Hon Elizabeth Stewart	Exeter Cathedral	S	GPC
3.	†1839	Marsh family member	Sturminster Newton, Dorset		Pevsner, *Dorset*, 1972, 406
4.	†1843	Canon E Heberden (designed by John Hayward)	Whimple, Devon		Pevsner, *Devon*, 1989, 905
5.	†1847	Dr George Barnes	Exeter Cathedral	S	GPC
6.	†1853	Rev Matthew Vicars	Exeter Cathedral		RG/JP, 7, 1212v
7.	†1854	General Gage Hall	Exeter Cathedral	S	GPC
8.	†1857	Rev Edward Bartlett	Exeter Cathedral		RG/JP, 7, 1212v
9.	†1865	Eleanor Roberts	Untraced		RG/JP, 7, 1212v

Architectural Sculpture

10.	1838	Canopies above central figures and openwork parapet	s	Exeter Cathedral, Devon, west front	Pevsner, *Devon*, 1989, 375
11.	1841	Reredos		St Andrew, Exwick, Exeter, Devon	Pevsner, *Devon*, 1989, 390
12.	1842	Ornamental stonework		St Andrew, Exwick, Exeter, Devon	*GM*, 1842, ii, 523; *Gunnis* 1968, 333
13.	1843	Font		Broadclyst, Devon	Pevsner, *Devon*, 1989, 215
14.	1843	Font (designed by John Hayward) Payment(s): nearly £100		Exeter Cathedral	*Builder* 1843, 37
15.	1845	Pulpit, reading desk and font	s	Holy Trinity, Barnstaple, Devon	*GM*, 1845, ii, 186
16.	1846	Freestone work		St Michael and All Angels, Heavitree, Exeter, Devon	*Builder* 1846, 393
17.	*c*1848	Font (designed by John Hayward)		St Swithun, Sandford, Devon	Pevsner, *Devon*, 1989, 718
18.	*c*1850	Font		St Mary, Bicton, Devon	Pevsner, *Devon*, 1989, 174
19.	nd	Unspecified ornaments	s	Fredericton Cathedral, New Brunswick, Canada	RG/JP, 7, 1213

ROWLANDSON, Thomas 1757–1827

The famous caricaturist, watercolourist, draughtsman and engraver was awarded the Royal Academy Schools silver medal for a figure in bas relief in 1777.

Literary References: *Grove* 27, 1996, 277–9 (Rodgers); *ODNB* (Hayes)

Reliefs

1.	1777	A figure	[RA silver medal]; untraced	RA Premium list

ROYAL, Thomas fl 1770–77

He exhibited wax portraits at the Society of Artists, 1770–1776, giving his address as 'At Mr. Brown, hairdresser, in St. Clement's churchyard' and '19 Borough'. In 1777 a wax-modeller called Ryal, who was an honorary exhibitor, showed a 'portrait of a gentleman in wax' (cat 332). It seems likely that he was the same man.

Literary References: *Gunnis* 1968, 333; *Pyke* 1973, 124

Miscellaneous

1.	1770	Unidentified lady	w	[Exhib Soc of Artists, London, 177]; untraced	*Graves* 1907, 219
2.	1775	Unidentified gentleman	w	[Exhib Soc of Artists, London, 209]; untraced	*Graves* 1907, 220
3.	1775	Unidentified lady, 'small whole length' portrait	w	[Exhib Soc of Artists, London, 210]; untraced	*Graves* 1907, 220
4.	1776	Unidentified gentleman	w	[Exhib Soc of Artists, London, 288]; untraced	*Graves* 1907, 220

ROYCE, Nathaniel, of Bury St Edmunds –1769

Nothing is known of his parentage but his wife was named Anne and she had six children born between 1716 and 1736 including Nathaniel, who became a mason. Royce signs the 'large and important monument' to Jacob Harvey at Cockfield, Suffolk (1). It is nearly 18 feet high and features a 'well-carved bust of a young man, clad in a coat and scarf and wearing his own hair' set upon a sarcophagus. This is housed within an architectural frame, with Corinthian pillars and pilasters of variegated marble supporting a heavy triangular pediment with a large coat of arms at the apex. This work shows that Royce was a 'skilled and competent statuary'.

Literary References: *Gunnis* 1968, 333

Archival References: Parish registers, St John Maddermarket and St Mary, Bury St Edmunds

Funerary Monuments

1.	†1723	Jacob Harvey	Cockfield, Suffolk	S	Pevsner, *Suffolk*, 1974, 171

RUBENS, Peter fl 1735

Architectural Sculpture

1.	1735	Two terms, Hercules and Deianeira Payment(s): £21	[for Kew Palace, Surrey]; untraced	Accounts of Frederick Prince of Wales, vol V, 1735, Duchy of Cornwall, in GPC

RUCK (or RUCH), William fl 1737–*c*1740

He was made free of the Masons' Company on 30 June 1737 after serving his apprenticeship with Samuel Sheemson. He evidently continued working with Sheemson after that date since in a list of London masons, *c*1740, he is noted as 'working with Mr Sheemsons'.

Archival References: Masons' Co, *Freemen*, fol 64; *Assistants*, fol 8

RUMPH, G fl 1775

For further information the reader is referred to *Pyke* 1973, 125

RUSH, John fl 1763

He was working as a mason in South Street, Berkeley-Square in 1763.

Literary References: *Mortimer* 1763, 49

RUSH (or RUST), Edmund –1708

He was probably based in Aylsham, Norfolk. He is known only for one monument, a large wall tablet described by Gunnis as 'an ambitious work, 9 ft high, with an urn surmounting a curved pediment and flaming lamps to left and right. The coat of arms at the base has elaborate mantling'. A bill of 170s from Edmund Rush to a Mr Carey 'for a Cornish at the front of his house' (£4 5s) is likely to be from this sculptor. The inscription on the memorial tablet to him and his wife outside Reepham church relates that he died on 28 May 1702, aged 70 and concludes "Edmund their son Facit". (Inf. Jon Bayliss)

Funerary Monuments

1.	†1708	Isaac Preston	Beeston St Lawrence, Norfolk	S	Pevsner, *Norfolk: N E & Norwich*, 1997, 381

RUSHWORTH, Edward, of Beverley fl *c*1775–1819

Funerary Monuments

1.	†1775	Rev John Holme	Skeffling, E R Yorks		Pevsner, *Yorks: E R & York*, 1995, 683
2.	†1778	Henry Holme	Skeffling, E R Yorks		Pevsner, *Yorks: E R & York*, 1995, 683
3.	†1781	Margaret Reaston	Skeffling, E R Yorks		Pevsner, *Yorks: E R & York*, 1995, 683
4.	†1800	Elizabeth Knowsley	Langtoft, E R Yorks		Pevsner, *Yorks: E R & York*, 1995, 592
5.	†1802	E S Brearey	Middleton-on-the-Wolds, E R Yorks		Pevsner, *Yorks: E R & York*, 1995, 615
6.	?1811	Anna Fox	Etton, E R Yorks	S	*Gunnis* 1968, 333
7.	†1816	William Wilson	Etton, E R Yorks	S	Pevsner, *Yorks: E R & York*, 1995, 410
8.	†1819	John Williams	Skirlaugh, E R Yorks		Pevsner, *Yorks: E R & York*, 1995, 689

RUSSELL, T H 1809–

He lived in Birmingham, where he sent two works to the exhibition of the Society of Artists in 1829 (1, 3). In 1832 he joined the Royal Academy Schools and exhibited *Innocence* at the Academy (2). He was then living at 7 Charlotte Street, Bloomsbury.

Literary References: *Gunnis* 1968, 333

Statues

1.	1829	Achilles	[Exhib Birmingham Soc of A]; untraced	*Gunnis* 1968, 333
2.	1832	Innocence	[Exhib RA, London, 1155]; untraced	*Graves* VI, 1905–6, 395

Busts

3.	1829	Unidentified lady	[Exhib Birmingham Soc of A]; untraced	*Gunnis* 1968, 333

RUSSELL, William, of Gloucester fl c1842

Funerary Monuments

1.	†1842	Jane Velley	a	Gloucester Cathedral	S	

RYLAND, Joseph fl 1787

For further information the reader is referred to *Pyke* 1973, 125

RYLEY fl 1782?

In St Peter, Cornhill, is a monument to the memory of the seven children of James and Mary Woodmason, who died during a fire at their home in Leadenhall Street in 1782. It takes the form of an oval tablet carved with seven winged cherubs' heads and Augustus Hare states that it is by an artist called Ryley (*Hare* 1878, I, 361). This may well be an error. Francesco Bartolozzi prepared an engraving of the monument based on a drawing by the painter Charles Reuben Ryley (1752–1798), which was published in Robert Wilkinson's *Londina Illustrata.*

Literary References: *Gunnis* 1968, 333

RYLEY, C H, of Louth fl c1832–33

Funerary Monuments

1.	1832	John Emeris		Alvingham, Lincs	S	Pevsner, *Lincs*, 1989, 99
2.	†1833	Rev Francis Mead		Candlesby, Lincs	S	Pevsner, *Lincs*, 1989, 210

RYLEY, E fl 1833–37

He exhibited a number of portrait busts at the Royal Academy between 1833 and 1837 and at the Liverpool Academy in 1836, from addresses in Dean Street, Soho; George Street, Euston Square; and Southampton Row.

Literary References: *Gunnis* 1968, 333

Funerary Monuments

1.	†1833	Rev Rowland Hill		Rowland Hill's tabernacle, Wotton-under-Edge, Glos	S	Pevsner, *Glos: Cotswolds*, 1999, 757

Busts

2.	1833	Unidentified gentleman	m	[Exhib RA, London, 1211]; untraced		*Graves* VI, 1905–6, 398
3.	1834	George Birkbeck		[Exhib RA, London, 1040]; untraced		*Graves* VI, 1905–6, 398
4.	1834	Miss Birkbeck		[Exhib RA, London, 1096]; untraced		*Graves* VI, 1905–6, 398
5.	1834	Rev J Fox		[Exhib RA, London, 1074]; untraced		*Graves* VI, 1905–6, 398
6.	1834	Rev J Leifchild		[Exhib RA, London, 1100]; untraced		*Graves* VI, 1905–6, 398
7.	1834	Thomas Wilson		[Exhib RA, London, 1073]; untraced		*Graves* VI, 1905–6, 398
8.	1834	Unidentified man	tc	Dr Williams Library, Gordon Square, London		RG/JP, 7, 1215
9.	1835	Daniel Harvey MP		[Exhib RA, London, 1064]; untraced		*Graves* VI, 1905–6, 398
10.	1835	Rev B Mardon		[Exhib RA, London, 1109]; untraced		*Graves* VI, 1905–6, 398
11.	1835	Rev J Tate		[Exhib RA, London, 1067]; untraced		*Graves* VI, 1905–6, 398
12.	1835	Sir John Bowring		[Exhib RA, London, 1125]; untraced		*Graves* VI, 1905–6, 398
13.	1835	William Frend		[Exhib RA, London, 1068]; untraced		*Graves* VI, 1905–6, 398
14.	1836	Rev J Yates	m	[Exhib Liverpool Ac, 1836]; untraced		*Graves* VI, 1905–6, 398; *Morris and Roberts* 1998, 531
15.	1837	Andrew Amos, for London University		[Exhib RA, London, 1248]; untraced		*Graves* VI, 1905–6, 398
16.	1837	John T Rutt		[Exhib RA, London, 1269]; untraced		*Graves* VI, 1905–6, 398

RYSBRACK, Michael 1694–1770

Michael Rysbrack was one of the leading sculptors working in England between 1720 and 1740 and was in steady demand throughout his long career. Although he never travelled to Italy he was the master of a restrained classical style that found favour with aristocrats and arbiters of taste of all political persuasions.

Rysbrack was a Fleming, baptised into the Catholic church at Sint Joriskerk, Antwerp, on 27 June 1694. He was the eighth or ninth child of Pieter Rysbrack, a landscape painter, who had visited England during the 1670s, but had been forced to return home because of the persecution facing Catholics after the Popish Plot of 1678.

In 1706 Rysbrack was apprenticed to Michael van der Voort, a successful Antwerp sculptor, known for his work in the classical idiom. He left the van der Voort workshop in 1712, became a master of the Antwerp Guild of St Luke in 1715 and took his first two apprentices in 1716. Rysbrack also worked in Brussels. No work from his Flemish years has been identified, but when he arrived in England in October 1720, he was already a confident master with an individual style. Rysbrack soon met the diarist and engraver George Vertue, who became an admirer and friend. Vertue's extensive notes from the principal contemporary source for Rysbrack's career. He was particularly impressed by Rysbrack's clay models, which he considered 'excellent & shows him to be a great Master *tho' young* (about 26 years old). he was recommended to Mr Gibbs. Architect' (*Vertue* 1, 76).

Rysbrack's association with James Gibbs, a fellow Catholic, began shortly thereafter. Gibbs almost certainly introduced Rysbrack to Edward, Lord Harley, later 2nd Earl of Oxford, a member of the Tory Opposition and a noted connoisseur, who became Rysbrack's patron (**7, 138, 145, 199, 291, 296** and perhaps **4**). Sarah, Duchess of Marlborough, whose son's bust, 1722, (**135**) was a very early commission, may well also have voiced her approval. Lord and Lady Harley were confident in recommending the sculptor to other Tory aristocrats, Henry, Viscount Bolingbroke (**169**), Thomas, Baron Foley (**42**), and the Bristol philanthropist, Sir Edward Colston (**11, 149**). Rysbrack's early Whig patrons included the First Minister, Sir Robert Walpole (**154, 215, 268, 274, 289, 290, 293, 297, 302**), Lord Chief Justice King (**30**), a member of the Pelham family (**161**) and Sir Gilbert Heathcote (**27**), an influential supporter in the City of London. The sculptor's comfortable relationship with clients throughout his career is particularly evident in his association with the banker, Henry Hoare (**120, 122, 127, 252, 216, 217**), which had begun by 1727 and ended only at Rysbrack's death. In his will, dated 5 March 1768, the sculptor left Hoare 'the model of the Hercules I made for him and the Drawing by me of Judas's last Kiss to our Saviour'. Another client who felt easy in his company was Hoare's cousin, Sir Edward Littleton of Teddesley Hall, near Penkridge, Staffs (**240, 243–5, 286**). 23 conversational letters from Rysbrack to Littleton, written during 1750s and 1760s, deal with the progress of work in hand for Littleton and other patrons, discuss technical procedures in the preparation of terracottas and tell of Rysbrack's indifferent health with increasing age. The last, written in February 1766, ends 'I think the Esteem which You and Mr. Hoare have for me, I shall never forget' (*Webb* 1954, 209).

Gibbs raised Rysbrack's professional standing by choosing him to execute his own designs for sculpture. The sculptor worked with Gibbs on at least eight monuments during the 1720s, most of them in London's most prestigious place of burial and commemoration, Westminster Abbey (**4, 6, 7, 10, 11, 14, 16, 80**). Rysbrack carved the surround and life-sized figures of *Clio* and *Euterpe* flanking a portrait bust of Matthew Prior by Antoine Coysevox, 1714, on the monument to the poet, 1723, in Poets' Corner (**7**). James Ralph, a terse critic, felt that the bust was 'hurt' by the statues flanking it (*Ralph* 1734, 79). Vertue thought that Gibbs had treated Rysbrack shabbily by paying him only £35 for each figure (he would later command 35 guineas for a portrait bust in marble).

Ralph was uncharacteristically generous in his response to two other Rysbrack monuments designed by Gibbs. The wall tablet for Ben Jonson, the playwright (**4**), has a relief portrait 'executed with great happiness' and a surround with the 'few, proper and elegant' ornaments that became characteristic of much of Rysbrack's later output (*Ralph* 1734, 78). Ralph also singled out the memorial to John Smith (**6**) as 'designed and executed with great judgment and spirit' (*Ralph* 1734, 74). This has a portrait medallion held by a weeping female attendant, a composition adopted widely for monuments later in the century. The collaboration with Gibbs ceased in the early 1730s, but Gibbs's *Book of Architecture*, published in 1728, to which Rysbrack subscribed, provided the inspiration for numbers of small monuments carved by Rysbrack (*Eustace* 1982, 78–80; eg **35**). Gibbs and Rysbrack continued to meet socially and carried on their respective businesses from comfortable terraced houses on either side of the Oxford Chapel (St Peter, Vere Street) on Lord and Lady Oxford's estate. Rysbrack began paying rates at Vere Street between 12 May and 26 August 1725 and he remained there throughout his life; the house was later numbered 3 Vere Street.

A second architect who collaborated with Rysbrack was William Kent. The sculptor probably met Kent through Lord Burlington, the champion of Palladian classicism, who commissioned statues of Andrea Palladio and Inigo Jones from Rysbrack for the principal front of his villa at Chiswick in 1723 (**100**). Kent was employed as decorator of the new state rooms at Kensington Palace and Rysbrack's overmantel relief of *A Roman Marriage* for the cube room (now cupola room) was ordered by the board of works on 22 January 1724 (**275**). The subject, which may have been determined by Kent, came from an ancient Roman source, accessible to artists in England through an engraving. Kent and Rysbrack also worked together in the state rooms at Houghton Hall, Sir Robert Walpole's country seat in Norfolk, where Rysbrack carved a series of classical reliefs from engraved sources (**268, 274, 297**). The two again worked in close association at Stowe: Kent designed a number of garden temples and Rysbrack provided busts of British Worthies (**159**) and statues of seven Anglo-Saxon deities, inventive figures that suggest a knowledge of medieval manuscripts (**105**). They also worked together on Queen Caroline's new library at St James's, London (**210**), the source of much confusion in the Rysbrack literature.

He executed designs by Kent for three of the most important funerary monuments in England in the first half of the 18th century. The memorial to Sir Isaac Newton, England's greatest scientist and astronomer, was completed in 1731 (**17**) and sited in a focal position on the north side of the screen separating the nave and choir of Westminster Abbey. Kent provided the inventive design. The composition is triangular and has a reclining effigy on a sarcophagus with *putti* at his feet, holding a scroll inscribed with a mathematical formula. Above them is a figure of *Astronomy* seated on a globe. Rysbrack made minor modifications to Kent's design, introducing a relief of boys with instruments on the sarcophagus. His finely detailed terracotta model for the Newton has survived and endorses Vertue's opinion of the sculptor's skill as a modeller in clay. A second ambitious monument commemorated John, Duke of Marlborough at Blenheim (**25**). It is an apotheosis of the great general in Roman military dress attended by his mourning family and by winged figures of *Fame* and *Victory*, either side of a sarcophagus. The lively relief on the pedestal records the moment of Marshall Tallard's surrender at the battle of Blenheim. The model for this historic scene is also intact (SJSM) and is remarkable for the way it conveys the tension between rival commanders and particularly the nervous movements of their horses. The third inventive monument, to James, Earl of Stanhope, 1731–33 (**24**), is set on the south side of the screen in Westminster Abbey, across from the Newton. This pictorial composition depicts Stanhope, the soldier, reclining in Roman armour in his tent. Kent's design was considered by Ralph to be 'trifling and absurd' (*Ralph* 1734, 72), though the execution is superb. Rysbrack's enhanced status is reflected in the patron's arrangements and in payments disbursed: Kent earned £50 for his design, but the contract between Rysbrack and Stanhope's sister made it clear that the sculptor was in sole control, responsible for all aspects of the commission except the iron railings and that a sum of £670 would be paid for his work and the cost of materials.

In 1732, Vertue listed 60 busts by Rysbrack, 'modelld from the life' or from painted portraits or engraved sources. These were of friends, artists, historic personalities, aristocrats and King George II, who twice sat to him. Heading Vertue's list was the image of Daniel, 2nd Earl of Nottingham, a clay model which was translated to marble *c*1723 (**137**). This has recently been called 'a landmark in English sculpture' (*Whinney* 1988, 166), because it was one of the first attempts in this country at portraiture in the Roman manner. Rysbrack advertised his unequivocal mastery of both the classical and contemporary idiom in 1726 with two marble busts of Gibbs, one *all'antica* with a bald head (**139**) and the other a contemporary image, *en negligé*, with a curled wig and open shirt (**140**).

The 1730s were Rysbrack's most secure years. His professional reputation was at its height and his company was sought by artists and collectors. In 1733 he became a member of the learned Spalding Gentleman's Society, founded by Lord Oxford, and on 4 December 1734 he joined the Club of St Luke, an exclusive dining club of which Gibbs and Vertue were also members. Rysbrack hosted their dinner in 1735, the last before the club closed in 1743. In 1735 he was included in a conversation-piece by Gawen Hamilton with members of another club, the virtuosi who met at the King's Arms in New Bond Street. Members of the latter included the Swedish portrait painters, Hans Hysing and Michael Dahl, the landcape architect Charles Bridgeman, John Wootton, the sporting and landscape painter, Matthew Robinson, a dilettante and amateur artist, William Thomas, steward of the Marylebone estate (on which several of them lived), Gibbs, Kent and Vertue. Rysbrack carved busts of seven of the 13 Virtuosi depicted in

Hamilton's painting. He also joined the larger and more loosely-knit Rose and Crown Club, which flourished for about 40 years until May 1745. Rysbrack was one of the first artists to rally around Captain Thomas Coram, founder of the Foundling Hospital, and he donated a work for permanent exhibition in the Court Room (**280**). He became a governor on 27 March 1745 and 15 other artists followed in December 1746.

Rysbrack's outstanding public memorial of the 1730s was the commanding equestrian figure of King William III, a technical masterpiece in bronze for the new Queen Square in Bristol (**108**). The contract, from leaders of Bristol's mercantile community, went to competition. Rysbrack and **Peter Scheemakers** submitted gilt models, to be 'Viewd [in London] by judges of Art & horses', whilst the Bristol community struggled to raise £1,500 to pay for the statue (*Vertue* III, 61). Bronze casting was costly and difficult, so the work in progress aroused considerable interest and Queen Caroline was among those who went to see it shortly before it was shipped to Bristol. The loyal Vertue noted that experts in casting considered it 'the best statue [in the medium] ever made in England' (*Vertue* III, 66).

By the 1740s Rysbrack's position as London's leading sculptor was under threat. Scheemakers attracted a following after the unveiling of his monument to William Shakespeare in Westminster Abbey and **Louis François Roubiliac** challenged the supremacy of formal classical sculpture with a figure of the composer, Handel, in the guise of *Apollo*. Vertue noted a decrease in Rysbrack's business, epitomised in 1745 by his failure to win the prestigious contract for the Duke of Argyll's monument in Westminster Abbey, which went to Roubiliac (**54**).

At this difficult period Rysbrack turned to a potential new market: he prepared models for statuettes of three famous artists, to be marketed as plaster multiples and advertised at seven and a half guineas a set (**114–16**). In 1744 he sought to attract public attention with another model, a statuette of *Hercules* (**117**), the acknowledged classical ideal of virility, and he combined a variety of sources in his new interpretation. The proportions of the figure were taken from the ancient *Farnese Hercules*, the pose from an engraving after an Italian baroque painter, Pietro da Cortona, and the musculature from a number of the best-proportioned boxers and bruisers in contemporary London. The figure was a success: Rysbrack's loyal patron, Henry Hoare, ordered a colossal marble version for his pantheon at Stourhead in 1747 and was so pleased with the work that he gave the sculptor a bonus of £50. In March 1759 he commissioned a marble statue of *Flora*, also adapted from the Antique, to stand beside it (**127**). Horace Walpole considered the *Hercules* to be Rysbrack's masterpiece, 'the principal ornament of Stourhead' (*Anecdotes* 1786, IV, 211). Hoare later bought five drawings and three basso relievos at Rysbrack's 1765 sale. The workshop continued to turn out considerable numbers of monuments and to provide a steady flow of portrait busts throughout the 1740s and 1750s. Rysbrack's preparatory model of the head of the 4th Duke of Beaufort for his effigy on the monument at Badminton, 1756, survives and shows that Rysbrack had lost none of his skill in conveying a sitter's personality (**78**).

If there was a diminution in Rysbrack's reputation in the 1740s, it was restored during the following decade, when he collaborated several times with the architect, Robert Adam, adapting successfully to the new neoclassical style. In 1755 Adam wrote to Lord Hopetoun from Rome sending a design for a grand chimneypiece (**285**) and recommending that it should be carved in London by Rysbrack or Roubiliac, both of whom could be relied on 'to follow the Antique Taste' and not fall into 'French littleness' (Linlithgow, NRA (S) 888 fol 621). Rysbrack won the contract. Two monuments to Adam's designs followed as late as 1763 (**95, 97**) and showed no diminution in quality. By this date Rysbrack had to contend with financial problems and also declining health: a letter sent on 11 July 1763 to the dilatory James West (the 2nd Earl of Oxford's executor), who had ordered a bust of Shakespeare in 1759 (**249**), but had still not given instructions for the inscription on the pedestal, ends 'I have nothing to live on but my Business I want Money and am at too great Expenses to continue where I am without business' (West Papers, Alscot, box 42). He wrote to Littleton on 30 November 1765 that he had entirely left off business. He died at home, on 8 January 1770, and was buried in the graveyard of the parish church of St Marylebone.

Rysbrack had a considerable reputation, not only as a sculptor but as a draughtsman, and was the author of a number of highly finished drawings of historical subjects that were not intended for translation to marble, but were regarded as independent works of art and were framed by patrons. In his practice as a sculptor he seems always to have prepared preliminary drawings for monuments himself, as well as models in clay, wood and plaster, or wax. The carving of marble components by his assistants was closely supervised by Rysbrack, who was an early riser, attending to his team and working with them from five or six in the morning until late at night. Most of his known assistants, cast-makers and suppliers seem to have been of Netherlandish origin. His foremen were Peter Classius or Claessens (†1749) and **Gaspar Vanderhagen** 'who did live with me' and was left £50 in his will. **Samuel Chaplin**, carver, of Oxford Chapel Court (whose son, John, was Rysbrack's godson), and Anna Maria, the wife of his cast-maker, **Peter Vanina**, were also beneficiaries. It is clear that Rysbrack also maintained links with his early master, for a godson, Peter Vandervoort, a carpenter, was left a small bequest. The executors were both connected with the sculpture trade: John Arnold Wallinger owned the marble importing firm who supplied his materials, and James Devaux was either a sculptor or a practioner in an allied trade and was related to the sculptor **John De Veaux**.

Rysbrack's work had an impact on that of his contemporaries, particularly on the more florid style of **Sir Henry Cheere**, and on **Thomas Carter II** and **William Tyler**. Provincial masons were quick to imitate his architectural wall tablets, particularly those which had their origins in Gibbs's *Book of Architecture*. He was admired above all for his portrait busts, which were faithful to the spirit of his sitters, but by the time of his death, his reputation was already in eclipse and he had no obituary. In 1805 Flaxman dismissed him as 'a mere workman, too insipid to give pleasure, and too dull to offend greatly', because he considered Rysbrack's work to be insufficiently grounded in the Antique (*Address to the President and Members of the Royal Academy on the Death of Thomas Banks, R.A., Sculptor*). His reputation was restored in 1954 with Webb's biography and reinforced by an exhibition with a major catalogue held in Bristol in 1982 and arranged by Katharine Eustace.

IR

Literary References: *Vertue* I, III, V *passim*; *Mortimer* 1763, 24; *Pub Ad*, April 18, 1767, 3; *Anecdotes* 1786, IV, 209; *Webb* 1954; *Webb* 1958 (1), 329; *Gunnis* 1968, 333–8; *Physick* 1969, 77–109; *Eustace* 1982; *JKB* 1983, 216–9; *Friedman* 1984, *passim*; *Wilson* 1984, *passim*; *Whinney* 1988, *passim*; *Lord* 1990 (2), 866–70; *Craske* 1992, *passim*; *Grove* 27, 466–9 (Eustace); *Colvin* 1995, 399–407, 580–6; *Eustace* 1997, 743–52; *Eustace* 1998, 31–40; *Baker* 2000, 95–118; *Balderston* 2000, 175–205; *Balderston* 2001, 1–28, esp. n19; *Ency of Sc* III, 1489–90 (Giometti); *ODNB* (Eustace); *Keynes* 2005

Archival References: PR, St Marylebone, 12 May and 26 August 1725, WCA 332 and 346; Hoare Private Accts, 1750–66, 16 July 1757, 19 Feb 1765; GPC
Wills: FRC PROB 11/954, quire 28, 223 verso-quire 29, 225 verso, 5 March 1768

Miscellaneous drawings: Design for the Mansion House pediment 'together with an explanation of the figures' (CLRO Mansion House Committee Minutes, 14 March 1744) untraced; eight designs for monuments, Chicago AI R306/1140, 1149, 1159, 1164, 1171, 1174, 1183–4; *Joseph and Potiphar's wife*, Chicago AI, RX16751/10; *Rest on the flight into Egypt*, Ashm (*Eustace* 1982, 185, repr); four, for a monument, perhaps to the 2nd Duke of Beaufort, Beaufort Papers (*Eustace* 1982, 151–3, repr); *The triumph of Alexander*, Bristol MAG K 4017 (*Eustace* 1982, 190–1, repr); *St Joseph holding the bridle of the ass*, BM Fawkener 44.5211; 15 classical and biblical subjects exhib Free Soc, 1765–9; *Maiden with a Pitcher, Tobias and the Angel, Joseph and his Brethren*, ink and wash, Harris P516, 517, 518; *Briseis restored to Achilles* and an unidentified monument, HMI 19/1988, 17/1991 (*Friedman* 1993, cat 1, 18, repr); *Two nymphs, huntresses*, Louvre, Paris, Département des Arts graphiques 20434; several, unidentified monuments and biblical scenes, ex coll Charles Rogers, Cottonian Coll, CMAG, Plymouth (*Eustace* 1982, 115–6, 126–7, 133, 179–80, 184–5, 186–7); misc designs, principally for monuments, Soane, vol 37; *The baptism of St John*; *Saul and the witch of Endor*; *A sacrifice*; *The punishment of a banditto*; *The contest between Aeneas and Diomedes, The entombing of our Saviour with Joseph of Arimathea*, exhib Soc of A, 1763, 1765; ten classical and biblical subjects including *Menelaus wounded, The surgeon extracting the dart from the wound of Menelaus, Judas's last kiss to our Saviour* (left to Henry Hoare in Rysbrack's will), *The Entombing of our Saviour, Saul and the Witch of Endor, The Witch of Endor raising the ghost of Samuel*, NT, Stourhead (*Webb* 1954, 185; *Eustace* 1982, 188–91, repr); misc designs, principally for monuments, VAM 93E, 27 A–D (principally vol A); misc design, VAM 4248; design, perhaps for a monument to Arthur Onslow, VAM 4910.58; design for a monument to Dr Arthur Johnston, VAM 8933.37 (*Physick* 1989, 60, 62, repr); design for an unidentified monument showing the influence of James Gibbs's design for the Craggs monument, exec Guelfi, inscr '£625', VAM E.434-1946; study of a horse's head, Nat Gall of Victoria, Melbourne (*Eustace* 1982, 97–8, repr); Henry Herbert, Earl of Carnarvon and his younger brother, William, portrait heads, chalk on buff paper, Wilton Archives (*Webb* 1954, 185, untraced 2002); 14 drawings of classical and biblical subjects sold Langford 14 Feb 1767, lots 22–28, 65–71; four designs for chimneypieces, 1759, VAM E.459-61, 463-1946 (*Physick* 1969, 101–3); two designs for chimneypieces, 1761, VAM E.464-1946 (*Physick* 1969, 101–3)

Auction Catalogues: Rysbrack 1764; Rysbrack 1765; Rysbrack 1766; Rysbrack 1767 (1); Rysbrack 1767 (2); Rysbrack 1772; Rysbrack 1774

Portraits of the sculptor: John Vanderbank attrib, *c*1728, oil on canvas, NPG 1802 (*Eustace* 1982, 64 repr), engraving by W Finden, *Anecdotes* 1876, III 33; John Faber after John Vanderbank, 1734, mezzotint (*Eustace* 1982, 64–5 (repr); Gawen Hamilton, *A Society of Artists*, c1730, oil on canvas, Ashm; Gawen Hamilton, *A Conversation of Virtuosis. . .at the Kings Armes*, oil on canvas, raffled on 15 April 1735, NPG 1384 (*Eustace* 1982, 62–3 repr); Andrea Soldi, 1753, oil on canvas, YCBA, Paul Mellon Coll, B1976.7.75 (*Eustace* 1982, 43, 192 repr); Jonathan Richardson, profile sketch, pencil, nd, VAM E1-1942 (*Eustace* 1982, 66–7 repr)

The following list of works was prepared by Gordon Balderston

Funerary Monuments

1.	*c*1721	Samuel Butler (†1680)	Westminster Abbey, London, south transept		*Dart* 1, 1723, 76–7 (repr); *Vertue* III, 57; *Webb* 1954, 213
2.	†1720	Dean Drelincourt (designed by W Coleburne)	Armagh Cathedral	S	*Potterton* 1975, 59, 76 (repr)
3.	†1720	Sir John Wentworth	South Kirkby, W R Yorks	S	Pevsner, *Yorks: W R*, 1967, 492
4.	1723	Ben Jonson (†1637) (designed by James Gibbs) Drawing(s): Ashm III, 104; BM PDL 1913-12-16-11	Westminster Abbey, London, south transept		*Dart* 2, 1723, 61–2 (repr facing 61); *Friedman* 1984, 99–100, 314 (repr)
5.	1723	Edward Eliot (†1722)	St Germans, Cornwall	S	*Craske* 1992, 34 (repr)
6.	*c*1723	John Smith (†1718) (designed by James Gibbs)	Westminster Abbey, London, nave, south aisle		*Dart* 2, 1723, 93–4; *Friedman* 1984, 92–3, 314–5 (repr)
7.	1721–1723	Matthew Prior (†1721), bust by Antoine Coysevox, 1714 (designed by James Gibbs) Drawing(s): Soc of Ant, MS 263; VAM 8933.51	Westminster Abbey, London, south transept		*Dart*, 1723, II, repr p 61; *Friedman* 1984, 99–102, 314 (repr); *Physick* 1989, 54; *Whinney* 1988, 165 (repr); *Balderston* 2001, 20–1, nn4, 16; *Balderston* 2002, 29m, n2
8.	1723	Sir Edward Ward, Lord Chief Baron of the Exchequer (†1714) Drawing(s): VAM 8933.210 Model(s): sold 25 Jan 1766, lot 49; untraced	Stoke Doyle, Northants		*Webb* 1954, 174, 226 (repr)
9.	1726	Andrew Innys (†1723)	St John, Bristol	S	*Webb* 1954, 218; *Eustace* 1982, 75, 195 (repr)
10.	1727–1728	Katherine Bovey (†1727) (designed by James Gibbs)	Westminster Abbey, London, nave, south aisle		*Friedman* 1984, 96–8, 313 (repr); *Colvin* 1995, 406
11.	1729	Edward Colston (†1721) (designed by James Gibbs) (co-sculptor: Michael Sidnell)	All Saints, Corn St, Bristol		*Eustace* 1982, 18–22, 70, 72, 75 (repr); *Friedman* 1984, 92–94 (repr)
12.	†1729	Thomas Southeby	Birdsall, E R Yorks	S	Pevsner, *Yorks: E R & York*, 1995, 326
13.	†1730	Ann Oldfield	Westminster Abbey, London, nave, south aisle		*MacMichael* 1977, 15
14.	1728–1730	Sir Edward Seymour Bt (†1707) (designed by James Gibbs) (co-sculptor: Walter Lee) Payment(s): £500 Drawing(s): Ashm, Gibbs 52a, 52b	Maiden Bradley, Wilts		*Eustace* 1982, 80–81 (repr); *Friedman* 1984, 95; 325; *Colvin* 1995, 407
15.	1723–1730	Sir Godfrey Kneller (†1723) (designed by Kneller, perhaps with modifications by Rysbrack and Robert, Lord Bingley) Model(s): 'a sketch of Sir Godfrey Kneller's monument', Rysbrack sale 24 Jan 1766, lot 18, clay	Westminster Abbey, London, south choir aisle; formerly west end of north nave aisle	S	FFB, 1726; Vertue III, 47; *Griffith* 1922, 182, nos 230–1; *Webb* 1954, 30, 43, 51–2, 86, 219 (repr); *Douglas Stewart* 1978, 215–22
16.	1730–1731	Dr John Freind (†1728) (designed by James Gibbs)	Westminster Abbey, London, south aisle	S	*Friedman* 1984, 99, 313 –4; *Colvin* 1995, 406
17.	1731	Sir Isaac Newton (†1727) (designed by William Kent) Drawing(s): VAM E.424-1946 (Kent's design); VAM A.1-1938; VAM 4910.19; r CMAG Plymouth; BM PDL 1859-7-9-100 Model(s): for Newton's effigy, VAM A 1-1938, clay; (sketch sold 24 Jan 1766, lot 42)	Westminster Abbey, London, nave	S	WAM (59); *Webb* 1954, 78–85 (repr); *Physick* 1969, 80–84 (repr); *Eustace* 1982, 127; *Whinney* 1988, 172–3 (repr), *Bilbey* 2002, 133–4

No.	Date	Subject		Location		References
18.	1732	Anthony, 1st Earl of Shaftesbury (†1683) Drawing(s): SJSM	m	Wimborne St Giles, Dorset Other versions: fired clay with painted surfaces, coll Earl of Shaftesbury		*Webb* 1954, 179, 224 (repr)
19.	†1732	Bennet, 1st Earl of Harborough		Stapleford, Leics	S	*Nichols* 1795–1815, 1, 342, pl LXVI; *Whinney* 1988, 177 (repr)
20.	1732	Daniel Pulteney (†1731) (designed by Giacomo Leoni)		Westminster Abbey, London, cloisters, east walk		*MacMichael* 1977, 104; *Balderston* 2000, 205, n168
21.	1732	John Palmer, Archdeacon of Northampton (†1672) Model(s): model of Palmer's bust, private coll, London		Ecton, Northants	S	Pevsner, *Northants*, 1973, 207; Christie, London, 6 Dec 1988, lot 128 (repr); *Balderston* 2000, 203 n139
22.	pre-1732	Sir Richard Newdigate (†1727) Payment(s): £132 Drawing(s): RIBA Drawings L5/2		St Mary, Harefield, Middx		*Webb* 1954, 176; *Eustace* 1982, 107–8 (repr)
23.	1731–1732	Sir William Strickland, 3rd Bt (†1724) Payment(s): £54 6s	s	Boynton, E R Yorks		Sir William Strickland 4th Bt (†1735), *Green Book*, Boynton archives, 28 June 1731, 12 May 1732
24.	1733	James, 1st Earl Stanhope (†1721) (designed by William Kent) Payment(s): £684 3s Drawing(s): BM 1859-7-9-99 (William Kent's design); VAM 8933.251 (Rysbrack's design) Model(s): 'A laying figure of General Stanhope', Rysbrack sale, 25 Jan 1766, lot 18		Westminster Abbey, London, nave	S	*Webb* 1954, 82–4 (repr); *Physick* 1969, 82–5 (repr)
25.	1730–1733	John, 1st Duke of Marlborough (†1722) (designed by William Kent) Drawing(s): Chicago AI, R306/1148, 1159, 1162–3, 1165–7, 1170, 1172–3 Model(s): SJSM BR28, relief; two trophies, two angels, a group of the Duke and Duchess, Rysbrack sale 24 Jan 1766, lots 11, 46, 47; the monument, 'in small', Rysbrack sale 14 Feb 1767, lot 64		Blenheim Palace, Oxon, chapel		*Green* 1971 (1), 26–8; *Whinney* 1988, 173–176 (repr); *Craske* 1992, 169–77
26.	†1733	Mr Knight and his wife (†1756) (perhaps begun by G-B Guelfi) Model(s): 'A group of Mr Knight and his lady, for a Monument', Rysbrack sale, 25 Jan 1766, lot 27		Gosfield, Essex		*Webb* 1954, 174–5, 177, 219 (repr)
27.	1732–1733	Sir Gilbert Heathcote (†1724)		[Normanton, Rutland]; Edith Weston, Rutland		*Lord* 1990 (2), 869–70 (repr)
28.	†1734	Arabella Oxenden Drawing(s): VAM 4247, signed 'CL 1740' (*Lord* 1990, 2, repr 59)		Rockingham, Northants		*Lord* 1990 (2), 868 (repr)
29.	†1734	Edward Newdigate		St Mary, Harefield, Middx		*Webb* 1954, 176; *White* 1995, 4
30.	†1734	Peter, Lord King, Baron of Ockham, Lord Chancellor Drawing(s): VAM 4910.8 Model(s): one in wood with the figures in burnt clay and another in wax, Rysbrack sale, 18 April 1767, lot 18		Ockham, Surrey, mausoleum		*Physick* 1969, 88–90 (repr); *Whinney* 1988, 451 n33
31.	†1734	Richard Chauncy		Edgcote, Northants		*Gunnis* 1968, 338; Pevsner, *Northants*, 1973, 209
32.	1734	Sir John Newton		Heydour, Lincs	S	*Lord* 1990 (2), 867 (repr)
33.	1736	John Gay (†1732) Drawing(s): Chicago AI, R306/1139 Model(s): relief used as a pattern for his monument, tc, Rysbrack sale, 24 Jan 1766, lot 12; untraced		Westminster Abbey, London, triforium	S	*Webb* 1954, 87, 215; *Whinney* 1988, 177, 178 (repr); *Pearson* 1991, 139 (repr)
34.	†1736	John Welby		Denton, Lincs		*Lord* 1990 (2), 867–8 (repr)
35.	†1736	Mary Edwards		St James, Bristol		*Eustace* 1982, 78–80 (repr)
36.	1737	Sir Nathaniel (†1719) and Lady Curzon (†1727) Drawing(s): Soane, Vol. 37/8		Kedleston, Derbys		*Read's Weekly Miscellany*, 29 July 1737; Pevsner, *Derbys*, 1986, 254
37.	†1737	Sir Richard and Charles Pye		Clifton Campville, Staffs	S	*Webb* 1954, 223
38.	1738	Baldwin Duppa (†1737)		Hollingbourne, Kent	S	Pevsner, *Kent: N E & E*, 1983, 355
39.	1738	Dean Henry Finch (†1728) and Canon Edward Finch (†1737)		York Minster, south choir aisle	S	*Whinney* 1971, 36; *Friedman* 1995, 75, n33
40.	1738	John Milton (†1674) Drawing(s): VAM E.442-1946		Westminster Abbey, London, south transept		*GM*, April 1738; FFB, 1738; *Physick* 1989, 58, 59, 61–2 (repr)
41.	†1738	Sir Thomas Crosse		St Margaret, Westminster, London		*Friedman* 1984, 348 n42

42.	1735–1738	Thomas, 1st Baron Foley (†1732) and family Drawing(s): VAM 4910.1; possibly related VAM E.430-1946 Model(s): for Lady Foley, Rhode Island School of Design; two figures, part of the monument, Lord Foley, his Lady and child, Rysbrack sale, 25 Jan 1766, lots 22, 23, 60	Great Witley, Worcs		*Baker* 1987, 261–8 (repr); *Baker* 2000, 108–118 (repr)
43.	c1739	Brigadier-General Richard Kane (†1736)	Westminster Abbey, London, north transept	S	FFB, 1739; *MacMichael* 1977, 85
44.	c1740	Children of Toby Chauncy	Edgcote, Northants		Pevsner, *Northants*, 1973, 209
45.	1740	Nicholas Rowe (†1718) and his daughter, Charlotte (†1739) Drawing(s): VAM E.441-1946; Chicago AI, R306/1149 Model(s): of Charlotte Fane, née Rowe, Fitz, SD 1740, clay	Westminster Abbey, triforium; formerly south transept	S	*Physick* 1969, 91–3 (repr); *Whinney* 1988, 451 n34
46.	1740	Sir Peter Delme (†1738)	St Margaret Pattens, City of London	S	*Webb* 1954, 214; Pevsner, *London: City*, 1997, 236
47.	c1740	William Chauncy (†1644)	Edgcote, Northants		Pevsner, *Northants*, 1973, 209
48.	†1741	Elizabeth Serle	Eling, Hants		Pevsner, *Hants & Isle of Wight*, 1967, 208
49.	1742	John, 3rd Lord Culpeper (†1719)	Hollingbourne, Kent	S	Pevsner, *Kent: N E & E*, 1983, 355; RG/JP 7, 1244
50.	1740–1742	Monument to an unknown subject contracted by Ann, Dowager Lady Abergavenny	[for Fletching, Sussex]; untraced		Contract, Sackville, 2 July 1740
51.	†1742	Sir John Tynte	Goathurst, Somerset		*Eustace* 1982, 107 (repr)
52.	†1743	Admiral Sir John Jennings	Barkway, Herts	S	*Webb* 1954, 188, 218 (repr)
53.	c1744	Anthony (†1737), Gertrude, Thomas and Anna Methuen	Holy Trinity, Bradford-on-Avon, Wilts	S	*Eustace* 1982, 112–3, 193 (repr)
54.	1744	John, 2nd Duke of Argyll and Greenwich (†1743), model for *Historia* (monument by L-F Roubiliac) Drawing(s): three, VAM 4910.3; CMAG Plymouth n8381 Model(s): *History* exhib Soc of A, London, 1765, 180	[Rysbrack sale (3), 1766]; Museum of Fine Arts, Boston, USA, 1997.142	SD	*Physick* 1969, 119; *Eustace* 1982, 129–32 (repr)
55.	1745	John, 1st Earl Poulett (†1743)	Hinton St George, Somerset	SD	Pevsner, *Somerset: S & W*, 1958, 198
56.	by 1745	Sigismond Trafford (†1740)	Tydd St Mary, Lincs		*Lord* 1990 (2), 870 (repr)
57.	†1745	Thomas, Lord Wyndham	Salisbury Cathedral, Wilts	S	*Whinney* 1988, 230
58.	1746	John Wyndham (†1724) and his wife Alice Drawing(s): VAM 8933.49 (?)	Alvediston, Wilts	S	*Eustace* 1982, 106–7 (repr)
59.	†1746	Mr and Mrs Bartholomew Clarke (he †1746) and Hitch Younge (†1759)	Hardingstone, Northants	S	*Webb* 1954, 176, 213, 227; Pevsner, *Northants*, 1973, 353; *Eustace* 1982, 177
60.	c1746	William (†1746) and Elizabeth (†1753) Powlett	West Grinstead, Sussex	S	Pevsner, *Sussex*, 1965, 371; *Craske* 1992, 98 (repr)
61.	†1747	Charles Colebourn	St Thomas, Lymington, Hants	S	Pevsner, *Hants & Isle of Wight*, 1967, 325
62.	1747	Charlotte (†1726) and Mary Pochin (†1732) Drawing(s): VAM 4230	Barkby, Leics	S	*Physick* 1969, 96–97 (repr)
63.	†1749	John, 2nd Viscount St John	Lydiard Tregoze, Wilts		Pevsner, *Wilts*, 1975, 318
64.	†1749	Rt Hon Lord Thomas Bertie and Albinia, Duchess of Ancaster and Kesteven (†1745)	St Nicholas, Chislehurst, Kent	S	
65.	1749	Sir John Dutton (†1743) and his wives Drawing(s): possibly related, VAM E.434-1946 Model(s): 'A figure of Sir John Dutton, leaning on an urn' Rysbrack sale 24 Jan 1766, lot 70	Sherborne, Glos	SD	*Whinney* 1988, 229 (repr); *Balderston* 2000, 180–81, nn68–9, 71–72 (repr)
66.	†1750	Sir Samuel Pennant	St Michael Paternoster Royal, City of London	S	Pevsner, *London: City*, 1997, 252
67.	1746–1750	Theophilus, 9th Earl of Huntingdon (†1746) and his wife, Selena (designed by William Kent) (co-sculptor: Joseph Pickford)	Ashby-de-la-Zouche, Leics	S	*Wilson* 1984, 258, n24; *Colvin* 1995, 586
68.	1751	Sir Chaloner Ogle	St Mary, Twickenham, Middx	SD	Pevsner, *London: S*, 1983, 539
69.	1751	Sir William and Sarah Young Model(s): 'A group of William Young, Esq: and his lady', Rysbrack sale, 25 Jan 1766, lot 57	Chartham, Kent	SD	*Webb* 1954, 175–6, 227
70.	1751	The Hon Harriot Bouverie (†1750) Drawing(s): VAM E.448-1946; VAM 4910.27	Coleshill, Berks	SD	*Webb* 1954, 176, 212 (repr); *Physick* 1969, 33 (repr)
71.	1752	John Sympson	Canterbury Cathedral, Kent	SD	*Physick* 1969, 87
72.	1752	Sir John Bridgeman	Llanyblodwel, Salop	SD	*Webb* 1954, 212; Pevsner, *Salop*, 1958, 171

73.	1753	John Bradhyll	Carshalton, Surrey	SD	*Webb* 1954, 212
74.	1753	Rev Thomas Busby (†1725) and his wife Ann (†1745) Drawing(s): VAM 4235	Addington, Bucks	SD	*Ashmolean* 1967, cat 33; *Physick* 1969, 86–87 (repr); *Eustace* 1982, 109–110 (repr)
75.	1753	Robert Elwes (†1752)	Throcking, Herts	SD	Pevsner, *Herts*, 1977, 364
76.	1753	Robert Holden	Aston, Birmingham	SD	*Webb* 1954, 217
77.	†1753	Susanna Serle	Eling, Hants	S	Pevsner, *Hants & Isle of Wight*, 1967, 208
78.	1754	Henry, 2nd Duke of Beaufort (†1714), his wife Rachel (†1709) and their son Henry, the 3rd Duke (†1745) Drawing(s): VAM 4910.45; eight designs relating to Beaufort monuments, Badminton portfolio 13 Model(s): Duke Henry, Beaufort coll, clay; 'two figures of the Dukes of Beaufort, Father and Son' Rysbrack sale, 24 Jan 1766, lot 60	Great Badminton, Glos	SD	*Physick* 1969, 98–100 (repr); *Eustace* 1982, 148–9, 151–7 (repr)
79.	1754	Hon John Hay (†1751)	Westminster Abbey, London, cloisters, south walk	SD	*Webb* 1954, 217
80.	1754	Sir Watkin Williams Wynn Bt (†1749) (designed by James Gibbs) Payment(s): £486 Drawing(s): VAM E.426-1946; VAM 4239; CMAG Plymouth	Ruabon, Denbighs	SD	*Eustace* 1982, 120–3 (repr)
81.	†1756	Charles, 4th Duke of Beaufort Drawing(s): eight designs relating to Beaufort monuments, Badminton portfolio 13 Model(s): for bust, Beaufort coll	Great Badminton, Glos		*Eustace* 1982, 150–1, 158–9 (repr)
82.	1756	James Kendall (†1751) and his wife, Jane (†1769)	Holy Trinity, Stratford-upon-Avon, Warks	SD	*Webb* 1954, 118, 219
83.	†1757	Elizabeth Long	Dunston, Norfolk	S	Pevsner, *Norfolk: N W & S*, 1999, 313
84.	1757	Rev William Wynne Drawing(s): VAM 8933.28	St Mary, Mold, Flint	S	Pevsner, *Clwyd*, 1994, 391
85.	1744–1758	The Rt Hon John (†1706) and the Rt Hon Sir Paul Methuen (†1757) Drawing(s): VAM 4910.15; related designs VAM D.1043-1887, 93 E 27 E and 4238	Westminster Abbey, London, nave, south choir aisle	S	*Eustace* 1982, 112–3 (repr)
86.	†1758	Thomas Rolt	Sacombe, Herts		Pevsner, *Herts*, 1977, 287
87.	†1760	Caroline, Countess of Bessborough	Derby Cathedral		Pevsner, *Derbys*, 1978, 170
88.	1760	Richard Chauncy	Edgcote, Northants		Pevsner, *Northants*, 1973, 209
89.	†1760	Roger Townshend	St Nicholas, Chiselhurst, Kent		Pevsner, *London: S*, 1983, 177
90.	1760	Sir James Reade Bt (†1701), Sir John Reade Bt (†1712) and Lady Reade Drawing(s): VAM 4910.31; E.1183-1965	St Etheldreda, Hatfield, Herts	SD	*Physick* 1969, 104–7 (repr); *Douglas Stewart* 1978, 218 221–2 (repr); *Balderston* 2000, 199, n66
91.	†1761	John Palmer (co-sculptor: Henry Cox of Northampton)	Ecton, Northants	S	*Webb* 1954, 222; Pevsner, *Northants*, 1973, 207
92.	?1761	John Roan	St Alfege, Greenwich		*Gunnis* 1968, 338
93.	†1761	Margaret, Countess of Coningsby	Heydour, Lincs	S	*Lord* 1980 (2), 870 (repr)
94.	1763	Admiral Edward Vernon (†1757) Payment(s): £625 Drawing(s): VAM E.433-1946; possibly related VAM 4910.7, 4910.11, E 431-1946 Model(s): Rysbrack sale (3), 1766, lot 9; *Fame*, VAM, A.1-1969, SD 1760, clay	Westminster Abbey, London, north transept	SD	*Physick* 1969, 72–3, 108–9 (repr); *Kerslake* 1977, 285 (bust repr); *Eustace* 1982, 182–4 (repr); *Bilbey* 2002, 141–2 (tc repr)
95.	1763	Admiral the Hon Edward Boscawen (†1761) (designed by Robert Adam) Drawing(s): Soane, Adam Vol 19/1,2,3,4,5,23	St Michael Penkevil, Cornwall	SD	*Webb* 1954, 120, 183, 188, 212 (repr)
96.	†1764	Brian Duppa Drawing(s): VAM E.455-1946	Hollingbourne, Kent		Pevsner, *Kent: N E & E*, 1983, 355
97.	1763–1764	Sir Nathaniel Curzon (†1758) (designed by Robert Adam) Drawing(s): Soane, Adam vol 19/6,7,8; VAM D.162-1886 Model(s): Two figures and an urn for a monument, Rysbrack sale 2 Jan 1766, lot 57	Kedleston, Derbys	SD	*Colvin* 1995, 61
98.	nd	Miss Stanley (designed by William Kent) Drawing(s): VAM E.453-1946	[Holyrood, Hants]; destroyed		*Webb* 1954, 225
99.	nd	Two 'original models' for an unspecified monument in Westminster Abbey	[Advertised for sale in the *Caledonian Mercury*, 14 March 1778, by the decorative painter Alexander Weir]; untraced		*Pearson* 1991, 45

Statues

No.	Date	Subject	Medium	Location		Literature
100.	1723	Inigo Jones, Andrea Palladio (designed by William Kent) Drawing(s): VAM 8933.103 (Inigo Jones) Model(s): 'original models', Rysbrack sale, 24 Jan 1766, lot 69 (Webb 1954, 102–3)	m	[Chiswick, Lord Burlington's bagnio]; Chiswick Villa, Middx, principal front Other versions: Henry Hoare, plaster, 1727, size unknown, bill for £1 10s, 10 Oct 1727 Inigo Jones, full size, before 1761, 4 St James's Square, London Inigo Jones, gilt statuette, Wilton House		*Webb* 1954, 101–9, 218, 222; *Physick* 1969, 7–9 (repr); *Grove* 27, 466
101.	*c*1724	Caroline, Princess of Wales (on four columns) Model(s): Rysbrack sale (3), 1766, lot 40	s	Stowe, Bucks, gardens		*JKB* 1985, 21; *Eustace* 1998, 32–4 (repr)
102.	1724	George, Prince of Wales (on a column of the Composite order) Payment(s): £80 Model(s): Rysbrack sale (3), 1766, lot 40		[Stowe Gardens, Bucks]; John Aspinall Wild Park, Port Lympne, Kent (now on a pedestal)		*Eustace* 1998, 31, 33, 39 n12 (repr)
103.	1727–1728	King George II Payment(s): £80 Model(s): 'a Model of the Kings face in Wax' finished by August 1728, Rysbrack sale (3) 1766, lot 521	s	[Royal Exchange, London, line of kings on the façade of the piazza]; untraced		*Vertue* III, 35, 36; *Esdaile* 1922, 165; *Roscoe* 1998, 173, 178–80 (repr); *Ward-Jackson* 2003, 317–8
104.	pre-1730	Goat lying down, after the Antique Model(s): purchased 1765 by Sir Edward Littleton, Teddesley Hall, Staffs; now at Anglesey Abbey, Cambs, clay	s	[Chiswick House, Middx, until 1928]; Chatsworth, Derbys		*Esdaile* 1932 (2), 43; *Webb* 1954, 117, 193, 206–9, 216
105.	pre-1731	Seven Anglo-Saxon Deities; Sunna, Mona, Tiw, Woden, Thor, Friga, Seatern Model(s): 'a Saxon God', Rysbrack's sale 25 Jan 1766, lot 44	s	[Stowe, 'sylvan temple']; untraced		Stowe Sale 11 Oct 1922 (repr); *JKB* 1985, 220–7; *Davis* 1991, 75–82; *Jackson-Stops* 1992, 64–6; *Bilbey* 2002, 130–1
106.	1732	Water god Payment(s): £7 7s		Davenport House, Salop		*Gunnis* 1968, 337
107.	1735	King George II	m	Royal Hospital, Greenwich (ORNC), forecourt		*Blackwood* 1989, 40 (repr); *Bold* 2000 (2), 28, 30 (repr)
108.	1733–1735	King William III, equestrian Drawing(s): study, Chicago AI, RX16751/17; study for a horse's head, Nat Gall of Victoria, Melbourne Model(s): Hull Museum and Art Gallery, gilt plaster; another, formerly private coll, Bristol Museums, Galleries and Archives; cast, Rysbrack's sale, 18 April 1767, lot 89	b	Queen Square, Bristol		*Eustace* 1982, 23–34, 96–98 (repr); *Whinney* 1988, 178 (repr); *Darke* 1991, 99–100 (repr); *Baker* 2000, 88–90 (repr)
109.	pre-1735	Two models of boys		[Sale of property, 'A person of Note Abroad' *c*1735]; untraced		*Gunnis* 1968, 334
110.	1737	Sir Hans Sloane Model(s): sketch, Rysbrack sale 25 Jan 1766, lot 45		[Chelsea Physic Garden]; BM		*Dawson* 1999, 208 (repr)
111.	1735–1738	Queen Anne Model(s): 'a figure', Rysbrack sale, 24 Jan 1766, lot 41	m	Blenheim Palace, Oxon		*Webb* 1954, 163–4 (repr); *Green* 1971 (1), 26–8
112.	1736–1739	King George I Model(s): VAM A.1-1954; 'A figure of his majesty King George the First', Rysbrack sale, 25 Jan 1766, 33	m	[Senate House, Cambridge]; Cambridge University, law library	S	*Vertue* III, 95; *Webb* 1954, 161–2, 216; *Goodison* 1955, 22–3 (repr); *Kerslake* 1977, 86–7, 89
113.	*c*1740	Thomas, 3rd Earl of Strafford (†1739) Model(s): VAM A.1-1954, clay	m	Wentworth Castle, W R Yorks	S	*Whinney* 1971, 40–41 (repr); *Bilbey* 2002, 136–7
114.	1743	François Duquesnoy, statuette Model(s): Rysbrack sale, 14 Feb 1767, lot 63	tc	[Joseph Van Aken, London; 'Vanhaecken's sale, 11–27 Feb 1751]; untraced Other versions: Bristol City Art Gall, white terracotta (damaged)	SD	*Vertue* III, 116, 135; *Webb* 1954, 109–10; *Eustace* 1982, 141–4 (repr); *Whinney* 1988, 227
115.	1743	Sir Anthony Van Dyck, statuette	tc	[Joseph Van Aken, London; 'Vanhaecken's sale, 11–27 Feb 1751]; untraced Other versions: bronze, signed 'Miche Rysbrack, 1749' sold Christie 21 Nov 1955; untraced	SD	*Vertue* III, 116, 135; *Esdaile* 1922, 168, 251–2 (repr); *Webb* 1950, 315 (repr); *Webb* 1954, 109–10, 224, 226 (repr); *Whinney* 1971, 46 (repr); *Eustace* 1982, 51, 56–8, 141–4 (repr); *Whinney* 1988, 227; *Bilbey* 2002, 144
116.	1743	Sir Peter Paul Rubens, statuette	tc	[Joseph Van Aken, London; 'Vanhaecken's sale, 11–27 Feb 1751]; (coll Earl of Harrowby) Other versions: bronze, signed 'Miche Rysbrack, 1749' sold Christie 21 Nov 1955; untraced	SD	*Vertue* III, 116, 135; *Webb* 1954, 109–10, 224 (repr); *Whinney* 1971, 44 (repr); *Eustace* 1982, 56, 141–4 (repr); *Whinney* 1988, 227; *Bilbey* 2002, 143–4

117.	1744	Hercules, statuette	tc	[inherited from Rysbrack by Henry Hoare]; National Trust, Stourhead, Wilts	SD	*Vertue* III, 121–2; *Eustace* 1982, 11, 44, 160–2 (repr); *JKB* 1983 (2), 216–9 (repr); *Jackson-Stops*, 1985, 235 (repr); FRC PROB 11, microfilm 954, quire 28, 223v–225v
118.	1745	Charity, model for Charity relief, Foundling Hospital, London	tc	Indianapolis Museum of Art, Indiana, USA	SD	*Webb* 1954, 135 (repr)
119.	1744–1747	Dr John Radcliffe Payment(s): £220 Drawing(s): VAM 8423 93 E 27 Model(s): Rysbrack sale 25 Jan 1766, lot 45	m	Radcliffe Library, Oxford, niche at gallery level	S	*Gibbs* 1747; *Webb* 1954, 167–8 (repr); *Gillam* 1958; *Friedman* 1984, 245–6, 320 (repr); *Grove* 27, 468
120.	1751	Bacchus, 'whole figure, less than life and composed from different antiques' Payment(s): £71 18s 10d	m	[Stourhead, Wilts]; Calouste Gulbenkian Foundation Museum, Lisbon	SD	Hoare Partnership Ledger 1751–1764, f59; *Webb* 1954, 125–6, 211; *Eustace* 1982, 180–1 (repr)
121.	pre-1751	Two terms		[Van Aken sale, 1751]; untraced		*Gunnis* 1968, 335
122.	1747–1752	Hercules, on a pedestal Payment(s): £300 plus a gratuity of £50 Model(s): Stourhead, Wilts, SD Mich: Rysbrack 1744, clay; model for the head, lifesize, YCBA B 1977.14.28, clay	m	Stourhead, Wilts, Pantheon	SD	Hoare Private Accounts 1734–49, 3 July 1747; Hoare Partnership Ledger 1751–1764, fol 86; Hoare Private Accounts 1750–66, 9 July 1752, 16 July 1757; *Vertue* III, 162; *Webb* 1954, 121–5, 190, 217 (repr); *Eustace* 1982, 11, 44, 160–2 (repr); *JKB* 1783 (2), 216–8 (repr)
123.	c1754	Fame '(7 feet high)', holding a medallion of the late Duke of Cumberland, with a pedestal	s	[Rysbrack sale (4), 1767, lot 87]; Musées des Beaux-Arts Brussels		*Webb* 1954, 137, 215
124.	1750–1756	Charles, 6th Duke of Somerset, Chancellor of the University Model(s): Rysbrack's sale, 24 Jan 1766, lot 58; bust SD 1754, Rysbrack's sale, 20 April 1765, lot 42, clay	m	Senate House, Cambridge	SD	*Public Advertiser*, 20 July 1756; *Webb* 1954, 162, 168–9, 194 (repr); *Whinney* 1988, 228–9
125.	1756	Governor Henry Grenville Model(s): Rysbrack sale 25 Jan 1766, lot 55; untraced	m	[Barbados Town Hall, court room]; destroyed		*London Evening Post*, 13 Jan 1757; *Webb* 1954, 216; *Craske* 1992, 81
126.	1755–1758	John Locke Drawing(s): three, Chicago AI, R306/1161 Model(s): VAM 33-1867, SD 1755, clay	m	Christ Church, Oxford, library staircase; previously in the library Other versions: Welbeck Abbey (related bust)	SD	*Douglas Stewart* 1978, 215–22 (repr); *Eustace* 1982, 114–5
127.	1759–1760	Flora, on a pedestal Payment(s): £400; pedestal £82 Model(s): Rysbrack sale, 24 Jan 1766, lot 56; VAM A 9-1961, clay	m	Stourhead, Wilts, Pantheon	S	Hoare Private Accounts 1750–66, 11 Dec 1760; *Esdaile* 1932 (2), 42–3 (repr); *Webb* 1954, 126, 215; *Eustace* 1982, 164–6 (repr); *JKB* 1983, 216–9 (repr); *Bilbey* 2002, 140–1 (tc repr)
128.	1763	'Go and do thou likewise': John Willett (previously thought to be John Howard) Model(s): a figure, Rysbrack sale, 24 Jan 1766, lot 56	m	Musées des Beaux-Arts, Brussels	SD	*Webb* 1954, 160, 170–1, 218, 226 (repr); *Whinney* 1988, 231 (repr)
129.	pre-1765	'Hercules reposing; on a plinth of dove marble'	m	[Rysbrack sale, 20 April 1765, lot 71]; Fitzwilliam		*Webb* 1954, 217
130.	pre-1766	Dolphin and boys, cast		[William Atkinson sale, 25 July 1766, lot 44]; untraced		BM, PDB, Sc.5.9
131.	pre-1766	Duke and Duchess of Kent 'figures'	tc	Untraced		*Webb* 1954, 219; *Bryant* 2003, 79
132.	pre-1766	Flora, after the Antique, by François Duquesnoy, restored by Rysbrack	tc	[Rysbrack sale, 20 April 1765, lot 65]; untraced		*Esdaile* 1932 (2), 20; *Webb* 1954, 202; *Eustace* 1984, 164; *Bilbey* 2002, 140
133.	nd	Boys and young satyrs		[Wanstead House, Essex, sold 1822]; untraced		*Gunnis* 1968, 337
134.	nd	Genius of Architecture Payment(s): £46 4s		[Wanstead House, Essex, sold 1822]; untraced		*Gunnis* 1968, 337

Busts

135.	1722	Charles, 3rd Earl of Sunderland (marble by 1732)	tc	Blenheim Palace, Oxon, great gallery	SD	*Vertue* III, 17, 56; *Webb* 1954, 43, 50–1, 225; *Whinney* 1988, 163
136.	?c1723	Cleopatra		[Kensington Palace, London, cupola room]; untraced		*Martyn* 1767, 85
137.	1723	Daniel, 2nd Earl of Nottingham	m	[Nottingham House, London]; VAM A.6-1999		*Whinney* 1988, 166–7 (repr); NACF *Review* 1999, 131 (repr); *Bilbey* 2002, 127–8
138.	†1725	Lord Henry Cavendishe, new-born son of the Earl and Countess of Oxford		Private coll		*Gunnis* 1968, 334, *Balderston* 2002, 28–9
139.	1723–1726	James Gibbs, 'a bald head' Model(s): 1723, untraced	m	[coll James Gibbs]; Radcliffe Library, Oxford	SD	*Vertue* III, 13, 17, 56; *Friedman* 1984, 15; *Baker* 2000, 98–101 (repr); *Balderston* 2001, 4–5 (repr)

No.	Date	Subject	Material	Location	Signed/dated	Literature
140.	1723–1726	James Gibbs, 'with a wigg on' Model(s): 'Gibbs, a bald head', 1723, clay, used for this bust also	m	[coll James Gibbs]; VAM A.6-1988	SD	*Vertue* III, 13, 17, 56; *Esdaile* 1922, 249; *Friedman* 1984, 15 (frontispiece repr); *Balderston* 2001, 1–28, 75n2 (repr); *Bilbey* 2002, 128 (repr)
141.	c1727	Inigo Jones	m	[coll Richard, Earl of Burlington]; Chatsworth, Derbys Other versions: RIBA NMMG SJSM L1, plaster ex coll Henry Hoare, 1727–9; untraced		*Vertue* III, 57; *Webb* 1954, 101–4, 218 (repr); *Kerslake* 1977, 30; *Whinney* 1988, 172; *Baker* 2000, 98
142.	by 1727	Joseph Goupy, limner		Untraced		*Vertue* III, 31, 56; *Webb* 1954, 61, 216
143.	1727	Peter Tillemans	tc	[Little Haugh Hall, Norton, Suffolk]; YCBA, Paul Mellon Coll B 1977.14.35	SD	*Balderston* 2000, 184 (repr)
144.	1727	Richard Miller	m	St Martin-in-the Fields, London, Other versions: Queen's Coll, Oxford, SD 1727, terracotta		*Vertue* III, 56 'Mr Muller'; *Webb* 1954, 53–4, 221 (repr)
145.	by 1727	'Young Lady Margaret Harley'	m	Private coll		*Vertue* III, 56; *Balderston* 2002, 26–29 (repr)
146.	1728	Canon Edward Finch	tc	VAM A.27-1939	SD	*Vertue* III, 56; *Whinney* 1971, 36 (repr); *Bilbey* 2002, 129–30 (repr)
147.	1728	Edmund Waller (†1687)	m	Hall Barn, Beaconsfield, Bucks	SD	*Rogers* 1977, 352
148.	By 1728	King George II 'a model of the King's face in wax', for the statue formerly on the Royal Exchange	w	Untraced		*Vertue* III, 35, 56; *Esdaile* 1922, 165; *Webb* 1954, 155; *Roscoe* 1998, 179–80
149.	pre-1728	Sir Edward Colston	tc	Bristol MAG		*Eustace* 1982, 70 (repr)
150.	1730	Alexander Pope	m	[Coll James Gibbs]; NPG, London, 5854	SD	*Vertue* III, 56; *British Portraits* 1956–7, 181; *Friedman* 1984, 24 (repr); *Balderston* 2001, 1–28, 83 n2 (repr)
151.	pre-1730	John, 1st Duke of Marlborough	m	[Bodleian Library, Oxford]; Ashmolean WA 1926.32 Other versions: For Sarah, Duchess of Marlborough, destroyed NPG, London, coll Earl of Shaftesbury, Wimborne St Giles, Dorset; sold Christie's, London, 26 June 1980, lot 14 Syon House, Middx		*Webb* 1954, 58, 72, 95, 164, 220, (repr); *Whinney* 1988, 167; *Penny* 1992, III, 155 (repr)
152.	pre-1730	Sidney, 1st Earl of Godolphin	m	[Wimbledon House, 1785, coll Sarah, Duchess of Marlborough]; Althorp, Northants		*Webb* 1954, 72, 96, 216 (repr); *Balderston* 2000, 191, n160
153.	1727–1730	Sir Isaac Newton	m	[coll John Conduitt FRS]; Farleigh Wallop, Basingstoke, Hants Other versions: Mrs West, marble; untraced Welbeck Abbey, Notts [ex coll Sir Edward Littleton; Trinity College, Cambridge, Wren library Rysbrack sale, 20 April 1765, lot 75, bronze, bequeathed to Trinity College, Cambridge, on loan to Fitz		*Vertue* III, 57; *Esdaile* (2), 1932, 35–6; *Webb* 1954, 78–82, 117, 193–5, 221–2 (repr); *Keynes* nd, 13, 14
154.	1730	Sir Robert Walpole, 'a large head, broad face' Model(s): 16 June 1726, clay; untraced	m	Houghton Hall, Norfolk, stone hall, over the chimneypiece		*Webb* 1954, 127, 128, 129, 149, 226; *Whinney* 1988, 168 (repr)
155.	†1731	Henry Blaake	m	Lord Mayor's Chapel, Bristol	S	*Eustace* 1982, 104–6 (repr)
156.	pre-1732	Andrea Palladio	m	Chatsworth, Derbys		*Vertue* III, 57; *Webb* 1954, 101–4; *Whinney* 1988, 172; *Baker* 2000, 98 (repr)
157.	pre-1732	Anthony, 1st Earl of Shaftesbury	tc	[Wimborne St Giles, Dorset]; Christie, 6 July 2000, lot 27; private coll		*Webb* 1954, 179, 224 (repr)
158.	pre-1732	Ben Jonson		Untraced		*Vertue* III, 57; *Webb* 1954, 219
159.	by 1732	British Worthies; Queen Elizabeth I, Sir Francis Bacon, William Shakespeare, King William III, John Locke, Sir Isaac Newton, Inigo Jones (attrib, after 1732), John Milton, John Hampden (attrib)	s	[Stowe, surrounding the Gibbs Building or Belvedere]; Stowe, Bucks, Temple of British Worthies, by 1735		*Friedman* 1984, 181–2; *Whinney* 1988, 172, 450, n22; *Davis* 1991, 85–88 (repr); *Eustace* 1998, 33–37 (repr); *Baker* 2000, 129 (repr); *Bilbey* 2002, 129
160.	pre-1732	Captain Aubin	m	Untraced		*Vertue* III, 56; *Webb* 1954, 211
161.	pre-1732	Colonel James Pelham	m	Untraced		*Vertue* III, 56; *Webb* 1954, 222
162.	pre-1732	Dr Cheseldon		perhaps the unsigned bust, RCS, London		*Vertue* III, 56; *Webb* 1954, 57, 213
163.	pre-1732	Dr George Harbin	m	Longleat, Wilts		*Vertue* III, 56; *Webb* 1954, 217; *Whinney* 1988, 168–9 (repr)

164.	pre-1732	Dr John Freind		Untraced		*Vertue* III, 57; *Webb* 1954, 86, 215
165.	pre-1732	Edmund Spenser		Untraced		*Vertue* III, 57; *Webb* 1954, 225
166.	pre-1732	Edward, the Black Prince	m	[John, Duke of Argyll's Gall, Adderbury, Oxon (?)]; untraced		*Vertue* III, 57; *Baker* 2000, 131–4 (repr)
167.	pre-1732	Elisabeth and Judith Sambroke	m	Untraced		*Vertue* III, 56; *Webb* 1954, 224
168.	pre-1732	Henry, 1st Duke of Kent Model(s): Rysbrack sale, 24 Jan 1766, lot 39: 'Two [figures] of the Duke and Dutchess of Kent'	m	Untraced		*Vertue* III, 56; *Webb* 1954, 109, 219
169.	?1730–1732	Henry, 1st Viscount Bolingbroke	m	Petworth House, Sussex Other versions: Lydiard Tregoze, Glos, 1737	S	*Vertue* III, 56; *JKB* 1980, 68–71 (repr); *Eustace* 1982, 134–5 (repr)
170.	pre-1732	Jacob Bouverie, later Viscount Folkestone	tc	Longford Castle, Wilts		*Vertue* III, 57; *Gunnis* 1968, 336; *Eustace* 1982, 177; *Balderston* 2000, 203 n142
171.	pre-1732	John Milton	m	[coll Thomas Serjeant, Tower of London]; Milton monument, Westminster Abbey, London, south transept (by 1740)		*Vertue* III, 57, 100; *Webb* 1954, 112
172.	pre-1732	John Straughan, 'surveyor of Bristol'		Untraced		*Vertue* III, 57; *Webb* 1954, 225
173.	pre-1732	John Wootton		Untraced		*Vertue* III, 56; *Webb* 1954, 227; *Balderston* 2000, 186–8
174.	pre-1732	John, 2nd Duke of Argyll and Jane, his wife	m	[Possibly Duke of Argyll's Gall, Adderbury, Oxon]; untraced		*Vertue* III, 56; *Baker* 2000, 130–3 (repr)
175.	pre-1732	King George I clad in armour with the insignia of the order of the garter and the white horse of the House of Hanover Model(s): George I *all'antica*, NPG, London, 4156, clay	m	[to be sold by Ford at Raphael's Head, Haymarket, London]; Christ Church, Oxford, library (by 1766)	S	*Vertue* III, 56; *Public Advertiser*, 18 April 1757, 3; Pevsner, *Oxon*, 1974, 127; *Kerslake* 1977, 86–89 (repr)
176.	pre-1732	King George II 'twice sat to him'		Untraced		*Vertue* III, 57
177.	pre-1732	Lord Macclesfield		Untraced		*Vertue* III, 56; *Webb* 1954, 220
178.	pre-1732	Michael Dahl		Untraced		*Vertue* III, 56; *Webb* 1954, 61, 214
179.	pre-1732	Michelangelo		Untraced		*Vertue* III, 57; *Webb* 1954, 221
180.	pre-1732	Mr Booth, 'player' and Mrs Booth Model(s): medal, Rysbrack sale, 24 Jan 1766, lot 12, clay		Untraced		*Vertue* III, 56; *Webb* 1954, 212
181.	pre-1732	Mr Halsey		Untraced		*Vertue* III, 56; *Webb* 1954, 217
182.	pre-1732	Mr Holland, 'herald painter'		Untraced		*Vertue* III, 56; *Webb* 1954, 217
183.	pre-1732	Mr Mason		Untraced		*Vertue* III, 56; *Webb* 1954, 220
184.	pre-1732	Mr Milner	m	Untraced		*Vertue* III, 56; *Webb* 1954, 221
185.	pre-1732	Mr Morett		Untraced		*Vertue* III, 57; *Webb* 1954, 221
186.	pre-1732	Mr Muller (Richard Miller, 1727 ?)	m	Untraced		*Vertue* III, 56; *Webb* 1954, 221
187.	pre-1732	Mrs Davenport		Untraced		*Vertue* III, 57; *Webb* 1954, 214
188.	pre-1732	Mrs Nash, 'a Beautifull Gentlewoman by the life' Model(s): by 1727; untraced	m	Untraced		*Vertue* III, 31, 56; *Webb* 1954, 221
189.	pre-1732	Oliver Cromwell	tc	[Rysbrack's sale, 14 Feb 1767, lot 61]; NMM, Greenwich London Other versions: Marble, coll John Duke of Argyll, Adderbury, Oxon; the same or another, unsigned, sold Christie, London, 10 July 1978, lot 242 Bronze, Rysbrack sale, 20 April 1765, lot 74 ex coll Humphrey Whitbread, private coll ex coll O V Watney, Cornbury Park, Oxon, sold Christie, 22 May 1967, lot 6 (house sale); untraced Christie, London, 5 April 2001, lot 311		*Vertue* III, 57; *Esdaile* 1932, 37 (repr); *Webb* 1954, 117, 192, 213; *Baker* 2000, 131–4 (repr)
190.	pre-1732	Oliver Cromwell 'with a carved truss' Model(s): Rysbrack sales, (2) 1765, lot 74; (4) 1767, lot 61, clay	b	[Rysbrack sale 20 April 1765, lot 74]; Trinity College, Cambridge (on loan to Cecil Higgins Art Gallery, Bedford, 1967–2004		*Webb* 1954, 214; *Keynes* nd, 18
191.	pre-1732	Queen Caroline		Untraced		*Vertue* III, 57
192.	pre-1732	Samuel Butler, the poet	tc	Untraced		*Vertue* III, 56–7; *Webb* 1954, 213
193.	pre-1732	Sarah, Dowager Duchess of Marlborough or Henrietta, Duchess of Marlborough	m	Untraced		*Vertue* III, 56; *Webb* 1954, 96, 220

No.	Date	Subject	Material	Location		Literature
194.	pre-1732	Sir Thomas Hewett, surveyor, and Lady Hewett Model(s): Sir Thomas, 1723, clay; untraced	m	[Shireoaks Hall, near Workshop, Notts, banqueting house]; untraced		*Vertue* II, 36; III, 17, 33, 56; *Colvin* 1973–6, V, 72; *Baker* 2000, 102
195.	pre-1732	The Hon Mr Bridgman	m	Untraced		*Vertue* III, 56; *Webb* 1954, 212
196.	pre-1732	Thomas Ripley, architect	tc	[Rysbrack sale (2), 1765, lot 28]; untraced		*Vertue* III, 56; *Webb* 1954, 223; *Whinney* 1988, 168
197.	post-1732	William Bouverie, later 1st Earl of Radnor	m	Longford Castle, Wilts		*British Portraits* 1956–7, I, 182–3, no 592; II, repr 18; *Gunnis* 1968, 336; *Balderston* 2000, 203, n142
198.	pre-1732	William Kent, 'painter', two versions		Untraced		*Vertue* III, 56; *Kerslake* 1977, 162
199.	pre-1732	William Thomas 'Steward to the Earl of Oxford'		Untraced		*Vertue* III, 57, 71–2; *Balderston* 2001, 23–4, 50 n43; *Balderston* 2004, 287–307
200.	post-1733	Charles, 3rd Duke of Marlborough	m	Blenheim Palace, Oxon, long gallery		*Vertue* III, 57; *Balderston* 2000, 192
201.	1733	Francis Bacon, Lord Verulam	m	[Queen Caroline's grotto, Richmond]; Windsor Castle, library corridor		*Webb* 1954, 211
202.	1732–1733	George, 1st Earl of Orkney	m	Private coll		*Vertue* III, 57; *Baker* 2000, 142 (repr)
203.	1733	Matthew Tindall, from a death mask by the sculptor		Untraced		*Biographica Britannica*, 1763
204.	1734	John Cossins	m	[Redland Court, Somerset]; Redland Chapel, Bristol		*Eustace* 1982, 82–83 (repr)
205.	c1734	John Innys	m	Redland Chapel, Bristol		*Eustace* 1982, 88–89 (repr)
206.	1734	Martha Cossins	m	[Redland Court, Somerset]; Redland Chapel, Bristol		*Eustace* 1982, 83–84 (repr)
207.	c1734	William Innys	m	Redland Chapel, Bristol		*Eustace* 1982, 86–88 (repr)
208.	1730–1735	King William III Model(s): by 1732	m	YCBA B 1977.14.27		*Vertue* III, 70; *Waterhouse* 1977, 351; *Eustace* 1982, 32 (repr)
209.	1735–1736	King Alfred and Edward, the Black Prince Payment(s): £105 Model(s): Black Prince, clay, before 1732, untraced	m	[Frederick, Prince of Wales, Octagon in the garden of the Princess of Wales in Pall Mall, London]; untraced Other versions: Warwick Castle Royal Coll, Windsor Castle, RCIN 3706		*Vertue* III, 57; *London Mag* 1735, 390; *Webb* 1954, 156; *Colvin* 1973–76, V, 138; *Eustace* 1998, 38 n72 (repr); *Baker* 2000, 133
210.	1735–1737	Eleven kings, queens and princes of England Model(s): 1735–7, delivered to the office of the Board of Works after 23 Jan 1738; at Windsor Castle until 1906, when all but three irreparably damaged; Edward the Black Prince and Edward VI, SD 1738, Elizabeth I, Royal coll, Windsor Castle RCIN 53346	m	[Queen Caroline's library, St James's, London (demolished 1825)]; untraced	SD	*GM*, 30 June 1735, 331; *Vertue* III, 75; *Webb* 1954, 145–6; *Colvin* 1973–76, V, 242–3; *Eustace* 1982, 135–7 (repr); *Baker* 2000, 136; *Balderston* 2000, 194, n3
211.	1738	Dr Robert Freind	m	Christ Church, Oxford	SD	*Webb* 1954, 179–80, 187, 215 (repr)
212.	1738	King George II Model(s): Rysbrack sale, 14 Feb 1767, lot 57; Royal coll RCIN 1412, clay	m	[Rysbrack's sale, 14 Feb 1767, lot 57]; Royal Coll, Kensington Palace RCIN 31623 Other versions: Royal Coll Christ Church, Oxford Christie, New York, 10 Jan 1990, lot 199A (signed)	S	*Vertue* III, 84, 95; *Esdaile* 1932 (2), 41–2 (tc repr); *Webb* 1954, 154–6, 192, 216 (repr); *Kerslake* 1977, 94 (repr)
213.	?c1738	Queen Anne	m	[Rysbrack sale (2), 1765, lot 31]; Sotheby, New York, 11 Jan 1995, lot 157; untraced		*Webb* 1954, 210
214.	1738	Queen Caroline Model(s): Rysbrack's sale 14 Feb 1767, lot 58, SD, clay; Royal coll, Windsor	m	[Queen Caroline's library]; Royal Coll, Kensington Palace, London RCIN 1411 Other versions: Wallace coll, marble, signed, Rijksmuseum, Amsterdam BK-16709, terracotta, SD 1738		*Vertue* III, 84, 95; *Webb* 1954, 154–6, 192, 216 (repr); *Kerslake* 1977, 35, 94 (repr); *Rococo* 1984, 39 (repr); *Whinney* 1988, 167–8; *Balderston* 2000, 191, n151–2
215.	1738	Sir Robert Walpole	tc	NPG London, 2126		*Vertue* III, 91; *Kerslake* 1977, 197–8 (repr); *Moore* 2002, 343
216.	c1738	The old Milton Drawing(s): two, Chicago AI, R3672 / 5574, 5575 Model(s): ex coll Sir Edward Littleton, clay, SD 1738; Fitz	m	[Wilbury, Wilts, coll William Benson]; Stourhead, Wilts, library Other versions: Earlier version at Stowe, Bucks		*JKB* 1980, 71–74 (repr); *Eustace* 1982, 167–9 (repr)
217.	c1738	The young Milton	m	[coll William Benson]; Stourhead, Wilts, library		*JKB* 1980, 71–74 (repr); *Eustace* 1982, 170–1 (repr)
218.	1738	Virgil Model(s): Rysbrack's sale 14 Feb 1767, lot 60		[Vanina sale (1), 1770]; Fitzwilliam	SD	*Webb* 1954, 126, 226
219.	1739	Dr Arthur Johnston	tc	SNPG, Edinburgh	SD	*Webb* 1954, 100, 115–6, 218 (repr)
220.	c1739	Queen Caroline		Wallace coll, London Other versions: Royal Coll RCIN 31317	S	*Whinney* 1988, 168

No.	Date	Subject		Location		Literature
221.	c1740	One or more unidentified 'young patriot'		[Stowe, Bucks, Temple of Friendship]; untraced		*Friedman* 1984, 192
222.	1740	Portrait of an unidentified man	tc	NGI 8015	SD	*le Harivel* 1988, 581
223.	c1741	Francis (or William) Smith of Warwick Model(s): Radcliffe Library, Oxford, SD 1741, clay	m	Christie, 17 July 1988, lot 278; private coll		*Webb* 1954, 180 (repr); *Baker* 2000, 101 (repr); *Balderston* 2001, 21 n14
224.	1743	Admiral Edward Vernon	m	[Probably at Wimbledon House, on an inscribed column]; Sudbury Hall, Derbys		*JKB* 1980, 66–68 (repr); *Kerslake* 1977, 285 (repr)
225.	1743	William Murray, later 1st Earl of Mansfield (†1793)	m	Scone Palace, Perths		*Vertue* III, 57; *Walker* 1961, 45; *Pearson* 1991, unpag, 140 (repr)
226.	1744	Daniel, 7th (now 8th) Earl of Winchilsea and 3rd Earl of Nottingham		Sotheby, 22 April 1986, lot 72; Dr Gustav Rau	S	*Vertue* III, 57; *Balderston* 2001, 21 n17
227.	post-1744	Dr William Bernard, Bishop of Raphoe		Untraced		*Vertue* III, 57; *Balderston* 2001, 21, n17
228.	1744	John Bernard, or Barnerd, a boy Model(s): t-c, SD 1743, Christies King Street, 7.7.2005, lot 420	m	Met, NY, 1976.330	SD	*Vertue* III, 57; *Balderston* 2000, 188, 190 n134 (repr)
229.	pre-1744	Thomas Walker		Untraced		*Vertue* III, 57; *Balderston* 2000, 202, nn111, 114; *Balderston* 2001, 21, n17
230.	1745	Lady Jemima Dutton	m	Musées Royaux des Beaux-Arts, Brussels	SD	*Webb* 1954, 172, 214; *Balderston* 2000, 181, n73 (repr)
231.	pre-1745	Self-portrait (pendant to a bust of Peter Tillemans)	tc	[Little Haugh Hall, Norton, Suffolk]; KMSK, Antwerp	S	*Vertue* III, 57; *Balderston* 2000, 184–5 (repr)
232.	1745	Unidentified woman, possibly Jane Mary Reade, née Dutton	m	Met, NY	SD	*Balderston* 2000, 199, n73; *Bull MMA*, fall 2002, 24–5
233.	1743–1746	François Duquesnoy (Fiammingo) Model(s): [Rysbrack sale, 20 April 1765, lot 65]; ROM, Toronto, SD 1743	m	[Rysbrack's sale, 20 April 1764, lot 65]; Museo di Capodimonte, Naples		*Vertue* III, 116, 132; *Webb* 1954, 111, 215, 223 (repr); *Watson* 1963, 441–5 (repr)
234.	1748	Edward Salter, aged six	tc	[coll Thomas Salter]; Ashmolean, WA 1999.22	SD	*Balderston* 2000, 175–205 (repr)
235.	pre-1751	Proserpine, after Bernini		[Van Aken sale, 1751]; L A County Museum, Cal		*Gunnis* 1968, 335; *Eustace* 1982, 64
236.	1754	Charles, 6th Duke of Somerset	tc	[Rysbrack's sale, 20 April 1765, lot 42]; Musées des Beaux-Arts, Brussels, Belgium	SD	*Esdaile* 1932 (2), 42 (repr); Webb 1954, 168–9, 225
237.	?c1754	Henry, 2nd Duke of Beaufort	m	Badminton, Glos, drawing room	S	
238.	1754	William Augustus, Duke of Cumberland Model(s): 'The late Duke of Cumberland, after the Life 1754', Rysbrack sales 14 Feb 1767, lot 59; 18 April 1767, lot 39	m	Teresa, Viscountess Galway Other versions: several	SD	*Webb* 1954, 117, 149, 157, 192, 214 (repr); Kerslake 1977
239.	1755	Francis Bacon, Lord Verulam	tc	[coll Sir Edward Littleton, Teddesley Hall]; NMM, Greenwich, SCU0005 Other versions: others recorded (two at NMM)	SD	*Esdaile* 1932 (2), 38 (repr); *Webb* 1954, 117, 192–7, 211
240.	1755	John Locke (used as the portrait for the statue at Christ Church, Oxford)	tc	[Teddesley Hall, Staffs]; Welbeck Abbey, Notts		*Esdaile* 1932 (2), 38 (repr); *Webb* 1954, 117, 169, 194–7, 220
241.	pre-1756	Sir Hans Sloane	tc	BM		*Dawson* 1999, 208–210 (repr)
242.	pre-1757	John Hampden	m	[to be sold by Ford at Raphael's Head, Haymarket, London]; untraced		*Public Advertiser*, 18 April 1757, 1; cf *Eustace* 1998, 36, 39
243.	1757	Sir Walter Raleigh Payment(s): £199	tc	[Teddesley Hall, Staffs]; NMM Greenwich, London SCU0043	SD	*Esdaile* 1932, 38–9 (repr); *Webb* 1954, 117, 192, 194–201
244.	pre-1758	Sir Edward Littleton and Lady Littleton	tc	[Teddesley Hall, Staffs]; untraced Other versions: reproduced in plaster		*Esdaile* 1932 (2); *Webb* 1954, 117, 192, 199–201, 219; *Allen* 1987, cat 22; *Balderston* 2000, 200, n86, 202, n125
245.	1760	Alexander Pope	tc	[Teddesley Hall, Staffs]; Fitzwilliam	SD	*Esdaile* 1932, 36–7 (repr); *Webb* 1954, 117, 203–5, 223
246.	1760	King George II (after the bust made from life in 1738, tc)	m	VAM A.10-1932 Other versions: Royal Coll, nd, RCIN 31623 Christ Church, Oxford, library	SD	*Whinney* 1971, 52–3 (repr); *Bilbey* 2002, 141
247.	c1760	Sir Anthony van Dyck Model(s): Althorp, Northants, SD 1743	m	Hagley Hall, Worcs		*Vertue* III, 132; *Webb* 1950, 315 (repr); *Webb* 1954, 111 (repr); *Eustace* 1982, 138–41 (repr)
248.	c1760	Sir Peter Paul Rubens Model(s): SD 1743, Rysbrack sale 20 April 1765, lot 44; Christie, 29 June 1961, lot 17 (bt Marcussen)	m	Hagley Hall, Worcs		*Vertue* III, 132; *Webb* 1954, 111 (repr); *Eustace* 1982, 138–9 (repr)
249.	1760	William Shakespeare Payment(s): £45 5s with pedestal Model(s): for Sir Edward Littleton, Teddesley Hall, Staffs; untraced	m	[Alscot Park, Warks]; Birmingham CMAG 1987 P2	SD	*Esdaile* 1932, 39–40; *Webb* 1954, 117, 198–205, 224 (repr); *Whinney* 1988, 452 n29

No.	Date	Subject		Location		References
250.	1761	Sir Thomas Littleton	tc	[coll Sir Edward Littleton]; untraced		*Webb* 1954, 205
251.	1757–1762	Benjamin Franklin		[Felixkirk, near Thirsk, N R Yorks]; Christie, 24 April 1986, lot 89, unsold; untraced		*McKay* 1986, 16–17
252.	1764	King Alfred Payment(s): £100 including pedestal	m	Stourhead, Wilts, saloon	SD	Hoare Private Accounts 1750–66, 12 March 1764; *Webb* 1954, 116; *JKB* 1980, 72, 77–79 (repr); *Eustace* 1982, 171–4 (repr)
253.	pre-1765	Antinous	m	[Rysbrack sale (2), 1765, lot 40]; untraced		*Webb* 1954, 210
254.	pre-1765	Apollo Model(s): sold 24 Jan 1765, lot 15	m	[Rysbrack sale (2), 1765, lot 39]; untraced		
255.	pre-1765	Cicero	m	[Rysbrack sale (2), 1765, lot 38]; untraced		*Webb* 1954, 213
256.	pre-1765	Dr King 'of Oxford'	m	[Rysbrack sale, 20 April 1765, lot 30]; untraced		*Webb* 1954, 219
257.	pre-1765	Seneca	m	[Rysbrack sale (2), 1765, lot 64]; untraced		*Webb* 1954, 224
258.	pre-1765	Sir Francis Bland	m	[Rysbrack sale (2), 1765, lot 29]; untraced		*Webb* 1954, 211
259.	nd	Charles, 4th Duke of Beaufort		Badminton, Glos, drawing room	S	
260.	nd	Dr Sharp		[Ditchley Park, Oxon, saloon]; untraced		*Gunnis* 1968, 335 (3rd Earl of Lichfield's Inventory, 1772)
261.	nd	Estet (?), the poet		[Frank Standish sale, 29 March 1843]; untraced		RG/JP, 7, 1225
262.	nd	Inigo Jones, Andrea Palladio, Sir Isaac Newton, John Locke, Alexander Pope, William Shakespeare, John Milton	pb	Birmingham MAG, nv P.24-30'59		*Silber* 1987, 82–5, catnos 247–53 (examples repr)
263.	nd	John Hadley	m	[Christie, 24 Feb 1809]; untraced		*Gunnis* 1968, 336
264.	nd	John Palmer		[Ecton Rectory, Northants]; Hazlitt, Gooden and Fox, 6 Dec 1988		*The Independent*, 7 Dec 1988
265.	nd	Nine unnamed busts	m	[Sir Gregory Page sale, 23 April 1783, lots 50–53, bt Lloyd]; untraced		*Gunnis* 1968, 335–336
266.	nd	Sir James (†1698) and Sir John (†1775) Rushout, busts incorporated into J F Moore's monument		Blockley, Glos	S	*Webb* 1954, 224
267.	nd	Thomas, 3rd Earl of Coventry, aged nine	tc	Badminton, Glos, drawing room	S	*Eustace* 1982, 147–8 (repr); *Balderston* 2000, 203, n143
Chimneypieces						
268.	Des 1726	Sacrifice to Diana, overmantel relief after the Antique Drawing(s): one, signed 'W Kent 1726', Witt coll, 3217, Courtauld Institute, London	s	Houghton Hall, Norfolk, marble parlour (dining room)		HMC, *Duke of Portland*, vol IV, 1897, 171; *Webb* 1954, 108, 128, 228 (repr); *Gunnis* 1968, 337; *Moore* 1996, 113–5
269.	1727	'carving' on 'my two large Chimneypieces' (design attributed to James Gibbs) Payment(s): £20		[Sir Thomas Hanmer's house, 52 Grosvenor St, London]; untraced		*Friedman* 1984, 305
270.	pre-1728	Three, including one with Xenophon offering a tenth of his estate to Diana (designed by James Gibbs) Drawing(s): Ashm I.63; II.9 16, 49; III.53; VAM E.3631-1913 Model(s): of Xenophon, Rysbrack's sale, 14 Feb 1767, lot 62; Stourhead, Wilts, clay		[Bartholomew Clarke and Hitch Young's house, Roehampton, Surrey, later called Elm Grove]; destroyed		*Gibbs* 1728, xxi, repr 92 (lacking bull, executioner and man with urn of tc model); *Eustace* 1982, 177; *Friedman* 1984, 123–4, 323–4 (design repr)
271.	1729	'Britannia receiving the Riches of the East', overmantel relief after Artus Quellin the Elder's pediment relief, Amsterdam town hall Payment(s): £100	m	[Old East India House, London]; Foreign and Commonwealth Office, London		*Vertue* III, 37; *Webb* 1954, 131 (repr); *Archer* 1965, 402–3 (repr); *Eustace* 1982, 10, 35–36 (repr); *Bilbey* 2002, 132–3
272.	c1729	Xenophon offering a tenth of his estate to Diana and two overmantel reliefs in part after the Antique (related reliefs, Houghton hall)	m	Clandon Park, Surrey, marble hall, north and south side	S	*Webb* 1954, 130–1, 227 (repr); *Eustace* 1982, 36, 41, 80, 174 (repr); *JKB* 1983, 216; *Whinney* 1988, 178–9 (repr)
273.	1733	For Frederick, Prince of Wales	m	untraced		*Webb* 1954, 156
274.	pre-1733	Xenophon offering a tenth of his estate to Diana, two overmantel reliefs in part after the Antique (related reliefs, Clandon Park) Model(s): Rysbrack sale (3), lot 31	m	Houghton Hall, Norfolk, marble parlour		*Webb* 1954, 128, 228 (repr); Moore 1996, 38, 139–40; *Moore* 2002, 342 (repr)
275.	1734	A Roman Marriage, overmantel relief after the Antique	m	Kensington Palace, London, cupola room, RCIN 1436	S	TNA WORK 4/2, 22 Jan 1724; Vertue III, 19; *Colvin* 1973–76, V, 198–201 (repr 67); *Whinney* 1988, 163–5 (repr)
276.	c1735	Sacrifice to Apollo, overmantel relief, after the Antique	m	Godmersham Park, Kent		*Webb* 1954, 128, 228; *Eustace* 1982, 35

No.	Date	Description	Material	Location		References
277.	1735–1737	Incorporating boys in terracotta Model(s): Boys in clay, 'the original design for the great saloon at Bedford House' Edward Stevens's sale, 7 February 1776, lots 57, 58 (BM, PDB, Sc.A.5.9)		[Bedford House, Bloomsbury Square, London, great saloon]; Sotheby, 10 July 1998; untraced		Bedford Estate Archives, 19.12.1735, 9 April, 1737; Edward Stevens's sale, 7 Feb 1776, lots 57–8 (models); BM, P&D, Sc. A.5.9; Sotheby, London, 10 July 1998, 188–93; *Bilbey* 2002, 134–5
278.	c1738	Two Payment(s): £266 15s		Longford Castle, Wilts		*Gunnis* 1968, 337; *Webb* 1954, 228
279.	c1744	One		Longford Castle, Wilts		*British Portraits*, 1956–7, I, 182–3; *Gunnis* 1968, 337
280.	1745–1746	'Children employed in Navigation and Husbandry', an Allegory of Charity, overmantel relief Drawing(s): E 415-1975 A 243 Model(s): acquired 1756 by Sir Edward Littleton, Teddesley Hall, Staffs; the wood surround VAM A.58-1953; Charity, statuette, clay, SD 1745, Indianapolis Museum of Art, Indiana, USA	m	Foundling Hospital, London, court room	S	*Vertue* III, 132; *Webb* 1954, 131–5 (repr); *Whinney* 1971, 42 (repr); *Eustace* 1982, 35; *Balderston* 2000, 184 n83; *Bilbey* 2002, 137–8
281.	1755	Sacrifice to Apollo and Sacrifice to Diana, two overmantel reliefs after the Antique	s	[Rysbrack sale (4), 1767, lots 31, 62]; Woburn Abbey, Beds, west hall		*Webb* 1954, 128–30
282.	1755	'Statuary marble plinths added to raise the chimney piece (under the picture of St. Peter a fishing') which were an alteration after the same as intirely finished'		[Bedford House, Bloomsbury Square, London]; untraced		Bedford Estate Archives, Woburn Abbey, MS 4D-A1-2-35-5
283.	1756	'A nymph laying on the ground and a boy running to her, being frightened by a sea monster', tablet for insertion in a chimneypiece Payment(s): £220		Woburn Abbey, Beds, blue (or state) drawing room		Woburn Building Accts, 1748–62, Apr-May 1756; *Webb* 1954, 130, 228
284.	c1756	Two overmantel reliefs after the Antique, and another small one	s	Woburn Abbey, Beds, blue drawing room, saloon and Queen's drawing room		*Webb* 1954, 228
285.	1756–1758	With relief tablet of *Venus and Cupid*, flanked by gryphons and foliate arabesques and two caryatids (designed by Robert Adam and Charles-Louis Clérisseau) Payment(s): £600 Drawing(s): Marquess of Linlithgow; VAM E.459-480-1946 (*Eustace* 1997, 750 repr) Model(s): for a herm, perhaps related, MCAG, clay; for the relief tablet, sold 20 April 1765, lot 48	m	Hopetoun House, West Lothian, red drawing room		*Webb* 1954, 135, 196, 228 (repr); *Eustace* 1997 (1), 743–52 (repr)
286.	c1760	Overmantel relief of An Allegory of Charity (after the Foundling Hospital overmantel relief), with a chimneypiece decorated with a ram's head and garlands Drawing(s): VAM E.461 to 465-1946 (1756)	m	[Teddesley Hall, Staffs]; destroyed		*Webb* 1954, 196, 204–5; *Physick* 1969, 101–3 (repr); *Whinney* 1971, 42 (repr)
287.	pre-1766	Sacrifice of a bull and a bearded priest pouring a libation, overmantel relief after the Antique	m	Cams Hill, Hants Other versions: without bearded priest, Houghton Hall, Norfolk and Stourhead, Wilts		*Mansuelli* 1958, no 149; *Eustace* 1982, 39, 41 (repr)
288.	nd	Judgment of Hercules, overmantel relief (replicated in bronze by Peter Vanina) Drawing(s): VAM D.234-1901 Model(s): Rysbrack's sale, 14 Feb 1767, lot 64 'after Ann. Carracci'	m	[Vanina sale, 5 April 1770, lot 77]; Carlton Towers, N R Yorks		*Friedman and Clifford* 1974, 32; *Physick* 1974, 1068 (repr)
Architectural Sculpture						
289.	c1730	Pediment relief of Neptune and Britannia attended by Peace and Plenty Drawing(s): one, by William Kent, sold Christie, London, 20 Sept 1970 Model(s): 'Two sketches for figures, on a pediment, of Neptune and Britannia', Rysbrack sale, 25 Jan 1766, lot 32; two ditto, of Peace and Plenty, lot 43	s	Houghton Hall, Norfolk, on façade over original entrance		*Webb* 1954, 127–8; *Moore* 1996, 38 (repr)
290.	pre-1731	Eight 'boys' on pediments over doors Model(s): Rysbrack sale, 25 Jan 1766, lots 13, 30–32, 43		Houghton Hall, Norfolk, stone hall, marble parlour door (putti representing Time and Eternity); common parlour and secondary stairs doors (four reclining putti with garlands); grand stairs door (crawling and reclining putti eating grapes)		*Webb* 1954, 113, 127–8; *Moore* 1996, 113–4; *Moore* 2002, 37, 38 (repr)

291.	1733	Lord Oxford's armorial shield and supporters (designed by James Gibbs)	s	[Court House, St Marylebone, London, over entrance door]; destroyed		*Friedman* 1984, 206, 306
292.	1746–1747	Duke of Montagu's arms		[The Magazine, Plymouth]; untraced		Ordnance Declared Accts, TNA, AOI 1876, 1600
293.	1754	Plinth for the monument to Lady Catherine Walpole (†1737) (statue by F della Valle)		Westminster Abbey, London, Chapel of Henry VII		*Webb* 1954, 48, 226; *Whinney* 1988, 259–60

Reliefs

294.	1723	James Gibbs, a profile 'with a wigg on'	m	untraced		*Vertue* III, 13, 56; *Friedman* 1984, 15 (repr); *Balderston* 2001, 5
295.	*c*1727	Inigo Jones and Ben Jonson, ovals	m	[Jones: Rysbrack's sale, 20 April 1765, lot 13]; Broughton Castle, Oxon, gallery	S	*Gunnis* 1968, 334; *Liversedge* 1990, 870–3 (repr)
296.	by 1727	'Young Lady Margaret Harley'	m	Private coll		*Vertue* III, 56; *Balderston* 2002, 27
297.	1726–1730	Four rectangular overdoor reliefs after the Antique Model(s): Trajans, Rysbrack sale, 14 Feb 1767, lot 49, Stourhead, Wilts; Sacrifice of a bull, Rysbrack sale, 14 Feb 1767, lot 50, Stourhead, Wilts	s	Houghton Hall, Norfolk, stone hall		HMC, *Duke of Portland*, Vol. IV, 171; *Webb* 1954, 113, 127–8 (repr); *Eustace* 1982, 37–38, 174–6, 178 (repr)
298.	pre-1735	King George I, two Model(s): medal, Rysbrack's sale, 24 Jan 1766, lot 13, clay	m	[Sale of property, 'A person of Note Abroad' *c*1735]; untraced		*Webb* 1954, 128, 228; *Gunnis* 1968, 334
299.	1737–1739	Pegasus (arms of the Inner Temple) Payment(s): £100	m	Inner Temple Treasury, City of London		*Webb* 1954, 131, 228; *Ward-Jackson* 2003, 396
300.	pre-1765	King George II	m	[Rysbrack's sale, 20 April 1765, lot 14]; untraced		*Webb* 1954, 216
301.	pre-1766	Mr Booth, 'player' and Mrs Booth	tc	[Rysbrack's sale, 24 Jan 1766, lot 12]; untraced		*Vertue* III, 56; *Webb* 1954, 212
302.	pre-1766	'Two medals of the late Rt. Hon. Sir Robert Walpole, Earl of Orford, and his lady'	tc	[Rysbrack's sale, 24 Jan 1766, lot 14]; untraced Other versions: plaster casts, Houghton Hall, Norfolk		*Webb* 1954, 129, 226; *Moore* 2002, 342
303.	pre-1767	Three oval reliefs after the Antique, Sacrifice to Hercules, Sacrifice to Apollo and Sacrifice to Diana Model(s): for Hercules relief, Rysbrack sale, 14 Feb 1767, lot 63; untraced	m	[coll the sculptor]; Royal Coll, Windsor Castle		*Bober & Rubinstein* 1986, 214–6

Miscellaneous

304.	1734	Models for a silver cistern in clay and wax (designed by George Vertue and others, cast by Charles Kandler)		Hermitage, Leningrad (cistern)		*Young* 1983, 286–7 (repr); *Cameron* 1996, 487–99
305.	1732–1734	Several chimneypieces, interior ornaments and perhaps a pedestal with angels' heads for the gardens		[Kew Palace, Surrey]; untraced		*Jones* 1981, 9–10 (pedestal repr)
306.	1735–1740	Genii of the Arts and Sciences, models for ornaments on a clock, executed in silver		Royal Coll, Kensington Palace, London		*Rococo* 1984, 288–9
307.	pre-1766	A cow		[Rysbrack sale, 24 Jan 1766, lot 47]; untraced		*Webb* 1954, 205
308.	nd	A sacrifice, model		[Rysbrack sale, 14 Feb 1767, lot 50]; untraced		
309.	nd	An hunting, after the Antique, model		[Rysbrack sale, 14 Feb 1767, lot 49]; untraced		
310.	nd	Boys playing with a goat, model		[Rysbrack sale, 14 Feb 1767, lot 47]; untraced		
311.	nd	Reclining figure in classical dress, model	tc	CMAG, Plymouth		*Eustace* 1982, 114–5 (repr)
312.	nd	River god, model		[Rysbrack sale, 14 Feb 1767, lot 48]; untraced		

SABIN, Thomas, of Ashby-de-la-Zouch –1702

He was the mason who built Sir John Moore's school at Appleby, Leics. In 1697 he received a part-payment of £362 for this work. Moore clearly did not trust Sabin and wrote asking him for a detailed breakdown of his costs for 'each parcell of Stone work' (*Bolton* 1934, 101), which Sabin duly sent. He married Mary Holt at Ashby-de-la-Zouch, Leics, on 17 July 1690 and he was buried there on 19 February 1703.

Literary References: *Bolton* 1934, 100; *Gunnis* 1968, 339

Archival References: GPC (inf. G Chinnery, Leicester City Museum)

Architectural Sculpture

1.	1697	Carved stonework, including cornices, pediments, Doric pilasters and a crest	s	[Sir John Moore's School, Appleby, Leics]; untraced		*Bolton* 1934, 101; *Gunnis* 1968, 339

SALE, A fl *c*1824

He is known only for one altar-tomb in Surrey.

Funerary Monuments

1.	?1824	Rev John Jeffreys		Barnes, Surrey, churchyard	S	*Gunnis* 1968, 339

SALISBURY, John, of London fl 1827

Although no works by him have come to light, his name is in Pigot's *Directory* as 'statuary and mason, Highgate' (*Pigot* 1827, 204). In the churchyard of West Malling, Kent, is the tombstone of Elizabeth, 'wife of John Salisbury, statuary in this town and formerly both of Exeter', who died in 1832, aged 40.

Literary References: *Gunnis* 1968, 339

SALMON, Mary 1650–1740

For information the reader is referred to *Pyke* 1973, 126–7 and *Pyke* 1981, 36–7

SALT, James fl c1738

His tablet to Richard Roberts is a small architectural work with a broken pediment and urn, and a coat of arms at the base.

Funerary Monuments

1.	?1738	Richard Roberts		Pelynt, Cornwall	S	*Gunnis* 1968, 339

SAMS, Thomas, of Piccadilly fl 1810–36

His yard was in Down Street. In 1810 he was the mason in charge of rebuilding Coventry House, Piccadilly. His tablets are classical in design.

Funerary Monuments

1.	1813	Gordon family member (with family arms, supporters and ducal coronet) Payment(s): £316 5s including packing and carriage		Untraced		Gordon Castle Muniments, NAS, GD 44/51/169/15 (6)
2.	?1821	Charles Pieschell		St John's Wood Chapel, Marylebone, London		*Gunnis* 1968, 339
3.	?1822	August Pieschell		St John's Wood Chapel, Marylebone, London		*Gunnis* 1968, 339
4.	?1831	Thomas Hunter		Holy Trinity, Brompton, London		*Gunnis* 1968, 339
5.	?1836	Frances Lincoln		Holy Trinity, Brompton, London		*Gunnis* 1968, 339

Chimneypieces

6.	1810	'Five veined marble' Payment(s): 60 gns	m	[Coventry House, Piccadilly, London]; untraced		Archives, Earl of Coventry, quoted in *Gunnis* 1968, 339

SAMSON, Giles, of Westbury fl c1754

Funerary Monuments

1.	†1754	William Church, table tomb		Tibberton, Glos, churchyard	S	Pevsner, *Glos: Vale & Forest of Dean*, 1976, 383

SANDERS, J J fl c1812–88?

He was the son of 'J Sanders, a mason', but since there were several craftsmen with this name, identification is problematic. There was, for example, a Joseph Sanders who joined the Royal Academy as 'a sculptor' in April 1775, but against whose name is an entry 'to be discharged' (RA student register). A James Sanders, son of Joseph Sanders, goldsmith of Maiden Lane, was apprenticed to Samuel Newton in 1754 and became free in 1762.

J J Sanders was the mason who carried out repairs to St John, Westminster, in 1812 (Ch W). He can probably be identified with the 'Sanders of Fitzroy Square, New Road', who produced a large number of tablets. These are often carved with the popular draped urn motif, though one has a woman mourning (**19**), another *Fame* writing on a pyramid (**26**), and a third an amphora with flowers (**27**). In 1846 Sanders carved a more elaborate tablet to the memory of John Lydekker (**24**). The *Illustrated London News* described this as 'a neat marble memorial. . .a tablet, surmounted by a bold pediment on Italian trusses; flanked by two seamen, one with a fractured arm, and the other leaning on a crutch. The tablet rests on a cornice, beneath which, in a panel, is sculptured a scene from the Southern Whale Fishery; the base being a shell and some cleverly-executed foliage'. Gunnis regarded the monument to Walter Strickland (**17**) as his best but summarised Sanders's work as 'dull and uninteresting' (*Gunnis* 1968, 339). The firm must have extended to at least a second generation, since the Barker monument, signed 'Sanders, Euston Road', dates from 1888 or after (**32**).

Literary References: *Gunnis* 1968, 339

Funerary Monuments

1.	?1812	Thomas Dampier	Eton College, Windsor, Berks, chapel	S	*Gunnis* 1968, 339
2.	†1813	Henry Whitfield	Rickmansworth, Herts	S	Pevsner, *Herts*, 1977, 279
3.	?1822	Thomas Gibson	Shalford, Surrey	S	*Gunnis* 1968, 339
4.	†1828	Elizabeth Cartwright	Haugham, Lincs	S	Pevsner, *Lincs*, 1989, 372
5.	?1830	Mary Cullum	Hawstead, Suffolk	S	*Gunnis* 1968, 339
6.	?1831	Christina Kidd	Hartfield, Sussex	S	*Gunnis* 1968, 339
7.	†1831	William Phelps	St George, Bloomsbury, London		
8.	†1833	Emma Faulkner	Whiteparish, Wilts	S	Pevsner, *Wilts*, 1975, 572
9.	?1833	Mariana Brouncker	Cranborne, Dorset	S	*Gunnis* 1968, 339
10.	†1836	Frances Strickland	Standlake, Oxon	S	Pevsner, *Oxon*, 1974, 777
11.	?1837	Evan Roberts	St Matthew, Brixton, London	S	*Gunnis* 1968, 339
12.	?1837	James Lockhart	St George, Roseau, Dominica	S	GPC
13.	?1837	Major Keighly	Idlicote, Warks	S	*Gunnis* 1968, 339
14.	†1837	Rev Romaine Hervey	Quarrington, Lincs	S	Pevsner, *Lincs*, 1989, 605
15.	†1838	John Pedley	Caddington, Beds	S	Pevsner, *Beds, Hunts & Peterborough*, 1968, 62
16.	?1839	Alexander Robinson	St George, Roseau, Dominica	S	GPC
17.	?1839	Walter Strickland	Standlake, Oxon		*Gunnis* 1968, 339
18.	?1841	James and Ann Corlett	St George, Roseau, Dominica	S	GPC
19.	†1841	Richard Estcourt Cresswell	Sherston, Wilts	S	Pevsner, *Wilts*, 1975, 470
20.	†1841	Thomas Jenkins Gee (†1834), Elizabeth Gee, and family members	Aldenham, Herts	S	
21.	†1843	Baskervyle Glegg	Backford, Cheshire	S	Pevsner, *Cheshire*, 1971, 70

22.	†1843	Lieutenant General O'Loghlin	Chalfont St Peter, Bucks	S	
23.	†1843	Peter Payne	Irchester, Northants	S	
24.	1846	John Lydekker (designed by J Tite)	Royal Exchange, London	S	*ILN*, 26 Sept 1846, 208 (repr); *Gunnis* 1968, 339
25.	1847	Two, unidentified	St Mary Magdalene, Offley, Herts	S	Pevsner, *Herts*, 1977, 265
26.	†1850	Hon Richard Boyle Bernard	St Peter, Bandon, Co Cork	S	*Potterton* 1975, 76
27.	†1851	John Willans Newell	Bosley, Cheshire	S	Pevsner, *Cheshire*, 1971, 109
28.	†1851	Mrs Peniston La Tour	Boothby Graffoe, Lincs	S	Pevsner, *Lincs*, 1989, 151
29.	†1851	Rev Peniston La Tour	Boothby Graffoe, Lincs	S	Pevsner, *Lincs*, 1989, 151
30.	†1854	Catherine Filmer	East Sutton, Kent	S	*Gunnis* 1968, 339
31.	†1871	Jane, wife of William Adams, wall-tablet	Holy Trinity, Clapham, London	S	
32.	†1884	Alleyne and Marianne (†1879) Barker	Rickmansworth, Herts	S	
33.	nd	Two tablets, unidentified subjects	Stradsett, Norfolk		NP/RG

SANDS, William, of Spalding –1751

An architect and mason, he signs a couple of tablets. He was master of the local freemasons' lodge, and a member of the prestigious Gentlemans' Society of Spalding. As an architect he designed Moulton chapel, near Spalding, and Monks Hall, Gosberton, which was executed by John Proudlove. Sands was buried in Spalding church, where a monument to his memory was erected by his pupil, **Edward Hutchinson, of Spalding**. This disappeared when the church was restored.

Literary References: *Gunnis* 1968, 339; *Colvin* 1995, 847–8

Funerary Monuments

1.	†1732	Mrs Lacy	Weston, Lincs	S	*Colvin* 1995, 848
2.	?1735	Elizabeth Cox	Crowland Abbey, Lincs	S	*Gunnis* 1968, 339

SANGIOVANNI, Benedetto –1853

Sangiovanni was born in Naples. According to a catalogue note of 1853 he was 'employed for some years' under Joachim Murat's generals in their struggle against southern Italian brigands, which 'gave him an opportunity of studying their character and modelling their figures with so much vigour' (Christie, 28 June 1853, in GPC). His models of brigands and rustic Neopolitan scenes were exhibited at the Royal Academy from 1828. In 1830 his address was 15 Warren Street, London.

By 1844 he was established at 23 Nassau Street, near the Middlesex Hospital. That year the *Art Union* described him as 'an Italian gentleman who has been compelled by circumstances to adopt as "a business" the occupation which he long followed as an accomplishment'. The journal praised his exhibits at the Society of Artists that year: 'We have more than once had occasion to direct attention to the studio of this artist in Nassaustreet . . . We rejoice to see that examples of his genius have been placed where they can be seen and appreciated'. Sangiovanni's works were executed or finished in plaster, which the journal considered an unfortunate choice for the British audience, who would associate plaster with reproduction: 'the distinction will not be at once perceived between a work moulded with the hands . . . and a mere plaster cast of a similar object. The difference in cost between the two is consequently so great as at first to startle an admirer' (*AU* 1844, 97) In the following year Sangiovanni exhibited his *Contadina of the Province of Salerno*, which the same journal described as 'perfect in costume and character and modelled with the utmost nicety of execution' (**21**).

He died in Brighton in 1853 and his will was proved on 20 July that year.

Literary References: *Gunnis* 1968, 339–40; *Johnson* 1975, 411; *Pyke* 1981, 37

Archival References: GPC

Will: PROB 11/2176

Miscellaneous

1.	1828	Brigands of Calabria	[Exhib RA, London, 1177]; untraced	*Graves* VII, 1905–6, 18
2.	1828	Horse's head	[Exhib RA, London, 1164]; untraced	*Graves* VII, 1905–6, 18
3.	1830	Group of brigands	[Exhib Soc of BA, London, 873]; untraced	*Johnson* 1975, 411
4.	1838	A brigand	[Exhib RA, London, 1345]; untraced	*Graves* VII, 1905–6, 19
5.	1838	A dog	[Exhib RA, London, 1327]; untraced	*Graves* VII, 1905–6, 19
6.	1838	A lion	[Exhib RA, London, 1331]; untraced	*Graves* VII, 1905–6, 19
7.	1838	Queen Victoria	[Sangiovanni studio sale, Christie, 28 June 1853]; untraced	GPC; *Pyke* 1981, 37 (repr 250A)
8.	1844	A Brazilian greyhound	[Exhib Soc of BA, London, 749]; untraced	*Johnson* 1975, 411
9.	1844	A spaniel	[Exhib Soc of BA, London, 748]; untraced	*Johnson* 1975, 411
10.	1844	An Italian setter	[Exhib Soc of BA, London, 750]; untraced	*Johnson* 1975, 411
11.	1844	The farewell – Greeks of Albania	[Exhib Soc of BA, London, 747]; untraced	*Johnson* 1975, 411
12.	1845	A bloodhound lying	[Exhib Soc of BA, London, 827]; untraced	*Johnson* 1975, 411
13.	1845	A bloodhound sitting	[Exhib Soc of BA, London, 826]; untraced	*Johnson* 1975, 411
14.	1845	A boar and dogs	[Exhib Soc of BA, London, 817]; untraced	*Graves* 1875, 474; *Johnson* 1975, 411
15.	1845	A dead stag and dogs	[Exhib RA, London, 1422]; untraced	*Graves* VII, 1905–6, 19
16.	1845	A greyhound	[Exhib Soc of BA, London, 825]; untraced	*Johnson* 1975, 411
17.	1845	A Newfoundland dog	[Exhib Soc of BA, London, 822]; untraced	*Graves* 1875, 474; *Johnson* 1975, 411
18.	1845	A wild boar	[Exhib BI, London, 516]; untraced	*Graves* 1875, 474
19.	1845	An Albanian Greek	[Exhib Soc of BA, London, 820]; untraced	*Johnson* 1975, 411

No.	Date	Subject	Location	Reference
20.	1845	An Italian bandit chief	[Exhib RA, London, 1426]; untraced	*Graves* VII, 1905–6, 19
21.	1845	Contadina of the province of Salerno	[Exhib BI, London, 518]; untraced	*AU* 1845, 78; *Gunnis* 1968, 340
22.	1845	Greyhound and hare	[Exhib Soc of BA, London, 824]; untraced	*Johnson* 1975, 411
23.	1845	Group of spaniels	[Exhib Soc of BA, London, 823]; untraced	*Johnson* 1975, 411
24.	1845	Neapolitan peasant girl	[Exhib Soc of BA, London, 821]; untraced	*Johnson* 1975, 411
25.	1845	Neapolitan shepherd and wolf	[Exhib Soc of BA, London, 819]; untraced	*Johnson* 1975, 411
26.	1845	'Peasant woman and child – costume of the Kingdom of Naples'	[Exhib Soc of BA, London, 818]; untraced	*Johnson* 1975, 411
27.	1846	A greyhound	[Exhib Soc of BA, London, 772]; untraced	*Johnson* 1975, 411
28.	1846	A Neapolitan fruit seller waiting for his companion to assist him in loading his ass with store	[Exhib Soc of BA, London, 769]; untraced	*Johnson* 1975, 411
29.	1846	A Newfoundland dog	[Exhib Soc of BA, London, 770]; untraced	*Graves* 1875, 474; *Johnson* 1975, 411
30.	1846	A red deer	[Exhib Soc of BA, London, 773]; untraced	*Johnson* 1975, 411
31.	1846	A Turk	[Exhib RA, London, 1380]; untraced	*Graves* VII, 1905–6, 19
32.	1846	A wounded brigand chief supported by his wife	[Exhib Soc of BA, London, 768]; untraced	*Johnson* 1975, 411
33.	1846	An Albanian Greek and dog	[Exhib RA, London, 1365]; untraced	*Graves* VII, 1905–6, 19
34.	1846	An Italian herd boy and goat	[Exhib BI, London, 487]; untraced	*Graves* 1875, 474
35.	1846	Dog gnawing a bone	[Exhib Soc of BA, London, 771]; untraced	*Johnson* 1975, 411
36.	1846	Wild boar and young	[Exhib BI, London, 484]; untraced	*Graves* 1875, 474
37.	1847	A Greek	[Exhib BI, London, 559]; untraced	*Graves* 1875, 474
38.	1847	A greyhound	[Exhib Soc of BA, London, 717]; untraced	*Johnson* 1975, 411
39.	by 1847	A lioness, two models	[Sculptor's studio]; untraced	*AU* 1847, 335
40.	1847	An Albanian Greek	[Exhib Soc of BA, London, 715]; untraced	*Johnson* 1975, 411
41.	1847	An Arab of Morocco	[Exhib RA, London, 1311]; untraced	*Graves* VII, 1905–6, 19
42.	1847	An Athenian Greek	[Exhib Soc of BA, London, 716]; untraced	*Johnson* 1975, 411
43.	1848	A Turk	[Exhib Soc of BA, London, 793]; untraced	*Johnson* 1975, 411
44.	1848	An Italian woman	[Exhib BI, London, 464]; untraced	*Graves* 1875, 474
45.	1848	Italian brigand	[Exhib Soc of BA, London, 793]; untraced	*Johnson* 1975, 411
46.	1848	Two small dogs	[Exhib Soc of BA, London, 794*]; untraced	*Johnson* 1975, 411
47.	nd	Admiral Lord Nelson	[Sangiovanni studio sale, Christie 28 June 1853]; untraced	GPC
48.	nd	Arthur, 1st Duke of Wellington	[Sangiovanni studio sale, Christie 28 June 1853]; untraced	GPC
49.	nd	Sir Robert Peel	[Sangiovanni studio sale, Christie, 28 June 1853]; untraced	GPC

SANSBY, Richard, of Hull fl 1803–29

He signs three large wall-tablets at North Cave. The monument to Captain Barnard (2), who fell at Waterloo, has a 'well-cut' trophy of arms (*Gunnis* 1968, 340).

Funerary Monuments

No.	Date	Subject	Location	Signed	Reference
1.	1803	Charles Lewyns Barnard	South Cave, E R Yorks	S	*Hull Advertiser*, 19 March 1803
2.	†1815	Captain Charles Leuyns Barnard	South Cave, E R Yorks	S	*Gunnis* 1968, 340; Pevsner, *Yorks: E R & York*, 1995, 700
3.	†1815	Henry B Barnard	South Cave, E R Yorks	S	*Gunnis* 1968, 340; Pevsner, *Yorks: E R & York*, 1995, 700
4.	†1831	Sarah Elizabeth Barnard	South Cave, E R Yorks	S	*Gunnis* 1968, 340; Pevsner, *Yorks: E R & York*, 1995, 700

Busts

No.	Date	Subject	Location	Signed	Reference
5.	1829	D J Alderson of Hull, model	Untraced		*Pictures of Old Hull*, 1945

SANTLER, Richard 1761–

Born on 28 September 1761, he attended the Royal Academy Schools in December 1780, winning a medal two years later (1). He exhibited wax portraits at the Royal Academy, giving his addresses as 13 Long Acre in 1785, 22 Rathbone Place in 1786, and 125 Strand in 1787.

Literary References: *Graves* VII, 1905–6, 24; *Hutchison* 1960–62, 145; *Gunnis* 1968, 340; *Pyke* 1973, 128

No.	Date	Subject	Medium	Location	Reference
1.	1782	Academy figure or a bas-relief		[RA, London, silver medal]; untraced	RA Premium list
Busts					
2.	1785	'Portrait of a gentleman', model		[Exhib RA, London, 366]; untraced	*Graves* VII, 1905–6, 24
3.	1878	'Portrait of a lady', model		[Exhib RA, London, 630]; untraced	*Graves* VII, 1905–6, 24
Miscellaneous					
4.	1785	Cupid and Calypso, model		[Exhib RA, London, 354]; untraced	*Graves* VII, 1905–6, 24
5.	1786	King George III, model	w	[Exhib RA, London, 301]; untraced	*Graves* VII, 1905–6, 24; *Gunnis* 1968, 340
6.	1786	Princess Royal, model	w	[Exhib RA, London, 303]; untraced	*Graves* VII, 1905–6, 24; *Gunnis* 1968, 340

7.	1787	Cupid's forge		[Exhib RA, London, 638]; untraced	*Graves* VII, 1905–6, 24
8.	1787	Hercules, model		[Exhib RA, London, 540]; untraced	*Graves* VII, 1905–6, 24
9.	1787	Portrait of a nobleman, deceased, model		[Exhib RA, London, 645]; untraced	*Graves* VII, 1905–6, 24

SARGEANT, J fl 1824

He was living at 4 Burlington Place, Kent Road, London, in 1824 when he won a medal from the Society of Arts (1).

Busts

1.	1824	Plaster copy of a bust		[Soc of A, large silver medal]; untraced	RSA *Transactions*, 1824, vol 42, xlvi

SARSFIELD, John fl 1770–77

He was educated at the Dublin Society Schools, and was subsequently a pupil of **Patrick Cunningham**. In 1777, when exhibiting in Dublin, he gave his address as 64 Dame Street.

Literary References: *Strickland* 2, 1913, 321

Reliefs

1.	1770	The judgment of Paris	m	[Exhib Society of Artists, William Street, Dublin]; untraced	*Strickland* 2, 1913, 321

Miscellaneous

2.	1777	Portrait of a lady	w	[Exhib Society of Artists, William Street, Dublin]; untraced	*Strickland* 2, 1913, 321

SARTI fl 1822–51

There are numerous references to works by plaster modellers of this name, who were presumably members of the same family. At **Joseph Nollekens**'s sale of 4–5 July 1823, a 'Sarti' bought a number of casts and terracottas after the antique, as well as figures by **Michael Rysbrack** and Nollekens. Sarti took a mould of the 'antique dog', then owned by Noel Jennings and now in the British Museum.

In 1826 a 'Sarti' received a payment of 10s for unspecified work for **John Flaxman RA** (Flaxman Papers BL Ad MS 39791, fol 135–42). Flaxman produced an undated pencil drawing inscribed 'Portrait of Sarti', which shows a young man with a naked muscular torso. J T Smith records that Sarti had a business in Greek Street in 1828, and that he offered for sale 52 varieties of Fiamingo's children.

An 'Angelo Sarti' of Dean Street, a one-time employee of **Sir Richard Westmacott**, was employed by the British Museum in 1835 as its first official *formatore* (*Jenkins* 1992, 34, 36). His first task was to mould a new set of casts from the Elgin marbles. Sarti's business was apparently taken over by **James Loft**, though another account suggests that **William Scoular** 'purchased the business of Sarti, a well-known Italian figure-maker' (*Redgrave* 1878, 384).

A 'P Sarti' of Dean Street signed a number of busts at Wimpole (3), and the same man (described as a 'modeller') received a payment from the Goldsmiths' Company in 1835 (1). He is also responsible for at least one work in marble (2).

The will of Antonio Sarti of Spur Street, Leicester Square, 'modellist' was proved on 12 February 1851. He appointed Samuel Wells of Kew and Selina Isabella Sarti as his executors. The latter had 'for many years' had 'the management of my business' at the same address. Sarti described himself as a 'subject of the Grand Dukedom of Florence' and left property in London and Tuscany. This included 'anatomical and other models, plates and prints and specimens of considerable value', which were to be sold or used in the meantime for profit. His estate was to be divided in thirds between his wife, Susan and Selina Isabella Sarti, and a child who was living in Florence under the care of Sarti's sister, Carolina (PROB 11/2128/156).

Literary References: *Jenkins* 1992, 34, 36 *Clifford* 1992, 62–3

Archival References: GPC

Statues

1.	1835	Apollo and Diana (by P Sarti)	p	[Goldsmiths' Hall, London, staircase hall]; untraced		Goldsmiths, CB bk 18, 621; Goldsmiths' Abstract E.1.2.a.48f; *Bells Weekly Messenger* 1835, 2

Busts

2.	1833	Lord Tenterden (by P Sarti)	m	Untraced (poss Sir Edward Maufe 1958)		RG/JP, 7, 1252
3.	nd	Dryden, Milton, Locke (by P Sarti)	p	Wimpole Hall, Cambs	S	*Baker* 1995 (3), 118

SARTINI, Anthony fl 1785–99

His tradecard of 1785, decorated with an urn and an angel holding a trumpet, carries the information on an oval medallion 'Sartini Figure maker/ No 34/New Compton Street/ St Giles' (BM Banks, 106.26). He is described in the *Universal British Directory*, 1790–1, 1, 278 as Anthony Sartini 'Paris Figure-Maker, 34 New Compton Street' (*Clifford* 1992, 62).

He appears to be the 'Mr Sartine' who was working for **Charles Horwell** as a modeller in 1787. After modelling a figure for Horwell, apparently for a Vulliamy clock, he was taken on by Joseph Lygo and William Duesbery as a figure-modeller for the Derby porcelain works. He was paid 'cash in full for moulding 2 figures £3 13 6' on 15 March 1790; for 'moulding a figure £1 2 6' in June 1790; and received 'cash in full for plaister figs £2 6s' on 24 September 1790. The relationship appears to have turned sour five years later when Lygo wrote to Duesbery: 'I have been with Mr Sartine about the plaister casts and he is sorry the price does not meet your approbation as it is the same he charges to all the artists but rather then they should come back he will take two guineas for them but not one farthing less' (*Bricknell* 1995, 31, 33, 40, 83).

One of the 'artists' for whom the modeller worked was **John Flaxman RA**, who recorded regular payments to 'Sartini' made between 1796 and 1799 for plaster moulding. The first was a payment for 'Moulding, casting etc £10 6s 6d' (Flaxman Papers BL Ad MS 39791, fols 135–42).

Literary References: *Clifford* 1992, 62–3 *Bricknell* 1995, *passim*

SAUNDERS, F fl 1842–72

Busts

1.	1842	Admiral Lord Nelson		Hereford Town Hall	SD	*Gunnis* 1968, 340
2.	1872	Head of the Apollo Belvedere	m	NGI		*le Harivel* 1988, 590

SAUNDERS, P, of Windsor fl c1828

Funerary Monuments

1.	?1828	William Cook, large wall-tablet		Horton, Middx	S	*Gunnis* 1968, 340

SAUNDERS, Richard –1735

The orphaned son of Jeremiah Saunders of Ampthill, Beds, he was apprenticed to **Jonathan Maine (or Mayne)** in 1675 and became free of the Joiners' Company in 1682. He lived in King Street, Cheapside. He did much work for the corporation of the City of London and also served as a captain in the City trained bands. In 1705 his name occurs in the minutes of the committee appointed to undertake repairs to the Guildhall (3).

Saunders' most famous works were the statues of the mythical giants *Gog* and *Magog*, carved in fir, which stood in the Guildhall until they were destroyed in the Second World War (2). They were ordered on 17 December 1709, and though it is generally supposed that the Stationers' Company presented them to the city, an entry in the City Cash Account for 1713 indicates that it was the corporation who paid Saunders for them. The entry reads as follows: 'To Richard Saunders Carver in full of his Bill for Making and Carving the Giants and other work in Guildhall and his time and Expenses in and about the Same by Order of the Committee for repairing and beautifying Guildhall dated 17 December 1709' (City Cash Accts 01/27 fol 239r). In 1711 he also received money for further carved work (5). In 1717 Saunders was unsuccessful in the competition to choose a sculptor for the statue of George I in the Royal Exchange (see **Edward Stanton**). Saunders's wife, Dorothy, was buried in St Laurence, Jewry on 17 December 1719 and Saunders himself was buried in the middle aisle on 2 January 1735. He left four children.

Literary References: *Gunnis* 1968, 340; *Douglas Stewart* 1978, 219

Archival References: Joiners, Freedoms, vol 1, fol 124r

Funerary Monuments

1.	1704	Sir Robert (†1703) and Lady Geffrye (†1676)		[St Dionis Backchurch, City of London]; Geffrye Museum, Shoreditch	Pevsner, *London: N*, 1998, 522

Statues

2.	c1709	Gog and Magog Payment(s): £65	wd	[Guildhall, City of London]; destroyed	City Cash Accts 01/27 fol 239r; *Gunnis* 1968, 340

Architectural Sculpture

3.	c1705	Scrolls, pediments, arms, dragons and other ornaments Payment(s): £72		[Guildhall, London, chapel front]; untraced	City Corp Records, MS.117/3, in *Gunnis* 1968, 340
4.	1710–1714	Unidentified carving work Payment(s): £78		[Lord Ashburnham's house in St James's Square, London]; untraced	Ashburnham Accts in *Gunnis* 1968, 340

Miscellaneous

5.	1711	'carving about the City eighteen-oared barge' Payment(s): £25		Guildhall, London	City Cash Accts 01/27, fol 154r; *Gunnis* 1968, 340

SAUNDERS, Samuel –1742

The son of John Saunders, he became free of the Masons' Company in 1708 by patrimony. He was presumably a brother of **Richard Saunders**, and like him worked for Lord Ashburnham, who employed him at Ashburnham House, Westminster, in 1708 (Ashburnham Archives, quoted by *Gunnis* 1968, 340). Saunders, who in 1717 took as an apprentice Thomas, son of Thomas Thompson of Waltham Abbey, Essex (TNA IR 1/6), was renters warden of the Masons' Company in 1721 and master in 1726. He was also an officer in the City trained bands. He was decribed as 'Col Saml Saunders' in the record of his death in the Court Book of the Company (Masons' Co, Court Book, 1722–51, 20 October 1742).

Literary References: *Gunnis* 1968, 340

Archival References: Masons' Co, Court Book, 1695–1722 fol 88r (1708), fols 192 r&v (1720), Court Book, 1722–51 (1726)

SAUNDERS, William fl 1743–54

When Leicester House, London, was restored for Frederick, Prince of Wales, Saunders was responsible for most of the masonry work, receiving £370 in 1743. The house must have been in a poor state of repair as the total cost of reconstruction came to £4,000, of which the Prince paid £500 and Lord Leicester the balance (Streatfield Archives). In the Westminster Poll-Book of 1748 Saunders's address is given as Windmill Street. In 1754 he was working as a mason on repairs to Coutts' Bank, Strand (bank archives).

He must have died before 1767, for in that year his widow and son William were noted as living in St Pancras and the son was apprenticed to John Hinchliff I (see **Hinchliffe** or **Hinchliff** family). William became free on 12 January 1775.

Literary References: *Gunnis* 1968, 340

Archival References: Masons' Co, *Freemen*, fol 75; GPC

SCHADOW, Rudolph (Rudolf) 1786–1822

Schadow was born in Rome on 9 June 1786, a son of the great German sculptor Johann Gottfried Schadow. He trained in his father's studio in Berlin, before departing to work in Rome with his brother, Wilhelm. In 1811 he took over the studio of his compatriot, Daniel Christian Rauch. He is recorded in the memoirs of G A Guattani as completing a *Filatrice* for 'un signore inglese' before 1816 (quoted in *JKB* 1972 (3), 324). The patron is not identified, but several copies of the work were produced, one of which was bought by the 6th Duke of Devonshire (3). Devonshire also commissioned two reliefs from the German, which take their subject from Apollodorus (5). In a surviving letter, which demonstrates something of Schadow's care about the reception of his works, the sculptor asked that they should be displayed so that the light fell upon them from the left. All three works are neoclassical and show the influence of **Bertel Thorvaldsen**.

Schadow appears to have been one of the sculptors that a grand tourist would expect to visit in Rome. Around 1818 he was commissioned to produce a monument for an English patron (1). Gilbert, 2nd Earl of Minto visited the workshop with the poet Samuel Rogers early in 1822 and recorded that Schadow was 'a Prussian artist of merit: some good things' (quoted by Iain Gordon Brown in *Clifford* 1995, 75). He died on 31 January 1822 in Rome.

Literary References: *JKB* 1972 (3), 324–6, 331; *Springer* 1977, 249–276; *Chalmers Johnson* 1983, 113–117; *Schmitz* 1986, 320–321; *Schmitz* 1991, 60–61; *Spitzer* 1993, 58–73; *Clifford* 1995, 75; *Grove* 1996, 28, 45–6 (Jutta von Simson)

Funerary Monuments						
1.	1819	Barbara, Countess of Shaftesbury (†1811)		Wimborne St Giles, Dorset	S	Pevsner, *Dorset*, 1972, 470
Statues						
2.	1818	A girl fastening her sandal		Drapers' Hall, City of London, stairwell		Pevsner, *London: City*, 1997, 384
3.	1819	Filatrice (spinning girl)	m	Chatsworth, Derbys	SD	*JKB* 1972 (3), 324, 325, 330, 331 (repr)
4.	nd	A group, in ormolu, honouring the Duke of Wellington, modelled by Schadow		[Stowe House, Bucks]; untraced		*Rumsey Foster* 1848, 1398
Reliefs						
5.	1821	Castor and Pollux carrying off the Leucippides; Castor and Pollux fighting Lynceus and Idas	m	Chatsworth, Derbys, sculpture gallery		*JKB* 1972 (3), 324–5, 326, 331 (repr)

SCHEEMAKERS, Henry 1700–48

The son of the sculptor, Peeter Scheemaekers the Elder (1652–1714) and Catharina, née van der Hulst, he was christened in Antwerp Cathedral on 4 November 1700. He and his elder brother, **Peter Scheemakers**, were both less than five feet in height.

Henry probably had some training in his father's workshop, but he followed his brother to Copenhagen, where he worked for three years under the Danish court sculptor, Johann Adam Sturmberg (1683–1741). He was in London by 1726 and on 29 October 1727 he married Catharina Hennekin at the Portuguese Embassy chapel. Their son, Peter (†1765) was a sculptor and architect, who does not appear to have practised in England. In his will Henry's brother, Peter, mentions a nephew, Thomas Henry Scheemakers and his two sisters, who may have been Henry's children.

In 1726 he acquired a dwelling and premises in St Margaret's Lane, Westminster, near the east end of the Abbey and adjacent to the workshops of **Henry Cheere**, with whom he was working in 1727. The Westminster rate books list 'Mr. Skymaker' in St Margaret's Lane in 1729, and by 1732 he had two sets of premises, one of them a 'shop'. He evidently had a good reputation, for in 1727 **John Nost II**, one of the most respected sculptors in London, apprenticed his son **John Nost III** to Scheemakers at a fee of £40.

The first known collaborative work by Scheemakers and Cheere, is a small, undistinguished wall tablet to members of the Twyman family, *c*1728, at Westbere, Kent, which takes the form of a swagged escutcheon (1). It is signed by both sculptors. The monument to Robert, 1st Duke of Ancaster, at Edenham, Lincs, erected in 1728 and signed '*H.Scheemakers et H. Cheere Inven et Fecit*' was a more ambitious commission (2). The authoritative life-size standing effigy has cropped hair, the garb of a Roman general and a pronounced *contrapposto* pose, which causes the left hip to jutt forward awkwardly. He stands in a niche between Corinthian columns and above is a charming winged head with depending floral swags beneath a triangular pediment supporting reclining cherubs. Cheere and Scheemakers are known to have collaborated also on at least one chimneypiece (7).

Scheemakers's monuments executed alone reflect little interest in the growing fashion for classical sculpture, so successfully exploited by his brother, Peter. The large monument to Sir Francis and Lady Page, is well designed and of a high technical quality, but the composition of tiered reclining effigies in contemporary dress is dated (5). Another work that ignored the new taste is the tablet to John Bradbury (4). It presents a resurrection scene in relief, within a richly curved baroque frame: a kneeling boyish figure is helped heavenwards by a group of circling *putti*.

Scheemakers apparently failed to prosper in England, for in 1733 he held a sale of his possessions prior to his departure for Paris. It included models and designs said to be by **Denis Plumier** and the revered European sculptors, Bernini and Duquesnoy, as well as reliefs, statues, busts, chimneypieces, a monument and a variety of rich polychrome marbles. In France he was involved in decorative programmes in the châteaux of Dampierre and St-Cloud, where he died in 1748.

IR

Literary References: *Daily Post*, no 4320, 20 July 1733; *Vertue* III, 61; *Baert c*1870, 74; *Register of the Catholic Chapels*, 1941, 37; *Weilbachs Kunstnerleksikon*, 136; *Webb* 1957 (3), 115–120; *Gunnis* 1968, 341; *Whinney* 1988, 191–3; *Roscoe* 1990, 26, 29–30; *Craske* 2000 (2), 96

Archival References: Baptismal Records, OLV Zuid, 4 November 1700 (Antwerp City Archives, PR 19)

Will: Peter Scheemakers PROB 11.1082, 17 v-r, 19 June 1771

Funerary Monuments					
1.	†1727	Hammond (†1727) and Anthony Twyman (†1722) (co-sculptor: Sir Henry Cheere)	Westbere, Kent	S	*Webb* (3), 1957, 119, 121 (repr); Pevsner, *Kent, NE and E*, 1983, 490; *Lord* 2002, 109
2.	1728	Robert, 1st Duke of Ancaster (†1723) (co-sculptor: Sir Henry Cheere)	Edenham, Lincs	S	*Webb* 1957 (3), 119, 121 (repr); *Lord* 1986, 96–98 (repr); *Lord* 2002, 107–109 (repr)
3.	†1729	Richard Graves	Mickleton, Glos	S	*Webb* (3) 1957, 119, 121 (repr); Pevsner, *Glos and the Cotswolds*, 1979, 315
4.	†1731	John Bradbury	Wicken Bonhunt, Essex	S	*Webb* (3), 1957, 118, 120 (repr); Pevsner *Essex*, 1965, 424; *Penny* 1977 (2), 215, n53
5.	1730–1732	Mr Justice Francis Page (†1741) and Lady Page (†1730)	Steeple Aston, Oxon	S	*Webb* (3) 1957, 117, 120 (repr); *Whinney* 1988, 191–3, 453, n6 (repr)

Busts					
6.	1732	Antoninus Pius Payment(s): 8 gns		[for Earl Fitzwalter]; untraced	Mildmay Accounts, 1732
Chimneypieces					
7.	1731	Of carved stone; charged with two marble slabs (co-sculptor: Henry Cheere) Payment(s): £33 10s		[Moulsham Hall, Essex, drawing room]; untraced	*Edwards* 1977, 42
8.	1733	'with a mask and carved egg and anchor' Payment(s): £28 12s	m	[Moulsham Hall, Essex, drawing room]; untraced	*Edwards* 1977, 51
Miscellaneous					
9.	1728	Unspecified work for the Duke of Kent Payment(s): £44		Untraced	Hoare's customer ledger, 1725–1728, vol I, fol 318

SCHEEMAKERS, Peter 1691–1781

Peter Scheemakers played a major role in promoting the classical style in earlier 18th-century England and ran one of the most successful workshops of his generation. He was the eldest son of the sculptor Peeter Scheemaekers the Elder (1652–1714) and was baptised in Sint Jacobskerk, Antwerp on 10 January 1691. He was apprenticed without indenture to his father and may have visited Rome briefly in 1710, before spending three years around 1718 in Copenhagen with the court sculptor, Johann Adam Sturmberg (1683–1741). Scheemakers came to London *c*1720 and joined the studio of **Denis Plumier**, where he worked with **Laurent Delvaux**. Plumier died in 1721, soon after receiving the prestigious contract for a monument to the Duke of Buckingham in Westminster Abbey (**1**). The commission was executed by Scheemakers and Delvaux and it gave them the opportunity to advertise their confidence with the classical idiom: the Duke's effigy was one of the first Roman warriors on an English monument with cropped hair instead of the customary full-bottomed wig, as well as classical armour. Scheemakers then worked briefly for **Francis Bird** at St Paul's Cathedral on the west pediment relief and one of the colossal statues, before going into partnership with Delvaux from premises in Millbank, Westminster. Over the next six years they worked on two large monuments for country churches, using effigies clad *all'antica* (**2, 5**), at least one pair of seductive nude statuettes (**110**) and several pairs of garden figures after the Antique, in which each sculptor took responsibility for one statue (**107, 108, 114**).

In 1728 the two sculptors sold their collection of models and prints and advertised their intention of travelling to Italy 'to form & improve their studies' (*Vertue* III, p. 36). In Rome they took lodgings in the Palazzo Zuccari, near the Piazza di Spagna, where Scheemakers remained until 1730. He attracted the attention of English collectors: in a letter to Samuel Hill in Venice, Thomas Fonnereau, who was in Rome, noted '[there is] a very clever fellow. . .his name is Schielmaker. . .I was thinking as you had a mind for the Meleager that perhaps you'd be willing to have some good statue copied. If so, I believe you could not employ anyone more able. . .[He] has copied the Hermaphrodite of Borghese about 2 ft long which he asks 120 [cru?, francs?] for. . .if you have a mind for any of these I'll buy 'em for you and gett'em cheaper if they'll take less' (Cheshire RO DET 4674/36). Vertue noted the sculptor's unusual application to his studies in Rome and the fine quality of his models after the Antique, which were displayed in the London workshop soon after his return (**118**). These have not survived.

Scheemakers returned to London without Delvaux, set up again in Millbank, and by 1732 he had completed four major monuments, including one to Dr Hugh Chamberlen in Westminster Abbey, a reclining figure with personifications of *Hygeia* and *Longevity* at the head and feet (**7**). Delvaux carved the statue of *Longevity*, perhaps during one of his brief visits to London at that time. In 1733 Scheemakers lost the competition to provide an equestrian statue of King William III for Bristol to **Michael Rysbrack**. Failure was turned to success, for Scheemakers was given £50 in compensation by the Bristol patrons and then succeeded in selling his idea to the citizens of Hull, who ordered their own equestrian statue, completed in 1734 (**123**).

In 1732 Dr Richard Mead, who became the sculptor's most important patron, gave him the first of nearly a dozen commissions (**13**). Through Mead's influence the sculptor was commissioned to provide life-sized statues of two hospital founders, Thomas Guy, cast in bronze (**124**), and King Edward VI, realised in 'Dutch metal' (**128**). The sculptor's naturalistic head of Dr William Harvey (**168**) was presented by Mead to the Royal College of Physicians.

In 1736 the sculptor moved to Old Palace Yard, Westminster, and then at Christmas 1741 to larger premises in Vine Street, Piccadilly. This final move, prompted by the expansion of his workshop, presumably took place after his marriage to Barbara la Fosse, of whom nothing is known, and the birth of his only child, **Thomas Scheemakers**. A policy for £1,500, taken out with the Sun Insurance Company in 1746, gives clues to the property's layout: the modelling room was next to the living space and behind was a yard and workshops on two levels.

The work that brought Scheemakers particular recognition was the memorial to Shakespeare in Poets' Corner, Westminster Abbey (**46**), designed by William Kent, who was responsible to a 'committee of taste', of which Mead was a member. Raised in war time, this tribute to a great Englishman aroused a patriotic response and brought Scheemakers wide acclaim. During the next decade he was in constant demand, whilst his rival, Rysbrack, suffered a diminution in popularity. In comparing the work of the two sculptors, Vertue was disparaging of Scheemakers's use of a high surface polish, an economical substitute for textural variety. He also hinted that sharp practice allowed the sculptor to undercut Rysbrack's prices.

Praise and success clearly turned Scheemakers's head. He was impudent to Lord Oxford and arrogant with the City fathers when the commission for pedimental sculpture at the Mansion House went to competition in 1744 (**218**). Asked to provide a second model, he refused to do so, declaring he had carved enough sculpture to prove his talent. **Sir Robert Taylor** won the contract.

During the 1740s Scheemakers turned out nearly 40 monuments, including several in Westminster Abbey to heroes of the War of the Austrian Succession. These were formulaic compositions focussing on a portrait bust or pictorial relief above an inscription panel. In some of his civilian monuments he found room for invention:

Marwood William Turner's standing effigy at Kirkleatham (**50**), was a deliberate reworking of the Shakespeare memorial to honour a scholar, and the monument to Marmaduke Coghill, an eminent judge at Drumcondra, Co Dublin (**51**), made use of a seated effigy, an early example of a convention for representing advocates, that gained currency later in the century.

Between 1736 and 1742 the sculptor worked on garden sculpture at Stowe and then at Rousham, both schemes supervised by Kent. At Stowe he was responsible for a large rectangular high-relief depicting *Britannia receiving gifts from the four quarters of the world*, carved for the Palladian bridge (**220**). This was unsuccessful in the restricted site and was later re-used and adapted for the pediment of the Temple of Concord and Victory. He also provided busts and statues as ornaments for buildings in the Elysian Fields (**125, 128, 165**) and portrait heads of Lord Cobham and his political allies for the Temple of Friendship (**162, 170, 172**). At Rousham, the sculptor's knowledge of Roman sculpture put him in a strong position to supply terms and figures after the Antique for the upper lawn (**130–131**).

His first known set of library busts was for Richard Mead, who ordered heads of Shakespeare, Milton and Pope for his home in Great Ormond Street, London around 1734 (**163**). Two sets of heads of English poets for Frederick, Prince of Wales followed soon after, one of which was presented by the prince to Alexander Pope (**165**). The first commission for a university library, at Trinity College, Dublin, was for 14 marble busts of English and classical literary heroes (**178**); the size of the order was overwhelming, even for Scheemakers's large studio, and Horace Walpole suggests that six were supplied by **Louis François Roubiliac**, working in sub-contract. Near the end of his career there was another university commission, for Trinity College, Cambridge, where he carved four uninspired portraits of contemporary alumni (**185, 186, 188, 189**). Many of his busts and the heads for several statues were reproduced in plaster using the life-sized models to make moulds. This was a lucrative exercise which he apparently initiated in 1747, when he announced his intention of marketing sets of five plaster casts from his models made in Rome, to be sold at five guineas per set. His last surviving sale catalogue (6–7 June 1771) included 13 moulds and casts of statuettes from the antique as well as casts from a number of busts of contemporaries.

In 1751 the sculptor won his most lucrative contract, for the massive Shelburne monument at High Wycombe (**84**), a doubly satisfying prize since it was won in competition with Roubiliac, who was now emerging as a serious rival. It followed the sculptor's well-tried formula (albeit on a grand scale) of an architectural frame enclosing effigies in classical dress.

The sculptor's health deteriorated in the mid-1750s and he auctioned much of his property in 1755, 1756 and 1757, intending to reduce his practice and move to rural Isleworth in Middlesex. By 1759 however he had rallied and he then went into a profitable partnership with the architect, James Stuart, whose knowledge of the Antique now eclipsed his own.

Stuart's ambitious design for the monument to Admiral Watson in Westminster Abbey combined allegorical figures of captives with palm trees and a standing toga-clad effigy (**94**); more dignified is the monument to the Earl of Hardwicke at Wimpole (**96**), which has a massy sarcophagus flanked by Greek-inspired Virtues. Scheemakers also worked under Stuart's direction at Shugborough, where he carved a delicate relief for the Shepherd's Monument (**222**) and ornaments for the Triumphal Arch (**219**). A few commissions continued to be executed independent of Stuart, of which the most notable is a group of three statues of heroes of the United East India Company in Roman armour (**145**).

All work went out of the workshop in his name until 1771, when he left England, and Thomas Scheemakers continued to show models at exhibitions under his father's name until 1780. Scheemakers returned to Antwerp with savings estimated by Farington at £3,000–£4,000. Investments from property enabled him to live in the affluent quarter by St Jacobskerk, where he died on 12 September 1781. He was buried in St Jacobskerk.

Scheemakers's impressive output meant that he must have had a team of 20–30 assistants and apprentices, though most of their names at this period are unknown. During his early years in partnership with Delvaux, **Prince Hoare, Charles Stanley** and perhaps **Henry Cheere**, were workshop members and much later, in 1747, he broke a lifetime's habit by formally indenting an apprentice, **Charles Manning. Joseph Nollekens RA** joined the team in 1747 and stayed until 1762, working on the statue of Lord Clive shortly before he left for Italy. Thomas Scheemakers will have started his training around 1750 and was probably in control of the workshop by the later 1760s. Peter's will, drawn up on 19 June 1771, mentions Christopher Ffinny, 'my Mason' and 'Mr **Vandermeulen** Statuary', both of whom received ten guineas, the only beneficiaries other than family members and a servant.

Scheemakers became particularly interested in the classical style in the wake of his visit to Rome and, on his return, played a major role in promoting it in England. He was, however, often obliged to temper the austerity to his chosen to suit the tastes of his patrons and, ironically, it was a naturalistic figure, the Shakespeare for Westminster Abbey, which brought him fame. By the early 1750s, when Roubiliac's revolutionary compositions began to attract fashionable interest, most of Scheemakers's commissions were coming from conservative clients, but while there was a taste for the classical ideal in sculpture, his reputation remained solid. He has been out of favour since the late 19th century and is still compared unfavourably with his principal rival, Rysbrack, who worked in a similar style and sometimes provided a more distinguished product, but generally charged higher prices. Scheemakers deserves credit as an astute workshop master in tune with contemporary needs, prepared to shave his profit margins and adapt his classicism to suit a broadening clientele. Unlike his two principal rivals, he was in full employment throughout his long career.

IR

Literary References: *Vertue* I, 101, III, *passim*; *Farington* 7, 2494; *Anecdotes*, 1888, 376; *Smith* 2, 1828, *passim*; *Farington* III, 44; *Roscoe*, 1987, 1–10; *Whinney* 1988, 157–9, 182–90, 233–48; *Roscoe* 1990; *Roscoe* 1999, 163–304, repr 32–96; *ODNB* (Roscoe); *Sullivan* 2006, 388–94 (repr)

Archival References: WCA, ratebooks, St Margaret, Westminster, 1723–8 (E.344-E.348), 1731 (E.352), 1736 (E.362); ratebooks, St James, Piccadilly, 1767–73 (Watch Rates, E. 1721, D. 596-600); Rome, Vicariato Archive, *Stato d'Anime*, parish of S Andrea delle Fratte 1729, 1730, fols 53, 54; Sun Insurance, 1746, 1756, 1761

Will: PROB 11/1082 178 v-r

Miscellaneous Drawings: sketchbook of designs made in Rome, 1728–30, Huntington libr, San Marino, California, USA, 75.14.1975 (*Roscoe* 1990, Appendix 1); HMI, Leeds, 17/1991 (*Leeds* 1999, 57, repr); Soane, research lib, vol 37; VAM, P&D, D.1039-1887, D.1044-1887, D.1046-1887, D.1050-1887; 8947; 8408–2

Auction Catalogues: Scheemakers and Delvaux 1728; Scheemakers 1755; Scheemakers 1756; Scheemakers 1757; Scheemakers 1771(1); Scheemakers 1771 (2)

Portraits of the Sculptor: William Hoare, profile drawing, *c*1738, etching, B.M., PDB, 1931–4; A B de Quertenmont, canvas with a statuette of Shakespeare in the background, Antwerp, 1776, NPG London 2675

Funerary Monuments

1.	1721–1722	John, 1st Duke of Buckingham (†1721) (designed by Denis Plumier) (co-sculptor: Laurent Delvaux) Payment(s): £500 Drawing(s): by Plumier, Soane AL31.E(46) Model(s): sold 16 April 1728, lots 11, 31, 69, 52, 72; 6 June 1771, lot 64	Westminster Abbey, London, Henry VII's Chapel	S	*Dart* 1, 1723, 162–3 (repr); *Vertue* I, 101; *Avery* 1980, 158–9; *Roscoe* 1999, 178–80 (repr 32, 33)
2.	1724–1725	Lewis, 1st Earl of Rockingham (†1724) and his wife Katharine (co-sculptor: Laurent Delvaux) Payment(s): £400 Drawing(s): VAM 8408-1	Rockingham, Northants	S	*Lord* 1986, 155–58 (repr 169); *Roscoe* 1999, 180–1 (repr 34, 35)
3.	pre-1728	Figure for a monument	[Delvaux/Scheemakers sale, 16 April 1728, lot 18]; untraced		*Roscoe* 1999, 293
4.	pre-1728	Model of a monument	[Delvaux/Scheemakers sale, 16 April 1728, lot 8]; untraced		*Roscoe* 1999, 293
5.	1727–1728	Sir Samuel Ongley (†1726) (co-sculptor: Laurent Delvaux) Drawing(s): VAM 8949; Musées Royaux des Beaux-Arts, Brussels	Old Warden, Beds	S	*Physick* 1969, 112–3 (repr); *Roscoe* 1999, 181–2 (repr 36–38)
6.	pre-1728	Sir Thomas Grantham (†1718) (co-sculptor: Laurent Delvaux) Payment(s): £100 earmarked in Grantham's will	St Eadburg, Bicester, Oxon	S	*Roscoe* 1999, 182–3
7.	1728–1731	Dr Hugh Chamberlen (†1728) Model(s): VAM A.6-1927	Westminster Abbey, London, north choir aisle	S	*Roscoe* 1999, 184–6 (repr 40, 42); *Bilbey* 2002, 146–7 (repr)
8.	*c*1731	John Dryden (bust only)	Westminster Abbey, London, south transept	S	*Friedman* 1974, 98–100, (repr 92); *Roscoe* 1999, 187
9.	†1731	Judge Francis Bernard Model(s): VAM A.1-1989	Ballymoden, Co Cork	S	*Roscoe* 1999, 188–9; *Bilbey* 2002, 146–7
10.	1731	Mountague Garrard Drake (†1728) Payment(s): £525 Drawing(s): Bucks RO, D/DR/10/11	St Mary, Amersham, Bucks	S	*Roscoe* 1999, 186–7 (repr 43–4)
11.	1731–1732	Dr John Woodward (†1728) Drawing(s): VAM D.1055-1877	Westminster Abbey, London, nave		*Roscoe* 1999, 189
12.	1728–1732	Sir Michael Warton (†1725) Payment(s): 300 gns	Beverley Minster, E R Yorks	S	*Neave and Woodward* 1979, 1231–35; *Roscoe* 1999, 183 (repr 39)
13.	1732	Topham Foot (†1712)	St John the Baptist, Windsor, Berks	S	*Roscoe* 1999, 188
14.	†1732	William Douglas	St Laurence, Reading, Berks	S	*Roscoe* 1999, 190
15.	†1733	Samuel Mead	[Temple Church, London, wall in rounds]; destroyed		*Esdaile* 1933, 38–9 (repr XVIII); *Roscoe* 1999, 190–1
16.	†1733	Sir John Potenger	Broad Blunsdon, Wilts	S	*Roscoe* 1999, 191–2
17.	1734	Thomas Graham (†1733)	St Mary, Harrow-on-the-Hill, Middx	S	*Roscoe* 1999, 191
18.	1735	Francis Meyrick (†1734)	Westminster Abbey, London, cloisters		*Roscoe* 1999, 192
19.	†1736	James Belchier	All Saints, Kingston-upon-Thames, Surrey	S	*Roscoe* 1999, 194
20.	1736	John Meller of Erddig (†1733) Drawing(s): Erddig MSS, Clwyd R O, D/E/1542/74 (By H Cheere?)	Marchwiel, Denbighs		*Roscoe* 1999, 193
21.	pre-1736	John, Lord Somers (†1716), design only (monument attrib Sir Robert Taylor)	VAM D1060-1887		*Physick* 1969, 110–1 (repr); *Roscoe* 1999, 250
22.	†1736	Prebendary John Grant	Exeter Cathedral, Devon	S	*Roscoe* 1999, 194–5
23.	†1737	Canon Charles Fleetwood	Ely Cathedral, Cambs	S	*Roscoe* 1999, 196
24.	†1737	Matthew Howard	[St Mary-le-Bow, London]; destroyed		*Roscoe* 1999, 196–7
25.	†1737	Nathaniel Piggott	St Mary, Twickenham, Middx	S	*Roscoe* 1999, 197
26.	†1737	Sir George Beaumont Bt	Stoughton, Leics	S	*Roscoe* 1999, 195–6
27.	1735–1737	Sir Henry Belasyse (†1717)	Westminster Abbey, London, St Paul's Chapel	S	*Roscoe* 1999, 192–3
28.	†1737	Susanna, Lady Newton	Heydour, Lincs	S	*Lord* 1986, 204–5; *Roscoe* 1999, 195
29.	1737	Thomas Jordan (†1736)	[Westminster Abbey, London, cloisters]; untraced		*Roscoe* 1999, 193–4
30.	†1738	Samuel Palmer	All Saints, Wandsworth, Surrey	S	*Roscoe* 1999, 199
31.	†1739	John Rudge	Wheatfield, Oxon	S	*Roscoe* 1999, 201–2
32.	†1739	Mary Hanger	Bray, Berks	S	*Roscoe* 1999, 201
33.	1739	Richard Brodrepp (†1737) Drawing(s): VAM D.1040-1887	Mapperton House, Dorset, chapel	S	*Roscoe* 1999, 197–8 (repr 46)
34.	1739	Sarah Fountaine	Narborough, Norfolk		*Roscoe* 1999, 198
35.	1739	Sir Thomas (†1737) and Lady Reeve	St John the Baptist, Windsor, Berks	S	*Roscoe* 1999, 198–9
36.	†1739	William Eyre Archer Drawing(s): VAM D.1045-1887	Theydon Garnon, Essex		*Roscoe* 1999, 200
37.	†1740	John Bullock	Faulkbourne, Essex	S	*Roscoe* 1999, 204
38.	?*c*1740	Thomas Brightwell	Padworth, Berks	S	*Roscoe* 1999, 201
39.	†1740	Ursula Fortrye	Northfleet, Kent	S	*Roscoe* 1999, 204–5

40.	†1740	Vice-Admiral Salmon Morrice	Betteshanger, Kent	S	*Roscoe* 1999, 205 (repr 53)
41.	†1741	Anne Colleton Drawing(s): VAM D.1053-1887	[All Hallows, Barking, Essex]; destroyed		*Physick* 1969, 114–5 (repr 79, 80); *Roscoe* 1999, 205–6
42.	†1741	Charles Savile	Methley, W R Yorks		*Roscoe* 1999, 210–11
43.	†1741	George Duncombe	Downton, Wilts	S	*Roscoe* 1999, 209
44.	†1741	Lady Susanna Hare	Stow Bardolph, Norfolk	S	*Roscoe* 1999, 209–210 (repr 68)
45.	†1741	Thomas Pindar Drawing(s): *Pennant* 1825, ii (Westminster public lib)	Burgh-on-Bain, Lincs	S	*Roscoe* 1999, 213 (repr 75)
46.	1740–1741	William Shakespeare (designed by Willam Kent)	Westminster Abbey, London, south transept	SD	*Roscoe* 1994, 72–82 (repr)
47.	†1742	Abraham Sharp	Bradford Cathedral, W R Yorks	S	*Roscoe* 1999, 212
48.	†1742	Christopher Tilson	Hampton Poyle, Oxon	S	*Roscoe* 1999, 212–3
49.	†1742	Jane Pusey	Pusey, Berks	S	*Roscoe* 1999, 216–7 (repr 67)
50.	1741–1742	Marwood William Turner (†1739) (designed by James Gibbs) Drawing(s): Soane Vol. 37/21; VAM D.1041-1887; Cleveland Co Archives PR/KRL (2) 4/5	Kirkleatham, N R Yorks	S	*Friedman* 1980, 61–5; *Roscoe* 1999, 206–7 (reprs 49, 50)
51.	1743	Dr Marmaduke Coghill (†1739)	Drumcondra, Dublin	S	*Loeber* 1970, 22–23 (repr); *Roscoe* 1999, 211–2
52.	1741–1743	Lieutenant-General Percy Kirke (†1741)	Westminster Abbey, London, north transept	S	*Whinney* 1988, 234–5 (repr); *Roscoe* 1999, 207–8
53.	post-1743	Sir Christopher Powell (†1742) Drawing(s): Soane Vol 37/9	Boughton Monchelsea, Kent	S	*Roscoe* 1999, 208–9
54.	†1744	Francis Sherwood	[All Hallows, Barking, Essex]; destroyed		*S of L*, XV, II, 83 (reprs 95, 96); *Roscoe* 1999, 219
55.	†1745	Anne Cox Drawing(s): VAM E.961-1965	Kilkenny Cathedral		*Potterton* 1975, 76–7; *Roscoe* 1999, 220
56.	†1745	David Petty	St Mary, Wanstead, Essex	S	*Roscoe* 1999, 219
57.	1743–1745	Lord Aubrey Beauclerk (†1740) Drawing(s): VAM D.1042-1887; VAM D.1058-1887	Westminster Abbey, London, north transept		*Physick* 1969, 116–7 (repr); *Roscoe* 1999, 213–4 (reprs 53, 54)
58.	†1745	William Plaxton	[Temple Church, London, south wall of the rounds]; destroyed	S	*Esdaile* 1933 (2), 85–6; *Roscoe* 1999, 222
59.	1745–1746	Charles Wathen (†1721)	[All Hallows, Barking, Essex]; destroyed		*S of L*, XV, 83–84 (reprs 97, 98); *Roscoe* 1999, 218
60.	†1746	Dorothy Snell Drawing(s): VAM D.1059-1887	St Mary de Crypt, Gloucester, Glos	S	*Roscoe* 1999, 223–4 (repr 72)
61.	1743–1746	General George Monck, Ist Duke of Albemarle (†1670) (designed by William Kent) Drawing(s): Soane, Vol 37/16; VAM D.1050-1887	Westminster Abbey, London, Henry VII's Chapel	S	*Roscoe* 1999, 214–5 (reprs 56–58)
62.	1744–1746	Rear-Admiral Sir John Balchen (†1744) Drawing(s): VAM D.1054-1887	Westminster Abbey, London, north transept	S	*Roscoe* 1999, 217–8
63.	†1746	Samuel Rolle	Chittlehampton, Devon	S	*Roscoe* 1999, 223
64.	1746	Sir Michael Newton (†1743)	Heydour, Lincs	S	*Lord* 1986, 206–7 (repr 99); *Roscoe* 1999, 219–20 (repr 41)
65.	1743–1747	Admiral Sir Charles Wager (†1743) Drawing(s): Soane, vol. 37/19	Westminster Abbey, London, north transept	S	*Kingzett*, 1980–2, 29; *Roscoe* 1999, 215–6 (reprs 59, 60)
66.	†1747	Ann Haydon	St Lawrence, Reading, Berks	S	*Roscoe* 1999, 224–5
67.	1746–1747	Captain William Horneck (†1746) Drawing(s): VAM D.1051-1887; Soane, vol 37/18	Westminster Abbey, London, north west tower		*Roscoe* 1999, 221–2 (reprs 61, 62)
68.	1747	Thomas Lewis (†1746) Drawing(s): VAM D.1048-1887	Soberton, Hants	S	*Roscoe* 1999, 222–3
69.	1748	Francis Dickins (†1747) Drawing(s): VAM D.1057-1887; VAM D.1056-1887	Cowlinge, Suffolk	S	*Roscoe* 1999, 224 (reprs 69, 70)
70.	†1748	Harwood Awbrey	St Giles, Reading, Berks	S	*Roscoe* 1999, 225–6
71.	†1748	Mary Gardiner Drawing(s): VAM D.1049-1887	St George Tombland, Norwich, Norfolk		*Roscoe* 1999, 226
72.	†1749	Ann Barker Bell	St Mary, Aylesbury, Bucks		Pevsner, *Bucks*, 1994, 153
73.	1749	Captain the Hon William Berkeley	Bruton, Somerset	S	*Roscoe* 1999, 225
74.	†1749	Elizabeth Carcassonnett	All Saints, Huntingdon	S	*Roscoe* 1999, 227
75.	1750	Admiral Sir John Norris (†1749)	Benenden, Kent	SD	*Roscoe* 1999, 226–7
76.	c1750	Ive Whitbread	Cardington, Beds	S	*Roscoe* 1999, 229–30
77.	†1751	John Pigott	Grendon Underwood, Bucks	S	*Roscoe* 1999, 231
78.	1751	Magdalen Walsh (†1747)	Westminster Abbey, London, east walk of cloisters		*Roscoe* 1999, 229
79.	1752	Brook Bridges (†1715)	Goodnestone, Kent	S	*Roscoe* 1999, 230–1
80.	†1753	George Strode Model(s): HMI 13/86, clay	Beaminster, Dorset		*Roscoe* 1999, 231–2 (repr 77–78)
81.	†1753	Robert Tothill	Urchfont, Wilts	S	*Roscoe* 1999, 235
82.	†1753	Roger Jenyns	Clewer, Berks	S	*Roscoe* 1999, 235
83.	1754	Frances Shirley (†1746)	King's Chapel, Boston, USA		*Roscoe* 1999, 232–3
84.	1751–1754	Henry, Earl of Shelburne (†1751) Drawing(s): unexecuted design by Sir Robert Taylor Bt, TI, Arch Tay 2, f86 Model(s): Royal Museum of Edinburgh, clay	High Wycombe, Bucks		*Baker* 2000, 62–69, 172n (repr)
85.	1754–1755	Dr Richard Mead (†1754)	Westminster Abbey, London, nave	S	*Roscoe* 1999, 233–4

No.	Date	Subject		Location		References
86.	*c*1756	Lady Elizabeth Hastings (†1739) Payment(s): £400 Drawing(s): Soane, vol. 37/11, 13 (tw)		Ledsham, W R Yorks	S	*Scott* 1983, 114–8 (repr); *Roscoe* 1999, 235–7
87.	1756	Lady Margaret Feversham (†1755)		Downton, Wilts	S	*Roscoe* 1999, 237 (repr 66)
88.	†1757	Lady Frances Feversham		Downton, Wilts		*Roscoe* 1999, 239
89.	1757–1758	Robert, Baron Raymond (†1756) Drawing(s): Filmer Papers, Centre for Kentish Studies, U120/F19 Model(s): Charity, VAM A2-1985		Abbots Langley, Herts	S	*Roscoe* 1999, 237–9; *Bilbey* 2002, 148
90.	†1759	George Petre		Studley, Warks	S	*Roscoe* 1999, 240
91.	*c*1761	James Hamilton Drawing(s): VAM D.1050-1887; VAM H63		Bangor Abbey, Co Down	S	*Roscoe* 1999, 243 (reprs 71, 73)
92.	1759–1762	Brigadier-General George Augustus, Viscount Howe (†1758) (designed by James Stuart)		Westminster Abbey, London, nave, south aisle	S	*Roscoe* 1987, 178 (repr); *Roscoe* 1999, 239–40; *Sullivan* 2006, 388 (repr)
93.	1761–1762	Hon Catharine Yorke (†1759) (designed by James Stuart)		Wimpole, Cambs	SD	*Roscoe* 1999, 242–3 (repr 80)
94.	1760–1763	Admiral Charles Watson (†1757) (designed by James Stuart) Payment(s): £1,000 Model(s): Exhib Free Soc, 1765, 167–9; untraced		Westminster Abbey, London, north transept	S	*Roscoe* 1987, 179 (repr); *Groseclose* 1990, 492–4 (repr); *Roscoe* 1999, 241–2; *Sullivan* 2006, 388–9 (repr)
95.	*c*1766	Henrietta, Duchess of Gordon (†1760) Payment(s): £140 Drawing(s): VAM E.165-1942		Elgin Cathedral, Morayshire, Gordon enclosure, south wall	S	*Roscoe* 1999, 245
96.	1764–1766	Lord Chancellor Philip, 1st Earl of Hardwicke (†1764) (designed by James Stuart) Drawing(s): Staffs RO D.615.P (S)/1/6		Wimpole, Cambs	S	*Roscoe* 1987, 181–2 (repr); *Roscoe* 1999, 243–5 (reprs 79, 81); Sullivan 2006, 390–3 (repr)
97.	pre-1766	Model of a monument		[Exhib Free Soc, 1766, 150]; untraced		*Roscoe* 1999, 293
98.	post-1767	Sir Jemmett Raymond (†1754)		Kintbury, Berks		*Roscoe* 1999, 245–6
99.	1770	Hon Charles Yorke (†1770)		Wimpole, Cambs	S	*Roscoe* 1999, 246–7 (repr 76)
100.	1770	Sir Mark Pleydell (†1768)		[? Coleshill, Berks]; untraced		*Roscoe* 1999, 247
101.	nd	Basso relievo for a monument		[Exhib Soc of Artists, 1777, 279]; untraced		*Roscoe* 1999, 293
102.	nd	Model of a monument		[Scheemakers's sale, 6 June 1771, lot 65]; untraced		*Roscoe* 1999, 293
103.	nd	Model of a monumental figure		[Exhib Soc of Artists, 1780, 230]; untraced		*Roscoe* 1999, 293
104.	nd	Model of monumental figures		[Exhib Soc of Artists, 1780, 231]; untraced		*Roscoe* 1999, 293
105.	nd	Monuments of boys, models		[Scheemakers's sale, 6 June 1771, lot 61]; untraced		*Roscoe* 1999, 293
106.	nd	William Watts		Prestbury, Cheshire	S	*Roscoe* 1999, 247

Statues

No.	Date	Subject		Location		References
107.	1722	Omphale (companion to Laurent Delvaux's Hercules) Drawing(s): VAM D.1062-1887	m	[Wanstead House, Essex, principal front]; untraced		*Hodgkinson* 1970, 208–11; *Roscoe* 1999, 282–3
108.	1725–1728	Apollo and Venus (companion to Laurent Delvaux's Vertumnus and Pomona)	m	[Canons, Middx]; St Paul's Waldenbury, Herts		*Rumsey Foster* 1848, lot 781; *Avery* 1980, 161–1 (repr); *Roscoe* 1999, 283
109.	pre-1728	Cleopatra, statuette (companion to Laurent Delvaux's Ariadne) Model(s): 'Venus Sleeping', Scheemakers/Delvaux sale, 16 April 1728, lot 92; 'figure sleeping' Delvaux/Scheemakers sale, 16 April 1728, lot 51	m	YCBA B 1977.14.30	S	*Waterhouse* 1977, 351–2; *Roscoe* 1999, 265, 290
110.	pre-1728	Figure after the Antique, statuette		[Delvaux/Scheemakers sale, 16 April 1728, lot 52]; untraced		*Roscoe* 1999, 296
111.	pre-1728	Figure, Roman, statuette		[Delvaux/Scheemakers sale, 16 April 1728, lot 35]; untraced		*Roscoe* 1999, 296
112.	pre-1728	Hercules, model, statuette		[Delvaux/Scheemakers sale, 16 April 1728, lot 27]; untraced Other versions: copied in plaster		*Roscoe* 1999, 296
113.	pre-1728	Pluto, model, statuette		[Delvaux/Scheemakers sale, 16 April 1728, lot 26]; untraced		*Roscoe* 1999, 297
114.	1723–1728	Urania, with the attributes of Ceres (companion to Laurent Delvaux's Flora)	m	Private coll	S	*Roscoe* 1999, 283–4
115.	pre-1728	Vertumnus, model, statuette		[Delvaux/Scheemakers sale, 16 April 1728, lot 67]; untraced		*Roscoe* 1999, 298
116.	pre-1728	Zephyrus and Aurora, model		[Delvaux/Scheemakers sale, 16 April 1728, lot 34]; untraced		*Roscoe* 1999, 299
117.	post-1730	Apollo		[Chiswick House, Middx, gallery]; untraced		*Roscoe* 1999, 289
118.	1728–1730	Faunus, Young Bacchus, Centaur with Cupid on his back, Venus crouching, Venus and cockle shell, Gladiator, Flora, Ceres, 'Hermaphrodite & a woman one groupe, Laocoon & sons, some busts, sphinx and lions, Egyptian statue, 'one of the Fiamingp' &c, models	tc	[Modelled in Rome]; untraced Other versions: several of Ceres recorded in clay or marble others duplicated in plaster		*Vertue* III, 42–3

119.	1730–1731	Calydonian boar Model(s): Sold 10 March, 1756, lot 56; another sold 6 June 1771, lot 85	s	[Chiswick House, Middx]; Chatsworth House, Derbys		*Roscoe* 1999, 287, 288, 294
120.	1730–1731	Wolf	s	[Chiswick House, Middx, garden front]; Chatsworth, Derbys		*Roscoe* 1999, 289, 299
121.	1732	Apollino, statuette	i	Brussels, Musées Royaux d'Art et d'Histoire	SD	*Roscoe* 1996, 3 (repr 4); *Roscoe* 1999, 265, 290
122.	1732	Flora, statuette	i	Untraced	SD	*Roscoe* 1999, 265, 291
123.	1732–1734	King William III, equestrian	l	Kingston-upon-Hull, E R Yorks, marketplace		*Whinney* 1988, 178, 181 (repr); *Roscoe* 1999, 254–5
124.	1732–1734	Thomas Guy (†1724)	b	Guy's Hospital, Southwark, London		*Roscoe* 1999, 251–2 (reprs 83, 84); *Solkin* 1996, 467–84 (repr); *Cavanagh* forthcoming 2007 (Southwark, Dulwich to Walworth)
125.	c1735	Ancient Worthies, Lycurgus, Socrates, Homer and Epaminondas Drawing(s): VAM D.1065-1887	s	[Stowe, Bucks, Temple of Ancient Virtue]; Cottesbrooke Hall, Northants, gardens	S	*Roscoe* 1997, 42–50; *Roscoe* 1999, 284–5 (repr 93)
126.	1735	Four terms	s	[Carlton House, Kew]; Dutch House, Kew, Surrey, Queen's garden		*Roscoe* 1999, 284
127.	1737–1739	King Edward VI Drawing(s): Harris Art Gall, Preston, 528-1948; 529-1948	b	St Thomas's Hospital, London	S	*Whinney* 1988, 188 (repr); *Roscoe* 1999, 255–6 (repr 83, 85–6); *Cavanagh* forthcoming 2007 (Lambeth 2)
128.	c1740	Crouching Venus, on a pedestal Model(s): 1728–1730, Vertue III, 44; another sold 11 March 1756, lot 27	m	[Stowe, Elysian Fields, grotto]; untraced Other versions: copied in plaster		*Bickham*, 1750, 27–8; *Roscoe* 1999, 289–90, 298, 299
129.	1740	Hercules and Pan with lamb and jug	s	Rousham House, Oxon, praeneste, above balustrade	S	*Roscoe* 1999, 285–6
130.	1742	A lion attacking a horse	s	Rousham House, Oxon, bowling green		*Davis* 1991, 67–8 (pl 21, colour repr 19); *Roscoe* 1999, 286
131.	post-1742	Dying gladiator Drawing(s): by William Kent with pedestal in sarcophagus form, Chatsworth Archives, album 26A	s	Rousham House, Oxon, above praeneste arcade		*Davis* 1991, 90–1 (repr 90); *Roscoe* 1999, 286–7
132.	1743	Four seasons, with pedestals Payment(s): £70 1s 3d		[coll Lord Archibald Hamilton]; untraced		*Roscoe* 1999, 287
133.	1743–1744	William Shakespeare (designed by William Kent)	s	[Wilton House, great gateway, 1767]; Wilton House, Wilts, north entrance hall Other versions: marble sold 11 March 1756, lot 59, £43 1s; untraced	S	*Roscoe* 1999, 256–7; *Guilding* 2001, 42–3 (repr)
134.	1746	Captain Robert Sandes (†1721)	l	[Trinity almshouses, Mile End Road, London, quadrangle]; Trinity House, City of London, entrance hall		*Whinney* 1988, 233 (repr); *Roscoe* 1999, 252
135.	1746–1747	Sir John Barnard (†1754)	m	[Royal Exchange, London]; destroyed		*Roscoe* 1997, 180–181 (repr); *Ward-Jackson* 2003, 317–8
136.	from 1748	Hercules, Flora, Venus, Faunus, 'Zingara Egyptian Woman' statuettes, casts, sold as a series	p	Untraced		*Vertue* III, 139, 141
137.	pre-1755	Zingara, statuette	m	[Dr Richard Mead; Mead sale (2), 1755]; untraced Other versions: several recorded, marble and plaster		Mead sale (2), p 219; *Roscoe* 1999, 299
138.	pre-1756	Cupid and Psyche, model, statuette		[Scheemakers sale, 11 March 1756, lot 23]; untraced Other versions: copied in plaster		*Roscoe* 1999, 295
139.	pre-1756	Cupid on a Sphinx, model, statuette Drawing(s): for a sphinx, Rome Sketchbook, Huntington lib 75.14.1975		[Scheemakers sale, 10 March 1756, lot 19]; untraced		*Roscoe* 1999, 295
140.	pre-1756	Faun, young, 'in the villa Borghese', model		[Scheemakers sale, 11 March 1756, lot 24]; untraced Other versions: several known casts		*Roscoe* 1999, 295
141.	pre-1756	Flora, of the Capitol, statuette Model(s): Scheemakers sale (3) 1756, lot 78	m	[Scheemakers sale (3), 1756, lot 31]; untraced Other versions: cast in plaster		*Roscoe* 1999, 265, 296
142.	pre-1756	Laocoon, statuette Model(s): Prepared during Rome visit 1728–1730	m	[Scheemakers sale, 11 March 1756, lot 60, bt Lord Lincoln]; untraced Other versions: several recorded		*Roscoe* 1999, 265, 291, 296–7
143.	pre-1756	Old faun in the Villa Borghese, statuette	tc	[Scheemakers sale, 11 March 1756, lot 24]; untraced		*Roscoe* 1999, 295
144.	1762	Faunus, possibly a statuette Payment(s): £31		[Wentworth Woodhouse, W R Yorks]; untraced		*Roscoe* 1999, 295
145.	1760–1764	General Lord Robert Clive, Vice-Admiral Sir George Pococke, Major-General Stringer Lawrence	m	[United East India Company, Leadenhall Street, City of London]; Foreign and Commonwealth office, London	S	*Roscoe* 1999, 253–4 (reprs 87–88)
146.	nd	Apollino and the old faun, cast	p	[Scheemakers sale, 7 June 1771, lot 11]; untraced		*Roscoe* 1999, 294
147.	nd	Bacchus and Flora, a pair	s	Wrest Park, Beds	S	

No.	Date	Subject		Location		Literature
148.	nd	Bull, group, model or cast		[Scheemakers sale, 6 June 1771, lot 45]; untraced		*Roscoe* 1999, 294
149.	nd	Faun dancing, statuette	p	[Scheemakers sale, 6 June 1771, lot 70]; untraced		*Roscoe* 1999, 295
150.	nd	'Faun with Goat' [kid] Drawing(s): Rome Sketchbook, Huntington lib 75.14.1975		[Scheemakers sale, 6 June 1771, lot 70]; untraced		*Roscoe* 1999, 295
151.	nd	Lions, a pair Model(s): prepared during Rome visit, 1728–1730; untraced	b	[coll Dr Richard Mead]; untraced		Mead sale (2), p 236; *Roscoe* 1999, 265, 291, 297
152.	nd	Neptune, model		[Nollekens sale, 5 July 1823, lot 4]; untraced		*Roscoe* 1999, 297
153.	nd	Niobe; daughter of Niobe (casts)	p	[Scheemakers sale, 6 June 1771, 54, 50]; untraced		*Roscoe* 1999, 297
154.	nd	Papirius and his Mother, statuette	p	[Scheemakers sale, 6 June 1771, lot 68]; untraced Other versions: multiple casts		*Roscoe* 1999, 297
155.	nd	Paris seated, statuette	p	[Nollekens sale, 4 July 1823, lot 43]; untraced		*Roscoe* 1999, 297
156.	nd	Piping faun, model, statuette		[Nollekens sale (1), 1823, lot 1]; untraced Other versions: copied in plaster		*Roscoe* 1999, 295, 299
157.	nd	Proserpine	p	[Scheemakers sale, 6 June 1771, lot 66]; untraced		*Roscoe* 1999, 297
158.	nd	Saturn and child, model, statuette		[Nollekens sale (1) 1823, lot 51]; untraced		*Roscoe* 1999, 298
159.	nd	The wrestlers, statuette	p	[Scheemakers sale, 6 June 1771, lot 46]; untraced		*Roscoe* 1999, 289, 299
Busts						
160.	1733	Francis, 2nd Earl of Godolphin (†1766)	m	[Britwell House, Bucks]; YCBA B1979.36.1	S	*Roscoe* 1999, 257 (repr 89)
161.	1733	John, Lord Gower (†1781)	m	Dunrobin Castle, Sutherland		*Pearson* 1991, 140 (repr)
162.	c1733	Richard, Viscount Cobham (†1749)	m	[Stowe, Bucks, Temple of Friendship]; VAM A.1-1942	S	*Whinney* 1971, 60–1 (repr); *Whinney* 1988, 187 (repr)
163.	?c1734	William Shakespeare, John Milton, Alexander Pope	m	[Mead sale (2), 1755]; untraced		Mead sale (2), p 251; *Webster* 1970, 251; *Roscoe* 1999, 271–2
164.	1735	English Poets, John Milton, Edmund Spenser, John Dryden and William Shakespeare Payment(s): 10 gns each	m	[Alexander Pope's villa, Twickenham, Middx]; Hagley Hall, Worcs Other versions: series for Frederick, Prince of Wales; untraced Dryden sold Langford, 10–11 March 1756; untraced Dryden, ex coll Watson Taylor, Erlestoke sale, 25 July 1832, lot 164; untraced		*GM* 1744, 313; *Manchester Art Treasures* 1857, 135; *Beard* 1953, 4–6 (repr); *Roscoe* 1999, 272
165.	1736–1737	British Worthies, Alexander Pope, Sir Thomas Gresham, King Alfred, Edward the Black Prince, Sir Walter Raleigh, Sir Francis Drake, Sir John Barnard	s	Stowe, Bucks, Temple of British Worthies		*Eustace* 1998, 31–40; *Roscoe* 1999, 267–8
166.	1739	Alexander the Great	s	[Rousham House, praeneste]; Rousham House, Oxon, garden niche Other versions: Mead sale (2), p 224, marble; untraced	S	*Roscoe* 1999, 263–4
167.	c1739	Bacchante	s	[Rousham House, praeneste]; Rousham House, Oxon, garden niche	S	*Roscoe* 1999, 264
168.	1739	Dr William Harvey (†1657)	m	[R C of Physic, Warwick Lane, London, great hall]; R C Physic, St Andrew's Place, London	S	*Roscoe* 1999, 261–2
169.	c1740	Alexander Pope Model(s): sold 10 March 1756, lot 21	m	YCBA, B 1977.14.29		*Roscoe* 1999, 257–8 (repr 90)
170.	1741	Frederick, Prince of Wales	m	[Stowe, Bucks, Temple of Friendship]; RCIN 31169		*Roscoe* 1999, 273; *Roberts* 2002, 138 (repr)
171.	†1742	Sir Richard Ellys		[Lord Hobart's library, Blickling, Norfolk]; Nocton, Lincs		*Roscoe* 1999, 261
172.	1739–1742	Viscount Cobham's boy patriots, Allen, Earl Bathurst; Philip, Earl of Chesterfield; Richard, Earl Temple	m	[Stowe, Bucks, Temple of Friendship]; Chesterfield at Huntington Museum, Cal; others untraced		*Rumsey Foster* 1848, lots 769, 770, 772; *Roscoe* 1999, 268–9; *Bilbey* 2002, 147–8 (Cobham repr)
173.	?post-1742	William Shakespeare	s	[Rousham House, Oxon, praeneste]; untraced		*Roscoe* 1999, 263
174.	c1743	Meleager	s	Rousham House, Oxon, above praeneste arcade		*Roscoe* 1999, 265
175.	pre-1745	Three male and three female members of the Shirley family	m	[Staunton Harold, Leics, library]; male heads, Nat Gall of Victoria, NSW; female heads, Ditchingham Hall, Suffolk, library		*Roscoe* 1999, 269–70
176.	1745	Unidentified male subject	m	Private coll	SD	*Roscoe* 1999, 258
177.	1747	King Edward VI (supplied with a chimneypiece)	m	King Edward VI grammar school, Birmingham, Warks		*Roscoe* 1999, 262
178.	1743–1749	Men of Letters, Cicero, Demosthenes, Homer, Locke, Milton, 8th Earl of Pembroke, Shakespeare, Archbishop Ussher	m	Trinity College, Dublin, Long Room Other versions: several recorded in marble, bronze and plaster		*Anecdotes* 1878, 376; *Crookshank* 1986, 22; *Baker* 1995 (2), 821–31 (repr); *Roscoe* 1999, 270–1

No.	Date	Subject	Material	Location		Reference
179.	pre-1756	Antoninus Pius, model		Untraced		*Roscoe* 1999, 294
180.	pre-1756	Apollo Model(s): sold 10 March 1756, lot 29	m	[Scheemakers sale, 10 March 1756, lot 53]; untraced		*Roscoe* 1999, 264, 294
181.	pre-1756	Apollonius Tyanaeus, model		[Scheemakers sale, 11 March 1756, lot 20]; untraced		*Roscoe* 1999, 294
182.	pre-1756	Cicero Model(s): sold 11 March 1756, lot 19	b	[Scheemakers sale, 11 March 1756, lot 52]; untraced Other versions: reproduced in plaster		
183.	pre-1756	Justinian Minerva Model(s): sold 6 June 1771, lot 61	m	[Scheemakers sale (3), 1756, lot 48]; untraced		*Roscoe* 1999, 265, 297
184.	pre-1756	Satyr Model(s): sold 16 April, 1728, lot 92; a satyr by Scheemakers sold Nollekens' sale 5 July 1823, lot 77	m	[Scheemakers sale (3), 1756, lot 49]; untraced		*Roscoe* 1999, 266, 298
185.	1758	Dr Robert Smith	m	Trinity College, Cambridge, Wren Library	SD	*Baker* 1995 (3), 110–35 (repr 80)
186.	1758	Dr Roger Cotes	m	Trinity College, Cambridge, Wren Library	SD	*Baker* 1995 (3), 110–35 (repr 79)
187.	1763	Nymph		Corsham Court, Wilts, cabinet room	S	*Gunnis* 1968, 343
188.	1766	Edward Wortley Montagu Payment(s): £42 9s	m	Trinity College, Cambridge, Wren Library, entrance hall	SD	*Baker* 1995 (3), 110–35 (repr 78)
189.	1766	James Jurin MD	m	Trinity College, Cambridge, Wren Library	SD	*Baker* 1995 (3), 110–35 (repr 77)
190.	1765–1766	Sir Paul Methuen (†1757)	m	Corsham Court, Wilts, great room		*Webb* 1957 (4), 491–3; *Roscoe* 1999, 259–60
191.	1766	Unidentified subject		[Exhib Free Soc, 1766, no 151]; untraced		*Roscoe* 1999, 272
192.	nd	Anthony (†1699) and Ashley (†1771), 3rd and 4th Earls of Shaftesbury		Wimborne St Giles, Dorset		*Gunnis* 1968, 343
193.	nd	Antinous, model		[Scheemakers sale, 6 June 1771, lot 53]; untraced		*Roscoe* 1999, 294
194.	nd	Apollonius	m	[Scheemakers sale (3), 1756, lot 51];		*Roscoe* 1999, 264
195.	nd	Caracalla	m	[Scheemakers sale (3), 1756, lot 51]; untraced Other versions: several recorded		*Roscoe* 1999, 265, 294
196.	nd	Dean Jonathan Swift; John Milton		[coll Rt Hon H Labouchère, 1857]; untraced		*Manchester Art Treasures* 1857, 136
197.	nd	Emperor Hadrian		[Scheemakers sale, 6 June 1771, lot 54]; untraced		*Roscoe* 1999, 296
198.	nd	Erasmus	m	[Scheemakers sale (3), 1756, lot 54, £11]; untraced		*Roscoe* 1999, 262
199.	nd	Faustina	p	[Scheemakers sale, 6 June 1771, lot 50]; untraced		*Roscoe* 1999, 296
200.	nd	Girl's head, after the Antique	m	[coll Charles Jennens]; untraced		*Roscoe* 1999, 272
201.	nd	Inigo Jones	m	[Scheemakers sale (3), 1756, lot 56, 14 gns]; untraced		*Roscoe* 1999, 262
202.	nd	Lucius Verus	m	[Scheemakers sale (3), 1756, lot 61]; untraced		*Roscoe* 1999, 265
203.	nd	Sappho	m	[Scheemakers sale (3), 1756, lot 52]; untraced		*Roscoe* 1999, 266
204.	nd	Sir Isaac Newton	m	[Scheemakers sale, 6 June 1771, lot 21]; untraced		*Roscoe* 1999, 301
205.	nd	Urania	m	[Scheemakers sale (3), 1756, lot 54]; untraced		*Roscoe* 1999, 266
206.	nd	Venus de Medicis	m	[Scheemakers sale (3), 1756, lot 59]; untraced		*Roscoe* 1999, 266
207.	nd	Vestal	m	[Scheemakers sale (3), 1756, lot 60]; untraced		*Roscoe* 1999, 266
208.	nd	Young blackamoor	m	[Scheemakers sale (3), 1756, lot 51 (£5 12s)]; untraced		*Roscoe* 1999, 265
Chimneypieces						
209.	1765–1766	With relief of Bacchus and the Tyrrhenian pirates (probably designed by James Stuart)	m	Lichfield, House, St James's Square, London, drawing room		*Roscoe* 1999, 280
210.	1736	Description unavailable Payment(s): £16 16s		[St Thomas's Hospital, London, committee room]; untraced		*Roscoe* 1999, 280
211.	1747–1749	With swags and garlands	m	[King Edward's School, library]; King Edward's School, Birmingham, new boardroom		*Roscoe* 1999, 278–9
212.	post 1759	With central classical relief; cross-member supported by vertical fluted columns with capitals incorporating female masks		[Spencer House, London, saloon]; Althorp, Northants, great room		*Roscoe* 1999, 279
213.	1763–1764	Supported by caryatids Payment(s): £225	m	Corsham Court, Wilts, great room		*Webb* 1957 (4), 491–3; *Roscoe* 1999, 279
214.	1765–1766	With horizontal relief of Bacchus and the Tyrrhenian Pirates	m	Corsham Court, Wilts, cabinet room		*Webb* 1957, (4), 491–3 (repr); *Roscoe* 1999, 280
Architectural Sculpture						
215.	pre-1728	Vases with reliefs of sacrifice to Apollo and sacrifice to Hercules (companions to Delvaux's 'Sacrifice of Iphigenia' and 'Sacrifice to Bacchus')	m	[Wanstead House, Essex, sold 1822, lots 369, 370]; Anglesey Abbey, Cambs	S	*Davis* 1991, 235–8 (repr); *Roscoe* 1999, 292 (repr 95)
216.	1735	Low relief for a garden building Payment(s): £210s 6d	p	[coll Frederick, Prince of Wales]; untraced		*Roscoe* 1999, 277

217.	1739–1740	Narcissus and dolphins fountain	m	[for Richard, Viscount Cobham]; untraced		*Roscoe* 1999, 287
218.	1744	Mansion House pediment, design or model		Untraced		*Vertue* III, 122–23
219.	1762–1769	Ornaments for the Triumphal Arch	s	Shugborough, Staffs, park		*Tiernan* 1994, 3–15; *Roscoe* 1999, 275–6
Reliefs						
220.	1738–1742	Britannia receiving gifts from the four quarters of the world	s	[Stowe, Palladian bridge]; Stowe, Bucks, Temple of Concord and Victory	S	*Roscoe* 1997, 57–62 (repr); *Roscoe* 1999, 274
221.	1744–1745	Henry, Lord Herbert (designed by William Hoare) Payment(s): 12 gns	m	Wilton House, Wilts	SD	*Webb* 1957 (4), 493 (repr)
222.	1755–1759	The Shepherd's Monument (designed or supervised by James Stuart; after Nicolas Poussin)	m	Shugborough, Staffs, park		*Watkin* 1982, 27–8; *Roscoe* 1999, 275 (repr 96); *Coltman* 2004, 52–54, 56
223.	nd	Basso Relievo, after Fiamingo		[Scheemakers sale, 11 March 1756, lot 47]; untraced		*Roscoe* 1999, 272
224.	nd	Twelve, Roman Emperors	m	[Scheemakers sale (3), 1756, lot 49]; untraced		*Roscoe* 1999, 265
Miscellaneous						
225.	pre-1728	Virgil, model		[Delvaux/Scheemakers sale, 16 April 1728, lot 79]; untraced		*Roscoe* 1999, 298
226.	1762	Unidentified work Payment(s): £123 5s		[for John, 14th Lord Willoughby de Broke of Compton Verney, Warks]; untraced		C Hoare and Co, Ledgers, vol B, 287

SCHEEMAKERS, Thomas 1740–1808

The only son of **Peter Scheemakers**, he was born in July 1740, perhaps in the vicinity of Old Palace Yard, Millbank where his father had premises. His mother was probably Barbara, née La Fosse, Peter's widow, whose name i mentioned on her husband's death certificate. The paternal workshop moved to Vine Street, Piccadilly, late in 1740 where Thomas Scheemakers received his training and worked alongside **Joseph Nollekens**. In the mid-1760s h began to show with the exhibiting societies and in 1765 won a Society of Arts premium in the historical bas-relie class (**74**). The following year he gained the first premium with another classically inspired relief (**76**), beatin **Thomas Banks** into joint second place. He continued to exhibit regularly throughout his career.

All sculpture from the Scheemakers workshop went out in the father's name until 1771, when Peter retired t Antwerp, aged 80. Thomas Scheemakers must necessarily have taken a major hand in monuments from the early o mid-1760s, working to the designs of James Stuart, the fashionable Greek revival architect. Stuart lived nearby, firs in Vine Street and then round the corner in Glasshouse Street.

The first publicly-announced collaboration between Thomas and Stuart appeared in the catalogue of the Fre Society of Artists exhibition in 1765. Scheemakers exhibited two bas-reliefs 'designed by Stuart', and showed othe works to the architect's designs in 1770 and in the early 1780s (**22, 24, 48, 75, 89, 93, 94**). In 1771 the pair signed thei first collaborative monument, to the 4th Earl of Shaftesbury (**1**). It has a bust *all'antica* on a socle above sarcophagus, attended by winged boys. The following year Scheemakers briefly attended the Royal Academy school perhaps anxious about the future of the partnership, since Stuart was often ill. The pair nonetheless signed seve more monuments between *c*1773 and 1783, making use of a repetitive vocabulary of profile heads in roundel mounted on or over massy sarcophagi. The monument to Ralph Freman, †1772, is characteristic, for it takes the forn of a heavy, polychrome sarcophagus with a scrolled lid, adapted from an Antique original at Scopolo. It supports double portrait roundel of numismatic appearance, and there are other portrait roundels on the wall behind (**2**). Th design was repeated with minor modifications for the monument to Thomas Steavens, *c*1773 (**4**), while a pure version of the Scopolo sarcophagus, with strigil decoration and lion's feet was used for the monument to Josia Wedgwood's partner, Thomas Bentley (**21**). A drawing for this monument in Thomas's hand survives and suggest that Stuart's involvement may not have been extensive. The memorial to Joseph Cocks, †1778, is again a variant o the Freman, this time with the addition of a Greek key border (**12**). That to Mary Cocks, †1779, breaks from th sarcophagus theme, but is conventional in composition. It presents a Bible-carrying figure of *Hope*, in classical garb beside an urn, while a putto extinguishes a torch (**17**). The extent of Stuart's involvement in these competent bu unimaginative works is open to question. It seems likely that he provided only working sketches, for a sheaf o carefully finished hand-coloured designs for 25 memorials by Thomas, including the signed monuments, ha survived and testifies to his own dogged competence as a draughtsman.

By the early 1780s Stuart had lost interest in the partnership. Thomas was now sufficiently well-known to attrac his own clientele and he went on to produce more varied work. The monument to General Sir John Honywood †1781, has a fine bust *en negligé* (**20**) and the success of the work led to other Honywood commissions (**59, 67**). Hi most competent and imaginative monument, to Mary Russell, was completed in 1787 (**30**). This has a lovely round limbed, lightly draped effigy, reclining on a sarcophagus which is carved with a crisply-realised relief medallion o the deceased teaching music to a child. Musical trophies, including an organ, 'cello and harp, flank the medallior The monument to the noted blue-stocking, Lady Mary Wortley Montagu, 1789, is disappointing, given the characte of the subject commemorated. It has another grieving classical female, leaning against a fluted vase (**33**).

Scheemakers carved or modelled a number of portrait busts, but these are largely untraced, so his abilities in thi field cannot be evaluated, but given the extraordinary skill in portraiture displayed by his prolific contemporar Nollekens, Scheemakers must have struggled to compete. Several of his busts were reproduced in plaster, perhaps a a marketing experiment, since they seem to have been left on his hands (**66, 68, 69**).

Apart from his exhibition entries, nothing came out of the workshop at 6 Titchfield Street, Oxford Market after 179 On 21 May 1805 he sold up his entire collection of terracotta models, reliefs from the Antique, a 'Capital' marb chimneypiece and his working tools. **Peter Turnerelli** bought a number of his models and casts and some modellin equipment. Scheemakers, who was a Roman Catholic, died on 15 July 1808, and was buried in St. Pancras churchyard; the inscription on his tombstone spelt his name 'Sheemakers'. His wife Barbara, who died at the age of 63, survived him by two years and was buried in the same grave. There were no children and the sculptor appears to have died intestate.

Scheemakers's career reads as a series of missed opportunities, for he had a thorough training as the only son of a successful sculptor, he collaborated with a fashionable architect at the outset of his career, and he enjoyed the opportunities for publicity afforded by the new exhibiting societies. The challenge he could not surmount came from the more talented and energetic sculptors who were his rivals and who were elected Academicians, Nollekens, Thomas Banks and **John Bacon RA**.

IR/MGS

Literary References: *Gunnis* 1968, 344–5; *Roscoe* 1987, 178–84; *Sullivan* 2006, 394–401 (repr)

Archival References: Paving rates, Church Ward, St James, Piccadilly, 1768, WPL E.1721

Collections of Drawings: 25 designs (some identified), VAM 8408-1878, pen, ink and watercolour

Miscellaneous Drawings: monument to a woman, VAM 8408.19; wall monument, VAM 8408.23; unidentified monument HMI, 30/1989 (repr *Friedman* 1993, 90, cat 2)

Auction Catalogues: Scheemakers, Thomas, 1805

Funerary Monuments

1.	1771	Anthony, 4th Earl of Shaftesbury (†1771) (designed by James Stuart)		Wimborne St Giles, Dorset	S	Pevsner, *Dorset*, 1972, 470
2.	†1772	Ralph Freman (designed by James Stuart)		Braughing, Herts	S	*Webb* 1958 (1), 331 (repr); *Roscoe* 1987 (2), 184 (repr); *Whinney* 1988, 238; *Sullivan* 2006, 394–7 (repr)
3.	†1773	Jemmet (†1767) and Elizabeth Raymond		Kintbury, Berks		*Whinney* 1988, 238
4.	c1773	Thomas Steavens (designed by James Stuart) Drawing(s): VAM, 8408.14		Preston-on-Stour, Warks	S	*Physick* 1969, 134–5 (repr); Sullivan 2006, 397 (repr)
5.	1774	A finished model of two boys on a sarcophagus supporting arms on a larger scale		[Exhib Free Soc, 261]; untraced		*Graves* 1907, 227
6.	1774	Model for the portrait on the aforesaid monument		[Exhib Free Soc, 262]; untraced		*Graves* 1907, 227
7.	1774	Sketch for a monument (designed by James Stuart)		[Exhib Free Soc, 260]; untraced		*Graves* 1907, 227
8.	†1774	Thomas (†1774) and Catherine Wilson		Bungay, Suffolk		Pevsner, *Suffolk*, 1974, 122
9.	1775	Model for a boy leaning on a vase, for a monument		[Exhib Free Soc, 241]; untraced		*Graves* 1907, 227
10.	1775	Model for a monumental medallion		[Exhib Free Soc, 240]; untraced		*Graves* 1907, 227
11.	1778	Basso relievo for a monument, model		[Exhib Free Soc, 121]; untraced		*Graves* 1907, 227
12.	1778	Joseph Cocks (†1775) (designed by James Stuart)		Eastnor, Herefs		*Colvin* 1995, 942; *Sullivan* 2006, 399 (repr)
13.	1778	Model for a monumental medallion		[Exhib Free Soc, 122]; untraced		*Graves* 1907, 227
14.	1778	Rev William Langhorn		Folkestone, Kent		*Gunnis* 1968, 344
15.	1779	Archbishop of Cashel		Kilkenny Cathedral		*Gunnis* 1968, 344
16.	1779	Charles Fortescue		St Peter, Droitwich		*Gunnis* 1968, 344
17.	†1779	Mary Cocks (designed by James Stuart)		Eastnor, Herefs	S	*Colvin* 1995, 942; *Sullivan* 2006, 399–400 (repr)
18.	1779	Two boys for a sepulchral monument, models		[Exhib Free Soc, 149]; untraced		*Graves* 1907, 227
19.	1780	Monumental figure	m	[Exhib Free Soc, 154]; untraced		*Graves* 1907, 227
20.	†1781	General Sir John Honywood Model(s): bust exhib RA, London, 1782, 500	m	Elmsted, Kent Other versions: Cast and mould of the bust, Scheemakers's sale 1805, lot 21	S	Pevsner, *Kent: N E & E*, 1983, 313
21.	1781	Thomas Bentley (†1780) (designed by James Stuart) Drawing(s): VAM 8408		Chiswick, Middx		*Colvin* 1995, 942; *Sullivan* 2006. 397–8 (repr)
22.	1782	Model of a monument from a design of Mr Stuart		[Exhib RA, London, 542]; untraced		*Graves* VII, 1905–6, 42
23.	1782	Monumental figure of Faith		[Exhib RA, London, 538]; untraced		*Graves* VII, 1905–6, 42
24.	1783	'Sketch of a monument' (designed by James Stuart)		[Exhib Free Soc, 327]; untraced		
25.	1784	Anthony, Lord Feversham (†1763) Drawing(s): VAM 8408.11		Downton, Wilts	S	Pevsner, *Wilts*, 1975, 224
26.	1784	Model of a monument		[Exhib RA, London, 496]; untraced		*Graves* VII, 1905–6, 42
27.	1785	Mrs Cocks and Mrs Neale		North Mymms, Herts		Pevsner, *Herts*, 1977, 263
28.	†1785	William (†1762) and Dorothea Henley Drawing(s): VAM 8408.17		Otham, Kent	S	*Gunnis* 1968, 344
29.	1786	Hon and Rev George Talbot (†1785)	m	Temple Guiting, Glos		*GM* 1786, i, 439; Pevsner, *Glos: Cotswolds*, 1999, 683
30.	1787	Mary Russell (†1786)		Powick, Worcs	SD	*Whinney* 1988, 23–9 (repr)
31.	1788	Medallion for a monument, with portraits of a lady and child		[Exhib RA, London, 648]; untraced		*Graves* VII, 1905–6, 42
32.	1788	Model for a monument; figure of Friendship		[Exhib RA, London, 649]; untraced		*Graves* VII, 1905–6, 42
33.	1789	Lady Mary Wortley Montagu		Lichfield Cathedral, Staffs	S	Pevsner, *Staffs*, 1974, 187
34.	1789	Model of a monument		[Exhib RA, London, 490]; untraced		*Graves* VII, 1905–6, 42
35.	†1792	Sir William Fagg		Chartham, Kent	S	Pevsner, *Kent: N E & E*, 1983, 267, 269
36.	1793	Model of a monument		[Exhib RA, London, 785]; untraced		*Graves* VII, 1905–6, 42
37.	1795	Model of a monument		[Exhib RA, London, 677]; untraced		*Graves* VII, 1905–6, 42

38.	1796	A monumental figure representing Humility		[Exhib RA, London, 866]; untraced		*Graves* VII, 1905–6, 42
39.	1798	Monumental figure		[Exhib RA, London, 1038]; untraced		*Graves* VII, 1905–6, 42
40.	1799	Monumental figure		[Exhib RA, London, 1048]; untraced		*Graves* VII, 1905–6, 42
41.	1801	Monumental figure of a boy		[Exhib RA, London, 1025]; untraced		*Graves* VII, 1905–6, 42
42.	1803	Monumental figure of a boy		[Exhib RA, London, 940, 941]; untraced		*Graves* VII, 1905–6, 42
43.	1803	Two monumental figures of boys		[Exhib RA, London, 919]; untraced		*Graves* VII, 1905–6, 42
44.	1804	Monumental figure of Piety		[Exhib RA, London, 907]; untraced		*Graves* VII, 1905–6, 42
45.	nd	Mrs Ogilvy (two casts and the mould)		Untraced		Scheemakers sale, 1805, lot 14
Statues						
46.	1773	Arion, statuette	tc	[Exhib Free Soc, 199]; VAM 247-1869 Other versions: Cast and mould, Scheemakers's sale 1805, lot 37	SD	*Graves* 1907, 227; *Bilbey* 2002, 151 (repr)
47.	1782	Minerva, model		[Exhib Free Soc, 244]; untraced		*Graves* 1907, 227
48.	1782	Venus, figure (designed by James Stuart)		[Exhib Free Soc, 245]; untraced		*Graves* 1907, 227
Busts						
49.	1772	A lady	m	[Exhib Free Soc, 172]; untraced		*Graves* 1907, 227
50.	1772	Unidentified gentleman	m	[Exhib Free Soc, 172]; untraced		*Graves* 1907, 227
51.	1773	Portrait of an artist, model		[Exhib Free Soc, 200]; untraced		*Graves* 1907, 227
52.	1775	Portrait of a gentleman, model		[Exhib Free Soc, 239]; untraced		*Graves* 1907, 227
53.	1776	Portrait of a gentleman	m	[Exhib Free Soc, 198]; untraced		*Graves* 1907, 227
54.	1776	Portrait of a lady	m	[Exhib Free Soc, 199]; untraced		*Graves* 1907, 227
55.	1778	An artist, model		[Exhib Soc of Artists, 199]; untraced		*Roscoe* 1999, 272
56.	1779	A nobleman		[Exhib Free Soc, 147]; untraced		*Graves* 1907, 227
57.	1779	Admiral Keppel, model from life Model(s): exhib Free Soc, 1782, 239		[Exhib Free Soc, 148]; untraced		*Graves* 1907, 227
58.	1779	Lord Le Despencer		Untraced		*Gunnis* 1968, 344
59.	1781	General Philip Honywood	m	[at D'Agar and Gifford-Mead Antiques, London 1996]; untraced	SD	*Apollo*, Jan 1996, 15 (repr)
60.	1782	Dr James, model		[Exhib Free Soc, 240]; untraced		*Graves* 1907, 227
61.	1783	A child	m	[Exhib Free Soc, 328]; untraced		*Graves* 1907, 227
62.	1783	A gentleman, model		[Exhib Free Soc, 326]; untraced		*Graves* 1907, 227
63.	1788	A boy's head; from nature		[Exhib RA, London, 606]; untraced		*Graves* VII, 1905–6, 42
64.	1790	Portrait of a young lady		[Exhib RA, London, 663]; untraced		*Graves* VII, 1905–6, 42
65.	1801	A young lady		[Exhib RA, London, 995]; untraced		*Graves* VII, 1905–6, 42
66.	nd	Admiral Keppel (bust and mould)		Untraced		Scheemakers sale, 1805, lot 20
67.	nd	Filmer Honywood		Untraced		Scheemakers sale, 1805, lot 23
68.	nd	Mr Robertson (bust and mould)		Untraced		Scheemakers sale, 1805, lot 19
69.	nd	Two of the 'celebrated' Dr James, with the mould		Untraced		Scheemakers sale, 1805, lot 22
Chimneypieces						
70.	1777	Alterations to existing chimneypieces and two coats of arms for chimneypieces		[Coleshill, Berks, bed chamber, saloon and other rooms]; untraced		Earl of Radnor, Household Bills and Vouchers, D/EPB/A7/1 and 4; *Gunnis* 1968, 344
71.	1779–1780	Chimney-pieces, and possibly a number of tablets for chimneypieces Payment(s): £118		[West Wycombe Park, Herts]; untraced		*Gunnis* 1968, 344
72.	nd	With carved tablet, pilasters and blocking		Untraced		Scheemakers's sale, 1805, lot 49
Architectural Sculpture						
73.	*c*1775	Ornaments from the design of the Company's surveyor Mr John Gorham Payment(s): £72	s	[Drapers' Hall, pediment]; untraced		*GM* 1778, vol 48, 585; *Gunnis* 1968, 344
Reliefs						
74.	1765	Cincinnatus' 2nd Dictatorship, in clay		[Exhib Soc of A, premium, 10 gns]; untraced Other versions: Cast and mould, Scheemakers's sale, 1805, lot 38		RSA *Minutes*, 1764–65, seq 3 f61; *Dossie* 1782, 439; *Graves* 1907, 227
75.	1765	Dancing Nymphs, two bas reliefs (from a design by James Stuart)		[Exhib Free Soc, 170]; untraced Other versions: cast and mould, Scheemakers sale, 1805, lot 34		*Graves* 1907, 227
76.	1766	Paris and Helen depart	s	[Soc of A, premium, £50]; untraced		*Dossie* 1782, 440; *Graves* 1907, 227
77.	1767	The rape of Helen		[Exhib Free Soc, 243]; untraced		*Graves* 1907, 227
78.	1767	Two boys playing with birds		[Exhib Free Soc, 242]; untraced		*Graves* 1907, 227
79.	1769	Unidentified subject Payment(s): £42		[Longford Castle, Wilts]; untraced		*Gunnis* 1968, 344
80.	1770	Boys		[Exhib Free Soc, 225]; untraced		*Graves* 1907, 227
81.	1771	Jupiter and Europa, tablet	tc	[Exhib Free Soc, 214]; untraced		*Graves* 1907, 227
82.	1771	Tethys on a sea horse, tablet	tc	[Exhib Free Soc, 215]; untraced		*Graves* 1907, 227
83.	1776	Apollo and Cybele, tablet		[Exhib Free Soc, 200]; untraced		*Graves* 1907, 227
84.	1778	Satyr and goat, model for a tablet		[Exhib Free Soc, 124]; untraced		*Graves* 1907, 227
85.	1778	Sleeping Cupid, model for a tablet		[Exhib Free Soc, 123]; untraced		*Graves* 1907, 227
86.	1780	Jupiter and Europa	tc	[Exhib Free Soc, 155]; untraced		*Graves* 1907, 227
87.	1780	Thetys	tc	[Exhib Free Soc, 156]; untraced		*Graves* 1907, 227
88.	1783	'Basso relievo; A Modell'		[Exhib Free Soc, 296]; untraced		*Graves* 1907, 227
Miscellaneous						
89.	1765	Bacchus (designed by James Stuart)		[Exhib Free Soc, 171]; untraced		*Graves* 1907, 227
90.	1768	Adonis, model		[Exhib Free Soc, 189]; untraced		*Graves* 1907, 227

91. 1768	Two boys		[Exhib Free Soc, 190]; untraced		*Graves* 1907, 227
92. 1769	Ceres		[Exhib Free Soc, 194]; untraced		*Graves* 1907, 227
93. 1770	Two sea horses, models (designed by James Stuart)	tc	[Exhib Free Soc, 226]; untraced		*Graves* 1907, 227
94. 1770	Venus anointing herself after the bath, model (designed by James Stuart)	tc	[Exhib Free Soc, 226]; untraced		*Graves* 1907, 227
95. 1772	Two boys fighting, model	tc	[Exhib Free Soc, 173]; untraced		*Graves* 1907, 227

SCHROUDER, James fl 1763

He was listed as 'Modeller, and Papier Maché Manufacturer. Great Marlborough-Street, Carnaby Market' in *Mortimer* 1763 (p26).

SCHROWDER, Benjamin 1757–1826

Schrowder, who claimed to be a maternal descendant of the poet Milton, was born at Winchelsea on 15 November 1757. On 31 January 1772 he joined the Royal Academy Schools and in 1781 exhibited various wax portraits at the Academy, giving his address as 27 Carnaby Market (4, 5). He later settled in Dublin, where he was invited to work on the new Custom House and carved most of the emblematic river gods designed by **Edward Smyth** (2). Only one of his monuments has been identified with certainty, though Potterton attributes to him two more in Newport, Co Mayo, to Hugh O'Donnell, †1798 and James Moore O'Donnell, †1800.

His wife Lavinia died young and was buried in St George's churchyard. The sculptor subsequently married Anne Byrne, the grandmother of **J H Foley** and **E A Foley**. Schrowder's business was conducted from 6 Montgomery Street, where 'with his long silvery locks, and surrounded with his tools, models and marbles, [he] was a familiar and venerable figure in the eyes of the younger generation of the household, one of whom was destined to occupy a distinguished, and another a pre-eminent, position in the world of art' (*Atkinson* 1882, 7–8).

The sculptor died in 1826 and was buried near his wife. He carved a medallion portrait of himself on a black slab intended to form his monument. In the event the sum required to gain permission for this structure was too great and Schrowder is instead commemorated with a simple tombstone in the churchyard.

Literary References: *Atkinson* 1882, 7–8; *Strickland* II, 1913, 325; *Hutchison* 1960–62, 138; *Gunnis* 1968, 345; *Potterton* 1975, 77–78

Funerary Monuments					
1. †1809	Maria Browne		Newport, Co Mayo	S	*Potterton* 1975, 63, 78 (repr)
Architectural Sculpture					
2. nd	Keystone representing Irish rivers (co-sculptor: Edward Smyth)		Customs House, Dublin		*Gunnis* 1968, 345
Reliefs					
3. nd	Self-portrait, medallion		Untraced		*Atkinson* 1882, 8
Miscellaneous					
4. 1781	Several unidentified portraits	w	[Exhib RA, London, 279, 354, 355]; untraced		*Graves* IV, 1905–6, 53
5. 1781	Unidentified portrait	m	[Exhib RA, London, 280]; untraced		*Graves* IV, 1905–6, 53

SCHWANTHALER, Ludwig Michael von 1802–48

He was born in Munich, the son of the sculptor Franz Jakob Schwanthaler, and continued the very successful family workshop in the city. He was greatly influenced by **Bertel Thorvaldsen** during his periods of study in Rome, 1826–27 and 1832–34. In Munich he was a professor at the Akademie der Bildenden Künste, and he enjoyed a flow of royal commissions in Bavaria throughout his career. With his cousin, Franz Xaver Schwanthaler, he was also responsible for important monuments in Frankfurt, Vienna, Salzburg and a number of other European countries. He is perhaps best known for his colossal cast bronze statue of *Bavaria* in Munich, which was unveiled in 1850. He clearly enjoyed a reputation among the cognoscenti in England, too, since one work was acquired by the Duke of Devonshire for a considerable price (2). He died in Munich on 14 November 1848.

Statues					
1. 1847	Undine		Wentworth Woodhouse, W R Yorks		Pevsner, *Yorks: W R*, 1967, 542
2. 1848	Girl with woodman (Paris and Oenone, Schwanengesang) Payment(s): £500	m	Chatsworth, Derbys, sculpture gallery	SD	*Chatsworth Handlist*, 25; *JKB* 1972 (3), 329, 331
3. nd	Schwanhilda		Salford AG, Lancs		*Wells* 1999, 48, 51 (repr)
4. nd	Venus disarming Cupid	m	[coll R Dalgleish]; untraced		*Manchester Art Treasures* 1857, 134
Miscellaneous					
5. nd	Nymph of the Danube, Ceres and Proserpine, two colossal Victories, head of Bavaria, casts	p	[Crystal Palace, Sydenham, 1853]; untraced		*JKB* 2006, 177, 180, 183 (Bavaria repr)

SCOTT, J, of Penzance fl c1813–26

Gunnis described his tablets as 'carefully carved and carried out' (*Gunnis* 1968, 345), although Pevsner described his tablet to William Arundel Harris (6) as 'reactionary for its date'.

Funerary Monuments			
1. ?1813	James Pascoe	Gulval, Cornwall	*Gunnis* 1968, 345
2. ?1815	William Nicholls	Madron, Cornwall	*Gunnis* 1968, 345
3. ?1820	Mary Harrison	Helston, Cornwall	*Gunnis* 1968, 345
4. ?1821	John Rogers	Helston, Cornwall	*Gunnis* 1968, 345
5. ?1825	Philothea Thompson	Gulval, Cornwall	*Gunnis* 1968, 345
6. †1826	William Arundel Harris	Gulval, Cornwall	Pevsner, *Cornwall*, 1970, 76

SCOTT, James fl 1747–49

Between 1747 and 1749 Scott built the Surgeon's Theatre at the Old Bailey. 'This was a handsome building adjoining the Sessions House, and was ornamented with ionic pilasters and a double flight of steps to the front door. It was to this theatre that the bodies of executed criminals were brought to be anatomatised' (Archives Barber-Surgeons' Company in GPC).

SCOTT, John c1742–

Described by *Dossie* as an ornamental carver, he was a son of **Thomas Scott II**, who became free of his father in 1758, having duly served his time. He won a number of premiums from the Society of Arts as a young man and was 'under nineteen and a pupil of Mr. **Cuenot**' when he received his first, in 1760 (2). In 1764 he was described as resident 'at Mr Scott's in Christ's Hospital'. Later that year he moved to High Holborn. He exhibited at the Free Society, 1761–1762.

Literary References: *Dossie* 1782, 437; *Gunnis* 1968, 345

Archival References: Masons' Company, *Court Book*, 1758

Reliefs

1.	1761	Vase with flowers	tc	[Exhib Free Soc, London, 92]; untraced	*Graves* 1907, 228

Miscellaneous

2.	1760	Model of ornaments in clay		[Soc of A, premium, 5 gns]; untraced	RSA *Minutes*, 1758–60 seq 4 fol 49
3.	1761	Models of ornaments in clay, under 19 category		[Soc of A, premium, 7 gns]; untraced	RSA *Minutes*, 1760–61 seq 3 fol 48
4.	1762	Model of ornaments in clay, under 22 category		[Soc of A, premium, 8 gns]; untraced	RSA *Minutes*, 1761–62, seq 3 fol 64
5.	1762	'Piece of Flowers'	tc	[Exhib Free Soc, London, 175]; untraced	*Graves* 1907, 228
6.	1763	Model of ornaments in clay, under 22 category		[Soc of A, premium, 5 gns]; untraced	RSA *Minutes*, 1761–62, seq 2 fol 70; RSA *Premiums*, 1762, 33
7.	1764	Model of ornaments in clay, under 22 category		[Soc of A, premium, 8 gns]; untraced	RSA *Minutes*, 1761–62, seq 3, fol 64
8.	1765	Model of ornaments in clay, under 22 category		[Soc of A, premium, 3 gns]; untraced	RSA *Minutes*, 1764–65, seq 3 fol 61

SCOTT, Robert fl 1743–62

A son of **Thomas Scott II**, he became free of the Masons' Company by patrimony in January 1743. Three years later he was working as a mason at the Hampstead house of Christopher Arnold, one of the partners in Hoare's Bank and a payment of £36 for unidentified work is recorded in the partnership ledger. In 1748 Scott provided the monument to John Nichol, father of the Marchioness of Carnarvon (1). In 1762 he took his son Edward as an apprentice.

Literary References: *Gunnis* 1968, 345

Archival References: Hoare Partnership Ledger, 1742–1751, fol 352; Masons' Company, *Freemen*, 1742; *Court Book*, 1722–51, 18 Jan 1742/3

Funerary Monuments

1.	1748	John Nichol	['A church near London, possibly Colney']; untraced	Stowe archives cited in *Gunnis* 1968, 345

SCOTT, Robert Grieve fl c1794

He signs one monument with **F J Wilcoxson**.

Funerary Monuments

1.	†1794	Captain Francis Light (co-sculptor: F J Wilcoxson)	Penang Cathedral	S	RG/JP, 7, 1272

SCOTT, Thomas I c1678–c1723

He was apprenticed to Anthony Leonard in 1692 and became free of the Masons' Company in 1703. In 1714 he was appointed mason to the Inner Temple, receiving £80 that year for repairing the garden wall. Between 1719 and 1721 he was paid small sums for repairs at Hoare's Bank. In 1722 Scott's son, William, was apprenticed to him. Thomas probably died in the following year, since William was described as the 'son of the late Thomas Scott' in 1724 (Masons' Co, *Freemen*, fol 67).

Literary References: *Gunnis* 1968, 345

Archival References: Masons' Co, Apprentice binding book (1), 1692; Court Book, 1695–1722 (1722); Hoare Partnership Ledger 1719–1725, fols 58, 61, 68

SCOTT, Thomas II c1703–57

The son of **Thomas Scott I**, he was apprenticed to John Lucas in 1717 and became free of the Masons' Company in 1724. He had three sons, **Robert, John** and **James Scott**, who all became masons. Scott's address c1740 was in Whitefriars, where his practice remained until his death. He was Master of the Masons' Company in 1745 and his death is noted in their Court Book. His will was proved on 23 March 1758.

Between 1730 and 1742 he was mason to the Inner Temple, an appointment which had also been held by his father. Here his work included the circular steps 'at the great gate of the Great Garden', for which he was paid £181 5s in 1729. In 1741 he was paid £246 8s 9d for obelisks (2) and 'for work and materials done at various places including the terrace before the hall and library' (*Inderwick* 1896–1936, 4, 232, 454).

Literary References: *Gunnis* 1968, 345

Archival References: Masons' Co, Court Book, 1695–1722, fol 164v (1717); Freemen, 1724, 1757; Assistants, fol 1; Court Book, 1722–51 (14 June 1745); Court Book, 1758

Will: PROB 11/836

Funerary Monuments

1.	?1741	John Elliston		Gestingthorpe, Essex	S	*Gunnis* 1968, 345

Architectural Sculpture

2.	1741	Portland Stone obelisks	s	[Inner Temple, Inns of Court, London, terrace]; untraced		*Gunnis* 1968, 345

SCOTT, Thomas, of York –1834

He was apprenticed to **William Shout I of York** and succeeded him as the Minster's master mason. He was killed in 1834 by the collapse of some scaffolding (*York Gazette*, 27 December 1834).

Archival References: GPC

Architectural Sculpture

1.	nd	Altar-screen	York Minster	GPC

SCOULAR, William 1796–1854

Little is known of William Scoular's early life but he studied under John Graham at the Trustees School of Design in Edinburgh before moving to London in 1814. There he became a pupil of **Sir Richard Westmacott** and attended the Royal Academy schools from 2 August 1815. He was living in Clarendon Street, Somer's Town in 1816, when he received a silver medal from the Society of Arts for a copy of a large antique statue of *Faunus* and in 1817 gained the RA gold medal for a relief of the *Judgement of Paris* and a silver medal for a model of *Patroclus slain* (**1, 67, 3**). He applied for the RA travelling scholarship to Italy in 1818 but his request was rejected after Sir Thomas Lawrence argued that he had not shown sufficient ability. **John Flaxman** was among the Academicians who voted against him, though the portrait painter Thomas Phillips argued that the Academy acted inconsistently in refusing to send Scoular to Rome after awarding him the gold medal. He was living in Edinburgh in 1820 when he was again recognised by the Society of Arts and was awarded the Isis gold medal for a group entitled *Brutus and his son* (**4**).

In 1821 the Duke and Duchess of Clarence (the future King William IV) commissioned Scoular to take the death mask of their infant daughter, Princess Elizabeth (**77**). He also carved a small figure of the child asleep on a couch, now at Windsor Castle (**5**). He was appointed sculptor in ordinary to the Duke and Duchess in 1823. Two years later Scoular defeated **Joseph Gott** by four votes to win the RA travelling studentship and went to study in Rome. He remained there for several years and a writer in the *Literary Gazette* noted that 'his modest and retired habits estrange him from his countrymen visiting Rome' (*Lit Gaz*, 1829, cited by *Gunnis* 1968, 346). After his return to London in 1829–30 he bought the business of **Sarti**, 'a well-known Italian modeller' (*Redgrave* 1878, 384). The enterprise did not succeed and he had returned to work as a sculptor by 1836, when he sent four busts to the RA exhibition (**47–50**).

Scoular spent almost all his career in London, working from various addresses in the area around the Middlesex Hospital and in Soho. However, he continued to cultivate Scottish connections and in the early 1820s kept a studio in Mound Place Edinburgh, where Scottish patrons came to sit for him. Several of his works were issued as prizes by the Association for the Encouragement of the Fine Arts in Scotland and the Art Union of Scotland (**3, 6, 11**). He exhibited in London, at the RA (1815–1846), the British Institution (1816–1843) and the Society of British Artists (1824–1838) and in Edinburgh at the Royal Scottish Academy (1832–1847) and the Royal Institution for the Encouragement of the Fine Arts in Scotland (1821–1822).

Scoular's exhibits included a number of ideal works based on classical and biblical subject matter. A figure of *Narcissus*, shown at the RA in 1825 was warmly received by the *Literary Gazette*, whose reviewer wrote 'we have rarely seen a more beautiful model, chaste in design, just in its proportions and graceful in action' (*Lit Gaz*, 1825, cited by *Gunnis* 1968, 346). However, the sculptor's output was dominated by portraiture and in 1838 the same journal praised a marble statue of Sir Walter Scott, which appeared in that year's RA exhibition, remarking that Scoular had been 'fortunate in giving an elevation to the figure of this great writer correspondent with that of his genius' (*Lit Gaz*, 1838, 346, cited by *Lady Lever* 1999, 74). It can probably be identified with a seated figure of the author at the Lady Lever Art Gallery, in a relaxed attitude with his arm resting on a bookcase and his favourite dog at his knee (**10**). This work was formerly ascribed to **Sir Francis Chantrey** but it is closely similar in style and format to Scoular's statue of the Scottish engineer and scientist James Watt (**12**) and the two figures may have been conceived as a pair. The sculptor's bust of Prince Albert was less successful (**63**): the *Art Union* condemned it as 'among the worst portraits of the Prince we have seen' (*AU*, 1844, 171). Scoular died at Dean Street, Soho on 23 July 1854.

EH

Literary References: *GM*, 1854, ii, 316; *Redgrave* 1878, 384; *Gunnis* 1968, 345–6; *Pyke* 1973, 135; *Woodward* 1977, vol 1, pt 2, 210–3; *Farington* XIV, 5118; XV, 5153, 5154

Archival References: RA Premium list

Statues

1.	1816	Faunus		[Soc of A, silver medal]; untraced		RSA *Transactions*, 1816, vol 34, 29
2.	1816	Narcissus		[Exhib BI, London, 267]; untraced Other versions: exhib RA, London, 1825, 1050 exhib R Sc A, Edinburgh, 1841, marble		*Graves* 1875, 481; *Graves* VII, 1905–6, 64; *Laperriere* 4, 1991, 140
3.	1817	Patroclus slain		[RA silver medal]; untraced Other versions: awarded as prizes by the Assoc for the Encouragement of the Fine Arts in Scotland, 1838 marble exhib RA, London, 1843, 1494		*Graves* 1875, 481; *Graves* VII, 1905–6, 65; *Woodward* 1977, vol 1, pt 2, 211
4.	1820	Brutus and his son		[Soc of A, gold Isis medal]; untraced		RSA *Transactions*, 1820, vol 38, xxxiv
5.	1821	Princess Elizabeth of Clarence on a couch	m	Royal Coll	S	*Graves* VII, 1905–6, 64; Penny 1977 (1), 117; C Lib (repr)
6.	1824	Adam consoling Eve after the transgression		[Exhib RA, London, 1032]; untraced Other versions: several exhib 1825–1844 awarded as prizes by the Association for the Encouragement of the Fine Arts in Scotland, 1838		*Graves* VII, 1905–6, 64, 65; *Johnson* 1975, 416; *Woodward* 1977, vol 1, pt 2, 211; *Laperriere* 4, 1991, 140
7.	1824	The finding of Moses		[Exhib Soc of BA, London, 361]; untraced Other versions: another exhib R Sc A, Edinburgh, 1837, 374		*Johnson* 1975, 416; *Laperriere* 4, 1991, 140
8.	1826	Adam and Eve lamenting over the body of Abel		[Exhib RA, London, 1035]; untraced Other versions: several exhib 1837–1846 marble offered for sale at the Colosseum, Regents Park, London, 1849		*Graves* VII, 1905–6, 65; *Laperriere* 4, 1991, 140; GPC

No.	Date	Subject	Medium	Location	Bibliography
9.	1829	A girl playing a guitar, figure		[Scoular's studio, Rome]; untraced Other versions: marble figure of an Italian girl playing a guitar exhib RA, London, 1840 (1202) model offered for sale at the Colosseum, Regents Park, London, 1849	*Lit Gaz* 1829, 649; *Graves* VII, 1905–6, 65; *Gunnis* 1968, 346; GPC
10.	1838	Sir Walter Scott	m	[Badger Hall, Salop]; Christie, 5 May 1905, lot 231; Lever LL711	*Laperriere* 4, 1991, 140; *Morris and Roberts* 1998, 540; *Lady Lever* 1999, 71–4 (repr)
11.	1839	Italian shepherd boy (Arcadian shepherd)	m	[Exhib Liverpool Ac, 685]; untraced Other versions: several exhib 1839–1843 awarded as a prize by the Scottish Art Union 1840	*Graves* 1875, 481; *Graves* VII, 1905–6, 65; *Gunnis* 1968, 346; *Laperriere* 4, 1991, 140; *Morris and Roberts* 1998, 540
12.	1839	James Watt	m	[Christie, 9 May 1889]; Glasgow Museums S.149	*Graves* VII, 1905–6, 65; *Pearson* 1991, unpag; *Laperriere* 4, 1991, 140; *Morris and Roberts* 1998, 540
13.	1843	The rose	m	[Exhib R Sc A, Edinburgh, 581]; untraced	*Laperriere* 4, 1991, 140
14.	1845	David with the sword of Goliath		[Exhib RA, London, 1427]; untraced	*Graves* VII, 1905–6, 65; *Laperriere* 4, 1991, 140
Busts					
15.	1815	Dr Leach		[Exhib RA, London, 892]; untraced	*Graves* VII, 1905–6, 64
16.	1815	Unidentified gentleman		[Exhib RA, London, 1048]; untraced	*Graves* VII, 1905–6, 64
17.	1817	Mr J Littler		[Exhib RA, London, 948]; untraced	*Graves* VII, 1905–6, 65
18.	1818	Unidentified gentleman		[Exhib RA, London, 1042]; untraced	*Graves* VII, 1905–6, 64
19.	1818	Unidentified gentleman		[Exhib RA, London, 1092]; untraced	*Graves* VII, 1905–6, 64
20.	1818	William Shakespeare		Untraced	*Annals of the Fine Arts*, 1819, 631–2
21.	1819	Henry Sass		[Exhib RA, London, 1217]; untraced	*Graves* VII, 1905–6, 65; *Ormond* 1973, 410
22.	1819	John Britton		[Exhib RA, London, 1229]; untraced	*Graves* VII, 1905–6, 65; *Ormond* 1973, 56
23.	pre-1820	Sir Walter Scott		[coll Sir Walter Scott]; untraced	*Lady Lever* 1999, 71–4; *Graves* VII, 1905–6, 65
24.	1821	B Oakley		[Exhib RA, London, 1151]; untraced	*Graves* VII, 1905–6, 65
25.	1821	Dr Gregory		[Exhib RA, London, 1107]; untraced	*Graves* VII, 1905–6, 65; *Laperriere* 4, 1991, 140
26.	1821	Dr Monro		[Exhib RA, London, 1099]; untraced	*Graves* VII, 1905–6, 65
27.	1821	Dr Rutherford		[Exhib RA, London, 1129]; untraced	*Graves* VII, 1905–6, 65
28.	1821	Mrs Oakley		[Exhib RA, London, 1130]; untraced	*Graves* VII, 1905–6, 65
29.	1821	R Stevenson		[Exhib RA, London, 1141]; untraced	*Graves* VII, 1905–6, 65
30.	1821	Unidentified gentleman		[Exhib RA, London, 1135]; untraced	*Graves* VII, 1905–6, 64
31.	1821	Unidentified man	p	Edinburgh University	*Woodward* 1977, vol 1, pt 2, 213
32.	1823	D Bridges	m	[Exhib RA, London, 1106]; untraced	*Graves* VII, 1905–6, 65
33.	1823	Rev H Gray		[Exhib RA, London, 1120]; untraced	*Graves* VII, 1905–6, 65
34.	1823	Unidentified gentleman		[Exhib RA, London, 1077]; untraced	*Graves* VII, 1905–6, 64
35.	1824	J Graham		[Exhib Soc of BA, London, 350]; untraced	*Johnson* 1975, 416
36.	1824	J Harley		[Exhib Soc of BA, London, 351]; untraced	*Johnson* 1975, 416
37.	1824	J Sanders		[Exhib Soc of BA, London, 323]; untraced	*Johnson* 1975, 416
38.	1824	Richard Penn		[Exhib Soc of BA, London, 344]; untraced	*Johnson* 1975, 416
39.	1824	Sir James Carmichael Smyth Bt	m	[Exhib RA, London, 992]; untraced	*Graves* VII, 1905–6, 65
40.	1824	Unidentified gentleman		[Exhib Soc of BA, London, 346]; untraced	*Johnson* 1975, 416
41.	1824	Unidentified gentleman		[Exhib Soc of BA, London, 349]; untraced	*Johnson* 1975, 416
42.	1824	Unidentified gentleman		[Exhib Soc of BA, London, 355]; untraced	*Johnson* 1975, 416
43.	1825	F W Smith		[Exhib RA, London, 1058]; untraced	*Graves* VII, 1905–6, 65
44.	1825	H Weigal		[Exhib RA, London, 1068]; untraced	*Graves* VII, 1905–6, 65
45.	1825	Mary Wood (Miss Paton)		[Exhib RA, London, 1056]; untraced	*Graves* VII, 1905–6, 65
46.	1832	Unidentified young lady	m	[Exhib R Sc A, Edinburgh, 331]; untraced	*Laperriere* 4, 1991, 140
47.	1836	Mr Chambers		[Exhib RA, London, 1081]; untraced	*Graves* VII, 1905–6, 65; *Johnson* 1975, 416
48.	1836	Unidentified gentleman	m	[Exhib RA, London, 1096]; untraced	*Graves* VII, 1905–6, 65
49.	1836	Unidentified lady		[Exhib RA, London, 1082]; untraced	*Graves* VII, 1905–6, 65
50.	1836	Unidentified lady		[Exhib RA, London, 1084]; untraced	*Graves* VII, 1905–6, 65
51.	1838	W Salter		[Exhib RA, London, 1319]; untraced	*Graves* VII, 1905–6, 65
52.	1839	Matthew Anketel	m	[Exhib RA, London, 1348]; untraced	*Graves* VII, 1905–6, 65
53.	1839	Poetry	m	[Exhib Liverpool Ac, 703]; untraced	*Graves* 1875, 481; *Graves* VII, 1905–6, 65; *Laperriere* 4, 1991, 140; *Morris and Roberts* 1998, 540
54.	1839	Queen Victoria	m	[Exhib R Sc A, Edinburgh, 514]; untraced	*Laperriere* 4, 1991, 140; *Morris and Roberts* 1998, 540
55.	1839	Sir James Carmichael Smyth Bt		[Exhib RA, London, 1319]; untraced	*Graves* VII, 1905–6, 65
56.	1840	An artist		[Exhib RA, London, 1156]; untraced	*Graves* VII, 1905–6, 65
57.	1840	Cupid	m	[Exhib R Sc A, Edinburgh, 371]; untraced	*Graves* 1875, 481; *Graves* VII, 1905–6, 65; *Laperriere* 4, 1991, 140; *Morris and Roberts* 1998, 541
58.	1840	Head of a child in marble		[Exhib RA, London, 1112]; untraced	*Graves* VII, 1905–6, 65

59.	1840	Psyche	m	[Exhib R Sc A, Edinburgh, 376]; untraced		*Graves* VII, 1905–6, 65; *Laperriere* 4, 1991, 140; *Morris and Roberts* 1998, 541
60.	1841	Arthur, 1st Duke of Wellington	p	RDS, Dublin	SD	*White and Bright* 1998, 87
61.	1842	Dr Hope	m	[Exhib RA, London, 1377]; untraced		*Graves* VII, 1905–6, 65
62.	1843	An Italian greyhound, head		[Exhib BI, London, 439]; untraced		*Graves* 1875, 481; *Laperriere* 4, 1991, 140
63.	1844	Albert, the Prince Consort		[Exhib RA, London, 1372]; untraced		*Graves* VII, 1905–6, 65; *Laperriere* 4, 1991, 140
64.	nd	Sir John Dashwood King		West Wycombe Park		*Gunnis* 1968, 346
65.	nd	Unidentified man	p	Edinburgh University		*Woodward* 1977, vol 1, pt 2, 213
Reliefs						
66.	1816	Robert Skirving	w	VAM	S	*Pyke* 1973, 135
67.	1817	Judgement of Paris		[RA gold medal]; untraced		*Graves* VII, 1905–6, 64; *Gunnis* 1968, 345
68.	1843	John Hampden (†1643), portrait medallion, part of a monument	m	Old Watlington Road, Chalgrove, Oxon (site of the Battle of Chalgrove)		*ILN*, 17 June, 1843, 431–2; *Gunnis* 1968, 346
Miscellaneous						
69.	1815	Portrait of a gentleman		[Exhib RA, London, 956]; untraced		*Graves* VII, 1905–6, 64
70.	1817	Satan's contemplation		[Exhib RA, London, 1072]; untraced		*Graves* 1875, 481; *Graves* VII, 1905–6, 65
71.	1817	Silvia at the fountain		[Exhib BI, London, 242]; untraced		*Graves* 1875, 481
72.	1818	Portrait of a gentleman		[Exhib RA, London, 982]; untraced		*Graves* VII, 1905–6, 64
73.	1818	Portrait of a gentleman		[Exhib RA, London, 1007]; untraced		*Graves* VII, 1905–6, 64
74.	1818	Portrait of a lady		[Exhib RA, London, 1015]; untraced		*Graves* VII, 1905–6, 64
75.	1819	The death of Virginia		[Exhib RA, London, 1188]; untraced		*Graves* 1875, 481; *Graves* VII, 1905–6, 64
76.	1819	Unidentified gentleman	w	[Exhib RA, London, 1118]; untraced		*Graves* VII, 1905–6, 64
77.	1821	Princess Elizabeth, death mask		untraced		*Woodward* 1977, vol 1, pt 2, 211
78.	1821	Robert the Bruce		[Exhib BI, London, 317]; untraced		*Graves* 1875, 481
79.	1822	The judgement of Brutus on his two sons		[Exhib RA, London, 997]; untraced		*Graves* VII, 1905–6, 64
80.	by 1829	The deluge		Untraced		*Gunnis* 1968, 345
81.	1838	Paris and Helen		[Exhib RA, London, 1263]; untraced		*Graves* VII, 1905–6, 64
82.	1840	The infant Moses		[Exhib Liverpool Ac, 690]; untraced		*Graves* VII, 1905–6, 65; *Laperriere* 4, 1991, 140; *Morris and Roberts* 1998, 541

SCURRY, J fl 1850–52

His Royal Academy exhibition entries included busts of Professor Rodgers, of St George's School of Medicine (1) and William Essex, the son of W Essex, enamel painter to Queen Victoria (5). His address was given as 13 Wilmington Square in 1851.

Busts						
1.	1850	Professor Rogers		[Exhib RA, London, 1390]; untraced		*Graves* VII, 1905–6, 66; *Gunnis* 1968, 346
2.	1851	W Scurry, Senior	p	[Exhib RA, London, 1356]; untraced		*Graves* VII, 1905–6, 66
3.	1852	Louisa Pyne		[Exhib RA, London, 1474]; untraced		*Graves* VII, 1905–6, 66; *Gunnis* 1968, 346
4.	1852	Master George Rodger		[Exhib RA, London, 1461]; untraced		*Graves* VII, 1905–6, 66
5.	1852	William Essex		[Exhib RA, London, 1384]; untraced		*Graves* VII, 1905–6, 66; *Gunnis* 1968, 346
Reliefs						
6.	1851	G H McShail, medallion		[Exhib RA, London, 1387]; untraced		*Graves* VII, 1905–6, 66
7.	1852	A medallion		[Exhib RA, London, 1492]; untraced		*Graves* VII, 1905–6, 66
8.	1852	A medallion		[Exhib RA, London, 1428]; untraced		*Graves* VII, 1905–6, 66

SEABORNE fl *c*1772

He can perhaps be identified with **Seaborne of Birmingham**.

Funerary Monuments						
1.	†1772	Benjamin Palmer		St Alphege, Solihull, Warks	S	

SEABORNE, of Birmingham fl *c*1812–24

He signs a wall-tablet in the form of a sarcophagus to Benjamin Wilson (1), and a large Gothic monument to Isaac Spooner (2).

Literary References: *Gunnis* 1968, 346

Funerary Monuments						
1.	?1812	Benjamin Wilson		Burton-on-Trent, Staffs		*Gunnis* 1968, 346
2.	†1818	Isaac Spooner		Elmdon, Warks	S	Pevsner, *Warks*, 1966, 288
3.	?1824	Thomas Hill		Old Swinford, Staffs	S	GPC

SEAGER, of Rugby fl 1788?

He may perhaps be identified with **Peter Seager of Coventry**.

Funerary Monuments						
1.	?1788	Thomas Benn		Clifton, Warks		*Gunnis* 1968, 346

SEAGER, Peter, of Coventry fl *c*1819–30

He signs a number of tablets in Warwickshire. He may perhaps be identified with **Seager of Rugby** or **Peter Séguier**.

Funerary Monuments						
1.	†1819	Thomas Lant (†1780), his wife Catherine (†1818) and her brother		Berkswell, Warks	S	*Gunnis* 1968, 346
2.	?1821	Richard Abbey		Watford, Northants		*Gunnis* 1968, 346
3.	?1825	Frances Prince		Solihull, Warks	S	*Gunnis* 1968, 346
4.	?1826	Edward Wise		St Paul, Birmingham, Warks	S	*Gunnis* 1968, 346
5.	†1828	George Yates		St Peter & St Paul, Aston, Warks	S	Pevsner, *Warks*, 1966, 148; *Gunnis* 1968, 346
6.	?1830	Edward Hobson		St Paul, Birmingham, Warks	S	*Gunnis* 1968, 346

SEALEY, Thomas fl 1810

He was employed as a marble mason under Wyatt when Longleat, Wilts, was being re-built, receiving payments from 27 October 1810. He signs one known monument with a relief of *Hope.*

Archival References: Longford HA, 1800–1818

Funerary Monuments						
1.	1810	Mrs Kent		St Mary, Paddington, London		*Gunnis* 1968, 346

SEALY, John I 1749–1813

See **Coade Factory of Lambeth**

SEALY, John II ?1789–1817

He was the son of **John Sealy I.** He entered the Royal Academy Schools on 27 January 1808, aged 19, and exhibited at the British Institution and the RA between 1809 and 1811, giving his address as the **Coade Factory of Lambeth.**

Funerary Monuments						
1.	1813	Thomas Ramsden (†1813)		Charterhouse chapel, City of London	SD	
Busts						
2.	1810	Mr Sealy		[Exhib RA, London, 900]; untraced		*Graves* VII, 1905–6, 65
3.	1810	Portrait of a young lady		[Exhib RA, London, 607]; untraced		*Graves* VII, 1905–6, 65
4.	1811	An artist		[Exhib RA, London, 932]; untraced		*Graves* VII, 1905–6, 65
Miscellaneous						
5.	1809	A greyhound	m	[Exhib BI, London, 341]; untraced		*Graves* 1875, 483

SEARES, Daniel, of Maidstone fl 1825

His yard was in Stone Street. Gunnis listed only one tablet, described as his best and Seares apparently signed a few more in Kent.

Funerary Monuments						
1.	1825	Priscilla Crispe (†1823)		Sutton Valence, Kent	S	*Gunnis* 1968, 346; Pevsner, *Kent: W & Weald,* 1976, 558

SEARS, of 9 Strand, London fl *c*1828

He signs a large marble tablet (**1**): every letter of the long inscription is cast in bronze.

Funerary Monuments						
1.	?1828	Dugdale Family		Handsworth, Warks		*Gunnis* 1968, 346

SEDDON, C M, of Liverpool fl *c*1824–42

A Liverpool sculptor, he exhibited at the Liverpool Academy, giving his address as 3 Daulby Street in 1829, and Russel Street from 1837 to 1842. His monuments to Richard Phillips, Thomas Robinson and Vincent Glover are all tablets with figures of kneeling emblematic females (**1, 3, 4**). He was probably related to **James Seddon**.

Literary References: *Gunnis* 1968, 347; *Morris and Roberts* 1998, 542

Funerary Monuments						
1.	†1824	Richard Phillips		St Martin's, Salop	S	Pevsner, *Salop,* 1958, 239; *Gunnis* 1968, 347
2.	1837	'A monumental design'		[Exhib Liverpool Ac, 693]; untraced		*Morris and Roberts* 1998, 542
3.	†1837	Rev Thomas Robinson		St Peter, Liverpool, Lancs		Pevsner, *Lancs: S,* 1969, 154
4.	†1840	Rev Vincent Glover		St Peter, Liverpool, Lancs		Pevsner, *Lancs: S,* 1969, 154
5.	?1841	James Young		Halifax Cathedral, Nova Scotia		GPC
Busts						
6.	1824	Richard Jones		[Exhib ALRI, Liverpool, 168]; untraced		*Morris and Roberts* 1998, 542
7.	1837	A child	m	[Exhib Liverpool Ac, 689]; untraced		*Morris and Roberts* 1998, 542
8.	1840	Two ladies		[Exhib Liverpool Ac, 682, 695]; untraced		*Morris and Roberts* 1998, 542
9.	1842	Dr Baird		[Exhib Liverpool Ac, 572]; untraced		*Morris and Roberts* 1998, 542
10.	1842	Thomas Coglan		[Exhib Liverpool Ac, 579]; untraced		*Morris and Roberts* 1998, 542
11.	1842	W Lawson		[Exhib Liverpool Ac, 573]; untraced		*Morris and Roberts* 1998, 542
Reliefs						
12.	1837	Sir Walter Scott, portrait medallion		[Exhib Liverpool Ac, 684]; untraced		*Morris and Roberts* 1998, 542
Miscellaneous						
13.	1825	Homer chanting his poems, model		[Exhib ALRI, Liverpool, 170]; untraced		*Morris and Roberts* 1998, 542
14.	1827	David slaying Goliath		[Exhib ALRI, Liverpool, 276]; untraced		*Morris and Roberts* 1998, 542
15.	1829	Judgement of Paris		[Exhib ALRI, Liverpool, 319]; untraced		*Morris and Roberts* 1998, 542

SEDDON, James fl 1832–72

James Seddon, who was probably related to **C M Seddon**, was a Liverpool sculptor and cotton broker. He worked at 5 Daulby Street, Liverpool. By 1832 he had moved his business to 8 Queen Street, Edge Hill. In 1847 he was in partnership with **John Alexander Paterson Macbride.** He is last recorded in 1872 as a 'gentleman' of 17 Ivy Leigh, Tue Brook (*Liverpool Directory* in GPC).

SEDERBACH, Victor Alexander fl 1755–56

He was a modeller in terracotta. John Talbot wrote to his architect, Sanderson Miller, in January 1756 about his improvements to Laycock Abbey: 'The Foreigner who has been here ever since May has executed his Performance in a very Workmanlike manner and your Niches are filled by a set of Inhabitants worthy such Repositories. I presume you are acquainted with the method of making Models for Statues. He proceeds on the same principles, only Bakes them afterwards, by which means they become of a Red Colour and ring like a Garden Pot . . . I fancy Lord Shelburn will employ him on his arrival at London, where he goes next week; however, as so many of your friends are Connoisseurs, I would advise them seeing his Performances, which are both Easy and not Expensive. His name is sonorous, no less than Victor Alexander Sederbach and yet lodges at one King's a grocer in Green Street, near Castle Street, Leicester Fields. I am sorry he did not show all his Performances to the Gentleman you sent a note by, but on asking the Reason, was told that someone the day before had Broke a Figure, which made him extremely Captious' (*Letters to Sanderson Miller*, 308).

The busts at Laycock are mounted on brackets and the figures are set off by canopied quatrefoil niches (1). The subjects are obscure, though Britton believed them to be 'allusive to the history of the monastery' (*Britton 1801–1815*, 3, 242). They include a half-length bust of *Death* with arms outstretched. Pevsner published photographs of the works, which he felt to be German or Austrian in style, in the hope that the sculptor of these 'weird saints and this bust of ferocious death' would be the subject of future research (*Pevsner* 1958, 334). The last record of Sederbach is a note in the Miller letters of 1757 recording that Sederbach had an offer of work in Holland.

Literary References: *Gunnis* 1968, 347; *Pevsner* 1958, 332–4

Miscellaneous

1.	1755–1756	Several busts and figures	tc	Lacock Abbey, Wilts, hall	Pevsner, *Wilts*, 1975, 288

SEELEY, John 1789–

Seeley, who joined the Royal Academy Schools in 1808, later went into partnership with **Felix Austin**, and together they executed various monumental works. Like his partner Seeley chose good designers for his works, and like him, too, dealt in terracotta, though he called his material 'artificial lime-stone'. He executed a number of fountains to designs by architects.

See **Austin, Felix**

Literary References: *The Builder*, 26 July 1851, 474 ('List of Fountains executed in Artificial Lime Stone by John Seeley, 1–4 Keppel Row, New Road, Regent's Park')

Funerary Monuments

1.	1829	Anna Forster	Walsall, Staffs	S	*Gunnis* 1968, 347
2.	1848	John Gosling	St John's Wood Chapel, Marylebone, London	S	*Gunnis* 1968, 347
3.	†1851	Sir Gilbert Heathcote	Edenham, Lincs		Pevsner, *Lincs*, 1989, 269

Architectural Sculpture

4.	*c*1845	Fountain	[Birkenhead Market Hall]; Arrowe Hall, Birkenhead, Cheshire		*Builder*, 1851, 474; Pevsner, *Cheshire*, 1971, 107
5.	nd	Fountain	The dairy, Blenheim Palace		*Gunnis* 1968, 347
6.	nd	Fountain (designed by Charles Barry and J B Papworth)	Queen's Park, Brighton		*Builder* 1851, 474; *Gunnis* 1968, 347
7.	nd	Fountain (designed by Charles Barry and J B Papworth)	The Steyne, Brighton		*Builder*, 1851, 474; *Gunnis* 1968, 347
8.	nd	Fountain (designed by Charles Barry)	Tottenham House, Marlborough, Wilts		*Gunnis* 1968, 347

SEEST, Christian Carlsen fl 1734–57

When he left his native Denmark in 1734, he was described on his passport as 'sculptor-apprentice'. He travelled to Germany, Holland and other countries and was in Paris in 1742. It is not clear when he first came to England, but he made his second visit at Michaelmas 1750, when he modelled a bust of George Vertue (1), and worked as assistant to **L F Roubiliac**. Vertue wrote: 'a bust, a modell done of my own portrait, a head only, by one who was workman to Mr. Rubilliac. This man came from Denmark and had been some years in ~ and Holland, but first in England and lately has returned to England again. Now constantly works for Mr. Rubilliac, his name is Siste. He is an ingenious man, draws very well and modells in good manner and taste' (*Vertue* III, 154). Seest married Ann Brandreth in December 1750 at St Anne, Soho, Westminster, and their child, Christian Charles Siste, was christened on 25 May 1752 at St Martin-in-the-Fields. Seest worked under Roubiliac on the statue of Sir Isaac Newton for Trinity College, Cambridge.

On 16 September 1748 he was appointed Danish court sculptor, a post he held until 1768. From London he had sent drawings for monuments, etc., to the Danish King, Frederick V, and a bust of that monarch, which is probably his work, is at Ledreborg Castle. He was dead by June 1771, when 'Anne Siest widow of Christn Seest, Sculptor' was donated 8 guineas by the Royal Academy on the recommendation of G M Moser. She continued to receive aid from the Academy of sums varying between 3 and 4 guineas, nearly every year until 1797, when she probably died.

Literary References: *Weilbach* 1897, II; *Gunnis* 1968, 347

Archival References: IGI; RA Council Minutes, vol 1, fols 108, 136, 159, 180, 203, 136, 258, 273, 287, 305, 330, 345, 361; vol 2, fols 10, 29, 41, 61, 83, 108, 142, 182, 228, 228, 273, 325

Busts

1.	1750	George Vertue, model	Untraced	*Vertue* III, 154; *Gunnis* 1968, 347

SEGUIER, Peter fl later 18th century

The brother of David Séguier, picture-restorer, dealer and painter who trained under George Morland. Séguier was apprenticed to **Richard Hayward** and executed one known marble profile medallion of David Garrick on a dark marble background (1). He was the father of another William Séguier, the first keeper of the National Gallery. According to Laurence Cust, whose information came from the family, Seguier devoted 'himself chiefly to works of a monumental character' and 'kept steadily to that profession all his life' (*Cust* 1909, 158). Given Hayward's Warwickshire connections, it is possible that he may be identified with **Peter Seager of Coventry**.

Literary References: *Gunnis* 1968, 346

Archival References: AL/RG

Reliefs

1.	nd	David Garrick	Untraced	*Cust* 1909, 158

SELDEN, John –1715

He assisted **Grinling Gibbons** at Petworth, where he provided much robust wood-carving. The Selden family first appeared in the Petworth parish registers in the early 17th century. John Selden was working in the house in 1687 and he appeared in the accounts until they cease in 1697. He was several times paid a lump sum of £40, which may have been his year's wages. Like many other carvers, he appears to have been skilful at working both in stone and wood. In John Bowen's account roll for 1696 there are payments for sending letters to John Selden about Portland stone as well as a long detailed entry about various wood- and stone-carving including mouldings, festoons and even a periwig stand.

Vertue noted 'in the Carvd Room. richly adord with Sculpture. of flowers, festoons & fruit birds & boys-&c.. by Gibbons. & *Selden* who wrought there many Years. this man lost his life by saving the carving from being burnt when the house was on fire' (*Vertue* II, 81). He was buried at Petworth on 12 January 1715.

Literary References: *Beard* 1989 (1), 37, 39–40, 41, 192, 193

No.	Date	Work		Location		Reference
Funerary Monuments						
1.	nd	James Butler		Thakeham, Sussex	S	
Chimneypieces						
2.	1689–1690	'large. . .made with ffowles, ffishes and flowers' Payment(s): £30		Petworth House, Sussex, dining room		*Beard* 1989 (1), 39, citing West Sussex CRO, Petworth MS 245
3.	nd	Overmantel for central fireplace		Petworth Park, Sussex, carved room		*Esterly* 1998, 108
Architectural Sculpture						
4.	1689–1690	'a picture frame for the chimney in the said roome carved with fouldinge & Flowers conteyning 22 feet at 5s the foot' Payment(s): £5 10s	s	Petworth House, Sussex, dining room		*Beard* 1989 (1), 39, citing West Sussex CRO, Petworth MS 245
5.	1692	Coat of arms, and other decorative woodwork	wd	Petworth House, Sussex, marble hall		*Rowell* 2000 (2), 16–17 (repr)
6.	1692	Gate-piers, and 'a seat that stands in the lower rampier'		[Petworth Park, Sussex]; untraced		*Rowell* 2000 (2), 50
7.	*c*1692	Military trophy with the 6th Duke of Somerset's coat of arms		Petworth House, Sussex, carved room		*Esterly* 1998, 130, 132 (repr)
8.	1696	Polished table	m	[Petworth Park, Sussex, fountain house]; untraced		*Rowell* 2000 (2), 51

SELLERS, Joseph, of Stoke fl *c*1803

No.	Date	Work		Location		Reference
Funerary Monuments						
1.	†1803	Thomas Acton, wall-tablet		Bunbury, Cheshire	S	*Gunnis* 1968, 347

SELSEN fl 1770

Mr Selsen, carver and modeller, bound Abraham Bertaud, pupil of the Westminster French Protestant Charity School, in February 1770.

Literary References: *le May* 2001, 566

SEPHTON, Daniel 1714–59

The son of Henry Sephton, Gunnis considered him the best of the 18th-century Manchester statuaries. His monument to William Wright is a large architectural work, nearly 20 feet high, with a portrait-bust, and side consoles delicately carved with beetles, butterflies and flora (**6**). The tablet to Thomas Barron has a rococo cartouche against an obelisk (**4**), and another, to Sarah Jarvis, has a pyramid with an armorial shield above an inscription tablet (**2**).

Sephton died on 11 January 1759, and was commemorated on the same tablet as his father in St Mary, Walton, near Liverpool. The epitaph describes him as 'late of Manchester, eminent in carving'. His wife survived him and died in 1770.

Literary References: *Gunnis* 1968, 347–8; *Colvin* 1995, 857–8

No.	Date	Work		Location		Reference
Funerary Monuments						
1.	?1748	Francis Massy		St Elphin, Warrington, Lancs	S	*Gunnis* 1968, 347
2.	†1748	Sarah Jarvis		Chester Cathedral	S	*Gunnis* 1968, 347
3.	†1749	Francis Price		Overton, Flint	S	Pevsner, *Clwyd*, 1986, 411
4.	†1751	Thomas Barron		St Mary, Prescot, Lancs	S	Pevsner, *Lancs: S*, 1969, 366
5.	†1752	Edward Dicconson		Standish, Lancs	S	
6.	†1753	William Wright		St Mary, Stockport, Cheshire		*Gunnis* 1968, 347; Pevsner, *Cheshire*, 1971, 340

SEPHTON, Henry *c*1686–1756

A mason and architect of Manchester, he is best known for designing and building Ince Blundell Hall. He was also one of the principal masons at Knowsley (Earl of Derby's Archives, DDK. 2002/1–7). He and his partner, a Mr Brooker, were the master masons for the Liverpool Exchange, 1752–1755. In 1726 he was paid 10 guineas for drawing 'ye plan' of St George's Church, Liverpool (City Corporation Records in GPC). His only known monument is a cartouche tablet 'with excellent detail' (**1**) (*Gunnis* 1968, 348).

He died on 2 June 1756, and was buried in St Mary, Walton, Liverpool, but the monument to his memory was lost when the church was destroyed in the Second World War. His wife Esther died in 1750. Henry was the father of **Daniel Sephton** and possibly also of 'John Sephton, Liverpool, stone-cutter', who died on 19 August 1770, aged 37, to whom there was also a tablet in Walton church (inf. Liverpool Public Library in GPC).

Literary References: *Gunnis* 1968, 348; *Colvin* 1995, 857–8; *Findlay* 1996, 24–36; *Robinson* 1999, 70–3

No.	Date	Work		Location		Reference
Funerary Monuments						
1.	?1737	Robert Scarisbrick		Ormskirk, Lancs	S	*Gunnis* 1968, 348

SERVANT fl 1762

The catalogue of the Society of Free Artists for 1762 lists a statue of Ceres in white marble by Servant. This work is ignored by Graves in his *Exhibitors* at the *Society of Artists and Free Society*, though he does mention a '– Servant' exhibiting pictures in 1764.

Literary References: Free Soc Cat, 1762, NAL

No.	Date	Work		Location		Reference
Statues						
1.	1762	Ceres	m	[Exhib Free Soc]; untraced		*Gunnis* 1968, 348

SETTLE, John fl 1682–92

A mason-sculptor, he was renter warden of the Masons' Company in 1682. In 1684 he was paid for 'a marble stone layd over the grave of Mr. George Papillon' (1). His most notable monument was to Sir Lumley Robinson (2). It has a bowed inscribed tablet between two Corinthian columns with skulls beneath them. The broken pediment above originally contained a vase and the apron supported an heraldic shield held by a cherub. It was situated between the 'third and fourth pillars from the cloyster gates westward', but now lies dismantled (*Neale and Brayley*). The work is illustrated in Dart's *Westmonasterium*. It is described in an anonymous guide to the Abbey, published about 1840: 'The columns are supported by Death's heads, and the arms upon the base by a cherub. On the top is a vase and rising to the pediments, enrichments of laurel branches, etc' (*Gunnis* 1968, 348).

In 1689 Settle was paid £4 by the 1st Earl Fauconberg for work at his London house, and there are other payments recorded until 1692 (*Wombwell Archives* in GPC). Settle was paid £214 15s in 1680 for 'paving worke & stuffe done & used in ye Chapell' and hall of the Mercers' Company.

Literary References: *Gunnis* 1968, 348

Archival References: Masons' Co, Masters and Wardens; Mercers S & R W Accts; GPC

Funerary Monuments

1.	1684	George Papillon, gravestone Payment(s): £10	[St Katherine Coleman, London]; destroyed		Papillon Archives in GPC
2.	†1684	Sir Lumley Robinson	Westminster Abbey, triforium	S	*Dart* 1723, 2, 117; *Neale and Brayley* 1818–23, 2, 234; *Gunnis* 1968, 348
3.	1685	Albert Faber (†1684)	St Dunstan-in-the-West, City of London	S	Pevsner, *London: City*, 1997, 216

SHANAHAN, Michael fl *c*1770–95

He is thought to have come from Cork and was taken up when young by the Earl Bishop of Derry, whom he may have met in 1768, when the latter was Bishop of Cloyne. Shanahan travelled on the Continent in the early 1770s with the bishop, acting as tutor to his son and making drawings of several sites, later engraved by Dall'Acqua in Vicenza, but apparently never published. In the 1780s he established a marble business in Cork, where he carried out orders for marble chimneypieces and other work. He is thought to have designed St Patrick's Bridge and the city and county gaols, both in Cork.

Literary References: *Potterton* 1975, 78

Funerary Monuments

1.	†1795	Dr Joseph Moore (designed by Sir Richard Morrison)	Clonmel, Co Tipperary	S	*Potterton* 1975, 73

SHARLAND, John, of Torquay fl *c*1823–55

A mason of Madrepue Place, Torquay, his tablets are mostly neo-Hellenic.

Literary References: *Gunnis* 1968, 348

Archival References: RG/JP, 7, 1281

Funerary Monuments

1.	?1823	Viscountess Kilcoursie	Tormohun, Devon		*Gunnis* 1968, 348
2.	?1830	Elizabeth Hague	Barrow Gurney, Somerset		*Gunnis* 1968, 348
3.	?1834	Rev John Edwards	Berry Pomeroy, Devon		*Gunnis* 1968, 348
4.	†1841	Charlotte Townes	St Mary, Brixham, Devon		RG/JP, 7, 1282
5.	?1854	Caroline Blake	Holy Trinity, Gosport, Hants	S	GPC
6.	?1855	Mary Blake	Holy Trinity, Gosport, Hants	S	GPC

SHARMAN, Edward, of Peterborough 1773–1805

He was perhaps the son of John Sharman, a Peterborough builder. Sharman's monuments and tablets are 'good provincial work, the best being that to George Pochin which bas a relief of a mourning woman' (4); (*Gunnis* 1968, 348). His obituary in the *Gentleman's Magazine* says of him that his 'goodness of heart was rarely equaled' [*sic*] and his 'natural genius was far above his opportunity of cultivating it' (*GM* 1805, ii, 686).

Literary References: *Gunnis* 1968, 348; *Colvin* 1995, 860

Funerary Monuments

1.	?1791	Judd family	St Martin, Stamford, Lincs	S	*Gunnis* 1968, 348
2.	?1796	William Whitsed	Peakirk, Northants	S	*Gunnis* 1968, 348
3.	?1797	George Digby	Bourne, Lincs	S	*Gunnis* 1968, 348
4.	†1798	George Pochin	Bourne, Lincs	S	*Gunnis* 1968, 348; Pevsner, *Lincs*, 1989, 173

SHARP, George, of Gloucester fl 1822–37

He signs a number of tablets, including one with naval trophies (1).

Funerary Monuments

1.	1822	John Sharp	St Magnus, London Bridge, City of London	S	*Gunnis* 1968, 348
2.	†1836	Rev John Kelsall	Bredon, Worcs	S	
3.	1837	Miles Coverdale (†1568)	St Magnus the Martyr, City of London		Pevsner, *London: City*, 1997, 233
4.	nd	Unidentified subject, tablet	Christ Church, Gloucester	S	Pevsner, *Glos: Vale & Forest of Dean*, 1976, 230

SHARP, Thomas 1805–82

Sharp first exhibited at the Royal Academy in 1830, giving his address as 31 Tichbourn Street, London, and Paris. He entered the Royal Academy Schools at the advanced age of 26 in 1831, on the recommendation of **Sir Francis Chantrey**. That year he showed *Boy and lizard*, which depicts the child recovering from his surprise at the sight of the creature, mistaken for a serpent. The figure was praised in the *Library of Fine Arts* as 'well conceived, and its modelling good throughout', but the writer felt that the overall effect was ruined by the material: 'it was probably in utter unconsciousness of his own power' that the sculptor 'had chosen a piece of marble so veiny and imperfect as to offend the eye; thus, while we see all around abominations in the purest white marble, here is a work that would have done credit to almost any artist carved in the most objectionable material, and consequently scarcely noticed' (4).

Sharp won a medal from the Academy in 1835 (**46**), and continued to exhibit there until late in life. His practice appears to have been chiefly in busts, though he was responsible for some ideal works and for a statue of Lord Palmerston (**12**). His workshop was located at 22 Dean Street, Soho in 1832 and he then moved house half a dozen times, ending up at 101 Edgware Road in 1869.

Sharp was also a designer for silverware. In 1836 he exhibited 'A Bacchanalian subject, embossed in sheet silver' with the Society of British Artists (*Johnson* 1975, 417). A 'Shakespeare' cup was exhibited at the RA in 1842. His 'justice cup' had a bas-relief of 'Justice protecting the Innocent, and driving from the earth Violence, Fraud, and Discord' (*AJ Cat* 1851, 60). This was shown at the Great Exhibition with a chimneypiece to his design for Messrs Rine. It was carved of statuary marble and had cast metal ornaments, including the 'initials of the Queen and Prince Albert, formed with the stems of the rose, shamrock and thistle, which entwine them' (*AJ Cat* 1851, 81). The carver is not identified. He assisted **John Bell** with the Guards Memorial and the Wellington Monument, and continued to exhibit in his own right until 1869.

Literary References: *Graves* 1875, 485; *Graves* VII, 1905–6, 88–89; *Gunnis* 1968, 348–9; *Pyke* 1973, 135; *Johnson* 1975, 417–8; *Barnes* 1999, 61
Archival References: RA Admissions

Funerary Monuments						
1.	c1830	Anne Hardinge		Crowhurst, Sussex	S	*Gunnis* 1968, 348
2.	1832	Elizabeth Grope Model(s): exhib RA, London, 1832, 1114		St John Baptist, Windsor, Berks	S	*Graves* VII, 1905–6, 88; Pevsner, *Berks*, 1966, 299
3.	†1860	Ellen Powell		St John's Wood Chapel, Marylebone, London	S	RG/JP, 7, 1283
Statues						
4.	1831	Boy and lizard	m	[Exhib RA, London, 1193; bt Lady Colbourne]; untraced		*Library of Fine Arts*, vol I, 1831, 430; *Graves* VII, 1905–6, 88; *Gunnis* 1968, 348; *Johnson* 1975, 417
5.	?1834	Eve at the fountain (Eve seeing the shadow in the water)	m	Glasgow Museums S.10		*Graves* VII, 1905–6, 89; *Johnson* 1975, 417
6.	1835	David giving thanks for his victory over Goliath	m	[Exhib RA, London, 1074]; untraced		*Graves* 1875, 485; *Graves* VII, 1905–6, 88; *Gunnis* 1968, 348; *Johnson* 1975, 418
7.	1837	A group of orphans	m	[Exhib RA, London, 1157]; untraced		*Graves* 1875, 485; *Graves* VII, 1905–6, 88
8.	1837	'Affection', group		[Exhib RA, London, 1171]; untraced		*Graves* VII, 1905–6, 88
9.	1848	A vintager dancing, model		[Exhib RA, London, 1433]; untraced		*Graves* VII, 1905–6, 89
10.	1854	Christ blessing little children, model of a group		[Exhib RA, London, 1395]; untraced		*Graves* VII, 1905–6, 89
11.	1867	Henry, 3rd Viscount Palmerston, sketch for a recumbent effigy		[Exhib RA, London, 1090]; untraced		*Graves* VII, 1905–6, 89; *Ormond* 1973, 361
12.	1868	Henry, 3rd Viscount Palmerston	m	[Exhib RA, London, 1868, 1002]; Palmerston Park, Southampton	D	*Graves* VII, 1905–6, 89; *Gunnis* 1968, 348; *Ormond* 1973, 361
13.	1868	Stafford Price	m	[Exhib RA, London, 1083]; untraced		*Graves* VII, 1905–6, 89
Busts						
14.	1831	C Hayter Snr		[Exhib Soc of BA, London, 900]; untraced		*Johnson* 1975, 417
15.	1831	James Stewart		[Exhib RA, London, 1141]; untraced		*Graves* VII, 1905–6, 88
16.	1831	Unidentified gentleman		[Exhib RA, London, 1145]; untraced		*Graves* VII, 1905–6, 88
17.	1831	Unidentified lady		[Exhib RA, London, 1134]; untraced		*Graves* VII, 1905–6, 88
18.	1832	Daughter of Lord and Lady Frederick Fitzclarence		[Exhib RA, London, 1198]; untraced		*Graves* VII, 1905–6, 88
19.	1832	Lord Augustus FitzClarence		[Exhib RA, London, 1183]; untraced		*Graves* VII, 1905–6, 88; *Gunnis* 1968, 348
20.	1832	Unidentified gentleman, model		[Exhib Soc of BA, London, 871]; untraced		*Johnson* 1975, 417
21.	1834	Unidentified lady		[Exhib Soc of BA, London, 842]; untraced		*Johnson* 1975, 417
22.	1835	Bacchante	m	Chatsworth, Derbys, sculpture gallery		*Graves* 1875, 485; *Graves* VII, 1905–6, 88; *Chatsworth Handlist*, 26
23.	1840	Mrs P H Dickes		[Exhib RA, London, 1163]; untraced		*Graves* VII, 1905–6, 89
24.	1844	Henry, 3rd Viscount Palmerston	m	Broadlands, Hants		*AU*, 1844, 171; *Graves* VII, 1905–6, 89; *Ormond* 1973, 359
25.	1852	Daughter of Charles Reeves	m	[Exhib RA, London, 1390]; untraced		*Graves* VII, 1905–6, 89
26.	1852	J Durance George	m	[Exhib RA, London, 1446]; untraced		*Graves* VII, 1905–6, 89
27.	1854	A Bacchante	m	[Exhib RA, London, 1450]; untraced		*Graves* VII, 1905–6, 89
28.	1854	Flora	m	[Exhib RA, London, 1421]; untraced		*Graves* VII, 1905–6, 89
29.	1854	Rev Robert Ainslie, model		[Exhib RA, London, 1492]; untraced		*Graves* VII, 1905–6, 89
30.	1857	Rev James Eyre	m	[Exhib RA, London, 1291]; untraced		*Graves* VII, 1905–6, 89
31.	1858	Joseph Miles	m	[Exhib RA, London, 1304]; untraced		*Graves* VII, 1905–6, 89
32.	1863	Rev J Reynolds		[Exhib RA, London, 1194]; untraced		*Graves* VII, 1905–6, 89; *Gunnis* 1968, 348
33.	1864	Mrs George Lewis Phipps Eyre		[Exhib RA, London, 1051]; untraced		*Graves* VII, 1905–6, 89
34.	1867	Henry Revell Reynolds		[Exhib RA, London, 1126]; untraced		*Graves* VII, 1905–6, 89
35.	1868	J S Charlton		[Exhib RA, London, 1195]; untraced		*Graves* VII, 1905–6, 89
36.	1869	Earl of Lauderdale	m	[Exhib RA, London, 1169]; untraced		*Graves* VII, 1905–6, 89

Reliefs

37.	1833	Unidentified gentleman, medallic portrait	w	[Exhib RA, London, 1036]; untraced	*Graves* VII, 1905–6, 88
38.	1833	Unidentified lady, medallic portrait	w	[Exhib RA, London, 1052]; untraced	*Graves* VII, 1905–6, 88
39.	1834	Rev George Clayton, medallic portrait	w	[Exhib RA, London, 965]; untraced	*Graves* VII, 1905–6, 88
40.	1835	G Sharp, medallic portrait	w	[Exhib RA, London, 1017]; untraced	*Graves* VII, 1905–6, 88

Miscellaneous

41.	1830	Flora	m	[Exhib RA, London, 1225]; untraced	*Graves* 1875, 485; *Graves* VII, 1905–6, 88
42.	1832	The nymph Leucothea presenting the scarf to Ulysses		[Exhib Soc of BA, London, 867]; untraced	*Johnson* 1975, 417
43.	1833	'Monsieur Louel as a Troubadour, at the Egyptian Hall', model		[Exhib RA, London, 1133]; untraced	*Graves* VII, 1905–6, 88
44.	1833	Psyche contemplating the emblem of the soul		[Exhib BI, London, 551]; untraced	*Graves* 1875, 485
45.	1834	Rev John Reynolds, medallic portrait	w	[Exhib RA, London, 975]; untraced	*Graves* VII, 1905–6, 88
46.	1835	Model		[RA, London, silver medal]; untraced	RA Premium list
47.	1835	'Wax model of St Martin and the beggar, to be made in silver and presented to the Rev. Dr Richards of St Martin-in-the-Fields'	w	[Exhib RA, London, 902]; untraced	*Graves* VII, 1905–6, 88; RG/JP, 7, 1284
48.	1851	Christ's charge to Peter Model(s): 'Model of Christ's Charge to Peter' exhib RA, London, 1850, 1333		[Gt Exhib]; untraced	*Graves* VII, 1905–6, 89; *Gunnis* 1968, 348
49.	1862	'Non Angli sed Angeli'		[Int Exhib]; untraced	*Gunnis* 1968, 348
50.	1865	Hagar and Ishmael		[Exhib RA, London, 1032; Christie, 4 March 1872]; untraced	*Graves* VII, 1905–6, 89; GPC
51.	1866	Cupid in love	m	[Exhib RA, London, 851]; Christie, 4 March 1872; untraced	*Graves* VII, 1905–6, 89; GPC

SHARP & GILLSON fl 1790

They are listed in the *London Directory* of 1790, as having a 'chimney-piece and composition ornament factory' at 24 High Holborn (GPC).

SHARPE, Edward, of Stamford fl 1714–c1736

Sharpe became a freeman of Stamford in 1714 on payment of £4 and his widow was admitted to his house in Barn Hill, Stamford by manorial court in 1764. Sharpe's son, another Edward, was apprenticed to him and became a freeman of Stamford in 1749. The business may been considerable, for two earlier apprentices, Thomas Burbridge and William Bolland, had both become freemen of the town in 1732 (Stamford Archives).

Literary References: *Gunnis* 1968, 349

Archival References: JP, Misc Corr

Funerary Monuments

1.	?1736	Sir Brownlow Sherrard		North Witham, Lincs	*Gunnis* 1968, 349

SHARPE, P fl 1813

He appears to have come from the Liverpool area.

Literary References: *Gunnis* 1968, 349

Busts

1.	1813	Master Betty in Achmed		[Exhib Liverpool Ac, 318]; untraced	*Morris and Roberts* 1998, 547

SHAW, Aaron, of Kingston-on-Hull fl 1845–60

He contributed an image of Thorwaldsen to the Grand Polytechnic Exhibition at the Mechanics' Institute, Hull in 1845 (5). White's *Directory* of 1846 listed him as a stone and marble mason of 16 St John Street, at which time he was engaged on work at Brocklesby Park, Lincs, the home of the Earl of Yarborough (1). The *Hull Advertiser* announced the marriage of Aaron Shaw, sculptor, of Hyde Park, on 7 January 1860. (Inf. Gerardine Mulcahy)

Chimneypieces

1.	1846	Several Payment(s): £5 12s		Brocklesby Park, Lincs	Brocklesby Estate Accts, 1846, 172
2.	1848	'for resetting & polishing Chimney piece in Dining Room' Payment(s): £5 17s		Brocklesby Park, Lincs	Brocklesby Estate Accts, 1848, 272
3.	1848	Several of marble, with repairs to old ones and tables Payment(s): £208 7s 7d		Brocklesby Park, Lincs	Brocklesby Estate Accts, 1848, 266
4.	1850	Of marble, charged with labour Payment(s): £90 19s		Brocklesby Park, Lincs	Brocklesby Estate Accts, 1850, 306

Miscellaneous

5.	1845	Bertel Thorwaldsen		[Exhib Mechanics' Institute, Hull, 18]; untraced	Hull Polytechnic Exhib Cat, 1845

SHAW, Daniel, of King's Lynn fl 1628–75

In 1628 he became a freeman of King's Lynn and he later executed work in that town.

Statues

1.	1667	A unicorn and a boy	s	[probably for the exterior of the Charity School, Kings Lynn, Norfolk]; untraced	*Gunnis* 1968, 349

Architectural Sculpture

2.	1660	Town arms		[The schoolhouse, King's Lynn]; untraced	Chamberlain's Accts, Kings Lynn in *Gunnis* 1968, 349
3.	1675	Lion	s	King's Lynn, Norfolk, town cross	Chamberlain's Accounts, King's Lynn in *Gunnis* 1968, 349

SHAW, J, of Reading fl c1815–37

Funerary Monuments

1.	?1815	Hon Henry Bennett	Easthampstead, Berks	S	*Gunnis* 1968, 349
2.	?1837	Martha Fisher	Basildon, Berks	S	*Gunnis* 1968, 349

SHAW, James fl 1776–87

A wax modeller, he exhibited at the Royal Academy, giving his addresses as Charlotte Street, Rathbone Place in 1776 and Coventry Street in 1786.

Literary References: *Graves* VII, 1905–6, 94–5; *Gunnis* 1968, 349; *Pyke* 1973, 135

Miscellaneous

1.	1776	Unidentified portraits		[Exhib RA, London, 280]; untraced	*Graves* VII, 1905–6, 94
2.	1784	Mrs Shirley		[Exhib RA, London, 54]; untraced	*Graves* VII, 1905–6, 94
3.	1784	Rev Mr Shaw		[Exhib RA, London, 88]; untraced	*Graves* VII, 1905–6, 94
4.	1786	Unidentified gentleman	w	[Exhib RA, London, 372]; untraced	*Graves* VII, 1905–6, 95
5.	1787	Mucius Scaevola, model	w	[Exhib RA, London, 646]; untraced	*Graves* VII, 1905–6, 95

SHEEHAN, Cornelius –1761

He is probably the Mr Sheehan, 'an eminent stone-cutter' whose death in Marlborough Street, Dublin on 16 June 1761 is recorded in *Sleator's Gazetteer* (*Strickland* 2, 1913, 348–49). Potterton says that his monument to Gustavus Handcock shows that 'the sculptor had little or no knowledge of tomb design', though the architectural details are well carved (*Potterton* 1975, 78).

Funerary Monuments

1.	1759	Gustavus Handcock	Athlone, Co Roscommon	*Potterton* 1975, 78

SHEEHAN, David –1756

A Dublin sculptor and mason, he worked in Marlborough Street in the mid-18th century. He rebuilt the entrance to Dublin Castle in 1746 at a cost of £341 7s 7d, and worked on Doneraile House, 45 Kildare Street, between 1745 and 1750. His monument to Lieutenant-General Nevil closely follows a design by Robert Kidwell, who could conceivably have trained Sheehan (1). He worked with **John Houghton** on two monuments (**2, 3**). The Barrymore is 18 feet high and features a military bust in a niche between two Corinthian columns. That to Miss Rogers also has a bust in Italian marble. *Faulkner's Journal* of 28–31 July 1753 described the Barrymore monument as 'magnificent' and a good demonstration that 'performance of this nature need not now be purchased in other countries' (*Potterton* 1975, 79).

Sheehan died in 1756 and was buried in Drumcondra churchyard. In his will, proved on 13 February 1756, he mentions his 'stock of stones in Dublin, Cork, Kilkenny and elsewhere' (*Strickland* 2, 1913, 348). His eldest son was **Cornelius Sheehan**. Another member of the family was Mordecai Sheehan, who also worked as a stone-cutter in Marlborough Street, and went bankrupt in 1774 when his stock, including some 'capital chimneypieces' was sold. Strickland notes that Mordecai worked until about 1789.

Literary References: *Strickland* 2, 1913, 348–349; *Potterton* 1975, 78–9

Funerary Monuments

1.	1745	Lieutenant-General the Hon Clement Nevil		Tullow, Co Carlow	S	*Strickland* 2, 1913, 348; *Potterton* 1975, 24, 78 (repr)
2.	1753	James, 5th Earl of Barrymore (†1751) (co-sculptor: John Houghton)		Castelyons church, Co Cork	S	*Strickland* 2, 1913, 348; *Potterton* 1975, 79
3.	nd	Daughter of Dr Joseph Rogers (co-sculptor: John Houghton)		Christ Church, Cork		*Strickland* 2, 1913, 349; *Potterton* 1975, 79

Architectural Sculpture

4.	c1751	Unidentified work	s	[Trinity College, Dublin]; untraced		*Strickland* 2, 1913, 349

SHEEMSON, Samuel fl c1740

See **William Ruck** (or **Ruch**).

SHEFFIELD, William fl 1758–59

In 1758, when under 22 and apprenticed to **John Wildsmith**, he was awarded the first of two premiums by the Society of Arts.

Literary References: *Gunnis* 1968, 349

Miscellaneous

1.	1758	Birds, model	[Soc of A, premium]; untraced	*Gunnis* 1968, 349
2.	1759	Clay tablets, of unspecified subjects	[Soc of A, premium]; untraced	*Dossie* 1782, 437
3.	1759	Festoon in clay	[Soc of A, premium, 10 gns]; untraced	RSA *Minutes*, 1758–60, seq 1 fols 78,80

SHENTON, Henry Chawner 1825–46

He came of a family of artists, his father being Henry Shenton, an engraver, and his uncle, Luke Clennell, a painter. His maternal grandfather was Charles Warren, a line-engraver. Young Shenton was a pupil of **William Behnes** and attended the Royal Academy Schools in 1843. In 1844 he received a medal from the Society of Arts (**2**). In 1844 he exhibited his 'Burial of the Princes in the Tower' at Westminster Hall, which was described by the *Art Union* as possessing 'daring effect', though apparently it was not finished to a sufficiently high standard (**1**). The following year Shenton exhibited a figure of Archbishop Cranmer, which was noted in the same journal: 'This is a standing figure, plainly draped, and executed in style free and broad; and as the essay of a young artist, affords promise of much future excellence' (**3**).

Shenton was not to fulfil this promise, for he died prematurely on 7 February 1846. His last address was 11 St James's Terrace, Camden Town. Apparently he worked under very difficult conditions, for his first group was 'modelled in a stable with a roof so low that the ground had to be dug away to the depth of several feet, while the only light came through a narrow window in the wall'. It was 'to the damps and chill of this fireless work-room his friends attribute the first insinuation of that disease which has laid the sculptor in an early grave'. The journal paid the tribute 'we grieve to hear of the untimely death of a young sculptor, whose future eminence in the profession we have had more than one occasion to predict' (*Athenaeum*, 1846, 72).

Literary References: *Graves* VII, 1905–6, 107; *Gunnis* 1968, 349

Statues

1.	1844	Burial of the Princes in the Tower		[Exhib Westminster Hall, London, 153]; untraced	*AU*, 1844, 216
2.	1844	Sabrina, clay model		[Soc of A, silver Isis medal]; untraced	RSA *Transactions*, 1845, vol 55, 214
3.	1845	Archbishop Cranmer	p	[Exhib Westminster Hall, London, 119]; untraced	*Westminster* 1845, 15; *AU*, 1845, 258

Busts

4.	1846	J Stenson Major		[Exhib RA, London, 1478]; untraced	*Graves* VII, 1905–6, 107

Reliefs

5.	1845	The Penitent		[Exhib RA, London, 1355]; untraced	*Graves* VII, 1905–6, 107; *Gunnis* 1968, 349

Miscellaneous

6.	1843	Christ and Mary, group		Untraced	*Gunnis* 1968, 349

SHENTON, William fl 1768

He was described as a 'statuary' of 5 Cornhill in the *London Directory* for 1768.

Archival References: GPC

SHENTON, HULL & POLLARD, of Leicester fl *c*1807–18?

The following list is composed of those monuments that Gunnis considered their best. Two of the firm's members were presumably **Samuel Hull, of Leicester** and **Thomas Pollard**.

Literary References: *Gunnis* 1968, 349

Funerary Monuments

1.	?1807	Katherine Aynsworth		Sileby, Leics	*Gunnis* 1968, 349
2.	?1812	Thomas Smith		Bitteswell, Leics	*Gunnis* 1968, 349
3.	?1818	Ann Parkinson		Cosby, Leics	*Gunnis* 1968, 349

SHEPHERD, Edward, of Plymouth fl *c*1818–32

In 1818 he provided a pavement of marble and brass for the Duke of Bedford's temple of the graces at Woburn (**10**). It was composed of coloured marbles from Sandygate, Bickerton, and elsewhere on the Duke of Bedford's estates in south Devon. The *Gentleman's Magazine* described his fountain of black-and-white Devon marble for the Emperor of Brazil as 'magnificent' (**9**). The work was 25 feet high and weighed 18 tons (*GM* 1826, 96, 70). Shepherd's tablets, mostly in the neoclassical style, are condemned by Gunnis as 'dull'.

Literary References: *Gunnis* 1968, 349; *Clifford* 1995, 68

Funerary Monuments

1.	?1818	Sally Graham		Saltash, Cornwall	*Gunnis* 1968, 350
2.	?1823	Joseph Ede		Liskeard, Cornwall	*Gunnis* 1968, 350
3.	†1823	Rev John Darke		Kelly, Devon	Pevsner, *Devon*, 1989, 511
4.	?1824	Jane Michel		Lostwithiel, Cornwall	*Gunnis* 1968, 350
5.	?1825	James Glencross		St Budeaux, Devon	*Gunnis* 1968, 350
6.	?1829	Richard King		Tamerton Foliot, Devon	*Gunnis* 1968, 350
7.	?1832	Rev W Manley		Stoke Fleming, Devon	*Gunnis* 1968, 350
8.	nd	Unidentified subject		Egloshayle, Cornwall	Pevsner, *Cornwall*, 1970, 65

Architectural Sculpture

9.	1826	Fountain	m	[coll Emperor of Brazil]; untraced	*GM* 1826, 96, 2, 70; *Gunnis* 1968, 349

Miscellaneous

10.	1818	A variegated pavement composed of 1,238 pieces of marble further enriched by 102 brass figures	m	Temple of the graces, Woburn Abbey, Beds	*New Monthly Mag*, 1818, 173; *Gunnis* 1968, 349

SHEPHERD, Vincent 1750–1812

He was 'workman and architect' to the Duke of Northumberland and carried out a considerable amount of stone-carving for his patron. In the choir of Alnwick church he executed 'a piece of Gothic trellis work, which for elegance of fancy and superiority of workmanship has seldom been equalled and perhaps never excelled' (**1**). He died at Alnwick, and the author of his obituary opined 'in the sublime walks of the Gothic, he stood without a rival in the county of Northumberland. In his intercourse with the world, he was peculiarly placid and engaging; and in the relative duties of father, husband, and friend, few characters have been more exemplary' (*GM*, 1812, 601).

Literary References: *Gunnis* 1968, 350

Architectural Sculpture

1.	*c*1812	Gothic trellis work		[Alnwick Church, Northumberland, choir]; destroyed	*GM* 1812, 601

SHEPPARD, S, of Dublin fl *c*1836

Funerary Monuments

1.	†1836	Rev William Colles Moore		Carnew, Co Wicklow	S *Potterton* 1975, 79

SHERWOOD, James, of Derby *c*1779–

The son of Samuel and Jane Sherwood of Derby, he worked as a sculptor, spar manufacturer and marble mason in Derby and Buxton from 1800 to 1824 and from King Street, Derby, in 1822. In 1801 he married Elizabeth Smedley at St Alkmund, Derby. His second wife was named Catherine. Sherwood was noticed in the *Derby Mercury*, 1810–12, for a series of vases including a commemorative work for Lord Nelson, and another, decorated with cavalry scenes, 'which in beauty and novelty of design surpasses anything of the kind ever attempted' (**7, 6**). Another, by the 'ingenious Mr Sherwood', and 'more superb than either of the former', featured a *Triumph of Venus* and was 'a most beautiful scene of festive mirth' (**8**). It is clear from its description that it was intricately carved and richly decorated. He was responsible for a number of monuments. The best, according to Gunnis, was the 'delightful' memorial to Thomas Swanwick, a schoolmaster for 30 years (**3**). It was erected by his former pupils and has a relief of a master teaching a small boy seated on a pile of books, above which are terrestrial and celestial globes.

Literary References: Pigot's *Directory*, 1822; *Gunnis* 1968, 350

Archival References: GPC; IGI

Funerary Monuments

	Date	Subject		Location		Reference
1.	?1802	William Mills		Leek, Staffs	S	*Gunnis* 1968, 350
2.	†1809	Thomasine Buxton		Tissington, Derbys	S	*Gunnis* 1968, 350; Pevsner, *Derbys*, 1978, 345
3.	†1814	Thomas Swanwick		All Saints, Derby	S	*Gunnis* 1968, 350; Pevsner, *Derbys*, 1978, 171
4.	†1815	Ralph Clay		St Katharine Cree, City of London		Pevsner, *London: City*, 1997, 229
5.	?1821	Rev James Falconer		Lichfield Cathedral, Staffs	S	*Gunnis* 1968, 350
Architectural Sculpture						
6.	1810	Vase decorated with battle scenes		Untraced		*Derby Mercury*, 26 July 1810
7.	pre-1810	Vase, in honour of Lord Nelson		Untraced		*Derby Mercury*, 26 July 1810
8.	1812	Vase depicting the triumph of Venus	a	Untraced		*Derby Mercury*, 6 Feb 1812

SHIELDS, I, of Hull fl *c*1848

Funerary Monuments

	Date	Subject	Location	Reference
1.	†1848	John Walker	Foston-on-the-Wolds, E R Yorks	Pevsner, *Yorks: E R & York*, 1995, 425

SHILLITOE (or SHILTO), Daniel, of Wakefield fl 1761–69

He was a mason-carver. In 1761 he took an apprentice, Matthew Vertram.

Archival References: GPC

Architectural Sculpture

	Date	Subject	Location	Reference
1.	1764	'two large key stones over the coach house door and six top stones for the gate pillars to the street' Payment(s): £6	[Fairfax House, Castlegate, York]; untraced	Wombwell Archives in GPC
2.	1767–1769	All the carved work in wood and stone	[Thoresby Park, Notts]; untraced	Archives Earl Manvers, Nottingham Univ lib, 4420, in GPC

SHORTHOSE, John –1704

He was the son of Thomas Shorthose, citizen and mason, who was warden of the Masons' Company in 1676. John joined the livery in 1662. In 1669 he was paid £100 for restoration work at the Guildhall and another £70 in the following year. In 1674 he was paid £130 for further work and materials for Guildhall, the Sessions house, and several other public buildings. With his partner, Robert Mortimer, he was the master-mason employed in rebuilding the Coopers' Hall, 1676–1682 (Company Archives). Shorthose also received numerous payments for work at Fleet Bridge.

He was employed under Wren on several of the City churches. He was the mason-contractor at St Olave, Jewry, where he was paid £3,366 between 1670 and 1679 (**2**). In the same capacity he, and his partner **John Crooke**, built Christ Church, Newgate (**3**), and both received £100 in July 1670, for mason's work on Ludgate. In May 1680 he agreed to be master-mason with **Edward Pearce** at St Clement Danes, where the pair were paid £500 for their work in 1681. His one known monument dates from 1680 (**1**). The chapter book of Rochester Cathedral carries a note describing him as 'mason & carver living in St Clement's Lane without Temple Barr'. Shorthose had brought a letter from the deceased's son, Henry Lee, regarding the 'placing of a monument'. The following December the work had 'begun to be sett up' (*Hope* 1900, 122–3).

In 1681 Shorthose became upper warden of the Masons' Company and he was master in 1685 and 1686. He married Mary (†1706), the daughter of **Humphrey Moyer**. Shorthose died in 1704 and his will was proved on 13 July that year.

Literary References: *Wren Soc*, 10, 108; *Weaver* 1915, 15; *Knoop and Jones* 1935, 31, n4; *Green* 1964 (1), 143

Archival References: TNA E.101. 475/2; Masons' Co, Masters and Wardens; Guildhall MSS 184/4 p7, 10v, 22r, 31r; GPC

Will: PROB 11/477, 13 July 1704

Funerary Monuments

	Date	Subject	Location	Reference
1.	1680–1681	Archdeacon Lee Warner (†1679)	Rochester Cathedral, Kent (moved from north-east transept to transept arch, 1825)	*Hope* 1900, 122–3; Pevsner, *Kent: W & Weald*, 1976, 483
Architectural Sculpture				
2.	1670–1679	'Roses, cherubim, festoons and the shield over the steeple door'	St Olave, Jewry, City of London	Bodleian Rawlinson MSS B 387 in *Gunnis* 1968, 350
3.	nd	Ten composite capitals, four pineapples, four urns for the steeple (co-sculptor: John Crooke) Payment(s): £130, £20, £36	[Christ Church, Newgate, London]; untraced	Bodleian Rawlinson MSS B 387 in *Gunnis* 1968, 350

SHORTHOSE, Thomas fl 1676–80

The father of **John Shorthose**, he was warden of the Masons' Company in 1676 and took an apprentice, Robert Wright of Burton-on-Trent, on 28 June 1670.

Literary References: *Webb* 1999, 37

Archival References: Masons' Co, Masters and Wardens

SHOUT, Benjamin –1811

Benjamin Shout was the uncle and partner of **Robert Shout**. He and his nephew were in business together by 1785, when their tradecard described them as 'Sculptors and Masons'. Benjamin appears to have had the freehold on both of the firm's yards, at 13 Eagle Street, St Andrew, Holborn, and at nearby 18 High Holborn. Benjamin had a number of business interests including a part share in a family shipping business, and he carried on trade as an 'oilman' from premises at Queen Street, Holborn.

He died early in 1811, leaving the premises in Eagle Street to his wife, Elizabeth, and arranging for his half share of the business, including all the 'stock of manufactured and unmanufactured' goods and materials, to be converted by Robert Shout into shares for his wife and his son, Benjamin.

In the following list, monuments to those who died before 1811 are assumed to be products of the partnership of Robert and Benjamin.

Literary References: *Gunnis* 1968, 350–1; *Clifford* 1992, 46

Archival References: Tradecard, Banks coll, BM, 106.27

Will: PROB 11/1521/303, proved 11 April 1811

Funerary Monuments

No.	Date	Subject		Location		Reference
1.	?1778	John Webber (co-sculptor: Robert Shout)		Bampton, Devon		*Gunnis* 1968, 350
2.	†1780	Lister family (†1738–80) (co-sculptor: Robert Shout)		Poole, Dorset		Pevsner, *Dorset*, 1972, 319
3.	†1787	Charles Brander and family (co-sculptor: Robert Shout) Drawing(s): VAM 93-H-137		Christchurch, Hants		C Lib (repr)
4.	?1789	Charles Bushby (co-sculptor: Robert Shout) Drawing(s): VAM E.3034-1980 (related)		Arundel, Sussex		*Gunnis* 1968, 350; C Lib (repr)
5.	?1790	Captain Baldon Swiney (co-sculptor: Robert Shout)		Hartfield, Sussex		*Gunnis* 1968, 350
6.	†1790	Younge (†1759), Martha (†1784) and Younge Willes (co-sculptor: Robert Shout)		Goring-by-Sea, Sussex	S	
7.	†1792	Elizabeth Cooper (co-sculptor: Robert Shout)		Sleaford, Lincs		Pevsner, *Lincs*, 1989, 653
8.	†1793	Mrs Lomax (co-sculptor: Robert Shout) Drawing(s): VAM E.3027-8-1980 (related)		Sleaford, Lincs		*Gunnis* 1968, 350
9.	?1794	Harriett Knatchbull (co-sculptor: Robert Shout) Drawing(s): VAM E.3081-1980 (related)		St Lawrence, Godmersham, Kent		*Gunnis* 1968, 350
10.	†1794	Thomas Knight (co-sculptor: Robert Shout) Drawing(s): VAM E.3081-1980 (related)		Godmersham, Kent	S	Pevsner, *Kent: N E & E*, 1983, 332
11.	?1795	Mrs Burrows (co-sculptor: Robert Shout)		Chalk, Kent		*Gunnis* 1968, 350
12.	?1799	William Carter (co-sculptor: Robert Shout)		St Dunstan, Canterbury		*Gunnis* 1968, 350
13.	?1800	Alexander Hoskins (co-sculptor: Robert Shout)		Melling, Lancs		*Gunnis* 1968, 350
14.	?1800	James Monypenny (co-sculptor: Robert Shout)		Rolvenden, Kent		C Lib (repr)
15.	?1801	Rev Stephen Barrett (co-sculptor: Robert Shout)		Hothfield, Kent		*Gunnis* 1968, 350
16.	?1804	Sarah Jeaffreson (co-sculptor: Robert Shout)		Dullingham, Cambs		*Gunnis* 1968, 350
17.	†1804	William Kemble (co-sculptor: Robert Shout)		Sidmouth, Devon		RG/JP, 7, 1291
18.	?1806	John Hinde (co-sculptor: Robert Shout)		Milton Regis, Kent		*Gunnis* 1968, 350
19.	†1806	Sir Matthew Blakiston (co-sculptor: Robert Shout)		Lymington, Hants	S	Pevsner, *Hants & Isle of Wight*, 1967, 325
20.	?1807	Harriet Stewart (co-sculptor: Robert Shout)		Portsmouth Cathedral		*Gunnis* 1968, 350
21.	1807	Sir Wolstan Dixie (†1767) (co-sculptor: Robert Shout)		Market Bosworth, Leics	S	*Gunnis* 1968, 350
22.	†1808	Mary Crop (co-sculptor: Robert Shout)		Dullingham, Cambs	S	Pevsner, *Cambs*, 1970, 332
23.	?1808	Sir William Yeo (co-sculptor: Robert Shout)		Wiveliscombe, Somerset		*Gunnis* 1968, 350
24.	?1809	John Stapleton (co-sculptor: Robert Shout)		Ottery St Mary, Devon		*Gunnis* 1968, 350
25.	?1809	Samuel Johnson (co-sculptor: Robert Shout)		St Ives, Hunts		*Gunnis* 1968, 350
26.	?1809	Thomas Cockayne (co-sculptor: Robert Shout)		Ickleworth, Herts		*Gunnis* 1968, 350

Busts

No.	Date	Subject		Location		Reference
27.	1798	Admiral Lord Nelson (co-sculptor: Robert Shout)		Reproduction in Lloyd's Bank, London, Nelson room Other versions: basalt reproductions by Wedgwood	SD	*Hughes* 1962, 360–1
28.	1806	Admiral Lord Nelson (co-sculptor: Robert Shout)	pb	John May, Grosvenor House Fair, London (1975); untraced	SD	*Clifford* 1992, 47 (repr)
29.	1806	Several (designed by Sir John Soane) (co-sculptor: Robert Shout)		[Lord Bridport's library]; untraced		*Gunnis* 1968, 350
30.	pre-1806	William Shakespeare, one of a series of British worthies (co-sculptor: Robert Shout)		Windsor Castle Other versions: Garrick Club, London, plaster, inv 7, 18 or 33, with Shout stamp		*Ashton* 1997, 522 (repr)

Architectural Sculpture

No.	Date	Subject		Location		Reference
31.	1803	Torchères, supported by three Graces (co-sculptor: Robert Shout)		Royal Pavilion, Brighton, Sussex	SD	*Clifford* 1992, 63
32.	1804	Tripod, with panther-heads (co-sculptor: Robert Shout)		Coll Timothy Clifford	SD	*Clifford* 1992, 63

33.	1806	A pair of bronzed greyhounds 'with 2 light candelabra' (co-sculptor: Robert Shout) Payment(s): £4 4s		[Blair Castle, Perths]; untraced		*Clifford* 1992, 63
34.	1806	Bronzed figure of Peace, on a marbled plinth supporting a three light candelabra (co-sculptor: Robert Shout) Payment(s): £5 5s		[Blair Castle, Perths]; untraced		*Clifford* 1992, 63
35.	1809	A pair of kneeling maidens for four-light candelabra, and a pair of standing figures supporting the same (co-sculptor: Robert Shout)	pb	Blair Castle, Perths	SD	*Clifford* 1992, 64

SHOUT, Charles Lutwyche 1794–1855

Charles was born in December 1794 and christened at St Andrew, Holborn, the son of **Robert Shout** and his first wife, Lucy. He was apprenticed to his father in 1809, and was taken into the business by 1820, when the firm was advertised as 'Robert Shout and Sons' in Robson's *London Directory* (*Clifford* 1992, 46). In 1823 he was listed under 'plaster cast makers' in Pigot's *Commercial Directory* and was living at 18 High Holborn. He acted as the sole executor and residuary legatee of his father's estate in 1843, and died at the family home, Treherne House, West End, Hampstead in 1855. He was the father of Robert Howard Shout (1823–82), a West Country restorer and architect. For a list of the firm's products see the entry for Robert Shout.

Literary References: *Gunnis* 1968, 350; *Clifford* 1992, 46; *Colvin* 1995, 867

Archival References: IGI

Wills: Robert Shout, proved 29 September 1843, PROB 11/1986/122; Charles Lidwyche Shout, proved 7 June 1855, PROB 11/2214

SHOUT, John 1738–81

The son of **Robert Shout**, he worked as a mason in Stockton-on-Tees, where he built the Tuscan column (1). In 1780–81 he was the harbour engineer of Sunderland. He died in Stockton on 13 June 1781.

Literary References: *Colvin* 1995, 867

Architectural Sculpture

1.	1768	Market cross	Stockton-on-Tees, Durham	Pevsner, *Durham*, 1983, 437

SHOUT, Robert *c*1760–1843

Shout had a business in monumental sculpture and also produced plaster busts, ornaments and casts after works by famous contemporaries. He must have been born around 1760, for in 1835 he gave his age as 75 (Shout/Peel) and he was probably the son of John Shout (1738–81), a mason of Stockton-on-Tees, and his wife Mary (†1814).

By 1785 Shout was working in partnership with his uncle, **Benjamin Shout**. Their tradecard, printed that year, describes them as 'Sculptors and Masons'. Shout married his first wife, Lucy, in or around 1794 and their child, **Charles Lutwyche Shout**, was christened at St Andrew, Holborn, in December that year. Benjamin and Robert's business was run from 18 High Holborn, where Robert lived, and from 13 Eagle Street, St Andrew's, Holborn. They remained in partnership until Benjamin's death in 1811.

Robert's earliest known design, for an unidentified wall-monument with a sarcophagus in relief, dates from May 1795. The surviving drawings are all signed by Robert Shout alone and he may have been chiefly responsible for the firm's designs. Neither they nor the works themselves are particularly noteworthy. Most are well-carved wall-monuments with the standard motif of a woman grieving over an urn or column and they often incorporate familiar neoclassical features, such as a sarcophagus with lion's feet, strigil decoration or a *tabula ansata* (or winged board).

By 1798, when Shout published his bust of Nelson (**41**), the partners were supplying works in plaster for the popular market. The venture appears to have been successful, despite competition from **John Flaxman I**, and later **Humphrey Hopper**. Among Shout's products in plaster were architectural ornaments, particularly lampstands (**52, 54–6**), and busts, sold singly or as a series (**43**).

Benjamin Shout died in 1811, leaving instructions in his will that his half-share in the business should be sold to Robert, to provide financial support for his own widow and son. The enforced purchase does not appear to have had an adverse effect on Robert's business, which he probably conducted alone until around 1820. He continued to produce monuments and casts of works by famous sculptors. In 1819 the *Annals of the Fine Arts* published a puff for the casts which Shout had recently produced of works by **Antonio Canova** (**37–40**). These were said to have been taken from the original works and were praised for the 'delicate precision' with which every detail had been reproduced. The article concluded by suggesting that Shout had given Canova's admirers an 'opportunity of gratifying themselves at a moderate expense' (*Annals of the Fine Arts* 1819, 632).

Shelley's poem, *Letter to Maria Gisborne*, 1820, not only assumed general acquaintance with Shout's plaster business, but also hinted that ownership of Shout's wares reflected taste and perhaps even integrity. Shelley wrote in a poem celebrating Leigh Hunt:

'his room no doubt
Is still adorned with many a cast from Shout,
With graceful flowers tastefully placed about;'

In 1820 the firm was described in Robson's *London Directory* as 'Robert Shout and Sons ... bronze figure manufactrs'. Little is known of Shout's work in bronze, and the only monument that makes mention of the next generation is signed 'Shout and Son' (**36**). This son, Charles Lutwyche Shout, may have taken control of the family's plaster business around 1823.

Shout's wife died in April 1822, and he married Sophia Morton in June that year. In 1835 he was living at Treherne House, West End, Hampstead. In a letter to Sir Robert Peel (in which he fulminated against the high levels of land tax) he described himself as 'possessed of independent property, consisting of land and houses' (Shout/Peel). Shout died in September 1843, and was given an obituary in *The Builder*. He left direction in his will that his name should be inscribed on his first wife's monument in Hampstead church, but that he should be buried as close as possible to his second wife in Kensal Green cemetery. He left £210 in mourning gifts, provision for his son-in-law Henry Brodie Morton and the residue of his property and estate to his son Charles Lutwyche Shout.

In the following list, monuments to those who died before 1811 are assumed to be by Robert and Benjamin, working in partnership.

MGS

Literary References: *Shelley* 1824, 65–6; *Builder*, v.42, Apr. 1 1882, 385; *Hughes* 1962, 360–1; *Gunnis* 1968, 350–1; *Clifford* 1992, 46; *Colvin* 1995, 867; *Curl* 2001, 102, 183, 211, 242; *Bilbey* 2002, 358

Archival References: Shout/Peel; tradecards in Banks coll, BM, 106.27 and Heal coll, BM 106.20; IGI

Wills: Benjamin Shout, proved 11 April 1811, PROB 11/1521/303; Robert Shout, proved 29 September 1843, PROB 11/1986/122

Collections of Drawings: Scrap-book of designs for identified and unidentified monuments and fireplaces, 1795–1819, VAM, P&D 93-H-137, including untraced, and possibly unexecuted designs for monuments to Ann Grigsby of Drinkslow, Suffolk, and John Walgan of Sunderland; a design for a chimneypiece for the Earl of Essex, Cashiobury, Herts, E.3046-1980; two designs for chimneypieces for Sir Robert Peel, Drayton Manor, Staffs E.3049-50-1980

Funerary Monuments

1.	?1778	John Webber (co-sculptor: Benjamin Shout)	Bampton, Devon		*Gunnis* 1968, 350
2.	†1780	Lister family (†1738–80) (co-sculptor: Benjamin Shout)	Poole, Dorset		Pevsner, *Dorset*, 1972, 319
3.	†1787	Charles Brander and family (co-sculptor: Benjamin Shout) Drawing(s): VAM 93-H-137 (authenticated by)	Christchurch, Hants		
4.	?1789	Charles Bushby (co-sculptor: Benjamin Shout) Drawing(s): VAM E.3034-1980 (related)	Arundel, Sussex		*Gunnis* 1968, 350; C Lib (repr)
5.	?1790	Captain Baldon Swiney (co-sculptor: Benjamin Shout)	Hartfield, Sussex		*Gunnis* 1968, 350
6.	†1790	Younge (†1759), Martha (†1784) and Younge Willes (co-sculptor: Benjamin Shout)	Goring-by-Sea, Sussex	S	
7.	†1792	Elizabeth Cooper (co-sculptor: Benjamin Shout)	Sleaford, Lincs		Pevsner, *Lincs*, 1989, 653
8.	†1793	Mrs Lomax (co-sculptor: Benjamin Shout) Drawing(s): VAM E.3027-8-1980 (related)	Sleaford, Lincs		*Gunnis* 1968, 350
9.	?1794	Harriett Knatchbull (co-sculptor: Benjamin Shout) Drawing(s): VAM E.3081-1980 (related)	Godmersham, Kent		*Gunnis* 1968, 350
10.	†1794	Thomas Knight (co-sculptor: Benjamin Shout) Drawing(s): VAM E.3081-1980 (related)	Godmersham, Kent	S	Pevsner, *Kent: N E & E*, 1983, 332
11.	?1795	Mrs Burrows (co-sculptor: Benjamin Shout)	Chalk, Kent		*Gunnis* 1968, 350
12.	?1799	William Carter (co-sculptor: Benjamin Shout)	St Dunstan, Canterbury		*Gunnis* 1968, 350
13.	?1800	Alexander Hoskins (co-sculptor: Benjamin Shout)	Melling, Lancs		*Gunnis* 1968, 350
14.	?1800	Elizabeth Pinnell (co-sculptor: Benjamin Shout)	Fittleworth, Sussex		*Gunnis* 1968, 350
15.	?1800	James Monypenny (co-sculptor: Benjamin Shout)	Rolvenden, Kent		C Lib (repr)
16.	?1801	Rev Stephen Barrett (co-sculptor: Benjamin Shout)	Hothfield, Kent		*Gunnis* 1968, 350
17.	?1804	Sarah Jeaffreson (co-sculptor: Benjamin Shout)	Dullingham, Cambs		*Gunnis* 1968, 350
18.	†1804	William Kemble (co-sculptor: Benjamin Shout)	Sidmouth, Devon		RG/JP, 7, 1291
19.	?1806	John Hinde (co-sculptor: Benjamin Shout)	Milton Regis, Kent		*Gunnis* 1968, 350
20.	†1806	Sir Matthew Blakiston (co-sculptor: Benjamin Shout)	Lymington, Hants	S	Pevsner, *Hants & Isle of Wight*, 1967, 325
21.	?1807	Harriet Stewart (co-sculptor: Benjamin Shout)	Portsmouth Cathedral		*Gunnis* 1968, 350
22.	1807	Sir Wolstan Dixie (†1767) (co-sculptor: Benjamin Shout)	Market Bosworth, Leics	S	*Gunnis* 1968, 350
23.	†1808	Mary Crop (co-sculptor: Benjamin Shout)	Dullingham, Cambs	S	Pevsner, *Cambs*, 1970, 332
24.	?1808	Sir William Yeo (co-sculptor: Benjamin Shout)	Wiveliscombe, Somerset		*Gunnis* 1968, 350
25.	?1809	John Stapleton (co-sculptor: Benjamin Shout)	Ottery St Mary, Devon		*Gunnis* 1968, 350
26.	?1809	Samuel Johnson (co-sculptor: Benjamin Shout)	St Ives, Hunts		*Gunnis* 1968, 350
27.	?1809	Thomas Cockayne (co-sculptor: Benjamin Shout)	Ickleworth, Herts		*Gunnis* 1968, 350
28.	†1812	Francis Valpy Drawing(s): VAM 93-H-137	St Brelade, Jersey	S	
29.	?1812	Francis Wheate	Glympton, Warks		RG/JP, 7, 1291
30.	†1814	Grace Sutton	Stockton-on-Tees parish church, Durham		Pevsner, *Durham*, 1983, 435

No.	Date	Subject	Material	Location	Signed	Reference
31.	†1819	Emma and Frederick (†1817) Waddington		Walkern, Herts	S	
32.	?1820	William Bennet		Emmanuel College, Cambridge, chapel		*Gunnis* 1968, 350
33.	†1824	Charles Edward Lambert		Whippingham, I of W	S	
34.	†1824	Martha (†1786) and William Wilshere		Welwyn, Herts		*Gunnis* 1968, 351
35.	?1826	Olive Western		Rivenhall, Essex		*Gunnis* 1968, 351
36.	1836–1838	James Morison, 'the Hygeist', design only (executed by William Milligan) Drawing(s): VAM E.3063-1980		Kensal Green Cemetery, London	S	*Curl* 2001, 102, 183 (repr)
Statues						
37.	1818	Hebe, cast (after Antonio Canova)	p	Untraced		*Annals of the Fine Arts* 1819, 632
38.	1818	Paris, cast (after Antonio Canova)	p	Untraced		*Annals of the Fine Arts* 1819, 632
39.	1818	Perseus, cast (after Antonio Canova)	p	Untraced		*Annals of the Fine Arts* 1819, 632
40.	1818	Venus, cast (after Antonio Canova)	p	Untraced		*Annals of the Fine Arts* 1819, 632
Busts						
41.	1798	Admiral Lord Nelson (co-sculptor: Benjamin Shout)		Untraced Other versions: basalt reproductions by Wedgwood, including one in Lloyds Bank, London, Nelson room	SD	*Hughes* 1962, 360–1
42.	1806	Admiral Lord Nelson (co-sculptor: Benjamin Shout)	pb	John May, Grosvenor House fair, London (1975); untraced	SD	*Clifford* 1992, 47 (repr)
43.	1806	Several (designed by Sir John Soane) (co-sculptor: Benjamin Shout)	p	[Lord Bridport's library]; untraced		*Gunnis* 1968, 350
44.	pre-1806	William Shakespeare, one of a series of British Worthies (co-sculptor: Benjamin Shout)		Windsor Castle Other versions: Garrick Club, London, plaster, inv 7, 18 or 33, with Shout stamp		*Ashton* 1997, 522 (repr)
45.	*c*1820	Sarah Siddons	p	VAM Dyce 3329 Other versions: Theatre museum, London, S.86-1978, plaster	S	*Bilbey* 2002, 358–9
46.	1820	Unidentified man	p	Timothy Millet (2003)	SD	
47.	1827	Unidentified busts	p	[Salters' Hall, City of London]; destroyed		*Gunnis* 1968, 350
48.	nd	Admiral Lord Nelson (after Anne Seymour Damer)	p	Royal Coll RCIN 79377 Other versions: attrib, NMM, Greenwich, SCU0083, *c*1798 gilt bronze		JM
49.	nd	Andrea Palladio, plaster patinated black	p	Knox/Longstaffe-Gowan coll	S	
50.	nd	John Milton (after Michael Rysbrack)	pb	Hughendon Manor, Bucks		AL/RG
51.	nd	Unidentified man	p	Untraced		*Gunnis* 1968, 350
Architectural Sculpture						
52.	1803	Torchères, supported by three Graces (co-sculptor: Benjamin Shout)		Royal Pavilion, Brighton, Sussex	SD	*Clifford* 1992, 63
53.	1804	Tripod, with panther-heads (co-sculptor: Benjamin Shout)		Coll Timothy Clifford	SD	*Clifford* 1992, 63
54.	1806	A pair of bronzed greyhounds 'with 2 light candelabra' (co-sculptor: Benjamin Shout) Payment(s): £4 4s		[Blair Castle, Perths]; untraced		*Clifford* 1992, 63
55.	1806	Bronzed figure of Peace, on a marbled plinth supporting a three light candelabra (co-sculptor: Benjamin Shout) Payment(s): £5 5s		[Blair Castle, Perths]; untraced		*Clifford* 1992, 63
56.	1809	A pair of kneeling maidens for four-light candelabra, and a pair of standing figures supporting the same (co-sculptor: Benjamin Shout)	pb	Blair Castle, Perth	SD	*Clifford* 1992, 64

SHOUT, Robert, of York 1702–74

A mason and architect from Helmsley, N R Yorks, in 1741 he carved the architrave of a window in the gallery wing a Gilling Castle for Lord Fairfax. He was paid £30 in 1749–50 for steps to the hall door, and £42 in 1752 for the summe house in the castle grounds. He was also responsible for unspecified work at Newburgh Priory, N R Yorks in 174 when he received 105 guineas (Wombwell Archives in GPC). From 1757 to 1765 he was surveyor of bridges for th North Riding of Yorkshire. He designed and built Elemore Hall, Co Durham, between 1749 and 1753.

Literary References: *Colvin* 1995, 867

SHOUT, William I, of York fl 1720–49

In 1720 and 1721 he built the north and south gateways at Castle Howard, as well as providing other carved work (2). In 1749 he built a small temple in the grounds of Hovingham Hall, N R Yorks, for Thomas Worsley (Archives, S William Worsley Bt).

Literary References: *Gunnis* 1968, 351

Architectural Sculpture

No.	Date	Subject	Location	Reference
1.	?1720–1721	Fluted obelisk	[Castle Howard, E R Yorks, south front]; untraced	Castle Howard archives, cited in *Gunnis* 1968, 351
2.	1720–1721	Vases and cartouches	[Castle Howard, N R Yorks]; untraced	Castle Howard archives, cited in *Gunnis* 1968, 351

SHOUT, William II, of York 1750–1826

The son of Henry Shout, he was appointed master-mason to the Minster in 1794, and in 1813 renewed and recut figures at the west end. He was buried at Huntington, near York, where his epitaph states: 'for forty years with credit to himself and satisfaction to his employers he conducted the repairs and restoration of York Minster'.

Literary References: *Gunnis* 1968, 351

Archival References: York Minster Library, Dean and Chapter Archives, E 10

SHROPSHIRE, John fl 1771?

He signs a 'large architectural tablet with excellently cut details' in Market Drayton.

Funerary Monuments

1.	?1771	John Smallwood	Market Drayton, Salop	S	*Gunnis* 1968, 351

SIBSON, Henry fl 1826–63

He first exhibited at the Royal Academy in 1826, giving his address as 84 Margaret Street. In 1844 he showed small statues of Marlborough and Bacon at Westminster Hall (**2, 3**). The *Literary Gazette* called them 'pretty pieces of costume – The Duke is all over in the Louis Quatorze fashion.' The *Art Union* remarked that though there was 'life and movement' in the figure of Marlborough 'whatever merit it possessed was annihilated by the heavy and graceless boots.' The same journal felt that the head of Bacon was 'successful as expressive of thought', but complained that Bacon's dress was inappropriate to the subject. Bacon was shown meditating corrections to his great work the *Novum Organum Scientarium*. 'We cannot believe', they wrote 'that Bacon wrote his Novum Organum in state robes, and therefore ought not to have been represented in such when mediating corrections.' Sibson's last recorded address, in 1863, was 9 Douro Cottages, St John's Wood.

Literary References: *Graves* VII, 1905–6, 121; *Gunnis* 1968, 351

Funerary Monuments					
1.	†1837	Anne Chamier	Chennai (Madras) Cathedral, India	S	*Gunnis* 1968, 173
Statues					
2.	1844	John, 1st Duke of Marlborough, statuette	[Exhib Westminster Hall, London, 103]; untraced		*AU*, 1844, 215; *Lit Gaz* 1844, 466
3.	1844	Sir Francis Bacon, statuette Model(s): Lord Bacon; half-sized model of a statue, exhib RA, London, 1863, 1200	[Exhib Westminster Hall, London, 104]; untraced		*AU*, 1844, 215; *Graves* VII, 1905–6, 121
4.	1851	Dying shipwrecked sea boy, recumbent life-size figure	[Gt Exhib 1851]; untraced		*Gunnis* 1968, 351
Busts					
5.	1833	R Franklin	[Exhib RA, London, 1141]; untraced		*Graves* VII, 1905–6, 121
Miscellaneous					
6.	1826	Satan calling up the infernal host	[Exhib RA, London, 1033]; untraced		*Graves* VII, 1905–6, 121
7.	1838	Part of a group, model for a silver centre piece	[Exhib RA, London, 1336 'presented to Sir Alexander Woodford, Bart, by the merchants of the Ionian Islands']; untraced		*Graves* VII, 1905–6, 121

SIDDONS, Sarah 1755–1831

The actress apparently took up modelling in 1789, because she did not think that the existing portraits of her were very accurate. She executed self-portraits, and a bust of her brother, John Kemble (**2**). J T Smith, quoting from *Dallaway* 1800, recorded 'The first tragedian of the English stage, Mrs Siddons, has executed the busts of herself and her brother, Mr John Kemble, with astonishing truth and effect' (*Smith* 1920 ed, 370). She was a friend of **Anne Seymour Damer**, with whom she practiced modelling on visits to Strawberry Hill and Mrs Damer's letters make numerous references to her sculptural work.

Literary References: *Bilbey* 2002, 358–9

Busts

1.	?1820s	Female head, probably a self-portrait, cast by Robert Shout	p	VAM, Dyce 3329 Other versions: Theatre Museum, London inv S.86-1978, nd	*Bilbey* 2002, 358 (repr)
2.	nd	John Kemble			*Smith* 1828, 1920 ed I, 370

SIDNELL, Michael, of Bristol fl 1718–50?

An architect and statuary, he became a freeman of Bristol on 2 December 1718 (City Archives in GPC). His monuments are architectural in design, and he makes much use of heraldic shields and coats of arms. The best, commemorating James Lyde stands about 12 feet high and has Doric pilasters supporting a broken pediment (**16**). The Cornelius Lyde is a baroque tablet with cherubs' heads carved at its foot (**2**). He made use of coloured marbles in the monument to Christopher Devonshire (**7**), and sent one known work to America (**14**).

Sidnell signed the fine monument to Edward Colston, though the semi-recumbent figure is by **Michael Rysbrack** (**5**). Sidnell must therefore have been responsible for the architectural elements or for setting it up when it was sent down from London. It was designed by James Gibbs and is illustrated in his *Book of Architecture*, 1728, to which Sidnell was a subscriber.

In 1742 the sculptor became bankrupt (*London Mag*, 1742, 518), but he continued to work. Between 1743 and 1745 he was the architect responsible for Westbury Court, Glos, and was described at that time as 'of the City of Bristol, master-workeman and architect' (Archives, Sir Francis Colchester-Wemyss in *Gunnis* 1968, 351). He also worked under **Thomas Paty** in 1744 at Redland chapel, Bristol.

A 'Daniel Sidnell of Bristol, Free Stone Cutter', became free of that city on 1 June 1739, on his marriage to Sarah, daughter of James Tanner, weaver, deceased (BRO, Burgess Books 04359, microfiche FC/BB/1 (m), 5 fol 155).

Literary References: *Gunnis* 1968, 351; *Friedman* 1984, 95, 290; *Colvin* 1995, 868

Funerary Monuments

1.	†1714	Henry Grinstead	Yatton, Somerset	S	Pevsner, *Somerset: N & Bristol*, 1958, 353
2.	†1717	Cornelius Lyde	Stanton Drew, Somerset	S	Pevsner, *Somerset: N & Bristol*, 1958, 262
3.	?1720	Captain Jacob Knight	Westbury, Glos	S	*Gunnis* 1968, 351
4.	?1729	Anna Maria Lyde	Stanton Drew, Somerset	S	*Gunnis* 1968, 351
5.	1728–1729	Edward Colston (†1721) (designed by James Gibbs, effigy by Michael Rysbrack)	All Saints, Corn St, Bristol	SD	*Eustace* 1982, 18–22, 68–72; *Friedman* 1984, 290 (repr)
6.	†1731	Anne Luttrell	Dunster, Somerset	S	Pevsner, *Somerset: S & W*, 1958, 156
7.	†1731	Christopher Devonshire	Alderley, Glos	S	Pevsner, *Glos: Cotswolds*, 1999, 133;
8.	?1731	John Frankland	St Stephen, Bristol		*Gunnis* 1968, 351
9.	?1732	Charles Pearson	Bredon, Worcs	S	*Gunnis* 1968, 351
10.	1733	Thomas and Jane Edwards	St James, Bristol		*Eustace* 1982, 78 (repr)
11.	†1734	William Mountjoy	Biddestone, Wilts	S	Pevsner, *Wilts*, 1975, 111
12.	?1736	Robert Earle	St Michael, Bristol		*Gunnis* 1968, 351
13.	?1737	Anthony Ellesdon	Charmouth, Dorset	S	*Gunnis* 1968, 351
14.	1737	Unidentified subject, wall-monument	St Peter New Kent County, Virginia, USA	S	GPC
15.	?1738	Freeman Partridge	St Augustine, Bristol		*Gunnis* 1968, 351
16.	?1738	James Lyde	Stanton Drew, Somerset		*Gunnis* 1968, 351
17.	?1750	Jane Symonds	Llangarren, Herefs		GPC

SIEVIER, Robert William 1794–1865

A man of parts who showed a talent for engraving and sculpture as a young man and in later life started his own manufacturing business. He was born in London on 24 July 1794 and became a competent draughtsman at an early age. In 1812, while living at Clarendon Square, Somer's Town, he was awarded the Society of Arts silver medal for a pen and ink drawing and, intending to become an engraver, he studied under John Young and then Edward Scriven. He was admitted to the Royal Academy Schools in 1818 and produced many successful engravings after famous artists.

To improve his depiction of the human form Sievier learnt to model in clay and he also studied under the anatomical lecturer, Joshua Brookes. By 1823 he had largely given up engraving and was concentrating on sculpture. One of his early works was a statue of a *Sleeping Bacchante*, which became part of the Grittleton House collection (**39**). That year Lord Chancellor Eldon sat for his bust (**62**). Other portrait commissions followed and Sievier's gift of seizing the likeness and characteristic expression of his sitters brought him many distinguished clients including Lord Harcourt, the Earl of Shaftesbury, and Sir Thomas Lawrence (**52, 60, 83**). In 1842 Prince Albert and Frederick William IV, King of Prussia both sat for him (**94, 95**).

In 1833 Sievier and **Richard Westmacott III** were commissioned by the 6th Duke of Devonshire each to make a chimneypiece for the new dining room at Chatsworth. Both followed a Bacchanalian theme and incorporated two life-sized figures (**104**). The Duke was disappointed with the results, noting 'They are clever and well-executed, but do not nearly approach the idea I wished to see realized. I wanted more abandon and joyous expression. I find these Baccanali too composed and sedate' (Chatsworth handbook, 1845, 83).

Sievier exhibited many times between 1822 and 1844 at the Royal Academy, the British Institution and the Royal Society of British Artists, showing principally busts, but also groups and a statue of Dr Jenner (**3**). He became a director of the General Cemetery Company in 1832 and in 1834 provided one of his first and most celebrated monuments in Kensal Green cemetery to the fraudulent doctor, John St John Long. This has a statue of *Hygeia*, the goddess of Medecine, beneath a domed canopy (**19**). The memorial to Sievier's family in the same cemetery is a touching depiction of family affection (**38**). Sievier's early training as an engraver is evident in many of his monuments which have scenic low-reliefs and whole scenes set in a small space. That to Robert Chessher, 1831, for example, has a relief of a graveyard with each tomb and gravestone minutely delineated, shadowed by weeping willows (**14**). The pedestal for the statue commemorating Lord Harcourt, 1832, presents battle scenes illustrating episodes in his career (**16**) and the Rev James Lyon is depicted on his monument administering communion to his parishioners (**27**).

Charles Abraham was one of Sievier's pupils, as he stated in a letter to the *Sidney Morning Herald* on 3 March 1845, '. . . I must be content to bear the responsibility of being and to be judged of as the pupil of no mean artist, R. Sievier Esq., at present Manager of the Polytechnic Institution, London'. Nothing is known of Sievier's connection with this post, but he had a lifelong interest in scientific matters and in 1831 took out a patent for 'the use of covered rubber threads for the manufacture of bags and ropes'. In 1841 he was made a Fellow of the Royal Society and by 1845 had ceased his artistic pursuits and started an India rubber works on his land in Holloway, North London, where he produced elastic fabrics and experimented in the manufacture of carpets. He also took an interest in electric telegraphy. Sievier and his wife Ann Eliza had a son, Robert Moore Sievier, born in 1827, who studied sculpture at the Royal Academy Schools in 1845. Sievier died on 28 April 1865 at 35 Rochester Road, Camden Town, and was buried with his parents in Kensal Green Cemetery.

Sylvia Allen

Literary References: *Graves* 1875, 491; *Graves* VIII, 1905–6, 123; *Bond* 1958, 91; *Gunnis* 1968, 351–2; *Redgrave* (1878), 1970, 304–5; *Johnson* 1975, 423; *Croot* 1985, 29–37; *Curl* 2000, 53, www.royalsoc.ac.uk

Archival References: GPC

Will: PPR, will with two codicils, 22 January 1866, fol 55, effects valued at under £200, revoked by decree 5 February 1867 and another will dated 18 January 1860 deposited at the PPR September 1867

Miscellaneous Drawings: 'from the battles of Le Brun', silver medal, Soc of A, 1812 (RSA *Transactions*, 1812, vol 30, 25)

Funerary Monuments

1.	†1820	John Dawson	Sedbergh, W R Yorks		Pevsner, *Yorks: W R*, 1967, 434
2.	†1825	Andrew Ffrench	Chennai (Madras) Cathedral, India	S	*Gunnis* 1968, 352; *Groseclose* 1995, 61

3.	1825	Dr Edward Jenner		Gloucester Cathedral	SD	*Graves* VII, 1905–6, 122; Pevsner, *Glos: Vale and Forest of Dean*, 1976, 218; *CIIA* 4/4/54 (repr)
4.	†1825	Jacob Dearden		St Chad, Rochdale, Lancs	S	Pevsner, *Lancs: S*, 1969, 375; *Johnson* 1975, 423
5.	1825	Sir George Paul (†1820)		Gloucester Cathedral	SD	Pevsner, *Glos: Vale & Forest of Dean*, 1976, 218; CIIA 4/4/51–2 (repr)
6.	†1826	Countess of Cardigan		Deene, Northants	S	Pevsner, *Northants*, 1973, 177
7.	†1826	Frances Ramsbotham		Stand, Lancs	S	
8.	†1826	Sir George Alderson		St Mary, Paddington, London	S	*Gunnis* 1968, 352
9.	1829	Charles Dibdin (†1814)	m	Royal Hospital (ORNC), Greenwich, Pensioners' Library		*Graves* 1875, 491; *Van Der Merwe* 1982, 82–5 (repr 4)
10.	†1829	John Bolland		Fetcham, Surrey		Pevsner, *Surrey*, 1971, 245
11.	1830	Isabella Fairlie		St Mary, St Marylebone, London	S	*Gunnis* 1968, 352
12.	†1830	William, 3rd Earl Harcourt		St Andrew, Windsor, Berks		Pevsner, *Berks*, 1966, 300
13.	†1830	William, 3rd Earl Harcourt		Stanton Harcourt, Oxon	S	Pevsner, *Oxon*, 1974, 781
14.	1831	Dr Robert Chessher (the first orthopaedist), with relief of a graveyard		Peckleton, Leics		*Gunnis* 1968, 352
15.	1832	Mr and Mrs Dearden of Rochdale		[Exhib RSBA, 1832]; untraced		*Johnson* 1975, 423
16.	1832	William, 3rd Earl Harcourt (†1830) Model(s): Stanton Harcourt church, Oxon, plaster, S		St George's Chapel, Windsor Castle	SD	*Graves* VII, 1905–6, 123; *Bond* 1999, 148; *Johnson* 1975, 423
17.	†1833	William Danby		Masham, N R Yorks		*Johnson* 1975, 423
18.	†1834	John Forster		St John, Lewisham, London		Pevsner, *London: S*, 1983, 414
19.	†1834	John St John Long		Kensal Green Cemetery, London		*Curl* 2001, 95, 103, 191, 214, 233 (repr)
20.	1834	Lieutenant Michael Smith and family		Holy Trinity, St Marylebone, London	S	Pevsner, *London: N W*, 1991, 600
21.	1834	Mrs Palmer, 'to be placed in Ham church'		[Exhib Soc of BA, London, 840]; untraced		*Johnson* 1975, 423
22.	1834	'The late Mrs Palmer, to be placed in Ham church'		[Exhib RSBA]; untraced		*Johnson* 1975, 423
23.	1835	'Part of a monument to J. Palmer, representing him upon a sofa, a few minutes before his death'		[Exhib RA, London, 1134]; untraced		*Graves* VII, 1905–6, 123
24.	†1835	Thomas Simpson		St Matthew, Brixton, London	S	Pevsner, *London: S*, 1983, 338
25.	†1836	John Tetlow		Middleton, Lancs		C Lib (repr)
26.	1836	Mary Barnard		Wolverstone, Suffolk	S	*Gunnis* 1968, 352
27.	1836	Rev James Lyon		Prestwich, Lancs		*Gunnis* 1968, 352
28.	†1837	Elizabeth Forster		St John, Lewisham, London		Pevsner, *London: S*, 1983, 414
29.	1837	'Mural monument to Mrs Cole'		[Exhib RA, London, 1183]; untraced		*Graves* VII, 1905–6, 123
30.	†1838	Rev Ferdinando Casson		Chester Cathedral	S	C Lib (repr)
31.	†1839	William Blathwayt		Dyrham, Glos	S	Pevsner, *Glos: Cotswolds*, 1999, 341
32.	†1840	Ann Sykes (†1835) and Martha Venn (†1840)		St John, Islington, London		Pevsner, *London: N*, 1998, 656
33.	†1840	Fletcher Raincock		St Martin, Bowness-on-Windermere, Westmorland		
34.	1842	Elizabeth Mott		Banstead, Surrey	S	*Gunnis* 1968, 352
35.	†1842	Lord James Townshend		Bintree, Norfolk	S	Pevsner, *Norfolk: N E & Norwich*, 1997, 393
36.	1843	Charles Bridge		Harwich, Essex	S	*Gunnis* 1968, 352
37.	c1845	George Brabins and many Brabins and Measure family members including Mary Measure (†1845)		Oinchbeck, Lincs	S	Pevsner, *Lincs*, 1989, 602
38.	nd	Sievier family		Kensal Green Cemetery, London		*Curl* 2001, 165, 224–5, 232 (repr)

Statues

39.	1824	Sleeping Bacchante	m	[coll Gwynn Ellis Esq]; untraced	SD	*Graves* VII, 1905–6, 122; *Grittleton Marbles* 1966, 16 (repr VII); *Read* 1982, 141, 199 (repr)
40.	1824	The three Graces, statuette	m	Birmingham MAG, inv P.1'66		*Silber* 1987, 86, cat no 259
41.	1828	Affection, group to be executed in marble (perhaps for the John and Frances Sievier monument)		[Exhib RA, London, 1212]; untraced		*Graves* VII, 1905–6, 123
42.	1829	Bacchus	m	[Exhib Soc of BA, London, 865]; untraced		*Johnson* 1975, 423
43.	1829	Reclining figure		[Exhib RSBA, London, 857]; untraced		*Johnson* 1975, 423
44.	1829	Reclining figure	m	[Exhib Soc of BA, London, 857]; untraced		*Johnson* 1975, 423
45.	1829	Undine		[The Colosseum, Regent's Park, London, conservatory]; untraced		*Gunnis* 1968, 352
46.	1830	Musidora	m	[coll Gwynn Ellis Esq]; untraced	SD	*Graves* VII, 1905–6, 123; *Graves* 1875, 491; *Grittleton Marbles* 1966, 17; *Read* 1982, 143, 207 (repr)
47.	1831	A faun	m	[Exhib RSBA, 884]; untraced		*Johnson* 1975, 423
48.	1831	A faun		[Exhib Soc of BA, London, 884]; untraced		*Johnson* 1975, 423
49.	1833	Captain Coram, statuette	p	Foundling Hospital, London	D	*Gunnis* 1968, 352
50.	nd	Sir William Curtis, statuette	p	Foundling Hospital, London		*Gunnis* 1968, 352; A&A (repr)

Busts

No.	Date	Subject	Material	Location	Signed	Literature
51.	1822	Daniel Moore FRS		[Exhib RA, London, 1038]; untraced		*Graves* VII, 1905–6, 122
52.	1822	William, 3rd Earl Harcourt		[Exhib RA, London, 1036]; untraced		*Graves* VII, 1905–6, 122
53.	1823	Lord Chief Justice Dallas		[Exhib RA, London, 1085]; untraced		*DNB*; *Graves* VII, 1905–6, 122
54.	1823	Mirza M Saleh		[Exhib RA, London, 1103]; untraced		*Graves* VII, 1905–6, 122
55.	1823	S Cartwright		[Exhib RA, London, 1083]; untraced		*Graves* VII, 1905–6, 122
56.	1823	S Satoore		[Exhib RA, London, 1071]; untraced		*Graves* VII, 1905–6, 122
57.	1823	Sir John Silvester, recorder of London 1803–1822	m	CL Coll, Guildhall, London, acc 1375		*Gunnis* 1968, 352; *Knight* 1986, 345 (repr); *Read* 1982, 172
58.	1823	W Horne		[Exhib RA, London, 1061]; untraced		*Graves* VII, 1905–6, 122
59.	1824	Charles Mills		[Exhib RA, London, 985]; untraced		*DNB*; *Graves* VII, 1905–6, 122
60.	1824	Cropley, 6th Earl of Shaftesbury, to be executed in marble		[Exhib RA, London, 973]; untraced		*Graves* VII, 1905–6, 122
61.	1824	Dr John Latham FRSP		St Bartholomew's Hospital, City of London		*Gunnis* 1968, 352
62.	1824	Lord Chancellor (and 1st Earl of) Eldon		St Giles, Dorset Other versions: duplicated (plaster, 1827, Windsor Castle)		*Library of Fine Arts* 1831, vol 1, 432–3; *Graves* VII, 1905–6, 122; *Gunnis* 1968, 352; *Johnson* 1975, 423
63.	1824	Lord Francis Gower		[Exhib RA, London, 990]; untraced		*Graves* VII, 1905–6, 122
64.	1824	William, 3rd Earl Harcourt	p	Private coll	S	C Lib (repr)
65.	1825	Joshua Brookes	m	Kensal Green Cemetery, catacombs	SD	
66.	1826	John Foster		[Exhib RA, London, 1043]; untraced		*Graves* VII, 1905–6, 122
67.	1826	Lord Francis Gower		[Exhib RA, London, 1059]; untraced		*Graves* VII, 1905–6, 122
68.	1826	Lord Rolle		[Exhib RA, London, 1088]; untraced		*Graves* VII, 1905–6, 123
69.	1828	John Abernethy	m	St Bartholomew's Hospital, London	S	*Graves* VII, 1905–6, 123; *Gunnis* 1968, 352
70.	1828	Unidentified gentleman		[Exhib RA, London, 1140]; untraced	S	*Graves* VII, 1905–6, 123
71.	1828	Unidentified lady		[Exhib RA, London, 1160]; untraced		*Graves* VII, 1905–6, 123
72.	1828	William, 3rd Earl Harcourt	m	Windsor Castle, RCIN 35847 Other versions: private coll, plaster, SD 1829	SD	*Gunnis* 1968, 352
73.	1829	Countess of Sheffield		[Exhib RA, London, 1176]; untraced		*Graves* VII, 1905–6, 123
74.	1829	Richard Clark, Chamberlain of London	m	CL Coll, Guildhall, City of London, acc 95		*Graves* VII, 1905–6, 123; *Knight* 1986, 346 (repr)
75.	1829	Unidentified gentleman		[Exhib RSBA, 874]; untraced		*Johnson* 1975, 423
76.	1829	Unidentified gentleman		[Exhib RSBA, 878]; untraced		*Johnson* 1975, 423
77.	1829	Unidentified gentleman		[Exhib Soc of BA, London, 874]; untraced		*Johnson* 1975, 423
78.	1829	Unidentified gentleman		[Exhib Soc of BA, London, 878]; untraced		*Johnson* 1975, 423
79.	1828–1830	Daniel Moore Payment(s): £94 10s	m	RI, London		
80.	1830	Henry, 1st Marquess of Anglesey	m	RDS, Dublin	SD	*Graves* VII, 1905–6, 123; *White and Bright* 1998, 53
81.	1830	Mrs W L Wellesley		[Exhib RA, London, 1211]; untraced		*Graves* VII, 1905–6, 123
82.	1830	Rt Hon W Long Wellesley		[Exhib RA, London, 1203]; untraced		*Graves* VII, 1905–6, 123
83.	1830	Sir Thomas Lawrence	m	SJSM		*Gunnis* 1968, 352; www.soane.org; *Johnson* 1975, 423
84.	1830	Sir William Bolland	m	Trinity College, Cambridge	SD	*Graves* VII, 1905–6, 123; *Gunnis* 1968, 352; *Johnson* 1975, 423
85.	1831	Dr Turton, Dean of Peterborough		Divinity School, Cambridge		*Graves* VII, 1905–6, 123; *Gunnis* 1968, 352
86.	1831	Lord Brougham and Vaux		[Exhib RA, London, 1229]; untraced		*Graves* VII, 1905–6, 123; *Johnson* 1975, 423
87.	1831	Thomas le Blanc		[Exhib RA, London, 1172]; untraced		*Graves* VII, 1905–6, 123
88.	1832	Richard Joddrell		[Exhib RA, London, 1186]; untraced		*Graves* VII, 1905–6, 123; *Johnson* 1975, 423
89.	1833	J Bolland		[Exhib RA, London, 1122]; untraced		*Graves* VII, 1905–6, 123
90.	1835	Professor Coleman		[Exhib RA, London, 1084]; untraced		*Graves* VII, 1905–6, 123
91.	1836	Rev James Lyon		Prestwich, Lancs		*Gunnis* 1968, 352
92.	1837	Sir Thomas Monro		[Exhib RA, London, 1231]; untraced		*Graves* VII, 1905–6, 123
93.	1838	J O Oughton		[Exhib RA, London, 1320]; untraced		*Graves* VII, 1905–6, 123
94.	1842	Albert, the Prince Consort		Royal Coll, Windsor Castle		*AU*, 1842, 127; *Ormond* 1973, 11; *Johnson* 1975, 423
95.	1842	Frederick William IV, King of Prussia		[Exhib RA, London, 1398]; untraced		*Graves* VII, 1905–6, 123
96.	1842	Sir William Horne		[Exhib RA, London, 1399]; untraced		*Graves* VII, 1905–6, 123
97.	1843	Mrs Ellis		[Exhib RA, London, 1517]; untraced		*Graves* VII, 1905–6, 123
98.	1843	Wynne Ellis		[Exhib RA, London, 1438]; untraced		*Graves* VII, 1905–6, 123
99.	1844	James Bourdieu		[Exhib RA, London, 1378]; untraced		*Graves* VII, 1905–6, 123
100.	1844	Mrs Oughton		[Exhib RA, London, 1371]; untraced		*Graves* VII, 1905–6, 123
101.	1844	Sir James Munro		Oriental Club, London		GPC
102.	nd	Lewis Duval	m	[Ex coll Lewis Duval (nephew)]		*DNB*
103.	nd	Unidentified subject		Trinity College, Cambridge		Pevsner, *Cambs*, 1970, 175

Chimneypieces

No.	Date	Subject	Material	Location	Signed	Literature
104.	1833	Flanked by bacchanalian figures, companion to one by Richard Westmacott III		Chatsworth, Derbys, dining room		Pevsner, *Derbys*, 1978, 137

Architectural Sculpture

No.	Date	Subject	Material	Location	Signed	Literature
105.	nd	Flora	sa	Terrace at the east end of the central avenue, Covent Garden		www.cgareatrust.org.uk
106.	nd	Low relief, subject unidentified		[Manor House, Elthorne Road, Holloway, London]; destroyed		*Croot* 1985, 29–37

Miscellaneous

No.	Date	Subject		Location		References
107.	1825	Pity, the daughter of love and sorrow		[Exhib RA, London, 992]; untraced		*Graves* VII, 1905–6, 122; *Graves* 1875, 491
108.	1826	Boy with tortoise		Private coll Other versions: Exhib RA, London, 1829, 1219; untraced		*Graves* 1875, 491; *Graves* VII, 1905–6, 123; *Gunnis* 1968, 352
109.	1829	A Turk		[Exhib BI, London, 540]; untraced		*Graves* 1875, 491
110.	1829	Bacchus	m	[Exhib RSBA, 865]; untraced		*Johnson* 1975, 423
111.	1829	Girl and lamb		[Exhib RA, London, 1170]; untraced		*Graves* 1875, 491; *Graves* VII, 1905–6, 123
112.	1831	Foliage		[Exhib Soc of BA, London, 915]; untraced		*Johnson* 1975, 423
113.	1834	Mother and child		[Exhib RA, London, 1078]; untraced		*Graves* VII, 1905–6, 123
114.	nd	Two Bacchantes				*Gunnis* 1968, 352

SILVESTER fl 1782–88

A modeller, he exhibited at the Free Society from 1782 from 44 Houndsditch. When he exhibited at the Royal Academy in 1788 he gave his address as Lyceum, Strand. He was presumably the Mr Silvester who took over the business of **Pingo,** who was rendered inactive by serious illness in 1800. Pingo's wife, Theodosia, told Wedgwood that Silvester's 'knowledge and diligence are well known' (Wedgwood/Pingo, L1/24, Theodosia Pingo to Wedgwood and Co, Feb 1800).

Literary References: *Gunnis* 1968, 352

Busts

No.	Date	Subject		Location		References
1.	1788	Frederick-Augustus, Duke of York and Albany		[Exhib RA, London, 655]; untraced		*Graves* VII, 1905–6, 125; *Gunnis* 1968, 352
2.	1788	John Wesley		[Exhib RA, London, 609]; untraced		*Graves* VII, 1905–6, 125; *Gunnis* 1968, 352
3.	1788	Lord Hood		[Exhib RA, London, 596]; untraced		*Graves* VII, 1905–6, 125; *Gunnis* 1968, 352
4.	1788	Lord Rodney		[Exhib RA, London, 656]; untraced		*Graves* VII, 1905–6, 125; *Gunnis* 1968, 352

Miscellaneous

No.	Date	Subject		Location		References
5.	1782	King George III		[Exhib Free Soc, London, 225]; untraced		*Graves* 1907, 234
6.	1782	Queen Charlotte		[Exhib Free Soc, London, 226]; untraced		*Graves* 1907, 234
7.	1782	Triumph of Cupid		[Exhib Free Soc, London, 236]; untraced		*Graves* 1907, 234
8.	1782	Unidentified subject	w	[Exhib Free Soc, London, 224]; untraced		*Graves* 1907, 234
9.	1782	Unidentified subject		[Exhib Free Soc, London, 235]; untraced		*Graves* 1907, 234
10.	1788	Unidentified subject	w	[Exhib Free Soc, London, 223]; untraced		*Graves* 1907, 234

SIMMONDS, of Blandford fl *c*1832

Funerary Monuments

No.	Date	Subject		Location		References
1.	†1832	Davis family member		Turnworth, Dorset		Pevsner, *Dorset*, 1972, 431

SIMMONDS, of Swindon fl *c*1802–03

He signs a 'curious' monument to the Fortescue children (1). This consists of a pyramid against which stand miniature statuettes about nine inches high of the three children in contemporary costume.

Funerary Monuments

No.	Date	Subject		Location		References
1.	1802	The three children of John and Maria Fortescue		Lambourn, Berks	S	*Gunnis* 1968, 352
2.	?1803	Joseph Walker		Bampton, Oxon	S	*Gunnis* 1968, 352

SIMON, Abraham

He was a medallist who used wax as a preliminary medium. For more information the reader is directed to *Pyke* 1973, 136, *Penny* 1992, III, 146 and *Gibson* 1998, 382.

SIMPKIN, John, of Bottesford 1749–1816

He had much of the Kesteven trade in slate headstones, signing 47 known works, 30 of them at Woolsthorpe, Lincs. They are competent but lack the ingenuity of **Francis Lamb,** who appears to have been his master.

Literary References: *Neave and Heron* 1969, 5

SIMPSON, Benjamin fl 1723–30

He worked as a stone-cutter at the Parliament House, Dublin (now the Bank of Ireland), from February 1729 to July 1730. His one known monument is signed 'Ben Simpson made this monument'.

Funerary Monuments

No.	Date	Subject		Location		References
1.	1723	Edward Croker		Cahercorney, Co Limerick	S	*Potterton* 1975, 79

SIMPSON, John fl 1723–25

A mason, he carried out work at Newby, near Baldersby, Yorks, then being rebuilt for Sir William Robinson.

Chimneypieces

No.	Date	Subject		Location		References
1.	1723–1725	Several		Newby, W R Yorks		Compton of Newby Archives in GPC

Architectural Sculpture

No.	Date	Subject		Location		References
2.	1723–1725	Architectural stonecarving	s	Newby, W R Yorks		Compton of Newby Archives in GPC

SIMPSON, of London Bridge fl 1799–1805?

He was mason to the Skinners' Company, 1801–4, and apparently died before 1808, since in that year a Mary Simpson of the same address, who was presumably his widow, was paid for repairs to the Fishmongers' Hall. Simpson's two signed monuments 'are pleasant and well-carved works' (*Gunnis* 1968, 352).

Archival References: Fishmongers PL, 2, 198

Funerary Monuments

No.	Date	Subject		Location		References
1.	†1799	Miles Stringer		St Magnus the Martyr, City of London	S	Pevsner, *London: City*, 1997, 233;
2.	?1805	Mrs Thomas White		St James, Garlickhithe	S	*Gunnis* 1968, 352

SIMPSON, William fl 1806

Funerary Monuments

1.	1806	Colonel Samuel Bagshawe (†1804) Payment(s): £58 16s		Chapel-en-le-Frith, Derbys, graveyard		Rylands Library, Bagshawe, 139/2/115–118 in GPC

SIMPSON & MALONE, of Hull fl c1844–61

James Simpson was employed as a marble carver by the **Earle family of Kingston-upon-Hull** before joining Malone to start the firm which became Hull's best known building contractors of the mid-Victorian period. White's *Directory* listed them at 31 Osborne Street in 1846. They executed many large works in Hull and elsewhere. (Inf. Gerardine Mulcahy).

Funerary Monuments

1.	†1844	William Athson		St James, Louth, Lincs	S	RG/JP, 7, 1299
2.	†1851	Ann Pulleine and John (†1858) Smith		Market Weighton, E R Yorks	S	Pevsner, *Yorks: E R & York*, 1995, 610
3.	†1854	George Baron		North Cave, E R Yorks	S	Pevsner, *Yorks: E R & York*, 1995, 625
4.	†1861	William Vernon Norman		Sculcoates, Hull, E R Yorks	S	

SIMSON, David 1803–74

A landscape painter and modeller, he was born in Dundee in 1803. He exhibited sculpture at the Royal Scottish Academy between 1831 and 1834, from addresses in North Hanover Street and Queen Street. After that date he appears to have concentrated on painting, exhibiting Scottish landscape views regularly between 1844 and 1864. An undated plaster bust by David Simson of his brother William Simson RSA, who was also a landscape painter, is in the Scottish National Portrait Gallery (**8**). Simson died at Edinburgh on 27 March 1874.

Literary References: *Woodward* 1977, vol 1, pt 2, 217–8

Busts

1.	1831	Unidentified boy		[Exhib R Sc A, Edinburgh, 369]; untraced	*Laperriere* 4, 1991, 164
2.	1831	Unidentified gentleman		[Exhib R Sc A, Edinburgh, 390]; untraced	*Laperriere* 4, 1991, 164
3.	1831	Unidentified lady		[Exhib R Sc A, Edinburgh, 392]; untraced	*Laperriere* 4, 1991, 164
4.	1831	Unidentified lady		[Exhib R Sc A, Edinburgh, 395]; untraced	*Laperriere* 4, 1991, 164
5.	1831	Unidentified painter		[Exhib R Sc A, Edinburgh, 379]; untraced	*Laperriere* 4, 1991, 164
6.	1832	Unidentified child		[Exhib R Sc A, Edinburgh, 321]; untraced	*Laperriere* 4, 1991, 164
7.	1834	Unidentified child		[Exhib R Sc A, Edinburgh, 346]; untraced	*Laperriere* 4, 1991, 164
8.	nd	William Simson (the sculptor's brother)	p	SNPG, Edinburgh	*Woodward* 1977, vol 1, pt 2, 217–8

Miscellaneous

9.	1832	Unidentified child	m	[Exhib R Sc A, Edinburgh, 316]; untraced	*Laperriere* 4, 1991, 164

SINGLETON, John, of Bury St Edmunds fl 1725–39

In the *Bury Post* of 14 March 1725 was a notice that at 'Mr. Singleton's the stone-cutter's shop in the Church Yard, Bury St. Edmunds, all persons may have Head and Feet Stones for graves at 10s. the pair; the headstone 4 foot long and 2 footbroad, with decent ornaments and a common inscription and proportionately for bigger or lesser sizes, performed by John Singleton, his father having wholly turned that branch of the trade to him'.

On 5 February 1738, John Singleton inserted a second notice in the same newspaper: 'whereas a report hath been spread that I am leaving my trade here in Bury, the better to prevent it gaining credit amongst those who have occassion for anything in my way of business, I am advised by my friends to declare to the Publick, that I have no such intention, but rather to inlarge it, having taken in Thomas Singleton my nephew partner with me, the better to enable me to give all my masters due attention'.

Archival References: GPC

Chimneypieces

1.	1739	Description not available		[Ickworth, Suffolk]; untraced	Account-book of the 1st Earl of Bristol in GPC; *Gunnis* 1968, 353

Architectural Sculpture

2.	1737	Coat of arms Payment(s): 30 gns		[Earl of Bristol's House, Bury St Edmunds, Suffolk, principal front]; untraced	Account-book of the 1st Earl of Bristol in GPC

SINGLETON, Robert, of Bury St Edmunds and Norwich 1682–

Nothing is known of Singleton's parentage, but he married Anne Crome on 28 April 1707, when both parties were aged 25. He was then described as a mason. There were nine or more children, at least five of whom died in infancy. He became a freeman of Norwich on 24 May 1716. Gunnis considered him a monumental sculptor of high rank and particularly admired his monument to Edmund Soames as an 'exciting and remarkable work' (1) It has a standing life-sized figure in armour, his helmet at his feet and his right hand holding his great cloak, 'which billows out and falls in folds behind him'. The cartouche tablet to Richard Manty 'is a delightful work' (4). The tablet to Thomas Pindar 'has a large figure of a cherub, an hourglass in his hand and with his head resting on a skull' (7).

In about 1729 he went into partnership with George Bottomley of the **Bottomley family of Norfolk and Cambridge**. Their monuments produced together are listed under Bottomley. An advertisement in the *Norwich Mercury* of 31 December 1737 announced that **Robert Page of Norwich** had bought the stock-in-trade of Singleton and Bottomley. (Add inf. Jon Bayliss)

Literary References: *Gunnis* 1968, 353

Archival References: Marriage licence bond, Norwich; parish registers of St John Timberhill and St John Maddermarket, Norwich, and St Mary and St James, Bury St Edmunds; Norwich freeman rolls TNA IRI 47/210, 49/47, 49/120; GPC

Funerary Monuments

1.	†1706	Colonel Edmund Soames	West Dereham, Norfolk		Pevsner, *Norfolk: N W & S*, 1999, 763
2.	1719	Jermyn Wyche and Maria Hungerford	Hockwold, Norfolk	S	Pevsner, *Norfolk: N W & S*, 1999, 410
3.	†1719	John Hungerford	Hockwold, Norfolk	S	Pevsner, *N-W & S Norfolk*, 1962, 199
4.	?1720	Richard Manty	St Martin's at Palace, Norwich		*Gunnis* 1968, 353
5.	?1720	Sir Dudley Cullum	Hawstead, Suffolk	S	*Gunnis* 1968, 353
6.	?1721	Mary Bateman	St Gregory, Norwich	S	*Gunnis* 1968, 353
7.	†1722	Thomas Pindar	St George Colegate, Norwich		Pevsner, *Norfolk: N E & Norwich*, 1997, 235

SINGLETON, Thomas, of Bury St Edmunds 1715–92

The son of a Thomas Singleton and probably the nephew of **Robert Singleton**, he was baptised at St John Maddermarket on 27 October 1715. He married Hannah Randall (†1788) and there were 11 children, all baptised at St Mary, Bury St Edmunds, in the years 1745–59. Singleton's yard was in Sparhawke Street, Bury St Edmunds, in premises now known as De Carle's yard. His six identified apprentices included his sons, Thomas (1763) and Charles (1770).

He was employed by Ambrose Crowley in 1753 on repairs to Barking Hall, Suffolk (Ashburnham Archives). In the same year he was the master mason making additions to Euston Hall, Suffolk under the architect Matthew Brettingham and was paid £228 (TNA c108/362). In 1778 he received £159 from Lord Archibald Hamilton for masonry work at Rendlesham Hall, Suffolk (Soane Archives). He worked under Robert Adam at Bury St Edmunds in 1775, where he built the town hall and carved reliefs which Gunnis found 'delightful' (**6**). In 1789–90, he repaired the Mansion House in the same town under Sir John Soane's direction.

In the *Bury Post* of 4 July 1792, he stated that he had 'disposed of his stock and premises to Messrs **John and Robert De Carle**'. He died in 1792, leaving his daughter Sarah as executrix. His obituary in the *Bury Post* of 24 October 1792 states he was advanced in age at the time of his death and had served as one of the burgesses of the Common Council. The writer added that 'few men have passed through a long life of active business more distinguished for ingenuity and integrity'. He was buried on 27 October 1792. The forthcoming sale of his household furniture and other effects was advertised in the *Bury & Norwich Post* on 13 March 1793. The notice stated that his 'good' dwelling house, yard and outbuildings 'together with the beneficial lease on part of the premises' were to be sold by private contract (inf. Jon Bayliss).

Gunnis commented that his monuments and tablets were not nearly as good as Robert Singleton's.

Literary References: *Gunnis* 1968, 353

Archival References: Parish registers, St John Maddermarket, Norwich, St Mary, Bury St Edmunds; Soane Bill Book 4, fols 21–5; Soane Priv Corr IV/9c/9, fol 35; GPC

Funerary Monuments

1.	?1740	Rev Thomas Knight	Bluntisham, Hunts		*Gunnis* 1968, 353
2.	†1748	Simon Kerrich	Redenhall, Norfolk		Pevsner, *Norfolk: N W & S*, 1999, 610
3.	?1748	Simon Kerrich	Harleston, Norfolk		*Gunnis* 1968, 353
4.	?1750	Valentine Muntee	Horringer, Suffolk		*Gunnis* 1968, 353
5.	nd	Lake family members	Goudhurst, Kent		*Gunnis* 1968, 353

Reliefs

6.	1775	Reliefs	Town Hall, Bury St Edmunds, exterior		Bury St Edmunds town archives in *Gunnis* 1968, 353

SKAE, Peter 1808–

He attended the Royal Academy Schools in April 1826 and later became an assistant to **Humphrey Hopper.** Gunnis noted that he was 'responsible for a few inferior busts' but identified none.

Literary References: *Hutchison* 1960–62, 178; *Gunnis* 1968, 353

SKELTON, Matthew, of York 1772–1844

Most of his tablets are neo-Hellenic in design. The monument to Ann and Elizabeth Simpson is a white marble tablet with fluted pilaster strips and a pediment with acroteria and consoles, and is surmounted by an urn (**11**). The Oldfield memorial is an architectural work with trophies (**23**), and the Joseph Johnson is a tablet with fluted pilasters (**26**). Gunnis described him as 'one of the least distinguished of the York statuaries' (*Gunnis* 1968, 353).

Funerary Monuments

1.	?1820	Joseph Emmot	Keighley, W R Yorks		*Gunnis* 1968, 353
2.	?1825	Francis Edmunds	Worsborough, W R Yorks		*Gunnis* 1968, 353
3.	†1825	Thomas Barmby	St Giles, Hull, E R Yorks		Pevsner, *Yorks: E R & York*, 1995, 510
4.	†1830	Sir Thomas Legard	Ganton, E R Yorks		Pevsner, *Yorks: E R & York*, 1995, 430
5.	†1831	John Grimston	Ripon Cathedral, W R Yorks	S	
6.	†1831	Rev William Jones	Sutton-upon-Derwent, E R Yorks		Pevsner, *Yorks: E R & York*, 1995, 716
7.	?1832	Elizabeth Alexander	Halifax, W R Yorks		*Gunnis* 1968, 353
8.	?1834	Samuel Wharton	Hackness, N R Yorks		GPC
9.	?1835	Ann Sleigh	Stockton, Durham	S	*Gunnis* 1968, 353
10.	†1835	Anna Maria Grimston	Ripon Cathedral, W R Yorks	S	
11.	†1836	Ann and Elizabeth Simpson	St Cuthbert, York		Pevsner, *Yorks: E R & York*, 1995, 165
12.	†1836	Varley Bealby	Unitarian Chapel, York		Pevsner, *Yorks: E R & York*, 1995, 179
13.	?1837	James Brooke	Barwick in Elmet, W R Yorks		*Gunnis* 1968, 353
14.	?1838	Charles Rickaby	Bridlington, E R Yorks		GPC
15.	†1838	Christopher Russell	All Saints, Muston, E R Yorks		Pevsner, *Yorks: E R & York*, 1995, 616
16.	†1838	Eliza Ellis	Yedingham, E R Yorks		Pevsner, *Yorks: E R & York*, 1995, 770

17.	†1838	Rev T Cutler Rudston-Read	Hayton, E R Yorks		Pevsner, *Yorks: E R & York*, 1995, 452
18.	?1840	Thomas Bland	Kippax, W R Yorks		*Gunnis* 1968, 353
19.	?1841	Francis Duffield	Bradford Cathedral, W R Yorks	S	*Gunnis* 1968, 353
20.	†1841	John and Ann Greame	Sewerby, E R Yorks		Pevsner, *Yorks: E R & York*, 1995, 678
21.	1850–1851	Thomas Dolman (†1589) and Robert Sothebie (†1594), restoration work	All Saints, Pocklington, E R Yorks		Pevsner, *Yorks: E R & York*, 1995, 649
22.	1852	Gee family member	St Oswald, Luddington, Lincs		Pevsner, *Lincs*, 1989, 546
23.	1852	Lieutenant Christopher Oldfield CB (†1850)	York Minster, south choir aisle	S	*Aylmer* 1977 466, 468 (repr); *Pattison and Murray* 2001, 121
24.	†1853	F O Smith	Sewerby, E R Yorks		Pevsner, *Yorks: E R & York*, 1995, 678
25.	†1856	John Wilkes Unett	St Oswald, Filey, E R Yorks		Pevsner, *Yorks: E R & York*, 1995, 416
26.	†1856	Joseph Johnson	Easingwold, N R Yorks	S	
27.	†1856	Yarburgh Yarburgh	Sewerby, E R Yorks		Pevsner, *Yorks: E R & York*, 1995, 678
28.	†1866	Mary Barmby	St Giles, Hull, E R Yorks		Pevsner, *Yorks: E R & York*, 1995, 510
29.	†1875	Martha and Joseph (†1875) Dent	Ribston Hall, W R Yorks, chapel	S	

SKIKELTHORPE, L, of Abridge, Essex fl 1842?

Funerary Monuments

1.	?1842	Emma Grosvenor, wall tablet	St Mary the Virgin, Wimbledon, Surrey	S	*Gunnis* 1968, 353

SKUTT, William, of York fl 1719–22

He was employed as a master-mason in 1719 at Castle Howard. Gunnis suggests that Skutt is probably a misspelling of Shout (**William Shout I**).

Chimneypieces

1.	1719–1722	Several	[Castle Howard, N R Yorks]; untraced	Castle Howard archives cited in *Gunnis* 1968, 353

Architectural Sculpture

2.	1719–1722	Pedestals and vases	[Castle Howard, N R Yorks, bowling green]; untraced	Castle Howard archives cited in *Gunnis* 1968, 353

SLATER, J R fl 1834–36

He exhibited two busts at the Royal Academy, giving his address in 1834 as 3 St James's Square, London.

Busts

1.	1834	J McRone	[Exhib RA, London, 1039]; untraced	*Graves* VII, 1905–6, 153; *Gunnis* 1968, 353
2.	1836	William Harrison Ainsworth	[Exhib RA, London, 1118]; untraced	*Graves* VII, 1905–6, 152; *Gunnis* 1968, 353

SLATER, Peter, of Edinburgh 1809–

He was born in Edinburgh, the son of John Slater, a marble and stone cutter of Picardy Place. Some time between 1823 and 1828 he entered the Edinburgh studio of **Samuel Joseph** as a carver and assistant. When Joseph moved to London in 1829 Slater accompanied him and he worked for Joseph over the next four years. On 26 April 1831 he was admitted to the RA schools on the recommendation of W Collins RA.

In 1833 Slater returned to Edinburgh where he lived at a number of addresses including 12 Union Street, 50 George Street, 27 Elder Street, 12 Elder Street and 52 Broughton Street. He returned to London in 1860. Slater exhibited at the Royal Scottish Academy, 1833–65 and at the Royal Academy in London, 1846–70, showing principally busts of Scottish worthies. His Royal Scottish Academy submissions for 1850 included an architectural design entitled *The house of Thespis*. In 1844 he sent a statue of *Canute reproving his flatterers* to the Westminster Hall Exhibition (7). The work was not well received, one reviewer observing tartly 'we must decline being one [a flatterer]', while another thought 'the general execution is coarse' (*Lit Gaz*, 27 July 1844, 482; *AU*, 1844, 215).

According to one 19th-century source, the statue of George Heriot on the Scott Monument, Edinburgh, was begun by Peter Slater and completed by a relative of the same name (*Colston* 1881, cited by *Woodward* 1977, vol 1, pt 2, 219). Woodward argues that this statement must be incorrect since the only other member of the Slater family who worked in the profession was Peter's father, John, who is not recorded in the *Edinburgh Post Office Directories* after 1816. She also suggests that Peter Slater can almost certainly be identified with Robert Slater, whom Samuel Joseph referred to as an ex-pupil in a letter written to William Lizars in 1833 (*Joseph/Lizars*). Peter exhibited a portrait of a Robert Slater at the RA in 1859 (59).

Literary References: *Gunnis* 1968, 353–4; *Woodward* 1977, vol 1, pt 2, 218–220

Archival References: RA Admissions

Funerary Monuments

1.	†1848	Alexander MacLeay		St James, King Street, Sydney, New South Wales	S	HMI Archive (repr)
2.	1855	Dr Ross Carson		St Giles Cathedral, Edinburgh		*Gunnis* 1968, 354; *Woodward* 1977, vol 1, pt 2, 220

Statues

3.	1836	David, model		[Exhib R Sc A, Edinburgh, 330]; untraced	*Laperriere* 4, 1991, 175
4.	1836	Sir Walter Scott, model	tc	[Exhib R Sc A, Edinburgh, 339]; untraced	*Laperriere* 4, 1991, 175
5.	1836	Unidentified subject, sketch		[Exhib R Sc A, Edinburgh, 342]; untraced	*Laperriere* 4, 1991, 175
6.	1839	'an attempt to accomodate the Highland costume for sculpture', sketch		[Exhib R Sc A, Edinburgh, 500]; untraced	*Laperriere* 4, 1991, 175

7.	1844	Canute reproving his flatterers		[Exhib Westminster Hall, London, 126]; untraced	*AU*, 1844, 215; *Gunnis* 1968, 353
8.	1844	Ellen Douglas	s	Scott monument, Princes Street, Edinburgh	*Woodward* 1977, vol 1, pt 2, 220
9.	1853	James Watt (after Sir Francis Chantrey)	s	[Adams Square, Edinburgh]; outside James Watt centre, Riccarton campus, Heriot-Watt University	*Gunnis* 1968, 353
10.	1854	George Heriot	s	Scott Monument, Princes Street, Edinburgh	*Gunnis* 1968, 354; *Woodward* 1977, vol 1, pt 2, 220; *Read* 1982, 117
Busts					
11.	1834	Miss Catherine Jameson		[Exhib R Sc A, Edinburgh, 337]; untraced	*Laperriere* 4, 1991, 175
12.	1834	Prof Jameson		[Exhib R Sc A, Edinburgh, 352]; untraced	*Laperriere* 4, 1991, 175
13.	1834	Robert Burns		[Exhib R Sc A, Edinburgh, 338]; untraced	*Laperriere* 4, 1991, 175
14.	1835	Miss Gibson		[Exhib R Sc A, Edinburgh, 351]; untraced	*Laperriere* 4, 1991, 175
15.	1835	Rev Dr Brown		[Exhib R Sc A, Edinburgh, 346]; untraced	*Laperriere* 4, 1991, 175
16.	1835	Robert Chalmers		[Exhib R Sc A, Edinburgh, 349]; untraced	*Laperriere* 4, 1991, 175
17.	1835	Unidentified child		[Exhib R Sc A, Edinburgh, 350]; untraced	*Laperriere* 4, 1991, 175
18.	1836	Ann McLaren	m	[Exhib R Sc A, Edinburgh, 331]; untraced	*Laperriere* 4, 1991, 175
19.	1836	Dr William Sharpey	p	[Exhib R Sc A, Edinburgh, 337]; untraced	*Laperriere* 4, 1991, 175
20.	1836	Unidentified lady		[Exhib R Sc A, Edinburgh, 354]; untraced	*Laperriere* 4, 1991, 175
21.	1837	Unidentified child		[Exhib R Sc A, Edinburgh, 377]; untraced	*Laperriere* 4, 1991, 175
22.	1839	Mrs Williams		[Exhib R Sc A, Edinburgh, 506]; untraced	*Laperriere* 4, 1991, 175
23.	1839	Rev James Marshall		[Exhib R Sc A, Edinburgh, 504]; untraced	*Laperriere* 4, 1991, 175
24.	1839	Unidentified gentleman	m	[Exhib R Sc A, Edinburgh, 492]; untraced	*Laperriere* 4, 1991, 175
25.	1842	John Napier, of Merchiston (†1617)		[coll Sir Alexander Johnston, of Carnsallach]; untraced	*Laperriere* 4, 1991, 175
26.	1844	Principal John Lee	m	Edinburgh University	*Woodward* 1977, vol 1, pt 2, 220; *Laperriere* 4, 1991, 175
27.	1844	T J Boyd		[Exhib R Sc A, Edinburgh, 569]; untraced	*Laperriere* 4, 1991, 175
28.	1845	Sir James Forrest	m	New College, Edinburgh	*Woodward* 1977, vol 1, pt 2, 220; *Laperriere* 4, 1991, 175
29.	1846	Alexander Goalen		[Exhib R Sc A, Edinburgh, 569]; untraced	*Laperriere* 4, 1991, 175, 176
30.	1846	Minna Troil, female head		[Exhib R Sc A, Edinburgh, 572]; untraced	*Laperriere* 4, 1991, 175
31.	1846	Prof Andrew Duncan	m	Edinburgh University Other versions: miniature bust exhib R Sc A, Edinburgh, 1848, 611	*Woodward* 1977, vol 1, pt 2, 220; *Laperriere* 4, 1991, 175, 176
32.	1846	Robert W Hamilton, of Edinburgh		[Exhib RA, London, 1484]; untraced	*Graves* VII, 1905–6, 153; *Laperriere* 4, 1991, 176
33.	1846	Unidentified gentleman		[Exhib R Sc A, Edinburgh, 568]; untraced	*Laperriere* 4, 1991, 175
34.	1847	Dr Joshua Davidson	p	R C Physic, Edinburgh	*Woodward* 1977, vol 1, pt 2, 220; *Laperriere* 4, 1991, 176
35.	1847	Rev Dr Bennie	m	Greyfriars church, Edinburgh	*Woodward* 1977, vol 1, pt 2, 220; *Laperriere* 4, 1991, 175, 176
36.	1847	Robert Bryson		[Exhib R Sc A, Edinburgh, 643]; untraced	*Laperriere* 4, 1991, 176
37.	1847	Sir John Gladstone, 1st Bt	p	Fasque, Kincardineshire	*Graves* VII, 1905–6, 153; *Woodward* 1977, vol 1, pt 2, 220; *Laperriere* 4, 1991, 175
38.	1848	E B Ramsay, Dean of Edinburgh		[Exhib R Sc A, Edinburgh, 614]; untraced	*Laperriere* 4, 1991, 176
39.	1848	Prof MacVey Napier	m	Edinburgh University	*Woodward* 1977, vol 1, pt 2, 220; *Laperriere* 4, 1991, 176
40.	1848	Unidentified man	m	Fasque, Kincardineshire	*Woodward* 1977, vol 1, pt 2, 220
41.	1849	Unidentified man	m	Fasque, Kincardineshire	*Woodward* 1977, vol 1, pt 2, 220
42.	1850	Charles Terrot, Bishop of Edinburgh	m	[Exhib RA, London, 1422]; untraced	*Graves* VII, 1905–6, 153; *Laperriere* 4, 1991, 176
43.	1850	Miss Gladstone		[Exhib R Sc A, Edinburgh, 478]; untraced	*Laperriere* 4, 1991, 175, 176
44.	1851	Prof George Dunbar	m	Edinburgh University	*Woodward* 1977, vol 1, pt 2, 220; *Laperriere* 4, 1991, 176
45.	1852	Prof James Pillans	m	Edinburgh University	*Graves* VII, 1905–6, 153; *Woodward* 1977, vol 1, pt 2, 220; *Laperriere* 4, 1991, 176
46.	1852	Robert Naysmith	m	[Exhib RA, London, 1422]; untraced	*Graves* VII, 1905–6, 153
47.	1853	Charles B Hornor		[Exhib RA, London, 1393]; untraced	*Graves* VII, 1905–6, 153
48.	1853	Lord Jeffrey	m	Faculty of Procurators, Glasgow	*Woodward* 1977, vol 1, pt 2, 220; *Laperriere* 4, 1991, 176
49.	1853	Mrs Robert Naysmith		[Exhib RA, London, 1394]; untraced	*Graves* VII, 1905–6, 153

50.	1853	Unidentified gentleman		[Exhib R Sc A, Edinburgh, 682]; untraced	*Laperriere* 4, 1991, 176
51.	1854	Unidentified lady	m	[Exhib R Sc A, Edinburgh, 720]; untraced	*Laperriere* 4, 1991, 176
52.	1855	J Ramsay McCulloch		Scotsman Newspaper Office, Edinburgh Other versions: Philosophical Institution, Edinburgh	*Graves* VII, 1905–6, 154; *Woodward* 1977, vol 1, pt 2, 220; *Laperriere* 4, 1991, 176
53.	1856	A Gillespie MD		[Exhib R Sc A, Edinburgh, 718]; untraced	*Laperriere* 4, 1991, 176
54.	1857	Head of Medusa	m	[Exhib R Sc A, Edinburgh, 684]; untraced	*Laperriere* 4, 1991, 176
55.	1857	Robert Bald	m	[Exhib RA, London, 1282]; untraced	*Graves* VII, 1905–6, 154; *Laperriere* 4, 1991, 176
56.	1858	George Brown	m	[Exhib RA, London, 1251]; untraced	*Graves* VII, 1905–6, 154
57.	1858	Leonard Horner	m	[coll Edinburgh School of Arts]; untraced	*Laperriere* 4, 1991, 176
58.	1859	David Dewar	m	[Exhib RA, London, 1312]; untraced	*Graves* VII, 1905–6, 154
59.	1859	Robert Slater	m	[Exhib RA, London, 1355]; untraced	*Graves* VII, 1905–6, 154
60.	1860	Alexander Grant		[Exhib RA, London, 1047]; untraced	*Graves* VII, 1905–6, 154
61.	1860	Robert Brown		Linnean Society, London	*Graves* VII, 1905–6, 154; *Ormond* 1973, 66; *Laperriere* 4, 1991, 176
62.	1861	Mrs Crichton of Edinburgh	m	[Exhib RA, London, 1054]; untraced	*Graves* VII, 1905–6, 154; *Laperriere* 4, 1991, 176
63.	1861	W S Lindsay MP		[Exhib RA, London, 1102]; untraced	*Graves* VII, 1905–6, 154
64.	1862	Capt Thomas Brown		[Exhib R Sc A, Edinburgh, 835]; untraced	*Laperriere* 4, 1991, 176
65.	1862	Prof Thomas Bell		[Linnean Club, London]; untraced	*Graves* VII, 1905–6, 154
66.	1863	Prof G G Stokes		[Exhib RA, London, 1167]; untraced	*Graves* VII, 1905–6, 154
67.	1863	William Anderson Ogg		[Exhib RA, London, 1018]; untraced	*Graves* VII, 1905–6, 154
68.	1864	John Thorpe	m	[Exhib RA, London, 989]; untraced	*Graves* VII, 1905–6, 154
69.	1864	Malvina	m	[Exhib RA, London, 1059]; untraced	*Graves* VII, 1905–6, 154
70.	1864	Robert Hepburn		[Exhib RA, London, 1054]; untraced	*Graves* VII, 1905–6, 154; *Laperriere* 4, 1991, 176
71.	1865	Dr F W Ramsay	m	[Exhib RA, London, 1018]; untraced	*Graves* VII, 1905–6, 154
72.	1865	Mrs William Wilson Hunter	m	[Exhib R Sc A, Edinburgh, 889]; untraced	*Laperriere* 4, 1991, 176
73.	1866	J S Bowerbank		[Exhib RA, London, 1035]; untraced	*Graves* VII, 1905–6, 154
74.	1867	Mrs John Stone		[Exhib RA, London, 1072]; untraced	*Graves* VII, 1905–6, 154
75.	1867	Mrs Wiltshire		[Exhib RA, London, 1022]; untraced	*Graves* VII, 1905–6, 154
76.	1868	Rev James Hamilton		[Exhib RA, London, 1135]; untraced	*Graves* VII, 1905–6, 154
77.	1869	Rev T Binney		[Exhib RA, London, 1176]; untraced	*Graves* VII, 1905–6, 154
Reliefs					
78.	1870	John Epps MD, commemorative medallion		[Exhib RA, London, 1071]; untraced	*Graves* VII, 1905–6, 154
Miscellaneous					
79.	1844	Monument for George Buchanan, model		[Exhib R Sc A, Edinburgh, 571]; untraced	*Laperriere* 4, 1991, 175
80.	1848	Brenda Troil		[Exhib R Sc A, Edinburgh, 600]; untraced	*Laperriere* 4, 1991, 176
81.	1848	Minna Troil		[Exhib R Sc A, Edinburgh, 610]; untraced	*Laperriere* 4, 1991, 176
82.	1856	The dying Alexander, sketch in marble	m	[Exhib R Sc A, Edinburgh, 731]; untraced	*Laperriere* 4, 1991, 176
83.	1859	The bard of Coila		[Exhib RA, London, 1253]; untraced	*Graves* VII, 1905–6, 154

SLATER, Robert

See **Peter Slater**.

SLAUGHTER, Mary

For information the reader is directed to *Pyke* 1973, 137

SLINGSBY FAMILY

Thomas Slingsby –*c*1778
John Slingsby –1808
Hannah Slingsby fl 1781–1808

Thomas Slingsby was the master-mason at Windsor Castle and appears to have retired or died in 1778, the year he carved the stonework of the portico on the north front (*Gunnis* 1968, 354, citing PRO Works 5/66). In 1778 he also built the Queen's Lodge, for which he was paid £2,261. He was succeeded by his son **John Slingsby**, who held the same post for 20 years. John assisted his father at the Queen's Lodge, working on the central buildings, the towers and the portico of the north front. In September 1778 he was given a bonus of £25 'for his extra care and attendance'. He also received payment for 'work at ye Equestrian statue in the great court yard' (TNA WORK 5/66), presumably the statue of Charles II by **Grinling Gibbons**. During the remodelling of the castle he was responsible for a considerable amount of mason's and stone carver's work, including new arches for the entrance tower, the removal of old stonework, work on the grand staircase and paving for Horn Court. Under James Wyatt he carried out work on the tomb house, including pinnacles and battlements. His work included a number of chimneypieces (1–5). He was paid over £4,000 between 1800 and 1805.

John appears to have run the firm with his wife, **Hannah Slingsby**. Between 1781 and 1808 they were paid £396 10s 3d for 'measured work' in the New Building at Queen's Lodge, Windsor (TNA WORK 5/67). After Slingsby's death in 1808 Hannah continued the business, receiving payment for the chimneypiece for the library (5) and a Portland stone staircase. He was succeeded as master-mason by **James Bedborough**.

Literary References: *Hope* 1913, 1, 348, 349, 351, 352; 2, 485; *Gunnis* 1968, 354
Archival References: GPC

Chimneypieces

No.	Date	Description		Location	Reference
1.	1781	Description not available (by John Slingsby)		[Prince of Wales's room, Windsor Castle]; untraced	*Gunnis* 1968, 354
2.	1800–1805	Dove-grey marble (by John Slingsby) Payment(s): £25	m	[Windsor Castle]; untraced	TNA WORK 5/67
3.	1800–1805	Marble reeded (by John Slingsby) Payment(s): £28	m	[Windsor Castle]; untraced	TNA WORK 5/67
4.	1800–1805	With pilasters of red marble (by John Slingsby) Payment(s): £20	m	[Windsor Castle]; untraced	TNA WORK 5/67
5.	1808	Red marble, with pilasters (payment to Hannah Slingsby) Payment(s): £60	m	[Windsor Castle, Berks, library]; untraced	TNA WORK 5/67

Architectural Sculpture

No.	Date	Description		Location	Reference
6.	1778	Unidentified carving (by John Slingsby)	s	Windsor Castle, principal front, portico	TNA WORK 5/66
7.	1794	Carved mouldings (by John Slingsby) Payment(s): £200		[Windsor Castle, picture gallery, windows]; untraced	*Gunnis* 1968, 354

LOCOMBE, Thomas fl 1830

Probably an Exeter mason, he built Bampfylde House, Exeter, in 1730 (Archives, Sir John Carew-Pole, in GPC).

LYTH, Isaac, of Colchester –1800

A stonemason, he worked in partnership with Messrs Roper and Doughty, of Ipswich, but became bankrupt a few months after leaving the firm in 1799 (*Chelmsford Chronicle*, 22 March 1799). He died in Colchester on 2 December 1800 (*Monthly Mag*, 1801, 11, 93).

Slyth was succeeded by his son James, who in 1812 advertised in the *Chelmsford Chronicle* that he had 'imported some very beautiful Italian marble and laid in a quantity of the newly discovered British marble', and also that he had a 'quantity of chimney-pieces fitted up for inspection'. The same paper reported James Slyth's death on 12 June 1816, stating that his widow intended to 'carry on the business for her children's benefit'.

The family continued in business as stone masons until the 20th century, but 'none of their tablets or gravestones ever rose above a low provincial level' (*Gunnis* 1968, 354).

Literary References: *Gunnis* 1968, 354
Archival References: GPC

MALLES fl *c*1779

His one known work is a marble inscription tablet set in a wooden ground.

Funerary Monuments

No.	Date	Subject	Location		Reference
1.	?1779	James Hulbert	Guiseley, W R Yorks		GPC

MALLMAN, J, of Bouldon fl *c*1772–80

He signs a large wall tablet with an arched pediment surmounted by an urn to Thomas Smyth (**2**), and another with pediment, draperies and a winged putto's head (**1**).

Funerary Monuments

No.	Date	Subject	Location		Reference
1.	†1772	Thomas and Elizabeth (†1769) Yate	Ashford Carbonell, Salop	S	
2.	1780	Thomas Smyth	Much Wenlock, Salop	S	*Gunnis* 1968, 354

MALLWELL, John fl –1706

He was a master joiner at Chatsworth with **Sir Charles Hopson** and **Roger Davis**, working under **Grinling Gibbons** and **William Emmett** in the chapel. He was with the same team under Gibbons at Whitehall, employed in the great chapel, and was one of those making models for elements of the choir at St Paul's Cathedral. He was also involved at Blenheim with the other board of works craftsmen in 1706.

Literary References: *Green* 1964 (1), 57–8, 62, 91, 126, 130

MART, James, of Guildford fl 1802–42

Between 1802 and 1804 he was the master-mason at Albury House, near Guildford, which was designed for Samuel Thornton by Soane. He and **L Moon of Goldalming** both sign a tablet (**4**), and must presumably have been in partnership.

Literary References: *Gunnis* 1968, 354
Archival References: Soane Bill Book D, fols 284–88

Funerary Monuments

No.	Date	Subject	Location		Reference
1.	?1826	Colonel Berkeley	Wotton, Surrey	S	*Gunnis* 1968, 354
2.	?1826	William Smith	Stoke-next-Guildford, Surrey	S	*Gunnis* 1968, 354
3.	†1835	Colonel Charles Henry Somerset	Old Woking, Surrey	S	*Gunnis* 1968, 354
4.	†1842	John Watts de Belin (co-sculptor: L Moon, of Godalming)	Holy Trinity, Guildford, Surrey	S	

MITH, Bernhard 1820–85

A little known artist, he was involved with the Pre-Raphaelites and specialised in carved portrait medallions until his early thirties, when he emigrated to Australia. He was born at Greenwich in 1820 to a family with maritime connections (three of his brothers served as naval officers). His mother's family, the Voases, had a substantial home at Analby, near Hull and were of some importance in that locality, but Bernhard's parents were not wealthy and the family lived frugally. He attended classes at Sass's Drawing School in Soho, London and by 1838 was drawing and modelling from the cast collection at the British Museum. During this period he also modelled portrait medallions and carved a tomb memorial to commemorate his sister (**5, 1**). He enrolled at the Royal Academy Schools in April 1840, but did not remain there long.

By October 1840 Smith was in Paris. He originally intended to study under **Pierre Jean David d'Angers**, whom he greatly admired, but was advised that David 'was too political a character and neglected his studio and schools for that profession' (letter to his mother, 21 Oct 1840, private coll, cited by *Read and Barnes* 1991, 13). Instead he joined the studio of Etienne Jules Ramey. Smith quickly impressed his new master, who set him to work modelling portrait medallions under his direct supervision, promoted him within the studio hierarchy and cast one of his works (17) Smith studied in the city's art galleries and libraries and made trips out, sketching from buildings and nature. He wa particularly interested in gothic architecture but also admired the paintings of Rubens and Claude and the sculptur of Jean Goujon. He returned to England in the summer of 1841.

By 1842 Smith was working from a studio in Great Ormond Street, London and that year he exhibited at the RA (**6, 7**). He soon became involved with the group of young artists and writers who later became known as the Pre Raphaelites. He was on close terms with the group: William Michael Rossetti later wrote affectionately of Bernhard' 'geniality of character and bearing' and the 'striking manly mould of his face and person' (Rossetti/Smith, cited b *Read and Barnes* 1991, 12). In 1847 he was sharing a studio in Stanhope Street, London with **Thomas Woolner** and in 1849 he signed a medallion portrait of Maria Gray with the initials 'P.R.B.' (**13**).

During the 1840s Smith produced a number of portrait medallions. These included depictions of members of hi own family and their immediate circle (**9–13, 15**), but Smith seems to have had difficulty in attracting wide patronage. The portrait medallion form was popular with the Pre-Raphaelites and these reliefs, with their minut realism and austere use of line, as exemplified in the portraits of Maria Gray and Emma Smith (**13, 15**), have stylisti affinities with Pre-Raphaelite works in various media. Smith's only surviving fully three-dimensional work is a smal seated figure known as *The schoolmaster* (**4**), inspired by Houdon's celebrated statue of Voltaire. Smith wa technically enterprising and showed interest in designing for manufacturers. He experimented in producing casts b an electroplating process using apparatus he had constructed himself in the studio he shared with Woolner. The *Ar Union* illustrated his design for a gas bracket in the form of a fairy sitting at the base of a convovulus as an exampl of graceful, yet practical, industrial design (*AU*, 1848, 321).

In the late 1840s Smith turned his attention briefly to painting, exhibiting a picture of water-elves at the RA in 1851 The following year he and Woolner emigrated to Australia where they hoped to make their fortunes prospecting fo gold. Both found the work gruelling, were shocked by the terrible living conditions and violence they witnessed an soon realised that they were unlikely to make much money. Smith abandoned the gold mines in mid-1853 and foun more congenial employment, first as a gold warden and then as a police magistrate. After his marriage to Olivi Boyes in 1863 he settled at Smythesdale in Victoria.

During most of this period he found little time for artistic activities but continued to sketch birds, flowers an fairy subjects. His only recorded Australian sculpture was a monument to the wife of the third Governor of Victoria Sir Henry Barkly (**2**) and a portrait medallion of one of his neighbours in Smythesdale, modelled in 1877 (**14**) neither of which has been traced. Towards the end of his life, Smith began to pursue art more seriously again. Afte 1878, when his duties as a magistrate frequently took him away from home, he spent his evenings working o elaborate large-scale tableaux in pen and ink, which were greatly influenced by the work of **John Flaxman RA** William Blake and Victorian fairy pictures. He was awarded a prize for his drawings when they were shown at th Melbourne International Exhibition of 1880. It is thought that he may have intended to realise some of these a sculpted reliefs, but this revival in his artistic career was cut short when he died of pneumonia on 7 October 188 contracted after he rescued two children from a flooded stream.

Smith produced few works of sculpture, of which only a handful can be traced today and is, as a consequence virtually unknown. In 1917 his daughter, Minnie, published a pamphlet in which she stretched the truth by claimin that her father was one of the original members of the Pre-Raphaelite Brotherhood. Her idiosyncratic an inaccurate account was discredited and may have damaged her father's reputation by compromising his status as serious subject for Pre-Raphaelite studies. In recent years Juliet Peers has re-assessed Smith's contribution to th movement, arguing that as a relatively experienced artist who had benefited from training in France he 'provide a backbone of artistic professionalism to the incipient group in the 1840s' (*Peers* 2004). She has suggested that hi knowledge of French sculpture and his interest in portrait medallions influenced the work of Thomas Woolne **Alexander Munro** and **John Hancock**.

EI

Literary References: *Gunnis* 1968, 354; *Fredeman* 1975, *passim*; *Smith* 1979, 82–4; *Read* 1984, 97–100, 109; *Read and Barnes* 1991, 12–20, 137–8 (Peers

Additional Manuscript Sources: Smith family papers

Miscellaneous Drawings: 'The Joyful Rain, The Solemn Rain', 1879, Australian National Gallery, Canberra (repr *Read and Barnes* 1991, 19 untitled pencil sketch from Minnie Bernhard Smith's book (repr *Smith* 1979, 83)

Portraits of the Sculptor: photo, anon, nd, Smith family papers (repr *Read and Barnes* 1991, 13)

Funerary Monuments

1.	1838–1840	The sculptor's sister		Untraced		*Read and Barnes* 1991, 137
2.	nd	Lady Barkly		Untraced		*Read and Barnes* 1991, 17

Statues

3.	1845	A dream		[Exhib Westminster Hall, London, 120]; untraced		*Westminster* 1845, 15
4.	1848	The schoolmaster	p	Private coll (descendant of the artist, Australia)	SD	*Read and Barnes* 1991, 16, 138 (repr)

Reliefs

5.	1838–1840	Unidentified subjects, portrait medallions		untraced		*Read and Barnes* 1991, 137
6.	1842	An old satyr extracting a thorn from the foot of a young man		[Exhib RA, London, 1303]; untraced		*AU*, 1842, 128; *Graves* VII, 1905–6, 166
7.	1842	Medallion portrait		[Exhib RA, London, 1390]; untraced		*Graves* VII, 1905–6, 167
8.	1842	Sir John Richardson, medallion	p	[coll Sir Joseph Dalton Hooker]; NPG, London Other versions: Scott Polar Research Inst, Cambridge, 1842 Coll Rev Edward Alston, 1842 Linnean Soc, stone, 1844		*Graves* VII, 1905–6, 167; *Ormond* 1973, 394 (pl 780)

9.	1843	Sir James Clark Ross, medallion	p	Linnean Soc, London Other versions: Scott Polar Research Inst, Cambridge, plaster NPG 887, plaster Royal Geographical Soc, London	SD	*Graves* VII, 1905–6, 167; *Read and Barnes* 1991, 137–8 (repr)
10.	1844	Lieutenant Henry Thomas Smith RN, medallion		[Exhib RA, London, 1347]; untraced		*Graves* VII, 1905–6, 167; *Read and Barnes* 1991, 137–8
11.	1848	L H Smith, medallion		[Exhib RA, London, 1311]; untraced		*Graves* VII, 1905–6, 167; *Read and Barnes* 1991, 14
12.	1848	Mrs Thomas Ringrose, medallion		[Exhib RA, London, 1305]; untraced		*Graves* VII, 1905–6, 167
13.	1849	Maria E Gray, medallion	p	[coll Minnie Smith]; untraced	S	*Read* 1982, 179 (repr); *Read and Barnes* 1991, 15 (repr)
14.	1877	'a fellow Smythesdale resident', medallion		Untraced		*Read and Barnes* 1991, 17
15.	nd	Emma A Smith, medallion	p	Untraced		*Read and Barnes* 1991, 15 (repr)
16.	nd	Frances E A Ince, medallion	p	Untraced		*Read and Barnes* 1991, 15 (repr)
Miscellaneous						
17.	1840–1841	Unidentified work, cast by Etienne Jules Ramey		Untraced		*Read and Barnes* 1991, 14
18.	1845	Edward Doubleday		[Exhib RA, London, 1466]; untraced		*Graves* VII, 1905–6, 167
19.	1845	Sir Rowland Hill		[Exhib RA, London, 1467]; untraced		*Graves* VII, 1905–6, 167; *Ormond* 1973, 226
20.	1846	Mrs Bell Smith		[Exhib RA, London, 1432]; untraced		*Graves* VII, 1905–6, 167
21.	1846	Unidentified lady		[Exhib RA, London, 1470]; untraced		*Graves* VII, 1905–6, 167
22.	1847	Christopher Rawdon		[Exhib RA, London, 1436]; untraced		*Graves* VII, 1905–6, 167
23.	1847	Edward Rushton		[Exhib RA, London, 1423]; untraced		*Graves* VII, 1905–6, 167
24.	1847	Fairie		[Exhib RA, London, 1411]; untraced		*Graves* VII, 1905–6, 167
25.	1847	John Gould FRS		[Exhib RA, London, 1428]; untraced		*Graves* VII, 1905–6, 167
26.	1847	William Rathbone		[Exhib RA, London, 1345]; untraced		*Graves* VII, 1905–6, 167

SMITH, Charles Edward fl 1845–65

A prolific Liverpool sculptor, he exhibited in Liverpool from 1845 to 1865. His address was given as 2 Lansdowne Place, St Domingo, Everton, from 1845 to 1859, and Mount Pleasant, Liverpool from 1860 to 1865. None of his many works has been traced.

Statues					
1.	1854	Infant son of the late Dr Turner, statuette		[Exhib Liverpool Ac, 755]; untraced	*Morris and Roberts* 1998, 557
2.	c1858	Eva		[coll G H Horsfall of Aigburth]; untraced	*Morris and Roberts* 1998, 557
3.	1865	Florence Bickersteth, model		[Exhib LAAI, Liverpool, 1086]; untraced	*Morris and Roberts* 1998, 557
Busts					
4.	1849	Rev William Withers Ewbank		[Exhib Liverpool Ac, 661]; untraced	*Morris and Roberts* 1998, 557
5.	1851	Ralph Randle Pickmere		[Exhib Liverpool Ac, 592]; untraced	*Morris and Roberts* 1998, 557
6.	1851	Rev David James		[Exhib Liverpool Ac, 591]; untraced	*Morris and Roberts* 1998, 557
7.	1852	Master Hatton Turner		[Exhib Liverpool Ac, 609]; untraced	*Morris and Roberts* 1998, 557
8.	1852	T A Ashcroft MD		[Exhib Liverpool Ac, 608]; untraced	*Morris and Roberts* 1998, 557
9.	1853	John Longton		[Exhib Liverpool Ac, 704]; untraced	*Morris and Roberts* 1998, 557
10.	1854	Hugh Fergie, model		[Exhib Liverpool Ac, 758]; untraced	*Morris and Roberts* 1998, 557
11.	1854	J A Pickmere		[Exhib Liverpool Ac, 765]; untraced	*Morris and Roberts* 1998, 557
12.	1854	John Graham, Bishop of Chester		[Exhib Liverpool Ac, 767]; untraced	*Morris and Roberts* 1998, 557
13.	1854	Rev T Major Lester		[Exhib Liverpool Ac, 766]; untraced	*Morris and Roberts* 1998, 557
14.	1855	Rev J Macnaught		[Exhib Liverpool Ac, 827]; untraced	*Morris and Roberts* 1998, 557
15.	1855	W W Ewbanks		[Exhib Liverpool Ac, 826]; untraced	*Morris and Roberts* 1998, 557
16.	1856	A lady		[Exhib Liverpool Ac, 878]; untraced	*Morris and Roberts* 1998, 557
17.	1857	Rev Holland Lomas		[Exhib Liverpool Ac, 883]; untraced	*Morris and Roberts* 1998, 557
18.	1858	A lady	p	[Exhib LSFA, Liverpool, 697]; untraced	*Morris and Roberts* 1998, 557
19.	1858	Rev H S Brown	p	[Exhib LSFA, Liverpool, 696]; untraced	*Morris and Roberts* 1998, 557
20.	1860	Unidentified gentleman		[Exhib LSFA, Liverpool, 767]; untraced	*Morris and Roberts* 1998, 557
21.	1861	Mrs Robinson		[Exhib LSFA, Liverpool, 801]; untraced	*Morris and Roberts* 1998, 557
22.	1861	Unidentified gentleman		[Exhib LSFA, Liverpool, 800]; untraced	*Morris and Roberts* 1998, 557
23.	1861	Unidentified lady		[Exhib LSFA, Liverpool, 894]; untraced	*Morris and Roberts* 1998, 557
24.	1861	Unidentified lady	m	[Exhib LSFA, Liverpool, 767]; untraced	*Morris and Roberts* 1998, 557
25.	1861	Unidentified lady		[Exhib LSFA, Liverpool, 894]; untraced	*Morris and Roberts* 1998, 557
26.	1862	A little boy		[Exhib LSFA, Liverpool, 684]; untraced	*Morris and Roberts* 1998, 557
27.	1862	A little girl		[Exhib LSFA, Liverpool, 683]; untraced	*Morris and Roberts* 1998, 557
28.	1862	Miss Williams		[Exhib LSFA, Liverpool, 328]; untraced	*Morris and Roberts* 1998, 557
29.	1862	Unidentified gentleman		[Exhib LSFA, Liverpool, 685]; untraced	*Morris and Roberts* 1998, 557
30.	1862	Unidentified gentleman, model		[Exhib LSFA, Liverpool, 686]; untraced	*Morris and Roberts* 1998, 557
31.	1863	Dr Bickersteth		[Exhib LIFA, Liverpool, 1227]; untraced	*Morris and Roberts* 1998, 557
32.	1863	Mrs Peter Bancroft	m	[Exhib LIFA, Liverpool, 1232]; untraced	*Morris and Roberts* 1998, 557
33.	1863	Unidentified gentleman, model		[Exhib LIFA, Liverpool, 1229]; untraced	*Morris and Roberts* 1998, 557
34.	1864	Infant daughter of Hugh N Nicholson	m	[Exhib LIFA, Liverpool, 1146]; untraced	*Morris and Roberts* 1998, 557
35.	1864	T Haigh		[Exhib LIFA, Liverpool, 1160]; untraced	*Morris and Roberts* 1998, 557
36.	1864	Unidentified gentleman, model		[Exhib LIFA, Liverpool, 1166]; untraced	*Morris and Roberts* 1998, 557
37.	1865	A lady		[Exhib LAAI, Liverpool, 1084]; untraced	*Morris and Roberts* 1998, 557
38.	1865	Mrs C K Prioleau, model		[Exhib LAAI, Liverpool, 1085]; untraced	*Morris and Roberts* 1998, 557
39.	1865	Peter Bancroft, model		[Exhib LAAI, Liverpool, 1083]; untraced	*Morris and Roberts* 1998, 557
Reliefs					
40.	1852	A child, portrait medallion		[Exhib Liverpool Ac, 594]; untraced	*Morris and Roberts* 1998, 557
41.	1852	A young gentleman, portrait medallion		[Exhib Liverpool Ac, 610]; untraced	*Morris and Roberts* 1998, 557
42.	1853	An infant, portrait medallion		[Exhib Liverpool Ac, 709]; untraced	*Morris and Roberts* 1998, 557
43.	1853	Arion rescued by the dolphin, medallion		[Exhib Liverpool Ac, 224]; untraced	*Morris and Roberts* 1998, 557
44.	1853	Infant son of G B Denton, portrait medallion		[Exhib Liverpool Ac, 708]; untraced	*Morris and Roberts* 1998, 557
45.	1853	Master J B N Longton, portrait medallion		[Exhib Liverpool Ac, 707]; untraced	*Morris and Roberts* 1998, 557

46.	1853	Miss P H Hilton, portrait medallion	[Exhib Liverpool Ac, 710]; untraced	*Morris and Roberts* 1998, 557
47.	1854	Infant son of J B Smith, portrait medallion	[Exhib Liverpool Ac, 756]; untraced	*Morris and Roberts* 1998, 557
48.	1855	Master R N Tweddle, portrait medallion	[Exhib Liverpool Ac, 825]; untraced	*Morris and Roberts* 1998, 557
49.	1855	'Medallion Head – a Study'	[Exhib Liverpool Ac, 824]; untraced	*Morris and Roberts* 1998, 557
50.	1855	Rev G Dover, portrait medallion	[Exhib Liverpool Ac, 823]; untraced	*Morris and Roberts* 1998, 557
51.	1856	A lady, portrait medallion	[Exhib Liverpool Ac, 873]; untraced	*Morris and Roberts* 1998, 557
52.	1857	Two sisters, portrait medallion	[Exhib Liverpool Ac, 879]; untraced	*Morris and Roberts* 1998, 557
53.	1859	Dr Stookes MD, portrait medallion	[Exhib LSFA, Liverpool, 743]; untraced	*Morris and Roberts* 1998, 557
54.	1859	Thomas Dawson, portrait medallion	[Exhib LSFA, Liverpool, 744]; untraced	*Morris and Roberts* 1998, 557
55.	1861	James and Margaret Dawson, portrait medallions	[Exhib LSFA, Liverpool, 788]; untraced	*Morris and Roberts* 1998, 557
Miscellaneous				
56.	1845	An infant sleeping in the vigour of health	[Exhib Liverpool Ac, 810]; untraced	*Morris and Roberts* 1998, 557
57.	1846	The infant St John	[Exhib Liverpool Ac, 808]; untraced	*Morris and Roberts* 1998, 557
58.	1848	Grecian flower girl	[Exhib Liverpool Ac, 688]; untraced	*Morris and Roberts* 1998, 557
59.	1848	Rev H V Hampton	[Exhib Liverpool Ac, 687]; untraced	*Morris and Roberts* 1998, 557
60.	1859	Rev Thomas Gardner	[Exhib LSFA, Liverpool, 781]; untraced	*Morris and Roberts* 1998, 557
61.	1859	W Gavin Herdman	[Exhib LSFA, Liverpool, 761]; untraced	*Morris and Roberts* 1998, 557
62.	1859	W Preston, Mayor of Liverpool	[Exhib LSFA, Liverpool, 755]; untraced	*Morris and Roberts* 1998, 557
63.	1861	Innocence	[Exhib LSFA, Liverpool, 775]; untraced	*Morris and Roberts* 1998, 557
64.	1862	Infant son of W J Harris, 'modelled portrait'	[Exhib LSFA, Liverpool, 162]; untraced	*Morris and Roberts* 1998, 557
65.	1864	'Posthumous cast of a child'	[Exhib LIFA, Liverpool, 1164]; untraced	*Morris and Roberts* 1998, 557

SMITH, Charles Harriott 1792–1864

He was born in London on 1 February 1792, the son of Joseph Smith, a monumental sculptor of Portland Road, Marylebone. He received only a basic education and left school at the age of 12 to work with his father. However, with the encouragement of Joseph Bonomi, the architect, he began to study 'higher branches of art than he was pursuing at home with his father as a stone mason' (*Builder*, 1864, 892). At first he practised drawing and modelling in his spare time, but in 1814 he entered the Royal Academy Schools, aged 22. There he showed unusual skill in drawing the human figure and in 1817 was awarded the gold medal for architecture for a design for a Royal Academy. He exhibited at the RA between 1809 and 1824, showing architectural drawings and several portrait busts (**33–35**).

Smith next turned his attention to architectural sculpture and carved the Corinthian capitals and other ornaments for University College London, the National Gallery and the Royal Exchange (**38–40**). He also executed ornamental stonework for Bridgewater House and a cornice and frieze at Dorchester House, London (**41, 43**). He provided a detailed full-scale model for the bronze parts of the capital of Nelson's Column in Trafalgar Square, London and these were cast at the Woolwich Arsenal foundry (**42**). Smith continued to work as a monumental sculptor, principally producing neo-Hellenistic wall tablets. Rupert Gunnis particularly admired a design consisting of 'an Attic plumed helmet in high relief with a great Homeric shield below it and crossed swords behind' which was used for example on the monument to George Deare (**8**). It is, Gunnis noted, 'a strictly classical work without any hint of an emblem of Christianity'.

Smith studied geology, mineralogy and chemistry, as well as architecture, and became as authority on appropriate stones for building use. In 1838 he was one of four commissioners appointed to identify the material most likely to stand the test of time for the new Houses of Parliament. Though in practice the selected stone decayed rapidly, the report of this commission won admiration as a great addition to professional knowledge, and Smith's zeal, intelligence and co-operation were commended. He also lectured and wrote many articles (notably in the *Builder*) on architectural and aesthetic topics and was, in his own words, 'a strange mongrel of art, science, literature and business' (*Builder, op cit*). He was an active member of the Society of Arts and was elected an honorary member of the Royal Institute of British Architects in 1855.

He died at his home, 24 Hatton Garden, London, on 27 October 1864 after a long illness. He left a wife, Fanny, and one son, Percy Gordon Smith, who was for many years architect to the local government board. One of his workmen said of him, 'He never grasped for money, but he did for knowledge which he held fast but nevertheless gave away abundantly' (*ibid*).

Literary References: *Builder*, 1864, 802; *Redgrave* 1878, 401; *DNB* (Carlyle); *Gunnis* 1968, 355; *Port* 1976, 97–8, 322 n3; *Dale-Jones and Lloyd* 1989, 57; *Colvin* 1995, 881; *ODNB* (Rev Goodall)

Additional Manuscript Sources: Smith/RIBA (1); Smith/RIBA (2); Smith Papers (1); Smith Papers (2)

Portraits of the Sculptor: F A Legé, bust, exhib RA, 1822 (untraced)

Funerary Monuments

1.	?1814	Nathaniel Crichton	Hendon, Mddx	S	*Gunnis* 1968, 355
2.	†1820	John Lewes	Llangeler, Carmarthen		*Dale-Jones and Lloyd* 1989, 57
3.	†1820	Sir Vicary Gibbs (monument in churchyard and tablet in church) (designed by Ignatius Bonomi)	Hayes, Kent		*Colvin* 1995, 141
4.	†1821	Ferdinand de Mierre	Chennai (Madras) Cathedral, India	S	
5.	?1821	Lieutenant-Colonel FitzGerald	St Mary, St Marylebone, London	S	*Gunnis* 1968, 355
6.	?1821	Robert Cotton	Reigate, Surrey	S	*Gunnis* 1968, 355
7.	?1822	Elizabeth Peters	Badby, Northants	S	*Gunnis* 1968, 355
8.	?1823	Lieutenant-General George Deare	St John's Wood Chapel, Marylebone, London	S	*Gunnis* 1968, 355
9.	†1824	Charles Harwood Higginson	Chennai (Madras) Cathedral, India	S	*Gunnis* 1968, 355
10.	†1824	John Beale Browne	All Saints, Salperton (in Hazleton), Glos	S	Pevsner, *Glos: Cotswolds*, 1999, 588
11.	?1824	John Francis	Badby, Northants	S	*Gunnis* 1968, 355
12.	?1824	Margaret Randall	Erith, Kent	S	*Gunnis* 1968, 355
13.	?1824	Stuckey Family	Langport, Somerset	S	*Gunnis* 1968, 355
14.	1824–1825	Mary and Anne Hoare, monument in churchyard and tablet in church (designed by Ignatius Bonomi)	Chislehurst, Kent		*Colvin* 1995, 141

15.	?1825	Rev Charles Tower		South Weald, Essex	S	*Gunnis* 1968, 355
16.	?1825	William Sleigh		Stockton-on-Tees, Durham	S	Pevsner, *Durham*, 1983, 435
17.	?1826	Georgina Chamier		Stoke-next-Guildford, Surrey	S	*Gunnis* 1968, 355
18.	?1827	Anthony Parker		Churchgate Street, Essex	S	*Gunnis* 1968, 355
19.	†1828	William Lewes		Llangeler, Carmarthen		*Dale-Jones and Lloyd* 1989, 57
20.	?1830	Rebecca Phipps		St Mary, St Marylebone, London	S	*Gunnis* 1968, 355
21.	†1837	William Staveley	s	Kensal Green Cemetery, London		*Curl* 2001, 198
22.	?1839	Rev Edward Meyrick		Ramsbury, Wilts	S	*Gunnis* 1968, 355
23.	†1841	Edward Scriven	s	Kensal Green Cemetery, London		*Curl* 2001, 178, 226 (repr)
24.	?1841	Henry Moreton-Dyer		St Mary, St Marylebone, London	S	*Gunnis* 1968, 355
25.	?1841	Richard Alsager		Tooting, Surrey	S	*Gunnis* 1968, 355
26.	†1842	Rev Francis Goode		Holy Trinity, Clapham, London	S	*Gunnis* 1968, 355
27.	?1846	Countess Beauchamp		St Mary, St Marylebone, London	S	*Gunnis* 1968, 355
28.	?1847	A R Freebairn		Highgate Cemetery, London	S	*Gunnis* 1968, 355
29.	?1853	John Pereira		Kensal Green Cemetery, London	S	*Gunnis* 1968, 355
30.	?1855	Henry Hickman		Newnham, Northants	S	*Gunnis* 1968, 355
31.	?1855	John Garden		Ringsfield, Suffolk	S	*Gunnis* 1968, 355
Statues						
32.	1850–1851	Farnese Hercules Payment(s): £150 17s	s	[Museum of Practical Geology, Jermyn Street, London]; British Geological Survey headquarters, Keyworth, Notts		*Gunnis* 1968, 355; *Haskell and Penny* 1981, 232; *TTSN* 1984, 107–9 (repr)
Busts						
33.	1818	Joseph Smith	w	[Exhib RA, London, 1096]; untraced		*Builder*, 1864, 802; *Graves* VII, 1905–6, 171
34.	1822	Unidentified lady		[Exhib RA, London, 993]; untraced		*Graves* VII, 1905–6, 171
35.	1824	The Hon and Rev E J Turnour		[Exhib RA, London, 988]; untraced		*Graves* VII, 1905–6, 171
36.	1851	Thomas Tredgold		Institution of Civil Engineers, London		RG/JP, 7, 1310
Chimneypieces						
37.	1839	Several Payment(s): £296		Rufford Abbey, Notts		Rufford Abbey Archives in GPC
Architectural Sculpture						
38.	c1828	Decorative carving	s	University College, London		*Gunnis* 1968, 354
39.	1832	Corinthian capitals and other Ornaments	s	NG, London		*DNB*; *Gunnis* 1968, 354–5
40.	post-1842	Decorative carving Payment(s): £6,500	s	Royal Exchange, London		*Builder* 1850, 305; *DNB*; *Port* 1997, 302
41.	1848	Decorative carving Payment(s): £1,349	s	Bridgewater House, London		*DNB*; *Gunnis* 1968, 355
42.	pre-1850	Capital for Nelson's Column, Trafalgar Square, London, model only (cast in bronze by Clarke at Woolwich Arsenal foundry)		Untraced		*Builder* 1850, 169
43.	1852	Decorative carving	s	[Dorchester House, Park Lane, London, façade]; destroyed		*Builder*, 1852, 550; *DNB*

SMITH, Charles Raymond –1888

He was the son of **James Smith II** and can perhaps be identified with a 'Chas Smith' who was born on 5 December 1798 and baptised on 31 March 1799, at St Marylebone parish church, London. The 1881 census however gives his age as 79, suggesting a birth date of about 1802. He trained under **William Tollemache** and **Josephus John Pinnix Kendrick** and at the Royal Academy Schools from 1816 onwards. In 1817 the Society of Arts awarded him a medal for an original model (**41**). This was followed by another medal for a model in the RA life class and the Society of Arts gold Isis medal for a group of two figures (**85**). He won the Society of Arts large gold medal for a group of *The fight for the body of Patroclus* in 1822 (**43**). He first exhibited at the Royal Academy in 1820, showing two portrait busts and giving his address as 57 Norton Street, Fitzroy Square (**59, 60**). In the later 1820s he worked from 37 George Street (now Bolsover Street) but by 1830 he had settled in Gloucester Place, New Road, where he remained until 1860 when he moved to premises at 246 Marylebone Road. J T Smith described him as 'a highly talented sculptor' and noted that he owned some models by his father's teacher **Giovanni Battista Locatelli** (*Smith* 1828, vol 2, 126).

Between 1838 and 1842 Smith carved a series of ten statues of Tudor kings, queens and other notables of the period in historical costume for Mamhead Park, Devon (**49, 50**). They remained in the gallery of this magnificent Tudor-style mansion until 1985, when all but two of the figures were sold. Further commissions for sculpture for country house settings followed, including two life-sized statues of Michelangelo and Raphael commissioned by Henry, 3rd Marquess of Lansdowne for Bowood (**44**). Smith exhibited the statue of Raphael, together with a *Falconer* carved for Mr Bulteel of Flete, in Devon, at Westminster Hall in 1844 (**45**). Both works were well received by the critics: the *Literary Gazette* considered the *Falconer* 'talented and full of pictorial character' (cited by *Gunnis* 1968, 359), while the *Art Union* thought that the Raphael had 'much merit' (*AU* 1844, 217). In the early 1850s Smith provided statues, a fountain and other ornaments for the formal gardens at Eaton Hall, Cheshire, laid out by William Andrews Nesfield for the 2nd Marquess of Westminster (**51, 52, 83**). He later worked with Nesfield at Holkham Hall, where he was responsible for the huge fountain featuring *Saint George slaying the dragon* (**82**). Smith received payments of £115 15s in January 1856, £300 on account in April 1856 and a further £936 2s 10d the following January, for the fountain, plus £542 for other, unspecified, sculptures for the terrace at Holkham (**90**).

Smith was also active as a sculptor of funerary monuments and examples of his work in that field include the life-sized semi-recumbent figures of Jacob Britton in Durham Cathedral and the Reverend Thomas Whitaker, at Whalley, Lancashire (**18, 39**). His best known work is the effigy of Grace Darling, the lighthouse-keeper's daughter, famous for courageously rowing out into stormy seas with her father to rescue the survivors of the wreck of the paddle steamer *Forfarshire* (**25**). The figure was part of a 13th-century-styled canopied tomb which was erected in 1844 beside her grave in Bamburgh churchyard, Northumberland. The stonework of the monument deteriorated rapidly in this exposed situation and in 1885 the effigy was replaced with a new figure of the heroine carved from Smith's model, which he had preserved in his studio. The original effigy is now inside St Aidan's church.

Smith died on 15 April 1888 and was buried in Kensal Green cemetery, where his grave is marked by a ledger stone. He left property valued at £2,110 17s 5d and his executors included his son, Charles John Thomas Smith, who was described as a sculptor. Smith's work has attracted little scholarly attention and his posthumous reputation has been affected by the considerable confusion that surrounds his identity. In his *Royal Academy Exhibitors* and *Exhibitors at the British Institution* Algernon Graves lists works by 'Charles Smith', 'Charles Raymond Smith' and 'R. Smith' (*Graves* 1875, 500; *Graves* VII, 1905–6, 169–70, 172, 189). Gunnis later included biographies of 'Charles R' and 'Raymond Smith', who he suggested were probably father and son, in his *Dictionary of British Sculptors*. It seems very likely that these were all the same sculptor and that Smith used his middle name from the 1840s onwards, perhaps to distinguish himself more clearly from **Charles Harriott Smith**.

EH

References: *Smith* 1828, II, 126; *Architect's, Engineer's and Building-Trades' Directory*, 1868; *Gunnis* 1968, 355–6, 359; *Curl* 2001, 242
Archival References: RA Premium list; 1881 census; GPC; IGI
Will: PPR, 12 May 1888, fol 418

Funerary Monuments

No.	Date	Subject		Location		References
1.	†1821	Rev Thomas Dunham Whitaker	s	Whalley, Lancs	S	*Graves* VII, 1905–6, 172; *Penny* 1977 (1), 85; *Gunnis* 1968, 355 (repr 27)
2.	?1823	Major Sayer		Clare, Suffolk	S	*Gunnis* 1968, 355
3.	1826	John Philip Kemble (†1823) design only		[Exhib RA, London, 1090]; untraced		*Graves* VII, 1905–6, 169; *Johnson* 1975, 427
4.	?1827	George Holroyd		Reigate, Surrey	S	*Gunnis* 1968, 355
5.	†1827	James Hudson		Newington-by-Sittingbourne, Kent	S	*Gunnis* 1968, 356
6.	†1828	Rev Richard Mytton		Guilsfield, Montgomery	S	Pevsner, *Powys*, 1979, 107
7.	†1828	William Williams		Chichester Cathedral, Sussex	S	*Gunnis* 1968, 356
8.	?1829	Countess of Clonmell		St Mary, St Marylebone, London	S	*Gunnis* 1968, 356
9.	?1829	Elizabeth Rose		Carshalton, Surrey	S	*Gunnis* 1968, 356
10.	?1830	Mary Walker		Sand Hutton, N R Yorks	S	*Gunnis* 1968, 356
11.	†1831	Francis and Anne Sanders		St George, Bloomsbury, London	S	
12.	†1831	Rev Francis Randolph		Banwell, Somerset		RG/JP, 7, 1313
13.	?1832	Rev Thomas Stephens		St John's Wood Chapel, London	S	*Gunnis* 1968, 356
14.	†1832	William J V Surtees		Sarratt, Herts	S	
15.	?1833	Rev Hugh Bailye		Hanbury, Staffs	S	*Gunnis* 1968, 356
16.	?1834	Jane Farquhar		St John's Wood Chapel, London	S	*Gunnis* 1968, 356
17.	1836	Rev Baptist Turner		Denton, Lincs	S	*Gunnis* 1968, 359
18.	1839	Jacob Britton (†1836) Model(s): exhib RA, London, 1839, 1293		Durham Cathedral	S	*Graves* VII, 1905–6, 170; Pevsner, *Durham*, 1983, 196
19.	?1839	Margaret Joliffe		Worth, Sussex	S	*Gunnis* 1968, 356
20.	†1839	Winthrop Mackworth Praed, with medallion portrait		Kensal Green Cemetery, London		*Ormond* 1973, 383
21.	†1842	Mary Westoby		St Pancras new parish church, London	S	
22.	†1843	Hesling B Yates		St Alphege, Solihull, Warks	S	
23.	†1843	William de St Croix	s	St George's chapel, Windsor, Berks	S	*Bond* 1999, 96
24.	c1844	Archbishop William Markham (†1807) (designed by Anthony Salvin) (co-sculptor: Thomas Willement)		York Minster	S	*Aylmer* 1977, 466–7; *Pattison and Murray* 2001, 103–4
25.	1844	Grace Darling, effigy		Bamburgh, Northumbs Other versions: Darling monument, Bamburgh churchyard, copy made in 1885		*Graves* VII, 1905–6, 189; *Usherwood* 2000, xiii, 12–13 (repr)
26.	1845	Countess Cadogan		St Luke, Chelsea, London	S	*Gunnis* 1968, 359
27.	†1846	Fulke Greville Howard		St Lawrence, Castle Rising, Norfolk		Pevsner, *Norfolk: N-W & S*, 1999, 254
28.	1848	Henry Baring		Felbrigg, Norfolk	S	*Gunnis* 1968, 359
29.	?1848	Sir William Richardson		Peartree Green, Southampton, Hants		GPC
30.	†1850	Anna Maria, 7th Countess of Scarborough		Saxby, Lincs	S	Pevsner, *Lincs*, 1989, 623
31.	†1850	Captain John Allen		St George's Chapel, Windsor Castle	S	*Bond* 1999, 5
32.	†1850	William Moriarty		St George, Hobart, Tasmania, Australia	S	
33.	†1852	George Emery		Banwell, Somerset		RG/JP, 7, 1313
34.	1852–1855	Aline Hoghton (†1852)		Farnworth, Lancs		NP/RG; *CIIA* 4/8/38–9 (repr)
35.	†1856	John, 8th Earl of Scarborough		Saxby, Lincs	S	Pevsner, *Lincs*, 1989, 622–3
36.	†1856	Mary Anne Ellis		St Thomas, Barbados, WI	S	
37.	?1863	Lady Rushout		Longborough, Glos		RG/JP, 7, 1313
38.	1872	Thomas Tryon		Bulwich, Northants	S	*Gunnis* 1968, 359
39.	1876	Rev Thomas Dunham Whitaker (†1821)		Holme in Cliviger, Lancs	S	*Graves* VII, 1905–6, 172; Pevsner, *Lancs: N*, 1969, 145
40.	†1881	Officers and men of HMS Doterel		Royal Hospital, Greenwich (ORNC), Chapel vestibule	S	

Statues

No.	Date	Subject		Location		References
41.	1817	'Original model of one figure'		[Soc of A, silver Isis medal]; untraced		RSA *Transactions*, 1817, vol 35, 29
42.	1821	Two figures, group		[Soc of A, gold Isis medal]; untraced		RSA *Transactions*, 1821, vol 39, xxxviii
43.	1822	The fight for the body of Patroclus, group	p	[Soc of A, large gold medal]; untraced		RSA *Transactions*, 1822, vol 40, xxxix; *Johnson* 1975, 427
44.	1841	Michelangelo and Raphael Model(s): exhib RA, London, 1841, 1229, 1238		Bowood, Wilts, entrance to walled garden		*Graves* VII, 1905–6, 170; *Gunnis* 1968, 355, 359; *Hiskey* 2001, 21
45.	1842	A Falconer Model(s): exhib RA, London, 1842, 1280		Flete, Devon		*Graves* VII, 1905–6, 172; Pevsner, *Devon*, 1989, 450

No.	Date	Subject		Location		Reference
46.	1842	A huntsman		Flete, Devon		Pevsner, *Devon*, 1989, 450
47.	1843	The warder		[Exhib RA, London, 1419]; untraced		*Graves* VII, 1905–6, 172
48.	1839–1844	Cardinal Wolsey and an unidentified bishop, two statues Model(s): exhib RA, London, 1840, 1095 (Wolsey)	s	Mamhead Park, Devon, gallery		*Graves* VII, 1905–6, 169, 170; Pevsner, *Devon*, 1989, 558
49.	1839–1844	King Henry VII, Queen Elizabeth of York, Lord Daubeny and Lady Daubeny, four statues Model(s): exhib RA, London, 1839, 1287 (King Henry VII) and 1844, 1288 (Queen Elizabeth of York)	s	[Mamhead Park, Devon, gallery]; Allerton Park, W R Yorks		*Graves* VII, 1905–6, 169, 170, 172; Pevsner, *Devon*, 1989, 558
50.	1839–1844	King Henry VIII, Lady Jane Seymour, Queen Elizabeth I and Sir Walter Raleigh, four statues Model(s): exhib RA, London, 1840, 1080 (King Henry VIII) and 1842, 1292 (Queen Elizabeth)	s	[Mamhead Park, Devon, gallery]; untraced		*Graves* VII, 1905–6, 169, 170, 172; Pevsner, *Devon*, 1989, 558
51.	1852	Odo, Bishop of Bayeux, Sir Robert de Grosvenor, Engulphus de Aquila and Joan of Eaton, four statues		Eaton Hall, Cheshire, gardens		*Builder* 1852, 595
52.	1852	Starting out for the chase and the death of the stag, two equestrian groups Payment(s): £500 each	s	Eaton Hall, Cheshire, gardens	S	*Builder* 1852, 595; Pevsner, *Cheshire*, 1971, 211
53.	1853	Eagle Payment(s): £140 (with river god)		[Bowood, terrace]; 'Perhaps that in the centre of the Diocletian wing'		GPC
54.	1853	River god Payment(s): £140 (with eagle)		Bowood, Wilts, terrace		GPC
55.	c1854	Egyptian lions, two statues	s	[Westfield, I of W, terrace]; untraced		*Gunnis* 1968, 359
56.	nd	Elements		Fonthill, Wilts		Pevsner, *Wilts*, 1975, 220; C Lib (repr)
57.	nd	Neptune and Amphitrite		[coll Marquess of Lansdowne]; untraced		*Architect's, Engineer's and Building-Trades' Directory* 1868
58.	nd	The seasons		Fonthill House, Wilts		Pevsner, *Wilts*, 1975, 220; C Lib (repr)

Busts

No.	Date	Subject		Location		Reference
59.	1820	Mr Myers		[Exhib RA, London, 1015]; untraced		*Graves* VII, 1905–6, 169
60.	1820	Mr Ricci		[Exhib RA, London, 1032]; untraced		*Graves* VII, 1905–6, 169
61.	1826	Unidentified gentleman		[Exhib RA, London, 1022]; untraced		*Graves* VII, 1905–6, 169
62.	1826	Unidentified gentleman		[Exhib RA, London, 1016]; untraced		*Graves* VII, 1905–6, 169
63.	1827	D Terry	m	[Exhib RA, London, 1116]; untraced		*Graves* VII, 1905–6, 169
64.	1827	Edward Goldsmith		[Exhib RA, London, 1121]; untraced		*Graves* VII, 1905–6, 169
65.	1829	Unidentified gentleman		[Exhib Soc of BA, London, 860]; untraced		*Johnson* 1975, 427
66.	1830	Colonel Dalrymple MP		[Exhib RA, London, 1191]; untraced		*Graves* VII, 1905–6, 169
67.	1830	J Devonport	m	[Exhib RA, London, 1242]; untraced		*Graves* VII, 1905–6, 169
68.	1830	Unidentified lady		[Exhib RA, London, 1193]; untraced		*Graves* VII, 1905–6, 169
69.	1830	W Upcott		[Exhib RA, London, 1212]; untraced		*Graves* VII, 1905–6, 169
70.	1831	Dr George Campbell		[Exhib RA, London, 1222]; untraced		*Graves* VII, 1905–6, 169; *Johnson* 1975, 427
71.	1834	C Buck		[Exhib RA, London, 1029]; untraced		*Graves* VII, 1905–6, 169
72.	1836	Charles Bushe		[Exhib Soc of BA, London, 893]; untraced		*Johnson* 1975, 893
73.	1841	Rev Thomas Gilsborne Model(s): exhib RA, London, 1841, 1296	m	[for Durham University]; untraced		*Graves* VII, 1905–6, 170
74.	c1841	Winthrop Mackworth Praed	m	coll Mrs Praed		*Graves* VII, 1905–6, 170; *Ormond* 1973, 383
75.	1855	William Nesfield	m	[Exhib RA, London, 1468]; untraced		*Graves* VII, 1905–6, 172

Chimneypieces

No.	Date	Subject		Location		Reference
76.	1839	Several Payment(s): £296		[Rufford Abbey, Notts]; untraced		GPC

Architectural Sculpture

No.	Date	Subject		Location		Reference
77.	1836	Reliefs for Manchester City Art Gallery, designs only		Untraced		*Malden* 1977, unpag
78.	1852	Fountain Payment(s): £43		Pynes, Upton Pyne, Devon		Pevsner, *Devon*, 1989, 885
79.	1852	Griffin (or dragon) fountain Payment(s): £300		Eaton Hall, Cheshire, gardens		GPC
80.	1852	Peace and war, two reliefs		[Bylaugh Hall, Norfolk, saloon]; untraced		*Builder* 1852, 517
81.	1852	Two bronze stags for gate piers Payment(s): £52	b	Pynes, Upton Pyne, Devon		*Gunnis* 1968, 355; Pevsner, *Devon*, 1989, 885
82.	1856	St George slaying the dragon, fountain Payment(s): £1,351 17s 10d	s	Holkham Hall, Norfolk		*Hiskey* 2001, 19–24 (repr)
83.	1857	Vases, pedestals and other ornaments Payment(s): £349 10s 1d		Eaton Hall, Cheshire, gardens		GPC
84.	1865	Statues representing Denmark, Portugal, Greece and others		Foreign and Commonwealth Office, London, façade		*Architect's, Engineer's and Building-Trades' Directory* 1868

Miscellaneous

No.	Date	Subject		Location		Reference
85.	1821	Unidentified subject, life class model		[Awarded RA silver medal]; untraced		RA Premium list
86.	1828	Cupid and Psyche		[Exhib RA, London, 1139]; untraced		*Graves* 1875, 500; *Graves* VII, 1905–6, 169
87.	1829	Mercury unveiling Pandora to Epimethus		[Exhib Soc of BA, London, 885]; untraced		*Johnson* 1975, 427

88.	1832	The murder of the innocents	[Exhib Soc of BA, London, 898]; untraced	*Johnson* 1975, 427
89.	1833	Love among the roses	[coll Duke of Sutherland]; untraced	*Architect's, Engineer's and Building-Trades' Directory* 1868; *Graves* 1875, 500
90.	1856	Ornamental garden sculpture Payment(s): £542	[Holkham Hall, Norfolk, terrace]; untraced	*Hiskey* 2001, 21

SMITH, Charlotte fl 1809

She won an award from the Society of Arts in 1809, at which time she lived in Bridge Row, Pimlico.

Miscellaneous

1.	1809	Bacchus, plaster cast	[Soc of A, silver palette]; untraced	RSA *Transactions*, 1809, vol 24, 20

SMITH, D, of Dundee fl 1827–32

He signs several carved memorials in the Dundee graveyard, the Houff. Those commemorating Alexander Miller, Charlotte Croom and the Brown family are among the more important.

Literary Reference: *Woodward* 1977 (vol 1, pt 2), 220

Funerary Monuments

1.	†1827	Alexander Miller	The Houff, Dundee	S	*Woodward* 1977, vol 1, pt 2, 220
2.	†1830	Charlotte Croom	The Houff, Dundee	S	*Woodward* 1977, vol 1, pt 2, 220
3.	1832	Brown family	The Houff, Dundee	S	*Woodward* 1977, vol 1, pt 2, 220

SMITH, Edwin, of Sheffield 1810–89

He was born in Sheffield on 8 April 1810, the son of an engraver, James Smith. At first he studied sculpture locally, but in 1836 he went to London to join the Royal Academy Schools and took lodgings in Bouverie Street. His son Theophilus was born in 1838 and *c*1840 Smith returned to Sheffield, where he set up as a sculptor.

Theophilus joined him in business at the Cemetery Road Marble and Stone Works, Little Sheffield, and between them they produced a large number of marble busts, medallions and other works of art for buildings in the vicinity, including the parish churches of Sheffield and Rotherham (**3, 6, 10**), Cutlers' Hall and the Infirmary (**14, 16, 17, 18, 20**). Many churches and cemeteries have specimens of their work in granite and bronze, as well as iron and marble. Among the local memorials mentioned in passing by Himsworth is one to George Bennet and another to 'Hunter of Hallamshire fame'. Two of the monuments, the Favell and Gilett, have medallion portraits (**6, 13**) and the Peel has a 'carefully and sentimentally carved rose' (**8**). Smith signs the fine monument with columns and pediment to William Bagshawe, which he perhaps restored (**1**). He was also responsible for the obelisk at Norton in memory of Sir Francis Chantrey (**22**).

Smith's most profitable work was a model in relief of Jerusalem on the scale of 18 inches to the mile, exhibited in a glass case on a mahogany stand (**26**). This was produced as a multiple and several booklets were issued by Smith to advertise the work. The publication of 1847, which has a key to the individual buildings shown numbered on a plan, also advertises its enthusiastic reception. There appear to have been about 200 subscribers, including members of the Royal Family, two archbishops, six bishops, Lord Fitzwilliam, and such local notables as the mayor of Sheffield and the master cutler.

Smith was clearly a man of unusual outlook, for not only did he advertise his stock of marble chimneypieces and side-boards, but also 'let out on hire rubber mattresses to be filled with water for the use of fever patients' and he took 'casts after death from which might be executed busts and medallions'. In 1862 he invented a machine for reproducing works of art in stone and wood by cutting from an original model.

Theophilus predeceased his father by two years. Himsworth judged Edwin a skilful sculptor and refined modeller and he was a pioneer of photography in the Sheffield area. He was living at 41 William Street, Sheffield when he died on 29 August 1889.

Literary References: *Himsworth* 1963, 13; *Gunnis* 1968, 356; *Pyke* 1973, 137–8; *Pyke* 1981, 38

Archival References: RA Admissions; RG/JP, 7, 1314

Will: Wakefield Probate Registry, 16 January 1890, personal estate valued at £1,041 18s 7d. He is described as an 'Ornamental Metal and Marble Worker'

Funerary Monuments

1.	†1702	William Bagshawe and family	Chapel-en-le-Frith, Derbys	S	GPC
2.	†1829	Rev Matthew Preston and his wife	Ecclesall, W R Yorks	S	
3.	1841	50 young persons killed in launching a vessel at Masbrough	All Saints, Rotherham, W R Yorks		Pevsner, *Yorks: W R*, 1967, 420
4.	†1845	Anne Willis Kent	Ecclesall, W R Yorks	S	
5.	?1845	Frederick Wilkinson	Newcastle-under-Lyme, Staffs	S	*Gunnis* 1968, 356
6.	?1846	Charles Favell, with medallion portrait	St Paul, Sheffield		*Gunnis* 1968, 356
7.	?1847	John Fullerton	Thrybergh, W R Yorks		GPC
8.	†1851	Elizabeth Peel	Wellow, Notts		Pevsner, *Notts*, 1979, 373
9.	?1851	William Bagshawe	Norton, Derbys	S	*Gunnis* 1968, 356
10.	?1854	Margaret Coward	All Saints, Rotherham, W R Yorks	S	*Gunnis* 1968, 356
11.	1854	Sir Francis Chantrey, obelisk	Norton, Derbys		GPC
12.	?1859	Henry Marwood Greaves	Chapel-en-le-Frith, Derbys	S	GPC
13.	?1862	Samuel Gilett, with medallion portrait	Norton, Derbys		*Gunnis* 1968, 356

Busts

14.	1834	James Silk Buckingham	Cutlers' Hall, Sheffield, W R Yorks		*Gunnis* 1968, 356; *Ormond* 1973, 78
15.	1836	James Watt	[Exhib Soc of BA, London, 890]; untraced		*Johnson* 1975, 429
16.	1839	Rev James Wilkinson	Royal Infirmary, Sheffield, W R Yorks		*Gunnis* 1968, 356
17.	?1843	James Montgomery	Cutlers' Hall, Sheffield, W R Yorks		*Gunnis* 1968, 356
18.	1845	William Jeffcock	Cutlers' Hall, Sheffield, W R Yorks		*Gunnis* 1968, 356
19.	?1853	Thomas Sutton	Sheffield Cathedral, W R Yorks	D	*Gunnis* 1968, 356
20.	?1854	Samuel Hadfield	Cutlers' Hall, Sheffield, W R Yorks		*Gunnis* 1968, 356
21.	?1861	Thomas Sutton	Bluecoat School, Sheffield, W R Yorks	D	*Gunnis* 1968, 356

Architectural Sculpture

22.	nd	Obelisk commemorating Sir Francis Chantrey		Norton, Sheffield, W R Yorks	GPC

Reliefs

23.	1837	William Younge, medallion	w	Untraced	*Gunnis* 1968, 356
24.	1839	Dr William Younge		Royal Hallamshire Hospital, Sheffield, W R Yorks	*Pyke* 1973, 138; *Pyke* 1981, 38
25.	1842	Unidentified man	w	Untraced (ex coll Mario Praz); untraced	*Pyke* 1973, 138
26.	pre-1847	Jerusalem, multiple versions		Dispersed	*Himsworth* 1963, 13–15

Miscellaneous

27.	1836	Medora		[Exhib Soc of BA, London, 865]; untraced	*Johnson* 1975, 429

SMITH, Francis, of Warwick 1672–1738

He was born on 4 January 1672, the third son of Francis Smith of Warwick, a bricklayer of The Wergs, near Tettenhall, Staffs. He and his brother William were brought up in the building trade, William as a bricklayer but Francis, apparently, as a mason. They often worked in partnership and by the time of William's death in 1724 they had become the leading master builders in the Midlands. Francis erected a monument to William at Tettenhall, on which the latter is described as an 'Architect Eminent in his profession'.

Francis established himself in Warwick, where in 1702 he married Anne Lea, a native of that town. Warwick had been devestated by fire in September 1694 and in 1696 Francis was appointed one of the two surveyors who were to regulate its rebuilding. Although it was this that gave him his first opportunities, in his subsequent career he relied on patronage from the Midlands gentry, many of whom employed him to build their country houses. Nearly all of them went up within a 50 mile radius of Warwick and there must have been years when he had three, four or even more houses in progress. Colvin lists 14 churches designed or built by the Smith brothers, and 53 houses. Their reputation for honesty and reliability were the qualities which stood them in good stead rather than any great distinction as architectural designers.

As a mason Francis maintained a yard at the Marble House in Warwick, from which he supplied chimneypieces and some statuary marble work, particularly the monument to Sir Justinian Isham, 1732, for which he received £87. This is an architectural composition with Corinthian pillars supporting an open pediment (**1**). Since the Smiths were prepared to undertake the construction of an entire building on behalf of the owner, Francis and his team of masons, which included **Henry Watson** in the 1730s, were inevitably responsible for much decorative carving, including chimneypieces. Gunnis suggests that he was responsible for those at Ombersley Court, Worcs, where he received regular payments between 1723 and 1726, amounting to some £1,500. He certainly supplied two chimneypieces for Lamport Hall, where he worked from 1732–8 (**2, 3**). Pevsner attributes four Northamptonshire monuments to him on stylistic grounds, including one to the Knightley family, 1728, at Fawsley, another to Mrs Knightley, †1730 at Woodford Halse, a third to Thomas Cave, †1733 at Stanford and one of coloured marbles to Robert Andrew, †1739, at Harlestone.

In his later years Francis grew corpulent though his energy seems to have been undiminished. When he died in April 1738 he left a flourishing business and an estate in Warwickshire that he had bought for £10,000. He had been twice mayor of Warwick (in 1713–14 and 1728–9). He was buried in St Mary, Warwick, but there is no record of any monument to his memory. He had four sons and a daughter, but only two sons survived him. William, the elder, to whom he left 'all my stock of Marble and Timber in my Marble Yard in Warwick' continued his father's business.

Literary References: *Isham* 1951, 442; *Gunnis* 1968, 356; Pevsner, *Northants*, 1973, 214, 247, 409, 468; *Colvin* 1995, 882–90; *Gomme* 2000

Will: PCC 162 BRODREPP

Portraits of the Sculptor: Unidentified artist, canvas, Court House, Warwick, nd (*Birmingham Arch Soc's Trans*, LIX, 1935, repr IV); W Winstanley, canvas, Bodleian, Oxford, nd (engraved by A Vanhacken); Michael Rysbrack, bust, tc, 1741, Radcliffe Library, Oxford

Funerary Monuments

1.	1732	Sir Justinian Isham Bt (†1730) Payment(s): £87		Lamport Hall, Northants	*Isham* 1951, 442; *Colvin* 1995, 883

Chimneypieces

2.	1732	Dove-grey marble	m	Lamport Hall, Northants	*Gunnis* 1968, 356
3.	1732	'of various coloured marbles with a cornice and two side-scrolls' Payment(s): £38 10s	m	Lamport Hall, Northants	Isham Archives in *Gunnis* 1968, 356

SMITH, Frederick William 1797–1835

He was born in Pimlico on 25 August 1797, the second son of Anker Smith, the engraver (1759–1819) and Charlotte Susannah Smith, and was christened on 18 October 1797 at St Ann Blackfriars. He joined the Royal Academy Schools in November 1815, winning medals in 1816 and 1821 (**15, 2**). He failed, however, to win the prize he really wanted, the three year scholarship to Rome. Smith was the first pupil of **Sir Francis Chantrey**, and remained with him, as his assistant and 'right-hand modeller' (*Builder*, 1863, 112). He lived in Bridge Row, Pimlico in 1818, at 1 Flask Row, Flask Lane in 1822 and at 8 Cecil Street, Strand in 1823. In the latter year Smith showed his bust of Chantrey's secretary, Allan Cunningham at the Academy (**9**). **John Flaxman RA**, who was arranging the works of art at Somerset House, said on seeing it that he would 'give this bust the best place in the exhibition, for in sentiment it surpasses any head I have seen here for some years' (*Athenaeum*, 1835, 75). The following year Smith showed a bust of Chantrey (**10**). Peter Cunningham, the sitter's son, was later to write of the two busts: 'Fred Smith knew by heart the features of the men he modelled; he saw them in all moods – in sunshine and in shade, – and has caught the two men, living as they thought and spoke, and sat and moved' (*Builder*, 1863, 112).

Smith exhibited busts and some ideal works at the Academy, giving his address as 21 Queen Street, Pimlico in 1824, and Ebury Cottage, Elizabeth Street in 1828. Peter Cunningham wrote that his 'soul was in his art' but his 'ambition was limited by the necessities of the week' (*Builder*, 1863, 112). He died young, in Shrewbury on 18 January 1835, after a long and distressing illness. His obituary in the *Athenaeum* stated that Smith's 'merits as an artist were of no ordinary kind; he had much force of conception, and singular ease and gracefulness of execution: in male figures such as his Ajax, he united natural action with great anatomical knowledge; and his female figures were remarkable for their unconstrained elegance of posture, the round softness of their limbs, and their perfect delicacy and truth of expression. We have seen little in English sculpture which surpassed the fleshy softness of his modelling' . . . . 'this young artist was frank, spirited, and kind-hearted, and was warmly beloved by all with whom he had intercourse: he was certainly the first of our second class of sculptors; nay, some of his works have a right to stand in the first rank' (*Athenaeum*, 1835, 75). A signed bust of Alderman Boydell (**6**) was carved after the model by **Thomas Banks.**

Literary References: *Athenaeum*, 1835, 75; *Builder*, 1863, 112; *Graves* VII, 1905–6, 176; *Hutchison* 1960–62, 168; *Gunnis* 1968, 356–7

Archival References: IGI

Funerary Monuments						
1.	1820	Alderman Boydell, bust (designed by Thomas Banks) Model(s): model by Banks exhib RA 1791		[St Olave, Jewry]; St Margaret Lothbury, City of London	S	Pevsner, *London: City*, 1997, 235
Statues						
2.	1821	Haemon and Antigone, group		[RA, London, gold medal]; untraced		RA Premium list; *Athenaeum*, 1835, 75; *Graves* VII, 1905–6, 176; *Gunnis* 1968, 356
3.	1824	'Mother and child, from the Massacre of the Innocents'		[Exhib RA, London, 982]; untraced		*Athenaeum*, 1835, 75; *Graves* VII, 1905–6, 176
4.	1827	Nymph and Cupid		[Exhib RA, London, 1118]; untraced		*Graves* VII, 1905–6, 176
5.	nd	The Deluge, group		Untraced		*Athenaeum*, 1835, 75
Busts						
6.	1818	A Smith ARA		[Exhib RA, London, 1102]; untraced		*Graves* VII, 1905–6, 176
7.	1820	An artist		[Exhib RA, London, 1054]; untraced		*Graves* VII, 1905–6, 176
8.	1822	John Keats		[Exhib RA, London, 1023]; untraced		*Graves* VII, 1905–6, 176; *Gunnis* 1968, 357
9.	1823	Allan Cunningham		[Exhib RA, London, 1060; 1826, 1042; coll Cunningham family, 1863]; untraced		*Builder*, 1863, 112; *Graves* VII, 1905–6, 176; *Ormond* 1973, 127
10.	1824	Sir Francis Legatt Chantrey Bt		[Exhib RA, London, 1023]; untraced Other versions: Burlington House, London, dated 1826		*Graves* VII, 1905–6, 176; *Gunnis* 1968, 357
11.	1824	Sir William Charles Ross		[Exhib RA, London, 1035]; untraced		*Graves* VII, 1905–6, 176; *Ormond* 1973, 403
12.	1827	Isambard Kingdom Brunel		[Exhib RA, London, 1094]; untraced		*Athenaeum* 1835, 75; *Graves* VII, 1905–6, 176; *Gunnis* 1968, 357
13.	1827	Mary, 2nd Countess of Liverpool	m	[coll Mrs Oliver Colthurst, intermediate owner]; untraced	SD	NP/RG
14.	1828	William Jerdan	m	[Exhib RA, London, 1167]; untraced		*Graves* VII, 1905–6, 176; *Ormond* 1973, 342
Reliefs						
15.	1816	The death of Pallas		[Soc of Arts, silver Isis medal]; untraced		RA Premium list
Miscellaneous						
16.	1821	Study from nature		[Exhib RA, London, 1111]; untraced		*Graves* VII, 1905–6, 176
17.	nd	Ajax		Untraced		*Athenaeum*, 1835, 75

SMITH, George 1782–1869

He provided many decorative elements for the principal entrance of the Royal Exchange (2), and made the altarpiece for St Michael, Queenhithe (1). Smith ran a large practice as an architect, working for James Wyatt and taking the post of district surveyor of the southern division of the City of London in 1810. In 1844–45 he was vice-president of the Institute of British Architects. As architect of the entrance front of the Royal Exchange, it seems likely that he designed rather than carved the exterior ornaments.

Literary References: *Gunnis* 1968, 357; *Colvin* 1995, 890–2

Architectural Sculpture				
1.	1823	Altarpiece	[St Michael Queenhithe, City of London]; untraced	*Elmes* 1827, 158; *Gunnis* 1968, 357
2.	1820–1826	Statues, reliefs, entablature and balustrade	[Royal Exchange, London, entrance front]; destroyed	*Elmes* 1827, 158; *Gunnis* 1968, 357
3.	1833	Pediment ornaments	Hertford County Hospital	GPC

SMITH, Gravas fl 1727–29

A woodcarver, he was employed on the Queen Anne Churches. He appears to have been in partnership with Thomas Darby.

Archival References: GPC

Architectural Sculpture				
1.	1727	Wood-carving (co-sculptor: Thomas Darby) Payment(s): £243	[Christ Church, Spitalfields, London]; untraced	Accounts for Queen Anne Churches, Lambeth Palace Library, in GPC
2.	1726–1729	Wood-carving (co-sculptor: Thomas Darby) Payment(s): £306	[St Mary Woolnoth, London]; untraced	Accounts for Queen Anne Churches, Lambeth Palace Library, in GPC

SMITH, H fl 1844

For information the reader is referred to *Pyke* 1973, 138

SMITH, H A fl 1827–57

He exhibited at the Royal Academy several times, giving his addresses as 57 Upper Norton Street in 1827 and 37 Gloucester Place, London in 1828. The former address was also **Charles Raymond Smith**'s, and it may be assumed that the two were related.

Literary References: *Graves* VII, 1905–6, 180; *Gunnis* 1968, 357; *Pyke* 1973, 138

Architectural Sculpture

1.	1857	Decorative stone work	s	Escrick, E R Yorks	*Builder* 1857, 392

Reliefs

2.	1844	Mrs Marsh, medallic portrait	w	[Exhib RA, London, 1255]; untraced	*Graves* VII, 1905–6, 180; *Gunnis* 1968, 357

Miscellaneous

3.	1827	A favourite spaniel (portrait)		[Exhib RA, London, 1102]; untraced	*Graves* VII, 1905–6, 180
4.	1828	Miss M Smith		[Exhib RA, London, 1065]; untraced	*Graves* VII, 1905–6, 180
5.	1828	Unidentified artist (portrait)		[Exhib RA, London, 1105]; untraced	*Graves* VII, 1905–6, 180

SMITH, J, of London fl *c*1791–95

He signs a number of monuments with **John Francis Moore**. Gunnis notes that three contemporary statuaries had this name, James, Joachim and Joseph, and he is inclined to think that the 'J' stands for James.

Literary References: *Gunnis* 1968, 264

Funerary Monuments

1.	?1791	Maria and John Chichester (co-sculptor: John Francis Moore)	Arlington, Devon	*Gunnis* 1968, 264
2.	?1793	Joseph Blunt (co-sculptor: J F Moore)	Mapledurham, Oxon	*Gunnis* 1968, 264
3.	?1795	Peter Oliver (co-sculptor: John Francis Moore)	Marylebone Chapel, London	*Gunnis* 1968, 264
4.	?1795	Thomas Wildman (co-sculptor: John Francis Moore)	St Mary, Twickenham, Middx	*Gunnis* 1968, 264

SMITH, James I –1705

Smith was the leading Scottish architect of his day. He was the son of a master-mason of the same name and he studied in Italy before returning to Scotland, where he married the daughter of **Robert Mylne I**. His father-in-law said of Smith that he was 'no contemptible sculptor' (*Colvin* 1995, 895). In 1683 a 'Mr James Smith statuary' was among those paid for recent works at Holyroodhouse. In 1685 Smith supplied the lead statue of King Charles II in Parliament Square, Edinburgh for £2,580. It seems unlikely that Smith was responsible for this work himself as the bill includes £38 for shipping the work in, presumably from a distance, but it demonstrates that Smith had good connections with sculptors. The statue had a chequered career. Henry Cockburn noted on 12 May 1835: 'I saw today for the first time the second Restoration of Charles II. – I mean of his statue, which has been replaced in the Parliament Square after a sleep in the prison for eleven years. A very respectable piece of Art. The horse had cracked at the fetlocks, but the legs are now mended, and his other frailties soldered, and his inside is sustained by a strong muscular system of oak, do he is expected to defy the weather, and remain sound for another century'.

In 1683 Smith was appointed surveyor of the Royal Works on the recommendation of the 1st Duke of Queensbury. He was responsible for improvements to Drumlanrig Castle, and contracted to build the Queensbury mausoleum at Durisdeer, ornamented with 'Mortheads, shankbones etc' all finished in polished marble. Smith was also the architect and contracting-builder at Hamilton Palace (Friedman 1987, 22).

In 1694 Anne, Duchess of Hamilton paid Smith £70 to procure marble in Holland for a monument to the Duke of Hamilton (**1**). Smith was employed to seek out a suitable sculptor in London but the design which he procured (probably by John Nost I) was rejected by the patron. Smith and his nephew, also James Smith, took on the commission, and their contract survives in the Scottish Record Office with their design (NRA (S) F1/685) (463/10/1). The finished work is grand and architectural, with twisted, fluted columns. It features statues of two mourning putti by an urn, behind which a 'small angill' pulls back a billowing curtain. The uneven execution suggests that the putti may have been the work of another sculptor, possibly Nost (ibid, 29). Smith died in Edinburgh on 6 November 1731. (Add inf. Helen Smailes)

Literary References: *Journal of Henry Cockburn* 1831–54, vol 1, 1874, 95; *Friedman* 1987, 22–31; Pevsner, *Edinburgh*, 1984, 203; *Colvin* 1995, 893–6

Funerary Monuments

1.	1696	William, Earl of Selkirk and 1st Duke of Hamilton (†1694) Payment(s): £600 Drawing(s): NRA, Scotland, Hamilton papers 332, F.1/685 (463/10/2)	[Hamilton, Lanarks]; St Bride, Bothwell	*Friedman* 1987, 22–31 (repr)
2.	1703	George, 15th Earl of Sutherland	Holyrood Abbey church, Edinburgh	Pevsner, *Edinburgh*, 1991, 140

SMITH, James II 1775–1815

A pupil of **Giovanni Battista Locatelli**, James Smith II attended the Royal Academy Schools from 1795. According to Farington he was awarded their silver medal for 'a Model of a Figure' in 1797 (*Farington*, 3, 943), though this was in fact a gold medal for *Venus wounded by Diomede*, a subject from Homer (**8**). In 1802 Smith applied to the RA for funding to travel to Italy, but appears to have been turned down. Instead he left the RA and worked briefly under **JCF Rossi** and later **John Flaxman RA**, with whom he stayed eight years as an assistant. During this time he was employed on various projects including Flaxman's monument in Westminster Abbey to Lord Mansfield.

Despite these connections, when Smith applied to undertake the monument in Guildhall to Admiral Lord Nelson (**3**) for the Corporation of London, neither Rossi nor Flaxman were generous in their support. After a visit from a Corporation delegation, Flaxman refused to endorse Smith's competence, in case 'it might hereafter be said that they had his authority for the ability of Smith in case of a failure in their expectations' (*Farington*, vol 7, 2760). Rossi considered Smith his professional inferior, but his lack of enthusiasm may also have stemmed from a desire to gain the Nelson commission himself. In this Rossi was supported by Alderman Boydell, but Smith's design was taken up by Boydell's political opponents on the court of Common Council and he was awarded the commission on 3 May 1806. Rossi seems to have recognised that Smith played no part in the political chicanery, affirming that Smith was 'a quiet man and not likely to have carried the point by intrigue' (*Farington*, 7, 2743). Smith's monument to Nelson cost £4,442 7s 4d, and was unveiled in 1810. It was 'generally deplored' (*Penny* 1976 (2), 548), and Gunnis called it 'an inferior mass of marble' (*Gunnis* 1968, 357). Smith also appears to have had problems in obtaining payment, and wrote to the Corporation to complain 'I am drained of all the money I had the honour of last receiving from the Corporation and I am now really left destitute of means to provide for the remaining sums that must be paid' (City Records, MS.95.2, cited by *Gunnis* 1968, 357). The Nelson memorial was Smith's only major commission for a monument, but he was responsible for a wall-mounted memorial with two seated figures to Giles Earle (**4**). There were also a few other memorials, chiefly in counties just north of London.

In 1808 a significant commission came in, for four chimneypieces ordered by the 5th Earl Cowper, son-in-law of the Prime Minister, Lord Melbourne, for the family home, Panshanger (**11–14**). Smith also executed a number of portrait busts, including one of the actress Mrs Siddons, 1813, which an advertisement claimed to be 'the only one of Mrs Siddons modelled from the life' (cited by *Gunnis* 1968, 357) (**9**). After being exhibited at the Royal Academy the bust was placed in the green room at Drury Lane theatre. Other notable sitters included the Poet Laureate Robert Southey (**10**).

In addition to sculptural works, Smith was the prefered modeller for the elaborate clocks, torcheres and other decorative objects in bronze produced in the early 1800s by the leading clockmakers, Vulliamy & Son. Outstanding examples of their work utilizing models by Smith are a set of 14 very large candelabra, each carried by three bronze putti, made for the Prince of Wales *c*1809–10 and still at Windsor Castle.

Smith's working life was relatively short, and he died on 28 April 1815 at the age of 41, leaving a wife and two sons, at least one of whom, **Charles Raymond Smith**, also became a sculptor. At his death James Smith had been under commission to produce a monument to General Le Marchant for St Paul's Cathedral, London, and this was completed by Rossi, who in turn sent the £200 payment he received to Smith's widow.

Michael Paraskos

Literary References: *GM*, 1819, i, 43; 1839, i, 547; *Smith*, 1828, II, 126; *Gunnis* 1968, 357–8; *Farington*, vol 3, 943; vol 7, 2760; *Whinney* 1988, 374; *Yarrington* 1988, 97–101

Archival References: RA Premium list

Will: PROB 11/1569

Funerary Monuments

1.	1809	Caroline Shuckburgh		Shuckburgh, Warks	S	*Gunnis* 1968, 357
2.	*c*1809	Hon G F Lake (†1808)		Westminster Abbey, London, nave, north aisle	S	WAM (17); Pevsner, *London: Westminster*, 1973, 454
3.	1806–1811	Admiral Lord Nelson (†1805) Payment(s): £4,442 7s 4d		CL Coll, Guildhall, City of London, great hall, acc 84		*Knight* 1986, 346; *Yarrington* 1988, 97–101 (pl 44); *Ward-Jackson* 2002, 386–94
4.	†1811	Giles Earle		St Mary, Hendon, Middx	S	Pevsner, *London: N*, 1998, 159
5.	1813	Brand family member		Hemingstone, Suffolk	S	Pevsner, *Suffolk*, 1974, 261
6.	†1813	Francis Evans		Mansell Gamage, Herefs	S	Pevsner, *Herefs*, 1963, 249
7.	1815	Thomas Barwis		All Saints, Wandsworth, London	S	*Gunnis* 1968, 357

Statues

8.	1797	Venus wounded by Diomede, group		[Awarded RA gold medal]; untraced		RA Premium list

Busts

9.	1813	Sarah Siddons		[Mrs Siddons's House]; Royal Shakespeare gall, Stratford-upon-Avon, Warks Other versions: replica at Guy's Cliff, Warwick		*Gunnis* 1968, 357
10.	1814	Robert Southey	p	[coll Robert Southey]; Knox/Longstaffe-Gowan coll (acq 1994)	D	*Graves* VII, 1905–6, 184; *Gunnis* 1968, 357

Chimneypieces

11.	1808	Black and yellow marble Payment(s): £278 (with others)	m	[Panshanger, Herts, library]; untraced		GPC
12.	1808	Dove marble with 'swell'd frieze and Pelasters with circular blocking' Payment(s): £278 (with others)	m	[Panshanger, Herts, dining room]; untraced		GPC
13.	1808	'Newcastle stone enrich'd with Gothic ornaments' Payment(s): £278 (with others)	s	[Panshanger, Herts, entrance hall]; untraced		GPC
14.	1808	Sienna marble Payment(s): £50	m	[Panshanger, Herts, drawing room]; untraced		GPC

Architectural Sculpture

15.	1808	Models of dragons for two mounted oriental vases supplied by Justin Vulliamy Payment(s): £6 12s		[Carlton House, London]; Royal Coll		*Carlton House* 1991–2, 96
16.	1811	Three models of partly draped female figures for a pair of candelabra supplied by Justin Vulliamy for Carlton House, London		Untraced		*Carlton House* 1991–2, 178
17.	1812	Hercules, model for candelabra manufactured by Benjamin Vulliamy		Untraced		*Murdoch* 2004, 98–9 (repr)

SMITH, Joachim *c*1737–

In 1758, when 'under twenty-two years of age' and an 'untaught designer and modeller,' he received a premium of ten guineas from the Society of Arts for a wax model of Alfred the Great. Dossie states that Smith had 'invented a composition in which colours being mixed up to the various tints and shades of human features, was rendered fit, from the fine texture and intimate commixtion of the ingredients to model portraits in miniature to a degree of delicacy'. It added 'the invention is now being carried on in an improved practice by the discoverer in Berners Street, near Middlesex Hospital' (*Dossie* 1782, 435). It was probably the new composition of coloured wax that was used for his exhibition entries at the Free Society in 1761 and 1762 (**40, 41**). Another premium was awarded to him in 1759 from the Society of Arts for a 'Drawing fit for any mechanical trade that requires taste by youths under the age of 22' (RSA *Minutes*, 1758–60 seq 1 fol 66, seq 2 fol 28). The minutes of the Society record further deliberations on his method of wax modelling (RSA *Minutes*, 1760–61, seq 3 fol 53).

In 1763 Smith made a celebrated model about four inches long of the infant Prince of Wales, given to the Prince's mother as a New Year present by the King (1). The *London Magazine* carried a lengthy notice of the work, which showed the baby 'naked . . . lying on a couch of crimson velvet' and noted the material: 'this amazing piece of art is done with a composition of wax in natural colours, without being painted, but blended, and incorporated in such manner, as to diffuse the various tints and softness of nature' (*London Mag* 1763, 32, 56). The piece was displayed under a bell-jar 18 inches high, designed by the London cabinetmaker William Vile.

That year Mortimer's *Director* included a lengthy puff for Smith, who was then living at King-Street, Bloomsbury. 'This ingenious young artist is an Englishman' it noted, to distinguish Smith from foreign-born wax-modellers like **Isaac Gosset**. He 'has given proofs of such uncommon ingenuity as are rarely met with in any country, for never having been instructed either in Drawing, Modelling or Mechanics, he is notwithstanding an undoubted Master of the two first and is equalled by few in his knowledge of the last' (*Mortimer* 1763, 26).

Evidence of Smith's knowledge of 'mechanics' can be found in a letter from the modeller, dated 16 May 1763, to Sir James Caldwell of County Fermanagh. In it Smith describes his 'new-invented-model of a ship', very different in design to vessels currently in use and 'perfectly agreeable in theory to the Laws of Hydrostatics' (Joachim Smith/Cladwell). Smith entered his model for a premium at the Society of Arts.

In 1765–66 Smith went to Bath, to find clients for his novel and affordable wax miniatures among the fashionable elite. In 1766, when he exhibited at the Society of Arts in London, he gave his addresses as 'Bath, and at the Raven and Anchor, Drury Lane'. He was subsequently recorded as living in Drury Lane at 'Mr Edward's,' presumably the publican, where he remained until 1772. It seems likely that his landlord was also his father-in-law, for the parish records of St Martin-in-the-Fields record that a Joachim Smith married a Miss Anne Edwards on 2 July 1758.

One of his works shown at the Society of Arts exhibition in 1766 was a portrait in coloured wax, intended 'for a ring' (*Graves* 1907, 238). The jewellery trade appears to have been a profitable market for Smith's wares, for a number of his portraits, including those of the Duke and Duchess of Gloucester, Governor and Mrs Johnstone and Mrs Fitzherbert (**12, 29, 31**) were used as models by gem-cutters and cameo-engravers.

In 1771 Smith was elected a fellow of the Society of Artists, he became a director in 1772 and treasurer in 1776. In 1772 he moved to 24 Henrietta Street, Covent Garden, and in 1774 to 34 Berners Street, Oxford Road.

In 1772 he began to model wax portraits, which were copied and produced by Wedgwood and Bentley in white biscuit-ware and later in white terracotta. These included likenesses of both Wedgwood and Bentley (**17, 19**). Smith also produced the finely modelled and distinguished portrait of Sir William Hamilton (**15**), which was presented to the sitter.

Smith appears to have been the first outside modeller to supply Wedgwood with wax portraits for reproduction. His connection with the firm was not free of problems: on 8 February 1775, Smith wrote to Wedgwood: 'the many accidents I have had with several moulds as well as with some of the models has been attended with a considerable loss of time and deprived me of the possibility of sending you anything for some months past. But there is a difficulty which naturally awaits on everything in its infancy – which with a little indulgence I hope to get the better of' (Wedgwood/Smith L1/47, 8 Feb 1775). In 1775 Wedgwood seems to have dispensed with Smith's services, apparently because he had heard that the modeller was working for the rival pottery at Derby. On 25 March 1779 his bankruptcy was announced in the *London Gazette*. (Inf. Roger Smith)

From 1781 Smith exhibited at the Royal Academy, where he showed as a 'sculptor.' He had a number of addresses in London including Wells Street, Oxford Road, and, finally, 57 Norton Street. He appears last to have exhibited at the RA in 1814 though from 1803 onwards Graves perhaps confused him with **James Smith II** (*Graves* VII, 1905–6, 184).

MGS

Literary References: *Graves* VII, 1905–6, 184; *Graves* 1907, 238; *Pyke* 1973, 138; *Pyke* 1981, 38; *Reilly* 1995, 395

Archival References: IGI

No.	Date	Subject			Location		References
Statues							
1.	1763	The infant Prince of Wales, model, statuette	w	[Buckingham House, London]; untraced			*London Mag*, 1763, 32, 56; *Gunnis* 1968, 358; *Pyke* 1973, 138
Busts							
2.	1812	'A decayed artist'		[Exhib RA, London, 902]; untraced			*Graves* VII, 1905–6, 184
3.	1812	Mr W Atkinson		[Exhib RA, London, 924]; untraced			*Graves* VII, 1905–6, 184
4.	1813	Lord Gray		[Exhib RA, London, 910]; untraced			*Graves* VII, 1905–6, 184
5.	1814	Robert Southey		[Exhib RA, London, 804]; untraced			*Graves* VII, 1905–6, 184
Reliefs							
6.	1762	'Picture in coloured wax' Payment(s): £6 11s	w	[for Miss Ingram]; untraced			*Pyke* 1973, 138
7.	1763	Hugh, Duke of Northumberland	w	Chicago A I			*Pyke* 1973, 138
8.	1765	Duchess of Newcastle	w	untraced		SD	*Pyke* 1973, 138
9.	1766	A lady, in coloured wax		[Exhib Soc of Artists, London, 239]; untraced			*Graves* 1907, 239
10.	1766	A young lady (in coloured wax 'for a ring')	w	[Exhib Soc of Artists, London, 215]; untraced			*Graves* 1907, 239
11.	1766	Thomas, 1st Duke of Newcastle (in coloured wax)	w	[Exhib Soc of Artists, London, 214]; untraced			*Graves* 1907, 239
12.	1766	William, Duke of Gloucester and the Duchess of Gloucester	w	M L			*Gunnis* 1968, 358; *Pyke* 1973, 138
13.	1771	Mr Smith	w	Private coll			*Pyke* 1973, 138
14.	1771	Unidentified man	w	Sotheby 24 July 1977, lot 51			*Pyke* 1981, 38
15.	1772	Sir William Hamilton (modelled for Wedgwood)		Untraced Other versions: Wedgwood ware, VAM			*Reilly* 1995, 395; *Young* 1995, 14, 59 (Wedgwood repr)

16.	1773	John Bradley (modelled for Wedgwood)	w	Untraced	*Gunnis* 1968, 358
17.	1773	Josiah Wedgwood (modelled for Wedgwood)	w	Untraced	*Gunnis* 1968, 358; *Reilly* 1995, 395
18.	1773	Lady Charlotte Finch and her daughter (modelled for Wedgwood)	w	Royal Coll	*Gunnis* 1968, 358; *Reilly* 1995, 395
19.	1773	Thomas Bentley (modelled for Wedgwood)	w	Untraced Other versions: Wedgwood ware, Wedgwood Museum, Barlaston, Staffs	*Gunnis* 1968, 358; *Bindman* 1979, 69 (Wedgwood version repr); *Reilly* 1995, 395
20.	c1774	Captain Edward Hamilton (modelled for Wedgwood)		Untraced	*Reilly* 1995, 395
21.	1776	Johann Reinhold Forster (modelled for Wedgwood)		Untraced	*Gunnis* 1968, 358; *Reilly* 1995, 395
22.	1776	John Bradby Blake (modelled for Wedgwood)		Untraced	*Reilly* 1995, 395
23.	?1778	Catherine Chichester-Constable	w	Private coll	*Pyke* 1973, 138
24.	c1778	John Chichester-Constable	w	Private coll	*Pyke* 1973, 138
25.	1791	Unidentified man	w	VAM	*Pyke* 1973, 138
26.	1795	Almon Hill	w	Chicago, A I	*Pyke* 1973, 138
27.	1797	Anne Harman Lyney	w	Chicago A I	*Pyke* 1973, 138
28.	1813	Portrait of Sarah Siddons		[Exhib RA, London, 916]; untraced	*Graves* VII, 1905–6, 184
29.	nd	Governor and Mrs Johnstone	w	Untraced	*Gunnis* 1968, 358
30.	nd	John Mayhew	w	VAM A.22-1970	*Pyke* 1973, 138; *Pyke* 1981, 38
31.	nd	Mrs Fitzherbert	w	Untraced	*Gunnis* 1968, 358
32.	nd	Unidentified man	w	VAM	*Pyke* 1973, 138
33.	nd	Unidentified man	w	Met NY	*Pyke* 1973, 138
34.	nd	Unidentified man	w	Met NY	*Pyke* 1983, 138
35.	nd	Unidentified man	w	Private coll, USA	*Pyke* 1981, 38
36.	nd	Unidentified man	w	Private coll	*Pyke* 1981, 38
37.	nd	Unidentified youth	w	Sotheby 15 Dec 1975, lot 3	*Pyke* 1981, 38
38.	nd	Viscount Fitzmaurice	w	Bowood, Wilts	*Gunnis* 1968, 358; *Pyke* 1973, 138
Miscellaneous					
39.	1758	Unidentified portrait	w	[Soc of A, London, premium]; untraced	*Gunnis* 1968, 358
40.	1761	A gentleman, model in coloured wax	w	[Exhib Free Soc, London, 104]; untraced	*Graves* 1907, 239
41.	1762	Flowers etc, model in coloured wax	w	[Exhib Soc of Artists, London, 173]; untraced	*Graves* 1907, 239
42.	1766	A gentleman, in coloured wax	w	[Exhib Soc of Artists, London, 216]; untraced	*Graves* 1907, 239
43.	1766	Frederick-Augustus, Duke of York and Albany	w	Royal Coll	*Gunnis* 1968, 358; *Pyke* 1973, 138 (repr 269)
44.	1766	Prince of Wales	w	Royal Coll	*Gunnis* 1968, 358; *Pyke* 1973, 138
45.	1767	A lady, in coloured wax	w	[Exhib Soc of Artists, London, 212]; untraced	*Graves* 1907, 239
46.	1767	Portrait of a child, in coloured wax	w	[Exhib Soc of Artists, London, 211]; untraced	*Graves* 1907, 239
47.	1768	A child, model in coloured wax	w	[Exhib Soc of Artists, London, 208]; untraced	*Graves* 1907, 239
48.	1769	A nobleman's child, model	w	[Exhib Soc of Artists, London, 246]; untraced	*Graves* 1907, 239
49.	1769	King of Denmark, in coloured wax 'from memory'	w	[Exhib Soc of Artists, London, 245]; untraced	*Graves* 1907, 239
50.	1770	A child, model in coloured wax	w	[Exhib Soc of Artists, London, 178]; untraced	*Graves* 1907, 239
51.	1771	A lady, model	w	[Exhib Soc of Artists, London, 226]; untraced	*Graves* 1907, 239
52.	1772	A child, model		[Exhib Soc of Artists, London, 292]; untraced	*Graves* 1907, 239
53.	1772	Lady 'in undress,' model		[Exhib Soc of Artists, London, 291]; untraced	*Graves* 1907, 239
54.	1772	Two gentlemen, models 'in imitation of ivory'		[Exhib Soc of Artists, London, 293–4]; untraced	*Graves* 1907, 239
55.	1772	Two gentlemen, models in coloured wax	w	[Exhib Soc of Artists, London, 295–6]; untraced	*Graves* 1907, 239
56.	1773	A gentleman, model in coloured wax	w	[Exhib Soc of Artists, London, 299]; untraced	*Graves* 1907, 239
57.	1773	A lady, model in coloured wax	w	[Exhib Soc of Artists, London, 298]; untraced	*Graves* 1907, 239
58.	1774	Two gentleman, portraits in coloured wax	w	[Exhib Soc of Artists, London, 256, 258]; untraced	*Graves* 1907, 239
59.	1774	Two ladies, portraits in coloured wax	w	[Exhib Soc of Artists, London, 257, 259]; untraced	*Graves* 1907, 239
60.	1777	Miniature portraits in compositions 'which will not suffer by Time or Fire'		[Exhib Soc of Artists, London, 286]; untraced	*Graves* 1907, 239
61.	1777	Unidentified sitter	w	[Exhib Soc of Artists, London, 288]; untraced	*Graves* 1907, 239
62.	1777	Unidentified sitter, in coloured wax	w	[Exhib Soc of Artists, London, 287]; untraced	*Graves* 1907, 239
63.	1778	A gentleman, in composition		[Exhib Soc of Artists, London, 214]; untraced	*Graves* 1907, 239
64.	1778	A lady, in composition		[Exhib Soc of Artists, London, 209]; untraced	*Graves* 1907, 239

65.	1778	A nobleman, 'from memory'		[Exhib Soc of Artists, London, 216]; untraced	*Graves* 1907, 239
66.	1778	A nobleman, in composition		[Exhib Soc of Artists, London, 215]; untraced	*Graves* 1907, 239
67.	1778	Two gentlemen, in composition		[Exhib Soc of Artists, London, 212–13]; untraced	*Graves* 1907, 239
68.	1778	Two ladies, in composition		[Exhib Soc of Artists, London, 210–11]; untraced	*Graves* 1907, 239
69.	1780	A clergyman, in coloured wax	w	[Exhib Soc of Artists, London, 237]; untraced	*Graves* 1907, 239
70.	1780	A young lady, in coloured wax	w	[Exhib Soc of Artists, London, 240]; untraced	*Graves* 1907, 239
71.	1780	Two gentlemen, in white wax	w	[Exhib Soc of Artists, London, 238–9]; untraced	*Graves* 1907, 239
72.	1780	Two ladies, models in coloured wax	w	[Exhib Soc of Artists, London, 235–6]; untraced	*Graves* 1907, 239
73.	1781	Mr Dingle, 'model in coloured composition'	w	[Exhib RA, London, 320]; untraced	*Graves* VII, 1905–6, 184
74.	1781	Mr West, 'model in coloured composition'		[Exhib RA, London, 329]; untraced	*Graves* VII, 1905–6, 184
75.	1781	Portrait of a boy, 'model in coloured composition'		[Exhib RA, London, 310]; untraced	*Graves* VII, 1905–6, 184
76.	1781	Portrait of a lady, 'model in coloured composition'		[Exhib RA, London, 298]; untraced	*Graves* VII, 1905–6, 184
77.	1783	A lady		[Exhib Soc of Artists, London, 233]; untraced	*Graves* 1907, 239
78.	1783	A young gentleman		[Exhib Soc of Artists, London, 239]; untraced	*Graves* 1907, 239
79.	1783	A young lady		[Exhib Soc of Artists, London, 234]; untraced	*Graves* 1907, 239
80.	1783	A young lady, 'done after death'		[Exhib Soc of Artists, London, 235]; untraced	*Graves* 1907, 239
81.	1783	Portrait 'for cameos for rings etc'		[Exhib Soc of Artists, London, 236]; untraced	*Graves* 1907, 239
82.	1783	Two gentlemen		[Exhib Soc of Artists, London, 230–1]; untraced	*Graves* 1907, 239
83.	1793	'Portrait of a gentleman'	w	[Exhib RA, London, 416]; untraced	*Graves* VII, 1905–6, 184
84.	1794	'Portrait of a gentleman'	w	[Exhib RA, London, 606]; untraced	*Graves* VII, 1905–6, 184
85.	1794	'Portrait of a gentleman'	w	[Exhib RA, London, 607]; untraced	*Graves* VII, 1905–6, 184
86.	1803	An angel casting Satan into the abyss		[Exhib RA, London, 1012]; untraced	*Graves* VII, 1905–6, 184
87.	1803	The nymph Laura rejecting the addresses of Mercury (from Ovid)		[Exhib RA, London, 1028]; untraced	*Graves* VII, 1905–6, 184

SMITH, John fl 1757

He described himself as an apprentice of **L F Roubiliac** when he submitted an model to the Society of Arts in 1757.

Statues

1.	1757	'Cast of St Andrew from a model of Fiamingo's'	[Soc of A, submission]; untraced	RSA Minutes 1757–58, fol 93

SMITH, John, of Darnick 1782–1864

He was the son of John Smith, a builder and mason of Darnick, near Melrose in Roxburghshire. He and his younger brother Thomas continued their father's business after his death. Their practice as architects and builders consisted chiefly in designing and enlarging small houses, rural churches, schools and manses. Local landowners who employed them included Sir Walter Scott, for whom they designed and built Chiefswood, Roxburghshire, as well as enlarging Abbotsford to the designs of William Atkinson. John Smith's own home, Darnlee, Darnick, was built to the brothers' designs. The intelligent and enterprising pair designed and built a number of bridges and prepared a paper describing an economical method of constructing bridges in whinstone rubble without the use of ashlar. This was published in the first volume of the *RIBA Transactions.*

John was also an occasional sculptor. He executed decorative carving at Abbotsford and in 1824 carved a portrait of Scott's deerhound, Maida (**2, 3**). His most famous work, a red sandstone statue of William Wallace, was commissioned by the 11th Earl of Buchan and erected at Dryburgh Abbey in 1814 (**1**). A contemporary report said that the statue was based on 'the authentic portrait painted of him in water colours, during his residence in France, which was purchased by the father of the late Sir Philip Ainslie of Pilt, Knt' (*GM*, 1817, i, 621). Woodward describes the figure, which is reputed to be the first monument to Wallace erected in Scotland, as 'poorly designed and crudely carved'.

Literary References: *Gunnis* 1968, 358; *Woodward* 1977, vol 1, pt 2, 220–1; *Colvin* 1995, 900–1

Additional Manuscript Sources: *Smith Diary*; *Smith of Darnick Family Papers*; *Smith/Scott*

Collections of Drawings: SRO RHP 5525, 7190–6, 7196, 8220–1, 8429–44 (architectural drawings)

Statues

1.	1814	William Wallace	s	Dryburgh Abbey, Berwickshire	*Pearson* 1991, 73, 77 (repr); *Colvin* 1995, 901
2.	1824	Maida (Sir Walter Scott's deerhound)		Abbotsford, Roxburghshire	*Woodward* 1977, vol 1, pt 2, 221

Architectural Sculpture

3.	nd	Decorative stone carving	s	Abbotsford, Roxburghshire	*Woodward* 1977, vol 1, pt 2, 221

SMITH, John, of Rye fl *c*1822–45

Gunnis notes that Smith's tablets are based on minor works by **John Bacon II**, but that considering he lived and worked in a small Sussex town 'they are surprisingly good and well above the average of the contemporary provincial sculptor'. In 1851 Smith and his son built the Gothic railway station at Battle, Sussex.

Literary References: *Gunnis* 1968, 357

Funerary Monuments

1.	?1822	Sarah Woodham	Udimore, Sussex	*Gunnis* 1968, 357
2.	?1826	William Woodham	Udimore, Sussex	*Gunnis* 1968, 357

3.	?1832	Rev John Lettice	Peasmarsh, Sussex		*Gunnis* 1968, 357
4.	?1845	Thomas Langford	Udimore, Sussex		*Gunnis* 1968, 357
Chimneypieces					
5.	1815	More than one	[Battle Abbey, Sussex]; untraced		Archives, Mrs Harbord, of Battle Abbey in *Gunnis* 1968, 357

SMITH, Joseph fl 1795–c1800

In 1795, Smith and his partner, George Cleverly, were paid £68 for masonry work which may have included carved stone at Bowood (Archives, Marquess of Lansdowne in GPC). His large monument to Lady Chapman features a sarcophagus surmounted by an urn.

Literary References: *Gunnis* 1968, 358

Funerary Monuments					
1.	?1800	Lady Chapman	Barkway, Herts		*Gunnis* 1968, 358

SMITH, Joseph, of Liverpool fl c1841

Funerary Monuments					
1.	?1841	Thomas Chadwick	Longton, Staffs	S	GPC

SMITH, Leonard, of York fl 1721–33

He was the son of Leonard Smith, 'freemason', who became a freeman of York in 1687. The elder Smith died on 25 November 1722 and was buried in the churchyard of All Saints, York (*Gent* 1730, 161). The son became free by patrimonial redemption in 1721, as did his younger brother, John, in 1725. In 1725 Leonard and his partner, James Disney, repaired the Barr wall at York. In 1729 Smith was appointed master-mason at the Assembly Rooms, but he was discharged for 'being negligent', early in 1731. His successor, **William Bateson of York** was even more unsatisfactory, and within the year Smith was reinstated to work on the portico, capitals and a chimneypiece (**2, 3**).

Literary References: *Gunnis* 1968, 358

Archival References: Assembly Rooms Directors' Minutes, Ledgers & Receipt Books, 1730–1925, York City Archives; GPC

Chimneypieces				
1.	1729	Description not available	[Guildhall, York]; untraced	York City Archives in *Gunnis* 1968, 358
2.	1733	Description not available	Assembly Rooms, York, 'circular room'	Assembly Rooms, directors' minutes, ledgers & receipt books, 1730–1925, York City Archives
Architectural Sculpture				
3.	1731	Portico, carved capitals (designed by 3rd Earl Burlington)	[Assembly Rooms, York]; untraced	Assembly Rooms, directors' minutes, ledgers & receipt books, 1730–1925, York City Archives

SMITH, Nathaniel c1741–3–after 1800

He was the father of **Joseph Nollekens**'s biographer, J T Smith, and was described in his son's obituary as a sculptor and afterwards, a printseller. Most of his work was produced as an assistant to more success sculptors. Nathaniel was the son of Thomas Smith, a Shropshire clothier and was christened at Eltham, near Woolwich, on 30 June 1738. J T Smith's obituary states that Nathaniel 'was the playfellow of Joseph Nollekens, R.A., and both learned drawing together at Shipley's school, then kept in the Strand, at the eastern corner of Castle-court, the house where the Society of Art had its first meeting'. On 7th Aug. 1755, Nathaniel Smith was placed with **L F Roubiliac**, and 'had the honour of working with him on some of the monuments of Westminster Abbey' (*GM* 1833, i, 641). The latter assertion should be treated with caution since it is likely to have come from J T Smith himself. Smith's Burrell monument has a medallion portrait backed by drapery (**1**) and derives from Roubiliac's Harvey monument at Hempstead (1758).

Nathaniel showed early promise, winning four premiums from the Society of Arts between 1758 and 1762 (**9–12**), by which time he was probably living in St Martin's Lane. From 1767–9 he was in Portland Place. After Roubiliac's death he became **Joseph Wilton's** assistant. According to J T Smith, the much admired bust of Philip Stanhope, 4th Earl of Chesterfield, 1757, was modelled by Wilton but actually carved by Nathaniel. The exact circumstances of the commission are unknown but the bust was presumably carved for Chesterfield House, London. Young Smith also claimed that his father spent three years carving the figures on Wilton's monument to General Wolfe in Westminster Abbey, and that he 'executed a great deal of the sculpture on Somerset House [some of it with **John Atkins**] for which Wilton received the money'. Whinney notes that Wilton's work there included statues of the four continents on the attic at the north side of the court and 4 of the 8 colossal masks of rivers on the Strand front, together with vases, lions and chimneypieces. Smith carved three heads of river gods, designed by J B Cipriani (**8**). By 1779 he had become Nollekens's principal assistant (inf. JKB).

Smith's early prize-winning relief, *Bringing down the stag*, is an astoundingly graphic and naturalistic work, a fine achievement which well endorses the decision of the Society of Arts to award him a premium (**10**). The model of Alderman Beckford for a statue in Guildhall was submitted in competition with **Agostino Carlini, John Flaxman RA** and others. **John Francis Moore** won the contract. It again endorses Smith's competence and invites speculation why such an obviously talented craftsman never gained an independent reputation. Graves notes a secondary career, describing him as a 'Sculptor and Miniature Painter', who showed miniatures at the Society of Artists in 1767–9 and 1773 (*Graves* 1907, 241).

Literary References: *Smith* II, 1828, 110; *Whinney* 1988, 198, 267, 461 n32; *Dawson* 1999, 10, 68; *Bilbey* 2002, 152–3; IGI

Will (?): PRO/FRC PROB 11/1493 (described as sculptor and printseller of Greenwich)

Miscellaneous Drawings: 'Drawings of figures from Models' premium, under 22 category, Soc of A, 27 Feb 1759 (RSA *Minutes*, 1758–60, seq 2 fol 27)

Auction: Smith 1803; Smith 1809

Portraits of the Sculptor: 'There is a portrait of him etched by Wilde; and small painting on panel by the same artist is also preserved'; untraced (*GM* 1833, i, 641)

Funerary Monuments					
1.	†1787	Sir Merrick Burrell	West Grinstead, Sussex	S	*Whinney* 1988, 461 n46

Statues

2.	1763	Time, figure 'imitating a bronze'		[Exhib Free Soc, London, 211]; untraced		*Graves* 1907, 241
3.	1770	Alderman Beckford in Guildhall, London, model Drawing(s): VAM 4910.12 (*Physick* 1968, 140, repr)	tc	VAM A.48-1929	SD	*Bilbey* 2002, 153
4.	1775	Alexander the Great (from a design by John Flaxman RA)	m	[coll Mr Knight, of Portland Place]; untraced		*Cunningham* 1829–33, vol 3, 288
5.	nd	William Pitt, Earl of Chatham, model	tc	Peter Norton sale, Christie, 11 Jan 1869, lot 1097; untraced		*Gunnis* 1968, 359
Busts						
6.	1763	Unidentified subject		[Exhib Free Soc, London, 210]; untraced		*Graves* 1907, 241
7.	1770	John Wesley	tc	Earls Colne, Essex, 1971	SD	*Van Oss* 1974, 307–308 (repr LXIX)
Architectural Sculpture						
8.	nd	Heads of three river gods (designed by Giovanni Baptista Cipriani)		Somerset House, London		*GM*, 1833, i, 64
Reliefs						
9.	1758	St Andrew	tc	[Soc of A, premium, 15 gns, under 22 class]; untraced		*Dossie* 1782, 438; *Wilson* 2007, 73–83
10.	1760	Bringing down the stag (Bucks and Dogs), model in black and gold wood frame	tc	[Soc of A, premium, under 22 class]; VAM 414: 1215–1885	SD	RSA *Minutes*, 1758–60, seq 4 fol 50, 53; *Bilbey* 2002, 152–3 (repr)
11.	1761	Continence of Scipio	tc	[Soc of A, premium, 15 gns; coll Lord Rockingham]; untraced		RSA *Minutes*, 1760–61, seq 3 fol 48; *Dossie* 1782, 438
12.	1762	Coriolanus and Volumnia	tc	[Soc of A, premium, 20 gns]; untraced		*London Mag*, 1762, 174; *Dossie* 1782, 438; RSA *Register* 1778, 31

SMITH, of Oxford

See **Garratt.**

SMITH, Robert –1698

The son of Luke Smith of East Greenwich, Kent, gentleman, he was apprenticed to **Abraham Story** on 10 January 1665. He was made free of the Masons' Company on 16 January 1672. His name appears in the Masons' Company yeomanry list of 1676 and in the assistants list of 1696. In the general search to locate freemen and apprentices working in the City conducted by the Masons' Company in September 1694, it was found that Mr Robert Smith of Pell Mell employed two apprentices and three journeymen. Two years later another search revealed that he still had the same number. His name appears in the assistants list of 1698 with 'mort' after it.

Another Robert Smith was renter warden of the Masons' Company in 1698 and upper warden in 1699. This may be the Robert Smith who was made free of the Masons' Company on 5 July 1687, having served under **William Stanton.**

Literary References: *Knoop and Jones* 1935, 30, n3

Archival References: Masons' Co, Masters and Wardens; Freemen, fol 66

SMITH, Robert Ormerod 1819–

He attended the Royal Academy Schools in 1838, but afterwards lived in Rome until at least 1855.

Literary References: *Gunnis* 1968, 359

Statues

1.	pre-1857	Rebekah	m	[Manc Art Treas Exhib, 1857, 61]; untraced	*Manchester Art Treasures* 1857, 134
2.	1857	The reaper	m	[Manc Art Treas Exhib, 27]; untraced	*Manchester Art Treasures* 1857, 133
3.	nd	Hebe		[Manley Hall sale, Christie, 15 March 1875]; untraced	GPC
4.	nd	The gleaner		[Manley Hall sale, Christie, 15 March 1875]; untraced	GPC
Busts					
5.	1855	Theophilus Isles Smith	m	[Exhib RA, London, 1509]; untraced	*Graves* VII, 1905–6, 190; *Gunnis* 1968, 359
6.	nd	Edward Rushton		Liverpool Town Hall, Lancs	GPC

SMITH, T, of Hertford fl *c*1847–56

Funerary Monuments

1.	†1847	Rev Henry Comyn	Bishops Hatfield, Herts	S
2.	†1856	Joseph (†1836) and Ann Field	Bishops Hatfield, Herts	S

SMITH, Thomas 1800–

He was the son of **James Smith II**, and the younger brother of **Charles Raymond Smith**. The family lived at 57 Norton Street, Fitzroy Square. He attended the Royal Academy Schools in 1817 and won medals in 1821 and 1822 from the Society of Arts (**10, 11**). From 1829 he ran his business from 6 Savoy Street, Strand. In 1830 he was appointed modeller of wax medallic portraits to William IV.

Smith had a practice also as a monumental sculptor. Gunnis thought his best works were the tablets to Robert Bevan and Eliza Russell, both of which have medallion portraits (**5, 7**). The Salusbury (**4**) and Banks (**3**) have busts and the latter also has reliefs of the Waterloo, Southwark and London bridges, all of which Banks built. By 1846 his business had moved to 10 Wellington Street and three years later he was at 30 Cranmer Place, Lambeth. In 1852 his address was 14 Hart Street, Bloomsbury. Graves identifies him with the Theophilus Smith, 'c/o 16 Cemetery Road, Sheffield' who exhibited at the Royal Academy in 1877 (*Graves* VII, 1905–6, 191)

Literary References: *Graves* 1875, 503; *Graves* VII, 1905–6, 191–192; *Gunnis* 1968, 359–60; *Pyke* 1973, 139

Archival References: RSA *Transactions*, 1822, vol 40, xxxix

Funerary Monuments						
1.	?1828	Lady Elizabeth Russell		North Ockendon, Essex		*Gunnis* 1968, 360
2.	?1833	Gilbert Jolliffe		Worth, Sussex Other versions: Merstham, Surrey		*Gunnis* 1968, 360
3.	†1835	Sir Edward Banks		Chipstead, Surrey	S	Pevsner, *Surrey*, 1971, 157
4.	?1835	Sir Thomas Salusbury		Great Offley, Hertfs		*Gunnis* 1968, 359
5.	?1837	Robert Bevan		Monmouth		*Gunnis* 1968, 359
6.	†1838	Dr Whitlock Nicholl		St Mary the Virgin, Wimbledon, Surrey	S	*Gunnis* 1968, 360
7.	†1838	Eliza Russell		North Ockendon, Essex	S	*Gunnis* 1968, 359
8.	?1839	Nicholas Mori		Kensal Green Cemetery, London		*Gunnis* 1968, 360
9.	†1841	John Hutton		Marske, N R Yorks	S	Pevsner, *Yorks: N R*, 1966, 238
Statues						
10.	1821	'a single figure'		[Soc of A, large silver medal]; untraced		RSA *Transactions*, 1821, vol 39, xxxviii
11.	1822	Oedipus and Antigone, an original group in plaster		[Soc of A, large silver medal]; untraced		RSA *Transactions*, 1822, vol 40, xxxix
Busts						
12.	1827	Unidentified lady		[Exhib RA, London, 995]; untraced		*Graves* VII, 1905–6, 191
13.	1828	Unidentified gentleman		[Exhib Soc of BA, London, 886]; untraced		*Johnson* 1975, 432
14.	1828	Unidentified gentleman		[Exhib Soc of BA, London, 896]; untraced		*Johnson* 1975, 432
15.	1828	Unidentified gentleman		[Exhib Soc of BA, London, 905]; untraced		*Johnson* 1975, 432
16.	1828	Unidentified gentleman		[Exhib Soc of BA, London, 908]; untraced		*Johnson* 1975, 432
17.	1829	J B Rondeaux		[Exhib RA, London, 1141]; untraced		*Graves* VII, 1905–6, 191; *Johnson* 1975, 432
18.	1829	J L Seager		[Exhib Soc of BA, London, 839]; untraced		*Johnson* 1975, 432
19.	1829	'– Joliffe Esq'		[Exhib Soc of BA, London, 849]; untraced		*Johnson* 1975, 432
20.	1829	Rev Dr Crombie		[Exhib Soc of BA, London, 835]; untraced		*Johnson* 1975, 432
21.	1829	Rev J Sloper		[Exhib Soc of BA, London, 882]; untraced		*Johnson* 1975, 432
22.	1829	W Gray		[Exhib Soc of BA, London, 853]; untraced		*Johnson* 1975, 432
23.	1830	Julia N Shelly		[Exhib Soc of BA, London, 838]; untraced		*Johnson* 1975, 432
24.	1830	Lord Archibald Hamilton		[Exhib RA, London, 1271]; untraced		*Graves* VII, 1905–6, 191; *Johnson* 1975, 432
25.	1830	Rev Dr Gaskin		[Exhib Soc of BA, London, 851]; untraced		*Johnson* 1975, 432
26.	1830	T Massy		[Exhib Soc of BA, London, 834]; untraced		*Johnson* 1975, 432
27.	1831	W Joliffe	m	[Exhib RA, London, 1189]; untraced		*Graves* VII, 1905–6, 191
28.	1832	P Hesketh Fleetwood		[Exhib Soc of BA, London, 863]; untraced		*Johnson* 1975, 432
29.	1832	Professor Headington		[Exhib Soc of BA, London, 874]; untraced		*Johnson* 1975, 432
30.	1833	J Leslie		[Exhib Soc of BA, London, 830]; untraced		*Johnson* 1975, 432
31.	1833	William James		[Exhib Soc of BA, London, 864]; untraced		*Johnson* 1975, 432
32.	1834	Duke of Buckingham		[Exhib Soc of BA, London, 814]; untraced		*Johnson* 1975, 432
33.	1834	Lady A Joliffe		[Exhib Soc of BA, London, 857]; untraced		*Johnson* 1975, 432
34.	1834	Mrs Pollock		[Exhib Soc of BA, London, 854]; untraced		*Johnson* 1975, 432
35.	1836	Thomas Sambrook		[Exhib Soc of BA, London, 862]; untraced		*Johnson* 1975, 432
36.	1837	Dellamark Banks		[Exhib RA, London, 1252]; untraced		*Graves* VII, 1905–6, 191
37.	1837	J Bingham		[Exhib RA, London, 1268]; untraced		*Graves* VII, 1905–6, 191
38.	1837	Mr Chippindale		[Exhib RA, London, 1261]; untraced		*Graves* VII, 1905–6, 191
39.	1838	Unidentified subject		[Exhib Soc of BA, London, 602]; untraced		*Johnson* 1975, 432
40.	1840	Signor Costa		[Exhib RA, London, 1089]; untraced		*Graves* VII, 1905–6, 191
41.	1840	Unidentified		[Exhib RA, London, 1168]; untraced		*Graves* VII, 1905–6, 191
42.	1841	J Holdham		[Exhib RA, London, 1297]; untraced		*Graves* VII, 1905–6, 191
43.	1841	Unidentified gentleman		[Exhib RA, London, 1315]; untraced		*Graves* VII, 1905–6, 191
44.	1842	Daughter of Dr Gully	m	[Exhib RA, London, 1362]; untraced		*Graves* VII, 1905–6, 191
45.	1843	Mr Marsh		[Exhib RA, London, 1445]; untraced		*Graves* VII, 1905–6, 191
46.	1844	F Bramah		[Exhib RA, London, 1357]; untraced		*Graves* VII, 1905–6, 191
47.	1844	J Wilson		[Exhib RA, London, 1351]; untraced		*Graves* VII, 1905–6, 191
48.	1844	Richard Cobden		[Exhib RA, London, 1358]; untraced		*Graves* VII, 1905–6, 191; *Ormond* 1973, 107
49.	1846	J French		[Exhib RA, London, 1473]; untraced		*Graves* VII, 1905–6, 191
50.	1846	Unidentified gentleman		[Exhib RA, London, 1471]; untraced		*Graves* VII, 1905–6, 191
51.	1849	Thomas Bull		[Exhib RA, London, 1294]; untraced		*Graves* VII, 1905–6, 191
52.	1850	Charles Holtzapffel		[Exhib RA, London, 1413]; untraced		*Graves* VII, 1905–6, 192
53.	1850	Unidentified gentleman		[Exhib RA, London, 1408]; untraced		*Graves* VII, 1905–6, 192
54.	1852	Mrs Edelmann		[Exhib RA, London, 1472]; untraced		*Graves* VII, 1905–6, 192
55.	nd	John Arthur Roebuck		Mappin Art Gallery, Sheffield, W R Yorks		*Ormond* 1973, 398

Reliefs

56.	1829	Mary Carr, medallic portrait		[Exhib RA, London, 1103]; untraced	*Graves* VII, 1905–6, 191
57.	1829	Miss Mary Augusta Carr, medallic portrait		[Exhib RA, London, 1066]; untraced	*Graves* VII, 1905–6, 191
58.	1829	R Evans, medallic portrait		[Exhib RA, London, 1081]; untraced	*Graves* VII, 1905–6, 191
59.	1830	J Debelle, medallic portrait	w	[Exhib RA, London, 1127]; untraced	*Graves* VII, 1905–6, 191
60.	1830	Miss Carr, medallion		[Exhib Soc of BA, London, 865]; untraced	*Johnson* 1975, 432
61.	1831	Mrs Depree, medallic portrait	w	[Exhib RA, London, 1033]; untraced	*Graves* VII, 1905–6, 191
62.	1831	Unidentified lady, medallic portrait	w	[Exhib RA, London, 1037]; untraced	*Graves* VII, 1905–6, 191
63.	1833	James Depree, medallic portrait		[Exhib RA, London, 1042]; untraced	*Graves* VII, 1905–6, 191
64.	1833	Unidentified gentleman, medallic portrait	w	[Exhib Soc of BA, London, 813]; untraced	*Johnson* 1975, 432
65.	1833	Unidentified lady, medallic portrait		[Exhib Soc of BA, London, 863]; untraced	*Johnson* 1975, 432
66.	1834	King George IV and Frederick-Augustus, Duke of York and Albany, medallic portrait		[Exhib RA, London, 970]; untraced	*Graves* VII, 1905–6, 191
67.	1834	'The lady of' William Rhoads, medallic portrait		[Exhib RA, London, 996]; untraced	*Graves* VII, 1905–6, 191
68.	1847	'Medallic portrait of a friend'		[Exhib RA, London, 1298]; untraced	*Graves* VII, 1905–6, 191
69.	1847	W Clowes, medallic portrait		[Exhib RA, London, 1303]; untraced	*Graves* VII, 1905–6, 191
70.	1850	Peter McLeod, medallic portrait	w	[Exhib RA, London, 1079]; untraced	*Graves* VII, 1905–6, 192
71.	1850	Unidentified lady, medallic portrait	w	[Exhib RA, London, 1078]; untraced	*Graves* VII, 1905–6, 192

Miscellaneous

72.	1827	Frederick-Augustus, Duke of York and Albany		[Exhib RA, London, 1040]; untraced	*Graves* VII, 1905–6, 191
73.	1828	Peter McIntosh	w	[Exhib RA, London, 1053]; untraced	*Graves* VII, 1905–6, 191
74.	1828	Samuel Joseph of Edinburgh	w	[Exhib RA, London, 1087]; untraced	*Graves* VII, 1905–6, 191; *Gunnis* 1968, 222; *Friedman* 1980 (1), 28, n15
75.	1829	G Henekey, model	w	[Exhib Soc of BA, London, 844]; untraced	*Johnson* 1975, 432
76.	1829	Mrs G Henekey	w	[Exhib Soc of BA, London, 888]; untraced	*Johnson* 1975, 432
77.	1829	Mrs Henekey, model	w	[Exhib Soc of BA, London, 841]; untraced	*Johnson* 1975, 432
78.	1829	The fair penitent		[Exhib BI, London, 537]; untraced	*Graves* 1875, 503
79.	1830	Macduff		[Exhib RA, London, 1192]; untraced	*Graves* VII, 1905–6, 191; *Johnson* 1975, 432
80.	1831	Miss Emma Murray as Spring	w	[Exhib RA, London, 1042]; untraced	*Graves* VII, 1905–6, 191; *Johnson* 1975, 432
81.	1831	The chameleon		[Exhib BI, London, 555]; untraced	*Graves* 1875, 503
82.	1834	James Dupree		[Exhib Soc of BA, London, 855]; untraced	*Johnson* 1975, 432
83.	1835	Mrs Rhodes	w	[Exhib Soc of BA, London, 774]; untraced	*Johnson* 1975, 432
84.	1872	R J Holland		[Exhib RA, London, 1496]; untraced	*Graves* VII, 1905–6, 192
85.	1877	Selim Rothwell		[Exhib RA, London, 1537]; untraced	*Graves* VII, 1905–6, 192
86.	1877	William Poole		[Exhib RA, London, 1533]; untraced	*Graves* VII, 1905–6, 192

SMITH, Thomas, of Stamford fl *c*1820–40

He was a general builder and marble mason who signed a number of mural monuments in churches in and around Stamford between *c*1820 and 1840. Most of these are neo-Hellenic in style. From 1828–32 he was the mason in charge at Burghley. In 1832 he set up business in the town, but on leaving Stamford in 1842, sold his stock (*Stamford Mercury*, 16 May 1834, 23 Sept 1842).

Literary References: *Gunnis* 1968, 354

Archival References: JP, Misc Corr

Funerary Monuments

1.	?1828	Francis Waters	Rippingale, Lincs	*Gunnis* 1968, 354
2.	†1831	George Parker	Edenham, Lincs	Pevsner, *Lincs*, 1989, 269
3.	†1834	Henry Williams	Witham-on-the-Hill, Lincs	Pevsner, *Lincs*, 1989, 807
4.	†1835	Martha Etough	St Martin, Stamford, Lincs	Pevsner, *Lincs*, 1989, 693
5.	†1835	Penelope Spurr	Sleaford, Lincs	Pevsner, *Lincs*, 1989, 653
6.	?1837	Emma Mason	Kingscliffe, Northants	*Gunnis* 1968, 354
7.	?1837	Rev William Hardyman	North Luffenham, Rutland	*Gunnis* 1968, 354
8.	nd	Several, unidentified subjects, tablets	St Mary, Stamford, Lincs	Pevsner, *Lincs*, 1989, 695

SMITH, W fl *c*1689

Probably a Durham artist, he signs the altar-tomb with a life-size recumbent figure of Michael Matthew, portrayed in contemporary costume with a book in his hand (1).

Literary References: *Gunnis* 1968, 360

Funerary Monuments

1.	†1689	Michael Matthew	s	Whitburn, Durham	S	Pevsner, *Durham*, 1983, 503

SMITH, William I fl *c*1726

He was probably a Liverpool craftsman and was the principal carver at St George's Church, Liverpool in 1726 (Liverpool City Corp cash book). He is possibly the 'W Smith' who was the master-mason for the church in 1715 (City Archives).

Literary References: *Gunnis* 1968, 360

Archival References: GPC

Architectural Sculpture

1.	1726	Decorative ornaments	[St George, Liverpool, Lancs]; untraced	GPC

SMITH, William II fl 1765–70

A William Smith signs the large architectural tablet with a broken pediment and flaming lamps to Ralph Manning (1). He may be the William Smith, son of Samuel Smith of Rochester, who was apprenticed in 1765 to Thomas Vidgeon. Three years later he was 'by order of the Lord Mayor and Court of Aldermen discharged from the said Thomas Vidgen, for his neglecting to inroll him', and was apprenticed instead to George Freshwater. Smith's new master 'turned him out of his Service and refused to receive him therein again', so that from 1770 he was obliged to finish his apprenticeship with John Wynne (Masons' Co, Court Book 1751–96, 19 Aug 1765, 5 July 1768, 25 Oct 1770).

In 1788 a William Smith, possibly the same, was paid £1,060 for mason's work when Chevening was rebuilt, this included carved stonework on both fronts (Stanhope Archives, Chevening).

Literary References: *Gunnis* 1968, 360; *Webb* 1999, 31

Archival References: GPC

Funerary Monuments

1.	†1769	Ralph Manning	Westerham, Kent	S	*Gunnis* 1968, 360

SMITH, William III c1758–

The son of John Smith, of Dunchurch, Warwick, he was apprenticed to **Thomas Beard** in 1772 and became free of the Masons' Company in 1785. His yard was in Jermyn Street, London. He signed a 'very pretty' tablet to Matthew Armstrong (1) (*Gunnis* 1968, 360).

Funerary Monuments

1.	?1801	Matthew Armstrong	St Magnus, London Bridge	S	*Gunnis* 1968, 360

SMITH, William IV 1790/1?–

A wax modeller. For further information the reader is referred to *Pyke* 1973, 139.

SMITH, William V 1808–

He attended the Royal Academy Schools in April 1826 on the recommendation of J Wood, giving his address as 21 John Street, Crutched Friars, London. He won silver medals in the following year and again in 1830.

Literary References: *Gunnis* 1968, *Hutchison* 1960–62, 179

Archival References: RA Admissions

SMITH, William, of Warwick 1705–47

He was the eldest surviving son of **Francis Smith of Warwick** and succeeded him in his business as an architect and master builder. After his father's death in 1738 he took over the contract for the masonry of the Radcliffe Library in Oxford, which he completed shortly before his death in April 1747, in conjunction with the Oxford mason, **John Townesend.** Colvin describes him as a competent provincial Palladian with some indebtedness to Gibbs. He was responsible for architectural work at 10 known significant houses in Derbys, Leics, Northants and Oxon, and also considerable rebuilding at Lamport church. In 1737 he provided a chimneypiece for Lamport Hall (1). In 1744, whilst working at Stoneleigh Abbey, he was paid for a fountain (2): he added to his bill 'I have charged nothing for ye designs and estimates of the Hall, nor any profits out of ye work at ye Chapell or ye Dog Kennell or anything else' (Archives, Lord Leigh cited by RG/JP, 7, 1326).

Literary References: *Gunnis* 1968, 360; *Colvin* 1995, 902–3

Chimneypieces

1.	1737	Dove marble	[Lamport Hall, Northants]; untraced	Isham Archives *in Gunnis* 1968, 360

Architectural Sculpture

2.	1744	Fountain	Stoneleigh Abbey, Warks	Archives Lord Leigh, quoted by RG/JP 7, 1326

SMITH, William, of York fl 1703–14

He worked in partnership with **John Elsworth** at Castle Howard between 1703 and 1714. A Major Smith, who may have been related to William, is also mentioned in the house accounts.

Literary References: *Gunnis* 1968, 141, 360; *Saumarez Smith*, 1990, 60

Archival References: Castle Howard Archives, G2/2 selected bills; Castle Howard Building Account Books G2/1/1–2

SMITH & COX fl 1799

Their tradecard of 1799 describes them as stone masons of Broadway, Deptford, providers of monuments, tombs, chimneypieces and headstones 'in the neatest manner' (Banks 106.29).

SMOOTE fl 1663–65

He was the master mason employed by the Duke of Richmond and Lennox for additions to Cobham Hall, Kent, in 1663–1665 (TNA, c.108/53). It is possible that he may have been the father of **John Smout** (or **Smoot**).

Archival References: GPC

SMOUT (or SMOOTE), John fl 1704–15

He was chiefly a carver of marble and stone chimneypieces. In 1704 he was paid for five chimneypieces at Chatsworth: the reference reads 'Paid James Smoot on Account of the Price of five Chimny peeces for ye West front of Chatsworth. £22.0.0'. In 1708 he was paid £555 7s 9d for stonework at the 'New Summerhouse at the lower end of the Garden' at Kensington Palace. This is thought to be the famous alcove now removed to the fountain garden at the head of the Serpentine. A 'Jno Smooter, mason', who may be the same man, received £629 2s 1d for other stonework in the same year. In 1712 he was paid for Purbeck paving at the lodgings in St James's Palace of Thomas Coke, Vice-Chamberlain to Queen Anne (Archives, Marquis of Lothian cited in *Gunnis* 1968, 360).

Literary References: *Bolton and Hendry* 1930, 189

Chimneypieces

1.	1704	Five	m	Chatsworth, Derbys, west front rooms	Chatsworth Accts, vol vii, 81
2.	1706	Portland stone and marble		[Whitehall Palace, London]; untraced	TNA WORK E 351/3312; *Gunnis* 1968, 360

3.	1706	Reigate and Portland stone	s	[Palace of Westminster, London]; destroyed	TNA WORK E 351/3312; *Gunnis* 1968, 360
4.	1709	Description not available		[Tower of London, City of London]; untraced	TNA AO 1/2248/38–40; *Gunnis* 1968, 360
5.	1709	Description unavailable		[Denmark House, London]; untraced	TNA AO 1/2248/38–40; *Gunnis* 1968, 360
6.	1710	Description unavailable		[St James's Palace, London]; untraced	TNA AO 1/2248/38–40; *Gunnis* 1968, 360
Architectural Sculpture					
7.	1715	'Great marble bason'		Bushy Park, London	TNA AO 1/2248/38–40; *Gunnis* 1968, 360
Miscellaneous					
8.	1710	Two veined marble tables	m	[Queen's closet, Newmarket Palace]; untraced	TNA AO 1/2248/38–40; *Gunnis* 1968, 360

SMYTH, Edward *c*1745–1812

Smyth was born in County Meath, reputedly the son of a stone-cutter who settled in Dublin *c*1750. He was apprenticed to **Simon Vierpyl** and in 1772, while employed by Vierpyl, he exhibited a competition-winning model for a statue of the patriot, Charles Lucas, which the merchants of Dublin had determined to erect in their new Royal Exchange (**6**). He exhibited the model in 1772. The statue, for which he was paid £300 was considered 'an astonishing performance for a young man of very limited opportunities' (*Crookshank*). Smyth next found employment with the stonecutter Henry Darley, carving plaques for chimneypieces and memorials such as the 'finely wrought' one to Lieutenant Dobbs in Lisburn Cathedral (**1**). With the exception of the Lucas statue and a more conventional one of the Marquis of Buckingham (**2**), his sculpture is principally architectural.

Darley was principal contractor for the Dublin Custom House, 1781–91, where an extensive scheme of decorative ornaments was proposed by its architect, James Gandon. Smyth made the models for the internal decoration of the cupola and these so impressed Gandon that he was awarded a number of independent commissions for the building, including four sets of the arms of Ireland, in which his design was judged superior to a proposal by **Agostino Carlini**. In Smyth's tour-de-force at the Custom House, 14 keystone heads emblematic of the rivers of Ireland, he was aided by **Benjamin Schrowder** (**11**). Gandon wrote warmly of Smyth's talents: 'Mr E Smyth a native of Ireland, a gentleman who without having the advantage of travel or the opportunity of seeing many specimens of sculpture, has given proof of abilities equal to any in the three kingdoms' (*Curran* 1947, 67).

His subsequent work for Gandon included keystone heads for Carlisle bridge (**14**), statues on the pediment of the House of Lords extension to the Parliament House (**13**), internal and external carving at the Four Courts (**17, 18**) and extensive work at the King's Inns (**16**). After Gandon's retirement, Smyth was taken up by the architect Francis Johnston, who commissioned the statue of St Andrew (**19**) and three statues on the Bank of Ireland (**20**). At the time of his death he was completing work on two other Johnston buildings, the Chapel Royal at Dublin Castle, where he was assisted by his son, **John Smyth**, and St George's church (**21, 23**).

Potterton considers his monuments 'extremely poor both in design and execution' by comparison with his architectural sculpture. The Handcock has a female figure, possibly the widow who erected the memorial, leaning on a medallion portrait, with a second medallion, of enormous size, around her neck (**5**). The Buckingham (**2**) is scarcely a sepulchral monument, since he is arrayed in the robes of the Order of St Patrick, instituted in 1783, when he was Viceroy of Ireland. Potterton attributes a number of monuments to Smyth including one to Major General Preston, †1788, at Kilmessan, Co Meath and another to Baron Lecale, †1810, in Bright, Co Down (*Potterton* repr 49), the latter of which which could also be by his son, John. Harbison, Potterton and Sheehy suggest that Smyth's workshop is likely to have been responsible for a number of chimneypieces in an Adamesque style. They particularly draw attention to one in the hall at Mount Kennedy, Co Wicklow, which has lions' masks, swags and an Irish harp in a roundel. The bust of George III is merely signed 'Smyth' and appears to have been carved in collaboration with his son (**9**).

In June 1811 Smyth was appointed master of the Dublin Society school of modelling and sculpture, a post which he held for only a short time. He died suddenly at his house at 36 Montgomery Street on 2 August 1812 and was buried in St Thomas's graveyard, Marlborough Street, Dublin, two days later. O'Dwyer describes him as 'shy and retiring but sociable among friends' and 'the most talented Irish sculptor of his day'. Apparently he had little interest in business matters and left his family scantily provided for (*Strickland*). The name of his wife is not known; they had several children.

Literary References: *Strickland* 2, 1913, 383–390; *Leask* 1945, 187–194; *Curran* 1947, 67–9; *Crookshank* 1966, 308–10; *Potterton* 1975, 79–81; *Harbison, Potterton and Sheehy* 1978, 176–7; *Hill* 1998, 54; *Grove* 29, 894 (Turpin); *ODNB* (O'Donoghue, O'Dwyer)

Miscellaneous Drawings: design for an unidentified monument, sd, Penrose-Wyatt designs, Nat Lib of Wales (*Potterton* repr 52).

Portraits of the Sculptor: J Camerford del, H Meyer sculpt, engraving, nd, *Archit Review* Feb 1947, 67

Funerary Monuments						
1.	1780	Lieutenant William Dobbs		Lisburn Cathedral, Co Antrim		*Potterton* 1975, 63, 80 (repr)
2.	1783	George, 1st Marquess of Buckingham, Viceroy of Ireland		St Patrick's Cathedral, Dublin		*Curran* 1947, 67; *Potterton* 1975, 80
3.	1788	Earl Temple, statue		St Patrick's Cathedral, Dublin		*ODNB*
4.	†1789	James, Viscount Clifton		Gowran, Co Kilkenny	S	*Potterton* 1975, 80
5.	†1794	William Handcock		Athlone, Co Roscommon		*Potterton* 1975, 80
Statues						
6.	1772	Charles Lucas Payment(s): £300		City Hall, Dublin		*Wright* 1821, 320–1; *Curran* 1947, 67 (repr); *Potterton* 1975, 79
Busts						
7.	1789	Professor William Clement MP		Trinity College, Dublin, Long Room		*Crookshank* 1986, 24, 28 (repr)
8.	1789	Thomas Parnell (†1718)		Trinity College, Dublin, Long Room		*Crookshank* 1986, 24
9.	?1809	King George III (perhaps by John Smyth)	m	NGI 8038	S	*Crookshank* 1966, 309, 310 (repr); *Harbison, Potterton and Sheehy* 1978, 176–7
10.	nd	Francis Johnston and wife (two)	m	Ulster Museum		*ODNB*

Architectural Sculpture

11.	post-1781	Fourteen riverine keystone heads, trophies of arms, figures of Plenty and Industry (formerly on south pediment); Hibernia and Britannia with Neptune in south tympanum (designed by Agostino Carlini); ox-head friezes, figure of Commerce and four heads surmounting dome (building designed by Joseph Gandon) Model(s): at least 2 sets of riverine heads prepared in wax, 12 exhib 1802, presented by Gandon to RHA, but destroyed 1916 uprising; another set Dublin Civic Museum		Dublin Custom House, restored after extensive damage	*Crookshank* 1966, 310–11 (keystone heads repr); *Harbison, Potterton and Sheehy* 1978, 176 (trophies repr); *Hill* 1998, 56–8; *ODNB*
12.	1789	Keystones and panels		Bishop's gate, Derry	*ODNB*
13.	pre-1789	Three		House of Lords extension, Parliament House, Dublin	*ODNB*
14.	by 1795	Two keystone heads (designed by James Gandon)		[Carlisle Bridge, Dublin]; unidentified building on Sir John Rogerson's quay, Dublin	*ODNB*
15.	1798–1799	Hibernia		[RDS, Hawkins St, Dublin]; RDS showground, Ballsbridge, entrance to jumping enclosure	*White and Bright* 1998, 85
16.	begun 1800	Three large figurative panels at attic level, west front, pair of caryatidic doorcases and statues in stucco for Benchers' dining room		King's Inns, Dublin	*Hill* 1998, 60; *ODNB*
17.	pre-1802	Four history panels, eight high-relief figures of Justice, Liberty, Eloquence, Punishment etc, eight medallions of law-givers, decorative frieze and other ornaments		[Four Courts, Dublin]; some destroyed 1922	*Curran* 1947, 67–9; *ODNB*
18.	pre-1802	Moses, Wisdom, Justice, Mercy and Authority, statues (designed by Joseph Gandon)		The Four Courts, Dublin, Ireland, surmounting façade (perhaps destroyed)	*Curran* 1947, 67–9; *Crookshank* 1966, 308
19.	1803	St Andrew		St Andrew, Dublin	*ODNB*
20.	1808	Three statues (designed by T Mulvany after Flaxman)		Bank of Ireland, Dublin, south pediment	*Crookshank* 1966, 308; *Hill* 1998, 58–9 (Liberty and Hibernia repr); *ODNB*
21.	1807–1812	Heads, angelic terms, figures of Faith, Hope and Charity, the Evangelists for the exterior, and interior stucco work (designed by Francis Johnston)		Dublin Castle, Chapel Royal	*Curran* 1947, 67–8; *ODNB*
22.	nd	Frieze (designed by Ensor and Richard Johnston)		Rotunda, Dublin	*Curran* 1947, 67–8
23.	nd	Three keystones representing Faith, Hope and Charity (designed by Francis Johnston)		St George, Dublin	*Curran* 1947, 67–8; *ODNB*

Miscellaneous

24.	1782	Crucifix	wd	Navan, Co Meath	*ODNB*

SMYTH, George 1818–

The younger son of **John Smyth ARHA**, he worked with his brother, **William Smyth**. He had a son, also George, who was still living in 1913 and working as a sculptor, chiefly on ecclesiastical decoration, from premises at 193 Great Brunswick Street, Dublin.

Literary References: *Strickland* 2, 1913, 392

SMYTH, John, ARHA *c*1773–1840

Born in Dublin, the son of **Edward Smyth**, he studied with his father at 36 Montgomery Street and enrolled in the Dublin Society's figure drawing school in 1791. In 1809 he showed a bust of George III at the exhibition in Hawkins Street, a work probably carved in collaboration with his father (**17**). He apparently exhibited busts again in 1811, 1813, 1815, 1817 and 1819.

Like his father, he was responsible for a number of statues for public buildings in Dublin, but his work, though of merit, is inferior to Edward's (**28, 29, 31**). He completed his father's work at Dublin Castle in 1814 (**27**) and succeeded him in the mastership of the Dublin Society's modelling school in 1812. His most important piece of stucco work was the *Ascension*, a large figurative composition in the apse of the Pro-cathedral (**29**).

He was also responsible for a number of monuments showing considerable variety, though Crookshank says they are notable chiefly for the curious proportions of the figures. The Thompson (**7**) has a life-size figure of *Religion* seated by an urn and pedestal and the Carpendale, a personification of *Science* in front of a pyramid, with book and doused torch (**8**). The MacDowell makes use of a relief of an angel, kneeling at an altar with the staff of Aesculapius (**11**).

Commissions for statues were very sparse. Hill suggests that Smyth may have carved the figure of John Switzer in a niche in the gardens of St James's Asylum, Kilkenny and the sculptor certainly repaired the statue of William III on College Green after it was blown up in 1836, replacing the left arm and leg, and the head which he modelled from a bust by **John Nost III** (**16**). His only identified chimneypiece is noted by Crookshank as having a panel of great charm (**26**).

In 1824 Smyth became one of the original associates of the Royal Hibernian Academy and contributed to its exhibitions in 1826, 1830 and 1831, resigning his associateship in 1834. His wife was named Mary and he had two sons, **William Smyth** and **George Smyth**. He died in March 1840.

Literary References: *Strickland* 2, 1913, 390–392; *Crookshank* 1966, 310; *Potterton* 1975, 81–82); *Harbison, Potterton and Sheehy* 1978, 177–9, 218; *ODNB* (O'Donoghue, O'Dwyer); *Hill* 1998, 74–5 (repr)

Funerary Monuments

1.	†1812	Rev Dubourdieu	Lisburn, Co Antrim	S	*Potterton* 1975, 82
2.	†1813	Elizabeth Phibbs	St Anne, Dublin	S	*Potterton* 1975, 81
3.	†1814	Brigadier Arthur Gore	Goresbridge, Co Kilkenny		*Potterton* 1975, 82
4.	†1814	John Boardman	[Grand Lodge of Freemasons of Ireland]; St Patrick's Cathedral, Dublin		*Potterton* 1975, 81
5.	†1814	Rt Hon George Ogle	St Patrick's Cathedral, Dublin		*Potterton* 1975, 81
6.	1817	John Ball, Serjeant-at-Law †1813	St Patrick's Cathedral, Dublin		*Strickland* 2, 1913, 392; *Potterton* 1975, 81
7.	†1818	Acheson Thompson	Newry, Co Down		*Potterton* 1975, 82
8.	1818	Rev Thomas Carpendale	Armagh Cathedral		*Potterton* 1975, 81
9.	1819	Major-General Henry Davis	Newry, Co Down		*Potterton* 1975, 29, 82 (repr)
10.	†1833	Sir Charles Giesecke	St George, Dublin		*Potterton* 1975, 69, 81 (repr)
11.	†1835	Dr Ephraim MacDowell	St George, Dublin		*Potterton* 1975, 81
12.	†1835	Rev Thomas Elrington	Ferns Cathedral, Co Wexford		*Potterton* 1975, 29, 81–82 (repr)
13.	†1836	Sarah Hamilton	Newry, Co Down		*Potterton* 1975, 82
14.	†1837	Rev John Magee	Drogheda, Co Louth	S	*Potterton* 1975, 81
15.	nd	Rev Mr Brown	Trinity Church, Newport, Rhode Island, USA		GPC

Statues

16.	post-1836	King William III, repairs only	College Green, Dublin		*Strickland* 2, 1913, 391

Busts

17.	1809	King George III (co-sculptor: Edward Smyth)	[Exhib Dublin Soc]; NGI		*Crookshank* 1966, 309 (repr)
18.	1813	William Dease, surgeon	[Exhib Dublin]; RCS, Dublin		*Strickland* 2, 1913, 392
19.	1819	Charles, Earl Whitworth, Lord Lieutenant	[Exhib Dublin]; Secretary's office, General Post Office, Dublin (1913)		*Strickland* 2, 1913, 392
20.	1826	Hon George Knox	RHA, Dublin		*Strickland* 2, 1913, 392
21.	1826	John Shekleton	[Exhib RHA, Dublin]; RCS, Dublin		*Strickland* 2, 1913, 392
22.	1830	John Egan	RHA		*Strickland* 2, 1913, 392
23.	1831	John Hamilton of Annandale	RHA, Dublin		*Strickland* 2, 1913, 392
24.	nd	John Claudius Beresford	RDS		*Strickland* 2, 1913, 392
25.	nd	King George IV	RCS, Dublin		*ODNB*

Chimneypieces

26.	nd	with charming panel	RDS, Dublin		*Crookshank* 1966, 310

Architectural Sculpture

27.	to 1814	Carved ornaments (co-sculptor: Edward Smyth)	Dublin Castle, Chapel Royal		*ODNB*
28.	1817	Hibernia, Mercury and fidelity	General Post Office, Dublin, above portico		*Strickland* 2, 1913, 392
29.	*c*1823	Ascension	St Mary's Pro-cathedral, Dublin		*ODNB*
30.	1827	Aesculapius, supported by Minerva and Hygeia, and royal arms in tympanum	RCS, Dublin		*Strickland* 2, 1913, 392; *ODNB*
31.	nd	Heads of Palladio, Michelangelo and Raphael	RHA, Abbey St, Dublin, over entrance door and windows		*Strickland* 2, 1913, 392
32.	nd	Heads of Peace, Hibernia, Commerce, Plenty, River Liffey, Industry	Richmond Bridge, Dublin		*Strickland* 2, 1913, 392

SMYTH, William 1804–

The son of **John Smyth ARHA**, he entered the Dublin Society's modelling school in 1814 at the age of ten and afterwards worked in his father's studio, but did not gain any eminence in his profession. After his father's death in 1840 he was an unsuccessful candidate for the mastership of the Dublin Society's modelling school. He afterwards went to London and died there in obscurity.

Literary References: *Strickland* 2, 1913, 391

Architectural Sculpture

1.	nd	Decorative carving	Marlborough Street Church, Dublin		*Strickland* II, 1913, 391

SMYTHE, James, of Woodbridge 1771–

A Suffolk craftsman, he signed a pretty architectural tablet, with an urn and cockle-shells to left and right (1). His wife Ann, died a few weeks after her husband.

Literary References: *Gunnis* 1968, 361

Funerary Monuments

1.	?1816	John Higgs	Grundisburgh, Suffolk	S	*Gunnis* 1968, 361

SNELL, T M

For information the reader is referred to *Pyke* 1973, 139

SNOW, J, of Droitwich fl *c*1840–42

He was responsible for several plain tablets in the Droitwich area. (Inf. Mike Wall)

Funerary Monuments

1.	†1840	Coningsby Norbury	St Andrew, Droitwich, Worcs	S	
2.	†1840	Thomas Gale	St Andrew, Droitwich, Worcs	S	
3.	†1842	Elizabeth and Richard (†1832) Smith	St Andrew, Droitwich, Worcs	S	

SOANE, Charles 1690–1764

He was both a master builder and an architect, and in this dual capacity erected the parish church of St George Gravesend, in 1731, being paid £3,824 (TNA c.108/140). Soane is buried in the churchyard close to the west door.

Archival References: GPC

SOANES, Joseph fl 1764

He was an assistant to **John Francis Moore**.

Literary References: *Gunnis* 1968, 361

Chimneypieces

1.	1764	Several	[Audley End, Essex]; untraced	Essex Record Office, D./DBY 243 in *Gunnis* 1968, 361

SOARE, Edward fl 1801

On a tradecard of 1801, decorated with a craftsman flanked by four different types of urn and two obelisks, Soar described his business as a 'Petrification manufactory'. Based at 25 Long Acre, London, he offered 'the most elegan assortment of Derbyshire Spar Ornaments, both natural and artificial, likewise all sorts of marble stands for Tim Pieces'. He also advertised 'Masons Work executed in the neatest manner' (BM Banks 106.30).

SOLDANI, Massimiliano 1656–1740

He was master of the Mint in Florence and in addition to medallions, produced full-size casts in bronze of ancien and renaissance statues as well as elaborate mythological subjects of his own. It was probably sculpture after th Antique and portrait medals that initially attracted English tourists to his studio opposite the entrance to the Uffizi Two commissions came in 1703 (**6, 7**) but his most influential portrait, of Sir Henry Newton, the British representativ at the Grand-ducal court, followed in 1707 (**8**). Newton proved to be a valuable go-between, introducing several fellov countrymen to Soldani.

One of Soldani's British patrons was Sir John Percival, later Earl of Egmont, who spent six months in Italy durin his grand tour. A letter to Percival from the grand-ducal chamberlain, Lorenzo Magnolfi, dated 22 November 170 mentions 24 heads and three statues ordered by Percival and packed up for dispatch. Avery suggests that the 'head may have been medals of Roman emperors and empresses (**10**). The letter also mentions sets of heads for two othe British buyers (**11, 12**).

In 1709 John, Duke of Marlborough began negotiations with the sculptor via the British consul in Leghorn Christopher Crowe, for a set of full-size bronze casts after the principle marble statues then in the Uffizi's Tribun (**1**). Soldani proposed all six, but two, the *Celestial Venus* and the *Venus Victrix*, were not required. The commissio is documented in a letter to Marlborough of 28 April 1710 from Sir John Vanbrugh, the architect of Blenheim, i which he refers to two letters recently received from Sir Henry Newton. Newton had obtained permission from th Grand Duke Cosimo III for the casts to be made and had immediately set Soldani to work. The Duchess howeve suspended work, pending further directions from the Duke. These must have been forthcoming and, since all fou bronzes bear the date 1711, they were probably completed and delivered to Blenheim that year. A pair of bronz statuettes after Renaissance marble statues by Benvenuto Cellini and Michelangelo also found their way to Blenheir and Avery conjectures that these may have been a present sent by Soldani after receiving a full payment equivalen to more than 1100 Spanish doubloons (**5**).

Lord Burlington visited Florence in 1715 and purchased a set of bronze narrative reliefs of *The seasons* fro Soldani (**9**). These were presented to George II at an unknown date. Other casts commissioned by Burlingto including a group of *Venus and Adonis*, a *Leda and the Swan* and a *Ganymede* which were never paid for, and so wer not forwarded to Burlington.

During his later years Soldani attempted to market a number of bronze statuettes in Britain through an agent i London named Zamboni, but perhaps without success.

Literary References: *Avery* 2005, 8–29

Statues

1.	1709–1711	The dancing faun, arrotino, the wrestlers and the Venus de' Medici	b	Blenheim Palace, Oxon, formerly all in the gardens, Venus de' Medici and dancing faun now in the marble hall	SD	*Treasure Houses* 1985, 292–3 (repr); *Avery* 2005, 11–14
2.	pre-1716	'A dozen', after statues in the Uffizi, statuettes	b	[coll Lord Burlington]; Chatsworth, Derbys		*Avery* 2005, 14 (Pomona repr)
3.	1717	Andromeda and the sea-monster, statuette for a table	b	Private coll		*Avery* 2005, 20–1 (repr)
4.	1717	Venus and Adonis Model(s): Cleveland Museum of Art, Ohio, clay	b	Syston Park, Lincs (1996)		*Avery* 2005, 17–19 (repr)
5.	nd	Ganymede and the eagle, and Bacchus, statuettes	b	Blenheim Palace, Oxon		*Avery* 2005, 14

Reliefs

6.	1703	Dr John Inglis, portrait medal	b	Untraced		*Avery* 2005, 9
7.	1703	William, 2nd Earl of Jersey, portrait medal	b	Untraced		*Avery* 2005, 9
8.	1707	Sir Henry Newton, portrait medal	b	Private coll, London		*Avery* 2005, 9 (repr)
9.	1715	The seasons	b	[coll Lord Burlington]; Royal Coll Other versions: Summer and Autumn, 1725, ex coll Sir Sampson Gideon; Spencer Museum of Art, Univ of Kansas at Lawrence		*Avery* 2005, 15

Miscellaneous

10.	1707	24 heads, perhaps medals, and three statues	b	[for Sir John Percival of Burton, Co Cork]; perhaps identifiable with a series of medals, private coll (repr *Avery* 2005, 10)		*Avery* 2005, 9–11

11.	1707	Sets of heads	b	[for Sir Thomas Samwell of Upton, Northants]; untraced	*Avery* 2005, 10–11
12.	1707	Sets of heads	b	[for Robert Furnese of Wildershare, Kent]; untraced	*Avery* 2005, 10–11

SOUTH, R, of London fl c1812

Funerary Monuments

1.	†1812	Francis Wheate	St Mary, Glympton, Oxon		RG/JP, 7, 1328v.

SOUTHERN, of Ditton fl c1840

Funerary Monuments

1.	c1840	Richard Patten and family	Much Wenlock, Salop		RG/JP, 7, 1328v.

SOWARD, John fl 1802?–c1845

Perhaps a son of George Soward, who is listed in the Westminster Poll Book of 1748 as having a mason's yard in Chapel Street and who carried out major repairs at St Anne's, Soho in 1761 (WPL, A.2312). John Soward's yard was in Tottenham Court Road. His monuments and tablets are 'not very exciting' (*Gunnis* 1968, 361). The best works are the large altar-tomb commemorating Eliza Harris (**1**), the tablet in coloured marbles to Spelman Swaine, and the tablet to Lady Sondes (**2, 5**). The Sondes has a well-carved relief of two angels guiding the deceased to heaven. The monument to James Sparrow is a large white marble plaque surmounted by a coat of arms on a black marble ground (**17**). The monuments to Miss Livermore and John Hooper, and the black and white marble memorial to John Sparrow, are signed 'J. Soward and Son' (**16–18**). Soward was also a heraldic painter and in 1831 executed two of the 4th Earl of Darnley hatchments, one for Cobham Hall and the other for his London house (Archives, Earl of Darnley).

Literary References: *Gunnis* 1968, 361

Funerary Monuments

1.	?1802	Eliza Harris	Hillingdon churchyard, Middx		*Gunnis* 1968, 361
2.	?1803	Spelman Swaine	Leverington, Cambs		GPC
3.	?1810	Shadrach Brise	Cavendish, Suffolk		*Gunnis* 1968, 361
4.	†1814	William Alexander	St George, Bloomsbury, London	S	
5.	†1818	Lady Sondes	St Mary, Norton, Kent		Pevsner, *Kent: N E & E*, 1983, 408
6.	?1821	Charlotte Prendergrass	St Giles-in-the-Fields, London		*Gunnis* 1968, 361
7.	?1821	Rev Joseph Jefferson	Witham, Essex		*Gunnis* 1968, 361
8.	†1821	Sir James Mansfield	St George, Bloomsbury, London	S	
9.	†1823	Rev Thomas (†1789) and Mrs Catherine Willis	Marshfield, Glos	S	Pevsner, *Glos: Cotswolds*, 1999, 469
10.	?1824	James Spawforth	Horbury, W R Yorks		*Gunnis* 1968, 361
11.	†1824	Thomas Leverton	St Giles-in-the-Fields, London	S	GPC
12.	?1827	Mrs Pedley	Everton, Beds		*Gunnis* 1968, 361
13.	†1828	Anthony (†1809) and Mary (†1828) Peacock	South Kyme, Lincs		Pevsner, *Lincs*, 1989, 665
14.	†1830	George Blake	St James Garlickhythe, City of London	S	RG/JP, 7, 1329
15.	?1831	Anne Burley	Basing, Hants		*Gunnis* 1968, 361
16.	?1831	Miss Livermore	St John, Hackney, London	S	*Gunnis* 1968, 361
17.	†1838	James Sparrow	Gosfield, Essex	S	*Gunnis* 1968, 361
18.	†1845	John Jefferies Hooper	Moreton-in-Marsh, Glos	S	Pevsner, *Glos: Cotswolds*, 1999, 489

SPANG, Michael Henry –1762

Little is known of Spang's origins, but he was a native of Denmark who came over to England about 1756 and remained here until his death. In 1758 he received a premium of 39 guineas for modelling the 'seal of the Society of Arts used for letters' from a design by Cipriani. He used wax as a preliminary medium in his work.

In 1759 Spang made chimneypieces for several parade rooms at Kedleston at a total cost of £990 (**11–13**). He drew a design for a painted ceiling in the drawing room, celebrating naval victories over the French, but this was not realised since Adam did not favour frescoed ceilings. In 1759 he also procured a model of a ship for Lord Scarsdale. In 1760 he carved the dolphins and prows of ships on the stone screen of the Whitehall entrance to the Admiralty (**14**), and in the same year executed three statues for the front of Spencer House, London (**15**).

His monument to James Thomson, †1748, was erected in Westminster Abbey about 1760. It has a life-size seated figure of Thomson in a toga, a book in one hand and the Cap of Liberty in the other. On the circular pedestal on which Thomson's arm rests are four enchanting reliefs of the seasons, commemorating his most famous poem (**1**).

Spang was on the list of artists who met at the Foundling Hospital in 1760 together with **William Tyler**, **Joseph Wilton**, **Richard Hayward** and Roubiliac (*Builder* 1859, 849). He exhibited with the Society of Artists from 1760–62 (**3, 8, 9, 16–19**). He signed a bronzed terra-cotta statuette of William Hogarth (**6**). Bilbey notes a reference in the VAM records to the similarity between the Hogarth and another statuette in the collection, previously identified as Matthew Prior and ascribed to **L F Roubiliac**, which may have been executed by Spang.

The sculptor left little or no money at his death. A sale of his belongings was held at Little Stanhope Street, near Mayfair Chapel, on 21 December 1762. Among the lots were various models and a marble bust. In 1768 the Society of Artists had to provide 11 guineas in order to apprentice his son, Henry, to a peruke-maker (Archives, Soc of Artists, ref untraced). Spang's widow, Mary, married a Mr Brown shortly after the death of her first husband, but on the recommendation of Sir William Chambers drew an annual pension from the Royal Academy from 1769 until her death in 1785. This varied from three to eight guineas (RA Council Minutes, vol 1, fols 27, 136, 159, 180, 203, 220, 241, 257, 273, 287, 305, 330, 345, 361).

Literary References: *Gunnis* 1968, 361; *Hardy and Hayward* 1978, 194–7; *Pyke* 1981, 38; *Kedleston* 1998, *passim*; *Bilbey* 2002, 155

Auction Catalogues: Spang 1762

Funerary Monuments

1.	1762	James Thomson (†1748) (designed by Robert Adam) Drawing(s): Soane, Adam Vol 19/24, 25, 26, 27, 28, 33	Westminster Abbey, London, south transept		Pevsner, *London: Westminster*, 1973, 445; *Colvin* 1995, 62

Statues						
2.	1758	Four classical figures; statuettes of painted wood Payment(s): £28		Kedleston, Derbys		*Kedleston* 1998, 55
3.	1760	Aeneas and Anchises, bronzed model		[Exhib Soc of Artists, London, 98]; untraced		*Graves* 1907, 242
4.	1761	Anatomy figure	b	[G M Moser sale, 1762, lot 19]; untraced		*Gunnis* 1968, 361
5.	1761	Anatomy figure, statuette	w	[Exhib Soc of Artists, London, 1761, 162]; Science Museum, London		*Graves* 1907, 242
6.	*c*1765	William Hogarth, bronzed statuette	tc	VAM 311-1885	S	*Bilbey* 2002, 155
7.	nd	Ecorché	b	[Commissioned by Dr William Hunter for the RA]; Science Museum, London Other versions: Spencer Museum of Art, University of Kansas		*Gunnis* 1968, 361
Busts						
8.	1761	Two, unidentified subjects		[Exhib Soc of Artists, London, 159 and 160]; untraced		*Graves* 1907, 242
9.	1762	Child's head, model		[Exhib Soc of Artists, London, 151]; untraced		*Graves* 1907, 242
10.	*c*1762	Unidentified subject	m	[Spang sale, 1762]; untraced		*Gunnis* 1968, 361
Chimneypieces						
11.	*c*1760	With central relief of 'Singing at a Greek Wedding'		Kedleston, Derbys, music room		Pevsner, *Derbys*, 1978, 257; *Kedleston* 1998, 16
12.	*c*1760	With two caryatids and a relief of 'Virtue rewarded by Riches and Honour'	m	Kedleston, Derbys, drawing room		Pevsner, *Derbys*, 1978, 257; *Kedleston* 1998, 24
13.	1765	With caryatid figures of 'Ceres and Bacchus' and relief of 'An Ancient Repast'	m	Kedleston, Derbys, dining room		*Kedleston* 1998, 46–7 (repr)
Architectural Sculpture						
14.	1760	Screen, dolphins and prows of ships	s	Admiralty, Whitehall, entrance		*Gunnis* 1968, 361
15.	1760	Three, unidentified subjects		Spencer House, St James's Park, London, façade		*Gunnis* 1968, 361
Reliefs						
16.	1761	Design for a medal commemorating 'The taking of Canada', model		[Exhib Soc of Artists, London, 163]; untraced		*Graves* 1907, 242
17.	1762	A sleeping boy, model		[Exhib Soc of Artists, London, 150]; untraced		*Graves* 1907, 242
Miscellaneous						
18.	1760	Cupid riding a dolphin	m	[Exhib Soc of Artists, London, 97]; untraced		*Graves* 1907, 242
19.	1761	King George III, model	w	[Exhib Soc of Artists, London, 161]; untraced		*Graves* 1907, 242; *Pyke* 1973, 140
20.	nd	'Anatomical-pathological work'	w	Untraced		*Pyke* 1981, 38

SPANGLER, John James 1755–

It is not known when Spängler arrived in England from Zurich, but he was resident modeller at the Derby Porcelain manufactory under William Duesbury from July 1790 to August 1792, engaged to make models for vases, groups, ornaments and vessels and to provide an original in porcelain from each of his models. Duesbury undertook to provide him with 'a fitting and convenient room' in the manufactory and to provide all things necessary for his use. Spängler agreed for his part to work exclusively for the Derby Works in London or any other part of the country as directed (Agreement, 13 Sept 1790, in *Bricknell*, 1998, 37–8). The exclusivity clause was incorporated in the contract because the modeller had been associated with Benjamin Vulliamy, the clockmaker. This breach of practice continued and he was arrested for abscondment in 1792–3, receiving bail on several occasions. He appeared before the Court of King's Bench on 24 December 1793 and was fined for his misdemeanours. He was nonetheless re-employed in London in 1793 working under Duesbury's partner, Joseph Lygo. He returned to Derby in 1795, after which he disappeared from sight.

Literary References: *Bricknell* 1998, *passim*

SPARROW, George, of Grantham *c*1740–1822

Described by Neave and Heron as the most important Kesteven slate engraver, Sparrow was the son of **James Sparrow of Stamford.** He appears to have worked for 60 years or more as a monumental mason, though his occupation is often also given as 'painter'. In 1791 he advertised his shop in the High Street, Grantham, and his profession as coach, sign and house painter. He was made a freeman in 1792 and a year later advertised additionally as a supplier of monuments and chimneypieces. He moved to 'near Paul's Street' in 1797 and into Broad Street in 1806. The 90 slates where his signature can be deciphered are carved in a number of different styles. At first he was very much influenced by his father, and also later, like his father, he varied his style according to the fashion of the time. From the 1760s to the mid-1770s baroque and rococo motifs were common in his work, with angels' heads, shells acanthus leaves, scrolls and entwining snakes. Urns took over as the primary feature by 1780 and gradually the carving became shallower and more unimaginative, with frequent recourse to acorns and flowers.

He worked in Ancaster stone as well as slate: his signature can be seen on three stone memorials at Barrowby and although weathered, the rococo angels show that his work in stone was as skilled as that in slate. He was also responsible for a number of monuments inside Kesteven churches and elsewhere. Sparrow restored the monument to Francis Edwards (†1728), which stood in the churchyard of Welham, Leics, and also built a large chapel on the north side of the church, in which the monument was placed.

Literary References: Nicholls, *Leics*, 4, part 2, 1047; *Neave and Heron* 1969, 6, 14

SPARROW, George, of Stamford fl *c*1753–1811?

Gunnis lists a George Sparrow who flourished 1782–1811 and was perhaps a son of **James Sparrow of Stamford** (*Gunnis* 1968, 362). It seems possible that there were two sculptors named George Sparrow and that the earlier works listed below by Pevsner were by an earlier generation of the family.

Funerary Monuments

1.	†1753	William (†1745) and Rebecca (†1753) Pickworth	Caythorpe, Lincs		Pevsner, *Lincs*, 1989, 217
2.	†1760	Thomas Smith	St John the Baptist, Stamford, Lincs		Pevsner, *Lincs*, 1989, 691
3.	†1769	Noah Neale	St Martin, Stamford, Lincs		Pevsner, *Lincs*, 1989, 693
4.	?1782	Thomas Smith	St George, Stamford, Lincs	S	*Gunnis* 1968, 362
5.	†1790	Samuel Judd	St Martin, Stamford, Lincs		RG/JP, 7, 1332
6.	†1792	Henry Shield	Preston, Rutland	S	*Gunnis* 1968, 362
7.	†1795	1st Lord Sondes	Rockingham, Northants		*Gunnis* 1968, 362
8.	1796	James Oldershaw (†1796)	St George, Stamford, Lincs		Pevsner, *Lincs*, 1989, 690
9.	†1801	Theophilus Buckworth	Surfleet, Lincs	S	Pevsner, *Lincs*, 1989, 730
10.	†1802	Elizabeth Arundell	Irnham, Lincs	S	Pevsner, *Lincs*, 1989, 408
11.	†1804	Peter Lafargue	Greatford, Lincs		Pevsner, *Lincs*, 1989, 328
12.	1805	Margaret Thompson	St George, Stamford, Lincs	S	*Gunnis* 1968, 362; Pevsner, *Lincs*, 1989, 690
13.	†1806	Lewis, Baron Sondes	Rockingham, Northants		*Gunnis* 1968, 362
14.	?1808	George Hill	Rotherwell, Northants	S	*Gunnis* 1968, 362
15.	†1811	Rev R L Carr	St George, Stamford, Lincs		Pevsner, *Lincs*, 1989, 690

SPARROW, James, of Stamford 1716–

According to the town archives, he was born in May 1716 at Radcliffe-on-Trent, the son of **George Sparrow** of Stamford and his wife, Elizabeth. Neave and Heron state that Sparrow's work was of the highest quality and note that his earliest slate, at Foston, depicts two life-like angels. His corpus can be divided into four main phases, classical with clear lettering; baroque with winged cherubs, acanthus scrolls and other carved ornament, often in low-relief; rococo with Corinthian capitals, flaming torches, foliage, skulls, candles and crossed bones and finally classical revival with urns and festoons. There are only five slates by him in Kesteven, all near the Nottinghamshire border.

Literary References: *Gunnis* 1968, 362; *Neave and Heron* 1968, 5; IGI

Funerary Monuments

1.	†1744	Ann Hall	sl	Granby, Notts, churchyard	S	Pevsner, *Notts*, 1979, 134
2.	?1753	John and Mary Langston	sl	St Wulfram, Grantham, Lincs, churchyard	S	*Gunnis* 1968, 362
3.	†1776	Henry Green	sl	Flintham, Notts, churchyard	S	Pevsner, *Notts*, 1979, 129
4.	nd	Several, unidentified subjects	sl	Cropwell Bishop, Notts, churchyard		Pevsner, *Notts*, 1979, 109
5.	nd	Several, unidentified subjects	sl	Hickling, Notts, churchyard		Pevsner, *Notts*, 1979, 143
6.	nd	Several, unidentified subjects	sl	St John the Baptist, Nottingham, churchyard		Pevsner, *Notts*, 1979, 251
7.	nd	Several, unidentified subjects	sl	Plumtree, Notts, churchyard		Pevsner, *Notts*, 1979, 290
8.	nd	Several, unidentified subjects	sl	Radcliffe-on-Trent, Notts, churchyard		Pevsner, *Notts*, 1979, 291

SPEER, Thomas fl 1763

In 1763 he was listed as a carver of Garrard-Street, St Anne's, Soho (*Mortimer* 1763, 26).

SPELT, H, of Sandwich fl *c*1828–31

Only three tablets have been identified, all of marble on slate.

Funerary Monuments

1.	†1828	George Boys	St Clement, Sandwich, Kent	S
2.	†1829	Amy Hawley	St Clement, Sandwich, Kent	S
3.	†1831	George Sayer	St Clement, Sandwich, Kent	S

SPENCE, Benjamin Edward *c*1823–1866

He is believed to have been born in Liverpool, and was certainly baptised there, at St Peter's, in January 1823. He specialised in ideal representations, often of literary or allegorical figures and produced a small number of portraits.

Spence's father was the sculptor **William Spence** and his mother was named Elizabeth. William Spence was a partner, with **Samuel Franceys**, in the well-known Liverpool firm of monumental masons, Spence and Franceys, and it is likely Benjamin Spence gained his earliest sculptural training within the firm. Certainly when he entered the Liverpool Academy Schools in 1838 at the age of 15 he was already an accomplished stone-carver, and was to have a portrait bust, *A student at the Liverpool Academy*, exhibited at the annual Liverpool Academy exhibition later that year (**34**). This was the start of a long relationship with the Academy where Spence exhibited almost annually over the next decade.

In 1844 his statue *The death of the Duke of York at Agincourt* was exhibited at Westminster Hall, London, and a year later *Ulysses* was shown at the same venue (**4, 5**). Both are now lost, but the statue of the Duke of York was deemed worthy enough at the time to be awarded the Heywood silver medal by the Royal Manchester Institution. Such success may have persuaded Spence's father to send him to Rome later that year at the invitation of **John Gibson**. Although he initially entered Gibson's studio, Spence moved soon afterwards to work with **Richard James Wyatt**, perhaps because of Gibson's poor opinion of Spence's abilities. Writing to John Crouchley, on 23 June 1846, Gibson said that Spence was 'sadly behindhand in his art', and needed to undertake 'a regular ABC study of the figure from the antique'. Gibson also complained that Spence was in too much of a hurry to do his own work, and added that he 'seems to me a very good young man but I do not think he has genius for art' (NLW MS 4914-5D). Despite this, Gibson and Spence were to remain close, and together they formed the core of the British artists' colony in Rome in the final years of its influence over British sculpture.

In Wyatt's studio Spence adopted a soft neo-classical style, not unlike that of Wyatt himself, which suited the production of sentimental subjects popular in mid-19th century Britain. This included *Ophelia* in 1850 and *The angel's whisper* in 1857, the latter taken from Samuel Lover's parlour ballad of the same name (**10, 19**). When Wyatt died in 1850, Spence took over his studio in Rome and completed his unfinished commissions.

Although he made a pilgrimage each year to London to visit the Royal Academy annual exhibition, Spence was not a frequent exhibitor at the RA, and he seems to have harboured no serious desire to become an Academician. Most of his work was sold directly from his studio in Rome, or commissioned by well-heeled British visitors to the city. Indeed, Spence only exhibited at the RA six times, showing his first work, *Lavinia*, there in 1849 (**9**). Although versions of the statue are sometimes misidentified as the Old Testament figure, Ruth, the subject is taken from James Thomson's highly influential poem, *The Seasons*, and was commissioned by Samuel Holme, a builder of Liverpool, who rose to become an alderman and eventually lord mayor of the city. When it was shown at the RA the *Art Journal* stated that the 'statue is altogether a work that does great credit to so young a hand' (*AJ*, 1849, 95).

Lavinia is also a work typical of Spence's orchestration of the female figure, which can at times be formulaic. She is depicted in notionally classical dress, with downcast eyes and a demure pose that is undercut by the way her robe falls away to reveal one of her breasts. This compositional device appeared repeatedly in subsequent works, including *Innocence*, *Psyche*, and *Rebecca at the Well* (**12, 17, 21**). It also underpins one of Spence's most popular works, *Highland Mary*, 1852, although in this case the figure manages to remain fully clothed (**11**). *Highland Mary* is inspired by Robert Burns's poem dedicated to his late common-law wife, Mary Campbell. The work was subsequently mass-produced as a Parian ware figure, but Spence also made several replicas including a full-size version in 1853, commissioned by Albert, the Prince Consort, as a birthday present for Queen Victoria.

He carved very few monumental or public works, the principal exceptions being a figure representing *Liverpool* for the rebuilt Crystal Palace on Sydenham Hill, and a memorial to Jonathan Brooks for St George's Hall, Liverpool, 1856 (**13, 15**). Only three funerary monuments are known: the Gibson, carved in Rome and placed over his grave, was Spence's last work, for he died of consumption on 28 October 1866 in Livorno soon after its completion. He left a widow, Rosina, the daughter of George Henry Gower, British consul in Livorno.

Although he died young, at 43, Spence's gentle neoclassical style was already beginning to look old-fashioned by the time of his death since taste had moved on to more realistic forms. This is indicated by the otherwise complimentary obituary published in 1866 by *The Art Journal* which stated that Spence 'was not a great sculptor', and his works were 'characterised by great purity of feeling . . . rather than by much originality of design, or vigorous treatment' (*AJ*, 1866, 364). Four years later the sale of the contents of Spence's studio elicited little interest and notably low prices, prompting *The Art Journal* to comment: 'We feel ashamed to note down the prices paid for Spence's examples' (*AJ*, 1870, 221). That said, it is notable that Spence's *The angel's whisper* is one of the few works by a British artist to find a place in the Musée d'Orsay, Paris, purchased in 1993.

Michael Paraskos

Literary References: *AJ*, 1866, 221; *AJ*, 1870, 364; *DNB*, 1898, vol. LIII, 334; *Matthews*, 1911, 134; *Stevens*, 1971, 226–31; *Read*, 1982, 199; *Read* 1996 40–42; *ODNB* (Stevens); *Cavanagh*, 1997, 248–9

Archival References: Letters of John Gibson, NLW MS 4914-5D; Crouchley Papers, Harris M & A G, Preston

Auction Catalogues: Spence 1870

Portrait of the Sculptor: photo, repr *Stevens*, 1971, 226

Funerary Monuments

1.	1855	Lieutenant James Marshall		St Peter, Leeds, W R Yorks	S	*Gunnis* 1968, 362
2.	†1857	Julia Josephine Muspratt		St Mary, Flint	S	Pevsner, *Clwyd*, 1986, 350
3.	*c*1866	John Gibson		Protestant Cemetery, Rome		*Gunnis* 1968, 362

Statues

4.	1844	The death of the Duke of York at Agincourt		[Exhib Westminster Hall, London, 118]; untraced		*AU*, 1844, 215; *Gunnis* 1968, 362; *Morris and Roberts* 1998, 565
5.	1845	Ulysses		[Exhib Westminster Hall, London, 144]; untraced		*Westminster* 1845, 17; *Morris and Roberts* 1998, 565
6.	1846	Children of Mr A Holmes		[Exhib Liverpool Ac, 805]; untraced		*Morris and Roberts* 1998, 565
7.	1848	Mabel Atkinson		[Exhib Liverpool Ac, 672]; untraced		*Morris and Roberts* 1998, 565
8.	1848	Parting of Hector and Andromache		[Exhib Liverpool Ac, 678]; untraced		*Graves* VII, 1905–6, 215; *Gunnis* 1968, 363; *Cavanagh* 1997, 248–9; *Morris and Roberts* 1998, 565
9.	1849	Lavinia Model(s): ex coll Liverpool corp, plaster; untraced	m	[coll Mr Holme, of Liverpool]; untraced Other versions: Spence sale, Christie, London, 4 June 1870, lot 170; untraced Sotheby, London, 22 June 1990, lot 91, marble		*Gunnis* 1968, 362; *Cavanagh* 1997, 248; *Morris and Roberts* 1998, 565
10.	1850	Ophelia Model(s): ex coll Liverpool corp, plaster; untraced		[coll Thomas Brassey MP]; untraced		*Graves* VII, 1905–6, 215; *Gunnis* 1968, 362
11.	1852	Highland Mary	pb	[Spence sale, 1870]; Picton Ref Lib, William Brown Street, Liverpool, Lancs Other versions: ex coll Charles Meigh, of Grove House, Shelton marble, 1852; untraced Royal Coll, Osborne House, I of W, marble, SD 1854 Palm House, Sefton Park, Liverpool, by 1855, marble, S Sotheby, New York, 23 May 1997, lot 64, marble, SD 1859 ex coll Dick Coats, marble, signed; untraced Walker, Liverpool, marble Spence sale, Christie, London, 4 June 1870, lot 162, bt 'Vokins' for £12, untraced; lot 171, untraced		*Manchester Art Treasures* 1857, 133; *Atterbury* 1989, 41; *Cavanagh* 1997, 248–50 (repr)

No.	Date	Title	Material	Location	Signed	References
12.	By 1853	Innocence (the dove)		untraced		*Illustrated Art Journal*, 1853; *Gunnis* 1968, 362
13.	1854	Liverpool		[Crystal Palace, Sydenham]; untraced		*Gunnis* 1968, 362
14.	1855	Venus and Cupid		[Hooton Hall, Cheshire]; untraced		*Graves* VII, 1905–6, 215; *Gunnis* 1968, 362
15.	1856	Rev Jonathan Brooks (†1855) Payment(s): £1,200	m	St George's Hall, Liverpool, Lancs		*Read* 1982, 113; *Cavanagh* 1997, 272–3 (repr)
16.	pre-1857	Girl at the fountain	m	[coll Thomas Critchley]; untraced		*Manchester Art Treasures* 1857, 133
17.	By 1857	Psyche	m	[Spence sale, 1870]; untraced Other versions: Walker, Liverpool, marble, 1860 UCL, SD 1864 Spence sale, Christie, London, 4 June 1870, lot 165, bt Agnew (untraced), lot 169, bt Walter Savage (untraced) and lot 172 (untraced)		*Manchester Art Treasures* 1857, 133; C Lib (repr)
18.	pre-1857	Spring, summer, autumn, winter	m	[coll John Pender]; untraced Other versions: Spring, statuette, Spence sale, Christie, London, 4 June 1870, lot 175; untraced		*Manchester Art Treasures* 1857, 134
19.	By 1857	The angel's whisper	m	[Hafodunos Hall, Denbys]; Musée d'Orsay, Paris, France Other versions: ex coll Liverpool Corp, plaster; untraced Palm House, Sefton Park, Liverpool, marble, SD 1859 Christie, 18 July 1983, lot 29, marble; untraced	S	*Manchester Art Treasures* 1857, 133; *Read* 1982, 205 (repr), 206; *Cavanagh* 1997, 203–4 (repr); *Morris and Roberts* 1998, 565
20.	1860	Bacchus		[coll R B Preston]; untraced		*Morris and Roberts* 1998, 565
21.	1860	Rebecca at the well		Walker, Liverpool Other versions: ex coll Liverpool corp, plaster; untraced Sotheby, London, 20 Sept 1999, marble, SD 1866; untraced Spence sale, Christie, London, 4 June 1870, lot 167; untraced		*Gunnis* 1968, 363; *Read* 1982, 203 (repr); *Cavanagh* 1997, 248–9
22.	1861	The lady of the lake	m	Buckingham Palace, London Other versions: Royal Coll, Balmoral, marble, SD 1863 Sotheby, London, 12–13 Nov 1992, lot 177, marble, SD 1865; untraced Picton ref lib, William Brown Street, Liverpool, plaster Spence sale, Christie, London, 4 June 1870, lot 168; untraced	SD	*AJ* 1863, 188 (repr); *Cavanagh* 1997, 249–50 (repr)
23.	1862	Hippolytus		[coll Judge Josephson]; Art Gallery of New South Wales, Sydney	SD	*Graves* VII, 1905–6, 215; *Read* 1982, 201
24.	1862	Jeanie Deans before Queen Caroline		[Int Exhib, London]; untraced		*Gunnis* 1968, 363
25.	By 1864	The finding of Moses		[coll J Naylor, of Liverpool]; untraced Other versions: ex coll corp of Liverpool, plaster; untraced		*Gunnis* 1968, 363; *Cavanagh* 1997, 248–9
26.	1865	Flora Macdonald	m	[Spence sale, 1870]; destroyed Other versions: ex coll corp of Liverpool, plaster; untraced Spence sale, Christie, London, 4 June 1870, lot 164, bt Agnew; untraced	SD	*Read* 1982, 206, 207 (repr); *Cavanagh* 1997, 304 (repr)
27.	1865	Marine Venus		Hereford Town Hall		*Gunnis* 1968, 363
28.	1866	Oberon and Titania	m	[Spence sale, 1870]; VAM A.214-1969 Other versions: ex coll Liverpool corp, plaster; untraced Spence sale, Christie, London, 4 June 1870, lot 166, bt 'Vokins', £200; untraced	SD	*AJ*, 1870, 221; *Gunnis* 1968, 362; *Cavanagh* 1997, 248–9; *Bilbey* 2002, 360 (repr)
29.	nd	Boy and kid	pm	[Liverpool Corporation; presented to William Brown Museum, Liverpool, Lancs]; untraced		*Cavanagh* 1997, 248–9
30.	nd	Boy with a bird's nest, statuette		[Spence sale, Christie, London, 4 June 1870, lot 173]; untraced		
31.	nd	Boy with a flute, statuette		[Spence sale, Christie, London, 4 June 1870, lot 174]; untraced	S	
32.	nd	Jeanie Deans	pb	Picton Reference Library, William Brown Street, Liverpool, Lancs	S	*Cavanagh* 1997, 249 (repr)
33.	nd	Sabrina		[Spence sale, 1870, lot 163]; untraced		*Gunnis* 1968, 362

Busts

No.	Date	Title	Material	Location	Signed	References
34.	1838	Unidentified student of the Liverpool Academy		[Exhib Liverpool Ac, 672]; untraced		*Morris and Roberts* 1998, 565
35.	1839	Unidentified gentleman		[Exhib Liverpool Ac, 695]; untraced		*Morris and Roberts* 1998, 565
36.	1840	Unidentified lady		[Exhib Liverpool Ac, 683]; untraced		*Morris and Roberts* 1998, 565
37.	1843	Unidentified subject		[Exhib Liverpool Ac, 559]; untraced		*Morris and Roberts* 1998, 565
38.	1844	Unidentified child		[Exhib Liverpool Ac, 567]; untraced		*Morris and Roberts* 1998, 565

39.	1844	Unidentified gentleman		[Exhib Liverpool Ac, 566]; untraced		*Morris and Roberts* 1998, 565
40.	1849	Charles Holland		[Exhib RA, London, 1283]; untraced		*Graves* VII, 1905–6, 215
41.	1849	George Smith, model		[Exhib Liverpool Ac, 659]; untraced		*Morris and Roberts* 1998, 565
42.	1863	Peter Bancroft	m	[Exhib LIFA, Liverpool, 1226]; untraced		*Morris and Roberts* 1998, 565
43.	c1865	Sir Joseph Paxton, herm	m	Chatsworth, Derbys	S	
44.	nd	Mrs Thomas Brassey		[Normanhurst Court, Sussex]; untraced		*Gunnis* 1968, 362
45.	nd	Thomas Brassey		[Normanhurst Court, Sussex]; untraced Other versions: Grosvenor Museum, Chester ex coll Ted Few, marble; untraced		*Gunnis* 1968, 362
46.	nd	Unidentified gentleman	m	Christie, London, 15 July 1993, lot 236	S	
47.	nd	Unidentified lady	m	Coll B Dawkins (Cardiff)		C Lib (repr)
48.	nd	Venus, two		[Spence sale, Christie, London, 4 June 1870, lots 176 and 177]; untraced		
49.	nd	Young Augustus		[Spence sale, Christie, London, 4 June 1870, lot 178]; untraced		
Miscellaneous						
50.	1841	Three unidentified gentlemen		[Exhib Liverpool Ac, 659, 661, 663]; untraced		*Morris and Roberts* 1998, 565
51.	1844	Shepherd and dog		[Exhib Liverpool Ac, 555]; untraced		*Morris and Roberts* 1998, 565
52.	1846	A frame		Brocket Hall, Herts	SD	

SPENCE, William 1793–1849

A Liverpool sculptor, he specialised in funerary monuments and busts. Spence was born in Chester and moved t Liverpool c1808 to study under a wood-carver and drawing master, Mr Pether. In Liverpool he was befriended b **John Gibson**, then employed by **Samuel and Thomas Franceys**, a local firm of stonemasons. This friendship was t be of great importance for Gibson introduced Spence to the Franceys brothers who consequently engaged him as modeller. In 1819 Spence became a partner in their firm, renamed Messrs Franceys and Spence, and he took over th whole business in 1830.

A number of funerary monuments by Spence, largely in Wales, are to people who died before 1810. These are, i correctly identified as his work, likely to be later commissions, for his earliest known works are two lost pieces *Centaurs Pursuing Dante* and *Young Hymen*, 1812 (**137, 138**). They were exhibited at the Liverpool Academy, an attracted the attention of the Liverpool banker, MP and anti-slavery campaigner, William Roscoe, who was also major patron of Gibson. Roscoe commissioned a bust of himself from Spence, exhibited at the Liverpool Academ in 1813 and replicated in various materials (**76**). Roscoe made attempts to encourage Spence to go to Rome to exten his study of Antique sculpture, but Spence declined and did not visit Italy until much later in life, when his son, th sculptor **Benjamin Spence**, was studying there. Spence's loyalty to Liverpool made him a fixture in the regional ar establishment and he continued to exhibit at the city's Academy until the end of his life. In 1828 he was made maste of drawing from the Antique in the Academy's schools, and in 1845 he became the Academy's treasurer.

It was unusual for Spence to show outside Liverpool. Two known exceptions were *Caractacus before Caesar* an *Aristides showing the shell to the Vates*, shown at the Westminster Hall Exhibitions, London, in 1844 and 1845 respectivel (**71, 72**). It is worth noting that these rare forays into the London art world co-incided with exhibitions that helpe launch the career of his son Benjamin, suggesting filial influence. Spence also showed drawings and carved work at the Polytechnic Exhibition in Leeds in 1845, including busts of the Reverends Hugh McNeil, Dr Raffles an J Brooks (**104, 111, 117**).

An assessment of Spence's ability as a sculptor is limited, since little of his enormous output appears to hav survived. Most of his church monuments are still intact, but they are often repetitive and not generally considere to be his best work. Many may have been workshop pieces and Gunnis considered them dull. Almost all hi ideal works, busts and reliefs are lost or attributions, making it difficult to concur with J A Picton's view that Spenc was surpassed by few 'for quickness in modelling and readiness in catching the expressive lines of a countenanc (*Picton*, 1875, II, 218). He died in Liverpool on 6 July 1849, aged 56.

Michael Parasko

Literary References: *Lit Gaz*, 27 July 1844, 482; E Twycross, *Mansions of England and Wales (Lancs)*, 1847, vol II, 50; *A J*, 1849, 95; *GM*, 1849 II, 435; *Picton*, 1875, II, 218; *Redgrave* 1878, 408; *Gunnis*, 1968, 363; *Cavanagh*, 1997, 209–11; *Morris and Roberts*, 1998, 721

Archival References: Letters of John Gibson, NLW MS 4914-5D

Funerary Monuments						
1.	†1802	Margaret Hughes		Woodchurch, Cheshire		Pevsner, *Cheshire*, 1971, 106; C Lib (repr)
2.	†1805	Diana Yorke		Llansannan, Denbighs		Pevsner, *Clwyd*, 1986, 240
3.	†1807	Thomas, 1st Lord Newborough		Llandwrog, Carnarvon		GPC
4.	†1813	Rev Brownlow Yorke		Llansannan, Denbighs		Pevsner, *Clwyd*, 1986, 240
5.	1819	Rachel Roe		Christ Church, Macclesfield, Cheshire		*Gunnis* 1968, 363
6.	1822	The good Samaritan, monumental design		[Exhib ALRI, Liverpool, 167]; untraced		*Morris and Roberts* 1998, 566
7.	1822	'Thy Kingdom come', monumental design		[Exhib ALRI, Liverpool, 172]; untraced		*Morris and Roberts* 1998, 566
8.	1824	J Horrocks, model only		[Exhib ALRI, Liverpool, 173]; untraced		*Morris and Roberts* 1998, 566
9.	†1824	Thomas (†1823) and Henry Thomas		Whitford, Flints		Pevsner, *Clwyd*, 1986, 455
10.	1825	Alexander Butler (†1811) (co-sculptor: Samuel and Thomas Franceys) Model(s): exhib ALRI, Liverpool, 1825, 164		Kirkland, Lancs	S	Pevsner, *Lancs: N*, 1969, 151; *Morris and Roberts* 1998, 566; C Lib (repr)
11.	1825	'Model of a monument'		[Exhib ALRI, Liverpool, 207]; untraced		*Morris and Roberts* 1998, 566
12.	1827	A figure rising from the sea, monumental design		[Exhib ALRI, Liverpool, 275]; untraced		*Morris and Roberts* 1998, 566

No.	Date	Subject		Location		Reference
13.	†1827	John Fowler		Horton, Staffs		Pevsner, *Staffs*, 1974, 151
14.	†1827	Joseph Lowe		Barbados Cathedral, Bridgetown	S	
15.	†1828	Edward Lloyd Rowland		Ruabon, Denbighs	S	Pevsner, *Clwyd*, 1986, 270
16.	1829	Mary Williams		Corwen, Denbigh		*Gunnis* 1968, 363
17.	†1829	Rev William Williams Edwards		Llanynys, Denbighs		Pevsner, *Clwyd*, 1986, 247
18.	†1829	Robert Hawkinson		Our Lady & St Nicholas, Liverpool, Lancs	S	Pevsner, *Lancs: S*, 1969, 151
19.	†1829	Thomas (†1801) and Ann Snape		Billinge, Lancs		*CIIA* 4/8/22 (repr)
20.	†1830	Bishop Majendie		Longdon, Staffs		*Jeavons* 1960, 69
21.	†1830	Jane Bonnor		Llangedwyn, Denbighs		Pevsner, *Clwyd*, 1986, 214
22.	†1830	John Gore		St James's Cemetery chapel, Liverpool		*Gunnis* 1968, 363
23.	†1830	Mary Corry		Newry, Co Down	S	*Potterton* 1975, 83
24.	†1831	Margarette Golightly		Gresford, Denbighs	S	Pevsner, *Clwyd*, 1994, 173
25.	†1831	Richard Augustus Griffith		Henllan, Denbighs		Pevsner, *Clwyd*, 1994, 179
26.	?1832	Field Marshal Sir Alured Clarke		Mold, Flints		GPC
27.	?1832	Hepzibah Williams		Conway, Carnarvon		RG/JP, 7, 1336
28.	†1832	Ralph Fletcher		St Peter, Bolton, Lancs		C Lib (repr)
29.	†1832	Rev James Archer		St Leonard, Middleton, Lancs		Pevsner, *Lancs: S*, 1969, 347; *Morris and Roberts* 1998, 566
30.	?1833	Owen family		Beaumaris, Anglesey		GPC
31.	†1833	Thomas Vernon		Old St Chad, Tushingham, Cheshire		Pevsner, *Cheshire*, 1971, 365
32.	1834	Charity, monumental group		[Exhib Liverpool Ac, 432]; untraced		*Morris and Roberts* 1998, 566
33.	†1834	Eli Fletcher and family members		Ringley, Lancs	S	C Lib (repr)
34.	?1834	John and Henry Fletcher		Overton, Flints		*Gunnis* 1968, 363
35.	†1834	Mary (†1817) and Charles Sankey		St Winefride, Holywell, Flints	S	Pevsner, *Clwyd*, 1986, 374
36.	post-1834	Matthew Fletcher (†1808)		Ringley, Lancs		*Morris and Roberts* 1998, 566
37.	†1834	Richard Jebb Browne		Newry, Co Down		*Potterton* 1975, 83
38.	1835	Michael Heathcote		Ormskirk, Lancs		*Gunnis* 1968, 363
39.	?1836	Catherine Shufflebottom		Betley, Staffs		*Gunnis* 1968, 363
40.	†1836	Harriet Vyse		Holme Chapel, Cheshire		Pevsner, *Cheshire*, 1971, 241
41.	1836	Resignation, monumental figure		[Exhib Liverpool Ac, 658]; untraced		*Morris and Roberts* 1998, 567
42.	†1837	Pierce Wynne Yorke		Llansannan, Denbighs		Pevsner, *Clwyd*, 1986, 240
43.	1837	Sarah Vawdrey		Middlewich, Cheshire		*Gunnis* 1968, 363
44.	†1838	Margaret Hoskins		Melling, Lancs	S	Pevsner, *Lancs: N*, 1969, 177
45.	†1839	Ann and Joseph (†1851) Aston		Stourbridge Congregational church, Worcs	S	
46.	?1839	Elizabeth Latham		Sandbach, Cheshire		*Gunnis* 1968, 363
47.	†1839	John Ford		Sandbach, Cheshire		C Lib (repr)
48.	†1839	Trevor Owen Jones		Connah's Quay, Flints	S	Pevsner, *Clwyd*, 1986, 339
49.	†1840	John Bibby		Allerton, Liverpool, Lancs	S	C Lib (repr)
50.	*c*1841	Agnes (†1800) and Richard (†1813) Carr		Billinge, Lancs	S	*CIIA* 4/8/21 (repr)
51.	*c*1841	Dr Wainwright, model		[Exhib Liverpool Ac, 651]; untraced		*Morris and Roberts* 1998, 567
52.	†1842	Anne Goodwin		Gresford, Denbighs		Pevsner, *Clwyd* 1994, 172
53.	?1842	Thomas Parker		Colne, Lancs		*Gunnis* 1968, 363
54.	?1843	Rev Richard Loxham		Halsall, Lancs		GPC
55.	†1844	Granville Eliot		Athlone, Co Roscommon	S	*Potterton* 1975, 83
56.	?1844	Rev John Bird		Upholland, Lancs		GPC
57.	1845	Joseph Bradbury		St Peter, Huddersfield, W R Yorks	S	*Gunnis* 1968, 363
58.	†1820–1845	Lewis family members		Llanfair Dyffryn, Denbighs	S	Pevsner, *Clwyd*, 1986, 207
59.	†1845	Milborne Kemeys Tynte		Goathurst, Somerset	S	*Gunnis* 1968, 363
60.	nd	Henry Swetenham		Astbury, Cheshire		*Gunnis* 1968, 363
61.	nd	James Gregg		Londonderry Cathedral	S	*Potterton* 1975, 83
62.	nd	Trevor Corry		Newry, Co Down	S	*Potterton* 1975, 83
Statues						
63.	1824	Spring		[Exhib ALRI, Liverpool, 181]; untraced		*Morris and Roberts* 1998, 566
64.	1825	Nessus carrying off Deianeira, model	p	[Exhib ALRI, Liverpool, 161]; untraced		*Morris and Roberts* 1998, 566
65.	1828	Christ		[Exhib ALRI, Liverpool, 227]; untraced		*Morris and Roberts* 1998, 566
66.	1829	A Greek soldier watering his horse	m	[Exhib ALRI, Liverpool, 318]; untraced		*Graves* VII, 1905–6, 216; *Morris and Roberts* 1998, 566, 567
67.	1832	William Roscoe		[Exhib Liverpool Ac, 386]; untraced		*Morris and Roberts* 1998, 566
68.	1839	Vandenhoff as Coriolanus		[Exhib Liverpool Ac, 690]; untraced		RG/JP, 7, 1336; *Morris and Roberts* 1998, 567
69.	1840	Hannibal drinking the poison in the palace of Prusias		[Exhib Liverpool Ac, 692]; untraced		*Morris and Roberts* 1998, 567
70.	1843	The muse Clio	m	[Exhib Liverpool Ac, 552]; untraced		*Morris and Roberts* 1998, 567
71.	1844	Caractacus before Claudius Caesar, group		[Exhib Westminster Hall, London]; untraced		*Gunnis* 1968, 363
72.	1845	Aristides showing the shell to the Vates		[Exhib Westminster Hall, London, 121]; untraced		*Westminster* 1845, 15; *Morris and Roberts* 1998, 567
73.	1846	Hengist, the Saxon chief		[Exhib Liverpool Ac, 802]; untraced		*Morris and Roberts* 1998, 567
74.	nd	Boy with a bird's nest		[for Matthew Uzielli, of Hanover Lodge, Regent's Park, London; Christie, April 1861]; untraced	S	GPC
75.	nd	Girl feeding a bird		[for Matthew Uzielli, of Hanover Lodge, Regent's Park, London; Christie, April 1861]; untraced	S	GPC
Busts						
76.	1813	William Roscoe		[Exhib Liverpool Ac, 316]; Athenaeum Lib, Liverpool Other versions: Knox / Longstaffe-Gowan coll (1995), small bronze, *c*1820 Manchester CAG 1981.11, small bronze, nd Private coll, South Africa Walker, Liverpool		*Carlisle Ac Exhibs* 1973; *Morris and Roberts* 1998, 566
77.	1814	Arthur, Duke of Wellington		[Exhib Liverpool Ac, 296]; untraced		*Morris and Roberts* 1998, 566

78.	?1821	George Canning		Walker, Liverpool		*Graves* VII, 1905–6, 216; *Gunnis* 1968, 363; *Carlisle Ac Exhibs* 1973; *Morris and Roberts* 1998, 566
79.	1822	Thomas Leyland		[Exhib Liverpool Ac, 184]; untraced		*Morris and Roberts* 1998, 566
80.	1822	Unidentified child		[Exhib ALRI, Liverpool, 191]; untraced		*Morris and Roberts* 1998, 566
81.	1824	Benjamin Heywood	m	[Exhib ALRI, Liverpool, 171]; untraced		*Morris and Roberts* 1998, 566
82.	1824	John Gladstone		[Exhib ALRI, Liverpool, 165]; untraced		*Morris and Roberts* 1998, 566
83.	1824	'Mr Serj. Heywood'		[Exhib ALRI, Liverpool, 177]; untraced		*Morris and Roberts* 1998, 566
84.	1824	Two unidentified gentlemen		[Exhib ALRI, Liverpool, 170, 172]; untraced		*Morris and Roberts* 1998, 566
85.	1825	William Pitt the Younger (after Joseph Nollekens)		Parliament House, Canberra	SD	*Morris and Roberts* 1998, 566
86.	1827	Alderman P W Brancker		[Exhib ALRI, Liverpool, 216]; untraced		*Morris and Roberts* 1998, 566
87.	1827	John Foster		Walker, Liverpool		*Morris and Roberts* 1998, 566; C Lib (repr)
88.	1827	Two unidentified children		[Exhib ALRI, Liverpool, 278, 280]; untraced		*Morris and Roberts* 1998, 566
89.	1827	Unidentified lady	m	[Exhib ALRI, Liverpool, 274]; untraced		*Morris and Roberts* 1998, 566
90.	1827	William Hope		[Exhib ALRI, Liverpool, 273]; untraced		*Morris and Roberts* 1998, 566
91.	1827	William Latham		[Exhib ALRI, Liverpool, 289]; untraced		*Morris and Roberts* 1998, 566
92.	1828	D Stewart		[Exhib ALRI, Liverpool, 221]; untraced		*Morris and Roberts* 1998, 566
93.	1828	J B Hollinshead		[Exhib ALRI, Liverpool, 218]; untraced		*Morris and Roberts* 1998, 566
94.	1828	Unidentified lady		[Exhib ALRI, Liverpool, 236]; untraced		*Morris and Roberts* 1998, 566
95.	1829	Two unidentified gentlemen		[Exhib ALRI, Liverpool, 320, 321]; untraced		*Morris and Roberts* 1998, 566
96.	1831	Rev R H Roughsedge, Rector of Liverpool		[Exhib Liverpool Ac, 403]; untraced		*Morris and Roberts* 1998, 566
97.	1831	Unidentified child		[Exhib Liverpool Ac, 392]; untraced		*Morris and Roberts* 1998, 566
98.	1831	Unidentified gentleman		[Exhib Liverpool Ac, 390]; untraced		*Morris and Roberts* 1998, 566
99.	1831	William Huskisson		[Exhib Liverpool Ac, 391]; untraced		*Morris and Roberts* 1998, 566
100.	1834	Robert Preston		[Exhib Liverpool Ac, 434]; untraced		*Morris and Roberts* 1998, 566
101.	1834	Unidentified child		[Exhib Liverpool Ac, 443]; untraced		*Morris and Roberts* 1998, 566
102.	1834	Unidentified infant		[Exhib Liverpool Ac, 445]; untraced		*Morris and Roberts* 1998, 566
103.	1835	Two unidentified gentlemen		[Exhib Liverpool Ac, 557, 558]; untraced		*Morris and Roberts* 1998, 566
104.	1836	Rev Hugh McNeil		[Exhib Liverpool Ac, 651]; untraced		*Morris and Roberts* 1998, 567
105.	1836	Unidentified child		[Exhib Liverpool Ac, 656]; untraced		*Morris and Roberts* 1998, 567
106.	1836	Unidentified gentleman		[Exhib Liverpool Ac, 653]; untraced		*Morris and Roberts* 1998, 567
107.	1838	Unidentified child		[Exhib Liverpool Ac, 673]; untraced		*Morris and Roberts* 1998, 567
108.	1839	Two unidentified gentlemen		[Exhib Liverpool Ac, 694, 696]; untraced		*Morris and Roberts* 1998, 567
109.	1839	Unidentified clergyman	m	[Exhib Liverpool Ac, 693]; untraced		*Morris and Roberts* 1998, 567
110.	1839	Unidentified lady		[Exhib Liverpool Ac, 697]; untraced		*Morris and Roberts* 1998, 567
111.	1840	Dr T Raffles	m	[Exhib Liverpool Ac, 686]; untraced		*Morris and Roberts* 1998, 567
112.	1840	S Williamson		[Exhib Liverpool Ac, 684]; untraced		*Morris and Roberts* 1998, 567
113.	1841	Unidentified lady		[Exhib Liverpool Ac, 668]; untraced		*Morris and Roberts* 1998, 567
114.	1842	Unidentified young lady	m	[Exhib Liverpool Ac, 593]; untraced		*Morris and Roberts* 1998, 567
115.	1844	Mr Holden		[Exhib Liverpool Ac, 563]; untraced		*Morris and Roberts* 1998, 567
116.	1844	Unidentified gentleman		[Exhib Liverpool Ac, 565]; untraced		*Morris and Roberts* 1998, 567
117.	1845	Rev J Brooks		[Polytechnic Exhib, Leeds]; untraced		RG/JP, 7, 1336
118.	1847	Unidentified gentleman		[Exhib Liverpool Ac, 751]; untraced		*Morris and Roberts* 1998, 567
119.	1847	Unidentified subject		[Exhib Liverpool Ac, 759]; untraced		*Morris and Roberts* 1998, 567
120.	nd	A nymph		[Mrs Huskisson sale, Christie, 20 June 1857]; untraced	S	GPC
121.	nd	Benjamin Hicks		[Myton Hall, N R Yorks]; untraced		*Gunnis* 1968, 363
Architectural Sculpture						
122.	1848	Neptune and horses fountain (designed by Meyrick Bankes of Winstanley Hall) Model(s): exhib Liverpool Ac, 1848, 674		Winstanley Hall, Wigan, Lancs		*Morris and Roberts* 1998, 567; GPC
Reliefs						
123.	1825	Chiron instructing Achilles, model	p	[Exhib ALRI, Liverpool, 166]; untraced		*Morris and Roberts* 1998, 566
124.	1827	Portrait of a horse		[Exhib ALRI, Liverpool, 268]; untraced		*Morris and Roberts* 1998, 566
125.	1827	Portrait of a horse		[Exhib ALRI, Liverpool, 271]; untraced		*Morris and Roberts* 1998, 566
126.	1827	The good Samaritan		[Exhib ALRI, Liverpool, 267]; untraced		*Morris and Roberts* 1998, 566
127.	1827	The incredulity of St Thomas		[Exhib ALRI, Liverpool, 269]; untraced		*Morris and Roberts* 1998, 566
128.	1835	George Canning, portrait medallion		[Exhib Liverpool Ac, 564]; untraced		*Morris and Roberts* 1998, 566
129.	1835	William Huskisson		[Exhib Liverpool Ac, 565]; untraced		*Morris and Roberts* 1998, 566
130.	1836	Lord Sandon, portrait medallion		[Exhib Liverpool Ac, 659]; untraced		*Gunnis* 1968, 363; *Morris and Roberts* 1998, 567
131.	1837	Sir Walter Scott, portrait medallion		[Myton Hall, N R Yorks]; untraced		*Gunnis* 1968, 363; *Morris and Roberts* 1998, 567
132.	1837	William Shakespeare, portrait medallion		[Myton Hall, N R Yorks]; untraced		*Gunnis* 1968, 363; *Morris and Roberts* 1998, 567
133.	1844	Benjamin Hicks, portrait medallion	ir	[Exhib Liverpool Ac, 573]; untraced		*Morris and Roberts* 1998, 567
134.	1845	Five, unidentified subjects		[Polytechnic Exhib, Leeds]; untraced		RG/JP, 7, 1336
135.	nd	Three Cupids		[Myton Hall, N R Yorks]; untraced		*Gunnis* 1968, 363
136.	nd	William Roscoe, portrait medallion		[Myton Hall, N R Yorks]; untraced		*Gunnis* 1968, 363
Miscellaneous						
137.	1812	Centaurs pursuing Dante		[Exhib Liverpool Ac, 328]; untraced		*Morris and Roberts* 1998, 565
138.	1812	Young Hymen		[Exhib Liverpool Ac, 259]; untraced		*Morris and Roberts* 1998, 565
139.	1813	Cupid riding on a dolphin		[Exhib Liverpool Ac, 314]; untraced		*Morris and Roberts* 1998, 566
140.	1814	'Crib in the attitude of Boxing'		[Exhib Liverpool Ac, 296]; untraced		*Morris and Roberts* 1998, 566
141.	1821	Venus and Adonis		[Exhib RA, London, 1093]; untraced		*Graves* VII, 1905–6, 216
142.	1822	An angel leading Adam and Eve out of paradise		[Exhib ALRI, Liverpool, 177]; untraced		*Morris and Roberts* 1998, 566

143.	1822	Daedalus and Icarus		[Exhib ALRI, Liverpool, 168]; untraced	*Morris and Roberts* 1998, 566
144.	1822	David taking Saul's spear and cruise		[Exhib ALRI, Liverpool, 210]; untraced	*Morris and Roberts* 1998, 566
145.	1822	Orpheus and Pluto		[Exhib ALRI, Liverpool, 169]; untraced	*Morris and Roberts* 1998, 566
146.	1822	Palermo convicted of intemperance		[Exhib ALRI, Liverpool, 211]; untraced	*Morris and Roberts* 1998, 566
147.	1822	St Paul before Agrippa		[Exhib ALRI, Liverpool, 186]; untraced	*Morris and Roberts* 1998, 566
148.	1822	Theseus killing the centaur, sketch		[Exhib ALRI, Liverpool, 180]; untraced	*Morris and Roberts* 1998, 566
149.	1822	Ulysses bringing Briseis to Chryseis		[Exhib ALRI, Liverpool, 209]; untraced	*Morris and Roberts* 1998, 566
150.	1824	Britannia supported by Commerce and Genius		[Exhib ALRI, Liverpool, 184]; untraced	*Morris and Roberts* 1998, 566
151.	1824	Christ healing the blind		[Exhib ALRI, Liverpool, 55]; untraced	*Morris and Roberts* 1998, 566, 567
152.	1824	Four quarters of the globe bringing tribute to Britannia		[Exhib ALRI, Liverpool, 62]; untraced	*Morris and Roberts* 1998, 566, 567
153.	1824	Satan cursing the sun		[Exhib ALRI, Liverpool, 178]; untraced	*Morris and Roberts* 1998, 566, 567
154.	1825	A dog, property of John Foster		[Exhib ALRI, Liverpool, 177]; untraced	*Morris and Roberts* 1998, 566
155.	1825	Battle of centaurs and lapithae		[Exhib ALRI, Liverpool, 195]; untraced	*Morris and Roberts* 1998, 566, 567
156.	1825	The choice of Penelope		[Exhib ALRI, Liverpool, 194]; untraced	*Morris and Roberts* 1998, 566, 567
157.	1827	Chryses supplicating Agamemnon for Chryseis		[Exhib ALRI, Liverpool, 266]; untraced	*Morris and Roberts* 1998, 566
158.	1827	Hector borne to the funeral pile		[Exhib ALRI, Liverpool, 251]; untraced	*Morris and Roberts* 1998, 566
159.	1828	Liverpool arms		[Exhib ALRI, Liverpool, 219]; untraced	*Morris and Roberts* 1998, 566
160.	1828	Milo		[Exhib ALRI, Liverpool, 225]; untraced	*Morris and Roberts* 1998, 566
161.	1828	St John	tc	[Exhib ALRI, Liverpool, 234]; untraced	*Morris and Roberts* 1998, 566
162.	1828	St Paul		[Exhib ALRI, Liverpool, 220]; untraced	*Morris and Roberts* 1998, 566
163.	1828	Ulysses		[Exhib ALRI, Liverpool, 231]; untraced	*Morris and Roberts* 1998, 566
164.	1829	Pegasus fed by the Muses	m	[Exhib ALRI, Liverpool, 317]; untraced	*Morris and Roberts* 1998, 566
165.	1830	Christ and the woman of Samaria		[Exhib ALRI, Liverpool, 277]; untraced	*Morris and Roberts* 1998, 566
166.	1830	Faith, Hope and Charity		[Exhib ALRI, Liverpool, 271]; untraced	*Morris and Roberts* 1998, 566
167.	1830	The messiah		[Exhib Carlisle Acad, 259]; untraced	*Carlisle Ac Exhibs*, 1973
168.	1830	Venus presenting love to Jupiter		[Exhib ALRI, Liverpool, 279]; untraced	*Morris and Roberts* 1998, 566
169.	1831	An Olympic chariot race		[Exhib Liverpool Ac, 409]; untraced	*Morris and Roberts* 1998, 566
170.	1831	Portrait of a horse		[Exhib Liverpool Ac, 408]; untraced	*Morris and Roberts* 1998, 566
171.	1832	A flying cupid		[Exhib Liverpool Ac, 431]; untraced	*Morris and Roberts* 1998, 566
172.	1835	Arcadian shepherd		[Exhib Liverpool Ac, 554]; untraced	*Morris and Roberts* 1998, 566
173.	1836	A Greek soldier		[Exhib Liverpool Ac, 654]; untraced	*Morris and Roberts* 1998, 567
174.	1836	Anatomical study of a horse		[Exhib Liverpool Ac, 657]; untraced	*Morris and Roberts* 1998, 567
175.	1837	Piety		[Exhib Liverpool Ac, 683]; untraced	*Morris and Roberts* 1998, 567
176.	1838	Alexander and the physician		[Exhib Liverpool Ac, 663]; untraced	*Morris and Roberts* 1998, 567
177.	1838	Bacchus		[Exhib Liverpool Ac, 670]; untraced	*Morris and Roberts* 1998, 567
178.	1838	Ceres		[Exhib Liverpool Ac, 675]; untraced	*Morris and Roberts* 1998, 567
179.	1838	Faith		[Exhib Liverpool Ac, 685]; untraced	*Morris and Roberts* 1998, 567
180.	1838	Hope		[Exhib Liverpool Ac, 684]; untraced	*Morris and Roberts* 1998, 567
181.	1839	Julius Caesar about to cross the Rubicon		[Exhib Liverpool Ac, 687]; untraced	*Morris and Roberts* 1998, 567
182.	1841	Jacob raising a pillar over Rachel's grave		[Exhib Liverpool Ac, 660]; untraced	*Graves* VII, 1905–6, 216; *Morris and Roberts* 1998, 567
183.	1841	Rachel hiding the gods of her father in the camel bags		[Exhib Liverpool Ac, 658]; untraced	*Graves* VII, 1905–6, 216; *Morris and Roberts* 1998, 567
184.	1842	An angel appearing to Cornelius		[Exhib Liverpool Ac, 571]; untraced	*Morris and Roberts* 1998, 567
185.	1842	Berenger		[Exhib Liverpool Ac, 592]; untraced	*Morris and Roberts* 1998, 567
186.	1842	Paris		[Exhib Liverpool Ac, 591]; untraced	*Graves* VII, 1905–6, 216; *Morris and Roberts* 1998, 567
187.	1842	Richard Coeur de Lion		[Exhib Liverpool Ac, 588]; untraced	*Morris and Roberts* 1998, 567
188.	1842	Venus taking a thorn from Cupid's foot		[Exhib Liverpool Ac, 586]; untraced	*Morris and Roberts* 1998, 567
189.	1843	Aeneas bearing his father from the ruins of Troy		[Exhib Liverpool Ac, 549]; untraced	*Morris and Roberts* 1998, 567
190.	1843	An Amazon striking down a soldier, sketch		[Exhib Liverpool Ac, 547]; untraced	*Morris and Roberts* 1998, 567
191.	1843	Hero and Leander		[Exhib RA, London, 1441]; untraced	*Graves* VII, 1905–6, 216; *Morris and Roberts* 1998, 567
192.	1843	Hylas and the nymphs, sketch		[Exhib Liverpool Ac, 550]; untraced	*Morris and Roberts* 1998, 567
193.	1843	Peteus and Aruice, sketch		[Exhib Liverpool Ac, 548]; untraced	*Morris and Roberts* 1998, 567
194.	1843	Roman soldier diverting his child		[Exhib Liverpool Ac, 551]; untraced	*Morris and Roberts* 1998, 567
195.	1843	Ulysses watching Argus die		[Exhib RA, London, 1490]; untraced	*Graves* VII, 1905–6, 216; *Morris and Roberts* 1998, 567
196.	1847	Untitled work		[Exhib Liverpool Ac, 758]; untraced	*Morris and Roberts* 1998, 567

SPENCER fl 1763

He was listed in 1763 as a mason at 'the corner of Purpool-lane, in Grays-inn-lane, Holborn' (*Mortimer* 1763, 49).

SPENCER, family, of Chester fl 1738–1809

The first mason member of the family appears to have been Richard, whose son and apprentice, Thomas, became a freeman in 1738–1739. On 3 September 1770, and 7 April 1784, respectively, Edward and Richard, sons of Thomas, in their turn became freemen of Chester (Archives, Masons' Company of Chester).

Their monuments and tablets are typical of the period, and they executed the Adamesque details in coloured marbles. In 1809 one of the Spencers was employed at Eaton Hall (**8**). In the previous year, C F Porden, Lord Grosvenor's architect, wrote to his patron: 'Last Spring I made Mr. Spencer an offer of new work and meant to give him any chimney-piece to do he might think proper to take, but he cut the matter short by saying he did not want work and he did not like trouble . . . . I fear if you Lordship employs him you will be sorry' (Grosveno Archives in GPC).

Literary References: *Gunnis* 1968, 363–4

Funerary Monuments

1.	?1775	Samuel Manning	Wrenbury, Staffs		*Gunnis* 1968, 364
2.	?1786	Lucy Jodrell (by Edward Spencer)	Chester Cathedral	S	GPC
3.	?1788	Priscilla Laurence	St Mary, Chester		*Gunnis* 1968, 364
4.	?1788	Sidney Lee	St John, Chester		*Gunnis* 1968, 364
5.	1790	Sir Robert Towneshend	Gresford, Denbighs		Pevsner, *Denbighs*, 1994, 173

6.	?1790	Spencer Family		Chester Cathedral	*Gunnis* 1968, 364
7.	†1796	Samuel Griffiths (by Edward Spencer)		Backford, Cheshire	Pevsner, *Cheshire*, 1971, 70
Chimneypieces					
8.	1809	Several Payment(s): £50		[Eaton Hall, Cheshire]; untraced	Grosvenor Archives in GPC

SPENCER & JONES, of New Road, Marylebone fl 1792

The following advertisement appeared in the *Daily Advertiser*, 4 June 1792: 'New-Road, Marybone, Artificial-Stone Manufactory. MESSRS. SPENCER and JONES beg Leave to inform their Friends and the Publick in general that the Partnership between them and THOMAS BRABHAM and JOSEPH DAY was dissolved by mutual Consent the 6th Day of June last, and that the said Trade is now carried on by themselves only in the New Road, Marybone, where Gentlemen may be served with all Sorts of Ornaments for Buildings, Statues, Busts, Coats of Arms, Vases, monumental and other Figures; they flatter themselves that the Specimens of their Manufactory already given, and the Punctuality and Dispatch with which all Orders have and will be executed, will entitle them to hope for a Continuation of their Patronage. All persons having any Demand on the late Firm are desired to deliver in their Bills to Mr. Spencer, at the Manufactory; and all Persons indebted to the said Firm are desired to pay no other Person but the said Mr. Spencer. Letters from any Part of the Country, Post-paid, will be regularly answered' (*Valpy* 1991, 231).

SPILL, Thomas fl 1697

Spill is listed with **John Thompson** and Richard Waters as supplying chimneypieces, marble tables and Purbeck paving at Kensington Palace in 1697 (**1, 2**).

Chimneypieces					
1.	1697	Description unavailable (co-sculptor: John Thompson (or Tompson))	m	[Kensington Palace, London]; untraced	TNA E.351/3466
2.	1697	Portland stone (co-sculptor: John Thompson (or Tompson))	s	[Kensington Palace, London, guard's room]; untraced	TNA E.351/3466

SPILLER, John 1763–94

A brother of James Spiller the architect, he was born on 23 December 1763. He first exhibited at the Royal Academy from an address at Highbury Place, Islington, in 1778, and enrolled in the Royal Academy Schools on 5 November 1781, giving his age as '18 23d next Decemr'. He later became a pupil of **John Bacon RA**. From 1786 until at least 179[illegible] his yard was at 8 Dyer's Buildings, Holborn.

His best-known work is the statue of Charles II which formerly occupied the centre of the piazza of the Royal Exchange and escaped the fire of 10 January 1838 (**2**). He also carved the Chauncy monument (**1**), which the *Gentleman's Magazine* described as 'a mural monument consisting of a pyramid of blue marble behind an urn, under which is a base' (*GM* 1794, 2, 592).

He died of consumption at Croydon on 17 May 1794. His wife, who was apparently a great beauty, succumbed to the same malady a few months later. The *Gentleman's Magazine* noted 'At Croydon, Surrey, in a deep decline, Mr John Spiller, mason of Temple-lane, Blackfriars, brother to the famous architect' (*GM* 1794, 2, 485). A much later romanticised account of the sculptor signed SMP appeared in the *Builder*, lamenting the early demise of this 'sculptor of great promise', adding that he was still working on his statue of Charles II in his last days: 'The enthusiasm of the young artist was so great, we are told, that, though consumption was doing its fatal work, he persisted in labouring at this statue, in spite of earnest advice to the contrary. He was willing, he said, to die at the foot of the statue. It was completed, and raised to its destined site. The young martyr to his profession gazed upon his finished work, returned home, and soon was known no more'. The elder D'Israeli said of him that 'the energy of his labour and the strong excitement of his feelings had already made fatal inroads into his constitution' (*Builder*, 1868, 415).

Literary References: *Euro Mag* 1794, 486; *GM* 1794, 2, 592; *Malcolm* 1803–7, 2, 442; *Builder*, 1868, 415 *Graves* VII, 1905–6, 221; *Hutchison* 1960–62, 146, *Gunnis* 1968, 364; *Pyke* 1973, 141

Archival References: GPC

Will: PROB 11/1258

Funerary Monuments					
1.	1791	Philip Chauncy		[Mercers' Hall, London, ante-chapel]; untraced	*GM* 1794, 2, 592; *Gunnis* 1968, 364
Statues					
2.	1789–1792	King Charles II	m	[Second Royal Exchange, centre of piazza]; third Royal Exchange, London, niche	*Builder*, 1868, 415; *Gibson* 1997, 157, 158 (repr); *Leith* 1997, 336, 340, 343
Chimneypieces					
3.	1792	Two, one of 'enriched veined marble,' the other of 'enriched statuary marble' Payment(s): £40 and £35	m	[Wimpole Hall, Cambs; returned to John Soane]; untraced	Bills in private poss, cited in *Gunnis* 1968, 364; GPC
Miscellaneous					
4.	1778	Portrait of Bacchus, model	w	[Exhib RA, London, 289]; untraced	*Graves* VII, 1905–6, 221
5.	1779	Portrait of an unidentified sitter, model	w	[Exhib RA, London, 310]; untraced	*Graves* VII, 1905–6, 221
6.	1785	Venus introducing Helen to Paris, after his combat with Menelaus		[Exhib RA, London, 494]; untraced	*Graves* VII, 1905–6, 221
7.	1786	Portrait of an unidentified artist		[Exhib RA, London, 499]; untraced	*Graves* VII, 1905–6, 221

SPILLER, Robert fl 1792–1827

A younger brother of **John Spiller**, he was employed by several architects on chimneypieces and ornamental details. Under Soane he made chimneypieces for Thomas Lewis, Lord Hardwicke, Lord Eliot, Samuel Thornton and for the Bank of England (**1–5**).

When Dance rebuilt the Royal College of Surgeons in 1807, Spiller was the master-mason (**7, 10, 15**). In 1803–10 Spiller was the master mason building Tollimore House, Herts, for a Robert Taylor, where he was paid £2,506 16s 6d for masonry work. He also worked as Dance's master-mason rebuilding Ashburnham Place, Sussex, from 1813. The bills record him as fashioning chimneypieces out of 'old marble', paving the staircase and 'making good brickwork to shelves in the Fish cellar', amongst other work. He charged £74 for chimneypieces in 1813–14 (**8, 9**). Payments to him totalled over £2,645.

Literary References: *Gunnis* 1968, 364

Archival References: Soane Priv Corr IV.10.6; Ashburnham Accts, ASH 2814, 1813–14; Ashburnham MS 1852, 2862, 2854, 2867; Ashburnham Accts with Artificers, ASH 2854 (to 31 Dec 1814)

Chimneypieces

1.	1792	'an enrich'd vein'd Marble Chimney Piece' (£40) and 'an enriched Statuary Marble Chimney Piece with Or molu' (£35)		Wimpole Hall, Cambs	Soane Wimpole Bill Bk, 1791–94, f50
2.	1794	Description not available Payment(s): £35		[Thomas Lewis's house at Palmer's Green]; untraced	Soane Ledger C, 3; *Gunnis* 1968, 364
3.	1799	Payment(s): £46	m	[for Lord Eliot, Down Ampney, Glos]; untraced	Soane bill book C, fol 11r; *Gunnis* 1968, 364
4.	1799	Three Payment(s): £102	m	[Bank of England, London]; untraced	Soane, Bank Acct 5, fol 174; *Gunnis* 1968, 364
5.	1802	Description not available Payment(s): £42 6s 6d		[for Samuel Thornton, Albury House, Surrey]; untraced	Soane bill book, D fol 289; *Gunnis* 1968, 364
6.	1803	Several Payment(s): £109		[Aynho Park, Northants]; untraced	Soane Abstract of Bills, 3 fol 124; *Gunnis* 1968, 364
7.	1807	All the chimneypieces, and all other carved work		[RCS, London]; untraced	*Gunnis* 1968, 364
8.	1813–1814	'Marble Portland Chimneys'		Ashburnham Place, Sussex	Ashburnham Archives, West Sussex RO, ASH 2867, 1813–14
9.	1813–1818	Some of the smaller chimneypieces	m	[Ashburnham Place, Sussex]; untraced	Ashburnham Archives West Sussex RO ASH 2814
10.	1827	Description unavailable		[RCS, London, library]; untraced	*Gunnis* 1968, 364
11.	nd	Description unavailable		[Bushy Park, London]; untraced	*Gunnis* 1968, 364
12.	nd	Description unavailable		[Lord le Despencer's London house]; untraced	*Gunnis* 1968, 364

Architectural Sculpture

13.	1803	Obelisk of Portland stone Payment(s): £310		[Reading marketplace, Berks]; untraced	Soane Abstract of Bills, 3 fol 119; *Gunnis* 1968, 364
14.	1809	Sepulchral urn (designed by Sir John Soane) Payment(s): £108	m	[Hagley, Worcs]; untraced	GPC
15.	1817	Terms for busts of Sir E Home and Sir W Blizzard		[RCS, London]; untraced	*Gunnis* 1968, 364

Miscellaneous

16.	1810	Sepulchral urn to a design by Sir John Soane and two inscribed tablets Payment(s): £108	m	[Lord Lyttleton's library, Macartney House, Blackheath]; untraced	Soane bill book G fol 42

PITTLE fl *c*1828

He was probably a Leicester statuary.

Funerary Monuments

1.	?1828	John Goodhall	Hungerton, Leics	S	*Gunnis* 1968, 364

PRATT, William *c*1709–

The son of William Spratt of Stepney, Middx, he was apprenticed to **Thomas Stayner I** on 2 August 1723, becoming free of the Masons' Company in February 1730. In a list of addresses of London masons, *c*1740, Spratt is stated as working with 'Mr. Horsnaile' (ie **Christopher Horsnaile I or II**). He signed the fine architectural monument to Mary Dawkins. A William Spratt, possibly his father, was made free by patrimony of the Masons' Company on 18 August 1703 after serving under another William Spratt.

Literary References: *Gunnis* 1968, 364; *Webb* 1999, 31

Archival References: Masons' Co, Court Book, 1722–51 (2 Aug 1723); Masons' Co, Freemen, fols 66, 67; Masons' Co, Assistants, fol 9; GPC

Funerary Monuments

1.	†1741	Mary Dawkins	South Mimms, Herts	S	*Gunnis* 1968, 364

PRINGALL, Robert, of Bletchington 1625–

In 1681 Springall gave evidence in a lawsuit between **Thomas Wood** and Richard Frogley, a carpenter. Then aged 56, he had served his apprenticeship with Thomas Barton, an Oxfordshire freemason about 40 years earlier. He had worked 'at his trade in Windsor Castle' where he supervised twenty '& sometimes more' workmen; he had worked for the late Duke of Richmond 'and now for the Lord Privie Seale at Bleshington, & like-wise for Esq Coghill there, for Chancellour Hyde at Cornebury, for Sr. Thomas Chamberlaine at Northbrooke, Esqr Dormer at Rowsam, & for Mr. Charte. at Brill, & for most of the Gentry of that side of ye. Sd Country [Oxfordshire], (OU, Chancellor's Ct Papers, Wood v Frogley, fol 9).'

Literary References: *Gunnis* 1968, 364

QUIRE, Richard, of Worcester 1700–86

A mason and monumental sculptor, he was considered by Gunnis to be one of the best of the Worcestershire statuaries. His tablets, which are architectural in design, are often executed in coloured marbles with well-designed and cut details. Classical motifs such as obelisks (**4, 12, 15**), putti (**2, 8**) and broken pediments with columns (**17**) are recuring decorative elements.

He died on 1 August, 1786, and was buried in the aisle of All Saints', Worcester (built 1738–42), where his epitaph on a ledger of touch commemorates 'Richard Squire, one of the master builders of this church, which with many

Memorial-works here, and throughout this County will be lasting Monuments of his Skill and Abilities'. In 173 Squire gave evidence before the House of Commons about the condition of the old church, and it is likely that h designed as well as built the new one. He also acted as building surveyor for the church at Upton-on-Severn, 1755–5; His son, Robert, was apprenticed to him in 1750. An earlier member of this family may be John Squire 'son of Richar Squire, of Evesham, mason', who was apprenticed to John Harbour, of London, mason, on 6 August 1714.

Literary References: *Gunnis* 1968, 365; *Colvin* 1995, 913–4; *Webb* 1999, 31

Funerary Monuments

1.	†1728	Elizabeth Cave	Evesham, Worcs	S	*Gunnis* 1968, 365
2.	†1728	Philip Bearcroft	St Helen, Worcester	S	
3.	†1739	Benjamin Scarlett	Hampton, Worcs		*Gunnis* 1968, 365
4.	†1740	James Smyth	All Saints, Worcester	S	*Gunnis* 1968, 365
5.	*c*1740	John Middlemore (†1698)	St Nicolas, King's Norton, Warks	S	Pevsner, *Warks*, 1966, 189
6.	†1741	Rev Thomas Hodgetts	Kingswinford, Staffs	S	
7.	†1746	Christianus Kendrick	Eckington, Worcs	S	*Gunnis* 1968, 365
8.	†1749	Mann family	Tewkesbury Abbey, Glos	S	Pevsner, *Glos: Vale & Forest of Dean*, 1976, 368
9.	†1752	Thomas Morres	Burford, Salop	S	*Gunnis* 1968, 365
10.	†1753	Henry Hope	St Swithun, Worcester	S	*Gunnis* 1968, 365
11.	†1758	Thomas Hopwood	St Andrew, Droitwich, Worcs	S	*Gunnis* 1968, 365
12.	†1765	Cocker Draper and family (†1716–1765)	All Saints, Worcester		*Gunnis* 1968, 365
13.	†1765	Josiah Weston	Powick, Worcs	S	*Gunnis* 1968, 365
14.	†1768	William Amphlett	Hadzor, Worcs	S	*Gunnis* 1968, 365
15.	1769	Robert and Bridget Cotton	St Helen, Worcester	S	
16.	†1771	Dorothy Holbeche	Dodderhill, Worcs	S	*Gunnis* 1968, 365
17.	†1780	Edward Lowbridge	All Saints, Worcester	S	*Gunnis* 1968, 365

Statues

18.	1724	King Charles I (repairs only)	Guildhall, Worcester, façade		City Archives in *Gunnis* 1968, 364

Architectural Sculpture

19.	1758	Marble table and a freestone font	Upton-on-Severn, Worcs		Ch W in *Gunnis* 1968, 364; *Colvin* 1995, 914

Miscellaneous

20.	*c*1765	Inscription with a seal alluding to Queen Anne's bounty, with the Queen's head in profile	All Saints, Worcester		*Gunnis* 1968, 365

ST GEORGE, Joseph fl 1815

At the exhibition of the works of Scottish artists held in Edinburgh in 1815 he showed a bust of Wellington (1). It wa favourably noticed by the *Scottish Magazine* as being 'freely modelled and the drapery very well cast'. The critic adde 'this young artist appears to be making rapid advancement and to feel his art'.

Literary References: *Gunnis* 1968, 339 quoting *Scottish Mag*, 1815, 100

Busts

1.	1815	Arthur, 1st Duke of Wellington	[Exhib Works of Scottish Artists, Edinburgh]; untraced		*Gunnis* 1968, 339

STACY (or STACEY) fl 1672–74

In 1672 a 'Mr Stacey the Carver' was paid £20 for carving at Vintners' Hall. He and **Young** were paid £8 in 1674 fo carving work about the door cases.

Archival References: Vintners, R W Accts, vol 5

STAFFORD, Francis, of Norwich 1688–1745

Stafford was a monumental mason and the clerk at Norwich Cathedral from 1711 until his death. On 26 June 1711 h married Rebecca Aldham and they had three children, including a son, Francis, a mason, who died in 1746–7, whil on the King's service in Canada. Stafford was parish clerk at St Mary-in-the-Marsh, Norwich for 34 years, and wa both general apparitor in the diocese of Norwich and beadle of the poor men at the time of his death. He had a hous in the Cathedral cloisters and a shop near Popinjay, Tombland, Norwich.

On 16 September 1732 he advertised in the *Norwich Mercury* that he sold 'Monuments and Grave-stones of all sor viz. Mural Monuments, Altar-Tombs, Black Marble Grave-Stones, with Coats of Arms well carved' and he adde 'Specimens of his Performance may be seen in the Cathedral Church of Norwich, and many other placed in the Cit and County'. A second notice in the *Norwich Gazette*, on 25 June 1743, announced that he had '. . . a stock of blac marble gravestone, a variety of Italian marble and a shipload of Portland Stone. He continues to sell monuments divers sorts of marble and other stone, altar tombs, gravestones, marble tables, coats of arms with their prop embellishments and all other ornaments for monuments or gravestones well carved'. His widow carried on th business from the same premises.

Gunnis said of him that 'his architectural monuments are well carved, the most interesting being to Mrs Hodgso (4) which has a central Corinthian column standing in front of a pyramid' (*Gunnis* 1968, 365). (Add. inf. Davi Cubitt, John Bayliss)

Literary References: *Linnell and Wearing* 1952, 15, 24, 30

Archival References: RG/JP, 8, 1340v

Will: PCC PROB 11/757 D&C will, vol V, fol 244

Funerary Monuments

1.	?1739	John Baron	Saxlingham Nethergate, Norfolk	S	*Gunnis* 1968, 365
2.	?1740	Ann Holmes	Wymondham, Norfolk	S	*Gunnis* 1968, 365
3.	*c*1740	Robert Wiggett	Guist, Norfolk	S	*Gunnis* 1968, 365
4.	†1743	Margaret Hodgson	Dersingham, Norfolk	S	Pevsner, *Norfolk: N W & S*, 1999, 297
5.	?1744	T Gurdon	Cranworth, Norfolk	S	*Gunnis* 1968, 365

STAFFORD, Thomas, of Norwich 1728–96

The son of **Francis Stafford**, he trained under his father and then under **James Chapling** and William Houghcraft. His marriage licence bond, dated 19 October 1754, names his wife as Elizabeth née Wells. Stafford was parish clerk at St Mary-in-the-Marsh for nearly 51 years and had a workshop near Norwich Cathedral.

Stafford later went into partnership with **John Athow**, and they signed a number of tablets together. An advertisement in the *Norwich Mercury* on 6 November 1773, advised the public that 'At Stafford and Athow's, Stone Masons, Near the Cathedral, Norwich Are made all Sorts of Monuments and Chimney-Pieces . . . also Black Marble Grave Stones, Portland Head Stones &c. with Arms and Inscriptions'.

He signed numerous tablets in Norfolk. The Colman has a rococo cartouche set against an obelisk (1). Stafford's death was noted in the *Bury Post* under 'Norwich' on 13 January 1796: 'Monday se'n night died Mr. Thos. Stafford, stone-mason, aged 68, in the precincts of the Cathedral.' (Add. inf. Jon Bayliss)

Literary References: *Gunnis* 1968, 365
Archival References: GPC
Will: Norwich D&C, vol 5, fol 244 (Francis Stafford)

Funerary Monuments

1.	†1758	Fysher Colman	Great Ellingham, Norfolk	S	Pevsner, *Norfolk: N W & S*, 1999, 366
2.	†1760	Hannah Curteis	Aylsham, Norfolk	S	*Gunnis* 1968, 365
3.	†1777	Abraham Robertson	St Swithin, Norwich, Norfolk	S	Pevsner, *Norfolk: N E & Norwich*, 1997, 253
4.	?1778	Robert Cremer	Wymondham, Norfolk	S	*Gunnis* 1968, 365
5.	†1780	Bartholomew Day (co-sculptor: John Athow, of Norwich)	Wicklewood, Norfolk		Pevsner, *Norfolk: N W & S*, 1999, 776
6.	†1788	Robert Plumptre (co-sculptor: John Athow, of Norwich)	Norwich Cathedral, Norfolk	S	Pevsner, *Norfolk, N E and Norwich*, 1997, 210
7.	1792	Dr George Horne, Bishop of Norwich (co-sculptor: John Athow, of Norwich)	Norwich Cathedral, Norfolk		Pevsner, *Norfolk: N E & Norwich*, 1997, 210
8.	?1795	William Fell (co-sculptor: John Athow, of Norwich)	Horsham St Faith, Norfolk	S	*Gunnis* 1968, 365

STAIG, of London fl 1826–29?

Staig, whose yard was in the Old Kent Road, signs the neo-Hellenic monument with a relief of a mourning angel to Sarah Drew (1) and a wall-tablet to another family member (2).

Funerary Monuments

1.	?1826	Sarah Drew	Streatham parish church, London	S	*Gunnis* 1968, 365
2.	?1829	Beriah Drew	Bermondsey parish church, London	S	*Gunnis* 1968, 365

STAINES, Sir William 1725–1807

He was born in the parish of St George, Southwark, the son of a stone-mason. As a young man he became a seaman and voyaged to Portugal, but on the return voyage was captured by the French, and spent six months in prison. After his return to England he was apprenticed to a stone-mason in Cannon Street and, on attaining his freedom, worked as a journeyman with **Daniel Pinder**. He set up for himself *c*1760 and won the contract to repair Bow steeple, a work which founded his fortune.

He became mason to the Royal Exchange, receiving nearly £1,700 between 1768 and 1772. In 1774, when described as a 'stone-mason and pavior', he designed and built St Alphage, Cripplegate, for which he received £1,350, 'the parish deeming the expense of an architect unnecessary' (*Allen* 1827–37, 3, 473). In 1784 he rebuilt the Barbican chapel, Cripplegate.

The account book of a provincial firm, Watts and Sons, stone masons of High Wycombe, Bucks, has a list of prices per foot for varieties of marble to be had at Staines's wharf in 1784. Among the marbles mentioned are:

Cube Statchuary	£1.6.0
Superficial Statchuary	6.0
Cube vain marble	14.0
Black marble ledgers	6.0
Cube Portland	1.10
Portland ledgers	1.8
Pirbeck ledgers	2.9
Sieanna Venears	2.9
Egyptian	6.0
Brocadilly	4.6

In the *London Directory* of 1787 Staines is described as a 'statuary of 23 Barbiccan'.

He was an Alderman of the City of London from 1793 to 1807, was knighted in 1796 and elected Lord Mayor of London in 1800. In an act of vanity he had Bow Church, the steeple of which he had repaired, painted in the background of one of the panels of the State coach. Staines died in Clapham on 10 September 1807, and was buried in Cripplegate churchyard.

Literary References: *Gunnis* 1968, 365; *Euro Mag* 1807, 2, 331–6
Archival References: GPC, inf, Howard Colvin
Will: PROB 11/1467, 25 September 1807

STANBOROUGH, William –1695

Stanborough supplied fittings for for St. Christopher le Stocks (1). In 1680 he was employed by the corporation of Trinity House at the 'Dagger house' (Trinity House Archives in GPC) and he was paid £36 in 1696 for mason's work at the Trinity Almshouses in Stepney. He died in 1695 and is buried in the north aisle of St Mary, Whitechapel. He was a renter warden of the Masons' Company in 1691, upper warden in 1692 and master in 1693. His son, also William Stanborough, was freed by patrimony on 5 April 1687.

Literary References: *Seymour* 1735, 2, 708; *Wren Soc*, vol XIX, 15; *Gunnis* 1968, 365

Archival References: Masons' Co, Masters and Wardens; Freemen, fol 66; GPC

Architectural Sculpture

1.	1673	Font, supplied with an hourglass Payment(s): £12 5s (font); 1s 6d (hourglass)	[St Christopher le Stocks, London]; untraced	*Wren Soc*, XIV, 15 quoting Vestry minutes; *Gunnis* 1968, 365

STANLEY, Charles 1703–61

A Danish-born sculptor and stuccoist, he spent two decades working in England. Stanley was born in Copenhagen on 12 December 1703 to an English father and a Danish mother. He was apprenticed in 1718 to the Danish court sculptor Johann Adam Sturmberg (1683–1741), who entrusted care of the young apprentice to one of his assistants, **Peter Scheemakers.** Stanley worked under Sturmberg on the elaborate stuccowork in Fredensborg Castle, 1720–22, and on two angels at the cornice of Sturmberg's monument to the statesman, Otto Krabbe, (†1719) in Roskilde Cathedral.

After completing his apprenticeship Stanley visited Germany and Holland before coming to London in 1727, where he spent a year as an assistant to Scheemakers and **Laurent Delvaux** at their Millbank workshop. When Scheemakers went to Rome in 1728, Stanley also considered making the journey south, but he decided instead to remain in London when he received a lucrative commission from Lord Wilmington to provide sumptuous stucco decorations in the state bedrooms at Compton Place, near Eastbourne. Among the ornaments provided for Wilmington was a ceiling panel with a characterised medallion portrait of the architect Colen Campbell (*Whinney* 1988, 255, repr).

On 21 May 1730 he married Mrs Anne Allen, the daughter of his landlord at Eastbourne, Sussex, where he lived whilst working on plaster ceilings at Compton Place. She died five years later and a second marriage took place on 2 August 1737 to Magdalene Margrethe Lindemann, the sister of the German chaplain to the Court of St James. The couple had a son, Carl Frederick Stanley (*c*1738–1813), who trained as a sculptor with his father and later had a successful career in Denmark, where he became a professor at the Copenhagen Academy.

Shortly after 1730 Stanley set up independently as a sculptor and plasterer in London, advised by Scheemakers, who had recently returned from Rome. A stream of decorative commissions and a few for sculpture followed. Working principally with the plasterer, Thomas Roberts of Oxford, he provided rich stucco ceilings at Langley Park, Norfolk (1740), the Radcliffe Camera (1744), Okeover Park, Staffs (*c*1745), Kirtlington Park, Oxon (*c*1745) and probably a number of other houses. In 1738, whilst living in the parish of St John the Evangelist, Westminster, 'Charles Stanley . . . plasterer' took an apprentice, John Dauson, at a fee of £10 (Apprenticeship Tax Roll index).

Stanley was responsible for two major monuments for the aristocratic Maynard family, who had large estates in Suffolk and Essex. The towering memorial to Thomas Maynard has a life-size standing effigy of Maynard in vigorous classical draperies, his left arm resting on an urn, while his right hand holds a book. His head recalls Scheemakers's work and on the pedestal is a large relief (**1**). The success of this commission led to a second, the monument to Charles, Lord Maynard and his ancestors (**3**). It also has a standing effigy garbed *all'antica* and grouped around him are three busts, three portrait medallions and a weeping *putto*. On the pedestal below is a fine high-relief tablet of three Cardinal and Christian Virtues, each attended by lively cherubs. Lord Maynard's response to the sculptor's work was expressed in an undated letter sent to Conyers Middleton: 'I can't say but I place a good deal of confidence in him' (Maynard/Middleton). Around 1744 Stanley also carved, though he did not sign, the monument in Ely Cathedral to Humphrey Smith, which has a naturalistic portrait bust of a heavy middle-aged subject, in a foliate oval frame, attended by a weary, standing cherub (**2**).

In the summer of 1746 he accepted an invitation from Frederick V to return to Copenhagen as court sculptor, a post he held until his death. He departed hastily for Denmark leaving his affairs in a confused state. Letters to Leeke Okeover from Joseph Sanderson, who was responsible for building work at Okeover, relate that Stanley left 'without settling with several of his acquaintances' and that he had failed to show Sanderson a bust, a chimneypiece (**4, 6**) and a gilt picture frame with ribbon and flowers, all prepared for Okeover (Sanderson/Okeover, 25.10.1746). A later letter adopted a more philosophical tone: 'One thing we must allow him [Stanley], is your ceiling is well done and cheap' (Sanderson/Okeover, 9 December 1746).

Soon after returning to Copenhagen Stanley began work on the elegant marble group, *Vertumnus, Pomona and Cupid*, *c*1749, derived from Delvaux's group for Wanstead (Copenhagen Stat Museum). When the Royal Danish Academy of Arts was founded in Copenhagen in 1752 he was appointed professor of sculpture. In his later years he continued to produce sculpture inspired by classical mythology. He was also responsible for a number of monuments.

Stanley had many skills. Whilst in England he probably become acquainted with the novelist Henry Fielding, a number of whose works he subsequently translated into Danish. In addition to his literary activities, Stanley composed various pieces of music including an oratorio. He also became a director of the Copenhagen porcelain factory.

IR

Literary References: *Buesching* 1754–7, I, 527, II, 193–9, III, 193–9; *Anecdotes* 1937, 144; *Esdaile* 1937, 348–53, 608–11; *Gunnis* 1968, 365–6; *Beard* 1981, 285; *Hare* 1990, 144; *Grove* 29, 540–1 (DBL)

Archival References: GPC (transcribed letters from Joseph Sanderson to Leake Okeover, 1745–46)

Funerary Monuments

1.	†1742	Thomas Maynard	Hoxne, Suffolk	S	*Esdaile* 1937, 352–3 (repr); *Whinney* 1988, 253; *Grove* 29, 540
2.	†1743	Humphrey Smith	Ely Cathedral, Cambs		Pevsner, *Cambs*, 1970, 365; *Grove* 29, 540
3.	1746	Charles, Lord Maynard (†1742) and his ancestors	Little Easton, Essex	S	Sanderson/Okeover 2 June 1745; *Whinney* 1988, 254; *Grove* 29, 540

Busts					
4.	c1745	A bust, perhaps of Mary Okeover	m	Okeover Hall, Staffs	*Treasure Houses* 1985, 295–6 (repr); *Avery* 1999, 29
Chimneypieces					
5.	c1745	Several		Okeover Hall, Staffs	*Treasure Houses* 1985, 295
6.	1746	Description unavailable		Okeover Hall, Staffs	Sanderson/Okeover, 25 Oct 1746
Architectural Sculpture					
7.	1746	Pediment ornaments		Okeover Hall, Staffs	Sanderson/Okeover, 16 Oct 1746

STANLEY, J, of Norwich fl 1845–c1858

Funerary Monuments					
1.	1845, 1852	Unidentified subjects, tablets	Sloley, Norfolk		Pevsner, *Norfolk: N E & Norwich*, 1997, 665
2.	†1855	John Blomfield	St Mary, Warham, Norfolk		Pevsner, *Norfolk: N & Norwich*, 1997, 707
3.	†1857	Rev John Toplis	St Lawrence, South Walsham, Norfolk		Pevsner, *Norfolk: N E & Norwich*, 1997, 669
4.	†1858	Thomas Clabburn	St Augustine, Norwich, Norfolk	S	Pevsner, *Norfolk: N E & Norwich*, 1997, 232

STANLEY, Rowles fl c1786

Gunnis wrote of his one known monument, a medallion-portrait hanging against a pyramid, that it was 'a very pretty work'.

Funerary Monuments					
1.	†1786	William Knight	St Laurence, Stroud, Glos	S	Pevsner, *Glos: Cotswolds*, 1999, 650

STANTON, Edward c1681–1734

Edward Stanton was a sculptor and mason, and the last successful head of the family workshop in Holborn. He was the ninth recorded child of **William Stanton** and was apprenticed to his father in June 1694. Before he completed his apprenticeship Edward had evidently assumed an important role within the workshop, since a payment for the monument to Richard and Isabel Shireburn was made to him in 1699. He and his brother, Thomas Stanton, became free of the Masons' Company by patrimony on 15 June 1702, and that year he was granted a licence to marry Sarah, a daughter of the mason **Samuel Fulkes.**

Edward Stanton took over the workshop after his father's death in May 1705. Like his father, he carried out masonry work at the Inner Temple, receiving £127 in 1707, and he retained the patronage of the Shireburns at Stonyhurst (**139, 141**). His assistant, **John Mason**, was still on site in 1715. In 1708 Stanton became mason to the City of London and in 1711 he was paid £273 for work at the Guildhall, and £520 for building 'Three Cranes Stairs' (City Cash Account 1/27). He secured the lucrative post of mason to Westminster Abbey, and in 1719 he and his family moved into a house with a wharf nearby (WA Muniments 65635). In December 1719 he entered into a written agreement with the Dean of Westminster to carry out repairs, with a bond penalty of £2,000 (WA Muniments 65663). At Westminster Abbey he was principally employed in rebuilding the north front: between 1720 and 1723 and was responsible for all the carved stonework, for which he received no less than £6,038 (**143**). In 1723 he subscribed to Dart's *Westmonasterium* and the Stanton coat-of-arms was appended to his name in the list of supporters. In 1726 he subscribed to Dart's *History of the Cathedral of Canterbury.* He was still supervising masonry work at the Abbey in 1726, on this occasion making good the damage caused by workmen erecting **G B Guelfi**'s monument to James Craggs. In 1721 he worked at Leicester House, London.

Stanton ran one of the most successful masonry businesses in London and in 1719, having served as a renter warden in 1713–14, and as an upper warden 1716–17, he became the third successive head of the family firm to become master of the Masons' Company. He was also a captain of the City's trained bands, a position of some status, and was often called 'Captain Stanton' in documents relating to his work. Other masonry contracts followed, for the parsonage of St John's, Clerkenwell in 1725 (PRO c108/140) and for the demolition of Bishopsgate in 1730–2.

He was one of the most prolific monumental statuaries of his time and provided the antiquary John le Neve with the inscribed texts for approximately 160 memorials supplied by the Stantons. These were incorporated in *Monumenta Anglicana*, published in five volumes in 1717–19. It is evident that more than two thirds of those memorials were produced whilst Edward was in charge of the workshop. Most of the surviving monuments are unsigned and many are minor works such as ledger slabs. The texts provide important evidence of the extent and range of his monumental production. Like his father, Edward was principally in demand for inscribed tablets, often carved with a panel simulating drapery, framed with columns or pilasters and topped with a pediment or arch. Ornaments such as crossed palm branches and garlands of fruit and flowers enlivened some compositions. Sir Justinian Isham, who had employed the sculptor's father, returned in March 1714, to order a monument for Elizabeth, Lady Isham, his late wife (**94**). Having settled, in writing, the terms of the contract, Isham said of Edward Stanton 'I believe the man to be fair dealing in his profession, and therefore may be trusted in what he saies, which makes me not so strict in drawing up the agreement' (quoted in *Isham* 1951, 440).

Stanton was capable of more elaborate work. Sir Francis Russell's reclining effigy was presented craning his neck to look into the eyes of his kneeling widow, as both gesture to the inscription tablet behind them (**17**). The monuments to Sir William Lytton and Sir George Strode (**9, 25**) both feature reclining figures of the deceased and are similar in composition to William Stanton's monument for Lord Coventry. Another notable monument is Richard Acton's, which has half-length figures of the deceased and his wife (**106**).

Stanton's wife died in October 1717 and in April 1718 he married Lucy Child at St Anne and St Agnes, Aldersgate. In 1717, also, he won an important commission, in competition with **Richard Saunders, Andrew Carpenter, Robert Hartshorne I** and a Mr Bushnell, to execute the statue of King George I for the Royal Exchange (**130**). A payment of

£60 'in full for making his Majesty's Statue set upp in the Royal Exchange' was recorded in the City Cash Accounts on 19 December 1718. The payment to **Michael Rysbrack** for his Exchange statue of George II, 1729, was disbursed through Stanton, who as city mason, was responsible for disbursements for public buildings (City Cash Accounts 2/35 1729, fol 63b).

Around 1720 Stanton went into partnership with **Christopher Horsnaile I**, and together they provided a number of chimneypieces, carried out masonry work, such as the building of a new dormitory at Westminster School, 1726–1730, and signed a series of monuments. These are chiefly architectural wall-monuments incorporating ornaments such as a festooned urn, bat-winged skulls, putti, and floral scrolls. The monument to Jacob Wishart is surrounded by an array of naval trophies and a relief of a man of war (**118**). More ambitious is the monument to Thomas Vernon, which features a stumpy effigy in wig and robes, flanked by two female virtues under a grand pediment (**115**).

In May 1730 Stanton's second wife died at their home in Hampstead, and he married Jane Churchill, daughter of the mason **Robert Churchill**. Stanton clearly had a sound reputation at this time, for the *St James' Evening Post* reported his second wife's death and referred to him as 'a great stone-cutter' (quoted in *Esdaile* 1930, 166). He died in May 1734 and in his will, proved on 20 June, he left over £1,740, including £40 to his 'honest and industrious copartner', Christopher Horsnaile. He asked to be buried 'by daylight in the north churchyard of St Andrew's, Holborn, towards the enginehouse door'. His library was sold in November 1735.

Stanton's eldest son, William, became master mason to the Mint and the Navy by 1727 and sold marble and stonework from the family premises. In 1735 William fell into debt and was declared bankrupt. His property went to auction in May 1736. Another son, Edward, was apprenticed to Joseph Selby, 'Citizen and Fishmonger' for seven years in May 1737 at a fee of £150. An Edward Stanton was on the livery of the Masons' Company *c*1740, when his address was given as 'the Star in Smithfield' (List of Masons' Assistants, fol 3).

His brother, Thomas, appears to have spent most of his life in Italy and left for Leghorn after joining the Masons' Company. In 1742 he was removed from his post as assistant to the Masons' Company, having been one of the court of assistants for 40 years without, latterly, attending their meetings. Another brother, William, became beadle of the Company and died in 1753, when his widow was granted a pension. Yet another family member, also William, had a mason's yard 'near Bloomsbury Church' in 1763, while a 'Mrs. Stanton, widow' was a pensioner of the Company until her death in 1785.

Gunnis and Whinney both considered Edward Stanton to be less skilled and sensitive as a sculptor than his father. Conversely, Colvin, in assessing Stanton's large and varied output as a whole, calls him 'one of the greatest of the eighteenth-century sculptor-masons' (*Colvin* 1995, 916).

MGS

Literary References: *Le Neve*; *Inderwick* 1896–1936, vol 3, 406; *Esdaile* 1930, 149–169; *Bolton* 1934, 43; *Knoop and Jones* 1935, 21; *Isham* 1951, 440–2; *Webb* 1957 (3), 115; *Gunnis* 1968, 366–7; *Physick* 1969, 26, 52, 64–5; *Douglas Stewart* 1978, 219; *Friedman* 1979–80, 75–90; *Whinney* 1988, 84, 135, 138, 139–42, 248, 446 n2; *Colvin* 1995, 916; *Roscoe* 1997, 179–80; *Ingamells* 1997, 889–90; *Craske* 2000 (2), 97; *Bilbey* 2002, 156; *ODNB*, Stanton, William (Fisher)

Archival References: Masons' Co, *Assistants*, fol 3; *Freemen*, fol 66; City Cash Accounts 1/27, 2/35 1729, fol 63b; WA Muniments 65635; Minutes of WA Chapter Meeting, 16 Feb 1726/7; Westminster Abbey Archives; Archives, Lord De L'Isle; PRO c108/140; IGI

Will: PROB 11/665, fols 368–9, signed 31 March 1733

Drawings: Design with contract, 1713, for a monument to Sir Edward Bagot, Staffs RO D3259/5/45

Auction Catalogues: Library sold with two others as *Bibliotheca Splendidissima*, 17 November 1735 (*Colvin* 1995, 916)

Funerary Monuments

1.	†1654	Sir Thomas Holte Bt	Aston, Warks		*Le Neve* 1650–1718, 22–3; C Lib (repr)
2.	†1681	John Wagstaffe and his wife, Alice	Bishop's Tachbrook, Warks		*Le Neve* 1680–1699, 19; C Lib (repr)
3.	†1696	Thomas Willington	Tamworth, Staffs		*Le Neve* 1680–1699, 175; C Lib (repr)
4.	†1702	George Vernon	Sudbury, Derbys		*Le Neve* 1700–1715, 43–4; Pevsner, *Derbys*, 1978, 331; C Lib (repr)
5.	†1704	Mary Chester	Barkway, Herts		*Le Neve* 1700–1715, 67; Pevsner, *Herts*, 1977, 87; C Lib (repr)
6.	†1704	Sir Samuel Astry	Aust, Glos		*Le Neve* 1700–1715, 79; Pevsner, *Glos: Vale & Forest of Dean*, 1976, 92; C Lib (repr)
7.	†1705	Lucy Monoux	Untraced		*Le Neve* 1700–1715, 81–2; C Lib (repr)
8.	†1705	Richard Bourne	Ufford, Soke of Peterborough		*Le Neve* 1700–1715, 99; C Lib (repr)
9.	†1705	Sir William Lytton	Knebworth, Herts	S	*GM*, 1790, 985; *Esdaile* 1930 (repr pl XI); Pevsner, *Herts*, 1977, 220; *Whinney* 1988, 139
10.	†1705	Thomas Bromsal	Blunham, Beds		*Le Neve* 1700–1715, 98; Pevsner, *Beds, Hunts & Peterborough*, 1968, 58
11.	†1705	Thomas Edwards	Wisbech, Cambs		*Le Neve* 1700–1715, 98; *Gunnis* 1968, 367
12.	†1706	Anna Comyns, ledger stone	[Writtle, Essex]; untraced		*Le Neve* 1700–1715, 97
13.	†1706	Elizabeth, Lady Chauncey	Ardeley, Herts		*Le Neve* 1700–1715, 112–3
14.	†1706	Frances, Lady Wagstaffe	Bishop's Tachbrook, Warks		*Le Neve* 1700–1715, 111–2; *Gunnis* 1968, 367
15.	†1706	Jane Pye	Faringdon, Berks		*Le Neve* 1650–1718, 211; Pevsner, *Berks*, 1966, 140; C Lib (repr)
16.	†1706	Rev John Hutchinson	Lichfield Cathedral, Staffs		*Le Neve* 1700–1715, 100–1; Pevsner, *Staffs*, 1974, 185

17.	†1706	Sir Francis Russell Bt and his wife	Strensham, Worcs		*Le Neve* 1700–1715, 93–4; *Kemp* 1985, 27 (repr)
18.	1706	Sir John Assheton Bt (†1697)	Downham, Lancs		*Le Neve* 1680–1699, 181; *Gunnis* 1968, 368
19.	†1707	Bishop Simon Patrick	Ely Cathedral, Cambs	S	*Le Neve* 1700–1715, 124; Pevsner, *Cambs*, 1970, 366; C Lib (repr)
20.	†1707	Edward Webbe	[Newton Bagpath, Glos]; untraced		*Le Neve* 1700–1715, 136–7
21.	†1707	James Sidgrave, ledger stone	Chapel of the Charterhouse, London		*Le Neve* 1700–1715, 139; *Gunnis* 1968, 367
22.	†1707	Rev James Hancox	['Worvil', Salop-probably Morville]; untraced		*Le Neve* 1700–1715, 117
23.	†1707	Rev Thomas Smoult	Barkway, Herts		*Le Neve* 1700–1715, 131–2; *Gunnis* 1968, 367
24.	1707	Robert Wynne of Garthewin (†1682) and his sisters Margaret (†1695) and Katherine (†1704)	Untraced		*Le Neve* 1680–1699, 32–3
25.	†1707	Sir George Strode	Knebworth, Herts	S	*GM*, Nov 1790, 985; *Esdaile* 1930, pl XII; Pevsner, *Herts*, 1977, 220; C Lib (repr)
26.	†1707	Sir John Francklin	Bolnhurst, Beds		*Le Neve* 1700–1715, 127–8
27.	†1707	Sir Philip Monoux Bt	Wootton, Beds		*Le Neve* 1700–1715, 125; Pevsner, *Beds, Hunts & Peterborough*, 1968, 172; C Lib (repr)
28.	†1707	Sir Thomas Brograve Bt, ledger stone	Braughing, Herts		*Le Neve* 1700–1715, 125
29.	†1707	Sir William Bury	Grantham, Lincs		*Le Neve* 1700–1715, 115; Pevsner, *Lincs*, 1989, 320
30.	†1707	Thomas (†1664) and Elizabeth Stanton	Wolverton, Warks		*Le Neve* 1650–1718, 58
31.	1707	Thomas Farrer (†1703) and family	Aylesbury, Bucks		*Le Neve* 1700–1715, 61–2; Pevsner, *Bucks*, 1994, 153; C Lib (repr)
32.	†1707	Thomas Mansfield	West Leake, Notts		*Le Neve* 1700–1715, 114; C Lib (repr)
33.	†1707	Thomas Walker, ledger stone	[Burnham Overy, Norfolk]; untraced		*Le Neve* 1700–1715, 137
34.	†1707	William Coldwell	Welwyn, Herts		*Le Neve* 1700–1715, 114–5; Pevsner, *Herts*, 1977, 393; C Lib (repr)
35.	†1708	Dr Edward Tyson	[All Hallows, Lombard Street, City of London]; All Hallows, Twickenham, Middx	S	*Le Neve* 1700–1715, 154; *Whinney* 1988, 142 (repr)
36.	1708	Hervey Bagot (†1699)	Blithfield, Staffs		*Le Neve* 1680–1699, 202–3; C Lib (repr)
37.	1708	Rev William Coldwell (†1702)	[Wisbech, Cambs]; untraced		*Le Neve* 1700–1715, 47
38.	†1708	Sir Brian Broughton Bt	[Broughton, Staffs]; untraced		*Le Neve* 1700–1715, 145
39.	† to 1708	Sir George Wenyeve (†1706) and family	[Brettenham, Suffolk]; untraced		*Le Neve* 1700–1715, 111
40.	†1708	Sir William Craven, ledger stone	Winwick, Northants		*Le Neve* 1700–1715, 127; Pevsner, *Northants*, 1973, 464; C Lib (repr)
41.	†1708	Thomas Fountayne	[Barkway, Herts]; untraced		*Le Neve* 1700–1715, 151–2
42.	1708	William Dansey	Brinsop, Herefs	SD	Pevsner, *Herefs*, 1963, 87; C Lib (repr)
43.	†1709	Mary Plummer	Eastwick, Herts		*Le Neve* 1700–1715, 174
44.	†1709	Rev Thomas Boteler	[Hatfield Broad Oak, Essex]; untraced		*Le Neve* 1700–1715, 158
45.	†1709	Sir John Burgoyne Bt	Sutton, Beds		*Le Neve* 1700–1715, 166–7; Pevsner, *Beds, Hunts & Peterborough*, 1968, 152; C Lib (repr)
46.	†1709	Sir Thomas Wagstaffe	Bishop's Tachbrook, Warks		*Le Neve* 1700–1715, 149; *Gunnis* 1968, 367; C Lib (repr)
47.	†1709	William Hesketh (†1703) and son	North Meols, Lancs		*Le Neve* 1700–1715, 60–1
48.	†1710	Henry Baldwin	Rickmansworth, Herts		*Le Neve* 1650–1718, 238–9
49.	1710	John Norton and family	St Mary, Warwick		*Le Neve* 1600–1649, 163
50.	†1710	Nathaniel Fowler	Southill, Beds		*Le Neve* 1700–1715, 194; *Gunnis* 1968, 367
51.	†1710	Olivia, Lady Smith	Edmondthorpe, Leics		*Le Neve* 1700–1715, 189; *Gunnis* 1968, 367; C Lib (repr)
52.	†1710	Rev Thomas Rayner	Untraced		*Le Neve* 1700–1715, 198–9
53.	†1710	Sir Charles Hoghton, 4th Bt	[Walton-le-Dale, Lancs]; untraced		*Le Neve* 1700–1715, 188; C Lib (repr)
54.	†1710	Sir Robert Kemp	Gissing, Norfolk		*Gunnis* 1968, 367; Pevsner, *Norfolk: N-W & S*, 1999, 362
55.	†1710	Sir Thomas Broughton Bt	Broughton, Staffs		*Le Neve* 1700–1715, 187–8; C Lib (repr)
56.	†1710	Sir William Milard	Houghton Regis, Beds		*Le Neve* 1700–1715, 168–9
57.	†1710	Thomas Fountayne	[Barkway, Herts?]; untraced		*Le Neve* 1700–1715, 170–1
58.	†1710	Thomas Robinson	Untraced		*Le Neve* 1650–1718, 236
59.	† to 1710	William Fisher (†1707) and family	Chawton, Hants		*Le Neve* 1700–1715, 138–9; *Gunnis* 1968, 367
60.	†1711	Constance, Lady Burgoyne	[Sutton, Beds]; untraced		*Le Neve* 1700–1715, 212
61.	†1711	Dorothy Fisher	[Yateley, Hants]; untraced		*Le Neve* 1700–1715, 197
62.	†1711	Henry Limbry	Untraced		*Le Neve* 1700–1715, 220

63.	†1711	John Bendish (†1707) and his wife	Bylaugh, Norfolk		*Le Neve* 1700–1715, 134; Pevsner, *Norfolk: N E & Norwich*, 1997, 423; C Lib (repr)
64.	†1711	John Sneyd	Wolstanton, Staffs		*Le Neve* 1700–1715, 193; C Lib (repr)
65.	†1711	Ralph Bromsal	Blunham, Beds		*Le Neve* 1700–1715, 220; Pevsner, *Beds, Hunts & Peterborough*, 1968, 58
66.	†1711	Rev Matthew Hutton	Aynho, Northants		*Le Neve* 1700–1715, 215; Pevsner, *Northants*, 1973, 97; C Lib (repr)
67.	†1711	Rev Thomas Evans, ledger stone	Untraced		*Le Neve* 1650–1718, 242–3
68.	†1711	Sibill (†1710) and Rupert Browne	Greenford, Middx		*Le Neve* 1700–1715, 196; *Gunnis* 1968, 367; C Lib (repr)
69.	1712	Denny family	Bishops Stortford, Herts		*Le Neve* 1650–1679, 90–1
70.	†1712	Elizabeth Skrymsher	Ladbroke, Warks		*Le Neve* 1700–1715, 245–6
71.	†1712	Joseph Wetham, ledger stone	Untraced		*Le Neve* 1700–1715, 242–3
72.	†1712	Mary Jones	St Alkmund, Shrewsbury, Salop		*Le Neve* 1700–1715, 246; C Lib (repr)
73.	† to 1712	Ralph Sneyd and family	Keele, Staffs		*Le Neve* 1700–1715, 59–60; C Lib (repr)
74.	†1712	Rev Nathaniel Blake	Harborough Magna, Warks		*Le Neve* 1700–1715, 247; C Lib (repr)
75.	†1712	St John Astry	Henbury, Glos		*Le Neve* 1700–1715, 241–2; C Lib (repr)
76.	†1712	Thomas Sturt	Untraced		*Le Neve* 1700–1715, 248
77.	†1712	Thomas Swallow	[Thaxted, Essex]; destroyed		*Le Neve* 1700–1715, 247–8; *Gunnis* 1968, 367
78.	†1713	Catherine Belenson, ledger stone	Wrotham, Kent		*Le Neve* 1700–1715, 266
79.	†1713	Felix Calvert	Hunsdon, Herts		*Le Neve* 1700–1715, 265; Pevsner, *Herts*, 1977, 212; C Lib (repr)
80.	†1713	Isaac Millner	St Mary-at-Hill, City of London		*Le Neve* 1700–1715, 267–8; Pevsner, *London: City*, 1997, 246; C Lib (repr)
81.	†1713	John Peck, ledger stone	['Bedford']; untraced		*Le Neve* 1700–1715, 268
82.	†1713	Judith Benet	Babraham, Cambs		*Le Neve* 1700–1715, 260; Pevsner, *Cambs*, 1970, 294
83.	†1713	Penelope Bate, ledger stone	Untraced		*Le Neve* 1700–1715, 266
84.	†1713	Rebecca, Lady Winche	Untraced		*Le Neve* 1700–1715, 236
85.	†1713	Sir Edward Smyth Bt	Theydon Mount, Essex		*Le Neve* 1700–1715, 253; *Gunnis* 1968, 367; Pevsner, *Essex*, 1965, 386; C Lib (repr)
86.	†1713	Sir Salathiel Lovell	Harlestone, Northants	S	*Le Neve* 1700–1715, 261; Pevsner, *Northants*, 1973, 247; C Lib (repr)
87.	†1713	Tollemache Duke, ledger stone	[Bentley, Suffolk]; untraced		*Le Neve* 1700–1715, 264
88.	†1714	Anne, Lady Poyntz	[North Ockendon, Essex]; untraced		*Le Neve* 1700–1715, 277
89.	†1714	Anne, Lady Swinnerton Dyer, ledger stone	[Dunmow, Essex]; untraced		*Le Neve* 1700–1715, 277
90.	†1714	Charles May	[Basingstoke, Hants]; untraced		*Le Neve* 1700–1715, 259
91.	†1714	Edward Billingsley	Great Stanmore, Middx, churchyard		*Le Neve* 1700–1715, 282
92.	†1714	Elizabeth Manningham	Chichester Cathedral, Sussex		*Le Neve* 1650–1718, 257; *Gunnis* 1968, 367
93.	†1714	Elizabeth Pilling	[Iver, Bucks]; untraced		*Le Neve* 1700–1715, 269
94.	c1714	Elizabeth, Lady Isham (†1713) Payment(s): £55 Drawing(s): Northants R O, I. L.3079/C 16	Lamport, Northants		*Le Neve* 1700–1715, 259; *Isham* 1951, 440–2 (repr); *Isham* 1965, 4
95.	†1714	Francis Williams	[St Mary's, Warwick]; untraced		*Le Neve* 1650–1718, 256–7
96.	†1714	Henry Cooley	Ivinghoe, Bucks		*Le Neve* 1700–1715, 286–7; Pevsner, *Bucks*, 1994, 417; C Lib (repr)
97.	†1714	Mary Stephens, ledger stone	Untraced		*Le Neve* 1700–1715, 265
98.	†1714	Nicholas Alexander	Chipping Ongar, Essex		*Le Neve* 1700–1715, 258; Pevsner, *Essex*, 1965, 125
99.	†1714	William Helder	Untraced		*Le Neve* 1700–1715, 260
100.	†1715	Charles Whitaker	St Nicholas, Ipswich, Suffolk		*Le Neve* 1700–1715, 264; C Lib (repr)
101.	†1715	George Lewis	[Carmarthen]; untraced		*Le Neve* 1700–1715, 268
102.	†1715	Henry Colman	[Harpley, Norfolk]; untraced		*Le Neve* 1700–1715, 296
103.	†1715	Hugh Marchant	[St Giles-in-the-Fields, London, churchyard]; untraced		*Le Neve* 1650–1718, 262
104.	†1715	James Pedley, ledger stone	[Bishops Stortford, Herts]; untraced		*Le Neve* 1700–1715, 287
105.	†1715	Rev John Smith	St John's College, Cambridge, chapel		*Le Neve* 1650–1718, 266–7; Pevsner, *Cambs*, 1970, 154
106.	1715	Richard Acton (†1704) and wife	Acton Round, Salop	S	Pevsner, *Salop*, 1958, 52; *Kemp* 1980, 117 (repr); C Lib (repr)
107.	1716	Elizabeth and Alice Eardley	[Audley, Staffs]; untraced		*Le Neve* 1650–1718, 263–4
108.	† to 1716	Galliard family	Edmonton, Middx		*Le Neve* 1650–1718, 183
109.	†1716	John Morgan	[Machen, Monmouths]; untraced		*Le Neve* 1650–1718, 268
110.	†1716	Thomas Orme	Longdon, Staffs		*Le Neve* 1650–1718, 274–5; Pevsner, *Staffs*, 1974, 197; C Lib (repr)

No.	Date	Subject		Location		Bibliography
111.	†1717	Thomas Stanton (†1674), his wife Frances (†1689), William Stanton (†1705), his wife Dorothy (†1707), Sarah (†1717) wife of the sculptor, and other members of the Stanton family		[St Andrew, Holborn, London, churchyard]; untraced		*Le Neve* 1650–1718, 104–5; *Esdaile* 1930, 149–169
112.	†1719	Anne, Lady Hodgson (co-sculptor: Christopher Horsnaile I)		Marston, Lincs	S	Pevsner, *Lincs*, 1989, 558; C Lib (repr)
113.	†1719	Robert Pleydell		Ampney Crucis, Glos		Pevsner, *Glos: Cotswolds*, 1999, 140
114.	†1721	Alice, Lady Brownlow (co-sculptor: Christopher Horsnaile I)		Belton, Lincs	S	*Lord* 1986, 103; Pevsner, *Lincs*, 1989, 134; C Lib (repr)
115.	†1721	Thomas Vernon (co-sculptor: Christopher Horsnaile I)		Hanbury, Worcs	S	Pevsner, *Worcs*, 1968, 184; *Whinney* 1988, 139; C Lib (repr)
116.	† to 1722	Cressener family (co-sculptor: Christopher Horsnaile I)		Earls Colne, Essex	S	*Gunnis* 1968, 210; C Lib (repr)
117.	†1722	Thomas Renda (co-sculptor: Christopher Horsnaile I)		Wallingford, Berks	S	Pevsner, *Berks*, 1966, 248; C Lib (repr)
118.	†1723	Admiral Sir James Wishart (co-sculptor: Christopher Horsnaile I)		Leatherhead, Surrey	S	Pevsner, *Surrey*, 1971, 339; *Whinney* 1988, 139
119.	†1723	Bishop Fleetwood (co-sculptor: Christopher Horsnaile I)		Ely Cathedral, Cambs	S	Pevsner, *Cambs*, 1970, 365; C Lib (repr)
120.	†1723	Gregory Geering (co-sculptor: Christopher Horsnaile I)		Denchworth, Berks	S	C Lib (repr)
121.	†1724	Sir John Sherard (co-sculptor: Christopher Horsnaile I)		North Witham, Lincs	S	*Lord* 1986, 103; Pevsner, *Lincs*, 1989, 589
122.	†1726	Sir John Blencowe (co-sculptor: Christopher Horsnaile I)		Marston St Lawrence, Northants	S	Pevsner, *Northants*, 1973, 302; C Lib (repr)
123.	†1726	William Brownlow (co-sculptor: Christopher Horsnaile I)		Belton, Lincs	S	*Lord* 1986, 103; Pevsner, *Lincs*, 1989, 134; C Lib (repr)
124.	†1726	William East (co-sculptor: Christopher Horsnaile I)		Witham, Essex	S	Pevsner, *Essex*, 1965, 429; C Lib (repr)
125.	†1727	Elizabeth, Lady Benet (co-sculptor: Christopher Horsnaile I)		Warminghurst, Sussex	S	Pevsner, *Sussex*, 1965, 363; C Lib (repr)
126.	1729	William Beaumont (†1718) (co-sculptor: Christopher Horsnaile I)		Great Dunmow, Essex	S	Pevsner, *Essex*, 1965, 202
127.	1720–1730	Bartholomew Layton (†1702) (co-sculptor: Christopher Horsnaile I)		Ringwood, Hants	S	*Gunnis* 1968, 210
128.	1720–1730	Maude family († to 1703) (co-sculptor: Christopher Horsnaile I)		St Mary, Kilkenny	S	*Potterton* 1975, 83; C Lib (repr)
129.	†1730	Sir Richard Sherard (co-sculptor: Christopher Horsnaile I)		North Witham, Lincs	S	*Lord* 1986, 103; Pevsner, *Lincs*, 1989, 589
Statues						
130.	1717–1719	King George I Payment(s): £60		[Royal Exchange, London]; untraced		Minutes of the George I statue & picture committee, 1716–18, CLRO, Alchin box H, item 106; *Douglas Stewart* 1978, 219; *ODNB*
Chimneypieces						
131.	1704	Description unavailable		[Aynho Park, Northants, south-west chamber]; untraced		*Gunnis* 1968, 366 citing Cartwright Archives
132.	1707	Description unavailable		[Aynho Park, Northants, closet above white parlour]; untraced		*Gunnis* 1968, 366 citing Cartwright Archives
133.	1708	For an unidentified room Payment(s): £13	m	[Aynho Park, Northants]; untraced		*Gunnis* 1968, 366 citing Cartwright Archives
134.	1708	'Marble Chimney piece and dutch tiles', billed with a marble slab for a sideboard table		Aynho Park, Northants		Cartwright Accounts
135.	1715	Several Payment(s): £34	m	Milton House, Northants		Fitzwilliam Letters
136.	1724	Description unavailable		[Knowsley, Lancs]; untraced		*Gunnis* 1968, 366 citing Derby Archives
137.	1726	Two, with black fluted Corinthian columns and white capitals (co-sculptor: Christopher Horsnaile I)		Ditchley Park, Oxon, library		Pevsner, *Oxon*, 1974, 575
138.	*c*1727	With cross-member carved with mask and garlands and term supports (designed by William Kent?) (co-sculptor: Christopher Horsnaile I) Payment(s): £64 15s	m	Ditchley Park, Oxon, hall		*Friedman* 1984, 121, 318–9; *Gomme* 1989, 89–90 (repr 9)
Architectural Sculpture						
139.	1705	Unicorn's head and helmet Payment(s): £30 including part payment for mason's wages		[Stonyhurst, gardens, head of stone stairs in the court]; Stonyhurst College, Boys' Refectory		*Stonyhurst* 1964, 480
140.	1708	Tablet inscribed with the details of the Clopton bequest		Guild chapel, Stratford-upon-Avon, Warks		RG/JP, 8, 1350–1
141.	1709	Crest and Shireburn coat of arms Payment(s): £6, £10		Stonyhurst College, Lancs, hall stairs, and perhaps refectory		*Stonyhurst* 1964, 480
142.	1709	'my Lady Charleton's inscription' Payment(s): £7 14s 6d		[Almshouses, Cartington, Northumbs]; untraced		*Stonyhurst* 1964, 480
143.	1720–1723	Capitals, pinnacles, cherubim heads, 'the College Arms,' 'Two Portcullis and Chains' and other work Payment(s): £6,038		Westminster Abbey, London		*Gunnis* 1968, 366

STANTON, James, of London fl 1810?–*c*1812

Funerary Monuments

1.	?1810	Theodosia Richards	Sidmouth, Devon	S	*Gunnis* 1968, 367
2.	†1812	Rev Philip Wroughton	Chaddleworth, Berks	S	HMC

STANTON, Robert fl 1738–39

He was a London carver who worked for **Henry Watson**. A payment of £1 3s 6d to him on 29 April 1738 is recorded in Watson's account book. He also worked for Watson at Wentworth Woodhouse in 1739.

Literary References: *Brighton* 2001, 72

STANTON, Thomas *c*1610–74

Thomas Stanton is the earliest recorded member of a family of masons and sculptors active until well into the 18th century, chiefly known for memorials, although they also took on some important masonry contracts. He was born in 1609 or 1610 and was apprenticed to Christopher Kingsfield, becoming free of the Masons' Company in February 1631, a warden in 1657 and master in 1660. By May 1638 he was living in the parish of St Andrew, Holborn, and by about 1639 he had premises next to St Andrew's church where he lived until his death.

His first documented work is a floor slab with a relief carving to Jane Isham, at Lamport, for which a signed design survives (Northants RO I.L.1635) (1). The memorial to Judith Combe, described by Vertue as of 'tolerable taste' and by Whinney as 'conservative' has two half-length figures holding hands (2). Stanton's most ambitious work is the monument to Dame Jane Bacon, at Culford, a large black and white tomb dominated by a seated figure of the deceased with a child on her lap, with a row of little girls standing to either side. The stiff effigy of her husband is below (4). Whinney considered the work heavy and clumsy, but commented that the design is a welcome change from the wide-spread type with kneeling figures. The contract relates that Stanton was paid £300 for the monument, but the client was responsible for freight and its setting up (HMC Verulam MSS (1906) 54). It was to be executed 'according to the best skill of a stone-cutter, alle in whit and black marble without the addition of any other ston whatsoever'. The agreement also survives for the Heath monument at Brasted, with receipts for payments in 1664 and 1666 (BM Egerton MS 2985 fols 94, 95). Brasses formed a significant part of Stanton's output.

White lists ten monuments attributed to the sculptor on stylistic grounds. These include the Thomasine Benet (†1645) at Wroughton, Wilts; Symeon Brograve and his wife (she †1645) at Braughing, Herts; Sir Henry Audley, 1648 at Berechurch, Essex; Edward Boys (†1649) at Betteshanger, Kent; William Draper and wife (she †1652) at St Paulinus, Crayford; Charles and Francis Tufton (†1652 and 1657) at Bobbing, Kent; Sir Richard Halford, 1659, at Wistow, Leics; Laetitia Boys (†1660), at Betteshanger, Kent; Sir William Cornwallis at Oakley, Suffolk and Sir William Wiseman and wife (she † 1662) at Great Canfield, Essex. Stanton died on 24 May 1674 and was buried in the family tomb in Holborn. His son Thomas, who was apprenticed to him on 20 August 1668, predeceased him, and he was succeeded in business by his nephew **William Stanton**. In his will Stanton left his lands at Aldington, Kent, to his wife Frances and legacies to his grandchildren, Thomas, Elizabeth, and Robert, the children of his dead son Thomas. Stanton's probate inventory lists his workshop and yard contents. In the shop were seven black marble gravestones, twelve black pilasters, five chimneypieces and other lumber. Eight more black marble grave stones were in the yard, but no identifiable sculpture was listed.

Literary References: *Vertue* IV 138; *Esdaile* 1930, 152; *Knoop and Jones* 1935, 21; *Whinney* 1988, 84, 135, 437 n58; *Lack et al*, 1994, 86–7, 118–9; *Colvin* 1995, 915–6; *White* 1999, 108–112; *Webb* 1999, 31

Will: PROB 4/14203

Funerary Monuments

1.	†1639	Jane Isham	Lamport, Northants		*White* 1999, 108 (repr 21, 22)
2.	†1649	Judith Combe and her betrothed	Holy Trinity, Stratford-upon-Avon, Warks	S	*Vertue* IV, 138; *White* 1999, 108
3.	†1656	Nicholas Fowle	Rotherfield, Sussex	S	*White* 1999, 109
4.	1657–1658	Dame Jane Bacon and family Payment(s): £300	Culford, Suffolk		*HMC* 1906, 54; *Esdaile* 1930, 153 (repr 1); *Whinney* 1988, 84, 437 n58; *White* 1999, 108
5.	†1665	Jane Robinson	Pangbourne, Berks	S	*White* 1999, 108
6.	1664–1666	Sir Robert Heath (†1649) and his wife Payment(s): £60	Brasted, Kent		Pevsner, *Kent: W & Weald*, 1976, 177–8; *White* 1999, 108

STANTON, William 1639–1705

William Stanton was a mason, sculptor and architect and was for 30 years the proprietor of one of London's leading workshops. He was born on 6 April 1639, the nephew of **Thomas Stanton** and the son of Edward Stanton (1596–1686), who may have been the craftsman responsible for setting up the clock at the Royal Exchange. William was apprenticed to his uncle and became free of the Masons' Company on 30 June 1663. His first monument appears to have been to John Byde (2) and he took his first apprentice in 1666. In 1674 he inherited his deceased uncle's business.

In 1678 he was employed nine men and ran what was then the largest mason-sculptor's premises in London, at St Andrew's, Holborn. Monumental sculpture formed a significant part of his wide-ranging business. The output ranged from minor building works (such as the columns erected in the cloister of the Inner Temple in 1680 for £20), to major contracts. He was the mason at Gray's Inn from 1672 until his death. Stanton was involved with **Edward Pearce** in rebuilding St Andrew, Holborn, to designs by Sir Christopher Wren, at a cost of £4,050. He also built Belton House, Lincs for Sir John Brownlow between 1685 and 1688, earning over £5,000. Like his uncle, Stanton was able to rise through the ranks of the Masons' Company, becoming a renter warden in June 1681, an upper warden in October 1683, and master in 1688–89.

Stanton's funerary sculpture ranges from inscriptions on ledger stones to large figural compositions but he was chiefly in demand for architectural wall monuments. Typically these consist of an inscribed tablet, sometimes carved to emulate hanging drapery, flanked by columns or pilasters and often surmounted by a segmental scrolled pediment. Other recurring features are putti, large floral scrolls and flaming urns. The monuments ranged in cost from £10, the price for the monument to Dr Balcanqual (**15**), to £64, the fee for Sir Justinian Isham's memorial, which has twisting columns of dove marble (**59**). On occasion a monument incorporated superbly executed figural elements, such as the two half-length effigies on the monument to Sir John and Lady Brownlow (**20**), or the naval trophies and relief of a ship on Lieutenant-Colonel Spencer Broughton's memorial (**74**). There are dozens of contemporary unsigned works all over England which make use of Stanton's combination of motifs, and which probably also emanate from the Holborn workshop.

From 1670 onwards Stanton produced large-scale effigial memorials. The Harison monument incorporates a kneeling and a standing figure (**25**) and the Lucy, a cross-legged recumbent effigy watched by his wife reclining on one elbow, and their son, who stands beside them in a long wig and large-cuffed coat (**44**). The reclining figures of Earl Rivers (**39**) and Lord Coventry (**60**) have considerable grace, the former posed beneath a marble canopy held up by black Corinthian columns, the latter gesturing towards a crown and flanked by two angels.

His most impressive sequence of figures was perhaps produced for the Shireburn family at Stonyhurst. Soon after 1695 Sir Nicholas Shireburn embarked on an extravagant programme of improvements to his house and Stanton was engaged to provide building and sculptural work, to which end he sent his man, **John Mason**, to Lancashire for extensive periods (**97–99**). In 1699 Stanton was paid for four effigies for the family church in Mitton which reflect the Royalist Catholic leanings of the family, both in the wording of the inscriptions and in the use of traditional, recumbent figures (**51–53**). A later monument, to Richard Francis Shireburn, depicts the pathetic figure of the last of the Shireburns, a boy of nine, who starts back in fear from a skull and crossbones, emblems of mortality (**77**).

The Masons' Company search of September 1694 recorded that Stanton employed eight men at his 'shop' in Holborn, including **William Holland**, a future master of the Masons' Company. Over the course of his career Stanton took 24 apprentices, including **William Atkins I** and **Thomas Hill II, Robert Hartshorne I**, who came to the workshop as an assistant, and **John Thompson**, his master-mason at Belton. His ninth child, **Edward Stanton**, was apprenticed to him in 1694 and became free in 1702. The payment for the monument to Richard and Isabel Shireburn, 1699 (**51**), is made out to Edward, which suggests that the younger Stanton had taken on an important role in the workshop by that date. It is not always possible to disentangle the early work of Edward Stanton from that of his father, and in the following list, memorials to persons who died before 1705 are treated as works of William Stanton, as head of the business until his death in that year, unless there is contrary evidence (Edward Stanton's signature, documentation or style).

Stanton's last known work was the quirky monument to the 4th Earl of Leicester, 1704, which has two angels, apparently running towards a central, festooned urn (**85**). This was completed by **William Woodman I**. Stanton died on 30 May 1705 and was buried two days later at St Andrew, Holborn. He was survived by his wife Dorothy (1640–1707), whom he married *c*1665, and who was described on the family tombstone as 'a prudent tender wife and mother' (*Le Neve* 1650–1718, 104–5). In his will, witnessed by two of his employees (John Sumners and Robert Swift), Stanton appointed his wife sole executrix and left her his personal estate, goods and property. He left £400 to his son, Thomas Stanton, who had also been apprenticed to his father and had become free in 1702. Whether Thomas took any later role in the family trade is unclear, for he soon departed for Livorno, Italy. The business was taken over by Edward Stanton, who continued to run the family workshop with success.

MGS

Literary References: *Le Neve* 1650–79, 1680–99, 1700–15, 1650–1718 *passim* (memorials are authenticated as Stanton works if their inscriptions are printed in Le Neve with Stanton credits); *Builder* 1846, vol 4, n152, 2; *Inderwick* 1896–1936, vol 3, 157; *Esdaile* 1930, 149–69; *Knoop and Jones* 1935, 20–1, 69, 78; *Isham* 1951, 440; *Gunnis* 1968, 367–8; *Physick* 1969, 14, 16, 24, 26, 28, 48–53; *Whinney* 1988, 84, 93, 135–8, 251, 445 n67, 446 n2–3; *Colvin* 1995, 916; *ODNB* (Fisher)

Archival References: Masons' Co, Masters and Wardens; Stanton/Isham; Stanton/Hatton; Stanton/Masons' Co; Stanton-Isham Agreement

Will: PROB 11/483, 152, 2 June 1705 (transcribed in *Esdaile* 1930, 156)

Collections of Drawings: 21 attributed designs for monuments, VAM 93.B.41 (D.1114-8-98, D.11120-32-98, D.1138-98, D.1140-1-98)

Funerary Monuments

1.	†1664	Francis (†1635) and John Conyers	Easington, Durham	S	*Surtees* I, 1816–40, 13–14
2.	1665	John Byde and family	[St Leonard, Shoreditch, London]; Bengeo, Herts	S	Pevsner, *Herts*, 1977, 93
3.	†1666	Sir Thomas Guybon	Thursford, Norfolk	S	Pevsner, *Norfolk: NE & Norwich*, 1997, 697
4.	†1666	Sir Thomas Lyttelton Bt (†1650) and wife	Worcester Cathedral	S	*White* 1999, 111, n49
5.	†1668	Captain Thomas Sondes	Throwley, Kent	S	*Whinney* 1988, 93
6.	†1669	John Skynner	Hitchin, Herts	S	
7.	†1670	Hon Penelope Egerton	Westminster Abbey, London, north west tower (formerly north aisle)	S	*Gunnis* 1968, 368
8.	1670	Sir Henry (†1625) and Lady Bridget Kingesmill (†1672)	Kingsclere, Hants	S	
9.	†1672	John Bowyer	Colwich, Staffs		*Le Neve* 1650–1679, 153
10.	†1673	Sir Edward Bagot Bt	Blithfield, Staffs		*Le Neve* 1650–1679, 155
11.	†1674	Carola Harsnett, Lady Morland	Westminster Abbey, London, nave, south aisle	S	Pevsner, *London: Westminster*, 1973, 458
12.	†1674	John Bromley of Holt Castle	Worcester Cathedral	S	*Gunnis* 1968, 368
13.	†1675	Sir John and Lady Dormer (†1673)	Quainton, Bucks	S	Pevsner, *Bucks*, 1994, 608
14.	†1677	Edmund Gybbon	Temple Church, London	S	
15.	1678	Dr Walter Balcanqual	Chirk, Denbighs		Chirk Castle Archives, transcribed in *Myddleton* 1931, vol. 3, 125
16.	†1678	Elizabeth Davies	Monken Hadley, Herts	S	Pevsner, *London: N*, 1998, 184
17.	†1679	Charles Holloway	St Mary the Virgin, Oxford	S	Pevsner, *Oxon*, 1974, 286
18.	†1679	Dame Margaret Turnor	Stoke Rochford, Lincs		*Le Neve* 1650–1718, 143–4
19.	†1679	George Wylde	Temple Church, London	S	Pevsner, *London: City*, 1997, 270

No.	Date	Subject	Location		Bibliography
20.	†1679	Sir John (†1679) and Lady Alicia (†1676) Brownlow Payment(s): £100	Belton, Lincs		*Esdaile* 1930, 161; *Physick* 1969, 52; *Kemp* 1985, 19 (repr)
21.	†1680	Ann Filding, Lady Morland	Westminster Abbey, London, nave, south aisle	S	Pevsner, *London: Westminster*, 1973, 458
22.	†1682	Bishop Robert Morgan (†1673) and daughter	Bangor Cathedral, Carnarvonshire		*Le Neve* 1650–1679, 156–7
23.	†1682	Susanna Warton Payment(s): Freight 23s, cost of monument unknown	Beverley Minster, E R Yorks		*Neave and Woodward* 1979, 1233
24.	1683	Sir John Archer (†1682), monument and gravestone Payment(s): £30	Theydon Garnon, Essex		Monson Accounts in GPC; C Lib (repr)
25.	†1683	Sir Richard and Philip Harison	St Nicholas Hurst, Berks	S	Pevsner, *Berks*, 1966, 210
26.	†1684	Elizabeth, Lady Brownlow Payment(s): £166 17s	Old Somerby, Lincs		*Esdaile* 1930, 161; *Gunnis* 1968, 367
27.	†to 1684	Members of the Hatton family, two similar tablets	Gretton, Northants		BL Ad MS 29560, fols 275, 315, 352, 374, 381; *Esdaile* 1930, 157–9; Pevsner, *Northants*, 1973, 242
28.	†1685	Sir Richard (†1678) and Lady Juliana Newdigate	Harefield, Middx	S	*Kemp* 1980, 119 (repr); Pevsner, *London: NW*, 1991, 318
29.	1689	Michael Warton (†1688) Payment(s): £50, freight £5 15s (sent with two of Stanton's men)	Beverley Minster, E R Yorks		*Neave and Woodward* 1979, 1230–3 (repr)
30.	† to 1691	Dayrell family	Hinxton, Cambs		*Le Neve* 1650–1679, 133–6
31.	1691	Samuel Langford	St Margaret, Westminster, London	S	
32.	†1692	Dorothy, Lady Smithson	Stanwick, N R Yorks	S	*Butler* 2000, 65–70 (repr)
33.	†1692	Thomasina Bownds	[Chelmsford, Essex]; untraced		*Le Neve* 1680–1699, 135
34.	†1692	William Palmer	Wanlip, Leics		*Le Neve* 1680–1699, 134
35.	†1693	Ralph Bromsal	[Blunham, Beds]; untraced		*Le Neve* 1680–1699, 140
36.	†1695	Charles Hutchinson	Owthorpe, Notts		*Le Neve* 1680–1699, 167
37.	†1695	Jane, Lady Bagot	Blithfield, Staffs		*Le Neve* 1680–1699, 162; *Physick* 1968, 90; Pevsner, *Staffs*, 1974, 72
38.	†1696	Abraham Stanyon	Harefield, Middx		*Le Neve* 1680–1699, 177; *Gunnis* 1968, 368
39.	1695–1696	Thomas, 3rd Earl Rivers (†1694) Payment(s): £370	St Michael (formerly All Hallows), Macclesfield, Cheshire	S	Earl Rivers Accounts; *Physick* 1968, 90; *Le Neve* 1680–1699, 154–5; *Whinney* 1988, 446 n3
40.	†1697	George Nodes	Shephall, Herts		BL Harley MS 3615, f87R
41.	1697	Isabella Shireburn (†1688), ledger stone	Rothbury, Northumbs		Lulworth Castle archives, Dorset cited in RG/JP 8, 1353
42.	†1697	Ralph Skynner	Hitchin, Herts	S	*Le Neve* 1680–1699, 180–1; *Gunnis* 1968, 368; Pevsner, *Herts*, 1977, 199
43.	†1698	Catherine, Lady Raynsford, ledger stone	Dallington, Northants		*Le Neve* 1680–1699, 188; Pevsner, *Northants*, 1973, 356
44.	†1698	Rev Richard Lucy (†1690) and his son, Gam	Christ College Chapel, Brecon		*Le Neve* 1680–1699, 175–6; Pevsner, *Powys*, 1979, 295 (repr)
45.	1698	Sir Richard Atkins Bt Payment(s): £15	[Newport Pagnell, Bucks]; untraced		Atkins Family Papers, Herts RO65435
46.	†1698	Thomas Ravenscroft	Hawarden, Flints		*Le Neve* 1680–1699, 188
47.	†1699	Captain John Smith	Bunhill Fields, London		*Le Neve* 1680–1699, 193
48.	†1699	Dorothy, Lady Williamson	Monkwearmouth, Durham		*Le Neve* 1680–1699, 202; *Gunnis* 1968, 368
49.	† to 1699	Emmott family	Colne, Lancs		*Le Neve* 1680–1699, 44
50.	†1699	Frances Hempson	Untraced		*Le Neve* 1680–1699, 201
51.	1699	Richard (†1689) and Isabel (†1693) Shireburn Payment(s): £253 with the monuments to Richard Shireburn (+1667), and that to Richard Shireburn (+1690)	Mitton, W R Yorks		*Stonyhurst* 1894, 68; *Esdaile* 1930, 160 (repr pl IV); Pevsner, *Yorks: W R*, 1967, 370; *Whinney* 1988, 136, 446 n2 (repr)
52.	1699	Richard Shireburn (†1667) Payment(s): £253 with the monuments to Richard and Isabel Shireburn, and that to Richard Shireburn (+1690)	Mitton, W R Yorks		*Stonyhurst* 1894, 68; Pevsner, *Yorks: W R*, 1967, 370
53.	1699	Richard Shireburn (†1690) Payment(s): £253 with the monuments to Richard Shireburn (+1667), and that to Richard and Isabel Shireburn	Mitton, W R Yorks		*Stonyhurst* 1894, 68; Pevsner, *Yorks: W R*, 1967, 370
54.	†1699	Sir John Newton Bt	Bitton, Glos		*Le Neve* 1680–1699, 195–6; *Neave and Woodward* 1979, 1235
55.	†1699	Sir Thomas Rokeby	Kirk Sandal, W R Yorks		*Le Neve* 1680–1699, 204–5
56.	†1699	William Hall	Untraced		*Le Neve* 1680–1699, 201
57.	†1700	Edmund Waller (†1687) and wife	Beaconsfield, Bucks, churchyard		BL Harley MS 3615, f48v
58.	†1700	John, Viscount Lonsdale	Lowther, Westmorland		*Le Neve* 1700–1715, 3–4; Pevsner, *Cumberland & Westmorland*, 1967, 273 (repr 92); *Kemp* 1980, 112 (repr)
59.	1700	Sir Justinian Isham Bt (†1675) and family	Lamport, Northants		*Physick* 1968, 88 (repr); *Isham* 1951, 440; *Isham* 1965, 2
60.	*c*1700	Thomas, 1st Earl of Coventry (†1699) Drawing(s): Epitaph design, Croome Court archives	Elmley Castle, Worcs	S	*Le Neve* 1680–1699, 198; *Physick* 1968, 90 (repr); *Whinney* 1988, 136, 137 (repr)

61.	†1700	William Lyngwood		[Stisted, Essex]; untraced		*Le Neve* 1680–1699, 208–9
62.	†1701	Simon Packe, ledger stone		Prestwold, Leics		*Le Neve* 1700–1715, 26
63.	†1702	Brooke Bridges		Wadenhoe, Northants		*Le Neve* 1700–1715, 41–2; Pevsner, *Northants*, 1973, 439
64.	†1702	Dean Henry Fairfax		Norwich Cathedral, Norfolk	S	*Le Neve* 1700–1715, 39–40; Pevsner, *Norfolk: N E & Norwich*, 1997, 212
65.	†1702	Sir Edward Sebright Bt		[Besford, Worcs]; untraced		*Le Neve* 1700–1715, 36–7
66.	†1702	William Mellish (†1690) and wife, Dorothy		St Andrew, Holborn, City of London (formerly at Ragnall, Notts)		*Le Neve* 1680–1699, 118; Pevsner, *Notts*, 1979, 291
67.	†1703	Anne Williams		Halkyn, Flints		*Le Neve* 1700–1715, 67
68.	†1703	E Cheselden (†1688) and wife		Braunston, Rutland		*Le Neve* 1680–1699, 99
69.	†1703	Elizabeth Langton		Doynton, Glos	S	
70.	†1703	Elizabeth Tollet, ledger stone		[St Martin-in-the-Fields, London]; untraced		*Le Neve* 1700–1715, 46
71.	†1703	Godfrey Thacker, ledger stone		[Writtle, Essex]; untraced		*Le Neve* 1700–1715, 60
72.	†1703	Judeth Chester		Barkway, Herts	S	*Le Neve* 1700–1715, 45; *Gunnis* 1968, 368; C Lib (repr)
73.	+1703	Lambert Bagot		[Blithfield, Staffs]; untraced		*Le Neve* 1700–1715, 44–5
74.	†1703	Lieutenant-Colonel Spencer Broughton		Broughton, Staffs		*Le Neve* 1700–1715, 43
75.	†1703	Meriel Williams		Meifod, Montgomerys		*Le Neve* 1700–1715, 45–6
76.	†1703	Owen Bold		Wrexham, Denbighs	S	*Le Neve* 1700–1715, 62–3; Pevsner, *Clwyd*, 1986, 302
77.	1703	Richard Francis Shireburn (†1702) Payment(s): £177, with lions and eagles for Stonyhurst		Mitton, W R Yorks		*Le Neve* 1700–1715, 44; *Esdaile* 1930, 165 (repr VII); *Stonyhurst* 1964, 480; Pevsner, *Yorks: W R*, 1967, 370; *Whinney* 1988, 136
78.	†1703	Sir Thomas Williamson Bt, ledger stone		[Monkwearmouth, Durham]; untraced		*Le Neve* 1700–1715, 56
79.	1703	Thomas Howard (†1701) and son, Thomas (†1703) Payment(s): £35		St Giles, Ashtead, Surrey		*Le Neve* 1700–1715, 23–4; *Gunnis* 1968, 368, citing Elford Hall MSS, Birmingham ref lib, 24 Sept, 1703,; *Beard* 1952 (1), 364 (repr); Pevsner, *Surrey*, 1971, 98
80.	†1704	Ann Barnham		Warminghurst, Sussex		*Le Neve* 1700–1715, 82–3; *Gunnis* 1968, 367
81.	†1704	Hannah Bownd		[Chelmsford, Essex]; untraced		*Le Neve* 1700–1715, 84
82.	†1704	Isaac Motham		Hethersett, Norfolk	S	*Gunnis* 1968, 368; Pevsner, *Norfolk: N-W & S*, 1999, 397
83.	†1704	John Walker		Monken Hadley, Herts		*Le Neve* 1700–1715, 61
84.	†1704	Peter Lee		Untraced		*Le Neve* 1700–1715, 80
85.	1704	Robert, 4th Earl of Leicester (†1702) (co-sculptor: William Woodman the Elder)		Penshurst, Kent		*Whinney* 1988, 138; *Wilson* 2002, 94–5 (repr)
86.	†1704	Sir Anthony Abdy		Kelvedon, Essex		*Le Neve* 1700–1715, 77; Pevsner, *Essex*, 1965, 254
87.	†1704	Sir Roger L'Estrange		St Giles-in-the-Fields, Holborn, London		*Le Neve* 1700–1715, 79; Pevsner, *London: N*, 1998, 259
88.	†1704	Ursula Taylor		Clapham, Beds		*Le Neve* 1700–1715, 68–9
89.	nd	Elizabeth and Ann Beane		Hythe, Kent	S	Pevsner, *Kent: NE & E*, 1983, 360
Busts						
90.	nd	Hugh Sexey, bust with arms		Sexey's Hospital, Bruton, Somerset	S	Pevsner, *Somerset: S & W*, 1958, 106; *Gunnis* 1968, 368
Architectural Sculpture						
91.	1686	'Cornish in ye withdrawing-roome' Payment(s): £8		[Belton, Lincs]; untraced		*Gunnis* 1968, 367, citing Brownlow Archives, Lincs RO
92.	1686	'Five cornishes with freezes to ten chimney-pieces' Payment(s): £30		[Belton, Lincs]; untraced		*Gunnis* 1968, 367
93.	1686	Paving		[Belton, Lincs, hall and staircase]; untraced		*Gunnis* 1968, 367
94.	1686	'Two scollop shells' Payment(s): £26		[Belton, Lincs]; untraced		*Gunnis* 1968, 367 citing archives, Lord Brownlow (Lincs RO)
95.	1687	Font Payment(s): £25	m	St Andrew, Holborn, London		Guildhall MS 4256, pp84–5
96.	1686–1688	Six friezes for chimneypieces, 'a Cornish in ye withdrawing roome' (£8), scallop shells and other carved work		Belton House, Lincs		Brownlow Papers BNLW 2/1/1/4/29 (cornice); *Gunnis* 1968, 367
97.	1701	Reigate stone lions Payment(s): £4 16s	s	[Stonyhurst, Lancs]; untraced		*Gunnis* 1968, 368 citing Shireburn Stonyhurst archives
98.	1703	Coat of Arms Payment(s): £30		Stonyhurst, Lancs, over front door		*Stonyhurst* 1964, 480; *Stonyhurst* 1894, 72
99.	1703	Lions and Eagles Payment(s): £30		Stonyhurst, Lancs, gardens, formerly Court Stairs		*Stonyhurst* 1894, 72 n3; *Stonyhurst* 1964, 480

STAVELEY, William fl 1723–49

He was employed as a mason at Ditchley Park, Oxon. The Dillon Accounts for 14 January 1723 carry the entry 'Paid Mr. Staffley towards Chimneypieces £12:12:0' and again, on 2 February 1749, 'for Mason's work on two Marble

Chimney pieces', paid at 2/- a day. He may be the Staveley of Woodstock responsible for a signed monument to Edward Perrott, 1731, at North Leigh, Oxon.

Literary References: *Gunnis* 1968, 369; Pevsner, *Oxon*, 1974, 721

Archival References: Dillon, DIL Ip/li and I/p/ly

Chimneypieces

1.	1749	Two, of marble	Ditchley Park, Oxon	Dillon Archives

STAVELEY FAMILY, of Melton Mowbray

Stephen Staveley 1705–1775
Edward Staveley –1837
Christopher Staveley I 1726–1801
Christopher Staveley II 1759–1827

The family produced four generations of monumental masons and surveyors. **Steven Staveley** who married Dorothy Loasby in 1741, worked in a similar style to **Francis Lamb** and **James Sparrow. Christopher Staveley I,** Steven's son, provided fine masonry and carving at Grantham church and churchyard and at several other churches, as well as carrying out extensive repairs at Stapleford Hall, making it habitable again. His tomb in Melton churchyard records his death on 31 January 1801, in his 75th year. His slates are often large and are probably the most flamboyant in the county, combining architectural features and ornamental devices. Two of the finest are to James Rubins and Robert Wing (**6, 8**). He also executed some good architectural monuments with excellent lettering. Among them Gunnis notes the altar tomb to Richard Huthwaite and the tombstone to Mary Blower with its charming relief of *Charity* (**5, 11**). **James Wallis of Newark** was apprenticed to him. **Edward Staveley** was surveyor to the corporation of Nottingham and remodelled the New Exchange in that city in 1814–15. **Christopher Staveley II** practiced as an architect, engineer and surveyor who worked for several canal companies. He repaired the tower and spire of St Mary, Stamford, and probably designed Leadenham House, Lincs (1790–91), for an entry in an 18th-century rent book preserved in the house, dated 26 April 1791, details 'Chrisr. Staveley, Surveyor, 15. 15. 0'. Oswald conjectures that this was enough for plans and elevations, but notes that there are no further payments to indicate that he supervised the building's construction.

Literary References: *Oswald* 1965, 1528–31, 1592–5; *Gunnis* 1968, 369; *Neave and Heron* 1969, 5; *Aston* 1987, 230–1; *Colvin* 1995, 919

Funerary Monuments

1.	†1728	John Hopkinson (by Stephen Staveley)	s	Hickling, Notts, churchyard	Pevsner, *Notts*, 1979, 143
2.	1739	Harlaxton family member (†1738), headstone (by Christopher Staveley I)	sl	Kesteven, Lincs	*Neave and Heron* 1969, 5
3.	†1751	Randolph Clarke		St Wulfram, Grantham, Lincs	Pevsner, *Lincs*, 1989, 320
4.	†1751	Rev Richard Stevens		St Wulfram, Grantham, Lincs	Pevsner, *Lincs*, 1989, 320
5.	†1752	Richard Huthwaite	sl	St Wulfram, Grantham, Lincs, churchyard	Pevsner, *Lincs*, 1989, 320
6.	1765	James Rubins, headstone (by Christopher Staveley II)	sl	Grantham, Lincs	*Neave and Heron* 1969, 5
7.	1767	Coleby family member (†1761), headstone (by Christopher Staveley I)	sl	Kesteven, Lincs	*Neave and Heron* 1969, 5
8.	1770	Robert Wing, headstone (by Christopher Staveley II)		Denton, Lincs	*Neave and Heron* 1969, 5
9.	1771	Jane Stevens		St Wulfram, Grantham, Lincs	*Gunnis* 1968, 369
10.	?1772	Joseph Osbourn (by Christopher Staveley)		St Wulfram, Grantham, Lincs, churchyard	*Gunnis* 1968, 369
11.	1781	Mary Blower	sl	St Wulfram, Grantham, Lincs, churchyard	Pevsner, *Lincs*, 1989, 320

STAYNER (or STAINER), of Warwick fl 1730–51

Gunnis notes that a 'Mr. Stayner, carver', was paid in 1730 for work on the court house at Warwick (1), and was still living in the town in 1751 (*Gunnis* 1968, 369). Since **Thomas Stayner I** is thought to have carved the figure of *Justice* for the Court House *c*1730, it might well be conjectured that the two men are one and the same, but this is not the case since Thomas Stayner I died in 1733.

Architectural Sculpture

1.	1730	Coat of arms	Court House, Warwick	*Gunnis* 1968, 369

STAYNER (or STAINER), Thomas I *c*1665–1733

The son of Thomas Stayner, a deceased mason of St Giles-in-the-Fields, and his wife Marjorie, Stayner was apprenticed to Michael Todd on 3 February 1683 and became free of the Masons' Company on 24 July 1690. By 1694 he had two apprentices, one of them his brother Anthony, who joined him in 1693. Two of his sons trained under their father, **Thomas Stayner II**, who was apprenticed to him in 1702 and became free in 1709 and William, who joined him in 1710. In 1697 Stayner lived in Goodman's Fields, but by 1712 he had moved to Stratford-le-Bow.

He made rapid progress in the Masons' Company for he was an assistant in 1691, the year after he became free, renter warden in 1703, upper warden in 1706 and master in 1709. An entry in the Company's Court Book states that in 1720 he behaved improperly at the Lord Mayor's Day dinner by 'affronting the Master Wardens and Company'. He was obliged to appear before the Court 'to show cause why he should not be discharged from being an assistant for the misdemeanour by him committed', but 'purged his offence' with a payment of 6s. 8d (Masons Co Court Book, 1695–1722, fols 201r & v).

Whinney brackets Stayner with **Edward Stanton** and **Thomas Green of Camberwell** as mason-sculptors who used baroque elements with little understanding of baroque design. This is perhaps over-dismissive of Stayner, for he was responsible for several lively and arresting monuments including an altar-tomb to Richard Winwood erected in 1689, which has a crisply carved near-recumbent effigy in wig and plate armour, attended by a solicitous wife in quasi-medieval head-dress (1). The monument to Sir William Benson, 1712, now destroyed, made use of an urn on a square pedestal with cherubs either side and, in front of the pedestal, a kneeling skeleton with a laurel wreath, holding an armorial shield (3). Dr Thomas Turner's memorial, 1716, is considered by Gunnis to be his most ambitious and remarkable monument (4). An architectural frame divides it into three parts: in the centre is an illusory winding-sheet carrying the inscription, knotted to curtains hanging from a *baldacchino*. Turner's standing effigy in clerical robes is on one side and on the other is the twisting figure of *Faith*, wearing gracefully disposed draperies, carrying a church. The monument to Sir Henry Bendyshe, †1717, has twisted barley-sugar columns framing a reclining effigy of Sir Henry with a baby beside him (5).

Stayner is likely to have been responsible for other funerary sculpture, not yet identified. A memorandum of an agreement for a monument, with a design on the back dated 1 June 1725, survives in private hands: William Dunster commissioned Thomas Stayner of Bow Bridge, mason, to make a monument for his kinsman, Giles Dunster, for All Saints, Hertford. It is not known whether this was executed (Bosanquet MSS 72, cited by RG/JP, 8, 1359). By coincidence, it was on 8 November that year that the *Northampton Mercury* reported that a Thomas Stayner, mason, had been declared bankrupt. Since several branches of the family appear to have been involved in the craft and Thomas was a recurring family name, it is not certain that this report relates to the sculptor under discussion.

On 13 February 1727, a Mr Rice Williams wrote to Samuel Sandys MP from Pyrgo informing him that 'Mr Stayner, a stone-cutter upon Bowbridge' had 'lay'd the stone upon Mrs. Cheeke in Pyrgo Chapel'. The writer, who was clearly concerned about the cost, continued: 'The dimensions of the stone are six foot six inches by three foot two inches, so that the whole stone will be near twenty foot, which at ten shillings a foot, a penny a letter for cutting and about three pounds for the coat of arms brings the whole to about 14 pounds if you have the same sort of stone with Mrs. Cheeke . . . If you please to stop on Bow Bridge you may talk with this Mr. Stayner yourselves and I think he may be brought a little lower in his prices' (Archives, Lord Sandys in *Gunnis* 1968, 369). The letter refers to the ledger stone in Pyrgo chapel, Essex, for Samuel's mother-in-law, Lady Tipping, who was a daughter of Thomas Cheke of Pyrgo (9).

The names of a number of apprentices other than family members are recorded in the Masons' Company registers. 'Thomas Stainer' or 'Stainer' took on Robert Price, who had initially been apprenticed to **William Woodman I** in 1692; John Atkins joined Stayner in 1705; Abel Lindel and John Sherman in 1716; Richard Daye in 1723 and John Holden in 1730, after the latter had spent three years under **Robert Taylor**. The number of men at his disposal supports the idea that Stayner was responsible for a considerable amount of unidentified work, perhaps including building contracts. A payment was certainly made to him in 1721 for work apparently undertaken at Ambrose Page's brewery at Bow (S S Co Ambrose Page, no 4 in 3, p18).

Stayner died on 7 October 1733 at West Hampton, Essex. In his will the 'Westham' home and other property in the neighbourhood was left to his widow, Dorothy, and after her death to his favourite daughter, Mary. According to custom his goods, chattels and personal estate in the City of London were divided into three equal parts, a third of which went to his widow, another third to his six children and the final part, customarily at the testator's disposal, to his daughter, Mary. A statue of 'King William on Horseback' was to be set aside since it had already been sold to Mary.

IR

Literary References: *Gunnis* 1968, 369–70; *Whinney* 1988, 140, 142; *Webb* 1999, 1, 10, 20, 27, 31; IGI
Archival References: Masons' Co, Apprentices, 1702, 1710; Freemen, fol 66 (1690, 1709); Court Book, 1677–94, fol 67r; Masters and Wardens; GPC
Will: PROB 11/820 (proved 10 Oct 1733)

Funerary Monuments

1.	1689	Richard Winwood (†1688)	Quainton, Bucks	S	*Gunnis* 1968, 369; Pevsner, *Bucks*, 1994, 608
2.	†1700	Grace, Viscountess Ardmagh	St Luke, Charlton, Middx	S	
3.	†1712	Sir William Benson	[St Mary, Bromley, Poplar, London]; Destroyed		Bodleian, Rawlinson MS B 389B, ff 140v-141r; *Survey of London* 1, 8
4.	1716	Dr Thomas Turner (†1714)	Stowe-Nine-Churches, Northants	S	*Gunnis* 1968, 369; *Whinney* 1988, 140, 142 (repr)
5.	†1717	Sir Henry Bendyshe Bt and his infant son, Henry	St Mary, Steeple Bumpstead, Essex		*Kemp* 1985, 20 (repr); *Whinney* 1988, 142
6.	1721	Sir Ralph Radcliffe (†1720)	St Mary, Hitchin, Herts		Delme-Radcliffe archives, Herts RO D E 3574 (contract), 31 Aug 1721
7.	†1723	Lady Margaret Gostlin	Morningthorpe, Norfolk		Pevsner, *Norfolk: N W & S*, 1999, 546
8.	1723	Sir Richard Hoare (†1719) and Dame Susanna Hoare (†1720)	St Dunstan-in-the-West, City of London		Hoare's Bank archives, 1725, in *Gunnis* 1968, 369
9.	*c*1727	Lady Tipping, ledger stone	Pyrgo Chapel, Essex		*Gunnis* 1968, 369

Architectural Sculpture

10.	1731	Figure of Justice, with royal crest above and Warwick coat of arms below	Court House, Warwick, central niche		Pevsner, *Warks*, 1966, 458; *Noszlopy* 2003, 104–5 (repr)

STAYNER (or STAINER), Thomas II *c*1690–after 1750

He was apprenticed to his father, **Thomas Stayner I**, on 30 June 1702 and became free of the Masons' Company on 29 October 1709. Thomas was living at Bow Bridge, Essex, perhaps in his father's house, around 1740 (Masons' Company Assistants fol 8), though the Masons' Company Court Book also records that he inherited his father's property at West Hampton, Essex, where Stayner was living in 1750.

A number of apprentices to a Thomas Stayner, who may be Thomas Stayner II, are recorded in the Masons' Company Apprenticeship Registers. They include William Cooley, apprenticed to 'Thomas Stainer jnr' in 1724; Anthony Hanson apprenticed in 1740 but turned over to Isaac Dent, a merchant tailor, in 1746; Thomas Duprée (1741); Thomas Parker, taken in 1743 but turned over to George Drewitt in 1749; Billy Lucas (1744) and William Stayner, the son of Richard Stayner, a sailmaker (1750).

Literary References: *Gunnis* 1968, 369; *Webb* 1999, 8, 11, 15, 21, 23, 25; IGI
Archival References: Masons' Co, Apprentices, 1702; Masons' Co, Court Book

Funerary Monuments

1.	1714	Thomas Stayner (perhaps by Thomas Stayner I)	Bromley St Leonard, Essex	S	*Georgian Group Journal*, vol XII, 2002, 7 (repr)

STEAD, Samuel, of Ludlow 1804–61

He was one of a family of masons and statuaries active in Shropshire. He designed the Assembly Rooms in Ludlow. He died on 20 January 1861.

Literary References: *Gunnis* 1968, 370; *Colvin* 1995, 920

Funerary Monuments

1.	post-1801	Richard Edwards	Clunbury, Salop	S	
2.	?1828	Thomas Green	Ashford Bowdler, Salop	S	*Gunnis* 1968, 370
3.	?1833	Rev John Bright	North Lydbury, Salop	S	GPC

STEAD, William, of York fl 1766–1822?

He was apprenticed to **Joseph Atkinson of York** in 1766 and became free in 1773. In 1799 he purchased from the widow of Christopher Dalton, 'stone mason', his yard and business (*York Herald*, 4 April, 1799). In 1805 he advertised himself in the *York Courant* as a marble and stone cutter. In 1823 he took his son William into partnership. William the younger died in 1823, aged 41 (*York Gazette* 8 Feb 1823). A handful of monuments signed 'Stead and Sons', including a wall tablet with a gadrooned sarcophagus (**13**), are assumed to be by this firm.

Literary References: *Gunnis* 1968, 370

Archival References: GPC

Funerary Monuments

1.	†1791	Mary Boucher	St Mary and All Saints, Chesterfield, Derbys		Pevsner, *Derbys*, 1978, 144
2.	†1792	Henry Jubb	Holy Trinity, Micklegate, York	S	Pevsner, *Yorks: E R & York*, 1995, 163
3.	†1792	Thomas Kilby	St Cuthbert, York		Pevsner, *Yorks: E R & York*, 1995, 165
4.	?1793	Samuel Lister	Bradford Cathedral, W R Yorks	S	*Gunnis* 1968, 370
5.	?1794	Rev Guy Fairfax	Newton Kyme, W R Yorks	S	
6.	†1795	Unidentified subject, tablet (by Stead & Sons)	Cherry Willingham, Lincs		Pevsner, *Lincs*, 1989, 219
7.	?1797	Matthew Smith	Newton Kyme, W R Yorks	S	
8.	?1799	James Lord	Sowerby, N R Yorks	S	*Gunnis* 1968, 370
9.	†1802	Peter Belt	Bossall, N R Yorks	S	
10.	?1804	Charles Sharp	Bradford Cathedral, W R Yorks	S	*Gunnis* 1968, 370
11.	†1809	Unidentified subject, tablet (by Stead & Sons)	Cherry Willingham, Lincs		Pevsner, *Lincs*, 1989, 219
12.	?1815	William Markham	Aberford, W R Yorks	S	*Gunnis* 1968, 370
13.	†1822	Rev Robert Benson (by Stead & Sons)	St Martin-cum-Gregory, York		Pevsner, *Yorks: E R & York*, 1995, 170
14.	nd	Unidentified subject, tablet	Gate Helmsley, N R Yorks		Pevsner, *Yorks: N R*, 1966, 165

Chimneypieces

15.	1793	Several, 'important'	Sledmere House, E R Yorks		GPC

STEELL, Sir John 1804–91

John Robert Steell was the first Scottish sculptor to achieve an international reputation without leaving his native land. He came from an artistic family: his father John Steell was a carver and gilder, his younger brother Gourlay Steell RSA (1819–94) became animal painter for Scotland to Queen Victoria and his nephew David George was an eminent Scottish painter. His son William had a successful practice as an architect.

Steell was born in Aberdeen on 18 September 1804. His family moved to Edinburgh about a year after his birth and at the age of 14 he was apprenticed to his father as a woodcarver, whilst studying at the Trustees' Academy under the landscape painter, Andrew Wilson. In 1826 he married Elizabeth, the daughter of an Edinburgh merchant, John Graham.

After completing his apprenticeship in 1827, Steell went into partnership with his father at 6 Hanover Street, but his ambitious, even driven character and his personal charm marked him out for greater things. He began to work on independent sculpture projects and studied drawing at the Edinburgh Life Academy, which had been founded by his friend, the painter, David Scott. In 1827 Steell began work a colossal statue of Saint Andrew in wood for the North British Fire Insurance corporation (**37**). This work was the first of 58 submissions to Royal Scottish Academy exhibitions.

In 1829 Steell travelled to Rome, where he studied for at least five months and is known to have carved 'ideal' works, but once back in Edinburgh he was overwhelmed by a wave of commissions, principally for busts. He moved into premises at 23 Dundas Street and during the next 12 years changed address several times, before moving to 1 Randolph Place, which remained his studio from 1842 to 1888.

In 1830 he began work on a model of *Alexander taming Bucephalus* (**39**), which brought him to public attention and for which in 1833 he received a special prize of £50 from the Board of Manufactures, the governing body of the Trustees School of Design. Later that year it was shown in London, where it was highly praised, in particular by **Sir Francis Chantrey**, who urged Steell to move to London and offered to help him do so. Steell declined, saying that he preferred to remain in his native country and to concentrate on improving the quality of Scottish sculpture.

His influential early patrons included Thomas Thomson, Lord Meadowbank and the 5th Duke of Buccleuch, and Steell's rapid rise to success may be attributed at least in part to their encouragement. In 1838 he became the first sculptor resident in Scotland to obtain royal patronage, receiving several sittings at Windsor Castle from Queen Victoria for a portrait bust (**86**) and a colossal statue (**43**) for the roof of the Royal Institution (Royal Scottish Academy), the first statue of the monarch raised in the British Isles after her accession to the throne. In 1838 he was appointed sculptor in ordinary to Her Majesty for Scotland. Royal patronage and support from the professional classes and members of the aristocracy gave Steell dominance of the Edinburgh market, and he received at least 28 commissions for large scale public monuments.

Steell's seated figure of Sir Walter Scott for the Scott Monument in Princes Street, Edinburgh, 1840–46, is thought to be the first marble statue ever commissioned in Scotland from a native artist (**44**). Steell was responsible also for the first bronze statue cast in Scotland, the national monument to the Duke of Wellington, 1840–1852 (**47**).

Work on this commission obliged him to open a foundry at his own expense in 1849, at 75 Grove Street, Edinburgh. The Grove foundry remained open until 1889 and was made regularly available to other sculptors. Many of Steell's works, including his most imaginative composition, the Albert Memorial in Charlotte Square, Edinburgh, 1865–76 (**61**) were cast at the foundry.

Several of his commissions went abroad: in 1863 he carved a tympanum group of *The wise and foolish virgins* for the Standard Life Assurance building in Dublin (**170**) and in 1867 he sent relief sculpture to Canada for the pediment of the Bank of Montreal (**172**). A statue of Sir Walter Scott (**60**) was erected in Central Park, New York in 1872 and versions of his statue of Robert Burns, 1880, also for Central Park (**63**), went to Dunedin (where the unveiling of their statue drew a crowd of more than 8,000 New Zealanders), as well as London and Dundee.

Steell was knighted by the Queen in 1876, the first sculptor to be so honoured since **Sir Francis Chantrey**, on the evening of the inauguration ceremony for his Scottish national monument to the Prince Consort (**61**). In 1884 a bronze version of his *Alexander taming Bucephalus*, previously reproduced only as a statuette, was erected as a public testimony to him. He continued to work for another decade, but retired through ill-health in 1887, when he was given an annual pension of £100 from the civil list. He died at 24 Greenhill Gardens, his home for 37 years, on 15 September 1891 and was buried in Old Calton cemetery, Edinburgh. He received lengthy and respectable obituaries and coverage in the *Dictionary of National Biography*.

He does not appear to have had students, apprentices, or assistants who became sculptors. Instead he employed skilled artisans in his studio and foundry, including William Young, who had worked for Chantrey and **Richard James Wyatt**, and became Steell's first master caster in 1852.

Steell's style was grounded in neo-classicism but he was abreast of metropolitan trends. He was a brilliant portraitist, whose attention to detail and use of contemporary dress make him a major precursor of later 19th-century realism. His achievement, forgotten for a century after his death, was recognised in 1991 in the exhibition *Virtue and Vision: Sculpture in Scotland, 1540–1990*. In her catalogue entry Fiona Pearson, summarised his achievement: 'Steell was the sculptor . . . of the first and last Victorian monuments in Scotland; he was the native school'.

Rocco Lieuallen

Literary References: *Scotsman*, 16 Sept 1891, 7 (obit); *Gunnis* 1968, 370–1; *Banford* 1973, 376–80; *Read* 1982, *passim*; *Pearson* 1991, 73–7; *Woodward* 1977, 226–36; *Grove* 29, 1996, 584–5 (Pearson); *Stocker* 1999, 11–24; *Lieuallen* 2002

Archival References: Steell Press Cuttings, 4 vols, NLS MS.FB.m.55. Compiled by John Steell's younger brother, Gresholm, these consist of news cuttings, photographs, pamphlets and longhand entries relating to the sculptor *c*1829–1877 and are the principal sources for Steell's career. They are arranged chronologically.

Auction: Account of his studio sale (which listed some works and equipment), *The Scotsman*, 14 March 1888, 6

Portraits of the sculptor: Robert Scott Lauder, oil on canvas, 1827, Univ of Dundee; Robert Scott Lauder, oil on canvas, 1832, SNPG; George Reid, oil on canvas, 1883 Aberdeen Art Gallery; Hill & Adamson calotype, *c*1843–7, SNPG; J G Tunney photo, 1854, Royal Scottish Academy; unknown photographer, *c*1860

Funerary Monuments

1.	1828	Mary Westwood Lewins (†1828)		St Mary's kirkyard, Haddington, East Lothian	S	*Lieuallen* 2002, 106 (repr)
2.	1837	Rev Dr Inglis, bust		High Tolbooth church, Edinburgh		*Woodward* 1977, vol 1, pt 2, 233
3.	1837	Rev Dr William Muir, bust		St Stephen, Edinburgh	SD	*Lieuallen* 2002, 65 (repr)
4.	1838	Sir Walter Scott (†1832) and his dog, competition model		Abbotsford, Roxburghshire		*Pearson* 1991, 74, 80 (repr)
5.	1839	Robert Jamieson (†1834)	s	St Cuthbert's churchyard, Edinburgh		*Woodward* 1977, vol 1, pt 2, 235; *Lieuallen* 2002, 103 (repr)
6.	1845	Dr Archibald Tait Alison (†1839)		St Paul and St George, Edinburgh	SD	Pevsner, *Edinburgh*, 1991, 281; *Lieuallen* 2002, 94 (repr)
7.	1847	John Smart	b	[Dean Cemetery, Edinburgh]; untraced		*Lieuallen* 2002, 130
8.	1847	Monteith Douglas Campbell (†1847)		Inchinnan, Renfrewshire	S	*Lieuallen* 2002, 97 (repr)
9.	1849	Elizabeth, Countess of Elgin (†1843)		Spanish Town Cathedral, Jamaica		*Graves* VII, 1905–6, 245; *Lieuallen* 2002, 7 (repr)
10.	1850	Francis Barry Hermitage (†1850)		Dean Cemetery, Edinburgh	S	Pevsner, *Edinburgh*, 1991, 390; *Lieuallen* 2002, 102 (repr)
11.	1850	Officers and men of the 78th Highland regiment		St Giles's Cathedral, Edinburgh	SD	Pevsner, *Edinburgh*, 1991, 116; *Lieuallen* 2002, 122 (repr)
12.	1851	Francis, Lord Jeffrey (†1850)	s	Dean Cemetery, Edinburgh		*Lieuallen* 2002, 104 (repr)
13.	1851	Lieutenant Sprot (†c1851)		[St Giles's Cathedral, Edinburgh]; untraced		*Lieuallen* 2002, 130
14.	1852	Thomas Thomson MD (†1852)	b	Dean Cemetery, Edinburgh	S	*Lieuallen* 2002, 115 (repr)
15.	1854	Andrew, Lord Rutherfurd (†1854) and Lady Sophia Frances Rutherfurd (†1852)	b	Dean Cemetery, Edinburgh		Pevsner, *Edinburgh*, 1991, 390; *Lieuallen* 2002, 112 (repr)
16.	1857	John Wilson (†1849), the vocalist		Dean Cemetery, Edinburgh		*Gunnis* 1968, 370; *Lieuallen* 2002, 117 (repr)
17.	1857	Lieutenant-Colonel Robert Gordon (†1853)		St Andrew's kirk, Chennai (Madras), India	SD	
18.	1858	John Gibson Lockhart (†1854)	b	Dryburgh Abbey, Berwickshire, graveyard		*Lieuallen* 2002, 107 (repr)
19.	1859	34th Cumberland regiment, Crimean memorial		Carlisle Cathedral	SD	*CJ*, 4 and 24 June 1861; *Lieuallen* 2002, 119 (repr)
20.	1859	Alexander, Viscount Balgonie (†1857)		Monimail, Fife	SD	*Lieuallen* 2002, 95 (repr)
21.	1859	Officers and men of the 93rd Sutherland Highlanders, Crimean memorial		Glasgow Cathedral	SD	Pevsner, *Glasgow*, 1990, 134; *Lieuallen* 2002, 123 (repr)
22.	1860	Henry, Lord Cockburn (†1854)		Dean Cemetery, Edinburgh		*Lieuallen* 2002, 98 (repr)
23.	1861	Hugh William Williams (†1829)	b	Canongate Cemetery, Edinburgh	S	*The Scotsman*, 20 Oct 1861; *Lieuallen* 2002, 116
24.	1864	Professor James Miller (†1864)	b	Grange Cemetery, Edinburgh		*Lieuallen* 2002, 108 (repr)
25.	1865	David, 8th Earl of Leven (†1860) and his wife, Elizabeth Anne (†1863)		Monimail, Fife		*Lieuallen* 2002, 105 (repr)

No.	Date	Subject	Material	Location		References
26.	1866	George, 6th Duke of Atholl (†1864)		St Bride, Old Blair, Perth		*Gunnis* 1968, 371; *Lieuallen* 2002, 111 (repr)
27.	1866	Lieutenant-Colonel J Drysdale (†1866)	b	Kirk of St Nicholas kirkyard, Strathbrock, Uphall, Linlithgow		*Gunnis* 1968, 371; *Lieuallen* 2002, 99 (repr)
28.	1866	Rev James Macfarlane, bust		High Tolbooth church, Edinburgh		*Woodward* 1977, vol 1, pt 2, 233
29.	1867	Rev Dr Robert Gordon (†1853)		Free Church college, Edinburgh	SD	*Gunnis* 1968, 371; *Lieuallen* 2002, 50 (repr)
30.	1869	Rev Dr William Muir (†1869)		Dean Cemetery, Edinburgh	S	*Lieuallen* 2002, 109 (repr)
31.	1872	Officers and men of the 42nd Highland regiment ('The Black Watch')		Dunkeld Cathedral, Perth	SD	*Pearson* 1991, 72, 73 (repr); *Lieuallen* 2002, 120–1 (repr)
32.	1873	Henry, 18th Earl of Shrewsbury (†1868)		Ingestre, Staffs	SD	*Lieuallen* 2002, 30 (repr)
33.	1874	John L H McFarlane (†1874)		Dean Cemetery, Edinburgh	S	*Lieuallen* 2002, 108 (repr)
34.	1876	Jane Tennant (†1866)		Traquair, Peeblesshire	S	*Lieuallen* 2002, 114 (repr)
35.	1876	Rev Edward Bannerman Ramsay (†1872), bust		St John the Evangelist episcopal church, Edinburgh Other versions: SNPG, nd, plaster	SD	*Gunnis* 1968, 371; *Woodward* 1977, vol 1, pt 2, 234
36.	1885	Robert Burns (†1796), bust		Westminster Abbey, London, south transept	S	*Goodwillie* 1911, 62; *Read* 1982, 349; *Lieuallen* 2002, 39 (repr)
Statues						
37.	1827–1829	St Andrew	wd	[North British Fire Insurance company, Princes Street, Edinburgh]; untraced Other versions: Dalkeith masonic lodge, plaster	SD	*Woodward* 1977, vol 1, pt 2, 233; *Pearson* 1991, 74
38.	1831	Reclining horse	s	Royal School of Veterinary Studies, Edinburgh, parapet		*Woodward* 1977, vol 1, pt 2, 233
39.	1833	Alexander taming Bucephalus, model, reproduced in bronze	p	[Steell's studio, until 1883]; destroyed Other versions: St Andrew's Square, Edinburgh, 1837, bronze, statuette, Dalmeny House, Edinburgh, 1837 statuette, private coll, London, *c*1837, bronze, SD statuette, private coll, Scotland, *c*1837, bronze, SD statuette, private coll, Scotland, *c*1837, bronze		*Pearson* 1991, unpag; *Lieuallen* 2002, 124 (repr)
40.	1837	Sphinxes	s	Royal Scottish Academy building, Edinburgh		*Lieuallen* 2002, 29 (repr)
41.	*c*1840	St Andrew	s	[North British Insurance Company, Princes Street, Edinburgh]; Botanical Gardens, St Andrews		*Lieuallen* 2002, 21 (repr)
42.	1844	Lord Provost James Blaikie	m	[St Nicholas kirk, Aberdeen]; Town House, Aberdeen	SD	*Lieuallen* 2002, 21 (repr)
43.	1844	Queen Victoria, seated, and eight sphinxes (designed by William Playfair)	s	Royal Scottish Academy, Prince's Street, Edinburgh, parapet		NAS NG 1/2/9; *Lieuallen* 2002, 14 (repr)
44.	1840–1846	Sir Walter Scott and Maida (Gothic surround by G M Kemp) Drawing(s): NGS D2699 (three)	m	Scott Monument, Princes Street, Edinburgh	SD	*Woodward* 1977, vol 1, pt 2, 232; *Read* 1982, 114 (repr), 116–7; *Lieuallen* 2002, 28 (repr)
45.	*c*1849	Monumental figure of Lady Melville		Untraced		*The Scotsman*, 31 March 1849; *Lieuallen* 2002, 130 (repr)
46.	1850	Sir Walter Scott, statuette	b	Huntly House Museum, Edinburgh Other versions: SNPG, 1850, Parian ware Abbotsford House, Glasgow, nd, parian ware Lady Stairs House, Edinburgh, parian ware SNPG, 1850, plaster Huntly House Museum, Edinburgh, nd, bronze		*Lieuallen* 2002, 126–7 (repr)
47.	1840–1852	Arthur, 1st Duke of Wellington, equestrian, for the Scottish National Monument	b	Princes Street, Edinburgh		NAS GD, 224/511/8–9; *Ward-Jackson* 1990, 851n, 858 (repr 37); *Pearson* 1991, 74–5 (reprs); *Lieuallen* 2002, 28 (repr)
48.	1854	Admiral Lord James de Saumarez Drawing(s): NGS D4443	m	[Greenwich, Naval College, painted hall]; NMM, Greenwich, upper court, SCU0048	S	*Gunnis* 1968, 370; *Lieuallen* 2002, 14 (repr); NMM Newsletter 2004
49.	1855	Francis, Lord Jeffrey Drawing(s): NGS D4442; another, Steell scrapbooks	m	Parliament House, Edinburgh	SD	Pevsner, *Edinburgh*, 1991, 123; *Lieuallen* 2002, 16 (repr)
50.	1857	Robert, 2nd Viscount Melville	b	Melville Crescent, Edinburgh		Pevsner, *Edinburgh*, 1991, 376; *Lieuallen* 2002, 15 (repr)
51.	1860	David, Lord Boyle, Lord President of the Court of Session Model(s): SNPG, Edinburgh, 1863, plaster (1865 version)	m	Parliament Hall, Edinburgh	SD	*Read* 1982, 10–11; *Lieuallen* 2002, 5, 6 (repr)
52.	1863	James, 10th Earl and 1st Marquess of Dalhousie Model(s): SNPG, plaster, full size	m	[Government House, Kolkata (Calcutta)]; Victoria Memorial Hall, Kolkata Other versions: Statuette, SNPG, nd, plaster		*Steggles* 2000, 74–5 (repr); *Lieuallen* 2002, 19 (model repr)

53.	1863	Sir David Baxter	m	[Baxter Park, Dundee]; McManus Galleries, Dundee	SD	*Gunnis* 1968, 370; *Lieuallen* 2002, 3 (repr)
54.	1865	Allan Ramsay, with four portrait reliefs on the pedestal of Lord Murray, Lady Campbell, General Ramsay and Mrs Allan Ramsay	m	Princes Street Gardens, Edinburgh	SD	*Woodward* 1977, vol 1, pt 2, 232; *Read* 1982, 115 117, 147 (repr)
55.	1865	David, Lord Boyle, Lord President of the Court of Session Model(s): SNPG, plaster, full size	b	Low Green, Irvine, Low Green, Irvine, Ayrshire		*Lieuallen* 2002, 5, 6 (repr)
56.	1865	James Wilson	m	[Dalhousie Institute, Kolkata (Calcutta)]; The Economist building, London	SD	*Lieuallen* 2002, 32 (repr)
57.	1865	Onesipherus Tyndall Bruce	b	[Falkland palace, Fife]; Falkland parish church, Fife	SD	*Lieuallen* 2002, 8 (repr)
58.	1863–1865	Professor John Wilson	b	East Princes Street Gardens, Edinburgh Other versions: Fine Art Soc, Edinburgh, nd, Parian ware	SD	*Read* 1982, 117; *Lieuallen* 2002, 33 (repr)
59.	1872	George Kinloch MP	b	George Square, Dundee	SD	*Lieuallen* 2002, 17 (repr)
60.	1872	Sir Walter Scott and Maida, replica of the Edinburgh statue (companion to Robert Burns, [63])	b	Literary Walk, Central Park, New York Other versions: George Square, Dundee, 1880 The Octagon, Dunedin, New Zealand, 1884 Victoria Embankment gardens, London, 1884		*Gunnis* 1968, 370; *Lieuallen* 2002, 23 (repr)
61.	1865–1876	Albert Memorial (Scottish National Memorial of the Prince Consort), (equestrian figure and four reliefs, with groups at the corners by Brodie, Stevenson and Clark Stanton) Drawing(s): Royal Archives, Windsor Castle, BAS GD 224/511/8–9	b	Charlotte Square, Edinburgh		*Read* 1982, 153, 156–8 (repr); *Read* 1982, 50, 153, 156–7 (repr); *Lieuallen* 2002, 24–7 (repr)
62.	1878	Rev Dr Thomas Chalmers	b	George Street, Edinburgh		*Read* 1982, 117; *Lieuallen* 2002, 13 (repr)
63.	1880	Robert Burns (companion to Sir Walter Scott [60])	b	Literary Walk, Central Park, New York Other versions: George Square, Dundee, 1880 The Octagon, Dunedin, New Zealand, 1884, bronze (4 copies in Dunedin, 1887, Timary, 1913, Auckland, 1921, Hokitika, 1933) Victoria Embankment Gardens, London, 1884		*Lieuallen* 2002, 39 (repr); *Stocker* 1999, 11–24 (repr)
64.	1883	Alexander taming Bucephalus, cast from the model of 1833 [39]	b	[St Andrew's Square, Edinburgh]; City Chambers, Edinburgh	S	*Woodward* 1977, vol 1, pt 2, 233; *Read* 1982, 56, 57 (repr), 59; *Pearson* 1991, 74; *Lieuallen* 2002, 2 (repr)
65.	nd	Colonel Robert Bruce	b	Destroyed		*Lieuallen* 2002, 132
66.	nd	John Bruce		Destroyed		*Lieuallen* 2002, 132 (repr)
67.	nd	Lord Justice General Boyle, statuette	p	[Steell's studio; sold 1888]; SNPG		*Woodward* 1977, vol 1, pt 2, 234
Busts						
68.	1828	John Baird		[Exhib GDS, 272]; untraced		*Lieuallen* 2002, 129
69.	1828	John Robison		[Exhib GDS, 268]; untraced		*Lieuallen* 2002, 129
70.	1828	Unidentified child		[Exhib GDS, 271]; untraced		*Lieuallen* 2002, 129
71.	1828	Unidentified lady		[Exhib GDS, 267]; untraced		*Lieuallen* 2002, 129
72.	1829	Unidentified architect		[Exhib R Sc A, 292]; untraced		*Lieuallen* 2002, 129
73.	1829	Unidentified artist		[Exhib R Sc A, 303]; untraced		*Lieuallen* 2002, 129
74.	1830	Unidentified gentleman		[Exhib R Sc A, 329]; untraced		*Lieuallen* 2002, 129
75.	1831	David Scott RSA, diploma work	m	R Sc A, Edinburgh Other versions: plaster, SNPG, 1831	SD	*Gunnis* 1968, 370; *Lieuallen* 2002, 78, 129 (repr)
76.	1832	Miss M Smith		[Exhib R Sc A, 322]; untraced		*Lieuallen* 2002, 129
77.	1834–1835	William Leigh Canning Sinclair		Aberdeen art gallery AG009584	S	*Lieuallen* 2002, 80 (repr)
78.	1836	Mrs Francis Grant		[Exhib R Sc A, 357]; untraced		*Lieuallen* 2002, 129
79.	1836	Robert Brown of Newhall		[Exhib R Sc A, 358]; untraced		*Lieuallen* 2002, 129
80.	1837	Charles, 2nd Earl Grey, 'to be placed in the Council Hall, Edinburgh'		[Exhib RA, London, 1264]; Howick Hall, Northumbs		*Graves* VII, 1905–6, 245; *Ormond* 1973, 203; *Lieuallen* 2002, 51 (repr)
81.	1837	Lady Stuart of Allanbank	m	[Exhib RA, London, 1260]; Edinburgh NGS		*Graves* VII, 1905–6, 245; *Woodward* 1977, vol 1, pt 2, 234
82.	1838	Alexander, Lord Meadowbank		[Exhib R Sc A, 401]; untraced		*La Perriere* 1991, vol 4, 238
83.	1838	George Chalmers	m	[Exhib R Sc A, 402]; Chalmers Hospital, Edinburgh		*Laperriere* 4, 1991, 238; *Lieuallen* 2002, 41 (repr)
84.	1838	Hon Charles Barrington		[Exhib R Sc A]; untraced		*La Perriere* 1991, 4, 238
85.	1838	Lady Katherine Steuart of Allanbank	m	NGS, Edinburgh	S	*Lieuallen* 2002, 82 (repr)
86.	1838	Queen Victoria	p	[Exhib RA, London, 1839, 1332]; SNPG, Edinburgh Other versions: c1840, sold Bonham, London, 29 Oct 2002		*Graves* V, 1905–6, 245, *Ormond* 1973, 481; *Pearson* 1991, 74; *Lieuallen* 2002, 88 (repr)

87.	1838	Unidentified woman	m	Untraced		*Woodward* 1977, vol 1, pt 2, 233
88.	1838	Wardlaw Ramsay		[Exhib R Sc A, 403]; untraced		*Gunnis* 1968, 370; *La Perriere* 1991, vol 4, 238
89.	1838	William Speirs of Elderslie		[Exhib R Sc A, 404]; untraced		*La Perriere* 1991, vol 4, 238
90.	1839	Baroness Stratheden	m	[Exhib RA, London, 1386]; untraced		*Graves* VII, 1905–6, 245
91.	1839	Charles, 2nd Earl Grey	m	Council Chambers, Edinburgh	S	*Ormond* 1973, 203; *Lieuallen* 2002, 51 (repr)
92.	1839	Lord Panmure		[for Dundee town hall]; National Library of Scotland		*Steell Scrapbooks*, 1, 41; *Lieuallen* 2002, 130
93.	1841	Master A Reginald Forbes	m	[Exhib R Sc A, 544]; untraced		*La Perriere* 1991, vol 4, 238
94.	1841	Neill Ballingall		[Exhib R Sc A, 545]; untraced		*La Perriere* 1991, 4, 238
95.	1842	Sir James Fergusson, 4th Bt	m	Kilkerran, Argyllshire		*Woodward* 1977, vol 1, pt 2, 233
96.	1843	Arthur, 1st Duke of Wellington		Cirencester Park, Glos Other versions: Private coll, Scotland, SD, 1843 Upper school, Eton, Windsor, Berks, 1845 SNPG, Edinburgh, 1845, SD, marble Wellington Museum, Apsley House, London, 1845 (1447–1948) Callender coll, Preston Hall, Kent, 1845 Royal Scottish Museum, Edinburgh, 1845		*Gunnis* 1968, 371; Pevsner, *London: Westminster*, 1973, 504; *Lieuallen* 2002, 89, 90 (repr)
97.	1843	John, 1st Baron Campbell	m	SNPG	SD	*Smailes* 1990, 55; *Lieuallen* 2002, 40 (repr)
98.	1843	Sir William Maynard Gomm	m	Keble College, Oxford, library	SD	*Ormond* 1973, 189; *Lieuallen* 2002, 49 (repr)
99.	1844	Dr Patrick Neill	m	Royal Botanical Gardens, Edinburgh	SD	*Lieuallen* 2002, 66 (repr)
100.	1844	Professor Thomas Charles Hope	m	University of Edinburgh	SD	*Read* 1982, 128; *Lieuallen* 2002, 55 (repr)
101.	1844	Rev John Brown		[Exhib R Sc A, 558]; untraced		*Lieuallen* 2002, 130
102.	1844	Thomas Thomson MD	m	Faculty of Advocates, Edinburgh Other versions: SNPG, 1844, plaster another, 1843; untraced		*Lieuallen* 2002, 86, 130 (repr)
103.	1845	Professor Robert Jameson	m	University of Edinburgh	SD	*Lieuallen* 2002, 56 (repr)
104.	1845	Unidentified man	m	Christie, 15 July 1993, lot 239; untraced	SD	*Lieuallen* 2002, 92 (repr)
105.	1846	Charlotte Anne, Duchess of Buccleuch	m	[Dalkeith Palace, Edinburgh]; private coll, Scotland	SD	*Graves* VII, 1905–6, 245; *Gunnis* 1968, 371; *Lieuallen* 2002, 87 (repr)
106.	1846	Dr John Abercrombie	m	RCS, Edinburgh Other versions: RC Physic, Edinburgh, SD 1846, marble	SD	*Lieuallen* 2002, 34 (repr)
107.	1846	Elizabeth Graham Steell, the sculptor's wife, as a young girl	m	Museum services, University of Dundee		*Lieuallen* 2002, 83 (repr)
108.	1846	Lady Isabella Gordon	m	[Exhib RA, London 1515]; untraced		*Graves* VII, 1905–6, 2453
109.	1846	Rev Dr Thomas Chalmers Model(s): SNPG, Edinburgh, SD, marble	m	[Dalmeny House, Edinburgh]; Museum of Scotland, Edinburgh Other versions: SNPG, SD 1846, plaster, Edinburgh university, 1875 New College, Edinburgh, SD 1877, marble SNPG, 1883, marble	SD	*Pearson* 1991, unpag; *La Periere* 1991, vol 4, 238; *Lieuallen* 2002, 42–3 (repr)
110.	1847	James, 10th Earl and Marquess of Dalhousie	m	Colstoun trust (Captain Colin Broun-Lindsay, Colstoun) Other versions: coll Marquess of Tweeddale, 1861, marble	SD	*Graves* 1905–6, VII, 245; *Ormond* 1973, 129; *Lieuallen* 2002, 74
111.	1847	Robert Graham Speirs	m	Sheriff's Court Library, Edinburgh	SD	*Lieuallen* 2002, 81 (repr)
112.	1849	Ferooza McNeill		[Exhib R Sc A]; untraced		*Lieuallen* 2002, 130
113.	1849	Robert Scott Lauder RSA	m	Private coll, Scotland	SD	*Lieuallen* 2002, 58 (repr)
114.	1849	Sir Walter Scott, with a relief on the socle	m	Perth Museum and Art Gallery Other versions: replicated in porcelain by Copeland	SD	*Lieuallen* 2002, 79 (repr)
115.	1849	Unidentified boy		Private coll, Scotland	SD	*Lieuallen* 2002, 92 (repr)
116.	c1850	Sir Robert Peel Bt	p	SNPG		*Ormond* 1973, 373; *Lieuallen* 2002, 70 (repr)
117.	1851	Henry, Lord Cockburn	m	Faculty of Advocates, Edinburgh Other versions: SNPG, 1851, s, plaster	SD	*Laperriere* 4, 1991, 238; *Lieuallen* 2002, 44 (repr)
118.	1851	Unidentified woman	m	Beningbrough Hall, N R Yorks	SD	*Lieuallen* 2002, 92 (repr)
119.	1852	Francis, Lord Jeffrey	m	Faculty of Advocates, Edinburgh	SD	*Lieuallen* 2002, 57 (repr)
120.	1852	John Archibald, Lord Dalmeny	m	Dalmeny House, Edinburgh	SD	*Lieuallen* 2002, 71 (repr)
121.	1852	John, Lord Fullerton	m	Faculty of Advocates, Edinburgh Other versions: Signet Library, Edinburgh, SD 1852, marble SNPG, SD 1852, plaster	SD	*Lieuallen* 2002, 48 (repr)
122.	c1852	Lady Susan Hay	m	Private coll, Scotland		*Lieuallen* 2002, 54 (repr)
123.	1853	Lady Sophia Rutherfurd	m	Christie, 20 Feb 1992, lot 158; untraced	SD	*Lieuallen* 2002, 77 (repr)
124.	1855	Alexander Cowan	m	[Exhib R Sc A, 749]; Lockhouse Farm, Beattock, Dumfriesshire		*Woodward* 1977, vol 1, pt 2, 100, 233 (repr 50)
125.	1855	Joshua, Lord Mackenzie	m	Faculty of Advocates, Edinburgh	SD	*Lieuallen* 2002, 61 (repr)
126.	1855	Rev Dr Robert Gordon		Free Church College, Edinburgh		*Woodward* 1977, vol 1, pt 2, 233

127.	1856	Duncan, Lord Colonsay and Oronsay	m	Faculty of Advocates, Edinburgh Other versions: SNPG, SD 1856, plaster Court House, Inverary, 1874, marble	SD	*Ormond* 1973, 113; *Lieuallen* 2002, 62 (repr)
128.	1856	Lord President McNeill	m	Faculty of Advocates, Edinburgh		*Woodward* 1977, vol 1, pt 2, 233
129.	1856	Professor Edward Forbes	m	University of Edinburgh Other versions: SNPG, SD 1856, plaster Linnean Soc, London, 1856	SD	*Ormond* 1973, 176; *Lieuallen* 2002, 47, 176 (repr)
130.	1856	Rev Dr Thomas Guthrie, model (cast in bronze 1873)		SNPG Other versions: private coll, London, 1856, stone		*Woodward* 1977, vol 1, pt 2, 233
131.	1857	Mrs Prevost		[Exhib R Sc A, 686]; untraced		*Lieuallen* 2002, 130
132.	1858	George Wauchope Hunter Blair, a child	m	Private coll, Scotland	SD	*Lieuallen* 2002, 38 (repr)
133.	1859	Albert Edward, Prince of Wales, later King Edward VII	p	SNPG Other versions: ex coll Royal High School, Edinburgh; reported destroyed		*Lieuallen* 2002, 46 (repr)
134.	1859	Florence Nightingale	m	Royal United Service Institution, London Other versions: Wilton House, Wilts, SD 1865, marble Derby Art Gall, 1862		*Gunnis* 1968, 371; *Woodward* 1977, vol 1, pt 2, 234
135.	1859	Lady Susan Ramsay	m	Private coll, Scotland	SD	*Lieuallen* 2002, 75 (repr)
136.	1859	Queen Victoria, colossal	m	[Exhib R Sc A, 708]; untraced		*Lieuallen* 2002, 130
137.	1859	Rt Hon Sir James Wilson	m	SNPG, Edinburgh	SD	*Ormond* 1973, 518; *Lieuallen* 2002, 91 (repr)
138.	1859	Sir John McNeill	m	SNPG Other versions: Scottish development department, 21 George St, Edinburgh	SD	*Woodward* 1977, vol 1, pt 2, 233; *Gunnis* 1968, 371; *Lieuallen* 2002, 63 (repr)
139.	1861	Colonel Baker, chief secretary of the military department	m	Untraced		*Scotsman*, 23 March 1861
140.	1861	Professor James Miller	m	University of Edinburgh	SD	*Lieuallen* 2002, 64 (repr)
141.	1862	Albert, the Prince Consort		[Chamber of Commerce, Dundee, Tayside]; untraced Other versions: Royal Coll, 1878 another, for Dundee, nd; untraced	SD	*Steell Scrapbooks*, II, 98; *Ormond* 1973, 15; *Lieuallen* 2002, 35, 131 (repr)
142.	1862	Alfred, Duke of Edinburgh	m	Royal High School, Edinburgh Other versions: University of Edinburgh, 1865, marble SNPG, 1865, plaster	SD	*Woodward* 1977, vol 1, pt 2, 233
143.	1862	Florence Nightingale	b	Kaiserswerth Hospital, Dusseldorf Other versions: SNPG, 1862, plaster National Army Museum, London, SD 1862, bronze, Florence Nightingale Museum, London, SD 1862, bronze		*Lieuallen* 2002, 67–8 (repr)
144.	1862	George, Lord Patton	m	Faculty of Advocates, Edinburgh	SD	*Lieuallen* 2002, 69 (repr)
145.	1864	George Ross	m	Faculty of Advocates, Edinburgh Other versions: Royal High School, Edinburgh, nd, marble	SD	*Woodward* 1977, vol 1, pt 2, 234; *Lieuallen* 2002, 76 (repr)
146.	1864	William Small RSA	m	Joanna Barnes Fine Arts, 1989	SD	*Lieuallen* 2002, 131 (repr)
147.	1865	William Thomas Thomson	m	Standard Life Assurance Company, Edinburgh	SD	*Lieuallen* 2002, 87 (repr)
148.	1866	Jeanie Steell, probably the artist's daughter Jane, as a young girl	m	Museum services, University of Dundee		*Woodward* 1977, vol 1, pt 2, 234
149.	1866	Rev James McFarlane	m	Christie, London, 25 Sept 1991, lot 115	SD	*Lieuallen* 2002, 131
150.	1867	Unidentified man	m	Private coll, London	SD	*Lieuallen* 2002, 93
151.	1875	Rev John Cook	m	[High Tolbooth church, Edinburgh]; untraced		*Woodward* 1977, vol 1, pt 2, 233; *Lieuallen* 2002, 131
152.	1875	Thomas de Quincey	m	SNPG Other versions: NPG 822, 1875, SD, plaster Worcester Coll, Oxford, 1882, marble, SD	SD	*Graves* VII, 1905–6, 245; *Ormond* 1973, 135; *Lieuallen* 2002, 45 (repr)
153.	1877	Dr James Warburton Begbie	m	R C Physic, Edinburgh Other versions: Royal Infirmary, Edinburgh, 1877, marble	SD	*Gunnis* 1968, 371; *Lieuallen* 2002, 37 (repr)
154.	1877	Lady Anna Stirling-Maxwell	m	Christie, May 1995; untraced	SD	*Lieuallen* 2002, 84 (repr)
155.	1879	'Gracie'		[Exhib R Sc A, 747]; Sotheby, 23 Nov 1990, lot 219; J R Findlay		*Lieuallen* 2002, 131
156.	1880	Mrs William Allan		[Exhib R Sc A, 781]; untraced		*Lieuallen* 2002, 131
157.	1882	Unidentified man	m	Private coll, Carmel, California	SD	*Lieuallen* 2002, 93 (repr)
158.	1885	Robert Burns, Burns monument Model(s): plaster, Burns Cottage, Alloway	m	Alloway, Ayr	SD	*Lieuallen* 2002, 39 (repr)
159.	1889	Mrs James Stewart		[Exhib R Sc A, 774]; untraced		*Lieuallen* 2002, 131
160.	nd	John Gibson, writer to the signet	m	Signet Library, Edinburgh		RG/JP, 8, 1363; *Lieuallen* 2002, 131 (repr)
161.	nd	Mr Plenderleath, treasurer of the Destitute Sick society		Untraced		*Lieuallen* 2002, 131

162.	nd	Mr Venebles		[for Calcutta (Kolkata)]; untraced		*Steell Scrapbooks*, vol III, 91; *Lieuallen* 2002, 131
163.	nd	Professor John Thomson	m	Department of Pathology, University of Edinburgh		*Lieuallen* 2002, 85 (repr)
164.	nd	Professor Sir John Leslie (after Samuel Joseph)	m	University of Edinburgh, old library		*Lieuallen* 2002, 60 (repr)
165.	nd	Sir Neil Douglas		[Report of Steell's sale]; untraced		*The Scotsman*, 14 March 1888, 6; *Lieuallen* 2002, 131
166.	nd	Sir Robert Cautley		[Kolkata (Calcutta) town hall]; untraced		RG/JP, 8, 1363; *Lieuallen* 2002, 131
167.	nd	Sir Thomas Dick Lauder	p	SNPG		*Smailes* 1990, 171; *Lieuallen* 2002, 59 (repr)
168.	nd	The dowager Marchioness of Lothian		[Report of Steell's sale]; untraced		*The Scotsman*, 14 March 1888, 6; *Lieuallen* 2002, 131
Architectural Sculpture						
169.	1833	Ceres, allegorical group	s	[Scottish Widows, St Andrew's Square, Edinburgh, façade]; Historic Scotland's Stenhouse conservation centre (1979)		*Glasgow Gazette*, 9 June 1860, 6; *Lieuallen* 2002, 129
170.	1839	The wise and foolish virgins, tympanum relief	s	[Standard Life Assurance Building, George Street, Edinburgh]; untraced Other versions: Standard Assurance Office, Upper Sackville St, Dublin		*Read* 1982, 220, 221; *Pearson* 1991, 70 (repr); *Lieuallen* 2002, 118
171.	*c*1860	Allegorical group		[Scottish Widows' Fund Life Assurance Society, Buchanan Street, Glasgow, Lanarks]; destroyed		*McKenzie* 2002, 434–5
172.	1867	The history of Commerce, pediment group	s	Bank of Montreal, St Jacques Street, Montreal, Canada		*Gunnis* 1968, 370; *Lieuallen* 2002, 96 (engraving repr)
173.	nd	Royal arms, pediment sculpture	s	Customs House, Leith, Edinburgh		*Woodward* 1977, vol 1, pt 2, 234
Reliefs						
174.	1844	Adam and Eve		[coll Denise, Lady Kilmarnock]; Christie, London, 15 Feb 1990, lot 154		*Lieuallen* 2002, 130 (repr)
175.	1855	Hamilton mausoleum, west chapel door, copies of 6 panels from Ghiberti's baptistry gates, Florence (after Ghiberti)	b	Hamilton, Lanarks		*Lieuallen* 2002, 101 (repr)
176.	1855	Isabella Robertson Fullarton	m	Aberdeen City Arts Dept, Galls and Museums		*Pearson* 1991, unpag, 159 (repr); *Lieuallen* 2002, 110 (repr)
177.	1861	Hugh William Williams, portrait medallion	m	NGS		*Pearson* 1991, unpag; *Lieuallen* 2002, 116 (repr)
178.	1850–1871	Unidentified man, draped	m	Aberdeen City Arts Dept, Galls and Museums		*Pearson* 1991, unpag
179.	1886	Sir Walter Scott, medallion portrait		First division court, Parliament House, Edinburgh, corridor Other versions: Faculty of Advocates, Parliament House, 1886, SD	SD	*Read* 1982, 349 (repr); *Lieuallen* 2002, 113 (repr)
Miscellaneous						
180.	1836	Boy fishing	m	[Exhib R Sc A, 356]; untraced		*Pearson* 1991, 74; *Lieuallen* 2002, 129 (repr)
181.	1885	Nelson monument: relief of the San Josef	b	Calton Hill, Edinburgh		*Woodward* 1977, vol 1, pt 2, 235
182.	nd	Daniel in the lion's den		Untraced		*Pearson* 1991, 74
183.	nd	Hebe		Untraced		*Pearson* 1991, 74
184.	nd	Sir Walter Scott, Copeland porcelain group		City of Edinburgh Museums and Galleries		*Pearson* 1991, unpag

STEFFANY fl 1770–93

Catherine, the widow of 'Steffany Sculptor' was awarded a donation of 5 guineas by the Royal Academy in June 177 on the recommendation of **William Tyler RA**. She continued to receive sums of between 2 and 5 guineas until 179

Archival References: RA Council Minutes, 1, fols 80, 109, 137, 159, 181, 204, 220, 242, 273, 286, 306, 330, 345, 361; 2, fols 10, 29, 41, 142, 165, 182

STEGGLES, William, of Bury St Edmunds 1767–1859

Steggles was a monumental mason. He was assisted in the business by his son, William Henry Steggles, who died i 1843 at the age of 31. Steggles himself died on 12 July 1859, and was buried in the Abbey graveyard at Bury St Edmund His wife Maria died on 4 July 1851, aged 72.

Literary References: *Gunnis* 1968, 371

Archival References: GPC

Funerary Monuments

1.	?1809	Rev Beriah Brook	Stansfield, Suffolk	S	*Gunnis* 1968, 371
2.	?1829	James Oakes	St Mary's, Bury St Edmunds, Suffolk	S	*Gunnis* 1968, 371
3.	?1834	Thomas Robins, ledger stone	Isleham, Cambs		*Gunnis* 1968, 371

STELT, W fl *c*1842

He signs a tablet in black and white marble.

Funerary Monuments

1.	†1842	Charles Robert Streatfield Nixon	Ash, Kent	S

STEPHAN, Pierre fl 1769–95

A Frenchman, he was evidently associated with the Tournai porcelain factory before coming to England, for a bi dated 14 October 1769 in the Tournai archives reads '4 figures elemens de Stephan'. On 17 September 1770 he signe a three-year agreement with William Duesbury to work for him at the Derby porcelain factory (MS NAL) wher was paid a good wage, of £2 12s 6d per week, for modelling and repairing porcelain. At the termination of hi agreement he went to Wirksworth, about 12 miles from Derby, and then approached Josiah Wedgwood. On 9 May 1774 he wrote to Wedgwood: 'I was informed some time agoe by several persons (particularly Mr. Gardiner of Derby the architect) that you gave great encouragements to Artists in Modelling branch, at which time I was then engag'd with Mr. Duesbury of Derby and since then with the china factory at Wirksworth, both of which I am now disengaged from and have some thought of goeing to London, but first take the liberty of informing you that if I coud meet with agreeable Employment and that encouragement my work may deserve; I should be glad to have an Opportunity of being Employ'd by persons of taste and meriets [*sic*] which I hear is the Character of your Manufactory, but at the same time should chuse to have some part of my Employment in London on account of having a greater Opportunity of improveing my Ideas in the art of Modelling; but hope you will be so kind as to favour me with a line as soon as possible as I shall leave this Plase in a fortnight or three weeks at the farthest. N.B. I work in figures, vasses, or any sort of Useful as Business may require' (Wedgwood/Stephan corr E2/1347). From May 1774 he worked for Wedgwood though based in London, making moulds and models. Stephan did not receive unqualified approval from his employer: Wedgwood wrote of two wax models of *Hope* and *The Conquer'd province* 'the drapery is hard and unfinished and the characters of the faces are those of common mortals of the lower class' (Wedgwood/Stephan E25/18554, Wedgwood/Bentley, 22 August 1774).

He apparently continued to work for Duesbury whilst employed by Wedgwood and, confusingly, Bricknell claims that he was resident modeller at Derby from 1770 to 1778 (*Bricknell* 1995, 125). When called upon in 1819 to give evidence in a lawsuit brought against Michael Kean by the heirs of William Duesbury II, Stephan stated: 'for the space of about 7 years he was employed as a Modeller in the service of the late William Duesbury of Derby . . . the Moulds and Models made . . . by this Deponent alone . . . were in constant use and in the judgment and opinion of this Deponent, were well worth to the said Manufactury the sum if £1500' (Dawson quoting *Bricknell* 1995, 101). It seems clear that he worked on a free-lance basis and it is recorded that he provided moulds for the Derby factory at least once more, around April 1795, when he requested payment for them. He was then living in Staffordshire. He wrote to Duesbury: 'Sir / Hope you have received the moulds in good condition, as I took the procation for there Savety. Sir, as am much necessitated for mony this particular time, your remitance would greatly oblige most humble Servant / P. Stephan / Shelton the 4 april 1795' (*Bricknel* 1995, 87). There are references to 'Old Mr Stephan' in documents relating to a lawsuit brought by Duesbury against Michael Kean 1814–1819.

Pierre's brother, John Charles Stephan, married in Derby in August 1773 and baptized his daughter two months later at Wirksworth. He was in Derby in December 1774 and in 1776. His signature appears on a bill for modelling ornamental wares and two dogs at Wirksworth. John Charles is not otherwise known to have created figures.

Literary References: *Gunnis* 1968, 371; *Jottrand* 1977, 133, 135 appendix III; *Bricknell* 1995, 87, 99, 100–2, 125; *Dawson* 1999, 234–7

Archival References: GPC

Statues

1.	nd	Admiral Rodney, two versions, one in black basalt and the other in dark grey clay		Untraced	S	*Dawson* 1999, 236
2.	nd	Admiral, Lord Howe (previously thought to be General Drinkwater), unglazed ceramic figure		[Rev Waldo Sibthorp]; untraced	S	*Dawson* 1999, 236
3.	nd	Hope and the conquered province, models	w	Untraced		*Gunnis* 1968, 371

Busts

4.	*c*1775	Unidentified young woman, porcelain		BM, MLA 1936, 7–15, 19	S	*Dawson* 1999, 234–7 (repr)

STEPHEN, John fl 1844

One of the partnership Scott, Stephen and Gale of Glasgow.

Funerary Monuments

1.	1844	Rev Robert Muter (†1842)	Glasgow Necropolis	Pevsner, *Glasgow*, 1990, 140–1

STEPHENS, Edward Bowring ARA 1815–82

He was born in Exeter on 10 December 1815, the son of James Stephens, a local mason. He began his artistic training under the draughtsman and landscape painter John Gendall, but then moved to London and in 1835 became a pupil of **E H Baily RA**. In 1837, while living at 78 Charlotte Street, Fitzroy Square, he won a silver medal from the Society of Arts for a model (**13**) and entered the Royal Academy Schools. The following year he was awarded the Academy's silver medal for an original model of *Ajax defying the Gods* (**14**). Stephens exhibited regularly at the RA from 1838 onwards, showing principally portrait busts and ideal works based on classical, biblical and literary subject matter. Between 1838 and 1858 he showed sporadically at British Institution exhibitions. In 1839 he travelled to Italy and spent time working in Rome before returning to Exeter nearly three years later, when he executed a life-size seated statue in marble of the Devonshire landowner and politician John, Baron Rolle (**16**).

In 1842 Stephens returned to London, where he resumed his studies at the RA Schools and in 1843 he was awarded the gold medal for a small relief model depicting the *Battle of the centaurs and lapithae* (**106**). He attracted public attention with three works sent to the Westminster Hall exhibitions of 1844 and 1845 (**19, 20, 21**), but it was the group of *Hagar and Ishmael in the wilderness* (**18**) that was particularly admired by one commentator. He considered Stephens 'one of the most rising sculptors of the day, one whom we confidently expect to see placed in the highest seat the profession supplies' (*AU*, 1844, 216). Stephens contributed statues of *Satan tempting Eve* and *Satan Vanquished* to the Great Exhibition of 1851 and another entitled *Preparing for the chase* to the Manchester Art Treasures Exhibition of 1857 (**26, 27, 30**). In that year his group of *Mercy on the battlefield* was issued as a small bronze by the Art Union of London (**29**).

Stephens maintained close links with his native county throughout his career. In 1861 he carved a statue of the politician and philanthropist, Sir Thomas Dyke Acland, for Northernhay Gardens, Exeter (**34**) and several commissions for public statues of Devon worthies followed (**36, 39, 46, 53**). In 1865 he carved two statues for the west front of Exeter Cathedral and in 1870 donated a statue of Albert, the Prince Consort to the Royal Albert Memorial Museum, Exeter (**104, 41**). His bronze group *The deerstalker*, generally regarded as his finest work, was purchased by public subscription and erected in Northernhay Gardens in 1878 (**45**). At a banquet held to mark this occasion the sculptor gave a speech in which he said that Acland and William, 10th Earl of Devon 'above all others were the founders of his professional career, and his first friends, who helped him on cheerfully and hopefully to try and do big things' (*Builder*, 1882, ii, 669).

As an established sculptor Stephens secured several significant institutional commissions. He provided a statue of Joseph Priestley for the Oxford University Museum in 1860 (**32**). The following year he started work on a figure of *Alfred the Great in the neatherd's cottage*, commissioned by the Corporation of London for the Egyptian Hall in the Mansion House (**35**). In 1873 he carved statues of Leonardo da Vinci, Sir Christopher Wren and Sir Joshua Reynolds for the façade of Burlington House, which had recently become the home of the Royal Academy (**105**). Stephens was elected an ARA in 1864, but it was generally believed that his election came about because he was confused with **Alfred Stevens**.

He died of bronchitis, at his home, 110 Buckingham Palace Road, London, on 9 November 1882. His grave in Kensal Green cemetery is marked with a simple ledger and a low headstone. Soon after his death, Samuel Carter Hall, editor of the *Art Journal*, described Stephens as 'a man of large worth in private life – a sculptor of the highest genius' (*Hall* II, 1883, 243–4). George Pycroft, the author of *Art in Devonshire*, remembered him as 'one of those genuine, unpretending, honest beings that are always appreciated' (*Pycroft* 1883, cited by *Gunnis* 1968, 372). His works have nonetheless been little studied.

EH

Literary References: *AJ*, 1882, 379; *Builder* 43, 1882, 669; *Hall* II, 1883, 242, 243–4; *DNB* (Graves); *Gunnis* 1968, 371–2; *Avery and Marsh* 1985, 333; *Curl* 2001, 242; *ODNB* (Rev. Worthington)

Archival References: RA Premium list

Wills and Administrations: PPR, will, 4 January 1883, fol 79, estate valued at £1,566 0s 4d

Funerary Monuments

1.	†1815	Jane Spence		Berrynarbor, Devon	Pevsner, *Devon*, 1989, 165
2.	†1841	Sir John Bayley		Meopham, Kent	Pevsner, *Kent: W & Weald*, 1976, 418
3.	?1843	Charles Goring		Cartmel, Lancs	RG/JP, 8, 1371
4.	†1843	Edward Lloyd Kenyon		Aylesbeare, Devon	Pevsner, *Devon*, 1989, 145
5.	†1843	Edward Lloyd Kenyon		Ruabon, Denbighs	Pevsner, *Clwyd*, 1986, 270
6.	†1844	Rev Thomas Putt		Gittisham, Devon	Pevsner, *Devon*, 1989, 457
7.	†1846	Sir Humphrey Davie		Sandford, Devon	Pevsner, *Devon*, 1989, 718
8.	*c*1849	Rev Richard Lewis (†1843)		St Paul, Honiton, Devon	*Graves* VII, 1905–6, 250; Pevsner, *Devon*, 1989, 494
9.	†1855	Captain John Newcombe		Moretonhampstead, Devon	Pevsner, *Devon*, 1989, 577
10.	1869	Elizabeth, Countess of Devon		Powderham, Devon	*Graves* VII, 1905–6, 251; *Gunnis* 1968, 372; Pevsner, *Devon*, 1989, 692
11.	1871	In Memoriam; part of a marble mural monument		[Exhib RA, London, 1294]; untraced	*Graves* VII, 1905–6, 251
12.	nd	Several, unidentified subjects		Tawstock, Devon	Pevsner, *Devon*, 1989, 791

Statues

13.	1837	Figure, model		[Soc of A silver medal]; untraced	RSA *Transactions*, 1838, vol 52, xv
14.	1838	Ajax defying the Gods, model		[RA silver medal]; untraced	*Graves* 1875, 517; *DNB*; *Gunnis* 1968, 371
15.	1838	Maternal love		[Exhib RA, London, 1281]; untraced	*Graves* 1875, 517; *Graves* VII, 1905–6, 250; *Gunnis* 1968, 372
16.	1841	John, Baron Rolle		Lupton House, Torbay, Devon, entrance hall Other versions: Bicton College of Agriculture, Devon, entrance hall, 1844	*AU*, 1844, 170; *Gunnis* 1968, 371; *Graves* VII, 1905–6, 250; Pevsner, *Devon*, 1989, 172, 833
17.	1842	Phrygian hunter		[Exhib RA, London, 1276]; untraced	*AU*, 1842, 128; *Graves* VII, 1905–6, 250
18.	1843	Hagar and Ishmael in the wilderness		[Exhib RA, London, 1414]; Westminster Hall, London, 1844, 164]; untraced	*AU*, 1844, 216; *Graves* VII, 1905–6, 250; *Gunnis* 1968, 372
19.	1844	Alfred the Great propounding his code of the law		[Exhib Westminster Hall, London, 173]; untraced	*Athen*, 1844, 674; *Builder*, 1844, 368
20.	1844	The wanderer's home Model(s): sketch exhib BI, London, 1847, 557		[Exhib Westminster Hall, London, 129]; untraced	*Westminster* 1845, 16; *Graves* 1875, 517; *Johnson* 1975, 440
21.	1845	Pastoral Apollo		[Exhib Westminster Hall, London, 128]; untraced	*Westminster* 1845, 16; *AU*, 1845, 258; *Builder*, 1845, 316; *Graves* 1875, 517
22.	1846	A deerstalker in pursuit	p	[Exhib RA, London, 1421]; untraced	*AU*, 1846, 188–9; *Graves* VII, 1905–6, 250
23.	1847	Comus offering the cup to the lady	m	[Shobrooke Park, Devon, coll T H Hippesley]; untraced	*AU*, 1847, 200; *Graves* VII, 1905–6, 250; *Gunnis* 1968, 372
24.	1848	Diana		[Beech Hill, Essex, coll Mr Soames]; untraced	*Gunnis* 1968, 372
25.	1850	Charity		[Exhib RA, London, 1323]; untraced	*Graves* 1875, 517; *Graves* VII, 1905–6, 250
26.	1851	Satan tempting Eve		[Gt Exhib, London]; untraced	*DNB*; *Gunnis* 1968, 372
27.	1851	Satan vanquished		[Gt Exhib, London]; untraced	*DNB*; *Gunnis* 1968, 372
28.	1856	Euphrosyne and Cupid		[Exhib RA, London, 1234]; untraced	*Graves* VII, 1905–6, 251

29.	1857	Mercy on the battlefield		[Exhib RA, London, 1349]; untraced Other versions: bronze statuette issued by the Art Union of London		*Graves* VII, 1905–6, 251; *Avery and Marsh* 1985, 333
30.	1857	Preparing for the chase	m	[Manc Art Treas Exhib, 34]; untraced		*Manchester Art Treasures* 1857, 133
31.	1859	General Lord Saltoun		Fraserburgh, Inverness		*DNB*; *Gunnis* 1968, 372
32.	1860	Joseph Priestley		Oxford University Museum		*Gunnis* 1968, 372; *Read* 1982, 235
33.	1861	Evening, going to the bath	m	[Exhib RA, London, 999]; untraced		*Graves* VII, 1905–6, 251
34.	1861	Sir Thomas Dyke Acland Model(s): exhib RA, London, 1862, 1028		[Northernhay Gardens, Exeter]; City walls, Exeter, Devon		*Graves* VII, 1905–6, 251; *Gunnis* 1968, 372
35.	1861–1863	Alfred the Great in the neatherd's cottage	m	CL Coll, Mansion House, City of London, Egyptian Hall, acc 127	D	*Graves* VII, 1905–6, 251; *Knight* 1986, 346 (repr); *Ward-Jackson* 2002, 556–7
36.	1863	Hugh, 2nd Earl Fortescue Model(s): exhib RA, 1863, London, 1062		Castle Yard, Exeter, Devon		*Graves* VII, 1905–6, 251; Pevsner, *Devon*, 1989, 401; *ODNB*
37.	1863	William, 2nd Earl of Lonsdale	m	Lowther mausoleum, Cumbria		*Graves* VII, 1905–6, 251; *Gunnis* 1968, 372
38.	1864	Francis, 7th Duke of Bedford Model(s): exhib RA, London, 1864, 910	b	Abbey precincts, Tavistock, Devon	SD	*Graves* VII, 1905–6, 251; *Gunnis* 1968, 372; PMSA NRP database; Pevsner, *Devon*, 1989, 783
39.	1864	John Dinham Model(s): exhib RA, London, 1866, 852	m	Northenhay Gardens, Exeter, Devon		*Graves* VII, 1905–6, 251; *Gunnis* 1968, 372; Pevsner, *Devon*, 1989, 403
40.	1865	Euphrosyne and Cupid	m	[Exhib RA, London, 896]; untraced		*Graves* VII, 1905–6, 251
41.	1868	Albert, the Prince Consort	s	Royal Albert Memorial Museum and Art Gall, Exeter, Devon		*Read* 1982, 95; *Derby and Smith* 1983, 80; Pevsner, *Devon*, 1989, 402
42.	1871	Zingari	m	[Brighton, Sussex, coll Captain Hill]; untraced		*Graves* VII, 1905–6, 251; *Gunnis* 1968, 372
43.	1873	Athlete (wrestler preparing for the grip)		Sold Sotheby, Belgravia, 6 April 1973, lot 49		*Graves* VII, 1905–6, 251–2; C Lib (repr)
44.	1875	A bowler		Sold Sotheby, Belgravia, 6 April 1973, lot 49		*Graves* VII, 1905–6, 252; C Lib (repr)
45.	1876	The deerstalker	b	Northenhay Gardens, Exeter, Devon Other versions: marble exhib RA, London, 1873, 1504		*Graves* VII, 1905–6, 252; *DNB*; *Gunnis* 1968, 372; Pevsner, *Devon*, 1989, 403
46.	1878	Alfred Rooker		Plymouth, Devon		*Graves* VII, 1905–6, 252; *DNB*; *Gunnis* 1968, 372
47.	1878	Sir John Cordy Burrows		[Brighton Pavilion grounds]; Old Steine, Brighton, Sussex		*Graves* VII, 1905–6, 252; *Gunnis* 1968, 372
48.	1878	The bathers		Russell-Cotes AG, Bournemouth, Dorset		*Graves* VII, 1905–6, 252; *Gunnis* 1968, 372
49.	1878	The little carpenter, statuette	m	[Exhib RA, London, 1509]; untraced		*Graves* VII, 1905–6, 252
50.	1879	Lady Godiva, statuette	m	[Exhib RA, London, 1529]; untraced		*Graves* VII, 1905–6, 252
51.	1879	Ophelia, statuette	m	[Exhib RA, London, 1526]; untraced		*Graves* VII, 1905–6, 252
52.	1879	Science and Literature		Melbourne, Australia		*Gunnis* 1968, 372
53.	1879	William, 11th Earl of Devon	b	[Bedford Circus Garden, Exeter]; Bedford Street, Exeter, Devon		*Graves* VII, 1905–6, 252; *Gunnis* 1968, 372; Pevsner, *Devon*, 1989, 419
54.	1880	The lecturer, model		[Exhib RA, London, 1519]; untraced		*Graves* VII, 1905–6, 252
55.	1882	Shielding the helpless		Burlington House, London		*Graves* VII, 1905–6, 252; *Gunnis* 1968, 372
Busts						
56.	1838	Blanche Sheffield		[RA, London, 1839, 1342]; untraced		*Graves* VII, 1905–6, 250; *Gunnis* 1968, 371
57.	1838	James Viney		[Exhib RA, London, 1371]; untraced		*Graves* VII, 1905–6, 250
58.	1842	John, Baron Rolle		[Exhib RA, London, 1335]; untraced		*Graves* VII, 1905–6, 250
59.	1842	Sir William Follett MP	m	Devon and Exeter Institution, Exeter		*AU*, 1842, 128; *Graves* VII, 1905–6, 250; *Ormond* 1973, 176
60.	1842	William, 10th Earl of Devon		Powderham Castle, Devon		*Graves* VII, 1905–6, 250; *Gunnis* 1968, 372
61.	1843	Baldwin Fulford		Fulford Park, Devon		*Gunnis* 1968, 372
62.	1843	Countess of Devon		Doncaster Art Gall, WR Yorks		*Graves* VII, 1905–6, 250; RG/JP, 8, 1370
63.	1843	Dean of Exeter	m	[Exhib RA, London, 1450]; untraced		*Graves* VII, 1905–6, 250
64.	1843	P Miller Esq MD	m	[Exhib RA, London, 1449]; untraced		*Graves* VII, 1905–6, 250
65.	1844	Sir Thomas Dyke Acland Bt MP	m	[Exhib RA, London, 1407]; untraced		*Graves* VII, 1905–6, 250
66.	1845	Colonel Fulford	m	[Exhib RA, London, 1414]; untraced		*Graves* VII, 1905–6, 250
67.	1845	General Gage Hall	m	[Exhib RA, London, 1408]; untraced		*Graves* VII, 1905–6, 250
68.	1845	Henry Phillpots, Bishop of Exeter	m	[Exhib RA, London, 1407]; untraced		*Graves* VII, 1905–6, 250
69.	1846	J B Creswell	m	[Exhib RA, London, 1481]; untraced		*Graves* VII, 1905–6, 250
70.	1846	W S Kelsall	m	[Exhib RA, London, 1466]; untraced		*Graves* VII, 1905–6, 250
71.	1847	General Sir Benjamin D'Urban	m	[Exhib RA, London, 1381]; untraced		*Graves* VII, 1905–6, 250
72.	1847	Sir Humphrey Davie	m	[Exhib RA, London, 1365]; untraced		*Graves* VII, 1905–6, 250
73.	1847	T S Kelsall	m	[Exhib RA, London, 1420]; untraced		*Graves* VII, 1905–6, 250
74.	1849	Infant son of Alfred T Jay	m	[Exhib RA, London, 1250]; untraced		*Graves* VII, 1905–6, 250
75.	1849	Samuel Fletcher	m	[Exhib RA, London, 1261]; untraced		*Graves* VII, 1905–6, 250
76.	1850	Sir John Bayley		Eton College, Windsor, Berks, upper school		*Gunnis* 1968, 372
77.	1851	Dealtry, Bishop of Madras	m	Kolkata (Calcutta) Cathedral		*Graves* VII, 1905–6, 250; *Gunnis* 1968, 372
78.	1851	Henry, 3rd Viscount Palmerston	m	Broadlands, Hants		*Graves* VII, 1905–6, 251; *Gunnis* 1968, 372

79.	1851	John Aitkens	m	[Exhib RA, London, 1333]; untraced	*Graves* VII, 1905–6, 251
80.	1854	William Courtenay	m	Powderham Castle, Devon	*Graves* VII, 1905–6, 251; *Gunnis* 1968, 372
81.	1855	Unidentified subject	m	[Exhib RA, London, 1540]; untraced	*Graves* VII, 1905–6, 251
82.	1857	Viscount Ebrington MP		[Exhib RA, London, 1330]; untraced	*Graves* VII, 1905–6, 251
83.	1859	James Anderton		[Exhib RA, London, 1318]; untraced	*Graves* VII, 1905–6, 251
84.	1861	Hugh, 2nd Earl Fortescue	m	Barnstaple Infirmary, Devon	*Graves* VII, 1905–6, 251; *Gunnis* 1968, 372
85.	1861	William Adams	m	[Exhib RA, London, 1041]; untraced	*Graves* VII, 1905–6, 251
86.	1866	Arthur W Jaffray	m	[Exhib RA, London, 865]; untraced	*Graves* VII, 1905–6, 251
87.	1866	Gerald Stanhope		Elvaston Castle, Derbys	RG/JP, 8, 1370
88.	1866	John Tyrrell	m	[Exhib RA, London, 913]; untraced	*Graves* VII, 1905–6, 251
89.	1870	Mrs Henry Fortescue	m	[Exhib RA, London, 1163]; untraced	*Graves* VII, 1905–6, 251
90.	1870	Sir John Bowring	m	Exeter Unitarian Church, Devon	*Graves* VII, 1905–6, 251;
91.	1871	Henry Fortescue	m	[Exhib RA, London, 1300]; untraced	*Graves* VII, 1905–6, 251
92.	1872	Henry, 3rd Viscount Palmerston	m	[Exhib RA, London, 1537]; untraced	*Graves* VII, 1905–6, 251; *Ormond* 1973, 361
93.	1872	William, 2nd Earl of Lonsdale	m	Hughenden, Bucks	*Graves* VII, 1905–6, 252
94.	1873	Lord Lister		St Thomas's Hospital, London	*Gunnis* 1968, 372
95.	1873	Samuel Solly FRS	m	[Exhib RA, London, 1430]; untraced	*Graves* VII, 1905–6, 252
96.	1879	C C Whiteford		Plymouth Town Hall, Devon	*Gunnis* 1968, 372
97.	1879	Rt Hon Peter Erle	m	[Exhib RA, London, 1467]; untraced	*Graves* VII, 1905–6, 252
98.	1881	R S Gard		Exeter Art Gall, Devon	*Gunnis* 1968, 372
Chimneypieces					
99.	1846	Description unavailable	m	Buckingham Palace, London, summer pavilion	*Gunnis* 1968, 372
Architectural Sculpture					
100.	1852–1854	Pair of Atlantes (designed by C R Cockerell)	s	St George's Hall, Liverpool, Lancs	*Cavanagh* 1997, 292 (repr)
101.	1854	'Parthenon' frieze	p	St George's Hall, Liverpool, Lancs, north entrance hall	*Cavanagh* 1997, 292–3
102.	1857	Sarcophagus	m	Lowther Mausoleum, Cumbria	*Gunnis* 1968, 372
103.	1861	Angel (for a mausoleum)		[Exhib RA, London, 1029]; untraced	*Graves* VII, 1905–6, 251
104.	1865	William the Conqueror and James the Less	s	Exeter Cathedral, Devon, west front	Pevsner, *Devon*, 1989, 375
105.	1873	Leonardo da Vinci, Sir Christoper Wren, Sir Joshua Reynolds		Burlington House, London, façade	*Gunnis* 1968, 372; *Read* 1982, 226
Reliefs					
106.	1843	Battle of the centaurs and lapithae, model		[Awarded RA gold medal]; untraced	*AU*, 1844, 170; *DNB*; *Graves* VII, 1905–6, 250
107.	1845	The attendant spirit disguised as Thyrsis and the lady	m	Buckingham Palace, London, summer temple	*Graves* VII, 1905–6, 250; *Gunnis* 1968, 372
108.	1859	Balaclava Model(s): exhib RA, London, 1861, 1098	b	Morris memorial obelisk, Hatherleigh Moor, Devon	*Graves* VII, 1905–6, 251; *Gunnis* 1968, 372; Pevsner, *Devon*, 1989, 475
109.	1868	Raising of the widow's son		All Saints, Kenton, Devon	*Gunnis* 1968, 372; Pevsner, *Devon*, 1989, 517
Miscellaneous					
110.	1838	Arcadian nymph		[Exhib RA, London, 1275]; untraced	*Graves* VII, 1905–6, 250
111.	1838	Narcissus		[Exhib RA, London, 1270]; untraced	*Graves* VII, 1905–6, 250
112.	1839	Diana		[Exhib RA, London, 1289]; untraced	*Graves* VII, 1905–6, 250
113.	1842	Eve		[Exhib RA, London, 1317]; untraced	*Graves* VII, 1905–6, 250
114.	1847	The lady, seated in the enchanted chair, refusing the cup		[Exhib RA, London, 1327]; untraced	*Graves* VII, 1905–6, 250
115.	1852	Young shepherdess by the brook side Payment(s): 80 gns (model); 250 gns (marble)		[Exhib RA, London, 1329]; untraced	*Graves* 1875, 517; *Graves* VII, 1905–6, 251
116.	1853	Eve contemplating death		[Exhib RA, London, 1317]; untraced	*Graves* VII, 1905–6, 251
117.	1867	Cupid's cruise		[Exhib RA, London, 1008]; untraced	*Graves* VII, 1905–6, 251
118.	1867	Lady Godiva		[Exhib RA, London, 1007]; untraced	*Graves* VII, 1905–6, 251
119.	1868	Blackberry picking – the thorn		[Exhib RA, London, 960]; untraced	*Graves* VII, 1905–6, 251
120.	1868	Coaxing		[Exhib RA, London, 945]; untraced	*Graves* VII, 1905–6, 251
121.	1869	Saved from the wreck		[Exhib RA, London, 1227]; untraced	*Graves* VII, 1905–6, 251
122.	1873	Eve's dream		[Exhib RA, London, 1541]; untraced	*Graves* VII, 1905–6, 252
123.	1874	Leander preparing to cross the Hellespont		[Exhib RA, London, 1513]; untraced	*Graves* VII, 1905–6, 252
124.	1875	Evening, Lord teach me how to pray		[Exhib RA, London, 1313]; untraced	*Graves* VII, 1905–6, 252
125.	1875	Morning, Lord, teach my heart Thy love to sing		[Exhib RA, London, 1315]; untraced	*Graves* VII, 1905–6, 252

STEPHENS, John fl 1759

He had a business as a mason in Longacre, and may be the J Stephens who supplied a 'carved bath grate' to Croom Court, Worcs in June 1759 (*Beard* 1993, 92).

Literary References: *Mortimer* 1763, 49

STEPHENS, Joseph I and II, of Worcester

Joseph Stephens I 1773–1834
Joseph Stephens II 1808–

Joseph Stephens I was the son of **William Humphries Stephens**. Gunnis notes that his monuments have little of th[e] charm of those designed and carved by his father. Many are plain tablets, occasionally embellished with ornament[s] such as a relief of *Hope* by an altar (on the Joseph Roberts (**3**), which Gunnis considers his best work), an urn (**7**), o[r] a bust above the inscription (**18**). He died on 14 July, 1834, and was buried at St Andrew, Worcester. His wif[e] Elizabeth, predeceased him, dying on 13 August, 1809, at the age of 36.

His son, **Joseph Stephens II** was born in 1808 and attended the Royal Academy Schools in 1828, on th[e] recommendation of **Sir Francis Chantrey**. At this time he was living at 11 Winchester Place. In the following yea[r] he received a large silver medal from the Society of Arts for a bust (**64**), and in 1830, after returning to Worcester, exhibited a model of a monument for St Nicholas, Worcester at the Birmingham Society of Artists (**28**). He appears to have lived in London between 1833 and 1845, first at 8 Buckingham Street, Adelphi, and then at 15 East Street, Red Lion Square (1834). In 1845 he went back again to Worcester and in 1853 took casts of the monuments in Worcester Cathedral for the sculpture gallery at the Crystal Palace.

Like his father he was a prolific statuary. Gunnis singles out the Brace and Corles as good tablets (**45, 55**) but most were conventional in composition: the Willis has an obelisk with a draped urn (**39**), the Charlett and Nash have a sarcophagus in relief (**41, 47**), the Ballard and Venables is personalised with masonic symbols (**43**) and the Thomas and Cameron are scrolled tablets (**51, 53**). He branched out into the making of busts and even an ideal work (**74**).

Works known to have been provided before 1834 have been accredited to the father as senior partner.

Literary References: *Graves* VII, 1905–6, 252; *Gunnis* 1968, 372–3

Archival References: RA Admissions

Funerary Monuments

1.	†1795	Hon and Rev Andrew St John (by Joseph Stephens I)	Worcester Cathedral	S	
2.	†1800	Catherine Yarndel (by Joseph Stephens I)	Malvern, Worcs		*Gunnis* 1968, 373
3.	†1806	Joseph Roberts (by Joseph Stephens I)	Saintbury, Glos	S	*Gunnis* 1968, 373
4.	†1807	Rev Edward Toldervy (†1761) and his wife, Margaret (by Joseph Stephens I)	Cleobury Mortimer, Salop	S	GPC
5.	†1808	Mrs Palmer (by Joseph Stephens I)	Spetchley, Worcs		*Gunnis* 1968, 373
6.	†1809	F B Thomas (by Joseph Stephens I)	Stretton Grandison, Herefs	S	RG/JP, 8, 1372
7.	†1814	Cossley Saunders (by Joseph Stephens I)	St Helen, Worcester	S	
8.	†1814	John Baker (by Joseph Stephens I)	Hartlebury, Worcs	S	GPC
9.	†1815	Archdeacon Thomas Evans (by Joseph Stephens I)	Worcester Cathedral	S	RG/JP, 8, 1371v.
10.	†1817	Arthur Onslow and wife (†1825) (by Joseph Stephens I)	Worcester Cathedral	S	RG/JP, 8, 1372
11.	†1817	Eleanor Bradley (by Joseph Stephens I)	St Bartholomew, Wolverhampton, Staffs	S	Pevsner, *Staffs*, 1974, 323; GPC
12.	†1817	William Wheeler (by Joseph Stephens I)	Chaddesley Corbett, Worcs	S	RG/JP, 8, 1372
13.	†1818	William Allies (by Joseph Stephens I)	Alfrick, Worcs	S	
14.	†1819	Herbert Fidkin (by Joseph Stephens I)	Hartlebury, Worcs	S	RG/JP, 8, 1371v.
15.	†1820	Thomas Davis (by Joseph Stephens I)	All Saints, Worcester	S	
16.	†1821	Jane Cazalet (by Joseph Stephens I)	Worcester Cathedral	S	AL
17.	†1821	Richard Bourner Charlett (by Joseph Stephens I)	Worcester Cathedral	S	
18.	†1821	Thomas Foley (by Joseph Stephens I)	Kempsey, Worcs		Pevsner, *Worcs*, 1968, 203
19.	†1822	Ambrose St John (by Joseph Stephens I)	Worcester Cathedral	S	
20.	†1823	John Yates and wife (by Joseph Stephens I)	Untraced		RG/JP, 8, 1372
21.	†1823	Margaret Ewing (by Joseph Stephens I)	All Saints, Worcester	S	
22.	†1823	Rev Slade Nash (by Joseph Stephens I)	St Peter, Droitwich, Worcs	S	*Gunnis* 1968, 373
23.	†1824	R Wilkes (by Joseph Stephens I)	Enville, Staffs	S	*Gunnis* 1968, 373
24.	†1825	John Wingfield (by Joseph Stephens I)	Worcester Cathedral	S	RG/JP, 8, 1372
25.	†1826	Richard (†1825), Sarah (†1797) and Margaret Nash (by Joseph Stephens I)	St Helen, Worcester	S	
26.	†1828	Elizabeth Wall (by Joseph Stephens I)	Quatt, Salop	S	RG/JP, 8, 1372
27.	†1830	Ann Prattenton and others (by Joseph Stephens I)	Hartlebury, Worcs	S	RG/JP, 8, 1372
28.	1830	'Model of a monument for St Nicholas's Church, Worcester' (by Joseph Stephens II)	[Exhib Birmingham Soc of A]; untraced		*Gunnis* 1968, 373
29.	†1831	Edward Wallwyn	Much Marcle, Herefs		*Gunnis* 1968, 373
30.	†1831	George, 7th Earl of Coventry	Croome d'Abitot, Worcs	S	*Gunnis* 1968, 373
31.	†1831	James West	Mathon, Herefs	S	RG/JP, 8, 1372
32.	†1831	Rev Charles Wigley	Mamble, Worcs	S	RG/JP, 8, 1372
33.	†1832	Rev J Fleming St John	Worcester Cathedral	S	RG/JP, 8, 1371v
34.	†1833	Edmund Greswolde	Mamble, Worcs	S	GPC
35.	†1833	Hon Sir William Russell	Chaddesley Corbett, Worcs	S	GPC
36.	†1835	Frances Carr (by Joseph Stephens II)	Hartlebury, Worcs	S	RG/JP, 8, 1372
37.	†1835	Jane Perrott (by Joseph Stephens II)	Fladbury, Worcs	S	*Gunnis* 1968, 373
38.	†1835	Rev Samuel Picart (by Joseph Stephens II)	Hartlebury, Worcs	S	GPC
39.	†1837	Frances Fermor and Frances Willis (by Joseph Stephens II)	Claines, Worcs	S	

40.	†1837	Percy family (by Joseph Stephens II)		Chaddesley Corbett, Worcs	S	RG/JP, 8, 1372
41.	†1838	James Charlett (by Joseph Stephens II)		Hanley William, Worcs	S	Pevsner, *Worcs*, 1968, 189
42.	†1838	Rosa Elizabeth Wheeler (by Joseph Stephens II)		Worcester Cathedral	S	
43.	†1839	John Severn Ballard and Anne Venables (†1839) (by Joseph Stephens II)		St Helen, Worcester	S	
44.	†1840	Dr John Jenkinson (by Joseph Stephens II)		Worcester Cathedral	S	RG/JP, 8, 1372
45.	1840	Frances Brace (by Joseph Stephens II)		Leominster, Herefs	S	*Gunnis* 1968, 373
46.	†1840	Frances Holmes (by Joseph Stephens II)		Stretton Grandison, Herefs	S	RG/JP, 8, 1371v.
47.	†1840	George Nash (by Joseph Stephens II)		Martley, Worcs	S	Pevsner, *Worcs*, 1968, 221
48.	†1841	Viscount Valentia (by Joseph Stephens II)		Upper Arley, Worcs	S	Pevsner, *Worcs*, 1968, 281
49.	†1843	Catherine Prattenton (by Joseph Stephens II)		Hartlebury, Worcs	S	RG/JP, 8, 1372
50.	†1843	George, 8th Earl of Coventry (by Joseph Stephens II)		Croome d'Abitot, Worcs		*Gunnis* 1968, 373
51.	†1844	John Thomas (by Joseph Stephens II)		Claines, Worcs	S	
52.	†1844	Marianne Wood (by Joseph Stephens II)		Ribbesford, Worcs	S	RG/JP, 8, 1372
53.	†1846	Archibald Cameron (by Joseph Stephens II)		St Helen, Worcester	S	
54.	†1848	Rev William Moore (by Joseph Stephens II)		Tasley, Salop	S	GPC
55.	†1848	William Corles (by Joseph Stephens II)		Worcester Cathedral	S	
56.	†1852	Rev John Cawood (by Joseph Stephens II)		Dowles, Worcs	S	RG/JP, 8, 1372
57.	†1854	Lady Winnington (by Joseph Stephens II)		Stanford, Worcs	S	*Gunnis* 1968, 373
58.	†1854	Thomas (†1820) and James Grove (†1854) (by Joseph Stephens II)		Enville, Staffs	S	RG/JP, 8, 1372
59.	†1855	Rev A Hopkins (by Joseph Stephens II)		Clent, Worcs	S	RG/JP, 8, 1372
60.	†1858	Lieutenant-Colonel T O W Ingram (by Joseph Stephens II)		Ribbesford, Worcs	S	RG/JP, 8, 1372
61.	†1858	Rev E Dudley (by Joseph Stephens II)		Broome, Worcs	S	RG/JP, 8, 1372
62.	†1866	Edward Corles (by Joseph Stephens II)		Worcester Cathedral	S	*Gunnis* 1968, 373
63.	†1871	Eliza Stock (†1827), John Reynolds Cassop (†1832), Elizabeth Beahan (†1839) and Mary Ann Stock (†1871) (by Joseph Stephens II)		St Helen, Worcester	S	
Busts						
64.	1829	'from nature' (by Joseph Stephens II)		[Soc of A large silver medal]; untraced		RSA *Transactions*, 1829, vol 47, xxii
65.	1830	Unidentified subject (by Joseph Stephens II)		[Exhib Soc of BA, London, 856]; untraced		*Johnson* 1975, 440
66.	1832	H Liversege (by Joseph Stephens II)		[Exhib Soc of BA, London, 841]; untraced		*Johnson* 1975, 440
67.	1833	Mr Longcroft (by Joseph Stephens II)	p	Mere Hall, Worcs		GPC
68.	1833	Son of J Malden, MD (by Joseph Stephens II)	m	[Exhib RA, London, 1184]; untraced		*Graves* VII, 1905–6, 252
69.	1833	Unidentified gentleman (by Joseph Stephens II)		[Exhib Soc of BA, London, 831]; untraced		*Johnson* 1975, 440
70.	1845	John Nash (by Joseph Stephens II)	m	[Exhib RA, London, 1459]; untraced		*Graves* VII, 1905–6, 252
71.	1850	Mrs Longcroft (by Joseph Stephens II)	p	Mere Hall, Worcs		GPC
72.	1852	Hon J Leslie (by Joseph Stephens II)		[Exhib RA, London, 1469]; untraced		*Graves* VII, 1905–6, 252
Architectural Sculpture						
73.	1759	'A carved bath grate with sup. fine marble fronts' (by Joseph Stephens I)		[for the Earl of Coventry]; untraced		Coventry Archives in GPC
Miscellaneous						
74.	1834	Innocence (by Joseph Stephens II)		[Exhib Soc of BA, London, 828]; untraced		*Johnson* 1975, 440

STEPHENS, William and Joseph, of Exeter fl 1807–68

The firm, whose tablets are the usual provincial productions of earlier 19th century, flourished for some 60 years in the West Country. Gunnis considered their best work to be the monument to Sir Bouchier Wray at Tawstock, which has well-carved classical details (7).

Literary References: *Gunnis* 1968, 373

Funerary Monuments

1.	†1807	Sarah Carne	Chaceley, Glos	S	
2.	†1815	Jane Spence	Berrynarbor, Devon	S	
3.	†1816	Susannah Buckle	Chaceley, Glos	S	
4.	†1819	Anna Stanhope	Exeter Cathedral, Devon	S	
5.	1822	Rev William Hole	Swimbridge, Devon	S	*Gunnis* 1968, 373

6.	†1825	John Whittall	Cefullys, Radnor	S	Pevsner, *Powys*, 1979, 225
7.	1826	Sir Bouchier Wray	Tawstock, Devon	S	*Gunnis* 1968, 373
8.	*c*1830	The Hawkesley Family	Crewkerne, Somerset	S	*Gunnis* 1968, 373
9.	†1832	Rev Thomas Bartlam	Exeter Cathedral, Devon	S	
10.	1833	Samuel Wills	Crewkerne, Somerset	S	*Gunnis* 1968, 373
11.	†1840	Francis Bond	Holy Trinity, Exeter, Devon	S	
12.	†1841	George, 2nd Earl of Mountnorris (by Joseph Stephens)	Upper Arley, Worcs	S	Pevsner, *Worcs*, 1968, 281
13.	†1842	Admiral William Shield	Holy Trinity, Exeter, Devon	S	
14.	†1842	Mary Brutton	St David, Exeter, Devon	S	
15.	†1848	Joseph Ratcliff	St Mary Major, Exeter, Devon	S	
16.	†1852	Elizabeth Pitman	Dunchideock, Devon	S	
17.	†1868	Catherine Pitman	Dunchideock, Devon	S	

STEPHENS, William Humphries, of Worcester 1737–

He was the son of Joseph Stephens, a stone-cutter, and was apprenticed to his father in 1751, becoming free in 1760 (Worcester Corp Archives). Early in his career he went into partnership with a Mr Bott and the tablet to Richard Canwardine (**5**) is signed with both their names. Stephens was joined by his son **Joseph Stephens I** when the latter completed his apprenticeship. The tablet to the Rev Hudson Boyce which is signed 'Stephens and Co' is probably their joint work (**29**). Another William Stephens (1692–1748), who may have been a relation, was one of the master-masons responsible for building Ombersley, near Worcester, 1724–1727 (Archives, Lord Sandys).

Stephens's works include the Eaton monument which has a sarcophagus and a relief of a family group in Grecian apparel (**32**), the Brace, with its relief of a female mourning over an urn and an image of *Hope* standing by an altar (**33**). He repeated several of his designs. In Gunnis's opinion 'William Stephens is the best of the Worcester school of statuaries. His tablets, with their various-coloured marbles and well-carved details, are a delight to the eye and are models of eighteenth-century good taste'.

Literary References: *Gunnis* 1968, 373

Funerary Monuments

1.	?1751	Thomas Parker	Longdon, Worcs		*Gunnis* 1968, 373
2.	†1761	Edward Toldervy	Cleobury Mortimer, Salop	S	
3.	†1761	Henry Roberts	Broadwas, Worcs	S	Pevsner, *Worcs*, 1968, 101
4.	†1763	Ann Bateson	Bourton-on-the-Hill, Glos	S	Pevsner, *Glos: Cotswolds*, 1999, 187
5.	†1763	Richard Canwardine (†1763) and John Thornborough (co-sculptor: Bott)	St John, Bedwardine, Worcs	S	*Gunnis* 1968, 373
6.	†1766	William Romney	Suckley, Worcs	S	
7.	†1770	Rev Robert Harrison	St-John-in-Bedwardine, Worcester	S	
8.	†1771	Rev Samuel Pritchett	Wichenford, Worcs	S	
9.	†1771	William Hankins	Dymock, Glos	S	Pevsner, *Glos: Vale & Forest of Dean*, 1976, 176
10.	†1773	Armell Green Browning	Martley, Worcs	S	
11.	?1777	Thomas Dunn	All Saints, Evesham, Worcs		*Gunnis* 1968, 373
12.	?1779	Arthur Charlett	Fladbury, Worcs		*Gunnis* 1968, 373
13.	?1779	Robert Bateson	Bourton-on-the-Water, Glos		RG/JP, 8, 1373
14.	†1780	Mrs Easton	Kempsey, Worcs	S	
15.	†1780	Robert Woodward	Fladbury, Worcs	S	*Gunnis* 1968, 373
16.	†1780	Sarah Hall	Ledbury, Herefs	S	*Gunnis* 1968, 373
17.	†1781	John Clements	St Swithun, Worcester	S	
18.	†1781	Mary Wakeman	St Swithun, Worcester	S	
19.	†1782	Edward Whitcombe	Cleobury Mortimer, Salop	S	
20.	†1782	Mary Astley	Fladbury, Worcs	S	*Gunnis* 1968, 373
21.	†1783	Bartholomew Barneby	Bromyard, Herefs	S	
22.	1783	Thomas Carter Phillips	[Jackfield, Salop]; untraced		BL Ad MS 21237 fol 376
23.	†1783	William Stephens	St Martin, Worcester		
24.	†1784	James Dansie	Bromyard, Herefs	S	GPC
25.	†1785	Rev Robert Bargis	Elmley Lovett, Worcs	S	
26.	†1785	William Batch	Leominster, Herefs	S	
27.	†1786	Charles Lucy	Ledbury, Herefs	S	
28.	1786	Rebecca Yarnold	Claines, Worcs	SD	
29.	†1786	Rev Hudson Boyce	Fladbury, Worcs	S	*Gunnis* 1968, 373
30.	†1789	John Hodgetts	Kinver, Staffs		GPC
31.	†1790	Mary Corbett	Bobbington, Staffs		GPC
32.	†1790	Mrs Eaton	Kempsey, Worcs	S	Pevsner, *Worcs*, 1968, 203
33.	†1792	Francis Brace	Leominster, Herefs	S	
34.	†1792	Jonathan Green	Ashford Bowdler, Salop	S	Pevsner, *Salop*, 1958, 61;
35.	†1792	Mary Clarke	Gloucester Cathedral	S	Pevsner, *Glos: Vale & Forest of Dean*, 1976, 218
36.	1792	Rev James Gyles	Powick, Worcs		*Gunnis* 1968, 373
37.	†1792	Rev Talbot Harris	Upton Warren. Worcs	S	
38.	†1793	Jane Blew	Bromyard, Herefs	S	
39.	†1793	John Bearcroft	Hanbury, Worcs	S	
40.	?1794	Mary Hall	Worcester Cathedral		*Gunnis* 1968, 373
41.	†1794	Thomas Parker	Longdon, Worcs		Pevsner, *Worcs*, 1968, 216; *Gunnis* 1968, 373
42.	†1795	Francis Best	Whittington, Worcs	S	
43.	†1795	Richard Harrison	Hallow, Worcs		Pevsner, *Worcs*, 1968, 182
44.	†1795	Thomas Freeman	Suckley, Worcs	S	
45.	?1796	Rev George Martin	Overbury, Worcs		*Gunnis* 1968, 373
46.	†1796	Richard Clarke	Gloucester Cathedral		*Gunnis* 1968, 373
47.	†1797	Daniel Ellis	Elmore, Glos	S	Pevsner, *Glos: Vale & Forest of Dean*, 1976, 180
48.	†1797	Robert Dangerfield	Mathon, Herefs	S	
49.	†1798	Joseph Berwick	St Nicholas, Worcester		*Gunnis* 1968, 373
50.	†1798	Mr and Mrs Whitcombe	Cleobury Mortimer, Salop		GPC

51.	†1800	Captain Norbury		Dodderhill, Worcs	S	*Gunnis* 1968, 373
52.	†1800	Catherine Yarnold		Great Malvern Priory, Worcs	S	
53.	†1800	John Ellis		Claines, Worcs		
54.	†1800	John Wall		Leominster, Herefs	S	
55.	†1801	Rev Richard Baty		Claines, Worcs		
56.	†*c*1802	Alexander Montgomerie		Great Malvern Priory, Worcs	S	
57.	†1802	Grace Collet		Ledbury, Herefs	S	
58.	†1802	Grace Colt		Great Malvern Priory, Worcs	S	
59.	†1803	Ann Wall		Leominster, Herefs	S	
60.	†1803	William Bellers		Ledbury, Herefs	S	
61.	†1804	Ellen Callow		Bishampton, Worcs		
62.	†1804	Robert Berkeley		Spetchley, Worcs	S	
63.	†1805	Joseph Severne		Bromyard, Herefs	S	
64.	†1806	Jane Roberts		Saintbury, Glos	S	Pevsner, *Glos: Cotswolds*, 1999, 587
65.	†1807	Sarah Carne (co-sculptor: J Stephens)		Chaceley, Glos	S	Pevsner, *Glos: Vale & Forest of Dean*, 1976, 119
66.	†1808	Bishop Hurd		Worcester Cathedral		Pevsner, *Worcs*, 1968, 314
67.	1808	Lord Somers (†1806)		Eastnor, Herefs	S	Pevsner, *Herefs*, 1963, 123
68.	†1811	Elizabeth (†1795) and James Newport		Claines, Worcs		
69.	†1811	John Stone		Longdon, Worcs		RG/JP, 8, 1374
70.	†1815	Mary Beardsley (†1802) and Sophia Matthews		Oddingley, Worcs		
71.	†1816	Susanna Buckle (co-sculptor: J Stephens)		Chaceley, Glos	S	Pevsner, *Glos: Vale and Forest of Dean*, 1975, 119
72.	†1819	Patience Turner and family members (†1759–1819)		All Saints, Worcester		*Gunnis* 1968, 373
73.	†1826	John Williams and family members (†1793–1826)		All Saints, Worcester		*Gunnis* 1968, 373
74.	†1826	William (†1803) and Mary Thomas		Claines, Worcs		
75.	†1840	George Nash		Martley, Worcs	S	

STEPHENS AND BOTT fl *c*1781

Funerary Monuments

1.	†1781	Martha Farmer		Grimley, Worcs		Pevsner, *Worcs*, 1968, 175

STEPHENS AND SON fl 1819

Presumably a firm of plaster manufacturers, their premises were at 186 Drury Lane.

Busts

1.	1819	Several	p	Lamport Hall, Northants, library	S	GPC

STEPHENSON, William, of Liverpool fl 1752–56

In 1752 Liverpool town council engaged Stephenson to carry out work on the Town Hall. They were not satisfied an paid the sculptor 80 guineas, instead of a larger sum originally mentioned. In 1756 Stephenson petitioned the counci for a further £20, but they refused his request, stating that the relief was 'ill-executed' and that 'Mr. Stephenson ha been already paid more than he deserved and that they would pay him no more' (City Archives in *Gunnis* 1968, 373). It seems possible that the sculptor is the William Stephenson who remodelled the relief by **Peter Scheemakers** for th Palladian bridge at Stowe, which was incorporated in the pediment of the Temple of Concord and Victory in 1762.

Literary References: *Gunnis* 1968, 373; *Roscoe* 1999, 274–5

Reliefs

1.	1752	Tympanum sculpture Payment(s): £84		[Town Hall, High Street, Liverpool, Lancs]; untraced		*Gunnis* 1968, 373; *Cavanagh* 1997, 303

STEVENS, Alfred 1817–75

Stevens is a curious figure in the history of 19th-century British sculpture because he was highly regarded during hi lifetime and remained the object of a certain degree of respect long after his death, even among some 20th-centur modernists. Yet he was an artist who produced relatively little sculptural work, and even less was fully completed.

He was born at Blandford Forum, Dorset, on 28 January 1818, the second son of George and Susan Stevens. Hi father was a joiner and decorator which may be why much of Stevens's own work was for domestic and publi decorative art schemes. According to one of his modernist admirers, Eric Underwood, Stevens 'received n schooling after the age of ten, instead entering his father's workshop as an assistant' (*Underwood* 1933, 128). H remained there until the age of 16 when the Rev Samuel Best, rector of St Mary, Blandford Forum, made attempt to steer him towards a career in the fine arts. Initially he tried to place Stevens in the studio of the painter Edwi Landseer, but this failed because Landseer demanded a fee of £500. Best then solicited funds from the local gentr to send Stevens to Italy, where he remained for nine years, travelling to Venice, Siena, Naples, Milan, Bologna Florence and Rome to study the Renaissance masters. In Florence Stevens briefly attended the Accademia di Bell Arti, before moving to Rome where in 1841–2 he worked as an assistant in the studio of **Bertel Thorvaldsen**.

He returned to England in 1843, the year he made four plaster reliefs for another rector in Blandford Forum, th Rev John West (**22**). A major commission followed in 1848 from the British Geological Survey for a pair of large bronz doors for headquarters of the Museum of Practical Geology in Jermyn Street, London. These would have formed th centrepiece of an overwhelming neo-Renaissance front to the building, designed by the architect James Pennethorne but for reasons that are unclear they were never cast. There may have been financial problems, though Stevens was t gain a reputation for a 'procrastinating love of perfection' which meant that a number of projects were never realized

In 1845 he was appointed by Henry Cole to teach at the newly established Government School of Design (later th Royal College of Art) at Somerset House. Yet he and Cole were to soon fall out over whether a one could lear the principles of design without first studying art. Stevens thought one could not and resigned his teaching post i 1847. In essence this disagreement sums up Stevens's own artistic practice and beliefs for he, like later artist-designer such as William Morris, Roger Fry and Eric Gill, fully integrated art and design into a single congruent creativ practice. It is unsurprising, therefore, that in 1850 Stevens was apparently happy to join the Sheffield iron manufacture

Messrs Henry Hoole and Co, on a salary of £20 a year, to design a range of household products including firebacks, firedogs, hunting knives, railings and stoves (27). Among the most well-known products produced by Stevens at this time were the much-copied railings of the British Museum. He and Hoole were to win several awards for their work including a council medal at the 1851 Great Exhibition in London, and a silver medal at the Paris Universal Exhibition of 1855. Stevens gained a reputation as a difficult artist for manufacturers to work with, not least because of his apparent unwillingness to abide by tight financial constraints. Lavish interior decorative schemes for the royal waiting rooms at Paddington station and the dome of the Reading Room at the British Museum Library failed for lack of funds, and very few sculptural commissions came his way at this time.

Yet in 1857 Stevens won the commission to produce the Wellington Monument for St Paul's Cathedral (1). It was to prove a pyrrhic victory. Although Stevens had originally lost this competition to **William Calder Marshall**, he was still able to gain the commission through the influence of friends and a willingness to undertake the work for a foolishly low fee of £14,000. In one of the longest sagas in sculptural history, the monument took 55 years to complete, and arguably cost Stevens his life. His painfully slow rate of progress and his disdain for the Cathedral's commissioner of works, A S Ayrton, even resulted in dismissal in 1870, though he was reinstated under the financial supervision of his close friend, the designer Leonard Collmann. By then, however, Stevens was ageing and only limited progress could be made. The main body of the monument was completed in 1878 by Hugh Stannus, and the figure of Wellington on horseback, in 1912, by John Tweed. Yet from this fiasco came two of the finest works by any 19th-century British sculptor, the larger than life-size plaster figures of *Truth and falsehood* and *Valour and cowardice*, now in the V&A, which have a strong sense of drama and dynamism showing Stevens at his best.

In 1860 he gained another important commission, this time from Robert Holford, to produce interior ornaments for the dining room at Dorchester House, London. His models for that location are among his best works (**13–19**). As with the Wellington Monument, numerous two- and three-dimensional studies exist, many of them showing an almost expressionistic handling of the human figure. This is particularly the case with the two caryatid figures on either side of the fireplace. The influence of his time in Italy is clear, for there are echoes of Michelangelo's work on the tombs of Guiliano and Lorenzo de Medici, in San Lorenzo, Florence. If the finished chimneypiece, now in the V&A, lacks some of the vitality of Stevens's studies for it, particularly the breathtaking verve of the half-scale plaster model, this may be put down to the inevitable distancing that occurs when a sculptor's ideas are transferred from one material to another. Equally Stevens's indecisiveness may have been to blame. Certainly the work took far longer to complete than it should have done, and, as with the Wellington monument, other sculptors had to complete the commission after Stevens's death.

Stevens was rare among British Victorian sculptors for he was a cult figure during his lifetime and the idolisation was evident after his death. An influential group of people campaigned to have the Wellington monument completed as close to Stevens's original design as possible. They also ensured that other examples of his fairly small sculptural output were preserved for the nation, much of it ending up in the Tate gallery before transfer to the V&A. Stevens's wild looks and temperamental character fitted well with the notion of the romantic artist as a misunderstood genius. So did his death in poverty. As an obituary notice in *The Times* stated 'he would destroy model after model and sketch after sketch while he was eating only a crust of bread' (*The Times*, 4 May 1875). His reputation was bolstered by the posthumous promotion of friends such as Frederic Leighton and James Abbott McNeill Whistler. Some recent critics have suggested that this has led to an overestimation of Stevens's talent, perhaps an unfair revision of history. There is no doubt that he was a significant precursor of the New Sculpture, and even aspects of Art Nouveau, and it is possible that had he possessed the social skills and business acumen of Rodin he might now be seen more fully as a precursor of aspects of modernism. He was unmarried and died at his home in Hampstead on 1 May 1875. His estate was valued at £2,000.

Michael Paraskos

Literary References: *AJ*, vol 37, 1875, 232; *Mag of Art*, vol 15, 1891–2, 303–8; *Underwood* 1933, 128; *Towndrow* 1939, 81 and *passim*; *Sheppard* 1960, 271–84; *Physick* 1970; *Ormond* 1973, 431; *Pyke* 1973, 142; *Beattie* 1975, *passim*; *Read* 1982, 194–7, 275–6; *Read* 1985, 63; *Read* 1992, 57; *Grove* 1996, website (Stocker); *Cavanagh* 1997, 338–9; *Bilbey* 2002, 375–85; *ODNB*; *Ward-Jackson* 2004, 120–8

Portraits of the Sculptor: Self portrait, oil on canvas, Tate, 1832; photo, NPG, *c*1867; R Townroe, death mask, 1875, plaster, NPG; W Ellis, bust, 1876, marble, Mappin, Sheffield; various self portrait drawings, Tate, various dates.

Funerary Monuments

1.	1857–1875	Arthur, 1st Duke of Wellington Model(s): VAM (25, including competition model and full-size plasters); Walker, Liverpool, Lancs (models); two pairs of full-sized models, VAM		St Paul's Cathedral, London Other versions: allegorical groups reproduced in bronze and in bronzed plaster by J W Singer & Sons	*Towndrow* 1951, 18–19 (repr); *Physick* 1970; *Read*, 1982, 93–5, 194–7, 276, 277, 294 (repr); *Bilbey* 2002, 375–85 (repr); *Ward-Jackson* 2004, 120–28

Statues

2.	*c*1844	Three struggling figures, model	p	[coll Charles Ricketts]; VAM A.19-1912 Other versions: VAM A.13-1975, bronze, 1812 (cast taken from A.19-1912)	*Bilbey* 2002, 400–1 (repr)
3.	*c*1857	Great Exhibition memorial, competition model only		[coll James Gamble]; VAM 318-1880	*Bilbey* 2002, 405–6 (repr)
4.	*c*1862	David, Jael, Judith, St John, St Mark (models for proposed redecoration of St Paul's Cathedral)	p	[coll Reuben Townroe]; VAM A.86-1911 Other versions: VAM A.11-1975, bronze	*Bilbey* 2002, 388 (repr)
5.	*c*1866	Nude with raised arms, fountain figure		[9 Eaton Villas, Haverstock Hill, London, garden]; untraced Other versions: VAM A 18-1912, plaster VAM A 14-1975, bronze	*Bilbey* 2002, 399–400 (repr)

No.	Date	Subject	Medium	Location	Literature
Busts					
6.	c1852	Leonard Collmann	p	[coll Reuben Townroe]; VAM 758-1899 Other versions: Tate Britain NO 2932, c1860, bronze ex coll Mrs Stannus, plaster; untraced	*Bilbey* 2002, 404–5 (repr)
7.	c1854	Herbert Collmann	p	[ex coll Reuben Townroe]; VAM 757-1899 Other versions: Tate Britain NO 2932, 1860, bronze ex coll Mrs Stannus, plaster; untraced	*Read* 1982, 276; *Bilbey* 2002, 405 (repr)
8.	c1866	Unidentified young woman (study for the Wellington monument?)	p	[ex coll James Nesfield Forsyth]; VAM 1357-1900 Other versions: VAM A.26-1975, bronze VAM A.24-1975, bronze, 1950 (cast from A.26-1975) ex coll James Gamble, plaster; untraced	*Bilbey* 2002, 383–4 (repr)
Chimneypieces					
9.	c1856	Models for a fireplace, manufactured by the Coalbrookdale Company	p	[for James Gamble]; VAM A.54-1911, A.65-1911, A.68-1911, A.73-1911	*Bilbey* 2002, 373–4 (repr)
10.	1860–1869	With crouching female caryatids Model(s): VAM 129-1879, 130-1879, A.23-1911, A.25-1934, A.26-1934, A.27-1934, A.15-1975, A.29-1975	m	[Dorchester House, London, dining room]; VAM A.2-1976	*Bilbey* 2002, 390–3 (repr)
Architectural Sculpture					
11.	?pre-1846	Classical scenes, reliefs copied from Thorwaldsen		Chettle House, Dorset, main hall, above doorway	*Read* 1982, 275
12.	1852	Lion sejant (model for British Museum forecourt railings)		Untraced Other versions: VAM A.21-1945, A.8-1975, A.9-1975 Ely House, Dover Street, London Wellington memorial railings, consistory chapel, Westminster Abbey, London, 1892–1912; untraced Walker, Liverpool Law Society railings, Chancery Lane, London	*Bilbey* 2002, 403–4 (repr); *Ward-Jackson* 2002, 206
13.	c1863	Door-knocker, model for Dorchester House	p	[for Reuben Townroe]; VAM 311-1895 Other versions: VAM A.23-1975, bronze	*Bilbey* 2002, 394, 407 (repr)
14.	c1863	Head of a mirror frame, model for Dorchester House	p	[for Reuben Townroe]; VAM 312-1895	*Bilbey* 2002, 394 (repr)
15.	c1863	Mirror frame, model for Dorchester House	p	[for John R Clayton]; VAM 594-1890	*Bilbey* 2002, 393–4 (repr)
16.	1850–1863	Ornaments		[Dorchester House, London]; destroyed	Pevsner, *London I*, 1973, 617
17.	c1863	Pilaster, model for sideboard at Dorchester House	p	[for James Gamble]; VAM A.33-1911 Other versions: VAM 961-1903, p	*Bilbey* 2002, 398–9 (repr)
18.	c1863	Roundels for door panels at Dorchester House, 5 models	p	[for the Holford family]; VAM A.18-22-1975	*Bilbey* 2002, 397–8 (repr)
19.	c1863	Roundels for door panels at Dorchester House, six models	p	[for James Gamble]; VAM A.16-21-1911	*Bilbey* 2002, 394–7 (repr)
20.	c1865	Medusa's head, model for decorative frieze at Westonbirt House	p	[for the Holford family]; VAM A.17-1975	
21.	1855–1870	Unidentified models for ornamental details (19)	p	VAM	*Bilbey* 2002, 408–12 (repr)
Reliefs					
22.	1842	Four	p	Chettle House, Dorset	*Grove* website (Stocker)
23.	1855–1870	Reclining figure, sketch model	p	[for James Gamble]; VAM A.24-1911	*Bilbey* 2002, 407 (repr)
Miscellaneous					
24.	c1850	Models for dagger sheaths, produced by George Westenholm & Son Ltd for the Great Exhibition	p	[coll James Gamble/Reuben Townroe]; VAM A.49-1911, A.50-1911, A.89-1911, A.90-1911	*Bilbey* 2002, 401–2 (repr)
25.	1853	Firedog figure	b	Walker, Liverpool	*Towndrow* 1951, 81
26.	1853	Rape of Proserpine, fireback	ir	[Great Exhib]; Walker, Liverpool Other versions: VAM, 1853	*Towndrow* 1951, 13 (repr); *Beattie* 1975, 27 (repr)
27.	1850–1857	Models for stoves and other metalwork manufactured by Henry Hoole & Co	p	VAM (37 examples)	*Bilbey* 2002, 361–73 (repr)
28.	1842–1865	Model for a toy cannon	p	[coll James Gamble]; VAM A.51-1911 Other versions: VAM A.79-1911, wood cast in brass by Henry Hoole & Co for the son of Alfred Pegler	*Bilbey* 2002, 400 (repr)

STEVENS, Joseph fl 1829

He was living at 11 Pentonville Place, Pentonville in 1829, when he was awarded a medal by the Society of Arts.

STEVENSON, Charles 1821–79

Born at Greenock in 1821, he worked in the Greenock and Gourock area all his life. He married Margaret Graham and they had one child, a son named Robert, who died at the age of 11 months. Stevenson died on 3 June 1879 and was buried in Greenock cemetery. His wife predeceased him by nine years. His monuments commemorating William Marshall and John Barr Cumming both have reliefs of allegorical figures (**1, 2**).

Literary References: *Woodward* 1977, vol 1, pt 2, 236–7

Funerary Monuments

1.	†1854	William Marshall	s	Greenock Cemetery, Renfrewshire	*Woodward* 1977, vol 1, pt 2, 237
2.	†1860	John Barr Cumming	s	Greenock Cemetery, Renfrewshire	*Woodward* 1977, vol 1, pt 2, 237

Busts

3.	nd	John Wilson	s	Greenock Art Gall, Renfrewshire	*Woodward* 1977, vol 1, pt 2, 237

TEWARD fl 1818

The journal of the Rev John Barwis has the following entry: '8 June 1818 in the evening came Steward a Scotchman to put a monument to Mrs Barwis in Bramfield Church. Went to see him at work in the evening. 9 June 1818 . . . work done by 11 o'clock and Steward went away'.

Literary References: *Transactions of the Cumberland Ant & Archaeological Society*, new series, vol xlv, 83

TEWART fl –1784

On 27 March 1784, Christie held the retirement sale of 'Mr. Stewart, statuary and mason, quitting business, at his house, No.14, on the west side of Princes Street, near Great George Street, Westminster'. Among the lots were '50 drawings for tablets, tombs, etc.' and 'drawings for chimney-pieces' (*Gunnis* 1968, 374).

Chimneypieces

1.	pre-1784	Four	m	[Princes Street, near George Street, London]; untraced	*Gunnis* 1968, 374

TEWART, James, of Dublin fl *c*1767–89

Funerary Monuments

1.	†1767	Anne Preston	Heversham, Westmorland	S	Pevsner, *Cumberland & Westmorland*, 1967, 251
2.	†1789	Rev William Preston	Ferns Cathedral, Co Wexford	S	*Potterton* 1975, 83

TEWART, John Guise –1844

His widow, Mary Ann, applied to the AGBI for assistance after her husband's death. She stated that Stewart had worked for **W G Nicholl, Samuel Nixon** and 'Mr. Smith of New Road'. He died on 20 June 1844, leaving a widow and four children. That year he exhibited a 'group of flowers in wax'.

Literary References: *Pyke* 1973, 142

TEWART, Richard –1847

He is described as 'Stone and Wood carver' in the *Dublin Directory* of 1831. Stewart applied to the AGBI for financial assistance in 1846 stating that he had left Dublin in 1843 to come to London, bringing with him his work *King John signing Magna Charta*, but had failed to sell this work or to find employment in the metropolis. He also stated that he had executed 'several works at Windsor under Sir Jeffery Wyatville', and had made stone figures for the Duchess of Leinster. He had also apparently given instructions in modelling to the Countess of Verulam, Earl of Auckland and many others of the Nobility. As a specimen of his work he sent to the AGBI a model 'of a work designed to be set up in Lloyd's Coffee Room, Royal Exchange'. There is no evidence that the benevolent fund came to his aid. Stewart died in April 1847, leaving a widow, Jane.

Literary References: *Gunnis* 1968, 374

Archival References: RG/JP

TEWART, Robert fl 1777–83

He exhibited at the Society of Artists, giving his address in 1777 as 15 Milman Street, Bedford Row and as 287 Holborn in 1778–83. In addition to his sculptural submissions he showed a sketch from a gem in 1777, a portrait of a lady in chalks in 1780, and a lion engraved on glass in 1780.

Literary References: *Gunnis* 1968, 374; *Pyke* 1973, 142

Reliefs

1.	1783	Duchess of Devonshire, medallion		[Exhib Soc of Artists, London, 309]; untraced	*Graves* 1907, 246
2.	1783	Lord Thurlow, medallion		[Exhib Soc of Artists, London, 308]; untraced	*Graves* 1907, 246

Miscellaneous

3.	1777	Frederick, Lord North	w	[Exhib Soc of Artists, London, 299]; untraced	*Graves* 1907, 246
4.	1778	'A Madonna'	w	[Exhib Soc of Artists, London, 298]; untraced	*Graves* 1907, 246
5.	1778	Unidentified lady		[Exhib Soc of Artists, London, 299]; untraced	*Graves* 1907, 246
6.	1780	Virgin and child	w	[Exhib Soc of Artists, London, 232]; untraced	*Graves* 1907, 246

TEWERT, James fl 1767

In 1767 he exhibited a bust at the Free Society, giving his address as Wardour Street, Soho.

Busts

1.	1767	Unidentified lady	m	[Exhib Free Soc, London, 255]; untraced	*Graves* 1907, 246

TIMSON fl *c*1808–26

Funerary Monuments

1.	†1808	George Rye	St James, Grimsby, Lincs	Pevsner, *Lincs*, 1989, 338
2.	†1826	Thomas Moore Williamson	St James, Grimsby, Lincs	Pevsner, *Lincs*, 1989, 338

TIRLING, Edwin 1819–67

He was born at Dryburgh in Scotland, on 27 July 1819. According to the *Art Journal* his prowess as a modeller was noted when still a boy: Sir David Erskine, who lived in the neighbourhood, discovered clay models by the child in a local field and arranged for Stirling to be apprenticed to a stone-carver at Darnick. Having gained his freedom h went to Edinburgh, where he found employment and attended the School of Art.

After three years working in Ulverston, Lancs, he settled in Liverpool, where he worked for a Mr Canovan, wh subsequently became his partner in an architectural carving business. In 1857 he executed most of the Venetian-sty decorative carving on the offices of the Liverpool and London and Globe Insurance Company (3). In this endeavou he worked with **William Grinsell Nicholl**.

Stirling died on 6 January 1867 and was buried in the Liverpool necropolis, where a monument commemorat him and his infant son. The *Art Journal* said of him that Liverpool was indebted to Stirling 'for a considerable portic of the best ornamental sculpture which has, in the last few years, added to the architectural beauty of the tow His works, they said, 'all bear witness to his skill and taste' (*AJ* 1867, 84).

Literary References: *AJ* 1867, 84; *Gunnis* 1968, 374

Statues					
1.	1867	Unidentified figures		[Horton Hall, Cheshire, south front]; untraced	*AJ* 1867, 84; *Gunnis* 1968, 374
Busts					
2.	1865	Dr Raffles, model	p	[Exhib LAAI, Liverpool, 1089]; untraced	*Morris and Roberts* 1998, 577
Architectural Sculpture					
3.	1855–1857	Decorative carving (co-sculptor: William Grinsell Nicholl)		Liverpool and London and Globe Insurance Company, Dale Street, Liverpool, Lancs	*Builder* 1857, 40; *Cavanagh* 1997, 31 (repr)
4.	1861–1863	Atlantes	s	[Brown's buildings, Water Street, Liverpool, flanking main entrance]; Calderstones Park, Liverpool, Lancs, Harthill estate entrance gateposts	*Cavanagh* 1997, 10–13 (repr)
5.	1863	Prince Albert, the Prince Consort, statue		[Albert Memorial clock tower and drinking fountain, Hastings, Sussex]; 'a greenhouse in a local park'	*Gunnis* 1968, 374; *Darby and Smith* 1983, 90
6.	1861–1863	The four seasons, statues	s	[Brown's buildings, Water Street, Liverpool, façade]; Calderstones Park, Liverpool, Lancs, surmounting walls adjacent to Harthill Estate entrance	*Cavanagh* 1997, 11–13 (repr)

STOKES fl *c*1772

Funerary Monuments				
1.	1772	Sir George Kelley (†1772) Payment(s): £76 18	[Speldhurst, Kent]; destroyed	GPC

STONE, John 1620–67

The third and youngest son of Nicholas Stone (1586/7–1647), master mason in the Office of Works under King Charl I, Vertue relates that he was 'brought up' at Oxford and was destined for a career in the church. Vertue also notes th he fought on the royalist side in the Civil War but escaped when the King was routed and lived for a year in his fathe house in Long Acre, Westminster, until he had the opportunity to go to France. At the Restoration he claimed enduring loyalty to the monarchy and petitioned the new king for his father's old post as master mason in the Offi of Works. This went instead to his rival, **Edward Marshall**, but in August 1660 he was appointed master mason Windsor Castle. Ill-health appears to have prevented him from carrying out his duties and he is said to have sold h position either to Edward Marshall or to Edward's son, **Joshua Marshall**. He ended his days at St Cross Hospit Winchester. Since there is no proof that Stone had any formal training as a sculptor it is suggested by Spiers that h commissions were delegated to his foreman, **C G Cibber**. This is questioned by White. Stone is said by Spiers have been an 'Excelent Architectt' and it is very likely that he designed Chesterton House, Warks, *c*1655–62. Only o monument has been identified from the Restoration period.

Literary References: *Spiers*, 1918–19, 27–8, 40, 34, 138; *Knoop & Jones*, 24–5; *White* 1999, 115–8

Funerary Monuments				
1.	*c*1650	Sir John Heigham	Barrow, Suffolk	*White* 1999, 115
2.	1653	Jacob, Lord Astley (co-sculptor: Henry Stone)	All Saints, Maidstone, Kent	*White* 1999, 115
3.	1653	Lionel Bacon and his second wife, Anne	Hessett, Suffolk	*White* 1999, 116
4.	1654	Anne, Lady Clarke	Sonning, Berks	*Whinney* 1988, 80; *White* 1999, 116
5.	*c*1654	Cary Williams	Sonning, Berks	*White* 1999, 116
6.	1654	Sir John Bankes	Christ Church Cathedral, Oxford	*White* 1999, 116
7.	1655	Edward Martyn	St Mary, Putney	*White* 1999, 116
8.	1655	John and Elizabeth Cresswell	Newbottle, Northants	*Whinney* 1988, 80
9.	1655	Sir John Osborn and his wife	Campton, Beds	*White* 1999, 116
10.	1655	Sir Peter Osborn and his wife	Campton, Beds	*White* 1999, 116
11.	1656	Elizabeth Blosse	Belstead, Suffolk	*White* 1999, 116
12.	1656	Sir Edward Spencer (†1655)	Great Brington, Northants	*Bailey* 1996, 34 (repr); *White* 1999, 116
13.	1656	Sir Edward Spencer (†1656)	Great Brington, Northants	*Whinney* 1988, 80; *White* 1999, 116
14.	1656	Sir Francis Mansell Bt	[St Gregory by St Paul's, City of London]; destroyed	*White* 1999, 116
15.	1656	Thomas Williams	[Temple Church, London]; destroyed	*White* 1999, 116
16.	?1656	Tobias Blosse and his wife	Belstead, Suffolk	*White* 1999, 116
17.	1657	Charles and Elizabeth Rich Drawing(s): BCH LDS 5286	Sonning, Berks	*White* 1999, 116
18.	1660	Edward Peyto (†1658), floor slab	Chesterton, Warks	*White* 1999, 116

STOREY, George, of Norwich fl *c*1733–59

Storey appears to have been involved with building work at Holkham Hall, Norfolk, in 1742–3. **Andrews Jelfe**, w also worked there, wrote to Matthew Brettingham, the architect, in July 1743: 'after I had parted with you at Norwic

I talked to George Storey, who I don't like and will have no further dealings with' (BL, Ad MS 27587, fol 141). Storey's monument to Davy Durrant (3) did not impress Gunnis: 'this a clumsy work, 18 ft. high, consisting of a pyramid with an urn at the apex, and is only impressive because of its size'. In 1751 a James Storey was apprenticed to **John Ivory**, and in 1774 Andrew Storey, who may have been a son of George Storey, was apprenticed to **Robert Page**, becoming free in 1781.

Literary References: *Gunnis* 1968, 375

Archival References: GPC

Funerary Monuments

1.	†1733	Thomas and Mary Till	St Peter Mancroft, Norwich	S	*Gunnis* 1968, 374
2.	?1743	John Newdigate	Holt, Norfolk	S	*Gunnis* 1968, 374
3.	†1759	Davy Durrant	Scottow, Norfolk	S	*Gunnis* 1968, 375; Pevsner, *Norfolk: N E & Norwich*, 1997, 658

STOREY, William, of London –1825

He was probably the son of William Storey, a mason of Mount Street, Grosvenor Square, whose will was proved on 7 October 1793 (PROB 11/1238). Storey carried out repairs in 1805 to Lord Radnor's house at 6 Grosvenor Street (Archives, Longford Castle in *Gunnis* 1968, 375). Two years later he was the master mason responsible for building a house for Thomas Coutts, where he supplied chimneypieces (16). His tablets are mostly classical. He was still in Mount Street at the time of his death.

In later life he was assisted by his son, Charles Henry. Another son, William Clayton Storey, became a liveryman of the Masons' Company in 1812. The monument to William Nicholay (15) may well be by one of the sons.

Literary References: *Gunnis* 1968, 375

Archival References: GPC

Will: PROB 11/1698, proved 18 April 1825

Funerary Monuments

1.	?1805	John Croft		Woodbridge, Suffolk		*Gunnis* 1968, 375
2.	?1806	Mrs Wilkes		Grosvenor chapel, London		*Gunnis* 1968, 375
3.	?1812	Hugh Dive		St Mary, Paddington, London		*Gunnis* 1968, 375
4.	?1817	John Cazenove		St John the Baptist, Croydon, Surrey, churchyard		GPC
5.	?1817	Soloman Knobel		St Mary, Paddington, London		*Gunnis* 1968, 375
6.	?1818	Colonel William Kelly		Chilton Foliat, Berks		*Gunnis* 1968, 375
7.	?1819	Lady Croft		Thornton Watlass, N R Yorks	S	GPC
8.	†1821	Joseph Akcock		Threddlethorpe All Saints, Lincs		Pevsner, *Lincs*, 1989, 755
9.	?1821	William Robinson		St George, Roseau, Dominica	S	GPC
10.	†1822	Elizabeth de Beauvoir		Basildon, Berks		*Gunnis* 1968, 375
11.	†1822	Mrs Benyon		St Bartholomew, Basildon, Berks		Pevsner, *Berks*, 1966, 76
12.	?1822	Sarah Hugford		Tonbridge, Kent		*Gunnis* 1968, 375
13.	?1823	Hugh Shortrudge		Great Bookham, Surrey		*Gunnis* 1968, 375
14.	?1824	James Brown		St George, Roseau, Dominica	S	GPC
15.	?1836	William Nicholay		St George, Roseau, Dominica	S	GPC
Chimneypieces						
16.	1807	Description not available	m	[Thomas Coutts's London house, corner of Stratton Street and Piccadilly]; untraced		Archives, Coutts Bank in *Gunnis* 1968, 375

STOREY (or STORY), Abraham –*c*1696

He worked at London Bridge in October 1652 at a wage of 18d a day, which was the rate normally paid to an apprentice, so it is not improbable that he was bound to Henry Wilson, the chief bridge mason, as Knoop and Jones suggest. Storey was admitted to the livery of the Masons' Company in 1663, he was warden in 1673 and master in 1680.

In 1663 he received £39 for stone supplied to St James's Palace. By 1669 he was apparently his own master, for he tendered for the masonry work at Brewers' Hall, then about to be rebuilt after the Great Fire (Archives, Brewers' Company, cited by Gunnis). He was paid £2,884 for masons' work at St Edmund the King, 1670–79, and £1,632 for masons' work at St Peter, Cornhill, 1677–87. In 1676–84 he and **John Barratt** were the masons building St James, Piccadilly. He apparently had a contract at St Paul's Cathedral in April 1678 for the search of 22 April shows that he was employing 20 men there. Since his name does not appear in the St Paul's Cathedral accounts for 1677–78, Knoop and Jones suggest that he was probably acting on behalf of Joshua Marshall's executors, Marshall having died on 16 April. As a master-mason under Wren he built the church of St Edmund the King, London, 1677–1679, receiving £2,884 (Bodleian, Rawlinson, B.387). There were also non-ecclesiastical commissions. He was the developer at Storey's Gate, a street in Westminster. In 1674 he was paid for work at the Royal College of Physicians and on 7 March 1677 the architect Robert Hooke wrote in his diary that he had agreed with Storey to build John Hervey's London house for £5,000. On 26 June, Hooke recorded that 'Mr Harvey paid Storey for the house and square' (*Robinson and Adams* 1935, 277, 298). Storey also worked for Hervey at 6 and 7 St James's Square, 1676–77, and in Strand, where he built five houses in 1678).

He is known to have been responsible for two major monuments. The most ambitious is the Crofts (2), which has a life-sized reclining effigy in peer's robes on a shelf, with his wife below, raised on her elbow to gaze up at her husband. On the front of the substructure is a large armorial shield. Whinney noted dryly that the figures show some attempt at animation. The Hewytt is an elaborate architectural structure (1). Several other monuments have been attributed to the sculptor including the Henry Gorges, †1674, at Stetchworth, Cambs (attrib Pevsner, citing Esdaile), which has a semi-reclining effigy with wig and Roman costume, again set on a tomb-chest. The Robert Coke, †1679 at Tittleshall, Norfolk, accredited by Pevsner, is a black and white tomb chest and reredos, and the Sir Edward de Carteret, at Holy Trinity, St Helier, is attributed by Edmund Esdaile because of its resemblance to the Crofts. The monuments to Richard le Neve, †1673 and Edward Carteret, †1677, both in Westminster Abbey have recently been attributed to the sculptor (Pevsner). A chalice at Swanage, Dorset, is inscribed as 'Given by Mrs. Elizabeth Toop, wife of Abraham Storey, Citizen and Mason of London, 1693' (inf Edmund Esdaile).

No less than nine apprentices are listed in the records of the Masons' Company. Robert Smith joined him in 1665, John Barratt in 1669, Drew Thomas in 1672, Thomas Thornton of Claybrooke, Leics in 1674, Anthony Hart in 1678, Charles Cawthorne in 1680, Christopher Page in 1686, Charles Corner of Lincoln in 1690, and Richard Woodley, who was with him in 1687 before being turned over to **Thomas Hill I**. None of these is known to have had an independent career as a mason-sculptor.

Literary References: *Knoop and Jones* 1935, 21; *Gunnis* 1968, 374; Pevsner, *Cambs*, 1970, 460; *Whinney* 1988, 446 n6; *Esdaile* 1991, 558–559; *Webb* 1999, 2, 7, 8, 11, 16, 24, 30, 33, 36; Pevsner, *Norfolk: N W & S*, 1999, 735; Pevsner, *London 6, Westminster*, 275, 584

Archival References: Masons' Co, Masters and Wardens

Funerary Monuments

1.	†1662	Sir Thomas Hewytt Bt		Sawbridgeworth, Herts	S	*Gunnis* 1968, 374; Pevsner, *Herts*, 1977, 335
2.	*c*1678	Lord (†1677) and Lady Crofts (†1672)		Little Saxham, Suffolk	S	*Gunnis* 1968, 374 (repr 23, opp 352); *Whinney* 1988, 446; *Knoop and Jones*, 21

Chimneypieces

3.	1672	Description unavailable Payment(s): £15	m	[Wrest Park, Beds]; untraced		*Gunnis* 1968, 374 citing archives Lady Lucas and Dingwall

Architectural Sculpture

4.	1669–1671	Stone work and carving Payment(s): £220	s	[Trinity House, Water Lane, City of London]; destroyed		GPC
5.	1673	Coat of arms Payment(s): £9 10s		[Almshouses, Deptford, London, over the gate]; Trinity House, London		GPC

STORY, John 1777–1801

A carver and gilder of Hull, he was the son of Edward Story, a builder. He executed the pediment sculpture for Hull library (1). His obituary in the *Hull Advertiser* on 13 January 1801 reads merely 'On Monday last, aged 24, Mr John Story of the Town Carver and Gilder' (Inf. Gerardine Mulcahy).

Archival References: Hull City Archives SFFW (box 3), the Foot Walker coll (notes on Hull sculptors).

Architectural Sculpture

1.	1801	Pediment figures		[Subscription library, Parliament Street, Hull, ER Yorks]; Wilberforce House Museum (in store)		*Hull, Advertiser*, 12 Sept 1801 (photos, Town Docks Museum, Sculptors' file)

STORY, William Wetmore 1819–95

A prolific American sculptor, he was invited with **J H Foley, Carlo Marochetti, William Theed II, Joseph Durham** and **Thomas Woolner** to submit designs in competition for the seated bronze statue of George Peabody, an American philanthropist who had given £250,000 for the 'benefit of the industrious poor of London' (1). In deference to the nationality of Peabody, Story, who had spent a large part of his life in Rome, was selected in 1867 and was paid £2,300 in July 1869. The result was described by Susan Beattie as 'stark [and] all but devoid of artistic identity' and as typical of the growing number of similarly undistinguished pieces in towns throughout England.

Literary References: *Beattie* 1983, 203; *Leith* 1987, 344

Miscellaneous Drawings: two of Elizabeth Barratt Browning, 1869, coll Mrs Nicholson (G R Hudson *Browning to his American Friends*, 1965, repr between pp 136–7)

Statues

1.	1869	George Peabody		Royal Exchange, London	SD	*Leith* 1997, 344 (repr)
2.	1872	Electra, a 'Semiramis in plaster'		Untraced		*Carlisle Express & Examiner*, 8 June 1872, 6

Busts

3.	1861	Elizabeth Barrett Browning		Keats and Shelley Memorial Museum, Rome		*Ormond* 1973, 70

STOTHARD, Alfred Joseph 1793–1864

Stothard specialised in medallion portraiture and became a noted medallist. He was one of 11 children of the celebrated painter and antiquarian, Charles Stothard RA (1755–1834). One of his brothers, Charles Alfred, was the author of *Monumental Effigies of Great Britain* and another, **Henry Stothard**, studied under **John Flaxman**, but was unable to follow his chosen career after suffering a stroke. Alfred Joseph born on 27 August 1793. In October 1820 he married Sophia Pinheiro, the daughter of a Whitechapel tobacconist and they had at least seven children over the next 20 years.

One of Stothard's early works was the tablet to Sir Gervase Clifton, *c*1815 (1). Thanks to his father's friendship with the artist John Constable, this was followed by a monument with a medallion portrait to the memory of the Rev Dr Durand Rhudde, rector of East Bergholt and the grandfather of Constable's wife, Maria Bicknell (2). Constable paid for the tablet. The Lane and Collins monuments also have medallion portraits (3, 4).

In 1823 Stothard won a silver medal from the Royal Academy for a model (30). Between 1824 and 1829 he created medallic portraits for the series celebrating great men, published by Samuel Parker. It included George Canning, Sir Walter Scott and James Watt, each after a bust by **Sir Francis Chantrey** (7, 8, 29); **John Flaxman** after a bust by **Edward Hodges Baily** (12) and the Duke of York after **Joseph Nollekens** (9). His work was recognized for the 'extreme correctness' of his translation (*Grant* 1934, 98–9) and Sir Walter Scott wrote a letter to Samuel Parker saying that although he couldn't be a judge of his own portrait, his family thought it 'very like' (www.gutenberg.org). In 1827 Stothard was appointed medal engraver in ordinary to George IV and the following year he produced designs for a medal celebrating the restoration of Windsor Castle (11). Two years later he provided designs along similar lines for two medals to mark the death of the King who died at Windsor Castle on 26 June 1830 (13). In 1828 he was given the contract to supply bas-reliefs to decorate the walls above the grand staircase of the newly extended Buckingham Palace. These were four panels, each 20 feet in length, designed by his father, depicting the four seasons. The designs were published in the *Literary Gazette* in 1829 (10).

Robert William Sievier approached Stothard in 1832 with the suggestion that he should submit a design for a common seal for the newly formed General Cemetery Company of which he was a director. His first suggestion was rejected but an alternative showing the foot of a sarcophagus with a curved lid flanked by seated gryphons proved acceptable (**15**). He also produced a design for the Company's share certificate. On 23 December 1833 he was elected a member of the Artists' Annuity Fund.

Stothard provided a medal of John Lee, a celebrated numismatist, in 1838 (**21**). He was less optimistic about a projected second medal, portraying John Yonge Ajerman, another numismatist (**24**), stating that it was perhaps a little premature to celebrate a second well-known coin-collector. This anxiety make have cloaked concern about payments. Stothard had agreed to provide 100 medals for Lee at 7s 6d each, on condition that advances would be made regularly. The work for Lee came to a complete standstill for lack of funds. In two letters to Lee he appealed to the patron's better nature by stating that without financial support the medallic art would die out completely (*Pickup* 1986, 19–20 quoting Hartwell Papers, Bucks RO D/LE/HI/42 and D/LE/HI/43). He was concerned about fees again when invited to provide a commemorative medal of George Carrington, chairman of the Aylesbury Railway Company, sponsored by the directors (**23**). Stothard stated in a letter that it was customary for the engraver to be paid separately for the dies and the manufacture of the medals, but as an alternative he would take responsibility for the whole process for an inclusive 12s 6d for 80 bronze medals or 10s 6d for 100. The estimate was provided on the understanding that he was supplied with a miniature or bust from which he could take the likeness. Since none was forthcoming it was Stothard's task to make a profile of Carrington, so he travelled out to Missenden, Bucks, but Carrington was too busy to allow sufficient time for a sitting. Stothard offered to withdraw if Carrington wished, but he did not. Stothard also complained of the quality of the accommodation and high prices at the inn and the subscribers informed him he must pay for the accommodation himself. The medal was somehow completed, but his last letter repeated the request for reimbursement of expenses incurred by him and also stated that he had received physical injury to his chest from a blow received from the coinage press (Stothard Corr, 8 Feb–14 Nov 1840, Bucks RO D/LE/IT.1/26–41).

He became medal engraver to the Queen by 1839 and in 1840 produced a portrait of the Queen and Prince Albert for a medal commemorating the birth of their first child, the Princess Royal (**22**). In 1842 Prince Albert laid the foundation stone of the new Royal Exchange building in London. A medal was struck to mark this event and Alfred produced a portrait of Prince Albert and another of the proposed building for the verso (**25**).

Stothard exhibited 30 medals and many impressions from dies at the Royal Academy between 1821 and 1845, from various London addresses. Although he produced little in later years, he described himself as a medal engraver until the end of his life. In 1861 he appears to have been living apart from his wife in Sheffield, whilst she lived with a son in Islington. When Stothard died in 1864 his wife was given accommodation at Fuller's Almshouses in Shoreditch.

Sylvia Allen

Literary References: *DNB*; *Graves* VII, 1905–6, 281–2; *Grant* 1934, 98–9; *Gunnis* 1968, 375; *Pyke* 1973, 142; *Taylor* 1978, 1043–1047; *Pyke* 1981, 39; *Pickup* 1986, 19–20; *Pickup* 1988, 17–28; *Curl* 2001, 75, 76

Archival References: AAF, Proposals 23663/1, fol 50 v

No.	Date	Subject		Location		References
Funerary Monuments						
1.	*c*1815	Gervase Clifton		Clifton, Notts	S	GPC
2.	1819	Dr D Rhudde Payment(s): £15 Drawing(s): design ex coll R Gunnis; untraced		East Bergholt, Suffolk	S	*Gunnis* 1968, 375; *John Constable Corr*, 262 facsimile, www.ancestry.co.uk
3.	?1827	Charles Lane Drawing(s): exhib RA 1832		Arundel, Sussex		*Gunnis* 1968, 375
4.	1831	Richard Collins		Fareham, Hants		*Graves* VII, 1905–6, 281; *Gunnis* 1968, 375
Busts						
5.	1836	Rev Edward Ward		[Exhib RA, London, 1114]; untraced Other versions: plaster cast, 1835, Wadham College, Oxford, SD		*Graves* VII, 1905–6, 282; GPC
Reliefs						
6.	1824	Lord Byron (medallic portrait)		[Exhib RA, London, 1825, 967]; BM, inv 1231		*Graves* VII, 1905–6, 281; *Pickup* 1988, 20 (repr)
7.	1826	George Canning	b	BM, inv 1256 Other versions: exhib ALRI, Liverpool, 1829 (310)		*Pickup* 1988, 20 (repr)
8.	1826	Sir Walter Scott	b	BM, inv 1260 Other versions: exhib ALRI, Liverpool, 1829 (309)		RG/JP, 8, 1384
9.	1827	Frederick, Duke of York, medallic portrait	b	BM, inv 1285		*Pickup* 1988, 22
10.	1828	Four seasons (designed by Thomas Stothard) Payment(s): £584		Buckingham Palace, London, grand staircase		*Lit Gaz*, 657, 22 Aug 1829, 555; PRO Works Cited by *Gunnis* 1968, 375 (ref untraced)
11.	1828	King George IV, medallic portrait with Windsor Castle on verso		BM, inv 1337 Other versions: exhib ALRI, Liverpool, 1829 (307)		*Pickup* 1988, 22
12.	1829	John Flaxman RA, medallic portrait		[Exhib ALRI, Liverpool, 308]; untraced		*Graves* VII, 1905–6, 281; *Morris and Roberts* 1998, 579
13.	1830	King George IV, medallic portrait marking his death (two)		BM, inv 1363; BM, inv 1364		*Pickup* 1988, 22
14.	1831	Lord Brougham, medallic portrait	b	BM, inv 1527		*Pickup* 1988, 26 (repr)
15.	*c*1832	Seal of the General Cemetery Company, depicting a sarcophagus end with classical ornaments Payment(s): £29 7s 6d (design)		GCC.MC F 131200		*Curl* 2001, 75–6 (repr)

16.	1833	Master Henry Scobel (medallic portrait)		[Exhib RA, London, 1038]; untraced	*Graves* VII, 1905–6, 282
17.	1833	Master Scobel (medallic portrait)		[Exhib RA, London, 1048]; untraced	*Graves* VII, 1905–6, 282
18.	1833	Miss Scobel (medallic portrait)		[Exhib RA, London, 1073]; untraced	*Graves* VII, 1905–6, 282
19.	1834	Unidentified friend (medallic portrait)		[Exhib RA, London, 971]; untraced	*Graves* VII, 1905–6, 282
20.	1835	Rev Hunter Francis Fell (medallic portrait)		[Exhib RA, London, 1015]; untraced	*Graves* VII, 1905–6, 282
21.	1838	John Lee, medallic portrait	b	BM	*Pickup* 1986, 19 (repr)
22.	1840	Birth of the Princess Royal, medallic portrait representing her parents	b	BM, inv 1953	*Pickup* 1988, 26 (repr)
23.	1841	George Carrington, medallic portrait	b	[Exhib RA, London, 1130]; Bucks County Museum	*Graves* VII, 1905–6, 282; *Pickup* 1988, 17 (repr)
24.	1841	John Yonge Akerman, white metal		BM	*Pickup* 1986, 19 (repr)
25.	1842	Albert, the Prince Consort, silver medallic portrait, with new Royal Exchange on verso		BM, inv 2077	*Pickup* 1988, 26 (repr)
26.	1842	Mehemet Ali Pasha, silver		BM	*Pickup* 1988, 26 (repr)
27.	1843	Espartero, Regent of Spain	b	BM	*Pickup* 1988, 28 (repr)
28.	1845	Sir Joshua Reynolds, for the Art Union of London		BM, inv 2207	*Pickup* 1988, 28 (repr)
29.	nd	James Watt		Untraced (?BM)	*Grant* 1934, 98–9 (repr)
Miscellaneous					
30.	1823	Model in the Antique Academy		[RA silver medal]; untraced	RA Premium list
31.	nd	Unidentified clergyman	w	Untraced	*Gunnis* 1968, 375

STOTHARD, Henry 1795–1847

The third son of **Thomas Stothard RA** and a brother of Alfred Stothard. He was a pupil of **John Flaxman RA** and entered the Royal Academy Schools in February 1811, winning a silver medal in 1813 (1). He later became incapacitated through paralysis and was forced to give up sculpture. The influence of Queen Adelaide secured him admission to the Charterhouse, where he died on 26 February 1847. This personal information about the life of Stothard was recorded in Gunnis from the Artists Annuity Fund Archives, but a search of the archives has failed to find the precise source. His younger brother, Robert Thomas Stothard, who was born in 1797, also attended the Academy schools, as a painter, in 1823.

Literary References: *Hutchison* 1960–62, 166, 176; *Gunnis* 1968, 375

Miscellaneous					
1.	1813	Model from the Antique Academy		[RA, London, silver medal]; untraced	RA Premium list

STOWERS, Charles 1788–

He was born on 8 October 1788 and christened on 5 November at St Sepulchre, London. His father was Thomas Stowers (†1817), a painter, who exhibited landscapes at the Royal Academy from 1778 to 1811. Stowers became a liveryman of the Masons' Company in 1810. He went on to exhibit, like his father, at the Academy, giving his address in 1811 as the family home, 22 Charterhouse Square. By 1818 he had moved his premises to 20 Wellington Street, Pentonville, and in 1821 he was at 11 Angel Row, Hammersmith. He signs some 'undistinguished tablets' (*Gunnis* 1968, 375).

Literary References: *Graves* VII, 1905–6, 286; *Gunnis* 1968, 375

Archival References: IGI

Will: Thomas Stowers, PROB 11/1590

Funerary Monuments					
1.	?1810	Mary Hughes	Merstham, Surrey	S	*Gunnis* 1968, 375
2.	?1811	Elizabeth Randolph	Walcot, Bath, Somerset	S	*Gunnis* 1968, 375
3.	?1817	Mary Glendining	Lympsone, Devon	S	*Gunnis* 1968, 375
4.	?1819	Spencer Perceval Payment(s): £177 8s	Lincoln's Inn Chapel, London		Lincoln's Inn Archives in *Gunnis* 1968, 375
Busts					
5.	1811	Unidentified young nobleman	[Exhib RA, London, 915]; untraced		*Graves* VII, 1905–6, 286; *Gunnis* 1968, 375
6.	1821	W Bromet MD	[Exhib RA, London, 1162]; untraced		*Graves* VII, 1905–6, 286; *Gunnis* 1968, 375
Miscellaneous					
7.	1818	Death of a stag	[Exhib RA, London, 1099]; untraced		*Graves* VII, 1905–6, 286

STOWEY, Philip fl 1789

In 1789, when the decision was made to build a county gaol in Dorset, a request was sent to Cornwall for a copy of the agreement made for building Bodmin prison, which was duly dispatched. It states that Philip Stowey with his partner, Thomas Jones of St Paul's, Exeter, agreed to build the Cornish prison for £5,165, and that they carried out the work in a 'satisfactory manner' (Dorset County Archives in GPC).

STRAKER fl 1797

He was probably a Coventry statuary.

Chimneypieces					
1.	1797	Description not available	m	[Arbury Hall, Warks]; untraced	GPC

STRETTON, William, of Nottingham 1755–1828

The son of Samuel Stretton, a builder of Nottingham, who erected Colwick Hall in 1776 and the grandstand on Nottingham racecourse in the following year. In 1778 the younger Stretton, who had just married, took over the yard of **F Radcliffe** at Nottingham, and advertised in the local press that he made 'monuments, chimney-pieces, marble sideboards, Indian inkstands, etc' (*Gunnis* 1968, 375).

He joined his father *c*1787, and together they were responsible for a number of buildings, including Arkwright's cotton-mill at Hockley in 1790 and the park gateway for Lord Middleton at Wollaton Hall, Notts. In Nottingham itself they built the Assembly Rooms in 1790 (to designs by John Carr of York), the seven-arched bridge over the River Trent in 1796, and the barracks from 1792 until 1799, the last named at a total cost of £20,000. He succeeded to the family business after the death of his father and on his own account built the church of St James, Standard Hill, Notts. He also rebuilt and ornamented the Nottingham Exchange in 1815 (**6**).

He signs the well-executed wall-monument, with roundels of bluejohn at its base, to Mary Bambrigge (**1**). According to the *Stretton Manuscripts*, privately published by G C Robertson in 1910, he was also responsible for other Nottinghamshire tablets (**2–5**).

Stretton was also an antiquary, archaeologist, surveyor, cartographer and collector. He died at his home, Lenton Priory, and his obituary in the *Nottingham Journal* states that in him 'antiquarians had lost a fund of general and useful knowledge' (*Gunnis* 1968, 376).

Literary References: *Stretton* 1910; *Gunnis* 1968, 375–6; *Colvin* 1995, 933

Funerary Monuments

1.	?1779	Mary Bambrigge	Lockington, Leics	S	*Gunnis* 1968, 376
2.	?1787	Jane Francis	Ruddington, Notts		*Gunnis* 1968, 376
3.	?1797	John Lindley	Skegby, Notts		*Gunnis* 1968, 376
4.	nd	Mary Williamson	Ruddington, Notts		*Gunnis* 1968, 376
5.	nd	'Two tablets to the memory of the present and late Rectors'	Nuthall, Notts		*Gunnis* 1968, 376

Architectural Sculpture

6.	1815	Carved stonework	s	[Nottingham Exchange]; untraced	*Gunnis* 1968, 375

STRONG, Edward I 1652–1724

The younger brother of **Thomas Strong**, from whom he inherited the family building and quarrying business, Edward was apprenticed to his brother on 2 January 1672 and no doubt assisted Thomas in his work on several of the City churches. He was described as 'of [the] City of London, Freemason' on 1 April 1675, when he married Martha, the sister of **Ephraim Beauchamp**, of the parish of St Thomas, Southwark (*Lic Vic Gen*). There were four children, the eldest of whom was **Edward Strong II**. Edward I was made free of the Masons' Company by redemption on 6 April 1680, the same day as his younger brother, John (†1725). He became renter warden in 1692 and master in 1796. In 1691, when he bound his son Edward II, his address was given as St Benet Paul's wharf, a convenient location for receiving stone from the family's Oxfordshire quarries.

Strong took over Thomas's contracts after his death in 1681. He completed several of his brother's churches and was himself responsible for the masonry and carved stonework of several more, representing contracts amounting to over £11,000. These included St Michael Paternoster Royal, St Mary Magdalen, Old Fish Street, St Mildred, Bread Street and St Clement, Eastcheap (**3–6**). He also worked at Winchester Palace (**2**), where, according to his own account, he 'had all the designs of all the masons' work committed to his care, by Sir Christopher Wren, the surveyor' (*Colvin* 1995, 936).

His principal London commission was as a master mason at St Paul's Cathedral, where he took a prominent part, supplying large quantities of Burford stone and contracting for the east end, the north portico, the north side of the nave and part of the done. In 1694 he was employing 65 masons at St Paul's (listed in the Masons' Company general search of September that year), more than twice the number working under his fellow-contractors, **Christopher Kempster** and Ephraim Beauchamp. He and his son were together responsible for the lantern. The contract included a considerable amount of carved stonework (**8**).

Strong's other work as a mason-contractor included Morden College, Blackheath, the Palace of Whitehall and in 1696, the first mason's contract at Greenwich Hospital, where he worked in partnership with **Thomas Hill.** In 1705 he and his son Edward took the chief mason's contract at Blenheim Palace, where they erected the whole of the main building at a reputed cost of £10,958 (**10**). They had recourse to litigation to attempt to recover the considerable sums owing to them when work came to a standstill in 1712 as the result of a dispute between the architect John Vanbrugh and the Duchess of Marlborough. They appear to have been unsuccessful in recouping their costs and the whole contract was clearly an unhappy business since the Duchess habitually intervened and changed her mind.

The indentures of a number of Strong's apprentices are recorded in the Masons' Company registers: John Miller and Richard Cowdry began their training under Thomas Strong and were turned over to Edward on Thomas's death; Richard Duffill joined Strong's team in 1682; Richard Webb of Burford (who trained first under John Miller) was turned over to Strong in 1690; Edward Strong II is listed in 1691, Mathew Bancks in 1692, Thomas Atkins in 1700, Edward Beacham (Beauchamp) of Burford in 1705 and William Prosser in 1717.

Strong took full advantage of the opportunities for a master mason and quarry owner at a time when unprecedented building activity offered great rewards for a man of his experience. The fortune he accumulated enabled him to establish himself as a landowner in Hertfordshire, where he bought the manors of Hyde at Abbots Langley and Herons at Wheathampstead. He lived at a house called New Barns on the River Vere, near St Albans. Strong died on 8 February 1724 and was buried in St Peter's church, St Albans, where there is a monument with a portrait bust. His lengthy epitaph states that he worked at St Paul's 'even from its foundations to his laying the last stone' and adds that, with Wren and Compton, Bishop of London, 'he shared the felicity of seeing both the beginning and finishing of that stupendous fabrick'.

IR

Literary References: *Builder*, 24 Sept 1864, 700–1; *Knoop and Jones* 1935, 20 n2, 75–6; Wren Soc XV, *passim*; *Green* 1964 (1), 62, 98–9, 126–8, 132, 133; *Gunnis* 1968, 376; *Colvin* 1995, 936; *Webb* 1999, *passim*

Archival References: Masons' Co, Freemen, fol 66, 6 April 1680; Masons' Co, Masters and Wardens

Additional MS Sources: Bodleian, Rawlinson MS, 387

Will: PCC 45 BOLTON

Portraits: Bust, marble, Strong monument, St Peter, St Albans; canvas, artist unknown, United Grand Lodge of England (*Colvin* 1995, 936)

Chimneypieces

1.	1688	Of Egyptian marble	[Queen's withdrawing room, Palace of Whitehall]; destroyed	PRO Works 5/42; *Gunnis* 1968, 376

Architectural Sculpture

2.	1682–1686	Pilasters, columns, 'ornaments on several pilasters and carving ye tops of ye capitals'		[Winchester Palace, Hants]; destroyed	TNA E.351/3460; *Gunnis* 1968, 376
3.	1686–1694	'Cherubim heads and keystones'	s	[St Michael Paternoster Royal, City of London London]; untraced	*Gunnis* 1968, 376
4.	1681–1694	'Fourteen Spandril Flowers' Payment(s): 18 gns	s	[St Mary Magdalen, City of London]; untraced	*Gunnis* 1968, 376
5.	1681–1694	'Two death's heads'	s	[St Clement, Eastcheap, City of London]; untraced	*Gunnis* 1968, 376
6.	1681–1694	'Ye Vine and two pineapples' Payment(s): £24	s	[St Mildred, City of London]; untraced	*Gunnis* 1968, 376
7.	1707	'Pedestal for the dial in the great garden steps' Payment(s): £25		[Inner Temple, London]; untraced	*Gunnis* 1968, 376
8.	1675–1710	Carved stonework	s	St Paul's Cathedral, London	*Colvin* 1995, 936; *Gunnis* 1968, 376
9.	1705–1712	Carved stonework (co-sculptor: Edward Strong II)	s	[Greenwich Palace, London]; untraced	TNA ADM 68/672; *Gunnis* 1968, 376
10.	1705–1712	Carved stonework (co-sculptor: Edward Strong II)		Blenheim Palace, Oxon	*Green* 1964 (1) 126–8; *Gunnis* 1968, 376; *Colvin* 1995, 936

STRONG, Edward II 1676–1741

The eldest son of **Edward Strong** I, he was apprenticed to his father on 30 July 1691 and became free of the Masons' Company on 18 October 1698. He was twice a warden of the Company, in 1712 and 1715, and became master in 1718. Strong married Susanna, the daughter of Joseph Roberts, serjeant plumber, in 1699, by whom he had four daughters and one son, Edward, who died of smallpox at the age of 20. His eldest daughter married Sir John Strange, Master of the Rolls. Strong lived at Greenwich for many years. Shortly after gaining his freedom of the Masons' Company he went abroad, travelling through France, Italy and Holland with Christopher Wren, the son of the architect.

In 1702 Strong provided a model and won the contract to build the north gate of St Bartholomew's Hospital, Smithfield. He assisted his father at Greenwich Hospital and at St Paul's Cathedral in 1706–8, where together they built the lantern. The younger Strong laid the marble pavement beneath the dome and transepts. He also built the 'lanterns' or spires of several City churches including Christchurch, Newgate Street; St Vedast, Foster Lane; St Stephen Walbrook; St Michael, College Hill and St James Garlickhythe, and the steeple of St Michael, Cornhill.

He worked in partnership with **Edward Tufnell** at St Alphege, Greenwich, 1712–1714 (**3**) and at St George, Wapping, 1715–1723 (**5**). The pair also collaborated on five of the new churches erected between 1712 and 1733 by the Commissioners for Building Fifty New Churches, for which they received a total of £5,000. These were St John, Westminster (**4**); St Paul, Deptford (**1**); St George in the East; St Anne, Limehouse and St George, Bloomsbury, which was begun by both men in 1717 and carried on by Strong after Tufnell's death in 1719. At St George, Bloomsbury they were responsible for a considerable amount of decorative carving including an eleven foot high statue of King George I, which surmounts the spire and for which they were paid £90 (**8**).

Strong went into partnership for a time with **Christopher Cass I** and **Andrews Jelfe**. After the death of **Edward Shepherd** in October 1727, Strong and Cass were paid £2,997 for finishing St Luke, Old Street, London, largely built by Shepherd. The association with Cass was terminated on 31 December 1728.

Strong took on a number of contracts to build private houses, including Addiscombe, Surrey, for William Draper, 1702–3, Marlborough House, London, 1712, and the north front of Canons, Middx, in 1715. He was master-mason at the Queen's House, Greenwich, where he worked on the west colonnade and provided a doorcase.

He died on 10 October 1741, leaving property in Hertfordshire to be divided among his daughters. Other family members continued as masons at Stanford, Berks, throughout the 18th century. As late as 1866 it was remembered that some of the best tombstones in the churchyard were 'the workmanship of a family of the name of Strong, who for many years were masons at Stanford, and who were famous in the country round' (LG Maine, *A Berkshire Village, its History and Antiquities*, 1866, 54, quoted by *Colvin* 1995, 937). An Edward Strong became an assistant of the Masons' Company 'at Greenwhich Street' *c*1740.

IR

Literary References: *Gunnis* 1968, 376–7; RG/JP 8, 1390; *Colvin* 1995, 935–8; *Friedman* 2004, 36–8

Archival References: Masons' Co, Apprentice binding book (1), 1691; Freemen, fol 66 18 October 1698; Assistants fol 1, *c*1740; Court Book, 1695–1722 (1718); TNA ADM 68/874, 68/875 (masonry work and repairs, Queen's House, Greenwich)

Additional Manuscript Sources: Strong and Tufnell's Book of Entry for Masons' Work, (Five New Churches) RIBA Library; BL Stowe MS, 412, no 77 (termination of agreement with Cass and Jelfe)

Will: PCC 184 Spurway (proved October 1741)

Portraits of the Sculptor: Charles Philips, group portrait of Strong and family, s&d 1732, Met NY

Chimneypieces

1.	1723	For the vestry, sacristy and elsewhere Payment(s): £314	St Paul, Deptford, London	RG/JP, 8, 1389

Architectural Sculpture

2.	1697	Dove and gloria with cherubs' heads	St Vedast, Foster Lane, City of London	Pevsner, *London* I, 1973, 180
3.	1712–1714	Four stone altars, with cherubs and festoons (co-sculptor: Edward Tufnell)	St Alphege, Greenwich, in front of the portico	TNA A 01.437-2; *Gunnis* 1968, 377
4.	1713–1719	Carved work including roses, husks, scrolls, fluting and cartouches (co-sculptor: Edward Tufnell) Payment(s): £80 for the 'scrools' and £180 for the capitals	St John, Westminster, London	*Friedman* 2004, 36–38
5.	pre-1723	Carved work including '32 Festoons in the 8 altars' (co-sculptor: Edward Tufnell) Payment(s): £64 for festoons	St George, Wapping, London	RG/JP, 8, 1389

6.	1724	Font Payment(s): £12	[St John, Clerkenwell, London]; untraced	TNA, AOI, 437/2 (Lambeth Palace Library)
7.	1713–1726	Ornaments including Doric capitals with rose husks, 129 cartouches in the cornices of the towers and pediment ornaments (co-sculptor: Edward Tufnell)	St Margaret, Westminster, London	*Friedman* 2004, 36–38
8.	1725–1726	Statue of King George I; two lions and two unicorns (£200); four festoons between the lions and unicorns (£30 each); four crowns (£7 each)	St George, Bloomsbury, London	St George, Bloomsbury, Bills of Work, 25 March 1724–25 March 1725 (OS); *Downes* 1959, repr 68b, 69c

STRONG, Thomas *c*1634–81

One of a family of masons active throughout the 17th and early-18th centuries. He was the eldest son of Valentine Strong (†1662), a mason and quarry owner of Taynton, Oxon, and his wife Anne Margetts of Charlbury and was the brother of **Edward Strong I**. Thomas carried on the family business after his father's death, completing the house which his father had been building at Fairford, Glos for Andrew Barker. In about 1663 he built the stables at Cornbury House, Oxon, designed by Hugh May for the Earl of Clarendon and in 1665–6, the east front, again to May's designs. At the same time he was engaged in work on the first part of the quadrangle at Trinity College, Oxford, designed by Sir Christopher Wren and completed in 1668.

After the Great Fire of 1666 Strong went to London with a team of assistants, where he obtained several important building contracts and also sold large quantities of stone to other masons. In 1670, taking advantage of the act for rebuilding the City, which permitted 'foreign' artificers to take up their freedom, Strong was made free of the Masons' Company and of the City by redemption. Strong undertook to build three City churches including St Stephen Walbrook, 1672–8, designed by Wren, a contract received jointly with **Christopher Kempster**. They were paid £1,489 17s 8d in 1674, including £112 for '16 Corinthian Capitalls', £4 for '7 small cherubins heads' and £1 10s for 'A Mask-head upon the west dore' (Bodl MS Rawlinson B 387). In 1679 Strong undertook to provide 'a convenient font' of marble (*Wren Soc* XX, 113). In May that year he, Kempster and Wren were guests of the parishioners at the vestry dinner at the Boar's Head Tavern.

Strong became one of the principal contractors at St Paul's Cathedral when work began in 1675, laying the foundation stone 'with his own hands' on 21 June that year. During the next six years his bills for masonry work and decorative ornaments (**4, 5, 7**) totalled nearly £4,000, a quarter of which was probably owing to him at his death in the summer of 1681. Whilst working at St Paul's he was also working on a new front for Lord Craven's house at Hampstead Marshall, Berkshire. He died unmarried, leaving everything to his brother Edward, who was his sole executor.

Literary References: *Wren Soc* X, XIII, XIV, *passim*; *Gunnis* 1968, 377; *Colvin* 1995, 934–6

Will: PCC 99 NORTH

Chimneypieces					
1.	1676	Three, for the Office of Works '& ye roomes below' Payment(s): £9 13s 5d	s	[St Paul's Cathedral, City of London]; untraced	*Wren Soc* XIII, 81
Architectural Sculpture					
2.	1672	'Mask-head to the west door' (co-sculptor: Christopher Kempster) Payment(s): £1 10s		St Stephen Walbrook, City of London	*Gunnis* 1968, 377
3.	1672	Sixteen Corinthian capitals (co-sculptor: Christopher Kempster) Payment(s): £122		St Stephen Walbrook, City of London	*Gunnis* 1968, 377
4.	1677	'one great Escallop' and other ornaments		St Paul's Cathedral, London	*Wren Soc* XIII, 87–8
5.	1678	Decorative carving including husks and scrolls under the windows		St Paul's Cathedral, London, north west vestry	*Wren Soc* XIII, 109
6.	1679	Font	m	St Stephen Walbrook, City of London	*Wren Soc* XX, 113; *Gunnis* 1968, 377
7.	pre-1681	Extensive decorative carving		St Paul's Cathedral, London	*The Builder*, 24.9.1864, 700; *Gunnis* 1968, 377

STUBINGTON, James, of Bishops Waltham fl *c*1748–53

The architectural tablet to Jane Wright is about 7 feet high, with an urn at the apex of a triangular pediment (**2**). Stubbington also provided a pedimented tablet to Edward Wynn (**1**).

Literary References: *Gunnis* 1968, 377

Funerary Monuments					
1.	†1748	Edward Wynn	Southwick, Hants		Pevsner, *Hants & Isle of Wight*, 1967, 605
2.	†1753	Jane Wright	Bishops Waltham, Hants	S	Pevsner, *Hants & Isle of Wight*, 1967, 105

STURDY, William, of Romford fl *c*1825–41?

He signs tablets to William Ford (**1**), with a relief of two charity children playing by a tombstone; to William Stone (**2**) with a well-carved relief of a woman mourning by an urn; and a classical one to the Fanshawe family (**3**). Sturdy may possibly be the son of the 'Mr William Sturdy, stone-mason' of Romford who died in 1800 (*Monthly Mag*, 1800, 9, 199).

Literary References: *Gunnis* 1968, 377

Funerary Monuments					
1.	?1825	William Ford	Dagenham, Essex	S	*Gunnis* 1968, 377
2.	?1839	William Stone	Dagenham, Essex	S	*Gunnis* 1968, 377
3.	?1841	Fanshawe Family	Dagenham, Essex	SD	*Gunnis* 1968, 377

STURGES, John –1763

A carver, he died in Hanover Lane, Dublin, in May 1763.

Literary References: *Strickland* 2, 1913, 417

SUMMERS, Charles 1825–78

The son of a mason, George Summers, he was born on 27 July 1825 at Charlton Mackrell, Somerset, the second eldest of eight children. His brother Joseph was a successful musician attaining the degree of doctor of music despite his artisan background. Charles received little education but showed an early talent for sketching portraits. Since the family income was precarious he worked with his father at menial jobs from the age of eight in Bristol and South Wales. Work was then found in Wells, building the Union Workhouse, and then, hearing of Brunel's need for labourers to construct the railway line, he and his father moved to Weston-super-Mare. While employed at that seaside resort erecting a monument he attracted the attention of **Henry Weekes**, who took him into his studio as a polisher. Each night he practised the craft of pointing marble. Summers also worked for **M L Watson**, and after the latter's death helped complete the colossal group of Lord Eldon and Lord Stowell, now in the library of University College, Oxford. On 16 December 1848 he was admitted as a student in the Royal Academy Schools and in 1849 he won a silver medal for a model (**88**). Two years later he was awarded both the silver and the gold for a group entitled *Mercy interceding for the vanquished* (**9**). In the same year his *Boy playing with a shell* won a bronze medal at the Great Exhibition (**8**). He was apparently the first student of sculpture to win both prizes simultaneously, and he also received a grant of £500 to enable him to continue his studies in Rome, an opportunity he did not take up.

On 9 July 1851 he married Augustine Amiot, the daughter of a farmer. They lived at 8 Brewer Street, with a studio in Warwick Street, Pimlico. Having been diagnosed with suspected tuberculosis he was advised to travel to Australia (in the wake of his father and brothers) and in 1852 arrived at Melbourne, where he built a house in Docker Street, Richmond. He took out a claim on a coalfield but had no success and, having seen an advertisement for modellers for the new Houses of Parliament, returned to Melbourne where he subsequently obtained employment as an architectural sculptor modelling the rich figurative decoration (**82**). Henceforth Summers, with a studio in Collins Street, was to be a central figure in artistic circles in Victoria. During the 1860s he became the most important sculptor in colonial Australia, monopolising local sculptural commissions. He also became a high-profile public figure attending civic balls dressed as Michelangelo and, more seriously, was appointed to official government positions such as that of chairman overseeing drawing instruction at the local schools (1864). He was active in promoting the earliest artists' society in Melbourne, the Victorian Society of Fine Arts.

His work as a sculptor encompassed portrait busts, prize medallions and large free-standing works including the neoclassical group *The sure friend*, which was used as the logo for the Australian Mutual Provident Society over the next century (**10**). His undoubted masterpiece was the memorial to the ill-fated explorers, Burke and Wills, reputed to be the largest bronze hitherto cast in Australia (**12**). Summers had never before worked in bronze and had to construct his own furnace, which makes the achievement the more remarkable. His first design, published in November 1861, showed a complex figurative group, with the explorers supported by a camel, surrounded by free-standing statues of Aboriginal people and decorative bas-reliefs. The simpler design, as completed, a 13 foot-high bronze group with reliefs below, was unveiled in 1865.

Summers's position and esteem was such that even though he returned to England in 1866 and settled in Rome in 1867, he continued to produce work for Australia as well as England. In Rome he established a studio that reputedly employed up to 20 assistants at the time of his death. He exhibited regularly at the Royal Academy, showing mostly portraiture. At the Paris Exhibition of 1867 the government of the state of Victoria, Australia, showed a collection of heads cast by Summers from live models at the Coranderk Aboriginal Mission. Several sets of casts were made, since the busts aroused much interest. In 1876 he executed life-size seated figures in marble of Queen Victoria and the Prince Consort as they had appeared *c*1860 and the Prince and Princess of Wales as they looked contemporaneously (**18–20**).

His best-known pupils were Charles Stanford (who was serving a term in Pentridge prison when he came to Summers's notice) and Margaret Thomas, an early woman sculptor, painter and art-writer. His son, Charles Francis Summers (b 1857), became a sculptor and worked closely with the Italian neo-classical sculptors G B Lombardi and G M Benzoni.

He died after an operation on 24 November 1878 at Neuilly-sur-Seine, France, and was buried in the Protestant cemetery in Rome, leaving less than £300. The characteristically ungenerous Palgrave wrote in 1866 of the sculptor 'Several heads by Mr C Summers afford proof that our colonies are willing as yet to put up with the lowest standard of native manufacture – When will friends and corporations learn that to be unsuccessfully done on a large scale is no compliment to any man?' (86). His obituary in the *Builder* dwelt on the manner of his death and reminisced on his early Australian activities as a gold-digger. The recent biography in the *ODNB* has done much to rehabilitate this remarkably resilient and successful sculptor.

EH

Literary References: *Thomas* 1879; *Gunnis* 1968, 377–8; Evans 1978; *Read* 1982, 120; *ODNB* (Harris and Peers)

Portraits of the Sculptor: M Thomas, canvas, 1860–69, State Library of Victoria, Melbourne, La Trobe picture coll; M Thomas, marble bust, 1880, Shire hall, Somerset; engraving, State Library of Victoria

Funerary Monuments

1.	?1865	William MacLeary	St James, Sydney, Australia		GPC
2.	1870	Lady MacLeay	[Exhib RA, London, 1143]; Godstone, Surrey	SD	*Graves* VII, 1905–6, 303; *Gunnis* 1968, 378
3.	1870	Unidentified figure	[Exhib RA, London, 1065]; untraced		*Graves* VII, 1905–6, 303
4.	1879	Lieutenant-General Sir Edward MacArthur (†1872)	Paramatta, New South Wales, Australia		Evans 1978, unpag
5.	nd	Guardian angel	Melbourne Cemetery		*Evans* 1978, unpag
6.	nd	Resignation	Melbourne Cemetery		*Evans* 1978, unpag

Statues

7.	*c*1847	Lord Eldon and Lord Stowell, group (co-sculptor: Musgrave Lewthwaite Watson)	University College, Oxford, library		*Gunnis* 1968, 378
8.	1851	Boy playing with a shell	[Gt Exhib]; untraced		*Gunnis* 1968, 378
9.	1851	Mercy interceding for the vanquished	[RA gold medal]; untraced		RA Premium list

10.	c1863	The sure friend		Destroyed		*ODNB*
11.	1863	William Shakespeare		Melbourne, Australia		*Gunnis* 1968, 378
12.	1861–1865	Robert O'Hara Burke and William John Wills Payment(s): £4,000	b	Melbourne, Australia		*Gunnis* 1968, 378; *Read* 1982, 120; *ODNB*
13.	1868	The signal of war, an Australian aboriginal, statuette	b	[Exhib RA, London, 1050]; untraced		*Graves* VII, 1905–6, 303
14.	1871	A mother (group)		[Exhib RA, London, 1265]; untraced		*Graves* VII, 1905–6, 303
15.	1873	Unidentified group	m	[Exhib RA, London, 1531]; untraced		*Graves* VII, 1905–6, 303
16.	1873	Unidentified group	m	[Exhib RA, London, 1535]; untraced		*Graves* VII, 1905–6, 303
17.	1875	Lynceus and Hypermnestra	m	[Exhib RA, London, 1312]; destroyed 1882 in Crystal Palace Fire		*Graves* VII, 1905–6, 303; *Evans* 1978, unpag
18.	1876	Albert Edward, Prince of Wales and Alexandra, Princess of Wales		Sailor's Rest, Geelong, Shire of Alexandra Other versions: State Library, Melbourne, Australia		*Evans* 1978, unpag
19.	c1878	Queen Victoria	m	State Library, Melbourne, Victoria Other versions: Royal Agricultural Soc, Victoria		*Evans* 1978, unpag; GPC
20.	By 1879	Albert, the Prince Consort		Royal Agricultural Soc of Victoria showgrounds, Melbourne, Australia		*Darby and Smith* 1983, 114 n96
21.	pre-1884	Maternal affection	m	State Library, Melbourne, Victoria		GPC
22.	nd	Rebecca		Exeter Art Gallery, Devon		*Gunnis* 1968, 378
Busts						
23.	1849	F Hutchinson Synge		[Exhib RA, London, 1269]; untraced		*Graves* VII, 1905–6, 302
24.	1850	J K Haberfield		[Exhib RA, London, 1416]; untraced		*Graves* VII, 1905–6, 302
25.	1851	George Dollond FRS	p	[Exhib RA, London, 1366]; Royal Hospital School, Holbrook, Suffolk		*Graves* VII, 1905–6, 302
26.	1851	Henry Lawson FRS	m	[Exhib RA, London, 1377]; Royal Hospital School, Holbrook, Suffolk		*Graves* VII, 1905–6, 302
27.	1852	Charles Lockey	m	[Exhib RA, London, 1443]; untraced		*Graves* VII, 1905–6, 303
28.	1852	Charles Moody MP		[Exhib RA, London, 1410]; untraced		*Graves* VII, 1905–6, 302
29.	1852	Master Arthur Loring	m	[Exhib RA, London, 1475]; untraced		*Graves* VII, 1905–6, 303
30.	1852	Master Pigott		[Exhib RA, London, 1459]; untraced		*Graves* VII, 1905–6, 303
31.	1853	Commander Robert Jenner RN		[Exhib RA, London, 1428]; untraced		*Graves* VII, 1905–6, 303
32.	1853	E F S P		[Exhib RA, London, 1366]; untraced		*Graves* VII, 1905–6, 303
33.	by 1854	W B Burnley		[Exhib Melbourne]; untraced		*Evans* 1978, nd
34.	by 1857	Charles Summers, self-portrait, miniature bust		[Exhib Victorian Soc of Fine Art, Melbourne, 1857]; untraced		*Graves* VII, 1905–6, 302
35.	by 1857	J G Knight		[Victorian Exhib, Melbourne, 1857]; untraced		*Evans* 1978, unpag
36.	1860	Richard Woolcott	m	L O Rumley, Victoria		*Evans* 1978, unpag
37.	pre-1860	Sir Redmond Barry KCMG	m	State Library, Melbourne, Victoria		*Evans* 1978, unpag
38.	1862	Richard Woollcott	p	Ballarat municipal art gallery, Australia		
39.	1862	Viscount Canterbury	m	State Library, Melbourne, Victoria		*Evans* 1978, unpag
40.	1864	Hon John O'Shaughnessy MP	m	[Exhib RA, London, 978]; untraced		*Graves* VII, 1905–6, 303; *Evans* 1978, unpag
41.	1864	Hon John Pascoe Fawkner	m	State Library of Victoria		*Graves* VII, 1905–6, 303; *Evans* 1978, unpag
42.	1864	Rev Thomas Binney	m	State Library of Victoria		*Graves* VII, 1905–6, 303; *Evans* 1978, unpag
43.	by 1866	Sir Charles Darling, Governor of Victoria		[Intercolonial Exhib, Melbourne, 1866]; untraced		*Evans* 1978, nd
44.	1866	Sir Henry Barkly, Governor of Victoria	m	State Library, Melbourne, Victoria		*Evans* 1978, unpag
45.	1867	Heads from live models at the Coranderk Aboriginal mission		Museum of Victoria, NSW Other versions: Jardin des Plantes, Paris BM		*ODNB*
46.	1868	Charles Sturt	m	[Exhib RA, London, 1015]; Art Gall of South Australia, Adelaide (1899)		*Graves* VII, 1905–6, 303; *Ormond* 1973, 438
47.	1868	Frederick Goodall RA		[Exhib RA, London, 1134]; untraced		*Graves* VII, 1905–6, 303
48.	1869	Gustavus Vaughan Brooke	m	Shrubland Hall, Suffolk Other versions: Theatre Royal, Melbourne, Australia State Library, Melbourne, Australia		GPC; *Evans* 1978, nd
49.	1869	James Macarthur	m	Parliament House, Sydney, Australia Other versions: Camden Park, NSW, Australia, 1870		*Graves* VII, 1905–6, 303; *Evans* 1978, unpag
50.	1869	Lady Macarthur	m	Parliament House, Sydney Other versions: Camden Park, NSW, Australia, 1870		*Graves* VII, 1905–6, 303; GPC
51.	1870	Sir Roger Therry	m	Mitchell Library, Sydney		*Graves* VII, 1905–6, 302; *Evans* 1978, unpag
52.	1870	William Sharp Macleay	m	Linnean Soc	SD	*Graves* VII, 1905–6, 303; *Evans* 1978, unpag
53.	1871	Admiral Sir George Brooke Middleton	m	[Exhib RA, London, 1214]; untraced		*Graves* VII, 1905–6, 303
54.	1871	Lady Broke-Middleton	m	Shrubland Hall, Suffolk		*Graves* VII, 1905–6, 303; *Evans* 1978, unpag
55.	1871	Mrs C William Siemens	m	[Exhib RA, London, 1199]; untraced		*Graves* VII, 1905–6, 303
56.	1871	Mrs Verdon	m	[Exhib RA, London, 1255]; untraced		*Graves* VII, 1905–6, 303
57.	1871	Professor Sir Richard Owen	m	[Exhib RA, London, 1186]; untraced		*Graves* VII, 1905–6, 303; *Ormond* 1973, 353
58.	1871	William Sharp Maclean	m	[Exhib RA, London, 1306]; untraced		*Graves* VII, 1905–6, 303
59.	1872	Admiral Sir George Broke-Middleton	m	Shrubland Hall, Suffolk	SD	*Evans* 1978, nd
60.	1872	Sir George Macleay KCMG	m	State Library, Melbourne, Victoria Other versions: Art Gall of South Australia, Adelaide		*Evans* 1978, unpag

61.	1873	Admiral Sir Philip Broke	m	Shrubland Hall, Suffolk		*Graves* VII, 1905–6, 303; *Evans* 1978, unpag
62.	1873	Alfred, Duke of Edinburgh	m	[Exhib RA, London, 1521]; Art Gallery, Melbourne, Australia		*Graves* VII, 1905–6, 303; *Gunnis* 1968, 378
63.	1873	C Williams Siemens FRS DCL	m	[Exhib RA, London, 1545]; untraced		*Graves* VII, 1905–6, 303
64.	1873	Colonel Sir Andrew Clarke KCMG	m	[Exhib RA, London, 1427]; untraced		*Graves* VII, 1905–6, 303
65.	1873	Miss Flora A Pond	m	[Exhib RA, London, 1517]; untraced		*Graves* VII, 1905–6, 303
66.	1875	Rev Edward Steane DD		[Exhib RA, London, 1263]; untraced		*Graves* VII, 1905–6, 303
67.	1876	Edwin Norris		Taunton Shire Hall, Somerset	SD	
68.	1876	Lilian, daughter of Jas H Randall	m	[Exhib RA, London, 1388]; untraced		*Graves* VII, 1905–6, 303
69.	1876	Rt Rev Charles Perry, 1st Anglican Bishop of Melbourne		Harrow School, speech room	SD	*Gunnis* 1968, 378
70.	pre-1877	Sir Charles Gavin Duffy		State Library, Melbourne, Victoria		GPC
71.	1878	William Wilkinson Wardell	m	V A Wardell, New South Wales		*Evans* 1978, unpag
72.	by 1888	Sir Charles Sladen	m	State Library, Melbourne, Victoria		*Evans* 1978, unpag
73.	nd	A Roman peasant woman		State Library, Melbourne, Victoria		GPC
74.	nd	Captain Charles Sturt		Mitchell Library, Sydney Other versions: Art Gall of South Australia, Adelaide State library of Victoria		*Ormond* 1973, 438
75.	nd	Edward Smyth-Pigott	m	Woodspring Museum, Weston-super-Mare, Somerset		*Evans* 1978, unpag
76.	nd	Henry Weekes	m	RA, London	S	*Evans* 1978, unpag
77.	nd	John Hugh Smyth-Pigott	m	Woodspring Museum, Weston-super-Mare, Somerset		*Evans* 1978, unpag
78.	nd	Joseph Edgar of Swiss Villa, Weston	m	Woodspring Museum, Weston-super-Mare, Somerset		*Evans* 1978, unpag
79.	nd	Sir Archibald Michie	m	State Library, Melbourne, Victoria		*Evans* 1978, unpag
80.	nd	Sir Francis Murphy KB	m	State Library, Melbourne, Victoria		*Evans* 1978, unpag
81.	nd	Sir James Bruce	m	Untraced		*Evans* 1978, nd
Architectural Sculpture						
82.	post-1852	Neo-rococo ornaments		Houses of Parliament, Melbourne, legislative chamber		*ODNB*
83.	1858	Frieze of putti		[for Bank of New South Wales, Melbourne]; Melbourne Public Library		*Evans* 1978, unpag
84.	nd	Albion, figure		[Over Commercial Hotel, Bridge Road, Richmond, Melbourne]; destroyed		*Evans* 1978, unpag
85.	nd	'Amicus Certus in Re Incerta', emblematic group		[Australian Mutual Provident Soc, 98 Pitt St, Sydney]; destroyed		*Evans* 1978, unpag
86.	nd	River god fountain		Melbourne, Australia		*ODNB*
87.	nd	The good Samaritan, high relief	s	Weston-super-Mare Hospital, Somerset		*Evans* 1978, unpag
Reliefs						
88.	1849	Silenus and the infant Bacchus, model		[RA silver medal]; untraced		*Evans* 1978, unpag
89.	1849	Unidentified subject (medallion)		[Exhib RA, London, 1221]; untraced		*Graves* VII, 1905–6, 302
90.	1850	W Stucker (medallion)		[Exhib RA, London, 1430]; untraced		*Graves* VII, 1905–6, 302
91.	1851	George Summers (medallion portrait)		[Exhib RA, London, 1312]; untraced		*Graves* VII, 1905–6, 302
92.	1852	T H Syng (medallion)		[Exhib RA, London, 1424]; untraced		*Graves* VII, 1905–6, 303
93.	1859	Elijah and Hannah Summers, double profile portrait		K Scarlett, Melbourne		*Evans* 1978, unpag
94.	1867	Richard Henry Horne, medallion	p	NPG, London		*Ormond* 1973, 233 (repr 451)
95.	nd	Mr and Mrs Brice of Weston, plaque with relief profiles	m	Woodspring Museum, Weston-super-Mare, Somerset		*Evans* 1978, unpag
96.	nd	Robert Gregory, medallion	p	Woodspring Museum, Weston-super-Mare, Somerset		*Evans* 1978, unpag
Miscellaneous						
97.	1851	Model from life		[RA silver medal]; untraced		*Evans* 1978, unpag
98.	1870	Playmates	m	[Exhib RA, London, 1128]; untraced		*Graves* VII, 1905–6, 303

SUMPTER, of Irthlingborough fl *c*1784–99

An article in the *Gentleman's Magazine* of 1799 states that he made the tablet to John Perkins (1), who was '27 years organist of the Church'. A correspondent signing himself 'A Traveller' gives details of the inscription, the last line being '*Sumpter, Irtlingbro*'. Another correspondent, signing himself 'D.' adds 'Sumpter is the stone-mason's name on the edge'. Sumpter carved the tablet topped with a basket of fruit to Thomas Wylde (2), and in 1799 built an obelisk for Sir English Dolben (3).

Funerary Monuments						
1.	†1784	John Perkins		Finedon, Northants		*GM*, 1799, 939 and 1103; *Gunnis* 1968, 378
2.	?1792	Thomas Wylde	s	Yeldon, Hunts	S	*Gunnis* 1968, 378
Architectural Sculpture						
3.	1799	Obelisk		Finedon, Northants		*Gunnis* 1968, 378

SUTTON, S fl 1811

He won a silver medal from the Society of Arts in 1811, at which date he lived at 8 New Road, opposite Fitzroy Square, London.

Miscellaneous				
1.	1811	Plaster cast of Hercules rescuing Deianeira from the centaur Nessus, 'modelled from a rude sketch of an Italian master'	[Soc of A, silver medal]; untraced	RSA *Transactions*, 1811, vol 29, 23

SUTTON, William fl 1757

Probably a Nottingham mason, he was paid £60 for building the 'Great Arch in the Parterre' at Thoresby, Notts, in 1757 (Archives Earl Manvers in GPC).

SUTTON, William, of Southport, Lancs 1752–1840

He originally came from Rossall and was in service with Mr B F Hesketh. In 1792 he erected a small inn on the sea-shore, near the Birkdale boundary, for the convenience of those who came for the sea bathing. This was the foundation of Southport. He later became the village gravestone cutter and was buried in the churchyard of St Cuthbert, North Meols, 'where yet may be seen many excellent specimens of his work; a large number of them being distinguishable by the skull and cross-bones; a favourite device of his'. He was known as 'Duke Sutton', and was buried at Churchtown (*Bland* 1888, 119).

SUTTON FAMILY, of Maidstone

James Sutton I 1774–1828
James Sutton II 1798–

James Sutton I signed a number of tablets in Kent. He died in 1828 and is buried in the churchyard of Maidstone parish church. He was succeeded in business by his nephew **James Sutton II**, the son of Mary Sutton of Maidstone, a widow, and was apprenticed to his uncle in 1812 (Town Archives in *Gunnis* 1968, 378). The younger Sutton is described by Gunnis as a prolific statuary, though he lists only a few monuments. Sutton II also made the 'very fine Portland stone façade' of the Kent Insurance Company in Maidstone (Company's Archives in GPC).

Literary References: *Gunnis* 1968, 378

Funerary Monuments

1.	?1813	Ann Argles (by James Sutton I)	Maidstone, Kent	S	*Gunnis* 1968, 378
2.	†1821	Thomas Turner and family (by James Sutton I)	Hunton, Kent	S	*Gunnis* 1968, 378
3.	†1826	Lieutenant Dering Addison	All Saints, Maidstone, Kent		RG/JP, 8, 1394
4.	?1828	Edward Usborne (by James Sutton II)	Staplehurst, Kent		*Gunnis* 1968, 378
5.	?1831	Joseph Sharpe (by James Sutton II)	Detling, Kent		*Gunnis* 1968, 378
6.	?1831	Robert Rugg (by James Sutton II)	Detling, Kent		*Gunnis* 1968, 378
7.	?1832	George, Viscount Torrington (by James Sutton II)	Mereworth, Kent		*Gunnis* 1968, 378
8.	†1834	George Harris (by James Sutton II)	All Saints, Maidstone, Kent		RG/JP, 8, 1394
9.	†1836	Anne Wandesforde (by James Sutton II)	Ulcombe, Kent	S	
10.	†1836	Charles Bathurst (by James Sutton II)	All Saints, Maidstone, Kent		RG/JP, 8, 1394
11.	†1843	Rebecca Hodges (by James Sutton II)	Benenden, Kent	S	
12.	†1846	Catherine du Bois (by James Sutton II)	All Saints, Maidstone, Kent		RG/JP, 8, 1394
13.	†1871	Frances Richardson Alkin and family members (by James Sutton II)	Hunton, Kent	S	

SWAN, William fl 1730

Architectural Sculpture

1.	1730	Decorative stonework, including shields and carving around windows and attic cornice Payment(s): £200 (shields at £3 each)	s	[Queen Anne's Court, Greenwich]; untraced	TNA, ADM 68/171

SWEET, William fl 1665

William Sweet and **M Miles** sign the large monument with a life-size reclining figure of Sir Edward Hales (**1**). They were probably local craftsmen, for 'the carving of the effigy is rather crude and coarse' (*Gunnis* 1968, 378).

Literary References: *White* 1999, 139

Funerary Monuments

1.	1665	Sir Edward Hales (†1654) (co-sculptor: M Miles)	Tunstall, Kent	*Gunnis* 1968, 378

SWIFT, of Shrewsbury fl 1765–69

He was employed by **T F Pritchard.**

Funerary Monuments

1.	1769	Richard Ward Offley (†1762) (designed by Thomas Farnolls Pritchard) (co-sculptor: Nelson and Van der Hagen) Drawing(s): Pritchard Drawing Book (AIA 64)		Pontesbury, Salop	*Ionides* 1999, 236 (repr)

Chimneypieces

2.	1765–1769	Five, for the drawing room, dressing room, common parlour, best chamber and dining parlour (designed by Thomas Farnolls Pritchard) (co-sculptor: Nelson and Van der Hagen) Drawing(s): Pritchard Drawing Book (AIA 29, 58, 59, 60, 62)	wd	Hatton Grange, Salop	*Ionides* 1999, 130–3, 331, 334, 379, 409–11, 413 (repr)
3.	1765–1769	For Miss Egerton's room (designed by Thomas Farnolls Pritchard) (co-sculptor: Nelson and Van der Hagen) Drawing(s): Pritchard Drawing Book (AIA 41)		[for Samuel Egerton, of Tatton Park, Cheshire]; untraced	*Ionides* 1999, 150, 332, 392 (repr)

4.	c1769	Six, of various designs (designed by Thomas Farnolls Pritchard) (co-sculptor: Nelson and Van der Hagen) Drawing(s): Pritchard Drawing Book (AIA 69, 72–77)		[Tern Hall, Salop]; untraced	*Ionides* 1999, 212, 335–7, 420, 423–8 (repr)
5.	1765–1769	Two (designed by Thomas Farnolls Pritchard) (co-sculptor: Nelson and Van der Hagen) Drawing(s): Pritchard Drawing Book (AIA 36, 37)		[for John Ashby, High Street, Shrewsbury]; untraced	*Ionides* 1999, 158, 331, 387–8 (repr)
6.	1765–1769	Two, for the common parlour and hall (designed by Thomas Farnolls Pritchard) (co-sculptor: Nelson and Van der Hagen) Drawing(s): Pritchard Drawing Book (AIA 19, 57)		[Gaines, Worcs]; untraced	*Ionides* 1999, 105–6, 329, 334, 369, 408 (repr)
7.	1765–1769	Two, with classical and gothic decoration (designed by Thomas Farnolls Pritchard) (co-sculptor: Nelson and Van der Hagen) Drawing(s): Pritchard Drawing Book (AIA 34, 63)	wd	Bitterley Court, Salop	*Ionides* 1999, 126–7, 333, 335, 384, 414 (repr)
8.	February 1769	With 'laurell leafe and ribbon' frieze (designed by Thomas Farnolls Pritchard) (co-sculptor: Nelson) Drawing(s): Pritchard Drawing Book (AIA 65)		[for Mr Good, of Shrewsbury]; untraced	*Ionides* 1999, 23, 335, 416 (repr)
9.	1765–1769	With birds in the frieze (designed by Thomas Farnolls Pritchard) (co-sculptor: Nelson and Van der Hagen) Drawing(s): Pritchard Drawing Book (AIA 17)		[for Mr Haycock in Wales]; untraced	*Ionides* 1999, 329, 367 (repr)
10.	1765–1769	With classical motifs (designed by Thomas Farnolls Pritchard) (co-sculptor: Nelson and Van der Hagen) Drawing(s): Pritchard Drawing Book (AIA 46)		[for Bartholomew Barnaby, of Brockhampton House, Herefs]; untraced	*Ionides* 1999, 99, 333, 397 (repr)
11.	1765–1769	With classical mouldings (designed by Thomas Farnolls Pritchard) (co-sculptor: Nelson and Van der Hagen) Drawing(s): Pritchard Drawing Book (AIA 79)		[for John Wilkinson, of The Lawns, Broseley, Salop]; untraced	*Ionides* 1999, 172, 337, 430 (repr)
12.	1765–1769	With foliage in the frieze (designed by Thomas Farnolls Pritchard) (co-sculptor: Nelson and Van der Hagen) Drawing(s): Pritchard Drawing Book (AIA 20)		[for Mr Burton of Longner Hall, Salop]; untraced	*Ionides* 1999, 330, 370 (repr)
13.	1765–1769	With frieze of scrolling foliage (designed by Thomas Farnolls Pritchard) (co-sculptor: Nelson) Drawing(s): Pritchard Drawing Book (AIA 27)	wd	[Kinsham Court, common parlour]; Kinsham Court, Herefs, dining room (now part of an overmantel)	*Ionides* 1999, 110–1, 330, 377 (repr)
14.	1765–1769	With frieze of scrolling foliage (designed by Thomas Farnolls Pritchard) (co-sculptor: Nelson and Van der Hagen) Drawing(s): Pritchard Drawing Book (AIA 38)	wd	Broseley Hall, Salop	*Ionides* 1999, 171, 332, 389 (repr)
15.	1765–1769	With Jacobean style details (designed by Thomas Farnolls Pritchard) (co-sculptor: Nelson and Van der Hagen) Drawing(s): Pritchard Drawing Book (AIA 24)	wd	Benthall Hall, Salop, drawing room	*Ionides* 1999, 172, 330, 374 (repr)
16.	1765–1769	With lion's head and grapes, for the best parlour (designed by Thomas Farnolls Pritchard) (co-sculptor: Nelson and Van der Hagen) Drawing(s): Pritchard Drawing Book (AIA 35)	wd	Kinsham Court, Herefs	*Ionides* 1999, 110–1, 331, 385 (repr)

No.	Date	Description	Material	Location	Reference
17.	1765–1769	With palmette and garlands of husks (designed by Thomas Farnolls Pritchard) (co-sculptor: Nelson and Van der Hagen) Drawing(s): Pritchard Drawing Book (AIA 22)	wd	[Gaines, Worcs, bed chamber]; unidentified house, Sussex	*Ionides* 1999, 105–6, 330, 372 (repr)
18.	1765–1769	With scrolls and flowers in the frieze (designed by Thomas Farnolls Pritchard) (co-sculptor: Nelson and Van der Hagen) Drawing(s): Pritchard Drawing Book (AIA 78)		[for Mr Good, of Shrewsbury]; untraced	*Ionides* 1999, 23, 337, 429 (repr)
19.	1765–1769	With waterleaf coving and frond-like branches (designed by Thomas Farnolls Pritchard) (co-sculptor: Nelson and Van der Hagen) Drawing(s): Pritchard Drawing Book (AIA 41)	wd	[for Mr Harley]; Kinsham Court, Herefs, dining room (now part of an overmantel)	*Ionides* 1999, 110–1, 332, 392 (repr)

Architectural Sculpture

No.	Date	Description	Material	Location	Reference
20.	1765–1769	'29 Stair Case Brackets in Oak' (designed by Thomas Farnolls Pritchard) (co-sculptor: Nelson) Drawing(s): Pritchard Drawing Book (AIA 42)	wd	Hatton Grange, Salop	*Ionides* 1999, 332, 393 (repr)
21.	1765–1769	Gothic columns, eight (designed by Thomas Farnolls Pritchard) (co-sculptor: Nelson and Van der Hagen) Drawing(s): Pritchard Drawing Book (AIA 54)		Gaines, Worcs	*Ionides* 1999, 106–8, 334, 405 (repr)

Miscellaneous

No.	Date	Description	Material	Location	Reference
22.	May 1768	'2 Frames for Shell pieces' (designed by Thomas Farnolls Pritchard) (co-sculptor: Nelson and Van der Hagen) Drawing(s): Pritchard Drawing Book (AIA 28)		[for Rev Mr Fowler, of Atcham rectory, Salop]; untraced	*Ionides* 1999, 330–1, 378 (repr)
23.	1765–1769	Glass frame (executed under the direction of Thomas Farnolls Pritchard) (co-sculptor: Nelson and Van der Hagen)		[for Mr Walcot, of Bitterley Hall, Salop]; untraced	*Ionides* 1999, 337, 432

SWINTON, Archibald, of Cambridge fl 1728?

Funerary Monuments

No.	Date	Description	Location		Reference
1.	?1728	John Whitechurch	Harlton, Cambs	S	*Gunnis* 1968, 378

SWITZER, Stephen *c*1618–*c*1669

He was apprenticed to Guy Glandinning in 1632 and was warden of the Masons' Company in 1660 and 1664, becoming master in 1665. In 1664 he was the mason responsible for building Clarendon House in Piccadilly and a year later he and his partner, **Thomas Wise I**, were working at Greenwich Palace, where they executed some of the carved stonework (1). Switzer had himself been sent to Portland in 1660 to select suitable stone for building the palace (*Gunnis* 1968, 378–9 incorrectly cites PRO, AO1, 2487/357). Six years later Switzer provided Portland stone to the value of £53 0s 6d for restoration work at the 'Chapell' of the Guildhall (Guildhall MSS 184/4, p12r). He may have been the father of the Stephen Switzer who was one of the apprentices of **Thomas Burman** and was left 40s in his master's will.

Literary References: *Knoop and Jones* 1935, *passim*; *Gunnis* 1968, 378–9

Architectural Sculpture

No.	Date	Description	Material	Location	Reference
1.	1667	Carved capital of a pilaster and other stonework (co-sculptor: Thomas Wise I) Payment(s): £13	s	[Greenwich Palace, London, 'south end towards the park']; untraced	TNA WORK 5, 9, fol 327; 329, fol 333; *Gunnis* 1968, 378–9

SYER, John fl 1781–84

He was employed by Henry Cornwell Legh to rebuild his home (1).

Architectural Sculpture

No.	Date	Description	Location	Reference
1.	1781–1784	Architectural ornament, including coat of arms in the pediment	[High Legh Hall, Cheshire]; untraced	Legh Archives, John Rylands Library, Manchester in GPC

SYLVESTER, Mr and Mrs fl 1780–94

For further information the reader is referred to *Pyke* 1973, 144 and *Pyke* 1981, 39

SYMONDS, Esther –1806

The *Hereford Journal* for 16 March 1791 recorded the death 'on Saturday last, Mr. **Thomas Symonds** stonemason of this city', and a week later that '**E. Symonds**', wife of Thomas, was carrying on the business. The journal carried the report on 20 April 1791 that Esther Symonds, widow of the late Thomas Symonds, architect and carver had 'engaged a person of acknowledged abilities in the business from London'. On 27 July 1803 it was announced that she had relinquished the business to **Thomas Wood**, statuary and mason 'at the established premises at Church St'. Esther Symonds died in the early part of 1806 at Hereford (*Monthly Mag*, 1806, 21, 94).

Funerary Monuments

No.	Date	Description	Location	Reference
1.	nd	Philip Turner	Rington, Herts	RG/JP 8, 1396

SYMONDS, of Swindon fl c1802

Funerary Monuments

1.	†1802	Fortescue children	Lambourn, Oxon	S	

SYMONDS, Thomas, of Hereford –1791

An architect and monumental mason, who became a freeman of Hereford in 1753, he was described by Gunnis as an excellent provincial statuary. He was responsible for some fine monuments, examples of which can be seen in many local churches. The large Thomas Symonds monument, 1760, has a fine medallion portrait (3), whilst the Somerset, 1764, is an impressive architectural work with a sarcophagus set against a pyramid (4). The Machen has a weeping child with a portrait medallion on a small sarcophagus before an obelisk (10).

He was for many years surveyor to the dean and chapter of Hereford and endeavoured without success to get them to take effective steps to prevent the collapse of the west end of the Cathedral, which finally occurred on Easter Monday, 1786. He was not dismissed as ineffectual from his post after the collapse of the tower 1786 (as suggested by Richard Garnier and Richard Hewlings in *CL* 21 Sept 1989). Instead he retired from his post.

In 1775 he was acting as clerk of works for Richard Payne Knight at Downton Castle, Wilts and major schemes followed at the county gaol, the infirmary, Allensmore Court, Herefs, and The Lodge, Ludlow, Salop, where his designs for its enrichment included portrait medallions, the device used on a number of his monuments.

The *Hereford Journal* for 16 March 1791 recorded the death 'on Saturday last, Mr. Thomas Symonds stonemason of this city', and a week later that 'E. Symonds', wife of Thomas, was carrying on the business. The journal carried the report on 20 April 1791 that **Esther Symonds**, widow of the late Thomas Symonds, architect and carver had 'engaged a person of acknowledged abilities in the business from London'.

Literary References: *Gunnis* 1968, 379; *Whitehead* 1989, 103; *Colvin* 1995, 945–6; *Aylmer and Tiller* 2000, 256–265

Funerary Monuments

1.	?1752	John Davies	Bullingham, Herefs		*Gunnis* 1968, 379
2.	?1760	Isabella Davies	Kingsland, Herefs		*Gunnis* 1968, 379
3.	†1760	Thomas Symonds	Sellack, Herefs		Pevsner, *Herefs*, 1963, 287;
4.	†1764	Anne Somerset	Pauntley, Glos	S	Pevsner, *Glos: Vale & Forest of Dean*, 1976, 320
5.	?1766	William Bach	Leominster, Herefs		*Gunnis* 1968, 379
6.	?1769	Rev Josiah Smart	Bodenham, Herefs		*Gunnis* 1968, 379
7.	?1772	Edmund Brydges	Tyberton, Herefs		*Gunnis* 1968, 379
8.	?1773	William Barnesley	Eardisley, Herefs		*Gunnis* 1968, 379
9.	?1775	Bridget Monnington	Sarnesfield, Herefs		*Gunnis* 1968, 379
10.	†1778	Edward Machen	English Bicknor, Glos	S	Pevsner, *Glos: Vale & Forest of Dean*, 1976, 183
11.	?1781	John Woodcock	Byford, Herefs		*Gunnis* 1968, 379
12.	?1788	Mary Trahern	Lugwardine, Herefs		*Gunnis* 1968, 379
13.	?1789	William Tolderly	Leominster, Herefs		*Gunnis* 1968, 379
14.	?1798	Philip Turner	Rington, Herefs		GPC

TABARY, James fl 1682–86

A French carver, he was admitted to the franchise of the City of Dublin in 1682. A John Tabary 'sculptor' and Louis Tabary 'carver' were admitted to the franchise in 1685 (*Strickland* 2, 1913, 422).

Architectural Sculpture

1.	1686	Rail panels and communion table Payment(s): £250	wd	Royal Hospital, Kilmainham, chapel	*Strickland* 2, 1913, 422

TACONET, Charles 1766–93

He joined the Royal Academy Schools in November 1788, winning a silver medal the following year (2). In 1790 he was awarded the gold medal for a biblical subject (1), submitted with a 'sketch' of *Dares & Entellus*. In 1790 he was described in the RA catalogue as a medallist of 12 Queen Anne Street. He died in 1793 and his widow, Martha, was granted a small pension by the Academy (Academy Archives in *Gunnis* 1968, 380).

Literary References: *Hutchison* 1960–62, 150; *Gunnis* 1968, 380

Statues

1.	1790	A part of the history of Samson	[RA, London, gold medal]; untraced	RA Premium list

Reliefs

2.	1791	Design for a medal with a portrait of Burke	[Exhib RA, London, 278]; untraced	*Graves* VII, 1905–6, 317

Miscellaneous

3.	1789	Model of an academy figure or a bas-relief	[RA, London, silver medal]; untraced	RA Premium list
4.	1790	The Death of Milo	[Exhib RA, London, 522]; untraced	*Graves* VII, 1905–6, 317
5.	1790	Venus instructing Cupid in archery	[Exhib RA, London, 535]; untraced	*Graves* VII, 1905–6, 317
6.	1792	Atlas	[Exhib RA, London, 720]; untraced	*Graves* VII, 1905–6, 317

TADOLINI, Adamo 1788–1868

One of an Italian family of sculptors, he worked in Bologna and then in Rome where he was considered to be **Antonio Canova**'s best pupil. The group of *Ganymede and the eagle* was ordered by the 6th Duke of Devonshire on 10 December 1822 after he saw the model in Tadolini's studio in Rome (1). His son Scipione was responsible for a group of *Venus and Cupid* in Joseph Neeld's collection, describes as showing 'the result of rigorous academic training' (*JKB* 1966, 712).

Literary References: *Grove* vol 30, 233 (Stefani)

Statues

1.	1823	Ganymede with the eagle of Jove Payment(s): 350 luigi	m	Chatsworth, Derbys	*Devonshire Diaries*, 19 Dec 1822, 20 Dec 1822; New Building, Chatsworth; *JKB* 1972 (3), 326, 327, 331 (repr)

TAIRE, of Kendal fl 1817?

He was responsible for a large tablet with a heavenly crown, descending dove, palm branches, Bibles, etc. 'so typical of the period' (*Gunnis* 1968, 380).

Funerary Monuments

1.	?1817	Margaret Chippindale		Skipton, W R Yorks	S	*Gunnis* 1968, 380

TANNER, John Sigismund fl 1706–75

For further information the reader is referred to *Pyke* 1973, 145–6

TARAGNOLA, Chevalier G fl c1818–20

He exhibited at the Royal Academy, 1815–1820. Garves describes him as 'painter and sculptor'. There are variant spellings of his name: 'J Targnola' showed from 89 High Holborn in 1815; 'Targnola' gave his address as 4 Rathbone Place in 1816; 'Chev. G Taragnola' was at 4 Rathbone Place in 1818 and 'C G Taragnola' was still at 4 Rathbone Place in 1820.

Literary References: *Graves* VII, 1905–6, 320–1

Funerary Monuments				
1.	1818	Model for a monument of a British hero	[Exhib RA, London, 1088]; untraced	*Graves* VII, 1905–6, 321; *Gunnis* 1968, 380
Reliefs				
2.	1816	Bas-relief of 'Victory Presenting two Dying British Heroes to Britannia'	[Exhib RA, London, 920]	*Graves* VII, 1905–6, 321; *Gunnis* 1968, 380
Miscellaneous				
3.	1815	Jacob deceived by Laban	[Exhib RA, London, 529]; untraced	*Graves* VII, 1905–6, 320
4.	1820	Bacchus and Ariadne	[Exhib RA, London, 400]; untraced	*Graves* VII, 1905–6, 321

TARRANT, of Swindon fl c1782

Funerary Monuments

1.	?1782	Frances Tyrell	s	Harwell, Berks	S	*Gunnis* 1968, 380

TATE, Christopher J A, of Newcastle-on-Tyne 1812–41

He was apprenticed to **R G Davies of Newcastle** and after he became free he worked as an assistant to **David Dunbar II** in Newcastle. After a few years in the latter's studio, he set up for himself as a sculptor and produced first a *Dying Christ Suitable for Catholic Chapels* (**9**), and later a statue of 'Blind Willie' (**3**).

Tate then turned his attention to busts, and carved, among others, likenesses of the Duke of Northumberland, Lord Byron, Henry Phillips, the singer, and Sheridan Knowles (**4, 5, 6, 7**). Apparently he met with some success, for the *Gentleman's Magazine* in its obituary, which is the principal source for his life, opined that 'for execution, precision and arrangement', the busts could 'scarcely be surpassed'. The same article also mentioned his *Judgement of Paris* and *Musidora* (**10, 11**) which, the writer thought, 'would have done credit to an artist of greater experience'.

In 1838 the sculptor carved the very fine Royal coat of arms in the pediment of Newcastle theatre (**8**). At the time of his death he was working on a statue of the Duke of Northumberland, to be erected in front of the Master Mariners' Asylum at Tynemouth (**2**), but the figure had to be completed by his former master, R G Davies.

Tate, who was a consumptive, went to Malta in an attempt to regain his health, but sailed for home when he realized that his end was near. He died on 22 March 1841, aged 29, soon after his ship reached London, leaving his widow and children totally unprovided for. The obituary notice concluded 'his store of information was inexhaustible and whatever the subject under discussion, Mr. Tate was always able to take a prominent part' (*GM*).

Literary References: *GM*, XVI, July 1841, 102; *Gunnis* 1968, 380; *Usherwood* 2000, 336

Funerary Monuments					
1.	†1836	Robert Wastney		St Thomas, Newcastle upon Tyne, Northumbs	Pevsner, *Northumbs*, 1992, 430
Statues					
2.	1839–1841	Hugh, 3rd Duke of Northumberland (co-sculptor: R G Davies, of Newcastle)	s	Master Mariners' asylum, Tynemouth, Northumbs	*Usherwood* 2000, 210–11 (repr)
3.	nd	Blind Willie		Untraced	*Gunnis* 1968, 380
Busts					
4.	c1841	Hugh, 3rd Duke of Northumberland		Untraced	*Gunnis* 1968, 380
5.	nd	George, Lord Byron		Untraced	*Gunnis* 1968, 380
6.	nd	Henry Phillips, the singer		Untraced	*Gunnis* 1968, 380
7.	nd	Sheridan Knowles		Untraced	*Gunnis* 1968, 380
Architectural Sculpture					
8.	1856	Royal Arms	s	Theatre Royal, Newcastle, Northumbs, pediment	*Usherwood* 2000, 118 (repr)
Miscellaneous					
9.	nd	'Dying Christ Suitable for Catholic Chapels'		Untraced	*Gunnis* 1968, 380
10.	nd	Judgement of Paris		Untraced	*Gunnis* 1968, 380
11.	nd	Musidora		Untraced	*Gunnis* 1968, 380

TATE, W K, of London fl 1828–34

His name is transcribed variously: he is listed among RA exhibitors as 'Tate, W Christopher', then as 'W K Tate' and finally as 'W H Tate'. He lived at 4 Ryder's Court, Leicester Square from 1828 to 1833.

Literary References: *Graves* VII, 1905–6, 323; *Gunnis* 1968, 380

Busts

1.	1828	George, Lord Byron	[Exhib Soc of BA, London, 882]; untraced	*Mag of Art* 1893–4, 258; *Johnson* 1975, 452
2.	1828	Sir Walter Scott	[Exhib Soc of BA, London, 880]; untraced	*Johnson* 1975, 452
3.	1828	Unidentified gentleman	[Exhib RA, London, 1163]; untraced	*Graves* VII, 1905–6, 323
4.	1828	Unidentified gentleman	[Exhib RA, London, 1165]; untraced	*Graves* VII, 1905–6, 323

5.	1829	Hon George Agar-Ellis MP, FRS		[Exhib RA, London, 1208]; untraced		*Graves* VII, 1905–6, 323; *Gunnis* 1968, 380
6.	1829	Major Bridgeman		[Exhib RA, London, 1213]; untraced		*Graves* VII, 1905–6, 323; *Gunnis* 1968, 380
7.	1829	Miss Judd		[Exhib RA, London, 1185]; untraced		*Graves* VII, 1905–6, 323
8.	1829	Miss Tennison		[Exhib RA, London, 1188]; untraced		*Graves* VII, 1905–6, 323
9.	1833	John Lawless		[Exhib RA, London, 1193]; untraced		*Graves* VII, 1905–6, 323
10.	1834	Henry Philip Hope	b	Ex coll Rupert Gunnis; untraced		*Gunnis* 1968, 380
11.	nd	Maria de Gloria, Queen of Portugal	w	Hughenden, Bucks	S	GPC
Miscellaneous						
12.	1827	Arthur, 1st Duke of Wellington	w	Royal Coll	SD	*Pyke* 1973, 174

TATEM, Edward fl *c*1785

Funerary Monuments						
1.	†1785	John Marris		Hough-on-the-Hill, Lincs	S	Pevsner, *Lincs*, 1989, 400

TATHAM, Benjamin and William, of Folkingham fl *c*1810–39

Funerary Monuments						
1.	†1810	William Farmer		Hough-on-the-Hill, Lincs		Pevsner, *Lincs*, 1989, 400
2.	1811	Mary Eastland		Folkingham, Lincs	S	*Gunnis* 1968, 381
3.	1825	Jackson Farmer (†1810)		Hough-on-the-Hill, Lincs	S	Pevsner, *Lincs*, 1989, 400
4.	?1831	Rebecca Chamberlain		Billingborough, Lincs	S	GPC
5.	1839	George Wakefield		East Stoke, Notts	S	*Gunnis* 1968, 381

TATHAM, Frederick 1805–78

The eldest son of the architect, Charles Heathcote Tatham (1772–1842), he worked as a sculptor and miniature painter. Tatham entered St Paul's School in the City of London on 5 May 1817 and in due course married Harriet Williams, the daughter of a well-known button maker of St Martin's Lane, London, by whom he had three children. He was living at 1 Queen Street, Mayfair in 1824, the year he was awarded the silver palette from the Society of Arts (**4**), but it was not until 1833 that he joined the Royal Academy Schools, aged 28, on the recommendation of J Phillips, RA. At this time he gave his address as 72 Newman Street. He exhibited a large number of portrait miniatures at the RA, but between 1829 and 1836 he was active as a sculptor, and showed nearly 40 portrait busts at the Academy. He also showed at the British Institution (**1, 46, 47**). The head of an antique warrior (**8**) is a severe, hard-edged portrait, almost certainly modelled from life. *The Library of Fine Arts* found a portrait of Lord Eldon equally forbidding (**9**), writing 'Why do artists give so grim an expression to the features of Lord Eldon? . . . any stranger, unacquainted with the features of the noble Earl, would take him for a headsman' (vol 1, 1832, 432).

The Tathams were close friends of William Blake and his wife. When Mrs Blake was taken mortally ill, she sent for Harriet Tatham and died in her arms. An undated letter survives from Tatham to Soane in which he says that 'at the demise of the Widow of the celebrated William Blake' he had become possessed 'of all the residue of his Works, being Drawings sketches & Copper Plates'. These he offered to sell to Soane (Soane, Priv Corr II T 2/1). Tatham attached himself to the Irvingites and became an itinerant preacher, usually speaking in Regents Park, London. Towards the end of his life he gave up art, and was employed exclusively by the sect. (Add inf. Mrs Knapp, née Tatham)

Literary References: RSA *Transactions*, 1824, vol 42, xlvi; *Gunnis* 1968, 380; *Penny* 1992, III, 166

Archival References: RA Admissions; GPC

Funerary Monuments						
1.	1828	A monumental sketch		[Exhib BI, London, 519]; untraced		*Graves* 1875, 528
2.	†1831	Ponsonby family members, tablet		Fiddown, Co Kilkenny	S	*Potterton* 1975, 83
3.	1831	The orphans, 'study for a monument'		[Exhib RA, London, 1152]; untraced		*Graves* VII, 1905–6, 325
Statues						
4.	1824	Model of a figure after the antique	p	[Soc of A, silver palette]; untraced		RSA *Transactions*, 1824, vol 42, xlvi
5.	1829	John, 1st Earl of Eldon (†1838)		Eldon Schools, Vauxhall, London		*Gunnis* 1968, 380
Busts						
6.	1829	A negro's head		[Exhib Soc of BA, London, 863]; untraced		*Johnson* 1975, 452
7.	1830	C H Tatham	m	[Exhib RA, London, 1262]; untraced		*Graves* VII, 1905–6, 325
8.	1830	Head of an antique warrior	m	Ashmolean WA 1988.301	SD	*Penny* 1992, III, 166 (repr)
9.	1830	John, 1st Earl of Eldon 'as Chancellor' Model(s): extant	m	[Exhib RA, London, 1831, 1215]; NPG, London 181	S	*Library of Fine Arts* 1831, vol 1, 432; *Graves*, VII, 1905–6, 325; *Gunnis* 1968, 380
10.	1830	Unidentified clergyman		[Exhib Soc of BA, London, 849]; untraced		*Johnson* 1975, 452
11.	1831	John Colley	m	[Exhib RA, London, 1200]; untraced		*Graves* VII, 1905–6, 325; *Gunnis* 1968, 380
12.	1832	'the Earl of Eldon, ex-Chancellor of Great Britain'.		[Exhib RA, London, 1133]; untraced		*Graves* VII, 1905–6, 325
13.	1835	Edward Foss		[Exhib RA, London, 731]; untraced		*Graves* VII, 1905–6, 325
14.	1835	Hon George Neville		[Exhib RA, London, 525]; untraced		*Graves* VII, 1905–6, 325; *Gunnis* 1968, 380
15.	1835	Robert Snow		[Exhib RA, London, 549]; untraced		*Graves* VII, 1905–6, 325
16.	1835	Robert Snow Junr		[Exhib RA, London, 427]; untraced		*Graves* VII, 1905–6, 325
17.	1836	Edward Irving MA		[Exhib RA, London, 551]; untraced		*Graves* VII, 1905–6, 325; *Gunnis* 1968, 380
18.	1836	Edward Walpole		[Exhib RA, London, 892]; untraced		*Graves* VII, 1905–6, 325; *Gunnis* 1968, 380
19.	1837	Charles Tatham		Lord Northampton's almshouses, Greenwich	D	*Gunnis* 1968, 380
20.	1839	Henry Knyvett		[Exhib RA, London, 873]; untraced		*Graves* VII, 1905–6, 325
21.	1839	Miss Bicknell		[Exhib RA, London, 789]; untraced		*Graves* VII, 1905–6, 325
22.	1839	Montagu Tatham		[Exhib RA, London, 627]; untraced		*Graves* VII, 1905–6, 325
23.	1840	T Conway Helps		[Exhib RA, London, 785]; untraced		*Graves* VII, 1905–6, 325
24.	1842	Hon Captain Cavendish		[Exhib RA, London, 820]; untraced		*Graves* VII, 1905–6, 325

25.	1842	Mrs Garnier		[Exhib RA, London, 680]; untraced	*Graves* VII, 1905–6, 325
26.	1842	Rt Hon General Sir George Hewett, Bart, GCB		[Exhib RA, London, 598]; untraced	*Graves* VII, 1905–6, 325
27.	1842	The Very Rev Thomas Garnier		[Exhib RA, London, 644]; untraced Other versions: Exhib RA, London, 1854, 994	*Graves* VII, 1905–6, 325
28.	1843	Charles Deacon		[Exhib RA, London, 713]; untraced	*Graves* VII, 1905–6, 325
29.	1843	Mrs Hatchard		[Exhib RA, London, 972]; untraced	*Graves* VII, 1905–6, 325
30.	1843	Robert Tatham		[Exhib RA, London, 652]; untraced	*Graves* VII, 1905–6, 325
31.	1843	Signor Lablache		[Exhib RA, London, 1160]; untraced	*Graves* VII, 1905–6, 325
32.	1844	Henry Hodding		[Exhib RA, London, 898]; untraced	*Graves* VII, 1905–6, 325
33.	1844	J Grove, MD		[Exhib RA, London, 902]; untraced	*Graves* VII, 1905–6, 325
34.	1844	Joseph Martineau		[Exhib RA, London, 945]; untraced	*Graves* VII, 1905–6, 325
35.	1845	George Palmer		[Exhib RA, London, 688]; untraced	*Graves* VII, 1905–6, 325
36.	1845	Hon Frederick Walpole		[Exhib RA, London, 978]; untraced	*Graves* VII, 1905–6, 325
37.	1845	Samuel Manning		[Exhib RA, London, 1059]; untraced	*Graves* VII, 1905–6, 325
38.	1846	Albert, the infant son of Viscount Sandon		[Exhib RA, London, 1106]; untraced	*Graves* VII, 1905–6, 326
39.	1846	Captain Hart		[Exhib RA, London, 1152]; untraced	*Graves* VII, 1905–6, 326
40.	1846	Hugh, the eldest son of the Hon Frederick Ryder		[Exhib RA, London, 748]; untraced	*Graves* VII, 1905–6, 326
41.	1846	Mrs Hart		[Exhib RA, London, 728]; untraced	*Graves* VII, 1905–6, 325
42.	1853	Mrs Marsh		[Exhib RA, London, 909]; untraced	*Graves* VII, 1905–6, 326
43.	1853	Rev T Protheroe		[Exhib RA, London, 943]; untraced	*Graves* VII, 1905–6, 326
44.	1854	David Veasy		[Exhib RA, London, 1043]; untraced	*Graves* VII, 1905–6, 326
Miscellaneous					
45.	1829	The angel Gabriel, sketch		[Exhib Soc of BA, London, 847]; untraced	*Johnson* 1975, 452
46.	1829	The dying warrior		[Exhib BI, London, 541]; untraced	*Graves* 1875, 528
47.	1829	The enslaved tyrant		[Exhib BI, London, 535]	*Graves* 1875, 528
48.	1837	My comrade's grave		[Exhib RA, London, 578]; untraced	*Graves* VII, 1905–6, 325
49.	1839	'– Bowler'		[Exhib RA, London, 590]; untraced	*Graves* VII, 1905–6, 325

TAUNTON AND BROWN fl *c*1793

Funerary Monuments

1.	†1793	John Barnfather	St Giles-in-the-Fields, Holborn	S	Pevsner, *London: N*, 1998, 259

TAYLER, Theophilus fl *c*1830

For further information the reader is referred to *Pyke* 1973, 148 and *Pyke* 1981, 40.

TAYLOR, Burder fl 1763

He was paid for work at Staunton Harold Hall, Leics in 1763 when it was being rebuilt.

Architectural Sculpture

1.	1763	Keystone profile and Ionic capitals	s	[Staunton Harold Hall, Leics, south west front (keystone), doorcase (capitals)]; untraced	Archives, Earl Ferrers in GPC

TAYLOR, E, of Stratford-on-Avon fl *c*1829

Funerary Monuments

1.	?1829	Philip Wren	Wroxall, Warks	S	*Gunnis* 1968, 383

TAYLOR, H 1805–

He joined the Royal Academy Schools in 1825, and in 1843, whilst living at 16 Dover Street, he showed a model at the Academy.

Literary References: *Graves* VII, 1905–6, 336; *Gunnis* 1968, 381

Statues

1.	1843	Model of a horse	[Exhib RA, London, 1461]; untraced	*Graves* VII, 1905–6, 336; *Gunnis* 1968, 381

TAYLOR, Henry, of London fl 1724

Chimneypieces

1.	1724	Description not available	m	[Parson's house, St John Camberwell, Red Lion Square, London]; untraced	TNA C108/40 in GPC

TAYLOR, James, of Sheffield fl 1797

His figures of *Faith* and *Charity*, modelled in wax, were in the window of Robert Ramsay of Sheffield, a carver and gilder, when they attracted the attention of the young **Francis Chantrey** in 1797, and caused him to apprentice himself to Ramsay. Taylor later carved these two works for Sheffield Infirmary. While still an apprentice Chantrey accompanied Taylor to Renishaw, Derbys and to Wentworth Woodhouse in Yorkshire, where Taylor was engaged on decorative work.

Archival References: GPC citing John Holland, *Memorials of Sir Francis Chantrey*

Statues					
1.	nd	Faith and Charity, figures	s	[Sheffield Infirmary, W R Yorks]; untraced	GPC
Architectural Sculpture					
2.	nd	Decorative work (co-sculptor: Sir Francis Legatt Chantrey RA)		[Renishaw, Derbys]; untraced	GPC
3.	nd	Decorative work (co-sculptor: Sir Francis Legatt Chantrey RA)		[Wentworth House, W R Yorks]; untraced	GPC

TAYLOR, John fl 1764

Reliefs

1.	1764	Model for a medallion depicting 'Asia' and 'Asiatics offering presents. . .to Britannia their protectress'	[Soc of A, premium, 10 gns]; untraced	RSA *Minutes*, 1763–64, seq 3 fol 83

TAYLOR, Michael, of York 1760–1848

A prolific maker of church monuments, principally in Yorkshire, he was born at Felton, Northumbs. He became a freeman of York in 1803 and from 1801–10 was responsible for much stone-carving at York Minster, including foliage on the west front, figures of significant historical figures from the north of England, and a statue of Henry VI for the organ-screen, described by Hargrove as 'most admirably executed by Mr Michael Taylor, a sculptor of considerable merit' (**60, 61**). Aylmer notes that he worked with **Francis Bernasconi** on repair work including a statue and finial on the canopy gable of Archbishop Greenfield's tomb in St Nicholas's chapel. In 1814–18 he was employed in restoration work at Skelton church, where he was responsible for all the stone-carving (**62**). A correspondent in the *Builder*, who saw him just before he died, described all the workmen employed by Graham, the architect, as 'well skilled in Gothic art and accustomed to it from boyhood' and Taylor as 'one of the most intelligent and careful of these'. This writer met him when 'a very old man' and felt after his meeting that the accuracy of the restoration 'may be fully relied on' (*Builder* 1846, 317).

Taylor also produced a large number of monuments and tablets featuring a conventional vocabulary of urns, sarcophagi, draperies and paterae. Gunnis singles out the Goodriche, with its charming swags of flowers and the Kingston, which has a relief of a mourning woman (**13, 21**).

In the 1841 census, compiled when he was 80, he was described as a sculptor, living with a general servant at Liberty of Mint Yard, York. He was buried at St Lawrence, York, where his tombstone stated that he died on 16 November 1848, and that he was 'for many years a skilful sculptor in the City'.

Literary References: 1841 census; *Gunnis* 1968, 381; *Aylmer* 1977, 182, 260, 462, 464–5

Will: PRO/FRC PROB 11/2049

Funerary Monuments

1.	†1774	Unidentified subjects, tablets	Kirkby Moorside, N R Yorks		Pevsner, *Yorks: N R*, 1966, 215
2.	?1782	Rev John Scott	Holy Trinity, Leeds, W R Yorks		GPC
3.	†1789	Thomas Comber and family members	Stonegrave, N R Yorks		Pevsner, *Yorks: N R*, 1966, 360
4.	1795	John Farr Abbott (†1794)	York Minster, north choir aisle		*Aylmer* 1977, 462, n65
5.	†1796	Theophilus Davye Garencières	St Helen, York	S	Pevsner, *Yorks E R & York*, 1995, 167
6.	?1797	Susannah Lloyd	Swillington, W R Yorks		*Gunnis* 1968, 381
7.	†1798	Edward Tipping	York Minster, All Saints Chapel	S	*Aylmer* 1977, 463, n65; *Pattison and Murray* 2001, 101
8.	†1798	Lady Mary Hoar	York Minster, south choir aisle		*Aylmer* 1977, 462–3, n65
9.	?1799	Aretas Akers	Fulford, N R Yorks		GPC
10.	†1800	Christopher Wormley	Riccall, E R Yorks		Pevsner, *Yorks: E R & York*, 1995, 655
11.	?1800	John Lea	Sowerby, W R Yorks		*Gunnis* 1968, 381
12.	†1800	Mrs Frances Legard	Etton, E R Yorks		Pevsner, *Yorks: E R & York*, 1995, 410
13.	†1801	Rev Henry Goodriche	Sutton-on-the-Forest, N R Yorks		Pevsner, *Yorks: N R*, 1966, 361
14.	?1803	Christopher Oxley	Ripon Cathedral, W R Yorks		*Gunnis* 1968, 381
15.	?1803	James Saunders	All Saints, Pavement, York		*Gunnis* 1968, 381
16.	†1803	John Edwards	Market Weighton, E R Yorks		Pevsner, *Yorks: E R & York*, 1995, 610
17.	?1803	Mary Walker	Darfield, W R Yorks		GPC
18.	†1803	Tate Wilkinson	All Saints, Pavement, York		Pevsner, *Yorks: E R & York*, 1995, 160
19.	†1805	Mr and Mrs Wharton	Scalby, N R Yorks		Pevsner, *Yorks: N R*, 1966, 319
20.	†1806	Emily Cleaver	Nunnington, N R Yorks		Pevsner, *Yorks: N R*, 1966, 274
21.	*c*1806	Evelyn, 2nd Duke of Kingston (†1773)	Holme Pierrepont, Notts		*Gunnis* 1968, 381; Pevsner, *Notts*, 1979, 147
22.	?1807	Samuel Waterhouse	Halifax, W R Yorks		*Gunnis* 1968, 381
23.	†1808	Thomas Hartley	St Helen, York		Pevsner, *Yorks: E R & York*, 1995, 167
24.	?1809	Thomas Kilvington	Ripon Cathedral, W R Yorks		*Gunnis* 1968, 381
25.	?1810	Sir Walter Vavasour	Roman Catholic Chapel, Sutton-on-the-Forest, N R Yorks		*Gunnis* 1968, 381
26.	†1810	Timothy Hutchinson	Old Church, Eggleston, Durham		Pevsner, *Durham*, 1983, 263
27.	?1810	William Comber	Stonegrave, N R Yorks		*Gunnis* 1968, 381
28.	†1811	Thomas Terry	Ripon Cathedral, W R Yorks	S	
29.	†1812	Mary Bagwell	Clonmel, Co Tipperary		*Potterton* 1975, 83
30.	†1813	Charles W Thompson	St Mary, Cottingham, E R Yorks		Pevsner, *Yorks: E R & York*, 1995, 387
31.	†1815	Unidentified subject, tablet	All Saints, Northallerton, N R Yorks		Pevsner, *Yorks: N R*, 1966, 271
32.	†1816	Rev J Minithorpe	Folkton, E R Yorks		Pevsner, *Yorks: E R & York*, 1995, 423
33.	†1816	Rev John Forth	Terrington, N R Yorks		Pevsner, *Yorks: N R*, 1966, 364
34.	†1818	Unidentified subject, tablet	Bolton-upon-Swale, N R Yorks		Pevsner, *Yorks: N R*, 1966, 82
35.	?1819	Anna Crompton	Guisley, W R Yorks		GPC
36.	†1819	Rev George Skelding	Market Weighton, E R Yorks		Pevsner, *Yorks: E R & York*, 1995, 610
37.	†1819	Rev John Clark	Goodmanham, E R Yorks		Pevsner, *Yorks: E R & York*, 1995, 438
38.	?1820	John Babley	Masham, N R Yorks		*Gunnis* 1968, 381
39.	†1820	Thomas Norcliffe	Langton, E R Yorks		Pevsner, *Yorks: E R & York*, 1995, 593
40.	†1823	William Briggs	St Cuthbert, York		Pevsner, *Yorks: E R & York*, 1995, 165
41.	?1824	John Raper	Aberford, W R Yorks		*Gunnis* 1968, 381
42.	†1826	Alexander Mather	Elvington, E R Yorks		Pevsner, *Yorks: E R & York*, 1995, 404
43.	†1826	John Robinson Foulis	West Heslerton, E R Yorks		Pevsner, *Yorks: E R & York*, 1995, 745
44.	†1826	John Roper	St Olave, York		Pevsner, *Yorks: E R & York*, 1995, 175

No.	Date	Subject		Location		Reference
45.	†1826	Unidentified subject, tablet		Bridlington Priory, E R Yorks		Pevsner, *Yorks: E R & York*, 1995, 346
46.	†1827	Elizabeth Hill Darwin		Elston, Notts		Pevsner, *Notts*, 1979, 122
47.	†1827	Unidentified subject, tablet		St Stephen, York		Pevsner, *Yorks: E R & York*, 1995, 177
48.	*c*1828	Hon Dorothy Langley (†1824)		York Minster, north choir aisle	S	*Aylmer* 1977, 465, n75; *Pattison and Murray* 2001, 113–4
49.	†1828	Thomas Ewbank		Settrington, E R Yorks		Pevsner, *Yorks: E R & York*, 1995, 676
50.	?1828	Thomas Lloyd		Pickering, N R Yorks		GPC
51.	?1828	Thomas Norcliffe		Langdon, Durham		*Gunnis* 1968, 381
52.	†1830	David Poole		St Olave, York		Pevsner, *Yorks: E R & York*, 1995, 175
53.	†1832	George Strickland		Wintringham, E R Yorks		Pevsner, *Yorks: E R & York*, 1995, 760
54.	†1832	Joshua Crompton		Holy Trinity, Micklegate, York		Pevsner, *Yorks: E R & York*, 1995, 163
55.	?1833	Countess Harcourt		Masham, N R Yorks		*Gunnis* 1968, 381
56.	?1835	Thomas Eadon		Selby, W R Yorks		*Gunnis* 1968, 381
57.	†1838	Rev Thomas Harrison		Westow, E R Yorks		Pevsner, *Yorks: E R & York*, 1995, 747
Statues						
58.	1810	King Henry VI		York Minster, organ screen		*Hargrove* 1818, 2, 77; *Allen* 1829, 284; *Aylmer* 1977, 182; Pevsner, *Yorks E R & York*, 1995, 144
Chimneypieces						
59.	1802–1803	'stonework for the Chimney-piece in the Gallery' Payment(s): £3 10s		Castle Howard, N R Yorks		Castle Howard archives in GPC; *Carlisle Ac Exhibs*, 1973
Architectural Sculpture						
60.	1802	Percy and Vavasour, figures	s	York Minster, central doorway		*Gunnis* 1968, 381
61.	1801–1816	Statuettes and foliage (restoration)		York Minster, west front		Pevsner, *Yorks: E R & York*, 1995, 138
62.	1814–1818	Stone carving (repairs)	s	Christ the Consoler, Skelton, W R Yorks		*Gunnis* 1968, 381

TAYLOR, of Dublin fl *c*1810

Potterton says of him: 'He was presumably just a mason-stonecutter, as this memorial [to the Kearneys (**1**)] displays little or no knowledge of monumental design. He may well have executed chimneypieces; and certainly the manner in which he arranges his motifs rather resembles the arrangement of ornaments on a mantleshelf' (*Potterton* 1975, 83).

No.	Date	Subject	Location		Reference
Funerary Monuments					
1.	†1810	James Kearney	Gowran, Co Kilkenny	S	*Potterton* 1975, 83

TAYLOR, of Shug Lane, London

An undated trade card for 'Taylor Statuary Mason &c upper end of Shug Lane next to the Haymarket' is pasted into AM Broadley *The Story of the Haymarket*, 1911, (MSS, CWAC, fol 565).

TAYLOR, Robert I *c*1690–1742

He was the father of the sculptor-architect **Sir Robert Taylor** (1714–1788) and a successful master mason and monumental sculptor in his own right. The son of a yeoman from Campden, Taylor was apprenticed to the mason Richard Garbut on 6 December 1705, and became free of the Masons' Company on 2 October 1712. He was master of the Company in 1733 and clearly took his civic responsibilities seriously for he became a captain in the City's trained bands. In 1723 he subscribed to John Dart's *Westmonasterium* as 'Mr R. T., Mason, in Greyfriars' and in 1726 enodorsed Dart's *History of the Cathedral Church of Canterbury* in like manner.

Taylor worked for several of the City Livery Companies. He was paid £19 7s for unspecified masonry, commissioned by the Ironmongers' Company in 1722, and his work for Masons' Hall included a chimneypiece (**15**). He received £69 from the Grocers' Company for decorative carving undertaken in 1735–1736 (**18**) and Gunnis suggests that he acted as master-mason for the Barber Surgeons when their theatre was rebuilt to designs by Lord Burlington. From 1725–39 he was mason for the Royal College of Physicians and he was also responsible for a good deal of building work at St Bartholomew's Hospital, 1728–40 (**14, 16**). In 1728 he rented two tenements in Duck Lane from the governors of the latter Hospital. When the contract to build the London Mansion House went to tender on 16 May 1738 Taylor, **Christopher Horsnaile II** and a haberdasher, John Townsend, competed with a rival team of masons headed by **Thomas Dunn** and **John Devall**. After much jockeying all five shared the contract, providing obelisks, plinths and paving in addition to structural work.

Records of Taylor's contribution to domestic buildings are scant but the Hoare partnership ledgers record a chimneypiece supplied to Stourhead in 1724 (**13**). In 1732 he received a further £150 for unidentified work at Stourhead and in 1733 another £98. Gunnis thinks these payments were probably for chimneypieces, but tentatively suggests that Taylor may have had something to do with the building of Alfred's Tower in the grounds, or with the carving of King Alfred's statue.

Taylor was responsible for a number of elaborate, if repetitive, monuments in which he made use of a range of coloured marbles. The Kidder (**1**) has a reclining female in a skimpy shift gesturing towards the plain slab behind her, which is framed by a curtain, winged cherubs' heads and sunbeams within composite columns. The Askel (**2**) is a wall monument with pilasters, flaming lamps, and cherubs at either side, one clasping a skull. Gunnis considers the Deacon (**7**) his best work and Whinney notes that it is in the manner of Francis Bird. It has a reclining effigy in contemporary dress, with a baroque flourish to the draperies covering the lower body. Deacon again gestures at the inscription slab behind him and he clasps a skull in the other hand. The Corinthian frame is decorated with heads of *putti* backed by clouds, and sunbeams slant through. The Raymond (**4**) is an architectural wall-tablet with an armorial shield and winged cherub-heads on the apron, and the Napier (**9**) uses a similar vocabulary of ornaments, but includes two stocky females on either side of the architectural frame. The Chester (**12**) is a little different, for it has a relief panel of Chester's widow and children above the inscription tablet. The classical pilasters are flanked by seated cherubs and two boys sit at the bottom of the slab on the gadrooned base. All the figures gesticulate dramatically.

The names of several apprentices are listed in the archives of the Masons' Company. John Percy joined him in 1715, **Francis Cunningham** in 1722 and **John Mallcott** in 1730. Charles, 'son of Robert Taylor of Christchurch, London, Mason' was apprenticed on 23 June 1737 to Thomas Fletcher of Chipping Campden.

The obituary, written by Horace Walpole in the *Gentleman's Magazine* of the son, Sir Robert Taylor, notes 'His father was the great stone-mason of his time; like Devall in the present day he got a vast deal of money; but again, unlike him altogether, he could not keep what he got. When life was less gaudy than it is now, and when the elegant indulgences of it were rare, old Taylor the mason enjoyed them all. He revelled at a villa in Essex; and as a villa is imperfect without a coach, he thought it necessary to have that too. To drive on thus, at a good rate, is generally thought pretty pleasant by most men; but it is not apt to be pleasant to their heirs. It was so here. For excepting some common schooling; a fee, when he went pupil to **Sir Henry Cheere**, and just enough money to travel on a plan of frugal study to Rome, Robert Taylor got nothing from his father.' (*Anecdotes* 1937, 192). (Add inf, AL/RG)

IR/MGS

Literary References: *Webb* (3), 1957, 116; *Gunnis* 1968, 381; *Whinney* 1988, 248–9; *Jeffery* 1993, 49–50, 67–8, 297, 300; *Colvin* 1995, 962; *Webb* 1999 9, 19, 21, 25, 32

Archival References: Ironmongers, WA, vol 10, fol 19; Masons' Co, Freemen, fol 68; Masons' Co, Court Book, 1705; Court Book, 1722–51 (29 Oct 1742); Apprenticeship Lists, 1737; Charles Taylor, Hoare partnership ledger, 1725–34, 1725–34, fol 272, 22 Dec 1732 (£150); fol 282, 4 July 1733, Joseph Cox's bill to Robert Taylor (£98)

Funerary Monuments

1.	†1703	Bishop Richard Kidder	Wells Cathedral, Somerset	S	C Lib (repr)
2.	1713	Michael Askel (†1697), John Askel (†1697), Susannah Askel (†1698) and Michael Askel (†1712)	Chadshunt, Warks	S	Pevsner, *Warks*, 1966, 226; C Lib (repr)
3.	†1716	Jane Brewer	West Farleigh, Kent	S	Pevsner, *Kent: W & Weald*, 1976, 598; C Lib (repr)
4.	†1720	Raymond family	Belchamp Walter, Essex	S	*Esdaile* 1948 (1), 63; Pevsner, *Essex*, 1965, 83; C Lib (repr)
5.	*c*1720	Sir John Garrard (†1700)	Wheathampstead, Herts	S	Pevsner, *Herts*, 1977, 404
6.	†1721	Abraham Hill	Sutton-at-Hone, Kent	S	Pevsner, *Kent: W & Weald*, 1976, 557; C Lib (repr)
7.	†1721	Thomas Deacon	Peterborough Cathedral, Northants	S	*Esdaile* 1948 (1), 63; *Gunnis* 1968, 381; *Whinney* 1988, 248–9; C Lib (repr)
8.	†1724	Francis Barrell	Rochester Cathedral, Kent	S	Pevsner, *Kent: W & Weald*, 1976, 485; C Lib (repr)
9.	1725	Sir Nathaniel Napier Bt (†1708) and his two wives, Jane (†1692) and Catherine (†1724)	Minterne Magna, Dorset	SD	*Gunnis* 1968, 381; Pevsner, *Dorset*, 1972, 295; C Lib (repr)
10.	†1727	Lady Pennyman	Stainton, N R Yorks	S	Pevsner, *Yorks: N R*, 1966, 353
11.	†1729	William Phillipps	Shepshed, Leics	S	Pevsner, *Leics & Rutland*, 1984, 376
12.	†1732	Robert Chester	Hunsdon, Herts	S	*Esdaile* 1948 (1), 63; *Gunnis* 1968, 381; C Lib (repr)

Chimneypieces

13.	1723	'Chimneypiece &c' Payment(s): £40	[Stourhead, Wilts]; untraced	*Gunnis* 1968, 381
14.	1730	Description unavailable Payment(s): £62	[St Bartholomew's Hospital, City of London]; untraced	*Gunnis* 1968, 381
15.	1732	Description unavailable	[Masons' Hall, City of London]; untraced	*Gunnis* 1968, 381

Architectural Sculpture

16.	1728–1740	Decorative work including 'leaves at the bottom of the scrolls'	[St Bartholomew's Hospital, City of London]; untraced	*Gunnis* 1968, 381, quoting Hospital archives

Miscellaneous

17.	1732–1733	Unidentified work Payment(s): £248	[Stourhead, Wilts]; untraced	*Gunnis* 1968, 381
18.	1735–1736	Decorative carving Payment(s): £69 10s	[Grocers' Hall, London]; untraced	Grocers WA 1735–6, 14; *Gunnis* 1968, 381

TAYLOR, Sir Robert 1714–88

Though best remembered as a distinguished architect, Taylor trained as a sculptor and practised the profession with considerable success for nearly 30 years. He was born in Woodford, Essex in 1714, the son of **Robert Taylor I.** After 'some common schooling' (*Anecdotes* 1937, 192) he was apprenticed in 1732 to **Sir Henry Cheere** at a fee of £105. Taylor was still working for his master in 1736–37, when payments were recorded to the younger man in Cheere's account at Hoare's Bank. To gain 'more pretension in his profession' (*Farington* vol 16, 5744) Taylor travelled to Rome in the early 1740s 'on a plan of frugal study' (*Anecdotes* 1937, 192), but felt compelled to return home when he heard that his father had fallen ill. He was unable to get passports because of the continental wars and so disguised himself as a friar and crossed hostile territory in the company of a Franciscan monk. He apparently kept his ecclesiastical apparel as a keepsake until his death.

Taylor's father died in October 1742, leaving considerable debts. Although Taylor later told a friend that he had only eighteen pence in his pocket at the time, he was soon able to set up a thriving sculptural practice, thanks to hard work and good connections. He received financial help from the Godfreys of Woodford, a family of distinguished

East India Company merchants to whose memory he later erected a large marble column (**34**). In the mid 1740s he took premises in Spring Gardens near the King's Mews, to the east of Cheere's workshop. On 3 August 1744 he became free by patrimony of the Masons' Company.

In the same year, despite competition from the more established sculptors, **L F Roubiliac, Peter Scheemakers**, Henry Cheere and **Michael Rysbrack**, Taylor won the contract to carve the pediment group for the Mansion House in the City of London (**42**). Vertue suggested that Taylor (who was so unfamiliar to the writer that he mistakenly called him 'Carter') was chosen because he was English, a 'Cittizen & son of a Mason' (*Vertue* III, 122). Taylor executed a large allegorical relief extolling the benefits of trade in London. In April 1746 the architect George Dance told the Mansion House committee that the work was 'very well done' (CLRO Minutes, quoted in *Ward-Jackson* 2003, 242). Interpretations of the iconography appeared in the *London Magazine* and the *Gentleman's Magazine.*

In 1747 Taylor was chosen, apparently without a competition, to carve the monument in Westminster Abbey to Captain Cornewall, a victim of the Battle of Toulon (**22**). This monument was the first in the Abbey to a war hero financed with parliamentary funds and was intended to salvage some glory from a battle which had resulted in two court-martials. The design, depicting *Fame* and *Britannia* on either side of a palm tree above a rocky base, was felt by a French critic, Grosley, to be closer in spirit to the magnificence of a *pompe célebre* than a standing monument (*Grosley* 1772, vol 2, 67). When it was unveiled in February 1755, *The Gentleman's Magazine*, less-concerned with its iconographical qualities than its political significance, called it an 'illustrious instance of national gratitude as well as of good policy' (*GM*, vol 25, 89).

Taylor's other Abbey monument, to Joshua Guest (**17**) was considered by Horace Walpole to be his finest memorial (*Anecdotes* 1937, 193) and Vertue praised the work, adding that the ornaments and the multicoloured marbles had brought Taylor some reputation. Vertue added that Taylor had 'infinitely polishd his work beyond comparison this being another English artist who made the tour of Italy' (*Vertue*, III, 161). In his church monuments Taylor developed an innovative and distinctive vocabulary of motifs: he presented portrait busts *en negligé* (**4, 6, 19**), and made use of medallion portraits (**29, 30**), praying putti precariously placed on a pedestals (**21, 25, 31**) and one almost grotesque weeping widow (**15**). The monuments often incorporated polychrome marbles (**17, 19**) and were framed with floral rococo ornaments (**11, 12, 16**), oak sprigs (**21**), crossed palm branches (**21, 27, 28, 30**), and egg and dart carving (**20, 26**). Taylor may well have repeated these designs. There are several more unsigned works in the British Isles and the former colonies which closely resemble these signed works or else Taylor's surviving drawings. His most ambitious design was for the monument to Henry, Earl of Shelburne at High Wycombe, a multi-figured baroque fantasy which drew heavily on modern Roman models. This was rejected in favour of a design by Peter Scheemakers but Taylor was paid £20 for his trouble. In addition to the identified works he is credited with the monument to Thomas and Robert Crosse, *c*1745, at Nettleswell, Essex and to John, Lord Somers, †1716, at North Mymms, Herts (*Baker* 2000, 51–2, 57, 60, 172 n33, repr; *Bilbey* 2002, 157, repr).

The executed works rarely match the designs in quality and Walpole hinted at one good reason: Taylor's method 'was to *bost*, as they call it, to hew out his heads from the block; and except some few finishing touches, to leave the rest to his workmen' (*Anecdotes* 1937, 193). **Bartholomew Cheney** is his only identified assistant: Smith remembered that Cheney was paid £4 15s a week for carving the figures on the Cornewall monument (*Smith* 1828, vol 1, 151).

Taylor produced some remarkable 'Chinese Chippendale' designs for chimneypieces, a book of which survives at the Taylorian Institute, Oxford. These reproduce in multiple form the floral motifs used on his monuments. In 1750 he supplied a chimneypiece for the London house of Peter Du Cane, a Director of the Bank of England and the East India Company (**38**) as part of a larger project of building and renovation, and this is Taylor's first datable architectural work. Taylor still described himself as a 'statuary' in 1758 (*Survey of London*, vol 29, 141), and he continued to produce monuments until the late 1760s, but his business moved steadily into the field of architecture.

Working chiefly for a City clientele of bankers, East and West Indian merchants, government financiers and lawyers, Taylor became one of the two leading architects of his day. Thomas Hardwick wrote that before Robert Adam entered the lists, Taylor and James Paine 'nearly divided the profession between them' (*Hardwick* 1825, 13). Taylor's architecture, like his sculptural work, made use of recurring elements, such as astylar elevations, vermiculated rustication, cantilevered staircases and rich rococo chimneypieces. His particular strength lay in his designs for compact houses for rich city dwellers and he is often credited with moving the Palladian style towards neoclassicism. His only major public building was the Bank of England (1765–87), now demolished. Walpole said Taylor was responsible for the statue of *Britannia*, pouring coins from a cornucopia, which survives on the pediment of one of the current buildings. This claim is brought into question by a press report of 1733 which records that the commission was originally given to Sir Henry Cheere.

By 1768 Taylor had amassed a fortune of £40,000 and his professional income was £8,000 a year. This is a remarkable achievement, bearing in mind that his first £15,000 was used to clear family debts. At the time of his death he was said to be worth £180,000. Much of this wealth came from his position as surveyor of several London estates, including the Duke of Grafton's. He was surveyor to the Bank of England, the Admiralty, the Foundling Hospital, Greenwich Hospital and Lincoln's Inn. He also held a number of posts in the Office of Works. In 1782 he was knighted, on the occasion of his election as Sheriff of London.

Contemporary sources construct Taylor as a paragon of stoical and devout professionalism. He ate little meat, abstained from alcohol, devoted all his evenings to his wife and a handful of sensible friends, and rarely slept beyond four in the morning. According to Farington he had three rules for growing rich 'viz; rising early, – keeping appointments, – and regular accounts' (*Farington* vol 3, 841). He was said to be attentive to his pupils, and he trained many of the most successful architects of the next generation, notably Samuel Pepys Cockerell and John Nash.

Taylor died on 27 September 1788 at the home in Spring Gardens, London which he had built in 1759. He fell ill after attending the funeral of his friend, the banker and one-time Lord Mayor, Sir Charles Asgill, and died a few days later of a 'violent mortification in the bowels' (*Anecdotes* 1937, 197). After a grandiose funeral attended by over a hundred people, Taylor was laid to rest in a vault near the north-east corner of St Martin-in-the-Fields. The bulk of his fortune was left to the University of Oxford to found an institution for the teaching of modern languages. His will was challenged by Taylor's son, Michel Angelo Taylor MP, but after his death in 1834 the Taylorian Institute was founded in accordance with Taylor's wishes. It houses Taylor's library of architectural books and two volumes of his drawings. Michael Angelo Taylor later commissioned Thomas Malton the Younger to draw and engrave a set of 32 plates of his father's architectural designs (1790–2, SJSM, Ashmolean).

A cenotaph was erected in Poets' Corner, Westminster Abbey asserting that Taylor's 'works entitle him to a distinguished rank in the first Class of British architects.' This verdict has been endorsed by later architectural historians but much less attention has been given to his achievement as a sculptor. Whinney dismissed Taylor's oeuvre as 'clumsy' and 'foolish,' but her view fails to do justice to the Cornewall and Mansion House commissions, nor does it take into account the innovative nature of Taylor's monumental designs. Baker has drawn attention to Taylor's assimilation of continental influences from the works of Gille-Marie Oppenard (1672–1742), Juste Aurele Meissonnier (1695–1750) and Sebastien-Antoine Slodtz (1695–1754), and has concluded that Taylor was one of the three major artists, who, with Sir Henry Cheere and Roubiliac, evolved the rococo style in English sculpture (*Rococo* 1984, 282–3)

MGS

Literary References: *Vertue*, III, 122, 161; *GM*, vol 18, pt 2, 1788, 930–1, reproduced with other obituaries of Taylor in *Anecdotes* 1937, 191–198; *Hardwick* 1825, 13; *Smith* 1828, I, 151; *Builder* 1846, no 194, 505; *Esdaile* 1948 (1), 63–6; *Survey of London*, vol 29, 141; *Gilson* 1975; *Farington passim; Summerson* 1980, 2–5; *Rococo* 1984, 277–309; *Binney* 1984; *Whinney* 1988, 248–9; *Colvin* 1995, 962–7; *Grove* 30, 1996 385–7 (White); *Coutu* 1997, 79, 85; *Craske* 2000 (2), 106; *Ward-Jackson* 2003, 239–41; *ODNB* (Baker)

Collections of Drawings: TI (Arch Tay 1), book of 54 designs, 52 of which are for monuments, pen, pencil, chalk, ink and wash, *Rococo* 1984 297–298, 308 (repr), *Baker* 2000, 65 (repr), *Garstang* 2003, 853 (repr), photos of about 50 of these drawings, Conway; TI (Arch Tay 2) 12, highly finished designs for chimneypieces, pen, ink and wash, *Binney* 1984, reprs 59–62, *Esdaile* 1948 (1), 66 (repr), C Lib (repr); TI (Arch Tay 3), a book of 'Problems in Geometry and Mensuration with Diagrams,' red and black ink.

Portraits of the Sculptor: Anon (possibly William Miller), half length portrait, RIBA, *Binney* 1984, repr 1; Anon, half length portrait, TI (similar to that in RIBA)

Funerary Monuments

1.	†1730	Eldest daughter of Francis Marston Drawing(s): TI, Arch Tay 1, fols 57, 103	Dunstable, Beds		C Lib (repr)
2.	?1741	Robert and Ann Young	Stoke Dameral, Devon		GPC
3.	†1741	William Marshe and family (last member †1741) Drawing(s): TI, Arch Tay 1, fols 30, 58	Dunstable, Beds	S	C Lib (repr)
4.	†1745	Robert Shippen	Brasenose College, Oxford, chapel	S	*Gunnis* 1968, 382
5.	†1745	Sir James Pennyman	Stainton, N R Yorks	S	Pevsner, *Yorks: N R*, 1966, 353
6.	†1746	Christopher (†1745) and John (†1746) Emmott	Colne, Lancs	S	Pevsner, *Lancs: N*, 1969, 106; C Lib (repr)
7.	†1746	Thomas Clarke Drawing(s): TI, Arch Tay 1, fols 30, 58 (work authenticated by drawing)	St Mary, Walthamstow, Essex		C Lib (repr)
8.	†1747	Francis Dickinson	Dunstable, Beds	S	*Esdaile* 1948 (1), 64; Pevsner, *Beds, Hunts & Peterborough*, 1968, 78; C Lib (repr)
9.	†1748	Rev John Finch	All Saints, West Ham, Essex	S	*Physick* 2000–1, 7
10.	†1748	William Phipps	[Westbury, Wilts]; untraced	S	*Whinney* 1988, 248 (repr); *Elliot* 2000, 13
11.	†1749	Elizabeth, Lady Cocks and six children Drawing(s): TI, Arch Tay 1, fol 99 (work authenticated by drawing)	Dumbleton, Glos		C Lib (repr)
12.	†1749	Richard Osborne Drawing(s): TI, Arch Tay 1, fol 99	Wotton-under-Edge, Glos	S	Pevsner, *Glos: Cotswolds*, 1999, 757; C Lib (repr)
13.	?1749	Thomas Panuwell	Tonbridge, Kent	S	*Gunnis* 1968, 382
14.	†1750	Leonard (†1746) and Sarah Gale Drawing(s): TI, Arch Tay 1, fols 30, 58 (monument authenticated by drawing)	Worth, Sussex		C Lib (repr)
15.	†1750	Mary Chetwynd	Grendon, Warks	S	*Whinney* 1988, 249; C Lib (repr)
16.	†1750	Thomas Withers	Barbados Museum and Historical Society	S	
17.	1752	Lieutenant-General Joshua Guest (†1747) Drawing(s): ?TI, Arch Tay 1, fol 90	Westminster Abbey, London, north transept	S	*Vertue* III, 161; *Whinney* 1988, 249, 458 n12; *Rococo* 1984 285, 287 (repr)
18.	†1752	Sir Henry Penrice	Offley, Herts	S	*Baker* 2000, 172 n33; *Whinney* 1988, 249 (repr)
19.	†1752	Thomas Marsh	Womenswold, Kent	S	*Esdaile* 1948 (1), 63; Pevsner, *Kent: N E & E*, 1983, 502; C Lib (repr)
20.	†1753	Anne Pyott Drawing(s): TI, Arch Tay 1, fols 57, 59, 103	St Martin, Canterbury, Kent	S	*Gunnis* 1968, 382; C Lib (repr)
21.	†1754	Elizabeth Townsend Drawing(s): TI, Arch Tay 1, fol 88r	Thorpe, Surrey	S	*Gunnis* 1968, 382; *Whinney* 1988, 458–9, n13; *Craske* 1992, 42 n8; C Lib (repr)
22.	1747–1755	Captain James Cornewall (+1743), with a relief of the Battle of Toulon	Westminster Abbey, London, cloisters, Dean's Yard; formerly nave, south west tower	S	*Rococo* 1984, 284–5, 297 (repr); *Bindman and Baker* 1995, passim (repr); *Baker* 2000, 14–15, 65 (repr); *Garstang* 2003, 851–3 (repr)
23.	†1755	Rev Alexander Young	Wickhambreaux, Kent	S	Pevsner, *Kent: N E & E*, 1983, 497; C Lib (repr)
24.	1756	Richard Freeman Drawing(s): TI, Arch Tay 1, fol 99 (monument authenticated by drawing)	Batsford, Glos		Pevsner, *Glos: Cotswolds*, 1999, 160

25.	1757	Edward Hunter Drawing(s): TI, Arch Tay 1, fol 88r		Maidstone, Kent		*Craske* 1992, 42 n8
26.	†1758	Elizabeth Hamby Drawing(s): TI, Arch Tay 1, fols 57, 103 (monument authenticated by drawing)		Ipswich, Suffolk		
27.	?1759	George Gordon (†1739) Drawing(s): TI, Arch Tay 1, fol 88r		Rochester, Kent		*Craske* 1992, 42, n8; C Lib (repr)
28.	1760	Theophilus Salwey Drawing(s): TI, Arch Tay 1, fol 88r		Ludlow, Salop		*Rococo* 1984, 308; *Craske* 1992, 42, n8
29.	†1761	Richard Emmott Drawing(s): TI, Arch Tay 1, fol 85r		Colne, Lancs	S	*Gunnis* 1968, 382; *Rococo* 1984, 308; C Lib (repr)
30.	†1763	Daniel Adey (†1752), Elizabeth Adey (†1717), Mrs Bridget Adey (†1740), Daniel Adey		Wotton-under-Edge, Glos	S	*Esdaile* 1948 (1), 63, 65 (repr); Pevsner, *Glos: Cotswolds*, 1999, 757
31.	†1763	Joseph Townsend Drawing(s): TI, Arch Tay 1, fol 88r		Honington, Warks		*Whinney* 1988, 458–9, n.13
32.	†1767	Edmund Auberry		St John the Baptist, Pinner, Middx	S	*Binney* 1984, 24; Pevsner, *London: NW*, 1991, 284
33.	†1769	George (†1766) and Philip Jackson Drawing(s): TI, Arch Tay 1, fol 10 (monument authenticated by drawing)		Great Stanmore, Middx, churchyard		
34.	nd	Edward Godfrey and family Payment(s): £1500		Woodford, Essex, churchyard		*Esdaile* 1948 (1), 63, 64; *Gunnis* 1968, 382; *Colvin* 1995, 963
35.	nd	John Fisher Drawing(s): TI, Arch Tay 1, fols 123, 127		Hayes, Middx	S	*Gunnis* 1968, 381; C Lib (repr)
36.	nd	Robartes family, two identical tablets		Dumbleton, Glos	S	*Esdaile* 1948 (1), 63
Chimneypieces						
37.	1750	'Chimneypieces etc' Payment(s): £131		[Longford Castle, Wilts]; untraced		*Gunnis* 1968, 382
38.	1748–1750	Statuary marble; also general repairs to the house Payment(s): £267 plus £167 for repair work	m	[Peter du Cane's residence, St James's Square, London]; untraced		Du Cane Accts, 14 March 1750, Essex RO, D/DDc. A.18, fol 1; *Gunnis* 1968, 382; *Binney* 1984, 24
39.	1751	Description unavailable		[Peter du Cane's residence, Braxted Lodge, Essex]; untraced		*Binney* 1984, 24
40.	c1758	Description unavailable Drawing(s): TI, Arch Tay 2, fol 7r (work authenticated by drawing)		Barlaston Hall, Staffs, west room		*Gomme* 1968, 979 (repr); *Rococo* 1984, 309
41.	1765–1774	Three		[Bank of England, City of London, court room]; untraced		*Binney* 1984, 74
Architectural Sculpture						
42.	1744–1745	The City of London trampling Envy and receiving the benefits of Plenty brought to London by the River Thames, pediment relief Payment(s): £421 18s Drawing(s): Soane	s	Mansion House, City of London		*Jeffery* 1993, 84–85; *Ward-Jackson* 2003, 239–242 (repr)
43.	c1750	Ornaments		Longford Castle, Wilts, north west front		Pevsner, *Wilts*, 1975, 304
Miscellaneous						
44.	1757	Lord Mayor's coach (designs only)		Museum of London		*Binney* 1978, 1596–8 (repr)

TAYLOR, Robert, of Melton Mowbray fl 1706–10

He was employed to build a house in Melton Mowbray, in 1708 for Thomas Coke, but apparently had difficulty in getting Coke to pay him, writing to Coke: 'I was fain to hire many men when your Honour was down and I have paid them as far as I am able and I desire you to consider my condition and relieve me, as I have not neglected your business night nor day, but have left all business to serve you. I beg you to send me an order as speedily as you can' (Archives, Marquess of Lothian). While working at Melbourne, Derbys, Taylor seems to have taken his son, also Robert Taylor, into partnership, for various payments are made out to both men.

Literary References: *Gunnis* 1968, 382

TAYLOR, T, of Soho, Birmingham fl 1818–30

A wax modeller and prize winner, he can perhaps be identified with **W H Taylor of Birmingham**.

Miscellaneous					
1.	1818	Princess Charlotte of Wales	w	[Soc of A, gold Isis medal]; untraced	RSA *Transactions*, 1818, vol 36, xxxii
2.	1826	'Miniature whole length portrait'	w	[Soc of A, gold Isis medal]; untraced	RSA *Transactions*, 1826, vol 44, xliii
3.	1830	'Model of James Watt'		[Exhib Birmingham Soc of A]; untraced	*Gunnis* 1968, 383

TAYLOR, Thomas, of Nottingham fl c1738–before 1755

Lord notes that the two most accomplished local sculptors in the Lincs-Notts area in the mid-18th century were Taylor and **Edward Poynton**, both of Nottingham. Taylor was employed as a carver in marble, stone and wood at Welbeck Abbey, 1743–1745. There he was responsible for ornamental work, including a carved stone doorcase and two chimneypieces, one for the alcove room costing £41 and another at £127. The latter was quite elaborate, combining lions' masks, snakes, two shields and two columns and capitals (**3**).

He signed a large monument with putti holding a medallion portrait of Sir John Bennett (**1**). The Gregory (**2**) is a tablet with volutes at the sides and at the foot, a skull, bats' wings, an hourglass and a serpent biting its tail, all symbols of *Time* and *Eternity*. In 1769–70 Sir Robert Burdett paid considerable sums to 'Thomas Taylor, mason' for work at Foremark Hall, Derbys. This could be Taylor of Nottingham (Berks CRO D/EBU A 9/1).

Literary References: *Gunnis* 1986, 383; *Lord* 1990 (2), p 868, n15

Funerary Monuments

1.	†1738	Sir John Bennett	St Mary, Melton Mowbray, Leics	S	Pevsner, *Leics & Rutland*, 1984, 318
2.	pre-1755	Susanna Gregory	Denton, Lincs	S	Pevsner, *Lincs*, 1989, 251

Architectural Sculpture

3.	1743–1745	Carved stone doorcase, two chimneypieces Payment(s): £41 and £127 for chimneypieces	[Welbeck Abbey, Notts]; untraced		*Gunnis* 1968, 383, citing Welbeck Abbey archives

TAYLOR, Thomas, of Stratford-on-Avon fl 1833?

Funerary Monuments

1.	?1833	Robert Middleton	Snitterfield, Warks	S	*Gunnis* 1968, 383

TAYLOR, W H, of Birmingham fl 1830

Miscellaneous

1.	1830	King George IV, model	[Exhib Birmingham Soc of A]; untraced		*Gunnis* 1968, 383

TAYLOR, William

The stock in trade of the bankrupt William Turner, carver and mason of Tottenham Court Road, was sold b Willoughby on 11 December 1777 (BM, PDB, Sc. A.5.9). Among the lots were chimneypieces.

TAYLOR, William, of London fl 1767–77

Knight's chimneypiece was an expensive item and must have been of marble (2). Taylor or possibly a son signed th Slingsby wall tablet (1). It is not clear whether this mason can be identified with the **William Taylor** whose stock i trade was forcibly sold in 1777.

Funerary Monuments

1.	1837	Mrs Slingsby	All Saints, Camden Town, St Pancras, London	S	*Gunnis* 1968, 383

Chimneypieces

2.	1767–1768	Description unavailable Payment(s): £128 4s 6d	[for Edward Knight of Wolverley]; untraced		GPC quoting Edward Knight Accts, Kidderminster Public Library, MSS 285–292

TEASDALE FAMILY

John Teasdale I 1777–*c*1809
John Teasdale II fl 1801–*c*1809
Michael Teasdale fl 1823

John Teasdale I was born at Greystoke in Cumberland in 1777. When the Duke of Norfolk resolved to rebuild Arunde Castle he is said to have selected a number of young men from his estate who had shown creative skills and had ther trained in London workshops. Both Teasdale and his brother James Teasdale, the architect, were selected in thi manner. John Teasdale was to become 'a sculptor of ornaments in marble' at Arundel, carrying out a good deal c work there, including a 'Saxon' doorway (2). **John Teasdale II** joined the Royal Academy Schools to study sculptur in 1801. He and his father were two of the chief stone-carvers employed during the restoration of King Henry VII chapel in Westminster Abbey. A **Michael Teasdale**, who may have been a relation, was awarded a silver palette fo sculpture by the Society of Arts in 1823, when his address was 1 Bond Street, Vauxhall (1). He later settled in Bath an is described as 'a sculptor' in a directory of 1842 (*Gunnis* 1968, 383).

Literary References: *Hutchison* 1960–62, 160; *Gunnis* 1968, 383; *Colvin* 1995, 969; *Woodburn and Guy* 2005–6, 24

Busts

1.	1823	Plaster copy of a head (by Michael Teasdale)	[Soc of A, silver palette]; untraced		RSA *Transactions*, 1823, vol 41, xxxix

Architectural Sculpture

2.	*c*1790	'Much of the ornamental work' (by John Teasdale I)	[Arundel Castle, West Sussex]; untraced		*Dallaway* 1819, 2, 1, 162; *Gunnis* 1968, 383
3.	1809	Restoration work, stone-carving (by John Teasdale I and II)	[King Henry VII's Chapel, Westminster Abbey, London]; untraced		*Neale and Brayley* 1818–23, 1, 2, 26; *Gunnis* 1968, 383

TEMPLETON, Elizabeth Upton 1747–1823

Gunnis writes that Lady Templeton provided a number of designs for Josiah Wedgwood between 1783 and 178 These dates are no doubt taken from the only surviving letter between Wedgwood and Lady Templeton and fron the 1787 Wedgwood catalogue. The catalogue includes the statement 'I have lately been enabled to enrich it with som charming groups, which Lady Diana Beauclerk and Lady Templeton, whose taste is universally acknowledged, hav honoured me with the liberty of copying from their designs' (Cat, Wedgwood Museum, Barlaston).

Literary References: *Gunnis* 1968, 383

Archival References: Letter, Josiah Wedgwood I to Lady Templeton, Wedgwood Museum E26/18958, 27 June 1783

Busts

1.	nd	John, 1st Marquess of Bristol	Ickworth Park, Suffolk		*Gunnis* 1968, 383
2.	nd	Lady Augusta Seymour	Ickworth Park, Suffolk		*AJ*, 1864, 256; *Gunnis* 1968, 383
3.	nd	Marquess of Bristol	Ickworth Park, Suffolk		*AJ*, 1864, 256; *Gunnis* 1968, 383

TEMPLETON, George fl 1811–47

He was born in Liverpool, and was living in Olive Street when he exhibited at the Liverpool Academy in 1811 (3). I 1844 he showed a statue of St John at Westminster Hall, which the *Literary Gazette* considered 'exactly like Westall *Spirit of the Storm*', and the *Art Union* 'poor and faulty to a degree' (1). Graves lists the artist as 'Templeton, P. A Sculptor, living at 16 Wellesley Street, Euston Square' in 1847, the year he showed a bust at the Royal Academy (2).

Literary References: *Gunnis* 1968, 383; *Graves* VII, 1905–6, 345

Statues

1.	1844	St John the Divine		[Exhib Westminster Hall, London, 96]; untraced	*Lit Gaz*, 1435, 20 July 1844, 466; *AU*, 1844, 215

Busts

2.	1847	Unidentified subject	m	[Exhib RA, London, 1378]; untraced	*Graves* VII, 1905–6, 345; *Gunnis* 1968, 383

Miscellaneous

3.	1811	Venus rising from the sea		[Exhib Liverpool Ac, 160]; untraced	*Morris and Roberts* 1998, 590

TENERANI, Pietro 1789–1869

An Italian sculptor, from 1803 he studied at the Academy at Carrara and he won the Rome prize in 1813. After a brief period studying with **Antonio Canova** he joined the studio of **Bertel Thorvaldsen** in 1815, with whom he was associated for the next 15 years, while also retaining a private practice. His reception piece presented to the Accademia di San Lucca in 1824 was a herm bust of Thorvaldsen. After Thorvaldsen's departure from Rome in 1838 he was regarded as the most important sculptor in the city, becoming President of the Accademia in 1857 and Director of the Museums in 1860. His most accessible works in Rome are a *Deposition* in St John Lateran, 1838–44, and the monument to Pius VII in St Peter's basilica, 1866.

Though he exhibited at the Royal Academy (**6, 12**) and executed work for a number of English clients, he did not become well known in this country. Travellers to Italy however visited his studio. The 2nd Earl of Minto was there in February 1822 and recorded in his diary that Tenerani promised 'great things' (*Clifford* 1995, 75). Having visited **John Gibson**'s studio in 1852, Caroline Stopford Sackville and her husband went 'Next to Tenerani's where the studio is large – a pretty group of Ld. Carnarvon's childn. (**8**) – some very fine likenesses – one of Canova's brother – a small one of Count Rossi's in a chair – & a larger one – a beautiful Pieta – & an Archangel Gabriel starting to sound the last Trump, the attitude of expectation very fine, & the wings beautifully done, also a monument to a child of the Ld. Vivian (**3**) of which the copy (wch is what we saw) is going to Rachel' (CSC, *Journal*, 12 Nov 1852). In 1854 the *Art Journal*, in an article signed 'Fiorentia' entitled 'A Walk Through the Studios of Rome' again linked Tenerani with Gibson, perhaps because their studios were near one another: 'our own classic Gibson with characteristic modesty pronounces as the first of modern sculptors. . . Tenerani is not known in England as he ought and deserves to be, principally because he was one of the few great living artists who did not contribute any work to our own exhibition. . . Very beautiful is Tenerani's "Flora" (**7**), executed for our own Queen, represented as a nymph of extreme youth, charmingly beautiful, joyously advancing, like a "returning diver gleeful with his pearls; her lap piled with flowers, which seem to drop around her, she lightly skims on the ambrosial gales, shedding forth streams of rich distilled perfume" ' (*AJ*, 1854, 350–1).

The monument to Margaret, Marchioness of Northampton (**2**) is described by Gunnis as having 'a charming relief, although his heroic angel commemorating the second Marquess, 1866, in the same church is rather overpowering' (**4**).

Literary References: *Neoclassicism* 1972, 283–4; *K-Browne* 1972 (3), 326, 328, 330, 331; *Penny* 1977 (1), 164; Grove Art Online

Funerary Monuments

1.	†1824	Mary Bold, Princess Sapieha		Farnworth, Lancs		*CIIA* 4/8/36–7 (repr)
2.	1836	Margaret, 2nd Marchioness of Northampton (†1830)		Castle Ashby, Northants		*Penny* 1977 (1), 164–5 (repr); Grove Online
3.	post-1852	Jesse Vivian (†1848)		Sketty, Swansea, Glamorgan		Pevsner, *Glamorgan*, 1995, 618
4.	1866	Spencer, 2nd Marquess of Northampton (†1851)		Castle Ashby, Northants		*CIIA* 4/3/32 (repr)

Statues

5.	1825	Cupid removing a thorn from the foot of Venus Payment(s): 2,000 scudi	m	Chatsworth, Derbys Other versions: Several, for European and Russian patrons	SD	*JKB* 1972 (3), 326, 328, 331; Grove Online, 1996
6.	1846	Psyche	m	[Exhib RA, London, 1397]; untraced		*Graves* VII, 1905–6, 346; *Gunnis* 1968, 383
7.	1848	Flora		Royal Coll	D	*Gunnis* 1968, 383
8.	c1852	Group of the two sons of Lord Carnarvon		Untraced		CSC, Journal, 12 Nov 1852
9.	c1855	'Wentworth'		Sydney University, New South Wales, Australia		*Read and Barnes* 1991, 36–7

Busts

10.	1844	Henri, Duc de Bordeaux	m	Burton Constable Hall, E R Yorks, staircase hall		*Mulcahy* 2006, 20–21 (repr)
11.	1848	Pope Pius IX	m	Chatsworth, Derbys, sculpture gallery	SD	*JKB* 1972 (3), 331
12.	1854	Lady Arbuthnot		[Exhib RA, London, 1448]; untraced		*Graves* VII, 1905–6, 346; *Gunnis* 1968, 383
13.	nd	Prince Woronzow		Wilton House, Wilts		*Gunnis* 1968, 383

Reliefs

14.	nd	Classical relief		61 Green St, Park Lane, London, outer wall		Pevsner, *London I*, 1973, 619
15.	nd	The three daughters of the Marquess of Abercorn		Untraced		RG/JP, 8, 1411

TERNOUTH, John 1796–1848

The name Ternouth originated in Cornwall, but John Ternouth's immediate ancestors were Plymouth stonemasons. The sculptor's parents were married in London, at St John the Evangelist, Westminster, in 1792, and he was born in Andover, Hants, on 30 January 1796. He moved to London c1810, possibly to begin his apprenticeship. On 13 August 1814 he married Sarah Abbot at St Marylebone. Their first child, William, was born the following May. Three more sons and five daughters were born between 1816 and 1830 and two orphaned nieces joined the sculptor's family in 1839. Shortly after his marriage Ternouth carved a portrait medallion of his wife to adorn their home in Chapel Street, Vincent Square, Westminster (**92**).

He entered the Royal Academy Schools in 1820, winning a silver medal the following year, and became a pupil o **Sir Francis Chantrey**. He was a regular exhibitor at the RA from 1819 onwards, showing principally portrait busts He also sent works to the British Institution in 1825 and to the Society of British Artists' exhibitions at the Suffol Street galleries between 1825 and 1838.

Needing more room for his growing family, Ternouth moved to Elizabeth Place, Pimlico, in 1821, and then t Westbourne Street, Chelsea, in 1824. As he was doing more work for Chantrey the family moved again in 1827 to Lower Belgrave Place, close to Chantrey's workshops at 13 Ecclestone Street and his home at 30 Lower Belgrave Place Meanwhile, Ternouth was establishing himself as an independent sculptor, securing commissions for portrait bust and funerary monuments. Examples include a memorial with a 'well-carved relief of an angel ascending to heaven' a St Mary Abbots, Kensington (**1**) and several with life-sized figures (**7, 9, 10, 24**). His growing success enabled him t buy premises in St James's Street in 1835, while retaining his Lower Belgrave Place address. About two years later friend of A E Gregory, whose 'very elegant bust' Ternouth had recently completed, commented on the sculptor' cheerful disposition, expressing the hope that 'his honest fresh face will wear many an additional smile for you honouring his genius' (Letter to A E Gregory, Feb 1837, Ternouth Papers) (**70**).

Ternouth also achieved some critical success. In 1825 he exhibited a bust of the radical politician John Can Hobhouse, which was praised as 'a facsimile of the features of that independent senator' (*The Times*, 16 May 1825, 3 (**48**). A version of his statue of a reclining *Nymph*, exhibited at the Society of British Artists in 1837, was particularl well-received (**43**). The *Observer* described it as 'one of the most faultlessly beautiful figures that can be imagined (*Observer*, 19 March 1837), while *The Times* considered it one of 'the most striking performances' in the sculptur room (*The Times*, 20 March 1837, 3). In 1844 he sent statues of *The Penitent* and of Thomas Henry Somerset Conway an officer in the Madras Army, to the Westminster Hall Exhibition, held to select artists to provide works of art fo the new Palace of Westminster (**36, 44**). The *Literary Gazette* considered the Conway statue a 'commanding figure both in figure and countenance' (*Lit Gaz*, 20 July 1844, 466), but *The Penitent* elicited a mixed response. The *Literar Gazette* condemned it as 'very carelessly done and wanting in feeling', while the *Art Union* felt the subject had bee 'treated in a spirit which appeals to our sympathies' (*AU* 1844, 216).

During the 1840s Ternouth was employed in overseeing the cleaning and repair of monuments in Westminster Abbe and reporting on their condition and safety. He was recommended for this post by the architect Edward Blore. Blor also employed him at Buckingham Palace, where he carved figures of *St George* and *Britannia* for the East front (**90**).

Ternouth's best known work is a bronze relief, *The Battle of Copenhagen*, one of the four depicting Nelson' victories at the base of Nelson's Column in Trafalgar Square (**94**). The others were modelled by **Musgrave Lewthwait Watson, John Edward Carew** and **William Frederick Woodington**. The choice of sculptors was influenced b the results of the 1844 Westminster Hall exhibition and both Ternouth and Watson were recommended for thi commission by the prime minister, Sir Robert Peel. The subject seems to have presented problems for Ternouth sinc the battle apparently lacked heroic incidents suitable for portrayal in sculpture. He chose to depict the triumphan Admiral sealing the peace treaty on an enemy canon after his successful bombardment of the city. While Ternout was still at work on the relief it was rumoured that the sculptor had died. However, the *Athenaeum* of 14 Novembe 1846, reported 'Mr Ternouth has written to say he is not dead and we give him the benefit of the assertion'. The sam journal commented pessimistically that 'the long slumber' in the progress of the Nelson Column had led to rumour that everyone involved was dead and that 'Mr Ternouth's very announcement of his life, in connexion with thi premature ruin, has a posthumous sound' (*Athenaeum*, 14, 1846, 1168). The plaster was ready by June 1848 and Princ Albert visited Ternouth's studio to inspect the work on 1 July 1848.

The sculptor did not survive to see the finished bronze installed at the base of the column. He contracted typhu and died on 13 December 1848, aged 52. His grave in Kensal Green cemetery is marked by a Carrara marble *stela* wit a classical relief of a grieving draped woman embracing an urn-topped pedestal. This may be one of his own works Shortly after Ternouth's death his medallion portrait of Robert Allen, the youngest son of the Bishop of Ely, wa exhibited at the RA and his memorial to Lady Madden was erected at Jacobstowe (**95, 40**). Ternouth's own deat seems to have passed without comment in the press and his posthumous reputation suffered from the generally lov regard for mid-19th century sculpture. (Add inf. Yolande Ternouth and her sons, John and Rowland)

EI

Literary References: *The Times*, 7 November 1846, 5; 3 July 1848, 4; *Redgrave* 1878, 426; *Hutchison* 1960–2, 173; *Gunnis* 1968, 383–4; *Potterton* 1975 83–4; *Mace* 1976, 100–107; *Curl* 2001, 207, 242–3

Archival References: Westminster Monuments Receipt; Westminster Monuments Report; Ternouth Letter; Ternouth Papers

Additional Manuscript Sources: Sun Insurance 11936/499/1019699 (9 September 1824); 11936/515/1065045 (23 August 1827)

Portraits of the Sculptor: plaster bust and 2 ivory reliefs, private coll, London

Will: PROB 11/208

Funerary Monuments

1.	1821	Bennett family	St Mary Abbots, Kensington, London	S	*Gunnis* 1968, 384
2.	1822	'A monumental alto-relievo, in marble'	[Exhib RA, London, 1045]; untraced		*Graves* VII, 1905–6, 347
3.	†1823	William Kinnersly	Ashley, Staffs	S	Pevsner, *Staffs*, 1974, 63
4.	1824	Lord Charles Murray	Dunkeld Cathedral, Perth		GPC
5.	†1825	Sarah Tyrell	Boreham, Essex	S	*Gunnis* 1968, 384
6.	†1826	Margaret Collett	St Mary, Hemel Hempstead, Herts	S	
7.	†1827	Henry Davidson	All Saints, Kingston upon Thames, Surrey	S	Pevsner, *London: S*, 1983, 312
8.	†1829	Charles Frederick Bond	Boreham, Essex	S	
9.	†1829	Lady Charlotte Bulkeley	Beaumaris, Anglesey		*Library of Fine Arts*, vol I, 1831, 430; *Graves* VII, 1905–6, 347; *Penny* 1977 (1), 73, 213 n9
10.	1829	Rev W D Shipley, Dean of St Asaph's	St Asaph's Cathedral, Flint		*Graves* VII, 1905–6, 347; Pevsner, *Clwyd*, 1986, 440
11.	?1830	Admiral Sir James Nicoll Morris	Marlow, Bucks	S	*Gunnis* 1968, 384
12.	†1831	Ann Rishton Ray	Boreham, Essex	S	

13.	†1831	Colonel Mark Wilks		Grosvenor Chapel, Mayfair, London	S	*Gunnis* 1968, 384
14.	†1831	Jean Miller		[Kensal Green Cemetery, London, colonnade]; untraced	S	*Curl* 2001, 237
15.	†1831	Lord Charles Henry Somerset		St Andrew, Waterloo Road, Hove, Sussex		Pevsner, *Sussex*, 1965, 429
16.	?1832	Rev Henry Ridley		Hambleden, Bucks	S	*Gunnis* 1968, 384
17.	†1832	William Ogilvie		Ardglass, Co Down		*Potterton* 1975, 83
18.	1833	'Part of a monument'		[Exhib RA, London, 1139]; untraced		*Graves* VII, 1905–6, 347
19.	†1833	Sir George Dallas		St Andrew, Waterloo Road, Hove, Sussex	S	Pevsner, *Sussex*, 1965, 429
20.	1834	Elizabeth Arbuthnot		Ockley, Surrey	S	*Gunnis* 1968, 384
21.	1834	John Kaye, Bishop of Lincoln		Brasenose College, Oxford, chapel		*Graves* VII, 1905–6, 347; Pevsner, *Oxon*, 1974, 107
22.	†1834	Rev Sir John Filmer Bt and Dame Charlotte Filmer (†1818) Model(s): exhib Soc of BA, London, 1838, 630		East Sutton, Kent	S	*Gunnis* 1968, 384; *Johnson* 1975, 457
23.	†1835	Jeremiah and Rose Milles		Sawbridgeworth, Herts	S	Pevsner, *Herts*, 1977, 334
24.	1835	John, 4th Duke of Atholl (†1830)		Dunkeld Cathedral, Tayside		*Graves* VII, 1905–6, 347; *Gunnis* 1968, 384; *Johnson* 1975, 457
25.	1835	Pelham Warren		Worting, Hants	S	*Gunnis* 1968, 384
26.	†1836	John Phillips		Wootton Wawen, Warks	S	Pevsner, *Warks*, 1966, 481
27.	†1837	Captain William Pryce Cumby RN		Heighington, Durham		NMM Maritime Memorials
28.	1837	Sir Peter and Lady Warburton		Great Budworth, Cheshire	S	*Gunnis* 1968, 384
29.	?1837	Susannah Newton		Great Hallingbury, Essex	S	*Gunnis* 1968, 384
30.	†1838	Henry and Louisa Ann (also †1838) Desborough, wall-tablet		Holy Trinity, Clapham, London	S	
31.	1838	Model of a monumental statue erected in North Wales		[Exhib Soc of BA, London, 646]; untraced		*Johnson* 1975, 457
32.	?1838	Rev William Heath		St George, Grenada, WI	S	*Gunnis* 1968, 384
33.	?1839	Frances Popham		Chilton Foliat, Wilts		*Gunnis* 1968, 384; *Penny* 1977 (1), 208 n28
34.	†1840	Marianne Maurice (designed by Sir Frances Chantrey RA)		St Peter and St Paul, Marlborough, Wilts	S	Pevsner, *Wilts*, 1975, 334
35.	†1842	John Ireland, Dean of Westminster		Westminster Abbey, London, nave, south aisle		Pevsner, *London I, Westminster*, 1973, 458
36.	1844	Thomas Henry Somerset Conway (†1837)		St Mary, Fort St George, Chennai (Madras), India		*Lit Gaz*, 20 July 1844, 466; *Graves* VII, 1905–6, 348; *Steggles* 2000, 56–57 (repr)
37.	1844	Thomas Lane		St George's Cathedral, Chennai (Madras), India	S	*Gunnis* 1968, 384
38.	†1845	Bishop Allen		Ely Cathedral, Cambs		Pevsner, *Cambs*, 1970, 368
39.	1848	Prudence Lamb (†1843)		Meeth, Devon	S	Pevsner, *Devon*, 1989, 565
40.	†1849	Lady Ellen Madden		Jacobstowe, Devon	S	Pevsner, *Devon*, 1989, 511
41.	†1852	General Sir Henry Wheatley		Erith, Kent		RG/JP, 8, 1423

Statues

42.	1826	Major Cartwright, sketches		[Exhib Soc of BA, London, 756 and 758]; untraced		*Johnson* 1975, 457
43.	1834	Nymph		[Exhib RA, London, 1042]; untraced Other versions: [Exhib Soc of BA, London, 1837, 618]; untraced [Exhib Westminster Hall, London, 1845, 135]; untraced		*Westminster* 1845, 16; *Graves* VII, 1905–6, 347; *Johnson* 1975, 457
44.	1844	The penitent		[Exhib Westminster Hall, London, 158]; untraced		*Lit Gaz*, 20 July 1844, 466; *AU*, 1844, 216

Busts

45.	1819	Mrs Chester		[Exhib RA, London, 1184]; untraced		*Graves* VII, 1905–6, 347
46.	1820	Unidentified lady		[Exhib RA, London, 1018]; untraced		*Graves* VII, 1905–6, 347
47.	1825	Colonel Hughes MP		[Exhib RA, London, 1019]; untraced		*Graves* VII, 1905–6, 347; *Johnson* 1975, 457
48.	1825	John Cam Hobhouse MP FRS		[Exhib RA, London, 1040]; untraced		*Graves* VII, 1905–6, 347; *Gunnis* 1968, 384; *Johnson* 1975, 457
49.	1826	Unidentified gentleman		[Exhib Soc of BA, London, 751]; untraced		*Graves* VII, 1905–6, 347; *Johnson* 1975, 457
50.	1827	Hudson Gurney MP	m	[Exhib RA, London, 1115]; untraced		*Graves* VII, 1905–6, 347
51.	1827	Mrs Hudson Gurney	m	[Exhib RA, London, 1086]; untraced		*Graves* VII, 1905–6, 347; *Johnson* 1975, 457
52.	1827	Sir Francis Burdett Bt, MP	m	[Exhib RA, London, 1111]; Palace of Westminster, London, members' entrance	SD	*Graves* VII, 1905–6, 347–348; *Walker* 1961, 9, cat. no.12; *Johnson* 1975, 457
53.	1828	Eldest son of Rowland Alston	m	[Exhib RA, London, 1199]; untraced		*Graves* VII, 1905–6, 347
54.	1828	Rev Peter Fraser	m	Christ's College, Cambridge		*Graves* VII, 1905–6, 347; *Gunnis* 1968, 384; *Johnson* 1975, 457
55.	1828	Rev W D Shipley, Dean of St Asaph		[Exhib Soc of BA, London, 897]; untraced		*Johnson* 1975, 457
56.	1828	Unidentified gentleman		[Exhib Soc of BA, London, 910]; untraced		*Johnson* 1975, 457
57.	1829	'An infant daughter of Colonel Tyrell'		[Exhib RA, London, 1168]; untraced		*Graves* VII, 1905–6, 347; *Johnson* 1975, 457
58.	1829	Miss M Tyrell		[Exhib RA, London, 1164]; untraced		*Graves* VII, 1905–6, 347; *Johnson* 1975, 457
59.	1829	Sir John Tyrell Bt		[Exhib RA, London, 1138]; untraced		*Graves* VII, 1905–6, 347; *Gunnis* 1968, 384; *Johnson* 1975, 457
60.	1830	A Marjoribanks		[Exhib RA, London, 1188]; untraced		*Graves* VII, 1905–6, 347

No.	Date	Subject	Mat.	Location		References
61.	1830	Mr Baxter		[Exhib RA, London, 1200]; untraced		*Graves* VII, 1905–6, 347
62.	1832	John Crabb		[Exhib RA, London, 1147]; untraced		*Graves* VII, 1905–6, 347; *Johnson* 1975, 457
63.	1832	Miss Tyrell		[Exhib RA, London, 1137]; untraced		*Graves* VII, 1905–6, 347
64.	1832	Sir Francis Burdett		formerly coll Rupert Gunnis; untraced		*Graves* VII, 1905–6, 347
65.	1832	Sir Richard William Bulkeley Bt		[Exhib RA, London, 1168]; untraced		*Graves* VII, 1905–6, 347; *Johnson* 1975, 457
66.	1833	Thomas Gardiner Bramston		[Exhib Soc of BA, London, 869]; untraced		*Johnson* 1975, 457
67.	1836	George Arbuthnot Jnr		[Exhib Soc of BA, London, 888]; untraced		*Johnson* 1975, 457
68.	1836	Lord George Murray, Bishop of Rochester	p	Blair Castle, Perths	SD	*Graves* VII, 1905–6, 347
69.	1836	William, 2nd Viscount Melbourne		Melbourne Hall, Derbys	SD	*Graves* VII, 1905–6, 347; *Ormond* 1973, 314
70.	1837	A E Gregory		[Exhib RA, London, 1283]; untraced		*Graves* VII, 1905–6, 348
71.	1837	Eva, third daughter of the Hon Rice Trevor MP		[Exhib RA, London, 1250]; untraced		*Graves* VII, 1905–6, 347
72.	1837	Mark Wilks Buchan		[Exhib RA, London, 1237]; untraced		*Graves* VII, 1905–6, 347
73.	1837	Miss Dorothy Gregory		[Exhib RA, London, 1199]; untraced		*Graves* VII, 1905–6, 347
74.	1837	Miss Gregory		[Exhib RA, London, 1257]; untraced		*Graves* VII, 1905–6, 347
75.	1837	Miss Perceval		[Exhib Soc of BA, London, 580]; untraced		*Johnson* 1975, 457
76.	1838	Mrs Jago		[Exhib Soc of BA, London, 598]; untraced		*Johnson* 1975, 457
77.	1838	Rowland Alston MP	m	[Exhib RA, London, 1361]; untraced		*Graves* VII, 1905–6, 348
78.	1838	Thomas Hopper	m	[Exhib RA, London, 1298]; untraced		*Graves* VII, 1905–6, 347; *ODNB*
79.	1839	General Sir Ronald C Ferguson		[Exhib RA, London, 1368]; untraced		*Graves* VII, 1905–6, 348
80.	1840	Lady Sudeley	m	Untraced		Ternouth Letter
81.	1841	John, 1st Earl Russell		[Exhib RA, London, 1318]; untraced		*Graves* VII, 1905–6, 348
82.	1842	George Arbuthnot		[Exhib RA, London, 1336]; untraced		*Graves* VII, 1905–6, 348
83.	1842	Hon Mrs Robert Drummond		[Exhib RA, London, 1323]; untraced		*Graves* VII, 1905–6, 348
84.	1842	Lord Bridport		[Exhib RA, London, 1401]; untraced		*Graves* VII, 1905–6, 348
85.	1842	W E Oliver		[Exhib RA, London, 1356]; untraced		*Graves* VII, 1905–6, 348
86.	1843	Colonel Vans Agnew KCB		[Exhib RA, London, 1504]; untraced		*Graves* VII, 1905–6, 348
87.	1844	George Pilcher		[Exhib RA, London, 1325]; untraced		*Graves* VII, 1905–6, 348
88.	1845	Edward Blore DCL FRS	m	University Press, Cambridge		*Graves* VII, 1905–6, 348; *Ormond* 1973, 42
89.	nd	John, Duke of Atholl; Lord Dinorben; Mr Arbuthnot; Sir E Bulwer		[offered for sale at the Colosseum, Regent's Park, London, 1849]; untraced		RG/JP, 8, 1412
Architectural Sculpture						
90.	1847	St George and Britannia, figures flanking a shield		[Buckingham Palace, London, east front]; destroyed		*ILN*, 9 March 1850, 168; *Smith* 1931, 55; *Colvin* VI, 1973–6, 301
Reliefs						
91.	*c*1810	Mary Magdalene washing the feet of Jesus	p	Private coll (London)		
92.	*c*1816	Sarah Ternouth (the sculptor's wife)		Private coll (London)		
93.	1821	Bacchanalian scene with putti, grapes and half-barrel	sl	Private coll, Sussex	SD	
94.	1845–1849	Battle of Copenhagen Model(s): Nelson receiving the surrender of Copenhagen, plaster trial model, sold Sotheby, London, 5 Oct 2005, lot 220	b	Nelson's Column, Trafalgar Square, London, base		*Colvin* VI, 1973–6, 493, 494 nl; *Read* 1982, 90; *Yarrington* 1988, 317 (pl 113)
95.	1849	Robert Allen, son of the Bishop of Ely, medallion		[Exhib RA, London, 1246]; untraced		*ILN*, 7 Dec 1850, 444; *Graves* VII, 1905–6, 347
Miscellaneous						
96.	1821	Specimen of sculpture in Penryn slate		[Exhib RA, London, 1088]; untraced		*Graves* VII, 1905–6, 347
97.	1824	Study from nature		[Exhib RA, London, 1037]; untraced		*Graves* 1875, 533; *Graves* VII, 1905–6, 347; *Johnson* 1975, 457
98.	1847	Musidora		[Exhib RA, London, 1336]; untraced		*Graves* VII, 1905–6, 348

TERRY, Ralph

He presented to the Society of Arts a 'Tablet with Flowers and Foliage, delicately carved in wood' for which he was 'gratified' with a bounty of 3 guineas (*Dossie* 1782, 438).

THEAKSTON, Charles Delatre 1804–

Son of **Joseph Theakston**, he was christened on 1 August 1804 at St George, Hanover Square. He entered the Royal Academy Schools in January 1820, and the following year, whilst living in Queen's Row, Pimlico, he received a medal from the Society of Arts (1). He was living in Belgrave Place, Pimlico when he exhibited at the Royal Academy in 1825 (3). He showed again at the Royal Academy in 1831, apparently for the last time (2). In November 1842 he and his six siblings were equal legatees of his father's estate.

Literary References: RSA *Transactions*, 1821, vol 39, xxxix; *Graves* VII, 1905–6, 351; *Hutchison* 1960–2, 173

Archival References: Society of Arts; IGI;

Will: Joseph Theakston, PROB 11/1971/233

No.	Date	Subject	Mat.	Location	References
Statues					
1.	1821	Laocoon	p	[Soc of A, silver Isis medal]; untraced	RSA *Transactions*, 1821, vol 39, xxxix
2.	1831	Arthur, 1st Duke of Wellington, 'cabinet statue'		[Exhib RA, London, 1175]; untraced	*Graves* VII, 1905–6, 351
Busts					
3.	1825	Edward Hind (posthumous)		[Exhib RA, London, 1067]; untraced	*Graves* VII, 1905–6, 351

THEAKSTON, Christopher, of Doncaster fl 1753–85?

He was apprenticed to **Christopher Richardson of Doncaster** in 1753 and later became his assistant. On 14 February 1765 he married Harriet, the daughter of his former master. She died on 19 January 1808, aged 61. Theakston and Richardson were employed at Wentworth Woodhouse in 1762 (**5**). On 6 July 1774, Theakston became a freeman of Doncaster and in the same year he carved the figure of *Justice* for Newark Town Hall (**6**). In 1773, working on his own account, he received payment for chimneypieces at Nostell Priory (**4**): an estimate and an agreement was drawn up on 17 May 1773 stipulating that they were 'to be compleated in the best manner with white freestone for £73, subject to alterations by Robert Adam' (*Brockwell* 1915, 19). In 1769 Theakston, described as a 'Carver in wood and stone', took a John Carter as his apprentice.

Literary References: *Gunnis* 1968, 384

Archival References: GPC

Funerary Monuments					
1.	1777	'Mrs Cook's father', tombstone	[Warmsworth, W R Yorks, churchyard]; untraced		GPC
2.	†1777	William Bilbie	Blidworth, Notts	S	Pevsner, *Notts*, 1979, 76
3.	?1785	Osborne family	Ravenfield, W R Yorks		GPC
Chimneypieces					
4.	1773	Two Payment(s): £73	Nostell Priory, W R Yorks, front hall		*Gunnis* 1968, 384
Architectural Sculpture					
5.	1762	Unidentified work	Wentworth Woodhouse, W R Yorks		*Gunnis* 1968, 384, citing Fitzwilliam Archives
6.	1774	Justice	[Newark Town Hall, Notts]; untraced		*Gunnis* 1968, 384
7.	1777	Carving	[Burton Hall, Lincs]; untraced		Archives, Lord Monson in GPC
8.	1777	Greyhounds	[Castle Howard, N R Yorks, front of stable block]; untraced		GPC
9.	1781	Pedestal Payment(s): £8 13s	[Castle Howard, N R Yorks]; untraced		GPC
10.	1783	Unidentified work	Wentworth Woodhouse, W R Yorks		*Gunnis* 1968, 384, citing Fitzwilliam Archives
Miscellaneous					
11.	1771	Carved work, including the great dining room chimneypiece Payment(s): £148 'for carved work'	Serlby Hall, Notts		Pevsner, *Notts*, 1979, 308; RG/JP, 8 1415

THEAKSTON, John Henry 1809–

The son of **Joseph Theakston** and the younger brother of **Charles Delatre Theakston**, he was born 25 November 1809 and christened on 17 December at St Marylebone, London. He exhibited at the Royal Academy in 1832, giving his address as 35 Gillingham Street, Pimlico. His father's will of April 1842 stated that he had 'some years since left this country' with his brother George Alfred Theakston, and both were assumed by their father to be dead.

Literary References: *Graves* VII, 1905–6, 352

Archival References: IGI

Will: Joseph Theakston, PROB 11/1971/233

Busts				
1.	1832	Daughter of Joseph Hoskins MD	[Exhib RA, London, 1142]; untraced	*Graves* VII, 1905–6, 352

THEAKSTON, Joseph 1772–1842

Theakston was born on 14 December 1772, the son of John Theakston, and was christened a week later at Saint Michael Spurriergate, York. His father died when he was young and his mother, Sarah, apprenticed him in 1786 to **John Fisher I**. He became free in 1794 and shortly afterwards went to London, where he became one of the last assistants to **John Bacon RA**, by whom he was well paid. According to the *Gentleman's Magazine* he 'formed his style on the amenities of that eminent artist' (*GM* 1842, vol 17, pt 1, 672). He subsequently worked for **John Flaxman RA** and **E H Baily**.

In 1809 he exhibited a design for a monument at the Royal Academy (**1**), giving his address as 10 New Road, Fitzroy Square, and in 1813 he showed a bust from a new address in Winchester Street, Pentonville (**43**). His earliest dateable monument depicts the dying Susannah Boutflower and her family in very high relief (**3**). In 1817 he competed to provide four monuments for St Paul's Cathedral, but failed to gain any of the commissions (**4–7**). The following year he began to work with with one of the successful competitors, **Sir Francis Chantrey**. There he remained until the end of Chantrey's life.

According to Peter Cunningham, who knew him well, Theakston became one of Chantrey's three most prized assistants, together with **Frederick William Smith** and **James Heffernan**. Chiefly responsible for the carving of draperies, Theakston 'was a consummate master in making marble convey the qualities and surfaces of silks and satins, velvets and ermines' (*Builder* 1863, 112), and unlike others in the studio he was happy for visitors to the studio to watch him at work. As a result the writer of his obituary in the *Gentleman's Magazine* was able to give a lengthy description of the working practice of the sculptor, whose hand 'scarcely seemed to move; few could imagine the rapidity of his execution from his quiet manner of handling his tools. . . When he began to carve a statue he knew perfectly well what was required of him and cut away the superfluous marble at once. He had not to try again, and again, like most artists, and by frequent touching and retouching accomplish his object' (*GM* 1842, vol 17, pt 1, 672).

Theakston was able to pursue his own successful practice despite his responsibilities to Chantrey. In 1821 he undertook 'the Herculean task' of restoring and cleaning the railings in Westminster Abbey (*English Chronicle* 20 Dec 1821), and the same year he executed a statue of a late chief magistrate of Weymouth for that town's Guildhall (**39**). He had a thriving practice as a monumental statuary, producing chiefly Hellenistic tablets, though the memorial to Anthony Hamond has a full-size statue of an angel above a sarcophagus (**9**), and another to William Davey has a medallion-portrait (**19**). The monument to Roger Wilson has reliefs of five Preston churches which were erected largely on his initiative (**36**). Following his master's lead Theakston produced a number of busts, including one in 1830 of either George IV or William IV, which he appears to have carved at Snelston Hall, the home of his patron John Harrison (**46**). He was also responsible for architectural sculpture (**49**) and his magnificent chimneypiece for Buckingham Palace has been described by Gunnis as the most imposing in the building (**48**). In addition he apparently 'had more than common skill in Gothic architecture' (*GM* 1842, vol 17, pt 1, 672), although no specimens of his work in this style or medium are known.

After 1825 he lived in Belgrave Place, Pimlico, where he died on 14 April 1842. He was buried in the Anglican chapel in Kensal Green cemetery near his wife Elizabeth (**28**). In his will he directed that his estate should be sold and the proceeds shared between seven of his eight children. He died waiting for the full payment of 'a considerable sum or the balance of an account for work and labour done for the late Sir Francis Chantrey' and directed that his executor Hugh James, a tailor of Bond Street, should 'apply to my friend **Allan Cunningham** and promise his assistance in settling and adjusting the said account.' He also directed that 'my present assistant John Thomas [**John Evan Thomas?**] complete any work which may be in hand and unfinished' Two of the sculptor's children, **Charles Delatre Theakston** and **John Henry Theakston**, followed his profession.

Peter Cunningham said of Theakston that he was 'a fine, venerable, kind-hearted man, ever prompt with a kind word and a kind smile' (*Builder* 1863, 112), whilst the *Gentleman's Magazine* described him as 'by nature gentle and affectionate, yet firm, as most calm hearts are'. Of his work the same writer adjudged Theakston 'perhaps, the ablest drapery or ornamental carver of his time, as he was certainly the most rapid' (*GM* 1842, vol 17, pt 1, 672).

MGS

Literary References: *Graves* 1875, 534; *Graves* VII, 1905–6, 351–2; *Gunnis* 1968, 384–5; *Chantrey Ledgers* 1991–2, 10; *Curl* 2001, 242
Archival References: IGI; York App Reg D15, 19 Oct 1767, 71; Flaxman Papers BL Ad MS 39784
Will: PROB 11/1971/233

Funerary Monuments

1.	1809	'Britannia at the tomb of her departed hero, referring you to History for his achievements'	[Exhib RA, London, 759]; untraced		*Graves* VII, 1905–6, 351
2.	†1812	Reymundo Putt	Gittisham, Devon	S	Pevsner, *Devon*, 1989, 457
3.	1815	Susannah Boutflower (†1810)	Seamer, N R Yorks		Pevsner, *Yorks: N R*, 1966, 336
4.	1817	Major-General Andrew Hay, sketch (for a monument in St Paul's Cathedral, commission won by Humphrey Hopper)	[Exhib RA, London, 1058]; untraced		*Graves* VII, 1905–6, 351
5.	1817	Major-General Sir Edward Pakenham and Major-General Samuel Gibbs, sketch (for a monument in St Paul's Cathedral, commission won by Sir Richard Westmacott)	[Exhib RA, London, 1037]; untraced		*Graves* VII, 1905–6, 351
6.	1817	Major-General Sir Robert Rollo Gillespie (†1814), sketch (for a monument in St Paul's Cathedral, commission won by Sir Francis Chantrey)	[Exhib RA, London, 1012]; untraced		*Graves* VII, 1905–6, 351
7.	1817	Major-General A Gore and General J B Skerett, sketch (for a monument in St Paul's Cathedral, commission won by Sir Francis Chantrey)	[Exhib RA, London, 1817, 1019]; untraced		*Graves* VII, 1905–6, 351
8.	†1820	William Shedden	Hardmead, Bucks	S	Pevsner, *Bucks*, 1994, 371; C Lib (repr)
9.	†1822	Anthony Hamond	West Acre, Norfolk	S	Pevsner, *Norfolk: N W & S*, 1999, 760
10.	†1822	Sir William Herschel	Upton, Bucks	S	Pevsner, *Bucks*, 1994, 641
11.	?1823	Robert Dorner	Budbrook, Warks	S	*Gunnis* 1968, 385
12.	†1825	Lady Sophia Heathcote	Edenham, Lincs		Pevsner, *Lincs*, 1989, 269
13.	1825	'Part of a monument to be placed in Great Saling Church, Essex, by an only child, Miss M B Shedden, to the memory of her parents'	[Exhib RA, London, 995]; untraced		*Graves* VII, 1905–6, 352
14.	1825	Peter Elmsley	Christchurch Cathedral, Oxford	S	*Gunnis* 1968, 385
15.	?1825	Thomas Hetherington	Walthamstow parish church, London	S	*Gunnis* 1968, 385
16.	†1826	Reginald Heber, Bishop of Calcutta	St Peter, Colombo, Sri Lanka (Ceylon)	S	*Gunnis* 1968, 385; C Lib (repr)
17.	†1826	Robert Sheddon	Paulerspury, Northants	S	Pevsner, *Northants*, 1973, 371
18.	?1827	Mary Inglis	Wartling, Sussex	S	*Gunnis* 1968, 385
19.	†1827	William Davey	Redruth, Cornwall		Pevsner, *Cornwall*, 1970, 150
20.	?1828	Archbishop Manners Sutton	Addington, Surrey	S	*Gunnis* 1968, 385
21.	†1828	Georgiana Elizabeth Smith	Cherry Hinton, Cambs	S	
22.	?1828	Sophia Matlock	Bramley, Surrey	S	*Gunnis* 1968, 385
23.	1829	Bishop Lloyd	Christchurch Cathedral, Oxford	S	*Gunnis* 1968, 385
24.	†1829	Lord Charles Fitzroy	Euston, Suffolk	S	
25.	?1830	Frances Goring	Wiston, Sussex	S	*Gunnis* 1968, 385
26.	?1831	John Christie	Broxbourne, Herts	S	*Gunnis* 1968, 385
27.	?1831	Marmaduke Ramsay	Jesus College Chapel, Cambridge	S	*Gunnis* 1968, 385
28.	†1833	Elizabeth Theakston	Kensal Green Cemetery, Anglican Chapel, colonnade	S	*Curl* 2001, 242
29.	†1833	Mary Platt	Forthampton, Glos	S	Pevsner, *Glos: Vale & Forest of Dean*, 1976, 188
30.	?1834	Frederick Page	Speen, Berks	S	*Gunnis* 1968, 385
31.	?1835	Ann Pearce	Cherry Hinton, Cambs	S	*Gunnis* 1968, 385
32.	+1835	John, 7th Earl of Scarborough	Saxby, Lincs		Pevsner, *Lincs*, 1989, 622
33.	†1836	Turner Macan	Armagh Cathedral		*Potterton* 1975, 84
34.	†1837	Mary Serocold	Cherry Hinton, Cambs	S	

35.	1839	Anne Wynter		Lanlivery, Cornwall	S	Pevsner, *Cornwall*, 1970, 92
36.	†1839	Rev Roger Carus Wilson		St John the Divine, Preston, Lancs	S	Pevsner, *Lancs: N*, 1969, 194; C Lib (repr)
37.	†1844	Francis Leigh Balfour		St John's Cathedral, Belize (formerly British Honduras)	S	*Hammond* 1999, 131, 135; *Hammond* 2000, 89
38.	nd	C P Serocold		Cherry Hinton, Cambs	S	
Statues						
39.	1821	Samuel Watson Model(s): Sketch exhib RA, London, 1820, 1057	m	Guildhall, Weymouth, Dorset		*Graves* VII, 1905–6, 351; Pevsner, *Dorset*, 1972, 452
40.	1837	'Sketch for a statue of Admiral Lord Nelson'		[Exhib RA, London, 1204]; untraced		*Graves* VII, 1905–6, 352
41.	1838	George, 1st Duke of Sutherland		Golspie, Sutherland		*Gunnis* 1968, 385
42.	nd	St Anthony of Padua		[Fonthill, Wilts]; Wardour Castle, Wilts, chapel gardens		*Storer* 1812, unpag (repr); *Lees-Milne* 1976, 76 (repr)
Busts						
43.	1813	R Walker		[Exhib RA, London, 901]; untraced		*Graves* VII, 1905–6, 351
44.	1817	Colossal head of a British warrior		[Exhib RA, London, 1022; exhib BI, London, 1819, 4]; untraced		*Graves* 1875, 534; *Graves* VII, 1905–6, 351
45.	1818	Charles Henry Schwanfelder, 'animal painter to HRH the Prince Regent'		[Exhib RA, London, 1069]; untraced		*Graves* VII, 1905–6, 351
46.	1830	'His Majesty'		[Exhib RA, London, 1235, executed for John Harrison of Snelston Hall, Derbys]; untraced		*Graves* VII, 1905–6, 352
47.	1851	Dr Peter Murray	p	Scarborough Museum, N R Yorks		GPC
Chimneypieces						
48.	1829–1832	With winged female figures supporting a roundel fitted with a clock, surmounted by bust of King George IV Payment(s): £1,000	m	Buckingham Palace, London		TNA WORK 19/3; *Smith* 1931, 131, repr 123; *Gunnis* 1968, 385; *Colvin* VI, 299
Architectural Sculpture						
49.	*c*1826	Six statues Payment(s): £50 each		[Grosvenor House, London, parapet over Rubens gallery]; untraced		*Allen* 1827–37, 362; *Survey of London*, vol 40, 246
Miscellaneous						
50.	1813	Hunting faun, after the antique		[Exhib BI, London, 206]; untraced		*Graves* 1875, 534
51.	1813	The interment of a warrior		[Exhib BI, London, 204]; untraced		*Graves* 1875, 534
52.	1822	Laughing girl		[Exhib North Soc, Leeds, W R Yorks]; untraced		GPC
53.	1829	Innocence reposing	m	[Exhib RA, London, 1210]; untraced		*Graves* VII, 1905–6, 352
54.	1831	Sleeping infant	m	[Exhib Soc of BA, London, 841]; untraced		*Johnson* 1975, 458

THEED, William I 1764–1817

He was a respected sculptor, a Royal Academician and a designer of ceramics and silver, who spent much of his career working for Josiah Wedgwood and then Rundle and Bridge. Few of his works are known today. He was born in 1764, the son of a wig-maker in Wych Street (*Farington* III, 719), an area of notorious mediaeval alleyways off Strand, London where Aldwych now stands. Theed entered the RA Schools in 1786 and began his career as a painter of portraits and classical subjects, exhibiting a canvas portrait of a gentleman at the Academy in 1789.

In 1790 he travelled to Florence with John Frearson, a friend and fellow painter. He returned to England briefly, but in January 1791 he was in Genoa and by February he had rejoined Frearson in Rome. Theed was neither happy nor successful in Rome: in 1792 he wrote to his father, 'you will imagine I have taken up my residence here for life – but be assured that this is not the case for every day increases my detestation of the people and the place; and were it not for the beauties in art which exist here I believe I should settle my concerns in ten minutes and be off' (*Theed Letters*, 18 July 1792, cited by *Ingamells* 1997, 934). He chose an unfortunate time to be in the city, for, as he later told Farington, living in Rome had become expensive and the Napoleonic Wars had reduced the number of English travellers visiting the city and commissioning art (*Farington* III, 719). The landscape painter, William Sandby RA, felt that the visit had nonetheless benefited Theed, for in his account of the history of the Royal Academy he observed that Theed was inspired to take up sculpture by the classical works he saw in Rome. He also struck up a friendship with **John Flaxman RA**. In 1795 Theed travelled to Naples, where, Sandby records, he married a French woman, Frances Rougeot. He was one of the group of young artists in Rome who signed a letter to Flaxman in January 1796, thanking him for interceding on their behalf with the Treasury to facilitate the import of their study collections of casts, prints and other artifacts into England, without paying the customary taxes. In July 1796 he was in Venice and he may then have spent time travelling in France and Germany, before returning to London by December 1796.

Theed showed a painting of *Venus and Cupids* at the RA in 1797, giving his address as 44 Long Acre, Covent Garden. The following year he exhibited a sketch of *Abraham offering Isaac* and a portrait of a woman and child, which Farington condemned as 'wretched performances' (*Farington* III, 996).

In 1799 he applied to work as a modeller for Wedgwood at the Etruria factory at Hanley, Staffs. His future employers were clearly cautious about entering into a fixed contract, for the younger Josiah Wedgwood wrote to Theed 'it appears very desirable that we should know each other better before we bind ourselves to one another for three years. You will be better able to understand what are our wants and expectations, and we should have a probability of their being fulfilled' (*Wedgwood Papers* E11-9411, 26 December 1799). Theed responded by offering to make and send a number of models to show his capabilities (*Wedgwood Papers* E11-9412). The models evidently found satisfaction for in 1800 he worked on ornamental details for Wedgwood in London, and by May 1801 he was in Etruria. It is not clear how long he worked for Wedgwood and little is known about the models he produced. In 1803 he advertised his intention to give drawing lessons in Newcastle-under-Lyme (*Staffordshire Advertiser*, 10 and

17 Dec, 1803) and by the time his son, **William Theed II**, was born in 1804, the family were living nearby at Trentham They may have returned to London soon after, for in 1805 Theed exhibited a wax model (**6**) at the RA, giving hi address as 11 Royal Hill, Greenwich. This was later realised in bronze. He maintained some connections wit Wedgwood and in 1811 modelled a portrait medallion of Thomas Byerley (**10**), a partner in the firm.

In London Theed found employment with Rundell and Bridge, making models for presentation plate. Farington late recorded a conversation with Theed: 'He spoke of the vast concerns of Rundle and Bridge, Silversmiths, with whom H is concerned in business He making models to be executed in Gold and Silver. He mentioned some inconvenience whic He suffered from their intruding their opinions in matters of taste and design, & sd. He could always go on better if h had access to the Noblemen or Gentlemen who gave them the Commissions and were easily led to adopt his opinion (*Farington* XII, 4292). It may have been intended that Theed should prepare the model for the *Shield of Achilles* fo Rundell and Bridge to a design by Flaxman. The silversmiths wrote to William Hayley, the poet and an associate c Flaxman, 'we trust that Mr Theed under the occasional inspection, which you have been kind enough to promise, wi be able to execute this exquisite design' (*Hayley Letters*, fol 98, 29 Oct 1810). It is now thought that the model for the shiel was eventually executed by **William Pitts**. Sandby relates that Theed remained with the firm for the remainder of his lif and that his employers provided him with a house and a handsome salary (*Sandby* II 1862, 383).

Theed was elected an associate of the Royal Academy in 1811, after apparently canvassing for votes. He called o Farington, who was an influential member of the RA's Council, and invited him to his studio in Dean Street, Soh on several occasions. Theed's supporters included Flaxman and **Sir Richard Westmacott RA**, but **J C F Ros** considered Theed's works 'ingenious but incorrect in execution' and thought that there were other sculptors wh would make better Associates (*Farington* XI 3984). Two years later, after further assiduous canvassing, Theed wa elected an Academician. His diploma work was a *Bacchanalian group* in bronze (**7**).

In 1817 he exhibited the relief of *Charity* for the monument to Thomas Westfaling at the RA (**3**). This has bee described as one of the finest works of sculpture of the period (*Penny* 1977 (1), 221 n62). Later that year he died, age 53. Sandby says that he left 'a small fortune' to pay for the education of his three children. His widow applied to th RA for a pension and was granted £50, but she died soon after (*Sandby* II 1862, 383).

EI

Literary References: *Farington, passim*; *Sandby* II 1862, 382–3; *DNB*, LVI 1898, 108; *Gunnis* 1968, 385–6; *Haggar* 1975, 22–9; *Penny* 1992, 6 *Ingamells* 1997, 934

Additional Manuscript Sources: *Theed Letters*

Will: PROB 11/1601

Collections of Drawings: Album of drawings connected with Rundle and Bridge, VAM, P&D E.70-124-1964, some perhaps by Theed

No.	Date	Work		Location		Sources
Funerary Monuments						
1.	1816	'A sepulchral monument'		[Exhib RA, London, 966]; untraced		*Graves* VII, 1905–6, 353
2.	1816	Thomas (†1792) and Mary Bridge (†1779)		Piddletrenthide, Dorset	S	RG/JP, 8, 1419
3.	1817	Thomas Westfaling		St Mary, Ross-on-Wye, Herefs		*Graves* VII, 1905–6, 353; Pevsner, *Herefs*, 1963, 278; *Penny* 1977 (1), 221 n62
4.	1816–1820	Major-General Sir William Ponsonby (†1815) (co-sculptor: Edward Hodges Baily)		St Paul's Cathedral, London		*Whinney* 1988, 470, n31; Pevsner, *London: City*, 1997, 182
Statues						
5.	1799	Nessus and Deianeira, model	p	[Exhib RA, London, 1001]; untraced		*Graves* 1875, 534; *Graves* VII, 1905–6, 352
6.	1805–1812	Thetis returning from Vulcan with arms for Achilles (cast by Rundell, Bridge and Rundell in 1829) Model(s): small wax exhib RA, London, 1805, 695	b	Wrest Park, Beds Other versions: ex coll Thomas Hope; untraced Royal Coll, RCIN 71833, cast	S	*Sandby* 1862, 383; *Graves* 1875, 534; *Graves* VII, 1905–6, 352–3; *Holland Park* 1957, unpag (repr)
7.	1813	Bacchanalian group (diploma work)	b	[RA, Burlington House, Piccadilly, London]; untraced		*Gunnis* 1968, 386
8.	1813	Mercury		[Exhib RA, London, 893]; untraced		*Graves* VII, 1905–6, 353
Architectural Sculpture						
9.	1806	Vase and pedestal in memory of Lord Nelson		[Exhib RA, London, 937]; untraced		*Graves* VII, 1905–6, 352
Reliefs						
10.	1811	Thomas Byerley, portrait medallion		untraced		*Gunnis* 1968, 385; *Haggar* 1975, 25–6
Miscellaneous						
11.	1800	Cephalus and Aurora		[Exhib RA, London, 92]; untraced		*Graves* VII, 1905–6, 352
12.	1809	A fawn; part of a group of figures, executed in ornamental plate		[Exhib RA, London, 865]; untraced		*Graves* VII, 1905–6, 352
13.	1811	The death of Eurydice		[Exhib RA, London, 912]; untraced		*Graves* 1875, 534; *Graves* VII, 1905–6, 352; *Morris and Roberts* 1998, 591
14.	1811	The death of Nessus		[Exhib RA, London, 914]; untraced		*Graves* VII, 1905–6, 352
15.	1811	Victory conducting the horses of war		[Exhib RA, London, 913]; untraced		*Graves* VII, 1905–6, 352
16.	1814	Bacchanalian group, for part of a piece of plate for the Prince Regent		[Exhib RA, London, 791]; untraced		*Graves* VII, 1905–6, 353
17.	1814	Model for a piece of plate for the Prince Regent		[Exhib RA, London, 790]; untraced		*Graves* VII, 1905–6, 353

THEED, William II 1804–91

Theed was a prominent and prolific sculptor, whose reputation was considerably enhanced by a close associatio with Albert, the Prince Consort. He produced a number of posthumous portraits of the Prince, some of whic reached a popular market as reproductions in other materials.

He was born at Trentham, Staffs and christened in nearby Newcastle-under-Lyme on 2 May 1804, the son c **William Theed I** and his French wife Frances, née Rougeot. The family set up in London and Theed received som education in Ealing before beginning his training as a sculptor with his father and then spending several years working in the studio of **E H Baily**. In January 1820 he entered the Royal Academy Schools, where he won a silver medal in 1822. He also won two prizes from the Society of Arts (**41, 186**). He first exhibited at the RA in 1824 (**89**), giving his address as 76 Dean Street, Soho.

In 1826 Theed went to Rome, where he studied under **Bertel Thorvaldsen, John Gibson, R J Wyatt** and **Pietro Tenerani**. He took lodgings at 9 Vicolo degli Incurabili and sent a number of works, mostly busts, to London to the Academy exhibitions. In 1844–5, after nearly 20 years in Rome he received a commission which marked a turning point in his career. When Prince Albert resolved to commission a series of ten statues for the interior of Osborne House he sought advice on eligible sculptors from Gibson, and Theed was one of those recommended. Theed carved two ideal figures, *Psyche lamenting the loss of Cupid* (**47**) and *Narcissus* (**46**), both completed in 1847.

He returned to England in 1848 and soon established a highly successful practice from his studio at 12 Henrietta Street, Covent Garden. He showed a number of ideal works at the Great Exhibition (**46, 48, 51, 52, 53**) and three appeared in the Manchester Art Treasures Exhibition of 1857 (**46, 48, 56**). Further commissions for the Prince Consort included a Sappho (**53**) a bust of Periander (**130**) and decorative work at Buckingham Palace. In 1856 he completed a major contract which included six busts after the antique for the gallery above the grand staircase (**133**), reliefs for the banqueting room and lunette reliefs above the doors in a small gallery adjoining the dining room (**179, 180**). The *Art Journal* praised the decorative scheme and paid tribute to Theed's contribution: 'we think its general elevation in no small degree results from the happy character of Mr Theed's statuary and bassi-relievi; these by their purity of form and graceful contour, give boldness and vigour to the general design of the apartments, which no flat painting could effect' (*AJ*, 1856, 192). Elsewhere, he modelled a series of 12 reliefs of scenes from Tudor history, which were cast in bronze by Elkington and Co, for the newly rebuilt Palace of Westminster (**185**) and executed a statue of *The bard* for the Egyptian Hall of the Mansion House (**64**).

The mainstays of Theed's production were portraiture and funerary monuments. He received commissions for many commemorative statues during his career, with examples in London, Manchester, Liverpool, Huddersfield, Grantham, Mumbai and Kolkata (**49, 55, 60, 61, 63, 65, 69, 73, 74, 77, 79, 80, 83–85**). His principal church monuments include those to Sir James Mackintosh and Sir Herbert Benjamin Edwardes in Westminster Abbey and to Henry Hallam in St Paul's Cathedral (**18, 36, 29**). The monument to Humphrey Chetham in Manchester Cathedral is a richly carved seated figure in elaborate Jacobean dress (**14**). It was reproduced in parian ware by Copeland, who also made small-scale ceramic versions of some of his most popular statues and busts (**48, 53, 56, 75, 142, 145, 158, 160**).

One of his most prestigious contracts outside London was the series of bronze statues and busts for Wellington College, Berks, executed between 1858 and 1862 (**67, 148**). The College had patriotic resonance as a memorial to the Duke of Wellington, founded to educate the sons of officers killed on active service. The Prince Consort originally envisaged an ambitious series of statues of all the generals closely associated with Wellington, together with busts of 103 of his officers, each to be financed by the families of the individual depicted. Theed offered to execute the busts at a modest charge of about £50 each. It soon became clear however that many of the busts could not be funded and only 33 were completed, 27 of them by Theed.

On 14 December 1861 Prince Albert died of typhoid fever. Queen Victoria immediately set about commemorating her husband, bringing in Theed to make his death mask and casts of his hands (**189**) which the Queen kept by her bedside. Within two weeks of Albert's death Theed was at Osborne, starting work on his first posthumous bust of the Prince (**148**). It was placed in the blue room at Windsor, where the Prince had died. A second bust, with draperies over one shoulder, was also completed that year (**147**). It was displayed in the entrance hall at Osborne, on an elaborate pedestal designed by Princess Alice and executed by Theed.

Theed was responsible for several commemorative statues of the Prince during the 1860s. The first, in Highland dress with a deerhound at his side, was inspired by John Phillip's painting of 1858 (**68**). A marble version was placed below the principal staircase at Balmoral and a larger one, cast in bronze by Elkington & Co, was presented by the Queen to the tenants of the Balmoral estate and erected close to the castle on a rough-hewn rock plinth. The Queen gave yet another statue, of the Prince in Garter robes and holding a field marshal's baton to the city of Coburg, Albert's birthplace (**72**). Theed's most romantic portrait of the Prince is the group of the royal couple in Anglo-Saxon costume at Frogmore, entitled *The parting* (**76**). The costume symbolises the close links between the English and German people, originating in the Anglo-Saxon period and re-inforced in recent years through the royal marriage. A version of the Coburg statue was erected in Sydney, Australia, and the Queen gave copies of the draped bust to several family members and loyal servants.

Theed was one of several leading sculptors involved in the Albert Memorial, 1864, in Kensington Gardens, London. Groups representing the Continents were executed by **John Henry Foley, John Bell, Patrick MacDowell**, and Theed, who contributed the colossal group of *Africa* (**70**). Theed's initial model was considered the least satisfactory of the four by Sir Charles Eastlake, who oversaw the commission on the Queen's behalf. He felt the composition lacked 'a principal view' of proper breadth and simplicity and among major changes he insisted on the substitution of a lion for a dromedary at the centre of the group (Royal Archives, Add H2/944, 1087–8 cited by *Brooks* 2000, 172, 177). Theed made the required modifications.

Theed continued to work well into the 1880s. The 1881 census returns show that he then lived at Campden Lodge, Kensington with his wife, Mary, and his son, the sculptor, Frank Theed, who exhibited busts and portrait medallions at the RA between 1873 and 1888. Theed died at Campden Lodge on 9 September 1891, aged 87.

His sculpture was praised in glowing terms in the 1862 International Exhibition catalogue, which paid tribute to his fusion of traditional practice with 'a certain touch of common nature, and an unbending towards domestic affection, which serve to bring cold marble down from her chilly heights into the warmer sphere of human sympathies' (*AJ Cat* 1862, 322). Approval was not however universal. F T Palgrave disliked his elaborate use of surface detail, particularly evident in the model for Prince Albert in Highland dress (**68**): the critic felt that the figure and head had been 'sacrificed to the accoutrements' (*Palgrave* 1866, 81–2). More recently Greenwood, commenting on the sculptor's varied output, judged that 'Despite his early immersion in the studios of the neo-classical sculptors in Rome, Theed developed into versatile and eclectic sculptor who was equally at ease with classicizing ideal works, historical realism and modern life portraiture' (ODNB).

EH

Literary References: *Palgrave* 1886, *passim*; *Athenaeum*, 1891, ii, 393; *The Times*, 11 Sept 1891, 7; *DNB* LVI, 1898, 108–9; *Gunnis* 1968, 386–7; *Baker* 1979, *passim*; *Bayley* 1981, 103–7; *Read* 1982, *passim*; *Darby and Smith* 1983, *passim*; *Grove* 30, 1996, 703 (Stocker); *Brooks* 2000, *passim*
Wills and Administrations: PPR, will with two codicils, 30 September 1891, fol 976 (personal estate £40, 508 6s 9d)

Funerary Monuments

1.	†1821	Mary Somerville		Kentstown, Navan, Co Meath	S	
2.	†1823	General Sir Eyre Coote GCB, KC		Rockbourne, Hants	S	Pevsner, *Hants & Isle of Wight*, 1967, 476
3.	†1824	Cecilia Windham		Felbrigg Hall, Norfolk	S	*Gunnis* 1968, 387
4.	c1825	Elizabeth, Lady Hare (†1823) and Sir Thomas Hare (†1834)		Stow Bardolph, Norfolk	S	*Graves* VII, 1905–6, 353; Pevsner, *Norfolk: N W & S*, 1999, 674; C Lib (repr)
5.	1828	Robert Hanbury		Little Berkhampstead, Herts		*Gunnis* 1968, 387
6.	†1831	Sir Marcus Somerville		Kentstown, Navan, Co Meath		*Potterton* 1975, 84
7.	†1837	Sophia, Lady de L'Isle and Dudley		Penshurst, Kent	S	Pevsner, *Kent: W & Weald*, 1976, 674
8.	†1843	Lady Maria Harriet Somerville		Kentstown, Navan, Co Meath		*Potterton* 1975, 84
9.	†1847	Major-General Archibald Robertson		Kensal Green Cemetery, London		*Curl* 2001, 192
10.	1848	John and Jane Lloyd (†1842)		Gwernaffield, Flint	SD	*Graves* VII, 1905–6, 353; Pevsner, *Clwyd*, 1986, 357–8
11.	†1849	Sir John and Lady Henrietta Frances Shelley-Sidney (†1811) and other family members		Penshurst, Kent	S	*Gunnis* 1968, 387
12.	1851	John Williams of Gwersyllt Park (†1848) Model(s): exhib RA London, 1852, 1343 (model of statue 'Resignation')		Gresford, Denbighs	S	*Graves* VII, 1905–6, 353; *Penny* 1977 (1), 74; C Lib (repr)
13.	1851	Monumental statue of a lady		[Exhib RA, London, 1258]; untraced		*Graves* VII, 1905–6, 353
14.	1853	Humphrey Chetham (†1653)		Manchester Cathedral, Lancs Other versions: reproduced in Parian ware by Copeland		*Graves* VII, 1905–6, 353; *Read* 1982, 108, 112, 164, 165 (repr); *Atterbury* 1989, 159 (repr)
15.	1853	Rev William Turner (†1879)	s	Trent, Dorset	SD	Pevsner, *Dorset*, 1972, 428; C Lib (repr)
16.	1854	Jane Smith (†1852)		Knowl Hill, Berks	SD	Pevsner, *Berks*, 1966, 163
17.	†1855	Major-General William Nairn Forbes		St Paul's Cathedral, Kolkata (Calcutta)		*Groseclose* 1995, 40
18.	1855	Sir James Mackintosh (†1832) Model(s): 'Genius of British Literature', relief, exhib RA, London, 1855, 1441; model for bust exhib RA, London, 1855, 1519		Westminster Abbey, London, nave, north west tower		*Graves* VII, 1905–6, 254; WAM (18); Pevsner, *London: Westminster*, 1973, 454; C Lib (repr)
19.	c1856	Captain Lempriere		Newton Valence, Hants		*ILN*, 8 March 1856, 256; C Lib (repr)
20.	†1856	Countess de Salis		Harlington, Middx	S	*Graves* VII, 1905–6, 354; RG/JP, 8, 1424, 1428
21.	†1857	Louisa Eliza Bright, of Civitavecchia		Kensal Green Cemetery, London		*Gunnis* 1968, 387; *Curl* 2001, 237
22.	1859	James, 1st Lord Sherborne (†1820) and his wife Elizabeth (†1854)		Sherborne, Glos	S	*CIIA* 4/4/92–3 (repr); Pevsner, *Glos: Cotswolds*, 1999, 602; C Lib (repr)
23.	?1860	David Williams		Winchester Cathedral, Hants		RG/JP, 8, 1428
24.	1860	Henry Denison (†1858)		All Souls College, Oxford		*Gunnis* 1968, 387
25.	1860	Lady Eardley		Little Berkhampstead, Herts		*Gunnis* 1968, 387;
26.	1859–1860	Princess Mary, Duchess of Gloucester (†1857) (designed by Sir George Gilbert Scott)		St George's Chapel, Windsor Castle	S	*Graves* VII, 1905–6, 354; *Bond* 1999, 223
27.	1861	Captain Sir William Peel (†1858)		Sandy, Beds		*Gunnis* 1968, 386; C Lib (repr)
28.	†1862	Elizabeth Graham Croft		Doddington, Kent	S	
29.	1862	Henry Hallam (†1859)		St Paul's Cathedral, London	SD	*Graves* VII, 1905–6, 354; *Ormond* 1973, 209; Pevsner, *London: City*, 1997, 182; C Lib (repr)
30.	†1862	Sir John Croft		Doddington, Kent	S	*Gunnis* 1968, 387
31.	1863	Caroline Hanbury		Thundridge, Herts		*Gunnis* 1968, 387
32.	1864	Albert, the Prince Consort (†1861) (designed by A J Humbert)		Whippingham, I of W		*ILN*, 16 July 1864, 77 (repr); *Darby and Smith* 1983, 22–3
33.	†1864	Hon and Rev Richard Cust		Belton, Lincs	S	
34.	1864	Victoria Mary Louise, Duchess of Kent (†1861) Model(s): Royal coll RCIN 90573, plaster		Royal Coll, Frogmore RCIN 60770	SD	C Lib (repr)
35.	†1865	Stapleton, Viscount Combermere		Wrenbury, Cheshire	S	*Read* 1982, 191, 197; C Lib (repr)
36.	†1868	Major-General Sir Herbert Edwardes KCB		Westminster Abbey, London, north transept		*Ormond* 1973, 157
37.	†1868	Robert (†1866) and Laura Hanbury		Essendon, Herts		*Gunnis* 1968, 387; *Penny* 1977 (1), 116; C Lib (repr)
38.	c1868	Robert Culling-Hanbury Model(s): exhib RA, London, 1868, 1099 (model of Faith); RA, London, 1868, 1012 (portrait of Culling Hanbury)		Thundridge, Herts		*Graves* VII, 1905–6, 355; *Gunnis* 1968, 387
39.	1875	Lieutenant-Colonel George Hussey Packe (†1874)		Prestwold, Leics	SD	*Gunnis* 1968, 387; C Lib (repr)
40.	1884	Archdeacon Grant		St Albans Cathedral, Herts	SD	C Lib (repr)

Statues

No.	Date	Title	Material	Location	SD	References
41.	1820	Hercules, copy of a figure from the British Museum		[Soc of A, silver palette]; untraced		RSA *Transactions* 1820, vol 38, xxxv
42.	1830–1831	Spring and Summer	m	Sold Sotheby, 14 July 1996; untraced	SD	
43.	1837	Diana the Huntress (A nymph preparing her bow for the chase)	m	Seago, Pimlico Road, London (March 1997)	SD	*Graves* VII, 1905–6, 353
44.	1841	Hebe		John Harris sale, Christie, 4 March 1872; untraced		RG/JP, 8, 1425
45.	pre-1844	Terpsichore		[Theed's studio, Rome]; untraced		*Le Grice* 1844, II, 232
46.	1847	Narcissus	m	Buckingham Palace, London RCIN 69002 Other versions: Anglesey Abbey, Cambs, gardens, 1848, marble Temple Newsam House, Leeds, WR Yorks, 1848	SD	*AJ Cat* 1851, 322; *Manchester Art Treasures* 1857, 133; *Holland Park* 1957, unpag (repr); *Read* 1982, 133, 201; *Leeds* 1996, 10 (repr); *Laing* 2001, 37 (repr
47.	1847	Psyche lamenting the loss of Cupid	m	Buckingham Palace, London RCIN 2044	SD	*Graves* VII, 1905–6, 353; Pevsner, *London I*, 1973, 509; *Grove* 30 1996, 703
48.	1847	Rebecca (Rebekah looking at her bracelet)		[coll Miss Rundell]; untraced Other versions: Sotheby, 22 March 1985, lot 326, marble statuette, SD 1868 (as a pair with Ruth) Mansion House, London, plaster Reproduced in Parian ware, by Copeland, 1851		*Manchester Art Treasures* 1857, 134; *Graves* 1875, 534; *Graves* VII, 1905–6, 353; *Holland Park* 1957, unpag (repr); *Gunnis* 1968, 386; *Atterbury* 1989, 151 (repr)
49.	1848	Charles Norris	m	[Mumbai Cathedral]; Asiatic Society, Mumbai (Bombay), India (formerly Town Hall)	SD	*Graves* VII, 1905–6, 353; *Groseclose* 1995, 134 n14; *Steggles* 2000, 149; C Lib (repr)
50.	1848	Demosthenes, statuette		[coll Richard Cobden]; Dunford House, Heyshott, Sussex, now YMCA	SD	
51.	1850	The prodigal son, 'Father I have sinned', group	m	[coll Lord Yarborough]; Usher Art Gallery, Lincoln Other versions: SD 1850, ex Nidd Hall, W R Yorks; sold Sotheby, 26 Nov 1996, lot 1 Burnley Museum, Lancs, statuette, SD 1867, marble		*AJ*, 1851, 218; *Graves* VII, 1905–6, 353; *Friedman and Stevens* 1972, 34; *Atterbury* 1989, 558 (repr)
52.	1851	Prometheus	m	[Gt Exhib, London]; untraced		*Graves* VII, 1905–6, 353; *Gunnis* 1968, 386
53.	1851	Sappho Payment(s): £157 10s	m	Buckingham Palace, London RCIN 2079 Other versions: Reproduced in Parian ware by Copeland, 1851 and 1869	SD	*AJ Cat* 1851, 2–3 (repr); *AJ* 1855, 30 (repr); *Atterbury* 1989, 155 (repr)
54.	1853	Napoleon, seated figure, model for Copeland Parian ware		Untraced		*Atterbury* 1989, 144 (repr)
55.	1855	John Dalton (after Sir Francis Chantrey)	b	Manchester Metropolitan University, Lancs, outside John Dalton Building		*CIIA* 4/6/141 (repr); *Read* 1982, 112
56.	pre-1855	Ruth	m	[Manc Art Treas Exhib, 35]; untraced Other versions: Sotheby, 22 March 1985, lot 326, marble statuette, SD 1868 (pair with Rebekah) reproduced in Parian ware, by Copeland		*AJ*, 1855, 300 (repr); *Manchester Art Treasures* 1857, 133; *Atterbury* 1989, 151 (repr)
57.	1856	An Indian officer, design		[Exhib RA, London, 1327]; untraced		*Graves* VII, 1905–6, 354
58.	1857	Boadicea		[coll Sir M Peto]; untraced		*Gunnis* 1968, 386
59.	1857	Hon Evelyn Cornwallis Anderson Pelham		[Exhib RA, London, 1237]; untraced		*Graves* VII, 1905–6, 354
60.	1857	James Watt (after Sir Francis Chantrey)	b	Piccadilly Garden, Manchester, Lancs		*CIIA* 4/6/64 (repr); Pevsner, *Lancs: S*, 1969, 296
61.	1858	Edmund Burke (†1797) Model(s): exhib RA, London, 1858, 1179	m	Palace of Westminster, London, St Stephen's Hall	SD	*ILN*, 5 June 1858, 568 (repr); *Graves* VII, 1905–6, 354; *Walker* 1961, 10, cat 13
62.	1858	Morning and Evening, seated figures for Queen's Gate, Hyde Park, models only		Untraced		*Gunnis* 1968, 386
63.	1858	Sir Isaac Newton Model(s): exhib RA, London, 1859, 1261	b	St Peter's Hill, Grantham, Lincs Other versions: New College, Oxford, plaster statuette, SD 1857	SD	*ILN*, 2 Oct 1858, 299, 315–6 (repr); *Graves* VII, 1905–6, 354; *Gunnis* 1968, 386; Pevsner, *Lincs*, 1989, 322
64.	1856–1858	The bard (inspired by Thomas Gray's poem) Model(s): exhib RA, London, 1857, 1225	m	CL Coll, Mansion House, City of London, inv 148	SD	*Graves* VII, 1905–6, 354; *Knight* 1986, 347 (repr); *Ward-Jackson* 2003, 252–3 (repr)
65.	1860	Captain Sir William Peel VC	m	[Greenwich Naval Gallery, painted hall]; NMM, Greenwich, upper court, SCU 0040	SD	*ILN*, 19 Jan 1861, 68 (repr); *Graves* VII, 1905–6, VII, 354; *Gunnis* 1968, 386; NMM Friends Neswletter, 2004
66.	1861	Malcolm Canmore (electrocast by Elkington & Co) Model(s): exhib RA, London, 1861, 1046	b	Royal Coll	SD	*Graves* VII, 1905–6, 354
67.	1858–1862	Nine generals, Wellington's allies and subordinates in the Napoleonic Wars (cast by Elkington & Co)	b	Wellington College, Berks		*Baker* 1979, 1–9

68.	1861–1863	Albert, the Prince Consort in Highland dress Model(s): exhib RA, London, 1864, 867	m	Royal Coll, Balmoral Other versions: Royal Coll, Balmoral, 1863, bronze Royal Coll, Osborne, SD 1863, bronze Cliveden, Bucks, SD 1865, bronze (in store) reproduced as a statuette by Elkington & Co (eg Coburg coll)		*Graves* VII, 1905–6, 354; *Ormond* 1973, 14; *Darby and Smith*, 1983, 11–13 (repr)
69.	1863	Captain Sir William Peel	m	[Eden Gardens, Kolkata (Calcutta)]; Temple of Fame, Barrackpore (1970s)		*ILN*, 12 Dec 1863, 592; *Steggles* 2000, 156
70.	1864	Africa		Albert Memorial, Kensington Gardens, London		*Bayley* 1981, 103, 105–7, 114–5 (repr); *Brooks* 2000, *passim* (repr)
71.	1864	Prince Albert as a Christian knight, silver statuette		Royal Coll Other versions: coll Royal Green Jackets, 1867, silver		*Darby and Smith* 1983, 16, 17 (repr)
72.	1865	Albert, the Prince Consort (cast by Lenz & Heoldt, Nuremberg)	b	Coburg, Germany, market place Other versions: Grimsby Docks, Lincs Roenau, Germany ex Royal Albert Infirmary, Bishop's Waltham, 1865, terracotta (cast by Blashfield), destr *c*1914 Sydney, Australia, SD 1866	SD	*Darby and Smith* 1983, 76–78, 114 n84 (repr)
73.	1861–1866	King George IV	m	[Westminster Hall, London]; Central Criminal Court (Old Bailey), City of London, entrance hall		*Ward-Jackson* 2003, 73 (repr)
74.	1861–1866	King William IV	m	[Westminster Hall, London]; Central Criminal Court (Old Bailey), London, entrance hall		*Ward-Jackson* 2003, 73–4 (repr)
75.	1866	Musidora	m	[Marlborough House, London]; untraced Other versions: reproduced in Parian ware by Copeland, 1867		*Graves* VII, 1905–6, 354; *Gunnis* 1968, 387; *Atterbury* 1989 153 (repr)
76.	1862–1867	Queen Victoria and Albert, the Prince Consort, in Saxon dress ('The Parting') Model(s): Plaster, Royal Coll, on loan NPG 69045	m	Royal mausoleum, Frogmore, Berks, RCIN 60778	SD	*Graves* 1905–6, VII, 354–5; *Ormond* 1973, 14, 489; *Darby and Smith* 1983, 13–15 (repr)
77.	1867–1869	Edward, 14th Earl of Derby Payment(s): £1,000	m	St George's Hall, Liverpool, Lancs Other versions: Hughenden Manor, Bucks	SD	*ILN*, 14 Aug 1869, 169; *Ormond* 1973, 137; *Cavanagh* 1997, 277–8 (repr)
78.	1871	Angel writing on a shield; Angel with a dragon	s	Windsor Castle, RCIN 29983, 29984	SD	
79.	1872–1873	Sir Robert Peel		[Huddersfield, W R Yorks]; removed 1949		*ILN*, LXII, 14 June 1873, 561 (repr); *Ormond* 1973, 373
80.	1874	Henry Booth		[William Brown library, Liverpool, Lancs, great hall]; St George's Hall, Liverpool, Lancs, north vestibule		*Cavanagh* 1997, 292–4 (repr)
81.	1874	Margaret Roberts	m	[Exhib RA, London, 1500]; untraced		*Graves* VII, 1905–6, 355
82.	1876	Hagar and Ishmael		[coll Lord Cowdray]; untraced		*Gunnis* 1968, 387
83.	1876	Hon Charles Pelham Villiers MP	m	Manchester Town Hall, Lancs Other versions: West Park, Wolverhampton, Staffs		*Read* 1982, 113; C Lib (repr)
84.	1878	John Bright		Manchester Town Hall, Lancs	D	*Graves* VII, 1905–6, 355; *Gunnis* 1968, 387; *Read* 1982, 110, 112–3 (repr)
85.	1879	William Ewart Gladstone		Manchester Town Hall, Lancs		*Gunnis* 1968, 387; *Read* 1982, 111, 113 (repr)
86.	*c*1885	Dancing girl	m	Dunorlan Park, Tunbridge Wells, Kent (in the gardens until 1958)		*Gunnis* 1968, 387
87.	nd	The Seasons, four figures, models for Copeland Parian ware		Untraced		*Atterbury* 1989, 168 (repr)
88.	nd	Torso of Psyche, copy after an antique fragment	m	NGS		*Pearson* 1991, unpag
Busts						
89.	1824	Unidentified gentleman		[Exhib RA, London, 1029]; untraced		*Graves* VII, 1905–6, 353
90.	1825	'A young lady'		[Exhib RA, London, 986]; untraced		*Graves* VII, 1905–6, 353
91.	1826	Unidentified gentleman		[Exhib RA, London, 1100]; untraced		*Graves* VII, 1905–6, 353
92.	1833	Edward Swinburne	m	[Exhib RA, London, 1183]; untraced		*Graves* VII, 1905–6, 353
93.	1839	Cupid	m	[Exhib RA, London, 1329]; untraced		*Graves* VII, 1905–6, 353
94.	1839	Duke of Lucca Model(s): exhib RA, London, 1839, 1318		Ducal Palace, Lucca		*Graves* VII, 1905–6, 353; *Gunnis* 1968, 387
95.	1839	Prince Charles of Capua, model		[Exhib RA, London, 1382]; untraced		*Graves* VII, 1905–6, 353
96.	1839	Princess of Capua	m	[Exhib RA, London, 1380]; untraced		*Graves* VII, 1905–6, 353
97.	1839	Psyche	m	[Exhib RA, London, 1344]; untraced		*Graves* VII, 1905–6, 353
98.	1839	Young woman	m	[Ted Few sale, London, 1995]; untraced	SD	
99.	1841	Unidentified young man	m	Knox/Longstaffe-Gowan coll (acq 1993)	SD	
100.	1842	Unidentified gentleman	m	[Exhib RA, London, 1312]; untraced		*Graves* VII, 1905–6, 353
101.	1844	Helen, Psyche, Emperor Lucius Verus, Emperor Marcus Aurelius		[Hendersyde Park, Roxburgh, coll Mr Waldie]; untraced		RG/JP, 8, 1421
102.	1844	James William Farrer	m	Heim Gallery, London	SD	*Graves* VII, 1905–6, 353

No.	Date	Subject	Medium	Location	Signed/Dated	Literature
103.	1844	Thomas William Helps (?)	m	Colnaghi Gallery, London (1986)	SD	*Graves* VII, 1905–6, 353; *The British Face* 1986, 104–1 (repr)
104.	1845	James Scott	m	[Exhib RA, London, 1433]; untraced		*Graves* VII, 1905–6, 353
105.	1845	Lady Culling Smith		[Exhib RA, London, 1428]; untraced		*Graves* VII, 1905–6, 353
106.	1845	Mrs Williams Helps	m	[Exhib RA, London, 1431]; untraced		*Graves* VII, 1905–6, 353
107.	1845	Sir Culling Eardley Smith		[Exhib RA, London, 1437]; untraced		*Graves* VII, 1905–6, 353
108.	1845	Sir Robert Dundas	m	Armiston House, Midlothian	SD	
109.	1845	Unidentified bearded man	m	[Sotheby, 27 Nov 1984, lot 463]; untraced	SD	
110.	1847	A gentleman (probably a member of the Morrison family)	m	[Siegfried Sassoon sale, Phillips, Bath, 1994]; untraced	SD	
111.	1847	Unidentified lady	m	[Exhib RA, London, 1409]; untraced		*Graves* VII, 1905–6, 353
112.	1848	James Silk Buckingham		[Exhib RA, London, 1458]; untraced		*Graves* VII, 1905–6, 353
113.	1848	Thomas William Tatton	m	[Wythenshawe Hall, Lancs]; Manchester CAG 1986.9	S	
114.	1848	Unidentified man	p	St George's Hospital, London, medical school library	SD	*Gunnis* 1968, 386
115.	1849	James Morrison	m	[Exhib RA, London, 1282]; sold Phillips, Bath, 1994; untraced	SD	*Graves* VII, 1905–6, 353
116.	1850	Paris		[Hendersyde Park, Roxburgh, coll Mr Waldie]; untraced		RG/JP, 8, 1421
117.	1851	Edward Riddle FRAS	m	[coll Edward Riddle]; Officers' mausoleum, Old Greewich Hospital burial ground, London	S	*ILN*, 29 May 1852, 436; C Lib (repr)
118.	1851	Mrs Pickersgill	m	[Exhib RA, London, 1360]; untraced		*Graves* VII, 1905–6, 353
119.	1851	Sir Charles Bell	m	[Exhib RA, London, 1358]; untraced		*Graves* VII, 1905–6, 353
120.	1852	John Gibson RA		Conway parish church, Carnarvon Other versions: RA, London, 03/3725, *c*1852 NPG, London, inv 1795, *c*1868, marble Stanford Hall, Leics, coll Lord Braye, c1868	SD	*Graves* VII, 1905–6, 353, 355; *Ormond* 1973, 186–7 (repr 353)
121.	1852	William Clifford	m	[Exhib RA, London, 1458]; untraced		*Graves* VII, 1905–6, 353
122.	1853	Helen of Troy Payment(s): 35 gns	m	[Exhib BI, London, 589]; untraced		*Graves* 1875, 534
123.	1853	James Stewart Mackenzie, of Seaforth	m	[Exhib RA, London, 1445]; untraced		*Graves* VII, 1905–6, 354
124.	1853	Lieutenant-General Guy George Carlton L'Estrange	m	[Exhib RA, London, 1407]; Christie, 24 Sept 1987, lot 172; untraced		*Graves* VII, 1905–6, 354
125.	1853	Sappho Payment(s): £35	m	[Exhib BI, London, 589]; untraced		*Graves* 1875, 534
126.	1854	Elizabeth, Lady Eastlake	m	[Exhib RA, London, 1497]; untraced		*Graves* VII, 1905–6, 354
127.	1854	Lady Cranworth	m	[Exhib RA, London, 1464]; untraced		*Graves* VII, 1905–6, 353–4
128.	1854	William Foster	m	[Exhib RA, London, 1496]; untraced		*Graves* VII, 1905–6, 354
129.	1855	F M Copeland	m	[Exhib RA, London, 1457]; untraced		*Graves* VII, 1905–6, 254
130.	1855	Periander, after the antique	m	Royal Coll, Osborne House, I of W, RCIN 41031	SD	C Lib (repr)
131.	1855	Rev Dr Francis Hessey		[Exhib RA, London, 1511]; untraced		*Graves* VII, 1905–6, 254
132.	1856	Hon Evelyn Anderson Pelham		Brocklesby Park, Lincs		RG/JP, 8, 1426
133.	1856	Six classical busts Payment(s): £504	m	Buckingham Palace, London	SD	
134.	*c*1857	Venus and Cupid		[Hendersyde Park, Roxburghshire]; untraced		RG/JP, 8, 1421
135.	1858	Edmund, Baron Lyons		National Army Museum, London		*Ormond* 1973, 284
136.	1858	Flora	m	Bowood, Wilts, private apartments	SD	*Gunnis* 1968, 387; C Lib I (repr)
137.	1859	Albert, the Prince Consort	m	Buckingham Palace, London RCIN 2068	SD	*Graves* VII, 1905–6, 354; *Ormond* 1973, 13
138.	1860	Albert, the Prince Consort		Grocers' Hall, City of London		*Ormond* 1973, 13
139.	1860	Bacchus		Christie, 14 May 1897; untraced		RG/JP, 8, 1427
140.	1860	Classical subject, female	m	Christie, 14 May 1987, lot 230; untraced	SD	
141.	1860	Queen Anne (after Michael Rysbrack)	m	Royal Coll, RCIN 31320	SD	
142.	1860	Queen Victoria	m	Grocers' Hall, City of London Other versions: Wellington College, Berks, library, marble Royal Coll RCIN 2145, SD 1863, bronze (cast by Elkington & Co) reproduced in Parian ware by Copeland, 1864		*Graves* VII, 1905–6, 354; *Ormond* 1973, 488; *Baker* 1979, 13–14; *Atterbury* 1989, 182 (repr)
143.	1861	Frederick, Crown Prince of Prussia (after a model by the Crown Princess of Prussia)	m	Buckingham Palace, London, RCIN 2100	SD	*Gunnis* 1968, 387
144.	1861	John Laird Lawrence, 1st Baron Lawrence	m	Grocers' Hall, City of London	SD	*Graves* 1905–6, VII, 354; *Ormond* 1973, 265
145.	1861	Victoria Mary Louise, Duchess of Kent	m	Royal Coll, Osborne House, I of W, RCIN 41222 Other versions: Reproduced in Parian ware by Copeland, 1874 (eg, Royal Coll RCIN 24424)	SD	*Atterbury* 1989, 184 (repr)
146.	1858–1862	27 officers of the Duke of Wellington's Regiment (cast by Elkington & Co) Payment(s): £50 each (approx) Model(s): Sandhurst Military Academy	b	Wellington College, Berks, quadrangles		*Baker* 1979, 9–14

No.	Date	Subject		Location		References
147.	1862	Albert, the Prince Consort, draped	m	Royal Coll, Osborne House, I of W Other versions: Royal Coll, several egs in marble and bronze RSA, London, SD, 1862 Schloss Callenberg, Coburg, Germany, 1863 Wellington College, Berks, library, marble Royal College of Surgeons, Dublin, 1863 Surrey County Hospital, Guildford, 1866 VAM, 1864, bronze (cast by Elkington & Co) Reproduced in Parian ware, by Copeland, 1864	SD	*Graves* VII, 1905–6, 354; *Ormond* 1973, 14; *Baker* 1979, 13–14; *Read* 1982, 130, 132, 171 (repr); *Darby and Smith* 1983, 7–10 (repr); *Atterbury* 1989, 182 (repr); *Bilbey* 2002, 414 (repr)
148.	1861–1862	Albert, the Prince Consort, with bare shoulders	m	Royal Coll, Osborne House, I of W Other versions: Royal Coll, Buckingham Palace, SD 1862 Howick coll (presented to Hon Charles Grey 1862)		*Darby and Smith* 1983, 7–10 (repr)
149.	1864	Henry Hallam		Royal Coll RCIN 70076	SD	
150.	1864	Unidentified lady	m	[Exhib RA, London, 939]; untraced		*Graves* VII, 1905–6, 354
151.	c1865	George, 1st Earl of Aberdeen (†1860)	p	Royal Military Academy, Sandhurst		*Ormond* 1973, 3
152.	1867	E Buckley, model for Copeland Parian ware		Untraced		*Atterbury* 1989, 183 (repr)
153.	1867	George, 1st Earl of Aberdeen (two, identical)	b	Harrow School, Middx	S	
154.	1868	Edward, 14th Earl of Derby		Knowsley Hall, Lancs		*Graves* VII, 1905–6, 355; *Ormond* 1973, 137
155.	1869	William, 5th Earl of Dartmouth		[Exhib RA, London, 1286]; untraced		*Graves* VII, 1905–6, 355; *DNB*, LVI, 1898, 109
156.	1868–1872	Sir William Tite Model(s): RIBA, SD 1868	m	Guildhall, Bath, entrance hall	SD	*Graves* VII, 1905–6, 355; *Gunnis* 1968, 387
157.	1873	Admiral Sir Augustus Clifford	m	[Exhib RA, London, 1429]; untraced		*Graves* VII, 1905–6, 355
158.	1873	Feodora, Princess of Hohenlohe-Langenburg	m	Royal Coll, RCIN 13102 Other versions: Royal Coll, RCIN 45136 Reproduced in Parian ware by Copeland, 1875	SD	*Atterbury* 1989, 187 (repr)
159.	1873	Sir Henry Holland, 1st Bt	m	[coll Sir Henry Holland]; NPG, London, 1067	SD	*Graves* VII, 1905–6, 355; *Ormond* 1973, 228–9 (pl 438)
160.	1874	Baron Sylvain van der Weyer	m	Royal Coll RCIN 29916 Other versions: Reproduced in Parian ware by Copeland, 1874	SD	*Atterbury* 1989, 187 (repr)
161.	1875	Sir Charles Lyell		Westminster Abbey, London, nave Other versions: Royal Soc, London		*Ormond* 1973, 280; C Lib (repr)
162.	1877	General, Lord William Sandhurst	m	[Exhib RA, London, 1405]; untraced		*Graves* VII, 1905–6, 355; *Graves* II, 1913–15, 1303
163.	1877	Lady Augusta Stanley	m	Royal Coll		*Gunnis* 1968, 387
164.	1878	William Ewart Gladstone		Lady Lever, Port Sunlight, Lancs, inv LL 320	SD	*Graves* VII, 1905–6, 355; *Lady Lever* 1999, 75–7 (repr)
165.	1879	Augustus Frederick, Duke of Sussex	m	Royal Coll RCIN 2004	SD	*Gunnis* 1968, 387; C Lib (repr)
166.	1879	Robert Arthur, 3rd Marquis of Salisbury	m	[Hatfield House, Herts]; Palace of Westminster, London (on loan since 1982)	SD	*Graves* VII, 1905–6, 355; *Ayerbach and Adams*, 1971, 241; C Lib (repr)
167.	1879	Sir Francis Goldsmid	m	Benchers' Hall, Lincoln's Inn, London	SD	*Graves* VII, 1905–6, 355; *Gunnis* 1968, 387; C Lib (repr)
168.	1879	William Pitt the Younger (after Nollekens)	m	Lincoln's Inn, London	SD	*Gunnis* 1968, 387; C Lib (repr)
169.	1881	Augustus Frederick, Duke of Sussex	m	Royal Coll RCIN 31622	SD	
170.	1881	Rowland Hill	m	Manchester Town Hall, Lancs	SD	*Gunnis* 1968, 387; C Lib (repr)
171.	1886	General Gordon	m	CL Coll, Guildhall, City of London, inv 291		*Knight* 1986, 347 (repr)
172.	1888	Unidentified man		Christie, 14 May 1987; untraced	SD	RG/JP, 8, 1427; C Lib (repr)
173.	nd	Autumn and ?Spring	m	Royal Coll RCIN 2007, 2006		
174.	nd	Field Marshal, Lord Henry Hardinge	p	NAM		*Ormond* 1973, 214
175.	nd	George Frederick Handel (after L-F Roubiliac), model for J Ridgeway Bates & Co, Parian ware		Untraced		*Atterbury* 1989, 240 (repr)
176.	nd	Napoleon, model for Copeland Parian ware		Untraced		*Atterbury* 1989, 183 (repr)
Architectural Sculpture						
177.	c1851	Sea allegories surrounding Andromeda fountain (fountain by John Bell)		Royal Coll, Osborne House, I of W		Pevsner, *Hants & Isle of Wight*, 1967, 758
178.	1856	Five statues emblematic of cities: Manchester, Glasgow, Belfast, Dublin, Edinburgh		Somerset House, London, new wing		*Gunnis* 1968, 386; C Lib (repr)

179.	1856	Reliefs, some on the theme of Cupid and Psyche		Buckingham Palace, London, banqueting room		*Gunnis* 1968, 386
180.	1856	The birth of Venus and Venus bringing armour to Achilles, two reliefs		Buckingham Palace, London, west gallery		*Gunnis* 1968, 386; Pevsner, *London: Westminster*, 1973, 509
181.	1859–1860	Hercules and the Thracian Horse Payment(s): £330		Buckingham Palace, London, riding house pediment		*Colvin* 1973–76, V, 301, 307; *Whinney* 1988, 471 n61; C Lib (repr)
182.	1867	Reredos		St John, Croydon, Surrey		*Gunnis* 1968, 386
183.	1869	John Locke, Sir Francis Bacon, Adam Smith, statues in niches		Former University of London Headquarters, Burlington Gardens, London, façade		*Read* 1982, 226 (repr)
184.	1884	Camel caravan (Peek Bros trademark)	s	Peek House, Eastcheap, City of London	SD	*Ward-Jackson* 2003, 99 (repr)
Reliefs						
185.	1853–1856	Scenes from Tudor history, twelve reliefs (cast in bronze by Elkington & Co)	b	Prince's chamber, Palace of Westminster, London		*Graves* VII, 1905–6, 353–4; *Bond* 1980, 66, 68–74 (repr)
Miscellaneous						
186.	1822	Plaster copy of a single figure		[Soc of A, silver Isis medal]; untraced		RSA *Transactions* 1822, vol 40, xxxviii
187.	1855	Robert Clive MP	m	[Exhib RA, London, 1539]; untraced		*Graves* VII, 1905–6, 254
188.	1857	Right hand and wrist of Princess Alice, aged 14	m	Royal Coll RCIN 35479		
189.	1861	Death mask and casts of hands of Albert, the Prince Consort		[coll Queen Victoria]; untraced		*Darby and Smith* 1983, 6
190.	1862	Figure of a dead child		Churchgate Street parish church, Essex, window-sill	SD	*Gunnis* 1968, 386
191.	1877	George Clive MP	m	[Exhib RA, London, 1438]; untraced		*Graves* VII, 1905–6, 355

THOM, James 1802–50

Thom was one of a group of Scottish mason sculptors, whose direct and often humorous depictions of popular subjects from Scottish history and literature enjoyed a vogue in the early 19th century (others included **John Greenshields, Robert Forrest, David Anderson**, and **John Currie**). He was born on 17 April 1802 at Skeoch Farm near Lochlee in Tarbolton parish, Ayrshire, and baptized at Tarbolton church on 19 April, the second of three sons of James Thom, a farm worker, and his wife, Margaret Morrison. The family later moved to Meadowbank in the adjoining parish of Stair, where Thom attended the local school until he and his younger brother, **Robert Thom**, were apprenticed to Howie and Brown, builders of Kilmarnock. When his apprenticeship ended Thom was employed by the firm as an ornamental carver and it was while renovating a tombstone at Crosbie Kirkyard, Troon in 1827 that he attracted the attention of his first and most influential patron, David Auld, the custodian of the Burns monument at Alloway. At Auld's suggestion Thom carved a bust of Robert Burns after the portrait by Alexander Nasmyth that hung at the Burns Monument (**10**).

Auld was so impressed with the bust that he encouraged the sculptor to attempt a more ambitious work and in 1828, while residing with Auld at Doonbrae Cottage in the gardens of the Burns monument, Thom carved a life-size statue of Burns's *Tam o' Shanter* (**1**). He did not make preliminary sketches but carved the figure directly from a block of rough-grained sandstone supplied by his patron from a neighbouring quarry. A companion statue of *Souter Johnnie* funded by a local subscription soon followed (**2**).

In July 1828, before placing the statues at the Burns Monument Auld exhibited them in Ayr, where they met great success. They were then displayed in Edinburgh, where they were admired by Sir Walter Scott, and also in Glasgow. In April 1829 they were sent to London, where the critics at once hailed them as inaugurating a new era in sculpture. They were seen as works of untutored genius unconstrained by academic convention and perfectly capturing the spirit of Burns's poetry. Viewers found their homely naturalism, expressive attitudes and humour particularly appealing. An admission fee of 1s- was charged to see the works and the substantial profits, variously stated as between £900 and £2,000, were divided three ways between Auld, Thom and the trustees of the Burns Monument. In addition Thom received a special award of 20 guineas from the Board of Manufactures in Scotland. Moreover the popularity of the exhibition is said to have resulted in 16 orders for replicas of the statues and also led to the production of small scale copies in stone by both Thom and his brother Robert.

Encouraged by this success Thom carved statues of the *The landlord* and *The landlady* (from *Tam O'Shanter*) which he displayed grouped together with *Tam O'Shanter* and *Souter Johnnie* (**5, 6**). Further works based on the writings of Burns and Scott and a statue of Burns soon followed (**3, 4, 8, 9**). Towards the end of 1829 he received the commission for a statue of William Wallace for Ayr and on 11 September 1830 he was given a public dinner at the Burns Monument hotel celebrating the work's completion (**7**). Five years later a second exhibition of Thom's work was held in London, but was not well received.

Around 1836 Thom went to America in pursuit of his agent, who had gone there to exhibit some of Thom's works and embezzled the proceeds. He recovered most of the money owed to him and settled in Newark, New Jersey, where he continued to work as a sculptor, producing replicas of many of his groups and carving ornamental details and decorative statues for gardens. He is also credited with discovering the freestone quarries at Little Falls, New Jersey, which provided stone for a number of major buildings. These included Trinity Church, New York (**11**), where, according to his obituary, Thom 'made an advantageous contract to do the stone-cutting, and executed much of the fine carving for that costly Gothic edifice' (*GM*, 1850, ii, 98). Having amassed a considerable fortune, he purchased a farm at Ramapo, Rockland County, New York, where he built a house to his own design. He died of consumption at a lodging house in New York City on 17 April 1850, leaving a widow and two children. His son James Crawford Thom (1835–1898) became an artist, specialising in landscape and genre paintings.

Literary References: *GM*, 1850, ii, 98; *Builder* 1851, 48; *Gunnis* 1968, 387–8; *Woodward* 1977, vol 1, pt 2, 249–53; *Forbes* 2000, 92–3; *ODNB* (Greenwood)

Statues

1.	1827	Tam O'Shanter	s	Burns National Heritage Park, Alloway, Ayrshire Other versions: Souter Johnnie's cottage, Kirkoswald, Ayrshire (NTS) ex Beauport Park, Sussex; untraced many replicas and small scale copies	*Gunnis* 1968, 388; *Woodward* 1977, vol 1, pt 2, 252; *Pearson* 1991, 73, 76 (repr)
2.	1828	Souter Johnnie	s	Burns National Heritage Park, Alloway, Ayrshire Other versions: Souter Johnnie's cottage, Kirkoswald, Ayrshire (NTS) ex Beauport Park, Sussex; untraced many replicas and small scale copies	*Gunnis* 1968, 388; *Woodward* 1977, vol 1, pt 2, 252; *Pearson* 1991, 73, 76 (repr)
3.	1830	Old Mortality	s	Untraced Other versions: Laurel Hill cemetery, Fairmount Park, Philadelphia, USA, *c*1836	*GM*, 1850, ii, 98; *Gunnis* 1968, 388; *ODNB*
4.	1830	Robert Burns		Untraced Other versions: one executed USA; untraced	*Gunnis* 1968, 388; *ODNB*
5.	*c*1830	The landlady	s	Burns National Heritage Park, Alloway, Ayrshire Other versions: Souter Johnnie's cottage, Kirkoswald, Ayrshire (NTS) several, including one for Lord Cassillis; untraced	*Gunnis* 1968, 388; *Woodward* 1977, vol 1, pt 2, 252
6.	*c*1830	The landlord	s	Burns National Heritage Park, Alloway, Ayrshire Other versions: Souter Johnnie's cottage, Kirkoswald, Ayrshire (NTS) several, including one for Lord Cassillis; untraced	*Gunnis* 1968, 388; *Woodward* 1977, vol 1, pt 2, 252
7.	1830	William Wallace	s	Wallace Tower, Ayr	*Gunnis* 1968, 388; *Woodward* 1977, vol 1, pt 2, 252
8.	*c*1830	Willie brew'd a peck o' maut	s	Untraced	*ODNB*
9.	nd	The Jolly Beggars, eight figures	s	[Gunnersbury Park, Ealing, 1849]; untraced	GPC

Busts

10.	1827	Robert Burns		Untraced	*Gunnis* 1968, 387; *ODNB*

Architectural Sculpture

11.	1839–1846	Decorative carving	s	Trinity church, Broadway at Wall St, New York	*GM*, 1850, ii, 98; *Gunnis* 1968, 388

THOM, Robert, of Glasgow 1805–95

Born in 1805 near Lochlee, he was three years younger than his brother **James Thom**. Like his brother he served his apprenticeship with the building firm of Howie and Brown in Kilmarnock. In the early 1830s he assisted James in making small scale reproductions of his statues of *Souter Johnnie* and *Tam o' Shanter*. In 1839 he erected an obelisk commemorating the victory of the Covenanters over the dragoons of Graham of Claverhouse at Drumclog (1). The *Art Union* considered it did 'great credit' to Thom's 'taste and talent' (*AU*, 1839, 153). He died after a street accident in Glasgow on 21 November 1895, leaving three sons and a daughter. One of his sons, John, worked as a architectural carver between about 1870 and 1900.

Literary References: *Gunnis* 1968, 388; *Woodward* 1977, vol 1, pt 2, 253–4

Architectural Sculpture

1.	1839	Covenanters monument, obelisk	Drumclog, Lanarks	*AU*, 1839, 153; *Gunnis* 1968, 388

THOMAS, G, of Yatton fl *c*1775

Funerary Monuments

1.	†1775	John Gaisford	Axbridge, Somerset	S	

THOMAS, G W, of Bristol fl *c*1828–66

Funerary Monuments

1.	†1828	Robert, 2nd Earl of Liverpool	Hawkesbury, Glos	S	Pevsner, *Glos: Cotswolds*, 1999, 409
2.	†1866	Walter Broad	St Andrew, Burnham-on-Sea	S	RG/JP, 8, 1431

THOMAS, John 1813–62

A versatile and prolific artist, he was primarily an architectural sculptor, best known as the executant of Charles Barry's elaborate gothic revival designs for the Palace of Westminster (the Houses of Parliament), but his sculptural activities included portraiture and 'ideal' works. Thomas was also a successful architect and designer of interior schemes. He was born at Chalford, Glos, perhaps to an hotel-keeper's wife, and was left an orphan at the age of 12 or 13. He was apprenticed to a local stonemason and, since he was put to work restoring gravestones, he must have been familiar with many of the medieval churches in his neighbourhood. Thomas was a hardworking and flexible young craftsman, who painted portraits and signboards and engraved brass plates in his spare time. The course of his career was influenced by a visit to Oxford to see an elder brother, William, an architect. There he was apparently so impressed by the buildings that he decided to concentrate his attention on drawing and carving architectural ornaments.

After completing his apprenticeship Thomas settled in the Birmingham area, near his brother. He found abundant work as an architectural carver and was perhaps for a short time an architect's assistant. A report in the *Art Journal*

(1849, 340) relates that Charles Barry was so impressed by an unidentified gothic monument by Thomas in Huntingdon that he engaged the young man to carve all the architectural ornaments in wood and stone for King Edward VI's Grammar School in New Street (**55**). An alternative explanation for his early association with Barry was given in an obituary, which suggested that Thomas obtained work at the grammar school by his own efforts and was there set to work carving ornamental bosses from wax models. There was a shortage of models, so the resourceful young man made one of his own. This was shown to Barry 'who at once saw that the designer was a man of very superior abilities' (*ILN*, 30 Aug 1862, 431). It was the sustained quality of Thomas's work at King Edward's School, built between 1832 and 1837, that led Barry to appoint him as overseer of decorative carving at the new Palace of Westminster (**80**).

Meanwhile Thomas travelled to Belgium, where he studied late gothic secular buildings including the town halls of Ghent, Bruges, Louvain and Ypres. He returned to England with numerous sketches of architectural details. By May 1841 he was supervising carving at the Palace of Westminster, though he was not formally appointed superintendent of stone carving until 1846. By 1843 work was well advanced and Barry reported to the Office of Works that a large quantity of carved stonework was ready to be fixed into position on three fronts (PRO Work 11/9/7, fols 3, 5). That year Thomas showed a painting, *View of the workshops at the new Houses of Parliament*, at the Royal Academy. The sculptural programme for the palace was extensive and complex: figures of monarchs, angels, saints, heraldic animals and coats of arms were sited on all major elevations, set off by rich gothic ornament. The decoration extended into the grand ceremonial spaces within. Thomas worked closely with Barry, producing detailed drawings from the architect's outline designs, supervising the modelling workshop and directing the stone carvers. The team working directly under Thomas at Westminster included **Robert Jackson**, his chief assistant, **James Mabey**, foreman in the modelling shop and **Thomas Garland**, an architectural modeller. Several sculptors who later developed their own successful practices worked on the extensive decorative scheme. They included **Alexander Munro, John Lawlor, Alexander Handyside Ritchie, Henry Hugh Armstead** and **John Birnie Philip.**

John Thomas took on commissions for other architectural sculpture in various styles while work progressed at Westminster and after its completion in 1853. His sculpture for classical buildings included a pediment group and a series of reliefs representing the cities and towns served by the North Western railway for Philip Charles Hardwick's Euston Square station (**69, 71**), as well as a tympanum relief depicting *The City of Leeds encouraging Commerce and Industry and fostering the Arts and Sciences* for Cuthbert Broderick's Leeds Town Hall (**92**). The Free Trade Hall in Manchester, built in a restrained Renaissance revival style to the designs of Edward Walters, is decorated with allegorical figures of the Continents, Trade, Industry, Commerce and the Arts (**87**). The former West of England and South Wales district bank in Corn Street Bristol, designed by W B Gingell and T R Lysaght 'in a glorious Venetian Cinquecento', is encrusted in decorative sculpture including a frieze 'bulging with putti in various pursuits and coats of arms' (Pevsner).

Thomas's success as an architectural sculptor encouraged him to venture into the realm of fine art, an unusual step for a craftsman without formal fine art training. His portraiture included a number of busts exhibited at the Academy (**41–46**), a statue of Thomas Attwood for Birmingham (**32**) and two statues, of Stephen Langton, the medieval Archbishop of Canterbury (**29**) and William Longespee, Earl of Salisbury (**30**) for the chamber of the House of Lords. The Langton and Longespee were not part of the scheme controlled by Barry but were commissioned by the Royal Fine Art commissioners, who also ordered statues from well-established sculptors like **Patrick MacDowell** and **Thomas Thornycroft.** Thomas's ideal works include a group of *Boadicea* (**25**) commissioned by Sir Morton Peto, who made and lost his fortune in the construction industry, a figure of *Rachel the daughter of Laban* (**26**) and a plaster equestrian statue of *Lady Godiva*, now at Maidstone museum (**33**). Thomas also submitted a design in competition for the national memorial to Arthur, Duke of Wellington, for St Paul's Cathedral (**9**), which was praised in the *Builder*. He exhibited regularly at the RA from 1842 onwards and showed a statuette of *Ariel directing the storm* at the British Institution in 1850 (**17**).

Among his important architectural commissions are two Jacobean revival style mansions: Somerleyton Hall, Suffolk, which was extended and adapted for Sir Morton Peto, and Preston Hall, Aylesford, Kent, built for Peto's business partner Edward Ladd Betts. Thomas was also employed as an interior designer by John Houldsworth, the industrialist and patron of the arts, decorating his new town house at 1 Park Terrace, Glasgow in an eclectic mix of fashionable styles including Elizabethan and Gothic. When the Corporation of Brighton bought the Royal Pavilion from Queen Victoria in 1850 John Thomas designed nine chimneypieces to replace the original Regency ones which had been removed (**49**). He designed a fantastic Chinoiserie chimneypiece and large dragons and griffons above chandeliers in the music room, made in papier-maché by **Charles F Bielefield.**

One of his most discerning patrons was Prince Albert, who commissioned numerous works for the Royal palaces. The exterior walls of Balmoral are enlivened with Thomas's fanciful, medieval inspired reliefs of St Andrew, St George and St Hubert and his depiction of the Royal family attending the Highland Games (**88**). He designed elaborate interior schemes for the private audience chamber and Royal print room at Windsor Castle and for the Royal dairy at the home farm, Frogmore. They are richly embellished with plasterwork, woodwork, painted decoration, ceramic tiles and fountains, all executed from his designs.

Thomas married twice. He died at his home in Blomfield Road, Maida Vale, at the age of 49, leaving a widow and one daughter and was buried in Kensal Green Cemetery. Soon after his death several major works went on display at the International Exhibition (**33, 35, 39, 40, 54, 100**). Initially the exhibition authorities prevaricated about displaying his model for a colossal monument to Shakespeare and it was suggested by a writer in the *Builder* (1862, 275) that the stress attendant on this disappointment hastened his death. He was still working on several projects, including statues of Sir Hugh Myddelton and Joseph Sturge when he died (**36, 38**).

During his lifetime Thomas was admired for his versatility and energy and he produced an enormous quantity and range of work in relatively few years, generally to a high standard. One critic suggested that his diversity was his weakness: 'His best works were not equal to the best works of Foley, Bailey, Durham and such men; it was impossible that they could be. These men devote their whole lives to producing a small number of works of a highly refined character. Thomas's works on the contrary are innumerable; and in every material – stone, wood, glass, porcelain, iron and brass; on wood and on paper; now a palace then a church or a Royal dairy; a whole village of labourers' cottages, an armchair, a pulpit, a sideboard, a stained glass window, a garden seat or a splendid reception room in the palace of the Queen of England' (*ILN*, Aug 30, 1862, 232).

EH

Literary References: *AJ*, 1849, 340, 1862, 144; *Heffer* 1861–62, 111–120; *Builder*, 1862, 275; *ILN*, 30 Aug 1862, 231–2; *DNB*, LVI, 1898, 184–5; Pevsner, *Somerset: N & Bristol*, 1958, 424; *Gunnis* 1968, 388–90; *Physick* 1970, 50, 163–4; *Read* 1976, 232–245; *Read* 1982, *passim*; *Smith* 1998, 266–278; *Read* 2000, 253–269; *Curl* 2001, 243; *ODNB* (Stevens)

Will: PPR, 26 April 1862, fol 248, effects under £25,000

Collections of Drawings: two albums of photographs, drawings and engravings of his works, compiled by a family member, probably around the time of his death, RIBA Drawings Coll, THOMAS, J, 2 vols (RIBA *Drawings Cat* 15, 1972–84, 35–9)

Miscellaneous Drawings: design for staircase lamp pedestals for Somerleyton Hall, VAM P&D pressmark H.2-d; design for a claret jug, to be decorated with reliefs by Maclise, pencil, VAM P&D E.5909-1910; design for a claret jug decorated with *The Triumph of Bacchus*, 2 sheets, pencil, VAM P&D E.5910, 5911-1910

Portraits of the Sculptor: Charles Louis Baugniet, 1847, lithograph, RIBA Drawings Coll, THOMAS, J, vol I, fol 1; self portrait, marble relief c1850, Knox/Longstaffe-Gowan Coll; anon, engraving (*Read* 1976, 241 repr)

Funerary Monuments

No.	Date	Subject	Material	Location	Signed	References
1.	1830	Rev William Owen		Castleton, Dorset	S	*Gunnis* 1968, 388
2.	†1841	Elizabeth Twitt (†1800) and others		Kewstoke, Somerset		RG/JP, 8, 1433v.
3.	†1841	Lieutenant Richard Creed		Westminster Abbey, London, nave, south choir aisle		*MacMichael*, 1977, 34
4.	†1842	Mary Peto		St Paul, Clapham, London		
5.	1844	Dr Thomas Arnold (†1842)	s	Rugby School, Warks, chapel		Pevsner, *Warks*, 1966, 389
6.	1851	Brooks mausoleum		St Mary, Prestwich, Lancs		*AJ Cat* 1851, 94 (repr); *Read* 1982, 188 (repr)
7.	†1852	Richard Selby Thomas		Christ Church, Chalford, Glos	S	*CIIA* 4/4/9 (repr); Pevsner, *Glos: Cotswolds*, 1999, 212
8.	1854	Houldsworth mausoleum		Glasgow Necropolis		*Graves* VII, 1905–6, 359; *McKenzie* 2002, 302–3 (repr)
9.	1857	Arthur, 1st Duke of Wellington (†1852) national memorial, model only (monument by Alfred Stevens) Drawing(s): RIBA		[Exhib Westminster Hall, London]; untraced		*Heffer* 1861–2, 117; *Physick* 1970, 50, 163–4 (repr); *Read* 1982, 29

Statues

No.	Date	Subject	Material	Location	Signed	References
10.	1845	Imogen	m	[Exhib RA, London, 1421]; untraced		*Graves* VII, 1905–6, 359
11.	1845	Queen Victoria		Lincoln's Inn, London, library, south end		*Gunnis* 1968, 389
12.	1845	St Michael		Sowton, Devon		*Gunnis* 1968, 389
13.	1848	Miranda	m	[Exhib RA, London, 1380]; untraced		*Graves* VII, 1905–6, 359
14.	1849	Musidora		[Exhib RA, London, 1340]; untraced Other versions: reproduced in Parian ware		*Heffer* 1861–2, 118; *Graves* VII, 1905–6, 359; *Gunnis* 1968, 389; *Read* 1982, 207
15.	1849	Triton	s	Lowestoft, Waveney, Suffolk		www.imagesofengland.org.uk
16.	1850	Amphitrite, model		[Exhib RA, London, 1312]; untraced		*Graves* VII, 1905–6, 359
17.	1850	Ariel directing the storm, statuette	b	[Exhib BI, London, 493]; Bonham, 25 Nov 1993, lot 161; untraced		*AJ Cat* 1851, 94–5 (repr); *Graves* 1875, 534
18.	1850	Henry Handley	s	Handley memorial, South St, Sleaford, Lincs		Pevsner, *Lincs*, 1989, 655
19.	1851	Rosamunda		[Gt Exhib, London]; untraced		*AJ Cat* 1851, 94–5 (repr)
20.	1853	Night, statuette	m	[Exhib RA, London, 1308]; untraced		*Graves* VII, 1905–6, 359
21.	pre-1854	Oliver Cromwell	p	[Crystal Palace, Sydenham, cast]; untraced		*JKB* 2007, 195 (repr)
22.	1854	Pleading for the innocent and Feeding the young, two groups (portraits of the children of E L Betts)		Preston Hall, Aylesford, Kent, grounds		*Graves* VII, 1905–6, 359
23.	1855	The Sire and his enemy and the Dam and her pets, two groups	m	Preston Hall, Aylesford, Kent, grounds		*Graves* VII, 1905–6, 359
24.	1856	Augustus Frederick, Duke of Sussex		Royal Free Hospital, London		*Gunnis* 1968, 389;
25.	1856	Queen Boadicea, group	m	[coll Sir S Morton Peto]; untraced Other versions: BMAG, bronze		*Manchester Art Treasures* 1857, 134; *Graves* VII, 1905–6, 359; *Read* 1982, 145–6
26.	1856	Rachel, the daughter of Laban, with a lamb at her feet	m	VAM 257-1885	SD	*Graves* VII, 1905–6, 359; *Bilbey* 2002, 415 (repr)
27.	1853–1856	Two saints		St Martin, the Bullring, Birmingham, tower		*Gunnis* 1968, 389; *Read* 1982, 258
28.	1844–1857	Reclining figures of Night and Day; groups of a huntsman with hounds and a huntsman with a stag; unidentified statuary on the loggia; deer on the gateposts at the main entrance		Somerleyton Hall, Suffolk, grounds		*Heffer* 1861–2, 114; *Read* 1982, 143–5 (repr)
29.	1847–1858	Stephen Langton, Archbishop of Canterbury (†1228)	b	Palace of Westminster, London, House of Lords		*Walker* 1961, 44, 97–8, cat 47
30.	1847–1858	William Longespee, Earl of Salisbury (†1225) Model(s): exhib RA, London, 1850, 1322	b	Palace of Westminster, London, House of Lords		*Graves* VII, 1905–6, 359; *Walker* 1961, 64, 97–8, cat. 67
31.	1858–1859	Apollo, Thetis, Briseis, Penelope and Calypso	m	[ex coll John Houldsworth, 1 Park Terrace, Glasgow]; untraced		*Graves* VII, 1905–6, 360; *Smith* 1998, 270
32.	1859	Thomas Attwood (†1856) Payment(s): £900	m	[Stephenson Place, Birmingham, Warks]; Larches Green, Highgate Road, Sparkbrook, Birmingham		*Noszlopy* 1998, 72–3 (repr)

No.	Date	Description	Material	Location		Literature
33.	1861	Lady Godiva	pm	Maidstone Museum and Art Gallery, Kent Other versions: reproduced in Parian ware		*Graves* VII, 1905–6, 360; *Gunnis* 1968, 389; *Read* 1982, 26–7, 37
34.	1861	Naiad (water nymph)	m	Windsor Royal Dairy, Frogmore, Berks Other versions: reproduced in Minton Parian ware		*Graves* VII, 1905–6, 360; *Gunnis* 1968, 389
35.	1861	Una and the lion Drawing(s): RIBA		[Exhib RA, London, 1083]; untraced		*Graves* VII, 1905–6, 360
36.	1862	Joseph Sturge (†1859) Payment(s): £1,000 Drawing(s): RIBA	s	Five Ways, Harborne Road, Birmingham		*Noszlopy* 1998, 70 (repr)
37.	1862	Queen Victoria, in a gothic canopy (the Randall fountain) Drawing(s): RIBA	m	Maidstone, Kent		*Gunnis* 1968, 389; *Read* 1982, 164 (repr)
38.	1862	Sir Hugh Myddelton, above a fountain with putti and vases Payment(s): £900 Drawing(s): RIBA	m	Islington Green, London		*Read* 1982, 145, 164 (repr); *Blackwood* 1989, 156–7 (repr); *Darke* 1991, 66–7 (repr)
39.	1862	William Shakespeare monument, model Drawing(s): RIBA	p	[Int Exhib, London]; untraced		*ILN*, 28 June 1862, 663 (repr); *ILN*, 30 April 1864, 416 (repr); *AJ*, 1862, 144; *Builder*, 1862, 275; *Gunnis* 1968, 389; C Lib (repr)
40.	nd	Undine Drawing(s): RIBA		Untraced		*ILN*, 30 Aug 1862, 232

Busts

No.	Date	Description	Material	Location		Literature
41.	1858	William Thomas	m	[Exhib RA, London, 1312]; untraced		*Graves* VII, 1905–6, 360
42.	1859	Daniel Maclise, on a pedestal with a relief of Hibernia (two versions)	m	NGI 8113, 8184	SD	*Graves* VII, 1905–6, 360; *le Harivel* 1988, 599 (repr)
43.	1859	William Powell Frith	m	Tate Britain, London (NO2061)	S	*Graves* VII, 1905–6, 360; www.tate.org.uk
44.	1855–1860	Albert, the Prince Consort	m	[Midland Institute, Birmingham, Warks]; Birmingham MAG, inv 695'38	D	*Graves* VII, 360; *Ormond* 1973, 13; *Silber* 1987, 90, cat 273
45.	1860	John Phillip RA	m	[Exhib RA, London, 1021]; untraced		*Graves* VII, 1905–6, 360
46.	1860	Study of a head	m	[Exhib RA, London, 1003]; untraced		*Graves* VII, 1905–6, 360

Chimneypieces

No.	Date	Description	Material	Location		Literature
47.	1847	Description unavailable		[Exhib RA, London, 1233]; untraced		*Graves* VII, 1905–6, 359
48.	1849	Figures of Comedy and Tragedy for an Elizabethan fireplace		[The 'Shakespeare Gallery' at Mr Brunel's home]; untraced		*AJ*, 1849, 340
49.	1851	Nine Drawing(s): Royal Pavilion, Brighton		Royal Pavilion, Brighton, Sussex		
50.	1851	With reliefs of Dorigene and Griselda, and a medallion portrait of Geoffrey Chaucer for Preston Hall, Kent		[Gt Exhib, London]; untraced		*AJ Cat* 1851, 94–5 (repr); *ILN* 6 Sept 1851, 300 (repr)
51.	1844–1857	Description unavailable		Somerleyton Hall, Suffolk, tea room		*Heffer* 1861–2, 114; *Read* 1982, 145
52.	1844–1857	Two, with inset medallions of Raphael, James Watt, Beethoven and Shakespeare, and standing figures of Art, Science, Music and Poetry		Somerleyton Hall, Suffolk, drawing room		*Heffer* 1861–2, 114; *Read* 1982, 145
53.	1858–1859	Several		[for John Houldsworth, 1 Park Terrace, Glasgow]; untraced		*Smith* 1998, 268
54.	1862	Decorated with relief figures of Oberon and Titania, busts of two children, and a roundel depicting Little Red Ridinghood Drawing(s): RIBA		Windsor Castle		*AJ Cat* 1862, 124 (repr); *ILN*, 24 May 1862, 538 (repr); *Gunnis* 1968, 389

Architectural Sculpture

No.	Date	Description	Material	Location		Literature
55.	1837	Decorative carving	s	[King Edward VI Grammar School, New Street, Birmingham, Warks]; destroyed		*ILN*, 30 Aug 1862, 231; *Gunnis* 1968, 388; *Read* 1982, 231–2
56.	1837–1839	Coats of arms and heraldic devices		Capesthorne Hall, Cheshire		*AJ*, 1849, 340; *Heffer* 1861–2, 113
57.	*c*1840	Coats of arms and heraldic devices		Crewe Hall, Cheshire		*AJ*, 1849, 340; *Heffer* 1861–2, 113
58.	1837–1840	Lions		[Warwick House, New Street, Birmingham]; untraced		*Heffer* 1861–2, 113
59.	*c*1840	Panels filled with shields and armorial bearings		Several stations on the North Midland railway		*Heffer* 1861–2, 113
60.	1845	Pulpit	s	Sowton, Devon		Pevsner, *Devon*, 1989, 755
61.	1846	Font		St Peter Bolton-le-Moors, Bolton, Lancs		*Gunnis* 1968, 389
62.	1843–1846	King Edward III, Alderman Whitson, Edward Colston, Rt Hon John Dunning, Sir Michael Foster and Queen Victoria, figures Drawing(s): RIBA		Guildhall, Bristol, between first-floor windows	S	*Read* 1982, 235 (repr)
63.	1847	Commerce, Plenty and coat of arms Drawing(s): RIBA (II, f.20)	s	[National Bank, Queen Street, Glasgow]; Langside Public Hall, Pollockshaws Road, Glasgow, Lanarks		*McKenzie* 2002, 273–4 (repr)
64.	1847	Font		Davington Priory, Kent		Pevsner, *Kent: N E & E*, 1983, 280
65.	1847	Font		St John, Westminster, London		*ILN*, 2 Oct 1847, 220 (repr); *Gunnis* 1968, 389

66.	1848	Lions		Britannia Bridge, Menai Straits, Anglesey		*AJ*, 1849, 340; *Gunnis* 1968, 389
67.	c1848	Ornamental stonework		General Station, Chester, Cheshire		Pevsner, *Cheshire*, 1971, 159
68.	1848	Peace and War (two reliefs) Drawing(s): RIBA (War)		Buckingham Palace, London, main staircase hall		*AJ*, 1849, 340; *ILN*, 4 Feb 1854, 104 (repr); *Gunnis* 1968, 389
69.	1847–1848	The chief cities and towns connected with the North-Western Railway Drawing(s): RIBA		[Euston Station, London, great hallway]; untraced		*AJ*, 1840, 340; *Gunnis* 1968, 389; *Read* 1982, 228
70.	1849	A fountain, designed for S Morton Peto		[Exhib RA, London, 659]; untraced		*Graves* VII, 1905–6, 359
71.	1849	Pediment group, Britannia accompanied by a lion, a ship, the Arts, Sciences and Mercury		Euston station, St Pancras, London	SD	*Read* 1982, 228, 229 (repr)
72.	1850	Decorative details		Bridgewater House, Cleveland Row, St James's, London		*Gunnis* 1968, 389
73.	c1850	Figures of bishops, judges and others connected with Lincoln's Inn	wd	Lincoln's Inn, London, dining hall		*AJ*, 1849, 340
74.	pre-1850	Ornaments		Imperial Fire Office, London		*AJ*, 1849, 340
75.	1845–1850	Pulpit, carved with an angel and gothic ornament		All Saints, Wigan, Lancs		*Read* 1982, 249
76.	1845–1850	Reredos, carved with two standing angels and gothic ornament		All Saints, Wigan, Lancs		*Read* 1982, 249
77.	c1850	Vases and other garden ornaments		Preston Hall, Aylesford, Kent, grounds		*AJ Cat* 1851, 104 (repr)
78.	1851	Fountain, with a group of Acis and Galatea	m	Preston Hall, Aylesford, Kent, grounds		*AJ Cat* 1851, 94–5 (repr); *Heffer* 1861–2, 115; *Graves* VII, 1905–6, 359; Pevsner, *Kent: W & Weald*, 1976, 141
79.	1852–1853	Decorative sculpture	s	PRO, City of London, central block		*Ward-Jackson* 2003, 303
80.	1841–1853	Figures, heraldic beasts, coats of arms, bosses and other ornamental carving Drawing(s): RIBA Model(s): formerly Crystal Palace, Sydenham (destroyed 1936)		Palace of Westminster, London		*Heffer* 1861–2, 113–4; *Read* 1976, 232–245 (repr)
81.	1853	Ornaments		Windsor Station, Berks		*Gunnis* 1968, 389
82.	1851–1853	Peace, Plenty, Industry and Science, pediment figures		Great Western Hotel, Paddington, London		*Graves* VII, 1905–6, 359; *Read* 1982, 228; Pevsner, *London: N W*, 1991, 683
83.	1854	Decorative work		[Crystal Palace, Sydenham]; destroyed		*Gunnis* 1968, 389
84.	1855	Exterior carving		Carlton Club, London		GPC
85.	1855	King Edward III, figure		[High Cross, College Green, Bristol, Somerset]; untraced		*Liversidge* 1978, 13–5, 21 n36
86.	1855–1856	Relief panels and pediment scenes of commercial activities, keystone heads (co-sculptor: Alexander Handyside Ritchie)		Former Commercial Bank of Scotland, 2–16 Gordon St, Glasgow		*McKenzie* 2002, 177–8 (repr)
87.	1853–1856	The Continents, Trade, Industry, Commerce and the Arts		Free Trade Hall, Manchester, Lancs, tympana, upper floor		*CIIA* 4/6/106–15 (repr); *Read* 1982, 230 231 (repr)
88.	c1856	The Royal Family at the Highland Games, relief; the Conversion of St Hubert, relief; St George; St Andrew		Balmoral Castle, Aberdeen, façade		*Ames* 1967, 103–4; *Pearson* 1991, 160 (repr)
89.	1857	Statues of Sir Joshua Reynolds and John Flaxman; lunette ornaments and figure group		Royal West of England Academy, Bristol		*Gunnis* 1968, 389
90.	1858	Frieze		United Services Club, London		*Gunnis* 1968, 389
91.	1854–1858	Frieze, spandrel figures and other ornaments		West of England and South Wales Bank (now Lloyds), Corn Street, Bristol		Pevsner, *Somerset: N & Bristol*, 1958, 424; *Read* 1982, 230–1 (repr)
92.	c1858	The City of Leeds encouraging Commerce and Industry and fostering the Arts and Sciences		Leeds Town Hall, W R Yorks, tympanum		*Read* 1982, 213, 215, 228 (repr)
93.	1858–1859	Small statues of historical figures for octagonal fountain (designed by Charles Doyle)		Holyrood Palace, Edinburgh		Pevsner, *Edinburgh*, 1991, 141
94.	1859	St Andrew, Faith, Hope and Charity		Masonic Hall, Edinburgh		*ILN*, 5 March 1859, 236 (repr); *AJ*, 1862, 144
95.	1860	Carving		Crimean Arch, Brompton barracks, Chatham, Kent		GPC
96.	1850–1860	Great Atlas fountain		Castle Howard, N R Yorks		Pevsner, *Yorks: N R*, 1966, 114
97.	1861	Urns, fountain figures, four roundels depicting the Seasons, portrait medallions of Queen Victoria and Prince Albert and other architectural decoration		Water gardens at the head of the Serpentine, Hyde Park, London	S	*Gunnis* 1968, 389; *Read* 1982, 229 231 (repr)
98.	1850–1862	Decorative sculpture		[Buckingham Palace, London, entrance gate piers]; untraced		*ILN*, 30 Aug 1862, 231; *Gunnis* 1968, 389
99.	1850–1862	Sculptural decoration		Sultan's Palace, Istanbul, Turkey		*ILN*, 30 Aug 1862, 231; *Gunnis* 1968, 389
100.	1862	St George fountain Drawing(s): RIBA		[Int Exhib, London]; destroyed		*AJ Cat* 1862, 209 (repr)

101. nd	Decorative work		Life Assurance Building, Edinburgh	*AJ*, 1862, 144
102. nd	Frieze, kings' heads		Windsor Castle, private audience chamber	*Read* 1982, 132
Reliefs				
103. c1850	John Thomas, self portrait	m	Palace of Westminster, London, WOA S240	*Read* 2000, 253 (repr)
104. 1856	Ariel	b	Balmoral Castle, Aberdeen	*Gunnis* 1968, 389
105. 1860	Mrs John Thomas, medallion	m	[Exhib RA, London, 975]; untraced	*Graves* VII, 1905–6, 360
Miscellaneous				
106. 1842	Edgar disguised as 'Mad Tom'		[Exhib RA, London, 1357]; untraced	*Graves* VII, 1905–6, 359
107. 1842	'Lear act 4, scene 6'		[Exhib RA, London, 1382]; untraced	*Graves* VII, 1905–6, 359
108. 1845	Coriolanus		[Exhib RA, London, 1352]; untraced	*Graves* VII, 1905–6, 359
109. 1847	An attendant on the chase; a model to be executed in stone		[Exhib RA, London, 1338]; untraced	*Graves* VII, 1905–6, 359
110. 1847	The water-lily; a model, part of a fountain to be executed in marble		[Exhib RA, London, 1388]; untraced	*Graves* VII, 1905–6, 359
111. 1852	Coats of arms on the funeral car of the Duke of Wellington		St Paul's Cathedral, on loan to the Duke of Wellington, Stratfield Saye, Hants	*Gunnis* 1968, 389
112. 1853	Happy hours		[Exhib RA, London, 1326]; untraced	*Graves* VII, 1905–6, 359
113. 1854	Preparing for the bath; portrait of the artist's infant daughter		[Exhib RA, London, 1469]; untraced	*Graves* VII, 1905–6, 359
114. 1856	Cleopatra		[Exhib RA, London, 1261]; untraced	*Graves* VII, 1905–6, 359

THOMAS, John & Son, of Brecon fl c1813–45

It is possible that the following works are by **John Thomas of Brecon** and his son **John Evan Thomas.**

Funerary Monuments			
1. †1813	Rev Lewis Williams	Myddfai, Carmarthen	*Dale-Jones and Lloyd* 1989, 57
2. †1814	John Bowen	Cynwyl Gaeo, Carmarthen	*Dale-Jones and Lloyd* 1989, 57
3. †1819	David Williams	Llandovery, Carmarthen	*Dale-Jones and Lloyd* 1989, 57
4. †1828	Mary Lewis	Llanwrda, Carmarthen	*Dale-Jones and Lloyd* 1989, 57
5. †1829	Magdalen Price	Myddfai, Carmarthen	*Dale-Jones and Lloyd* 1989, 57
6. †1834	Lewis family	Llanddeusant, Carmarthen	*Dale-Jones and Lloyd* 1989, 57
7. †1835	Rice and Anne Price	Myddfai, Carmarthen	*Dale-Jones and Lloyd* 1989, 57
8. †1838	Rev William Morgan	Cynwyl Gaeo, Carmarthen	*Dale-Jones and Lloyd* 1989, 57
9. †1840	Gwynne-Holford children	Myddfai, Carmarthen	*Dale-Jones and Lloyd* 1989, 57
10. †1842	Elizabeth Johnes	Abergwili, Carmarthen	*Dale-Jones and Lloyd* 1989, 57
11. †1845	Enoch children	Cynwyl Gaeo, Carmarthen	*Dale-Jones and Lloyd* 1989, 57
12. †1845	Rev Joshua Davies	[Llanbydder, Carmarthen]; untraced	*Dale-Jones and Lloyd* 1989, 57

THOMAS, John Evan 1810–73

John Evan Thomas senior and his wife, Jane, of Brecon, South Wales, were the parents of three gifted sons. John Evan Thomas, the eldest, was born on 15 January 1810 and by the age of 14 showed such a talent for carving fruits and flowers in stone that he was sent to London to study under **Sir Francis Chantrey. William Meredyth Thomas** followed his elder brother into Chantrey's studio and James Lewis Thomas became a successful architect and eventually chief surveyor to the War Office.

Thomas spent some time on the Continent before returning to London to take a studio in Belgrave Place and by 1830 was producing funerary monuments, mostly for Welsh clients. He first exhibited at the Royal Academy in 1838, showing a bust of Daniel Jones, a benefactor of the Cardiff Infirmary (**66**). In 1840 he married Mary Gunter who came from a distinguished Welsh family and by this time William Meredyth had joined him as his assistant, an arrangement that was to last for 30 years. In 1842 John Evan became a fellow of the Society of Antiquaries, proposed, among others, by Admiral William Henry Smyth and the architect, George Godwin, who later became editor of the *Builder*.

A statue of the Marquess of Londonderry was commissioned by the Marquess's brother for Westminster Abbey (**37**). It was exhibited at Westminster Hall in 1844 and then displayed on the staircase at Holderness House during a banquet, where it was 'universally admired'. In 1848 Thomas provided a statue of Sir Charles Morgan MP for Bridge Street, Newport (**53**). During the same period Thomas executed two statues for Charles Barry's new Palace of Westminster, Henri de Londres, Archbishop of Dublin, (**57**) and the Earl of Pembroke (**64**), both signatories of Magna Carta. In 1848 also he showed his *Death of Tewdric, King of Gwent and Morganwg* at the Abergavenny Eisteddfod and won a prize of 70 guineas for 'the best model in plaster illustrative of Cambro-British History' (**55**). This was later cast in bronze by Elkington & Co and shown as part of their display at the Great Exhibition of 1851. Thomas, who was one of the original guarantors of the exhibition, showed a statue of the Marquess of Bute destined for Cardiff (**59**) and a plaster relief, *Science unveiling ignorance* (**107**). In 1852 he produced a bust of Sir Benjamin Hall (**93**), the chief commissioner for works at the time of the rebuilding of the Palace of Westminster, for whom the great bell in the clock tower was named 'Big Ben'.

Following the death of the Duke of Wellington in 1852 Thomas was commissioned by the corporation of Brecon to design a statue to his memory for the town, incorporating a relief showing the death at Waterloo of the Welsh hero, General Picton (**63**). Thomas himself contributed £700 towards the cost of the memorial which was unveiled in 1856.

James Lewis Thomas was treasurer to the Most Honourable and Loyal Society of Ancient Britons which owned a school in London for children of Welsh parentage. When the school moved to its present site in Ashford in 185, John Evan Thomas was given the commission to produce a statue of the Prince of Wales for the entrance hall (**61**). The young prince, accompanied by his father, went to the sculptor's studio for sittings.

Thomas moved back to Wales in 1857 but kept a London studio in Buckingham Palace Road. He bought a house at Lanspyddid near Brecon where he served as a magistrate and in 1862 became a deputy lieutenant of the county. In 1868 he was high sheriff of Brecknockshire.

In 1864, after the death of the Prince Consort, the mayor of Tenby decided that Wales should follow England, Scotland and Ireland and erect its own national memorial. The commission was entrusted to John Evan Thomas, who advised that the work should be executed in Sicilian marble rather than bronze, which was inclined to look 'heavy and dwarf everything around it'. He said the marble statue would be 'light and hard as metal' and 'much less common than one in bronze'. The memorial, the design of which was approved and revised personally by Queen Victoria, was unveiled on Castle Hill, Tenby, by the 15-year old Prince Arthur in 1865 (**65**).

Thomas continued to exhibit at the Royal Academy until 1870. He died in London on 9 October 1873 and was buried in Brompton cemetery. His nephew later wrote affectionately of his uncle, recounting how he 'identified himself with the interests and progress of his country'. He said that 'Mr Evan Thomas' social qualities endeared him to a large circle of friends, and his conversational powers and fund of anecdotes, as well as his mature judgement of all matters concerning art, made him an honoured guest in all the houses of the great in rank, literature and opulence'. (Add inf. Adrian James)

Sylvia Allen

Literary References: 1851 & 1871 Census; *Poole* 1886, 495; *Jones* 1909, 1911, 1930; *Graves* VII, 1905–6, 360–1; *Harley Thomas* 1936; *Dict Welsh Biography*, 1959, 955; *Darby & Smith* 1983, 76, 78; *ODNB* (Evans)

Portraits of the Sculptor: William Meredyth Thomas, bust, exhib RA, 1848, untraced

Funerary Monuments

No.	Date	Subject		Location		Reference
1.	†1826	Charlotte de Winton		Llanfrynach, Brecon	S	Pevsner, *Powys*, 1979, 341
2.	†1829	Rev Thomas Watkins		Brecon Cathedral		Pevsner, *Powys*, 1979, 290
3.	†1831	David Edwards		St George, Bloomsbury, London	S	
4.	?1831	William Bailey		Mitcham, Surrey		*Gunnis* 1968, 390
5.	†1834	Frederick Jones		Brecon Cathedral	S	Pevsner, *Powys*, 1979, 291
6.	?1835	Sir Charles Cunningham		Eye, Suffolk		*Gunnis* 1968, 390
7.	†1835	Sir Charles Tyler		St Nicholas, Glamorgan	S	Pevsner, *Glamorgan*, 1995, 570
8.	†1837	Mary Powell		Cowbridge, Glamorgan	S	Pevsner, *Glamorgan*, 1995, 331
9.	†1839	Rev Rice Rees		Llandovery, Carmarthen		*Dale-Jones and Lloyd* 1989, 43, 57
10.	†1839	Rev Thomas Williams		Llanfrynach, Brecon		*Jones*, 1909–30, IV, 46
11.	†1840	David Jones		Cilycwm, Carmarthen		*Dale-Jones and Lloyd* 1989, 57
12.	*c*1840	John Powell (†1809)		Brecon Cathedral	S	Pevsner, *Powys*, 1979, 291
13.	†1840	John, 1st Marquess Camden		Brecon Cathedral		*Gunnis* 1968, 390
14.	†1840	Walter de Winton		Glasbury, Brecon	S	Pevsner, *Powys*, 1979, 321
15.	†1841	Daniel Jones		St Hilary, Glamorgan	S	Pevsner, *Glamorgan*, 1995, 564
16.	1841	Fountain Woodyeare		Conisborough, W R Yorks		GPC
17.	†1841	Lady Frances Elizabeth Somerset		Great Badminton, Glos	S	
18.	†1841	Maria, Marchioness of Bute		Kirtling, Cambs	S	*Gunnis* 1968, 390; Pevsner, *Cambs*, 1970, 420
19.	†1841	Richard de Winton		Llanfrynach, Brecon	S	Pevsner, *Powys*, 1979, 341
20.	†1842	Lieutenant-Colonel Thomas Basset and his wife Elizabeth (†1835)		St George's Chapel, Windsor, Cloisters		*Bond* 1999, 19
21.	†1842	William Morgan		Llandovery, Carmarthen		*Dale-Jones and Lloyd* 1989, 57
22.	†1843	Bishop Farrer		St Peter, Carmarthen		*Dale-Jones and Lloyd* 1989, 57
23.	†1843	David Jones		Llandovery, Carmarthen		*Dale-Jones and Lloyd* 1989, 57
24.	†1843	George Price Watkins Model(s): City Hall, Cardiff, plaster, S		Brecon Cathedral		
25.	1843	John Mitchell		Kington, Radnor		GPC
26.	†1843	Thomas Kynnersley		Leighton, Salop	S	Pevsner, *Salop*, 1958, 165
27.	1844	Admiral Benbow		St Mary, Shrewsbury, Salop	SD	Pevsner, *Salop*, 1958, 256
28.	†1844	Anne Jones		Cilycwm, Carmarthen		*Dale-Jones and Lloyd* 1989, 57
29.	1844	Bishop Farrar		St Peter, Carmarthen		GPC
30.	?1845	Hannah Bowen		Carew, Pembrokes		*Gunnis* 1968, 390
31.	†1845	Thomas Maybery (†1829) and Frances Wilkins		Brecon Cathedral	S	Pevsner, *Powys*, 1979, 291
32.	†1846	Sir Charles Morgan		Bassaleg, Monmouthshire		*Gunnis* 1968, 390
33.	†1848	John, 2nd Marquess of Bute		Kirtling, Cambs	S	*Read* 1982, 190 (repr)
34.	?1849	Rev William McDouall		Luton, Beds		*Gunnis* 1968, 390
35.	†1850	John Lewis		St Isan, Llanishen, Cardiff, Glamorgan	S	Pevsner, *Glamorgan*, 1995, 294
36.	†1850	Joseph Bailey		St Mary Magdalene, Little Hereford, Herefs		Pevsner, *Herefs*, 1963, 236
37.	1844–1850	Robert, Marquess of Londonderry (†1822) Model(s): exhib Westminster Hall, London, 1844, 161		Westminster Abbey, London, north transept		*ILN*, 6 June 1849, 405, 406 (repr); *MacMichael* 1977, 87
38.	†1851	Alfred Homfray		Tredegar, Monmouths	S	Pevsner, *Gwent/Monmouths*, 2000, 559
39.	†1851	Sophia Watkins		Brecon Cathedral	S	Pevsner, *Powys*, 1979, 290–1 (repr)
40.	†1852	Morgan Lloyd		Llangadog, Carmarthen		*Dale-Jones and Lloyd* 1989, 42, 57
41.	†1852	Rev William Borrows		St Paul, Clapham, London	S	Pevsner, *London: S*, 1983, 381
42.	†1854	Robert Graham Polhill		Renhold, Beds	S	Pevsner, *Beds, Hunts & Peterborough*, 1968, 137
43.	†1855	Eliza Watkins		Brecon Cathedral		C Lib (repr)
44.	†1855	Jane Loveden		Llanbadarnfawr, Radnor		GPC
45.	1856	John Nicholl (†1853)		Llandaff Cathedral, Cardiff, Glamorgan	S	Pevsner, *Glamorgan*, 1995, 252
46.	†1856	John Pearce		Llanspyddid, Brecon, churchyard		Pevsner, *Powys*, 1979, 354
47.	†1856	Sir William Temple (copy of John Flaxman's Palmerston monument)		Romsey Abbey, Hants		Flaxman Account Book 1794–1810, 81; Pevsner, *Hants*, 1967, 486
48.	?1858	Michael Williams		Gwennap, Cornwall		*Gunnis* 1968, 390
49.	†1858	Sir Joseph Bailey		Penmyarth, Brecon	S	Pevsner, *Powys*, 1979, 366
50.	nd	Several, Dr Coke's family		Dr Coke Memorial Church, Brecon		Pevsner, Powys, 1979, 299

Statues

No.	Date	Subject		Location		Reference
51.	1840	Arthur, 1st Duke of Wellington	m	[coll Joseph Bailey, of Glanusk]; untraced		*Graves* VII, 1905–6, 360
52.	1845	The afflicted mother (probably for the memorial to George Price Watkins)		[Exhib Westminster Hall, London, 122]; untraced		*Westminster* 1845, 15

No.	Date	Subject	Material	Location		Literature
53.	1848	Sir Charles Morgan Bt Model(s): exhib RA, London, 1850, 1341	b	Bridge Street, Newport, Monmouthshire Other versions: bust exhib RA, London, 1847, 1360 cabinet statue, m, exhib RA, London, 1848, 1335		*ILN*, 3 June 1848, 363 (repr); *Graves* VII, 1905–6, 360, 361; Pevsner, *Gwent/Monmouths*, 2000, 449
54.	1848	Sir William Nott, design		[Exhib RA, London, 1337]; untraced		*Graves* VII, 1905–6, 360
55.	1849	The Death of Tewdric, King of Gwent, at the moment of Victory over the Saxons Model(s): exhib RA, London, 1849, 1220	b	NMW, Cardiff	S	*ILN*, 11 Aug 1849, 109 (repr); *Manchester Art Treasures* 1857, 135; *Graves* VII, 1905–6, 360; *Read* 1982, 208, 209 (repr)
56.	1851	Sir Robert Peel, statuette		[Exhib RA, London, 1304]; untraced		*Graves* VII, 1905–6, 361; *Ormond* 1973, 372
57.	1847–1852	Henri de Londres, Archbishop of Dublin (†1228)		Palace of Westminster, London, House of Lords, Chamber		*Walker* 1961, 44, 97–8, cat. 48
58.	1852	Musidora	m	[Exhib RA, London, 1327]; untraced		*Graves* VII, 1905–6, 361
59.	1853	John, 2nd Marquess of Bute	b	St Mary Street/Wood Street, Cardiff, Glamorgan	SD	*ILN*, 19 March 1853, 213 (repr); *Gunnis* 1968, 390; Pevsner, *Glamorgan*, 1995, 215
60.	1853	Sir Joseph Bailey		Glanusk, Monmouthshire		*Graves* VII, 1905–6, 361; *Gunnis* 1968, 390
61.	1857	Albert Edward, Prince of Wales		St David's School, Ashford, Middlesex		*Gunnis* 1968, 390
62.	1857	James H Vivian Model(s): exhib RA, London, 1857, 1229	b	[Old Guildhall, Swansea, Courtyard]; Ferrara Square, Swansea		*Graves* VII, 1905–6, 361; Pevsner, *Glamorgan*, 1995, 605
63.	1858	Arthur, 1st Duke of Wellington Payment(s): £1,200 Model(s): bust exhib RA, London, 1853, 1437 Death of General Sir Thomas Picton, design for bronze panel, exhib RA, London, 1855, 1432	b	The Bulwark, Brecon		*Graves* VII, 1905–6, 361; *Darke* 1991, 111 (repr)
64.	1847–1858	William Marshal, Earl of Pembroke (†1219)		Palace of Westminster, London, House of Lords		*Walker* 1961, 53, 97–8, cat. no. 58
65.	1863	Albert, the Prince Consort Payment(s): £2,250	m	Castle Hill, Tenby, Pembrokes		*Gunnis* 1968, 390; *Darby and Smith* 1983, 72–4, 76 (repr)
Busts						
66.	1838	Daniel Jones	m	[Cardiff Infirmary]; NMW, Cardiff		*Graves* VII, 1905–6, 360
67.	c1840	George Price Watkins		NMW, Cardiff		*Graves* VII, 1905–6, 360
68.	1840	J G	m	[Exhib RA, London, 1153]; untraced		*Graves* VII, 1905–6, 360
69.	1840	Lancelot Morgan, of Brecon	m	[Exhib RA, London, 1144]; untraced		*Graves* VII, 1905–6, 360
70.	1840	Sir Charles Morgan		Tredegar Park, Monmouthshire		*Graves* VII, 1905–6, 360; *Gunnis* 1968, 390
71.	1840	Sir Watkin Williams-Wynn MP		[Welsh Institution, London]; St David's School, Ashford, Middx, board room	S	*Graves* VII, 1905–6, 360; *Gunnis* 1968, 390
72.	1841	John, 2nd Marquess of Bute		[Exhib RA, London, 1379]; untraced Other versions: another exhib RA 1844, 1340; untraced another exhib RA, London, 1848, 1435; untraced		*Graves* VII, 1905–6, 360
73.	1841	Maria, Marchioness of Bute		[Exhib RA, London, 1367]; untraced		*Graves* VII, 1905–6, 360
74.	1841	Sir Charles Morgan		Tredegar Park, Monmouthshire	D	*Gunnis* 1968, 390
75.	1841	Sir Joseph Bailey		[Exhib RA, London, 1280]; untraced		*Graves* VII, 1905–6, 360
76.	1843	Walter de Winton MP		[Exhib RA, London, 1443]; untraced		*Graves* VII, 1905–6, 360; *Johnson* 1975, 458
77.	1844	Sir J L Knight Bruce		[Exhib RA, London, 1395]; untraced		*Graves* VII, 1905–6, 360
78.	1844	Undientified clergyman		[Exhib Soc of BA, London, 758]; untraced		*Johnson* 1975, 458
79.	1844	Unidentified lady		[Exhib RA, London, 1402]; untraced		*Graves* VII, 1905–6, 360
80.	1845	Canon M Williams, of St David's		[Exhib RA, London, 1400]; untraced		*Graves* VII, 1905–6, 360
81.	1845	Lancaster Baugh Allen		[Exhib RA, London, 1430]; untraced		*Graves* VII, 1905–6, 360
82.	1845	Robert, Lord Clive	m	Powis Castle, Montgomery		*Graves* VII, 1905–6, 360, 361; *Gunnis* 1968, 390
83.	1846	George Price Watkins		[Exhib RA, London, 1430]; untraced		*Graves* VII, 1905–6, 360
84.	1846	Robert Gardner		[Exhib RA, London, 1492]; untraced		*Graves* VII, 1905–6, 360
85.	1848	Colonel Gwynne		[Exhib RA, London, 1439]; untraced		*Graves* VII, 1905–6, 360
86.	1848	Viscount Hereford		[Exhib RA, London, 1441]; untraced		*Graves* VII, 1905–6, 360
87.	1849	Claude Bernard	p	Wellcome Museum, London	SD	
88.	1849	Rt Hon Knight Bruce		[Exhib RA, London, 1314]; untraced		*Graves* VII, 1905–6, 361
89.	1850	John Parry de Winton		[Exhib RA, London, 1375]; untraced		*Graves* VII, 1905–6, 361
90.	c1850	Thomas Phillips		Llandovery College, Carmarthen		*Graves* VII, 1905–6, 360; *Dale-Jones and Lloyd* 1989, 59
91.	1851	Joseph Bailey Jnr MP		[Exhib RA, London, 1332]; untraced		*Graves* VII, 1905–6, 361
92.	1852	Joseph Bailey (†1850)		Hereford Cathedral		*ILN*, 2 April 1853, 261 (repr); *Gunnis* 1968, 390
93.	1852	Sir Benjamin Hall MP		[Exhib RA, London, 1401]; untraced		*Graves* VII, 1905–6, 361
94.	1853	Bishop Ollivant, of Llandaff		[Exhib RA, London, 1431]; untraced		*Graves* VII, 1905–6, 361
95.	1853	Dean W D Conybeare, of Llandaff		[Exhib RA, London, 1390]; untraced		*Graves* VII, 1905–6, 361
96.	1855	Rear-Admiral Price		[Exhib RA, London, 1512]; untraced		*Graves* VII, 1905–6, 361
97.	1856	Clement Tudway Swanston QC	m	Lincoln's Inn, London	SD	*Gunnis* 1968, 390
98.	1856	John Propert, for the Royal Medical Benevolent Coll, Epsom		[Exhib RA, London, 1307]; untraced		*Graves* VII, 1905–6, 361
99.	1856	Unidentified gentleman		[Exhib RA, London, 1313]; untraced		*Graves* VII, 1905–6, 361

100.	1857	Albert Edward, Prince of Wales		St David's School, Ashford, Middx, board room	S	*Graves* VII, 1905–6, 361
101.	1857	John Pearce Church		[Exhib RA, London, 1286]; untraced		*Graves* VII, 1905–6, 361
102.	1857	Lord James Stuart MP		[Exhib RA, London, 1263]; untraced		*Graves* VII, 1905–6, 361
103.	1862	Charles Crofts Williams	m	Town Hall, Cardiff		*Graves* VII, 1905–6, 361; *Gunnis* 1968, 390
104.	1862	Lord James Stuart, MP		[Exhib RA, London, 1032]; untraced		*Graves* VII, 1905–6, 361
Chimneypieces						
105.	nd	With figures		Penpont, Breconshire		Pevsner, *Powys*, 1979, 368
Architectural Sculpture						
106.	*c*1840	External stonework		Arley Hall, Nantwich, Cheshire		GPC
Reliefs						
107.	1851	Science Unveiling Ignorance, plaster model		[Exhib Gt Exhib]; Cardiff City Hall		*Gunnis* 1968, 390; *ODNB*
Miscellaneous						
108.	1856	The racquet player, model, to be cast in bronze		[Exhib RA, London, 1251]; untraced		*Graves* VII, 1905–6, 361
109.	1862	J Parry de Winton		[Exhib RA, London, 1037]; untraced		*Graves* VII, 1905–6, 361
110.	1862	Joseph Bailey MP		[Exhib RA, London, 1122]; untraced		*Graves* VII, 1905–6, 361

THOMAS, John, of Bristol fl *c*1832–50

Funerary Monuments					
1.	†1832	William Day (designed by S C Fripp)	St Philip & St Jacob, Bristol		Pevsner, *Somerset: N & Bristol*, 1958, 408
2.	†1842	John Alway	Iron Acton, Glos	S	Pevsner, *Glos: Vale & Forest of Dean*, 1976, 277
3.	†1843	J Hunt AM	Almondsbury, Glos	S	
4.	†1850	Francis and William Dovell	Molland, Devon		Pevsner, *Devon*, 1989, 572

THOMAS, Mary, of Exmouth fl 1814–16?

Funerary Monuments					
1.	1814	Charles Fanshawe	[Temple Church, London]; destroyed World War II		*Gunnis* 1968, 388
2.	?1816	Heathfield Family, large wall-tablet	Cullompton, Devon	S	*Gunnis* 1968, 388

THOMAS, S, of Brecon fl *c*1792

Funerary Monuments					
1.	†1792	James Baskerville	Aberedw, Radnor	S	Pevsner, *Powys*, 1979, 217

THOMAS, William Meredyth 1819–77

He was born on 13 July 1819 in Brecon, South Wales, the younger brother of **John Evan Thomas**, in whose footsteps he followed by becoming a pupil of **Sir Francis Chantrey**, before enrolling at the Royal Academy, where he specialised in studies from the antique. By 1840, his brother was established at a studio in Belgrave Place, London. William Meredyth joined him there as his assistant and for more than 30 years assisted his brother with all his major works.

In response to a competition at the 1848 Abergavenny Eisteddfod, John Evan Thomas provided a design for a statue depicting *The death of Tewdrig*. This was modelled by William Meredyth, cast in bronze by Elkington & Co and shown at the Great Exhibition in 1851. William Meredyth first exhibited at the Royal Academy in 1848 showing a bust of his brother (**13**). This was followed in 1850 by a bust of the Welsh historian and poet Thomas Price (**14**), one of the organisers of the Abergavenny Eisteddfod. In 1866 he exhibited the model for Thomas Price's monument, intended for Abergavenny priory church, but apparently never executed (4). He showed a model for a posthumous bust of Sir George Cornwall Lewis, MP for the Radnorshire Boroughs in 1864 (**17**).

Another organiser of the Eisteddfod was Lady Llanover who became an important patron. Over the years he produced busts and medallions of various members of her family (**19, 23, 24, 29–31, 33**). In 1871 he carved a medallion portrait of the popular actress, Clara Dowse, who was known to her admirers as 'the beautiful Mrs Rousby' (**25**). William Meredyth might well have become an actor himself for he was possessed of a retentive memory and loved to entertain friends and family with long recitations from English literature.

John Evan Thomas died in 1873 and William Meredyth completed all his brother's outstanding works. He then devoted himself to the creation of ideal works, among which were *The lament of Llewellyn over his dog Gelert* (**37**) and *The Welsh harper* (**38**). He never married and outlived his brother by only four years, dying suddenly of a stroke on 7 September 1877. He is buried in the family vault at Brompton cemetery. It was said of him that he had 'a purity and truth of style which distinguished his works and would have given him a prominent place amongst his contemporaries in the art had he chosen to strike out a separate path from that of his brother' (*Poole* 1886, 232).

Sylvia Allen

Literary References: *Poole* 1886, 323–4; *Graves* 1905–6, VII 365; *Harley Thomas*, 1936, *passim* (original in Brecon Museum); *Dale-Jones and Lloyd*, 1989, 88

Funerary Monuments					
1.	†1850	Charles and Eliza Griffiths	Llanon, Carmarthen		*Dale-Jones and Lloyd* 1989, 58
2.	†1850	John Maund	Llanelly, Brecon	S	Pevsner, *Powys*, 1979, 335
3.	1860	James Beek	Cynwyl Gaeo, Carmarthen		*Dale-Jones and Loyd* 1989, 58
4.	1866	Rev Thomas Price MA	[Exhib RA, London, 1040]; untraced		*Graves* VII, 1905–6, 365
Statues					
5.	1844	Prince Henry	[Exhib Westminster Hall, London, 163]; untraced		*AU*, 1844, 216; *Gunnis* 1968, 391
6.	1856	Cricket player, a sketch, statuette	[Exhib RA, London, 1269]; untraced		*Graves* VII, 1905–6, 365
7.	nd	Resignation, Purity and Hope, figures	Untraced		*Poole* 1886, 323–4
8.	nd	The bathers, statuette	Untraced		*Poole* 1886, 323–4
9.	nd	The music lesson	Untraced		*Poole* 1886, 323–4
10.	nd	The racket player, statuette	Untraced		*Gunnis* 1968, 391
11.	nd	The students, statuette	Untraced		*Poole* 1886, 323–4

Busts

12.	c1845	Rev Thomas Price		Llandovery College, Carmarthen	*Dale-Jones and Lloyd* 1989, 59
13.	1848	John Evan Thomas, the sculptor's brother		[Exhib RA, London, 1404]; untraced	*Graves* VII, 1905–6, 365
14.	1850	Rev Thomas Price		[Exhib RA, London, 1418]; untraced	*Graves* VII, 1905–6, 365
15.	1855	Unidentified boy		[Exhib RA, London, 1475]; untraced	*Graves* VII, 1905–6, 365
16.	1863	M H Lax Marianne Smallwood	m	[Exhib RA, London, 1144]; untraced	*Graves* VII, 1905–6, 365
17.	1864	Sir George Cornwall Lewis Bt, MP, model		[Exhib RA, London, 937]; untraced	*Graves* VII, 1905–6, 365; *Ormond* 1973, 270
18.	1865	Joseph Leyton Elms Spearman	m	[Exhib RA, London, 931]; untraced	*Graves* VII, 1905–6, 365
19.	1870	Master Stephen Herbert		[Exhib RA, London, 1137]; untraced	*Graves* VII, 1905–6, 365
Architectural Sculpture					
20.	1859	St Andrew, relief		Edinburgh Masonic hall	GPC
Reliefs					
21.	1856	Miss Fugion, medallion portrait		[Exhib RA, London, 1341]; untraced	*Graves* VII, 1905–6, 365
22.	1865	Ariel		[Exhib RA, London, 962]; untraced	*Graves* VII, 1905–6, 365; *Gunnis* 1968, 391
23.	1868	Hon Mrs Herbert, medallion		[Exhib RA, London, 1092]; untraced	*Graves* VII, 1905–6, 365
24.	1868	Master Bleiddian Herbert (medallion)		[Exhib RA, London, 1094]; untraced	*Graves* VII, 1905–6, 365
25.	1871	Mrs Rousby, portrait medallion		[Exhib RA, London, 1325]; untraced	*Graves* VII, 1905–6, 365
Miscellaneous					
26.	1846	Sabrina rising from the lake attended by water nymphs		[Exhib Soc of BA, London, 775]; untraced	*Gunnis* 1968, 391; *Johnson* 1975, 458
27.	1854	Heloise		[Exhib RA, London, 1473]; untraced	*Graves* VII, 1905–6, 365
28.	1864	William Rawlins		[Exhib RA, London, 987]; untraced	*Graves* VII, 1905–6, 365
29.	1868	Master Arthur Herbert		[Exhib RA, London, 1086]; untraced	*Graves* VII, 1905–6, 365
30.	1868	Master Herbert		[Exhib RA, London, 1098]; untraced	*Graves* VII, 1905–6, 365
31.	1868	Miss Florence Herbert		[Exhib RA, London, 1089]; untraced	*Graves* VII, 1905–6, 365
32.	1869	Hilda de Bunsen		[Exhib RA, London, 1273]; untraced	*Graves* VII, 1905–6, 365
33.	1869	Hon Mrs Herbert	m	[Exhib RA, London, 1308]; untraced	*Graves* VII, 1905–6, 365
34.	1869	Miss Herbert		[Exhib RA, London, 1309]; untraced	*Graves* VII, 1905–6, 365
35.	1871	Master Claud Alexander	m	[Exhib RA, London, 1301]; untraced	*Graves* VII, 1905–6, 365
36.	nd	Puck seated on the toad's stool		Untraced	*Poole* 1886, 323–4
37.	nd	The lament of Llewellyn over his dog Gelert		Untraced	*Gunnis* 1968, 391
38.	nd	The Welsh harper		Untraced	*Gunnis* 1968, 391

THOMAS FAMILY, of Sherborne fl *c*1775–1805

C Thomas of Sherborne signs wall-tablets in Somerset. He was succeeded in the business by his son, J Thomas (1742–1805) who repaired the monuments to the Williams family at Wotton Glanville, Dorset, in 1805. Unusually he signed one monument 'J Thomas pinxit, Sherborne' (2).

Literary References: *Monthly Mag*, 1805, 197; *Gunnis* 1968, 368

Funerary Monuments

1.	1775	John Gaisford (by C Thomas)	Axbridge, Somerset	S	*Gunnis* 1968, 388
2.	1785	Rev William Preston (†1742) (by J Thomas)	[Bradford Abbas, Dorset]; untraced	S	*Hutchins* 1870, 124; *Gunnis* 1968, 388
3.	1785	Thomas Pearson (by C Thomas)	Queen Camel, Somerset	S	*Gunnis* 1968, 388

THOMASON, Sir Edward 1769–1849

The son of a Birmingham buckle manufacturer, he was baptized in Birmingham on 14 November 1769. He served as an apprentice in Matthew Boulton's factory in Soho, Birmingham and, after his father's retirement in 1793, began making gilt and plated buttons on his own account from premises in Church Street. The range soon expanded to include medals, tokens and works in gold, silver and bronze and in 1810, to plating steel cutlery. He was an eccentric character, taking out patents for inventions and presenting medals, mainly of classical or biblical subjects, to all the crowned heads of Europe. As a result he was appointed to the office of vice-consul for Birmingham to 8 foreign governments. His triumph came in 1832 when he was knighted by William IV.

In 1845 he produced an egotistical two-part advertisement which he called his Memoirs. In it he writes that in 1813 the Earl of Warwick had finally consented to have a copy made of the antique marble Warwick Vase, but had stipulated that it should be entirely of silver. The project was abandoned but in 1816 Thomason persuaded the Earl to allow a facsimile to be made in bronze instead of silver and finally, in 1820, the cast of this huge vase was made in iron, not bronze (3). There were problems with corrosion and a new finish had to be applied, but when Thomason was entirely satisfied, he struck two celebratory medals, in bronze and white metal. Although the vase attracted much attention in Thomason's showroom it was never sold and after many years Thomason presented it to the Royal Birmingham Society of Artists, where it remained until 1867. It was then moved to Aston Hall, Birmingham in a badly rusted state.

Thomason cast the first life-size statue in Birmingham of George IV (1), at a cost exceeding £1,500. He never found a customer and it was eventually sold in 1880 for £150, its scrap value. It was considered a very good likeness of the King. The statue disappeared and was probably melted down by its buyer. Other reports suggest it may have been sent to the Westminster Hall exhibition of 1844, where the *Literary Gazette* dismissed it as 'Brummagen and contemptible' (*Lit Gaz*, 1844, 466). He also made a bronze bust of the Duke of Wellington, which his widow presented to the 'Cavalry of England' and which is now in the Cavalry barracks at Canterbury (2). He died on 29 May 1849 at his home in Jury Street, Warwick. He is buried in St Philip's, Birmingham. An account of his copy of the Warwick Vase featured in his obituary in the *Gentleman's Magazine*.

Literary References: *GM*, vol XXXII, Oct 1849, II, 430; *Penzer* 1956, 71; *Gunnis* 1968, 391; *Noszlopy* 1998, 206; *ODNB* (Attwood)

Statues

1.	1823	King George IV Payment(s): over £1,500	b	Destroyed	*Noszlopy* 1998, 175
Busts					
2.	nd	Arthur, 1st Duke of Wellington	b	Cavalry barracks, Canterbury, Kent	*Gunnis* 1968, 391

Architectural Sculpture

3.	1816–1820	Warwick Vase, facsimile	ir	Aston Hall, Birmingham		*Penzer* 1956, 71–2
4.	1824	Models of the horses of Lysippus		[Thomason's manufactory, Colmore Row, Birmingham, Warks, pediment]; untraced		*Noszlopy* 1998, 162

THOMPSON fl 1780?

He may perhaps be identified with **John Thompson, of Lichfield** and signs a 'charmingly carved' tombstone, with a relief of a dove bearing an olive-branch (**1**).

Funerary Monuments

1.	?1780	Jane Bannister	Hanbury, Staffs	S	*Gunnis* 1968, 392

THOMPSON, Charles and William fl *c*1800–45

Thompson, who was later assisted by his son William, had his studio in Osnaburgh Street, London. The wall monuments of the firm are typical of their period, with heavily draped urns, branches of cypress and reliefs of weeping widows. The King memorial however has a relief of a man-of-war with a voluminous sail (**11**). The Prettejohn makes use of a classical Virtue (now decapitated), leaning on an urn, set off by a black ground (**3**).

Literary References: *Gunnis* 1968, 391

Funerary Monuments

1.	*c*1800	George Cuthbert	Portsmouth Cathedral, Hants		*Gunnis* 1968, 391
2.	?1800	Josias Du Pre	Beaconsfield, Bucks		*Gunnis* 1968, 391
3.	†1803	John Prettejohn	St George, Bridgetown, Barbados	S	*Gunnis* 1968, 391
4.	?1822	Dorothy Twopenny	Tunstall, Kent		*Gunnis* 1968, 391
5.	†1825	Rev Arthur and Susan (†1823) Crichton	Badlesmere, Kent	S	
6.	?1828	Amelia Barnett	Great Hormead, Herts		*Gunnis* 1968, 391
7.	?1828	Martha Lovibond	Hatfield Peverel, Essex		*Gunnis* 1968, 391
8.	?1833	Mr and Mrs Knightley	Offchurch, Warks		GPC
9.	†1834	Sir Richard King (by Charles Thompson)	Eastchurch, Kent		Pevsner, *Kent: N E & E*, 1983, 304
10.	?1837	Lady Duckworth	St Mary, Paddington, London		*Gunnis* 1968, 391
11.	?1841	Charles King	Sutton, Surrey		*Gunnis* 1968, 391

Statues

12.	1845	Classical figures, casts	[Colosseum, Regent's Park, London]; untraced		*Gunnis* 1968, 391

THOMPSON, John Daines, of Aylsham, Norfolk –1826

Nothing is known of his parentage but in 1824 he married Mary Anne, the daughter of **Charles Abbott**, and she eventually took over the business after his death. He became a freeman of Norwich on 19 June 1809 and took premises in Aylsham in 1819, advertising in the *Norfolk Chronicle* on 4 September 1819 that he had taken over the premises of 'Mr Warden', where he intended to carry on in business as a stone and marble mason and could provide 'Monuments, Marble and Stone Chimney Pieces, Tombs, and Grave-stones, executed or cleaned in the neatest manner, and in the shortest notice'. He also offered barn flooring 'on reasonable terms'. He was listed as a stone and marble mason in Pigot's directory for Norfolk in 1822–23. Mary Anne Thompson of Cromer Road appeared in the directory for Norfolk & Suffolk in 1830. (Add inf. Jon Bayliss)

Archival References: Aylsham and St John Timberhill, Norwich, parish registers; Norwich freemen rolls; GPC

THOMPSON, John, of Lichfield fl 1780?–1807?

He may be the 'Thompson' who signs a charmingly carved tombstone with a relief of a dove bearing an olive-branch, to Jane Bannister, 1780, at Hanbury, Staffs.

Funerary Monuments

1.	?1801	John Fern	St Chad, Lichfield, Staffs	S	*Gunnis* 1968, 392
2.	?1803	John and Catherine Barker, tablet	St Michael, Lichfield	S	GPC
3.	?1807	John Bramall, tablet	St Michael, Lichfield		GPC

THOMPSON, John, of Peterborough fl *c*1841

His only identified work is an elaborate gothic tablet.

Funerary Monuments

1.	†1841	Rev John Shillibeer	Oundle, Northants		Pevsner, *Northants*, 1973, 363

THOMPSON, of London fl 1781?

Gunnis says of his one known monument, 'This is very competent and better than anything I imagine that **Charles Thompson** could have done' (GPC).

Funerary Monuments

1.	?1781	Daniel Lascelles	Goldsborough, W R Yorks	S	GPC

THOMPSON, of Newcastle-upon-Tyne fl 1786–96

He built the church of All Saints, Newcastle 1786–1796, receiving £3,282 for stone masonry.

Literary References: *Sopwith* 1826, 72

THOMPSON, William, of Birmingham fl *c*1790–1817?

Funerary Monuments

1.	†1790	William and Rebecca (†1781) Grice	Birmingham Cathedral	Pevsner, *Warks*, 1966, 108
2.	?1798	John Clare	Wolverley, Worcs	GPC
3.	?1802	Jane Simpson	Dudley, Worcs	*Gunnis* 1968, 392
4.	?1802	Thomas Brooke	Aston, Birmingham, Warks	*Gunnis* 1968, 392
5.	?1805	Rev Richard Yates	Solihull, Birmingham, Warks	*Gunnis* 1968, 392
6.	?1809	Henry Morris	Birmingham Cathedral	GPC
7.	?1811	Sobieski Brookshaw	Birmingham Cathedral	*Gunnis* 1968, 392
8.	?1817	Moxham family	Bromyard, Hereford	GPC

HOMPSON (or THOMSON), Mary fl 1843–52

She is listed as 'Thomson, Mrs Mary, of 25 New Bond Street', in the lists of exhibitors at the Royal Academy and British Institution. Her B I exhibits all appear to be paintings: in 1849 she showed *A sail! A sail!*; in 1852 *A peep from the terrace* and in 1852 *A shipwrecked group on a raft*.

Literary References: *Graves* 1875, 536; *Graves* VII, 1905–6, 375–6

Busts

1.	1843	Clementina Pike (portrait)		[Exhib RA, London, 241]; untraced	*Graves* VII, 1905–6, 375; *Gunnis* 1968, 392
2.	1844	Unidentified subject; in composition		[Exhib RA, London, 1262]; untraced	*Graves* VII, 1905–6, 376
3.	1852	Unidentified lady		[Exhib RA, London, 1386]; untraced	*Graves* VII, 1905–6, 376
4.	1852	Unidentified lady		[Exhib RA, London, 1391]; untraced	*Graves* VII, 1905–6, 376

HOMPSON (or TOMPSON), John *c*1655–1700

Gunnis notes that he was apprenticed to Francis Clarke and became free in 1667. He was about 36 on 12 March 1691 when he was described as of 'St. Sepulchre's, Lond. Carver, Bachr' at the time of his marriage to Mary Aylward (Lic Vic Gen). He was the contractor under Wren for several of the City churches and was also paid for carved decorative stonework. He built St Magnus with George Dowsewell (4) and the tower of St Mary-Le-Bow with **Thomas Cartwright I** (3). In 1685 he was paid £600 for repairs to the chapel of Lincoln's Inn. Outside London, he was master-mason under **William Stanton** at Belton House, Grantham, in 1686, and he appears to be the Thompson who supplied a chimneypiece to the Duke of Beaufort (1).

Thompson built St Dionis Backchurch and All Hallows', Lombard Street, receiving payments totalling nearly £6,000 for work at St Dionis (1670–86), and more than £8,000 at All Hallows (1686–94) (6, 7). He also worked in some capacity at St Vedast, Foster Lane (1670–73) and at St Bartholomew by the Exchange (1674–86), where he was paid over £5,000 (5). In 1683 he was employed at Winchester Palace, and in 1691 carried out work at a total cost of £1,308 in the gardens of Hampton Court. He earned £600 in 1685 for rebuilding the chapel at Lincoln's Inn. From 1688–1700 Thompson was at St Paul's, where his most important contribution to the building was the great doorcase at the west end of the Cathedral (8). There he was assisted by **Joseph Catterns**, who was found 'with Mr Tompson' when the general search was carried out in 1678, together with three other masons of whom nothing is known, Robert Parnecutt, John Lockett and Richard Hill, 'formerly an appr. in Sussex now turned over to Mr Tompson by a Scrivener' (*Knoop and Jones* 1935, 69).

At Kensington Palace, he and two other partners, **Thomas Hill I** and **Richard Walters**, were responsible for 25 marble chimneypieces and 221 of Portland stone for lesser rooms (2) (TNA E 351/3466). Payments for these and for several carved door-cases were made to them between 1689 and 1700. Thompson can perhaps be identified with a craftsman of the same name who was responsible for several reliefs on the walls of London churches, one of them, at least, in boxwood. This is the signed *Last Judgment* formerly on a gateway at St Stephen, Coleman Street, London (9). It was probably accompanied by a series of six rectangular reliefs depicting scenes from the *Life of Christ* and a larger relief of the *Nativity*.

He was renter warden of the Masons' Company in 1683 and 1684, upper warden in 1685 and 1686 and master in 1690. His apprentices came from afar: in 1670 he took on Elias Dodson of Collyweston; Richard Perkes of Sontrilloe, Co Edernion joined him in 1670 and John Magnus of Wells-next-the-Sea in 1681. He apparently took Theophilus, son of **Peter Allen** as a pupil in 1686 (GPC).

Literary References: *Wren Soc* X, 46, 48, 52 (All Hallows, Lombard St, St Bartholomew, Exchange, St Magnus, London Bridge, St Vedast, Foster Lane); *Wren Soc* XIX, 16–17 (St Dionis Backchurch); *Gunnis* 1968, 391–2; *Whinney* 1988, 446 n7; *Bilbey* 2002, 20

Chimneypieces

1.	1689	Description not available Payment(s): £13 10s	m	[for the Duke of Beaufort]; untraced	Childe's Bank, Ledger 1688–1732, fol 30
2.	1689–1700	25 of marble and 221 of Portland stone for lesser rooms (co-sculptor: Thomas Hills I and Richard Walters)		Kensington Palace, London	(TNA E 351/3466)

Architectural Sculpture

3.	1671–1672	Four pinnacles, four flaming urns and other carving (co-sculptor: Thomas Cartwright) Payment(s): £250 plus £20 for urns		St Mary-le-Bow, City of London, tower	*Gunnis* 1968, 391 citing Bodleian, Rawlinson MS B 387; *Wren Soc* X, 33, 69–74, 89, 50
4.	1667–1680	Eight Ionic capitals and two Portland scrolls, with much mason's work (co-sculptor: George Dowsewell) Payment(s): £24		St Magnus the Martyr, City of London	*Wren Soc* XIX, 26–7; *Gunnis* 1968, 391 citing Bodleian, Rawlinson MS B 387
5.	1674–1686	Eight cherub heads and other work Payment(s): £6		[St Bartholomew by the Exchange, City of London]; destroyed	*Gunnis* 1968, 391
6.	1670–1686	Four great festoons and other stone work Payment(s): £15		[St Dionis Backchurch, City of London, east front]; destroyed	*Gunnis* 1968, 391
7.	1686–1694	Frieze ornaments Payment(s): £10		[All Hallows, Lombard Street, City of London]; destroyed	*Gunnis* 1968, 391
8.	1688–1700	Great doorcase for the west end, festoons about tower windows, carved tribune above the west end of the chapel and other ornaments Payment(s): £60 for festoons, £100 for the tribune and chapel carving		St Paul's Cathedral, London, west end	*Wren Soc* XIV, 83; XV, 49, 51–2, 60–2 (repr 37, 52); *Gunnis* 1968, 391

Reliefs

9.	1680–1700	The Last Judgment	wd	[St Stephen, Coleman St, London]; VAM A.48-1932	*Bilbey* 2002, 20 (repr)

THOMSON, of Cambridge fl 1792–1803

The *Norwich Mercury* reported on 9 July 1803 that 'The famous statue of the Goddess Ceres, lately brought from the Temple of Elensis, by Messrs Clarke and Cripps, of Jesus College, and presented by those gentlemen to the University was on Friday last placed at the entrance to the Library at the stair-case. The pedestal was designed by Flaxman, and executed by Thomson of this town [Cambridge] . . .'. Thomas Tomson was paid £90 for repairs to Caius College Cambridge, in 1792–3. See also **Tomson, Jeffs & Dawson**.

Archival References: Soane Bill Book 3, fols 298–301; GPC

THORNE fl ***c*****1703**

The Burkitt memorial has an inscription panel in the form of a heavy, gold-fringed curtain, bunched at the corner 'The large acanthus leaf at the base of the monument is boldly carved' (Pevsner, *Essex*, 1965, 157)

Funerary Monuments

1.	†1703	William Burkitt		Debden, Essex	S

THORNE, James, of Westminster fl 1769

Described as a 'carver' of St James, Westminster, he was appointed the legal guardian of the children of **Oliver Alker** in April 1769. A similar duty was entrusted to **Richard Lawrence**.

Literary References: *Beard* 1981, 241; *Beard* 1985, 693

Will: PROB 11/947/119

THORNTHWAITE, John fl 1772–76

The son of Andrew Thornthwaite, an architect, he was a modeller, die-maker and seal engraver. He exhibited wax portraits, giving his address as Goodwin's Court, St Martin's Lane, London.

Literary References: *Gunnis* 1968, 392; *Pyke* 1973, 148

Reliefs					
1.	1773	Duke of Gloucester	w	[Soc of A, London, 325]; untraced	*Graves* 1907, 258
Miscellaneous					
2.	1772	Three unidentified models	w	[Exhib Soc of A, London, 329–31]; untraced	*Graves* 1907, 258
3.	1773	Unidentified gentleman	w	[Exhib Soc of A, London, 327]; untraced	*Graves* 1907, 258
4.	1773	Unidentified ladies, two	w	[Exhib Soc of A, London, 326]; untraced	*Graves* 1907, 258
5.	1776	A head, coloured	w	[Exhib Soc of A, London, 281]; untraced	*Graves* 1907, 258

THORNTON, Herbert, of Gainsborough fl ***c*****1792**

Gunnis notes that the Cole wall-monument has pretty details.

Funerary Monuments

1.	†1792	Gervase Cole		Kettlethorpe, Lincs	*Gunnis* 1968, 392; Pevsner, *Lincs*, 1989, 413

THORNYCROFT, Mary 1809–95

Mary Thornycroft's name was established through her position as a favourite sculptor of Queen Victoria and Prince Albert. Her posthumous reputation hinges principally on her maternal link with her more famous son, William Hamo Thornycroft, who became a leading protagonist of the New Sculpture movement at the end of the 19th century.

She was born in Thornham, Norfolk in 1809, the daughter of **John Francis**, who trained his daughter in his studio in Albany Street, London with his male apprentices, who included **Matthew Noble, Joseph Durham** and **Thomas Thornycroft**. Mary and Thornycroft married at St Pancras church, London on 29 February 1840. They had seven children, four of whom studied at the Royal Academy, including (Mary) Alyce (1844–1906), who became a sculptor and painter and (William) Hamo Thornycroft (1850–1925).

Mary first exhibited at the Royal Academy in 1835 showing a *Bust of a gentleman* (**12**). The following year she produced the first of many child studies, *Sleeping infant* (**61**), and in 1839 her life-sized idealised figure, *Orphan flower girl* (**3**) attracted warm praise from the critics: the *Art Union* noted that it displayed 'so much knowledge, and skill, and, ability, that there can be no question as to the fair artist's right to class high in a profession which demands genius, thought, and industry of no common order' (*AU*, 1 June 1839, 85–6).

In 1842, whilst expecting her second child, Mary accompanied her husband on the arduous sea voyage to Rome where they became acquainted with **Bertel Thorvaldsen** and **John Gibson**. The couple remained in Rome only a few months and by the time of their return Mary had her first commission from Queen Victoria, a set of marble limbs of the infant Princess Victoria, the Princess Royal and Albert Edward, Prince of Wales (**63**). It was her father who brought Mary's talents to the Queen's attention, for he brought the *Orphan flower girl* to Windsor to be viewed by the Royal couple in 1843 when he was applying the finishing touches to a bust of Prince Albert.

In 1845 Mary was invited to carve a life size statue of the royal couple's third child, Princess Alice. This work was later incorporated into the group for which Mary is perhaps best remembered, *The four seasons* (**4**). These allegorical portraits of the four oldest royal children are still in the room for which they were commissioned, the drawing room at Osborne House. They were reproduced as engravings and, on a reduced scale, in Parian ware, as were a number of her later statues, including Princess Helena and Princess Louise as *Peace* and *Plenty* (**8**) and Prince Leopold as a fisher boy (**9**). In 1863 she carved a marble bust of Alexandra, Princess of Wales (**40**), which was copied in Parian as an Art Union prize the following year. Mary's commissions were received principally from the Royal circle, but reached a wider public through this popular ceramic medium.

She found constant employment throughout her long career, but relied heavily on assistance from her husband Thomas, who often found himself chiefly employed as his wife's assistant. Mary exhibited regularly at the Royal Academy between 1835 and 1886, and at the British Institution between 1845 and 1868. She was a member of the Society of Women Artists and the Society of Lady Artists between 1857 and 1868, but her most enviable showcases were the Great Exhibition of 1851 and the International Exhibition of 1862.

She is best remembered for ideal neoclassical figures of children and portrait busts in contemporary dress. It was her ability to create a balance between the extremes of idealism and naturalism that ensured her sustained success. Her skill in execution, coupled with an ability to render a credible likeness kept Mary in favour with the Queen and brought employment at a time when many of her male contemporaries were struggling. The royal couple's trust led them to engage her to instruct the royal princesses in the art of modelling, and when Princess Louise displayed aptitude, Mary went so far as to rough out her designs for her from the block. Her repertoire was perhaps limited by her royal patrons' taste for domestic subjects, the genre which established her reputation, but occasionally she escaped from this narrow field, for instance with the *Poets' fountain* (**59**), a work produced in collaboration with her husband and her son, Hamo.

Portraits of Mary Thornycroft reveal a striking and elegant artist, admired for her handsome looks as much as her loyalty and devotion to family and friends. She was clearly a strong character, nicknamed Minerva by young fellow sculptors in her father's workshop, and her self-discipline and 'uncompromising attitude towards weakness of character' made her a formidable matriarch, but Hamo's wife Agatha recalled that inspite of her 'fiery eye' she was kind and delightful (*Manning* 1982, 26–7). She was intelligent and well-read and to her family she was a 'trusty jewel in an emergency . . . inspired more than most with good judgement' (Note from Hamo Thornycroft to Agatha Cox, 17 Nov 1883, HMI). Mary retired in 1880 and spent her later years living with her daughter Theresa Georgina, a painter and the mother of the poet Siegfried Sassoon. She died of pneumonia in 1895, and is buried beside her husband in Chiswick old churchyard.

Fiona Darling-Glinski

Literary References: *Stephens* 1895, 305–7; *Manning* 1932, *passim*; *Manning* 1982, *passim*; *McCracken* 1997, 3–8; *Darling-Glinski* 2004, 55–68

Archival References: Thornycroft Archive, HMI, Leeds

Selected portraits of the sculptor: TB Wirgman, canvas, nd; Alyce Thornycroft, bronze bust, c1892, NPG 4065; Roger Fenton, *Mary Thornycroft and Princess Helena as Peace*, nd, one of several photographs, HMI, Leeds (*Darling-Glinski* 2004, repr 3)

No.	Date	Subject	Material	Location	References
Funerary Monuments					
1.	†1851	John Hamilton-Martin, recumbent figure of a child (co-sculptor: Thomas Thornycroft)		Ledbury, Herefs	Pevsner, *Herefs*, 1963, 217
2.	1865	Sarah, Baroness Braye (†1862) (co-sculptor: John Gibson)		Stanford, Northants	*Darling-Glinski* 2004, 66 (repr)
Statues					
3.	1839	Orphan flower girl	m	[Exhib RA, London, 1304]; untraced	*Graves* 1875, 197; *Graves* III, 1905–6, 161; *Johnson* 1975, 460; *Darling-Glinski* 2004, 56, 59
4.	1846	The seasons (Princess Alice, the Princess Royal, Prince Alfred and the Prince of Wales)	m	Royal Coll, Osborne House, I of W Other versions: Royal Coll (Buckingham Palace), 1847, bronze reproductions in Copeland Parian ware, statuettes, (shown at 1849 Birmingham Exhib and Gt Exhib, 1851)	*Manchester Art Treasures* 1857, 135; *Graves* 1875, 537; *Graves* VII, 1905–6, 384; *Holland Park* 1957, unpag (repr); *Atterbury* 1989, 163 (reprs 542–544A); *Darling-Glinski* 2004, 57–60 (repr); C Lib (repr)
5.	1849	Sleeping child guarded by a spaniel (sleeping child and dog)	m	[Exhib BI, London, 509]; untraced	*Graves* 1875, 537; *Darling-Glinski* 2004, 57
6.	1854	The skipping girl (the skipping rope)		Royal Coll, Osborne House, I of W Other versions: Salford Art Gall, Lancs, plaster, destroyed reproduced in Minton Parian ware (shown at 1862 Int Exhib)	*AJ Cat* 1862, fol 168 (repr); *Graves* 1875, 537; *Graves* VII, 1905–6, 384, 385; *Atterbury* 1989, 112 (repr 373); *Morris and Roberts* 1998, 594; *Darling-Glinski* 2004, 66, 67 (repr)
7.	1858	The cradle (Princess Beatrice)	m	Royal Coll Other versions: reproduced in Minton Parian ware, 1867 Royal Coll, versions in plaster and Parian ware	*Graves* VII, 1905–6, 384; *Atterbury* 1989, 80 (repr 121); C Lib (repr)
8.	1855–1860	Peace (Princess Helena) and Plenty (Princess Louise)	m	Royal Coll Other versions: both reproduced in Minton Parian ware (shown at 1862 Int Exhib) reproductions of Plenty issued in Copeland Parian ware by the Art Union of London from 1871	*Darling-Glinski* 2004, 60; *Atterbury* 1989, 34, 111 (reprs 49, 370, 371); C Lib (repr)
9.	by 1864	Fisher boy (Prince Leopold) and hunter (Prince Arthur)	m	Royal Coll Other versions: both reproduced in Minton Parian ware (shown at 1862 Int Exhib)	*Read* 1982, 132 (repr); *Atterbury* 1989, 114 (reprs 380, 381); C Lib (repr)
10.	1865	Portrait group of three sisters		[Exhib RA, London, 964]; untraced	*Graves* VII, 1905–6, 385
11.	1877	Princesses Victoria, Maud and Louise, daughters of the Prince and Princess of Wales		Untraced	*Gunnis* 1968, 392
Busts					
12.	1835	Unidentified gentleman		[Exhib RA, London, 1100]; untraced	*Graves* VII, 1905–6, 161
13.	1836	Charles Sharpe		[Exhib RA, London, 1080]; untraced	*Graves* VII, 1905–6, 161
14.	1840	John Lander		[Exhib RA, London, 1088]; untraced	*Graves* VII, 1905–6, 384
15.	1840	Queen Victoria		Royal Coll	*Gunnis* 1968, 392
16.	1840	Sappho	m	[Exhib RA, London, 1307]; untraced	*Graves* 1875, 537; *Graves* VII, 1905–6, 384
17.	1840	Unidentified gentleman		[Exhib RA, London, 1167]; untraced	*Graves* VII, 1905–6, 384
18.	1841	Isaac Thornycroft, Thomas Thornycroft's brother	m	Untraced	*Darling-Glinski* 2004, 56 (repr)

19.	1846	Albert Edward, Prince of Wales	m	Royal Coll		*AU*, 1847, 200; *Graves* VII, 1905–6, 384; *Gunnis* 1968, 392
20.	1847	Duchess of Kent	m	Royal Coll Other versions: reproduced in Minton Parian ware	SD	*Gunnis* 1968, 392; *Atterbury* 1989, 125 (repr 448)
21.	1848	Prince Alfred		[Commissioned by Queen Victoria]; untraced		*Graves* VII, 1905–6, 384
22.	1850	Princess Louise		[Presented to Queen Victoria by the Duchess of Kent]; untraced		*Darling-Glinski* 2004, 60, 68 n22
23.	1851	Head of Psyche	m	[Exhib BI, London, 538]; untraced		*Graves* 1875, 537
24.	1852	A lady, probably Viscountess Mahon	m	HMI 1997.0001		*Graves* VII, 1905–6, 384; *Leeds* 2001, 10 (repr); *Morris and Roberts* 1998, 594
25.	1852	Hon Miss Stanhope		[Exhib RA, London, 1460]; untraced		*Graves* VII, 1905–6, 384
26.	1852	Lord Clanmaurice	m	[Exhib RA, London, 1478]; untraced		*Graves* VII, 1905–6, 384
27.	1853	Countess of Hardwicke	m	[Exhib RA, London, 1440]; untraced		*Graves* VII, 1905–6, 384; *Darling-Glinski* 2004, 65
28.	1853	Duchess of Gloucester		Royal Coll		*Graves* VII, 1905–6, 384; *Gunnis* 1968, 392
29.	1853	Queen Victoria	m	[Exhib RA, London, 1303]; untraced		*Graves* VII, 1905–6, 384; *Morris and Roberts* 1998, 594; *Darling-Glinski* 2004, 65
30.	1854	Marquess of Lorne		[coll Duke of Argyll]; untraced Other versions: exhib RA, London, 1857, 1319, bronze		*Graves* VII, 1905–6, 384
31.	1855	Lord Petersham		[coll Countess of Harrington]; untraced		*Graves* VII, 1905–6, 384
32.	1857	Ann Thornycroft, the sculptor's daughter	m	[Exhib RA, London, 1269]; untraced		*Graves* VII, 1905–6, 384; *Darling-Glinski* 2004, 62, 65 (repr)
33.	1858	Princess Royal		Royal Coll		*Graves* VII, 1905–6, 384; *Gunnis* 1968, 392; *Morris and Roberts* 1998, 594
34.	1859	Annie, daughter of Roger Fenton	m	[Exhib RA, London, 1316]; untraced		*Graves* VII, 1905–6, 384
35.	1859	Lady Elizabeth York	m	[Exhib RA, London, 1354]; untraced		*Graves* VII, 1905–6, 384
36.	1860	'Marble Head, a study for a statue'	m	[Exhib BI, London, 637]; untraced		*Graves* 1875, 537
37.	1860	Unidentified lady	m	[Exhib RA, London, 1022]; untraced		*Graves* VII, 1905–6, 384
38.	1861	Princess Alice		Royal Coll Other versions: reproduced in Parian ware by Minton (shown 1862 Int Exhib) and Copeland (30 copies issued 1879 after her death)		*Gunnis* 1968, 392; *Atterbury* 1989, 125, 181 (reprs 447, 590); *Darling-Glinski* 2004, 65
39.	1862	Mrs Thornycroft		[Exhib RA, London, 1016]; untraced		*Graves* VII, 1905–6, 384
40.	1863	Alexandra, Princess of Wales		[Commissioned by Queen Victoria]; untraced Other versions: copies in Copeland Parian ware issued by the Art Union of London		*Graves* VII, 1905–6, 384; *Atterbury* 1989, 34, 181 (reprs 48, 590) *Darling-Glinski* 2004, 65
41.	1863	Mrs Wallace	m	[Exhib RA, London, 1053]; untraced		*Graves* VII, 1905–6, 384
42.	1863	Princess Louise of Hesse	m	[Commissioned by Queen Victoria]; untraced		*Graves* VII, 1905–6, 384; *Morris and Roberts* 1998, 594
43.	1864	'D. S. S. Esq.'	m	[Exhib RA, London, 985]; untraced		*Graves* VII, 1905–6, 385
44.	1864	Head of a boy	m	[Exhib BI, London, 648]; untraced		*Graves* 1875, 537
45.	1864	Mrs Sassoon		[Exhib RA, London, 1011]; untraced		*Graves* VII, 1905–6, 385
46.	1865	Miss Thornycroft		[Exhib RA, London, 959]; untraced		*Graves* VII, 1905–6, 385
47.	1866	Abraham Bensusan		[Exhib RA, London, 986]; untraced		*Graves* VII, 1905–6, 385
48.	1868	Unidentified young girl	m	[Exhib RA, London, 975]; untraced		*Graves* VII, 1905–6, 385
49.	1870	Alderman Pochin, mayor of Salford		[coll Salford Corporation]; untraced		*Graves* VII, 1905–6, 385
50.	1870	George Baird	m	[Exhib RA, London, 1173]; untraced		*Graves* VII, 1905–6, 385
51.	1870	Prince Albert of Schleswig-Holstein		Royal Coll		*Gunnis* 1968, 392
52.	1870	Princess Louise, Duchess of Argyll	m	Royal Coll Other versions: reproduced in Copeland Parian ware		*Graves* VII, 1905–6, 385; *Atterbury* 1989, 181 (repr 590); *Darling-Glinski* 2004, 64, 65 (repr)
53.	1871	Edward Baird		[Exhib RA, London, 1299]; untraced		*Graves* VII, 1905–6, 385
54.	1874	Princess Helena		Royal Coll		*Gunnis* 1968, 392
55.	1875	Princess Christian of Schleswig-Holstein	m	[Exhib RA, London, 1254]; untraced		*Graves* VII, 1905–6, 385
56.	1875	Princess Louise, Marchioness of Lorne		[Executed for Queen Victoria]; untraced		*Graves* VII, 1905–6, 385
57.	1876	Duchess of Edinburgh		Royal Coll		*Graves* VII, 1905–6, 385; *Gunnis* 1968, 392
58.	nd	Lady Peel		[Avington Park, Hants]; untraced		*Gunnis* 1968, 392

Architectural Sculpture

59.	1875	Poets' fountain (co-sculptor: Thomas and William Hamo Thornycroft)		[Junction of Park Lane and Hamilton Place, London]; Renishaw Hall, Derbys [fragment]		*Gunnis* 1968, 393; *Read* 1982, 39

Reliefs

60.	1873	Mrs Frances Tagart, medallion	m	[Exhib RA, London, 1595]; untraced		*Graves* VII, 1905–6, 385

Miscellaneous

61.	1836	Sleeping infant, a study		[Exhib RA, London, 1099]; untraced		*Graves* III, 1905–6, 161
62.	1837	Unidentified boy, a portrait		[Exhib RA, London, 1238]; untraced		*Graves* III, 1905–6, 161
63.	1843–1845	Limbs of Royal children	m	Royal Coll, Osborne House, I of W		*Darling-Glinski* 2004, 58
64.	1858	Jepthah's daughter		[Exhib BI, London, 588]; untraced		*Graves* 1875, 537
65.	1869	A young cricketer		[Exhib RA, London, 1226]; untraced		*Graves* VII, 1905–6, 385
66.	1872	Melpomene		[Exhib RA, London, 1415]; untraced		*Graves* VII, 1905–6, 385

THORNYCROFT, Thomas 1816–85

He was born into a farming family at Great Tidnock Farm, Gawsworth, Cheshire. His father died when he was six leaving his mother Ann with three young sons. Thomas showed no aptitude for farming and spent his spare time carving models of animals, using home-made tools until he and his youngest brother Isaac were sent to Congleton grammar school, leaving the middle son, William, at home to learn how to run the farm. On leaving school, his mother apprenticed him to a Macclesfield surgeon but it was not long before the surgeon complained that young Thomas was not suited to the medical profession as he spent his time using the scalpels to carve pieces of marble. His mother sought the advice of another local surgeon, WB Dickenson, a connoisseur of coins and medals, who recognised the young man's talents. He arranged through Edward Davenport, an influential Whig MP, for Thomas to have an interview with the Duke of Sussex, who after seeing some of his carvings suggested that he should become a pupil in the London studio of his protégé **John Francis**.

In August 1835 Thornycroft arrived at 56 Albany Street, Regents Park, London where Francis lived with his family and two other pupils, **Matthew Noble** and **Joseph Durham.** Before long Francis wrote to a delighted Mrs Thornycroft praising her son's talents and offering 'Thorny', a nickname he was to keep all his life, a four year apprenticeship at a fee of £100 per year.

Thomas exhibited at the Royal Academy for the first time in 1836 (**58**) and in 1837 showed a marble bust of *Melancholy* (**29**), which sold for 40 guineas. During the next few years he spent periods at home whilst working on commissions for Cheshire benefactors. He executed two works for WB Dickenson, a bust and a medallion portrait of his recently deceased wife (**30, 1**). Edward Davenport, who had an interest in phrenology, commissioned a bust of his young son Arthur and was anxious that the bumps on his head should be faithfully recorded (**32**). Whilst Thomas was away from London, he wrote letters to John Francis's daughter, **Mary Francis**, and in 1839 they became engaged. That year Thomas returned to Cheshire to organise an exhibition of some of his and Mary's works in Macclesfield and he showed a bust of John Ryle of Henbury Hall, Cheshire at the Royal Academy (**31**).

Thomas and Mary were married on 29 February 1840 at St Pancras church. The following two years were difficult for the couple, as commissions were scarce. Thomas's statue of *Orpheus Abandoned* was rejected by the Royal Academy and he was so dismayed that he left the piece 'on a strange doorstep, rang the bell and rushed away!' (*Manning* 1982, 25). A meeting with Thomas Page, who had worked as assistant to Isambard Kingdom Brunel, began a lifelong interest in engineering and, with time on his hands, he produced a steam threshing machine for his brother's farm.

In November 1842, hoping to gain more experience, Thomas and Mary went to Rome where they met **John Gibson** and other sculptors in the English colony. They took lodgings in the Via Felice and, as there was no heating, Thomas immediately set to work to build a stove. On 1 February 1843 when Mary gave birth to a son, Thomas acted as midwife, prompting her sister to write saying 'You are lucky to have a husband who can do everything'. They both began to work and Thomas started on a dark subject, *The jealousy of Medea* (**5**). There was soon to be good news. John Gibson had been asked by Prince Albert to provide sculpted portraits of the Royal children and since he had no wish to leave Rome he recommended Mary for the task. In 1844 the couple returned to England and took a house at 39 Stanhope Street.

Mary gradually began to receive more commissions from the Royal family while for a time Thomas found it difficult to get work, which caused friction between them. However, Prince Albert soon began to show an interest in him and in 1847 he was commissioned to produce statues for the new House of Lords of two signatories of the Magna Carta (**15, 17**). In 1853 Mary gave birth to her seventh child, a daughter, Georgiana, thus completing their family.

Thornycroft always claimed that during discussions with Prince Albert about art, he had encouraged the Prince to admit sculpture to the Great Exhibition. The sculptor was then asked to produce an equestrian statue of Queen Victoria to be displayed there (**8**). It depicts the Queen, on her favourite horse, in a dashing close-fitting riding habit, wearing a small crown. It was given Royal approval and placed in a prominent position just inside the exhibition's entrance, prompting Thomas to say that 'you see the Queen riding out as you enter'. The composition did not receive universal approval and no new commissions followed. After some modifications, including the substitution of a plumed hat for the crown, the work was chosen as the model for a limited edition Art Union bronze statuette. In 1869 the revised statue was cast in bronze and erected in Liverpool as a companion to the Thornycroft memorial statue to the Prince Consort (**24**). In 1857 Thomas entered a competition to find a design for a memorial to the Duke of Wellington for St Paul's Cathedral. His design was much admired but the commission finally went to **Alfred Stevens.**

Although the death of the Prince Consort in 1861 was a blow to the many sculptors he had sponsored and encouraged in his lifetime, it opened the door to a mass of commemorative commissions. Nearly every town wanted a memorial to the Prince and Thomas's equestrian statue for Liverpool was adapted for Halifax and Wolverhampton (**24**). The Liverpool statue depicts the Prince wearing civilian dress, but for Wolverhampton the Queen requested that he should be shown in a field marshal's uniform. The statue was considered 'one of the most faithful and characteristic likenesses yet produced', due to the fact that the sculptor had been personally acquainted with the Prince over many years.

Soon after the Prince Consort's death, it was decided to commission a national memorial to stand on the site of the Great Exhibition. Gilbert Scott's Gothic design was chosen, comprising a seated statue of the Prince under an ornate canopy, presiding over various sculptural groups. Thomas was selected to execute the group representing *Commerce* (**23**) to accompany *Agriculture, Manufactures* and *Engineering*, all skills which were 'furthered and promoted by the International Exhibitions . . . which claim the Prince Consort as their great originator'. The *Art Journal* described *Commerce* as 'a group of much elegance, combined with spirited and life-like action' (*AJ* 1871, 208).

In 1856 Thornycroft had conceived the idea of a colossal group depicting *Boadicea and her Daughters* (**28**) and Prince Albert had encouraged him by lending horses from the Royal mews, visiting the studio frequently to give advice and expressing a wish that the completed work should eventually be erected over the central arch to the entrance to Hyde Park. After the Prince's death the work was abandoned until the 1870s when there was hope of a new commission. Thomas set the whole family to work, his daughters acting as models and his son William (Hamo) working on models of the horses. No commission was forthcoming and the huge plaster model was put into storage.

It was not until 1902, when his eldest son John Isaac Thornycroft donated the model to the recently formed Londo County Council, that the statue was eventually realised and erected at the west end of Westminster bridge.

In 1871 a Mrs Mangini Brown set up a competition for sculptors to produce a design for a monument to the glorie of English poetry to be set up in Park Lane, opposite her house. Despite tough competition, Thomas won th commission and the family set to work again on *The poets' fountain* (54). Whilst Mary worked on *Melpomene* an Hamo tackled *Thalia*, Thomas concentrated on *Milton*, and various members of the family again acted as models The fountain, erected in 1875, stood until the Second World War. It was around this time that Thomas lost interes in sculpture and turned his attention entirely to engineering. From 1864 he had experimented with the building o steam launches at Church wharf, Chiswick, where his eldest son John Isaac eventually founded a successful boat building works, John Thornycroft & Co. Thomas began to spend more of his time at Chiswick working with his so and navigating the Thames in his own steam launch, *Waterlily*. In 1885 he died at the home of his daughter i Brenchley, Kent, of sunstroke caused by falling asleep on the *Waterlily*. He was buried at St Nicholas, Chiswick within sound of the hammers of the boat builders and ten years later Mary was laid beside him, leaving their son Hamo Thornycroft (1850–1925), by now an accomplished sculptor in his own right, to ensure that the name o Thornycroft remained influential in the world of sculpture.

Sylvia Alle

Literary References: *Sassoon* 1938, 35; *Physick* 1970, 29–30, 48–49, 159–161; *Bayley* 1981 87–9; *Manning* 1982, *passim*; *Darby & Smith*, 1983, 74–5 *Newark* 1985, p12; *Blackwood* 1989, 58–69; *Ward-Jackson* 2003, 70–72

Funerary Monuments

No.	Date	Subject		Location		References
1.	†1851	Mrs William Dickenson		Twycross, Leics		*Gunnis* 1968, 393
2.	1853	Hon Elliott Yorke, model		[Exhib RA, London, 1313]; untraced		*Graves* VII, 1905–6, 383
3.	1856–1857	Wellington monument, competition model		Untraced		*ILN*, 29 Aug 1857, 225

Statues

No.	Date	Subject		Location		References
4.	?1842	Orpheus abandoned		Untraced		*Manning* 1982, 25
5.	1844	The jealousy of Medea		[Exhib Westminster Hall, London, 1844, 172]; untraced		*Graves* 1875, 537; *Graves* VII, 1905–6, 383; *Gunnis* 1968, 393
6.	1848	Prince Albert's favourite greyhound		Royal Coll		*L'Illustration*, 1 May 1851, 273
7.	1850	Alfred the Great encouraged in the pursuit of learning by his mother		[Exhib RA, London, 1299]; untraced		*AJ Cat* 1851, 315 (repr); *Graves* VII, 1905–6, 383
8.	1851	Queen Victoria, equestrian	p	[Gt Exhib]; destroyed		*Cavanah* 2000, 96
9.	1853	Queen Victoria, equestrian statuette	b	[Exhib RA, London, 1854, 1417]; Walker, Liverpool Other versions: 49 Art Union statuettes cast by Thornycroft YCBA B2001.2.360	SD	*Graves* VII, 1905–6, 384; *Cavanagh* 1997, 95–7
10.	1855	The knitting girl	m	[Exhib RA, London, 1418]; untraced		*Graves* VII, 1905–6, 384
11.	1856	A young girl Payment(s): £300 in books and work, etc	m	[Exhib BI, London, 544]; untraced		*Graves* 1875, 537
12.	1857	G B Thornycroft	m	Wolverhampton, Staffs		*Graves* VII, 1905–6, 384; *Gunnis* 1968, 393
13.	1857	George Washington, statuette	b	[Exhib RA, London, 1252]; untraced		*Graves* VII, 1905–6, 384; *Morris and Roberts* 1998, 594
14.	1857	Industry	m	[Manc Art Treas Exhib, 57]; untraced		*Manchester Art Treasures* 1857, 134
15.	1847–1858	Henry, Earl of Hereford (†1220)		Palace of Westminster, London, House of Lords		*Graves* VII, 1905–6, 383; *Walker* 1961, 39, 97–8, cat 41; *Read* 2000, 260 (repr)
16.	1858	Lady Anne Chandos-Pole Model(s): exhib RA, London, 1858, 1175	m	Radbourne Hall, Derbys		*Graves* VII, 1905–6, 384
17.	1847–1858	Roger le Bigod, Earl of Norfolk (†1221)		Palace of Westminster, London, House of Lords		*Walker* 1961, 47, 97–8, cat 52
18.	1859	'Lady Harrington and her son, Lord Petersham; sketch for a portrait group'		[Exhib RA, London, 1245]; untraced		*Graves* VII, 1905–6, 384
19.	1860	'Sketch for a staue of Havelock'		[Exhib RA, London, 966]; untraced		*Graves* VII, 1905–6, 384
20.	1860	The young student	b	[Exhib BI, London, 647]; untraced		*Graves* 1875, 537
21.	1863	King James I (co-sculptor: Mary Thornycroft)	m	[Westminster Hall, London]; Central Criminal Court, Old Bailey, London, entrance hall	D	*ILN*, 29 July 1867, 648; *Graves* VII, 1905–6, 384; *Walker* 1961, 107; *Read* 1982, 121
22.	1861–1864	King Charles I (co-sculptor: Mary Thornycroft)	m	[Westminster Hall, London]; Central Criminal Court, Old Bailey, London, entrance hall		*Graves* VII, 1905–6, 384; *Walker* 1961, 107; *Read* 1982, 121, 164; *Ward-Jackson* 2003, 72
23.	1865	Commerce, group Model(s): sketch exhib RA, London, 1868, 1096		Albert Memorial, Kensington Gardens, London, inner corner		*ILN*, 27 July 1872; *Graves* VII, 1905–6, 384; *CIIA* 4/1/88–9 (repr); *Read* 1982, 100 (repr)
24.	1866	Albert, the Prince Consort, equestrian statue (gun metal) Payment(s): £10,000		St George's Plateau, Liverpool, Lancs Other versions: Halifax, W R Yorks, 1864 Wolverhampton, Staffs, 1866	SD	*ILN*, 20 Nov 1866, 376; *Graves* VII, 1905–6, 384; *Read* 1982, 113, 365; *Darby and Smith* 1983, 74–5 (repr); *Cavanagh* 1997, 91–5 (repr)
25.	*c*1869	Queen Victoria, equestrian (gun metal)		St George's plateau, Liverpool, Lancs	SD	*Read* 1982, 113, 365; *Cavanagh* 1997, 95–7 (repr)
26.	1869	Richard, 2nd Marquess of Westminster		Grosvenor Park, Chester, Cheshire		*Graves* VII, 1905–6, 384; *Gunnis* 1968, 393

27.	1872–1875	Robert, 6th Earl of Mayo, equestrian (co-sculptor: William Hamo Thornycroft RA)	b	[Chowringhee Road, Kolkata (Calcutta)]; Temple of Fame, Barrackpore, 1974 Other versions: bronze statuette exhib RA, London, 1874; untraced		*ILN*, 25 April 1896, 530; *ILN*, 22 Jan 1898, 105; *Steggles* 2000, 132–4 (repr)
28.	1856–1897	Boadicea and her daughters in their chariot	b	Westminster Bridge, London		*Graves* VII, 1905–6, 384; *Read* 1982, 57, 59, 133, 209 (repr)
Busts						
29.	1837	Melancholy	m	[Exhib RA, London, 1270]; untraced		*Graves* VII, 1905–6, 383
30.	1838	William Burley Dickenson	m	[Exhib RA, London, 1358]; untraced		*Graves* VII, 1905–6, 383
31.	1839	John Ryle of Henbury Hall, Cheshire	m	[Exhib RA, London, 1388]; untraced		*Graves* VII, 1905–6, 383
32.	1840	Arthur Davenport	m	[Exhib RA, London, 1196]; private coll		*Graves* VII, 1905–6, 383
33.	1840	Il Penseroso (companion to 36)	m	[Exhib BI, London, 451]; private coll	S	*Manchester Art Treasures* 1857, 136; *Graves* 1875, 537; *Morris and Roberts* 1998, 594
34.	1840	Mrs Hibbert of Mirtly Hall, Cheshire	m	[Exhib RA, London, 1151]; untraced		*Graves* VII, 1905–6, 383
35.	1841	Albert, the Prince Consort		[Coll Duke of Sussex]; untraced Other versions: Royal Coll, 1844		Leeds Archive handlist
36.	1841	L' Allegro (companion to 33)	m	[Exhib RA, London, 1284]; private coll	S	*Graves* 1875, 537; *Graves* VII, 1905–6, 383; *Morris and Roberts* 1998, 594
37.	1841	Samuel Thompson		[Exhib RA, London, 1319]; untraced		*Graves* VII, 1905–6, 383
38.	1842	Edward Hawkins FRS, MSA	m	[Exhib RA, London, 1354]; untraced		*AU*, 1842, 129; *Graves* VII, 1905–6, 383
39.	1842	Mrs Glendinning of Ash Grove, Kent	m	[Exhib RA, London, 1373]; untraced		*Graves* VII, 1905–6, 383
40.	1842	S Thompstone	m	[Exhib RA, London, 1365]; untraced		*Graves* VII, 1905–6, 383
41.	1844	Medea	m	[Exhib RA, London, 1342]; untraced		*Graves* VII, 1905–6, 383
42.	1845	Brian Houghton Hodgson	m	[Model exhib RA, London, 1392]; Asiatic Soc, Kolkata (Calcutta)		*Graves* VII, 1905–6, 383; *Ormond* 1973, 227
43.	1846	Medea		Royal Coll, Osborne House, I of W Other versions: Royal Coll, 1849	SD	*Gunnis* 1968, 393
44.	1853	John Brocklehurst MP	m	[Exhib RA, London, 1408]; untraced		*Graves* VII, 1905–6, 383
45.	1855	Osberga, mother of King Alfred; part of an historical group	m	[Exhib RA, London, 1517]; untraced		*Graves* VII, 1905–6, 384
46.	1861	John Marshall FRS		[Exhib RA, London, 1057]; untraced		*Graves* VII, 1905–6, 384
47.	1863	'Albert, the Prince Consort; heroic size, from the model of a public statue, revised by Queen Victoria'		[Exhib RA, London, 1011]; untraced		*AJ*, 1863; *Graves* VII, 1905–6, 384; *Cavanagh* 1997, 92; *Darby and Smith* 1983, 116 n63; *Morris and Roberts* 1998, 594
48.	1865	David Dracksford	m	[Exhib RA, London, 965]; untraced		*Graves* VII, 1905–6, 384
49.	1866	Charles, 7th Earl of Harrington (†1881)		Elvaston Castle, Derbys		GPC
50.	1866	Leicester, 5th Earl of Harrington		[Exhib RA, London, 862]; untraced		*Graves* VII, 1905–6, 384
51.	1869	George Baird	m	[Exhib RA, London, 1164]; untraced		*Graves* VII, 1905–6, 384
52.	1869	P H Humberstone		[Exhib RA, London, 1261]; untraced		*Graves* VII, 1905–6, 384
53.	nd	A young princess ('classical or ancient subject')		Sotheby, 29 March 1983, lot 211; untraced	S	
Architectural Sculpture						
54.	1875	Poets' fountain (co-sculptor: Sir Hamo and Mary Thornycroft)		[junction of Park Lane and Hamilton Place, London]; Renishaw Hall, Derbys [fragment]		*Graves* VII, 1905–6, 383; *Gunnis* 1968, 393; *Read* 1982, 39
Reliefs						
55.	1837	Ann Thornycroft, the sculptor's mother	m	Gawsworth Hall, Cheshire	SD	*Gawsworth Guide*, 44
56.	1838	Unidentified lady, medallion	m	[Exhib RA, London, 1291]; untraced		*Graves* VII, 1905–6, 383
57.	nd	Dr Dickenson of Macclesfield		Gawsworth Hall, Cheshire		*Gawsworth Guide*, 44
Miscellaneous						
58.	1836	Study		[Exhib RA, London, 1148]; untraced		*Graves* VII, 1905–6, 383

THORPE, John, of Bakewell fl 1706–28

He was much employed by Thomas Coke of Melbourne, where in addition to mason's work, he supplied chimneypieces. In 1706 Mr Sergeant, Coke's Derbyshire agent, wrote to his master in London: 'John Thorpe has brought three chimney-pieces from Bakewell' (**1**). Two years later Coke agreed with Thorpe for two more (**2**) and in 1723 Thorpe was paid for another chimneypiece, apparently for Coke's London house, for Coke wrote to his agent that it was to be 'carefully putt up and to be sent by water to London directed to me' (**7**).

Another important client was the 3rd Earl of Carlisle. Around 1712 Thorpe worked at Castle Howard on chimneypieces and door surrounds (**3, 4, 8, 9**). In 1721 he supplied marble for the building of Knowsley Hall, a seat of the Earl of Derby (Lancashire County Archives, D.D.K. 2002/1) and in 1727 returned to Yorkshire, where he was employed by Lord Bingley at Bramham Park. There the steward addressed him as 'Mr. Thorpe, marble-cutter' and informed him that 'My Lord will pay your bill if you will come hither on the five and twentieth day of September, but you must be punctual to your time because you cannot have your money before and within three or four days after My Lord goes to London' (**10**).

Thorpe's widow may have carried on the business for in 1739 a payment of £11 9s was made to Mrs Thorpe for a marble chimneypiece (Account book of the Duke of Kingston, Nottingham Univ Library, 4550). James Thorpe, perhaps a son of John Thorpe, supplied a chimneypiece for Lord Fairfax at Gilling Castle, N R Yorks, in 1730 (Wombwell Archives in GPC). Another John Thorpe had marble works at Ashford, Derbys, which he sold to **Henry Watson** in 1742.

Literary References: *Gunnis* 1968, 393–4; *Brighton* 2001, 55

Archival References: Castle Howard Building Accts, G2/2/2, fols 61, 93, 1713–19; GPC

Chimneypieces

No.	Date	Description		Location	Source
1.	1706	Three		Melbourne Hall, Derbys	*Gunnis* 1968, 393
2.	1708	Two, of grey marble		Melbourne Hall, Derbys	*Gunnis* 1968, 393
3.	1712	Description unavailable Payment(s): £23	m	Castle Howard, N R Yorks, saloon	Castle Howard Building Accts, G2/1/1, fol 123v; *Saumarez Smith* 1990, 111
4.	1712	Description unavailable Payment(s): £37		Castle Howard, N R Yorks, 'Bewfett'	Castle Howard Building Accts, G2/1/1, fol 123v
5.	1717	Several	m	[Sir Charles Hotham's house, Beverley, ER Yorks]; untraced	Archives, Lord Hotham in GPC
6.	1717	'Two great chimney pieces' Payment(s): £40		[Duke of Newcastle's house, London]; untraced	Archives, Lord Hotham in GPC
7.	1723	Description unavailable Payment(s): £11 6s 3d		[Probably Thomas Coke's house, St James's Place, London]; untraced	*Gunnis* 1968, 393 quoting archives, Marquess of Lothian

Architectural Sculpture

No.	Date	Description		Location	Source
8.	post-1711	Door surrounds	m	Castle Howard, N R Yorks, saloon	*Saumarez Smith* 1990, 110–1
9.	?1712	Double doorcase for dining room and another in marble for drawing room		Castle Howard, N R Yorks, dining room and drawing room	Castle Howard Building Accts G2/1/1 (?)
10.	1727	Unspecified work		Bramham Park, W R Yorks	*Gunnis* 1968, 393 quoting Lane Fox archives

THORVALDSEN, Bertel 1770–1844

Thorvaldsen's severe, hellenizing style marks the final phase of the neoclassical movement. He is remembered in Britain for his portrait busts, considered by some patrons to excel the work of **Antonio Canova**, and because his career was saved through the intervention of an English patron, Thomas Hope.

The sculptor's early years were spent in Copenhagen. He was the son of an Icelandic wood-carver, Gotskàl Thorvaldsen and his wife, Karen Dagnes, a schoolmaster's daughter from Jutland. Thorvaldsen had a sketchy early education, but joined the flourishing Royal Academy of Fine Arts in Copenhagen in 1781. His teachers included two artists who had benefited from a period spent in Rome, the painter Nicolai Abraham Abildgaard, who noticed and fostered his talent, and the sculptor, Johannes Widewelt, who knew about the early stages of the Greek revival since he had shared lodgings in Rome with Winckelmann during the 1750s. In 1793 Thorvaldsen won the Academy's gold medal and gained a travelling scholarship to Italy, which he took up in 1796.

He arrived in Rome in March 1797 intent on studying the antiquities, but chose an unfortunate moment, since Napoleon's troops were about to invade the city. Soon after his arrival the most famous excavated statues in the Vatican were packed up in readiness to be sent to France by the terms of the treaty of Tolentino. He also discovered that the wealthy English tourists who had been leading purchasers of neo-classical sculpture were returning home. The lively group of British artists who might have provided advice and contacts, **John Flaxman RA, Sir Richard Westmacott RA, Christopher Hewetson** and the painter, Gavin Hamilton, were leaving, or died shortly after his arrival. Thorvaldsen, who admired and collected Flaxman's spare, linear illustrations to the classics, took the studio formerly used by Flaxman in the Strada Babuino, near the Teatro d'Aliberti.

Although Thorvaldsen was obliged to forego study of the masterworks of antiquity there was a wealth of ancient sculpture in Rome and he became familiar with classical forms, iconography and methods of composition by making numerous drawings. As in later life, he took time to create sculpture and produced little of note during his first years. The professors of the Copenhagen Academy grew impatient and warned that they might suspend his grant if he failed to produce a substantial work. Thorvaldsen's consequent anxiety forced him to concentrate on modelling a colossal statue, *Jason with the golden fleece* (**12**). The severe, uncluttered lines of the heroic figure, caught at the moment between rest and movement, marked it out as a new interpretation of the classical style. Canova was one of many visitors to Thorvaldsen's studio and he generously paid tribute to its innovative nature.

In the wake of the short-lived Peace of Amiens, 1802, British visitors returned briefly to Rome and renewed the practice of visiting the leading sculpture studios as a part of their itinerary. Thomas Hope, a wealthy banker and one of the most influential and discerning connoisseurs of his time, saw the *Jason* and ordered a marble to be made from the model. In his characteristically business-like manner, Hope drew up a contract and made a down-payment which alleviated Thorvaldsen's immediate financial problems and polarised attention on his radical work. Hope was obliged to wait a quarter of a century before he received his statue.

His reputation grew steadily during the Napoleonic era, thanks to support from fellow countrymen and then from leaders of European society. In 1812 his career received a boost for a plaster frieze of 17 low-reliefs depicting *The triumphant entry of Alexander into Babylon* was ordered for the Quirinal Palace in Rome, prior to an expected visit by Napoleon. The portrait painter Sir Thomas Lawrence, who considered Canova to be the ablest sculptor since the classical Greek era, conceded that Thorvaldsen 'had executed [the frieze] with ability' (*Farington* XVI, 5675, 6 June 1821). It was copied in marble for the Christiansborg Palace, Copenhagen and for the Villa Carlotta on Lake Como. By 1815 Thorvaldsen had enough commissions for statues and reliefs to justify renting three small houses near the Piazza Barberini as a workshop.

One of his first British clients after the cessation of hostilities was the 6th Duke of Bedford, who arrived in Rome with his family in December 1814. Bedford was considering converting a conservatory at Woburn Abbey into a sculpture gallery, where he would eventually assemble a major collection of antiquities and modern works, presided over by Canova's *Three Graces*, 1817–19. He commissioned two reliefs from Thorvaldsen, *The wrath of Achilles*, taken from a model prepared in 1803–5 (**57**), and a new work, *The embassy of Priam*, which is closely related to antique compositions and may have been inspired by a classical gem in Thorvaldsen's collection (**56**). Bedford considered Thorvaldsen's reliefs of sufficient importance to be grouped with nine antique panels in his gallery. Whilst the family were in Rome Thorvaldsen modelled the head of the Duke's daughter, Georgiana, for a marble statue, one of his most charming portraits (**6**). This formed a pendant to a statue of Georgiana's elder sister provided by **Sir Francis Chantrey** for Woburn in 1819.

Another British aristocrat intent on creating a sculpture gallery at his country seat was the 6th Duke of Devonshire. With this in mind he went to Rome in 1819 together with his step-mother, Elizabeth, Duchess of Devonshire, and there commissioned a number of works from Canova. He also ordered a *Venus* from Thorvaldsen (**9**) and paid half the asking price on 19 May 1819. The receipt confirmed that the statue would be finished in a year and Devonshire was fortunate since it was dispatched only a little late, in August 1821. By contrast, a *Venus* ordered by Lord Lucan in 1816 was still awaited in 1824 (**10**). Devonshire's *Venus* was damaged at the customs and repaired under the supervision of **Allan Cunningham**, later to become known for his *Lives of the Artists*. The Duke was slighting about the *Venus*, which he described as a 'perfect woman, not at all goddess' (6th Duke's *Handbook to Chatsworth* and Hardwick, 1844, quoted by *JKB* (2), 324), but he returned to Thorvaldsen on two subsequent visits. In 1822, he noted archly: 'Thorvaldsen showed me his grand works but I look on him as a modellist and not a sculptor' (*ibid*). By then he was finishing four reliefs which went to Chatsworth, copies of the Woburn *Achilles* reliefs and two new subjects, *Night* and *Day* (**56–58**). The *Achilles* reliefs had been ordered by another English patron, the historian George Agar Ellis, when he sat for his bust in 1818 (**36**), but who then declined to take them. On a third visit to Rome in 1824, Devonshire ordered a bust of Cardinal Ercole Consalvi, secretary of state to Pope Pius VII (**42**). This was copied from the bust on Consalvi's newly erected monument by Thorvaldsen in the Pantheon, a memorial ordered by Devonshire's step-mother.

The British passion for portraiture gave Thorvaldsen the task of synthesizing realism and classical ideals. The sculptor's busts for European clients during the Napoleonic era reflected his careful studies of antique precedents. His heads of Cicero and Agrippa were severe portraits with closely cropped hair, sharply defined lips and bare, squared-chest sections. The heads modelled after 1814 are more individualised. Male sitters often presented a challenge to notions of ideal portraiture with their bloated faces, forward-swept hair and side-whiskers that grew more pronounced with the passage of time, but Thorvaldsen nonetheless provided refinement and dignity without sacrificing likeness. He varied the treatment of the upper torso: Edward Divett, a Devonshire squire, and Thomson Henry Bonar, a boy, were presented with deep chests and classical draperies (**25, 34**); George Agar Ellis, was given a severely square, naked chest (**36**), Lord Byron had shoulders draped in a toga (**26**) and Thomas Maitland was garbed in Roman imperial armour fastened with a pin on the right shoulder (**40**). The ladies presented fewer problems, since the taste for ringlets framing the face and hair swept into a chignon provided a suitably classical aura, whilst a bare neck conformed with contemporary fashions in dress. The French novelist Stendhal, who preferred the work of Canova to Thorvaldsen, nonetheless conceded that the Dane's busts were excellent, whilst criticizing his Roman rival for imbuing his sitters with too much ideal grace.

Thomas Hope returned to Rome in 1816 with several family members. On a visit to the sculptor's studio he sat for a portrait characterised by its calm dignity (**41**). Thorvaldsen also modelled a head of Hope's wife Louisa, and one son, Adrian (**24, 32**), and he prepared a model for the head of a second son, Henry, which he later presented to Hope (**28**). Hope raised the matter of his statue of *Jason*, now 13 years overdue and Thorvaldsen suggested that since it was a juvenile work, Hope might prefer another subject. Hope was unmoved and demanded to have the subject which the sculptor had contracted to carve. In April 1819 Hope felt obliged to hand negotiations over to the bankers Torlonia and Company, who were encouraged to exert the severest pressure on Thorvaldsen. The statue finally arrived at The Deepdene, Hope's country house, in the spring of 1828. With it came peace-offerings, the bust of young Henry and two low reliefs, *Art and the genius of light* and *Cupid received by Anacreon* (**55, 61**) a composition described by Hope's biographer, David Watkin as 'a work of considerable elegance, closely based on antique models' (*Watkin* 1968, 38). Eventually Hope appears to have owned at least nine, and probably eleven, works by Thorvaldsen (**5, 11, 12, 24, 28, 32, 41, 49, 55, 60, 61**) which remained at The Deepdene until 1917, when Lord Francis Hope was obliged to sell them and they were acquired by the Thorvaldsen Museum in Copenhagen.

The 2nd Earl of Minto, a Whig politician and diplomat, was in Rome with his family in 1821–22 and kept a diary of his visit, in which he debated the rival merits of Canova and Thorvaldsen. His initial enthusiasm for Canova was tempered after visiting Thorvaldsen's studio, where he ordered a version of the *Shepherd boy* (see **11**). Minto admired Canova's mastery of the calmly posed female nude and his skill with surface textures, but he pronounced Thorvaldsen's low reliefs to be the finest he had seen since the Elgin Marbles. On 7 January 1822 Minto noted: 'am more than ever confirmed in my opinion of his [Canova's] great inferiority to Torwaldsen [*sic*] in every thing except the surface he gives his marble. Scarcely any one figure of Canova's is free from affectation . . . Torwalson's [*sic*] compositions, on the contrary, are full of genius'. (*Minto Diaries*, Nat Lib of Scotland, MSS 11986-7, quoted by *Gordon Brown* 1995, 75). Minto's *Shepherd Boy* was probably not completed since he was still enquiring about it five years later.

Thorvaldsen's many commissions for busts and statues of classical subjects freed him from the need to rely on church monuments as his mainstay and he produced only one great work in the genre, the monument to Pope Pius VII, 1824–25, in St Peter's, Rome. He was responsible for a number of tomb reliefs and drew on a British motif, recently explored by Flaxman, for two monuments to European subjects, Baroness Chaudoir, 1818 (location unknown, plaster model, Thorvaldsen Museum, Copenhagen), and the children of Princess Helena Poniñska, 1834–5 (State Museum, Lvov, Ukraine). These have souls of human form rising in the air in the manner of Flaxman's monument to Agnes Cromwell, 1800. His three English monumental reliefs all have Christian narrative content (**1–3**). Two other monuments, ordered by English clients of whom little is known, failed to materialise. Colonel Thomson Bonar, who obtained a marble bust of his young son from Thorvaldsen in 1817 (**34**) ordered a grave relief from him in the same year depicting *The three Marys at the tomb of Christ*. Edward Cooper was unusual among Thorvaldsen's clients in providing a detailed programme for his wife's monument: he specified that the relief was to depict Cooper kneeling by her deathbed with two angels hovering above, about to welcome the deceased to heaven, in the form of an angel.

During his last decade in Rome, Thorvaldsen received a prestigious commission from England, for a commemorative statue of Lord Byron (**13**). Byron's portrait bust by Thorvaldsen was well known to the British through marble replicas and plaster casts and he was the logical choice of sculptor when in 1829 a committee chaired by Sir John Hobhouse, who had originally introduced the poet to Thorvaldsen, elected to erect a monument to

Byron. Two years earlier Hobhouse had written to Thorvaldsen asking whether he would be prepared to carv Byron's statue for a fee of £1,000, with a further £500 to be set aside to cover the cost of a plinth, freight and custom duties. Thorvaldsen responded with enthusiasm, offering to provide both the statue and a pedestal relief for th proposed £1,000. No site was specified at this date though Hobhouse airily promised that it would be housed i Westminster Abbey, St Paul's, the British Museum or the National Gallery. Hobhouse sent the payment to Rom with a letter suggesting that the poet should be represented seated, to disguise his clubfoot. Thorvaldsen concurre not because of the deformed foot but for the more lofty reason that he considered poetry a contemplative art. Th source for Thorvaldsen's initial sketch was an antique seated statue of the muse Urania, but with Byron presente in modern dress. A number of modifications were introduced as the work evolved, particularly to the head, whic follows the earlier bust. When the statue arrived in England in 1835 none of the proposed sites were prepared t house it, since objections had been raised to Byron's profligate life-style. A decade later it was installed in the librar of Byron's old college, Trinity, Cambridge.

When Thorvaldsen returned to Copenhagen in 1838, after 40 years in Rome, he had completed most of h commissions, including a large number of marble copies, executed by assistants, sometimes with little supervisio He was received home with honour, given the use of an apartment in the Academy at Charlottenburg, received visi from members of the royal family and died on 8 March 1844 in his usual seat at the Royal theatre. The Crown Princ was at his funeral.

Thorvaldsen's reputation in England was considerable in the years following his death. Casts of 37 of his work were exhibited in the Courts of Modern Sculpture at the Crystal Place in 1851, more than any other sculpto including Canova. Several English sculptors made copies of his work: the **Coade factory** reproduced Alexand Baring's *Mercury* (**8**), **E H Baily** copied reredos figures for Leigh Delamere, Wilts and **Thomas Earle** copied his reli of *Night* for the Minerva masonic lodge in Hull.

Thorvaldsen's large team of assistants included several with English associations. **John Gibson** became a pup after the death of Canova and was much influenced by Thorvaldsen's style, **William Theed II**, who was in Rome i 1826, studied under him, **Joseph Hermann** of Dresden was a pupil for ten years and has one signed English work t his credit, and **J H D Kaehler** worked under Thorvaldsen before leaving for London in 1826. **Alfred Stevens** worke in his studio, which survived in Rome until 1844.

His estate made provision for a natural daughter, Elisa, the child of his long-term mistress, Anna Maria Magnan but in 1837 he presented the bulk of his fortune, his works and collection of paintings and Antiquities to the city c Copenhagen. The Thorvaldsen Museum, which was built to house them, was well advanced when the sculptor die He was buried in a burial chamber in the centre of the museum's courtyard lined with paintings after the Antiqu A considerable sum was set aside to enable local sculptors to carve marble copies of his casts and their style becam progressively less classical with changing taste. These copies damaged his reputation. Finally, in 1916, the fund wa redirected to the purchase of Thorvaldsen's original work when it came on the market. Thomas Hope's collectio was followed by a steady succession of acquisitions, most of them from England. The purchase of these works ha restored his reputation as one of the two leading sculptors of the neoclassical movement.

The following list includes only works commissioned or acquired by British patrons.

I

Literary References: *Sass* III, 1965, *passim; Watkin* 1968, *passim; Hodgkinson* 1970, 74; *Neoclassicism* 1971, 284–9; *JKB* 1972 (3), 322–35; *Sutton* 197 176–97; *Salling* 1972, 214–9; *Helsted* 1972, 228–34; *Janson* 1977, 107–28; *Read* 1982, 32–3, 37, 70, 275; *Laing* 1983, 186–8; *Gordon Brown* 1995, 73–8 *Jørnæs* 1993, *passim; Floryan* 2003, 43–74

Collection of Drawings: Thorvaldsen Museum, Copenhagen; Cupid and Psyche, nd, pen and ink, Witt

Selected Portraits of the Sculptor: self-portrait, 1810, charcoal, Ny Carlsberg Glyptotek (*Sutton* 1972, 177, repr 2); self-portrait, bust, 1810, marbl Royal Danish Academy of Art, Copenhagen (*Sutton* 1972, 177, repr 4); C W Eckersberg, 1814, oil on canvas, Royal Danish Academy of Art (*Salli* 1972, 222 (repr); **A H Ritchie**, bust, 1830, untraced; E M Ward, *Thorvaldsen in his studio in Rome*, 1838, pen and ink, Thorvaldsen Museum Copenhagen (*Sass* III, 47, repr): self-portrait, statue, 1839, plaster, Thorvaldsen coll, *Nysø* (*Helsted* 1972, 231, repr)

Funerary Monuments

1.	†1817	Sir Charles Drake Garrard and wife, Anne Model(s): *Man and wife reunited in Heaven*, plaster relief, Thorvaldsen Museum A620		Wheathampstead, Herts	S	Pevsner, *Herts*, 1977, 404; *Jørnæs* 1993, 70; *Jansen* 1977, 112
2.	1818	Anthony, Earl of Newburgh (†1814), relief Model(s): *The genius of death and a woman kneeling at a tombstone*, plaster relief, Thorvaldsen Museum A622, A740, A889		Slindon House, Arundel, Sussex	S	*Sass* 1, 1963, 425–8; III, 79; Pevsner, *Sussex*, 1965, 327; *Janson* 1977, 112; *Jørnæs* 1993, 70, 76
3.	1828	Lady Jane Lawley (†1816) Model(s): *Woman kneeling between two angels*, plaster relief, Thorvaldsen Museum A623		Escrick, E R Yorks	S	Pevsner, *Yorks: E R & York*, 1995, 406; *Jørnæs* 1993, 70

Statues

4.	1806	Hebe		[coll Samuel Boddington]; Thorvaldsen Museum, Copenhagen A875 Other versions: Chatsworth, Derbys, nd Thorvaldsen Museum, Copenhagen A 874 (ex coll Alexander Baring)		*JKB* 1972, (3) 327, 331 n18; *Jørnæs* 1993, 23, 86
5.	1806	Psyche with the jar of beauty Model(s): plaster, Thorvaldsen Museum A26	m	[The Deepdene, Dorking, Surrey; Hope sale, 1917, lot 1163]; Thorvaldsen Museum, Copenhagen A821 Other versions: Lyne House, Surrey, chapel, nd	SD	*Watkin* 1968, 38, 170 (repr 62); *Jørnæs* 1993, 83

No.	Date	Work	Material	Location		Literature
6.	1815	Lady Georgiana Russell Model(s): plaster bust, first model for the statue, Thorvaldsen Museum A315		Woburn Abbey, Beds		*Sass* I, 1963, 224–8 (repr); III, 73; *Jørnæs* 1993, 34, 46, 79 (repr)
7.	?1817	Ganymede and Jupiter's eagle	m	Waddesdon Manor, Bucks Other versions: Private coll, Prince's Gate, London Minneapolis School of Art, USA Thorvaldsen Museum, Copenhagen		*Hodgkinson* 1970, 74–5 (repr); *Sutton* 1972, 185, 188 (repr)
8.	1818	Mercury about to kill Argus Drawing(s): Thorvaldsen Museum, Copenhagen (*Sass* III, 26–7, 29 (repr)	m	[coll Alexander Baring]; Thorvaldsen Museum, Copenhagen A873 Other versions: Chatsworth, Derbys, the park, nd ex coll Dukes of Sutherland, nd, Cliveden, Ilex grove,	S	*JKB* 1972 (2), 327, 331 n18; *Helsted* 1990, 76–77 (repr)
9.	1819–1821	Venus (Venere Vincitrice) Payment(s): 2,000 scudi	m	Chatsworth, Derbys		*JKB* 1972 (3), 323, 325, 331 (repr)
10.	1813–1824	Venus with the apple awarded by Paris Model(s): plaster, Thorvaldsen Museum A12	m	[coll Lord Lucan]; Hearst Castle, St Simeon, Cal Other versions: Chatsworth, Orangery (Chatsworth Handlist, 28) ex coll Henry Labouchère, Thorvaldsen Museum, Copenhagen A853, 1829	S	*Sass* III, 1965, 26–7, 28 (repr); *JKB* 1972 (2), 323; *Laing* 1983, 188, repr; *Helsted* 1990, 76–77 (repr)
11.	1822–1825	A shepherd boy with his dog Model(s): plaster, 1817, Thorvaldsen Museum, Copenhagen A177	m	[The Deepdene, Dorking, Surrey]; Manchester CAG Other versions: Waddesdon Manor, Bucks Chatsworth, Derbys, the park Heaton Park, Manchester Drapers' Hall, City of London, Drawing Room, 1822–25 Roundhay Hall, Leeds, W R Yorks		*Watkin* 1968, 38; *Hodgkinson* 1970, 250–1 (repr); *Helsted* 1990, 80–81 (repr)
12.	1802–1828	Jason with the golden fleece Model(s): plaster, Thorvaldsen Museum A51	m	[The Deepdene, Dorking, Surrey; Hope sale 1917, lot 1168]; Thorvaldsen Museum, Copenhagen A822	S	*Janson* 1977, 107–8; *Watkin* 1968, 37–8 (repr); *Helsted* 1990, 50–1 (repr 9); *Thorvaldsen Museum Bulletin*, 2003 (202pp)
13.	1829–35	George Gordon, Lord Byron Model(s): plaster, Thorvaldsen Museum A133 (sketch)	m	Trinity College, Cambridge, library		*Neoclassicism* 1972, 289; *Helsted* 1972, 229–30 (repr); *Janson* 1977, 113, 127, 128 (repr); *Helsted* 1990, 101
14.	nd	Cupid playing with a lyre	m	Private coll, Henley-on-Thames, Oxon		Thorvaldsen Museum checklist 1996
15.	nd	Singing Angels	m	[coll Francis Edwards]; untraced		*Manchester Art Treasures* 1857, 235
16.	nd	Theseus		Heaton Park, Manchester, Lancs, entrance hall		Pevsner, *Lancs: S*, 1969, 329
Busts						
17.	1814	Admiral Edward Pellew, later 1st Viscount Exmouth Model(s): plaster, Thorvaldsen Museum A260	m	Canonteign, Devon	SD	*Sass* I, 1963, 213 (repr); III, 72–3; *Jørnæs* 1993, 41
18.	1815	Catharina de Branciforte, Mrs George Wilding Model(s): plaster, Thorvaldsen Museum A276	m	Thorvaldsen Museum, Copenhagen	SD	*Jørnæs* 1993, 43, 88
19.	1815	George William Wilding Model(s): plaster, Thorvaldsen Museum A275	m	Thorvaldsen Museum, Copenhagen	SD	*Jørnæs* 1993, 42, 88
20.	1816	Alexander Baillie Model(s): plaster, Thorvaldsen Museum A262	m	Royal Soc of Sciences and Letters, Trondhjem, Norway		*Sutton* 1972, 194 (repr); *Jørnæs* 1993, 42
21.	c1816	Lord William Cavendish-Bentinck, later Governor General of India Model(s): plaster, Thorvaldsen Museum A261	m	Welbeck Abbey, Notts		*Sass* I, 1963, 223; III, 73; *Jørnæs* 1993, 43
22.	1816	Mary Ann, Countess of Sandwich, model	p	Thorvaldsen Museum, Copenhagen A267	D	*Sass* I, 1963, 245, 249; *Sutton* 1972, 195 (repr); *Jørnæs* 1993, 42
23.	?1816	William Haldimand, modelled in Rome		Untraced		*Sass* III, 1965, 75; *Gunnis* 1968, 394
24.	c1817	Adrian Hope, aged six	m	[The Deepdene, Dorking, Surrey]; Thorvaldsen Museum, Copenhagen A826		*Sass* I, 1963, 281, 292–301 (repr), II, 403, III, 75–6; *Helsted* 1990, 71 (repr)
25.	1817	Edward Divett of Bystock, Devon	p	Thorvaldsen Museum, Copenhagen A263		*Jørnæs* 1993, 42
26.	1817	George Gordon, Lord Byron Model(s): plaster, Thorvaldsen Museum A257	m	[coll Lord Byron]; Thorvaldsen Museum, Copenhagen A256 Other versions: Lord Kinnaird of Inchtire, c1817, marble Royal Coll, Windsor Castle, Berks, 1817 Chatsworth, Derbys, nd Sir John Murray, London, nd	SD	*British Portraits* 1956–7, 117; *Janson* 1977, 113; *Adams* 1996, 205–19
27.	1817	George, Lord Gower Model(s): plaster, Thorvaldsen Museum A259	m	Cliveden, Bucks	SD	*Sutton* 1972, 195 (repr); *Jørnæs* 1993, 41

28.	1817	Henry Hope Model(s): plaster, Thorvaldsen Museum A265, A266	m	[The Deepdene, Dorking, Surrey]; Thorvaldsen Museum, Copenhagen A825		*Watkin* 1968, 37; *Neoclassicism* 1971, 284–5; *Jørnæs* 1993, 42, 83
29.	1816–1817	Lady Elisabeth Bingham	m	[Longniddry, East Lothian]; Daniel Katz showroom, 2003		*Sass* I, 1963, 368–80 (repr)
30.	1816–1817	Lady Georgiana Bingham Model(s): plaster, Thorvaldsen Museum A313	p	[coll Richard, 2nd Earl of Lucan]; Daniel Katz showroom, 2003		*Sass* I, 1963, 370, 379 (repr); *Jørnæs* 1993, 46
31.	1817	Lady Harriet Pellew Model(s): plaster, Thorvaldsen Museum A309	m	Canonteign, Devon	SD	*Jørnæs* 1993, 45
32.	1817	Louisa Hope Model(s): plaster, Thorvaldsen Museum A824	m	[The Deepdene, Dorking, Surrey]; Thorvaldsen Museum, Copenhagen	SD	*Sass* I, 1963, 283 (repr); *Watkin* 1968, 38; *Jørnæs* 1993, 42, 83
33.	1816–1817	'Madama Vernot', probably Lady Elizabeth Vernon, née Bingham	p	Thorvaldsen Museum, Copenhagen A311		*Sass* I, 1963, 380–3 (repr); III, 78; *Jørnæs* 1993, 45
34.	1817	Thomson Henry Bonar	m	Thorvaldsen Museum, Copenhagen	SD	*Jørnæs* 1993, 88
35.	1818	Francis, 1st Baron de Dunstanville Model(s): plaster, Thorvaldsen Museum A297	m	[Tehidy, Cornwall]; untraced	D	*Farington* XVI, 5675 (June 1821); *Sass* I, 1963, 451ff; III, 80; *Jørnæs* 1993, 44
36.	1818	George Agar Ellis, later Baron Dover Model(s): plaster, Thorvaldsen Museum A299		Holdenby House, Northants		*Sass* I, 1963, 411, 412 (repr); III, 79; *Jørnæs* 1993, 45
37.	*c*1818	Giovanna Nugent, model	p	Thorvaldsen Museum, Copenhagen A239		*Sass* I, 1963, 469, 470 (repr); III, 81; *Jørnæs* 1993, 40
38.	1818	Jane Craufurd Model(s): plaster, Thorvaldsen Museum A307	m	[Swindridge Muir, Ayrshire]; Thorvaldsen Museum, Copenhagen A898	D	*Sass* I, 1963, I, 446–50 (repr); II, 393, 404, 405; III, 80; *Jørnæs* 1993, 45, 89
39.	1817–1818	'Valletort'; probably either William Richard, Viscount Valletort, or his brother Ernest Augustus, Viscount Valletort	p	Untraced		*Sass* III, 1965, 81
40.	1818–1820	Sir Thomas Maitland, lord high commissioner of the Ionian Isles, with bronze relief on a pedestal of Minerva protecting Virtue and revealing Vice Model(s): Thorvaldsen Museum A258, colossal	p	[Island of Zakynthos]; Thorvaldsen Museum, Copenhagen A268, A600		*Sass* I, 1963, 414–23 (repr); III, 79; *Jørnæs* 1993, 41, 67
41.	1822–1823	Thomas Hope Model(s): plaster, Thorvaldsen Museum A298	m	[The Deepdene, Dorking, Surrey]; Thorvaldsen Museum, Copenhagen, A825	SD	*Sass* I, 1963, 281–96 (repr); III, 75; *Watkin* 1968, 38, (repr 8); *Neoclassicism* 1972, 284
42.	1824	Cardinal Ercole Consalvi Payment(s): 100 louis	m	Chatsworth, Derbys		*Neoclassicism* 1972, 288; *JKB* 1972 (3), 331
43.	1824	Ghazi 'l-Din Haidar, King of Oudh Model(s): plaster, Thorvaldsen Museum A280	m	Thorvaldsen Museum, Copenhagen	SD	*Jørnæs* 1993, 87
44.	1816–1824	Lady Anne Bingham Model(s): plaster, Thorvaldsen Museum A308	m	[Longniddry, East Lothian]; Daniel Katz, 2003		*Sass* I, 1963, 368–80 (repr); III, 78; *Jørnæs* 1993, 45
45.	1828	Henry Labouchere MP, later Baron Taunton	p	Thorvaldsen Museum, Copenhagen A294	SD	*Sass* II, 1965, 162–3, 183–9, 377, 384 (repr); III, 95; *Jørnæs* 1993, 44
46.	1828	Sir George Barlow Bt, Governor General of India Model(s): plaster, Thorvaldsen Museum A289	m	Thorvaldsen Museum, Copenhagen A892, 1950 Other versions: The cottage, Thruxton, Andover, Hants, marble	S	*Sass* II, 1963, 165 (repr); III, 94; *Jørnæs* 1993, 44, 88
47.	*c*1829	Eliza, Lady Glenorchy Model(s): plaster, Thorvaldsen Museum A268	m	[Taymouth Castle, Berwicks]; untraced	S	*Sass* II, 1963, 240ff; III, 98; *Jørnæs* 1993, 42
48.	*c*1829	John, Lord Glenorchy Model(s): plaster, Thorvaldsen Museum A303	m	[Taymouth Castle, Berwicks]; untraced	S	*Sass* II, 1963, 238–48 380 (repr); III, 97–8; *Jørnæs* 1993, 45
49.	1829	Lord Wriothesley Russell Model(s): plaster, Thorvaldsen Museum A285	m	[Probably The Deepdene, Dorking, Surrey]; untraced		*Sass* II, 1965, II, 194–200 (repr); III, 95–6; *Watkin* 1968, 38; *Jørnæs* 1993, 44
50.	1831	Dr John Wyllie Model(s): plaster, Thorvaldsen Museum A283	m	Town Hall, Forfar, Tayside	SD	*Sass* II, 1963, 259, 260–1 (repr); III, 99; *Jørnæs* 1993, 43
51.	*c*1832	Charles James Patrick Mahon MP(?), model	p	Thorvaldsen Museum, Copenhagen A286		*Sass* II, 1963, 289, 291; III, 100; *Jørnæs* 1993, 44
52.	1832	John O'Brien of Fitzwilliam Square, Dublin	p	Untraced		*Sass* III, 1965, 100
53.	*c*1832	Sir Walter Scott (†1832)	m	NPGS Other versions: cast, Thorvaldsen Museum, Copenhagen A255		*Sass* II, 1963, passim; III, 1965, 99–100; *Jørnæs* 1993, 41; *Knox and Longstaffe-Gowan* 1993, 75–81
54.	nd	Louisa Sandwich	m	Hinchinbrooke, Huntingdon		Thorvaldsen Museum checklist 1996

Reliefs

55.	1808	Art and the genius of light	m	[The Deepdene, Dorking, Surrey]; Thorvaldsen Museum, Copenhagen A828	D	*Watkin* 1968, 37 (repr 7); *Jørnæs* 1993, 84 (repr)
56.	1815	The embassy of Priam to Achilles Model(s): plaster, 1815	m	[coll Duke of Bedford]; Woburn Abbey, Beds Other versions: Thorvaldsen Museum, Copenhagen A 792 Chatsworth, Derbys, sculpture gall, 1827–32		*Sass* III, 1965, 41; *Neoclassicism* 1972, 286–7; *Angelicoussis* 1992, 21, 38 (repr)

57.	1815	The wrath of Achilles Model(s): plaster, 1803, Thorvaldsen Museum	m	[coll Duke of Bedford]; Woburn Abbey, Beds Other versions: Thorvaldsen Museum, Copenhagen A789 Chatsworth, Derbys, sculpture gall, 1827–32	*Neoclassicism* 1972, 286–7; *Helsted* 1990, 52–3 (repr); *Angelicoussis* 1992, 21, 38 (repr)
58.	1822	Night with her children, Sleep and Death; Day: Aurora with the genius of light Payment(s): 500 scudi Model(s): plaster, 1815 (Aurora: Thorvaldsen Museum)	m	Chatsworth, Derbys, sculpture gallery Other versions: Walker Art Gall, Liverpool VAM, 1842, marble (on loan from Thorvaldsen Museum) Thorvaldsen Museum, Copenhagen	*JKB* 1972 (3), 324, 331; Thorvaldsen Museum checklist 1996; *Chatsworth Handlist*, 25
59.	1823	Morning		[Exhib Carlisle Ac, 162]; untraced	*Carlisle Ac Exhibs*, 1823, 13
60.	1823	Night		[Exhib Carllisle Ac 163; perhaps the version acquired by Thomas Hope for The Deepdene, Dorking, Surrey, lilac room]; untraced	*Carlisle Ac Exhibs*, 1823, 13; *Watkin* 1968, 38
61.	1823–1824	Cupid received by Anacreon	m	[The Deepdene, Dorking, Surrey]; Thorvaldsen Museum, Copenhagen A827	*Watkin* 1968, 37; *Neoclassicism* 1972, 285 (repr); *Helsted* 1990, 94–5 (repr); *Jørnæs* 1993, 84
62.	1824	The ages of love	m	[coll P C Labouchère]; Danish Embassy, London	*Laing* 1983, 188 (repr)
63.	nd	Bacchante and satyr	m	61 Green Street, London	Thorvaldsen Museum checklist, 1996
64.	nd	Charity		[coll Henry, 3rd Marquess of Lansdowne]; untraced	*Gunnis* 1968, 394
65.	nd	Cupid complains to Venus	m	Laleham House, Middx	Thorvaldsen Museum checklist, 1995
66.	nd	Cupid's dominion over the Elements, four panels	m	[coll Henry Labouchère]; Stoke Park, Stoke Poges, Bucks, eating room	*Laing* 1983, 187–8 (repr)
67.	nd	Four, from the Alexander frieze	m	Laleham House, Middx	Thorvaldsen Museum checklist, 1995
68.	nd	Hercules and Hebe	m	London, 61 Green Street	Thorvaldsen Museum checklist, 1996
69.	nd	Homer reciting	p	[coll Henry Labouchère]; Thorvaldsen Museum, Copenhagen	*Laing* 1983, 188 (repr)
70.	nd	Mercury brings Bacchus to Ino	m	Laleham House, Middx	Thorvaldsen Museum checklist, 1996
71.	nd	Minerva and Prometheus		London, 61 Green Street	Thorvaldsen Museum checklist, 1996
72.	nd	Vulcan forging the arrows of love, and love dominating the four continents	m	[coll Henry Labouchère]; Stoke Park, Stoke Poges, Bucks, eating room	*Laing* 1983 187–8 (repr); Pevsner, *Bucks*, 1994, 656

HRUPP, Frederick 1812–95

Frederick Thrupp was born in Paddington Green, Middx, the second youngest child of Joseph and Mary Thrupp and a half-brother of the noted English hymn writer Dorothy Ann Thrupp. He had a long and not unsuccessful life as a sculptor, providing ideal works, reliefs and busts for both public and private patrons, as well as a smaller number of monuments and architectural pieces. He also undertook several commissions for lithographic works, including engravings for an edition of Milton's *Paradise Lost* in 1879.

Thrupp first studied art at Henry Sass's Academy in Bloomsbury, London, where he learnt modelling and drawing, winning a Society of Arts silver medal in 1829 for a chalk drawing. In 1830 he was admitted to the Royal Academy Schools, where he first exhibited a sculptural work in 1832 entitled *The prodigal returned* (**97**). In 1837 he travelled to Rome, remaining there four years, during which time he met many of the best-known sculptors of the time, including **William Theed II, R J Wyatt** and **Bertel Thorvaldsen**. The most notable friendship he struck up was perhaps with **John Gibson**, who is said to have 'obtained several commissions' for Thrupp (ODNB). Returning to London in 1842, Thrupp settled at his now widowed mother's house, 15 Paddington Green, where he lived until her death in 1845, then moving with two of his sisters to 232 Marylebone Road (also called New Road), a home in which he was to remain for the next 40 years. Although he appears initially to have kept a studio at 30 Gloucester Place, Marylebone, in 1858 he established both studio and showroom at 232 Marylebone Road.

Thrupp worked principally on ideal works and reliefs. These often had a religious theme, for instance *The Magdalene* made for the John, 1st Baron Coleridge, the lord chief justice, *c*1841; *Christ blessing the children* of 1860; and a reredos of *The Last Supper* for St Clement's, York, *c*1874 (**9, 30, 71**). Retallick suggests that these reflected a lifelong aim 'to create an English School of Religious Art' (*Retallick*, 81), which can be seen as contiguous with a number of religious tracts written by Thrupp, including *The Angelic Nature*, published in 1879, in which he discussed the relationship between Christianity and art. Thrupp also undertook ideal works based on secular subjects and Greek mythology, and a number of portrait busts and statues. Amongst the most notable statues were two for the Palace of Westminster, 1847–58, of Baron Fitzwalter and the 3rd Earl of Oxford, the leaders of the 'Magna Carta Barons' (**22, 28**). These two works are unusual because they were produced in zinc using an electro-deposition process that Elkington and Co had only recently put into commercial service.

Thrupp was rarely commissioned to produce funerary monuments, perhaps because of two controversial commissions for Westminster Abbey obtained early in his career, the memorials to Sir Thomas Fowell Buxton and William Wordsworth (**1, 2**). Buxton had been a prominent anti-slavery campaigner and member of parliament, and the Westminster monument was commissioned in 1846, a year after his death. Unfortunately for Thrupp, his achievement in gaining the commission was 'marred by rumours of favouritism' (*Greenwood*, 1999, 3). His friend, the painter George Richmond, was on the selection committee. There was much hostile press coverage, including a scathing report in *The Art Union* which claimed Thrupp's entry had been 'the worst statue of all' chosen in a way which disgusted 'our best artists with competitions' (*AU*, 1846, 264). Thrupp's success in winning the commission for the Wordsworth memorial in 1851 was similarly problematic. Not only did the Wordsworth family dislik the idea of having a monument in Westminster Abbey, but the Dean and Chapter were opposed to having an more in the Abbey and only accepted the Wordsworth memorial because 'In this particular instance they *could* nc refuse' (*Robinson*, vol 2, 751). Thrupp's insistence that the monument should be placed in the baptistry instead c Poets' Corner did not help: the *Athenaeum* commented that in this location the seated figure appeared 'literall entombed' (*Athenaeum*, 1854, 1467). However, it was again the initial competition that caused most disquiet, fc there was a strong suspicion that Thrupp had won despite submitting an inferior entry. The monument present a seated figure of the poet with a pensive expression and is allegedly based on a drawing of Wordsworth by Haydo made in 1819, though some sources claim the likeness came from the death-mask of Wordsworth cast by **Chantre** Forty-one other sculptors entered the competition, including **Thomas Woolner**, who had carved the memori tablet to Wordsworth at St Oswald's, Grasmere, but according to the *Art Journal* the refusal to allow the public t see and compare the competition entries for themselves suggested 'there must have been some lack of fair play the successful artist was not successful enough to show his design' (*AJ*, 1851, 222). That these scandals may have hu Thrupp's reputation is perhaps indicated by the fact that he received only one further significant publi commission, *Timon of Athens*, for the Corporation of London in 1853 (**26**).

In 1868 Thrupp exhibited a pair of doors at the Royal Academy. These were inspired by Ghiberti's baptistry doors i Florence and comprise ten bas-relief panels showing scenes from John Bunyan's *The Pilgrim's Progress* (**70**). These wer purchased for the Bunyan meeting house in Bedford by the 9th Duke of Bedford in 1876. Narrative panels were t become something of a speciality for Thrupp, and he produced another set of doors with 10 panels depicting the poetr of George Herbert in 1878, which were erected in 1888 at Selwyn divinity school, Cambridge, and a third set of 10 reli panels depicting scenes from Milton's *Paradise Lost* c1880 (**72, 86**).

In 1885 Thrupp married Sarah Frances and began a series of extensive tours of North Africa and Europe, includin Algeria in 1885–86, Italy and southern Europe in 1887 and Westphalia and the Low Countries in 1889. By this time h had virtually stopped sculpting, and in 1887 he left his London home and studio for good, to settle in Upton nea Torquay. Here Thrupp negotiated the disposal of the remaining contents of his studio, with most of it going to th city of Winchester in 1894 for display in a 'Thrupp Gallery' at Abbey House. Thrupp died of pneumonia the followin year and was buried in Torquay. After his death his reputation fell rapidly, as evidenced by Winchester's ungraciou return to his family of Thrupp's gift to the city in 1911. The gift was passed on to Torquay borough council later tha year, and augmented in 1916 by an additional bequest to Torquay from Thrupp's widow. This included numerou unsold works, models in clay and plaster, drawings, etchings and notebooks, as well as studio effects. In 1932 muc of this gift was placed on display at Torre Abbey, Torquay, where the collection remains to this day.

Michael Parasko

Literary References: *AU* 1846, 264; *AJ* 1851, 222; *Athenaeum* 1854, 1467; *Palgrave* 1866, 250; *DNB* 1898 335–36 (Dodgson); *Robinson* 1938, 75 *Gunnis* 1968, 394; *Read* 1982, 79–80, 103–4; *Retallick* 1998, 80–81; *Greenwood* 1999, 1–12; *Matthews* 2004, 181–85, *ODNB* (Greenwood)

Archival References: Parish Register, St James, Paddington; 1861 census

Miscellaneous Drawings: chalk drawing of a bust, silver medal, Soc of A, 1829 (RSA *Transactions*, vol 47, xxiii)

Portraits of the Sculptor: photo, c1890–95 (repr *Greenwood* 1999, 1)

Funerary Monuments

1.	1846–47	Sir Thomas Fowell Buxton (†1845)		Westminster Abbey, London, nave	S	*Graves* VII, 1905–6, 389; *Read* 1982, 79–80; *Greenwood* 1999, 3
2.	1854	William Wordsworth (†1850) Model(s): numerous maquettes, Torre Abbey, Torquay, Devon		Westminster Abbey, London, south transept	S	*Read* 1982, 103–4, 105 (repr); *Greenwood* 1999, 1–3, 7 (repr)
3.	†1857	James Forster Drawing(s): Torre Abbey, Torquay, Devon		Stisted, Essex	S	C Lib (repr)
4.	1879	Lady Jane Coleridge (†1878)		Ottery St Mary, Devon Other versions: Private coll, Devon (statue)	SD	*Kemp* 1980, 150, 152 (repr); *Greenwood* 1999, 4
5.	1883	Canon Hugh Pearson		Sonning, Berks		*Gunnis* 1968, 394; Pevsner, *Berks*, 1966, 219
6.	nd	Unidentified cleric, sketch model only	p	Torre Abbey, Torquay, Devon		C Lib (repr)

Statues

7.	?1837	The young hunter	p	Torre Abbey, Torquay, Devon		*Graves* VII, 1905–6, 388; *Greenwood* 1999, 6
8.	1840	Arethusa Payment(s): £150	m	[coll Earl Grosvenor]; untraced Other versions: exhib Westminster Hall, London, 1844 ex coll John, 1st Baron Coleridge, marble; untraced		*Graves* 1875, 537; *Graves* VII, 1905–6, 388; *Greenwood* 1999, 3
9.	?1841	The Magdalene	m	[coll John, 1st Baron Coleridge]; untraced		*Graves* 1875, 537; *Graves* VII, 1905–6, 388; *Greenwood* 1999, 4
10.	1843	Hope	m	[Exhib RA, London, 1416]; untraced		*Graves* 1875, 537; *Graves* VII, 1905–6, 388
11.	1844	Hebe followed by the eagle, statuette	m	Torre Abbey, Torquay, Devon	SD	*AU*, 1844, 171; *Graves* VII, 1905–6, 388; *Greenwood* 1999, 6
12.	1844	Hindu throwing a javelin		[Exhib Westminster Hall, London]; untraced		*Greenwood* 1999, 3
13.	1844	Two boys over a basket of fruit	m	Torre Abbey, Torquay, Devon	S	*Graves* VII, 1905–6, 388
14.	1845	Flora scattering flowers		[Exhib Westminster Hall, London, 134]; untraced		*Westminster* 1845, 16
15.	1845	Hunter returning home with a child on his back		[Exhib Westminster Hall, London, 117]; untraced		*Westminster* 1845, 15; *AU*, 1845, 258

No.	Date	Title	Mat	Location		Literature
16.	?1846	The prodigal son, statuette	m	Torre Abbey, Torquay, Devon	S	*Graves* VII, 1905–6, 389; *Greenwood* 1999, 6
17.	1847	Nymph and Cupid (The maid and the mischievous boy)	p	Torre Abbey, Torquay, Devon		*AJ Cat* 1851, 92 (repr); *AJ Cat* 1862, 315 (repr); *Graves* VII, 1905–6, 389; *Greenwood* 1999, 3, 6 (repr)
18.	1847	Two boys	m	[Exhib BI, London, 545]; untraced		*Graves* 1875, 537
19.	?1848	Girl playing with a bird	p	Torre Abbey, Torquay, Devon		*Graves* VII, 1905–6, 389
20.	1849	Ariel		[Exhib Birmingham Soc of A]; untraced		*Gunnis* 1968, 394
21.	1850	Boy catching a butterfly Model(s): exhib RA, London, 1847, 1387	m	City Art Gallery, York		*Manchester Art Treasures* 1857, 133; *Graves* VII, 1905–6, 389; *Read* 1982, 43; *Gunnis* 1968, 395
22.	1847–1852	Robert, Baron Fitzwalter (†1235)		Palace of Westminster, London, House of Lords		*Walker* 1961, 27, 97–8, cat no 29
23.	1853	Two boys with a pipe	p	[Exhib RA, London, 1319]; untraced		*Graves* VII, 1905–6, 389
24.	1854	Flora Model(s): Torre Abbey, Torquay, Devon	p	CL Coll, Mansion House, City of London		*Graves* VII, 1905–6, 389; *Holland Park* 1957, unpag (repr)
25.	1855	Reaper, statuette		[Exhib RA, London, 1499]; untraced		*Graves* VII, 1905–6, 389
26.	1853–1855	Timon of Athens Drawing(s): Torre Abbey, Torquay, Devon Model(s): plaster, C of L coll, Guildhall Art Gallery, City of London, acc 147; two studies, Torre Abbey, Torquay, Devon	m	CL Coll, Mansion House, City of London, Egyptian Hall, acc 146	SD	*Knight* 1986, 348 (repr); *Greenwood* 1999, 3, 7 (repr); *Ward-Jackson* 2002, 546–8
27.	1858	Girl by the seashore	m	[Exhib RA, London, 1194]; untraced		*Graves* VII, 1905–6, 389
28.	1847–1858	Robert de Vere, Earl of Oxford (†1221)		Palace of Westminster, London, House of Lords		*Walker* 1961, 49, 97–8, cat 54
29.	1859	Mercy making garments to give to the poor	m	Torre Abbey, Torquay, Devon	S	*Graves* VII, 1905–6, 389
30.	1860	Christ blessing the children, statuette Model(s): Torre Abbey, Torquay, Devon, plaster	m	Torre Abbey, Torquay, Devon	SD	*Greenwood* 1999, 6
31.	1861	Boy making a flute Model(s): Torre Abbey, Torquay, Devon, plaster	m	[Exhib RA, London, 1065]; untraced		*Graves* VII, 1905–6, 389
32.	1861	The good shepherd, statuette Payment(s): 110 gns	m	Torre Abbey, Torquay, Devon Other versions: ex Torquay cemetery, Devon, clay; untraced	SD	*Graves* 1875, 537; *Graves* VII, 1905–6, 389; *Greenwood* 1999, 4, 6, 8 (repr)
33.	1862	Girl going from the spring (Girl carrying a pitcher), statuette	m	[Exhib BI, London, 642]; untraced		*Graves* 1875, 537; *Graves* VII, 1905–6, 389
34.	nd	Boy with a bird, statuette	b	Torre Abbey, Torquay, Devon	S	C Lib (repr)
35.	nd	Child running	p	Torre Abbey, Torquay, Devon		C Lib (repr)
36.	nd	Faith, statuette	p	Torre Abbey, Torquay, Devon		C Lib (repr)
37.	nd	Female nude with basket of fruit, statuette	m	Torre Abbey, Torquay, Devon	S	C Lib (repr)
38.	nd	Male nudes, two models		Torre Abbey, Torquay, Devon		C Lib (repr)
39.	nd	Nude youth holding a spear, statuette	m	Torre Abbey, Torquay, Devon		C Lib (repr)
40.	nd	Seated naked child, statuette	b	Torre Abbey, Torquay, Devon	S	C Lib (repr)
41.	nd	Striding nude youth with cloak, model		Torre Abbey, Torquay, Devon		C Lib (repr)
42.	nd	Striding nude youth, model		Torre Abbey, Torquay, Devon		C Lib (repr)
43.	nd	Woman reading with a child, model	p	Torre Abbey, Torquay, Devon		C Lib (repr)
44.	nd	Woman with child, statuette	p	Torre Abbey, Torquay, Devon		C Lib (repr)
Busts						
45.	1833	J H Pope		[Exhib RA, London, 1123]; untraced		*Graves* VII, 1905–6, 389
46.	1835	B E Hall		[Exhib RA, London, 1089]; untraced		*Graves* VII, 1905–6, 388
47.	1837	Lucy Gray		[Exhib BI, London, 440]; untraced		*Graves* 1875, 537
48.	1840	Head of the Saviour Payment(s): £30		Eaton Hall, Cheshire, chapel		GPC
49.	1840	Phyllis	m	[coll Earl Grosvenor]; untraced Other versions: Torre Abbey, Torquay, Devon, marble, nd		*Graves* VII, 1905–6, 388, 389
50.	1844	Ariel imprisoned in a pine tree Model(s): Torre Abbey, Torquay, Devon, plaster	m	Torre Abbey, Torquay, Devon		*Graves* 1875, 537; *Graves* VII, 1905–6, 388; *Greenwood* 1999, 6
51.	1846	Arethusa Model(s): Torre Abbey, Torquay, Devon, plaster	m	Torre Abbey, Torquay, Devon		*Graves* VII, 1905–6, 389; *Greenwood* 1999, 6
52.	1848	Samuel Hoare		[Exhib RA, London, 1422]; untraced		*Graves* VII, 1905–6, 389
53.	1849	Boy crowned with hops	m	[Exhib RA, London, 1251]; untraced		*Graves* VII, 1905–6, 389
54.	1849	Charles Cope	m	[Exhib RA, London, 1247]; untraced		*Graves* VII, 1905–6, 389
55.	1851	William Wordsworth	m	Wordsworth Trust, Grasmere, Westmorland Other versions: Torre Abbey, Torquay, Devon, plaster ex coll John, 1st Baron Coleridge, marble; untraced	SD	*Greenwood* 1999, 4
56.	1860	John Bunyan		[Exhib RA, London, 961]; untraced		*Graves* VII, 1905–6, 389
57.	1865	A child		[Exhib RA, London, 1077]; untraced		*Graves* VII, 1905–6, 389
58.	1874	Irene Farrar		[Exhib RA, London, 1600]; untraced		*Graves* VII, 1905–6, 389
59.	1876	Miss Richmond	tc	[Exhib RA, London, 1448]; untraced		*Graves* VII, 1905–6, 389

60.	post-1887	Edward Vivien		Untraced		*Greenwood* 1999, 4
61.	nd	Girl with a spaniel	m	Torre Abbey, Torquay, Devon		*Greenwood* 1999, 6
62.	nd	Head of a female classical figure	m	Torre Abbey, Torquay, Devon		C Lib (repr)
63.	nd	Head of a warrior	m	Torre Abbey, Torquay, Devon		C Lib (repr)
64.	nd	Unidentified boy		Torre Abbey, Torquay, Devon		C Lib (repr)
65.	nd	Unidentified child	p	Torre Abbey, Torquay, Devon		C Lib (repr)
66.	nd	Unidentified man	p	Torre Abbey, Torquay, Devon		C Lib (repr)
67.	nd	Unidentified old woman, sketch model	p	Torre Abbey, Torquay, Devon		C Lib (repr)
68.	nd	Unidentified woman	p	Torre Abbey, Torquay, Devon		C Lib (repr)
69.	nd	Unidentified young woman	p	Torre Abbey, Torquay, Devon		C Lib (repr)

Architectural Sculpture

70.	1868	Ten door panels, illustrating The Pilgrim's Progress Model(s): Torre Abbey, Torquay, Devon, plaster	b	Bunyan Meeting Free Church, Bedford		*Graves* VII, 1905–6, 389; *Greenwood* 1999, 3–4 (repr)
71.	c1874	The Last Supper, reredos		St Clement, York		*Gunnis* 1968, 394; *Greenwood* 1999, 4
72.	1888	Ten door panels illustrating George Herbert's poems Model(s): Torre Abbey, Torquay, Devon, plaster	b	Selwyn divinity school, Cambridge Other versions: Torre Abbey, Torquay, Devon, bronze		*Graves* VII, 1905–6, 389; *Greenwood* 1999, 4, 6

Reliefs

73.	1843	Faith shows the promises to the pilgrim kneeling at the foot of the cross	m	[Exhib RA, London, 1418]; untraced		*Graves* VII, 1905–6, 388
74.	1843	Nymphs (or hamadryads) bringing lilies to Alexis		Torre Abbey, Torquay, Devon		*Le Grice* 1844, II, 244–5; *Graves* VII, 1905–6, 388, 389; *Gunnis* 1968, 395; *Read* 1982, 19
75.	1846	The Saviour washing Peter's feet	p	Torre Abbey, Torquay, Devon Other versions: Torre Abbey, Torquay, Devon, terracotta, SD 1873		*Graves* VII, 1905–6, 389
76.	1846	Thetis bringing armour to Achilles, who is mourning over the body of Patroclus		[Exhib RA, London, 1414]; untraced		*Graves* VII, 1905–6, 389
77.	1853	Unidentified subject		[St Martin's Hall, Long Acre, London]; untraced		*Gunnis* 1968, 394
78.	1855	Girls at a fountain	w	[Exhib RA, London, 1551]; untraced		*Graves* VII, 1905–6, 389
79.	1855	'The muse, the poet never found her . . .'	w	[Exhib RA, London, 1558]; untraced		*Graves* VII, 1905–6, 389
80.	1856	Grace before meat	p	Torre Abbey, Torquay, Devon Other versions: gilt bronze exhib RA, London, 1877, 1496	S	*Graves* VII, 1905–6, 389
81.	1863	Girl and child	b	Torre Abbey, Torquay, Devon	SD	C Lib (repr)
82.	1865	Girl feeding calves Model(s): Torre Abbey, Torquay, Devon, plaster	m	[Exhib RA, London, 1011]; untraced Other versions: Torre Abbey, Torquay, Devon, bronze, S		*Graves* VII, 1905–6, 389
83.	1871	James Thrupp, medallion	b	[Exhib RA, London, 1338]; untraced		*Graves* VII, 1905–6, 389
84.	1873	A group of women making music	tc	Torre Abbey, Torquay, Devon	SD	C Lib (repr)
85.	1873	The vision of the Saviour in the Holy Communion		[Exhib RA, London, 1221]; untraced		*Graves* VII, 1905–6, 389
86.	1880–1885	Panels illustrating Milton's *Paradise Lost*, several Model(s): Death triumphing over the Saviour exhib RA, London, 1871, 871; Prevenient Grace descending from above exhib RA, London, 1874, 1234; Death, Sin and Satan exhib RA, London, 1876, 1178	m	[ex coll John, 1st Baron Coleridge]; untraced		*Graves* VII, 1905–6, 389; *Greenwood* 1999, 4
87.	nd	Cincinnatus		Torre Abbey, Torquay, Devon		C Lib (repr)
88.	nd	Classical subjects, three	p	Gunnersbury Park, Middx, temple		C Lib (repr)
89.	nd	Mother with two children, sketch model	tc	Torre Abbey, Torquay, Devon		C Lib (repr)
90.	nd	Mother with two children, sketch model	p	Torre Abbey, Torquay, Devon		C Lib (repr)
91.	nd	Mourning female figure, model	p	Torre Abbey, Torquay, Devon		C Lib (repr)
92.	nd	The Annunciation, model	p	Torre Abbey, Torquay, Devon		C Lib (repr)
93.	nd	The return of the prodigal son	b	Torre Abbey, Torquay, Devon	S	C Lib (repr)
94.	nd	To Zion	b	Torre Abbey, Torquay, Devon	S	C Lib (repr)
95.	nd	Unidentified subject (Satan tempting the Saviour?)	p	Torre Abbey, Torquay, Devon	S	C Lib (repr)
96.	nd	Unidentified woman, medallion, model	p	Torre Abbey, Torquay, Devon		C Lib (repr)

Miscellaneous

97.	1832	The prodigal returned		[Exhib RA, London, 1126]; untraced		*Graves* VII, 1905–6, 388
98.	1835	A mother bending over her sleeping infant		[Exhib RA, London, 1066]; untraced		*Graves* VII, 1905–6, 388
99.	1836	Contemplation		[Exhib RA, London, 1088]; untraced		*Graves* VII, 1905–6, 388
100.	1837	Mother and children		[Exhib RA, London, 1222]; untraced		*Graves* VII, 1905–6, 388
101.	1850	The shepherd		[Exhib RA, London, 1338]; untraced		*Graves* VII, 1905–6, 389
102.	1859	Ariel laden with glistering apparel	m	[Exhib BI, London, 580]; untraced		*Graves* 1875, 537
103.	1860	A soldier of Gideon's army		[Exhib RA, London, 956]; untraced		*Graves* VII, 1905–6, 389

104.	1861	Our Saviour led into the wilderness		[Exhib RA, London, 1112]; untraced	*Graves* VII, 1905–6, 389
105.	1865	The angel of peace		[Exhib RA, London, 961]; untraced	*Graves* VII, 1905–6, 389
106.	1866	A river nymph	m	[Exhib RA, London, 924]; untraced	*Graves* VII, 1905–6, 389
107.	1866	Sherborne Farrer		[Exhib RA, London, 968]; untraced	*Graves* VII, 1905–6, 389
108.	1869	The young schoolmistress		[Exhib RA, London, 1137]; untraced	*Graves* VII, 1905–6, 389
109.	1870	St John blessing little children	m	[Exhib RA, London, 1091]; untraced	*Graves* VII, 1905–6, 389
110.	1873	Penelope		[Exhib RA, London, 1453]; untraced	*Graves* VII, 1905–6, 389
111.	1874	Irene Farrer	m	[Exhib RA, London, 1600]; untraced	*Graves* VII, 1905–6, 389
112.	1876	Maiden meditation		[Exhib RA, London, 1467]; untraced	*Graves* VII, 1905–6, 389
113.	1880	Satan tempting the Saviour		[Exhib RA, London, 1338]; untraced	*Graves* VII, 1905–6, 389

THURLOW, Thomas, of Saxmundham 1813–99

He is celebrated locally as the creator of memorials in several churches in Suffolk and particularly for the monument with a portrait bust to the poet, George Crabbe (3). He was born on 23 October 1813, the son of John Thurlow, a builder and stonemason of Saxmundham and his wife, Rebecca. Thurlow went to school in nearby Brook Cottage and early showed his manual dexterity. As a teenager he would turn his hand to wood and plaster carving, stone-polishing, and he even made a violin, succeeding at the second attempt. At the age of 23 he left home for London where he was engaged by a monument manufacturer in Regent Street. During his spare time he took lessons in oil painting, something he pursued throughout his life (some of his paintings are in the Moot Hall, Aldeburgh, Suffolk). After a time employed with the **London Marble Works**, where he gained valuable experience of stone carving, Thurlow returned to Suffolk first opening a business in Halesworth and then settling back in Saxmundham in 1839. He was living with his parents at the time of the 1841 census on the east side of Turnpike Road. He became active in the town being appointed secretary and manager of the Saxmundham gas works. He was an overseer for the parish, was the town surveyor, and in 1847 he acquired the license for photography for the county of Suffolk, which he practised for a time. He is reported to have given 'penny readings' in the market hall, reciting from Dickens to packed audiences. In 1881 he and his wife lived in the High Street, Saxmundham, and he described himself as a sculptor in the census records.

His largest monument is the niched statue of Samuel Clouting, which reminded Gunnis of the Duke of Wellington, with its beaky nose and almost military cloak (7). His other monuments are varied in composition. The King has a medallion portrait (1), the Blois is a tablet with standing angels (4), the Gooch has a relief of the three Christian Virtues in classical garb (6), the Garrett, a bust (10) and the Crampin, an elaborate Gothic frame (11).

He is buried with his father and other family members in Saxmundham churchyard.

Literary References: Census records, 1841, 1881; *Gunnis* 1968, 395; Pevsner, *Suffolk*, 1974, *passim*

Website: http://www.saxmundham.org/aboutsax/people.html

Funerary Monuments						
1.	†1842	Robert King		Witnesham, Suffolk		Pevsner, *Suffolk*, 1974, 496
2.	†1846	Ann and Catherine (†1839) Lawson		Aldeburgh, Suffolk	S	
3.	1847	George Crabbe (†1832)		Aldeburgh, Suffolk	S	*ILN*, 2 Oct 1847, 220 (repr); Pevsner, *Suffolk*, 1974, 72
4.	†1850	Sir Charles Blois		Yoxford, Suffolk		Pevsner, *Suffolk*, 1974, 511
5.	?1850	William Shuldham		Marlesford, Suffolk		*Gunnis* 1968, 395
6.	†1851	Sir Thomas Gooch		Benacre, Suffolk		Pevsner, *Suffolk*, 1974, 97
7.	†1852	Samuel Clouting		Kelsale, Suffolk		Pevsner, *Suffolk*, 1974, 313
8.	?1853	Susanna Mayhew		Saxmundham, Suffolk		*Gunnis* 1968, 395
9.	†1860	Frederick Bell		Aldeburgh, Suffolk	S	
10.	†1866	Richard Garrett		Leiston, Suffolk		*Gunnis* 1968, 395
11.	†1869	John Crampin		Saxmundham, Suffolk		Pevsner, *Suffolk*, 1974, 412
Busts						
12.	1846	Hon Clara Vanneck		[Exhib RA, London, 1494]; untraced		*Graves* VII, 1905–6, 390
Architectural Sculpture						
13.	1873	Reredos		Saxmundham, Suffolk		*Gunnis* 1968, 395
Reliefs						
14.	1841	Flowers		[Exhib BI, London, 397]; untraced		*Graves* 1875, 537
Miscellaneous						
15.	1864	The weary traveller	m	[Exhib RA, London, 935]; untraced		*Graves* VII, 1905–6, 390
16.	1864	Winter	m	[Exhib RA, London, 1030]; untraced		*Graves* VII, 1905–6, 390
17.	1865	Shepherd and dog		[Exhib RA, London, 972]; untraced		*Graves* VII, 1905–6, 390
18.	1872	Homeless and friendless		[Exhib RA, London, 1401]; untraced		*Graves* VII, 1905–6, 390

TIDD, of Sleaford fl 1780?

Funerary Monuments						
1.	?1780	Thomas Wiles	s	Ruskington, Lincs	S	GPC

TILNEY, J, of York fl c1822–44

His tablets are mostly neo-Hellenic in design, the best, in Gunnis's opinion, being the wall tablets to Ann Eglin, Isabella Serjeantson, Henry Sidgwick, John Todd, and Harriet Carr (1–5). The Carr has a relief of a kneeling allegorical figure by an urn. Tilney took his son Charles as an apprentice in 1833.

Literary References: *Gunnis* 1968, 395

Funerary Monuments				
1.	†1822	Ann Eglin (†1822) and Toft Richardson (†1827)	Riccall, E R Yorks	*Gunnis* 1968, 395; Pevsner, *Yorks: E R & York*, 1995, 655
2.	?1834	Isabella Serjeantson	Snaith, W R Yorks	*Gunnis* 1968, 395
3.	?1835	Henry Sidgwick	Brompton, N R Yorks	*Gunnis* 1968, 395
4.	?1837	John Todd	St Michael-le-Belfrey, York	*Gunnis* 1968, 395
5.	†1841	Harriet Carr	St Peter and St Leonard, Horbury, W R Yorks	Pevsner, *Yorks: W R*, 1967, 269
6.	†1842	Clough family member	Newbald, E R Yorks	Pevsner, *Yorks: E R & York*, 1995, 622
7.	†1844	Clough family member	Newbald, E R Yorks	Pevsner, *Yorks: E R & York*, 1995, 622

TILNEY, T, of Leeds fl c1819–42

Funerary Monuments

1.	?1819	Thomas Cookson	St John, Leeds, W R Yorks	S	GPC
2.	†1842	Robinson family (†1827, 1842)	Hemingbrough, E R Yorks	S	

TILSTON, John, of Chester 1671–1723

The son of Modland Tilston, of Gresford, Denbigh, he was apprenticed to Thomas Davies of Chester, and became a freeman of that city in 1695. In about 1710 he rebuilt Pemberton's Parlour, Watergate, Chester, which had been virtually destroyed during the Civil War, and he was responsible for two fine cartouches on it depicting the Royal and City coats of arms (**2**). The rebuilding work cost upwards of £1,000. He also carved the statue of Queen Anne for the front of Chester Exchange (**1**). He died in 1723 and was buried in the south aisle of St John's church. His grandson, John Tilston, was also a carver and became free of the Masons' Company of Chester in 1732.

Literary References: *Gunnis* 1968, 395

Statues				
1.	nd	Queen Anne	Chester Exchange, Chester	*Gunnis* 1968, 395
Architectural Sculpture				
2.	c1710	Two cartouches	Pemberton's Parlour, Watergate, Chester	www.bwpics.co.uk/martins.html

TIMBRELL, Henry 1806–49

He was born in Dublin, the son of James Timbrell, clerk in the ordinance. He began his studies under the Irish sculptor, **John Smyth** in 1823 and executed a bust of his master (**10**). In 1825 he entered the Royal Dublin Society Schools and after winning several prizes and exhibiting at the Royal Hibernian Academy, he went to London in 1831. There he entered the studio of **E H Baily**, for whom he worked for many years, whilst studying at the Royal Academy. He appears also to have worked with **William Behnes.** When he first exhibited at the Royal Academy in 1833 he gave his address as 7 Carburton Street. He soon moved to a warmer climate: when he put down his name for the Royal Academy Schools, to which he had been recommended by **Thomas Denman**, he gave his address as 40, Via Laurina, Rome. Previously he had lived at 90 Tottenham Court Road (RA Admissions). He married Susan Flather on 3 February 1838 at St Pancras, and joined the Artists' Annuity Fund in 1842, giving his address as Upper John Street, Fitzroy Square (AAF, CM, 23667/5,9).

Timbrell was an outstanding student at the Royal Academy, winning the gold medal in 1836, and his *Hercules throwing Lycas into the sea* (**22**) gained him the travelling scholarship and enabled him to travel to Rome again in 1843. Nearly two years later he executed a life-size marble group of a mother teaching two children which he sent to the Royal Academy. The ship carrying the work was wrecked on its way to England and the group almost completely ruined (**5**). His only known monument, to Walter Long, was executed in Rome and has a relief of a young woman with a baby and angels (**2**).

He died of pleurisy and inflammation of the lungs in Rome on 10 April 1849, leaving unfinished statues for the House of Lords of the heavily bearded Earl of Hertford in chain mail and long surcoat (**8**), and of the Count of Aumale, with sword and shield (**9**). He also left unfinished a statue, *Lamp of the Ganges* for Queen Victoria (**6**), to whom he had been recommended by **John Gibson**. About 20 artists in Rome, including Gibson, **R J Wyatt, Joseph Gott** and **John Hogan**, attended his funeral. According to his obituary in the *Art Journal*, 'had he lived, Mr. Timbrell was an artist certain to have attained the highest point in his profession. In his early years he was a most ardent student, labouring in search of knowledge with zeal and intelligence, aiming to attain the highest qualities in Art. In private life he was esteemed for his amiability of manner, his goodness of heart, and integrity of friendship' (*AJ* 1849, 198).

Literary References: *Graves* 1875, 538; *Graves* VII, 1905–6, 396; *Strickland* 2, 1913, 448–449; *Gunnis* 1968, 395; *Read* 1982, 69, 120

Funerary Monuments						
1.	1835	'Sorrow, sketch for a monument'		[Exhib RA, London, 1093]; untraced		*Graves* VII, 1905–6, 396
2.	1848	Walter Long (†1847)		St John Evangelist, West Ashton, Wiltshire	SD	Pevsner, *Wilts*, 1975, 559
Statues						
3.	1827	Figure of a Grecian warrior		[Exhib RHA, Dublin]; untraced		*Strickland* 2, 1913, 447
4.	1836	Mezentius tying the living to the dead, group		[Exhib RA, London, 1067, gold medal]; untraced		RA Premium list; *Graves* VII, 1905–6, 396; *Strickland* 2, 1913, 447
5.	1845	Life-size group of a mother teaching two children	m	Untraced		*AJ* 1849, 198; *Strickland* 2, 1913, 447; *Gunnis* 1968, 395
6.	c1849	Lamp of the Ganges		Untraced		*Gunnis* 1968, 395
7.	c1849	Seated Indian girl, from 'Lalla Rookh', (finished by R J Wyatt and John Gibson)	m	Royal Coll RCIN 41025		*AJ*, 1855, 260 (repr); *Strickland* 2, 1913, 447; *Gunnis* 1968, 395
8.	1848–50	Richard de Clare, Earl of Hertford (†1217)		Palace of Westminster, London, House of Lords		*Walker* 1961, 39, 97–8, cat 42
9.	1847–1858	William de Forz, Count of Aumale (†1241) (co-sculptor: James Sherwood Westmacott)		Palace of Westminster, London, House of Lords		Walker 1961, 3, 97–8, cat. no. 6
Busts						
10.	1828	John Smyth		[Exhib RHA, Dublin]; untraced		*Strickland* 2, 1913, 447
11.	1838	Unidentified gentleman		[Exhib RA, London, 1297]; untraced		*Graves* VII, 1905–6, 396
12.	1838	Unidentified lady		[Exhib RA, London, 1296]; untraced		*Graves* VII, 1905–6, 396
13.	1839	John Fletcher		[Exhib RA, London, 1359]; untraced		*Graves* VII, 1905–6, 396
14.	1841	J Hutton		[Exhib RA, London, 1274]; untraced		
15.	1842	A child		[Exhib RA, London, 1352]; untraced		*Graves* VII, 1905–6, 396
16.	1848	Joseph Strutt (after John Gibson)	m	Birmingham MAG, inv 148'38	SD	*Silber* 1987, 92, cat 288

Reliefs

17.	1834	Satan in search of the earth		[Exhib RA, London, 1071]; untraced	*Graves* VII, 1905–6, 396; *Johnson* 1975, 461–2
18.	1839	Grief	m	[Exhib RA, London, 1379]; untraced	*Graves* VII, 1905–6, 396
19.	1843–1849	Two bas-reliefs		[Buckingham Palace, London, garden house]; untraced	*Strickland* 2, 1913, 447; *Gunnis* 1968, 395

Miscellaneous

20.	1833	Phaeton	[Exhib RA, London, 1171]; untraced	*Graves* VII, 1905–6, 396
21.	1842	Psyche	[Exhib RA, London, 1369]; untraced	*Graves* 1875, 538; *Graves* VII, 1905–6, 396
22.	1843	Hercules throwing Lycas into the sea	[Exhib RA, London, 1409]; untraced	*Graves* VII, 1905–6, 396; *Strickland* 2, 1913, 447; *Gunnis* 1968, 396

TIMBRELL, James Christopher 1807–50

He was born in Dublin, a younger brother of **Henry Timbrell**. He entered the Schools of the Royal Dublin Society in 1825, where he studied painting. Five years later he went to London, but it was not until 1848 that he turned his attention to sculpture and exhibited a figure at the Royal Academy (1). He was at this time living at 50 Upper John Street.

He died at Portsmouth on 5 January 1850, apparently nearly penniless, for his widow was given a grant of £10 by the Royal Academy shortly after his death (Royal Academy Archives in *Gunnis* 1968, 396).

Literary References: *Strickland* 2, 1913, 448–449

Funerary Monuments

1.	1848	'Bas-relief, part of a monument to be erected in marble'	[Exhib RA, London, 1469]; untraced	*Graves* VII, 1905–6, 396; *Gunnis* 1968, 396

TINDALE, William fl 1761

In 1761 Sir Edward Littleton paid 'William Tindale, Carver in stone, for ye door case [at Teddesley Hall, Staffs] £7.16.' (GPC citing Staffs RO, Littleton, D/260/M/E.116).

TINKLER, of Derby fl 1759?

Funerary Monuments

1.	?1759	Herrick family, ledger with a coat of arms	Barrow-on-Soar, Leics	S	*Gunnis* 1968, 396

TIPPING, John fl 1763

He is listed as a mason of Mount Street, Grosvenor-Square in 1763.

Literary References: *Mortimer* 1763, 49

TOGNOLI, Giovanni, of Rome 1786–1862

He was drawing-master to **Antonio Canova** and made the font at Escrick, E R Yorks in 1844. This charming work takes the form of two angels supporting a bowl.

Literary References: *Gunnis* 1968, 396

Architectural Sculpture

1.	1844	Font	Escrick, E R Yorks	S	*Gunnis* 1968, 396

TOLEMAN, of Bristol fl *c*1848

Funerary Monuments

1.	†1848	Juliet Crawshay	St John, Cinderford, Glos	S	Pevsner, *Glos: Vale & Forest of Dean*, 1976, 159

TOLLEMACHE (or TALLEMACH), William 1782–1816

Nothing is known of his early training but it is possible that he was the son of 'William Tallemach, stone mason of Kingston-upon-Thames', whose will was proved 9 January 1810 (PROB 11/1507). Tollemache enrolled at the Royal Academy Schools in June 1800, aged 18. In 1804 he was a prize winner (2) and again the following year, with a subject from Aeschylus (3). In the latter year he also submitted a sketch, presumably in pencil, of *Hercules and Omphale.* In 1813 he was awarded a silver medal by the Society of Arts (5). 'Tallmach' also submitted a letter to the Society, published in the *Transactions*, detailing his method of casting, the nature of the mould and the materials used. His address was then Castle Street, Oxford Street. A model by him was already in the Society's repository.

He exhibited at the Academy and at the British Institution, 1814–1816, showing various small models in wax, to be cast in bronze. His name was given as 'Tallemach' and his address in 1816 as 64 Upper Charlotte Street. He also won a prestigious commission from the Committee of Taste, for a monument in St Paul's Cathedral to General Gore and General Skerett but the work was executed by **Sir Francis Chantrey** owing to Tollemache's early demise. The work is inscribed 'W. Tallimache inv./F. Chantrey sc'.

He died on 18 November 1816, leaving a wife, Harriet (née Gilchrist) and five children. In the year of his death his widow wrote to the Academy 'stating her great distress and petitioning for assistance'. The Academy's Council awarded her a pension amounting to £127 10s, paid out between 1817 and 1835. She was also paid an annuity between February 1817 and October 1841 by the Artists' Annuity Fund. She had married Tollemache at St James, Piccadilly, on 21 August 1804. She died in Liverpool on 28 October 1841.

Literary References: *Graves* 1875, 528; *Gunnis* 1968, 396; *Pyke* 1973, 144

Archival References: AAF, CM, 23667/1, p at rear of volume; 4, 153; AAF, AB; RSA *Transactions*, 1813, vol 31, 23; RA/GA *passim*; GPC

Funerary Monuments

1.	†1807	Amelia Gooch	Beaconsfield, Bucks	S	*Gunnis* 1968, 396

Statues

2.	1804	An academy figure	[RA, London, silver medal]; untraced	RA Premium list
3.	1805	Group of Prometheus chained to the rock	[RA, London, gold medal]; untraced	RA Premium list; *Gunnis* 1968, 396
4.	1812	King George II, to be executed in bronze	[Exhib RA, London, 906]; untraced	*Graves* VII, 1905–6, 318
5.	1813	Venus disarming Cupid, bronze cast	[Soc of A, silver medal, 20 gns premium]; untraced	RSA *Transactions*, 1813, vol 31, 23; *Graves* 1875, 528

Chimneypieces

6.	1802	Description not available		[Coome House (the seat of Lord Hawkesbury)]; untraced	GPC citing SJSM archives
7.	1807	Description not available Payment(s): £50	m	[Lord Bute's villa, Petersham, Surrey]; untraced	Journals of Robert Mylne in GPC

Miscellaneous

8.	1814	Ariadne, model to be cast in bronze	w	[Exhib RA, London, 798]; untraced	*Graves* VII, 1905–6, 319; *Graves* 1875, 528
9.	1814	Bacchus, model to be cast in bronze	w	[Exhib RA, London, 196]; untraced	*Graves* VII, 1905–6, 319; *Graves* 1875, 528
10.	1816	Bacchantes (model)	w	[Exhib BI, London, 268]; untraced	*Graves* 1875, 528

TOLMIE, James –1866

As an ornamental stone-carver, he was employed at the Whitehall Club (6), the New City Club (2), the Inns of Court Hotel (7) and the Great Hotel at Buxton (8). Gunnis says that he was also responsible for some of the carving on the Prince Consort's mausoleum.

He married Ann Eaton on 4 October 1856 at St James, Westminster and the couple had two grown sons in 1881, when Ann, a widow aged 40, described as a paralysis invalid, was living at Lambeth. One son was a farrier and the other a cowman.

Winfrey describes Tolmie's two statues in Bradford, left unfinished at his death (1): 'On the left is Bishop Blaise, the patron saint of woolcombers, holding in his right hand a woolcomb which in fact was the implement used in his torture and subsequent martyrdom. On the left is King Edward IV, holding a sceptre and orb, who granted Bradford its trading charter. Both figures are slightly less than life size, but beautifully carved. The two high-relief portrait roundels on the Bradford Wool Exchange may be by the same sculptor'.

Tolmie died suddenly at his home in Lambeth in December 1866. The *Art Journal* paid him a tribute: 'His death is much regretted by a large circle of personal friends. In his profession Tolmie held a very high position. In private life he was a generous, open-handed man, had a warm affectionate heart, and by his happy conversational powers, he always won the esteem and regard of all with whom he came in contact' (*AJ*, 1867, 56).

Biographical References: Census records, 1881; *Gunnis* 1968, 396

Statues

1.	c1866	Two statues		[Interior, St George's Hall, Bradford]; Bradford Wool Exchange	*AJ*, 1867, 56; *Gunnis* 1968, 396; Winfrey, nd

Architectural Sculpture

2.	?1833–1834	Ornamental carving		[New City Club, City of London]; untraced	*Gunnis* 1968, 396
3.	1860	City arms		[Lowestoft Town Hall, Suffolk]; untraced	*Builder*, 1860, 173
4.	1862	Stone carving		[London Bridge Hotel, London]; untraced	*Builder* 1862, 164
5.	1863	Decorative stone work	s	[Wesleyan chapel, Lowestoft, Suffolk]; untraced	*Builder* 1863, 300
6.	1864–1866	Ornamental carving (designed by Parnell)	s	Whitehall Club, London	Pevsner, *London I*, 1973, 544
7.	nd	Ornamental carving		[Inns of Court Hotel, London]; untraced	*Gunnis* 1968, 396
8.	nd	Ornamental carving		['The hotel at Buxton']; untraced	*Gunnis* 1968, 396
9.	nd	'Some of the carving of the Prince Consort's mausoleum'		untraced	*Gunnis* 1968, 396

TOMBLING FAMILY, of London

Robert Tombling –1791
John Tombling fl 1790–1805

Robert Tombling worked as a mason at Corsham Court, Wilts, on various occasions between 1769 and 1786 (Archives, Lord Methuen in *Gunnis* 1968, 396). In 1786 he was paid £74 for repairs to the house of the Rt Hon Reginald Pole-Carew in New Cavendish Street, London (Archives, Sir John Pole-Carew Bt). By 1790 he had taken his son, John, into business and that year 'Tombling and Son' were paid £115 for masons' work at Lansdowne House, London (Archives, Marquess of Lansdowne in GPC). Robert Tombling died in 1791 a successful man. In his will he left to his two sons and three daughters, cash gifts and bank stocks, a dwelling house at 67 Edgware Road, another house and gardens in nearby Queen Street, a property in Orange Street, Bloomsbury, another in Mount Street, and two in Gray Street. Amongst items named in his will were a silver watch, silver tankard and silver tablespoons, and mahogany furniture. His premises, which were also in Mount Street, were left to his son John Tombling 'together with the yard, sheds and buildings'. The rent on the property was £40 per year, and Tombling left instructions that his son was to rebuild the walls and 'give up the firestone shed'. John was also bequeathed two-thirds of the stock-in-trade 'as shall be in rough materials also my working utensils and implements of all kinds used in and about my said trade together with such horse and mare and cart' (PROB 11/1205/183v).

John Tombling was employed on masonry work at Lord Delaval's house in Hanover Square, and also worked for the Duke of Leeds (2). As a mason he worked at Lord Brownlow's house in Hill Street in 1794 (Archives, Lord Brownlow in *Gunnis* 1968, 396) and in 1801 received £84 for work for Reginald Pole-Carew, presumably started by his father. He was responsible only for one known Hellenic wall-tablet (1). He appears to have had a professional or friendly relationship with **Robert Ashton I**, since he was named as executor in Ashton's will in December 1805. Tombling was left property in New Street, Kensington, in trust for Ashton's family and was bequeathed £20 for his trouble (PROB 11/1434).

Literary References: *Gunnis* 1968, 396

Archival References: GPC

Funerary Monuments

1.	?1803	Mrs Faran (by John Tombling)	Grosvenor Chapel, London	*Gunnis* 1968, 396

Architectural Sculpture

2.	1795	'Three marble tables with moulded edges' (by John Tombling)	[Duke of Leeds's residence, St James's Square, London]; untraced	Soane bill book, fol 167r; *Gunnis* 1968, 396

TOMKINSON, J fl c1813

Funerary Monuments

1.	†1813	Mary Auberry	St John the Baptist, Pinner, Middx		Pevsner, *London: N W*, 1991, 284

TOMLINSON, J, of Uxbridge fl c1806–19

Gunnis notes that most of his monuments and tablets are in the Regency style, though the Mary Auberry (5) is a copy of the pedimented tablet by Sir Robert Taylor erected in the same church in 1767 to Edmund Auberry.

Literary References: *Gunnis* 1968, 396

Funerary Monuments

1.	†1806	Jane Smith	East Bedfont, Hounslow, Middx		Pevsner, *London: N W*, 1991, 413
2.	?1806	Mrs Barry	East Bedfont, Middx		*Gunnis* 1968, 396
3.	?1811	Lieutenant-Colonel Hillard	Cowley, Middx		*Gunnis* 1968, 396
4.	?1813	Henry Pye	Pinner, Middx		*Gunnis* 1968, 396
5.	?1813	Mary Auberry	Pinner, Middx		*Gunnis* 1968, 396
6.	†1819	Arabella Popple	Burnham, Bucks	S	*Gunnis* 1968, 396

TOMLINSON, Richard 1779–

He joined the Royal Academy Schools in 1798 and won a silver medal in 1805 for a model of an Academy figure (RA Premium list). He was living that year at 7 Horsemonger Lane. From 1806 until 1810 he exhibited at the Academy, showing busts, including a fine marble one of William Beckwith. His relief of a shipwreck (which he also showed at the Academy) afterwards formed part of his monument to the memory of Captain Robert Scott, commander of HMS *Boreas*, which went down off Guernsey in 1807 (1). The will of a Richard Tomlinson, Sculptor of Saint Mary Newington, Surrey was proved on 4 July 1853.

Literary References: *Graves* VIII, 1905–6, 6; *Gunnis* 1968, 396–7

Archival References: RA Premium list

Will (?): PRO/FRC PROB 11/2176

Funerary Monuments

1.	†1807	Captain Robert Scott	Jesus Church, East Southampton, Hants		*Graves* VIII, 1905–6, 6; Pevsner, *Hants & Isle of Wight*, 1967, 593

Busts

2.	1806	Miss H Webster	[Exhib RA, London, 835]; untraced		*Graves* VIII, 1905–6, 6
3.	1807	William Beckwith	Foundling Hospital, London, office	D	*Graves* VIII, 1905–6, 6; *Gunnis* 1968, 396

TOMSON FAMILY, of Cambridge

Edward Tomson 1773–1829
Thomas Tomson 1775–1849

Edward Tomson carved the pedestal for an antique statue of *Ceres* from an Athenian temple, presented to the University of Cambridge by Messrs Clarke and Cripps (15). The design, by **John Flaxman RA**, was based on a pedestal from 'the original in the portico in the Temple of Minerva at Athens' (*Monthly Mag*, 1803, 16, 87). In 1815 Tomson was employed at the University on masonry work at Clare Hall.

He was assisted by his brothers Thomas and Lewis (1783–1832). **Thomas Tomson** worked under Sir John Soane at Caius College in 1792. He altered the west front of Clare Hall in 1815, and ten years later built Gisborne Court at Peterhouse. Edward Tomson's best monumental work, in Gunnis's opinion, is the large wall-tablet in coloured marbles to Joseph Clerke (1). He signs the Knight monument with Thomas (2), and Thomas signs a number of tablets alone. Edward died in 1829, and was buried at St Botolph, Cambridge. The business was continued by Thomas and his sons. Thomas died in 1849, and in his will, proved on 25 January 1850, he is described as a 'stone and marble mason' (PROB 11/2108).

An 'Edward Tomson, stone cutter', presumably an ancestor, was paid £5 3s 10d in 1754 for repairing the market cross in Cambridge (City Sessions Book in *Gunnis* 1968, 397). Another likely family member was the Mr Tomson who, with his partners, Jeffs and Dawson, was employed under Sir John Soane at the Senate House, Cambridge, in 1792. That year the firm was paid £494 for enclosing the Senate House, Cambridge University. Under the same architect but without his partners Tomson was paid £90 in 1792 for repairs to Caius College.

Literary References: *Willis and Clark* 1886, 1, 111, 39; *Gunnis* 1968, 397

Archival References: Soane Bill Book 3, fols 146–8; GPC

Will: Edward Tomson, PROB 11/1760, proved 8 August 1829

Funerary Monuments

1.	†1790	Joseph Clerke and family (by Edward Tomson)	Wethersfield, Essex	S	Pevsner, *Essex*, 1965, 422
2.	?1806	Samuel Knight (by Edward and Thomas Tomson)	Milton, Cambs	S	*Gunnis* 1968, 397
3.	†1808	Robert Martin (by Thomas Tomson)	St Mary, Ely, Cambs		RG/JP, 8, 1463v.
4.	†1811	Charles Skinner Matthews (by Edward Tomson)	St Benet, Cambridge	S	*Gunnis* 1968, 397
5.	†1812	Sir Thomas Hatton (by Edward Tomson)	Long Stanton, Cambs		Pevsner, *Cambs*, 1970, 432
6.	?1819	Thomas Sennett (by Thomas Tomson)	Newton, Cambs	S	*Gunnis* 1968, 397
7.	?1820	George Maltby (by Thomas Tomson)	Buckden, Hunts	S	*Gunnis* 1968, 397
8.	?1821	Thomas Marten (by Thomas Tomson)	Stow-cum-Quy, Cambs	S	*Gunnis* 1968, 397
9.	?1832	Mary Jennyns (by Thomas Tomson)	Bottisham, Cambs	S	*Gunnis* 1968, 397
10.	†1833	Anne Claydon (by Thomas Tomson)	Great St Mary, Cambridge	S	RCHM, *Cambs* II, 279

11.	?1833	Charlotte Gibbons (by Thomas Tomson)	West Wratting, Suffolk	S	*Gunnis* 1968, 397
12.	†1833	Rev B Bridges (by Tomson and Son)	Cherry Hinton, Cambs	S	
13.	†1837	Dorothy Spilsbury and Elizabeth Hollingworth (†1820) (by Thomas Tomson)	Grantchester, Cambs	S	
14.	†1844	Mary and William Layton (by Thomas Tomson)	St Mary, Ely, Cambs		RG/JP, 8, 1463v.
Architectural Sculpture					
15.	1803	Pedestal for a statue of Ceres (by Edward Tomson)	[Cambridge University]; untraced		*Monthly Mag*, 1803, 2, 87; *Gunnis* 1968, 397

TOMSON, JEFFS AND DAWSON

See **Tomson family, of Cambridge**

TOOKEY, W, of High Street, St Marylebone fl *c*1842

Funerary Monuments

1.	†1842	John Parker	All Saints, St John's Wood, London	RG/JP, 8, 1463v.

TOOLE, James

He was an assistant to **Sir Richard Westmacott RA**.

Literary References: *Busco* 1996, 175 n115

TOON, Charles fl 1776

Statues

1.	1776	Eagles	Quenby Hall, Leics, gardens	Pevsner, *Leics & Rutland*, 1984, 353

TORRE, Anthony fl 1761

The *Edinburgh Evening Courant* of 13 April 1761 carried the following announcement: 'To be Sold By Antony Torre, at the back of the Fountain-well, Edinburgh. A great Variety of Busts, Statues and Brackets, of different sizes, neatly made, and most of them brounced [*sic*] after the newest taste, all of Paris Plaister. Also great variety of Basso-Relievos, &c. fram'd and glaz'd. Any gentleman who hath Busts or Statues to be repair'd, or brounced, may depend upon having them carefully and neatly done. As the proprietor is to leave this place and go to London at Whitsunday, he will sell the stock he hath on hand at the very lowest prices.' (Inf. Helen Smailes)

TOUSEY (or TOWSEY), John fl 1763–75

Mortimer's directory lists 'John Tousey, Carver and Gilder, Bow-Street, Bloomsbury' (*Mortimer* 1763, 28). An entry in the Fair Minute books of the Marine Society for 27 April 1775 records that 'Jonas Hanway reported that in December 1773 some Gentlemen thought proper to have a Chimney piece that should be durable, elegant and expressive of the nature of the institution . . . not to exceed £36'. For this £26 had already been subscribed, and the entry is followed by a list of expenditure by Hanway, including 'For the Chimney piece paid Mr. Tousey £30 15s. 6d' (1). (Add inf. Cdr C R Burgess, secretary to the Marine Society)

Archival References: GPC

Chimneypieces					
1.	1775	Description unavailable Payment(s): £30 15s 6d		[Marine Soc]; untraced	GPC
Architectural Sculpture					
2.	1768	Picture frames Payment(s): £117 1s	m	[Croome Court, Worcs]; untraced	*Beard* 1993, 93, 95

TOVELL FAMILY, of Ipswich

Robert Tovell –1786
Edward Tovell fl 1733
George Tovell fl *c*1821–32?
Robert Tovell 1778–1840

The earliest known member of this family was **Robert Tovell**, 'stonemason', who died on 27 October 1786 and was buried at St Margaret, Ipswich. **Edward Tovell**, presumably a son of the above, was employed by **Robert Mylne II**, the architect, who noted in his diary 'Sept 18. 1791. Went to Wolverstone, examined with Mr. Berners situation for Obelisk, settled the business for it with Towell, Mason' (*Mylne Diary* in GPC). The obelisk is 96 feet high, with a staircase in the interior up to the top, which is surmounted by a globe encircled by rays. This was erected by Charles Berners to the memory of his father (7).

Edward Tovell was the father of **George** and **Robert Tovell**, who sign a good many tablets in Suffolk, 'though none of these is outstanding' (*Gunnis* 1968, 397). Robert married Sarah Thurston, also of Ipswich, on 17 November 1812. She died in 1831.

Literary References: *Gunnis* 1968, 397

Archival References: IGI; GPC

Funerary Monuments					
1.	?1818	Robert Green (by Robert Tovell)	Debenham, Suffolk	S	*Gunnis* 1968, 397
2.	?1821	Elizabeth Trotman (by George Tovell)	St Peter, Ipswich, Suffolk	S	*Gunnis* 1968, 397
3.	?1821	George Booth (by George Tovell)	St Clement, Ipswich, Suffolk	S	*Gunnis* 1968, 397
4.	?1824	Elizabeth Cobbold (by George Tovell)	St Mary-at-Tower, Ipswich, Suffolk	S	*Gunnis* 1968, 397
5.	?1832	James Ellis (by George Tovell)	Hunston, Suffolk	S	*Gunnis* 1968, 397
6.	?1834	Rev John Longe (by Robert Tovell)	Coddenham, Suffolk	S	*Gunnis* 1968, 397
Architectural Sculpture					
7.	1791–1793	Berners obelisk (designed by Robert Mylne II, erected by Edward Tovell)	[Woolverstone Hall, Suffolk]; destroyed		Mylne Diary in GPC

TOVEY, William –1771

On 30 September 1725 Tovey was made free by redemption of the Masons' Company 'by Virtue of an Order of the Court of the Lord Mayor and Aldren' (*Court Book*, 1722–5). In 1749 he sent in an estimate for £1,203 for mason's work on the principal storey of the Mansion House, but it was turned down in favour of **Christopher Horsnaile II**, whose estimate was only £900. Tovey worked as a mason to the Ironmongers Company from 1758 until 1767. He left a widow (or perhaps a daughter) named Sarah when he died in 1771 (Court-book, Masons' Co). She proceeded to carry on the business in partnership with a Mary Wheeler and their firm was responsible for mason's work at Skinners' Hall in 1771. They were appointed to work on masonry for the renovation in June 1773. In 1774 they were paid £139 17s 6d. Gunnis noted that this was the only example he had found in the 18th century of two women being partners and running a mason's business.

Literary References: *Gunnis* 1968, 397

Archival References: Masons' Co, Freemen, fol 68; Ironmongers, WA, vol 13; Skinners, Court Books, 2, 128, 140, 148

TOWNE, Joseph 1806–79

He was born at Royston, Cambs, on 25 November, 1806, the third of five sons of the Rev Thomas Towne, pastor to the New Meeting House and a director of the London Missionary Society. Little is known of his youth but he probably received much tuition at home since both parents were also teachers. He married a schoolteacher, Mary, and was living in 4 Holland Place, Lambeth at the time of the 1851 census, with two sons, five daughters and three servants. He was then described as an anatomical modeller and his eldest son, Joseph, was a medical student. In 1871 he was listed as a sculptor, living at 10 Holland Place, Lambeth, and by then the family had grown to nine.

Encouraged as a modeller by his father from childhood, in *c*1825 he took a 33 inch high wax model of a human skeleton to Cambridge to show the professor of anatomy, William Clark. Encouraged by his favourable reception in Cambridge, Towne took the model to London, and entered it in the Society of Arts competition (**25**). He was introduced to Sir Astley Cooper, a surgeon at Guy's Hospital, who authenticated the model as an accurate rendering of the human skeleton and he was subsequently engaged as a modeller for the new medical school. In 1827, when living at 8 High Street, the Borough, he was awarded a Society of Arts medal, again for an anatomical model (**26**).

During his 53 years' association with Guy's Hospital he completed a prodigious amount of work, producing over 200 anatomical wax models in the first 10 years. He gained an international reputation and received orders for models from countries all over the world, including America, Russia and Australia. Thomas Hodgkin, in a lecture on Towne and his anatomical models, said of him that 'he was an artist, who had the signal merit of having both created his art for himself and arrived at such a proficiency in it that his works, already numerous, rival, if not surpass, those of the best and most distinguished masters of Florence and Bologna'. Most of his models for Guy's have survived and are displayed in the medical school museum.

In 1834 he began exhibiting marble busts and occasional statues at the Royal Academy. Several had associations with the hospital, including heads of William Babbington, Thomas Addison and Sir Astley Paston Cooper, which has a large pedestal with a fine relief, also carved by Towne, of three youths carrying a sick man (**10, 21, 19**).

The Thwaytes monument had a relief in an architectural frame of Christ healing a blind boy (**2**). The wall tablet to Mary Faviell has a seated mourning husband and a little daughter at prayer (**3**). The Bishop Otter memorial (**4**) was singled out in the *Builder* in an article on Chichester Cathedral and its restoration: 'The fine marble bust in memory of the amiable and excellent Bishop Otter, is intact, a fact we mention with reference to the sad fall of the tower and spire. The bust is by Towne, and bears a strong resemblance to the good prelate.' Towne died on 25 June 1879.

Literary References: RSA *Transactions*, 1826, vol 44, xliv; Census records 1851, 1871; *Wilks and Bettany* 1892, 415; *Graves* VIII, 1905–6, 14; *Gunnis* 1968, 397–8; *Pyke* 1973, 149–50; *Pyke* 1981, 40; *ODNB* (Maynard)

Funerary Monuments

1.	?1837	Randal Jackson		[Temple Church, London]; untraced	S	*Gunnis* 1968, 398
2.	1841	William Thwaytes	m	[Clothworkers' Hall, City of London]; destroyed		*Graves* VIII, 1905–6, 14; *Gunnis* 1968, 398; *Wickham* 2001, vol 1, 254 (repr)
3.	1842	Mary Faviell		Rothwell, W R Yorks	SD	Pevsner, *Yorks: W R*, 1967, 423
4.	1844	Bishop William Otter (†1840)		Chichester Cathedral, Sussex (since 1861)	D	Pevsner, *Sussex*, 1965, 156

Statues

5.	1835	Arthur, 1st Duke of Wellington	m	[Exhib RA, London, 1073]; untraced		*Graves* VIII, 1905–6, 14; *Gunnis* 1968, 398
6.	1837	Duke of Kent, equestrian statuette		[coll Queen Victoria]; untraced		*Gunnis* 1968, 397
7.	1838	Arthur, 1st Duke of Wellington, small equestrian		Guy's Hospital, London		*Gunnis* 1968, 397
8.	1839	Sleeping child	m	[Exhib RA, London, 1305]; untraced		*Graves* VIII, 1905–6, 14

Busts

9.	1834	Benjamin Harrison	m	[Exhib RA, London, 1075]; untraced		*Graves* VIII, 1905–6, 14
10.	1834	William Babbington		Guy's Hospital, London		*Gunnis* 1968, 398
11.	1834	William Morgan	m	[Exhib RA, London, 1057]; untraced		*Graves* VIII, 1905–6, 14
12.	1836	Admiral Lord Nelson		Junior United Service Club, London		*Gunnis* 1968, 397
13.	1836	Sir Astley Cooper Bt Payment(s): £400	m	[Exhib RA, London, 1151]; untraced		*Graves* VIII, 1905–6, 14; *Gunnis* 1968, 397
14.	1837	Eldest son of Dr Ashwell	m	[RA, London, 1212]; untraced		*Graves* VIII, 1905–6, 14
15.	1838	Randal Jackson	m	[Exhib RA, London, 1318]; untraced		*Graves* VIII, 1905–6, 14
16.	1839	Unidentified young lady	m	[Exhib RA, London, 1333]; untraced		*Graves* VIII, 1905–6, 14
17.	1840	Rev Hugh J Rose	m	[Exhib RA, London, 1194]; untraced		*Graves* VIII, 1905–6, 14
18.	1840	Unidentified lady	m	[Exhib RA, London, 1158]; untraced		*Graves* VIII, 1905–6, 14
19.	1841	Sir Astley Paston Cooper, with relief on pedestal of three youths carrying a sick man Payment(s): 400 gns		Guy's Hospital, London		*GM*, XVII (ns), June 1842, 639
20.	1842	Arthur, 1st Duke of Wellington		Junior United Services Club, London		*Graves* VIII, 1905–6, 14; *Gunnis* 1968, 397

21.	1852	Thomas Addison		Guy's Hospital, London		*Gunnis* 1968, 398
22.	1856	Florence Nightingale		Repton School, Derbys	SD	GPC
23.	1866	John Frederick Gruning		[Exhib RA, London, 889]; untraced		*Graves* VIII, 1905–6, 14
24.	nd	A medical man	m	Birmingham MAG, inv P.55'79	S	*Silber* 1987, 94, cat 291
Miscellaneous						
25.	1826	Model of a skeleton		[Soc of A, large silver medal]; untraced		RSA *Transactions*, 1826, vol 44, xliv
26.	1827	Model in coloured wax of the human brain		[Soc of A, large gold medal]; untraced		RSA *Transactions*, 1827, vol 45, xxxii

TOWNESEND, George, of Bristol –1719

The eldest son of John Townesend I of Oxford, he became a freeman of Bristol on 29 June 1706, on marrying Margaret, the widow of Malachi Harford. In August 1705 he was paid £1 13s 'for work in the Councell Chamber ye Coves'. In 1709 he drew a frontispiece for the Bristol Council House and in January 1709 was paid £12 for it. In 1716 he agreed to complete the tower of All Saints', Bristol, for which he was paid £251 17s 6d in April 1717. Gunnis believes he may have provided urns and vases for the tower. Townesend signed a receipt for a 'Marble chimney piece for ye Vestry Room' on 4 January 1717 (4).

Townesend signs monuments to Sir Hugh Smyth and to Lady Smyth both in Long Ashton Church, Somerset (**1, 2**). The designs are similar, consisting of Corinthian pilasters supporting a pediment on which recline mourning cherubs. The coats of arms and other details are well carved.

George Townesend is probably to be associated with the 'Mr Towneseend' who is referred to by Sir John Vanbrugh in one of his letters as the mason 'who did Mr. Southwell's masonry' at Kings Weston, near Bristol (*Colvin* 1995, 982). He appears to have had no children and, by his will, proved on 14 May 1719, he left all his plate to his nephew John Townesend, son of **William Townesend of Oxford.**

See also **Townesend Family, of Oxford and London.**

Literary References: *Gunnis* 1968, 398; *Colvin* 1995, 982

Archival References: BRO, Burgess Books 14359, microfiche FC/BB/1 (j) 2, fol 16 (1705); Bristol Cash Books, fol or p.78 (1709); BRO All Saints, Churchwardens' Accts P/AS/Ch W 3b fol 88, 93; P/AS/ChW/5/3, fol 16 (1717)

Funerary Monuments					
1.	1697	Sir Hugh Smyth (†1680)	Long Ashton, Somerset	S	*Gunnis* 1968, 398
2.	†1715	Lady Smyth	Long Ashton, Somerset	S	*Colvin* 1995, 982
Chimneypieces					
3.	1704	Stone Payment(s): 9s	[Bristol Council House, Somerset, lower room]; untraced		*Colvin* 1995, 982
4.	1717	Marble	All Saints, Bristol, vestry		Churchwardens' Accts

TOWNESEND, William, of Oxford 1676–1739

William Townesend was the most prolific member of a leading family of Oxford master masons. The son of **John Townesend I**, he was baptised in St Giles's church on 17 December 1676. Working initially with his father, he carried out extensive masonry work at many Oxford colleges, as well as undertaking commissions for monumental and architectural sculpture throughout the county. By the time his father was elected mayor of Oxford in 1720, Townesend had taken his position as that city's mason of choice and was described by the antiquarian Thomas Hearne as having had 'a hand in all the Buildings in Oxford'; he was actively promoted by the university's leading architectural patrons, including Dr George Clarke. He continued the Oxford Townesend dynasty of masons, having by his wife, Mary, a son, John, and a daughter, Mary. He died in 1739 and was buried in the churchyard of St Giles, Oxford, on 22 September. In September 1739 the *London Magazine* noted the death 'At Oxford, Mr. Townsend, the great mason and builder'.

As a mason-contractor, Townesend erected many of the new buildings going up in Oxford and the surrounding county between 1700 and 1739, as the accounts of the Queen's College, Balliol, Christ Church, Trinity and Exeter Colleges reveal. In 1707 he was paid £15 4s 6d 'for worke at Carfax' (OU, Vice-Chancellor's Accts, WP-/21/6). In many cases, he built to the designs of others, such as Hawksmoor at the Clarendon Building and All Souls, Gibbs at the Radcliffe Library, and Vanbrugh at the grand bridge, Blenheim Palace. He was also however capable of architectural design, as at Oriel and Magdalen Colleges, and possibly Radley Hall, where he and Peisley were mason-contractors, at Britwell Salome and at Shotover.

His contribution to sculpture is harder to assess since he combined the roles of mason, sculptor, and contractor on many projects. Even Hiscock, Townesend's principal champion, was unable to unravel these varied strands. It is known that he provided carving at the Queen's College where payments appear from 1694 onwards to 'Lapidicidae Townsend', when was paid £11 5s 5d 'ut p billa'. He was paid £2,239 9s between 23 February 1714 and 1720 for work on the chapel and hall and a further £35 10s for carved decoration in the chapel in 1718. In 1733 he submitted an estimate of £1,000 for the 'Gate cupola & Cloysters in ye front of Queen's College, according to design given' with an addition signed by him of 'sixteen vases over the cloisters as one such in a printed design of the College' priced £30. On 28 August 1733, his son William addressed a proposal to the Provost, Dr Joseph Smith, to alter Hawksmoor's design 'for the new Cloyster'. Further payments for work at the College are listed until the year of his death. It emerges that Townesend was paying his carvers and statuaries direct and being reimbursed by the provost and College. From the presentation of his bills it misleadingly appears that he was doing the carving himself. But, for instance, on 22 December 1711 he 'paid Mr **Garratt** for work in Carving the pediment' and likewise 'Mr Smith' [**William Smith of Oxford?**], who was also paid for three statues, while a payment to **Henry Cheere** for pediment carving was endorsed by him (**10–12, 19, 20**).

He was also employed at All Souls (**17**), Corpus Christi (**9**) and Pembroke (**18**), as well assisting with the column of victory (designed by Flitcroft) and the chapel at nearby Blenheim Palace (**15, 16**). His work on screens, altarpieces, and embellishments contributes substantially to the enrichment of the grand interiors of the chapels of Queen's and Pembroke, and the hall of Corpus Christi.

Hearne cordially disliked Townesend, writing in 1721 that he was a 'proud, conceited Fellow, and a great many justly wonder that he should have been so much made use of by the University'. He reported that 'tis well known that he hath spoil'd most, if not all, the Buildings he hath been employ'd in' (*Hearne* 1906, 247). On the other hand, that notoriously stern critic, Sarah, Duchess of Marlborough, described him and his sometime partner Peisley as 'able & honest', though she was subsequently disappointed in the quality of the stonework at Blenheim (*Churchill* 1884–5, 5 & 12–13).

In recent years his achievement has been well endorsed. Pevsner noted the animation and excellent carving of the monument to David Gregory (4) and considered the memorial to James Narborough 'specially good' (3) whilst also praising the chapel screens at Queen's and Pembroke. Townesend's lively sculptural style and his great experience in stone working, architectural design, and large-scale construction contributed to his constant employment on all the major architectural projects of early 18th-century Oxford.

See also **Townesend family, of Oxford and London**.

Lucy Jessop and Kate Eustace

Literary References: *Churchill* 1884–5, 7, 12–13; *Hearne* 1906, 171, 247; *Hearne* 1914; *Hiscock* 1945, 99–107; *Hope* 1950, 237; *Gunnis* 1968, 399; *Jackson-Stops* 1972, 810–814; Pevsner, *Oxon*, 1974, 286, 122, 188 & 183; *Batey* 1977, 1978–1979; *Colvin* 1995, 984–987; *Grave* vol 31, 234–5 (Sturdy); *Colvin* 2000, 43–60.

Archival References: Parish Registers, St Giles', Oxford; QC, LRS; QC Wm Townesend Accts; QC 2W 222; 2W 128; 2W 64; 2W 125

Will: PCC 219 HENCHMAN

Funerary Monuments

1.	?1703	John Wallis		St Mary, Oxford	*Hiscock* 1946, 60; *Gunnis* 1968, 399; Pevsner, *Oxon*, 1974, 286
2.	1706	Sir Thomas Powell		Llanbadarn, Aberystwyth, Cardigan	*Gunnis* 1968, 400; *Colvin* 1995, 987
3.	†1707	James Narborough (†1707)		Christchurch Cathedral, Oxford	*Hiscock* 1946, 60; Pevsner, *Oxon*, 1974, 122; *Colvin* 1995, 987
4.	†1708	David Gregory		St Mary, Oxford	*Hiscock* 1946, 60; Pevsner, *Oxon*, 1974, 286; *Colvin* 1995, 987
5.	†1713	Henry, 2nd Duke of Beaufort		Christchurch Cathedral, Oxford	Pevsner, *Oxon*, 1974, 121
6.	1713	Lord Charles Somerset		Christchurch Cathedral, Oxford	*Hiscock* 1946, 60; *Colvin* 1995, 987
7.	†1728	John Townesend I		St Giles, Oxford, churchyard	*Hiscock* 1946, 60; *Colvin* 1995, 987

Chimneypieces

8.	1731	Marble		St John's College, Oxford, hall	Colvin 1995, 986

Architectural Sculpture

9.	1701–1705	Carved work on the hall screen including six shields and work in the chapel		Corpus Christi, Oxford	*Hiscock* 1946, 40; Pevsner, *Oxon*, 1974, 131
10.	*c*1716	18 Corinthian capitals, 4 cherubim-heads for 2 niches, 2 lions Payment(s): £36, £3, £18	s	The Queen's College, Oxford, chapel	QC, Wm Townesend Accts, fol 4; *Gunnis* 1968, 399
11.	1718	Entablature with escutcheons and metopes		The Queen's College, Oxford, between hall and chapel	QC, Wm Townesend Accts, f4 8; QC 2W 222; *Gunnis* 1968, 399
12.	1719	Altarpiece Payment(s): £293	m	The Queen's College, Oxford, chapel	*Gunnis* 1968, 399
13.	post-1720	Two door cases with columns and enriched entablatures (with Peisley II)		Blenheim Palace, Oxon	*Green* 1951, 159–60
14.	1721–1725	'A good deal of the carved stonework'		Radley Hall, Oxon (now Radley College)	*Gunnis* 1968, 399
15.	*c*1727	'Marble work in the Chapel'		Blenheim Palace, Oxon	*Gunnis* 1968, 399
16.	1727	Memorial column (designed by Henry Flitcroft)	m	Blenheim Palace, Oxon, park	*Churchill* 1884–5, 12–14; *Gunnis* 1968, 399
17.	1729	Carved screen, four coats of arms on the South side and 'the shield between the two pinacles'		All Souls College, Oxford	*Gunnis* 1968, 399
18.	1728–1732	Corinthian screen and marble altarpiece		Pembroke College, Oxford	*Hiscock* 1945, 105; Pevsner, *Oxon*, 1974, 183
19.	1733	16 vases over the Cloisters Payment(s): £30		The Queen's College, Oxford	QC, Wm Townesend Accts, 2W 60
20.	1733	'Gate cupola & Cloysters in ye front of Queen's College' Payment(s): £1,045		The Queen's College, Oxford	QC 2W 60; *Gunnis* 1968, 399

TOWNESEND FAMILY, of Oxford and London

John Townesend I, of Oxford	1648–1728
William Townesend, of Oxford	1676–1739
John Townesend II, of London	1678–1742
George Townesend, of Bristol	1681–1719
John Townesend III, of Oxford	1709–1746
John Townesend IV, of Oxford	–1784
Stephen Townesend, of Oxford	1755–1800

A well-known family of mason-contractors, they made their fortune during the great Oxford building boom of the early 18th century, during which period they were engaged in major works at 12 of the 19 colleges then in existence. In some cases it is impossible to determine which family member was responsible for a work since the records at Oxford simply say 'Townesend'. **William Townesend** and **George Townesend** have been accorded separate entries since their works can more clearly be identified.

John Townesend I was the son of a labourer, Thomas Townesend of Oxford, and was apprenticed to **Bartholomew Peisley** [II?], a mason of St Giles, Oxford, on 2 October 1674 (Hanaster EB, L.5.4). By the 1690s he had emerged as the most important of several relatively minor Oxford masons. He was responsible for building work on the front range and classical gate-tower at Pembroke College (1691–4), the library at the Queen's College (1692–5), the master's lodgings at Pembroke (1695), the classical gate tower at Exeter College (1701–3), the kitchen-court at Blenheim (1705–11) and part of the back quadrangle at the Queen's College (1707). One chimneypiece by a family member has been tentatively identified as his work (**8**) and the provision of chimneypieces may well have been a useful sideline for him and other family members. His monument in the churchyard of St Giles, Oxford is a dignified baroque sarcophagus surmounted by a flaming urn, and must have been a product of the firm (*Colvin* 2000, 52, repr). He had three sons who followed him in the business, William, John II and George.

John Townesend II was apprenticed in 1693 to **Samuel Fulkes**, a member of the Haberdashers' Company, and was in due course admitted to membership of that Company, as opposed to the Masons'. His yard was in London at St Paul's wharf, and from 1714 to 1717 he and his brother William were the mason contractors building St Mary-le-Strand. On 16 May 1738 'Messrs John Townsend, Citizen and Haberdasher, **Christopher Horsnaile** [II] and **Mr. Robert Taylor** [I], Citizens and Masons, proposed jointly to perform the Masons Work . . . for £18,000 at the Mansion House'. Their competitors were **Thomas Dunn** and **John Devall.** On 17 July 1739 it was decided that all five should work jointly at the Mansion House, for a sum not exceeding £17,000 (Mansion House Comm 01/1, pp151–2, 230–1). His death is noted in the *London Magazine* of April 1742 as follows: 'Died, Mr. John Townesend, one of the Common Council men for Castle Baynard Ward and brother to the late Mr. Townesend of Oxford, well known for his many noble structures in that place'. An Edward Townesend, who may have been a relation, became free in 1721, was steward of the Masons' Company in 1727 and master in 1738.

John Townesend III was the son and successor of William Townesend. He is described as a stone carver in the list of workmen employed on the Radcliffe Library and succeeded his father as one of the principal mason-contractors for that building in 1739. He also took his father's place as mason to the dean and chapter of Christchurch. In 1742 when James Gibbs went to Tetbury, Glos to report on the state of the church, he took with him John Townesend, 'an eminent master builder from Oxford'. John was at that time engaged in building the stone screen in the hall of St John's College, working to Gibbs's designs (**21**). Shortly before his death he resurfaced and raised the early Tudor main front of Corpus Christi College. When he died in 1746 he owned a 'large handsome House' in Oxford and considerable other property (PCC 25 POTTER). His son, William, entered the church.

The nature of **John Townesend IV**'s kinship to other family members has not been established. He continued building in Oxford on a large scale, finishing the masonry work of the Radcliffe Library (1751), completing the Queen's College (1757–9) and giving the convocation house under the Bodleian Library a fine fan vault (1758–9). He designed and built the graceful Ionic library at Exeter College (1779). He signed three local monuments including a graceful gothick plaque in St Mary's church commemorating Lady Pomfret, donor of the Arundel Marbles (**4**). His son was **Stephen Townesend**, another mason, whose work on Oxfordshire buildings included the tower of Woodstock church (1785), the rebuilding of Wheatley church (1793–5) and a gothic necessary house at Magdalen College. Towards the end of his life he lived at Court Place, Iffley, a large house near the church. His foreman, **Thomas Knowles I** took over the business in 1797.

IR

Literary References: *Gunnis* 1968, 398; *Jeffery 1993, passim* (John Townesend II); *Colvin* 1995 982–4; *Grove*, vol 31, 234–5 (Sturdy); *Colvin* 2000, 43–60)

Funerary Monuments

1.	?1740	John Clark (by John Townesend II ?)		Fighledean, Wilts	S	*Gunnis* 1968, 399
2.	†1741	John Stamp (†1728) and his wife (†1741) (by John Townesend II?)		St Peter & St Paul, Wantage, Berks	S	*Gunnis* 1968, 399; Pevsner, *Berks*, 1966, 253
3.	1757	Shield and inscription to commemorate Sarah Holmes, added to her husband, William's monument (by John Townesend III ?) Payment(s): £4 16s 1d		St John's College, Oxford, chapel		St John's Coll archives, annual accts, 28 Nov 1757; *Gunnis* 1968, 399
4.	†1762	Henrietta Luisa Fermor, Countess of Pomfret (by John Townesend IV)		St Mary, Oxford	S	*Penny* 1977 (1), 111 (repr); *Colvin* 1995, 984
5.	†1765	Henry Bowles (by John Townesend IV)		New College, Oxford, chapel	S	*Colvin* 1995, 984
6.	†1768	Richard Wykeham (†1751) and wife (by John Townesend IV)		Swalcliffe, Oxon	S	Pevsner, *Oxon*, 1974, 796; *Colvin* 1995, 984

Chimneypieces

7.	1715–1719	Description unavailable	m	Sudbrook House, Petersham, Surrey, saloon		*Friedman* 1984, 135–6, 323 (repr)
8.	1732	Marble (by John Townesend I ?) Payment(s): £80		St John's College, Oxford, hall		St John's Coll archives, ACC V.B.1 and ACC 1. A.85, 43
9.	1745	Description unavailable		St John's College, Oxford, library		St John's College Archives, ACC V.B.I

Architectural Sculpture

10.	1698	Carved stone hood over the door to the principal's lodgings (John Townesend I ?)		Jesus College, Oxford		*Colvin* 2000, 26 (repr)
11.	1714–1717	Four Corinthian capitals of the pillars under the organ gallery (by John Townesend II) (co-sculptor: William Townesend, of Oxford) Payment(s): £32	wd	St Mary-le-Strand, London		GPC

12.	1714–1717	'Scroles carv'd with Cherub Heads'; 'Corinthian Capitals'; 'Carv'd panels over windows of altar'; 'Capitals at the East End of the Church'; 'ye King's Arms'; '8 Cherub heads with wings extended' (by John Townesend II) (co-sculptor: William Townesend, of Oxford)	s	St Mary-le-Strand, London	GPC quoting Accounts for the building of the New Churches, Lambeth Palace Library (Loc cit Box VII)
13.	1718	Arms, etc (by John Townesend I ?) Payment(s): £6 16s 6d		[Sharlestone, W R Yorks]; untraced	Archives, the Earl of Westmorland in GPC
14.	1736	Doorcases (by John Townesend II)		[Codrington Library, Oxford]; untraced	GPC
15.	post-1736	'Two lions and two unicorn-heads, large gilloss-flowers in the centre of the arch, sixty-four octagon panels and carving a flower in the middle of each', pedestal, statues and the pediment (by John Townesend II ?) Payment(s): £25		The Queen's College, Oxford	QC, Wm Townesend draft Acct, 2W 128
16.	1737	Carved work (by John Townesend II) Payment(s): £6 5s 3d		[St Mary, Oxford]; untraced	RG/JP, 8, 1469 citing Vice-C's Accts
17.	1737	Tympanum carving (by John Townesend II ?) Payment(s): £25		The Queen's College, Oxford	*Gunnis* 1968, 398 quoting Bodl, Rawlinson, D.912, f528
18.	1737–1738	Stone and wood carving (by John Townesend III ?) Payment(s): £154	s	[Codrington Library, Oxford]; untraced	GPC
19.	1737–1738	Wood carving (by John Townesend II) Payment(s): £65		[Codrington Library, Oxford]; untraced	GPC
20.	c1739	32 Corinthian capitals (£384), eight festoons between columns (£32), 45 Ionic capitals (£105), and other work (by John Townesend III ?)		Radcliffe Library, Oxford	*Gunnis* 1968, 399, quoting Building Accts, Radcliffe Lib, Bodleian
21.	1742–1743	Screen (by John Townesend III?) (designed by James Gibbs) Payment(s): £120		St John's College, Oxford, hall	St John's College Archives, ACC V.B.1 and ACC I.A.96, pp 45, 47
22.	1745	'Niche, where statue of Queen Philippa stood' (by John Townesend II ?)		The Queen's College, Oxford	*Gunnis* 1968, 398, citing College archives
23.	1757–1759	'pediment with a sitting figure draped, with insignia and carved with festoons of Fruit and Flowers and with a Shield & Arms' (by John Townesend III ?) Payment(s): £41		The Queen's College, Oxford, east wing	College Archives in GPC
24.	nd	'Carving the greate gate . . . in the Bowling Green' (by John Townesend III ?) Payment(s): £13 14s (with repairs to statues)		[Oxford University [Queen's College?]]; untraced	Vice Chancellor's Accounts in GPC
Miscellaneous					
25.	1758	Gate piers with two pots of flowers (by John Townesend III ?) Payment(s): £4 10s		St John's College, Oxford, garden gate	St John's College archives, Annual Accts, 20 May 1758; *Gunnis* 1968, 399

TRENTANOVA, Raimondo, of Rome 1792–1832

He was born in Faenza and learned his profession from his father, Antonio. He studied for a time at the Accademia di Belle Arti di Carrara and in 1814 went to Rome where he entered the circle of **Antonio Canova**. Thanks to the influence of his famous colleague, he was able to obtain several commissions for private and public works. After Canova's death, Trentanove made a number of copies from his work. Several of his works were commissioned by English patrons.

Literary References: *Palgrave* 1866, 121; *Fehl* 1974, 123–151; *Panzetta* 1994, 270

Funerary Monuments						
1.	†1839	Sir John Elley		St George's Chapel, Windsor Castle		*Gunnis* 1968, 400; *Bond* 1991, 117
Statues						
2.	1823	Pensive Cupid (Cupid resting)	m	Chatsworth, Derbys, orangery		*JKB* 1972 (3), 326, 331
3.	1825	Group of Venus and Cupid		Private coll	SD	*Gunnis* 1968, 400
4.	nd	Plenty, Flora, Minerva, Nemosene	m	[for John Earl of Shrewsbury, Alton Towers sale, Christie, 1857 (£215)]; untraced		Sale cat
5.	nd	Princess Paulina Borghese, statuette after Canova	m	[Stowe House, Bucks]; untraced		*Rumsey Foster* 1848, lot 702; *Gunnis* 1968, 400
Busts						
6.	1820	J J Astor	m	Cliveden House, Bucks	SD	
7.	1824	Napoleon Bonaparte	m	United Service Club, London	SD	*Gunnis* 1968, 400
8.	1828	Anne Caroline la Touche of Marlay	m	[coll La Touche family]; private coll, Ireland	SD	C Lib (repr)
9.	1828	Unidentified youth	m	Balnagown Castle, Ross-shire	SD	C Lib (repr)

10.	nd	Charles, 4th Earl of Hardwicke (†1873)		Untraced	S	*CL*, 7 March 1957
11.	nd	Copy of Antonio Canova's self-portrait	m	Woburn Abbey, Beds Other versions: several recorded	S	C Lib (repr)
12.	nd	Lord Nugent	m	[Stowe House, Bucks]; untraced		*Rumsey Foster* 1848, lot 759
13.	nd	Richard, Marquess and later 1st Duke of Buckingham	m	[Stowe House, Bucks]; untraced		*Rumsey Foster* 1848, lot 757; *The Times*, 21 Aug 1848; *Gunnis* 1968, 400
14.	nd	Vestal, after Canova		Chatsworth, Derbys		*Gunnis* 1968, 400; *JKB* 1972 (3), 326, 331

TRIGG, John, of Kingston-upon-Thames fl c1837–43?

Funerary Monuments

1.	?1837	Edward Woods	Shere, Surrey	S	*Gunnis* 1968, 400
2.	†1841	Henry Wadham Diggle	Esher, Surrey	S	*Gunnis* 1968, 400
3.	?1843	William Sells	All Saints, Kingston-upon-Thames, Surrey	S	*Gunnis* 1968, 400

TRIQUET, Thomas fl 1793–94

He manufactured artificial stone in Chelsea, in partnership with Charles Taconet until Taconet's death in 1793, and then alone until his bankruptcy in 1794.

Literary References: *Valpy* 1991, 231–2

TRIQUETI, Henri, baron de 1804–74

A French sculptor and designer of Italian descent. Triqueti studied painting in Paris before embarking on a career as a sculptor. He was one of a new generation of romantic sculptors who rejected neo-classicism in favour of medieval and early renaissance models. He made his début at the Salon of 1831 with a bronze relief, *The death of Charles the Bold* (untraced) derived from early-15th century work. His most significant French commissions included a pair of bronze doors for the Madeleine, Paris, decorated with reliefs of the *Ten Commandments* inspired by the baptistry doors of Florence Cathedral (1834–4) and the memorial to Ferdinand Philippe, Duc d'Orleans, at Chapelle St Ferdinand, Neuilly-sur-Seine (1842–3), which he executed from designs by Ary Scheffer. He exhibited at the Royal Academy in London occasionally between 1840 and 1862, and attracted commissions from British patrons. The most important of these were the memorial to Prince Albert in the Albert memorial chapel at Windsor Castle (after 1865) and decorations in intarsia and in relief for University College, London (1865). Most of Triqueti's works destined for Britain date from after 1851 and therefore fall outside the scope of the present work and only those executed before that date are listed here. Triqueti's pupils included **Susan Durant**, who was also his lover and the mother of his son, Henry Paul Harvey. (Inf. Alastair Laing)

Literary References: *Grove* 31, 345–6 (Lemaistre); *Bellenger* 1996, 183–200; exhib cat, Musée Girodet, Montargis-Musée des Beaux-arts, Orléans, 3 Oct 2007–6 Jan 2008

Statues					
1.	1847	Faun playing cymbals to the Infant Bacchus, group	m	[Exhib 1847 Salon, coll Lord Ellesmere]; untraced	*Graves* VIII, 1905–6, 21; *Lami* 1921, 318–24
2.	1848	Sappho & Cupid, group	i	Royal Coll	*Lami* 1921, 318–24
Busts					
3.	1844	Miss Wellesley		Draycot Cerne, Wilts	*Lami* 1921, 318–24
Reliefs					
4.	1838	Virgin holding the Christ-Child in her arms	m	[Exhib 1838 Salon, coll Lord Lansdowne]; untraced	*Lami* 1921, 318–24
5.	1839	Sir Thomas More (cast by Richard, Eck & Durand)	b	[Exhib 1839 salon; exhib RA 1984, 1073]; untraced	*Lami* 1921, 318–24; *Graves* VIII, 1905–6, 21
6.	1848	A small ewer in bronze, the bas-relief representing children at play		[Exhib RA, London, 1848, 1419]; untraced	*Graves* VIII, 1905–6, 21
7.	1848	Allegory of divine grace	b	[coll Lady Byron]; untraced	*Lami* 1921, 318–24
8.	1848	Infant Jesus feeding birds, as an emblem of divine providence	m	[Exhib RA, London, 1848, 1342]; untraced	*Graves* VIII, 1905–6, 21
9.	1848	Infant Moses saved from the waters	s	[Exhib RA, London, 1848, 1369]; untraced	*Graves* VIII, 1905–6, 21
10.	1848	Vase in bronze, the bas-relief representing Bacchus arriving in Gaul		[Exhib RA, London, 1848, 1418]; untraced	*Graves* VIII, 1905–6, 21
11.	1850	M Smith, medallion		Untraced	*Lami* 1921, 318–24
Miscellaneous					
12.	1850	Grape-harvesters	i	[coll Lord Ellesmere]; untraced	*Lami* 1921, 318–24

TROSCHEL, Julius 1806–63

Troschel, who came from Berlin and was a pupil of Schadow and Rauch, settled in Rome c1833, where he worked with **Bertel Thorvaldsen**. His statue of *La Filatrice*, acquired by Queen Victoria and the Prince Consort, is a group of three figures, two scantily dressed women, one borne up by the other and both supported by a reclining hero, perhaps *Hercules*, since he lies on a lion's pelt (3). Troschel was also responsible for two monuments in England. The Shuldham has a small statue of an angel (1).

Literary References: *Gunnis* 1968, 400; *Hubert* 1966, 466–9; *Read* 1982, 132, 135, 139

Funerary Monuments					
1.	1841	Gilbert Shuldham	Lea, Lincs	S	Pevsner, *Lincs*, 1989, 429
2.	?1846	Lady Elizabeth Feilding	Laycock, Wilts		*Gunnis* 1968, 400
Statues					
3.	1845	La Filatrice Addormentata	[Osborne House, I of W, billiard room]; Windsor Castle		*Read* 1982, 132, 134 (repr)

TROY, Richard James fl 1827–34

He lived in Stafford Street in 1827, and afterwards at Merchant's quay and Arran quay in Dublin. He exhibited 11 busts at the Royal Hibernian Academy between 1827 and 1834, two of which are listed by Strickland.

Literary References: *Strickland* 2, 1913, 461

Busts

1.	1827	Robert Lucius West	[Exhib RHA, Dublin]; untraced	*Strickland* 2, 1913, 461
2.	1831	Henry Aaron Baker, architect	[Exhib RHA, Dublin]; untraced	*Strickland* 2, 1913, 461

TROYE fl c1820

The identity of this signatory of two relief portraits has not been discovered, although there are several possible candidates. One is Jean Baptiste Troy (or Troye), who is known to have been in England in the early-19th century.

Literary References: *Gunnis* 1968, 400; *Ormond* 1973, 50; *Pyke* 1973, 150

Reliefs						
1.	c1820	William Thomas Brande	p	NPG, London	S	*Ormond* 1973, 50, pl 79
Miscellaneous						
2.	c1820	Henrietta, Countess of Stamford	w	coll Earl of Stamford, Altrincham	S	*Gunnis* 1968, 400; *Pyke* 1973, 150

TRUBSHAW, Charles Cope, of Stafford 1715–72

He was born on 13 September 1715, the son of Richard Trubshaw, the mason who built Bangor-Iscold steeple in 1726. He trained in London apparently under **Peter Scheemakers**, but later returned to Stafford where he set up for himself and made marble chimney-pieces for houses in the neighbourhood (**9, 10, 12, 13**). He lived at 'The Mount'.

In 1765 **Michael Rysbrack** carved a figure of a goat for Sir Edward Littleton, which was damaged on the way from London to Teddesley. In a letter to Sir Edward, written on 30 November that year, Rysbrack assured him that he need not 'be uneasy about the goat, because when Mr. Trubshaw has mended it, it will be just the same as it was before' (*Webb* 1954, 207).

In a history of her family, Susannah Trubshaw refers to the ledgers of Charles Cope Trubshaw, which appear not to have survived. They record that Trubshaw charged £3 for 12 days' work, and that he carved chimneypieces and monuments at his yard in Haywood from marble supplied by an agent in Westminster. Patrons provided with unspecified work include the Rev Bagot, J Barry, Sir William Bagot, Sir Thomas Boughton, Viscount Chetwynd, Hon Mr Clifford, Thomas Fitzherbert, Sir Byron Boughton-Delves, Sir Edward Littleton, the Lord Kilmorey, Messrs Mainwaring and Whitmore, the Hon Mr Talbot, Talbot Hoarcross, George Venables Vernon, Mr Whitby and George Adams. An involvement at Swinnerton parsonage, 1760, and with Trentham bridge, 1766 is also recorded as is his building of the *Temple of the Winds* for Thomas Anson. A pocket book for the years 1754–55 survives in the National Library of Wales (MS 16635). Trubshaw died on 22 December 1772 and is commemorated by a monument on the south wall of Colwich churchyard.

Literary References: *Trubshaw* 1876, *passim*; *Whitehouse* 1924, 110, 135; *Gunnis* 1968, 400; *Colvin* 1995, 990–2

Funerary Monuments						
1.	?1745	Acton Moseley		Enville, Staffs		*Gunnis* 1968, 400
2.	†1764	Christopher Horton		Croxall, Staffs		*Colvin* 1995, 990
3.	1767	Mr Talbot of Hoar Cross		Croxall, Staffs		*Colvin* 1995, 990
4.	1770	Mr Lucas		Croxall, Staffs		*Colvin* 1995, 990
5.	?1820	John Collins		Hints, Staffs	S	*Gunnis* 1968, 400
Chimneypieces						
6.	c1741	Several		Wolterton Hall, Norfolk		Pevsner, *Norfolk: N E & Norwich*, 1997, 731
7.	1756	Description unavailable		[Bellaport, Market Drayton, Salop]; untraced		RG/JP, 8, 1473
8.	1756	Two		Brand Hall, Norton-in-Hales, Salop		RG/JP, 8, 1473
9.	nd	Description unavailable	m	Keele Hall, Stafford		*Gunnis* 1968, 400
10.	nd	Description unavailable	m	Himley Hall, Staffs		*Gunnis* 1968, 400
11.	nd	Description unavailable	m	Raven Inn, Shrewsbury, Salop		*Gunnis* 1968, 400
12.	nd	Description unavailable	m	[coll Mr Talbot]; Hoarcross Hall, Staffs		*Gunnis* 1968, 400
13.	nd	Description unavailable		Tixall Hall, Staffs		*Colvin* 1995, 990
Architectural Sculpture						
14.	1759	Decorative carving		[for Madame Boswell]; untraced		*Colvin* 1995, 990
15.	1766–1767	Carved work in the colonnade Payment(s): £237 16s 4d	s	[Teddesley Hall, Staffs]; untraced		Lord Hatherton's Archive, Staffs CRO, E116
16.	1776	Unidentified carving Payment(s): £112		[Teddesley Hall, Staffs]; untraced		Lord Hatherton's Archive, Staffs CRO, E116
17.	nd	Decorative carving		[for Sir Lynch Cotton]; untraced		*Colvin* 1995, 990
Miscellaneous						
18.	nd	Sideboard	m	[for Mr Corbet of Sundorn Hall, Salop]; untraced		*Colvin* 1995, 990

TRUBSHAW, James 1777–1853

The son of James Trubshaw (1746–1808) and a grandson of **Charles Cope Trubshaw**, he was born on 13 February 1777. He studied sculpture in London under **Richard Westmacott I**, who afterwards found him a post as the foreman supervising building work at Fonthill Abbey. He was later employed at Windsor Castle and at Buckingham Palace, where he assembled the grand staircase.

Trubshaw returned to Stafford to marry in 1800 and around this time he built Ilam Hall, near Ashbourne. In 1809–1811 he was working at Ingestre Hall, Staffs, receiving over £1,500 (Archives, Earl of Shrewsbury in GPC). In 1827 he built the Grosvenor bridge over the Dee at Chester, which had the largest span in Europe.

He was apparently a man of great physical strength for when he was working at Ilam, his employer, Watts Russell, matched him in a race with his children's tutor. On eyeing his opponent, who was slight, Trubshaw offered to run with **Sir Francis Chantrey** on his back, the latter being a guest of the family at the time. This was agreed and in spite of so great a handicap, he won the race.

Trubshaw signed a number of Staffordshire wall-tablets. That to the Hales family (**13**) is signed 'J and C Trubshaw'. At the end of his life he was contemplating a scheme to erect an enormous obelisk, larger than Cleopatra's needle, to the memory of George Stephenson. He died on 28 October 1853 and is commemorated as 'civil engineer and architect' on his tablet at Colwich, Staffs, which notes Grosvenor Bridge as his 'enduring monument'. His obituary appeared in the *Gentleman's Magazine* in January 1854 and a posthumous bust of Trubshaw by **E W Wyon** was shown at the Royal Academy in 1857.

Literary References: *Trubshaw* 1876, *passim*; *Whitehouse* 1924, 64, 126; *Gunnis* 1968, 400; *Bayliss* c1978; *Stamp* 1981, 357–379; *Colvin* 1995, 992–5

Archival References: GPC

Funerary Monuments

1.	?1802	Hannah Moreton	Wolstanton, Staffs		RG/JP, 8, 1474
2.	?1807	James Chetwynd	Baswich, Staffs		RG/JP, 8, 1474
3.	?1813	Margaret Sheppard	Uttoxeter, Staffs		GPC
4.	?1818	Elizabeth Sparrow	Colwich, Staffs		RG/JP, 8, 1474
5.	?1820	Rev. E Dickenson	St Mary, Stafford		RG/JP, 8, 1475
6.	?1820	Samuel Wolferton	Stratford, Staffs		RG/JP, 8, 1475
7.	?1820	Thomas Brome	Colwich, Staffs		GPC
8.	?1821	John Sparrow	Colwich, Staffs	S	*Gunnis* 1968, 400
9.	?1821	Thomas Mills	Barlaston, Staffs		RG/JP, 8, 1475
10.	?1834	Ralph Moreton	Wolstanton, Staffs	S	*Gunnis* 1968, 400
11.	?1836	Mary Myott	Biddulph, Staffs		RG/JP, 8, 1475
12.	?1838	M A Whyle	Rocester, Staffs		RG/JP, 8, 1475
13.	?1841	Hales family (co-sculptor: C. Trubshaw)	Stoke-on-Trent parish church, Staffs	S	*Gunnis* 1968, 400
14.	?1842	George Lander	St James, Longton, Staffs		GPC

TRUEMAN, Edward, of Worcester fl *c*1791–*c*1812

He signs a pedimented tablet to John Bourne with shell motifs and gadrooning (**1**), and a tablet with a weeping figure by an urn to John Groves (**2**). Trueman's son by his wife, Ann, was christened George Clewer Trueman on 21 January 1780 at Ribbesford, Worcester. This son was apprenticed to him and became free in 1807.

Literary References: *Gunnis* 1968, 401

Archival References: IGI

Funerary Monuments

1.	†1791	John Bourne	St Andrew, Droitwich, Worcs	S	
2.	†1797	John Groves	Wichenford, Worcs	S	
3.	†1812	Ann Wickens	All Saints, Worcester	S	*Gunnis* 1968, 401

TRUMAN fl *c*1688

Funerary Monuments

1.	†1688	George Lucas	Llandyfodwg, Glamorgan	S	Pevsner, *Glamorgan*, 1995, 381

TRUMAN, Edward, of Bewdley fl *c*1741–80

Funerary Monuments

1.	†1741	Humphrey Bate (†1741) and Thomas Bate (†1775)	Wolverley, Worcs	S	GPC
2.	†1780	Rowland Hill (†1780) and wife (†1831)	Tasley, Salop		GPC

TUCKEY, E, of Banwell, Somerset fl *c*1753

Funerary Monuments

1.	†1753	Hannah Hemens	Banwell, Somerset		RG/JP, 8, 1474v.

TUFFNELL FAMILY

John Tuffnell 1643–1697
Edward Tuffnell 1678–1719
Samuel Tuffnell –1765

John Tuffnell and his son Edward were members of a family of masons and master-builders. John may have been the son of Edward Tuffnell and Catherine Moorecocke of Christ Church, Newgate, London, who were married at St Martin-in-the-Fields on 8 October 1638. John was the master-mason at Westminster Abbey for 23 years and was also employed on repairs to St Margaret, Westminster in 1674 and later. He died on 18 February 1697, and was buried 'near the east end of the south Cloister' of the Abbey on 23 February (*Chester* 1876, 241, 297 n5). His wife, Dorothy née Smythe, whom he had married in 1673, afterwards became the wife of a Mr Noble and died in 1720.

Edward Tuffnell, who succeeded his father as Abbey mason, was baptised at St Margaret, Westminster, on 21 February 1678. He was apprenticed to **Christopher Kempster** on 14 June 1692. In 1697 he married Anne Browne, the daughter and co-heiress of Samuel Browne of St Margaret's, Westminster. He worked at the Abbey as master-mason for 22 years and his epitaph relates that during that time he restored and redecorated the south and east sides of the building. In 1702 he received £12 15s for 'laying 21 ft of marble around the mouth of the vault and also 12ft of new marble to make good what was broken' when the Royal vault in Henry VII's chapel was opened to receive the coffin of King William III (TNA WORK 5/53 fol 400). He also worked with **Edward Strong II** at St Alphege, Greenwich, 1712–14, at St Anne, Limehouse, 1712–24, St Paul, Deptford, 1712–30, St Margaret, Westminster 1713–26, St John, Westminster, 1714–28 and St George, Wapping, 1715–23 (TNA, A 01.437/2). The two received a total of £5,000 for work on these six new churches erected by the Commissioners for building Fifty New Churches.

On 14 October 1717 Edward was appointed one of four auditors of the Westminster Fire Company. In the same year he made a model of one of the new churches designed by Nicholas Hawksmoor (Lambeth Palace Library, Bill Book for the New Churches in GPC). He died on 2 September 1719 and, like his father, was buried in the cloisters, where a large monument with a portrait-bust (presumably the work of his son Samuel) was erected to his memory (**7**). Tuffnell is described on his epitaph as an architect, and is depicted in the soft cap sometimes associated with artists. In 1721 his widow remarried a merchant, Thomas Mytton, of St Leonard's, Shoreditch. She died seven years later.

Samuel Tuffnell was the son of Edward Tuffnell and followed in the family trade. The *Northampton Mercury* of 27 September 1725 noted that the 'magnificent altarpiece for Bath Abbey' was to be seen at his yard in Westminster (GPC). The work was removed in 1833, despite the very high quality of its design and execution, and now adorns a private house in Bath (**12**). He was the master-mason at St John, Horsleydown, from 1728 until 1733. He also made marble chimneypieces (**9, 10**). He succeeded **Christopher Horsnaile I** as mason at Westminster Abbey in December 1737. The extensive repair work on the Abbey continued until 1745 when the west towers were completed.

In 1743 Samuel became a director of the Westminster Fire Company (WFO, MB 343/7, 20 Oct 1743). He signed a number of monuments, usually architectural in character, such as that to Henry Phillips (**1**). It is a tall tablet of coloured marbles with Corinthian pilasters, a broken segmental pediment enclosing a rich cartouche, and an apron with a winged cherub's head between fluted black ogee consoles. His monument to the Cart family was formerly in St Mary-le-Bow, but was destroyed when the church was bombed in 1940 (**8**). The antiquary Thomas Allen described this as 'a plain sarcophagus surmounted by a well-executed bust of the deceased in the undress costume which marks the likeness of Thomson and other poets. At the back of the bust are four Corinthian Columns, sustaining a broken elliptical pediment. On the base is J. Potter arch. S. Tuffnell sculp'. Samuel died in 1765 and was buried with his wife Ann (née Mytton) in the churchyard of St Giles, Camberwell, London.

Edward and Samuel Tuffnell had another brother, William (1680–1733), who worked as a master-builder and bricklayer for the New River Company. A William Tuffnell, presumably another family member, became a director of the Westminster Fire Office on 27 October 1737, and a monument to a Samuel Tuffnell, who died in 1748, was carved by **Sir Henry Cheere** for Pleshey, Essex. Several members of the family served on the vestry of St Margaret, Westminster, and rose to high-ranking positions in the Middlesex militia.

The family seem to have had the right to be buried in Westminster Abbey, for as late as 1832 Ann White, Samuel's grand-daughter, was buried in the west cloister, and her grave was reopened in 1839 on the death of her daughter, Emmeline-Eliza.

MGS

Literary References: *Chester* 1876, 241, 297 n5; *Tuffnell* 1924, 66; *Gunnis* 1968, 401; *Craske* 1992, 69; *Baker* 1995 (1), 100; *Webb* 1999, 33; *Baker* 2000, 74; *Friedman* 2004, 36–38, 42, 45

Archival References: WFO, DMB; MB, 343/6; WAM Chapter Books; GPC

Will: Edward Tufnell, mason of St Margaret, Westminster, 9 January 1720, PROB 11/572

Funerary Monuments

1.	†1714	Henry Phillips (by Samuel Tuffnell)		St Mary, Aylesbury, Bucks		*Gunnis* 1968, 401
2.	†1714	Newdigate Owsley (by Samuel Tuffnell)		Leyton, Essex	S	*Gunnis* 1968, 401; Pevsner, *Essex*, 1965, 268
3.	†1727	Bishop George Hooper (by Samuel Tuffnell)		Wells Cathedral, Somerset	S	Pevsner, *Somerset: N & Bristol*, 1958, 312
4.	?1728	Abigail Hooper (by Samuel Tuffnell)		Wells Cathedral, Somerset	S	*Gunnis* 1968, 401
5.	?1728	Francis Wilkinson (by Samuel Tuffnell)		Feltham, Middx	S	*Gunnis* 1968, 401
6.	?1730	Benjamin Hucks (by Samuel Tuffnell)		Abingdon, Berks		GPC
7.	1726–1730	Edward Tuffnell (†1719) (by Samuel Tuffnell)		Westminster Abbey, London, cloisters, south walk		*Gunnis* 1968, 401; *Baker* 2000, 97 (repr)
8.	nd	James Cart and family (by Samuel Tuffnell, designed by John Potter)		[St Mary-le-Bow, London]; destroyed World War II	S	*Allen* 1827–37, 3, 437; *Gunnis* 1968, 401

Chimneypieces

9.	1719	Description unavailable (by Samuel Tuffnell)	m	[for Lord Derby, Knowsley, Lancs]; untraced		Derby Archives in *Gunnis* 1968, 401
10.	1725	Description unavailable (by Samuel Tuffnell, designed by Nicholas Dubois)	m	Stanmer House, Sussex		Newcastle Archives in *Gunnis* 1968, 401

Architectural Sculpture

11.	1671	Sundial (by John Tuffnell) Payment(s): 15s		Cleave's almhouses, Kingston-upon-Thames, Surrey		Archives, Cleave's almhouses in *Gunnis* 1968, 401
12.	1725	Altarpiece, architectural elements only (by Samuel Tuffnell) Payment(s): £1500		[Bath Abbey, Somerset (removed 1833)]; Grosvenor Villa, Bath		*Sloman* 1991, 507–510 (repr); GPC
13.	1713–1726	Ornaments including Doric capitals with rose husks, 129 cartouches in the cornice of the towers and pediment ornaments (by Edward Tufnell) (co-sculptor: Edward Strong II)		St Margaret, Westminster, London		*Friedman* 2004, 36–38

TUPPER, John Lucas ?1823–79

John Lucas Tupper was an anatomical draughtsman, teacher, poet and sculptor, closely linked to the Pre-Raphaelite movement. He showed an interest in becoming an artist at an early age and was encouraged by his father, George Frederick Tupper, a printer in the City of London. His earliest artistic efforts included models of cats and satyrs (**20**), chalk portraits of his family and copies after Old Master prints. In 1836 he enrolled as a student at the British Museum, where he studied ancient Greek and Roman sculpture. A few years later he was admitted to the Royal Academy Schools on the strength of a relief of the *Discobolus* (**3**). (Tupper later gave the date of entry as 1840 but the RA records state that he became a student in 1838). He was disappointed by Academic practice, which obliged him to spend most of his time copying casts rather than working from nature. Tupper had modest success whilst still a student: he was paid ten guineas for a portrait medallion of a lawyer in 1840 and then modelled another of the lawyer's daughter and of a doctor (**5–7**). He also produced designs inspired by a poem of Robert Burns and a relief after Shelley's *Witch of Atlas*, but these works have not been traced and they are they are unlikely to have survived (**23, 4**).

During his time as a Royal Academy student Tupper met and formed lasting friendships with Frederick George Stephens and William Holman Hunt, both of whom went on to become founding members of the Pre-Raphaelite Brotherhood. Tupper was introduced to Dante Gabriel Rossetti and the other group members by Hunt and he frequently attended PRB meetings during the late 1840s and early 1850s. William Michael Rossetti later described him as 'a meagre young man, hardly up to middle height, with pale visage, abundant dark hair, vivid dark eyes and very mobile eyebrows' adding that he was 'not handsome, but got wonderfully improved and not a little picturesque by growing, as he was approaching middle age, a very copious beard.' (*Rossetti* 1906, I, 161, cited by *Read and Barnes* 1991, 67) Tupper's father and two brothers, George and Alexander, also became involved in the movement and their firm printed the Pre-Raphaelite periodical, *The Germ*, to which John contributed a two part essay on *The Subject in Art* and several poems.

In 1849 Tupper found work as an anatomical draughtsman at Guy's Hospital, London. This work suited him well, for he was much interested in science and the close observation of nature. Some of his anatomical drawings, which were much admired, were lithographed by his father's firm and published in *Guy's Hospital Reports* between 1847 and 1864 and Dr John Hilton engaged him to illustrate his book, *On the Influence of Mechanical and Physiological Res[t] and the Diagnostic Value of Pain*, published in 1863.

In 1851 he submitted a relief illustrating a passage in *The Merchant's Second Tale* by Chaucer for exhibition at the RA but it was rejected (**8**). WM Rossetti considered the work, which depicted the merchant playing chess with an old man met in a strange city, too radical for the Academy: he described it as being 'at the extremest edge of P.R.B.ism, most conscientiously copied from Nature, and with good character'. Rossetti suggested however that in his bid to represent nature without compromise, Tupper failed to pay heed to 'the requirements peculiar to the particular form of art adopted'. Judged by the ideals of the Academy he had produced 'a perfect sculpturesque heresy, whose rejection – especially seeing it is the *introductory* sample of the P.R.B. system in sculpture – cannot be much wondered at, though most unjustifiable' (*PRB Journal*, 16–23 May 1851, cited by *Fredeman* 1975, 96). The work was placed in St George's Chess Club, St James's, London, where the first international chess tournament took place that year, but is now lost and has probably perished. The Academicians were more tolerant of Tupper's portraiture and he exhibited at the RA between 1854 and 1868, showing principally portrait medallions, including one of Hunt (**16**) and several of eminent medical men (**10, 11, 15**).

Tupper's largest and most important sculptural work was a statue of the 18th-century Swedish botanist, Carl Linnaeus for the great hall of the Oxford University Museum (**2**). D G Rossetti had written to Tupper in April 1856 urging him to approach the architect Benjamin Woodward, about the commission which, although poorly paid, might lead to further opportunities. WM Rossetti later described Tupper's statue as 'a work of the most conscientious order in realism of intention and unsparing precision of detail' (*Tupper* 1897, ix, cited by *Read and Barnes* 1991, 68). It adheres to Pre-Raphaelite principles of 'Truth to Nature' in its faithful depiction of the botanist's apparel (including a fur coat which was probably taken from Rossetti's goat-skin jacket) and the plants and flowers at his feet. Several Pre-Raphaelites contributed to the decoration of the Museum, including **Thomas Woolner** and **Alexander Munro** who also provided statues.

Tupper left Guy's Hospital in 1863, perhaps due to illness, or in order to concentrate on his sculpture. However he failed to attract influential patrons and was unable to make a living as a sculptor, so he soon sought new employment. In 1865 he took up the post of master of scientific drawing at Rugby School after Hunt recommended him to the head master, Frederick Temple. There Tupper dedicated himself to the development of art education, publishing a pamphlet on the theme and establishing an art museum at the school. Meanwhile he continued to write and sculpt and he maintained contact with the Pre-Raphaelites. At the inaugural exhibition of the Rugby School Museum in 1879 Tupper's own work was represented by pencil drawings of Arthur Durham and Leigh Sotheby and two portrait medallions (**16, 19**). Sculpture by Woolner was also exhibited. Tupper's position at Rugby provided him with financial security which enabled him to marry Annie French, whom he had met while teaching drawing, in December 1871. The first of their two children was christened John Holman after Tupper's steadfast friend. Tupper did not have many years as a family man: he suffered from periods of poor health throughout the latter part of his life, became seriously ill in October 1878 and died on 29 September 1879.

In the introduction to an edition of Tupper's poetry published in 1897, WM Rossetti noted that his sculpture had never attracted much public attention, adding 'The tendency of his mind was certainly quite as much scientific as artistic; and, though I conceive him to have been fully capable of producing sound works of art, had circumstances been favourable, he did in fact pass through life without realizing anything considerable in sculpture, if we except the life-sized statue of Linnaeus' (*Tupper* 1897, viii–ix, cited by *Read and Barnes*, 70). Apart from the Linnaeus, the only surviving works by Tupper that have been traced to date are two typically Pre-Raphaelite portrait medallions (**10, 13**). The limited nature of his output meant that Tupper was virtually unknown until his correspondence with Holman Hunt and F G Stephens came to light during the 1970s (for his correspondence with Hunt, now in the Huntington Library, see *Coombs* 1986, *passim*). More recently he has attracted some scholarly attention because of his close involvement with the Pre-Raphaelites.

EH

Literary References: *Fredeman* 1975, *passim*; *Kapoor* 1984, 70–85; *Read* 1984, 97, 98–100, 101, 109; *Coombs* 1986, *passim*; *Kapoor* 1986, 37–43; *Landow* 1986, 63–8 (including list of Tupper's unpublished writings); *Read and Barnes* 1991, 66–70, 139–140

Additional MS Sources: Rossetti/Tupper; Tupper Corr; Tupper/Stephens

Portraits of the Sculptor: Anon, photo, nd (repr *Read and Barnes* 1991, 66)

Will: PPR, 27 November 1879, fol 960, personal estate valued at under £60

Statues

1.	1838	Theseus, model		Untraced		*Read and Barnes* 1991, 66
2.	1856–1858	Carl Linnaeus	s	Oxford University Museum	S	*Read* 1982, 180 (repr); *Read and Barnes* 1991, 68–9 (repr)

Reliefs

3.	1838	Discobolus, model		Untraced		*Read and Barnes* 1991, 66
4.	c1840	Scene from Shelley's *Witch of Atlas*		Untraced		*Read and Barnes* 1991, 66
5.	1841	A lawyer, portrait medallion		Untraced		*Read and Barnes* 1991, 66, 70
6.	1841	Dr S, portrait medallion		Untraced		*Read and Barnes* 1991, 66, 70
7.	1841	Lawyer's daughter, Miss A, portrait medallion		Untraced		*Read and Barnes* 1991, 66, 70
8.	1851	Chessplaying		[St George's Chess Club]; untraced		*Read and Barnes* 1991, 67–8
9.	1854	J Callaway, portrait medallion		[Exhib RA, London, 1525]; untraced		*Graves* VIII, 1905–6, 27
10.	1854	John Hilton, portrait medallion	p	RCS, London	S	*Graves* VIII, 1905–6, 27; *Read and Barnes* 1991, 139 (repr)
11.	1855	Dr Gall, portrait medallion		[Exhib RA, London, 1487]; untraced		*Graves* VIII, 1905–6, 27
12.	1855	Edward Cock, portrait medallion	m	[Exhib RA, London, 1488]; untraced		*Graves* VIII, 1905–6, 27
13.	1856	Thomas Bell, portrait medallion	p	Linnean Soc, London	S	*Graves* VIII, 1905–6, 27; *Read and Barnes* 1991, 70, 140 (repr)

14.	1857	A young lady, portrait medallion	[Exhib RA, London, 1362]; untraced	*Graves* VIII, 1905–6, 27
15.	1857	J Patient, portrait medallion	[Exhib RA, London, 1364]; untraced	*Graves* VIII, 1905–6, 27
16.	1857	William Holman Hunt, portrait medallion	[Exhib RA, London, 1301]; untraced	*Graves* VIII, 1905–6, 27
17.	1862	The image of pity	Untraced	*Read and Barnes* 1991, 70
18.	1869	William Michael Rossetti, portrait medallion	Untraced	*Read and Barnes* 1991, 68
19.	1879	Annie Tupper, portrait medallion	[Exhib Rugby School Museum and Art Gallery]; untraced	*Read and Barnes* 1991, 70
Miscellaneous				
20.	pre-1838	Cats and satyrs, models	Untraced	*Read and Barnes* 1991, 70
21.	1841	Antinous, model	Untraced	*Read and Barnes* 1991, 70
22.	1841	Dancing Faun, model	Untraced	*Read and Barnes* 1991, 70
23.	1841	Design based on a poem by Burns	Untraced	*Read and Barnes* 1991, 66, 70
24.	1841	Germanicus, model	Untraced	*Read and Barnes* 1991, 70
25.	1856	A portrait	[Exhib RA, London, 1371]; untraced	*Graves* VIII, 1905–6, 27
26.	1867	James Salter	[Exhib RA, London, 1185]; untraced	*Graves* VIII, 1905–6, 27
27.	1868	Dr Hyde Salter	[Exhib RA, London, 1164]; untraced	*Graves* VIII, 1905–6, 27

TURNBULL fl *c*1803

His only known work is signed 'Turnbull Sculptor London'. He may have been related to **Robert Turnbull**, or possibly to the James Turnbull 'mason of St Martin in the Fields' whose will was proved on 20 May 1791 (PROB 11/1205).

Funerary Monuments

1.	1803	John Aldridge	Nuthurst, Sussex

TURNBULL, Robert fl 1748–*c*1750

His yard was in Brick Street, Piccadilly (Westminster Poll Book, 1748). He built the grotto and circular Corinthian temple at Ascot Park, Berks. This was evidently a work of some bravado, as the historian Hakewill described it as 'almost entirely covered with a white spar, intermixed with curious and unique specimens of polished pebbles and petrifactions. . . the whole, when under the influence of a strong sun, has an almost magical effect'. Hakewill added of the sculptor: 'The carving with which he has enriched the Corinthian Temple and a Gothic seat at no great distance from it gives very sufficient proof of his skill and ingenuity' (*Hakewill* 1813, 292–3).

Literary References: *Gunnis* 1968, 401

Architectural Sculpture

1.	*c*1750	Grotto, and Corinthian temple ornaments	[Ascot Park, Berks]; untraced	*Gunnis* 1968, 401

TURNER, C fl 1837

In 1837, while living at 13 Turnham Place, Curtain Road, London, he was awarded a medal from the Society of Arts (1).

Miscellaneous

1.	1837	'Carving in wood of flowers'	[Soc of A, silver medal]; untraced	RSA *Transactions*, 1838, vol 52, xvi

TURNER, Joseph, of Chester –1807

He was admitted to the freedom of Chester by order of Assembly on 22 October 1774, and in 1782 became a sheriff of the city. In the same year he was the architect responsible for Bridge Gate. Turner became an alderman of Chester and died on 6 February 1807. He was buried at Hawarden, Flint, where there is a tablet to his memory, which records that 'the many splendid and Public Works in which he was concerned in the counties of Flint, Denby and Chester, will be a lasting memorial of his taste and abilities as an architect'.

Turner's monuments are mostly architectural in character, the most imposing being the Cotton, which has a large urn set against a pyramid (1). The monument to Susanna Price has an urn on a corbelled casket, and that to Mary Hughes has an elegant urn against an obelisk (7, 8).

Literary References: *Hemingway* 1831, 1, 369; *Gunnis* 1968, 401–2; Pevsner, *Clwyd*, 1986, 275

Archival References: Chester Corporation Archives in *Gunnis* 1968, 401–2

Funerary Monuments

1.	?1777	Sir Lynch Cotton	Wrenbury, Cheshire	S	*Gunnis* 1968, 402
2.	?1785	Charles Legh	Prestbury, Cheshire	S	*Gunnis* 1968, 402
3.	?1789	J Harrison	Aldford, Cheshire	S	*Gunnis* 1968, 402
4.	?1791	Mr and Mrs Kelsall	Dodleston, Cheshire		GPC
5.	?1792	George Hawkshaw	Chester Cathedral, Cheshire	S	*Gunnis* 1968, 402
6.	?1792	Shakerley family	Gresford, Denbighs		GPC
7.	1796	Susanna Price	St Collen, Llangollen, Denbighs	S	Pevsner, *Clwyd*, 1986, 220
8.	†1798	Mary Hughes	Ruthin, Denbighs	S	*Gunnis* 1968, 402; Pevsner, *Clwyd*, 1986, 275

TURNER, Thomas, of London fl 1837?

His only known monument is a Hellenic wall-tablet (1). His yard was in Somerset Place, Whitechapel.

Funerary Monuments

1.	?1837	Elizabeth Peters	St Luke, Chelsea, London	S	*Gunnis* 1968, 402

TURNER, William, of London fl 1804–22

Turner's address was Richmond Buildings in 1804 and 7 Union Street, Berkeley Square in 1813. The Mount Edgcumbe monument is an Hellenic wall-tablet in polychrome marbles (1). The Grant tablet is a smaller variant (2).

Literary References: *Graves* VIII, 1905–6, 42; *Gunnis* 1968, 402

Funerary Monuments					
1.	?1806	Countess of Mount Edgcumbe	Maker, Cornwall	S	*Gunnis* 1968, 402
2.	?1814	Anne Grant	Farnborough, Hants	S	*Gunnis* 1968, 402
Busts					
3.	1804	Unidentified old lady	[Exhib RA, London, 929]; untraced		*Graves* VIII, 1905–6, 42
4.	1813	Mr T Brown	[Exhib RA, London, 894]; untraced		*Graves* VIII, 1905–6, 42

5.	1814	Unidentified artist		[Exhib RA, London, 762]; untraced	*Graves* VIII, 1905–6, 42
6.	1815	J Shaw		[Exhib RA, London, 908]; untraced	*Graves* VIII, 1905–6, 42; *Gunnis* 1968, 402
7.	1819	Mrs Phillips of Tean Hall		[Exhib RA, London, 1243]; untraced	*Graves* VIII, 1905–6, 42; *Gunnis* 1968, 402
Chimneypieces					
8.	1819	Veined marble Payment(s): £42 12s	m	[Bank of England]; untraced	Soane bank acct, vol 11, fol 429; *Gunnis* 1968, 402
9.	1822	Two, of marble Payment(s): £44		[Earl St German's residence, Charles St, St James's Square, London]; untraced	Soane Bill Book 1, fol 555
Miscellaneous					
10.	1813	Mr Tucker (portrait)		[Exhib RA, London, 545]; untraced	*Graves* VIII, 1905–6, 42

TURNERELLI, James fl 1796

James Turnerelli, or Tognarelli, was an Italian modeller and figure-maker, the son of a political refugee from Italy and the father of **Peter Turnerelli**. He worked in Belfast and Dublin, and anglicised his name to 'Turnerelli'. After the death of his wife, a Protestant Irishwoman, he moved to London. He was mentioned as a modeller in a letter from Joseph Lygo to William Duesbury in January 1796, and then in an article about his son in the *European Magazine* of 1821, which described him as a modeller 'of considerable talent and ingenuity' (*Euro Mag* 1821, 79, 387). None of his works has yet come to light.

Literary References: *Gilmartin* 1967, 3; *Bricknell* 1995, 9

TURNERELLI, Peter 1774–1839

Turnerelli was one of the most noted portraitists of his time. He was born in Belfast in 1774, the grandson of a political refugee from the Papal States. His father, James Tognarelli, was a modeller and figure-maker who had married an Irishwoman. When Peter was young the family moved to Dublin to be close to his mother's relations, and he studied at the Roman Catholic Academy in Saul's Court, founded by the Jesuit Father Betagh, whose monument Turnerelli later executed (**8**). Turnerelli was intended for the priesthood but the situation altered in 1792 when his mother died and the family moved to London. He joined them the following year.

He joined the Royal Academy Schools in October 1794 and in 1799 was awarded a silver medal by unanimous decision for a model of an Academy figure (**141**), though Farington recorded that the competition that year was not strong. The entrants 'are in general very bad,' he wrote in his diary (*Farington* IV, 1312). Whilst at the Academy Schools Turnerelli worked in the studio of the modeller **P F Chenu** in Wardour Street, and it was assumed that he, too, would be a modeller. In January 1796 he was assessed as a possible employee by Joseph Lygo of the Derby manufactory. Lygo subsequently wrote a poor appraisal to William Duesbury: 'Young Tognerelle' he said 'knew very little of moulding. One would think from his being brought up by his father till at the age of one or two and twenty, and since that time has been with Mr Chenu, he would have understood moulding well, but from what I can learn . . . he has been principally imployed in repairing his best figures and some times modelling' (letter, Derby Local Studies Library, DL82 1/468 quoted in *Bricknell* 1995, 95).

After completing his studies Turnerelli is said to have spent a brief period in Rome, but by 1802 he was back in London, living at 9 Poland Street, Soho. One of his first patrons was the 2nd Lord Heathfield who employed him to produce busts of Francis Drake and General Eliot modelled from portraits (**128, 129, 135**). He also came to the attention of Sir Thomas Lawrence, who recommended him to the royal family to teach modelling to the young Princess Charlotte. In 1802 Turnerelli received payment from the Prince of Wales for a portrait of that princess (**29**). He was subsequently appointed teacher and sculptor to the Queen, a post he held for 3 years, and at the end of that time he became sculptor-in-ordinary to the Royal family. He was twice offered a knighthood, which he refused on both occasions.

In 1809 Turnerelli modelled the 'Jubilee bust' of George III, a naturalistic depiction of the monarch in contemporary dress with bowl-cut hair and an open-mouth (**46**). According to the *European Magazine* of 1821 over 80 copies of this work were subsequently ordered in marble by private patrons and public bodies, and its success ensured that Turnerelli became the most popular sculptor of the day. The magazine was also convinced that it was Turnerelli's gift for conveying expressive likeness in 'a style of elegance and happy simplicity' which ensured widespread appreciation of his work (*Euro Mag* 1821, vol 79, 388–9).

Turnerelli subsequently executed a second bust of the King in the guise of a Roman emperor (**53**) and a crisply carved statue in wig and full robes of state (**24**). He also produced a matronly portrait of Queen Charlotte, begun by the sitter herself, as a companion piece to the Jubilee bust of her husband and completed by the sculptor (**75**). Princess Charlotte and Prince Leopold sat for their 'Nuptial busts' on the morning of their wedding in 1816 (**67, 73**). The death of the Princess soon after appears to have given the work an added sentimental appeal, and Turnerelli incurred the wrath of Prince Leopold by producing numerous copies of the work for general sale.

According to Strickland, the Duke of Wellington sat for the second of two portraits by Turnerelli in 1814 (**49, 59**). One of these earlier versions did not please **Joseph Nollekens**, who complained to Joseph Farington in July 1813 that the Irishman had copied his bust of Lord Wellington 'and now sold it as his own performance' (*Farington* vol 12, 4408). Turnerelli also carved portraits of the heroes of the Russian and Prussian forces, Platov and Blücher (**63, 64**), both depicted in high-necked collars with turned heads and full military regalia. The Prince Regent paid £472 10s for a set of all three for Carlton House in 1816. Turnerelli's European reputation increased as a result of these works: orders came from the Czar of Russia and the King of Prussia. In 1816 Louis XVIII, the restored King of France, sat for Turnerelli at the Tuileries and the impact of this French visit is perhaps present in Turnerelli's later busts, which have a French Empire feeling. The artist Edward Bird, who was painting Louis XVIII at the same time, noticed that Turnerelli 'spoke to the King with a most unbecoming familiarity, indeed his whole deportment was brutally improper' (*Farington* 14, 4841). Around this time he also became sculptor to the King of Portugal.

Turnerelli was at the height of his fame in 1821, when the *European Magazine* appraised his achievement, noted the dissemination of his works throughout Europe, and compared his commemorative portraits in contemporary dress to the modern history paintings of his friend Benjamin West. The journal also gave notice of a forthcoming exhibition of his work. Turnerelli's meteoric rise to fame appears not to have endeared him to his artistic colleagues. He failed in his attempts to be elected an ARA in 1807 and again in 1811. In 1812 the Royal Academy rejected a model of a statue of *Apollo* that he had sent for exhibition. Benjamin West remonstrated with the committee in vain that the work 'was a commission from a country gentleman, to be executed in marble, and that Tonarelli might lose £1500 if it shd be rejected' (*Farington* 11, 4113).

Turnerelli married Margaret Tracy, the heiress to the Tracy peerage, whom he met at a soirée in Charlemont House, Dublin. Their son, Edward Tracy, was born in 1813. The couple lived at 67 Newman Street, London, but Turnerelli made frequent visits to Ireland, where he educated his son, and he sculpted many leading Irish figures. His bust of the statesman Henry Grattan (**51**), said to have been completed in one 11-hour sitting at Tinnahinch, was reportedly praised by **Antonio Canova** as the best modern bust he had seen in England. Turnerelli produced busts of Archbishops Troy and Doyle (**69, 101**), and carved the high altar for Dublin Cathedral (**140**). In 1828 he produced a bust of the Catholic lawyer and political agitator Daniel O'Connell, of which 10,000 plaster copies were reportedly sold in Ireland (**99**).

Although he was chiefly a portraitist Turnerelli created a number of monuments. Perhaps the most notable is the statue of Robert Burns, which attempts to convey the poet's untutored genius by representing him, like Elijah, receiving inspiration at a plough (**25**). Others are variants on the popular theme of a female grieving at an urn or a sarcophagus (**5, 9**), and include the memorial to Lord Nelson's widow (**15**) which Rupert Gunnis considered 'more like the work of a "New Road statuary" than of a distinguished sculptor' (*Gunnis* 1968, 403). More innovative is the monument to Bishop Moylan, where the grieving female has been transformed into a nun, mourning at the shrine of the prelate (**4**). Another in the series, to the bookseller James Edwards, has a little still-life of vases and a selection of antiquarian books (**6**).

Turnerelli's first wife died in 1835, and in the same year, on 28 December, he married Mary O'Connor, a relation of the Earl of Clare, at St Thomas's, Dublin. He had two children by his second marriage. He died of apoplexy in London on 18 March 1839 at 62 Newman Street, Marylebone and was buried in the graveyard of St John's Wood Chapel. He was intestate and a sale was held of the contents of his studio, when many of his moulds and models were bought by the **Manzoni** firm, who issued numerous reproductions. His widow and her infant children, Charles and Mary, received annual grants from the Artists' Annuity Fund from 1840. The provident Turnerelli had clearly been an active member of the Society, paying a subscription of 10 guineas or more in 1837.

The *Gentleman's Magazine*, in its obituary, noted that Turnerelli was a 'charming singer, with a voice of singular quality and sweetness' (*GM* 1839, 548). This talent was also noted by Farington, who heard Turnerelli and some musical friends singing 'catches and glees' with 'professional excellence' at a party in January 1807 (*Farington* 8, 2951–2). The obituary also opined that the list of eminent and distinguished people that Turnerelli had portrayed would 'long preserve his name and memory from oblivion' (*GM* 1839, 548). Whilst this has proved true, assessments of Turnerelli's abilities have differed: John Gilmartin has praised him as a great Irish sculptor, in the forefront of the neoclassical revival. Friedman dismissed his busts of the Royal family as shallow, immobile and artificial and compared his work unfavourably with that of his contemporaries Nollekens and **Sir Francis Chantrey**. What is not in dispute, however, is Turnerelli's contemporary fame, his extensive array of national and international clients, and his status as the favoured sculptor of the British monarchy in the early-19th century.

MGS

Literary References: *Farington, passim*; *Euro Mag* 1821, vol 79, 387–393; *GM* 1839, Part I, 548; *DNB*; *Graves* VIII, 1905–6, 43–5; *Strickland* 2, 1913, 466–470; *Wellesley* 1935, 48; *Hutchison* 1960–2, 155; *Gilmartin* 1967, 1–19; *Friedman* 1974 (1), 12–18; *Potterton* 1975, 84–85; *Bricknell* 1995, 95; *Grove* 31, 477 (Turpin)

Archival References: RA Council Minutes, vol 5, fol 42; PRO, LC 9/367; AAF, Proposals, p 1; AAF, MGM 23666/2

Portraits of the Sculptor: James Thomson, after Samuel Drummond, stipple engraving, published 1821, *Euro Mag*, 387 (*Gilmartin* 1967, 2 repr); NGI, 11278 (repr *le Harivel* 1988, 551)

Funerary Monuments

1.	†1808	Lieutenant-Colonel John Stuart Model(s): part of monument exhib RA, London, 1810, 844	Canterbury Cathedral, Kent	S	*Euro Mag* 1821, vol 79, 391; *Graves* VII, 1905–6, 43; *Gunnis* 1968, 403
2.	†1813	Sarah Parkinson	Asgarby, Lincs		Pevsner, *Lincs*, 1989, 104
3.	?1814	Pearson Walsh	King's Chapel, Gibraltar		GPC
4.	†1815	Bishop Moylan	Shandon RC church, Cork	S	*Euro Mag* 1821, vol 79, 391; *Potterton* 1975, 84; C Lib (repr)
5.	†1815	John Willett Willett	Canford Magna, Dorset	S	*Euro Mag* 1821, vol 79, 391; Pevsner, *Dorset*, 1972, 126
6.	†1816	James Edwards	St Mary, Harrow-on-the-Hill, Middx		Pevsner, *London: N W*, 1991, 262; C Lib (repr)
7.	†1816	Sophia Parry	Redland Chapel, Bristol		*Gunnis* 1968, 403; C Lib (repr)
8.	1817	Father Thomas Betagh (†1811)	SS Michael and John, Arran Quay, Dublin	S	*Gilmartin* 1967, 14, 15 (repr); *Potterton* 1975, 85; *Harbison, Potterton and Sheehy* 1978, 178–9 (repr)
9.	1819	John and Patrick Stirling (both †1816)	Dunblane Cathedral, Perth	S	*Gunnis* 1968, 403; C Lib (repr)
10.	*c*1820	Samuel Moorat	['lately sent to the West Indies']; untraced		*Euro Mag* 1821, vol 79, 391
11.	*c*1822	Rear-Admiral Sir George Hope (†1818)	Westminster Abbey, London, north west tower		*Euro Mag* 1821, vol 79, 391; WAM; (8) *MacMichael* 1977, 22
12.	†1825	John (†1803), Anna Maria and John Warburton (†1801) Aldridge	Nuthurst, Sussex	S	
13.	?1825	Rev Robert Montgomery	Beaulieu, Co Louth		GPC
14.	†1826	Rev Charles Jervis	St Mary, Cheltenham, Glos		*CIIA* 4/4/11 (repr)
15.	†1831	Frances, Viscountess Nelson	Littleham, Devon		*Gunnis* 1968, 403; Pevsner, *Devon*, 1989, 538
16.	?1832	Mary Ackroyd	Erith, Kent		GPC
17.	?1833	T Roper	St Mary, The Boltons, London		*Gunnis* 1986, 403
18.	†1836	Thomas Pensick	St Nicholas, Liverpool, Lancs	S	Pevsner, *Lancs: S*, 1969, 154

No.	Date	Subject	Medium	Location	Signed	Sources
19.	nd	Officers and privates of the Royal York Rangers who fell at Guadaloupe under Sir George Beckwith		Untraced		*Euro Mag* 1821, vol 79, 391
Statues						
20.	1802	A nest of cupids		[Exhib RA, London, 958]; untraced		*Graves* VIII, 1905–6, 43
21.	1811	'Caro, a favourite Venetian greyhound for the Countess of Breadalbane'		[Exhib RA, London, 955]; untraced		*Graves* VIII, 1905–6, 44; *Gunnis* 1968, 403
22.	1812	Apollo, model		['for a country gentleman']; untraced		*Farington* XI, 4113
23.	1813	King George III, equestrian statuette, model	p	SJSM M873		SJSM Inventory; *Gilmartin* 1967, 5, 17 (repr); *Dorey* 2004, 62
24.	1813–1815	King George III	m	King's College, London	SD	*Euro Mag* 1821, vol 79, 389; *Graves* VIII, 1905–6, 44; *Strickland* 2, 1913, 467; *British Portraits* 1956–7, 105; C Lib (repr)
25.	1816	Robert Burns Payment(s): £10,000		National Monument, Dumfries		*Euro Mag* 1821, vol 79, 391; *Graves* VIII, 1905–6, 44; *Gilmartin* 1967, 9, 10 (repr); *Gunnis* 1968, 403
26.	1819	St Peter and St Paul, two		Roman Catholic chapel, Bath		*Gunnis* 1968, 403
27.	1830	Henry Grattan, statuette		[Exhib RHA]; untraced		*Strickland* 2, 1913, 467
Busts						
28.	1801	Lord Hood		Coll Lord Bridport		*Gunnis* 1968, 403
29.	1802	Charlotte, Princess of Wales	p	Royal Coll		*Graves* VIII, 1905–6, 43; *Gilmartin* 1967, 7, 8, 17 (repr); *Gunnis* 1968, 403; *Friedman* 1974, 18
30.	1802	Rev Arthur O'Leary		[Exhib RA, London, 1056]; untraced		*Graves* VIII, 1905–6, 43
31.	1804	Admiral Gell		[Exhib RA, London, 848]; untraced		*Graves* VIII, 1905–6, 43
32.	1804	Jeremy Bentham	b	[coll Samuel and Anne Romilly]; untraced Other versions: BM 1897, 4–15, 1 Parkes family coll		*Graves* VIII, 1905–6, 43; *Dawson* 1999, 40–2 (version repr)
33.	1805	Admiral Lord Nelson	p	Lewes Town Hall, Sussex		*Gunnis* 1968, 403
34.	1805	Charles Townley		[Exhib RA, London, 724]; untraced		*Graves* VIII, 1905–6, 43
35.	1805	Mr C Dignum		[Exhib RA, London, 812]; untraced		*Graves* VIII, 1905–6, 43
36.	1806	Arthur Murphy		[Exhib RA, London, 852]; untraced		*Graves* VIII, 1905–6, 43; *Strickland* 2, 1913, 470
37.	1807	Henry, 1st Viscount Melville		Albury, Surrey		*Euro Mag* 79, 1821, 388; *Graves* VIII, 1905–6, 44; *Strickland* 2, 1913, 470; *Gilmartin* 1967, 17; GPC
38.	1807	Unidentified man	m	Syon House, Middx	D	C Lib (repr)
39.	1807	William Pitt (†1806)		[Goodwood House, Sussex]; untraced Other versions: Albury, Surrey Syon House, Middx, marble, 1807		*Graves* VIII, 1905–6, 43; GPC; C Lib (repr)
40.	1808	Mr J Watts		[Exhib RA, London, 865]; untraced		*Euro Mag* 1821, vol 79, 391; *Graves* VIII, 1905–6, 43
41.	1808	Mr Oakley	m	[Exhib RA, London, 883]; untraced		*Graves* VIII, 1905–6, 43
42.	1808	Sir Thomas and Lady Proctor		[Langley Park, Norfolk]; untraced		*Gunnis* 1968, 403
43.	1809	Colonel Burr, 'late Vice-President of America'		[Exhib RA, London, 788]; untraced		*Graves* VIII, 1905–6, 43; *Gunnis* 1968, 403
44.	1809	Colonel Gwyllym Lloyd Wardle		Untraced		*Strickland* 2, 1913, 470
45.	1809	Ernest August, Duke of Cumberland	m	Trinity College, Dublin, Long Room		*Graves* VIII, 1905–6, 43; *Gilmartin* 1967, 18; *Crookshank* 1986, 24; C Lib (repr)
46.	1809	George III, jubilee bust Model(s): exhib RA, London, 1810, 883; small model for the national bust of George III exhib RA, London, 1812, 908; RA, London, 1818, 1093	m	NPG, London 3903 Other versions: VAM A.62-1965, marble, S Windsor Castle, £63 paid in Jan 1811 Bank of England, 1812 Bank of Ireland Royal coll RCIN 11910, SD 1812 Penicuik House, near Edinburgh, marble, SD 1813 Goodwood, Sussex, marble Apsley House, London, marble, SD 1814 coll Lord Normanton	SD	*Euro Mag* 1821, vol 79, 388; *Graves* VIII, 1905–6, 44; *Strickland* 2, 1913, 467, 470; *Gilmartin* 1967, 17; *Gunnis* 1968, 402; *Friedman* 1974 (1), 12, 14, 18 (repr); *Bilbey* 2002, 423 (repr)
47.	1809	Mr Fitzsimmons		[Exhib RA, London, 790]; untraced		*Graves* VIII, 1905–6, 43
48.	1809	Mrs Seabright		[Exhib RA, London, 877]; untraced		*Graves* VIII, 1905–6, 43
49.	1812	Arthur, 1st Duke of Wellington	p	Sotheby, 2 April 1985	SD	C Lib (repr)
50.	1812	Bishop Douglass		RC Chapel, Ware, Herts		*Gunnis* 1968, 403
51.	1812	Henry Grattan	m	NGI 8107 Other versions: plaster, without shoulders, SD 1812, NPG 1341 Bank of Ireland, marble, 1813 Wardour Castle, marble, S, 1820 exhib RA, London, marble, 1821 Royal Dublin Society, Ball's Bridge, plaster	S	*Euro Mag* 1821, vol 79, 389; *Graves* VIII, 1905–6, 44; *Gilmartin* 1967, 6, 7, 17 (repr); *Barrett* 1971, 94 (repr 30); *le Harivel* 1988, 600 (repr); *Morris and Roberts* 1998, 604
52.	1812	Hon Henry Erskine	m	Parliament House, Edinburgh		*Euro Mag* 1821, vol 79, 390; *Graves* VIII, 1905–6, 44; C Lib (repr)

53.	1812	King George III, with laurel wreath	m	BL Other versions: Newark Town Hall Royal coll RCIN 31167, 1955, SD 1813 VAM A.11-1937, marble, S Trinity College, Dublin, Long Room, SD 1813	SD	*Crookshank* 1986, 24; *Bilbey* 2002, 422 (repr)
54.	1812	King William III		Bank of England, City of London		*Graves* VIII, 1905–6, 44; *Gunnis* 1968, 403
55.	1812	Lord President Blair, of Scotland		[Exhib RA, London, 890]; untraced		*Euro Mag* 1821, vol 79, 390; *Graves* VIII, 1905–6, 44
56.	1813	Dr Elrington, Provost of Trinity College, Dublin		[Exhib RA, London, 940]; untraced		*Euro Mag* 1821, vol 79, 390; *Graves* VIII, 1905–6, 44; *Gilmartin* 1967, 7
57.	1813	Rev J Archer		[Exhib RA, London, 900]; untraced		*Graves* VIII, 1905–6, 44
58.	1813	Rev W V Fryer, chaplain to the Portuguese Embassy		[Exhib RA, London, 938]; untraced		*Graves* VIII, 1905–6, 44
59.	1814	Arthur, 1st Duke of Wellington		Original unknown Other versions: Royal Coll, Walmer Castle, marble, SD, 1814 Hasfield Court, Glos, SD, 1814 Guildhall, London, marble, 1814 Blair Castle, Perthshire, marble, SD 1815 BL (ex Foreign and Commonwealth Office, London), 1815 Bank of Ireland Ombersley Court, Worcs, 1816 NGI, marble, SD, 1816 Ordered for Carlton House in 1816 with busts of Blücher and Platov for £472 10s (PRO, LC 9/367) Goodwood, Sussex, SD 1817 Victoria Memorial Hall, Calcutta Castle Coole, Ireland		*Graves* VIII, 1905–6, 44; *Strickland* 2, 1913, 470; *Wellesley* 1935, 48; *Gilmartin* 1967, 17; *Gunnis* 1968, 402–3; *Archer* 1986, 104–5; *Friedman* 1974 (1), 12; *Knight* 1986, 348 (repr); *Carlton House* 1991–2, 31, 50, 54; *le Harivel* 1988, 601 (repr); *Morris and Roberts* 1998, 604
60.	1814	Mr R Elsam		[Exhib RA, London, 766]; untraced		*Graves* VIII, 1905–6, 44
61.	1814	Sir Joseph Banks Payment(s): £105		RCS, London Other versions: NMM, Greenwich, London SCU0006		*Graves* VIII, 1905–6, 44; *Strickland* 2, 1913, 469; *Gunnis* 1968, 403; *Morris and Roberts* 1998, 604
62.	1815	Brownlow North, Bishop of Winchester		Abbey House, Winchester, Hants		*Euro Mag* 1821, vol 79, 389; *Graves* VIII, 1905–6, 44; GPC
63.	1815	Count Matvei Ivanovich Platov	m	Windsor Castle, RCIN 35416 Other versions: Blair Castle, Perthshire, marble, SD 1816 (£150 with the busts of Wellington and Blücher) Ordered for Carlton House in 1816 with busts of Blücher and Wellington for £472 10s (PRO, LC 9/367) Hermitage, St Petersburg, 1816 The Tuileries, Paris For the King of Portugal; untraced	SD	*Graves* VIII, 1905–6, 44; *Strickland* 2, 1913, 470; *Gilmartin* 1967, 5, 18; *Carlton House* 1991–2, 31, 50, 54; C Lib (repr)
64.	1815	Field-Marshal Gebhard Lebrecht von Blücher Payment(s): £157 10s Model(s): SJSM M119, plaster	m	Windsor Castle, RCIN 35402 Other versions: replica ordered 1814 by Emperor Alexander of Russia replica ordered by the King of Prussia Blair Castle, Perthshire, SD 1816 (£150 with the busts of Wellington and Platov) Ordered for Carlton House in 1816 with busts of Platov and Wellington for £472 10s (PRO, LC 9/367) NGI, marble	SD	*Euro Mag* 79, 1821, 389; *DNB*; *Graves* VIII, 1905–6, 44; *Strickland* 2, 1913, 466–470; *Gilmartin* 1967, 5; *le Harivel* 1988, 601 (repr); *Thornton and Dorey* 1992, 52 (plaster repr)
65.	1815	John Philpott Curran	p	RDS, Dublin		*Euro Mag* 1821, vol 79, 391; *Strickland* 2, 1913, 469; *Gilmartin* 1967, 7; *White and Bright* 1998, 87–8
66.	1816	Charles Kendal Bushe (1767–1843)	p	NGI 8188	SD	*le Harivel* 1988, 600 (repr)
67.	1816	Charlotte Augusta, Princess of Wales	m	NPG, London, 4470 Other versions: Royal coll RCIN 31319, SD 1817 ex Forbes Gall, 60 Fifth Avenue, NY, marble, SD 1817	SD	*Euro Mag* 1821, vol 79, 389; *Farington* XV, 5306; *Graves* VIII, 1905–6, 44; *Gilmartin* 1967, 18; *Gunnis* 1968, 403; *Friedman* 1974 (1), 18
68.	1816	Duke of Atholl		Blair Castle, Perths		GPC
69.	1816	John Thomas Troy, Archbishop of Dublin (1739–1823)		[Exhib RA, London, 965]; untraced Other versions: NGI 8199, plaster, SD 1816		*Euro Mag* 1821, vol 79, 391; *Graves* VIII, 1905–6, 44; *Potterton* 1975, 84; *le Harivel* 1988, 601 (repr)
70.	1816	King Louis XVIII		[Exhib RA, London, 959]; untraced		*Farington* XIV, 4841; *Graves* VIII, 1905–6, 44; *Gunnis* 1968, 402
71.	1816	Unidentified man	p	NGI 8078		*Wynne and White* 1975, 47
72.	1817	George Frederick Brooke of Somerton		Coll John Gilmartin, Dublin		*Gilmartin* 1967, 18

73.	1817	Prince Leopold, later King of the Belgians	m	Royal Coll RCIN 37141	SD	*Graves* VIII, 1905–6, 44; *Gilmartin* 1967, 7; *Friedman* 1974 (1), 18; C Lib (repr)
74.	1818	King George III		Royal College of Maynooth, Ireland		*Graves* VIII, 1905–6, 44; *Gilmartin* 1967, 18; *Gunnis* 1986, 403
75.	1818	Queen Charlotte	m	LMG, W R Yorks inv 33/71 Other versions: Blair Castle, Perthshire, plaster cast, publ 21 Dec 1818 Col and Mrs Rupert Alec-Smith, Winestead Hall, marble, SD 1818	SD	*Euro Mag* 1821, vol 79, 388; *Friedman* 1974 (1), 12–18 (repr); *Leeds* 1996, 6 (repr); GPC
76.	1819	Bishop Bathurst of Norwich		[Exhib RA, London, 1206]; untraced		*Euro Mag* 1821, vol 79, 390; *Graves* VIII, 1905–6, 44
77.	1820	Bishop of Jerusalem		[Exhib RA, London, 1040]; untraced		*Graves* VIII, 1905–6, 44
78.	1820	Edward, Duke of Kent and Strathearn		Royal Coll Other versions: SNPG, marble, signed		*Graves* VIII, 1905–6, 44; *Gilmartin* 1967, 18; *Gunnis* 1968, 403; *Friedman* 1974 (1), 14, 15, 18 (repr
79.	1820	Lord and Lady Audley		[Exhib RA, London, 1031 and 1036]; untraced		*Graves* VIII, 1905–6, 44; *Gunnis* 1968, 403
80.	1820	Unidentified man	m	Mawley Hall, Salop	SD	C Lib (repr)
81.	1821	Duchess of Kent		Untraced		*Euro Mag* 1821, vol 79, 390
82.	1821	Lady Caroline Lamb		[Exhib RA, London, 1113]; untraced		*Graves* VIII, 1905–6, 44; *Gunnis* 1968, 403
83.	1821	Mr J Logier		[Exhib RA, London, 1137]; untraced		*Graves* VIII, 1905–6, 44
84.	pre-1821	Prince of Saxe-Coburg		Untraced		*Euro Mag* 1821, vol 79, 389
85.	1821	Princess (later Queen) Victoria, aged 2 years		[Exhib RA, 1823, London, 1072]; untraced		*Euro Mag* 1821, vol 79, 390 (repr); *Graves* VIII, 1905–6, 44; *Ormond* 1973, 479
86.	1821	Rev G Edwards		Coll Sir Carne Rasch, Bt		GPC
87.	1821	Unidentified female with pearls in her hair	m	Private coll	SD	C Lib (repr)
88.	1821	Unidentified man Model(s): plaster, NGI, S 'P. Turnerelli fecit/16 Jan. 1816' (*le Harivel* 1988, 600, repr)	m	YCBA B 1977.14.32	SD	*Waterhouse* 1977, 352
89.	1823	H S Johnston		[Exhib RA, London, 1075]; untraced		*Graves* VIII, 1905–6, 44
90.	1823	Sir R Phillips		[Exhib RA, London, 1069]; untraced		*Graves* VIII, 1905–6, 44
91.	1824	Dr Gall, craniologist		[Exhib RA, London, 989]; untraced		*Graves* VIII, 1905–6, 44
92.	1824	Rt Rev Dr Poynter, deceased		[Exhib RA, London, 998]; untraced		*Graves* VIII, 1905–6, 44
93.	1825	Alderman Waithman		[Exhib RA, London, 1004]; untraced		*Graves* VIII, 1905–6, 44
94.	1825	J Collitch		[Exhib RA, London, 1055]; untraced		*Graves* VIII, 1905–6, 44
95.	1825	William Jerdan		[Exhib RA, London, 1038]; untraced		*Graves* VIII, 1905–6, 44; *Ormond* 1973, 342
96.	1826	Countess of Newburgh	m	[Exhib RA, London, 1078]; untraced		*Graves* VIII, 1905–6, 44
97.	1826	Thomas Bellamy		[Exhib RA, London, 1023]; untraced		*Graves* VIII, 1905–6, 44
98.	1827	Catherine, Countess of Essex (Miss Stephens)	m	[Exhib RA, London, 1084]; untraced		*Graves* VIII, 1905–6, 44; *Ormond* 1973, 163
99.	1828	Daniel O'Connell		[Exhib RA, London, 1153]; untraced		*Euro Mag*, 1821, 1, 387; *DNB*; *Graves* VIII, 1905–6, 44; *Strickland* 2, 1913, 467, 470; *Potterton* 1975, 84
100.	1828	Henry, 1st Marquess of Anglesey	m	Royal Coll RCIN 20748	SD	*Graves* VIII, 1905–6, 44; *Gilmartin* 1967, 18; *Gunnis* 1968, 403; C Lib (repr)
101.	1828	James Doyle, Bishop of Kildare		[Exhib RA, London, 1155]; Cathedral sacristy, Carlow		*Graves* VIII, 1905–6, 44; *Strickland* 2, 1913, 469; *Gilmartin* 1967, 7, 18
102.	1828	Sir George Farrant		[Exhib RA, London, 1204]; untraced		*Graves* VIII, 1905–6, 44
103.	1829	Donna Maria II, Queen of Portugal	m	[Exhib RA, London, 1205]; untraced		*Graves* VIII, 1905–6, 44; *Gunnis* 1968, 403
104.	1829	John, Earl of Ossory, afterwards 2nd Marquess of Ormonde	m	[Exhib RA, London, 1166]; Christie, 6 July 1993, lot 90	SD	*Graves* VIII, 1905–6, 44; *Strickland* 2, 1913, 470
105.	1830	Charles Kendal Bushe, Lord Chief Justice of Ireland		[Exhib RA, London, 1182]; untraced		*Graves* VIII, 1905–6, 45
106.	1831	Princess Adelaide Carolath, Queen Victoria's god-daughter		[Exhib RA, London, 1129]; untraced		*Graves* VIII, 1905–6, 45
107.	1831	Princess Lucy Carolath		[Exhib RA, London, 1155]; untraced		*Graves* VIII, 1905–6, 45
108.	1831	Sydney, Lady Morgan		[Exhib RA, London, 1147]; untraced		*Graves* VIII, 1905–6, 45; *Ormond* 1973, 325
109.	1832	Admiral George Parker	m	Gawsworth Hall, Cheshire	SD	*Graves* VIII, 1905–6, 45; *Gawsworth Guide*, 44; C Lib (repr)
110.	1832	Fanny Kemble		[Exhib RA, London, 1223]; untraced		*Graves* VIII, 1905–6, 45
111.	1832	Hon Mrs Edward Pellew		[Exhib RA, London, 1127]; untraced		*Graves* VIII, 1905–6, 45
112.	1832	Mrs George Parker	m	[Gawsworth Hall, Cheshire]; Knox/Longstaffe-Gowan coll	SD	*Graves* VIII, 1905–6, 45; *Gawsworth Guide*, 44; C Lib (repr)
113.	1832	Viscount Nevill		[Exhib RA, London, 1228]; untraced		*Graves* VIII, 1905–6, 45
114.	1833	Rt Rev Dr Bramston		[Exhib RA, London, 1220]; untraced		*Graves* VIII, 1905–6, 45
115.	1833	Sir Henry Halford Bt Payment(s): £84	m	Wistow, Leics	SD	*Graves* VIII, 1905–6, 45; C Lib (repr)
116.	1834	Henry Phillpotts, Bishop of Exeter		[Exhib RA, London, 1050]; untraced		*Graves* VIII, 1905–6, 45
117.	1834	Lord Stafford		[Exhib RA, London, 1111]; untraced		*Graves* VIII, 1905–6, 45

118.	1835	N A Vigors		[Exhib RA, London, 1070]; untraced	*Graves* VIII, 1905–6, 45
119.	1835	Thomas Attwood MP		[Exhib RA, London, 1002]; untraced	*Graves* VIII, 1905–6, 45
120.	1835	Viscount Frankfort de Montmorency		[Exhib RA, London, 1124]; untraced	*Graves* VIII, 1905–6, 45; *Gunnis* 1968, 403
121.	1836	H Woodthorpe, town clerk to the City of London	tc	[Exhib RA, London, 1078]; untraced	*Graves* VIII, 1905–6, 45
122.	1837	Chevalier Buckhausen, consul-general of Russia		[Exhib RA, London, 1224]; untraced	*Graves* VIII, 1905–6, 45
123.	1838	Constantine, Earl of Mulgrave, afterwards 1st Marquess of Normanby		[Exhib RA, London, 1363]; untraced	*Graves* VIII, 1905–6, 45; *Strickland* 2, 1913, 470; *Ormond* 1973, 344
124.	1838	Mr Hicks, surgeon		[Exhib RA, London, 1338]; untraced	*Graves* VIII, 1905–6, 45
125.	1838	Rt Hon William Saurin		[Exhib RA, London, 1339]; untraced	*Graves* VIII, 1905–6, 45; *Strickland* 2, 1913, 470
126.	nd	Arthur, 1st Duke of Wellington, *all'antica*	m	Gov Art coll 3312 Other versions: Christie, London 10 May 1990, plaster, S Sotheby 10 Dec 2002, marble	Sotheby Cat 10 Dec 2002 (repr)
127.	nd	Earl of Fingal		Untraced	*Strickland* 2, 1913, 469
128.	nd	General Eliot		[coll 2nd Lord Heathfield]; untraced Other versions: for George, Prince of Wales, 1805	Windsor Castle Accts 26703; *Euro Mag* 1821, vol 79, 388; *Strickland* 2, 1913, 467; *Friedman* 1974 (1), 18
129.	nd	George, Lord Heathfield		[coll 2nd Lord Heathfield]; untraced Other versions: Colnaghi (1993), signed 'P Tognarelli', plaster	*Gunnis* 1968, 402; C Lib (repr)
130.	nd	Hon Thomas Erskine		Ferens Art Gall, Hull, E R Yorks	GPC
131.	nd	Lady Melville		Untraced	*Euro Mag* 1821, vol 79, 388
132.	nd	Lord Aberdeen		Untraced	*DNB*
133.	nd	Lord Whitworth	p	Knole, Kent	GPC
134.	nd	Rev Barnaby Murphy		Untraced	*Strickland* 2, 1913, 470
135.	nd	Sir Francis Drake		[coll 2nd Lord Heathfield]; untraced	*Strickland* 2, 1913, 467; *Gunnis* 1968, 402
136.	nd	Sir Henry Holland Bt	m	(coll K Freemantle, Wistow)	*Ormond* 1973, 229
137.	nd	Unidentified male sitter		Mussenden temple, County Londonderry	*Gilmartin* 1967, 18

Architectural Sculpture

138.	1806	An Egyptian candelabrum		[Exhib RA, London, 837]; untraced	*Graves* VIII, 1905–6, 43
139.	1808	Figures of Comedy and Tragedy, for candelabra		[Exhib RA, London, 860, 893]; untraced	*Graves* VIII, 1905–6, 43
140.	1828–30	High altar, with bas-relief of two angels in prayer, either side of a monstrance	m	St Mary's Pro-Cathedral, Marlborough Street, Dublin	*Gilmartin* 1967, 11 (repr); *Gunnis* 1968, 402; *Potterton* 1975, 84

Miscellaneous

141.	1799	Academy figure, model		[RA silver medal]; untraced	RA Premium list; *Farington*, IV, 1312, 1322
142.	1805	An Egyptian Goddess		[Exhib RA, London, 782]; untraced	*Graves* VIII, 1905–6, 43
143.	1809	Figure of Vesta for a candelabrum		[Exhib RA, London, 777]; untraced	*Graves* VIII, 1905–6, 43
144.	1810	A Madonna		[Exhib RA, London, 769]; untraced	*Graves* VIII, 1905–6, 43
145.	1813	Crucifix	i	[Exhib RA, London, 933]; untraced	*Graves* VIII, 1905–6, 44
146.	1813	'Sacrifice, being part of a work to be executed for Spetchley Hall, near Worcester, the seat of R. Berkley, Esq.'		[Exhib RA, London, 902]; untraced	*Graves* VIII, 1905–6, 44; *Gunnis* 1968, 403

TUSSAUD, Francis Babington 1829–58

Busts

1.	1855	Charles John Kean		[Exhib RA, London, 1471]; untraced	*Ormond* 1973, 247

TUSSAUD, Marie 1761–1850

For further information the reader is referred to *Pyke* 1973, 151 and *Pyke* 1981, 40

TYLER, William RA c1728–1801

Tyler was an accomplished monumental sculptor and architect and a founder member of the Royal Academy. From references in Joseph Farington's *Diary* his date of birth can be fixed as being between 1727 and 1729. Tyler's family background is obscure although he described himself as the 'son and grandson of a citizen [of London]' (CLRO MSS 5.18 quoted in *Roscoe* 1997 (2), 181), and it is known that his mother died, aged 88, in January 1795. His family must have been well-to-do, as Tyler was sent to Westminster School, and was subsequently placed with the leading sculptor of the day, **Louis François Roubiliac**, with whom he studied for 'many years' (*ibid*).

Tyler married when he was 22 and **Joseph Nollekens RA** later recalled that in about 1760 he 'lived in Dean Street nearly opposite Anne's Church, where his wife kept a shop and sold watch springs or something of the kind' (*Farington*, vol 4, 1316). Tyler must already have had an established business as a sculptor by this time for in the early 1760s he applied for two of the most lucrative commissions of the day. In 1760, in competition with his former master, he submitted a design for the monument in Westminster Abbey to General Wolfe (5) and in January 1762 he offered himself as a candidate for the statue of George III in the Royal Exchange. In both cases the commission went to **Joseph Wilton RA**.

Tyler played a role in all the fledgling art institutions of the capital. In 1760 he was one of the sculptors involved in the programme of arts connected with the Foundling Hospital, and he exhibited at the Society of Artists exhibitions from their inception in 1760. In 1765 he became one of the Society's directors, and in December 1768 he was one of the 40 artists whose names appear on the 'Instrument of Foundation' of the Royal Academy. The only other sculptors to achieve the latter distinction were Wilton and **Agostino Carlini**.

From 1763 to 1784 Tyler had premises in Vine Street, Piccadilly. His earliest known work is a very competent multi figured relief of *Diogenes*, carved in several gradations (**72**). He appears to have specialised in monuments of a modes size, sometimes working in collaboration with the architects Robert Adam (**10**) and Henry Keene (**27, 41**). Working to Keene's design he carved the remarkable rococo monument to the 3rd Earl of Lichfield which has two urns in recessed oval niche, set in a convex frame of yellow marble and surmounted by a white marble oak tree (**27**). Severa of his earliest known monuments have expressive portrait busts in the manner of Roubiliac, for instance the memorials to Joseph Smith, Samuel Vassall and Thomas Jones (**2, 12, 18**). His use of multi-coloured marbles and livel *putti* suggests he was also influenced by **Sir Henry Cheere** and **Sir Robert Taylor**. Elements in Tyler's composition were sometimes repeated: cherubs decorating an urn with garlands appear on the monuments to the 4th Earl o Lichfield and the 2nd Viscount Ashbrook (**41, 50**) and were later used by Nollekens. The detailing and finish of Tyler' monuments is always of a very high standard.

He also sent out chimneypieces, including one to a design by Sir William Chambers for Milton Hall, 1772 (**67**). A this time Tyler's business must have been in difficulties, for Chambers wrote to Lord Fitzwilliam enclosing Tyler's bi and adding 'If it is convenient to your Lordship, Mr. Tyler will, I believe, be very thankful for the money as he tol me in confidence he was as poor as could be' (Chambers's Letter-Books, BL Add MS 41133). In another lette Chambers passed on Tyler's thanks to Lord Fitzwilliam for looking after Tyler's man, who had fallen sick whe working at Milton (*ibid*). In about 1773 Tyler embarked on a tour of Derbyshire and Yorkshire with the painte Francis Cotes and the author Theodosius Forrest. An anonymous account of the tour records that Tyler used the tri to find business, securing a commission for a chimneypiece from Lady Rockingham at Wentworth Woodhouse (**68**)

Some time after 1779 he appears to have gone into partnership with his former pupil, **Robert Ashton I**, with whon he signed several monuments (**47, 48, 56, 57**). Their greatest achievement together is the monument to Dr Marti Folkes (**56**), which has a full-size seated statue of the dignified scholar leaning on his publications.

In the 1780s Tyler practised increasingly as an architect, designing the Villa Maria at Kensington for the Duches of Gloucester (now demolished), and making alterations to a house in Hampton Court for the Duke, for whom h also acted as an 'agent' (*Farington*, vol 3, 796, 14 March 1797). He worked on two gaols, Maidstone and Dorchester and designed the town hall in Bridport. Colvin believed his finest work as an architect was the Ordnance Office i Westminster, 1779–80, which was demolished in 1805. Tyler may also have worked on a project in Derby, where h travelled with Sir John Soane in 1796. Nollekens told Joseph Farington that Tyler was appointed mason or bricklaye to the Board of Ordnance by Lord Amherst (*Farington* vol 4, 1316), for whose family Tyler also produced two churc monuments (**51, 58**).

Tyler was a prominent member of the Royal Academy in the 1790s, despite suffering from fevers, rheumatism an diabetes. He played a role in the attempted removal of Sir Joshua Reynolds as president in 1790 and contributed man reminiscences to Farington's projected history of the progress of the arts in England. In 1796 he and his friend Georg Dance (whose portrait of Tyler hangs in Burlington House) became the Academy's first auditors. They put the financia affairs of the Academy onto a more professional footing and several of their reforms are still in force. In 1799 Tyle was presented with a silver cup for his efforts. He wrote a short account of his own life for the first volume of Dance' *Portraits of Academicians* in 1798.

Tyler died in his house in Caroline Street, Bedford Square, on 6 September, 1801. In his will he requested to be burie in the family vault in the churchyard of Tottenham High Cross. He left £1,000 in shares to pay for the apprenticeshi of his son William Jackson, who was then ten years old and lived with his mother Mary Jackson at Overton, nea Ellesmere, Salop. Despite early finahcial difficulties, Tyler's practice in sculpture and architecture had ultimately bee profitable: he left property in Upper Seymour Street, Portman Square, Gower Street and Bedford Square, and a sun of £2,450 in named and numbered gifts, including £100 to **Robert Ashton II**. He also left provision for his sister, Mary On seeing the press report of the death of his 'worthy friend,' Farington, wrote a brief tribute in his diary to a 'cheerful and 'good-humoured' man whose 'convivial and social turn of mind' had done much to bring harmony to an ofte factious Royal Academy (*Farington*, vol 5, 1618).

The reactions of other contemporaries were less generous, for Tyler's artistic abilities were not felt to be equal t his status as an Academician. **Nathaniel Marchant** said he 'was no artist,' whilst King George III, in conversation wit Benjamin West after Tyler's death, was baffled as to how such 'an odd man' came to be an Academician at a (*Farington*, vol 3, 827; vol 6, 2214). The short notice of Tyler in the DNB (1885–1900) dismissed him as a sculptor o little ability, and Whinney has subsequently called him 'relatively unimportant' (*Whinney* 1988, 269). Gunnis howeve felt that Tyler's busts were 'extremely well modelled' and that his monuments had 'great charm' (*Gunnis* 1968, 404) More recently Baker has provided a new biography for the ODNB and he concludes that Tyler's monuments ar stylistically progressive and show a high quality of execution, whilst Tyler himself deserves recognition for his role i the institutions which shaped sculptural practice in the late-18th century. (Inf. Roger Smith)

MG

Literary References: *Mortimer* 1763, 28; *Farington, passim; Builder* 1859, 849; *Graves* IV, 1905–6, 50; *Graves* 1907, 262; *Gunnis* 1968, 403–4 *Hutchison* 1986, 28, 56, 245; *Whinney* 1988, *passim; Colvin* 1995, 999; *Bindman and Baker* 1995, 170, 221, 336; *ODNB* (Baker)

Archival References: Forrest's *Tours*, fols 22–56

Miscellaneous Drawings: Denison of Ossington Papers, Notts Univ library, MSS and Special Colls, De 2 P/14–16, proposed designs for the monument to William Denison with an estimate of £412 (unexecuted)

Will: PROB 11/1363/619, 19 September 1801

Portraits of the sculptor: Johan Zoffany *Life Class at the Royal Academy* 1771–2, oil on canvas (Royal Coll); George Dance, Royal Academy Library

Funerary Monuments

1.	†1725	Colonel John Davis, President of the Council of the Island of St Christopher	Westminster Abbey, London, nave		WAM; *MacMichael* 1977, 24
2.	†1756	Joseph Smith	The Queen's College, Oxford	S	*Gunnis* 1968, 404
3.	†1759	Elizabeth Wake	Thurning, Norfolk	S	Pevsner, *Norfolk: N E & Norwich*, 1997, 696

4.	†1759	Thomas Spencer	Guisborough, N R Yorks		Pevsner, *Yorks: N R*, 1966, 179
5.	1760	Design for General Wolfe's monument	[Exhib Soc of Artists, London, 99]; untraced		*Graves* 1907, 262
6.	†1761	Bishop Francis Gastrell	Christchurch Cathedral, Oxford	S	*Gunnis* 1968, 404
7.	†1761	Thomas Crosfield	Northallerton, N R Yorks		Pevsner, *Yorks: N R*, 1966, 271
8.	?1762	Ann Wyndham	Earsham, Norfolk		*Gunnis* 1968, 404
9.	1765	Monumental medallion; a model	[Exhib Soc of Artists, London, 181]; untraced		*Graves* 1907, 262
10.	1765	Sir Wyndham Knatchbull (†1763) (designed by Robert Adam) Payment(s): £37 6s 6d	Mersham, Kent		Archives, Lord Brabourne in *Gunnis* 1968, 404; Pevsner, *Kent: W & Weald*, 1976, 425; *Colvin* 1995, 61
11.	1765	Thomas Crosfield	Northallerton, N R Yorks		*Gunnis* 1968, 404
12.	1766	Samuel Vassall	King's Chapel, Boston, USA	S	*London Mag*, 1766, 436; *Whinney* 1988, 270–1 (repr)
13.	†1766	Thomas Carew and his two wives Mary (†1738) and Mary (†1757)	Crowcombe, Somerset	S	Pevsner, *Somerset: S & W*, 1958, 142; C Lib (repr)
14.	†1766	Thomas Marriott	Finchingfield, Essex	S	Pevsner, *Essex*, 1965, 181
15.	†1767	Richard Smith	Chichester Cathedral, Sussex	S	*Gunnis* 1968, 404; C Lib (repr)
16.	†1768	John Somner	Aston Clinton, Bucks	S	AL/RG
17.	†1769	Charles Holland	St Nicholas, Chiswick		Pevsner, *London: N W*, 1991, 394
18.	1770	Rev Thomas Jones (†1762)	Southwark Cathedral, London	S	*Whinney* 1988, 271; C Lib (repr)
19.	1770	Robert Dinwiddie	Clifton, Bristol		*Gunnis* 1968, 404
20.	†1770	Sir John Cust Bt	Belton, Lincs	S	*Whinney* 1988, 271; C Lib (repr)
21.	†1771	Francis Colman (†1733), his wife Mary Gumley (†1767) and Sarah Colman	St Mary Abbots, Kensington, London	S	Pevsner, *London: N W*, 1991, 460
22.	†1771	Richard (†1735) and Anne Acland	St George, Beckenham, Kent	S	
23.	†1771	Sir Henry John Packer	Tredington, Warks	S	
24.	†1772	Anne Thomas	Bletchingley, Surrey	S	*Gunnis* 1968, 404; C Lib (repr)
25.	1772	Barton Booth (†1733)	Westminster Abbey, London, south transept	SD	Pevsner, *London: Westminster*, 1973, 443; C Lib (repr)
26.	1772	Figure of Piety, for unidentified monument	[Exhib RA, London, 260]; untraced		*Graves* VIII, 1905–6, 50
27.	†1772	George, 3rd Earl of Lichfield (designed by Henry Keene)	Spelsbury, Oxon	S	Pevsner, *Oxon*, 1974, 775; *Kemp* 1985, 12 (repr); *ODNB*
28.	†1772	Lady Clayton	Bletchingley, Surrey		Pevsner, *Surrey*, 1971, 115
29.	1772	Lady Cust	Belton, Lincs	S	RG/JP, 8, 1489
30.	†1772	Savile Cockayne Cust	St George, Stamford, Lincs		*Gunnis* 1968, 404; Pevsner, *Lincs*, 1989, 690; C Lib (repr)
31.	1773	Anne Jemima Yorke (†1770)	Marchwiel, Flint		*Whinney* 1988, 271; C Lib (repr)
32.	†1773	Lucy, Countess of Rochford	St Osyth, Essex	S	Pevsner, *Essex*, 1965, 342
33.	?1775	Bishop Smyth	Lincoln Cathedral		*Gunnis* 1968, 404
34.	1775	Humility and Modesty for an unspecified monument, model	[Exhib RA, London, 315]; untraced		*Graves* VIII, 1905–6, 50
35.	1775	John Harris (†1768)	Georgeham, Devon	SD	Pevsner, *Devon*, 1989, 455; C Lib (repr)
36.	†1775	Major-General Stringer Lawrence	Dunchideock, Devon	S	Pevsner, *Devon*, 1989, 342; C Lib (repr)
37.	†1775	Major-General Stringer Lawrence Payment(s): £705 5s	Westminster Abbey, London, nave	S	E I Co, Ct Minutes, 2 Oct 1776, 9 April 1777, 236, 688; *Whinney* 1988, 271
38.	?1775	Richard Astell	Everton, Beds		*Gunnis* 1968, 404
39.	1775	Sir Richard Hoare (repairs only; monument by Thomas Stayner) Payment(s): £7 12s 6d	St Dunstan-in-the-West, City of London		Hoare Private Accts, 1752–1778, 2 Feb 1775; *Gunnis* 1968, 404
40.	†1775	William Pym	Sandy, Beds	S	*Gunnis* 1968, 404; C Lib (repr)
41.	†1776	Robert, 4th Earl of Lichfield (designed by Henry Keane)	Spelsbury, Oxon	S	*Gunnis* 1968, 404; C Lib (repr)
42.	1777	Commodore John Watson (†1774) Payment(s): £110 6s 6d	Mumbai (Bombay) Cathedral, India	S	E I Co, Cash Journal, 1777, 10 March 1777; C Lib (repr)
43.	*c*1777	Dr Zachary Pearce, Bishop of Rochester (†1774) Model(s): bust exhib RA 1777, 351	Westminster Abbey, London, nave	S	*Whinney* 1988, 271, 461 n43; C Lib (repr)
44.	†1777	Sarah Boteler	Eastry, Kent	S	Pevsner, *Kent: N E & E*, 1983, 308
45.	†1777	Thomas Lewis	Old Radnor, Radnorshire	S	*Gunnis* 1968, 404
46.	?1778	Charles and Mary Long	Saxmundham, Suffolk		*Gunnis* 1968, 404
47.	†1778	William Pym (co-sculptor: Robert Ashton I)	Sandy, Beds	S	*Gunnis* 1968, 404; C Lib (repr)
48.	†1779	Elizabeth Yorke (co-sculptor: Robert Ashton I)	Marchwiel, Flint	S	*Gunnis* 1968, 404
49.	1780	Faith and Hope, design for an unidentified monument	[Exhib RA, London, 469]; untraced		*Graves* VIII, 1905–6, 50
50.	†1780	William, 2nd Viscount Ashbrook	Shillingford, Berks	S	Pevsner, *Berkshire*, 1966, 215; *Whinney* 1988, 271; C Lib (repr)

51.	1781	Admiral John Amherst and Lieutenant-General William Amherst		Sevenoaks, Kent	S	Pevsner, *Kent: W & Weald*, 1976, 511; C Lib (repr)
52.	1781	Religion, medallion for an unidentified monument		[Exhib RA, London, 50]; untraced		*Graves* VIII, 1905–6, 50
53.	†1784	George Perrot (†1780) and his wife		Laleham, Surrey		Pevsner, *Surrey*, 1971, 338
54.	post-1784	Rear-Admiral John Storr (†1783)		Westminster Abbey, London, Chapel of St John the Evangelist		*MacMichael* 1977, 50
55.	†1785	Beeston Long		Saxmundham, Suffolk	S	Pevsner, *Suffolk*, 1974, 412
56.	1790	Dr Martin Folkes (†1754) (co-sculptor: Robert Ashton I)		Westminster Abbey, London, nave	S	*Whinney* 1988, 271 (repr)
57.	?1790	William Franks (co-sculptor: Robert Ashton I)		Kentish Town parish church, London	S	*Gunnis* 1968, 404
58.	†1797	Field Marshal Jeffrey, Lord Amherst		Sevenoaks, Kent	S	Pevsner, *Kent: W & Weald*, 1976, 511; C Lib (repr)
59.	†1797	Thomas Lewis		Old Radnor, Radnorshire		Pevsner, *Powys*, 1979, 264
Statues						
60.	1784	Admiral Lord Rodney, model with bas-reliefs on the pedestal (commission won by John Bacon RA)		[Exhib RA, London, 466]; untraced		*Graves* VIII, 1905–6, 50
Busts						
61.	1761	Two, of unidentified sitters		[Exhib Soc of Artists, London, 164, 165]; untraced		*Graves* 1907, 262
62.	1767	Unidentified gentleman		[Exhib Soc of Artists, London, 213]; untraced		*Graves* 1907, 262
63.	1770	A clergyman, model		[Exhib RA, London, 190]; untraced		*Graves* VIII, 1905–6, 50
64.	1771	Unidentified gentleman, model		[Exhib RA, London, 200]; untraced		*Graves* VIII, 1905–6, 50
65.	1773	A philosopher, 'a study from nature'		[Exhib RA, London, 297]; untraced		*Graves* VIII, 1905–6, 50
66.	1776	An officer, model		[Exhib RA, London, 306]; untraced		*Graves* VIII, 1905–6, 50
Chimneypieces						
67.	1772	Designed by Sir William Chambers Payment(s): £282		[Milton Hall, Peterborough, Northants]; untraced		*Chambers's Letter-Books*, 41133; *Gunnis* 1968, 404
68.	*c*1773	An 'elegant chimneypiece . . . for one of the best rooms'		[Wentworth Woodhouse, W R Yorks]; untraced		Forrest's *Tours*, fol 42
Reliefs						
69.	1764	The story of Narcissus, a model for a bas-relief		[Exhib Soc of Artists, London, 159]; untraced		*Graves* 1907, 262
70.	1765	A lion couchant, model		[Exhib Soc of Artists, London, 183]; untraced		*Graves* 1907, 262
71.	1765	Bacchus sleeping, a model for a tablet		[Exhib Soc of Artists, London, 182]; untraced		*Graves* 1907, 262
72.	1765	Diogenes	tc	Sotheby, NY, 10–11 Jan 1995, lot 74	SD	
73.	1769	'An Indian, representing North America, offering the produce of that country to Britannia', bas-relief	m	[Exhib RA, London, 116]; untraced		*Graves* VIII, 1905–6, 50
Miscellaneous						
74.	1766	'A model of the Thames, with his commercial attributes'		[Exhib Soc of Artists, London, 218]; untraced		*Graves* 1907, 262 untraced

TYLEY, James and Thomas & Sons, of Bristol

Thomas Tyley I	*c*1788–after 1881
James Tyley	*c*1792–
Jabez Tyley	*c*1824–
Thomas Tyley II	*c*1826–
Henry Tyley	*c*1845–
William Tyley	active *c*1834

The Tyley family maintained their business as monumental masons in Bristol over more than a century. **Thoma Tyley** I was born in Bath and married Eliza (born *c*1809), perhaps as his second wife. In 1881 (aged 93) he was livin (as he seems to have done through most of his life), at Under Bank tenement in the parish of St Augustine, Bristo Pigot's *Directory for Bristol*, 1830, lists Tyley & Son (not Sons), stone and marble masons, at this address. Thomas had at least three sons, **Jabez, Thomas II** and **Henry**, all marble masons living in the vicinity of St Augustine's. Jabe is credited with the tympanum sculpture on the principal front of the Victoria Rooms, Bristol (now part of th university), *c*1841, which has a relief of *Dawn in a chariot, with floating genii in attendance* (**137**). In 1881 he describe himself as a 'retired sculptor'.

The Bristol sculptor James Harvard Thomas (1854–1921) was trained in the workshop. J H Thomas's obituar notes that he once said 'To learn marble carving I went to Thomas Tyley's in St Augustine's, who was then a very ol man and had been a pupil of Bacon Jnr [**John Bacon II**] and retained many of the traditions of the Englis eighteenth century sculpture' (letter, Bristol City Archives, inf. Douglas Merritt). **James Tyley** was probably th brother of Thomas I. There were other Tyley marble masons: James, born *c*1819 and Thomas, *c*1820, both spent thei mature years in London.

A Thomas Tyley, whose kinship to the above listed family members is unclear, ventured out of the monument field. He won a Silver Isis Medal in 1811 from the Society of Arts for a group entitled *Christ healing the sick*, at whic date he lived at 23 Upper Marylebone, London (**132**). In 1830 he carved the dove on the pediment of Holy Trinit Clifton (**136**) and in 1839 carved a statue of Sir Charles Wetherell (**133**). Another member of this generation was Jame Tyley II, who was apprenticed to **John Dunn** on 14 March 1807.

The firm was still active in 1864, for in that year it received a commission for a proposed sculpture gallery of Britis worthies (**134, 135**). On 22 October 1864 the *Builder* carried a report of the venture (p 783): 'In accordance with proposition in the Builder that busts or portraits of local worthies might usefully be placed in the respective publi buildings of the localities in which they lived, it has been proposed by Mr. R. A. Kinglake to form a sculpture gallery of Somerset worthies in the Shire-hall. He has commissioned Messrs. Tyley of Bristol to execute a memorial bust of "Good Bishop Ken" well remembered in the diocese of Bath and Wells. The Marquis of Bath permitted Messrs. Tyeley to make a photograph of the portrait of Ken in the portrait-gallery at Longleat; and Scheffer's painting of Ken in the Palace, Wells, was also copied for the same purpose, by favour of Lord Auckland. Another subject of sculpture is a memorial bust of the celebrated loyalist, the Rev. Henry Byam, D. D., Rector of Luccombe, Somerset, and chaplain to Charles II. in his exile'.

There are many monuments executed by the Tyleys in the West Country and the list below is not comprehensive. They are by no means all stock compositions. Gunnis considered the best to be the Gore, which has a medallion portrait between two figures of officers in full regimentals (**24**). Potterton notes of the Stock that it 'has a figure of a mourning Religion kneeling at an altar, but bored by mourning alone, she is now engrossed in the book which is her attribute' (**22**). The Worrall, a tablet to a four-year old child, has a relief of the sleeping child above a touching poem, the whole encased in a black frame (**60**). Penny illustrates the Rogers, which has a conventional, but crisply carved, broken Ionic column from which sprouts a luxuriant willow tree (**75**). The Lawless is a cartouche supported by a kangaroo and what may be an ostrich (**122**).

Literary References: Census returns 1841, 1861, 1881; *Potterton* 1975, 85; *Penny* 1977 (1), 29, 31, 119; *Read* 1982, 220

Funerary Monuments

1.	†1746	Mary Chichester and Mary, Lady Constable (†1825)	[Unidentified church in Bristol or Bath]; Church of the Holy Sacrament, Burton Constable, E R Yorks	S	
2.	†1763	Nicholas Wolferstan	St Nectan, Hartland, Devon	S	Pevsner, *Devon*, 1989, 473
3.	†1771	John and Jane (†1749) Shoare	Warminster, Wilts	S	
4.	†1782	Frances Osborne	West Littleton, Glos	S	Pevsner, *Glos: Cotswolds*, 1999, 713
5.	?1792	John Tucker (by Thomas Tyley I)	St Dogwell, Pembrokes	S	*Gunnis* 1968, 404
6.	†1793	Walter Rice	Llandovery, Carmarthen	S	*Dale-Jones and Lloyd* 1989, 58
7.	?1798	Shiercliffe family	St Augustine, Bristol	S	*Gunnis* 1968, 405
8.	†1799	Ann and Mary Hill	Banwell, Somerset	S	RG/JP, 8, 1491
9.	post-1800	Rev Charles Huntley (†1728) and his wife Anne (†1761)	Boxwell, Glos	S	Pevsner, *Glos: Cotswolds*, 1999, 194
10.	c1800	Thomas Blagey	Hinton St George, Somerset	S	
11.	†1804	Henry Trotman	St George, Bridgetown, Barbados	S	*Gunnis* 1968, 405
12.	†1805	Drusilla Richens	St John, Slimbridge, Glos	S	Pevsner, *Glos: Vale & Forest of Dean*, 1976, 340
13.	†1805	Selwyn James	St Mary, Tidenham, Glos	S	Pevsner, *Glos: Vale & Forest of Dean*, 1976, 384
14.	†1807	Louisa Lucas	Wraxall, Somerset	S	RG/JP, 8, 1491
15.	†1808	Edward and Mary Mansel	St Elli, Llanelly, Carmarthen	S	*Dale-Jones and Lloyd* 1989, 58
16.	†1808	Thomas and Catherine Cosby	Tenby, Pembrokes	S	RG/JP, 8, 1491
17.	?1809	Laurence Cook	Penally, Pembrokes	S	*Gunnis* 1968, 405
18.	†1810	Caroline Rice	Llandovey, Brecon	S	*Dale-Jones and Lloyd* 1989, 58
19.	†1810	William Davies	Slimbridge, Glos	S	Pevsner, *Glos: Vale and Forest of Dean*, 1976, 340
20.	†1811	Rev Walter Davies	Laugharne, Carmarthen	S	*Dale-Jones and Lloyd* 1989, 58
21.	†1811	Richard King	Ugborough, Devon	S	Pevsner, *Devon*, 1989, 879
22.	†1813	Bishop Stock	Waterford Cathedral	S	*Potterton* 1975, 85
23.	†1813	Unidentified subject, tablet	Backwell, Somerset	S	Pevsner, *Somerset: N & Bristol*, 1958, 84
24.	†1814	Major William Gore	Bristol Cathedral	S	Pevsner, *Somerset: N & Bristol*, 1958, 383
25.	†1814	Mary Senior	Iron Acton, Glos	S	Pevsner, *Glos: Vale & Forest of Dean*, 1976, 277
26.	c1815	Mary MacDonell Chichester	Church of the Holy Sacrament, Marton, near Burton Constable, E R Yorks	S	Pevsner, *Yorks: E R & York*, 1995, 613; *Mulcahy* 2006, 35–6 (repr)
27.	post-1817	Councelletta Lloyd and son	Cilybebyll, Glamorgan	S	Pevsner, *Glamorgan*, 1995, 332
28.	†1817	John Campbell	Bristol Cathedral	S	Pevsner, *Somerset: N & Bristol*, 1958, 381
29.	†1817	John Lucas	Wraxall, Somerset	S	Pevsner, *Somerset: N & Bristol*, 1958, 347
30.	†1817	John Maggs	Axbridge, Somerset	S	
31.	?1818	Charles Hawker	Chester Cathedral, Cheshire	S	*Gunnis* 1968, 405
32.	†1818	Maria Henderson	Banwell, Somerset	S	RG/JP, 8, 1491
33.	?1818	Susannah Henning	Wells Cathedral, Somerset	S	*Gunnis* 1968, 405
34.	†1819	Captain John Gardes	St Stephen, Bristol	S	*Gunnis* 1968, 405
35.	?1819	James Ley	Bideford, Devon	S	*Gunnis* 1968, 405
36.	†1819	Jane Mountague	St James, Montego Bay, Jamaica	S	
37.	†1819	John Emery	Banwell, Somerset	S	RG/JP, 8, 1491
38.	†1819	Louise Davies	St Cyr, Stonehouse, Glos	S	Pevsner, *Glos: Vale & Forest of Dean*, 1976, 352
39.	†1819	Sarah Hillier (†1819)	West Littleton, Glos	S	Pevsner, *Glos: Cotswolds*, 1999, 713
40.	†1820	Mary Down	Holy Trinity, Ilfracombe, Devon	S	RG/JP, 8, 1491
41.	?1820	William Mullins	Barnstaple, Devon	S	*Gunnis* 1968, 405
42.	†1821	John Thomas	Llanon, Carmarthen	S	*Dale-Jones and Lloyd* 1989, 58
43.	†1821	Samuel Worrall	Almondsbury, Glos	S	
44.	†1822	Anne Mallory	Tenby, Pembrokes	S	RG/JP, 8, 1491
45.	†1822	Betty Broad	St Andrew, Burnham-on-Sea, Somerset	S	RG/JP, 8, 1491
46.	†1822	Osborne family member	West Littleton, Glos	S	Pevsner, *Glos: Cotswolds*, 1999, 713
47.	†1822	Warlow Teague Gwyther	Tenby, Pembrokes	S	RG/JP, 8, 1491
48.	†1823	Rachel Fry	Axbridge, Somerset	S	
49.	†1824	Ann Toll (by Thomas Tyley)	St Mary, Thornbury, Glos	S	

50.	†1825	James (†1820) and Frances Ackland	Tenby, Pembrokes	S	RG/JP, 8, 1491
51.	†1826	Henry Emery	Banwell, Somerset	S	RG/JP, 8, 1490v.
52.	†1826	John Edwardes and sons	Laugharne, Carmarthen	S	*Dale-Jones and Lloyd* 1989, 58
53.	†1827	John George and family members	Cherington, Glos	S	*Gunnis* 1968, 405
54.	†1827	Martinus Andrée	Banwell, Somerset	S	RG/JP, 8, 1491
55.	†1829	Anthony Peacock	South Kyme, Lincs	S	Pevsner, *Lincs*, 1989, 665
56.	†1829	Richard Newman (by Thomas Tyley)	St Mary, Thornbury, Glos	S	
57.	?1830	John Thring	Alford, Somerset	S	*Gunnis* 1968, 405
58.	†1830	Robert Harkness	Wells Cathedral	S	GPC
59.	†1831	Walter and Mary Powell	Llanboidy, Carmarthen	S	*Dale-Jones and Lloyd* 1989, 58
60.	†1832	Georgiana Worrall	Bristol Cathedral	S	*Penny* 1977 (1), 118–119 (repr)
61.	?1832	Lord de Clifford	Henbury, Glos	S	*Gunnis* 1968, 405
62.	?1833	Catherine and Grace Hickman	Tenby, Pembrokes	S	*Gunnis* 1968, 405
63.	†1833	Elizabeth Emery	Banwell, Somerset	S	RG/JP, 8, 1491
64.	†1834	Emma Atholl Murray	Olveston, Glos	S	
65.	†1834	Emma Chester-Master	Almondsbury, Glos	S	Pevsner, *Glos: Vale & Forest of Dean*, 1976, 83
66.	†1834	Thomas Richardson	Iron Acton, Glos	S	Pevsner, *Glos: Vale and Forest of Dean*, 1976, 277
67.	?1835	Wolferston family	Hartland, Devon	S	*Gunnis* 1968, 405
68.	†1836	Sir William Henry Robinson (by Thomas Tyley)	St Mary, Thornbury, Glos	S	
69.	†1836	William Smyth	St Mary the Virgin, Oxford	S	RG/JP, 8, 1491
70.	?1837	George Hibbert	Aldenham, Herts	S	*Gunnis* 1968, 405
71.	†1837	Mary Mytton	Guilsfield, North Powys	S	RG/JP, 8, 1491
72.	?1837	Sophia Phillips	Hope-under-Dinmore, Herefs	S	*Gunnis* 1968, 405
73.	†1835–1838	Three Darwin children	Elston, Notts	S	Pevsner, *Notts*, 1979, 122
74.	†1839	Danvers Ward	Olveston, Glos	S	
75.	†1840	George Rogers	Bristol Cathedral	S	*Penny* 1977 (1), 28, 29 (repr)
76.	?1840	William Phillips	Lilleshall, Salop	S	*Gunnis* 1968, 405
77.	c1842	Frances (†1842), Charles (†1840), and Arthur (†1840) Lamb	Bristol Cathedral	S	*Penny* 1977 (1), 31, 32 (repr)
78.	†1842	Hester Purnell	Dursley, Glos	S	Pevsner, *Glos: Cotswolds*, 1999, 335
79.	†1843	Jane Harkness	Weston-super-Mare, Somerset	S	GPC
80.	†1843	Richard, Mary (†1839) and Elizabeth Gilling (by Thomas Tyley)	St Andrew Cheddar, Somerset	S	
81.	†1844	Captain Thomas Maitland	Weston-super-Mare, Somerset	S	GPC
82.	†1844	Elizabeth Fry	Axbridge, Somerset	S	
83.	†1844	Frederick Hickes	Berkeley, Glos	S	Pevsner, *Glos: Vale & Forest of Dean*, 1976, 101
84.	†1845	Alice Southwell and Frances Bearcroft (†1845)	Pitminster, Somerset	S	
85.	†1845	Anne Hewitt	St Peter, Bandon, Co Cork	S	GPC
86.	†1845	John Lax	Wells Cathedral, Cloisters	S	RG/JP, 8, 1492
87.	†1845	Margaret Lippincott	Almondsbury, Glos	S	Pevsner, *Glos: Vale & Forest of Dean*, 1976, 83
88.	†1846	George Jenner	Stone, Glos	S	Pevsner, *Glos: Vale & Forest of Dean*, 1976, 352
89.	†1846	Joseph Hume	St Mary, Thornbury, Glos	S	
90.	†1846	Rev George Law	Wells Cathedral, Cloisters	S	RG/JP, 8, 1491v.
91.	†1847	George Coates and Elizabeth Lane (†1848)	Holy Trinity, Ilfracombe, Devon	S	RG/JP, 8, 1492
92.	1847	Unidentified subject, tablet	Hempsted, Glos	S	Pevsner, *Glos: Vale & Forest of Dean*, 1976, 268
93.	†1848	Thomas Smyth Upton	Long Ashton, Somerset	S	
94.	†1849	Helen Somerset	Tormarton, Glos	S	Pevsner, *Glos: Cotswolds*, 1999, 699
95.	†1851	Arabella Chavasse	St Thomas, Barbados	S	
96.	†1851	Blanche, Adela and Frederick Lawrence	Olveston, Glos	S	Pevsner, *Glos: Vale & Forest of Dean*, 1976, 316
97.	?1851	Emma and Edward Prichard	Dowles, Worcs	S	RG/JP, 8, 1492
98.	†1851	Lord William Somerset	Tormarton, Glos	S	Pevsner, *Glos: Cotswolds*, 1999, 699
99.	†1851	Mary Merle	Congresbury, Somerset	S	Pevsner, *Somerset: N & Bristol*, 1958, 176
100.	†1852	Elizabeth Cookson	Bristol Cathedral	S	*Gunnis* 1968, 405
101.	†1852	Richard Goodenough Newman (by Thomas Tyley)	St Mary, Thornbury, Glos	S	
102.	†1853	George and Charlotte Vigor	St David, Carmarthen	S	*Dale-Jones and Lloyd* 1989, 58
103.	†1854	Eliza Smith and others (†1860)	Weston-super-Mare, Somerset	S	RG/JP, 8, 1492
104.	†1854	Grace and Thomas (†1850) Buller	Old Milverton, Warks	S	
105.	†1773–1854	Hunt family	Warminster, Wilts	S	
106.	†1855	Captain Frederick Smith	Weston-super-Mare, Somerset	S	GPC
107.	†1855	Elizabeth Hamilton	Hill, Glos	S	Pevsner, *Glos: Vale & Forest of Dean*, 1976, 272
108.	†1855	John Eagles	Bristol Cathedral	S	*Gunnis* 1968, 405
109.	†1855	Sarah Capell and Georgina Capel (†1856)	Worle, Somerset	S	GPC
110.	†1855	William Ellis	Berkeley, Glos	S	Pevsner, *Glos: Vale & Forest of Dean*, 1976, 101
111.	†1856	Mary Anne Cole	Acton Turville, Glos	S	Pevsner, *Glos: Cotswolds*, 1999, 130
112.	?1856	Rev M Leacock	Sierra Leone Cathedral	S	*Gunnis* 1968, 405
113.	†1856	Sir James Meek	Holy Trinity, Ilfracombe, Devon	S	RG/JP, 8, 1492
114.	†1857	Charles James	Evenlode, Glos	S	Pevsner, *Glos: Cotswolds*, 1999, 359
115.	†1858	Bowen family	Llanlilwni, Carmarthen	S	*Dale-Jones and Lloyd* 1989, 58
116.	†1858	Grantham Hodgson	Withern, Lincs	S	Pevsner, *Lincs*, 1989, 809

117.	†1858	Lord Proby	Elton, Hunts	S	Pevsner, *Beds, Hunts & Peterborough*, 1968, 238
118.	1859	Rev Henry Beva (†1854) and others	Congresbury, Somerset	S	RG/JP, 8, 1492
119.	*c*1859	Unidentified subjects, two tablets	Horsley, Glos	S	Pevsner, *Glos: Cotswolds*, 1999, 416
120.	†1860	John Brown	Paramatta, New South Wales, Australia	S	GPC
121.	†1863	Major-General Sir W Sleeman	Falmouth Parish Church, Devon	S	RG/JP, 8, 1491v.
122.	†1865	Paul and John Lawless	Cloyne Cathedral, Co Cork	S	*Potterton* 1975, 85
123.	†1867	John and Anne Clement	Kidwelly, Carmarthen	S	*Dale-Jones and Lloyd* 1989, 58
124.	†1867	Martha Byam, wife of Sir William Byam, president of Antigua	Parham, Antigua	S	
125.	?1868	Annie Hodgson	Alderley, Glos	S	RG/JP, 8, 1492
126.	†1869	Maria and Thomas Morris	St Peter, Carmarthen	S	*Dale-Jones and Lloyd* 1989, 58
127.	†1881	Mary Selena Wathen	Long Ashton, Somerset	S	
128.	†1884	William Hall and others	Holy Trinity, Cheltenham, Glos	S	RG/JP, 8, 1492
129.	†1886	Morris family	Llanstephan, Carmarthen	S	*Dale-Jones and Lloyd* 1989, 58
130.	nd	Unidentified subject, tablet	Christ Church, Gloucester, Glos	S	Pevsner, *Glos: Vale & Forest of Dean*, 1976, 230
131.	nd	Unidentified subjects, tablets	Beachley, Glos	S	Pevsner, *Glos: Vale & Forest of Dean*, 1976, 98

Statues

132.	1811	Christ healing the sick, group (by a Thomas Tyley)	[Soc of A, silver Isis medal]; untraced		*Gunnis* 1968, 404
133.	1839	Sir Charles Wetherell (by a Thomas Tyley)	Clifton, Bristol		*G M*, new series vol XXVI, Oct 1846, II, 430

Busts

134.	1864	Bishop Ken, commissioned for a proposed sculpture gallery of British Worthies	[coll Mr Robert Arthur Kinglake]; untraced		*Builder*, 1864, 783; *Gunnis* 1968, 405
135.	1864	Rev Henry Byam, commissioned for a proposed sculpture gallery of British Worthies	Untraced		*Builder*, 1864, 783; *Gunnis* 1968, 405

Architectural Sculpture

136.	1830	Dove (by a Thomas Tyley)	Holy Trinity, Clifton, Bristol, pediment		*Chilcott* 1840, 273; *Gunnis* 1968, 404
137.	*c*1841	Dawn in a chariot, pediment group (by Jabez Tyley) (co-sculptor: Musgrave Lewthwaite Watson)	Victoria rooms, Bristol		Pevsner, *Somerset: N & Bristol*, 1958, 418

YLEY, of Colerne fl *c*1784

He is known only for one tablet at Corsham. It is possible that he was related to the **Tyley family of Bristol**.

Funerary Monuments

1.	†1784	John Leir	Corsham, Wilts	S	*Gunnis* 1968, 404

NWINS, Thomas, of Liverpool, ARA fl 1831

Busts

1.	1831	Nathaniel Philips	m	[Exhib Liverpool Ac, 399]; untraced	*Gunnis* 1968, 405; *Morris and Roberts* 1998, 606

AGO, L A

Busts

1.	nd	Admiral Lord Nelson, after Flaxman's original	pm	[ex coll Rupert Gunnis]; untraced	GPC

ALADIER, Luigi 1726–85

The leading bronze founder in later 18th century Rome, he specialised in large bronze figures after the antique. These included several casts from works in the Louvre and one of the *Dying gladiator*, purchased by the 1st Duchess of Northumberland in 1773 for £300 (**2**). The Duchess obtained two other bronzes (**1, 3**). Valadier is not known to have modelled portrait busts, but he signed and dated a bronze bust of Sir Thomas Gascoigne of Parlington, Yorks in 1778 (**6**). At that time Gascoigne was in Rome with friends, Henry and Martha Swinburne, whose unsigned bronze heads relate closely in style to the Gascoigne bust (**4, 5**). The Swinburnes' small daughter, Martha, died in Rome and her marble wall tablet by **Christopher Hewetson** was commissioned and set up in the English College in Rome late in 1778. It is reasonable to assume that Hewetson modelled heads of the Swinburnes and Gascoigne whilst working on the memorial and that Valadier cast them. The Swinburne busts appear in a portrait of Gascoigne by Pompeo Batoni, painted in 1779, at Lotherton Hall, W R Yorks.

Literary References: *Friedman* 1976 (1), 16–23

Statues

1.	1770	Borghese Silenus with the Infant Bacchus Payment(s): 1,300 scudi	b	Syon House, Middx	S	*Thompson* 1991, 166–7 (repr)
2.	pre-1773	Dying gladiator, after the Capitoline statue	b	Syon House, Middx, entrance hall	S	*Haskell and Penny* 1981, 225 (repr 49); *Thompson* 1991, 166–7 (repr)
3.	nd	Belvedere Antinous	b	Syon House, Middx	S	*Thompson* 1991, 166–7 (repr)

Busts

4.	1778	Henry Swinburne, probably after a model by Christopher Hewetson	b	LMG, Lotherton Hall, W R Yorks		*Friedman* 1976 (1), 16–23 (repr)
5.	1778	Martha Swinburne, probably after a model by Christopher Hewetson	b	LMG, Lotherton Hall, W R Yorks		*Friedman* 1976 (1), 16–23 (repr)
6.	1778	Sir Thomas Gascoigne, probably after a model by Christopher Hewetson	b	LMG, Lotherton Hall, W R Yorks Other versions: VAM Wentworth Woodhouse sale, July 1949, lot 614; untraced	SD	*Friedman* 1976 (1), 16–23 (repr); *Penny* 1991 (2), 19, 34 n97

VALDRE, Vincenzo 1742–

Born in Faenza, he probably met his future patron, George Grenville, the heir to Stowe, in Italy in 1774. He worked a Stowe for a decade from 1778, employed largely in decorative painting and architectural design. In his 1773 guide t Stowe, J B Seely described Valdre's saloon ornaments as 'A rich cornice and an attic on which is a marble decoratio which runs round the whole room representing a triumph and a sacrifice consisting of above 300 figures in reliev Gibbon suggests that these figures were probably designed but not carved by Valdre. He later settled in Ireland wher he rebuilt the debating chamber of the Irish House of Commons.

Literary References: *Seely* 1773; *Gibbon* 1965, 238–42; *Gibbon* 1966, 260–3; *Tite* 2001, 143

Architectural Sculpture

1.	pre-1773	Frieze with more than 300 figures in relief	m	Stowe House, Bucks		*Gibbon* 1965, 238–42

VALENTINE, J, of Birmingham fl 1829

Busts

1.	1829	Rev E Dales		[Exhib Birmingham Soc of A]; untraced		*Gunnis* 1968, 406

VALLE, Filippo della 1698–1768

Horace Walpole, in wishing to erect a monument to his mother in Westminster Abbey, ordered a figure of a Roma matron from della Valle in the early 1740s. Michael Rysbrack provided a drawing of the statue set in a pedimente frame. The attenuated draped figure, copied from an antique image of *Pudicity*, arrived in England in 1743, but wa not erected by Rysbrack until 1754 and now stands on a pedestal with no frame (1). Eight statues after the antiqu were made for Lord Rockingham at Wentworth Woodhouse in Rome by **Joseph Wilton, Simon Vierpyl, G B Main** **Bartolomeo Cavaceppi** and della Valle (3).

Literary References: *Whinney* 1988, 259–60, 459–60, n9

Funerary Monuments

1.	pre-1743	Lady Catherine Walpole, first wife of Sir Robert Walpole		Westminster Abbey, London, Henry VII's Chapel		*MacMichael* 1977, 78; *Haskell and Penny* 1981, 300; *Whinney* 1988, 259–60, 460–1, n9 (repr)
2.	1730	Sir Thomas Robinson (Lady Robinson's bust only)		Westminster Abbey, London, south transept		*Baker, Harrison, Laing* 2000, 752–62

Statues

3.	1749–1750	Flora and Germanicus	m	Wentworth Woodhouse, W R Yorks, originally in the great hall, moved to niches in the marble saloon (1967)	S	Pevsner, *Yorks: W R*, 1967, 650

VALOIS fl 1770

His trade card, engraved by Littret in 1770, states that he lived at 368 Oxford Street. It has a column with a portrai bust lying at its base together with the tools of the sculptor's trade (Heal, BM 106.21).

VAN DER HAGEN, Alexander fl 1763

Statues

1.	1763	Two figures Payment(s): £63	s	[Kedleston Hall, Derbys]; untraced		*Gunnis* 1968, 406

VAN DER HAGEN, Gaspar –1769

A carver in ivory and marble, Van der Hagen was a long-term assistant to **Michael Rysbrack**. His date of birth i unknown and no information has surfaced on his training, but he had relatives in Antwerp. He was in London by 174 when the *Daily Advertiser* made reference to 'Mess. Claessens and Ven Hagen, at Mr Rysbrack's in Vere Street, nea Oxford Chapel'. Claessens was Rysbrack's foreman who died on 4 December 1749. In 1747 Vertue noted 'Mr Vande Hagen. Sculptor works for Mr Rysbrack. has done several heads portraits in Ivory.—very well. but not meeting wit propper encouragement did not continue' (*Vertue* III, 135). The lack of encouragement must have been temporary, fo Van der Hagen was still exhibiting ivory portraits nearly 20 years later. His small bust of the Duke of Cumberland i a very assured, minutely detailed and textured rendering of a larger marble work by his master (4). It suggests that Va der Hagen had considerable talent.

He was still lodging with his master in Vere Street, Oxford Road in 1766, and four works by him were sold in th auction of Rysbrack's collection held by Langford on 14 February 1767 (**2, 6, 10, 11**). The *Sacrifice to Hercules*, whic resurfaced in 2002 (**6**) is a competent work after a terracotta model by Rysbrack, itself based on a relief on the Arc of Constantine in Rome.

Rysbrack bequeathed £50 to 'Gaspar Vanderhagen Statuary who did live with me' in his will, dated 5 March 1768 and an undated codicil adds 'Gaspar Vanderhagen dyed before me'. In fact Vanderhagen was still alive in 1768, but ha moved to York, where he died in 1769. The timing was unfortunate for Van der Hagen appears to have lived out hi last days in penury. In 1768 he applied to the Society of Artists for support, 'being in great necessity', and received fou guineas (Society of Artists' Archives, Burlington House).

His goods were administered by his sisters Isabella and Catherine (Harman), both of whom lived in Antwerp These executors held a sale of their brother's work on 17 April 1771. Van der Hagen was described in the catalogue a the 'principal assistant to the late Mr. Rysbrack,' and the sale included 'several fine heads and figures in ivory, bass relievos in marble, books of prints, &c' (*Anecdotes* 1937, 154–5).

In the letters of administration Van der Hagen is described as a 'bachelor', so it is perhaps unlikely tha **Vanderhagen of Shrewsbury** was, as Gunnis supposed, his immediate offspring. The Royal Academy pension pai to a Mr Vanderhagen between 1769 and 1775, and subsequently to the widow of the same until 1781, also relates t another family.

After **Jean Cavalier** and **David le Marchand**, with whom he shares some stylistic similarities, Van der Hagen i currently the best documented ivory carver of the 18th century. However the large corpus of works includes man attributions, not here listed. Among them are an oval medallion of John Milton, signed 'VDHN' (VAM) as well as many unsigned works and others with the incongruous signatures, '**GVD**,' '**GVDR**' and '**GVR**.' (Add inf. Gordon Balderston, Marjorie Trusted)

MGS

Literary References: *Graves* 1907, 263; *Webb* 1954, 68, 186, 189; *Gunnis* 1968, 406; *Davis* 1970 (1), 16; *Davis* 1971 (4), 1223

Archival References: SAA SA/34/1; SA/37/6

Wills and Administrations: Administration of the will of Jasper otherwise Gaspard Vanderhagen, 17 July 1769, FRC PROB 6/145/27; will of Michael Rysbrack PROB 11/954/224–6

Auction Catalogues: Van der Hagen 1771

Funerary Monuments					
1.	nd	Mrs Richard Lyster		Alderbury, Salop	S
Busts					
2.	pre-1767	Blackmoor's head		[coll Michael Rysbrack]; untraced	*Baker* 2000 77, 173 n31; Rysbrack 1767 (4), lot 45
3.	1767	King Alfred Payment(s): £7		[coll Lord Radnor]; untraced	*Gunnis* 1968, 406
4.	1767	William Augustus, Duke of Cumberland (†1765)	i	[Exhib Free Soc, London, 271]; VAM A.84-1937	*Graves* 1907, 263
Reliefs					
5.	1766	Nymph and Genii	m	[Exhib Free Soc, London, 176]; untraced	*Graves* 1907, 263
6.	1766	Sacrifice to Hercules, bas-relief (after Michael Rysbrack)	m	[coll Michael Rysbrack]; YCBAB2003.6	*Graves* 1907, 263; *Baker* 2000 77, 173 n31; Rysbrack 1767 (4), lot 44
7.	1767	Anthony Van Dyck, medal		[Exhib Free Soc, London, 274]; untraced	*Graves* 1907, 263
8.	1767	Oliver Cromwell, medal		[Exhib Free Soc, London, 275]; untraced	*Graves* 1907, 263
9.	1767	Peter Paul Rubens, medal		[Exhib Free Soc, London, 273]; untraced	*Graves* 1907, 263
10.	pre-1767	Venus and Cupid, bas-relief (after Michael Rysbrack)		[coll Michael Rysbrack]; untraced	*Baker* 2000 77, 173 n31; Rysbrack 1767 (4), lot 43
11.	pre-1767	Venus, and a boy frightened by a monster		[coll Michael Rysbrack]; untraced	*Baker* 2000 77, 173 n31; Rysbrack 1767 (4), lot 46
Miscellaneous					
12.	by 1747	'Several head portraits in ivory very well'	i	Untraced	*Vertue*, III, 135
13.	1767	Two girls, after Fiamingo	i	[Exhib Free Soc, London, 272]; untraced	*Graves* 1907, 263

VAN DER HAGEN, of Shrewsbury –c1790

Nothing is known of Van der Hagen's early life except that, according to his own advertisements, he trained at 'European Academies' (inf. James Lawson). He is unlikely to have been a direct descendant of **Gaspar Van Der Hagen** who was described as 'a bachelor' in the administration letter of his will, but he may have been connected in some way to another Van der Hagen, who received a Royal Academy pension from 1769 until 1775, when the payments were transferred to his widow. He had certainly settled in Shrewsbury by 1765, where he was employed as a carver by **Thomas Farnolls Pritchard** and established his own business as a monumental mason.

An album of Pritchard's designs in the American Institute of Architects in Washingon DC (reproduced in full by *Ionides* 1999) includes information on the craftsmen responsible for their execution. It shows that Van der Hagen frequently worked in collaboration with **John Nelson** and **Swift** and occasionally with **Danders** and **Halley**, carving chimneypieces, frames and other decorative features in various styles for Pritchard. Van der Hagen, Nelson and Swift were all employed on Pritchard's monument to Richard Ward Offley at Pontesbury (**2**) and it seems likely that the same team was responsible for carving the large wall-monument, designed by Pritchard, to Richard Lyster at Alberbury, which Gunnis thought 'exactly like, and very nearly equal to, the work of **Sir Henry Cheere**' (*Gunnis* 1968, 406). Their involvement in the Lyster cannot be confirmed, though Van der Hagen's signature appears on the small, simple tablet to the memory of Lyster's wife which was added at the base of the monument at a later date.

Van der Hagen's most important independent works are the monuments commemorating Maria Lloyd, 1780, at Corwen, Merioneth, and William Vaughan, 1786, at Llanddwywe in the same county, both of which have medallion portraits (**8, 15**). He appears to have died about 1790 for the following year **John Carline I** and his partner John Tilley announced that they had purchased Van der Hagen's stock in trade and intended to carry on his business in monuments and chimneypieces (*Shrewsbury Chronicle* 1791, inf. James Lawson).

Literary References: *Gunnis* 1968, 406; *Rococo* 1984, 207; RG/JP, 8, 1495; *Ionides* 1999, *passim*

Wills and Administrations: Administration of the will of Jasper otherwise Gaspard Vanderhagen, FRC 17 July 1769

Funerary Monuments					
1.	?1767	Thomas Jenkins	Shrewsbury Abbey, Salop	S	*Gunnis* 1968, 406
2.	1769	Richard Ward Offley (†1762) (designed by Thomas Farnolls Pritchard) (co-sculptor: Nelson and Swift) Drawing(s): Pritchard Drawing Book (AIA 64)	Pontesbury, Salop		*Ionides* 1999, 236 (repr)
3.	?1770	John Corser	Moreton Say, Salop	S	*Gunnis* 1968, 406
4.	c1770	Mrs Hanmer	Overton, Flint	S	Pevsner, *Clwyd*, 1986, 411;
5.	?1772	Margaret Vaughan	Llanddwywe, Merioneth	S	*Gunnis* 1968, 406
6.	?1778	Sir John Markham	Moreton Say, Salop, churchyard	S	*Gunnis* 1968, 406
7.	?1779	Lewis Nanney	Dolgelley, Merioneth	S	*Gunnis* 1968, 406
8.	?1780	Maria Lloyd	Corwen, Merioneth		*Gunnis* 1968, 406
9.	†1780	Owen Wynne	Overton, Flint	S	Pevsner, *Clwyd*, 1986, 411
10.	†1782	Rev Richard Congreve	Iscoed; Flint		Pevsner, *Clwyd*, 1986, 379
11.	†1784	Dr Cheney Hart	St Giles, Shrewsbury, Salop, churchyard		RG/JP, 8, 1495

No.	Date	Description	Material	Location		Literature
12.	†1784	Sir Thomas Kyffyn		Llanddoged, Denbighs		Pevsner, *Clwyd*, 1994, 190
13.	†1784	Thomas Trevor		Oswestry, Salop	S	*Gunnis* 1968, 406
14.	†1786	John Amler		Ford, Salop	S	
15.	?1786	William Vaughan		Llanddwywe, Merioneth	S	*Gunnis* 1968, 406
Chimneypieces						
16.	?1765	Baroque chimney frame (designed by Thomas Farnolls Pritchard) (co-sculptor: Nelson and Halley) Drawing(s): Pritchard Drawing Book (AIA 3)	wd	Shipton Hall, Salop, library		*Ionides* 1999, 122, 123, 327, 353 (repr)
17.	?1765	Chimney frieze with wreath and leaves (designed by Thomas Farnolls Pritchard) (co-sculptor: Nelson) Drawing(s): Pritchard Drawing Book (AIA 10)	wd	Croft Castle, Herefs, Bishop's room		*Ionides* 1999, 52, 91, 328, 360 (repr)
18.	?1765	Gothic chimney frame (designed by Thomas Farnolls Pritchard) (co-sculptor: Nelson) Drawing(s): Pritchard Drawing Book (AIA 4–5)	wd	[Croft Castle, Herefs, library]; Croft Castle, Herefs, ante-room		*Ionides* 1999, 47, 52, 91–2, 327, 354–5 (repr)
19.	November 1765	With cornucopia and phoenix heads in the frieze (designed by Thomas Farnolls Pritchard) (co-sculptor: Nelson) Drawing(s): Pritchard Drawing Book (AIA 7)	wd	27 Broad Street, Ludlow, Salop		*Ionides* 1999, 166–9, 327, 357 (repr)
20.	1765–1766	Three, for the dining room, parlour and attick storey (designed by Thomas Farnolls Pritchard) (co-sculptor: Nelson) Drawing(s): Pritchard Drawing Book (AIA 12)		[for Mr Bather, of Mardol, Shrewsbury, Salop]; untraced		*Ionides* 1999, 328, 362 (repr)
21.	1765–1769	Four, of various designs (designed by Thomas Farnolls Pritchard) (co-sculptor: Nelson and Danders) Drawing(s): Pritchard Drawing Book (AIA 13, 33, 45)		[Condover Hall, Salop]; untraced		*Ionides* 1999, 328, 331, 332, 363, 383, 396 (repr)
22.	*c*1769	Six, of various designs (designed by Thomas Farnolls Pritchard) (co-sculptor: Nelson and Swift) Drawing(s): Pritchard Drawing Book (AIA 69, 72–77)		[Tern Hall, Salop]; untraced		*Ionides* 1999, 212, 335–7, 420, 423–8 (repr)
23.	1765–1769	Three, for the common parlour, Mr Freeman's chamber and the hall (designed by Thomas Farnolls Pritchard) (co-sculptor: Nelson and Swift) Drawing(s): Pritchard Drawing Book (AIA 19, 21, 57)		[Gaines, Worcs]; untraced		*Ionides* 1999, 105–6, 329, 334, 369, 371, 408 (repr)
24.	1765–1769	Three, for the drawing room, dressing room and dining parlour (designed by Thomas Farnolls Pritchard) (co-sculptor: Nelson and Swift) Drawing(s): Pritchard Drawing Book (AIA 29, 58, 69)	wd	Hatton Grange, Salop		*Ionides* 1999, 131–3, 331, 334, 379, 409, 420 (repr)
25.	1765–1769	Three, with classical, rococo and gothic decoration (designed by Thomas Farnolls Pritchard) Drawing(s): Pritchard Drawing Book (AIA 34, 47, 63)	wd	Bitterley Court, Salop		*Ionides* 1999, 126–7, 331, 333, 335, 384, 398, 414 (repr)
26.	1765–1769	Two (designed by Thomas Farnolls Pritchard) (co-sculptor: Nelson and Swift) Drawing(s): Pritchard Drawing Book (AIA 36, 37)		[for John Ashby, High Street, Shrewsbury]; untraced		*Ionides* 1999, 158, 331, 387, 388 (repr)
27.	1765–1769	Two for the great room (designed by Thomas Farnolls Pritchard) Drawing(s): Pritchard Drawing Book (AIA 8)		[Red Lion Inn, Wolverhampton]; demol *c*1960		*Ionides* 1999, 174, 327, 358 (repr)
28.	1765–1769	Two, including one for Miss Egerton's room (designed by Thomas Farnolls Pritchard) (co-sculptor: Nelson and Swift) Drawing(s): Pritchard Drawing Book (AIA 40, 41)		[for Samuel Egerton, of Tatton Park, Cheshire]; untraced		*Ionides* 1999, 47, 150, 332, 391, 392 (repr)
29.	1765–1769	With a scallop shell (designed by Thomas Farnolls Pritchard) (co-sculptor: Nelson) Drawing(s): Pritchard Drawing Book (AIA 53)		[for Mr Bather, of Mardol, Shrewsbury, Salop]; untraced		*Ionides* 1999, 333, 404 (repr)

30.	1765–1769	With birds in the frieze (designed by Thomas Farnolls Pritchard) (co-sculptor: Nelson and Swift) Drawing(s): Pritchard Drawing Book (AIA 17)		[for Mr Haycock in Wales]; untraced	*Ionides* 1999, 329, 367 (repr)
31.	1769	With classical decoration (designed by Thomas Farnolls Pritchard) Drawing(s): Pritchard Drawing Book (AIA 70)	wd	Broseley Hall, Salop	*Ionides* 1999, 171, 336, 421 (repr)
32.	1765–1769	With classical motifs (designed by Thomas Farnolls Pritchard) (co-sculptor: Nelson and Swift) Drawing(s): Pritchard Drawing Book (AIA 46)		[for Bartholomew Barnaby, of Brockhampton House, Herefs]; untraced	*Ionides* 1999, 99, 333, 397 (repr)
33.	1765–1769	With classical mouldings (designed by Thomas Farnolls Pritchard) (co-sculptor: Nelson) Drawing(s): Pritchard Drawing Book (AIA 11)		[for Mr Pritchard]; untraced	*Ionides* 1999, 328, 361 (repr)
34.	1765–1769	With classical mouldings (designed by Thomas Farnolls Pritchard) (co-sculptor: Nelson and Swift) Drawing(s): Pritchard Drawing Book (AIA 79)		[for John Wilkinson, of The Lawns, Broseley, Salop]; untraced	*Ionides* 1999, 172, 337, 430 (repr)
35.	1765–1769	With foliage in the frieze (designed by Thomas Farnolls Pritchard) (co-sculptor: Nelson and Swift) Drawing(s): Pritchard Drawing Book (AIA 20)		[for Mr Burton, of Longner Hall, Salop]; untraced	*Ionides* 1999, 330, 370 (repr)
36.	1765–1769	With frieze of oak leaves and acorns (designed by Thomas Farnolls Pritchard) (co-sculptor: Nelson) Drawing(s): Pritchard Drawing Book (AIA 80)		High Hatton Hall, Salop	*Ionides* 1999, 135–6, 337, 431 (repr)
37.	1765–1769	With frieze of scrolling foliage (designed by Thomas Farnolls Pritchard) (co-sculptor: Nelson and Swift) Drawing(s): Pritchard Drawing Book (AIA 38)	wd	Broseley Hall, Salop	*Ionides* 1999, 171, 332, 389 (repr)
38.	1765–1769	With Jacobean style details (designed by Thomas Farnolls Pritchard) (co-sculptor: Nelson and Swift) Drawing(s): Pritchard Drawing Book (AIA 24)	wd	Benthall Hall, Salop, drawing room	*Ionides* 1999, 172, 330, 374 (repr)
39.	1765–1769	With lion's head and grapes, for the best parlour (designed by Thomas Farnolls Pritchard) (co-sculptor: Nelson and Swift) Drawing(s): Pritchard Drawing Book (AIA 35)	wd	Kinsham Court, Herefs	*Ionides* 1999, 110, 111, 331, 385 (repr)
40.	1765–1769	With mask of Diana the huntress and dogs (designed by Thomas Farnolls Pritchard) (co-sculptor: Nelson) Drawing(s): Pritchard Drawing Book (AIA 14)		[for Bartholomew Barnaby, of Brockhampton House, Herefs]; untraced	*Ionides* 1999, 99, 328, 364 (repr)
41.	1765–1769	With oak leaf moulding (designed by Thomas Farnolls Pritchard) (co-sculptor: Nelson) Drawing(s): Pritchard Drawing Book (AIA 9)		[for Mr Powis, Gravel Hill]; untraced	*Ionides* 1999, 327, 359 (repr)
42.	1765–1769	With palmette and garlands of husks (designed by Thomas Farnolls Pritchard) (co-sculptor: Nelson and Swift) Drawing(s): Pritchard Drawing Book (AIA 22)	wd	[Gaines, Worcs, Bed Chamber]; Unidentified house, Sussex	*Ionides* 1999, 105–6, 330, 372 (repr)
43.	1765–1769	With scallop shell and scrolling foliage (designed by Thomas Farnolls Pritchard) (co-sculptor: Nelson) Drawing(s): Pritchard Drawing Book (AIA 16)		[for Mr Scot Draper, Grope Lane, Shrewsbury, Salop]; untraced	*Ionides* 1999, 329, 366 (repr)
44.	1765–1769	With scrolls and flowers in the frieze (designed by Thomas Farnolls Pritchard) (co-sculptor: Nelson and Swift) Drawing(s): Pritchard Drawing Book (AIA 78)		[for Mr Good, of Shrewsbury]; untraced	*Ionides* 1999, 23, 327, 429 (repr)

45.	1765–1769	With waterleaf coving and frond-like branches (designed by Thomas Farnolls Pritchard) (co-sculptor: Nelson and Swift) Drawing(s): Pritchard Drawing Book (AIA 41)	wd	[for Mr Harley]; Kinsham Court, Herefs, dining room (now part of an overmantel)	*Ionides* 1999, 110–1, 332, 392 (repr)
Architectural Sculpture					
46.	?1765	Two door friezes with lion's head masks and branches (designed by Thomas Farnolls Pritchard) (co-sculptor: Nelson) Drawing(s): Pritchard Drawing Book (AIA 10)		[Croft Castle, 'Mr Johnes dressing room']; Croft Castle, Herefs, saloon	*Ionides* 1999, 52, 93–4, 328, 360 (repr)
47.	?1765	Two door friezes with scrolling foliage (designed by Thomas Farnolls Pritchard) (co-sculptor: Nelson) Drawing(s): Pritchard Drawing Book (AIA 10)		Croft Castle, Herefs, saloon	*Ionides* 1999, 52, 93, 328, 360 (repr)
48.	1765–1769	Doorcase (designed by Thomas Farnolls Pritchard) Drawing(s): Pritchard Drawing Book (AIA 44)		[Condover Hall, Salop]; untraced	*Ionides* 1999, 332, 395 (repr)
49.	1765–1769	Eight gothic columns (designed by Thomas Farnolls Pritchard) (co-sculptor: Nelson and Swift) Drawing(s): Pritchard Drawing Book (AIA 54)		Gaines, Worcs	*Ionides* 1999, 106–8, 334, 405 (repr)
Reliefs					
50.	1779	A view of the Rialto		[Exhib Free Soc]; untraced	*Graves* 1907, 263
Miscellaneous					
51.	May 1768	'2 Frames for Shell pieces' (designed by Thomas Farnolls Pritchard) (co-sculptor: Nelson and Swift) Drawing(s): Pritchard Drawing Book (AIA 28)		[for Rev Mr Fowler, of Atcham Rectory, Salop]; untraced	*Ionides* 1999, 330–1, 378 (repr)
52.	1765–1769	Frame for Lord Bath's picture (designed by Thomas Farnolls Pritchard) (co-sculptor: Nelson) Drawing(s): Pritchard Drawing Book (AIA 6)		[Red Lion Inn, Wolverhampton]; demol *c* 1960	*Ionides* 1999, 327, 356 (repr)
53.	1765–1769	Glass frame (executed under the direction of Thomas Farnolls Pritchard) (co-sculptor: Nelson and Swift)		[for Mr Walcot, of Bitterley Hall, Salop]; untraced	*Ionides* 1999, 337, 432
54.	1765–1769	Mahogany shield for a bookcase (designed by Thomas Farnolls Pritchard) (co-sculptor: Nelson) Drawing(s): Pritchard Drawing Book (AIA 15)		[for Mr Bather, of Mardol, Shrewsbury, Salop]; untraced	*Ionides* 1999, 329, 365 (repr)
55.	1765–1769	Rococo glass frame (designed by Thomas Farnolls Pritchard) (co-sculptor: Nelson) Drawing(s): Pritchard Drawing Book (AIA 11)		[for Mr Pritchard]; untraced	*Ionides* 1999, 328, 361 (repr)
56.	1765–1769	'Three frames in Burnished Gold for a Dessart Table' (designed by Thomas Farnolls Pritchard) (co-sculptor: Nelson) Drawing(s): Pritchard Drawing Book (AIA 55)		[for Mr Lee, of Coton Hall, Salop (?)]; untraced	*Ionides* 1999, 334, 406 (repr)

VAN DER MEULEN, John Ferdinand fl 1765–80

Though Van der Meulen showed extensively with the Free Society and other exhibiting societies between 1765 and 1780, none of his works appears to have survived. On 24 May 1765 he received a premium from the Society of Arts (**8**) and another followed in 1767 (**9**), at which time he lived in Little Castle Street, Oxford Road. In 1768 he sent in a model for the statue of Sir William Harpur to be erected at Bedford School, but was unsuccessful and the commission was given to **Benjamin Palmer** (**2**). He was a minor beneficiary in **Peter Scheemakers**'s will and conceivably worked for him before Scheemakers departed for Antwerp in 1771. The son, **Van der Meulen II**, lived in Castle Street with his father in 1778–80.

Literary References: *Graves* 1907, 263–4; Gunnis 1968, 406

Will: PROB 11/ 1082, 17 v-r (Peter Scheemakers)

Funerary Monuments				
1.	1769	Unidentified subject, monumental medallion, model	[Exhib Free Soc, London, 226]; untraced	*Graves* 1907, 263
Statues				
2.	1768	Sir William Harpur (†1552), for Bedford School, model only	[Exhib Free Soc, London, 1769, 223]; untraced	*Graves* 1907, 263; *Gunnis* 1968, 406

Busts					
3.	1769	Unidentified young gentleman	tc	[Exhib Free Soc, London, 224]; untraced	*Graves* 1907, 263
4.	1774	A young fawn	m	[Exhib Free Soc, London, 298]; untraced	*Graves* 1907, 264
5.	1775	Unidentified young lady, model		[Exhib Free Soc, London, 278]; untraced	*Graves* 1907, 264
Architectural Sculpture					
6.	1774	Sketch for a fountain	pm	[Exhib Free Soc, London, 299]; untraced	*Graves* 1907, 264
7.	1775	Design for a pediment	tc	[Exhib Free Soc, London, 277]; untraced	*Graves* 1907, 264
Reliefs					
8.	1765	Supplication of Veturia to Coriolanus	tc	[Soc of Arts, premium, 50 gns]; untraced	RSA Minutes, 1764–65, seq 3 fol 62; *Dossie* 1782, 440
9.	1767	Abimelech restoring Sarah to Abraham	m	[Soc of A, premium, 30 gns]; untraced Other versions: tc exhib Free Soc, London, 1779, 171	RSA *Premiums*, 1766–67, PR/GE/112/12/8 seq 3 fols 34, 36; *Graves* 1907, 263, 26
10.	1768	Unidentified subject	m	[Exhib Free Soc, London, 233]; untraced	*Graves* 1907, 263
11.	1769	Cupid and Psyche, model for a tablet	tc	[Exhib Free Soc, London, 225]; untraced	*Graves* 1907, 263
12.	1770	Jupiter and Leda, a tablet	tc	[Exhib Free Soc, London, 259]; untraced	*Graves* 1907, 264
13.	1771	Apollo rewarding Merit, after the Antique	m	[Exhib Free Soc, London, 254]; untraced	*Graves* 1907, 264
14.	1772	The four seasons, model	tc	[Exhib Free Soc, London, 199]; untraced	*Graves* 1907, 264
15.	1773	Unidentified young lady, medallion, model		[Exhib Free Soc, London, 252]; untraced	*Graves* 1907, 264
16.	1775	The marriage of Cupid and Psyche, tablet	m	[Exhib Free Soc, London, 276]; untraced	*Graves* 1907, 264
17.	1775	Unidentified subject, medallion in stucco		[Exhib Free Soc, London, 279]; untraced	*Graves* 1907, 264
Miscellaneous					
18.	1768	Genii playing with a dog, model	tc	[Exhib Free Soc, London, 233]; untraced	*Graves* 1907, 263
19.	1770	Madonna and child, model	tc	[Exhib Free Soc, London, 256]; untraced	*Graves* 1907, 263
20.	1770	St John the Evangelist, model	tc	[Exhib Free Soc, London, 258]; untraced	*Graves* 1907, 263
21.	1770	St Matthew, model	tc	[Exhib Soc of Artists, London, 257]; untraced	*Graves* 1907, 263
22.	1772	Feeling, model	tc	[Exhib Free Soc, London, 196]; untraced	*Graves* 1907, 264
23.	1772	Hearing, model	tc	[Exhib Free Soc, London, 195]; untraced	*Graves* 1907, 264
24.	1772	Seeing, model	tc	[Exhib Free Soc, London, 194]; untraced	*Graves* 1907, 264
25.	1772	Smelling, model	tc	[Exhib Free Soc, London, 198]; untraced	*Graves* 1907, 264
26.	1772	Tasting, model	tc	[Exhib Free Soc, London, 197]; untraced	*Graves* 1907, 264
27.	1773	Unidentified young gentleman, model		[Exhib Free Soc, London, 251]; untraced	*Graves* 1907, 264
28.	1775	The four seasons, in stucco		[Exhib Free Soc, London, 280]; untraced	*Graves* 1907, 264
29.	1776	Unidentified gentleman	w	[Exhib Free Soc, London, 212]; untraced	*Graves* 1907, 264
30.	1776	Unidentified gentlemen		[Exhib Free Soc, London, 213 and 214]; untraced	*Graves* 1907, 264
31.	1776	Unidentified lady	w	[Exhib Free Soc, London, 211]; untraced	*Graves* 1907, 264
32.	1776	Unidentified lady	w	[Exhib Free Soc, London, 215]; untraced	*Graves* 1907, 264
33.	1776	Unidentified nobleman	w	[Exhib Free Soc, London, 210]; untraced	*Graves* 1907, 264
34.	1778	Unidentified 'great personage'	w	[Exhib Soc of Artists, London, 243]; untraced	*Graves* 1907, 263
35.	1778	Unidentified children, two portraits	w	[Exhib Soc of Artists, London, 247]; untraced	*Graves* 1907, 263
36.	1778	Unidentified gentleman	w	[Exhib Soc of Artists, London, 246]; untraced	*Graves* 1907, 263
37.	1778	Unidentified nobleman	w	[Exhib Soc of Artists, London, 244]; untraced	*Graves* 1907, 263
38.	1778	Unidentified young lady	w	[Exhib Soc of Artists, London, 245]; untraced	*Graves* 1907, 263
39.	1779	Unidentified 'great personage'	w	[Exhib Free Soc, London, 165]; untraced	*Graves* 1907, 264
40.	1779	Unidentified child	w	[Exhib Free Soc, London, 168]; untraced	*Graves* 1907, 264
41.	1779	Unidentified gentleman	w	[Exhib Free Soc, London, 166]; untraced	*Graves* 1907, 264
42.	1779	Unidentified lady	w	[Exhib Free Soc, London, 167]; untraced	*Graves* 1907, 264

43.	1779	Unidentified young lady	w	[Exhib Free Soc, London, 169]; untraced	*Graves* 1907, 264
44.	1780	Captain James Cook	w	[Exhib Soc of Artists, London, 277]; untraced	*Graves* 1907, 263
45.	1780	Unidentified artist	w	[Exhib Soc of Artists, London, 276]; untraced	*Graves* 1907, 263
46.	1780	Unidentified boy	w	[Exhib Free Soc, London, 179]; untraced	*Graves* 1907, 264
47.	1780	Unidentified gentleman	w	[Exhib Free Soc, London, 178]; untraced	*Graves* 1907, 264
48.	1780	Unidentified lady	w	[Exhib Soc of Artists, London, 275]; untraced	*Graves* 1907, 263
49.	1780	Unidentified young lady	w	[Exhib Free Soc, London, 177]; untraced	*Graves* 1907, 264
50.	1780	Unidentified young lady	w	[Exhib Free Soc, London, 180]; untraced	*Graves* 1907, 264

VAN DER MEULEN (or VANDERMUELEN), Laurens 1645–1719

He was born in Malines in 1645, the son of Pierre and Elizabeth Schuermans and entered the workshop of Pierre van der Stock on 10 November 1665. Neefs records that a note in his hand gives details of his journey to London in 1675. He married Cornélie Thérèse, née de Croes, 1702.

Among the names mentioned in the 'License to Forainers employed at Windsor to remaine here wth. out molestation' dated 16 November 1678, are 'Laurence Vandermuelen and Antony Verhencke servants to Mr. **Grinling Gibbons**, the carver' (TNA *Domestic Entry Book*, Car II, vol LI, 77, Sp 44/51, fols 77–79). Vertue notes that Gibbons 'was neither well skill'd or practis'd in Marble or in Brass, for which works he imployd the best Artists he could procure'. These included Vandermuelen 'of Brussels' and **A Dievot of Malines**. The two men apparently 'modelld & made' Gibbons's bronze statue of King James II, originally in the Privy Garden at Whitehall (*Vertue* V, 59, 61).

In his notes covering the years 1713–21, Vertue stated that 'Laurence' and Dievot were 'still Living at Antwerp' at that time (*Vertue* I, 61). They had 'left England in the troubles of the Revolution [1688] & retird to their own Country. where Laurence became wealthy. did many Curious works. not only in the Statuary way but also carving Ornaments of wood' (*Vertue* IV, 50). He died on 26 October 1719.

Literary References: *Vertue* I, 61; IV, 50; *Neefs* 1876, 219–24; *Gunnis* 1968, 406–7; *Beard* 1989, 52, 61, 197; *Gibson* 1997 (1), 179; *Gibson* 1999, 22; *Baker* 2000, 86

VAN DER MEULEN II fl 1772–80

The son of **John Ferdinand Van der Meulen**, he too showed regularly with the Free Society, working in marble, clay and wax. For further information the reader is referred to *Pyke* 1973, 91.

Busts

1.	1774	Venus	m	[Exhib Free Soc, London, 300]; untraced	*Graves* 1907, 264
2.	1775	'A Madona'	m	[Exhib Free Soc, London, 281]; untraced	*Graves* 1907, 264
3.	1776	Unidentified subject, 'a small bust'	m	[Exhib Free Soc, London, 216]; untraced	*Graves* 1907, 264
4.	1780	'A Madona'	m	[Exhib Soc of Artists, London, 278]; untraced	*Graves* 1907, 264
5.	1780	Unidentified subject, 'small bust'	m	[Exhib Free Soc, London, 185]; untraced	*Graves* 1907, 264

Reliefs

6.	1773	'A Madona'	m	[Exhib Free Soc, London, 254]; untraced	*Graves* 1907, 264
7.	1773	Head of Our Saviour	m	[Exhib Free Soc, London, 253]; untraced	*Graves* 1907, 264
8.	1773	St John the Evangelist	m	[Exhib Free Soc, London, 255]; untraced	*Graves* 1907, 264
9.	1773	St Luke	m	[Exhib Free Soc, London, 256]; untraced	*Graves* 1907, 264

Miscellaneous

10.	1772	'A Madona', model	tc	[Exhib Free Soc, London, 200]; untraced	*Graves* 1907, 264
11.	1773	Bacchus, model	tc	[Exhib Free Soc, London, 257]; untraced	*Graves* 1907, 264
12.	1774	The four Evangelists	m	[Exhib Free Soc, London, 301]; untraced	*Graves* 1907, 264
13.	1778	Two fancy heads	w	[Exhib Soc of Artists, London, 248 and 249]; untraced	*Graves* 1907, 264
14.	1779	Boy's head (after Bernini)	w	[Exhib Free Soc, London, 172]; untraced	*Graves* 1907, 264
15.	1780	Unidentified child	w	[Exhib Free Soc, London, 184]; untraced	*Graves* 1907, 264
16.	1780	Unidentified young lady	w	[Exhib Free Soc, London, 183]; untraced	*Graves* 1907, 264

VAN DER VOORT, Michiel 1667–1737

He was born, practiced and died in his native Antwerp, spending three years studying in Italy, 1690–93. Like most of his fellow countrymen his work was principally commissioned for an ecclesiastical context though he was responsible also for some imposing baroque portrait busts. It is not clear how the Duke of Argyll's group arrived in Britain (1).

Literary References: *Sculpture. . .Rubens*, 1977, 219–42

Statues

1.	1713	Perseus and Andromeda	[Whitton Place, Middx]; Inveraray Castle, Argyll Other versions: Hotel Osterrieth, Antwerp	*Pearson* 1991, 41, 45

VAN PENNEN, Theodore fl 1725

Statues

1.	1725	Two	[Canons, Middx]; untraced	*Collins Baker* 1949, 142

VAN SANT VOORT, Jan fl 1677–79

A Dutch carver living in Leith, he may have supplied the architect Sir William Bruce with 'robust enrichments of festoons, trophies and cornucopia' especially around the doorway to the west front and on the eastern gate of Bruce's house in Kinross, Fife. He certainly supplied Bruce with a carved heraldic doorway in 1679 (2). Sant Voort also worked under Bruce's supervision at the Palace of Holyroodhouse (1).

Literary References: *Pearson* 1991, 13, 19 n25

Chimneypieces

1.	1677	With lion headed caryatid jambs and swagged overmantel drapery, supplied with other carved work	Holyrood Palace, King's bed chamber and closet	Pevsner, *Edinburgh*, 1991, 145

Architectural Sculpture

2.	1679	Heraldic overdoor	[Kinross, Fife]; untraced	*Pearson* 1991, 13

VAN SPANGEN, I fl 1800–28

See **Austin, Felix**

Statues

1.	1801	Faith, Hope and Charity	[Freemasons' Charity School for female children, St George's Fields, Southwark, London]; untraced	*Euro Mag*, Aug 1801, 105–6; *Gunnis* 1968, 408; *Cavanagh* forthcoming 2007 (lost or removed works)

VAN SPANGEN, Nicholas and Company

Their tradecard describes them as 'Artificial stone manufacturers, near the Old Globe, Mile End Road, where the public may be supplied with all kinds of beautiful statues, ornaments for buildings and which for beauty and durability far exceed stone. Also stones or lumps to any size or dimensions for firework' (BM Heal, 106.22/2).

VAN SPANGEN, Richard fl 1677

He was described as 'of St Bride's, London, Carver, abt. 25' in 1677 when he married Martha Garland (Lic Vic Gen, 18 Sept 1677). See **Van Spangen (or Spanger), Richard, of Camberwell.**

VAN SPANGEN (or SPANGER), Richard, of Camberwell –1757

A mason and haberdasher of Camberwell, Surrey, in 1728 he subscribed to James Gibbs's *Book of Architecture* and the following year carved a font to Gibbs's design (2). This was commissioned by a Mr Hume whose memorandum reads 'Sept 1729 I agreed with Mr Van Spangen to make me a font to the dimensions and form of the draught made by Mr Gibbs architect. The Bason and pedestal to be of the best white veined marble. The plinth of black marble vein'd with gold, and the step of Portland stone. The whole to be perforated with a brass stop-cock to carry off the water into a cistern below, and to be set up in Dulwich College Chapel' (*Young* 1889, 2, 346).

He is likely to be the 'Mr Spangor' who provided the monument for Lord Trevor, commissioned by the 3rd Baron Trevor (1). It has an armorial shield with helm, crest and supporters, and a cushion of white marble supporting the baron's coronet. The Rev Benjamin Rogers noted in his diary 'Some of the marble cost Mr. Spangor the Statuary in the block in Italy 18s. per foot, which stood him in 26s. per foot when brought to London, this was black with yellow veins' (*Harvey* 1872–8, 68). It was completed on 25 October 1732.

Spangen appears to have had some association with a *Thomas Dunn*, who names him as 'Richard Spanger other Spangen' of Camberwell in his will. Van Spangen acted as an executor and was left £5 (PROB 11/747/12–15).

Gunnis possessed a letter from Van Spangen, dated 19 December 1749, addressed to a Mr Hooper of Hailsham, Sussex, enclosing three drawings for monumental tablets. The current whereabouts of this letter is unknown, but Gunnis quoted it at length. Spangen wrote 'the enclosed sketches I have made according to your direction, the expense will be about what you mention; they are drawn to a small scale but when executed will be about 8 ft. high and breadth proportionate. Materials to be of the best white and Veined and statuary marble'. It continues, 'the inscription to be engraved and painted black, and the coat of arms in proper colours and executed in a workmanlike manner'. It is not known if Mr Hooper ever ordered from one of these designs and there is no sign of any work resembling them in Hailsham church.

Van Spangen's will was proved on 14 February 1757. The sale of a collection of paintings owned by a Mr Van Spangen was held at Fords, 2–4 March 1742.

Literary References: *Lugt*, 552; *Gunnis* 1968, 361; *Craske* 2000 (2), 105, 112 n27–8

Archival References: RG/JP, 8, 1501

Will: PROB 11/828

Funerary Monuments

1.	1732	Lord Trevor Payment(s): £250	Bromham, Beds	*Harvey* 1872–8, 68; *Gunnis* 1968, 361

Architectural Sculpture

2.	1729	Font, marble bowl on baluster (designed by James Gibbs)	Dulwich College, London, chapel	*Friedman* 1984, 305
3.	1754	Dial and pedestal Payment(s): £6 10s 6d	[Glynde, Sussex]; untraced	GPC

VANDER HAGEN, M fl 1851

When he exhibited at the Great Exhibition he was described in the *Art Journal* as 'a Belgian sculptor settled in London' (*AJ Cat* 1851, 72). The writer was impressed with the work which it described as 'very symmetrical in its proportions, and the drapery is arranged in an easy flowing style, that gives grace and firmness to the principal figure' (1).

Statues

1.	1851	Virgin and child	[Gt Exhib, London]; untraced	*AJ Cat* 1851, 72 (repr)

VANDERSTAINE (or VAN DER STEIN), John fl 1678–1700

He was a stonecarver, servant and housekeeper to **Grinling Gibbons**. On 16 November 1678 a licence was granted for him to be employed under the architect Hugh May in the King's service at Windsor Castle. A further permit from the Privy Council, dated 21 May 1679, allowed him to 'remaine here wth out molestation together with John Oastes [**John Nost I**] and Arnold Luellan [**Arnold Quellin**]' and 'to go freely about the cities of London and Westminster until further orders' (TNA *Domestic Entry Book*, Car II, Vol LI, SP 44/51 fol 77–79). Three days later Hugh May certified that Vanderstaine was one of the men employed at Windsor Castle (TNA, Privy Council Register, PC, 2/68). There he worked on the elaborate royal throne, cutting slaves, a figure of *Justice* and two of *Fame*, as well as 'three pieces of Trophies' (*Hope* 1913, 318) (**3**). He also provided a pedestal for the King's statue and sundry other work (**4**).

In 1684–5 he was in Oxford. 'Mr Vanderstene Carver' was paid £26 10s for unidentified work at the Physick Garden and the following year he was paid a further £7 12s for 'cutting the Earl of Danby's Statue, and for other Worke at the Physick Garden' (Oxford, V-C's Accts, Archive WP /21/5 unfol) (**1**). In c1693 he received £8 for models of classical philosophers (**2**) and in 1694 a payment for 'fretwork in the New Library' (**5**). In 1696 he was also paid for carving the eight statues on the west front of the building, and for 'two eagles and eight keystones' (**6**).

Literary References: *Green* 1964 (1), 54, 82–3, 84; *Gunnis* 1968, 407; *Whinney* 1988, 443 n34, 445 n67; *Beard* 1989 (2), 51–2, 58

Statues

1.	1694–1696	King Charles I, King Charles II, Earl of Danby Payment(s): £26 10s	s	Oxford Physic Gardens, entrance archway	Oxford, V-C's Accts; *Gibson* 1997 (1), 374
2.	1693–1696	Statues, including four philosophers Payment(s): £178 1s		Queen's College Library, Oxford, garden front	QCL, Ms 475 (Smith Ms 98) fol 234c; *Magrath* II 1921, 70, n4; Pevsner, *Oxon*, 1974, 186

Architectural Sculpture

3.	1678	Carver's work for the Royal throne Payment(s): £197 10s	wd	[Windsor Castle, Berks]; untraced	*Hope* 1913, 318; *Gunnis* 1968, 407
4.	1678	'For drawing and making of several designs, models and figures in clay for ye pedestall under His Majesty's statue and for carving ye stone eagles that the brasse dyall is set upon'		[Windsor Castle, Berks]; untraced	TNA A01/2478/271; *Gunnis* 1968, 407
5.	1694	Fretwork in the new library		[The Queen's College, Oxford]; untraced	*Gunnis* 1968, 407 quoting Queen's Coll archives (entry untraced)

Miscellaneous

6.	1696	'Two eagles and eight keystones'		[The Queen's College, Oxford]; untraced	*Gunnis* 1968, 407 quoting Queen's Coll archives (entry untraced)

VANGELDER, Peter Mathias *c*1742–1809

Vangelder was born in Amsterdam, but nothing is known of his parentage, early life or training. He was first recorded in London in September 1769, when he entered the Royal Academy schools, giving his age as 27. He was an outstanding student, winning a silver medal in the same year and a gold medal for a bas-relief in 1771 (**39, 40**). In the competition for the latter he also submitted a 'sketch' (perhaps a drawing) of *Samson and Delilah*. In May 1772 the Royal Academy council wrote to Van Gelder, along with three other students asking if he wanted to be considered as a candidate 'to be sent abroad on his Majesty's pension'. In the event the scholarship was won by **Thomas Banks** (RA Council Minutes, vol 1, 1772, fol 135).

He was employed in the busy workshop of **Thomas Carter II** from 1769. **John Deare**, who was apprenticed to Carter in 1776, recorded in June that year that Vangelder had carved a 'large figure' for Carter which was currently in the shop and that the Dutchman was 'considered one of the best hands in London at foliage' (*Smith* 1828, vol 2, 306). This skill was most clearly demonstrated in the monument to Mary Frampton (**1**), which the antiquary John Hutchins described in 1774 as 'esteemed by connoisseurs one of the completest pieces of sculpture in this Kingdom' (*Hutchins* 1, 1861, 403). The monument is a simple wall-slab in a frame carved with wild and cultivated flowers. Its appeal was lasting: Gunnis called it 'one of the most enchanting works of art in any English church' (*Gunnis* 1968, 407).

Vangelder appears to have begun working independently whilst employed at Carter's workshop. Deare wrote that Vangelder 'was seven years in saving a thousand pounds, by keeping men at work at his own house, while he got two guineas a week at Mr Carter's' (*Smith* 1828, vol 2, 306). By June 1776 he had set up his own premises in Riding House Lane.

In April 1775 he married Martha Evans at St Marylebone. The connection was to prove useful: she was the daughter of the carpenter and architect Charles Evans, who subsequently employed Vangelder to carve sculptural ornaments for 20, Upper Grosvenor Street, London and for St Michael, Badminton, which Evans rebuilt for the 5th Duke of Beaufort (**35**).

Vangelder was the executant of several monuments designed by the architect Robert Adam. The memorial commemorating Mary, Duchess of Montagu (**3**), which was at least part-designed by Adam, takes the form of a semi circular platform decorated with low-relief carvings of women, one engaged in painting, another in sewing and a third holding an inverted torch. Ionic pilasters and festoons set off the figures. On this platform is a sculptural scene reflecting the Duchess's most admired virtue, charity. An angel shows the seated Duchess the path to Heaven, while two orphans and a widow mourn her death. The monument to Major John André has a relief carving of the British officer soliciting pardon from George Washington, who had ordered André's execution as a spy during the American War of Independence (**5**). The monument to Robert Child has a pyramid flanked by finely-carved candelabra (**6**).

Vangelder's business was diverse, like many another traditional mason-sculptor. As a building contractor he put up houses in Bedford Square (1781), Riding House Lane (1786) and Devonshire Place (1793), and he was responsible for a considerable amount of architectural sculpture for the City livery companies. He provided chimneypieces a

Northwick Park (**26**) 'in a superior style of elegance' (*GM*, vol 63, 1793, 298) and supplied at least one chimneypiece for Adam at Culzean Castle (**30**). His wall-monuments typically comprise pyramids, above inscription tablets flanked by fluted borders to suggest the edges of a sarcophagus (**2, 13, 15**). There were variations: the monument to James West has a gothic, almost oriental arch (**12**), whilst Alexander Hume's has two large dolphins either side of an altar tomb (**11**).

Vangelder died on 3 September 1809, in Upper Norton Street, Marylebone. His obituary states that he was 70 (*GM*, 1809, vol 79, pt II, 392). He entrusted his properties in Gower Street to William Meredith of Harley Place and William Winfield of St Martin's Lane. Mary Franklin of Cricklewood Farm was left £2,500 in annuities, and £200, also in annuities, went to the son of his surgeon. All Vangelder's household goods and furniture, including his jewellery, china, glassware, books, prints, wines and liquors were left to his wife, Martha. She died on 6 March 1814, at Upper George Street, Portman Square (*GM*, 1814, pt1, 414), and parts of Vangelder's estate remained unadministered until 1842.

MGS

Literary References: *Hutchison* 1960–2, 123; *Gunnis* 1968, 407; *Penny* 1977 (1), 192, 224 n43; *Whinney* 1988, 313; *Colvin* 1995, 355
Archival References: RA Premium list; Middx Sessions Colls of Records, MR/B; IGI
Will: PROB 11/1506/494–8

Funerary Monuments

1.	+1762	Mary Frampton (under the direction of Thomas Carter II)		Moreton, Dorset		*Hutchins* 1774, I, 149 (repr); *Hutchins* 1861, vi, 403–4; *Gunnis* 1968, 407; *Whinney* 1988, 315
2.	†1775	Catherine Jekyll		Arthingworth, Northants	S	*Whinney* 1988, 465 n22
3.	1775	Mary, Duchess of Montagu (†1771) (designed by Robert Adam) Payment(s): £2000		Warkton, Northants	S	Pevsner, *Northants*, 1973, 443; *Penny* 1977 (1), 192, 224 n43; *CIIA* 4/3/122–38; *Whinney* 1988, 313–5 (repr)
4.	1778	Edward Fulham (†1694) and family		Compton, Surrey		Pevsner, *Surrey*, 1971, 168
5.	c1782	Major John André (†1780) (designed by Robert Adam) Drawing(s): Soane, Adam, Vol 19/29, 30, 31, 32		Westminster Abbey, London, nave	S	*Malcolm* 1803–7, 167; *Sherborn* 1955, 617 (repr); *MacMichael* 1997, 18 (repr); *Whinney* 1988, 315
6.	†1782	Robert Child (designed by Robert Adam) Drawing(s): VAM E.973-1965; Soane, Adam Vol 19/79, 80, 81, 82		Heston, Middx	S	*Physick* 1969, 142–3 (drawing and monument repr); Pevsner, *London: N W*, 1991, 423; *Colvin* 1995, 63
7.	†1786	Henry Read		Ramsbury, Wilts	S	*Gunnis* 1968, 407; Pevsner, *Wilts*, 1975, 379
8.	†1786	Selina Newland		Havant, Hants	S	Pevsner, *Hants & Isle of Wight*, 1967, 277; *Gunnis* 1968, 407
9.	1796	Margaret Emma, Lady Orde (†1790)		Hanwell, Middx	S	*Gunnis* 1968, 407; Pevsner, *London: N W*, 1991, 183
10.	?1797	Henry Southby		Buckland, Berks	S	*Gunnis* 1968, 407
11.	†1800	Alexander Hume		Wormley, Herts, churchyard		*Malcolm* 1803–7, 167; *Gunnis* 1968, 408
12.	1800	James West and family		Preston-on-Stour, Warks		C Lib (repr)
13.	†1800	John, Lord Northwick		Blockley, Glos	S	*Gunnis* 1968, 407; *Whinney* 1988, 315; Pevsner, *Glos: Cotswolds*, 1999, 183
14.	+1801	Frances Read		Ramsbury, Wilts	S	*Gunnis* 1968, 407; Pevsner, *Wilts*, 1975, 379
15.	†1802	John Fleming		North Stoneham, Hants	S	*Gunnis* 1968, 407; Pevsner, *Hants & Isle of Wight*, 1967, 359
16.	†1802	Mary Puleston		St Giles, Wrexham, Denbighs	S	Pevsner, *Clwyd*, 1986, 301–2
17.	?1802	Robert Davies		Wrexham, Denbighs	S	*Gunnis* 1968, 407
18.	†1804	Frances Puleston		St Giles, Wrexham, Denbighs	S	Pevsner, *Clwyd*, 1986, 301
19.	?1804	Richard Puleston		Wrexham, Denbighs	S	*Gunnis* 1968, 407
20.	†1805	Elizabeth Hatsell		All Saints, Fulham, London	S	Pevsner, *London: N W*, 1991, 231
21.	1806	Marmaduke Tomline (†1803) (designed by E Tomline)		Riby, Lincs		Pevsner, *Lincs*, 1989, 611
22.	?1808	Newton Barton		Broadwater, Sussex	S	*Gunnis* 1968, 408

Chimneypieces

23.	c1760	A pair for the saloon ('highly finished') and another with caryatid figures of nymphs, and ornamented with the triumph of Venus, for the gallery		Harewood House, W R Yorks		*Jewell* 1822, 30, 32
24.	1777	Description unavailable Payment(s): £16 7s 5d	m	[30 Upper Grosvenor Street, London]; untraced		RG/JP, 8, 1498 (quoting archives, Lord Braye of Stanford, untraced)
25.	1776–1778	One, with other ornamental carving in the hall Payment(s): £691 1s 2d		[Drapers' Hall, London, court room]; untraced		Drapers' Co Ledger 1770–9, AL16
26.	c1778	Two		[Northwick Park, Glos, breakfast and drawing rooms]; untraced		*GM*, vol 63, 1793, 298; Pevsner, *Glos: Cotswolds*, 1999, 523
27.	1779	Statuary marble		[Beaufort House, Grosvenor Square, London]; untraced		Beaufort Papers QA 2/5/2
28.	1782	Drawing room and back parlour Payment(s): £264 15s 6d with other work	m	[Duke of Beaufort, probably for his London house]; untraced		RG/JP, 8, 1498 quoting archives, Duke of Beaufort
29.	1786	One Payment(s): £54 5s (?part payment)		Oakly Park, Ludlow, Salop		SRR 552/Powis coll
30.	1791	With statuary marble mantel and jambs with carved wood dressings	m	[Culzean Castle, Ayrshire]; untraced		*Harris* 2001, 366 n55

31.	1793	Several, including two, each with a large sphinx as a central tablet and tripods with elephant heads as the side panels Payment(s): £168	m	Sledmere House, E R Yorks, gallery (£168), drawing room and perhaps other rooms	Sykes/Rose, March 1791, 31 May 1793
32.	1800	Several		[Grocers' Hall, London]; untraced	Grocers, Ledger, p230; *Gunnis* 1968, 407;
33.	1809	Description unavailable		[Mr Coutts's house, Stratton Street, Piccadilly]; untraced	*Gunnis* 1968, 407
34.	nd			[Shugborough, Staffs]; untraced	*Robinson* 1989, 37
Architectural Sculpture					
35.	1783–1785	Decorative carving Payment(s): £73 16s 9d		St Michael, Great Badminton, Glos	Building Accounts, Badminton Church, Glos RO D2700/RA2/1/19 and 20
36.	1790	Urn Payment(s): 17 gns	m	[Sledmere House, E R Yorks]; untraced	RG/JP, 8, 1498 quoting Sykes archives
37.	1789–1792	Various, including four Portland stone capitals for the colonnade, the King's Arms over the Master's chair and 'two boys holding two dolphins' Payment(s): £296 in all, Including £60, £38 and £24 respectively for the specified work	s	[Fishmongers' Hall, London]; untraced	Fishmongers P L, 1, pp 107, 111, 156
38.	1794	Marble plaque	m	[Audley End, Essex, library]; untraced	Essex RO D/DBy A225; *Gunnis* 1968, 407
Reliefs					
39.	1769	Unidentified subject, model		[RA Silver Medal]; untraced	RA Premium list; *Hutchison* 1960–2, 134
40.	1771	The choice of Hercules, bas-relief		[RA Gold Medal]; untraced	*Press Cuttings* 1723–1800, fol 117; RA Premium list

VANINA (or VANNINI), Peter fl 1753–70

Vanina produced plaster casts of antiquities, historic and contemporary subjects. He rented premises at 6 St James's Street, London, from George James, which he kept until June 1765. Soon after Vanina was granted a 14-year extension to his lease by John Finlayson, a coal merchant, he was approached by James Lock, a hatter. Lock offered him £520 plus £52 10s p.a. to sell him the sublease. Vanina accepted Lock's offer in December 1764 and he had moved out by Midsummer's Day 1765, when Lock first paid rates for 6 St James's Street. On 19 December 1767 Vanina placed a notice in the *Public Advertiser* in which he described himself as a 'caster in Dover-Street, Piccadilly, formerly in St James's Square' (p 4). It announced his intention to sell by subscription sets of figures in plaster of paris 'by the best masters, about two and a half feet high, taken from original models recently purchased and brought from Rome, including Castor and Pollux after the antique, a young Mars ditto, and a Venus de Medicis after Legros'. This set was to be marketed at five guineas. A second set comprising a David and Goliath, a Samson after the antique, and a 'Susannae after Fiamingo' would be offered at four guineas the set. Clients were informed that half the payment should be made on subscribing and the rest on delivery. He also advertised as available at the same premises several large statues from original models and bronzes.

In 1758 when Sir Edward Littleton approached **Michael Rysbrack** for plaster copies of his own portrait bust, Rysbrack replied that making multiples was 'a thing Entirely out of my way', going on to say that he had consulted 'Mr Vannini, the Caster in Plaster of Paris. (Whom I Employ when I want) what the expense will be, of a Mould off of your Honour's Bust, and each Cast out of it . . . For the Mould the Expence will be three Guineas, and each cast, out of it; will be 16 Shillings' (*Webb* 1954, 199 quoting Rysbrack's letter of 21 January). A second letter, dated 28 February, assured Littleton that Vannini was confident that making a mould from his bust would not damage it (*ibid*). A payment of £15 10s to a 'Peter Vannine' in **L F Roubiliac**'s bank account on 26 March 1756 suggests that he too occasionally employed Vanina. There may also have been a connection with **Peter Scheemakers**, for Staffordshire figures of Shakespeare after Scheemakers's monument in Westminster Abbey often bear the incised mark 'P.V' on the back of the pedestal, indicating that they are taken from a signed plaster model by Vanina. Scheemakers had himself marketed sets of plaster casts of his own models from the antique in 1748 and it is conceivable either that Vanina was responsible for those, in which case he was working in England earlier than available documentation indicates, or that Vanina capitalised on Scheemakers's business venture. It is also possible that Vanina made scaled-up versions in plaster of the clay models prepared by sculptors, so that dimensions could be translated accurately to marble.

Vanina had a wide selection of plaster busts and figures, some of them of a considerable size (**5, 21**). He had a repertoire of finishes, including 'plaster bronzes' and 'figures bronzed'. Plaster bronzes may simply have been coloured with bronze filings to resemble bronze, but 'figures bronzed', if different, may have been a more elaborate technique whereby copper was applied to the surface of the plaster, a method which had been used on Italian terracottas since the 15th century. He coloured at least one to imitate terracotta (**37**). There is no evidence that he worked in materials other than plaster.

James Christie held two auctions at Vanina's house in Dover Street in 1770, selling his stock in trade on 4–5 April 1770 and his household possessions on 3 July 1770. The first catalogue carried the information that Vanina was going abroad. It listed 'a great variety of plaister figures, busts, brackets, basso relievos, equestrian statues in bronze and white; also, all his models, by the most esteemed artists, together with some real bronzes, two fine schiola marble tables, &c / The statues are original casts from the Antique'. There were 90 lots. The purchasers included **John Cheere** and **Richard Parker**.

Vanina and his wife were named as legatees in Michael Rysbrack's will of 5 March 1768. Rysbrack left Vanina one guinea in his will, but £25 to his wife, Anna Maria Vanina (PROB 11, microfilm 954, quire 28, 223).

Gordon Balderston/IR

Literary References: *Vertue* III, 141; *Webb* 1954, 190, 193, 199, 201; *Survey of London*, XXIX–XXX, Parish of Westminster, pt 1, south of Piccadilly, 3 vols, 1960, 433–58; *Gunnis* 1968, 408; *Clifford* 1992, 64–5; *Bindman and Baker* 1995, 250, 385 n12; *Dawson* 1999, 154

Auction Catalogues: Vanina 1770 (1); Vanina 1770 (2)

Statues					
1.	1759	Apollo Payment(s): 7 gns	p	[Croome Court, Worcs]; untraced	*Beard* 1993, 92; GPC
2.	Before 1760	Lions and other figures		[for Charles Rogers]; untraced	*Melton* 1961, 366
3.	1761	Two		[Glynde, Sussex, coll Richard Trevor, Bishop of Durham]; untraced	*Gunnis* 1968, 408 quoting archives, Humphrey Brand of Glynde; *Clifford* 1992, 64
4.	nd	A figure of St Jerome and 8 boys		bt John Cheere; untraced	Vanina sale (2), day 2, lot 6, £1 10s
5.	nd	Antique boxer, six feet high		bt Oliver; untraced	Vanina sale (2), day 2, lot 46
6.	nd	Apollo, Venus de Medici, Mercury, Antinous, Brutus and Celeste 'original statues'		[Vanina sale (1), 1770]; untraced	*Gunnis* 1968, 408
7.	nd	Castor and Pollux, and two other figures		Untraced	Vanina sale (1), lot 6
8.	nd	David and Goliath's head, two		bt Richard Parker; untraced	Vanina sale (2), day 2, lots 29 and 36
9.	nd	Dryden	p	bt Oliver; untraced	Vanina sale (2), day 2, lot 25
10.	nd	Flora		[Vanina sale (1), 1770]; bt John Flaxman I; untraced	*Gunnis* 1968, 408
11.	nd	Flora, Hercules, Susannah, Venus, Sampson, St Andrew (part of repertoire)	p	Untraced	*Clifford* 1992, 65
12.	nd	Hercules, Ceres and Venus, figures		bt John Cheere; untraced	Vanina sale (2), day 2, lot 3, 15s
13.	nd	Homer	p	bt Oliver; untraced	Vanina sale (2), day 2, lot 24
14.	nd	Horses, sphinxes, lions (part of repertoire)	pb	Untraced	*Clifford* 1992, 65
15.	nd	King Louis XIV and King William III, equestrian		[Vanina sale (1), 1770]; untraced	*Gunnis* 1968, 408
16.	nd	Rhinoceros		bt Richard Parker; untraced	Vanina sale (2), day 2, lot 14
17.	nd	Rubens and Vandyck, statuettes, probably after Rysbrack		[Vanina sale (2), 1770]; untraced	*Gunnis* 1968, 408
18.	nd	Sampson with the lion		Untraced	Vanina sale (1), lot 13
19.	nd	St Elizabeth and St John on her knee		bt John Cheere; untraced	Vanina sale (2), day 2, lot 6, 12s
20.	nd	Two, of Susannah	p	bt John Cheere; untraced	Vanina sale (2), day 2, lot 28, £1 10s and lot 45, £1 10s
21.	nd	'Venus Celeste, from the Tuscan gallery, five feet four inches high'		bt John Cheere; untraced	Vanina sale (2), day 2, lot 57, £8 10s
22.	nd	Venus de Medicis	p	bt Oliver; untraced	Vanina sale (2), day 2, lot 46
23.	nd	'Venus with the Crawfish'		Untraced	*Clifford* 1992, 65
Busts					
24.	1759	Homer and Seneca		[Croome Court, Worcs]; untraced	GPC quoting Archives, Earl of Coventry
25.	nd	3 large plaster busts and 4 bronzed ditto		Untraced	Vanina sale (1), lots 4 and 5
26.	nd	Duke of Cumberland	p	bt Richard Parker; untraced	Vanina sale (2), day 2, lot 53
27.	nd	Horace and Pope, with brackets	pb	bt Richard Parker; untraced	Vanina sale (2), day 2, lot 18
28.	nd	Madonna, Vestal, Apollo, Julius Caesar, Antinous, Seneca, Demosthenes, William Shakespeare, Matthew Prior, William Congreve, John Milton, Sir Walter Raleigh, Ben Jonson, and the Duke of Cumberland		[Vanina sale (1), 1770]; untraced	*Gunnis* 1968, 408; *Clifford* 1992, 65
29.	nd	Mithridates, Lord Halifax, King Alfred		Untraced	*Clifford* 1992, 65
30.	nd	Niobe, Caracalla, Antinous, Cupid and Psyche, Castor and Pollux, Hercules and Atlas	p	Untraced	*Clifford* 1992, 65
31.	nd	Sir Isaac Newton		Untraced	*Clifford* 1992, 65; *Dawson* 1999, 152–4
32.	nd	Venus and Tiberius		[Vanina sale (1), 1770]; untraced	*Gunnis* 1968, 408
Reliefs					
33.	nd	'of boys and a dolphin', and 'Two ditto'		bt John Cheere; untraced	Vanina sale (2), day 2, lot 57, £1 10s; lot 58, £1 10s
34.	nd	The Virgin Mary Visiting St Elizabeth	pb	[Vanina sale (1), 1770, lot 69]; bt John Cheere; untraced	*Gunnis* 1968, 408
35.	nd	'Two barso relievos (plaister)'		bt John Cheere; untraced	Vanina sale (2), day 2, lot 56, £1 10s
Miscellaneous					
36.	nd	Group of figures, Hercules, medallion and model		Untraced	Vanina sale (1), lot 7
37.	nd	St James 'plaister coloured like terracotta'		Untraced	*Clifford* 1992, 65
38.	nd	Two vases		bt Richard Parker; untraced	Vanina sale (2), day 2, lot 13
39.	nd	Two vases		bt Richard Parker; untraced	Vanina sale (2), day 2, lot 40
40.	nd	Watch-case in basso relievo, ditto tablet, two busts and brackets		Untraced	Vanina sale (1), lot 8

VANPOOK, of Brussels fl *c*1790

The Petrie monument has a large, sparingly framed relief of a woman reclining on a couch, with children at her feet and an allegorical female at her head (1). Gunnis considered it magnificent. It was sent over from Brussels *c*1790 and erected on the north side of the organ, where it was fixed in position by **Thomas Banks**. In 1795 Banks provided the companion monument to Margaret Petrie on the south side of the organ.

Literary References: *Gunnis* 1968, 408

Funerary Monuments				
1.	†1787	Anne Petrie	St Mary, Lewisham, London	*Gunnis* 1968, 408; Pevsner, *London: S*, 1983, 415

VANVELT –1773

On 20 September 1773 the *Public Advertiser* announced 'Yesterday Morning early died, at his House in Piccadilly, Mr Vanvelt, an eminent Carver and Statuary' (p 2).

VARDY, Thomas fl 1755–89

Vardy was a furniture carver and the brother of the architect John Vardy. In 1763 he was described in Mortimer's *Universal Director* as a 'carver' of Park Street, Grosvenor Square (p 28).

On 9 July 1755 he submitted an estimate of £450 for executing all the carving designed by George Dance (1695–1768) for the great hall of the Mansion House, but his estimate was not accepted. The contract went to **John Fowler Nicholl** and **William How** who quoted £437 (Mansion Hse Comm 01/01/2 p 764). In 1767 Vardy carved tablets for chimneypieces at Hill Park (1), then being built for Lord Hillsborough by the architect Henry Holland (Holland's account-book, SJSM). He also made several chimneypieces for Cobham Hall, Kent, including 'a very pretty one' in 1773 for the blue damask room (2) (Archives, Earl of Darnley, cited by *Gunnis* 1968, 408).

In 1774 Thomas's daughter, Sarah, married **Richard Westmacott I**. In 1789 Thomas took his grandson, **Sir Richard Westmacott RA**, as an apprentice (Joiner's Apprentice Bindings, Guildhall, London, vol 7, 215, 24 June 1789). The will of **Richard Westmacott I** describes Sarah Vardy (Westmacott's wife) as 'Sarah, daughter of the late Thomas Vardy of Park Street.'

Literary References: *Gunnis* 1968, 408; *Busco* 1994, 6

Will: PROB 11/1483, 253–4, proved July 1808 (Richard Westmacott I)

Chimneypieces

1.	1767	Two tablets		[Hill Park, Westerham, Kent]; untraced	Soane Case 128, fols 10–11; 129, unfol, c ff68–9; *Gunnis* 1968, 408
2.	1773	Several		Cobham Hall, Kent	*Gunnis* 1968, 408

VARIGNE fl 1703

In 1703 William Wynde, the architect, wrote to Lady Mary Bridgwater concerning lead figures: 'Madam since my laste I have enquired about a statue fitt for yr Ladys garden, and in order thereunto I was at Mr Nostes [**John Nost I**]; Mr lasons [**Lasons**], Mr Varigne and Mr Ansgood [**Richard Osgood** ?]; who has the best Leaden figures 3 of wch I picked on . . . a Venus and Cupide wch will cost about 12 pound, if single, withe out a Cupid 8 pound, the next is Juno . . . about 10 but ye besy figure is an Extraordinary figur but one oor two of ye moulds have been [illegible] very good pieces with fine mantel or drapery caste very loosely over him . . . this is the best of all the figures, they are moderne . . .' (Weston Hall, Staffs, Earl of Bradford MSS 18/4).

VASSALLI, Francesco fl 1723–63

A decorative plasterer, he was one of a family long settled at Riva St Vitale, near Lugarno. He was in England by 1724 and provided ornaments in a number of English houses including Sutton Scarsdale, Derbys; Aske Hall, Yorks and Townley Hall, Lancs. At Castle Howard, he was paid 2 guineas 'for drawing a design for finishing ye temple' in 1736 (5th Book of Disbursements, 7 Sept). The following year he earned £141 for work 'at ye inside of ye Temple' [of the Winds] in stucco and scagliola (Castle Howard Building Accts, G2/1/4, fol 151r, 152v; G2/2/54). In 1723 Sir John Dutton paid 'Sig. Vassalli' for 14 busts, again no doubt of plaster (1). In 1724 he made a number of plaster figures and busts for Ditchley Park, Oxon (4). His last known English commission, completed in 1763, was for stucco work in the library and dining room at Shugborough, Staffs.

Literary References: *Gunnis* 1968, 408; *Beard* 1981, 288–9

Busts					
1.	1723	14, of unidentified subjects Payment(s): £20 9s		[coll Sir John Dutton]; untraced	*Gunnis* 1968, 408 citing Archives, Lord Sherborne
Architectural Sculpture					
2.	1724	Plaster-work	p	[Sutton Scarsdale, Derbys]; untraced	*Gunnis* 1968, 408
3.	1761	Stucco work	p	[Croome Court, Worcs]; untraced	*Beard* 1993, 92
Miscellaneous					
4.	1724	Several figures and busts	p	Ditchley Park, Oxon, great hall	GPC citing Dillon Archives

VAUGHAN, William fl *c*1671

Funerary Monuments

1.	†1671	Dame Sarah Wynn		Llanrwst, Denbighs	Pevsner, *Clwyd*, 1986, 235

VAUGHAN & CO, of Southwark fl 1846

Statues

1.	1846	Theobald Mathew	s	Cork	*ILN*, IX, 1846, 109 (repr as woodcut); *Ormond* 1973, 306

VEALE, John Richard, of Plymouth fl 1747–74

His known monuments are large and architectural and have an elaborate and well-carved shield and coat of arms at the base. Richard Veale of Plymouth, who was perhaps a son of J R Veale was paid nearly £100 for repairs to Antony House, Cornwall, in 1818 (Archives, Sir John Carew-Pole Bt, in GPC).

Literary References: *Gunnis* 1968, 409

Funerary Monuments						
1.	?1747	Adrian Swete		Ermington, Devon	S	*Gunnis* 1968, 409
2.	1749	John Clarke		St Dominic, Cornwall	S	Pevsner, *Cornwall*, 1970, 168
3.	†1753	Thomas Saltren		Parkham, Devon	S	Pevsner, *Devon*, 1989, 624
Chimneypieces						
4.	1733	Description unavailable Payment(s): £9 13s 6d	m	[John Tremayne's house, Sydenham, Devon, dining room]; untraced		GPC citing Archives Air-Vice Marshal Sir Philip Babbington

VEALE, of Plympton St Mary, Devon fl 1725?

Funerary Monuments

1.	?1725	John Harrys	Plymstock, Devon	S	*Gunnis* 1968, 409

VERDIER fl 1755–61?

Verdier was one of the carvers, like **Gaspar Van der Hagen**, who worked for Rysbrack and may be identical with the ivory carver who signs himself '**GVDR**.' An 'Ayme Vedeau' was rated in Green Street South, London, at £35 between 1755 and 1761

Archival References: Cleansing Street Rates F5907 1881; F5983 1887; F5991 1887

VERE, William, of Stratford-by-Bow fl 1762–90

The son of Thomas Vere, a corn-factor of Barking, Essex, he was apprenticed to Thomas Vidgeon on 5 October 1762, becoming free of the Masons' Company in 1775. In 1787 he was appointed steward of the Masons' Company, but asked to be allowed to refuse the office as he had met with an accident and hurt his leg. The Court would not accept this excuse and ordered their clerk to write 'peremptorily to him to attend' (Masons' Co, *Court Book*, 1751–96, 4 Oct 1787). His son, also William, became a liveryman of the Masons' Company and took two apprentices under its auspices, Thomas Humphrey (1786) and Robert Cooke (1795). The Feake monument is 12 feet high and has a pyramid, in front of which stands a large urn with a well-carved relief of an East Indiaman in full sail (**2**).

Literary References: *Gunnis* 1968, 409; *Webb* 1999, 8, 18, 34

Archival References: Masons' Co, Freemen, fol 70, 17th Jan 1776; GPC

Funerary Monuments

1.	†1782	Chester Moor Hall (†1771) and his wife, Martha	Sutton, Essex	S	
2.	1790	Samuel Feake	Henham, Essex	S	Pevsner, *Essex*, 1965, 239

VERHUKE, Anthony fl 1670–1719

He was one of the foreign crafstmen employed at Windsor Castle by King Charles II, who was given a permit from the Privy Council on 21 May 1679 to 'remaine here wth out molestation together with John Oastes [**John Nost I**] and Arnold Luellan [**Arnold Quellin**]' and 'to go freely about the cities of London and Westminster, until further orders' (TNA *Domestic Entry Book*, Car II, Vol LI, SP 44/51 fols 77–79). He, **Laurens Vandermeulen** and **Arnold Quellin** were described as 'servants to **Grinling Gibbons**, the Carver'.

VERNON, John fl 1713

Statues

1.	1713	Two griffins	s	[probably for Wentworth Woodhouse, W R Yorks]; untraced	*Gunnis* 1968, 409, citing BM Add. MS, 22,257

VERSCHAFFEN (or VERSCHAFFELT), Peter Anton 1710–93

As chief sculptor to the Elector Palatine, he chose, perhaps surprisingly, to exhibit at the Free Society in 1765 (**3**). Lord Rockingham bought his busts of *Homer* and *Mithridates* from John Shackleton in March 1762 (**1, 2**). George Bubb Doddington recorded in his diary for 27 June 1752 'Mr Verschaffelts dined here, and I paid him 100 l. in part, for his statue'. No information has emerged on this work. (Inf. Gordon Balderston)

Literary References: *Wyndham* 1764, 146; *Gunnis* 1968, 409; *Penny* 1991 (2), 15, 32 n68

Busts

1.	1762	Homer Payment(s): £52 with Mithridates	m	[Wentworth Woodhouse, Yorks]; untraced	W W Muniments, M2, SCL; *Penny* 1991 (2), 15, 16 (repr)
2.	1762	Mithridates Payment(s): £52 with Homer	m	[Wentworth Woodhouse, Yorks]; untraced	W W Muniments, M2, SCL; *Penny* 1991 (2), 15, 16 (repr)

Reliefs

3.	1765	Large marble relief	m	[Exhib Free Soc, London, 192]; untraced	*Graves* 1907, 267

VIALLS, Thomas fl 1763

Mortimer's *Director* recorded in 1763 that Vialls was a carver of Great Newport-Street (p 28).

VICK, of Hereford fl 1798–1825

Gunnis notes that the tablets commemorating Lacon Lambe and Thoms Woodward both have well carved details.

Funerary Monuments

1.	?1798	Mary Wotton	Withington, Herefs	S	RG/JP, 8, 1504
2.	†1799	Unidentified subject, tablet	St Mary, Linton-by-Ross, Herefs	S	Pevsner, *Herefs*, 1963, 234
3.	?1805	Penelope Butler	Preston Wynne, Herefs	S	RG/JP, 8, 1504
4.	?1807	Lacon Lambe	Dilwyn, Herefs	S	*Gunnis* 1968, 409
5.	?1822	Thomas Woodward	Ledbury, Herefs	S	*Gunnis* 1968, 409

VIDLER FAMILY, of Battle fl 1780–1827

The family were the leading masons in Battle, Sussex over several generations. In 1780 John Vidler was paid £300 for building the Webster family vault in Battle church-yard. He was succeeded by his son, Thomas, who, between 1811 and 1818, was responsible for all the alterations and additions to Battle Abbey, and also in 1817 for building the stables. Vidler was paid £1,950 by Sir Godfrey Webster in the first year or two, but after that found it impossible to extract any more money from his patron; as late as 1827 he was writing to the Webster lawyer in London trying to get his claim settled. Vidler appears also to have been an architect, as in the same letter he stresses that his claim on Sir Godfrey also involved 'superintending the whole of the works at Battle Abbey from the year 1812 and drawing all plans and working drawings'. He was succeeded by his son, John. In 1775 'Messrs. Inskip and Vidler' repaired the House of Correction at Battle, Sussex (County Archives, Lewes).

Literary References: *Gunnis* 1968, 409 citing Archives, Mrs Harbord of Battle Abbey and County Archives, Lewes

VIDLER, John, of Westminster fl 1775–1804

In 1790 Vidler's yard was in Millbank Street, Westminster. He was variously employed at Richmond Palace in 1796, and carved the capitals of the piers for the gateway into the Botanic Gardens (**2**). In 1804 he claimed £1,255 for sundry work carried out at the White Lodge, Richmond (TNA, WORK, 19.25/9 fol 17). Gunnis suggests that he may be the Vidler who signed the 'very pretty' monument to William Lowndes, which has a portrait relief in an oval medallion (**1**).

Literary References: *Gunnis* 1968, 409

Archival References: RG/JP, 8, 1505

Funerary Monuments

1.	†1775	William Lowndes	Astwood, Bucks	S	*Gunnis* 1968, 409; Pevsner, *Bucks*, 1994, 147

Architectural Sculpture

2.	1796	Capitals	[Botanic Gardens, Richmond Palace, gate piers]; untraced		*Gunnis* 1968, 409

VIDLER, Major, of Hastings fl 1823–29?

Gunnis describes his three known tablets as 'rather dull'.

Funerary Monuments

1.	?1823	Edmund Cartwright	Battle, Sussex	S	*Gunnis* 1968, 409
2.	?1826	Elizabeth Barnouin	All Saints, Hastings, Sussex	S	*Gunnis* 1968, 409
3.	?1839	Richard Greenland	Winchelsea, Sussex	S	*Gunnis* 1968, 409

VIERPYL, Simon *c*1725–1810

He was born in London and after studying under **Peter Scheemakers** went to Rome in 1748, where he remained until 1756. He was much patronised by English and particularly Irish tourists wanting copies of the antique masterpieces. Throughout his stay he had rooms in the Palazzo Zuccari above the Spanish Steps, where his former master and a number of other English sculptors lodged during their Rome years. In 1750 he shared lodgings with **Joseph Wilton** and in 1752 with **Francis Harwood**. His popularity with tourists in the city is suggested by his inclusion with Lord Charlemont and other Irish patrons in the *Parody of the School of Athens* which Sir Joshua Reymolds painted in Rome in 1751 (NGI).

Vierpyl's first Italian commission came in the summer of 1749 from Lord Malton, acting for his father, the Earl of Rockingham. He ordered copies of the *Apollino* and *Clapping faun* in the Uffizi Galleries (**3**). Duplicates of both, together with marble tables and gesso busts, were commissioned by Ralph Howard (later Lord Wicklow), who paid Vierpyl a first installment for his work on 15 February 1752 (signed receipt, Wicklow Papers, noted by *Ingamells* 1997, 968, n3) (**4**). On 18 March the antiquary James Russel, who acted as Howard's agent in Rome, reported: 'Vierpyl, by working very hard, had reduc'd his block, into something of a human shape' and on 20 September Howard heard from another source that the marble of the statues was flawless and 'ye workmanship wont be disagreeable'. They were not completed until October 1753. When Russel wrote confirming their dispatch on 25 December he added 'your statues have been extremely admired and prais'd by Gentlemen and Connoisseurs, from whence no small advantage has accru'd to Mr Vierpyle [who has] since had commissions to do the fighting & the dying Gladiator, the former for Lord Charlemont, and the latter for Lord Pembroke (**6, 8**), as likewise several busts for Lord Bolingbroke & other Gentlemen'. Henceforth Vierpyl's activities were largely confined to making copies from antiquities in the Capitoline Museum and the French Academy in Rome, where he gained access thanks to the powerful influence of Cardinal Albani.

James, 1st Earl of Charlemont gave Vierpyl several commissions. On 26 July 1755 his agent John Parker reported that Vierpyl had yet to execute the 'busts of Brutus, Pompey and Caesar in bronze, that he was to do, the busts too in red marble', but the *Gladiator*, for which he had been paid on account, was 'very forward' (**12, 6**). On 24 December Parker wrote that Vierpyl was shortly to go to Carrara with gessos of 'the little Apollo' and the Mercury in the Farnese Gallery and in May 1756 Vierpyl wrote from Carrara that the two statues were 'almost in a state of being forwarded to Dublin' and he had sent twelve blocks of marble to await his arrival there.

Vierpyl's largest commission, which occupied him from 1751 to 1755, came from Edward Murphy, Lord Charlemont's tutor. It was for terracotta copies of 22 statues and 78 busts of Roman Emperors and others in the Capitoline Museum (**5, 11**). These were all sent to Dublin in 1755. Nearly two decades later, on 15 August 1774, Vierpyl discussed his work with Murphy in a letter: 'your happy, and, I believe, singular thought (Of getting the whole series copied, and then by one artist only) has never before, nor to this day, been executed by any sculptor, except me. So that your imperial series is the only one of the kind now in the world'. He added: 'an equal series will never again be made; for I am certain that no eminent artist will hereafter stand four years, winter and summer (as I have done) in the chilling Capitoline museum to model so many busts and statues with his own hand'. He undertook various other commissions and appears to have acted as an agent for collectors of antiquities since items such as a marble intaglio table and an excavated cinerary urn went to England from Rome at his direction.

He left Rome early in 1756, travelled to Venice and then to Ireland probably at Charlemont's behest. He settled in Dublin, first in Marlborough Street, then Henry Street and finally at 41 (now 2) Bachelor's Walk. On 26 December 1758 he married Frances Dickson, who was agreeable and had a fortune, though she met her death by throwing herself out of a window in the house in Bachelor's Walk. There were two sons, William and Charles, both of whom were brought up as sculptors. Vierpyl took a second wife, Mary Burrowes, on 30 August 1779.

His principal work for Lord Charlemont in Ireland was on the casino at Marino House, Clontarf, near Dublin, designed by Sir William Chambers (**20**). Vierpyl was supervising mason and clerk of works, in charge of the construction of the casino and it is probably to him that the credit goes for the quality of the stonework, the precision of the dressing and all the fine carved detail. Chambers had dismissed Vierpyl to Lord Hopetoun in 1755 as 'an Englishman [in Rome], many degrees inferior to those now at London as a maker of chimneypieces' (*Allen* 1983, 201). He evidently revised his opinion for in his *Treatise* of 1791, he wrote of the casino 'it was built by Mr Verpyl with great neatness and taste after models made here'. Vierpyl may also have worked under Chambers at Castletown, Co Kildare, for Thomas Conolly.

Vierpyl found other clients in Ireland. Two busts were commissioned for the Long Room at Trinity College, Dublin (**13, 14**). Claudius Gilbert is presented naturalistically in his own curled hair, with a double chin and a chest tapering into a triangle. His image was placed above the collection of 13,000 books he had bequeathed to the library.

The *Gentleman's Magazine* noted 'It is the workmanship of Mr Verpoil; and for expression and elegance does great honour to the taste and skill of the statuary' (*GM* 4 Feb 1758, 91). The second bust in the Library, of Provost Baldwin, is also characterised. This frontal image in wig and robes, has a small o-shaped mouth and again a tapering torso. A third, of the Bishop of Clogher, was bequeathed to the library in the early 19th century and it too is a round-jowled image, in clerical robes (17).

His only recorded monument, to Lady Donneraile, in St Patrick's Cathedral, closely follows **Henry Cheere**'s monument to Viscount Donneraile in Donneraile, Co Cork. It has a central seated figure in an attitude of grief holding a portrait medallion. The surrounding arch has two tapering Corinthian columns supporting a pediment with an armorial shield flanked by two *putti* (1).

IR

Literary References: *Charlemont Corr*, HMC 1891, 225–6 (*Gladiator*), 227 (dispatch of 12 blocks of marble from Carrara); *Strickland* II, 1913, 488–490; *Harris* 1970, 43, 67, 201; *Stainton* 1983, 11, 35; *Cornforth* 1988, 70–3; *Byrne* 1995 (1), 31–56; *Byrne* 1995 (2); *Ingamells* 1997, 967–8; *Casey* 1999, 42–50

Portraits of the Sculptor: *Strickland* II, 1913, repr LXI (detail from Reynolds's portrait)

Funerary Monuments						
1.	1762	Lady Donneraile (†1761)		St Patrick's Cathedral, Dublin	S	*Loeber* 1970, 24, 27 (repr); *Potterton* 1975, 87; C Lib (repr)
Statues						
2.	*c*1750	Silenus and the infant Bacchus, cast for a marble copy		[for Lord Charlemont]; untraced		*Haskell and Penny*, 1981, 307
3.	1749–1751	Apollino and Clapping faun	m	Wentworth Woodhouse, W R Yorks, marble saloon, niches (1967)	SD	*Haskell and Penny* 1981, 206, 208 n27; *Whinney* 1988, 259; *Penny* 1991 (2), 7
4.	1752–1753	Apollino and the Clapping Faun, commissioned with two marble tables and six gesso busts		[for Ralph Howard]; untraced		*Ingamells* 1997, 967
5.	1751–1755	22 statues after the antique		[coll Edward Murphy]; Irish Royal Academy (1768)		*Ingamells* 1997, 968
6.	1755	'Fighting Gladiator' (Borghese gladiator)		[for Lord Charlemont]; Irish Royal Academy (1868)		Charlemont Corr. 1, 1891, 225–6; *Ingamells* 1997, 968
7.	1756	'Little Apollo' (Apollino) and Farnese Mercury		[for Lord Charlemont]; Irish Royal Academy (1868)		*Ingamells* 1997, 968
8.	pre-1769	Dying gladiator (Dying Gaul)		Wilton House, Wilts (? still *in situ*)		*Gunnis* 1968, 410
Busts						
9.	?*c*1752	Pythagoras (perhaps connected with a mould taken with Cardinal Albani's assistance and packed for shipping to England with Lord Dartmouth's heads of Seneca and Cicero		[coll Lord Brudenell]; untraced Other versions: Pythagoras 'and other work' for the 10th Earl of Huntingdon mentioned in corr, 24 Dec 1755, 22 May 1756		*Gunnis* 1968, 410; *JKB* 1983 (1), 65; *Ingamells* 1997, 968
10.	1747–1754	Seneca and Cicero, after originals in Florence	m	[coll Lord Dartmouth]; untraced		*JKB* 1983 (1), 65 123; *McKay* 1992–3, 268
11.	1751–1755	78, of Roman Emperors		[coll Edward Murphy]; Royal Irish Academy (37 or more)		*Potterton* 1975, 87; *Ingamells* 1997, 968
12.	1755–1756	Brutus, Pompey and Caesar, in bronze and another set in red marble		[for Lord Charlemont]; untraced		*Ingamells* 1997, 967–8
13.	1758	Dr Claudius Gilbert Payment(s): £34 2s 6d	m	Trinity College, Dublin, Long Room		*Crookshank* 1986, 23 (repr); C Lib (repr)
14.	1761	Provost Baldwin (†1758) Payment(s): £34 2s 6d		Trinity College, Dublin, Long Room		*Crookshank* 1986, 23; C Lib (repr)
15.	by 1768	Epicurus and Pythagoras		[Donington Park, Leics, seat of the 10th Earl of Huntingdon]; untraced		Hastings Corr, Huntingdon HA 13303 (Box 91); HA Box 42 (7); Box 42 (10). Walpole, *Country Seats*, 1928, 64
16.	nd	Commodus, Marcus Aurelius, Caracalla, Faustina	m	[for Stephen Beckingham]; untraced		*Ingamells* 1997, 968
17.	nd	Robert Clayton, Bishop of Clogher (†1785)	m	Trinity College, Dublin, Long Room		*Crookshank* 1986, 23; C Lib (repr)
18.	nd	Three of the Farnese Homer (conceivably not executed)	p	Untraced		*Ingamells* 1997, 968
Chimneypieces						
19.	1773	Description unavailable		[for Lord Charlemont at Clontarf]; untraced		Sir William Chambers's Letterbook, 15 May 1773, BL Ad MS 41133, fol 101
Architectural Sculpture						
20.	1756	Ornaments for the casino for Lord Charlemont		Marino, Clontarf, Dublin		*Cornforth* 1988, 70–3 (repr)
21.	post-1773	Ornamental stone carving		King's Hospital, Dublin (former Bluecoat School)		*Loeber* 1970, 24
22.	1769–1779	Ornamental stone carving		City Hall, Dublin		*Loeber* 1970, 24
23.	nd	Ornamental stone carving		St Thomas, Marlborough Street, Dublin		*Strickland* II, 1913, 489
24.	nd	Ornamental stone carving		Royal Exchange, Dublin		*Strickland* II, 1913, 489

VINE, James and Thomas fl early 19th century

Thomas (1788–1840) and James (1798–1831) were the sons of 'Mr. Vine, of Bury, mason', who died in 1827, aged 70; together they sign the monument to Sir Thomas Cullum, 1830. Gunnis notes that their obituaries appeared in the *Bury Post.*

Funerary Monuments					
1.	?1830	Sir Thomas Cullum	Hawstead, Suffolk	S	*Gunnis* 1968, 410

VINER, C, of Bath fl *c*1779–1814

Gunnis notes that his monuments are quite well executed but not particularly interesting, the best being that to Lady Dundonald, which is a large work in coloured marbles (1). The diary of Sir Charles Throckmorton of Coughton Court, Warks contains the entry '14 April, 1795. Agreed with Mr. Viner, of Morford Street, Bath, to erect a marble monument in the Abbey Church of Bath to the memory of Mr. Metcalfe according to the draught given in, for £15' (*Beard* 1951, (2), 1641). In 1814 Viner was paid £133 for black marble for the staircase hall and, two years later, for the chimneypieces for Doddington Park, Glos, then being rebuilt by Christopher Codrington.

Literary References: *Gunnis* 1968, 410

Funerary Monuments

1.	†1779	Lady Dundonald	m	Weston, Somerset		*Gunnis* 1968, 410
2.	?1788	Robert Coe		Walcot, Bath, Somerset	S	*Gunnis* 1968, 410
3.	†1790	Brigadier-General Joseph Smith		Weston, Somerset		RG/JP, 8, 1506
4.	?1791	Theophilus Ponting		Norton St Philip, Somerset	S	*Gunnis* 1968, 410
5.	?1795	Charlotte Wicker		Weston, Somerset	S	*Gunnis* 1968, 410
6.	1795	Mr Metcalfe Payment(s): £15	m	[Bath Abbey, Somerset]; untraced		*Gunnis* 1968, 410
7.	?1806	John Taylor		Newton St Loe, Somerset	S	*Gunnis* 1968, 410
8.	?1817	John Dick		Devizes, Wilts		RG/JP, 8, 1507

Chimneypieces

9.	1816	Several		[Doddington Park, Glos]; untraced		GPC quoting Codrington Archives

VINO & PERONNE

Their tradecard carries the information 'Vino and Peronne MODELLERS AND DESIGNERS At the Golden Vase No 155 HIGH HOLBORN Make ornaments for ceilings, Frames for/ Glasses, Girandoles and all sorts of Decorations in Papier Mache both Antique and Modern NB all sorts of Paper Hangings' (Heal Coll, BM 106.23).

VON LÜCKE, Johann Christoph Ludwig fl *c*1757–61

A German ivory carver, active in Britain from *c*1757 to 1760/1. An ivory bust of a man thought to be by him was sold at Holloways, Oxon, on 30 November 2004, but it is uncertain whether the sitter was English (Inf. Marjorie Trusted).

Literary References: *Theuerkauff* 1986, 194

VOSE, Mrs fl 1819

She lived in Liverpool in 1819.

Busts

1.	1819	John Gibson RA		[Exhib RA, London, 1190]; untraced		*Graves* II, 1905–6, 93; *Ormond* 1973, 186

VOUSDEN, Samuel, of Clapham fl *c*1823–38?

He gave his address as Manor Street on the monument to Thomas Cattley (2). Gunnis notes that he signed a few Hellenic tablets, of which the three best are the Charrington, Withington and Chancellor (4, 5, 1).

Funerary Monuments

1.	?1823	Katharine Chancellor		St Matthew, Brixton, London	S	*Gunnis* 1968, 410
2.	†1824	Thomas and Frances (†1841) Cattley		Holy Trinity, Clapham, London	S	
3.	†1829	Thomas Kettlewell, wall-tablet		Holy Trinity, Clapham, London	S	
4.	?1832	William Charrington		St Leonard, Streatham, London	S	*Gunnis* 1968, 410
5.	?1838	Thomas Withington		St Leonard, Streatham, London	S	*Gunnis* 1968, 410

VOYEZ, John *c*1740–

Voyez was a modeller, who also worked with glass, wood, ivory and marble. He probably came from a family of engravers and metalworkers living near Amiens in the 18th century and appears to have worked for at least a year in a French pottery before coming to England. In 1768, whilst living in Long Acre, he carved a fine glass cameo of King George III in order to qualify as a master. He is also known to have produced a coloured wax model of the royal coach in association with **Capizzoldi** and he had some connection with an artificial stone manufactury in Goldstone Square, Whitechapel around 1768. His given addresses when exhibiting with the Society of Artists and the Free Society were 'At Mr West's Princes Street, St Ann's' (1767), Hanley, Staffs (1771) and 'the Music Shop, Saville Passage, Saville Row' (1791).

In 1768 Voyez was offered employment by Wedgwood, who apparently had great hopes of him, for he wrote to his partner, Bentley, on 31 March, that he had 'hired a modeller for three years, the best I am told in London. He served his time with a silversmith, has worked several years at a china works, has been two or three years carving in wood and marble for Mr. Adam the famous architect, is a perfect master of the antique style in ornaments, vases, etc., and works with equal facility in clay, wax, wood or stone' (Wedgwood to Bentley, 31 March 1768, Wedgwood/Voyez E25/18197). Wedgwood treated Voyez extremely well, paying his debts in London and transporting him and his wife to Burslem. Voyez seemed aware of his good fortune, for when he wrote to Wedgwood's London agent, Mr Cox, on 19 August, 1768, he spoke of 'Mr. Wedgwood's exceeding genteel behaviour to me, who, on my arrival here, entertained us in his own house until our house was gotten ready which was by the usiall diligance or rather delays of joiner Show kept back longer than it otherwise might have been' (Jean Voyez to William Cox, Wedgwood/Voyez L1/55). In spite of this good beginning, Voyez was in trouble in less than a year and was sentenced to seven years transportation, then commuted, for allegedly stealing clay models and plaster moulds from his master. Wedgwood then apparently regretted having committed Voyez to prison for in a letter to Bentley he ruefully reflected 'What then do our competitors stand in most need of to enable them to rival us effectively? Some person to instruct them to compose good forms, & to ornamt. them with tolerable propriety. V . . . can do this much more effectually than all the Potters in the country put together, & without much personal layout, as the ornaments may be bot or modeld by others'. Whilst in prison Voyez carved a figure of *Prometheus*, chained to the rock with a vulture preying on his liver (5). He later used the same motif on a large vase, modelled for the potter, Humphrey Palmer, which bears his signature and Palmer's stamp (4).

Wedgwood produced his first vases, including the results of Voyez's labours, at Etruria in June 1769. These were very successful, but nonetheless anxious about competition from Voyez, Wedgwood tried to coerce him into leaving Staffordshire. Cox wrote indignantly to Bentley on 17 June 1769, to inform him that 'I have not seen Mr. Voyez and have desired our people to keep him out of here if he should dare to call when I am out' (Cox to Wedgwood, Wedgwood/ Voyez E5/30867). Voyez later left Palmer for another potter, T Hales of Cowridge, for whom he modelled, among other works, a plaque with classical motifs (1). He also provided models for Ralph Wood, including the *Fair Hebe* jug, which is thinly cast in the form of a tree-trunk, on which stand several figures with bumpers of ale (14).

This versatile artist was involved in several other activities. In 1773 he published a catalogue of his cameos and intagalios after the antique, describing himself as 'J Voyez, Member of the Royal Society of Artists of Great Britain' and gave his address as Cowbridge, near Newcastle, Staffs. To the catalogue, which lists 200 subjects, can be added upwards of 7000 ciphers and seals advertised in 1776, many of them produced with James Tassie. The monopolistic Wedgwood wrote to Bentley on 24 February 1776 'Mr Tassie and Voyez between them have made terrible depredations upon our Seal trade' (*Grundy* 1958, 113). Voyez also worked as enameller for the firm of Philip Rundell and his works in ivory include a number of small boxes with reliefs of classical subjects. He was clearly a talented and perhaps restless character, temperamentally incapable of accepting the disciplined anonymity that Wedgwood and other manufacturers sought to impose on him. Nothing is known of him after 1773.

MGS

Literary References: *Graves* 1907, 269; *Grundy* 1958, 110–5; *Hutchinson* 1966, 212–15; *Gunnis* 1968, 410; *Pyke* 1981, 41

Reliefs

1.	nd	Plaque with two mermaids holding a garland either side of an elaborate classical vase, model		BM (painted ceramic cast)	S	*Grundy* 1958, 111–2 (repr)

Miscellaneous

2.	1767	'A piece of flowers in wax'		[Exhib Free Soc, 294]; untraced		*Graves* 1907, 269
3.	1768	Two festoons of flowers	sa	[Exhib Soc of A, 210]; untraced		*Graves* 1907, 269
4.	1769	Model for a vase, ornamented with a relief of Prometheus		Holborne of Menstrie Museum, Bath	S	*Grundy* 1958, 112
5.	1769	Prometheus	i	Holborne of Menstrie Museum, Bath		*Grundy* 1958, 112
6.	1771	'A whole length portrait of a lady in the character of Diana in coloured wax'		[Exhib Free Soc, 281]; untraced		*Graves* 1907, 269
7.	1771	Two pieces of flowers; on white wax		[Exhib Free Soc, 282]; untraced		*Graves* 1907, 269
8.	1772	Judith with the head of Holfernes, in coloured wax		[Exhib Free Soc, London, 210]; untraced		*Graves* 1907, 269
9.	1772	'Two composition turned frames'		[Exhib Free Soc, London, 211]; untraced		*Graves* 1907, 269
10.	1772	Unidentified subject, 'a model in composition'		[Exhib Free Soc, London, 207]; untraced		*Graves* 1907, 269
11.	1772	Unidentified subject, 'a model in composition'		[Exhib Free Soc, London, 208]; untraced		*Graves* 1907, 269
12.	1772	Unidentified subject, 'a model in composition'		[Exhib Free Soc, London, 209]; untraced		*Graves* 1907, 269
13.	1772	Unidentified subject, 'a model in composition'		[Exhib Free Soc, London, 206]; untraced		*Graves* 1907, 269
14.	1788	'Fair Hebe' jug		VAM, Schreiber coll		*Grundy* 1958, 112–3 (repr)
15.	1791	A lady; model in coloured wax		[Exhib Soc of A, 208]; untraced		*Graves* 1907, 269

VULLIAMY, Benjamin 1780–1854

A clockmaker, his name is included in this dictionary as an illustration of collaboration between the crafts in 18th and 19th century Britain. He employed **John Bacon RA, J C F Rossi, Charles Peart** and **John Deare** to model figures for his clocks.

Literary References: *Kelly* 1968, 152–63; *Clifford* 1990, 226–37

WADDILOVE, J fl 1795?

The Tate monument has an Adam-style urn and well-carved details.

Funerary Monuments

1.	?1795	Martha Tata		Mitcham, Surrey	S	*Gunnis* 1968, 411

WADE, Henrietta 1789–1851

For further information the reader is referred to *Pyke* 1981, 41.

WADE, John fl 1717

Architectural Sculpture

1.	1717	Carved doorway		St Michael, Cornhill, City of London		*Gunnis* 1968, 411

WADE, Joseph *c*1664–1743

He executed work in both wood and stone in partnership with **Richard Chichley** between 1719 and 1728 (1, 2). In 1729 Wade was employed on his own at Greenwich Palace, receiving a total of £2,595 2s 9d. This included £101 for decorative work on the south pavilion of Queen Anne's Court, £8 a 'face' for Corinthian capitals, £21 10s for 43 modillions and £3 each for two scrolls, carved to a depth of 2 feet (TNA ADM 68/708) (3). He received £121 9s 1d in 1740 for carved work on the Duke of Kingston's new yacht, 'Mary' (4).

He died on 22 November 1743, aged 79, and was buried at St Mary, Rotherhithe, London, where a cartouche tablet states that he was 'King's carver in His Majesty's Yards at Deptford and Woolwich' and adds that he was 'Equalled by few and excelled by none' in his profession.

Literary References: *Gunnis* 1968, 411; *Penny* 1992, 20

Archival References: GPC

Architectural Sculpture

1.	1719–1720	Carved work (co-sculptor: Richard Chichley)	wd	[St Paul, Deptford, London]; untraced		GPC citing Lambeth Palace Library, New Churches, box VII

2.	1726–1728	Great Pediment carving (co-sculptor: Richard Chichley)	s	[Greenwich Palace, South Pavilion]; untraced		*Gunnis* 1968, 100; *Penny* 1992, 20
3.	1729	Decorative work	s	Queen Anne's Court, Greenwich Palace, south pavilion		*Gunnis* 1968, 411 citing PRO Ad., 68/708 (untraced)

Miscellaneous

4.	1740	Ornaments for the Duke of Kingston's yacht	wd	Untraced		GPC quoting Archives, Lord Manvers

WADE, W, of Eaton Ford fl 1832?

Funerary Monuments

1.	?1832	James Plumpton		Great Gransden, Cambs		RG/JP, 8, 1509

WAKE, J Hall fl 1792

He acted as foreman to **Henry Wood I** and in 1792 worked under him at Woburn Abbey.

Archival References: Woburn Cash Book 1791–92, BLARS R5/1297

Architectural Sculpture

1.	1792	Unidentified stone carving Payment(s): £100	s	Woburn Abbey, Beds		*Gunnis* 1968, 411

WALDIN (or WALLDIN), Samuel, of Winchester *c*1730–1804

The son of Samuel Waldin, a Winchester farmer, he was apprenticed to **John Blake** in 1744, but did not trouble to take up his freedom until 30 years later. In 1781 he was employed on repair work at Winchester Palace. The Knollys monument is a large tablet with a pediment and garlands (1). The Chernocke tablet has an urn and two allegorical figures under a large willow tree (3). On Waldin's death his son, Samuel, took over the business (*Monthly Mag* 1804, II, 370).

Literary References: *Gunnis* 1968, 411

Funerary Monuments

1.	1751	Thomas Knollys		Nursling, Hants		Pevsner, *Hants & Isle of Wight*, 1967, 361
2.	†1770	Robert Eyre		Winchester Cathedral	S	*Gunnis* 1968, 411
3.	†1779	Villiers Chernocke		Winchester Cathedral		Pevsner, *Hants & Isle of Wight*, 1967, 684

WALKER fl 1825?

He can perhaps be identified with **Walkers of Nottingham.**

Funerary Monuments

1.	†1825	Thomas Roberts		St Mary, Nottingham		NP/RG

WALKER, A E fl 1830

His address was given as 42 Paternoster Row in 1830 (*Graves*).

Reliefs

1.	1830	F P Becker (medallic portrait)		[Exhib RA, London, 1132]; untraced		*Graves* VIII, 1905–6, 102; *Gunnis* 1968, 411

WALKER, R, of Bath fl 1852?

He may perhaps be connected to **R Walker, of Bristol.**

Funerary Monuments

1.	?1852	John Rundall		St Mary, Fort St George, Chennai (Madras), India	S	*Gunnis* 1968, 411

WALKER, R, of Bristol fl *c*1817–35

Possible connected with **R Walker, of Bath.** The 'ambitious' Palmer monument has a life-size figure of a woman kneeling by an urn (2). The Kater is a neo-Greek tablet (3).

Literary References: *Gunnis* 1968, 411

Funerary Monuments

1.	†1817	Admiral John Thomas		Llanlilwni, Carmarthen		*Dale-Jones and Lloyd* 1989, 58
2.	†1834	Lucy Palmer		Brixton, Devon	S	Pevsner, *Devon*, 1989, 214
3.	†1835	Elizabeth Kater		Cold Ashton, Glos	S	Pevsner, *Glos: Cotswolds*, 1999, 291
4.	†1835	Mary Thomas and others		Wick, Somerset		RG/JP, 8, 1509v.

WALKER, Theresa Snell fl 1841

Statues

1.	1841	Kertamaroo, a native of South Australia, model		[Exhib RA, London, 1140]; untraced		*Graves* VIII, 1905–6, 102
2.	1841	Mocatta, or Pretty Mary, a native of South Australia, model		[Exhib RA, London, 1136]; untraced		*Graves* VIII, 1905–6, 102

WALKER, William fl 1847–49

Little is known about this Leith sculptor except that he studied at the Trustees Academy in the 1840s and showed at the Royal Scottish Academy, 1847–49. His exhibits in 1847 included a marble medallion of **Bertel Thorvaldsen** perhaps suggesting that he had travelled to Rome (2).

Literary References: *Woodward* 1977 (vol 1, pt 2), 259

Architectural Sculpture

1.	1848	Vase		[Exhib R Sc A, Edinburgh, 620]; untraced		*Laperriere* 4, 1991, 369

Reliefs

2.	1847	Bertel Thorvaldsen, medallion	m	[Exhib R Sc A, Edinburgh, 645]; untraced		*Laperriere* 4, 1991, 369

Miscellaneous

3.	1847	Blind buff		[Exhib R Sc A, Edinburgh, 638]; untraced		*Laperriere* 4, 1991, 369
4.	1849	The golden age		[Exhib R Sc A, Edinburgh, 617]; untraced		*Laperriere* 4, 1991, 369

WALKERS, of Nottingham fl *c*1825–65

There are a number of tablets in St Mary, Lace Market, Nottingham signed either 'WALKERS' (**2, 4, 6**) or 'WALKERS' (1). Thomas Roberts's memorial has a draped urn above the inscription and acanthus ornament below, while the

Watson has only a draped urn (**1, 4**). The Hill and Sarah Roberts are even plainer: the former has a small coat of arms above the tablet and the latter stylised acanthus ornament (**2, 6**).

Funerary Monuments

1.	†1825	Thomas Roberts	St Mary, Lace Market, Nottingham	S
2.	†1835	Thomas Hill	St Mary, Lace Market, Nottingham	S
3.	†1838	Martin (†1836) and Salacia Roe	St Peter, Nottingham	S
4.	†1851	Elizabeth Watson	St Mary, Lace Market, Nottingham	S
5.	?1851	Margaret Clarke	Worfield, Salop	S
6.	†1851	Sarah Roberts	St Mary, Lace Market, Nottingham	S
7.	†1865	Mary Stubbs	St Peter, Nottingham	S

WALLACE & WHITE, of Edinburgh fl 1828–74

This firm of marble cutters was established at Shrub Place, Leith in 1828. They were also known at various times by the names Wallace, White and Son and Andrew Wallace and Co.

Literary References: *Woodward* 1977, vol 1, pt 2, 260

Funerary Monuments

1.	†1833	Thomas Ogier	First Presbyterian Church, Charleston, South Carolina, USA	S	*Hershey* 1970, 804 (repr)
2.	1841	Sir Henry Moncrieff Wellwood	St Cuthbert, New Town, Edinburgh		Pevsner, *Edinburgh*, 1991, 276
3.	†1864	Robert Latta	Warriston Cemetery, Edinburgh		*Woodward* 1977, vol 1, pt 2, 260
4.	1874	Rev Robert Nisbet	St Giles Cathedral, Edinburgh		*Woodward* 1977, vol 1, pt 2, 260

WALLIS, James, of Newark c1748–1824

He was apprenticed to **Christopher Staveley I** of Melton Mowbray, 'stonecutter', in 1761 (PRO, IRI/22, 203), and subsequently established himself himself as a builder and monumental mason in Newark, Notts, where he is said to have designed several houses. His nine surviving slates in Kesteven were influenced by Staveley's work but are less florid. Gunnis describes his monuments as 'neat and pleasant' works, mostly in coloured marbles, and considers the best to be that to Richard Fydell, a large tablet with a profile portrait medallion on an obelisk (**7**). Pevsner describes the Edward Smith as a tablet with good lettering (**5**), but does not consider the Darwin to be 'up to much artistically' (**24**). Examples of his slate gravestones can be found at Caythorpe, Claypole, Cranwell (two), Foston, Grantham, North Witham and Woolsthorpe.

Wallis later went into partnership with **R Marshall** and together they sign a number of tablets (**20, 21, 25–29**) as well as slate gravestones at Caythorpe and Claypole. Wallis died on 6 January 1824, aged 76, and Marshall erected a large monument to him, now in the north transept of St Mary Magdalen, Newark. The inscription describes him as an architect. Marshall continued the business after Wallis's death.

Literary References: *Gunnis* 1968, 411; *Neave and Heron* 1969, 5; *Colvin* 1995, 1019

Funerary Monuments

1.	†1766	George Smith	Fulbeck, Lincs	S	Pevsner, *Lincs*, 1989, 291
2.	c1770	Gilbert Charlton	Staunton-in-the-Vale, Notts	S	*Gunnis* 1968, 411
3.	c1770	Thomas and Mary Kelham	Staunton-in-the-Vale, Notts	S	*Gunnis* 1968, 411; GPC
4.	?1778	Joseph Sykes	Balderton, Notts	S	*Gunnis* 1968, 411
5.	†1779	Edward Smith	Caythorpe, Notts		Pevsner, *Lincs*, 1989, 217
6.	?1779	Rev John Ferrand	Messingham, Notts	S	*Gunnis* 1968, 411
7.	†1780	Richard Fydell	St Botolph, Boston, Lincs		*Gunnis* 1968, 411; Pevsner, *Lincs*, 1989, 161
8.	†1781	John Hallilay	Carlton-le-Moorland, Lincs		Pevsner, *Lincs*, 1989, 212
9.	c1782	John and Susanna Peachell	Carlton Scroop, Lincs		Pevsner, *Lincs*, 1989, 213
10.	†1783	Elizabeth Fydell	St Botolph, Boston, Lincs		Pevsner, *Lincs*, 898, 161
11.	†1785	Rev John Calthorp	Gosberton, Notts		GPC
12.	†1792	Arabella Ashton	Hough-on-the-Hill, Lincs		Pevsner, *Lincs*, 1989, 400
13.	?1792	Francis Foss	Everton, Notts	S	*Gunnis* 1968, 411
14.	†1795	Francis Atkinson	Fulbeck, Lincs		Pevsner, *Lincs*, 1989, 291
15.	?1798	Rev B Clarkham	Sleaford, Lincs	S	*Gunnis* 1968, 411
16.	?1798	Rev Thomas Wakefield	East Stoke, Notts	S	*Gunnis* 1968, 411
17.	?1803	Margaret Spragging	St Mary Magdalen, Newark, Notts	S	*Gunnis* 1968, 411
18.	†1805	Thomas Atkinson	Fulbeck, Lincs		Pevsner, *Lincs*, 1989, 291
19.	†1806	Anne Smith	Caythorpe, Lincs		Pevsner, *Lincs*, 1989, 217
20.	?1806	George Smith (co-sculptor: R Marshall)	Fulbeck, Lincs	S	*Gunnis* 1968, 411
21.	†1811	Robert (†1795) and Elizabeth Tange (co-sculptor: R Marshall)	Carlton-le-Moorland, Lincs		Pevsner, *Lincs*, 1989, 213
22.	†1812	William Shield	Caythorpe, Lincs		Pevsner, *Lincs*, 1989, 217
23.	?1814	Thomas Spragging	St Mary Magdalen, Newark, Notts	S	*Gunnis* 1968, 411
24.	1789–1816	Darwin family members	Elston, Notts		Pevsner, *Notts*, 1979, 122
25.	?1817	Elizabeth Withers (co-sculptor: R Marshall)	Barnby, Notts	S	*Gunnis* 1968, 411
26.	†1818	Rev John Rowland Litchford (co-sculptor: R Marshall)	Boothby Pagnell, Lincs		Pevsner, *Lincs*, 1989, 152
27.	†1819	Elizabeth Beers (co-sculptor: R Marshall)	South Muskham, Notts		Pevsner, *Notts*, 1979, 316
28.	?1819	Mary Boucher (co-sculptor: R Marshall)	Coddington, Notts	S	*Gunnis* 1968, 411
29.	?1820	William Underwood (co-sculptor: R Marshall)	Melton Mowbray, Leics	S	*Gunnis* 1968, 411

WALLIS, John fl 1789–91

As a mason and stone-carver he was employed at Carlton House in 1789–90 (*Gunnis* 1968, 412, incorrectly cites PRO, HO 73/24). In the following year he received £89 2s for sundry works at Woburn Abbey, the second receipt signed by his son W Wallis. His trade card is among the papers of George Selwyn at Castle Howard; on it he describes himself as a 'mason', living at 6 Market Lane, Pall Mall, with a yard near the turn-pike, Pimlico.

Literary References: *Gunnis* 1968, 412

Archival References: Woburn Building Accts 1789–1791, BLARS R3/2114/497, 27 April 1791 (£50), 6 September 1791; BLARS R5/1105, 24 Dec 1790 (£89 2s); GPC

Chimneypieces

1.	1791	Several	m	Woburn Abbey, Beds	*Woburn Building Accts*; *Gunnis* 1968, 412

WALLIS, Thomas W 1821–

A woodcarver, his self-portrait, aged 35, with a sample of his work is at Wilberforce House, Kingston-upon-Hul ER Yorkshire (inf. Terry Friedman).

WALMSLEY, John, of Liverpool *c*1765–1812

The son of Isaac Walmsley, a mason of Liverpool, he had a considerable business as a builder and statuary mason owning his own stone and marble quarries at Toxteth Park, near Liverpool, and at Kilkenny in Ireland. In hi *Memorials of Liverpool*, J A Picton says that he was 'a man of considerable taste' and records that in 1798 he designe and built handsome new premises in Berry Street for himself (*Picton* ii, 1875, 280). He also designed the octagona Unitarian chapel in Paradise Street, 1791. Only one monument is recorded.

Literary References: *Colvin* 1995, 1019–20

Funerary Monuments

1.	?1796	John Plumb	Aughton, Lancs	*Gunnis* 1968, 412

WALSH, J Henry fl 1830

In 1830, while living at 3 St James's Square, he received a medal from the Society of Arts.

Miscellaneous

1.	1830	Coloured anatomical model	[Soc of A, gold Isis medal]; untraced	RSA *Transactions*, 1831, vol 48, xxiv

WALSH, John fl 1757–77

In 1757 he won a premium for a cast of a clay model of the *Dying gladiator* at the Society of Arts, at which time h said he was an apprentice of 'Mr Carter' (**9**). A second premium of five guineas followed in 1759 for a model c *Bacchus* (**11**), but was withdrawn after it was shown that he (and **Joseph Nollekens**) had been assisted in their worl by **Joseph Wilton**. Walsh gave his address as South Street, Berkeley Square in 1757 and was described as a 'statuary of St George's, Hanover Square' in the apprenticeship registers of 1769.

Richard Trevor, Bishop of Durham, paid Walsh £26 in 1764 for his coat of arms in Portland stone (**16**). This wa placed on an exterior wall of Glynde chapel, Sussex, which was designed that year by Sir Thomas Robinson. H appears also to have worked for Sir William Chambers and hoped to execute three chimneypieces under the architect supervision for a Mr Errington, whose new house near Hexham had been designed by Chambers. Errington also ha a house in St James's stable yard, London, and the chimneypieces may alternatively have been intended for tha residence (**13**). Chambers wrote to Errington in 1770–1, saying that he believed 'Mr. Walsh's proposals about th chimney-pieces are reasonable and if he will send me the size of the tablet, I will make a drawing for it. In a day o two I shall have the drawings done for your other two chimney-pieces, and I will send for Mr. Walsh to hear hi proposals. I think he will execute them very well' (Chambers's Letter-Books, Ad MS 41133, fol 31).

Walsh evidently had a thriving practice for he had a number of apprentices. In 1769 he took on Charles Hoswell an George Egellstone. **William Braithwaite** joined him in 1771, Philip Colley in 1772, Andrew Leicester and Charles Flemin in 1775 and Russell Brown, Eyre Crotty and Thomas Baily in 1776. His output included several architectura monuments: that to Stephen Soame at Little Thurlow, Suffolk has a portrait-medallion of Mrs Soame and her child (7).

In 1777 Walsh was commissioned to provide a wall monument to commemorate the architect Sir Thoma Robinson in Westminster Abbey (**8**). Robinson had stipulated in his will that the work was to incorporate busts c himself and the Dowager Lady Lechmere, executed in Rome in 1730 by **Filippo della Valle** and Edmé Bouchardo respectively. Walsh's monument combined several kinds of veined marble with a statuary urn, fasces and sarcophagus with strigil decoration.

In October 1775, a John Walsh, who may have been a relation, became free of the Masons' Company by redemption having served his apprenticeship with **Thomas Carter II**.

Literary References: *Graves* 1907, 275; *Gunnis* 1968, 412; RG/JP, 8, 1513; *Baker, Harrison, Laing* 2000, 752–62

Archival References: Masons' Co, *Freemen*, fol 7

Funerary Monuments

1.	†1763	Thomas Amphlett		Enville, Staffs	S	*Gunnis* 1968, 412
2.	?1764	Joseph Percival		St Michael, Bristol	S	*Gunnis* 1968, 412
3.	?1765	Sir Ralph Assheton		Middleton, Lancs	S	*Gunnis* 1968, 412
4.	†1768	Henry, 4th Earl of Stamford		Enville, Staffs	S	*Gunnis* 1968, 412
5.	†1770	Pratt Mawbey		Chertsey, Surrey	S	Pevsner, *Surrey*, 1971, 148
6.	†1771	Sir John Rous		Wangford, nr Southwold, Suffolk	S	Pevsner, *Suffolk*, 1974, 475
7.	†1771	Stephen Soame		Little Thurlow, Suffolk	S	Pevsner, *Suffolk*, 1974, 339
8.	*c*1778	Sir Thomas Robinson and Lady Lechmere (busts by Filippo della Valle and Bouchardon)		Westminster Abbey, London, south transept	S	*Worsley* 1999, 12–13; *Baker, Harrison, Laing* 2000, 752–62 (repr)

Statues

9.	1757	'Cast of a gladiator from a model of Scheemakers'		[Soc of A, 1757; 'The Dying Gladiator', Soc of A premium, 1761, 5 gns]; untraced		RSA *Minutes* 1757–58, fol 150
10.	1757	Dying gladiator, clay model		[Exhib Free Soc 1761, 94]; untraced		*Graves* 1907, 275; *Gunnis* 1968, 412
11.	1759	Bacchus, after Michelangelo, model	tc	[Soc of A, premium, 5 gns]; untraced		RSA *Minutes* 1757–58, seq 1 fol 77; RSA *Minutes* seq 1 fol 79

Busts

12.	1763	A lady		[Exhib Free Soc, 237]; untraced		*Graves* 1907, 275

Chimneypieces

13.	1762	Three, designed by Sir William Chambers		[for 'Mr Errington']; Warwick House, Cleveland Row, London (one only)		Chambers's Letter-Books, Ad MS 41133, fol 31; *Gunnis* 1968, 412; Pevsner *London: Westminster*, 2003, 608; GPC

14.	1770	Several Payment(s): £150	m	[Thoresby Hall, Notts]; untraced		Archives, Earl Manvers, Nottingham University Library, 4421; GPC
15.	1771–1772	Three		[Hallingbury Place, Essex]; untraced		GPC
Architectural Sculpture						
16.	1764	Coat of arms (designed by Sir Thomas Robinson) Payment(s): £26	s	Glynde, Sussex, chapel, external elevation		*Gunnis* 1968, 412, citing Archives, Brand of Glynde
Miscellaneous						
17.	1764	'A model in clay'		[Exhib Free Soc, 201]; untraced		*Graves* 1907, 275

WALSH & DUNBAR, of Leeds fl c1817–36

The firm flourished 1816–40, producing 'heavy, unexciting monuments and tablets' at their yard in Park Row. Gunnis considered the best to be the Brackenbury, a tablet with a relief sarcophagus, the Alcott, the Lindley, the Beckett and the Ramsden (**3, 4, 5, 8**). The Nichols tablet has a mourning female by an altar with an urn (**2**). Walsh & Dunbar may have been connected with another Leeds firm, **Walsh & Lee.**

Literary References: *Gunnis* 1968, 412

Funerary Monuments					
1.	†1817	Ann Bellhouse	Holy Trinity, Leeds, W R Yorks	S	GPC
2.	†1818	Northend Nichols	Elland, W R Yorks		Pevsner, *Yorks W R*, 1967, 193
3.	†1819	Charles Brackenbury	Scremby, Lincs		*Gunnis* 1968, 412; Pevsner, *Lincs*, 1989, 629
4.	?1824	John Allcott	South Kirby, W R Yorks		*Gunnis* 1968, 412
5.	1825	Anne Lindley	Whitkirk, W R Yorks		*Gunnis* 1968, 412
6.	?1826	Charles Nainby	Barnoldby le Beck, E R Yorks	S	GPC
7.	†1826	Sir John Beckett	Corringham, Lincs		Pevsner, *Lincs*, 1989, 234
8.	1836	John Ramsden	Brotherton, W R Yorks		*Gunnis* 1968, 412

WALSH & LEE, of Leeds fl 1830–60

Perhaps connected with the rival Leeds firm, **Walsh & Dunbar**, they flourished 1830–60 and had premises in Waterloo Street, Leeds. Their known works are all in Yorkshire and include a large Gothic tablet to Sir John Ramsden (**1**) and a Hellenic wall monument to John Wilkinson (**5**). They were also responsible for the 15 foot high Crimean War memorial in Leeds Parish Church, which was erected by public subscription and had an image of *Victory* crowning a British soldier, leaning on his hand in the agony of death (**6**). Only the inscription tablet survives.

There are references in the Leeds Town Hall committee minutes to work by **Walsh & Lee, Lee and Walsh** and **Dennis, Lee and Welsh**, who are clearly interconnected. They read as follows: '26 Nov 1858. Lee and Welsh paid £33 4s for marble pedestals; 18 June 1865 Lee and Walsh paid £4 10s for a marble mantle piece; 27 Feb 1865. Dennis Lee and Welsh paid £7 15s 6d for cleaning statues; 1 Feb 1867. Dennis Lee and Welsh paid £29 9s for cleaning statues and marble' (HMI, misc file).

Literary References: *Gunnis* 1968, 412; *Jeavons* 1960, 70

Funerary Monuments					
1.	†1839	Sir John Ramsden Bt	Brotherton, W R Yorks		*Gunnis* 1968, 412; Pevsner, *Yorks: W R*, 1967, 149
2.	?1844	John Starkey	St Peter, Huddersfield, W R Yorks		*Gunnis* 1968, 412
3.	?1845	Thomas Pearson Crossland	St Peter, Huddersfield, W R Yorks		*Gunnis* 1968, 412
4.	?1849	John Hill	Holy Trinity, Leeds, W R Yorks	S	GPC
5.	?1850	John Wilkinson	Barwick-in-Elmet, W R Yorks		*Gunnis* 1968, 412
6.	1859	Crimean War Memorial	[St Peter, Leeds, W R Yorks]; destroyed c1951		*Rusby* 1896; *Gunnis* 1968, 412

WALSHA, George, of Wakefield fl c1814–16

He signs a number of tablets in Yorkshire, only two of which are listed by Gunnis.

Funerary Monuments					
1.	?1814	George Clerk	Barnsley, W R Yorks	S	*Gunnis* 1968, 412
2.	?1816	Thomas Cotton	Darton, W R Yorks	S	*Gunnis* 1968, 412

WALTERS, Richard fl 1691–1701

A London sculptor, Walters is known chiefly as a carver of chimneypieces, including 121 at Kensington Palace, supplied with his partners, **Thomas Hill** and **John Thompson.** Together they received £2,321 for various works at that palace. In 1700 the executors of Thomas, Lord Crewe made Walters a payment of £179 for Crewe's monument (**1**). Lord notes that such a large sum suggests a considerable reputation for such items and that he should therefore be viewed as a major monumental sculptor. The Crewe monument has been variously misattributed to **Joseph Catterns** and **Edward Stanton.**

Literary References: *Wren Soc* VII, 177; *Gunnis* 1968, 412; *Lord* 1986, 100

Funerary Monuments					
1.	1700	Thomas, Lord Crewe (†1697) Payment(s): £179		Steane, Northants	Lincs RO, ANC 9/A; *Lord* 1986, 100
Chimneypieces					
2.	1701	Description unavailable	m	['My Lord's bedchamber', Powys House, London]; untraced	*Gunnis* 1968, 412 (incorrectly citing PRO Works 5/51).
Miscellaneous					
3.	1691	96 chimneypieces in Portland stone, 25 others, three tables and a 'cisterne' in marble (co-sculptor: Thomas Hill) Payment(s): £2,321		Kensington Palace, London	*Gunnis* 1968, 412

WALTON, Frederick, of Staines 1799–1834

He was responsible for the large wall-tablet to Henry Wood (**1**) and the square Hellenistic tomb with an urn to Alexander Urquhart (**2**). Walton himself is buried in the churchyard of Kingston-upon-Thames under a tomb of his own design, for the inscription states that beneath it lies 'Frederick Walton, by whom this tomb was composed and erected' (3). His wife, Charlotte, survived him and died in 1839.

Funerary Monuments

1.	?1827	Henry Wood	Chertsey, Surrey	*Gunnis* 1968, 413
2.	?1829	Alexander Urquhart	Churchyard, Long Ditton, Surrey	*Gunnis* 1968, 413
3.	†1834	Frederick Walton	All Saints, Kingston-upon-Thames, Surrey	*Gunnis* 1968, 413

WALTON, of Wisbech fl *c*1719

Funerary Monuments

1.	†1719	John Trafford	Tidd St Mary, Lincs	S

WARD, H, of the Marble Works, Pentonville Hill, London fl *c*1839–45

Probably a prolific manufacturer though only two of his works are recorded.

Funerary Monuments

1.	†1839	Dr Arthur Quartley	Christchurch Priory, Hants	S
2.	†1782–1845	Elizabeth Reekes and others	Christchurch Priory, Hants	S

WARD, Robert, of Liverpool fl 1824–29

Ward showed regularly at the Liverpool Academy in the years 1824–29, giving his address as 'London' (1824–8) and then Harford Street. Picton writes 'Not long after [**John**] **Gibson**'s departure for Rome [1815] a young man named Robert Ward entered Messrs. [**Samuel and Thomas**] **Franceys**'s studio. He was the son of a worthy Liverpool burgess well-known in his day, named Jonah Ward. The youth displayed considerable ability as a modeller and sculptor. I have in my possession a bas-relief of a sleeping Venus from his hand which displays great capability (6). A bust executed by him of William Huskisson, M.P. for Liverpool (2) is well known from the casts which have been sold. His early death nipped in the bud the germs of early promise which were rapidly developing.'

Literary References: *Picton* 1875, II, 217; *Morris and Roberts* 1998, 628

Busts

1.	1827	General Gascoyne	[Exhib ALRI, Liverpool, 287]; untraced	*Morris and Roberts* 1998, 628
2.	1827	William Huskisson	[Exhib ALRI, Liverpool, 288]; untraced Other versions: multiple casts	*Gunnis* 1968, 413; *Morris and Roberts* 1998, 628
3.	1829	Dr Birkbeck	[Exhib ALRI, Liverpool, 339]; untraced	*Morris and Roberts* 1998, 628
4.	1829	Rev E Hull	[Exhib ALRI, Liverpool, 340]; untraced	*Morris and Roberts* 1998, 628
5.	1829	Unidentified gentleman	[Exhib ALRI, Liverpool, 347]; untraced	*Morris and Roberts* 1998, 628

Reliefs

6.	nd	Sleeping Venus	[J A Picton (intermediate owner)]; untraced	*Picton* 1875, II, 217

Miscellaneous

7.	1824	Diomed	[Exhib ALRI, Liverpool, 193]; untraced	*Morris and Roberts* 1998, 628
8.	1824	Discobolus	[Exhib ALRI, Liverpool, 187]; untraced	*Morris and Roberts* 1998, 628
9.	1824	Haeman and Antigone	[Exhib ALRI, Liverpool, 208]; untraced	*Morris and Roberts* 1998, 628
10.	1824	Ilyssus	[Exhib ALRI, Liverpool, 194]; untraced	*Morris and Roberts* 1998, 628
11.	1825	Model from the statue of Niobe	[Exhib ALRI, Liverpool, 169]; untraced	*Morris and Roberts* 1998, 628
12.	1825	Model of a Cupid, copy	[Exhib ALRI, Liverpool, 167]; untraced	*Morris and Roberts* 1998, 628
13.	1825	Model of the Apollo Belvidere	[Exhib ALRI, Liverpool, 168]; untraced	*Morris and Roberts* 1998, 628
14.	1825	Model, copy from the Antique	[Exhib ALRI, Liverpool, 171]; untraced	*Morris and Roberts* 1998, 628
15.	1827	Unidentified subject	[RA silver medal]; untraced	RA Premium list
16.	1828	Venus and Adonis	[Exhib ALRI, Liverpool, 242]; untraced	*Morris and Roberts* 1998, 628
17.	1829	Ganymede	[Exhib ALRI, Liverpool, 342]; untraced	*Morris and Roberts* 1998, 628

WARD, Thomas fl 1739

A carver, who worked at Wentworth Woodhouse for **Henry Watson** in February 1739. His name is recorded in Watson's account book (Bodleian MS Eng Misc fols 383, 144).

WARD, William, of Scarborough fl *c*1820–28

Known currently only for two monuments, the Musham is described by Pevsner as having good lettering on an oval tablet (1). The Shepherd is a tablet with a draped urn (2).

Funerary Monuments

1.	†1820	Elizabeth Musham	Burton Agnes, E R Yorks	S	Pevsner, *Yorks: E R & York*, 1995, 366
2.	*c*1828	Robert Shepherd (†1813)	St Oswald, Filey, E R Yorks	S	Pevsner, *Yorks: E R & York*, 1995, 416

WARE, Walter James fl 1750–60

He was the son of Elizabeth, née Richards, and Isaac Ware, the architect, and the grandson of **James Richards** who employed him. In August 1750 the Board of Works received and approved a petition from Richards the master carver, to perform the carver's work with his grandson 'James Ware'. In Richards's will, proved in January 1760, he set aside a sum not to exceed £200 to pay Ware's 'debts', in order to set himself at liberty 'that he may by his industry get his living.' The sum was reduced to £100 in a codicil. He was also left £1,000 in securities.

Literary References: *Colvin* V, 1973–76, 438

Will: James Richards, PROB 11/852/282–3

1.	1750–1751	Decorative ornaments, including small pineapples and fasces (co-sculptor: James Richards)	Horse Guards, Whitehall, London, west front	Board of Works/Horseguards, HOR/1/3 i; *Colvin* 1973–76, V, 438

WARING, John

See **Robert Jones**.

WARNER, I & R fl 1827

Statues

1.	1827	Frederick-Augustus, Duke of York and Albany, statuette	b	Knox/Longstaffe-Gowan coll (acq 1996)	SD	

WARNER, W fl 1827

In 1827, while living at 22 New North Street, Red Lion Square, he was awarded a gold Isis medal for an intaglio gem-engraving of a group.

Literary References: RSA *Transactions*, 1727, vol 45, xxxii

WARREN, Josiah, of Southampton fl *c*1808–22?

He seems to have started business in Southampton, but later moved to Wareham, Dorset.

Literary References: *Gunnis* 1968, 413

Funerary Monuments

1.	?1808	Eliza Stewart		North Stoneham, Hants	S	*Gunnis* 1968, 413
2.	?1814	Sarah Wilt		East Stoke, Dorset	S	*Gunnis* 1968, 413
3.	?1822	John Card		Wareham, Dorset	S	*Gunnis* 1968, 413

WARREN, U fl *c*1801

The Bromfield monument appears to be signed 'U. Warren. Mason', though the craftsman could well be **Josiah Warren of Southampton**.

Funerary Monuments

1.	†1801	John Arnold Bromfield MA		Boldre, Hants	S	

WARREN, William, of Glasgow fl 1824–36

William Warren designed the statue of John Knox carved by Robert Forrest for the Glasgow necropolis in 1825. He was a carver and gilder who worked in Maxwell Street, Glasgow from 1824 to 1836.

Literary References: *Woodward* 1977 (vol 1, pt 2), 261

Statues

1.	1825	John Knox (†1572), model for monument in Glasgow necropolis (designed by Thomas Hamilton and executed by Robert Forrest)		Untraced		*McKenzie* 2002, 293–7 (repr)

WARREN, William, of Hitchin fl *c*1790–1828

In 1826 he was employed by Countess de Grey at Wrest Park, Beds, where he received £90 for repairing the statues and £75 for carving and erecting stone piers for the gates. Two years later he made vases, columns and statues in Portland stone for the bowling green house in the garden. The Wilshire family monument is a large wall-tablet (1) and the Price is a tablet with an urn (2).

Literary References: *Gunnis* 1968, 413

Funerary Monuments

1.	*c*1790	Wilshire family		Welwyn, Herts	S	*Gunnis* 1968, 413
2.	?1820	Catherine Price		Knebworth, Herts	S	*Gunnis* 1968, 413
3.	nd	Jane and Martha Sibley		Wheathampstead, Herts	S	

Architectural Sculpture

4.	1826	Gate piers Payment(s): £75	s	[Wrest Park, Beds]; untraced		*Gunnis* 1968, 413, citing Wrest Archives

Miscellaneous

5.	1828	Vases, columns, statues	s	[Wrest Park, Beds, Bowling Green House]; untraced		*Gunnis* 1968, 413 citing Wrest Archives

WARRINGTON, Joseph fl 1686

With his partner **Ezra Horson** he was employed at Grimsthorpe in 1686.

Architectural Sculpture

1.	1686	Windows, cornices, chimney-panels and a doorcase (co-sculptor: Ezra Horson)	s	[Grimsthorpe Castle, Lincs]; untraced		Wentworth Woodhouse Archives, cited in *Gunnis* 1968, 211

WATERWORTH, Thomas I and II, of Doncaster

Thomas Waterworth I 1753–1829
Thomas Waterworth II 1788–1835

Thomas I was the son of Thomas Waterworth of Sutton-on-Derwent and Rebecca, née Whittal. In 1767 he was apprenticed to **Christopher Richardson of Doncaster**, whose daughter he later married. She had previously been married to **Christopher Theakston**. Thomas I was responsible for all the decorative stone-carving of the mausoleum, erected in 1788 at Wentworth Woodhouse by Lord Rockingham (9). He signed several monuments as 'Thomas Waterworth of Doncaster' including one with a portrait-bust, to William Dixon (2). The Simpson has an urn (3) and the Busk is a restrained tablet (1).

Gunnis assumed that **Thomas II** was responsible for the monument Captain Charles White, 1814, which has a relief of the graves of the Captain and his brother-officers at Bayonne (5). He died on 21 December 1835, aged 47, and was buried at Doncaster. His widow died on 11 September 1837, aged 42.

Literary References: *Gunnis* 1968, 413

Archival References: GPC citing Doncaster Corporation Archives

Funerary Monuments

1.	?1777	Martha Busk		Darfield, W R Yorks	S	GPC
2.	†1783	William Dixon (by Thomas Waterworth I)		Loversall, W R Yorks	S	*Gunnis* 1968, 413; Pevsner, *Yorks W R*, 1967, 357
3.	†1784	Rev John Simpson (by Thomas Waterworth I)		Babworth, Notts	S	Pevsner, *Notts*, 1979, 63

4.	1800	John Jarrett		Bradford, W R Yorks	S	*Gunnis* 1968, 413
5.	1814	Captain Charles White		Tuxford, Notts	S	*Gunnis* 1968, 413
6.	1816	Lord Effingham		All Saints, Rotherham, W R Yorks	S	*Gunnis* 1968, 413
Architectural Sculpture						
7.	*c*1780	Cavendish arms (by Thomas Waterworth I) Payment(s): £65	s	The Crescent, Buxton, Derbys	S	Pevsner, *Derbys*, 1978, 114
8.	*c*1782	Urn (by Thomas Waterworth I)		[Well House, Buxton]; Devonshire Royal Hospital, Buxton, Derbys	S	Pevsner, *Derbys*, 1978, 114
9.	1788	Decorative carving (by Thomas Waterworth I)	s	[coll Charles, 2nd Marquess of Rockingham]; Wentworth Woodhouse, W R Yorks, mausoleum		*Gunnis* 1968, 413, citing Fitzwilliam Archives
10.	nd	Justice, statue		Sheffield, W R Yorks, head of the Shambles		GPC

WATKIN, Daniel fl before 1751

The *Northampton Mercury* for 10 June 1751 carried an advertisement that the 'Stone Quarry Pit at Taternhoe nea Dunstable, Bedfordshire', which had belonged to the late Daniel Watkin, was 'now opened by Mrs. Watkin' and tha 'Chimney-pieces, monuments, tombs and headstones' could be obtained at reasonable prices'. (Inf. Bruce Bailey)

WATKINS, Henry, of Newport fl 1838–51

Watkins either died or left Newport in 1852, for his name ceases to appear in local directories after that date.

Literary References: *Gunnis* 1968, 413

Funerary Monuments						
1.	1838	Martha Davies, large wall-tablet		Newport, Monmouths		*Gunnis* 1968, 413
Statues						
2.	1851	The death of Llewllyn, the last Prince of Wales, group	m	[Gt Exhib, Fine Arts, class 30, 187]; untraced		*Great Exhib* 1861 (2), 151; *Gunnis* 1968, 413

WATKINS, John fl *c*1780–92

It is not clear whether the John Watkins who signed the Davies monument at Lyonshall is the author of the Joh Thomas at Radnor.

Funerary Monuments						
1.	1780	Catherine and James Davies		Lyonshall, Herefs	S	*Gunnis* 1968, 413
2.	†1792	John Thomas and others		Bleddfa, Radnor		GPC

WATKINS, John, of Ringwood fl 1795–*c*1813

The architectural monument about 8 feet high to James Mowbray has an Adamesque urn and gadrooned base (1 Gunnis considered it an extremely competent piece of carving for a local craftsman. The Hackman family memori is a circular wall-tablet (2). Watkins was a Calvinist.

Funerary Monuments						
1.	1801	James Mowbray		Ringwood, Hants	S	*Gunnis* 1968, 413
2.	1811	Hackman family		Ringwood, Hants	S	*Gunnis* 1968, 413
3.	†1813	Mrs Eyre		Burley Meeting House, New Forest, Hants	S	GPC
Architectural Sculpture						
4.	1795	Dial		Burley Meeting House, New Forest, Hants, north end		GPC

WATKINS, W fl *c*1752

Funerary Monuments						
1.	†1752	Ezekial Williams		Disserth, Radnor	S	Pevsner, *Powys*, 1979, 230

WATSON, Edward fl 1777

He was paid £23 13s 6d in 1777 by the 5th Earl of Carlisle for 'carving' (GPC quoting Castle Howard Archives).

WATSON, Henry 1714–86

Watson was baptised at Heanor, Derbys on 22 April 1714. He was the elder surviving son of **Samuel Watson** and hi wife Katherine. His brother, **Samuel Watson II**, is known to have worked with Henry in the 1730s.

He was apprenticed to **Edward Poynton of Nottingham** in 1729. During the 1730s he produced a number c monuments which are known from surviving drawings. One design in Derbyshire Record Office, Matlock, is for monument, nine feet in height, with volutes on either side, above which is a segmental pediment. The design i inscribed by Watson 'June 13. 1736. This is ye 3rd monument I have performed after this design, the last was erecte at Didsbury near Manchester in memory of Sir John Bland's mother, ye others I did for him in memory of hi ancestors at Kippax' (3; GPC). Annotations on another design indicate that Watson also carried out carving in woo for a chimneypiece designed by the architect Giacomo Leoni (8).

Henry Watson's account book in the Bodleian Library shows that he travelled widely in connection with his work His assistants, including **William Owen, John James** and **Robert Stanton**, operated from London and early in 173 Watson recorded a journey on horseback from his base in Derbyshire to Nottingham, Oxford and the capital, befor travelling to Wentworth Woodhouse in Yorkshire to work for Lord Malton. He then travelled to Warwick to 'mode the busto for Sir Verney Cave's monument' (4), a project which involved him with **Francis Smith of Warwic** (Bodleian MS Eng. Misc fol 383, quoted in *Brighton* 2001, 72). He received payments from Smith at Oxford in 173 and 1739, possibly for architectural carving at the Radcliffe Library, where Smith was joint contractor together wit **William Townesend**. Watson also worked for Smith at Wingerworth Hall and Sutton Scarsdale, Derbys, and a Trentham Hall, Staffs (**15, 16**).

Watson purchased a marble works in Ashford-in-the-Water, Derbys from **John Thorpe of Bakewell** in 1742. In 174 there, on the River Wye, he constructed water-powered mills for sawing, grinding and polishing Derbyshire 'marble from the local mines. The mills were the first of their kind in the country and in 1751 Watson successfully applied fo a royal patent for his invention. Around the same date Watson extended his business to premises in Bakewell. A notic advertising the move described his products as 'marble and other monuments, with their proper embellishments, tables curiously inlaid and decorated with a variety of colours in stone, the produce of this island; vases, obelisks and other curiosities in radix amethysti, &c ornamented either in the material itself or with d'Or Moulu, &c with a variety of other articles' (quoted in *Tomlinson* 1996, 12–13).

The Duke of Devonshire, who owned the mines worked by Watson, employed the sculptor to lay a tessellated floor of black and white marbles at Chatsworth (**19**). Watson also supplied plinths to Matthew Boulton of Birmingham for ormolu ornaments. He evidently maintained London contacts for in 1775 he wrote to Jacob Houblon, the owner of Hallingbury, saying that 'he hopes Mr. Houblon has seen his mosaic table at Mr. Devall's, mason, in Little Portland Street, Cavendish Square' (GPC). This was **John Deval II**, who was presumably selling Watson's wares through his London premises.

It seems that the marble mines, despite their innovative nature, failed to bring Watson the rewards he might have expected. In 1802 the antiquarians John Britton and E W Brayley recorded his achievement but added that 'though a patent was obtained to secure the profits of the invention, the advantages were not commensurate with the expectations that had been formed' (*Britton and Brayley* 1802, 3, 484).

Watson died on 24 October 1786 and is buried at Holy Trinity, Ashford-in-the-Water. A tablet in Derbyshire Black marble records that 'he established the marble-works near this place: and was the first who formed into ornaments The *Fluors* and other *Fossils* Of this County.' Watson's successor as owner of the Ashford marble works was **John Platt of Rotherham**. Watson's nephew, **White Watson**, worked briefly at the mills.

MGS

Literary References: *Britton and Brayley* 1802, 3, 484; *Glover* 1831–3, 2, 260; *Thompson* 1949, 115; *Gunnis* 1968, 414; *Penny* 1977 (1), 9; *Tomlinson* 1996, *passim*; *Brighton* 2001, 49–55

Archival References: GPC

Portraits of the Sculptor: White Watson, silhouette, Derbys RO D859Z/Z85, in *Brighton* 2001, 54 (repr)

Funerary Monuments					
1.	1733	Mr Turnbull, cartouche Drawing(s): ex Welbeck Abbey; untraced		['to be erected at Bedsworth church']; untraced	*Gunnis* 1968, 414
2.	1736	Mr Murgatroyd Drawing(s): ex Welbeck Abbey; untraced		[All Saints, Dewsbury, W R Yorks]; untraced	*Gunnis* 1968, 414; GPC
3.	1736	Sir John Bland's mother Drawing(s): Derbys RO D589Z/Z85		[Didsbury, near Manchester]; untraced	*Gunnis* 1968, 414; GPC
4.	1738	Sir Verney Cave, bust		[Stanford Hall, Northants]; untraced	*Brighton* 2001, 51
5.	1740	Mr Fairfax Drawing(s): ex Welbeck Abbey; untraced		[Wakefield, W R Yorks]; untraced	*Gunnis* 1968, 414
6.	nd	Ancestors of Sir John Bland		[Kippax, W R Yorks]; untraced	GPC
7.	nd	Mr Bagshaw's family Drawing(s): ex Welbeck Abbey; untraced		[Norton, E R Yorks]; untraced	*Gunnis* 1968, 414
Chimneypieces					
8.	1738	With a broken pediment (designed by Giacomo Leoni) Drawing(s): Derbys RO D589Z/Z85, annotated 'This design was made by Mr Leoni, the ornaments I performed in wood for Peter Bold' Esq	wd	[for Peter Bold]; untraced	*Gunnis* 1968, 414; *Brighton* 2001, 51
9.	1749	Description unavailable Payment(s): £65 10s	m	[Welbeck Abbey, Notts, north-east room]; unidentified	*Turberville* 1938–9, 1 394; *Gunnis* 1968, 414
10.	1757	Gothic (co-sculptor: Daniel Sephton)		Tissington Hall, Derbys	*Brighton* 2001, 51
11.	1775	Of 'various stones set in an antique mosaic' Payment(s): £53		[Hallingbury Place, Essex, lady's dressing room]; untraced	GPC quoting Archives Puxley of Welford, Berks
Architectural Sculpture					
12.	post-1739	Pediment carving	s	Radburne Hall, Derbys	Pevsner, *Derbys*, 1978, 301
13.	1747	Carved work Payment(s): £19 12s		[Kirtlington Park, Oxon]; untraced	GPC
14.	*c*1763	Coat of arms		Chatsworth, Derbys, stables	Pevsner, *Derbys*, 1978, 137; *Brighton* 2001, 52, 57
Miscellaneous					
15.	*c*1737	Carved chairs		[Wingerworth Hall, Derbys, hall and best parlour]; untraced	*Brighton* 2001, 71
16.	*c*1737	Unidentified work Payment(s): £5 5s		[Sutton Scarsdale, Derbys]; untraced	*Brighton* 2001, 71
17.	1738–1739	Unspecified carving		[Wentworth Woodhouse, W R Yorks]; untraced	*Brighton* 2001, 72
18.	*c*1775	Mosaic table		['at Mr Devall's, mason, in Little Portland Street, Cavendish Square']; untraced	GPC quoting Archives Puxley of Welford, Berks
19.	1779	Mosaic floor of black and white marble	m	Chatsworth, Derbys, painted hall	*Glover* 1831–3, 2, 260; *Thompson* 1949, 115; *Brighton* 2001, 53 (drawing repr)
20.	nd	Vases in blue John Drawing(s): Derbys RO		[for Mrs Legge of Grindlesmith Gate, Nottingham]; untraced	*Gunnis* 1968, 414

WATSON, James, of Norwich 1800–49

Gunnis believed there were two James Watsons, father and son, perhaps because the monument to Elizabeth Clarke, † 1793 (**1**) is in the mid-18th century style. It was however clearly made to match the tablet to her husband, Samuel,

†1761, also in the north transept at East Dereham. The second Watson monument at East Dereham, to the Clarkes daughter and her husband, Peter Stoughton, is little more than an inscription (2). The signature on both is 'J WATSON. NORWICH'.

There appears to be no mention of a James Watson in Norwich newspapers or other documents before 1825 Inscriptions recorded in the church of St Peter Parmentergate, Norwich, give dates for the death of Susanna, wife of James Watson, statuary and mason, late of Thorner in the county of York, in 1838 aged 41; James Watson himself in 1849, aged 49; and James Clemshaw Watson, their only surviving son, in 1851, aged 22. The IGI confirms that Watson was baptised in Thorner on 3 May 1801, less than a year after his parents married there, his father being named Robert.

Gunnis described tablets which he took to be by the elder Watson as quite well carved, but in no way outstanding and considered the best to be the pair in East Dereham (1, 2). In 1825 Watson formed a partnership with another stone and marble mason, Samuel Blythe of 89 Pottergate Street, Norwich (*Norwich Mercury*, 18 June). This may have been short-lived for it is Watson's signature that appears on the 'competent' wall-tablets listed below. These include the 'very chaste monument of white marble' put up by James Watson of Castle Meadow to commemorate his kinsman William Moore (8) (*Norwich Mercury*, 30 Oct 1841).

On 1 June 1844 the *Norwich Mercury*, reported that James Watson had contracted with Mr Donthorn, the successful entrant in the competition for the Leicester monument (13), 'to erect that column and all its ornament' except for the bronze bas reliefs, which are by **John Henning II.**

The business was continued to 1857 or later by Watson's second wife, Ann and her son by a previous marriage.

Jon Bayliss

Literary References: *Gunnis* 1968, 414

Funerary Monuments

1.	†1793	Elizabeth Clarke	East Dereham, Norfolk	S	*Gunnis* 1968, 414
2.	†1805	Peter Stoughton and his wife, Elizabeth	East Dereham, Norfolk	S	*Gunnis* 1968, 414
3.	†1810	William Jary	South Walsham, Norfolk		Pevsner, *Norfolk: N E & Norwich*, 1997, 668
4.	?1824	Rev John Warren	Tacolneston, Norfolk	S	*Gunnis* 1968, 414
5.	?1832	Thomas Talbot	Wymondham, Norfolk	S	*Gunnis* 1968, 414
6.	?1835	Rev Bartholomew Riston	St Margaret, Lowestoft, Suffolk	S	*Gunnis* 1968, 414
7.	?1841	George Smith	Mattishall, Norfolk	S	*Gunnis* 1968, 414
8.	1841	William Moore (†1839)	[St Andrew, Norwich, Norfolk]; untraced	S	*Norwich Mercury*, 30 Oct 1841
9.	†1844	Mary Alexander	Cromer, Norfolk	S	RG/JP, 8, 1519
10.	†1848	Frederick Skoulding	Wymondham Abbey, Norfolk	S	RG/JP, 8, 1519
11.	?1848	Samuel Stone	St Andrew, Norwich, Norfolk	S	*Gunnis* 1968, 414
12.	?1851	Lord Berners	Ashwellthorpe, Norfolk	S	*Gunnis* 1968, 414

Architectural Sculpture

13.	1844	Column commemorating the Earl of Leicester	Holkham Hall, Norfolk		*Norwich Mercury*, 1 June 1844

WATSON, John I –1771

The son of another John Watson (†1757), a mason and surveyor of bridges in the West Riding of Yorkshire, Watson followed his father's profession. In 1759–61 he and his partner, John Gott, built the stone bridge which carries the public road past Nostell Priory. The bridge was designed by Sir George Savile and cost nearly £800 (Nostell Archives cited in GPC). He also built a pavilion at Seaton Delaval, Northumbs in 1756 (Seaton Delaval Archives, Newcastle Public Library, Box 4, no 1). Between 1760 and 1770 he was the master-mason responsible for building Serlby Hall, Notts, receiving payments as a mason and carver. Watson's son, Charles (*c*1770–1836) was responsible for much architectural work in Yorkshire.

Literary References: Pevsner, *Notts*, 1979, 306 n; *Colvin* 1995, 1024–6

Archival References: GPC

Chimneypieces

1.	1753	Description unavailable	m	[Cusworth Hall, W R Yorks, library]; untraced	GPC citing Cusworth Hall archives, Leeds Public Library
2.	1760–1770	Two Payment(s): £38	m	[Serlby Hall, Notts, drawing room and dining room]; untraced	GPC

WATSON, John II fl 1808–29

Gunnis notes that he did a considerable amount of work at the Royal Hospital at Greenwich, building the 'New Helpless Ward' in 1808 and the Infirmary four years later. There he was apparently responsible for all the carved stonework and the marble chimneypieces (1, 2). In 1812–14 he completed the west front of King Charles's Building, and in 1815 received £7,000 for new offices, eastward of Greenwich Palace. In 1825 he built the out pension office at St Mary Axe, and in 1828–29 the Royal Hospital Schools at Greenwich (*Gunnis* 1968, 414, incorrectly cites PRO, ADM 882-Ad. 887).

Chimneypieces

1.	1812	Several, including one of veined marble and another of black Payment(s): £20 16s; £16 4s	[Infirmary, Greenwich Hospital]; untraced	*Gunnis* 1968, 414

Architectural Sculpture

2.	1812	Carved stonework	[Infirmary, Greenwich Hospital]; untraced	*Gunnis* 1968, 414

WATSON, Musgrave Lewthwaite 1804–47

Musgrave Lewthwaite Watson might have become one of the great sculptors of the 19th century, but he died at the age of 43, having completed only a small number of works. He was born at Hawksdale Hall, in the Caldew valley, near Carlisle, on 24 January 1804, the second son of Thomas Watson, a small-holder who had travelled to the West Indies as young man and made sufficient capital to set up as a farmer on his return. Thomas married

Mary Lewthwaite and became a partner in the cotton mill of his father-in-law, Musgrave Lewthwaite, at Dalston and had interests in the Dalston forge which was also owned by his father-in-law (CRO LT/20, Covens Textile Mill, schedule of deeds). Musgrave went to a village school at nearby Raughton Head, where the master, Rev R Monkhouse, considered him an outstanding pupil. The boy soon showed his artistic talent and spent much of his time drawing, wood-carving and metal-engraving. He wanted to become a sculptor, but his family insisted on a career in the law and articled Watson to a Carlisle solicitor, Major Mounsey. Mounsey encouraged him to pursue his artistic interests in his spare time, allowing him to study his own significant art collection. He also attended modelling classes at the Carlisle Academy of Arts in Finkle Street, which had recently founded by a small group of local artists, led by the sculptor **David Dunbar**.

After his father's death in 1823, Watson left Carlisle for London. There he showed his drawings and models to **John Flaxman RA** and on his advice entered the Royal Academy Schools, submitting the model of a *Shepherdess* as his probationary work (**54**). Watson also studied briefly under **Robert William Sievier**, together with **William Frederick Woodington**, and he attended an informal art school started up by a few young sculptors for their 'mutual improvement' (*Lonsdale* 1866, 55). He sent four reliefs and an engraving of *Cupid and Psyche*, to the second exhibition of the Carlisle Academy in 1824 (**40–43**). The following year he went to Italy, where he remained for three years, living for much of that time among the French and German students in Rome and studying languages as well as art. Watson had a range of artistic talents: he could etch, carve, design cameos and paint in watercolours, skills which enabled him to support himself during his travels.

In 1828 Watson returned to London. He stayed with Woodington for some months before going back to Carlisle, where he executed a number of statues and busts, including a portrait of the naturalist John Heysham, which was shown in 1828 at the Carlisle Exhibition of Painting and Sculpture (**32**). Among Watson's earliest works in his home county is a simple tablet commemorating his former school master, surmounted by a charming, naïve figure of a mourning student (**2**). A more sophisticated subject, an allegory of the Fates, was used for the memorial to Watson's father, carved in Rome a few months earlier (**1**). This was inspired by Fuseli's painting, *The three witches* (1783).

Opportunities for sculptors were limited in Carlisle and since Watson's family remained unsympathetic to his choice of career, he returned to London, where he took studios near the British Museum, first in Museum Street and then in Rathbone Place. He exhibited regularly at the Royal Academy from 1829, concentrating principally on poetic works including a small terracotta sketch, *The madness of Hercules* (**57**) and a bronze statue of *Sigismunda* (**14**). His practice failed to prosper and by 1832 Watson was living in penury. His belongings were seized when he failed to pay his rent and a model of *Hercules* (**16**) on which he had worked for many months was broken up so that the clay could be sold.

In 1833 Watson found work as a modeller in **Francis Chantrey**'s studio, but he left when Chantrey refused to increase his wages. He then became an assistant to **William Behnes**, modelling the figure, but not the head, of Dr William Babington's statue for St Paul's Cathedral (**3**). This was widely considered to be the most successful of Behnes's statues, praised by FT Palgrave for its beautiful drapery (*Palgrave* 1866, 223). Watson was again dissatisfied with his earnings and left Behnes to work in the studio of **Edward Hodges Baily**, where he was more content. He was also employed by **William Croggon** at the **Coade Factory** in Lambeth making models for artificial stone ornaments, apparently including friezes for the Wyndham family, statues of *Esculapius* and *Hygeia* for a hall in Liverpool and other groups for Dublin (**63**).

During the early 1840s he was working more or less independently, with a studio at 13 Upper Gloucester Place, Marylebone. In 1842 he completed a frieze celebrating *Commerce* for Moxhay's Hall of Commerce in Threadneedle Street, London (**38**). Shortly afterwards he received the commission that was to be his greatest work, a colossal group of two brothers, Lord Eldon and Lord Stowell, for University College, Oxford (**24**). This commission would have gone to Chantrey, but his death intervened and, on the advice of Allan Cunningham, Watson was called in. Gunnis considered the work to be one of the most important portrait groups of the nineteenth century. Among Watson's other major works at this time was a relief, *The Battle of St Vincent*, for the base of Nelson's Column in Trafalgar Square (**49**). He also executed a series of statues, two for Carlisle Assize Courts (**19, 22**), Elizabeth I for the Royal Exchange (**21**) and John Flaxman (**23**), now at University College, London. He continued to exhibit at the Royal Academy, showing a relief of *Sleep and death bearing off the body of Sarpedon* (**46**) in 1844. A plaster version of this acclaimed work was later shown at the 1862 International Exhibition at the instigation of **John Henry Foley**.

The successful years were pitifully short, for Watson died from heart disease at his home in London on 28 October 1847. The stress and physical labour involved in the design and execution of the Eldon and Stowell group had taken its toll on his frail physique. He was buried in Highgate cemetery and his monument, with a portrait medallion by his assistant **George Nelson**, was erected in Carlisle Cathedral. Watson had married for the *Carlisle Journal* of 18 February 1832 gives the obituary 'Near Hampstead, London, on the 29 ult, Ellen wife of Mr ML Watson, deservedly lamented'.

Towards the end of his life Watson destroyed many of the models in his studio that he found unsatisfactory. Other models and sketches were sold from his studio on 14 September 1848. A number of works were unfinished at his death, including the Eldon and Stowell group, Flaxman's statue and the monument to the 50th Regiment in Canterbury Cathedral (**10**). These were all completed by Nelson, whilst the relief of the *Battle of St Vincent* was finished by Woodington.

Watson was a complex personality, who quarrelled frequently with patrons and employers. He was sensitive and intelligent but prone to depression and he became increasingly embittered by professional disappointments. Lonsdale suggests that his advancement may have been hampered by his irregular domestic arrangements, for he lived with the daughter of a Carlisle publican but never married her. Her early death was a further blow. Watson was admired by contemporary sculptors, including **Allan Cunningham, John Henry Foley** and **John Gibson**, but he had little success in public competitions and no influential patrons, so many of his works never advanced beyond the model stage. After his death, he was seen as a sculptor of great promise, whose career had been cut short when success was within reach: 'Alas for the fame of the gifted! Mr. Watson lived long enough to achieve, but not to enjoy, fam… It is the old story over again; genius lives in poverty, and then all at once the world wakes up to the knowledge th… a great spirit has gone out of its portals' (*Illus Exhib*, 1851, 14). (add inf. Denis Perriam)

EI…

Literary References: *Athenaeum*, 1847, 1154; *AU*, 1848, 27; *AJ*, 1856, 193; *Lonsdale* 1866, *passim*; *Palgrave* 1866, *passim*; *Weekes* 1880, 297; *DNB* L… 1899, 21–2; *Archit Rev* 1967, 406; *Gunnis* 1968, 414–5; *Perriam* 1975, 300, 302; *Read* 1982, *passim*; *Grove* 32, 1996, 911 (Stocker); *ODNB* (Stocker)
Additional MS Sources: *Flaxman Papers*, 1825, 1843, 1844, Add MSS 39781 fol 235, 39783, fols 285, 291, 293
Will: PROB 11/2072
Collections of Drawings: designs for monuments, VAM P&D, H.6.a
Auction Catalogue: *Lonsdale* 1866, 223–4

Funerary Monuments

1.	†1823	Thomas Watson		Sebergham, Cumberland	S	Pevsner, *Cumberland & Westmorland*, 1967, 188 (repr 57); *Archit Rev* 1967, 466 (repr)
2.	c1828	Rev Robert Monkhouse (†1822)		Raughton Head, Cumberland	S	Pevsner, *Cumberland & Westmorland*, 1967, 180; *Archit Rev* 1967, 466 (repr)
3.	1837	Dr William Babington (†1833) (co-sculptor: William Behnes)		St Paul's Cathedral, London		*Lonsdale* 1866, 85–6; *Graves* I, 1905–6, 168; *Read* 1982, 67
4.	1843	Major Francis Aglionby (†1840)		Ainstable, Cumberland	SD	Pevsner, *Cumberland & Westmorland*, 1967, 59; *Read* 1982, 290, 291 (repr)
5.	c1845	Allan Cunningham (†1842)		St Michael, Dumfries	S	*Gunnis* 1968, 415
6.	c1845	Allan Cunningham (†1842)		Kensal Green Cemetery, London		*Lonsdale* 1866, 185–6; *Graves* VIII, 1905–6, 170; *Gunnis* 1968, 415
7.	†1845	Sir Thomas Fowell Buxton, for Westminster Abbey, small model (monument executed by Frederick Thrupp)		Untraced		*Lonsdale* 1866, 135–6
8.	†1846	Rev Walter Fletcher		Dalston, Cumberland		Pevsner, *Cumberland & Westmorland*, 1967, 118; *Read* 1982, 190, 191 (repr)
9.	1847	Dr Archibald Cameron Model(s): exhib RA, London, 1847, 1339	s	[Savoy Chapel, London]; destroyed		*AU*, 1847, 200; *Lonsdale* 1866, 169–76 (repr); *Graves* VIII, 1905–6, 170
10.	1848	Officers and men of the 50th Regiment (co-sculptor: George Nelson)		Canterbury Cathedral, Kent	SD	Pevsner, *Kent: N E & E*, 1983, 211; C Lib (repr)
11.	nd	Admiral Sir Thomas Williams		Kensal Green Cemetery, London		*Lonsdale* 1866, 215

Statues

12.	1828	Clytie, statuette	m	[coll G G Mounsey]; untraced		*Lonsdale* 1866, 76–8
13.	1828	Lord Eldon (co-sculptor: Frederick William Woodington)		[Unidentified school, New Road, London]; untraced		*Lonsdale* 1866, 81
14.	1829	Sigismunda	b	[Exhib RA, London, 1184]; untraced		*Graves* VIII, 1905–6, 169–70
15.	1830	Napoleon, statuette	b	[Carlisle Exhib]; untraced		*Lonsdale* 1866, 79
16.	1832	Hercules, model		Destroyed		*Lonsdale* 1866, 112
17.	c1839	Nelson memorial, designs only (executed by Railton and E H Baily)		Untraced		*Lonsdale* 1866, 95–8
18.	1842	Sir David Wilkie, for the National Gallery, model (statue executed by Samuel Joseph)	p	[Watson sale, 1848]; untraced		*Lonsdale* 1866, 187–9; *Gunnis* 1968, 415
19.	1843	Major Francis Aglionby		Assize Courts, Carlisle, Cumberland	SD	*Lonsdale* 1866, 180–3; Pevsner, *Cumberland & Westmorland*, 1967, 101; *Read* 1982, 166–167 (repr)
20.	By 1843	Mrs Brougham (the mother of Lord Henry Bougham), model		[Watson sale, 1848]; untraced		*Lonsdale* 1866, 134–5
21.	1844	Queen Elizabeth I	s	Royal Exchange, City of London		*Lonsdale* 1866, 179–80; *Leith* 1997, 340; *Ward-Jackson* 2003, 325–6 (repr)
22.	1845	William, 1st Earl of Lonsdale		Assize Courts, Carlisle, Cumberland, outside principal front	S	*CJ*, 13 Aug 1847; *Lonsdale* 1866, 180–3; Pevsner, *Cumberland & Westmorland*, 1967, 101; *Read* 1982, 167
23.	1843–1847	John Flaxman	m	UCL, library		*CJ*, 11 and 18 June 1847; *Lonsdale* 1866, 199–206 (repr); Pevsner, *London: N*, 1998, 272
24.	1842–1848	John, 1st Lord Eldon and William, 1st Lord Stowell, group (co-sculptor: George Nelson) Drawing(s): University College, Oxford		University College, Oxford		*CJ*, 6 Oct 1848; *Lonsdale* 1866, 151–68 (repr); Pevsner, *Oxon*, 1974, 212; *Read* 1982, 50
25.	nd	Chaucer, Spenser, Jonson, Shakespeare, Beaumont and Fletcher, statuettes		Untraced		*Lonsdale* 1866, 98–104 (Chaucer repr); *Graves* VIII, 1905–6, 169
26.	nd	Girl and lizard, design only		Untraced		*Lonsdale* 1866, 87
27.	nd	Iris Model(s): 'sketch' exhib Soc of BA, London, 1830, 862	b	[ex coll G G Mounsey]; untraced		*Lonsdale* 1866, 78; *Johnson* 1975, 488
28.	nd	Jolly or Crutched friars, statuette		Carlisle Museum and Art Gallery, Cumberland		*Lonsdale* 1866, 85, 91–5 (repr); *Read* 1982, 209, 212; *Grove* 32, 1996, 911

29.	nd	The chimney sweep, model		Untraced		*Lonsdale* 1866, 184 (repr); *Read* 1982, 212
30.	nd	The outcasts (mother and children in a storm), small model		Untraced		*Lonsdale* 1866, 118–22 (repr)
Busts						
31.	*c*1825	Arthur, 1st Duke of Wellington	m	Gov Art Coll (1971)	S	Gov Art Coll Archives
32.	1828	John Heysham	m	[Exhib Carlisle Acad, 195]; untraced		*Lonsdale* 1866, 71, 76; *Gunnis* 1968, 414
33.	1828	Major Hodgson	m	[Carlisle Exhib]; untraced		*Lonsdale* 1866, 76
34.	1840	Miss Greaves	i	[Exhib RA, London, 1150]; untraced		*Graves* VIII, 1905–6, 169
Chimneypieces						
35.	1842	Poetry and Painting, frieze for a mantelpiece	b	[Exhib RA, London, 1349]; untraced		*Graves* VIII, 1905–6, 169
Architectural Sculpture						
36.	?*c*1822	Busts of Benjamin West, Christopher Wren and Francis Chantrey, and in a niche over the entrance, 'a sculptured sculptor in his artist's frock coat, in the act of finishing the bust of a princess'		[Carlisle Acad of Art]; untraced		*The Citizen*, 1 May 1830, 677
37.	*c*1840	Dawn in a chariot, pediment group (co-sculptor: T Tyley)		Victoria Rooms, Bristol		*Lonsdale* 1866, 130–2; *Read* 1982, 218, 219 (repr)
38.	1842	The Benefits of Commerce, frieze		[Moxhay's Hall of Commerce, Threadneedle St, City of London]; Napier Terrace, Islington, walls of recreation area		*ILN*, 30 July 1842, 180 (repr); *Lonsdale* 1866, 137–50 (repr); *Leith* 1997, 340 *Gunnis* 1968, 415
39.	1847	Font		[for Ryde church, I of W]; untraced		
Reliefs						
40.	1824	A nymph		[Second Carlisle Exhib]; untraced		*Lonsdale* 1866, 55
41.	1824	Adoration, a Roman head		[Second Carlisle Exhib]; untraced		*Lonsdale* 1866, 55
42.	1824	Cupid bearing down the arms of Mars		[Second Carlisle Exhib]; untraced		*Lonsdale* 1866, 55
43.	1824	Melpomene, a study		[Second Carlisle Exhib]; untraced		*Lonsdale* 1866, 55
44.	1835	The dream of Io		[Exhib RA, London, 1059]; untraced		*Lonsdale* 1866, 78; *Graves* VIII, 1905–6, 169
45.	1837	Dante and Beatrice		[Exhib RA, London, 1196]; untraced		*AU*, 1848, 27; *Lonsdale* 1866, 104; *Graves* VIII, 1905–6, 169
46.	1844	Sleep and death bearing off the body of Sarpedon, model		Carlisle Museum and Art Gallery, Cumberland		*AU*, 1844, 171; *Lonsdale* 1866, 123–30 (repr); *Graves* VIII, 1905–6, 170; *Grove* 32, 1996, 911
47.	1845	'Little children come unto me' (Christ blessing little children)	tc	[A school near Holland House, London]; untraced		*Lonsdale* 1866, 115–6; *Graves* VIII, 1905–6, 170
48.	1847	Hebe and Iris		Bowood, Wilts, gates		*AU*, 1847, 200; *Lonsdale* 1866, 105; *Graves* VIII, 1905–6, 170; *Gunnis* 1968, 415
49.	1850	Battle of St Vincent (co-sculptor: William Frederick Woodington)	b	Nelson's Column, Trafalgar Square, London, base	S	*Lonsdale* 1866, 190–2; *CIIA* 4/2/30 (repr); *Read* 1982, 90: *Yarrington* 1988, 317 (pl 112)
50.	nd	Dante and Raphael, medallions		Untraced		*AU*, 1848, 27; *Lonsdale* 1866, 104
51.	nd	Lucifer and Cain in the abyss of space		Untraced		*Lonsdale* 1866, 211–5 (repr)
52.	nd	Man's first sacrifice		Untraced		*Lonsdale* 1866, 207–10 (repr)
53.	nd	Night		Untraced		*Lonsdale* 1866, 78
Miscellaneous						
54.	1824	Shepherdess, model		Untraced		*Lonsdale* 1866, 54
55.	1828	Happiness	m	[Carlisle Exhib]; untraced		*Lonsdale* 1866, 76
56.	1828	Simplicity	m	[Carlisle Exhib]; untraced		*Lonsdale* 1866, 76; *Graves* VIII, 1905–6, 169
57.	1828	The madness of Hercules	tc	[Carlisle Exhib]; untraced		*Lonsdale* 1866, 76
58.	1829	Hagar and Ishmael, model		[Exhib RA, London, 1830, 1250]; untraced		*Lonsdale* 1866, 78, 79–80; *Graves* VIII, 1905–6, 169
59.	1829	Melancholy, sketch		[Exhib Soc of BA, London, 845]; untraced		*Johnson* 1975, 488
60.	1829	Musidora		[Exhib RA, London, 1207]; untraced		*Graves* VIII, 1905–6, 169
61.	*c*1830	Compositions from Homer, Chaucer and Spenser		untraced		*Lonsdale* 1866, 98–9; *Gunnis* 1968, 414
62.	1841	'Design in bronze for an Egyptian priest; cast in one piece by the Electrotype'		[Exhib RA, London, 1146]; untraced		*Graves* VIII, 1905–6, 169
63.	nd	Models for the Coade Factory (including friezes for the Wyndham family, statues of Esculapius and Hygeia for a hall in Liverpool, groups for Dublin)		Untraced		*Lonsdale* 1866, 89

WATSON, R, of Dartford fl 1802–18?

Gunnis considers his best work to be the large wall-tablet to George Sharp which has a relief of a wreathed urn on a column (3). The Heathcote tablet 'has good details and a coat of arms engraved on brass' (1).

Funerary Monuments					
1.	?1802	Thomas Heathcote	Stone, Kent		*Gunnis* 1968, 415
2.	?1809	Enoch Holden	Crayford, Kent	S	*Gunnis* 1968, 416
3.	?1810	George Sharp	Stone, Kent		*Gunnis* 1968, 415
4.	?1811	Lady Gordon	West Tilbury, Essex	S	*Gunnis* 1968, 416
5.	?1818	Miss Pritchard	West Tilbury, Essex	S	*Gunnis* 1968, 416

WATSON, Samuel I 1662–1715

A talented carver whose work was similar in style to **Grinling Gibbons**, he is chiefly remembered for his immense amount of carving of a very high standard at Chatsworth, Derbys, which was for many years misattributed to Gibbons (**2–20, 22–27**).

Watson was born at Heanor, Derbys, the son of Ralph Watson, a husbandman of Heanor, and his wife, Bridget née Townsend, and was baptised there on 2 December 1662. Little is known of his early life but his grandson, **White Watson**, stated that he was 'a pupil of Mr. Charles Oakey, carver, in the parish of St Martin's in the fields' (*Lyson* 1806–22, V, 153). Oakey or Okey was employed by the 1st Duke of Beaufort on the remodelling of Badminton House in 1683 and it is possible that Watson worked there too. He is known to have worked under the London carver **Thomas Young** for the Earl of Exeter at Burghley House and for George Vernon at Sudbury Hall. Since Gibbons was also employed at Badminton, Burghley and Sudbury, Watson must have had many opportunities to study his work.

By 1690–91 Young and Watson were employed by the Earl of Exeter's brother-in-law, the 4th Earl (and later 1st Duke) of Devonshire at Chatsworth. There they were joined by **Joel Lobb** and his assistant **William Davis.** By 1692 Young had left and Watson and Davis were both working as Lobb's assistants, while other carvers including **Nadauld** and **C G Cibber**, came and went. In that year, following a dispute over pay, the Earl dismissed his architect, John Talman, and most of his London and foreign craftsmen, but Watson was kept on and he rose to become principal carver. He worked at Chatsworth until 1711 and as well as carving, he assisted Sir Christopher Wren in his independent valuation of the work done by Talman's team.

Much of Watson's work at Chatsworth is well-documented: numerous payments to him for carving in limewood, stone, alabaster and marble are recorded in the accounts and many drawings relating to his work have survived. George Vertue, his contemporary, commented on 'The Ornaments Carvd in wood & foliages by Watson sculptor in wood & stone. The boys in the Chapel and other parts of his works. very fine . . . a most ingenious artist' (*Vertue* II, 37). It is certain that Gibbons never worked at Chatsworth but by the mid-18th century his name had become associated with carving there. In 1744 the Earl of Egmont noted that there was 'a good deal of fine carving in wood by the late Grinlin Gibbons' in the chapel (HMC Egmont MSS, in *Green* 1964, 118) and in 1760 Horace Walpole mentioned 'Much carving here [in the Chapel] & about the house by Gibbins & Watson his scholar' (*Walpole, Country Seats*, 28). With Walpole's authority behind it, this myth has persisted until the present day, though documents proving Watson's contribution were revealed by his descendants in the early 19th century and several historians have pointed to the lack of evidence linking Gibbons to the house.

In addition to his work at Chatsworth Watson may have provided stone carving in the painted hall and grotto, and the ornamental parts of the alabaster reredos in the chapel, thought to have been designed by Cibber. Brighton also attributes to Watson a famous assemblage of limewood carving, featuring a portrait medallion, a point-lace cravat and a dead woodcock, long thought to be the work of Grinling Gibbons. The medallion is of particular interest since it may be the only surviving likeness of Watson.

Elsewhere, Watson carved ornamental vases for Thomas Coke of Melbourne Hall (**21**). In 1806 he wrote to Coke: 'I have according to your order sent you two designs of vases, which I take to bee something after ye manner your worship spoke of att Melborn; but if you would have any alteration in either of them as to cartouches instead of festoons or in any other part, be pleased to give me your directions which shall bee observed to my uttermost power' (Archives, Marquess of Lothian, in *Gunnis* 1968, 416). Gunnis notes that a number of stone vases which are perhaps Watson's work survive in the gardens at Melbourne.

Collections of Watson's drawings are kept at Chatsworth, the Derbyshire record office at Matlock, the Bodleian Library, Oxford, and Alnwick Castle, Northumberland. These volumes include Watson's own designs, sketches by other artists and drawings by Watson of the work of his contemporaries at Chatsworth and elsewhere. A drawing of the Ferrers monument at Tamworth, Staffs, falls into the last category. Gunnis cited this drawing as proof that the monument was by Watson but it was subsequently shown to be the work of Gibbons and **Arnold Quellin.** Watson does appear to have undertaken some monumental work for a payment of £17 was made to him in 1698 for 'cutting a monument in alabaster for His Grace the Duke of Newcastle' (**1**).

Towards the end of his life Watson married Katherine Greensmith, a woman 17 years his junior, from Pilsey, a Chatsworth estate village, and they settled at Heanor. Their first son died in infancy in 1711, but a second son was born in 1714 and Katharine was pregnant with another when her husband died of a stroke in 1715. Samuel was buried at Heanor on 31 March 1715. His sons **Henry Watson** and **Samuel Watson II** both trained as carvers, as did his grandson, White Watson. As part of the rehabilitation of his grandfather, White Watson erected a monument to his memory at Heanor about a century after his death.

EH

Literary References: *Glover* 1831–3, 255–8; *Thompson* 1949, *passim*; *Green* 1964 (1), *passim*; *Gunnis* 1968, 416; *Tomlinson* 1996, 12, 32, 48; *Brighton* 1998, 811–8; *Esterly* 1998, *passim*; *Brighton* 2001, 47–9, 60–70; *ODNB* (Brighton)

Archival References: Chatsworth Accts, vol ix

Additional MS Sources: Chatsworth Building Accts; Watson/Chatsworth; Watson Notebooks

Collections of Drawings: Derbys RO; Alnwick Castle, Northumbs

Funerary Monuments

1.	1698	'Ffor cutting a monument in Allablster 2 [pieces?] for His Grace the Duke of Newcastle Payment(s): £17	a	Untraced	Chatsworth Building Accts, IX, 5 Sept 1698

Architectural Sculpture

2.	1692	Carved ornaments, including urns, cherubs, a scroll and a pulpit		Chatsworth, Derbys, chapel	*Brighton* 2001, 48
3.	1692–1694	Carved ornaments (working with Lobb and Davis)	wd	Chatsworth, Derbys, state rooms	*Glover* 1831–3, 255; *Thompson* 1949, 149–50; *Green* 1964 (1), repr 169–71; Pevsner, *Derbys*, 1978, 135

4.	1694	Carved ornaments (working with Lobb)	wd	Chatsworth, Derbys, Queen of Scots apartments	*Thompson* 1949, 150, 170; Pevsner, *Derbys*, 1978, 136
5.	1696	Carved ornaments, including architrave and cornice, pilaster capitals, a picture frame and 'the Spandrills of 2 Ovall frames'		Chatsworth, Derbys, library (some still in situ)	*Thompson* 1949, 167–8
6.	1698	'ffor 2 Large Festoons on ye East Side Chatsworth £20'; ffor Carving 2 pedestalls in the Garden 3£ Each £06.0.0'		Chatsworth, Derbys	Chatsworth Building Accts, IX, 5 Sept 1698
7.	1699	'for carving 7 foot of moulding . . . at 3d' Payment(s): 1s		[Chatsworth, Derbys, dining room]; untraced	*Thompson* 1949, 143
8.	1699	'for raising Stone Masoning and Carving 8 basons in the Willow Tree grove at 6£ each'; for Carving 2 Vanes on ye Peirs at ye Bird houses £2.10.0' Payment(s): £48 (basons and masonry)		Chatsworth, Derbys	Chatsworth Building Accts, vol X, 4
9.	1701	'14 Mask heads in the Terrase Wall and making 2 Flower Potts set upon 2 Peers going to the Bowling green' Payment(s): £34 5s		Chatsworth, Derbys	Chatsworth Building Accts, vol vi, 23
10.	1701	Capitals (£4 10s and £3 each), ornaments over windows (£4 each) and other ornaments	s	Chatsworth, Derbys, west front	*Glover* 1831–3, 255–6; *Gunnis* 1968, 416
11.	1701	Thirteen urns for the roof Payment(s): £84		Chatsworth, Derbys	*Green* 1964 (1), 119 n2
12.	1701	Urn for the altar Payment(s): £2 15s		Chatsworth, Derbys, chapel	*Green* 1964 (1), 119 n2
13.	1703	Carved ornaments (designed by Thomas Archer)	s	Chatsworth, Derbyshire, cascade house	*Devonshire* 1999, 16–17 (repr)
14.	1703	Cornice, doorcase and scallops in niches on top landing		Chatsworth, Derbys, west stairs	*Thompson* 1949, 184; *Gunnis* 1968, 416, *Murdoch* 1988, 240
15.	1704	Arms Payment(s): £55		Chatsworth, Derbys, west pediment	Pevsner, *Derbys*, 1978, 131
16.	1705	Buffet fountain Payment(s): £8	s	[Chatsworth, Derbys, buffet room]; Thornbridge Hall, Derbys	*Thompson* 1949, 179, 181–2; Pevsner, *Derbys*, 1978, 340
17.	1705	Cornices and window mouldings Payment(s): £38 1s 10d; £6 1s 8d; £6 16s; £1 7s 3d		Chatsworth, Derbys, second floor bedrooms, west front	*Thompson* 1949, 188–9
18.	1705	Mouldings in the window		[Chatsworth, Derbys, south west closet]; untraced	*Thompson* 1949, 159
19.	1706	Carved cornice Payment(s): £8 16s 7d		[Chatsworth, Derbys, buffet room]; untraced	*Thompson* 1949, 179
20.	1706	Dolphins for the 'Bathing Roome' Payment(s): £14 part payment		Chatsworth, Derbys, grotto	*Murdoch* 1988, 240
21.	1706	Vases	s	Melbourne Hall, Derbys, gardens	*Gunnis* 1968, 416
22.	1705–1707	Carved ornaments to designs 'drawne by Mr Archer' Payment(s): £95		Chatsworth, Derbys, north front	*Glover* 1831–3, 256; *Thompson* 1949, 70, 77–8; *Brighton* 1998, 815
23.	1707	Carving Payment(s): £19 18s 9d		[Chatsworth, Derbys, 'at the cascade']; untraced	GPC
24.	1708	Pilasters and ornament at base of niches on the top landing		Chatsworth, Derbys, west stairs	*Thompson* 1949, 184–5
25.	1711	'For carving 10 forms in ye Garden att 3 pound each £30'		Chatsworth, Derbys, gardens	Chatsworth Building Accts, vol IX, 29 Sept 1711
26.	1711	Two mask heads Payment(s): £1 10s	a	[Chatsworth, Derbys, lower dining room]; untraced	GPC
27.	nd	'48 foot running in the great Member of the Cornish'	wd	[Chatsworth, Derbys, first library]; destroyed	*Thompson* 1949, 166

WATSON, Samuel II 1715–78

He was born in June 1715, at Heanor, Derbys, the posthumous son of **Samuel Watson I**. His father left £100 to his wife, Katherine, who was to raise the child on the interest. During the 1730s he worked with his brother **Henry Watson** carving chairs for Wingerworth Hall; Derbys (Henry Watson's Accounts, Watson Notebooks, in *Brighton* 2001, 71). He is described as a carver in a financial document of June 1741 (White Watson, *Collections for a History of Derbyshire*, Chatsworth Library, cited by *Brighton* 2001, 50). As the head of a team of joiners and carpenters employed at Chatsworth in 1756, he received £115 18s 8d for 'sashes for ye South Front, the Queen of Scots apartment, the Hall, 2 windowes in ye East Front and one in ye great apartment' (Chatsworth MSS Vouchers L95/7 in *Brighton* 2001, 55). In the following year, heading the same team at Hardwick Hall, he was paid £121 19 4d for 'work done to 26 sashes to west front and to taking down the woodwork and making good again' (*ibid*).

He was living at Whiteley Woods, Fulwood, near Sheffield, when his son **White Watson**, was born in 1760 and two years later he moved to Baslow. By then he had established a thriving mill-stone cutting business, which he eventually passed on to another son, Samuel. In 1774 he patented a portable milling machine.

Literary References: *Brighton* 2001, 55–6

Portraits of the Sculptor: White Watson, silhouette, Derbys RO D589Z/Z85 (repr *Brighton* 2001, 59)

WATSON, White 1760–1835

White Watson was a sculptor, marble-worker, geologist and mineral-dealer who lived in Bakewell, Derbys throughout most of his life. He was born at Whiteley Wood Hall, near Sheffield, on 10 April 1760, the son of

Samuel Watson II and the nephew of **Henry Watson**. During his boyhood White paid frequent visits to his uncle' marble mill and shop, and from an early age took an interest in the collections of fossils and minerals whic his uncle sold from time to time. He kept his uncle supplied by visiting local quarries and mines and soo started his own collection. He left Sheffield School at the age of 14 and on 31 May 1774 went to live with his uncl who had retired to Bakewell in 1773. For some years White helped carry on his uncle's business and in 178 he advertised himself as a sculptor and engraver. When Henry Watson died in 1786 the marble mill was sold, bu White continued to trade as a dealer and finisher of marble products. He sold these, together with articles in blu john and alabaster, in his museum-shop at the Bath House in Bakewell. A trade card of 1825 states that he, 'execute monuments, tombs, &c. / Gives Lessons on Geology and Minerology; / And Furnishes Collections./ AFFORD INFORMATION TO ANTIQUARIANS; / And Amusement to Botanists' (repr *Tomlinson* 1996, 48).

Gunnis notes that Watson signs a number of tablets, mostly in Derbyshire, and that his 'most importan monumental work is the semi-Corinthian column, 15 feet high, with a central inscription-tablet in the form of parchment, which commemorates Sir Sitwell Sitwell' (**18**). Watson's account book, which is in private ownershi records payments for further monuments, chimneypieces, ornaments in Derbyshire spar, collections of fossils an other items. Among those who purchased collections of fossils from him between 1796 and 1802 were Alexande Hume, the Duke of Rutland, Sir Joseph Banks, Mr Wedgwood, the Marquess of Blandford and Viscount Charvill He was paid £66 18s 9d for 'designing the grotto and for fossils' for Chatsworth in 1798 and in the same year receive £21 for 'Lectures on minerology given to the three young ladies and the Marquess of Hartington' (Watson Accoun in GPC). Watson is probably best known for his unusual inlaid marble specimen panels using polychrome rock from Derbyshire and adjoining counties. He produced nearly 100 of these geological 'tablets', which were supplie with explanatory pamphlets. Purchasers included Sir Thomas Woollaston, the Earl of Newburgh, the Duke of Leed and Berriah Botfield, who bought two for £34 (*ibid*). Examples survive at Chatsworth House, Derby Museum, th Oxford University Museum and elsewhere (see *Ford* 1995, 164 for a full list).

In addition to these activities, Watson published a number of geological books including catalogues of hi collections and *A Delineation of a Section of the Strata in Derbyshire* (1811). He kept records of the weather, and mad botanical and horticultural observations which earned him a fellowship of the Linnean Society in 1795. He was note locally for his ability to record human profiles, either in ink or as marble inlays, and he occasionally wrote poetr He was an assiduous collector and preserver of family records and it is thanks to his efforts that so many of th drawings and papers of his uncle and grandfather, **Samuel Watson I**, have been preserved. He died on 8 August 183 and was buried in Bakewell churchyard.

Literary References: *Ford* 1960, 349–363; *Gunnis* 1968, 416; *Ford* 1995, 157–164; *Tomlinson* 1996, 25, 32, 48–9, 84–90; *Brighton* 1998, *passim*; *Brighto* 2001, 55, 56–9

Portraits of the Sculptor: Tradecard with portrait silhouette (repr *Tomlinson* 1996, 48)

Funerary Monuments

1.	?1795	Richard Roe	All Saints, Bakewell, Derbys	S	*Gunnis* 1968, 416
2.	1796	'Mr Sutton, Heanor' Payment(s): £17 10s 6d	Untraced		Watson Accounts in GPC
3.	1796	'Tomb for Mr Charlesworth at Longor' Payment(s): £15 15s	Untraced		Watson Accounts in GPC
4.	1797	'Monument erected in Chesterfield Church to Mr and Mrs Walliff'	Untraced		Watson Accounts in GPC
5.	?1799	Richard Jackson	Sandbach, Cheshire	S	*Gunnis* 1968, 416
6.	1800	'Mr and Mrs Wilkinson, Chesterfield Church' Payment(s): 10 gns	Untraced		Watson Accounts in GPC
7.	1801	William Milnes (†1797) Payment(s): £26 5s	Chesterfield, Derbys	S	Watson Accounts in GPC
8.	1802	'Errected by Mr Thomas Roe to his father in Bakewell Church' Payment(s): 6 gns	Untraced		Watson Accounts in GPC
9.	1802	'Hon Robert Hamilton-Lindsay, Buxton Church' Payment(s): £11 11s	Untraced		Watson Accounts in GPC
10.	1802	'Sir Peter Fretchville, Staveley Church' Payment(s): £5 12s	Untraced		Watson Accounts in GPC
11.	1802	Sir Roger Manners (†1632), repairs only	Whitwell, Derbys		Derby Public Library, MS9626, in GPC
12.	1803	'Rev Thomas and Mrs Thwaites, Wortley Church'	Untraced		Watson Accounts in GPC
13.	1806	John Sutton (†1803) Payment(s): £16	Heanor, Derbys	S	Watson Accounts in GPC; Pevsner, *Derbys*, 1978, 243
14.	†1807	G, E and A Riddiard (†1754, 1738 and 1807)	All Saints, Bakewell, Derbys	S	
15.	†1807	R, M and A Roe (†1798, 1776 and 1807)	All Saints, Bakewell, Derbys	S	
16.	†1811	J and A Chapman	All Saints, Bakewell, Derbys	S	
17.	1812	'Lowndes family, Chesterfield Church' Payment(s): £72	Untraced		Watson Accounts in GPC
18.	1812	Sir Sitwell Sitwell (†1811) Payment(s): £300	Eckington, Derbys		Watson Accounts in GPC; *Gunnis* 1968, 416; Pevsner, *Derbys*, 1978, 204
19.	1815	'Burrell family, Winkbourne Church' Payment(s): £45	Untraced		Watson Accounts in GPC
20.	1818	Rev Richard Chapman (†1816)	All Saints, Bakewell, Derbys	SD	*Gunnis* 1968, 416
21.	?1821	Emma Sgambella	Bradley, Derbys	S	*Gunnis* 1968, 416
22.	1821	'J A Alsop, Hartington Church' Payment(s): £36	Untraced		Watson Accounts in GPC

23.	1821	'Mrs Hoult, Longstone Church' Payment(s): £40	Untraced		Watson Accounts in GPC
24.	T1822	Edward Buxton	Great Longstone, Derbys	S	
25.	1823	'Evans family, Bonsal Church' Payment(s): £71	Untraced		Watson Accounts in GPC
26.	?1823	Frances Kirkby	Broadwater, Sussex	S	*Gunnis* 1968, 416
27.	1810–1823	Samuel Watson (†1815) Drawing(s): Watson/Chatsworth	Heanor, Derbys		ATTRIB Trevor Brighton
28.	1824	'Rev George Brossley, Chesterfield Church' Payment(s): £61	Untraced		Watson Accounts in GPC
29.	1825	'Mrs Rhodes, Barlborough Church' Payment(s): £42 6s	Untraced		Watson Accounts in GPC
30.	?1826	Thomas Rawson	Ecclesfield, W R Yorks	S	*Gunnis* 1968, 416
31.	?1827	Benjamin Pearson	Hope, Derbys	S	RG/JP, 8, 1527
32.	1831	'Mr Alsop, Lea Chapel' Payment(s): £35	Untraced		Watson Accounts in GPC
33.	1832	'Ms Chesshyre, Manchester (Sr Peters)'	Untraced		Watson Accounts in GPC
34.	nd	Sir Godfrey Foljambe (†1377) and wife (restoration only)	All Saints, Bakewell, Derbys		*Ford* 1960, 351

Chimneypieces

35.	nd	Description unavailable Payment(s): £15 15s	[for Mr Nodder]; untraced		Watson Accounts in GPC
36.	nd	Description unavailable Payment(s): £7 17s 6d	[for Dr Denman]; untraced		Watson Accounts in GPC
37.	nd	Description unavailable Payment(s): £20	[for Bache Thornhill]; untraced		Watson Accounts in GPC
38.	nd	Description unavailable Payment(s): £19 12s 6d	[ordered by the Duke of Devonshire for the steward's room, Chatsworth, Derbys]; untraced		Watson Accounts in GPC
39.	nd	Description unavailable	[for the Misses Milnes of Ashover]; untraced		Watson Accounts in GPC
40.	nd	Description unavailable	[for John Alsop of Leek]; untraced		Watson Accounts in GPC
41.	nd	Description unavailable	[for Sir Francis Darwin]; untraced		Watson Accounts in GPC
42.	nd	Several	Hassop Hall, Hassop, Derbys		Pevsner, *Derbys*, 1978, 239

Architectural Sculpture

43.	*c*1789	Inlaid plaque commemorating the restoration to health of King George III	St George's Chapel, Windsor, Berks		*Ford* 1960, 351
44.	1792	Font	[All Saints, Bakewell, Derbys]; untraced		*Gunnis* 1968, 416
45.	1793	Sundial (designed by Mr Gauntley)	All Saints, Bakewell, Derbys		Pevsner, *Derbys*, 1978, 73
46.	nd	Font Payment(s): £18 4s	[for Richard Arkwright of Sutton Scarsdale]; untraced		Watson Accounts in GPC
47.	nd	Rutland arms	s	[Rutland Arms Inn, Bakewell, Derbys]; untraced	*Gunnis* 1968, 416

WATTS, and Sons, of High Wycombe fl 1738–1854

Gunnis notes in the possession of Mr E Harris (before 1966) four volumes of accounts of the Watts family covering, with only one break, the years between 1738 and 1854. They were begun by **Thomas Watts**, whose father, Thomas, the son of another Thomas, was murdered on 8 June 1740. **Banister Watts** was the younger brother of Thomas, deputed from 11 March 1745 'to Look after the Bisness for my Mother'. **William Watts** was another brother: on 28 July 1755 Banister wrote, 'William Watts came into partners with me at Sr. Francis Dashwood at that Jobb'.

William died on 21 December 1778, aged 41. The name of William Neale, who was bound apprentice to Mr Slingsby for five years on 3 March 1778, first appears in the accounts in 1784. Neale eventually took over the business, and from him it passed to William Broughton in 1833. Tablets and gravestones by the firm can be found in a number of churches around High Wycombe and in 1752 Banister Watts erected the obelisk at High Wycombe (**6**). In 1743 the firm made a temple for Sir William Stanhope.

Archival References: GPC

Funerary Monuments

1.	?1756	Margery Jones Payment(s): £20 11s 7d		Great Missenden, Bucks	Watts Family Accts in GPC

Chimneypieces

2.	1740	Description unavailable		[for William Stanhope of Eythorpe]; untraced	Watts Family Accts
3.	1743	Description unavailable		[for Mr Tipping]; untraced	Watts Family Accts
4.	1776	Description unavailable		[for Sir John Warren]; untraced	Watts Family Accts

Architectural Sculpture

5.	1740	'Blue marble touch-stone with a coat of arms'	m	[for Joseph Lowndes, of Winslow]; untraced	Watts Family Accts
6.	1752	Obelisk (by Banister Watts)		High Wycombe, Bucks	Watts Family Accts

WAUDBY, John and Sons, of Hull and York fl 1820–56

On 26 April 1833 John Waudby advised readers of the *Hull Advertiser* that he sold British chimneypieces 'from 30 shillings' at his premises in Waltham Street, Hull. He had an outlet also in York and perhaps at Scarborough. Gunnis dismisses most of his tablets as heavy and clumsy works in the Hellenic manner, of which the best are a gothic wall monument to Joseph Eggington, and identical tablets with draped urns to Charlotte and Henry Willoughby (**3, 12**). Five wall tablets to the Bell family of Portington Hall in the classical and gothic styles, record them as active Methodists (**28**). The Delpratt is a retarded composition with winged angels' heads (**25**). At least one of the firm's monuments went to the West Indies (**26**). (Inf. Gerardine Mulcahy)

Literary References: *Gunnis* 1968, 416

Funerary Monuments

1.	†1820	Rev Robert Gilbert	Settrington, E R Yorks	S	Pevsner, *Yorks: E R & York*, 1995, 676
2.	†1829	Thomas Carter	Howden, E R Yorks	S	Pevsner, *Yorks: E R & York*, 1995, 489
3.	†1830	Joseph Egginton	Kirk Ella, E R Yorks	S	*Gunnis* 1968, 416; Pevsner, *Yorks: E R & York*, 1995, 585
4.	?1833	Charles and Edward Dodsworth	Thornton Watlass, N R Yorks	S	GPC
5.	†1835	Nathaniel Holmes	Pocklington, E R Yorks	S	Pevsner, *Yorks: E R & York*, 1995, 649
6.	1835	Rev W Jolland (†1831)	Louth, Lincs	S	GPC
7.	?1837	Christopher Alderson	Askrigg, N R Yorks	S	RG/JP, 8, 1528
8.	†1837	Mary Norcliffe Best	Langton, E R Yorks	S	Pevsner, *Yorks: E R & York*, 1995, 593
9.	†1841	James Dowker	North Dalton, E R Yorks	S	
10.	†1841	James Dowker	North Dalton, E R Yorks		Pevsner, *Yorks: E R & York*, 1995, 628
11.	†1845	Anna Maria Greenwood Clyton	Bierley, W R Yorks	S	
12.	†1845	Charlotte and Henry Willoughby, two identical tablets	Birdsall, E R Yorks	S	Pevsner, *Yorks: E R & York*, 1995, 326
13.	†1845	H W Legard	Ganton, E R Yorks	S	Pevsner, *Yorks: E R & York*, 1995, 430
14.	†1845	Unidentified subject, Grecian tablet	Holtby, N R Yorks	S	Pevsner, *Yorks: N R, 1966*, 191
15.	†1846	Mary Dewsberry	Pocklington, E R Yorks	S	Pevsner, *Yorks: E R & York*, 1995, 649
16.	†1846	Samuel Coverley	Bempton, E R Yorks		Pevsner, *Yorks: E R & York*, 1995, 276
17.	†1847	Alexander Bosville	Rudston, E R Yorks	S	Pevsner, *Yorks: E R & York*, 1995, 664
18.	†1847	Joseph Agar	Centenary Methodist Church, St Saviourgate, York	S	Pevsner, *Yorks: E R & York*, 1995, 178
19.	1847	Robert Dunn	Howden, E R Yorks	S	*Gunnis* 1968, 416
20.	†1847	Unidentified subject, tablet	Bridlington Priory, E R Yorks	S	Pevsner, *Yorks: E R & York*, 1995, 346
21.	†1848	William Robinson Gilbey	Beverley Minster, E R Yorks	S	
22.	1849	Henry Willoughby	Birdsall, E R Yorks	S	*Gunnis* 1968, 416
23.	†1850	Harriet Clough	Ripon Cathedral, W R Yorks	S	
24.	†1852	Mary Rivis	Burythorpe, E R Yorks	S	Pevsner, *Yorks: E R & York*, 1995, 380
25.	†1852	Sarah Delpratt	South Cave, E R Yorks	S	Pevsner, *Yorks: E R & York*, 1995, 700
26.	†1853	Henry Higginson Haynes	St John, Hackleton's Cliff, Barbados	S	
27.	1854	R Debank Sneyd	Ipstones, Staffs	S	*Jeavons* 1960, 70
28.	†1839–1855	Henry Bell (†1839) and other family members, five tablets	Eastrington, E R Yorks	S	*Gunnis* 1968, 416; Pevsner, *Yorks: E R & York*, 1995, 399
29.	†1856	Charles Whitaker	Welton, E R Yorks	S	Pevsner, *Yorks: E R & York*, 1995, 740
30.	†1856	George Fletcher	St Mary, Scarborough, N R Yorks	S	
31.	†1857	Elizabeth Hornsby	St Mary, Scarborough, N R Yorks	S	
32.	1850–1858	Ann Turner (†1833) and family members	St John, Wolverhampton, Staffs	S	*Jeavons* 1960, 70
33.	†1860	Francis Coverley	Bempton, E R Yorks	S	Pevsner, *Yorks: E R & York*, 1995, 276

WAUDSBY, T, of Hull fl 1835

Funerary Monuments

1.	1835	Wolley Jolland (designed by Sir Francis Chantrey RA)	St James, Louth, Lincs		Pevsner, *Lincs*, 1989, 540

WAUGH, Alexander

For further information the reader is referred to *Pyke* 1973, 155 and *Pyke* 1981, 41–2.

WEALE, William, of Bilston and Wolverhampton fl c1810–46?

It seems that William Weale, marble mason and statuary of Oxford Street, Bilston, and William Weale, marble mason, statuary and engraver of Darlington Street, Wolverhampton, were the same man. He signs a number of tablets in Staffordshire.

Literary References: *Gunnis* 1968, 417; *Jeavons* 1960, 59

Funerary Monuments

1.	†1810	William Brueton and his wife Mary (†1815)	St Leonard, Bilston, Staffs		*Jeavons* 1960, 59
2.	?1829	Joseph Percival	St Leonard, Bilston, Staffs		*Jeavons* 1960, 59
3.	†1835	Sarah Riley	St Leonard, Bilston, Staffs	S	*Gunnis* 1968, 417
4.	1837	Rowlinson family (†1811–1836)	St Peter, Wolverhampton, Staffs	S	*Jeavons* 1960, 59
5.	†1843	Mrs R Thompson	St Leonard, Bilston, Staffs		RG/JP, 8, 1528
6.	?1844	Thomas Brueton	St Leonard, Bilston, Staffs		*Jeavons* 1960, 59
7.	?1846	Valentine Vickers	Adbaston, Staffs		*Jeavons* 1960, 59

WEARING, John fl 1695–99

In 1695–96 he was paid £402 for stone work at the Trinity almshouses in Stepney (1). He was almost certainly responsible for some of the very fine stone carving there, but as **Robert Jones** was also employed as a carver it is difficult to know which of the shields of arms, swags of fruit and flowers, cartouches, drapery, foliage, lyres and rudders were carved by Wearing and which by Jones.

Archival References: GPC citing Trinity House Archives

Architectural Sculpture

1.	1695–1696	Carved stonework	Trinity Almshouses, Stepney, London	RG/JP, 8, 1528; RG/JP, 9, 1529
2.	1699	'finishing the marble fountain & stairs', and 'finishing staircase in West Court and fountain in the inner court and steps in the gatehouse' Payment(s): £15, £55 1s 5d	Chatsworth, Derbys	Chatsworth Building Accts, 1699–1700, 1, 10; *Gunnis* 1968, 417

WEBB, Edward William 1811–

He attended the Royal Academy Schools in 1829 and won a silver medal four years later. A bust by 'Webb' was in an anonymous sale held by Christie's on 22 June 1861 (1).

Literary References: *Gunnis* 1968, 417

Busts

1.	nd	Dr Adam Clarke	Christie, 22 June 1861; untraced	GPC

WEBB, R D fl 1826–27

He gave his address as 12, Charles Street, Middlesex Hospital in 1826 when he was awarded a silver palette from the Society of Arts, and a silver Isis medal followed in 1827. He did not exhibit at the Royal Academy and nothing more is known of him.

Literary References: *Gunnis* 1968, 417

Statues

1.	1826	'A figure in the round, a copy'	[Soc of A, silver palette]; untraced	RSA *Transactions*, 1826, vol 44, xliii

Miscellaneous

2.	1827	'A copy in bas relief of an entire figure'	[Soc of A, silver Isis medal]; untraced	RSA *Transactions*, 1827, vol 45, xxxi

WEBB, Thomas fl 1800–30

For further information the reader is referred to *Pyke* 1981, 42.

WEBB, Thomas, of Tetbury fl 1776–86

Presumably a local statuary, he signs two monuments at Tetbury, the Romney, which has a portrait bust (1) and the Wickes (3), with its urn and draped pyramid. He appears to have been the son of Walter Webb of Isleworth, mason, and was apprenticed to John Boreman, 'citizen and mason' on 9 November 1736.

Literary References: *Webb* 1999, 35

Funerary Monuments

1.	†1611	Sir William Romney	m	Tetbury, Glos	S	*Gunnis* 1968, 417
2.	c1783	Thomas Davis (†1749) and family		Horsley, Glos	S	Pevsner, *Glos: Cotswolds*, 1999, 416
3.	†1786	Joseph Wickes (†1764) and the Rev Thomas Croome Wicks (†1786)		Tetbury, Glos	S	Pevsner, *Glos: Cotswolds*, 1999, 686

WEBBER, Henry 1754–1826

A sculptor and modeller, Webber was born in London in July 1754, the third son of Abraham Wäber. His father was a Swiss sculptor who had settled in England sometime before 1744 and married an Englishwoman named Mary Quant, at St George, Hanover Square. Henry Webber's elder brother was the painter John Webber, who was later to become known for scientific illustrations made during Captain Cook's last voyage.

In 1772, at the age of 17, Webber enrolled at the Royal Academy Schools to study sculpture, winning a silver medal two years later (19). He first exhibited at the Royal Academy in 1775, giving his address as 4 Down Street, Piccadilly. In 1776, by unanimous decision, he won a gold medal for a highly competent relief of *The judgment of Midas* (7). In addition he submitted a sketch (presumably in pencil) of *Pyrrhus killing Priam.*

In 1779 he exhibited a classical relief at the Royal Academy from 28 Great Portland Street, Cavendish Square (8). Little information has emerged on Webber's work at this time, though he is known to have studied under **John Bacon RA**, whose background in modelling for manufacturers may have influenced the course of Webber's own career. On 8 May 1782 Webber signed a contract to work for Josiah Wedgwood at a wage of eight guineas a month, apparently recommended by Sir Joshua Reynolds and Sir William Chambers. Wedgwood called Webber 'the first in his profession in England' (quoted in *Tattersall* 1985, 36) and immediately bought from him a sketchbook of classically-derived designs, at a cost of £16 9s. On 1 January 1785 he signed another contract, this time for seven years and was appointed head of the ornamental department at Wedgwood's factory at Etruria, with an annual salary of £250. He left London, by his own account, in too much of a hurry even to pay his debts.

In July 1787 Wedgwood sent Webber to Rome, partly to garner antique sources from the Capitoline Museum for future use at the factory, but also to act as a *cicerone* to his employer's 21 year old son, John Wedgwood. The agreement made it clear that Webber was to go 'for the purpose of making models, drawings and other improvements in the art of modelling and designing for the benefit of the said Josiah Wedgwood' (Webber-Wedgwood agreement). Webber and Wedgwood Junior travelled to Rome via Paris, Geneva, Genoa and Florence, and spent nine months in the Eternal City. Whilst there Webber bought copies after the antique and set up a modelling school which commissioned works from Italian artists such as **Camillo Pacetti, Giuseppe Angelini** and **Allesandro Cades**. He must also have worked with **John Flaxman RA** and **John De Vaere**, who were employed by Wedgwood in Rome at this time.

On his return to England in 1789 Webber modelled the Wedgwood copy of the Barberini Vase (22), known in England as the Portland vase after its ducal owner. Webber retained a position of considerable authority at Etruria until 1794 and must have had overall control over the artistic design of the factory's products. Nevertheless it remains difficult to identify with certainty the works which Webber himself modelled. His *magnum opus* is thought to be the statuette of *Britannia triumphant*, developed from a statue of Minerva, which appears on John Bacon's monument to Lord Chatham in Westminster Abbey.

By August 1794 Webber had parted company with Wedgwood and wrote to offer his services to William Duesbury of the Derby porcelain manufactory, citing as a reference only 'the general approbation with which the public have honour'd the numerous various studies I have produc'd both at Rome, and at Etruria' (*Bricknell* 1995, 77). Webber appears from the subsequent correspondence to have been in a strong professional position at this time, having an offer of work abroad and 'fortune enough to live on without any employment' (*ibid*, 87–8). Despite a desire to continue to work he seems to have been in a poor state of health, and hoped to avoid doing so in London. In the course of guarded negotiations with Duesbury's representative, Joseph Lygo, in May the next year Webber agreed to take a part-time post at the Derby works at an annual salary of £100. He also produced a design for the Derby works to accompany their *Palamor and Lavinia*. In the event Webber never took up the job, postponing the appointment in a letter to Duesbury in July 1795 because he had recently won a commission 'for a monument to be plac'd in Westminster Abbey' (*ibid*, 91).

This unnamed monument was the work commemorating David Garrick (1), and was awarded to Webber following the sudden death of **John Hickey**, who was the original choice as sculptor. Despite some initial difficulties in confirming the commission and receiving a first payment, the monument was completed and unveiled in May 1797. It shows Garrick, in Vandyck costume, taking his last curtain between two columns of the Abbey's arcading, whilst figures of *Tragedy* and *Comedy* mourn his exit. This was an innovative adaptation of dramatic Baroque motifs to emphasise Garrick's profession, the *Universal Magazine* considered it worthy of the sculptor's 'improved talents' and added that it afforded 'a happy earnest of what in future may be expected from them' (*Univ Mag* 1797, Pt II, 73). This was not the view of Charles Lamb, who took a turn in the Abbey and found himself 'not a little scandalised at the introduction of theatrical airs and gestures into a place set apart to remind us of the saddest realities' (quoted in *Gunnis* 1968, 417).

Only one other monument by Webber is known, to Henry Askew and his wife in Newcastle (2). It has two female figures and a child garlanding an urn decorated with profile portrait medallions of the deceased. The additional motif of a pelican feeding its young is drawn directly from the work of John Bacon RA. Despite the artistic influence which his former master had on his work, Webber and Bacon appear not to have liked one another. In January 1796, in conversation with Joseph Farington, Bacon said that Webber 'never seemed to have the feelings of honour or principle' nor was he 'even anxious to preserve the appearance of it' (*Farington* 2, 473).

In 1802 Webber began to invest in property and his sculpture dried up, which suggests that he was happy to enjoy a more sedentary life, relying on his investments. In 1821 he was living at 36 Great Coram Street and owned two properties in Lisson Grove, Marylebone and two more in Great Portland Street. He died in the afternoon of 7 August 1826 at the home of a Mrs Kincaid at 11 South Crescent, Bedford Square. A 'very old friend' of Webber, Captain William Small, communicated the news of his death to Webber's former charge, Josiah Wedgwood II, in a letter which survives in the Wedgwood archives (Small/Wedgwood).

Webber appears to have had no family and in his will he left annual sums of £150 to two London hospitals, to be funded by the rents on two of his properties. His two other dwellings were bequeathed to a spinster, Eliza Tuigrouis of the Strand. He left four gifts of £100, one of them to John Wedgwood, who was his executor. A gold watch, which he habitually wore, was left to the master of the Mint in Bern, Switzerland. He also requested that £500 be paid to **Sir Francis Chantrey** to provide a suitable monument for his brother John, who had died in 1793. Chantrey was indeed paid for the monument in 1831, though its location has not been ascertained.

Assessments of Webber's abilities and his contribution to British sculpture have not been uniform. Margaret Whinney summarily dismissed Webber's work, including the remarkable monument to Garrick, and bemoaned the lack of influence which the time in Rome had had on the sculptor. Bruce Tattersall has more recently posited Webber as an unjustly neglected sculptor whose eclectic sensibility produced, in the Garrick, one of the most striking monuments of the eighteenth century. Tattersall argues furthermore that Webber was 'the first art director in the English ceramic industry' and as such presages the most important 19th-century developments in industrial artistic production (*Tattersall* 1985, 36).

MGS

Literary References: *Farington* vol 2, 473; *Graves*, VIII, 1905–6, 186; *Graves* 1907, 274; *Hutchison* 1960–62, 138; *Gunnis* 1968, 417–8; *Pyke* 1973, 155; *Bindman* 1979, 48; *Tattersall* 1 985, 36–42; *Clifford* 1985, 294; *Whinney* 1988, 316, 318; *Chantrey Ledgers* 1991–2, 249; *Bricknell* 1995, 77, 78, 87–8, 90, 91, 92; *Reilly* 1995, 459; *Young* 1995, 55, 90; *Ingamells* 1997, 984; *Hauptman* 1999, 41–52

Archival References: RA Premium list; Webber/Byerley

Additional MS Sources: Papers, including memoranda, accounts, receipts and sketches (c100 items) 1782–1826, Wedgwood Archives, Keele University Library

Portraits of the Sculptor: *Portrait of a Sculptor* (? Webber), by John Webber, Kunstmuseum, Bern, *Hauptman* 1999, 41–52 (repr)

Miscellaneous Drawings: Designs for Wedgwood, including the *Triumph of Mars*, four statues, a *Marine Venus* and over 30 other unidentified subjects, untraced but recorded in a memorandum in the Wedgwood archives (*Young* 1995, 41 and *Tattersall* 1985, 36); design for the Sydney Cove medallion (for Wedgwood), 1789, modelled by **William Hackwood** (*Tattersall* 1985, 38, repr)

Will: PROB 11/1717/79

Funerary Monuments

1.	1795–1797	David Garrick (†1779)		Westminster Abbey, London, south transept	S	*Neale and Brayley* 1818–23, 253; *Tattersall* 1985, 39, 40 (repr); *Whinney* 1988, 316, 318 (repr); *Bricknell* 1995, 91
2.	1801	Henry Askew (†1796) and his wife Dorothy (†1792)		Newcastle Cathedral	SD	Pevsner, *Northumbs*, 1992, 422 (repr 71); *Tattersall* 1985, 40, 41 (repr)

Statues

3.	c1782	Cupid, 'in the round' (model for Wedgwood) Payment(s): 10 gns		Untraced		*Tattersall* 1985, 37
4.	1802	Britannia triumphant, statuette (model for Wedgwood)		Untraced		*Tattersall* 1985, 40–2 (Wedgwood repr); *Gustafson* 1991, 1070 (Wedgwood repr); *Miller* 1993, 22–36 (Wedgwood repr)
5.	nd	Hercules holding Cerberus, model (after Augustin Pajou)	p	SJSM M 405		*Gunnis* 1968, 417; *Tattersall* 1985, 42

Reliefs						
6.	1776	Model of a senatorial figure		[Exhib RA, London, 315]; untraced		*Graves* VIII, 1905–6, 186
7.	1776	The judgement of Midas, bas-relief		[RA gold medal]; SJSM SC23	S	RA Premium list; *Gunnis* 1968, 417; *Tattershall* 1985, 36 (repr); *Dorey* 2004, 57, 70
8.	1779	Bacchus and Ariadne		[Exhib RA, London, 340]; untraced		*Graves* VIII, 1905–6, 186
9.	c1782	A boy leaning on his quiver (model for Wedgwood)	tc	Untraced		*Tattersall* 1985, 37
10.	c1782	Apollo and Daphne (model for Wedgwood)		Untraced		*Tattersall* 1985, 37; *Reilly* 1995, 459
11.	c1782	Cupid drawing his dart (model for Wedgwood)		Untraced		*Tattersall* 1985, 37
12.	c1782	Hebe (model for Wedgwood)		Untraced		*Tattersall* 1985, 37
13.	c1782	Sacrifice to Concordia, roundel (model for Wedgwood) Payment(s): 3 gns	p	Wedgwood Museum, Barlaston, Staffs		*Tattersall* 1985, 37 (repr)
14.	c1782	Sacrifice to Hymen, roundel (model for Wedgwood) Payment(s): 3 gns	p	Wedgwood Museum, Barlaston, Staffs		*Tattersall* 1985, 37 (repr)
15.	1788	Sacrifice of the bull, large bas-relief (model for Wedgwood)		Untraced		*Tattersall* 1985, 39
16.	1789	The Sydney Cove medallion (model for Wedgwood)		Wedgwood Museum, Barlaston, Staffs		*Bindman* 1979, 66
17.	nd	The Muse Erato	w	Lady Lever, Liverpool		*Pyke* 1973, 155 (pl 296)
Miscellaneous						
18.	1773	Head of an old man, model	w	[Exhib Soc of Artists, London, 369]; untraced		*Graves* VIII, 1905–6, 186; *Graves* 1907, 274
19.	1774	An academic figure or bas-relief		[RA silver medal]; untraced		RA Premium list
20.	1775	Soldiers in conversation, model	w	[Exhib RA, London, 330]; untraced		*Graves* VIII, 1905–6, 186
21.	1788	Unspecified design from a work in the Capitoline Museum, Rome (model for Wedgwood)		Untraced		*Tattersall* 1985, 39
22.	1786–1789	Copy of the Barberini (or 'Portland') vase (model for Wedgwood)		Untraced		*Gunnis* 1968, 417; *Bindman* 1979, 65–6 (Wedgwood repr); *Tattersall* 1985, 38 (Wedgwood repr)
23.	nd	Candlestick representing the seated Minerva, model for Josiah Wedgwood		Untraced		*Bindman* 1979, 65

WEBSTER, C, of Lichfield fl c1764–c1802

Jeavons comments that Webster was 'a good craftsman and his monuments are well above the usual standard of the local masons', adding that the monument to Samuel Peach, 1801, at Trysull, Staffs, is 'undoubtedly by Webster' although it is not signed (*Jeavons*, 1960, 59). The Perrott has a pyramid, from which hangs a coat of arms (3).

Funerary Monuments					
1.	1764	Samuel Wilkes, gravestone	Bloxwich, Staffs, Churchyard	S	*Jeavons* 1960, 59
2.	1793	Mary Cobb	St Michael, Lichfield, Staffs		*Jeavons* 1960, 59
3.	1802	John Perrott	Brewood, Staffs		*Gunnis* 1968, 418

WEBSTER, Francis and Sons, of Kendal

Francis Webster I 1767–1827
George Webster 1797–1864
Francis Webster II 1805–80

Francis Webster I was the son of Robert Webster (1726–1827), a mason of Quarry Flat, near Cartmel. By 1788 he had moved to Kendal where he established a marble yard in New Inn Yard, off Highgate, and developed a highly successful business as an architect, builder and mason, specialising in the production of monuments and marble chimneypieces. At first he worked in partnership with a local mason called William Holme and a directory of 1790 describes them as 'builders and marble cutters' (*Universal British Directory*, 1790–1, in *Taylor* 2004, 49).

Webster seems to have embraced technological advances. Around 1800 the firm introduced water-powered machinery for cutting and polishing marble at their mill at Helsington Laithes, on the river Kent, south of Kendal. In 1829 a local directory commented: 'This machinery is brought to such a state of perfection, that every description of mouldings, whether straight or circular, is now wrought by it with more accuracy than manual labour, and the flutings of diminishing columns are furnished by it in a most beautiful and regular style' (*Parson and White* 1829, 638–9, in *Taylor* 2004, 49). Webster was particularly well known for producing chimneypieces of highly polished Kendal Fell limestone, although he was not the first to utilise this material as has been suggested. The business also benefited from improvements to the transportation network. In 1819 the Lancaster Canal, which linked Kendal to Lancaster, Preston and Manchester, was completed and Webster moved his marble yard to new premises in Miller's Close, near the canal basin.

As an architect, Webster designed such buildings as workhouses, mills, bridges and the firm's own offices and showrooms at Bridge House in Kendal. Between 1796 and 1802 he was responsible for an abortive scheme to rehabilitate the gutted Lowther Hall for the 1st Earl of Lonsdale, who eventually employed Robert Smirke to design an entirely new house. He was also a prominent figure in the public life of Kendal and served as mayor in 1823–24. He retired in 1826 and moved to Eller How, a country house near Lindale which he had bought some years earlier. He died there on 10 October 1827 and is commemorated both by a tombstone in Kendal churchyard and a tablet at Lindale which was probably made by his firm.

Webster and his wife, Janet née Slater, of Spital Farm near Kirkby Lonsdale, had three sons and four daughters between 1793 and 1805. Their eldest son, Robert, died in 1810 when he was 15 or 16 years old, but the younger sons, **George Webster** and **Francis Webster II**, assisted and then succeeded their father in the business. Unlike his father,

George Webster must have had a professional training in an architect's office and after his father's death in 1827 he concentrated on his architectural work, building up a considerable practice in north-west England, while Francis oversaw the marble works. George Webster's architectural designs included classical public buildings and gothic churches, but his most important and innovative buildings were Jacobean Revival country houses, such as Eshton Hall, Gargrave and Underley Hall, near Kirkby Lonsdale.

The Websters appear to have run an extensive masonry business. In 1829 they opened a second showroom in Bold Street, Liverpool, and by 1861 they apparently had a third, in Preston. In order to keep up with the steady demand for chimneypieces and memorial tablets they recruited both apprentices and mature masons. In 1809 the 14-year old Thomas Lindsay of Ravenstonedale was apprenticed to Francis Webster I and he was still with the firm in 1841. In 1826 'Six or Eight Stout Active Youths' of about 14 were offered apprenticeships at 7 guineas each and the firm also advertised for 'a number of Marble Masons who have served an apprenticeship to stonemasons [to] find immediate and constant employment at very liberal wages' (*Westmorland Gazette*, 29 April 1826, in *Taylor* 2004, 51). **Thomas Duckett** managed the Websters' sculpture department for several years in the 1830s and was probably responsible for the few examples of figurative sculpture produced by the firm. A weeping figure with an urn in memory of Francis Webster I which once stood in the garden at Eller How and the heads on the windows of St George's, Kendal, have been attributed to Duckett (*Taylor* 2004, 51) and he was probably responsible for the mourning soldier on the monument to Captain Considine in Chester Cathedral (**117**).

In 1845 Miles Thompson, who had been employed by the Websters as a draghtsman since the 1820s, was taken into partnership and the firm became 'Webster and Thompson'. Thompson signs a number of monuments (**149, 162–6, 173**). George Webster retired the following year and died at Eller How on 16 April 1864. Francis continued in charge of the marble works until 1880 but the business declined during the second half of the 19th century and the firm seems to have produced few monuments after the 1850s.

In addition to the signed and documented works listed below, the Websters were probably responsible for decorative carving and chimneypieces for the buildings they designed and constructed, and about 80 additional monuments have been attributed to the firm (see *Taylor* 2004, *passim*).

EH

Literary References: *GM*, 1827, ii, 381; *Cooper* 1973, 762–4; *Colvin* 1995, 1032–5; *Taylor* 2004, *passim*

Funerary Monuments

1.	†1756	William Tomlinson	Kirkby Lonsdale, Westmorland	S	*Taylor* 2004, 170
2.	†1781	Catherine Gregg	Cartmel, Lancs	S	*Taylor* 2004, 167
3.	†1785	Thomas Cartmel	Beetham, Westmorland	S	*Taylor* 2004, 166
4.	†1787	Edward Burns	Colton, Lancs	S	*Taylor* 2004, 167
5.	†1788	James Wilkinson	Slaidburn, W R Yorks	S	*Taylor* 2004, 171
6.	?1792	Daniel Dickinson	St Mary, Crosthwaite, Westmorland	S	*Taylor* 2004, 168
7.	?1792	General William Peachey	St Kentigern, Crosthwaite, Cumberland	S	*Taylor* 2004, 168
8.	?1793	Robert Myers	Cartmel, Lancs	S	*Taylor* 2004, 167
9.	?1800	Oglethorpe Wainman	Holy Trinity, Skipton, W R Yorks	S	*Taylor* 2004, 171
10.	?1800	Rev Alan Chambre	Heversham, Westmorland	S	*Taylor* 2004, 169
11.	?1800	William Brownrigg	St Kentigern, Crosthwaite, Cumberland	S	*Taylor* 2004, 168
12.	†1801	Edward Suart	St Mary, Lancaster	S	*Taylor* 2004, 170
13.	?1803	Joseph Maude	Holy Trinity, Kendal, Westmorland	S	*Taylor* 2004, 169
14.	†1804	Elizabeth Carus	Holy Trinity, Kendal, Westmorland	S	*Taylor* 2004, 169
15.	?1804	Jackson Harrison	Holy Trinity, Kendal, Westmorland	S	*Taylor* 2004, 169
16.	?1804	Richard Nelson	Heversham, Westmorland	S	*Taylor* 2004, 169
17.	†1805	Joseph T Senhouse	Calder Bridge, Cumberland	S	*Taylor* 2004, 167
18.	†1807	Anthony Jackson	[Holy Trinity, Kendal, Westmorland]; untraced	S	*Taylor* 2004, 169
19.	†1808	Nicholas Halstead	St Peter, Burnley, Lancs	S	*Taylor* 2004, 167
20.	?1811	William Fairer	Great Asby, Westmorland	S	*Taylor* 2004, 169
21.	?1816	Arthur Shepherd	Grayrigg, Westmorland	S	*Taylor* 2004, 168
22.	?1816	John Preston	Heversham, Westmorland	S	*Taylor* 2004, 169
23.	?1817	Barbara Fleming	St Martin, Windermere, Westmorland	S	*Taylor* 2004, 172
24.	?1817	Thomas Hodgson	Brookhouse, Lancs	S	*Taylor* 2004, 166
25.	†1817	Thomas Ireland	Holy Trinity, Kendal, Westmorland	S	*Taylor* 2004, 170, 296 (repr)
26.	?1818	Joseph Burn	Orton, Westmorland	S	*Taylor* 2004, 171
27.	†1818	Thomas Lyon	St Elphin, Warrington, Cheshire	S	*CIIA* 4/8/138 (repr)
28.	†1819	John Park	Bolton-le-Sands, Lancs	S	*Taylor* 2004, 166
29.	?1819	John Wordsworth	Barton, Westmorland	S	*Taylor* 2004, 166
30.	1819	Thomas Hinde (†1798)	St Mary, Lancaster	S	*Taylor* 2004, 170
31.	?1820	Rev Isaac Denton	St Kentigern, Crosthwaite, Cumberland	S	*Taylor* 2004, 168
32.	?1820	Rev John Bolton	Millom, Cumberland	S	*Taylor* 2004, 171, 294 (repr)
33.	?1820	Richard Scrambler	Ambleside, Westmorland	S	*Taylor* 2004, 166
34.	?1821	James King	Finsthwaite, Lancs	S	*Taylor* 2004, 168
35.	?1821	William Atkinson	Dalton-in-Furness, Lancs	S	*Taylor* 2004, 168
36.	?1822	David Murray	Melling, Lancs	S	*Taylor* 2004, 171
37.	†1822	Frances Parke	St Mary, Lancaster	S	*Taylor* 2004, 170
38.	?1822	Peggy Taylor	Whalley, Lancs	S	*Taylor* 2004, 172
39.	†1822	Rev Christopher Goodwill	Richmond, N R Yorks	S	*Taylor* 2004, 171
40.	†1822	Rev Thomas Edmondson (†1797) and son	St Mary, Threlkeld, Cumberland	S	*Taylor* 2004, 172
41.	?1822	Robert Michaelson	Cartmel, Lancs	S	*Taylor* 2004, 167
42.	?1822	Thomas Hargreaves	St James, Accrington, Lancs	S	*Taylor* 2004, 166
43.	?1822	Thomas Kilner	St Mary, Ulverston, Lancs	S	*Taylor* 2004, 172
44.	†1822	William St Clare	St John the Divine, Preston, Lancs	S	*Taylor* 2004, 171
45.	†1822	William Steele	Market Drayton, Salop	S	*Taylor* 2004, 170
46.	?1823	Charles Gibson	Brookhouse, Lancs	S	*Taylor* 2004, 166
47.	?1823	Edward Greenhalgh	St Michael-on-Wyre, Lancs	S	*Taylor* 2004, 171
48.	?1823	Elizabeth Fetherstonhaugh	Kirkoswald, Cumberland	S	*Taylor* 2004, 170
49.	†1823	Elizabeth Rawstorne	Penwortham, Lancs	S	*Taylor* 2004, 171
50.	?1823	John Edmonson	St Kentigern, Crosthwaite, Cumberland	S	*Taylor* 2004, 168

51.	?1823	John Jones	Holy Trinity, Kendal, Westmorland	S	*Taylor* 2004, 170
52.	?1823	Sir Alan Chambre	Holy Trinity, Kendal, Westmorland	S	*Taylor* 2004, 170
53.	†1823	Strethill Harrison	Holme Chapel, Cheshire	S	*Taylor* 2004, 169
54.	?1823	William Dawson	Warton, Lancs	S	*Taylor* 2004, 172
55.	†1824	Countess of Lonsdale	Lowther, Westmorland	S	*Taylor* 2004, 170
56.	?1824	Daniel Wilson	Beetham, Westmorland	S	*Taylor* 2004, 166
57.	?1824	Mary Halstead	Church, Lancs	S	*Taylor* 2004, 167
58.	?1824	Rev James Thomas	St Mary, Lancaster	S	*Taylor* 2004, 170
59.	?1824	Rev Oliver Cooper	St Laurence, Chorley, Lancs	S	*Taylor* 2004, 167
60.	†1825	Elizabeth Crawshay	Llandaff Cathedral, Glamorgan	S	*Gunnis* 1968, 418
61.	?1825	John Parr	Kirkby Lonsdale, Westmorland	S	*Taylor* 2004, 170
62.	1825	Thomas Parkin (†1808)	Ecclesfield, W R Yorks	S	*Taylor* 2004, 168
63.	?1825	William Atkinson	Burton-in-Kendal, Westmorland	S	*Taylor* 2004, 167
64.	?1826	Agnes M Hinde	St Mary, Lancaster	S	*Taylor* 2004, 170
65.	?1826	Richard Wilkinson	Slaidburn, W R Yorks	S	*Taylor* 2004, 171
66.	†1827	Margaret Taylor	Finsthwaite, Lancs	S	*Taylor* 2004, 168, 295 (repr)
67.	?1827	Rev James Satterthwaite	Lowther, Westmorland	S	*Taylor* 2004, 170
68.	?1827	Richard Thompson	St Mary, Lancaster	S	*Taylor* 2004, 170
69.	†1828	Anne Moffett	Holy Trinity, Kendal, Westmorland		*Taylor* 2004, 170
70.	†1828	Susannah Rigge	Northallerton, N R Yorks	S	*Taylor* 2004, 171, 297 (repr)
71.	1829	Benjamin Wilson (†1749)	St James, Accrington, Lancs	S	*Taylor* 2004, 166
72.	?1829	Rev Philip Knipe	Field Broughton, Lancs	S	*Taylor* 2004, 168
73.	?1829	Rev Thomas Bowman	Hawkshead, Lancs	S	*Taylor* 2004, 169
74.	1829	Richard Hankins (†1807)	Ledbury, Herefs	S	*Taylor* 2004, 170
75.	?1829	Thomas A Beck	Hawkshead, Lancs	S	*Taylor* 2004, 169
76.	1829	William Pritchard (†1803)	St John the Divine, Preston, Lancs	S	*Taylor* 2004, 171
77.	?1830	John Oddie	St Mary Magdalene, Clitheroe, Lancs	S	*Taylor* 2004, 167
78.	1830	Richard Orford (†1791)	Prestbury, Cheshire	S	*Gunnis* 1968, 418; *Taylor* 2004, 171
79.	?1831	Elizabeth B Scott	Preston Patrick, Westmorland	S	*Taylor* 2004, 171
80.	?1831	Elizabeth Clapham	Clapham, W R Yorks	S	*Taylor* 2004, 167
81.	?1831	John Procter	Melling, Lancs	S	*Taylor* 2004, 171
82.	?1831	Richard Tinkler	Bolton-on-Eden, Westmorland	S	*Taylor* 2004, 166
83.	?1831	Sarah Nelson	Gressingham, Lancs	S	*Taylor* 2004, 169
84.	†1831	Thomas Smith	Melling, Lancs	S	*Taylor* 2004, 171
85.	?1832	Mary Assheton	Downham, Lancs	S	*Taylor* 2004, 168
86.	?1832	Michael King	Slaidburn, W R Yorks	S	*Taylor* 2004, 172
87.	†1832	R Litler	Newchapel, Staffs		*Jeavons* 1960, 70
88.	?1832	Thomas Berry	Brookhouse, Lancs	S	*Taylor* 2004, 167
89.	†1832	William Higginson	Tyldesley, Lancs	S	*CIIA* 4/8/109 (repr)
90.	1832	William Taylor (†1819)	Warton, Lancs	S	*Taylor* 2004, 172
91.	†1833	Rev Thomas Watson	Edenhall, Cumberland	S	*Taylor* 2004, 168
92.	1834	Alexander Worswick (†1814) and family Payment(s): £25 10s	Warton, Lancs		Suffolk RO MS 449/5/15/17
93.	?1834	Christopher Netherwood	Holy Trinity, Skipton, W R Yorks	S	*Taylor* 2004, 171
94.	?1834	Henry G Poulett Thomson	St Martin, Windermere, Westmorland	S	*Taylor* 2004, 172
95.	?1834	James Hargreaves	St Peter, Burnley, Lancs	S	*Taylor* 2004, 167
96.	?1834	John Hargreaves	Holme (Cliviger), Lancs	S	*Taylor* 2004, 169
97.	?1834	John Jackson	St Kentigern, Crosthwaite, Cumberland	S	*Taylor* 2004, 168
98.	†1834	Musgrave family	Edenhall, Cumberland		Pevsner, *Cumberland & Westmorland*, 1967, 123
99.	?1834	Rev Henry Robinson	Otley, W R Yorks	S	*Taylor* 2004, 171
100.	†1834	Rev John Raws	St Peter, Burnley, Lancs	S	C Lib (repr)
101.	†1834	William and Mary (†1832) Sugden	Keighley, W R Yorks	S	*Gunnis* 1968, 418; *Taylor* 2004, 169
102.	?1835	John Dugdale	St Bartholomew, Great Harwood, Lancs	S	*Taylor* 2004, 169
103.	?1835	Rev John Pedder	Garstang, W R Yorks	S	*Taylor* 2004, 168
104.	?1835	Thomas Dicey Cotton	Burton-in-Kendal, Westmorland	S	*Taylor* 2004, 167
105.	?1836	Lady Julia Barrie	Over Kellert, Lancs	S	*Taylor* 2004, 171
106.	?1837	Edward Burrell	Holy Trinity, Kendal, Westmorland	S	*Taylor* 2004, 170
107.	†1837	Ralph Fisher	New Hutton, Westmorland	S	*Taylor* 2004, 171
108.	†1837	Richard Haydon	Broughton, Oxon	S	*Gunnis* 1968, 418
109.	?1838	Lady Mary Musgrave	Edenhall, Cumberland	S	*Taylor* 2004, 168
110.	†1838	Richard Botcherby	Darlington, Co Durham		*Taylor* 2004, 168
111.	?1839	John Wilkinson	Slaidburn, W R Yorks	S	*Taylor* 2004, 172
112.	?1839	Mr and Mrs Clayton	Leyland, Lancs		GPC
113.	?1840	Frank H Standish	St Laurence, Chorley, Lancs	S	*Taylor* 2004, 167
114.	?1840	Thomas Coward	St Laurence, Chorley, Lancs	S	*Taylor* 2004, 167
115.	?1840	Thomas Fisher	Holy Trinity, Ulverston, Lancs	S	*Taylor* 2004, 172
116.	1841	Ambrose Gillison (†1742) and family	St Mary, Lancaster	S	*Taylor* 2004, 170
117.	†1841	Captain William Considine	Chester Cathedral, Cheshire	S	*Taylor* 2004, 51, 167
118.	?1841	Joseph Pedder	Garstang, Lancs	S	*Taylor* 2004, 168
119.	?1841	Martha S Sugden	Keighley, W R Yorks	S	*Taylor* 2004, 169
120.	?1841	Nancy Hargreaves	St James, Accrington, Lancs	S	*Taylor* 2004, 166
121.	†1841	Philip Bedingfield	Northallerton, N R Yorks	S	*Taylor* 2004, 171
122.	?1841	Rev William Ponsonby	Great Urswick, Lancs	S	*Taylor* 2004, 169
123.	†1841	William C Lister	Addingham, W R Yorks	S	*Taylor* 2004, 166, 293 (repr)
124.	?1842	Jane Smythe	Whalley, Lancs	S	*Taylor* 2004, 172
125.	?1842	John Robinson	Colton, Lancs	S	*Taylor* 2004, 168
126.	†1842	Lady Jane Gardener	Whalley, Lancs	S	*Taylor* 2004, 172
127.	?1842	Rev George Lawson	Heversham, Westmorland	S	*Taylor* 2004, 169
128.	?1843	John Hull	Poulton-le-Fylde, Lancs	S	*Taylor* 2004, 171
129.	1843	Rev John Bowstead (†1841)	Bampton, Westmorland	S	*Taylor* 2004, 166
130.	1843	Rev John Crosse (†1816)	Bradford Cathedral, W R Yorks	S	*Taylor* 2004, 166
131.	?1843	Rev John Hudson	Holy Trinity, Kendal, Westmorland	S	*Taylor* 2004, 170

No.	Date	Subject		Location		Reference
132.	?1843	Sarah M Wilson		Beetham, Westmorland	S	*Taylor* 2004, 166
133.	1843	Thomas Mann (†1811)		Bradford Cathedral, W R Yorks	S	*Taylor* 2004, 166
134.	?1843	William Atkinson		Cockerham, Lancs	S	*Taylor* 2004, 167
135.	?1844	James Everard		Lowick, Lancs	S	*Taylor* 2004, 170
136.	?1844	Rev Joseph Thexton		Beetham, Westmorland	S	*Taylor* 2004, 166
137.	1844	Sir Frederick Vane (†1832)		St Bega, Bassenthwaite, Cumberland, exterior	S	*Taylor* 2004, 166
138.	?1844	Thomas J Scales		Ambleside, Westmorland	S	*Taylor* 2004, 166
139.	?1844	William W Atkinson		Burton-in-Kendal, Westmorland	S	*Taylor* 2004, 167
140.	†1845	Ann Redhead		Cartmel, Lancs	S	*Taylor* 2004, 167, 294 (repr)
141.	?1845	James Clarke		Cockerham, Lancs	S	*Taylor* 2004, 167
142.	?1846	James Atkinson		Dalton-in-Furness, Lancs	S	*Taylor* 2004, 168
143.	?1846	John Thwaites		St Laurence, Chorley, Lancs	S	*Taylor* 2004, 167
144.	†1848	James Farington		Leyland, Lancs		GPC
145.	1848	Joseph Nelson (†1792)		Holy Trinity, Kendal, Westmorland	S	*Taylor* 2004, 170
146.	?1848	Leonard Wilkinson		Slaidburn, W R Yorks	S	*Taylor* 2004, 172
147.	?1849	Rev Ralph W Fisher		New Hutton, Westmorland	S	*Taylor* 2004, 171
148.	?1850	Christopher Robinson		Holy Trinity, Kendal, Westmorland	S	*Taylor* 2004, 170
149.	?1850	Henry Shepherd (signed by Miles Thompson)		Grayrigg, Westmorland	S	*Taylor* 2004, 168
150.	†1850	James Thompson		St Mary Magdalene, Clitheroe, Lancs	S	*Taylor* 2004, 167, 295 (repr)
151.	†1850	Laurence Rawstorne		Penwortham, Lancs	S	*Read* 1982, 188, 190 (repr)
152.	?1850	Sir Charles Richardson		Bampton, Westmorland	S	*Taylor* 2004, 166
153.	?1852	Edward Thurtell		Brookhouse, Lancs	S	*Taylor* 2004, 167
154.	?1852	Rev William Burn		Lowther, Westmorland	S	*Taylor* 2004, 170
155.	1852	Richard M Nonely (†1839)		Marjet Drayton, Salop	S	*Taylor* 2004, 171
156.	?1853	Rev John Lodge		Askrigg, N R Yorks	S	*Taylor* 2004, 166
157.	†1817–1854	Edward Buckley and family		St Mary, Lancaster	S	*Taylor* 2004, 170
158.	?1854	John Braithwaite		St Martin, Windermere, Westmorland	S	*Taylor* 2004, 172
159.	?1855	Thomas Hartley		Egremont, Cumberland	S	*Taylor* 2004, 168
160.	?1856	Thomas Dixon (signed by Thomas Dixon)		Colton, Lancs	S	*Taylor* 2004, 168
161.	†1856	Timothy Fetherstonhaugh		Kirkoswald, Cumberland	S	*Taylor* 2004, 170, 296 (repr)
162.	1857	Ann Relph (†1825) (signed by Miles Thompson)		St Mary, Crosthwaite, Westmorland	S	*Taylor* 2004, 168
163.	?1857	Edmund Atkinson (signed by Miles Thompson)		Natland, Westmorland	S	*Taylor* 2004, 171
164.	?1859	Hornby Roughsedge (signed by Miles Thompson)		High Bentham, W R Yorks	S	*Taylor* 2004, 169
165.	1859	John Gibson (†1834) (signed by Miles Thompson)		Cartmel Fell, Lancs	S	*Taylor* 2004, 167
166.	?1860	Rev George Wilson (signed by Miles Thompson)		Grayrigg, Westmorland	S	*Taylor* 2004, 169
167.	?1868	Rev Robert Fenwick		Tunstall, Lancs	S	*Taylor* 2004, 172
168.	?1869	Lucy Rothwell		Yealand Conyers, Lancs	S	*Taylor* 2004, 173
169.	?1869	Robert G Bradley		Bolton-le-Sands, Lancs	S	*Taylor* 2004, 166
170.	?1872	Sir George Musgrave		Edenhall, Cumberland	S	*Taylor* 2004, 168
171.	?1872	Thomas Wright		Yealand Conyers, Lancs	S	*Taylor* 2004, 173
172.	?1873	Lady Charlotte Musgrave		Edenhall, Cumberland	S	*Taylor* 2004, 168
173.	?1876	Thomas Read (signed by Miles Thompson)		Natland, Westmorland	S	*Taylor* 2004, 171
174.	nd	William Richardson		St John the Divine, Preston, Lancs	S	*Taylor* 2004, 171
Chimneypieces						
175.	c1790	Five, including at least one of Kendal Fell limestone		Assembly Rooms and Market House, Hawkshead, Lancs		*Taylor* 2004, 8–9, 50
176.	1801	Description unavailable	m	[Union Newsroom, Liverpool]; untraced		*Gunnis* 1968, 418
177.	1805	Several		[Cockermouth Castle, Cumberland]; untraced		*Taylor* 2004, 50
178.	1805	Several		[Eaton Hall, Cheshire]; untraced		Grovenor Archives in GPC
179.	1796–1811	Several Payment(s): £1,293		[Lowther Hall, Westmorland]; untraced		*Taylor* 2004, 50
180.	1816			[Cuerdon Hall, Preston, Lancs]; untraced		*Taylor* 2004, 53
181.	1826	Description unavailable	m	[for Sir Charles Ibbetson]; untraced		*Gunnis* 1968, 418
182.	1839	Several		[Holker Hall, Cark-in-Cartmel, Lancs]; untraced		*Taylor* 2004, 53
183.	1842	Several, one of 'Italian vein marble' and one of 'Kendal Dark Imperial'		[Haverthwaite vicarage, Lancs]; demol		*Taylor* 2004, 53
Architectural Sculpture						
184.	1788	Obelisk comemorating the centenary of the Glorious Revolution		Castle Howe, Westmorland		*Taylor* 2004, 8, 49

WEEKES, Henry RA 1807–77

Henry Weekes was one of the leading portrait sculptors of the mid-19th century. He was professor of sculpture at the Royal Academy for many years and his published lectures and art criticism provide valuable insights into the theory and practice of sculpture during that period. He was born in Canterbury, the only son of Capon Weekes, a bank clerk, and was educated at the King's School. He was a studious pupil who did well academically, although 'he was not a favourite with his schoolfellows, who, after the manner of boys, did not comprehend his retiring, thoughtful ways.' (*Weekes* 1880, 1). From an early age he showed an interest in art, which his father encouraged him to pursue. His first recorded work, a model of *St George and the dragon* based on the image on a coin, was made when he was about 12 years old (**198**). In 1822, at the age of 15, he was apprenticed to **William Behnes**, who had a studio in Dean Street, London. There Weekes 'learned more holding a candle for Behnes while modelling than by any actual instruction he received from him' (*Weekes* 1880, 3). The following year he became a student at the Royal Academy Schools, where he regularly attended the evening life class and won a silver medal for a model from the antique in 1826.

When his apprenticeship came to an end in 1827, Weekes became an assistant to **Francis Chantrey RA**. He remained in Chantrey's employment until that sculptor's death, about 14 years later. Chantrey provided Weekes with accommodation and a small studio near to his own in Pimlico, and soon Weekes began to undertake independent commissions in addition to his work for Chantrey. In 1838 Queen Victoria commissioned a bust of herself from Weekes as a gift for the Duchess of Kent (**95**). It was the first sculpted portrait of the young Queen to be executed after her accession. Weekes oversaw the completion of Chantrey's unfinished works after his death in 1841, including a statue of the Duke of Wellington for the Royal Exchange. He put the sum of £1000 left to him by his former employer towards purchasing Chantrey's studio.

Commissions came quickly, principally for portrait busts and funerary monuments. Like Chantrey he varied the format of his many portrait busts to accord with the subject: a classical herm was considered appropriate for a representation of Henry William Whitbread (**149**), whilst Edmund Hammond was depicted in classical drapery (**172**) and Dr Mead's bust is enlivened by picturesque historical costume (**168**). The monument to Samuel and Elizabeth Whitbread is considered particularly successful (**29**): Nicholas Penny has commented 'The heavy draperies, the bold modelling, and also the sentiment mark this as a work of an artist profoundly influenced by Chantrey' (*Penny* 1977 (1), 79). Weekes's best known monument is the dramatic group commemorating Percy Bysshe Shelley, erected by the poet's son at Christchurch Priory, Hampshire in 1854 (**35**). It depicts the drowned man lying amid broken pieces of rock, as if just washed ashore, supported by an idealized figure of his wife.

Weekes executed a number of works for public and institutional patrons. The council of the Royal College of Surgeons acquired six busts of officials of the College between 1844 and 1863 (**106, 128, 136, 147**) and was presented with a statue of John Hunter, funded by public subscription, for its Hunterian Museum in 1864 (**68**). In 1856 the Corporation of London commissioned a figure of *Sardanapalus*, the Assyrian king celebrated by Byron (**64**). This is one of an important of series of statues based upon English literature which ornament the Egyptian Hall of the Mansion House. It was exceptional for a civic institution to purchase ideal sculpture on such a scale and Weekes was fortunate to receive this high-profile commission. He provided statues of Sir Francis Bacon and Dr William Harvey for Eton College and the Oxford University Museum (**53, 67**). His flamboyant statue of King Charles II in contemporary dress (**74**) was originally intended for the Royal gallery at the new Palace of Westminster, where it was to be sited near statues of English monarchs by **Thomas Thornycroft, William Theed II, Thomas Woolner RA** and **Alexander Munro**. When the statues were completed they were found to be too large for their designated niches and after some years in Westminster Hall, the series was transferred to the Old Bailey.

Weekes also contributed to the most important and elaborate public commemorative scheme of the period, the Albert Memorial. He was chosen to execute the group symbolising *Manufactures* (**69**) after **Patrick MacDowell**, who was originally to have carved it, was assigned one of the larger groups of the Continents in place of **John Gibson**. The group includes idealized representations of an iron worker, a potter and a textile factory girl, 'too well favoured in every way, it is to be feared, to have been modelled after nature', grouped around the allegorical figure of *Manufactures*. Later, together with **H H Armstead**, he supervised the casting of the bronze statue of the Prince Consort, the focus of the memorial, following the death of **J H Foley RA** before its completion.

Weekes exhibited at the RA between 1828 and 1877 and at the British Institution from 1850 to 1866. In addition to portraiture he showed a small number of ideal works, including *The suppliant* (**57**) and the *Young naturalist* (**63**). He was elected an associate of the Academy in 1850 and a full member in 1862, when he deposited, as his diploma work, a bust of Joseph Henry Green, the Academy's professor of anatomy (**147**).

Weekes also enjoyed considerable success as a writer and teacher. In 1852 he was awarded a gold medal for his essay, *Fine Arts at the Great Exhibition*. In 1869 he joined the staff of the RA Schools as professor of sculpture and travelled to Italy to study classical art in preparation for this new role. His Royal Academy lectures were published posthumously as *Lectures on Art*, prefaced by a biography of the sculptor by John Ernest Weekes. Half the lectures explored the themes of composition, beauty, taste, style, idealism and realism in sculpture, colour in sculpture, education and portraiture. The latter part of the book is principally an historical survey. Weekes viewed the reconciliation of idealism and realism in sculpture as a key issue. The two extremes, an ossified and increasingly irrelevant neo-classicism as practiced by **John Gibson RA** and the excessive, flamboyant realism exemplified in the work of **Carlo, Baron Marochetti**, seemed equally unsatisfactory to him and he advised his students to follow a middle path. He discussed the training of sculptors, stressing the importance of having both a practical and an intellectual education and lamented the inadequacy of the teaching and facilities offered to sculptors at the RA Schools. His lectures have been described as 'the most consistent and intelligent exposition of sculptural thinking in the Victorian era and, as far as the published material goes, exceptional if not unique' (*Read* 1982, 16–7).

In 1876 Weekes, who was now in poor health, retired to Ramsgate. There he formed a friendship with Sir Moses Montefiore, a leading Jewish businessman and philanthropist, who had established a synagogue on his estate in Ramsgate. Two of his last works were busts of the Archbishop of Canterbury and his wife for St Peter's Orphanage at Broadstairs in Kent (**176, 180**). When his health deteriorated further Weekes returned to London, where he died on 28 May 1877. He was buried in Kensal Green cemetery in a grave marked by a simple red granite ledger-stone. His biography in the preface to the essays described him as, 'about the middle height, his head large, the forehead high and square, features rugged and irregular, but thoughtful and expressive. Upright and true in thought, word, and deed, he expressed his opinions fearlessly and with decision on all subjects within the scope of his experience; while his simple kindly manner, remarkable powers of conversation, and freshness of idea gave a charm to his society, rare as it was delightful' (*Weekes* 1880, 9–10).

The acerbic contemporary critic, F T Palgrave, dismissed the sculptor as a follower of Chantrey's 'coarse and careless style in modelling and execution' (*Palgrave* 1866, 293) and condemned the exaggerated features of his portraits, singling out the bust of Sir George Cornewall Lewis in Westminster Abbey (**45**), which he called 'as unpleasant a caricature of a fine head as any we can remember' (*Palgrave* 1866, 85). However, as an enthusiastic supporter of Thomas Woolner Palgrave was often severe in his criticisms of his rivals and clearly his views were not typical for Weekes had little difficulty in attracting patronage. Like many sculptors of the mid-century, Weekes' reputation declined soon after his death and has not revived, though he has been described as 'an unjustly forgotten figure' and 'the finest English portrait sculptor of his day' (*Radcliffe* 1969, 50).

EH

Literary References: *Sandby* II, 1862, 351–2; *Palgrave* 1866, 37, 82, 84–6, 122, 225, 293; *Weekes* 1880, *passim; DNB*, LX, 1899, 148; *Radcliffe* 1969, 50–1; *Penny* 1977 (1), 11, 79, 160–1, 195, 205 n22; *Read* 1982, *passim*; *Grove* 33, 1996, 24 (Turpin); *Curl* 2001, 243; *ODNB* (Stevens)

Additional Manuscript Sources: Chantrey/Lewis; Foley/Weekes; Weekes/Ansdell; Weekes/Cunningham

Wills and Administrations: PPR, will with codicil, 25 June 1877, fol 535, effects under £25,000, re-sworn January 1878, effects under £30,000

Auction Catalogues: Weekes and others 1880

Portraits of the Sculptor: self-portrait, bust, untraced (185)

Funerary Monuments

1.	1830	Joseph Stewart (†1828)	Sandwich, Kent		*Gunnis* 1968, 420
2.	†1836	George, 4th Viscount Midleton	Peper Harrow, Surrey	S	Pevsner, *Surrey*, 1971, 408
3.	1836	James Stephen Lushington (+1832)	St George's Cathedral, Chennai (Madras), India	S	*Graves* VIII, 1905–6, 192; *Steggles* 2000, 127–8 (repr)
4.	†1837	Daniel Corrie, Bishop of Madras	St Peter (the garrison church), Colombo, Sri Lanka (formerly Ceylon)	SD	*Gunnis* 1968, 420
5.	†1837	Daniel Corrie, Bishop of Madras	Lahore Cathedral, India		RG/JP, 9, 1540
6.	1837	Sarah Hyder (†1836)	Seasalter, Kent	S	Pevsner, *Kent: N E & E*, 1983, 454
7.	1839	Captain Frederick McGillivray (†1838)	Mumbai (Bombay) Cathedral, India	SD	
8.	†1840	Charles Kemp	St Matthew, Brixton, London		Pevsner, *London: S*, 1983, 338
9.	1840	John Wordsworth	Trinity College, Cambridge, chapel		Pevsner, *Cambs*, 1970, 168
10.	1842	Daniel Corrie, Bishop of Madras (†1837)	St George's Cathedral, Chennai (Madras), India		*Weekes* 1880, 5; *Graves* VIII, 1905–6, 192; *Groseclose* 1995, 95, 96 (repr); *Steggles* 2000, 67–69 (repr)
11.	?1842	Henry Hoare	Mitcham, Surrey		*Gunnis* 1968, 420
12.	†1842	Rev Dr Joseph Goodall	[Eton College chapel]; Eton College, Windsor, Berks, churchyard	S	*Weekes* 1880, 5; *Graves* VIII, 1905–6, 192; Pevsner, *Bucks*, 1994, 307
13.	1844	Emily Smyth Pigott (†1838)	St John the Baptist, Weston-super-Mare, Somerset		*AU*, 1844, 170; *Graves* VIII, 1905–6, 192; Pevsner, *Somerset: N & Bristol*, 1958, 337; *Gunnis* 1968, 420
14.	?1844	Richard Gibbs	Tooting, Surrey		*Gunnis* 1968, 420
15.	†1845	Anne Tyrwhitt Drake	St Mary, Amersham, Bucks		Pevsner, *Bucks*, 1994, 132–3
16.	†1845	John Dent	St George's Cathedral, Chennai (Madras), India		*Archer* 1984, 51; *Groseclose* 1985, 80–2 (repr)
17.	*c*1845	Robert Southey (†1843)	Westminster Abbey, London, south transept		Pevsner, *London I*, 1973, 444; *Read* 1982, 103, 172
18.	*c*1845	Zachary Macaulay (†1838)	Westminster Abbey, London, nave	S	WAM (5); Pevsner, *London* I, 1973, 454
19.	1846	Edward Tatham (†1834) Payment(s): £800	All Saints, Oxford		Pevsner, *Oxon*, 1974, 289
20.	1846	Sir Edward Barnes (†1838)	St Peter (the garrison church), Colombo, Sir Lanka (formerly Ceylon)		*Gunnis* 1968, 419; *Ormond and Rogers* 2, 1979–81, 13
21.	†1846	Sir George Wombwell, 2nd Bt	St Mary, Battersea, London		*Gunnis* 1968, 420
22.	?1847	Inigo Thomas	Willingdon, Sussex		*Gunnis* 1968, 420
23.	1847	Sir Thomas Fowell Buxton, design only (monument executed by Frederick Thrupp)	[Exhib RA, London, 1329]; untraced		*Graves* VIII, 1905–6, 193
24.	†1848	Charles Buller	Westminster Abbey, London, north transept Other versions: Reform Club, London (bust)		*Graves* VIII, 1905–6, 193; Pevsner, *London I*, 1973, 450
25.	†1848	Edmund Kennedy	St James, King Street, Sydney, Australia	S	
26.	†1849	George, Earl of Auckland	Beckenham, Kent	S	
27.	1849	Lieutenant-Colonel Sir George Gipps (†1847)	Canterbury Cathedral, Kent	SD	*Graves* VIII, 1905–6, 193; Pevsner, *Kent: N E & E*, 1983, 214
28.	†1849	Rev E S P Serocold	Cherry Hinton, Cambs	S	
29.	1849	Samuel (†1815) and Elizabeth Whitbread (†1846)	Cardington, Beds	SD	*Graves* VIII, 1905–6, 193; *Penny* 1977 (1), 79–80 (repr); *Grove* 33, 1996, 24
30.	1849	William, Lord Auckland (†1814)	St George, Beckenham, Kent	S	Pevsner, *London: S*, 1983, 159
31.	†1850	Charles Arkwright	Cromford, Derbys		Pevsner, *Derbys*, 1978, 159
32.	†1850	Frederick, 1st Duke of Cambridge	Royal female orphan asylum, Beddington, Surrey		*Gunnis* 1968, 419
33.	†1852	Robert Cary Elwes	Great Billing, Northants	S	*CIIA* 4/3/90 (repr)
34.	?1853	Mary Innes	Leyton, Essex		*Gunnis* 1968, 420
35.	1854	Percy Bysshe Shelley (†1822)	Christchurch Priory, Hants		*Graves* VIII, 1905–6, 193; *Read* 1982, 178, 179 (repr)
36.	1854	Thomas Tyrwhitt Drake (†1852)	St Mary, Amersham, Bucks	S	Pevsner, *Bucks*, 1994, 132
37.	1858	Dr William Buckland, Dean of Westminster (†1856)	Westminster Abbey, London, nave Other versions: Oxford University Museum, bust Geological Museum, London, bust ex coll NPG, plaster bust; untraced		*Graves* VIII, 1905–6, 194; *Gunnis* 1968, 419; *Ormond* 1973, 79, pl 131; *MacMichael* 1977, 16
38.	†1858	Sir Charles Abney Hastings, 2nd Bt	Willesley, Leics		*Gunnis* 1968, 420

No.	Date	Subject	Material	Location	Signed	Literary references
39.	†1858	William Hyder		Seasalter, Kent	S	
40.	?1859	Charles Hoare		Morden, Surrey		*Gunnis* 1968, 420
41.	†1862	Captain William Hyder		Seasalter, Kent	S	
42.	1862	Guards' memorial, design only (monument executed by John Bell)		[Exhib RA, London, 1031]; untraced		*Graves* VIII, 1905–6, 194
43.	1864	Richard Gibbs		St Matthew, Brixton, London		*Gunnis* 1968, 420
44.	1864	Richard Gibbs		St Peter, Cornhill, London		RG/JP, 9, 1541
45.	1864	Sir George Cornewall Lewis Bt (†1863)		Westminster Abbey, London, north transept	SD	*Graves* VIII, 1905–6, 194; Pevsner, *London I*, 1973, 450; *Ormond* 1973, 270
46.	1864	William Whitmore (†1858)		Quatt, Salop		RG/JP, 9, 1541
47.	1865	Military trophies, part of a monument to John Bridge (†1863)		Piddletrenthide, Dorset	SD	
48.	1866	Rt Hon Dr John Sumner, Archbishop of Canterbury (†1862)		Canterbury Cathedral, Kent		*Graves* VIII, 1905–6, 194; *Ormond* 1973, 439; Pevsner, *Kent: NE & E*, 1983, 211
49.	†1871	Sir Roderick Murchison		Bathampton, Dorset		RG/JP, 9, 1541
50.	1875	Charles Richard Sumner, Bishop of Winchester (†1874)		Winchester Cathedral, Hants		*Weekes* 1880, 9; *Gunnis* 1968, 420
Statues						
51.	1831	Sleeping infant		[Exhib RA, London, 1160]; untraced		*Graves* VIII, 1905–6, 192
52.	1845	Richard, Marquess Wellesley	m	[East India Company, Leadenhall Street, City of London, board room]; Foreign and Commonwealth Office, London		*Weekes* 1880, 5, fol 224 (repr); *Graves* VIII, 1905–6, 192; Pevsner, *London I*, 1973, 548
53.	1845	Sir Francis Bacon		Trinity College, Cambridge, chapel	SD	*Weekes* 1880, 5; Pevsner, *Cambs*, 1970, 168; *Read* 1982, 128
54.	1847	George, 1st Earl of Auckland Model(s): exhib RA, London, 1847, 1395	b	[Kolkata (Calcutta)]; Aotea Square, Auckland, New Zealand		*Weekes* 1880, 5, fol 200 (repr); *Graves* VIII, 1905–6, 193; *Steggles* 2000, 39–40
55.	1850	Girl with the hoop ('Resting after a run', the daughter of Frederick Reed)	m	Tenenbaum coll sale, NY (26 May 1994, lot 72)	SD	*AJ Cat* 1851, 88 (repr); *Graves* VIII, 1905–6, 193
56.	?c1850	John Flaxman		Tate Gallery, London		*Gunnis* 1968, 419
57.	1850	The suppliant		[Exhib RA, London, 1304]; untraced Other versions: Sotheby, London, 1998, small bronze		*AJ Cat* 1851, 208 (repr); *Weekes* 1880, 6, fol 405 (repr); *Graves* VIII, 1905–6, 193; *Penny* 1977 (1), 195, 224 n54
58.	1852	A shepherd		[Exhib RA, London, 1319]; untraced		*Graves* VIII, 1905–6, 193
59.	1852	Sir Robert Peel, design only		[Exhib RA, London, 1350]; untraced		*Graves* VIII, 1905–6, 193
60.	1854	Arthur, 1st Duke of Wellington, equestrian, design only		[Exhib RA, London, 1377]; untraced		*Graves* VIII, 1905–6, 193
61.	1855	Infant son of George Beaufoy	m	[Exhib RA, London, 1411]; untraced		*Graves* VIII, 1905–6, 193
62.	1857	The mother's kiss	m	Sotheby, 21 Nov 1995, lot 111	S	*Weekes* 1880, 7, fol 87 (repr); *Graves* VIII, 1905–6, 193, 194; *Morris and Roberts* 1998, 635
63.	1857	Young naturalist	m	Private coll, Scotland Other versions: RDS, Dublin, plaster, nd LMG, W R Yorks 85/04, marble, 1870 small bronzes produced by Elkington		*Manchester Art Treasures* 1857, 135; *Graves* 1875, 574; *Graves* VIII, 1905–6, 193; *Leeds* 1996, 11 (repr); *CL*, 3 June 1999, 142 (repr)
64.	1856–1861	Sardanapalus Model(s): C of L Coll, acc no 151, plaster	m	CL Coll, Mansion House, City of London, Egyptian Hall, acc 150		*Graves* VIII, 1905–6, 194; *Knight* 1986, 350 (repr); *Ward-Jackson* 2002, 555–6
65.	1863	Ariel		[Exhib RA, London, 1044]; untraced		*Graves* VIII, 1905–6, 194
66.	1863	Play: Miss Hartree and dog	m	[Exhib RA, London, 1040]; untraced		*Graves* VIII, 1905–6, 194
67.	1864	Dr William Harvey (†1657) Model(s): exhib RA, London, 1864, 917	m	Oxford University Museum	S	*Graves* VIII, 1905–6, 194; *Read* 1982, 235
68.	1864	John Hunter	m	RCS, London		*Graves* VIII, 1905–6, 194; *Read* 1982, 20–1, 123, 164 (repr); *Grove* 33, 1996, 24
69.	1864	Manufactures	m	Albert Memorial, Kensington Gardens, London	S	*Bayley* 1981, 55, 87–91 (reprs 48, 55, 56); *Brooks* 2000, 177, 178, 180, 224–6 (repr)
70.	1865	Sleeping child and dog Model(s): exhib BI, London, 1854, 575 (5 gns)	m	[Weekes and others, sale, 1880 (£152)]; Christie, London, 26 Feb 1998, lot no 404	SD	*Graves* 1875, 574; *Gunnis* 1968, 419
71.	1866	Luna	m	[Exhib RA, London, 847]; Canterbury Museum, Kent	SD	*Graves* VIII, 1905–6, 194
72.	1867	True friends	m	[Exhib BI, London, 625]; untraced		*Graves* 1875, 574
73.	1869	Cleopatra, statuette		[Exhib RA, London, 1283]; untraced		*Weekes* 1880, fol 155 (repr); *Graves* VIII, 1905–6, 194
74.	1865–1871	King Charles II Model(s): exhib RA, London, 1809, (763), 1869, (1242)	m	[Westminster Hall, London]; Central Criminal Court (Old Bailey), City of London, entrance hall	S	*Graves* VIII, 1905–6, 194; *Read* 1982, 121 (repr); *Ward-Jackson* 2002, 195–7
75.	1875	Queen Victoria Model(s): exhib RA, London, 1869, 1218	b	[Kolkata (Calcutta), India]; Delhi; formerly Durbar, now School of Art		*Graves* VIII, 1905–6, 194; *Ormond* 1973, 490
76.	nd	Mother and child		Southill, Beds		*Gunnis* 1968, 419
Busts						
77.	1828	An infant	m	[Exhib RA, London, 1192]; untraced		*Graves* VIII, 1905–6, 192
78.	1828	John Plumptree		[Exhib RA, London, 1142]; untraced		*Graves* VIII, 1905–6, 192
79.	1829	Lord Darnley		Cobham Hall, Kent		*Graves* VIII, 1905–6, 192; *Gunnis* 1968, 419

80.	c1829	William, 2nd Baron Harris		Untraced		*Weekes* 1880, 4; *Gunnis* 1968, 418
81.	1830	Dr Richard Bagot, Bishop of St Asaph		[Exhib RA, London, 1224]; untraced		*Graves* VIII, 1905–6, 192
82.	1830	Unidentified gentleman		[Exhib RA, London, 1183]; untraced		*Graves* VIII, 1905–6, 192
83.	1831	Unidentified lady	m	[Exhib RA, London, 1166]; untraced		*Graves* VIII, 1905–6, 192
84.	1832	'A young lady'	m	[Exhib RA, London, 1215]; untraced		*Graves* VIII, 1905–6, 192
85.	1833	Unidentified child	m	[Exhib Soc of BA, London, 871]; untraced		*Johnson* 1975, 492
86.	1833	William Master	m	[Exhib RA, London, 1203]; untraced		*Graves* VIII, 1905–6, 192
87.	1834	Rev Dr William Welfitt, Prebendary of Canterbury	m	Canterbury Cathedral, Kent		*Graves* VIII, 1905–6, 192
88.	1834	Stephen Rumbold Lushington	m	[Exhib RA, London, 1095]; untraced		*Graves* VIII, 1905–6, 192
89.	1834	Unidentified gentleman		[Exhib Soc of BA, London, 821]; untraced		*Johnson* 1975, 492
90.	1835	'A widow lady'	m	[Exhib RA, London, 1080]; untraced		*Graves* VIII, 1905–6, 192
91.	1836	George, 9th Earl of Winchilsea	m	[Eastwell Park, Kent]; Birmingham MAG, inv P.29'58	SD	*Graves* VIII, 1905–6, 192; *Gunnis* 1968, 419; *Silber* 1987, 96–7, cat no 301 (repr)
92.	1837	Dr Phillips Jones	m	[Exhib RA, London, 1236]; untraced		*Graves* VIII, 1905–6, 192
93.	?1837	Henry Maudslay (after Chantrey)	m	Institution of Mechanical Engineers, London Other versions: Science Museum, London, plaster		*Graves* VIII, 1905–6, 192; *Ormond and Rogers* 2, 1979–81, 145
94.	1837	John Martin		[Exhib RA, London, 1275]; untraced		*Graves* VIII, 1905–6, 192; *Ormond* 1973, 302; *Johnson* 1975, 492
95.	1838	Queen Victoria	m	[coll Duchess of Kent]; Mulgrave Castle, N R Yorks		*Weekes* 1880, 5; *Graves* VIII, 1905–6, 192; *Gunnis* 1968, 418; *Ormond* 1973, 481
96.	1839	Thomas Watson		Royal Infirmary, Sheffield, W R Yorks		*Gunnis* 1968, 419
97.	1840	Harriet, Viscountess Midleton	m	[Exhib RA, London, 1147]; Colnaghi, London (Nov 1987)	SD	*Graves* VIII, 1905–6, 192
98.	1840	Hugh Richard Fahie Hoare	m	LMG, W R Yorks 5/72	SD	*Graves* VIII, 1905–6, 192; *Ret to Life*, 2000, 16, 48, 62 (repr)
99.	1841	'A young lady'	m	[Exhib RA, London, 1312]; untraced		*Graves* VIII, 1905–6, 192
100.	1841	Charles Shaw Lefevre	m	[Exhib RA, London, 1330]; untraced		*Graves* VIII, 1905–6, 192
101.	1842	Allan Cunningham	m	SNPG, Edinburgh		*AU*, 1842, 129; *Graves* VIII 1905–6, 192; *Ret to Life*, 2000, 16, 62 (repr)
102.	1843	Baboo Dwarkanauth Tagore	m	[Exhib RA, London, 1467]; untraced		*ILN*, 3 June 1843, 399 (repr); *Graves* VIII, 1905–6, 192
103.	1843	Cropley, 6th Earl of Shaftesbury	m	St Giles, Dorset		*Graves* VIII, 1905–6, 192; *Gunnis* 1968, 419
104.	1844	George, 1st Earl of Auckland	m	Victoria Memorial Hall, Kolkata (Calcutta)		*Graves* VIII, 1905–6, 192; *Gunnis* 1968, 419
105.	1844	Henry Toby Prinsep	m	Victoria Memorial Hall, Kolkata (Calcutta)		*Graves* VIII, 1905–6, 192; *Gunnis* 1968, 419
106.	1844	Sir Astley Paston Cooper Payment(s): £113 8s (incl pedestal)	m	RCS, London		*AU*, 1844, 171; *Graves* VIII, 1905–6, 192; *Read* 1982, 59, 121
107.	1845	Charles Beckett Greenlaw	m	[Exhib RA, London, 1469]; untraced		*Graves* VIII, 1905–6, 192
108.	1845	Charles, 5th Duke of Richmond	m	Goodwood House, Sussex		*Graves* VIII, 1905–6, 192; *Gunnis* 1968, 419
109.	1845	John Travers	m	[Exhib RA, London, 1445]; untraced		*Graves* VIII, 1905–6, 192
110.	1846	Adam Sedgwick	m	Geological Society, London		*Graves* VIII, 1905–6, 193; *Ormond* 1973, 414
111.	1846	General Sir Edward Paget	m	[Exhib RA, London, 1456]; untraced		*AU*, 1846, 189; *Graves* VIII, 1905–6, 192
112.	1846	Jane, Duchess of Marlborough	m	Blenheim Palace, Oxon		*Graves* VIII, 1905–6, 193; *Gunnis* 1968, 419
113.	1846	John Forbes	m	[Exhib RA, London, 1499]; untraced		*Graves* VIII, 1905–6, 192
114.	1847	General Caulfield	m	[Exhib RA, London, 1429]; untraced		*Graves* VIII, 1905–6, 193
115.	1847	James S Forbes	m	[Exhib RA, London, 1446]; untraced		*Graves* VIII, 1905–6, 193
116.	1848	Dowager Countess of Dunmore	m	Knox/Longstaffe-Gowan coll (acq 1997)	SD	*Graves* VIII, 1905–6, 193
117.	1849	James, 1st Baron Abinger	m	[Exhib RA, London, 1257]; untraced		*Graves* VIII, 1905–6, 193
118.	1849	Unidentified woman (possibly Mrs George Forbes)	m	VAM A.9-1988	SD	*Graves* VIII, 1905–6, 193; *Bilbey* 2002, 426
119.	1850	Thomas Wilkinson	m	[Exhib RA, London, 1436]; untraced		*Graves* VIII, 1905–6, 193
120.	1850	William Amory	m	[Exhib RA, London, 1434]; untraced		*Graves* VIII, 1905–6, 193
121.	1851	A young boy	m	Christie, London (28 Jan 1988, lot 196)	SD	
122.	1851	Capon Weekes (the sculptor's father)		[Mrs Van Maurik, the sculptor's descendant]; untraced		*Graves* VIII, 1905–6, 193; *Gunnis* 1968, 418
123.	1851	Samuel Amery	m	[Exhib RA, London, 1330]; untraced		*Graves* VIII, 1905–6, 193
124.	1852	Henry Beaufoy, FRS	m	[Exhib RA, London, 1481]; untraced		*Graves* VIII, 1905–6, 193
125.	1852	Miss Georgina Peel	m	[Exhib RA, London, 1485]; untraced		*Graves* VIII, 1905–6, 193
126.	1852	Mrs Charles Mears	m	[Exhib RA, London, 1483]; untraced		*Graves* VIII, 1905–6, 193
127.	1852	Mrs Shelley		untraced		*Weekes* 1880, 6
128.	1853	James Moncrieff Arnott FRS Payment(s): £110	m	RCS, London		*Graves* VIII, 1905–6, 193; *Read* 1982, 59, 123
129.	1853	Louisa Nicholson	m	[Exhib RA, London, 1448]; untraced		*Graves* VIII, 1905–6, 193
130.	1853	Mrs Vaughan	m	[Exhib RA, London, 1437]; untraced		*Graves* VIII, 1905–6, 193
131.	1854	Horace Cust		Boughton, Northants		*Gunnis* 1968, 419
132.	1855	Lieutenant Greathed, RN	m	[Exhib RA, London, 1542]; untraced		*Graves* VIII, 1905–6, 193
133.	1855	Mrs Harrison Blair		[Exhib RA, London, 1541]; untraced		*Graves* VIII, 1905–6, 193
134.	1855	Unidentified gentleman	m	Knox/Longstaffe-Gowan coll	SD	
135.	1856	Mrs Charles Grey	m	[Exhib RA, London, 1324]; untraced		*Graves* VIII, 1905–6, 193

136.	1856	Sir Charles Bell	m	RCS, London Other versions: University College Hospital, medical school library, plaster, SD 1856		*Graves* VIII, 1905–6, 193; C Lib (repr)
137.	1856	Thomas, 1st Baron Truro	m	Palace of Westminster, London, Peers' Library, Truro Room Other versions: Middle Temple, London, nd	SD	*Graves* VIII, 1905–6, 193; *Walker* 1961, 71, cat 74
138.	1857	Anna Maria Lambert	m	[Exhib RA, London, 1272]; untraced		*Graves* VIII, 1905–6, 193
139.	1859	African head (? Mary Seacole)	m	Getty, Los Angeles 95.SA.82	SD	*Graves* 1875, 574; *Graves* VIII, 1905–6, 194; *Fusco* 1998, 116–7 (repr)
140.	1859	George, 6th Duke of Marlborough		Blenheim Palace, Oxon		*Graves* VIII, 1905–6, 194; *Gunnis* 1968, 419
141.	1859	John Perry		[Exhib RA, London, 1287]; untraced		*Graves* VIII, 1905–6, 194
142.	1859	Mrs James P Currie		[Exhib RA, London, 1348]; untraced		*Graves* VIII, 1905–6, 194
143.	1860	Mary Wollstonecraft		[Exhib RA, London, 1080]; untraced		*Graves* VIII, 1905–6, 194
144.	1861	Joseph Maudslay		[Exhib RA, London, 1056]; untraced		*Graves* VIII, 1905–6, 194
145.	1861	Walter, 5th Duke of Buccleuch		Boughton Hall, Northants		*Gunnis* 1968, 419; *Ormond and Rogers* 3, 1979–81, 29
146.	1862	Captain Robb RN	m	[Exhib RA, London, 1010]; untraced		*Graves* VIII, 1905–6, 194
147.	1863	Joseph Henry Green, FRS, RA		RA, Burlington House, London Other versions: R C Surg, London, 1865, £126 Others recorded		*Graves* VIII, 1905–6, 194; *Radcliffe* 1969, 50 (repr); *Read* 1982, 59, 121–3
148.	1863	Sir Benjamin Brodie	m	RCS, London		*Graves* VIII, 1905–6, 194; *Gunnis* 1968, 419
149.	1864	Henry William Whitbread	m	Southill Park, Beds		*Graves* VIII, 1905–6, 194; *Read* 1982, 171 (repr); *Grove* 33, 1996, 24
150.	1864	Unidentified gentleman	m	Christie, London, 16 June 1994, lot no 337	SD	
151.	1865	Peter Martin	m	[Exhib RA, London, 952]; untraced		*Graves* VIII, 1905–6, 194
152.	1865	Sir Tatton Sykes Bt	m	[Exhib RA, London, 938]; untraced		*Graves* VIII, 1905–6, 194
153.	1866	Joshua Field		[Exhib RA, London, 880]; untraced		*Graves* VIII, 1905–6, 194
154.	1866	Richard Gibbs	m	[Exhib RA, London, 872]; untraced		*Graves* VIII, 1905–6, 194
155.	1866	Thomas Martin		[Exhib RA, London, 870]; untraced		*Graves* VIII, 1905–6, 194
156.	1866	William Mulready RA	m	Tate Britain, London NO2076		*Graves* VIII, 1905–6, 194; *Ormond* 1973, 328
157.	1867	Charles Pearson	m	[Exhib RA, London, 1053]; untraced		*Graves* VIII, 1905–6, 194;
158.	1867	Sir William Lawrence Bt	m	RCS, London Other versions: St Bartholomew's Hospital, London, marble, SD 1867	S	*Graves* VIII, 1905–6, 194; *Graves* 1913–15, 1640; *Ormond* 1973, 265; C Lib (repr)
159.	1868	Nathaniel Crewe, Bishop of Durham (†1722)		Crewe Hall, Cheshire		*Gunnis* 1968, 420
160.	1868	Sir Randolph Crewe		Crewe Hall, Cheshire		*Gunnis* 1968, 419
161.	1868	Thomas Stothard RA	m	Tate Britain, London NO2075	S	*Graves* VIII, 1905–6, 194
162.	1870	George Jones RA	m	RA, London		*Graves* VIII, 1905–6, 194; *Ormond* 1973, 245
163.	1870	H Fenwick	m	[Exhib RA, London, 1193]; untraced		*Graves* VIII, 1905–6, 194
164.	1870	John Smith	m	[Exhib RA, London, 1217]; untraced		*Graves* VIII, 1905–6, 194
165.	1870	Unidentified gentleman	m	Christie, London, 24 Oct 1996, lot 216A	SD	
166.	1871	John Fleming, CSI	m	[Exhib RA, London, 1286]; untraced		*Graves* VIII, 1905–6, 194
167.	1871	Mrs Fleming	m	[Exhib RA, London, 1284]; untraced		*Graves* VIII, 1905–6, 194
168.	1871	Richard Mead		St Thomas's Hospital, London	SD	*Gunnis* 1968, 420; *Cavanagh* forthcoming 2007 (Lambeth 2); C Lib (repr)
169.	1871	Sir Roderick Murchison		Geological Museum, London Other versions: Royal Geographical Society, replica Royal Soc of Edinburgh, marble, SD 1871		*Graves* VIII, 1905–6, 194; *Graves* 1913–15, 1640; *Ormond* 1973, 330
170.	1871	Thomas Richards Harding	m	Christie, London, 20 March 1984, lot 20	SD	
171.	1871	William Cheselden (after Roubiliac)	m	St Thomas's Hospital, London	SD	*Gunnis* 1968, 420; *Cavanagh* forthcoming 2007 (Lambeth I); C Lib (repr)
172.	1872	Edmund, Baron Hammond	m	University College, Oxford Other versions: coll Mrs van Maurik (the sculptor's descendant) 1873; untraced Gov Art Coll, marble, SD 1874	SD	*Graves* VIII, 1905–6, 194; *Gunnis* 1968, 418; Gov Art Coll archives
173.	1872	John Flint South	m	St Thomas's Hospital, London	SD	*Graves* VIII, 1905–6, 194; *Gunnis* 1968, 420; *Cavanagh* forthcoming 2007 (Lambeth 2); C Lib (repr)
174.	1873	Field Marshal Sir George Pollock	m	Merchant Taylors' Company, City of London		*Graves* VIII, 1905–6, 194; *Ormond* 1973, 380
175.	1873	Richard Ansdell		Walker, Liverpool		*Graves* VIII, 1905–6, 194; *Gunnis* 1968, 420
176.	1874	Archibald Tait, Archbishop of Canterbury		[St Peter's orphanage, Thanet, Kent]; Untraced		*Graves* VIII, 1905–6, 194; *Loewe* II, 1983, 266–9

177.	1874	M T Smith		[Exhib RA, London, 1512]; untraced		*Graves* VIII, 1905–6, 194
178.	1874	Sir Joshua Reynolds	m	Leicester Square, London		*Gunnis* 1968, 420; *Read* 1982, 171; *Grove* 33, 1996, 24
179.	1875	Sir Francis Grant	m	coll T Lewis, 1904; untraced		*Ormond* 1973, 194
180.	1876	Catherine Tait		[St Peter's orphanage, Thanet, Kent]; untraced		*Loewe* II, 1983, 266, 286–7
181.	1877	Sir Moses Montefiore Bt	m	[coll Sir Moses Montefiore]; untraced		*Graves* VIII, 1905–6, 194; *Loewe* II, 1983, 290
182.	nd	Albert, the Prince Consort		Coll Mlle Mathys, Brussels, 1935; untraced Other versions: reproduced in biscuit ware, *c*1841		*Ormond* 1973, 15; *Brooks* 2000, 49, 431 n15 (repr)
183.	nd	Caroline Weekes (afterwards Mrs Collard)		[Mrs Van Maurik, the sculptor's descendant]; untraced		*Gunnis* 1968, 418
184.	nd	Elizabeth Cust		Boughton Hall, Northants		*Gunnis* 1968, 420
185.	nd	Henry Weekes (self-portrait)		[Victorian Exhib, New Gall, London, 1892, 1082]; untraced		*Graves* 1913–15, 1640
186.	nd	John Bennett	p	Linnean Soc		RG/JP, 9, 1540
187.	nd	Mary Weekes (afterwards Mrs Knight)		[Mrs Van Maurik, the sculptor's descendant]; untraced		*Gunnis* 1968, 418
188.	nd	Mrs Catherine Pfiel		[Mrs Van Maurik, the sculptor's descendant]; untraced		*Gunnis* 1968, 418
189.	nd	Portrait of an unidentified man	p	Ashmolean WA 1973.29	S	*Penny* 1992, III, 177 (repr)
190.	nd	Sir William Arbuthnot		Tunbridge Wells Public Library, Kent		*Gunnis* 1968, 418
191.	nd	Unidentified man	p	Royal Coll RCIN 2224	S	JM
Chimneypieces						
192.	1869	Description unavailable		Crewe Hall, Cheshire		*Gunnis* 1968, 418
Architectural Sculpture						
193.	1829	Column for a sundial	m	[Dane John Gardens, Canterbury]; untraced		*Weekes* 1880, 4; *Graves* VIII, 1905–6, 192; *Gunnis* 1968, 418
194.	1841–1843	Thomas Cranmer, Nicholas Ridley and Hugh Latimer (†1555–6) (memorial designed by Sir George Gilbert Scott)		Martyrs' memorial, Oxford, upper tier		Pevsner, *Oxon*, 1974, 314
195.	*c*1874	John Flaxman		RA, Burlington House, London, above window on second storey		Pevsner, *London*: I, 1973, 624
196.	*c*1874	Raphael		RA, Burlington House, London, above window on second storey		Pevsner, *London*: I, 1973, 624
197.	1876	Thomas Linacre, William Harvey and Thomas Sydenham, statues		R C Physic, London, portico		*Gunnis* 1968, 419
Reliefs						
198.	1819	St George and the dragon		Untraced		*Weekes* 1880, 2
Miscellaneous						
199.	1834	Study		[Exhib Soc of BA, London, 827]; untraced		*Johnson* 1975, 492

WEIGALL, Henry 1800?–1882

He exhibited portrait busts and a relief portrait at the Royal Hibernian Academy, the Society of British Artists and the Royal Academy between 1829 and 1853, from addresses in St James's Street, Somerset Street and Wimpole Street, London. His works included several busts of the Duke of Wellington (**1, 12, 20**). The last of these was a life-sized bronze, modelled from the life during sittings given in August and on 18 November 1851. The Duke died the following September and this was the last bust he sat for. In 1854 Weigall sent proofs to the RA of the 'Flaxman medal executed for the Art Union of London' and the 'Prize Gold Medal given by the Lord Bishop of London to King Edward IV's Grammar School at Bury St Edmund's'. Several of his works were put on display at the Crystal Palace in Sydenham during the 1850s (**10, 22, 23**).

A number of artists named Weigall exhibited at the RA during the 19th century and it is not always easy to distinguish between them. It is possible that Henry Weigall was responsible for a number of impressions from intaglio gems and a wax portrait of the Duke of York which Graves lists as the work of a painter, Charles Harvey Weigall. This was shown from addresses in Conduit Street during the 1820s (*Graves* VIII, 1905–6, 198–9). Pyke calls the sculptor 'C. Henry Weigall' and notes that he was gem-engraver to Their Royal Highnesses the Dukes and Duchesses of Cumberland and Cambridge.

In 1856 Weigall and his wife, a sister of Dr Thyre Smith, a celebrated preacher at the Temple Church, sailed with Sir Henry Barkly, Governor of Victoria, to Melbourne. He died on 14 August 1882, and was buried at Kyneto, Victoria (inf. Mitchell Lib, Sydney).

Literary References: *Gunnis* 1968, 420; *Pyke* 1973, 155–6; *Pyke* 1981, 42

Busts					
1.	1829	Arthur, 1st Duke of Wellington	b	Untraced Other versions: several duplicates	*Gunnis* 1968, 420
2.	1832	James Stewart		[Exhib Soc of BA, London, 893]; untraced	*Johnson* 1975, 493
3.	1832	Rev T Smith		[Exhib Soc of BA, London, 853]; untraced	*Johnson* 1975, 493
4.	1836	John Durant		[Exhib Soc of BA, London, 861]; untraced	*Johnson* 1975, 493
5.	1836	Thomas Stavely		[Exhib Soc of BA, London, 886]; untraced	*Johnson* 1975, 493
6.	1837	Sir Harris Nicholas KCMG		[Exhib RA, London, 1256]; untraced	*Graves* VIII, 1905–6, 199
7.	1848	Rev J H Howlett		[Exhib RA, London, 1464]; untraced	*Graves* VIII, 1905–6, 199

8.	1848	Richard Clarke of Kensington		[Exhib RA, London, 1406]; untraced		*Graves* VIII, 1905–6, 199
9.	1848	S Jarratt		Oxford University Museum		*Gunnis* 1968, 420
10.	1848	Thomas Carlyle		[Exhib RA, London, 1437]; untraced		*Graves* VIII, 1905–6, 199; *Ormond* 1973, 93
11.	1848	Unidentified gentleman		[Exhib RA, London, 1447]; untraced		*Graves* VIII, 1905–6, 199
12.	1849	Arthur, 1st Duke of Wellington	m	[Exhib RA, London, 1306]; untraced		*Graves* VIII, 1905–6, 199
13.	1849	Peter Laurie		[Exhib RA, London, 1321]; untraced		*Graves* VIII, 1905–6, 199
14.	1849	Samuel Warren FRS		[Exhib RA, London, 1271]; untraced		*Graves* VIII, 1905–6, 199
15.	1849	Sir David Davies KCH		[Exhib RA, London, 1337]; untraced		*Graves* VIII, 1905–6, 199
16.	1850	Apley Pellatt		[Exhib RA, London, 1444]; untraced		*Graves* VIII, 1905–6, 199
17.	1850	Edward N Dennys		[Exhib RA, London, 1404]; untraced		*Graves* VIII, 1905–6, 199
18.	1850	Samuel Phillips		[Exhib RA, London, 1450]; untraced		*Graves* VIII, 1905–6, 199
19.	1850	Viscount Mandeville MP		[Exhib RA, London, 1385]; untraced		*Graves* VIII, 1905–6, 199
20.	1851	Arthur, 1st Duke of Wellington	b	Lever LL318 Other versions: several, including BMAG, inv 3164'85	SD	*Graves* VIII, 1905–6, 199; *Silber* 1987, 98, cat 302; *Lady Lever* 1999, 77 (repr)
21.	1851	Dr Kelaart, of Ceylon		[Exhib RA, London, 1317]; untraced		*Graves* VIII, 1905–6, 199
22.	1851	William Yarrell		[Exhib RA, London, 1353]; untraced		*Graves* VIII, 1905–6, 199; *Handbook to the Crystal Palace*, 1854
23.	pre-1854	Charles James Blomfield, Bishop of London		[Crystal Palace, Sydenham, portrait gall]; untraced		*Ormond* 1973, 41
24.	nd	Cropley, 6th Earl of Shaftesbury (†1851)		St Giles, Dorset		*Gunnis* 1968, 420
Reliefs						
25.	1829	George Canning, model		[Exhib RHA, Dublin, 272]; untraced		*Stewart*, III, 1985, 261

WELCH fl 1780

A man of this name appeared in the trial, for highway robbery, of William Harding on 13 September 1780. He described himself as 'a statuary' and said he had employed the defendant many times 'to receive considerable sums of money for me.' **Richardson** appeared as a character witness in the same trial.

Literary References: *The Proceedings of the Old Bailey*, t17800913-11

WELLS, Thomas fl 1786–94

A sculptor, medallist and wax-modeller who worked in London and Birmingham. He exhibited wax portraits at the Royal Academy from 2 Fenwick Court, Holborn, London. He is listed at that address and described as 'Modeller and Chaser' in Wakefield's *Directory* of 1794 (inf. Hilary Young).

Literary References: *Gunnis* 1968, 420; *Pyke* 1973, 156

Miscellaneous					
1.	1786	Unidentified young lady	w	[Exhib RA, London, 253]; untraced	*Graves* VIII, 1905–6, 210
2.	1787	Unidentified lady, model	w	[Exhib RA, London, 632]; untraced	*Graves* VIII, 1905–6, 210
3.	1787	Unidentified lady, model	w	[Exhib RA, London, 636]; untraced	*Graves* VIII, 1905–6, 210
4.	1788	Unidentified artist, model		[Exhib RA, London, 616]; untraced	*Graves* VIII, 1905–6, 210
5.	1791	Unidentified lady, model	w	[Exhib RA, London, 657]; untraced	*Graves* VIII, 1905–6, 210

WESSEL, Gerhard George 1744–1811

He was born in Hollenstede and studied in Berlin before coming to England in 1773, encouraged by King George III. He entered the Royal Academy Schools on 31 December 1773 and was awarded a silver medal three years later (**3**). He exhibited at the RA, 1781–87, from 10 Little Titchfield Street and 8 Upper Marylebone Street, showing wax portraits and a figure of *Argos* in terracotta (**1**).

In 1787 he left England for Osnabrück, and in the following year the decorative artist Vernona wrote to the Hofmarschall, Count von Münster, that 'Her Royal Highness has just told me to inform you that she has sent from London to Osnabrück a very accomplished sculptor named Wessel; he has worked for fourteen years in London, but is a native of Osnabrück and prefers to work here'. Wessel was employed under Vernona, but his chief collaborator was the architect Hollenberg. He carried out a good deal of work at the Royal palace in Osnabrück, which then belonged to the English Crown, and various reliefs and wax portraits by him are now in the local museum.

Literary References: *Hutchison* 1960–62, 140; *Gunnis* 1968, 420; *Pyke* 1973, 156

Statues					
1.	1781	Argos	tc	[Exhib RA, London, 474]; untraced	*Graves* VIII, 1905–6, 212
Busts					
2.	1787	Mr Lunardie		[Exhib RA, London, 657]; untraced	*Graves* VIII, 1905–6, 212
Miscellaneous					
3.	1776	Academy figure or bas-relief		[RA silver medal]; untraced	RA Premium list
4.	1782	Unidentified subject, portrait, model	w	[Exhib RA, London, 356]; untraced	*Graves* VIII, 1905–6, 212
5.	1783	Unidentified foreign nobleman	w	[Exhib RA, London, 283]; untraced	*Graves* VIII, 1905–6, 212
6.	1783	Unidentified French nobleman	w	[Exhib RA, London, 354]; untraced	*Graves* VIII, 1905–6, 212
7.	1783	Unidentified gentleman	w	[Exhib RA, London, 351]; untraced	*Graves* VIII, 1905–6, 212
8.	1783	Unidentified gentleman	w	[Exhib RA, London, 352]; untraced	*Graves* VIII, 1905–6, 212
9.	1784	Unidentified gentleman	w	[Exhib RA, London, 238]; untraced	*Graves* VIII, 1905–6, 212
10.	1784	Unidentified gentleman	w	[Exhib RA, London, 242]; untraced	*Graves* VIII, 1905–6, 212
11.	1784	Unidentified lady	w	[Exhib RA, London, 246]; untraced	*Graves* VIII, 1905–6, 212
12.	1785	Unidentified gentleman, model	w	[Exhib RA, London, 365]; untraced	*Graves* VIII, 1905–6, 212
13.	post-1787	Unidentified work		Royal palace, Osnabrück, Germany	*Gunnis* 1968, 420

WESTMACOTT, Charles Molloy 1782–1868

The illegitimate second son of **Richard Westmacott I** and Susannah Molloy, a widow and landlady of the Bull and Horns Inn at Fulham. He was brought up as Westmacott's own son, went to St Paul's School, and trained at the Royal Academy. On the death of his father, Charles's half-brother, **Sir Richard Westmacott**, sent him away penniless. He later achieved considerable success and notoriety as the proprietor and editor of a scandalous Tory journal, *The Age*, and used this position to extort money from public figures keen to avoid adverse publicity. By 1834 he was prosperous enough to own a pretty cottage between Barnes and Richmond, the grounds of which were adorned with sculpture.

Westmacott's artistic background is reflected in some of his publications. *British Galleries of Painting and Sculpture* (1824) set out to describe all the 'Palaces, Mansions, and Galleries . . . in the Kingdom' and catalogue the works of art they contained. *A Descriptive and Critical Catalogue to the Exhibition of the Royal Academy . . . with a brief . . . Account of the Rise and Progress of the Arts of Painting and Sculpture in England* (1823) includes an attack on the Academicians who had wasted £4,000 on a banquet.

Literary References: *Gunnis* 1968, 421; *ODNB* (Draudt)

Archival References: GPC printout from *Frazer's Mag*, vol 9, 1834

Auction Catalogues: *Westmacott* 1832; *Westmacott* 1852

Busts

1.	1822	J P Kemble	[Exhib RA, London, 1016]; untraced		*Graves* VIII, 1905–6, 234

WESTMACOTT, George 1782–1868

A son of **Richard Westmacott I** and the brother of **Sir Richard Westmacott RA**, he exhibited at the Royal Academy, 1799–1820, and at the British Institution in 1808, showing sculpture and a design for a cottage. His recorded addresses were 5 Mount Street; 12 Lower Belgrave Place, Pimlico; 2 Ranelagh Walk, Pimlico; Avery Farm Row, Chelsea and 4 Vauxhall Road. He appears to have assisted his brother **Henry Westmacott**, for payments for the base of the *Achilles* statue in Hyde Park were made to them jointly. In his father's will he is described as George Westmacott of Portman Place in the Parish of St Mary le Bow. He inherited nothing as he was 'already provided for', perhaps as a beneficiary of the agreement whereby Sir Richard Westmacott took care of the family (PROB 11/1483, 253–4).

Literary References: *Gunnis* 1968, 421

Archival References: GPC

Funerary Monuments					
1.	1808	A monumental subject	[Exhib BI, London, 142]; untraced		*Graves* 1875, 580
2.	1810	Filial affection, a monumental figure	[Exhib RA, London, 738]; untraced		*Graves* VIII, 1905–6, 234
Statues					
3.	1818	'Sketch of a national monument to Sir T Picton'	[Exhib RA, London, 1106]; untraced		*Graves* VIII, 1905–6, 235
4.	1839	Young child with dog, statuette	Untraced	SD	C Lib (repr)
Busts					
5.	1804	Unidentified gentleman	[Exhib RA, London, 836]; untraced		*Graves* VIII, 1905–6, 234
6.	1818	J Harrison Esq	[Exhib RA, London, 1065]; untraced		*Graves* VIII, 1905–6, 235
7.	1818	Unidentified artist	[Exhib RA, London, 1049]; untraced		*Graves* VIII, 1905–6, 235
8.	1818	Unidentified lady	[Exhib RA, London, 1044]; untraced		*Graves* VIII, 1905–6, 235
9.	1819	C Goulding Esq	[Exhib RA, London, 1194]; untraced		*Graves* VIII, 1905–6, 235
10.	1819	Unidentified child	[Exhib RA, London, 1245]; untraced		*Graves* VIII, 1905–6, 235
11.	1819	Unidentified lady	[Exhib RA, London, 1211]; untraced		*Graves* VIII, 1905–6, 235
12.	1819	W A Sharp	[Exhib RA, London, 1201]; untraced		*Graves* VIII, 1905–6, 235
13.	1820	Unidentified child	[Exhib RA, London, 1070]; untraced		*Graves* VIII, 1905–6, 235
Miscellaneous					
14.	1814	'For Pity begg'd her keep her flitting breath . . .'	[Exhib RA, London, 811]; untraced		*Graves* VIII, 1905–6, 234–5

WESTMACOTT, Henry 1784–1861

Westmacott was christened on 13 October 1784 at St George, Hanover Square, London, the son of **Richard Westmacott I** and Sarah, née Vardy. He was the younger brother of **Sir Richard Westmacott RA**. He was probably trained by his father and had a moiety of the family workshop at 25 Mount Street at the time of his father's death in 1808. In his father's will it was stipulated that Henry was to continue the family business, one half of which was to belong to Henry's mother and be used for the maintenance of the younger members of the family. This arrangement was to continue for seven years,

In May 1810 he married Eliza Brodie Stewart, daughter of the town clerk of Montrose, who seems to have been the ward of Captain John Guise of the East India Company. Guise married Westmacott's sister, Maria, in August of the same year. Westmacott and his wife had five sons and four daughters, including **James Sherwood Westmacott**, who also became a sculptor, after which the business was to become Henry's own.

It continued along the lines set by Richard Westmacott I, producing chimneypieces, carrying out masonry work and providing wall-monuments. In 1808 he was paid £1,399 0s 10d for numerous chimneypieces at Kensington Palace (**78–81**) and others followed (**82, 83**). In 1810 he was employed as a mason at Somerset House and two years later in the same capacity, at the Fleet prison. In 1814 he received a large payment for architectural carving at Greenwich (**88, 89**) and in 1818–19 worked at Lord Carrington's house in Whitehall. Like his father, Westmacott collaborated with the architect James Wyatt, carrying out a range of carved work at Dodington Park (**85, 87**). His monument to Ernest Udny (**10**), like the elder Westmacott's to John Platt, has an inscription slab in the form of drapery hanging over an arrow with a putto below.

The sculptor appears very likely to have been the Westmacott who carried out architectural carving at Fonthill between 1807 and 1822 (**92**). The temperamental William Beckford, who referred to the carver as 'Rhinoceros', was intermittently delighted and exasperated by Westmacott's efforts. In 1817 Beckford was enraptured by the sight of 'Rhinoceros', 'on scaffolding, carving the ornaments of the Oriel divinely, incomparably' although by 1819 he had tired of this 'beast' who had, by his assessment 'neither taste nor a sense of proportion, and not the least knowledge of the true Gothic style' (*Alexander* 1957, 217, 221, 304).

Westmacott's monuments are, typically, crisply carved wall-slabs with some neoclassical decoration, but he signed a handful of more elaborate works in the 1820s. These incorporate figurative elements such as the mourning figures in high relief on the monument to George Ede (**42**) and the pilgrim grieving at a grave on the monument to Caleb Dickinson (**51**). This last was one of several works exported to Jamaica. Perhaps his most notable work in England is the full-length relief portrait of the deceased Lord William Gordon, shown in full highland dress with a sword, his hand resting on his hip (**50**).

Westmacott continued to take masonry contracts throughout the 1820s: in 1825 he built part of the Royal Mews at Pimlico and was also employed as a mason at Buckingham Palace and at the stationary office at Buckingham Gate.

He appears to have supplied paving in Langley Marish church, Bucks and in 1823 he and his brother **George Westmacott** were paid £801 for the base for the statue of *Achilles* in Hyde Park. This commemorated the victories of the Duke of Wellington and was the work of their more distinguished sibling, Sir Richard Westmacott.

In December 1827 Westmacott remarried, at St Clement Dane's, Hannah Wilkinson Rowe, a descendant of Nicholas Rowe (1673–1718), the poet laureate. The following year he appears to have moved to Edinburgh. In 1830 he exhibited at the Liverpool and Scottish Academies, giving his address as 8 West Lauriston Lane, Edinburgh. In 1832 he exhibited at the West of Scotland Academy from 22 Windsor Street, Edinburgh and in 1835 his address was 5 Royal Terrace in the same city. He appears to have been closely involved with the Scottish Academy, being employed as a drawing tutor in 1833 and donating casts of the *Apollo Belvedere* and *Diana* in the same year. He was also made an honorary member of the Academy.

It is noteworthy that Westmacott's Scottish sculpture appears to have been of a rather more elevated nature than his known work in London. A large proportion of his Edinburgh output was busts, a genre of sculpture which does not feature as part of his pre-1830 oeuvre, and these include some distinguished commissions, such as the portrait of President Jackson of the USA (**75**) and the bust of Sir Walter Scott (**74**). His bust of Nicolò Paganini, with hair and side whiskers animated like sea-creatures, was probably carved to mark the virtuoso violinist's visit to Britain in 1831–2 (**68**).

In 1836 he exhibited for the last time at the Scottish Academy, showing a model of a cenotaph for a monument to Sir Walter Scott, to be erected in New York. Westmacott died in 1861 at Newcastle-upon-Tyne. Gunnis's lukewarm verdict on Westmacott's work was that his monuments were 'competent, but not outstanding' (*Gunnis* 1968, 421).

MGS

Literary References: *Farington* vol 15, 5140; *Graves* VIII, 1905–6, 235; *Rinder and McKay* 1917, 415; *Gunnis* 1968, 421–2; *Colvin* VI, 1973–6, 131, 485; *Woodward* 1977 (vol 1, pt 2), 264; *Busco* 1994, 7; *Morris and Roberts* 1998, 643

Archival References: Westmacott/Harvey; Soane Bill Book G fols 205–6 (Lord Carrington's house); GPC; IGI

Additional MS Sources: Sun Insurance, policies for 25 Mount Street, 1820, 11936/483/962846–7, 966271–2; Westmacott/Cornewall

Will: Richard Westmacott I, PROB 11/1483/253–4

Funerary Monuments

1.	†1783	Sarah Beavis	Stadhampton, Oxon	S	Pevsner, *Oxon*, 1974, 776
2.	?1796	Henry Roberts	Swanscombe, Kent		*Gunnis* 1968, 421
3.	†1798	Sir Joseph Mawbey	Chertsey, Surrey		Pevsner, *Surrey*, 1971, 148
4.	?1799	John Cocks	Eastnor, Herefs		*Gunnis* 1968, 421
5.	?1800	Goodbehere family	St Mary, Lambeth, London		*Gunnis* 1968, 421
6.	?1800	John D'Oyly	Hambleden, Bucks		*Gunnis* 1968, 421
7.	c1800	Sir Nicholas Carew	Beddington, Surrey		*Gunnis* 1968, 421
8.	†1807	Martha Dear	[St Martin, Chichester, Sussex]; St Olave, Chichester, Sussex	S	Pevsner, *Sussex*, 1965, 179
9.	?1807	Thomas Davis	Horningsham, Wilts		*Gunnis* 1968, 421
10.	†1808	Ernest Udny	Chichester Cathedral, Sussex	S	*Kemp* 1985, 26 (repr)
11.	?1808	Mary Heaton	Wyddial, Herts		*Gunnis* 1968, 421
12.	?1808	Robert Donald	Norwood, Middx		*Gunnis* 1968, 422
13.	?1809	Lieutenant-Colonel Donaldson	Harwich, Essex		*Gunnis* 1968, 422
14.	1806–1810	Unspecified work in connection with Nelson's tomb Payment(s): £173	St Paul's Cathedral, London		*Gunnis* 1968, 421
15.	1811	Blencowe family	Hayes, Middlesex		GPC
16.	?1811	Elizabeth Tchitchagoff	Beddington, Surrey		*Gunnis* 1968, 422
17.	?1811	Hon Mrs Finch	Voelas, Denbighs		GPC
18.	1811	John Isham (†1746) Payment(s): £113 10s	Lamport, Northants	S	Isham Archives, Northants RO IL 1451; *Gunnis* 1968, 422; Pevsner, *Northants*, 1973, 286; C Lib (repr)
19.	†1811	Lady Rebecca Gibbons	Stanwell, Middx	S	
20.	?1812	James Garth	Mitcham, Surrey		*Gunnis* 1968, 422
21.	†1812	Lieutenant Harrington RN	Hartest, Suffolk		Pevsner, *Suffolk*, 1974, 250
22.	?1813	Jeremiah Dyson	Crowhurst, Sussex		*Gunnis* 1968, 422
23.	?1814	Dudley Wyatt	Heavitree, Devon		*Gunnis* 1968, 422
24.	†1814	Edmund Estcourt	Shipton Moyne, Glos	S	*CIIA* 4/4/91 (repr)
25.	†1814	Sarah Newton Kerr	St James, Montego Bay, Jamaica	S	*Gunnis* 1968, 422; C Lib (repr)
26.	?1815	Georgiana Reay	Hambleden, Bucks		*Gunnis* 1968, 422
27.	c1815	Lieutenant John Beresford (†1812)	Westminster Abbey, London, north transept		Pevsner, *London I*, 1973, 448
28.	?1815	Thomas Cuff	Teddington, Middx		*Gunnis* 1968, 422
29.	†1816	Philip Antrobus	Cheam, Surrey, Lumley chapel		Pevsner, *Surrey*, 1971, 145
30.	†1817	Sir John Palmer Bt	East Carlton, Northants		*CIIA* 4/3/62 (repr)
31.	1817	Thomas Palmer (†1810)	East Carlton, Northants	S	*CIIA* 4/3/61 (repr)
32.	?1818	John Hey	Passenham, Northants		RG/JP, 9, 1547
33.	†1818	John James	Hamstead Marshall, Berks		*Gunnis* 1968, 422
34.	†1818	Lieutenant Robert Ashmead Billamore	Mumbai (Bombay) Cathedral, India	S	*Groseclose* 1995, 133 n15; C Lib (repr)
35.	†1819	Henrietta Peere-Williams	Broxbourne, Herts	S	Pevsner, *Herts*, 1977, 114; C Lib (repr)
36.	?1819	Louisa Baldock	Southover, Sussex		*Gunnis* 1968, 422
37.	†1820	Edward Jones	Llandeilo's Fan, Powys	S	Pevsner, *Powys*, 1979, 333
38.	?1820	Rev Andrew Downes	Witham, Essex		*Gunnis* 1968, 422
39.	†1820	Richard Milles	North Elmham, Norfolk		Pevsner, *Norfolk: N-W & S*, 1999, 569
40.	1820	William Caxton	[intended for Westminster Abbey, but although completed, still unerected in 1823]; untraced		Abbey Muniments RC 0.2; Dibdin 1836, 386–9
41.	†1820	William Mills	Barford, Warks		Pevsner, *Warks*, 1966, 85
42.	†1821	George Ede	Jesus church, Pear Tree Green, Hants	S	Pevsner, *Hants & Isle of Wight*, 1967, 593; C Lib (repr)

No.	Date	Subject		Location		References
43.	?1821	Lucy Bayley		Little Stukeley, Hunts		*Gunnis* 1968, 422
44.	†1821	Samuel Goodbehere		St Mary, Lambeth, London		Pevsner, *London: S*, 1983, 337
45.	†1821	William Wilson		Nether Worton, Oxon	S	Pevsner, *Oxon*, 1974, 714; C Lib (repr)
46.	†1822	Joseph Smith		Newport, Essex		*Gunnis* 1968, 422; C Lib (repr)
47.	†1822	Sir Isaac Heard		St George's Chapel, Windsor, Berks	S	*Gunnis* 1968, 422; *Bond* 1999, 157
48.	†1823	Hardin Burnley and his two daughters (†1803 & 1804)		St Pancras new church, London	S	
49.	?1823	Sarah Stokes		Clifton Campville, Staffs		*Gunnis* 1968, 422
50.	†1824	Lord William Gordon		Whitkirk, W R Yorks	S	*Gunnis* 1968, 421; C Lib (repr)
51.	1828	Caleb Dickinson (†1821) Payment(s): £500 with the monument to Robert Hugh Munro		St John the Evangelist, Black River, Jamaica	S	*Lewis* 1965–1967, 17–18, 62 (repr); *Penny* 1977 (1), 197, n62; *Coutu* 1998, 50, n32
52.	1828	Robert Hugh Munro (†1798) Payment(s): £500 with the monument to Caleb Dickinson		St John the Evangelist, Black River, Jamaica	S	*Lewis* 1965–1967, 17, 62 (repr); *Penny* 1977 (1), 197, n62; *Coutu* 1998, 50, n32
53.	?1829	Richard Allnutt		Penshurst, Kent		*Gunnis* 1968, 422
54.	1832	Andrew Miller Model(s): Exhib R Sc A, 324, medallion only; untraced		St John the Evangelist, Black River, Jamaica		*Rinder and McKay* 1917, 415; *Lewis* 1965–1967, 62
55.	1832	Medallion portrait, model for a monument		[Exhib L'pool Ac, 380]; untraced		*Morris and Roberts* 1998, 643
56.	1832	Sketch for unspecified monument		[Exhib R Sc A, 334]; untraced		*Rinder and McKay* 1917, 416
57.	1833	Sir Walter Scott, granite cenotaph surmounted by a bust, model		[Exhib R Sc A, 321; 1836, 416 'to be erected by subscription at New York']; untraced		*Rinder and McKay* 1917, 416
Busts						
58.	1830	A lady		[Exhib L'pool Ac, 282]; untraced		*Morris and Roberts* 1998, 643
59.	1830	Dr Valpy		[Exhib L'pool Ac, 281]; untraced		*Morris and Roberts* 1998, 643
60.	1830	John Bowie		[Exhib IEFAS, 164]; untraced		*Rinder and McKay* 1917, 415
61.	1830	Miss Dougal		[Exhib IEFAS, 163]; untraced		*Rinder and McKay* 1917, 415
62.	1831	A glass case containing three small busts, the Duke of Kent, Dr Richard Valpy and a deceased artist	w	[Exhib L'pool Ac, 402]; untraced		*Rinder and McKay* 1917, 415; *Morris and Roberts* 1998, 643; *Gunnis* 1968, 421
63.	1831	A young midshipman in the East India Company's service		[Exhib L'pool Ac, 397]; untraced		*Morris and Roberts* 1998, 643
64.	1831	Unidentified gentleman		[Exhib L'pool Ac, 395]; untraced		*Morris and Roberts* 1998, 643
65.	1831	Unidentified woman		[Exhib R Sc A, 387]; untraced		*Rinder and McKay* 1917, 415
66.	1831	Unidentified woman		[Exhib R Sc A, 389]; untraced		*Rinder and McKay* 1917, 415
67.	1832	John Mackintosh, MD	m	[Exhib R Sc A, 333]; untraced Other versions: 'Miniature bust' (possibly identifiable with the above), exhib L'pool Ac, 398		*Rinder and McKay* 1917, 416; *Morris and Roberts* 1998, 643
68.	1832	Nicolò Paganini	m	[coll Sir Henry Tate]; VAM A.12-1955 Other versions: A miniature version, exhib L'pool Ac, 1832, 396	SD	*Graves* VIII, 1905–6, 235; *Rinder and McKay* 1917, 416; *Morris and Roberts* 1998, 643; *Bilbey* 2002, 428 (repr)
69.	1832	Rev Dr Grant	m	[Exhib R Sc A, 332]; untraced		*Rinder and McKay* 1917, 415
70.	1832	Young lady, model 'to be executed in marble'		[Exhib L'pool Ac, 385]; untraced		*Morris and Roberts* 1998, 643
71.	1833	Alexander Rowe, 'The Adonis of Devon'	m	[Exhib R Sc A, 319; Exhib RA, London, 1836, 1101]; private coll		*Graves* VIII, 1905–6, 235; *Rinder and McKay* 1917, 416; GPC
72.	1833	Mrs Captain James Archibald Campbell, posthumous		[Exhib R Sc A, 318]; untraced		*Rinder and McKay* 1917, 416
73.	1833	Rev John Sinclair, of Edinburgh		[Exhib R Sc A, 316]; untraced		*Rinder and McKay* 1917, 416
74.	1833	Sir Walter Scott, on a verd antique scagliola pedestal Payment(s): £23 3s in 1864		[Oppenheim sale, Christie, 4 June 1864, lot 59]; untraced		*Graves* VIII, 1905–6, 235; *Rinder and McKay* 1917, 416; *Gunnis* 1968, 421; *Morris and Roberts* 1998, 643
75.	1835	General Jackson, President of the United States, model 'to be executed in marble'		[Exhib R Sc A, 354]; untraced		*Rinder and McKay* 1917, 416
76.	1835	Peter Borthwick, MP		[Exhib R Sc A, 353]; untraced		*Rinder and McKay* 1917, 416
77.	nd	Unidentified man	m	Edinburgh College of Art, Scotland		*Woodward* 1977, vol 1, pt 2, 264
Chimneypieces						
78.	1808	Of 'bardiglio' marble	m	[Kensington Palace, London]; untraced		TNA WORK, 5/97-5/101; *Gunnis* 1968, 421
79.	1808	'Of spar marble inlaid with mouldings and ornaments of statuary marble in the frieze' Payment(s): £50		[Kensington Palace, London]; untraced		TNA WORK, 5/97-5/101; *Gunnis* 1968, 421
80.	1808	Several, one inlaid with mouldings and ornaments of statuary marble in frieze and pilasters Payment(s): £40		[Kensington Palace, London, drawing room]; untraced		TNA WORK 5/97; *Gunnis* 1968, 421
81.	1808	Two, with circular reeded profiles, moulded cornice, panelled frieze and pilaster Payment(s): £100	m	[Kensington Palace, London]; untraced		TNA WORK 5/97-5/101; *Gunnis* 1968, 421
82.	1809	Several, including two in marble with circular reeded profiles and bronze metal columns Payment(s): £222 (including £86 for the above named)		[Kensington Palace, London]; untraced		TNA WORK, 5/98; *Gunnis* 1968, 421

83.	1812	Seven Payment(s): £267		[Kensington Palace, London]; untraced	TNA WORK, 5/101; *Gunnis* 1968, 421
84.	1814	Description unavailable	m	[Stoneleigh Abbey, Warks]; untraced	Stoneleigh Accounts DR 18/17/40/25, 27
85.	1810–1820	Description unavailable	m	Dodington Park, Glos, drawing room	Codrington Accounts D1610/A96; GPC; Pevsner, *Glos: Cotswolds*, 1999, 318
86.	1823	Description unavailable Payment(s): £448	m	Brighton Pavilion, Sussex	*Gunnis* 1968, 421
Architectural Sculpture					
87.	1810–1812	Capitals and other work		Dodington Park, Glos	Codrington Accounts D1610/A77
88.	1814	Eighteen pilaster capitals Payment(s): £990		Royal Naval College, Greenwich (ORNC), King Charles quadrangle	TNA Ad. 68/884; *Gunnis* 1968, 421
89.	1814	Six Corinthian capitals of Portland stone Payment(s): £450	s	Royal Naval College, Greenwich (ORNC), King Charles quadrangle	TNA Ad. 68/884; *Gunnis* 1968, 421
90.	1816	Pyramid on the mausoleum (repairs only) Payment(s): Over £500		Cobham Hall, Kent	*Gunnis* 1968, 421
91.	1822	Marble plinth Payment(s): £32	m	[Brighton Pavilion, Sussex]; untraced	*Gunnis* 1968, 421
92.	1807–1822	Ornaments including carving on the oriel, a rose and a frieze		[Fonthill, Wilts]; untraced	*Alexander* 1957, 186, 189, 217, 221, 304
93.	1823	Pedestal for the statue of Achilles by Sir Richard Westmacott RA (co-sculptor: George Westmacott) Payment(s): £801		Hyde Park, London	*Gunnis* 1968, 421
94.	1831	Work 'on the sculpture to the triumphal arch at the new palace in St James's'		Buckingham Palace, London	TNA WORK Ad. 68/884 19/3 f180
Miscellaneous					
95.	c1817	Chimneypiece and masonry work Payment(s): £1,265		[Carlton House, London, gothic dining room]; destroyed	*Carlton House*, 1991–2, 222

WESTMACOTT, James Sherwood 1823–1900

He was born in London on 27 August 1823, the son of **Henry Westmacott** and Eliza, née Brodie Stewart. According to his contemporary, William Hooe, Westmacott was educated first in Edinburgh and then at the German city of Neuwied on the River Rhine. He subsequently studied sculpture at the Dresden Academy under Professor Ernst Rietschel, and in 1845 won a medal from the Academy for a figure of *Victory*, which he exhibited at the Royal Academy in London the following year (**12**).

Westmacott showed at the Westminster Hall exhibition of 1844 and his figures of King Alfred and Richard I won him favourable notice (**10, 11**). The *Literary Gazette* remarked that both works evinced 'much knowledge of the figure and spirit of execution' (*Lit Gaz* 1844, 467). Alfred's statue was singled out for attention by the German critic, Dr Forster, and by the *Art Union*, who called it 'one of the most elegant and impressive statues we have ever seen' (*AU* 1844, 215). In 1847 Westmacott was chosen to execute two of the statues commissioned for the House of Lords of barons who had signed Magna Carta (**23, 24**). Formidable in their chainmail and both grasping weapons, these were cast in zinc and coated with copper by Messrs Elkington, who were later to produce bronze replicas of Westmacott's *Satan overthrown* (**14**).

In 1849 Westmacott gave two addresses in the Royal Academy catalogue, Lauriston Cottage, Whetstone, Middx and Rome. He signed some works from the Eternal City: the Canova-esque *Penitent Magdalene* (**78**) and the statue of Geoffrey de Mandeville (**23**). His stay in Rome cannot have been a long one, however, for the following year he was back in London, living at 1, St John's Place, Lisson Grove.

Westmacott produced many miniature statues of biblical and literary subjects in the 1850s. Examples of the former are *Ruth at the well* (**15**), and of the latter, *The Peri at the gates of paradise* from Thomas Moore's *Lalla Rookh* (**18**). This has a single winged female figure and was praised in the Press as an accurate realisation in sculpture of the verse, 'perfectly fulfilled by the language of sorrow which is pronounced by the lineaments, and written on every tournure of the composition' (*AJ* 1855, 184). The work was exhibited at the Paris Exhibition in 1855 and at the International Exhibition of 1862, when it was reproduced in the *Illustrated London News* and again in the *Art Journal*. In the latter it was lauded as 'a favourable example of the delicious sentimentality which is now suffused into the marble illustrations of our popular lyrics and dramas' (*AJ Cat* 1862, 323).

In 1857 Westmacott was responsible for extensive work on the reredos in Newcastle Cathedral, which has numerous statues of various sizes, within an ornate Gothic frame (**58**). His monuments are relatively few in number, although well-carved and composed with decorum. That to Sir Gilbert East has the inscription written diagonally on a sail apparently before the wreck of a ship (**5**); the brackets take the form of sea shells. Louisa Brockman's monument has figures of *Hope* and *Religion* (**4**).

During the 1860s Westmacott appears to have been principally concerned with ideal works, most of them statuettes and two of his portraits were exhibited with lines from Byron (**51, 52**). Occasionally he won commissions for poetic works on a grander scale, for instance the cup-bearing statue of Alexander the Great, a *contrapposto* figure provided for the Mansion House, London (**28**) and the seated, heavily-draped figure of *Chryseis* (**32**).

The *Art Journal* recorded in 1860 how 'in the last few years' Westmacott 'has come prominently before the public' (*AJ* 1860, 172), and they illustrated and commented upon his work regularly over succeeding years. The *Fountain nymph* (**25**) was praised as a satisfactory rendering of the subject, *L'Allegro* for its originality, and the reliefs of *Mercy* and *Truth* for their 'fine feeling' (**66**) (*AJ* 1860, 172). The *Illustrated London News* was also alert to Westmacott's talents and illustrated his works on nine occasions. He exhibited at the Royal Academy until 1885.

Westmacott's studio was at 21 Wilton Place in 1858, the home also of his cousin, **Richard Westmacott III**. By 1876 he was at 49 Hugh Street, Eccleston Square. In 1881 he was living in Clapham, where the census records him as having three daughters, Fanny, Alice and Violet, and one servant. He died in Union Road on 16 September 1900, an was buried in Norwood cemetery. A side altar in St Peter, Manor Street, Clapham forms a memorial to him and wa donated by his son-in-law and daughter, Mr and Mrs O'Leary.

MG

Literary References: *AJ* 1853, 152; 1860, 172; *Graves* 1875, 1852; *Hooe* 1880, 24; *Graves* VIII, 1905–6, 235; *Gunnis* 1968, 422; *Read* 1982, 245–6; *Bilbe* 2002, 429

Archival References: Archives, Artists' Annuity Fund; GPC

Collections of Drawings: Album of 34 drawings on 20 sheets, dating 1844–1856, HMI 22/1992, (*Friedman* 1993, 90)

Funerary Monuments

1.	?1856	Rev George Vanbrugh		Aughton, Lancs		*Gunnis* 1968, 422
2.	†1858	Captain Thomas Thruston RN		Pennal, Merioneth		GPC
3.	†1859	William Rason		St Mary, Eastbourne, Sussex		GPC
4.	1866	Louisa Brockman (†1837)		Leybourne, Kent	S	C Lib (repr)
5.	†1866	Sir Gilbert East		Hurley, Berks	S	*Gunnis* 1968, 422; C Lib (repr)
6.	?1867	Martha Wethered		Marlow, Berks	S	*Gunnis* 1968, 422
7.	?1867	Owen Wethered		Marlow, Berks	S	*Gunnis* 1968, 422
8.	?1869	John Francis Bassett		Illogan, Cornwall	S	*Gunnis* 1968, 422
9.	?1881	W and E J Janson		Fairlight, Sussex		RG/JP, 9, 1552

Statues

10.	1844	Alfred the Great, small statue		[Exhib Westminster Hall, London, 120]; untraced		*AU* 1844, 215; *Lit Gaz*, 20 July 1844, 467; *Gunnis* 1968, 422
11.	1844	Richard I planting the standard of England on the walls of Acre, half-size		[Exhib Westminster Hall, London, 137]; untraced		*AU* 1844, 216; *Lit Gaz* 1844, 467; *Gunnis* 1968, 422
12.	1845	Victory in the act of rising to crown the victor, a figure Drawing(s): Pencil, HMI, Leeds, 22/1992		[Dresden Acad, gold medal; exhib RA, London, 1846, 1405]; untraced		*Graves* VIII, 1905–6, 235; *Friedman* 1993, 9, 90 cat 7 (drawing repr)
13.	1849	Joseph Baxendale, statuette	m	[Exhib RA, London, 1254]; private coll, London	S	*Graves* VIII, 1905–6, 235
14.	1849	Satan overthrown, statuette		[coll Mr Theophilus Burnand]; untraced Other versions: several cast in bronze by Messrs Elkington, 1853; untraced		*Graves* 1875, 580; *Gunnis* 1968, 422
15.	1852	Ruth at the well, statuette	m	untraced	SD	C Lib (repr)
16.	1853	Samson and the lion, group (lion modelled by Julius Haeknal)	p	[Exhib RA, London, 1310]; untraced		*AJ* 1853, 151; *Graves* VIII, 1905–6, 235
17.	1854	'Mary sat at Jesus' feet and heard his word' – Luke, x, 39, group	p	[Exhib RA, London, 1394]; untraced		*Graves* VIII, 1905–6, 235
18.	1855	The Peri at the gates of paradise, from Moore's 'Lalla Rookh' Payment(s): Silvered casts offered for 10 gns; marble for 100 gns	m	[Exhib RA, London, 1416; 1856, 1227; 1876, 1477; Exhib BI, 1861, 645; Paris Int Exhib]; untraced		*AJ* 1855, 184; *Manchester Art Treasurses* 1857, 133; *AJ Cat* 1862, 313, 323 (repr); *ILN* 30 Aug 1862, 240 (repr); *Graves* 1875, 580; *Graves* VIII, 1905–6, 235, 236
19.	1857	David playing before Saul, statuette	m	[Exhib BI, London, 567]; untraced		*Graves* 1875, 580
20.	1857	Rev Robert Philips, vicar of Yeovil, posthumous statuette	m	[Exhib RA, London, 1351]; untraced		*Graves* VIII, 1905–6, 235
21.	1858	Autumn, statuette Payment(s): Offered for 130 gns	m	[Exhib RA, London, 1858, 1254; 1867, 1009 Exhib BI, London, 1866, 648]; untraced		*Graves* 1875, 581; *Graves* VIII, 1905–6, 235, 236
22.	1858	Eve and the serpent, statuette Payment(s): Offered for £125	m	[Exhib BI, London, 586 Exhib RA, London, 1865, 892; ?1871, 1307; 1885, 2053]; untraced		*Graves* VIII, 1905–6, 236; *Graves* 1875, 580
23.	1847–1858	Geoffrey de Mandeville, Earl of Gloucester (†1216)		Palace of Westminster, London, House of Lords	S	*ILN*, 13 March 1852, 216 (repr); *Walker* 1961, 31, 97–8, cat no 32
24.	1847–1858	Saher de Quency, Earl of Winchester (†1219) Model(s): Gt Exhib, London, 1851		Palace of Westminster, London, House of Lords		*AJ Cat* 1851, 108 (repr); *AJ* 1853, 152; *Walker* 1961, 77, 97–8, cat 81; *Graves* VIII, 1905–6, 235
25.	1860	'Fair the greeting face ascends, like a naiad's daughter, when the gentle maiden bends to the trembling water', cabinet statue of a girl at a fountain (Fountain nymph) Payment(s): offered for 120 gns		[Exhib RA, London, 948; ?1864, 886; 1884, 1706 Exhib BI, London, 1865, 648]; untraced		*AJ* 1860, 172; 1862, 216 (repr); *Graves* 1875, 581; *Graves* VIII, 1905–6, 235; *Johnson* 1975, 496
26.	1860	Il Penseroso, statuette Payment(s): offered for £130	m	[Exhib BI, London, 635; exhib RA, London, 1862, 993]; untraced		*AJ* 1862, 137; *Graves* 1875, 580; *Graves* VIII, 1905–6, 235
27.	1860	L'Allegro, statuette Payment(s): offered for £130	m	[Exhib BI, London, 634; exhib RA, London, 1862, 995]; untraced		*AJ* 1862, 137; *Graves* 1875, 580; *Graves* VIII, 1905–6, 236
28.	1861–1863	Alexander the Great	m	CL Coll, Mansion House, City of London, Egyptian Hall, acc 126	S	*AJ* 1863, 116; *ILN* 23 May 1863, 569 (repr); *Graves* VIII, 1905–6, 236; *Knight* 1986, 350 (repr)
29.	1865	Adam, statuette	m	[Exhib RA, London, 902]; untraced		*Graves* VIII, 1905–6, 236
30.	1865	'Missie going to bed', portrait statuette of Miss L E Maling Wynch		[Exhib RA, London, 944]; untraced		*Graves* VIII, 1905–6, 236

31.	1866	Sappho, statuette	m	[Exhib RA, London, 918; 1879, 1534]; untraced		*Graves* VIII, 1905–6, 236
32.	1867	Chryseis		Laing Art Gallery, Newcastle-upon-Tyne	SD	*Graves* VIII, 1905–6, 236; *Read* 1982, 202, 203 (repr)
33.	1867	Modesty, statuette	m	[Exhib RA, London, 1017]; untraced		*Graves* VIII, 1905–6, 236
34.	1867	Resting	m	[Exhib RA, London, 1160]; untraced		*Graves* VIII, 1905–6, 236
35.	1867	Subject from Ovid: 'Here as I lay, and swelled with tears the flood, etc', statuette Payment(s): offered for 80 gns	m	[Exhib BI, London, 626]; untraced		*Graves* 1875, 581
36.	1868	Elaine (from Tennyson), statuette		[Exhib RA, London, 981]; untraced		*ILN* 9 May 1868, 464 (repr); *Graves* VIII, 1905–6, 236
37.	1868	Two sisters and their infant brother, portrait group	m	[Exhib RA, London, 952]; untraced		*Graves* VIII, 1905–6, 236
38.	1869	A child with a swan, group		[Exhib RA, London, 1193]; untraced		*ILN* 12 June 1869, 593 (repr); *Graves* VIII, 1905–6, 236
39.	1870	Enid (from Tennyson), statuette	m	[Exhib RA, London, 1144]; untraced		*Graves* VIII, 1905–6, 236
40.	1870	Jephthah's daughter, statuette	m	[Exhib RA, London, 1149]; untraced		*ILN* 16 July 1870, 176 (repr); *Graves* VIII, 1905–6, 236
41.	1870	The guardian angel, figure		[coll Mr Burnand of Lowndes Square]; untraced		*AJ*, 1871 (repr); *Gunnis* 1968, 422
42.	1872	Andromeda, statuette	m	[Exhib RA, London, 1398]; untraced		*ILN* 31 Aug 1872, 205 (repr); *Graves* VIII, 1905–6, 236
43.	1881	Poetry, statuette		[Exhib RA, London, 1507]; untraced		*Graves* VIII, 1905–6, 236
44.	1885	Atalanta, statuette	b	[Exhib RA, London, 2056]; untraced		*Graves* VIII, 1905–6, 236

Busts

45.	1853	Albert, the Prince Consort (in Copeland statuary porcelain)		Royal Coll, Osborne House, I of W Other versions: private coll	SD	
46.	1854	George Barnard	m	[Exhib RA, London, 1424]; untraced		*Graves* VIII, 1905–6, 235
47.	1858	Henry, 1st Marquess of Anglesey (†1854)	m	Plas Newyd, Anglesey	SD	*Graves* VIII, 1905–6, 235; *Marsden* 1999, 49
48.	c1862	Bomanjee Hormarjee Wasia (part of a monumental fountain and clocktower)		Perin Nariman St, Fort Mumbai, (Bombay), India Other versions: Sir J J Parsi Benevolent Institution, Bombay, marble Peoples' Native General Library, Dhobi Talao, marble Wadiaji Atash Behram, Bombay, marble		*Graves* VIII, 1905–6, 236; *Gunnis* 1968, 422; *Giara* 2000, 281–3
49.	1866	Asleep	m	[Exhib RA, London, 961]; untraced		*Graves* VIII, 1905–6, 236
50.	1866	Awake	m	[Exhib RA, London, 965]; untraced		*Graves* VIII, 1905–6, 236
51.	1867	Unknown sitter, exhibited with lines from Byron 'Sleep on and smile, thou young inheritor, etc' Payment(s): offered for 35 gns	m	[Exhib BI, London, 627]; untraced		*Graves* 1875, 581
52.	1867	Unknown sitter, exhibited with lines from Byron 'The morn is up again, etc' Payment(s): offered for 35 gns	m	[Exhib BI, London, 630]; untraced		*Graves* 1875, 581
53.	1869	Unidentified lady		[Exhib RA, London, 1174]; untraced		*Graves* VIII, 1905–6, 236
54.	1870	Mrs Ferdinand Rodewald	m	[Exhib RA, London, 1210; 1873, 1567]; untraced		*Graves* VIII, 1905–6, 236
55.	1871	Octavius H Smith	m	[Exhib RA, London, 1268]; untraced		*Graves* VIII, 1905–6, 236
56.	1872	Unidentified gentleman	m	[Exhib RA, London, 1444]; untraced		*Graves* VIII, 1905–6, 236
57.	1883	J Langdon Down, MD, FRCP	m	[Exhib RA, London, 1641]; untraced		*Graves* VIII, 1905–6, 236

Architectural Sculpture

58.	1857	35 figures on the reredos, including the Four Evangelists, St Aidan and angels		Newcastle Cathedral		*Read* 1982, 245 (repr), 246
59.	1858	Font, with angels on columns	s	St Mary, Stoke Newington		*ILN* 11 Sept 1858, 246 (repr); Pevsner, *London: N*, 1998, 535
60.	1862	Fountain, with a figure of a woman and two swans (designed by Richard Westmacott the Younger RA, and manufactured by Messrs Elkington) Model(s): ?Exhib RA, London, 1864, 925		Regent's Park, London, Broad Walk		*ILN* 12 July 1862, 59 (repr); *Graves* VIII, 1905–6, 236; *Gunnis* 1968, 428
61.	1868	Reredos		Little Walston, Bucks		*Gunnis* 1968, 422
62.	1869	Galen, Cicero and Aristotle		Former University of London Headquarters, Burlington Gardens, London, façade		*Read* 1982, 226

Reliefs

63.	1851	Sleep, bas-relief	m	[Exhib RA, London, 1286; 1863, 1046]; untraced		*AJ*, 1851, 162; *Graves* VIII, 1905–6, 235, 236
64.	1853	George Wightwick Rendel		Untraced		NPG cat
65.	1854	H Vignoles, medallion	p	[Exhib RA, London, 1462]; untraced		*Graves* VIII, 1905–6, 235
66.	1859	'Mercy and Truth are met together – Psalm lxxxv, 10', a pair of bas-reliefs Payment(s): £120 in marble with carved oak frame; £10 in plaster (minimum purchase of three), 'coloured like the original £3 extra'		[Exhib L'pool Ac Exhib RA, London, 1048]; untraced		*AJ* 1860, 172; *Graves* VIII, 1905–6, 235; *Morris and Roberts* 1998, 644
67.	1859	Unknown clergyman	p	Untraced	SD	C Lib (repr)
68.	1861	Sir John Franklin, medallion	p	Scott Polar Research Institute		*Ormond* 1973, 182
69.	1861	The east wind, medallion		[Exhib RA, London, 1109]; untraced		*Graves* VIII, 1905–6, 235

70.	1861	The north wind, medallion		[Exhib RA, London, 1110]; untraced		*Graves* VIII, 1905–6, 235
71.	1861	The south wind, medallion		[Exhib RA, London, 1111]; untraced		*Graves* VIII, 1905–6, 235
72.	1861	The west wind, medallion		[Exhib RA, London, 1108]; untraced		*Graves* VIII, 1905–6, 235
73.	c1872	The artist's daughter? (Constance Westmacott)	m	VAM A.12-1968		*Graves* VIII, 1905–6, 236; *Bilbey* 2002, 429 (repr)
74.	1873	Alice, alto-relievo	m	[Exhib RA, London, 1587]; untraced		*Graves* VIII, 1905–6, 236
75.	1878	Ecce homo, alto-relievo		[Exhib RA, London, 1434]; untraced		*Graves* VIII, 1905–6, 236
76.	1879	Alice Kendall, alto-relievo	m	[Exhib RA, London, 1451]; untraced		*Graves* VIII, 1905–6, 236
77.	1879	Francesca da Rimini, bas-relief	pb	[Exhib RA, London, 1468]; untraced		*Graves* VIII, 1905–6, 236
Miscellaneous						
78.	1849	Penitent Magdalene		[Exhib RA, London, 1850, 1349]; Christie, 14 May 1987, lot 219; untraced	SD	*Graves* VIII, 1905–6, 235
79.	1850	Evening		[Exhib RA, London, 1327]; untraced		*Graves* VIII, 1905–6, 235
80.	1850	Morning		[Exhib RA, London, 1330]; untraced		*Graves* VIII, 1905–6, 235
81.	1859	The triumph of Judith		[Exhib RA, London, 1232]; untraced		*Graves* VIII, 1905–6, 235
82.	1862	Queen Eleanor sucking poison from the arm of Edward I Payment(s): Copies in plaster offered for 10 gns each	p	[Exhib BI, London, 641]; untraced		*Graves* 1875, 581
83.	1869	Hypatia	m	[Exhib RA, London, 1204]; untraced		*Graves* VIII, 1905–6, 236
84.	1877	Arthur and Guinevere (from Tennyson)		[Exhib RA, London, 1453]; untraced		*Graves* VIII, 1905–6, 236
85.	1880	Grace Harvey (from Charles Kingsley's 'Two Years Ago')		[Exhib RA, London, 1523]; untraced		*Graves* VIII, 1905–6, 236

WESTMACOTT, Richard I 1746/7–1808

The first of a notable family of sculptors and architects, he was the son of Richard and Abigail Westmacott and was baptised at Stockport, Cheshire on 15 March 1746 or 1747. A later account says that he was educated at Brasenose College Oxford, but 'gave up all pursuit of the learned professions early in life and took to the business of a statuary' (*GM* 1856 Part II, 509). This suggestion may be mythical since no record has been found of his attendance at that college.

In September 1774 Westmacott married Sarah (1750–1826), the daughter of **Thomas Vardy**, at St George, Hanover Square, London. Their son, **Sir Richard Westmacott RA**, was born in July the following year, the first of at least 13 children. In 1776 he took an apprentice, **Edward Bone**.

Westmacott's workshop was in Ranelegh Street, Pimlico. His earliest datable works are chimneypieces and include one for Cobham Hall with rustic figures emblematic of *Music* (**69**), which he later adapted for a chimneypiece at Powderham Castle (**79**). In 1777, presumably to encourage custom, he published a set of 20 engraved designs for chimneypieces. The plates were engraved by B and JA Clowes and are rich Adamesque designs incorporating grotesques and rams' heads as well as classical reliefs depicting *Apollo, Flora* and other mythological subjects. Westmacott must have been competing with **Thomas Carter II**, with whose works his productions bear some affinities and Westmacott's prices appear to have been cheaper.

In January 1783 Westmacott held a sale of his stocks of marble and stone and moved to a studio at 25 Mount Street Grosvenor Square. He was responsible for many monuments of conventional design, sometimes featuring a kneeling female mourner (**4, 6**) or a standing figure draping an urn (**5**). He occasionally used multi-coloured marbles (**10, 64**) and the carving is usually of a high quality. His masterpiece is the monument to James Lenox Dutton, which has a life-sized angel with outspread wings draped over a double portrait medallion (**33**). From beneath the folds of drapery at her feet emerges an unusually animated and beautifully carved skeleton.

Westmacott's workshop also carried out masonry work. Between 1777 and 1784 he was one of the mastermasons (together with **John Wildsmith** and **Joseph Hawke**) at Gorhambury, near St Albans, which was being built to **Sir Robert Taylor**'s designs. In 1781 he laid down the marble floor in the Methuen chapel in the aisle of North Wraxall church, Somerset, and in 1790 he carried out work on Lord Cremorne's properties in Stanhope Street and Chelsea London. In 1796 he was granted a royal appointment as mason for Kensington Palace and at the turn of the century he was working at Woburn Abbey, where he repaired and polished antique columns, laid yellow and black marble paving, and created a mosaic marble floor.

In the 1790s Westmacott carved several monuments to designs by the architect James Wyatt. The compositions are simple and classical: the monument to Joseph May consists of an urn on an altar decorated with rams' heads (**47**) and the monument to the Earl of Pembroke is simply a severe sarcophagus (**39**). Wyatt appears to have been a friend as well as a collaborator. Farington recorded them dining together, and in June 1796 both were involved in canvassing for Sir Alan Gardner in the Westminster election against Charles James Fox and Horne Tooke. The connection proved helpful to the family as Wyatt later recommended Westmacott's son, Sir Richard, for several commissions.

Westmacott's business appears to have flourished in the 1790s, but foundered at the turn of the century and he was declared bankrupt in 1803. After a long illness he died on 27 February 1808. In his will, proved in July, he left all his goods, including the house in Mount Street and his cottage in Woodlands, to his wife Sarah. It appears that he and his son Richard had a prior agreement that Richard would provide funds for the upbringing of younger members of the family. The business would be owned jointly by Sarah and **Henry Westmacott** and be run by Henry in the interests of the family for seven years, after which time it was to belong exclusively to Henry. James Wyatt and his nephew Jeffrey were to be asked to act as mourners at the funeral.

Two of Westmacott's other children, **George Westmacott** and **Charles Molloy Westmacott** became sculptors, whilst Thomas (†1798), John and William Berners Westmacott trained as architects.

MGS

Literary References: *Westmacott* 1777; *Farington*, vol 2, 573, 577, 578, vol 3, 947; vol 4, 1310; Notices, *Monthly Mag*, 2, 1803, 58; *GM* 1856, part II 509; *Gunnis* 1968, 423; *Binney* 1984, 86; *Whinney* 1988, 316; *Busco* 1994, *passim*; *Clifford* 1995, 64; *Colvin* 1995, *passim*

Archival References: Apprenticeship Lists, PRO; *Methuen Archives; Westmacott-Cremorne Bills*; IGI

Will: PROB 11/1483, 253–4

Auction Catalogues: Westmacott R I, 1783

Funerary Monuments

1.	†1763	Elizabeth Egerton (designed by James Wyatt)	Rostherne, Cheshire	S	*Busco* 1994, 172 n17
2.	†1770	George Willy	Devizes, Wilts		*Gunnis* 1968, 423
3.	?1771	Richard Benyon	Margaretting, Essex		*Gunnis* 1968, 423
4.	?1773	Thomas Ashton	Bowdon, Cheshire		*Gunnis* 1968, 423
5.	†1774	Elizabeth Plampin	Shimpling, Suffolk		Pevsner, *Suffolk*, 1974, 416; *Gunnis* 1968, 423
6.	†1774	Thomas Assheton Smith	Bowdon, Cheshire	S	Pevsner, *Cheshire*, 1971, 110
7.	†1775	William Peareth	Newcastle Cathedral		Pevsner, *Northumbs*, 1992, 423
8.	†1776	Katherine A'Court (designed by James Wyatt)	St Mary, Cheltenham, Glos		*Colvin* 1995, 1120–1
9.	†1776	Mary Coxwell	Ryton, Salop	S	
10.	†1778	Elizabeth Jeaffreson	Dullingham, Cambs		*Penny* 1977 (1), 8 (repr)
11.	?1779	Prince Sutton	Devizes, Wilts		*Gunnis* 1968, 423
12.	†1780	Anne Dewes	St Mary, Cheltenham, Glos		RG/JP, 9, 1554
13.	?1780	Mary Edwards	St Mary Redcliffe, Bristol		*Gunnis* 1968, 423
14.	†1781	Sir Thomas Stapleton	Rotherfield Greys, Oxon		Pevsner, *Oxon*, 1974, 735; *Gunnis* 1968, 423
15.	?1782	Charles Rich	Grosvenor chapel, London		*Gunnis* 1968, 423
16.	†1782	Matthew Knapp	Little Linford, Bucks		Pevsner, *Bucks*, 1994, 440
17.	?1782	Sir James Burrow	Lingfield, Surrey		*Gunnis* 1968, 423
18.	†1783	Thomas Fowle	Charlton, Wilts	S	Pevsner, *Wilts*, 1975, 164
19.	†1784	Rev James Tattershall	Chipstead, Surrey	S	Pevsner, *Surrey*, 1971, 157
20.	1784	Sarah Shrimpton (†1783)	All Saints, High Wycombe, Bucks		Pevsner, *Bucks*, 1994, 386
21.	†1784	Unidentified subject	St John, Devizes, Wilts		Pevsner, *Wilts*, 1975, 207
22.	?1785	Lady Fagg	Chartham, Kent		*Gunnis* 1968, 423
23.	?1786	John Luther	Kelvedon Hatch, Essex		*Gunnis* 1968, 423
24.	?1787	Catherine Buckridge	Lichfield Cathedral, Staffs		*Gunnis* 1968, 423
25.	?1787	Elizabeth King	Longcot, Berks		*Gunnis* 1968, 423
26.	†1787	Richard Garth	Morden, Surrey	S	*Gunnis* 1968, 423
27.	?1788	William Handley	Newark, Notts		*Gunnis* 1968, 423
28.	†1789	Christopher Jeaffreson	Dullingham, Cambs		*Gunnis* 1968, 423
29.	†1790	Anthony Addington	St Michael, Fringford, Oxon		Pevsner, *Oxon*, 1974, 608; *Gunnis* 1968, 423
30.	1790	Rev Thomas Woolis	St Peter & St Paul, Fareham, Hants		Pevsner, *Hants & Isle of Wight*, 1967, 220
31.	1790	William Lowndes Stone (†1772) and wife, Catherine (†1789)	Brightwell Baldwin, Oxon	SD	*Gunnis* 1968, 423; Pevsner, *Oxon*, 1974, 485
32.	?1791	James and Mary Sutton	Devizes, Wilts		*Gunnis* 1968, 423
33.	1791	James Lenox Dutton and his second wife, Jane (both †1776)	Sherborne, Glos	SD	*Whinney* 1988, 316 (repr)
34.	†1791	Richard Heaton	St Marcella, Denbighs		Pevsner, *Clwyd*, 1994, 153
35.	†1792	Rev Edward Emily	Old Woking, Surrey	S	Pevsner, *Surrey*, 1971, 397
36.	†1793	Mary Elizabeth Crawford (designed by Joseph Bonomi)	King's Langley, Herts	S	Pevsner, *Herts*, 1977, 218; *Busco* 1994, 172 n17; *Colvin* 1995, 143
37.	†1793	William, Viscount Barrington (designed by James Wyatt)	Shrivenham, Berks	S	*Busco* 1994, 172 n17
38.	†1794	Catherine Knapp	Great Linford, Bucks		Pevsner, *Bucks*, 1994, 528
39.	†1794	Henry, 10th Earl of Pembroke and Montgomery (designed by James Wyatt)	Wilton, Wilts	S	*Penny* 1977 (1), 12 (repr); *Colvin* 1995, 1121
40.	†1794	John Griffith	Pentrefoelas, Denbighs		Pevsner, *Clwyd*, 1986, 259
41.	†1794	John Oglander (designed by James Wyatt)	New College, Oxford, chapel	S	Pevsner, *Oxon*, 1974, 172; *Busco* 1994, 172 n17
42.	1794	Sir Lister Holte (†1770)	St Peter & St Paul, Aston, Warks		Pevsner, *Warks* 1966, 148
43.	†1795	Henry Beaufoy	St Mary, Ealing, Middx		Pevsner, *London: N W*, 1991, 166
44.	†1795	Rev Samuel Dennis	St John's College, Oxford, chapel	S	Pevsner, *Oxon*, 1974, 197;
45.	?1795	Sir John Cotton and Sir John Hyde	Landwade, Cambs		*Gunnis* 1968, 423
46.	†1795	Sophia Knapp	Little Linford, Bucks		Pevsner, *Bucks*, 1994, 440
47.	†1796	Joseph May (designed by James Wyatt)	Hale, Hants	S	*Colvin* 1995, 1121
48.	?1796	Richard Benyon	Margaretting, Essex		*Gunnis* 1968, 423
49.	†1797	Cyril Jackson	Stamford, Lincs		Pevsner, *Lincs*, 1989, 692; *Gunnis* 1968, 423
50.	?1797	John Fletcher	Lichfield Cathedral		*Gunnis* 1968, 423
51.	1797	Richard Harrison	[Brompton Chapel, Knightsbridge, London]; destroyed		*GM*, 1797, 10; *Gunnis* 1968, 423
52.	c1798	Henry Blundell and family († to 1798)	Sefton, Lancs	S	
53.	†1798	Lady Lewisham	Compton Verney, Warks, chapel		Pevsner, *Warks*, 1966, 241
54.	?1798	Maria Tate	Mitcham, Surrey		*Gunnis* 1968, 423
55.	1799	Hughes family	Llanfwrog, Denbighs	SD	Pevsner, *Clwyd*, 1986, 213
56.	†1799	Mary, 4th Duchess of Beaufort	Great Badminton, Glos		*CIIA* 4/4/57 (repr)
57.	?1799	Mrs Bunbury	St James, Weybridge, Surrey		*Gunnis* 1968, 423
58.	c1799	Sir Richard Spry (†1775)	St Anthony-in-Roseland, Cornwall	S	Pevsner, *Cornwall*, 1970, 156
59.	?1802	John Colbourne	St Mary, Paddington, London		*Gunnis* 1968, 423
60.	†1802	John Platt	St Michael Cornhill, City of London		Pevsner, *London: City*, 1997, 251
61.	?1803	Mrs Goulburn	St Giles-in-the-Fields, London		*Gunnis* 1968, 423
62.	1804	George Jarvis (†1793)	Bredwardine, Herefs, churchyard	S	*Gunnis* 1968, 423
63.	?1805	Elizabeth Owen	Linton, Cambs		*Gunnis* 1968, 423
64.	1805	Lucy Knightley	Fawsley, Northants		Pevsner, *Northants*, 1973, 214
65.	†1806	Lieutenant William Grant	Garison Church, Portsmouth,	S	

No.	Date	Description		Location	Reference
Chimneypieces					
66.	*c*1774	Description unavailable		Milton Abbey, Dorset, ballroom	Pevsner, *Dorset*, 1972, 293
67.	1776	Several, including those for Miss Damer's dressing room and bedroom Payment(s): those named, £30 and £25 respectively Drawing(s): RIBA library K8/87; K8/89		Milton Abbey, Dorset	*Oswald* 1966, 208–12 (repr)
68.	1777	Several Payment(s): £89 15s 6d		[Gorhambury, Herts]; untraced	Gorhambury Building Accounts, I.B.12; *Gunnis* 1968, 423
69.	1778	With relief tablet and caryatid figures of a piping youth and a girl with a tambourine		Cobham Hall, Kent	*Dale* 1956, 23; *Whinney* 1988, 465
70.	1780	Description unavailable Payment(s): £50		Corsham Court, Wilts	Methuen Papers, 23 March and 20 May 1780; *Gunnis* 1968, 423
71.	1788	Several' Payment(s): £260 in toto (the above named £84 and £63 respectively)	m	[Admiralty coll]; untraced	TNA Ad 17/1; *Gunnis* 1968, 423
72.	1790	Description unavailable Payment(s): £37	m	[Woburn Abbey, Beds]; untraced	*Gunnis* 1968, 423 citing Bedford Archives
73.	*c*1790	Overmantel with relief		Bank of England, City of London, anteroom	Pevsner, *London: City*, 1997, 280
74.	*c*1790	With carvings in imitation of drapery Payment(s): £126	m	[Castle Coole, Fermanagh, library]; untraced	*Dale* 1956, 64
75.	1793	Several Payment(s): £147 with other work	m	[Uxbridge House, London]; untraced	LMA 446/H/29
76.	*c*1795	Description unavailable Payment(s): £48 5s 2d		[Oriel College, Oxford, east common room]; untraced	*Dale* 1956, 85
77.	1796	Reeded Payment(s): £45		Plas Newydd, Anglesey, octagon room (?)	*Marsden* 1999, 36
78.	1796	White marble with panels of guilloche ornament Payment(s): £120		Plas Newydd, Anglesey, saloon (?)	*Marsden* 1999, 40
79.	*c*1796	With large frieze of musical shepherd and shepherdess flanking a relief frieze		Powderham Castle, Devon, music room	Pevsner, *Devon*, 1989, 694 (repr 131)
80.	1790–1806	White marble and ormulu	m	Shugborough, Staffs, red drawing room	*Robinson* 1989, 37 (repr)
81.	1810–1820	Several	m	Dodington Park, Glos	Pevsner, *Glos: Cotswolds*, 1999, 318
82.	nd			[Howick Hall, north library]; untraced	Wyatt/Grey, 16 Nov 1809
83.	nd	Tablet with 'birds in a nest, and festoons of flowers and foliage in high relief' (reproduced in blue jasper for Wedgwood) Payment(s): jasper sold for £98 in 1877		[Sibson sale, Christie, 1877, lot 247]; untraced	Sale cat
84.	nd	'Verd' antique and white marble		Warwick Castle, Queen Anne's bedroom	*Field* 1815, 193; Pevsner, *Warks*, 1966, 456
85.	nd	With relief		Tatton Park, Tatton Park, Cheshire, dining room	Pevsner, *Cheshire*, 1971, 355
Reliefs					
86.	*c*1789	Five, representing the salutation of the Virgin Mary, the nativity, the deposition, the resurrection and the ascension	m	New College, Oxford, chapel, over altar	*Dugdale* IV, 1819, 94; Pevsner, *Oxon*, 1974, 170
Miscellaneous					
87.	1775	'Model of a boy for a monument'		[Exhib Soc of Artists, London, 290]; untraced	*Graves* 1907, 275; *Gunnis* 1968, 423

WESTMACOTT, Sir Richard RA 1775–1856

Sir Richard Westmacott was the most significant member of a family of successful sculptors and won the lion's shar of public commissions during the first three decades of the 19th century. He was born in London on 15 July 177 the eldest son of **Richard Westmacott I** and Sarah, née Vardy. He probably received some training at his father workshop in Mount Street before being apprenticed at the age of 14 to his grandfather, the furniture carver **Thoma Vardy**. He also received teaching from the Italian sculptor **Castoro Casoni** before leaving England with Casoni in th winter of 1792. After a brief stay in Paris they travelled to Rome, arriving in January 1793.

Westmacott appears to have led a productive life during his three years in Italy. He lived in the Palazzo Zuccari o the Strada Gregoriana and spent his mornings and evenings modelling at the Accademia di San Luca. He sketche in the Vatican, the Capitoline Museum and the Museo Pio Clementino with Casoni and sometimes with the painte Joseph Gandy. He appears to have met **John Flaxman RA** and his wife socially. Westmacott worked as an agent i Italy for the architect Henry Holland, buying and selling antique fragments. It was in the context of this trade an through an introduction by the Abbate Carlo Bonomi that he met **Antonio Canova**, with whom he struck up friendship that persisted for 25 years.

Westmacott spent the summer months in Florence, where he sketched at the Uffizi and received the first priz from the Florentine Academy for a model in a life class (**288**). His earliest surviving work in marble was a copy c the Uffizi *Apollino*, bought by an English patron, J S B Morritt (**287**), but he was also working on original work

In May 1795 he won the Pope's medal from the Florentine Academy for his classicizing relief, *Joseph confiding Benjamin to Juda* (**357**). Westmacott was helped by his friendship with the sculptor Vincenzo Pacetti, who not only corrected defects in the work but also sat on the committee awarding Westmacott the prize.

In the autumn of 1795 Westmacott went with Gandy to look at antiquities in Abruzzo and Calabria, moving on to Lake Fucino, Naples, Portici, Pompeii and Herculaneum. In April 1796 he was making preparations to leave Rome when was robbed of his possessions by armed assailants in the Via Flaminia. After recuperating the sculptor travelled north through Florence, Bologna, Venice, Trieste, Vienna, Dresden and Berlin, arriving in England late in 1796. He was elected a member of the Florentine Accademia del Disegno *in absentia* on 24 September 1797.

Westmacott set up his studio in London next to his father's house and on 20 February 1798 he married 'wisely and well', choosing Dorothy Margaret Wilkinson, daughter of Dr William Wilkinson of Barbados (*AJ* 1856, 315). Their wedding was at St George's, Hanover Square. Westmacott had good connections, including family ties with the influential architect, James Wyatt, who attempted to win public commissions for the sculptor, and he soon attracted distinguished patrons. Among his first exhibited works was a bust of Sir William Chambers and a statue for William Beckford (**325, 289**). In April 1803 Farington noted that Westmacott had work in hand worth £16,000, and by 1806 he employed an Italian assistant (*Farington*, vol 6, 2162; vol 7, 2715).

In 1803 Westmacott won the contract for Sir Ralph Abercromby's monument in St Paul's Cathedral, his first memorial financed by public subscription (**83**). It is a dramatic tableau illustrating the moment when the Lieutenant-General fell dying from his horse at the Battle of Alexandria. Seven other monuments by Westmacott followed, commissioned by the Committee of Taste which was set up to oversee the erection of public monuments in Westminster Abbey and St Paul's Cathedral (**70, 86, 128, 131, 141, 149, 213**). The *Gentleman's Magazine* later described the cathedral as 'a sort of gallery of the works of Sir Richard Westmacott' (*GM*, vol 201, 1856, 510). His commissions from the committee would earn him £29,300 in the next 20 years, but his rise to prominence inevitably caused jealousy among rivals: in 1807 **Nathaniel Marchant** spoke of his work 'with much disapprobation, saying the parts of his figures were without form,' and he suggested that **Joseph Nollekens** and the collector Charles Townley had 'puffed him into notice' (*Farington*, vol 8, 3084).

In 1803 Westmacott began work on his statue of the essayist, Joseph Addison, for Westminster Abbey (**82**), a monument noteworthy for the severe classical relief of the muses on the cylindrical pedestal. Several other early works, particularly the monuments to the Earl of Ilchester and Philip Yorke, have figures with heavy-hooded eyes, broadly carved draperies and an aura of classical purity almost unique in British sculpture of the day (**32, 54**).

Westmacott's first public statue in bronze was of the 5th Duke of Bedford for Russell Square (**291**). *The Times* called it 'the most magnificent work . . . ever cast in England' and Westmacott soon gained a reputation as Britain's foremost sculptor in bronze. The commemorative urge which swept through Britain's institutions during and after the Napoleonic Wars proved immensely beneficial to Westmacott's business. He designed, modelled and cast two statues of Nelson for Birmingham and Bridgetown (**290, 292**) and modelled and cast **M C Wyatt**'s complex baroque allegory commemorating Nelson for Liverpool (**293**). He is best known, however, for the statue of Achilles, 18 feet high, in Hyde Park. This was raised to celebrate the Duke of Wellington's victories and was financed by subscription from patriotic British women, led by Lavinia, Countess Spencer (**298**). The Achilles is a modified version of one of the antique horse-tamers on the Quirinale in Rome, a scholarly quotation lost on the British press, who found hilarious the concept of high-born patriotic women erecting a colossal bronze statue of a naked man.

Westmacott hoped that the Achilles would foster a more widespread knowledge of classical sculpture and thus improve British taste. He was an acknowledged expert on the antique, who collected Roman works, such as the *Westmacott athlete* (BM) and dealt in antiquities with other connoisseurs, like the 4th Earl of Egremont, who nicknamed him 'Westmacotteles.' The sculptor was a member of the Society of Dilettanti and the Society of Antiquaries, and his views were sought by the Elgin Marbles committee. He, John Flaxman and **William Pistell** also helped to construct a temporary display for the Elgin and Phigaleian marbles at Burlington House. In 1815 Westmacott visited Paris to view the works of art looted by Napoleon and there met up again with Canova, who subsequently visited England and was received as an honoured guest in numerous country houses in Westmacott's company. From 1816 he also acted as an unofficial advisor on antiquities and purchases to the Trustees of the British Museum. Westmacott also involved himself in depictions of British history, carving an unusual sequence of full-length statues for Ashridge Park, of historic personalities associated with the house (**348, 350**).

He became an ARA in 1805 and a full academician in February 1811. In 1818 his premises were no longer large enough to house the business and he moved to 14 South Audley Street, where he remained for the rest of his life. The property was soon extended and by 1820 he had set up his own bronze foundry in Pimlico. He employed several assistants, including **M L Watson** and **John Carew**. Carew was a valued employee, who was given piece-work between 1809 and 1827, which Westmacott estimated to be worth £800 to £1,200 per annum (*Carew v Burrell 1840*, 42). In 1838–39 Carew helped Westmacott sell 20 cases of antique statues, busts and fragments to the 4th Earl of Egremont, at an asking price of £1,137 (Orchard Wyndham MSS, 15 Nov 1838, 25 Jan and 25 Feb 1839). Other assistants included **James Toole, T Clark of Bristol, James Trubshaw, William Griggs, William Scoular** and **Vincent Gahagan**.

In December 1822 Westmacott was the subject of a five-page memoir in the *European Magazine*. That year he worked on a bronze statue of George III in the pose of Marcus Aurelius (**311**) and his monument to Charles James Fox was erected in Westminster Abbey (**122**). It depicted the Whig leader cradled by a severely classical *Liberty* and mourned by a kneeling African. By the early 1820s, Westmacott was acknowledged as leader in the field for public statues and major church monuments and he had the financial security and enlightened patronage to turn to ideal works, considered an artist's highest achievement. His *Psyche*, shown opening a real ivory casket, appears to owe something to Canova and his asking price of 1,000 guineas was close to the Italian's exorbitant charges (**301**). *The Dream of Horace*, a relief inspired by one of the poet's odes, was exhibited with a long Latin quotation at the Royal Academy. It illustrates an episode from the poet's infancy, when Horace was protected from wild animals by supernatural grace (**362**).

Westmacott's monumental practice continued to be extensive, varied in style and occasionally innovative. Th ponderous Greek revival mode of his early monuments gave way to a greater eclecticism: graceful mourning female appeared on several monuments (**216**, **226**), he used deathbed scenes reminiscent of the work of **Thomas Banks** (**99** and he echoed Flaxman with his angels escorting or exhorting the dead to heaven (**135**, **252**). He also revived an adapted medieval conventions, representing the Dukes of Montpensier and Cleveland as recumbent effigies (**241**, **282**

One of Westmacott's notable introductions to funerary sculpture was a sentimental rustic realism. Th monument to Lord Penrhyn at Llandegai has a full-length figure of a slate-worker, complete with apron, crowba and hatchet, accompanied by a Welsh girl. Together they mourn over the sarcophagus of the rural reformer (**165** During the 1820s Westmacott also produced a relief of 'afflicted peasants' in the style of Raphael for the 7th Earl c Bridgwater's monument (**192**). His monument to Elizabeth Warren, 1824, features a statue of a ragclad Irish migrar with her naked infant, grieving for the loss of her benefactress (**198**). This much appealed to contemporary taste In 1832 he exhibited a figure of a gypsy with a child, apparently modelled from the life (**312**). The *Gentleman Magazine* later commented that Westmacott was essentially a naturalistic sculptor, and his achievement was t 'represent thought and emotion . . . under their modern and national types' (*GM* vol 201, 1856, 510).

Public works remained a part of Westmacott's practice. In the 1820s he worked on the Waterloo Vase (**351**), carve from 20 tons of Carrara marble presented by the Grand Duke of Tuscany to George IV, who commissioned relief celebrating Napoleon's defeat (*GM* vol 159, 1836, 186). Westmacott was still depicting British victories at Trafalgar an Waterloo in 1830, when he provided reliefs for the Marble Arch (**353**). His imposing bronze statue of the Duke c York, on a column 112 feet high, was an important precursor of Nelson's Column (**316**).

In 1827 Westmacott was elected professor of sculpture at the Royal Academy, receiving £60 annually for deliverin six lectures. These were said to be 'treatises of considerable archaeological research, interspersed with practica remarks of great force and shrewdness and accompanied by admirable drawings' (*GM*, vol 201, 1856, 510). Othe public honours followed: in 1836 he received an honorary doctorate from Oxford University and on 19 July 183 he was knighted by Queen Victoria. In 1840 Westmacott estimated that he and **Sir Francis Chantrey** commande the highest prices for sculpture in England (*Burrell v Carew* 1840, 48).

His notable later works included *The sleeping infant*, a sentimental monument to Lady Susan Murray (**278**) and statue to the former Governor-General of India, Lord William Bentinck (**319**), his last work in bronze. Like the earlie monument to Warren Hastings in Calcutta (**309**), the Bentinck stresses the contribution of the Britis administration to the people of India. Hastings is depicted on a raised pedestal flanked by a Hindu brahmin and muslim, whilst Bentinck's monument includes a relief commemorating the outlawing of the practice of suttee.

Westmacott's pediment group for the British Museum was clearly intended to be his crowning achievement, testament to his scholarship and vision (**356**). It traces the progress of mankind from rude savagery to civilizatio and the accompanying creation of art. It makes reference to contemporary debates over the use of colour in Gree sculpture by its modest use of polychromy: the tympanum was tinted blue and some of the ornaments were gilde

As a grandee of the British art establishment, Westmacott served on a number of public bodies. In 1843 he was on of the judges in the parliamentary fresco competition and in 1845 he reported on the condition of tombs in Canterbur Cathedral for the office of woods and forests. In 1849 the same department appointed him to supervise the erection c **E H Baily**'s Nelson monument in Trafalgar Square. In 1850 he was the leading candidate for the presidency of the Roya Academy but declined in favour of the painter, Sir Charles Eastlake. He acted as a commissioner for the Grea Exhibition in 1851 and in 1853 testified as a witness for the select committee on the National Gallery. In 1855 he serve on the Committee for English Sculpture at the International Exhibition in Paris, where he exhibited *The housele traveller*, *The nymph unclasping her zone* and *The sleeping infant* (**198**, **308**, **278**).

Some associates regarded the ageing artist as pompous, but the painter Benjamin Robert Haydon, who was know for his waspish comments, found him mellow and generous. The diarist Caroline Fox, who visited Westmacott studio in June 1842, saw him as 'a man of extreme energy and openness of countenance, real enthusiasm for his ar and earnest to direct its aim as high as heaven' (*Fox* 1882, vol 2, 317, quoted in *Busco* 1994, 6). The most vivi illustration of his commitment to art came in 1834, when, at the age of 61, his physical exertions helped prevent th destruction of Westminster Hall during the fire at the Houses of Parliament.

Westmacott remained healthy until a few weeks before his death at South Audley Street on 2 September, 1856. H was buried at Chastleton, Glos, where he had the living and his son, Horatio, was the rector. Westmacott had alread settled part of his fortune on his children on marriage, but in his will he left a settlement of £12,500 on his tw daughters, Dorothy and Eliza, £1,100 to his son Spencer and £100 per annum to another son, Robert Marsh. He lef numerous properties in London, his advowson at Chastleton and a large collection of works of art. These include a painting by Rembrandt, a portrait by Sebastiano del Piombo, a collection of papal medals and more than 4,00 prints and drawings by Stothard. The house in South Audley Street was made over to his son **Richard Westmacot III RA**, who appears to have taken an increasing role in the monumental business during the 1840s.

Westmacott was in virtual retirement for most of the last two decades of his life and his obituaries suggest that hi work had already become old-fashioned. It was recognised nonetheless that for many years Westmacott and Chantre had enjoyed the highest reputation accorded to any British sculptors at home or abroad. His output was considerabl and since it spanned more than 55 years and several styles, writers of his obituaries and later scholars found it har to categorise. Whinney was one who found his work puzzling and disappointing. In recent years, Penny and Busc have provided a more balanced appraisal of a man who was Britain's principal official sculptor for thirty years.

MG

Literary References: *Farington, passim; Euro Mag* 1822, vol 82, 493; *GM* 1836, vol 159, 186; *Carew v Burrell* 1840, 42–59; *GM* 1856, vol 201, 509–1 *AJ* 1856, 316; *Honour* 1963, 368–76; *Gunnis* 1968, 423–8; *Colvin* 1973–6, vol 6, 404–5; *Penny* 1974, 492–3; *Penny* 1975 (1), 314–32; *Penny* 1975 (2), 120– *Penny* 1977, *passim*; *Read* 1982, *passim*; *Whinney* 1988, *passim*; *Busco* 1988 (2); *Busco* 1989, 776; *Penny* 1991 (1), 255–264; *Jenkins* 1992, *passim*; *Bus* 1994; *Ingamells* 1997, 993; *JKB* 2006, 181–2

Archival References: Westmacott family archive (HMI 2000/80); Westmacott Corr, BL; Westmacott Corr, Yale; Westmacott Corr, VAM Westmacott Corr, Met NY; Orchard Wyndham MSS; Westmacott/Elmes; Westmacott/Wellesley; Westmacott/Canova; Westmacott/Duke Newcastle; Westmacott/Knighton; Westmacott/Nash; Westmacott/Adam; Westmacott/Lincoln; Westmacott/SDUK; Westmacott/RIEFAS; IGI;

Will: PROB 11/2245, 345v-238v

Collections of drawings: 96 studies of sculpture and architecture and English landscape watercolours, including views of Woburn Abbey, most inscribed and some dated circa 1848 (HMI A/S3 3); an album of 128 landscape sketches made on the Continent 1820–1824 and 1826 (HMI A/S1 4); 36 landscape views, studies of castles and churches in pencil, pen and ink and sepia wash, some landscape watercolours (HMI A/D1 7); Diary and sketchbook, c1835, detailing a journey in Scotland (HMI A/S2 19); 36 sketches of landscape views in Italy and Britain (HMI A/D1 32)

Miscellaneous drawings: Sketch after Raphael, ink, private coll, *Busco* 1994, 108 (repr); Sketch after a portrait of Edward VI, ink and pencil, private coll; sketch of a figure on Gloucester Cathedral, ink and watercolour, private coll; Two angels and a dying girl, watercolour, private coll, *Busco* 1994, 151 (repr); four designs (documented or attributed) including an equestrian statue of King George III for Windsor, Royal Coll, RL 24112, 24126, 17489, 23232

Auction Catalogues: Westmacott 1857 (1); Westmacott 1857 (2); Westmacott 1859

Portraits of the Sculptor: J Thomson, engraving in the *Euro Mag*, vol 82, December 1822, *Busco* 1994, vi; Charles Benezech, 1792, chalk, NPG 731, *Busco* 1994, 7; George Scharf I, *Westmacott's lecture at the Royal Academy*, 1836, pencil drawing, BM, P&D, 1862,0614.179; William Brockedon, chalk and pencil, 1844 NPG 2515 (95); Charles Hutton Lear, pencil, c1845; NPG 1456 (27); Eliza Westmacott, c1846–50, watercolour, private coll, *Busco* 1994, 20

Funerary Monuments

1.	†1795	George Errington (†1769) and his son George	Ashbourne, Derbys	S	Pevsner, *Derbys*, 1978, 62
2.	†1796	Dr William Fowle	St James, Montego Bay, Jamaica	S	*Busco* 1994, 127–8 (repr)
3.	†1796	Henry Roebuck	Swanscombe, Kent		Pevsner, *Kent: W & Weald*, 1976, 562; C Lib (repr)
4.	c1796	Hon William Paget (†1794)	King's Chapel, Gibraltar		*Busco* 1994, 10, 126–7 (repr)
5.	1796	Joseph Price	Monmouth parish church		*Gunnis* 1968, 425
6.	c1796	William (†1768) and Olivia Barker (†1780)	Sonning, Berks	S	*Busco* 1994, 126–8 (repr)
7.	1797	Catherine Pennant	Monken Hadleigh, Herts	S	*Gunnis* 1968, 425; Pevsner, *Herts*, 1977, 249; C Lib (repr)
8.	†1797	James West Payment(s): £124 18s 10d	Preston-on-Stour, Warks		*Busco* 1994, 125–6; C Lib (repr)
9.	†1797	John Parry	Gresford, Denbighs	S	*Busco* 1994, 127–8 (repr)
10.	1798	Martha James	Mitcham, Surrey		*Gunnis* 1968, 425
11.	†1798	Thomas Pennant	Whitford, Flint		Pevsner, *Clwyd*, 1986, 455
12.	†1799	Dorothy Eveleigh	St Mary, Oxford		Pevsner, *Oxon*, 1974, 287
13.	†1799	Elizabeth Pinder	St John, Hackleton's Cliff, Barbados		*Whinney* 1988, 393
14.	?1799	Ninian Home	St George, Grenada		*Gunnis* 1968, 425
15.	†1799	Rev Henry Evans and family	Pembridge, Herefs		Pevsner, *Herefs*, 1963, 268; *Gunnis* 1968, 426
16.	†1799	Sir James Eyre	Ruscombe, Berks		Pevsner, *Berks*, 1966, 209
17.	1799	Thomas Fettiplace (†1767)	Swinbrook, Oxon		Pevsner, *Oxon*, 1974, 800
18.	1800	Benjamin Kinton	Stepney parish church, London		*Gunnis* 1968, 426
19.	†1800	Caroline Somerset	Great Badminton, Glos	S	C Lib (repr)
20.	1800	John Warren, Bishop of Bangor (†1800)	Westminster Abbey, London, north transept		*Busco* 1994, 135, 138 (repr)
21.	†1800	Lord Lilford	Achurch, Northants		*Gunnis* 1968, 426
22.	?1800	Peter Brown	St Leonard, Streatham, London		*Gunnis* 1968, 426
23.	†1800	Philip, 7th Lord Wenman	Thame Park, Oxon, Chapel		Pevsner, *Oxon*, 1974, 812
24.	†1800	Russell Manners	St Mary, Battersea, London	S	*Gunnis* 1968, 426; C Lib (repr)
25.	†1800	Sir Benjamin Hammet	Wilton, Wilts	S	
26.	†1801	Hon John Yorke	Wimpole, Cambs	S	*Whinney* 1988, 390–1 (repr); *Busco* 1994, 129–30 (repr)
27.	†1801	James Sutton	St John, Devizes, Wilts	S	Pevsner, *Wilts*, 1975, 207
28.	1801	'Part of a monument to be erected in Ireland'	[Exhib RA, London, 998]; untraced		*Graves* VIII, 1905–6, 236
29.	†1801	Sir George Warren	St Mary, Stockport, Cheshire	SD	Pevsner, *Cheshire*, 1971, 340; C Lib (repr)
30.	†1802	Augustus Leveson-Gower Payment(s): £65 5s 1d	Kingston, Jamaica		*Busco* 1994, 125
31.	†1802	Dorothy Harrison	St John, Hampstead, London		Pevsner, *London: N*, 1998, 202
32.	†1802	Henry, 2nd Earl of Ilchester	Farley, Wilts		*Busco* 1994, 140, 142 (repr)
33.	1802	Hon Mrs Bruce	[Relief exhib RA, London, 1031]; Chennai (Madras) Cathedral, India		*Graves* VIII, 1905–6, 237; *Gunnis* 1968, 426
34.	1802	Mather Byles	St George, Grenada		*Gunnis* 1968, 426
35.	1803	Benjamin Kenton (†1800)	[Exhib RA, 1801, 1023]; St Dunstan, Stepney, London		*Graves* VIII, 1905–6, 236; *Busco* 1994, 152, 154 (repr)
36.	1803	Elizabeth Hughes	Ruthin, Denbighs		*Gunnis* 1968, 426
37.	†1803	Henry, 5th Duke of Beaufort	Great Badminton, Glos	S	*CIIA* 4/4/58 (repr)
38.	?1803	John Cushnie	West Kirk, Aberdeen		RG/JP, 9, 1565
39.	†1803	John Gawler	Weyhill, Hants		Pevsner, *Hants & Isle of Wight*, 1967, 649
40.	†1803	Mary, Countess of Darnley	Bidborough, Kent, churchyard		Pevsner, *Kent: W & Weald*, 1976, 167
41.	†1803	Milburg Alpress	Englefield, Berks	S	C Lib (repr)
42.	†1803	Rev Henry Newcome	Gresford, Denbighs		*Busco* 1994, 138–9 (repr)
43.	†1803	Sarah Goulburn	St Giles-in-the-Fields, London	S	*Busco* 1994, 13, 138–9 (repr)
44.	†1803	Sir William Atherton	Prescot, Lancs		Pevsner, *Lancs: S*, 1969, 366
45.	†1804	Ann Champain	St Helen, Abingdon, Berks	S	*Gunnis* 1968, 426' C Lib (repr)
46.	†1804	Henry Lee-Warner	Little Walsingham, Norfolk		*Busco* 1994, 143
47.	?1804	Lucy Clarke	St Helena, Jamestown		RG/JP, 9, 1565
48.	†1804	Mary Sergison	Cuckfield, Sussex	S	*Busco* 1994, 131–2 (repr)
49.	1805	Captain Marriott	Horsham, Sussex		*Gunnis* 1968, 426
50.	1805	Hon Mrs Cocks	Shute, Devon		*Gunnis* 1968, 426; Pevsner, *Devon*, 1989, 731; C Lib (repr)
51.	1805	Hon Reginald Cocks	Mylor, Cornwall		Pevsner, *Cornwall*, 1970, 125
52.	†1805	Mary Henson	Bainton, Northants	S	Pevsner, *Beds, Hunts & Peterborough*, 1968, 207
53.	1805	Mary Hill	Sheldwich, Kent		*Gunnis* 1968, 426

54.	1805	Philip Yorke (†1804) Payment(s): £150	Marchwiel, Denbighs		*Busco* 1994, 126, 128 (repr)
55.	†1805	Sir James Whalley Smythe Gardiner	Whalley, Lancs		*Busco* 1994, 128 (repr)
56.	†1806	Captain George Dyson	Spanish Town Cathedral, Jamaica	S	C Lib (repr)
57.	†1806	Frances Browne	Frampton, Dorset	S	Pevsner, *Dorset*, 1972, 213; C Lib (repr)
58.	†1806	Francis and Catherine (†1798) Canning	Ilmington, Warks	S	Pevsner, *Warks*, 1966, 317; C Lib (repr)
59.	†1806	George Hotham	Binfield, Berks		Pevsner, *Berks*, 1966, 87
60.	†1806	John Turton	Brasted, Kent		Pevsner, *Kent: W & Weald*, 1976, 178
61.	1806	William Savage	Little Samford, Essex		*Gunnis* 1968, 426
62.	†1807	Dame Jane Trafford Southwell	Orsett, Essex		*Busco* 1994, 130–1 (repr)
63.	†1807	Edward Atkyns	Ketteringham, Norfolk	S	*Busco* 1994, 131 (repr)
64.	†1807	Elizabeth Leigh	Rostherne, Cheshire		Pevsner, *Cheshire*, 1971, 324
65.	†1807	1st Lord Brownlow	Belton, Lincs	S	*Penny* 1977 (1), 30, 31, 43 (repr)
66.	1807	Jemima Pole-Carew Payment(s): £50	Antony, Cornwall		Pevsner, *Cornwall*, 1970, 37
67.	1807	John Cotton	Madingley, Cambs		*Gunnis* 1968, 426
68.	1807	Richard Veale	Titchfield, Hants		*Gunnis* 1968, 426
69.	†1807	Thomas Liell	Clent, Worcs		RG/JP, 9, 1566
70.	†1807	Thomas Newton	St Paul's Cathedral, London		*Busco* 1994, 156–7 (repr)
71.	1808	Andrew Newton (†1806)	Lichfield Cathedral, Staffs	SD	*Busco* 1994, 133–4 (repr)
72.	†1808	Charles, 1st Earl of Liverpool	Hawkesbury, Glos	S	Pevsner, *Glos: Cotswolds*, 1999, 409
73.	†1808	Lieutenant-General William Anne Villettes	St Andrew, Jamaica		*Gunnis* 1968, 426; C Lib (repr)
74.	†1808	Lieutenant-General William Anne Villettes	Westminster Abbey, London, Chapel of St Andrew	S	*Gunnis* 1968, 426
75.	†1808	Mary, Lady Morgan	Bassalleg, Gwent		*Busco* 1994, 134–5 (repr)
76.	†1808	Phillips Lloyd Fletcher	Overton, Flint	S	Pevsner, *Clwyd*, 1986, 411
77.	†1808	Robert Scott	Medmenham, Bucks	S	Pevsner, *Bucks*, 1994, 468
78.	?1808	Sarah Popham	Shanklin, I of W		RG/JP, 9, 1566
79.	†1808	William (†1801) and Ann Bowles	Longworth, Berks	S	Pevsner, *Berks*, 1966, 172; C Lib (repr)
80.	1809	Blencowe family	Hayes, Middx		*Gunnis* 1968, 426
81.	†1809	Hon Henry Neville	Waltham St Lawrence, Berks	S	Pevsner, *Berks*, 1966, 251
82.	1803–1809	Joseph Addison (†1719) Payment(s): £1000	Westminster Abbey, London, south transept		*Busco* 1994, 85–7 (repr)
83.	1803–1809	Lieutenant-General Sir Ralph Abercromby (†1801) Payment(s): £6,300 Model(s): study for part of the group exhib RA, London, 1804, 897	St Paul's Cathedral, London	S	*Graves* VIII, 1905–6, 237; *Busco* 1994, 13, 35–8 (repr)
84.	†1809	William Walmesley	St Lawrence, Marston St Lawrence, Northants	S	*CIIA* 4/3/102 (repr)
85.	†1810	Beatrix Outram	Birmingham Cathedral		*Penny* 1977 (1), 32, 34 (repr)
86.	c1810	Captain John Cooke (†1805) Payment(s): £1,575	St Paul's Cathedral, London, crypt		*Busco* 1994, 40–1 (repr)
87.	1810	George Mangles	Weybridge, Surrey		*Gunnis* 1968, 426
88.	c1810	John Symons	Bathford, Somerset		*Gunnis* 1968, 426
89.	†1810	Mary Turton	Brasted, Kent		*Gunnis* 1968, 426
90.	†1810	Sir Charles Turner	St Cuthbert, Kirkleatham, N R Yorks		Pevsner, *Yorks: N R*, 1966, 219
91.	1810	William Burgh (†1808)	York Minster, south choir aisle	S	*Aylmer* 1977, 463–4, 468 (repr); *Busco* 1994, 138–9 (repr); *Pattison and Murray* 2001, 104–5
92.	1811	Anne Marriott	Finchingfield, Essex		Pevsner, *Essex*, 1965, 181
93.	†1811	Bishop Percy	Dromore Cathedral, Co Down		*Potterton* 1975, 87
94.	†1811	Captain James Newman Model(s): 'Model for a monument to Captain Newman, killed in the Hero man-of-war' exhib RA, London, 1813, 907, *Graves* 1905–6, 237; untraced	Fareham, Hants		Pevsner, *Hants & Isle of Wight*, 1967, 220
95.	†1811	James and Elizabeth (†1805) Bernard	Crowcombe, Somerset		Pevsner, *Somerset: S & W*, 1958, 142 (repr 37a); *Whinney* 1988, 393
96.	1811	Job Staunton Charlton (†1788)	Staunton-in-the-Vale, Notts		Pevsner, *Notts*, 1979, 338; C Lib (repr)
97.	†1811	Provost George Carter	Oriel College, Oxford, chapel		Pevsner, *Oxon*, 1974, 179
98.	†1811	Sir Henry Worsley Holmes	Arreton, I of W		Pevsner, *Hants & Isle of Wight*, 1967, 731
99.	†1811	Ursula Mary, Viscountess Sidmouth	St Mary, Mortlake, Surrey		*Busco* 1994, 143–4 (repr)
100.	1812	'I know that my redeemer liveth', relief for an unidentified monument – Job, xix, 25	[Exhib RA, London, 914]; untraced		*Graves* VIII, 1905–6, 237
101.	†1812	James Esdaile	St Laurence, Upminster, Essex		Pevsner, *Essex*, 1965, 398
102.	†1812	Jemima Clough	Llanrhudd, Denbighs		Pevsner, *Clwyd*, 1986, 233
103.	†1812	John Hunter	Sidmouth, Devon		*Gunnis* 1968, 426
104.	†1813	Charles S Watkins	Clifton Campville, Staffs		Pevsner, *Staffs*, 1974, 105
105.	†1813	Chief Justice Edward Long	Slindon, Sussex		Pevsner, *Sussex*, 1965, 327
106.	†1813	Francis Otter	Clayworth, Notts		Pevsner, *Notts*, 1979, 99
107.	1813	George Hall (†1810)	St George, Barbados	SD	*Gunnis* 1968, 426
108.	1813	J Pares, Esq, of Leicester ('Thou shalt come to thy grave in a full age, etc')	[Exhib RA, London, 942]; untraced		*Graves* VIII, 1905–6, 237
109.	1813	John Antrobus	Cheam, Surrey, Lumley chapel		*Gunnis* 1968, 426

110.	1813	Lieutenant-Colonel G Williamson	[Exhib RA, London, 939 ('Take heed that ye despise not one of these little ones, etc – Matthew, xviii)]; Duke of York's School, Chelsea, London		*Graves* VIII, 1905–6, 237; *Gunnis* 1968, 426
111.	1813	Rev Henry Peach	Cheam, Surrey, Lumley Chapel		*Gunnis* 1968, 426
112.	†1813	Sir Henry Vane Tempest	Long Newton, Durham		Pevsner, *Durham*, 1983, 355
113.	1813	Thomas Wilson	Clitheroe, Lancs		*Gunnis* 1968, 426
114.	†1813	William Hoskins	North Perrott, Somerset		Pevsner, *Somerset: S & W*, 1958, 260
115.	c1814	Brownlow, 5th Duke of Ancaster (†1809)	Swinstead, Lincs		Pevsner, *Lincs*, 1989, 739; *Whinney* 1988, 393
116.	†1814	Kathleen Long	Whaddon, Wilts		Pevsner, *Wilts*, 1975, 571
117.	1814	Mrs Cottrell	Crayford, Kent		*Gunnis* 1968, 426
118.	†1814	Robert Myddleton Biddulph	Ledbury, Herefs		*Busco* 1994, 131 (repr)
119.	†1814	Sir Richard Fleming Worsley Holmes	Arreton, I of W		Pevsner, *Hants & Isle of Wight*, 1967, 731
120.	†1814	William Stratton	St Mary, Teddington, Middx		Pevsner, *London: S*, 1983, 535
121.	†1815	Caroline, Lady Cholmondeley	Malpas, Cheshire		Pevsner, *Cheshire*, 1971, 274
122.	1809–1815	Charles James Fox (†1806) Payment(s): £6,000	Westminster Abbey, London, nave (installed c1822)		WAM (22); *Busco* 1994, 70–72 (repr)
123.	†1815	Elizabeth Bennett	High Wycombe, Bucks		C Lib (repr)
124.	†1815	Frederick Howard Payment(s): £59 4s (Castle Howard Archives)	St Leonard, Streatham, London		Pevsner, *London: S*, 1983, 391
125.	†1815	Harriet West Payment(s): £176 12s 11d	Preston-on-Stour, Warks		*Busco* 1994, 125
126.	1815	John Eardley-Wilmot	Berkswell, Warks		*Gunnis* 1968, 426
127.	†1815	John Sawrey Morritt	Rokeby, N R Yorks		Pevsner, *Yorks: N R*, 1966, 310
128.	c1815	Major-General Sir Isaac Brock (†1812) Payment(s): £1,575 Drawing(s): PRO, MPD 78, with agreement and bond Model(s): exhib RA, 1815, 876, *Graves* 1905–6, 237	St Paul's Cathedral, London	S	*Busco* 1994, 38 (repr)
129.	†1815	Rev Matthias D'Oyly	Buxted, Sussex	S	*Gunnis* 1968, 426
130.	†1815	Sir Francis D'Oyly	Buxted, Sussex	S	*Gunnis* 1968, 426
131.	1807–1815	William Pitt (†1806) Payment(s): £6,300	Westminster Abbey, London, nave	SD	*Whinney* 1988, 384–6, 472 n6 (repr); *Busco* 1994, 75–6 (repr)
132.	1816	Captain H Bagot	Blithfield, Staffs		*Gunnis* 1968, 426
133.	†1816	Captain John Westmacott (the sculptor's brother), tombstone	Halifax, Nova Scotia, Canada		RG/JP, 9, 1559
134.	1816	Charles Dunster	Petworth, Sussex		*Gunnis* 1968, 426
135.	†1816	Elizabeth Stanhope	Bristol Cathedral	S	*Busco* 1994, 148–9 (repr)
136.	†1816	Henrietta Madan	Thorpe Constantine, Staffs	S	*Gunnis* 1968, 426; C Lib (repr)
137.	1816	John Thornton (†1790)	St Paul, Clapham, London		*Gunnis* 1968, 426
138.	†1816	Michael Cheese	St John, Kolkata (Calcutta)		*Gunnis* 1968, 426; *Busco* 1994, 191 n71
139.	1816	Rev J Townsend	Pewsey, Wilts		*Gunnis* 1968, 426
140.	†1816	Sir Henry Bradford	Storrington, Sussex		Pevsner, *Sussex*, 1965, 343
141.	1814–1816	Spencer Perceval MP (†1812), with a relief of his assassination Payment(s): £5,250 Drawing(s): PRO, MPD. 78	Westminster Abbey, London, nave		WAM (50); *Busco* 1994, 76–8 (repr); *Whinney* 1988, 386, 472 n7 (repr)
142.	1816	William Lloyd (†1793), William Lloyd (†1816) and Elizabeth Lloyd (†1816)	St Giles, Wrexham, Denbighs		Pevsner, *Clwyd*, 1986, 301; C Lib (repr)
143.	1817	A sepulchral monument – 'But I trusted in thee, O Lord', etc' – Psalm xxxi	[Exhib RA, London, 1065]; untraced		*Graves* VIII, 1905–6, 237
144.	†1817	Ann Fryer	St Giles, Wrexham, Denbighs	S	Pevsner, *Clwyd*, 1986, 301; C Lib (repr)
145.	†1817	Caroline Gresley	St Nicholas, Kenilworth, Warks		*Busco* 1994, 145 (repr)
146.	1817	George Woodyatt	Ledbury, Herefs		*Gunnis* 1968, 426
147.	1817	H Coulthurst	St John, Halifax, W R Yorks		*Gunnis* 1968, 426
148.	1817	Selina Smith	Hampton, Middx		*Gunnis* 1968, 426
149.	1811–1817	Vice-Admiral Cuthbert, Lord Collingwood (†1810) Payment(s): £4,200	[Relief of 'Progress of Navigation' exhib RA, London 1813, 941 with iconographical interpretation]; St Paul's Cathedral, London	S	*Read* 1982, 90–1; *Busco* 1994, 41–2 (repr)
150.	†1818	Charles Fox-Maitland	Trinity College, Cambridge, chapel		*Busco* 1994, 151 (repr)
151.	†1818	Charles Garth Colleton	['Maternal Affection' (Charity) exhib RA, London, 1818, 1045]; Hurst, Berks		*Graves* VIII, 1905–6, 238; *Busco* 1994, 143 (repr)
152.	†1818	Charlotte Baker	Orsett, Essex		*Whinney* 1988, 394
153.	†1818	Elizabeth Emma Eardley-Wilmot	Berkswell, Warks		*Busco* 1994, 150–1 (repr)
154.	†1818	Ellen Nicholas	St Mary, Perivale, Ealing	S	Pevsner, *London: N W*, 1991, 190
155.	1818	'He shall give his angels charge over thee' (Psalm xci), relief for the monument to an unidentified subject	[Exhib RA, London, 1110]; untraced		*Graves* VIII, 1905–6, 238
156.	†1818	John James	Hampstead Norris, Berks		Pevsner, *Berks*, 1966, 151
157.	†1818	John, 2nd Earl of Upper Ossory	St James, Grafton Underwood, Northants		*Busco* 1994, 134–6 (repr)
158.	†1818	Lady Caroline Rushout	Burford, Salop	S	Pevsner, *Salop*, 1958, 92
159.	1818	Penelope Biddulph	Ledbury, Herefs		*Gunnis* 1968, 427
160.	1818	Sir Stephen Cottrell	Crayford, Kent		*Gunnis* 1968, 427

161.	†1818	Thomas, Viscount Anson	Colwich, Staffs		*Penny* 1977 (1), 209 n32; C Lib (repr)
162.	†1819	Charlotte (†1794) and John Coker	Bicester, Oxon		Pevsner, *Oxon*, 1974, 454
163.	†1819	John Bannerman	St George, Penang		*Gunnis* 1968, 427
164.	†1819	John, 4th Earl Poulett	Hinton St George, Somerset	S	Pevsner, *Somerset: S & W*, 1958, 198; *Gunnis* 1968, 427
165.	1819	Richard Pennant, Lord Penrhyn (†1808), and his wife Anne Susannah (†1816) Payment(s): £2000 set aside in Baroness Penrhyn's will for the monument: exact cost unknown	[Relief and female figure exhib RA, London, 1819, 1179 and 1238]; Llandegai, Gwynedd		*Graves* VIII, 1905–6, 238; *Busco* 1994, 126, 164–5 (repr)
166.	†1819	Sophia Musters	Annesley, Notts		
167.	†1819	Vere, 3rd Earl Poulett (†1788) and his wife	Hinton St George, Somerset	S	*Gunnis* 1968, 427
168.	1820	Anne Birch	Weobley, Herefs		*Gunnis* 1968, 427
169.	1820	Benjamin Tate	Loughborough, Leics		*Gunnis* 1968, 427
170.	1820	Geoffrey Chaucer (†1400)	St Margaret, Westminster, London		RG/JP, 9, 1569
171.	†1820	Hon Kean Osborn	St Peter of the Alley, Vere, Jamaica	S	*Busco* 1994, 135–6 (repr)
172.	?1820	James Shottowe	Lacock, Wilts		*Gunnis* 1968, 427
173.	†1820	Jeremiah Ives	Old Catton, Norfolk	S	Pevsner, *Norfolk: N E & Norwich*, 1997, 627
174.	†1820	Rev Charles Prescot	St Mary, Stockport, Cheshire		Pevsner, *Cheshire*, 1971, 340; C Lib (repr)
175.	1821	Alexander Colvin (†1818) Model(s): plaster of the the Hindu girl, Ashm	[Hindu girl exhib RA, London, 1821, 1085]; St John, Kolkata (Calcutta) Other versions: statue of seated Hindu girl, marble, Chelminski Gallery, London, 2003		*Graves* VIII, 1905–6, 238; *Archer* 1984, 53; *Penny* 1992, III, 178 (repr); *Busco* 1994, 139–41 (repr)
176.	†1821	Arthur Evans	Darley Abbey, Derbys		Pevsner, *Derbys*, 1978, 193
177.	c1821	James Perry (†1821)	St Mary, Wimbledon, Surrey		*Busco* 1994, 18
178.	†1821	Lady Elizabeth Townsend	Honington, Warks		Pevsner, *Warks*, 1966, 315
179.	1821	Mrs Tate	Mitcham, Surrey	S	Pevsner, *Surrey*, 1971, 370
180.	1821	Rev Colston Carr	Feltham, Middx		*Gunnis* 1968, 427
181.	†1821	Richard Cosway	St Mary, St Marylebone, London		*Busco* 1994, 154–5 (repr)
182.	†1821	Sarah, Countess of Mexborough (with relief of the raising of Lazarus)	Methley, W R Yorks		*Whinney* 1988, 394; C Lib (repr)
183.	1821	Sir Henry Carr	Feltham, Middx		*Gunnis* 1968, 427
184.	†1822	Dr Woolcombe	St Andrew, Plymouth, Devon		Pevsner, *Devon*, 1989, 642
185.	†1822	George Tate	All Saints, Loughborough, Leics		Pevsner, *Leics & Rutland*, 1984, 281
186.	†1822	Major George Cruttenden	St John, Kolkata (Calcutta)		*Archer* 1984, 52–3 (repr); *Busco* 1994, 166
187.	†1822	Richard Drax Grosvenor (†1819) and his wife Sarah Erle Drax	Charborough, Dorset	S	Pevsner, *Dorset*, 1972, 140
188.	†1822	Thomas, Viscount Warren Bulkeley	St Mary, Beaumaris, Anglesey		*Busco* 1994, 135, 137 (repr)
189.	†1823	Elizabeth Burton	Spanish Town Cathedral, Jamaica	S	*Gunnis* 1968, 427; C Lib (repr)
190.	†1823	Elizabeth Leigh	St John the Baptist, Knutsford, Cheshire		Pevsner, *Cheshire*, 1971, 251
191.	†1823	John, 1st Earl of St Germans	St Germans, Cornwall		*Busco* 1994, 132
192.	†1823	John, 7th Earl of Bridgewater ('The afflicted peasants') Model(s): plaster, Chastleton House, Glos, CHS/SC/1	[Relief exhib RA, London, 1043]; Little Gaddesden, Herts	S	*Graves* VIII, 1905–6, 238; *Busco* 1994, 31, 165–6 (repr)
193.	1823	Major-General Sir Edward Pakenham and Major-General Samuel Walsh Payment(s): £2,100	St Paul's Cathedral, London		*Whinney* 1988, 373 (repr); *Busco* 1994, 38–9 (repr)
194.	†1823	Mary Pares	Ockbrook, Derbys		Pevsner, *Derbys*, 1978, 293
195.	†1823	Sarah Woodward	St Thomas Becket, Framfield, Sussex		Pevsner, *Sussex*, 1965, 506
196.	†1823	William Daniell	Burton Bradstock, Dorset	S	*Gunnis* 1968, 427
197.	1824	Augusta Kirkland	St Mary, St Marylebone, London		*Gunnis* 1968, 427
198.	1822–1824	Elizabeth Southwell Warren (†1816) ('The houseless traveller')	[Exhib RA, London, 989]; Westminster Abbey, London, north transept Other versions: Bowood, Wilts, marble, 1823, £500 for Mrs Ferguson of Raith for her home in Beal, Scotland; untraced	S	*Graves* VIII, 1905–6, 238; *Busco* 1992, 3–10; *Busco* 1994, 95, 167–9 (repr)
199.	†1824	Henry Peirse and his daughter Harriet, Lady Beresford (†1825)	Bedale, N R Yorks		*Busco* 1994, 156, 158 (repr)
200.	†1824	Hon Charlotte Seymour	Woburn Abbey, Beds		*Penny* 1977 (1), 215
201.	1824	John Sheppard	Campsey Ash, Suffolk		*Gunnis* 1968, 427
202.	†1824	Lieutenant-General Christopher Jeaffreson	Dullingham, Cambs		*Busco* 1994, 159–61 (repr)
203.	†1824	Mary May	Hale, Hants		*Busco* 1994, 151–2 (repr)
204.	1824	Sir Arscott Molesworth Bt (†1823)	Egloshayle, Cornwall	S	Pevsner, *Cornwall*, 1970, 65; C Lib (repr)
205.	?1824	Streynsham Myers	Mitcham, Surrey		RG/JP, 9, 1570
206.	†1824	Thomas Pares	Ockbrook, Derbys		Pevsner, *Derbys*, 1978, 293
207.	?1824	William Raikes	St Mary, Walthamstow, London		*Gunnis* 1968, 427
208.	†1825	Daniel Ellis Saunders	Ledbury, Herefs		Pevsner, *Herefs*, 1963, 217
209.	†1825	Lady Fowler	St Modwen, Burton-on-Trent, Staffs		Pevsner, *Staffs*, 1974, 84
210.	†1825	Lady Mary Wildman	St Mary, Twickenham, Middx		Pevsner, *London: S*, 1983, 539
211.	†1825	Robert Bateson Harvey	Langley Marish, Bucks	S	Pevsner, *Bucks*, 1994, 639
212.	?1825	William Fairlie	St Mary, St Marylebone, London		*Gunnis* 1968, 427

No.	Date	Subject	Location		Bibliography
213.	1823–1826	Admiral, Viscount Duncan Payment(s): £2,000	St Paul's Cathedral, London		*Busco* 1994, 38–40 (repr)
214.	?1826	Edward Morris	Chenies, Bucks		*Gunnis* 1968, 427
215.	?1826	Gore Townsend	Honington, Warks		*Gunnis* 1968, 427
216.	†1826	Henrietta, Viscountess Gormanston	Dullingham, Cambs	S	*Busco* 1994, 132–3 (repr)
217.	†1826	John Rawson	St John, Halifax, W R Yorks		Pevsner, *Yorks: W R*, 1967, 231
218.	†1826	Lord Carteret	Haynes, Beds		Pevsner, *Beds, Hunts & Peterborough*, 1968, 96
219.	†1827	Elizabeth Mallett	Hampton, Middx	S	*Whinney* 1988, 395
220.	†1827	Francis, 8th Earl of Bridgewater Model(s): plaster, Chastleton House, Glos	Little Gaddesden, Herts		*Busco* 1994, 151–2 (repr)
221.	†1827	George Augustus, 11th Earl of Pembroke and Montgomery	Wilton, Wilts Other versions: Ashm, plaster copy	S	*Penny* 1992, III, 182 (repr); *Busco* 1994, 166, 168 (repr)
222.	1827	Hon John Adam (†1825)	St John, Kolkata (Calcutta)	S	*Busco* 1994, 138–40 (repr)
223.	?1827	Isabella Peyton	Bainton, Northants		*Gunnis* 1968, 427
224.	†1827	Louisa (†1826) and Lucy Boyle	Frome, Somerset		*Busco* 1994, 156, 158 (repr)
225.	†1827	Major Hugh Falconer	Storrington, Sussex		Pevsner, *Sussex*, 1965, 343; *Busco* 1994, 133; C Lib (repr)
226.	1827	Rev John Chetwynd Talbot (†1825)	Ingestre, Staffs	SD	C Lib (repr)
227.	†1827	Richard Baker	Orsett, Essex		*Busco* 1994, 151, 153 (repr)
228.	†1827	Sir Nelson Rycroft	Farnham, Surrey	S	*Busco* 1994, 151, 153 (repr)
229.	†1827	Thomas Philip Bagge	Stradsett, Norfolk	S	*Busco* 1994, 132–3 (repr)
230.	†1828	Charles Hutchinson	St Mary, Ealing, Middx		Pevsner, *London: N W*, 1991, 166
231.	†1828	Commander Charles Cotton	Madingley, Cambs	S	Pevsner, *Cambs*, 1970, 435
232.	†1828	John James, Bishop of Calcutta	Christ Church Cathedral, Oxford	S	*Gunnis* 1968, 428; C Lib (repr)
233.	?1828	Mary Hawes	Shalstone, Bucks		*Gunnis* 1968, 427
234.	†1828	Paul Francis Benfield	St Mary de Castro, Leicester	S	C Lib (repr)
235.	?1828	William Rawson	St John, Halifax, W R Yorks		*Gunnis* 1968, 427
236.	†1829	George Evelyn	Wotton, Surrey		Pevsner, *Surrey*, 1971, 543
237.	?1829	George Todd	St John, Hampstead, London		*Gunnis* 1968, 427
238.	?1829	Jane Brown	St Leonard, Streatham, London		*Gunnis* 1968, 427
239.	?1829	Mrs Knyvett and Mrs Aldous	Feltham, Middx		*Gunnis* 1968, 427
240.	?1829	Wilson Roberts	Packwood, Warks		*Gunnis* 1968, 427
241.	1830	Antoine Philippe, Duc de Montpensier (†1807) Payment(s): Cost estimated at £1,200, final price unknown	[Exhib RA, London, 1170]; Westminster Abbey, London, Henry VII's Chapel		*Graves* VIII, 1905–6, 239; *Busco* 1994, 126, 159–60, 162 (repr)
242.	†1830	Frances Crosbie Fairfield	St Nicholas, Brighton, Sussex		Pevsner, *Sussex*, 1965, 428
243.	1830	John Dandridge (†1785) and family members	Malvern Priory, Great Malvern, Worcs		*Penny* 1977 (1), 34, 35
244.	†1830	Mary Elizabeth Chichester	Derby Cathedral	S	Pevsner, *Derbys*, 1978, 170; C Lib (repr)
245.	†1831	John Thomas Batt	Nunton, Wilts		*Busco* 1994, 138, 140 (repr)
246.	†1831	Sir Thomas Mantell	Chilham, Kent		*Busco* 1994, 131–2 (repr)
247.	†1832	Roger Pettiward	Great Finborough, Suffolk		*Busco* 1994, 152, 154 (repr)
248.	1832	Timothy Tyrrell	St Anne, Kew, Surrey		*Gunnis* 1968, 427
249.	†1833	Eliza Woodhouse	King's Caple, Herefs		Pevsner, *Herefs*, 1963, 204
250.	1833	Georgiana, Duchess of Newcastle (†1822)	Milton mausoleum, Notts		*Penny* 1977 (1), 91 (repr); *Busco* 1994, 145–7 (repr)
251.	1833	Walter Nisbet	Kolkata (Calcutta) Cathedral		*Archer* 1984, 53
252.	†1834	Ann Bankes	St Denys, Sleaford, Lincs		Pevsner, *Lincs*, 1989, 653; C Lib (repr)
253.	?1834	Augusta Biddulph	Ledbury, Herefs		*Gunnis* 1968, 427
254.	?1834	Charles Shakerley	Astbury, Cheshire		*Gunnis* 1968, 427
255.	†1834	Dorothy Margaret Westmacott	St Nicholas, Brighton, Sussex		*Busco* 1994, 154, 156 (repr)
256.	†1834	Grace Bagge	Stradsett, Norfolk	S	*Penny* 1977 (1), 215–6 n.66; *Whinney* 1988, 395 (repr)
257.	?1834	Joshua Knowles	St Mary, Wanstead, Essex		*Gunnis* 1968, 427
258.	1834	Sir Benjamin Carew	Beddington, Surrey		*Gunnis* 1968, 427
259.	†1834	Sir William Clayton	Marlow, Bucks		*Gunnis* 1968, 427
260.	*c*1835	Anne Lee-Warner (†1819)	Walsingham, Norfolk	S	*Gunnis* 1968, 427; C Lib (repr)
261.	†1835	Charles Burrell Massingberd	South Ormsby, Lincs		*Penny* 1977 (1), 208 n27; C Lib (repr)
262.	†1835	Frances Annabella Assheton	Downham, Lancs	S	Pevsner, *Lancs: N*, 1969, 115; C Lib (repr)
263.	?1835	Frances Ives	Old Catton, Norfolk		*Gunnis* 1968, 427
264.	†1835	Francis, Lord de Dunstanville	Illogan, Cornwall		Pevsner, *Cornwall*, 1970, 83
265.	†1835	George Brettle	St Peter, Belper, Derbys		Pevsner, *Derbys*, 1978, 89
266.	†1835	George Brettle	St Matthew, Brixton, London		*Gunnis* 1968, 427
267.	†1835	Henry, 6th Baron Middleton	Wollaton, Notts		Pevsner, *Notts*, 1979, 274
268.	†1835	Henry, 6th Baron Middleton	Birdsall, E R Yorks		Pevsner, *Yorks: E R & York*, 1995, 326
269.	†1835	Mr Pennant	Whitford, Flint	S	Pevsner, *Clwyd*, 1986, 455
270.	†1835	Rev William, 1st Earl Nelson	Cricket St Thomas, Dorset		*Busco* 1994, 146
271.	1835	Sir John Williams Bt (†1830) and Lady Margaret Williams	St Asaph's Cathedral, Flint	S	*Penny* 1977 (1), 216 n66
272.	†1837	Sir Charles Cockerell	Longborough, Glos	S	*Busco* 1994, 135, 137 (repr)
273.	1837	William Myers	Mitcham, Surrey		*Gunnis* 1968, 427
274.	†1838	Charles, Lord Farnborough	Saxmundham, Suffolk		Pevsner, *Suffolk*, 1974, 412; *Gunnis* 1968, 428
275.	†1838	Charles, Lord Farnborough and his wife	Wormley, Herts	S	Pevsner, *Herts*, 1977, 409; C Lib (repr)
276.	†1838	John Aldborough Dennis	Holy Trinity, Stratford-upon-Avon, Warks	S	Pevsner, *Warks*, 1966, 413

No.	Date	Subject	Medium	Location		Bibliography
277.	†1838	Sir Abraham Hume		Wormley, Herts		Pevsner, *Herts*, 1977, 409
278.	1839	Lady Susan Murray ('The sleeping infant')		Scone Palace, Perth		*Graves* VIII, 1905–6, 239; *Busco* 1994, 158–9 (repr)
279.	?1839	Mary Warrington		Wyke Regis, Dorset		*Gunnis* 1968, 428
280.	?1840	Francis Bower		St Anne, Kew, Surrey		*Gunnis* 1968, 428
281.	†1842	Mary Jervoise		Shalstone, Bucks		Pevsner, *Bucks*, 1994, 617
282.	1844	William, Duke of Cleveland (†1842) Payment(s): ? £1086		St Mary, Staindrop, Durham		*Busco* 1994, 161–3, 191 n92 (repr)
283.	1819–1845	Henry, 3rd Lord Holland (†1840), Lady Holland (†1845) and Georgiana Holland (†1815)		Millbrook, Beds		*Busco* 1994, 143–4 (repr)
284.	†1846	Edward Bagge		Islington, Norfolk	S	
285.	nd	John Daddridge and family		Malvern priory, Worcs		*Penny* 1977 (1), 34, 35 (repr)
286.	nd	Model for an unidentified naval monument with two allegorical figures	p	Chastelton House, Glos		*Busco* 1994, 23; C Lib (repr)
Statues						
287.	1794	Apollino	m	Rokeby Park, N R Yorks, saloon	D	*Busco* 1994, 9 (repr)
288.	1794	Model from a life class		[Accademia di San Luca, Florence, first prize]; untraced		*Busco* 1994, 9
289.	1799	La Madonna della Gloria, for Fonthill		[Exhib RA, London, 1006]; untraced		*Graves* VIII, 1905–6, 236; *Busco* 1994, 12
290.	1806–1809	Admiral Lord Nelson (†1805) Payment(s): £2,500	b	Bull Ring, Birmingham, Warks		*Yarrington* 1983, 315–29; *Busco* 1994, 43–4 (repr); *Noszlopy* 1998, 116–7 (repr)
291.	1809	Francis, 5th Duke of Bedford	b	Russell Square, Holborn, London		*Busco* 1994, 88–9 (repr)
292.	1810–1813	Admiral Lord Nelson Payment(s): £1,414	b	National Heroes Square, Bridgetown, Barbados (2002)		*Busco* 1994, 43–4 (repr)
293.	1806–1813	Admiral Lord Nelson (†1805) (co-sculptor: Matthew Cotes Wyatt) Payment(s): £8,000 (8 per cent to M C Wyatt)	b	Liverpool, Lancs		*Yarrington* 1983, 315–29; *Busco* 1994, 47–51 (repr); *Cavanagh* 1997, 51–5 (repr)
294.	1809–1813	Robert Milligan (†1809) Payment(s): £1,100	b	[Royal Docks, London, north quay entrance]; Docklands Museum, London, store [pedestal relief lost]		*Busco* 1994, 89–90 (repr)
295.	1810–1814	Charles James Fox	b	Bloomsbury Square, London Other versions: Brooks's Club, bust, bronze Holland House, bust, bronzed plaster ex Alscot House, sold Christie, 15 July 1986, lot 77 bust, marble, SD 1818; untraced		*Busco* 1994, 19, 72–3 (repr)
296.	1815–1818	William Pitt (†1806) Model(s): Exhib RA 1818, 1046, *Graves* 1905–6, 238	b	[National debt redemption office, London]; Pembroke College, Oxford		*Busco* 1994, 74–5 (repr)
297.	1821	Resignation	m	[Exhib RA, London, 1084]; untraced		*Graves* VIII, 1905–6, 238
298.	1814–1822	Achilles (monument to the Duke of Wellington) Payment(s): £10,000	b	Hyde Park, City of Westminster, London		*Busco* 1988, 920–4; *Busco* 1994, 51–55 (repr); *Read* 1982, 91, 92 (repr); *Yarrington* 1988, 54, 217, 221–6 (reprs 76, 77)
299.	1818–1822	King George III, equestrian Payment(s): £5,000 Drawing(s): Liverpool PRO 731 GEO	b	London Road, Liverpool, Lancs		*Busco* 1994, 65–8 (repr) *Cavanagh* 1997, 103
300.	1822	Mary, Queen of Scots Payment(s): £350	s	[for William, 6th Duke of Devonshire]; Hardwick Hall, Derbys		*Busco* 1994, 93, 116 (repr)
301.	1822	Psyche	m	Woburn Abbey, Beds Other versions: Castle Howard, plaster ex coll John, Lord Burghersh, British ambassador to Florence, plaster; untraced		*Graves* VIII, 1905–6, 238; *Busco* 1994, 93, 96–99 (repr)
302.	1823	Cupid	m	Woburn Abbey, Beds		*Graves* VIII, 1905–6, 238; *Busco* 1994, 98–99 (repr)
303.	1825	Madonna and Child (The happy mother) Drawing(s): Private coll	m	[Exhib RA, London, 1065]; Church of the Transfiguration, 1, East 29th St, NY	S	*Graves* VIII, 1905–6, 238; *Busco* 1994, 106–8 (repr)
304.	1826	Lord Thomas Erskine (†1823)	m	[Lincoln's Inn, London, hall]; Lincoln's Inn, Holborn, London, library		*Graves* VIII, 1905–6, 238; *Busco* 1994, 19, 80–1 (repr)
305.	1827	Cupid made prisoner	m	Petworth House, Sussex		*Graves* VIII, 1905–6, 238; *Busco* 1994, 103–4 (repr)
306.	1828	Euphrosyne Payment(s): £500	m	[Clumber House, Notts, library]; Christie, 12–14 June 1989, lot 914; untraced		*Graves* VIII, 1905–6, 239; *Busco* 1994, 95, 104–5 (repr); *Fletcher* 2001, 68
307.	1825–1828	Nymph and Zephyr Payment(s): 750 gns Drawing(s): **Private coll**	m	[Sir John Leicester, Lord de Tabley, Grosvenor House, London, Gallery]; Eaton Hall, Cheshire Other versions: Ashm, plaster, later truncated		*Penny* 1992, vol 3, 180–1; *Busco* 1994, 95, 101–3 (repr)
308.	1823–1828	Venus attiring (A nymph unclasping her zone)	m	[Castle Howard, E R Yorks]; destroyed Other versions: Ashm, bust, plaster SJSM HR3, plaster Copies in Coadestone		*Graves* VIII, 1905–6, 238; *Thornton and Dorey*, 1992, 49 (plaster repr); *Busco* 1994, 100 (plaster repr); Dorey 2004, 60–1 (repr)
309.	1828	Warren Hastings	m	[Town hall, Kolkata (Calcutta)]; Victoria Memorial Gardens, Kolkata		*Graves* VIII, 1905–6, 238; *Busco* 1994, 82–3 (repr)

310.	1831	Frances Penelope Rawson (†1825)	m	[Nidd Hall, Harrogate, W R Yorks]; Christie, 24 Sept 1987, lot 175; untraced	S	*Busco* 1994, 30 (repr)
311.	1824–1831	King George III, equestrian Payment(s): £19,600 Drawing(s): RL 17489 (attrib)	b	Snow Hill, Windsor Great Park, Berks		*Darke* 1991, 152–3 (repr); *Busco* 1994, 68–9 (repr)
312.	1832	Gypsy with a child	m	[Orchard Wyndham, Somerset or Silverton Park, Devon]; untraced Other versions: Ashm, plaster fragment, *Penny* 1992, 183 (repr)		Orchard Wyndham MSS, 28 Jan 1840; *Graves* VIII, 1905–6, 239; *Busco* 1994, 108–9 (repr)
313.	1827–1832	Rt Hon George Canning (†1827) Payment(s): 7,000 gns	b	Parliament Square, City of Westminster, London, formerly New Palace Yard		*Busco* 1994, 79–80 (repr)
314.	1833	Dr John Alderson (†1829) Payment(s): £300	s	Royal Infirmary, Hull, ER Yorks		*Busco* 1994, 87; C Lib (repr)
315.	1832–3	Eleanor Cross, statues		Waltham Cross, Herts		Pevsner, *Herts*, 1977, 374
316.	1829–1834	Frederick-Augustus, Duke of York and Albany (column designed by Benjamin Dean Wyatt) Payment(s): £4,000	b	Duke of York column, Carlton House Terrace, London		*Yarrington* 1988, 17, 266–272 (reprs 97, 98); *Busco* 1994, 63–4 (repr)
317.	?1809–1834	John Locke	m	University College, Holborn, London, library		*Graves* VIII, 1905–6, 239; *Busco* 1994, 19, 87 (repr)
318.	1835	Devotion	m	[Exhib RA, London, 1045]; untraced		*Graves* VIII, 1905–6, 239
319.	1839	Lord William Bentinck (†1835), with a pedestal relief of the abolition of the suttee	b	[Pedestal relief exhib RA, London, 1288]; Victoria Memorial, Kolkata (Calcutta)		*Graves* VIII, 1905–6, 239; *Busco* 1994, 84–5 (repr); *Groseclose* 1990, 509–11 (repr)
320.	1840	Hindoo girl, originally intended for the monument to Alexander Colvin		[The sculptor's studio]; untraced		Orchard Wyndham MSS, 28 Jan 1840
321.	nd	Copy of an Antique group of Priapos and a Maenad	p	Chastleton House, Glos		*Busco* 1994, 22–3 (repr)
322.	nd	The Magdalen		[Alfred Cooper, of Enfield; sold Phillips 20 Oct 1884]; untraced		RG/JP, 9, 1562
323.	nd	Venus and Cupid		[formerly Trentham Hall]; untraced		*Gunnis* 1968, 425
Busts						
324.	1797	Henry Disney-Roebuck	m	Walker, Liverpool	D	*Busco* 1994, 11 (repr)
325.	1797	Sir William Chambers	m	[Office of Works, London]; SJSM	D	*Graves* VIII, 1905–6, 236; *Colvin* 1973–6, vol 6, 98; *Busco* 1994, 10–11 (repr)
326.	1803	A child		[Exhib RA, London, 918]; untraced		*Graves* VIII, 1905–6, 237
327.	1807	Thomas Newton	m	Royal Literary Fund, London		*Graves* VIII, 1905–6, 237; *Busco* 1994, 14
328.	1808	David Williams	m	Royal Literary Fund, London		*GM*, 1816, 2, 90; *Graves* VIII, 1905–6, 237; *Busco* 1994, 14
329.	1810	Henry, Viscount Sidmouth	b	[Exhib RA, London, 892]; Royal Albert Memorial Museum, Exeter, Devon		*Graves* VIII, 1905–6, 237; *Busco* 1994, 14–15 (repr)
330.	1820	Arthur, 1st Duke of Wellington	b	Alameda Gardens, Gibraltar		RG/JP, 9, 1563
331.	nd	King George III	m	Belton House, Lincs		C Lib (repr)
332.	nd	Lord Pembroke		Voronzov Palace, Aloupka, Crimea		RG/JP, 9, 1563
333.	nd	Robert Otway Cave		Stanford Hall, Leics		RG/JP, 9, 1563
Chimneypieces						
334.	1790	Statuary marble Payment(s): £41 19s 9d		Woburn Abbey, Beds		Woburn Building Accts, 1787–91, BLARS R5/1105
335.	1791	Statuary marble Payment(s): £41 19s		Woburn Abbey, Beds		Woburn Building Accts, BLARS R3/2114/495
336.	1805	'a dove marble piece' Payment(s): 16 gns		[Carlton House, London, for 'her majesty's sitting room']; untraced		TNA WORK 5/94
337.	1805	Dove grey marble Payment(s): 16 gns	m	[Windsor Castle, Queen's sitting room]; untraced		TNA WORK 5/94 – *Gunnis* 1968, 424
338.	1805	Two, of dove grey marble inset with scagliola by Bartoli (designed by James Wyatt) Payment(s): £140		[Carlton House, London, circular dining room]; untraced		TNA WORK 5/94; *Carlton House* 1991–2, 215
339.	1807	Four, of grey marble Payment(s): £192	m	[Kensington Palace, London, drawing room and saloon of the Duke of York's apartments]; untraced		TNA WORK 5/96; *Gunnis* 1968, 424
340.	*c*1808	Description unavailable		[Howick, Northumbs, north library]; untraced		RG/JP, 9, 1557
341.	*c*1812	More than one, of statuary marble	m	[Bretby House, Derbys, saloon]; untraced		*Glover* 1831–3, 188
342.	1814	Two, large, one of statuary marble with inlay and 'ornamented with ormulu' in a Gothic style (designed by James Wyatt) Payment(s): £140		[Carlton House, London]; untraced		*Gunnis* 1968, 424; *Colvin* 1973–6, vol 6, 315
343.	1818	Description unavailable		Woburn Abbey, Beds, inner library		Pevsner, *Beds, Hunts & Peterborough*, 1968, 169; C Lib (repr)
344.	1816–1818	Dragon chimneypiece (designed by Crace and sons, with mounts by Benjamin Vulliamy) Payment(s): £1244 2s 6d	m	[Royal Pavilion, Brighton, music room]; Buckingham Palace, London		*Roberts* 1939, 134–5; *Busco* 1994, 26, 176 n137; C Lib (repr)
345.	1831	Two of sculptured marble		Buckingham Palace, London		TNA Ad. 68/884, fol 361

Architectural Sculpture

No.	Date	Work	Material	Location		References
346.	1800	'Suffer little children', sketch for an altar piece		[Exhib RA, London, 1058]; untraced		*Graves* VIII, 1905–6, 236
347.	*c*1818	Dancing putti, relief Model(s): 'Cupids; model for a relief for the Temple of the Graces at Woburn Abbey', exhib RA, London, 1818, 1111; untraced	m	Woburn Abbey, Beds, Temple of the Graces, exterior wall		*Graves* 1905–6, 238; *Busco* 1994, 118–120 (repr)
348.	1815–1818	Queen Elizabeth	s	[Ashridge Park, Little Gaddesden, Herts, exterior]; Harrow School, Speech House exterior		*Busco* 1994, 115, 117 (repr)
349.	*c*1818	The progress of mankind	m	Woburn Abbey, Beds, Temple of Liberty, exterior wall		*Busco* 1994, 118–120 (repr)
350.	1815–1823	King Edward VI; Richard, Earl of Cornwall (1209–1272); Edmund, Earl of Cornwall; Senchia of Provence; Edward the Black Prince (1330–1376); unidentified monk; St Benedict of Nunsia (480–530); Thomas de Canteloupe, Bishop of Hereford; Richard of Watford	s	Ashridge Park, Little Gaddesden, Herts, staircase hall		*Busco* 1994, 114–118 (repr)
351.	1820–1827	Waterloo vase Drawing(s): VAM E.963-1965	m	[NG, London]; Buckingham Palace, London, gardens		*GM*, 1836, vol 159, 186; *Busco* 1994, 55–57 (repr)
352.	1827–1828	Three reliefs: King Alfred driving the Danes to their ships, King Alfred publishing the laws, and Patriotism encouraging youth in martial exercises Payment(s): £700	s	Buckingham Palace, London, west front		TNA Ad.68/884 f317; *Colvin* 1973–6, vol 6, 298, 301; *Busco* 1994, 58
353.	1828	Two relief panels: England, Scotland, Wales and Peace with trophies of war; six Victories in spandrels and three keystones	m	Marble Arch, London		*Colvin* 1973–6, vol 6, 293–302; *Yarrington* 1988, 229–45; *Busco* 1994, 57–61 (repr)
354.	*c*1830	Friezes of the battles of Trafalgar and Waterloo (originally intended for Marble Arch)	m	Buckingham Palace, London, east front, attic		*Colvin* 1973–6, vol 6, 293–302; *Yarrington* 1988, 229–45; *Busco* 1994, 58–61 (repr)
355.	*c*1830	Section of frieze depicting Napoleon's retreat from the Battle of Waterloo (originally intended for Marble Arch)	m	[Manor of Littleton, Shepperton, Middx]; Christie, 13 Dec 1985, lots 207–8; untraced		*Colvin* 1973–6, vol 6, 293–302; *Yarrington* 1988, 229–45; *Busco* 1994, 61–2 (repr)
356.	1847–1851	Progress of civilization Drawing(s): pen and ink, BL Ad MS 56068 f1 (with agreement)	s	BM, pediment of entrance front		*Busco* 1994, 120–4 (repr); *Read* 1982, 218, 219 (repr)

Reliefs

No.	Date	Work	Material	Location		References
357.	1795	Joseph confiding Benjamin to Juda	tc	Academia Nazionale de San Luca, Rome, Italy		*Busco* 1994, 8–9 (repr)
358.	1811	Ganymede and the eagle	m	RA, London (diploma work)		RA Archives AND/XVI/166; *Busco* 1994, 16–17 (repr)
359.	1820	Hero receiving Leander (pendant to Hector reproaching Paris)	m	[Exhib RA, London, 1820, 1026]; Woburn Abbey, Beds		*Graves* VIII, 1905–6, 238; *Busco* 1994, 95 (repr)
360.	1821	Hector reproaching Paris (pendant to Hero Receiving Leander)	m	Woburn Abbey, Beds		*Busco* 1994, 96 (repr)
361.	1821	Hero and Leander		Petworth, Sussex		*Gunnis* 1968, 425
362.	1823	The dream of Horace	m	Petworth House, Sussex, north gallery		*Graves* VIII, 1905–6, 238; *Busco* 1994, 110–3 (repr)
363.	1818–1824	The trial of Socrates Payment(s): £361 6s od Model(s): Ashm, plaster	m	Holkham Hall, Norfolk	S	*Hassal and Penny* 1977, 207–11 (repr); *Penny* 1992, vol 3, 179 (repr); *Busco* 1994, 112–3 (repr)

Miscellaneous

No.	Date	Work	Material	Location		References
364.	1802	'And I heard a voice from Heaven, saying unto me, "write, blessed are the dead which die in the Lord" ' - Rev xiv, 13		[Exhib RA, London, 1024; 1814, 810]; untraced		*Graves* VIII, 1905–6, 237
365.	1803	Repairs to 'two oriental marble columns' Payment(s): £20		[Castle Howard, N R Yorks]; untraced		Castle Howard Archives
366.	1804	Unspecified work, possibly including chimneypieces Payment(s): £275		[Cobham Hall, Kent]; untraced		Archives, Earl of Darnley, in *Gunnis* 1968, 424
367.	1815	Model of a national monument to Major-General Sir Isaac Brooks		[Exhib RA, London, 876]; untraced		*Graves* VIII, 1905–6, 237
368.	1818	Unspecified work Payment(s): £68		[for Lord Carlisle, Castle Howard, N R Yorks]; untraced		Castle Howard Archives
369.	*c*1820	The dying gladiator, bronze cast	b	Woburn Abbey, Beds		*Gunnis* 1968, 425
370.	*c*1820	The fighting gladiator, bronze cast	b	Woburn Abbey, Beds		*Gunnis* 1968, 425

WESTMACOTT, Richard III RA 1799–1872

The most notable of the third generation of Westmacott sculptors, he was also a prolific writer on the art. He was the eldest son of **Sir Richard Westmacott RA** and Dorothy Margaret Wilkinson and was baptised in Grosvenor Square, London. He was sent to the then fashionable Ealing School and in his youth hoped to become a barrister, although eventually he acceded to his father's wishes and trained as a sculptor in the latter's studio. In March 1818 he entered the Royal Academy Schools and in 1820 his father paid for him to go to Italy, where he spent six years studying Greek and Roman art.

A sketchbook of this period reveals that Westmacott travelled widely in Italy, looking at a number of northern cities as well as Venice, Florence and Rome. He was visited in his Rome studio by the Duke of Devonshire, for whom he designed a statue of a seated cymbal player, which he executed in marble on his return to London (**88**). In 1825 he completed the standing monument to a renowned beauty, Rosa Bathurst, the young daughter of a diplomat, who had drowned in the River Tiber (**6**). Westmacott's memorial, which has reliefs of an angel ferrying the girl to heaven from the waters, became a noted site for visiting English tourists. A drawing of Westmacott in Rome depicting him as a Byronic figure holding a modelling tool was executed by John Partridge.

After his return to England Westmacott lived at the family home at 14 South Audley Street, where he executed chimneypieces for Buckingham Palace and worked with his father on a relief intended for the Marble Arch (**148, 151**). In 1827 he exhibited at the Royal Academy for the first time, showing a figure of a girl with a bird (**86**), which the *Art Journal* subsequently described as 'characterised by considerable grace and purity of feeling' (*AJ* 1872, 167).

By 1830 he had set up his own studio at 21 Wilton Place, sending out monuments, busts, chimneypieces and, on occasion, ideal works. His most notable monument of the 1830s was to John Wycliffe, the celebrated the 14th-century ecclesiastical reformer (**31**). The relief, ordered for Wycliffe's local church at Lutterworth, Leics, depicts the Bible translator preaching animatedly to a cross-section of English society.

Westmacott's busts include the herm of Davies Gilbert (**101**) and the austere neoclassical representation of Dr Friedrich August Rosen, a Professor of Oriental Languages at University College, London (**104**). A letter from Westmacott to one of his clients, Lord John Russell, who sat for his portrait (**120**) stipulates that his charge for a bust was 60 guineas. He worked with **R W Sievier** at Chatsworth, where he disappointed the 6th Duke of Devonshire with a chimneypiece adorned with Bacchanalian figures, supplied in 1833. 'I wanted more abandon, and joyous expression' the Duke complained in his handbook to his collection, 'I find these baccanali too composed and sedate' (**149**) (*Cavendish* 1846, 83). Westmacott provided two reliefs for Bowood on classical and literary themes (**156, 157**) and reliefs for the Earl of Ellesmere (**158, 159**). The latter works included *Blue bell*, a curious representation of a bare-breasted, winged female seated in a flower, was illustrated in the *Art Journal* and was praised for its 'flowing wavy grace' and elegance of conception (*AJ* 1849, 56).

In 1838 Westmacott was elected an ARA and in 1849 an RA. In the 1840s he produced a number of monuments with life-sized recumbent effigies (**55, 56, 59, 69, 78, 80**), including one to a 15-year old Eton schoolboy, Charles Packe (**48**). Other effigial monuments incorporate effete angels, for instance one standing over and blessing the dead child, Charlotte Egerton (**58**). The angel guarding the family vault of the Baring family was singled out by both the *Builder* and the *Art Journal* as one of Westmacott's finest works (**65**).

His most notable sculpture from this period is probably the pediment relief for the Royal Exchange (**152**). A group of 17 figures representing the progress of world trade and Britain's divinely providential status at its heart, it was entitled 'The Earth is the Lord's and the Fulness Thereof'. Its centrepiece is a ten foot high statue of *Commerce* between interacting trading groups composed of the mayor and aldermen of the City, a Turk, an Armenian, two Asiatics, one Greek, one Persian, a black slave, a Levantine sailor and representatives of the British Navy. According to the *Illustrated London News*, who disapproved of Westmacott's inclusion of an allegorical figure at the centre of the composition, Westmacott chose to carve all the figures in the round, even though the contract had stipulated figures in relief.

In 1845 Westmacott married an heiress, Caroline Elizabeth Edgell, and his father settled a considerable sum on him. Although he must now have been well off he continued to work and his monument to Joseph Ridgway is one of his most simple and affecting compositions, featuring a statue of a female kneeling before an altar on a raised plinth, with her finger marking her page in the Bible (**70**). At about this time Westmacott appears to have begun to write on the history of sculpture, contributing an article on the practice of medieval sculpture in England to the *Archaeological Journal* in 1846.

In 1856 Westmacott's father died, leaving his son the property in Audley Street, together with his library and the bulk of his paintings, medals and prints. In June 1857 the Royal Academy appointed Westmacott to succeed his father as professor of sculpture, and he appears increasingly to have devoted his energies to the academic study of sculpture rather than its practice. In addition to his course of lectures for students he wrote a *Handbook of Sculpture Ancient and Modern* (1864), which was originally composed for the *Encyclopaedia Britannica* and he contributed numerous articles on the history of sculpture to the *Archaeological Journal* and the *Builder*. His literary efforts extended also to farces for the stage. He enthusiastically carried out his duties as advisor on sculpture to the British Museum, drawing on his knowledge of European galleries and offering extensive and sometimes controversial advice on the sculptural displays. The *Art Journal* said of him that he was 'indeed learned in his art, and accepted as an authority on all matters connected with it' (*AJ* 1872, 167).

Westmacott's health failed noticeably in the last years of his life, and a fall in 1871 left him unable to use his right hand, though he then apparently trained himself to write with his left. He died on 19 April 1872 at his home, a highly decorated and asymmetrical multi-storey corner house at 1 Kensington Gate, Hyde Park. In his will he left effects to the value of nearly £25,000. A monument, incorporating one of his own reliefs, was erected to his memory in St Mary Abbots, Kensington (**83**).

The obituarists were in no doubt that the artistic community had lost a very learned and esteemed sculptor. The *Art Journal* compared his work unfavourably with his father's, but nonetheless conceded the younger man's merit as both sculptor and scholar. The *Builder*, mourning a 'friend and valued contributor' felt that Westmacott shared his father's grace and tenderness in conception, 'purity of feeling' and classical severity, and added that the son's 'genius was of a graver character, and he excelled in monumental and devotional subjects, and in fancies of a thoughtful and reflective cast' (*Builder* 1872, 380). Although clearly a sculptor of some note in his day, his work appears not to have been received much commendation since. Gunnis, who was not a devotee of Victorian sculpture, dismissed Westmacott's monuments as 'competent, though uninspired' (*Gunnis* 1968, 428), while Whinney tartly described the sculptor's works as 'a pale reflection of those of his father, and not, unfortunately, of his father at his best' (*Whinney* 1988, 397).

MGS

Literary References: *AJ* 1872, 167; *Builder* 1872, 380; *Graves* VIII, 1905–6, 239–40; *Hutchison* 1960–2, 171; *JKB* 1972 (3), 329; *Penny* 1977 (1), 106; *Perry* 1978, 292–7; *Haskell and Penny* 1981, 336; *Read* 1982, 16; *Jenkins* 1992, 50; *Busco* 1994, *passim*

Archival References: Westmacott Family Archive; Westmacott III/Russell; RA/GA 10 April 1850; IGI

Additional MS Sources: Westmacott III, Letters

Wills: Richard Westmacott III RA, PPR 18 May 1872; Sir Richard Westmacott RA PROB 11/2245/234–8

Collections of Drawings: (1) Sketchbook, HMI Wes/A/S4, 263, studies, two of which are signed 'Rome', dated 1823 and 1825. Included are numerous other drawings made in Italian cities, also sketches of works by Chinard, Bernini, Botticelli, Kessel, **Pietro Tenerani** and **Antonio Canova**. There are also sketches of the Bishop Hough monument by **L-F Roubiliac**, and works by **Sir Francis Chantrey** and **Bertel Thorvaldsen** at Woburn Abbey, Beds. (2) Sketchbook HMI Wes/DS6, including a sketch of the statue of Duncan Forbes by L-F Roubiliac, landscape sketches and drawings of family groups. (3) Sketchbook HMI D/S2 2, 22 watercolour views of Tunbridge Wells and Southend, most inscribed, one dated 1863

Miscellaneous Drawings: *Christ appearing to the two disciples journeying to Emmaus*, design, probably for bas-relief, signed with monogram, RW, inscribed with title, pencil, pen and ink, VAM E.963-1965; design for the swan fountain in Regent's Park, 1862, untraced, the work executed by his cousin **James Sherwood Westmacott** (*ILN* 12 July 1862, 59); designs for a moral allegory, *The Fighte of Free Wille*, published 1839, HMI D/E1 8

Representations of the Sculptor: John Partridge, 1825, pencil on paper, signed 'Rome', NPG 3944/4; **Alfred, Count D'Orsay**, 1831, pencil and black chalk, NPG 4026/59, and another, ditto in profile (both reproduced in *Ormond* 1973, reprs 980 and 981)

Funerary Monuments

1.	†1798	Bartholomew Tipping	Chaddleworth, Berks	S	Pevsner, *Berks*, 1966, 112
2.	†1806	Stephen Cosser	[St John, Smith Square, London]; untraced		RG/JP, 9, 1578
3.	†1820	William Burslem	Worcester Cathedral	S	Pevsner, *Worcs*, 1968, 311
4.	†1822	Caroline Rushout	Burford, Salop	S	
5.	†1824	Caroline, Countess Brownlow	Belton, Lincs, Brownlow chapel	S	
6.	1825	Rosa Bathurst (†1824) Drawing(s): Sketchbook D, p148, private coll	Protestant Cemetery, Rome		*Perry* 1978, 292–7 (repr)
7.	†1826	Eleanor, daughter of the Earl of Ripon	Nocton, Lincs		Pevsner, *Lincs*, 1989, 577
8.	†1827	Elizabeth Rushout	Burford, Salop	S	*Kemp* 1985, 28 (repr)
9.	†1827	Sir George Tomline, Bishop of Winchester	Winchester Cathedral, Hants		*Graves* VIII, 1905–6, 239; Pevsner, *Hants & Isle of Wight*, 1967, 684
10.	†1828	Rev William Pemberton	Newton, Cambs		Pevsner, *Cambs*, 1970, 443
11.	†1828	Sacharissa Hibbert	Exeter Cathedral, Devon	S	Pevsner, *Devon*, 1989, 383
12.	†1828	Samuel Osborn	St Peter Vere of the Alley, Jamaica	S	
13.	†1829	J T James	Christ Church Cathedral, Oxford,		Pevsner, *Oxon*, 1974, 121
14.	†1831	Roger Leigh	St Peter, Leeds, W R Yorks	S	Pevsner, *Yorks: W R*, 1967, 312; *Pullan* 2006, 171
15.	†1831	Sir Mannaseh Lopes	Bickleigh (nr Plymouth), Devon		Pevsner, *Devon*, 1989, 169
16.	†1832	Lissey Anne Powys	Berwick, Salop	S	
17.	†1832	Sir James Macdonald and his infant son (†1831)	St Mary, Bramshott, Hants	S	*Graves* VIII, 1905–6, 239; Pevsner, *Hants & Isle of Wight*, 1967, 141
18.	†1833	Andalusia, Countess of Carnwath Drawing(s): private coll	Storrington, Sussex	S	*Gunnis* 1968, 429
19.	1833	Dr John Wooll	Rugby School, Warks, chapel	S	Pevsner, *Warks*, 1966, 389
20.	*c*1833	George Tierney (†1830)	Westminster Abbey, London, north west tower		WAM (12); *MacMichael* 1977, 22
21.	†1833	Lady Elizabeth Barbara Halford Drawing(s): private coll	Wistow, Leics		Pevsner, *Leics & Rutland*, 1984, 425
22.	†1833	Lord King	Ockham, Surrey		Pevsner, *Surrey*, 1971, 394
23.	1834	Emma Scott	Medmenham, Bucks		*Gunnis* 1968, 429
24.	?1834	Sir Michael McCreagh	Holy Trinity, Leeds, W R Yorks		GPC
25.	†1834	Sir William Clayton	All Saints, Marlow, Bucks		Pevsner, *Bucks*, 1994, 457
26.	†1835	Joseph Drury	St Mary, Harrow-on-the-Hill, Middx		Pevsner, *London: N W*, 1991, 262
27.	1835	Sir George Cornewall	Moccas, Hereford		*Gunnis* 1968, 429
28.	†1836	Anna, Duchess of Buckingham	Wotton Underwood, Bucks		RG/JP, 9, 1577
29.	†1836	Jemima Newman	Littlemore, Oxon		Pevsner, *Oxon*, 1974, 689; *Howell* 1983–4, 51–6 (repr)
30.	†1836	Penelope Lucas	Paramatta, New South Wales, Australia	S	GPC
31.	1837	John Wycliffe memorial (†1384) Drawing(s): private coll	St Mary, Lutterworth, Leics	SD	*Graves* VIII, 1905–6, 239; Pevsner, *Leics & Rutland*, 1984, 300
32.	1837	Mary Denman	St Luke, Chelsea, London		*Gunnis* 1968, 429
33.	†1837	Paul Mildmay Methuen	North Wraxall, Wilts		Pevsner, *Wilts*, 1975, 360; *Gunnis* 1968, 428
34.	†1837	Richard F Acton	[Aldenham Park, Salop, chapel]; untraced		Pevsner, *Salop*, 1958, 57
35.	†1838	Charles Leslie	Ballybay, Co Monaghan	S	*Potterton* 1975, 87
36.	†1838	James Roberts West	Preston-on-Stour, Warks	S	Pevsner, *Warks*, 1966, 375
37.	†1838	James Smith	Brasenose College, Oxford, chapel	S	*Gunnis* 1968, 429; Pevsner, *Oxon*, 1974, 108; C Lib (repr)
38.	?1838	Tyrrell family	St Anne Kew, Surrey		GPC
39.	†1838	William Hayward	St Benet, Cambridge	S	*Gunnis* 1968, 429
40.	1839	Archdeacon Henry Berners	Woolverstone, Suffolk		*Graves* VIII, 1905–6, 239; Pevsner, *Suffolk*, 1974, 504; *Gunnis* 1968, 428
41.	1839	Charles James Packe	Prestwold, Leics		Pevsner, *Leics & Rutland*, 1984, 349;

42.	†1839	Robert Holford (†1838) and George Holford		Westonbirt, Glos	S	*CIIA* 4/4/168 (repr)
43.	†1839	Sir John Vaughan		Wistow, Leics		Pevsner, *Leics & Rutland*, 1984, 425
44.	†1840	Francis Bauer		Kew, Surrey	S	Pevsner, *London: S*, 1983, 504
45.	1840	William Henry Cooper		Cobham, Surrey		*Gunnis* 1968, 429
46.	†1841	Dame Eleanor Elliott Drake		Buckland Monachorum, Devon		Pevsner, *Devon*, 1989, 233
47.	†1841	Lady Anne Fitzpatrick		Grafton Underwood, Northants	S	*Penny* 1977 (1), 166 (repr); *CIIA* 4/3/85, 87–9 (repr)
48.	†1842	Charles Hussey Packe		Prestwold, Leics		*Penny* 1977 (1), 126, 218 n64; C Lib (repr)
49.	†1842	Hon Sampson Salter Blowers		Halifax Cathedral, Nova Scotia		*Harris* 1949, repr 9
50.	†1843	Charles, 5th Duke of Dorset		Lowick, Northants		*CIIA* 4/3/96–100 (repr)
51.	†1843	Hon Henry George Monck Browne		Crossboyne, Co Mayo	S	*Potterton* 1975, 87
52.	†1843	Isabella, Countess of Cork		St John, Frome, Somerset	S	Pevsner, *Somerset: N & Bristol*, 1958, 196
53.	†1843	Lieutenant Charles Newton		Holy Trinity, Tunbridge Wells, Kent		*Penny* 1977 (1), 36 (repr)
54.	1844	Marianne Packe		Prestwold, Leics		*Gunnis* 1968, 428
55.	1844	Philip, 3rd Earl of Hardwicke (†1834)		Wimpole, Cambs	S	*Gunnis* 1968, 429; Pevsner, *Cambs*, 1970, 493; *Penny* 1977 (1), 123–4 (repr)
56.	†1844	Robert Otway Cave		Stanford, Northants		*Read* 1982, 191, 194; *CIIA* 4/3/111–5 (repr)
57.	†1844	Sir Henry Halford		Wistow, Leics		Pevsner, *Leics & Rutland*, 1984, 425
58.	†1845	Charlotte Egerton		Rostherne, Cheshire		*Penny* 1977 (1), 126–7 (repr)
59.	1845	Lord Glentworth (†1844)		Limerick Cathedral	S	*Potterton* 1975, 87
60.	†1846	Ann Birch		Weobley, Herefs		Pevsner, *Herefs*, 1963, 313; *Gunnis* 1968, 429
61.	1846	Prayer and Resignation, part of a monument to be placed in a rich Gothic recess in a church in Glos		[Exhib RA, London, 1415]; untraced		*AJ* 1872, 167; *Builder* 1872, 380; *Graves* VIII, 1905–6, 240
62.	†1846	Sir Henry Fetherstonhaugh		Harting, Sussex	S	Pevsner, *Sussex*, 1965, 238
63.	†1847	Henry Villebois		Marham, Norfolk		Pevsner, *Norfolk: N W & S*, 1999, 533
64.	†1848	1st Earl of Strafford (†1860) and officers of the Worcestershire Regiment		Worcester Cathedral		*Gunnis* 1968, 429; Pevsner, *Worcs*, 1968, 314
65.	1848	Baring family		Northington, Hants		*Builder* 1872, 380; *AJ* 1872, 167; *Graves* VIII, 1905–6, 240; Pevsner, *Hants & Isle of Wight*, 1967, 356
66.	1848	Captain John Moore Napier (†1848)		Chester Cathedral, Cheshire		*ILN* 15 Jan 1848, 18 (repr)
67.	†1848	Dr Howley, Archbishop of Canterbury (effigy only)		Canterbury Cathedral, Kent		*AJ* 1850, 177; *Graves* VIII, 1905–6, 240; Pevsner, *Kent: N E & E*, 1983, 206
68.	†1848	Lieutenant-Colonel William Havelock		All Saints, Maidstone, Kent		Pevsner, *Kent: W & Weald*, 1976, 399
69.	†1849	Charles, 2nd Earl Talbot		Ingestre, Staffs		*Gunnis* 1968, 429
70.	post-1849	Joseph Ridgway (†1842)		Horwich, Lancs	S	Pevsner, *Lancs: N*, 1969, 147; *CIIA* 4/9/81–6 (repr)
71.	†1850	Lieutenant-Colonel John King		Maidstone, Kent	S	
72.	†1850	Mary Ann Henson Drawing(s): private coll		St James, Cheltenham, Glos	S	*CIIA* 4/4/13 (repr)
73.	1852	Brigadier-General Cureton CB (†1848)		St Mary, Shrewsbury, Salop	S	*Graves* VIII, 1905–6, 240; Pevsner, *Salop*, 1958, 255
74.	†1852	Geraldine (†1850) and Henry Jervoise		Shalstone, Bucks		Pevsner, *Bucks*, 1994, 617
75.	†1852	Lady Margaret Milbank		Well, N R Yorks		Pevsner, *Yorks: N R*, 1966, 380; *Gunnis* 1968, 429
76.	1854	Rev Dr George Butler		Harrow, Middx		*ILN* 16 Sept 1854, 257 (repr)
77.	†1855	Robert Phelips		Yeovil, Somerset		Pevsner, *Somerset: S & W*, 1958, 355
78.	1856	John, 1st Baron Stanley of Alderley (†1850)		Nether Alderley, Cheshire		Pevsner, *Cheshire*, 1971, 292; *Gunnis* 1968, 429
79.	?1856	Sir William Petty		Romsey Abbey, Hants		GPC
80.	1857	John Kaye, Bishop of Lincoln		Lincoln Cathedral		Pevsner, *Lincs*, 1989, 479; *Gunnis* 1968, 429
81.	†1858	Georgiana, Lady Gordon		Chenies, Bucks		Pevsner, *Bucks*, 1994, 231
82.	1858–1859	Sir John Franklin		Royal Hospital, Greenwich (ORNC), chapel, vestry stairwell (formerly painted hall)		*ILN* 8 Jan 1859, 36 (repr); GPC
83.	†1872	Richard Westmacott III RA (the sculptor)		St Mary Abbots, Kensington, London	S	
84.	nd	Female statue kneeling on cushion, arms crossed over chest, presumably for a monument	p	Wetheral, Cumberland	S	

Statues

85.	*c*1825	Diana		Rokeby Park, Co Durham		*Busco* 1994, 172 n32
86.	1827	Girl with a bird	m	[Exhib RA, London, 1089]; untraced		*AJ*, 1872, 167; *Graves* VIII, 1905–6, 239
87.	1829	A reaper	m	[Exhib RA, London, 1139 'The Young Reaper' exhib BI, London, 544]; untraced		*Graves* 1875, 581; *Graves* VIII, 1905–6, 239
88.	1832	The cymbal player Drawing(s): sketchbook D, p149, private coll, SD 'Rome 1823'	m	Chatsworth, Derbys, sculpture gallery		*Graves* VIII, 1905–6, 239; *JKB* 1972 (3), 329, 331; *Busco* 1994, 185 n6

89.	1833	Narcissus	m	[Exhib RA, London, 1212 Exhib BI, London, 557]; untraced		*Graves* 1875, 581; *Graves* VIII, 1905–6, 239
90.	1835	George, eldest son of Mr and Lady Agnes Byng	m	[Exhib RA, London, 1081]; untraced		*Graves* VIII, 1905–6, 239
91.	1840	The captive, group Drawing(s): Pencil and wash, private coll	m	[Exhib RA, London, 1102]; untraced		*Graves* VIII, 1905–6, 239–40; *Gunnis* 1968, 428
92.	1841	Ariel		[Exhib RA, London, 1225]; untraced		*Builder* 1872, 380; *Graves* VIII, 1905–6, 240
93.	1841	T Williams	m	[Exhib RA, London, 1317]; untraced		*Graves* VIII, 1905–6, 240
94.	1844	An angel, part of a group		[Exhib Westminster Hall, London, 146]; untraced		*The Athenæum*, 1844, 674
95.	1849–1852	Odo, Bishop of Bayeux; Ernulph de Aquila; Sir Robert Grosvenor; Joan of Eaton Payment(s): £250 each		[Eaton Hall, Cheshire]; Saighton Grange, nr Chester		GPC
Busts						
96.	1829	Admiral Sir Sidney Smith		[Exhib RA, London, 1177]; untraced		*Graves* VIII, 1905–6, 239
97.	1829	C H Moore		[Exhib RA, London, 1134]; untraced		*Graves* VIII, 1905–6, 239
98.	1829	Dr J Thomson		[Exhib RA, London, 1163]; untraced		*Graves* VIII, 1905–6, 239
99.	1829	E Foxhall		[Exhib RA, London, 1158]; untraced		*Graves* VIII, 1905–6, 239
100.	1830	John Lodge		[Exhib L'pool Ac, 276]; untraced		*Gunnis* 1968, 428; *Morris and Roberts* 1998, 644;
101.	1833	Davies Gilbert, FRS	m	Pembroke College, Oxford Other versions: Royal Society, London	S	*Graves* VIII, 1905–6, 239; *Gunnis* 1968, 428
102.	1834	W E Tomlyne MP	m	[Exhib RA, London, 1068]; untraced		*Graves* VIII, 1905–6, 239
103.	1835	Rev Sydney Smith		St Paul's Cathedral, London, library		*Graves* VIII, 1905–6, 239; Pevsner, *London: City*, 1997, 182
104.	1838	Dr Friedrich August Rosen	m	BM	SD	*Dawson* 1999, 179–80 (repr)
105.	1838	Hon Adelaide Lister		Coll Mrs Basil Willett (1953) Other versions: medallion, exhib RA, London, 1294	SD	*Graves* VIII, 1905–6, 239; GPC
106.	1838	Villiers Lister	m	[Exhib RA, London, 1359]; untraced		*Graves* VIII, 1905–6, 239
107.	1839	Female in a shawl	m	Christie South Kensington, 10 Oct 2001	SD	C Lib (repr)
108.	1839	Mrs Henry Milman	m	[Exhib RA, London, 1376]; untraced		*Graves* VIII, 1905–6, 239
109.	1840	'A young lady'	m	[Exhib RA, London, 1191]; untraced		*Graves* VIII, 1905–6, 240
110.	1840	Lady Chatterton	m	[Exhib RA, London, 1197]; untraced		*Graves* VIII, 1905–6, 240
111.	1840	Viscount Fordwich	m	[Exhib RA, London, 1182]; untraced		*Graves* VIII, 1905–6, 240
112.	1841	Amorino	m	[Exhib RA, London, 1286]; untraced		*Graves* VIII, 1905–6, 240
113.	1841	Cardinal John Henry Newman	m	[Exhib RA, London, 1342]; untraced		*Graves* VIII, 1905–6, 240; *Ormond* 1973, 340
114.	1841	George Byng MP	m	[Exhib RA, London, 1324]; untraced Other versions: Woburn Abbey, Beds, marble, SD 1846		*Graves* VIII, 1905–6, 240; *British Portraits* 1956–7, 121; *Gunnis* 1968, 425
115.	1841	Lady Eleanor Elliott Drake	m	Christie 3 July 1985, lot 248	SD	*Graves* VIII, 1905–6, 240
116.	1842	Lady Harriet Baring		[Exhib RA, London, 1406]; untraced		*Graves* VIII, 1905–6, 240
117.	1842	Miss Egerton		Tatton Park, Cheshire		*Graves* VIII, 1905–6, 240; *Gunnis* 1968, 428
118.	1842	Wilbraham Egerton		Tatton Park, Cheshire		*Graves* VIII, 1905–6, 240; *Gunnis* 1968, 428
119.	1843	B Greenough FRS		[Exhib RA, London, 1529]; untraced		*Graves* VIII, 1905–6, 240
120.	1843	John, 1st Earl Russell		Woburn Abbey, Beds		*Graves* VIII, 1905–6, 240; *Walker* 1961, 63; *Gunnis* 1968, 428; *Ormond* 1973, 407
121.	1843	Lieutenant-General Sir Howard Douglas Bt		[Exhib RA, London, 1526]; untraced		*Graves* VIII, 1905–6, 240
122.	1844	Francis, Marquess of Tavistock, later 8th Duke of Bedford	m	Woburn Abbey, Beds		*Gunnis* 1968, 428
123.	1844	Major-General Lord William George Russell	m	[Exhib RA, London, 1464]; untraced	SD	*Graves* VIII, 1905–6, 240
124.	1844	Rev Lord Wriothesley Russell	m	Woburn Abbey, Beds	SD	*Graves* VIII, 1905–6, 240; *Gunnis* 1968, 428
125.	1845	Charles William Packe		Prestwold Hall, Leics		*Graves* VIII, 1905–6, 240; GPC; C Lib (repr)
126.	1845	Edward, 1st Earl of Wharncliffe		[Exhib RA, London, 1849, 1333]; Falconhurst, Hever, Kent		*Graves* VIII, 1905–6, 240; GPC
127.	1845	John Edward Gray FRS	m	BM	SD	*Dawson* 1999, 106–8 (repr)
128.	1845	Sir Francis Burdett		Untraced Other versions: marble, Coutts Bank, S		*AJ* 1872, 167; *Graves* VIII, 1905–6, 240; *Gunnis* 1968, 428
129.	1845	T Hildyard, of Flintham Hall	m	[Exhib RA, London, 1391]; untraced		*Graves* VIII, 1905–6, 240
130.	1846	Charles, 2nd Earl Talbot		Falconhurst, Hever, Kent		*Graves* VIII, 1905–6, 240; GPC
131.	1846	Marianne Packe		Prestwold Hall, Leics		*Graves* VIII, 1905–6, 240; GPC; C Lib (repr)
132.	1847	'A young lady, posthumous'	m	[Exhib RA, London, 1426]; untraced		*Graves* VIII, 1905–6, 240
133.	1847	Francis, 7th Duke of Bedford		Woburn Abbey, Beds	SD	*AU* 1846, 189; *Graves* VIII, 1905–6, 240; *Gunnis* 1968, 428
134.	1847	Robert Williams, of Bridehead	m	[Exhib RA, London, 1424]; untraced		*Graves* VIII, 1905–6, 240
135.	1847	Sir Roderick Murchison	p	SNPG		*AU* 1848, 180; *Graves* VIII, 1905–6, 240; *Ormond* 1973, 329

136.	1848	A Sidebottom, Esq		[Exhib RA, London, 1461]; untraced		*Graves* VIII, 1905–6, 240
137.	1848	'A young lady'		[Exhib RA, London, 1445]; untraced		*Graves* VIII, 1905–6, 240
138.	1848	G Purefoy Tervoise		[Exhib RA, London, 1463]; untraced		*Graves* VIII, 1905–6, 240
139.	1848	Lord Charles Townshend		[Exhib RA, London, 1324]; untraced		*Graves* VIII, 1905–6, 240
140.	†1848	Unidentified male (inscribed 'G.P.J')		Untraced	S	GPC
141.	1850	Sir Robert Peel		[coll Alderman Copeland]; untraced		GPC
142.	1854	Mrs Crole Wyndham	m	[Exhib RA, London, 1505]; untraced		*Graves* VIII, 1905–6, 240
143.	1854	Rev Crole Wyndham	m	[Exhib RA, London, 1504]; untraced		*Graves* VIII, 1905–6, 240
144.	1855	Richard Ellison, of Sudbrooke Holme, Lincoln		[Exhib RA, London, 1544]; untraced		*Graves* VIII, 1905–6, 240
145.	nd	9th Duke of Bedford	m	Woburn Abbey, Beds		C Lib (repr)
146.	nd	Hon Algernon Russell Gayleard Stanhope (1838–1847)	m	NGI 8209		*le Harivel* 1988, 604 (repr)
147.	nd	Lady Ribblesdale (†1838)		Private coll (1953)		GPC
Chimneypieces						
148.	1829	Two, carved marble Payment(s): £600		[Buckingham Palace, London]; untraced		TNA WORK 19/3 fol 361; *Gunnis* 1968, 428
149.	1833	Flanked by bacchanalian figures (co-sculptor: Robert William Sievier)		Chatsworth, Derbys, dining room		*Cavendish* 1846, 83; *Thompson* 1949, 199; Pevsner, *Derbys*, 1978, 137; *Busco* 1994, 185 n6
150.	nd	With portraits of the two daughters of the Duchess of Sutherland as caryatids		[Stafford House, London]; untraced		*Gunnis* 1968, 428
Architectural Sculpture						
151.	1828–1832	Relief of Fame displaying Britain's military and naval triumphs (originally intended for Marble Arch)		Buckingham Palace, London, west front attic		*Colvin* 1973–6, vol 6, 301; *Busco* 1994, 58, 180 n97
152.	1842–1844	'The Earth is the Lord's And the Fulness thereof,' group representing Commerce and the History of Trade	s	Royal Exchange, City of London, exterior pediment		*ILN* 17 Feb 1844, 104 (repr); *Read* 1982, 215, 215–6 (repr); *Busco* 1994, 124 (repr); *Ward-Jackson* 2002, 687–91
153.	nd	Reredos, central panel		North Perrott, Somerset		Pevsner, *Somerset: S & W*, 1958, 260
Reliefs						
154.	1831	Venus carrying away Ascanius		Bridgewater House, City of London		*Passavant* 1836, vol 2, 281–2; *AJ* 1872, 167; *Graves* 1875, 581; *Graves* VIII, 1905–6, 239; *Gunnis* 1968, 428; Pevsner, *London: Westminster*, 1973, 573
155.	1834	Hope, alto-relievo	m	[Exhib RA, London, 1113]; untraced		*Graves* VIII, 1905–6, 239
156.	1837	Mercury introducing Pandora to Prometheus		[Bowood, Wilts, entrance hall]; Sotheby, Belgravia, 6 June 73 lot 56; private coll, N Y	SD	*Graves* VIII, 1905–6, 239; Sotheby's Belgravia, 6 June 1973 (repr); C Lib (repr)
157.	1837	Paolo and Francesca Model(s): Sotheby 12 May 1995	m	Bowood, Wilts Other versions: Replica, Nostell Priory, W R Yorks, D 1838		*AJ* 1872, 167; *Builder* 1872, 380; *Graves* VIII, 1905–6, 239; *Gunnis* 1968, 428; GPC
158.	1836–1838	Blue bell Model(s): plaster, SD, Feb 1836, sold Christie, Belgravia, 15 Feb 1990		[coll Earl of Ellesmere]; untraced		*AJ* 1849, 56 (repr); *AJ Cat* 1862, fol 1 (repr); *Builder* 1872, 380; *Graves* VIII, 1905–6, 239; *Gunnis* 1968, 428
159.	1836–1838	The butterfly Model(s): Exhib RA, London, 1288, family coll	m	[coll Earl of Ellesmere]; untraced		*Builder* 1872, 380; *AJ*, 1872, 167; *Graves* VIII, 1905–6, 239; *Morris and Roberts* 1998, 644
160.	1838	Venus instructing Cupid		Bridgewater House, City of London		*AJ* 1872, 167; *Graves* VIII, 1905–6, 239; *Gunnis* 1968, 428; Pevsner, *London: Westminster*, 1973, 573
161.	1842	A child's head, from life		[Exhib L'pool Ac, 567]; untraced		*Morris and Roberts* 1998, 644
162.	1847	'The soul enslaved by sin, unable to join the spirits of the blessed', a sketch		[Exhib RA, London, 1451]; untraced		*Graves* VIII, 1905–6, 240
163.	nd	Bacchus and Ariadne	m	Chatsworth, Derbys	S	*Busco* 1994, 185 n6
Miscellaneous						
164.	1829	Girl with a fawn, group	m	[Exhib RA, London, 1200]; untraced		*Graves* VIII, 1905–6, 239
165.	1831	Mischief (Cupid with an arrow)		[Exhib RA, London, 1225 Exhib BI, 1832, 586]; untraced		*Passavant* 1836, vol 2, 281–2; *Graves* 1875, 581; *Graves* VIII, 1905–6, 239; *Library of Fine Arts* 1831, vol 1, 432
166.	1849	'Go, and sin no more'		[Exhib RA, London, 1850, 1320, Diploma Work]; Burlington House, London	SD	*Builder* 1872, 380; *Graves* VIII, 1905–6, 240; *Gunnis* 1968, 428
167.	1855	A study		[Exhib RA, London, 1547]; untraced		*Graves* VIII, 1905–6, 240
168.	1855	'Sketch for an enriched salver in gold and ivory; the groups of children, with the foliage form letters'		[Exhib RA, London, 1433]; untraced		*Graves* VIII, 1905–6, 240
169.	nd	Cupid and wasp		Eaton Hall, Cheshire		*Gunnis* 1968, 428
170.	nd	David slaying Goliath		[Crystal Palace, Sydenham]; untraced		*AJ* 1872, 167; *Builder* 1872, 380; *Graves* VIII, 1905–6, 240;GPC
171.	nd	Head of a girl		County Museum, Carmarthen		GPC

WESTMINSTER MARBLE COMPANY fl *c*1848–52

The firm's authoritative name, coupled with the fact that they sent at least one monument to the West Indies (**3**), suggests a flourishing company, though few of their works have been identified. In 1852 their yard was in Earl Street, London. See **Patent Marble Works of Westminster** and **Westminster Marble Works.**

Funerary Monuments

1.	†1848	Enoch Durant	St Peter, Arkley, Barnet		Pevsner, *London: N*, 1998, 110
2.	†1852	W Tierney Clark	St Paul, Hammersmith, London	S	Pevsner, *London: N W*, 1991, 205
3.	†1852	William Swanston	Trinity, Palmetto, St Kitts	S	

WESTMINSTER MARBLE WORKS fl *c*1848

Possibly an alternative name for the **Westminster Marble Company** or **Patent Marble Works of Westminster.**

Funerary Monuments

1.	†1848	Anne Burmester	Holy Trinity, Tunbridge Wells, Kent	Pevsner, *Kent: W & Weald*, 1976, 580

WESTON fl 1704

In 1704 Browne Willis, the antiquary, whilst at Bletchley, paid Weston £3 for restoring Lord Grey's monument (**1**). Two inscribed slabs were also laid in the chancel floor to Willis's parents and Gunnis notes that the armorials are surprisingly well carved (**2**).

Literary References: *Gunnis* 1968, 429, citing *Records of Bucks*, XII, 246

Miscellaneous

1.	1704	'New cutting over the Lord Grey's monument' (Lord Grey of Wilton †1447) Payment(s): £3	Bletchley, Bucks	*Gunnis* 1968, 429; Pevsner, *Bucks*, 1987, 67
2.	1704	'Two black marble stones laid over the body of Thomas Willis, Esq. [†1699] and Alice his wife and cutting the arms and inscription'	Bletchley, Bucks	*Gunnis* 1968, 429; Pevsner, *Bucks*, 1987, 68

WESTON, John, of Exeter –before 1748

Nothing is known of Weston's training but he became one of the most accomplished West Country sculptors of the earlier 18th century. His monuments are ambitious and wide-ranging in style, and several of the best incorporate *Last judgment* reliefs with large numbers of twisting figures (**1, 6, 8, 10**). Gunnis notes that the figures 'have all the grace and movement of the Italian Renaissance, while the design anticipates the work of William Blake'.

The first recorded reference to Weston was on 2 February 1723 when the dean and chapter of Exeter rented out to him a shed and courtlage in the Close at an annual rent of 25/-. The land tax assessment for 1730 valued his house in the parish of St Mary Major at £6 10s. That year John Weston, freeman, became surveyor and clerk of works to the dean and chapter and was accorded a loft and workshop in the cloisters, valued at £6 10s. This appointment terminated in 1741 or 1742. In 1745 he became a member of the Exeter Association in support of King George II. Three years later he had evidently died for the land tax records refer to the 'late Mr Weston's house'.

His signed works include wall tablets (**3, 5**) and architectural monuments with full-sized attendant figures (**1, 4, 8, 10**). The Ivie monument, originally a much larger work, was first erected in St Kerrian, Exeter, but when the church was pulled down the relief was moved to St Petrock (**6**). According to Cresswell, it was signed by Weston and its architectural surround was probably similar to those of the Kelland (now dismantled) and Scobell monuments (**1, 10**). The tablet to Francis Pengelly is also an architectural composition and flanking the monument are symbolic figures of *Learning* and *Justice* (**8**). The Hobbs has a *baldacchino* with hanging curtains, raised on either side by figures to reveal the inscription tablet. Below is a shield carved with spades, scythes, coronets, a skull and crossed bones (**7**). A late work, the memorial to a sailor, John Taylor, reflects the deceased man's occupation: it has a portrait medallion, naval trophies, medals of Queen Anne and King George I and below, a fine relief of Taylor's ship engaging 4 triremes, probably manned by Moorish pirates (**11**).

Easter doubts that Weston is the author of the monument to Benjamin Dolen, †1700, in Exeter Cathedral, questioning Gunnis's claim that it is signed. It has an uncharacteristic bust above a heavily moulded frame adorned with a wealth of swirls and foliage and a ship in profile in the lowest curve. Easter suggests however that the memorial to Sir Thomas Northmore, †1713, at St Thomas, Exeter, may well be Weston's work since it too has a characteristic relief of the *Last judgment.* He argues also for the William Williams, †1713, at St Thomas, Exeter, on stylistic grounds.

Literary References: *Cresswell* 1908, 147; *Gunnis* 1952 (2), 1337; *Little* 1952, 1659; *Gunnis* 1968, 429–50; *Easter* 1995, 84–89

Funerary Monuments

1.	†1712	John Kelland	Ashprington, Devon until *c*1960. The relief perhaps identifiable with a *Last judgment* panel sold Bonham, London, 25 Oct 1990	S	*Gunnis* 1968, 429
2.	*c*1712	The Last Judgement, panel from an unidentified monument, possibly the Kelland	Royal Albert Memorial Museum, Totnes		*Easter* 1995, 85–6
3.	†1713	Nicholas Sayer	Morebath, Devon	S	
4.	†1715	Philip Hooper	St Martin, Exeter, Devon	SD	Pevsner, *Devon*, 1989, 391
5.	1715	Rev John Newte	Tiverton, Devon	S	*Gunnis* 1968, 430
6.	†1717	Jonathan and Elizabeth Ivie	[St Kerrian, Exeter]; St Petrock, Exeter, Devon	S	Pevsner, *Devon*, 1989, 395; *Easter* 1995, 86
7.	1718	Edward Hobbs	Gerrans, Cornwall		*Gunnis* 1968, 430
8.	†1722	Francis Pengelly (or Pengelley)	Whitchurch, Devon	S	*Little* 1952, 1659; *Easter* 1995, 86, 87 (repr)
9.	†1727	Roger Vavasour (†1696) and son	St Saviour, Dartmouth, Devon	S	Pevsner, *Devon*, 1989, 324
10.	1729	Henry Scobell (†1727)	St Blazey, near St Austell, Cornwall	S	Pevsner, *Cornwall*, 1970, 159; *Easter* 1995, 87 (repr)

11.	1736	John Taylor (†1733)	Denbury, Devon	S	Pevsner, *Devon*, 1989, 334; *Easter* 1995, 88
12.	nd	Fragment, mourning cherubs, coat of arms, perhaps from the monument to Francis Weller	Honiton Clyst, Devon	S	*Gunnis* 1968, 430

WHEELER, I, of Reading fl *c*1844

The Arnold monument is described by Pevsner as a sumptuous Gothic shrine without effigy.

Funerary Monuments

1.	†1844	George Henry Arnold	Ashby St Ledgers, Northants	S	Pevsner, *Northants*, 1973, 90; *CIIA* 4/3/8-18 (repr)

WHEELER, John, of Beaulieu fl *c*1806

Funerary Monuments

1.	1806	Lady Cope, neo-Hellenic wall-tablet	Eversley, Hants		*Gunnis* 1968, 430
2.	nd	Unidentified subjects, tablets	South Warnborough, Hants	S	*Gunnis* 1968, 430

WHEELER, of Bristol and Gloucester fl *c*1833

Funerary Monuments

1.	†1833	Eliza Watson	Hutton, Somerset		RG/JP, 9, 1580v

WHISSELL, Brandon fl 1750–90

He was responsible for a great deal of building at Ragley Hall, Warks, receiving over £500 in 1749–50 for mason's work; this payment included £96 for 'Pillasters, rustics and mouldings'. In 1780 he repaired the chancel of St James, Arrow, Warks and in 1787 he was again the principal mason for alterations to Ragley Hall under the architect James Wyatt, receiving £344.

Archival References: GPC quoting Archives, Marquess of Hertford

WHITE, C, of London fl 1808

Funerary Monuments

1.	1808	John Hooper	Shoreham, Sussex		*Gunnis* 1968, 430

WHITE, G P fl 1844–49

The Hobart monument (1) has an arched surround and two kneeling women at prayer.

Funerary Monuments					
1.	†1846	Rev H L Hobart, Dean of Windsor	Nocton, Lincs		Pevsner, *Lincs*, 1989, 578
Architectural Sculpture					
2.	1844–1845	Heads and figures on canopies of chapter house seats	York Minster		Pevsner, *Yorks E R & York*, 1995, 135
3.	*c*1849	Capitals	St Stephen, Rochester Row, Westminster, London		Pevsner, *London: Westminster*, 1973, 501

WHITE, of Bath fl *c*1808–55

Funerary Monuments

1.	†1808	Sarah Tuck	St Lawrence, Didmarton, Glos	S	Pevsner, *Glos: Cotswolds*, 1999, 314
2.	†1837	Elizabeth Adey	St Mary the Virgin, Wotton-under-Edge, Glos	S	Pevsner, *Glos: Cotswolds*, 1999, 757
3.	†1855	George (†1847), Sarah (†1854) and Hannah Ireland	South Cerney, Glos	S	Pevsner, *Glos: Cotswolds*, 1999, 619
4.	†1855	Sarah Redwood	South Cerney, Glos	S	

WHITE, of Vauxhall Bridge Road, London fl *c*1850–54

Since he sent monuments as far afield as Herts and Staffs it seems likely that he had a substantial practice.

Funerary Monuments

1.	†1850	Peel family member	Drayton Bassett, Staffs		Pevsner, *Staffs*, 1974, 117
2.	†1854	Thomas, Ethelbert and Frederick Halsey	Great Gaddesdon, Herts	S	

WHITE, Richard *c*1615–64/5

He was apprenticed to Nicholas Stone, Master Mason to King Charles I, in 1629–30, under the auspices of the Masons' Company and is listed among the Company's yeomanry until his death. In 1638 White subcontracted to him a 'statua in whitt marbell', probably the effigy of Penelope, Lady Spencer on Stone's monument at Great Brington, Northants. He agreed also to complete a Corinthian capital, probably intended for the canopy. There are no recorded works after 1660.

Literary References: *Knoop and Jones* 1935, 24; *White* 1999, 140–1

WHITE, Sampson, of York fl 1755

He was employed by Richard Weddell at Newby Hall, W R Yorks, in 1755.

Funerary Monuments				
1.	1755	'marble grave stone' for an unidentified subject Payment(s): £19 4s 6d	Untraced	GPC citing Archives, Compton of Newby
Chimneypieces				
2.	1755	'Apollo and Marygold'	[Newby Hall, W R Yorks]; untraced	GPC citing Archives, Compton of Newby

WHITE, Simon, of Oxford 1619–

Baptised in 1619, the son of Abraham White, he was the principal stone-carver working on the library and chapel at Brasenose College, Oxford, both before the Restoration and later. He was described as a carver for marbles when he received a payment of £30 from the College in 1665. A year later he was paid a further £52 for laying the marbles (*Allfrey* 1909, 3, 20–22). In 1669 White received £5 for a marble altar (1), which was placed with the Arundel Marbles.

Literary References: *Cole* 1949, 64; *Gunnis* 1968, 430

Architectural Sculpture

1.	1669	Marble altar Payment(s): £5	m	Untraced	*Gunnis* 1968, 430 quoting Wood *Life and Times*, IV, 69

WHITE, Thomas, of Canterbury fl 1764–1801

From 1764 until 1801 he was the master-mason at Canterbury Cathedral, and in 1791 carried out extensive repairs, receiving £271 for his work on 'Bell Harry' (Treasurer's Accounts, Cathedral Library quoted by *Gunnis* 1968, 430). In the previous year he had been paid £890 for rebuilding St Augustine, Brookland, Kent. He was succeeded by his nephew **Thomas Longley**.

WHITE, Thomas, of Worcester *c*1674–1748

White was a carver and, according to several commentators, an architect, though he described himself in his will as a statuary, a claim endorsed by the quantity and quality of his known sculpture. He was well regarded by early historians of his native Worcester where he executed much of his work, but he also had premises in Shrewsbury. He was probably trained in London where he was apprenticed to a 'statuary and stone-cutter in Piccadilly' (*Green* 1796, 89). He may conceivably be the Thomas White made free of the Masons' Company as a 'Foreign Member' on 13 January 1690.

He was working in Worcester by 1709 when he became a freeman of that city having made 'a handsome effigie of the Queen to ye well likeing of the Mayor and Aldermen' (**15**) and in 1712 he repaired statues of Charles I and Charles II (**16**). His work must have impressed the city elders: when rebuilding work began at Worcester Guildhall in 1721, White worked on the sculptural programme. The two statues of Stuart kings were positioned on the façade with his figure of Queen Anne and the pediment was exuberantly carved with trophies, statues and reliefs (**20**). In 1724 the Corporation granted him an annuity of £30 in recognition of this work. As a good citizen he stipulated in his will that any outstanding monies from the annuity should be used by the Worcester Infirmary.

His practice encompassed funerary monuments, both tablets and figurative compositions, and he built several churches in Worcester. He died in 1748 and was buried at Kempsey, near Worcester. In his will, proved on 14 September that year, he left property to his servant Mary Rudsbey and to several family members.

Colvin describes him as a 'very competent draughtsman' and notes that he was responsible for the 'elaborate' Worcester guildhall pediment, but other commentators have been less kind. Whiffen dismissed him as 'not a great architect, and still further from being a great sculptor' (*Whiffen* 1945, 1005). Pevsner thought the tablet to Bridges Nanfan at Birtsmorton 'nothing special' and refused to consider White as author of the splendid neighbouring monument to William Caldwell, despite a convincing attribution by Buchanan-Dunlop. Pevsner described the extensive sculptural programme at Worcester Guildhall as bellicose and barbaric in its splendour, though it clearly makes a substantial and positive contribution to the grandeur of the building. Whatever the merit of his funerary monuments, White's work at the Guildhall marks him out as one of Worcester's most significant artistic figures.

Lucy Jessop

Literary References: *Nash* 1791, *passim*; *Green* 1796, 89; *Watkin* 1907, 1–80, 147–78; *Griffiths* 1932, 93; *Wren MS* 1941, 204; *Buchanan-Dunlop* 1943, 17, 18, 19; *Buchanan-Dunlop* 1944 (1), 64; *Whiffen* 1945, 1002; Pevsner, *Worcs*, 1968, 92, 323; *Shaw* 1976, I, *passim*; *Colvin* 1995, 1004

Archival References: Masons' Co, *Freemen*, fol 72

Will: PROB 11/764/349

Funerary Monuments

1.	†1698	Adam Cave	All Saints, Evesham	S	*Buchanan-Dunlop* 1943, 19
2.	1704	Bridges and Catherine Nanfan	Birtsmorton, Worcs	S	*Buchanan-Dunlop* 1944 (1), 64; *Whiffen* 1945, 1005 (repr)
3.	1707	Sir John Turton	Alrewas, Staffs	S	*Gunnis* 1968, 430; Pevsner, *Staffs*, 1974, 53; *Shaw* 1976, 1, 129
4.	*c*1710	Bishop William Thomas (†1689)	Worcester Cathedral	S	*Buchanan-Dunlop* 1943, 19; *Whiffen* 1944, 127; *Whiffen* 1945, 1005; *Gunnis* 1968, 430
5.	†1718	Jane Jeffreyes	Clifton-on-Teme, Worcs	S	Nash 1791, 1, 242; *Wren* MS, 4, 15–17; *Buchanan-Dunlop* 1943, 19; Pevsner, *Worcs*, 1968, 122
6.	†1719	Henrietta Wrottesley	Worcester Cathedral	S	*Buchanan-Dunlop* 1943, 18; *Gunnis* 1968, 430
7.	1719	Lady Ursula Bridgeman Drawing(s): Staffs RO D1287/8/8 temp listing P267	Llanyblodwel, Salop	S	*Watkin* 1907, 57; Pevsner, *Shrops*, 1958, 171; *Gunnis* 1968, 430; *Colvin* 1995, 1044
8.	†1725	Captain Samuel Skynner	Ledbury, Herefs	S	*Whiffen* 1944, 127 (repr); Pevsner, *Herefs*, 1963, 217
9.	1727	Rev Josiah Foster	Aston, Birmingham	S	*Buchanan-Dunlop* 1943, 19; *Gunnis* 1968, 431
10.	†1730	Mary Lyster and family members	St Mary, Shrewsbury, Salop	S	*Buchanan-Dunlop* 1943, 19; *Whiffen* 1945, 1005; Pevsner, *Salop*, 1958, 256
11.	1735	John Holt	Ripple, Worcs	S	*Buchanan-Dunlop* 1944 (1), 65; *Whiffen* 1945, 1005; *Gunnis* 1968, 431
12.	post-1736	Roger Matthews (†1673)	Llanyblodwel, Salop	S	*Watkin* 1907, 57; *Buchanan-Dunlop* 1943, 19; *Colvin* 1995, 1044
13.	†1742	Dr George Peyton	Tewkesbury Abbey, Glos	S	*Buchanan-Dunlop* 1943, 19; Pevsner, *Glos: Vale & Forest of Dean*, 1976, 368
14.	†1742	John Brydges	Holy Trinity, Bosbury, Herefs	S	*Buchanan-Dunlop* 1944 (1), 65; *Whiffen* 1945, 1005 (repr); Pevsner, *Herefs*, 1963, 80; *Gunnis* 1968, 431

Statues

15.	1709	Queen Anne	New Guildhall, Worcester, niche over door (formerly Worcester Town Hall)		*Green* 1796, 1, 90; *Wren* MS 1941, 204; *Gunnis* 1968, 431; *Colvin* 1995, 1044
16.	1712	King Charles I and King Charles II 'repaired and beautified'	Guildhall, Worcester		*Buchanan-Dunlop* 1943, 17; *Gunnis* 1968, 430
17.	nd	Britannia	Alice Ottley School, Worcester (formerly Britannia House)		*Buchanan-Dunlop* 1943, 23 (repr); *Whiffen* 1945, 1002–3 (repr); *Gunnis* 1968, 430

Busts

18.	nd	Bishop Hough	[All Saints, Worcester]; untraced		*Wren* MS 1941, 204; *Buchanan-Dunlop* 1943, 20
19.	nd	King George II	[Edgar's Tower, Worcester]; untraced		*Wren* MS 1941, 204; *Buchanan-Dunlop* 1943, 20

Architectural Sculpture

20.	1722	Tympanum sculpture and other ornaments	Guildhall, Worcester	SD	*Whiffen* 1945, 1002–3 (repr); *Gunnis* 1968, 430; *Colvin* 1995, 1044

WHITE, W Joseph fl 1761

He lived in Great Portland Street, Cavendish Square in 1761, when he carved a statue of George III (inf. Claude Blair).

Statues

1.	1761	King George III	Untraced		Guildhall MS.70.2 and MS. 5.18

WHITEHEAD, J fl *c*1881

Funerary Monuments

1.	†1888	William Wainwright	Old Woking, Surrey	S	

WHITEHEAD, J & Co fl *c*1849

Funerary Monuments

1.	†1849	Wright family member	Acton Trussell, Staffs		Pevsner, *Staffs*, 1974, 52

WHITEHEAD, J and M

Funerary Monuments

1.	nd	Unidentified subject, tablet with the figure of a mourning woman	Kentish Town parish church, London	S	*Gunnis* 1968, 431

WHITEHEAD, J T, of Cheltenham fl *c*1813

Funerary Monuments

1.	†1813	Robert Arkell	Boddington, Glos	S	Pevsner, *Glos: Vale & Forest of Dean*, 1976, 113

WHITEHEAD, James, of London fl *c*1799–1817

Funerary Monuments

1.	†1799	Mrs Brandreth	Redbourn, Herts	S	GPC
2.	†1815	Edward Matthews	Chipping Norton, Oxon	S	GPC
3.	1818	Lieutenant-General William St Leger	St Mary, St Marylebone, London	S	*Gunnis* 1968, 431

Chimneypieces

4.	1817	Several Payment(s): £123	[Battle Abbey, Sussex]; untraced		*Gunnis* 1968, 431, citing Archives, Mrs Harbord, of Battle Abbey

WHITEHEAD, John, of the New Road, Fitzroy Square fl 1814

Miscellaneous

1.	1814	Aeneas flying from Troy, plaster-cast p	[Soc of A, silver palette]; untraced		RSA *Transactions*, 1815, vol 32, 23; *Gunnis* 1968, 431

WHITEHEAD, Peter fl 1739

A carver who worked at Wentworth Woodhouse for **Henry Watson** in March 1739. His arrival is recorded in Watson's account book (Bodleian MS Eng Misc fols 383, 152).

Literary References: *Brighton* 2001, 72

WHITEHEAD, W, of London fl *c*1859

Funerary Monuments

1.	†1859	Hon George Fox-Strangways	Farley, Wilts	S	*Gunnis* 1968, 431; Pevsner, *Wilts*, 1975, 243

WHITELAW, William, of London fl 1786–*c*1843

Gunnis described him as a prolific monumental statuary, most of whose works are dull. The Tew monument however has a fully clothed genius with wings, rising against a black slab (**6**), the St Vincent has a portrait bust (**13**) and the Wykeham, a weeping woman kneeling over an urn (**14**). 'Wm Whitelaw-Statuary &c- Bath Place [Fitzroy Square, London]' appears several times in the Longleat archives (**32**). By 1842 he was living in New Road, London.

Literary References: *Gunnis* 1968, 431; *Potterton* 1975, 87

Archival References: Longleat HA 1800–1818

Funerary Monuments

1.	†to 1786	Lister family	Burwell, Lincs	S	Pevsner, *Lincs*, 1989, 202
2.	†1805	Mrs Forrester	All Saints (disused), Leicester	S	*Gunnis* 1968, 431; Pevsner, *Leics & Rutland*, 1984, 210
3.	†1814	Matthew Flinders	Donington, Lincs	S	Pevsner, *Lincs*, 1989, 256
4.	?1816	Frederick Pitcher	[St James, Hampstead Road, London]; untraced	S	*Gunnis* 1968, 431
5.	?1816	Richard Sowdon	St Mary, Reading, Berks	S	*Gunnis* 1968, 431
6.	†1817	Edward Tew	Eton College, Windsor, Berks	S	Pevsner, *Bucks*, 1994, 307

7.	?1817	Robert Powney	St Mary, St Marylebone, London	S	*Gunnis* 1968, 431
8.	?1818	Lady Bayly	Stoke d'Abernon, Surrey	S	*Gunnis* 1968, 431
9.	†1818	Rev Thomas Taylor	Debden, Essex	S	*Gunnis* 1968, 431; Colvin/Gunnis corr, HMI
10.	†1820	James Grave and Anthony Littledale	Baldock, Herts	S	*Gunnis* 1968, 431
11.	†1821	James (†1808) and Rebecca Seager	Poole, Dorset	S	RG/JP, 9, 1585
12.	?1822	Hon Samuel Ongley	Sandy, Beds	S	*Gunnis* 1968, 431
13.	†1823	Lord St Vincent	Stone, Staffs		*Gunnis* 1968, 431; Pevsner, Staffs, 1974, 268;
14.	†1823	Mrs Wykeham	Kingsey, Bucks	S	Pevsner, *Bucks*, 1994, 421
15.	1824	Sir Thomas Reid Bt FRS	St Michael, Dumfries	SD	*Gunnis* 1968, 431
16.	†1826	Hon Samuel Trench Ongley	Christ Church Cathedral, Dublin		*Potterton* 1975, 87
17.	?1827	General Sir Edward Howorth	Banstead, Surrey	S	*Gunnis* 1968, 431
18.	†1828	Simon Taylor	All Souls College, Oxford, chapel	S	RG/JP, 9, 1585
19.	†1829	Charles Gordon	St Peter, Berkhamsted, Herts	S	*Gunnis* 1968, 431; Pevsner, *Herts*, 1977, 97
20.	?1832	Rev John Templer	Teigngrace, Devon	S	*Gunnis* 1968, 431
21.	†1833	Sarah Bourne	Hilderstone, Staffs		*Jeavons* 1960, 70
22.	†1834	Robert Hopkins	Tidmarsh, Berks		Pevsner, *Berks*, 1966, 241
23.	†1835	Ralph Bourne	Hilderstone, Staffs		*Jeavons* 1960, 70
24.	†1836	James, Lord de Saumarez	Town church, St Peter Port, Guernsey	S	
25.	?1837	Edward Jacob	Faversham, Kent	S	*Gunnis* 1968, 431
26.	?1837	Lucy Monoux	Evershot, Beds	S	*Gunnis* 1968, 431; RG/JP, 9, 1585
27.	†1841	Frances, Lady Ongley	Old Warden, Beds	S	RG/JP, 9, 1585
28.	†1842	Sir Joseph Littledale	St George, Bloomsbury, London	S	
29.	†1843	John Fam Timins and family members	Aldenham, Herts	S	
Chimneypieces					
30.	1809	Description unavailable	[Panshanger, Herts]; untraced		Panshanger Archives in GPC
31.	1812	Description unavailable	[Ombersley Court, Worcs]; untraced		Archives, Lord Sandys, in *Gunnis* 1968, 431
32.	1807–1812	Several, statuary marble Payment(s): £182	[Longleat, Wilts]; untraced		Longleat HA, 1800–1818, 12.12.1807 (fol 14r); 6.8.1808 (fol 22r); *Gunnis* 1968, 431
Architectural Sculpture					
33.	1817	Stone carving	Knebworth, Herts, mausoleum		GPC

WHITING fl *c*1765

Possibly related to **John Whiting of Northampton**.

Funerary Monuments					
1.	†1765	John Orlebar	Podington, Beds	S	

WHITING, John, of Northampton 1782–1854

An earlier member of the family seems to have been William Whiting who, in the *Northampton Mercury* of 31 July 1775, advertised that, together with John Middleton and a Mr John Lickfield, he wanted stone cutters for a quarry at Dunstan Heath, near Northampton. This quarry belonged originally to the Lumleys and the Whitings seem to have married into that family. John Whiting purchased his freedom of the town of Northampton on 15 March 1806, and his subsequent monumental work was almost exclusively for local patrons. Gunnis considered it on the whole 'very uninteresting'. The Kerr tablet has a relief of the county hospital at the top (**9**) and the Samwell has a 'well-cut' relief of a mourning woman (**11**). He was apparently also responsible for a number of chimneypieces at Lamport Hall, Northants (**14**).

The following advertisement appeared in the *Northampton Mercury* of 14 June 1817: 'Handsome Marble Monuments and Entablators, adapted for the deceased of both sexes in the best manner, on Terms remarkably cheap. A variety of Marble Chimney Pieces, for Drawing Rooms, Libraries, &c. of various dimensions; to be seen at J. Whiting's, Statuary, Derngate, Northampton. N.B. Marble Mortars, Teneriffe filtering Stone, slate Cisterns, a Quantity of plain white Dutch Tiles, &c. &c.'

Literary References: *Gunnis* 1968, 431

Archival References: GPC

Funerary Monuments					
1.	?1807	Katherine Thornton	Brockhall, Northants	S	*Gunnis* 1968, 431
2.	?1808	Daniel Knightley	Hardingstone, Northants	S	*Gunnis* 1968, 431
3.	?1810	Benjamin Laver	Hardingstone, Northants	S	*Gunnis* 1968, 431
4.	?1810	Robert Fleetwood	St Peter, Northampton	S	*Gunnis* 1968, 431
5.	?1814	Rev E Isham	Lamport, Northamptonshire	S	*Gunnis* 1968, 431
6.	?1821	Thomas Foster	Newport Pagnell, Bucks	S	*Gunnis* 1968, 431
7.	†1823	Sir Justinian Isham (†1818) and his wife Susanna	Lamport, Northants	S	*Isham* 1965, 7c
8.	?1824	John Yates	Brackley, Northants	S	*Gunnis* 1968, 431
9.	?1824	William Kerr	Church of the Holy Sepulchre, Northampton		*Gunnis* 1968, 431
10.	?1829	Mary Dawson	Clapham, Beds	S	*Gunnis* 1968, 431
11.	1835	Thomas Samwell	St Michael, Upton, Northants		*Gunnis* 1968, 431; Pevsner, *Northants*, 1973, 438
12.	?1838	Mary Hayne	Spratton, Northants	S	*Gunnis* 1968, 431
13.	?1840	Joseph Brookes	Clifton-Reynes, Bucks	S	*Gunnis* 1968, 431
Chimneypieces					
14.	nd	Several including one in the cabinet room	Lamport Hall, Northants		RG/JP, 9, 1585

WHITING, Robert, of Cambridge fl *c*1790?

Funerary Monuments					
1.	?*c*1790	Thomas Price, large wall-tablet	Astwell, Northants	S	*Gunnis* 1968, 431

WHITLEY, W

For further information the reader is referred to *Pyke* 1973, 157 and *Pyke* 1981, 42.

WHITTLE, Benjamin, of Liverpool fl 1816

Funerary Monuments

1.	1816	Rev W Keyt, wall-tablet with an urn and coat of arms	Runcorn, Cheshire	S	*Gunnis* 1968, 431

WHITTLE, James –1759

A successful mason and wood carver of Great St Andrews Street, Soho, he was in business with his son Thomas from 1752–55, when Thomas died. The father and son were responsible for extensive work, particularly pediment sculpture at Woburn Abbey (**1, 2**). In 1754 the cabinet-maker William Hallett appears to have steered Whittle's daughter, Ann, towards marriage with **Samuel Norman**, Hallett's nephew, who had his own carving and gilding business in King Street, Soho. It is not clear when Whittle and Norman went into partnership but Whittle received payments totalling £1,219 15s from the Earl of Egremont at Petworth between December 1755 and February 1759 and thereafter it was Norman's name that appeared in the books (**3**). Whittle and Norman were together responsible for much interior ornament in wood at Woburn (**4**). In June 1759 the pair considered expanding the masonry side of their business and bought a large piece of marble which was inspected by their sub-contractor, William Long, and was to have been made into chimneypieces and table slabs. The venture proved short-lived for the material was spoilt in a fire in the King Street premises. Whittle died shortly beforehand, on 10 December 1759. He left half his estate to his wife and the residue with his stock in trade, to Norman, who inherited about £6,000. Norman had no children and eventually half his now reduced estate went to Whittle's grandson.

Literary References: *Kirkham* 1969, 501–10; *Beard and Hayward* 1988, 395

Architectural Sculpture

1.	1754	A very rich shield carved with star & garter and two very large dolphins Payment(s): £67 15s	Woburn Abbey, Beds, secondary pediment		*Beard and Hayward* 1988, 395
2.	1754	Ducal arms and rich ornaments Payment(s): £75 10s	Woburn Abbey, Beds, front pediment		*Beard and Hayward* 1988, 395
3.	1755–1757	Substantial unidentified work including a picture frame of carved and gilt wood (co-sculptor: Samuel Norman) Payment(s): £1,420	Petworth, Sussex		*Jackson-Stops* 1977, 362
4.	1755–60	Architectural ornaments, chairs and a grand state bed (co-sculptor: Samuel Norman)	Woburn Abbey, Beds, state rooms		*Coleridge* 1964, 125, 127 (repr); *Kirkham* 1969, 504 (repr 32); *Beard and Hayward* 1988, 394–5 (repr)

WHITTON, Robert, of Ripon fl 1830–34?

Both known monuments are large Hellenic tablets.

Funerary Monuments

1.	?1830	Edward Oxley	Ripon Cathedral	S	*Gunnis* 1968, 431
2.	?1834	John Small	Ripon Cathedral	S	*Gunnis* 1968, 431

WHITTON FAMILY, of Beverley fl *c*1827–62

The Barkworth (**5**) is a Gothic wall tablet. The two tablets commemorating Constable family members both have a framed inscription topped by a sarcophagus (**3, 10**).

Funerary Monuments

1.	?1827	Adolphus Bayard	Bridlington, E R Yorks		GPC
2.	†1836	William Stephenson	St Mary, Beverley, E R Yorks		Pevsner, *Yorks: E R & York*, 1995, 299
3.	†1839	Lucy Constable (by R Whitton)	Sigglesthorne, E R Yorks		Pevsner, *Yorks: E R & York*, 1995, 682
4.	†1839	Simpson family member	Brantingham, E R Yorks		Pevsner, *Yorks: E R & York*,
5.	†1851	Mary Barkworth (by R Whitton)	Hessle, E R Yorks		Pevsner, *Yorks: E R & York*, 1995, 468
6.	†1851	Susan Gertrude Collet	Beverley Minster, E R Yorks	S	
7.	†1854	Richard Foster	Kirkburn, E R Yorks		Pevsner, *Yorks: E R & York*, 1995, 583
8.	†1856	Robert Walker	St Mary, Beverley, E R Yorks		Pevsner, *Yorks: E R & York*, 1995, 299
9.	†1859	Robert Kenningham (by R Whitton)	St Mary, Beverley, E R Yorks		Pevsner, *Yorks E R & York*, 1995, 299
10.	†1862	Constable family members (by R Whitton)	Sigglesthorne, E R Yorks		Pevsner, *Yorks: E R & York*, 1995, 682
11.	†1862	Rev John Blanchard	Lund, E R Yorks		Pevsner, *Yorks: E R & York*, 1995, 607

WICKSTEAD (or WICKSTEED), James fl 1779–1824

A gem-engraver, he exhibited at the Royal Academy and the Suffolk Street Galleries a number of times between 1779 and 1824. His address was May's Buildings, St Martin's Lane in 1779, whence he moved to Charing Cross, then Henrietta Street, Covent Garden, then Holborn and finally Denmark Street, Soho.

Literary References: *Graves* VIII, 1905–6, 263–4, *Gunnis* 1968, 432

WIDDISON, of Edwinstone fl 1845

Funerary Monuments

1.	1845	Robert Millhouse (the poet)	Nottingham Cemetery		*Builder*, 1845, 117

WILCOX, G fl *c*1831

Only one monument has been identified, signed in tandem with **Robert Blore II**.

Funerary Monuments

1.	†1831	Montague Cholmeley (co-sculptor: Robert Blore II)	Stoke Rochford, Lincs	S	Pevsner, *Lincs*, 1989, 720

WILCOXSON, F J fl *c*1794

Funerary Monuments

1.	†1794	Captain Francis Light (co-sculptor: Robert Grieve Scott)	Penang Cathedral, Malaysia	S	RG/JP, 9, 1587

WILD, H fl 1777

Gunnis suggests that he was probably a Manchester mason.

Funerary Monuments

1.	1777	George Clarke, wall-tablet	Stockport, Cheshire	S	*Gunnis* 1968, 432

WILDING, R fl *c*1714

Presumably a Shrewsbury artist, his memorial to Thomas Jones takes the form of a brass plate with a long inscription, while above are three repoussé coats of arms very well cast in bronze (1). The Fowler is a small brass with an engraved coat-of-arms (2).

Literary References: *Gunnis* 1968, 432

Funerary Monuments

1.	1714	Thomas Jones	St Alkmund, Shrewsbury		*Gunnis* 1968, 432
2.	nd	Sir Richard Fowler	Cound, Salop	S	RG/JP, 9, 1587

WILDSMITH, John fl 1760–69

Gunnis suggests he may have been an apprentice of Thomas Carter, presumably **Thomas Carter II**. He was responsible for a number of chimneypieces, particularly for the 6th Earl of Coventry, who also ordered exotic tables from him (2–4, 14–16). Binney states that he was one of the master masons at Gorhambury, Herts, built in 1777–84 to the designs of **Sir Robert Taylor**, which seems an unlikely departure, particularly since he became bankrupt in 1669 and was obliged to sell his stock in trade. The sale catalogue described him as a carver and mason, and the auction took place at his yard and premises in Piccadilly, near the church of St James. It included models of chimneypieces and 'curious carvings'.

Literary References: *Gunnis* 1968, 432; *Binney* 1984, 86

Archival References: GPC

Auction Catalogues: Wildsmith 1769

Busts

1.	1769	'A rock abby bust of a Venus'	[Wildsmith sale, day 1, lot 38]; untraced	Wildsmith sale cat

Chimneypieces

2.	1760	'Mantelpieces'	[Croome Court, Worcs]; untraced	*Beard* 1993, 92
3.	1760	'Rich Statuary Marble Chimney Piece with Turtle Doves in frieze and festoons, highly finished' Payment(s): £86 9s	[Croome Court, Worcs]; untraced	GPC quoting Coventry Archives
4.	1760	'Rich Truss Chimney Piece with Antick Caps. and Statuary Ornaments laid on Merona Grounds, highly finished' Payment(s): £35 10s	[Croome Court, Worcs]; untraced	GPC quoting Coventry Archives
5.	1761	Statuary marble with jasper columns Payment(s): £108 11s 6d	Dunkeld House, Perth, drawing room	GPC quoting Archives, Duke of Atholl
6.	1762	Description unavailable Payment(s): £34 5s	[for the Duke of Atholl]; untraced	GPC quoting Archives, Duke of Atholl
7.	1763	Several	[Sir Richard Littleton's house, Piccadilly, London]; untraced	*Gunnis* 1968, 432
8.	1763	'Statuary and black marble' Payment(s): £39	[Croome Court, Worcs]; untraced	GPC citing Archives, Duke of Atholl
9.	1766	'Coln. Ionic Chimney Piece. . . with a plain Dentile cornice'	[for Edward Knight, of Wolverley, Worcs]; untraced	Edward Knight's account book. Kidderminster Public Library, MSS 285–292
10.	1769	'Statuary tablet of Flora, polished'	[Wildsmith sale, day I, lot 38]; untraced	Wildsmith sale cat
11.	by 1769	'Tablet of Boys and Sheep'	[Wildsmith sale, 1769]; untraced	*Gunnis* 1968, 432
12.	by 1769	'Tablet of Diana'	[Wildsmith sale, 1769]; untraced	*Gunnis* 1968, 432
13.	by 1769	'Tablet of Shepherd and Wolf'	[Wildsmith sale, 1769]; untraced	*Gunnis* 1968, 432

Miscellaneous

14.	1759	Inlaid marble table 'in squairs of all the curious sorts' Payment(s): £42 10s	[Croome Court, Worcs]; Met NY	*Beard* 1993, 92, 94, 111 (repr)
15.	1759	Marble table of lapis lazuli and one square of 'plumb pudding stone' Payment(s): £3 13s	[Croome Court, Worcs]; untraced	*Beard* 1993, 94
16.	1760	Two jasper marble tables Payment(s): £42 10s	[Croome Court, Worcs]; untraced	GPC citing Archives, Earl of Coventry
17.	1769	Three marble boxes inlaid with different sorts of marble	[Wildsmith sale]; untraced	*Gunnis* 1968, 432

WILFORD, R fl *c*1796

Funerary Monuments

1.	†1796	Thomas Dupuis	Westminster Abbey, London, cloisters	S	GPC

WILKES, of Birmingham fl *c*1830–38

Funerary Monuments

1.	?1830	Abraham Spooner	Elmdon, Warks	S	*Gunnis* 1968, 432
2.	?1838	Countess of Rosse	Elmdon, Warks	S	*Gunnis* 1968, 432

WILKINS, of Beaminster fl 1837–39

Gunnis notes that he signs a few tablets in Dorset, the best commemorating Captain Bowles, which has military trophies (1). The large, heavy Hall monument has a relief of a dragoon and his horse (2).

Funerary Monuments

1.	1837	Captain Bowles	Netherbury, Dorset	S	*Gunnis* 1968, 432
2.	1839	Edmund Hall	Broadwindsor, Dorset	S	*Gunnis* 1968, 432

WILKINS, S and C fl *c*1843

The Ennis tablet in Mumbai is decorated with an urn and several fronds of weeping willow. (Inf. Steven Allen)

Funerary Monuments

1.	†1843	Captain E M Ennis	Mumbai (Bombay) Cathedral, India	S

WILKINSON, Christopher, of Durham

See **James OLIPHANT, of Durham.**

WILKINSON, of Ketton fl 1698

Lord Ashburnham wrote to John Hutton (perhaps his agent) on 24 June 1698 'I have received a letter from Wilkinson the stone mason of Ketton wherein he informs me that he has sent up twenty tunn of paving stone to Bedford and that he would have 12⁸=advanced him in money to pay the carriage, which I have consented to gratifye him inn. . . Wilkinson does allsoe desire that a shedd may be made for his workmen to stand under' (Ashburnham Letterbook ASH 841, p 409).

WILLCOX, of Bath

Busts

1.	nd	Albert, the Prince Consort, walnut	wd	Royal Coll RCIN 42891	S

WILLEMS (or WILLIAMS), Joseph *c*1715–66

Willems was born in Brussels *c*1715 and married Marie Joseph Lahaize at Tournai in 1739. He came to England around the middle of the 18th century and worked as a modeller at the Chelsea porcelain factory, run by Nicholas Sprimont. It has been suggested that the emergence of an interest in figurative models at Chelsea after 1749 and the development of a house style of modelling from about 1753 onwards may be linked to Willems's arrival at the factory. However, his presence in England cannot be confirmed until 1755–8 when 'Mr Williams or Mr Sprimont' are mentioned in the Chelsea rate books as tenants of a house there. A pair of terracotta dancing figures at the Ashmolean Museum are signed 'WILLEMS 1749' but it is not certain that they were made in Britain and the veracity of the inscription has been called into question (*Penny* III, 1992, 185) (1).

He exhibited models at the annual exhibitions of the Society of Artists between 1760 and 1766 and Mortimer's *Universal Director* for 1763 carried the notice, 'Williams, Joseph, Modeller, at the Brussels Coffee-house, Chelsea. This artist teaches drawing and modelling; and has modelled for the Chelsea china manufactory for many years' (*Mortimer* 1763, 29). He left England soon after February 1766, invited to the Tournai porcelain factory by its director, and died in Tournai on 1 November. A posthumous inventory of his effects included 'plusiers grouppes de ronde bosse de terre cuite et colorées en blanc de sa composition, et par lui modelées' (*Lane* 1960, 247). Several of the models exhibited by Willems at the Society of Arts, or recorded as being in his possession at his death, appear to correspond to surviving Chelsea porcelain figures.

The death of 'Mrs Mary Williams, wife of Mr Williams, Modeller at the Chelsea Manufactury' was reported in the *London Chronicle* for 24–27 July 1764 (*Lane* 1960, 247 n12). Willems apparently remarried soon after, for on 25 July 1769 the *Chiswick Times* announced the death of 'Mrs Mary Williams, widow of Mr Williams, for a long time Modeller at the Chelsea Manufactory'. It is possible that his second wife was Mary Anne Nollekens, the mother of **Joseph Nollekens**, for one account states that her second husband was 'a person of the name of Williams an inferior statuary, who modelled for the Chelsea Porcelain Manufactory, and who went to Flanders, where he died, his widow surviving him for four years' (*Annual Biography and Obituary*, 1824 and *Gould* 1838, 368, in GPC).

Literary References: *Tapp* 1938, 176–82; *Lane* 1960, 245–51; *Gunnis* 1968, 432; *Watney* 1972, 818–28; *Penny* III, 1992, 185–6

Statues

1.	1749	Lady and gentleman dancing	tc	Ashmolean WA 1959.231-2	SD	*Penny* 1992, III, 184–5 (repr)
2.	1760	Charity		[Exhib Soc of Artists, London, 100]; untraced		*Graves* 1907, 282
3.	1762	A boy, after nature		[Exhib Soc of Artists, London, 155]; untraced		*Graves* 1907, 282
4.	1762	Generosity		[Exhib Soc of Artists, London, 152]; untraced		*Graves* 1907, 282
5.	1762	Heroic virtue		[Exhib Soc of Artists, London, 153]; untraced		*Graves* 1907, 282
6.	1762	Seneca		[Exhib Soc of Artists, London, 154]; untraced		*Graves* 1907, 282
7.	1763	Cleo		[Exhib Soc of Artists, London, 149]; untraced		*Graves* 1907, 282
8.	1763	Honour, emblematic figure		[Exhib Soc of Artists, London, 148]; untraced		*Graves* 1907, 282
9.	1763	Leda, model		[Exhib Soc of Artists, London, 147]; untraced		*Graves* 1907, 282
10.	1764	A young student and a country girl sleeping		[Exhib Soc of Artists, London, 160]; untraced		*Graves* 1907, 279
11.	1765	Charity, model		[Exhib Soc of Artists, London, 184]; untraced		*Graves* 1907, 279
12.	1753–1766	Models of figures for the Chelsea porcelain factory		Untraced		*Gunnis* 1968, 432

Busts

13.	1761	Mr Martinelli		[Exhib Soc of Artists, London, 166]; untraced		*Graves* 1907, 282
14.	1764	Unidentified gentleman		[Exhib Soc of Artists, London, 161]; untraced		*Graves* 1907, 279

Miscellaneous

15.	1766	Sincerity, model	[Exhib Soc of Artists, London, 219]; untraced	*Graves* 1907, 279

WILLIAMS, B, of Cowbridge fl *c*1809

The Jones monument is an oval tablet with an urn and sarcophagus.

Funerary Monuments

1.	†1809	Mary Jones	Llandow, Glamorgan	S	Pevsner, *Glamorgan*, 1995, 379

WILLIAMS, Caleb

For further information the reader is referred to *Pyke* 1973, 157.

WILLIAMS, Edward 1746–1826

Edward Williams (better known in his fatherland as Iolo Morganwg), was a prime force behind the cultural revival that saw the birth of modern Wales, though during his chequered and multi-faceted life he also struggled as a provincial poet in London, as a medievalist, and as a source of druidic knowledge. He was a manipulator and victim of the world of literary patronage, an opium eater and for a time, a marble mason. He was born in Penon, Glamorganshire, the stone of a stone mason. His mother, whose maiden name was Mathews, was of good birth and education. As a boy he was too weak to attend school and from the age of nine until his mother's death in 1770 he worked desultorily at his father's trade. He then left Glamorgan and for about seven years worked as a journeyman mason in various parts of England, before returning home and marrying Margaret Roberts of Marychurch in 1781.

His trade card of 1779 has survived: on it he advertised himself as 'Edward Williams, jun./ Marble Mason / at Flimston, near Cowbridge' and added that he could make 'all sorts of Chimney-pieces, Monuments, Tombs, Head-stones, and every other Article in MARBLE and FREESTONE-MASONRY in the newest and neatest Manner'. Williams also stated that he had 'for many years regularly followed this trade in London and other capital towns under the best Masters' and that 'as there are various Sorts of good Marble found in many parts of GLAMORGAN, Tables, Chimney-pieces, &c of it may be had very cheap (Banks 106.31).

He signs an undated oval wall-tablet to Anthony Jones at Llantwit, Glamorgan; this was erected about 1800 and is very like the contemporary work of **Thomas King of Bath.**

Literary References: *DNB*; Univ of Wales website

Archival References: GPC

Collections of Drawings: National Lib of Wales (including many original designs for wall-monuments etc)

Funerary Monuments

1.	?*c*1800	Anthony Jones, oval wall-tablet	Llantwit, Glamorgan	*Gunnis* 1968, 432

WILLIAMS, Emanuel fl 1761–78

A carver and mason, he became free by redemption of the Masons' Company on 1 October 1761. In 1763 he lived in Eastcheap and when he became bankrupt in 1778, his address was Glean Alley, Tooley Street, Southwark. On 18 and 19 January the following year his stock-in-trade was put up for auction. The lots included a great deal of marble, chimneypieces, monuments, and tablets, which suggests that he must have had a considerable business. Gunnis traced references in the Guy's Hospital archives to extensive building activity at the hospital, noting that in 1774–77 Williams was paid £1,425 for his work on the west wing, and in 1777–78, £1,474 for the centre building.

Literary References: *Mortimer* 1763, 49; *Gunnis* 1968, 432

Archival References: Masons' Co, *Freemen*, fol 73

Auction Catalogues: Williams 1779

WILLIAMS, Hugh, of Holyhead fl 1831

Funerary Monuments

1.	1831	Gromo Owen	[Bangor Cathedral]; untraced	*Gunnis* 1968, 432 citing the *Cambrian Mag*, III, 507

WILLIAMS, J, of Llandeilo fl *c*1827–67

Funerary Monuments

1.	†1827	Rev William Williams	Llanfynydd, Carmarthen	*Dale-Jones and Lloyd* 1989, 58
2.	†1867	Margaretta Gwynne Hughes	Llanfynydd, Carmarthen	*Dale-Jones and Lloyd* 1989, 58

WILLIAMS, James, of Ipswich 1798–1888

His commissions in Suffolk included reredoses, fonts and gable crosses as well as busts of well-known men. The son of a Monmouthshire smallholder, he was one of the many migrant poor who settled in Ipswich in the early 19th century, at a time when the stimulus of the Oxford Movement brought employment for stone masons in a growing number of church restorations. After a few years in Wickham Market, where he and his wife kept a general shop, he moved to Ipswich in 1845 where he rented a house, shop and warehouse in Queen Street. He appears to have learnt the rudiments of his art as a sculptor through church restoration. After restoring 13 fonts by removing the whitewash and 'amending' carvings destroyed by the Puritans, he made an octagonal font of his own, copied from one at Newbourne, with compartments filled with angels alternating with Evangelical symbols, illustrating what could be done in imitation of medieval sculpture.

Turning from his work as a restorer of church interiors he experimented with portraits busts which he exhibited in Queen Street (**2**). From the 1851 census it is known that he employed 6 men and 13 labourers, but had no assistants, which suggests that he took on refined carving work himself. He modelled busts in clay from which moulds and casts were produced (**3**). His burgeoning success enabled him to invest in land and by 1854 he owned seven properties; two years later he moved to a spacious house in the vicinity, Tintern Villa. Concurrent with the busts, he continued his ecclesiastical work. In 1857 he made an ambitious stone reredos for the Manchester Art Treasures Exhibition (**9**). The exhibition committee rejected it since 'works in stone were not anticipated', but the indignation voiced in the *Ipswich Journal* brought him attention and the following year the rector of St Mary, Brome, bought a reredos from him that sounds very like the one intended for Manchester (**10**). Williams provided another reredos for the International

Exhibition of 1862 (**13**). The main section was finished in time for an exhibition held by the Suffolk Institute of Archaeology at the Athenaeum, Bury St Edmunds in 1861, and was shown in a prime position at the head of the room, where it attracted considerable attention. The *Bury Free Press* of 24 August 1861 noted 'I would invite your special notice to the considerable effort . . . the work of a Suffolk artist. . .It is for the reredos of a church and is the work of Mr Williams of Ipswich. I think you will agree with me in according to it the meed of your praise'. It was duly exhibited in 1862, attracted the attention of churchmen and led to further ecclesiastical commissions.

He continued to model or carve busts, some of them as large as 33 inches in height (**5, 6**). A demand for images of more modest proportions was met with a half-sized head of James Ransome, copied from a full-sized model produced several years earlier (**8**).

Advancing years and failing sight stemmed the flow. Williams died on 23 January 1888, aged 89 and was survived by his third wife. His lengthy obituary concluded: 'His studio was a "study". At every turn you met with the faces of Suffolk and Ipswich men who occupied prominent positions . . . and here and there were to be seen the "mortal remains" of some of his bolder ventures, such as a marble reredos with saintly figures, mythological subjects and a good deal of other work . . . By his death Suffolk loses a sculptor of great skill' (*Ipswich Journal*, 3 Feb 1888). In tracing his development from a stone mason and decorative carver working in the context of the rapidly expanding world of church restoration to a figurative fine art sculptor, Read summarises his career: 'Williams it seems to me was a competent, solid, honest Victorian sculptor. His career mirrors at a local scale that of national figures and his art reflects the age in which he lived'. Read concludes 'There is surely no reason why this should not be a compliment to any artist'.

Literary References: *Brown, Reynolds and Read* 1985, 21–30

Statues

1.	c1864	The Seasons, four	s	[Summer and Winter commissioned for Shrubland Park, Suffolk]; Stoke Park, Suffolk	*Brown, Reynolds and Read* 1988, 24

Busts

2.	1848	J T Nottidge, James Ransome, J E Sparrowe	tc	[Exhib Queen Street, Ipswich]; untraced	*Brown, Reynolds and Read* 1988, 21
3.	1852	Sir Robert Peel, Arthur, Duke of Wellington, Lord John Russell, 'Uncle Tom'	tc	[Exhib Suffolk Fine Art Soc]; untraced Other versions: reproduced extensively in plaster	*Brown, Reynolds and Read* 1985, 22
4.	1864	Archdeacon Lord Arthur Hervey (president, Suffolk Inst of Archaeology)	p	Untraced	*Brown, Reynolds and Read* 1988, 24
5.	1870	Mrs Ogilvie		[Sizewell House, Leiston, Suffolk]; untraced	*Brown, Reynolds and Read* 1988, 25
6.	1871	Cardinal Wolsey	m	Ipswich Town Hall, Suffolk	*Brown, Reynolds and Read* 1988, 25 (repr Vb)
7.	by 1871	Lieutenant General Sir Stephen Lakeman		[Stoke Park, Suffolk]; untraced	*Brown, Reynolds and Read* 1988, 24–5
8.	1875	James Ransome	m	Untraced	*Brown, Reynolds and Read* 1988, 25

Architectural Sculpture

9.	1857	Reredos depicting the Crucifixion flanked by 'The Prayer in the Garden' and 'The Resurrection'		[intended for the Exhibition of Art Treasures, Old Trafford, Manchester]; untraced	*Brown, Reynolds and Read* 1985, 22
10.	1858	Reredos: Agony, Crucifixion, Resurrection, Christ appearing to his disciples	s	St Mary Brome, Suffolk	*Brown, Reynolds and Read* 1985, 22–3
11.	1859–1861	Altar-rail (£15), sedilia (£15), font (£20), pulpit and desk (£75), about 96 corbels and work on the south and circular windows	s	St Mary, Brome, Suffolk	*Brown, Reynolds and Read* 1985, 22–3
12.	1862	Reredos	s	St Lawrence, Ipswich, Suffolk	*Brown, Reynolds and Read* 1988, 24
13.	1861–1862	Reredos, 'The Last Supper'		[Int Exhib]; untraced	*Brown, Reynolds and Read* 1988, 23–4

WILLIAMS, M, of Forden fl c1779

Funerary Monuments

1.	†1779	Charles Rocke	Welshpool, Montgomery	S	RG/JP, 9, 1590v.

WILLIAMS, of Brighton fl 1803–32

Gunnis notes that he signed a few tablets in Sussex, of which the best were the Ingram and the Payne, the latter carried out in coloured marbles (**1, 2**).

Funerary Monuments

1.	1803	John Ingram	Chailey, Sussex	S	*Gunnis* 1968, 432
2.	1805	John Payne	Patcham, Sussex		*Gunnis* 1968, 432
3.	†1832	William (†1829), Sarah (†1824) and Elizabeth (†1832) Falconer	Henfield, Sussex	S	

WILLIAMS, of Haverfordwest fl 1824?

Funerary Monuments

1.	?1824	Cozens family	Walwyns Castle, Pembrokes	S	RG/JP, 9, 1590

WILLIAMS, of New Road, London fl c1802–08

The Colston has a relief of cherubs with an urn (**1**).

Funerary Monuments

1.	†1802	Sophia Colston	St Peter & St Paul, Broadwell, Oxon	S	Pevsner, *Oxon*, 1974, 490
2.	†1807	Peter Kennedy	Sarratt, Herts	S	
3.	†1808	William (†1758), Ann (†1790) and Henrietta Beach	Fittleton, Wilts	S	

WILLIAMS, of Plymouth fl 1808–18

He was responsible for three tablets at Egg Buckland, the best of which commemorates William Harris.

Funerary Monuments

1.	†1816	William Harris	Egg Buckland, Devon	S	*Gunnis* 1968, 432

WILLIAMS, Richard 1799–

The son of Solomon Williams, an Irish historical and portrait painter, he studied at the Dublin Society Schools unde **John Smyth**, winning the first prize for sculpture in 1816. In 1815, 1817 and 1819, while still studying, he exhibited a Hawkins Street. In 1820 he moved to London and joined the Royal Academy Schools, winning silver medals in 182 and 1823 (**6, 8**). He exhibited at the RA between 1822 and 1832, showing both portraits and ideal works, from severa addresses: 1 York Street, Foley Place; 41 York Square, Diorama; 99 Grove Street, Camden Town; and 7 Cadogan Stree Sloane Street. He was elected a member of the Artists' Annuity Fund in 1822. He was probably the 'Mr Williams' who while working as an assistant to **J C F Rossi**, carved a seated female figure with her arms around her legs for the Ear of Egremont (**1**). This was based on a model by **Joseph Nollekens** bought by the Earl at Nollekens's posthumous sale Williams became became blind in 1841 (AGBI Archives, in *Gunnis* 1968, 433).

Literary References: *Strickland* II, 1913, 536; *Smith* II, 1920, 5–6; *Hutchison* 1960–2, 173; *Gunnis* 1968, 233

Archival References: AAF, Proposals, 51

Statues

1.	c1823	Sitting Venus, after Joseph Nollekens (working as assistant to J C F Rossi)	[coll Lord Egremont]; Petworth, Sussex	*Smith* II, 1920, 5–6

Busts

2.	1822	Unidentified gentleman	[Exhib RA, London, 1003]; untraced	*Graves* VIII, 1905–6, 292
3.	1824	John Charles Felix Rossi RA	[Exhib RA, London, 1022]; untraced	*Graves* VIII, 1905–6, 292
4.	1826	Model of a head in wax	[Exhib RHA, Dublin, 369]; untraced	*Stewart* III, 1985, 294

Reliefs

5.	1826	Unidentified gentlemen, two medallic portraits	[Exhib RA, London, 939 and 943]; untraced	*Graves* VIII, 1905–6, 292

Miscellaneous

6.	1820	Model in the Antique academy	[RA silver medal]; untraced	RA Premium list
7.	1823	Milo	[Exhib RA, London, 1092]; untraced	*Graves* VIII, 1905–6, 292
8.	1823	Unidentified subject	[RA silver medal]; untraced	RA Premium list
9.	1828	Bacchus	[Exhib RA, London, 1137]; untraced	*Graves* VIII, 1905–6, 292
10.	1832	Haidée recovering Juan	[Exhib RA, London, 1116]; untraced	*Graves* VIII, 1905–6, 292

WILLIAMS, W, of Merthyr fl c1804

Funerary Monuments

1.	†1804	Lewis Thomas, oval wall-tablet	Brecon Cathedral	*Gunnis* 1968, 433

WILLIAMS, W, of St Florence fl c1807–49

A Pembrokeshire mason whose known works are all in the vicinity. Sir Richard Steele's monument at Carmarthen i a six-foot high slate slab with a ten line eulogistic poem (**3**).

Funerary Monuments

1.	†1807	Robert Phillips		St Florence, Pembrokes	S	RG/JP, 9, 1592
2.	†1808	Rev John Jordan		Steynton, Pembrokes	S	RG/JP, 9, 1592
3.	c1810	Sir Richard Steele	sl	Llangunnor, Carmarthen	S	*Dale-Jones and Lloyd* 1989, 58
4.	†1828	Augusta Lloyd		Manorbier, Pembrokes	S	RG/JP, 9, 1592
5.	†1834	Colonel Elliot Voyle		Tenby, Pembrokes	S	RG/JP, 9, 1592
6.	†1837	Henry Williams		Tenby, Pembrokes	S	RG/JP, 9, 1592
7.	†1849	Marianne Lloyd		Tenby, Pembrokes	S	RG/JP, 9, 1592

WILLIAMS, William fl 1824–37

He described himself as a sculptor and architect when he exhibited architectural plans and portrait busts at the Roya Academy, 1824–1839. During this period he changed address several times, giving St Alban's Place, St James's (1824) 1 Lion Street, New Kent Road (1832); 72 Judd Street (1834); 33 Berkeley Street, Lambeth Walk (1835); 13 Windmi Street, Lambeth Walk (1838). He signed the monument to John Mortimer in Huddersfield parish church.

Literary References: *Graves* VIII, 1905–6, 295

Funerary Monuments

1.	1829	John Mortimer	St Peter, Huddersfield, W R Yorks	S	*Gunnis* 1968, 433

Busts

2.	1833	Unidentified gentleman	[Exhib RA, London, 1168]; untraced	*Graves* VIII, 1905–6, 295
3.	1834	Unidentified gentleman	[Exhib RA, London, 1066]; untraced	*Graves* VIII, 1905–6, 295
4.	1835	Unidentified gentleman	[Exhib Soc of BA, London, 792]; untraced	*Johnson* 1975, 507
5.	1836	Unidentified gentleman	[Exhib Soc of BA, London, 866]; untraced	*Johnson* 1975, 507
6.	1838	Unidentified gentleman	[Exhib RA, London, 1350]; untraced	*Graves* VIII, 1905–6, 295
7.	1839	Unidentified gentleman	[Exhib RA, London, 1338]; untraced	*Graves* VIII, 1905–6, 295

Reliefs

8.	1833	Unidentified lady (medallic portrait)	[Exhib RA, London, 1040]; untraced	*Graves* VIII, 1905–6, 295
9.	1834	Unidentified gentleman (medallic portrait)	[Exhib RA, London, 972]; untraced	*Graves* VIII, 1905–6, 295
10.	1837	Unidentified clergyman (medallic portrait)	[Exhib RA, London, 1143]; untraced	*Graves* VIII, 1905–6, 295

Miscellaneous

11.	1832	Unidentified gentleman (portrait)		[Exhib RA, London, 1083]; untraced	*Graves* VIII, 1905–6, 295
12.	1832	Unidentified lady (portrait)		[Exhib RA, London, 1078]; untraced	*Graves* VIII, 1905–6, 295
13.	1833	Unidentified gentleman		[Exhib Soc of BA, London, 818]; untraced	*Johnson* 1975, 507
14.	1833	Unidentified lady	w	[Exhib Soc of BA, London, 868]; untraced	*Johnson* 1975, 507

15.	1833	Unidentified subject, a portrait		[Exhib Soc of BA, London, 860]; untraced		*Johnson* 1975, 507
16.	1834	Unidentified lady	w	[Exhib Soc of BA, London, 860]; untraced		*Johnson* 1975, 507
17.	1835	Unidentified gentleman (portrait)		[Exhib RA, London, 997]; untraced		*Graves* VIII, 1905–6, 295
18.	1837	Unidentified subject (portrait)		[Exhib RA, London, 1159]; untraced		*Graves* VIII, 1905–6, 295

WILLIAMS, William and Thomas, of Middleton Stoney fl 1715–24

They sign the large and important monument at Kirtlington erected to the Dashwood family in 1724. This impressive architectural work has a broken pediment with a fluted urn in the centre, and two mourning cherubs standing at the base of the inscription-tablet. It is an extremely advanced and elaborate production for provincial (indeed, almost village) masons.

Literary References: *Gunnis* 1968, 433

Funerary Monuments

1.	1724	Dashwood family	St Mary, Kirtlington, Oxon	S	*Gunnis* 1968, 433; Pevsner, *Oxon*, 1974, 676

Chimneypieces

2.	1715	One	Aynho Park, Northants, little parlour		*Gunnis* 1968, 433 citing Cartwright Archives
3.	1716	One	Aynho Park, Northants, unidentified room		*Gunnis* 1968, 433 citing Cartwright Archives

Architectural Sculpture

4.	1706	Capitals	[Aynho Park, Northants, greenhouse]; untraced		*Gunnis* 1968, 433 citing Cartwright Archives

WILLIS, Matthew fl *c*1848

He was employed in modelling figures on the south side of Lichfield Cathedral, and at the Houses of Parliament. He went to Sydney in 1848, and opened a school of modelling, but met with little success (inf. Mitchell Lib., Sydney).

Archival References: RG/JP, 9, 1593

WILLOUGHBY, G, of Malton *c*1767–1835

He probably had an extensive practice since his death, aged 68, was noted in the *York Gazette* of 31 January 1835. Only two works have been identified, the Greek revival Worsley monument (2) and a tablet to Nathaniel Bruton with naval trophies at the base (1). The business was perhaps inherited by **J and C Willoughby**, 'stone masons', who worked at Everingham Hall in East Yorkshire.

Literary References: *Gunnis* 1968, 433

Archival References: GPC

Funerary Monuments

1.	1815	Nathaniel Bruton	Stockton, Durham		*Gunnis* 1968, 433
2.	?1824	Thomas Worsley and others	Hovingham, N R Yorks		*Gunnis* 1968, 433; Pevsner, *Yorks: N R*, 1966, 194

WILLOUGHBY, J and C, of York fl 1838–44

John and C Willoughby provided fittings for the chapel at Everingham Hall between 1838 and 1844. (Inf. East Yorks NADFAS)

Architectural Sculpture

1.	1838–1844	Altar, credences and fittings (designed by Leonardi)	Chapel of the Virgin, Everingham Hall, E R Yorks	S	

WILLOUGHBY, W, of Howden fl *c*1794–1822

Known only for two wall tablets, the Whitaker is described by Gunnis as being large, with careful, well-cut details (1).

Funerary Monuments

1.	†1794–1803	Ann Whitaker and family members	Howden, E R Yorks		*Gunnis* 1968, 433; Pevsner, *Yorks: E R & York*, 1995, 489
2.	†1822	Rev Thomas Kipling	Holme-upon-Spalding-Moor, E R Yorks		Pevsner, *Yorks: E R & York*, 1995, 474

WILLS, Sampson fl 1806

Probably a local stone mason he was paid £1,542 in 1806 by Sir William Fellowes for rebuilding Ramsey Abbey, Hunts, designed by Sir John Soane.

Archival References: Soane Bill Book D fols 500–03

WILLS & SON, J, of New Road, London fl *c*1841–47

Though only three of their works are here recorded, it seems likely that Wills & Son were a successful commercial firm, since their work went out to at least one colonial outpost (1). The Lewis wall tablet follows a standard design, featuring a weeping woman by a draped urn, above a sarcophagus with acroteria. The Fergusson tablet makes use of a similar formula though here the sarcophagus is surmounted by a cross and palm-leaves (2). W J Wills, who may be one of the family, exhibited a teracotta bust at the RA in 1867, no 1027 (*Ormond* 1973, 108). W J and T Wills were responsible for an 8 foot marble statue of Richard Cobden on a large pedestal, erected in 1868 at the south end of Camden High Street, London (*Blackwood* 1989, 183, repr).

Funerary Monuments

1.	†1841	Robert Lewis	Mumbai (Bombay) Cathedral, India	S	
2.	†1845	John Fergusson	Kensal Green Cemetery, catacombs	S	
3.	†1847	Catherine Monro	East Sutton, Kent	S	

WILLSON, Daniel William, of London fl 1824–34

He seems to have specialised in wall monuments featuring women. The Bainbridge (1) is described by Gunnis as having a relief of a seated mourning woman in the manner of **John Bacon II**. The Sikes has figures of *Hope* and *Faith* (2) and the Peach, a weeping woman seated by an urn (4). Wilson's yard was at Bath Place, New Road.

Literary References: *Gunnis* 1968, 433

Funerary Monuments

1.	†1827	Elizabeth Bainbridge	St Laurence, Chobham, Surrey	S	Pevsner, *Surrey*, 1971, 158
2.	†1828	Mary Sikes	Balderton, Notts		Pevsner, *Notts*, 1979, 65
3.	?1829	Lord Colchester	St Swithun, East Grinstead, Sussex	S	*Gunnis* 1968, 433
4.	1833	Francis Peach (†1832)	Ketteringham, Norfolk	S	*Gunnis* 1968, 433; Pevsner, *Norfolk: NW & S*, 1999, 455
5.	?1834	Benjamin Burton	St Mary, St Marylebone, London	S	*Gunnis* 1968, 433

WILMOT, Thomas, of Wolverhampton fl *c*1791–1860

This firm appears to have been run by a father and then his son. In 1818 the son, Thomas Wilmot, stone and marble mason, had a yard in Bell Street and by 1828 he had moved to Castle Street.

Literary References: *Jeavons* 1960, 60

Funerary Monuments

1.	†1791	Thomas Hayes	Penkridge, Staffs	S	*Jeavons* 1960, 60
2.	†1815	Henry Wood	St John, Wolverhampton, Staffs	S	*Jeavons* 1960, 60
3.	†1791–1828	Moss family	St Leonard, Bilston, Staffs	S	*Jeavons* 1960, 60
4.	†1830	Mary Jeavons	St John, Wolverhampton, Staffs	S	*Jeavons* 1960, 60
5.	†1831	George Smith	St Lawrence, Darlaston, Staffs	S	*Jeavons* 1960, 60
6.	†1831	Joseph Reed	St John, Wolverhampton, Staffs	S	*Jeavons* 1960, 60
7.	†1842	William Yates	St Lawrence, Darlaston, Staffs	S	*Jeavons* 1960, 60
8.	†1852	George Bailey	St Lawrence, Darlaston, Staffs	S	*Jeavons* 1960, 60
9.	†1853	Herbert family	St John, Wolverhampton, Staffs	S	
10.	†1800–1860	Foster family	St Lawrence, Darlaston, Staffs	S	*Jeavons* 1960, 60

WILSON, H fl *c*1841

Funerary Monuments

1.	†1841	John Thomas, Charles James (†1838) and Elizabeth (†1839) James	Littlebourne, Kent	S	

WILSON, J K fl 1837–38

Graves gives his address as 7 Cleveland Street (1837) and 2 Percy Street (1838), both in London.

Busts

1.	1838	Sir Robert Harry Inglis Bt		[Exhib RA, London, 1295]; untraced	*Graves* VIII, 1905–6, 311; *Gunnis* 1968, 433

Reliefs

2.	1837	Unidentified subjects, medallion portraits	m	[Exhib RA, London, 1213 and 1215]; untraced	*Graves* VIII, 1905–6, 311; *Gunnis* 1968, 433

WILSON, J, of Leeds fl *c*1822

Funerary Monuments

1.	†1822	John Beverley	St John, Leeds, W R Yorks	S	GPC

WILSON, John

A medallist, cameo engraver and wax modeller and the partner of William Tassie, who continued the business after Wilson retired. For further information the reader is referred to *Pyke* 1973, 163.

WILSON, of Exeter fl *c*1850

His one identified monument gives his address as Magdalen Street.

Funerary Monuments

1.	†1850	James Cresswell	Holy Trinity, Exeter, Devon	S	RG/JP, 9, 1593v.

WILSON, of Wellingborough fl *c*1781

Funerary Monuments

1.	†1781	Jane Roberts	Fineden, Northants	*GM*, vol LXIX, Nov 1799, II, 939

WILSON, Robert Acton fl 1850

Miscellaneous

1.	1850	Model in the life academy	[RA silver medal]; untraced	RA Premium list

WILSON, Sir William 1641–1710

The Midlands architect and carver was a native of Leicester and can probably be identified with William, baptised in St Nicholas, Leicester on 16 May 1641, the son of William Wilson, a baker. He appears to have served his apprenticeship with a statuary mason and is said to have carved the statue of King Charles II which was set up on the west front of Lichfield Cathedral shortly before 1699, when Bishop Hacket's restoration was completed. It was taken down in 1877 and is now in the north west tower. Between 1670 and 1673 he was working as a carver at Sudbury Hall, Derbys, then being rebuilt by George Vernon (**8**, **9**). In or about 1671 he provided several Wilbraham monuments at Weston for Lady Elizabeth Wilbraham, who recorded the agreement in her copy of Palladio's *First Book of Architecture*, which is preserved in the library at Weston Park (**1**).

Wilson later carved an equestrian statue of the Duke of Newcastle, for the north-east front of Nottingham Castle (**4**). In 1831 the castle was sacked and set alight during riots which broke out after the Reform Bill was rejected by the House of Lords. Apparently 'the mob . . . carried off the figure as a glorious trophy of the destructive work on which they had been engaged' (*Builder*, 8 Sept 1900, 210) but some fragments of the statue remain *in situ*. Charles Deering, the Nottingham historian, notes that soon after the completion of this work Wilson was 'for a time spoiled for a statuary because a Leicestershire widow lady, the Lady Pudsey, who was possessed of a very large jointure falling deeply in love with him, got him knighted and married him, but he living up to the extent of his apron-string estate, and his lady dying before him, Sir William returned to his former occupation, and the publick recovered the loss of an eminent artist' (*Deering* 1751 in *Wren Soc* XI, 108). The lady was in fact Mrs Jane Pudsey the widow, of Henry Pudsey, of Langley, near Sutton Coldfield, Warks, who had died in 1677. It has been plausibly suggested that Wilson executed the monument to Mr Pudsey, which features busts of him and his wife within a draped recess, for the church at Sutton Coldfield (*Edwards* 1950, 45, repr). The date of Wilson's marriage has not been established but he was knighted at Whitehall on 8 March 1681/2 and two days later was admitted to the fellowship of the freemasons at Masons' Hall, London.

As an architect and surveyor Wilson supervised the erection of the Free School, at Appleby, Leics for Sir John Moore, 1693–97. The original plans were drawn up by Wren but Wilson made drastic alterations to them, producing a building which, while it conformed to Wren's general plan, had, with its mullioned and transomed windows, the appearance of a Jacobean structure of the first half of the 17th century. In the end Moore found that the school cost more than he had anticipated and Wilson had some difficulty in obtaining payment for his work as surveyor and for the founder's statue which he had executed and set up in a pedimented niche in what was then the main schoolroom (**6**). Wilson provided designs for rebuilding St Mary, Warwick, after the fire of 1694 and received payments for carving there in 1700 and 1706 (**10, 12**). In 1707 he was paid a further £10 'for the Marble Monuments on which two brass figures are fixt in the Church of St Maryes in Warwick over againt the South Isle in the sd. Church' (Warwick Fire Commissions, Warks RO CR 1618/WA4/270). This must refer to the slab on which the medieval brasses of Thomas Beauchamp, Earl of Warwick (†1401) and his wife and his wife were placed after the fire of 1694 (inf. GMD Booth). In 1697 he was employed by Thomas Coke in measuring the foundations of Melbourne Hall, Derbys and a 'gauche elevation of baroque character' mentioned in the Melbourne archives, inscribed 'alteration for Melbourne by Sir Wm. Wilson' was probably made at that time (*Colvin* 1995, 1064). He also designed the 'agreeable Baroque chapel' at Hall Green, Yardley, near Birmingham, which was consecrated in 1704 and several houses in Warwickshire are attributed to him (*ibid*).

Lady Wilson died in 1697 and was buried in Sutton Coldfield. Her husband died there at the age of 69 on 3 June 1710, and is commemorated by a tablet in the church. In his will he provided for a benefaction to the poor of St Nicholas parish, Leicester. It was later reported that Wilson's lowly birth so offended his wife's relations that they refused to contemplate his being buried in the vault with her. Wilson was aware of this and, when a friend commiserated with him, facetiously replied that he was not worried, for he would be buried outside the church, directly opposite the Pudsey vault. Then, he said, 'there will be only a single stone wall betwixt us, and as I am stonemason there will be no kind of labour or difficulty in cutting my road through the wall to my old bedfellow' (*Sutton Coldfield* 1762, in *Gunnis* 1968, 434).

Literary References: *Churches of Warwick* 1847, 1, 34; *Builder*, 8 Sept 1900, 210; *Wren Soc*, XI (1934), 108–113; *Edwards* 1950, 44–5; *Brandon-Jones* 1954, 177–8; *Beard* 1954, 780; *Gunnis* 1968, 433–4; *Whitehead* 1992, 79–81; *Colvin* 1995, 1063–64

Archival References: GPC

Funerary Monuments

1.	c1671	Wilbraham ancestors, tablets		St Andrew, Weston-under-Lizard, Staffs	*Beard* 1954, 780; Pevsner, *Staffs*, 1974, 307
2.	†1687	John Clobery	a	Winchester Cathedral, Hants	*Edwards* 1950, 45 (repr); Pevsner, *Hants & Isle of Wight*, 1967, 677
3.	†1699	Sir Thomas Gresley Drawing(s): Gresley papers, Derbys RO D77/Box 39 (box file 1)		Church Gresley, Derbys	Pevsner, *Derbys*, 1978, 153

Statues

4.	c1680	William, Duke of Newcastle, equestrian	wd	Nottingham Castle	*Deering* 1751, in *Wren Soc*, XI, 108; Pevsner, *Notts*, 1979, 227
5.	1697	Peace and Plenty Payment(s): 12 gns	s	Castle Bromwich Hall, Warks, over entrance porch	*Beard* 1954, 780 (repr); *Colvin* 1995, 1064; *Noszlopy* 2003, 198–9 (repr)
6.	1700	Sir John Moore Payment(s): £50	s	Sir John Moore's School, Appleby Magna, Leics, assembly hall	*Cavanagh* 2000, 2–4 (repr)
7.	1707	King Edward VI Payment(s): £25		[Edward VI Grammar School, Birmingham, Warks, tower]; untraced	*Carlisle* 1818, II, 644

Chimneypieces

8.	1670–1673	Description unavailable Payment(s): £20	a	Sudbury Hall, Derbys, Queen's room	Pevsner, *Derbys*, 1978, 334; *Beard and Knott* 2000, 44

Architectural Sculpture

9.	1670–1673	Frontispiece; carved ornaments on south front and cupola		Sudbury Hall, Derbys	Pevsner, *Derbys*, 1978, 332; *Beard and Knott* 2000, 43, 44 (repr)
10.	1700	'Carving work'		St Mary, Warwick	*Gunnis* 1968, 434
11.	1701	Coat of arms Payment(s): £5		Sir John Moore's School, Appleby Magna, Leics, exterior	*Gunnis* 1968, 434
12.	1706	'Carving church windows'		St Mary, Warwick	*Gunnis* 1968, 434

WILSON, William, of London fl 1746

In 1746 he was working at Welbeck Abbey with his partner, **John Draper**.

Architectural Sculpture

1.	1746	'a large ornament with festoons of fruit and flowers and a keystone with a lion's head in front' (co-sculptor: John Draper)	[Welbeck Abbey, Notts]; untraced	Archives, Duke of Portland in *Gunnis* 1968, 132

WILTON, Joseph RA 1722–1803

Innovative in his work, a gentleman in his lifestyle and the fortunate possessor of a Continental training, Wilton was, for a time, England's foremost sculptor and a leading figure in the newly-formed Royal Academy. He was born in London on 16 July 1722, and christened at St Martin-in-the-Fields on 8 August, the eldest son of **William Wilton**, an entrepreneurial plasterer who owned an ornament manufactory, with premises near Cavendish Square and Charing Cross. Joseph appears to have received some instruction in the decorative arts in his father's workshops, but William Wilton's contacts and wealth enabled Joseph to have a privileged training as a sculptor. In 1739 he was sent at his father's expense to Nivelles, Belgium, where he joined the workshop of **Laurent Delvaux**. Wilton is recorded in his master's surviving account-books as working for 53 and a half days on Delvaux's oak pulpit for th Carmelite church in Nivelles, completed in 1744.

Following a path taken by several of Delvaux's pupils, Wilton then went to Paris, where he learned to carve marbl in the studio of Jean-Baptiste Pigalle (1714–1785) and won a silver medal, presumably from the French Academy According to the engraver Thomas Major, who shared Wilton's lodgings in Paris in 1746, the sculptor passed himse off as a Fleming in order to avoid detainment as an English Protestant during the War of the Austrian Succession.

Wilton later told Joseph Farington that he first went to Italy in 1747 (*Farington* 2, 403), but the earliest record o the sculptor's presence in Rome is in January 1749, when he was recommended by the English politician, Georg Bubb Doddington, to Cardinal Albani. Wilton lived in the Palazzo Zuccari on the Strada Felice with **Simon Vierpy** between 1749 and 1751 and acted as an intermediary for Vierpyl with an English client on at least one occasion Wilton became involved in the making and supplying of plaster casts after the antique with **Matthew Brettingham** who also lodged in the Palazzo Zuccari. In 1750 Wilton became the first Englishman to win a premium from th Academy of St Luke, the gold medal awarded by Pope Benedict XIV in his jubilee year (**160**). Wilton's Rom sketchbook includes drawings of ornaments in churches and a study of Bernini's monument to Pope Alexander VI in St Peter's. He made his way however by copying excavated sculpture, and his early patrons were English and Iris tourists, including the avid collector, Lord Malton, later 2nd Marquess of Rockingham (**47**). According to J T Smith Wilton also had a close friendship with William Locke of Norbury Park, one of the most noted Englis connoisseurs and theorists of the antique of his day.

Wilton lived in Florence from 1751 to 1755, paying frequent visits to Rome. On 9 January 1752 he was elected to th Florentine Accademia del Disegno. By June 1753 he was living in a house belonging to the British envoy, Sir Horac Mann, on the Via de' Bardi, and that September Mann wrote proudly to Horace Walpole of this 'ingenious modes sculptor' whose work 'is admired by all the professors as well as connoisseurs' (*Lewis* 1937–1983, vol 20, 391–2). Wilto became a familiar figure with British visitors in Florence and acted as a guide to the collections of the Palazzo Pitt and the Uffizi galleries, where he met many of his future patrons. Joshua Reynolds painted his portrait in 1752, an Robert Adam reported to his brother in 1755 that he had been skating on the Arno with Wilton, and found hin 'sensible, civil and good-hearted' (*Eustace* 1997, 743). Wilton's practice was still chiefly confined to copying antiquitie for visitors like Lord Edgcumbe and Lord Tylney (**75, 48**), but he also gave his opinion on artistic matters, found ar antique marble altar for Horace Walpole, and advised Robert Adam on the design and execution of a chimneypiec (carved by **Michael Rysbrack**) for Hopetoun House.

In 1755 Wilton returned to London in the company of **G B Capezzuoli**, the painter G B Cipriani and the architec Sir William Chambers, with whom he would collaborate extensively in later years. Wilton had attracted the notice o numerous aristocratic patrons in Italy, and much was expected of him in London. His copies of ancient sculptur had been 'mentioned with encomiums' in *The London Daily Advertiser and Literary Gazette* (*Lewis* 1937–1983, vol 20 391–2), and as early as 1753 Reynolds had urged him to return home and 'begin a reputation in London' (*Postle* 1995 17). In addition to his excellent training and connections, Wilton was also a skilful and inventive sculptor. His bus of Dr Antonio Cocchi, 1755–56, a portrait without wig or draperies, combines the severity of an antique bust wit features and skin texture treated with an unflinching naturalism (**78**). A puff in the *Critical Review* of 1756 (vol 1, 387 announced that the bust was 'almost finished' and that Wilton combined 'the strength and accuracy of a Bona Rot with all taste and delicacy of a Bernini'.

In London, Wilton worked from his father's premises in Charing Cross, where he remained until 1761. He marrie Frances Lucas of Bishopsgate on 9 June 1757 in St Martin-in-the-Fields and their first child, Frances, was born nin months later. Wilton continued to churn out copies from the antique (**81–83**), but he also carved innovative portrai busts, notably Lord Chesterfield's head, 1757 (**80**), which again combined classical and naturalistic elements. He als maintained a public profile through the press and was singled out for his 'perfect power of Dorick elegance an simplicity' in a pamphlet of 1761 entitled *A Call to the Connoisseurs*.

Wilton took an active role in several nascent artistic institutions. In the years 1756–59, with Brettingham, h supplied the plaster casts for the 3rd Duke of Richmond's Gallery in London, having, it seems, selected suitabl subjects for the Duke whilst in Italy (**51, 52, 79, 85**). His bill of 1758 included itemised casts of Trajan's column Giambologna's *Samson and the Philistine*, and the feet of Michelangelo's *David* (**162**). He also carved a marble cop of the *Apollo Belvedere* for the entrance (**54**). When the gallery was opened to boys over the age of 12 as a drawin school in February 1758, Wilton and Cipriani were appointed directors. Wilton also became one of the first artis members of the Society of Arts, Commerce and Manufactures in February 1757, and he was on the committee of th Society of Artists, who met in 1759 to organise London's first art exhibition. In 1760 he was among the group of artist who gave work for display in the Foundling Hospital.

Wilton's connections brought a prestigious reward in 1760, when he won the commission for General Jame Wolfe's monument in Westminster Abbey (**24**), in competition with such formidable rivals as **Louis François Roubiliac**, Rysbrack and **Sir Henry Cheere**. Wilton had already been commissioned to produce an image of Wolf for the Duke of Richmond in 1759 (**52**), after studying the corpse's physiognomy on its arrival in Portsmout (*Anecdotes* 1937, 156), and he may already have carved a bust of Wolfe in Roman military armour (**87**). Funds fo this first publicly-financed monument were voted in September 1759 by the House of Commons, led by Willian Pitt the Elder, one of Wilton's patrons (**86**). Wilton's innovative design for the monument presents the General a a near-naked Pietà figure, expiring in the arms of a uniformed grenadier, who receives a laurel wreath from ar angel, symbolising the victory at Quebec where Wolfe lost his life. Although not finally erected until 1772 the desig prefigured Benjamin West's supposedly revolutionary depiction of the same scene in contemporary dress. Th monument reflects Wilton's ambitious approach, demonstrates the assimilation of French influences, and show his ability to innovate within the traditions of Baroque monumental theatricality. Cappezuoli, who was living wit Wilton in April 1774, executed the fine relief on the pedestal.

In 1760 Wilton made the model and began carving a new royal coach (**163**) and in 1761, the year in which a flattering poem appeared in the *London Magazine* calling Roubiliac and Wilton 'names as high as Phidias of antiquity' he was appointed statuary to the King. A series of commissions for royal statues followed. In November the Corporation of London resolved to erect a marble figure of the new King on the Royal Exchange and Wilton wrote an obsequious letter to the committee offering his services as sculptor (Wilton/City Corp). The commission appears to have been awarded to him without competition (**57**). The statue was the subject of a spirited tirade in the *Royal Magazine* in April 1764, when the stiff pose and Roman habit were interpreted as dangerously expressive of the 'haughty air of a tyrant'. Wilton was encouraged to reply to the criticisms in print, but answered that 'an altercation with thousands of people who understand nothing of the matter' would endanger his reputation and leave him open to prejudicial equivocation. Instead he answered each criticism levelled at his work in a letter (Wilton/City Corp), in which he suggested that the connoisseurs should be referred to antique precedents in the Capitoline Museum.

Wilton's other royal monuments elicited varied responses Horace Walpole described the statue of George II at Cambridge (**59**) as 'most vile' (*Anecdotes* 1937, 156), but William Mason called the lead equestrian statue of George III in Berkeley Square 'Phidian' (**60**) (*Lewis* 1937–1983, vol 28, 472). It collapsed under its own weight in the early 19th century like other of Wilton's publicly displayed portraits. The statue of George III erected in New York (**65**) became an inevitable early victim of the American War of Independence, and a bust of the King, commissioned by the philanthropist, Jonas Hanway, for the main square in Montreal was also destroyed (**100**). The Royal Exchange statue was taken down in a state of dilapidation in 1827, and was last seen in the studio of **J G Bubb**.

By the latter part of 1761 Wilton had erected extensive workshops in Queen Anne Street East, opposite Marylebone Fields, and occupied a large adjoining house on Portland Street. From here he ran a multi-faceted workshop, dealing in imported marble, urns and vases (**145–9**), supplying numerous chimneypieces, carrying out restoration work on antique sculpture (**72**), and turning out monuments of high quality. He employed many assistants including **Nathaniel Smith**, **John Atkins** and **A Beaupré**, a French sculptor recommended to him by Pigalle. Many of his works were produced in collaboration with Sir William Chambers, who had worked with Wilton's father. Wilton's eclectic training, his use of many assistants and his collaborative approach allowed him to move effortlessly between different styles. The influence of Delvaux has been detected in the arboreal frames to the Hales and Wolfe monuments (**7, 24**), the influence of Roman sculpture in the Berniniesque excess of the Bedford monument (**22**), whilst the memorials to Sir Hans Sloane, Christopher Griffith and Sir Robert Long are early examples of a cool, restrained neoclassicism (**11, 16, 18**).

The collaboration of Chambers and Wilton appears to have been the guiding force behind the foundation of the Royal Academy in 1768. The two resigned as directors of the Society of Artists that year and it was at a meeting at Wilton's house that it was decided to offer the presidency of a new institution under the monarch's protection to Sir Joshua Reynolds (*Farington* vol 6, 2469). These three leading figures in the artistic world were later depicted together in a painting by J F Rigaud celebrating the union of architecture, sculpture and painting. When Somerset House was built to Chambers's design between 1776 and 1790 to house the Royal Academy and other bodies, Wilton's workshop undertook a large share of the sculptural decoration (**117, 140, 141, 151–6**).

In 1768 Wilton's father died, leaving his estate to his eldest son, Joseph. In addition, three properties in Mortimer Street, Cavendish Square, were left in trust to be administered by Wilton and Chambers in the interests of Joseph's children. Wilton had acquired the trappings of a gentleman, including houses in town, on the Mall at Hammersmith, and at Snaresbrook, near Wanstead. His two sons, John and Joseph, were educated at Westminster School and young Joseph went on to University College, Oxford. His daughter, Frances, married Sir Robert Chambers, who had recently been appointed a judge of the Supreme Court of Judicature in Bengal. J T Smith, whose father had worked for Wilton, doubted that any man 'supported a more liberal table' (*Smith* 1828, 2, 177), and his guests included Lord Charlemont, one of his patrons (**164**), Joseph Baretti, who published puffs of Wilton's work, and Dr Johnson, who refers to Wilton's family in his correspondence, and who wrote the epitaph on the monument to Hester Salisbury (**26**). Many years later, when Wilton read Boswell's biography of Johnson, he bemoaned the fact that he, Wilton, hadn't kept a diary of things 'worth recording of himself and those he knew' (*Farington* 2, 415).

Wilton's social standing no doubt helped him to secure regular commissions and throughout the 1770s and '80s he produced a steady flow of church monuments. Protean in style, these incorporate elements borrowed from the previous century of British sculpture, from the reclining figure awaiting the Last Judgement in the Mexborough monument (**35**) to the severe neoclassical urns on the monument to the three wives of Lord Guildford (**40**). His finest achievement in the field was probably, however, the testament to Lady Anne Dawson, erected in a temple on her husband's estate in County Monaghan (**27**). Its arrival in Ireland was announced in the *Hibernian Journal* in August 1774. Wilton and Chambers had used the theme of an angel escorting the deceased to heaven in their monument to the Countess of Mountrath (**23**), and then returned to it for the Dawson memorial, which has an angel appearing to Lady Dawson's widower and son as they grieve over her urn. The angel appears in a swirl of draperies and clouds, causing the little boy to clasp his father in terror at the apparition. Despite the grandeur of the concept, the composition is relatively simple, tense and effective.

Wilton appears to have had financial difficulties in the late 1780s and J T Smith wrote that in June 1786 he sold his premises and studio contents. No sale catalogue has surfaced, so it is difficult to ascertain the reasons for the sale, or its size, although there were blocks of marble, models, casts, busts and several 'elegantly ornamented chimney-pieces, which had been executed upon speculation' (*Smith* 1828, vol 2, 180). In 1790 he was appointed keeper of the Royal Academy in succession to Carlini and he moved into a suite of rooms at Somerset House. His financial decline continued and on 22 June 1793 the *Universal Magazine* carried news of Wilton's bankruptcy (vol XCII, 472). He continued to work during these difficult years, was paid for more ornaments at Somerset House (largely the work of assistants, according to Smith), and in 1796 he dedicated his model for the bravura statue of Archbishop Tillotson (**69**) to George Stansfield, who supervised the monument's erection in Yorkshire, signing himself 'Joseph Wilton, RA, Statuary to the King and Keeper of His Majesty's Royal Academy in London.'

Although now over 70, Wilton was in general good health, and appears to have carried out effectively such dutie as vetting students for the plaster Academy at the RA. At this period he also began to write down particulars of hi life, largely for Farington. He continued to be sociable, dining with guests in his rooms and receiving visits fron his family, including his son who had become an Episcopalian vicar in Haddington, Scotland. Wilton's wife died i September 1794 (*GM*, Sept 1794, 866) and he appears to have re-married for Farington recorded in January 1800 tha Wilton's 'wife's mother has £1,000 a year which must come to His family after Her decease. She is 70 years of age - He expects soon to have a good living' (*Farington*, 4, 1357). Farington reported that Wilton's health was failing in 179 but he survived another four years dying on 25 November 1803. He was buried in the graveyard at St Mary, Wanstead above the inscribed slab is a tall stone watch-house, locally known as the 'watchers-box', said to be a replica o the entrance to the holy sepulchre in Jerusalem. Wilton's obituary in the *Gentleman's Magazine* described him a 'an artist of very considerable merit. In his private life he was universally beloved, being of a placid temper, mild i his manners, benevolent, and hospitable; an indulgent and affectionate parent, and a kind master; all his habits wer temperate, which contributed very much to his longevity' (*GM*, Nov 1803, 1099).

J T Smith's response to the sculptor was similar: he gave a vivid picture of the 'portly and well-looking' sculpto 'always dressed in the height of fashion' and carrying a gold cane, whose perfectly gentlemanlike manners 'rendere him an agreeable companion' (*Smith* 1828, 2, 183). Horace Mann was less charitable about his former lodger. In 176 after Wilton had failed to maintain correspondence with the consul, he described the sculptor as 'a low-born fello without education or gratitude' (*Lewis* 1937–1983, vol 22, 418–9). In 1796, the generous-spirited Wilton told Faringto that 'there was no just ground of reproach against the late Sir Horace Mann' (*Farington*, vol 2, 524).

A similar ambivalence is evident in evaluations of Wilton's art. James Dallaway suggested that 'the works of Bacon Banks, Nollekins [*sic*], Wilton and Flaxman, will rescue the present age from being totally indebted to foreigners fo perfection in statuary' (*Dallaway* 1800, 402). Later critics have been less charitable: Baker notes that mos commentators have treated Wilton's variety of styles and genres as evidence of a lack of a strong sculptura personality (*Baker* 2000, 26). **Allan Cunningham** considered Wilton to be possessed of 'little original merit as sculptor' and condemned him for his dependence on Chambers and his inability to produce poetic works whe Wilton, unlike other sculptors, had the financial independence to do so (*Cunningham* 1829–33, vol 3, 81). Mor recently, Whinney has professed herself baffled and disappointed by Wilton's inability to shake off the baroque styl he had learnt under Delvaux and to embrace wholly the neo-classical ethos. His achievement is hard to summaris but his career and output confirms that he was an innovative, skilled and eclectic sculptor, who played a pivotal rol in British artistic communities from his days as a *cicerone* in Rome to his Keepership of the Royal Academy. As sculptor, a friend of aristocrats and literati, and a crusader for institutions to support fellow artists, he occupie a unique role in the history of British 18th-century art.

MG

Literary References: *Critical Review*, I, 1756, 387; *GM*, 1761, 431; *Mortimer* 1763, 29; *GM*, 1774, 141; *Farington, passim*; *GM*, 1790, 962; *Univ Ma* XCII, 22 June 1793, 472; *GM*, 1803, 1099; *Smith* 1828, 2, 167–184; *Cunningham* 1829–33, III, 68–81; *Builder* 1859, 849; *Graves* 1907, 283; *Walpole So* 1917–18, 116; *Whitley* 1928, I, 96; *Anecdotes* 1937, 5; *Lewis* 1937–1983, vol 20, 391–2, vol 22, 418–9, vol 23, 567, vol 28, 472; *Gunnis* 1961, 13–1 *Hodgkinson* 1967, 73–80; *Nat Sculpt Rev*, 1974, 13; *Allen* 1983, 196; *JKB* 1983 (2), 41–44; *Whinney* 1988, *passim*; *Sunderland* 1988, 131 and repr 4 *Coutu* 1992, 59–67; *Allan and Abbott* 1992, 118; *Coutu* 1993, *passim*; *Postle* 1995, 11–18; *Bindman and Baker* 1995, *passim*; *Grove* 33, 1996, 22 (Murdoch); *Coutu* 1996, 175–185; *Eustace* 1997, 743; *Jacobs* 1997, 58–66; *Ingamells* 1997, 1009; *Baker* 1998 (3), 223–5; *Leeds* 1999, 62; *Baker* 2000, 2 *Bilbey* 2002, 161–64; *ODNB* (Coutu); Baker 2007, 219–25

Portraits of the Sculptor: Sir Joshua Reynolds, 1752, oil on canvas, NPG 4810; L F Roubiliac, bust of Wilton, *c*1761, RA; Johann Zoffany 'Th Academicians of the Royal Academy' 1773, Royal coll); Charles Grignion, 1773, chalk, NPG 4314; John Francis Rigaud, *Sir William Chamber Joseph Wilton and Sir Joshua Reynolds*, oil on canvas, 1782, NPG 987; John Hamilton Mortimer, *Self-portrait with Joseph Wilton and a studen* oil on canvas, *c*1765, RA; John Hamilton Mortimer *Caricature Group*, nd, YCBA

Archival References: Wilton Archive; Wilton/Bedford (see *Harris* 1970, 201, 247); letter to Lord Charlemont, 17 May 1773 with detailed bill, *HM* 1891, vol 1, 314–5; Wilton/City Corp (transcribed in *Roscoe* 1997, 186–7); Chambers's Letter-Books 41133, fol 1, 94 (letters to Wilton relating to th trust set up by Wilton's father); Goodwood bills; IGI

Will: William Wilton, PROB 11/935, p316r

Miscellaneous Drawings: Continental sketchbook, ex coll Christopher Powney, 26 drawings chiefly of sculptural decoration, including M notes and a sketch of a work by Pigalle (C Lib repr). Four studies from this notebook are of interior decoration in S Ignazio, Rome; a study o a papal monument; designs for or studies of a monument and a study of the nave decoration in S Maria in Vallicella, now HMI, 27.1 to 27.4/7 (*Leeds* 1999, 62); sketch of the tomb of Pope Alexander VII, St Peters, Rome, private coll (*Grove* 1996, 227, C Lib repr); design for a carved gi mirror, three designs for garden urns, seven designs for unidentified monuments VAM E496-1964, E497-499-1964, E502, 505-7-1964, E1185-1187 1965; design for a vase, Stanford SC; chimneypiece design for Osterley House, signed by Wilton, Soane v22/201 (*Harris* 1970, 42, 240)

Auction Catalogues: *Wilton* 1786

Funerary Monuments

1.	post-1788	Stephen Hooker (†1775) and wife (†1788)	Brenchley, Kent	S	Pevsner, *Kent: W & Weald*, 1976, 180
2.	†1755	Admiral Graves Drawing(s): VAM E.503-1964	Antony, Cornwall		Pevsner, *Cornwall*, 1970, 37
3.	1756	Pyke Crouch	Layston, Herts		*Gunnis* 1968, 437
4.	†1761	Bishop Benjamin Hoadley Drawing(s): E 964-1965 (SD 1762)	Winchester Cathedral		*Royal Magazine*, 1763, 244; Pevsner, *Hants & Isle of Wight*, 1967, 682
5.	1761	Vice-Admiral Temple West (†1757)	Westminster Abbey, London, nave		WAM (66); *Whinney* 1988, 262 (repr)
6.	†1762	Charlotte St Quintin Drawing(s): VAM E.501-1964	St John of Beverley, Harpham, E R Yorks	S	*Physick* 1969, 91; Pevsner, *Yorks: E.R. & York*, 1995, 450
7.	1762	Dr Stephen Hales (†1761)	Westminster Abbey, London, south transept	S	*Whinney* 1988, 264–5, 460n (repr); *Jacobs* 1997, 61–2 (repr)
8.	†1762	Maria Margaretta Elibank Drawing(s): VAM, signed 'J: Wilton Sculp: invet'	Aberlady, East Lothian		*Coutu* 1993, repr 54
9.	†1763	John Wood	SS Peter and Paul, Tonbridge, Kent	S	
10.	†1763	Lady Browne (?designed by Sir William Brown)	Hillington, Norfolk		Pevsner, *Norfolk: N W & S*, 1999, 403

11.	1763	Sir Hans Sloane (†1753)	Chelsea Old Church (All Saints), London, churchyard		*Anecdotes* 1937, 156; Pevsner, *London: N W*, 1991, 558; *Colvin* 1995, 241
12.	†1764	Leak and Mary Okeover	Okeover, Staffs	S	*Oswald* 1964, 176, 227 (repr); Pevsner, *Staffs*, 1974, 216
13.	c1764	Rear-Admiral Charles Holmes (†1761)	Westminster Abbey, London, Chapel of St John the Baptist	S	*Whinney* 1988, 265
14.	c1766	Robert Byerley and family	Goldsborough, W R Yorks	S	*Roscoe and Hempel* 1997, 49–57 (repr)
15.	†1766	Sir Edward and Lady (†1770) Turner	St Eadburg, Bicester, Oxon	S	Pevsner, *Oxon*, 1974, 454
16.	†1767	Christopher Griffith	Padworth, Berks		Pevsner, *Berks*, 1966, 191
17.	1767	Elizabeth Ottley (†1766)	Antigua Cathedral, WI		*Coutu* 1993, 327, cat. 247
18.	†1767	Sir Robert Long	Draycott Cerne, Wilts	S	Pevsner, *Wilts*, 1975, 226
19.	1767	William, 1st Earl of Bath (†1764)	Westminster Abbey, London, Chapel of St John the Baptist	S	Pevsner, *London: Westminster*, 1973, 446
20.	†1768	Henry Archer	Hale, Hants	S	Pevsner, *Hants & Isle of Wight*, 1967, 264
21.	†1769	Grace Trecothick	St Mary, Addington, Surrey		Pevsner, *London: S*, 1983, 204
22.	1765–9	Wriothesley, 2nd Duke of Bedford (†1711) and his duchess, Elizabeth (designed by Sir William Chambers) Payment(s): £1,000	Chenies, Bucks	S	*Whinney* 1988, 266, 267 (repr); *Coutu* 1996, 181–2 (repr)
23.	1766–71	Algernon, 6th Earl (†1744) and Diana, Countess of Mountrath (†1766) (designed by Sir William Chambers and G B Cipriani) Payment(s): £2, 162 15s 9d Drawing(s): by Sir William Chambers sold Christie, 6 June 1811, 87; 6 June 1817, 55	Westminster Abbey, London, Chapel of St Michael (partly dismantled)	S	Chambers's Letter-Books, 41133, fol 40; *Harris* 1970, 233; *Coutu* 1996, 181–2 (repr); *Colvin* 1995, 241
24.	1760–1772	General James Wolfe (†1759) (relief of 'The Taking of Quebec' by Capezzuoli) Drawing(s): pen and wash, formerly Parson's (*Baker* 2000, 46, repr)	Westminster Abbey, London, north ambulatory		*GM*, Nov 1772, 517–8, Dec 1773, 616; *Whinney* 1988, 265 (repr); *Baker* 2000, 11–15, 45–6 (repr)
25.	†1772	Sir John St Aubyn	Crowan, Cornwall		Pevsner, *Cornwall*, 1970, 60
26.	†1773	Hester Salisbury, mother of Mrs Thrale (epitaph by Dr Johnson)	Streatham, London	S	Pevsner, *London: S*, 1983, 391
27.	1774	Lady Anne Dawson (†1769) Drawing(s): VAM E.500-1964	Dartrey, Co Monaghan, mausoleum	S	*Potterton* 1975, 64, 65, 87 (repr); *Penny* 1977 (1), 47–50 (repr)
28.	c1774	Sir Thomas Street (†1696)	Worcester Cathedral		Pevsner, *Worcs*, 1968, 312
29.	†1774	Sir William Browne (?designed by Sir William Brown)	Hillington, Norfolk		Pevsner, *Norfolk: N W & S*, 1999, 403
30.	1775	Robert Wood (†1771), epitaph by Horace Walpole Drawing(s): Private coll	Putney New Cemetery, London		*Lewis* 1937–1983, vol 41, 317–8 (repr)
31.	†1777	Jane Day	Horsford, Norfolk	S	Pevsner, *Norfolk: N E & Norwich*, 1997, 564
32.	1778	John Lockwood (†1778)	Lambourne, Essex	D	*Nichols* 1812–15, 8, 637; Pevsner, *Essex*, 1965, 257; *Whinney* 1988, 268–9
33.	†1778	Sir John James Markham	Market Drayton, Salop	S	Pevsner, *Salop*, 1958, 194
34.	†1780	George Montagu	Kimbolton, Huntingdon	S	Pevsner, *Beds, Hunts & Peterborough*, 1968, 276
35.	1780	John, 1st Earl of Mexborough (†1778)	Methley, W R Yorks	SD	Pevsner, *Yorkshire: W R*, 1967, 365; *Whinney* 1988, 269
36.	1780	Richard Gipps (bust)	All Saints, West Harling, Norfolk		*Nichols* 1812–15, vol 8, 679; Pevsner, *Norfolk: N W & S*, 1999, 765
37.	1780	Sir James Denham Bt	Westminster Abbey, London, nave		*Gunnis* 1968, 437
38.	1782	Elizabeth Bacon and Peter Standly Drawing(s): VAM E.504-1964 (*Physick* 1969, 136 repr)	Linton, Cambs		*Physick* 1969, 136–7 (reprs); Pevsner, *Cambs*, 1970, 425; *Whinney* 1988, 269
39.	1782	John Ingram and family	Wakefield Cathedral, W R Yorks	SD	*Butler* 1998, 107–8 (repr)
40.	1783	Lucy (†1734), Katherine (†1766) and Elizabeth (†1745), the three wives of 1st Lord Guilford Drawing(s): pen and wash, Met NY 49.56.51 (*Harris* 1963, 222)	All Saints, Wroxton, Oxon	SD	Pevsner, *Oxon*, 1974, 861
41.	1783	Matthew (†1779) and Lucretia (†1750) Gregory	Spanish Town Cathedral, Jamaica	SD	*Lewis* 1965–7, April 1966, 124–5 (repr); *Jacobs* 1997, 63–4 (repr)
42.	†1786	Rev Philip Barton	Great Brickhill, Bucks		Pevsner, *Bucks*, 1994, 345
43.	†1787	Lucy Smith (†1781) and Anne Wilton (†1787), daughters of the sculptor	All Saints, Chelsea	S	Pevsner, *London: N W*, 1991, 558
44.	1787	Sir Basil Keith (†1777)	St Catherine, Jamaica	S	*Dossie* 1782, 440; *Lewis* 1965–7, April 1966, 126–7 (repr); *Coutu* 1998, 47–8, n6
45.	c1788	Design for the monument to Thomas Guy (commission awarded to John Bacon RA) Payment(s): £31 10s	Untraced		*Cox-Johnson* 1961, 13
46.	1795	General Sir Archibald Campbell (†1791)	Westminster Abbey, London, south transept	S	Pevsner, *London I:* 1973, 446

Statues

No.	Date	Work		Location		Reference
47.	1749–50	Medici Venus and the Queen of Sweden's faun		Wentworth Woodhouse, W R Yorks, marble saloon (1967)		*Penny* 1991 (2), 7; Pevsner, *Yorkshire: W R*, 1967, 650
48.	pre-1753	Bacchus ('of his own invention,' according to Horace Mann)		[coll Lord Tylney]; untraced		*Lewis* 1937–1983, vol 20, 398
49.	1752–3	Venus Payment(s): 300 crowns		[coll Ralph Howard]; untraced		*Ingamells* 1997, 1009
50.	pre-1753	Venus (made in Florence)		[coll Charles, 2nd Marquess of Rockingham]; untraced Other versions: Sir Horace Mann's residence, Florence		*Lewis* 1937–1983, vol 20, 397
51.	c1755	Medicean faun Payment(s): £150	m	[coll 3rd Duke of Richmond]; untraced		*Whinney* 1988, 260
52.	1759	General James Wolfe		[coll 3rd Duke of Richmond]; untraced		*Anecdotes* 1937, 156
53.	1760	Two classical female figures		Brensett, Pembury, Kent (1961); untraced	SD	C Lib (repr)
54.	1758–61	Apollo Belvedere Payment(s): £300	m	[Duke of Richmond's gallery, Whitehall, doorway]; untraced Other versions: Wilton House, Wilts, marble, nd Sledmere House, ER Yorks		*Anecdotes* 1937, 156; Pevsner, *Yorks E R & York*, 1995, 695; *Coutu* 1996, 176; *Guilding* 2001, 43 (repr)
55.	1761	Bacchus (after Michelangelo) Payment(s): £300	m	Syon House, Middx		*Allen* 1983, 200
56.	1762	'Two small statuettes' Payment(s): 50 gns		[coll Charles, 2nd Marquess of Rockingham]; untraced		*Penny* 1991 (2), 16
57.	1761–4	King George III Payment(s): £300	m	[Royal Exchange, London, line of kings on the façade of the piazza]; untraced		*Anecdotes* 1937, 157; *Roscoe* 1997, 173, 181–2, 186–7
58.	1765	Peace, model		[Exhib Soc of Artists, 187]; untraced		*Graves* 1907, 284
59.	1766	King George II		[Senate House, Cambridge]; Old University Library, Cambridge	S	Pevsner, *Cambs*, 1970, 204; *Whinney* 1988, 460 n27
60.	1766	King George III, equestrian statue (modelled by A Beaupré)	l	[Berkeley Square, London]; removed 1827		*Royal Mag*, 4 June 1766; *Smith* 1828, vol 2, 181; *Grove* 1996, 227
61.	by 1766	Medicean lion (plinth designed by Samuel Wyatt)	s	Kedleston Hall, Derbys		*Jackson-Stops* 1987 (1), 792 (repr); *Kedleston* 1998, 64–5 (repr)
62.	1762–6	Unnamed statue and other unidentified work (£400)		[Syon House, Middx]; untraced		*Allen* 1983, 200 n48
63.	1766	William Pitt, 1st Earl of Chatham		[Cork Town Hall]; Municipal art gall, Cork		*Walker* 1961, 13; *Coutu* 1993, fig 48
64.	1768	Peace, model		[Exhib Soc of Artists, London, 161]; untraced		*Graves* 1907, 284
65.	1770	King George III, equestrian	l	[Bowling green, opposite Fort George, New York]; destroyed		*Public Advertiser*, 23 Feb. 1770; *Fehl* 1972, 12; *Nat Sculpt Rev* 1974, 13 (repr); *Marks* 1981, 61–82
66.	1766–70	William Pitt, 1st Earl of Chatham	m	[New York, intersection of Wall and William Streets]; NYHS 1864.5	S	*Fehl* 1972, 11–13; *Craven* 1975, 36, 41; *Coutu* 1993, cat. 9; www.nyhistory.org
67.	1766–70	William Pitt, 1st Earl of Chatham	m	[Charlestown, South Carolina]; City Hall Park, Columbia, South Carolina		*Fehl* 1972, 17–18 (repr); *Nat Sculpt Rev* 1974, 13; *Craven* 1975, 41 (repr); *Coutu* 1993, 317–26, cat 27
68.	pre-1779	Hermaphroditus 'very capital after the antique'		[ex coll 'A man of fashion']; untraced		Earl Ferrers sale, Christie, 2–3 June 1779, lot 80
69.	1796	Archbishop John Tillotson (†1694) (inscription carved by Joseph Nollekens RA) Drawing(s): VAM E 1184-1965 (*Physick* 1969, 139, repr) Model(s): Huntington Art Colls, San Marino		Sowerby, W R Yorks		MS Inscriptions, 91; *Whinney* 1988, 268–9 (repr); *Bindman and Baker* 1995, 254
70.	pre-1801	Apollo and Venus (two)		[Earl of Bessborough; Christie, 7 April 1801]; untraced		Bessborough Sale, Christie, 7 April 1801 (£130, £105)
71.	nd	Flora		[Wanstead House, Essex]; untraced		*Gunnis* 1968, 436
72.	nd	Jupiter (restorations only – arms and attributes)		[Holkham Hall, Norfolk, portico in the billiard-room]; untraced		*Dallaway* 1800, 277
73.	nd	Venus and Apollo		Wilton House, Wilts		*Gunnis* 1968, 436
74.	nd	Venus de' Medici, copy	m	Wilton House, Wilts, entrance hall Other versions: Charlemont House; untraced		*Smith* 1828, vol 2, 181; *Guilding* 2001, 43 (repr)

Busts

No.	Date	Work		Location		Reference
75.	1752	Julius Caesar		[coll Lord Edgcumbe]; untraced Other versions: Christie, 17 Feb 1781, lot 36		*Postle* 1995, 12
76.	pre-1753	(Either for or of) Mr Swift, 'an original'		[Sir Horace Mann's residence, Florence]; untraced		*Lewis* 1937–1983, vol 20, 397
77.	pre-1753	Homer ('most glorious' according to Horace Mann)		[Sir Horace Mann's residence, Florence]; untraced		*Lewis* 1937–1983, vol 20, 397
78.	1755	Dr Antonio Cocchi	m	[Donington Park, Leics]; VAM A.9 1966 Other versions: Cocchi's funerary monument, Santa Croce, Florence, bronze Lewis Walpole library, Farmington, Conn, bronze	SD	*Hodgkinson* 1967, 73; *Whinney*, 1971, 98–99 (repr); Baker forthcoming

No.	Date	Subject	Material	Location	Sig	References
79.	1756	Trajan Payment(s): £50	m	[coll 3rd Duke of Richmond]; untraced		RG/JP, 9, 1598
80.	1757	Philip, 4th Earl of Chesterfield	m	BM		*Dawson* 1999, 66–68 (repr)
81.	1758	Bearded immortal		[Wentworth Woodhouse, W R Yorks]; untraced	D	*Penny* 1991 (2), 20
82.	1758	Bust of a man (after the antique Demosthenes)	m	[Wentworth Woodhouse, W R Yorks]; Getty, Los Angeles	SD	*Penny* 1991 (2), 20 (repr)
83.	1758	Laocoon		VAM A.84-1949	SD	
84.	1758	Thomas Sydenham MD Payment(s): £73	m	R C Physic, London		*Wolstenholme* 1964, 404–5 (repr)
85.	1759	Hercules, Alexander, Ariadne, Demosthenes		[coll 3rd Duke of Richmond]; untraced		Goodwood Estate Archives, WSRO
86.	1759	William Pitt, 1st Earl of Chatham		SNPG, Edinburgh (replica Peper Harow, Surrey)	SD	*Walker* 1961, 13; *Whinney* 1988, 261
87.	*c*1760	General James Wolfe	p	NPG 4415 Other versions: Dalmeny House, Lothian, Scotland, *c*1760, signed		*Whinney* 1988, 262, 263 (repr)
88.	1760	Unidentified subject	m	[Exhib Soc of Artists, 101]; untraced		*Graves* 1907, 283
89.	1761	Francis, 10th Earl of Huntingdon	m	[Castle Donington, Leics]; Gov Art Coll	SD	*Smith* 1828, vol 2, 174; Gov Art Coll archives
90.	1761	Louis-François Roubiliac	m	[Exhib Soc of Artists, London, 167]; NPG 2145		*Graves* 1907, 283; *Rococo* 1984, 302–3; *Kerslake* 1977, 236
91.	1762	Leak Okeover		Okeover Hall, Staffs	SD	*Oswald* 1964, 176, 227 (repr); *Treasure Houses* 1985, 295
92.	1762	Oliver Cromwell (†1658) Model(s): t-c, VAM, A.72-1965, Gunnis bequest, *Whinney* 1971, 102 (repr)	m	VAM A 32-1930 Other versions: Castle Donington, Leics, hall (1789), marble Gov Art Coll, 1947, marble British Embassy, Lisbon, Portugal	SD	*Throsby* 1789, vol 1, 173; *Walker* 1961, 20; *Whinney* 1971, 100 (repr)
93.	1762	Sir Isaac Newton	m	Bodleian, on loan to History Faculty library, 2002	SD	*Keynes* nd, 29
94.	*c*1762	Thomas Hollis	m	[coll The sitter]; Sotheby NY, 10–11 Jan, 1995 Other versions: Sotheby, 8 July 2003, lot 145, marble (catalogue repr)		*Smith* 1828, vol 2, 174; *Wilson* 2005, 4–26
95.	1762	Unidentified subject	m	[Exhib Soc of Artists, London, 168]; untraced		*Graves* 1907, 283
96.	*c*1763	Omphale Model(s): YCBA, New Haven B1977.14.34, clay	m	coll Sir Walter Bromley-Davenport	S	*Neoclassicism* 1992, 292–3; C Lib (repr)
97.	1763	Unidentified gentleman, model		[Exhib Soc of Artists, London, 151]; untraced		*Graves* 1907, 283
98.	1763	Unidentified gentleman, model		[Exhib Soc of Artists, London, 152]; untraced		*Graves* 1907, 283
99.	1764	Unidentified gentleman		[Exhib Soc of Artists, London, 162]; untraced		*Graves* 1907, 283
100.	pre-1766	King George III	m	[Place d'Armes, Montreal]; MMCH, 15885		*Coutu* 1992, 59–67 (repr)
101.	pre-1766	Sir Hugh Smithson, later 1st Duke of Northumberland	m	Syon Park, Middx, hall		*Treasure Houses* 1985, 16 (repr)
102.	1766	Unidentified gentleman	m	[Exhib Soc of Artists, London, 220]; untraced		*Graves* 1907, 284
103.	1766	Unidentified man		Fitzwilliam M65-1937	SD	
104.	*c*1766	William Pitt, 1st Earl of Chatham	m	NPG 6081 Other versions: Fitzwilliam M65-1937	S	*Curtis* 2000, 16, 57, 62 (repr)
105.	1767	Lord Bacon, model		[Exhib Soc of Artists, 214 (the same, or another, model of Lord Bacon exhib. 1768 Soc of A, 160)]; untraced		*Graves* 1907, 284
106.	1767	Lord Camden	m	[Exhib Soc of Artists, London, 215]; untraced		*Smith* 1828, vol 2, 174; *Graves* 1907, 284
107.	1769	Unidentified lady	m	[Exhib RA, London, 125]; untraced		*Graves* VIII, 1905–6, 316
108.	1770	Unidentified gentleman, model	m	[Exhib RA, London, 204]; untraced		*Graves* VIII, 1905–6, 316
109.	1771	King Alfred	m	[Lord Radnor]; University College, Oxford, Oxon		Pevsner, *Oxon*, 1974, 212; *Gunnis* 1968, 437
110.	1771	Unidentified man	m	Bromley-Davenport coll	SD	*British Portraits* 1956–1957, 77, n213
111.	1771	Unidentified gentleman	m	[Exhib RA, London, 224]; untraced		*Graves* VIII, 1905–6, 316
112.	1772	Unidentified nobleman		[Exhib RA, London, 277]; untraced		*Graves* VIII, 1905–6, 316
113.	1777	Unidentified gentleman	m	[Exhib RA, London, 380]; untraced		*Graves* VIII, 1905–6, 316
114.	pre-1779	Laocoon, Homer, Caracalla, Faustino, Sir Isaac Newton, Alexander, Julius Caesar		[Coll 'A man of fashion', Christie, 2 June 1779]; untraced		Earl Ferrers's Sale, Christies, 2–3 June 1779, lots 72–9
115.	1780	William Pitt, 1st Earl of Chatham (†1778)	m	Belvoir Castle, Rutland Other versions: marble replica, Palace of Westminster, London, Norman porch	SD	*Walker* 1961, 13, 14a, cat. no. 90; *British Portraits* 1956–1957, 77, cat 214
116.	by 1781	'Bust of Alexander, very capital, from the antique, executed at Rome from the original by Wilton'		[Coll 'a gentleman in Norfolk'; Christie 16 Feb 1781]; untraced		Christie, London, 16 Feb 1781
117.	pre-1781	Michelangelo, Sir Isaac Newton Model(s): Sir Isaac Newton (marked as 'special' in the catalogue), Exhib Soc of A, 159, 1768, *Graves* 1907, 284		Somerset House, London, over ceremonial doors		*Coutu* 1996, 185

118.	1781	Unidentified man, *en negligé*	m	VAM A.160-1969	SD	*Baker* 1995 (2), 827 (repr)
119.	1781	William Pitt, 1st Earl of Chatham		[Hon Anne Pitt]; Private coll, Cornwall	SD	
120.	1782	Medici Venus	m	[ex coll Earl of Abercorn]; Daniel Katz, July 1998; untraced	SD	C Lib (repr)
121.	1770–1783	Thomas, 1st Baron Dartrey (later 1st Viscount Cremorne)	m	YCBA, B 1977.14.33	S	*Waterhouse* 1977, 351
122.	pre-1786	Masks of Garrick, Roubiliac and Hogarth Payment(s): £2 7s		[Wilton sale, June 8–9, 1786, lot 40]; untraced		*Smith* 1828, vol 2, 180
123.	nd	Classical head		Wentworth Woodhouse, W R Yorks	S	C Lib (repr)
124.	nd	Frederick, Bishop of Derry and 4th Earl of Bristol (†1803)		Ickworth Park, Suffolk		*Gunnis* 1968, 437
125.	nd	Marquess of Rockingham		[Charlemont House]; untraced		*Smith* 1828, vol 2, 181
126.	nd	Martinelli		Untraced		*Smith* 1828, vol 2, 174
127.	nd	Milo Crotoniates		[Blenheim, Oxon]; untraced		*Dallaway* 1800, 394
128.	nd	Roman emperor	m	Wentworth Woodhouse, W R Yorks	S	C Lib (repr)

Chimneypieces

129.	*c*1760	Designed by Sir William Chambers Drawing(s): Met. NY	m	[Richmond House, London]; untraced		*Harris* 1970, 62, 235
130.	*c*1760	With bas-relief of Cupid and Psyche		Kedleston Hall, Derbys, library		*Kedleston* 1998, 29
131.	1762	Two Payment(s): £175 15s 3d		[Styche Hall, Salop]; untraced		*Harris* 1970, 53, 248
132.	1763	'plain, flatt' (designed by Sir William Chambers)		[Walcot House, Salop]; untraced		*Harris* 1970, 53, 250 citing Clive MSS, India Office library
133.	1766	'Composed of statues representing Nymph of Flora, holding a wreath' Payment(s): £300	m	Croome Court, Worcs, long gallery		*Harris* 2001, 72 (repr)
134.	1767	'in the vestibule' Payment(s): £217 Drawing(s): Soane 22:39		[Syon House, Middx]; untraced		*Allen* 1983, 200; *Eustace* 1997 (1), 750
135.	*c*1768	For the entrance hall		Manrésa House (Garnett College), Roehampton		*Harris* 1970, 245; Pevsner, *London: S*, 1983, 693
136.	*c*1768	Two, one with tablet representing Bacchus and a tiger (designed by Sir William Chambers)		Peper Harow House, Surrey, dining and drawing rooms		Pevsner, *Surrey*, 1971, 408
137.	pre-1769	Several, in Siena and statuary Payment(s): £100	m	[Kirkleatham, N R Yorks, gallery and dining room]; untraced		*Russell and Price* 1759, vol 2, 158
138.	1772	Designed by Sir William Chambers	m	Blenheim, Oxon, Duchess of Marlborough's dressing-room		Chambers's Letter-Books, 41133, fol 75, 76; Pevsner, *Oxon*, 1974, 471
139.	1780	(possibly made originally for Somerset House)		Burlington House, London, council room		Pevsner, *London: Westminster*, 1973, 625; *Valentine* 1991, 29
140.	1786	Several		Somerset House, London, east and west return buildings and main building		Chambers/Somerset Hse, box 7, CHA/3/2
141.	1780–92	Several Drawing(s): Soane 42/6/4–7, 11–12 and 42/5/131		Somerset House, London, RA council room (£1,097), treasury offices, unidentified rooms, mezzanines and attics		Chambers/Somerset Hse, CHA, box 6, 3/1/8, fo 270, 271; CHA box 7, CHA/3/2, fo 144; TNA AO1/2495–2498; *Harris* 1970, 229–32; *Coutu* 1996, 183, 218 n55
142.	nd	Description unavailable Drawing(s): VAM E.495-1964		Milton Abbey, Dorset		*Allen* 1983, 201 fn56
143.	nd	Statuary marble on a ground of verd antique, caryatids and reliefs on the frieze	m	[Sandbeck Park, W R Yorks, great room]; untraced		*Miller* 1804, 311

Architectural Sculpture

144.	1757	Head of a river god Payment(s): £5 5s	wd	[Kew bridge, Surrey]; untraced		Kew Accounts, Duchy of Cornwall office, XLI, Nov 1757; *Harris* 1970, 34 n12
145.	1758	Pair of small white vases of 'oval form with ox-skulls'		[coll 3rd Duke of Richmond]; untraced		Goodwood Estate Archives, WSRO in RG/JP, 9, 1598
146.	1758	Pair of Tuscan alabaster vases Payment(s): £16	a	[coll 3rd Duke of Richmond]; untraced		WSRO, Papers of the Duke of Richmond, Box 36/7
147.	1760	'Bianco e nero' tables	m	[Egremont House]; Petworth House, Sussex (?)		*Rowell* 2000 (2), 30
148.	1759–60	Supply of lapis lazuli (for a table finished by John Wildsmith)		[Croome Court, Worcs]; untraced		*Beard* 1993, 92
149.	1764–7	'Two alabaster urns' Payment(s): 4 gns		[Walcot House, Salop]; untraced		*Harris* 1970, 250
150.	*c*1772	Neo-classical tripod (designed by Sir William Chambers)		[Blenheim, Oxon, flower garden]; untraced		*Harris* 1970, 198–9 (pl. 193)
151.	1778	Four colossal statues of Asia, America, Africa and Europe (designed by Sir William Chambers) Payment(s): £484 including carriage and erection	s	Somerset House, Strand elevation, courtyard façade		*Coutu* 1996, 183–5 (repr); *Jenkins* 2000–1, 28
152.	1778	Keystones depicting the Ocean and the rivers Thames, Humber, Mersey, Medway and Tweed Payment(s): £126 for keystones Model(s): four keystone models at Chambers's house at Whitton Place, valued at £4 4s	s	Somerset House, London		*Harris* 1970, 101–2 (repr 158); *Jenkins* 2000–1, 24, 27 (repr)

153.	1781	'Two semi-circular niches in Portland stone'		Somerset House, London	RIBA Library, MS 335A; TNA AO1/2495–2498; *Gunnis* 1968, 435
154.	1784	Eight large oval medallions representing the Winds and the Seasons Payment(s): £176 (£22 each)	s	Somerset House, London	Chambers/Somerset Hse, box 7, CHA/3/2, fo 144; *Jenkins* 2000–1, 28
155.	1787	Eight vases with emblematical figures and ornaments and trophies 'allusive to different offices' Payment(s): £678 including materials and erection	s	Somerset House, London, recesses in south front and the great court	*Coutu* 1996, 185; *Jenkins* 2000–1, 28
156.	1790	Two lions in Portland stone Payment(s): £200, including the cost of a model in plaster	s	Somerset House, London, eastern watergate of great terrace	*Coutu* 1996, 185; *Jenkins* 2000–1, 28
Reliefs					
157.	1754	'Model of a woman's head in bass relievo from ye antique'		[ex coll Matthew Brettingham]; untraced	*JKB* 1983 (2), 86
158.	1765	Friendship, monumental bas-relief		[Exhib Soc of Artists, 186]; untraced	*Graves* 1907, 284
159.	1765	Neptune bringing treasure to Britannia	m	[Exhib Soc of Artists, 185]; untraced	*Graves* 1907, 283
Miscellaneous					
160.	1750	Cain killing Abel		[Accademia di San Luca, gold medal]; untraced	*Ingamells* 1997, 1009
161.	1757	Plaster casts after the antique	p	[Kedleston Hall, Derbys]; untraced	*JKB* 1983 (2), 44
162.	1758	Numerous plaster casts after Michelangelo, Giambologna and the antique		[3rd Duke of Richmond's gallery of painting and sculpture, Whitehall, London]; untraced	Goodwood Estate Archives, WSRO
163.	1760	Model and carving of royal state coach (designed by Sir William Chambers and G B Cipriani) Payment(s): £2,500 Model(s): presentation model, modelled by Capezzuoli and John Voyez, Worshipful Company of Coachmakers (*Coutu* 1996, 180, repr)		Royal Coll	*Coutu* 1996, 179–81 (reprs)
164.	1768	Table veneered with Sicilian jasper, marble pedestal 'for Lord Chesterfield's busto' and other unidentified decorative work (with Cipriani, under direction of William Chambers)		[coll Lord Charlemont]; untraced	*HMC* 1891, vol 1, 314–5
165.	c1770	Pedestal, originally for an equestrian statue of King George III (by Charles MacKubin Lefferts), later used as a tomb slab for Major John Smith of the British Army	m	[Bowling green, New York]; NYHS, 1874.6	www.nyhistory.org
166.	1771	Keystones for the Bridge (designed by Sir William Chambers)		[Woburn Abbey, Beds]; untraced	Chambers's Letter-Books, 41133
167.	1772	Hymen, model	tc	[Exhib RA, London, 278]; untraced	*Graves* VIII, 1905–6, 316
168.	1773	Casts of a relief of a sacrifice, two oval reliefs of the Seasons (Spring and Winter)	p	[Wentworth Woodhouse, W R Yorks]; untraced	*Penny* 1991 (2), 13
169.	1773	Mucius Scaevola before Porsena, model		[Exhib RA, London, 315]; untraced	*Graves* VIII, 1905–6, 316
170.	1772–3	Pier-table in lapis-lazuli with scalloped border (£146 6s 3d) Payment(s): £146 3s 3d		[for Lord Charlemont]; untraced	Chambers's Letter-Books, 41133, f75; *HMC* 1891, vol 1, 314–5
171.	1774	Model for a senatorial figure		[Exhib RA, London, 318]; untraced	*Graves* VIII, 1905–6, 316
172.	1781	Monumental figure of Hope		[Exhib RA, London, 539]; untraced	*Graves* VIII, 1905–6, 316
173.	1783	Monumental figure of Hope ('lately executed')		[Exhib RA, London, 431]; untraced	*Graves* VIII, 1905–6, 316
174.	1784	Two chimneypieces of statuary and Siena marble, architectural ornaments and tablets of fine Siena Payment(s): £129		Somerset House, London, Navy board room, Navy office	Chambers/Somerset Hse, box 7, CHA/3/2, fo 144
175.	1786	Chimneypiece of statuary and Ponsevera marbles, moulded cornice, enriched capitals to pilasters, mantle and jambs of Ponsevera Payment(s): £55		Somerset House, London, commissioning room for auditing public accounts	Chambers/Somerset Hse, Box 7, CHA/3/2

WILTON, William –1768

An ornamental plasterer, nothing is known of his early life or training, except that he took a wife, Elizabeth, before 1722, when his first son, **Joseph Wilton** was born. In 1737 he worked with **Thomas Carter I** providing plasterwork for a building belonging to William Pulteney in Chandos Place, London and he was also responsible for the elaborate rococo plasterwork ceilings of the Foundling Hospital (4).

By the 1740s Wilton must have been relatively affluent since he paid for an expensive Continental training for his son in the Nivelles workshop of **Laurent Delvaux**. Delvaux and Wilton may have had business dealings for in his notebooks of 1740–1 the Flemish sculptor refers to 'Mr Wllm. Wilton,' then living in Margaret Street, near Cavendish Square (*Jacobs* 1997, 58).

Wilton founded a highly-profitable factory producing papier-mâché ornaments for chimneypieces and mirror frames. J T Smith wrote that the workshops employed 'hundreds of people, including children' (*Smith* 1828, 2, 167). In addition to his Cavendish Square premises, Wilton also had works on the south-west corner of Hedge Lane, Charing Cross. He later retired to Wanstead, Essex, and he was buried in Wanstead parish church, Essex on 27 January 1768.

In his will he left three residential properties in Cavendish Square jointly to his friend, the architect Williar Chambers, and to his son Joseph. From the profits made on leasing them, the beneficiaries were instructed to pay a annuity of £50 to another son, William Wilton II, and to support the education of Wilton's three grandchildrei Frances Wilton, and two boys. He also left three guineas to his nephew and former pupil **Thomas Collins** to buy ring. Administration of the trust occasioned some spirited correspondence between Chambers and Joseph Wilton

Literary References: *Builder* 1859, 849; *Survey of London* 1970, vol 36, 264; *Allen* 1983, 196; *Coutu* 1996, 175–85

Archival References: Chambers's Letter-Books Add MS 41133, fols, 94

Miscellaneous Drawings: Three designs for unidentified monuments VAM E 1185-87-1965

Will: PROB 11/935/316–318

Architectural Sculpture

1.	1751	Unidentified work Payment(s): £52	p	[Okeover Hall, Staffs]; untraced	*Oswald* 1964, 227
2.	1762	Unidentified work	p	[Styche, Salop]; untraced	*Harris* 1970, 53, 248
3.	*c*1768	Unidentified work	p	[Manresa House (Garnett College), Roehampton (formerly Parkstead House)]; untraced	*Harris* 1970, 245
4.	nd	Decorated ceiling	p	Foundling Hospital, London	*Whinney* 1988, 460

WINBURY fl 1690–1710

He re-cut **Stephen Baldwyn**'s statue of Charles I or Charles II in Worcester. In 1690 there is an order that Mr Alderma Haines 'doe agree with Winbury the stonecutter for the takinge downe of the King's picture and settinge it up again while in the audit of accounts for that year there is a payment of £5 to Winbury for 'work done to and settinge up th King's picture'. In 1710 he received a further payment for putting a new hand on the statue (Worcester City Accounts

Literary References: *Gunnis* 1968, 437; *Gibson* 1997 (1), 165, 370

WINCHESTER, William *c*1715–72

The son of Henry Winchester of Wimbledon, he was apprenticed to **Thomas Dunn** on 30 April 1729 and became fre of the Masons' Company on 14 June 1739, at which time he 'live[d] with Mr. Dunn' (Masons' Co Assistants, fol 10 In 1763 he was listed in Mortimer's *Director* as a citizen and mason of Holborn (p 49). He took three apprentices, tw of them family members, through the auspices of the Masons' Company. Henry, the son of Henry Winchester, mason, joined him in 1757, and Henry Winchester, the son of a butcher, in 1765. James Fleming of Whitechapel als arrived in 1765. Winchester signs the large churchyard monument to James Adams, 1765, a work that Gunnis not illustrated in Palm's *Stifford and Its Neighbourhood* (1872).

Literary References: *Gunnis* 1968, 437; *Webb* 1999, 13, 36

Archival References: Masons' Co, Court Book, 1722–51 (1729); Freemen, fol 73 (1739); Court Book, 1751–96 (1 Oct 1772)

Funerary Monuments

1.	1765	James Adams	Stanford-le-Hope, Essex, churchyard	S	*Gunnis* 1968, 437

WINDOVER (or WENDOVER), J, of Andover fl 1810–30

Only two monuments have been identified, a large wall-tablet with fluted pilasters supporting a plain pediment t John Carter (1), and a smaller one to the Rev John Blair (2). Windover was later assisted by his son, James.

Literary References: *Gunnis* 1968, 437

Funerary Monuments

1.	1810	John Carter	Kingsclere, Berks	S	*Gunnis* 1968, 437
2.	1830	Rev John Blair	Whitchurch, Hants	S	*Gunnis* 1968, 437

WINFIELD, James, of Leicester fl *c*1795–96

Winfield was one of the best of the Leicestershire slate-workers and his productions are frequently found in th county. Gunnis lists only two, both tablets.

Funerary Monuments

1.	?1795	Lucretia King	Barrow-on-Soar, Leics	S	*Gunnis* 1968, 437
2.	?1796	Langley Bankes	Loughborough, Leics	S	*Gunnis* 1968, 437

WING, John, of Bedford 1756–1826

He was the eldest son of John Wing, an architect and mason of Hallaton, Leics, who moved to Bedford about 179 where he died four years later (*GM*, LXIV, July 1794, II, 675). Wing was born in July 1756. Early in the 1780s John Win junior moved to Bedfordshire, where his father had recently acquired a stone-quarry at Totternhoe. He settled Bedford, took over the quarry, and soon became the leading architect and builder in the county, frequently acting a surveyor of bridges, and erecting most of the public buildings in Bedford. He was employed as a mason during th rebuilding of Woburn Abbey, 1789–1792, receiving nearly £5,000 for masonry and carved stone work. He also erecte the stables and the main entrance-lodge, the latter at a cost of £1,278 3s 6d.

He took an interest in civic affairs, becoming a prominent member of the corporation and holding the office mayor three times. In 1799 he married Elizabeth Tracy, by whom he had five sons, none of whom followed his caree He died at Bedford on 2 December 1826, aged 70, and was buried in St Mary's, where there is an inscription to h memory in the south aisle.

His tablets are architectural and occasionally have well-carved details in coloured marbles.

Literary References: *Gunnis* 1968, 437–8; *Colvin* 1995, 1069–70

Archival References: Woburn Building Accts 1789–1792, BLARS R3/2114/469–71, R5/1102, R5/1297, R5/1105

Funerary Monuments

1.	1786	Henry Palmer	Northill, Beds		*Gunnis* 1968, 438
2.	1788	Robert Battisson	St Paul, Bedford		*Gunnis* 1968, 438
3.	?1790	John Green	St Mary, Bedford	S	GPC
4.	†1794	Mrs Bull	Godmanchester, Hunts	S	*Gunnis* 1968, 438
5.	1794	Rev John Crowe	St Paul, Bedford		*Gunnis* 1968, 438
6.	1797	George Edwards	Henlow, Beds		*Gunnis* 1968, 438
7.	†1800	Henry Shuttleworth and his second wife (†1806)	Great Bowden, Leics	S	

8.	1800	Richard Raynsford	Henlow, Beds		*Gunnis* 1968, 438
9.	1803	Martha Monoux	Sandy, Beds		*Gunnis* 1968, 438
10.	1807	William Wright	Apsley Guise, Beds		*Gunnis* 1968, 438

Miscellaneous

11.	1789–1792	Masonry and carved stonework Payment(s): £5,000	Woburn Abbey, Beds		*Gunnis* 1968, 437

WINSER, Edward, of Newton Abbot fl 1810–17

Funerary Monuments

1.	1810	Banfill family	Townstal, Devon	S	*Gunnis* 1968, 438
2.	?1813	William Pilcher	St Clement, Dartmouth, Devon	S	
3.	1817	William Banfill	Townstal, Devon	S	*Gunnis* 1968, 438

WIRMADGE, of Leicester fl 1786

Gunnis describes him as a worker in slate and the author of the signed slab to Henry Payne, which has a well-carved figure of *Hope* at the top. It seems likely that the sculptor was in fact **William Firmadge of Leicester**.

Literary References: *Gunnis* 1968, 438

Funerary Monuments

1.	1786	Henry Payne, slate slab	Market Bosworth, Leics	S	*Gunnis* 1968, 438

WISE, Thomas I –1685

Wise, who was admitted to the freedom of the Masons' Company by redemption in 1672 and became master in 1681, held the post of master mason to the Crown at Windsor Castle and in the office of works from 6 June 1678 until his death in December 1685. Nothing is known of his origins but he seems to have had connections with the Isle of Portland. He is first recorded in 1665, working with **Stephen Switzer** at Greenwich Palace, where their work included stonecarving (4). In 1681 he was employed at the Tower of London, where he supplied a chimneypiece for Lord Alington's apartment (1). The following year he made improvements to the Queen's chapel at St James's Palace, and in 1685 he was employed at Chelsea Hospital.

He had considerable employment at Whitehall where, in 1682, he made a Portland stone chimneypiece for the Queen's Room in 'King Charles's new building' (2) and 'laid down Purbeck paving in the Duke of York's passage' (TNA WORK 5/37 fols 39, 91). In 1684 he supplied marble for three chimneypieces in the Duchess's lodgings among sundry other works (TNA WORK 5/38, fols 11, 19, 28, 59, 70, 79). By October 1685 he was working on the privy gallery building, where he received a number of payments including £23 19s for Portland stone 'in the little front leading to the Chapell and the Corbell over the arch in the great Staircase' and £3 4s, made for 'carving in the Architrave 4 cherubim's heads' (TNA WORK 5/54 fols 42, 81). He worked at Whitehall until his death and the last payments were made to the 'Executors for Thomas Wise. Late Master Mason' in July 1686 (TNA WORK 5/54 fols 42, 81, 105).

Wise worked under Wren on rebuilding the City churches, receiving total payments of £1,019 at St Michael Wood Street between March 1670 and October 1687, £3,141 at St Nicholas Cole Abbey between November 1671 and June 1681, and £2,658 at St Benet Gracechurch, built between August 1681 and August 1687. His work at these churches included some carved stonework (**5, 8, 9**).

He was also a mason contractor at St Paul's Cathedral. In December 1678 he agreed to 'continue the building of the S.W Leggs of the Dome with the Great Staircase from the midle of the Window on the W. Side of the S. Cross Isle from the Stoole of the Window upwards to the height of the Stay-barrs' and a year later signed a contract for work on a part of the building 'from the midle of the W. Window of the S. Portico so farr South Westwards as he shall be directed, together with the S.W Corner of the Dome, and the Great Round Staires soe high as he shall be directed' (*Wren Soc*, XVI, 17–8). This work included ornamental sculpture, such as 'Masoning and carving 6 Cartouches over ye Doore & Neeches' for £9, 'carving 4 ffestoones 10 feet long each at £20 p. piece' and 'Carving 36 Pannells with fflowers & enrichments of ye Mouldings at £3. 5s. each Pannell £117' (*Wren Soc*, XIII, 146). In a further contract of April 1681, Wise undertook, together with **Thomas Strong, Edward Pearce** and **Jasper Latham**, to carve 'the great Capitells of the Pilasters both for the Inside & the Outside' (*Wren Soc*, XVI, 20) (**6**). He continued to work at St Paul's until his death and during the period he and his executors received a total of £5,616 18s 10d.

Wise, who was described as late of Whitefriars, London, widower, in his will, is commemorated by a monument at St Mary, Winkfield, Berks. He left three sons, two of whom, **Thomas Wise II** and **William Wise**, were masons. Wise's pupils included Benjamin, son of Giles Pearce, of the Isle of Portland, mason, who was apprenticed to him in 1672.

Literary References: *Weaver* 1915, 15, 16, 20; *Knoop and Jones* 1935, 35–6; *Wren Soc*, VII, X, XI, XIII, XIV, XV, XVI, XVIII, XIX, *passim*; *Colvin* V, 1973–6, 249, 471, 478; *Gunnis* 1968, 438

Archival References: Masons' Co, Freedom Register, 1663–94; Court Book, 1677–94, fol 41v; RG/JP, 9, 1610

Will: PROB 11/382 (proved 22 Feb 1685/6)

Chimneypieces

1.	1681	White marble Payment(s): £13	[Tower of London, Lord Alington's apartment]; untraced		PRO Works 5/36, unlocated ref cited by *Gunnis* 1968, 438
2.	1682	Portland stone	[Whitehall Palace, London, 'King Charles's new building', Queen's room]; destroyed		TNA WORK 5/37 f39
3.	1685	38 in Portland stone, 'Rigate' and marble	[Privy Gallery Building, Whitehall Palace, London]; destroyed		*Wren Soc* VII, 108–9

Architectural Sculpture

4.	1665	Carved stonework (co-sculptor: Stephen Switzer)	[Greenwich Palace]; untraced		TNA WORK 5, 9, fols 327, 329, 333
5.	1671–1681	Four urns	[St Nicholas Cole Abbey, City of London, corners of the steeple]; untraced		Bodleian, Rawlinson 387, in *Gunnis* 1968, 438
6.	1678–1685	Carved ornaments	St Paul's Cathedral, London	s	*Wren Soc*, XIII, XIV, *passi*
7.	1685	Carved ornaments	[Privy gallery building, Whitehall Palace, London]; destroyed		*Wren Soc* VII, 95, 101–2

8.	1670–1685	Four Ionic capitals	s	[St Michael Wood Street, City of London]; untraced		Bodleian, Rawlinson, 387 in *Gunnis* 1968, 438
9.	1681–1685	Two palm branches		[St Benet Gracechurch, City of London]; untraced		Bodleian, Rawlinson, 387 in *Gunnis* 1968, 438

WISE, Thomas II fl 1678–94

The son of **Thomas Wise I**, he ran a large Portland stone business for many years and was a mason-contracto employed on the construction of St Paul's Cathedral. Wise and his partner Thomas Gilbert supplied Portland ston for St Paul's from 1678 onwards, for Winchester Palace in 1683 and for the water gallery at Hampton Court as late a 1690. The Winchester Palace stone contract describes the partners as 'of the Isle of Portland' but a contract fc St Paul's Cathedral, dated 23 December 1680, refers to them as 'Thomas Gilbert of ye Isle of Portland and Thoma Wise of St Olave's, Southwark' (*Wren Soc*, VII, 32–3; XVI, 19).

Wise was made free of the Masons' Company in 1684, probably by patrimony. He became an upper warden in 169 and master of the Company in 1698. He he seems to have been working with his father at St Paul's in 1685, since ther is a note by Thomas Wise I in the Acquittance Book, under the date 4 July 1685, authorising a payment to his son. I December 1685 Wise took over his father's work at the Cathedral, in partnership with **Thomas Hill I**. At the time c the general search in 1694 Wise and Hill employed 16 masons at St Paul's. In 1698 they contracted to carry out th stonework of the south west quarter of the dome and they continued to work on the building until 1707. Betwee them they received payments of £24,509. Their work included carved stonework, such as scrolls, festoons, capitals a £15 a face, 'window scrowles' at £6 each, the keystone of the great window on the inside of the portico and some c the shields in the wreaths of the nave cupolas (**2**).

It was probably **Thomas Wise II** (not his father) who succeeded **Joseph Cartwright** as mason for the Bridg House, London Bridge, in 1684. He received an annual salary of £4 and regularly supplied stone and effected repair In 1685 he was paid £50 for the 'Neece' for the statue of Charles II at Southwark town hall (Bridge House Rental 1682–86) (**1**). Thomas Wise was still master mason at the Bridge at the end of September 1694. Samuel Pearemar who began work at the Bridge in July 1684, was apprenticed to him the following October. Two further apprentice are recorded: Thomas's son, John Wise, was bound to him on 4 December 1689 and he was joined by Robert Blak on 24 November 1690. Both worked at the Bridge.

Literary References: *Knoop and Jones* 1935, 38–9; *Wren Soc*, IV, VII, XIII, XIV, XV, VXI, *passim*; *Gunnis* 1968, 438; *Webb* 1999, 4, 25

Archival References: Masons' Co, Court Book, 1695–1722, fol 31 r; Masons' Co, Masters and Wardens

Architectural Sculpture

1.	1685	Richly carved niche 'on St Margaretts Hill' for the statue of Charles II Payment(s): £50	[Southwark Town Hall, London]; untraced		*Bridge House Rentals*, 1685; *A New View of London*, 1708, 801; *Gunnis* 1968, 438
2.	nd	Carved ornaments (co-sculptor: Thomas Hill)	St Paul's Cathedral, London		*Wren Soc* XIV, XV, *passim*

WISE, William fl 1673–1703

He was the second son of **Thomas Wise I** and was apprenticed to his father in 1673, becoming free of the Mason Company on 5 October 1680. He became renter warden of the Masons' Company in 1695, upper warden in 1696 an master in 1703. In 1683 he and his partner, **Samuel Fulkes** worked as masons at Winchester Palace.

Literary References: *Knoop and Jones* 1935, 35–6; *Wren Society*, VII, 23, 36–8, 61, 62–4, 66; XIV, 16–7; XV, 10; *Gunnis* 1968, 438

Archival References: Masons' Co, Apprentice binding book (1), 1673; Freemen, fol 72; Masters and Wardens

WITHENBURY (or WYTHINBURY), James, of Worcester –1725

He was a mason and also, at the time of his death, proprietor of the King's Head inn in Worcester. Gunnis note that the contract for the monument to Bishop Lloyd is published in A Tindal Hart's *Life of Lloyd, Bishop of Worceste* (p 258). It was to be of marble, to cost £140, to be completed by 1 August 1718, and erected in Fladbury church Worcs. The bishop's widow was specific about the composition which was to comprise a half figure of the bisho in an architectural setting. When the church was restored in 1865 the monument was dismembered. It has no however been restored. Pevsner describes it as a standing monument with elaborate flowers and foliage.

Literary References: *Gunnis* 1968, 438; *Colvin* 1995, 1071

Funerary Monuments

1.	1718	Lloyd, Bishop of Worcester (†1717) Payment(s): £140	Fladbury, Worcs		Pevsner, *Worcs*, 1968, 154

WITHERS, Robert fl *c*1777?

The Davison wall tablet has a draped urn in front of a pyramid.

Funerary Monuments

1.	?1777	William Davison	Milverton, Somerset	S	*Gunnis* 1968, 439

WOLFE (or WOOLFE), Bartholomew *c*1654–1720

He was the son of Bartholomew Woolfe, of Bromley, Kent, a yeoman, and was apprenticed to John Palmer in 166 becoming free in 1675. He later became one of the leading City masons and worked for several of the City Companie including the Fishmongers, for whom he executed masonry work in 1717–18. He was again at Fishmongers' Hall i 1720 when he was paid £5 10s. His executors received a further payment of £170 for the period 1720–21.

Literary References: *Gunnis* 1968, 439

Archival References: Fishmongers P W Accts, 157, 187, 209

WOLFF, Emil fl 1839–44

His address in 1839 was Quattro Fontane, Rome (*Graves* VIII, 1905–6, 328). Le Grice visited the studio in 1844 an described the works on display with reverent admiration. All were classical subjects. Le Grice listed twelve with the intended destinations. Wolff's patrons included the King and Crown Prince of Prussia and several Russia aristocrats, but a number of the statues were for English clients (**1, 3, 4, 5**).

Literary References: *Le Grice* 1844, vol I, 120–5; vol II, 249–52

Statues						
1.	by 1844	A youth fishing		[for the Duke of Sutherland; sculptor's studio, Rome, 1844]; untraced		*Le Grice* I, 1844, 124
2.	1844	Albert, the Prince Consort		Royal Coll, Osborne House, I of W Other versions: Buckingham Palace, London, marble, SD 1846		*Harris, de Bellaigue, Millar* 1968, 186 (repr); *Read* 1982, 30 (repr), 32
3.	1844	Greek warrior putting on his greaves		[for Richard Holt Esq; sculptor's studio, Rome]; untraced		*Le Grice* I, 1844, 124
4.	1844	Hunter with a spear		[for Richard Holt Esq; sculptor's studio, Rome]; untraced		*Le Grice* I, 1844, 124
5.	1844	Shepherdess with a kid		[for Yates of Liverpool; sculptor's studio, Rome]; untraced		*Le Grice* I, 1844, 124
6.	pre-1857	Cupid as Hercules	m	[coll E Leatham]; untraced		*Manchester Art Treasures* 1857, 134
7.	nd	Love the conqueror	m	Scottish Youth Hostels Assoc		*Pearson* 1991, unpag
8.	nd	Pan	m	Birmingham MAG, inv P.225'77	S	*Silber* 1987, 100, cat no 311
9.	nd	Youthful satyr	m	Scottish Youth Hostels Assoc		*Pearson* 1991, unpag
Busts						
10.	1839	Albert, the Prince Consort	m	Royal Coll		*Ormond* 1973, 10
11.	1841	Sir Thomas Fowell Buxton Bt	m	[Exhib RA, London, 1257]; untraced		*Graves* VIII, 1905–6, 328; *Ormond* 1973, 83
Miscellaneous						
12.	1839	Girl with a goat and tambourine		[Exhib RA, London, 1306]; untraced		*Graves* VIII, 1905–6, 328

WOLSTENHOLME, John, of York fl 1793–1843

He was the son of Francis Wolstenholme, a carver and gilder of York, who died on 13 April 1833 (*Yorkshire Gazette*, 20 April 1833). In 1793 John provided the decorative woodwork for the organ at Sledmere for Sir Christopher Sykes (3). His statue of *Minerva* on High Petergate is painted and gilded (1).

He was employed on repair work at York Minster after the fire of 1829; among payments to him is one of £411 in 1843 for carvied bosses in American yellow pine for the ceiling of the nave 'chiefly from the drawings of Mr. J Brown' (2) (GPC, ref untraced). His name appears in the lease records for a house in Petergate in August 1843, when he paid £14 11s 3d in rent (York Minster Library, Dean and Chapter Archives, E4e). A Mr Wolstenholme, perhaps the same man, received £505 in 1811 for work at Eaton Hall, Cheshire (Grosvenor Archives).

Archival References: GPC

Statues						
1.	1801	Minerva		Corner of Minster gates and High Petergate, York, exterior of building	SD	
Architectural Sculpture						
2.	1843	Bosses		York Minster, nave ceiling		Minster Archives cited in GPC
Miscellaneous						
3.	1793	Organ casing	wd	Sledmere, E R Yorks		RG/JP, 9, 1612

WOLSTENHOLME, Thomas, of York 1759–1812

He was related to **John Wolstenholme**. The epitaph on his tombstone in the churchyard of St Olave, York, describes him as a sculptor. It gracefully adds 'His Genius shone with graceful taste attir'd / His works spoke merit and the Age admired'.

Archival References: GPC

WOOD, Enoch 1759–1840

Perhaps the most notable of a distinguished family of Staffordshire potters, he was apprenticed to Josiah Wedgwood of Burslem and Humphrey Palmer of Hanley. In 1784 he founded Enoch Wood and Company in Burslem: this became Wood and Caldwell in 1790 and Enoch Wood and Sons in 1818. He was also in partnership with his cousin, the figure-maker Ralph Wood, around 1783. One of the earliest collectors of English pottery, Wood seems first to have exhibited in 1816 at a dinner celebrating the 50th anniversary of the cutting of the Trent and Mersey Canal. His museum, housed in his factory, contained almost 700 pieces and was internationally known. His self-portrait bust, executed at the age of 61, is a confident, characterised statement, well reflecting his skill as a modeller (2).

Literary References: *Dawson* 1999, 88

Busts					
1.	1818	George Washington	Stoke-on-Trent, MAG		Grove Art Online (Mawer)
2.	1821	Enoch Wood, unglazed white earthenware	BM	SD	*Dawson* 1999, 229–232
Reliefs					
3.	1777	Christ on the Cross, two large octagonal earthenware plaques	Stoke-on-Trent, City Museum and Art Gall, inv 18a 1910 and Schreiber Coll, VAM		*Dawson* 1999, 229, 232 n6

WOOD, George, of Gloucester and Cheltenham fl *c*1734?–1823?

The *Gloucester Journal* of 5 January 1807 states 'On Thursday last was married at St Mary de Crypt, Mr George Wood, statuary, of the Black friars, to Miss Mary Bryan, youngest daughter of the late Mr. **John Bryan**, of this City'.

Almost all his monuments are found in the close vicinity of Gloucester. Gunnis considers his best to be to Charles George, which has a pretty relief of a mourning widow standing by an urn, while her little daughter clutches at her skirt (**15**). His stock monumental motif was the draped urn (**2, 9, 14, 19, 24, 30**) though there were occasional neo-Greek compositions (**28, 29**). His bankruptcy notice, which described him as a marble mason, was announced in the *European Magazine* on 8 July 1820 (*Euro Mag* 1820, 77, 561). He had a second yard in Cheltenham.

Funerary Monuments					
1.	†1734	Henry Adey	St James, Dursley, Glos	S	Pevsner, *Glos: Cotswolds*, 1999, 335
2.	*c*1783	Richard Rogers (†1757)	Dowdeswell, Glos	S	Pevsner, *Glos: Cotswolds*, 1999, 323

3.	†1784	Captain William Moore	St James, Dursley, Glos	S	Pevsner, *Glos: Cotswolds*, 1999, 334
4.	?1785	Dr John Bosworth	Tortworth, Glos	S	*Gunnis* 1968, 439
5.	?1785	John de la Bere	St Mary, Cheltenham, Glos	S	*Gunnis* 1968, 439
6.	†1794	Samuel Adey	St James, Dursley, Glos	S	Pevsner, *Glos: Cotswolds*, 1999, 335
7.	†1801	James Daubeny	Stratton, Glos	S	Pevsner, *Glos: Cotswolds*, 1999, 646
8.	†1802	Richard Brereton (co-sculptor: John Bryan II)	Edgeworth, Glos	S	
9.	†1802	Thomas Clutterbuck	Avening, Glos	S	Pevsner, *Glos: Cotswolds*, 1999, 150
10.	†1803	Martha Browne	Salperton, Glos		RG/JP, 9, 1613
11.	†1803	Thomas Martin	Hindlip, Worcs	S	
12.	†1804	Rev John Craven	Sevenhampton, Glos	S	Pevsner, *Glos: Cotswolds*, 1999, 597
13.	†1805	Thomas Heynes	Chipping Norton, Oxon	S	RG/JP, 9, 1613
14.	†1806	Thomas Went	Uley, Glos	S	Pevsner, *Glos: Cotswolds*, 1999, 703
15.	†1807	Charles George	Rodmarton, Glos	S	Pevsner, *Glos: Cotswolds*, 1999, 582
16.	†1809	John Smyth	Gloucester Cathedral	S	*Gunnis* 1968, 439
17.	†1810	Edward Rogers	Dowdeswell, Glos		Pevsner, *Glos: Cotswolds*, 1999, 323
18.	†1810	John Lucas	St Mary, Cheltenham, Glos	S	RG/JP, 9, 1613
19.	†1811	Ann Stephens	St Peter, Winchcombe, Glos	S	Pevsner, *Glos: Cotswolds*, 1999, 729
20.	†1811	Jane Webb	Gloucester Cathedral	S	Pevsner, *Glos: Vale & Forest of Dean*, 1976, 218
21.	†1812	5 Browne children (†1803–1812)	Salperton, Glos	S	Pevsner, *Glos: Cotswolds*, 1999, 588
22.	†1813	Eliza Crawshay	Kinver, Staffs		*Jeavons* 1960, 70
23.	†1813	Esther Hayward	South Cerney, Glos	S	Pevsner, *Glos: Cotswolds*, 1999, 619
24.	†1815	Giles Greenaway	Little Barrington, Glos	S	Pevsner, *Glos: Cotswolds*, 1999, 449
25.	1816	Unidentified subject, tablet	Hempsted, Glos	S	Pevsner, *Glos: Vale & Forest of Dean*, 1976, 268
26.	†1817	James Steers	Upton St Leonard's, Glos	S	Pevsner, *Glos: Vale & Forest of Dean*, 1976, 396
27.	†1817	Martha Taylor	St Mary, Charlton Kings, Glos	S	Pevsner, *Glos: Vale & Forest of Dean*, 1976, 120
28.	†1817	Rev Thomas Bayley	St George, King's Stanley, Glos	S	Pevsner, *Glos: Cotswolds*, 1999, 431
29.	†1818	Elizabeth and Abraham Birch	St Mary, Cheltenham, Glos		RG/JP, 9, 1613
30.	†1819	John Warren Wynniatt	Stanton, Glos	S	Pevsner, *Glos: Cotswolds*, 1999, 625
31.	†1819	Rev Isaac Edwards	South Cerney, Glos	S	Pevsner, *Glos: Cotswolds*, 1999, 619
32.	?1821	Capel Molyneux	Prestbury, Glos	S	*Gunnis* 1968, 439
33.	?1823	Lady Robert Somerset	Great Badminton, Glos	S	*Gunnis* 1968, 439

WOOD, H fl 1769–*c*1844

Presumably a Yorkshire craftsman, his large tombstone to Hannah Jennet has a well-cut angel's head at the top (**1**). The inscription relates that she was housekeeper to the Marquis of Rockingham.

Funerary Monuments

1.	1769	Hannah Jennet	Wentworth, W R Yorks, churchyard		*Gunnis* 1968, 439
2.	†1775	Rachel Turton	Olveston, Glos	S	Pevsner, *Glos: Vale & Forest of Dean*, 1976, 316
3.	†1844	William Tonge	Olveston, Glos	S	Pevsner, *Glos: Vale & Forest of Dean*, 1976, 316

WOOD, Henry I and II, of Bristol fl *c*1764–*c*1876?

Henry Wood I was a monumental mason working in London and then in Bristol from the later eighteenth century until about 1830, when he was succeeded by his son, **Henry Wood II**. Little is known about the pair and their dates of birth and death have not been discovered, but they left behind them a sizeable body of work, consisting of both church monuments and designs for monuments and chimneypieces. These are contained in two albums, the *Paty Copy Book* and *Wood's Monumental Masonry*.

From the 1770s until the mid-1790s Henry Wood I, who was then resident in Chelsea, worked for the architect Henry Holland, carrying out ornamental stone carving at a number of country houses, including Althorp, Claremont and Woburn, and at the Prince of Wales's London residence, Carlton House (**69, 72, 74–7**). In 1794–96 he built the pyramidal mausoleum at Blickling Park, Norfolk, to the designs of Joseph Bonomi, and he was probably the 'Wood' who designed the church of St Margaret at Thorpe Market in the same county, which was rebuilt in 1796. In 1801 he supplied a marble fireplace for The Mote, near Maidstone (**71**).

In the same year Wood bought the yard and business of **William Paty** and settled in Bristol. An advertisement, dated Bristol, 16 March 1801, announced: 'The Public are respectfully informed, Mr HENRY WOOD, <u>ARCHITECT AND STATUARY</u>, from London, having engaged and succeeded to the business of the late Mr. WILLIAM PATY continues and carries on the same, <u>At his House and Yards, College-place</u>. His engagements in many of the first buildings in the Kingdom enable him to say, those who may honour him with employment in the Architectural, Statuary and Building Line, may depend upon having their business in those several departments executed with propriety and taste. All letters and orders addressed to Mr. WOOD, Architect, College-Place, will be duly attended to' (*Felix Farley's Bristol Journal*, 28 March and 4 April 1801).

Wood carried out building work at Ashton Court, near Bristol, in 1802 and in 1806–8 he designed and built Merthyr Mawr, a small country house in Glamorganshire, for Sir John Nicholl. However, after the move to Bristol he seems to have concentrated on his monumental business, which flourished in this prosperous port. Gunnis comments: 'Wood's monuments and tablets, which are quite pleasant, must have been much admired in his day, for they are not only found all over England, but also in Ireland and the West Indies'. Among the most ambitious are a pair of elegant tablets at New Ross, County Wexford (3, 4). The Arabella Tottenham has a relief figure of her husband mourning over an urn beneath a weeping willow. Her husband's monument features a portrait relief of the deceased attended by diminutive grieving figures of his three sons.

Further light is thrown on the firm's activities by the album *Wood's Monumental Masonry*. It was put together over a long period as a copybook from which prospective customers could select designs. Most of the 223 drawings are by Henry Wood I and probably his son, but a few were inherited from the Paty family and some are by other, unidentified, draughtsmen. Evidence of another member of the Wood family is provided by drawings inscribed 'I. WOOD, Sculr BRISTOL' (fol 207) and 'I. WOOD, Ft. BATH' (fol 145, left). The monuments are carefully arranged by design, size and materials and many are annotated with dimensions and prices, ranging from about £20 for the most modest tablets to as much as £99 for large wall monuments in coloured marbles. Some of the drawings include inscriptions which show that while most of the firm's patrons came from the landed gentry, they also included clergymen, professionals and aristocrats. The Woods were not innovative designers and the monuments represented tend to be repetitive. Few include figures or elaborate decorative detailing but a range of fashionable styles, including Greek, Egyptian and Gothic, were available. Indeed the designs are typical of the conventional repertory employed among late-Georgian sculptors across Britain and it is likely that similar albums were in use in many other workshops.

The business survived into the 20th century and in 1923 the Bristol historian, C F W Dening noted that Henry Wood II's grandson was still operating from the workshop originally occupied by the Paty family (*Dening* 1923, 139). It is possible that some of the later works listed below were produced by Henry Wood II's successors.

EH

Literary References: *Gunnis* 1968, 439; *Potterton* 1975, 88; *Haslam* 1984, 1276–1280; *Dale-Jones and Lloyd*, 1989, 59; *Friedman* 1993, 12, 91, cat 16–17; *Colvin* 1995, 1071–2; Friedman/Woods *c*2000; *Priest* 2003, *passim*

Archival References: Woburn Cash Book 1791–92, BLARS R5/1297; Woburn Building Accts, 1789–01, BLARS R5/1105; Friedman typescript (HMI)

Collections of drawings: *Paty Copybook*; Wood's *Monumental Masonry*

Funerary Monuments

1.	†1764	John Thomas	Llangan, Glamorgan		Pevsner, *Glamorgan*, 1995, 383
2.	†1785	John Bosworth	Tortworth, Glos	S	Pevsner, *Glos: Vale & Forest of Dean*, 1976, 389
3.	†1795	Arabella Tottenham	New Ross, Co Wexford		*Potterton* 1975, 88
4.	†1795	Charles Tottenham	New Ross, Co Wexford		*Potterton* 1975, 88
5.	†1796	Charles Powell	Llanfinangel Fechan, Brecon	S	Pevsner, *Powys*, 1979, 360
6.	†1796	Thomas Bullock Lloyd	Brecon Cathedral		Pevsner, *Powys*, 1979, 294
7.	†1797	J Davis	Chepstow, Monmouths		RG/JP, 9, 1613v
8.	†1798	Herbert Ball	St Peter, Carmarthen		*Dale-Jones and Lloyd*, 1989, 59
9.	†1800	Catherine Smith	Barbados Cathedral, Bridgetown	S	*Gunnis* 1968, 439
10.	†1803	James Hughes	St Peter, Carmarthen		*Dale-Jones and Lloyd*, 1989, 59
11.	†1803	William Clarkson	Alvington, Glos	S	Pevsner, *Glos: Vale & Forest of Dean*, 1976, 85
12.	†1804	David Bernard	St James, Montego Bay, Jamaica	S	RG/JP, 9, 1614
13.	†1804	Henry Tonge	Ebrington, Glos	S	Pevsner, *Glos: Cotswolds*, 1999, 352
14.	1806	Mrs Tottenham	New Ross, Co Wexford	S	*Gunnis* 1968, 439
15.	†1807	Mary Hill	Laugharne, Carmarthen		*Dale-Jones and Lloyd*, 1989, 59
16.	†1807	William Perry	Winterbourne, Glos	S	Pevsner, *Glos: Vale & Forest of Dean*, 1976, 409
17.	1808	Rev Thomas Pentycross	Wallingford, Berks	S	*Gunnis* 1968, 439
18.	†1809	Rev John Pelly	Weston-sub-Edge, Glos	S	Pevsner, *Glos: Cotswolds*, 1999, 719
19.	†1810	William Jones	United Reform church, Thornbury, Glos	S	
20.	?1811	Thomas Browne	Church Stoke, Montgomery	S	*Gunnis* 1968, 439
21.	†1814	Catherine and Thomas Rees	St Clears, Carmarthen		*Dale-Jones and Lloyd*, 1989, 59
22.	†1815	Bingham Hamilton	Laugharne, Carmarthen		*Dale-Jones and Lloyd*, 1989, 59
23.	†1815	Clement Tudway Drawing(s): Wood's *Monumental Masonry*, fol 166	St Cuthbert, Wells, Somerset	S	*Gunnis* 1968, 439; *Friedman/Woods*, 2
24.	?1815	Francis Smith	Shepton Mallet, Somerset	S	*Gunnis* 1968, 439
25.	†1815	Lady Henry Somerset	Great Badminton, Glos	S	
26.	†1815	Margaret Ann Dunn	Barbados Cathedral, Bridgetown	S	
27.	†1813–1815	Thomas and James Rich Drawing(s): Woods *Monumental Masonry*, fol 206	St Peter & St Paul, Over Stowey, Somerset		Pevsner, *Somerset: S & W*, 1958, 270; *Friedman/Woods*, 6
28.	?1815	Thomas Taylor	Marlow, Bucks	S	*Gunnis* 1968, 439
29.	1816	Frances (†1793) and Lucy (†1815) Ireland Drawing(s): Wood's *Monumental Masonry*, fol 190	Christ Church, Broad St, Bristol	S	*Gunnis* 1968, 439; *Friedman/Woods*, 6
30.	†1818	Alexander Jaffray	St Mary, Cheltenham, Glos	S	Pevsner, *Glos: Vale & Forest of Dean*, 1976, 126
31.	†1818	Elizabeth Huggins	St George, Gingerland, Nevis	S	
32.	†1818	Samuel Norman	Shepton Mallet, Somerset	S	
33.	?1819	Arabella Schaw	St Mary Redcliffe, Bristol	S	*Gunnis* 1968, 439
34.	?1820	Richard Turville	Ewenny, Glamorgan	S	*Gunnis* 1968, 439
35.	?1821	Richard Goodlad	Droxford, Hants	S	*Gunnis* 1968, 439
36.	†1822	Lord Edward Somerset	Great Badminton, Glos	S	Pevsner, *Glos: Cotswolds*, 1999, 386

No.	Date	Subject		Location		Reference
37.	†1823	Louisa Somerset		Great Badminton, Glos	S	Pevsner, *Glos: Cotswolds*, 1999, 386
38.	†1824	Sir Hugh Smyth Drawing(s): Wood's *Monumental Masonry*, fol 72		Long Ashton, Somerset	S	*Gunnis* 1968, 439; *Friedman/Woods*, 3
39.	?1825	Gertrude Allen		Jeffreston, Pembrokes	S	*Gunnis* 1968, 439
40.	†1826	John Fletcher		Cranham, Glos	S	Pevsner, *Glos: Cotswolds*, 1999, 306
41.	†1826	Rev Edward Mansfield		Bisley, Glos	S	Pevsner, *Glos: Cotswolds*, 1999, 175
42.	†1827	Hall Wake		[St John, Smith Square, London]; destroyed		RG/JP, 9, 1614
43.	†1828	5th Duchess of Beaufort		Great Badminton, Glos		Pevsner, *Glos: Cotswolds*, 1999, 386
44.	†1829	Maria Jane Ward and family		Barbados Cathedral, Bridgetown	S	*Gunnis* 1968, 439
45.	1830	Robert Howe Drawing(s): Paty Copybook, 17, perhaps by Thomas Paty		St Stephen, Bristol		*Priest* 2003, 147
46.	†1831	Lady Isabella Kingscote		Great Badminton, Glos	S	Pevsner, *Glos: Cotswolds*, 1999, 428
47.	†1831	Maria Lloyd		Llanstephan, Carmarthen		*Dale-Jones and Lloyd* 1989, 59
48.	†1833	Rev John Frere Pilgrim		St John, Hackleton's Cliff, Barbados	S	
49.	†1834	Henry Rees		Roch, Pembrokes		
50.	†1835	Henry Knight		Newton Nottage, Glamorgan		RG/JP, 9, 1613v
51.	†1835	James and Mary May (†1837)		Worle, Somerset		RG/JP, 9, 1613v
52.	†1835	Rear-Admiral James Bowen		Holy Trinity, Ilfracombe, Devon		RG/JP, 9, 1613v
53.	1837	General Kinsey		Abergavenny, Monmouths	S	*Gunnis* 1968, 439
54.	†1838	Charlotte Ricketts		St Lawrence, Didmarton, Glos	S	Pevsner, *Glos: Cotswolds*, 1999, 315
55.	?1840	Lant Carpenter Drawing(s): Wood's *Monumental Masonry*, fol 61		Lewins Mead chapel, Bristol	S	*Gunnis* 1968, 439; *Friedman/Woods*, 5
56.	†1840	William Lloyd		Llanstephan, Carmarthen		*Dale-Jones and Lloyd* 1989, 59
57.	†1841	Martha Croome		St John the Baptist, Cirencester, Glos	S	
58.	†1842	George A Dean		St John, Hackleton's Cliff, Barbados	S	
59.	†1842	William Dalzell		[Barbados Cathedral, Bridgetown]; untraced		GPC
60.	†1843	Thomas (†1842) and Elizabeth Disdee		Hutton, Somerset (?)		RG/JP, 9, 1613v
61.	†1847	Samuel Maynard Alleyne		St Thomas, Barbados	S	*Gunnis* 1968, 439
62.	†1850	Hester and John Williams		Llandybie, Carmarthen		*Dale-Jones and Lloyd* 1989, 59
63.	†1850	Mary Castle		Worle, Somerset		RG/JP, 9, 1613v.
64.	†1859	Walter Rice and family		Llandovery, Carmarthen		*Dale-Jones and Lloyd* 1989, 59
65.	†1861	Thomas Westcott		St Clears, Carmarthen		*Dale-Jones and Lloyd* 1989, 59
66.	†1867	Valentine Lewes		Llandovery, Carmarthen		*Dale-Jones and Lloyd* 1989, 59
67.	†1876	William James		Lewins Mead chapel, Bristol	S	
68.	nd	Unidentified subject, tablet		Congregational Church, Upper Cam, Glos	S	Pevsner, *Glos: Cotswolds*, 1999, 210
Chimneypieces						
69.	1783–1789	Two and 'a rich stove in veined marble for the lower octagon' Payment(s): £80; £42 10s; £55		[Carlton House, London, bow room and lower eating room]; untraced		*Gunnis* 1968, 439 incorrectly cites PRO HO 73/24
70.	1796	Two of French marble Payment(s): £34 2s	m	[Cleveland House, London]; untraced		*Gunnis* 1968, 440
71.	1801	Description unavailable	m	The Mote, Maidstone, Kent		*Gunnis* 1968, 440
Architectural Sculpture						
72.	1771–1772	Capitals, six lions' heads in the frieze on the portico, 'two therme' and three masks of satyrs		[for Lord Clive, Claremont, Surrey]; untraced		Soane Case 127, fols 73–4; 128, fols 54–5; *Gunnis* 1968, 439
73.	1775	Six Ionic capitals for the pilasters on the front of the house	s	Benham Park, Berks		*Gunnis* 1968, 439
74.	1783–1789	Carved stonework	s	[Carlton House, London, Riding House]; untraced		*Gunnis* 1968, 439 incorrectly cites PRO HO 73/24
75.	1790	Corinthian capitals for the pilasters of the central front	s	Althorp, Northants		GPC
76.	1790–1792	Stone and wood carving		[Woburn Abbey, Beds]; untraced		*Gunnis* 1968, 440
Miscellaneous						
77.	1783–1789	A 'rich stove in veined marble for the lower octagon' Payment(s): £55		[Carlton House]; untraced		*Gunnis* 1968, 439

WOOD, J fl 1822

He was living at 3 High Street, Whitechapel in 1822 when he was awarded a medal from the Society of Arts (1).

No.	Date	Subject		Location	Reference
1.	1822	Adam and Eve lamenting over the body of Abel	pm	[Soc of A, gold Isis medal]; untraced	RSA *Transactions*, 1822, vol 40, xxxix

WOOD, J, of Bristol fl *c*1815

Funerary Monuments

No.	Date	Subject	Location	Reference
1.	†1815	Reynold Deere	Llanfrynach, Glamorgan	Pevsner, *Glamorgan*, 1995, 382

WOOD, Joseph fl 1766–*c*1772

He was the master-mason in charge of rebuilding Thoresby Park, Notts, for the Duke of Kingston from 1766 to 1769 (Archives, Earl Manvers, Nottingham Univ library, 4420). The Hornby is a large architectural wall-tablet of marble and stone, with Doric pilasters supporting a plain pediment surmounted by an urn, while flaming lamps stand to left and right.

Literary References: *Gunnis* 1968, 440; GPC

Funerary Monuments

1.	†1772	Catherine Hornby	St Mary & St Martin, Blyth, Notts	S	*Gunnis* 1968, 440; Pevsner, *Notts*, 1979, 79

WOOD, L F fl *c*1822

Funerary Monuments

1.	†1822	George de Ligne Gregory	Harlaxton, Lincs		Pevsner, *Lincs*, 1989, 361

WOOD, Lancelot Edward, of Chelsea fl 1804–29

Wood worked as a mason and was paid in 1810 for covering flues in Kew Peach house and for relaying paving and repairing coping in the kitchen garden. Gunnis describes his tablets as competent but dull and lists those he considers best. It is noteworthy that one of his works was sent out to Canada (**6**). His yard was in the King's Road.

Literary References: *Gunnis* 1968, 440

Archival References: TNA WORK 5/99 (Kew)

Funerary Monuments

1.	†1804	Lady Caroline Leigh	Adlestrop, Glos	S	*Gunnis* 1968, 440; Pevsner, *Glos: Cotswolds*, 1999, 132
2.	?1807	Josiah Tead	Bridport, Dorset	S	*Gunnis* 1968, 440
3.	?1808	John Mansfield	Portisham, Dorset	S	*Gunnis* 1968, 440
4.	?1809	Levett Ibbetson	Castor, Northants	S	*Gunnis* 1968, 440
5.	?1822	George Gregory	Harlaxton, Lincs	S	*Gunnis* 1968, 440
6.	†1823	Peter Waterhouse	Halifax Cathedral, Nova Scotia	S	GPC
7.	1824	Bishop Richard Beadon	Wells Cathedral, Somerset	S	*Gunnis* 1968, 440
8.	†1826	Sarah Black	Braughing, Herts	S	

Statues

9.	†1823	James Henry Leigh	Adlestrop, Glos	S	Pevsner, *Glos: Cotswolds*, 1999, 132

Chimneypieces

10.	1809	Veined-marble with reeded pilasters Payment(s): £22	Hampton Court Palace, Middx		TNA WORK 5/99; *Gunnis* 1968, 440
11.	1812	With a 'water-leaf design' Payment(s): £30	Hampton Court Palace, Middx		TNA WORK 5/99; *Gunnis* 1968, 440
12.	nd	Description unavailable	[for Earl Spencer, Althorp, Notts]; untraced		RG/JP, 9, 1616 (inf Bruce Bailey)

WOOD, of Newark fl *c*1839

He signs an Hellenic wall-monument with **John Nicholson** (1).

Funerary Monuments

1.	†1839	Hon Lady Bromley (co-sculptor: John Nicholson)	East Stoke, Notts	S	Pevsner, *Notts*, 1979, 117

WOOD, R fl 1826

Funerary Monuments

1.	1826	J Phillips	Dilwyn, Herefs		*Gunnis* 1968, 440

WOOD, Ralph –1730/43

Surtees notes that there was in Stockton churchyard a tomb with the inscription 'Ralph Wood who departed this life Oct. 22. 1730 in the 67th year of his age. Here lies the body of Ralph Wood aged 67, 1743. "We that have made tombs for others Now here we lie, Once we were two flourishing Woods But now we die." '

Literary References: *Surtees* 1816–40, 3, 186

WOOD, Richard, of Oxford –1700

He was the brother of **Thomas Wood of Oxford**. Nothing is known of his work as a stonecutter, but he was involved in parish affairs at St Mary Magdalen, Oxford and worked in civic affairs as a bailiff in the 1680s and as mayor of Oxford in 1694. In 1696 he submitted a bill to the council for a sundial he had made on the south bridge (**2**). Pevsner notes that the Matthew monument is a 'broad, gristly white cartouche, rather 1665 than 1685 in style' (**1**). Gunnis notes that the work is not unlike the stone tablets of **William Byrd of Oxford**.

Literary References: *Cole* 1949, 65

Archival References: GPC

Funerary Monuments

1.	†1687	John Matthew	Upton Grey, Hants		Pevsner, *Hants & Isle of Wight*, 1967, 633

Architectural Sculpture

2.	1696	Sundial	Oxford, south bridge		*Cole* 1949, 65

WOOD, T, of Hereford fl 1787–1803?

Gunnis considers his best tablets to be the Allen and Lane (**1, 2**). An 'R Wood of Leominster' signed a tablet to J Phillips, 1826, at Dilwyn, in the same county.

Literary References: *Gunnis* 1968, 440

Funerary Monuments

1.	1787	Elizabeth Allen	Kinnersley, Herefs	S	*Gunnis* 1968, 440
2.	1799	Thomas Lane	Leominster, Herefs	S	*Gunnis* 1968, 440
3.	?1803	Abigail Barneby	Bromyard, Herefs	S	GPC

WOOD, Thomas, of Bingham 1760–1841

He appears to have been chiefly a maker of slate headstones for Nottinghamshire churchyards. Pevsner refers to three, one at Cropwell Bishop, another at Granby carved with an urn and pastoral scenes, and a third at Screveton with masonic emblems. Neave and Heron describe a slate at Caythorpe, 1815, depicting at the top, two fine pheasants, and another at Foston, 1812, with 'one of his typical rustic scenes', which has a lady weeping against a large urn, a sheep, trees and houses and a grassy hill behind. Gunnis mentions others at Bingham (1794), Whatton (1815) and

Lowdham (1785, 1799, 1820, 1826). The White has 'a delightful engraving of the Day of Resurrection, showing church, houses, while from a tomb in the churchyard emerges a figure with a crown in its hand' (1). The Timm is classical altar-tomb (4).

Wood was buried at Bingham, where his epitaph describes him as 'well-known for more than half a century as a ingenious carver of tombs and gravestones'.

Literary References: *Gunnis* 1968, 440; *Neave and Heron* 1969, 5–6; Pevsner, *Notts*, 1979, 109, 134, 304

Funerary Monuments

1.	†1773	Robert White		Bingham, Notts	S	GPC
2.	†1788	Robert Levers	sl	East Bridgford, Notts		GPC
3.	?1812	Children of Samuel White	sl	Bingham, Notts, churchyard		GPC
4.	?1822	William Timm		Bingham, Notts, churchyard	S	GPC

WOOD, Thomas, of London *c*1760–

He was the son of John Wood, mason, of 'Rose Street, St Luke's, Old Street', who had become free by redemption i 1770. Young Wood was bound apprentice to his father on 6 October 1774 and later went into partnership with **Joh Gilliam**. From 1793 onwards they did a great deal of masonry work at Somerset House, receiving a total payment £1,797 for that year alone, a period when they were also employed at the Rolls House (*Gunnis* 1968, 441 incorrectl cites PRO, Works 5/82). From 1808–1810 Wood (now on his own) was employed at the Chapel Royal, Whitehall, whe he received £1,695 for sundry work including 'Pedestalls, ballustrades, and the coping'. From 1812 until 1815 he worke under James Wyatt at the Palace of Westminster (2).

He may conceivably be the Thomas Wood whose tradecard of 1795 is engraved with a putto carving the followin on a plinth: 'Thomas Wood Statuary. Monuments and Chimney Pieces, executed in the neatest manner/ No 2 Palace Street/ Pimlico/ near Buckingham Gate'. Two putti dance around a column with ribbons inscribed with th words 'Carving and Guilding Executed' (BM Heal 106.24).

Literary References: *Gunnis* 1968, 440; *Webb* 1999, 36

Chimneypieces					
1.	1808	Unidentified	m	[Palace of Westminster]; untraced	*Gunnis* 1968, 441
Architectural Sculpture					
2.	1812–1815	Carved stonework	s	[Palace of Westminster]; untraced	*Gunnis* 1968, 441 incorrectly cites PRO, AO 435/2499
Miscellaneous					
3.	1805	Chimneypiece, baths and tables	m	[New bath house, the Pantiles, Tunbridge Wells, Kent]; untraced	RG/JP, 9, 1619

WOOD, Thomas, of Oxford 1646–

Wood worked as a journeyman under **William Byrd** together with his brother **Richard Wood of Oxford** in 166 when Byrd paid him a wage of £8. He was described as aged 22 and 'of St. Peter's in the East, Oxford, Sculptor', whe in 1668, he took out a licence to marry Alice Beach, of Patchall, Herefs, at St Margaret, Westminster. In 1685 he live next door to William Byrd at the corner of Smith Street, Oxford. His widow continued in the same tenement lon after Thomas's death. They seem to have had no children and took lodgers to supplement their income.

In 1679 Wood was engaged by Richard Frogley, a carpenter of the city, to work on masonry for the Bishop of Oxford new palace at Cuddesdon, which Frogley had contracted to build. Besides providing the stonework of the walls, Woo also supplied the doorcase of Burford stone in front of the house, but he was unable to get his money, and in 168 brought an action against his employer. In the course of the evidence it appeared that Frogley had also commissione a stone chimneypiece from Wood for 'Esquire Lenttall's house at Hasely' (3) and 'Cornish work' at Newington.

In 1679–83 he was the mason responsible for building 'Dr Ashmole's Repository', and was paid £1,006 0s 11d i 1679–80 'towards the building of the same' (Oxford, V-Cs Accts, fol 58). Two years later he provided a chimneypiece fo the repository (4). In 1693 he received £10 for setting up a chimneypiece at Water Eaton, near Oxford (5). In 1671 h carved the tablet commemorating John Myddelton at Brasenose (1), and in 1679–80 was paid £20 for the monume to Francis Junius at Windsor, erected at the University of Oxford's expense (2). Nothing is known of him after 1693.

Literary References: *Cole* 1949, 65; *Gunnis* 1968, 440

Archival References: Wood v Frogley, OU, Chancellor's Ct Register, HYO/A/49; Chancellor's Ct Papers, 1680–81, fols 1 and 1v

Funerary Monuments					
1.	1671	John Myddelton		Brasenose College, Oxford, cloisters	*Gunnis* 1968, 440, quoting Chirk Castle Archives
2.	1680	Francis Junius (†1677)		St George's Chapel, Windsor, Berks	Oxford, V-C's Accts, Archive WO, fol 58; *Colvin* 1995, 1076–7; *Bond* 1999, 189
Chimneypieces					
3.	1681	'of Burford stone hansomly wrought'	s	[Esquire Lenttall's house, Hasely, Oxon]; untraced	OU, Chancellor's Ct Papers, 1680–1, 1v; *Gunnis* 1968, 440
4.	1682	Of stained marble		[Ashmolean, Oxford]; untraced	Oxford, VC's Accts, fol 70v; *Gunnis* 1968, 440
5.	1693	Of white marble Payment(s): £10	m	['At Water Eaton for the Lord Lovelace']; untraced	*Gunnis* 1968, 440 citing BM Ad. MS 22,188
Architectural Sculpture					
6.	1676	'Carving of anticks' and other work		St Mary, Oxford, Adam Brome's Chapel	OU, Vice-C's Accts, WP - /21/5 fol 41; *Gunnis* 1968, 440
7.	1677	'Cutting Oriel College Arms in Adam Brome's Chapell' and laying a pavement Payment(s): £1 10s		[Oriel College, Oxford, chapel]; untraced	Oxford, V-C's Accts fols 41, 42; *Gunnis* 1968, 440
Miscellaneous					
8.	1675–1676	'Laying ye marbles' Payment(s): £87 19s 2d		['St Maire's Church', Oxford]; untraced	*Gunnis* 1968, 440 citing Vice-C's Accounts

WOODALL, Christopher, of Carlisle 1795–1859

The Hildebrand tablet has a portrait relief.

Funerary Monuments

1.	†1842	William Hildebrand	Carlisle Cathedral	S	*Gunnis* 1968, 441

WOODALL, John *c*1670–1735

Woodall was a master mason working with **Benjamin Jackson** at Drayton Hall, Northants in 1702. A contract between Sir John Germaine and Benjamin Jackson was drawn up on 24 August that year for an elaborate façade for the great hall and new offices, to be built as 'set down in the ground plat of Mr. [William] Tallman'. Initial payments were to Jackson, but from March 1703 to April 1704 they were made to Woodall (Drayton Archive MM/A/674). Woodall returned to Drayton in September 1710 to build colonnades on each side of the entrance courtyard, flanking Talman's façade. Payments continued until May 1711 (MM/A/674). Both colonnades have elaborate carved details and Woodall may have been involved with these (inf. Bruce Bailey).

He worked as a mason at several of the royal palaces and carved at least one chimneypiece (**1**). In the PRO is Woodall's contract, dated 1723, in which he stated 'I doe hereby oblige myself faithfully to serve His Majesty and in the best and most workmanlike manner to doe and performe all such mason's work (as shall be decided by this board [of Works] to be done) at the rates and prizes aforementioned for one year' (TNA WORK 5/145 fol 263, 26 Feb 1723). He was also the mason responsible for repairs to Hicks Hall (the Middlesex Sessions House) from 1723 to 1728 (Parliamentary Report, 1731 cited by *Gunnis* 1968, 441). In 1726 he was paid £73 for work at the Arlington Street house of Evelyn, Duke of Kingston (Accounts of the trustees of the Duke of Kingston, Archives, Lord Monson cited in GPC).

In the Earl of Westmorland's archives is a letter from John Fane of Mereworth, written in 1730 to Lord Westmorland about a matter to which he had given some thought, namely, a sculptor for the monument to Lady Westmorland. 'It is but just come into my head', he says, 'and I will send by the next post to Mr. Woodall my mason, the same draught and order him to make an estimate of it'. It is not known if the work materialised.

He died on 4 September 1735 and was buried at Kingston-on-Thames (*GM*, vol 5, Sept 1735, 559). The *Northampton Mercury* for 21 September reported the death of 'Mr. Woodhill', master mason to George I. The epitaph on his monument stated that his death occurred at his house in Mount Street near Grosvenor Square and stated that he was born in the parish of Rotherham, was mason to his majesty's board of works in the reign of George I, and died aged 65.

Literary References: *Gunnis* 1968, 441

Archival References: GPC

Chimneypieces

1.	1715	Marble	[Countess of Schulemberg's apartment, St James's Palace]; untraced	*Gunnis* 1968, 441 citing PRO, AO 1, 3448/149

WOODBRIDGE, T W fl 1839

For further information the reader is referred to *Pyke* 1973, 158.

WOODHILL

See **Woodall, John**

WOODINGTON, William Frederick ARA 1806–93

A sculptor and painter, Woodington was born at Sutton Coldfield, Warks, on 10 February 1806. He moved to London in 1815 and was apprenticed in about 1820 to **Robert William Sievier**, who was at that time working as an engraver. A few years later Woodington followed his master's example by abandoning engraving to concentrate on sculpture. Early in his career he worked for the **Coade Factory of Lambeth**, modelling a colossal lion which was cast in artificial stone for the Lion brewery in Belvedere Road, Lambeth (**4**). This cast is now on Westminster bridge.

He first came to public attention with two submissions sent to the Westminster Hall Exhibition in 1844, *Milton dictating to his daughters* and *The deluge* (**7, 8**). One reviewer praised them as 'able groups, designed with much skill and beautifully executed'. He considered the mother and son of *The deluge* group 'finely imagined' and admired the 'calm earnestness' of Milton and the 'sweet simplicity' of his daughters (*Lit Gaz*, 1844, 466). Three years later Woodington was commissioned to sculpt figures of the medieval Earls of Kent and Sussex for the chamber of the House of Lords (**12, 13**). Another prominent public work followed in 1850, when he was invited to prepare models for one of the four bronze reliefs at the base of Nelson's Column in Trafalgar Square. He provided the relief of the *Battle of the Nile* and completed another, of the *Battle of St Vincent*, which was left unfinished at his friend **Musgrave Lewthwaite Watson**'s death (**27, 26**).

In 1857 Woodington was awarded the second prize of £500 in the competition for the national memorial to the Duke of Wellington (**2**). His design for a seated statue of the Duke, supported by figures symbolising *Energy*, *Decision*, *Devotion* and *Order*, elicited various critical responses. Several writers praised the portrait of Wellington and one thought that the sculptor had produced 'a consummate likeness of the aged warrior and statesman as we saw him three months before his death' (*Building News*, 7 August 1857, cited by *Physick* 1970, 154). Others were impressed by the careful execution of the model and the simplicity of the composition. Woodington's failure to include any direct reference to the Duke's military achievements and the vague symbolism of the supporting figures were however criticised. The competition results were discredited when it became clear that the judges, who lacked artistic expertise, had made no attempt to assess the suitability of the designs for the intended site in St Paul's Cathedral and, after months of wrangling, the commission was finally awarded to **Alfred Stevens**. Woodington and **William Calder Marshall**, the first prize-winner, provided a series of reliefs for the chapel where the monument was eventually placed (**30**).

Woodington continued to take on demanding commissions until he was well into his sixties. In 1867 he carved a series of six statues of explorers and a pediment relief depicting *Wisdom sending forth her messengers to the nations of the earth* for T H Wyatt's New Liverpool Exchange (**24**). It was demolished and replaced with a new building in 1937, when the statues were presented to the Liverpool Corporation. All have been lost or destroyed. In 1869 he was commissioned to provide three more statues of historical figures for the façade of 6 Burlington Gardens, London, the headquarters of the University of London (**25**). These figures were part of a substantial sculptural programme which included statues by **Patrick MacDowell, William Theed II, Joseph Durham, Edward William Wyon, James Sherwood Westmacott** and **Matthew Noble**. Woodington's colossal marble bust of the architect and engineer Sir Joseph Paxton was unveiled outside his most famous building, the Crystal Palace at Sydenham, in June 1873, when the sculptor was 67 (**21**).

Woodington was a frequent contributor to Royal Academy exhibitions between 1825 and 1882. He showed many figures and reliefs of biblical, mythological and literary subjects, as well as a number of oil paintings and a few portrait busts. He occasionally exhibited at the Society of British Artists, the British Institution and the Liverpool Academy and sent ideal sculpture to the Great Exhibition of 1851 and the Manchester Art Treasures Exhibition of 1857 (**9, 11**). He was appointed curator of the RA sculpture school in 1851 and was elected an associate Academician in 1873. Towards the end of his life Woodington, who was unmarried, lived at 51 Hayter Road, Brixton, with a sister, a niece and one domestic servant. He died at home on 24 December 1893 and was buried nearby in Norwood cemetery. A few years later F M O'Donoghue, who provided a brief biography for the DNB, described his 'fancy figures and reliefs of sacred and poetical subjects' as 'deficient in the highest qualities of art' but 'composed with much grace and feeling'. The 1881 census records that another sculptor called William F Woodington, who was born in London about 1831, lived with his family at 25 Knowle Road, Lambeth. It is not known whether the two men were related.

EH

Literary References: *Lonsdale* 1866, *passim*; *AJ*, 1894, 61; *DNB*; *Gunnis* 1968, 441–2; *Read* 1982, 22, 84, 89, 90, 120, 226; *Physick* 1970, *passim*; *Friedman* 1993, 13, 91; *ODNB* (O'Donoghue, rev. Barnes)

Archival References: IGI

Additional MS Sources: Woodington/Riddel

Collections of Drawings: Album of 42 drawings, HMI 44/1990

Funerary Monuments

No.	Date	Subject		Location		References
1.	?1839	Henry and Mary Cogswell		Halifax Cathedral, Nova Scotia		GPC
2.	1857	Arthur, 1st Duke of Wellington, national memorial, design only (monument executed by Alfred Stevens)		[Exhib Westminster Hall, London]; untraced		*Physick* 1970, *passim* (repr)

Statues

No.	Date	Subject		Location		References
3.	1828	Lord Eldon (co-sculptor: Musgrave Lewthwaite Watson)		[Unidentified school, New Road, London]; untraced		*Lonsdale* 1866, 81
4.	1837	Lion, model for Coade Factory of Lambeth, cast in artificial stone		[Lion brewery, Lambeth]; Westminster Bridge, London		*Kelly* 1990, 393, 408 (repr)
5.	1842	The mother		[Exhib RA, London, 1272]; untraced		*AU*, 1842, 127; *Graves* VIII, 1905–6, 345
6.	1843	Nymph and Zephyr, statuette (after Sir Richard Westmacott RA)		[for the Art Union of London]; untraced		*Avery and Marsh* 1985, 328–37 (repr)
7.	1844	Milton dictating to his daughters		[Exhib Westminster Hall, London, 108]; untraced		*AU*, 1844, 215
8.	1844	The deluge		[Exhib Westminster Hall, London]; untraced		*Gunnis* 1968, 441
9.	1851	A girl at a spring		[Gt Exhib, London]; untraced		*AJ Cat* 1851, 252 (repr)
10.	1856	James Steel		[for Carlisle]; untraced		*CJ*, 20 June 1856, 4; *Gunnis* 1968, 441
11.	1857	See-saw	m	[Manc Art Treas Exhib, 37]; untraced		*Manchester Art Treasures* 1857, 135
12.	1847–1858	Hubert de Burgh, Earl of Kent (†1243)		Palace of Westminster, London, House of Lords	S	*Walker* 1961, 42, 97–8, cat 45
13.	1847–1858	William d'Aubigny, Earl of Sussex and Arundel (†1221) Model(s): exhib RA, London, 1849, 1219		Palace of Westminster, London, House of Lords		*Graves* VIII, 1905–6, 345; *Walker* 1961, 3, 97–8, cat 5; *Read* 1982, 120

Busts

No.	Date	Subject		Location		References
14.	1825	G Forster		[Exhib RA, London, 1054]; untraced		*Graves* VIII, 1905–6, 345
15.	1828	Unidentified gentleman		[Exhib RA, London, 1152]; untraced		*Graves* VIII, 1905–6, 345
16.	1832	A child	m	[Exhib RA, London, 1210]; untraced		*Graves* VIII, 1905–6, 345
17.	1838	A Spedding	m	[Exhib RA, London, 1309]; untraced		*Graves* VIII, 1905–6, 345
18.	1846	King George III (after John Bacon RA)		[for Eton Coll, Upper School]; untraced		*Gunnis* 1968, 441
19.	1847	Henry Fielding		[Exhib RA, London, 1422]; untraced		*AU*, 1847, 200; *Palgrave* 1866, 82; *Graves* VIII, 1905–6, 345, 346
20.	1862	Patrick Macdowell RA		Burlington House, London	D	*Graves* VIII, 1905–6, 346; *Gunnis* 1968, 441
21.	1873	Sir Joseph Paxton		[Crystal Palace, Sydenham]; National Sports Centre, Crystal Palace, London, entrance		*The Times*, 11 June 1873
22.	1873	Unidentified lady	m	[Exhib RA, London, 1558]; untraced		*Graves* VIII, 1905–6, 346

Architectural Sculpture

No.	Date	Subject		Location		References
23.	1840	Sea-gods in lunettes, papier-maché		Fishmongers' Hall, City of London, banqueting hall		Pevsner, *London: City*, 1997, 388
24.	1867	Pediment group and statues of Christopher Columbus, Galileo, Sir Francis Drake, Captain James Cook, Sir Walter Raleigh and Mercator Model(s): Columbus exhib RA, London, 1869, 1269; design for pediment exhib RA, London, 1874, 1153		[New Liverpool Exchange, Liverpool, Lancs, façade]; untraced		*Graves* VIII, 1905–6, 346; *Cavanagh* 1997, 301–3 (repr)
25.	1869	Plato, Archimedes and Justinian, statues		Former University of London buildings, Burlington Gardens, London, façade		*Read* 1982, 226

Reliefs					
26.	1850	Battle of St Vincent (co-sculptor: Musgrave Lewthwaite Watson)	b	Nelson's Column, Trafalgar Square, London, base	*Lonsdale* 1866, 190–2; *CIIA* 4/2/30 (repr); *Yarrington* 1988, 317 (repr 112)
27.	1850	Battle of the Nile	b	Nelson's Column, Trafalgar Square, London, base	*Read* 1982, 89, 90 (repr); *Yarrington* 1988, 317
28.	1852	Happy days		[Exhib RA, London, 1341]; untraced	*Graves* VIII, 1905–6, 345
29.	1860	The captive	m	[Exhib RA, London, 1083]; untraced	*Graves* VIII, 1905–6, 346
30.	1861	'Blessed be the most high God, which hath delivered mine enemies' and 'Thou hast covered my head in the day of battle'		St Paul's Cathedral, London, consistory chapel	*Graves* VIII, 1905–6, 346; *Gunnis* 1968, 441; Ward-Jackson 2004, 126–7 (repr)
31.	1865	Ariel		[Exhib RA, London, 894]; untraced	*Graves* VIII, 1905–6, 346
32.	1865	Lady in the enchanted chair		[Exhib RA, London, 923]; untraced	*Palgrave* 1866, 122; *Graves* VIII, 1905–6, 346
33.	1865	Miranda		[Exhib RA, London, 901]; untraced	*Graves* VIII, 1905–6, 346
34.	1866	Youth and innocence	m	[Exhib RA, London, 863]; untraced	*Graves* VIII, 1905–6, 346
Miscellaneous					
35.	1825	A nymph		[Exhib RA, London, 1063]; untraced	*Graves* VIII, 1905–6, 345
36.	1825	Lavinia		[Exhib Soc of BA, London, 366]; untraced	*Johnson* 1975, 518
37.	1826	A naiad		[Exhib RA, London, 1020]; untraced	*Graves* 1875, 607; *Graves* VIII, 1905–6, 345
38.	1827	Maria		[Exhib RA, London, 1125]; untraced	*Graves* VIII, 1905–6, 345; *Johnson* 1975, 518
39.	1830	Boy bathing		[Exhib BI, London, 509]; untraced	*Graves* 1875, 607
40.	1831	Virginius, a sketch		[Exhib RA, London, 1207]; untraced	*Graves* VIII, 1905–6, 345
41.	1832	Affection		[Exhib BI, London, 595]; untraced	*Graves* 1875, 607
42.	1833	The orphans		[Exhib RA, London, 1163]; untraced	*Graves* VIII, 1905–6, 345
43.	1836	Oedipus parting with his daughters		[Exhib RA, London, 1000]; untraced	*Graves* VIII, 1905–6, 345
44.	1837	Spring		[Exhib RA, London, 1182]; untraced	*Graves* VIII, 1905–6, 345
45.	1839	Milton's dream		[Exhib RA, London, 1292]; untraced	*Graves* VIII, 1905–6, 345
46.	1841	Christ raising the widow's son		[Exhib RA, London, 1235]; untraced	*Graves* VIII, 1905–6, 345
47.	1843	Music, for a silver salver		[Exhib RA, London, 1463]; untraced	*Graves* VIII, 1905–6, 345
48.	1846	Captivity		[Exhib RA, London, 1503]; untraced	*Graves* VIII, 1905–6, 345
49.	1858–1860	Ariel		[coll James Heyshom]; untraced	*Graves* VIII, 1905–6, 346
50.	1865	Viola	m	[Exhib RA, London, 936]; untraced	*Graves* VIII, 1905–6, 346
51.	1869	Humility	m	[Exhib RA, London, 1172]; untraced	*Graves* VIII, 1905–6, 346
52.	1872	The gentle shepherd	m	[Exhib RA, London, 1531]; untraced	*Graves* VIII, 1905–6, 346
53.	1877	The first sorrow		[Exhib RA, London, 1467]; untraced	*Graves* VIII, 1905–6, 346
54.	1878	The rose-bud	m	[Exhib RA, London, 1474]; untraced	*Graves* VIII, 1905–6, 346

WOODLEY, John, of Torquay –1862

He not only made monuments in his yard by St Mary Church, near Torquay, but also carried on a flourishing business in local marbles, manufacturing 'columns, vases, chimney-pieces and a variety of other ornamental articles' (*AJ*, 1856, 4). Under the heading 'British Industries – Devonshire Marbles' was the announcement 'At the Marble Works of Mr Woodley, at St. Mary Church, near Petit Tor, and Babbacombe may be inspected every variety of these limestones – worked into columns, chimneypieces, and a variety of other ornamental articles'. He signed a number of minor monuments and tablets. The most important, to Mary Bloxsome, has a relief of a woman leaning on a broken column, with its Corinthian capital lying at her feet (**4**).

Woodley died on 27 February 1862 and was buried in St Mary's parish churchyard, where his wife Elizabeth joined him on 10 May 1872. He was probably a son of Daniel Woodley, a marble merchant with premises near Babbacombe Road.

Literary References: *Gunnis* 1968, 442

Archival References: GPC

Funerary Monuments					
1.	†1812	John Gilliard	St John, Paignton, Devon	S	RG/JP, 9, 1622v.
2.	†1821	John Limbery	St John, Paignton, Devon		RG/JP, 9, 1622v.
3.	†1840	Elizabeth Belfield	St John, Paignton, Devon		RG/JP, 9, 1622v.
4.	†1840	Mary Bloxsome	St James, Dursley, Glos	S	Pevsner, *Glos: Cotswolds*, 1999, 335

WOODMAN, William I c1654–?1731

Woodman was a mason-sculptor whose monuments were largely conservative in character, though in his late career he was responsible for one that showed sound knowledge of the latest compositional trends (**8**). He was apprenticed in 1668 to a haberdasher, Francis Devonshire, but then chose to become a mason and was turned over to William Mathews, becoming free of the Masons' Company in January 1678. In 1689 he became an assistant of the Company, he was renter warden in 1702, upper warden in 1703 and master in 1708. Woodman's wife, Elinor, assisted him in the business and they had a son, **William Woodman II**. The entry 'Mr Woodmans in Queen Street' appears in the list of masons living in the City recorded in the general search of 1694, together with 'William Woodmans man at work in Fanchurch St' (*Knoop and Jones* 1935, 73, 78).

Woodman's building work included the Resurrection Gate at St Giles-in-the-Fields, 1687, in which was set a wooden relief of the *Resurrection of the dead*, carved by an otherwise unknown carver named Love. In 1705 Woodman and his son William built a house for Lord Ashburnham at Brockborough Park, Beds. On 1 December that year Ashburnham sent instructions to 'William Woodman Senior & William Woodman Junior att the Dairy House in Brockborough Park' to pay the bricklayer, John Rentham, for his services. They were also instructed to pay £20 to Francis Bushby, the carpenter (Ashburnham Letterbook, ASH 845, 271).

In the early 1700s he supplied marble work for Sir John Germaine's buffet room at Drayton House, Northants. A receipt for £5 7s 6d signed by Woodman 'on Acct. of marble work' is dated July 1705 and Elinor Woodman signed a receipt for £11 18s 6d in May 1704 'for four Marble tables' (**9**). An unsigned bill with comparable handwriting lists 'the Ritch Italian veind Marble Chimney peece in the Great Hall at Drayton by Agreemt. £40.00.00' and adds 'fo Loading and Carrying of the Marble Table and Cistern and Rd. carryage to Westmstr. £00.16.06'. The bill includes smal sums for 'rubing stoping pollishing and Glazeing ye Marble Table' and for 'pollishing stoping and Glazeing ye Marble Cistern' (**10**). Parts of the buffet room marble work still exist at Drayton, notably the two cisterns and portions of cornice work. There is also a receipt signed by Henry Gates 'for the use of my Master Mr Wyman' for a chimneypiece priced £4 5s and this may well refer to Woodman (Stopford Sackville Archive MM/A/466). All this supports an attribution to Woodman of Sir John Germaine's monument (†1718) in St Peter, Lowick, which has a reclining figure in armour.

In 1704 Woodman finished the monument to the 4th Earl of Leicester at Penshurst, said to have been begun by **William Stanton**, though the style suggests that Stanton had no involvement with the executed work (**4**). Several of Woodman's signed monuments are tablets with decorative embellishments (**2, 6**), but a few are more ambitious: that to the Earl of Romney (†1704), damaged in World War II, is nonetheless an imposing work with its great trophy of arms and a shield of Medusa. A curious feature is pair of twisted columns joined at the base by clasps in the form of earls' coronets (**3**). The monument to Nicholas Monck, Bishop of Hereford (a brother of General Monck), has a fashionable pyramid (**7**).

Woodman's acknowledged masterpiece commemorates Viscount and Viscountess Newhaven (**8**) and was probably inspired by the monument to John, Duke of Buckingham in Westminster Abbey, 1721–22, carved by the Flemish sculptors **Laurent Delvaux** and **Peter Scheemakers**. The viscount is a relatively stiff reclining figure in state robes, reminiscent of effigies carved at the turn of the 18th century by **Grinling Gibbons**. He lies on a sarcophagus and behind him is a pyramid. By contrast his wife's effigy, seated at his feet, is posed in a vital, informal manner and carved with extraordinary skill. The monument was probably commissioned soon after Newhaven's death in 1728 but the remarkable image of Lady Newhaven appears to have been added after her death in 1732, by which time Woodman had also died. It was probably carved by **Henry Cheere**. Gunnis noted that this 'remarkable' memorial in its rarely-visited church 'is one of the most outstanding monuments in England'.

Gunnis brought to light a curious minute penned in the Court Book of the Masons' Company in 1719. It desired Woodman to visit a certain Mr Robinson 'who alleages to have Discovered an Art to Glaze Corner Stones for Chimneys and prevail with him if he can to produce a specimen to the Company of one of these stones 4. ffoot long, and then this Court will further consider of the Proposition by him made to the Company' (Masons Co, 1695–1722, fol 185r).

Woodman evidently ran a large workshop, engaged in a range of activities. Seven of his assistants are recorded in the Masons' Company apprenticeship lists, none of whom appear to have worked independently as sculptors. Robert Price joined him in 1686 and was turned over to **Thomas Stayner** in 1692; Edward Walker was described as his 'clerk' in 1696; John Baker was apprenticed in 1703, William Clare in 1715, Charles Wright in 1719, John Bishop in 1720 and Robert Webbe in 1721.

A number of fine drawings confidently attributed to Woodman is listed below and suggests a more extensive practice than hitherto established. (Inf. Bruce Bailey)

IR

Literary References: *Notes & Queries*, vol 5, 23 Jan, 1864, 67 (Resurrection Gate); *Gunnis* 1968, 442; *Whinney* 1988, 251, 253; *Webb* 1999, *passim*

Archival References: Masons' Co, Freemen, fol 72, 21 Jan 1678; Masons' Co, Masters and Wardens

Attributed Drawings: Design for a monument to Sir Robert Clayton, his wife and infant son, c1703: HMI/Leeds City Art Galleries, 1999.0008 (*Leeds* 2001, 12, repr); design for a cartouche monument, VAM D.1100-98; design for the monument to Lady Brownlow, †1700, at Sutton, Surrey VAM D.1104-98; design for a monument with a standing figure of a man in chancellor's robes, D.1105-98; unfinished design for a monument VAM D.1113-98; monument design based on S Gribelin, *A Book of Ornaments*, 1700, pl 1, VAM D.1139-98; design for a monument to Lady Roberts, †1690, at St Mary by Bow, London, VAM E.959-1965

Funerary Monuments

1.	†1681	Edward Mansell	Westminster Abbey, London, nave	S	Pevsner, *London: I*, 1973, 453
2.	?c1700	Sir Thomas Fotherley, his son Thomas and grandson Sir Thomas	Rickmansworth, Herts	S	Pevsner, *Herts*, 1977, 279
3.	†1704	Henry, Earl of Romney	St James Piccadilly, London	S	Pevsner, *London: Westminster*, 1973, 491
4.	1704	Robert, 4th Earl of Leicester (†1702)	Penshurst, Kent		*Whinney* 1988, 138; *Wilson* 2002, 94–5 (repr)
5.	†1712	John Nicholas	Winchester Cathedral, Hants	S	*Gunnis* 1968, 442
6.	†1715	Elizabeth Calnent	All Saints, Maidstone, Kent	S	*Gunnis* 1968, 442
7.	1726	Nicholas Monck, Bishop of Hereford (†1661)	Westminster Abbey, London, Chapel of St Edmund	S	FFB, 1725/6; *MacMichael* 1977, 82
8.	1732–1735	William, 2nd Viscount (†1728) and Gertrude, Viscountess Newhaven (†1732)	Drayton Beauchamp, Bucks		*London Evening Post*, 7 March 1732; *Gunnis* 1968, 442; *Whinney* 1988, 251, 254 (repr)

Miscellaneous

9.	1705	Four tables Payment(s): £11 18s 6d	m	[Drayton House, Northants, buffet room]; untraced	Drayton Archive, MM/A/466
10.	1705	Two cisterns	m	Drayton House, Northants, buffet room	Drayton Archive, MM/A/466
11.	1713	Pavement (co-sculptor: William Woodman II) Payment(s): £46	m	Whitchurch Church, Salop, chancel	*Gunnis* 1968, 442
12.	nd	Cistern	m	[Dowager Lady Leicester's house, London]; untraced	*Gunnis* 1968, 442

WOODMAN, William II fl 1713–c1741

The son of **William Woodman I** and his wife Elinor, he carried on the family business after the death of his father c1731 In 1713 he and his father provided the marble pavement for the chancel of St Alkmund, Whitchurch (4), but it was not until many years later that the younger Woodman sent in his account for £46. Writing to Alexander Duncombe in October, 1733, he explained that 'being under an extream fitt of the Gout, I could not go to render the bill and was forc'd to send one of my Dautrs who this day recd the money' (Bridgewater Archives, cited by *Gunnis* 1968, 442).

His father's monument to Viscount and Viscountess Newhaven, *c*1728–35, was still in preparation when the elder Woodman died. The female effigy was probably carved by **Henry Cheere**, no doubt because it was considered beyond the younger Woodman's competence.

Only two of William II's monuments have been identified: the *Northampton Mercury* of 22 January 1733, reporting the will of Christopher Rawlinson of Cartmel, Lancs, said that he desired to be buried at St Alban's and that he left £200 for a monument 'to be made by Mr. Woodman a Freemason in Holborn'. The wall monument has a flat obelisk above a sarcophagus and below that is a cornice and consoles enclosing the inscription. A seated mourning woman, carved in the round, sits on the sarcophagus ledge (1). The monument to Daniel Dodson has a pedimented frame enclosing a life-size, cross-legged effigy in toga and sandals, leaning against an urn (3). It was inspired by **G-B Guelfi**'s monument to James Craggs in Westminster Abbey, 1724–7, which provided a pattern for monuments by a number of other sculptors.

Literary References: *Gunnis* 1968, 442; *Whinney* 1988, 251–3

Archival References: GPC

Funerary Monuments

1.	†1733	Christopher Rawlinson Payment(s): £200	St Albans Cathedral, Herts		*Northampton Mercury*, 22 Jan 1734; Pevsner, *Herts*, 1977, 311
2.	*c*1734	Dr Edward Wetenhall (†1733)	Westminster Abbey, London, south transept		Pevsner, *London I: Westminster*, 1973, 446
3.	†1741	Daniel Dodson Drawing(s): VAM 8933.152 (?), attrib	Cheshunt, Herts	S	*Whinney* 1988, 253

Miscellaneous

4.	1713	Marble pavement (co-sculptor: William Woodman I) Payment(s): £46	Whitchurch, Salop, chancel		*Gunnis* 1968, 442

WOODROFFE, George fl 1662

Architectural Sculpture

1.	1662	St John, figure	St John's College, Cambridge, gatehouse		Pevsner, *Cambs*, 1970, 144

WOODRUFFE, Edward

He was to be admitted a freeman of Oxford in 1667 without fine if he could 'in a workmanlike manner cutt or carve the King's Arms or such other signes for the use of the City as the Mayor or his brethren shall direct' (*Gunnis* 1968, 443, quoting Oxford Council Acts, 1666–1701, OHS p 6). A payment which may be connected with this agreement was made to him in 1669 for 'making a mould for ye University Arms' (Vice-Chancellor's Accounts quoted in GPC).

WOODRUFFE, Francis *c*1657–

The son of William Woodruffe, a yeoman, he was apprenticed to **John Woodruffe** on 16 January 1672. In the account-book of Sir Charles Kemeys (in Gunnis's possession in 1966) is a payment to Francis Woodruff for a chimneypiece for an unnamed house (2). Woodruffe signed an architectural monument to Edward Cotton, described by Pevsner as having two black columns, an open scrolling pediment and no figures (1).

Literary References: *Gunnis* 1968, 442–3; *Webb* 1999, 36

Archival References: Masons' Co, Court Book, 1677–94, fol 38r

Funerary Monuments

1.	†1682	Edward Colton	All Saints, Wokingham, Berks	S	Pevsner, *Berks*, 1966, 308

Chimneypieces

2.	nd	Unidentified	[for Sir Charles Kemeys Bt]; untraced		*Gunnis* 1968, 442

Architectural Sculpture

3.	1693	Miscellaneous carving Payment(s): £31	[Brewers' Hall, London]; untraced		*Gunnis* 1968, 442 citing Archives, Brewers' Company

WOODRUFFE, John, of Windsor –1728

Woodruffe was paid £23 by Lord Weymouth for work at his house in Old Windsor (*Gunnis* 1968, 443, citing Longleat Accts). He was buried in St John the Baptist, Windsor and his son John II succeeded to the family business. A letter to John II from Thomas Gayfere II dated 1743, reminded him that he owed money to Gayfere's master, **Andrews Jelfe**. Gayfere wrote 'My master imagines that it may have slipt your memory, so desires you would order ye payment and send him word by next post' (BM Ad MS 27, 587).

Literary References: *Gunnis* 1968, 443

WOODRUFFE, William fl 1685

He provided carved work in St Matthew, Friday-Street together with a John Lawrence, invoiced on 22 October 1685 (1). Another invoice from Woodruffe dated 22 Oct 1685 was for joiner's work and came to £210 18s 9d.

Archival References: St Matthew, Friday Street, Accts

Miscellaneous

1.	1685	'a lion and unicorn & fflower potts'	[St Matthew, Friday Street, City of London]; untraced		Church Accts

WOODS, T, of Titchfield fl 1804

Funerary Monuments

1.	1804	G A Thomas, large wall-tablet	Wickham, Hants	S	*Gunnis* 1968, 443

WOODWARD, Edward, of Chipping Campden *c*1697–1766

He was one of a family of master-masons and quarry owners. His father was Thomas Woodward (*c*1672–1748) who worked on the churches at Squinton, Warks, and Blockley, Worcs, and in 1719 leased Westington quarries. Edward worked in partnership with his brother Thomas (1699–1761) during the 1730s, rebuilding Alcester church, Warks (1730), St John the Baptist, Gloucester (1732–34), St Swithin, Worcester (1735–36) and the nave of Llandaff Cathedral (*c*1736).

Several earlier 18th-century Warwickshire houses have been attributed to the brothers. Between 1750 and 1764 Edward was employed by the antiquary James West to reconstruct Alscot Park, Warks and to remodel the neighbouring church of Preston-on-Stour. In 1752 Woodward submitted plans to rebuild the church in an elaborate gothic style but his patron rejected the proposal and instead Woodward remodelled the building piecemeal over the next few years.

In addition to his building work, Edward practised as a monumental mason and he signed several monuments. These are largely architectural works decorated with heraldry and carved *putti*, but he also carved a cartouche tablet in memory of his grandparents and built the family tomb in Chipping Campden churchyard (**2, 6**). The unusual gothic monument to Samuel Sanson (†1750) in the churchyard at Ilmington, Warks, was probably designed by him too. Colvin describes it as 'a buttressed tomb chest surmounted by a miniature tower and spire, complete with pinnacles and battlements very similar to those shown in Wooward's design for Preston Church' (*Colvin* 1995, 1080; *Colvin* 1999, 241, repr).

In 1845 Edward's son Richard worked with his uncle Thomas to build St Anne's, Bewdley, Worcs. The family was also responsible for rebuilding the upper part of the tower of Fladbury church, Worcs, which has a stone inscribed with Richard Woodward's name and the date 1750. Richard died, aged 32, in 1755. Edward died on 24 March 1766, aged 69, leaving a widow and three sons. Most of his property was left to Edward, apparently a younger son, who carried on the family business for some years, but became bankrupt in January 1777.

Literary References: *Colvin* 1948, 95–8; *Beard and Piper* 1951, 706–7; *Gunnis* 1968, 443; *Colvin* 1993, 75–7; *Colvin* 1995, 1079–81; *Colvin* 1999, 230–243, 244 n30

Funerary Monuments

1.	†1711	Edward Croft (†1706) and his wife Jane	s	Blockley, Glos	S	Pevsner, *Glos: Cotswolds*, 1999, 183
2.	†1716	Thomas Woodward and wife (the sculptor's grandparents)	s	Mickleton, Glos	S	Pevsner, *Glos: Cotswolds*, 1999, 476
3.	†1720	Robert Martin		Pebworth, Glos	S	*Gunnis* 1968, 443
4.	1721	Graves family	s	Mickleton, Glos		Pevsner, *Glos: Cotswolds*, 1999, 476
5.	†1724	John Brandis		Alcester, Warks		*Gunnis* 1968, 443
6.	†1766	Edward Woodward (the sculptor) and family		Chipping Campden, churchyard		*Gunnis* 1968, 443; *Colvin* 1995, 1080

WOODWARD, John fl 1720–23

In 1720 he executed carved woodwork in the University Schools, Cambridge, receiving £4 'for two pillaster cappatalls, very large, after the Corinthian order' and £24 for six similar double pilasters (**1**). Eight years later he was paid for cutting stone for the same building.

Literary References: *Gunnis* 1968, 443

Architectural Sculpture

1.	1720	Carved work	wd	Old Schools building, University of Cambridge, 'dome room'	*Gunnis* 1968, 443 citing Vice-C's Accounts
2.	1723	Arms of Sir Walter Mildmay (the founder of the college) Payment(s): £150		Westmorland Building, Emmanuel College, Cambridge	Emmanuel College Mag, vol II (2), 1898, 88 (BL PP.6119)

WOODWARD, of Bakewell fl 1818?

Funerary Monuments

1.	?1818	Benjamin Newton	Wortley, W R Yorks	S	*Gunnis* 1968, 443

WOOLCOTT, of Bristol fl *c*1819–50

The Gimblett is a tablet surmounted by an urn on a black ground (**6**).

Funerary Monuments

1.	†1819	Charles Court	St Briavels, Glos	S	Pevsner, *Glos: Vale & Forest of Dean*, 1976, 332
2.	†1831	Sarah Lawrence	St Andrew Cheddar, Somerset	S	
3.	†1835	Drummond Thatcher	St Mary, Tidenham, Glos	S	Pevsner, *Glos: Vale & Forest of Dean*, 1976, 384
4.	†1839	Julie Roberts and others	Tintern, Monmouths	S	RG/JP, 9, 1626v.
5.	*c*1841	Bassett family	Bonvilston, Glamorgan	S	Pevsner, *Glamorgan*, 1995, 157
6.	†1850	William and Sarah (†1837) Gimblett	Watchett, Somerset	S	

WOOLES, William 1804–35

The son of William Wooles, a Bristol surveyor, he came to London as a boy and entered the studio of **E H Baily**. In 1827, while living at 154 High Holborn, he won a gold medal from the Society of Arts, and two years later joined the Royal Academy Schools, gaining a silver medal for a model in 1830 (**12, 14**). He exhibited at the Society of British Artists' Suffolk Street Galleries between 1828 and 1834 and at the RA 1830–33, from addresses given as 38 Newman Street; 15 Frith Street, Soho Square; 44 Ludgate Hill and 7 Cleveland Street, Fitzroy Square. He died on 4 May 1835 and a short obituary appeared in the *Gentleman's Magazine* the following month (*GM*, 1835, i, 667).

Literary References: RSA *Transactions*, 1827, vol 45, xxxi; *Gunnis* 1968, 443; *Pyke* 1973, 158

Busts

1.	1829	Unidentified child		[Exhib Soc of BA, London, 884]; untraced	*Johnson* 1975, 518
2.	1830	Alfred the Great		[Exhib Soc of BA, London, 853]; untraced	*Johnson* 1975, 518
3.	1831	William Wooles (the sculptor's father)		[Exhib RA, London, 1130]; untraced	*Graves* VIII, 1905–6, 353; *Johnson* 1975, 518

Reliefs

4.	1829	Unidentified gentleman	w	[Exhib Soc of BA, London, 889]; untraced	*Johnson* 1975, 518
5.	1830	Unidentified gentleman, medallic portrait		[Exhib RA, London, 1092]; untraced	*Graves* VIII, 1905–6, 353
6.	1830	Unidentified lady, medallic portrait		[Exhib RA, London, 1095]; untraced	*Graves* VIII, 1905–6, 353

7.	1832	Unidentified gentleman, medallion		[Exhib Soc of BA, London, 886]; untraced	*Johnson* 1975, 518
8.	1832	Vice-Admiral Sir Robert Otway KCB	w	[Exhib RA, London, 1051]; untraced	*Graves* VIII, 1905–6, 353; *Johnson* 1975, 518
9.	1833	H E Kendall Jnr, medallic portrait		[Exhib RA, London, 810]; untraced	*Graves* VIII, 1905–6, 353
10.	1834	H E Kendall	w	[Exhib Soc of BA, London, 817]; untraced	*Johnson* 1975, 518
11.	1834	King William IV, medallion portrait in silver		[Exhib Soc of BA, London, 815]; untraced	*Johnson* 1975, 518
Miscellaneous					
12.	1827	Original model of an historical group		[Soc of A, gold medal]; untraced	RSA *Transactions*, 1827, vol 45, xxxi
13.	1828	Perseus rescuing Andromeda		[Exhib Soc of BA, London, 883]; untraced	*Johnson* 1975, 518
14.	1830	Unidentified subject, model		[RA silver medal]; untraced	RA Premium list
15.	1832	The wounded knight, sketch		[Exhib RA, London, 1197]; untraced	*Graves* VIII, 1905–6, 353
16.	1833	Portrait of Swap, a celebrated racer		[Exhib Soc of BA, London, 865]; untraced	*Johnson* 1975, 518
17.	1833	The repose of the templar		[Exhib Soc of BA, London, 849]; untraced	*Johnson* 1975, 518
18.	1833	The tourney, sketch		[Exhib RA, London, 1157]; untraced	*Graves* VIII, 1905–6, 353

WOOLNER, Thomas RA 1825–92

Woolner was a sculptor, poet and founder member of the Pre-Raphaelite Brotherhood. There has been increasing interest in his work in recent years as it has been reassessed in the light of his Pre-Raphaelite connections.

He was born at Hadleigh, Suffolk, on 17 December 1825, the son of Thomas and Rebecca Woolner and went to school in Ipswich until he was about ten, when the family moved to London, where his father took a job with the Post Office. His artistic talent was apparent from an early age and when he was about 13 he was sent to study with the painter Charles Behnes. Behnes died soon after and Woolner was then taken on by his brother **William Behnes**. Woolner must already have made a good impression on the well-established Behnes, for he was accepted as a pupil without fee, provided that when Woolner was sufficiently advanced he should work for a period at a reduced rate of pay. Woolner remained in Behnes's studio, at Osnaburgh Street, Regent's Park, for about six years.

In 1842, while still employed by Behnes and with his encouragement, Woolner joined the Royal Academy Schools. He later claimed to have learned little at the Schools since he had already received all the formal training he needed from Behnes. The following year he showed his first work at the Royal Academy (**173**), an exhibiting space he would continue to use regularly throughout his life.

In 1844 he exhibited a model, *The death of Boadicea* (**35**) at Westminster Hall, hoping to obtain sculptural commissions for the Houses of Parliament. This attracted considerable attention: one reviewer praised Woolner's dramatic treatment and the powerful emotions aroused by the figure (*Athenæum*, 1844, 674) and another noted that the work was 'produced under extraordinary disadvantages' and greeted it as 'an earnest of better things' (*Lit Gaz*, 1844, 483). This comment probably refers to Woolner's straitened circumstances during his early career, when no financial support could be provided by his family.

The sculptor, who was then living at 15 Mary Street, Regent's Park, won the Society of Arts silver medal in 1845 for a relief of *Affection* (**174**). He showed several ideal pieces through the exhibiting societies over the next few years, including *Puck* (**39**), a rare surviving early work, but was increasingly obliged to turn to portraiture as a means of making a living. His first portrait medallion, of the poet Coventry Patmore (**179**), was cast in 1849. Another of Mrs Patmore followed (**181**) and elicited warm praise from her husband. Patmore introduced Woolner to Tennyson and helped arrange sittings for his first representation of the poet laureate, completed in 1850. These small scale images of well-known figures were particularly lucrative as they could be cast and sold in large numbers.

Woolner was the only sculptor among the seven original members of the Pre-Raphaelite Brotherhood (PRB), formed in 1848. They believed that they could find in Nature 'the one means of purifying modern art' and aimed to produce work of 'excelling truthfulness and strong poetic spirit' (*Hunt* I 1905, 112–3, 118). He participated actively in the group's activities and published poetry in the Pre-Raphaelite journal, *The Germ*.

Woolner's dedication to these principles is evident in two monuments to William Wordsworth and in much of his later work. The memorial in Grasmere church (**2**) is another profile portrait, flanked by meticulously carved spring flowers. It was admired both for its verisimilitude and as a depiction of the poet's intellectual character. He provided a second, more complex design, in which he sought symbolically to 'embody the "Individual Mind" of Wordsworth' (*Graves* VIII, 1905–6, 355) for the national memorial to be raised in Westminster Abbey. The poet's statue was to be flanked by allegorical groups representing 'Control of Passion (Being the basis of Law)' and 'Nature contemplated to the Glory of God (Being the Basis of Religion)' (*ibid*). Despite his lofty aspirations, Woolner lost in competition to **Frederick Thrupp**, a more established but now less well regarded artist.

This disappointment and, perhaps, an unhappy love affair caused Woolner to depart for Australia. He set sail from Gravesend on 24 July 1852, hoping to make his fortune in the gold fields. Among the friends who saw him off was Ford Madox Brown, whose painting *The Last of England* was inspired by the event. Woolner soon discovered that it was not easy to make money as a prospector and started to work as a sculptor in Australia. In spite of problems in obtaining materials, he opened a studio in Melbourne and built up a successful practice in portrait medallions. He wrote to his father on 10 July 1853, 'I have my tools a little in order now and mean to work hard. I get 25 pounds for a medallion here. In England they would not give me 25 pence' (*Woolner* 1917, 61). In 1853–54 Woolner modelled some 24 medallions of Australian colonists. He then returned to England, hoping to secure the commission for a statue of W C Wentworth for Sydney. Again he was unsuccessful, in spite of the popularity of his earlier medallion of this leading Australian statesman (**211**).

Woolner's fortunes now improved, for he received several commissions for portraits and ideal works. His busts and medallions of Tennyson (**73, 123, 126, 180, 214, 229**), Carlyle (**96, 184, 213, 255**) and Browning (**219**) established his reputation as a portrait sculptor. A first bust of Tennyson (**73**), acquired by Trinity College, Cambridge, made a favourable impression and led to further commissions, including statues of Macaulay (**46**) and Whewell (**53**) for the college. His bust of W E Gladstone, 1866, on a pedestal with reliefs from *The Iliad* (**97**), a memorial commissioned for Oxford University, further increased his reputation. Many of Woolner's sitters, including Tennyson, whom he much admired, became close friends and furthered his career.

His first major public statue, of Sir Francis Bacon (**43**), completed in 1857, was for the Oxford University Museum, a building project to which several members of the PRB contributed. This was followed by statues for India (**52, 55, 56, 59**), New Zealand (**47**), Australia (**64**) and Singapore (**69**), admired for their realism, characterisation and the sculptor's handling of contemporary costume. There were also failures: a late work, the statue of George Dawson for Birmingham, 1881 (**67**) was thought 'so ludicrously bad that after the deceased's fellow townsmen had laughed at it for several years they agreed to take it down' (*ILN*, 15 Oct 1892, 475).

Woolner's most poignant works are *Brother and sister* (**44**), completed in 1862 for the International Exhibition and *Mother and child*, which took more than a decade to materialise, in 1867 (**49**). The first, commissioned by the collector and organiser of the Manchester Art Treasures Exhibition, Sir Thomas Fairbairn, is a portrait of his two children, described 'almost as a manifesto of Woolner's particular artistic ideas and skills' (*Read and Barnes* 1991, 29). It is a sensitive psychological portrait of the two deaf and dumb children which clearly shows the bond between them. The second is an ideal work, a full size statue of a mother teaching her child the Lord's Prayer and this image of Christian maternal tenderness is contrasted with relief scenes on the plinth of pre-Christian barbarism. The group was commissioned by Lady Pauline Trevelyan, who was herself an artist and critic, as part of an ambitious Pre-Raphaelite decorative scheme at Wallington Hall, Northumbs. Many of these works were disseminated to a wider audience through photographic reproductions.

Whilst working on *Mother and child*, Woolner married Alice Gertrude Waugh, a model for that composition and the sister of Fanny, who became the wife of Holman Hunt. They had two sons and three daughters and lived at Welbeck Street, London and Mayfield, Sussex.

Late in his career, in 1872, he was elected an associate of the Academy and he became a full member three years later, depositing as his diploma work a version of the relief of *Achilles and Pallas shouting from the trenches* from the Gladstone memorial (**97**). In 1877 he was appointed professor of sculpture on the death of **Henry Weekes RA**, but he claimed never to have lectured and resigned in 1879.

As a young man Woolner conformed physically to PRB ideals of beauty, with his robust, square-featured, noble face, thick masses of brownish auburn hair and penetrating eyes (F G Stephens, *AJ*, 1894, 82). He was considered energetic, honest and dedicated to his work and his extensive correspondence is full of gossip, anecdote and humour. He could also be blunt, which made him some enemies. His obituary focussed on his dedication to perfectionism, irrespective of financial considerations. 'In life as in art he was the uncompromising foe of sham, of claptrap and of superficiality' (*The Times*, 8 October 1892, 10).

The demand for Woolner's work remained high until the end of his life and he supplemented his income by dealing in pictures, so he died in comparative wealth, leaving an estate valued at £64,000. In his last decade, Woolner's naturalistic style was challenged by the work of the New Sculptors and his last work, *The housemaid* (**71**), completed in plaster only a few weeks before his death, can be seen as his response. The life-sized figure of a servant girl wringing out a cloth combines realism with a restrained classical grace and contrasts with the more dramatic effects achieved by the New Sculptors. Until recently Woolner had little place in the extensive Pre-Raphaelite literature; '*The Last of England* might as well have been *The Last of Woolner*' (*Read* 1984, 97–8). It is now acknowledged however that his close involvement in the Brotherhood, the truth to nature that was so characteristic of his work, his contributions to a number of Pre-Raphaelite decorative schemes and his prolific output make him a key figure in the movement.

EH

Literary References: *Palgrave* 1866, 83, 206, 208–10, 221, 224–5, 253–4, 260, 294–5; *Athenæum* 1892, 522–3; *Magazine of Art* 1892–3, 71–2, viii; *AJ* 1894, 80–6; *Graves* VIII, 1905–6, 354–7; *Woolner* 1917, *passim*; *DNB* XXI, 905–7; *Ormond* 1967, 25–7; *Gunnis* 1968, 443–5; *Cox* 1977–8, 64–75; *Trevelyan* 1978 (1), *passim; Trevelyan* 1978 (2), 200–5; *Trevelyan* 1978–9, 1–37; *Ormond and Rogers* 3, 1979–81, 226; *Cox* 1981, 1–27; *Cox* 1981–2, 1–21; *Ormond* 1981, 1–31; *Read* 1982, *passim*; *Bronkhurst* 1983, 586–97; *Read* 1984, 97–110; *Read and Barnes* 1991, *passim*; *Parris* 1994, 41; *Grove* 33, 1996, 373–5 (Stocker); *ODNB* (Stevens); *Lukitsh* 2005, 1–16

Additional MS Sources: Corr and misc papers, BL MSS, Brotherton MSS, Bodl, Fitz, John Rylands, Co-Op MSS, Robinson, Wordsworth Lib, Tennyson RC, SRO, Rosenbach, Stanford, Mass Hist Soc, NSW Lib, Durham Univ Lib GB-0033-Add-838; Woolner's notes for Palgrave's *Golden Treasury*, 1860–61, BL MSS, Add 42126; Studio diaries for 1864 and 1874, HMI; MS of *My Beautiful Lady*, Bodl, MS Eng poet e 58; papers concerning commission of statues in the Museum Court, Oxf Univ Mus, history of the building archive; Woolner's Australian Journal, 31 Oct 1852 – 25 May 1854 (photocopy), Bodl, Ms Facs d 152

Administration: PPR, 7 February 1893, effects £65,866 19s 3d, resworn November 1894 £65,766 19s 3d

Auction Catalogues: Woolner 1875; Woolner 1883, Woolner 1895; Woolner 1913; Woolner and others 1895; Woolner and others 1913 (1); Woolner and others 1913 (2)

Portraits of the Sculptor: 'Mr B -'s Tyger', a caricature of Thomas Woolner when a young man in William Behnes's studio, *Woolner* 1917, fol 14; Dante Gabriel Rossetti, 1852, pencil drawing, NPG 3848; Dante Gabriel Rossetti, 16 April 1853, sketch in a letter, Thomas Woolner as 'Fire Fiend', *Woolner* 1917, 56; photo, *c*1860–1865, *Ormond* 1981, 5 (repr); Ernest Edwards, photo for *Men of Eminence*, vol II, 1864, NPG; J P Mayall, photo, Woolner at work on the bust of Tennyson in 1873, NPG x13286; Alphonse Legros, 1874, painting, Ipswich borough museums and galls; Lock and Whitfield, photo for *Men of Mark*, 1877, NPG; A C Gow, 1883, painting, Aberdeen art gall; after T B Wirgman, woodcut, for *Century Mag*, 1883, BM; Ralph Winwood Robinson, 1889, platinum print, NPG x7402; J M Johnstone, after a photo, woodcut, *Mag of Art* 1891; Ralph W Robinson, 1891, photo, NPG x7402; engraving, *AJ*, 1894, 81; photo, 'Thomas Woolner, The Sculptor among his Men', *Woolner* 1917, fol 119; 170 studio photos, HMI; various photos, NPG x5126-44

Funerary Monuments

1.	1851	William Wordsworth (†1850), design only (monument by Frederick Thrupp)	pm	[Exhib RA, London, 1852, 1353]; Wordsworth Trust, Grasmere (central figure only)		*Read* 1984, 106–8; *Read and Barnes* 1991, 22 (repr)
2.	1851	William Wordsworth (†1850), with medallion portrait		St Oswald, Grasmere, Westmorland	S	*Read* 1982, 182–3 (repr); *Read* 1984, 105–8 (repr)
3.	1860	The Palmer cross		Untraced		*Read and Barnes* 1991, 28

4.	1861	Cawnpore memorial cross, model	p	Untraced		*Read and Barnes* 1991, 28 (repr)
5.	1861	John Ashley Warre		Ramsgate, Kent		*Woolner* 1917, 202, 338
6.	1865	Design for the Spofforth cross		Untraced		*Woolner* 1917, 338
7.	†1865	Sir William Hooker		Kew, Surrey Other versions: NPG 1866, medallion only VAM, medallion only	S	*Ormond* 1973, 232 (repr 449)
8.	1866–1867	Mary Ellen (†1863) and Archibald Peel (†1860) (with a relief of 'Heavenly Welcome')		[Model exhib RA, London, 1867, 1068]; St Giles, Wrexham, Denbighs		*Read and Barnes* 1991, 157–9 (repr)
9.	?1867	William Prescott		Bockleton, Worcs		*Gunnis* 1968, 445
10.	1869	Design for the Neave memorial		Untraced		*Woolner* 1917, 340
11.	1870	Design for the Ogle cross		Untraced		*Woolner* 1917, 340
12.	1870	Galt family member, a novelist		Greenock, Renfrewshire		*Woolner* 1917, 340
13.	1870	William Dobson (†1868)		Cheltenham College, Glos, chapel		*CIIA* 4/4/16–7 (repr)
14.	1871	John, Baron Lawrence (†1879), bust		Westminster Abbey, London, nave		*Read* 1982, 103 (repr); *Steggles* 2000, 123
15.	1871	Samuel (†1870) and Elizabeth Bright (†1880)		Unitarian church, Ullet Road, Liverpool, Lancs	S	*Woolner* 1917, 840; C Lib (repr)
16.	1872	John Keble (†1866)		Westminster Abbey, London, south transept		Pevsner, *London: Westminster*, 1973, 446; C Lib (repr)
17.	1873	John W S Wyllie, officiating foreign secretary to the government of India; part of a tablet for Cheltenham College chapel		[Exhib RA, London, 1588]; untraced		*Graves* VIII, 1905–6, 356
18.	1873	Sir John Simeon, cross		Newport, I of W		*Gunnis* 1968, 444; C Lib (repr)
19.	?1874	Mr Meynell-Ingram		Laughton, Lincs		RG/JP, 9, 1636
20.	†1874	Sir William Fairbairn		[Cross Street chapel, Manchester]; destroyed.		*Bronkhurst* 1983, 587 n11
21.	1875	Henrietta Elizabeth Froude (†1874)		St Laurence, Ramsgate, Kent	S	*Woolner* 1917, fol 207, 341 (repr); *Gunnis* 1968, 445
22.	1875	John Coleridge Patteson, Bishop of Melanesia (†1871)		Merton College, Oxford, chapel	SD	*Gunnis* 1968, 445; C Lib (repr)
23.	1875	Ransom memorial vase		Untraced		*Woolner* 1917, 341
24.	1876	Charles Kingsley (†1875)		Westminster Abbey, London, nave Other versions: bust, plaster, NPG		*Graves* VIII, 1905–6, 356; Pevsner, *London: I*, 1973, 444; C Lib (repr)
25.	?1876	Daniel Hanbury		La Mortola, near Menton, France		*Read* 1982, 183
26.	1880	Sir Francis Grant		[Melton Mowbray, Leics, churchyard]; untraced		*Woolner* 1917, 343
27.	?1881	Hepworth Dixon		Highgate Cemetery, London		*Curl* 2001, 237
28.	1881	John (†1889) and Grace Percy (†1880)		Kensal Green Cemetery, London	S	*Woolner* 1917, 343; *Curl* 2001, 203, 208
29.	1882	Sir Edwin Landseer (†1873)		St Paul's Cathedral, London		*Read and Barnes* 1991, 23
30.	1882	The Percival cross		Holywell Cemetery, Oxford		*Read* 1982, 349; C Lib (repr)
31.	1884	Gleadhall family member		Foundling Hospital, London		*Woolner* 1917, 344
32.	1885	Lord Frederick Cavendish (†1882)		Cartmel priory church, Lancs		*Graves* VIII, 1905–6, 357; *Read* 1982, 349
33.	1887	Design for the Brook cross		Untraced		*Woolner* 1917, 344
34.	1887	John Jackson, Bishop of London (1885)		St Paul's Cathedral, London		*Read* 1982, 349; Courtauld photo B84/1493
Statues						
35.	1844	The death of Boadicea, model	p	[Exhib Westminster Hall, London, 154]; untraced		*Read and Barnes* 1991, 21–2
36.	1847	Feeding the hungry, statuette	p	[Exhib RA, London, 1394]; untraced		*Graves* VIII, 1905–6, 355; *Read and Barnes* 1991, 143
37.	1847	Little Red Riding Hood, statuette		Untraced Other versions: reproduced in Parian ware		*Read and Barnes* 1991, 142–3 (repr)
38.	1847	'Lo, one generation passeth away, and another cometh'		Untraced		*Read* 1984, 99
39.	1847	Puck, statuette	pb	[Exhib BI, London, 550]; Tate Britain, London Other versions: four recorded		*Read and Barnes* 1991, 141–2 (repr)
40.	1848	Eros and Euphrosyne		[Exhib RA, London, 1339]; Woolner coll		*Graves* VIII, 1905–6, 355; C Lib (repr)
41.	1848	Titania and the Indian boy, group	p	[Exhib BI, London, 473]; untraced		*Graves* 1875, 610; *Gunnis* 1968, 443
42.	1856	Love, statuette	p	[Exhib RA, London, 1342]; Ipswich Borough Museums and Galls Other versions: several recorded	S	*Read and Barnes* 1991, 28–9, 149 (repr)
43.	1857	Sir Francis Bacon	s	Oxford University Museum		*Read* 1982, 123 (repr); *Read and Barnes* 1991, 25–6 (repr)
44.	1857–1862	Brother and sister (The Fairbairn group; Constance and Arthur; Deaf and dumb)		[Int Exhib, 1862]; private coll	SD	*Read* 1982, 8–10, 179, 185 (repr)
45.	1864	Albert, the Prince Consort	s	Oxford University Museum		*Read* 1982, 122, 123, 169 (repr)
46.	1866	Thomas Babington, 1st Baron Macaulay	m	Trinity College, Cambridge, chapel		*Read* 1982, 81, 128 (repr)
47.	1867	John Robert Godley	b	Christchurch, New Zealand		*Stocker* 1985, 19–25 (repr)
48.	1862–1867	King William III	m	[Westminster Hall, London]; Central Criminal Court, Old Bailey, London, entrance hall		*Walker* 1961, 107; *Read* 1982, 121 (repr); *Ward-Jackson* 2003, 74–5 (repr)

No.	Date	Subject	Medium	Location		Literary references
49.	1856–1867	Mother and child (The Lord's prayer; Civilization) Payment(s): £1,500		[coll Sir Walter Trevelyan]; Wallington Hall, Northumbs		*Read* 1982, 55, 63–5 184–6, 204, 206 (repr)
50.	1868	Elaine with the shield of Sir Launcelot, statuette	m	[Dunster House, Rochdale; Nield sale, 1879 (£178)]; untraced		*Art J*, 1894, 84; *Graves* VIII, 1905–6, 356; *Woolner* 1917, 339
51.	1868	Ophelia, statuette	m	Royal Shakespeare Theatre, Stratford-upon-Avon, Warks Other versions: several recorded		*Graves* VIII, 1905–6, 356; *Read* 1982, 207; *Read and Barnes* 1991, 159 (repr)
52.	1869	David Sassoon	m	[Exhib South Kensington Museum, 1869]; Mumbai (Bombay) University, India		*Read and Barnes* 1991, 26 (repr); *Steggles* 2000, 172
53.	1872	Dr William Whewell Model(s): Newnham Coll, Cambridge; Fitz, Cambridge	m	[Exhib RA, London, 1873, 1516]; Trinity College, Cambridge, chapel	D	*Read* 1982, 124, 128, 176, 177 (repr); *Read and Barnes* 1991, 162 (repr)
54.	1872	Guinevere, statuette	m	[Exhib RA, London, 1503; Nield sale, 1879, £136]; private coll, London		Nield sale, Christie, 3 May 1879 (£136); *Graves* VIII, 1905–6, 356; *Woolner* 1917, fol 178, 341 (repr); *Read* 1982, 207
55.	1868–1873	Sir Henry Bartle Frere Bt Model(s): NPG, London, 1670, plaster	m	[Exhib RA, London, 1872, 1513]; Asiatic Soc, Mumbai (Bombay), India (formerly town hall)	D	*Steggles* 2000, 95–96 (repr)
56.	1875	John, Baron Lawrence Model(s): exhib RA, London, 1876, 1442	b	[Government House, Kolkata (Calcutta), India]; Old Flagstaff House, Barrackpore, India		*Read and Barnes* 1991, 166–7; *Steggles* 2000, 123
57.	1875	The Coleridge memorial prize, a group of Bluecoat boys, Samuel Taylor Coleridge, Thomas Fanshaw Middleton and Charles Lamb	b	Christ's Hospital, Horsham, Surrey		*Read and Barnes* 1991, 162–3 (repr)
58.	1876	Henry, 3rd Viscount Palmerston	b	Parliament Square, London	SD	*Walker* 1961, 105; *CIIA* 4/7/124–5 (repr)
59.	1876	Sir Cowasji Jehangir		Mumbai (Bombay), India		*ILN*, 19 July 1890, 79; *Gunnis* 1968, 444; C Lib (repr)
60.	1877	Edwin Field	m	[Exhib RA, London, 1462]; Law Courts, London		*Graves* VIII, 1905–6, 357; *Read and Barnes* 1991, 27
61.	1878	John Stuart Mill Model(s): William Morris Gallery, Waltham Forest, London, painted plaster	b	Thames embankment, London		*Read* 1982, 355; *Read and Barnes* 1991, 26–7 164–5 (repr)
62.	1878	Lady Godiva, statuette	m	[Exhib RA, London, 1482]; Herbert Art Gallery and Museum, Coventry, Warks		*Graves* VIII, 1905–6, 357; *Victorian Nude* 2001, 76–7 (repr)
63.	1878	Sir Thomas White, Lord Mayor of London	m	Merchant Taylors' Company, City of London		*Graves* VIII, 1905–6, 357; *Woolner* 1917, 342
64.	1879	Captain James Cook, on a column	b	Hyde Park, Sydney, Australia	SD	*Read and Barnes* 1991, 27, 37–8 (repr)
65.	1880	James Whiteside, Lord Chief Justice of Ireland	m	[Four Courts, Dublin]; untraced		*Woolner* 1917, 343; *Gunnis* 1968, 444
66.	1881	Enid, statuette	m	Untraced		*Read* 1982, 207; *Read and Barnes* 1991, 30
67.	1881	George Dawson	m	Chamberlam Square, Birmingham, Warks		*Noszlopy* 1998, 31 (repr)
68.	1883	Queen Victoria	m	[Exhib RA, London, 1541]; Council House, Birmingham, Warks	S	*Noszlopy* 1998, 143 (repr)
69.	1887	Sir Thomas Stamford Raffles Model(s): exhib RA, London, 1888, 1915	b	[Padang, Singapore]; Victoria Memorial Hall, Singapore Other versions: Marble replica, North Boat quay, Singapore		*Steggles* 2000, 159–61 (repr)
70.	1888	James Fraser, Bishop of Manchester	b	[Model exhib RA, London, 1929]; Albert Square, Manchester, Lancs		*CIIA* 4/6/47–51 (repr); *Read* 1982, 349, 359
71.	1892	The housemaid	b	Salters' Company Other versions: Christchurch mansion, Ipswich	SD	*Read* 1982, 211 (repr), 212, 349; *Read and Barnes* 1991, 167 (repr)
72.	nd	Sir Cawasjee Jehanghier Readymoney Payment(s): 22,000 rupees		University of Mumbai (Bombay), India, gardens		*Giara* 2000, 107
Busts						
73.	1856–1857	Alfred, Lord Tennyson, unbearded	m	Trinity College, Cambridge Other versions: ex coll Charles Jenner; Westminster Abbey	SD	*Manchester Art Treasures* 1857, 136; *Read* 1982, 64–5, 123, 179 (repr); *Read and Barnes* 1991, 42–4, 149–50 (repr)
74.	1859	Edward Henry Lushington	m	[Exhib RA, London, 1353]; untraced		*Graves* VIII, 1905–6, 355; *Woolner* 1917, 338
75.	1858–1859	Sir James Brooke, Rajah of Sarawak	m	[coll Sir Thomas Fairbairn]; private coll Other versions: Bodelwyddan Castle, Wales NPG, London	SD	*Read and Barnes* 1991, 150–1 (repr)
76.	1859	Sir William Hooker		Royal Botanic Gardens, Kew Other versions: two plaster casts, NPG and Linnean Soc		*Graves* VIII, 1905–6, 355; *Ormond* 1973, 232 (repr 448)

77.	1860	Prof Adam Sedgwick	m	Trinity College, Cambridge, library Other versions: NPG 1669, plaster Dept of Geology, Cambridge	SD	*Read and Barnes* 1991, 153–4 (repr)
78.	1861	John Stevens Henslow	m	[coll H Christy]; Fitzwilliam	SD	*Woolner* 1917, 338; *Gunnis* 1968, 445; C Lib (repr)
79.	1861	Julius Hare	m	Wren Library, Trinity College, Cambridge	SD	*Graves* VIII, 1905–6, 356; *British Portraits* 1956–7, 137; *Read* 1982, 123–8; C Lib (repr)
80.	1861	Rev Frederick Denison Maurice		['for the Working Women's College']; untraced Other versions: replicas at Westminster Abbey and Senate House, Cambridge		*Ormond* 1973, 310; C Lib (repr)
81.	1861	William Shaen	m	[Exhib RA, London, 1080]; Senate House, University of London		*Graves* VIII, 1905–6, 355; *Woolner* 1917, 338; C Lib (repr)
82.	1862	Sir William Brooke Fairbairn	m	[Exhib RA, London, 1048]; private coll, USA Other versions: NPG, London		*Graves* VIII, 1905–6, 355; *Read and Barnes* 1991, 152; C Lib (repr)
83.	1862	William Miller Christy	m	Witt Library, Courtauld Institute of Art, London		*Woolner* 1917, 338; C Lib (repr)
84.	1863	Arthur Hugh Clough	m	Rugby School, Warks, Temple Reading Room and Museum Other versions: NPG, London, plaster		*Woolner* 1917, 338; *Read and Barnes* 1991, 24; C Lib (repr)
85.	1863	Thomas Combe	m	Ashmolean WA 1894.21	SD	*Graves* VIII, 1905–6, 356; *Penny* 1992, III, 188 (repr)
86.	1864	William Spottiswoode	m	Royal Soc, London		*Woolner* 1917, 338; *Gunnis* 1968, 445; C Lib (repr)
87.	1865	John Kemble		Trinity College, Cambridge		*Gunnis* 1968, 445
88.	1865	Professor Cockerell		Untraced		*Woolner* 1917, 338
89.	1865	Richard Cobden		[coll Emperor Napoleon III]; untraced		*Ormond* 1973, 107
90.	1865	William Bingham, 2nd Baron Ashburton	m	Castle Ashby, Northants	SD	*Read and Barnes* 1991, 155–7 (repr)
91.	1866	Cardinal John Henry Newman	m	[Exhib RA, London, 1867, 1035]; Keble College, Oxford Other versions: two plaster casts: NPG, Trinity College	SD	*Webb* 1953 (1), 242 (repr 13); *Ormond* 1973, 339, 340 (repr 670)
92.	1866	Dr Symonds of Clifton	m	Untraced		*Woolner* 1917, 339
93.	1866	John Fowler	m	LMG, Armley Mills, Leeds, W R Yorks	SD	*Woolner* 1917, 339
94.	1866	Mr Cox		Untraced		*Woolner* 1917, 339
95.	1866	Richard Cobden	m	[coll Mrs Cobden]; Brighton Art Gall, Sussex Other versions: Westminster Abbey, London Brighton Art Gallery, Sussex NPG, London, 219	D	*Ormond* 1973, 107
96.	1866	Thomas Carlyle	m	Castle Ashby, Northants Other versions: University Library, Edinburgh, marble other recorded versions	SD	*Graves* VIII, 1905–6, 356; *Ormond* 1973, 91–2
97.	1866	William Ewart Gladstone on a pedestal with scenes from the *Iliad* (the Gladstone memorial)	m	[Bodleian, Oxford]; Ashmolean WA 1926.33 Other versions: Another made for Hawarden for WE Gladstone	SD	*Penny* 1992, 189–90 (reprs)
98.	1867	Captain Francis Fowke (produced by Minton & Co from Woolner's model)	tc	VAM 37-1867 Other versions: VAM 1155-1868, gilt bronze, SD 1866 (cast by Elkington & Co)	SD	*Bilbey* 2002, 435–6 (repr)
99.	1867	Hon William Edward Frere, formerly of Bombay	m	[Exhib RA, London, 1868, 1001]; Asiatic Soc, Mumbai (Bombay), India (formerly town hall)	SD	*Graves* VIII, 1905–6, 356; *Woolner* 1917, 340
100.	1868	Dr Robert Haines	m	Mumbai (Bombay), India		*Woolner* 1917, 340
101.	1868	Dr William Hey	m	[Leeds Infirmary, W R Yorks]; Armley mills, Leeds (2002)		*Gunnis* 1968, 445
102.	1868	Edward Wilson	m	Victoria State Lib, Melbourne, LTS 43	SD	*Graves* VIII, 1905–6, 356; *Gunnis* 1968, 445
103.	1868	Henry Christy	m	BM, London	SD	*Dawson* 1999, 69–71 (repr)
104.	1868	Robert Leslie Ellis		[Exhib RA, London, 1029]; Trinity College, Cambridge, library		*Graves* VIII, 1905–6, 356; *Woolner* 1917, 340
105.	1868	Sir Henry Bartle Frere	p	NPG, London Other versions: University of Bombay, India, library, SD 1869		*Gunnis* 1968, 445
106.	1868	Sir Mark Cubbon	m	India		*Woolner* 1917, 340
107.	1869	Charles Darwin	m	[Exhib RA, London, 1870, 1198]; University of Cambridge, botany department Other versions: Darwin family, marble RCS, plaster Shrewsbury School, plaster	SD	*Read and Barnes* 1991, 160–1 (repr)

108.	pre-1869	David Sassoon	m	Dr Bhau Daji Lad Museum, Mumbai (Bombay), India		*Steggles* 2000, 172–3 (repr)
109.	1869	Frederick Temple	m	Rugby School, Warks, Temple Reading Room and Museum	SD	*Read and Barnes* 1991, 24 (repr)
110.	1869	Hatley Frere	m	Untraced		*Woolner* 1917, 340
111.	1869	Joseph Pease, of Darlington	m	[Exhib RA, London, 1241]; untraced		*Graves* VIII, 1905–6, 356; *Woolner* 1917, 340
112.	1869	Sir Bartle Frere, late Governor of Bombay	m	[Exhib RA, London, 1285]; untraced		*Graves* VIII, 1905–6, 356; *Woolner* 1917, 340
113.	1870	Dr Rees	m	Untraced		*Woolner* 1917, 340
114.	1870	Sir James Hope Grant		[Exhib RA, London, 1115]; untraced		*Graves* VIII, 1905–6, 356; *Woolner* 1917, 340
115.	c1870	Sir Jonathan Frederick Pollock		Inner Temple, London		*Ormond* 1973, 381
116.	1871	Dr Bayer (?)	m	Untraced		*Woolner* 1917, 340
117.	1871	Dr Temple, Bishop of Exeter	m	[Exhib RA, London, 1282]; untraced		*Graves* VIII, 1905–6, 356
118.	1872	Charles Dickens	m	[Exhib RA, London, 1560]; private coll, USA	SD	*Graves* VIII, 1905–6, 356; C Lib (repr)
119.	1872	Mr Tilleard	p	Untraced		*Woolner* 1917, 341
120.	1872	Mrs Miles Gaskell	m	[Exhib RA, London, 1546]; untraced		*Graves* VIII, 1905–6, 356
121.	1872	Professor De Morgan	m	[Exhib RA, London, 1873, 1549]; Senate House, University of London	SD	*Graves* VIII, 1905–6, 356; C Lib (repr)
122.	1872	Sir John Simeon	p	Untraced		*Woolner* 1917, 341
123.	1873	Alfred, Lord Tennyson, bearded		Art Gall of Southern Australia, Adelaide Other versions: NPG, London, 1667 Usher art gall, Lincoln, 1876, marble Lincoln central lib, plaster St Margaret, Somersby, bronze		*Graves* VIII, 1905–6, 357; *Ormond* 1973, 452 (repr 906); *Read and Barnes* 1991, 45
124.	1873	Dr Henry Bence Jones	m	R I, London		*Gunnis* 1968, 445; C Lib (repr)
125.	1873	W W Pearce	m	[Exhib RA, London, 1576]; untraced		*Graves* VIII, 1905–6, 356
126.	1874	Alfred, Lord Tennyson, wearing a cloak	p	Untraced		*Ormond* 1981, 18
127.	1874	Dr John Hunter	m	Leicester Square, Westminster, London		*Woolner* 1917, 341; *Read* 1982, 171; C Lib (repr)
128.	1874	James Milnes-Gaskell	m	Untraced		*Woolner* 1917, 341
129.	1874	Mrs Alfred Morrison	m	[Exhib RA, London, 1454]; untraced		*Graves* VIII, 1905–6, 356; *Woolner* 1917, 341
130.	1874	Ophelia	m	[Exhib RA, London, 1878, 1417; Nield sale, 1879 (£220)]; Christchurch Museum and Art Gall, Ipswich, Suffolk		*Woolner* 1917, fols 200, 341 (repr); *Read* 1982, 171; *Read and Barnes* 1991, 159
131.	1875	Thomas Hewitt Key	m	[Exhib RA, London, 1876, 1423]; University College, London	SD	*Read and Barnes* 1991, 164 (repr)
132.	1876	Dudley, Viscount Sandon	m	Sandon Park, Staffs		*Graves* VIII, 1905–6, 357; C Lib (repr)
133.	1877	Edmund Law Lushington	m	[Exhib RA, London, 1444]; Glasgow University		*Graves* VIII, 1905–6, 357; *Gunnis* 1968, 445
134.	1877	Edwin Wilkins Field	m	Gov Art Coll	SD	Gov Art Coll archives
135.	1877	Professor Thomas Huxley		Charing Cross Hospital, London		*Graves* VIII, 1905–6, 357; *Gunnis* 1968, 445
136.	1877	William Fuller Maitland	m	[Exhib RA, London, 1443]; untraced		*Graves* VIII, 1905–6, 357; *Woolner* 1917, 342
137.	1878	Sir John Quain		Middle Temple, London		*Gunnis* 1968, 445
138.	1878	Sir John Simon	m	RCS, London		*Graves* VIII, 1905–6, 357; *Gunnis* 1968, 445; C Lib (repr)
139.	1878	Sir Redmond Barry, Chancellor of Melbourne University	m	[Exhib RA, London, 1472]; NPG, Canberra; on loan from Victoria State Lib, Melbourne	SD	*Graves* VIII, 1905–6, 357; *Woolner* 1917, 343; *Gunnis* 1968, 445; *Read and Barnes* 1991, 34
140.	1879	Cookson family member	m	Peterhouse, Cambridge		*Woolner* 1917, 342
141.	1879	J T Knowles	m	[Exhib RA, London, 1486]; untraced		*Graves* VIII, 1906, 357
142.	1879	James Aikin	m	[Liverpool Town Hall, Lancs]; Walker, Liverpool	SD	*Woolner* 1917, 343; RG/JP, 9, 1636; C Lib (repr)
143.	1879	John Torr MP	m	Walker, Liverpool	SD	*Woolner* 1917, 343
144.	1879	John, Baron Lawrence	b	[coll Mrs Buxton, Lawrence's daughter]; untraced		*Read and Barnes* 1991, 166–7
145.	1879	Sir William Gull Bt	m	[Exhib RA, London, 1483]; untraced		*Graves* VIII, 1906, 357
146.	1879	William George Clark	m	Trinity College, Cambridge		*Woolner* 1917, 343; *Gunnis* 1968, 445
147.	1880	Dr John Percival	m	Clifton College, Bristol		*Graves* VIII, 1905–6, 357; *Gunnis* 1968, 445; *Read* 1982, 349; C Lib (repr)
148.	1880	Henry Dudley Ryder	m	Sandon Park, Staffs		*Graves* VIII, 1905–6, 357; C Lib (repr)
149.	1880	Judge Keogh	m	Untraced		*Woolner* 1917, 343
150.	1880	Mr Cammell (?)	m	Untraced		*Woolner* 1917, 343
151.	1882	Edward M Barry, RA	m	RA, London		*Graves* VIII, 1905–6, 357; *Gunnis* 1968, 445
152.	1882	Richard, 3rd Earl of Clanwilliam	m	[Exhib RA, London, 1675]; untraced		*Graves* VIII, 1906, 357
153.	1882	Sir Henry Parkes		Untraced		*Cox* 1981–2, 8
154.	1882	William Ewart Gladstone	m	[Guildhall, City of London]; destroyed Other versions: NPG, London		*Graves* VIII, 1905–6, 357; *Read* 1982, 174; *Read and Barnes* 1991, 157; C Lib (repr)

No.	Date	Subject	Mat.	Location	Sig.	Literature
155.	1883	Miss Hankey	p	Untraced		*Woolner* 1917, 344
156.	1883	William Erle, for the Temple library	m	[Exhib RA, London, 1580]; untraced		*Graves* VIII, 1905–6, 357
157.	1884	Sir Donald Currie, KCMG	m	University College Hospital, London	SD	*Graves* VIII, 1905–6, 357; *Woolner* 1917, 344; RG/JP, 9, 1636; C Lib (repr)
158.	1885	Henry, 3rd Viscount Palmerston	b	Untraced		*Woolner* 1917, 344
159.	1885	Richard Quain	m	RCS, London	SD	*Woolner* 1917, 344; *Gunnis* 1968, 445; C Lib (repr)
160.	1886	Lady Currie	m	Untraced		*Woolner* 1917, 344
161.	1886	Professor Munro	m	Trinity College, Cambridge		*Gunnis* 1968, 445
162.	1887	Andrew Knowles	m	Untraced		*Woolner* 1917, 344
163.	1889	Professor Harrison	m	Muir College, Allahabad		*Gunnis* 1968, 445
164.	1889	Rev Coutts Trotter	m	Trinity College, Cambridge		*Graves* VIII, 1905–6, 357; *Woolner* 1917, 344
165.	1883–1890	Four British Prime Ministers		[Commissioned by Henry Parkes]; Parliament House, Sydney, Australia		*Read and Barnes* 1991, 38
166.	1890	Sir Thomas Elder	m	[Exhib RA, London, 2079]; Adelaide University, Australia		*Graves* VIII, 1906, 357; *Gunnis* 1968, 445
167.	1891	Thomas Rawlinson, KCB	m	[Exhib RA, London, 2076]; untraced		*Graves* VIII, 1905–6, 357

Architectural Sculpture

No.	Date	Subject	Mat.	Location	Sig.	Literature
168.	1858	Moses, David, St John the Baptist, St Paul, relief panels Model(s): Moses exhib RA, London, 1858, 1203; John the Baptist exhib RA, London, 1858, 1204	s	[Pulpit, Llandaff Cathedral]; destroyed		*Read* 1982, 39, 182, 258, 259 (repr), 261; *Read and Barnes* 1991, 7–8, 27, 151 (repr)
169.	1861–1867	11 English historical figures and three reliefs (the Judgement of Solomon, and two historical subjects). (co-sculptor: Imhof)		[Assize Courts, Manchester, Lancs]; Destroyed		*Read* 1982, 237–8, 239 (repr); *Grove* 33, 1996, 375
170.	1855–1868	Ornamental sculpture: Adam and Eve and an angel holding a nucleating cell (designed by James Hungerford Pollen)		Oxford University Museum, main entrance		*Read* 1982, 235; C Lib (repr)
171.	1876	Reredos	m	[Exhib RA, London, 1419]; Luton Hoo, Beds, private chapel		*Graves* VIII, 1905–6, 8, 356; RG/JP, 9, 1629, 1632
172.	1876	Reredos, the crucifixion	m	St John the Evangelist, Liverpool, Lancs	S	*Woolner* 1917, f244, 342 (repr)

Reliefs

No.	Date	Subject	Mat.	Location	Sig.	Literature
173.	1843	Eleanora sucking the poison from the wound of Prince Edward, model		[Exhib RA, London, 1442]; untraced		*Graves* 1875, 610; *AJ*, 1894, 81; *Graves* VIII, 1905–6, 355
174.	1845	Affection	p	[Soc of A, silver medal]; untraced		RSA *Transactions*, 1845, 30, xv
175.	1846	Alastor	p	[Exhib RA, London, 1447]; untraced		*AJ*, 1894, 81; *Graves* VIII, 1905–6, 355
176.	1846	Edwin Adolphus Ashford, medallion	p	[Exhib RA, London, 1461]; untraced		*AJ*, 1894, 81; *Graves* VIII, 1905–6, 355; *Woolner* 1917, 336
177.	1848	A gentleman, medallion		[Exhib RA, London, 1411]; untraced		*Graves* VIII, 1905–6, 355
178.	1848	The rainbow	p	[Exhib RA, London, 1414]; untraced		*AJ*, 1894, 82; *Graves* VIII, 1905–6, 355
179.	1849	Coventry Patmore, medallion	p	Untraced		*Ormond* 1981, 3
180.	1849–1850	Alfred, Lord Tennyson, medallion	b	Usher art gall, Lincoln Other versions: several recorded		*Parris* 1994, 82 (repr)
181.	1850	Mrs Coventry Patmore, medallion	p	Untraced	SD	*Woolner* 1917, 9, 336; *Gunnis* 1968, 444; C Lib (repr)
182.	1851	Mrs Orme, medallion	p	Untraced		*Woolner* 1917, 336
183.	1851	Rosaline Orme, medallion	b	Untraced		*Woolner* 1917, 336
184.	1851	Thomas Carlyle, medallion		[Exhib RA, London, 1852, 1396]; untraced		*Graves* VIII, 1905–6, 355; *Ormond* 1973, 91; C Lib (repr)
185.	1851	William Wordsworth, medallion	b	[Exhib RA, London, 1852, 1397]; private coll	SD	*Read and Barnes* 1991, 143 (repr); C Lib (repr)
186.	1852	Design for a medal – 'Competition of the Lever'		[Exhib RA, London, 1346]; untraced		*Graves* VIII, 1905–6, 355
187.	1852	Design for a medal – 'England rewards Agriculture'		[Exhib RA, London, 1344]; untraced		*Graves* VIII, 1905–6, 355; *Woolner* 1917, 336
188.	1852	Unidentified lady, medallion		[Exhib RA, London, 1398]; untraced		*Graves* VIII, 1905–6, 355
189.	1853	Charles Joseph Latrobe, medallion	b	Victoria State Lib, Melbourne Other versions: NPG, London, reduced size many others recorded	SD	*Read and Barnes* 1991, 145 (repr)
190.	1853	Farquahar Cole	p	Victoria State Lib, Melbourne, H26352	SD	
191.	1853	Rev James H Clow, medallion	p	Victoria State Lib, Melbourne, H36	SD	RG/JP, 9, 1634
192.	1853	Thomas Anne Cole	p	Victoria State Lib, Melbourne, H26352	SD	*Read and Barnes* 1991, 15
193.	1853–1854	A lady, medallion	b	Untraced		*Woolner* 1917, 337
194.	1853–1854	Admiral Philip Parker King, medallion	b	NPG, Canberra, Australia		*Woolner* 1917, 337; C Lib (repr)
195.	1853–1854	Charley Howitt, medallion	b	Untraced		*Woolner* 1917, 337
196.	1853–1854	Dr Bland	b	Untraced		*Woolner* 1917, 337
197.	1854	Edward William Terrick Hamilton, medallion	b	Mitchell lib, Sydney Other versions: City of Ballarat fine art gall, plaster others recorded in plaster	SD	*Read and Barnes* 1991, 146 (repr)
198.	1853–1854	George MacLeay, medallion	b	Untraced		*Woolner* 1917, 337

199.	1853–1854	George Ward Cole, late of Melbourne, Victoria	p	[Exhib RA, London, 1856, 1285]; Victoria State Lib, Melbourne, H 10583 LTS 18		*Graves* VIII, 1905–6, 355
200.	1854	James Macarthur, medallion	b	Mitchell Library, Sydney Other versions: Australiana Fund, Kirribilli House, plaster others recorded	SD	*Woolner* 1917, 337; *Read and Barnes* 1991, 146 (repr)
201.	1853–1854	Miss Edith Howitt	b	Untraced		*Woolner* 1917, 337
202.	1853–1854	Mr and Mrs John Pinney Bear, pair of medallions	p	Christie, 20 Feb 1992, lot 156; untraced		*Woolner* 1917, 337
203.	1853–1854	Mr Reynolds, medallion	b	Untraced		*Woolner* 1917, 337
204.	1853–1854	Octavius Browne	b	Untraced		*Woolner* 1917, 337
205.	1854	Oriana Fanning	p	Joanna Barnes Fine Arts, London	SD	*Read and Barnes* 1991, 148 (repr)
206.	1854	Sir Charles Augustus Fitzroy, medallion	b	Mitchell Lib, Sydney Other versions: University of Sydney, Australia	SD	*Read and Barnes* 1991, 145 (repr)
207.	1853–1854	Sir Charles Nicholson, medallion	b	Untraced		*Woolner* 1917, 337
208.	1854	Sir James Martin, medallion	b	Mitchell Lib, Sydney Other versions: University of Sydney others recorded		*Read and Barnes* 1991, 36, 147–8 (repr)
209.	1853–1854	Thomas Barker	b	Untraced		*Woolner* 1917, 337
210.	1853–1854	W Macarthur, medallion	b	Untraced		*Woolner* 1917, 337
211.	1854	William Charles Wentworth, plaque	b	[Exhib RA, London, 1856, 1282]; Birmingham MAG P.9 '97 Other versions: replicated	SD	*Read and Barnes* 1991, 147 (repr)
212.	1853–1854	William Fanning, medallion	p	Christie, 3 July 1985, lot 230; private coll		*Woolner* 1917, 337; *Read and Barnes* 1991, 148; C Lib (repr)
213.	1855	Thomas Carlyle, medallion	p	[Exhib RA, London, 1856, 1370]; SNPG Other versions: Carlyle's House, London, bronze SNPG, 1855, plaster NPG, 1241, plaster Gov Art Coll, 1855, plaster Walker, Liverpool, plaster Lion Foundry Co Kirkintilloch, private coll, iron plaque		*Graves* VIII, 1905–6, 355; *Ormond* 1973, 91 (repr 152)
214.	1855–1856	Alfred, Lord Tennyson, medallion	b	Private coll Other versions: NPG 3847, plaster Tate Britain, plaster others recorded	SD	*Read and Barnes* 1991, 40–1, 42, 49 (repr)
215.	1856	Charles Ernest Howitt, medallion		[Exhib RA, London, 1283]; untraced		*AJ*, 1894, 83; *Graves* VIII, 1905–6, 355
216.	1856	Emily Tennyson, medallion		[coll Tennyson family]; untraced Other versions: private coll		*Read and Barnes* 1991, 42
217.	1856	Helen F Orme		[Exhib RA, London, 1852, 1369]; untraced		*Graves* VIII, 1906, 355; *Woolner* 1917, 337
218.	1856	Mrs Neville, medallion		Untraced		*Woolner* 1917, 337
219.	1856	Robert Browning, medallion	b	Birmingham MAG inv P.97'47 Other versions: Wallington Hall, plaster Baylor University, Waco, Texas, bronze London art market, London, 1990, bronze J S Maas & Co, 1970, plaster cast Australian national gall, plaster Bronze, Sotheby, Billingshurst, 6 & 15 Nov 1990, lot 620.	SD	*Read and Barnes* 1991, 148 (repr); *Silber* 1987, 102–3, cat 317 (repr)
220.	1857	Robert Brownrigg, medallion		[Exhib RA, London, 1367]; untraced		*Graves* VIII, 1905–6, 355
221.	1857	Sir Thomas Fairbairn, medallion	b	[coll Sir Thomas Fairbairn]; private coll	SD	*Read and Barnes* 1991, 152 (repr)
222.	1859	Alexander A Knox, medallion	b	[Exhib RA, London, 1860, 993]; untraced		*Graves* VIII, 1906, 355; *Woolner* 1917, 338
223.	1859	Emily Tennyson, medallion	p	[Exhib RA, London, 1859, 1380]; Art Gall of South Australia, Adelaide Other versions: private coll, plaster	SD	*Read and Barnes* 1991, 42, 153 (repr)
224.	1859	George Warde Norman, medallion		[Exhib RA, London, 1379]; NPG, London (plaster cast)	S	*Graves* VIII, 1905–6, 355; C Lib (repr)
225.	1859	Rt Hon Stephen Lushington, medallion		Untraced		*Woolner* 1917, 338
226.	1860	Edward H T Crawford, MP, medallion	b	[Exhib RA, London, 992]; untraced		*Graves* VIII, 1905–6, 355
227.	1861	Rev William George Clark, medallion		[Exhib RA, London, 986]; untraced		*Graves* VIII, 1905–6, 355; *Woolner* 1917, 338
228.	1861	Sir Francis Palgrave, medallion	p	NPG, London	SD	*Graves* VIII, 1905–6, 355; *Ormond* 1973, 354 (repr 695)
229.	1864	Alfred, Lord Tennyson, portrait medallion		[Exhib RA, London, 1867, 1091]; Usher art gallery, Lincoln (examples in bronze and marble)		*Graves* VIII, 1905–6, 356; *Ormond* 1973, 452, 455
230.	1864	Rev W Gifford Palgrave, medallion	p	NPG, London		*Graves* VIII, 1905–6, 356; www.npg.org.uk

231.	1865	Emily Rhodes, medallion	p	Untraced		*Woolner* 1917, 338
232.	1867	Henry Christy, medallion	m	BM	S	*Woolner* 1917, 399; *Dawson* 1999, 71–2 (repr)
233.	1869	Charles Darwin, medallion (replicated by Wedgwood)	b	[Woolner sale, 1913, lot 123]; untraced		*Read and Barnes* 1991, 161
234.	1869	Mrs Hall, medallion		Untraced		*Woolner* 1917, 340
235.	1870	A H Novelli, medallion		Untraced		*Woolner* 1917, 340
236.	1870	'In Memoriam' (Four children in paradise)	p	[Exhib RA, London, 1222]; Nat gall of Victoria, Melbourne		*Read and Barnes* 1991, 161 (repr)
237.	1871	Feeding the hungry; Clothing the naked; Visiting the afflicted; Teaching the ignorant (The four acts of mercy)		['Instructing the ignorant' exhib RA, London, 1872, 1468]; Moore memorial fountain, Wigton, Cumberland		*Graves* VIII, 1905–6, 356; *Read* 1982, 163–4 (repr)
238.	1871	Mrs Hichins, medallion		[Exhib RA, London, 1295]; untraced		*Graves* VIII, 1905–6, 356
239.	1871	Virgilia bewailing the banishment of Coriolanus	m	St Mary's College, Strawberry Hill, Twickenham		*Graves* VIII, 1905–6, 356; *Read and Barnes* 1991, 30–2 (repr)
240.	1872	Frederick Denison Maurice, death mask, medallion	tc	NPG, London, 1397		*Ormond* 1973, 309–19 (repr 618)
241.	1872	In Memoriam G B		[Exhib RA, London, 1469]; untraced		*Woolner* 1917, fols 171, 341 (repr); *Graves* VIII, 1905–6, 356
242.	1872	Mercury teaching a shepherd boy to sing; design for the Charles Lucas medal for the Royal Academy of Music	p	[Exhib RA, London, 1576]; untraced		*Read and Barnes* 1991, 162–3 (silver version repr)
243.	1872	Mrs William Cleverly Alexander, medallion	m	[Exhib RA, London, 1570]; untraced		*Graves* VIII, 1905–6, 356
244.	1874	Achilles and Pallas shouting from the trenches	m	[Exhib RA, London, 1417, diploma work]; RA, London		*Graves* VIII, 1905–6, 356; *Gunnis* 1968, 444
245.	1874	The listening boy, sketch for an imaginary memorial to a deaf child	p	Untraced		*Woolner* 1917, fols 213, 341 (repr); *Read and Barnes* 1991, 32
246.	1875	Sir Cowasji Jehangir	m	[Exhib RA, London, 1876, 1422]; Edinburgh University	SD	*Read* 1982, 126, 128 (repr)
247.	1875	Winterbotham family member, medallion		Untraced		*Woolner* 1917, 342
248.	1876	Dr John Tyndall, medallion	b	[Exhib RA, London, 1490]; RI, London Other versions: RI, marble	SD	*Read and Barnes* 1991, 165; C Lib (repr)
249.	1877	Cockerell family member, medallion		Untraced		*Woolner* 1917, 342
250.	1878	John Owens, medallion	m	Owens College, Manchester, Lancs		*Woolner* 1917, 342
251.	1880	Joseph Chamberlain, medallion	m	Chamberlain memorial fountain, Chamberlain Square, Birmingham		*Noszlopy* 1998, 30 (repr)
252.	1881	Head of Bunyan	s	Untraced		*Woolner* 1917, 343
253.	1881	Head of Cromwell	s	Untraced		*Woolner* 1917, 343
254.	1881	Shakespeare		Untraced		*Woolner* 1917, 343
255.	1881	Thomas Carlyle		Birmingham, Warks		*Woolner* 1917, 343
256.	1882	Dorothy Woolner, the sculptor's daughter, b 1873, medallion	m	Birmingham MAG, inv P.51'48	SD	*Graves* VIII, 1905–6, 357; *Silber* 1987, 102–3, cat 318 (repr); *Read and Barnes* 1991, 166 (repr)
257.	1882	James Spedding, medallion	m	[Exhib RA, London, 1637]; Trinity College, Cambridge, chapel		*Graves* VIII, 1905–6, 357; *Ormond* 1973, 425
258.	1882	John, Baron Lawrence, commemorative medal (co-sculptor: Joseph Moore)	b	Birmingham MAG		*Read and Barnes* 1991, 166–7 (repr)
259.	1882	Science research medal, University College School, London		[Exhib RA, London, 1617]; untraced		*Graves* VIII, 1905–6, 357
260.	1882	Unidentified gentleman	m	Joanna Barnes Fine Art, London (1991)	SD	*Read and Barnes* 1991, 165 (repr)
261.	1883	Alice Gertrude Woolner (the sculptor's wife) medallion		Untraced		*Cox* 1981–2, 10, 12 n4
262.	1883	Clare Woolner, medallion		Untraced		*Woolner* 1917, 344
263.	1883	Phyllis Woolner, medallion		Untraced		*Woolner* 1917, 344
264.	1883	Walcott Leigh Browne, medallion	m	Untraced		*Woolner* 1917, 344
265.	1884	The water lily	b	Aberdeen art gall, DB 642-11		*Graves* VIII, 1905–6, 357; *Woolner* 1917, f306, 344 (repr)
266.	1885	James William Barclay, MP	b	[Exhib RA, London, 2089]; untraced		*Graves* VIII, 1905–6, 357; *Woolner* 1917, 344
267.	1885	Miss Currie, medallion	m	Untraced		*Woolner* 1917, 344
268.	1885	Mrs Barclay, medallion	b	[Exhib RA, London, 2085]; untraced		*Graves* VIII, 1905–6, 357
269.	1885	Mrs Mirrilees, medallion	m	[Exhib RA, London, 2093]; untraced		*Graves* VIII, 1905–6, 357; *Woolner* 1917, 344
270.	1889	Sir Joseph Whitworth, medallion	m	Manchester University, Lancs		*Graves* VIII, 1905–6, 357
Miscellaneous						
271.	1849	Grace dancing		Untraced		*Read* 1982, 53

WOONS, John fl 1761

An advertisement in the *Norwich Mercury*, on 26 September 1761, announced that John Woons, lately foreman to **Lock**, carver and gilder in St Andrew's, Norwich, had set up on his own account at premises facing St Peter's Hungate and proposed to carve in wood and stone.

WRAY, of Lincoln fl *c*1828–31

The Savage monument is a tablet in the Greek taste (1).

Funerary Monuments

1.	†1828	Poole Savage	Bassingham, Lincs	S	Pevsner, *Lincs*, 1989, 128
2.	†1832	Richard, 6th Earl of Scarborough	Saxby, Lincs	S	Pevsner, *Lincs*, 1989, 622; GPC

WRAY, Robert Bateman 1715–79

For further information the reader is referred to *Pyke* 1973, 158.

WRIGHT fl 1672–82?

Gunnis suggests that he may possibly be identified with a 'William Wright', who was apprenticed to **John Shortho** and became free in 1672. Webb lists this man as a husbandman to Shorthose on 27 April 1677.

Literary References: *Gunnis* 1968, 445; *Webb* 1999, 37

Chimneypieces

1.	1680	More than one, in cedar wood Payment(s): £120	[coll Duke of Newcastle]; untraced	*Throsby* 1795, 22
2.	*c*1680	More than one, in marble Payment(s): £52	[Nottingham Castle]; untraced	*Throsby* 1795, 22

WRIGHT, John, of Chester fl *c*1824–29

As a mason he was responsible for building St. Bridget's church, Chester, in 1827, executing the work 'in a superi style of elegance' (*Hemingway* 1931, II, 116). Gunnis notes that the monuments are Hellenistic in style and uninspiri in workmanship though Hemingway calls the Shaw family tablet (5) a beautifully executed work (*op cit*, 118). He w in partnership at one time with **Elizabeth Harrison of Chester** (3).

Funerary Monuments

1.	?1824	Margaret Hallon	Chester Cathedral	S	*Gunnis* 1968, 445
2.	?1826	Simeon Leet	St Oswald, Chester	S	*Gunnis* 1968, 445
3.	?1827	John Edgworth (co-sculptor: Elizabeth Harrison of Chester)	Marchwiel, Flint	S	*Gunnis* 1968, 189
4.	†1829	Jane Hughes	Llanfwrog, Denbighs	S	Pevsner, *Clwyd*, 1986, 213
5.	?1829	Shaw family	St Bridget, Chester	S	*Gunnis* 1968, 445

WRIGHT, Joseph fl 1778

Reliefs

1.	1778	Bas-relief, model	[RA silver medal]; untraced	RA Premium list

WRIGHT, of Derby fl 1704–12

Between 1704 and 1707 Wright was responsible for the architectural cutting of the exterior of Calke Abbey, for whi he received £176. In 1712 he was paid £88 for 'the new steps in the garden on the North east side of the house' (Harpu Crewe Archives, Calke Abbey, quoted in GPC).

WRIGHT, Patience 1725–86

A sculptor, wax modeller and wax-work manager, she was born in Bordentown, USA, and died in London. Py records that she was the earliest wax modeller in America. In 1769, after her husband died, she moved to New Yor where in 1771, she advertised the public exhibition of wax figures made by herself and her sister Rachel Wells in Ne York City. Early in 1772 after most of the wax figures had been destroyed by fire she came to London to set up h waxworks. Her recorded addresses were Great Suffolk Street, Strand and Pall Mall. She was employed by Wedgwo to model a portrait in wax of Benjamin Franklin. A number of wax medallions have been attributed to her.

In 1776 the *Gentleman's Magazine* published the following account of her activities: 'As it is now the general seas for exhibition, give me leave, through the channel of your Magazine, to recommend to the notice of the public t performances of a lady of very singular genius. Mrs. Wright of Chudleigh court, Pall-Mall, is one of the mo extraordinary women of the age. As an artist she stands alone; for it is not in memory, that there now exists a pers possessed of her abilities as a modeller in wax. In her present exhibition, if the busts of the King and Queen, the Du of Cumberland, Lord North, Lord Chatham, Lord Effingham, Lord Temple, Jonas Hanway, Dr. Wilson, John Wilk and others, were not sufficient proofs of her skill, that of the Rev. Mr. Gostling, of Canterbury, lately finished, wou be an incontestible evidence of her happy talent of preserving an admirable likeness, and coming the nearest to representation of life of any artist that ever attempted modelling . . . Mrs. Wright in the opinion of all who have se it, has acquitted herself incomparably in the bust of Mr. Gostling, having given his immediate appearance, witho the smallest deviation from the original' (*GM* 1776, 214–5).

Literary References: *Pyke* 1973, 158–9

Busts

1.	1773	Mr Hanway, model	w	[coll Marine Soc]; untraced	GPC
2.	1774	John, 3rd Duke of Atholl Payment(s): 12 gns		[coll Duke of Atholl]; untraced	GPC

Reliefs

3.	1774	George III and Queen Charlotte, two cameos	[coll Duke of Atholl]; untraced	RG/JP, 9, 1638 citing Archives, Duke of Atholl

Miscellaneous

4.	?pre-1772	Benjamin Franklin	[for Josiah Wedgwood]; untraced	Pyke 1973, 158

WRIGHT, Robert fl 1677–78

He was made free of the Masons' Company by service to **Thomas Shorthose** on 15 January 1677. When he marri Judith Jennings on 18 July 1678 he was described as 'of St. John's Street, London, Cit. and Mason, Bachr. about 2 (Lic Vic Gen).

Archival References: Masons' Co, *Freemen*, fol 72; GPC

WYATT, Edward 1757–1833

The first of his family to display a talent for wood carving, Wyatt was much involved in decorative schemes for roy palaces in the neoclassical, revived Gothic and Restoration styles. He was the son of John Wyatt, whose occupati is not known, and Sarah, née Fieldhouse. Wyatt married Ann Maddox and had four talented sons, William Madd who became clerk to the Office of Works, Edward, who followed in his father's profession, Henry John, an archite and **Richard James Wyatt**. His wider family included **Matthew Cotes Wyatt** and **James Wyatt**. Edward Wyatt ow much of his success to support from the architects James Wyatt the Elder, Jeffry Wyatville and Lewis Wyatt, all whom were kinsmen.

He began his career as a maker of picture frames with a shop at 360 Oxford Street, next to James Wyatt the Elder's fashionable assembly rooms, the Pantheon. In addition to picture frames he carved pier-glasses, girandoles and furniture. In 1798, through the influence of James Wyatt, who had recently become surveyor general and comptroller of the Office of Works, Wyatt was appointed carver and gilder to the Office of Works. Between 1800 and 1822 he was engaged on carving and gilding at Windsor Castle and Carlton House (**3, 7, 10, 12, 16, 17**). At Windsor he provided an exquisitely carved emblematic panel in limewood for the Queen's audience chamber (**7**) and in 1805, panels for a gallery in St George's Hall and other sundries, for which he charged £30 9s (TNA WORK 5/94). He worked again at Windsor under Wyatville *c*1824 (**17**).

His contribution to the redecoration of Carlton House for the Prince Regent was his greatest achievement (**16**). It entailed the total remodelling of the ground floor rooms as well as further adornment of the State Rooms, which had been created by the architect Henry Holland in the late 18th century and were further embellished under the supervision of James Wyatt. Edward designed some of the ornaments himself, including roundels for the ceilings in the scagliola room and panels depicting the Elements, Seasons and Virtues, executed in stucco for the drawing room. For the throne room he designed and executed four overdoors representing the Orders of the Garter, the Bath, St Patrick and St George in the form of swags made of their insignia. The blue velvet rooms were enhanced by Wyatt's elaborate pier glass frames and by 24 ornamented door panels, which were salvaged after the demolition of Carlton House in 1826 and rehung in the private apartments at Windsor Castle. John Martin Robinson has described them as among the most magnificent in England. Wyatt's principal source of inspiration was French 17th- and 18th-century woodcarving, probably known to him from engravings, though he spoke the language and may have visited France.

Wyatt was responsible for much other work for the Office of Works. As a stone carver, he provided gateposts with lions' heads and flowers for St James's Park, now incorporated in the forecourt screen of Buckingham Palace (**9**). In 1817 he was responsible for all the gothic woodwork, pews, pulpit and reading-desk in the new City church of St Dunstan-in-the-East and the following year he worked under Sir John Soane at Westminster Hall, where he repaired carved angels and completed the roof at the north end. Forty loads of well-seasoned oak from broken-up ships were used for this exercise.

His private commissions were largely under the aegis of his architect cousins (**11, 13, 14**). At Hackwood he carved four great swags of fruit and flowers to supplement carvings by Grinling Gibbons already in the house (**13**). These are among the earliest examples of the Restoration revival in England and have mistakenly been attributed to Gibbons, but Wyatt's accounts prove that he produced them in 1815 (Guildhall MS 3070A, Chesterfield House account book, cited by *Robinson*, 160 n8).

The success of his business enabled him to retire during the 1820s, when he bought a small country estate at Merton in Surrey. He also bought a property at Weybridge for William Maddox Wyatt, his eldest son. When he died on 5 January 1833 he bequeathed his house and farm to his wife, while to each of his five children he left £11,000. His second son, Edward (†1860) carried on the business. A tablet commemorating Wyatt and his wife Ann, who died in 1835, is on the exterior wall of Merton church, Surrey, at the south east corner.

IR

Literary References: *Gunnis* 1968, 446; *Colvin* VI, 1973–6, 58, 312–5, 376 n2; *Robinson* 1979 (2), 157–60; *Roberts* 1990, 168–71; *Colvin* 1995, 1107

Archival References: TNA WORK 5/103 (carving and gilding in seven parade rooms, Carlton House); TNA WORK 5/94 (carving panels for gallery in St George's Hall and mouldings to bookcase in His Majesty's Library £30 9s)

Portraits of the Sculptor: Sir Thomas Lawrence, nd, untraced (*Robinson* 1979 (2), 160; James Godby after Sir Thomas Lawrence, nd, coll John Martin Robinson (*Robinson* 1979 (2), repr 95)

Busts

1.	nd	Lady Catherine Stanhope	m	Chevening, Kent (1956)	S	GPC
2.	nd	Philip Henry, 4th Earl Stanhope	m	Chevening, Kent (1956)	S	GPC

Architectural Sculpture

3.	*c*1800	Rearrangement and extension of Grinling Gibbons's carvings	wd	Windsor Castle, state apartments	*Gunnis* 1968, 446; *Robinson* 1979 (2), 156
4.	1801–1802	Door frieze Payment(s): £3 13s 6d	wd	Castle Howard, N R Yorks, long gallery	Castle Howard archives, F4/9/37, p29
5.	1805	Pulpit Payment(s): £100 (part-payment)	wd	[St Paul's Cathedral, City of London]; untraced	Robert Mylne's Journals, cited in GPC
6.	1805	Pulpit		St Paul's Cathedral, London	GPC
7.	1807	Panel with Royal arms surrounded by emblems Payment(s): £176	wd	[Windsor Castle, Queen's audience chamber]; Royal Coll	*Roberts* 1990, 168–71
8.	1808	Altar piece and other work (under James Wyatt the Elder) Payment(s): £245 12s 7d	wd	[Doddington church, Worcs]; untraced	GPC citing Codrington Papers
9.	1808	Gate posts with nine lions' heads and twenty-four flowers	s	[St James's Park]; Buckingham Palace, London, forecourt screen	*Gunnis* 1968, 446; *Robinson* 1979 (2), 158
10.	1811	20 carved and gilded door panels, and pier glass frames	wd	[Blue velvet room, Carlton House, London]; Windsor Castle (doors only)	*Robinson* 1979 (2), 158–9 (repr)
11.	1801–1813	Gothic columns with foliage and animals (under James Wyatt the Elder)	s	Belvoir Castle, Rutland	*Robinson* 1979 (2), 158
12.	1806–1813	Gothic work for the grand staircase		Windsor Castle, state apartments	*Robinson* 1979 (2), 157
13.	1815	Drops representing the Seasons, in the style of Grinling Gibbons (under Lewis Wyatt)	wd	Hackwood Park, Hants, entrance hall	*Robinson* 1979 (2), 158, 160–1 (repr); Roberts 1990, 168
14.	1815	Stalls with pinnacled canopies in the chapel and other work (under Sir Jeffry Wyatville) Payment(s): £200	wd	[Ashridge Park, Bucks]; untraced	*Gunnis* 1968, 446; *Robinson* 1979 (2), 158
15.	1817	Pews, pulpit and reading desk in the Gothic style	wd	[St Dunstan-in-the-East, City of London]; destroyed	*Robinson* 1979 (2), 158

16.	1802–1822	Adornments to the ground-floor and State Rooms (under James Wyatt the Elder)	wd	[Carlton House, London]; destroyed	*Robinson* 1979 (2), 157–8 (designs repr 92)
17.	*c*1824	Carving and gilding (under Sir Jeffry Wyatville)	wd	Windsor Castle	*Robinson* 1979 (2), 157

WYATT, Henry fl 1814

Miscellaneous

1.	1814	Model after the Antique	[RA silver medal]; untraced	RA Premium list

WYATT, James 1808–93

James Wyatt was the second son of the sculptor **Matthew Cotes Wyatt**. His three brothers became architects bu James trained to be a sculptor so that he might join his father's practice, where he remained until Matthew Cote died in 1862. He also worked independently. James inherited a considerable fortune from his father and then retire from the business. He first married a widow, Mrs Read, by whom he had three children, two daughters and a so who became an engineer. The second marriage, to Miss Florence King, took place when he was 80.

Wyatt assisted his father from an early age. In 1849 he claimed to have spent 29 years 'upon works of ver considerable importance' sent out in his father's name and he listed the monument to Princess Charlotte in St George' Chapel, Windsor, 1826 and 'works' at Belvoir Castle including the statue of the 5th Duchess of Rutland, for which h was paid £500 for three years' labour at the age of 18 (letter from James Wyatt to Alfred Padley, 28 Jan 1849, BM Egerto MS 3515, quoted by *Robinson* 1979 (2), 188). He also apparently assisted with the statue of King George III in Cockspu Street, London, 1836, the controversial figure of the Duke of Wellington for Hyde Park Corner, 1838–46 'and work for George III and the late Lord Dudley' (*ibid*). He was particularly interested in equestrian subjects and designed th eight moulds used for casting the colossal Wellington statue.

He exhibited for the first time at the Royal Academy in 1838 with a marble statue of his young daughter entitle *Lilla asleep* (**3**). Two equestrian works were shown at the Academy in the 1840s (**4, 5**) and in 1844 he submitted a equestrian figure of Richard Coeur de Lion to the Westminster Hall exhibition, which was organised with the view of choosing sculptors to provide sculpture for the new Houses of Parliament (**6**). The statue was praised as 'a bol and spirited horse and rider, the former amazingly life-like, the action of the King just and appropriate' (*Lit Gaz* 1844, 482). The *Builder* (1844, 367) considered it 'of considerable beauty', but no commission for Parliament followed

Wyatt evidently inherited his father's taste for the theatrical, for in 1838 he was responsible for designing monument to Begum Sombre, a former dancing girl whose husband ruled the principality of Sirdhana in India (**2**) Allegorical figures adapted from Bernini's sculpture are placed in a crinkle-crankle gothic chapel, which has angel ascending above the altar. Nothing came of the project.

In 1848 he submitted a design for a bronze statue of Lord George Bentinck for the proposed Bentinck Memoria in the market-place at Mansfield, Notts (**7**). Since funds for the statue failed to materialise, the elaborate Gothi canopy designed by the architect Edward Davis was built without Bentinck's image inside.

Wyatt showed three works at the Great Exhibition of 1851, a model of a quadriga intended for a triumphal arch and equestrian statues of Queen Victoria and Prince Albert (**9, 10, 14**). *The Times* said of the prince's horse that it wa 'admirably modelled and comes nearer to life than any which quite recent art has produced' (*Gunnis*). It was late bought by the owner of the Coliseum, who displayed it outside the building.

James Wyatt had talents as a draftsman and sculptor, but was indolent, allowed himself to be overshadowed by hi more famous father, and comfortably settled to the life of a gentleman after Matthew Cotes died.

Sylvia Alle

Literary References: *Gunnis* 1968, 446; *Linstrum* 1974, 18; *Penny* 1977, 58–9; *Robinson* 1979 (2), 188–91; *Read* 1982, 93; *Munsell* 1991, 21, 24, 25, 73, 8

Miscellaneous Drawings: Album including drawings for and of sculpture, domestic sketches of the artist's family, and a design for a monumen to 'W Venables', perhaps Edward Frederick Venables (†1858) a hero of the Indian Mutiny, VAM E.1896-1948, 40, 118, 119, 164; *Mercury tying sandal*, nd, chalk, RIBA (*Robinson* 1979 (2), 189)

Funerary Monuments

1.	†1837	John Vanderspar, administrator in Ceylon		Untraced	S	RG/JP, 9, 1644
2.	1838	Begum Sombre (†1836) (designs only)		RIBAD; VAM 92D59		*Linstrum* 1974, 18; *Penny* 1977 (2), 58–9

Statues

3.	1838	Lilla asleep	m	[Exhib RA, London, 1254]; private coll, USA	*Graves* VIII, 1905–6, 374; *Robinson* 1979 (2), 189–91 (repr)
4.	1843	Mazeppa		[Exhib RA, London, 1460]; untraced	*Graves* VIII, 1905–6, 374; *Robinson* 1979 (2), 189
5.	1844	An Arab and his steed		[Exhib RA, London, 1334]; untraced	*Graves* VIII, 1905–6, 374; *Robinson* (2), 1979, 189
6.	1844	Richard Coeur de Lion		[Exhib Westminster Hall, London, 140]; untraced	*Lit Gaz*, 1436, 27 July 1844, 482; *Gunnis* 1968, 446; *Robinson* 1979 (2), 189
7.	1848	Lord George Bentinck, for the Bentinck memorial, Mansfield, design only		Untraced	*Robinson* 1979 (2), 189
8.	1850	Duke of Rutland (design only, monument by Edward Davis)		Untraced	*Robinson* 1979 (2), 180
9.	1851	Albert, the Prince Consort, equestrian		[Exhib Gt Exhib]; untraced	*Gunnis* 1968, 446; *Ormond* 1973, 12
10.	1851	Queen Victoria, equestrian		[Exhib Gt Exhib]; untraced	*Gunnis* 1968, 446; *Linstrum* 1974, 18, 24 n219
11.	nd	Field Marshall, Henry Viscount Hardinge, equestrian statuette		[Bank of Scotland, Edinburgh]; untraced	*Ormond* 1973, 214

Busts

12.	*c*1848	Lord George Bentinck	Untraced	*ILN*, 1 Nov 1848, 300; *Robinson* 1979 (2), 189

Architectural Sculpture

13.	1843–1846	Fruitfulness accompanied by Trade and Navigation, pediment sculpture, designed by Wyatt, executed by Alexander Handyside Ritchie Drawing(s): VAM 92D59; RIBAD, Wyatt MSS; BL Egerton MS 3515	Royal Bank of Scotland, George Street, Edinburgh	*ILN*, 18 June 1846; Robinson 1979 (2), 189
14.	1851	Model of a quadriga for a triumphal arch	[Exhib Gt Exhib]; untraced	*Gunnis* 1968, 446

WYATT, Matthew Cotes 1778–1862

Matthew Cotes Wyatt, one of the most controversial sculptors of his age, came from a creative family, several of whom practised as sculptors, painters and architects. He was born in London on 30 April 1778, the son of the architect, James Wyatt, and had a happy youth receiving his schooling at Eton College and idling away the summers at Hanworth. In 1801 he married Maria McClellan, a wealthy widow, who bore him four talented sons, three architects and the sculptor, **James Wyatt**, who became his assistant and executed most of his father's later designs.

Wyatt showed an early talent for miniature painting, which perhaps encouraged his father to enrol him at the Royal Academy Schools, where he studied drawing and painting. His first drawing, *Study for Head of Cerberus*, was exhibited at the Academy in 1800. His father's contacts as surveyor general soon brought commissions for Wyatt and in 1805 he began work on a lengthy and prestigious contract for decorative ceiling paintings in the newly remodelled state apartments at Windsor Castle. These were destroyed during restoration work directed by his cousin, Jeffrey Wyatville. Wyatt was also invited to paint 28 life-sized portraits of founding members of the order of the Garter for a new chapter house in St George's chapel. Plans to convert the adjacent Wolsey chapel for this purpose were not executed and none of the 21 portraits he completed have survived. He received £1,323 for these paintings.

In 1807, again supported by his father, who had influence with leaders of the Liverpool community, Wyatt submitted a design for the Nelson monument, to be sponsored by public subscription and sited in front of the new Exchange buildings (7). Several celebrated sculptors, including **John Flaxman RA, JCF Rossi RA, Joseph Nollekens RA, John Bacon RA, (Sir) Richard Westmacott RA** and a strong local contender, **George Bullock**, were invited to submit suggestions, but Wyatt's design, his first known drawing for a work of sculpture, was chosen. His dramatic concept was for an apotheosis of Nelson, accompanied by *Victory* and *Death*, enveloped in swirling captured flags. This group was set on a drum decorated with four reliefs of Nelson's greatest victories, interspersed with figures of shackled prisoners of war. Since the execution of the design was beyond Wyatt's powers at this time, Westmacott cast the bronze statue. The monument was prepared in Westmacott's studio and visitors commended him for successfully completing the largest and best executed work of its kind (*Liverpool Mercury*, 22 October 1813, cited by *Yarrington* 1988, 127). It was unveiled on the 21 October 1813, the eighth anniversary of Nelson's death at Trafalgar.

After the death of Wyatt's father in 1813, commissions for paintings from the Office of Works abruptly ceased. Wyatt decided to concentrate his energies on sculpture by teaching himself modelling and carving. Little is known about this period of his life except that he went to wrestling matches to make close studies of human anatomy.

In 1815 the Government invited leading artists to submit designs for a national *tropheum* to celebrate the nation's victories during the Napoleonic Wars. Wyatt and his younger brother Philip presented a grandiose design for a pyramid 360ft high consisting of 22 terraces, each decorated with bronze reliefs commemorating a year of the conflict. This was to be surmounted by a statue of George III and placed in the King's Mews next to St Martin-in-the-Fields (**24**). It was not executed.

On 6 November 1817, the Prince Regent's only child, Princess Charlotte Augusta, died in childbirth. Such was the nation's sorrow that a fund was opened for a memorial, to be raised by public subscription, limited to 1/- a head. The appeal brought in over £12,000. Wyatt provided the model for a proposed memorial and his personal connexions with the royal family gained him the commission (5). The group, which was originally intended to be placed in a temple, perhaps in a public park, was almost complete by April 1820, when it could be viewed in the sculptor's studio in Henrietta Street. In February 1824 it was decided to house it in the Urswick chantry in St George's Chapel, Windsor, despite objections that this was not a sufficiently public site. It was finally unveiled in 1826. Wyatt created a startling image, which had no real precursor in English funerary art, but may have been inspired by Arthur William Devis's painting of the *Apotheosis of Princess Charlotte* in St George's church, Esher, Surrey. The Princess lies covered by a shroud with the fingers of one limp hand protruding to macabre effect. She is attended by four, completely veiled, kneeling figures, thought at the time to represent the four quarters of the globe (*GM*, 1826, 350). Above the pitiful scene and in sharp contrast, the Princess bursts theatrically from an open tomb and soars upwards, accompanied by two angels, one of whom holds her child. Wyatt's intention, to express the grimness of death and boldly assert Christian hopes of resurrection, met the public mood and made his reputation.

After the death of George III in 1820 a committee was formed to erect a memorial to his memory, by public subscription (**15**). Wyatt was invited to submitted a design because of 'the long connection of his family with the late King' (*GM*, 1822, pt 1, 268–9). His sketch of the king standing in a quadriga attended by two angels was rejected as too costly and a simpler design, an equestrian portrait of the King on his favourite charger, *Adonis*, was instead chosen. Waterloo Place was selected as the appropriate site for the statue until the committee realised that a statue of the Duke of York on a column nearby would overshadow his father's memorial, whilst also turning his back upon it. When Cockspur Street was chosen as an alternative location, a banker in Pall Mall took out an injunction against the erection of the statue opposite his premises. Much time and expense was wasted before the Lord Chancellor gave his verdict that the Cockspur Street plan should be implemented. There were further problems when a section of the mould for the horse was sabotaged and part of the statue had to be recast. On 3 August 1836, 14 years after its inception, the statue was eventually unveiled by the unpopular Duke of Cumberland and the ceremony was disrupted by an unruly mob. It was described as a 'burlesque effigy' (*The Times*, 4 August 1836), and the king's image, in a pigtailed riding wig, earned Cockspur Street the nickname Pigtail Place.

The Duke and Duchess of Rutland were loyal patrons of the Wyatt family and they employed Matthew Cotes an his brothers Benjamin and Philip in the restoration of Belvoir Castle after a fire. M C Wyatt, assisted by his son Jame designed the new Elizabeth saloon, providing painted ceilings and a marble statue of the duchess (**9**). He supplied *trompe-l'oeil* table for an immense silver wine cooler for the dining room (**29**) and a marble fireplace for the rege gallery (**22**). The duchess died unexpectedly in 1825 and the Wyatt brothers were commissioned to build a gran mausoleum at the Castle. M C Wyatt's memorial to the Duchess was completed by 1829 and depicts her rising fro the tomb with arms extended to greet her four dead children (**4**). It is lit through richly coloured stained glass, whic gives drama to the darkened interior of the mausoleum. The monument has been described as Wyatt's masterpiec but better seen from a distance since the modelling does not stand up to close scrutiny (*Robinson* 1979 (2), 188).

In 1831 Wyatt was approached by Lord Dudley to have his favourite Newfoundland dog, Bashaw, immortalised i marble (**11**). Wyatt was asked to produce not only a good likeness but also his best work, regardless of cost. There wa a promise of extensive further patronage at his lordship's estate at Himley. Bashaw himself sat for the sculptor o numerous occasions in London and the statue was nearly complete when Lord Dudley died in 1833. His trustees an executors refused to honour the agreement to pay Wyatt the expected 5,000 guineas. The extraordinary statue cause a stir when it became the centrepiece of an exhibition in Wyatt's studio, for it was unprecedented in intricacy. The life sized dog had a coat carved from black, grey and white marble, eyes composed of gems and, beneath its foot, a bronz boa-constrictor with a forked tongue and protruding ruby eyes. Wyatt felt that the matter of payment should b referred to the courts, but nothing was done. The dog was exhibited at Wyatt's show of his own work held in the gre room, 21 Old Bond Street, London in 1834, where he also showed a 'lay figure' of a horse with metallic pivots on whic the joints turned, so that a number of attitudes could be contrived. The dog was then forgotten until it was exhibite at the Great Exhibition in 1851 with the title *The Faithful Friend of Man Trampling underfoot his most Insidious Enem* Wyatt remained bitter about his treatment by Lord Dudley's executors and added a clause to his will stipulating th if any descendant of Lord Dudley should wish to buy the figure they should be obliged to pay the full 5,000 guinea

In 1837 the City of London resolved to erect a statue of the Duke of Wellington, in recognition of his assistance wi the London Bridge Approaches Act of 1827. Wyatt was proposed as executant, but the contract went to **Sir Franc Chantrey RA**. Later in the same year it was decided to erect a memorial commemorating the Duke of Wellington military achievements and a Wellington military memorial committee was duly set up, chaired by the Duke Rutland. By 1838, £14,000 had been raised by subscription and it was resolved that the memorial should take the for of a bronze equestrian statue, to be placed above the triumphal arch at Hyde Park Corner (**17**). Wyatt was selected sculptor but angry letters appeared in the papers condemning the selection of artist without competition and the u of a great triumphal arch as a mere pedestal. Wyatt nonetheless started work on a design, choosing to depict the Duk seated on his favourite horse, *Copenhagen*, at the close of the battle of Waterloo. The committee approved the desig and Wyatt signed a contract which accorded him £30,000.

Before work could start, a special studio with a roof 30 feet high had to be constructed next to his studio in Harro Road, Paddington. Wyatt and his son James spent the next two years working on a huge model in plaster of paris. It too three years to cast the statue, in eight pieces, using bronze from French cannon captured at Waterloo. When complete the statue weighed over 40 tons and was large enough for a party of eight people to dine comfortably within the bod of the horse. In September 1846 the roof and one wall of the foundry were removed and the statue was manoeuvred ont a special carriage designed by Wyatt, weighing nearly twenty tons. On 28 September the statue made its one and a ha hour journey to Hyde Park Corner hauled by 29 dray horses and accompanied by military detachments and their band

It was greeted with derision. Every newspaper was hostile, questions were asked in Parliament and the RIB condemned both the equestrian figure and its position on the arch, calling for its removal, a view endorsed by th Queen and Prince Albert. At this stage the duke himself made it known that he would consider the removal the statue a personal insult and he threatened to resign as commander-in-chief. Faced with this prospect, th controversy collapsed and the statue remained on the Arch. Over the next 37 years Londoners became accustomed t seeing it and even came to regard it with some affection. In 1883, when Parliament resolved to make improvemen to Hyde Park Corner, the statue was finally removed from the arch. It remained at ground level for a year before bein offered to the army who re-sited it at Aldershot.

Wyatt did not live to see the banishment of the most controversial of all his works. He died at his home at Dudle Grove House, Harrow Road, Paddington, on 3 January 1862 and was buried at Highgate Cemetery. He had amasse a fortune of just under £80,000, thanks in part to family connections and a judicious marriage, but principally to successful career. It is now generally recognised that his principal talent was as an imaginative designer, but that th finished works, which were executed largely by assistants, were at times disappointing.

Sylvia Alle

Literary References: *GM* 1862, 241 (brief notice of death); *Tallis* 1951, III, 11; *Gunnis* 1968, 446–8; *Physick* 1969, 42; *Linstrum* 1974, 17; *Penny* 19 (1), 314–32; *Penny* 1977 (1), 11, 12, 13, 56–9, 214 n48; *Robinson* 1979 (2), 173–88; *Yarrington* 1983, 315–29; *Yarrington* 1988, 124–8, 267; *Whinney* 198 422; *Colvin* 1995, 730, 1105, 1110; *Grove* 33, 1996, 447–8 (Robinson); *Cavanagh* 1997, 51–5; *Phillimore*, 2002, XIV; *Bilbey* 2002, 437–8; *ODN* (O'Donoghue, rev. JM Robinson)

Archival References: Agreement between Westmacott and the committee for Nelson's monument, Liverpool, 25 April 1818, Liverpool PRO 73 /Ge 2/11, cited by *Yarrington* 1988, 124; Wyatt family papers, RIBA drawings coll WY 3/1/28; family corr, NAL MSL/1948/3143–3144, (including lette from Wyatt to John, Duke of Rutland and to Charles, Marquis of Londonderry; payments for paintings for the Wolsey Chapel, St George Chapel, Windsor, TNA WORK 5/103; decorative work for the Royal Mint, PRO Works 5/112; sketch for an heraldic crest in the shape of a quatre foil, 26 July 1862, RIBA drawings, J13/68; sketch for a jewelled coronet, RIBA drawings, J13/69; James Wyatt the Younger, album of drawings of ar for sculpture including several relating to the Wellington statue, one of Queen Victoria exhib 1851, one of *St George and the dragon*

Additional MS Sources: Two letters from Soane to Wyatt, NAL, cited in the catalogue of non-illuminated MSS, National Art Lib, 1975, 89

Will: Draft, 10 November 1858, RIBA Wy Fam/1/10; FRC, Eyre and Spottiswood, Microfiche 6/98

Miscellaneous Drawings: Design for a low relief in St George's Hall, Windsor, Royal Coll RL 17613; design for a monument to George III in th form of a quadriga, RIBAD

Handbill for Wyatt's exhibition at the great room, 21 Old Bond St in 1834, coll Derek Linstrum (xerox HMI)

Auction Catalogues: M C Wyatt (1), 16 June 1860 (untraced); M C Wyatt (2), 20 June 1862 (untraced); M C Wyatt (3), 2–3 July 1862; M C Wya (4) 25 February 1881

Funerary Monuments

No.	Date	Subject		Location		Literature
1.	†1813	Rt Hon Isaac Corry		Newry, Co Down	S	*Potterton* 1975, 88; *Robinson* 1979, (2), 179, 250
2.	†1821	Robert Darling Willis MD and Francis Willis (†1831)		Greatford, Lincs	S	Pevsner, *Lincs*, 1989, 328
3.	†1823	Charlotte Pigott		Quainton, Bucks	S	*Robinson* 1979 (2), 250; Pevsner, *Bucks*, 1994, 608
4.	†1825	Elizabeth, 5th Duchess of Rutland		Belvoir Castle, Leics, mausoleum		*Gunnis* 1968, 447; *Penny* 1977 (1), 56–9 211, n32 (repr); *Robinson* 1979 (2), 188, 250; *Yorke* 1994, 6205
5.	1818–1826	Princess Charlotte Augusta (†1817) Drawing(s): RIBA J13/74 (1–2), 1817–18		St George's Chapel, Windsor Castle	S	*Graves* 1875, 612; *Gunnis* 1968, 446; *Linstrum* 1974, 17; *Liscombe* 1976, 35, 37 (repr); *Robinson* 1979, (2), 180–2, 250 (repr 106); *Bond* 1999, 67
6.	*c*1834	Richard Thompson (†1820)		Escrick, E R Yorks	S	Pevsner, *Yorks: E R & York*, 1995, 406

Statues

No.	Date	Subject		Location		Literature
7.	1807–1813	Admiral Lord Nelson (co-sculptor: Sir Richard RA Westmacott RA) Model(s): exhib BI 1808, 486; great room, 21 Old Bond St, London, 1834	b	[Liverpool Town Hall, quadrangle]; Exchange flags, Liverpool, Lancs		*Graves* 1875, 611; *Linstrum* 1974, 17, 24n 207; *Penny* 1976 (2), 547–8; *Robinson* 1979, (2), 177–9, 250; *Read* 1982, 91; *Yarrington* 1983, 315–28; *Yarrington* 1988, 124–8; *Busco* 1994, 29, 43, 46–51 (repr); *Morris* 2002, 26–8 (repr)
8.	1821	Henry, 1st Marquess of Anglesey, equestrian statuette	i	['Study in ivory, from the Marquess of Anglesea' exhib BI, London, 1821, 319]; untraced		*Graves* 1875, 612; *Gunnis* 1968, 448
9.	1826	Elizabeth, 5th Duchess of Rutland	m	Belvoir Castle, Leics, Elizabeth saloon		*Gunnis* 1968, 447; *Penny* 1977 (1), 58–9; *Robinson* 1979, (2), 186; *Yorke* 1994, 62–5
10.	1831	Frederick-Augustus, Duke of York and Albany, for Duke of York's column, model, competition design		Untraced		Stratfield Saye MSS, Corr; *Robinson* 1979 (2), 250
11.	1831–1834	Bashaw, 'the faithful friend of man', Lord Dudley's favourite Newfoundland dog Payment(s): asking price: £5,000		[Sculptor's studio, until 1862]; VAM A.4-1960		RIBA WyFam/1/3–10; Wyatt exhibition handbill, 1834; *Harris* 1957, 1085; *Robinson* 1979, (2), 184–6, 250 (repr 109); *Bryant* 1983 (2); *Cavanagh* 1997, 51–5; *Bilbey* 2002, 437–8 (repr) *Linstrum* 1974, 18, 24 nn212–5
12.	by 1834	Head of a horse, coloured		[Wyatt's exhibition, great room, 21 Old Bond Street, London]; untraced		Wyatt exhibition handbill, 1834
13.	by 1834	Horse, colossal, perhaps a model for the statue of King George III erected in Cockspur Street	p	[Wyatt's exhibition, the great room, 21 Old Bond Street, London]; untraced		Wyatt exhibition handbill, 1834
14.	by 1834	'lay' figure of a horse with metallic pivots allowing the joints to turn in various directions		[Wyatt's exhibition, the great room, 21 Old Bond Street, London]; untraced		Wyatt exhibition handbill, 1834
15.	1835–1836	King George III, equestrian Payment(s): £4,000	b	Cockspur St, London		*GM* 1822, pt 1, 268–9 (repr); RIBA Wy Fam/1/3–10; *Gunnis* 1968, 446–7; *Linstrum* 1974, 18, 24 nn 216–7; *Robinson* 1979, (2), 182–4, 250 (repr 107); *Yarrington* 1988, 254–5; *Blackwood* 1989, 48–9 (repr); *Ward-Jackson* 2003, 330–34
16.	1844	St George and the dragon, intended for St George's Hall, Windsor; horse and dragon without St George cast 1844 Drawing(s): RIBA J13/70; Stratfield Saye		[Incomplete model, sculptor's studio until 1851, when cast in bronze for the Great Exhibition]; Stratfield Saye, Hants		Wyatt Exhibition handbill, 1834; *CH*, 1951, 1195; *Gunnis* 1968, 447; Pevsner, *Hants & Isle of Wight*, 1967, 615; *Robinson* 1979, (2), 184, 250
17.	1838–1846	Arthur, 1st Duke of Wellington, equestrian (co-sculptor: James Wyatt the Younger) Drawing(s): VAM E.1896 (146) -1948 (by M C Wyatt); RIBA (by James Wyatt)	b	[Constitution Arch, Hyde Park Corner, London]; Round Hill, Aldershot, Hants (since 1883)		RIBA WyFam/1/9/12–15 and 1/3–10; *Physick* 1966 (1), 1076–7 (repr); *Physick* 1969, 42, 183–5 (repr); *Robinson* 1979, (2), 186–8, 250; *Read* 1982, *passim* (repr); *Munsell* 1991, *passim*; *Morris* 2002, 34; *Ward-Jackson* 2003, 330–34

Busts

No.	Date	Subject		Location		Literature
18.	1810	King George III Payment(s): £157 10s	b	[Treasury Board Room, London; Wyatt sale, 1862]; Gov Art Coll, 156 Other versions: for the board room at the treasury, 1811; now at British Embassy, Lisbon Wyatt sale, 20 June 1862; untraced		NAL,MSL/1948/3143/38 (1810); *Graves* 1905–6, VIII, 375; *Gunnis* 1968, 448; *Robinson* 1979 (2), 179, 250
19.	1821	Princess Charlotte Augusta	m	Manchester CAG 1984.28	SD	

20.	1820–1824	Princess Charlotte Augusta		Brighton Pavilion, Sussex		*Robinson* 1979 (2), 250
21.	c1826	Elizabeth, 5th Duchess of Rutland	m	Castle Howard, N R Yorks Other versions: Belvoir, Leics, stairwell, c1826	S	*Gunnis* 1968, 448; *British Portraits* 1956–7, 106; *Robinson* 1979 (2), 250
Chimneypieces						
22.	c1826	Marble		Belvoir Castle, Leics, regent gallery		*Robinson* 1979, (2), 186
23.	1829	Two Payment(s): £1,050	m	[Buckingham Palace, London, armouries]; untraced		*Colvin* VI, 1973–6, 299
Architectural Sculpture						
24.	1815	Waterloo monument, designs only, by Wyatt and his brother Philip		[for the King's Mews, Charing Cross, London]; Royal Lib, drawings and corr, 12168		*Robinson* 1979 (2), 179–80, 250 (repr 105)
25.	1816	Decorative work		[Royal Mint, London]; untraced		TNA WORK 5/112; *Gunnis* 1968, 446
Reliefs						
26.	nd	Two small portraits of horses, high relief	b	[ex coll King George IV]; untraced		*Gunnis* 1968, 448
Miscellaneous						
27.	1811	Seal depicting Commerce		Corporation of Liverpool		*Robinson* 1979 (2), 250
28.	1832	A horse's head, studied from nature and executed in bronze	b	[Exhib Soc of BA, London, 844]; untraced		*Johnson* 1975, 524
29.	nd	Trompe l'oeil side table for a punch bowl	m	Belvoir Castle, Leics, dining room		*Gunnis* 1968, 447; *Robinson* 1979, (2), 186, 250 (repr 110); *Yorke* 1994, 62–5

WYATT, Richard James 1795–1850

A member of the Wyatt family of architects and sculptors, Richard James Wyatt was the fourth son of the carver Edward Wyatt and Ann Maddox. He was born above his father's shop in Oxford Street, London on 3 May 1795 and was apprenticed in 1809 to J C F Rossi, who gave him a good practical grounding. Whilst with Rossi, Wyatt carved a number of marble chimneypieces and simple memorial tablets, the stock in trade of an English sculptor (1, 2). He entered the Royal Academy Schools in 1812 and in 1815 won the silver medal for the best model from life. His first life-size classical group, a *Judgement of Paris* (14) was exhibited in 1818, when he was perhaps formulating an ambition to go to Rome and complete his training under Antonio Canova. Sir Thomas Lawrence, who had met Canova in London in 1815, recommended Wyatt to him and the Italian apparently intimated that he might find Wyatt a place in his studio.

In 1820 Wyatt left England for Paris where he spent a period in the studio of the distinguished sculptor, Baron François-Joseph Bosio. Bosio was known for the smooth, warm surfaces of his statues and probably taught Wyatt something of his technique. He arrived in Rome early in 1821 with letters of introduction to Canova both from Sir Thomas Lawrence, and from a cousin, the architect, Sir Jeffry Wyatville. Canova took Wyatt into his studio, where he met another ex-patriot sculptor, **John Gibson**, who had already been in Rome for four years. They became lifelong friends. After Canova died in 1822 Gibson and Wyatt worked briefly under **Bertel Thorvaldsen** before setting up independently in studios opposite one another in the Via della Fontanella Barberini. Gibson, who was five years older than Wyatt and acted as his protector, described Wyatt at this time as 'remarkably modest, retiring and very shy, an excellent judge of art' (*Matthews* 1911, 134) The two young sculptors formed part of the expatriot community in Rome which included **Joseph Gott, William Theed II** and **George Rennie**.

Wyatt was known for his extraordinarily long working hours. He rose early and breakfasted daily with Gibson at the Caffé Greco at 86, Via Condotti, the haunt of writers, musicians and artists visiting the city. The two sculptors read the newspapers before walking on the Pincio and returning to their studios for a day's work. Wyatt often remained in his studio until after midnight. In his early years he worked without assistants. Gibson noted that it was his habit to make a preliminary model which he put away for six or more months, before assessing its potential. If it then pleased him he translated it to a small plaster model and then to a full-size plaster model with scale-marks to guide the marble-carver. Even at the end of his career when he was in high demand, he finished his works himself, unlike many of his contemporaries who left all the marble carving to assistants.

Soon after setting up on his own Wyatt had the fortune to receive an order from the Duke of Devonshire, who visited Rome in 1822 with Sir Jeffry Wyatville. This was for a marble version of Wyatt's plaster of *Musidora*, a subject from Thomson's *Seasons*, that would be re-interpreted endlessly by sculptors over the next 20 years (**15**). It was dispatched to Chatsworth in 1824. Though the Duke was well pleased with his statue, it was several years before further commissions came to Wyatt. In 1829, the year Wyatt had a riding accident which left him lame for life, an unidentified visitor, who contributed to the *Literary Gazette*, saw several works to the studio ordered by English clients (**5, 16, 18**). By 1830 he was in considerable demand for ideal statues and groups and from 1831 until his death he exhibited a new work every year at the Royal Academy, though he had a poor opinion of the way sculpture was displayed there. He was proposed for membership of the Academy by his friend Charles Eastlake, later director of the National Gallery, but the proposal was over-ruled by **Sir Francis Chantrey** on the grounds that Wyatt was not a British resident. Since the qualification had been waived in John Gibson's case, Chantrey's opposition was probably caused by jealousy. The hostility was mutual: the outspoken Wyatt felt Chantrey lacked taste and was a poor carver of draperies. Wyatt also expressed a poor opinion of the sculptors who had supplied monuments for St Paul's Cathedral, particularly **Sir Richard Westmacott RA**.

Wyatt's art came to maturity during the 1830s. He was responsible for some fine monuments and busts, but it was as a virtuoso carver of life-size figures and groups, particularly single female figures, that he became best-known. He made copies of his most popular subjects, often several years after completing the original work. The statue of a *Nymph going to the bath* (**19**) was repeated at least seven times for British clients over a 13-year span and he produced two variants, *Nymph at the bath* and *Nymph coming out of the bath* (**28, 34**) both of which were replicated. Another popular subject, a *Nymph of Diana*, was re-worked with various animals, a leveret, a leveret and greyhound and a dead bird (**18, 26, 47**). These groups were based on antique originals but also responded to the contemporary enthusiasm for the depiction of animals. Wyatt's portrait busts were noted for their realism, particularly the head of Lord Selsey, (**64**), now lost but considered a striking likeness by a contemporary, Lady Anne Murray, and the portrait of the Marquess of Anglesey, which presents the sitter with stern features and the heroic aura of a Roman general (**63**).

Wyatt's debt to his masters in Italy is evident in his works of the 1830s. The *Musidora, Ino and Bacchus, Flora and Zephyr*, and *Shepherd boy protecting his sister from the storm* are all reminiscent of Canova's ideal works (**15, 17, 25, 27**). The model for the group of the *Shepherd boy* was apparently coloured, and since it prefigures Gibson's first attempts in polychromy by three years, it suggests that Wyatt had some interest in experiment. His monument to Charlotte Buller (**6**) is reminiscent of Canova's monument to the Marchesa di Haro, 1806–8 at Possagno: it is a death-bed scene with a recumbent effigy attended by two mourners, one kneeling and the other leaning over her. The relief tablet to Ellen Legh (**7**) is more ambitious: she is met by an angel pointing to Heaven and turns away from her husband who mourns, hand on brow, holding their child. The influence of Thorvaldsen, whose plaster models were accessible to Wyatt, is evident in Wyatt's statues of children (**20, 23, 24**), which owe debts to the Dane's statue of Lady Georgiana Russell, 1815, at Woburn Abbey. The source for Wyatt's relief tablet to Ellen Legh is probably Thorvaldsen's monument to Philip Bethman-Hollweg, 1814, at Frankfurt-am-Main. Wyatt's monument has an angel leading Mrs Legh away, while her grieving husband is left behind with the baby. It has been described by John Martin Robinson as 'a masterpiece with its perfect composition and austerely understated emotion' (*Robinson* 1979 (2), 166).

He reached his zenith in the 1840s. In 1841 he visited England for the only time since settling in Rome, the city he so loved. The Prince Consort commissioned a statue of *Penelope* for the entrance to the Queen's apartments at Windsor Castle (**41**), the first of five works for or bought by Queen Victoria (**26, 40, 41, 46, 47**). Wyatt's obituary in the *Art-Journal* in 1850 singles out the *Penelope* as the work most admired by his friends in Rome.

In 1848, the year of revolutions, there was a major political upheaval in Rome, culminating in Garibaldi's triumphal entry into the city and an upsurge of Italian nationalist feeling. English artists suffered: Gibson left the city and Wyatt was asked to release his studio in the Via della Fontanella. Though he took a new one in the Via dei Incurabile he never moved there. The proposed eviction upset him greatly and further distress was caused by bombardment of the city by the French, and then by a grenade which exploded in his studio, inflicting minor injuries on him and destroying some of his plaster casts. When Queen Victoria heard from Gibson of the misadventure she ordered another statue from Wyatt as recompense.

Wyatt died on 28 May 1850 from a neglected cold, which led to a throat infection and subsequent suffocation. He was buried in the English cemetery in Rome and his funeral was attended by nearly 50 artists and friends. Gibson carved his tombstone with a medallion portrait and the effusive epitaph 'His works were universally admired for their purity of taste, grace and truth of nature. The productions of his genius adorn the Royal Palaces of England, St Petersburg and Naples as well as the residences of the nobility and gentry of his own country' (*Matthews* 1911, 136).

He died intestate but is computed to have executed works in his lifetime worth at least £20,000. The Liverpool sculptor **Benjamin Spence** took over his studio in the Via dei Incurabile and he and Gibson completed Wyatt's unfinished works, a *Nymph of Diana* for the Queen, Lord Charles Townsend's version *of A Nymph taking a thorn out of a greyhound's foot* and a version of the *Nymph coming out of a bath* for Mr Foot of Read Hall, Lancs (**26, 46, 34**). The few statues left in the old studio were sold at Christie's on 22 June 1861. His personal possessions, including the Royal Academy silver medal won in 1815, went to his niece. In 1851 a number of casts of his statues were shown at the Great Exhibition, as well as the *Glycera* from the Royal collection and *The Infant Bacchus* (**40, 44**). He was awarded one of the four first-class gold medals retrospectively.

During his later years Wyatt was much revered, particularly for the delicate beauty of his female figures, his mastery of composition and the excellent surface finish of his works. Since his largely aristocratic patrons continued to clamour for Wyatt's figures in the tradition of Canova over a 20-year span, his style developed astonishingly little. The declining interest in neoclassicism in the later 19th century inevitably led to a loss of enthusiasm for his work, which is still current. The only recent survey of his life and achievement forms a part-chapter in John Martin Robinson's biography of the Wyatt family, subtitled 'An Architectural Dynasty'.

IR

Literary References: *A J*, 1850, 246–7; 1854, 352; *Matthews* 1911, 110–12, 130–36; *Gunnis* 1968, 448–9, *Linstrum* 1974, 18; *Penny* 1975 (1), 322; *Robinson* 1979 (2), 160–73; *Read* 1982, 37; *Grove* 33, 448–9 (Robinson)

Archival References: Wyatville/Canova, 5 Feb 1821; GPC

Miscellaneous Drawings: 'Tuning' (two figures with lyre and pipe, for a relief), NPG, *c*1850

Portraits of the Sculptor: John Partridge, 1825, NPG (3944/19) George K Childs, engraving, nd, *AJ*, 1850, 246; attrib S Pearce, oil on canvas, nd (*Robinson* 1979 (2), repr 96)

Auction Catalogue: Wyatt, R J, 1861

Funerary Monuments

1.	pre-1815	Unidentified subject	[St John's Wood Chapel, Marylebone, London]; untraced		*Robinson* 1979 (2), 254
2.	†1819	Captain Hughes RN and his wife Maria	St George, Esher, Surrey		*Robinson* 1979 (2), 163, 254
3.	1819	Lady Ann Hudson (†1818) Model(s): Exhib RA, London, 1819, 1240	Bessingby, E R Yorks	S	*Graves* VIII, 1905–6, 376; *Robinson* 1979 (2), 163, 254; Pevsner, *Yorks ER & York*, 1995, 277
4.	†1827	C R Beaumont	Kirkheaton, W R Yorks		GPC
5.	1829	Lady Barrington	[Artist's studio, Rome]; untraced		*Lit Gaz*, no 652, 18 July 1829, 746; *Robinson* 1979 (2), 254
6.	1829–1831	Charlotte Buller (†1829)	Poltimore, Devon		*Lit Gaz*, no 652, 18 July 1829, 746; *Penny* 1975 (1), 322; *Robinson* 1979 (2), 251; Pevsner, *Devon*, 1989, 688; C Lib (repr)

7.	†1831	Ellen Legh		Winwick, Lancs	S	*Penny* 1975 (1), 49, 322–3 repr; *Robinson* 1979, 166, 254 (repr 103); *CIIA* 4/8/139–144 (repr)
8.	1832	Members of the family of Captain James Cook		Merton, Surrey	SD	*Gunnis* 1968, 449; *Robinson* 1979 (2), 254
9.	1832	Rear-Admiral Isaac Smith and three family members		Merton, Surrey	SD	Pevsner, *London: S*, 1983, 438
10.	1835	Monumental alto-relievo	m	[Exhib RA, London, 1133]; untraced		*Graves* VIII, 1905–6, 376
11.	1835	Relief for an unidentified monument	m	[Exhib RA, London, 1133]; untraced		*Graves* VIII, 1905–6, 376
12.	1838	Elizabeth Bayley (†1830)		Meopham, Kent	SD	Pevsner, *Kent: W & Weald*, 1976, 418; *Robinson* 1979 (2), 255
13.	By 1844	Figure of Resignation, part of a design for a monument		Untraced		*Le Grice* 1844, I, 92

Statues

14.	1818	Judgement of Paris, model		[Exhib RA, London, 1107]; untraced		*Graves* VIII, 1905–6, 376; *Robinson* 1979 (2), 163, 254
15.	1822–1824	Musidora Payment(s): 250 louis	m	Chatsworth, Derbys		*GM* ii, 1844, 71; *Le Grice* 1844, II, 255–6; *Gunnis* 1968, 448; *JKB* 1972 (3), 331; *Robinson* 1979 (2), 164–5, 254
16.	c1829	A group		[Artist's studio, Rome, intended for Sir Robert Lawley]; untraced		*Gunnis* 1968, 448
17.	1829	Ino and the Infant Bacchus	m	[coll Sir Robert Peel]; Fitz M.1-1975 Other versions: ex coll G Cornwall Legh, Chester County Hall; untraced coll Marquess of Abercorn, exhib Manc Art Treasures 1857, 79 ex coll Miss Webb, sold Christie, 2 May 1878, untraced ex coll J Neeld, Grittleton House, 1845, sold 1966, signed		*Graves* VIII, 1905–6, 376; *JKB* 1966, 712 (repr); *Gunnis* 1968, 448; *Grittleton Marbles* 1966, 15 (repr V); *Robinson* 1979 (2), 166, 254 (repr 101)
18.	1829	Nymph of Diana with leveret and greyhound Payment(s): £140		[coll Matthew Ridley]; untraced Other versions: ex coll Earl Fitzwilliam, 1848, signed, untraced Museo di Capodimonte, Naples, signed Huntress with leveret and greyhound exhib RA, 1850, 1294		*Lit Gaz*, no 652, 18 July 1829, 746; *Graves* VIII, 1905–6, 376; *Gunnis* 1968, 448; *Robinson* 1979 (2), 254, 255; *Read* 1982, 132
19.	1831	Nymph going to the bath	m	[Duke of Leuchtenberg; Christie 1861]; untraced Other versions: ex Colebrooke Park, Co Fermanagh, 1831; untraced Camellia House, Chiswick, Mddx, c1841, marble, S ex coll Lord Wenlock, untraced by 1844 Lord Canning, 1844 Chatsworth, Derbys, Orangery, marble, nd Earl de Grey, Wrest Park, Beds, nd (ex coll H N Sandbach, Hafodunos), nd; Walker, Liverpool		*Library of Fine Arts*, vol I, 1831, 430; *Le Grice* I,1844, 90, 91; *Manchester Art Treasures* 1857, 134; *Graves* VIII, 1905–6, 376; *Stevens* 1971 (1), 150–1; *Robinson* 1979 (2), 165, 254 (repr 99, Colebrooke version)
20.	1831	Richard Lawley (later 2nd Baron Wenlock) and his brother Stephen, group	m	[Escrick Park, E R Yorks]; private coll	SD	*Graves* VIII, 1905–6, 376; *Robinson* 1979 (2), 254
21.	1832	Lady Caroline Wenlock	m	[Exhib RA, London, 1154]; private coll	SD	
22.	1832	Sleeping Cupid	m	Sotheby, 13 Nov 1975, lot 185; untraced	SD	
23.	1833	Infant daughter of Sir Michael Shaw Stewart		[Exhib RA, London, 1181]; untraced		*Graves* VIII, 1905–6, 376; *Robinson* 1979 (2), 254
24.	1833	Infant son of Sir Michael Shaw Stewart		[Exhib RA, London, 1210]; untraced		*Graves* VIII, 1905–6, 376; *Robinson* 1979 (2), 254
25.	1834	Flora and Zephyr (Cupid and Psyche) Payment(s): £400	m	[Lord Wenlock]; Nostell Priory, W R Yorks Other versions: ex coll Lord Otho Fitzgerald; untraced		*Le Grice* 1844, I, 91; *Graves* VIII, 1905–6, 376; *Robinson* 1977–8, 30–34 (repr); *Robinson* 1979 (2), 166, 172, 254 (repr 97, Nostell version)
26.	1835	Nymph of Diana with leveret	m	Royal Coll RCIN 2130		*Graves* VIII, 1905–6, 1047; *Robinson* 1979 (2), 254
27.	1836	A shepherd boy protecting his sister from the storm Model(s): one, apparently coloured	m	[Exhib RA, London, 1241]; untraced		*Le Grice* 1844, I, 91; *Graves* VIII, 1905–6, 376; *Robinson* 1979 (2), 254
28.	1837	Nymph at the bath	m	[Exhib RA, London, 1180; Christie, 1861]; untraced Other versions: replica, H J Hope sale 1917, lot 1170 Lord Townshend, replica ex Byng family, sold Christie, Wrotham Park, Herts, 2 Oct 1990; untraced		*Graves* VIII, 1905–6, 376; *Robinson* 1979 (2), 254

No.	Date	Title	Material	Location	Signed	Literature
29.	1839	Hebe Payment(s): £200 Drawing(s): Earl de Grey		[Wrest Park, Beds]; untraced Other versions: for Earl Grosvenor (£200)		*Le Grice* 1844, I, 91; *Graves* VIII, 1905–6, 376; *Gunnis* 1968, 449; *Robinson* 1979 (2), 255; GPC
30.	1840	Girl with kid	m	[Manley Hall, Manchester]; Essie, 62 Piccadilly, London, (2002) Other versions: 'Shepherdess with kid' sold Sotheby, London, 21 June 1988 'Young girl with lamb' sold Sotheby, N Y, 1 May 2001, signed	SD	*AJ*, 1850, 249; *GM*, II, 1850, 99; *Gunnis* 1968, 449; C Lib (repr)
31.	1841	Apollo as a shepherd boy		[Colebrooke, Co Fermanagh]; untraced Other versions: Duke of Sutherland, Trentham, Staffs, gardens ex coll Sir Robert Peel; untraced		*Gunnis* 1968, 449; *Robinson* 1979 (2), 172, 255 (repr 98)
32.	1841	Flora		[Sir Arthur Brooke Bt, Colebrooke, Co Fermanagh]; sold Osborne King of Belfast, 1974; untraced		*Le Grice* 1844, I, 91; *Robinson* 1979 (2), 166, 172, 253
33.	1841	Hunter with his dog		Untraced		*Le Grice* 1844, I, 91; *Robinson* 1979 (2), 255
34.	1841	Nymph coming out of a bath	m	[coll Mr Wild]; untraced Other versions: Mr Foot, replica Lord Canning, 1847 Sir Arthur Brooke Sudeley House, Liverpool Camelia House, Chiswick		*Graves* VIII, 1905–6, 376; *Robinson* 1979 (2), 255
35.	*c*1842	Apollo as the shepherd boy of Admetus		[ex coll Duke of Sutherland]; untraced Other versions: Replicas by Copeland in 'statuary-porcelain' including one in the Royal Coll		*AU* 1846, 298 (repr)
36.	1842	Nymph		[for the Emperor of Russia; Huskisson sale, Christie, 20 June 1857 (£3110s)]; untraced Other versions: Christie, London, 20 June 1857; untraced ex coll Claude Wilde; untraced R J Wyatt's studio, 1841; untraced Syon House, Middx		GPC
37.	*c*1844	A flower-girl		Untraced		*GM*, ii, 1844, 71
38.	1844	Bacchante crowned with flowers		Untraced		*GM*, ii, 1844, 71; *Robinson* 1979 (2), 255
39.	1844	Bacchante with a cup		Untraced		*GM*, ii, 1844, 71; *Robinson* 1979 (2), 255
40.	1844	Glycera		Royal Coll, Osborne House, I of W Other versions: coll Duke of Westminster, Eaton Hall, Cheshire, replica (£250)	S	*Holland Park* 1957, unpag (repr); *Gunnis* 1968, 449; *Robinson* 1979 (2), 169, 170; *Bryant* 2003, 22–3 (repr)
41.	1841–1844	Penelope with the bow of Ulysses Payment(s): £350		[Osborne House, I of W]; Windsor Castle RC 71423	S	*GM* ii, 1844, 71; *Gunnis* 1968, 448; *Read* 1982, 132–3 (repr); *Robinson* 1979 (2), 169, 255 (repr 100)
42.	By 1844	Shepherd boy lamenting the death of a young kid		Untraced		*Le Grice* 1844, I, 92
43.	1847	Venus and Cupid, for Mr Holford		Untraced		*Gunnis* 1968, 449
44.	1848	The infant Bacchus	m	[Hadzor House, Droitwich, Cheshire]; Sotheby, 8 July 2003; untraced	S	*Graves* VIII, 1905–6, 376; *Robinson* 1979 (2), 169, 172, 255
45.	1848	The nymph Eucharis and Cupid, group	m	[Dorchester House]; untraced		*Graves* VIII, 1905–6, 376; *Robinson* 1979 (2), 255
46.	1834–1849	Diana taking a thorn from a greyhound's foot	m	Capodimonte, Naples, Italy Other versions: Buckingham Palace, replica Lord Charles Townshend, replica; in the sculptor's studio at his death Temple Newsam, W R Yorks 2441/67, replica		*Graves* VIII, 1905–6, 376; *Robinson* 1979 (2), 255 (Temple Newsam version, repr 102); *Leeds* 1996, 10 (repr)
47.	*c*1850	Nymph of Diana with a dead bird and quiver	m	Royal Coll RCIN 2052 Other versions: Marble, signed, sold Christie, 14 May 1987, lot 237 Marble, sold Sotheby, 13 June 1988	S	C Lib (repr)
48.	1850	Youth mourning a dead kid		Untraced		*AJ*, 1851, 95; *Robinson* 1979 (2), 255
49.	nd	Bacchante and child	m	[Gunnerside, N R Yorks, library]; untraced		*AU*, 1846, 304; *Gunnis* 1968, 448
50.	nd	Cupid and Psyche		[Baron Wenlock of Escrick]; Nostell Priory, W R Yorks Other versions: ex coll Lord Otho Fitgerald, sold Christie, 10 May 1878		*Gunnis* 1968, 448; Pevsner, *Yorks: W R*, 1967, 381
51.	nd	Innocence		[Lord Charles Townshend; Christie, 22 April 1852]; untraced		

52.	nd	Seated nymph		[Mrs Huskisson; Christie, 20 June 1857 (£230)]; untraced		GPC
53.	nd	The little dreamer	m	[offered for sale at the Colosseum, Regent's Park, 1849]; untraced		GPC
54.	nd	Two figures of Nymphs		[coll Earl de Grey]; Wrest Park, Beds		*Gunnis* 1968, 448
Busts						
55.	c1824	Lady Anne Cullum	m	[coll Cullum family]; Manor House Museum, Bury St Edmunds, Suffolk	S	*Gunnis* 1968, 449
56.	1830	Unidentified boy		T Knox & T Longstaffe-Gowan	SD	C Lib (repr)
57.	c1831	Lady Beilby Thompson		[Escrick Park, E R Yorks]; private coll		*Robinson* 1979 (2), 254
58.	1831	Unidentified lady		Private coll	SD	C Lib (repr)
59.	1832	Unidentified lady	m	[Exhib RA, London, 1154]; untraced		*Graves* VIII, 1905–6, 376
60.	1835	Barber Beaumont	m	[Exhib RA, London, 1092]; untraced		*Graves* VIII, 1905–6, 376; *Robinson* 1979 (2), 254
61.	1835	Countess Sydney	m	[Exhib RA, London, 1108]; sold Frognal, Chislehurst, Sept 1915, lot 2072; untraced		*Graves* VIII, 1905–6, 376; *Robinson* 1979 (2), 254; GPC
62.	c1835	Flora (after the statue)		BADA Antiques Fair, Olympia, March 1998; untraced Other versions: Bust of a nymph, possibly Flora, signed, sold Christie 10 Dec 1991		
63.	1835	Henry, 1st Marquess of Anglesey		[Hinchinbrooke Castle, Huntingdon]; untraced		*Graves* VIII, 1905–65, 376; *Robinson* 1979 (2), 254 (repr 104
64.	1835	Lord Selsey		Untraced		*Robinson* 1979 (2), 254
65.	1835	Mrs Barber Beaumont		Private coll, Yorks		*Robinson* 1979 (2), 254
66.	1837	Sir John Bayley		[Exhib RA, London, 1218]; untraced		*Graves* VIII, 1905–6, 376; *Robinson* 1979 (2), 254
67.	1838	Lady Wilhelmina Stanhope	m	[Exhib RA, London, 1357]; untraced		*Graves* VIII, 1905–6, 376
68.	1838	Philip, 4th Earl Stanhope	m	Chevening House, Kent Other versions: BM signed, plaster, nd		*Robinson* 1979 (2), 255; *Dawson* 1999, 212–5 (repr)
69.	nd	Arthur, 1st Duke of Wellington	b	[Wellington College, pedestal in front quad]; Wellington College, Berks, roof of great school		*Baker* 1979, 8–9
70.	nd	Duke of Northumberland		Syon House, Middx		GPC
71.	nd	George Lushington, cast	p	Raby Castle, Durham		*Gunnis* 1968, 449; *Robinson* 1979 (2), 255
72.	nd	Hyacinth Mary, Lady Hatherton		Private coll	S	
73.	nd	John, 1st Lord de Tabley	m	Tabley House, Manchester University	S	
74.	nd	Lady Catherine Stanhope, later Duchess of Cleveland		Chevening House, Kent	S	GPC
75.	nd	Penelope		[The sculptor's studio; Wyatt sale, 1861]; untraced		*Robinson* 1979 (2), 255
76.	nd	Sir Thomas Cullum		[coll Cullum family]; Manor House Museum, Bury St Edmunds, Suffolk	S	*Gunnis* 1968, 449
77.	nd	Susanna Arethusa Cullum		[coll Cullum family]; Manor House Museum, Bury St Edmunds, Suffolk		
78.	nd	Unidentified man		Syon House, Middx, courtyard, under staircase	S	
79.	nd	Unidentified woman	m	LMG, W R Yorks 19/81	S	*Ret to Life*, 2000, 17, 62 (repr)
80.	nd	Young Paris		[Sculptor's studio; Wyatt sale, 1861]; untraced		*Robinson* 1979 (2), 255
Chimneypieces						
81.	pre-1815	Several	m	Untraced		*Robinson* 1979 (2), 163
82.	1819	With frieze representing the four seasons and flanking figures emblematical of Music and Drawing		[Hackwood Park, Hants]; untraced		*Robinson* 1979 (2), 254
Miscellaneous						
83.	1815	Unidentified subject		[RA silver medal for best model from life]; untraced		*Robinson* 1979 (2), 160, 254
84.	nd	Child with a Dead Hare		[Wentworth Woodhouse, W R Yorks]; untraced		GPC

WYATT, Richard P fl 1802–22

In 1821–2 Wyatt was paid £596 for mason's work at Wotton House, Bucks, then being altered for the Marquess Buckingham by Sir John Soane (Soane, Abstract of Bills, 5 fol 16). In 1802 Thomas and Richard Wyatt 'Mason an Bricklayers' were paid £2,529 for alterations to Aynho Park under Sir John Soane (Soane, Abstract of Bills 3, fol 124 Richard appears to have no connection with the well-known Wyatt dynasty.

Archival References: GPC

WYLLIE, James, of Aberdeen fl 1753–54

In 1753 he was paid 5 guineas for making a niche at Gordon's College, Aberdeen to house **John Cheere**'s statue Robert Gordon. In 1763 he was the master-mason building the West Kirk under James Gibbs, also in Aberdeen. Th Strachan monument is a 'pretty tablet'.

Archival References: GPC

Funerary Monuments

1.	†1754	William Strachan		Aberdeen Cathedral	S	RG/JP, 9, 1649

WYNN, William

Wynn's tradecard describes him as 'Statuary at Shakespeare's Head, Henrietta Street COVENT GARDEN La Apprentice to Mr [**Benjamin**] **Rackstrow**'. It adds 'Takes off Gentlemen and Ladies Faces from the Life with th greatest ease and safety and forms them into Busts to an exact likeness. Likewise makes all sorts of figures, bust vases, etc, for Halls, staircases, Dining Rooms, etc in plaister of Paris to represent either Marble, Stone or Bronzes, etc. Likewise mends, Gilds, Paints & Bronzes Old Figures, etc. NB Leaden figures, Vases, etc for Gardens made and mended' (Banks 106.33). There are two other trade cards in the collection, neither of which elaborate on the above notice (Banks 106.22; Banks 103.22).

WYNNE, Robert, of Ruthin –1731?

He lived at Ruthin from 1715 until 1731 and there are various payments to him in the Chirk Castle archives for work carried out for the Myddeltons. This included carving Robert Myddelton's coat of arms in the 'new seat' in Ruthin church (**8**), and 'beautifying the coats of arms and other ornaments of the old monuments of Chirk Church' (**7**). He was also responsible for the family monument erected at Chirk by Mary Myddelton (**5**). This 'striking' work, with its three life-size effigies, is unsigned, but in the family archives there is a payment in 1721 of £180 to 'Mr. Robert Wynne stone-cutter in Ruthin . . . being ye remainder of £400 in full for ye monument in Chirk'.

The Wynn memorial (**4**) also has three life-sized effigies. Gunnis calls this 'impressive' and describes the blind Henry Wynn standing in his lawyer's robes, extending his blessing over the flanking kneeling figures of Jane and John. Pevsner is less generous: he describes Henry on a pedestal 'in ludicrous pose'. Pevsner attributes two other monuments to the sculptor, one to Maurice Jones (†1702) at Llanrhaeadr, Denbighs and another to Gabriel Goodman (†1673) and Roger Mostyn (†1712) at Ruthin, Denbighs.

On 2 September 1669 Simon, son of Guallott Wynne, gentleman of Llanbedr, Denbighs, was apprenticed to Peter Roberts under the auspices of the Masons' Company. Gunnis suggests that it is possible that Simon and Robert were one and the same, for there is no trace of Robert ever having been apprenticed in London, although the carving of his figures suggests a City training.

Literary References: *Gunnis* 1968, 449; Pevsner, *Clwyd*, 1994, 231, 274; *Webb* 1999, 37

Funerary Monuments

1.	*c*1700	Sir John Owen (†1666)	Penmorfa, Carnarvon		GPC
2.	?1705	Thomas Powell	Llanbadarnfawr, Cardigan	S	*Gunnis* 1968, 449
3.	*c*1708	Thomas Bulkeley of Dinas	Llanwnda, Carnarvon		RG/JP, 9, 1650
4.	1719	Henry Wynn (†1671), Jane Wynn (†1675) and John Wynn (†1718)	Ruabon, Denbighs	S	*Gunnis* 1968, 449; Pevsner, *Clwyd*, 1986, 270
5.	?1721	Mary Myddleton's father, mother and brother Payment(s): £400	Chirk, Denbighs		*Gunnis* 1968, 449
6.	1721	Sir Richard and Lady Myddleton and their son, William	Chirk, Denbighs	S	Pevsner, *Clwyd*, 1994, 128–9 (repr)
7.	1728	Restoration work on the monuments	Chirk, Denbighs		*Gunnis* 1968, 449

Architectural Sculpture

8.	1723	Myddleton coat of arms	[Ruthin church, Denbighs]; untraced		*Gunnis* 1968, 449

WYNNE, T fl *c*1705–32

Funerary Monuments

1.	†1705	Thomas Powell	Llanbadarn Fawr, Cardigan	S	GPC
2.	†1708	Thomas Bulkeley	Llanwnda, Carnarvon	S	GPC
3.	1731	Mostyn family	Cilcain, Flint	S	Pevsner, *Clwyd*, 1986, 337
4.	1732	David Morris	Llansilin, Denbighs	S	GPC

WYON, Anne fl 1821

In 1821 Anne Wyon of Vauxhall Walk, London was awarded a silver Isis medal from the Society of Arts (**1**). She must have been related to the Wyon family of die-engravers and medallists for **Benjamin Wyon** was living at the same address when he was awarded a gold Isis medal for a medal die in the same year (RSA *Transactions*, 1821, vol 39, xxxvix).

Miscellaneous

1.	1821	Composition of flowers in wax	[Soc of A, silver Isis medal]; untraced		RSA *Transactions*, 1821, vol 39, xxxvix

WYON, Benjamin 1802–58

A die engraver and chief engraver of seals at the Mint, he used wax as a preliminary medium. He was the brother of **Edward William Wyon**. For further information the reader is referred to *Pyke* 1973, 160 and *ODNB* (Attwood). See also **Anne Wyon**.

WYON, Edward William 1811–85

The third son of Thomas Wyon the Elder (1767–1830), chief engraver of the seals, he was born in Blackfriars, London on 12 January 1811 and christened on 27 February at Christ Church, Southwark. Wyon joined the Royal Academy Schools on 22 April 1829 on the recommendation of a Mr Cooper (not **EH Baily**, as Gunnis thought), giving his address as Nassau Street. In 1830 he exhibited at the Birmingham Society of Artists and in 1831 at the Royal Academy, by which time he was living at 28 Gloucester Street, Queen's Square, London (**18**). In 1833 he won a silver medal from the Royal Academy for a model.

His early works appear chiefly to have been portraits, including some relief profiles in wax. Among his subjects were the poets Robert Southey and William Wordsworth (**72, 92, 106**) and the diplomats Baron Blöme and James Colquhoun (**70, 104**). In the 1840s he produced ideal works from Shakespeare and Edmund Spenser (**83, 120, 115**) and a number of monuments, including one designed by Henry Corbould, which incorporates a low relief of the deceased, Caroline Stevens, kneeling in prayer (**1**). The monument to the missionary Josiah Pratt (**4**) has a low relief of an angel instructing 'barbarous nations', which the *Art Journal* felt to be 'beautifully allusive to the charities of the Missionary Society' (*AJ* 1846, 188).

Wyon worked for the Art Union of London, modelling a miniature version of **John Flaxman RA**'s *St Michael slaying Satan* which was reproduced many times in bronze (**8**) and a tazza modelled on a Greek design, which was exhibited at the Great Exhibition (**116**). The modelling of works for reproduction was a recurring feature in Wyon's art of the 1850s. He modelled a statuette of Marquess Dalhousie (**9**) in modern dress, leaning on an altar, for a founder called Mr Collis, one of a series of statuettes of eminent men commissioned by the Nepalese Ambassador. Wyon also produced statuettes of literary subjects and a bust of the Duke of Wellington for reproduction by Wedgwood (**31**).

He continued to receive favourable reviews from the *Art Journal*, who described his bust of Harriet, Duchess of Sutherland (**33**), as a 'work of elevated character' (*AJ* 1853, 152), and he was sufficiently well known to receive one of the Mansion House commissions for statues of literary subjects. His figure of *Britomart* is a classicised rendering of a female from Spenser's *Fairie Queene* (**12**) which stands in the Egyptian Hall with works by **Joseph Durham, E C Marshall** and **Henry Weekes**. Further notable commissions for public spaces followed: in 1865 he modelled a statue of Richard Green, having already executed a bust of the shipowner and philanthropist two years earlier (**14, 50**). Gunnis felt the statue possessed 'considerable merit' (*Gunnis* 1968, 450). It shows Green sitting in an armchair caressing a Newfoundland dog whose head rests on his knee. In 1869 Wyon carved three statues of notable thinkers for London University (**65**).

His largest commission is the series of more than a dozen reliefs for the interior of Drapers' Hall, London, provided in the late 1860s (**66**). These are designed with a good deal of skill and cover a wide iconographic range.

By 1865 the *Art Journal* had become less enthusiastic about Wyon's work, saying of his sentimental depiction, *Mending the net* (**125**) that it was 'in treatment merely pictorial and picturesque, unprejudiced by even the first principles of the sculpture art' (*AJ* 1865, 172).

He continued to exhibit at the Royal Academy until 1873, when he showed a bust of the Dean of St Paul's, a characterised portrait with half-closed eyes and luxuriant whiskers (**58**). Wyon died in 1885.

MGS

Literary References: *Graves* VIII, 1905–6, 389; *Hutchison* 1960–2, 181; *Gunnis* 1968, 449–50; *Pyke* 1973, 160
Archival References: IGI; RA Admissions; RA Premium list

No.	Date	Subject		Location		References
Funerary Monuments						
1.	†1840	Caroline Stevens (designed by Henry Corbould)		Bradfield Church, Berks		*Gunnis* 1968, 450
2.	†1844	Barbara Hofland		St Mary Magdalene, Richmond, Surrey		Pevsner, *Surrey*, 1971, 433
3.	*c*1844	Rev Watts Wilkinson (†1840) Model(s): exhib RA, London, 1844, 1410		St Margaret Lothbury, City of London		*AU*, 1844, 171; *Graves* VIII, 1905–6, 389; Pevsner, *London: City*, 1997, 235
4.	1846	Rev Josiah Pratt, with bas-relief Model(s): exhib RA, London, 1846, 1406		St Stephen, Coleman Street		*AU* 1846, 188; *Graves* VIII, 1905–6, 389; *Gunnis* 1968, 450
5.	1853	'Charity, a monumental sketch'		[Exhib RA, London, 1416]; untraced		*Graves* VIII, 1905–6, 390
6.	1853	Rev Frederick Robertson (two bronze plaques only, showing the deceased preaching, and teaching in a Mechanics' Institute)		Brighton Cemetery		*Gunnis* 1968, 450
7.	†1858	Sir Belford Hinton Wilson	s	Kensal Green Cemetery, London		*Curl* 2001, 259n
Statues						
8.	1842	St Michael slaying Satan, statuette (after John Flaxman RA)	b	[for the Art Union of London]; Sotheby, 16 April 2002	SD	
9.	1853	James, 1st Marquess Dalhousie, statuette		[Commissioned by the Nepalese Ambassador, Jung Bahadoor]; untraced		*ILN*, 22 Jan 1853, 61 (repr); *Ormond* 1973, 129
10.	*c*1853	Titania, Oberon, Hope and the Nubian Water-Carrier (models for Wedgwood, to be executed in Parian ware)		Untraced		*AJ*, 1853, 152; *Graves* VIII, 1905–6, 390; *Gunnis* 1968, 449
11.	1854	'Sketch, submitted to the Committee of the Manchester Wellington Memorial'		[Exhib RA, London, 1408]; untraced		*Graves* VIII, 1905–6, 390
12.	1856–1861	Britomart	m	CL Coll, Mansion House, City of London, Egyptian Hall, acc 128	SD	*Knight* 1986, 351 (repr); *Ward-Jackson* 2003, 241, 351–2 (repr)
13.	1862	Briseis		[Exhib RA, London, 1005]; untraced		*Graves* VIII, 1905–6, 390
14.	1865–1866	Richard Green	b	Poplar public baths, East India Dock Road, London	SD	*ILN* 19 May 1866, 494; *Gunnis* 1968, 450; *Blackwood* 1989, 90–1 (repr); *Darke* 1991, 69 (repr)
15.	1867	A woman of the Delta, Egypt, statuette	m	[Exhib RA, London, 1188]; untraced		*Graves* VIII, 1905–6, 391
16.	1870	Night, statuette	m	[Exhib RA, London, 1157]; untraced		*Graves* VIII, 1905–6, 391
Busts						
17.	1830	Rev William Orme, of Camberwell		[Exhib Birmingham Soc of A]; untraced		*Graves* VIII, 1905–6, 389; *Gunnis* 1968, 450
18.	1831	General Frederick Maitland		[Exhib RA, London, 1133]; untraced		*Graves* VIII, 1905–6, 389; *Johnson* 1975, 526
19.	1832	Mrs Lyndon		[Exhib Soc of BA, London, 870]; untraced		*Johnson* 1975, 526
20.	1833	G W Lyndon		[Exhib RA, London, 1117]; untraced		*Graves* VIII, 1905–6, 389
21.	1833	Sir George Chetwynd		[Exhib RA, London, 1112]; untraced		*Graves* VIII, 1905–6, 389
22.	1837	Rev John Wilcox		[Exhib RA, London, 1207]; untraced		*Graves* VIII, 1905–6, 389
23.	1838	Portrait of a gentleman		[Exhib RA, London, 586]; untraced		*Graves* VIII, 1905–6, 389
24.	1839	Portrait of a young gentleman in the naval service of the Hon East India Company		[Exhib RA, London, 1273]; untraced		*Graves* VIII, 1905–6, 389
25.	1840	Sir William Charles Ross		[Exhib RA, London, 1123]; untraced		*Graves* VIII, 1905–6, 389
26.	1841	J Preston Neal		[Exhib RA, London, 1320]; untraced		*Graves* VIII, 1905–6, 389
27.	1848	Unidentified lady		[Exhib RA, London, 1428]; untraced		*Graves* VIII, 1905–6, 390
28.	1850	John Milton	p	Birmingham MAG, 69'42b	SD	*Silber* 1987, 104, cat 321
29.	1850	Robert Belford Wallis		[Exhib RA, London, 1098]; untraced		*Graves* VIII, 1905–6, 390
30.	1850	William Shakespeare	p	Birmingham MAG, inv 69'42a	SD	*Silber* 1987, 102, cat 320

No.	Date	Subject	Medium	Location	Signed	Literary references
31.	1852	Arthur, 1st Duke of Wellington (reproduced in Parian ware for Wedgwood)		Untraced		*ILN* 7 May 1853, 357 (repr); *Gunnis* 1968, 449
32.	1853	General Sir Charles Napier		Untraced		*ILN* 3 Sept 1853, 192
33.	1853	Harriet, Duchess of Sutherland		[Exhib RA, London, 1458]; untraced		*AJ*, 1853, 390; *Graves* VIII, 1905–6, 390; *Ormond* 1973, 441
34.	1854	George Richardson Porter		[Exhib RA, London, 1493]; untraced		*Graves* VIII, 1905–6, 390
35.	1854	John Lewis Ricardo MP		[Exhib RA, London, 1481 Exhib RA, London, 1855, 1442]; untraced		*Graves* VIII, 1905–6, 390
36.	c1855	George Parker Bidder	m	NPG 5163	S	*Manchester Art Treasures* 1857, 136; *Graves* VIII, 1905–6, 390
37.	1855	James Meadows Rendel Model(s): t-c, formerly Institute of Civil Engineers; untraced	m	[coll J Scott Russell Esq]; untraced		*Manchester Art Treasures* 1857, 136; *Graves* VIII, 1905–6, 390
38.	1855	Robert Stephenson	p	Birmingham MAG (Science Museum) Other versions: Newcastle Literary Soc, SD 1855, marble Institution of Mechanical Engineers, Parian ware ex Euston Railway Station; untraced	SD	*ILN* 11 Dec 1858, 555 (repr); *Manchester Art Treasures* 1857, 136; *Graves* VIII, 1905–6, 390; *Gunnis* 1968, 450; *Read* 1982, 123; *Silber* 1987, 104, cat 322
39.	1857	James Trubshaw	m	[Exhib RA, London, 1336]; untraced		*Graves* VIII, 1905–6, 390
40.	1858	Dr David Livingstone		[Exhib RA, London, 1234]; untraced		*AJ*, 1858, 172; *Graves* VIII, 1905–6, 390
41.	1859	George Stephenson	m	[Exhib RA, London, 1859 (1330)]; untraced Other versions: Institution of Mechanical Engineers, Parian ware		*ILN* 11 Dec 1858, 555 (repr); *Graves* VIII, 1905–6, 390; GPC
42.	1859	Joseph Locke, MP	tc	[Exhib RA, London, 1371]; untraced		*ILN* 3 Nov 1860, 428 (repr); *Graves* VIII, 1905–6, 390; GPC
43.	1860	John Hawkshaw Model(s): Another exhib RA 1863 (1153)	tc	[Exhib RA, London, 1861 (1055)]; untraced		*Graves* VIII, 1905–6, 390; GPC
44.	1860	John Wichcord, cast		Maidstone Museum, Kent	SD	*Gunnis* 1968, 450
45.	1861	Isambard Kingdom Brunel		Institution of Mechanical Engineers, London Other versions: Paddington railway station, London; untraced		*Graves* VIII, 1905–6, 390; RG/JP, 9, 1651–2
46.	1862	Admiral Moorson		[Exhib RA, London, 1107]; untraced		*Graves* VIII, 1905–6, 390
47.	1862	Robert Hawthorn	m	[Exhib RA, London, 1085]; untraced		*Graves* VIII, 1905–6, 390
48.	1863	Daniel Gooch	m	[Paddington railway station, London]; untraced		*Graves* VIII, 1905–6, 390; GPC
49.	1863	Mrs Gooch	m	[Exhib RA, London, 1164]; untraced		*Graves* VIII, 1905–6, 390
50.	1863	Richard Green		Kenswick Manor, Worcs		*Gunnis* 1968, 450
51.	1863	William Fairbairn	p	Birmingham MAG (Science Museum)	SD	*Silber* 1987, 104, cat 323
52.	1864	Sir Joseph Paxton		[Exhib RA, London, 979]; untraced		*Graves* VIII, 1905–6, 390
53.	c1865	Henry, 3rd Viscount Palmerston (Parian ware)		NPG 4508	S	*Ormond* 1973, 358 (pl 709)
54.	1867	N Griffiths	m	[Exhib RA, London, 1147]; untraced		*Graves* VIII, 1905–6, 391
55.	1867	Robert Napier		[Exhib RA, London, 1167]; GAGM		*Graves* VIII, 1905–6, 391; *Gunnis* 1968, 450
56.	1868	Henry Bessemer	m	[Exhib RA, London, 966]; Institution of Civil Engineers, London		*Graves* VIII, 1905–6, 391; *Gunnis* 1968, 450
57.	1869	John Probert	m	[Exhib RA, London, 1166 Royal Medical Benevolent College]; untraced		*Graves* VIII, 1905–6, 391
58.	1873	The Very Rev Henry Longueville Mansel	m	[Exhib RA, London, 1437]; St John's College, Oxford		*Graves* VIII, 1905–6, 391; *Ormond* 1973, 300
59.	nd	Admiral Moorson		[Euston railway station, London]; untraced		RG/JP, 9, 1652
60.	nd	James Watt		Institution of Mechanical Engineers, London		RG/JP, 9, 1651
61.	nd	John Sims Reeves	b	ex coll E F Croft-Murray; untraced		*Ormond* 1973, 392
62.	nd	Robert Stevenson		Euston Station, London		GPC
63.	nd	Unidentified male subject		Private coll		C Lib (repr)
Architectural Sculpture						
64.	1837	Model of a fountain, to be executed in stone for Earl Ducie		[Exhib Soc of BA, London, 616]; untraced		*Johnson* 1975, 526
65.	1869	Galileo, Goethe, and La Place		University of London former headquarters, Burlington Gardens, London, façade		*Builder* April 17, 1869, 303; *Read* 1982, 226
66.	1869–1871	Reliefs of Science taught by Truth, the Earth, the Heavens, Charity, Prayer, Faith, Praise, Hope, Asia, America, Africa, Europe, Mathematics, History, Commerce; statues of Edward III and Queen Philippa on façade; keystones of Plato, Pliny?, an ancient Chaldean, Moses, St Matthew, St John, St Luke, St Mark, an ironworker, Queen Victoria, a shepherd, Michelangelo, a reaper, Archimedes, North American Indian, Herodotus, ancient Egyptian, a Turk's head, Jason, Strength and Renown		Drapers' Hall, City of London		Drapers' Company Archives a.1109, a.596; *Gunnis* 1968, 450
67.	1874	Caryatids		Fitzwilliam, dome lantern		Pevsner, *Cambs*, 1970, 211; *Gunnis* 1968, 450

Reliefs

No.	Date	Subject		Location		Reference
68.	1833	Mr Serjeant Wilde, medallic portrait		[Exhib RA, London, 1206]; untraced		*Graves* VIII, 1905–6, 389
69.	1833	Thomas, Baron Truro, medallic portrait		[Exhib RA, London, 1206]; untraced		*Ormond* 1973, 470
70.	1835	Baron Blöme	w	[Exhib Birmingham Soc of A; exhib RA, London, 389]; untraced		*Graves* VIII, 1905–6, 389; *Gunnis* 1968, 450
71.	1835	Henry, 4th Duke of Newcastle, medallic portrait	b	[Exhib RA, London, 1132]; untraced		*Graves* VIII, 1905–6, 389
72.	1835	Robert Southey	w	NPG 2681 Other versions: ex coll E J Pyke, London; untraced Bristol MAG Madame Tussaud's, London		*Gunnis* 1968, 450; *Pyke* 1973, 160
73.	1836	John Marshall, portrait medallion		[Exhib RA, London, 984]; untraced		*Graves* VIII, 1905–6, 389; *Morris and Roberts* 1998, 673
74.	1836	Mrs H Turner, medallion		[Exhib Soc of BA, London, 897]; untraced		*Johnson* 1975, 526
75.	1837	James, 5th Earl Cornwallis, medallic portrait	w	[Exhib RA, London, 1140]; untraced		*Graves* VIII, 1905–6, 389
76.	1837	Miss Mitford, medallic portrait		[Exhib RA, London, 1142]; untraced		*Graves* VIII, 1905–6, 389
77.	1837	Rajah Rahmohun Roy, portrait medallion		[Exhib Liverpool Ac, 673]; untraced		*Morris and Roberts* 1998, 673
78.	1838	Edward, Baron Lytton, medallion portrait		[Exhib Birmingham Soc of A]; untraced		*Ormond* 1973, 287
79.	1840	Rev T B Buller, medallic portrait		[Exhib RA, London, 1084]; untraced		*Graves* VIII, 1905–6, 389
80.	1841	John, 1st Earl of Durham, medallic portrait		[Exhib RA, London, 1128]; untraced		*Graves* VIII, 1905–6, 389
81.	1841	Sir Benjamin Collins Brodie Bt, medallic portrait		Knox/Longstaffe-Gowan coll (acq 1995)		
82.	1841	Sir Henry Taylor, medallic portrait		[Exhib RA, London, 1127]; untraced		*Graves* VIII, 1905–6, 389
83.	1842	Oberon and Titania, bas-relief		[Exhib RA, London, 1288; 1848, 1312]; untraced Other versions: Private coll, wax, SD 1848		*AU*, 1842, 128; *Graves* VIII, 1905–6, 389, 390
84.	1843	Rev Joseph Clark, medallic portrait		[Exhib RA, London, 1354]; untraced		*Graves* VIII, 1905–6, 389
85.	1844	Deceased lady, medallic portrait	w	[Exhib RA, London, 1247]; untraced		*AJ*, 1844, 171; *Graves* VIII, 1905–6, 389
86.	1844	Venus and Adonis, medallion		[Exhib RA, London, 1247]; untraced		*AJ*, 1844, 171; *Graves* VIII, 1905–6, 389
87.	1845	A child, medallion	b	[Exhib RA, London, 1356]; untraced		*Graves* VIII, 1905–6, 389
88.	1847	Madame Anaide Castellane, medallic portrait		[Exhib RA, London, 1291]; untraced		*Graves* VIII, 1905–6, 389
89.	1847	W Vincent Wallace, medallic portrait		[Exhib RA, London, 1299]; untraced		*Graves* VIII, 1905–6, 390
90.	1848	Unidentified classical subject	w	Stanton Harcourt, Oxon		*Pyke* 1973, 160
91.	1848	Unidentified classical subject	w	Private coll, Rome		*Pyke* 1973, 160
92.	pre-1861	Portraits, illustrating 'The Authors of England' by Achille Collas, publ 1861: Mrs Hemans, Lord Byron, Dr Southey, Coleridge, Edward Bulwer Lytton, Lady Morgan, Shelley, Thomas Moore, Miss Mitford and Thomas Campbell	w	Untraced		*Morris and Roberts* 1998, 672–3; *Johnson* 1975, 526
93.	1863	Mrs F Pavey, medallion	m	[Exhib RA, London, 1202]; untraced		*Graves* VIII, 1905–6, 390
94.	1866	John Devonshire Ellis, medallion		[Exhib RA, London, 1036]; untraced		*Graves* VIII, 1905–6, 391
95.	1866	William Bragge, medallion		[Exhib RA, London, 844]; untraced		*Graves* VIII, 1905–6, 390
96.	1878	Unidentified youth	w	Stanton Harcourt, Oxon		*Pyke* 1973, 160
97.	nd	Col Frederick Clinton	w	[ex coll Rupert Gunnis]; untraced		*Pyke* 1973, 160
98.	nd	General Sir Charles Colville	w	[ex coll Rupert Gunnis]; untraced		*Pyke* 1973, 160
99.	nd	King George IV	w	Hammond Museum, North Salem, New York		*Pyke* 1973, 160
100.	nd	The Princess, from Tennyson		Forbes Magazine Coll, 60 Fifth Avenue, New York	S	

Miscellaneous

No.	Date	Subject		Location		Reference
101.	1832	An Italian greyhound, the property of Mrs Poidevin of Bayswater, study		[Exhib RA, London, 1196]; untraced		*Graves* VIII, 1905–6, 389; *Johnson* 1975, 526
102.	1832	Model of a stone fountain, for Lord Ducie		[Exhib Suffolk St, London]; untraced		RG/JP, 9, 1652
103.	1834	Group of unidentified children		[Exhib Soc of BA, London, 845]; untraced		*Johnson* 1975, 526
104.	1835	James Colquhoun		[Exhib RA, London, 1061]; untraced		*Graves* VIII, 1905–6, 389
105.	1835	Other, 6th Earl of Plymouth	w	[Exhib RA, London, 992]; untraced		*Graves* VIII, 1905–6, 389
106.	1835	William Wordsworth	w	NPG 2680 Other versions: Madame Tussaud's, London		*Graves* VIII, 1905–6, 389; *Gunnis* 1968, 450; *Pyke* 1973, 160
107.	1836	Miss Shepherd		[Exhib RA, London, 986]; untraced		*Graves* VIII, 1905–6, 389
108.	1836	Rev John Jowett		[Exhib RA, London, 979]; untraced		*Graves* VIII, 1905–6, 389
109.	1836	Robert Southey		[Exhib RA, London, 982]; untraced		*Graves* VIII, 1905–6, 389
110.	1838	Henry Marshall		[Exhib RA, London, 573]; untraced		*Graves* VIII, 1905–6, 389
111.	1838	John Marshall jnr		[Exhib RA, London, 569]; untraced		*Graves* VIII, 1905–6, 389
112.	1839	Study from nature		[Exhib RA, London, 1271]; untraced		*Graves* VIII, 1905–6, 389
113.	1843	Infant child of Pedro de Zuluetá		[Exhib RA, London, 1397]; untraced		*Graves* VIII, 1905–6, 389
114.	1845	John Baptist Cramer, 'for a medal now executing by B Wyon'		[Exhib RA, London, 1387]; untraced		*Graves* VIII, 1905–6, 389
115.	1847	Speranza		[Exhib RA, London, 1847]; untraced		*Graves* VIII, 1905–6, 389–90
116.	1851	Tazza 'modelled from a Greek design for the Art Union of London'		[Exhib Gt Exhib, 86]; untraced		*Great Exhib* 1851 (1), vol 2, 846
117.	1858	Hon James Thomason		[Exhib RA, London, 1227]; untraced		*Graves* VIII, 1905–6, 390
118.	1859	John Propert		[Exhib RA, London, 1309]; untraced		*AJ*, 1859, 172; *Graves* VIII, 1905–6, 390

119.	1861	Oberon		[Exhib RA, London, 994]; untraced		*Graves* VIII, 1905–6, 390
120.	1861	Prospero and Miranda		[Exhib RA, London, 988]; untraced		*Graves* VIII, 1905–6, 390
121.	1862	Miranda		[Exhib RA, London, 1118]; untraced		*Graves* VIII, 1905–6, 390
122.	1864	Nicholas Wood	m	[Exhib RA, London, 1050]; Sold Tennant's of Leyburn, 10 April 2003, lot 768 Other versions: Cluny Castle, Aberdeen, 1864	SD	*Graves* VIII, 1905–6, 390; GPC
123.	1864	William Fairbairn		[Exhib RA, London, 994]; untraced		*Graves* VIII, 1905–6, 390
124.	1865	Charles M Palmer		[Exhib RA, London, 1019]; untraced		*Graves* VIII, 1905–6, 390
125.	1865	Fisherman's daughter (Mending the net)	m	[Exhib RA, London, 911]; untraced Other versions: Phillips Son and Neale, April 1976, Parian ware, SD 1873		*AJ*, 1865, 172; *Graves* VIII, 1905–6, 390
126.	1866	John Brown, Master Cutler of Atlas Steel Works, Sheffield		[Exhib RA, London, 1005]; untraced		*Graves* VIII, 1905–6, 390
127.	1866	William Fairbairn		[Exhib RA, London, 850]; untraced		*Graves* VIII, 1905–6, 390
128.	1868	Edward Headland		[Exhib RA, London, 1143]; untraced		*Graves* VIII, 1905–6, 391
129.	1870	John Penn	m	[Exhib RA, London, 1188]; untraced		*AJ*, 1870, 172; *Graves* VIII, 1905–6, 391
130.	1874	Rector of St Marylebone	m	[Exhib RA, London, 1557]; untraced		*Graves* VIII, 1905–6, 391
131.	1875	Miss Chadwick	m	[Exhib RA, London, 1362]; untraced		*Graves* VIII, 1905–6, 391

WYON, James 1804–68

He worked as an assistant to his cousin **William Wyon** and was probably the 'J Wyon' of Birmingham who was awarded a silver Isis medal from the Society of Arts in 1820 for a copy of a head in miniature (RSA *Transactions*, 1820, vol 38, xxxv).

Literary References: *Pyke* 1973, 160, 161; *ODNB* (Attwood)

WYON, Leonard Charles 1826–91

A son of **William Wyon**, he was a die-engraver and medallist who used wax as a preliminary medium. In addition to medals and models for medals, his Royal Academy exhibits included a *Head of the Apollo Bevedere*, for which he was awarded a medal in 1845 (1). For further information the reader is referred to *Pyke* 1973, 160–1, *Pyke* 1981, 43 and *ODNB* (Attwood).

Busts

1.	1845	Apollo Belvedere	[RA silver medal]; untraced	*Graves* VIII, 1905–6, 394

WYON, Thomas I 1767–1830

A silver-chaser and die-engraver who also modelled in wax and was the father of **Edward William Wyon**. For further information the reader is referred to *Pyke* 1973, 161, *Pyke* 1981, 43 and *ODNB* (Attwood).

WYON, Thomas II 1767–1830

A brother of **Edward William Wyon**, he was a die engraver and medallist who used wax as a preliminary medium. He attended the Royal Academy Schools, winning medals for two models (1, 2). For further information the reader is referred to *Pyke* 1973, 161, *Pyke* 1981, 43 and *ODNB* (Attwood).

Miscellaneous

1.	1812	Model from the Antique Academy	[RA silver medal]; untraced	RA Premium list
2.	1813	Model from the Life Academy	[RA silver medal]; untraced	RA Premium list

WYON, William 1795–1851

A medallist who used wax as a preliminary medium and the brother of **Thomas Wyon I**. For further information the reader is referred to *Pyke* 1973, 161–2, *Pyke* 1981, 43 and *ODNB* (Attwood).

XAVERI fl 1734

Perhaps identifiable with **Xavery, A.**

Busts

1.	1734	The Prince of Orange	untraced	*Northampton Mercury*, 11 Feb 1734

XAVERY, A fl 1711

Perhaps identifiable with **Xaveri**, he signs one of two pairs of children 'A Xavery, 1711'.

Architectural Sculpture

1.	1711	Two pairs of children	m	Olantigh, Wye, Kent, in niches flanking the portico	SD	Pevsner, *Kent: N E & E*, 1983, 508

YATES fl 1717–40?

The name Yates recurs in records of the Masons' Company. Joseph Yates bound Sepherus, son of Thomas Yates, citizen and mason, on 4 July 1717, and also Francis Thomas Yates of St Saviour, Southwark on 6 April 1722. A Joshua Yates, 'mason in Mountague Court, Southwark' was on a list of assistants and livery of the Masons' Company, *c*1740 (Masons' Co Assistants, fol 9).

Literary References: *Webb* 1999, 33, 37

YATES, D, of Leicester fl 1830–40

Known only for two undistinguished tablets. He may be connected with **J Yates of Leicester**.

Funerary Monuments

1.	†1831	John Pares	Scraptoft, Leics	S	*Gunnis* 1968, 451
2.	†1836	Thomas Whiteman	Peckleton, Leics	S	*Gunnis* 1968, 451

YATES, J, of Hereford fl 1801–22

He was responsible for a number of tablets in Herefordshire churches. These include an architectural tablet with two *putti* heads to Joseph Sterling (1) and a large Hellenic wall-monument to Thomas Farrington (3). There is a small tablet to John Berrow, 1809, at Burghill, Herefs, signed 'T. Yates, Junior', which may be by a family member.

Literary References: *Gunnis* 1968, 451

Funerary Monuments

1.	†1781	Joseph Sterling	Bromyard, Herefs	S	RG/JP, 9, 1658
2.	†1791	Thomas Cook	Much Cowarne, Herefs		RG/JP, 9, 1658
3.	†1801	Thomas Farrington	Burghill, Herefs	S	*Gunnis* 1968, 451
4.	?1805	Elizabeth (†1771) and George Godsall	Ashperton, Herefs	S	RG/JP, 9, 1658
5.	?1807	Robert Homes	Ashperton, Herefs	S	RG/JP, 9, 1658
6.	1808	James Godsall	Ashperton, Herefs	S	RG/JP, 9, 1658
7.	†1811	William Hardwick	Madley, Herefs	S	*Gunnis* 1968, 451
8.	?1823	Thomas Knill	Humber, Herefs		RG/JP, 9, 1658
9.	?1824	John Palmer	Withington, Herefs		RG/JP, 9, 1658

YATES, J, of Leicester fl *c*1844

Funerary Monuments

1.	†1844	Hon Caroline Russell	Kirkby Mallory, Leics	S	

YATES, John fl 1827

He was probably a Maidstone mason.

Chimneypieces

1.	1827	Several (by John Yates)	[Kent Insurance Company offices, Maidstone, Kent]; untraced	RG/JP, 9, 1658

YEOMANS, T, of Bodenham fl 1797–1830

A village mason, he signed a number of stone wall-tablets in Wellington church, Herefs. These are dated between 1797 and 1830 and Gunnis notes that they are of pleasant, though rather crude, workmanship. Yeomans was succeeded in the business by his son Richard, who signed other tablets in the same church.

Literary References: *Gunnis* 1968, 451

YOUING, of Barnstaple

Funerary Monuments

1.	nd	Unidentified subjects, tablets	Tawstock, Devon	Pevsner, *Devon*, 1989, 791

YOUNG fl 1673–74

In 1673 a 'Mr Younge the Carver' was paid £10 for work at Vintners' Hall. He and **Stacey** were paid £8 in 1674 for carving work about the doorcases.

Archival References: Vintners, RW Accts, vol 5

YOUNG, J fl 1788?

Funerary Monuments

1.	?1788	William Tabburn	Portsmouth Cathedral	S	*Gunnis* 1968, 451

YOUNG, J, of Ewell fl 1814–32?

Gunnis notes that the large wall-tablet to Sir George Glyn has carefully cut details (**1**).

Funerary Monuments

1.	?1814	Sir George Glyn Bt	Ewell, Surrey	S	*Gunnis* 1968, 451
2.	?1832	William Payne, small wall-tablet	Sutton, Surrey	S	*Gunnis* 1968, 451

YOUNG, John I –1679

Young worked in turbulent times, beginning his career as a mason during the reign of Charles I, surviving the Commonwealth and coming into his own after the Restoration. Having been 'made sinisterly free of ye Weavers', he was taken and presented for disfranchisement together with his master in 1636 (*Knoop and Jones* 1935, 31). He then wooed the Masons' Company and agreed to pay £5 for his translation from the Weavers, £3 being paid on 16 May 1637 and the balance of 40s in 1637–8. In 1652 and again in 1655, he was a warden of the Masons' Company and was appointed master in 1657.

In 1638–40 he was one of the masons responsible for building the tower of Goudhurst church, Kent. He was also working at the Inner Temple where he received £140 for repairs to the Temple Church. Further payments totalling £14 7s were made for unspecified work and £1 12s for taking down the staircase of the steeple and scaffolding the same. In 1640 he began work on the new Temple bridge receiving a first payment of £100 and in 1641 he was paid a further £335 for stonework. In 1655 another £33 18s was made over for work 'about the Garden Gate and Stairs' (*Inderwick* 1896–1936, 2, 321). A new contract was drawn up for repairs in 1663, by which time Young was working in partnership with his son **Nicholas Young.** He had designed and built the new church at Berwick-upon-Tweed by 1653.

From 1664–69 Young and **Joshua Marshall** worked in partnership at Greenwich Hospital, building first the north end and later the east front, where they also provided quantities of Portland stone for paving. They carried out a good deal of decorative carving (**2, 3**).

Young was the master-mason at Mercers' Hall, building it and its chapel in the years 1668–75, to designs by John Oliver. In 1669 he was paid £100 for work at St Paul's School and on the schoolmasters' houses. In 1669 he made the great gateway and in 1670 he and his son Nicholas were paid £50 for statues of the Christian Virtues (**3**) and a further £350 for building the chapel gate and setting up the figures. He was assisted in other work by **Thomas Cartwright I**: Young and Cartwright were paid £500 in January 1673 for stonework on the porch and columns. £100 was paid solely to Young in April 1674 for 'plaistering the cupilo' and that year he earned a further £100 for work on the clerk's house. In 1669 the Grocers' Company commissioned 'Mr Young, Mason' to carve a statue of Sir John Cutler, but for some reason Young did not comply. There is an obscure reference in Robert Hooke's diary to a visit in May 1674 by Sir John Cutler 'about Young and theater'. Later the same month Hooke 'View'd Young's work for Sir J Cutler' (*Robinson and Adams* 1935, 101, 102). He was the master mason building the Apothecaries' Hall in 1667–9: apparently the Company was in financial difficulties and offered one of the building plots on the site of their old hall to Young, who in return agreed to make the grand staircase to the new hall 'for his own credit and gratefuly for the Company'. In 1673 he was paid £147 for paving the courtyard. In October 1670 he carried out 'tiling about the Church' and other work at St Dunstan-in-the-East. He was employed at Bethlem Hospital in 1675, for Robert Hooke noted in his diary on 1 April that year that he had 'signed Young's bills for carvings' (*Robinson and Adams* 1935, 156). He died in March 1679 leaving two sons, Nicholas and **John Young II**, both of whom followed their father's craft.

Literary References: *Inderwick* 1896–1936, 2, 246, 247, 258, 263; 3, 21; *Wren Soc* XIX, 18; *Knoop and Jones* 1935, 31; *Gunnis* 1968, 451; RG/JP, 9, 1660; *Colvin* 1995, 1136

Archival References: TNA A.O.l 2487/357 fol 3 (paving: Greenwich Palace); Mercers Misc Ms 17.1; Mercers Acts of Ct 1669 fols 7v & 12r (St Paul's School and school masters' houses); Mercers S & R W Accts (chapel, hall, and clerk's house); Mercers' Acts of Ct, fols 126, 128 (plastering the cupola); GPC

Architectural Sculpture

1.	1663	Repairs to the Temple bridge (co-sculptor: Nicholas Young)		Inner Temple, London	*Gunnis* 1968, 451
2.	1667	'Ballastrades and rails'		[Greenwich Hospital, London (ORNC), pavilion]; untraced	*Gunnis* 1968, 451
3.	1665–1667	Carved work including 'two capitals carved for 3 quarter columns' (£36) and 'flower stands over the keystones of the windows wrought with abacus moulding' (£1 4s) (co-sculptor: Joshua Marshall)		Greenwich Hospital, London (ORNC)	TNA WORK 5/9 fol 332; *Gunnis* 1968, 451; *Bold* 2000 (2), 124
4.	1670	Drapery and flying putti bearing a bust of Flora		Town Hall, Swanage, Dorset, façade	Pevsner, *Dorset*, 1972, 411
5.	1671	Faith, Hope and Charity (co-sculptor: Nicholas Young) Payment(s): £50		[Mercers' Hall, London, chapel porch]; Town Hall, Swanage, Dorset (1878)	Mercers, Misc Ms 17.1; *Gunnis* 1968, 451
6.	1675	'Carvings'		[Bethlem Hospital, London]; untraced	*Robinson and Adams* 1935, 156; *Gunnis* 1968, 451

YOUNG, John II *c*1649–95

The son of **John Young I** and brother of **Nicholas Young**, he became free of the Masons' Company by patrimony in 1671. 'John Young, jun. of St. Anne, Blackfriars, Cit. & Mason, Bachr. ab. 26' married 'Alice Harvey, of Edmonton, c. Middlesex, Spr. abt. 20' on 24 January 1676. She was the daughter of George Harvey, a feltmaker (*Armytage* 1892 (Lic Vic Gen), vol 34, 1669–1679, 159). Young was warden of the Masons' Company in 1685 and 1686, upper warden in 1687 and master in 1695, but died during his year of office. In 1695 he was paid £100 for stone work at the Trinity almshouses at Stepney. In January 1696 his widow was paid the balance of £178 owing to him at Stepney.

Literary References: *Gunnis* 1968, 451; RG/JP, 9, 1660

Archival References: Masons' Co, Masters and Wardens

Chimneypieces

1.	1684	Description unavailable Payment(s): £15	m	[for Thomas Thynne]; untraced	Longleat Archives quoted in *Gunnis* 1968, 451

YOUNG, Nicholas fl 1663–87

Young, who was admitted to the Masons' Company in 1663, was the son of **John Young I**, with whom he worked as an assistant or partner. Inderwick quotes an agreement of 1 August 1663, between Sir Heneage Finch, treasurer of the Inner Temple, and 'John Younge and Nicholas Younge his son, Citizens and Freemasons' for repairs to the Temple bridge (*Inderwick* 1896–1936, 3, 21). Similarly, the Court Book of the Mercers' Company notes a payment of £50 to 'John Young and his sonne Nicholas' in 1670.

Working under Sir Christopher Wren, Nicholas Young was employed as a master-builder at several of the City churches, including St Andrew-by-the-Wardrobe and St Michael, Cornhill (1670–77). He also provided a certain amount of stone-carving, making a festoon measuring 18 feet, for the front of St George, Botolph Lane (5), as part of a major masonry contract worth around £10,000, and four pillars costing £120 for St Martin, Ludgate Hill (4). He also worked at St Mary-at-Hill in 1670–76, and under Wren at Ludgate in 1680.

He was warden of the Masons' Company in 1674 and in 1679, becoming master in 1682. Gunnis felt that his finest work of sculpture was the bust of Gideon De Laune (1). His son, John Young III, was made free from the Masons' Company by patrimony on 12 October 1699.

Literary References: *Knoop and Jones* 1935, 31; *Robinson and Adams* 1935, 442; *Gunnis* 1968, 452; *Colvin* 1995, 1136

Archival References: Masons' Co, Masters and Wardens; Masons' Co, Freemen, fol 74

Portraits of the Sculptor: ex coll Derek Sherburn, untraced (C Lib repr)

Busts					
1.	nd	Gideon De Laune		Apothecaries' Company	*Gunnis* 1968, 452
Chimneypieces					
2.	1686	Several Payment(s): £21	m	[Gray's Inn, London, library]; untraced	Treasurer's Accounts; RG/JP, 9, 1661
Architectural Sculpture					
3.	1681	'Two bases and two columns'		[Sir William Turner's house, Slingsby, N R Yorks]; untraced	RG/JP, 9, 1661
4.	1677–1687	Four pillars Payment(s): £120		[St Martin, Ludgate Hill]; untraced	*Wren Soc* XIX, 29; *Gunnis* 1968, 452
5.	nd	Festoon		[St George, Botolph Lane, London]; untraced	*Wren Soc* XIX, 20; *Knoop and Jones* 1935, 31; *Gunnis* 1968, 452

YOUNG, Thomas fl 1672–85

A London wood-carver who worked in the naturalistic style associated with **Grinling Gibbons**, his first recorded payment, of £40, was made by Sir Robert Clayton for unspecified work in August 1672. In the 1680s he had a loosely-knit partnership with **Jonathan Maine**: on four occasions between 2 February 1683 and 19 December 1684 they received payments totalling £432 3s 11d from the 5th Earl of Exeter for work connected with the restoration of Burghley House, Northants. Young moved on to Chatsworth, where William Talman was rebuilding the south and east fronts for the 4th Earl (later 1st Duke) of Devonshire. There he joined **Samuel Watson**, the resident house carver, **William Davis** and **Joel Lobb**. Lobb and Young together provided a richly carved overmantel with heads of *putti* and garlands of flowers for the state music room. Young also worked at Kiveton, W R Yorks, a house possibly by Talman, at Subury, Derbys and in the London churches of St Mary-at-Hill (1672) and St Mary Magdalene, Old Fish Street (1685).

Literary References: *Green* 1964 (1), 112, 113, 119, 120, 123; *Beard* 1985, 688, 690

Archival References: Clayton & Morris fol 242v, Aug 1672; James Whildon's Accts, Chatsworth, 1685–99, 76

YOUNG, William fl 1731–33

The *Daily Post* of 23 April, 1731, refers to him as 'that ingenious statuary at the Eagle and Rock, near Hyde Park Corner'. In December 1731 Henry Hoare paid him 6 guineas for a 'plaister figure' (1) and a second sum of £21 for unspecified work followed in January 1733 in respect of 'Johs Cox's bill to Wm Young'.

Literary References: *Gunnis* 1968, 452

Archival References: Hoare Partnership Ledger, 1725–34, fol 261, 20 Dec 1731; fol 274 25 Jan 1732/3

Statues

1.	1731	Plaster figure	[for Henry Hoare]; untraced	Hoare Partnership Ledger

YOUNG & COLE fl *c*1855

Funerary Monuments

1.	†1855	George Johnston	Holy Trinity, Berwick-upon-Tweed, Northumbs	Pevsner, *Northumbs*, 1992, 172

ZUDOWIG fl 1768

Miscellaneous

1.	1768	'His late Majesty cut in ivory, from the life'	Untraced	Press Cuttings 1723–1800, fol 117

APPENDIX

SCULPTORS' AND COLLECTORS' SALES CATALOGUES

Sale/Status/Reason	Owner/Address	Auctioneer/Date	Contents	Catalogue
Adam 1818 Collector	Robert Adam	Christie 22 May 1818	Classical statuary, also original architectural work by Bacon, Locatelli, Collins and Ceracchi	Christie Picture Cats XII 1816–19 (NAL II. RC.DD.27), 6pp
Adams 1900 Sculptor Deceased	George Gamon Adams, 126 Sloane Street, London	Sotheby July 1900	Medals (near-complete set)	*Forrer* 1904–1930, I, 25
Anon 1807 Collector		Christie 23–24 Jan 1807	A work of sculpture by Locatelli	Christie Archives
Anon 'Man of Fashion' 1793 Collector		Christie 14 May 1793	Two life-size statue in Orco stone by Locatelli, unsold	Christie Archives
Arminger 1794 Sculptor Deceased	William Arminger	Greenwood 6 March 1794	Prints, library, models, pictures etc	VAM NAL 23.L
Atkinson 1766 Sculptor Deceased	William Atkinson, Piccadilly, London	24–25 July 1766	Part stock in trade	BM, P&D Sc. A.5.9.
Atkinson 1767 Sculptor Deceased	William Atkinson, Piccadilly, London	Burnsall 2–3 April 1767	Stock in trade	BM, P&D, Sc.5.9.
Banks 1805 Sculptor Deceased	Thomas Banks, 5 Newman Street, London	Christie 22 May 1805	Original models in terra cotta, moulds and casts	NAL II.RC DD.1, f12
Beckford 1830 Collector	William Beckford, Fonthill, Wilts	Sotheby 19–20 March 1830	14 works of sculpture (etc)	NAL 23.XX
Bicknell 1863 Collector	Elkanah Bicknell, Herne Hill, London	Christie 25 April 1863	English pictures and sculpture	NAL 23X
Bird 1751 Sculptor Deceased (1731)	Francis Bird, Lincolns Inn Fields, London	Langford 30 April–4 May 1751	'Models, Casts, Prints, Books of Prints and Drawings of Mr Francis Bird'	BM, P&D Sc. A.5.9.
Bird 1771 Marble merchant Bankrupt	Edward Chapman Bird, Millbank, London	Christie 18 March 1771	Chimneypieces, materials, busts, bas-reliefs	BM, P&D, Sc. A.5.9.
Blanchard 1860 Sculptor	Mark H Blanchard, Westminster Road, London	Christie 27 March 1860	Stock in trade	GPC
Blanchard 1861 Sculptor	Mark H Blanchard, Westminster Road, London	Christie 5 April 1861	Stock in trade	GPC
Blanckley 1770 Collector Deceased	Blanckley, Crutched Friars, London	Bristow 1770	Ancient coins, medals, busts and basso relievos, inc models for Roubiliac's George II and the Shelburne monument	BM, P&D, Sc. A.5.9.

SALE/STATUS/REASON	OWNER/ADDRESS	AUCTIONEER/DATE	CONTENTS	CATALOGUE
Boydell 1805 Collector	Alderman John Boydell	Christie 17 May 1805	'the . . . pictures . . of the Shakespeare Gallery' (including works by Anne Damer and Thomas Banks)	NAL II.RC. DD.1, fol.11
Bridges 1775 Sculptor Quitting business	I Bridges, Knightsbridge, London	Christie 26 May 1775	'the remaining stock in trade of artificial stone'	Christie Archives
Brodie 1881 Sculptor Deceased	William Brodie, Edinburgh	Dowell's, Edinburgh 16–19 Dec 1881	Studio equipment and stock-in-trade	DNB
Bullock 1806 Sculptor	George Bullock, 48 Church Street, Liverpool	3–7 March 1806	Sale of stock	*Bullock* 1988, 156
Bullock 1812 (1) Sculptor	George Bullock, Manchester	3 Feb 1812	Workshop contents	*Bullock* 1988, 157
Bullock 1812 (2) Sculptor Moving to London	George Bullock, Bold Street, Liverpool	28 Aug 1812		*Bullock* 1988, 157
Bullock 1812 (3) Sculptor	George Bullock, Bold Street, Liverpool	11 Sept 1812	Paintings	*Bullock* 1988, 157
Bullock 1814 Sculptor Moving to London	George Bullock, Bold Street, Liverpool	21 Nov 1814	Final sale of Liverpool stock and premises	*Bullock* 1988, 157
Bullock 1819 (1) Sculptor Deceased	George Bullock, 4 Tenterden Street, Hanover Square	24–25 March 1819	Pictures, library, shares in Liverpool's public institutions	*Bullock* 1988, 158
Bullock 1819 (2) Deceased	George Bullock, 4 Tenterden Street, Hanover Square	Christie 13–15 May 1819	Unmanufactured stock in trade	Christie Archives
Carlini 1791 Sculptor Deceased	Agostino Carlini, 14 Carlisle Street, Soho, London	Greenwood 13 Jan 1791	Prints, a few pictures, models of monuments, copper-plates, &c	NAL 23L, transcribed in *Trusted* 1992, 784
Carpenter 1736 Sculptor Concentrating on stone carving	Andrew Carpenter, Portugal Row, Piccadilly, London	Jan 1736	Entire stock of statues or figures in hard lead, vases, pots and pedestals	*Daily Journal*, 26 Jan 1736
Carpenter 1744 Sculptor Deceased	Andrew Carpenter, Hyde Park Corner, London	May 1744	Metal statues or figures in hard metal . . . together with his moulds, models and casts in plaister	*Daily Ad*, May 1744
Carr 1768 Mason Deceased	Joseph Carr, Millbank, London	Skinner 13 Sept 1768	Materials	BM, P&D, Sc. A.5.9.
Carter II 1777 (1) Sculptor	Thomas Carter, Stangate Wharf, Westminster Bridge, south side	Willoughby 2 Jan 1777	Marble blocks	BM, P&D, Sc. A.5.9, f.80
Carter II 1777 (2) Sculptor Quitting premises	Thomas Carter, Hyde Park Corner, London	Willoughby 18 Dec 1777	Stock in trade	BM, P&D, Sc. A.5.9, f.495
Carter II 1777 (3) Sculptor Moving house	Thomas Carter, Hyde Park Corner, London	Willoughby 19 Dec 1777	Stock in trade	BM, P&D, Sc. A.5.9, f.54
Chandos 1747 Collector Deceased	James, Duke of Chandos, Canons, Middx	Cock, London 16 June 1747 and 11 days ff	Materials of the Dwelling-House, Out-Houses etc	Huntington
Chantrey 1842 Sculptor	Sir Francis Legatt Chantrey	Christie 10–12 May 1842		*Lugt*
Chantrey 1861 Sculptor	Sir Francis Legatt Chantrey	Christie 15 June 1861		*Lugt*

Sale/Status/Reason	Owner/Address	Auctioneer/Date	Contents	Catalogue
Cheere 1788 Sculptor Deceased	John Cheere, Piccadilly, dwelling and yard	Greenwood 11 Feb 1788 ff	'All the superb and valuable assemblage of casts in lead and plaister, exquisite models and moulds, &c., of the late John Cheere, Esq.'	*Anecdotes*, 1937, V, 144 (quoting unnamed newspaper of 15 Jan 1788)
Cheere 1770 Sculptor Retired	Sir Henry Cheere	Langford 26–27 March 1770	'the Entire large and valuable Collection of Statuary, Busts, basso Relievos, &c. in marble, terracota, and Gess, of an eminent Statuary'	BM, P&D, Sc. A.5.9
Coade Factory 1779 Sculptor Clearing premises	Eleanor Coade, Knightsbridge, London	Jan 1779	Artificial stone and equipment	*Daily Ad*, 24 Dec 1778 and 7–9 Jan 1779
Coade Factory 1834 Sculptor	Coade Factory of Lambeth, Palace Row, New Road	30 July 1834	'the surplus and splendid collection of sculpture in Coade's Imperishable Stone: Sculptured Statues and Groups, Busts, Animals, Medallions, Chimneypieces, etc'	Soane SC 2/35
Coade Factory 1843 Sculptor Ceased trading	Coade Factory of Lambeth, Belvedere Road, Lambeth, London	Rushworth and Jarvis 21–24 July 1843	'valuable works in Terracotta of Coade's Celebrated Manufactory'	Minet Lib, Lambeth, 12/24, 12/64
Damer 1828 Sculptor Deceased	Ann Seymour Damer	1828	Library contents	Warks RO CR 341/266–270
Davy 1768 (1) Sculptor	George Davy, Goulston Square, Whitechapel, London	Moreing March 1768	Works in artificial stone	*Daily Ad*, 23–4 March 1768
Davy 1768 (2) Sculptor	George Davy, Goulston Square, Whitechapel, London	Moreing 9 June 1768	Artificial stone	*Daily Ad*, 27 May and 4 June 1768
Davy 1768 (3) Sculptor Goods from previous sale	George Davy, Goulston Square, Whitechapel, London	Moreing 15 June–2 July 1768	Artificial stone	*Daily Ad*, 15 June 1768
Davy 1768 (4) Sculptor	George Davy, Goulston Square, Whitechapel, London	Moreing 12–14 Dec 1768	Artificial stone	*Daily Ad*, 12 Dec 1768
Davy 1770 Sculptor	George Davy, Goulston Square, Whitechapel, London	Blyth 15–16 Feb 1770	Works in artificial stone	*Daily Ad*, 12–16 Feb 1770
Davy 1771 Sculptor	George Davy, Goulston Square, Whitechapel, London	Blyth 29 April 1771 (postponed from 19 April)	Works in artificial stone	*Daily Ad*, 17–19, 27 & 29 April 1771
Delvaux and Scheemakers 1728 Sculptors Going abroad	Laurent Delvaux and Peter Scheemakers, Millbank, Westminster	Cooper 16–17 April 1728	'Models, by Fiamingo, and other masters . . . and also their collection of prints and drawings'	R Delvaux, Brussels
Dickenson 1726 Sculptor	Richard Dickenson	1726	The 'Curious Stock'	BM Anderdon Cuttings, 1-303, fol 13
Dickenson 1736 Sculptor Deceased	Richard Dickenson	1736	'a great variety of statues, bustos, bass relievos etc in hard metal and finely finished and in particular a very fine gladiator in hard metal' as well as plasters'	*Baker* 2000, 120
Dixon 1775 Sculptor	Dixon's, Wharf, Pedlars Acre, Lambeth	Hathwell 13–15 Dec 1775	Stock in trade	BM, P&D, Sc. A.5.9.
Douglas 1783 Mason		Willoughby 20 March 1783	Materials	BM, P&D, Sc. A.5.9.

Sale/Status/Reason	Owner/Address	Auctioneer/Date	Contents	Catalogue
Durham 1878 Sculptor Deceased	Joseph Durham, London	Christie, Manson and Woods 18 March 1878	Works and collection	Conway Lib photocopy
Erlestoke 1832 Collector	George Watson Taylor, MP, Erlestoke, Wilts	Robins, London 9 July–1 Aug 1832	Sculpture by Banks, Roubiliac, Scheemakers, Gibson, Baily and G Gibbons	NAL 23.E, Courtauld Inst
Fenton 1840 Collector	Miss Fenton, Chandos House, Bath	F Curtis, Machine Printer, 4 Quiet Street, Bath 1840	'Figures and Statuettes; by the late L. Gahagan, Sculptor'	RA Library AND/XVI/166
Flaxman 1803 Sculptor	John Flaxman I	Winstanley 17 June 1803		Getty Br-205
Flaxman 1828 (1) Sculptor Deceased	John Flaxman RA	Christie 12 June 1828	Antique drawings	BM, P&D
Flaxman 1828 (2) Sculptor Deceased	John Flaxman RA	Christie 1 July 1828	Designs, sc, bronze, marble (etc)	BM, P&D
Folkes 1755 Collector Deceased	Martin Folkes	Langford 7–8 May 1755	48 works of sculpture etc	NAL 23D
Forrest 1876 Sculptor Eviction	Robert Forrest, Calton Hill, Edinburgh	Lyon and Turnbull 6 Nov 1876	Coll of sculpture exhibited at the National Monument, Calton Hill, Edinburgh	Edinburgh Public Library
Grittleton 1966 Collector	J Bourne coll	Christie, London 22 Sept 1966	'The Grittleton Marbles'	NAL 23.ZZ
Harris 1790 Sculptor	Charles Harris, 'opposite to the New Church in the Strand, London'	*c*1790	Current stock	NAL 1 37 Y
Hayward 1783 (1) Sculptor	Richard Hayward, London	March 1783	Misc	list in Hofstede de Groot Coll, RKD; *Lugt*
Hayward 1800 (2) Sculptor Deceased	Richard Hayward, London	Mr Smith 4–6th Nov 1800	Misc	Courtauld Book Lib, *Lugt*
Hope 1917 Collector	Thomas Hope, The Deepdene, Dorking, Surrey	Humbert and Flint, 11 Serle St, Lincoln's Inn 12–19 Sept 1917	Contents of the Mansion. . .Statue Gallery and other rooms	VAM 23D
Jelfe 1772 Mason Deceased	William Jelfe	Godfree 9 Jan 1772	Stock and utensils	BM, P&D, Sc. A.5.9.
Langstaff 1778 Mason Bankrupt	Thomas Langstaff, Edward St, Marylebone and George St, Portman Sq.	Willoughby 10 March 1778	Stock in trade	BM, P&D, Sc. A.5.9.
Lawrence 1830 (1) Artist Deceased	Sir Thomas Lawrence PRA, 65 Russell Square, London	Christie 6 July 1830	Medals and casts of works by Gott, Flaxman, Baily, Mrs Damer, Canova and Scheemakers	NAL 23XX
Lawrence 1830 (2) Artist Deceased	Sir Thomas Lawrence PRA, 65 Russell Square, London	Christie 17–19 June 1830	'The remaining part of the valuable collection' including four busts of artists by E H Baily, a 'Sleeping Venus' and a 'Group of four figures' by Joseph Gott and several terracottas by Joseph Nollekens	NAL 23XX
MacDowell 1871 Sculptor Deceased	Patrick MacDowell	Foster 14 July 1871	139 works of sculpture	*Lugt*
Marochetti 1868 (1) Sculptor Deceased	Charles, Baron Marochetti	Sotheby 31 March–3 April 1868	Engravings and etchings	NAL 23.XX

Sale/Status/Reason	Owner/Address	Auctioneer/Date	Contents	Catalogue
Marochetti 1868 (2) Sculptor Deceased	Charles, Baron Marochetti	Christie 7 May 1868	Studio contents	NAL 23.XX
McCulloch 1867 Collector Deceased	Horato McCulloch	T Chapman, Edinburgh 28 Nov 1867 and 4 days following	'Catalogue of the Extensive, Varied & Interesting Collection of Objects of Vertu. . .Medals. . . Miniatures. . .Marble Bust of Dickens by Patric Park'	NLS X.44.g.4 (4)
Mead 1755 (1) Collector Deceased	Dr Richard Mead	Langford, Baker 11–19 Feb 1755	Sculpture, Vases, etc	NAL 2482
Mead 1755 (2) Collector Deceased	Dr Richard Mead	Langford 11–15 March 1755	63 sc, 49 bronzes etc	NAL 23L
Mercer 1772 Sculptor	Bolsover St and Chandos St, Cavendish Square	Bennett 20 May 1772	Materials and utensils	BM, P&D, Sc. A.5.9.
Monti 1855 Sculptor Bankrupt	Raffaelle Monti, 45 Great Marlborough Street, London	Christie 22 June 1855	24 statues by Monti and 21 more 'finished' by him	NAL 23.XX
Nield 1879 Collector	Jonathan Nield, Dunster House, Rochdale	Christie 3 May 1879	'The Valuable Collection of Modern Pictures and Sculpture of Dunster House, Rochdale'	Christie Archives
Noble 1879 Sculptor Deceased	Matthew Noble	Christie 7 June 1879	44 works of sculpture by Noble and other sculptors	*Lugt*
Nollekens 1823 (1) Sculptor Deceased	Joseph Nollekens RA, 9 Mortimer Street, Marylebone, London	Christie 3–5 July 1823	Models and marbles	NAL 23.XX
Nollekens 1823 (2) Sculptor Deceased	Joseph Nollekens RA, 9 Mortimer Street, Marylebone, London	Evans 4–5 Dec 1823	Prints and Drawings	NAL 23.L
Nollekens 1823 (3) Sculptor Deceased	Joseph Nollekens RA, 9 Mortimer Street, Marylebone, London	Evans 18–19 Dec 1823	Library contents	BM, P&D
Nost 1712 (1) Sculptor Deceased	John Nost I, Hyde Park Road, London	8–9 April 1712	Plasters by several eminent sculptors, abundance of models of monuments by Nost	*Spectator*, 31 March 1712 (BM C71.g.1)
Nost 1712 (2) Sculptor Deceased	John Nost I, Hyde-Park-Road 'near the Queen's Mead-house', London	17 April 1712	Lead vases and figures, marble chimneypieces etc	BL Cup.645.e.5 (1) transcribed in *O'Connell* 1987, 805–6
Nost 1712 (3) Sculptor Deceased	John Nost I, near Hyde Park Corner, London		'fine inlaid tables, marble chimneypieces, figures etc'	*The Guardian* (no 60, 20 May 1713)
Oppenheim 1864 Collector Deceased	Johann Moritz Oppenheim	Christie 4 June 1864	'the highly important collection of Ancient and Modern pictures, bronzes and sculpture' incl a bust by Henry Westmacott	NAL 23XX
Paine 1830 Collector Deceased	James Paine	Christie 12 March 1830	Coll, including terra-cotta model by Thomas Banks	Christie and VAM II. RC. DD.29, f227
Pearce 1696 Sculptor Deceased	Edward Pearce	Feb 1696	A '*curious collection of Books, Drawings, Prints, Models and Plaster Figures*' sold with the collection of Thomas Manby, landscape painter	*Colvin* 1995, 755 quoting *London Gazette*, 3156, 30 Jan–3 Feb 1695/6
Peel heirlooms 1900 Collector	Sir Robert Peel and descendants	Robinson and Fisher, Dublin		

Sale/Status/Reason	Owner/Address	Auctioneer/Date	Contents	Catalogue
Phillipson 1785 Sculptor Deceased	Phillipson, Great Castle Street, Cavendish Square	Christie 12 Dec 1785	Stock in trade	*Gunnis* 1968, 301
Pincot and Davy 1767 Sculptor	Daniel Pincot and George Davy, Goulston Square, Whitchapel, London	Christie Dec 1767	Stock in trade	Christie Archives
Pistrucci 1855 Sculptor Deceased	Benedetto Pistrucci, Englefield Green, Surrey	Foster 30 Nov 1855	Unfinished works in marble, moulds, casts	ODNB
Pond 1759 Artist	Arthur Pond	Langford 17 March 1759	Casts from the antique and modern masters	BM, P&D, Sc. A.5.9.
Read 1787 Sculptor Deceased	Nicholas Read, 65, St Martin's Lane	William Booth 2 Aug 1787	Workshop contents (inc shop front)	NAL II.RC.Q.25
Rossi 1835 Sculptor Retirement	John Charles Felix Rossi, Grove Place, Lisson Grove North, London	Robins 3–4 March 1835	Studio contents	NAL 23L
Rossi 1840 Sculptor Unknown	Frederick Orton Rossi	Mr Coates, Portman Square 10 July 1840 (?)	Raffle of 24 original models by the late Charles Rossi, RA	J C F Rossi Archive, Guildhall PMD
Roubiliac 1762 (1) Sculptor Deceased	Louis-François Roubiliac, St Martin's Lane, London	Langford 12 May 1762 and 3 days following	Models, moulds, casts and busts	*Bindman and Baker*, 362–7
Roubiliac 1762 (2) Sculptor Deceased	Louis-François Roubiliac, St Martin's Lane, London	Langford 12 June 1762	Marble stocks, utensils	*Bindman and Baker*, 368–9
Rysbrack 1764 (1) Sculptor Retiring	Michael Rysbrack, Vere Street, Oxford Road, London	Langford 15 Feb 1764 and 10 evenings following	Drawings and books of prints of Mr. Michael Rysbrack	*Lugt*; BM, P&D
Rysbrack 1765 (2) Sculptor Retiring	Michael Rysbrack, Vere Street, near Oxford Chapel, London	Langford 20 April 1765	The 'genuine and curious collection'	*Lugt*
Rysbrack 1766 (3) Sculptor Retiring	Michael Rysbrack, Vere Street, near Oxford Chapel, London	Langford 24–25 Jan 1766	The 'Genuine, Large and Curious Collection of Models, &c'	BL C.119.h.3 (61)
Rysbrack 1767 (4) Sculptor Retiring	Michael Rysbrack, Vere St, Oxford Road, London	Langford 14 Feb 1767	'pictures, marble bustos and vases, fine models of basso relievos and monuments'	*Lugt*
Rysbrack 1767 (5) Sculptor Retiring	Michael Rysbrack, Vere St, near Oxford Chapel, London	Langford 18 April 1767	'A catalogue of the curious and well-chosen collection of plaister figures, heads, hands, feet &c'	*Lugt*
Rysbrack 1772 (6) Sculptor Deceased	Michael Rysbrack	Langford April 1772	Drawings, sketches, miniatures, books and aquatints	BL, Library
Rysbrack 1774 (7) Sculptor Deceased	Michael Rysbrack	Christie 7–9 Feb 1774	'the reserved collection of capital drawings, prints, and books of prints, of the late ingenious Mr. Rysbrack'	*Lugt*
Scheemakers 1733 Sculptor Going abroad	Henry Scheemakers, St Margaret's Lane, Westminster	20 July 1733	Stock, including statues, busts, reliefs, pedestals, chimneypieces, a monument	*Daily Post*, 20 July 1733
Scheemakers 1755 Sculptor Intending to retire	Peter Scheemaker, Vine St, Piccadilly, London	Langford 10 Dec 1755 and 6 evenings following	'The Genuine, Entire and Curious Collection of Prints and Drawings, bound and unbound of Mr. Peter Scheemaker'	BL, c.119.h.3 (32)
Scheemakers 1756 Sculptor Moving to Isleworth	Peter Scheemakers, Vine St, Piccadilly, London	Langford 10–11 March 1756	A Catalogue of the Genuine, large and Curious Collection of Models and Marbles in Groupes, Figures, Busts, &c [and] Pictures	BL c.119.h.3 (33)

Sale/Status/Reason	Owner/Address	Auctioneer/Date	Contents	Catalogue
Scheemakers 1757 Sculptor Intended retirement	Peter Scheemakers, Vine St, Piccadilly, London	Langford 18–19 May 1757	Marbles, models and casts	*Daily Ad*, 6 May 1757
Scheemakers 1771 (1) Sculptor Retirement	Peter Scheemakers, Vine St, Piccadilly, London	Langford and son 6–7 June 1771	Models and casts	BM, P&D, A.5.9. Sc.
Scheemakers 1771 (2) Sculptor Retirement	Peter Scheemakers, Vine St, Piccadilly, London	1771	Busts, vases, figures	BM MSS D-7854 i 17 (8); destroyed
Scheemakers 1805 Sculptor Retirement	Thomas Scheemakers, 6 Titchfield St, Oxford Market, London	Christie 21 May 1805	Models in terracotta, bas reliefs, stocks of marble, working tools	Christie Archives
Scheemakers and Delvaux 1728 Sculptors Going abroad	Peter Scheemakers and Laurent Delvaux, Millbank, Westminster	Cooper 16–17 April 1728	Models, by Fiamingo, and other masters . . . and also their collection of prints and drawings	R Delvaux, Brussels
Sibson 1877 Collector	Francis Sibson	Christie 7 March 1877	'The extensive and beautiful collection of Old Wedgwood', wax models and drawings by J. Flaxman, also work by Westmacott I	*Priced cats, NAL[1]; Christie Archives
Smith 1803 (1) Sculptor	Nathaniel Smith	Wells 8 Oct 1803	Misc	Getty prov index Br-216
Smith 1809 (2) Sculptor	Nathaniel Smith	Dodd's 26 April–4 May 1809	Misc	Getty prov index Br-665
Spang 1762 Sculptor Deceased	Michael Henry Spang, Little Stanhope St, London	21 Dec 1762	Household furniture, models, moulds and stock in trade	BM, P&D, Sc. A.5.9
Spence 1870 Sculptor Deceased	Benjamin Edward Spence, Rome	Christie, Rome 4 June 1870	Statues, statuettes and busts	GPC
Stewart 1784 Sculptor Quitting business	Robert Stewart, 14 Prince's Street, near Great George Street, London	Christie 27 March 1784	50 drawings for tablets, tombs etc; drawings for chimneypieces	*Gunnis* 1968, 374
Stowe sale 1921 Collection		Jackson Stops July 4–28, 1921	Entire contents; numerous pieces of work by British sculptors	H Shaw ed, *The Stowe House Sale Cat*
Stowe sale 1922 Collection		Jackson Stops Oct 1922	Remaining contents; numerous pieces of work by British sculptors	H Shaw ed, *The Stowe House Sale Cat*
Taylor 1777 Sculptor Bankrupt	William Taylor	Willoughby 11 Dec 1777	Materials, chimneypiece, utensils	BM, P&D, Sc. A.5.9.
Van Aken (Vanhaecken) 1751 Artist Deceased	Joseph Van Aken, Southampton Rd, Bloomsbury, London	Langford 11 February and following 14 days	Entire coll, models, terracottas, plasters, including several by Rysbrack	BM, P&D, Sc. A.5.9.
Van der Hagen 1771 Sculptor Deceased	Gaspar Van der Hagen,	Langford and Son, Great Piazza, Covent Garden 20 April 1771	'by order of the executors of Mr Vanderhagen, carver, deceased, principal assistant to the late Mr Rysbrack, several fine heads and figures in ivory, basso-relievos in marble, books and prints etc'	*Walpole* 1937, 154–5
Van Spangen 1748 Sculptor (?) Deceased	John Van Spangen	Cock and Langford, London 10–12 Feb 1748	'purchased lately in Holland' Sc, paintings, curios	*Lugt*
Vanina 1770 (1) Sculptor Going abroad	Peter Vanina, Dover Street, Piccadilly, London	Christie 3–4 April 1770	Stock in trade	BM, P&D, Sc. A.5.9.

Sale/Status/Reason	Owner/Address	Auctioneer/Date	Contents	Catalogue
Vanina 1770 (2) Sculptor 'Going abroad'	Peter Vanina, Dover St, Piccadilly, London	Christie 3 July 1770	Stock in trade	*Gunnis* 1968, 408
Watson 1848 Sculptor Deceased	Musgrave Lewthwaite Watson, Upper Gloucester Place, London	14 Sept 1848	Sketches, casts etc	*Gunnis* 1968, 415
Weekes and others 1880 Sculptor Deceased	Henry Weekes and others	Christie 29 May 1880	48 sculptures	*Lugt*
Westmacott 1783 Sculptor Removing to Mount St, London	Richard Westmacott I	Willoughby 28 January 1783	Stocks of marble and stone	BM, P&D, Sc. A.5.9.
Westmacott 1828 Sculptor	George Westmacott	Christie 5 Aug 1828	59 works of sculpture, '109 marbles'	Christie Archives
Westmacott 1832 Sculptor	Charles Molloy Westmacott	Phillips, London 29 May and 2 June 1832	251 items including 116 paintings, bronze, porcelain and furniture	*Lugt*
Westmacott 1852 Sculptor	Charles Molloy Westmacott	Puttick, London 2 March 1852	Statuettes and other objets d'art	*Lugt*
Westmacott 1857 Sculptor Deceased	Sir Richard Westmacott (and others)	Sotheby 13–17 July 1857	Paintings, drawings, books and porcelain (over 1000 lots)	*Lugt*
Westmacott 1859 Sculptor	Sir Richard Westmacott (and others)	Christie, London 7 May 1859	111 paintings and 5 sculptures	NAL 23.XX
Wildsmith 1769 Sculptor Bankrupt	John Wildsmith, Piccadilly, near St James's, London	Webster 31 July and 1 Aug 1769	Stock in trade	BM, P&D, Sc. A.5.9.
Williams 1779 Sculptor Bankrupt	Emanuel Wilson	Willoughby 18–19 Jan 1779	Stock in trade	BM, P&D, Sc. A.5.9.
Wilton 1786 Sculptor	Joseph Wilton RA	8–9 July 1786	Sale of premises and studio contents, including blocks of marble, models, casts, busts and several 'elegantly ornamented chimney-pieces, which had been executed upon speculation'	*Smith* 1828, vol 2, 180
Woolner 1913 Sculptor Deceased	Thomas Woolner, 29 Welbeck Street, London	Knight, Frank and Rutley 22 April 1913	Models, works in marble and bronze, sculptor's tools	NAL 23.L
Wyatt 1861 Sculptor Deceased (1850)	Richard James Wyatt	Christie 22 June 1861	Studio contents (53 sculptures)	*Lugt*
Wyatt 1862 Sculptor Deceased	Matthew Cotes Wyatt	Foster 20 June 1862	Personal belongings, including a large bronze bust of George III, an ivory statuette of the Marquess of Anglesea and a large coll of precious stones	RH/JP 9, 1644 (info Miss E Wyatt), untraced

BIBLIOGRAPHY and ABBREVIATIONS

A&A
www.artandarchitecture.org.uk/images/conway/1a01af9e.html

AAF
Artists' Annuity Fund

AAF, AB
Artists' Annuity Fund, the Annuitants Book, from 1810 (Guildhall, 23676)

AAF, CM
Artists' Annuity Fund, Committee Minutes, 1825–28; 1836–42; 1842–47 (Guildhall, 23667)

AAF, MGM
Artists' Annuity Fund, Minutes of General Meetings, 1839–54 (Guildhall, 23666)

AAF, Proposals
Artists' Annuity Fund, Proposals for Membership, 1812–41 (Guildhall, 23663/1)

Abbey Muniments
Westminster Abbey Muniments, 700–present (Westminster Abbey Muniment Room and Library)

Abbot 1988
Abbot, W W, ed, *The Papers of George Washington: Colonial Series, vol 6, 6 Sept 1758–Dec 1760* (Charlottesville VA: 1988) p 355

Abel Smith 1986
Abel Smith, Julia, 'Great Saxham Hall, Suffolk: The home of Lady Stirling', *Country Life*, vol 180, no 4658 (27 Nov 1986) pp 1698–702

Abramson 1993
Abramson, Daniel, 'Money's Architecture: The Building of the Bank of England, 1731–1833' Ph D Diss (Harvard: 1993)

Acquisitions 1981
'Recent Acquisitions (VAM)', *Burlington Magazine*, vol 123 (1981) p 63

Adams 1968
Adams, John, 'Bastards of Blandford', *Architectural Review*, vol 143 (June 1968) p 445

Adams 1991
Adams, Adeline, 'Early American Sculpture Reflected', *Sculpture Review*, vol 40, no 4 (1991) pp 20–7

Adams 1996
Adams, Bernard, 'The Thorvaldsen Bust of Byron', *Keats–Shelley Review*, (Spring 1996) pp 205–19

Adams Papers (1)
Personal and family papers of George Gamon Adams, 1844–1899 (Getty Research Institute, Los Angeles, California, MSS 870072)

Adams Papers (2)
Papers relating to George Gamon Adams, including photographs of the sculptor and his works, notes and press cuttings, *c*1820–1979 (VAM, AAD/1997/12)

Addleshaw 1967
Addleshaw, G W O, 'Architects, Sculptors, Painters, Craftsmen, 1660–1960, Whose Work is to be Seen in York Minster', *Architectural History*, vol 10 (1967) pp 89–119

AGBI (1)
Artists' General Benevolent Fund, Applicants Registers, 6 vols (Burlington House, London)

AGBI (2)
Artists' General Benevolent Institution

AGNSW
Art Gallery of New South Wales, Sydney

Aislabie Papers
Aislabie Papers, 1732–1753 (West Yorks CRO, VR 285)

AJ
Art Journal, initially *Art Union*

AJ Cat 1851
The Great Exhibition of the Works of Industry of all Nations: The Art Journal Illustrated Catalogue, facsimile of official catalogue published London, 1851 (Newton Abbott: 1970)

AJ Cat 1862
The Art Journal Illustrated Catalogue of the International Exhibition 1862, facsimile edition (Wakefield: 1973)

AL/RG
Alastair Laing, annotated Gunnis

Albrizzi 1821–4
Albrizzi, Isabella Teotochi, *Opere di Scultura e di Plastica di Antonio Canova* (1821–1824; reprinted in 4 vols with an introduction by Gianni Venturi and Manlio Pastore Stocchi 2003)

Alcock 1980
Alcock, J P, 'Sir William Chambers and the Building of Parkstead House, Roehampton', *Sussex Archaeological Collections*, vol 72 (1980) pp 197–219

Aldsworth 1982
Aldsworth, F G, 'The May Family Vault and the Lady May Monument', *Sussex Archaeological Collections*, vol 120 (1982) p 231

Alexander 1957
Alexander, Edward Boyd, *Life at Fonthill 1807–1822* (1957)

Alfonso 1989
Alfonso, S L, *Palácio de Quelez, Jardins* (Lisbon: 1989)

Alfonso and Delaforce 1986
Afonso, S L and Delaforce, A, *Palace of Queluz: The Gardens* (Lisbon: 1986)

All Saints, Bristol, Ch W Accts
Churchwardens' Accounts, All Saints, Bristol, 1717 (BRO, P/AS/ChW)

All Souls, Coll Buildings
College Buildings (All Souls, Oxford, Bodl MSS DD)

Allan 1975
Allan, D G C, 'Caleb Whitefoord', *Connoisseur*, vol 190, no 765 (Nov 1975) pp 194–99

Allan 1979
Allan, D G C, *William Shipley. Founder of the Royal Society of Arts* (1979)

Allan 1984
Allan, D G C, 'Artists and the Society in the 18th Century (i) The Foundation and Henry Cheere's Plan for an Academy (ii) Members and Premiums in the First Decade, 1755–64 (iii) The Second Decade, 1765–74 (iv) Members and Premiums in the Years after 1775', *Royal Society of Arts Journal*, vol 132, no 5331–4 (May 1984) pp 204–207, 401–406

Allan and Abbott 1992
Allan, D G C, and Abbott, John L, *The Virtuoso Tribe of Arts and Sciences* (1992)

Allderidge 1977
Allderidge, P, *Cibber's Figures from the Gates of Bedlam*, V&A "Masterpieces", 14 (1977)

Allen 1826
Allen, Thomas, *History of Lambeth* (1826)

Allen 1827–37
Allen, Thomas, *The History and Antiquities of London*, 5 vols (1827–37)

Allen 1829
Allen, Thomas, *A New and Complete History of the County of York*, 2 vols (1829)

Allen 1958
Allen, Cynthia, 'John Graham Lough and the Neo-Classic Tradition' BA Diss (Univ of Newcastle-upon-Tyne: 1958)

Allen 1981
Allen, Brian, 'Jonathan Tyers' Other Garden', *Journal of Garden History*, vol 1, no 3 (1981) pp 215–38

Allen 1983
Allen, Brian, 'Joseph Wilton, Francis Hayman and the Chimney-Pieces from Northumberland House', *Burlington Magazine*, vol 125 (April 1983) pp 195–202

Allen 1987
Allen, Brian, *Francis Hayman* (New Haven and London: 1987)

Allen and Dukelskaya 1996–7
Allen, Brian, and Dukelskaya, Larissa, *British Art Treasures from Russian Imperial Collections in the Hermitage* (Yale Center for British Art, New Haven: 1996–97)

Allfrey 1909
Allfrey, E W, 'III. The architectural history of the college', in *Brasenose Quartercentenary Monographs*, vol I (Oxford Historical Society, 1909)

ALRI
Academy of the Liverpool Royal Institution

Am Archi 1933
'Grinling Gibbons, 1648–1721', *American Architect and Architecture*, vol 143 (March 1933) pp 29–30

Ambrose 1990
Ambrose, Jamie, 'Restoring Grinling Gibbons; An American at the Court of King William', *Apollo*, no 132 (Nov 1990) pp 340–41

Anderdon Cuttings
Cuttings collected by J H Anderdon, 1869 (BM)

Anderson 1855
Anderson, John Corbet, *Monuments and Antiquities of Croydon Church, in the County of Surrey* (1855)

Anderson 1980
Anderson, Patricia, *Promoted to Glory; The Apotheosis of George Washington*, exhib cat (Northampton, MA: 22 Feb–6 April 1980)

Anecdotes 1762–71
Walpole, Horace, *Anecdotes of Painting in England*, 4 vols (1762–71)

Anecdotes 1782
Walpole, Horace, *Anecdotes of Painting in England*, 5 vols (1782)

Anecdotes 1876
Walpole, Horace, *Anecdotes of Painting in England*, ed Ralph N Wornum, 3 vols (London: 1876)

Anecdotes 1888
Walpole, Horace, *Anecdotes of Painting in England*, 3 vols (1888)

Anecdotes 1937
Walpole, Horace, *Anecdotes of Painting in England*, vol 5 (1937)

Angelicoussis 1992
Angelicoussis, Elizabeth, *The Woburn Abbey Collection of Classical Antiquities* (Mainz am Rhein: 1992)

Ann Saunders typescript
Ann Saunders (née Cox-Johnson), John Bacon RA and John Bacon the Younger, unpublished monograph, *c*1960 (HMI)

Annals of the Fine Arts
Elmes, James, ed, *Annals of the Fine Arts*, 5 vols (1817–20)

Anspach 1826
Margravine of Anspach, Elizabeth, *Memoirs of the Margravine of Anspach*, 2 vols (1826)

Antiques 1952
'Flaxman's Wedgwood Vase Decorations: Homer, Virgil', *Antiques Magazine*, vol 61 (May 1952) p 403

Apollo 1938
'Wedgwood Medallion Portrait', *Apollo*, vol 27 (May 1938) p 249

Apollo 1953
'Mirror Frame; The Work of Grinling Gibbons?', *Apollo*, vol 58 (Sept 1953) pp 74–75

Apollo 1963
Editorial, 'The Neo-Classic Ideal', *Apollo*, no 78 (Nov 1963) p 335

Apollo 1968
'Two Empire Sculptures to Ottowa', *Apollo*, no 88 (Sept 1968) p 227

Apollo 1981
'Bust of Sir Hans Sloane (British Museum) (Terracotta)', *Apollo*, no 114 (Nov 1981) p 328

Apollo 1989
Editorial, 'How to Recognise a Third-Class Nation: Works of Art Leaving the Country', *Apollo*, no 130 (Oct 1989) pp 224–25

Apollo 1990
Editorial, 'Saving the Graces', *Apollo*, no 131 (Feb 1990) p 76

Apollo 1994
'Acquisition of the Year: The Three Graces by Antonio Canova', *Apollo*, no 140 (Dec 1994) pp 18–23

Apollo 2002
'Lord Cobham's monument at Stowe, Buckinghamshire', *Apollo*, vol 154, no 478 (April 2002) p 7

Apprenticeship Tax Roll Index
Index to the Apprenticeship Roll, 1738 (PRO, IR 1/15 fol 226)

APR
Artists' Papers Register

Apted 1984
Apted, M R, 'Arnold Quellin's Statues at Glamis Castle', *Antiquaries Journal*, vol 64, no 1 (1984) pp 53–61

AQ
Art Quarterly

ARA
Associate Member of the Royal Academy, London

Archer 1965
Archer, Mildred, 'East India Company and British Art', *Apollo*, no 82 (Nov 1965) pp 401–9

Archer 1984
Archer, Mildred, 'Neo-classical Sculpture in India by British Artists', *Apollo*, vol 120, no 269 (July 1984) pp 50–5

Archer 1986
Archer, Mildred, *The India Office Collection of Paintings and Sculpture* (1986)

Archit Rev 1944
'Argyll Monument in Westminster Abbey', *Architectural Review*, vol 95 (Feb 1944) pp 52–3

Archit Rev 1967
'Cumberland Sculpture', *Architectural Review*, vol 141 (June 1967) p 466

Archit Rev 1968
'Stone's Sculpture', *Architectural Review*, vol 144 (Oct 1968) pp 248–49

Archit Rev 1969
'Rysbrack and Roubiliac', *Architectural Review*, vol 145 (Feb 1969) pp 88–89

Archit Rev 1970
'Emperors Restored: Emperors' Heads Surrounding the Sheldonian Theatre at Oxford', *Architectural Review*, vol 148 (Nov 1970) pp 280–1

Arciszewska 2000
Arciszewska, Barbara, 'Re-Casting George I. Sculpture, the Royal Image and the Market', in *The Lustrous Trade: Material Culture and the History of Sculpture in England and Italy, c.1700–c.1860*, ed Sicca, Cinzia and Yarrington, Alison (2000) pp 27–48

Arias Angles 1985
Arias Angles, Enrique, 'Influencias de John Flaxman y Gavin Hamilton en Jose de Madrazo y Nueva Lectura de La Muerte de Viriato', *Archivo Espanol de Arte Madrid*, vol 58, no 232 (Oct–Dec 1985) pp 351–62

Armstead Albums
Albums of Henry Hugh Armstead (RA)

Armstead Archive
Papers of Henry Hugh Armstead (HMI)

Armstead Death Duty Accounts
Death Duty Accounts of Henry Hugh Armstead, 1905–6 (TNA, IR 59/237)

Armstead Letter
Letter, Henry Hugh Armstead (CWAC, Acc 988/1)

Armstead/Craik
Correspondence between Henry Hugh Armstead and George Lillie Craik, Macmillan Papers 1888–1895 (BL, Add MS 61895 fols 96–117)

Armstead/Cusins
Letter from Henry Hugh Armstead to Sir W G Cusins, concerning a bust of Beethoven, Royal Philharmonic Society Archive 1871 (BL, RPS MS 333 fols 242–45)

Armstead/Dilke
Letter from Henry Hugh Armstead to Emilia Francis, 2nd Lady Dilke, Dilke Papers 1879 (BL, Add MS 43908, fol 66)

Armstead/Fildes
Letter from Henry Hugh Armstead to Luke Fildes, Fildes Corr 1901 (NAL, MSL/1972/6977/9)

Armstead/Gosse
Letters (thirteen) from Henry Hugh Armstead to Edmund Gosse, Gosse Papers 14 June 1880–21 Nov 1897 (Brotherton MSS, BC Gosse Correspondence)

Armstead/Layard
Letters from Henry Hugh Armstead to Sir Austen Henry Layard, Layard Papers 1866, 1867 (BL, Add MS 38992 fol 254, 38993 fol 27, 38994 fols 51–109)

Armstead/Pascal
Letter from Henry Hugh Armstead to C Pascal, 1903 (NAL)

Armstead/Philip
Letter from Henry Hugh Armstead to John Birnie Philip regarding podium sculpture for the Albert Memorial, Whistler Papers 16 April 1864 (University of Glasgow Special Collections, MS Whistler A194)

Armstead/Scott
Copies of correspondence between Henry Hugh Armstead and Sir George Gilbert Scott, Layard Papers 1869 (BL, Add MS 38996 fols 86–9)

Armstead/Spielmann (1)
Letters from Henry Hugh Armstead to Isidore Spielmann, Spielmann Correspondence 1897–1904 (NAL, MSL/1999/2/95–100)

Armstead/Spielmann (2)
Letter from Henry Hugh Armstead to I Spielmann, Isidore Spielmann collection of autograph letters of British artists 1900 (NAL, MSL/1917/229/10)

Armstead/VAM
Correspondence between Henry Hugh Armstead and the Victoria and Albert Museum, 1870–1900 (VAM AAD, MA/1/A834)

Art Dig 1931
'Washington's Sculptor was Napoleon's Foe', *Art Digest*, vol 5 (Sept 1931) p 19

Art Dig 1933
'Marble Bust by Joseph Nollekens of Charles James Fox', *Art Digest*, vol 8 (15 Nov 1933) p 10

Art in Am 1994
'Three Graces Not California Bound', *Art in America*, vol 82 (Oct 1994) p 160

Art News 1934
'Bust of Spenser is Given to Yale', *Art News*, vol 32 (19 May 1934) p 13

Art News 1935
'Grinling Gibbons Staircase Bought by Metropolitan', *Art News*, vol 34 (23 Nov 1935) p 13

Art News 1938
'Indianapolis: The Outline Drawings of John Flaxman', *Art News*, vol 36 (19 Mar 1938) pp 18–19

Art Newsp 1994
'In Legal Limbo; Getty Trust Appeal for Legal Review of Secretary of State's Export Ban on Canova's Three Graces', *Art Newspaper*, vol 5 (Oct 1994) p 5

Art Newsp, 1994 Apr
'The Three Graces are not just a National Matter', *Art Newspaper*, vol 5 (Apr 1994) p 1

ASA
Association of Scottish Artists (held in Edinburgh, various locations), 1808–1813

Ashburnham Abstract of Bills
Lord Ashburnham, Abstract of Bills for Sundry Works at Dover Street, 1819 (East Sussex RO, ASH 2877)

Ashburnham Accts
Lord Ashburnham, Bills, Ashburnham Archives 1812–1817 (East Sussex RO, ASH 2804, 2805, 2806, 2812, 2814, 2816, 2820, 2824, 2829, 2835, 2836, 2850, 2851, 2853, 2855)

Ashburnham Letterbook
John, Lord Ashburnham, Letterbook, Ashburnham Archives 9 March 1696–28 Aug 1698; 24 Aug 1698–23 Feb 1699; 24 July 1704–12 Dec 1705; Dec 1705–Feb 1707 (East Sussex RO, ASH 841–847)

Ashburnham MS
Lord Ashburnham, Masons' Work at Ashburnham Place, 1815–1818 (East Sussex RO, MS 1852, 2862)

Ashburnham, Accts with Artificers
Lord Ashburnham, Statement of Account with Artificers at Ashburnham, 1813–1815 (East Sussex RO, 1862, 1854, 2867)

Ashby 1913
Ashby, T, 'Thomas Jenkins in Rome', *Papers of the British School in Rome*, vol 6 (1913) p 487

Ashmolean
Ashmolean Museum, Oxford

Ashmolean 1967
Drawings by English Sculptors 1680–1810, exhib cat (Ashmolean, Oxford: 1967)

Ashton 1980
Ashton, Geoffrey, *Shakespeare's Heroines in the Nineteenth Century*, exhib cat (Buxton Museum and Art Gallery: 22 July–17 Aug 1980)

Aslet 1984
Aslet, Clive, 'Stoneleigh Abbey, Warwickshire, I, II: the Seat of Lord Leigh', *Country Life*, vol 176, no 4557 (20 Dec 1984) pp 1934–37

Aslet 1989
Aslet, Clive, 'Early History of Allerton Park', *Country Life*, vol 183, no 4 (26 Jan 1989) pp 92–95

Ass Univ Presses
Associated University Presses

Aston 1987
Aston, Nigel, 'Patronage of a Parson-Peer: Church of the 4th Earl of Harborough', *Country Life*, vol 181, no 49 (3 Dec 1987) pp 230–32

Atholl Accounts
Blair Castle Accounts, 1756 (Archives Duke of Atholl, Blair Castle, Perthshire, Scotland)

Atkinson 1858
Atkinson, S, 'John Hogan', *Irish Quarterly Review*, vol 8, no 30 (July 1858) pp 493–588

Atkinson 1882
A[tkinson], S, *Arts and Industries in Ireland. I John Henry Foley, R A. A sketch of the life and works of the Sculptor of the O'Connell Monument* (Dublin: 1882) pp 1–34

Atterbury 1989
Atterbury, Paul, ed, *The Parian Phenomenon. A Survey of Victorian Parian Porcelain Statuary and Busts* (1989)

Atterbury and Wainwright 1994
Atterbury, Paul, and Wainwright, Clive, *Pugin: a Gothic passion*, published to accompany VAM exhib (New Haven and London: 1994)

AU
Art Union

Audley End Archives
Audley End Archives, 1763–4 (Essex CRO, D/DBy, A248)

Auque 1992
Auque, Hubert, 'Deux Oeuvres de Louis François Roubiliac, 1705?–1762: Les Tombreaux du Duc et de la Duchesse de Montagu', *Revue du Nord*, vol 74, no 297–298 (1992) pp 593–98

Australia 1979
Tomory, Peter A, *The Poetical Circle. Fuseli and the British*, exhib cat (travelling exhib, Australia and New Zealand: 1979)

Aveling 1970
Aveling, J C H, *Catholic Recusancy in the City of York, 1558–1791* (Catholic Record Society, 1970)

Avery 1972
Avery, Charles, 'From David d'Angers to Rodin – Britain's National Collection of French Nineteenth-Century Sculpture', *Connoisseur*, vol 179 (Apr 1972) pp 230–39

Avery 1974
Avery, Charles, 'John Cheere at Marble Hill', *Burlington Magazine*, vol 116 (1974) pp 551–53

Avery 1975
Avery, Charles, 'Neo-Classical Portraits by Pistrucci and Rauch', *Apollo*, no 102 (July 1975) pp 36–43

Avery 1977
Avery, Charles, 'Bernardo Vecchietti and the Wax Models of Giambologna', in *Ceroplastica nella Scienza e nell'Arte*, conference proceedings (Firenze: 1977) pp 461–76

Avery 1980
Avery, Charles, 'Laurent Delvaux's Sculpture in England', *National Trust Studies*, vol 2 (1980) pp 150–70

Avery 1981
Avery, Charles, *Studies in European Sculpture* (Christie, 1981)

Avery 1983
Avery, Charles, 'Laurent Delvaux's Sculpture at Woburn Abbey', *Apollo*, vol 118 (Oct 1983) pp 312–21

Avery 1984
Avery, Charles, 'David Le Marchand – Huguenot Ivory Carver', *Proceedings of the Huguenot Society of London*, vol 24, no 2 (1984) pp 113–18

Avery 1985
Avery, Charles, 'Missing Presumed Lost; Some Ivory Portraits by David Le Marchand', *Country Life*, vol 177, no 4581 (6 June 1985) pp 1562–64

Avery 1987
Avery, Charles, 'Finding the Second Version of Biblis and Caunus by Laurent Delvaux', *Apollo*, no 126 (Dec 1987) p 454

Avery 1996
Avery, Charles, *David le Marchand, 1674–1726 "An Ingenious Man for Carving in Ivory"*, exhib cat (1996)

Avery 1999
Avery, Charles, 'David le Marchand, Precursor of Eighteenth Century English Portrait Sculpture', *British Art Journal*, vol 1, no 1 (1999) pp 27–34

Avery 2002
Avery, Charles, 'John Deare's Marble Reliefs for Sir Andrew Corbet Corbet Bt', *British Art Journal*, vol III, no 2 (Spring 2002) pp 50–57

Avery 2005
Avery, Charles, 'Soldani's Mythological Bronzes and his British Clientele', *The Sculpture Journal*, vol 14 (2005) pp 8–29

Avery and Laing 1981
Avery, Charles, and Laing, Alastair, *Fingerprints of the artist: European terra-cotta sculpture from the Arthur M Sackler collections*, exhib cat (National Gallery of Art, Washington: 1981)

Avery and Marsh 1985
Avery, Charles, and Marsh, Madeleine, 'The Bronze Statuettes of the Art Union of London: the Rise and Decline of Victorian Taste in Sculpture', *Apollo*, no 121 (May 1985) pp 328–37

Ayerbach and Adams, 1971
Ayerbach, Ena and Kingsley Adams, C, *Paintings and Sculpture of Hatfield House* (1971)

Aylmer 1977
Aylmer, G E, 'Funeral Monuments and other Post-Medieval Sculpture', in *A History of York Minster*, ed G E Aylmer and A Cant (Oxford: 1977) pp 430–86

Aylmer and Tiller, 2000
Aylmer, G E and Tiller, J E, *Hereford Cathedral: The Architectural History of the Cathedral since the Reformation* (2000)

Ayres 1997
Ayres, Patrick, *Classical Culture and the Idea of Rome in Eighteenth-Century England* (1997)

B'ham R L
Birmingham Reference Library

B'ham Soc of A
Birmingham Society of Artists

Baarsen 1998
Baarsen, Reinier, 'High Rococo in Holland: William IV and Agostino Carlini', *Burlington Magazine*, vol 140 (Mar 1998) pp 172–83

Bacchi 1994
Bacchi, Andrea, 'L'Andromeda di Lord Exeter', *Antologia di Belle Arti*, no 48–51 (1994) pp 64–70

Bacchi 1995
Bacchi, Andrea, ' "L'Operazione con li Modelli": Pierre Etienne Monnot et Carlo Maratta a Confronto', *Ricerche di Storia dell'Arte*, no 55 (1995) pp 39–52

Bach-Nielson 1985
Bach-Nielson, Carsten, 'Der Bildhauer Thomas Quellin und das Hochbarock in Morden', *Analecta Instituti Danici*, vol 45 (1985)

Bacon Family Papers
Bacon family papers, including letters and diaries of the 18th and 19th centuries (family coll)

Bacon Property Papers
Documents relating to London properties owned by the Bacon family, formerly Messrs Kennedy, Ponsonby and Prideaux 18th and 19th century (LMA E/BN/16–46)

Bacon Reminiscences 1847–50
Reminiscences of the Late John Bacon Esquire RA and other persons of his time; as far as an old treacherous memory may be relied on, 1847–50 (family coll)

Bacon the Younger 1843 (1)
Bacon, John II, 'Remarks on Monumental Architecture', *Transactions of the Exeter Diocesan Society*, vol 1 (1843) pp 117–26

Bacon the Younger 1843 (2)
Bacon, John II, *A Letter to the Right Hon. Sir Robert Peel, Bart, MP on the appointment of a commission for promoting the cultivation and improvement of the fine arts: with some suggestions respecting a former commission, denominated 'The Committee of Taste'*, pamphlet (London: 1843)

Bacon/Anon
Letter from John Bacon II to unnamed correspondent, 1810 (NLW, MS 16599E, fol(s) 57)

Bacon/Hoare
Two letters from John Bacon II to Prince Hoare, Osborn Coll 11 and 18 Oct 1804 (Beinecke Library, Yale University)

Bacon/Howard
Letters and Papers concerning John Bacon's statue of John Howard, 1792–1797 (BL, Add MS 26055, fol(s) 74–82, 87–91, 94)

Bacon/Long
John Bacon RA, letter to Edward Long of Aldermaston House, Reading, regarding the Wolmer monument, for which Long provided the inscription, 19 Aug 1789 (BL, Add MS 22677, fol(s) 81)

Bacon/M C Wyatt
Letter from John Bacon II to Matthew Cotes Wyatt, 1808 (BL MSS, Eg 3515, fol(s) 163)

Bacon/Mackenzie
Letters from John Bacon RA to Francis Humberston Mackenzie, Seaforth Muniments 1796–97 (National Archives of Scotland, GD 46)

Bacon/Normanton
John Bacon II, letter to Countess of Normanton, Cartwright of Aynho, Papers relating to Offices and Public Work, 1 Jan 1813 (NRO, C(A) 8267)

Bacon/Tracy
Letter from John Bacon RA to Dr Tracy, Warden of All Souls, Oxford concerning the statue of William Blackstone, Aug 1784 (All Souls, Oxford, MSS Box E, Bundle U, 348e, p 402a)

Bacot and Lambdin 1977
Bacot, H Parrott, and Lambdin, B B, 'Edwin Lyon, an Anglo-American Sculptor in the Lower Mississippi River Valley', *Antiques Magazine*, vol 111 (March 1977) pp 554–59

Baert, *c*1870
P Baert, 'Memoires sur les Sculpteurs et Architectes des Pays-Bas', *c*1870 (VAM, 86.WW.64)

Bailey 1958–9
Bailey, Bruce A, 'London Sculptors of the Eighteenth Century in Northamptonshire', *Records & Papers of the Northamptonshire Antiquarian Society*, vol 62 (1960) pp 25–36

Bailey 1969
Bailey, T D S, 'Lady Mary May's monument in Mid-Lavant Church', *Sussex Archaeological Collections*, vol 107 (1969) pp 1–11

Bailey 1996
Bailey, Bruce A, ed, *Northamptonshire in the Early Eighteenth Century; the Drawings of Peter Tillemans and Others*, Publications of the Northamptonshire Record Society, vol 39 (Northampton: 1996)

Bailey 1997
Bailey, Martin, 'Mona, Tiw, Wooden, Thor, Friga, Seatern. . . but shall we lose Sunna?', *Art Newspaper*, vol 8 (Apr 1997) p 3

Bailey and Isham 1968
Northamptonshire Museums & Art Gallery, *Sculpture in England since the seventeenth century, with special reference to Northamptonshire*, exhib cat (1968)

Baily Biog Coll
Collection of notes, letters, extracts and cuttings from newspapers and magazines, engravings and portraits made by Joseph Riddel *c*1883–1884, for an intended biography of his father-in-law Edward Hodges Baily (BL, Add MS 38678)

Baily Corresp
Miscellaneous correspondence concerning Edward Hodges Baily, 1819 (Mitchell Library, Glasgow, AL3 104)

Baily/RA Council (1)
Letter from E H Baily to the President and Council of the RA, submitting Eve as diploma work, 31 Oct 1821 (RA Lib, London, 1039)

Baily/RA Council (2)
Letter from E H Baily to the President and Council of the RA deploring the effect on British Sculptors of unfair competition from Italy, 15 Nov 1833 (RA Lib, London, 1039)

Baily/RA Council (3)
E H Baily, request to the RA Council for financial assistance, 6 Dec 1837 (RA Library, London, 1039)

Baily/RA Council (4)
E H Baily, letter defending himself against allegations by students that he had worked on models by students in the Antique school who were candidates for prizes, Nov 1843 (RA Library, London, 1039)

Baily/White
E H Baily, letter to J White, 1833 (Edinburgh City Library, BRS/qwN 45/Box)

Baird 1998
Baird, Rosemary, 'Cobras and Crocodiles Return to Goodwood', *Country Life*, vol 192, no 17 (23 Apr 1998) pp 84–87

Baker 1822–30
Baker, George, *History and Antiquities of the County of Northampton*, 2 vols (1822–30)

Baker 1949
Baker, Charles Henry Collins, *The Life and Circumstances of James Brydges, first Duke of Chandos; Patron of the Liberal Arts* (1949)

Baker 1979
Baker, Mark, 'So Noble a Work; Sculpture at Wellington College', (1979, pamphlet)

Baker 1983
Baker, Malcolm, 'European Sculpture over Three Centuries', *Apollo*, vol 118, no 262 (1983) pp 471–75

Baker 1984 (1)
Baker, Malcolm, 'Roubiliac and his European Background', *Apollo*, no 120 (Aug 1984) pp 106–13

Baker 1984 (2)
Baker, Malcolm, 'A Piece of Wondrous Art: Giambologna's Samson and Philistine and its Later Copies', *Antologia di Belle Arti*, no 23–24 (1984) pp 62–71

Baker 1986 (1)
Baker, Malcolm, 'Roubiliac's Models and 18th Century English Sculptor's Working Practices', in *Entwurf und Ausführung in der Europäischen Barockplastik: Beiträge zum Internationalen Kolloquium des Bayerischen Nationalmuseums und des Zentralinstituts für Kunstgeschichte München*, ed Volk, Peter, (München: 1986)

Baker 1986 (2)
Baker, Malcolm, 'Sir Henry Cheere and the Response to the Rococo in English Sculpture', in *The Rococo in England: A Symposium*, ed Hind, Charles (VAM, 1986) pp 143–60

Baker 1987
Baker, Malcolm, 'Rysbrack's Terracotta Model of Lady Foley and her Daughter and the Foley Monument at Great Whitley', *Stadel Jahrbuch*, vol 11 (1987) pp 261–68

Baker 1990 (1)
Baker, Malcolm, 'Lord Shelburne's Costly Fabrick: Scheemakers, Roubiliac and Taylor as Rivals', *Burlington Magazine*, vol 132 (Dec 1990) pp 841–48

Baker 1990 (2)
Baker, Malcolm, 'Portrait Busts of Architects in Eighteenth Century Britain', in *New Light on English Palladianism: Papers Given at the Georgian Group Symposium 1988*, conference proceedings, ed Hind, Charles (Georgian Group, 1990) pp 14–30

Baker 1992
Baker, Malcolm, 'Roubiliac's Argyll Monument and the Interpretation of Eighteenth-Century Sculptors' Designs', *Burlington Magazine*, vol 134 (Dec 1992) pp 785–97

Baker 1995 (1)
Baker, Malcolm, 'Roubiliac and Cheere in the 1730s and 40s: Collaboration and Sub-Contracting in Eighteenth-Century English Sculptors' Workshops', *Journal of the Church Monuments Society*, vol 10 (1995) pp 90–108

Baker 1995 (2)
Baker, Malcolm, 'The Making of Portrait Busts in the Mid-Eighteenth Century: Roubiliac, Scheemakers and Trinity College, Dublin', *Burlington Magazine*, vol 137 (Dec 1995) pp 821–31

Baker 1995 (3)
Baker, Malcolm, 'The Portrait Sculpture', in *The Making of the Wren Library, Trinity College, Cambridge*, ed McKitterick, David, (1995) pp 110–37

Baker 1996
Baker, Malcolm, 'The Production and Viewing of Bronze Sculpture in Eighteenth-Century England', *Antologia di Belle Arti*, no 52–55 (1996) pp 144–53

Baker 1997
Baker, Malcolm, 'Roubiliac and Chelsea in 1745', *English Ceramic Circle Transactions*, vol 16, no 2 (1997) pp 222–25

Baker 1998 (1)
Baker, Malcolm, 'Tyers, Roubiliac and a Sculpture's Fame: A Poem About the Commissioning of the Handel Statue at Vauxhall', *The Sculpture Journal*, vol 2 (1998) pp 41–45

Baker 1998 (2)
Baker, Malcolm, 'Limewood, Chiromancy and Narratives of Making. Writing about the Materials and Processes of Sculpture', *Art History*, vol 21, no 4 (Dec 1998) pp 498–530

Baker 1998 (3)
Baker, Malcolm, 'Augustin Pajou [exhib review]', *Burlington Magazine*, vol 140 (March 1998) pp 223–25

Baker 2000
Baker, Malcolm, *Figured in Marble: The Making and Viewing of Eighteenth Century Sculpture* (2000)

Baker 2007
Baker, Malcolm, 'An Anglo-French Sculptural Friendship: Pigalle and Wilton' in G Bresc and G Scgerf, eds, *La Sculpture en Occident, Etudes offerts a Jean-René Gaborit* (Paris 2007) pp 217–25

Baker, Harrison, Laing 2000
Baker, Malcolm, Harrison, Colin, and Laing, Alastair, 'Bouchardon's British Sitters: Sculptural Portraiture in Rome and the Classicising Bust around 1730', *Burlington Magazine*, vol 142, no 1173 (Dec 2000) pp 752–62

Balderston 1985
Balderston, Gordon, 'Roubiliac and Lord Chesterfield', *Apollo*, no 121 (Mar 1985) p 189

Balderston 2000
Balderston, Gordon, 'The Genesis of Edward Salter Aetatis 6', *Georgian Group Journal*, vol 10 (2000) pp 175–205

Balderston 2001
Balderston, Gordon, 'Rysbrack's Busts of James Gibbs and Alexander Pope from Henrietta Street', *Georgian Group Journal*, vol 11 (2001) pp 1–28

Balderston 2002
Balderston, Gordon, 'Young Lady Margaret Harley', *The Sculpture Journal*, vol 7 (2002) pp 26–29

Balderston 2004
Balderston, Gordon, 'William Thomas, steward of the 'Marylebone' estate', *Georgian Group Journal*, vol 14 (2004)

Balderston 2008
Balderston, Gordon, 'Giovanni Battista Guelfi: five busts for Queen Caroline's Hermitage in Richmond', *The Sculpture Journal*, vol 18 (2008)

Baldwin 1955
Baldwin, Mary, 'Appleby Magna, Sir John Moore's School', *Architectural Journal*, vol 112 (1955) pp 167–68

Ballantyne 1989
Ballantyne, Andrew, 'Downton Castle: Function and Meaning', *Architectural History*, vol 32 (1989) pp 105–30

Ballarat 1976–7
Early Australian Sculpture (Ballarat Fine Art Gallery, Australia: 1976–1977)

BAM 1929
'Sur un Sculpteur Bien Oublié', *Beaux Arts Magazine*, vol 7 (April 1929) p 29

Banford 1973
Banford, F, 'Edinburgh's Sober Statues', *Country Life*, vol 154, no 3972 (9 Aug 1973) pp 376–80

Banks
Banks Trade Cards, Sculptors and Masons (BM, PDL, 106)

Banks 1979
Banks, Ada Shadmi, 'Two Letters from Girodet to Flaxman', *Art Bulletin*, vol 61, no 1 (Mar 1979) pp 100–1

Banks/Cumberland
Correspondence between Thomas Banks and George Cumberland, 1796–1804 (BL, Add MSS 36498–500)

Banks/Hastings
Thomas Banks, Letters to Warren Hastings, 1794, 1798 (BL, Ad MSS 29173, 29175)

Banks/Upscott
Thomas Banks, Misc Letters, Upscott MSS (RA, II, nos 67–8, 74–5)

Barker 1982
Barker, Felix, and Hyde, Ralph, *London as it Might Have Been* (1982)

Barker 1993
Barker, Godfrey, 'How the Getty Gets', *Art News*, vol 92 (Dec 1993) p 34

Barnard and Fenlon 2000
Barnard, Toby and Fenlon, Jane, *The Dukes of Ormonde* (2000)

Barnes 1991
Barnes, Trevor, 'New Life for Grinling Gibbons' Carving', *Fine Woodworking*, no 89 (July–Aug 1991) p 100 ff

Barnes 1996
Barnes, Joanna, 'An Unknown Bust by Christopher Hewetson', *Antologia di Belle Arti*, vol 52–55 (1996) pp 166–69

Barnes 1999
Barnes, Richard, *John Bell, The Sculptor's Life and Works* (1999)

Barnes 2001
Barnes, Richard, *The Year of Public Sculpture, Norfolk* (2001)

Barrett 1971 (1)
Barrett, Cyril, *Irish Art in the 19th Century*, exhib cat (Crawford Municipal School of Art, Cork: 31 Oct–29 Dec 1971)

Barrett 1971 (2)
Barrett, Cyril, 'Irish Art in the Nineteenth Century', *Connoisseur*, vol 178 (Dec. 1971) pp 230–37

Barrett and Thorpe 1971
Barrett, Franklin Allen, and Thorpe, Arthur L, *Derby Porcelain 1750–1848* (1971)

Barron 1913
Barron, James, *The Northern Highlands in the Nineteenth Century*, III (Inverness: 1913)

Bartell 1800
Bartell, Edmund, *Observations upon the Town of Cromer, Considered as A Watering Place, and the Picturesque Scenery in its Neighbourhood* (1800)

Bartolini 1978
Lorenzo Bartolini, Mostra del Attività del Tutela (Florence, Prato, Palazzo Pretorio: 1978)

Bassett 1981
Bassett, Richard, 'Barlaston Reborn', *Architect's Journal*, vol 174, no 55 (11 Nov 1981) pp 920–22

Bate 2003
Bate, Jonathan, *John Clare, A Biography* (London: 2003)

Bates 1955
Bates, Rachel, 'A Westmoreland Sculptor', *Manchester Guardian* (2 May 1955)

Batey 1977
Batey, Mavis, 'Shotover's Continuity with the Past: An early Naturalistic Garden, parts I, II', *Country Life*, vol 162, no 4199 (29 Dec 1977) pp 1978–79

Baum 1934
Baum, Richard M, 'Joseph Nollekens: A Neo-Classical Eccentric; Two Water-Colour Drawings Attributed to Thomas Rowlandson in the Widener Memorial Collection', *Art Bulletin*, vol 16 (Dec 1934) pp 385–95

Bayley 1981
Bayley, S, *The Albert Memorial: The Monument and its Social and Architectural Context* (1981)

Bayliss c1978
Bayliss, Anne, *The Life and Work of James Trubshaw (1777–1853), Staffordshire Builder, Architect, and Civil Engineer* (Stockport: c1978)

Bazarov 1979
Bazarov, K, and Collis, L, 'Flaxman', *Art and Artists*, vol 14, no 6 (Oct 1979) pp 21–23, 48–50

BB
Bruce Bailey

BCH
Burton Constable Hall, E R Yorks

Beard 1951 (1)
Beard, Geoffrey, 'A Monument in Bath Abbey', *Country Life*, vol 109, no 2836 (25 May 1951)

Beard 1951 (2)
Beard, Geoffrey, 'Thomas White's Work at Castle Bromwich', *Country Life*, vol 110, no 2844 (20 July 1951) pp 204–7

Beard 1952 (1)
Beard, Geoffrey, 'Monument by Stanton', *Country Life*, vol 111, no 2873 (1952) p 364

Beard 1952 (2)
Beard, Geoffrey, 'White of Worcester', *Country Life*, vol 111, no 2881 (4 Apr 1952) p 1005

Beard 1952 (3)
Beard, Geoffrey, 'Castle Bromwich Hall, Warwickshire. A Property of the Earl of Bradford', *Country Life*, vol 111, no 2886 (9 May 1952) pp 1408–11

Beard 1953
Beard, Geoffrey, 'Alexander Pope's Bequest: Busts of Dryden, Spenser, Shakespeare and Milton', *Apollo*, vol 57 (Jan 1953) pp 4–6

Beard 1954
Beard, Geoffrey, 'Sculpture by Sir William Wilson', *Country Life*, vol 115 (18 Mar 1954) p 780

Beard 1956
Beard, Geoffrey, 'Monument by James Paget', *Country Life* (9 Aug 1956) p 289

Beard 1960
Beard, Geoffrey, 'A Family's 50-Year Supremacy', *Country Life*, vol 128 (8 Dec 1960) pp 1428–29

Beard 1963
Beard, Geoffrey, 'Belton House: The Lincolnshire Home of Lord Brownlow', *Connoisseur*, vol 152 (April 1963) pp 213–19

Beard 1964
Beard, Geoffrey, 'Italian Stuccoists in England', *Apollo*, no 80 (July 1964) pp 48–56

Beard 1975
Beard, Geoffrey, *Decorative Plasterwork in Britain* (1975)

Beard 1981
Beard, Geoffrey, *Craftsmen and Interior Decorators in England, 1660–1820* (1981)

Beard 1985
Beard, Geoffrey, 'Some English Wood-Carvers', *Burlington Magazine*, vol 127, no 991 (Oct 1985) pp 686–94

Beard 1986
Beard, Geoffrey, 'William Kent's Furniture Designs and the Furniture Makers', *Antiques Magazine*, vol 129 (June 1986) pp 1278–91

Beard 1989 (1)
Beard, Geoffrey, *The Work of Grinling Gibbons* (1989)

Beard 1989 (2)
Beard, Geoffrey, 'Grinling Gibbons', *Antiques Magazine*, vol 135 (June 1989) pp 1444–55

Beard 1993
Beard, Geoffrey, 'Decorators and Furniture Makers at Croome Court', *Furniture History*, vol 29 (1993) pp 88–113

Beard 2004
Beard, Geoffrey, 'Wood Carvers in England, *c*1660–1880', *Antiques (New York)*, vol VLXV, no 6 (June 2004) pp 73–83

Beard and Gilbert 1986
Beard, Geoffrey, and Gilbert, Christopher, eds, *Dictionary of English Furniture Makers 1660–1840* (1986)

Beard and Hayward 1988
Beard, Geoffrey, and Hayward, Helena, 'Interior Design and Furnishings at Woburn Abbey', *Apollo*, no 127 (June 1988) pp 393–400

Beard and Knott 2000
Beard, Geoffrey, and Knott, Cherry Anne, 'Edward Pearce's Work at Sudbury', *Apollo*, vol 151, no 458 (Apr 2000) pp 43–48

Beard and Piper 1951
Beard, Geoffrey, and Piper, J A, 'An Architectural Discovery', *Country Life*, vol 109 (9 Mar 1951) pp 706–7

Beattie 1983
Beattie, Susan, *The New Sculpture* (1983)

Beaufort Accts, 1704–6
Beaufort Accounts, 1704–6 (Glos RO, 53.15 QB3/2/1)

Beaufort Accts, 1714
Beaufort Accounts, 1714 (Badminton House, Glos, PA1/1, PA 1/2/26, PA 2/23)

Beaufort Accts, 1749
Beaufort Accounts, 1749 (Badminton House, Glos, FmJ3/12)

Beaufort Papers
Beaufort Papers (Glos RO, QA 2/5/2 and 3)

Beaumont 1995
Beaumont, Mary Rose, 'Amazing Graces: Controversy Surrounding Canova's The Three Graces', *Art News*, vol 94 (Jan 1995) pp 138–39

Beckett 1990
Beckett, Alison, 'Amazing Graces', *Art and Antiques*, vol 7 (April 1990) p 22

Beckford 1976
Clark, Kenneth et al, *William Beckford*, exhib cat (Compton Press, 1976)

Beddard 1984
Beddard, R A, 'Wren's Mausoleum for Charles I and the Cult of the Royal Martyr', *Architectural History*, vol 27 (1984) pp 36–49

Beds RO
Bedfordshire and Luton Archives and Record Service

Behnes Papers
Correspondence and papers of William and Charles Behnes, Fairfax Murray Coll 1819–1861 (John Rylands Library, English MS 1283)

Behnes/Hone
William Behnes, draft of a letter from William Hone, Hone Papers 1826 (BL, Add MSS 40120, fol(s) 275)

Behnes/Panizzi
William Behnes, Letters to Sir Antonio Panizzi, McCrimmon Coll 1856–1857 (BL, Add MS 70847, fol(s) 35–6)

Beinecke
Beinecke Rare Book and Manuscript Library, Yale University

Belcher 2001
Belcher, Margaret, ed, *The Collected Letters of A W N Pugin*, vol 1, 1830–1842 (2001)

Bell 1938
Bell, Charles Francis, *Annals of Thomas Banks* (1938)

Bell Scott 1892
Minto, W, ed, *Autobiographical Notices of the Life of William Bell Scott . . . 1830 to 1882* (1892)

Bell/Gosse
Eleven letters from John Bell to Sir Edmund Gosse, 11 Oct 1881–3 July 1889 (Brotherton MSS, Leeds Univ, Gosse Corr)

Bell/Holland
John Bell, Three letters to John Holland, concerning the statue of James Montgomery, 1856–1870 (Sheffield Archives, SLPS 222. 46–8)

Bell/Lubbock
John Bell, Letter to Sir John Lubbock, 1st Baron Avebury, Avebury Papers 1889 (BL, Add MS 49678 A fol 58)

Bell/Soden-Smith
John Bell, memoranda and letters to R H Soden-Smith chiefly concerning Bell's statue of Cromwell; two copies of a printed leaflet and a photograph, 1888 (NAL, MSL/1890/1109)

Bellenger 1996
Bellenger, Sylvain, 'Henri de Triqueti et l'Angleterre', in *La Scultura II: Studi in Onore di Andrew S Cirehamanowisetri, Antologia di Belle Arti* (1996)

Belsey 1980
Belsey, Hugh, 'A Newly Discovered Work by Francesco Harwood', *Burlington Magazine*, vol 122, no 922 (Jan 1980) pp 65–66

Bence-Jones 1972
Bence-Jones, Mark, 'The Monuments at Cashel', *Country Life*, vol 152 (24, 31 Aug 1972) pp 438–40, 521–24

Bénezit
Bénezit, E, *Dictionnaire des Peintres, Sculpteurs, Dessinateurs at Graveurs*, 14 vols (1999)

Benforado 1986
Benforado, Susan, 'Anne Seymour Damer (1748–1828), Sculptor' Ph D Diss (Univ of New Mexico: July 1986)

Benge 1984
Benge, Glenn F, 'Barye, Flaxman and Phidias', in *Congrès International d'Histoire de l'Art*, Atti del XXIV Congresso, vol 6 (Bologna: 1984)

Bennett 1998
Bennett, Susan, 'Art in the Square: Links Between the RSA and Trafalgar Square', *Royal Society of Arts Journal*, vol 146, no 3 (1998) p 130

Bentley 1981
Bentley, Gerald Eades, 'Flaxman in Italy: A Letter Reflecting the Anni Mirabiles, 1792–93', *Art Bulletin*, vol 63, no 4 (Dec 1981) pp 658–64

Benyon Accounts
Account Books of Richard Benyon of Gidea Hall (Berks RO, D/EBy A.3)

Beresford 1924–31
Beresford, John, ed, *The Diary of a Country Parson: the Reverend James Woodforde*, 5 vols (1924–1931)

Berge 1994
Berge, Willem, *Heimwee Naar de Klassieken: de Beelden van Mathieu Kessels en zijn Tijdgenoten, 1815–1840*, exhib cat (Zwolle: Noorbrabants Museum, 1994)

Berks RO
Berkshire Record Office

Berman 1974
Berman, Harold, *Bronzes: Sculptors and Founders, 1800–1930* (Chicago: 1974)

Berry Journals 1865
Lewis, Theresa, ed, *Journals and Correspondence of Miss Berry*, 3 vols (1865)

Bershad 1984
Bershad, D L, 'Pierre-Etienne Monnot; Newly Discovered Sculpture and Documents', *Antologia di Belle Arti*, nos 23–24 (1984) pp 72–75

Bertelli 1976
Bertelli, C, 'Visita a Santa Maria del Priorato', *Paragone*, vol 27, no 317–19 (1976) pp 180–88

Bertram 1985
Bertram, Michael, *Die Präraffaelitische Fotografie: Eine Ausstellung aus Grossbritannien*, exhib cat (Berlin, Galerie am Weidendamm, and Dresden, Galerie Rähnitzgasse: 1985)

Beulah 1985
Beulah, G K, 'Pistrucci's Great Waterloo Medal', *Medal*, vol 7 (Winter 1985) pp 12–14

Bewley 1998
Bewley, Christina, and Bewley, David, *Gentleman Radical, A Life of John Horne Tooke 1736–1812* (1998)

BGM
Bethnal Green Museum, London

BHO
British History Online

BI
British Institution, London

Bialostocki 1973
Bialostocki, Jan, 'The Door of Death. Survival of a Classical Motif in Sepulchral Art', *Jahrbuch der Hamburger Kunstsammlungen*, vol 18 (1973) pp 7–32

Bialostocki 1974
Bialostocki, Jan, *Polska i Anglia; Stosunki Kulturalno-Artystyczne. Pamietnik Wystawy Sztuki Angielskiej* (Warszawa: Muzeum Narodowe, 1974)

Bickham 1750
Bickham, George, *The Beauties of Stow* (1750)

Bicknell coll 1863
Catalogue of the Renowned Collection of English Pictures and Sculpture, of Elkanah Bicknell Esq, sale catalogue (London: Christie, 25 April 1863)

Bilbey 2002
Bilbey, Diane and Trusted, Marjorie, *British Sculpture 1470 to 2000 A Concise Catalogue of the Collection at the Victoria and Albert Museum* (2002)

Bilcliffe 1992
Bilcliffe, Roger, ed, *The Royal Glasgow Institute of the Fine Arts 1861–1989* (Glasgow: 1992)

Bills 2001
Bills, M ed, *Art in the Age of Queen Victoria: A Wealth of Depictions* (Bournemouth: 2001)

Bilodeau 1970
Bilodeau, Francis W, 'American Art at the Cibbes Art Gallery in Charleston', *Antiques Magazine*, vol 98 (Nov 1970) p 782

Bimson 1986
Bimson, Mavis, 'Some Recent Research on Coade Stone', *English Ceramic Circle Transactions*, vol 12, no 3 (1986) pp 203–5

Bindman 1970
Bindman, David, *European Sculpture from Bernini to Rodin* (1970)

Bindman 1973
Bindman, David, 'John Flaxman's Funerary Monument', *Neoclassicism* (1973) pp 9–13

Bindman 1979
Bindman, David, ed, *John Flaxman RA*, exhib cat (London, RA: 1979)

Bindman 1981
Bindman, David, 'Roubiliac in Westminster Abbey', *Oxford Art Journal*, vol 4, no 2 (Nov. 1981) pp 14–16

Bindman 1986 (1)
Bindman, David, 'Roubiliac: Some Problems', in *The Rococo in England: A Symposium*, ed Hind, Charles (1986) pp 134–42

Bindman 1986 (2)
Bindman, David, 'The Consolation of Death: Roubiliac's Nightingale Tomb', *Huntington Library Quarterly*, vol 49 (1986) pp 25–46

Bindman 1997
Bindman, David, 'Roubiliac's Statue of Handel and the Keeping of Order in Vauxhall Gardens in the Early Eighteenth Century', *The Sculpture Journal*, vol 1 (1997) pp 22–31

Bindman 2000
Bindman, David, 'Thomas Banks's 'Caractacus before Claudius': New Letters to and from Ozias Humphry', *Burlington Magazine*, vol 142, no 1173 (Dec 2000) pp 769–72

Bindman 2003
Bindman, David, ed, *John Flaxman 1755–1826, master of the purest line*, exhib Soane, UCL (2003)

Bindman and Baker 1995
Bindman, David, and Baker, Malcolm, *Roubiliac and the Eighteenth-Century Monument* (1995)

Binney 1969 (1)
Binney, Marcus, 'Sharpham House, Devon', *Country Life*, vol 145 (17, 24 April 1969) pp 952–55, 1014–17

Binney 1969 (2)
Binney, Marcus, 'From the Sentimental to the Sublime; Exhibition of Neoclassical Drawings at Ickworth', *Country Life*, vol 145, no 3769 (29 May 1969) pp 1360–61

Binney 1969 (3)
Binney, Marcus, 'Sir Robert Taylor's Bank of England', *Country Life*, vol 146 (13 Nov, 20 Nov 1969) pp 1244–48, 1326–30

Binney 1970
Binney, Marcus, 'Packington Hall, Warwickshire – III', *Country Life*, vol 148, no 3822 (23 July 1970)

Binney 1973
Binney, Marcus, 'Upton House, Tetbury, Gloucestershire', *Country Life*, vol 153 (15 Feb 1973) pp 390–94

Binney 1975
Binney, Marcus, 'Chicheley Hall, Buckinghamshire', *Country Life*, vol 157 (13 Feb 1975) pp 378–81

Binney 1977
Binney, Marcus, 'No Taking Wing (Two Wings of Clifton Campville, near Tamworth in Staffordshire)', *Country Life*, vol 161 (26 May 1977) p 1410

Binney 1978
Binney, Marcus, 'Apotheosis of the Rococo; the Lord Mayor's Coach', *Country Life*, vol 164, no 4245 (16 Nov 1978) pp 1596–98

Binney 1981
Binney, Marcus, 'Sir Robert Taylor's Grafton Street – I, II', *Country Life*, vol 170, nos 4395, 4396 (12 Nov, 19 Nov 1981) pp 1634–37, 1766–69

Binney 1984
Binney, Marcus, *Sir Robert Taylor: From Rococo to Neoclassicism*, Genius of Architecture, 4 (1984)

Binney 1998
Binney, Marcus, 'Barlaston Hall, Staffordshire, the Home of Mr and Mrs James Hall', *Country Life*, vol 192, no 31 (30 July 1998) pp 52–55

Biography Handbook Papers
Letters, with corrected proofs of memoirs, addressed to Charles Griffin, publisher of the 'Handbook of Contemporary Biography' 1860 (BL, Add MSS 28509–28512)

Birmingham 1972
Birmingham Public Library, *Statues, Public Memorials and Sculpture in the City of Birmingham*, Publication no 35 (Birmingham: 1972)

Birmingham CMAG
Birmingham City Museum and Art Gallery

BL
British Library

BL MSS Cat
British Museum Manuscripts Catalogue

Bla
Blackmansbury

Bla 1964
'Thomas Farnolls Pritchard', *Blackmansbury*, vol 1, no 3 (1964) p 15

Black c1872
Black, *Guide to Ireland* (c1872)

Blackmore 1989
Blackmore, Howard L, 'Sculptors and Gunmakers', *Apollo*, no 29 (Feb 1989) pp 105–9

Blackwood 1989
Blackwood, John, *London's Immortals* (1989)

Blair Castle misc tradesmen's accts
Duke of Atholl, Bills from tradesmen, 1740–61 (Blair Castle, Perthshire, Scotland, misc bundles, uncatalogued)

Blakiston 1957
Blakiston, Noel, 'Notes on British Art from Archives, iv', *Burlington Magazine*, vol 99 (1957) p 57

Blakiston 1973
Blakiston, J M G, 'Flaxman's Monument to Joseph Warton: Its Genesis and Evolution', *Winchester Cathedral Record*, vol 42 (1973) p 9

Bland 1888
Bland, E, *Annals of Southport and District. A Chronological History of North Meols 1086–1886* (Manchester: 1888)

BLARS
Bedfordshire and Luton Archives and Records Service

Blatchly and Fisher 2000
Blatchly, John, and Fisher, Geoffrey, 'Thomas Essington at Brightwell and the Identity of his Sculptor', *Proceedings of the Suffolk Institute of Archaeology and History* (2000)

Blatchly and Fisher 2004
Blatchly, John, and Fisher, Geoffrey, 'The Itinerant Italian Artist Diacinto Cawcy, and the Genesis of the Barrow Monument at Westhorpe', *Proceedings of the Suffolk Institute of Archaeology and History*, vol 40, no 4 (2004) pp 443–54

Blickling 1987
National Trust, *Blickling Hall, Norfolk* (National Trust, 1987)

Blomefield 1745
Blomefield, Francis, *The History of the City and County of Norwich*, vol 2 of *An Essay towards a Topographical History of Norfolk* (Norwich: 1745)

Blühm 1996
Blühm, Andreas, *The Colour of Sculpture 1840–1910*, exhib cat (Van Gogh Museum, Amsterdam and Henry Moore Institute, Leeds: 1996)

Blunt 1923
Blunt, Reginald, ed, *Mrs Montagu, 'Queen of the Blues,' her Letters and Friendships from 1762 to 1800*, 2 vols (1923)

BM
British Museum, London

BM Harleian 1618
Accounts to the Board of Works, from 1664 (BM, BL, Harleian 1618)

BM PDL
British Museum, London, Prints and Drawings

BMAG
Birmingham Museum and Art Gallery

BMQ 1932
'Pistrucci's Model of the St George for the Sovereign', *British Museum Quarterly*, vol 7 (Sept 1932) pp 52–53

Board of Works/Whitehall
Board of Works, Accounts for the New Building at the Horseguards, Whitehall, 1750–1759 (RIBA, VAM)

Boase 1956
Boase, Thomas Sherrer Ross, 'St George's Chapel: Some Changes in English Taste', *Annual Report of the Society of the Friends of St George*, (1956) pp 18–26

Boase 1959
Boase, Thomas Sherrer Ross, *English Art, 1800–1870* (1959)

Boase 1960
Boase, Thomas Sherrer Ross, 'John Graham Lough, a Transitional Sculptor', *Journal of the Warburg and Courtauld Institutes*, vol 23 (July 1960) pp 277–90

Bodleian
Bodleian Library, Oxford

Bold 1988
Bold, John, *Wilton House and English Palladianism: Some Wiltshire Houses* (1988)

Bold 2000 (1)
Bold, John, 'Greenwich Revived', *Country Life*, vol 194, no 47 (23 Nov 2000) pp 46–53

Bold 2000 (2)
Bold, John, *Greenwich An Architectural History of the Royal Hospital for Seamen and the Queen's House* (2000)

Bolton 1922
Bolton, Arthur T, *The Architecture of Robert and James Adam (1758–1794)*, 2 vols (1922)

Bolton 1934
Bolton, Arthur T, 'Designs of Sir Christopher Wren for Westminster Abbey, the New Dormitory, Westminster School, 1708–31', *Wren Society*, vol 11 (1934) pp 35–45

Bolton 1939
Bolton, Arthur T, and Hendry, Duncan, 'Drawings and Models of the Construction of St Paul's Cathedral', *Wren Society*, vol 16 (1939)

Bolton 1942
Bolton, Arthur T, 'Tom Tower, Christchurch, Oxford; Sir Christopher Wren Architect, 1681–2, Christopher Kempster, Mason', *Wren Society*, vol 19 (1942) pp 90–91, 100–2

Bolton and Hendry 1930
Bolton, Arthur T, and Hendry, Duncan, 'The Royal Palaces of Winchester, Whitehall, Kensington, and St James', *Wren Society*, vol 7 (1930)

Bolton and Hendry 1940
Bolton, Arthur T, and Hendry, Duncan, 'Designs and drawings with appendices: the domestic work of Sir Christopher Wren', *Wren Society*, vol 17 (1940)

Bolton and Hendry 1942
Bolton, Arthur T, and Hendy, Duncan, 'The City churches, vestry minutes and churchwardens' accounts', *Wren Society*, vol 19 (1942)

Bond 1980
Bond, Maurice, *Works of Art in the House of Lords* (1980)

Bond 1999
Bond, Shelagh M, ed, *The Monuments of St George's Chapel, Windsor Castle*, Historical Monographs Relating to St George's Chapel (Windsor: 1999)

Bonomi Autograph 1
Note signed by Joseph Bonomi, nd (Edinburgh Central Library, BRS/qwN 45/Box)

Bonomi Autograph 2
Autograph of Joseph Bonomi, nd (Exeter University MSS, Marshall Papers 37)

Bonomi Miscellanea
Two letters and a portrait of Joseph Bonomi, Misc letters 1842, 1845, 1865 (BL, Add MS 35057 fols 119, 121, 140)

Bonomi Papers
Correspondence and papers of Joseph Bonomi, *c*1820–1880 (Cambridge University Library, Dept of MSS, Add MS 9389)

Bonomi/Catherwood
Letter from Joseph Bonomi to F Catherwood, Sherborn Autographs 1853 (BL, Add MS 42575 fol 140)

Bonomi/Douce
Letter from Joseph Bonomi to Douce (Bodleian, MSS Douce d 27)

Bonomi/Eastlake
Letter from Joseph Bonomi to Sir Charles Eastlake, 1826 (NAL, MSL/1922/416/2)

Bonomi/Hay (1)
Letters from Joseph Bonomi to Robert Hay, Miscellaneous original letters and papers 19 March 1833–28 March 1863, with a few undated (BL, Add MS 38510 fols 136–233)

Bonomi/Hay (2)
Letters from Joseph Bonomi to Robert Hay, Correspondence of Robert Hay 1830–1863 (BL, Add MS 38094 fols 7, 15, 41, 61–5, 67, 71, 105, 130, 138, 141, 152–7, 160, 164–179, 187–196, 199)

Bonomi/Hérékyan Bey
Paper on Egyptian Archaeology and letters from Joseph Bonomi to Joseph Hérékyan Bey, Correspondence and papers of Joseph Hérékyan Bey 1845, 1862 (BL, Add MS 37462 fol 25, 37463 fols 190, 192, 199, 205, 210)

Bonomi/Lee 1
Letters from Joseph Bonomi to John Lee, Lee Papers 1848–1850 (BL, Add MS 47491 A, fols 193, 198, 211–14, 227, 232, 243–45)

Bonomi/Lee 2
Correspondence between Joseph Bonomi and John Lee, 1861–1863 (Centre for Buckinghamshire Studies, D/X720)

Bonomi/Lee 3
Letters from Joseph Bonomi to John Lee, 1860–1861 (Durham University MSS, Add MSS 350–99)

Bonomi/Panizzi
Letter from Joseph Bonomi to Antonio Panizzi, Correspondence and papers of Antonio Panizzi 1859 (BL, Add MS 36719 fol 105)

Bonomi/Smythe
Letter from Joseph Bonomi to Rear Admiral Smythe, 1861 (NAL, MSL/1985/8/11)

Bonomi/Trevelyan
Letter(s) from Joseph Bonomi to Sir Walter and Lady Pauline Trevelyan, 1826–1873 (Newcastle University MSS, WCT 88)

Bonomi/Wornum
Letter from Joseph Bonomi to R N Wornum, Sherborn Autographs, 1864 (BL, Add MS 42575 fol 72)

Booth-Jones 1966
Booth-Jones, Margaret, *The Church of St Mary, Hale. A Visitor's Guide* (priv printed, 1966)

Borean 1999
Borean, Linda, 'John Bushnell in Venice', *Journal of the Church Monuments Society*, vol 14 (1999) pp 88–103

Borg 1975
Borg, Alan, 'Two Studies in the History of the Tower Armouries', *Archaeologia*, vol 15 (1975) pp 317–52

Boringdon 1818
Anon, *Some Account of Lord Boringdon's Accident* (1818)

Borowitz 1979
Borowitz, Helen O, 'Two Nineteenth-Century Muse Portraits', *Country Life*, vol 66 (Sept 1979) pp 246–67

Bostrom 1999
Bostrom, A, *Cliveden Sculpture Catalogue* (1999)

Bostrom 2000
Bostrom, A, 'Giovanni Maria Benzoni, Randolph Rogers and the Collecting of Sculpture in Nineteenth Century Detroit', *The Sculpture Journal*, vol 4 (2000) pp 151–59

Bott 1995–7
Bott, Gerhard, 'Die Künstlerfamilie Eckstein Emigriert 1793 nach Amerika', *Aachener Kunstblatter*, vol 61 (1995–1997) pp 417–28

Bourne 1736
Bourne, Henry, *The History of Newcastle upon Tyne* (Newcastle: 1736)

Boustead 1952
Boustead, Mervyn, 'Smith of Warwick in Shropshire', *Country Life*, vol 110 (18 July 1952) p 194

Bowdler 1993
Bowdler, Roger, 'Rococo in Lee: The Fludyer Tomb by Robert Chambers', *Georgian Group Journal*, (1993) pp 91–93

Bowdler 2002
Bowdler, Roger, 'The Speaker's Sepulchre: Chaloner Chute's Tomb at the Vyne', *Apollo*, vol 154, no 482 (April 2002) pp 46–50

Bower/Strafford Accts, 1738–39; 1742; 1744
Bills of Work done for the Right Hon the Earl of Strafford at Wentworth Castle by Joseph Bower Junior, Dec 1738–Sept 1739; to Dec 1742; to Nov 1744 (BL, Add MS 22,241)

Bowron and Rishel, 2000
Bowron, Edgar Peters and Rishel, Joseph J, eds, *Art in Rome in the Eighteenth Century* (London and Philadelphia: 2000)

Boyle 1892
Boyle, J R, *County of Durham: its Castles, Churches and Manor-Houses* (1892)

Boynton 1971
Boynton, I, and Boynton, Lindsay, 'Some Documented Pieces of English Furniture', *Antiques Magazine*, vol 99 (Apr 1971) p 562

Boynton 1990
Boynton, Lindsay, 'Benjamin Jackson's Will and Inventory', *Furniture History*, vol 26 (1990) pp 20–26

Brand 1789
Brand, John, *History and Antiquities of the Town and County of the Town of Newcastle* (1789)

Brandon-Jones 1954
Brandon-Jones, J, 'Sir John Moore's School at Appleby, or, When is a Wren Building not a Wren Building?', *Architecture and Building News*, vol 205 (11 Feb 1954) pp 177–78

Brea 1994
Brea, Leticia Azcue, *La Escultura en la Real Academia de Bellas Artes de San Fernando, Madrid* (Madrid: 1994)

Brettingham 1773
Brettingham, Matthew, *The Plans, Elevations and Sections of Holkham ... to which are added the ceilings and chimneypieces ... not in the former edition* (1773)

Breward 2004
Breward, Christopher, *Fashioning London* (Oxford: 2004)

Bricknell 1995
Bricknell, Brian, *Derby Modellers 1786–1796, Extracts from Original Documents* (The Derby Porcelain International Society, 1995)

Bricknell 1998
Bricknell, Brian, *William John Coffee, 1773–c1846: Modeller, Sculptor, Painter and Ornamentalist: His Life and Work Reviewed* (Derby Porcelain International Society, 1998)

Bridge House Comm.
CLRO, Journal of the Bridge House Committee

Bridge House Rentals
Corporation of London, Rentals of the Bridge House, 1681–86; 1682–96 (CLRO Guildhall, LMA CLA/007/ FN/02/20; ibid 02/29)

Bridgman Records
Ledgers, day books, cash books, accounts, order books, wage books, letter books and patterns of C F Bridgman, stonemasons of Lewes, 1794–1959 (East Sussex RO, AMS 5836)

Brighton 1998
Brighton, Trevor, 'Samuel Watson, Not Grinling Gibbons at Chatsworth', *Burlington Magazine*, vol 140, no 1149 (Dec 1998) pp 811–18

Brighton 2001
Brighton, Trevor, 'The Watsons: Some further notes on Derbyshire's ingenious family of craftsmen', *Journal of the Bakewell and District Historical Society*, vol 28 (2001)

Bristol Burgess Books
Bristol Burgess Books, 1713–26, 1759–68, 1774–80 (Bristol RO, 04359/6; 14359/13; 04359/15)

Bristol Cash Books
Cash Books, Bristol City (BRO, 04029/2)

Bristol MAG
Bristol Museum and Art Galleries

British Portraits 1956–1957
British Portraits, exhib cat (RA: 1956–1957)

Britton 1801–1815
Britton, John, *The Beauties of Wiltshire, displayed in Statistical, Historical and Descriptive Sketches*, 3 vols (1801)

Britton 1801–1818
Britton, John, *The Beauties of Britain* (1801–1818)

Britton and Brayley 1802
Britton, John, and Brayley, Edward Wedlake, *The Beauties of England and Wales* (1802)

Britton and Pugin 1823–1828
Britton, John, and Pugin, Augustus Charles, *Illustrations of the Public Buildings of London*, 2 vols (1823–1828)

BRO
Bristol Records Office

Brock 1996
Brock, David, 'The Improvement of Coombe Place', *Georgian Group Journal*, vol 6 (1996) pp 74–84

Brocklesby Estate Accts
Brocklesby Park, Estate Accounts, 1846–1850 (Lincs RO, YARB/52/9–1)

Brockwell 1915
Brockwell, Maurice W, *Catalogue of the Pictures and Other Works of Art in the Collection of Lord St Oswald at Nostell Priory* (1915)

Brodie Correspondence
Correspondence of William Brodie, 1852–1890 (NLS)

Broeder 1973
Broeder, Frederick den, ed, *The Academy of Europe; Rome in the Eighteenth Century*, exhib cat (Benton Museum of Art, Univ of Connecticut: 13 Oct–21 Nov 1973)

Bronkhurst 1983
Bronkhurst, Judith, 'Fruits of a Connoiseur's Friendship: Sir Thomas Fairbairn and William Holman Hunt', *Burlington Magazine*, vol 125 (Oct 1983) pp 586–95

Brooks 2000
Brooks, Chris, ed, *The Albert Memorial. The Prince Consort National Memorial: its History, Contexts and Conservation* (2000)

Brotherton MSS
University of Leeds, Brotherton Library, Dept of MSS and Special Colls

Brown 1963
Brown, William, 'William and Henry Haworth: Woodcarvers from London', *Connoisseur*, vol 153 (May 1963) pp 21–24

Brown 1978
Brown, Iain Gordon, ' "The Resemblance of a Great Genius"; Commemorative Portraits of Robert Adam', *Burlington Magazine*, vol 120, no 904 (July 1978) pp 444–51

Brown 1980
Brown, Laurence, *A Catalogue of British Historical Medals 1760–1960* (1980)

Brown 1999
Brown, Sarah, *Sumptuous and richly adorn'd, the decoration of Salisbury Cathedral* (1999)

Brown, Reynolds and Read 1985
Brown, Cynthia, Reynolds, Bernard, and Read, Benedict, 'James Williams 1798–1888: Profile of a Victorian Sculptor', *Proceedings of the Suffolk Institute of Archaeology and History*, vol 36, no 1 (1988) pp 21–30

Brownell 1978
Brownell, Morris R, *Alexander Pope and the Arts of Georgian England* (1978)

Brownlow Papers BNLW 2/1/1/4
'A bill of masons worke Done for the Right Worshipfull Sr John Brownlowe Bart at Belton by Wm Stanton', Brownlow Papers, June 1686–May 1688 (Lincs RO, BNLW 2/1/1/4)

Brugnoli 1960
Brugnoli, Maria Vittoria, 'Due Bozzetti del Seicento: Ercole Ferrata e Pierre Etienne Monnot', 4, *Bollettino d'Arte*, vol 45 (Oct 1960) pp 339–45

Brumbaugh 1958
Brumbaugh, Thomas Brendle, 'Ball Hughes Correspondence', *Art Quarterly*, vol 21, no 4 (Winter 1958) pp 422–27

Brumbaugh 1973
Brumbaugh, Thomas, 'John Gibson in Rome: An Unpublished Letter', *Connoisseur*, vol 183 (June 1973) pp 122–27

Brushe 1981
Brushe, John, 'Further Light on Cole Green House', *Architectural History*, vol 24 (1981) pp 53–58

Brussels, Mus A Anc
Musée d'Art Ancien, Brussels

*Bryant c*1982
Bryant, Julius, 'Bashaw by Matthew Coates Wyatt', V&A (*c*1982)

Bryant 1983 (1)
Bryant, Julius, 'Mourning Achilles: A Missing Sculpture by Thomas Banks', *Burlington Magazine*, vol 125 (1983) pp 742–45

Bryant 1983 (2)
Bryant, Julius, 'Bashaw', *V&A Masterpiece Sheet*, (1983)

Bryant 1985
Bryant, Julius, 'The Church Memorials of Thomas Banks', *Journal of the Church Monuments Society*, vol 1 (1985) pp 49–64

Bryant 1991
Bryant, Julius, 'Thomas Banks's Anatomical Crucifixion', *Apollo*, vol 133 (1991) pp 409–11

Bryant 2002
Bryant, Julius, 'Bergonzoli's Amori degli Angeli: The Victorian Taste for Contemporary Latin Sculpture', *Apollo*, vol 156, no 487 (Sept 2002) pp 16–21

Bryant 2003
Bryant, Julius, ed, *English Heritage, Collections Review*, vol 4 (2003)

Bryant 2005 (1)
Bryant, Julius, 'The Royal Academy's 'violent democrat'. Thomas Banks', *British Art Journal*, no 3 (Winter 2005) pp 51–58

Bryant 2005 (2)
Bryant, Julius, *Thomas Banks, 1735–1805. Britain's First Modern Sculptor* (Sir John Soane's Museum: 2005)

Brydges 1789–91
Brydges, Sir Samuel Egerton, *The Topographer, for the Year 1789, containing a variety of original articles, illustrative of the local history and antiquities of England*, 4 vols (1789–91)

Buchanan Dunlop 1943
Buchanan Dunlop, W R, 'Thomas White of Worcester (*c*1674–1748), Sculptor and Architect', *Worcestershire Archaeological Society*, new series vol 20 (1943) pp 15–25

Buchanan Dunlop 1944 (1)
Buchanan Dunlop, W R, 'Thomas White of Worcester (*c*1674–1748), Sculptor and Architect; A Supplementary Note', *Worcestershire Archaeological Society*, new series new series vol 21 (1944) pp 64–65

Buchanan Dunlop 1944 (2)
Buchanan Dunlop, W R, 'Thomas White', *Burlington Magazine*, vol 85 (Aug 1944) p 206

Buckeridge 1706
Buckeridge, B, *An Essay towards an English-school, with the lives and characters of above 100 painters*', in Roger de Piles, *The art of painting, and the lives of painters . . .* (London, 1706: NAL Special Colls)

Bucks RLSS
Buckinghamshire Records and Local Studies Service

Bueschting 1754–7
Bueschting, A F, *Nachrichten van dem Zustande der Wissenschaften und Kunste in den Koniglichen Danischen Reichen*, 3 vols (1754–57)

Builder
The Builder: An Illustrated Weekly Magazine, 1842–1966, 210 vols

Builder 1859
'Social Bridges: The Foundling and the Arts', *Builder*, vol 17, no 882 (31 Dec 1859) p 849

Builder 1951
'Archbishop Tenison's Throne, Canterbury Cathedral: A Remarkable Work of Reconstruction', *Builder*, vol 180 (Mar. 23 1951) pp 407–10

Building Accounts, Badminton Church
Accounts for the Building of Badminton Church, Beaufort Papers 1783–85 (Glos RO, fol(s) QA 2/5/2–4)

Bull BMFA 1958
'Some Recent Accessions', *Bulletin of the Museum of Fine Arts, Boston*, vol 56, no 305 (Autumn 1958) pp 92–115

Bull LACM 1980
'Three Decades of Collecting: Gifts of Anna Bing Arnold', *Bulletin of the Los Angeles County Museum*, no 26 (1980) pp 34–35

Bull MIA 1970
'Rafaello Monti: The Veiled Lady', *Bulletin of the Minneapolis Institute of Arts*, vol 59 (1970) pp 36–37

Bull MMA 1948
'Terracotta Bust by G Ceracchi', *Bulletin of the Metropolitan Museum of Art, New York*, no 6 (March 1948) p 195

Bull PMA 1933
'Bust of Fox by Nollekens', *Bulletin of the Philadelphia Museum of Art*, vol 29 (Nov 1933) p 9

Bull PMA 1947 (1)
'Wax Miniatures', *Bulletin of the Philadelphia Museum of Art*, vol 42 (March 1947) pp 49–63

Bull PMA 1947 (2)
'Wax Portrait by J Flaxman', *Bulletin of the Philadelphia Museum of Art*, vol 42 (March 1947) p 60

Bull Rijks 1997
'Ruiterstandbeeld van Stadhouder-Koning Willem III', *Bulletin van het Rijksmuseum*, vol 45, no 1 (1997) pp 68–70

Bull RISD 1958
'Bust after Mrs Damer', *Bulletin of the Rhode Island School of Design*, vol 44 (May 1958) p 6

Bullock 1988
George Bullock Cabinet Maker (Sudley Art Gallery, Liverpool: 1988)

Burgess 1960
Burgess, Frederick, 'Artificial Stone', *Country Life*, vol 127, no 3290 (24 March 1960) p 639

Burgess 1963
Burgess, Frederick, *English Churchyard Memorials* (1963)

Burghley Artificers, 1798–1803
Artificers Accounts, Burghley House, Northants April 1798–June 1803

Burke 1976
Burke, Joseph, *English Art 1714–1800* (1976)

*Burke c*1968
Burke, Joseph, 'Hogarth, Handel and Roubiliac. A Note on the Interrelationships of the Arts in England', *Eighteenth Century Studies*, vol 3, no 2 (*c*1968)

Burl 1932
R R T, 'Rysbrack's Terracottas, at Messrs Spink', *Burlington Magazine*, vol 61 (July 1932) p 45

Burl 1966
'Roubiliac's 'Handel': A Terracotta Restored', *Burlington Magazine*, vol 108 (Sept 1966) p 475

Burl 1970
'Paintings and Sculpture of the Baroque; Heim Gallery, London', *Burlington Magazine*, vol 112 (Dec 1970) p 838

Burl 1975
'Notable Works of Art Now on the Market', *Burlington Magazine*, vol 117 (Dec 1975) supp pp 1–34

Burl 1988
'Bust of Isaac Ware Acquired by the Detroit Institute of Arts', *Burlington Magazine*, vol 130 (June 1988) pp 497–98

Burl 1990
'Pro Bono Privato', *Burlington Magazine*, vol 132 (April 1990) p 243

Burl 1993
Editorial, 'Sculpture and the Graceless British', *Burlington Magazine*, vol 135 (Dec 1993) p 795

Burl 1997
'Acquisitions at the Ashmolean Museum, Oxford, 1985–97', *Burlington Magazine*, vol 139 (May 1997) pp 363–68

Burl 2003
'Acquisitions at York Art Gallery 1991–2003', *Burlington Magazine*, vol 145 (Dec 2003) pp 893–900

Burlowe/Clare
Letters from Henry Behnes Burlowe to John Clare, 1827–1832 (BL, Egerton MSS 2247–2249)

Bury 1962
Bury, Shirley, 'Prince Consort and the Royal Plate Collections', *Burlington Magazine*, vol 104 (Aug 1962) pp 352–55

Bury 1966
Bury, Shirley, 'Lengthening Shadow of Rundell's', *Connoisseur*, vol 161 (March 1966) pp 152–58

Bury 1967
Bury, Shirley, 'Felix Summerly's Art Manufactures', *Apollo*, (1967) pp 28–33

Bury 1979
Bury, Shirley, 'Antiquarian Plate of George IV: A Gloss on E A Jones', *Burlington Magazine*, vol 121 (June 1979) pp 343–51

Busco 1988 (1)
Busco, Marie, 'The Achilles in Hyde Park', *Burlington Magazine*, vol 130 (Dec. 1988) pp 920–24

Busco 1988 (2)
Busco, Marie, 'The Sculptor Sir Richard Westmacott (1775–1856): Life and Works' Ph D Diss (New York Univ: 1988)

Busco 1989
Busco, Marie, 'Letter', *Burlington Magazine*, vol 131, no 1040 (Nov 1989) p 776

Busco 1992
Busco, Marie, 'The Houseless Traveller and Related Sculptures by Sir Richard Westmacott', in Essays in Honour of Gert Schiff *Source*, vol 11, no 3–4 (Spring–Summer 1992) pp 3–10

Busco 1994
Busco, Marie, *Sir Richard Westmacott, Sculptor* (1994)

Busiri Vici 1981
Busiri Vici, A., 'Un Inedito Ritratto Marmoreo del Cardinale Giacomo Antonelli', *Strenna dei Romanisti*, vol 42 (1981) pp 96–100

Butler 1998
Butler, Lawrence, 'The Monuments in Wakefield Cathedral', *Journal of the Church Monuments Society*, vol 13 (1998) pp 106–9

Butler 2000 (1)
Butler, Lawrence, 'The Smithson Monument at Stanwick, North Yorkshire', *Journal of the Church Monuments Society*, vol 15 (2000) pp 65–70

Butler 2000 (2)
Butler, Ruth, *European Sculpture of the Nineteenth Century* (Washington: 2000)

Byrne 1995 (1)
Byrne, Helen, 'The Speculative Building Activities of Simon Vierpyl', *Bulletin of the Irish Georgian Society*, vol 37 (1995) pp 31–56

Byrne 1995 (2)
Byrne, Helen, 'Simon Vierpyl (*c*1725–1810), New Light on His Work in Ireland' MA Diss (University College, Dublin: 1995)

Byron 1978
Byron, Arthur, *Josiah Wedgwood; "the Arts and Sciences United"; Correspondence, Experiment Books and the Ceramic Products*, exhib cat (Science Museum, London: 21 March–24 Sept 1978)

Byrth 1851
Byrth, Thomas, *Travel in Italy, 1844–49* (1851)

C and B Company Roll
Carpenters and Bricklayers' Company Roll (Shrewsbury Records and Research Centre, 6000/13487)

C H 1951
C H, 'Vicissitudes of a St George; His Horse and Dragon by Matthew Cotes Wyatt at Stratfield Saye', *Country Life*, vol 109, no 2831 (20 April 1951) p 1195

C Lib (repr)
Conway Library, Courtauld Institute, London; Gunnis's photographic archive

C of L Coll
Corporation of London Permanent Collection of Works of Art

C v B 1840
Report of the Trial of the cause, Carew against Burrell, Bt. and another, Executors of the late Earl of Egremont, at the Sussex Spring Assizes, held at Lewes, on Wednesday March 18, BL 1243.i.21.

C v B, 1842
Report of the proceedings in the Court for the Relief of Insolvent Debtors, in the matter of John Edward Carew, an Insolvent Debtor, on the opposition entered by Sir Charles Merrick Burrell, Bart. and Colonel George Wyndham, Executors of the late Earl of Egremont. Appendix, of the Bill of discovery filed by the Executors of the late Earl of Egremont against Mr Carew, with his answer thereto, both BL 1243.i.21; the appendix separately paginated (London: 1842)

Calderini 1828
Calderini, M, *Carlo Marochetti* (Turin: nd [?1828])

Cameron 1959
Cameron, Roderick, 'Flaxman et Wedgwood', *L'Oeil*, no 53 (May 1959) pp 38–55

Cameron 1996
Cameron, Peter, 'The Kandlers and the Client who changed his Mind', *Silver Society Journal*, no 8 (Autumn 1996) pp 487–99

Campbell 1958
Campbell, Malcolm, 'Alternative Design for a Commemorative Monument by John Flaxman', *Record of the Art Museum (Princeton University)*, vol 17, no 2 (1958) pp 65–73

Campbell 1993
Campbell, Richard J, *Visions of Antiquity: Neoclassical Figure Drawings*, exhib cat (Los Angeles County Museum: 1993)

Campbell/Buccleuch Letters
Letters from Thomas Campbell to the Duke of Buccleuch, 1835–45 (Dalkeith Palace Muniments)

Campitelli 1993–1994
Campitelli, Alberta, ed, *Giardino del Lago a Villa Borghese: Sculture Romane dal Classico al Neoclassico*, exhib cat (Roma Palazzo delle Esposizioni: 17 Nov 1993–31 Jan 1994)

Cannons Garden Accounts
His Grace Ye Duke of Chandos's Garden Account at Cannons, vol 2, Stowe Papers, Jan 1720–Sept 1724 (Huntington Library, MS ST 63, San Marino, California)

Cannons, Accts/Trades
Cannons, Accounts with Tradesmen, 1722–1732 (Huntington Library, MS ST 82, San Marino, California)

Canova/Aberdeen
Letter from Antonio Canova to George, Lord Aberdeen, 1806 (BL, Add MS 43229, fol(s) 169)

Canova/Bedford
Letter from Antonio Canova to John, 6th Duke of Bedford, 1815 (Bedford Estate Archives)

Canova/Castlereagh
Correspondence between Antonio Canova and Robert, 1st Viscount Castlereagh, 1819 (BL, Add MS 52311, fol(s) 14–17)

Canova/Cawdor
Correspondence between Antonio Canova and John, Lord Cawdor, Cawdor MSS (Carmarthens RO)

Canova/Hamilton
Nineteen letters from Antonio Canova to William Richard Hamilton, 1816–22 (private coll, GB)

Canova/Lansdowne
Letter from Canova to Henry, 3rd Marquess of Lansdowne, 1821 (VAM NAL, MSL/1930/642)

Canova/Lawrence
Correspondence between Antonio Canova and Sir Thomas Lawrence (RA, LAW)

Canova/Sir Richard Westmacott NY Met
Letter from Antonio Canova to Sir Richard Westmacott RA (NY Met, 920, vol 52, p 133)

Canova/Sir Richard Westmacott VAM
Letter from Antonio Canova to Sir Richard Westmacott RA, 1819 (VAM NAL, MSL/1998/7/2)

Canova/Wellington
Letter from Antonio Canova to Arthur, Duke of Wellington, 1815 (Museo-Biblioteca-Archivio, Bassano del Grappa, E25/bis/5611)

Cansick 1869–72
Cansick, Frederick Teague, *A collection of curious and interesting epitaphs, copied from the monuments of distinguished and noted characters in the ancient church and burial grounds of Saint Pancras, Middlesex*, 2 vols (1869–1872)

Cansick 1875
Cansick, Frederick Teague, *A collection of curious and interesting epitaphs . . . in the churches and churchyards of Hornsey, Tottenham, Edmonton, Enfield, Friern Barnet and Hadley, Middlesex* (London: 1875)

Cantabrigia Depicta 1763
Cantabrigia Depicta. A Concise and accurate description of the university and town of Cambridge (Cambridge: 1763)

Caputo Calloud 1981
Caputo Calloud, Annarita, 'Note su Luigi Pampaloni', *Ricerche di Storia dell'Arte*, vol 13–14 (1981) pp 57–70

Caputo Calloud 1984
Caputo Calloud, Annarita, 'Niccolò Puccini, Luigi Pampaloni e gli Orfani sulla Rupe: Cronistoria e Significati Romantici', *Ricerche di Storia dell'Arte*, no 23 (1984) pp 93–99

Carline 1958
Carline, Richard, 'Corbet and the Carlines – Shrewsbury Painter, Sculptors and Architects of the Early 19th Century', *Shropshire Magazine*, (March 1958) pp 13–15

Carline Order Book
John Carline II, of Shrewsbury, Order Book, 1801–2 (Salop CRO, Longueville Coll, Box 20)

Carline/Downward
Letters from John Carline II, of Shrewsbury, to Mr Downward, of the Citadel Hawkstone, on business affairs (Shrewsbury Public Library)

Carlisle 1818
Carlisle, Nicholas, *A concise description of the endowed grammar schools of England and Wales*, 2 vols (1818)

Carlisle 2000
Carlisle, Carol Jones, *Helen Faucit: Fire and Ice on the Victorian Stage* (2000)

Carlisle Ac Exhib, 1823
A Catalogue of the Exhibition of the Painting and Sculpture at the Academy of Arts, Finkle-Street, Carlisle (1823)

Carlisle Acad
Carlisle Academy of Fine Arts, Cumberland

Carlisle Exhib
Carlisle Exhibition of Painting and Sculpture

Carlisle Exhibs 1973
The Carlisle Exhibitions 1823–1850, exhib cat (Carlisle MAG: 1973)

Carlisle MAG
Carlisle Museum and Art Gallery

Carlisle Pat
The Carlisle Patriot

Carlton House 1991–2
Carlton House, The Past Glories of George IV's Palace (The Queen's Gallery, Buckingham Palace, London: 1991–92)

Carpenter/Carlisle list
Andrew Carpenter's list of available subjects, Castle Howard, NR Yorks (Castle Howard Muniments, G2/2/51)

Carr 1975
Carr, Malcolm Stuart, 'Tommaso and Luigi Saulini', *Connoisseur*, vol 190, no 765 (Nov 1975) pp 170–81

Carr 1990
Carr, J L, *Churches in Retirement: A gazetteer* (1990)

Carswell and Dralle, 1965
Carswell, John and Dralle, Lewis Arnold, eds, *The Political Journal of George Bubb Dodington* (Oxford: 1965)

Carter I Bank Account
Thomas Carter I's bank account, Drummond's Bank, 1756 (Royal Bank of Scotland, Drummond's branch, Charing Cross, London)

Carter I/Kay
Letter from Thomas Carter I to William Kay regarding a design for a 'Gothick' chimneypiece, Archives, Duke of Portland 1746

Carter/Okeover MS
Payments to Thomas Carter I's mason, Richard Kay 1745; letter from Thomas Carter I to Leak Okeover 13 October 1747, Okeover Archives 1745–7 (Derbys RO D231)

Cartwright Accounts
Household Accounts, Cartwright of Aynhoe 1704–8 (Northants RO, C(A)3489)

Cartwright Accts
Thomas Cartwright the Elder, Account Book, MS Rawlinson Jan 1657–Nov 1659 (Bodleian, Oxford, c 495)

Casey 1995
Casey, Christine, 'A Wax Bas-Relief by Patrick Cunningham', *Irish Arts Review*, vol 11 (1995) pp 117–118

Casey 1999
Casey, Christine, 'Newly Discovered Building Accounts for Charlemont House and the Casino at Marino', *Apollo*, vol 149, no 448 (June 1999) pp 42–50

Castan 1888
Castan, A, *Le Sculpteur Francais Pierre-Etienne Monnot ... sur la vie et ses ouvrages* (1888)

Cavanagh 1997
Cavanagh, Terry, *Public Sculpture of Liverpool* (Liverpool: 1997)

Cavanagh 2000
Cavanagh, Terry, *Public Sculpture of Leicestershire and Rutland* (Liverpool: 2000)

Cavanagh 2007
Cavanagh, Terry, *Public Sculpture of South London* (Liverpool: 2007)

Cavendish 1846
Cavendish, W G S, 6th Duke of Devonshire, *Handbook of Chatsworth* (1846)

CCHA
Canadian Catholic Historical Association

Ceccopiero Maruffi 1973
Ceccopiero Maruffi, F, 'Epistolario Neoclassico', *Urbe*, vol 36, no 4 (1973) pp 35–36

Cecil 1801
Cecil, Richard, *Memoir of John Bacon, Esq. RA: with reflections drawn from a review of his moral and religious character* (1801)

Ceracchi exhib cat, 1989
Giuseppe Ceracchi, Scultore Giacobino, 1751–1801, exhib cat (Roma, Palazzo dei Conservatori: 1989)

CERC
The Church of England Record Centre, London

CH Accounts, 1770–1816
Annual Accounts, Castle Howard 1770–1816 (Castle Howard Muniments, F4/9/1–50)

CH Building Accts
Castle Howard, Building Account Books, 1705–6 (Castle Howard Muniments, G1/1; G1/2)

CH Cash Books, 1761–1815
Cash Books, Castle Howard 1761–1815 (Castle Howard Muniments, F4/11/2–25)

CH G2/1
3rd Earl of Carlisle, Building Account Books (Castle Howard Archives, CH G2/1)

CH Letters
Michael Jackson (Carlisle's London agent) to Lord Carlisle, Castle Howard, NR Yorks 6 Dec 1731 (Castle Howard Muniments, J8/34/234)

CH Masons/Carvers
Castle Howard, An estimate of the masons and carvers bills, 1706 (Castle Howard Muniments, G2/2/28)

CH selected bills
3rd Earl of Carlisle, Selected bills, to 1760 (Castle Howard Archives, G2/2; G3/3)

Ch W
Churchwardens' Accounts

Ch W St Margaret, Westminster
Churchwardens' Accounts, St Margaret, Westminster 1762 (Westminster Public Library, London, E 136, E 3293/5)

Chalmers Johnson 1983
Chalmers Johnson, D, 'Rudolf Schadows Sandalenbinderin in Rom und Amerika', *Forschungen und Verichte Staatliche Museen zu Berlin*, vol 23 (1983) pp 113–17

Chamb London Accts
GL, Chamberlain of London's Accounts

Chamberlain 1957
Chamberlain, Georgia S, 'Portrait Busts of Robert Ball Hughes', *Art Quarterly*, vol 20, no 4 (Winter 1957) p 382

Chamberlain 1958
Chamberlain, Georgia S, 'Robert Ball Hughes, Sculptor and the U S Silver Coinage of 1840', *Numismatist*, vol 71 (Aug 1958) pp 923–32

Chambers 1855
Chambers, Robert, *Biographical Dictionary of Eminent Scotsmen* (1855)

Chambers Letter-Books
The Letter-Books of Sir William Chambers, 1769–1774 (BL MS, Add MS 41133–41136)

Chambers Letters, RIBA
Sir William Chambers, Letters (RIBA, VAM)

Chambers/Somerset Hse
Sir William Chambers, Somerset House Accounts, 1776–1798 (RIBA, VAM, 8 boxes)

Chan 1981
Chan, Victor, 'Blake, Goya, Flaxman, Romney, and Fuseli: Transcriptions and Transformations of a Dantesque Image', *Arts Magazine*, vol 55, no 7 (March 1981) pp 80–84

Chan 1983
Chan, Victor, 'Note on Gericault, Flaxman, and Michelangelo', *Arts Magazine*, vol 57 (Feb 1983) p 88

Chan 1984
Chan, Victor, 'Rebellion, Retribution, Resistance, and Redemption: Genesis and Metamorphosis of a Romantic Giant Enigma', *Arts Magazine*, vol 58 (June 1984) pp 80–95

Chancellor 1911
Chancellor, Beresford Edwin, *The Lives of the British Sculptors, and Those Who Have Worked in England from the Earliest Days to Sir Francis Chantrey* (1911)

Chandos Cat
A Catalogue of all the Materials of the Dwelling-House, Outhouses etc of his Grace James Duke of Chandos, 16 June 1747 and 11 days following (Huntington Library, San Marino, California)

Chantrey Ledgers 1991–92
Yarrington, Alison, Baker, Malcolm, Lieberman, Ilene and Potts, Alex, eds, *An Edition of the Ledger of Sir Francis Chantrey, R.A., at the Royal Academy, 1809–1841* (Walpole Society, vol 56, 1991–1992)

Chantrey/Lewis
Letter from Francis Chantrey to John Lewis, 28 Nov 1838 (Cambridge University Library, Dept of MSS, Fitzwilliam, MS 23-1949)

Charlemont Corr, HMC 1891
Historical Manuscripts Commission, *The Manuscripts and Correspondence of James, First Earl of Charlemont*, 2 vols (1891)

Charleston 1956
Charleston, R J, and Wills, Geoffrey, 'The Bow 'Flora' and Michael Rysbrack', *Apollo*, vol 63 (April 1956) pp 125–27

Charleston 1958
Charleston, R J, 'Chinese Face-Makers', *Antiques Magazine*, vol 73 (May 1958) pp 459–61

Chatsworth Accts, vol i
James Whildon's Accounts, Disbursements, 1685 to 1689 (Devonshire Archives, Chatsworth, vol 1)

Chatsworth Accts, vol ix
Chatsworth Accounts: Designs, Agreements and Bills of Carved-work executed at Chatsworth by Samuel Watson, 1690–1712 (Devonshire Archives, Chatsworth, vol ix)

Chatsworth Accts, vol vi
Household, Garden, Husbandry and Building at Chatsworth, 1700–1705 and part of 1706 (Devonshire Archives, Chatsworth, vol vi)

Chatsworth Accts, vol vii
Chatsworth Accounts, West Front and North Front, 1700–05 and part of 1706 (Devonshire Archives, Chatsworth, vol vii)

Chatsworth Accts, vol viii
Chatsworth Building Accts, Receipted Bills-Tradesmen and Craftsmen, 1687–1694 (Devonshire Archives, Chatsworth, vol viii)

Chatsworth Building Accts, vols ii, iii, iv, v
Designs Agreements and Bills, of Carved-work executed at Chatsworth, 1686–94, 1695–96, 1697–98, 1699–1700 (Devonshire Archives, Chatsworth)

Chatsworth Handbook, 1845
William, 6th Duke of Devonshire, *Handbook to Chatsworth & Hardwick* (1845)

Chatsworth Handlist
Chatsworth: Handlist of Paintings and Sculpture (nd)

Chatwin 1922
Chatwin, P, 'Monumental Effigies in the County of Warwick, Part III', *Transactions of the Birmingham Archaeological Society*, vol 18 (1922) p 136

Chatwin 1949
Chatwin, Philip B, 'The Rebuilding of St Mary's Church, Warwick', *Transactions of the Birmingham Archaeological Society*, vol 65 (1949) pp 1–40

Chenies Accts
Chenies Chapel Accounts (Bedford and Luton Archives and Records Service)

Chester 1876
Chester, Joseph Lemuel, *The Marriage, Baptismal and Burial Registers of Westminster Abbey* (Harleian Society, 1876)

Chester 1887
Chester, Joseph Lemuel, *Allegations for Marriage Licences issued by the Bishop of London*, 2 vols (Harleian Society, 1887)

Chester Inventory 1721
The Particular and Inventory of Robert Chester, Esq, one of the late Directors of the South Sea Company (1721)

Chicago A I
Art Institute of Chicago, Illinois

Chilcott 1840
Chilcott, J, *Descriptive History of Bristol*, 4th ed (1840)

Childe-Pemberton 1925
Childe-Pemberton, William S, *The Earl Bishop. The Life of Frederick Hervey, Bishop of Derry, Earl of Bristol*, 2 vols (1925)

Christ's H, TAB
Christ's Hospital, Treasurer's Account Book, 1667–81; 1680–96; 1695–1717; 1748–55 (Guildhall, 12819)

Christensen 1987
Christensen, Annie, 'The Horse and the Lion', *Journal of Garden History*, vol 15, no 2 (Autumn 1987) pp 110–14

Churches of Warwicks 1847
Anon, *Notices of the Churches of Warwickshire, Deanery of Warwick* (1847)

Churchill 1884–5
Churchill, Walter J, 'Some Unpublished Letters of Sarah, Duchess of Marlborough, relating to the Building of Blenheim Palace', *Birmingham and Midland Institute Archaeological Section, Transactions, Excursions and Reports*, vol 1884–85, pp 1–15

Chute 1954
Chute, Sir Charles L, 'A Monument by Thomas Carter [II]', *Country Life*, vol 115, no 2993 (27 May 1954) p 1733

CIIA
Read, Benedict and Ward-Jackson, Philip, eds, *Archive 4: Late 18th and 19th Century Sculpture in the British Isles*, Courtauld Institute Illustration Archives (London: 1976 ff)

City Cash Accts
Corporation of London, City Cash Accounts, 1665–67, 1668–70, 1696–98; 1707; 1705–7, 1708–10, 1711–13 (CLRO, Guildhall, City of London, LMA COL/CHD/CT/01/12; 01/13; 01/22; 01/25, 01/27)

City Lands Comm Papers
Corporation of London, City Lands Committee Papers, 1666–79 (CLRO Guildhall, LMA COL/CC/CLC/04/1)

City Lands Comm, Order Books
Corporation of London, Order Books, City Lands Committee 1676 (CLRO, Guildhall, City of London)

City Lands, Rough Minutes
Corporation of London, City Lands Committee, Rough Minutes, 1668–73 (CLRO Guildhall, LMA COL/CC/CLC/03/001)

CJ
Carlisle Journal

CKS
Centre for Kentish Studies, Maidstone

CL
Country Life

CL 1966
'Staircase Under Sentence of Death', *Country Life*, vol 140 (18 Aug 1966) p 382

CL 1970
'Oxford Lar', *Country Life*, vol 148 (31 Dec 1970) p 1280

CL 1972
'Talking About Salesrooms', *Country Life*, vol 151 (16 March 1972) p 610

CL 1981
'Saving Langley Hall's Ceiling', *Country Life*, vol 170, no 4385 (3 Sept 1981) p 767

CL coll
City of London Collections

CL, CR
City of London, Corporation Records

Clark 1889–99
Clark, Andrew, ed, *Survey of the antiquities of the city of Oxford, compiled in 1661–6 by Anthony Wood*, vols I–III, Oxford Historical Society, vols 15, 17 and 37 (1889–1899)

Clark 1891–90
Clark, Andrew, ed, *The life and times of Anthony Wood, antiquary of Oxford, 1632–1695, described by himself*, vols I–V, Oxford Historical Society, vols 19, 21, 26, 30, 40 (1891–1900)

Clark 1957
Clark, Anthony M, *The Age of Canova*, exhib cat (Rhode Island School of Design: 6 Nov–15 Dec 1957)

Clark 1983
Clark, Jane ed, *The Great Eighteenth-Century Exhibition* (Victoria, New South Wales: 1983)

Clarke 1830
Clarke, G R, *The History and Description of the Town and Borough of Ipswich* (1830)

Clarke 1973
Clarke, George, 'Grecian Taste and Gothic Virtue', *Apollo*, (June 1973)

Clarke 1974
Clarke, Michael, 'Victorian Sculpture at York: Patronage and Survival', Preview 107 *City of York Art Gallery Quarterly*, vol 27 (July 1974) pp 954–59

Clarke 1990
Clarke, G B, ed, *Descriptions of Lord Cobham's Gardens at Stowe (1700–1750)* (Bucks Records Society, 1990)

Claydon 2002
National Trust, *Claydon House, Buckinghamshire* (2002)

Clayton 1913
Clayton, E W, 'Richard Morton Paye', *Connoisseur*, vol 37 (1913) pp 229–36

Clayton & Morris
Clayton & Morris, Business Ledgers, 4 vols, 1669–1680 (Guildhall MSS, City of London, 6428/1–4)

Cleaver 1963
Cleaver, Dale Gordon, 'Concept of Time in Modern Sculpture', *Art Journal*, vol 22, no 4 (Summer 1963) pp 232–36

Clement and Hutton 1879
Clement, Clara, and Hutton, Laurence, *Artists of the nineteenth century and their works: a handbook containing two thousand and fifty biographical sketches*, 2 vols (1879)

Cleveland 1975–6
Aspects of Sculpture, exhib cat (Cleveland Museum of Art: 1975–76)

Clifford 1970
Clifford, Timothy, 'Thomas Hope's Shepherd Boy', *Connoisseur*, vol 175 (Sept 1970) pp 12–16

Clifford 1976
Clifford, Timothy, 'James Jefferys, Historical Draughtsman (1751–84)', *Burlington Magazine*, vol 118, no 876 (1976) pp 148–55

Clifford 1978
Clifford, Timothy, 'Some English Vases and their Sources', *English Ceramic Circle Transactions*, vol 10, no 3 (1978) pp 159–73

Clifford 1985
Clifford, Timothy, 'John Bacon and the Manufacturers', *Apollo*, vol 122, no 284 (Oct 1985) pp 288–304

Clifford 1990
Clifford, Timothy, 'Vulliamy Clocks and British Sculpture', *Apollo*, no 132 (Oct. 1990) pp 226–37

Clifford 1992
Clifford, Timothy, 'The Plaster Shops of the Rococo and Neo-Classical Era in Britain', *Journal of the History of Collections*, vol 4, no 1 (1992) pp 39–65

Clifford 1995
Clifford, Timothy et al, *The Three Graces: Antonio Canova* (Edinburgh: 1995)

Clifford 2000
Clifford, Jane, 'Miss Berry and Canova. A Singular Relationship', *Apollo* (Sept 2000)

Clough-Williams 1960
Clough-Williams, Ellis, 'Hercules in bronze', *Country Life*, vol 127, no 3302 (16 June 1960) p 1394

CLRO
Corporation of London Records Office

Clutterbuck
Clutterbuck, J, *Hertfordshire*, 2 vols (c1826)

Clyde Bust Papers
Letters and papers relating to bust of Baron Clyde by George Gamon Adams, 1863–1864 (Mitchell Library, City of Glasgow, No 104)

CM
Journal of the Church Monuments Society

Co-op MSS
Co-operative Union Archive, Manchester

Coade 1784
A Descriptive Catalogue of Coade's Artificial Stone Manufactory (1784)

Coade 1799
Coade and Sealey, *Coade's Gallery or Exhibition in Artificial Stone* (1799)

Coade c1808
Description of the grand model of Neptune giving up the body of Nelson, with the dominion of the sea, into the arms of Britannia, executed from a design of Benjamin West, Esq, for Greenwich Hospital, at Coade and Sealy's ornamental stone manufactory, Lambeth (London: c1808)

Coade Papers
Coade Factory Order, Day and Letter Books, 1813–1821 (PRO, C111/106)

Cobb 1948
Cobb, Gerald, *The Old Churches of London* (1948)

Cocke 1995
Cocke, Thomas, *900 Years: the Restorations of Westminster Abbey* (1995)

Cockerell Diary
Diaries of Charles Robert Cockerell, 1821–1832 (coll Mrs B J Crichton)

Codrington Accounts
Documents relating to the building of Dodington House, Glos, by James Wyatt for C B Codrington, Codrington Archives 1796–1813 (Glos RO, D1610)

Cole 1949
Cole, J C, 'William Byrd, Stonecutter and Mason', *Oxoniensia*, vol 14 (1949) pp 63–74

Cole 1952–3
Cole, J C, 'The Painting or Staining of Marble as Practised by William Byrd of Oxford and Others', *Oxoniensia*, vol 17–18 (1952–1953) pp 193–99

Coleridge 1964
Coleridge, Anthony, 'Some Mid-Georgian Cabinet-Makers at Holkham', *Apollo*, no 79 (Feb 1964) pp 122–28

Coleridge 2000
Coleridge, Anthony, 'English Furniture Supplied for Croome Court: Robert Adam and the 6th Earl of Coventry', *Apollo*, vol 51, no 456 (Feb 2000) pp 8–19

Collard 1969
Collard, Elizabeth, 'Nelson in Old Montreal: A Coade Memorial', *Country Life*, vol 146 (24 July 1969) pp 210–11

Collectanea Ægyptiaca
Letters, drawings and other papers of Joseph Bonomi, James Burton's 'Collectanea Ægyptiaca' 1820–1839 (BL, Add MSS 25629 fol 51 25636; fol 17, 25638; fol 81, 25651, 25658; fols 50, 50b, 67–77, 25663; fols 42–107)

Collins 1957
Collins, F J, 'Eleanor Coade, 1733–1821', *Museums Journal*, vol 57 (May 1957) pp 37–38

Collins Baker 1949
Collins Baker, C H, *The Life and Circumstances of James Brydges, 1st Duke of Chandos* (1949)

Collins/Constable 1768
William Constable, Bill for relief of Pan & the Graces from William Collins, Burton Constable Papers 1768 (East Yorks RO, DDCC/2/52)

Collins/Constable 1769
William Constable, bill from William Collins, Burton Constable Papers 1769 (East Yorks RO, DDCC/2/53)

Collinson 1975
Collinson, H, *Country Monuments: Their Families and Houses* (1975)

Colston 1881
Colston, James, *History of the Scott Monument, Edinburgh, to which is prefixed a biographical sketch of Sir Walter Scott* (Edinburgh: 1881)

Coltman 2004
Coltman, Viccy, 'Thomas Anson's sculpture collection at Shugborough: 'living good and pleasing' or 'much taste a turn to Roman splendour'', *The Sculpture Journal*, vol 12 (2004) pp 35–56

Colton 1974
Colton, J, 'Kent's Hermitage for Queen Caroline at Richmond', *Architectura* (Munich/Berlin), (1974, pt 2) pp 181–91

Colton 1976
Colton, J, 'Merlin's cave and Queen Caroline: garden art as propaganda', *Eighteenth-Century Studies*, vol 10 (Fall 1976) pp 1–20

Columns
Columns, Newsletter of the Friends of Christ Church Spitalfields, (2003)

Colville 1869
Colville, F L, *The Worthies of Warwickshire* (1869)

Colvin 1947
Colvin, Howard, 'The Bastards of Blandford: Architects and Master-Builders', *Archaeological Journal*, vol 104 (1947) pp 178–95

Colvin 1948
Colvin, Howard, 'Gothic Survival and Gothic Revival', *Architectural Review*, vol 103 (March 1948) pp 91–98

Colvin 1954
Colvin, Howard, 'The Bishop's Palace, Lichfield', *Country Life*, vol 116 (30 Dec 1954) pp 2312–15

Colvin 1955
Colvin, Howard, 'Roubiliac's Bust of Isaac Ware', *Burlington Magazine*, vol 97 (May 1955) pp 150–51

Colvin 1972/3
Colvin, Howard, 'Francis Smith of Warwickshire, 1672–1738', *Warwickshire History*, vol 2, no 2 (1972/3) pp 3–13

Colvin 1973–76
Colvin, Howard and Newman, John, eds, *History of the King's Works*, vols V–VI (1973–1976)

Colvin 1978
Colvin, Howard, 'A Monument by Robert Adam', *Architectural History*, vol 21 (1978) p 94, reprs 32a,b

Colvin 1981
Colvin, Howard, 'The Church of St. Mary Aldermary and its Rebuilding after the Great Fire of London', *Architectural History*, vol 24 (1981) pp 24–31

Colvin 1984
Colvin, Howard, 'Letters and Papers relating to the Rebuilding of Combe Abbey, Warwickshire', *Walpole Society*, vol 50 (1984) pp 248–309

Colvin 1985
Colvin, Howard, *Calke Abbey, Derbyshire. A Hidden House Revealed* (National Trust, 1985)

Colvin 1988
Colvin, Howard, *The Canterbury Quadrangle, St John's College, Oxford* (1988)

Colvin 1993
Colvin, Howard, 'Bell-Guttae and the Woodwards of Chipping Camden', *Georgian Group Journal*, (1993) pp 75–7

Colvin 1995
Colvin, Howard, *A Biographical Dictionary of British Architects, 1600–1840*, 3rd edition (Yale, 1995)

Colvin 1999
Colvin, Howard, 'Gothic Survival and Gothic Revival', in *Essays in English Architectural History* (1999)

Colvin 2000
Colvin, Howard, 'The Townesends of Oxford: A Firm of Georgian Master-Masons and its Accounts', *Georgian Group Journal*, vol 10 (2000) pp 43–60

Colvin and Oswald 1954
Colvin, Howard and Oswald, A, 'The Bishop's Palace, Lichfield', *Country Life* (30 Dec 1954) pp 2312–15

Comstock 1936
Comstock, H, 'Carving by Grinling Gibbons; Panel of Carved Limewood Showing a Variety of Fruit and Flower Forms', *Connoisseur*, vol 97 (March 1936) p 159

Comstock 1939
Comstock, H, 'Discovery of Flaxman Drawings', *Connoisseur*, vol 103 (Feb 1939) pp 98–99

Comstock 1940 (1)
Comstock, H, 'Architectural Elements from the Hearst Collection', *Connoisseur*, vol 106 (Oct 1940) pp 160–61

Comstock 1940 (2)
Comstock, H, 'Wax Miniature by Samuel Percy', *Connoisseur*, vol 106 (Dec 1940) pp 258–59

Conc 1975
'Historic Concrete', no 12 *Concrete*, vol 9, no 8 (Aug 1975) p 23

Condor 1894
Condor, Edward Jnr, *Records of the Hole Crafte and Fellowship of Masons* (1894)

Conn
Connoisseur

Conn 1936
'Portrait Medallion by J Flaxman', *Connoisseur*, vol 98 (July 1936) p 31

Conn 1941
'Footnote to Grinling Gibbons', *Connoisseur*, vol 108 (Aug 1941) p 74

Conn 1946
'Portrait Bust by Nollekens', *Connoisseur*, vol 118 (Sept 1946) p 28

Conn 1949
'Bust by J Bushnell', *Connoisseur*, vol 123 (March 1949) p 53

Conn 1954
'Portrait by Nollekens', *Connoisseur*, vol 133 (May 1954) p 180

Conn 1954 June
'Roubiliac at Hagley; Monument to the Memory of Lucy Lyttleton', *Connoisseur*, vol 133 (June 1954) p 256

Conn des Arts
Connaissance des Arts

Connor 1975
Connor, T, 'The Building of Campsmount (Flaxman's Yarborough Monument)', *Yorkshire Archaeological Journal*, vol 47 (1975) pp 121–32

Connor 1979
Connor, Patricia, and Lambourne, Lionel, *Derby Day 200*, exhib cat (Royal Academy: 1979)

Constable 1927
Constable, William George, *John Flaxman* (1927)

Constable Accts
Constable Papers, Account Book, 1763–1766; 1766–1768 (East Yorks CRO, DDCC)

Conway Microform 1987
The Conway Library, The Courtauld Institute of Art. Part IV Sculpture Microform (Haslemere: 1987)

Cook 1984
Cook, B F, *The Elgin Marbles* (1984)

Coombs 1986
Coombs, James H, ed, *A Pre-Raphaelite Friendship. The Correspondence of William Holman Hunt and John Lucas Tupper* (Ann Arbor, Michigan: UMI Research Press, 1986)

Cooper 1971
Cooper, Jeremy, 'John Gibson and his Tinted Venus', *Connoisseur*, vol 178 (Oct 1971) pp 84–92

Cooper 1973
Cooper, Nicholas, 'Kendal, Westmorland', *Country Life*, vol 154 (20, 27 Sept 1973) pp 762–64, 892–96

Cooter 1984
Cooter, Roger, *The cultural meaning of popular science: phrenology and the organization of consent in nineteenth-century Britain* (1984)

Cooter 1989
Cooter, Roger, *Phrenology in the British Isles: An Annotated, Historical Biobibliography and Index* (Metuchen N J and London: 1989)

Coppel Areizaga 1997
Coppel Areizaga, Rosario, 'Relieves que Deocran los Pedestales de las Esculturas de la Reina Cristina de Suecia', *Archivo Espanol de Arte*, vol 70, no 279 (July/Sept 1997) pp 310–15

Corbet and Carline 1958
Exhibition of Works of the Corbet and Carline Families, exhib cat (Shrewsbury Art Gallery: 1958)

Cork Hist Soc Journal 1895
J C, 'Biographical Sketches of Persons Remarkable in Local History. XIV. John Hogan, the Sculptor', *Cork Historical Society Journal*, vol 1 (1895) pp 207–18

Cornforth 1961
Cornforth, John, 'Seventeenth-Century Panelling in a School Hall', *Country Life*, vol 129 (May 11 1961) pp 1102–4

Cornforth 1964
Cornforth, John, 'Charity on a Noble Scale', *Country Life*, vol 135 (16 April 1964) pp 902–5

Cornforth 1968 (1)
Cornforth, John, 'Hatton Grange, Shropshire', *Country Life*, vol 143 (29 Feb 1968) pp 466–70

Cornforth 1968 (2)
Cornforth, John, 'Houses by T F Pritchard', *Country Life*, vol 143 (4 April 1968) p 815

Cornforth 1970 (1)
Cornforth, John, 'Uncertain Future of Sutton Scarsdale: The Ruins of this Great Georgian House in Derbyshire are in Danger of Collapse', *Country Life*, vol 147 (16 April 1970) pp 850–51

Cornforth 1970 (2)
Cornforth, John, 'Dublin Castle', *Country Life*, vol 148 (20 Aug 1970) pp 458–59

Cornforth 1971
Cornforth, John, 'Artistic Rivalries in Seventeenth Century London', *Country Life*, vol 150 (14 Oct 1971) pp 976–78

Cornforth 1972
Cornforth, John, 'Bowood, Wiltshire, Revisited', *Country Life*, vol 151 (8, 15, 22 June 1972) pp 1448–51; 1546–50; 1610–13

Cornforth 1977
Cornforth, John, 'Kirkleatham, Cleveland', *Country Life*, vol 161, no 4149 (6 Jan 1977) pp 18–21

Cornforth 1979
Cornforth, John, 'Dudmaston, Shropshire. Parts I, II, III', *Country Life*, vol 165, no 4263 (22 March 1979) pp 818–21

Cornforth 1984
Cornforth, John, 'The Building of Crichel: Dorset, England', *Architectural History*, vol 27 (1984) pp 268–69

Cornforth 1988 (1)
Cornforth, John, 'The Casino at Marino – I, II', *Country Life*, vol 182, no 5, 6 (11 and 18 Feb 1988) pp 70–73, 94–97

Cornforth 1988 (2)
Cornforth, John, 'Ditchley Park, Oxfordshire', *Country Life*, (17 and 24 Nov 1988)

Cornforth 1989
Cornforth, John, 'Hagley Hall, Worcestershire I and II', *Country Life*, vol 183, no 17 and 18 (27 April and 4 May 1989) pp 136–39; 152–55

Cornforth 1994
Cornforth, John, 'Hillsborough Castle, Co Down – I', *Country Life*, vol 188, no 30 (July 28, 1994) pp 64–67

Cornforth and Glin 1977
Cornforth, John, and Glin, Knight of, 'Kilruddery, Co Wicklow', *Country Life*, vol 162, no 4176–7 (14 July 1977) pp 78–81, 146–49

Corti 1977
Corti, Gino, 'Canova's Funeral Monument and the Galleria Borghese: Letters from Leopoldo Cicognara and the Countess of Albany', *Burlington Magazine*, vol 119 (July 1977) p 500

Cosin Letters 1870
Cosin, John, 'The Letters of John Cosin', *Surtees Society*, vol 55 (1870)

Cossa 1982
Cossa, Frank, 'Josiah Wedgwood: his Role as a Patron of Flaxman, Stubbs and Wright of Derby' Ph D Diss (Rutgers, New Jersey: *c* 1982)

Cossa 1983
Cossa, Frank, 'Josiah Wedgwood, Potter and Patron', *Portfolio*, vol 5, no 2 (March–April 1983) pp 116–17, 119–20

Costeloe 2006
Costeloe, Michael P, 'William Bullock and the Mexican Connection', *Mexican Studies* (2006), pp 275–309

Court Minutes, Merchant Taylors
Merchants Taylors' Company, Court Minutes, 1837–1838 (Corporation of London, MS 34010/20)

Coutu 1992
Coutu, Joan, 'Philanthropy and Propaganda: the Bust of George III in Montreal', *Revue d'Art Canadienne, Canadian Art Review*, vol 19, no 1/2 (1992) pp 59–67

Coutu 1993
Coutu, Joan, 'Eighteenth Century British Monuments and the Politics of Empire' Ph D Diss (University Coll, London: 1993)

Coutu 1996
Coutu, Joan, 'William Chambers and Joseph Wilton', in *Sir William Chambers, Architect to George III*, exhib cat ed Harris, John and Snodin, Michael (Courtauld: 1996) pp 175–85

Coutu 1997
Coutu, Joan, 'Carving Histories: British Sculpture in the West Indies', *Journal of the Church Monuments Society*, vol 12 (1997) pp 77–85

Coutu 1998
Coutu, Joan, 'The Rodney Monument in Jamaica and an Empire Coming of Age', *The Sculpture Journal*, vol 2 (1998) pp 46–57

Cox 1773
Cox, James, *A Descriptive Inventory of the several exquisite and magnificent pieces of mechanism and jewelry, comprised in the schedule annexed to an Act of Parliament*. . . (1773)

Cox 1875–9
Cox, John Charles, *Notes on the churches of Derbyhire*, 4 vols (1875–79)

Cox 1881
Cox, John Charles, *Chronicles of the Collegiate Church of Free Chapel of All Saints' Derby* (1881)

Cox 1973
Cox, John Francis, 'An Annotated Edition of Selected Letters of Thomas Woolner, Pre-Raphaelite Poet and Sculptor' Ph D Diss (Arizona State University: 1973)

Cox 1977–8
Cox, J F, 'Thomas Woolner Pre-Raphaelite Prospector: a Record of his Early Phase', *Pre-Raphaelite Review*, vol 1, no 2 (1977–1978) pp 64–75

Cox 1981
Cox, J F, 'Some Letters of Thomas Woolner to Mr and Mrs Henry Adams. 1', *Journal of Pre-Raphaelite Studies*, vol 1, no 2 (1981) pp 1–27

Cox 1981–2
Cox, J F, 'Thomas Woolner's Letters to Mr and Mrs Henry Adams. 2', *Journal of Pre-Raphaelite Studies*, vol 2, no 1 (1981–1982) pp 1–21

Cox-Johnson 1959
Cox-Johnson, Ann, 'Gentleman's Agreement', *Burlington Magazine*, vol 101 (June 1959) pp 236–43

Cox-Johnson 1961
Cox-Johnson, Ann, 'John Bacon RA', *St Marylebone Society Publication*, vol 4 (1961)

Cox-Johnson 1962
Cox-Johnson, Ann, 'Patrons to a Sculptor: The Society and John Bacon', *Royal Society of Arts Journal*, vol 110 (Aug 1962) pp 705–9

CP
Cumberland Pacquet

CR
Christopher Ridgeway, Librarian and archivist, Castle Howard, E R Yorks

Cram and Allen 1998–9
Cram, Jean, and Allen, Sylvia, *Report of the Society of the Friends of St George's and the Descendants of the Knights of the Garter*, vol VII, 10 (1998–9) pp 418–24

Cranston 1957
Cranston, Maurice, *John Locke, a biography* (1957)

Craske 1992
Craske, Matthew J, 'The London Trade in Monumental Sculpture and the Development of the Imagery of the Family in Funerary Monuments of the Period 1720–1760' Ph D Diss (Queen Mary and Westfield College, London: 1992)

Craske 2000 (1)
Craske, Matthew, 'Entombed like an Egyptian: An Eighteenth Century Surgeon's Extravagant Mausoleum to Preserve his Mortal Remains (John Blake)', *Journal of the Church Monuments Society*, vol 15 (2000) pp 71–88

Craske 2000 (2)
Craske, Matthew, 'Contacts and Contracts. Sir Henry Cheere and the Formation of a New Commercial World of Sculpture in Mid-Eighteenth-Century London', in *The Lustrous Trade: Material Culture and the History of Sculpture in England and Italy, c.1700–c.1860*, ed Sicca, Cinzia and Yarrington, Alison (2000) pp 95–113

Craven 1963
Craven, Wayne, 'Horatio Greenough's Statue of Washington and Phidias' Olympian Zeus', *Art Quarterly*, vol 26, no 4 (1963) pp 429–40

Craven 1975
Craven, Wayne, '1776 – How America Really Looked: Sculpture', *American Art Journal*, vol 7 (May 1975) pp 34–42

Craven 1977
Craven, Wayne, 'Origins of Sculpture in America: Philadelphia, 1785–1830', *American Art Journal*, vol 9 (Nov 1977) pp 4–33

Crawford MAG
Crawford Municipal Art Gallery, Cork

Crawford MSA
Crawford Municipal School of Art, Cork

Creasey 1970
Creasey, E, 'Unique Memorial', *Country Life*, vol 148 (13 Aug 1970) p 406

Cremoncini 1994
Cremoncini, Roberta, 'Alcune note su Francis Harwood', *Gazetta Antiquaria* (Dec 1994) pp 68–73

Cresson 1957
Cresson, Margaret, 'First in Toga, First in Sandals: Statue of George Washington', *American Heritage*, vol 8 (Feb 1957) pp 46–47

Cresswell 1908
Cresswell, Beatrix F, *Exeter Churches. Notes on the History, Fabrics and Features of Interest in the Churches of the Deanery of Christianity, Devon* (1908)

Crichton 1971
Crichton, Fenella, 'Canova to Tiffany at Bethnal Green', *Apollo*, no 93 (Mar 1971) pp 222–24

CRO
Cumbria Records Office, Carlisle

Croft-Murray and Hulton 1960
Croft-Murray, Edward, and Hulton, Paul, *Catalogue of British Drawings*, British Museum, 2 vols (1960)

Croggon/Soane
Letter from William Croggon John Soane, 28 February 1834 (Soane, Private Corr I.C.15.2)

Crook 1973
Crook, John Mordaunt, 'Strawberry Hill Revisited', *Country Life*, vol 154 (14 June 1973) pp 1726–30

Crookshank 1966
Crookshank, Anne, 'Irish Sculptors from 1750 to 1860', *Apollo*, no 84 (Oct. 1966) pp 306–13

Crookshank 1986
Crookshank, Anne, 'The Long Room', in *Treasures of the Library, Trinity College, Dublin*, ed Fox, Peter (Dublin: 1986) pp 16–28

Croome
Croome Court, Bills from John Cheere, 1767–1781 (Croome Court Archives, Carter Jonas Estate office, The Builders Yard, High Green, Severn Stoke, Worcs WR8 9JS, F 60)

Croot 1985
Croot, Patricia, *History of the County of Middlesex*, vol 8, VCH (1985)

Crossley 1939
Crossley, F H, 'Post-Reformation Effigies of Cheshire', *Transactions of the Historical Society of Lancashire and Cheshire*, vol 91 (1939) p 1

Crossman 1991
Crossman, Carl L, *The Decorative Arts of the China Trade* (Woodbridge: 1991)

Cruickshank 1954
Cruickshank, I, 'The Monument in Hafod Church', *Country Life*, vol 116, no 3017 (11 Nov 1954) p 1673

Cruickshank 1969
Cruickshank, Anne, *Irish Portraits 1660–1860*, exhib cat (NGI, Dublin: 1969)

CSC, Journal
Journal of Caroline Harriet Stopford Sackville, 1851–1855 (Drayton Archive, Drayton House, Northants)

CUL
Cambridge University Library, Dept of MSS and University Archives

Cullen 1982
Cullen, Finton, 'Hugh Douglas Hamilton in Rome 1779–92', *Apollo*, vol 115, no 240 (1982) pp 86–91

Cumberland Artists 1971
Cumberland Artists 1700–1900, exhib cat (Carlisle MAG: 1971)

Cummings 1968
Cummings, Frederick, 'Boothby, Rousseau, and the Romantic Malady', *Burlington Magazine*, vol 110 (Dec 1968) pp 659–67

Cundall 1926
Cundall, F, 'The Rodney Memorial in Jamaica', *Connoisseur*, vol 76 (1926) pp 34–37

Cunningham 1820
Cunningham, Allan, 'Francis Chantrey, Sculptor', *Blackwood's Edinburgh Magazine*, vol 37 (April 1820) pp 3–10

Cunningham 1829–33
Cunningham, Allan, *Lives of the Most Eminent British Painters, Sculptors and Architects*, 6 vols (1829–1833)

Cunningham 1843
Cunningham, Allan, *The Life of Sir David Wilkie* (1843)

Cunningham 1990
Cunningham, John F, 'The "Soviet at Galway" and the Downfall of Dunkellin', *Journal of the Wesport Historical Society*, vol 10, no 1 (1990) pp 115–23

'Curious Crowe' 1942
'Curious Crowe', 'The Oldest Theatre', *Country Life*, vol 91 (Jan. 1942) p 211

Curl 2001
Curl, James, ed, *Kensal Green Cemetery, the Origins and Development of the General Cemetery of All Souls, Kensal Green, London, 1824–2001* (Chichester: 2001)

Curran 1947
Curran, C P, 'Edward Smythe, Sculptor, Dublin', *Architectural Review*, vol 101 (Feb 1947) pp 67–69

Curtis 1989
Curtis, Penelope, ed, *Patronage and Practice: Sculpture on Merseyside* (Liverpool, Tate Gallery: 1989)

Curtis 2000
Curtis, Penelope et al, *Return to Life A New Look at the Portrait Bust* (Leeds, Henry Moore Institute: 2000)

Cust 1908
Cust, Laurence, 'A Terra-Cotta Bust of Thomas, Third Earl of Coventry, by John Michael Rysbrack', *Burlington Magazine*, vol 13 (1908)

Cust 1909
Cust, Laurence, 'William Séguier, First Keeper of the National Gallery', *Proceedings of the Huguenot Society of London*, vol 8 (1909) pp 157–64

Cust 1914
Cust, Lionel, *History of the Society of Dilettanti* (1914)

Cust 1915
Cust, Lionel, 'The Bust [of Lord Byron] by Thorvaldsen', *Burlington Magazine*, vol 27 (May 1915) pp 59–65

Cuzner 1866–7
Cuzner, Samuel, *Handbook to Froome-Selwood* (1866–67)

CWAC
City of Westminster Archives Centre

Daily Ad
Daily Advertiser

Dale 1956
Dale, Antony, *James Wyatt* (1956)

Dale 1961
Dale, Antony, 'Coade Stone Monuments', *Country Life*, vol 129, no 3348 (4 May 1961) pp 1034–35

Dale-Jones 1989
Dale-Jones, Edna, 'Daniel Mainwaring, statuary and marble mason-builder of the Picton monument', *Carmarthenshire Antiquary*, (1989)

Dale-Jones and Lloyd 1989
Dale-Jones, Edna, and Lloyd, Thomas, 'Sculpture in Carmarthenshire', *Carmarthenshire Antiquary*, (1989) pp 35–60

Dallaway 1800
Dallaway, James, *Anecdotes of the Arts in England* (1800)

Dallaway 1819
Dallaway, James, *A history of the western division of the county of Sussex* (1819)

Danby Papers
Danby Papers, Account Books for Swinton Castle, 1764, 1793–94 (North Yorks CRO, ZS 2290)

Darby 1981
Darby, E S, 'John Gibson, Queen Victoria, and the Idea of Sculptural Polychromy', *Art History*, vol 4, no 1 (1981) pp 37–53

Darby 1983 (1)
Darby, Michael, *The Islamic Perspective, An Aspect of British Architecture and Design in the 19th century* (Leighton House Gallery: World of Islam Festival Trust, 1983)

Darby 1983 (2)
Darby, Elisabeth, 'Statues of Queen Victoria and Prince Albert' Ph D Diss (London Univ: Courtauld Institute, 1983)

Darby and Smith 1983
Darby, Elisabeth, and Smith, Nicola, *The Cult of the Prince Consort* (1983)

Darke 1991
Darke, Jo, *The Monument Guide to England and Wales* (London and Sydney: 1991)

Darling-Glinski 2004
Darling-Glinski, Fiona, 'The Privilege of Patronage: Mary Thornycroft and the Sculptural Aesthetic', *The Sculpture Journal*, vol XI (2004), pp 55–68

Darlington 1955
Darlington, Ida, 'Coade's Artificial Stone in St George's Chapel', *Annual Report of the Society of the Friends of St George*, (1955) pp 13–18

Dart 1723
Dart, John, *Westmonasterium or the History and Antiquities of the Abbey Church of St Peter's Westminster* (2 vols, 1723)

Datchet Parish Registers
Datchet Parish Registers (Bucks RLSS, PR 60/1/3)

Davey 1910
Davey, F Hamilton, 'Neville Northy Burnard', *Royal Cornwall Polytechnic Society Annual Report*, vol 1, part 2 (1910)

Davidson 1969
Davidson, R, 'European Sculpture in Canada', *Antiques Magazine*, vol 95 (May 1969) p 658

Davidson 1970
Davidson, R, 'European Art: Accessions of the Cleveland Museum of Art', *Antiques Magazine*, vol 97 (Mar 1970) p 356

Davies 1992
Davies, Glenys, ed, *Plaster and Marble: The Classical and Neo-Classical Portrait Bust: The Edinburgh Albacini Colloquium*, conference proceedings (Edinburgh, National Gallery of Scotland: 1992)

Davies 2000
Davies, William, ed, *Joseph Edwards Merthyr Sculptor* (Merthyr Tydfil Historical Society, 2000)

Davis 1970 (1)
Davis, Frank, 'Talking about Sales-Rooms', *Country Life*, vol 148 (2 July 1970) p 16

Davis 1970 (2)
Davis, Frank, 'Talking about Sales-Rooms', *Country Life*, vol 148 (13 Aug 1970) p 400

Davis 1970 (3)
Davis, Frank, 'Talking about Sales-Rooms', *Country Life*, vol 148 (8 Oct 1970) pp 896–97

Davis 1971 (1)
Davis, Frank, 'Talking About Sales-Rooms', *Country Life*, vol 149 (14 Jan 1971) p 64

Davis 1971 (2)
Davis, Frank, 'Talking About Sales-Rooms: A Golden Age of Sculpture', *Country Life*, vol 149 (8 April 1971) p 818

Davis 1971 (3)
Davis, Frank, 'Talking about Salesrooms: the Astonishing Grinling Gibbons', *Country Life*, vol 149 (6 May 1971) p 1092

Davis 1971 (4)
Davis, Frank, 'Talking about Sales-Rooms', *Country Life*, vol 149 (20 May 1971) p 1223

Davis 1971 (5)
Davis, Frank, 'Busiest Sculptor in England', *Country Life*, vol 150 (11 Nov 1971) p 1272

Davis 1971 (6)
Davis, Frank, 'Talking About Salesrooms', *Country Life*, vol 150 (25 Nov 1971) pp 1440–41

Davis 1977 (1)
Davis, Frank, 'Against the Evidence: Follies and Fakes of the Art World', *Country Life*, vol 161 (24 Feb 1977) pp 444–45

Davis 1977 (2)
Davis, Frank, 'Talking about Salesrooms; Gibbons as a Furniture-Maker', *Country Life*, vol 161 (5 May 1977) p 1150

Davis 1991 (1)
Davis, John, *Antique Garden Ornament. 300 years of creativity: artists, manufacturers & materials* (Woodbridge: 1991)

Davis 1991 (2)
Davis, John, '19th Century Artificial Stone Garden Ornaments', *Antique Collecting*, vol 26, no 4 (Sept 1991) pp 15–18

Davy/Northumberland
Letter from George Davy to the Duke of Northumberland regarding payment of bill for various items in artificial stone, Northumberland Archives 5 Oct 1773 (Alnwick Castle, Syn V I 28)

Dawes Album
Album of drawings and poetry by Nevil Northey Burnard presented to the Dawes family of Crow's Nest, St Cleer, 1875–1876 (private coll, Berks)

Dawson 1981
Dawson, Aileen, 'Three Friends; Joseph Banks, Josiah Wedgwood and Thomas Bentley', *English Ceramic Circle Transactions*, vol 11, no 1 (1981) pp 21–32

Dawson 1999
Dawson, Aileen, *Portrait Sculpture. A Catalogue of the British Museum Collection c1675–1975* (1999)

DBI 1960–2000
Dizionario Biografico degli Italiani, 55 vols (Rome: 1960–2000)

De Bellaigue 1997
De Bellaigue, Geoffrey, 'Samuel Parker and the Vulliamys, Purveyors of Gilt Bronze', *Burlington Magazine*, vol 139 (Jan 1997) pp 26–37

De Breffny 1986
De Breffny, B, 'Christopher Hewetson, a Preliminary Catalogue Raisonné', *Irish Arts Review*, vol 111 (1986) pp 52–75

De Carle Cash Book
Cash and wages book of John de Carle and John Ivory, 1776–1816 (Suffolk CRO, Bury St Edmunds, 505/1)

De Carle Day Books
Three day books of John de Carle, 1792–1805, 1814–1824, 1818–1844 (Suffolk CRO, Bury St Edmunds, 505/2–4)

De Carle Letter Book
Letter book of John and Benjamin de Carle, 1794–1836 (Suffolk CRO, Bury St Edmunds, 468/1)

De Carle Obelisk Bill
Bill for the erection of an obelisk as a monument to 4th Earl of Bristol, by John de Carle, Hervey family Archives (Suffolk CRO, Bury St Edmunds, 941/83/3)

de Montfort 1993
de Montfort, Patricia, ed, *The Patons – An Artistic Family* (St Andrews, Crawford Arts Centre: 1993)

De Seta 1994
De Seta, Cesare, 'Parthenopean Panopticon: Edgar George Papworth', *FMR Journal*, vol 14 (June 1994) pp 97–126

Deare Inventory
Inventory of the contents of John Deare's studio, inserted into the Giornale of Vincenzo Pacetti, 1798 (Biblioteca Alessandrina, Rome, MS 321)

Death Certificate of Samuel Joseph
Death certificate of Samuel Joseph, 1 July 1850 (General Register Office, London, DA 716728 death no 446)

Deering 1751
Deering, Charles, *Nottinghamia Vetue et Nova, or an Historical Account of the Ancient and Present State of the Town of Nottingham* (1751)

Deitz 1993
Deitz, Paula, 'The King's Apartments Reborn at Hampton Court', *Antiques Magazine*, vol 143, no 6 (1993) pp 876–85

Delaforce 2002
Delaforce, Angela, *Art and Patronage in Eighteenth Century Portugal* (Cambridge: 2002)

Delattre 1978
Delattre, J L, *Laurent Delvaux, 1696–1778. Exposition*, exhib cat (Nivelles: 1978)

Dell 1962
Dell, R F, *The Building of the County Hall, Lewes, 1808–12* (Sussex Archaeological Soc, 1962)

Demoriane 1969
Demoriane, Helene, 'Canova: Napoleon l'Admirait', *Connaissance des Arts*, no 209 (July 1969) pp 26–37

Dening 1923
Dening, C F W, *The Eighteenth-Century Architecture of Bristol* (1923)

Denvir 1956
Denvir, Bernard, 'Sir Francis Chantrey Reconsidered', *Country Life*, vol 120, no 3126 (13 Dec 1956) pp 1416–18

Derby Mech Exhib
Derby Mechanics Exhibition

Derby Mech Inst
Derby Mechanics Institute

Desportes 1963
Desportes, Ulysse, 'Guiseppe Ceracchi in America and his Busts of George Washington', *Art Quarterly*, vol 26, no 2 (Summer 1963) pp 140–79

Desportes 1964
Desportes, Ulysse, 'Ceracchi's Design for a Monument', *Art Quarterly*, vol 27, no 4 (1964) pp 475–89

Desportes 1969
Desportes, Ulysse, ' "Great Men of America" in Roman Guise, Sculptured by Giuseppe Ceracchi', *Antiques Magazine*, vol 96 (July 1969) pp 72–75

Desportes Doctorat nd
Desportes, Ulysse, 'Giuseppe Ceracchi 1751–1801' Deuxième question auxiliaire par le Doctorat (Université de Paris: nd)

Deuchar 1984
Deuchar, Stephen, *Paintings, Politics and Porter. Samuel Whitbread II (1764–1815) and British Art* (Museum of London: 1984)

Deuter 1989
Deuter, Jorg, 'Rom von Oldenburg aus Gesehen: Friedrich Leopold Graf Stolberg und die Kenotaphe für St. Lamberti', *Niederdeutsche Beitrage zur Kunstgeschichte*, vol 28 (1989) pp 161–93

Devigne 1924
Devigne, Marguerite, Esdaile, Katharine, and Toynbee, Margaret, 'Notes on Bernini, Rysbrack and Roubiliac', *Burlington Magazine*, vol 44 (1924) pp 93–97

Devizes 1859
Anon, *History of Devizes* (1859)

DeVoe 1975
DeVoe, Shirley Spaulding, *English Papier Mâché of the Georgian and Victorian Periods* (1975)

Devonshire 1991
Devonshire, Duchess of, *Treasures of Chatsworth* (1991)

Devonshire 1998
Devonshire, Duchess of, *Chatsworth* (Derbyshire Countryside Ltd, 1998)

Devonshire 1999
Devonshire, Duchess of, *Chatsworth Gardens* (Derbyshire Countryside Ltd, 1999)

Devonshire Building Accounts
Charges for Statues at Thoresby by Caius Gabriel Cibber, 1st Duke of Devonshire's Building Accounts 1688 (Devonshire Archives, Chatsworth, VIII, p 5A)

Devonshire Diaries
Diaries of the 6th Duke of Devonshire, early 19th century (Devonshire Archives, Chatsworth)

Dew 1933
Dew, Roderick, *Kilkhampton Church* (Hartland: 1933)

Dibdin 1836
Dibdin, Thomas Frognall, *Reminiscences of a Literary Life* (1836)

Dillon
Dillon Archives (Oxfordshire R O, DIL (1)–(6))

Ditner 1988
Ditner, David, 'Nineteenth-Century English Portrait Sculpture in the National Gallery of Canada', *Apollo*, vol 127, no 315 (May 1988) pp 334–38

Dix Hamilton 1956
Dix Hamilton, M L, 'Rysbrack's Bust of Lord Orkney', *Country Life*, vol 120, no 3126 (13 Dec 1956) pp 1411–12

DNB
Stephen, L and Lee, S, eds, *Dictionary of National Biography*, 63 vols, 3 supplements and index (1885–1900)

Dodsley 1761
Dodsley, Robert, and Dodsley, J, *London and its Environs Described*, 6 vols (1761)

Dommasch 1989
Dommasch, Hans S, and Silversides, Brock, 'Scott Archer and the Collodion Process', *Photography Journal*, vol 129 (July 1989) pp 334–36

Dorey 2004
Dorey, Helen, 'The union of architecture, sculpture and painting: Sir John Soane (1753–1837) as a collector of sculpture', *The Sculpture Journal*, vol 12 (2004) pp 57–70

Dorment 1985
Dorment, Richard, *Alfred Gilbert* (1985)

Dormer 1934
Dormer, Ernest W, 'Coats of Arms in Berkshire Churches', *Berkshire Archaeological Society Journal*, vol 38 (1934) pp 133–49

Dossie 1782
Dossie, John, *Memoirs of Agriculture, and other Oeconomical Arts*, 2 vols (London: 1782), RSA SC/EL/1/204)

Dossie 1787
Dossie, John, *Memoirs of Agriculture, and other Oeconomical Arts*, vol 3 (1787)

Douglas Stewart 1963
Stewart, J Douglas, 'Some Unrecorded Gibbons Monuments', *Burlington Magazine*, vol 105 (March 1963) pp 124–26

Douglas Stewart 1976
Stewart, J Douglas, 'New Light on the Early Career of Grinling Gibbons', *Burlington Magazine*, vol 118 (July 1976) p 508

Douglas Stewart 1978
Stewart, J Douglas, 'New Light on Michael Rysbrack: Augustan England's 'Classical Baroque' Sculptor', *Burlington Magazine*, vol 120 (Apr 1978) pp 215–22

Douglas Stewart 1997
Stewart, J Douglas, 'A Militant Stoic Monument: the Wren–Cibber–Gibbons Charles I Mausoleum Project', in *The Restoration Mind* (London: 1997)

Downes 1959
Downes, Kerry, *Hawksmoor* (1959)

Drakard 1815
Drakard, *Guide to Burghley* (1815)

Drake 1736
Drake, Francis, *Eboracum: or, the History and Antiquities of the City of York*, 2 vols (1736)

Drake 1886
Drake, Henry H, *Hasted's History of Kent, corrected, enlarged, and continued to the present time, from the MS collection of the late Rev Thomas Streatfeild. Part 1, the Hundred of Blackheath* (1886)

Draper 1993
Draper, James David, 'A New Bozzetto by Canova', *Burlington Magazine*, vol 135 (Dec 1993) pp 825–26

Draper 1994
Draper, James David, 'Antonio Canova: Venus and Cupid', *Bulletin of the Metropolitan Museum of Art, New York*, vol 52 (Fall 1994) p 40

Drapers' Court Minutes
Court of Assistants Minutes, Worshipful Company of Drapers 1640–1667, 1667–1705 (Drapers' Hall, City of London, MB14, MB15)

Drapers' Declarations
Master and Wardens Declarations, Worshipful Company of Drapers 1689–1876 (Drapers' Hall, City of London, MDI)

Drapers' Dinner Book
Dinner Book, Worshipful Company of Drapers 1693–1760 (Drapers' Hall, City of London, DB 3)

Drapers' Rebuilding
Minute Book for the rebuilding of Drapers' Hall, Worshipful Company of Drapers 1667–1672 (Drapers' Hall, City of London, M B /T 1)

Drayton Archive
Stopford Sackville Archive (Drayton House, Northants)

Dreier 1996
Dreier, Franz Adrian, 'Landgrave Carl of Hesse-Kassel as a Patron of the Arts', *Journal of Glass Studies*, vol 38 (1996) pp 17–20

Dreyer 1973
Dreyer, Peter, 'James Durno, Beitrage zu Seiner Zeichenkunst und zu Seinen Entwurfen fur die Ausmalung der Sala Grande im Palazzo Ducale in Genua von 1783', *Jahrbuch der Berliner Museen*, vol 15 (1973) p 38

Drummond 1879
Drummond, P R, *Perthshire in Bygone Days* (1879)

Drummond 1979
Drummond, Caroline, 'Four London Horses (The Equestrian Monument in London 1830–1930)' MA Report (University of London: 1979)

Drury 1984
Drury, P J, 'Joseph Rose Senior's Site Workshop at Audley End, Essex: Aspects of the Development of Decorative Plasterwork Technology in Britain during the Eighteenth Century', *Antiquaries Journal*, vol 64, no 1 (1984) pp 62–83

Duchamp 1995
Duchamp, Michel, 'L'Histoire de Trois Trouvailles', *Mercers' Company Archives*, no 49 (Dec 1995) pp 9–13

Duchamp 1998
Duchamp, Michel, 'Numismatique et Glyptique: Les Soeurs de Napoléon, Pistrucci et Mastini', *Medal*, vol 32 (Spring 1998) pp 44–49

Dugdale 1819
Dugdale, J, *The New British Traveller, or Modern Panorama of England and Wales* (1819)

Dugdale 1987
Dugdale, 'Nottinghamshire and Derbyshire Visitation Papers', *Harleian Society*, vol 6, new series (1987)

Dukelskaya 1979
Dukelskaya, Larissa, ed, *The Hermitage, English Art, Sixteenth to Nineteenth Century* (St Petersburg: 1979)

Dunbar 1977
Dunbar, John, 'Carvers in Restoration Scotland', *Country Life*, vol 162, no 4180 (1977) pp 372–73

Dunbar/RMI
Two letters from David Dunbar I to the Royal Manchester Institution, Royal Manchester Institution Archive 8 August and 14 Nov 1834 (Royal Manchester Institution Archive, M6/1/55/186, 228)

Dunkerley 1995
Dunkerley, S, *Francis Chantrey, Sculptor: From Norton to Knighthood* (Sheffield: 1995)

Durbé c1987
Durbé, Dario, intro, *Giovanni Fattori: Dipinti, 1854–1906 / A Cura di Giuliano Matteucci, Raffaele Monti, Ettore Spalletti*, exhib cat (Firenze: c1987)

Duyckaerts 1987
Duyckaerts, Etienne, *Le Sculpteur Laurent Delvaux (1696–1778)* (Liège: 1987)

E F
Eric Foster

E I Co
East India Company

E I Co Cash Journal
East India Company, Cash Journal, 1773–79 (BL, IOR: L/AG/1/5/20)

E I Co, Ct Minutes
East India Company, Minutes of Court of Directors, 1776–77 (BL, IOR B/92)

Earl of Radnor, Household Bills and Vouchers
Mark, 1st Earl of Radnor's Household Bills and Vouchers, Pleydell-Bouverie Papers 1777–1778 (Berks RO, D/DPB/A7/1; D/DPB/A7/4)

Earl Rivers' Accounts
Accounts of Earl Rivers, Bank Ledger, Child's Bank 1685–1713 (Williams and Glyn's Bank, Child's branch, Fleet Street, London, fol(s) 353)

Easter 1995
Easter, Clive, 'John Weston of Exeter and the Last Judgement', *Journal of the Church Monuments Society*, vol 10 (1995) pp 84–89

Easter 2001
Easter, Clive, 'Notes on the Monuments and Career of Thomas Green of Camberwell: Some Recent Discoveries', *Journal of the Church Monuments Society*, vol 16 (2001) pp 65–78

Eastlake 1870
Eastlake, Charles Lock, *Contributions to the Literature of the Fine Arts . . . with a Memoir compiled by Lady Eastlake* (1870)

Eclipse Scrapbook
Scrapbook of eclipse expedition to Spain, including passport, newspaper cuttings, drawings and photographs, 1860 (Royal Astronomical Society, Add MS 56)

ECS
Eighteenth Century Studies

Edmonds 1956
Edmonds, J M, 'White Watson; Information Wanted', *Museums Journal*, vol 56 (Oct 1956) p 182

Edwards 1950
Edwards, T, 'Sir William Wilson: An Obscure Craftsman', *Country Life*, vol 108, no 2790 (7 July 1950) pp 44–45

Edwards 1951
Edwards, Tudor, 'Georgian Birmingham', *Country Life*, vol 110 (16 Nov 1951) pp 1626–27

Edwards 1969
Edwards, Ralph, 'George Bullock as Sculptor and Modeller', *Connoisseur*, vol 171 (July 1969) pp 172–73

Edwards 1977
Edwards, A C, ed, *The Account Books of Benjamin Mildmay, Earl Fitzwalter* (1977)

Edwards 1978
Edwards, Geoffrey, 'Figure – Lalage', *Art Bulletin of Victoria, New South Wales*, vol 19 (1978) pp 74–75

Egremont 1985
Egremont, Max, 'The Third Earl of Egremont and his Friends', *Apollo*, no 122 (Oct 1985) pp 280–87

Egremont/Drummond
Lord Egremont's Accounts, Drummonds Bank 1763 (Royal Bank of Scotland, Drummond's branch, Charing Cross, London)

Eidelberg 2003
Eidelberg, Martin, 'More about Old Nollekens', *Apollo*, vol 157, no 493 (March 2003) pp 22–26

Eimer 1998
Eimer, Christopher, *The Pingo Family and Medal Making in 18th Century Britain* (London: British Art Medal Trust, 1998)

Eland 1931
Eland, G, ed, *Purefoy Letters 1735–1753* (London: 1931)

Elkins 1990
Elkins, James, 'Clarification, Destruction, and Negation of Pictorial Space in the Age of Neoclassicism, 1750–1840', *Zeit fur Kunst*, vol 53, no 4 (1990) pp 560–82

Elliot 2000
Elliot, Rev Ben, 'The Monument by Sir Robert Taylor to Sir William Phipps died 1748 in All Saints Church, Westbury, Wilts', *Journal of the Church Monuments Society*, vol 16, no 1 (2000) p 13

Ellison 1989
Ellison, Leslie, 'Carving Out a Career', *Country Life*, vol 183, no 20 (18 May 1989) pp 240–41

Elmes 1827
Elmes, James, *Metropolitan Improvements; or London in the Nineteenth Century* (1827)

Elwyn 1934
Elwyn, E G, 'Samuel Percy's Rustic Scenes in Wax', *Connoisseur*, vol 93 (May 1934) pp 320–24

Emmerson 1995
Emmerson, Robin, 'Wax Models by Pacetti and Angelini in the Lady Lever Art Gallery', *Ars Ceramica*, vol 12 (1995) pp 22–33

Encyc Sc
Bostrom, Antonia, ed, *Encyclopedia of Sculpture* (Chicago: 2004)

Eng Misc
English Miscellany

Enggass 1976 (1)
Enggass, Robert, *Early eighteenth century sculpture in Rome* (Pennsylvania: 1976)

Enggass 1976 (2)
Enggass, Robert, 'Un Probleme du Baroque Romain Tardif. Projets de Sculptures par des Artistes non Sculpteurs', *Revue de l'Art*, no 31 (1976) pp 21–32

Enggass 1981
Enggass, Robert, 'Settecento Sculpture in St Peter's: an Encyclopedia of Styles', *Apollo*, vol 113, no 228 (Feb 1981) pp 74–81

englishorigins
www.englishorigins.com

ERAO
East Riding Archive Office (Beverley)

Eriksen 1994
Eriksen, Jorgen, 'Paolo og Francesca', *Passepartout* [aka *Skulptur*], vol 2, no 3 (April 1994) pp 25–32

Erwood 1996
Erwood, Maurice, 'The Equestrian Statue of Charles II at Gautby', *Lincolnshire Past and Present*, vol 25 (1996) pp 4–8

ESC
Edinburgh Sheriff Court

Esdaile 1922
Esdaile, Katharine, 'Studies of the English Sculptors from Pierce to Chantrey', *The Architect*, vols 10, 11 (3 March and 7 April 1922) pp 164–68; 249–52

Esdaile 1923
Esdaile, Katharine, 'Roubiliac and Rysbrack', *Burlington Magazine*, vol 42 (April 1923) pp 197–99

Esdaile 1924 (1)
Esdaile, Katharine, *Roubiliac's Work at Trinity College Cambridge* (1924)

Esdaile 1924 (2)
Esdaile, Katharine, 'Flaxman's Design for the Monument to Lord Mayor Beckford at the Guildhall', *Burlington Magazine*, vol 45, no 258 (Aug 1924) pp 81–86

Esdaile 1924 (3)
Esdaile, Katharine, 'Bust of William Hamilton by Michael Foye', *Burlington Magazine*, vol 45, no 258 (Aug 1924) p 87

Esdaile 1924 (4)
Esdaile, Katharine, 'Note on Michael Foye', *Burlington Magazine*, vol 45, no 260 (Nov 1924) p 237

Esdaile 1926–7
Esdaile, Katharine, 'John Bushnell, Sculptor', *Walpole Society*, vol 15 (1926–27) pp 21–45

Esdaile 1927
Esdaile, Katharine, *English Monumental Sculpture since the Renaissance* (1927)

Esdaile 1928
Esdaile, Katherine, *The Life and Works of Louis François Roubiliac* (1928)

Esdaile 1929 (1)
Esdaile, Katharine, 'Bubb; Life and Work', *Artwork*, vol 5, no 17 (1929) pp 33–40

Esdaile 1929 (2)
Esdaile, Katharine, 'A Seventeenth Century Model of an English Monument', *Burlington Magazine*, vol 55 (Oct 1929) pp 195–97

Esdaile 1930
Esdaile, Katharine, 'The Stantons of Holborn', *Archaeological Journal*, vol 85 (1930) pp 149–69

Esdaile 1931
Esdaile, Katharine, 'Statuette of Inigo Jones', 3 *RIBA Journal*, vol 38 (7 Feb 1931) pp 220–21

Esdaile 1932
Esdaile, Katharine, *The Art of Michael Rysbrack in terracotta* (London: Spink and Son, 1932)

Esdaile 1932–3
Esdaile, Katharine, 'English Sculpture at Cambridge from 16th to 18th Century', *Proceedings of the Cambridge Antiquarian Society*, vol 34 (1932–3) pp 1–16

Esdaile 1933 (1)
Esdaile, Katharine, 'Additional Notes on John Bushnell', *Walpole Society*, vol 21 (1933) p 105

Esdaile 1933 (2)
Esdaile, Katharine, *Temple Church Monuments* (1933)

Esdaile 1933 (3)
Esdaile, Katharine, 'The Tomb of Sir Justinian Isham at Lamport', *RIBA Journal*, vol 40, no 5 (14 Jan 1933) pp 174–75

Esdaile 1934
Esdaile, Katharine, 'English Sculpture in Cambridge from the Sixteenth to the Eighteenth Century', *Proceedings of the Cambridge Antiquarian Society* (1934) p 1

Esdaile 1935
Esdaile, Katharine, 'New Light on Hubert Le Sueur and his Collaborators', *Burlington Magazine*, vol 66 (April 1935) pp 177–84

Esdaile 1937
Esdaile, Katharine, 'A Georgian Sculptor Discovered, I and II', *Country Life*, vol 82 (2 Oct and 11 Dec) pp 348–53, 608–11

Esdaile 1938
Esdaile, Katharine, 'Two Busts of Charles I and William III', *Burlington Magazine*, vol 72 (April 1938) pp 164–68

Esdaile 1939 (1)
Esdaile, Katharine, 'Bacon's George III, the River Thames at his Feet, at Somerset House', *Burlington Magazine*, vol 75 (Oct 1939) p 168

Esdaile 1939 (2)
Esdaile, Katharine, 'Post-Reformations Monuments, Mostly in Derbyshire', *Journal of the Derbyshire Archaeological and Natural History Society*, vol 40, no 13 (1939) pp 84–104

Esdaile 1940 (1)
Esdaile, Katharine, 'Statuette of William III at South Kensington', *Burlington Magazine*, vol 76 (April 1940) pp 122–24

Esdaile 1940 (2)
Esdaile, Katharine, 'Coade Stone', *The Architect and Building News*, vol 161 (19, 26 Jan 1940) pp 94–96, 112–14

Esdaile 1940 (3)
Esdaile, Katharine, 'Sculpture and Sculptors in Yorkshire', *Yorkshire Archaeological Journal*, vol 35 and 36 (1940–43 and 1944–47) pp 362–88 and 78, 137

Esdaile 1941
Esdaile, Katharine, 'English Sculpture in Some Berkshire Churches', *Berkshire Archaeological Society Journal*, vols 45 and 46 (1941) pp 45, 86 and 22, 69

Esdaile 1942
Esdaile, Katharine, 'Some Annotations on John Le Neve's Monumenta Anglicana (1717–1719)', *Antiquaries Journal*, vol 22 (1942) pp 176–97

Esdaile 1943
Esdaile, Katharine, 'The Gunpowder Plot in Needlework', *Country Life*, vol 93 (18 June 1943) p 1094

Esdaile 1944 (1)
Esdaile, Katharine, 'So-Called Aged Wren Proves to be Richard Miller by Rysbrack', *Architectural Review*, vol 95 (June 1944) pp 142–43

Esdaile 1944 (2)
Esdaile, Katharine, 'Group of Terracotta Models by Joseph Nollekens, R.A.', *Burlington Magazine*, vol 85 (Sept 1944) pp 220–23

Esdaile 1946
Esdaile, Katharine, *English Church Monuments, 1510–1841* (1946)

Esdaile 1947 (1)
Esdaile, Katharine, 'The Royal Sisters, Mary II and Anne in Sculpture', *Burlington Magazine*, vol 89 (1947) p 254

Esdaile 1947 (2)
Esdaile, Katharine, 'Arnold Quellin's Charles II', *Architectural Review*, vol 102 (Nov 1947) pp 174–75

Esdaile 1947 (3)
Esdaile, Katharine, 'Christopher Hewetson and His Monument to Dr. Baldwin in Trinity College, Dublin', *Journal of the Royal Society of Antiquaries of Ireland*, vol 77, no 2 (1947)

Esdaile 1948 (1)
Esdaile, Katharine, 'Sir Robert Taylor as Sculptor', *Architectural Review*, vol 103 (Feb 1948) pp 63–66

Esdaile 1948 (2)
Esdaile, Katharine, 'Signor Guelfi, An Italian', *Burlington Magazine*, vol 90 (Nov 1948) pp 317–21

Esdaile 1991
Esdaile, Edmund, 'The De Carteret Monument in the Parish Church of Holy Trinity', *Annual Bulletin Societé Jersiaise*, vol 25, no 3 (1991) pp 558–59

Esdaile and Toynbee 1956
Esdaile, Katharine, and Toynbee, M, 'More Light on English Quellin', *Transactions of the London and Middlesex Archaeological Society*, vol 19, no 1 (1956) p 34

Esdaile Typescript
Esdaile, Katharine, *Typescript for an unpublished dictionary of sculptors*, 5 vols, LMG, HMI Archive; another NAL, London MSL/1977/4462 (nd, unpag)

Essex Review 1934
WGB, 'Edward Stanton, Sculptor', *Essex Review*, vol 43, no 169 (Jan 1934) p 122

Essex RO
Essex Record Office, Chelmsford

Esterly 1994
Esterly, David, 'Grinling Gibbons: The Final Experiments in Hampton Court Palace, London', *Apollo*, no 140 (Aug 1994) pp 32–38

Esterly 1998
Esterly, David, *Grinling Gibbons and the Art of Carving* (1998)

Esterly 1999
Esterly, David, 'Grinling Gibbons in Retrospect', *Burlington Magazine*, vol 141, no 1155 (June 1999) pp 355–56

Ettinger 1924
Ettinger, P, 'Portraits of Charles Fox at the Hermitage', *Burlington Magazine*, vol 45, no 258 (Aug 1924) p 88

Euro Mag
The European Magazine and London Review, (87 vols, Jan 1782–June 1825)

Eustace 1982
Eustace, Katharine, *Michael Rysbrack; Sculptor 1694–1770*, exhib cat (Bristol Mus Art Gallery: 1982)

Eustace 1997 (1)
Eustace, Katharine, 'Robert Adam, Charles-Louis Clerisseau, Michael Rysbrack and the Hopetoun Chimneypiece', *Burlington Magazine*, vol 139 (Nov 1997) pp 743–52

Eustace 1997 (2)
Eustace, Katherine, *Canova Ideal Heads* (Oxford, Ashmolean: 1997) pp 9–38, 66–125

Eustace 1998
Eustace, Katharine, 'The Politics of the Past: Stowe and the Development of the Historical Portrait Bust', *Apollo*, vol 148, no 437 (July 1998) pp 31–40

Evans 1828
Evans, Rev John, *The New Guide, or Picture of Bristol*, 4th edition (1828)

Evans 1978
Evans, Jane, *Charles Summers 1827–1878*, exhib cat (Woodspring Museum and Art Gallery, Weston-Super-Mare: 1978)

Evelyn 1959
de Beer, E S, ed, *John Evelyn, Diary*, 6 vols (Oxford: 1959)

Every/Guise
Letter from Sir Simon Every to Lady Guise, regarding Carter's monument to his brother Sir Henry Every, 1734 (Derbys RO)

Exhib Cat SBA
The Exhibition of the Society of British Artists, Suffolk Street, Pall Mall East, 2 vols, bound in VAM, volume 1 1824–1839, vol 2 1840–1857 (1824–1857)

Exhib Cat, Mechanics' Inst
Catalogue of the Exhibition at the Mechanics' Institute, George Street, Hull (1842)

Eyres 1997
Eyres, Patrick, *The Political Temples of Stowe* (1997)

Eyres 2001
Eyres, Patrick, 'Celebration and Dissent, Thomas Hollis, The Society of Arts, and Stowe Gardens (John Pingo and James Lovell)', *Medal*, no 38 (2001) pp 31–50

Faber 1926
Faber, Harald, *Caius Gabriel Cibber, 1630–1700, His Life and Work* (Oxford: 1926)

Farington
Garlick, K and Mackintyre, A (1–6), and Cave, K (7–16), eds, *The Diary of Joseph Farington* (1978–84)

Farnley archives
Farnley Hall archives (West Yorks RO, uncatalogued)

Fastnedge 1949
Fastnedge, R, 'Jean Voyez and Wedgwood', *Apollo*, vol 49 (Jan 1949) pp 22–23

Faulkner 1845
Faulkner, Thomas, *The History and Antiquities of Brentford, Ealing and Chiswick* (1845)

Feeke 2000
Feeke, Stephen, *Hounds in Leash: The Dog in Eighteenth and Nineteenth Century Sculpture*, exhib cat (HMI Leeds: 2000)

Feely 1996
Feely, Martin, Lidwell, Jerry, and Monaghan, Dominic, 'Mrs Coade's Stone: a Late 18th Century Addition to Co. Galway's Architectural Heritage', *Journal of the Galway Archaeological and Historical Society*, vol 48 (1996) pp 92–97

Fehl 1972
Fehl, Philip, 'John Trumbull and Robert Ball Hughes's Restoration of the Statue of Pitt the Elder', *New York Historical Society Quarterly*, vol 56, no 1 (1972) pp 7–28

Fehl 1974
Fehl, Phillip, 'The Account Book of Thomas Appleton of Livorno, A Document in the History of American Art', *Winterthur Portfolio*, vol 9 (1974) pp 123–51

Ferrey 1978
Ferrey, Benjamin, *Recollections of A.W.N. Pugin and his father Augustus Pugin*, first published 1861 (London: 1978)

Festing 1984
Festing, S, 'Pulham has done his work well', *Journal of Garden History*, vol 12, no 2 (Autumn 1984) pp 138–58

Festing 1988
Festing, S, 'Great credit upon the ingenuity and taste of Mr Pulham', *Journal of Garden History*, vol 16, no 1 (Spring 1988) pp 90–102

FFB
Westminster Abbey, Funerary Fees Books

Ffoukes 1916
Ffoukes, Charles, *Armouries of the Tower of London*, 2 vols (1916)

Field 1815
'WF' [Field, William], *An Historical and Descriptive Account of the Town and Castle of Warwick* (1815)

Field 1995
Field, Marcus, 'London Docklands Looks to its Past as Well as its Future', *Architect's Journal*, vol 202 (3 Aug 1995) pp 20–23

Filler 1996
Filler, Martin, 'True to his Coade', *House Beautiful*, vol 138, no 3 (March 1996) pp 102–9, 148

Finch 1901
Finch, Pearl, *History of Burley-on-the-Hill* (1901)

Finch 1966
Finch, R H C, 'The Life and Work of J E Carew', *Bulletin of the Irish Georgian Society*, vol 9, no 3–4 (1966) pp 84–96

Finch 2000
Finch, Jonathan, *Church Monuments in Norfolk before 1850. An Archaeology of Commemoration*, British Archaeological Reports, British Series 317 (2000)

Findlay 1996
Findlay, Donald, 'The Pious Works of Henry Sephton', *Georgian Group Journal*, vol 6 (1996) pp 24–36

Finer and Savage 1965
Finer, A and Savage, C, eds, *The Selected Letters of Josiah Wedgwood* (1965)

Finn 1979
Finn, David, 'Canova', *National Sculpture Review*, vol 28, no 1 (Spring 1979) pp 20–23

Firmadge/King
Letters from William Firmadge, of Leicester, to his sister, Ann King, of Baltimore, Maryland (1811–1836) and from Mrs King's son to his aunt Mrs Firmadge (1837), King Family Papers 1811–1910 (Maryland Historical Society, MS 2701)

Fisher & Newman 1985
Fisher, Geoffrey, and Newman, John, 'A fountain design by Inigo Jones', *Burlington Magazine*, vol 127 (1985) pp 531–32

Fisher Letters
Fisher Letters, 1806 (CLRO, Misc MSS 207)

Fishmongers PL
Corporation of London, Fishmongers' Company, Payment Ledger, 1785–1802; 1808–23 (CLRO Guildhall, 5566/1; 5566/2)

Fishmongers, PW Accts
Corporation of London, Fishmongers' Company, Prime Warden's Accounts, 1636–1682, 1682–1706, 1706–24, 1724–33, 1738–56, 1785–1802 (CLRO, Guildhall, 5561/1–8)

Fishmongers' PW and W Accts
Corporation of London, Fishmongers' Company, Prime Wardens' and Wardens' Account Books, Worshipful Company of Fishmongers 1646–1688 (CLRO Guildhall, 5562/1–2)

Fitzgerald 1957
Fitzgerald, Brian, ed, *Correspondence of Emily, Duchess of Leinster*, 3 vols (Dublin: 1957)

Fitzgerald 1968
Fitz-Gerald, Desmond, 'A Sheraton designed bookcase and the Giannellis', *Bulletin of the Victoria and Albert Museum*, vol 4, pt 1 (1968)

FitzGerald 2002
FitzGerald, John Edward, 'The "Year of Joy" and Centenary Renovations to the Cathedral, St. John's, Newfoundland, 1953–1955', *Canadian Catholic Historical Association*, no 68 (2002) pp 44–65

Fitzpatrick 1855
Fitzpatrick, W J, *The Life and Times of Lord Cloncurry* (1855)

Fitzwilliam
Fitzwilliam Museum, Cambridge

Fitzwilliam Letters
Fitzwilliam Papers, Fitzwilliam, misc unsorted letters 1710–44 (NRO, Milton)

Flaxman 1799
Flaxman, John RA, *A Letter to the Committee for raising the Naval Pillar, or Monument, under the Patronage of his Royal Highness the Duke of Clarence, by John Flaxman, Sculptor (plates engraved by William Blake)*, pamphlet (1799)

Flaxman 1838
Flaxman, John RA, *Lectures on Sculpture*, 2nd edition (1838)

Flaxman 1980
Flaxman, Vivien, 'Flight of Satan from Paradise and Adam and Eve: John Flaxman's Last Works', *Burlington Magazine*, vol 122, no 931 (Oct 1980) pp 687–90

Flaxman Account Book 1794–1810
Croft-Murray, Edward, 'An Account Book of John Flaxman', *Walpole Society*, vol 28 (1940) pp 51–93

Flaxman Account Book 1809–26
Account Book of John Flaxman RA, 1809–1826 (Columbia University, NY, Collections D 430 394 F61)

Flaxman Leases
Leases on property taken by John Flaxman I, 16 Aug 1776, 24 Dec 1799, 1 March 1803, 24 June 1803 (LMA, BRA 723/41; 723/52–6)

Flaxman Papers
Correspondence and other papers of John Flaxman RA and his household, which included Ann Flaxman (née Denman), Mary Ann Flaxman and Maria Denman, 11 vols and 39 notebooks (BL, Add MSS 39780–39792)

Flekel' 1986
Flekel', M, 'Risunok Skul'ptora', *Hud*, no 4 (1986) pp 46–58

Fleming 1956
Fleming, John, 'Pluras of Turin and Bath; with French Summary', *Connoisseur*, vol 138 (Dec 1956) pp 175–81, 198

Fleming 1962 (1)
Fleming, John, *Robert Adam and his Circle* (1962)

Fleming 1962 (2)
Fleming, John, 'Robert Adam, Luc-Francois Breton and the Townshend Monument in Westminster Abbey', *Connoisseur*, vol 150 (July 1962) pp 163–71

Fleming and Honour 1968
Fleming, John, and Honour, Hugh, 'An English Sculptor in XVIII Century Florence', *Festschrift Ulrich Middeldorf (Berlin)*, (1968) pp 510–16

Fletcher 1972
Fletcher, Hans, 'John Gibson, an English Pupil of Thorvaldsen', *Apollo*, no 96 (Oct 1972) pp 336–40

Fletcher 1974
Fletcher, Hans, 'John Gibson's Polychromy and Lord Londonderry's Bacchus', *Connoisseur*, vol 187 (Sept 1974) pp 2–5

Fletcher 1977
Fletcher, Hans, 'John Gibson's Narcissus', *Connoisseur*, vol 196 (Sept 1977) pp 60–62

Fletcher 2001
Fletcher, John, ed, *Where Truth Abides: Diaries of the 4th Duke of Newcastle-under-Lyme (1822–1850)* (Bakewell: 2001)

Floryan 2003 (1)
Floryan, Margrethe, 'Meddeleser fra Thorvaldsens Museum', *Thorvaldsen's Museum Bulletin*, (2003)

Floryan 2003 (2)
Floryan, Margrethe, 'Om Thomas Hope, hans huse og hobbies', in *Thorvaldsens Museum Bulletin* (2003) pp 43–74

Flynn 1997
Flynn, Tom, 'Canova: Ideal Heads in Oxford', *Apollo*, vol 146 (Nov 1997) pp 57–58

Fogelman 1990
Fogelman, Peggy, 'Flaxman's Relief of Satan's Flight from Paradise', *Burlington Magazine*, vol 132, no 1042 (1990) p 31

Fogelman 1994
Fogelman, Peggy, 'S'eri tu in Viso Qual ti Feo Canova: Canova's Herm of a Vestal Virgin', *J Paul Getty Museum Journal*, vol 22 (1994) pp 43–55

Fogelman 2000
Fogelman, Peggy, Fusco, Peter, and Stock, Simon, 'John Deare (1759–1798): A British Neo-Classical Sculptor in Rome', *The Sculpture Journal*, vol 4 (2000) pp 85–126

Foley/Weekes
Letter from J H Foley to Henry Weekes, Sydney Smirke Papers 1872 (BL, Add MS 60745, fol 55)

Forbes 2000
Forbes, Duncan, ' "Dodging and watching the natural incidents of the peasantry," genre painting in Scotland 1780–1830', *Oxford Art Journal*, vol 23, no 2 (2000) pp 79–94

Ford 1960
Ford, Trevor D, 'White Watson (1760–1835) and his Geological Sections', *Proceedings of the Geologists' Association*, vol 71 (1960) pp 349–63

Ford 1962
Ford, Trevor D, 'White Watson – Pioneer Derbyshire Geologist', *Bulletin of the Peak District Mines Historical Society*, vol 1, no 7 (1962) pp 27–32

Ford 1974
Ford, Brinsley, 'The Earl-Bishop, an Eccentric and Capricious Patron of the Arts', *Apollo*, vol 99, no 148 (1974) pp 426–34

Ford 1995
Ford, Trevor D, 'White Watson (1760–1835) and his Geological Tablets', *Mercian Geologist*, vol 13, no 4 (1995) pp 157–64

Forrer 1904–30
Forrer, L, *Biographical dictionary of medallists: coin-, gem-, and seal-engravers, mint-masters, &c., ancient and modern: with references to their works, B.C. 500 – A.D. 1900*, facsimile reprint, originally published 1904–1930, 8 vols (London: 1979–1980)

Forrest's Tours
Forrest's Tours [including a Tour into Derbyshire with William Tyler RA] (BL, Add MS 42232)

Forsyth Album
Album of photographs collected by James Forsyth (HMI, 21/86)

Fosbrooke 1819
Fosbrooke, Thomas Dudley, *An Original History of the City of Gloucester* (1819)

Foster 1887
Foster, J, ed, *London Marriage Licences 1521–1869* (1887)

Fothergill 1984
Diary of Charles Fothergill, Yorkshire Archaeological Society Record Series, 142 (1984)

Fox 1882
Pym, Horace, ed, *Memories of old friends. Being extracts from the journals and letters of Caroline Fox of Penjerrick, Cornwall 1835–1871*, 2 vols (1882)

Fox 1923
Earl of Ilchester, Giles, *The Journal of the Hon Henry Edward Fox* (1923)

Fox Strangways Papers
Account Book of Sir Stephen Fox's Household, 1677/8–1682–3, Fox Strangways Papers (Dorset RO, Dorchester, D/FSI/box 211)

Francastel 1933
Francastel, Pierre, 'Le Marmorbad de Cassel et les Lazienski de Varsovie', 6 *Gazette des Beaux-Arts*, vol 9 (March 1933) pp 138–56

FRC
Family Records Centre, 1 Myddleton St, London EC1R 1UW

Fredeman 1975
Fredeman, William E, ed, *The P.R.B. Journal. William Michael Rossetti's diary of the Pre-Raphaelite Brotherhood, 1849–1853, together with other Pre-Raphaelite documents* (Oxford: 1975)

Free Soc
Free Society of Artists

Freestone 1985
Freestone, I C, Bimson, M, and Tite, M S, ' "The Constitution of Coade Stone", Ancient Technology to Modern Science', *Bulletin of the American Ceramics Society* (1985)

Frew 1984
Frew, John, 'Gothic in Transition: Wyatt and Bernasconi at New College Chapel, Oxford, 1788–94', *Burlington Magazine*, vol 126 (Nov 1984) pp 683–85

Frick, NY
Frick Collection, New York

Friedman 1972
Friedman, Terry, 'Aspects of Nineteenth Century Sculpture in Leeds 1. The Northern Society Exhibitions and 2. Patronage of the Benjamin Gott Family', *Leeds Arts Calendar*, no 70 (1972) pp 22–28

Friedman 1973 (1)
Friedman, Terry, 'A Noble Magnificent Statue', *Leeds Arts Calendar*, no 72 (1973) pp 5–13

Friedman 1973 (2)
Friedman, Terry, 'John Cheere's Busts and Statuettes from Kirkleatham Hall', *City of York Art Gallery Quarterly*, vol 26 (1973) p 923

Friedman 1973 (3)
Friedman, Terry, *Immortal Fame. An Anthology of Drawings and Models for English Sculpture*, exhib cat (1973)

Friedman 1974 (1)
Friedman, Terry, 'Turnerelli's Bust of Queen Charlotte', *Leeds Arts Calendar*, vol 75 (1974) pp 12–18

Friedman 1974 (2)
Friedman, Terry, 'A Decorative Sculptor's Tradecard', *Leeds Arts Calendar*, no 75 (1974) pp 29–32

Friedman 1976 (1)
Friedman, Terry, 'Sir Thomas Gascoigne and his Friends in Italy', *Leeds Arts Calendar*, vol 78 (1976) pp 17–23

Friedman 1976 (2)
Friedman, Terry, 'Foggini's Statue of Queen Anne', *Kunst des Barock in der Toskana*, (1976) pp 41–46

Friedman 1979–80
Friedman, Terry, 'The Rebuilding of Bishopsgate: a Case of Architecture and Corruption in Eighteenth Century London', *Guildhall Studies*, vol 4, no 2 (1979–1980) pp 75–90

Friedman 1980 (1)
Friedman, Terry, 'Samuel Joseph Phrenologized', *Leeds Arts Calendar*, no 86 (1980) pp 20–28

Friedman 1980 (2)
Friedman, Terry, 'Scheemakers's Monument to the Best of Sons', *Burlington Magazine*, vol 122, no 922 (Jan. 1980) pp 61–65

Friedman 1981 (1)
Friedman, Terry, 'A Conveniant and Pleasant Habitation', *Leeds Arts Calendar*, no 89 (1981) pp 5–13

Friedman 1981 (2)
Friedman, Terry, 'Cavalier's Charles II on Horseback', *Leeds Arts Calendar*, vol 88 (1981) pp 4–13

Friedman 1984
Friedman, Terry, *James Gibbs* (New Haven and London: 1984)

Friedman 1985
Friedman, Terry, 'A "Beautifull True Genteel Likeness" ', *Leeds Arts Calendar*, no 97 (1985) pp 15–22

Friedman 1987
Friedman, Terry, 'Nost at Bothwell', *Journal of the Church Monuments Society*, vol 2 (1987) pp 22–31

Friedman 1991
Friedman, Terry, 'Samuel Joseph and the Sculpture of Feeling', in *Virtue and Vision Sculpture and Scotland 1540–1990*, ed Pearson, Fiona, (1991) pp 58–63

Friedman 1993
Friedman, Terry, *Four Centuries of Sculptor's Drawings from the Collection of Leeds City Art Galleries* (1993)

Friedman 1995
Friedman, Terry, 'The Transformation of York Minster, 1726–42', *Architectural History*, vol 38 (1995) pp 69–90

Friedman 1997
Friedman, Terry, *Church Architecture in Leeds 1700–1799* (Thoresby Society, 1997)

Friedman 1998
Friedman, Terry, 'William Halfpenny's Designs for an "Early Christian" Cathedral at Waterford', *Irish Architectural and Decorative Studies*, vol 1 (1998) pp 8–33

Friedman 2004
Friedman, Terry, *The Georgian Parish Church* (Reading: 2004)

Friedman (Winifred) 1976
Friedman, Winifred H, *Boydell's Shakespeare Gallery* (1976)

Friedman and Clifford, Leeds, 1974
Friedman, Terry and Clifford, Timothy, *The Man at Hyde Park Corner: Sculpture by John Cheere* (exhib cat, Leeds and Greater London Council: 1974)

Friedman and Stevens 1972
Friedman, Terry, and Stevens, Timothy, *Joseph Gott, 1786–1860, Sculptor*, exhib cat (Temple Newsam, Leeds, and Walker Art Gallery, Liverpool: 1972)

Friedman/Woods
Friedman, Terry F, 'Looking into the Woods', typescript, HMI (c2000)

FRS
Fellow of the Royal Society

Fry 1999
Fry, Terry, *Nottingham's plaques and statues* (Nottingham Civic Society, 1999)

Fuchs 1997
Fuchs, Thomas, *Tradition und Innovation im Werk des Pierre-Etienne Monnot: das Marmorbad in Kassel* (Weimar: 1997)

Fulton 2001
Fulton, Moira, 'John Cheere Statuary, His Workshop Practice and output' MA Diss (Univ of York: 2001)

Fulton 2003
Fulton, Moira, 'John Cheere, the Eminent Statuary, his Workshop and Practice, 1737–1787', *The Sculpture Journal*, (2003) pp 21–39

Fulton 2004
Fulton, Moira, 'John Cheere at Queluz Palace', *The Sculpture Journal*, vol 12 (2004) pp 102–3

Furnese General Expenditure
General Expenditure of Arabella Furnese, North family, Earls of Guilford 1715–1727 (East Kent Archives Centre, EK/U471/A49)

Fusco 1988
Fusco, Peter, 'Pierre-Etienne Monnot's Inventory after Death', *Antologia di Belle Arti*, no 33–34 (1988) pp 70–77

Fusco 1998
Fusco, Peter, Fogelman, Peggy Anne, and Cambereri, Marietta, *European Sculpture*, Masterpieces of the J Paul Getty Museum (1998)

G Misc
Guildhall Miscellany

Gabriels 1930
Gabriels, Jullane, *Artus Quellien de Oude, Kunstryck Beelthower* (Antwerp: 1930)

Gage 1838
Gage, John, *The History and Antiquities of Suffolk. Thingoe Hundred* (1838)

GAGM
Glasgow Art Gallery and Museum

Galvin 1990
Galvin, Carol, 'The Construction of Roubiliac's Shelburne and Argyll Models', *Burlington Magazine*, vol 132 (Dec 1990) pp 849–50

Galvin and Lindley 1988
Galvin, Carol, and Lindley, Phillip, 'Pietro Torrigiano's portrait bust of King Henry VII', *Burlington Magazine*, vol 130 (1988) pp 892–902

Gardner 1938
Gardner, Bellamy, 'Sophie Roubiliac in Chelsea Porcelain', *Connoisseur*, vol 102 (Aug 1938) pp 58–61

Gardner 1948
Gardner, Albert Ten Eyck, 'Fragment of a Lost Monument: Marble Bust of Washington', *Bulletin of the Metropolitan Museum of Art, New York*, no 6 (March 1948) pp 189–97

Garnier 1993
Garnier, Richard, 'Clermont Lodge, Norfolk', *Country Life*, vol 187, no 38 (23 Sept 1993) pp 78–81

Garnier 1997
Garnier, Richard, 'Two "Crystalline" Villas of the 1760s', *Georgian Group Journal*, vol 7 (1997) pp 9–25

Garnier 1998
Garnier, Richard, 'Gatton Town Hall' and 'Arno's Grove, Southgate', *Georgian Group Journal*, vol 8 (1998) pp 72–75, 122–34

Garnier and Hewlings 1989
Garnier, Richard, and Hewlings, Richard, 'The Salwey Saga', *Country Life*, vol 183, no 38 (21 Sept 1989) pp 208–13

Garratt 1991
Garratt, Pat, 'Re-incarvation', *World of Interiors* (Oct 1991) pp 43–44

Garstang 1988
Garstang, Donald, 'Finding–Piamontini v Harwood: A Rediscovered Terracotta by G B Piamontini', *Apollo*, no 128 (Sept 1988) pp 179–81

Garstang 2003
Garstang, Donald, 'Sir Robert Taylor and Camillo Rusconi: the source of "Britannia" on the Cornewall monument in Westminster Abbey', *Burlington Magazine*, vol 145 (Dec 2003) pp 851–53

Gatley Corr
Letters from friends and family transcribed by Alfred Gatley, started in Rome and including account of visit to Florence, 1853 and years following (private coll)

Gatley/Atkinson
Letter from Alfred Gatley to J B Atkinson, nd (BM, Add 42712 fol 195)

Gatley/Bollington
'Alfred Gatley: Kerridge boy who became famous sculptor', *Bollington Festival Programme* (1964)

Gatley/Cope
Handwritten transcript of notes on Alfred Gatley by Dr John Cope (Bollington Library, Macclesfield, Cheshire)

Gatley/Rathbone
Transcript of Gatley's Letters and Diaries by Mrs Rathbone (untraced)

Gatty 1921
Gatty, Charles T, *Mary Davies and the Manor of Ebury*, 2 vols (1921)

Gaunt 1960
Gaunt, Arthur, 'An Art Patron's Village Birthplace', *Country Life*, vol 128, no 3316 (22 Sept 1960) pp 626–27

Gaunt 1963
Gaunt, William, 'Set of Drawings by John Flaxman', *Connoisseur*, vol 153 (Aug 1963) pp 250–54

Gawsworth Guide
Gasworth Hall Macclesfield, 10th edition (nd)

Gayle 1979
Gayle, M, 'Iron Bridge: 200 and Going Strong', *Historic Preservation*, vol 31, no 4 (1979) pp 40–42

Gaz-Beaux
Gazette des Beaux-Arts

Gaz-Beaux 1958
'Portrait Bust by J Bushnell', *Gazette des Beaux-Arts*, vol 51 series 6 (April 1958) p 240

GB
Gordon Balderston

GDS
Glasgow Dilettanti Society

Gehren 1982
Gehren, G von, 'Josiah Wedgwood und die Kunst Seiner Zeit', *Weltkunst (Munich)*, vol 52, no 17 (1982) pp 2283–84

Gennaccari 1996
Gennaccari, Cristina, 'Museo Pio Cristiano: Documenti Inediti di Rilavorazioni e Restauri Settecenteschi Sui Sarcofagi Paleocristiani', *Bollettino–Monumenti Musei e Gallerie Pontificie*, vol 16 (1996) pp 153–285

Gent 1730
Gent, Thomas, *History of York* (1730)

Gerdts 1971
Gerdts, William H, 'Marble and Nudity: Neo-Classic Nineteenth Century Sculpture in America', *Art in America*, vol 59 (May 1971) p 60ff

Gerdts 1978
Gerdts, William H, 'Medusa of Harriet Hosmer', *Bulletin of the Detroit Institute of Arts*, vol 56, no 2 (1978) pp 96–107

Gere 1963
Gere, John A, 'Alexander Munro's Paolo and Francesca', *Burlington Magazine*, vol 105 (Nov 1963) pp 508–10

GF
Geoffrey Fisher

GGW
Gahagan genealogical website <www.geogahagan.org>

Giara 2000
Giara, Marzban J, *Parsi Statues* (Dhunmai Building, 667 Jehangir Road, Dadar, Bombay: 2000)

Gibbon 1969
Gibbon, Michael, 'The Queen's Temple at Stowe', *Country Life*, vol 145 (9 Jan 1969) pp 78–80

Gibbs 1747
Gibbs, James, *Bibliotheca Radcliviana: or, a Short Description of the Radcliffe Library at Oxford* (London: 1747)

Gibbs 1728
Gibbs, James, *A Book of Architecture, Containing Designs of Buildings and Ornaments* (London: 1728)

Gibson 1997 (1)
Gibson, Katharine, ' "Best Belov'd of Kings", The Iconography of King Charles II' (Ph D Diss, London Univ: 1997)

Gibson 1997 (2)
Gibson, Katharine, ' "The Kingdom's Marble Chronicle": The Embellishment of the First and Second Buildings, 1600 to 1690', in *The Royal Exchange*, ed Saunders, Ann (London Topographical Society, 1997) pp 138–73

Gibson 1999
Gibson, Katharine, 'The Emergence of Grinling Gibbons as a "Statuary" ', *Apollo*, vol 150, no 451 (Sept 1999) pp 21–29

Gibson 2000
Gibson, Katharine, 'Jan Wyck c1645–1700 A Painter with "a Grate Deal of Fire" ', *British Art Journal*, vol 2, no I (Autumn 2000) pp 3–13

Gibson 2001
Gibson, Katharine, 'The Trials of John Bushnell', *The Sculpture Journal*, vol VI (2001) pp 49–60

Gibson Albums
Two albums of material relating to the life and work of John Gibson, including manuscripts, press cuttings, sketches and prints (NLW, 4914–4915D)

Gibson Letters
John Gibson, Miscellaneous letters to various correspondents, 1839–1865 (NLW, MSS 657D, 3292E, 3294E, 4507C, Edward Hall Purchase 1969)

Gibson Papers (1)
Miscellaneous papers relating to John Gibson (NLW, MS 20568E)

Gibson Papers (2)
John Gibson, Correspondence and papers, 1821–1866 (RA, GI/1–5)

Gibson/Blair
John Gibson, letter to Mrs Hunter Blair, 24 Oct 1833 (CUL, Fitz, MS 78-1949)

Gibson/Ellis
Letter from Solomon Gibson to Sir H Ellis, 6 July 1826 (BL, Add MS 41312, fol 47)

Gibson/Hall
John Gibson, letter to Samuel Carter Hall concerning an engraving by John Roffe of Gibson's bas relief 'Cupid and Psyche', with a pencil sketch, 1855 (NAL, MSL/1941/421)

Gibson/Horner
John Gibson and Penry Williams, letter to Susan Horner and others (NAL, MSL/1942/862)

Gibson/Lawrence
John Gibson, letters to Mrs Lawrence, bound vol of approx 100, 27 Sept 1821–20 June 1865 1821–1865 (Walker, A14)

Gibson/Lyttelton
John Gibson to Lord Lyttelton, eight letters, 1836–1847 (Herts Archives and Local Studies, C3/113–7, C4/113–4)

Gibson/Mozley
John Gibson to Miss Edith Mozley, letter concerning a bust (NAL, MSL/1971/3520)

Gibson/Rogers
John Gibson, letter to Rogers, 1832 (BL, Add MS 37951 fol 79)

Gibson/Sandbach
John Gibson, 171 letters to Margaret and Henry Sandbach of Liverpool and Hafodunos, April 1839–July 1865 (NLW, MSS 20566E)

Gibson/Shaw
John Gibson, signed receipt to Sir Michael Shaw Stewart for statue of Cupid disguised as a Shepherd, 27 Nov 1835 (CUL, Fitz, MS 2-1949, no 36)

Gibson/Thomas
John Gibson, letter to John Thomas, Letters to John Thomas ('Pencerdd Gwallia') 1843–1901 1855 (NLW, MS 21822D fol 47)

Gibson/Thrupp
John Gibson, letter to Frederick Thrupp regarding prints and his bust of Queen Victoria, 2 Oct 1850 (Torquay Museum, AR.704)

Gifford 1995
Gifford, John, 'The Duchess-Countess of Sutherland and Dunrobin Castle', in *Scottish Country Houses, 1600–1914*, ed Gow, Ian and Rowan, Alistair (1995) pp 248–260

Gilbert 1889–1922
Gilbert, John Thomas and Gilbert, Lady Rosa, eds, *Calendar of Ancient Records of Dublin in the Possession of the Municipal Corporation of that City*, 18 vols (1889–1922)

Gilbert 1962–63
Gilbert, C, 'A Newly-Discovered Monument by John Nost in Leeds', *Leeds Arts Calendar*, vol 50–1 (1962–63) p 4

Gilbert 1978
Gilbert, Christopher, *Furniture at Temple Newsam House and Lotherton Hall*, 2 vols (NA-CF and LACF, 1978)

Gildard 1892
Gildard, Thomas, 'On the late John Mossman, Hon. Royal Scottish Academician', Read before the Architectural Section, 14th March, 1892 *Proceedings of the Philosophical Society of Glasgow*, vol 23 (1891–1892) pp 291–302

Gillam 1958
Gillam, Stanley G, *The Building Accounts of the Radcliffe Camera* (Oxford Historical Society XIII, 1958)

Gillow 1973
Gillow, N, 'Some Flaxman Drawings at York', *Preview*, vol 26, no 102 (1973) pp 915–19

Gilmartin 1967
Gilmartin, J, 'Peter Turnerelli, Sculptor (1774–1839)', *Bulletin of the Irish Georgian Society*, vol 4 (1967) p 1 ff

Gilson 1975
Gilson, David, *Books from the library of Sir Robert Taylor in the library of the Taylorian Institution, Oxford: a checklist* (1975)

Giometti 1999
Giometti, Cristiano, 'Giovanni Battista Guelfi: New Discoveries', *The Sculpture Journal*, vol 3 (1999) pp 26–43

Giometti 2000
Giometti, Cristiano, 'Gentlemen of Virtue: Morality and Representation in English Eighteenth-Century Tomb Sculpture', in *The Lustrous Trade: Material Culture and the History of Sculpture in England and Italy, c.1700–c.1860*, ed Sicca, Cinzia and Yarrington, Alison (2000) pp 79–95

Girouard 1958
Girouard, Mark, 'Alscot Park, Warks', *Country Life*, vol 123 (15 May, 29 May 1958) pp 1064–67, 1184–87

Girouard 1960
Girouard, Mark, 'Picton Castle', *Country Life* (14 Jan 1960)

Girouard 1965
Girouard, Mark, 'Sandbeck Park, Yorks', *Country Life*, vol 138 (7, 14 and 21 October 1965) pp 880–83, 966–69, 1024–27

Girouard 1966 (1)
Girouard, Mark, 'English Art and the Rococo I; Coffee at Slaughter's', *Country Life*, vol 139, no 3593 (13 Jan 1966) pp 58–61

Girouard 1966 (2)
Girouard, Mark, 'English Art and the Rococo II; Hogarth and his Friends', *Country Life*, vol 139, no 3595 (27 Jan 1966) pp 188–90

Girouard 1966 (3)
Girouard, Mark, 'English Art and the Rococo III; The Two Worlds of St Martin's Lane', *Country Life*, vol 139, no 3596 (3 Feb 1966) pp 224–27

Girouard 1971
Girouard, Mark, 'Town Houses for the Wealthy: Kensington Palace Gardens I', *Country Life*, vol 150, no 3883 (11 Nov 1971) pp 1268–70

Girouard 1989
Girouard, Mark, *Hardwick Hall* (National Trust, 1989)

GL
Guildhall Library

Gladstone Diaries
Foot, M R D and Matthew, H C G, eds, *The Gladstone Diaries*, 14 vols (Oxford: 1968–1994)

Gladstone Papers
William Ewart Gladstone, Correspondence, literary manuscripts and other papers (BL, Add MSS 44086-44835)

GLC
Greater London Council

GLC 1971
Greater London Council, *Grinling Gibbons* (1971)

Gleichen 1928
Gleichen, Lord Edward, *London's Open-Air Statuary* (1928)

Glenn 1979
Glenn, Virginia, 'George Bullock, Richard Brigdens and James Watts Regency Furnishing Schemes', *Furniture History*, vol 15 (1979) pp 54–67

Gloucester Council Minutes
Council Minutes, 1700–1716; 1716–1760; 1760–1783 (Gloucester Borough Council, GBR B3/8; GBR B3/9–10; GBR B3/11)

Gloucester Freemen
Register of Freemen, 1653–1726 (Gloucester Borough Archives, GBR C9/7)

Glover 1831–33
Glover, Stephen, *The History and Gazeteer of the County of Derby*, 2 vols (1831–33)

GM
Gentleman's Magazine

gns
guineas

Godwin 1850
Godwin, George, *Buildings and Monuments, Modern and Medieval* (1850)

Gold 1984
Gold, S, 'The Reredos Which Slipped Through the Net', *Transactions of the Ancient Monuments Society, Bristol*, vol 28 (1984) pp 93–113

Goldmiths Freedom
Corporation of London, Goldsmiths' Company, Freedom Book, vol 3, 1781–1810 (CLRO Guildhall)

Goldsmith 1974
Goldsmith, R F K, *The Military Memorials in Winchester Cathedral* (1974)

Goldsmiths Abstract
Corporation of London, Goldsmiths' Company, Abstract of Contractors' Accounts, 1831–1835 (CLRO Guildhall)

Goldsmiths CB
Corporation of London, Goldsmiths' Company, Committee Book, vols 18, 19, 1823–37; 1837–46 (CLRO Guildhall)

Goldsmiths Ct Bk
Corporation of London, Goldsmiths' Company, Court Book, vol 9, 1682–88 (CLRO Guildhall)

Gomme 1968
Gomme, Andor, 'The Architect of Barlaston Hall', *Country Life*, vol 143 (18 Apr 1968) pp 975–79

Gomme 1971
Gomme, Andor, 'Stoneleigh Abbey', *Archaeological Journal*, vol 188 (1971) pp 246–51

Gomme 1981
Gomme, Andor, 'Genesis of Sutton Scarsdale', *Architectural History*, vol 24 (1981) pp 34–38

Gomme 1984
Gomme, Andor, 'Badminton Revisited', *Architectural History*, vol 27 (1984) pp 163–82

Gomme 1988
Gomme, Andor, 'Stoneleigh after the Grand Tour', *Antiquaries Journal*, vol 68, no 2 (1988) pp 265–86

Gomme 1989
Gomme, Andor, 'Architects and Craftsmen at Ditchley', *Architectural History*, vol 32 (1989) pp 85–104

Gomme 1992
Gomme, Andor, 'Smith and Rossi', *Architectural History*, vol 35 (1992) pp 183–91

Gomme 2000
Gomme, Andor, *Smith of Warwick: Francis Smith, Architect and Master-Builder* (2000)

Goode 1970
Goode, Basil, 'Gibbon's Masterpiece Restored; Font in All Hallows by-the-Tower', *Country Life*, vol 148 (22 Oct 1970) p 1047

Goodison 1955
Goodison, J W, *Cambridge Portraits* (1955)

Goodison 1974 (1)
Goodison, Nicholas, *Ormolu: the Work of Matthew Boulton* (1974)

Goodison 1974 (2)
Goodison, Nicholas, 'Persian Slave', *Connoisseur*, vol 187 (Oct 1974) pp 98–103

Goodison 1985
Goodison, Nicholas, 'Urania Observed', *Furniture History*, vol 21 (1985) pp 241–42

Goodwillie 1911
Goodwillie, Edward, *The World's Memorials of Robert Burns* (Detroit: 1911)

Goodwood Bills
Joseph Wilton and Matthew Brettingham, bills, Goodwood Estate Archives 1756–9 (WSRO, 230/38, fol(s) 113, 131, 139, 178, 221)

Gordon Brown 1995
Gordon Brown, Iain, 'Canova, Thorvaldsen & the Ancients', in *The Three Graces: Antonio Canova*, ed Clifford, Timothy, (Edinburgh: 1995) pp 72–112

Gorely 1955
Gorely, Jean, 'Flaxman's Work for Wedgwood; With Lists', *Antiques Magazine*, vol 68 (Dec 1955) pp 568–72

Gorhambury Building Accts
Building Accounts, Gorhambury, Herts, 1777 (Hertfordshire Archives and Local Studies, I.B.12)

Gosse 1883
Gosse, Edmund W, 'Living Sculptors', *The Century Magazine*, vol 26, no 2 (June 1883) pp 163–85

Gosse 1894
Gosse, Edmund, 'The New Sculpture 1879–1894', *Art Journal*, (1894) pp 138–42, 199–203, 277–82, 306–11

Gosset 1888–91
Gosset, Mary H, 'A Family of Modellers in Wax', *Proceedings of the Huguenot Society of London*, vol 3 (1888–1891) pp 540–68

Gottesman 1970
Gottesman, R S, *The Arts and Crafts in New York 1726–1776* (1970)

Gould 1834
Gould, John, *Biographical Sketches of Eminent Artists* (1834)

Gov Art Coll
Government Art Collection

GPC
Gunnis Papers, mss etc intended for incorporation in a third edition of *Gunnis*, Conway Library, Courtauld Institute, Library

GPC
Notes, Addenda, Letters and other papers collected by Rupert Gunnis (Conway Library, Courtauld Institute, London)

Grace 1980
Grace, Priscilla, 'Wax Miniature of Joseph Boruwlaski', *Journal of the Metropolitan Museum of Art, New York*, vol 15 (1980) pp 175–82

Graham 1871
Graham, John Murray, *British Literature and Art* (1871)

Graham ed
Graham, Malcolm, ed, *Oxford City Apprentices, 1697–1800* (Oxford Historical Society, series XXXI, nd)

Graham/Collier Accts
Accounts of Richard Graham and Jabez Collier (on behalf of Lord Burlington), 1719–1722 (Chatsworth MSS)

Grano and Grossi Grano 1990
Grano, L, and Grossi Grano, B, *Giovanni Battista Comolli, Scultore Valenziano. L'Uomo e l'Artista*, exhib cat (Valenza: 1990)

Grant 1934
Grant, Maurice, 'English Medallist, Alfred Joseph Stothard', *Connoisseur*, vol 94 (Aug 1934) pp 98–99

Grant 1953
Grant, Maurice Harold, *A Dictionary of British Sculptors from the Seventeenth Century to the Twentieth Century* (1953)

Grantham Corr
Correspondence between Thomas Robinson, 2nd Baron Grantham and brother Frederick, regarding work produced by John Flaxman the Elder, 14, 17 and 21 Dec 1785 (Beds RO, L30/14/333/334; L30/15/54/295; L30/14/333/337)

Granville 1841
Granville, Augustus Bozzi, *Spas of England and Principal Sea-bathing Places*, 3 vols (1841)

Graves 1875
Graves, Algernon, *The British Institution 1806–1867: A Complete Dictionary of Contributors and their Work from the Foundation of the Institution*, facsimile of the 1875 edition (Bath: 1969)

Graves 1901
Graves, Algernon, *Dictionary of Artists who have exhibited Works in the Principal London Exhibitions from 1760 to 1893*, facsimile 1901 (3rd) edition (Weston-super-Mare: 1969)

Graves 1905–6
Graves, Algernon, *The Royal Academy of Arts: a Complete Dictionary of Contributors and their Work from its Foundation in 1769 to 1904*, 8 vols (London: 1905–6)

Graves 1907
Graves, Algernon, *The Society of Artists of Great Britain, 1760–1791, the Free Society, 1761–1783: a complete dictionary of contributors and their work from the foundation of the Societies to 1791*, facsimile of 1907 edition (Bath: 1969)

Graves 1913–15
Graves, Algernon, *A Century of Loan Exhibitions 1813–1912*, 3 volumes, facsimile of 1913–1915 edition (Bath: 1970)

Gray 1889
Gray, John, *Catalogue of the Scottish National Portrait Gallery*, 3rd ed (1889)

Great Exhib 1851
Great Exhibition of the Works of Industry of all Nations: Official Descriptive and Illustrated Catalogue, 3 vols (London: 1851)

Green 1796
Green, Valentine, *The History and Antiquities of Worcester*, 2 vols (1796)

Green 1902
Green, Mowbray Aston, *The Eighteenth Century Architecture of Bath* (Bath: 1902)

Green 1951
Green, David, *Blenheim Palace* (London: 1951)

Green 1962
Green, David, 'A Lost Grinling Gibbons Masterpiece', *Country Life*, vol 131, no 3386 (25 Jan 1962) pp 164–66

Green 1963
Green, David, 'A Peapod Myth Exploded', *Country Life*, vol 134 (8 Aug 1963) pp 328–29

Green 1964 (1)
Green, David Brontë, *Grinling Gibbons: His Work as Carver and Statuary, 1648–1721* (1964)

Green 1964 (2)
Green, David, 'Paintings that Inspired Gibbons', *Country Life*, vol 135 (11 June 1964) pp 1481–83

Green 1971 (1)
Green, David, 'Rysbrack at Blenheim', *Country Life*, vol 149 (7 Jan 1971) pp 26–28

Green 1971 (2)
Green, David, 'In Pursuit of Grinling Gibbons', *Connoisseur*, vol 177 (July 1971) pp 190–93

Green 1973
Green, David, 'Carving at Petworth', *Country Life*, vol 154 (6 Sept 1973) p 626

Greenwich Hospital Bills
Corporation of London, bills of work done at Greenwich Hospital, 1699–1708 (CLRO Guildhall, 233)

Greenwood 1999
Greenwood, Martin, *Frederick Thrupp (1812–1895): Survivals from a Sculptor's Studio*, Essays in the Study of Sculpture, published to accompany the exhibition at the Henry Moore Institute 21 Jan–28 Feb 1999 (Leeds: Henry Moore Sculpture Trust, 1999)

Greifenhagen 1985
Greifenhagen, Adolf, 'William Martin Leake, 1777–1860: ein Portrat in Danischem Privatbesitz', *Pantheon*, vol 43 (1985) pp 123–25

Grenside 1953–4
Grenside, Dorothy, 'The Weybridge Monument on the Village Green', *Surrey Archaeological Collections*, vol 54 (1953–4) pp 143–5

Gresham Reps.
Mercers' Company Archives, Gresham Repertories

Grey 1980
Earl de Grey, *Memoirs*, Bedfordshire Historical Society, vol 59, 1980 (1846)

Griffith 1922
Griffith, Reginald H, *Alexander Pope. A bibliography*, vol 1, part I. Pope's own Writings, 1709–1734 (Austin, Texas: 1922)

Griffiths 1932
Griffiths, R G, 'The History of Clifton-on-Teme', *Worcestershire Archaeological Society*, vol 9 (1932) pp 75–99

Grigson 1960
Grigson, Geoffrey, 'Masters of West Country Memorials', *Country Life*, vol 128, no 3324 (17 Nov 1960) p 1182

Grittleton Marbles 1966
Catalogue of the Grittleton Marbles . . . Statuary and Garden Ornaments, sale catalogue (Christie, London: 22 Sept 1966)

Groce 1946
Groce, George, 'William John Coffee, Long-Lost Sculptor', *American Collector*, vol 15 (May 1946) pp 14–15

Grocers WA
Corporation of London, Grocers' Company, Warden's Accounts, 1671–81; 1681–97; 1697–98; 1699–1700; 1712–22; 1732–42 (CLRO Guildhall, 11571/16; 11571/17; 11571/18; 11571/20; 11571/22)

Grocers, Ledger
Corporation of London, Grocers' Company, Ledger, 1785–1817 (CLRO Guildhall, 11572/2)

Groseclose 1980
Groseclose, Barbara, 'Harriet Hosmer's Tomb to Judith Falconet: Death and the Maiden', *American Art Journal*, vol 12, no 2 (1980) pp 78–89

Groseclose 1990
Groseclose, Barbara, 'Imag(in)ing Indians: Indian Figures on British Sculpture', *Art History*, vol 13 (Dec 1990) pp 488–515

Groseclose 1995
Groseclose, Barbara, *British Sculpture and the Company Raj: Church Monuments and Public Statuary in Madras, Calcutta, and Bombay to 1858* (Delaware: 1995)

Grosley 1772
Grosley, Pierre Jean, *A Tour of London, or new observations on England and its inhabitants. . translated by Thomas Nugent*, 2 vols (1772)

Grove 1996
Turner, Jane, ed, *The Dictionary of Art*, 34 vols (1996)

Grub-St
The Grub-Street Journal

Grundy 1958
Grundy, Anne, 'John Voyez – Some Masterpieces of Craftsmanship', *Apollo*, vol 68 (Oct 1958) pp 110–15

GS
Guildhall Studies

Gt Exhib
Great Exhibition, 1851

Guildh MSS
Guildhall MSS, City of London

Guildh PMD
Guildhall Library, Prints, Maps and Drawings Section, City of London

Guildhall Committee/J C F Rossi
Guildhall Committee, letter to J C F Rossi, Documents relating to William Pitt the Younger's monument, Guildhall 1806 (CLRO, Guildhall, City of London, MS 95.2)

Guildhall Committee/Lawrence Gahagan
Guildhall Committee, letter from Lawrence Gahagan, Documents relating to William Pitt the Younger's monument, Guildhall 1806 (CLRO, Guildhall, City of London, MS 95.2)

Guildhall restoration
Payments for the Restoration of Guildhall etc, 1666–1675 (Guildhall MSS, City of London, 184/4)

Guilding 2001
Guilding, Ruth, ' "Grecian gods and demi-gods in niches . . . fit for the Castle of Otranto": Wilton House in the early nineteenth century', *Apollo*, vol 154, no 477 (Nov 2001) pp 42–48

Guillum Scott 1942
Guillum Scott, Judith, *The Story of St Mary Abbots* (1942)

Guinness 1981
Guinness, Desmond, 'Castletown, County Kildare, Ireland', *Antiques Magazine*, vol 120 (Oct 1981) pp 896–905

Gunnis 1948
Gunnis, Rupert, 'Some of the Nave Monuments and their Sculptors', *Friends of Rochester Cathedral Report*, vol 6 (May 1948) pp 20–27

Gunnis 1949
Gunnis, Rupert, 'Signed Monuments in Kentish Churches', *Archaeologia Cantinana*, vol 62 (1949) pp 57–86

Gunnis 1951
Gunnis, Rupert, 'A Derbyshire Sculptor', *Country Life*, vol 109, no 2821 (9 Feb 1951) p 393

Gunnis 1952 (1)
Gunnis, Rupert, 'Mason and Statuary', *Country Life* (18 Jan 1952)

Gunnis 1952 (2)
Gunnis, Rupert, 'A Provincial Sculptor', *Country Life*, vol 111, no 2885 (2 May 1952) p 1337

Gunnis 1953 (1)
Gunnis, Rupert, *Dictionary of British Sculptors, 1660–1851* (London: 1953)

Gunnis 1953 (2)
Gunnis, Rupert, 'Sculptor to the Crown', *Country Life*, vol 113 (16 April 1953) p 1168

Gunnis 1954 (1)
Gunnis, Rupert, 'Monuments by Nollekens', *Country Life*, vol 115, no 2977 (4 Feb 1954) p 293

Gunnis 1954 (2)
Gunnis, Rupert, 'Sculpture by Thomas Carter', *Country Life*, vol 116, no 3022 (16 Dec 1954) p 2191

Gunnis 1955
Gunnis, Rupert, 'Sculpture by John Cheere', *Country Life*, vol 117, no 3043 (12 May 1955) p 1243

Gunnis 1957
Gunnis, Rupert, 'Richard Fisher: A Yorkshire Sculptor', *Country Life*, vol 122, no 3161 (15 Aug 1957) pp 309–10

Gunnis 1958
Gunnis, Rupert, 'The Carters, Georgian Sculptors', *Architectural Review*, vol 123 (May 1958) p 334

Gunnis 1959 (1)
Gunnis, Rupert, 'Key to Monument Sculpture', *Country Life*, vol 125, no 3234 (Jan 8, 1959) p 72

Gunnis 1959 (2)
Gunnis, Rupert, 'Monuments by John Flaxman in Sussex', *Sussex Archaeological Collections*, vol 97 (1959) pp 82–88

Gunnis 1960 (1)
Gunnis, Rupert, 'Chimney-Pieces at Langley Park', *Country Life*, vol 127, no 3293 (14 April 1960) p 818

Gunnis 1960 (2)
Gunnis, Rupert, 'Prolific Scottish Sculptor', *Country Life*, vol 127, no 3304 (30 June 1960) p 1508

Gunnis 1960 (3)
Gunnis, Rupert, 'Austin's Artificial Stone', *Country Life*, vol 127, no 3287 (3 March 1960) p 441

Gunnis 1961
Gunnis, Rupert, 'Some Irish Memorials', *Bulletin of the Irish Georgian Society*, vol 4, no 1 (Jan–March 1961)

Gunnis 1963
Gunnis, Rupert, 'Georgian Monuments in Irish Churches', *Country Life*, vol 134 (7 Nov 1963) p 1174

Gunnis 1968
Gunnis, Rupert, *Dictionary of British Sculptors 1660–1851*, 2nd ed (London: 1968)

Gunnis and Whinney 1967
Gunnis, Rupert, and Whinney, Margaret, *Collection of Models by John Flaxman, R.A., at University College London* (1967)

Gunther 1928
Gunther, Robert William Theodore, *The Architecture of Sir Roger Pratt* (1928)

Gur 1994
Gur, Michael E., 'Artist vs. Connoisseur: The Committee of National Monuments and the Arbitration of Taste', *Southeastern College Art Conference Review*, vol 12, no 4 (1994) pp 259–64

Gurrieri 1972
Gurrieri, F, 'Lorenzo Bartolini a Londra', *Prato*, vol 13, no 34–35 (1972) pp 158–61

Gustafson 1991
Gustafson, Eleanor H, 'Museum Accessions: Britannia Triumphant Acquired for the Birmingham Museum of Art, Alabama', *Antiques Magazine*, vol 139 (June 1991) p 1070 ff

H and B
Rates, Highways and Bridges

Haberdashers, Freedom
Corporation of London, Haberdashers' Company, Freedom Register, 1642–1772 (CLRO Guildhall, 15857)

Haberdashers, Minutes
Corporation of London, Haberdashers' Company, Minute Book, 1689–97 (CLRO Guildhall, 15845)

Hadfield 1960
Hadfield, Miles, 'Artificial Stone of the Nineteenth Century', *Country Life*, vol 127, no 3284 (11 Feb 1960) p 280

Hadley 1788
Hadley, G H, *A New and Complete History of the Town and County . . . of Kingston-upon-Hull* (1788)

Haggar 1950
Haggar, Reginald, 'Pattison of Lane End, and Notes on Tittensor and Voyez', *Apollo*, vol 51 (Jan 1950) pp 18–19

Haggar 1951
Haggar, Reginald, 'John Bacon the Elder Unrecorded Wood Figure: Cupids Quarrelling Over a Human Heart Adapted from Cayot's Bronze', *Apollo*, vol 53 (March 1951) pp 83–84

Haggar 1975
Haggar, R, 'William Theed and Wedgwood', *Proceedings of the Wedgwood Society*, no 9 (1975) pp 22–30

Hagstrum 1978
Hagstrum, Jean, 'Blake and British Art; The Gifts of Grace and Terror', in *Images of Romanticism; Verbal and Visual Affinities*, ed Kroeber, Karl and Walling, William (1978) pp 61–80

Hakewill 1813
Hakewill, James, *The History of Windsor, and its Neighborhood* (1813)

Hall 1839
Hall, George, *History of Chesterfield* (1839)

Hall 1883
Hall, Samuel Carter, *Retrospect of a Long Life: From 1815 to 1883*, vol 2 (London: 1883) pp 236–44

Hall 1953
Hall, Henry Cecil, *Artists and Sculptors of Nottingham and Nottinghamshire, 1750–1950; A Biographical Dictionary* (Nottingham: 1953)

Hall 1970
Hall, Ivan, *An exhibition of paintings, sculpture, prints, furniture, books and scientific instruments collected during the eighteenth century by William Constable of Burton Constable, East Riding* (Ferens Art Gallery, Hull: 1970)

Hall 1976 (1)
Hall, Ivan, 'Furniture at Burton Constable', *Country Life*, vol 159 (3 June 1976) p 1476 ff

Hall 1976 (2)
Hall, Ivan, 'Jeremiah and Joseph Hargrave of Hull; Architects, Carvers, Furniture Makers', *Furniture History*, vol 12 (1976) pp 51–58

Hall 1979
Hall, Marshall, *The Artists of Cumbria; an illustrated dictionary of Cumberland, Westmoreland, North Lancashire . . . painters, sculptors . . .*, Artists of the Regions, vol 2 (1979)

Hall 1990
Hall, Michael, 'Brockhampton, Herefordshire: a Property of the National Trust', *Country Life*, vol 184, no 1 (1990) pp 46–51

Hall 1991
Hall, Michael, 'In the Right Setting', *Country Life*, vol 185, no 47 (21 Nov 1991) pp 98–99

Hall 1995
Hall, Melanie, *Leeds Statues Trail*, pamphlet (Leeds Civic Trust and Leeds City Council, 1995)

Hall 1996
Hall, Michael, '27 Broad Street, Ludlow, Shropshire, the Home of Mr. and Mrs. George Williams', *Country Life*, vol 190, no 30 (25 July 1996) pp 58–63

Hallé 1909
Hallé, Charles E, *Notes from a Painter's Life, including the founding of two galleries* (1909)

Halsema Kubes 1976
Halsema Kubes, Willy, 'Laurent Delvaux' Grafmonument voor Leonard Mathias van der Noot en Helena Catharina de Jonghe', *Bulletin van het Rijksmuseum*, vol 24, no 3 (1976) pp 123–39

Hamburg 1979
Hofmann, Werner, and Bindman, David, *John Flaxman, Mythologie und Industrie: Kunst um 1800*, exhib cat (Hamburg: 1979)

Hamilton 1839
Hamilton, G, *Gallery of British Artists; from the days of Hogarth to the present time*, 4 vols (Paris: 1839)

Hamilton 1954
Hamilton, S B, 'Coade Stone', *Architectural Review*, vol 116 (Nov 1954) pp 295–98

Hammond 1999
Hammond, Norman, 'Outpost of Empire: Church Monuments in Belize', *Church Monuments*, vol 14 (1999) pp 129–39

Hammond 2000
Hammond, Norman, 'Beyond the Mexique Bay: Church Monuments on Belize, Part II', *Church Monuments*, vol 15 (2000) pp 89–102

Hamper (ed) 1827
Hamper, William, ed, *The Life and Correspondence of Sir William Dugdale* (1827)

Hanaster EB
Oxford City Archive, OCA Hanasters Enrollment Book, 1699–1780 (Oxfordshire RO, unpag)

Hand-in-Hand
Hand-in-Hand Fire Insurance Records, 1685–1696 (Guildhall MSS, City of London, 9674/1–150)

Handley Read 1970 (1)
Handley Read, Lavinia, 'Legacy of a Vanished Empire: Design of the India Office, the West Side of Whitehall', *Country Life*, vol 148 (9 July 1970) pp 110–12

Handley Read 1970 (2)
Handley Read, Lavinia, 'Whitehall Sculpture', *Architectural Review*, vol 148 (Nov 1970) pp 276–79

Hands c1770
Hands, John, *A Brief Description of the Collegiate Church and Choir of St Mary, in the Borough of Warwick* (Warwick: c1770)

Harbison, Potterton and Sheehy 1978
Harbison, Peter, Potterton, Homan, and Sheehy, Jeanne, *Irish Art and Architecture from Prehistory to the Present* (1978)

Hardwick 1825
Hardwick, Thomas, *A Memoir of the Life of Sir William Chambers* (1825)

Hardwick 1857
Hardwick, Charles, *History of the Borough of Preston and its Environs, in the County of Lancaster* (1857)

Hardy 1978
Hardy, John, 'Robert Adam and the Furnishing of Kedleston Hall', *Connoisseur*, vol 198, no 797 (July 1978) pp 198–207

Hardy 1981
Hardy, John, 'The Essence of "Etruscan" Style', *Connoisseur*, vol 208, no 837 (Nov 1981) pp 224–27

Hardy 1989
Hardy, John, 'Fonthill Splendens: An Iconographic Chimneypiece Rediscovered', *Apollo*, no 130 (July 1989) pp 40–42

Hardy 1996
Hardy, George, 'Turner, Lawrence, Canova and Venetian Art: Three Previously Unpublished Letters', *Apollo*, vol 144 (Oct 1996) pp 25–32

Hardy and Hayward 1978
Hardy, John, and Hayward, Helena, 'Kedleston Hall, Derbyshire', *Country Life*, vol 163, no 4203 (26 Jan 1978) pp 194–97

Hare 1990
Hare, Susan, *Paul de Lamerie* (1990)

Hargrove 1789
Hargrove, Ely, *The History of the Castle, Town and Forest of Knaresborough* (York: 1789)

Hargrove 1818
Hargrove, W M, *History and Description of the Ancient City of York*, 2 vols (York: 1818)

Harley Thomas 1936
Harley Thomas, G T, *Some Reminiscences of the Breckonshire Sculptor by his Nephew*, typescript, National Museum of Wales (1936)

Harris 1949
Harris, V, *The Church of St Paul, Halifax, Nova Scotia 1749–1949* (Toronto: 1949)

Harris 1956
Harris, John, 'A Link with John Lumley', *Country Life*, vol 120 (29 Nov 1956) p 1239

Harris 1957
Harris, John, 'The Story of the Marble Dog', *Country Life*, vol 122 (21 Nov 1957) p 1085

Harris 1957–58
Harris, John, 'The Building of Denham Place', *Records of Buckinghamshire*, vol 16, no 3 (1957–58) pp 193–97

Harris 1963
Harris, John, 'Some English Architectural and Decorative Drawings in the Museum's Collection', *Bulletin of the Metropolitan Museum of Art, New York*, no 21 (Feb 1963) p 214

Harris 1966
Harris, J, 'Fonthill, Wiltshire, I', *Country Life*, vol 140 (1966) p 1370

Harris 1968
Harris, John, 'Pritchard Redivivus', *Architectural History*, vol 11 (1968) pp 17–24

Harris 1969
Harris, John, 'Diana Fountain at Hampton Court', *Burlington Magazine*, vol 111 (July 1969) p 444 ff

Harris 1970
Harris, John, *Sir William Chambers, Knight of the Polar Star* (London: 1970)

Harris 1971
Harris, John, *A Catalogue of British Drawings for Architecture, Sculpture and Landscape Gardening 1500–1900 in American Collections* (1971) p 111

Harris 1981
Harris, John, *The Palladians*, RIBA Drawings Series (1981)

Harris 1982
Harris, John, *William Talman, Maverick Architect* (London: 1982)

Harris 1985
Harris, John, 'Harley, the Patriot Collector', *Apollo*, vol 122, no 283 (1985) pp 198–203

Harris 1987
Harris, Leslie, *Robert Adam and Kedleston; The Making of a Neo-Classical Masterpiece* (National Trust: 1987)

Harris 1998
Harris, Kate, 'A New Grinling Gibbons Document', *Burlington Magazine*, vol 140, no 1149 (Dec 1998) pp 829–32

Harris 2001
Harris, Eileen, *The Genius of Robert Adam, his Interiors* (2001)

Harris and Snodin 1996
Harris, John, and Snodin, Michael, *Sir William Chambers, Architect to George III*, exhib cat (Courtauld: 1996)

Harris M and AG
Harris Museum and Art Gallery, Preston, Lancs

Harris, de Bellaigue, Millar 1968
Harris, John, de Bellaigue, Geoffrey, and Millar, Oliver, *Buckingham Palace and its Treasures* (New York: 1968)

Harrison 2004
Harrison, John, 'The Prince, the Baron and the Knight: Baron Carlo Marochetti and the Black Prince', *British Art Journal*, vol 5, no 2 (Autumn 2004) pp 62–68

Hartmann 1955
Hartmann, J Birkedal, 'Canova, Thorvaldsen and Gibson', *English Miscellany* (1955) pp 205–35

Hartmann 1969
Hartmann, Jorgen, 'Die Genien des Lebens und des Todes; zur Sepulkralikonographie des Klassizismu', *Romisches Jahrbuch fur Kunstgesichte*, vol 12 (1969) pp 9–38

Harvey 1872–78
Harvey, William Marsh, *The History and Antiquities of the Hundred of Willey, in the County of Bedford* (1872–78)

Harvey 1965
Harvey, J H, 'Edward Pearce's will (abstract)', *Journal of the British Archaeological Association*, vol 28, 3rd series (1965) p 127

Haskell 1975
Haskell, F, 'Un monument et ses mystères', *Revue de l'Art*, vol 30 (1975) pp 61–79, 104–10

Haskell and Penny 1981
Haskell, Francis, and Penny, Nicholas, *Taste and the Antique; The Lure of Classical Sculpture 1500–1900* (New Haven and London: 1981)

Haskell and Penny exh.
Haskell, Francis, and Penny, Nicholas, *The Most Beautiful Statues; the Taste for Antique Sculpture*, exhib cat (Oxford, Ashmolean: 1981)

Haslam 1984
Haslam, Richard, 'Merthyr Mawr House, Mid-Glamorgan: the Home of Mr and Mrs Murray McLaggan', *Country Life*, vol 176, no 4550 (1 Nov 1984) pp 1276–80

Haslem 1876
Haslem, John, *The Old Derby China Manufactory* (1876)

Hassal and Penny 1977
Hassal, W O, and Penny, Nicholas, 'Political Sculpture at Holkham', *Connoisseur*, vol 195, no 785 (July 1977) pp 207–11

Hatesaul 1990
Hatesaul, Kathrin, Schmidt, Martin and Vogel, Dietmar, eds, *Schülergabe für Prof. Dr. Peter Bloch zum 65. Geburtstag* (Berlin: 1990)

Hatton 1958
John Flaxman R.A., Sculptor, exhib cat (Hatton Gallery, Durham: Feb 1958)

Hauptman 1999
Hauptman, William, 'Henry Webber and Johann Friedrich Funk: Observations on Two Portraits by John Webber', *Zeitschrift für Schweizerische Archaologie und Kunstgeschichte*, vol 56, no 1 (1999) pp 41–52

Havill 1986
Havill, John, *Eleanor Coade: Artificial Stone Manufacturer, born Exeter 1733 and died London 1821* (Exeter, Devon: c1986)

Hawley 1969
Hawley, Henry, 'Antonio Canova: Terpsichore', *Country Life*, vol 56 (Oct 1969) pp 287–305

Hawthorne Notebooks
Stewart, Randall, ed, *The English Notebooks by Nathaniel Hawthorne* (1941)

Hay Expedition Papers
Views, water-colour drawings, sketches of buildings and monuments, and copies of mural paintings, inscriptions, and antiquities in Egypt, made by Joseph Bonomi and others, during an expedition organised by Robert Hay, 1826–1838 (BL, Add MSS 29812–29860)

Haydon Autobiography 1853
Taylor, Tom, ed, *Life of Benjamin Robert Haydon Historical Painter from his Autobiography and Journals*, 3 vols (1853)

Haydon Autobiography 1926
Taylor, Tom, ed, *The Autobiography and Memoirs of Benjamin Robert Haydon* (1926)

Hayes 1977
Hayes, John, *Treasures in the National Portrait Gallery* (1977)

Hayley Letters
Volume of autograph letters to William Hayley (Cambridge University Library, Dept of MSS, Fitzwilliam)

Hayward 1971
Hayward, J F, 'Rundell, Bridge and Rundell, 'Aurifices Regis' ', *Antiques Magazine*, vol 100 (July 1971) pp 110–15

Hayward's List and Sales Catalogues MS
Richard Hayward's list of visitors to Rome and collection of sales catalogues, some annotated (BM, A.5.9.Sc.)

Hayward/Horsnaile Lease
Deeds of Lease and Release between Richard and Mary Hayward to transfer property in Weston in Arden to Christopher Horsnaile the Younger, 1748/9 (Warks CRO, CR2973/4–6)

Hayward/Newdigate
Richard Hayward, two letters to Sir Roger Newdigate (Warks CRO, CR 136/B1730–33; B1736)

HCA, vol 110
Hampton Court Album, c1690 (Soane Museum, London, vol 110, 30)

Headley 1994
Headley, Janet A, 'The Monument without a public: The case of the Tripoli monument', *Winterthur Portfolio*, vol 29, no 4 (1994) pp 247–64

Headley 2000
Headley, Janet, ' "Something of my own invention": Horatio Greenough, Sir Joshua Reynolds, and Sculptural Originality', *The Sculpture Journal*, vol 4 (2000) pp 141–50

Heal
Heal Tradecards, Sculptors and Masons (BM, PDL, 106)

Hearn, Upstone, Waterfield, 1998
Hearn, Karen, Upstone, Robert, and Waterfield, Giles, *The Art of the Country House* (Tate, London: 1998)

Hearne 1906
Hearne, Thomas, 'Remarks and Collections of Thomas Hearne, vol VII (9 May 1719–22 Sept 1722)', *Oxford Historical Society*, vol 65 (1906)

Hearne 1914
Hearne, Thomas, 'Remarks and Collections of Thomas Hearne, vol IX (10 Aug 1725–26 March 1728)', *Oxford Historical Society*, ed H E Salter, vol 65 (1914)

Heath 1799
Heath, Charles, *Excursion Down the Wye* (1799)

Heber Percy/Hodnet
Heber Percy archives, Hodnet Hall, Rentals 1755–57 (Heber Percy family)

Heffer 1861–62
Heffer, Edward A, 'A Short Account of the Life and Works of the late John Thomas, Esq, Sculptor and Architect', *Liverpool Architectural and Archaeological Society*, vol 14 (1861–62) pp 111–20

Heighway 1994
Heighway, C M, 'Investigations at St Kenelm's Church, Sapperton', *Transactions of the Bristol and Gloucestershire Archaeological Society*, vol 112 (1994) pp 111–26

Heim 1976
Powney, Christopher, and Bindman, David, *John Flaxman*, exhib cat (Heim Gallery, London: 1976)

Helsted 1972
Helsted, Dyveke, 'Thorvaldsen's Technique', *Apollo*, (Sept 1972) pp 228–33

Helsted 1990
Helsted, Dyveke, Henschen, Eva and Jornaes, Bjarne, *Thorvaldsen* (Copenhagen: 1990)

Hemingway 1831
Hemingway, Joseph, *History of the City of Chester, from its foundation to the present time*, 2 vols (1831)

Hendersyde 1859
A catalogue of the pictures, statues, busts, antique columns, bronzes, fragments of antique buildings . . . at Hendersyde Park, 2nd ed (printed for private circulation by R Stewart, 1859)

Hendricks 1984
Hendricks, Ella, 'The First Patron of John Flaxman', *Burlington Magazine*, vol 126 (Oct 1984) pp 618–25

Henning I/David Murray
Letter from John Henning I to David Murray, 10 Dec 1847 (Marylebone Public Library, 384 Misc D.97)

Henning I/Wedgwood
Letters from John Henning I to Josiah Wedgwood, Wedgwood Archives 13 Sept 1813 and 19 Oct 1813 (University of Keele, Etruria MSS 2617-3; 2618-3)

Herbert 1939
Herbert, Sidney Charles (Baron Herbert), ed, *Henry, Elizabeth and George (1734–81). Letters and diaries of Henry Tenth Earl of Pembroke and his circle* (1939)

Herbert 1972
Herbert, G, 'The Portable Colonial Cottage', *Journal of the Society of Architectural Historians*, vol 31, no 4 (1972) pp 261–75

Herding 1998
Herding, Klaus, 'Reflecting on Sculpture as Theatre', *Art History*, vol 21, no 2 (June 1998) pp 268–72

Herefs RO
Herefordshire Record Office

Hershey 1970
Hershey, Constance, 'Mortuary Art in Charleston Churches', *Antiques Magazine*, vol 98 (Nov 1970) pp 800–7

Herts ALS
Hertfordshire Archives and Local Studies

Hervey 1749
Hervey, J, *Meditations and Contemplations* (1749)

Hervey 1894
Hervey, Sydenham A H, ed, *The Diary of John Hervey, first Earl of Bristol. With extracts from his book of expences . . . 1688–1742* (1894)

Heseltine 1916
Heseltine, John Postle, *Trifles in Sculpture, from the collection of JPH* (private print, 1916)

Hewlings 1980
Hewlings, R, 'Wortley Hall', *Archaeological Journal*, vol 137 (1980) pp 397–406

Hewlings 1981
Hewlings, Richard, 'Ripon's Forum Populi', *Architectural History*, vol 24 (1981) p 47

Hewlings 2003
Hewlings, Richard, 'The Rysbrack statues at Chiswick House', unpublished typescript (2003)

Heyert 1979
Heyert, Elizabeth, *The Glass-House Years; Victorian Portrait Photography 1839–1870* (1979)

Hibbert 1983
Hibbert, C, 'Royal Spendthrift. George IV Believed that Great Monarchies Required Great Settings', *Connoisseur*, vol 213, no 858 (1983) pp 94–99

Hibern Mag
The Hibernian Magazine: or, Compendium of Entertaining Knowledge, (1775)

Hiesinger 1978
Hiesinger, Ulrich W, 'Canova and the Frescoes of the Galleria Chiaramonti', *Burlington Magazine*, vol 120 (Oct 1978) pp 654–63

Hiesinger 1981
Hiesinger, Ulrich W, and Percy, Ann, *A Scholar Collects; Selections from the Anthony Morris Clark Bequest*, exhib cat (Philadelphia Museum of Art: 2 Oct 1980–4 Jan 1981)

Higgott 2004
Higgott, Gordon, 'The revised design for St Paul's Cathedral, 1685–90: Wren, Hawksmoor and Les Invalides', *Burlington Magazine*, vol CXLVI (August 2004)

Hill 1952
Hill, J W F, ed, *The Letters and Papers of the Banks Family of Revesby Abbey 1704–1760*, Lincoln Record Society, vol 45 (1952)

Hill 1998
Hill, Judith, *Irish Public Sculpture: A History* (Dublin: 1998)

Hill and Midgley 1929
Hill, Joseph, and Midgley, William, *The History of the Royal Birmingham Society of Artists* (Birmingham: 1929)

Himsworth 1963
Himsworth, J B, 'Edwin Smith and Theophilus His Son, of Cemetery Road Marble and Stone Works, Little Sheffield', *Transactions of the Hunter Archaeological Society*, vol 8 (1963) p 13

Hinks 1962
Hinks, Roger, 'Le Bicenteniere de Louis François Roubiliac', *Etudes Anglaises, Grand-Bretagne, Etats-Unis*, vol 15, no 1 (Jan–March 1962)

Hiscock 1945
Hiscock, W G, 'Mason and Architect of Oxford', *Architectural Review*, vol 98 (Oct 1945) pp 99–107

Hiscock 1946
Hiscock, W G, *A Christ Church Miscellany* (1946)

Hiscock 1948
Hiscock, W G, 'Jonathan Maine, Woodcarver; His Work at Oxford', *Country Life*, vol 104, no 2711 (31 Dec 1948) pp 1398–1401

Hist Reg
Sun Fire Office, 'The Historical Register, containing an impartial relation of all transactions foreign and domestic (chronological register for the year 1717–1738)', 23 vols (1717–1739)

HM Comm, Portland, 1897
Report on the manuscripts of His Grace the Duke of Portland, preserved at Welbeck Abbey, Fifteenth Report, appendix, part IV (Historical Manuscripts Commission, 1897)

HMC
Historical Manuscripts Commission

HMC 1896
Historical Manuscripts Commission, *The Manuscripts of the Earl of Dartmouth*, vol 3 (1896)

HMC 1906
Historical Manuscripts Commission, *Report on the Manuscripts of the Earl of Verulam, preserved at Gorhambury* (1906)

HMI
Henry Moore Institute, Leeds

HMSO
Her Majesty's Stationery Office

Hoare
Hoare's Bank (C Hoare and Co), 37 Fleet Street, London

Hoare 1809
Hoare, Prince, *Academic Annals of Painting, Sculpture and Architecture, Published by the Authority of the RA 1805–6, 1807, 1808–9* (1809)

Hoare Customer Ledger
Hoare Customer Ledger (Hoare's Bank, Fleet St, London)

Hoare Partnership Ledger, 1719–1725
Hoare Family Partnership Ledger, 1719–1725 (Hoare's Bank, Fleet St, London)

Hoare Partnership Ledger, 1725–34
Henry Hoare II, Partnership Ledger, 1725–34 (Hoare's Bank, Fleet St, London)

Hoare Partnership Ledger, 1734–42
Henry Hoare II, Partnership Ledger, 1734–42 (Hoare's Bank, Fleet St, London)

Hoare Partnership Ledger, 1742–1751
Hoare Family Partnership Ledger, 1742–1751 (Hoare's Bank, Fleet St, London)

Hoare Private Accounts, 1714–31
Henry Hoare I, Private Account Book ('An Account of Money paid for building my House at Stourton'), 1714–31 (Hoare's Bank, Fleet St, London)

Hoare Private Accounts, 1734–49
Henry Hoare II, Private Account Book (The Wilberry Account Book), 1734–49 (Hoare's Bank, Fleet St, London)

Hoare Private Accounts, 1750–66 (1)
Henry Hoare II, Private Account Book, 1750–66 (Wilts CRO, 383.6)

Hoare Private Accounts, 1750–66 (2)
Henry Hoare II, Private Account Book, 1752–78 (Hoare's Bank, Fleet St, London)

Hobbs 1960
Hobbs, John L, 'Famous Shropshire Architects – 3, Carlines – Architects, Builders and Sculptors', *Shropshire Magazine* (March 1960) pp 17–18

Hobbs 1974
Hobbs, Thomas C, *Sculpture and Sculptors; a Bibliography*, Ledoux Library. Bibliography 7 (Louisiana: 1974)

Hobhouse 1934
Hobhouse, Edmund, ed, *Diary of a West Country Physician* (1934)

Hobson and Salter 1933
Hobson, M G and Salter, H E, eds, *Oxford Council Acts, 1626–1665*, Oxford Historical Society, vol 95 (1933)

Hodgkinson 1947
Hodgkinson, Terence, 'Sketch in Terracotta by Roubiliac; Model for the Monument to John, Second Duke of Montagu', *Burlington Magazine*, vol 89 (Sept 1947) p 258

Hodgkinson 1952–54
Hodgkinson, Terence, 'Christopher Hewetson, an Irish Sculptor in Rome', *Walpole Society*, vol 34 (1952–54) pp 42–54

Hodgkinson 1965 (1)
Hodgkinson, Terence, 'Handel at Vauxhall', *Bulletin of the Victoria and Albert Museum*, vol 1, no 4 (Oct 1965) pp 1–13

Hodgkinson 1965 (2)
Hodgkinson, Terence, 'An Ingenious Man for Carving in Ivory', *Bulletin of the Victoria and Albert Museum*, vol 1, no 2 (1965) pp 29–32

Hodgkinson 1967
Hodgkinson, Terence, 'Joseph Wilton and Doctor Cocchi', *Bulletin of the Victoria and Albert Museum*, vol 3, no 2 (April 1967) pp 73–80

Hodgkinson 1969
Hodgkinson, Terence, 'John Lochée, Portrait Sculptor', *Victoria and Albert Museum Yearbook*, vol 1 (1969)

Hodgkinson 1971–2
Hodgkinson, Terence, 'Monuments from Faxton Church, Northamptonshire, in the Victoria and Albert Museum', *Northamptonshire Past and Present*, vol 4, no 6 (1971–72) p 334

Hodgkinson 1970
Hodgkinson, Terence, *The James A. De Rothschild Collection at Waddesdon Manor, Sculpture* (Office du Livre, 1970)

Hodgson/Lonsdale
William Hodgson, Letter to the Earl of Lonsdale, 1832 (Cumbria RO, Carlisle, D/LONS/LI/2/119)

Hodson 1992
Hodson, Harry, 'The Iron Bridge: Its Manufacture and Construction', *Industrial Archaeology Review*, vol 15, no 1 (Autumn 1992) pp 36–44

Hoebankx 1986
Hoebankx, J J, 'Laurent Delvaux et les Carmes de Nivelles', *Annales de la societé archaeologique ... de Nivelles*, vol 8 (1986) pp 75–81

Hofmann 1979
Hofmann, Werner, *John Flaxman; Mythologie und Industrie*, exhib cat (München: 1979)

Hogan Papers
Correspondence and papers of John Hogan, 3 July 1823–27 Feb 1824 (Public Record Office of Northern Ireland, Belfast, D/1537/6)

Hogg 1875
Hogg, David, *Life of Allan Cunningham, with Selections from his Works and Correspondence* (Dumfries: 1875)

Holden 1811
Holden, William, *Holden's Triennial Directory 1809–1811* (1811)

Holland 1851
Holland, John, *Memorials of Sir Francis Chantrey* (1851)

Holland 1869
Holland, John, *Or old churchyard: a paper read before Sheffield Literary and Philosophical Society, October 5th 1869* (Sheffield: 1869)

Holland Park 1957
Sculpture 1850 and 1950, London County Council Exhibition (Holland Park, London: May–September 1957)

Hollins Notebook
Notebook, ex coll Peter Hollins, containing instructions for making scagliola and for polishing, together with a recipe for making modelling wax (Birmingham City Archives, MS 1554)

Holt 1730
Holt, Richard, *A Short Treatise of Artificial Stone As 'tis now made, And converted into all Manner of Curious Embellishments, and Proper Ornaments of Architecture; containing The most Beautiful, the Strongest and the Cheapest Method, of Adorning Buildings of all Sorts. Being an Excellent and most useful Art, well known to the Ancients, but lost to the world for many Ages* (1730)

Holt Formula
Richard Holt's Invention for Making Artificial Stone, Miscellaneous Papers and Letters 3 March 1731/2 (BL, Add MS 11394)

Holt Patent
Ripley and Holt's Patent: Compound Metal for Manufacturing Artificial Stone and Marble, 31 May 1722 (Patent Office, 447/1722)

Holyoake 1980
Holyoake, Gregory, 'London's Charity Children's Statues [Eustace, T and Coade, E]', *Country Life*, vol 168, no 4343 (13 Nov 1980) pp 1787–91

Honour 1958 (1)
Honour, Hugh, 'Canova Anniversary', *Connoisseur*, vol 140 (Jan 1958) p 248

Honour 1958 (2)
Honour, Hugh, 'English Patrons and Italian Sculptors in the first half of the Eighteenth Century', *Connoisseur*, vol 141 (June 1958) pp 220–26

Honour 1958 (3)
Honour, H, 'Count Giovanni Baratta and his brothers', *Connoisseur*, vol 142 (1958) pp 170–77

Honour 1959
Honour, Hugh, 'Antonio Canova and the Anglo-Romans, pts 1 and 2', *Connoisseur*, vol 143 (June and Aug 1959) pp 241–45 and 225–31

Honour 1962
Honour, Hugh, 'An Italian monument to Nelson: Canova's unexecuted commission', *Country Life*, (1962) pp 137–38

Honour 1963
Honour, Hugh, 'Rome of Vincenzo Pacetti: Leaves from a Sculptor's Diary', *Apollo*, no 78 (Nov 1963) pp 368–76

Honour 1964
Honour, Hugh, 'Italian Empire Style', *Apollo*, no 80 (Sept 1964) pp 226–36

Honour 1968
Honour, Hugh, *Neoclassicism* (1968)

Honour 1969
Honour, Hugh, 'Canova's Theseus and the Minotaur', *Victoria and Albert Museum Yearbook*, vol 1 (1969) pp 1–15

Honour 1972 (1)
Honour, Hugh, 'Canova's Studio Practice', *Burlington Magazine*, vol 114 (April 1972) pp 214–29

Honour 1972 (2)
Honour, Hugh, 'Canova's Statues of Venus', *Burlington Magazine*, vol 114 (Oct 1972) pp 658–70

Honour 1972 (3)
Honour, Hugh, 'Canova and David', *Apollo*, no 96 (Oct 1972) pp 312–17

Honour 1973
Honour, Hugh, 'Canova's Napoleon', *Apollo*, no 98 (Sept 1973) pp 180–84

Honour 1976 (1)
Honour, Hugh, 'Eight Letters from Antonio Canova (in the Lugt Collection)', *Apollo*, no 104 (Oct 1976) pp 290–97

Honour 1976 (2)
Honour, Hugh, 'L'Image de Christophe Colomb', *Revue du Louvre et des Musées de France*, vol 26, no 4 (1976) pp 255–67

Honour 1991
Honour, Hugh, 'A Bust of Sappho by Antonio Canova', *Artibus et Historiae*, no 24 (1991) pp 193–200

Honour 1994
Honour, Hugh, 'Canova's Amorini for John Campbell and John David La Touche', ns *Antologia di Belle Arti*, nos 48–51 (1994) pp 129–40

Honour 1995
Honour, Hugh, 'Canova and His Printmakers', *Print Quarterly*, vol 12 (Sept 1995) pp 253–75

Honour (ed) 1994
Honour, Hugh, ed, *Edizione Nazionale delle Opere di Antonio Canova*, vol 1, Scritti (Rome: 1994)

Honour and Mariuz (eds) 2002
Honour, Hugh, and Mariuz, Paolo, eds, *Edizione Nazionale delle Opere di Antonio Canova: Epistolario 1816–1817*, 2 vols (2002)

Hood 1991
Hood, Graham, 'Early Neoclassicism in America', *Antiques Magazine*, vol 140 (Dec 1991) pp 978–85

Hooe 1880
Hooe, William, *Sculptors of the day: a list of the profession in 1880* (1880)

Hoole 1924
Hoole, B H, 'Edward Law, a Notable Sheffield Sculptor of the Past', *Transactions of the Hunter Archaeological Society*, vol 2 (382–83) p 1924

Hoole 1925
Hoole, B, *Sheffield Portraiture in Sculpture, Painting and Engraving* (1925)

Hope 1900
Hope, W H St John, *Cathedral Church and Monastery of St Andrew at Rochester* (1900)

Hope 1913
Hope, John, 'Windsor Castle: An Architectural History', *Country Life* (1913)

Hope 1950
Hope, V, 'The Architect of Radley Hall', *Country Life*, no 107 (27 Jan 1950) p 237

Horn 1797
Horn, J, *A History or description, general and circumstantial, of Burghley House, the seat of the Right Honorable the Earl of Exeter* (1797)

Horsfield 1835
Horsfield, Thomas Walker, *History, Antiquities and Topography of the County of Sussex* (1835)

Houfe 1971
Houfe, Simon, 'New Light on Ampthill Park', *Country Life*, vol 150 (21 Oct 1971) pp 1085–86

Houfe 1978
Houfe, Simon, *The Dictionary of British Book Illustrators and Caricaturists* (Antique Collectors' Club, 1978)

Howard 1964
Howard, Seymour, 'Boy on a Dolphin: Nollekens and Cavaceppi', *Art Bulletin*, vol 46 (June 1964) pp 177–89

Howard 1998
Howard, Maurice, *The Vyne*, National Trust (1998)

Howell 1983–84
Howell, P, 'Newman's Church at Littlemore', *Oxford Art Journal*, vol 6, no 1 (1983–84) pp 51–56

Howell and Pritchard 1972
Howell, Peter, and Pritchard, T W, 'Wynnstay, Denbighshire', *Country Life*, vol 151 (23 March 1972) pp 686–88

Hubert 1964
Hubert, Gérard, *Les Sculpteurs Italiens en France sous la Révolution l'Empire et la Restauration 1790–1830* (1964)

Hubert 1972
Hubert, Gérard, 'Arte Neoclassica: Atti del Convegno Venezia-Roma, Istituto per la Collaborazione Culturale', *Gazette des Beaux-Arts*, vol 79 series 6 (May 1972) pp 39–40 (supp)

Hubert 1976
Hubert, Gérard, 'Sculptures and Bronzes of the First Empire', *Apollo*, vol 103, no 172 (June 1976) pp 464–71

Hudson 1979
Hudson, Margaret, 'Pillar of Patriotism', *Country Life*, vol 166, no 4303 (27 Dec 1979) pp 2460–61

Hughes 1952
Hughes, Edward, *North Country Life in the Eighteenth Century*, 2 vols (Durham: 1952)

Hughes 1955
Hughes, Bernard, 'Wax Portraits by Samuel Percy', *Country Life*, vol 117, no 3043 (12 May 1955) pp 1255–57

Hughes 1962
Hughes, Bernard, 'Portrait Busts in Black Basaltes', *Country Life*, vol 132, no 3415 (16 Aug 1962) pp 360–61

Hughes 1974
Hughes, J, 'Bromleys of Keswick, a family business', Transactions of the Cumberland & Westmorland Antiquarian & Archaeological Society (1974)

Hughson 1806–11
Hughson, David, *London, being an Accurate History and Description of the British Metropolis and its Neighbourhood*, 6 vols (1806–11)

Hulton 1969
Hulton, P H, 'Royal Academy: A Little-Known Cache of English Drawings', *Apollo*, no 89 (Jan 1969) p 52

Hunt 1846
Hunt, Frederick Knight, *The Book of Art* (1846)

Hunt 1905
Hunt, William Holman, *Pre-Raphaelitism and the Pre-Raphaelite Brotherhood* (1905)

Hunterian
Hunterian Art Gallery, University of Glasgow

Huntington
Henry E Huntington Library, Art Gallery and Botanical Gardens, San Marino, California

Hurtado 1994
Hunter Hurtado, Shannon, MA Diss (Univ of Manitoba, Canada: 1994)

Hurtado 2002
Hunter Hurtado, Shannon, 'Genteel Mavericks: Women Sculptors in Victorian Britain' Ph D Diss (Univ of Manitoba, Canada: 2002)

Hurtig 1982
Hurtig, Judith W, 'Seventeenth-Century Shroud Tombs: Classical Revival and Anglican Context', *Art Bulletin*, vol 64 (1982) pp 217–28

Hurtig 1983
Hurtig, Judith W, 'Death in Childbirth: Seventeenth-Century English Tombs and their Place in Contemporary Thought', *Art Bulletin*, vol 65 (Dec 1983) pp 603–15

Hussey 1947
Hussey, Christopher, 'The Library of Christ Church, Oxford', *Country Life*, vol 101 (6 April 1947) pp 612–13

Hussey 1953
Hussey, Christopher, 'Ashburnham Place, Sussex', *Country Life*, vol 113 (16, 23, 30 April 1953) pp 1158–60, 1246–49, 1334–38

Hussey 1958
Hussey, Christopher, 'A Gibbs–Rysbrack Monument', *Country Life*, vol 124, no 3226 (13 Nov 1958) pp 1124–25

Hussey 1960
Hussey, Christopher, 'Althorp, Northamptonshire', *Country Life*, vol 127 (19 May 1960) pp 1122–25

Hutchins 1774
Hutchins, John, *The History and Antiquities of the County of Dorset*, 2 vols (1774)

Hutchins 1861; Hutchins 1863
Hutchins, John, *The History and Antiquities of the County of Dorset* (1861; 3rd ed 1863)

Hutchins 1870
Hutchins, John, *The History and Antiquities of the County of Dorset*, 4 vols (London: 1870)

Hutchison 1960–62
Hutchison, Sidney C, 'The Royal Academy Schools, 1768–1830', *Walpole Society*, vol 38 (1960–62) p 123 ff

Hutchison 1986
Hutchison, Sidney, *History of the Royal Academy 1768–1986* (2nd ed, 1986)

Hutton 1783
Hutton, William, *An history of Birmingham* (Birmingham: 2nd ed, 1783)

HWC
Lewis, Wilmarth Sheldon, ed, *Horace Walpole's Correspondence*, 48 vols (Yale: 1937–1983)

Hyland 1986
Hyland, Douglas, 'Lorenzo Bartolini and Italian Influences on American Sculptors in Florence, 1825–1850' Ph D Diss (Univ of Delaware: Outstanding Dissertations in the Fine Arts, 1986)

I of W
Isle of Wight

Ickworth Building Accounts
Correspondence and accounts for building work and alterations to Ickworth House, Hervey Family Archives 1795–1921 (Suffolk CRO, Bury St Edmunds, 941/30)

IEFAS
Institution for the Encouragement of the Fine Arts in Scotland

IGI
International Genealogical Index

ILN
Illustrated London News

ILN 1949
'Portrait Bust by John Bushnell', *Illustrated London News*, vol 214 (26 Feb 1949) p 282

ILN 1955
'Flaxman's Bicentenary Honoured', *Illustrated London News* (9 April 1955) p 655

ILN 1956
'Portrait Bust by F. Chantrey', *Illustrated London News*, vol 228 (21 Jan 1956) p 91

ILN 1957
'Grinling Gibbons Carved Staircase Newly Installed in the Metropolitan Museum of Art', *Illustrated London News*, vol 231 (6 July 1957) p 19

Impey 1998
Impey, Oliver, *Four Centuries of Decorative Arts from Burghley House* (Alexandria, Virginia: 1998)

Inderwick 1896–1936
Inderwick, F A, *A Calendar of the Inner Temple Records*, 5 vols (1896–1936)

Ingamells 1972
Ingamells, John, *The Noble City of York* (1972)

Ingamells 1974
Ingamells, John, 'Andrea Soldi', *Connoisseur*, vol 185–86 (1974) pp 192–200, 178–85

Ingamells 1997
Ingamells, John, *A Dictionary of British and Irish Travellers in Italy, compiled from the Brinsley Ford Archive by John Ingamells* (1997)

Ingamells 2007
Ingamells, John, *Dulwich Picture Gallery: British* (2007)

Ingamells 2009
Ingamells, John, *National Portrait Gallery: Later Stuart Portraits 1685–1714* (2009)

Ingram 1951
Ingram, M Edward, 'A Note on Admiral Medley's Monument in York Minster', *Yorkshire Archaeological Journal*, vol 37 (1951) pp 258–61

Ingram 1952
Ingram, M Edward, 'A Gothic Fantasy by Carr of York: Grimston Garth, Yorkshire', *Country Life*, vol 112 (17 Oct 1952) pp 1186–88

Ingram 1955
Ingram, M Edward, 'A Further Note on Henry Cheere', *Yorkshire Archaeological Journal*, vol 38 (1955) pp 2–6

INPG
Irish National Portrait Gallery

Int Exhib
International Exhibition, 1862

Interiors 1957
'Grinling Gibbons' Staircase', *Interiors*, vol 117 (Aug 1957) p 12

Inverness Guide
A Guide to Inverness House (nd)

Ionides 1997
Ionides, Julia, 'Bitterley Court, Shropshire, the Home of Mr and Mrs John Wheeler', *Country Life*, vol 191, no 37 (11 Sept 1997) pp 106–11

Ionides 1998
Ionides, Julia, 'Summer Living in the Quietest Country Under the Sun', *Country Life*, vol 192, no 26 (25 June 1998) pp 106–11

Ionides 1999
Ionides, Julia, *Thomas Farnolls Pritchard of Shrewsbury: Architect and "Inventor of cast Iron Bridges"* (Ludlow: 1999)

Ironmongers, W A
Corporation of London, Ironmongers' Company, Wardens' Accounts, 1734–41; 1741–52; 1752–70 (CLRO Guildhall, 16988/11–13)

Irwin 1959 (1)
Irwin, David, 'Flaxman: Italian Journals and Correspondence', *Burlington Magazine*, vol 101 (June 1959) pp 212–17

Irwin 1959 (2)
Irwin, David, 'Reviving Interest in John Flaxman', *Connoisseur*, vol 144 (Nov 1959) pp 104–5

Irwin 1961
Irwin, David, 'English Neo-Classical Art: Views and Taste of the Principal Artists' Ph D Diss (Univ of London: 1961)

Irwin 1966
Irwin, David, *English Neoclassical Art: Studies in Inspiration and Taste* (1966)

Irwin 1968
Irwin, David, 'Decline of Garden Sculpture', *Apollo*, no 88 (Sept 1968) p 215 ff

Irwin 1972 (1)
Irwin, David, 'Unclassical Neo-Classicism: Sentiment and Gothic', *Connoisseur*, vol 181 (Sept 1972) pp 18–24

Irwin 1972 (2)
Irwin, David, 'Neo-Classical Design: Industry Plunders Antiquity', *Apollo*, no 96 (Oct 1972) p 288

Irwin 1977
Irwin, David, 'Death, Sentiment and Pity in Tombs at the End of the Eighteenth Century', *British Society for Eighteenth Century Studies* (Feb 1977) pp 37–40

Irwin 1979
Irwin, David, *John Flaxman, 1755–1826, Sculptor, Illustrator, Designer* (1979)

Isham 1951
Isham, Gyles, 'Edward Stanton's Monument to Elizabeth Lady Isham in the Isham Chapel, All Saints Church Lamport', *RIBA Journal*, vol 58 (Sept 1951) pp 440–42

Isham 1965
Isham, Gyles, 'The Isham Chapel at the Church of All Hallows, Lamport', (publ privately 1965)

Isham and Bailey 1970
Isham, Gyles, and Bailey, Bruce, 'Cottesbrooke Hall Revisited: the Home of Sir Reginald and the Hon. Lady Macdonald-Buchanan', *Country Life*, vol 147 (19 Feb 1970) pp 434–37

Ison 1948
Ison, W, *The Georgian Buildings of Bath* (1948)

ITC
Inner Temple Catalogue

ITC 1915
Catalogue of the Paintings, Engravings, Serjeants' Rings, Plate, Stained Glass, Sculptures etc belonging to the Honourable Society of the Inner Temple (1915)

Ivon Jones 1973
Ivon Jones, B, 'Regency Splendour 1810–1820: The Achilles Silver-Gilt Shield', *Apollo*, no 97 (April 1973) p 447

Ivory Stock Valuation
Valuation of stock (marble, stone and tools) of John Ivory taken by himself and John de Carle, March 1776 (Suffolk CRO, Bury St Edmunds, 492/1)

Ivory/de Carle Indentures
Partnership indentures of John Ivory and John de Carle, 1 April 1776 (Suffolk CRO, Bury St Edmunds, HD553/1060/1)

J C F Rossi Catalogue 1833
Rossi, John Charles Felix, *A Catalogue of Seven Groups and Statues in Marble and Bronze and Other Works of Art* (15 Shoe Lane, Fleet Street: W Guthrie, 1833)

J Warb & Court
Journal of the Warburg and Courtauld Institutes

Jackson-Stops 1972
Jackson-Stops, Gervase, 'Britwell Salome, Oxfordshire', *Country Life*, vol 152 (5 Oct 1972) pp 810–14

Jackson-Stops 1974
Jackson-Stops, Gervase, 'Harrowden Hall, Northamptonshire', *Country Life*, vol 156 (17 Oct 1974) pp 1086–89

Jackson-Stops 1976
Jackson-Stops, Gervase, 'Pusey House, Berkshire', *Country Life*, vol 160 (30 Dec 1976) pp 1958–61

Jackson-Stops 1977 (1)
Jackson-Stops, Gervase, 'Furniture at Petworth', *Apollo*, no 105 (May 1977) pp 358–66

Jackson-Stops 1977 (2)
Jackson-Stops, Gervase, 'Aldenham Park, Salop. Parts I, II, III', *Country Life*, vol 162, no 4175 (7 July 1977) pp 18–21

Jackson-Stops 1978 (1)
Jackson-Stops, Gervase, 'Acton Round, Salop', *Country Life*, vol 163 (9 March 1978) pp 614–17

Jackson-Stops 1978 (2)
Jackson-Stops, Gervase, *Drayton House, Northamptonshire* (1978)

Jackson-Stops 1980
Jackson-Stops, Gervase, 'Broadlands, Hampshire; the Home of Lord and Lady Romsey', *Country Life*, vol 168, no 4348 (18 Dec 1980) pp 2334–37

Jackson-Stops 1987 (1)
Jackson-Stops, Gervase, 'Figures in a Landscape: Sculpture in the British Garden', *Antiques Magazine*, vol 132 (Oct 1987) pp 782–97

Jackson-Stops 1987 (2)
Jackson-Stops, Gervase, 'New Deities for Old Parterres: The Painting of Lead Statues', *Country Life* (1987) p 92

Jackson-Stops 1987 (3)
Jackson-Stops, Gervase, *Felbrigg Hall*, National Trust (1987)

Jackson-Stops 1988 (1)
Jackson-Stops, Gervase, Archer, Michael, and Mitchel, David, 'The Decorative Arts Catalog for Christie's Exhibition, London', *Journal of Garden History*, vol 8 (April / Sept 1988) pp 305–23

Jackson-Stops 1988 (2)
Jackson-Stops, Gervase, 'Newbridge Restored', *Country Life*, (18 Feb 1988)

Jackson-Stops 1989
Jackson-Stops, Gervase, ed, *The Fashioning and Functioning of the British Country House* (Washington: 1989)

Jackson-Stops 1992
Jackson-Stops, Gervase, 'John Michael Rysbrack, a Saxon Goddess Saved', *National Arts Collection Fund Review*, vol 88 (1992) pp 64–66

Jacobs 1996
Jacobs, Alain, 'L'Archange Raphael et L'Ange Tutelaire du Royaume du Portugal Sculptes a Rome vers 1730–1732 par Laurent Delvaux. Contribution a L'Etude des Sculptures de la Basilique de Mafra', *Gazette des Beaux-Arts*, vol 128, series 6 (Sept 1996) pp 71–90

Jacobs 1997
Jacobs, Alain, 'Joseph Wilton's Nivelles Years and the Influence of Laurent Delvaux', *Journal of the Church Monuments Society*, vol 12 (1997) pp 58–66

Jacobs 1999 (1)
Jacobs, Alain, *Laurent Delvaux* (Paris: 1999)

Jacobs 1999 (2)
Jacobs, Alain, 'Pierre-Denis Plumier', *Revue Belgique*, vol 68 (1999) pp 113–70

Jacobs 2000
Jacobs, Alain (et al), eds, *Terracottas 17th and 18th Century. The Van Herck Collection* (King Baudoin Foundation: 2000)

Jaffe 1974
Jaffe, Michael, *The European Fame of Isaac Newton*, exhib cat (Fitzwilliam, Cambridge: 1974)

JAIA 1947
'The Octagon's Coade Mantels', *Journal of the American Institute of Architects*, vol 7 (March 1947) pp 130–34

James 1952
James, R G, 'Thread', in *History of the Rubber Industry*, ed Schidrowitz, P and Dawson, T R (Cambridge: 1952)

Janson 1976
Janson, H W, *Aspects of 19th-Century Sculpture*, exhib cat (Cleveland Museum of Art: 1976)

Janson 1977
Janson, H W, 'Thorvaldsen und England', *Kolner Berichte zur Kunstgeschichte Koln*, vol 2 (1977) pp 107–28

Janson 1981
Janson, H W, 'Pars Pro Toto; Hands and Feet as Sculptural Subjects before Rodin', in *Shape of the Past; Studies in Honour of Franklin D. Murphy*, ed Buccellati, Giorgio, Speroni, Charles and Young, Charles (California: 1981) pp 289–304

Janson 1984
Janson, H W, ed, *La Scultura nel XIX Secolo*, Comité International d'Histoire de l'Art. Atti del XXIV Congresso Internazionale di Storia dell'Arte, 6 (Bologna: 1984)

Jeavons 1951–53
Jeavons, S A, 'The Monumental Effigies of Staffordshire, parts I–III', *Transactions of the Birmingham Archaeological Society*, vol 69–71 (1951–1953)

Jeavons 1959
Jeavons, S A, 'The monumental effigies of Staffordshire, part IV', *Transactions of the Birmingham Archaeological Society*, vol 75 (1959) pp 49–84

Jeavons 1960
Jeavons, S A, 'The monumental effigies of Saffordshire, part V', *Transactions of the Birmingham Archaeological Society*, vol 76 (1960) pp 51–83

Jeffery 1993
Jeffery, Sally, *The Mansion House* (1993)

Jelfe Letter Book
A Jelfe, Letter-Book relating to Westminster Bridge, 1734–1744 (BL, Add MS 27,587)

Jenkins 1992
Jenkins, Ian, *Archaeologists and Aesthetics in the Sculpture Galleries of the British Museum 1800–1939* (1992)

Jenkins 1997
Jenkins, Simon, 'England's Thousand Best Churches: Warwick St Mary', *Country Life*, vol 191, no 49 (4 Dec 1997) pp 122–23

Jenkins 2000–1
Jenkins, Susan, 'The external sculptural decoration of Somerset House and the documentary sources', *British Art Journal*, vol 2, no 2 (Winter 2000–1) pp 23–28

Jenkins 2005
Jenkins, Susan, 'An Inventory of His Grace The Duke of Chandos's Seat att Cannons taken June the 19th 1725 by John Gilbert', *Walpole Society*, vol 67 (2005) pp 93–192

Jervis 1973
Jervis, S S, 'Evocation of Walpole', *Country Life*, vol 154 (20 Dec 1973) p 2117

Jervis 1986
Jervis, Simon, 'A Seventeenth-Century Book of Engraved Ornament', *Burlington Magazine*, vol 128, no 1005 (Dec 1986) pp 893–903

Jevons 1960 (1)
Jevons, John H W, 'Chimney-Pieces by Cheere', *Country Life*, vol 127, no 3288 (10 March 1960) p 505

Jevons 1960 (2)
Jevons, John H W, 'Cheere in Norwich', *Country Life*, vol 127, no 3293 (14 Apr 1960) p 821

Jewell 1822
Jewell, John, *The Tourist's Companion, or the History and Antiquities of Harewood*, 2nd edition (1822)

Jewitt 1878
Jewitt, Llewellyn, *The Ceramic Art of Great Britain*, 2 vols (1878)

JKB
John Kenworthy-Browne

JKB 1966
Kenworthy-Browne, John, 'Marbles from a Victorian Fantasy', *Country Life*, vol 140 (22 Sept 1966) pp 708–12

JKB 1970
Kenworthy-Browne, John, 'The Sculpture at Chatsworth' MA Diss (Univ of London: 1970)

JKB 1971
Kenworthy-Browne, John, 'Pauline and the Bachelor Duke', *Country Life*, vol 149 (28 Jan 1971) p 208

JKB 1972 (1)
Kenworthy-Browne, John, 'Age of Marblemania', *Country Life*, vol 151 (27 Jan 1972) pp 206–8

JKB 1972 (2)
Kenworthy-Browne, John, 'Sculpture by Bartolini', letter and photo *Country Life*, vol 151 (4 May 1972) p 1102

JKB 1972 (3)
Kenworthy-Browne, John, 'A Ducal Patron of Sculptors', *Apollo*, no 96 (October 1972) pp 322–31

JKB 1973 (1)
Kenworthy-Browne, John, 'Some English Funeral Monuments, *c.*1780–1820', in *Neoclassicismo*, conference proceedings (London: 1973) pp 55–57

JKB 1973 (2)
Kenworthy-Browne, John, 'Drawings and Models by Thorvaldsen', *Connoisseur*, vol 184, no 742 (1973) pp 256–60

JKB 1973 (3)
Kenworthy-Browne, John, 'Lord Egremont and his Sculptors; the Collection at Petworth House, Sussex', *Country Life*, vol 154 (7 June 1973) pp 1640–43

JKB 1974 (1)
Kenworthy-Browne, John, 'Patroness of the Arts; the Duchess of Devonshire in Rome', *Country Life*, vol 155 (25 April 1974) pp 982–84

JKB 1974 (2)
Kenworthy-Browne, John, 'Man at Hyde Park Corner', *Country Life*, vol 156 (1 Aug 1974) pp 305–6

JKB 1975
Kenworthy-Browne, John, 'Taken from the Marble: Portraits in Plaster, by Nollekens', *Country Life*, vol 157 (5 June 1975) pp 1509–10

JKB 1977 (1)
Kenworthy-Browne, John, 'Monument to Three Captains (in Westminster Abbey)', *Country Life*, vol 161 (27 Jan 1977) pp 180–82

JKB 1977 (2)
Kenworthy-Browne, John, 'Third Earl of Egremont and Neo-Classical Sculpture', *Apollo*, vol 105, no 183 (May 1977) pp 367–73

JKB 1977 (3)
Kenworthy-Browne, John, 'A Marble Bust by Nollekens', *North Carolina Museum of Art Bulletin*, vol 14, no 1 (1977) pp 1–13

JKB 1977–78
Kenworthy-Browne, John, 'Rise and Demise of a Wren Church; The Reredos from S. Matthew Friday Street at Polesdon Lacey', *National Trust Yearbook* (1977–1978) pp 63–74

JKB 1978
Kenworthy-Browne, John, 'Sculptor and Revolutionary; British Portraits by Bartolini', *Country Life*, vol 163 (8 June 1978) pp 1655–56

JKB 1979
Kenworthy-Browne, John, 'Joseph Nollekens: The Years in Rome', *Country Life*, vol 165 (7, 14 June, 1979) pp 1844–48, 1930–31

JKB 1980
Kenworthy-Browne, John, 'Portrait Bust by Rysbrack', *National Trust Studies* (1980) pp 66–79

JKB 1981
Kenworthy-Browne, John, '"Pure Emanation of British Genius"; Portraits by Chantrey at the NPG', *Country Life*, vol 169, no 4358 (26 Feb 1981) pp 530–31

JKB 1983 (1)
Kenworthy-Browne, John, 'Matthew Brettingham's Rome Account Book 1747–1754', *Walpole Society*, vol 49 (1983) pp 37–132

JKB 1983 (2)
Kenworthy-Browne, John, 'Rysbrack, 'Hercules', and Pietro da Cortona', *Burlington Magazine* (April 1983) pp 216–19

JKB 1985
Kenworthy-Browne, John, 'Rysbrack's Saxon Deities', *Apollo*, no 122 (Sept 1985) pp 220–27

JKB 1989
Kenworthy-Browne, John, 'The Temple of Liberty at Woburn Abbey', *Apollo*, no 130 (July 1989) pp 27–32

JKB 1993
Kenworthy-Browne, John, 'Designing around the Statues, Matthew Brettingham's casts at Kedleston', *Apollo*, no 137 (1993)

JKB 1998
Kenworthy-Browne, John, 'Terracotta Models by Joseph Nollekens, R.A.', *The Sculpture Journal*, vol 2 (1998) pp 72–84

JKB 2006
Kenworthy-Browne, John, 'Plaster Casts for the Crystal Palace, Sydenham', *The Sculpture Journal*, vol 15.2 (2006) pp 173–98

JM
Jonathan Marsden

JM 2006
Marsden, Jonathan, *Catalogue of the Royal Collections* (2006)

Joachim Smith/Caldwell
Letter from Joachim Smith to Sir James Caldwell, Bagshawe Muniments 16 June 1763 (John Rylands Library, University of Manchester, 3/16/324)

Jodidio 1994
Jodidio, Philip, 'Albion et les Trois Graces', *Connaissance des Arts*, no 510 (Oct 1994) p 141

Joekes 1982
Joekes, Rosemary, ' "A Briefe Life", The Memorial to Thomas Sackville', *Country Life*, vol 172, no 4435 (19 Aug 1982) pp 535–38

John Rylands
Manchester University, John Rylands Library

Johns 1989 (1)
Johns, Christopher, 'French Connections to Papal Art Patronage in the Rome of Clement XI', *Storia dell'Arte*, no 67 (Sept–Dec 1989) pp 279–85

Johns 1989 (2)
Johns, Christopher, 'Antonio Canova's Drawings for Hercules and Lichas', *Master Drawings*, vol 27 (Winter 1989) pp 358–67

Johns 1998
Johns, Christopher, 'Ecclesiastical Politics and Papal Tombs: Antonio Canova's Monuments to Clement XIV and Clement XIII', *The Sculpture Journal*, vol 2 (1998) pp 58–71

Johnson 1975
Johnson, Jane, *Works exhibited at the Royal Society of British Artists 1824–1893 and the New English Art Club 1888–1917* (Woodbridge: 1975, reprinted 1987)

Johnson 1993
Johnson, Jane, *Works exhibited at the Royal Society of British Artists 1824–1893 and The New English Art Club 1888–1917* (1993)

Joiners, Apprentices
Corporation of London, Joiners' Company Apprentices, 1678 (CLRO Guildhall, 8051/1; 8052/4)

Joiners, Freedoms
Corporation of London, Joiners' Company, Freedoms, 1651–87 (CLRO Guildhall, 8051/1)

Joiners, Minutes
Corporation of London, Joiners' Company, Minutes, 1698–1707 (CLRO Guildhall, 8046/3)

Joiners' Co, Master and Wardens
Corporation of London, Joiners Company, Master and Warden's Accounts, 1621–1684 (CLRO Guildhall, 8041)

Jones 1909
Jones, Theophilus, *A History of the County of Brecknock*, 4 vols (1909, 1911, 1930)

Jones 1934
Jones, Edward, 'Forgotton English Sculptor and Silversmith', *Apollo*, vol 19 (May 1934) pp 248–50

Jones 1959
Jones, M U, 'George III in Coade Stone', *Country Life*, vol 126, no 3278 (31 Dec 1959) p 1314

Jones 1981
Jones, Stephen, *Frederick, Prince of Wales and his Circle*, exhib cat (Sudbury, Gainsborough's House: 1981)

Jones 1990
Jones, Mark, Craddock, Paul, and Barker, Nicholas, *Fake? The art of deception*, exhib cat (British Museum: 1990)

Jones Memoirs 1951
Jones, Thomas, 'Memoirs of Thomas Jones', *Walpole Society*, vol 32 (1951)

Jones, Mercantile Directory, 1863–4
Jones, *Mercantile Directory of the Shipping Port of Hull* (1863–64)

Jornaes 1993
Jørnaes, Bjarne, Melander, Torben, and Urne, Anne Sophie, *Thorwaldsens Italienske Elever*, exhib cat (København: Thorwaldsens Museum, 1993)

Jornoes 1995
Jornoes, Bjarne, Melander, Torben and Urne, Anne Sophie, *The Thorvaldsen Museum* (Copenhagen: 1995)

Joseph/Lizars
Letter from Samuel Joseph to William Lizars, 1833 (NLS, MS 1831 fol 17)

Joseph/Mathews
Letter from Samuel Joseph to Charles Mathews, 19 April 1822 (Fitz, MS 111–1949)

Jottrand 1977
Jottrand, M, 'Tournai Porcelain and English Ceramics', *English Ceramic Circle Transactions*, vol 10, no 2 (1977) pp 130–41

Jouin 1878
Jouin, Henry, *David d'Angers, sa vie, son oeuvre, ses écrits at ses contemporains*, vol 2 (Paris: 1878)

Joy 1977
Joy, Edward T, *English Furniture 1800–1851* (London: 1977)

JP Misc Corr
John Physick, Miscellaneous Correspondence, Henry Moore Institute, Leeds

JP/IM
Physick, John, ed, *Inventory of Monuments, Westminster Abbey*, typescript (Westminster Abbey Muniment Room: nd)

JPGM
J Paul Getty Museum, Malibu, California

JSA
Journal of the Society of Arts

JT Smith 1862
Smith, J T, *The Streets of London*, first published as 'An Antiquarian Ramble in the Streets of London', 1815 (1862 ed)

Julius 1926
Julius, Arvid, *Jean Cavalier och några andra elfenbensnidare studier i elfenbenplastik i Sverige* (Uppsala: 1926)

Kader 1996
Kader, Alexander, 'Four Marble Busts of Artists by Edward Hodges Baily', *Antologia di Belle Arti*, no 52–55 (1996) pp 177–82

Kagan and Neverov 2000
Kagan, Yulia and Neverov, Oleg, *Treasures of Catherine the Great* (Somerset House, London: 2000) p 132

Kane 1979
Kane, Eileen, 'The Golden Age of Irish Plasterwork', *Art of Ireland*, vol 1, no 2 (1979) pp 18–21

Kane 2000
Kane, Eileen, 'From Rome to Dublin in 1848: A Madonna for St. Audoen's', *Irish Arts Review*, vol 16 (2000) pp 150–56

Kaplan 1970
Kaplan, Julius, 'Gustave Moreau's Jupiter and Semele', *Art Quarterly*, vol 33, no 4 (Winter 1970) pp 393–414

Kapoor 1984
Kapoor, Sushma, 'John L Tupper, to 1863: "King of the Cadaverals" ', *Journal of Pre-Raphaelite Studies*, vol 4, no 2 (1984) pp 70–86

Kapoor 1986
Kapoor, Sushma, 'John Lucas Tupper, 1865–79: The Rise of Outis', *Journal of Pre-Raphaelite Studies*, vol 6, no 2 (1986)

Kasson 1990
Kasson, Joy S, *Marble Queens and Captives: Women in Nineteenth Century American Sculpture* (New Haven and London: 1990)

Kedleston 1998
Kedleston Hall, Derbyshire (National Trust, 1998)

Keith 1933
Keith, William Grant, 'Six Houses in Search of an Architect; John Webb and the Marshalls', 3 *RIBA Journal*, vol 40 (22 July 1933) pp 732–33

Kelly 1968
Kelly, Alison, 'Vuillamys, Wedgwoods and Georgian Clocks', *Proceedings of the Wedgwood Society* (1968)

Kelly 1973
Kelly, Alison, 'Decorative Stonework in Disguise: Plaques and Medallions in Coade Stone', *Country Life*, vol 154, no 3988 (29 Nov 1973) pp 1797–1800

Kelly 1974
Kelly, Alison, 'Furnishings from the Coade Factory in Lambeth', *Furniture History*, vol 10 (1974) pp 68–70

Kelly 1977 (1)
Kelly, Alison, 'Mrs Coade's Gothic', *Country Life*, vol 161, no 4170 (2 June 1977) pp 1514–16

Kelly 1977 (2)
Kelly, Alison, 'Imitating Mrs Coade: Ceramic Artificial Stone Makers', *Country Life*, vol 162 (10 Nov 1977) p 1430 ff

Kelly 1978
Kelly, Alison, 'Mrs Coade's Stone', *Connoisseur*, vol 197, no 791 (Jan 1978) pp 14–25

Kelly 1979
Kelly, Alison, 'A Camouflage Queen by the River; Mrs Coade at Greenwich', *Country Life*, vol 165, no 4255 (25 Jan 1979) pp 244–45

Kelly 1980
Kelly, Alison, 'Coade Stone at National Trust Houses', *National Trust Studies* (1980) pp 94–111

Kelly 1982
Kelly, Alison, 'Mrs Coade's Stone', *English Ceramic Circle Transactions*, vol 11, no 2 (1982) pp 102–8

Kelly 1984
Kelly, Alison, 'An Expensive Present: the Adam Screen in Rio de Janeiro', *Burlington Magazine*, vol 126, no 978 (Sept 1984) pp 548–53

Kelly 1985
Kelly, Alison, 'Coade Stone in Georgian Architecture', *Architectural History*, vol 28 (1985) pp 71–101

Kelly 1988 (1)
Kelly, Alison, 'Coade Stone in Georgian Gardens', *Journal of Garden History*, vol 16, no 2 (Autumn 1988) pp 109–33

Kelly 1988 (2)
Kelly, Alison, 'Coade Stone in Sussex', *Sussex Archaeological Collections*, vol 126 (1988) pp 179–93

Kelly 1989 (1)
Kelly, Alison, 'Sir John Soane and Mrs Eleanor Coade', *Apollo*, vol 129, no 326 (April 1989) pp 247–53

Kelly 1989 (2)
Kelly, Alison, 'Josiah Wedgwood and Eleanor Coade', *Ars Ceramica*, vol 6 (1989) pp 18–22

Kelly 1990
Kelly, Alison, *Mrs Coade's Stone* (Upton-upon-Severn: 1990)

Kelly 1992
Kelly, Alison, 'Eleanor Coade at Stowe', *Georgian Group Journal*, (1992) pp 97–100

Kelly 1993
Kelly, Alison, 'Coade Stone in Georgian Gardens', *Antiques Magazine*, vol 143, no 6 (June 1993) pp 912–21

Kelly 1995
Kelly, Anne, 'Van Nost's Equestrian Statue of George I', *Irish Arts Review*, vol 11 (1995) pp 103–7

Kelly 1997
Kelly, Alison, 'Coade Stone at Croome', *Apollo*, vol 145, no 422 (April 1997) pp 21–23

Kemp 1980
Kemp, Brian, *English Church Monuments* (1980)

Kemp 1985
Kemp, Brian, *Church Monuments* (1985)

Kempster Misc Bills
Christopher Kempster, Miscellaneous bills, 1705–1717 (TNA, C106/145, parts 1 and 2)

Kendrick/Westm Abbey
Letter from Josephus John Pinnix Kendrick to the Dean and Chapter of Westminster Abbey proposing the erection of a statue of Sir James Leith with a sketch and some 20th century correspondence, 1819 (WAM, 66182, 66183, 66183–91)

Kent's Directory
Kent's Original London Directory (1814–1827)

Kenwood 1959
Eighteenth Century Portrait Busts, exhib cat (Iveagh Bequest, Kenwood: June–Sept 1959)

Kerslake 1966 (1)
Kerslake, John, '1965 – A Vintage Year for the National Portrait Gallery', *Connoisseur*, vol 161 (March 1966) p 159

Kerslake 1966 (2)
Kerslake, John, 'Roubiliac's Handel, a Terracotta Restored', *Burlington Magazine*, vol 108 (1966) p 475

Kerslake 1977
Kerslake, John, *Early Georgian Portraits*, 2 vols (London: 1977)
Kessels 1955
Kessels, S H, 'Coade Stone: A Lost Secret', *Country Life*, (1955) p 141
Keutner 1969
Keutner, Herbert, *Sculpture: Renaissance to Rococo* (New York Graphic Society: 1969)
Keynes 2005
Keynes, Milo, *The Iconography of Sir Isaac Newton to 1800* (2005)
Killanin and Duignan 1967
Killanin, Lord, and Duignan, M V, *The Shell Guide to Ireland* (1967)
King 1950
King, P G, 'Augustan Manner of John Michael Rysbrack', *Art Quarterly*, vol 13, no 3 (1950) pp 196–210
King Edward's School 1924–74
Records of King Edward's School, Birmingham, Dugdale Society Publications, 6 vols (Oxford: 1924–1974)
Kingzett 1982
Kingzett, Richard, 'A Catalogue of the Works of Samuel Scott', *Walpole Society*, vol 48 (1980–82)
Kirby 1892
Kirby, T F, *Annals of Westminster College* (1892)
Kirkham 1969
Kirkham, Pat, 'Samuel Norman: A Study of an Eighteenth Century Craftsman', *Burlington Magazine*, vol 111 (Aug. 1969) pp 500–11
Kirkham 1988
Kirkham, Pat, 'The London Furniture Trade 1700–1870', *Furniture History*, vol 24 (1988) pp vii-219
Kloss 1988
Kloss, William, *Samuel F B Morse* (New York: 1988)
KMSK, Antwerp
Koninklijk Museum voor Schone Kunsten, Antwerp
Knight 1843
Knight, Charles, ed, *London*, vol 5 (1843)
Knight 1986
Knight, Vivien, *The Works of Art of the Corporation of London; A Catalogue of Paintings, Watercolours, Drawings, Prints and Sculpture* (Cambridge: 1986)
Knoop and Jones 1935
Knoop, D, and Jones, G P, *The London Mason in the Seventeenth Century, including Masons' Company General Search Listings, 1678, 1694* (London: 1935)
Knox 1996
Knox, Tim, 'Losing Thorvaldsen's Leveson-Gower: The Rediscovery of Earl Gower's Bust at Clivedon', *Apollo*, vol 143 (April 1996) pp 37–43
Knox 1998
Knox, Tim, 'Portrait of a Collector: Rupert Gunnis at Hungershall Lodge and his Bequest to the Victoria and Albert Museum', *The Sculpture Journal*, vol 2 (1998) pp 85–96
Knox 1999
Knox, Tim, 'The obsequies of a Victorian grandee: the 1st Earl Brownlow's Chapelle Ardente at Belton House', *Apollo* (April 1999)
Knox 2001
Knox, Tim, 'Sculpture in Trust: The National Trust as the Guardian of Outdoor Sculpture', *Apollo*, vol 154, no 475 (Sept 2001) pp 26–31
Knox and Longstaffe-Gowan 1993
Knox, Tim, and Longstaffe-Gowan, Todd, 'Thorvaldsen's "Valrescot". A Lost Bust of Sir Walter Scott Discovered', *Apollo*, vol 137 (Feb 1993) pp 75–81
Knuth 1999
Knuth, Michael, 'Korrigierte Attributionen: Zu Zuschreibungs-problemen bei Berliner Bildwerken', *Museums Journal (Berlin)*, vol 13, no 1 (Jan 1999) pp 43–45
Kramer 1998
Kramer, Miriam, 'Grinling Gibbons: Aspects of his Style and Technique', *Antiques Magazine*, vol 154, no 4 (Oct 1998) pp 494–501
KULSC
Keele University Library Special Collections
Kurtz 1997
Kurtz, Donna, *Canova Ideal Heads* (Ashmolean, 1997) pp 43–46
La Belle 1990
La Belle, Jenijoy, 'Blake's Bald Nudes', *Blake*, vol 24, no 2 (Fall 1990) pp 52–58
LA County Museum
Los Angeles County Museum, California
La Perriere 1991
de la Perriere, Charles, ed, *The Royal Academy Exhibitors 1826–1990*, 4 vols (Wiltshire: 1991)
la Roche 1933
la Roche, Sophie von, *Sophie in London, 1786 . . . a translation of the portion referring to England of 'Tagebuch einer Reise durch Holland und England'* trans Clare Williams (1933)
LAAI
Liverpool Academy and Art Institute (combined exhibition)
LAC
Leeds Arts Calendar
Lack et al, 1994
Lack, W, Stuchfield, H M, and Whittemore, P, *The Monumental Brasses of Buckinghamshire* (1994)
Lady Lever 1999
British Sculpture in the Lady Lever Art Gallery (National Museums and Galleries on Merseyside, 1999)
Lady's Mag
Lady's Magazine, or Entertaining Companion for the Fair Sex, (1809)
Laing 1983
Laing, Alastair, 'Sculpture at Stoke Poges; Clubhouse Neo-Classicism', *Country Life*, vol 173, no 4458 (27 Jan 1983) pp 186–88
Laing 1985
Laing, Alastair, 'Fischer von Erlach's Monument to Wenzel, Count Wratislaw von Mitrowicz and its Place in the Typology of the Pyramid Tomb', *Umeni*, vol 33 (1985) p 204
Laing 2001
Laing, Alastair, 'The Ozymandias Solution', *Apollo*, vol 154, no 475 (Sept 2001) pp 32–37
Laing 2003
Laing, Alastair, '3rd Earl of Egremont as a Collector of Modern Sculpture', *Conference paper, Collectors in the Round, Wallace Collection and Anglesey Abbey* (19–20 May 2003)
Lami 1914–21
Lami, Stanislas, *Dictionnaire des sculpteurs de l'ecole Francais au dix-neuvieme siecle*, 4 vols (Paris: 1914–1921)
Lancaster 1970
Lancaster, Clay, 'Precedents for a Stair Design', *Country Life*, vol 147 (25 June 1970) p 1264
Landi 1994
Landi, Ann, 'Saving Graces: Two British Museums Keep Three Graces in the United Kingdom', *Art News*, vol 93 (Oct 1994) pp 61–62
Landow 1986
Landow, George P, 'A Check List of the Writings of John Lucas Tupper, Friend of the Pre-Raphaelites', *Journal of Pre-Raphaelite Studies*, vol 7 (1986) pp 63–68
Lane 1960
Lane, Arthur, 'Chelsea Porcelain Figures and the Modeller Joseph Willems', *Connoisseur*, vol 145 (June 1960) pp 245–51
Lane 1961
Lane, Arthur, *English Porcelain Figures of the Eighteenth Century* (New York: 1961)
Lane 1993
Lane, Joan, 'Umberslade Hall, Warwickshire: a Tale of Architects and Craftsmen', *Apollo*, no 138 (July 1993) pp 37–39
Langford 1873
Langford, John Alfred, *Modern Birmingham and its Institutions: a chronicle of local events from 1841–1871*, 2 vols (?1873)
Lankheit 1962
Lankheit, K, *Florentinishe Barockplastik, 1670–1743* (Munich: 1962)
Laperriere 1991
de Laperriere, Charles Baile, *The Royal Scottish Academy Exhibitors 1826–1990, a dictionary of artists and their work in the annual exhibitions of the Royal Scottish Academy* (1991)

Laperriere 1996
de Laperriere, Charles Baile, *The Society of Female Artists Exhibitors 1855–1996* (1996)

Larkin 1954
Larkin, Oliver W, *Samuel F B Morse and American Democratic Art* (Boston: 1954)

Latimer 1893
Latimer, John, *The annals of Bristol in the eighteenth century* (Bristol: 1893)

Law 1988
Law, Brian R, *Building Oxford's Heritage: Symm and Company from 1815* (Oxford: 1998)

Lawley 1980
Lawley, Ian, 'Art and Ornament in Iron; Design and the Coalbrookdale Company', in *Design and Industry; The Effects of Industrialisation and Technical Change on Design*, History of Design ed Hamilton, Nicola and Newport, Roger (London: Design Council, 1980) pp 18–21

Lawson and Waterson 1975–6
Lawson, J, and Waterson, M, 'Pritchard as Architect and Antiquary at Powis', *National Trust Yearbook*, (1975–76) pp 8–11

Layard Papers
Correspondence and papers of Sir Henry Austen Layard (BL, Add MSS 38931-39164, 58149-58202)

Le Fanu 1960
Le Fanu, William, *A Catalogue of the Portraits and Other Paintings, Drawings and Sculptures in the Royal College of Surgeons in England* (1960)

Le Grice 1844
Le Grice, Count Hawks, *Walks through the Studii of the Sculptors at Rome*, 2 vols (Rome: 1844)

le Harivel 1988
le Harivel, Adrien, *Illustrated Summary Catalogue of Prints and Sculptures* (National Gallery of Ireland, 1988)

le May 2001
le May, Keith, 'The Westminster French Protestant Charity School: apprenticeships of former pupils, 1750–1815', *Proceedings of the Huguenot Society of London*, vol 27, no 4 (2001) pp 561–72

Le Neve
le Neve, John, *Monumenta Anglicana*, volumes covering 1600–1649, 1650–1679, 1680–1699, 1700–1715 and 1650–1718 (1717–19)

Le Neve MSS
John Le Neve, Monumenta Anglicanum, Harleian MSS (BM, 3605–3616, 5321, 6405–6418)

Leach 1976
Leach, Joseph, 'Harriet Hosmer; Feminist in Bronze and Marble', *Feminist Art Journal*, vol 5, no 2 (Summer 1976) pp 9–13

Leach 1978
Leach, Peter, 'Doncaster Mansion House, Yorkshire', *Country Life*, vol 164, no 4226 (6 July 1978) pp 18–21

Leach 1984
Leach, Peter, 'James Paine Junior: An Unbuilt Architect', *Architectural History*, vol 27 (1984) pp 392–405

Leask 1945
Leask, H G, 'Dublin Customs House: The Riverine Sculptures', *Journal of the Royal Society of Antiquaries of Ireland*, vol 75 (1945) pp 187–94

Lederer 1934
Lederer, P, 'Portraits in wax: the collections of Mrs A E Hamill', *Connoisseur*, vol 93 (1934)

Leeds 1996
Curtis, Penelope and Friedman, Terry, eds, *Leeds' Sculpture Collections, Illustrated Concise Catalogue* (1996)

Leeds 1999
Taylor, Dorcas, ed, *Leeds' Sculpture Collections: Works on Paper: Concise Catalogue* (Leeds: The Henry Moore Sculpture Trust, 1999)

Leeds 2001
Withey, Matthew, Wood, Jon and Curtis, Penelope, eds, *Leeds' Sculpture Collections: Supplement to the Concise Catalogue: Sculptures and works on paper acquired 1996–2000* (Leeds: Henry Moore Institute, 2001)

Leeds Archives 1988
An Illustrated Guide to Leeds District Archives 1938–1988 (1988)

Leeds Man 1868
A Leeds Man, *Memoirs of Eminent Men of Leeds* (Leeds: 1868)

Leeds Polytechnic exhib cat, 1845
The Journal of the Leeds Polytechnic Exhibition for providing Public Walks and Baths (Exhibition Rooms, Music-Hall, Leeds: Monday 9 June 1845)

Lees-Milne 1962
Lees-Milne, James, *Earls of Creation. Five great patrons of eighteenth-century art* (London: 1962, reprinted 2001)

Lees-Milne 1973
Lees-Milne, James, 'Stouts Hill, Uley and Hardwicke Court, Gloucestershire', *Country Life*, vol 154 (5 July 1973) pp 16–20

Lees-Milne 1976
Lees-Milne, James, *William Beckford* (Wiltshire: 1976)

Lees-Milne, 1998
Lees-Milne, James, *Through Wood and Dale* (1998)

Legg 1985
Legg, Polly, 'A Bastard Barometer', *Dorset Natural History and Archaeological Society Proceedings*, vol 107 (1985) pp 1–5

Legg 1994
Legg, Polly, 'The Bastards of Blandford: An Inventory of their Losses in the Fire of 1731', *Furniture History*, vol 30 (1994) pp 15–42

Legouix 1975
Legouix, Susan, 'John Cheere's Statue of George II', *Connoisseur*, vol 188, no 758 (April 1975) pp 278–83

Leith 1997
Leith, Ian, 'The Sculpture of the Third Exchange', in *The Royal Exchange*, ed Saunders, Ann (London Topographical Society, 1997) pp 336–48

Lenehan 1989–90
Lenehan, P, 'Edward Smyth, Dublin's Sculptor', *Irish Arts Review* (1989–1990) p 68

LEP
London Evening Post

Letters to Sanderson Miller
Dickins, Lilian, and Stanton, Mary, eds, *An Eighteenth Century Correspondence . . . letters . . . to Sanderson Miller* (1910)

Lever
Lady Lever Art Gallery, Liverpool

Levey 1977
Levey, Michael, *A Royal Subject; Portraits of Queen Charlotte*, exhib cat (National Gallery, London, 1977)

Levin 1954
Levin, Hugh, 'A Monument by Nollekens', *Country Life*, vol 115, no 2981 (4 March 1954) p 599

Levy 1989
Levy, Martin, 'George Bullock's partnership with Charles Fraser 1813–1818 and the stock in trade sale, 1819', *Furniture History*, vol 25 (1989) pp 145–213

Lewer and Dark, 1997
Lewer, D, and Dark, R, *The Temple Church in London* (1997)

Lewis 1837
Lewis, Samuel, *A Topographical Dictionary of Ireland* (London: 1837)

Lewis 1953
Lewis, Shelagh M, 'A Family of Stone Carvers, the Coxes of Northamptonshire', *Northamptonshire Past and Present*, vol 1, no 6 (1953) pp 19–38

Lewis 1961
Lewis, L, *Connoisseurs and Secret Agents in Eighteenth Century Rome* (1961)

Lewis 1965–1967
Lewis, Lesley, 'English Commemorative Sculpture in Jamaica', 16 articles *Commemorative Art* (Nov 1965–Feb 1967) pp (Nov 1965) 317; (Dec) 365–73; (Jan 1966) 19–28; (Feb) 55–62; (Mar) 77–86; (April) 124–57; (May) 158–66; (Jun) 196–201; (July) 231–37; (Aug) 254–61; (Sept) 292–99; (Oct) 326–34; (Nov) 369–75; (Dec) 405–9; (Jan 1967) 17–22; (Feb) 54–57

Lewis 1966
Lewis, Lesley, 'Wilton Monument in Jamaica', *Burlington Magazine*, vol 108 (Jan. 1966) pp 20–23

Lewis 1967
Lewis, Lesley, 'Elizabeth, Countess of Home, and her House in Portman Square', *Burlington Magazine*, vol 109 (Aug 1967) pp 443–51

Leyland 1954
Leyland, Mary, 'The Leyland Family', *Halifax Antiquarian Society Transactions* (1954) pp 29–48

Leyland 1963
Leyland, Mary, 'Letters of J B Leyland, Sculptor', *Halifax Antiquarian Society Transactions* (1963) pp 91–107

Leyland MSS
Letters (20) from Patrick Branwell Brontë to Joseph Bentley Leyland and a bound volume of transcripts of these letters with an introduction by C W Hatfield, 1842–1848, 1925 (Brotherton MSS, Leeds University MS 19c Brontë B4 and B4.1)

LGI
Leeds General Infirmary, W R Yorks

Library of the Fine Arts
Library of the Fine Arts or Repository of Painting (London: 1831–34)

Lic Vic Gen
Armytage, George J, ed, *Allegations for marriage licences issued by the vicar-general of the Archbishop of Canterbury*, Harleian Society, 4 vols (1890–92)

Licht 1967
Licht, Fred, *Sculpture: 19th and 20th Centuries* (1967)

Licht 1982
Licht, Fred, 'Eine Reduction des Grabmals der Chiara Maria Rosa Spinucci', *Weltkunst (Munich)*, vol 52, no 9 (1 May 1982) p 1259

Licht 1983
Licht, Fred, *Canova* (1983)

Liddell 1945
Liddell, Donald, 'Counterfeit Flaxman Chessmen', *Antiques Magazine*, vol 47 (May 1945) pp 276–77

LIE 1862
London International Exhibition, Official Catalogue of the Fine Art Department, London (1862)

Liebermann 1983
Liebermann, Ilene, 'The Church Monuments of Sir Francis Chantrey, R.A.', Ph D Diss (Princeton University, 1983)

Liebermann 1989
Liebermann, Ilene, 'Sir Francis Chantrey's Monument to George Washington: Sculpture and Patronage in Post-Revolutionary America', *Art Bulletin*, vol 71 (June 1989) pp 254–68

Liebermann 1990
Liebermann, Ilene, 'Sir Francis Chantrey's Early Monuments to Children, and Neoclassical Sensibilities', *Journal of the Church Monuments Society*, vol 5 (1990) pp 70–80

Liebert 1960
Liebert, Herman W, *Johnson's Head: the Story of the Bust of Dr. Samuel Johnson Taken from the Life by Joseph Nollekens, RA, in 1777* (The Johnsonians, 1960)

Liebert 1974
Liebert, Herman W, 'Portraits of the Author; Lifetime Likenesses of Samuel Johnson', in *English Portraits of the Seventeenth and Eighteenth Centuries; Papers Read at a Clark Library Seminar, April 14, 1973*, conference proceedings (Los Angeles: 1974) pp 47–95

Lieuallen 2002
Lieuallen, Rocco, 'A Sculptor for Scotland: The Life and Work of Sir John Steell, R.S.A. (1804–1891)' Ph D Diss (Edinburgh University, 2002)

LIFA
Liverpool Institution of Fine Arts

Life of Haydon 1853
Taylor, Tom, ed, *Life of Benjamin Robert Haydon historical painter from his autobiography and journals*, 3 vols (1853)

Linnell 1955
Linnell, E L S, 'Suffolk Church Monuments: A Preliminary Survey', *Proceedings of the Suffolk Institute of Archaeology and History*, vol 27 (1955) pp 1–24

Linnell and Wearing 1952
Linnell, Charles Lawrence Scruton, and Wearing, Stanley J, *Norfolk Church Monuments* (Ipswich: 1952)

Linstrum 1974
Linstrum, Derek, *A Catalogue of the Drawings Collection of the Royal Institute of British Architects: the Wyatt Family* (Farnborough: 1974) pp 17–18

Lippert 1981
Lippert, Catherine, 'An Altar Dedicated to Bacchus', *Decorative Arts Society News*, vol 2, no 4 (Dec 1981) pp 1–6

Lipscomb 1847
Lipscomb, George, *The History and Antiquities of the County of Buckingham*, 4 vols (1847)

Lipscombe 1987
Lipscombe, R W, 'The "Diffusion of Knowledge and Taste", John Flaxman and the Improvement of the Study Facilities at the Royal Academy', *Walpole Society*, vol 53 (1987) pp 226–38

Liscombe 1976
Liscombe, Rhodri Windsor, 'Commencement of Real Art', *Apollo*, no 103 (Jan 1976) pp 34–39

Liscombe 1977
Liscombe, Rhodri Windsor, 'Canova, Aberdeen and the Pitt Monument', *Burlington Magazine*, vol 119 (Oct 1977) pp 700–3

Lister 1981
Lister, R, *George Richmond: a critical biography* (London: 1981)

Lit Gaz
Literary Gazette

Little 1952
Little, Bryan, 'A Provincial Sculptor', *Country Life*, vol 111, no 2889 (30 May 1952) p 1659

Little 1966
Little, Bryan, 'Britain's Oldest Theatre', *Architecture and Building News*, vol 229, no 20 (18 May 1966) pp 889–90

Liverpool Ac
Liverpool Academy

Liversedge 1990
Liversedge, M J H, 'Two Portrait Medallions by Michael Rysbrack', *Burlington Magazine*, vol 132, no 1053 (Dec 1990) pp 870–73

Liversidge 1978
Liversidge, M. J. H., *The Bristol High Cross* (Bristol: Bristol Branch of the Historical Association, 1978)

Llanover 1861
Llanover, Lady, ed, *The Autobiography and Correspondence of Mary Granville, Mrs Delany: with interesting reminiscences. . .*, 3 vols (1861)

Lloyd 1995
Lloyd, Thomas, 'Carmarthen Town Hall: the Architect Revealed!', *Georgian Group Journal* (1995) pp 125–26

LMA
London Metropolitan Archives

LMA, Cavendish Square Accounts
Carving Bills for 18 Cavendish Square, 'Plans etc Cavendish Square House by Henry Keene for Thomas Bridges' (LMA, 85/223–264)

LMG
Leeds Museum and Art Galleries

Loch 1934
Loch, Gordon, *The family of Loch* (Edinburgh: 1934)

Lock 1944
Lock, Max, 'Roubiliac's Handel', *Architectural Review*, vol 95 (Jan 1944) p 27

Loeber 1970
Loeber, Rolf, 'An Introduction to the Dutch Influence in Seventeenth and Eighteenth Century Ireland: An Unexplored Field', *Bulletin of the Irish Georgian Society*, vol 13, nos 2 and 3 (April–Sept 1970) pp 19–29

Loeber 1983
Loeber, Rolf, 'Arnold Quellin's and Grinling Gibbons' Monuments for Anglo-Irish Patrons', *Studies-Dublin*, vol 72, no 285 (1983) pp 84–101

Loewe 1983
Loewe, Louis, ed, *Diaries of Sir Moses and Lady Montefiore. A facsimile of the 1890 edition introduced by Professor Raphael Loewe with a new index by Walter Schwab*, 2 vols (London: Jewish Historical Society of England, 1983)

Loire 1998
Loire, Stephane, 'La Donation Lemme au Musee du Louvre', *Revue du Louvre*, vol 48, no 1 (Feb 1998) pp 18–19

Lond Stu 1944 (1)
'Bust by A Carlini', *London Studio*, vol 27, no 127 (March 1944) p 73

Lond Stu 1944 (2)
'Portrait by E Landseer', *London Studio*, vol 27, no 127 (March 1944) p 80

London Fine Art 1968
British Sculpture 1850–1914. A Loan Exhibition of Sculpture and Medals Sponsored by the Victorian Society, exhib cat (London Fine Art Society, 1968)

London Mag
London Magazine, or Gentleman's Monthly Intelligencer

London Marriage Licences
Calendar of the Bishop of London's Marriage Licences, 1740–45 (Guildhall MSS, 10091G/16)

London Topog Soc
London Topographical Society

Longleat HA, 1687–1712
Thomas Thynne, Ist Viscount Weymouth, House Archives (Longleat, Wilts, Warminster, 275; 1 Jan 1687–23 April 1712)

Longleat HA, 1800–1818
Thomas Thynne, 2nd Marquess of Bath, House Archive, 1800–1818 (Longleat, Wilts, Warminster, NMR 0 WMR 0)

Longridge 1954
Longridge, Richard, *Parish Church of St Nicholas, Silton, Dorset* (Silton: 1954)

Longstaffe 1854
Longstaffe, W, *History and Antiquities of the Parish of Darlington* (London and Newcastle: 1854)

Lonsdale 1866
Lonsdale, Henry, *The Life and Works of Musgrave Lewthwaite Watson* (London: 1866)

Lord 1986 (1)
Lord, John, 'Patronage and Church Monuments 1660–1794: A Regional Study', *Journal of the Church Monuments Society*, vol 1, no 2 (1986) pp 95–105

Lord 1986 (2)
Lord, John, 'The Patronage of Sculpture in Lincolnshire 1660–1800' Ph D Diss (University of Leeds, 1986)

Lord 1988
Lord, John, 'Joseph Nollekens and Lord Yarborough: Documents and Drawings', *Burlington Magazine*, vol 130 (Dec 1988) pp 915–19

Lord 1990 (1)
Lord, John, 'A Pugilist's Monument: The Parkyns Tomb at Bunny, Nottinghamshire', *Journal of the Church Monuments Society*, vol 5 (1990) pp 64–69

Lord 1990 (2)
Lord, John, 'J. M. Rysbrack and a Group of East Midlands Commissions', *Burlington Magazine*, vol 132 (Dec. 1990) pp 866–70

Lord 1992
Lord, John, 'The Building of the Mausoleum at Brocklesby, Lincolnshire', *Journal of the Church Monuments Society*, vol 7 (1992) pp 85–96

Lord 1994
Lord, John, 'Repairing and Cleaning of the Said Burying Places', *Journal of the Church Monuments Society*, vol 9 (1994) pp 83–92

Lord 1997
Lord, John, 'Richard Hayward: An Early and Some Later Commissions', *Journal of the Church Monuments Society*, vol 12 (1997) pp 67–76

Lord 2000
Lord, Peter, *Imaging the Nation: The Visual Culture of Wales*, vol. 2 (2000)

Lord 2002
Lord, John, 'A Decade of Bertie Memorials in Lincolnshire', *Journal of the Church Monuments Society*, vol 17 (2002) pp 107–13

Lough and Merson, 1987
Lough, John, and Merson, Elizabeth, *John Graham Lough, 1798–1876: A Northumbrian Sculptor* (Woodbridge: 1987)

Lough/Forster
John Graham Lough, letters to John Forster, Forster Collection 1854–1856 (NAL, Forster Coll)

Lough/Howard
Letter from John Graham Lough to Henry Howard, *c*1856 (State University of New York, Buffalo)

Louvre 1988
Musee du Louvre, Nouvelles Acquisitions du Departement des Sculptures, 1984–1987 (Paris: 1988)

Louvre 1992
Baker, Malcolm, 'Nouvelles Acquisitions du département des Sculptures 1988–1991', *Revue du Louvre et des Musées de France* (1992) pp 71–73

Loveday 1957
Loveday, A Knight, 'Statuary at Stowe', *Country Life*, vol 122, no 3160 (8 Aug 1957) p 267

Lovejoy 1946
Lovejoy, Edward Daland, 'Poker drawings of Ball-Hughes', *Antiques Magazine*, vol 50 (Sept 1946) p 175

Lovell 1986
Lovell, V M E, 'Benjamin Gott of Armley House, Leeds, 1762–1840; Patron of the Arts', Miscellany, vol 18, part 2 *Proceedings of the Thoresby Society*, vol 59, part 2, no 130 (1986) pp 177–221

Lowe 1986
Lowe, Jill, 'Newby Hall: Two Late Eighteenth-Century Inventories', *Furniture History*, vol 22 (1986) pp 135–75

Lowther Drawings
Colvin, Howard, Mordaunt Crook, J, and Friedman, Terry, *Architectural Drawings for Lowther Castle, Westmorland*, Society of Architects of Great Britain (1980)

LPL
Lambeth Palace Library

LSFA
Liverpool Society of Fine Arts

Lucas 1870
Lucas, Richard Cockle, *An essay on art; especially that of painting, done by R.C. Lucas, sculptor, in the sky parlour of his Tower of the Winds, Chilworth, Romsey, Hants* (1870)

Lucas 1910
Lucas, Perceval, *Heathfield Memorials: Collected from the Parish Records and other Unpublished Manuscripts* (1910)

Lucas Autobiography
'The Life of an Artist; Being the Autobiography of R. C. Lucas, Sculptor of Chilworth Tower, Hants', 1861 (Southampton City Cultural Services)

Lucas Fragment
Fragment of autobiographical pieces by Richard Cockle Lucas, 1863 (Hartley Library, University of Southampton, Cope cabinet 73 LUC)

Lucas Miscellanea
Chilworth Tower and Richard Cockle Lucas, selected items from information collected by M L Durrant, typescripts, MSS and photocopies of articles, 1980 (Hartley Library, University of Southampton, Cope quarto CHL 72 TOW)

Lucas Monument
'My Monument', an autobiography by Richard Cockle Lucas, with several views of his studio or gallery, 1878 (BM P&D, inv no 1919-8-5-1)

Lucas/Owen
Letter from Richard Cockle Lucas to Sir Richard Owen, nd (BL, Add MS 39954 fol 311)

Lucas/Peel
Letters from Richard Cockle Lucas to Sir Robert Peel, Peel Papers 1845–1846 (BL, Add 40579 fols 388, 389; 40588, fol 274)

Lucie-Smith 1979
Lucie-Smith, Edward, 'Flaxman in Context', *Illustrated London News*, vol 267, no 6975 (1979) p 131

Lugt
Lugt, Frits, *Repertoire des Catalogues des Ventes* (The Hague: 1953)

Lukitsh 2005
Lukitsh, Joanne, *Thomas Woolner: seeing sculpture through photography*, Henry Moore Institute Essays on Sculpture, no 49, published to accompany the exhibition at the Henry Moore Institute, 5 Nov 2005–5 Jan 2006 (2005)

Lutyens 1968
Lutyens, Mary, 'Portraits of Effie', *Apollo*, no 87 (March 1968) pp 190–97

Lysons 1792–1811
Lysons, Rev Daniel, *The Environs of London*, 7 vols (1792–1811)

Lysons 1806–22
Lysons, Daniel, *Magna Britannia: being a concise topographical account of the several counties of Great Britain*, 6 vols (1806–1822)

Ma 1996
Ma, J F, 'Church Monuments in Norfolk and Norwich Before 1850: A Regional Study in Medieval and Post-Medieval Material Culture' Ph D Diss (University of East Anglia, 1996)

Macdonald 1982
Macdonald, Katharine, 'Alexander Munro, the Pre-Raphaelite Brotherhood and the "Unmentionable" ', *Apollo*, no 115 (March 1982) pp 190–97

Mace 1976
Mace, Rodney, *Trafalgar Square: Emblem of Empire* (London: 1976)

Mace 1998
Mace, Angela, *Architecture in Manuscript 1601–1996* (1998)

Mackay 1995
Mackay, James A, *Dictionary of Sculptors in Bronze* (Woodbridge: Antique Collectors Club, 1995)

Mackenzie 1825
Mackenzie, E, *An historical, topographical, and desriptive view of the county of Northumberland*, 2 vols (2nd ed, 1825)

Mackenzie 1827
Mackenzie, Eneas, *Description and Historical Account of Newcastle*, 2 vols (1827)

Mackenzie Reminiscences
Reminiscences of Samuel Mackenzie, typescript, by J Mackenzie (Royal Scottish Academy Library)

Mackerness 1978
Mackerness, Eric, 'Art and Instruction in a Nineteenth-Century City: Sheffield', *Art History*, vol 1, no 3 (Sept 1978) pp 253–62

MacMichael 1977
MacMichael, N H, *Westminster Abbey Official Guide* (1977)

MacPherson 1878
MacPherson, Gerardine, *Memoirs of the Life of Anna Jameson* (1878)

Macready Diaries
Toynbee, William, ed, *The Diaries of William Charles Macready*, 2 vols (London: 1912)

Maddison 2001
Maddison, John, *Felbrigg Hall* (National Trust, *c*.2001)

Madocks Family Papers
Papers of William Alexander Madocks (1773–1828) and his family, Portmadock Archive (NLW, MSS 1–512)

Mag Antiq 1945
'Wedgwood Medallion Profile by J Flaxman', *Antiques Magazine*, vol 47 (Jan 1945) p 29

Mag Antiq 1947
'Wax Portraits by Ball-Hughes in Philadelphia Museum', *Antiques Magazine*, vol 52 (July 1947) p 58

Mag Antiq 1952
'Flaxman's Wedgwood Vase Decorations: Homer, Virgil', *Antiques Magazine*, vol 61 (May 1952) p 403

Mag Antiq 1954
'Portrait in Pink and White Wax Ascribed to J. C. Lochee', *Antiques Magazine*, vol 65 (March 1954) p 199

Mag Antiq 1955 (1)
'Study by Ball Hughes in Norfolk', *Antiques Magazine*, vol 68 (July 1955) p 76

Mag Antiq 1955 (2)
'Wedgwood Portrait Medallion by Flaxman', *Antiques Magazine*, vol 68 (Dec 1955) p 569

Mag Antiq 1957
'Portrait by E Landseer', *Antiques Magazine*, vol 71 (May 1957) p 446

Mag Antiq 1958
'Bust of George III by John Nost the Younger', *Antiques Magazine*, vol 74 (July 1958) p 73

Mag Antiq 1967
'Statuary for an Adam House', *Antiques Magazine*, vol 91, no 2 (Feb 1967) p 186

Magrath 1921
Magrath, J R, *The Queen's College*, 2 vols (Oxford: 1921)

Mainstone 1976
Mainstone, Madelaine, *Roubiliac's Handel*, V&A "Masterpieces", no 4 (1976)

Malcolm 1803–7
Malcolm, James Peller, *Londinium Redivivum or an Ancient History and Modern Description of London*, 4 vols (1803–7)

Malden 1977
Malden, John, *John Henning 1771–1851 – ". . A Very Ingenious Modeller . ."* (Paisley: Renfrew District Council, Museum and Art Galleries Dept, 1977)

Mallet 1962
Mallet, J V G, 'Some Portrait Medallions by Roubiliac', *Burlington Magazine*, vol 104 (April 1962) pp 153–58

Mallet 1967
Mallet, J V G, 'Hogarth's Pug in Porcelain', *Bulletin of the Victoria and Albert Museum*, vol 3, no 2 (April 1967)

Mallet 1974
Mallet, J V G, 'Wedgwood and the Rococo', *Apollo*, no 99 (May 1974) pp 320–31

Manc A
Manchester Academy

Manc Art Treas Exhib
Manchester Art Treasures Exhibition

Manc Inst
Manchester Institution

Manc Inst Letter Book
Out letter Book, Royal Manchester Institution 30 Oct 1848–21 Sept 1853 (Manchester Archives, M6/1/49/5)

Manc Cont Art Exhib
Manchester Contemporary Art Exhibition

Manchester Art Treasures 1857
Catalogue of the Art Treasures of the United Kingdom (Manchester: 1857)

Manchester CAG
Manchester City Art Galleries

Manco 1991
Manco, Jean, and Kelly, Francis, 'Lulworth Castle from 1700', *Architectural History*, vol 34 (1991) pp 145–170

Mander 1964
Mander, R, 'Best Dressed Woman', *Apollo*, no 79 (March 1964) p 250

Manners 1930
Manners, Lady Victoria, 'Garden Sculpture by Caius Gabriel Cibber', *Country Life*, vol 68 (1930) p 382

Manning 1932
Manning, Elfrida, *Thomas Thornycroft, Bronze & Steel: The Art & Life of Thomas Thornycroft, Sculptor & Engineer* (Shipston-on-Stour: 1932)

Manning 1982
Manning, Elfrida, *Marble & Bronze: The Art & Life of Hamo Thornycroft* (London: 1982)

Marchand 1973–94
Marchand, Leslie A, ed, *Byron's Letters and Journals*, 13 vols (London: 1973–94)

Mariacher 1975
Mariacher, Giovanni, 'Unfamiliar Masterpieces of North Italian Sculpture', *Apollo*, no 102 (Sept 1975) pp 174–89

Marks 1981
Marks, Arthur, 'Statue of King George III in New York and the Iconology of Regicide', *American Art Journal*, vol 13, no 3 (Summer 1981) pp 61–82

Marochetti/Ashburton
Four letters from Carlo, Baron Marochetti and his family to Louisa, Lady Ashburton, Ashburton Papers 1859–1868 (NLS, 11388)

Marsden 1992
Marsden, Jonathan, *Plas Newydd* (National Trust, 1999)

Marsden 1998
Marsden, Jonathan, 'William Penn and Sir Francis Dashwood's Sawmill', *Georgian Group Journal*, vol 8 (1998) pp 143–50

Marsden and Hardy 2001
Marsden, Jonathan, and Hardy, John, ' "O fair Britannia Hail": The "most superb" state coach', *Apollo*, vol 153, no 468 (Feb 2001) pp 3–12

*Marsh c*1996
Marsh, Michael, *Benedetto Pistrucci, Principal Engraver and Chief Medallist of the Royal Mint: 1783–1855* (Cambridge: *c*1996)

Marshall 1894
Catalogue of the Works of the Late William Calder Marshall exhibited at his studio, 115 Ebury Street, London, S.W. (London: 1894)

Marshall 1895
Catalogue of the works of the late William Calder Marshall, R.A., H.R.S.A., Chev. Leg. Hon. exhibited at his studios 115, Ebury Street, London, S.W. (London: 1895)

Marshall Album
Some of the Works of W. Calder Marshall, R.A. (Born 1813. Died 1894). From Photographs by his Son Charles J. Marshall, A.R.I.B.A., 1894 (HMI)

Marshall Journals
Journals of William Calder Marshall, 1836–1838 (NLS)

Marshall Papers (1)
Household and studio accounts, travel documents and miscellaneous papers of William Calder Marshall, 1839–1860 (HMI)

Marshall Papers (2)
Diaries, notes and account books of William Calder Marshall, 1871–1878 (RA)

Marshall/Smirke
Letters from William Calder Marshall to Sydney Smirke, Smirke correspondence 1867–1868 (BL, Add MS 60745 fol 78, 60756 fol 119)

Marshall/Stephens
Letters from William Calder Marshall to F G Stephens, Miscellaneous letters and papers 1884 (BL, Add 41567 ff 95, 96)

Martin 1972
Martin, R A, 'The Life and Work of Richard James Wyatt (1795–1850), Sculptor' BA Diss (University of Leeds, 1972)

Martin 1974
Martin, G, 'Founding of the National Gallery in London', *Connoisseur*, vol 187 (Sept 1974) pp 48–53

Martin 1978
Martin, M, *A Wayward Genius: Neville Northy Burnard, Cornish Sculptor, 1818–1878, A Study* (Padstow: 1978)

Martin 2000
Martin, Frank, 'Camillo Rusconi in English Collections', in *The Lustrous Trade: Material Culture and the History of Sculpture in England and Italy, c1700–c1860*, ed Sicca, Cinzia and Yarrington, Alison (2000) pp 49–66

Martin Gonzalez 1971
Martin Gonzalez, Juan Jose, 'La Escultura en el Museo de Arte del Siglo XIX', *Goya*, no 104 (Sept 1971) pp 112–13

Martyn 1767
Thomas, Martyn, *The English Connoisseur* (1767)

Martyn 1980
Martyn, C A, 'Thomas Gray's Notes on Painting and Sculpture made during a Tour of Italy, 1739–1741' Ph D Diss (Leicester University, 1980)

Maruffi Ceccopieri 1993
Maruffi Ceccopieri, Franco, 'Il Soggiorno Romano di John Gibson e i Suoi Rapporti Artistici con Vincenzo Camuccini', *Strenna dei Romanisti*, (1993) pp 63–72

Masnsion House Comm
Corporation of London, Mansion House Committee, 1735–55; 1755–77 (CLRO Guildhall, LMA COL/MH/ MSH/01/01/1)

Mason 1811
Mason, William, *The Works of William Mason*, 4 vols (1811)

Mason 1839
Mason, William Hayley, *Goodwood . . . with a catalogue raisonné* (1839)

Mason 1937
Mason, Frances Norton, *John Norton and Sons, Merchants of London and Virginia.. Papers from their Counting House* (Richmond, Virginia: 1937)

Masons' Co, App binding bk (1)
Masons' Co, Apprentice binding book, 1663–94; 1694–1756; 1772–96 (Guildhall Lib, 5313)

Masons' Co, App binding bk (2)
Masons' Co, Apprentice binding book, 1772–96 (Guildhall Lib, 5310)

Masons' Co, App binding bk & orphans' tax book
Masons' Co, Apprentice binding book & orphans' tax book, 1694–1856 (Guildhall Lib, 5312)

Masons' Co, Apprentices
Masons' Co, Alphabetical list of apprentices, 1694–1795 (Guildhall Lib, 5309)

Masons' Co, Assistants
List of Assistants and the Livery of the Mason's Company, c1740 (Guildhall MSS, 9470)

Masons' Co, Court Books
Masons' Co, Court Books, 1677–94; 1695–1722; 1722–51; 1751–96; 1784–1805; 1805–39 (Guildhall Lib, 5303/1; 5304/1; 5304/2; 5304/3; 5304/4; 5304/5; 5304/6)

Masons' Co, Freedom Register
Masons' Co, Freedom register, 1663–94 (Guildhall Lib, 5313)

Masons' Co, Freedom register & stamp duty book
Masons' Co, Freedom register & stamp duty book, 1694–1948 (Guildhall Lib, 5307)

Masons' Co, Freemen
Masons' Company List of Freemen 1677–1795 (Guildhall, MS 5308)

Masons' Co, List of Company Members
Masons' Co, List of Company Members, 1708 (Guildhall Lib, 5987/1 & 2)

Masons' Co, Livery Lists
Masons' Co, Livery Lists, c1685 & 1708–34 (Guildhall Lib, 5982)

Masons' Co, Masters and Wardens
A List of the Masters and Wardens of the Company of Masons London from 1675–1708 (Guildhall Lib, MS 5981)

Masons' Co, Quarterage book (1)
Masons' Co, early quarterage book (Guildhall Lib, 5303/1)

Masons' Co, Quarterage book (2)
Masons' Co, Quarterage book, 1663–76, 1696–1702 (Guildhall Lib, 5313)

Masons' Co, Quarterage book (3)
Masons' Co, Quarterage book, 1714 (Guildhall Lib, 5987/3)

Masons' Co, Rebuilding accounts
Masons' Co, Rebuilding accounts (Guildhall Lib, 5322)

Masons' Co, Rough minutes & accts
Masons' Co, Rough minutes & accounts, 1732 (Guildhall Lib, 5979/13)

Mass Hist Soc
Massachusetts Historical Society

Massingberd/Chester
Letters from Sir John Chester to Burrell Massingberd, papers of the Massingberd-Mundy family of Ormsby 1710–1724 (Lincs RO, 2-MM/B/21)

Masterpieces 1994
Roscoe, Ingrid, and others, *Masterpieces from Yorkshire Houses* (York City Art Gall: 1994)

Matthews 1820
Matthews, Henry, *The diary of an invalid: being the journal of a tour in pursuit of health in Portugal, Italy, Switzerland and France in the years 1817, 1818 and 1819* (London: John Murray, 1820)

Matthews 1911
Matthews, T, *The Biography of John Gibson, R.A., Sculptor, Rome* (London: Heinemann, 1911)

Matthews 2004
Matthews, Samantha, *Poetical Remains: Poets' Graves, Bodies and Books in the Nineteenth Century* (Oxford: Oxford University Press, 2004)

Matucci 2003
Matucci, Benedetta, *Aristodemo Costoli. 'Religiosa Poesia' nella scultura dell'Ottocento* (2003)

Mauchline 1992
Mauchline, Mary, *Harewood House* (Moorland Publishing, second ed, 1992)

Maynard/Middleton
Correspondence from Lord Maynard to Conyers Middleton of Stanley, nd (BL, Add MS 32,457-32,455, fol 166)

MC
Mercers' Company Archives

MC, GR
Gresham Repertories, Worshipful Company of Mercers 16 vols, 1629–1860 (Mercers' Hall, Ironmonger Lane, City of London)

MCAG
Manchester City Art Galleries

McCarthy 1973 (1)
McCarthy, Michael, 'James Lovell and his Sculptures at Stowe', *Burlington Magazine*, vol 115 (April 1973) pp 220–32

McCarthy 1973 (2)
McCarthy, Michael, 'Sir Roger Newdigate: Drawings for Copt Hall, Essex and Arbury Hall, Warwickshire', *Architectural History*, vol 16 (1973) pp 26–36

McCarthy 1979
McCarthy, Michael, 'Sir Roger Newdigate, Arbury Hall, Copped Hall and John Conyers', *Burlington Magazine*, vol 121, no 915 (June 1979) p 382

McCarthy 1994
McCarthy, Steve, *The Crystal Palace Dinosaurs: the Story of the World's first Prehistoric Sculptures* (Crystal Palace Foundation, London, 1994)

McCoubrey 1990
McCoubrey, John, 'The Hero of a Hundred Fights: Turner, Schiller and Wellington', *Turner Studies*, vol 10, no 2 (Winter 1990) pp 7–11

McCracken 1997
McCracken, Penny, 'Sculptor Mary Thornycroft and her Artist Children', *Women's Art Journal*, vol 17, no 5 (Fall/Winter 1997) pp 3–8

McDowall 1876
McDowall, William, *Memorials of St Michael's, the Old Parish Church, and of Dumfries* (Edinburgh: 1876)

McEvansoneya 1993
McEvansoneya, Philip, 'A Note on Hubert le Sueur and Isaac Besnier', *Burlington Magazine*, vol 135 (Aug 1993) pp 532–35

McEvansoneya 2001
McEvansoneya, Philip, 'Lord Egremont and Flaxman's "St Michael Overcoming Satan" ', *Burlington Magazine*, vol 143, no 1179 (June 2001) pp 351–59

McEwan 1994
McEwan, Peter J M, *Dictionary of Scottish Art and Architecture* (Woodbridge: 1994)

McKay 1986
McKay, I, 'Franklin bust on the block', *Maine Antique Digest*, vol 14, no 4 (April 1986) pp 16–17

McKay 1992–3
McKay, Peter, 'A Patron of Promise: Charles, 7th Earl of Northampton', *Northamptonshire Past and Present*, vol 8, no 4 (1992–93) pp 263–73

McKendry 1962
McKendry, John J, 'Antiquity Smith', *Bulletin of the Metropolitan Museum of Art, New York*, no 20 (Feb 1962) pp 202–11

McKenzie 1999
McKenzie, Ray, *Sculpture in Glasgow*, an illustrated handbook (1999)

McKenzie 2002
McKenzie, Ray, *Public Sculpture of Glasgow*, Public Sculpture of Britain 5 (Liverpool: 2002)

Mclean 1991
Mclean, Rita, 'A Matthew Boulton Medal: a Recent Acquisition for Birmingham', *Medal*, no 19 (Autumn 1991) pp 43–45

McParland 1976
McParland, Edward, 'Cherishing A Palladian Masterpiece, The Provost's House, Trinity College, Dublin – II (Hewetson)', *Country Life*, vol 160 (1976) p 1106

McParland 1994
McParland, Edward, 'A Monument by Grinling Gibbons', *Irish Arts Review*, vol 10 (1994) pp 108–9

Meara 1991
Meara, D, *A W N Pugin and the Revival of Memorial Brasses* (1991)

Meldrum 1987
Meldrum, Edward, *Aberdeen of Old* (1987)

Meller 1978
Meller, H, 'Edward Blore (1787–1879); From Engraver to Architect', *Country Life*, vol 164, no 4241 (19 Oct 1978) pp 1205–6

Mellor 1999
Mellor, Hugh, *London Cemeteries* (1999)

Melton 1961
Melton, James, 'Charles Rogers and his Furniture', *Apollo*, vol 73 (Feb 1961)

Melville 1967
Melville, R, 'Drawings for Sculptural Projects Made in England Between 1680 and 1860 Shown in Print Room of the Victoria and Albert Museum', *Architectural Review*, vol 141 (Feb 1967) p 140

Menai Francis essay
'From Obscurity to Fame. John Gibson RA, the world-famous Welsh marble sculptor', essay in Welsh, by Rev B Menai Francis (NLW, MS 12622B)

Mercers Acts of Ct
Corporation of London, Mercers' Company, Acts of Court, 1669–1675 (CLRO Guildhall)

Mercers Misc Ms
Corporation of London, Mercers' Company, Misc Ms, 1670–71 (CLRO Guildhall, 17.1)

Mercers S & R W Accts
Corporation of London, Mercers' Company, Second & Renter Wardens Accounts, 1666–71; 1671–76; 1676–82 (CLRO Guildhall)

Mercers' Acts of Court
Marginal Notes from the Acts of Court, Committee for Rebuilding the Hall & Chapel, Mercers' Company 1669–1675 (Mercers' Hall, City of London)

Merkel 1994
Merkel, Kerstin, 'Pierre-Etienne Monnot: das Marmorbad in Kassel', *Gartenkunst*, vol 6, no 2 (1994) pp 249–80

Meslay 2004
Meslay, Olivier, *English Art in the Collections of the Institut de France* (Chantilly, Musée Condé, 2004)

Met NY
Metropolitan Museum of Art, New York

Metcalfe 1977
Metcalfe, P, *The Halls of the Fishmongers' Company* (1977)

Meteyard 1866
Meteyard, Eliza, *Life of Josiah Wedgwood*, 2 vols (1866)

Methuen Accounts
Paul Methuen, Personal Day Account Books, 1760–73; 1774–95 (Wilts and Swindon R O, 1742/8113; 1742/8113)

Metzl 1954
Metzl, Ervine, 'John Flaxman, English Designer and Illustrator', *American Artist*, vol 18 (Nov 1954) pp 38–43

Meyer 1976
Meyer, Jerry D., 'Benjamin West's St Stephen Altar-Piece: A Study in Late Eighteenth-Century Protestant Church Patronage and English History Painting', *Burlington Magazine*, vol 118 (Sept 1976) pp 634–41

MFAB
Museum of Fine Arts, Boston

MHCM
Mansion House, London, Committee Minutes, 1734; 1755–77 (CLRO, Guildhall)

Michalski 1996
Michalski, Sergiusz, 'Drzwi Smierci w Sepulkralnej Rzezbie Francuskiej XVIII Wieku', *Ik*, vol 11 (1996) pp 81–88

Mildmay Accounts
Mildmay Account Book, 1732–32 (Hants RO, 15M50/31)

Millar 1995
Millar, Oliver, 'Artists and Craftsmen in the service of Sir Stephen Fox and his family', *Burlington Magazine*, vol 137 (August 1995) pp 518–28

Miller 1804
Miller, Edward, *The History and Antiquities of Doncaster and its Vicinity* (Doncaster: 1804)

Miller 1993
Miller, Lynn, 'Britannia', *Proceedings of the Wedgwood Society*, (1993) pp 22–36

Milles 1735
Milles, Jeremiah, *Description of Stowe* (1735)

Milton 1947
Milton, E R, 'An eighteenth century cathedral craftsman', *Lincoln Diocesan Magazine*, vol 63 (1947) pp 212–14

Missirini 1824
Missirini, Melchior, *Della Vita di Antonio Canova Libri Quattro* (Prato: 1824; reprinted with an introduction by F Leone, Bassano 2004)

Mitchell 1992
Mitchell, L G, *Charles James Fox* (1992)

ML
Museum of London

MMAG
Maidstone Museum and Art Gallery, Kent

MMCH
McCord Museum of Canadian History, Montreal

Mobus 2003
Mobus, Melody, 'Christopher Kempster 1627–1715: His Place in Contemporary Architecture' BA Diss (OUDCE, Oxford University, 2003)

MOD
Ministry of Defence

Molesworth 1951
Molesworth, Hender Delves, *Sculpture in England: Renaissance to Early 18th Century* (1951)

Molesworth 1954
Molesworth, Hender Delves, *Baroque, Rococo and Neoclassical Sculpture*, V&A Large Picture Book, 2 (1954)

Mongan 1947
Mongan, Agnes, 'Ingres and the Antique', *Journal of the Warburg and Courtauld Institutes*, vol 10 (1947) pp 1–13

Monkhouse 1875
Monkhouse, W Cosmo, *The Works of John Henry Foley, R.A. Sculptor* (London: ?1875)

Monson Accounts
Lord Monson, Accounts, *c*1683 (Lincs CRO, 28B/6/1/17)

Monthly Mag
The Monthly Magazine; or, British Register, 1796–1826

Moore 1851
Moore, William, *The Gentleman's Society at Spalding: its origin and progress* (London: 1851)

Moore 1877
Moore, R W, *A History of the Parish Church of Leeds* (1877)

Moore 1934
Moore, William, *The Story of Australian Art*, 2 vols (1934)

Moore 1985 (1)
Moore, Susan, 'Hail! Gods of our Fore-fathers; Rysbrack's "Lost" Saxon Deities at Stowe', *Country Life*, vol 177, no 4563 (31 Jan 1985) pp 250–51

Moore 1985 (2)
Moore, Andrew, *Norfolk & the Grand Tour* (Norfolk Museums Service, 1985)

Moore 2002
Moore, Andrew and Dukelskaya, Larissa, *A Capital Collection, Houghton Hall and the Hermitage* (New Haven and London: 2002)

Moore Family Pictures
'Family Pictures of William Moore Esq left to go with the estate and not yet delivered to Lord North,' including details of a painting lent to Thomas Carter I, North Archives *c*1735 (Bodl, C14, F19)

Morden 1897
Morden, William Edward, *The history of Tooting-Graveney: compiled from original documents* (London: 1897)

Morescalchi 1955
Morescalchi, Bernardo, introd, *Mostra di Benedetto Pistrucci (1784–1855)*, exhib cat (Palazzo Braschi, Roma: 1955–56)

Morn Post
Morning Post

Morris 1971
Morris, Edward, 'John Gibson's Satan', *Journal of the Warburg and Courtauld Institutes*, vol 34 (1971) p 397

Morris 1987
Morris, Barbara, 'Flaxman's Illustrations to Homer as a Design Source for Glass Decoration in the 1870s', *Burlington Magazine*, vol 129 (May 1987) pp 318–21

Morris 2002
Morris, Edward, 'The public sculpture of Britain', *The Sculpture Journal*, vol 8 (2002) pp 25–35

Morris and Roberts 1998
Morris, Edward, and Roberts, E, *The Liverpool Academy and other Exhibitors of Contemporary Art in Liverpool 1774–1867* (Liverpool: 1998)

Mortimer 1763
Mortimer, Thomas, *The Universal Director; or, the Nobleman's and Gentleman's True Guide to the Masters and Professors of the Liberal and Polite Arts. . .* (1763)

Morton and Wess 1993
Morton, Alan Q, and Wess, Jane A, *Public and Private Science: the King George III Collection* (1993)

Moser 1803
Moser, Joseph, 'Jervase, the Painter, and Carter, the Sculptor', Vestiges, Collected and Recollected by Joseph Moser, *European Magazine*, vol 44 (Sept 1803) pp 178–79

Mossman & Co Papers
Papers of J & G Mossman & Co, monumental masons, including balance sheets, sales ledgers, day books, job books and orders, 1833–1967 (Private coll)

Mossman Job Book
Job book of William Mossman (photocopy), 1835–39 (Glasgow City Archives, GB243/TD110)

Mote Building Accs
Accounts for building the Mote, near Maidstone, Kent, Earls of Romney manuscripts 1793–1801 (Centre for Kentish Studies, U1644/A2)

Mottley 1734–35
Mottley, John, *A Survey of the Cities of London and Westminster, Borough of Southwark, and parts adjacent . . . by Robert Seymour Esq*, 2 vols (1734–35)

Mowl 1991
Mowl, Timothy, *To Build the Second City: Architects and Craftsmen of Georgian Bristol* (Bristol: 1991)

Mowl 1994
Mowl, Timothy, 'Welford Park, a New House for John Jackson', *Georgian Group Journal* (1994) pp 51–54

MS Inscriptions
Collection of Inscriptions upon monuments, and under busts, executed by Joseph Nollekens, Esq (Beinecke Library, Yale University)

Mulcahy 2000 (1)
Mulcahy, Gerardine, 'Hull Sculptors', in *Artists and Craftsmen of Hull and East Yorkshire*, ed Credland, Arthur G, (Hull Museums and Art Gallery, 2000) pp 41–60

Mulcahy 2000 (2)
Mulcahy, Gerardine, 'The Earles and the Keyworths: two Nineteenth-Century families of Sculptors from Kingston-upon-Hull' Ph D Diss (University of Leeds: 2000)

Mulcahy 2001
Mulcahy, Gerardine, 'An Eminent Sculptor: William Day Keyworth Jun. of London & Hull', *Journal of the Church Monuments Society*, vol 16 (2001) pp 126–34

Mulcahy 2006
Mulcahy, Gerardine, *A Country House Sculpture Trail, Burton Constable, Burton Agnes & Sledmere* (Burton Constable Foundation, 2006)

Munby 1946
Munby, Alan, 'Letters of British Artists of the XVIIIth and XIXth Centuries', *Connoisseur*, vol 118 (Sept 1946) pp 24–28

Munby 1948
Munby, A N L, 'Letters of British Artists; Letter from Woolner to Robert Browning', *Connoisseur*, vol 122 (Dec 1948) pp 101–3

Munro Papers
Correspondence of Alexander Munro (Munro family collection)

Munro/Brown
Alexander Munro, letter to John Brown, or to his son James Roberts Brown, John Brown Correspondence (BL, Add MS 42713, fol(s) 232)

Munro/Gladstone
Alexander Munro, letters to Sir Thomas Gladstone, Glynne-Gladstone MSS 1854–5 (St Deniols Library, Hawarden, 450)

Munro/Hamilton
Alexander Munro, letters to William Richard Hamilton, Letters to W R Hamilton 1857 (BL, Add MSS 50132, fols 68–69)

Munro/Trevelyan
Alexander Munro, letters to Sir Walter and Lady Trevelyan (Robinson, WCT)

Munsell 1991
Munsell, F Darrell, *The Victorian Controversy Surrounding the Wellington War Memorial* (1991)

Murat 1992
Murat, Laure, 'La Modernite Selon Canova', *Connaissance des Arts*, no 484 (June 1992) pp 74–81

Murdoch 1980
Murdoch, Tessa, 'Roubiliac as an Architect? The Bill for the Warkton Monuments', *Burlington Magazine*, vol 122 (Jan 1980) pp 40–46

Murdoch 1982
Murdoch, Tessa, *Huguenot Artists, Designers and Craftsmen in Great Britain and Ireland, 1680–1760* (1982)

Murdoch 1983
Murdoch, Tessa, 'Louis François Roubiliac and his Huguenot Connections', *Proceedings of the Huguenot Society of London*, vol 24, no 1 (1983) pp 26–45

Murdoch 1985
Murdoch, Tessa, 'Roubiliac's Monuments to Bishop Hough and the Second Duke and Duchess of Montagu', *Journal of the Church Monuments Society*, vol 1 (1985) pp 34–48

Murdoch 1988
Murdoch, Tessa, 'Carving a Brighter Niche: Nadauld the Sculptor', *Country Life*, vol 182, no 41 (13 Oct 1988) pp 240–42

Murdoch 1992
Murdoch, Tessa, 'A Mirror Designed by Robert Adam: An Adam Mirror for Coventry House Returns to London', *National Arts Collection Fund Review*, vol 88 (1992) pp 44–47

Murdoch 2004
Murdoch, Tessa, 'London ormolu lighting from George II to George IV', *Antiques Magazine*, vol 165, no 3 (2004) pp 92–99

Murdoch 2006
Murdoch, Tessa, 'A French Carver at Norfolk House: The Mysterious Mr Cuenot', *Apollo*, vol 163, no 252 (June 2006)

Murdoch and Burton 1974
Murdoch, John, and Burton, Anthony, *Byron*, exhib cat (VAM, 1974)

Murdoch and Hebditch 1985
Murdoch, Tessa, and Hebditch, Max, *The Quiet Conquest; The Huguenots 1685–1985* (Museum of London, 1985)

Murdoch and Snodin 1993
Murdoch, Tessa, and Snodin, Michael, 'Admiral Keppel's Freedom Box from the City of London', *Burlington Magazine*, vol 135, no 922 (June 1993) pp 403–10

Murphy 1991–2
Murphy, Paula, 'Terence Farrell', *Irish Arts Review* (1991–92) pp 73–79

Murphy 1992
Murphy, Paula, 'Thomas Farrell, Dublin Sculptor 1827–1900' Ph D Diss (University College, Dublin, 1992)

Murphy 1993
Murphy, Paula, 'Thomas Farrell, Sculptor', *Irish Arts Review*, vol 9 (1993) pp 196–207

Murphy 1995
Murphy, Paula, 'John Henry Foley's O'Connell Monument', *Irish Arts Review*, vol 11 (1995) pp 155–56

Murphy 1996
Murphy, Paula, 'The O'Connell Monument in Dublin: The Political and Artistic Context of a Public Sculpture', *Apollo*, vol 143, no 409 (March 1996) pp 22–26

Murphy 1999
Murphy, Paula, 'British Sculpture at the Early Universal Exhibitions: Ireland Sustaining Britain', *The Sculpture Journal*, vol 3 (1999) pp 64–73

Murphy 2001
Murphy, Paula, 'Rejecting Public Monuments in Dublin', *Apollo*, vol 154, no 475 (Sept 2001) pp 40–47

Murray 1991
Murray, Peter, *The Crawford Municipal Art Gallery, Cork* (City of Cork VEC, 1991)

Murrell 1994
Murrell, Jim, 'The Technique of British Wax Portraits: The Visual Evidence', *Conservator*, vol 18 (1994) pp 41–49

Mus City NY
Museum of the City of New York

Mus J 1990
'Government Gracefully Wriggling', *Museums Journal*, vol 90 (June 1990) p 37

Musgrave 1899–1901
Musgrave, W, *Obituary Prior to 1800* (1899–1901)

Musgrave 1966
Musgrave, Clifford, 'Arbury, Warks: A Gothic Fantasy of the English Midlands', *Connoisseur*, vol 163 (Sept 1966)

Musgrave 1972
Musgrave, Clifford, 'Living With Antiques. Mawley Hall, Shropshire', *Antiques Magazine*, vol 101 (June 1972) pp 1000–5

Musson 1996
Musson, Jeremy, 'Hatfield Priory, Essex, I: the Home of Mr and Mrs Adrian Cowell', *Country Life*, vol 190, no 20 (1996) p 16

Musson 1999
Musson, Jeremy, 'In the House of Snapped-Up Trifles', *Country Life*, vol 193, no 22 (3 June 1999) pp 136–41

Myddleton 1931
Myddleton, W M ed, *Chirk Castle Accounts, 1666–1753* (St Albans: 1931)

Myerscough 1975
Myerscough, Corita, 'Missing God', *Country Life*, vol 158 (17 July 1975) p 152

Myerscough 1996
Myerscough, Corita, 'The Fishers of York – A Provincial Carver's Workshop in the 18th and 19th Centuries' Ph D Diss (University of York: 1996)

Myerscough 2000
Myerscough, Corita, 'Carver and Customer – The Fishers of York and their Customers', Annual Report *York Georgian Society*, (2000) pp 24–33

Mylne 1893
Mylne, Robert Scott, *The Master Masons to the Crown of Scotland and their works* (Edinburgh: 1893)

Myrone 1998
Myrone, M D, 'Body-Building: British Historical Artists in London and Rome and the Remaking of the Heroic Ideal, *c*1760–1800' Ph D Diss (Courtauld Institute, London, 1998)

N&Q
Notes and Queries

Nachmani 1968/1969
Nachmani, Cynthia, 'Early English Cottage Book', *Marsyas*, vol 14 (1968/1969) pp 67–76

NADFAS
National Association of Decorative & Fine Art Societies, Church Recordings Team

NAL
National Art Library, Victoria and Albert Museum

NAM
National Army Museum, London

Nares 1953 (1)
Nares, Gordon, 'Aynhoe Park, Northamptonshire', *Country Life*, vol 114 (2, 9, 16 July 1953) pp 42–45; 122–25; 202–5

Nares 1953 (2)
Nares, Gordon, 'Arbury Hall, Warwickshire – II', *Country Life*, vol 114 (15 Oct 1953) pp 1210–13

NAS
National Archives of Scotland, Edinburgh

Nash 1791
Nash, *The History and Antiquities of Worcestershire*, 2 vols (1791)

Nash MS
John Nash MS, Shide Hill Ledger from 1814 (RIBA, VAM)

Nason 1983
Nason, Pippa, 'John Pinney's Georgian House; Building, Bristol-Fashion', *Country Life*, vol 173, no 4468 (7 April 1983) pp 886–88

Nat Sculpt Rev 1974
'Statues that Started it All', *National Sculpture Review*, vol 23, no 3 (Autumn 1974) p 13

Naylor 1839
Naylor, S, *Ceracchi, a Drama* (1839)

Neale 1819
Neale, John Preston, *Views of the Seats of Noblemen and Gentlemen in England, Wales, Scotland and Ireland*, 2 vols (1819)

Neale and Brayley 1818–23
Brayley, Edward Wedlake, and Neale, John Preston, *The History and Antiquities of the Abbey Church of St Peter, Westminster*, 2 vols (1818–23)

Neave and Heron 1969
Neave, D, and Heron, V, 'Kesteven Slate Headstones and Their Engravers 1700–1825', *Lincolnshire History and Archaeology*, vol 4 (1969) p 3

Neave and Woodward 1979
Neave, David, and Woodward, David, 'Memorials to a Yorkshire Family', *Country Life*, vol 166 (Oct 1979) pp 1231–35

Neefs 1876
Neefs, Emmanuel, *Histoire de peinture et de sculpture a Malines*, 2 vols (1876)

Nelson 1811
Nelson, John, *The History of Islington*, A facsimile of the first edition (1811) together with 79 additional illustrations and an introduction by Julia Melvin (London: 1980)

Neoclassicism 1972
Council of Europe, *The Age of Neoclassicism*, exhib cat (RA and VAM: London, Arts Council of Great Britain, 1972)

Neverov 2000–1
Neverov, Oleg, 'Catherine the Great; Public and private collector', *British Art Journal*, vol 2, no 2 (Winter 2000–1) pp 121–33

New Building, Chatsworth
Papers relating to the New Building at Chatsworth, 1845 (Devonshire Archives, Chatsworth, B8)

New Churches Report Book
Tenders for Building Regent Square Chapel, Surveyor's Report Book, Commissioners for the Building of New Churches 29 March 1822 (Church of England Record Centre, 15 Galleywall Road, Bermondsey, London SE16 3PB, CBC/SR 1, p 97)

New Monthly Mag
The New Monthly Magazine and Universal Register

New View of London 1708
Anon, *A New View of London*, 2 vols (1708)

Newark 1985
Newark, Tim, 'The Barbarians: The Artistic Portrayal of Warriors of Yore', *Art and Artists*, no 228 (Sept 1985) pp 10–13

Newby 1986
Newby, Evelyn, 'The Hoares of Bath', in *Bath History*, vol 1 (1986) pp 90–127

Newcastle Exhib 1831
Dunbar, David, *Exhibition of Sculpture of Foreign and British Sculptors* (1831)

Newcastle Exhib 1832
Dunbar, David, *Exhibition of Sculpture of Foreign and British Sculptures* (1832)

Newdigate Accts, 1751–52
Sir Roger Newdigate, Account Book, Michaelmas 1751–Michaelmas 1752 (Warks CRO, CR 136/V 156)

Newdigate Accts, 1763–96
Sir Roger Newdigate, Account Book, 1763–96 (Warks CRO, CR 136/V119)

Newdigate Accts, 1796–1802
Sir Roger Newdigate, Account Book, 1796–1802 (Warks CRO, CR 136/B2634)

Newdigate Archives
Sir Roger Newdigate, Miscellaneous bills, agreements, contracts, letters (Warks CRO, CR 136/B)

Newman 1974
Newman, R F, 'Roubiliac's Marriage', *Burlington Magazine*, vol 116 (Aug 1974) pp 478–79

NG
National Gallery, London

NGC
National Gallery of Canada, Ottawa

NGI
National Gallery of Ireland, Dublin

NGS
National Gallery of Scotland, Edinburgh

Nichols 1795–1815
Nichols, John, *The History and Antiquities of the County of Leicester*, 4 vols (1795–1815)

Nichols 1812–15
Nichols, John, *Literary Anecdotes of the Eighteenth Century*, 9 vols (1812–15)

Nicholson 1972
Nicholson, Benedict, ed, *The Treasures of the Foundling Hospital* (1972)

Ninnis 1974
Ninnis, B J, 'The Hewer Memorial at Clapham', *Antiquaries Journal*, vol 54, no 2 (1974) pp 257–67

Nixon/Brayley 1845
Samuel Nixon, Letter to E Wedlake Brayley, 1845 (BL, Add MS 52481, fol(s) 66)

NLS
National Library of Scotland, Edinburgh

NLW
National Library of Wales, Aberystwyth

NMG Merseyside
National Museums and Galleries, Merseyside

NMM
National Maritime Museum, Cambridge

NMM, Gr
National Maritime Museum, Greenwich

NMS
National Museums of Scotland

NMW
National Museum of Wales, Cardiff

Noble 1901
Noble, Margaret Elizabeth, *History of the Parish of Bampton* (1901)

Noble 1908
Noble, Percy, *Anne Seymour Damer A Woman of Art and Fashion 1748–1828* (1908)

Noe 1997
Noe, Enrico, 'Gessi Canoviani Restaurati Alle Gallerie dell'Accademia di Venezia', *Bollettino d'Arte*, vol 82, no 101/102 (July–Dec 1997) pp 107–28

Nollekens Corr BL
Nollekens to H I Legge, letter 1812; Nollekens to M I Lee, letter 1813, 1812–1813 (BL, Add MS 37907, fol 76; Add MS 36594)

Nollekens Corr Yale
Three letters from Joseph Nollekens to Charles Burney, 1803–15, Burney Collection, 971, 1340–1; letter to Henry Crowe, November 27, 1812, Osborn Collection; letter to Mr Bond, May 17, 1811, FW Hilles Collection, Britton 15, 1803–1815 (Beinecke Library, Yale)

Nollekens Family Papers
Nollekens Family Papers, 1710–1825 (PRO, Kew, London, C112/183)

Nollekens Leasehold Assignments
Copy of an assignment of two leasehold houses in Marylebone, Middlesex, 1792 (VAM NAL, MSL/1987/2)

Nollekens Lecture Ticket
Royal Academy lecture ticket, signed by Joseph Nollekens (Mitchell Library, City of Glasgow, AL3)

Nollekens Note on Cowper Bust
Note concerning the Lord Cowper's sittings for his bust by Joseph Nollekens (VAM NAL, MSL/1979/5116/390)

Nollekens/Polley
Joseph Nollekens, letter to Polley Nollekens, 1780 (VAM NAL, MSL/1979/8184)

Norfolk RO
Norfolk County Record Office

Norman-Wilcox 1965
Norman-Wilcox, G, 'Two Figures from Croome Court', *Bulletin of the Los Angeles County Museum*, vol 17, no 3 (1965) pp 14–31

North Soc
Northern Society, Leeds

Northampton 1968
Sculpture in England since the Seventeenth Century: with special reference to Northamptonshire (Central Museum and Art Gallery, Northampton, England, 27 April to 23 May, 1968)

Northcote 1813
Northcote, James, *Memoirs of Sir Joshua Reynolds* (1813)

Norton 1963
Norton, P F, 'Daylesford: S. P. Cockerell's Residence for Warren Hastings; Two Chimney Pieces by Thomas Banks', *Journal of the Society of Architectural Historians*, vol 22 (Oct 1963) pp 131–32

Nost I/Coke
John Nost I, letter to Thomas Coke of Melbourne Hall, 1 July 1699 (Melbourne Hall Archives, Melbourne, Derbys, 219/4/6)

Nost II Casting Warrant
John Nost II, warrant from the Lord Chamberlain allowing the sculptor to make a cast of Hubert Le Sueur's horse, June 1719 (PRO, Kew, London, LC/5157, 241)

Nost II Hopetoun contract
John Nost II and the Earl of Hopetoun, contract for garden statuary, 24 May 1718 (Linlithgow Muniments, Hopetoun House, West Lothian, NRAS 888 Bundle 2964; receipt NRAS 888)

Nost II/Dryden
John Nost II, letter to Edward Dryden, Papers relating to Canons Ashby 1713 (NRO, Dryden D (CA) 938)

Nost/Hopetoun list
John Nost I, list of available works sent to Charles Hope, Ist Earl of Hopetoun, 1709 (Linlithgow Munimemts, Hopetoun House, West Lothian, NRA [S] 888, bundles 630, 2964)

Nost/Hopetoun MS
List of available works sent by John Nost I to Charles Hope, Ist Earl of Hopetoun (1709); Contract between John Nost II and Earl of Hopetoun for garden statuary (24 May 1718); Shipping order for works by John Nost II to Charles Hope, Ist Earl of Hopetoun (1719), 1709–1719 (Linlithgow Munimemts, Hopetoun House, West Lothian, NRAS 888 Bundle 630 and 2964)

Nost/Hopetoun shipping
John Nost II, shipping order for Charles Hope, Ist Earl of Hopetoun, 1719 (Linlithgow Muniments, Hopetoun House, West Lothian, NRA [S] 888, Bundle 1964)

Noszlopy 1998
Noszlopy, George T, *Public Sculpture of Birmingham: Including Sutton Coldfield*, Public Sculpture of Britain 2 (Liverpool: 1998)

Noszlopy 2003
Noszlopy, George, *Public Sculpture of Warwickshire: with Solihull and Coventry*, Public Sculpture of Britain 6 (Liverpool: 2003)

Novotny 1960
Novotny, Fritz, *Painting and Sculpture in Europe 1780–1880* (1960)

NP/RG
Nicholas Penny, Annotated Gunnis

NPG
National Portrait Gallery, London

NRA
National Register of Archives

NRAS
National Register of Archives, Scotland

NRM
National Railway Museum, York

NRO
Northamptonshire Record Office

NRP database
National Recording Project, attached to Public Monuments and Sculpture Association

NSW
New South Wales, Australia

NSW Lib
New South Wales State Library, Australia

NT
National Trust

NTS
National Trust for Scotland

Numis 1953
'Biographical Note: Benedito Pistrucci', *Numismatist*, vol 66 (May 1953) p 457

NY
New York

NYCRO
North Yorkshire Records Office

NYHS
New York Historical Society

O'Connell 1987
O'Connell, Sheila, 'The Nosts: A Revision of the Family History', *Burlington Magazine*, vol 129 (Dec 1987) pp 802–6

O'Connor 1986
O'Connor, Cynthia, 'Furnishing for the Casino at Marino, Co. Dublin: A Chimney-Piece Made in Florence for Lord Charlemont', *Burlington Magazine*, vol 128 (Sept 1986) pp 670–72

O'Donoghue 1896
O'Donoghue, D J, *The Life of William Carleton* (1896)

O'Neill 1998
O'Neill, C, 'In Search of Bossi', Irish Architectural and Decorative Studies *Journal of the Irish Georgian Society*, vol 1 (1998)

OAJ
Oxford Art Journal

ODNB
Matthew, Colin and Harrison, Brian, eds, *Oxford Dictionary of National Biography* (Oxford: 2004)

Odom 1926
Odom, William, *Hallamshire worthies: characteristics and work of notable Sheffield men and women* (Sheffield: 1926)

Oliver 1829
Oliver, George, *The History and Antiquities of the Town and Minster of Beverley* (Beverley: 1829)

Olsen 1970
Olsen, C, 'Kopenhagen: Thorvaldsen-Museum', *Pantheon*, vol 28 (March 1970) pp 150–51

Oman 1966
Oman, Charles, 'A Problem of Artistic Responsibility: the Firm of Rundell, Bridge and Rundell', *Apollo*, vol 83 (March 1966) pp 174–82

'One of the People' 1857
'One of the People', *On the Designs for the Wellington Memorial*, pamphlet (London: 1857)

Oppé 1950
Oppé, A P, *English Drawings Stuart and Georgian Periods in the Collection of His Majesty the King at Windsor Castle* (London: 1950)

Orchard Wyndham MSS
Correspondence between J E Carew and 4th Earl of Egremont and Sir Richard Westmacott and the 4th Earl, with other papers, particularly lists of Antiquities sold by Westmacott to Egremont, 1838–41 (Orchard Wyndham House, Somerset)

Oriel Accts
Oriel College Accounts (Oxfordshire Record Office, OCA L 5.5)

Ormond 1967
Ormond, Richard L, 'Portraits to Australia, a Group of Pre-Raphaelite Drawings', *Apollo*, no 85 (Jan 1967) pp 25–27

Ormond 1973
Ormond, Richard, *Early English Victorian Portraits, Catalogue of the National Portrait Gallery Permanent Collection* (1973)

Ormond 1981
Ormond, Leonée, *Tennyson and Thomas Woolner* (Lincoln, England: Tennyson Society, 1981)

Ormond and Rogers 1979–81
Ormond, Richard and Rogers, Malcolm, eds, *Dictionary of British Portraiture*, 4 vols (London: 1979–81)

ORNC
Old Royal Naval College (Greenwich)

Osbourne and Fisher 1951
Osborne, E, and Fisher, F, 'A Derbyshire Gibbons Monument', *Journal of the Derbyshire Archaeological and Natural History Society*, vol 24, no 71 (1951) p 81

Oswald 1949
Oswald, Arthur, 'Blair Castle, Perthshire – the Seat of the Dukes of Atholl – II', *Country Life*, vol 106 (11 Nov 1949) pp 1434–38

Oswald 1952
Oswald, Arthur, 'Davenport House, Shropshire [Smith, F. of Warwick]', *Country Life*, vol 112 (27 June, 4, 7 July 1952) pp 1996–99, 40–43, 114–17

Oswald 1953 (1)
Oswald, Arthur, 'Ombersley Court, Worcestershire', *Country Life*, vol 113 (2, 9, 16 Jan 1953) pp 34–37, 94–97, 152–55

Oswald 1953 (2)
Oswald, Arthur, 'Came House, Dorset', *Country Life*, vol 113 (1953) pp 490–93, 572–75

Oswald 1954
Oswald, Arthur, 'William Baker of Audlem, Architect', *Collections for a History of Staffordshire (Staffs Record Society)*, vol 1950–51 (1954) pp 107–36

Oswald 1964
Oswald, Arthur, 'Okeover Hall, Staffs', *Country Life*, vol 135 (23, 30 Jan, 12, 19 March 1964) pp 172–76, 224–28, 569–75, 645–49

Oswald 1965
Oswald, Arthur, 'Leadenham House, Lincolnshire', *Country Life*, vol 137, nos 563, 564 (17, 24 July 1965) pp 1528–31, 1592–95

Oswald 1966
Oswald, Arthur, 'Milton Abbey, Dorset V', *Country Life*, vol 140 (28 July 1966) pp 208–12

OU Museum Papers
Correspondence and other papers concerning statues for the Oxford University Museum, c1856–1866 (Oxford University Museum Archives, The History of the Building of the Museum, Box 2, Parts 4–5)

OUA Chancellor's Ct Papers
Oxford University, Chancellor's Court Papers, Wood v Frogley, 1680–1681

OUA, V-C's Accts 1666–97
Vice-Chancellor's Accounts, University of Oxford 1666–97

OUA V-C's Accts 1697–1735
Vice-Chancellor's Accounts, University of Oxford 1697–1735

Oughton 1979
Oughton, Frederick, *Grinling Gibbons and the English Woodcarving Tradition* (1979)

Ox
Oxoniensa

Oxf Univ MHS
Oxford University, Museum of the History of Science

Oxf Univ Mus
Oxford University, Museum of Natural History

Oxford CCP
Chancellor's Court Papers, University of Oxford 1680–81

Oxford Guide 1805
A New Pocket Companion for Oxford; or Guide through the University (Oxford: 1805)

Oxford H S
Oxford Historical Society

Paine 1767
Paine, James, *Plans, Elevations and Sections of Noblemen and Gentlemen's Houses* (1767)

Paine 1783
Paine, James, *Plans, elevations and sections of buildings executed in the counties of Nottingham, Essex, Wiltshire. . .* (1783)

Painter-Stainers 1723
Company Terrier, Worshipful Company of Painter-Stainers 1723 (Guildhall MSS, City of London, 11505)

Palazzo Pitti 2003
Capecchi, Gabriella, *Palazzo Pitti: la reggia rivelata*, exh cat (Florence: 2003)

Palgrave 1862
Palgrave, F T, *Catalogue of the International Exhibition* (1862)

Palgrave 1866
Palgrave, Francis Turner, *Essays on Art* (London and Cambridge: 1866)

Palmer 1932
Palmer, William Mortlock, ed, *Monumental Inscriptions and Coats of Arms from Cambridgeshire ... Recorded by John Layer c1632 and William Cole between 1742 and 1782* (Cambridge: 1932)

Palmerston/Granville
Letter from Lord Palmerston to to Earl Granville concerning a civil list pension for Richard Cockle Lucas in return for donating works to the South Kensington Museum, 10 July 1865 (VAM NAL)

Palumbo-Fossati 1982
Palumbo-Fossati, C, *Gli Stuccatori Ticinesi Lafranchini in Inghilterra e in Irelando nel Secolo XVIII* (Lugano: Fondazione Ticino Nostro, 1982)

Panzetta 1994
Panzetta, Alfonso, *Dizionario degli Scultori Italiani dell'Ottocento e del Primo Novecento* (Turin: 1994)

Papworth Letters
Signed note and letter describing five busts, both by Edgar George Papworth, nd, April 1839 (Edinburgh Central Library, BRS/qwN 45/Box)

Paris Int Exhib
International Exhibition, Paris, 1855

Park Correspondence
Correspondence of Patric Park, 1832–1855 (National Library of Scotland, Edinburgh, Acc 100097)

Park/Brown
Correspondence between Patric Park and Robert Brown (Private coll)

Park/Napier
Letters from Patric Park to Sir Charles James Napier, Napier Papers 1848 (BL MSS, Add 54557, ff 56, 70, 192)

Park/Peel
Letters from Patric Park to Sir Robert Peel, Peel Papers 1845–1846 (BL MSS, Add 40580 ff 101, 165; Add 40592 f 251)

Park/Wellington
Letter from Patric Park to the Duke of Wellington, Peel Papers 1844 (BL MSS, Add 40547 f 198)

Parker 1957
Parker, James, 'Staircase by Grinling Gibbons from Cassiobury Park', *Bulletin of the Metropolitan Museum of Art, New York*, no 15 (15 June 1957) pp 228–36

Parker 1958
Parker, James, 'Staircase by Grinling Gibbons', *Connoisseur*, vol 141 (May 1958) pp 192–96

Parris 1994
Parris, Leslie, *The Pre-Raphaelites*, exhib cat (London: Tate Gallery Publications, 1994)

Parry 1997
Parry, Graham, 'The John Talman Letter-Book', *Walpole Society*, vol 59 (1997)

Parry-Jones 1981
Parry-Jones, Brenda, 'Peter Hollins at the Warneford Hospital', *Leeds Arts Calendar*, vol 88 (1981) pp 24–32

Parson and White 1829
Parson, William, and White, William, *History, Directory and Gazeteer of the Counties of Cumberland and Westmoreland* (1829)

Parsons Accounts
Accounts of Parsons of Lewes (photocopies), 1794–1802 (East Sussex RO, ACC4031)

Parsons Records
Financial and other records of Parsons of Lewes, 1794–1932 (East Sussex RO, ACC8262)

Pascoli 1736
Pascoli, L, *Vite de' Pittori, Scultori ed Architetti moderni* (Rome: 1736)

Pasquin 1786
Pasquin, Anthony, *The Royal Academicians: A Farce* (1786)

Pasquin 1796
Pasquin, Anthony, *A Critical Guide to the Royal Academy for 1796* (1796)

Passavant 1836
Passavant, Johan David, and Bailey, Colin J, *Tour of a German Artist in England* (1836, reprint 1978)

Passeggia 2000
Passeggia, Luisa, 'The marble trade: the Lazzerini workshop and the arts, crafts and entrepreneurs of Carrara in the early nineteenth century', in *The Lustrous Trade: Material Culture and the History of Sculpture in England and Italy, c.1700–c.1860*, ed Sicca, Cinzia and Yarrington, Alison (2000) pp 156–73

Paterson 1854
Paterson, James, *Memoir of the Late James Fillans, Sculptor, W.S.A., S.E.S. and S.A., London* (Paisley: 1854)

Pattison and Murray 2000
Pattison, Ian R, and Murray, Hugh, *Monuments in York Minster: an illustrated inventory* (York: The Friends of York Minster, 2001)

Paty Copybook
Funerary Monuments and Chimneypieces, Patterns by Paty family members and Henry Wood, c1715–1815 (Bristol University, RWA School of Architecture, DM1874)

Paty/Morgan 1787
Letter from Thomas Paty and Sons to Charles Morgan Esq, 24 April 1787 (Glamorgan Archive Service, Cardiff, D/D Xgc 54)

Pauli 1931
Pauli, Gustav, 'Die Geschichte der Florabuste im Kaiser Friedrich-Museum zu Berlin', *Belvedere*, vol 10, no 7/8 (1931) pp 1–11

Paulson 1996
Paulson, Ronald, 'Roubiliac and Hogarth: Representations of Temporality and Eternity', *Eighteenth Century Studies*, vol 20, no 2 (May 1996) pp 104–26

Pavanello 1976
Pavanello, Giuseppe, *L'Opera Completa del Canova* (Milan: 1976)

Pavanello 1997
Pavanello, Giuseppe, and Stringa, Nico, 'I Due Primi Testamenti di Antonio Canova', *Arte Veneta*, vol 51 (1997) pp 115–25

Pawson/Accounts
Pawson MSS, Account Book, 1740–42 (West Yorks CRO, uncat)

Payne 1889
Payne, John Orlebar, *Records of English Catholics of 1715* (1889)

PBS 1984
Pirzio Biroli Stefanelli, Lucia, 'Benedetto Pistrucci (Roma 1784–Englefield Green 1855): Tre Cere del Museo di Roma', *Bolletino dei Musei Communali di Roma*, vol 31 (1984) pp 92–96

PBS 1989
Pirzio Biroli Stefanelli, Lucia, *I Modelli in Cera di Benedetto Pistrucci* (Roma, Museo della Zecca: 1989)

PBSR
Papers of the British School in Rome

Pearson 1981
Pearson, Fiona, 'Phrenology and Sculpture 1820–1855', *Leeds Arts Calendar*, no 88 (1981) pp 14–23

Pearson 1991
Pearson, Fiona, ed, *Virtue and Vision: Sculpture and Scotland, 1540–1990* (with unpaginated room list) (1991)

Pearson 1995
Pearson, David, 'A Late Eighteenth-Century Binding with an Intaglio Gemstone Clasp', *Book Collector*, vol 44, no 3 (1995) pp 371–73

Pearson/Armstead
Copy of a letter to Henry Hugh Armstead from J L Pearson, Macmillan Papers 1895 (BL, Add MS 61896 fol 113)

Peat 1957
Peat, W D, 'Statuette by Rysbrack: Charity', *Bulletin of the Art Association of Indianapolis, Indiana*, vol 44 (April 1957) pp 3–4

Peck 2005
Peck, Linda Levy, *Consuming Splendour: Society and Culture in Seventeenth-Century England* (2005)

Peel Papers
Correspondence and papers of Sir Robert Peel (BL, Add MSS 40181–40617)

Peisley/Blenheim
Papers Respecting the Building of Blenheim, 1706–1748 (BL, Add MS 24,327)

Pelham
Pelham Account Book, 1750 (RIBA, VAM)

Pellegrini 1991
Pellegrini, Giorgio, 'Meleagro Risorto: Un Modello Antico nell'Iconografia del Neoclassicismo', *Annali della Facolta di Lettere e Filosofia dell'Universita di Cagliari*, vol 49 (1991) pp 187–217

Pennant 1825
Pennant, Thomas, *London*, 2 vols (1825)

Penny 1974
Penny, Nicholas, 'Monuments to Early Reformers; Sir Richard Westmacott's Sculpture', *Country Life*, vol 155 (7 March 1974) pp 492–93

Penny 1975 (1)
Penny, Nicholas, 'English Church Monuments to Women who died in Childbed between 1780 and 1835', *Journal of the Warburg and Courtauld Institutes*, vol 38 (1975) pp 314–32

Penny 1975 (2)
Penny, Nicholas, 'Sculpture of Sir Richard Westmacott', *Apollo*, vol 102, no 162 (Aug 1975) pp 120–27

Penny 1975 (3)
Penny, Nicholas, 'Themes and Conventions in English Commemorative Sculpture, c1780–c1840' Ph D Diss (Courtauld Institute, London, 1975)

Penny 1976 (1)
Penny, Nicholas, 'Dead Dogs and Englishmen', *Connoisseur*, vol 142, no 774 (Aug 1976) pp 298–303

Penny 1976 (2)
Penny, Nicholas, 'Grand and National Obsequies', *Country Life*, vol 160, no 4130 (26 Aug 1976) pp 547–48

Penny 1976 (3)
Penny, Nicholas, 'The Whig Cult of Fox', *Past & Present*, vol 70 (Feb 1976) pp 94–105

Penny 1977 (1)
Penny, Nicholas, *Church Monuments in Romantic England* (1977)

Penny 1977 (2)
Penny, Nicholas, 'To Honour Pitt the Younger; Nollekens' Statue in the Cambridge Senate House', *Country Life*, vol 161 (19 May 1977) pp 1336–37

Penny 1986
Penny, Nicholas, *Reynolds*, exhib cat (Royal Academy, 1986)

Penny 1990
Penny, Nicholas, 'Book Review: Mrs Coade's Stone. By Alison Kelly', *Burlington Magazine* (Dec 1990) pp 879–80

Penny 1991 (1)
Penny, Nicholas, 'Chantrey, Westmacott and Casts after the Antique', *Journal of the History of Collections*, vol 3, no 2 (1991) pp 255–64

Penny 1991 (2)
Penny, Nicholas, 'Lord Rockingham's Sculpture Collection and The Judgement of Paris by Nollekens', *J Paul Getty Museum Journal*, vol 19 (1991) pp 5–34

Penny 1992
Penny, Nicholas, *Catalogue of European Sculpture in the Ashmolean Museum, 1540 to the Present Day*, 3 vols (1992)

Penny 1995 (2)
Penny, Nicholas, 'Edinburgh: Canova's Three Graces', *Burlington Magazine*, vol 137 (Dec 1995) pp 861–62

Penry Williams Letters
Penry Williams, Letters to William Theed, the painter William Cooke and an unnamed correspondent, including references to John Gibson, 1844–1876 (NLW, MS 21796B)

Penzer 1955
Penzer, N M, 'Two-Handled Cup or Vase of Silver-Gilt Known as the Theocritus Cup', *Apollo*, vol 62 (Sept 1955) p 66

Penzer 1956
Penzer, N M, 'Copies of the Warwick Vase, Part III', *Apollo*, vol 63 (March 1956) pp 71–75

Perceval Accts
Sir John Perceval, Day Book of Expenses, from 20 Sept 1712 (BL, Add MS 47047)

Perks 1922
Perks, S, *History of the Mansion House* (1922)

Perowne 1951
Perowne, Stewart, 'Monuments in Barbados', *Country Life*, (7 Dec 1951) pp 1940–42

Perriam 1975
Perriam, D R, 'Carlisle Academy of Fine Art', *Connoisseur*, vol 189 (Aug 1975) pp 300–5

Perriam 1992
Perriam, D R, *Carlisle: an illustrated history* (1992)

Perry 1899
Perry, M, 'The Origin, progress and present state of the Spalding Gentlemen's Society', *Journal of the British Archaeological Association* (1899) pp 39–50

Perry 1978
Perry, Marilyn, ' "La Pauvre Miss Bathurst" Memorials to a Tragedy in Stendhal's Rome', *Connoisseur*, vol 197, no 794 (April 1978) pp 292–97

Pesci 1934
Pesci, Costanza Gradara, 'Cronache Estere: Un Artista Romano a Londra Sulla Fine del '700', *Emporium*, vol 80 (Sept 1934) pp 170–74

Peter Du Cane Accounts
Accounts of Peter Du Cane relating to his house in St James's Square, London, 1748–50 (Essex RO, D/DDC.A.18)

Petit and Spedding 2002
Petit, Alexander, and Spedding, Patrick, eds, *Eighteenth Century British Erotica* (2002)

Pevsner
Pevsner, Nikolaus and others, *The Buildings of England* (Harmondsworth: 1958–2005)

Pevsner 1958
Pevsner, Nikolaus, 'Georgian Sculptors; Victor Alexander Sederbach', *Architectural Review*, vol 123 (May 1958) pp 332–34

Pevsner 1968
Pevsner, Nikolaus, 'Architectural Setting of Jane Austen's Novels', *Journal of the Warburg and Courtauld Institutes*, vol 31 (1968) pp 404–22

Pevsner and Metcalf 1985
Pevsner, Nikolaus, and Metcalf, P, *The Cathedrals of England*, 2 vols (1985)

Phelps 1839
Phelps, Rev William, *History and Antiquities of Somersetshire* (1839)

Phillimore 2002
Phillimore, Andrea Cameron, *Feltham, Hanworth & Bedfont*, pamphlet (2002)

Phillips 1779
Phillips, Thomas, *The History and Antiquities of Shrewsbury* (Shrewsbury: 1779)

Phillips 1964
Phillips, H, *Mid-Georgian London: Topographical and Social Survey of Central and Western London about 1750* (London: 1964)

Phillips 1970
Phillips, John Goldsmith, 'Canova's Reclining Naiad', *Bulletin of the Metropolitan Museum of Art, New York*, vol 29 (Summer 1970) pp 1–10

PHSL
Proceedings of the Huguenot Society of London

Physick 1957
Physick, John, 'A Sculptor Identified', *Country Life*, vol 122, no 3159 (1 Aug 1957) p 223

Physick 1966 (1)
Physick, John, 'The Banishment of the Bronze Duke', *Country Life*, vol 140 (27 Oct 1966) pp 1076–77

Physick 1967
Physick, John, 'Some Eighteenth Century Designs for Monuments in Westminster Abbey', *Bulletin of the Victoria and Albert Museum*, vol 3, no 1 (1967) p 26

Physick 1968
Physick, John, 'Tracing the Work of William Stanton', *Country Life*, (1968) pp 88–91

Physick 1969
Physick, John, *Designs for English Sculpture 1680–1860* (London: 1969)

Physick 1970
Physick, John, *The Wellington Monument* (London: HMSO, 1970)

Physick 1973
Physick, John, *Five Monuments from Eastwell, Kent*, V&A Brochures, 3 (1973)

Physick 1974
Physick, John, 'Cheere and Rysbrack', *Country Life*, vol 155 (2 May 1974) p 1068

Physick 1977
Physick, John, 'Monuments', in *Change and Decay; the Future of Our Churches*, ed Binney, Marcus (1977) p 75

Physick 1982
Physick, John, 'Cheere in the China Trade Room?', *Country Life*, vol 172, no 4452 (16 Dec 1982) p 1966

Physick 1986
Physick, John, 'The Sculpture', in *Westminster Abbey*, ed Wilson, Christopher (1986)

Physick 1989
Physick, John, 'Westminster Abbey: Designs for Poet's Corner and a New Roubiliac in the Cloister', *Journal of the Church Monuments Society*, vol 4 (1989) pp 54–63

Physick 1991
Physick, John, 'The Sondes Monuments at Throwley, Kent', *Journal of the Church Monuments Society*, vol 6 (1991) pp 42–46

Physick 1995 (1)
Physick, John, 'The Oxenden Monument Judgement, 1978', *Archaeologia Cantiane*, vol 115 (1995) pp 29–44

Physick 1995 (2)
Physick, John, 'The Monument to Dr Richard Busby in Westminster Abbey', *Journal of the Church Monuments Society*, vol 11, no 1 (Summer 1995) pp 7–8

Physick 2000–1
Physick, John, 'A Monument Uncovered', *Journal of the Church Monuments Society*, vol 16, no 2 (2000–1) p 7

Physick 2002
Physick, John, 'The Physick Family of Sculptors', *Magazine of the Friends of Kensal Green Cemetery*, no 30 (Feb 2002) pp 9–11

Physick 2004
Physick, John, 'Serendipity', *NADFAS, Church Recorders, News and Views* (2004)

Pickford/Newdigate
Letter from Joseph Pickford to Sir Roger Newdigate, Newdigate Archives 1755/1775?

Pickup 1986
Pickup, David, ' "Patrons they are but Few": Two Letters from a Nineteenth Century Medallist to his Patron', *Medal*, vol 10 (Winter 1986) pp 19–20

Pickup 1988
Pickup, David, 'Taking Mr. Carrington's Head Off: Correspondence between Alfred Stothard and John Lee', *Medal*, vol 12 (Spring 1988) pp 17–28

Picón 1985
Picón, C., 'Two Neo-Attic Pedestals at Newby Hall', *Burlington Magazine*, vol 127, no 991 (1985) pp 706–13

Picton 1875
Picton, J A, *Memorials of Liverpool* (London and Liverpool: 1875)

Pictures of Old Hull, 1945
Anon, *Pictures of Old Hull and Directory of Old Hull Artists* (Hull: 1945)

Pidgeon 1951
Pidgeon, H, *Memorials of Shrewsbury* (1837; enlarged edition 1851)

Pierpoint 1908
Pierpoint, Robert, *'History' The marble statue of Mrs Catherine Macauley in the entrance hall of Warrington Town Hall*, for private circulation (Warrington, 1908)

Pietrangeli 1976
Pietrangeli, C, 'I Ritratti "Redenti" ', *Spoletium Spoleto*, no 21 (1976) pp 3–6

Pigot 1826–7
Pigot and Co, *London and Provincial New Commercial Directory* (1826–1827)

Pigot 1827
Pigot and Co, *Metropolitan Directory* (1827)

Pigot 1830
Pigot and Co, *National Commercial Directory* (1830)

Pigot 1838
Pigot and Sons, *Directory of Manchester and Salford* (1838)

Pincot 1770
Pincot, Daniel, *An Essay on the Origin, Nature and Uses and Properties of Artificial Stone* (1770)

Pinkerton 1906
Pinkerton, G, 'Some Dublin Buildings: II', *Architectural Review*, vol 20, no 118 (1906) p 116

Pinkerton 1973
Pinkerton, John, 'Roubiliac's Statue of Lord President Forbes', *Connoisseur*, vol 183 (Aug 1973) pp 274–79

Piper 1952
Piper, D, 'Chitqua; a Chinese Artist in England', *Country Life*, vol 112, no 2896 (18 July 1952) p 198

Piper 1963
Piper, David, *Catalogue of 17th Century Portraits in the National Gallery, London* (1963)

Pistrucci Medal Sketches
Three Pen sketches [perhaps by E W Wyon] derived from a medal by Benedetto Pistrucci, after 1837 (BL, Add MS 64082 fol 2)

Pistrucci Mint Papers
Papers relating to Benedetto Pistrucci's work as an engraver for the Royal Mint and related material (5 folders), 1821, 1823, 1830–7, 1851–2

Pistrucci/Gladstone
Correspondence between Benedetto Pistrucci and William Ewart Gladstone, Gladstone Papers 1843–1845 (BL, Add MSS 44360 fols 29, 46, 47, 90, 94; 44362 fol 34; 44527 fols 115, 116, 124, 138b, 141)

Pistrucci/Hamilton
Letter from Benedetto Pistrucci to William Richard Hamilton regarding a bust of the Duke of Wellington, nd (BL, Add MS 20132 fol 131–3)

Pistrucci/Herschel
Letters (23) from Benedetto Pistrucci to Sir John Frederick William Herschel, 1851–2 (Harry Ransom Humanities Research Center Library, University of Texas at Austin)

Platt Journal
Journal of John Platt, Jan 1763–Dec 1796 (Private coll, cited by Potts 1959, 10 ff)

Pleydell-Bouverie receipt book
Sir Mark Pleydell-Bouverie, signed receipt book, 1756 (Berks RO, D/EPB/E11)

Plot 1686
Plot, R, *Natural History of Staffordshire* (1686)

Plumptre 1996
Plumptre, George, 'Historic Gardens: Stowe in England; Epic Effort to Save a Celebrated Landscape', *Architectural Digest*, vol 53, no 5 (1996) pp 66, 70, 74, 76, 78, 83

*Plumptre c.*1989
Plumptre, George, *Garden Ornament: 500 Years of History and Practice* (*c*1989)

Plymouth CMAG
Plymouth City Museum and Art Gallery

PMSA
Public Monuments and Sculpture Association

PMSA NRP
Public Monuments and Sculpture Association National Recording Project

POB 1674–1834
Proceedings of the Old Bailey, 1674–1834

Pointon 1975–1976
Pointon, Marcia, 'W. E. Gladstone as an Art Patron and Collector', *Victorian Studies*, vol 19, no 1 (1975–76) pp 73–98

Pool 1996
Pool, David, 'List of monuments erected by the Fisher family in York Cemetery', in *Myerscough 1966 (appendix)*, Ph D Diss

Pool and Cash 1780
Robert, Pool, and Cash, John, *Views of the Most Remarkable Public Buildings, Monuments and other Edifices in the City of Dublin* (Dublin: 1780)

Poole
Poole, Rachael E M, ed, *Catalogue of the portraits in the possession of the university, colleges, city and county of Oxford*, 3 vols (Oxford Historical Society, vols 57 (1912); 81 (1925); 82 (1926))

Poole 1870
Poole, Benjamin, *Coventry: Its History and Antiquities* (1870)

Poole 1886
Poole, Edwin, *The Illustrated History and Biography of Brecknockshire* (Brecknockshire: 1886)

Poole 1912
Poole, Rachael E M, *Catalogue of portraits in the possession of the university, colleges, city and county of Oxford* (Oxford Historical Society, vol 57, 1912)

Poole 1922–23
Poole, R, 'Edward Pierce, the Sculptor', *Walpole Society*, vol 11 (1922–23) pp 32–45

Pope-Hennessy 1964
Pope-Hennessy, John, 'Sculpture for the Victoria and Albert Museum', *Apollo*, no 80 (Dec 1964) p 458

Pope-Hennessy 1972
Pope-Hennessy, John, 'The Tombs and Monuments', in *Westminster Abbey* (1972)

Popelier 1968
Popelier, Francoise, and De Wilde, Eliane, *Laurent Delvaux, Jacob De Wit*, exhib cat (Brussels, Musées Royaux, 1968)

Port 1997
Port, Michael, 'Destruction, Competition and Rebuilding: The Royal Exchange, 1838–1884', in *The Royal Exchange*, ed Saunders, Ann (London Topographical Society, 1997) pp 279–310

Portraits of Garrick 2003
Shawe-Taylor, Desmond, *Every Look Speaks: Portraits of David Garrick* (Holborne Museum of Art, Bath, *c*2003)

Postle 1995
Postle, Martin, 'An Early Unpublished Letter by Sir Joshua Reynolds', *Apollo*, vol 141, no 400 (June 1995) pp 11–18

Potterton 1972 (1)
Potterton, Homan, 'New Pupil of Edward Pierce: William Kidwell', *Burlington Magazine*, vol 114 (Dec. 1972) pp 864–67

Potterton 1972 (2)
Potterton, Homan, 'Little-Known Irish Memorial', *Country Life*, vol 152 (28 Dec 1972) pp 1784–85

Potterton 1972 (3)
Potterton, Homan, 'William Kidwell, Sculptor (c.1664–1736) and some Contemporary Mason-Sculptors in Ireland', *Bulletin of the Irish Georgian Society*, vol 15, no 3–4 (July–Dec 1972) pp 80–124

Potterton 1973
Potterton, Homan, *The O'Connell Monument*, Gatherum Series, no 3 (Ballycotton: 1973)

Potterton 1974 (1)
Potterton, Homan, 'Garrick as Roscius?', *Country Life*, vol 155 (7 Feb 1974) p 260

Potterton 1974 (2)
Potterton, Homan, 'The Sculpture Collection [of the National Gallery of Ireland]', *Apollo*, vol 99, no 144 (Feb 1974) pp 142–45

Potterton 1974 (3)
Potterton, Homan, 'Dublin's Vanishing Monuments', *Country Life*, vol 155, no 4012 (23 May 1974) pp 1304–5

Potterton 1975
Potterton, Homan, *Irish Church Monuments 1570–1880* (Ulster Architectural Heritage Society, 1975)

Potts 1959
Potts, John Douglas, *Platt of Rotherham, Mason-Architects, 1700–1810* (Sheffield: 1959)

Potts 1981 (1)
Potts, Alex, 'Chantrey as the National Sculptor of Early Nineteenth-Century England', *Oxford Art Journal*, vol 4, no 2 (1981) pp 17–27

Potts 1981 (2)
Potts, Alex, *Sir Francis Chantrey, 1781–1841, Sculptor of the Great*, exhib cat (London, NPG, 1981)

Potts 1981 (3)
Potts, Alex, 'Sculptor to an Age: the Public & the Private Image in Chantrey's Portrait Busts', in *Sir Francis Chantrey Sculptor to an Age 1781–1841*, ed Binfield, Clyde (University of Sheffield, 1981) pp 51–82

Powis 1993
Powis Castle, Powys, National Trust (1993)

Powney and Bindman 1976
Powney, C, and Bindman, David, *John Flaxman*, exhib cat (1976)

PPR
Principal Probate Registry, London

PR
Poor Rates

PRA
President of the Royal Academy, London

Prato 1978
'Neoclassical Sculpture: Englishmen in Italy 1750–1840', *Prato*, no 52–53 (1978) pp 4–7

Praz 1957
Praz, Mario, 'Canova, or the Erotic Frigidaire', *Art News*, vol 56 (Nov 1957) pp 24–27

PRB
Pre-Raphaelite Brotherhood

Press Cuttings
Press Cuttings, VAM PP.17.GBW

Press Cuttings 1686–1835
Press Cuttings, from English newspapers, on matters of artistic interest, especially notices of exhibitions, sale announcements 1686–1835, 6 vols (NAL, VAM: 1686–1835)

Press Cuttings 1723–1800
Press Cuttings, chiefly from the Public Advertiser, including notices and reports of sales. . . (VAM: NAL: 1723–1800)

Pressly 1979
Pressly, Nancy, *The Fuseli Circle in Rome: Early Romantic Art of the 1770s* (1979)

Pressly 1982
Pressly, Nancy L, 'Guy Head and his Echo Flying from Narcissus: A British Artist in Rome in the 1790s', *Bulletin of the Detroit Institute of Arts*, vol 60, no 3/4 (Winter 1982) pp 68–79

Priest 2003
Priest, Gordon, *The Paty Family: Makers of Eighteenth-century Bristol* (Bristol: 2003)

Priestley 1994
Priestley, Ursula, ed, *The Letters of Philip Stannard, Norwich Textile Manufacturer (1751–1763)*, Norfolk RO, vol 57, 1992 (1994)

Pritchard 1980
Pritchard, T W, 'An Architectural History of the Mansion of Wynnstay, Ruabon. 1', *Denbighshire Historical Society Transactions*, vol 29 (1980) pp 9–36

Pritchard D B
Album of designs for chimneypieces, decorative features and monuments by Thomas Farnolls Pritchard, 1765–1769 (AIA, Washington DC)

PRO
Public Record Office, Kew (now TNA)

PRO, NI
Public Record Office of Northern Ireland, Belfast

Proserpi 1987
Proserpi, Ivan, 'L'Attività degli Stuccatori Pozzi del Castel San Pietro in Alcune Regioni Nordalpine', *Unsere Künstdenmaler*, vol 38, no 2 (1987) pp 266–75

PSGB
'The Political State of Great Britain. Being an impartial account of the most material occurrences . . .', 60 vols (1711–1740)

Public Ad
Public Advertiser

Pullan 2006
Pullan, Margaret, *The Monuments of the Parish Church of St Peter-at-Leeds* (Thoresby Society, 2006)

Pycroft 1883
Pycroft, George, *Art in Devonshire, with biographies of artists born in that county* (Exeter: 1883)

Pyke 1973
Pyke, E J, *A Biographical Dictionary of Wax Modellers* (Oxford: 1973)

Pyke 1981
Pyke, E J, *A Biographical Dictionary of Wax Modellers (Supplement)* (London: 1981)

Pyke 1983
Pyke, E J, *A Biographical Dictionary of Wax Modellers (Supplement)* (1983)

Pyke 1986
Pyke, E J, *A Biographical Dictionary of Wax Modellers (Supplement)* (1986)

Pyne 1819
Pyne, William Henry, *The History of the Royal Residences*, 3 vols (1819)

Pyne 1823
Pyne, William Henry, *Wine and Walnuts; or after dinner chit-chat. By Ephraim Hardcastle* [pseud], 2 vols (1823)

QC
The Queen's College, Oxford

QC, FIR
The Queen's College, Fund for Internal Repairs, 1817–56 (Queen's College, unpaginated)

QC, LRJ
The Queen's College Archives, Oxford, Long Roll J, 1792–1818 (Queen's College, unpaginated)

QC, Wm Townesend Accts
The Queen's College, Oxford, William Townesend, Building Account Book, 1709–1715 (Queen's College)

QCA
The Queen's College Archives, Oxford

QCA LRE 1666–1713
The Queen's College, Oxford, Long Roll E, 1666–1713

QCA LRJ 1792–1818
The Queen's College, Oxford Long Roll J, 1792–1818

QCA, Building Accts
The Queen's College, Oxford Building Account Book, 1720–65

Quarre 1968
Quarre, Pierre, 'Musee des Beaux-Arts de Dijon: Acquisitions (1965–1968)', *Revue du Louvre et des Musées de France*, vol 18, no 6 (1968) pp 463–74

Queen's, Ms 475
The Queen's College, Oxford (Queen's College, library, 475, Smith MS 98)

Quieto 1996
Quieto, Pier Paolo, *Il Lapis Come Filo di Arianna: 100 Disegni della Raccolta Mela, in Firenze dal XVI al XIX Secolo* (A Pontecorboli: Florence, 1996)

R C of P Cash Book
Cash Book, 1664–1726 (Royal College of Physicians, MS 2041)

R C Physic, Cash Book
Royal College of Physicians; Cash Books, 1664–1726; 1726–1788; 1778–1863 (Royal College of Physicians, London, 2041–3)

R C Physic, Edinburgh
Royal College of Physicians, Edinburgh

R Sc A
Royal Scottish Academy, Edinburgh

R Sc A Art Property 1883
Anon, *Art Property in the Possession of the Royal Scottish Academy* (Edinburgh: privately printed, 1883)

R Soc
Royal Society

R Soc of Med
Royal Society of Medicine

RA
Royal Academy, Burlington House, London

RA Admissions
Student Admissions to the Royal Academy, 1825–90 (RA)

RA Council Minutes
Royal Academy Council Minutes, 1769 ff (Royal Academy, London)

RA Exhib Cat
Original Catalogues of Royal Academy Exhibitions (RA)

RA Premium List
A List of the Students of the Royal Academy who have obtained premiums of Gold and Silver Medals, in Painting, Sculpture and Architecture. The Subjects, Sketches &c and the years when given, 1769–1880 (Royal Academy Archives)

RA Student Register
Royal Academy Students' Register, 1769–1829 (RA)

RA/GA
Royal Academy, Index to Minutes of the Council and General Assembly of the Royal Academy, *c*1850 (Royal Academy, London)

RABASF, Madrid
Real Academia de Bellas Artes de San Fernando, Madrid

Radcliffe 1969
Radcliffe, Anthony, 'Acquisitions of Sculpture by the Royal Academy During its First Century', *Apollo*, no 89 (Jan 1969) pp 44–51

Radcliffe 1970
Radcliffe, Anthony, *Monti's Allegory of the Risorgimento*, V&A Museum Bulletin Reproductions (HMSO, 1970)

Raggio 1967
Raggio, Olga, 'Tarnowska Perseus by Canova', *Bulletin of the Metropolitan Museum of Art, New York*, vol 26 (Dec 1967) pp 185–91

Raggio 1968
Raggio, Olga, 'Metropolitan Marbles', *Art News*, vol 67 (Summer 1968) pp 45–49

Raggio 1969
Raggio, Olga, 'Canova's Triumphant 'Perseus' ', *Connoisseur*, vol 172 (Nov 1969) pp 204–12

Raggio 1977
Raggio, Olga, 'Sculpture in the Grand Manner: Two Groups by Anguier and Monnot', *Apollo*, no 106 (Nov 1977) pp 364–75

Raggio 1990
Raggio, Olga, 'Du Bernin a Bourdelle . . . au Metropolitan Museum of Art, New York', *Connaissance des Arts*, no 466 (Dec 1990) pp 110–19

Raggio 1991
Raggio, Olga, 'New Galleries for French and Italian Sculpture at the Metropolitan Museum of Art', 6 *Gazette des Beaux-Arts*, vol 118 (Dec 1991) pp 231–52

Raines 1976
Raines, R, 'An Art Collector of Many Parts: Rev. C. Macro', *Country Life*, vol 160 (1976) p 1692

Ralph 1734
Ralph, James or Benjamin, *A Critical Review of the Publick Buildings, Statues and Ornaments In, and about London and Westminster (1734)* (reprinted 1971)

Ralston 1929
Ralston, R, 'Two Black Basalt Figures of Historical Interest; Admiral Rodney and Admiral Hood by P. Stephen', *Bulletin of the Metropolitan Museum of Art, New York*, vol 24 (Sept 1929) pp 232–33

Ramage 1989
Ramage, Nancy H, 'Owed to a Grecian Urn: the Debt of Flaxman and Wedgwood to Hamilton', *Ars Ceramica*, vol 6 (1989) pp 8–12

Ramallo 1973
Ramallo, German, 'Christopher Hewetson, Tres Obras Suyas en Espana', *Archivo Espanol de Arte*, vol 46 (April 1973) pp 181–87

RAPFAS
Royal Association for the Encouragement of the Fine Arts in Scotland

Rasmusson 1948
Rasmusson, N L, 'Nytt on Jean Cavalier', *Fornvannen*, vol 43 (1948) pp 159–63, 191

Ray 1989
Ray, Sidney F, 'Frederick Archer: the Inventor of the Wet Collodion Process', *British Journal of Photography*, vol 136 (11 May 1989) pp 28–9

RBSA
Royal Birmingham Society of Artists

RBSA Index
Index of works exhibited at the RBSA compiled from the exhibition catalogues (Birmingham Central Library, Local Studies)

RC Physic
Royal College of Physicians

RCHM 1879
Seventh Report of the Royal Commission on Historical Manuscripts of Great Britain (1879)

RCHME
Royal Commission on the Historical Monuments of England

RCHME 1952–75
Royal Commission on the Historical Monuments of England, *An inventory of the historical monuments in Dorset*, vols 1–4 (London: HMSO, 1952–75)

RCHME 1980
Royal Commission on the Historical Monuments of England, *Ancient and historical monuments of the City of Salisbury*, vol 1 (London: HMSO, 1980)

RCHME 1987
Royal Commission on the Historical Monuments of England, *Churches of south-east Wiltshire* (London: HMSO, 1987)

RCIN
Royal Collection Inventory Number

RCS, Dublin
Royal College of Surgeons, Dublin

RCS, London
Royal College of Surgeons, London

RCS, Scotland
Royal College of Surgeons, Scotland

RDS
Royal Dublin Society

Read 1974
Read, Benedict, 'John Henry Foley', *Connoisseur*, vol 186, no 750 (Aug 1974) pp 262–71

Read 1976
Read, Benedict, 'The Palace of History and Art: 2. The Architectural Sculpture', in *The Houses of Parliament*, ed Port, Michael H (1976) pp 232–45

Read 1982
Read, Benedict, *Victorian Sculpture* (1982)

Read 1984
Read, Benedict, 'Was there Pre-Raphaelite Sculpture?', in *Pre-Raphaelite Papers*, ed Parris, Leslie (1984) pp 97–110

Read 1985
Read, Benedict, 'Victorian Sculpture and its Sources', in *Influences in Victorian Art and Architecture*, Occasional Paper (Society of Antiquaries of London) ed Macready, Sarah and Thompson, F H (1985) pp 59–64

Read 1992
Read, Benedict, introd, *Gibson to Gilbert: British Sculpture, 1840–1914, Including a Group of Comparative French Bronzes*, exhib cat (Fine Art Society, London, 1992)

Read 1996
Read, Benedict, 'La Revue du Musée d'Orsay' (3 Sept 1996)

Read 1997
Read, Benedict, 'The Colour of Sculpture, review', *The Sculpture Journal*, vol 1, no 1997, pp 67–71

Read 2000
Read, Benedict, 'Sculpture and the New Palace of Westminster', in *The Houses of Parliament: history, art, architecture*, ed Riding, Christine and Riding, Jacqueline (London: 2000) pp 253–69

Read and Barnes 1991
Read, Benedict and Barnes, Joanna, eds, *Pre-Raphaelite Sculpture; Nature and Imagination in British Sculpture 1848–1914*, exhib cat (1991)

Reading Room Papers
Applications and recommendations for admission to the British Museum Reading Room, British Museum Reading Room Papers 1831–1881 (BL, Add MSS 48340, 48341)

Reaney 1968
Reaney, A, 'Landseer of Sculpture', *Cheshire Life*, vol 34 (May 1968) pp 34–35

Records of Bucks
Records of Buckinghamshire, or Papers and Notes on the History, Antiquities and Architecture of the County (1854–)

Redfern 1977
Redfern, Roger, 'Chantreyland Revisited; Looking Back in a Sheffield Suburb', *Country Life*, vol 162, no 4196 (8 Dec 1977) pp 1751–52

Redgrave 1878
Redgrave, Samuel, *A Dictionary of the English School* (2nd ed, 1878)

Redland Chapel, Church Book
Redland Chapel, Church Book, *c*1740–1775 (Bristol RO, P.RG/T/1)

Register of the Catholic Chapels
'Register of the Catholic Chapels Royal and of the Portuguese Embassy Chapels, 1662–1829', *Catholic Record Society*, vol 38 (1941)

Reichner 1990
Reichner, Robert J, 'Wedgwood Chessmen', *Ars Ceramica*, no 7 (1990) pp 24–28

Reid 1971
Reid, William, 'Cumberland Tankard, Commemorating a Significant Military Event', *Connoisseur*, vol 178 (Nov 1971) pp 154–60

Reilly 1995
Reilly, Robin, *Wedgwood, the New Illustrated Dictionary* (1995)

Remnant 1962
Remnant, G L, 'Jonathan Harmer's Terracottas I', *Sussex Archaeological Collections*, vol 100 (1962) pp 142–48

Remnant 1964
Remnant, G L, 'Jonathan Harmer's Terracottas II', *Sussex Archaeological Collections*, vol 102 (1964) pp 52–54

Rendel 1972
Rendel, R, 'Francis Bird, 1667–1731, Sculptor', *Recusant History*, vol 11, no 4 (1972) pp 206–9

Renfrew 1990
Renfrew, Jane and Robbins, Michael, 'Tobias Rustat and his Monument in Jesus College Chapel, Cambridge', *Antiquaries Journal*, vol 70, no 2 (1990) pp 416–23

Retallick 1998
Retallick, Leslie, *Torre Abbey, Catalogue of the Art Collections* (Torquay: Torbay Council Education Services, 1998)

RG/AL
Gunnis, *A Dictionary of British Sculptors*, annotated by Alastair Laing

RG/HMC
Gunnis, *A Dictionary of British Sculptors*, 1968, annotated by Howard Colvin

RG/JP (1)
Gunnis, Rupert, *A Dictionary of British Sculptors, With Additions and Annotations by John Physick*, 9 vols, typescript (Leeds, Henry Moore Institute, 1965–75)

RG/JP (2)
Gunnis, *A Dictionary of British Sculptors*, John Physick revision (Leeds, Henry Moore Institute, 1975–93)

RG/NP
Gunnis, *A Dictionary of British Sculptors*, annotated by Nicholas Penny

RGIFA
Royal Glasgow Institute for the Fine Arts (founded 1861)

RHA
Royal Hibernian Academy, Dublin

Rhead 1924
Rhead, F A, 'Ireson in Wincanton', *Connoisseur*, vol 69 (1924) pp 147–53

Rheims 1977
Rheims, Maurice, *Nineteenth Century Sculpture* (New York: 1977)

RHS
Royal Horticultural Society, London

RI
Royal Institution

RIBA
Royal Institute of British Architects

RIBA Drawings Cat 1972–84
Royal Institute of British Architects Drawings Collection, *Catalogue of the Drawings Collection of the Royal Institute of British Architects*, 19 volumes (Farnborough: 1972–84)

RIBAD
Royal Institute of British Architects, Drawings

Rice 1983
Rice, D G, *Derby Porcelain* (1983)

Richard Norton Account
Richard Norton, bank account, 1694–5 (Hoare, Ledger D.2)

Richards 1947
Richards, Raymond, *Old Cheshire Churches* (1947)

Richardson 1776
Richardson, George, *A Book of Ceilings, composed in the style of the Antique Grotesque* (1776)

Richardson 1802–8
Richardson, George, *The New Vitruvius Britannicus*, 2 vols (1802–8)

Richardson 1933
Richardson, A E, and Esdaile, Katharine, 'Seventeenth-Century Buildings in Search of an Architect; With Reply by G. Webb', 3 *RIBA Journal*, vol 40 (17 June 1933) pp 24–34

Richardson 1980
Richardson, Joanna, *Keats and his Circle* (London: 1980)

Riches 1984
Riches, Anne, 'Mount Clare, Roehampton', *Architectural History*, vol 27 (1984) pp 255–62

Rickword 1942–45
Rickword, Gerald O, 'The rebuilding of the church of St Mary-at-the-walls, Colchester, 1713–14', *Transactions of the Essex Archaeological Society*, vol 23 (NS) (1942–45) pp 311–20

Riddell 1986
Riddell, Richard, 'Neo-Classical Designs for Medals by C. H. Tatham', *Apollo*, no 123 (Feb 1986) pp 116–22

Ridley 1958
Ridley, Ursula (Viscountess), *Cecilia: The Life and Letters of Cecilia Ridley 1819–1845* (London: 1958)

RIEFAS
Royal Institution for the Encouragement of the Fine Arts in Scotland (founded 1819, granted Royal Charter 1827)

Rijksmuseum Portraits 1995
Scholten, Frits, *Gebeeldhouwde Portretten/ Portrait Sculptures* (Rijksmuseum, Amsterdam: 1995)

Rinder and McKay 1917
Rinder, Frank, and McKay, William Darling, *The Royal Scottish Academy 1826–1916: a complete list of the exhibited works* (1917)

Rippingille 1859
Rippingille, E V, 'Personal recollections of the artists by the late E. V. Rippingille, no. 3: Burlowe the sculptor', *Art Journal*, vol 21 (1859) pp 201–2

Ritchie/Wyatt
Letter from Alexander Handyside Ritchie to James Wyatt, Wyatt Papers 1845 (BL, Add MSS Eg 3515, fol 231)

RKD
Rijksbureau voor Kunsthistorische Documentatie (Netherlands Institute for Art History)

RL
Royal Library

RMI
Royal Manchester Institution

RMI Exhib 1838
Royal Manchester Institution, *Catalogue of the Exhibition of Pictures by the Ancient and Deceased Masters of the Italian, Spanish, Flemish, Dutch and English Schools* (1838)

RMS, Edinburgh
Royal Museum of Scotland, Edinburgh

Roani Villani 1975
Roani Villani, Roberta, 'Innocenzo Spinazzi e l'Ambiente Fiorentino nella Seconda Meta del Settecento', *Paragone*, no 309 (1975) pp 53–85

Roani Villani 1991
Roani Villani, Roberta, 'Il Busto di Negro di Francis Harwood', *Paragone*, vol 42 (July 1991) pp 68–74

Roani Villani 1993
Roani Villani, Roberta, 'Copie dall'Antico: F. Harwood et G. B. Piamontini', *Antologia di Belle Arti*, no 43–47 (1993) pp 108–15

Roberson and Gerdts 1965
Roberson, Samuel A, and Gerdts, William H, 'Greek Slave', *Newark Museum Quarterly*, vol 17, no 1–2 (Winter–Spring 1965) pp 1–30

Roberts 1933
Roberts, R A, *A Calendar of the Inner Temple Records*, 5 vols (1933)

Roberts 1939
Roberts, Henry D, *History of the Royal Pavilion* (1939)

Roberts 1987
Roberts, Jane, *Royal Artists* (1987)

Roberts 1990
Roberts, Hugh, 'Soe Thinn the Wood', *Furniture History*, vol 26 (1990) pp 165–73

Roberts 2002
Roberts, Jane, ed, *Royal Treasures A Golden Jubilee Celebration* (The Royal Collection)

Robinson
Newcastle upon Tyne University, Robinson Library

Robinson 1886
Robinson, John, *Descriptive Catalogue of the Lough & Noble Models of Statues, Bas-reliefs, and Busts in Elswick Hall, Newcastle-on-Tyne* (Newcastle: 1886)

Robinson 1938
Robinson, Henry Crabbe, *Books and their Writers*, 3 vols (London: 1938)

Robinson 1976
Robinson, John, 'Farming on a Princely Scale: Estate Buildings of the Fifth and Sixth Dukes of Bedford at Woburn 1787–1839', *Architectural Review*, vol 160 (Nov 1976) pp 276–79

Robinson 1977–78
Robinson, John Martin, 'R J Wyatt's Flora and Zephyr at Nostell Priory', *National Trust Yearbook*, (1977–78) pp 30–34

Robinson 1978
Robinson, John Martin, 'Alresford House, Hampshire', *Country Life*, vol 163, no 4200 (5 Jan 1978) pp 18–21

Robinson 1979 (1)
Robinson, John Martin, 'A Catalogue of the Architectural Drawings at Carlton Towers, York', *Architectural History*, vol 22 (1979) pp 116–24

Robinson 1979 (2)
Robinson, John Martin, *The Wyatts: An Architectural Dynasty* (1979)

Robinson 1983
Robinson, John Martin, 'Magna Carta, and Pretty Ladies Maids', *Country Life*, (7 July 1983) pp 46–49

Robinson 1989
Robinson, John Martin, *Shugborough*, National Trust (1989)

Robinson 1990
Robinson, Walter, 'Britain Balks at Giving Up Graces', *Art in America*, vol 78 (July 1990) p 35

Robinson 1994
Robinson, John Martin, *Arundel Castle* (Chichester: 1994)

Robinson 1999
Robinson, John Martin, 'Knowsley Hall, Lancashire: A Seat of the Earl of Derby', *Country Life*, vol 193, no 15 (15 April 1999) pp 70–73

Robinson and Adams 1935
Robinson, Henry W and Adams, Walter, ed, *The Diary of Robert Hooke, MA, MD, FRS, 1672–1680, transcribed from the original in the possession of the City of London (Guildhall Library)* (1935)

Rock 2003
Rock, Joe, ' "An ingenious self-taught sculptor", Robert Forrest', *The Sculpture Journal*, vol 9 (2003) pp 62–71

Rockingham Vouchers
Vouchers for works of art, Papers of the Second Marquess of Rockingham, Wentworth Woodhouse Muniments (Sheffield City Library, WWM vouchers 1, 36, 54, 66, 77, 93)

Rococo 1984
Rococo, Art and Design in Hogarth's England (exhib cat, VAM: 1984) pp 277–309

Rogers 1778
Rogers, C, *A Collection of Prints in Imitation of Drawings* (London: 1778)

Rogers 1957
Rogers, Alan, 'A Masterpiece in Marble', *Country Life*, vol 122 (19 Dec 1957) p 1371

Rogers 1977
Rogers, M, 'Michael Rysbrack's Bust for Edmund Waller', *Burlington Magazine*, vol 119 (May 1977) p 352

Rogers and Cotton, 1974
Exhibition of Old Master and English Drawings and European Bronzes from the Collection of Charles Rogers and William Cotton (London, Sotheby: 1974)

ROM, Toronto
Royal Ontario Museum, Toronto

Roper 1913
Roper, Ida Mary, *The History and Memorials of St Marks Church, Bristol, Which is Now the Lord Mayor's Chapel* (Bristol: 1913)

Roper 1931
Roper, Ida Mary, *The Monumental Effigies of Gloucestershire and Bristol* (Gloucester: Printed for the author by H Osborne, 1931)

Roper 1964
Roper, Lanning, *The Gardens of Anglesey Abbey* (1964)

Roper 1967
Roper, A, *The Church of All Saints, Burmarsh* (Ashford: 1967)

Rorschach 1985
Rorschach, Kimerly, 'Frederick, Prince of Wales (1707–1751) as a Patron of the Visual Arts: Princely Patriotism and Political Propaganda' Ph D Diss (Yale University, 1985)

Roscoe 1980
Roscoe, Ingrid, 'The Decoration and Furnishing of Kirtlington Park', *Apollo*, vol 111, no 215 (Jan 1980) pp 22–29

Roscoe 1987 (1)
Roscoe, Ingrid, 'Peter Scheemakers at Rome: A Visit with Laurent Delvaux, Peter Angelles and William Hoare', *Gazette des Beaux-Arts*, vol 110 (July–Aug 1987) pp 1–10

Roscoe 1987 (2)
Roscoe, Ingrid, 'James "Athenian" Stuart and the Scheemakers family: a Lucrative Partnership between Architect and Sculptors', *Apollo*, vol 126 (Sept 1987) pp 178–84

Roscoe 1990
Roscoe, Ingrid, 'Peter Scheemakers and Classical Sculpture in early Georgian England' Ph D Diss (University of Leeds, 1990)

Roscoe 1992
Roscoe, Ingrid, 'Flemish Sculptors and Adjustments for the English Market: The Case of Peter Scheemakers', *Journal of the Church Monuments Society*, vol 7 (1992) pp 75–84

Roscoe 1994
Roscoe, Ingrid, 'The Monument to the Memory of Shakespeare', *Journal of the Church Monuments Society*, vol 9 (1994) pp 72–82

Roscoe 1995
Roscoe, Ingrid, ' "Of Statues, Obelisks, Dyals, and other Invegetative Ornaments": Sources and Meanings for English Garden Statues', *Apollo*, vol 141, no 395 (Jan 1995) pp 38–42

Roscoe 1997
Roscoe, Ingrid, ' "The Statues of the Sovereigns of England": Sculpture for the Second Building, 1695–1831', in *The Royal Exchange*, ed Saunders, Ann (London Topographical Society, 1997) pp 174–87

Roscoe 1999
Roscoe, Ingrid, 'Peter Scheemakers, Business Conduct and Workshop Practice with Catalogue Raisonné', *Walpole Society*, vol 61 (1999) pp 163–304

Roscoe 2001
Roscoe, Ingrid, 'Laurent Delvaux, 1696–1778, Reviver of a National School', review *The Sculpture Journal*, vol 5 (2001) pp 106–8

Roscoe and Hempel 1997
Roscoe, Ingrid, and Hempel, Kenneth, 'The Refreshment of Memory: Joseph Wilton's Byerley Monument, Restored', *Journal of the Church Monuments Society*, vol 12 (1997) pp 49–57

Rosenbach
Rosenbach Museum and Library, Philadelphia

Ross 1841
Ross, M, *Architectural and Picturesque Views in Newcastle upon Tyne* (1841)

Rossetti 1906
Rossetti, William Michael, *Some Reminiscences of William Michael Rossetti*, 2 vols (1906)

Rossetti/Smith
Fragments of a letter from William Michael Rossetti to Bernhard Alexander Smith, Smith family papers nd (State Library of Victoria, Melbourne, Australia, MS 10626 Box 2 25/f)

Rossetti/Tupper
Correspondence between the Rossetti and Tupper families, *c*1850–1906 (Brotherton MSS, University of Leeds, BC Rossetti Correspondence)

Rossi Archive
Two contracts; 'Description of the sketch for Lord Nelson's Monument'; 'Explanation of the Design of a monument to the memory of Captains Mosse and Riou'; Letter to Rossi' from the Jennerian Society; letter from Rossi to Committee for the Inspection of National Monuments, describing a proposed monument to commemorate Waterloo; Catalogue of a posthumous auction of his models held by his son, F O Rossi, *c*1801–1840 (Guildhall PMD, uncatalogued)

Rossi/Balfour
J C F Rossi, letter to E Balfour, requesting that the College Arms be given to the bearer, 3 May 1823 (Edinburgh University Library, Special Colls, La.II.426/375)

Rossi/Balmano
J C F Rossi, letter to Mr Balmano declining an invitation to dine, 5 May 1821 (Edinburgh University Library, Special Colls, La.II.426/374)

Rossi/Beckford
J C F Rossi, letter to William Beckford, Beckford MSS 8 Oct 1822 (Bodleian, C34 f.134)

Rossi/Newton
Letters from Charles Rossi to Francis Milner Newton, Secretary of the Royal Academy, requesting reimbursement for expense of transporting bas-relief of Ulysees from Rome to Leghorn, 29 April and 7 December 1785 (RA, 1184)

Rossi/Phillips
J C F Rossi, letter to Mr Phillips, 12 October 1822 (Edinburgh City Library, BRS/qwN/Box)

Rossi/Rigaud
J C F Rossi, letter to J F Rigaud, 1834–36 (Oxford University MHS, NRA 9532 Oxford Scientific)

Rowan 1968
Rowan, Alistair, 'Penicuik House, Midlothian – I', *Country Life* (15 Aug 1968) pp 383–87

Rowan 1973
Rowan, Alistair, 'Blairquhan, Ayrshire II', *Country Life*, vol 153, no 3951 (1973) pp 1154–58

Rowan 1985
Rowan, Alistair, 'Lord Derby's Reconstruction of The Oaks', *Burlington Magazine*, vol 127, no 991 (Oct 1985) pp 678–87

Rowell 2000 (1)
Rowell, Christopher, 'Grinling Gibbons's Carved Room at Petworth: 'The Most Superb Monument of his Skill' ', *Apollo*, vol 151, no 458 (April 2000) pp 19–26

Rowell 2000 (2)
Rowell, Christopher, *Petworth House*, National Trust (2000)

Rowell 2002
Rowell, Christopher, 'Turner at Petworth: The 3rd Earl of Egremont's carved room restored', *Apollo*, vol 155, no 484 (June 2002) pp 40–47

Roy Cornwall Soc
Royal Cornwall Polytechnic Society, Falmouth

Royal A
Royal Archives, Windsor Castle

Royal Inf
Royal Infirmary

Royal Mag
Royal Magazine

RSA
Royal Society of Arts (see also Soc of A)

RSA J. 1991
'Sale of Carlini Statue', *Royal Society of Arts Journal*, vol 139 (June 1991) p 433

RSA Minutes
Royal Society of Arts, Minutes of Various Premium Committees, 1757–58; 1758–60, 1761–62, 1762–63, 1763–64, 1764–65, 1765–66, 1766–67, 1767–68, 1768–69 (RSA, London, AD/MA/100/12/02 (1757–58); PR/GE/112/12/1–10 (1758–69)

RSA Premiums
Royal Society of Arts, Premiums by the Society established at London for the Encouragement of Arts, Manufactures and Commerce, (RSA, London: 1758–62, 1763, 1765, 1767, 1768–75, PR/GE/112/13/1–5)

RSA Register 1778
RSA London, A Register of the Premiums and Bounties given by the Society Instituted at London for the Encouragement of the Arts, Manufactures, and Commerce, from the Original Institution in the Year MDCCLIV, to the Year MDCCLXXVI Inclusive (James Phillips, in George-Yard, Lombard St, 1778, RSA PR.GE/112/13/225)

RSA Transactions
Transactions of the Society Instituted at London for the Encouragement of the Arts, Manufactures and Commerce (London: 1783–1851, RSA, PR.GE/112/13/11–67)

Ruch 1968
Ruch, John E., 'Regency Coade: A Study of the Coade Record Books, 1813–21', *Architectural History*, vol 11 (1968) pp 34–56

Ruch 1970
Ruch, John, 'Coade Stone in Ireland', *Bulletin of the Irish Georgian Society*, vol 13, no 4 (Oct–Dec 1970) pp 1–12

Rudolph 1980
Rudolph, Stella, 'Il Monumento Stuart del Canova: Un Committente Dimenticato e il Primo Pensiero Ritrovato', *Antologia di Belle Arti*, no 13–14 (1980) pp 44–54

Rudolph 1997–1998
Rudolph, William Keyse, 'The "Choice" of Hercules and Homer: Two Wedgwood Designs by John Flaxman', *Ars Ceramica*, vol 14 (1997–98) pp 24–34

Rumsey Foster 1848
Rumsey Foster, H, ed, *The Stowe Catalogue, Priced and Annotated* (London: 1848)

Rusby 1896
Rusby, James, *The History of Leeds Parish Church* (1896)

Ruskin 1903–12
Cook, E T and Wedderburn, Alexander, eds, *The Works of John Ruskin*, 39 vols (1903–12)

Russell
Russell Papers, 1675 (Bedford and Luton Archives and Records Service, box 262)

Russell 1954
Russell, Maud, 'For Identification; A Bust by Nollekens Dated 1797', *Country Life*, vol 115, no 2997 (June 24 1954) p 2105

Russell and Price 1759
Russell, P, and Price, Owen, *England Displayed. Being a New and Accurate Survey and Description of the Kingdom of England*, 2 vols (1759)

Russell Cotes Mu
Russell Cotes Museum, Bournemouth, Hants

Rutledge 1945
Rutledge, Anna, 'William John Coffee as a Portrait Sculptor', *Gazette des Beaux-Arts*, vol 28 ser 6 (Nov 1945) pp 297–312

S of L
Survey of London

S S Co, Inventories
South Sea Company Inventories (Francis Hawes, Sir Harcourt Masters, Sir John Fellowes, Ambrose Page), Guildhall Library (London: 1721)

SAA
Society of Artists Archives, Burlington House, London

Saabye 1977
Saabye, M., 'Literaturverzeichnis (Thorvaldsen)', *Kolner Berichte zur Kunstgeschichte Koln*, vol 2 (1977) pp 469–81

Sabin c1760
Sabin, John, *A Brief Description of the collegiate church and choir of St Mary, Warwick* (Coventry: c1760)

SAC
Sussex Archaelogical Collections

SAC 1929
Spokes, Sidney, 'Notes and Queries', *Sussex Archaeological Collections*, vol 70 (1929) pp 221–22

Sackler Priv Coll
Kenworthy-Brown, John, ed, *Private Collection of the Sackler family* (nd)

Sackville
Sackville Papers, 1677 (Centre for Kentish Studies, Maidstone, U 269 E 291/3; UO 51 C 244)

Sackville 2003
Sackville, Edward, 'The Sackville Monument: an evaluation' MA Diss (Edinburgh University, 2003)

Sadleir 1933
Sadleir, Michael, *Blessington-d'Orsay: a masquerade* (London: 1933)

SAG
Salford Art Gallery, Lancs

Sakula 1988
Sakula, A, *Royal Society of Medicine. Portraits, Paintings and Sculptures* (1988)

SAL
Society of Artists in Liverpool

Salling 1972
Salling, Emma, 'Canova and Thorvaldson, a Study in Contrasts', *Apollo*, no 96 (Sept 1972) pp 214–19

Salmon 1990
Salmon, Frank, 'British Architects and the Florentine Academy', *Mitteilungen des Kunsthistorischen Institutes in Florenz*, vol 34, no 1–2 (1990) pp 199–214

Salters Ct Mins
Corporation of London, Salters' Company, Court Minutes, 1821–1827 (CLRO Guildhall)

Salters, BCM
Salters' Company, Building Committee Minutes, 1821–1827 (Salters' Hall, City of London, E3/1/1)

Saltram 1992
Saltram, National Trust (1992)

Sampson ed, 1895
Sampson, J, ed, *Handlist of Books and Pamphlets of the Liverpool Royal Institution* (1895)

Sanchez-Jauregui 2001
Sanchez-Jauregui, Maria Dolores, 'Two Portraits of Francis Basset by Pompeo Batoni in Madrid', *Burlington Magazine*, vol 143, no 1180 (July 2001) pp 420–25

Sandby 1862
Sandby, William, *The History of the Royal Academy of Arts*, facsimile of 1862 edition, 2 vols (London: 1970)

Sanderson/Okeover
Leeke Okeover, Estate Correspondence, Okeover of Okeover Coll 1745–6 (Derbys RO, D231)

Sandstrom 1989
Sandstrom, Birgitta, 'A Rediscovered Marble Relief by John Flaxman', *Burlington Magazine*, vol 131 (Sept 1989) pp 631–33

SANG
South Africa National Gallery, Cape Town

Sankey 1999
Sankey, John, 'Thomas Brock and the Albert Memorial', *The Sculpture Journal*, vol 3 (1999) pp 87–92

Sarfatti 1939
Sarfatti, Margherita Grassini, 'Lorenzo Bartolini; with English Summary', *La Renaissance*, vol 22 (March 1939) pp 22–25, 48

Sargent 1949
Sargent, C, 'Battle Against the Academy Over the Chantrey Collection', *Art News*, vol 48 (March 1949) p 31ff

Sass I and II, 1963; Sass III, 1965
Else Kai, Sass, *Thorvaldsens Portraetbuster*, 3 vols (Copenhagen: 1963–65)

Sassoon 1938
Sassoon, Siegfried, *The Old Century and Seven More Years* (London: 1938)

Saumarez Smith 1990
Saumarez Smith, Charles, *The Building of Castle Howard* (London: 1990)

Saunders 1985
Saunders, Ann, 'Samuel Johnson's Funeral Monument', *Royal Society of Arts Journal*, vol 133, no 5349 (Aug 1985) pp 632–36

Saunders 1993
Saunders, Edward, *Joseph Pickford of Derby* (1993)

Saunders 1997
Saunders, Ann, 'The Second Exchange', in *The Royal Exchange*, ed Saunders, Ann (London Topographical Society, 1997) pp 121–35

Saunders 2001
Saunders, Ann, *St Paul's The Story of a Cathedral* (London: 2001)

Saur 1998
Saur, K G, *Allgemeines Künstlerlexicon. Die Bildenden Künstler aller Zeiten und Völker* (Munich and Leipzig: 1998)

Savanarola 1847
Savanarola, J, *Facts and Figures from Italy. Addressed during the last two winters to Charles Dickens, being an appendix to his 'Pictures'* (1847)

Sayce and Esterly 2000
Sayce, Lynda, and Esterly, David, ' "He Was Likewise Musical": An Unexplored Aspect of Grinling Gibbons', *Apollo*, vol 151, no 460 (June 2000) pp 11–21

SBA
Society of British Artists

Sborgi 1983–1985
Sborgi, F, 'Colombo, Otto Scultori e un Piedistallo', *Studi di Storia delle Arti*, vol 5 (1983–85) pp 329–47

SBT RO
Shakespeare Birthplace Trust Record Office, Warwicks

Sc J
The Sculpture Journal

Schaefer and Fusco 1987
Schaefer, Scott, and Fusco, Peter, *European Painting and Sculpture in the Los Angeles County Museum of Art* (1987)

Scheidemantel 1968
Scheidemantel, V, ' "The Apotheosis of Homer", a Wedgwood and Bentley Plaque', in *Festschrift Ulrich Middeldorf*, ed Kosegarten, Antje and Tigler, Peter (Berlin: 1968) pp 517–22

Schellekens 1995
Schellekens, Claudia, 'Strijd en Verzoening?: Het Iconografische Beeldprogramma van de Tuinen te Melbourne Hall, Derbyshire, Engeland', *Tuinkunst (Amsterdam)*, vol 1 (1995) pp 80–94

Schlegal 1974
Schlegel, Ursula, 'Bozzetti in Terracotta by Pietro Stefano Monnot', *Bulletin of the Museum of Fine Arts, Boston*, vol 72, no 367 (1974) pp 56–68

Schmitz 1986
Schmitz, Brigitte, 'Rudolf Schadow. Ein Lyriker unter den Klassizistischen Bildhauern', *Bildende Künst*, vol 34, no 7 (1986) pp 320–21

Schmitz 1991
Schmitz, Brigitte, 'Die Grazie der "Spinnerin": Eine Restaurierte Skulptur von Rudolph Schadow', *Museums Journal, Berlin*, vol 5, no 2 (April 1991) pp 60–61

Scholten 1995
Scholten, Frits, 'Canova in Delft: The Commission for the \funeral Monument to Willem George Frederick, Prince of Orange (1806) Reconstructed', *Journal of the Church Monuments Society*, vol 10 (1995) pp 109–22

Scholten 2003
Scholten, Frits, *Sumptuous Memories: Studies in Seventeenth-Century Dutch Tomb Sculpture* (Zwolle: 2003)

SCL
Sheffield City Libraries

Scott 1871
Scott, William Bell, *The British School of Sculpture* (1871)

Scott 1879
Scott, George Gilbert, *Personal and Professional Recollections*, a facsimile of the original edition [published 1879] with new material and critical introduction by Gavin Stamp (Stamford: 1995)

Scott 1983
Scott, Beatrice, 'Lady Elizabeth Hastings', *Yorkshire Archaeological Journal*, vol 15 (1983) pp 95–118

Scott 2000
Scott, Eliza, 'Romancing the Stone', *Garden Design*, vol 19, no 4 (June–July 2000) pp 68–73

Sculpture . . . Rubens, 1977
M M, *La Sculpture au Siecle de Rubens dans les Pay-Bas merid-ionaux et la principauté de Liege* (Musée d'Art Ancien, Brussels: 1977) pp 219–42

SD
signed and dated

SDA
Seventh Day Adventists, website <www.familysearch.org>

Seely 1773
Rivington, J, and Seely, J B, *A Description of Stowe, London and Buckingham* (1773)

Seidmann 1985
Seidmann, Gertrude, 'Studies in the Society's History and Archives. "A Very Ancient, Useful and Curious Art": The Society of Arts and the Revival of Gem-Engraving in Eighteenth Century England', *Royal Society of Arts Journal*, vol 133, no 5342 (1985) pp 150–53

Seidmann 1987
Seidmann, Gertrude, 'Nathaniel Marchant, Gem-Engraver', *Walpole Society*, vol 53 (1987) pp 1–105

Seidmann 1993
Seidmann, Gertrude, 'A Cornelian Intaglio Antinous by Edward Burch', *Antiquaries Journal*, vol 73 (1993)

Seidmann 1996
Seidmann, Gertrude, 'News About Marchant', *Jewellery Studies*, vol 7 (1996) p 89

Seidmann 1997
Seidmann, Gertrude, 'An Eighteenth Century Collector as Patron: the 4th Duke of Marlborough and the London Engravers', *Stud Hist Art*, vol 54 (1997) pp 262–79

Selincourt and Darbyshire 1947
Selincourt, E, and Darbyshire, H (eds), *Wordsworth: Poetical Works*, 4 vols (1947)

Semenzato 1967
Semenzato, Camillo, *La Scultura Veneta del Seicento e del Settecento* (1967)

Sessions House Minutes
Minutes of the Commission to rebuild the Middlesex Sessions House, 1779–82 (LMA)

Sewter 1939
Sewter, A C, 'Statue by Roubiliac: Religion, or Victory, in Leicester Museum', *Burlington Magazine*, vol 75 (Sept 1939) pp 120–23

Seymour 1735
Seymour, Robert, *A Survey of the Cities of London and Westminster*, 2 vols (1735)

Seymour 1952
Seymour, June, 'Edward Pearce: Baroque Sculptor of London', *Guildhall Miscellany*, vol 1 (Jan 1952) pp 10–18

Seymour 1962
Seymour, Howard, 'Some Eighteenth-Century Restorations of Myron's Discobolus', *Journal of the Warburg and Courtauld Institutes*, vol 25 (July 1962) pp 330–34

SFA
Society of Female Artists

Sgherzi 2003
Sgherzi, Michela, 'Ufficio Arte Sacra', *Rivista Diocesana Caslese*, no 3 (Maggio-Guigno 2003) pp 204–8

Sharf 1961
Sharf, Frederic Alan, 'Garden Cemetery and American Sculpture: Mount Auburn', *Art Quarterly*, vol 24, no 1 (Spring 1961) pp 80–88

Sharples 1991
Sharples, Joseph, *The Oratory, St James's Cemetery, Liverpool* (Liverpool: 1991)

Shaw 1911
Shaw, William, *Letters of Denization and Acts of Naturalisation 1603–1700* (Lymington: 1911)

Shaw 1935
Shaw, G, *History of the Humber Lodge of Freemasons* (Hull: 1935)

Shaw Sparrow, 1931
Shaw Sparrow, W, *A Book of Sporting Painters* (1931), pp 247–53

Sheahan 1868
Sheahan, J J, *History of the Town and Port of Kingston-upon-Hull*, 2nd ed (Beverley: 1868)

Shearstone c1980
Shearstone, Pauline, *Sheffield Sketches Including Norton and the Chantrey Story* (Sheffield: c1980)

Shedd 1992
Shedd, Meredith, 'A Mania for Statuettes: Achille Collas and other pioneers in the mechanical reproduction of Sculpture', *Gazette des Beaux-Arts*, vol 120 (1992) pp 36–48

Sheehy 1980
Sheehy, Jeanne, *The Early Celtic Revival* (Dublin, National Gallery of Ireland, 1980)

Shelley 1824
Shelley, Percy Bysshe, *Posthumous Poems* (1824)

Sheppard 1960
Sheppard, F H W, ed, *Survey of London: St James Westminster* (London: HBMCE, 1960)

Sherborn 1955
Sherborn, Derek, 'History in Marble', *Country Life*, vol 118, no 3062 (22 Sept 1955) p 617

Sherborn Autographs
Letter to John Bell, 1846; Letter to William Calder Marshall; John Henry Foley, letter to R N Wornum, 1866, Letters and papers collected by Charles Davies Sherborn, mainly 19th and 20th century (BL, Sherborn Autographs, Add MSS 42575 fol 47; 42576 fol 198; 42585 fol 270)

Sherburn 1956
Sherburn, George, ed, *The Correspondence of Alexander Pope* (1956)

Shields 1989
Shields, John, 'Josiah Wedgwood and the Ladies: the Lives and Careers of Lady Diana Beauclerk, Miss Emma Crewe, and Lady Elizabeth Templetown' MA Diss (Fashion Institute of Technology, 1989)

Shortt 1952
Shortt, H de S, 'Another Bust of Newton', *Country Life*, vol 111, no 2877 (7 March 1952) p 662

Shout/Peel
Letter from Robert Shout to Sir Robert Peel, 20 Jan 1835 (BL, Add MS 40410, fol(s) 306)

Sicca and Yarrington 2000
Sicca, Cinzia, and Yarrington, Alison, *The Lustrous Trade: Material Culture and the History of Sculpture in England and Italy, c.1700–c.1860* (2000)

Sidney 1834
Sidney, Edwin, *The Life of the Reverend Rowland Hill* (1834)

Silber 1987
Silber, Evelyn, *Sculpture in Birmingham Museum and Art Gallery: A Summary Catalogue* (1987)

Silvester and Pitman 1998
Silvester, Bob, and Pitman, Liz, 'Eighteenth-century stone masons in the Black Mountains', *Church Archaeology*, vol 2 (1998) pp 19–34

Simon 1981
Simon, Herta Babette, 'Millais Portrait Relief by Alexander Munro at the Ashmolean Museum, Oxford', *Apollo*, no 113 (Feb 1981) p 115

Simon 1986
Simon, Jacob, *Handel: a Celebration of his Life and Times*, exhib cat (NPG, 1986)

Simon 1992
Simon, Jacob, *Beningborough Hall*, National Trust (1992)

Simon 1993
Simon, Robin, 'British Art and Europe: Theme of the Grosvenor House Fair, London', *Apollo*, no 137 (June 1993) pp 348–62

Simon 1994
Simon, Jacob, 'Frame Studies II', *Burlington Magazine*, vol 136, no 1096 (July 1994) pp 444–55

Simpson 1895
Simpson, William, 'Joseph Bonomi, A.R.A., Architect, and his Son', 3rd series *RIBA Journal*, vol 2 (1895) pp 548–49

Simpson 1925
Simpson, William, *Inverness Artists. Some noted figures of the nineteenth century*, reprinted from the *Inverness Courier* of 30 Dec 1924 to 20 Jan 1925 (Inverness: 1925) pp 4–18

Simpson 1991
Simpson, Ian, *Anatomy of Humans, Including Works by Leonardo da Vinci, John Flaxman . . .* (1991)

Singer 1901–7
Singer, Isidore, ed, *The Jewish Encyclopaedia: a descriptive record of the history, religion, literature, and customs of the Jewish people from the earliest times to the present day*, 12 vols (New York: 1901–7)

Sir Richard Westmacott/Canova
Letters from Sir Richard Westmacott RA to Antonio Canova, 1796–1820 (Museo-Biblioteca-Archivio, Bassano del Grappa)

Sir Robert Smirke/New Church Commission
Letter from Sir Robert Smirke to Parliamentary Commissioners, Minute Book, HM Commission for Building New Churches 1821 (Lambeth Palace Library)

SIRIS
Smithsonian Institution Research Information System (http://www.siris.si.edu/)

SJSM
Sir John Soane's Museum, London

Skelton 1994–1996
Skelton, Andrew C, 'The Development of the Briggens Estate, Hunsdon, since 1720', *Hertfordshire Archaeology*, vol 12 (1994–96) pp 111–28

Skelton 1996
Skelton, Andrew C, 'New Light on the Development of Carshalton Church', *Surrey Archaeological Collections*, vol 83 (1996) pp 1–19

Skinner 1977
Skinner, Basil, 'Entering heaven politely, the Georgian way of death', *Country Life*, vol 161, no 4153 (3 Feb 1977) pp 258–59

Skinners, Ct Bks
Corporation of London, Skinners' Company, extracts from Court Books relating to Skinners' Hall (CLRO Guildhall, 31310 A, 1–2)

Slee 1966
Slee, John, 'Wren's Favoured Stone and Masons', *Country Life*, vol 139 (16 April 1966) pp 870–71

Slingsby Papers
Slingsby Papers, 1729 (Yorkshire Archaeological Soc, DD56, 148, 12)

Sloman 1932
Sloman, V, 'M. H. Spang en Dansk Billedhugger fra de 18 Aarhundrede', *Tilsk* (1932) p 12

Sloman 1991
Sloman, Susan Legouix, 'General Wade's Altar-Piece for Bath Abbey: a Reconstruction', *Burlington Magazine*, vol 133, no 1061 (Aug 1991) pp 507–10

Smailes 1987
Smailes, Helen, 'Thomas Campbell and the Camera Lucida: the Buccleuch Statue of the 1st Duke of Wellington', *Burlington Magazine*, vol 129 (Nov 1987) pp 709–14

Smailes 1990
Smailes, Helen, ed, *The Concise Catalogue of the Scottish National Portrait Gallery* (Edinburgh: 1990)

Small/Wedgwood
Letter from Captain William Small to Josiah Wedgwood II, Wedgwood Archive, 8 August 1826 (Keele University Library, E2/1396)

Smiles 1861
Smiles, Samuel, *Lives of the Engineers* (1861)

Smiles 1894
Smiles, Samuel, *Josiah Wedgwood* (1894)

Smith 1774
Smith, Charles, *The Ancient and Present State of the County and City of Waterford*, 2nd ed (Dublin: 1774)

Smith 1807
Smith, John Thomas, *Antiquities of Westminster* (1807)

Smith 1815
Smith, J T, *Antient Topography of London* (1815)

Smith 1828
Smith, J T, *Nollekens and his Times*, 2 vols (1828)

Smith 1846
Smith, J T, and Mackay, Charles, eds, *An Antiquarian Ramble in the Streets of London with Anecdotes of their more celebrated residents* (1846)

Smith 1905
Smith, J T, *A Book for a Rainy Day* (1905)

Smith 1916
Smith, A H, 'Lord Elgin and his Collection', *Journal of Hellenic Studies*, vol 36 (1916) pp 163–372

Smith 1920
Smith, J T, *Nollekens and his Times*, edited and annotated by Wilfred Whitten, 2 vols (1920)

Smith 1931
Smith, Harold Clifford, *Buckingham Palace: its Furniture, Decoration and History* (London and New York: 1931)

Smith 1945
Smith, H. Clifford, 'Henry Keene: A Georgian Architect', *Country Life*, vol 97 (30 March, 18 May, 1945) pp 556–57, 868

Smith 1957
Smith, E E, 'An Eighteenth Century London Mason', *Country Life*, vol 122 (10 Oct 1957) p 727

Smith 1979
Smith, Bernard, *Place, Taste and Tradition, a study of Australian art since 1788*, 2nd edition (1979)

Smith 1982
Smith, L R, 'Sir Joseph Banks – the First Wedgwood Portrait Medallion', *Proceedings of the Wedgwood Society*, no 11 (1982) pp 173–78

Smith 1996
Smith, Nicola, 'Great Nassau's Image, Royal George's Test', *Georgian Group Journal*, vol 6 (1996) pp 12–23

Smith 1998
Smith, George, 'Furniture and Plenishing for 1 Park Terrace, Glasgow: A Little-Known Commission Designed by John Thomas (1813–1862)', *Furniture History*, vol 34 (1998) pp 266–78

Smith 1999
Smith, Nicola, 'The Ludgate Statues', *The Sculpture Journal*, vol 3 (1999) pp 14–25

Smith 2000
Smith, Dan, 'Hopeful monsters: The Crystal Palace dinosaurs', *Things*, no 13 (Winter 2000–1) pp 29–45

Smith 2001
Smith, Nicola, *The Royal Image and the English People* (Aldershot: 2001)

Smith and Hall 2000
Smith, Ann, and Hall, Michael, 'Sherborne Castle, Dorset', *Country Life*, vol 194, no 32 (10 Aug 2000) pp 38–41

Smith Diary
Typescript extracts from the diary of John Smith, of Darnick, 1812–1854 (NLS, MS 8499)

Smith Family Papers
Papers of the family of Bernhard Smith, including correspondence, diaries and drawings, *c*1873–1929 (State Library of Victoria, Melbourne, Australia, MS 10626)

Smith of Darnick Family Papers
Family papers of John and Thomas Smith of Darnick (SRO, GD 241/250)

Smith Williams/Park
Letter from W Smith Williams of Kensington to Patric Park, 8 Sept 1841 (National Library of Scotland, 10098, vol 1, no 47)

Smith/Scott
Letter from John and Thomas Smith of Darnick to Sir Walter Scott, 1824 (NLS, MS 3899, fol 199)

Smyth 1839
Smyth, George Lewis, *The Monuments and Genii of St Paul's Cathedral and Westminster Abbey* (1839)

Smyth 1905–7
Smyth, Albert Henry, ed, *The Writings of Benjamin Franklin*, 10 vols (New York: 1905–7)

Snodin 1986
Snodin, Michael, 'Trade Cards and English Rococo', in *The Rococo in England, Symposium*, ed Hind, Charles (London: VAM, 1986) pp 82–103

Snodin and Styles 2001
Snodin, Michael, and Styles, John, *Design and the Decorative Arts, Britain 1500–1900* (VAM: 2001)

Snow 1932
Snow, Julia, 'Canova Commemorated on Staffordshire', *Antiques Magazine*, vol 22 (Oct 1932) pp 143–45

Snow 1941
Snow, J D S, 'Postscript to Canova Commemorated on Staffordshire; Evidence Implicating a Staffordshire Potter', *Antiques Magazine*, vol 40 (Oct 1941) p 218

SNPG
Scottish National Portrait Gallery

Soane 1986
Thornton, Peter, ed, *A New Description of Sir John Soane's Museum*, seventh edition (1986)

Soane Abstract of Bills
Abstract of bills paid by Sir John Soane (SJSM, Abstract of Bills, 3 books)

Soane Accts, 1781–86
Sir John Soane, Account Book, 1781–1786 (SJSM)

Soane Accts, 1792–1805
Sir John Soane, Account Book, 1792–1805 (SJSM)

Soane Bank Account
Sir John Soane, Bank Account with the Bank of England, 1777–1810 (SJSM, 11 vols)

Soane Bill Book
Sir John Soane, Bill Book, 1794–1797 (SJSM)

Soane Bills, 1785
Sir John Soane, Copies of Bills, 1785 (SJSM)

Soane Cupboard
Sir John Soane, Misc papers (SJSM, Soane Cupboard)

Soane Journal I
Sir John Soane, Journal I, 1787–1793 (SJSM)

Soane Journal II
Sir John Soane, Journal II, 1781–97 (SJSM)

Soane Priv Corr
Sir John Soane, Private Correspondence (SJSM)

Soane, Crawford Acct Bk
Sir John Soane, Account Book for John Crawford, 1793–1795 (SJSM, Cupboard F/xxx)

Soane, New Cavendish Acct Bk, 1781–4
Sir John Soane, Account Book for New Cavendish Street, 1781–1784 (SJSM, Cupboard F/vii)

Soane, Wimpole Bill Bk
Sir John Soane, Wimpole Bill Book, 1791–94 (SJSM, Cupboard F/xviii)

Soc Antiq
Society of Antiquaries, London

Soc of A
Society of Arts, Manufacture and Science, later Royal Society of Arts

Soc of Artists
Society of Artists, London

Soc of Artists Papers 1759–61
'The Papers of the Society of Artists of Great Britain', *Walpole Society*, vol 6 (1917–18) pp 113–30

Soc of BA
Society of British Artists

Soc of Dil
Society of Dilettanti

Solkin 1996
Solkin, David, 'Samaritan or Scrooge? The contested image of Thomas Guy in Eighteenth-Century England', *Art Bulletin*, vol 78 (Sept 1996) pp 467–84

Sopwith 1826
Sopwith, T, *An Historical and Descriptive Account of All Saints Church, Newcastle* (Newcastle: 1826)

Sotheby MSS
Sotheby, James, *Accountbook*, Sotheby Family Notebooks MSS (NAL 86KK Box 1: 1701–1704)

Souden 1991
Souden, David, *Wimpole Hall, Cambridgeshire*, National Trust (1991)

Southwick 1990
Southwick, Leslie, 'The Silver Vases Awarded by the Patriotic Fund', *Silver Society Journal*, vol 1 (1990) pp 27–49

Sparrow 1926
Sparrow, Walter Shaw, *A Book of British Etching, from Francis Barlow to Seymour Haden* (London: 1926)

Spencer 1977
Spencer, N, *Sculptured Monuments in Norfolk Churches* (1977)

Spencer-Longhurst 1998
Spencer-Longhurst, Paul, and Naylor, Andrew, 'Nost's Equestrian George I Restored', *The Sculpture Journal*, vol 2 (1998) pp 31–40

Spielmann 1901
Spielmann, M H, *British Sculpture and Sculptors of To-day* (London: 1901)

Spiers 1918–19
Spiers, Walter Lewis, 'The Notebook and Account Book of Nicholas Stone', *Walpole Society*, vol 7 (1918–19)

Spink 1976
Spink, Reginald, 'Sculptor of Gods and Madmen; Caius Gabriel Cibber, 1630–1700', *Country Life*, vol 159 (22 Jan 1976) pp 208–9

Spitzer 1993
Spitzer, Gerd, 'Zur Situation der Bildhauerei an der Dresdener Kunstakademie im Ersten Drittel des 19. Jahrhunderts', *Zeitschrift des Deutschen Vereins fur Kunstwissenschaft*, vol 47 (1993) pp 58–73

SPPDL
Society for Promoting Painting and Design in Liverpool

Springer 1977
Springer, P, 'Thorvaldsen und die Bildhauer der Berliner Schule in Rom', *Kolner Berichte zur Kunstgeschichte Koln*, vol 2 (1977) pp 249–76

SRO
National Archives of Scotland/Scottish Record Office

SRR
Shropshire Records and Research

SRR/Powis Coll
Building &c at Oakley Park (2nd Baron Clive), 1785–1790

SSAHST
South Staffordshire Archaeological and Historical Society Transactions

SSC
South Sea Company Directors, Inventories

SSC Directors' sale, 1722
A Catalogue of the Pictures, bustos, Antiquities & other valuable Curiosities lately belonging to C Joye, Sir L Blackwell, F Hawes and other Directors of the South Sea Company (1722)

St George, Bloomsbury, Bills of Work
St George, Bloomsbury, Bills of Work, Commission for Building Fifty New Churches in London and Westminster 1711–1759 25 March 1724–25 March 1725 (Lambeth Palace Library, MS 2700, p 64, MS 2718, fol 55)

St George, Kingswood, Book of Commissioners
The Book of the Commissioners, under an Act for erecting a Church in the outparish of St Philip and Jacob (Vicarage of St George), 1751–64 (Bristol RO, 04225/1)

St George, Kingswood, Chamberlain's cash accts
Chamberlain's Cash Accounts under an Act for erecting a church in the outparish of St Philip and Jacob (Vicarage of St George), 1752–64

St John's Coll Accts
Annual Accounts, 1730s to 1750s (St John's College, Oxford, ACC V.B.I and ACC 1.A.96)

St Matthew, Friday-Street, Accts
Corporation of London, St Matthew, Friday Street with St Peter, Eastcheap, Accounts, 1664–1806 (CLRO Guildhall, 543)

St Matthew, Friday-Street, Papers
Corporation of London, St Matthew, Friday Street with St Peter, Eastcheap, Papers, 1664–1806 (CLRO Guildhall, 3543)

St Paul's Monuments Costs
A list of proposed monuments for St Paul's and their estimated costs, annotated by King George III, c1796 (PRO, Kew, London, MPD 78 (50))

St Thomas's, Cash Books
Hospital Cash Books, St Thomas's Hospital, Southwark Sept 1671–Sept 1686 (London Metropolitan Archives, Faringdon, HO1/ST/D/07/003)

St Thomas's, Governors' Minute Books
Minute Books of the General Court of Governors, St Thomas's Hospital, Southwark Feb 1677–July 1735 (London Metropolitan Archives, Faringdon, HO1/ST/A/001/006)

Stafford 1982
Stafford, Melanie, 'Peel's Statue in Leeds – A First for Town and Country', *Leeds Arts Calendar*, no 90 (1982) pp 4–11

Staffs RO
Staffs and Stoke-on-Trent Archives Service

Stainton 1974
Stainton, Lindsay, 'Re-discovered Bas-reliefs by Thomas Banks', *Burlington Magazine*, vol 116, no 855 (June 1974) pp 327–31

Stainton 1983
Stainton, Lindsay, 'Hayward's List: British Visitors to Rome 1753–1775', *Walpole Society*, vol 49 (1983) pp 3–36

Staiti 1989
Staiti, Paul J, *Samuel F B Morse* (Cambridge: 1989)

Stamp 1981
Stamp, Gavin, 'British Architecture in India 1857–1947', *Royal Society of Arts Journal*, vol 129, no 5298 (May 1981) pp 357–79

Stanford SC
Stanford University, Special Collections, California

Stanton 1935
Stanton, G R, 'Ivory Miniature Sculpture', *Connoisseur*, vol 96 (Oct 1935) pp 210–12

Stanton-Isham Agreement
Agreement between William Stanton and Sir M Dayrell on behalf of Sir Justinian Isham for the monument in Lamport Church, Isham Archives 16 Feb 1699 (NRO, IL 1434)

Stanton/Hatton
William Stanton, letters to Lord Hatton, 1684 (BL, Add MS 29560, fol(s) 275, 315, 347, 352, 374, 381)

Stanton/Isham
William Stanton, letter to Sir Justinian Isham regarding arrangements for sending and setting up the monument in Lamport Church, Isham Correspondence 20 Aug 1700 (NRO, IC 1630)

Stanton/Masons' Co
Letter from William Stanton to the Masons' Company refusing to serve as master for the following year and agreeing to submit to a fine for standing down, Masons' Co 24 June 1690 (Guildhall MSS)

Stationers Accts, 1727–87
Stationers' Company, The Warden's Accounts, 1727–July 1787; 1788–1837 (The Worshipful Company of Stationers and Newspaper Makers, London)

Stato d'Anime
Stato d'Anime (Rome, Vicariato Archive)

Stebbing 1976
Stebbing, Shaw, *The History and Antiquities of Staffordshire*, 2 vols (1976 reprint)

Steggies 1993
Steggies, M A, 'The Empire Aggrandized: A Study in Commemorative Portrait Statuary Exported from Britain to her Colonies in South Asia, 1800 to 1939' Ph D Diss (Leicester University, 1993)

Steggles 1997
Steggles, Mary Ann, 'Art and Politics: the visualization of British imperialism in the Bombay presidency 1800–1927', in *From Bombay to Mumbai: Changing Perspectives*, ed Godrej, P, Rohatgi, P and Mehta, R (Bombay: 1997) pp 182–207

Steggles 2000
Steggles, Mary Ann, *Statues of the Raj* (Putney, London: British Association for Cemetaries in South Asia, 2000)

Steggles 2002
Steggles, Mary Ann, 'Victoria, Icon of the British Indian Empire', *The Sculpture Journal*, vol 8 (2002) pp 12–24

Stell 1973
Stell, G, 'Highland Garrisons, 1717–23. Bernera Barracks', *Public Monuments Association*, vol 7 (1973) pp 20–30

Stephens 1895
Stephens, F G, 'The Late Mrs Mary Thornycroft', *Magazine of Art*, (June 1895) pp 305–7

Stevens 1971 (1)
Stevens, Timothy, 'Nymph Preparing for the Bath by James Wyatt: Walker Art Gallery, Liverpool, Acquisition', *Connoisseur*, vol 176 (Feb 1971) pp 150–51

Stevens 1971 (2)
Stevens, Timothy, 'Roman Heyday of an English Sculptor', *Apollo*, no 94 (Sept 1971) pp 226–31

Stevens 1971 (3)
Stevens, Timothy, 'Leeds Sculptor', *Country Life*, vol 150 (21 Oct 1971) p 1060

Stewart 1985
Stewart, Ann M, *Royal Hibernian Academy of Arts: index of exhibitors and their works*, 3 vols (Dublin: 1985)

Stillman 1977
Stillman, Damie, 'Chimneypieces for the English Market: a Thriving Business in Late Eighteenth-Century Rome', *Art Bulletin*, vol 59, no 1 (1977) pp 85–94

Stillman 1978
Stillman, Damie, 'Death Defied and Honor Upheld: The Mausoleum in Neo-Classical England', *Art Quarterly*, vol 1, no 3 (1978) pp 175–213

Stirling 1911
Stirling, A M W, *Annals of a Yorkshire House: from the Papers of a Macaroni and his Kindred* (1911)

Stocker 1985
Stocker, Mark, 'Ready to Move and Speak: Thomas Woolner's Statue of Godley', *Bulletin of New Zealand Art History*, vol 9 (1985) pp 19–25

Stocker 1989
Stocker, Mark, 'John Graham Lough, Review of Lough and Merson, 1987', *Victorian Studies* (Spring 1989) pp 435–36

Stocker 1999
Stocker, Mark, ' "This beautiful statue of thee, Immortal Bard of Ayr": Sir John Steell's Statue of Robert Burns in Dunedin', *Bulletin of New Zealand Art History*, vol 20 (1999) pp 11–24

Stoke CMAG
Stoke City Museum and Art Gallery

Stone 1955–6
Stone, Lawrence, 'The Verney Tomb at Middle Clayton', *Records of Buckinghamshire*, vol 16 (1955–56) pp 67–82

Stoneleigh Accounts
Estate papers of the Leigh family of Stoneleigh Abbey, Warwicks, 1708–1924 (Shakespeare Birthplace Trust Records Office, DR 18/17/38–99)

Stonyhurst 1894
Gerard, John, *Stonyhurst College, its life beyond the seas, 1592–1794 and on English soil, 1794–1894*, Centenary Record (1894)

Stonyhurst 1964
T G H, 'Gleanings from Sir Nicholas Shireburn's Accounts', *The Stonyhurst Magazine*, vol 34, no 425 (Jan 1964) pp 478–81

Storer 1812
Storer, James, *A Description of Fonthill Abbey, Wiltshire* (1812)

Story 1892
Story, Alfred Thomas, *The Life of John Linnell*, 2 vols (1892)

Stow 1720
Stow, John, *A survey of the cities of London and Westminster . . . brought down from the year 1633 to the present time by John Strype*, 2 vols (London: 1720)

Stow 1754–5
Stow, John, *A Survey of the Cities of London and Westminster*, 2 vols (1754–55)

Stowe sale 1922
Stowe House Sale (11 Oct 1922 and two days following)

Strafford Papers
Accounts and Papers relating to Stainborough and Wentworth Castle, 1708–1785 (BL, Add MS 22, 241)

Stranger in Liverpool 1812
Anon, *The Stranger in Liverpool*, 3rd ed (1812)

Stratton 1920
Stratton, A, *The English Interior* (London: 1920)

Stratton 1993
Stratton, Michael, *The Terracotta Revival: Building Innovation and the Image of the City in Britain and North America* (London: 1993)

Stretton 1910
Stretton, William, of Lenton Priory, *The Stretton Manuscripts, edited by G C Robertson with an introduction by J T Godfrey* (1910)

Stretton 1961
Stretton, E N, 'Samuel Percy, Wax Modeller', *Apollo*, vol 73 (March 1961) pp 63–66

Strickland 1913
Strickland, W G, *Dictionary of Irish Artists*, 2 vols (1913)

Strien 2000
van Strien, Kees, 'Thomas Hollis and his Donation to Leiden University Library, 1759–1770', *Quaerendo*, vol 30, no 1 (2000) pp 4–34

Stukeley
The Family Memoirs of the Rev William Stukeley MD, Surtees Society, vol 80 (1887)

Sturdy 1997
Sturdy, David, *A History of Knowles and Son: Oxford Builders for 200 Years 1797–1997* (Oxford: 1997)

Suffolk St
Suffolk Street Galleries, London

Sullivan 1937
Sullivan, William, 'Illustrations by John Flaxman', *Bulletin of the Art Association of Indianapolis, Indiana*, vol 24 (Dec 1937) pp 17–30

Sullivan 2005
Sullivan, Matthew Greg, 'Brass Sculpture and the Ideology of Bronze in Britain 1660–1851', *The Sculpture Journal*, vol 14 (Oct 2005) pp 1–12

Sullivan 2006
Sullivan, M G, 'Stuart and the changing relationships between architects and sculptors in eighteenth-century Britain', in *James "Athenian" Stuart The Rediscovery of Antiquity*, ed Soros, Susan Weber (2006) pp 383–411

Summerson 1935
Summerson, John, *John Nash, Architect to King George IV* (London: 1935)

Summerson 1980
Summerson, John, *The Life and Work of John Nash, Architect* (1980)

Sumner 1885
Sumner, M S, 'Our Sculptor Friend: a biographical sketch', *Aunt Judy's Annual Volume* (1885) pp 722–36

Sumner 1996
Sumner, Anne, 'Diana and Endymion by Joseph Plura', *Apollo*, vol 144 (Nov 1996) p 61

Sun Insurance
Sun Insurance policy registers, 1710–1862 (Guildhall MSS, City of London, 11936/1–732)

Sunderland 1988
Sunderland, John, 'John Hamilton Mortimer His Life and Works', *Walpole Society*, vol 52 (1988)

SUNY
State University of New York

Surtees 1816–40
Surtees, Robert, *The History and Antiquities of the County Palatine of Durham*, 4 vols (1816–40)

Susson 1870
Cusson, John Edward, *History of Hertfordshire*, 3 vols (1870)

Sutton 1972
Sutton, Denys, 'Il Cavaliere Alberto', *Apollo* (Sept 1972) pp 176–97

Sutton Coldfield 1762
The History of Sutton Coldfield by an Impartial Hand (London: 1762)

Swift/Wedgwood
Letter from Peter Swift to Josiah Wedgwood regarding work by John Bacon RA, 21 March 1769 (Wedgwood Archives)

Sykes/Rose
Correspondence from Joseph Rose to Sir Christopher Sykes Bt of Sledmere, 1791–1794 (EYCRO, HUL DDSY 101/62 (1791–94); DDSY (3) 5/1 (1793))

Symes 1987
Symes, Michael, 'John Donowell's Views of Chiswick and other Gardens', *Journal of Garden History*, vol 7 (Jan–March 1987) pp 43–57

Symes 1996
Symes, Michael, *Garden Sculpture* (1996)

Symmons 1971
Symmons, Sarah, 'John Flaxman and Francisco Goya: Infernos Transcribed', *Burlington Magazine*, vol 113 (Sept 1971) pp 508–12

Symmons 1973 (1)
Symmons, Sarah, 'French Copies After Flaxman's Outlines', *Burlington Magazine*, vol 115 (Sept 1973) pp 591–99

Symmons 1973 (2)
Symmons, Sarah, 'Gericault, Flaxman and Ugolino', *Burlington Magazine*, vol 115, no 847 (Oct 1973) pp 669–72

Symmons 1975
Symmons, Sarah, 'Spirit of Despair: Patronage, Primitivism and the Art of John Flaxman', *Burlington Magazine*, vol 117, no 871 (Oct 1975) pp 644–50

Symmons 1979
Symmons, Sarah, 'J. A. D. Ingres: The Apotheosis of Flaxman', *Burlington Magazine*, vol 121, no 920 (Nov 1979) pp 721–25

Symonds 1941
Symonds, Robert, 'Grinling Gibbons, 1648–1720; The Supreme Wood Carver', *Connoisseur*, vol 107 (April 1941) pp 141–47

Synge Hutchinson 1964
Synge Hutchinson, Patrick, 'Unique Essay in English Ceramic Art', *Connoisseur*, vol 156 (June 1964) pp 86–87

Synge Hutchinson 1966
Synge Hutchinson, Patrick, 'Only Known Examples of Jean Voyez's Seals, a Major Discovery', *Connoisseur*, vol 161 (April 1966) pp 212–15

Szpila 1997
Szpila, Kathleen, 'An Eighteenth-Century English Artemisia: Sarah Churchill and the Invention of the Blenheim Memorials', in *Women and Art in Early Modern Europe: Patrons, Collectors and Connoisseurs*, conference proceedings (Pennsylvania State University Press, 1997) pp 189–206

T Carter II/Knatchbull
Thomas Carter II, letter to Sir Edward Knatchbull, with a draft response from Knatchbull, 1766 (CKS, U951 A18/57)

Taft 1930
Taft, Lorado, *History of American Sculpture* (New York: 1930)

Tallis 1852
Tallis, John, *History and Description of the Crystal Palace*, 3 vols (1852)

Tallowchandlers, WA
Corporation of London, Tallowchandlers' Company, Warden's Accounts, 1653–1703 (CLRO Guildhall, 6152/3)

Talman Letter Book
John Talman's Letter Book (Bodleian, English Letters E. 34)

Tapp 1943
Tapp, William, 'Some Ceramic Attributions', *Apollo*, vol 37 (Feb 1943) pp 28–30

Tassie 1791
Raspe, R E, *A Descriptive catalogue of a general collection of ancient and modern engraved gems, cameos as well as intaglios taken from the most celebrated cabinets in Europe; and cast in coloured pastes, white enamel and sulphur, by James Tassie, modeller* (1791)

Tattersall 1985
Tattersall, Bruce, 'Henry Webber: Art at the Service of Industry', *Apollo*, vol 122, no 281 (July 1985) pp 36–42

Taylor 1925
Taylor, John George, *Our Lady of Batersey. The Story of Battersea Church* (1925)

Taylor 1989
Taylor, Angus, 'The Dukery of Carlisle', *Country Life*, vol 183, no 35 (11 Aug 1989) pp 92–97

Taylor 2004
Taylor, Angus, *The Websters of Kendal* (Cumberland & Westmorland Architectural Society, 2004)

Taylor and Wakeling 2002
Taylor, Roger, and Wakeling, Edward, *Lewis Carroll Photographer: The Princeton University Library Albums* (Princeton, NJ: 2002)

Temple 1918
Temple, A G, *Guildhall Memories* (1918)

Tennyson RC
Lincoln Central Library, Tennyson Research Centre

Ternouth Letter
Letter from John Ternouth concerning busts on which he is engaged [recipient unidentified], 4 May 1840 (NAL, MSL/1979/5116/518)

Ternouth Papers
Papers and correspondence of John Ternouth (private coll, London)

The British Face 1986
Colnaghi, *The British Face. A View of Portraiture* (1986)

Theed Letters
Letters of William Theed and papers relating to his family, 1790–1924 (BL, Add MS 53790 and another in a private coll)

Theuerkauff 1984
Theuerkauff, Christian, *Elfenbein: Sammlung Reiner Winkler* (Munich: 1984)

Theuerkauff 1986
Theuerkauff, Christian, *Die Bildwerke in Elfenbein des 16.–19. Jahrhunderts* (Berlin: 1986)

Theuerkauff 1988
Theuerkauff, Christian, 'Von Dürer zu Lucas?: Zu Einigen Kleinreliefs von und in der Art des Georg Schweigger', *Kunst & Antiquitaten*, no 4 (1988) pp 68–73

Theuerkauff 1989
Theuerkauff, Christian, 'Laurent Delvaux: Biblis und Caunus nach der Antike: Neuer Werkung fur die Sculpturengaleries', *Jahrbuch Preussischer Kulturbesitz*, vol 26 (1989)

Thieme Becker
Thieme, Ulrich, and Becker, Felix, *Allgemeines Lexikon der bildenden Künstler*, 37 vols (Leipzig: 1905–50)

Thomas 1879
Thomas, Margaret, *A Hero of the Workshop and a Somerset Worthy* (1879)

Thomas 1936
Thomas, John, 'Wedgwood Ceramic Portraits', *Connoisseur*, vol 98 (July 1936) pp 29–35

Thomas 1967
Thomas, Clara, *Love and Work Enough. The Life of Anna Jameson* (1967)

Thomas 1973
Thomas, James, 'Lost Ceracchi Bust of Thomas Jefferson', *Antiques Magazine*, vol 104 (July 1973) pp 125–27

Thompson 1949
Thompson, Francis, *History of Chatsworth* (1949)

Thompson 1991
Thompson, Eleanor, and others, *Valadier* (1991)

Thomson 1931
Thomson, John H, 'A history of Oscott College', *Oscotian*, vol ns 2 (Whitsun 1931) pp 63–84

Thomson 1949
Thomson, Gladys Scott, *Family Background* (1949)

Thoresby 1715
Thoresby, Ralph, *Ducatus Leodiensis: or, the Topography of the Ancient and Populous Town and Parish of Leedes* (London: 1715)

Thoresby Diary
Hunter, Rev Joseph, ed, *The Diary of Ralph Thoresby, FRS (1677–1724)*, 2 vols (1830)

Thornton 1968
Thornton, Peter, 'Carvings by Sefferin Alken', *Country Life* (22 Feb 1968) pp 419–20

Thornton and Dorey 1992
Thornton, Peter, and Dorey, Helen, *A Miscellany of Objects from Sir John Soane's Museum* (London: 1992)

Thornycroft 1932
Thornycroft, Elfrida, *Bronze & Steel* (1932)

Thorpe 1946
Thorpe, William, 'Stoneleigh Abbey and its Furniture', *Connoisseur*, vol 118 (Dec 1946) pp 71–78

Thorvaldsen
Thorvaldsen Museum, Copenhagen, Denmark

Thorvaldsens Museum Bulletin 2003
Melander, Torben, and Miss, Stig eds, *Thorvaldsens Museum Bulletin* (2003)

Throsby 1789
Throsby, John, *Select Views in Leicestershire*, 2 vols (1789)

Throsby 1795
Throsby, John, *The History and Antiquities of the town and of the county of Nottingham* (1795)

Thynne Papers
Thynne Papers Book (Longleat House Archives, Wilts, 200)

TI
Taylorian Institution, Oxford

Tiernan 1994
Tiernan, John, 'The Triumphal Arch, Shugborough Park, Staffordshire: Repair Works, 1988–93', *Transactions of the Association for Studies of Historic Buildings*, vol 19 (1994) pp 3–15

Timbs 1855
Timbs, John, *Curiosities of London* (1855)

Tinniswood 1992
Tinniswood, Adrian, *Belton House*, National Trust (1992)

Tinted Venus Papers
Letters, papers, press cuttings, photographs and other illustrations relating to John Gibson's 'Tinted Venus', *c*1853–1869 (NLW, MS 6757D)

Tipping 1920
Tipping, H Avray, *English Homes*, period 4, vol 1, Late Stuart, 1649–1714 (London: 1920)

Tite 2001
Tite, Catherine M, 'Depicting the Elite Family in Situ: Portraiture, Likeness and English Visual Culture 1760–1789', Ph D Diss (University of Manchester, 2001)

TN
Temple Newsam Archives (West Yorks CRO)

TNA
The National Archive (formerly PRO)

Tomlinson 1990
Tomlinson, David, 'Threatened by a Bridge: Conservation in Action', *Country Life*, vol 184, no 23 (7 June 1990) p 173

Tomlinson 1996
Tomlinson, John Michael, *Derbyshire Black Marble*, Peak District Mines Historical Society Special Publication No. 4 (Matlock Bath: 1996)

Tooley 1895
Tooley, Sarah A, 'A Famous Lady Sculptor', *The Young Woman*, (1895) pp 361–67

Towndrow 1939
Towndrow, K R, *Alfred Stevens* (London: 1939)

Towneley, Burnley
Towneley Hall Art Gallery, Burnley, Lancs

Toynbee 1927
Toynbee, Paget Jackson, *Strawberry Hill Accounts; a record of expenditure in building, furnishing, &c, kept by Horace Walpole from 1747 to 1795* (Oxford: 1927)

Treasure Houses, 1985
Yakush, Mary, and Smyth, Frances, *The Treasure Houses of Britain* (National Gallery of Art, Washington DC, New Haven and London: 1985)

Treuherz 1983
Treuherz, Julian, 'Jonathan Hatfield of Manchester and Naples', *Apollo*, vol 117 (Feb 1983) pp 110–14

Trevelyan 1978 (1)
Trevelyan, Raleigh, *A Pre-Raphaelite Circle* (1978)

Trevelyan 1978 (2)
Trevelyan, Raleigh, 'Thomas Woolner: Pre-Raphaelite Sculptor – the Beginnings of Success', *Apollo*, vol 107, no 193 (March 1978) pp 200–5

Trevelyan 1978–79
Trevelyan, Raleigh, 'Thomas Woolner and Pauline Trevelyan', *Pre-Raphaelite Review*, vol 2, no 2 (1978–79) pp 1–37

Trinder 1978–79
Trinder, B., 'The First Iron Bridges', *Industrial Archaeology Review*, vol 3, no 2 (1978–79) pp 112–21

Tringham 1985–1986
Tringham, Nigel, 'Bishop's Palace, Lichfield Cathedral Close: Its Construction 1686–87', *South Staffordshire Archgaeological and Historical Society Transactions*, vol 27 (1985–86) pp 57–63

Trubshaw 1876
Trubshaw, Susanna, *Family Records* (Stafford: 1876)

Trumble 1999
Trumble, Angus, 'Gilbert Scott's "Bold and Beautiful Experiment", part I: The Tomb of Sir Charles Hotham in Melbourne', *Burlington Magazine*, vol 141, no 1161 (Dec 1999) pp 739–48

Trumble 2000
Trumble, Angus, 'Gilbert Scott's 'Bold and Beautiful Experiment', part II: The Tomb of Charlotte, Lady Canning', *Burlington Magazine*, vol 142, no 1162 (Jan 2000) pp 20–28

Trusted 1992
Trusted, Marjorie, ' "A Man of Talent": Agostino Carlini, *c*1718–90, pt I', *Burlington Magazine*, vol 134, no 1080 (Dec 1992) pp 776–84

Trusted 1993
Trusted, Marjorie, ' "A Man of Talent": Agostino Carlini, c.1718–90, pt. II', *Burlington Magazine*, vol 135, no 1080 (March 1993) pp 190–201

Tucker 1995
Tucker, Kevin, 'Harriet Goodhue Hosmer, a Portrait from Rome', *Collections, Columbia, South Carolina*, vol 7, no 1 (Winter–Spring 1995) pp 8–9

Tuffnell 1924
Tuffnell, E B, *Family of Tuffnell* (1924)

Tummers 1988
Tummers, Harry, 'The Medieval Effigal Tombs in Chichester Cathedral', *Church Monuments*, vol 3 (1988) pp 3–41

Tupper 1897
Tupper, John Lucas, *Poems*, selected and edited by W M Rossetti (1897)

Tupper Correspondence
Correspondence of John Lucas Tupper and his family, 1849–1900 (Bodleian, MS Eng lett d 308)

Tupper/Stephens
Letters from John Lucas Tupper to Frederick George Stephens, 1849–1879 (Bodleian, MS Don e 78)

Turberville 1938–39
Turberville, Arthur Stanley, *A History of Welbeck Abbey and Its Owners*, 2 vols (1938–39)

Turner Misc Accts
Miscellaneous Accounts, chiefly of clients, Sir William Turner coll 1662–74 (Guildhall Library, MSS, 05107/1)

Turpin 1979 (1)
Turpin, John, 'The Career and Achievement of John Henry Foley, Sculptor (1818–1874)', *Dublin Historical Record*, vol 32, no 2 (March 1979) pp 42–53

Turpin 1979 (2)
Turpin, John, 'Catalogue of the Sculpture of J. H. Foley', *Dublin Historical Record*, vol 32, no 3 (June 1979) pp 108–16

Turpin 1982 (1)
Turpin, John, *John Hogan, Irish Neoclassical Sculptor in Rome 1800–1858; A Biography and Catalogue Raisonné* (1982)

Turpin 1982 (2)
Turpin, John, 'John Hogan, Irish Sculptor, 1800–58', *Apollo*, no 115 (Feb 1982) pp 98–103

UCD
University College Dublin

UCL
University College London

Udy 1978
Udy, David, 'Piranesi's "Vasi", the English Silversmith and His Patrons', *Burlington Magazine*, vol 120 (Dec 1978) p 820

Underwood 1933
Underwood, Eric G, *A Short History of English Sculpture* (London: 1933)

Uns K
Unsere Künstdenmaler

Uppark 1999
Uppark, West Sussex, National Trust (1999)

Upstone 1990
Upstone, Robert, 'Private Graces', *Museums Journal,* vol 90 (April 1990) p 8

Urwin 1997
Urwin, A, 'The Second Earl of Kilmorey and his Mausoleum at St Margaret's, Twickenham', *Borough of Twickenham Local History Society,* no 75 (1997)

Usherwood 2000
Usherwood, Paul, Beach, Jeremy, and Morris, Catherine, *Public Sculpture of North-East England,* Public Sculpture of Britain 3 (Liverpool: 2000)

Valentine 1991
Valentine, Helen, *From Reynolds to Lawrence. The First Sixty Years of the Royal Academy and its Collections* (1991)

Valpy 1986
Valpy, Nancy, 'Advertisements for Artificial Stone in the *Daily Advertiser*', *English Ceramic Circle Transactions,* vol 12, no 3 (1986) pp 206–26

Valpy 1990
Valpy, Nancy, 'Extracts from the *Daily Advertiser* and Additional Manuscripts, Department of Manuscripts, British Museum', *English Ceramic Circle Transactions,* vol 14, no 1 (1990) pp 106–17

Valpy 1991
Valpy, Nancy, 'Extracts from the *Daily Advertiser,* 1792–1795', *English Ceramic Circle Transactions,* vol 14, no 2 (1991) pp 228–34

VAM
Victoria and Albert Museum, London

VAM Designs
VAM, *Designs for Monuments,* 4 vols (93.E.27 a–d)

VAM, AAD
Victoria and Albert Museum, Archive of Art and Design

VAM, NAL
Victoria and Albert Museum, National Art Library

VAM, P&D
Victoria and Albert Museum, Prints and Drawings

Van Der Merwe 1982
Van Der Merwe, Pieter, 'Gone Aloft: Charles Dibdon's Monument', *Theatre Notebook,* vol 26, no 2 (1982) pp 82–85

Van Oss 1974
Van Oss, Oliver, 'An Unrecorded Bust of John Wesley', *Antiquaries Journal,* vol 54, no 2 (1974) pp 307–8

Vaughan-Morgan 1979
Vaughan-Morgan, Julia, *Equestrian Monuments* (Oxford: 1979)

Vertue
Vertue, George, 'Notebooks I–VI; vol VI with integral index', *Walpole Society,* vol I, XVIII (1929–30); vol II, XX (1931–32); vol III, XXII (1933–34); vol IV, XXIV (1935–36); vol V, XXVI (1937–38); vol VI, index to I–V, XXIX (1940–42); vol VI with integral index, XXX (1951–52)

Vertue 1758
Vertue, George, *A description of Easton-Neston in Northamptonshire, the seat of the right honourable the Earl of Pomfret* (London: 1758)

Verulam 1959
Verulam, Earl of, 'Gorhambury and its Collections', *Connoisseur,* vol 143 (Feb 1959) pp 2–7

Victorian Church Art
Victorian Church Art, exhib cat (VAM, London: 19 Nov–Jan 1972)

Victorian Nude 2001
Smith, Alison, ed, *Exposed: The Victorian Nude* (Tate Britain, London: 2001)

Vincent 1955
Vincent, J A, 'Makers of Tradition: Gibbons and Marot, Co-Creators of Dramatic Restoration Interiors', *Interiors,* vol 114 (March 1955) pp 88–91

Vincent 1988
Vincent, Gilbert T, 'Fine Arts: A Collection Fitting the Nation', in *George Washington's Mount Vernon,* ed Garrett, Wendell, (New York: 1988) p 169

Vintners, R W Accts
Corporation of London, Vintners' Company, Renter-Warden's Accounts, 1658–87; 1790–1803 (CLRO Guildhall, 15333/5,10)

Visconti 1816
Visconti, Chevalier Ennio Quirino, *A Letter from the Chevalier Antonio Canova ... on the sculptures in the collection of the Earl of Elgin* (1816)

Vivian-Neal 1935
Vivian-Neal, A W, 'Sculptures by Grinling Gibbons and Quellin, originally in Whitehall, later in Westminster Abbey, now in the Church at Burnham-on-Sea', *Proceedings of the Somersetshire Archaeological and Natural History Society,* vol 71 (1935) pp 127–32

Vivien-Neal 1935
Vivien-Neal, A W, 'Sculptures by Grinling Gibbons and Quellin in the Church at Burnham-on-Sea', *Proceedings of the Somersetshire Archaeological and Natural History Society,* vol 81 (1935) pp 127–32

Volk 1980
Volk, Peter, 'Der Bildhauer Giuseppe Ceracchi und Kurfurst Karl Theodor', *Pantheon,* vol 38 (Jan 1980) pp 68–74

Voyage d'Angleterre, 1728
Voyage d'Angleterre, d'Hollande et de Flandre, fait en l'année 1728, anon, MS 86 NN2 1728 (VAM, MSL/1912/1255)

VS
Victorian Studies

Vyner MSS
Vyner MSS, 1732–1750 (West Yorks CRO)

W Ra
Westminster Ratebooks

WA
Westminster Abbey

Wadmore 1902
Wadmore, James Foster, *Some Account of the Worshipful Company of Skinners of London* (1902)

Wainwright 1975
Wainwright, Nicholas B, 'Nicholas Biddle in Portraiture', *Antiques Magazine,* vol 108 (Nov 1975) pp 956–64

Wainwright 1977
Wainwright, Clive, 'Walter Scott and the Furnishing of Abbotsford; or the Gabions of Jonathan Oldbuck Esq', *Connoisseur,* vol 194 (Jan 1977) pp 3–15

Wait 1977
Wait, Peter, ed, *Journal of a coutry curate: selections from the diary of Francis Kilvert 1870–1870* (London: 1977)

Wake 1988
Wake, Jehanne, *Princess Louise* (1988)

Walch 1965
Walch, Peter S, 'Chimney-piece at Daylesford', *Burlington Magazine,* vol 107 (Feb 1965) p 90

Waldeck Diary
Account of a visit to Benedetto Pistrucci's workshop with reference to the Waterloo Medal, Diaries of Johann Friedrich Maximilan, Baron de Waldeck 1823 (BL, Add MS 73164 fols 13–15)

Walker 1961
Walker, R J B, *A Catalogue of paintings, drawings, sculpture and engravings in the Palace of Westminster,* Part III. Sculpture (The Ministry of Works, London: 1961)

Walker 1965
Walker, R J B, *A Catalogue of Paintings, Drawings, Sculpture and Engravings in the Palace of Westminster,* supplement number I, 1959–1964 (Ministry of Public Building and Works, London: 1965)

Walker 1966
Walker, R J B, *A Catalogue of Paintings, Drawings, Sculpture and Engravings in the Palace of Westminster,* supplement number II, 1965 (Ministry of Public Buildings and Works, London: 1966)

Walker 1967
Walker, R J B, *A Catalogue of Paintings, Drawings, Sculpture and Engravings in the Palace of Westminster,* supplement number III, 1966–67 (Ministry of Public Buildings and Works, London: 1967)

Walker 1974
Walker, R J B, *A Catalogue of Paintings, Drawings and Sculpture in the Palace of Westminster,* supplement number VII, 1973 (Department of the Environment, London: 1974) p 10

Walker 1982
Walker, Corlette, *The Anglo-American Artist in Italy*, exhib cat (University of California Museum: 7 March–9 May 1982)

Walker 1985
Walker, Richard, *Regency Portraits* (London, National Portrait Gallery: 1985)

Walker 1994
Walker, Stefanie, 'The Sculptor Pietro Stefano Monnot in Rome 1695–1713' Ph D Diss (Institute of Fine Arts, New York University, 1994)

Walker, Liverpool
Walker Art Gallery, Liverpool

Walker, Liverpool, Annual Reports
Walker Art Gallery, Liverpool: Annual Reports and Bulletin, 4 vols (1970–74)

Wall 2008
Wall, John, '*That Most Ingenious Modeller'. The Life and Work of John Henning, Sculptor 1771–1851* (2008)

Walpole
Walpole Society volumes

Walpole 1784
Walpole, Horace, *A Description of the Villa of Mr Horace Walpole. . .* (1784)

Walpole 1798–1825
Walpole, Horace, *The Works of Horatio Walpole, edited by R. Berry*, 9 vols (1798–1825)

Walpole at Wolterton
Horace Walpole's Account Book, 1730–46 (Lord Walpole at Wolterton Hall, Box 41 L, 17/1/3)

Walpole, Country Seats
Toynbee, Paget, ed, 'Horace Walpole's Journals of Visits to Country Seats, &c', *Walpole Society*, vol 16 (1928) pp 9–81

Walton/Dunn Accts, Burton C
Walton and Dunn Accounts, Burton Constable Papers 1769 (East Yorks RO, DDCC20A/6)

WAM
Physick, John, ed, *Inventory of Abbey monuments, Westminster Abbey* (1990)

Wanley Diary 1966 ed
Wright, C E and Ruth C Wright, ed, *The Diary of Humfrey Wanley 1715–26*, 2 vols (1966)

Warburton, Whitelaw, and Walsh 1818
Warburton, J, Whitelaw, J and Walsh, Robert, *History of the City of Dublin* (1818)

Ward-Jackson 1985
Ward-Jackson, Philip, 'A-E Carrier-Belleuse, J-J Feuchere and the Sutherlands', *Burlington Magazine*, vol 127, no 984 (March 1985) pp 146–53

Ward-Jackson 1990 (1)
Ward-Jackson, Philip, 'Carlo Marochetti and the Glasgow Wellington Monument', *Burlington Magazine*, vol 132 (Dec 1990) pp 851–62

Ward-Jackson 1990 (2)
Ward-Jackson, Philip, 'Expiatory Monuments by Carlo Marochetti in Dorset and the Isle of Wight', *Journal of the Warburg and Courtauld Institutes*, vol 53 (1990) pp 266–80, repr 29–35

Ward-Jackson 1993
Ward-Jackson, Philip, 'The French background of Royal Monuments at Windsor and Frogmore', *Journal of the Church Monuments Society*, vol 8 (1993) pp 63–83

Ward-Jackson 1994
Ward-Jackson, Philip, 'Carlo Marochetti et les photographes', *Revue de l'Art*, no 104 (1994) pp 43–48

Ward-Jackson 2000
Ward-Jackson, Philip, 'Carlo Marochetti: Maintaining Distinction in an International Sculpture Market', in *The Lustrous Trade: Material Culture and the History of Sculpture in England and Italy, c.1700–c.1860*, ed Sicca, Cinzia and Yarrington, Alison (2000) pp 174–90

Ward-Jackson 2003
Ward-Jackson, Philip, *Public Sculpture of the City of London*, Public Monuments and Sculpture Association, vol 6 (2003)

Ward-Jackson 2004
Ward-Jackson, Philip, 'Carlo Marochetti and the Tombs of Napoleon at the Dome des Invalides, Paris, and the Duke of Wellington at St Paul's Cathedral, London', *The Sculpture Journal*, vol 19 (2004) pp 115–29

Ward-Jackson and Read 1979
Ward-Jackson, Philip, and Read, Benedict, 'Late 18th and 19th Century Sculpture in the British Isles. 9. Lancashire', *Courtauld Institute Illustrated Archive*, vol 4, no 9 (1979)

Waring 1863
Waring, J B, *Masterpieces of Industrial Art and Sculpture at the International Exhibition, 1862*, 3 vols (1863)

Wark 1954
Wark, Robert, 'Note on the Subject Matter of the Museum's Painting by Soest', *Bulletin of the Museum of Fine Arts, Boston*, vol 52 (Oct 1954) pp 63–64

Wark 1970
Wark, Robert, *Drawings by John Flaxman in the Huntington Collection* (San Marino, California: 1970)

Wark 1978
Wark, Robert, *British Silver in the Huntington Collection* (San Marino, California: 1978)

Waterfield 1982
Waterfield, Giles, 'The Illusion of Life; Rysbrack Exhibition in Bristol', *Country Life*, vol 171, no 4413 (1982) pp 700–1

Waterhouse 1977
Waterhouse, E K, 'Sculpture from the Paul Mellon Collection at the British Art Center at Yale', *Burlington Magazine*, vol 119 (May 1977)

Watkin 1907
Watkin, Isaac, 'History of the parish of Llanyblodwel', *Collections Historical and Archaeological . . . Montgomeryshire*, vol 34 (1907)

Watkin 1968
Watkin, David, *Thomas Hope 1769–1831 and the Neo-Classical Idea* (1968)

Watkin 1974
Watkin, David, *The Life and Work of C R Cockerell* (1974)

Watkin 1982
Watkin, David, *Athenian Stuart. Pioneer of the Greek Revival* (1982)

Watkin 1997
Watkin, David, 'The Master's Lodge, Peterhouse, Cambridge, the Home of Sir John Meurig and Lady Thomas', *Country Life*, vol 191, no 35 (28 Aug 1997) pp 34–37

Watney 1972
Watney, Bernard, 'Origins of Designs for English Ceramics of the Eighteenth Century', *Burlington Magazine*, vol 114 (Dec 1972) pp 818–28

Watney 1980
Watney, Bernard, 'Some Parallels and Prototypes in Ceramics', *English Ceramic Circle Transactions*, vol 10, nos 4–5 (1980) pp 350–68

Watson 1850
Watson, John F, *The Annals of Philadelphia and Pennsylvania in Olden Time*, 2 vols (1850)

Watson 1939–40
Watson, F J B, 'Thomas Patch', *Walpole Society*, vol 28 (1939–40)

Watson 1955
Watson, F J B, 'Flaxman: The Bicentenary of an English Neoclassicist', *Architectural Review*, vol 118 (Nov 1955) pp 285–89

Watson 1956
Watson, F J B, 'English Taste in the Eighteenth Century', *Connoisseur*, vol 124 (1956) p 124

Watson 1957
Watson, F J B, 'Canova and the English', *Architectural Review*, vol 122 (Dec 1957) pp 403–6

Watson 1963
Watson, F J B, 'A Bust of Fiammingo by Rysbrack Rediscovered', *Burlington Magazine*, vol 105 (1963) pp 441–45

Watson notebooks
Book of sketches and notes by Samuel Watson I and accountbook of Henry Watson (Bodleian, Oxford, Ms Eng. Misc. fol 383)

Watson/Chatsworth
Accounts and drawings of Samuel Watson I (Devonshire Archives, Chatsworth)

WCA
Westminster City Archives, London, City of Westminster Archives Centre

WCRO
Warwickshire County Record Office

Weaver 1909; *Weaver* 1972
Weaver, Lawrence, *English Leadwork: Its Art and History* (London: 1909; 2nd ed, New York: 1972)

Weaver 1915
Weaver, Lawrence, 'The Complete Building Accounts of the City Churches (parochial) designed by Sir Chritopher Wren', *Archaeologia*, vol 66 (1915) pp 1–60

Weavers, Subs
Corporation of London, Weavers' Company, subscription book for rebuilding the Hall, 1667 (CLRO Guildhall, 04650)

Webb 1925 (1)
Webb, Geoffrey, 'Robert Grumbold and the Architecture of the Renaissance in Cambridge Part I', *Burlington Magazine*, vol 47 (1925) pp 315–18

Webb 1925 (2)
Webb, Geoffrey, 'John and William Bastard of Blandford', *Burlington Magazine*, vol 47, no 270 (Sept 1925) pp 144–50

Webb 1926
Webb, Geoffrey, 'Robert Grumbold and the Architecture of the Renaissance in Cambridge Part II', *Burlington Magazine*, vol 48 (1926) pp 37–41

Webb 1950
Webb, M I, 'Sculpture by Rysbrack at Stourhead', *Burlington Magazine*, vol 92 (Nov 1950) pp 306–13

Webb 1951 (1)
Webb, M I, 'Michael Rysbrack, Sculptor', *Country Life*, vol 109, no 2816 (5 Jan 1951) pp 34–36

Webb 1951 (2)
Webb, M I, 'Augustan Manner of John Michael Rysbrack: Reply', *Art Quarterly*, vol 14, no 1 (1951) pp 72–73

Webb 1951 (3)
Webb, M I, *Southill, a Regency House* (1951)

Webb 1952
Webb, M I, 'Busts of Sir Isaac Newton', *Country Life*, vol 111 (1952) pp 216–18

Webb 1953 (1)
Webb, M I, 'English Sculpture on Exhibition in London', *Burlington Magazine*, vol 95 (July 1953) pp 242–43

Webb 1953 (2)
Webb, M I, 'The Monuments in Warkton Church', *Architectural Journal*, vol 110 (1953) p 199

Webb 1954
Webb, M I, *Michael Rysbrack: Sculptor* (1954)

Webb 1955 (1)
Webb, M I, 'Giovanni Battista Guelfi: An Italian Sculptor Working in England', *Burlington Magazine*, vol 97 (May 1955) pp 138–45

Webb 1955 (2)
Webb, M I, 'Craggs Monument in Westminster Abbey', *Burlington Magazine*, vol 97 (Aug 1955) p 260

Webb 1956 (1)
Webb, M I, 'Roubiliac's Busts at Wilton', *Country Life*, vol 119, no 3092 (19 April 1956) pp 804–5

Webb 1956 (2)
Webb, M I, 'Portraits of Bolingbroke', *Country Life*, vol 119 (24 May 1956) pp 1131–32

Webb 1956 (3)
Webb, M I, 'A Rysbrack Discovery', *Country Life*, vol 120, no 3123 (22 Nov 1956) p 1182

Webb 1957 (1)
Webb, M I, 'Sir Francis Chantrey Reconsidered', *Country Life*, vol 121, no 3131 (17 Jan 1957) p 112

Webb 1957 (2)
Webb, M I, 'French Antecedents of Louis-Francois Roubiliac', 6 *Gazette des Beaux-Arts*, vol 49 (Feb 1957) pp 81–88

Webb 1957 (3)
Webb, M I, 'Henry Cheere, Henry Scheemakers, and the Apprenticeship Lists', *Burlington Magazine*, vol 99 (Apr 1957) pp 115–20

Webb 1957 (4)
Webb, M I, 'Chimney-pieces by Scheemakers', *Country Life*, vol 121, no 3139 (14 March 1957) pp 491–93

Webb 1958 (1)
Webb, M I, 'Georgian Sculptors; Architect and Sculptor', *Architectural Review*, vol 123 (May 1958) pp 329–31

Webb 1958 (2)
Webb, M I, 'Henry Cheere, Sculptor and Businessman, and John Cheere', *Burlington Magazine*, vol 100 (Aug 1958) pp 232–40, 274–79

Webb 1996
Webb, C R, *An Index of Wills proved in the Archdeaconry Court of London, 1700–1807* (London: Society of Genealogists, 1996)

Webb 1999
Webb, Cliff, *London Livery Company Apprenticeship Registers: vol 27, Masons' Company 1663–1805* (London: Society of Genealogists, 1999)

Webb/Gunnis 1954
Webb, M I, 'Dictionary of British Sculptors, 1660–1851, by Rupert Gunnis', *Burlington Magazine*, vol 96 (1954) p 25

Webber-Wedgwood Agreement
Agreement between Henry Webber and Josiah Wedgwood, Wedgwood Archive 16 July 1787 (Keele University Library, L 155)

Webber/Byerley
Letter from Henry Webber to Thomas Byerley, Wedgwood Archive 30 April 1786 (Keele University Library, L1/152)

Weber 1987
Weber, Ingrid, 'Bacchus und Mänade', *Weltkunst (Munich)*, vol 57, no 23 (1987) pp 3583–85

Weber 1989
Weber, Ingrid, 'Geschnittene Steine nach Antiken Vorbild', *Weltkust*, vol 59, no 12 (15 June 1989) pp 1782–84

Webster 1970
Webster, Margaret, 'Taste of an Augustan Collector', *Country Life*, (29 Jan 1970) p 251

Webster 1978
Webster, M, *Neoclassicism in Celebration* (1978)

Webster et al 1971
Webster, Mary, Lightbown, R W, and Lightbown, W, 'Princely Friendship and the Arts: A Relief by Grinling Gibbons', *Apollo*, no 94 (Sept 1971) pp 192–97

Wedgwood 1977
Wedgwood, Alexandra, *A W N Pugin and the Pugin family*, Catalogue of the drawings collection of the Royal Institute of British Architects, vol 16 (1977)

Wedgwood-Bacon RA Receipt
Receipt for modelling undertaken for Wedgwood by John Bacon RA, 1769 (Keele University Library, Special Collections, L1-37)

Wedgwood/de Ville
Wedgwood/de Ville, Wedgwood Archives 1809 (Keele University, Special Colls and Archives, L1/215)

Wedgwood/Hackwood
Wedgwood/Hackwood, Wedgwood Archives 1777–1778 (Keele University, Special Colls and Archives, E2/1353A)

Wedgwood/J Cheere
Wedgwood/J Cheere, Wedgwood Archives 1774 (Keele University, Special Colls and Archives)

Wedgwood/Landré
Wedgwood/Landré, Wedgwood Archives 1769–1774 (Keele University, Special Colls and Archives, L1/56; L1/57)

Wedgwood/Lochee
Wedgwood/Lochee, Wedgwood Archives 1787–1788 (Keele University, Special Colls and Archives, L1/25; L1/27; L1/58; L1/47)

Wedgwood/Papera
Wedgwood/Papera, Wedgwood Archives 1802 (Keele University, Special Colls and Archives, L108/20403)

Wedgwood/Parker
Wedgwood/Parker, Wedgwood Archives 1769, 1774 (Keele University, Special Colls and Archives, L1/74)

Wedgwood/Peart (1)
Wedgwood/Peart, Wedgwood Archives 1787 (Wedgwood Museum, Barlaston, Staffs, E2/931; E2/1358)

Wedgwood/Peart (2)
Wedgwood/Peart, Wedgwood Archives 1788 (Keele University, Special Colls and Archives, L1/59)

Wedgwood/Pingo
Wedgwood/Pingo, Wedgwood Archives 1800 (Keele University, Special Colls and Archives, L1/24)

Wedgwood/Stephan
Wedgwood/Stephan, Wedgwood Archives 1774 (Keele University, Special Colls and Archives, E2/1347; E25/18554)

Wedgwood/Templetown
Wedgwood/Templetown, Wedgwood Archives 1783–1787 (Wedgwood Museum, Barlaston, Staffs, E26/18958)

Wedgwood/Voyez
Wedgwood/Voyez, Wedgwood Archives 1768–69 (Keele University, Special Colls and Archives, E/25/18197; L1/55; E5/30867)

Wedgwood/Hoskins
Wedgwood/Hoskins, Wedgwood Archives 1770–1779 (Keele University, Special Colls and Archives, E2/30950–30951; L1/115; L1/116)

Weekes 1880
Weekes, Henry, *Lectures on Art* (London: 1880)

Weekes/Ansdell
Letter from Henry Weekes to Richard Ansdell, 21 Jan 1850 (Cambridge University Library, Dept of MSS, Fitzwilliam, MS 1-1966, p 18)

Weekes/Cunningham
Letter from Henry Weekes to Allan Cunningham, nd (Cambridge University Library, Dept of MSS, Fitzwilliam, MS 24-1949)

Weilbach 1897
Weilbach, Phillip, *Nyt Dansk Kunstnerlexicon* (1897)

Weinhardt 1958
Weinhardt, Carl J jr, 'Indian Taste: The Museum's Exhibition of Prints and Drawings', *Bulletin of the Metropolitan Museum of Art, New York*, no 16 (March 1958) pp 208–16

Weisser 1974
Weisser, Michael, 'The Iron Bridge', *Bauwelt*, vol 65, no 45 (2 Dec 1974) pp 1490–91

Wellesley 1935
Wellesley, Gerald, Duke of Wellington, and Steegman, John, *The iconography of the first Duke of Wellington* (London: 1935)

Wells 1999
Wells, Pamela, 'The Salford Peel Park Sculpture Collection' MA Diss (University of Leeds, 1999)

Wells-Cole 1968
Wells-Cole, Anthony, 'John Flaxman and Benjamin Gott of Armley House, Leeds', *Leeds Arts Calendar*, no 63 (1968) pp 21–24

Wells-Cole 1987
Wells-Cole, Anthony, *Art and Decoration in Elizabethan and Jacobean England* (1987)

Wenley 2004
Wenley, Robert, 'The 4th Marquess of Hertford's "lost collection" of sculpture', *The Sculpture Journal*, vol 13 (2004) pp 71–85

Wentworth Castle Papers
Accounts and papers relating to Stainborough and Wentworth Castle, co York, belonging to the Earl of Strafford, Papers of the families of Johnson and Wentworth, Earls of Strafford 1708–1785 (BL, Add MS 22241)

Westm Abbey Notes 1819
Westminster Abbey, Chapter Clerk's notes for 20 July 1819 (WAM)

Westm Hall
Westminster Hall, London

Westmacott 1777
Westmacott, Richard I, *Designs for Chimneypieces* (1777)

Westmacott Corr BL
Sir Richard Westmacott RA Correspondence, BL: letters to Dr W Buckland, 1844, Add MS 40608 fol 223; to Sir W Knighton, 1830, Add MS 40300, fol 355; to Sir Henry Ellis, 1819–44, 1851, Add MS 41312 fols 33, 143, 220, Add MS 38626 fols 182, 198, 200; to Miss H Sotheby Add MS 70951 fol 66; to W Ayrton, 1833, Add MS 52338 fol 99; to D Colnaghi, 1836, Add MS 35255 fol 59; to 3rd Lord Hardwicke, 1819, Add MS 35652 fol 202; to Rev P Bliss, 1836, 1851, Add MS 34572 fol 59, Add MS 34578 fol 436; to Mrs Kerr, 1852, Add MS 42577 fol 309, 1809–52

Westmacott Corr Met NY
Sir Richard Westmacott RA, Correspondence (Met NY, NUC MS 60-920)

Westmacott Corr VAM
Sir Richard Westmacott RA, Correspondence: letter(s) to Henry Holland, 1794–6, Holland Papers D.1479-98, PDP; letters to William Mulready MSL/1961/4461/131–2; to Captain Young MSL/1980/59; to James Christie, Anon and William Wyon MSL/1979/7198/1–5; to Anon MSL/1979/7461/470–1; to Anon MSL/1980/103; to William Finden, Mr Burder and Mr Jepre MSL/1980/60–3; to Anon MSL/1973/4639; to Messrs Colnaghi MSL/1903/9000/155, 1818–42 (VAM NAL and PDP)

Westmacott Corr Yale
Sir Richard Westmacott RA, Correspondence: Letter(s) to T J Pettigrew, Caroline Fox and Lady Holland; to Sir William Chatterton, John Flaxman, anon, J E Carew, Miss Farron, J. Magrath, Charles Manby, Lewis Roberts, C Stokes, Robert Westmacott, Osborn coll and Gen MSS 1812–53 (Beinecke Library, Yale)

Westmacott Family Archive
Westmacott Family Archive: 9 sketchbooks, 91 drawings, *c*15 letters, 3 journals, 5 notes, 2 scrapbooks, 11 printed ephemera, 3 newspaper cuttings, 29 engravings, 3 miscellaneous, by Sir Richard Westmacott RA, Richard Westmacott III RA and other members of the family, *c*1820–*c*1900 (HMI, 2000/80)

Westmacott III Letters
About 15 letters from Richard Westmacott III to his brother, William Westmacott, from Italy, Westmacott Archive 1821–1824 (HMI, D/C1–15 18)

Westmacott III/Russell
Letter from Richard Westmacott III to Lord John Russell, Russell Papers 6 Feb 1838 (PRO, 30/22/3)

Westmacott-Cremorne Bills
Two bills from Richard Westmacott I for mason's work done on Lord Cremorne's houses in Stanhope Street and Chelsea, 1790 (LMA, ACC/2079/D3/009)

Westmacott/Adam
Sir Richard Westmacott RA, letters to William Adam (private coll)

Westmacott/Cornewall
Letter from Henry Westmacott to Sir George Cornewall, Records of the Moccas Estate Aug 1805 (Herefs RO, J56/III/111)

Westmacott/Duke of Newcastle
Sir Richard Westmacott RA, letter to the Duke of Newcastle, 26 May 1841 (University of Nottingham, Newcastle Papers NCC7-320a)

Westmacott/Elmes
Sir Richard Westmacott RA, letter to James Elmes, 25 Oct 1822 (RA, Jupp Catalogue 6/154–5)

Westmacott/Harvey
Letters from Henry Westmacott to Sir Robert Bateson Harvey regarding the paving of Langley Marish church, Langley Park Archives nd (Centre for Buckinghamshire Studies, D31/A/24)

Westmacott/Knighton
Sir Richard Westmacott RA, letters to Sir William Knighton, 8 Jan 1828 (Royal Archives, Windsor, RA 27070)

Westmacott/Lincoln
Sir Richard Westmacott RA, letters to Lord Lincoln on the restoration of monuments in Canterbury Cathedral (Nottingham University Library, MS and Special Collections)

Westmacott/Nash
Sir Richard Westmacott RA, letters to John Nash, 17 January 1829 (Treasury Papers, T.1/3489 f1682/29)

Westmacott/RIEFAS
Sir Richard Westmacott RA, letters to the Royal Institution for the Encouragement of the Fine Arts in Scotland, 1824–7 (SRO, NG.3/4/6–9)

Westmacott/SDUK
Sir Richard Westmacott RA, letters to the Society for the Diffusion of Useful Knowledge, 1835–44 (UCL, MS Room, GB 0103 SDUK)

Westmacott/Wellesley
Sir Richard Westmacott RA, letters to Rev Henry Wellesley, 12 Jan 1852 (Ashm, Department of Western Art)

Westminster 1845
Catalogue of Works of Art sent in, pursuant to the notices issued by Her Majesty's Commissioners on the Fine Arts, for exhibition in Westminster Hall (London: HMSO, 1845)

Westminster Fire Office, PR
Westminster Fire Office, Policy Register, 1717–19 (Westminster Archives Centre, 1971/43)

Westminster Monuments Receipt
Receipt from John Ternouth for half a year's work cleaning the monuments in Westminster Abbey (£30), Westminster Abbey Muniments 1847 (WAM General Vouchers 1847)

Westminster Monuments Report
Report on the state of the monuments in Westminster Abbey, prepared by Edward Blore for the Dean and Chapter, Westminster Abbey Muniments 14 June 1842

Westmorland 2003
El Westmorland Recuerdos del Grand Tour (Real Academia de Bellas Artes de San Fernando, Madrid: April–June 2003)

Westmorland Papers
Westmorland Papers (Northants RO, 1950/88, misc vol 1, 94/95)

WFO
Westminster Fire Office

WFO, DM
Westminster Fire Office, Meetings of the Directors, March 1726–March 1730 (Westminster Archives Centre, 343/4)

WFO, DMB
Westminster Fire Office, Directors' Minute Book, 1717–1721; 1721 ff (Westminster Archives Centre, 343/1)

WFO, GCB
Westminster Fire Office, General Court Book, 1717–1746 ff (Westminster Archives Centre, 343/75)

WFO, MB
Westminster Fire Office, Minute Book, March 1730–Dec 1735; Dec 1735–Oct 1741; 1741–45; 1745–50; 1759–64; 1764–68 (Westminster Archives Centre, 342/5; 343/6; 343/7; 343/8; 343/11; 343/12)

Wheatley 1891
Wheatley, Henry B., *London Past and Present, based upon the Handbook of London by the late Peter Cunningham*, 3 vols (1891)

Whiffen 1944
Whiffen, Marcus, 'Note on Thomas White of Worcester', *Burlington Magazine*, vol 84 (May 1944) pp 124–27

Whiffen 1945
Whiffen, Marcus, 'White of Worcester: A Local Architect of the Eighteenth Century', *Country Life*, vol 98, no 2551 (7 Dec 1945) pp 1002–5

Whinney 1948
Whinney, Margaret, *Gibbons in Cambridge* (1948)

Whinney 1956
Whinney, Margaret, 'Flaxman and the Eighteenth Century', *Journal of the Warburg and Courtauld Institutes*, vol 19 (July 1956) pp 269–82

Whinney 1964
Whinney, Margaret, *Sculpture in Britain 1530–1830*, Pelican History of Art (London: 1964)

Whinney 1965
Whinney, Margaret, 'Flaxman and Covent Garden', *About the House: the Magazine of the Friends of Covent Garden*, vol 1, no 10 (June 1965) pp 24–29

Whinney 1971
Whinney, Margaret, *English Sculpture 1720–1830* (London: 1971)

Whinney 1988
Whinney, Margaret, *Sculpture In Britain 1530–1830* (ed and revised John Physick, 1988)

Whinney and Millar 1957
Whinney, Margaret, and Millar, Oliver, *English Art, 1625–1714* (1957)

Whinyates 1894
Whinyates, F T, *Whinyates Family Records*, 2 vols (1894)

Whistler 1954
Whistler, Laurence, *The imagination of Vanbrugh and his fellow artists* (London: 1954)

Whistler 1997
Whistler, Catherine, 'The Sheldonian Theatre', *Apollo*, vol 145, no 423 (May 1997) p 21

Whistler Papers
Papers of James McNeill Whistler and his family, including John Birnie Philip, 1653–1956 (University of Glasgow, Special Colls, MS Whistler)

Whitbread and Croft-Murray 1961
Whitbread, Humphrey, and Croft-Murray, Edward, *George Garrard 1760–1826*, exhib cat (Cecil Higgins Museum, Castle Close, Bedford: 18 Feb–18 March 1961)

White 1834
White, William, *History, Gazeteer, and Directory of Staffordshire* (Sheffield: 1834)

White 1845
White, William, *History, Gazeteer, and Directory of Norfolk*, Reprint of 1845 issue (Newton Abbot, Devon: 1969)

White 1904
White, F G, *History of Walbrook Ward* (1904)

White 1978
White, Raymond, 'Application of Gas-Chromatography to the Identification of Waxes', *Studies in Conservation*, vol 23 (May 1978) pp 57–68

White 1981
White, R, 'The Architects of Bramley College, Kent', *Architectural History*, vol 24 (1981) pp 32–33

White 1986
White, Adam, 'Two Bronze Dogs from the Hope Collection', *Leeds Arts Calendar*, vol 98 (1986)

White 1995
White, A W A, *The Correspondence of Sir Roger Newdigate of Arbury, Warks* (1995)

White 1999
White, Adam, 'A Biographical Dictionary of London Tomb Sculptors c.1560–c.1660', *Walpole Society*, vol 61 (1999) pp 1–163

White and Bright 1998
White, James, and Bright, Kevin, *A Summary Catalogue of the Works of Art in the Collection of the Royal Dublin Society* (Dublin: 1998)

White's Directory, 1838; 1846
White, F, *General Directory of Kingston-upon-Hull* (1838; 1846)

Whitehall O/E, 1666–1667
Whitehall, Ordinary and Extraordinary Accounts, 1666–1667 (PRO, Kew, London, Work 5/9, 1 vol)

Whitehead 1989
Whitehead, David, 'The Skill of Symonds', *Country Life*, vol 183, no 47 (23 Nov 1989) p 104

Whitehead 1992
Whitehead, David, 'Job Marston's Chapel', *Georgian Group Journal*, (1992) pp 79–81

Whitehead 1999
Whitehead, Christopher, 'Archival Sources for the Study of the Eighteenth-Century Anglo-Italian Marble Trade', *The Sculpture Journal*, vol 3 (1999) pp 44–52

Whitehouse 1924
Whitehouse, Eva, *Guide and history of Haywood and its old church near Stafford* (Birmingham: 1924)

Whitley 1928
Whitley, William, *Artists and their Friends in England*, 2 vols (1928)

Whitley 1930
Whitley, William, *Art in England 1821–1837* (1930)

Whittingham 1993
Whittingham, Selby, 'Chantrey, Westmacott and Casts after the Antique', *Journal of the History of Collections*, vol 5, no 1 (1993) pp 89–92

Whitworth
Whitworth Art Gallery, University of Manchester

Whye 2002
Whye, John van, 'The History of Phrenology on the Web', http://pages.britishlibrary.net/phrenology/17.08.05 (2002)

Wickham 2000
Wickham, David, *Millennial History, the Clothworkers' Company* (2000)

Wilkins 1994
Wilkins, Charles, 'Recollections of Three Merthyr Artists', *Merthyr Historian*, vol 7 (1994)

Willett 1785
Willett, Ralph, *A Description of the Library at Merly in the County of Dorset* (1785)

Williams 1939
Williams, Marjorie, ed, *The Letters of William Shenstone* (1939)

Williams 1960
Williams, Iolo, 'Identification of Some Early Drawings by John Flaxman', *Burlington Magazine*, vol 102 (June 1960) pp 246–51

Williams 1967
Williams, Ben, 'A Raleigh, Caroline du Nord, un des Rares Musees Americains qui ne Soient pas dus a l'Initiative Privee', *L'Oeil*, no 155 (Nov 1967) pp 2–9

Williams 1971
Williams, M., 'Old Mortality', *Country Life*, vol 150 (11 Nov 1971) p 1280

Williamson 1936
Williamson, George Charles, 'Portrait Work in Wax', *Apollo*, vol 24 (July 1936) pp 27–33

Williamson 1996
Williamson, Paul, ed, *European Sculpture at the Victoria and Albert Museum* (1996)

Williamson and Engleheart 1902
Williamson, George C, and Engleheart, Henry L D, *George Engleheart 1750–1829, miniature painter to George III* (London: 1932)

Willis 1986
Willis, Peter, 'William Kent's Letters in the Huntington Library, California', *Architectural History*, vol 29 (1986) pp 158–67

Willis and Clark 1886
Willis, Robert, and Clark, Willis, *The Architectural History of the University of Cambridge* (1886, facsimile 1988)

Willows 2004
Willows, Denise, 'Lucas – Father and Son', *Winchester Cathedral Record*, vol 73 (2004) pp 56–72

Wills 1962
Wills, Geoffrey, 'Victorian Sculptor: Samuel James Bouverie Haydon', *Apollo*, no 76 (Dec 1962) pp 785–87

Wills 1979
Wills, Geoffrey, 'Two Wedgwood Aberrations', *Proceedings of the Wedgwood Society*, no 10 (1979) pp 123–24

Wilson 1971
Wilson, R G, *Gentlemen Merchants The Merchant Community in Leeds, 1700–1830* (1971)

Wilson 1976
Wilson, Arnold, 'Rysbrack in Bristol', *Apollo*, vol 103 (Jan 1976) pp 22–25

Wilson 1984
Wilson, Michael I, *William Kent, Architect, Designer, Painter, Gardener, 1685–1748* (London: 1984)

Wilson 1995
Wilson, Jean, ' "Two Names of Friendship, but One Starre": Memorials to Single-Sex Couples in the Early Modern Period', *Journal of the Church Monuments Society*, vol 10 (1995) pp 70–83

Wilson 1997
Wilson, Timothy, 'The Sheldonian Theatre', *Apollo*, vol 145, no 423 (1997) pp 20–21

Wilson 2002
Wilson, Jean, 'Dead Fruit: The Commemoration of Still-Born and Unbaptized Children in Early Modern England', *Journal of the Church Monuments Society*, vol 17 (2002) pp 89–106

Wilson 2003
Wilson, David, 'Nollekens and Fox in the Temple – The Armistead Bust', *British Art Journal*, vol 4, no 3 (Autumn 2003) pp 65–69

Wilson 2004
Wilson, Frances, *The Courtesan's Revenge* (2004)

Wilson 2005 (1)
Wilson, David, 'Naval gazing: a search for the true identity of a sculpted head by Michael Foye', *British Art Journal*, vol 6, no 2 (Autumn 2005) pp 31–39

Wilson 2005 (2)
Wilson, David, 'A bust of Thomas Hollis by Joseph Wilton RA. Sitter and bust revisited', *British Art Journal*, vol 5 (2005) pp 4–26

Wilson 2006 (1)
Wilson, David, 'The Year of the Fox', *Journal of Liberal History*, no 50 (Spring 2006) pp 4–11

Wilson 2006 (2)
Wilson, David, 'A Fox in sheep's clothing', *House Magazine, Houses of Parliament* (Autumn 2006) pp 20–25

Wilson 2006 (3)
Wilson, David, 'The Boy in the Temple – Joseph Nollekens's lost portrait bust of Bob St John', *British Art Journal*, vol 7, no 2 (Spring–Summer 2006) pp 17–24

Wilson 2006 (4)
Wilson, David, 'Roubiliac, the Earl of Pembroke, and the chancellor's discretion – preservation of the nation's heritage in the consistory courts of the Church of England', *Journal of the Church Monuments Society*, vol 21 (2006) pp 141–84

Wilson 2007
Wilson, David, 'New information from the Society of Arts: Roubiliac's model of *Hercules and Atlas*, and Nathaniel Smith's model of *St Andrew* after Duquesnoy', *Sculpture Journal*, vol 16.2 (2007)

Wilton 1973
Wilton, Andrew, 'An Early Drawing by John Gibson', *British Museum Quarterly*, vol 37, nos 3–4 (1973) pp 118–19

Wilton and Bignamini 1996
Wilton, Andrew, and Bignamini, Ilaria, *Grand Tour. The Lure of Italy in the Eighteenth Century*, exhib cat (Tate: 1996)

Wilton Archive
Papers of Joseph Wilton, including an autobiographical note (*c*1793) and some official documents (RA, Anderdon Catalogues, AND/27/167)

Wilton Ely 1976
Wilton Ely, John, 'Bust of Piranesi by Nollekens', *Burlington Magazine*, vol 118 (Aug 1976) pp 592–95

Wilton Ely 1985
Wilton-Ely, John, *A Tercentenary Tribute to William Kent*, exhib cat (Hull, Ferens Art Gallery: 1985)

Wilton/Bedford
Joseph Wilton, letter to the Duke of Bedford's agent; another to Percival Beaumont, 25 October 1766; 21 May 1769 (Bedford Office, London Rack 13/3/4 Box 523)

Wilton/City Corporation
Joseph Wilton, letter to the City Corporation, 1764 (CLRO, Guildhall, City of London, MSS 5.18)

Wimsatt 1965
Wimsatt, W, *The Portraits of Alexander Pope* (New Haven: 1965)

Winde/Bridgeman
William Winde to Lady Mary Bridgeman, letters relating to alterations at Castle Bromwich, Earl of Bradford MSS 1688–1703 (Staffs RO, D1287/18/4)

Winfrey, nd
Winfrey, Jan, *Bradford's Sculpture Trail* (nd)

Winn Accts
Miscellaneous Accounts, Winn family, Nostell Priory, Yorks (West Yorks CRO, NP)

Winter 1958
Winter, Carl, *The Fitzwilliam Museum, an illustrated survey* (1958)

Wischermann 1980
Wischermann, Heinfried, 'Canova's Pantheon – Uberlegungen zum Canoviano von Possagno', *Architectura*, vol 10, no 2 (1980) pp 134–63

WMF
World Monuments Fund

Woburn Abbey, Cash Book
Woburn Abbey, Cash Book, 1791–1792 (Luton Archives & Records Service, BLARS R5/1297)

Woburn Building Accts 1748–1762
Woburn Abbey, Building Accounts, 4 Nov 174 – 4 Aug 1762 (Luton Archives & Records Service, R5/1092)

Woburn Building Accts 1789–1791
Woburn Abbey Building Accounts, Nov 1789–Dec 1791 (Luton Archives & Records Service, BLARS ref R5/2114/494, 498–502; R5/1105)

Woburn Building Accts, 1770–73
Woburn Abbey, Building Accounts, 1770–1773 (Luton Archives & Records Service, BLARS R5/1093)

Woburn Building Accts, 1787–91
Woburn Abbey, Account of Building & Repairs, Nov 1787–Dec 1791 (Luton Archives & Records Service, BLARS R5/1105)

Woburn Building Accts, 1790–1791
Woburn Abbey, Building Accounts, detailed bills and loose receipts, 1790–1791 (Luton Archives & Records Service, R5/2114/496)

Wolstenholme 1964
Wolstenholme, G, ed, *The Royal College of Physicians of London Portraits* (1964)

Wolstenholme and Kerslake 1977
Wolstenholme, Gordon and Kerslake, John F, *The Royal College of Physicians of London, Portraits* (Excepta Medica, 1977)

Wolterton/Fisher
Wolterton Hall Archives, Fisher Letters, 1737 (Wolterton Hall, Norfolk)

Wolverhampton A G
Wolverhampton Art Gallery & Museum

Wombwell Archives
Wombwell Family Papers (Northallerton RO, ZDV)

Wood 1729
Wood, John, *Essay towards a description of Bath* (1729)

Wood 1745
Wood, John, *A Description of the Exchange of Bristol* (1745)

Wood 1749
Wood, John, *An Essay towards a description of Bath in four parts* (1749)

Wood 1765
Wood, John, *A Description of Bath*, 2 vols (Bath: 1765)

Wood 1971
Wood, M A, 'Memorial to Two Sisters; Sarah Losh's Church of St Mary, Wreay', *Country Life*, vol 150 (4 Nov 1971) pp 1230–31

Wood 1991 (1)
Wood, Lucy, 'George Brookshaw, the case of the vanishing cabinet-maker: Part 1', *Apollo*, vol 133, no 351 (May 1991) pp 301–6

Wood 1991 (2)
Wood, Lucy, 'George Brookshaw, 'Peintre Ebeniste par Extraordinaire', the case of the vanishing cabinet-maker: Part 2', *Apollo*, vol 133, no 352 (June 1991) pp 383–97

Wood 1993
Wood, Jeremy, 'The Architectural Patronage of Algernon Percy, 10th Earl of Northumberland', in *English Architecture Public and Private: Essays for Kerry Downes*, ed Bold, John and Chaney, Edward (1993) pp 55–80

Wood's *Monumental Masonry*
Wood's *Monumental Masonry*, c1801–30 (HMI, 13.84)

Woodbridge 1974 (1)
Woodbridge, Kenneth, 'Dream of Aeneas: A Rosa Source for Cheere's River God at Stourhead', *Burlington Magazine*, vol 116, no 861 (Dec 1974) p 756

Woodbridge 1974 (2)
Woodbridge, Kenneth, 'Kent's Gardening, the Rousham Letters', *Apollo*, vol 100, no 2 (Oct 1974) pp 282–91

Woodburn and Guy 2005–6
Woodburn, Bill, and Guy, Neil, 'Arundel Castle', *Castle Studies Group Journal*, vol 19 (2005–6) pp 9–24

Woodward 1976
Woodward, Robin, 'Scotland's Albert Memorial', *Country Life*, vol 160 (23 Dec 1976) pp 1908–9

Woodward 1977
Woodward, Robin, 'Nineteenth Century Sculpture in Scotland' Ph D Diss (University of Edinburgh, 1977)

Woodward 1998
Woodward, Christopher, 'William Beckford & Fonthill Splendens', *Apollo* (Feb 1998)

Woolner 1917
Woolner, Amy, *Thomas Woolner R.A. Sculptor and Poet: His Life in Letters* (London: 1917)

Woolner Diary
Thomas Woolner's Australian diary [a photocopy of the original MS, which was in private hands, made in 1971], 1852 (Bodleian MSS, Facs. d.152)

Worcs RO
Worcester Record Office

Wordsworth Lib
Wordsworth Library, The Wordsworth Trust, Grasmere, Cumbria

Worley 1993
Worley, M P, 'Identifying Pietro Cardelli (1776–1822) and his Oeuvre: From the Salon of 1804 in Paris to the Pediment of the Cabildo in New Orleans', *Gazette des Beaux-Arts*, vol 6, no 122 (July/Aug 1993) pp 41–50

Worsley 1986
Worsley, Giles, 'Mystery of the Seven Dials Resolved', *Country Life*, vol 179, no 4612 (9 Jan 1986) pp 78–79

Worsley 1988 (1)
Worsley, Giles, 'Berkley House, Somerset: the Home of Mr Michael Philips', *Country Life*, vol 182, no 20 (19 May 1988) pp 168–71

Worsley 1988 (2)
Worsley, Giles, 'Stapleford Park, Leicestershire', *Country Life*, vol 182, no 25 (23 Jun 1988) pp 160–63

Worsley 1988 (3)
Worsley, Giles, 'Alnwick Castle, Northumberland I', *Country Life*, vol 182, no 48 (1 Dec 1988) pp 174–78

Worsley 1989
Worsley, Giles, 'Cowick Hall, Yorkshire', *Country Life*, vol 183, no 12 (23 Mar 1989) pp 192–95

Worsley 1999
Worsley, Giles, 'New light on "Long Sir Thomas" ', *Georgian Group Journal*, vol 9 (1999)

WPL
Westminster Public Library, London

Wragg 1957
Wragg, R B, 'The History of Scagliola', *Country Life*, vol 122, no 3169 (10 Oct 1957)

Wragg 1959
Wragg, R B, 'Charles Clerici: Craftsman in Scagliola', *Architectural Review*, vol 126 (Dec 1959) pp 356–57

Wragg 1978–79
Wragg, R B, 'Four Monuments at Wentworth', *Transactions of the Ancient Monuments Society*, vol 23 (1978–79) pp 29–39

Wren MS 1941
Bolton, Arthur T, and Hendry, Harry, 'The Wren MS ... Together with Some Account of Thomas White of Worcester, Sculptor and Architect ...', *Wren Society*, vol 18 (1941) pp 3–204

Wren Soc
Wren Society Publications

Wren Soc V
'Designs of Sir Christopher Wren for Oxford, Cambridge, London etc', *Wren Society*, vol 5 (1928)

Wren Soc X
The Parochial Churches of Sir Christopher Wren, 1666–1718 (Wren Society Publication, 1933)

Wren Soc XIII
St Paul's Cathedral, Building Accounts, part I, 1675–85 (Wren Society Publication, 1936)

Wren Soc XIV
St Paul's Cathedral, Building Accounts, part II, 1685–95 (Wren Society Publication, 1937)

Wren Soc XV
St Paul's Cathedral, Building Accounts, part III, 1 October 1695 to 24 June 1713 (Wren Society Publication, 1938)

Wren Soc XIX
'The City Churches: Accounts and Minutes of the Vestries', *Wren Society*, vol 19 (1942) pp 1–56

Wrest (Lucas) Archive (1)
Wrest (Lucas) Archive (1), Account Book 1727 (Beds RO, L31/199)

Wrest (Lucas) Archive (2)
Wrest (Lucas) Archive (2), Letters 1730 (Beds RO, 130/8/39/7; L30/8/39/8; L30/8/39/9)

Wright 1821
Wright, George Newenham, *An Historical Guide to Ancient and Modern Dublin* (1821)

Wright 1886
Wright, Thomas, *The Town of Cowper or the literary and historical associations of Olney and its neighbourhood* (1886)

Wright 1984
Wright, Geoffrey N, 'Monument to the Ironmasters', *Country Life*, vol 176, no 4547 (11 Oct 1984) p 1032

Wright and Montgomery 1945
Wright, Harold Bunker, and Montgomery, Henry Close, 'The Art Collection of a Virtuoso in Eighteenth-Century England: Matthew Prior's Collection with Catalogue', *Art Bulletin*, vol 27 (Sept 1945) pp 195–204

Wrinch 1969
Wrinch, A M, 'A Sculptor of Children and Colossi – The Work of Alexander Handyside Ritchie', *Country Life*, vol 146, no 3780 (14 Aug 1969) pp 380–81

WSRO
West Sussex Record Office

Wunder 1991
Wunder, Richard P, *Hiram Powers: Vermont Sculptor, 1805–1873*, 2 vols (c1991)

WW
Steward's Papers, Wentworth Woodhouse Muniments (Sheffield City Library)

WW/Steward's Papers
Steward's Papers, Wentworth Woodhouse Muniments 1768, 1784–93 (West Yorks CRO)

Wyatt/Grey
Letter from George Wyatt to Lord Grey, 16 Nov 1809 (Durham University Library, GRE/B60/8/14)

Wyatville/Canova
Letter from Sir Jeffry Wyatville to Antonio Canova recommending Richard James Wyatt, Canova Papers 5 February 1821 (Biblioteca Civica, Bassano del Grappa, Italy, 1772)

Wyndham 1764
Wyndham, Henry P, *The Diary of the late George Bubb Dodington, Baron of Melcombe Regis: from March 8, 1748–49, to February 6, 1761* (London: 1784)

Wynne and White 1975
Wynne, Michael, and White, James, *Catalogue of the Sculptures* [of the National Gallery of Ireland] (Dublin: 1975)

Wynnstay Accounts
Account Book of Sir William Watkins Wynn, Wynnstay Papers 1775 (National Library of Wales, Aberystwyth, Box 115/7)

Yarrington 1983
Yarrington, Alison, 'Nelson the Citizen Hero: State and Public Patronage of Monumental Sculpture 1805–18', *Art History*, vol 6, no 3 (1983) pp 315–29

Yarrington 1988
Yarrington, Alison, 'The Commemoration of the Hero: Public Monuments to the British Victims of the Napoleonic Wars 1800–1864', Ph D Diss (Cambridge University, 1988)

Yarrington 1993
Yarrington, Alison, 'Chantrey's Monument to Frederick Iremonger', *Winchester Cathedral Record*, vol 62 (1993) pp 38–43

Yarrington 1997
Yarrington, Alison, 'The Female Pygmalion: Anne Seymour Damer, Allan Cunningham and the Writing of a Woman Sculptor's Life', *The Sculpture Journal*, vol 1 (1997) pp 32–44

Yarrington 2000
Yarrington, Alison, 'Anglo-Italian Attitudes Chantrey and Canova', in *The Lustrous Trade: Material Culture and the History of Sculpture in England and Italy, c1700–c1860*, ed Sicca, Cinzia and Yarrington, Alison (2000) pp 132–55

Yarrington 2002
Yarrington, Alison, 'The *Three Graces* and the Temple of Feminine Virtue', *The Sculpture Journal*, vol 7 (2002) pp 30–43

YAS
Yorkshire Archaeological Society

YCAG
York City Art Galleries

YCBA
Yale Center for British Art, New Haven, Connecticut

Yockney 1940
Yockney, Alfred, 'Agostino Aglio', *Apollo*, vol 32 (Nov 1940) pp 129–30

Yockney 1943
Yockney, Alfred, 'Aglio Family', *Apollo*, vol 38 (Nov 1943) pp 145–46

York App Reg
York Apprenticeship Registers, 1784–1814 (York Archives, Exhibition Square, York, D14, D15)

Yorke 1993
Yorke, James, 'Better than any Original', *Country Life*, vol 187, no 13 (April 1993) pp 54–55

Yorke 1994
Yorke, James, 'Belvoir Castle, Leicestershire, II: A Seat of the Duke of Rutland', *Country Life*, vol 188, no 26 (30 June 1994) pp 62–65

Yorke 1999
Yorke, James, 'The Work of John Henning Junior at Stafford House', *Apollo*, vol 149, no 443 (Jan 1999) pp 44–48

Young 1889
Young, William, *History of Dulwich College*, 2 vols (1889)

Young 1983
Young, Hilary, 'Thomas Heming and the Tatton Cup', *Burlington Magazine*, vol 125, no 962 (May 1983) pp 285–89

Young 1995
Young, Hilary, *Genius of Wedgwood*, exhib cat (V&A: 1995)

Young 1996
Young, Hilary, 'Philip Cornman: A Biographical Note', *Silver Society Journal*, no 8 (Autumn 1996) pp 481–86

Young 1999
Young, Hilary, *English Porcelain, 1745–95* (1999)

Yung and Pettman 1981
Yung, K K, and Pettman, Mary, *National Portrait Gallery: Complete Illustrated Catalogue* (London: 1981)

Zeitler 1955
Zeitler, Rudolf, 'Klassizismus und Utopia; Interpretationen zu Werken von David, Canova, Carstens, Thorvaldsen, Koch', *Journal of Aesthetics and Art Criticism*, vol 14 (Dec 1955) pp 278–79

Zock 2002
Zock, Katherine, *Daniel Katz Ltd, European Sculpture* (New York, 6–18 May 2002)

INDEX OF NAMES

Index of portrait sculpture (including plaques and memorials).
Peers, Peeresses and Baronets have been further identified according to given dates.
Bracketed dates (of death, or of the sculpture) may be given to distinguish similar names.

INDEX OF LOCATIONS

This index is in two parts: British Isles and Eire, pp. 1583–1617, and Other Countries, pp. 1617–20. Only when the location is unknown is an owner's name given (in italics). Names of some Counties are updated.

LONDON (Greater London)
Churches listed separately

OTHER COUNTRIES

AFRICA

AUSTRALIA